D1178346

PATTERSON'S

ELEMENTARY EDUCATION

2018 Edition
VOLUME XXX

Editorial Staff

Editor	Wayne Moody
Assistant Editor	Rita Ostdick
Assistant Editor	James Thiessen

EDUCATIONAL DIRECTORIES INC.

Educational Directories Inc.
PO Box 68097
Schaumburg IL 60168-0097
(847) 891-1250 or (800) 357-6183
www.ediusa.com

First edition published 1989. Thirtieth edition 2018

ISBN 978-0-9883500-1-4
ISSN 1044-1417
Library of Congress Catalog Card Number: SN89-646629
Printed in the United States of America

CONTENTS

How to Use This Directory iv

Guide to Editorial Style vi

Elementary Schools Alphabetically By State 1

Charter Schools 1018

Bureau of Indian Affairs Schools 1074

Department of Defense Dependent Schools 1076

Catholic School Superintendents 1077

Lutheran School Superintendents 1078

Seventh-Day Adventists School Superintendents 1079

HOW TO USE THIS DIRECTORY

Patterson's ELEMENTARY EDUCATION (published annually since 1989) is the first, single-volume, comprehensive, national directory to elementary schools and the second in a series of school directories published by Educational Directories Inc. Patterson's AMERICAN EDUCATION (published annually since 1904) is THE standard directory to secondary schools; and post-secondary schools available. The two volumes combined fulfill the need for a single, systematized, comprehensive directory to our nation's schools from kindergarten through post-graduate studies.

Patterson's ELEMENTARY EDUCATION contains more than 12,000 public school districts, more than 64,000 public, private and Catholic elementary schools and more than 15,700 middle schools in an easy-to-use and consistent format. It is an invaluable resource for anyone involved in education or educational research. School registrars, guidance counselors, principals, superintendents, directors of admissions, financial aid officers, schools of education, public libraries, government agencies, armed forces and business people find it a welcome replacement for the multitude of other directories required for national coverage of our nation's school systems with their variation in size, content, format and publishing date.

One of the primary objectives of this directory is to make available the latest, most comprehensive information about elementary schools in a condensed and easily accessible format. Its general organization is geographical. Entries are arranged alphabetically, by state, then by community (post office) and then by District and School name. Each state begins with a listing of the officials in its Department of Education followed by the head of the State Board of Education. If a state has intermediate superintendents (a level of superintendent between the state superintendent of schools and the superintendents who actually supervise the schools) they appear in a table preceding the community listings. Community listings follow and include the community name, county name, community population, district name, total district student enrollment, the superintendent's name, address, telephone, fax number and website where available followed by a listing of the district schools, showing their enrollment, grade range and the principal's name, address, telephone number and fax number. A district may be responsible for schools in more than one community. To achieve consistency, the district office is listed in the community in which it is located. A cross-reference is provided to and from the schools of the district located in other communities.

A short line may appear at the end of the listing of public elementary schools. This line separates the public schools from the private and Catholic elementary schools located in the community. Private and Catholic school listings include their enrollment, grade range and the principal's name, address, telephone number and fax number. Please refer to page vi, "Guide to Editorial Style," for an example of how these elements work together to provide an easy-to-use format.

Schools Listed

Patterson's ELEMENTARY EDUCATION lists the following types of schools:

- **Kindergarten Schools**
- **Primary Schools** usually teach any combination of the first three elementary grades.
- **Intermediate Schools** usually teach any combination of grades four through six.
- **Elementary Schools** usually teach a combination of the first four to the first eight grades.
- **Middle Schools** usually teach any combination of grades five through eight.
- **K-12 Schools**

The following are included:

- All graded state approved public elementary schools.
- All graded elementary schools belonging to the National Catholic Education Association.
- All graded, regionally accredited, private elementary schools.
- Private elementary schools belonging to the member associations of the Council of American Private Education.

Non-graded, special education schools, and other non-traditional elementary schools are not listed.

Patterson's AMERICAN EDUCATION lists Junior High Schools, Junior-Senior High Schools, Senior High Schools, High Schools and K-12 Schools.

ABBREVIATIONS

AVC. . . Area Vocational Center
CCSD. . Community Consolidated School District
CDC . . Child Development Center
CESD. . Consolidated Elementary School District
CISD . . City Independent School District
CSD. . . City School District
CUSD. . Community Unit School District
ECC. . . Early Childhood Center
ECCSD . Elementary Community Consolidated School District
EHSD. . Elementary-High School District
ES . . . Elementary School
ESD. . . Elementary School District
EVD. . . Exempted Village District
HS . . . High School
HSD. . . High School District
IS . . . . Intermediate School
ISD . . . Independent School District
JESD . . Joint Elementary School District
JHS. . . Junior High School
JSD . . . Joint School District
JSHS. . Junior-Senior High School
JUESD . Joint Unified Elementary School District
JUHSD . Joint Unified High School District
JUNESD Joint Union Elementary School District
JUNHSD Joint Union High School District
JUSD . . Joint Unified School District
JVSD . . Joint Vocational School District
K . . . . Kindergarten
MS . . . Middle School
MSHS. . Middle School High School
PS . . . Primary School
RHSD. . Rural High School District
RISD . . Rural Independent School District
RSD. . . Reorganized School District
S . . . . School
SAD. . . School Administrative District
SC . . . School Corporation
SD . . . School District
SHS. . . Senior High School
SSD. . . Separate School District
UESD. . Unified Elementary School District
UFD. . . Union Free District
UHSD. . Unified High School District
UNESD . Union Elementary School District
UNHSD . Union High School District
UNSD. . Union School District
USD. . . Unified School District
Vo/Tech. Vocational/Technical

GUIDE TO EDITORIAL STYLE

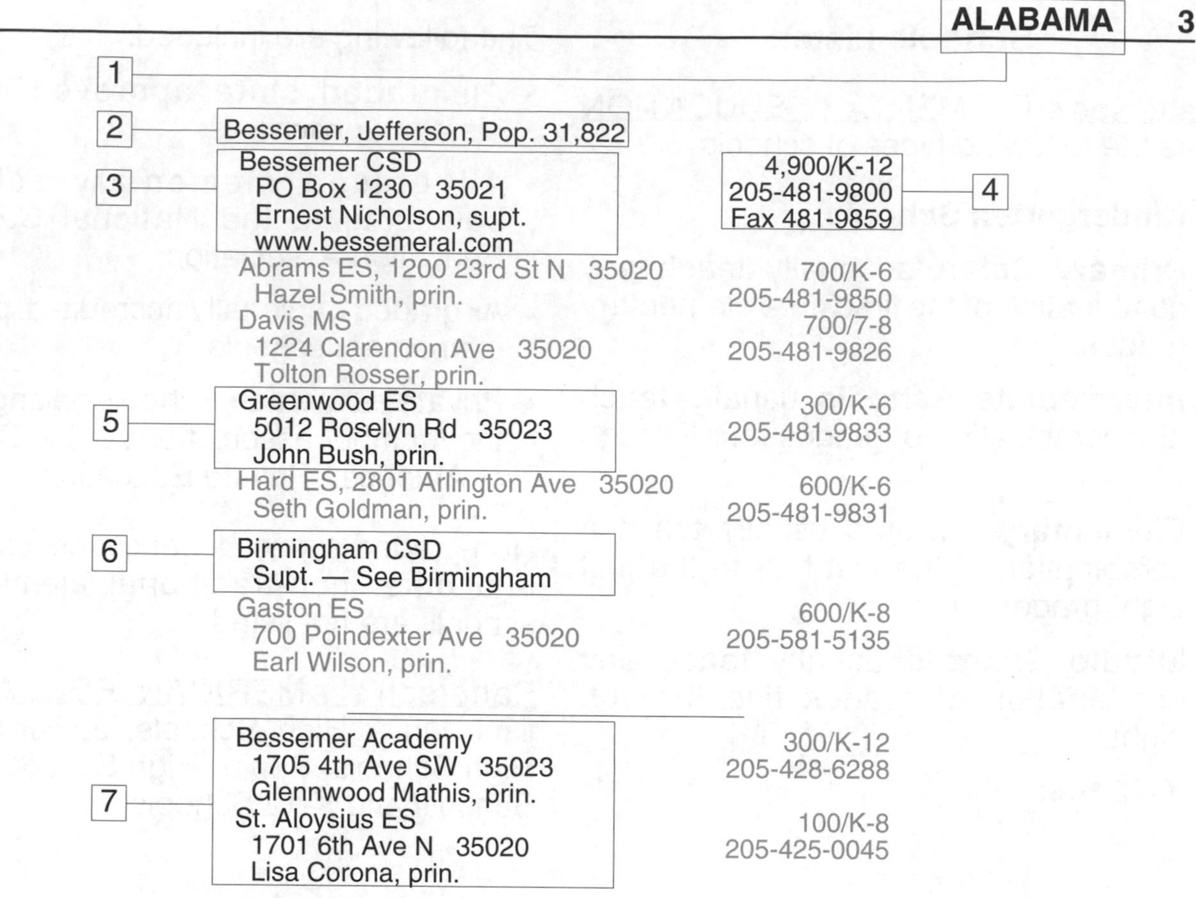

ALABAMA 3

1

2 Bessemer, Jefferson, Pop. 31,822

3 Bessemer CSD
PO Box 1230 35021
Ernest Nicholson, supt.
www.bessemeral.com

4 4,900/K-12
205-481-9800
Fax 481-9859

Abrams ES, 1200 23rd St N 35020 — 700/K-6
Hazel Smith, prin. — 205-481-9850

Davis MS — 700/7-8
1224 Clarendon Ave 35020 — 205-481-9826
Tolton Rosser, prin.

5 Greenwood ES — 300/K-6
5012 Roselyn Rd 35023 — 205-481-9833
John Bush, prin.

Hard ES, 2801 Arlington Ave 35020 — 600/K-6
Seth Goldman, prin. — 205-481-9831

6 Birmingham CSD
Supt. — See Birmingham

Gaston ES — 600/K-8
700 Poindexter Ave 35020 — 205-581-5135
Earl Wilson, prin.

7 Bessemer Academy — 300/K-12
1705 4th Ave SW 35023 — 205-428-6288
Glennwood Mathis, prin.

St. Aloysius ES — 100/K-8
1701 6th Ave N 35020 — 205-425-0045
Lisa Corona, prin.

1. State.
2. City, county and city population.
3. Community school districts - school district name (refer to page v for abbreviations), address, superintendent's name and website.
4. Enrollment, grade range, phone number and fax number.
5. Community schools - school name, address and principal's name.
6. If the school district office is not located in this city, a cross-reference will show office location.
7. Private and Catholic elementary schools appear below a short line in the cities where they are located.

ELEMENTARY SCHOOL COUNTS BY STATE

State	Public						Private	Catholic	Total
	Districts	K-4	K-6	K-8	5-8	K-12			
Alabama	137	154	465	61	261	67	146	33	1,324
Alaska	53	7	138	11	34	174	27	6	450
Arizona	193	62	518	297	200	5	112	48	1,435
Arkansas	232	185	307	2	181	6	74	23	1,010
California	860	185	4,415	686	1,258	10	1,159	529	9,102
Colorado	178	38	809	58	249	17	129	43	1,521
Connecticut	158	132	371	92	188	3	78	78	1,100
Delaware	15	20	79	2	37	0	45	17	215
District Of Columbia	1	2	62	13	14	0	21	13	126
Florida	67	41	1,633	119	508	15	983	162	3,528
Georgia	175	101	1,097	23	468	3	380	31	2,278
Hawaii	1	1	167	4	38	5	69	24	309
Idaho	114	43	284	13	97	16	50	15	632
Illinois	756	473	1,150	614	733	0	443	375	4,544
Indiana	290	207	784	33	333	2	181	153	1,983
Iowa	328	173	476	13	255	2	70	98	1,415
Kansas	286	104	567	44	227	3	66	87	1,384
Kentucky	173	50	582	68	222	10	86	96	1,287
Louisiana	71	125	451	71	225	59	159	132	1,293
Maine	143	80	168	89	96	9	43	12	640
Maryland	24	28	749	75	218	0	207	101	1,402
Massachusetts	271	278	635	86	315	1	192	129	1,907
Michigan	538	347	974	101	508	37	386	178	3,069
Minnesota	329	141	609	23	216	22	218	160	1,718
Mississippi	142	148	262	31	195	33	106	22	939
Missouri	516	218	837	99	369	5	161	184	2,389
Montana	300	41	270	106	222	1	39	18	997
Nebraska	244	61	452	22	118	8	75	84	1,064
Nevada	17	16	321	15	93	11	74	10	557
New Hampshire	153	66	156	49	86	2	56	21	589
New Jersey	495	389	760	253	450	0	242	174	2,763
New Mexico	89	33	361	17	145	0	70	26	741
New York	677	429	1,690	224	780	78	650	382	4,910
North Carolina	115	110	1,167	78	482	3	366	38	2,359
North Dakota	170	11	206	42	35	5	18	25	512
Ohio	610	479	983	155	658	8	253	310	3,456
Oklahoma	511	169	479	256	309	1	80	29	1,834
Oregon	178	40	521	93	201	17	138	45	1,233
Pennsylvania	499	382	1,036	138	504	2	368	333	3,262
Rhode Island	35	36	127	1	51	1	27	32	310
South Carolina	81	79	549	25	255	1	131	28	1,149
South Dakota	149	35	193	82	158	1	36	23	677
Tennessee	141	201	590	174	310	18	280	43	1,757
Texas	1,023	728	3,370	79	1,649	142	581	209	7,781
Utah	41	14	512	3	59	4	37	13	683
Vermont	56	24	127	61	29	10	27	10	344
Virginia	132	77	1,048	13	346	2	268	64	1,950
Washington	294	82	994	60	356	26	324	80	2,216
West Virginia	55	92	297	38	115	2	50	19	668
Wisconsin	409	199	715	116	350	12	352	265	2,418
Wyoming	48	32	147	16	60	8	16	6	333
Total	12,573	7,168	35,660	4,844	15,266	867	10,149	5,036	91,563

ELEMENTARY SCHOOLS

ALABAMA

ALABAMA DEPARTMENT OF EDUCATION

PO Box 302101, Montgomery 36130
Telephone 334-242-9700
Fax 334-242-9708
Website http://www.alsde.edu

State Superintendent of Education Ed Richardson

ALABAMA BOARD OF EDUCATION

PO Box 302101, Montgomery 36130

President Kay Ivey

PUBLIC, PRIVATE AND CATHOLIC ELEMENTARY SCHOOLS

Etowah County SD
Supt. — See Gadsden
Glencoe ES 400/K-4
207 N College St 35905 256-492-4709
Teresa Ashley, prin. Fax 492-4704

Abbeville, Henry, Pop. 2,658
Henry County SD 2,600/PK-12
300 N Trawick St 36310 334-585-2206
Chris Padget, supt. Fax 585-2551
www.henrycountyboe.org
Abbeville ES 400/PK-6
100 Elm St 36310 334-585-3679
Jill Barber, prin. Fax 585-1122
Other Schools – See Headland

Abbeville Christian Academy 200/K-12
PO Box 9 36310 334-585-5100
Melanie Carlisle, head sch Fax 575-5184

Adamsville, Jefferson, Pop. 4,485
Jefferson County SD
Supt. — See Birmingham
Adamsville ES 300/K-5
4600 Hazelwood Rd 35005 205-379-2400
Susan Remick, prin. Fax 379-2445
Minor MS 800/6-8
400 Hillcrest Rd 35005 205-379-2550
Taki Sarhaan, prin. Fax 379-2553

Addison, Winston, Pop. 756
Winston County SD
Supt. — See Double Springs
Addison ES 300/K-6
PO Box 660 35540 256-747-1665
Jeffery Scott, prin. Fax 747-1654

Alabaster, Shelby, Pop. 29,944
Alabaster CSD 6,100/K-12
1953 Municipal Way Ste 200 35007 205-663-8400
Dr. Wayne Vickers, supt. Fax 663-8408
www.alabasterschools.org
Meadow View ES 1,000/K-3
2800 Smokey Rd 35007 205-682-5740
Dr. Rachea Simms, prin. Fax 682-5745
Thompson IS 1,000/4-5
10019 Highway 119 35007 205-682-5720
Brent Byars, prin. Fax 682-5725
Thompson MS 900/7-8
1509 Kent Dairy Rd 35007 205-685-8100
Neely Woodley, prin. Fax 685-0446
Thompson Sixth Grade Center 500/6-6
10111 Highway 119 35007 205-682-5790
Dr. Daniel Steele, prin. Fax 682-5465
Other Schools – See Maylene

Evangel Classical Christian S 400/K-12
423 Thompson Rd 35007 205-216-0149
Kingwood Christian S 400/PK-12
1351 Royalty Dr 35007 205-663-3973

Alberta, Wilcox
Wilcox County SD
Supt. — See Camden
ABC ES 200/PK-6
3000 County Road 29 36720 334-573-2550
Laurette Gibson, prin. Fax 573-9361

Albertville, Marshall, Pop. 20,874
Albertville CSD 4,700/PK-12
107 W Main St 35950 256-891-1183
Dr. Ric Ayer, supt. Fax 891-6303
www.albertk12.org
Albertville ES 800/3-4
1100 Horton Rd 35950 256-894-4822
Mona Sheets, prin. Fax 891-6390
Albertville MS 600/7-8
600 E Alabama Ave 35950 256-878-2341
Lance Kitchens, prin. Fax 891-6334
Albertville PS 1,000/PK-2
1100 Horton Rd 35950 256-878-6611
Vanessa Fowler, prin. Fax 891-6390
Big Spring Lake K 500/K-K
257 Country Club Rd 35951 256-878-7922
Tracy Penney, prin. Fax 891-6386
Evans ES 700/5-6
901 W Mckinney Ave 35950 256-878-7698
Robert Sims, prin. Fax 891-7841

Marshall County SD
Supt. — See Guntersville
Asbury ES 500/PK-5
1966 Asbury Rd 35951 256-878-6221
Jean Wilks, prin. Fax 878-6205

Marshall Christian S 200/PK-12
1631 Brashers Chapel Rd 35951 256-279-0192
Roy Bryant, admin. Fax 891-4160

Alexander City, Tallapoosa, Pop. 14,759
Alexander City SD 3,100/K-12
375 Lee St 35010 256-234-5074
Dr. J. Darrell Cooper, supt. Fax 329-6547
www.alexcityschools.net
Alexander City MS 500/7-8
359 State St 35010 256-234-8660
Tracie Blakely, prin. Fax 234-8659
Pearson ES 700/K-2
1240 Scott Rd 35010 256-234-8625
Jamie Forbus, prin. Fax 234-8647
Radney ES 400/5-6
140 Alison Dr 35010 256-234-8636
John Prestridge, prin. Fax 234-8654
Stephens ES 400/3-4
851 Laurel St 35010 256-234-8631
April Neese, prin. Fax 234-8653

Alexandria, Calhoun, Pop. 3,872
Calhoun County SD
Supt. — See Anniston
Alexandria ES 900/K-4
PO Box 121 36250 256-741-4300
Derek Cobb, prin. Fax 820-7101
Alexandria MS 5-8
353 Stadium Dr 36250 256-741-4500
Shannon Finley, prin. Fax 820-7161

Aliceville, Pickens, Pop. 2,445
Pickens County SD
Supt. — See Carrollton
Aliceville ES 300/K-4
800 Columbus Rd NW 35442 205-373-8722
Russell Smart, prin. Fax 373-3337
Aliceville MS 300/5-8
1000 Columbus Rd NW 35442 205-373-6900
Fred Young, prin. Fax 373-8296

Altoona, Etowah, Pop. 916
Etowah County SD
Supt. — See Gadsden
West End ES 500/PK-6
6795 Highway 132 35952 256-622-1085
Michelle Moore, prin. Fax 622-1086

Andalusia, Covington, Pop. 8,865
Andalusia CSD 1,600/K-12
1201 C C Baker Ave, 334-222-3186
Ted Watson, supt. Fax 222-8631
andalusia.schoolinsites.com
Andalusia ES 800/K-6
1501 W Bypass 36420 334-222-1224
Alane Brunson, prin. Fax 427-7214
Andalusia JHS 300/7-8
408 4th Ave 36420 334-222-7569
Dr. Daniel Shakespeare, prin. Fax 222-5834

Covington County SD 3,100/PK-12
807 C C Baker Ave, 334-222-7571
Shannon Driver, supt. Fax 222-7573
www.cov.k12.al.us
Pleasant Home S 500/PK-12
12548 Falco Rd 36420 334-222-1315
Craig Nichols, prin. Fax 222-4415
Straughn ES 600/PK-5
29324 Straughn School Rd, 334-427-1311
Bettye Anne Older, prin. Fax 427-1401
Straughn MS 300/6-8
29324 Straughn School Rd, 334-222-4090
Cassandra Scott, prin. Fax 222-4132
Other Schools – See Lockhart, Opp, Red Level

Anniston, Calhoun, Pop. 22,755
Anniston CSD 1,800/PK-12
PO Box 1500 36202 256-231-5000
Darren Douthitt, supt. Fax 231-5073
www.annistonschools.com/
Anniston MS 400/6-8
4800 Mcclellan Blvd 36206 256-231-5020
Kimberly Garrick, prin. Fax 231-5024
Cobb Pre K Academy 100/PK-PK
1325 Cobb Ave 36201 256-231-5030
Sheila Ball, prin. Fax 231-5009
Golden Springs ES 200/PK-5
100 Feary Dr 36207 256-231-5050
Betty Merriweather, prin. Fax 231-5052
Randolph Park ES 200/K-5
2200 W 17th St 36201 256-231-5080
Teresia Hall, prin. Fax 231-5082
Tenth Street ES 300/K-5
1525 E 10th St 36207 256-231-5090
Dexter Copeland, prin. Fax 231-5044

Calhoun County SD 9,300/K-12
PO Box 2084 36202 256-741-7400
Joe Dyar, supt. Fax 237-5332
www.ccboe.us
Saks ES 500/K-4
31 Watson St 36206 256-741-6800
Amber Ray, prin. Fax 236-8181
Saks MS 300/5-7
32 Watson St 36206 256-741-6900
Jennifer Dothard, prin. Fax 236-9191
Wellborn ES 600/K-6
525 Cooper Cir 36201 256-741-7500
Jeanna Chandler, prin. Fax 236-3141
White Plains ES 500/K-4
5600 AL Highway 9 36207 256-741-7700
Jonathan Gilbert, prin. Fax 236-6008
White Plains MS 500/5-8
5800 AL Highway 9 36207 256-741-4700
Courtney Wilburn, prin. Fax 238-1715
Other Schools – See Alexandria, Jacksonville, Ohatchee, Weaver

Oxford CSD
Supt. — See Oxford
Coldwater ES 400/K-4
530 Taylors Chapel Rd 36201 256-241-3870
Christy Shepard, prin. Fax 236-6061
De Armanville ES 500/K-4
101 School Rd 36207 256-241-3918
Amy Copeland, prin. Fax 241-3921

Donoho S 400/PK-12
2501 Henry Rd 36207 256-237-5477
Faith Christian S 300/PK-12
4100 Ronnaki Rd 36207 256-236-4499
Chop Jones, head sch Fax 236-4673
IQRA Math and Science Academy 50/K-12
1821 McCall Dr 36207 256-403-6161
Sacred Heart S 200/PK-12
16 Morton Rd 36205 256-237-4231
Charlie Maniscalco, prin. Fax 237-2353
Sharp-Dean S of Continuing Studies 50/K-12
1910 Noble St 36201 256-238-0466

Arab, Marshall, Pop. 7,960
Arab CSD 2,600/PK-12
750 Arabian Dr NE 35016 256-586-6011
John Mullins, supt. Fax 586-6013
www.arabcityschools.org
Arab ES 600/3-5
241 8th Ave NE 35016 256-586-6085
Jessica McCrary, prin. Fax 931-0427
Arab JHS 600/6-8
911 Old Cullman Rd SW 35016 256-586-6074
John Ingram, prin. Fax 586-1348
Arab PS 600/PK-2
121 Mimosa St NE 35016 256-586-6005
Leah Keith, prin. Fax 586-0616

Marshall County SD
Supt. — See Guntersville
Brindlee Mountain ES 200/3-5
2233 Shoal Creek Rd 35016 256-753-2246
Amanda Hollaway, prin. Fax 753-6630

Ardmore, Limestone, Pop. 1,178
Limestone County SD
Supt. — See Athens
Cedar Hill ES 600/K-5
27905 Cedar Hill Rd 35739 256-423-5950
Glen Garner, prin. Fax 423-5970

Ariton, Dale, Pop. 752
Dale County SD
Supt. — See Ozark
Ariton S 700/K-12
PO Box 750 36311 334-445-5560
Joshua Herring, prin. Fax 445-5561

Arley, Winston, Pop. 344
Winston County SD
Supt. — See Double Springs
Meek ES 200/K-6
6613 County Road 41 35541 205-221-9425
Heather Tucker, prin. Fax 221-5886

Ashford, Houston, Pop. 2,133
Houston County SD
Supt. — See Dothan
Ashford ES 800/K-5
100 Barfield St 36312 334-899-5912
Denise Kohen, prin. Fax 899-4728

Ashland, Clay, Pop. 2,015
Clay County SD 1,500/K-12
PO Box 278 36251 256-396-1475
William Walker, supt. Fax 396-5415
www.claycoboe.org
Ashland ES 500/K-6
PO Box 128 36251 256-396-1466
Jared Wesley, prin. Fax 354-2512
Other Schools – See Lineville

First Assembly Christian S 200/PK-12
PO Box 697 36251 256-354-4090

Ashville, Saint Clair, Pop. 2,172
Saint Clair County SD 8,800/PK-12
410 Roy Dr 35953 205-594-7131
Jenny Seals, supt. Fax 594-4441
www.sccboe.org
Ashville ES 400/K-4
33225 US Highway 231 35953 205-594-5242
Lisa Glasgow, prin. Fax 594-2239
Ashville MS 400/5-8
33221 US Highway 231 35953 205-594-7044
Rusty St. John, prin. Fax 594-2241
Other Schools – See Moody, Odenville, Ragland, Springville, Steele

Athens, Limestone, Pop. 21,523
Athens CSD 3,800/PK-12
455 US Highway 31 N 35611 256-233-6600
Dr. Trey Holladay, supt. Fax 233-6640
www.acs-k12.org
Athens ES 400/PK-4
515 N Madison St 35611 256-233-6609
Cindy Davis, prin. Fax 230-2861
Athens IS 500/5-6
1916 US Highway 72 W 35611 256-230-2880
Mitzi Dennis, prin. Fax 230-9593
Athens MS 500/7-8
601 S Clinton St 35611 256-233-6620
Dr. Kerry Donaldson, prin. Fax 233-6623
Athens Renaissance School 500/K-12
405 South St E 35611 256-614-3708
Nelson Brown, prin. Fax 233-6640
Brookhill ES 300/K-4
320 Brookhill Dr 35611 256-233-6603
Jeff Mathheus, prin. Fax 230-2871
Newman ES 400/K-4
517 Julian Newman St 35611 256-233-6630
Sharla Birdsong, prin. Fax 230-2864
SPARK Academy at Cowart 300/K-4
1701 W Hobbs St 35611 256-233-6627
Dr. Beth McKinney, prin. Fax 230-2884

Limestone County SD 9,000/PK-12
300 S Jefferson St 35611 256-232-5353
Dr. Tom Sisk, supt. Fax 233-6461
www.lcsk12.org
Blue Springs ES 500/K-5
16787 Hardy Rd 35611 256-729-4092
Robert Baker, prin. Fax 729-4097
Johnson ES 300/K-5
21360 AL Highway 251 35613 256-233-6665
Fax 233-6673
Piney Chapel ES 200/K-6
20835 Elkton Rd 35614 256-233-6674
Rebecca Valenzuela, prin. Fax 233-6697
Other Schools – See Ardmore, Elkmont, Harvest, Lester, Tanner

---

Athens Bible S 300/K-12
507 Hoffman St 35611 256-232-3525
Randall L. Adams, prin. Fax 232-5417
Lindsay Lane Christian Academy 300/PK-12
1300 Lindsay Ln S 35613 256-262-5323
Stephen Murr M.Ed., hdmstr. Fax 232-0425

Atmore, Escambia, Pop. 10,046
Escambia County SD
Supt. — See Brewton
Escambia County MS 500/5-8
PO Box 1236 36504 251-368-9105
Deborah L. Bolden, prin. Fax 368-0969
Huxford ES 300/K-6
637 Huxford Rd 36502 251-294-5475
Leigh Ann Rowland, prin. Fax 294-5858
Patterson ES 400/K-2
1102 W Craig St 36502 251-368-4860
John Brantley, prin. Fax 368-0764

Escambia Academy 300/PK-12
268 Cowpen Creek Rd 36502 251-368-2080

Attalla, Etowah, Pop. 5,935
Attalla CSD 1,500/PK-12
101 Case Ave SE 35954 256-538-8051
David Bowman, supt. Fax 538-8388
www.attalla.k12.al.us
Attalla ES 300/PK-5
300 Cullman Ave SW 35954 256-538-7266
Greg Edge, prin. Fax 538-6064
Etowah MS 400/6-8
316 Jones St SE 35954 256-538-9221
Jeff Johnson, prin. Fax 538-3232

Etowah County SD
Supt. — See Gadsden
Duck Springs ES 200/K-6
10180 Duck Springs Rd 35954 256-538-6301
Suzanne Nance, prin. Fax 538-0037
Ivalee ES 200/K-6
840 Gallant Rd 35954 256-538-9781
Connie Stancil, prin. Fax 538-0831

Auburn, Lee, Pop. 52,538
Auburn CSD 7,300/K-12
PO Box 3270 36831 334-887-2100
Dr. Karen T. DeLano, supt. Fax 887-2107
auburnschools.org
Auburn Early Education Center 500/K-2
721 E University Dr 36830 334-887-4950
Dr. Shelley Aistrup, prin. Fax 887-2139
Dean Road ES 500/K-2
335 S Dean Rd 36830 334-887-4900
Dr. Jacquelynne Greenwood, prin. Fax 887-0599
Drake MS 1,200/6-6
655 Spencer Ave 36832 334-887-1940
Sarah Armstrong, prin. Fax 887-5302
East Samford S 7-7
332 Samford Ave 36830 334-887-1960
Duriel Barlow, prin. Fax 887-4160
Ogletree ES 400/3-5
737 Ogletree Rd 36830 334-887-4920
Dr. Mary Anna Martin-Smith, prin. Fax 826-1328
Pick ES 3-5
1320 N College St 36830 334-887-2110
Deborah Brooks, prin. Fax 887-8067
Richland ES 500/K-2
770 Yarbrough Farms Blvd 36832 334-887-1980
Jeffery J. Johnson, prin. Fax 502-2963
Woods ES 500/K-2
715 Sandorc St 36830 334-887-4940
Karen Snyder, prin. Fax 887-4172
Wrights Mill Road ES 500/3-5
807 Wrights Mill Rd 36830 334-887-1990
Karen Mason, prin. Fax 887-4180
Yarbrough ES 400/3-5
1555 N Donahue Dr 36830 334-887-1970
Jeffrey Pete Forster, prin. Fax 826-2516

Holy Trinity Day S 50/PK-K
100 Church Dr 36830 334-821-9838
Alyssa Northcutt, dir. Fax 887-9501
Lee-Scott Academy 600/PK-12
1601 Academy Dr 36830 334-821-2430
St. Michael Catholic Preschool 50/PK-PK
1100 N College St 36830 334-887-5540
Cindy Wilton, dir. Fax 887-5572

Autaugaville, Autauga, Pop. 858
Autauga County SD
Supt. — See Prattville
Autaugaville S 300/K-12
PO Box 99 36003 334-365-8329
Susan Butts, prin. Fax 365-8043

Axis, Mobile, Pop. 736
Mobile County SD
Supt. — See Mobile
North Mobile County S 600/K-8
1950 Salco Rd W 36505 251-221-2000
Melissa Mixon, prin. Fax 221-2004

Baileyton, Cullman, Pop. 598
Cullman County SD
Supt. — See Cullman
Parkside S 300/K-8
12431 AL Highway 69 N 35019 256-796-5568
Richard Orr, prin. Fax 796-5507

Banks, Pike, Pop. 174
Pike County SD
Supt. — See Troy
Banks S 400/PK-8
9769 N US Highway 29 36005 334-243-5514
Mattie Lee Scott, prin. Fax 243-5984

Bay Minette, Baldwin, Pop. 7,923
Baldwin County SD 29,900/PK-12
2600 Hand Ave 36507 251-937-0306
Eddie Tyler, supt. Fax 580-1856
www.bcbe.org
Bay Minette ES 600/PK-6
800 Blackburn Ave 36507 251-937-7651
Laura Moorer, prin. Fax 937-6983
Bay Minette MS 500/7-8
1311 W 13th St 36507 251-580-2960
Zachary Wigstrom, prin. Fax 580-5120
Delta ES 200/PK-6
10251 Whitehouse Fork Road 36507 251-937-3657
Keri Shofner, prin. Fax 937-3637
Pine Grove ES 500/PK-6
43980 Pine Grove Rd 36507 251-937-0453
Donnashele Bruister, prin. Fax 580-4188
Other Schools – See Bon Secour, Daphne, Elberta, Fairhope, Foley, Gulf Shores, Loxley, Orange Beach, Perdido, Robertsdale, Silverhill, Spanish Fort, Stapleton, Summerdale

Bayou La Batre, Mobile, Pop. 2,494
Mobile County SD
Supt. — See Mobile
Alba MS 600/6-8
14180 S Wintzell Ave 36509 251-824-4134
Rhonda Mayfield, prin. Fax 824-1324

Bear Creek, Marion, Pop. 1,062
Marion County SD
Supt. — See Hamilton
Phillips ES 200/K-6
160 School Ave 35543 205-486-5062
David Pruitt, prin. Fax 486-5011

Beatrice, Monroe, Pop. 301
Monroe County SD
Supt. — See Monroeville
Shields S 300/PK-12
17688 Highway 21 N 36425 251-789-2168
Ramona Dailey, prin. Fax 789-2715

Berry, Fayette, Pop. 1,134
Fayette County SD
Supt. — See Fayette
Berry ES 300/PK-6
341 School Ave 35546 205-689-4464
Darrell Thomas, prin. Fax 689-4463

Bessemer, Jefferson, Pop. 27,229
Bessemer CSD 3,000/PK-12
PO Box 1230 35021 205-432-3000
Dr. Keith Stewart, supt. Fax 432-3085
www.besskl2.org
Abrams ES 400/PK-5
1200 23rd St N 35020 205-432-3100
Armentress Robinson, prin. Fax 432-3147
Bessemer City MS 1,000/6-8
100 High School Dr 35022 205-432-3600
LaRhonda Aikerson, prin. Fax 432-3607
Greenwood ES 300/K-5
5012 Roselyn Rd 35022 205-432-3200
Deborah Billups, prin. Fax 432-3207
Hard ES 300/PK-5
2801 Arlington Ave 35020 205-432-3300
LaKeshya George, prin. Fax 432-3307
Jonesboro ES 700/K-5
125 Owen Ave 35020 205-432-3400
Sylvia Haslam, prin. Fax 432-3466
Westhills ES 400/K-5
710 Glenn Rd 35022 205-432-3500
Mildred Posey, prin. Fax 432-3502

Jefferson County SD
Supt. — See Birmingham
Concord ES 400/K-5
1886 Learning Ln 35023 205-379-3150
Lynn Vines, prin. Fax 379-3195
Greenwood ES 200/K-5
1219 School Rd SE 35022 205-379-3750
Dr. Gayle Gober, prin. Fax 379-3751
Lipscomb ES 200/K-5
5605 10th St S 35020 205-379-4550
Cheritta Hayes, prin. Fax 379-4571
Oak Grove ES 600/K-5
9000 Tiger Cub Trl 35023 205-379-2450
Randy McCarty, prin. Fax 379-2495

Bessemer Academy 300/PK-12
1705 4th Ave SW 35022 205-428-6288
St. Aloysius S 200/PK-8
751 Academy Dr Ste A 35022 205-425-0045
Stephanie Burke, prin. Fax 425-0046

Big Cove, Madison
Huntsville CSD
Supt. — See Huntsville
Goldsmith Schiffman ES 600/PK-5
1210 Taylor Rd SE 35763 256-428-7150
Jennifer Douthit, prin. Fax 428-7158

Billingsley, Autauga, Pop. 144
Autauga County SD
Supt. — See Prattville
Billingsley S 700/K-12
PO Box 118 36006 334-365-5516
Gregory Pittman, prin. Fax 755-1633

Birmingham, Jefferson, Pop. 210,274
Birmingham CSD 23,900/PK-12
PO Box 10007 35202 205-231-4600
Dr. Lisa Herring, supt.
www.bhamcityschools.org
Arrington MS 500/6-8
2101 Jefferson Ave SW 35211 205-231-1130
Bruce Roper, prin. Fax 231-1133
Avondale ES 500/K-5
4000 8th Ct S 35222 205-231-7130
Courtney Nelson, prin. Fax 231-7139
Barrett ES 400/K-5
7601 Division Ave 35206 205-231-8130
Wanda Birchfield, prin. Fax 231-8134
Brown ES 400/K-5
4811 Court J 35208 205-231-6860
Steve Brown, prin. Fax 231-6892
Bush ES 500/K-8
1832 Center Way S 35205 205-231-6000
Genita Matthews, prin. Fax 231-7231
Bush Hills Academy 500/PK-8
900 16th St W 35208 205-231-6370
Judith Ross, prin. Fax 231-6423
Central Park ES 500/K-5
4915 Avenue Q 35208 205-231-1250
Andra Walls, prin. Fax 231-1300
EPIC ES 400/K-5
1000 10th Ave S 35205 205-231-7370
Dr. Eleanor Stokes, prin. Fax 231-7419
Gaskins ES 500/K-5
200 Dalton Dr 35215 205-231-9200
Elvirita Finley, prin. Fax 231-9253
Glen Iris ES 900/K-5
1115 11th St S 35205 205-231-7440
Dr. Michael Wilson, prin. Fax 231-7443
Green Acres MS 300/6-8
1220 67th St W 35228 205-231-1370
Dr. Willie Goldsmith, prin. Fax 231-1414
Hayes K-8 S 900/K-8
505 43rd St N 35222 205-231-8900
Dr. Natasha Flowers, prin. Fax 231-8948

Hemphill ES 500/PK-5
714 12th St SW 35211 205-231-7500
Kristin Booker, prin. Fax 231-7499
Hudson S 800/PK-8
3300 FL Shuttlesworth Dr 35207 205-231-3000
Fred Stewart, prin. Fax 231-3072
Huffman Academy 700/K-5
1212 Cheyenne Blvd 35215 205-231-5800
Dr. Kathleen Lindsey, prin. Fax 231-5850
Huffman MS 300/6-8
517 Huffman Rd 35215 205-231-5370
WaShunda Gill, prin. Fax 231-5426
Inglenook S 400/K-8
4120 Inglenook St 35217 205-231-3310
Mario Lumzy, prin. Fax 231-3358
Jones Valley MS 500/6-8
2000 31st St SW 35221 205-231-1040
Carolyn Denson, prin. Fax 231-1088
Minor ES 400/K-5
2425 Avenue S 35218 205-231-6555
Terrell Brown, prin. Fax 231-6602
Mitchell MS 300/6-8
501 81st St S 35206 205-231-9400
Rameka Davis, prin. Fax 231-9464
Norwood ES 200/PK-5
3136 Norwood Blvd 35234 205-231-3440
Carolyn Russell-Walke, prin.
Oliver ES 200/K-5
6871 6th Ct S 35212 205-231-8620
Dr. Selena Florence, prin. Fax 231-8662
Oxmoor Valley ES K-5
3600 Sydney Dr 35211 205-231-1200
Melvin Love, prin. Fax 231-1220
Phillips Academy 700/PK-8
2316 7th Ave N 35203 205-231-9500
Dr. Emeka Nzeocha, prin. Fax 231-9580
Putnam MS 300/6-8
1757 Montclair Rd 35210 205-231-8680
Dr. Sakema Porterfield, prin. Fax 231-8685
Robinson ES 400/PK-5
8400 1st Ave S 35206 205-231-5555
Sandra Kindell, prin. Fax 231-5554
Smith MS 600/6-8
1124 Five Mile Rd 35215 205-231-5675
Dr. Demarcus Gates, prin. Fax 231-5899
South Hampton ES 600/PK-8
565 Sheridan Rd 35214 205-231-6689
Alicia Washington, prin. Fax 231-6683
Sun Valley ES 600/PK-5
1010 18th Ave NW 35215 205-231-5740
Albert LeBlanc, prin. Fax 231-5747
Tuggle ES 300/K-5
412 12th Ct N 35204 205-231-2675
Ann Jemison, prin. Fax 231-2718
Washington S 600/PK-8
115 4th Ave S 35205 205-231-7740
Antonia Ishman, prin. Fax 231-7800
West End Academy 800/PK-5
1840 Pearson Ave SW 35211 205-231-1742
Chandra Blackmon, prin. Fax 231-1788
Wilkerson MS 300/6-8
116 11th Ct W 35204 205-231-2740
Davida Hill-Johnson, prin. Fax 231-2790
Wylam S 500/PK-8
701 Erie St 35224 205-231-6800
Ashley Moore Samuels, prin. Fax 231-6830

Hoover CSD
Supt. — See Hoover
Berry MS 1,200/6-8
4500 Jaguar Dr 35242 205-439-2000
Dr. Christopher Robbins, prin. Fax 439-2001
Greystone ES 600/K-5
300 Village St 35242 205-439-3200
Stacey Stocks, prin. Fax 439-3201
Rocky Ridge ES 600/K-5
2876 Old Rocky Ridge Rd 35243 205-439-2900
Dr. Dilhani Uswatte, prin. Fax 439-2901

Jefferson County SD 35,600/K-12
2100 18th St S 35209 205-379-2000
Dr. Craig Pouncey, supt. Fax 379-2311
www.jefcoed.com
Center Point ES 700/K-2
4801 Indian Trl 35215 205-379-2900
Jay Gary, prin. Fax 379-2945
Chalkville ES 1,100/K-5
940 Chalkville School Rd 35215 205-379-2950
Rod Johnson, prin. Fax 379-2995
Crumly Chapel ES 300/K-5
2201 Pershing Rd 35214 205-379-3250
Jessica Hahn, prin. Fax 379-3295
Erwin IS 600/3-5
528 23rd Ave NW 35215 205-379-3350
Kirsten Logan-Marshall, prin. Fax 379-3395
Erwin MS 700/6-8
532 23rd Ave NW 35215 205-379-3430
Serra Peterson, prin. Fax 856-6663
Gresham ES 400/K-5
2650 Gresham Dr 35243 205-379-3830
Laura Kirkpatrick, prin. Fax 379-3846
Hillview ES 300/K-5
1520 Cherry Ave 35214 205-379-4050
Bert Stewart, prin. Fax 379-4095
Irondale MS 600/6-8
6200 Old Leeds Rd 35210 205-379-3800
Carita Venable, prin. Fax 379-3845
Minor Community ES 400/K-5
3006 Cora Ave 35224 205-379-4800
Dr. Angela Harris, prin. Fax 379-4845
Other Schools – See Adamsville, Bessemer, Brighton, Clay, Dora, Fultondale, Gardendale, Graysville, Hueytown, Irondale, Kimberly, Mc Calla, Morris, Mount Olive, Pinson, Pleasant Grove, Quinton, Trussville, Warrior

Shelby County SD
Supt. — See Columbiana
Inverness ES 700/K-3
5251 Valleydale Rd 35242 205-682-5240
Christine Hoffman, prin. Fax 682-5245
Mt. Laurel ES 700/K-5
1 Jefferson Pl 35242 205-682-7230
Celita Deem, prin. Fax 682-7235
Oak Mountain ES 700/K-3
5640 Cahaba Valley Rd 35242 205-682-5230
Debbie Horton, prin. Fax 682-5235
Oak Mountain IS 800/4-5
5486 Caldwell Mill Rd 35242 205-682-5220
Dr. Pat LeQuier, prin. Fax 682-5225
Oak Mountain MS 1,200/6-8
5650 Cahaba Valley Rd 35242 205-682-5210
Larry Haynes, prin. Fax 682-5215

Vestavia Hills CSD
Supt. — See Vestavia Hills
Vestavia Hills ES Cahaba Heights 400/K-5
4401 Dolly Ridge Rd 35243 205-402-5480
Alicia Hunsberger, prin. Fax 402-5499

Advent Episcopal S 300/PK-8
2019 6th Ave N 35203 205-252-2535
W. Palmer Kennedy M.A., hdmstr. Fax 252-3023
Alabama Waldorf S 200/PK-8
5901 Crestwood Blvd 35212 205-592-0541
Briarwood Christian S 1,900/PK-12
2204 Briarwood Way 35243 205-776-5800
Fax 776-5815
Bruno Montessori Academy 100/PK-8
5509 Timber Hill Rd 35242 205-995-8709
Central Park Christian S 200/K-12
1900 43rd St W 35208 205-786-4811
Cornerstone S of Alabama 300/PK-12
PO Box 320309 35232 205-591-7600
Dr. Nita Carr, pres. Fax 769-0063
Ephesus Academy 200/K-8
829 McMillon Ave SW 35211 205-786-2194
Highlands S 300/PK-8
4901 Old Leeds Rd 35213 205-956-9731
Kavita Vasil, head sch Fax 951-8127
Hilltop Montessori S 200/PK-8
6 Abbott Sq 35242 205-437-9343
Michele Scott Wilensky, head sch Fax 437-9344
Holy Family Catholic Academy 100/6-8
1916 19th Street Ensley 35218 205-780-5858
Sidney Moore, prin. Fax 785-2666
Hoover Christian S 100/PK-12
2113 Old Rocky Ridge Rd 35216 205-987-3376
Integrity Christian Academy 100/PK-6
216 Roebuck Dr 35215 205-833-4416
Venandee Hennington, admin. Fax 833-4450
Islamic Academy of Alabama 200/PK-12
1810 25th Ct S 35209 205-870-0422
Jefferson Christian Academy 200/PK-12
1500 Heritage Place Dr 35210 205-956-9111
McElwain Christian Academy 50/K-5
4445 Montevallo Rd 35213 205-957-2628
Lucy Bloodworth, admin. Fax 956-5910
Miles Jewish Day S 100/K-8
4000 Montclair Rd 35213 205-879-1068
Debra Abolafia, head sch Fax 879-6183
Our Lady of Lourdes K 100/PK-K
980 Huffman Rd 35215 205-836-1218
Jennifer Genereux, prin. Fax 836-5436
Our Lady of Sorrows Preschool 100/PK-PK
1703 29th Ct S 35209 205-380-2646
Lynne Stella, dir. Fax 380-2648
Our Lady of Sorrows S 400/PK-8
1720 Oxmoor Rd 35209 205-879-3237
Mary Jane Dorn, prin. Fax 879-9332
Our Lady of the Valley S 400/PK-8
5510 Double Oak Ln 35242 205-991-5963
Katie Zielinski, prin. Fax 995-1251
St. Barnabas S 100/PK-8
7901 1st Ave N 35206 205-836-5385
John Parker, prin. Fax 833-0272
St. Francis Xavier Preschool PK-PK
2 Xavier Cir 35213 205-879-5596
Meghan Hendrick, prin. Fax 871-1674
St. Francis Xavier S 200/K-8
2 Xavier Cir 35213 205-871-1687
Nathan Wright, prin. Fax 871-1674
St. Peters Child Development Center 100/PK-PK
2061 Patton Chapel Rd 35216 205-822-9461
Susan Wilkens, prin. Fax 822-9451
St. Rose of Lima S 200/PK-8
1401 22nd St S 35205 205-933-0549
Sr. Mary Elizabeth, prin. Fax 933-0591
Westminster S at Oak Mountain 600/K-12
5080 Cahaba Valley Trce 35242 205-995-9694

Blountsville, Blount, Pop. 1,659
Blount County SD
Supt. — See Oneonta
Blountsville ES 700/K-6
260 Page St 35031 205-429-2458
Shannon Lakey, prin. Fax 429-5540
Moore ES 700/K-6
3996 Susan Moore Rd 35031 205-466-5844
Bridgette Murphree, prin. Fax 466-3808

Boaz, Marshall, Pop. 9,410
Boaz CSD 2,200/PK-12
126 Newt Parker Dr 35957 256-593-8180
Dr. Shannon Stanley, supt. Fax 593-8181
www.boazk12.org
Boaz ES 400/PK-1
362 Collier St 35957 256-593-3481
Joshua Walker, prin. Fax 593-6738
Boaz IS 400/4-5
11 Newt Parker Dr 35957 256-593-9211
Dr. Todd Haynie, prin. Fax 593-9388
Boaz MS 500/6-8
140 Newt Parker Dr 35957 256-593-0799
Dr. Richard Rutledge, prin. Fax 593-0729

Corley ES 400/2-3
505 Mount Vernon Rd 35957 256-593-3254
Allison Haygood, prin. Fax 593-7833

Etowah County SD
Supt. — See Gadsden
Carlisle ES 500/K-6
8025 US Highway 431 35956 256-593-4613
Hope Harris, prin. Fax 622-1116
Sardis MS 400/6-8
1415 Sardis Dr 35956 256-622-1120
Chris Royal, prin. Fax 622-1119
Whitesboro ES 300/K-6
5080 Leeth Gap Rd 35956 256-593-5406
Kristy Towns, prin. Fax 593-5431

Bon Secour, Baldwin
Baldwin County SD
Supt. — See Bay Minette
Swift Consolidated ES 300/PK-6
PO Box 7 36511 251-949-6422
Sandra Thorpe, prin. Fax 949-7015

Brantley, Crenshaw, Pop. 786
Crenshaw County SD
Supt. — See Luverne
Brantley S 600/PK-12
PO Box 86 36009 334-527-8879
Kris Odom, prin. Fax 527-3405

Bremen, Cullman
Cullman County SD
Supt. — See Cullman
Cold Springs ES 600/K-8
PO Box 120 35033 256-287-1247
Amanda Johnson, prin. Fax 287-2775

Brent, Bibb, Pop. 4,909
Bibb County SD
Supt. — See Centreville
Brent ES 500/PK-4
160 4th St 35034 205-926-4993
Dr. Mechelle Hollifield, prin. Fax 926-5642

Brewton, Escambia, Pop. 5,355
Brewton CSD 1,100/K-12
811 Belleville Ave 36426 251-867-8400
Dr. Kenneth Varner, supt. Fax 867-8403
www.brewtoncityschools.org/
Brewton ES 400/K-4
901 Douglas Ave 36426 251-867-8410
Anne Lambert, prin. Fax 867-8408
Brewton MS 300/5-8
1384 Old Castleberry Rd 36426 251-867-8420
Madelyn Cave, prin. Fax 867-8422

Escambia County SD 4,300/K-12
PO Box 307 36427 251-867-6251
John J. Knott, supt. Fax 867-6252
www.escambiak12.net
Pollard-McCall S 200/K-8
3975 Old Highway 31 36426 251-867-4070
Stewart Powell, prin. Fax 867-6387
Other Schools – See Atmore, East Brewton, Flomaton

Bridgeport, Jackson, Pop. 2,317
Jackson County SD
Supt. — See Scottsboro
Bridgeport ES 200/K-4
1014 Jacobs Ave 35740 256-495-3147
Lauria Merritt, prin. Fax 495-3192
Bridgeport MS 200/5-8
629 Dr Lee Ave 35740 256-495-2967
Jonathan Colvin, prin. Fax 495-2850

Brighton, Jefferson, Pop. 2,927
Jefferson County SD
Supt. — See Birmingham
Brighton S 400/K-6
3400 Browns Cir 35020 205-379-2650
Donna King, prin. Fax 379-2695

Brilliant, Marion, Pop. 893
Marion County SD
Supt. — See Hamilton
Brilliant ES 200/K-6
10180 State Highway 129 35548 205-465-2323
Gary McCarley, prin. Fax 465-2473

Brookwood, Tuscaloosa, Pop. 1,803
Tuscaloosa County SD
Supt. — See Tuscaloosa
Brookwood ES 600/PK-5
16049 Highway 216 35444 205-342-2668
Michael Keeton, prin. Fax 342-2845

Brundidge, Pike, Pop. 2,052
Pike County SD
Supt. — See Troy
Pike County ES 400/PK-6
186 Hillcrest Dr 36010 334-735-2683
Tracey Arnold, prin. Fax 735-5660

Bryant, Jackson
Jackson County SD
Supt. — See Scottsboro
Bryant S 200/K-8
6645 AL Highway 73 35958 256-597-2203
Lloyd Ellison, prin. Fax 597-2851

Floral Crest SDA S 50/PK-8
1228 County Road 89 35958 256-597-2582
Mountain View Christian Academy 100/PK-12
3665 AL Highway 73 35958 256-597-3467

Buhl, Tuscaloosa
Tuscaloosa County SD
Supt. — See Tuscaloosa
Buhl ES 200/K-5
11968 Buhl School Rd 35446 205-342-2640
Vanessa Clay, prin. Fax 333-3951

Sipsey Valley MS 400/6-8
15817 Romulus Rd 35446 205-342-2870
Frank Kelly, prin. Fax 342-2871

Butler, Choctaw, Pop. 1,876
Choctaw County SD 1,700/PK-12
107 Tom Orr Dr 36904 205-459-3031
Dorothy Banks, supt. Fax 459-3037
www.choctawal.org
Choctaw County ES 500/PK-6
201 Tom Orr Dr 36904 205-459-3520
Marcus Dent, prin. Fax 459-7406
Other Schools – See Gilbertown

Patrician Academy 300/PK-12
901 S Mulberry Ave 36904 205-459-3605
Billy Burnham, hdmstr. Fax 459-4802

Calera, Shelby, Pop. 11,417
Shelby County SD
Supt. — See Columbiana
Calera ES 700/K-2
855 10th St 35040 205-682-6120
Genet Holcomb, prin. Fax 682-6125
Calera IS 600/3-5
8454 Highway 31 35040 205-682-6500
Haley Franks, prin. Fax 682-6505

Camden, Wilcox, Pop. 2,011
Wilcox County SD 1,900/PK-12
PO Box 160 36726 334-682-4716
Andre Saulsberry, supt. Fax 682-4179
www.wilcox.k12.al.us
Camden S of Arts & Technology 300/7-8
PO Box 698 36726 334-682-4514
Andre Davis, prin. Fax 682-5934
Hobbs ES 600/PK-6
PO Box 578 36726 334-682-9310
Shelton Frye, prin. Fax 682-9127
Other Schools – See Alberta, Pine Hill

Wilcox Academy 300/PK-12
PO Box 1149 36726 334-682-9619

Carbon Hill, Walker, Pop. 1,992
Walker County SD
Supt. — See Jasper
Carbon Hill S 600/PK-8
283 Bulldog Blvd 35549 205-924-4101
Mary Slaughter, prin. Fax 924-4199

Carrollton, Pickens, Pop. 1,006
Pickens County SD 2,700/K-12
377 Ladow Center Cir 35447 205-367-2082
Jamie Chapman, supt. Fax 367-8404
www.pickenscountyschools.net
Other Schools – See Aliceville, Gordo, Reform

Pickens Academy 300/PK-12
225 Ray Bass Rd 35447 205-367-8144

Castleberry, Conecuh, Pop. 571
Conecuh County SD
Supt. — See Evergreen
Conecuh County S 200/PK-8
2347 Cleveland Ave 36432 251-966-5411
Peggy Baggett, prin. Fax 966-2833

Cecil, Montgomery

Macon East Academy 400/PK-12
15396 Vaughn Rd 36013 334-277-6566

Cedar Bluff, Cherokee, Pop. 1,779
Cherokee County SD
Supt. — See Centre
Cedar Bluff S 600/K-12
3655 Old Highway 9 35959 256-779-6211
Aubrey Thrasher, prin. Fax 779-8328

Centre, Cherokee, Pop. 3,423
Cherokee County SD 4,000/PK-12
130 E Main St 35960 256-927-3362
Mitchell Guice, supt. Fax 927-3399
www.cherokeek12.org
Centre ES 600/K-4
725 E Main St 35960 256-927-3302
Wes Neyman, prin. Fax 927-4932
Centre MS 500/5-8
1920 E Main St 35960 256-927-5656
Casey Young, prin. Fax 927-4656
Other Schools – See Cedar Bluff, Gaylesville, Sand Rock, Spring Garden

Centreville, Bibb, Pop. 2,751
Bibb County SD 3,300/PK-12
721 Walnut St 35042 205-926-9881
Duane McGee, supt. Fax 926-5075
www.bibbed.org/
Centreville MS 500/5-8
1621 Montgomery Hwy 35042 205-926-9861
Dr. Ernie Cutts, prin. Fax 926-3917
Other Schools – See Brent, Randolph, West Blocton, Woodstock

Cahawba Christian Academy 100/PK-12
2415 Montevallo Rd 35042 205-926-4676

Chatom, Washington, Pop. 1,283
Washington County SD 3,100/K-12
PO Box 1359 36518 251-847-2401
John Dickey, supt. Fax 847-3611
www.wcbek12.org
Chatom ES 300/K-4
PO Box 1209 36518 251-847-2946
Benjamin Jones, prin. Fax 847-3903
Other Schools – See Fruitdale, Leroy, Mc Intosh, Millry

Chelsea, Shelby, Pop. 10,063
Shelby County SD
Supt. — See Columbiana
Chelsea MS 1,000/6-8
2321 Highway 39 35043 205-682-7210
Caroline Obert, prin. Fax 682-7215
Chelsea Park ES 800/K-5
9000 Chelsea Park Trl 35043 205-682-6700
Dr. Jennifer Galloway, prin. Fax 682-6705
Forest Oaks ES 600/K-5
1000 Hornet Pkwy 35043 205-682-7220
Sasha Baker, prin. Fax 682-7225

Cherokee, Colbert, Pop. 1,027
Colbert County SD
Supt. — See Tuscumbia
Cherokee ES 400/PK-6
1305 North Pike 35616 256-359-6422
Anthony Olivis, prin. Fax 359-6426

Chickasaw, Mobile, Pop. 6,039
Chickasaw CSD 900/PK-12
201 N Craft Hwy 36611 251-452-2256
Kathy Odom, supt. Fax 380-8380
www.chickasawschools.com
Chickasaw Early Learning Center 100/PK-PK
201 N Craft Hwy 36611 251-380-8114
Jodie McPherson, admin. Fax 380-8380
Chickasaw ES, 80 Grant St 36611 500/K-5
Christy Amick, prin. 251-452-6452

Childersburg, Talladega, Pop. 5,086
Talladega County SD
Supt. — See Talladega
Childersburg ES 200/K-4
235 Pinecrest Dr 35044 256-315-5525
Nicki Bryant, prin. Fax 315-5535
Childersburg MS 500/5-8
800 4th St SE 35044 256-315-5505
Jena Jones, prin. Fax 315-5520
Watwood ES 400/K-4
3002 Limbaugh Blvd 35044 256-315-5460
Dr. Scarlet Thomas, prin. Fax 315-5470

Citronelle, Mobile, Pop. 3,830
Mobile County SD
Supt. — See Mobile
Lott MS 500/6-8
17740 Celeste Rd 36522 251-221-2240
Jason Golden, prin. Fax 221-2247
McDavid-Jones ES 1,000/PK-5
16250 US Highway 45 36522 251-221-1510
Susan Dickinson, prin. Fax 221-1513

Clanton, Chilton, Pop. 8,519
Chilton County SD 7,700/PK-12
1705 Lay Dam Rd 35045 205-280-3000
Tommy Glasscock, supt. Fax 755-6549
www.chilton.k12.al.us
Clanton ES 700/PK-2
1000 Cloverleaf Dr 35045 205-280-2730
Rebecca Threlkeld, prin. Fax 755-8483
Clanton IS 700/3-5
825 Temple Rd 35045 205-280-2790
Louise Pitts, prin. Fax 280-2795
Clanton MS 700/6-8
835 Temple Rd 35045 205-280-2750
Carla White, prin. Fax 755-2446
Other Schools – See Jemison, Maplesville, Thorsby, Verbena

Clay, Jefferson, Pop. 9,594
Jefferson County SD
Supt. — See Birmingham
Clay ES 600/K-5
6745 Old Springville Rd 35048 205-379-3000
Dr. Sharon Gallant, prin. Fax 379-3045

Clayton, Barbour, Pop. 3,001
Barbour County SD 800/PK-12
PO Box 429 36016 334-775-3453
Dr. Matthew Alexander, supt. Fax 775-7301
www.barbourschools.org
Other Schools – See Louisville

Cleveland, Blount, Pop. 1,288
Blount County SD
Supt. — See Oneonta
Cleveland ES 500/K-6
115 Stadium Dr 35049 205-274-2223
Joseph Whited, prin. Fax 274-2224

Coker, Tuscaloosa, Pop. 978
Tuscaloosa County SD
Supt. — See Tuscaloosa
Westwood ES 300/K-5
11629 Westwood School Rd 35452 205-342-2666
Becky Brown, prin. Fax 347-4197

Collinsville, DeKalb, Pop. 1,945
De Kalb County SD
Supt. — See Rainsville
Collinsville S 900/K-12
802 S Valley Ave 35961 256-524-2111
Donny Jones, prin. Fax 524-7526

Columbiana, Shelby, Pop. 4,133
Shelby County SD 18,600/K-12
PO Box 1910 35051 205-682-7000
Randy Fuller, supt. Fax 682-7005
www.shelbyed.org
Columbiana MS 500/6-8
222 Joiner Town Rd 35051 205-682-6610
Dr. Kerry Rush, prin. Fax 682-6615
Hill ES 500/K-5
201 Washington St 35051 205-682-6620
Dr. Elizabeth Smith, prin. Fax 682-6625
Other Schools – See Birmingham, Calera, Chelsea, Helena, Montevallo, Shelby, Vincent, Wilsonville

---

Cornerstone Christian S 200/PK-12
24975 Highway 25 35051 205-669-7777

Coosada, Elmore, Pop. 1,216
Elmore County SD
Supt. — See Wetumpka
Airport Road IS 600/3-4
384 Blackmon Farm Ln 36020 334-285-2115
Marcia Stephens, prin. Fax 285-2116

Cordova, Walker, Pop. 2,077
Walker County SD
Supt. — See Jasper
Bankhead MS 300/5-8
110 School Rd 35550 205-483-7245
Amber Freeman, prin. Fax 483-7244
Cordova ES 400/PK-4
35 North St 35550 205-483-7666
Dianne Williams, prin. Fax 483-1026

Cottondale, Tuscaloosa
Tuscaloosa CSD
Supt. — See Tuscaloosa
Eastwood MS 600/6-8
6314 Mary Harmon Bryant Dr 35453 205-759-3613
Eric Hines, prin. Fax 759-3798

Tuscaloosa County SD
Supt. — See Tuscaloosa
Cottondale ES 400/K-5
2301 Cottondale Ln 35453 205-342-2642
Cindy Montgomery, prin. Fax 247-4168
Davis - Emerson MS 400/6-8
1500 Bulldog Blvd 35453 205-342-2750
Marlon Murray, prin. Fax 247-4169

Tuscaloosa Christian S 300/PK-12
1601 Prude Mill Rd 35453 205-553-4303
Dan Lancaster, prin. Fax 553-4259

Cottonwood, Houston, Pop. 1,266
Houston County SD
Supt. — See Dothan
Cottonwood S 700/K-12
663 Houston St 36320 334-691-2587
Paul Strange, prin. Fax 691-4200

Cropwell, Saint Clair
Pell City CSD
Supt. — See Pell City
Coosa Valley ES 300/K-4
3609 Martin St S 35054 205-338-7713
Jennifer Hannah, prin. Fax 338-0694

Crossville, DeKalb, Pop. 1,821
De Kalb County SD
Supt. — See Rainsville
Crossville ES 600/K-3
63 Justice St 35962 256-528-7859
Philip Bryan, prin. Fax 528-5407
Crossville MS 700/4-6
63 Justice St 35962 256-528-7859
Dewey DeBoard, prin. Fax 528-5407

Cuba, Sumter, Pop. 342
Sumter County SD
Supt. — See Livingston
Kinterbish JHS 200/K-8
5586 Kinterbish 10 36907 205-392-4559
Dr. Cynthia Jemison, prin. Fax 392-4566

Cullman, Cullman, Pop. 14,641
Cullman CSD 3,100/PK-12
301 1st St NE 35055 256-734-2233
Dr. Susan Patterson, supt. Fax 737-9621
www.cullmancats.net
Cullman City PS 500/PK-1
900 Hoehn Dr 35055 256-775-0234
Tricia Culpepper, prin. Fax 775-0238
Cullman MS 500/7-8
800 2nd Ave NE 35055 256-734-7959
Patrick Hill, prin. Fax 734-7711
East ES 600/2-6
608 4th Ave SE 35055 256-734-2232
David Wiggins, prin. Fax 734-2241
West ES 600/2-6
303 Rosemont Ave SW 35055 256-734-4271
Dr. Andrew Page, prin. Fax 775-5980

Cullman County SD 9,500/PK-12
PO Box 1590 35056 256-734-2933
Shane Barnette, supt. Fax 736-2486
www.ccboe.org
Fairview ES 600/K-5
700 Wesley Ave N 35058 256-796-6304
Marty Hardman, prin. Fax 796-0066
Fairview MS 300/6-8
841 Welcome Rd 35058 256-796-0883
Trina Walker, prin. Fax 796-0885
Good Hope ES 300/3-5
204 Good Hope School Rd 35057 256-734-3824
Susan Melton, prin. Fax 734-4985
Good Hope MS 400/6-8
216 Good Hope School Rd 35057 256-734-9600
Alan Dunkling, prin. Fax 734-9704
Good Hope PS 300/K-2
661 County Road 447 35057 256-734-0109
Tonya Cupp, prin. Fax 737-0680
Welti ES 200/PK-5
8545 County Road 747 35055 256-734-4956
Gina Webb, prin. Fax 734-4855
West Point ES 500/K-3
4300 County Road 1141 35057 256-775-6178
Angie Yarbrough, prin. Fax 734-5381
West Point IS 300/4-5
4541 County Road 1141 35057 256-734-8019
Michael Jones, prin. Fax 739-0749
Other Schools – See Baileyton, Bremen, Hanceville, Holly Pond, Logan, Vinemont

---

Sacred Heart S 100/PK-6
112 2nd Ave SE 35055 256-734-4563
Greg Hughes, prin. Fax 734-5882
St. Paul Lutheran S 100/PK-6
510 3rd Ave SE 35055 256-734-6580
Annette Creest, prin. Fax 841-1993

Dadeville, Tallapoosa, Pop. 3,198
Tallapoosa County SD 3,100/PK-12
679 E Columbus St 36853 256-825-0746
Joseph Windle, supt. Fax 825-8224
www.tallapoosak12.org
Dadeville ES 600/PK-6
670 E Columbus St 36853 256-825-6811
Dr. Chris Dark, prin. Fax 825-4068
Other Schools – See New Site, Notasulga

Daleville, Dale, Pop. 5,083
Daleville CSD 1,100/PK-12
626 N Daleville Ave 36322 334-598-2456
Dr. Diane Flournoy, supt. Fax 598-9006
www.daleville.k12.al.us
Windham ES 600/PK-6
626 N Daleville Ave 36322 334-598-4466
Christopher Mitten, prin. Fax 598-4467

Danville, Morgan
Lawrence County SD
Supt. — See Moulton
Speake ES 200/PK-6
7323 Highway 36 35619 256-905-0894
Tina Blankenship, prin. Fax 974-1404

Morgan County SD
Supt. — See Decatur
Danville MS 400/5-8
5933 Highway 36 W 35619 256-773-7723
Gary Walker, prin. Fax 773-7708
Danville-Neel ES 500/PK-4
8688 Danville Rd 35619 256-773-7182
Tara Murphy, prin. Fax 773-7718

Daphne, Baldwin, Pop. 21,279
Baldwin County SD
Supt. — See Bay Minette
Carroll IS 500/4-6
1000 Main St 36526 251-626-0277
Dana Horst Bottoms, prin. Fax 626-0488
Daphne East ES 1,000/K-6
26651 County Road 13 36526 251-626-1663
Mark Doherty, prin. Fax 625-2616
Daphne ES 600/K-3
2307 Main St 36526 251-626-2424
Jonathan Ellis, prin. Fax 626-6054
Daphne MS 600/7-8
1 Jody Davis Cir 36526 251-626-2845
Tiffany Irby, prin. Fax 626-0025

Bayside Academy 800/PK-12
303 Dryer Ave 36526 251-338-6300
Michael Papa, head sch Fax 338-6310
Christ the King S 500/PK-8
PO Box 1890 36526 251-626-1692
Maxwell Crain, prin. Fax 626-9976
Community S 100/PK-7
29964 Saint Basil St 36526 251-517-5590
Melanie Daw, admin.

Dauphin Island, Mobile, Pop. 1,225
Mobile County SD
Supt. — See Mobile
Dauphin Island ES 100/K-5
1501 Bienville Blvd 36528 251-861-3864
Diane Allgood, prin. Fax 861-8142

Deatsville, Elmore, Pop. 1,131
Autauga County SD
Supt. — See Prattville
Pine Level ES 900/K-5
2040 US Highway 31 N 36022 334-358-2658
Christen Harry, prin. Fax 358-2309

Elmore County SD
Supt. — See Wetumpka
Holtville ES 700/PK-4
287 Whatley Dr 36022 334-569-2925
Chris Holley, prin. Fax 569-1016
Holtville MS 500/5-8
655 Bulldog Ln 36022 334-569-1596
Lee Jackson, prin. Fax 569-3258

Decatur, Morgan, Pop. 54,679
Decatur CSD 8,500/PK-12
302 4th Ave NE 35601 256-552-3000
Dr. Michael Douglas, supt. Fax 552-3981
www.dcs.edu
Austinville ES 400/PK-5
2320 Clara Ave SW 35601 256-552-3050
Fax 552-4688
Banks-Caddell ES 500/PK-5
211 Gordon Dr SE 35601 256-552-3040
David McCollum, prin. Fax 552-4653
Brookhaven MS 400/6-8
1302 5th Ave SW 35601 256-552-3045
Anita Clarke, prin. Fax 552-3047
Cedar Ridge MS 900/6-8
2715 Danville Rd SW 35603 256-552-4622
Demond Garth, prin. Fax 552-4623
Chestnut Grove ES 400/PK-5
3205 Cedarhurst Dr SW 35603 256-552-3092
Luke Bergeson, prin. Fax 552-4646
Davis ES 200/PK-2
417 Monroe Dr NW 35601 256-552-3025
Dr. Aundrea Hanson, prin. Fax 552-4689
Eastwood ES 200/PK-5
1802 26th Ave SE 35601 256-552-3043
Beth Hales, prin. Fax 552-4696
Harris ES 400/PK-5
1922 McAuliffe Dr SW 35603 256-552-3096
Derrick Aikerson, prin. Fax 552-4659
Jackson ES 300/K-5
1950 Park St SE 35601 256-552-3031
Tamara Caudle, prin. Fax 552-4693
Nungester ES 400/PK-5
726 Tammy St SW 35603 256-552-3079
Shannon McCaskey, prin. Fax 552-4658
Oak Park MS 700/6-8
1218 16th Ave SE 35601 256-552-3035
Dr. Rachel Poovey, prin. Fax 552-3082
Sheffield ES 400/3-5
801 Wilson St NW 35601 256-552-3056
David Kross, prin. Fax 552-4690
Somerville Road ES 500/PK-5
1302 5th Ave SE 35601 256-552-3033
Dr. Theodoria Jackson, prin. Fax 552-4692
West Decatur ES 300/PK-5
708 Memorial Dr SW 35601 256-552-3027
Allen Malone, prin. Fax 552-4694
Woodmeade ES 300/PK-5
1400 19th Ave SW 35601 256-552-3023
Angie Whittington, prin. Fax 552-4695

Morgan County SD 7,800/PK-12
235 Highway 67 S 35603 256-309-2100
Bill Hopkins, supt. Fax 309-2180
www.morgank12.org
Priceville ES 700/K-5
438 Cave Spring Rd 35603 256-341-9202
Tanya McCain, prin. Fax 341-0776
Priceville JHS 400/6-8
317 Highway 67 S 35603 256-355-5104
Mary Speegle, prin. Fax 355-5932
Other Schools – See Danville, Eva, Falkville, Hartselle, Laceys Spring, Somerville, Trinity

---

Decatur Heritage Christian Academy 400/K-12
PO Box 5659 35601 256-351-4275
Scott Mayo, hdmstr. Fax 355-4738
St. Ann S 100/PK-8
3910A Spring Ave SW 35603 256-353-6543
David Weimer, prin. Fax 353-0705

Demopolis, Marengo, Pop. 7,436
Demopolis CSD 2,200/PK-12
PO Box 759 36732 334-289-1670
Kyle Kallhoff, supt. Fax 289-1689
www.dcsedu.com
Demopolis MS 600/6-8
300 E Pettus St 36732 334-289-4242
Brandon Kiser, prin. Fax 289-2670
Jones ES 500/3-5
715 E Jackson St 36732 334-289-0426
Leon Clark, prin. Fax 289-8456
Westside ES 500/PK-2
1720 Mauvilla Dr 36732 334-289-0377
Roshanda Jackson, prin. Fax 289-0337

Dixons Mills, Marengo
Marengo County SD
Supt. — See Linden
Marengo S 200/PK-12
212 Panther Dr 36736 334-992-2395
David Miller, prin. Fax 992-2197

Dora, Walker, Pop. 1,996
Jefferson County SD
Supt. — See Birmingham
Bagley ES 300/K-4
8581 Tate Mill Rd 35062 205-379-2500
Phil Ackerman, prin. Fax 379-2545

Dothan, Houston, Pop. 64,426
Dothan CSD 9,400/PK-12
500 Dusy St 36301 334-793-1397
Todd Weeks, supt. Fax 794-2034
www.dothan.k12.al.us
Beverlye Magnet MS 500/6-8
1025 S Beverlye Rd 36301 334-794-1432
Maria Johnson, prin. Fax 792-0886
Carver Magnet MS 600/6-8
1001 Webb Rd 36303 334-794-1440
Dr. Donnie Chambers, prin. Fax 794-1587
Cloverdale ES 300/PK-5
303 Rollins Ave 36301 334-794-1487
Christy Martin, prin. Fax 794-7451
Faine ES 400/PK-5
1901 Stringer St 36303 334-794-1455
Debra Wright, prin. Fax 671-7983
Girard ES 300/PK-5
522 Girard Ave 36303 334-794-1467
Glenda Sanders, prin. Fax 794-1468
Girard MS 500/6-8
600 Girard Ave 36303 334-794-1426
Darius McKay, prin. Fax 794-6373
Grandview ES 400/K-5
900 Sixth Ave 36301 334-794-1483
Tamika Fleming, prin. Fax 793-9012
Heard Magnet ES 400/K-5
201 Daniel Cir 36301 334-794-1471
Jeffrey Hatfield, prin. Fax 792-6971
Hidden Lake ES 600/K-5
1475 Prevatt Rd 36301 334-794-1491
Vanessa Gunn, prin. Fax 702-2997
Highlands ES 600/K-5
1400 S Brannon Stand Rd 36305 334-794-1459
Vicki Davis, prin. Fax 671-8163
Honeysuckle MS 600/6-8
1665 Honeysuckle Rd 36305 334-794-1420
Jeffrey Torrence, prin. Fax 678-6546
Kelly Springs ES 400/PK-5
1124 Kelly Springs Rd 36303 334-983-6565
Wanda Dismukes, prin. Fax 983-5822
Montana Magnet ES 500/K-5
1001 Montana St 36303 334-794-1475
Sue Clark, prin. Fax 794-1477
Pre-School / Head Start Center 100/PK-PK
900 W Powell St 36303 334-794-1447
Y. Denise Vincent, dir. Fax 712-9379
Selma Street ES 600/K-5
1501 W Selma St 36301 334-794-1463
Dionne Blair, prin. Fax 794-1464
Slingluff ES 400/K-5
4130 Westgate Pkwy 36303 334-794-1479
Christina Johnson, prin. Fax 793-1180
Houston County SD 6,300/PK-12
404 W Washington St 36301 334-792-8331
David Sewell, supt. Fax 792-1016
hcboe.us
Rehobeth ES 1,000/PK-5
5631 County Road 203 36301 334-677-3838
Greg Yance, prin. Fax 677-5947
Rehobeth MS 500/6-8
5631 County Road 203 36301 334-677-5153
Derrick Morris, prin. Fax 677-5947
Other Schools – See Ashford, Cottonwood, Newton, Webb

Bethel Christian Academy 50/K-8
3257 E Cottonwood Rd 36301 334-671-1567
Donna Skinner, prin. Fax 793-9581
Dothan Montessori S 50/PK-3
PO Box 5921 36302 334-671-7170
Emmanuel Christian S 500/PK-12
178 Earline Rd 36305 334-792-0935
Mark Redmond, admin. Fax 702-7410
Houston Academy 600/PK-12
901 Buena Vista Dr 36303 334-794-4106
Dr. Scott Phillipps, hdmstr. Fax 793-4053
Northside Methodist Academy 400/PK-12
2600 Redmond Rd 36303 334-794-7273
Providence Christian S 700/1-12
4847 Murphy Mill Rd 36303 334-702-8933
Emory Latta, head sch Fax 702-0700
Westgate Christian S 100/PK-8
617 Westgate Pkwy 36303 334-793-3399

Double Springs, Winston, Pop. 1,073
Winston County SD 2,600/PK-12
PO Box 9 35553 205-489-5018
Gregory Pendley, supt. Fax 717-3391
www.winstonk12.org
Double Springs ES 400/PK-4
PO Box 550 35553 205-489-2190
Keith Hood, prin. Fax 717-3392
Double Springs MS 300/5-8
PO Box 669 35553 205-489-3813
Ben Aderholt, prin. Fax 717-3392
Other Schools – See Addison, Arley, Lynn

Douglas, Marshall, Pop. 724
Marshall County SD
Supt. — See Guntersville
Douglas ES 500/3-5
PO Box 299 35964 256-593-4420
Wallace Young, prin. Fax 593-4423
Douglas MS 500/6-8
PO Box 269 35964 256-593-1240
Rita Walker, prin. Fax 593-1259

Duncanville, Tuscaloosa
Tuscaloosa County SD
Supt. — See Tuscaloosa
Duncanville MS 500/6-8
11205 Eagle Pkwy 35456 205-342-2830
Darrell Williams, prin. Fax 759-1998
Maxwell ES 500/K-5
11370 Monticello Dr 35456 205-342-2656
Ira Sullivan, prin. Fax 366-8625

Dutton, Jackson, Pop. 304
Jackson County SD
Supt. — See Scottsboro
Dutton S 200/K-8
PO Box 38 35744 256-228-4265
Craig Robbins, prin. Fax 228-3210

East Brewton, Escambia, Pop. 2,446
Escambia County SD
Supt. — See Brewton
Neal ES 600/K-4
701 Williamson St 36426 251-867-7674
Eric Tyrone Andrews, prin. Fax 809-2951
Neal MS 400/5-8
703 Williamson St 36426 251-867-5035
Dr. Laura Leigh Rambach, prin. Fax 867-5051

Eclectic, Elmore, Pop. 979
Elmore County SD
Supt. — See Wetumpka
Eclectic ES 600/K-4
35 Harden St 36024 334-541-2291
Timothy Turley, prin. Fax 541-4465
Eclectic MS 500/5-8
170 S Ann St 36024 334-541-2131
Blair Andress, prin. Fax 541-3556

Eight Mile, See Prichard
Mobile County SD
Supt. — See Mobile
Collins-Rhodes ES 700/PK-5
5110 Saint Stephens Rd 36613 251-221-1226
Veronica Coleman, prin. Fax 221-1732
Indian Springs ES 400/PK-5
4550 Highpoint Blvd 36613 251-221-1436
Teffine Petro, prin. Fax 221-1438

Elba, Coffee, Pop. 3,889
Coffee County SD 2,000/PK-12
400 Reddoch Hill Rd 36323 334-897-5016
Terry Weeks, supt. Fax 897-6207
www.coffeecountyschools.org
Other Schools – See Jack, Kinston, New Brockton

Elba CSD 700/K-12
131 Tiger Dr 36323 334-897-2801
Dennis Coe, supt. Fax 897-5601
www.elbaed.com
Elba ES 400/K-6
145 Tiger Dr 36323 334-897-2814
Debra Strickland, prin. Fax 897-2839

Elberta, Baldwin, Pop. 1,467
Baldwin County SD
Supt. — See Bay Minette

Elberta ES 500/PK-3
25820 US Highway 98 36530 251-986-5888
Jenny Breazeale, prin. Fax 986-3664

St. Benedict S 200/PK-8
12786 Illinois St 36530 251-986-8143
Leslie Mapp, prin. Fax 986-8144

Elkmont, Limestone, Pop. 433
Limestone County SD
Supt. — See Athens
Elkmont ES, 26010 Vaughn St 35620 400/K-5
Haley James, prin. 256-732-4291

Elmore, Elmore

Edgewood Academy 300/PK-12
PO Box 160 36025 334-567-5102
Clint Welch, head sch Fax 567-8316

Enterprise, Coffee, Pop. 25,851
Enterprise CSD 5,600/PK-12
PO Box 311790 36331 334-347-9531
Gregory S. Faught, supt. Fax 347-5102
www.enterpriseschools.net/
Coppinville JHS 500/7-8
301 N Ouida St 36330 334-347-2215
David West, prin. Fax 347-7895
Dauphin JHS 300/7-8
1271 Dauphin Street Ext 36330 334-347-1141
Judy Thomas, prin. Fax 347-0845
Enterprise Early Education Center 500/PK-K
6500 Boll Weevil Cir 36330 334-393-9542
Waller Martin, prin. Fax 393-9547
Harrand Creek ES 400/1-6
216 Morgan Ln 36330 334-347-5383
Ronnie Retherford, prin. Fax 347-0463
Hillcrest ES 700/1-6
400 E Watts St 36330 334-347-6858
Melissa Layton, prin. Fax 347-1322
Holly Hill ES 600/1-6
201 Pineview Dr 36330 334-347-9700
Christie Mitten, prin. Fax 347-0782
Pinedale ES 400/1-6
207 Plaza Dr 36330 334-347-5460
Twyla Pipkin, prin. Fax 347-0347
Rucker Boulevard ES 500/1-6
209 Regency Dr 36330 334-347-3535
Sheree Hardrick, prin. Fax 347-0610

St. John Catholic Montessori S 50/PK-PK
123 Heath St 36330 334-347-0413
Sandra Pellissier, dir. Fax 347-0849
Wiregrass Christian Academy 100/PK-6
209 W College St 36330 334-393-8972

Eufaula, Barbour, Pop. 13,021
Eufaula CSD 2,900/PK-12
333 State Docks Rd 36027 334-687-1100
Dr. Elisabeth Davis, supt. Fax 687-1150
www.eufaulacityschools.org
Eufaula Early Learning Center 200/PK-PK
333 State Docks Rd 36027 334-687-1100
Deltonya Warren, dir. Fax 687-1150
Eufaula ES 600/3-5
422 Sanford Ave 36027 334-687-1134
Jina Sanders, prin. Fax 687-1136
Eufaula PS 700/K-2
520 Pump Station Rd 36027 334-687-1140
Emily Jackson, prin. Fax 687-1142
Moorer MS 600/6-8
101 Saint Francis Rd 36027 334-687-1130
Jessica Morton, prin. Fax 687-1138

Lakeside S 300/PK-12
1020 Lake Dr 36027 334-687-5748

Eutaw, Greene, Pop. 2,918
Greene County SD 900/PK-12
220 Main St 35462 205-372-3161
Dr. James Carter, supt. Fax 372-3247
www.greene.k12.al.us
Brown MS 100/4-6
623 Mesopotamia St 35462 205-372-3269
Frederick Square, prin. Fax 372-4828
Brown MS 100/7-8
623 Mesopotamia St 35462 205-372-9021
Barbara Martin, prin. Fax 372-4828
Eutaw PS 300/PK-3
212 Eutaw Ave 35462 205-372-1051
Sharon Jennings, prin. Fax 372-1050

Eva, Morgan, Pop. 505
Morgan County SD
Supt. — See Decatur
Eva S 400/K-8
20 School Rd 35621 256-796-5141
David Estes, prin. Fax 796-7108

Evergreen, Conecuh, Pop. 3,925
Conecuh County SD 1,600/PK-12
1455 Ted Bates Rd 36401 251-578-1752
Zickeyous Byrd Ed.D., supt. Fax 578-7061
www.conecuh.k12.al.us
Evergreen ES 500/PK-5
821 W Front St 36401 251-578-2576
Peggy Grant, prin. Fax 578-7083
Lyeffion S 200/PK-8
7575 Highway 83 36401 251-578-2800
Rita Nettles-Armstrong, prin. Fax 578-5513
Marshall MS 200/6-8
428 Reynolds Ave 36401 251-578-2866
LaTonya Gill, prin. Fax 578-7067
Other Schools – See Castleberry, Repton

Sparta Academy 200/PK-12
300 Pierce St 36401 251-578-2852

Excel, Monroe, Pop. 708
Monroe County SD
Supt. — See Monroeville
Excel S 1,100/PK-12
PO Box 429 36439 251-765-2351
Marty Hanks, prin. Fax 765-9153

Fairfield, Jefferson, Pop. 11,062
Fairfield CSD 1,900/K-12
6405 Avenue D 35064 205-783-6850
Walter Curry Ph.D., supt. Fax 783-6805
fairfield.cyberschool.com
Donald ES 300/K-6
715 Valley Rd 35064 205-783-6823
Corvetta Vann, prin. Fax 783-6825
Forest Hills Community Development Ctr 300/7-8
610 Valley Rd 35064 205-264-9655
Shun Williams, prin.
Glen Oaks ES 400/K-6
1301 Highland Dr 35064 205-783-6837
David Bennett, prin. Fax 783-6763
Robinson ES 300/K-6
301 61st St 35064 205-783-6878
Tracy Ford, prin. Fax 783-6757

Mt. Pilgrim Christian Academy 50/PK-6
6746 Grasselli Rd 35064 205-780-5096
Eleashia Roper, prin. Fax 780-5098
Restoration Academy 300/K-12
PO Box 30 35064 205-785-8805
Brian Goessling, prin. Fax 785-8809

Fairhope, Baldwin, Pop. 15,206
Baldwin County SD
Supt. — See Bay Minette
Fairhope ES 700/1-3
408 N Section St 36532 251-928-8400
Julie Pierce, prin. Fax 928-9709
Fairhope IS 800/4-6
2 N Bishop Rd 36532 251-928-7841
Carol Broughton, prin. Fax 990-2227
Fairhope MS 800/7-8
2 Pirate Dr 36532 251-928-2573
Angie Hall, prin. Fax 990-0403
Newton ES 600/K-6
9761 County Road 32 36532 251-990-3858
Patrice Krueger, prin. Fax 990-9706

Bayshore Christian S 200/K-12
23050 US Highway 98 36532 251-929-0011

Falkville, Morgan, Pop. 1,257
Morgan County SD
Supt. — See Decatur
Falkville ES 400/K-5
72 Clark Dr 35622 256-784-5249
Brandon Bryan, prin. Fax 784-9070

Fayette, Fayette, Pop. 4,573
Fayette County SD 2,400/PK-12
PO Box 686 35555 205-932-4611
Jim Burkhalter, supt. Fax 932-7246
www.fayette.k12.al.us
Fayette ES 500/K-4
509 2nd St NE 35555 205-932-3161
Dr. Alicia Nalls, prin. Fax 932-5285
Fayette MS 500/5-8
418 3rd Ave NE 35555 205-932-7660
Rodney Hannah, prin. Fax 932-7661
Hubbertville S 400/PK-12
7360 County Road 49 35555 205-487-2845
Tim Dunavant, prin. Fax 487-3375
Other Schools – See Berry

Five Points, Chambers, Pop. 140
Chambers County SD
Supt. — See Lafayette
Five Points S 100/K-8
PO Box 98 36855 334-864-7615
Rhonda Givins, prin. Fax 864-7612

Flat Rock, Jackson
Jackson County SD
Supt. — See Scottsboro
Flat Rock S 200/K-8
788 County Road 326 35966 256-632-2323
Scotty Overdear, prin. Fax 632-6317

Flomaton, Escambia, Pop. 1,423
Escambia County SD
Supt. — See Brewton
Flomaton ES 400/K-8
1634 Poplar St 36441 251-296-5238
Diane Holmes, prin. Fax 296-3060

Florence, Lauderdale, Pop. 38,649
Florence CSD 4,400/PK-12
PO Box 10 35631 256-768-3000
Dr. Jimmy Shaw Ed.D., supt. Fax 768-3009
www.florencek12.org/
Florence MS 700/7-8
1603 Appleby Blvd 35630 256-768-3100
Dr. Aimee Rainey, prin. Fax 768-3105
Forest Hills ES 800/PK-4
101 Stovall Dr 35633 256-768-2500
Dr. Michael South, prin. Fax 768-2505
Harlan ES 500/K-4
2233 McBurney Dr 35630 256-768-2700
Janice Jackson, prin. Fax 768-2705
Hibbett S 700/5-6
1601 Appleby Blvd 35630 256-768-2800
Dr. Cindy Jackson, prin. Fax 768-2805
Weeden ES 500/K-4
400 Baldwin St 35630 256-768-2900
Dr. Joey Dawson, prin. Fax 768-2905

Lauderdale County SD 8,600/PK-12
PO Box 278 35631 256-760-1300
Dr. Jonathan Hatton, supt. Fax 766-5815
www.lcschools.org
Central S 1,400/PK-12
3000 County Road 200 35633 256-764-2903
Duane Keener, prin. Fax 764-5409
Kilby Laboratory ES 100/K-6
PO Box 5035 35632 256-765-4303
Dr. Chris James, prin. Fax 765-4167
Rogers S 1,200/PK-12
300 Rogers Ln 35634 256-757-3106
David Matthews, prin. Fax 757-9625
Underwood ES 400/K-6
4725 Highway 157 35633 256-764-8939
Kevin Moore, prin. Fax 766-5044
Wilson S 1,300/PK-12
7601 Highway 17 35634 256-764-8470
Gary Horton, prin. Fax 764-1304
Other Schools – See Killen, Lexington, Rogersville, Waterloo

Mars Hill Bible S 600/PK-12
698 Cox Creek Pkwy 35630 256-767-1203
Dexter Rutherford, pres. Fax 767-6304
Riverhill S 100/PK-6
2826 County Road 30 35634 256-764-8200
St. Joseph S 200/PK-8
115 Plum St 35630 256-766-1923
Kelley Dewberry, prin. Fax 766-1713
Shoals Christian S 200/PK-12
301 Heathrow Dr 35633 256-767-7070
Felicia Jones, head sch Fax 766-5677

Foley, Baldwin, Pop. 14,389
Baldwin County SD
Supt. — See Bay Minette
Foley ES 1,400/PK-4
450 N Cedar St 36535 251-943-8861
Danny McDuffie, prin. Fax 943-1732
Foley IS 400/5-6
2000 S Cedar St 36535 251-943-1244
Shannon McCurdy, prin. Fax 970-2004
Foley MS 700/7-8
201 N Pine St 36535 251-943-1255
Danny McDuffie, prin. Fax 943-8221
Magnolia ES 700/PK-6
1 Jaguar Loop 36535 251-965-6200
Debra Phillips, prin. Fax 965-6221

Snook Christian Academy 100/PK-12
18930 County Road 28 36535 251-989-2333

Fort Deposit, Lowndes, Pop. 1,336
Lowndes County SD
Supt. — See Hayneville
Fort Deposit ES 300/K-5
PO Box 250 36032 334-227-8704
Audra Stinson, prin. Fax 227-4735
Lowndes County MS 200/6-8
PO Box 393 36032 334-227-4206
Toriano Baker, prin. Fax 227-4125

Fort Mitchell, Russell
Russell County SD
Supt. — See Phenix City
Mt. Olive IS 500/3-5
454 Highway 165 36856 334-321-2235
Kimberly Core, prin. Fax 855-9483

St. Joseph Child Development Center PK-PK
1444 Highway 165 36856 334-855-4675
Silke Brede, dir. Fax 855-3115

Fort Payne, DeKalb, Pop. 13,756
De Kalb County SD
Supt. — See Rainsville
Ruhuma S 200/K-8
3371 County Road 81 35967 256-845-3377
Jordan Phillips, prin. Fax 845-3377

Fort Payne CSD 3,100/PK-12
PO Box 681029 35968 256-845-0915
James Cunningham, supt. Fax 845-4962
www.ftpayk12.org
Fort Payne MS 900/5-8
4910 Martin Ave NE 35967 256-845-7501
Shane Byrd, prin. Fax 845-8292
Williams Avenue ES 500/3-4
1700 Williams Ave NE 35967 256-845-0626
Heath Shaddix, prin. Fax 845-0147
Wills Valley ES 900/PK-2
4111 Williams Ave NE 35967 256-845-3201
Sally Wheat, prin. Fax 845-2909

Fosters, Tuscaloosa
Tuscaloosa County SD
Supt. — See Tuscaloosa
Myrtlewood ES 300/K-5
14701 Gainsville Rd 35463 205-342-2658
Michael Tilford, prin. Fax 247-4185

Fruitdale, Washington, Pop. 184
Washington County SD
Supt. — See Chatom
Fruitdale S 400/K-12
PO Box 448 36539 251-827-6655
Curtis Stagner, prin. Fax 827-6573

Fruithurst, Cleburne, Pop. 283
Cleburne County SD
Supt. — See Heflin
Fruithurst ES 300/PK-6
222 School St 36262 256-579-2232
Dr. Christy Hiett, prin. Fax 579-5094

Fultondale, Jefferson, Pop. 8,247
Jefferson County SD
Supt. — See Birmingham

Fultondale ES 800/K-6
950 Central Ave 35068 205-379-3450
Frances Finney, prin. Fax 379-3495

Fyffe, DeKalb, Pop. 992
De Kalb County SD
Supt. — See Rainsville
Fyffe S 1,000/K-12
PO Box 7 35971 256-623-2116
Ricky Bryant, prin. Fax 623-4388

Gadsden, Etowah, Pop. 36,211
Etowah County SD 9,100/PK-12
3200 W Meighan Blvd 35904 256-549-7560
Dr. Alan Cosby, supt. Fax 549-7589
www.ecboe.org
Gaston S 600/K-12
4550 US Highway 411 35901 256-547-0047
Tammy George, prin. Fax 543-7124
Highland ES 200/PK-6
3156 Tabor Rd 35904 256-546-7409
Lori Moss, prin. Fax 546-7158
Hokes Bluff ES 600/K-5
5375 Main St 35903 256-492-5571
Charles Gardner, prin. Fax 492-2513
Hokes Bluff MS 300/6-8
3121 Appalachian Hwy 35903 256-492-1963
Greg Watkins, prin. Fax 492-1950
Other Schools – See , Altoona, Attalla, Boaz, Glencoe, Rainbow City, Southside

Gadsden CSD 5,900/K-12
PO Box 184 35902 256-543-3512
Dr. Ed Miller, supt. Fax 549-2950
www.gcs.k12.al.us
Adams ES 300/K-5
919 Raley St 35903 256-492-4952
Tomasina Smitherman, prin. Fax 492-3008
Brown ES 400/K-5
1231 Alcott Rd 35901 256-546-0011
Katie Holland, prin. Fax 546-6855
Donehoo ES 300/K-5
1109 E Broad St 35903 256-546-3604
Hector Baeza, prin. Fax 547-9021
Floyd ES 400/K-5
601 Black Creek Rd 35904 256-546-0836
Nicole Chester, prin. Fax 546-9955
Gadsden MS 500/6-8
612 Tracy St 35901 256-547-6341
Joel Gulledge, prin. Fax 547-6323
Litchfield MS 200/6-8
1109 Hoke St 35903 256-492-6793
Dr. Charlie Parker, prin. Fax 492-4010
Mitchell ES 400/K-5
1501 Noccalula Rd 35904 256-546-2711
Roger Wilkinson, prin. Fax 549-2970
Sansom MS 500/6-8
2210 W Meighan Blvd 35904 256-546-4992
Kevin Young, prin. Fax 543-1060
Striplin ES 300/K-5
600 Cleveland Ave 35901 256-546-8616
Delsia Malone, prin. Fax 543-7905
Thompson ES 200/K-5
236 Goldenrod Ave 35901 256-546-7011
Patrice Maxwell, prin. Fax 546-7011
Walnut Park ES 300/K-5
3200 Walnut St 35904 256-546-4665
Kristen Woods, prin. Fax 546-9703

Coosa Christian S 300/PK-12
2736 Wills Creek Rd 35904 256-547-1841
St. James S 100/PK-8
700 Albert Rains Blvd 35901 256-546-0132
Michele Adams, prin. Fax 546-0134

Gardendale, Jefferson, Pop. 13,766
Jefferson County SD
Supt. — See Birmingham
Bragg MS 900/6-8
840 Ash Ave 35071 205-379-2600
Larry Robertson, prin. Fax 379-2645
Gardendale ES 900/K-5
860 Bauers Ln 35071 205-379-3550
Dr. Charles Yeager, prin. Fax 379-3595
Snow Rogers ES 200/K-5
2636 Snow Rogers Rd 35071 205-379-5400
Kathy Murray, prin. Fax 379-5445

Gaylesville, Cherokee, Pop. 143
Cherokee County SD
Supt. — See Centre
Gaylesville S 400/PK-12
760 Trojan Way 35973 256-422-3401
Scott Hays, prin. Fax 422-3165

Geneva, Geneva, Pop. 4,382
Geneva CSD 1,300/K-12
511 Panther Dr 36340 334-684-1090
Rhonda Stringham, supt. Fax 684-3128
www.genevacity.schoolinsites.com
Geneva MS 300/6-8
501 Panther Dr 36340 334-684-6431
Danny Bedsole, prin. Fax 684-0476
Mulkey ES 700/K-5
800 W Meadow Ave 36340 334-684-2294
Jami Seay, prin. Fax 684-2543

Geneva County SD 2,700/K-12
PO Box 250 36340 334-684-5690
Becky Birdsong, supt. Fax 684-5601
genevacounty.schoolinsites.com/
Other Schools – See Hartford, Samson, Slocomb

Georgiana, Butler, Pop. 1,722
Butler County SD
Supt. — See Greenville
Georgiana S 500/K-12
PO Box 680 36033 334-376-9130
Curtis Moorer, prin. Fax 376-2956

Geraldine, DeKalb, Pop. 882
De Kalb County SD
Supt. — See Rainsville
Geraldine S 1,200/K-12
13011 AL Highway 227 35974 256-659-2142
Steven Street, prin. Fax 659-4296

Gilbertown, Choctaw, Pop. 214
Choctaw County SD
Supt. — See Butler
Southern Choctaw ES 400/K-6
10935 Highway 17 36908 251-843-2461
Jonathan Johnson, prin. Fax 843-4646

Glencoe, Etowah, Pop. 5,099
Etowah County SD
Supt. — See Gadsden
Glencoe MS 300/5-8
809 Lonesome Bend Rd 35905 256-492-5627
Tisha Howell, prin. Fax 492-7076

Gordo, Pickens, Pop. 1,715
Pickens County SD
Supt. — See Carrollton
Gordo ES 700/K-6
535 4th St NW 35466 205-364-8480
Kenneth Holder, prin. Fax 364-0350

Goshen, Pike, Pop. 265
Pike County SD
Supt. — See Troy
Goshen ES 500/PK-6
23 County Road 2238 36035 334-484-3442
Wanda Corley, prin. Fax 484-3009

Grady, Montgomery

South Montgomery County Academy 100/PK-12
PO Box 10 36036 334-562-3235

Grand Bay, Mobile, Pop. 3,617
Mobile County SD
Supt. — See Mobile
Breitling ES 600/PK-5
8350 Grand Bay Wilmer Rd S 36541 251-865-0900
Amy Blake, prin. Fax 865-0902
Castlen ES 500/K-5
9960 School House Rd 36541 251-865-6733
Laura Dickens, prin. Fax 221-1099
Grand Bay MS 800/6-8
12800 Cunningham Rd 36541 251-865-6511
Jacob Butler, prin. Fax 221-2405

Grant, Marshall, Pop. 887
Marshall County SD
Supt. — See Guntersville
Smith DAR ES 400/PK-4
6077 Main St 35747 256-728-2226
Keith Buchanan, prin. Fax 728-8430
Smith DAR MS 400/5-8
6077 Main St 35747 256-728-5950
Tim Isbill, prin. Fax 728-8447

Graysville, Jefferson, Pop. 2,135
Jefferson County SD
Supt. — See Birmingham
Brookville ES 200/K-5
4275 Brookville School Rd 35073 205-379-2700
Paula Allen, prin. Fax 379-2745

Greensboro, Hale, Pop. 2,483
Hale County SD 2,300/PK-12
1115 Powers St 36744 334-624-8836
Osie Pickens, supt. Fax 624-3415
www.halek12.org
Greensboro ES 500/PK-5
1801 South St 36744 334-624-8611
Stephanie Richey, prin. Fax 624-8644
Greensboro MS 300/6-8
620 Carver St 36744 334-624-4005
Anthony Sanders, prin. Fax 624-0308
Other Schools – See Moundville

Southern Academy 200/PK-12
407 College St 36744 334-624-8111

Greenville, Butler, Pop. 8,092
Butler County SD 3,200/K-12
211 School Highlands Rd 36037 334-382-2665
Dr. John Strycker, supt. Fax 382-8607
www.butlerco.k12.al.us
Greenville ES 300/3-4
102 Butler Cir 36037 334-382-7614
Kent McNaughton, prin. Fax 382-7735
Greenville MS 700/5-8
300 Overlook Rd 36037 334-382-3450
Bryant Marlow, prin. Fax 382-0686
Parmer ES 600/K-2
100 Butler Cir 36037 334-382-8720
Jacqueline Thornton, prin. Fax 382-2425
Other Schools – See Georgiana, Mc Kenzie

Fort Dale Academy 400/PK-12
1100 Gamble St 36037 334-382-2606

Grove Hill, Clarke, Pop. 1,558
Clarke County SD 3,100/PK-12
PO Box 936 36451 251-275-3255
Larry Bagley, supt. Fax 275-8061
www.clarkecountyschools.org/
Grove Hill ES 400/PK-4
PO Box 907 36451 251-275-3423
Kathy Spidle, prin. Fax 275-4887
Wilson Hall MS 400/5-8
401 Carter Dr 36451 251-250-2140
Carolyn Taite, prin. Fax 275-4688
Other Schools – See Jackson

Clarke Preparatory S 300/PK-12
20100 Highway 43 36451 251-275-8576
Doug Bradford, hdmstr. Fax 275-8579

Guin, Marion, Pop. 2,339
Marion County SD
Supt. — See Hamilton
Guin ES 300/PK-6
PO Box 10 35563 205-468-3433
Josh Weatherly, prin. Fax 468-3575

Gulf Shores, Baldwin, Pop. 9,533
Baldwin County SD
Supt. — See Bay Minette
Gulf Shores ES 1,100/PK-6
1600 E 3rd St 36542 251-968-7375
Amy Hiller, prin. Fax 968-7217
Gulf Shores MS 500/7-8
450 E 15th Ave 36542 251-968-8719
Kyle McCartney, prin. Fax 967-1577

South Baldwin Christian Academy PK-12
6900 Highway 59 36542 251-968-1230

Guntersville, Marshall, Pop. 8,040
Guntersville CSD 2,000/PK-12
PO Box 129 35976 256-582-3159
Brett Stanton, supt. Fax 582-6158
www.guntersvilleboe.com
Cherokee ES 500/3-5
3300 Highway 79 S 35976 256-582-3908
Julie Ann McCulley, prin. Fax 582-3986
Guntersville ES 400/PK-2
1800 Lusk St 35976 256-582-3364
John Doyle, prin. Fax 582-0892
Guntersville MS 500/6-8
901 Sunset Dr 35976 256-582-5182
Susan Galante, prin. Fax 582-4477

Marshall County SD 5,600/PK-12
12380 US Highway 431 35976 256-582-3171
Dr. Cindy Wigley, supt. Fax 582-3178
www.marshallk12.org
Claysville ES 100/PK-4
140 Claysville School Rd 35976 256-582-4444
Tenna Anderton, prin. Fax 582-4454
Other Schools – See Albertville, Arab, Douglas, Grant, Horton, Union Grove

Gurley, Madison, Pop. 783
Madison County SD
Supt. — See Huntsville
Madison County ES 400/K-8
173 Wood St 35748 256-851-3290
Amy Mason, prin. Fax 851-3291

Hackleburg, Marion, Pop. 1,499
Marion County SD
Supt. — See Hamilton
Hackleburg ES 200/K-6
185 School St 35564 205-935-5156
Donna Palmer, prin. Fax 935-3951

Haleyville, Winston, Pop. 4,111
Haleyville CSD 1,700/PK-12
2011 20th St 35565 205-486-9231
Holly Sutherland, supt. Fax 486-8833
haley-k12.us
Haleyville ES 800/PK-5
2000 20th St 35565 205-486-3405
Christy Bice, prin. Fax 486-8960
Haleyville MS 400/6-8
2014 20th Ave 35565 205-486-9240
Richard Wilcoxson, prin. Fax 486-9244

Hamilton, Marion, Pop. 6,817
Marion County SD 3,500/PK-12
188 Winchester Dr 35570 205-921-3191
Ryan Hollingsworth, supt. Fax 921-7336
www.mcbe.net
Hamilton ES 700/K-4
784 10th Ave SW 35570 205-921-2145
Lynda Hall, prin. Fax 921-9857
Hamilton MS 600/5-8
400 Military St S 35570 205-921-7030
Norman Ballard, prin. Fax 921-3821
Other Schools – See Bear Creek, Brilliant, Guin, Hackleburg

Hampton Cove, Madison
Huntsville CSD
Supt. — See Huntsville
Hampton Cove ES 500/PK-5
261 Old Highway 431 35763 256-428-7180
Autumn Bray, prin. Fax 428-7181
Hampton Cove MS 600/6-8
261 Old Highway 431 Ste B 35763 256-428-8380
Yvette Coley-Smith, prin. Fax 428-8383

Hanceville, Cullman, Pop. 2,928
Cullman County SD
Supt. — See Cullman
Hanceville ES 500/K-5
799 Commercial St SE 35077 256-352-9196
Tony Johnson, prin. Fax 352-9221
Hanceville MS 300/6-8
805 Commercial St SE 35077 256-352-6175
Cynthia Roden, prin. Fax 352-9741

Harpersville, Shelby, Pop. 1,615

Coosa Valley Academy 300/K-12
PO Box 250 35078 205-672-7326
Pamela Lovelady, head sch Fax 672-7329

Hartford, Geneva, Pop. 2,582
Geneva County SD
Supt. — See Geneva
Geneva County ES 400/K-5
819 S 6th Ave 36344 334-588-2923
Ann Stafford, prin. Fax 588-0553
Geneva County MS 200/6-8
301 Lily St 36344 334-588-2943
Leslie Habbard, prin. Fax 588-3650

Hartselle, Morgan, Pop. 14,036
Hartselle CSD 2,600/PK-12
305 College St NE 35640 256-773-5419
Dr. Dee Dee Jones, supt. Fax 773-5433
www.hartselletigers.org
Barkley Bridge ES 300/PK-4
2333 Barkley Bridge Rd SW 35640 256-773-1931
Tina Towres, prin. Fax 751-5659
Burleson ES 400/PK-4
1100 Bethel Rd NE 35640 256-773-2411
Debra Queen, prin. Fax 751-5655
Crestline ES 400/PK-4
600 Crestline Dr SW 35640 256-773-9967
Karissa Lang, prin. Fax 751-5656
Hartselle IS 5-6
130 Petain St SW 35640 256-773-6094
Gaylon Parker, prin. Fax 751-5657
Hartselle JHS 500/7-8
904 Sparkman St SW 35640 256-773-5426
Dr. Robbie Smith, prin. Fax 751-5658

Morgan County SD
Supt. — See Decatur
Sparkman S 300/K-8
72 Plainview St 35640 256-773-6458
Layne Dillard, prin. Fax 751-1256

Harvest, Madison, Pop. 5,123
Limestone County SD
Supt. — See Athens
Creekside ES 1,000/3-5
15983 Sanderson Rd 35749 256-216-8702
Dana Rhinehart, prin. Fax 216-8704
Creekside PS 500/PK-2
16049 Sanderson Rd 35749 256-216-8702
Matt Scott, prin.

Madison County SD
Supt. — See Huntsville
Endeavor ES 700/PK-5
1997 Old Railroad Bed Rd 35749 256-851-4620
Karen Mardis, prin. Fax 851-4621
Harvest ES 700/K-5
8845 Wall Triana Hwy 35749 256-851-4590
Hydi Phelps, prin. Fax 851-4591

Hayden, Blount, Pop. 432
Blount County SD
Supt. — See Oneonta
Hayden ES 400/3-4
4111 State Highway 160 35079 205-647-6578
Anthony Marsh, prin. Fax 647-1386
Hayden MS 600/5-7
310 2nd Ave 35079 205-647-3083
Suzette Johnson, prin. Fax 861-1050
Hayden PS 500/K-2
160 Bracken Ln 35079 205-647-2103
Kimberly Harbison, prin. Fax 969-1130

Hayneville, Lowndes, Pop. 928
Lowndes County SD 1,700/K-12
PO Box 755 36040 334-548-2131
Dr. Daniel Boyd, supt. Fax 548-2161
www.lowndesboe.org/
Central ES 300/K-5
141 Main St 36040 334-563-7319
Tara Green, prin. Fax 563-7347
Hayneville MS 200/6-8
PO Box 307 36040 334-548-2184
Keith Scissum, prin. Fax 548-5237
Jackson-Steele ES 200/K-5
570 Freedom Rd 36040 334-872-0758
Bessie Morgan, prin. Fax 872-2923
Other Schools – See Fort Deposit

Hazel Green, Madison, Pop. 3,538
Madison County SD
Supt. — See Huntsville
Hazel Green ES 800/PK-4
14250 Highway 231 431 N 35750 256-851-4540
Dr. Sheila Jones, prin. Fax 851-4541
Meridianville MS 700/7-8
12975 Highway 231 431 N 35750 256-851-4550
David Manning, prin. Fax 851-4551

Headland, Henry, Pop. 4,460
Henry County SD
Supt. — See Abbeville
Headland ES 800/PK-5
305 Mitchell St 36345 334-585-7080
Carmen Neiswanger, prin. Fax 585-7082

Heflin, Cleburne, Pop. 3,431
Cleburne County SD 2,700/PK-12
141 Davenport Dr 36264 256-463-5624
Chad Young, supt. Fax 463-5709
www.cleburneschools.net
Cleburne County ES 400/PK-4
584 Evans Bridge Rd 36264 256-463-2654
Barbara Johnson, prin. Fax 463-5305
Cleburne County MS 300/5-7
661 Duke Dr 36264 256-463-2405
Sandy Butterworth, prin. Fax 463-2482
Pleasant Grove ES 200/PK-6
9855 Highway 9 36264 256-253-2146
Dr. Adam Dasinger, prin. Fax 253-2147
Other Schools – See Fruithurst, Ranburne

Helena, Shelby, Pop. 16,576
Shelby County SD
Supt. — See Columbiana
Helena ES 800/K-2
187 3rd St 35080 205-682-5540
Mary Cooper, prin. Fax 682-5545
Helena IS 900/3-5
3500 Highway 52 35080 205-682-5520
Kathy Paiml, prin. Fax 682-5525
Helena MS 900/6-8
1299 Hillsboro Pkwy 35080 205-682-5300
Andrew Gunn, prin. Fax 682-5305

Henagar, DeKalb, Pop. 2,306
De Kalb County SD
Supt. — See Rainsville
Henagar S 300/K-8
PO Box 69 35978 256-657-4483
Stevie Green, prin. Fax 657-4481

Higdon, Jackson
Jackson County SD
Supt. — See Scottsboro
North Sand Mountain S 700/K-12
PO Box 129 35979 256-597-2111
Dustin Roden, prin. Fax 597-2505

Highland Home, Crenshaw
Crenshaw County SD
Supt. — See Luverne
Highland Home S 800/PK-12
18434 Montgomery Hwy 36041 334-537-4379
Cliff Maddox, prin. Fax 537-9805

Holly Pond, Cullman, Pop. 794
Cullman County SD
Supt. — See Cullman
Holly Pond ES 400/K-5
120 New Hope Rd 35083 256-796-0046
Karen Sparks, prin. Fax 796-5753
Holly Pond MS 300/6-8
91 Buckner Rd 35083 256-796-5898
Dr. Chuck Gambrill, prin. Fax 796-0680

Hollywood, Jackson, Pop. 967
Jackson County SD
Supt. — See Scottsboro
Hollywood S 100/K-8
6369 County Road 33 35752 256-574-2054
Michael Wilborn, prin. Fax 259-0331

Homewood, Jefferson, Pop. 24,859
Homewood CSD 3,800/K-12
450 Dale Ave 35209 205-870-4203
Dr. Bill Cleveland, supt. Fax 877-4544
www.homewood.k12.al.us
Edgewood ES 800/K-5
901 College Ave 35209 205-423-2400
Dr. Matthew Kiser, prin. Fax 423-2406
Hall Kent ES 600/K-5
213 Hall Ave 35209 205-423-2430
Kiana Coleman, prin. Fax 423-2432
Homewood MS 900/6-8
395 Mecca Ave 35209 205-870-0878
Jimmie Pearson, prin. Fax 877-4573
Shades Cahaba ES 500/K-5
3001 Independence Dr 35209 205-871-1113
John Lowry, prin. Fax 871-1186

Creative Montessori S 200/PK-6
2800 Montessori Way 35209 205-879-3278

Hoover, Jefferson, Pop. 80,440
Hoover CSD 13,900/K-12
2810 Metropolitan Way 35243 205-439-1000
Dr. Kathy Murphy, supt. Fax 439-1001
www.hoover.k12.al.us
Bluff Park ES 600/K-5
569 Park Ave 35226 205-439-2800
Dr. Terry Lamar, prin. Fax 439-2801
Brock's Gap IS 800/5-6
1730 Lake Cyrus Club Dr 35244 205-439-1600
Scott Mitchell, prin. Fax 439-1601
Bumpus MS 900/7-8
6055 Fleming Pkwy 35244 205-439-2200
Dr. Tamala Maddox, prin. Fax 439-2201
Deer Valley ES 800/K-5
4990 Ross Bridge Pkwy 35226 205-439-3300
Dr. Wayne Richardson, prin. Fax 439-3301
Green Valley ES 400/K-5
3200 Old Columbiana Rd 35226 205-439-2500
Amy Gregory, prin. Fax 439-2501
Gwin ES 600/K-5
1580 Patton Chapel Rd 35226 205-439-2600
Dr. Kimberly White, prin. Fax 439-2601
Riverchase ES 600/K-5
1950 Old Montgomery Hwy 35244 205-439-3400
Dr. Alice Turney, prin. Fax 439-3401
Shades Mountain ES 300/K-5
2250 Sumpter St 35226 205-439-3100
Juli Feltham, prin. Fax 439-3101
Simmons MS 800/6-8
1575 Patton Chapel Rd 35226 205-439-2100
Brian Cain, prin. Fax 439-2101
South Shades Crest ES 600/K-4
3770 S Shades Crest Rd 35244 205-439-3000
Kara Scholl, prin. Fax 439-3001
Trace Crossings ES 500/K-4
5454 Learning Ln 35244 205-439-2700
Quincy Collins, prin. Fax 439-2701
Other Schools – See Birmingham

Heritage Christian Academy 400/PK-12
2290 Old Tyler Rd 35226 205-978-6001
Brian Willett, hdmstr. Fax 978-9120
Prince of Peace S 400/PK-8
4650 Preserve Pkwy 35226 205-824-7886
Connie Angstadt, prin. Fax 824-2093

Hope Hull, Montgomery
Montgomery County SD
Supt. — See Montgomery
Pintlala ES 200/K-5
215 Federal Rd 36043 334-288-9523
Charlesetta Robinson, prin. Fax 288-4185

Hooper Academy 400/PK-12
380 Fischer Rd 36043 334-288-5980

Horton, Marshall
Marshall County SD
Supt. — See Guntersville

Sloman PS 500/PK-2
200 Bethleham Rd 35980 256-593-4912
Scott Bonds, prin. Fax 593-4874

Hueytown, Jefferson, Pop. 15,960
Jefferson County SD
Supt. — See Birmingham
Hueytown ES 900/K-5
112 Forest Rd 35023 205-379-4100
Angela Watkins, prin. Fax 379-4145
Hueytown MS 800/6-8
701 Sunrise Blvd 35023 205-379-5150
Chris Anders, prin. Fax 379-5195
North Highland ES 300/K-5
2021 29th Ave N 35023 205-379-4950
Vicki Brasher, prin. Fax 379-4995

Valley Creek Academy 100/K-12
3253 Virginia Dr 35023 205-491-3330
Kim Dobbs, dir.

Huntsville, Madison, Pop. 175,870
Huntsville CSD 20,500/PK-12
PO Box 1256 35807 256-428-6800
Dr. Matt Akin Ed.D., supt. Fax 428-6817
www.huntsvillecityschools.org
Academy for Academics & Arts 500/PK-8
4800 Sparkman Dr NW 35810 256-428-7600
Amelia VanAllen, prin. Fax 428-7601
Academy for Science & Foreign Language 500/PK-8
3221 Mastin Lake Rd NW 35810 256-428-7000
Jeanne Greer, prin. Fax 428-7002
Blossomwood ES 600/PK-6
1321 Woodmont Ave SE 35801 256-428-7020
Jamie Burton, prin. Fax 428-7021
Chaffee ES 400/PK-5
7900 Whittier Rd SW 35802 256-428-7040
Christina Spivey, prin. Fax 428-7047
Challenger ES 600/PK-5
13555 Chaney Thompson Rd SE 35803 256-428-7060
Michele Wallace, prin. Fax 428-7064
Challenger MS 500/6-8
13555 Chaney Thompson Rd SE 35803 256-428-7620
Dr. Dianne Hasty, prin. Fax 428-7621
Chapman P-8 S 300/PK-8
2006 Reuben Dr NE 35811 256-428-7640
Paula Thompson, prin. Fax 428-7641
Dawson ES 400/PK-6
5308 Mastin Lake Rd NW 35810 256-428-7500
Deana Henson, prin. Fax 428-7501
Farley ES 300/PK-5
2900 Green Cove Rd SW 35803 256-428-7160
Towana Smith, prin. Fax 428-7165
Hereford ES K-6
2755 Wilson St 35816 256-428-7440
Mark McCrory, prin. Fax 428-7441
Highlands ES 400/PK-6
2500 Barney Ter NW 35810 256-428-7200
Amber Hall, prin. Fax 428-7201
Huntsville JHS 400/7-8
817 Adams St SE 35801 256-428-7700
Stephanie Wieseman, prin. Fax 428-7701
Jones Valley ES 500/PK-6
4908 Garth Rd SE 35802 256-428-7220
Taunya Smith, prin. Fax 428-7221
King ES 400/PK-5
3112 Meridian St N 35811 256-428-7100
Karen Melillo, prin. Fax 428-7101
Lakewood ES 500/PK-6
3501 Kenwood Dr NW 35810 256-428-7240
Fred Barnes, prin. Fax 428-7241
McDonnell ES 600/PK-5
4010 Binderton Pl SW 35805 256-428-7280
Laura Worshim, prin. Fax 428-7281
McNair JHS 400/7-8
5000 Pulaski Pike 35810 256-428-7660
Chrystapher Walker, prin. Fax 428-7661
Monte Sano ES 200/PK-6
1107 Monte Sano Blvd SE 35801 256-428-7300
Sharon Driggers, prin. Fax 428-7301
Montview ES 300/PK-5
2600 Garvin Rd NW 35810 256-428-7320
Marcia Sutton, prin. Fax 428-7321
Morris ES 600/PK-8
4801 Bob Wallace Ave SW 35805 256-428-7340
Patty Boyd, prin. Fax 428-7341
Mountain Gap P-8 S 700/PK-8
821 Mountain Gap Rd SE 35803 256-428-7720
Heather Bardwell, prin. Fax 428-7721
Providence ES 900/PK-5
10 Chalkstone St NW 35806 256-428-7125
Paul Bonner, prin. Fax 428-7139
Ridgecrest ES 500/PK-5
3505 Cerro Vista St SW 35805 256-428-7380
Denine Matthews, prin. Fax 428-7381
Rolling Hills ES 400/PK-6
2901 Hilltop Ter NW 35810 256-428-7400
Linda Burruss, prin. Fax 428-7401
Weatherly Heights ES 500/PK-5
1307 Cannstatt Dr SE 35803 256-428-7460
Debra West, prin. Fax 428-7468
Whitesburg P-8 S 800/PK-8
107 Sanders Rd SW 35802 256-428-7780
Dr. Bradley Scott Ed.D., prin. Fax 428-7781
Williams ES 500/PK-8
155 Barren Fork Blvd SW 35824 256-428-7540
Melissa Veasy-Lindsey, prin. Fax 428-7541
Other Schools – See Big Cove, Hampton Cove

Madison County SD 18,800/PK-12
PO Box 226 35804 256-852-2557
Matthew Massey, supt. Fax 852-2538
www.mcssk12.org
Central S 800/K-8
990 Ryland Pike 35811 256-851-4670
Alex Hughes, prin. Fax 851-4671

Monrovia ES 500/K-5
1030 Jeff Rd NW 35806 256-851-4570
Renee Headen, prin. Fax 851-4571
Monrovia MS 1,100/6-8
1216 Jeff Rd NW 35806 256-851-4580
Anthony Thompson, prin. Fax 851-4581
Mt. Carmel ES 600/PK-5
335 Homer Nance Rd 35811 256-851-4660
Julie Pool, prin. Fax 851-4661
Riverton ES 400/PK-4
2615 Winchester Rd NE 35811 256-851-4650
Jeff Malone, prin. Fax 851-4651
Riverton IS 800/4-6
399 Homer Nance Rd 35811 256-851-4640
Randy Hill, prin. Fax 851-4641
Other Schools – See Gurley, Harvest, Hazel Green, Madison, Meridianville, New Hope, New Market, Owens Cross Roads, Toney

---

Country Day S 100/PK-8
1699 Old Dry Creek Rd NW 35806 256-837-5266
Grace Lutheran S 100/PK-11
3405 Memorial Pkwy SW 35801 256-881-0553
Joshua Swartz, prin. Fax 881-0563
Holy Family S 200/K-8
2300 Beasley Ave NW 35816 256-539-5221
Dr. Libby Parker, prin. Fax 533-0747
Holy Spirit S 400/PK-8
619 Airport Rd SW 35802 256-881-4852
Beth Mattingly, prin. Fax 881-4904
Islamic Academy of Huntsville 100/PK-8
1645 Sparkman Dr NW 35816 256-722-9838
Montessori S of Huntsville 100/PK-6
15975 Chaney Thompson Rd SE 35803
256-881-3790
Oakwood Adventist Academy 300/K-12
7000 Adventist Blvd NW 35896 256-726-7010
Providence Classical S 300/K-12
605 Clinton Ave E 35801 256-852-8884
Pattie Steward, prin. Fax 852-8884
Randolph S 1,000/K-12
1005 Drake Ave SE 35802 256-799-6100
Jay Rainey, hdmstr. Fax 881-1784
Scruggs Child Development Center & Acad 100/PK-5
3509 Blue Spring Rd NW 35810 256-852-6673
Union Chapel Christian Academy 200/K-6
315 Winchester Rd NE Ste B 35811 256-489-4728
Anita Weathers M.A., prin. Fax 489-9025
Valley Fellowship Christian Academy 200/PK-12
3616 Holmes Ave NW 35816 256-533-5248
Patti Simon M.A., head sch Fax 533-5253
Whitesburg Christian Academy 400/PK-12
7290 Whitesburg Dr SW 35802 256-704-7373
Jerry Reeder, hdmstr. Fax 650-6115

Ider, DeKalb, Pop. 708
De Kalb County SD
Supt. — See Rainsville
Ider S 800/K-12
1064 Crabapple Ln 35981 256-632-2302
Wayne Lyles, prin. Fax 632-3481

Irondale, Jefferson, Pop. 12,191
Jefferson County SD
Supt. — See Birmingham
Grantswood Community ES 400/K-2
5110 Grantswood Rd 35210 205-379-3700
Ann Tillman, prin. Fax 379-3745
Irondale Community ES 400/3-5
225 16th St S 35210 205-379-4200
Ann King, prin. Fax 379-4245

Irvington, Mobile
Mobile County SD
Supt. — See Mobile
Booth ES 600/PK-5
17001 Hurricane Blvd 36544 251-824-1740
Lisa Williams, prin. Fax 221-1055
Dixon ES 500/PK-5
8650 Four Mile Rd 36544 251-824-4314
Glenda Warren, prin. Fax 221-1191
Haskew ES 600/K-5
7001 White Oak Dr 36544 251-221-1850
Catherine Coxe, prin. Fax 221-1855
Saint Elmo ES 400/K-5
8666 McDonald Rd 36544 251-957-6314
Sondra Roberts, prin. Fax 957-3693

Jack, Coffee
Coffee County SD
Supt. — See Elba
Zion Chapel S 800/PK-12
29256 Highway 87 36346 334-897-6275
Vohn Enloe, prin. Fax 897-5136

Jackson, Clarke, Pop. 5,191
Clarke County SD
Supt. — See Grove Hill
Gillmore ES 400/PK-2
133 Mayton Dr 36545 251-246-2525
Shannon Odom, prin. Fax 246-3171
Jackson IS 400/3-5
2950 Highway 43 36545 251-246-1599
Gwendolyn Wheeler, prin. Fax 246-7208
Jackson MS 400/6-8
235 College Ave 36545 251-246-3597
Adam Andrews, prin. Fax 246-6017

Jackson Academy 200/K-12
PO Box 838 36545 251-246-5552
Suzanne Bailey, head sch Fax 246-0202

Jacksonville, Calhoun, Pop. 12,298
Calhoun County SD
Supt. — See Anniston
Pleasant Valley ES 600/K-6
265 Mark Green Rd 36265 256-741-6600
Crystal Sparks, prin. Fax 782-0060

Jacksonville CSD 1,500/PK-12
123 College St SW 36265 256-782-5682
Mark Petersen, supt. Fax 782-5685
www.jcsboe.org
Stone ES 800/PK-6
1200 James Hopkins Rd 36265 256-782-5191
Yvonne Swift, prin. Fax 782-5978

Jacksonville Christian Academy 200/K-12
831 Alexandria Rd SW 36265 256-435-3333
Dr. Tommy Miller, prin. Fax 435-2059

Jasper, Walker, Pop. 14,147
Jasper CSD 2,800/PK-12
PO Box 500 35502 205-384-6880
Dr. Ann Jackson, supt. Fax 387-5213
www.jasper.k12.al.us
Maddox IS 600/4-6
201 Panther Trl 35501 205-384-3235
Marc Sargent, prin. Fax 387-5208
Memorial Park ES 500/2-3
800 10th Ave 35501 205-384-6461
Matthew Eric Rigsby, prin. Fax 387-5219
Simmons ES 500/PK-1
1001 Viking Dr 35501 205-387-2535
Jonathan Allen, prin. Fax 387-5216

Walker County SD 6,800/PK-12
PO Box 311 35502 205-387-0555
Dr. Jason Adkins, supt. Fax 221-5636
www.walkercountyschools.com
Curry ES 600/PK-5
85 Yellow Jacket Dr 35503 205-387-7845
Roy Martin, prin. Fax 387-7871
Curry MS 300/6-8
115 Yellow Jacket Dr 35503 205-384-3441
Barry Wilson, prin. Fax 384-1110
Valley ES 600/K-8
155 Valley School Rd 35504 205-483-9381
Joe Harrison, prin. Fax 483-9509
Other Schools – See Carbon Hill, Cordova, Nauvoo, Oakman, Parrish, Sumiton

Jemison, Chilton, Pop. 2,561
Chilton County SD
Supt. — See Clanton
Jemison ES 900/K-3
1495 County Road 44 35085 205-280-4820
Hayden Ingram, prin. Fax 688-2812
Jemison IS 500/4-6
1491 County Road 44 35085 205-280-4840
Kendall Jackson, prin. Fax 688-2302
Jemison MS 7-8
25125 US Highway 31 35085 205-280-4862
Kendall Jackson, prin. Fax 688-3202

Killen, Lauderdale, Pop. 1,097
Lauderdale County SD
Supt. — See Florence
Brooks ES 900/PK-6
100 School Ln 35645 256-757-2171
Jennifer Gray, prin. Fax 757-1265

Legacy Christian Academy 50/PK-6
PO Box 1054 35645 256-737-5345
Laurie Wilson, prin.

Kimberly, Jefferson, Pop. 2,694
Jefferson County SD
Supt. — See Birmingham
North Jefferson MS 600/6-8
8350 Warrior Kimberly Rd 35091 205-379-4000
Terry Henderson, prin. Fax 379-4045

Kinston, Coffee, Pop. 531
Coffee County SD
Supt. — See Elba
Kinston S 500/PK-12
201 College St 36453 334-565-3016
Jennifer Lee, prin. Fax 565-3494

Laceys Spring, Morgan
Morgan County SD
Supt. — See Decatur
Laceys Spring S 300/K-8
48 School Rd 35754 256-881-4460
Mark Edwards, prin. Fax 881-1748

Lafayette, Chambers, Pop. 2,991
Chambers County SD 3,800/PK-12
PO Box 408 36862 334-864-9343
Kelli Hodge, supt. Fax 864-0119
www.chambersk12.org
Lafayette Eastside ES 300/PK-5
300 Avenue A SE 36862 334-864-8274
Lakeyda Burnett, prin. Fax 864-9018
Powell MS 200/6-8
700 Martin Luther King Dr 36862 334-864-8876
Daron Brooks, prin. Fax 864-8169
Other Schools – See Five Points, Lanett, Valley

Chambers Academy 100/K-12
15048 US Highway 431 36862 334-864-9852

Lanett, Chambers, Pop. 6,366
Chambers County SD
Supt. — See Lafayette
Huguley ES 400/PK-5
3011 S Phillips Rd 36863 334-576-2572
Benjamin Mitchum, prin. Fax 576-7699

Lanett CSD 900/K-12
105 N Lanier Ave 36863 334-644-5900
Phillip Johnson, supt. Fax 644-5910
www.lanettcityschools.org
Lance ES 500/K-6
200 S 8th Ave 36863 334-644-5915
Jamie Heard, prin. Fax 644-5926
Lanett JHS 100/7-8
1301 S 8th Ave 36863 334-644-5950
Donna Bell, prin. Fax 644-5964

Springwood S 300/PK-12
PO Box 1030 36863 334-644-2191
Rick Johnson, hdmstr. Fax 644-2194

Leeds, Jefferson, Pop. 11,579
Leeds CSD 1,200/PK-12
PO Box 1029 35094 205-699-5437
John Moore, supt. Fax 699-6629
www.leedsk12.org/
Leeds ES 300/3-5
950 Ashville Rd 35094 205-699-4500
Justin Burns, prin. Fax 699-4504
Leeds MS 400/6-8
1771 Whitmire St 35094 205-699-4505
Dr. Bobby Byrd, prin. Fax 847-2027
Leeds PS PK-2
991 Park Dr 35094 205-702-2300
Wesley Graham, prin. Fax 702-4221

Leighton, Colbert, Pop. 711
Colbert County SD
Supt. — See Tuscumbia
Hatton ES 200/PK-6
2130 Hatton School Rd 35646 256-446-5679
David Isbell, prin. Fax 446-8063
Leighton ES 300/PK-6
8100 Old Highway 20 35646 256-446-8351
Vickie Osborn, prin. Fax 446-6668

Leroy, Washington, Pop. 902
Washington County SD
Supt. — See Chatom
Leroy S 700/K-12
PO Box 40 36548 251-246-2000
Danny Patterson, prin. Fax 246-2199

Lester, Limestone, Pop. 111
Limestone County SD
Supt. — See Athens
Sugar Creek ES 600/PK-PK, 5-
26595 Salen Minor Rd 35647
Cleo Miller, prin.

Lexington, Lauderdale, Pop. 728
Lauderdale County SD
Supt. — See Florence
Lexington S 900/K-12
101 School St 35648 256-229-6622
Willie Joiner, prin. Fax 229-6636

Lincoln, Talladega, Pop. 6,180
Talladega County SD
Supt. — See Talladega
Drew MS 300/7-8
78975 AL Highway 21 35096 256-315-5280
Dr. Rhonda Lee, prin. Fax 315-5290
Lincoln ES 800/K-6
79001 AL Highway 77 35096 256-315-5265
Jesse Hooks, prin. Fax 315-5275

Linden, Marengo, Pop. 2,103
Linden CSD 500/PK-12
PO Box 480609 36748 334-295-8802
Dr. Timothy Thurman, supt. Fax 295-8801
www.lindencity.org
Austin JHS 100/6-8
PO Box 480699 36748 334-295-5378
Marcus West, prin. Fax 295-5376
Linden ES 200/PK-5
PO Box 480579 36748 334-295-5860
Dr. Timothy Thurman, prin. Fax 295-5559

Marengo County SD 1,100/PK-12
PO Box 480339 36748 334-295-4123
Luke Hallmark, supt. Fax 295-2259
www.marengocounty.schoolinsites.com/
Other Schools – See Dixons Mills, Sweet Water, Thomaston

Marengo Academy 200/K-12
2103 S Main St 36748 334-295-4151

Lineville, Clay, Pop. 2,331
Clay County SD
Supt. — See Ashland
Central JHS of Clay County 7-8
1 Bob Riley Dr 36266 256-396-1401
Ray Sewell, prin. Fax 396-2452
Lineville ES 500/K-6
18 W Main St 36266 256-396-1420
Timothy Pilkington, prin. Fax 396-5335

Livingston, Sumter, Pop. 3,462
Sumter County SD 1,800/PK-12
PO Box 10 35470 205-652-9605
Dr. Tyrone Yarbrough, supt. Fax 652-9641
www.sumter.k12.al.us
Livingston JHS 600/PK-8
PO Box 370 35470 205-652-2125
Tramene Maye, prin. Fax 652-2174
Other Schools – See Cuba, Panola, York

Loachapoka, Lee, Pop. 179
Lee County SD
Supt. — See Opelika
Loachapoka ES 300/K-6
PO Box 60 36865 334-887-8066
Mary Ross, prin. Fax 887-2948

Lockhart, Covington, Pop. 512
Covington County SD
Supt. — See Andalusia
Harlan ES 300/K-6
PO Box 267 36455 334-858-3294
Joy Colvin, prin. Fax 858-3866

Locust Fork, Blount, Pop. 1,182
Blount County SD
Supt. — See Oneonta
Locust Fork ES 500/K-6
155 School Rd 35097 205-681-9512
Amy Williamson, prin. Fax 681-8479

Logan, Cullman
Cullman County SD
Supt. — See Cullman
Harmony S 200/K-8
4910 County Road 940 35098 256-747-1427
Kevin Sullins, prin. Fax 747-1043

Louisville, Barbour, Pop. 513
Barbour County SD
Supt. — See Clayton
Barbour County IS 300/3-6
PO Box 459 36048 334-266-6151
Kelvin James, prin. Fax 266-5991
Barbour County PS 300/PK-2
PO Box 429 36048 334-266-5643
Dr. Patrick Fenderson, prin. Fax 266-5195

Lower Peach Tree, Monroe
Monroe County SD
Supt. — See Monroeville
Monroe IS 100/K-8
3366 County Road 49 36751 334-636-2032
Coquesa Dotson, prin. Fax 636-0506

Lowndesboro, Lowndes, Pop. 112

Lowndes Academy 200/K-12
PO Box 99 36752 334-278-3366

Loxley, Baldwin, Pop. 1,614
Baldwin County SD
Supt. — See Bay Minette
Loxley ES 400/PK-6
4999 S Magnolia St 36551 251-964-5334
Misty Wilkinson, prin. Fax 964-7369

Luverne, Crenshaw, Pop. 2,775
Crenshaw County SD 2,200/PK-12
183 Votec Dr 36049 334-335-6519
Dr. Boyd English, supt. Fax 335-6510
crenshawcounty.schoolinsites.com
Luverne S 800/PK-12
194 First Ave 36049 334-335-3331
Jamie Howard, prin. Fax 335-2246
Other Schools – See Brantley, Highland Home

Crenshaw Christian Academy 200/K-12
608 Country Club Dr 36049 334-335-5749

Lynn, Winston, Pop. 651
Winston County SD
Supt. — See Double Springs
Lynn ES 200/K-7
531 E Main St 35575 205-893-5702
Jennifer Baker, prin. Fax 893-2484

Mc Calla, Jefferson
Jefferson County SD
Supt. — See Birmingham
McAdory ES 1,100/K-5
6251 Eastern Valley Rd 35111 205-379-4650
James McLeod, prin. Fax 379-4696
McAdory MS 800/6-8
5450 Yellow Jacket Blvd 35111 205-379-4730
Julie McAlister, prin. Fax 379-4745

Tuscaloosa County SD
Supt. — See Tuscaloosa
Lake View ES 600/K-5
21610 Youngblood Pkwy 35111 205-342-2951
Martha Roop, prin. Fax 247-4181

Mc Intosh, Washington, Pop. 237
Washington County SD
Supt. — See Chatom
McIntosh ES 300/K-5
PO Box 357 36553 251-944-2481
Dr. Edna Billingsley, prin. Fax 944-2001

Mc Kenzie, Butler, Pop. 519
Butler County SD
Supt. — See Greenville
Mc Kenzie S 400/K-12
PO Box 158 36456 334-374-2711
Miles Brown, prin. Fax 374-8108

Madison, Madison, Pop. 41,860
Madison CSD 9,600/PK-12
211 Celtic Dr 35758 256-464-8370
Dr. Robert Parker, supt. Fax 464-8291
www.madisoncity.k12.al.us
Columbia ES 700/K-6
667 Balch Rd 35758 256-430-2751
Jamie Hill, prin. Fax 430-2794
Discovery MS 800/7-8
1304 Hughes Rd 35758 256-837-3735
Kimberly Stewart, prin. Fax 837-1573
Heritage ES 800/K-6
11775 County Line Rd 35758 256-772-2075
Dr. Georginia Nelson, prin. Fax 772-6580
Horizon ES 600/K-6
7855 Madison Pike 35758 256-464-3614
Rodney Richardson, prin. Fax 464-3689
Liberty MS 700/7-8
281 Dock Murphy Dr 35758 256-430-0001
Shannon Brown, prin. Fax 430-0282
Madison ES 500/K-6
17 College St 35758 256-772-9255
Melissa Mims, prin. Fax 461-8300
Mill Creek ES 800/PK-6
847 Mill Rd 35758 256-774-4690
Carmen Buchanan, prin. Fax 774-4691
Rainbow ES 800/PK-6
50 Nance Rd 35758 256-824-8106
Stanley Givens, prin. Fax 824-8110
West Madison ES 500/PK-6
4976 Wall Triana Hwy 35758 256-837-1189
Dr. Daphne Jah, prin. Fax 837-1258

Madison County SD
Supt. — See Huntsville
Legacy ES 700/PK-5
165 Pine Grove Rd 35757 256-851-4630
Keith Trawick, prin. Fax 851-4631

Madison Academy 900/PK-12
325 Slaughter Rd 35758 256-469-6400
St. John the Baptist S 500/K-8
1057 Hughes Rd 35758 256-722-0772
Sherry Lewis, prin. Fax 722-0151
Westminster Christian Academy 200/PK-5
375 Mount Zion Rd 35757 256-705-8300

Maplesville, Chilton, Pop. 698
Chilton County SD
Supt. — See Clanton
Isabella S 700/K-12
11338 County Road 15 36750 205-280-2770
Ricky Porter, prin. Fax 755-8549
Maplesville S 500/K-12
1256 AL Highway 139 36750 205-280-4900
Steven Hunter, prin. Fax 366-2531

Marbury, Autauga, Pop. 1,390
Autauga County SD
Supt. — See Prattville
Marbury MS 500/6-8
PO Box A 36051 334-365-3522
Jerome Barrington, prin. Fax 755-3168

Marion, Perry, Pop. 3,671
Perry County SD 800/PK-12
PO Box 900 36756 334-683-6528
John Heard, supt. Fax 683-8427
www.perrycountyal.org
Marion S 400/PK-12
PO Box 150 36756 334-683-6741
Dr. Cathy Trimble, prin. Fax 683-8838
Other Schools – See Uniontown

Marion Academy 100/PK-12
1820 Prier Dr 36756 334-683-8204
Dr. Cynthia Stewart, prin. Fax 683-4938

Maylene, Shelby
Alabaster CSD
Supt. — See Alabaster
Creek View ES 1,000/K-3
8568 Highway 17 35114 205-682-5730
Charissa Cole, prin. Fax 682-5735

Mentone, DeKalb, Pop. 346
De Kalb County SD
Supt. — See Rainsville
Moon Lake ES 100/K-6
PO Box 166 35984 256-634-4113
Mary Lance, prin. Fax 634-4113

Meridianville, Madison, Pop. 5,896
Madison County SD
Supt. — See Huntsville
Fanning ES 500/K-3
8861 Moores Mill Rd 35759 256-851-4680
Tammie Burger, prin. Fax 851-4681

Midfield, Jefferson, Pop. 5,311
Midfield CSD 1,200/K-12
417 Parkwood St 35228 205-923-2262
Demica Sanders, supt. Fax 929-0585
www.midfield.k12.al.us/
Midfield ES 400/K-4
416 Parkwood St 35228 205-923-7727
Marshae Pelt, prin. Fax 929-0594
Rutledge MS 400/5-8
1221 8th St 35228 205-780-8647
Marcus Harris, prin. Fax 780-3664

Midland City, Dale, Pop. 2,267
Dale County SD
Supt. — See Ozark
Midland City ES 400/K-4
48 2nd St 36350 334-983-4591
Michael Smith, prin. Fax 983-1638

Millbrook, Elmore, Pop. 14,375
Elmore County SD
Supt. — See Wetumpka
Coosada ES 900/K-2
5260 Airport Rd 36054 334-285-0273
Janice Darty, prin. Fax 285-9231
Millbrook MS 1,300/5-8
4228 Chapman Rd 36054 334-285-2100
Ayena Jackson, prin. Fax 285-2102

Victory Baptist S 200/PK-12
5480 Main St 36054 334-285-0208
John Lopez, admin. Fax 285-0216

Millport, Lamar, Pop. 1,035
Lamar County SD
Supt. — See Vernon
South Lamar S 500/K-12
300 Sls Rd 35576 205-662-4411
Jason Williams, prin. Fax 662-4544

Millry, Washington, Pop. 541
Washington County SD
Supt. — See Chatom
Millry S 500/K-12
PO Box 65 36558 251-846-2987
John Carter, prin. Fax 846-2986

Mobile, Mobile, Pop. 192,396
Mobile County SD 57,500/PK-12
PO Box 180069 36618 251-221-4000
Martha Peek, supt. Fax 221-4399
www.mcpss.com
Austin ES 500/K-5
150 Provident Ln 36608 251-221-1015
Amanda Jones, prin. Fax 221-1018
Burns MS 1,000/6-8
6175 Girby Rd 36693 251-221-2025
Jason Laffitte, prin. Fax 221-2021
Calloway-Smith MS 700/6-8
350 N Lawrence St 36603 251-221-2042
D.H. Walton, prin. Fax 221-2041
Causey MS 1,500/6-8
2205 McFarland Rd 36695 251-221-2060
John Poiroux, prin. Fax 221-2062
Chastang-Fournier MS 400/K-8
2800 Berkley Ave 36617 251-221-2081
Bernard Everett, prin. Fax 221-2080
Clark-Shaw Magnet S 900/5-8
5960 Arlberg St 36608 251-221-2106
Mary Divincenzo, prin. Fax 221-2108
Collier ES 700/PK-5
601 Snow Rd N 36608 251-221-1120
Michelle Shropshire, prin. Fax 221-1123
Council Traditional ES 700/K-5
751 Wilkinson St 36603 251-221-1139
Hattie Alexander, prin. Fax 221-1140
Craighead ES 500/PK-5
1000 S Ann St 36605 251-221-1155
Tracey Hunter, prin. Fax 221-1151
Dawes IS 500/3-5
10451 W Lake Rd 36695 251-221-1485
Michele McClung, prin. Fax 221-1488
Denton Magnet S of Technology 700/6-8
3800 Pleasant Valley Rd 36609 251-221-2148
James Gill, prin. Fax 221-2152
Dickson ES 900/K-5
4645 Bit and Spur Rd 36608 251-221-1180
Katryna Kinn, prin. Fax 221-1185
Dodge ES 1,000/K-5
2615 Longleaf Dr 36693 251-221-1195
Dr. Suzanne Crist, prin. Fax 221-1197
Dunbar Magnet S 600/4-8
500 Saint Anthony St 36603 251-221-2160
Timesha Dumas, prin. Fax 221-2162
Eichold-Mertz ES 500/PK-5
2815 Government Blvd 36606 251-221-1210
Michelle Adams, prin. Fax 221-1212
Fonde ES 700/PK-5
3956 Cottage Hill Rd 36609 251-221-1240
Joy Gould, prin. Fax 221-1243
Forest Hill ES 500/K-5
4501 Moffett Rd 36618 251-221-1270
Sharon Smith, prin. Fax 221-1271
Gilliard ES 700/PK-5
2757 Dauphin Island Pkwy 36605 251-221-1820
Faith Lucy, prin. Fax 221-1824
Griggs ES 700/PK-5
6001 Three Notch Rd 36619 251-221-1330
Laura Hittson, prin. Fax 221-1335
Hall ES 500/PK-5
1108 Antwerp St 36605 251-221-1345
Melissa Mitchell, prin Fax 221-1348
Hollingers Island ES 300/K-5
2400 Hammock Rd 36605 251-221-1376
Deborah Torbert, prin. Fax 221-1375
Holloway ES 700/K-6
625 Stanton Rd 36617 251-221-1391
Metra Turner, prin. Fax 221-1393
Howard ES 500/PK-5
957 Dr Martin L King Jr Ave 36603 251-221-1406
Michelle Manzy, prin. Fax 221-1410
Hutchens ES 600/PK-2
10005 W Lake Rd 36695 251-221-1420
Katherine Gallop, prin. Fax 221-1425
Just 4 Developmental Lab S 300/PK-PK
2263 Saint Stephens Rd 36617 251-221-1450
Monique Baugh, prin. Fax 221-1452
Leinkauf ES 400/K-5
1410 Monroe St 36604 251-221-1495
Quentina Pruitt, prin. Fax 221-1498
Maryvale ES 600/PK-5
1901 N Maryvale St 36605 251-221-1810
June Stanford, prin. Fax 221-1812
Meadowlake ES 500/PK-5
8251 Three Notch Rd 36619 251-221-1529
Joi Miles, prin. Fax 221-1528
Morningside ES 500/K-5
2700 S Greenbrier Dr 36605 251-221-1540
Michelle Dumas, prin. Fax 221-1542
Old Shell Road Magnet S 400/K-3
3160 Heather St 36607 251-221-1557
Christi Brown, prin. Fax 221-1559
Orchard ES 400/K-5
6400 Howells Ferry Rd 36618 251-221-1571
LaTunga Ransom, prin. Fax 221-1570
O'Rourke ES 1,000/K-5
1975 Leroy Stevens Rd 36695 251-221-1585
Cheryl Chapman, prin. Fax 221-1586
Phillips Preparatory S 900/6-8
3255 Old Shell Rd 36607 251-221-2286
Brenda Hartzog, prin. Fax 221-2285
Pillans MS 500/6-8
2051 Military Rd 36605 251-221-2300
Jacinda Hollins, prin. Fax 221-2314
Scarborough MS 400/6-8
1800 Phillips Ln 36618 251-221-2323
Andrea Dennis, prin Fax 221-2321
Shepard ES 500/PK-5
3980 Burma Rd Ste B 36693 251-221-1645
Kay Smith, prin. Fax 221-1646
Spencer-Westlawn ES 600/PK-5
3071 Ralston Rd 36606 251-221-1705
Dianne Reynolds, prin. Fax 221-1710
Taylor-White ES 300/K-5
476 Eliza Jordan Rd N 36608 251-221-1465
Diana Shaw, prin. Fax 221-1466
Washington MS 300/6-8
1961 Andrews St 36617 251-221-2361
Angie Brown, prin. Fax 221-2367
Will ES 600/PK-5
5750 Summit Ave 36608 251-221-1750
Deidre Jefferson, prin. Fax 221-1752

Other Schools – See Axis, Bayou La Batre, Citronelle, Dauphin Island, Eight Mile, Grand Bay, Irvington, Mount Vernon, Prichard, Semmes, Theodore, Wilmer

---

Corpus Christi S 500/PK-8
6300 McKenna Dr 36608 251-342-5474
Kristy Martin, prin. Fax 380-0325
Cottage Hill Christian Academy 400/PK-8
4255 Cottage Hill Rd 36609 251-660-2427
Jimmy Messer, head sch Fax 660-0558
Covenant Christian S 200/PK-8
7150 Hitt Rd 36695 251-633-8055
Keith Currie, prin. Fax 633-5577
Faith Academy 1,900/PK-12
8650 Tanner Williams Rd 36608 251-633-7267
Tim Skelton, hdmstr. Fax 633-9133
Government Street Christian S 200/PK-8
3401 Government Blvd 36693 251-660-7444
Little Flower S 200/PK-8
2103 Government St 36606 251-479-5761
Alesa Weiskopf, prin. Fax 450-3696
Mobile Christian S 600/PK-12
5900 Cottage Hill Rd 36609 251-661-1613
David Pahman, hdmstr. Fax 661-1396
Mobile Jr. Academy 50/PK-8
1900 Cody Rd S 36695 251-633-8638
Wesley Gennick, prin. Fax 633-8639
Most Pure Heart of Mary S 200/PK-8
310 Sengstak St 36603 251-432-5270
Jamie Crain, prin. Fax 432-5271
Our Savior Preschool 50/PK-PK
1801 Cody Rd S 36695 251-633-3017
Rita Langan, dir. Fax 633-7790
Revelation Christian S 50/PK-5
1711 Taylor Ln 36605 251-473-2555
Patrice A. Casher M.Ed., prin. Fax 473-2727
St. Dominic S 500/PK-8
4160 Burma Rd 36693 251-661-5226
Laurie Michener, prin. Fax 660-2242
St. Ignatius S 500/PK-8
3650 Spring Hill Ave 36608 251-342-5442
Tori Miller, prin. Fax 344-0944
St. Luke's Episcopal Lower S PK-5
3975 Japonica Ln 36693 251-666-2991
St. Mary S 500/PK-8
107 N Lafayette St 36604 251-433-9904
Debbie Ollis, prin. Fax 438-9069
St. Paul's Episcopal S 1,300/PK-12
161 Dogwood Ln 36608 251-342-6700
Dr. Mark Foley, head sch Fax 342-1844
St. Pius X S 400/PK-8
217 S Sage Ave 36606 251-473-5004
Lauren Alvarez, prin. Fax 473-5008
St. Vincent De Paul S 200/PK-8
4980 St Vincent Dr 36619 251-666-8022
Daria McDonald Ph.D., prin. Fax 666-1296
Trinity Evangelical Lutheran S 100/PK-5
2668 Berkley Ave 36617 251-456-7960
Theron Florence, admin. Fax 456-7909
UMS Wright Preparatory S 1,300/PK-12
65 Mobile St 36607 251-479-6551
Dr. Doug Barber, head sch Fax 470-9010

Monroeville, Monroe, Pop. 6,440
Monroe County SD 3,700/PK-12
109 Pickens St 36460 251-575-2168
Gregory L. Shehan, supt. Fax 575-9353
www.monroe.k12.al.us/
Monroeville ES 600/PK-4
297 S Mount Pleasant Ave 36460 251-743-3474
Amy McCrory, prin. Fax 575-3723
Monroeville MS 500/5-8
201 York St 36460 251-575-4121
Valerie Stevens, prin. Fax 575-2934
Other Schools – See Beatrice, Excel, Lower Peach Tree, Uriah

Monroe Academy 500/PK-12
4096 S Alabama Ave 36460 251-743-3932

Montevallo, Shelby, Pop. 6,221
Shelby County SD
Supt. — See Columbiana
Calera MS 600/6-8
9178 Highway 22 35115 205-682-6140
Branden Vincent, prin. Fax 682-6145
Montevallo ES 700/K-5
171 Jeter Cir 35115 205-682-6420
Dr. Allison Campbell, prin. Fax 682-6425
Montevallo MS 300/6-8
235 Samford St 35115 205-682-6410
Sheila Lewis, prin. Fax 682-6415

Montgomery, Montgomery, Pop. 203,255
Montgomery County SD 31,300/K-12
PO Box 1991 36102 334-223-6700
Dr. Reginald Eggleston, supt. Fax 269-3076
www.mps.k12.al.us
Baldwin Arts & Academics Magnet S 600/6-8
410 S McDonough St 36104 334-269-3870
Jannette Wright, prin. Fax 269-3918
Bear Exploration Center ES 500/K-5
2525 Churchill Dr 36111 334-284-8014
Elizabeth Hill, prin. Fax 284-8096
Bellingrath MS 700/6-8
3350 S Court St 36105 334-269-3623
Sonya Floyd, prin. Fax 269-6173
Blount ES 600/K-5
1650 Ray Thorington Rd 36117 334-244-0078
Mona Green, prin. Fax 244-0237
Brewbaker IS 700/3-5
4455 Brewbaker Dr 36116 334-284-8006
Natasha Starr, prin. Fax 284-8067
Brewbaker MS 1,000/6-8
4425 Brewbaker Dr 36116 334-284-8008
Cameron Whitlow, prin. Fax 284-8052
Brewbaker PS 800/K-2
4445 Brewbaker Dr 36116 334-284-8005
Catherine Rogers, prin. Fax 284-8035
Capitol Heights MS 700/6-8
116 Federal Dr 36107 334-260-1000
Cheryl Smith-Fountain, prin. Fax 260-1049
Carr MS 800/6-8
1610 Ray Thorington Rd 36117 334-244-4005
Brittany Aarestad, prin. Fax 244-4009
Carver ES 500/K-5
3100 Mobile Dr 36108 334-269-3625
Calandra Hawkins, prin. Fax 269-3923
Catoma ES 300/K-5
1780 Mitchell Young Rd 36108 334-288-5799
Mary Markham, prin. Fax 281-8232
Chisholm ES 600/K-5
307 E Vandiver Blvd 36110 334-269-3643
Lolita Osborne, prin. Fax 269-3645
Crump ES 500/K-5
3510 Woodley Rd 36116 334-284-8020
Randy Shaw, prin. Fax 284-8024
Dalraida ES 800/K-5
440 Dalraida Rd 36109 334-260-1007
Michelle Harris, prin. Fax 260-1071
Dannelly ES 600/K-5
3425 Carter Hill Rd 36111 334-269-3657
Dwight Brooks, prin. Fax 269-3655
Davis ES 500/K-5
3605 Rosa L Parks Ave 36105 334-269-3662
Aleysia Alves, prin. Fax 241-5392
Dozier ES 400/K-5
200 Eastern Blvd 36117 334-260-1012
Eric James, prin. Fax 260-1010
Fitzpatrick ES 600/K-5
4055 Fitzpatrick Blvd 36116 334-284-8044
William Milledge, prin. Fax 284-8045
Flowers ES 400/K-5
3510 Harrison Rd 36109 334-260-1015
Ethel Barnes, prin. Fax 260-1050
Floyd ES 400/K-5
630 Augusta Ave 36111 334-284-7120
Tiffany Scissum, prin. Fax 284-7265
Floyd MS for Math Science & Technology 500/6-8
3444 Le Bron Rd 36111 334-284-7130
Vince Johnson, prin. Fax 284-7125
Forest Avenue Magnet ES 700/K-5
1700 W 5th St 36106 334-269-3673
Emily Little, prin. Fax 269-3963
Garrett ES 600/K-5
555 Mclemore Dr 36117 334-260-1090
Anissha Officer, prin. Fax 260-1092
Goodwyn MS 600/6-8
209 Perry Hill Rd 36109 334-260-1021
Curtis Black, prin. Fax 260-1079
Halcyon ES 600/K-5
1501 Parkview Dr S 36117 334-271-9000
Shannon Schmidt, prin. Fax 271-9002
Highland Avenue ES 400/K-5
2024 Highland Ave 36107 334-269-3690
Courtney Giles, prin. Fax 269-6151
Highland Gardens ES 500/K-5
2801 Willena Ave 36107 334-269-3685
Jessietta Thomas, prin. Fax 241-5329
Johnson ES 500/K-5
4550 Narrow Lane Rd 36116 334-284-8016
Bridgette Carter, prin. Fax 284-8056
King ES 400/K-5
4655 Gateway Dr 36108 334-284-8080
Booker MacMillian, prin. Fax 284-8085
MacMillan International Academy at McKee 300/K-5
4015 McInnis Dr 36116 334-284-7137
Faith Goshay, prin. Fax 284-7569
McKee MS 900/6-8
4017 McInnis Dr 36116 334-284-7528
Patrick Nelson, prin. Fax 241-5308
Morningview ES 500/K-5
2849 Pelzer Ave 36109 334-260-1028
Kenyetta Miller, prin. Fax 260-1029
Morris ES 500/K-5
801 Hill St 36108 334-223-6920
DeNitta Easterling, prin. Fax 241-5399
Nixon ES 500/K-5
1000 Edgar D Nixon Ave 36104 334-269-3012
Dana Williams, prin. Fax 269-3019
Southlawn ES 300/K-5
5225 Patricia Ln 36108 334-284-8028
Tamara Winston, prin. Fax 284-8069
Southlawn MS 700/6-8
5333 Mobile Hwy 36108 334-284-8086
Jarmar Muhammad, prin. Fax 284-8094
Vaughn Road ES 500/K-5
4407 Vaughn Rd 36106 334-260-1031
Brenda Lindsey, prin. Fax 260-1041
Wares Ferry Road ES 400/K-5
6425 Wares Ferry Rd 36117 334-260-1036
Marcus Roberts, prin. Fax 260-1035
Wilson ES 500/K-5
8900 Park Xing 36117 334-272-8819
Meredith Bishop, prin. Fax 395-8172
Other Schools – See Hope Hull, Pike Road, Ramer

Alabama Christian Academy 1,000/PK-12
4700 Wares Ferry Rd 36109 334-277-1985
Bethany Christian Academy 100/K-8
1765 Highland Ave 36107 334-264-1078
Cornerstone Classical Christian Academy 100/K-12
125 Calhoun Rd 36109 334-356-7788
Eastwood Christian S 400/K-12
1701 E Trinity Blvd 36106 334-272-8195
Evangel Christian Academy 300/PK-12
3975 Vaughn Rd 36106 334-272-3882
Rev. Scott Matthes, admin. Fax 272-5662
Montgomery Academy Lower S 300/K-5
1550 Perry Hill Rd 36106 334-272-8210
Jay Spencer, head sch Fax 270-1462
Montgomery Adventist S 50/1-8
4233 Atlanta Hwy 36109 334-398-8210
Montgomery Catholic Prep MS 200/7-8
5350 Vaughn Rd 36116 334-272-2465
Justin Castanza, prin. Fax 272-2330
Montgomery Catholic Prep - St. Bede 300/PK-6
3850 Atlanta Hwy 36109 334-272-3033
Laurie Gulley, prin. Fax 272-9394
Montgomery Catholic Prep S - Holy Spirit 100/PK-6
8580 Vaughn Rd 36117 334-649-4404
Nancy Foley, prin. Fax 649-4409
Montgomery Christian S 100/K-5
3265 McGehee Rd 36111 334-386-1749
Kathi Atkins, head sch Fax 262-4469
Resurrection Catholic S 100/PK-8
2815 Forbes Dr 36110 334-265-4615
Tamarcus Milner, prin. Fax 265-7988
St. James S 1,000/PK-12
6010 Vaughn Rd 36116 334-277-8033
Dr. Larry McLemore, head sch Fax 277-2542
Success Unlimited Academy 200/PK-12
2328 Fairlane Dr 36116 334-213-0803
Trinity Presbyterian S 900/PK-12
1700 E Trinity Blvd 36106 334-213-2100
Kerry Palmer, head sch Fax 213-2171
Valiant Cross Academy 100/6-8
301 Dexter Ave 36104 334-301-0478
Anthony Brock, prin.

Moody, Saint Clair, Pop. 11,564
Saint Clair County SD
Supt. — See Ashville
Moody ES 800/PK-3
1006 HL Blocker Cir 35004 205-640-2180
Kathy Tice, prin. Fax 640-4971
Moody JHS 400/7-8
600 High School Dr 35004 205-640-2040
Cassandra Taylor, prin. Fax 640-3036
Moody MS 500/4-6
696 High School Dr 35004 205-640-2190
Debra Allred, prin. Fax 640-7903

Morris, Jefferson, Pop. 1,853
Jefferson County SD
Supt. — See Birmingham
Bryan ES 700/K-5
600 Kimberly Cut Off Rd 35116 205-379-2750
Debra Campbell, prin. Fax 379-2795

Moulton, Lawrence, Pop. 3,330
Lawrence County SD 4,600/PK-12
14131 Market St 35650 256-905-2400
Jon Smith, supt. Fax 905-2406
www.lawrenceal.org
Moulton ES 700/K-4
412 Main St 35650 256-905-2450
Tiletha Shelton, prin. Fax 905-2480
Moulton MS 600/5-8
660 College St 35650 256-905-2460
Tiletha Shelton, prin. Fax 905-2481
Other Schools – See Danville, Mount Hope, Town Creek, Trinity

Moundville, Hale, Pop. 2,391
Hale County SD
Supt. — See Greensboro
Hale County MS 300/6-8
120 Wildcat Way 35474 205-371-7000
Eric Perry, prin. Fax 371-7099
Moundville ES 600/PK-5
537 Alabama Ave 35474 205-371-2679
Jonathan Posey, prin. Fax 371-4279

Tuscaloosa County SD
Supt. — See Tuscaloosa
Big Sandy ES 400/PK-5
11950 Upper Hull Rd 35474 205-342-2840
Glynis Rhodes, prin. Fax 247-4199

Mountain Brook, Jefferson, Pop. 20,299
Mountain Brook CSD 4,500/K-12
32 Vine St, Birmingham AL 35213 205-871-4608
Dr. Richard Barlow, supt. Fax 802-1630
www.mtnbrook.k12.al.us
Brookwood Forest ES 500/K-6
3701 S Brookwood Rd 35223 205-414-3700
Nathan Pitner, prin. Fax 969-8121
Cherokee Bend ES 500/K-6
4400 Fair Oaks Dr, Birmingham AL 35213
205-871-3595
Betsy Bell, prin. Fax 877-8312
Crestline ES 800/K-6
3785 W Jackson Blvd, Birmingham AL 35213
205-871-8126
Laurie King, prin. Fax 877-8324
Mountain Brook ES 500/K-6
3020 Cambridge Rd 35223 205-871-8191
Ashley McCombs, prin. Fax 877-8330

Mount Hope, Lawrence
Lawrence County SD
Supt. — See Moulton
Mount Hope ES 200/PK-6
8455 County Road 23 35651 256-905-2470
Jean Howard, prin. Fax 905-2471

Mount Olive, Jefferson, Pop. 4,057
Jefferson County SD
Supt. — See Birmingham
Mount Olive ES 400/K-5
1301 Brookside Rd 35117 205-379-4900
Judy Sullivan, prin. Fax 379-4945

Mount Vernon, Mobile, Pop. 1,556
Mobile County SD
Supt. — See Mobile
Calcedeaver ES 200/PK-6
20500 Patillo Rd 36560 251-221-1092
George Sullivan, prin. Fax 221-1094

Munford, Talladega, Pop. 1,274
Talladega County SD
Supt. — See Talladega
Munford MS, 360 Cedars Rd 36268 400/6-8
Angel Carter, prin. 256-315-5235
Munford ES 800/K-6
365 Cedars Rd 36268 256-315-5250
Angela Robinson, prin. Fax 315-5260

Muscle Shoals, Colbert, Pop. 12,952
Muscle Shoals CSD 2,900/PK-12
PO Box 2610 35662 256-389-2600
Dr. Brian Lindsey, supt. Fax 389-2605
www.mscs.k12.al.us
Highland Park ES 200/1-2
714 Elmhurst Ave 35661 256-389-2620
Wes Pounders, prin. Fax 389-2625
Howell Graves Preschool 300/PK-K
3201 Alabama Ave 35661 256-389-2630
Sheneta Smith, prin. Fax 389-2632
McBride ES 600/3-5
1400 Avalon Ave 35661 256-389-2610
Dr. Alan Willingham, prin. Fax 389-2613
Muscle Shoals MS 700/6-8
100 Trojan Dr 35661 256-389-2640
Kevin Davis, prin. Fax 389-2647
Webster ES 200/1-2
200 Webster St 35661 256-389-2650
Jason Simmons, prin. Fax 389-2655

Nauvoo, Walker, Pop. 220
Walker County SD
Supt. — See Jasper
Lupton S 500/K-8
1110 Prospect Rd 35578 205-384-5838
Corey Shubert, prin. Fax 387-0434

New Brockton, Coffee, Pop. 1,118
Coffee County SD
Supt. — See Elba
New Brockton ES 300/PK-6
PO Box 489 36351 334-894-6152
Jason Hadden, prin. Fax 894-0058

New Hope, Madison, Pop. 2,743
Madison County SD
Supt. — See Huntsville
New Hope S 600/K-8
5300 Main Dr 35760 256-851-3260
Vincent Edmonds, prin. Fax 851-3262

New Market, Madison, Pop. 1,576
Madison County SD
Supt. — See Huntsville
Buckhorn MS 700/7-8
4185 Winchester Rd 35761 256-851-3230
April McCutcheon, prin. Fax 851-3231
Moores Mill IS 4-6
1210 Walker Ln 35761 256-851-4700
Daniel Evans, prin. Fax 851-4701
New Market S 400/PK-6
PO Box 217 35761 256-851-3250
Keri Smith, prin. Fax 851-3251
Walnut Grove ES 200/PK-6
1961 Joe Quick Rd 35761 256-851-4690
Kathy Reynolds, prin. Fax 851-4691

New Site, Tallapoosa, Pop. 769
Tallapoosa County SD
Supt. — See Dadeville
Horseshoe Bend S 800/K-12
10684 Highway 22 E 36256 256-329-9110
James Aulner, prin. Fax 329-9119

Newton, Dale, Pop. 1,478
Dale County SD
Supt. — See Ozark
Newton ES 200/K-6
523 S College St 36352 334-299-3581
Patrick Reed, prin. Fax 299-6693

Houston County SD
Supt. — See Dothan
Wicksburg S 1,000/K-12
1172 S State Highway 123 36352 334-692-5549
Cheryl Smith, prin. Fax 692-3184

Northport, Tuscaloosa, Pop. 23,073
Tuscaloosa County SD
Supt. — See Tuscaloosa
Collins-Riverside MS 500/6-8
1400 3rd St 35476 205-342-2680
Clifton Henson, prin. Fax 752-8024
Crestmont ES 400/PK-5
2400 34th Ave 35476 205-342-2695
Lucretia Prince, prin. Fax 247-4171
Echols MS 700/6-8
2701 Echols Ave 35476 205-342-2884
Jason Stapp, prin. Fax 339-1064
Faucett-Vestavia ES 400/K-5
1150 Vestavia Cir 35473 205-342-2646
Genea Monroe, prin. Fax 247-4174
Flatwoods ES 400/PK-5
3800 66th Ave 35473 205-342-2648
Mary Sutton, prin. Fax 333-5814
Huntington Place ES 500/K-5
11601 Huntington Pl 35475 205-342-2652
Andrea Hamner, prin. Fax 247-4180
Matthews ES 400/K-5
1225 Rice Mine Rd 35476 205-342-2654
Dr. Tripp Marshall, prin. Fax 391-2169
Northport ES 600/PK-2
13695 Frankie Thomas Dr 35475 205-342-2862
John Campbell, prin. Fax 333-3955
Northside MS 400/6-8
19130 Northside Pkwy 35475 205-342-2740
Bobby Beasley, prin. Fax 247-4188
Walker ES 700/K-5
13051 Northside Rd 35475 205-342-2664
Marsha Johnson, prin. Fax 333-5491

Notasulga, Macon, Pop. 958
Macon County SD
Supt. — See Tuskegee
Notasulga S 300/PK-12
500 E Main St 36866 334-724-1240
Lasisi Hooks, prin. Fax 257-4228

Tallapoosa County SD
Supt. — See Dadeville
Reeltown ES PK-6
4085 AL Highway 120 36866 334-257-3784
Pam Langford, prin. Fax 257-2793

Oakman, Walker, Pop. 785
Walker County SD
Supt. — See Jasper
Oakman S 600/PK-8
PO Box 287 35579 205-622-3611
Christopher Walton, prin. Fax 622-2322

Odenville, Saint Clair, Pop. 3,535
Saint Clair County SD
Supt. — See Ashville
Margaret ES 600/K-5
200 Mustang Dr 35120 205-629-5034
Julie Talton, prin. Fax 629-6149
Odenville ES 400/PK-2
420 Alabama St 35120 205-629-6406
Christa Urban, prin. Fax 629-6408
Odenville IS 400/3-5
300 Burgess Dr 35120 205-629-2246
Mark Ford, prin. Fax 629-2249
Odenville MS 500/6-8
100 1st Ave 35120 205-629-2280
Walker Cook, prin. Fax 620-2282

Ohatchee, Calhoun, Pop. 1,146
Calhoun County SD
Supt. — See Anniston
Ohatchee ES 500/K-6
365 J St 36271 256-741-4800
Tesha Crump, prin. Fax 892-2040

Oneonta, Blount, Pop. 6,492
Blount County SD 8,300/K-12
PO Box 578 35121 205-625-4102
Rodney Green, supt. Fax 625-4100
www.blountboe.net
Appalachian S 600/K-12
350 County Highway 12 35121 205-274-9712
Jonathan Cleveland, prin. Fax 274-9706
Other Schools – See Blountsville, Cleveland, Hayden, Locust Fork, Remlap

Oneonta CSD 1,100/K-12
27605 State Highway 75 35121 205-625-4106
Dr. Timothy Nabors, supt. Fax 274-2910
www.oneontacityschools.com
Oneonta ES 700/K-5
27605 State Highway 75 35121 205-625-4108
Leslie Russell, prin. Fax 625-5509
Oneonta MS 6-8
27605 State Highway 75 35121 205-625-3018
Brad Newton, prin. Fax 625-3059

Opelika, Lee, Pop. 26,170
Lee County SD 8,800/K-12
2410 Society Hill Rd 36804 334-705-6000
James McCoy, supt. Fax 745-9822
www.lee.k12.al.us
Beauregard ES 700/K-4
300 Lee Road 431 36804 334-745-2972
Lisa Harris, prin. Fax 745-2287
Sanford MS 600/5-8
1500 Lee Road 11 36804 334-745-5023
Lura Reed, prin. Fax 745-5685
Other Schools – See Loachapoka, Salem, Smiths, Smiths Station, Valley

Opelika CSD 4,400/PK-12
300 Simmons St 36801 334-745-9700
Dr. Mark Neighbors, supt. Fax 745-9706
www.opelikaschools.org
Carver PS 400/PK-2
307 Carver Ave 36801 334-745-9712
Joe Hoss, prin. Fax 745-9722
Jeter PS 400/PK-2
700 Jeter Ave 36801 334-745-9723
David Carpenter, prin. Fax 745-9740
Morris Avenue IS 300/3-5
8 Morris Ave 36801 334-745-9734
Nino Mason, prin. Fax 745-9736
Northside ES 300/3-5
601 N 5th St 36801 334-745-9731
Laura Hartley, prin. Fax 745-9755
Opelika MS 1,000/6-8
1206 Denson Dr 36801 334-745-9726
Keith York, prin. Fax 745-9730
Southview PS 400/PK-2
2712 Marvyn Pkwy 36804 334-745-9711
Mary Patton, prin. Fax 745-9741
West Forest IS 300/3-5
2801 Waverly Pkwy 36801 334-745-9737
Dr. Pam Fourtenbary, prin. Fax 745-9739

Russell County SD
Supt. — See Phenix City
Dixie ES 200/PK-5
4914 US Highway 80 W 36804 334-321-2228
Paula Thompson, prin. Fax 298-0167

Trinity Christian S 200/K-12
PO Box 311 36803 334-745-2464

Opp, Covington, Pop. 6,581
Covington County SD
Supt. — See Andalusia
Fleeta S 200/K-8
27463 County Road 30 36467 334-493-6772
Seth Richards, prin. Fax 493-9813

Opp CSD 1,300/K-12
PO Box 840 36467 334-493-3173
Michael Smithart, supt. Fax 493-3060
www.oppcityschools.com
Opp ES 500/K-4
27098 Bobcat Dr 36467 334-493-6031
Shawn Short, prin. Fax 493-7082
Opp MS 400/5-8
303 E Stewart Ave 36467 334-493-6332
Sharon Spurlin, prin. Fax 493-1120

Orange Beach, Baldwin, Pop. 5,326
Baldwin County SD
Supt. — See Bay Minette
Orange Beach ES 500/K-6
4900 Wilson Blvd 36561 251-981-5662
Ryan Moss, prin. Fax 981-5684

Orrville, Dallas, Pop. 204
Dallas County SD
Supt. — See Selma
Salem ES 200/PK-5
3486 County Road 3 36767 334-996-8636
Chinita Irby, prin. Fax 996-3649

Owens Cross Roads, Madison, Pop. 1,475
Madison County SD
Supt. — See Huntsville
Owens Cross Roads ES 300/PK-6
161 Wilson Mann Rd 35763 256-851-3240
Mitchell Hampton, prin. Fax 851-3241

Big Cove Christian Academy 50/K-9
6354 Highway 431 S 35763 256-518-9642

Oxford, Calhoun, Pop. 21,062
Oxford CSD 4,200/K-12
PO Box 7670 36203 256-241-3140
Dr. Jeff Goodwin, supt. Fax 241-3938
www.oxfordcityschools.com
Hanna ES 700/5-6
1111 Watson Dr 36203 256-241-3896
Clint McCall, prin. Fax 241-3912
Oxford ES 700/K-4
1401 Caffey Dr 36203 256-241-3844
Jordan Weathers, prin. Fax 835-3043
Oxford MS 700/7-8
1750 US Highway 78 W 36203 256-241-3816
Michael Maniscalco, prin. Fax 241-3831
Other Schools – See Anniston

Ozark, Dale, Pop. 14,570
Dale County SD 3,000/K-12
202 S Highway 123 Ste E 36360 334-774-2355
Ben Baker, supt. Fax 774-3503
www.dalecountyboe.org
Other Schools – See Ariton, Midland City, Newton, Pinckard, Skipperville

Ozark CSD 1,700/PK-12
1044 Andrews Ave 36360 334-774-5197
Dr. Richard McInturf, supt. Fax 774-2685
www.ozarkcityschools.net
Lisenby PS 100/PK-2
860 Faust Ave 36360 334-774-4919
Charlotte Smith, prin. Fax 774-4960
Mixon IS 300/3-5
349 Sherril Ln 36360 334-774-4912
Maghen Lowery, prin. Fax 774-1402
Smith MS 500/6-8
994 Andrews Ave 36360 334-774-4913
Danelle Peterman, prin. Fax 774-0568

Panola, Sumter, Pop. 144
Sumter County SD
Supt. — See Livingston
North Sumter JHS 100/K-8
PO Box 99 35477 205-455-2422
Melissa Woods, prin. Fax 455-2582

Parrish, Walker, Pop. 961
Walker County SD
Supt. — See Jasper
Parrish ES 200/K-6
PO Box 109 35580 205-686-5061
Thomas Kyzer, prin. Fax 686-7998

Pelham, Shelby, Pop. 21,087
Pelham CSD 4,000/K-12
3113 Cummings St 35124 205-624-3700
Dr. Scott Coefield, supt. Fax 624-3980
www.pelhamcityschools.org
Pelham Oaks ES 700/K-5
2200 Highway 33 35124 205-682-5530
Deberah Miller, prin. Fax 682-5535
Pelham Park MS 700/6-8
2016 Pelham Park Blvd 35124 205-624-3702
Justin Hefner, prin. Fax 624-3990
Pelham Ridge ES 800/K-5
251 Applegate Pkwy 35124 205-624-3704
Robin Hollingsworth, prin. Fax 624-3999

Pell City, Saint Clair, Pop. 12,505
Pell City CSD 4,100/PK-12
3105 15th Ave N 35125 205-884-4440
Dr. Michael Barber, supt. Fax 814-1010
www.pellcityschools.net
Duran JHS 300/8-8
309 Williamson Dr 35125 205-338-2825
Richard Garris, prin. Fax 884-6502
Duran South JHS 300/7-7
813 16th St S 35128 205-884-7957
Cory O'Neal, prin. Fax 884-7959
Eden ES 400/PK-4
412 Wolf Creek Rd N 35125 205-338-6930
Laurie Funderburg, prin. Fax 338-8613
Kennedy ES 500/K-4
250 Otis Perry Dr 35128 205-338-7896
Leah Stover Ed.D., prin. Fax 338-1659
Roberts ES 500/K-4
810 Martin St N 35125 205-338-7312
Elizabeth Grimes, prin. Fax 884-0936
Williams IS 600/5-6
2000 Hardwick Rd 35128 205-338-4949
Holly Costello, prin. Fax 338-4953
Other Schools – See Cropwell

Victory Christian S 400/PK-12
PO Box 710 35125 205-338-2901

Perdido, Baldwin
Baldwin County SD
Supt. — See Bay Minette
Perdido S 500/PK-8
23589 County Road 47 36562 251-937-8456
Phillip Stewart, prin. Fax 937-3073

Phenix City, Russell, Pop. 32,176
Phenix City SD 6,700/PK-12
PO Box 460 36868 334-298-0534
Randy Wilkes, supt. Fax 298-2674
www.pcboe.net
Lakewood ES 500/3-5
24 Explorer Dr 36867 334-732-1173
Lanette Holmes, prin. Fax 732-0866
Lakewood PS 400/K-2
18 Explorer Dr 36867 334-664-9955
Sarah Kimmel, prin. Fax 664-9958
Meadowlane ES 200/K-5
709 Meadowlane Dr 36869 334-298-2568
Aretha McDonald, prin. Fax 291-3008
Phenix City ES 800/K-5
2307 S Railroad St 36867 334-732-1160
Sylvia Averett, prin. Fax 732-1165
Phenix City IS 1,000/6-7
2401 S Railroad St 36867 334-298-8744
Bobby Cook, prin. Fax 291-0824
Ridgecrest ES 800/K-5
1806 8th Pl S 36869 334-298-3004
Veatrice Thomas, prin. Fax 298-1763
Sherwood ES 500/K-5
706 Idle Hour Dr 36867 334-298-7097
Jeremy Suchman, prin. Fax 298-9429
South Girard S 500/8-8
521 Fontaine Rd 36869 334-298-2527
Kerry McDonald, prin. Fax 297-8274
Westview ES 400/K-5
1012 23rd St 36867 334-298-4507
Marceda Gordey-Lewis, prin. Fax 298-7891

Russell County SD 3,600/PK-12
PO Box 400 36868 706-321-2224
Dr. Brenda Coley Ed.D., supt. Fax 448-8314
myrcsd.org
Ladonia ES 500/PK-5
9 Woodland Dr 36869 334-321-2232
Pamela Simpson, prin. Fax 297-2189
Mt. Olive PS 400/K-2
PO Box 400 36868 706-321-2238
Larry Saulsberry, prin. Fax 855-9483
Other Schools – See Fort Mitchell, Opelika, Seale

Phil Campbell, Franklin, Pop. 1,134
Franklin County SD
Supt. — See Russellville
East Franklin S 200/PK-9
1815 Highway 89 35581 256-331-2140
Nancy Hallman, prin. Fax 331-2144
Phil Campbell ES 400/PK-6
PO Box 129 35581 256-331-2170
Jackie Ergle, prin. Fax 331-2171

Piedmont, Calhoun, Pop. 4,787
Piedmont CSD 1,200/K-12
502 W Hood St 36272 256-447-8831
Dr. Mike Hayes, supt. Fax 447-6486
www.piedmont.k12.al.us/
Piedmont ES 600/K-5
504 W Hood St 36272 256-447-7483
Brigett Stewart, prin. Fax 447-0130
Piedmont MS 300/6-8
401 N Main St 36272 256-447-6165
Chris Hanson, prin. Fax 447-8070

Pike Road, Montgomery, Pop. 5,366
Montgomery County SD
Supt. — See Montgomery
Washington MS 700/6-8
696 Georgia Washington Rd 36064 334-215-8290
Orlando Ledyard, prin. Fax 215-1304

Pike Road SD PK-10
500 Avenue of Learning St 36064 334-420-5310
Charles Ledbetter, supt.
www.pikeroadschools.org
Pike Road S PK-6
500 Avenue of Learning St 36064 334-420-5310
Ryan Kendall, prin.

Pinckard, Dale, Pop. 638
Dale County SD
Supt. — See Ozark
South Dale MS 400/5-8
PO Box D 36371 334-983-3077
Bucky Sconyers, prin. Fax 983-5882

Pine Hill, Wilcox, Pop. 972
Wilcox County SD
Supt. — See Camden
Ervin ES 300/PK-6
PO Box 220 36769 334-963-4702
Brenda Autry, prin. Fax 963-9060

Pinson, Jefferson, Pop. 7,099
Jefferson County SD
Supt. — See Birmingham
Johnson ES 800/3-5
8300 Kermit Johnson Rd 35126 205-379-4350
Christy Hamilton, prin. Fax 379-4395
Pinson ES 800/K-2
4200 School Dr 35126 205-379-5050
Karen Jones, prin. Fax 379-5095
Rudd MS 800/6-8
4526 Rudd School Rd 35126 205-379-5300
Susan Slaney, prin. Fax 680-8124

Pisgah, Jackson, Pop. 710
Jackson County SD
Supt. — See Scottsboro
Pisgah S 700/K-12
60 Metcalf St 35765 256-451-3241
Billy Duncan, prin. Fax 451-3457

Rosalie S 200/K-8
162 County Road 355 35765 256-451-3616
Bill Shelton, prin. Fax 451-3605

Plantersville, Dallas
Dallas County SD
Supt. — See Selma
Terry ES 100/K-6
70 Academy St 36758 334-366-2838
Robert Dolbare, prin. Fax 366-5325

Pleasant Grove, Jefferson, Pop. 10,034
Jefferson County SD
Supt. — See Birmingham
JCIB MYP 400/6-8
805 7th Ave 35127 205-379-5280
Sandy Jolivette, head sch Fax 379-5295
Pleasant Grove ES 600/K-5
601 Park Rd 35127 205-379-5200
Jay Jacks, prin. Fax 379-5245

Prattville, Autauga, Pop. 33,381
Autauga County SD 9,500/K-12
153 W 4th St 36067 334-365-5706
Spence Agee, supt. Fax 361-3828
www.acboe.net
Pratt ES 1,100/1-6
420 Harvest Loop 36066 334-361-6400
Julie Harrington, prin. Fax 358-2393
Prattville ES 600/3-4
134 Patrick St 36067 334-361-3885
Felissa Clemons, prin. Fax 361-3835
Prattville IS 700/5-6
1020 Honeysuckle Dr 36067 334-361-3880
Angela Landry, prin. Fax 361-3884
Prattville JHS 1,100/7-8
1089 Martin Luther King Dr 36067 334-365-6697
Janice Stockman, prin. Fax 361-3870
Prattville K 500/K-K
338 1st St 36067 334-361-3890
Jodi Womble, prin. Fax 361-3891
Prattville PS 600/1-2
216 Wetumpka St 36067 334-365-6277
Tammy Starnes, prin. Fax 365-0116
Other Schools – See Autaugaville, Billingsley, Deatsville, Marbury

---

Autauga Academy 300/PK-12
497 Golson Rd 36067 334-365-4343
East Memorial Christian Academy 300/PK-12
1320 Old Ridge Rd E 36066 334-358-4085
Bryan Easley, admin. Fax 358-9226
Prattville Christian Academy 700/PK-12
322 Old Farm Ln N 36066 334-285-0077

Prichard, Mobile, Pop. 22,453
Mobile County SD
Supt. — See Mobile
Grant ES 400/PK-5
535 Easterling St 36610 251-221-1319
Kimba Drakeford, prin. Fax 221-1315
Mobile County Training MS 200/6-8
800 Whitley St 36610 251-221-2267
Rashad Stallworth, prin. Fax 221-2269
Robbins ES 400/PK-5
2416 W Main St 36610 251-221-1600
Teronda Smith, prin. Fax 221-1605
Whitley ES 400/PK-5
528 Capt Leon C Roberts St 36610 251-221-1737
JaaDaa Holcombe, prin. Fax 221-1736

Emmanuel Christian Academy 50/K-9
520 Gilbert St 36610 251-478-1140
Prichard Preparatory S PK-5
743 Mt Sinai Ave, 251-380-7220
Lorie Minor, prin. Fax 380-7221

Princeton, Jackson
Jackson County SD
Supt. — See Scottsboro
Paint Rock Valley S 100/K-12
PO Box 150 35766 256-776-2628
Michael McBride, prin. Fax 776-0042

Quinton, Jefferson
Jefferson County SD
Supt. — See Birmingham
West Jefferson ES 200/K-6
4880 Freewill Dr 35130 205-379-5550
Dr. Brenda Cassady, prin. Fax 379-5595

Ragland, Saint Clair, Pop. 1,613
Saint Clair County SD
Supt. — See Ashville
Ragland S 500/K-12
1060 Main St 35131 205-472-2123
Jennifer Ball, prin. Fax 472-0086

Rainbow City, Etowah, Pop. 9,471
Etowah County SD
Supt. — See Gadsden
Jones ES 700/K-5
301 Lumbley Rd 35906 256-442-2900
Tanya Clark, prin. Fax 442-5060
Rainbow MS 700/6-8
454 Lumbley Rd 35906 256-442-1095
Matt Brooks, prin. Fax 442-1028

Westbrook Christian S 600/PK-12
100 Westminster Dr 35906 256-442-7457

Rainsville, DeKalb, Pop. 4,882
De Kalb County SD 8,700/K-12
PO Box 1668 35986 256-638-6921
Jason Barnett, supt. Fax 638-6972
www.dekalbk12.org
Plainview S 1,100/K-12
PO Box 469 35986 256-638-3510
Tony Richards, prin. Fax 638-6811

Other Schools – See Collinsville, Crossville, Fort Payne, Fyffe, Geraldine, Henagar, Ider, Mentone, Sylvania, Valley Head

Ramer, Montgomery
Montgomery County SD
Supt. — See Montgomery
Dunbar-Ramer S 200/K-8
56 Naftel Ramer Rd 36069 334-562-3250
James Owens, prin. Fax 562-3134

Ranburne, Cleburne, Pop. 406
Cleburne County SD
Supt. — See Heflin
Ranburne ES 300/K-4
181 Young Dr 36273 256-568-9722
Brenda Hall, prin. Fax 568-2607

Randolph, Bibb
Bibb County SD
Supt. — See Centreville
Randolph ES 200/PK-6
7259 Highway 36 36792 334-366-2897
Louise Carey, prin. Fax 366-5003

Red Bay, Franklin, Pop. 3,100
Franklin County SD
Supt. — See Russellville
Red Bay S 800/PK-12
PO Box 1518 35582 256-331-2270
Lance Mitchell, prin. Fax 331-2281

Red Level, Covington, Pop. 487
Covington County SD
Supt. — See Andalusia
Red Level ES 400/PK-6
PO Box D 36474 334-469-5315
Clifton Pace, prin. Fax 469-5317

Reform, Pickens, Pop. 1,691
Pickens County SD
Supt. — See Carrollton
Reform ES 300/K-6
815 7th Ave SW 35481 205-375-6351
Dr. Valerie Carter-Jackson, prin. Fax 375-6777

Remlap, Blount
Blount County SD
Supt. — See Oneonta
Southeastern S 600/K-12
18770 State Highway 75 35133 205-681-3964
Billy Puckett, prin. Fax 681-3975

Repton, Conecuh, Pop. 275
Conecuh County SD
Supt. — See Evergreen
Repton S 200/PK-8
2340 Conaly St 36475 251-248-2960
Tommy Dukes, prin. Fax 248-2371

Roanoke, Randolph, Pop. 6,021
Roanoke CSD 1,500/PK-12
PO Box 1367 36274 334-863-2628
Chuck Marcum, supt. Fax 863-2849
www.roanokecityschools.org/
Handley MS 600/4-8
PO Box 725 36274 334-863-4174
Lynn Robinson, prin. Fax 863-6129
Knight Enloe ES 400/PK-3
PO Box 685 36274 334-863-2237
Amy Moody, prin. Fax 863-6092

Robertsdale, Baldwin, Pop. 5,180
Baldwin County SD
Supt. — See Bay Minette
Central Baldwin MS 700/7-8
PO Box 930 36567 251-947-2327
Phillip Fountain, prin. Fax 947-1949
Elsanor ES 300/PK-6
23440 US Highway 90 36567 251-947-5401
Susan Runnels, prin. Fax 947-4966
Robertsdale ES 1,100/PK-6
1 Cub Dr 36567 251-947-4003
Faye Sheppard, prin. Fax 947-1919
Rosinton ES 300/PK-6
19757 County Road 64 36567 251-964-5210
Joseph Benton, prin. Fax 964-4421

Central Christian S 300/PK-12
17395 State Highway 104 36567 251-947-5043
Tim Shelton, admin. Fax 947-2572
St. Patrick S 200/PK-8
PO Box 609 36567 251-947-7395
Sr. Margaret Harte, prin. Fax 947-3860

Rockford, Coosa, Pop. 477
Coosa County SD 1,100/K-12
PO Box 37 35136 256-377-4913
Andi Wilson, supt. Fax 377-2385
www.coosaschools.k12.al.us
Central ES Coosa County 400/K-4
95 Coosa County Road 75 35136 256-377-1456
Kara Forbus, prin. Fax 377-1459
Central MS Coosa County 400/5-8
97 Coosa County Road 75 35136 256-377-1490
Dr. Nicole Ivey, prin. Fax 377-1493

Rock Mills, Randolph, Pop. 594
Randolph County SD
Supt. — See Wedowee
Rock Mills S 200/K-8
415 County Road 75 36274 334-885-6823
Chad Kendrick, prin. Fax 885-6806

Rogersville, Lauderdale, Pop. 1,248
Lauderdale County SD
Supt. — See Florence
Lauderdale County S 1,200/PK-12
201 Cedar St 35652 256-247-3414
Eric Cornelius, prin. Fax 247-3444

Russellville, Franklin, Pop. 9,705
Franklin County SD 3,200/PK-12
PO Box 610 35653 256-332-1360
Greg Hamilton, supt. Fax 331-0069
www.franklin.k12.al.us
Belgreen S 500/PK-12
14220 Highway 187 35653 256-332-1376
Ann Scott, prin. Fax 332-7209
Tharptown ES 400/PK-6
145 Highway 80 35654 256-332-3404
Kelby Daniel, prin. Fax 332-3402
Other Schools – See Phil Campbell, Red Bay, Vina

Russellville CSD 2,500/K-12
1945 Waterloo Rd 35653 256-331-2000
Heath Grimes, supt. Fax 332-7323
www.rcs.k12.al.us
Russellville ES 600/3-5
133 Chucky Mullins Memorial 35653 256-331-2123
Kristie Ezzell, prin. Fax 332-1880
Russellville MS 600/6-8
765 Summit St 35653 256-331-2120
Dr. Karen Thorn, prin. Fax 332-8453
West ES 700/K-2
1340 Clay Ave 35653 256-331-2122
Deanna Hollimon, prin. Fax 332-6124

Salem, Lee
Lee County SD
Supt. — See Opelika
Wacoochee ES 500/K-6
125 Lee Road 254 36874 334-664-4072
Tammy Senn, prin. Fax 745-3565

Samson, Geneva, Pop. 1,902
Geneva County SD
Supt. — See Geneva
Samson ES 300/K-5
823 N State Highway 87 36477 334-898-7439
Blakelynn Barker, prin. Fax 898-2473
Samson MS 200/7-8
209 N Broad St 36477 334-898-2371
Danny Branch, prin. Fax 898-7576

Sand Rock, Cherokee, Pop. 556
Cherokee County SD
Supt. — See Centre
Sand Rock S 900/K-12
1950 Sand Rock Ave 35983 256-523-3564
John East, prin. Fax 523-3507

Saraland, Mobile, Pop. 13,216
Saraland CSD 2,700/PK-12
4010 Lil Spartan Dr 36571 251-375-5420
Dr. Aaron Milner, supt. Fax 375-5430
www.saralandboe.org
Saraland Early Education Center PK-1
4000 Lil Spartan Dr 36571 251-602-8930
Kim Williams, prin. Fax 602-8931
Saraland ES 1,000/2-5
229 McKeough Ave 36571 251-679-5739
Stan Stokley, prin. Fax 679-5749
Saraland MS - Nelson Adams Campus 800/6-8
401 Baldwin Rd 36571 251-679-9405
Alex Crane, prin. Fax 679-9456

North Mobile Christian S 300/PK-8
1255 Industrial Pkwy 36571 251-679-3279

Satsuma, Mobile, Pop. 6,101
Satsuma City SD 1,100/PK-12
PO Box 939 36572 251-380-8200
Joe Walters, supt. Fax 380-8201
satsumacity.schoolinsites.com/
Lee ES 400/PK-6
251 Baker Rd 36572 251-380-8210
Brenda Sharp, prin. Fax 380-8211

Scottsboro, Jackson, Pop. 14,491
Jackson County SD 5,700/PK-12
PO Box 490 35768 256-259-9500
Dr. Kevin Dukes, supt. Fax 259-0076
www.jackson.k12.al.us
Skyline S 500/K-12
897 County Road 25 35768 256-587-6561
Anthony Davidson, prin. Fax 587-6562
Other Schools – See Bridgeport, Bryant, Dutton, Flat Rock, Higdon, Hollywood, Pisgah, Princeton, Section, Stevenson, Woodville

Scottsboro CSD 2,600/K-12
305 S Scott St 35768 256-218-2100
Fax 218-2190
www.scottsboroschools.net
Brownwood ES 300/K-4
305 Bingham St 35768 256-218-2400
Dr. Gary Speers, prin. Fax 218-2490
Caldwell ES 400/K-4
905 S Market St 35768 256-218-2500
Fax 218-2590
Collins IS 400/5-6
102 Legion Dr 35768 256-218-2700
Julie Petty, prin. Fax 218-2790
Nelson ES 200/K-4
202 Ida Moody Rd 35769 256-218-2600
Dale Hancock, prin. Fax 218-2690
Scottsboro JHS 400/7-8
1601 Jefferson St 35768 256-218-2300
Jason Hass, prin. Fax 218-2390

Seale, Russell
Russell County SD
Supt. — See Phenix City
Oliver ES 500/PK-5
77 Longview St 36875 706-321-2241
Alison Waldrop, prin. Fax 855-3201
Russell County MS 600/6-8
4716 Old Seale Hwy 36875 706-321-2261
Rebecca Johnston, prin. Fax 855-4487

Section, Jackson, Pop. 755
Jackson County SD
Supt. — See Scottsboro
Macedonia S 200/K-8
196 County Road 49 35771 256-228-4483
Steven Paradise, prin. Fax 228-7083
Section S 600/K-12
PO Box 10 35771 256-228-6718
Gene Roberts, prin. Fax 228-6252

Selma, Dallas, Pop. 20,594
Dallas County SD 3,400/PK-12
PO Box 1056 36702 334-875-3440
Hattie Shelton, supt. Fax 876-4497
www.dallask12.org
Brantley ES 200/PK-6
5585 Water Ave 36703 334-874-8185
Audrey Strong, prin. Fax 874-6541
Craig ES 300/3-5
108 Craig Industrial Park 36701 334-875-7937
Ebony Cox, prin. Fax 875-7937
Southside PS 300/K-2
3104 Old Montgomery Rd 36703 334-874-9566
Brenda Mitchell, prin. Fax 874-8226
Tipton MS 200/7-8
2500 Tipton St 36701 334-872-8080
Jackie Averhart, prin. Fax 872-8008
Other Schools – See Orrville, Plantersville, Valley Grande

Selma CSD 3,600/PK-12
PO Box 350 36702 334-874-1600
Arthur Capers, supt. Fax 874-1604
www.selmacityschools.org
Byrd First Class Early Learning Center 50/PK-PK
625 Lapsley St 36701 334-874-1620
Cheryl Randolph, prin. Fax 874-1648
Cedar Park ES 200/K-5
1101 Woodrow Ave 36701 334-874-1625
Dr. Doris Cureton, prin. Fax 874-1702
Clark ES 400/K-5
405 Lawrence St 36703 334-874-1630
Dyphelia Thrash, prin. Fax 874-1711
Edgewood ES 300/K-5
709 Highland Ave 36701 334-874-1640
Joe Peterson, prin. Fax 874-1641
Hudson MS 500/7-8
1701 Summerfield Rd 36701 334-874-1675
LaShonda Moorer, prin. Fax 874-1679
Kingston ES 200/K-5
2224 Selma Ave 36703 334-874-1635
Ozella Ford, prin. Fax 874-1637
Knox ES 200/K-5
1002 Mabry St 36701 334-874-1650
Dr. Lachonda Brown, prin. Fax 876-1403
Meadowview ES 300/K-5
1816 Old Orrville Rd 36701 334-874-1655
Concetta Burton, prin. Fax 874-1656
Payne ES 300/K-5
1529 Franklin St 36703 334-874-1660
Taurus Smith, prin. Fax 874-1662
School of Discovery Genesis Center 300/6-6
400 Washington St 36703 334-874-1670
Cicely Curtis, prin. Fax 874-1674

Ellwood Christian Academy 200/PK-12
1 Bell Rd 36701 334-877-1586
Meadowview Christian S 200/PK-12
1512 Old Orrville Rd 36701 334-872-8448
Morgan Academy 500/K-12
2901 W Dallas Ave 36701 334-875-4464

Semmes, Mobile
Mobile County SD
Supt. — See Mobile
Allentown ES 800/K-5
10330 Howells Ferry Rd 36575 251-221-1000
Ashtiny Roberts, prin. Fax 221-1003
Semmes ES 600/PK-5
10100 Blackwell Nursery S 36575 251-221-1630
Valerie Johnson, prin. Fax 221-1633
Semmes MS 1,600/6-8
4566 Ed George Rd 36575 251-221-2344
Wendell Ellis, prin. Fax 221-2347

Sheffield, Colbert, Pop. 8,895
Sheffield CSD 1,100/PK-12
300 W 6th St 35660 256-383-0400
Daniel Lankford, supt. Fax 386-5704
www.scs.k12.al.us
Sheffield JHS 200/7-8
1803 E 30th St 35660 256-386-5735
Eric Kirkman, prin. Fax 386-5706
Threadgill PS 300/PK-2
900 Annapolis Ave 35660 256-386-5720
Matthew Syesta, prin. Fax 386-5705
Willson ES 300/3-6
2200 E 31st St 35660 256-386-5730
Charles Willis, prin. Fax 386-5708

Shelby, Shelby, Pop. 1,031
Shelby County SD
Supt. — See Columbiana
Shelby ES 200/K-5
19099 Highway 145 35143 205-682-6630
Stacy Aderholt, prin. Fax 682-6635

Shorter, Macon, Pop. 469
Macon County SD
Supt. — See Tuskegee
Wolfe ES 100/K-6
4450 Cross Keys Rd 36075 334-727-1641
Carolyn Bradley, prin. Fax 727-9958

Silverhill, Baldwin, Pop. 701
Baldwin County SD
Supt. — See Bay Minette
Silverhill ES 400/PK-6
PO Box 190 36576 251-945-5188
Pamela Moorer, prin. Fax 945-5116

Skipperville, Dale
Dale County SD
Supt. — See Ozark
Long ES 500/K-6
2567 County Road 60 36374 334-774-0021
John Kelly, prin. Fax 445-5593

Slocomb, Geneva, Pop. 1,949
Geneva County SD
Supt. — See Geneva
Slocomb ES 600/K-5
108 S Hemby St 36375 334-886-2132
Christie Hughes, prin. Fax 886-9842
Slocomb MS 300/6-8
591 S County Road 9 36375 334-886-2008
Zeb Brown, prin. Fax 886-9889

Smiths, Lee, Pop. 3,456
Lee County SD
Supt. — See Opelika
East Smiths Station ES 900/K-6
171 Lee Road 728 36877 334-448-4422
Paul Kohler, prin. Fax 448-4499

Glenwood S 400/PK-12
5801 Summerville Rd 36877 334-297-3614

Smiths Station, Lee, Pop. 4,838
Lee County SD
Supt. — See Opelika
Smiths Station JHS 7-8
1100 Lee Road 298 36877 334-664-4070
Rick Harris, prin.
South Smiths Station ES 700/K-6
80 Lee Road 926 36877 334-298-8370
Kelley Smith, prin. Fax 298-8474
West Smiths Station ES 800/K-6
150 Lee Road 295 36877 334-298-6089
Bonnie Short, prin. Fax 214-0361

Somerville, Morgan, Pop. 713
Morgan County SD
Supt. — See Decatur
Cotaco S 500/PK-8
100 Cotaco School Rd 35670 256-778-8154
Bradley Stapler, prin. Fax 778-8148
Union Hill S 500/K-8
2221 Union Hill Rd 35670 256-498-2431
Robert Elliott, prin. Fax 498-3524

Southside, Etowah, Pop. 8,359
Etowah County SD
Supt. — See Gadsden
Southside ES 600/K-5
2551 Highway 77 35907 256-442-1090
Carrie Yancey, prin. Fax 442-1075

Spanish Fort, Baldwin, Pop. 6,701
Baldwin County SD
Supt. — See Bay Minette
Rockwell ES 800/K-5
10183 US Highway 31 36527 251-626-5528
Robert Owen, prin. Fax 621-7206
Spanish Fort ES 700/K-5
30900 State Highway 225 36527 251-626-9751
Rebecca Comer, prin. Fax 621-8018
Spanish Fort MS 900/6-8
33899 Jimmy Faulkner Dr 36527 251-625-3271
Oliver Sinclair, prin. Fax 626-7201

Spring Garden, Cherokee, Pop. 234
Cherokee County SD
Supt. — See Centre
Spring Garden S 500/K-12
PO Box 31 36275 256-447-7045
Michael Welsh, prin. Fax 447-6947

Springville, Saint Clair, Pop. 4,042
Saint Clair County SD
Supt. — See Ashville
Springville ES 900/PK-5
75 Wilson St 35146 205-467-6550
James Talton, prin. Fax 467-2716
Springville MS 500/6-8
6691 US Highway 11 35146 205-467-2740
James Talton, prin. Fax 467-2742

Stapleton, Baldwin
Baldwin County SD
Supt. — See Bay Minette
Stapleton ES 200/PK-6
35480 Harriot Ave 36578 251-937-2038
James Perry, prin. Fax 580-2001

Steele, Saint Clair, Pop. 1,031
Saint Clair County SD
Supt. — See Ashville
Steele S 200/K-8
105 McHugh St 35987 256-538-5489
Kelley Peoples, prin. Fax 538-5496

Stevenson, Jackson, Pop. 1,968
Jackson County SD
Supt. — See Scottsboro
Stevenson ES 400/K-4
930 Old Mount Carmel Rd 35772 256-437-2203
James Brooks, prin. Fax 437-8372
Stevenson MS 300/5-8
701 Kentucky Ave 35772 256-437-2945
Dr. Beverly Kenimer, prin. Fax 437-2747

Sulligent, Lamar, Pop. 1,890
Lamar County SD
Supt. — See Vernon
Sulligent S 800/K-12
PO Box 909 35586 205-698-9254
Dr. Lisa Stamps, prin. Fax 698-8497

Sumiton, Walker, Pop. 2,483
Walker County SD
Supt. — See Jasper

Sumiton ES K-4
71 1st St N 35148 205-648-5656
Dr. Kristy Wheeler, prin. Fax 648-5657
Sumiton MS 400/5-8
275 1st St N 35148 205-648-2390
Chris Stephenson, prin. Fax 648-0183

Sumiton Christian S 400/PK-12
155 Hosanna Dr 35148 205-648-6643
Cheryl Capps, prin. Fax 648-9893

Summerdale, Baldwin, Pop. 836
Baldwin County SD
Supt. — See Bay Minette
Summerdale S 500/PK-8
PO Box 9 36580 251-989-6850
Mark Pumphrey, prin. Fax 989-6611

Sweet Water, Marengo, Pop. 258
Marengo County SD
Supt. — See Linden
Sweet Water S 700/PK-12
PO Box 127 36782 334-994-4263
Phyllis Mabowitz, prin. Fax 994-4686

Sycamore, Talladega
Talladega County SD
Supt. — See Talladega
Sycamore ES 200/K-4
18101 AL Highway 21 35149 256-315-5450
Shareka Lee, prin. Fax 315-5455

Sylacauga, Talladega, Pop. 12,625
Sylacauga CSD 2,400/PK-12
43 N Broadway Ave 35150 256-245-5256
Michael Freeman, supt. Fax 245-6665
www.sylacauga.k12.al.us
Indian Valley ES 600/PK-2
1099 Oldfield Rd 35150 256-249-0397
Monte Abner, prin. Fax 245-9851
Nichols-Lawson MS 600/6-8
1550 Talladega Hwy 35150 256-245-4376
Gary Rivers, prin. Fax 245-4071
Pinecrest ES 500/3-5
615 Coaling Rd 35151 256-245-5700
Debbie Barnett, prin. Fax 245-2699

Talladega County SD
Supt. — See Talladega
Comer Memorial ES 500/K-6
803 Seminole Ave 35150 256-315-5430
Melia Brashear, prin. Fax 315-5445
Fayetteville S 700/K-12
170 WW Averitte Dr 35151 256-315-5550
Amy Smith, prin. Fax 315-5575

Knollwood Christian S 50/PK-11
PO Box 340 35150 256-249-4750

Sylvania, DeKalb, Pop. 1,781
De Kalb County SD
Supt. — See Rainsville
Sylvania S 900/K-12
133 Second St N 35988 256-638-2030
Westley King, prin. Fax 638-7839

Talladega, Talladega, Pop. 15,505
Talladega CSD 2,200/PK-12
PO Box 946 35161 256-315-5600
Terry Roller, supt. Fax 315-5606
www.talladega-cs.net
Ellis JHS 300/7-8
414 Elm St 35160 256-315-5700
Shari Dye, prin. Fax 315-5704
Graham ES 300/K-6
403 Cedar St 35160 256-315-5200
Dr. Melissa Kelley, prin. Fax 315-5781
Houston ES 400/PK-6
1310 Ashland Hwy 35160 256-315-5800
Marvin Moten, prin. Fax 315-5804
Salter ES 300/K-6
106 Brecon Access Rd 35160 256-315-5822
Micah Cook, prin. Fax 315-5826
Young ES 300/K-6
200 E Damon Ave 35160 256-315-5888
Linda Haynes, prin. Fax 315-5884

Talladega County SD 7,600/K-12
PO Box 887 35161 256-315-5100
Dr. Suzanne Lacey, supt. Fax 315-5126
www.tcboe.org
Stemley Road ES 400/K-6
2760 Stemley Bridge Rd 35160 256-315-5325
Michelle Barker, prin. Fax 315-5335
Other Schools – See Childersburg, Lincoln, Munford, Sycamore, Sylacauga

Tallassee, Elmore, Pop. 4,755
Tallassee CSD 1,900/K-12
308 King St 36078 334-283-6864
Wade Shipman, supt. Fax 283-4338
www.tcschools.com
Southside MS 600/5-8
901 EB Payne Sr Dr 36078 334-283-2151
Bruce Dean, prin. Fax 283-3577
Tallassee ES 800/K-4
850 Friendship Rd 36078 334-283-5001
Dr. Jose Reyes, prin. Fax 283-8661

Tanner, Limestone
Limestone County SD
Supt. — See Athens
Tanner ES, 12067 Dowd St 35671 400/PK-5
Angie Barnes, prin. 256-233-6682

Tarrant, Jefferson, Pop. 6,300
Tarrant CSD 1,100/PK-12
1318 Alabama St 35217 205-849-3700
Dr. Shelly Mize, supt. Fax 849-3728
www.tarrant.k12.al.us
Tarrant ES 300/PK-2
1269 Portland St 35217 205-841-7541
Walter Womack, prin. Fax 849-3716
Tarrant IS 300/3-6
1 Wildcat Dr 35217 205-849-0168
David Seale, prin. Fax 849-1545

Theodore, Mobile, Pop. 6,002
Mobile County SD
Supt. — See Mobile
Burroughs ES 400/PK-5
6875 Burroughs Ln 36582 251-221-1077
Dr. Julia Nelson, prin. Fax 221-1076
Davis ES 500/K-5
6900 Nan Gray Davis Rd 36582 251-221-1166
Eileen Mai, prin. Fax 221-1167
Hankins MS 800/6-8
5750 Katherine Hankins Dr 36582 251-221-2200
David Diaz, prin. Fax 221-2204

Thomaston, Marengo, Pop. 414
Marengo County SD
Supt. — See Linden
Johnson S 200/K-12
PO Box 67 36783 334-627-3364
William Martin, prin. Fax 627-3396

Thomasville, Clarke, Pop. 4,190
Thomasville CSD 1,500/PK-12
PO Box 458 36784 334-636-9955
Dr. Vic Adkison, supt. Fax 636-4096
www.thomasvilleschools.org/
Thomasville ES 500/PK-4
300 Quincy Ingram St 36784 334-636-0063
Sandra Williams, prin. Fax 636-0021
Thomasville MS 400/5-8
781 Gates Dr 36784 334-636-4928
Gerald McAnally, prin. Fax 636-4924

Thorsby, Chilton, Pop. 1,968
Chilton County SD
Supt. — See Clanton
Thorsby S 800/K-12
54 Opportunity Dr 35171 205-280-4880
Harold Clements, prin. Fax 646-2197

Toney, Madison
Madison County SD
Supt. — See Huntsville
Madison Cross Roads ES 900/K-5
11548 Pulaski Pike 35773 256-851-4600
Mitchell Hampton, prin. Fax 851-4601
Sparkman MS 800/6-8
2697 Carters Gin Rd 35773 256-851-4610
Russ O'Rear, prin. Fax 851-4611

Town Creek, Lawrence, Pop. 1,049
Lawrence County SD
Supt. — See Moulton
Hatton ES 400/K-6
6536 County Road 236 35672 256-685-4000
Brittney Morgan, prin. Fax 685-4004
Hazlewood ES 200/K-6
PO Box 699 35672 256-685-4020
Stacie Givens, prin. Fax 685-4008

Toxey, Choctaw, Pop. 137

South Choctaw Academy 300/PK-12
PO Box 160 36921 251-843-2426

Trinity, Morgan, Pop. 2,059
Lawrence County SD
Supt. — See Moulton
East Lawrence ES 400/K-4
263 County Road 370 35673 256-905-2513
Casey Tate, prin. Fax 905-2522
East Lawrence MS 400/5-8
99 County Road 370 35673 256-905-2420
Baine Garner, prin. Fax 905-2477

Morgan County SD
Supt. — See Decatur
West Morgan ES 600/K-4
571 Old Highway 24 35673 256-350-8818
Rebecca Burt, prin. Fax 350-5756
West Morgan MS 400/5-8
261 S Greenway Dr 35673 256-353-5214
Jill Jones, prin. Fax 355-8713

Troy, Pike, Pop. 17,799
Pike County SD 2,200/PK-12
101 W Love St 36081 334-566-1850
Dr. Mark Bazzell M.Ed., supt. Fax 566-2580
www.pikecountyschools.com
Other Schools – See Banks, Brundidge, Goshen

Troy CSD 1,900/K-12
PO Box 529 36081 334-566-3741
Lee Hicks, supt. Fax 566-1425
www.troyschools.net
Henderson MS 300/6-8
PO Box 925 36081 334-566-5770
Aaron Brown, prin. Fax 566-3071
Troy ES 900/K-5
PO Box 708 36081 334-566-1444
Teresa Sims, prin. Fax 566-8142

Pike Liberal Arts S 400/PK-12
PO Box 329 36081 334-566-2023

Trussville, Jefferson, Pop. 19,764
Jefferson County SD
Supt. — See Birmingham
Clay-Chalkville MS 1,000/6-8
6700 Trussville Clay Rd 35173 205-379-3100
Ron Tillman, prin. Fax 379-3145

Trussville City SD 3,400/K-12
113 N Chalkville Rd 35173 205-228-3018
Dr. Patricia Neill, supt. Fax 228-3001
trussvillecityschools.com/
Cahaba ES, 301 Parkway Dr 35173 K-5
Joy Tyner, prin. 205-228-3400
Hewitt-Trussville MS 1,000/6-8
5275 Trussville Clay Rd 35173 205-228-3700
Lisa Berry, prin. Fax 228-3701
Magnolia ES K-5
5400 Hidden Way Ln 35173 205-228-3500
Autumm Jeter, prin.
Paine ES 1,000/K-5
7600 Gadsden Hwy 35173 205-228-3200
J. Tygar Evans, prin. Fax 228-3201

Tuscaloosa, Tuscaloosa, Pop. 89,545
Tuscaloosa CSD 9,700/PK-12
PO Box 38991 35403 205-759-3700
Mike Daria, supt. Fax 759-3542
www.tusc.k12.al.us
Alberta S of Performing Arts 300/PK-8
2700 University Blvd E 35404 205-759-3564
Brenda Parker, prin. Fax 759-3753
Arcadia ES 300/K-5
315 McFarland Blvd E 35404 205-759-3567
Amy Elam, prin. Fax 759-3754
Central ES 400/PK-5
1510 Dinah Washington Ave 35401 205-759-3570
Monte Linebarger, prin. Fax 759-3755
King ES 300/K-5
2430 ML King Jr Blvd 35401 205-759-3619
Tyrone Jones, prin. Fax 759-3556
Northington ES 400/PK-5
1300 21st St E 35404 205-759-3622
Ingrid Edwards, prin. Fax 759-3761
Oakdale ES 300/PK-5
5001 25th St 35401 205-759-3626
Dr. Lucile Prewitt, prin. Fax 759-3762
Rock Quarry ES 600/K-5
2000 Rock Quarry Dr 35406 205-759-8347
Laura Jockisch, prin. Fax 759-8348
Rock Quarry MS 600/6-8
2100 Rock Quarry Dr 35406 205-759-3578
Lynda Ingram, prin. Fax 759-3582
Skyland ES 400/PK-5
2605 Southview Dr 35405 205-759-3638
Vertis Giles-Brown, prin. Fax 759-3764
Southview ES 500/K-5
2601 Southview Dr 35405 205-345-1325
Yosondra Lett, prin. Fax 554-1069
Tuscaloosa Magnet ES 300/K-5
315 McFarland Blvd E 35404 205-759-3655
Preeti Nichani, prin. Fax 759-3658
Tuscaloosa Magnet MS 100/6-8
315 McFarland Blvd E 35404 205-759-3653
Kristi Thomson, prin. Fax 759-3784
University Place ES 400/PK-5
2000 1st Ave 35401 205-759-3664
Nakelya Mullins, prin. Fax 759-3768
University Place MS 100/6-8
2010 1st Ave 35401 205-759-3631
Tom Danner, prin. Fax 759-3635
Verner ES 600/K-5
2701 Northridge Rd 35406 205-759-3667
Elizabeth Curtis, prin. Fax 759-3769
Westlawn MS 400/6-8
1715 ML King Jr Blvd 35401 205-759-3673
Tiffany Davis, prin. Fax 759-3770
Woodland Forrest ES 400/PK-5
6001 Hargrove Rd E 35405 205-759-3675
Terri North-Byrts, prin. Fax 759-3771
Other Schools – See Cottondale

Tuscaloosa County SD 17,800/PK-12
PO Box 2568 35403 205-758-0411
Dr. Walter Davie, supt. Fax 758-2990
www.tcss.net
Englewood ES 500/K-5
10300 Old Greensboro Rd 35405 205-342-2644
Tameka Rice, prin. Fax 247-4173
Hillcrest MS 600/6-8
401 Hillcrest School Rd 35405 205-342-2820
Karen Davis, prin. Fax 247-4177
Holt ES 400/K-5
1001 Crescent Ridge Rd NE 35404 205-342-2650
Debbie Crawford, prin. Fax 247-4176
Taylorville PS 500/K-2
350 Bobby Miller Pkwy 35405 205-342-2939
Keri Criss, prin. Fax 247-4193
Other Schools – See Brookwood, Buhl, Coker, Cottondale, Duncanville, Fosters, Mc Calla, Moundville, Northport, Vance

American Christian Academy 900/PK-12
2300 Veterans Memorial Pkwy 35404 205-553-5963
Dr. Dan Carden, hdmstr. Fax 553-5942
Capitol S 100/PK-12
2828 6th St 35401 205-758-2828
Holy Spirit S PK-6
711 James I Harrison Jr E 35405 205-553-9630
Lisa Corona, prin. Fax 553-8880
North River Christian Academy 300/PK-12
1785 McFarland Blvd N 35406 205-349-4881
Riverwood Classical School 50/K-11
501 Rice Valley Rd N 35406 205-758-5502
Tuscaloosa Academy 400/PK-12
420 Rice Valley Rd N 35406 205-758-4462
Dr. Bryan Oliver, hdmstr. Fax 758-4418

Tuscumbia, Colbert, Pop. 8,279
Colbert County SD 2,700/PK-12
PO Box 538 35674 256-386-8565
Dr. Gale Satchel, supt. Fax 381-9375
colbert.k12.al.us/
Colbert Heights ES 400/PK-6
1551 Sunset Dr 35674 256-381-6132
Alvie Shaw, prin. Fax 389-9980

New Bethel ES 100/PK-6
900 New Bethel Rd 35674 256-383-6471
Tom Windsor, prin. Fax 383-1098
Other Schools – See Cherokee, Leighton

Tuscumbia CSD 1,500/K-12
303 N Commons St E 35674 256-389-2900
Darryl Aikerson, supt. Fax 389-2903
www.tuscumbia.k12.al.us
Deshler MS 400/6-8
598 N High St 35674 256-389-2920
Bryan Murner, prin. Fax 389-2921
Thompson IS 300/3-5
829 Frankfort Rd 35674 256-389-2930
Robert Bissell, prin. Fax 389-2931
Trenholm PS 300/K-2
601 Joe Wheeler Dr 35674 256-389-2940
Veronica Bayles, prin. Fax 389-2941

Covenant Christian S 200/PK-12
1900 Covenant Dr 35674 256-383-4436
Donny Davis, admin. Fax 381-4437

Tuskegee, Macon, Pop. 9,751
Macon County SD 2,200/PK-12
PO Box 830090 36083 334-727-1600
Dr. Jacqueline Brooks, supt. Fax 724-9990
www.maconk12.org
Carver ES 500/PK-3
303 Union Springs Hwy 36083 334-727-2700
Norman Williams, prin. Fax 727-5520
Tuskegee Public ES 300/4-6
101 E Price St 36083 334-727-3222
Tiffany Williams, prin. Fax 727-3703
Other Schools – See Notasulga, Shorter, Tuskegee Institute

Tuskegee Institute, See Tuskegee
Macon County SD
Supt. — See Tuskegee
Tuskegee Institute MS 300/7-8
1809 Franklin Rd 36088 334-727-2580
Rosemary Wright, prin. Fax 727-5089

St. Joseph S 100/PK-8
2009 W Montgomery Rd 36088 334-727-0620
Marjorie Reese, prin. Fax 727-0642

Union Grove, Marshall, Pop. 77
Marshall County SD
Supt. — See Guntersville
Brindlee Mountain PS 200/PK-2
3685 Union Grove Rd 35175 256-753-2532
Terry Allen, prin. Fax 753-0021

Union Springs, Bullock, Pop. 3,959
Bullock County SD 1,500/K-12
PO Box 231 36089 334-738-2860
Elliott Harris, supt. Fax 738-2802
bullockcounty.schoolinsites.com
South Highlands MS 400/5-8
PO Box 111 36089 334-738-2896
Sean Dees, prin. Fax 738-5746
Union Springs ES 600/K-4
211 Conecuh Ave W 36089 334-738-2990
Marvin Lowe, prin. Fax 738-2923

Uniontown, Perry, Pop. 1,770
Perry County SD
Supt. — See Marion
Hatch S 400/PK-12
PO Box 709 36786 334-628-4061
Leslie Ford, prin. Fax 683-4935

Uriah, Monroe, Pop. 280
Monroe County SD
Supt. — See Monroeville
Blacksher S 700/PK-12
15933 Highway 21 S 36480 251-862-2130
Donald Baggett, prin. Fax 862-2808

Valley, Chambers, Pop. 9,430
Chambers County SD
Supt. — See Lafayette
Burns MS 700/6-8
292 Johnson St 36854 334-756-3567
Dr. Frankie Bell, prin. Fax 756-7511
Fairfax ES 500/PK-5
502 Boulevard 36854 334-756-2966
Fran Groover, prin. Fax 756-4749
Harding-Shawmut ES 200/PK-2
3301 23rd Dr 36854 334-768-3474
Alison Burton, prin. Fax 768-3475
Lafayette Lanier ES 300/3-6
6001 20th Ave 36854 334-756-3623
Russell Newton, prin. Fax 756-4809

Lee County SD
Supt. — See Opelika
Beulah ES 700/K-6
4747 Lee Road 270 36854 334-745-5028
Angela Arnett, prin. Fax 745-2401

Valley Grande, Dallas, Pop. 3,989
Dallas County SD
Supt. — See Selma
Martin MS 300/7-8
2863 County Road 81, 334-872-6417
William Reece, prin. Fax 875-4013
Valley Grande ES 500/K-6
2765 County Road 81, 334-872-7661
Erika Crum, prin. Fax 875-8834

Valley Head, DeKalb, Pop. 541
De Kalb County SD
Supt. — See Rainsville
Valley Head S 500/K-12
PO Box 149 35989 256-635-6228
William Monroe, prin. Fax 635-6229

Vance, Tuscaloosa, Pop. 1,508
Tuscaloosa County SD
Supt. — See Tuscaloosa
Brookwood MS 800/6-8
17021 Brookwood Pkwy 35490 205-342-2748
Daniel Bray, prin. Fax 553-9910
Vance ES 500/K-5
18202 Highway 11 N 35490 205-342-2697
Carolyn Wilson, prin. Fax 247-4195

Verbena, Chilton
Chilton County SD
Supt. — See Clanton
Verbena S 600/K-12
202 County Road 510 36091 205-280-2820
Todd Davis, prin. Fax 755-0393

Vernon, Lamar, Pop. 1,977
Lamar County SD 2,400/K-12
PO Box 1379 35592 205-695-7615
Vance Herron, supt. Fax 695-7678
www.lamarcountyschoolsal.net
Vernon ES 300/K-3
PO Box 1349 35592 205-695-7717
Tracy Walker, prin. Fax 695-8218
Other Schools – See Millport, Sulligent

Vestavia Hills, Jefferson, Pop. 33,714
Vestavia Hills CSD 6,700/K-12
PO Box 660826 35266 205-402-5100
Sheila Phillips, supt. Fax 402-5134
www.vestavia.k12.al.us
Liberty Park ES 600/K-5
17051 Liberty Pkwy 35242 205-402-5400
Ty Arendall, prin. Fax 402-5401
Liberty Park MS 500/6-8
17035 Liberty Pkwy 35242 205-402-5450
Tonya Rozell, prin. Fax 402-5450
Pizitz MS 1,100/6-8
2020 Pizitz Dr 35216 205-402-5350
Meredith Hanson, prin. Fax 402-5354
Vestavia Hills Central ES 700/4-5
1289 Montgomery Hwy 35216 205-402-5300
Marian Humphries, prin. Fax 402-5301
Vestavia Hills ES East 800/K-3
2109 Tyson Dr 35216 205-402-5200
Dr. Mark Richardson, prin. Fax 402-5211
Vestavia Hills ES West 800/K-3
1965 Merryvale Rd 35216 205-402-5151
Becky Patton, prin. Fax 402-5156
Other Schools – See Birmingham

Vina, Franklin, Pop. 354
Franklin County SD
Supt. — See Russellville
Vina S 300/PK-12
8250 Highway 23 35593 256-331-2260
James Pharr, prin. Fax 331-2292

Vincent, Shelby, Pop. 1,969
Shelby County SD
Supt. — See Columbiana
Vincent ES 400/K-5
40800 Highway 25 35178 205-682-7320
Dr. Tonya Borden-Hudson, prin. Fax 682-7325

Vinemont, Cullman
Cullman County SD
Supt. — See Cullman
Vinemont ES 500/K-5
PO Box 39 35179 256-734-0314
Kim Brown, prin. Fax 737-3083
Vinemont MS 200/6-8
170 High School Rd 35179 256-739-1943
Dr. Vicky Spear, prin. Fax 737-1664
West Point MS 400/6-8
4545 County Road 1141 35179 256-734-5904
Clark Farley, prin. Fax 736-2354

Wadley, Randolph, Pop. 735
Randolph County SD
Supt. — See Wedowee
Wadley S 400/K-12
105 Bailey St 36276 256-395-2286
Lori Carlisle, prin. Fax 395-4488

Warrior, Jefferson, Pop. 3,120
Jefferson County SD
Supt. — See Birmingham
Corner MS 300/5-8
10005 Corner School Rd 35180 205-379-3230
Michael Manning, prin. Fax 379-3246
Warrior ES 300/K-5
300 Montgomery St 35180 205-379-5450
Sandra Lyle, prin. Fax 379-5495

Waterloo, Lauderdale, Pop. 203
Lauderdale County SD
Supt. — See Florence
Waterloo S 300/PK-12
PO Box 68 35677 256-766-3100
Dr. Gary Dan Williams, prin. Fax 766-3194

Weaver, Calhoun, Pop. 2,963
Calhoun County SD
Supt. — See Anniston
Weaver ES 700/K-6
444 School Dr 36277 256-741-7100
Summer Davis, prin. Fax 820-4101

Webb, Houston, Pop. 1,416
Houston County SD
Supt. — See Dothan
Webb ES 500/K-6
178 Depot St 36376 334-792-5744
Marsha Shelley, prin. Fax 792-7967

Wedowee, Randolph, Pop. 821
Randolph County SD 2,200/K-12
182 Circle Dr 36278 256-357-4611
John Jacobs, supt. Fax 357-4844
www.randolphboe.org
Wedowee ES 300/K-3
940 Woodland Ave W 36278 256-357-4588
Lucille Burns, prin. Fax 357-4599
Wedowee MS 200/4-6
896 Woodland Ave W 36278 256-357-4636
Alan Robertson, prin. Fax 357-9576
Other Schools – See Rock Mills, Wadley, Woodland

West Blocton, Bibb, Pop. 1,231
Bibb County SD
Supt. — See Centreville
West Blocton ES 300/PK-4
828 Cahaba River Dr 35184 205-938-9005
Tammy Morton, prin. Fax 938-2653
West Blocton MS 500/5-8
4721 Truman Aldrich Pkwy 35184 205-938-2451
Dr. Greg Blake, prin. Fax 938-3261

Wetumpka, Elmore, Pop. 6,406
Elmore County SD 11,100/PK-12
100 H H Robinson Dr 36092 334-567-1200
Richard Dennis, supt. Fax 567-1405
www.elmoreco.com
Redland ES 900/K-6
495 Scholars Dr 36093 334-567-1248
Chad Walls, prin. Fax 567-1407
Wetumpka ES 1,000/PK-4
510 Micanopy St 36092 334-567-4323
Bonnie Sullivan, prin. Fax 567-1409
Wetumpka MS 1,000/5-8
1000 Micanopy St 36092 334-567-1413
Tremeca Jackson, prin. Fax 567-1408
Other Schools – See Coosada, Deatsville, Eclectic, Millbrook

Wilmer, Mobile, Pop. 545
Mobile County SD
Supt. — See Mobile
Tanner-Williams ES 300/K-5
13700 Tanner Williams Rd 36587 251-221-1675
Nancy Lowell, prin. Fax 221-1678
Turner ES 500/K-5
8361 Lott Rd 36587 251-221-1285
Lynn Huey, prin. Fax 221-1287
Wilmer ES 600/K-5
7456 Wilmer Georgetown Rd 36587 251-221-1780
Timothy Dollar, prin. Fax 221-1781

Wilsonville, Shelby, Pop. 1,805
Shelby County SD
Supt. — See Columbiana
Wilsonville ES 200/K-5
71 School St 35186 205-682-6640
Melody Byrne, prin. Fax 682-6645

Winfield, Marion, Pop. 4,666
Winfield CSD 1,300/K-12
PO Box 70 35594 205-487-4255
Dr. Keith Davis, supt. Fax 487-4603
www.winfield.k12.al.us
Winfield ES 500/K-4
601 County Highway 14 35594 205-487-2305
Roy Williams, prin. Fax 487-8907
Winfield MS 400/5-8
481 Apple Ave 35594 205-487-6901
Wendell Goodwin, prin. Fax 487-6258

Woodland, Randolph, Pop. 182
Randolph County SD
Supt. — See Wedowee
Woodland S 800/K-12
24574 Highway 48 36280 256-449-2315
Jeffery Thompson, prin. Fax 449-2316

Woodstock, Bibb, Pop. 1,414
Bibb County SD
Supt. — See Centreville
Woodstock ES 300/PK-4
19456 Eastern Valley Rd 35188 205-938-2028
Andrea Essman, prin. Fax 938-2044

Woodville, Jackson, Pop. 730
Jackson County SD
Supt. — See Scottsboro
Woodville S 600/PK-12
290 County Road 63 35776 256-776-2874
James Darwin, prin. Fax 776-4718

York, Sumter, Pop. 2,533
Sumter County SD
Supt. — See Livingston
York West End JHS 300/K-8
PO Box 127 36925 205-392-5901
Clifford Reynolds, prin. Fax 392-4700

Sumter Academy 200/PK-12
181 Sumter Academy Rd 36925 205-392-5238

ALASKA

ALASKA DEPARTMENT OF EDUCATION
PO Box 110500, Juneau 99811
Telephone 907-465-2800
Fax 907-465-4165
Website http://www.eed.state.ak.us/

Commissioner of Education Dr. Michael Johnson

ALASKA BOARD OF EDUCATION
PO Box 110500, Juneau 99811

Chairperson James Fields

PUBLIC, PRIVATE AND CATHOLIC ELEMENTARY SCHOOLS

Adak, Aleutians West, Pop. 290
Aleutian Region SD
Supt. — See Anchorage
Adak S 50/PK-12
PO Box 2083 99546 907-592-3820
Molly Lashier, lead tchr. Fax 592-2249

Akhiok, Kodiak Island, Pop. 51
Kodiak Island Borough SD
Supt. — See Kodiak
Akhiok S 50/PK-12
PO Box 5049 99615 907-836-2223
Kendra Bartz, prin. Fax 836-2206

Akiachak, Bethel, Pop. 621
Yupiit SD 400/PK-12
PO Box 51190 99551 907-825-3600
Rayna Hartz, supt. Fax 825-2404
www.yupiit.org
Akiachak S, PO Box 51189 99551 200/K-12
Tarik Malik, prin. 907-825-3616
Other Schools – See Akiak, Tuluksak

Akiak, Bethel, Pop. 339
Yupiit SD
Supt. — See Akiachak
Akiak S, PO Box 49 99552 100/PK-12
Teresa Cox, prin. 907-765-4600

Akutan, Aleutians East, Pop. 979
Aleutian East Borough SD
Supt. — See Sand Point
Akutan S 50/PK-12
PO Box 25 99553 907-698-2205
Kenneth Barbour, prin. Fax 698-2216

Alakanuk, Wade Hampton, Pop. 660
Lower Yukon SD
Supt. — See Mountain Village
Alakanuk S 200/PK-12
PO Box 9 99554 907-238-3312
Herbert Hooper, prin. Fax 238-3417

Aleknagik, Dillingham, Pop. 199
Southwest Region SD
Supt. — See Dillingham
Aleknagik S 50/K-8
PO Box 84 99555 907-842-5681
Audra Finkenbinder, prin. Fax 842-1094

Allakaket, Yukon-Koyukuk, Pop. 101
Yukon-Koyukuk SD
Supt. — See Fairbanks
Allakaket S 50/PK-12
PO Box 69 99720 907-968-2205
Larry Parker, prin. Fax 968-2250

Ambler, Northwest Arctic, Pop. 248
Northwest Arctic Borough SD
Supt. — See Kotzebue
Ambler S 100/PK-12
PO Box 109 99786 907-445-2154
Scott Lefebvre, prin. Fax 445-2159

Anaktuvuk Pass, North Slope, Pop. 294
North Slope Borough SD
Supt. — See Barrow
Nunamiut S 100/PK-12
PO Box 21029 99721 907-661-3226
Doni Newell, prin. Fax 661-3402

Anchorage, Anchorage, Pop. 265,438
Aleutian Region SD 50/PK-12
PO Box 92230 99509 907-277-2648
Joe Beckford, supt. Fax 277-2649
www.aleutregion.org
Other Schools – See Adak, Atka

Anchorage SD 47,800/PK-12
5530 E Northern Lights Blvd 99504 907-742-4000
Dr. Deena Bishop, supt. Fax 742-4318
www.asdk12.org
Abbott Loop ES 400/K-6
8427 Lake Otis Pkwy 99507 907-742-5400
Arthur Sosa, prin. Fax 742-5411
Airport Heights ES 300/PK-6
1510 Alder Dr 99508 907-742-4550
Mike Webb, prin. Fax 742-4570
Baxter ES 400/K-6
2991 Baxter Rd 99504 907-742-1750
Dawn Campbell, prin. Fax 742-1777
Bayshore ES 500/PK-6
10500 Bayshore Dr 99515 907-742-5360
Heidi Packer, prin. Fax 742-5399
Bear Valley ES 400/K-6
15001 Mountain Air Dr 99516 907-742-5900
Lisa Huffman, prin. Fax 742-5909
Begich MS 1,000/6-8
7440 Creekside Center Dr 99504 907-742-0500
Brian Singleton, prin. Fax 742-0510
Bowman ES 500/PK-6
11700 Gregory Rd 99516 907-742-5600
Patrick Freeman, prin. Fax 742-5611
Campbell ES 400/PK-6
7206 Rovenna St 99518 907-742-5560
Michelle Johansen, prin. Fax 742-5575
Central MS of Science 500/7-8
1405 E St 99501 907-742-5100
Joel Roylance, prin. Fax 742-5125
Chester Valley ES 200/PK-5
1751 Patterson St 99504 907-742-0335
Adrian Grenier, prin. Fax 742-0350
Chinook ES 500/PK-6
3101 W 88th Ave 99502 907-742-6700
Heather Jones, prin. Fax 742-6722
Chugach Optional ES 300/PK-6
1205 E St 99501 907-742-3730
Clare Fulp, prin. Fax 742-3747
Clark MS 1,100/6-8
150 Bragaw St 99508 907-742-4700
Cessilye Williams, prin. Fax 742-4756
College Gate ES 400/PK-6
3101 Sunflower St 99508 907-742-1500
Darrell Berntsen, prin. Fax 742-1515
Creekside Park ES 500/PK-5
7500 E 6th Ave 99504 907-742-1550
Tim Andrew, prin. Fax 742-1577
Denali Montessori S 400/PK-6
952 Cordova St 99501 907-742-4500
Ruth Dene, prin. Fax 742-4520
Fairview ES 400/PK-6
1327 Nelchina St 99501 907-742-7600
Dianne Orr, prin. Fax 742-7616
Goldenview MS 700/7-8
15800 Golden View Dr 99516 907-348-8626
David Nogg, prin. Fax 742-8273
Government Hill ES 500/K-6
525 E Bluff Dr 99501 907-742-5000
Mandy Clark, prin. Fax 742-5015
Hanshew MS 800/7-8
10121 Lake Otis Pkwy 99507 907-349-1561
Nancy Brain, prin. Fax 349-2835
Huffman ES 400/PK-6
12000 Lorraine St 99516 907-742-5650
Chris Opitz, prin. Fax 742-5660
Inlet View ES 200/K-6
1219 N St 99501 907-742-7630
Patricia Ahrens, prin. Fax 742-7650
Kasuun ES 400/PK-6
4000 E 68th Ave 99507 907-349-9444
Anita Stevens, prin. Fax 349-9402
Kincaid ES 500/PK-6
4900 Raspberry Rd 99502 907-245-5530
Shannon Gallagher, prin. Fax 245-5535
Klatt ES 400/PK-6
11900 Puma St 99515 907-742-5750
David Christal, prin. Fax 742-5757
Lake Hood ES 300/K-6
3601 W 40th Ave 99517 907-245-5521
Michael Thomas, prin. Fax 245-5528
Lake Otis ES 400/PK-6
3331 Lake Otis Pkwy 99508 907-742-7400
Douglas Gray, prin. Fax 742-7407
Mears MS 800/7-8
2700 W 100th Ave 99515 907-742-6400
Michael Perkins, prin. Fax 742-6444
Mountain View ES 300/K-5
4005 Mcphee Ave 99508 907-742-3900
Chris Woodward, prin. Fax 742-3911
Muldoon ES 400/PK-5
525 Cherry St 99504 907-742-1460
Leroy Grant, prin. Fax 742-1477
Northern Lights ABC S 600/K-8
2424 E Dowling Rd 99507 907-742-7500
Karen Wallace, prin. Fax 742-7530
North Star ES 400/PK-6
605 W Fireweed Ln 99503 907-742-3800
Julie Sery, prin. Fax 742-3822
Northwood ABC ES 400/PK-6
4807 Northwood Dr 99517 907-742-6800
Deanna Beck, prin. Fax 742-6822
Nunaka Valley ES 200/K-5
1905 Twining Dr 99504 907-742-0366
Tim Blake, prin. Fax 742-0393
Ocean View ES 400/PK-6
11911 Johns Rd 99515 907-742-5850
Dayna Durr, prin. Fax 742-5885
O'Malley ES 300/PK-6
11100 Rockridge Dr 99516 907-742-5800
Kelly Eagleton, prin. Fax 742-5822
Ptarmigan ES 400/K-5
888 Edward St 99504 907-742-0400
Lori Cheek, prin. Fax 742-0425
Rabbit Creek ES 400/PK-6
13650 Lake Otis Pkwy 99516 907-742-5700
Greg Balcao, prin. Fax 742-5711
Rogers Park ES 500/PK-6
1400 E Northern Lights Blvd 99508 907-742-4800
Nuri Johnsen, prin. Fax 742-4815
Romig MS 800/7-8
2500 Minnesota Dr 99503 907-742-5200
Carrie Sumner, prin. Fax 742-5252
Russian Jack ES 400/PK-5
4300 E 20th Ave 99508 907-742-1300
Elizabeth Hornbuckle, prin. Fax 742-1341
Sand Lake ES 700/K-6
7500 Jewel Lake Rd 99502 907-243-2161
Linson Thompson, prin. Fax 243-6025
Scenic Park ES 400/K-5
3933 Patterson St 99504 907-742-1650
Jennifer Schmitz, prin. Fax 742-1677
Spring Hill ES 400/PK-6
9911 Lake Otis Pkwy 99507 907-742-5450
Lana Bailey, prin. Fax 742-5477
Susitna ES 400/PK-5
7500 Tyone Ct 99504 907-742-1400
Diane Hoffbauer, prin. Fax 742-1418
Taku ES 400/PK-6
701 E 72nd Ave 99518 907-742-5940
Kelly Ramey, prin. Fax 742-5959
Trailside ES 400/PK-6
5151 Abbott Rd 99507 907-742-5500
Mary Ellison, prin. Fax 742-5511
Tudor ES 400/PK-6
1666 Cache Dr 99507 907-742-1050
Nicole Sommerville, prin. Fax 742-1066
Turnagain ES 500/PK-6
3500 W Northern Lights Blvd 99517 907-742-7200
Carissa Cote, prin. Fax 742-7207
Tyson ES 400/PK-5
2801 Richmond Ave 99508 907-742-8000
John Kito, prin. Fax 742-8008
Wendler MS 500/7-8
2905 Lake Otis Pkwy 99508 907-742-7300
Brendan Wilson, prin. Fax 742-7350
Williwaw ES 400/K-5
1200 San Antonio St 99508 907-742-2000
Likka McCauley, prin. Fax 742-2020
Willow Crest ES 400/K-6
1004 W Tudor Rd 99503 907-742-1000
Kristina Peterson, prin. Fax 742-1044
Wonder Park ES 300/K-5
5101 E 4th Ave 99508 907-337-1569
Sean Murphy, prin. Fax 337-2046
Wood ES 400/PK-6
7001 Cranberry St 99502 907-742-6760
Cindy Hemry, prin. Fax 742-6779
Other Schools – See Chugiak, Eagle River, Elmendorf AFB, Fort Richardson, Girdwood

Chugach SD 100/PK-12
9312 Vanguard Dr Ste 100 99507 907-522-7400
Fax 522-3399
www.chugachschools.com
Other Schools – See Chenega Bay, Tatitlek, Whittier

Anchorage Christian S 700/PK-12
6575 E Northern Lights Blvd 99504 907-337-9575
Thomas Cobaugh, admin. Fax 338-3903
Anchorage Junior Academy 50/PK-8
5511 OMalley Rd 99507 907-346-2164
Darne King, prin. Fax 346-1332
Anchorage Montessori S 200/PK-6
5001 Northwood Dr 99517 907-276-2240
Anchorage Waldorf S 100/PK-8
3250 Baxter Rd 99504 907-333-9062
Anchor Lutheran S 200/PK-8
8100 Arctic Blvd 99518 907-522-3636
Allison Chandler, admin. Fax 522-3359
Faith Lutheran S 100/K-8
5200 Lake Otis Pkwy 99507 907-563-3499
Tom Zarnstorff, prin. Fax 563-6057
Grace Christian S 600/K-12
12407 Pintail St 99516 907-868-1203
Randy Karlberg, supt. Fax 644-2261
Holy Rosary Academy 100/K-12
1010 W Fireweed Ln 99503 907-276-5822
Catherine Neumayr, prin. Fax 258-1055
Pacific Northern Academy 100/PK-8
9251 Lake Otis Pkwy 99507 907-333-1080
Laurie Hoefer, head sch Fax 333-1652
St. Elizabeth Ann Seton S 200/K-6
2901 Huffman Rd 99516 907-345-3712
Kathy Gustafson, prin. Fax 345-2910

Anchor Point, Kenai Peninsula, Pop. 1,850
Kenai Peninsula Borough SD
Supt. — See Soldotna
Chapman S 100/PK-8
PO Box 1109 99556 907-235-8671
Conrad Woodhead, prin. Fax 235-5460

Anderson, Denali, Pop. 234
Denali Borough SD
Supt. — See Healy
Anderson S 50/K-12
PO Box 3120 99744 907-582-2700
Jeni Mason, prin. Fax 582-2000

Angoon, Skagway-Hoonah-Angoon, Pop. 409
Chatham SD 200/K-12
PO Box 109 99820 907-788-3302
Bernie Grieve, supt. Fax 788-3252
chathamsd.schoolwires.net
Angoon S 100/K-12
PO Box 209 99820 907-788-3811
Jim Parkin, prin. Fax 788-3812
Other Schools – See Gustavus, Haines, Tenakee Springs

Aniak, Bethel, Pop. 452
Kuspuk SD 400/PK-12
PO Box 49 99557 907-675-4250
Bernard Grieve, supt. Fax 675-4305
www.kuspuk.org
Nicoli ES 100/PK-6
PO Box 29 99557 907-675-4363
Todd Boynton, prin. Fax 675-4305
Other Schools – See Chuathbaluk, Crooked Creek, Kalskag, Lower Kalskag, Sleetmute, Stony River

Anvik, Yukon-Koyukuk, Pop. 82
Iditarod Area SD
Supt. — See Mc Grath
Blackwell S 50/PK-12
PO Box 90 99558 907-663-6348
Conda Artega, prin Fax 663-6349

Arctic Village, Yukon-Koyukuk, Pop. 142
Yukon Flats SD
Supt. — See Fort Yukon
Arctic Village S 50/PK-12
PO Box 22049 99722 907-587-5211
Geoffrey Johnson, lead tchr. Fax 587-5210

Atka, Aleutians West, Pop. 61
Aleutian Region SD
Supt. — See Anchorage
Netsvetov S 50/K-12
PO Box 47050 99547 907-839-2210
Sonja Mills, lead tchr. Fax 839-2212

Atmautluak, Bethel, Pop. 277
Lower Kuskokwim SD
Supt. — See Bethel
Alexie Memorial S 100/PK-12
PO Box ATT 99559 907-553-5112
Kimberly Hankins, prin. Fax 553-5129

Atqasuk, North Slope, Pop. 231
North Slope Borough SD
Supt. — See Barrow
Meade River S 100/PK-12
PO Box 91030 99791 907-633-6315
Emily Roseberry, prin. Fax 633-6215

Barrow, North Slope, Pop. 3,772
North Slope Borough SD 2,000/PK-12
PO Box 169 99723 907-852-5311
Glen Szymoniak, supt. Fax 852-9503
www.nsbsd.org
Hopson MS 200/6-8
PO Box 509 99723 907-852-3880
LeeAnn Tyree, prin. Fax 852-7794
Ipalook ES 700/PK-5
PO Box 450 99723 907-852-4711
Jay Thomas, prin. Fax 852-4713
Other Schools – See Anaktuvuk Pass, Atqasuk, Kaktovik, Nuiqsut, Point Hope, Point Lay, Wainwright

Beaver, Yukon-Koyukuk, Pop. 83
Yukon Flats SD
Supt. — See Fort Yukon
Cruikshank S 50/PK-12
PO Box 24050 99724 907-628-6313
Fax 628-6615

Bethel, Bethel, Pop. 5,648
Lower Kuskokwim SD 4,300/PK-12
PO Box 305 99559 907-543-4800
Daniel Walker, supt. Fax 543-4904
www.lksd.org
Ayaprun Elitnaurvik S 200/PK-6
PO Box 1468 99559 907-543-1645
Zachary Bastoky, prin. Fax 543-1647
Jung ES 300/3-6
PO Box 800 99559 907-543-4440
Christopher Carmichael, prin. Fax 543-2533
Mikelnguut Elitnaurviat ES 400/PK-2
PO Box 900 99559 907-543-2845
Jazzmin Lavelle, prin. Fax 543-2429
Other Schools – See Atmautluak, Chefornak, Eek, Goodnews Bay, Kasigluk, Kipnuk, Kongiganak, Kwethluk, Kwigillingok, Mekoryuk, Napakiak, Napaskiak, Newtok, Nightmute, Nunapitchuk, Platinum, Quinhagak, Toksook Bay, Tuntutuliak, Tununak

Big Lake, Matanuska-Susitna, Pop. 3,191
Matanuska-Susitna Borough SD
Supt. — See Palmer
Big Lake ES 400/PK-5
PO Box 520049 99652 907-892-9700
Brenna Reintsma, prin. Fax 892-9780
Houston MS 400/6-8
PO Box 520920 99652 907-892-9500
Benjamin Howard, prin. Fax 892-9560

Brevig Mission, Nome, Pop. 377
Bering Strait SD
Supt. — See Unalakleet
Brevig Mission S 100/PK-12
General Delivery 99785 907-642-4021
Diane Crockett, prin. Fax 642-4031

Buckland, Northwest Arctic, Pop. 408
Northwest Arctic Borough SD
Supt. — See Kotzebue
Buckland S 200/PK-12
PO Box 91 99727 907-494-2127
Matthew Berlin, prin. Fax 494-2106

Cantwell, Denali, Pop. 205
Denali Borough SD
Supt. — See Healy
Cantwell S 50/K-12
PO Box 29 99729 907-768-2372
Jeni Mason, prin. Fax 768-2500

Chalkyitsik, Yukon-Koyukuk, Pop. 69
Yukon Flats SD
Supt. — See Fort Yukon
Tsuk Taih S 50/PK-12
1 Marten Hill 99788 907-848-8113
Vicki Salmon, lead tchr. Fax 848-8312

Chefornak, Bethel, Pop. 415
Lower Kuskokwim SD
Supt. — See Bethel
Chaputnquak S 200/PK-12
PO Box 50 99561 907-867-8700
Dustin Wright, prin. Fax 867-8727

Chenega Bay, Valdez-Cordova, Pop. 94
Chugach SD
Supt. — See Anchorage
Chenega Bay S 50/PK-12
PO Box 8030 99574 907-573-5123
Sarah Jones, lead tchr. Fax 573-5137

Chevak, Wade Hampton, Pop. 915
Kashunamiut SD 300/PK-12
PO Box 345 99563 907-858-7712
Norma Holmgaard, supt. Fax 858-6150
www.chevakschool.org
Chevak S 300/PK-12
PO Box 345 99563 907-858-7712
Minty Ruthford, prin. Fax 858-6150

Chignik, Lake and Peninsula, Pop. 87
Lake & Peninsula SD
Supt. — See King Salmon
Chignik Bay S 50/PK-12
PO Box 9 99564 907-749-2213
Kitza Durkop, prin. Fax 749-2261

Chignik Lagoon, Lake and Peninsula, Pop. 69
Lake & Peninsula SD
Supt. — See King Salmon
Chignik Lagoon S 50/PK-12
PO Box 60 99565 907-840-2210
Joe Ward, prin. Fax 840-2265

Chignik Lake, Lake and Peninsula, Pop. 71
Lake & Peninsula SD
Supt. — See King Salmon
Chignik Lake S 50/K-12
General Delivery 99548 907-845-2210
Robert Fagerquist, lead tchr. Fax 845-2254

Chiniak, Kodiak Island, Pop. 45
Kodiak Island Borough SD
Supt. — See Kodiak
Chiniak S 50/K-12
PO Box 5529 99615 907-486-8323
Kendra Bartz, prin. Fax 486-3185

Chuathbaluk, Bethel, Pop. 112
Kuspuk SD
Supt. — See Aniak
Crow Village Sam S 50/PK-12
PO Box CHU 99557 907-467-4229
Steven B. Porter, prin. Fax 675-4305

Chugiak, See Anchorage
Anchorage SD
Supt. — See Anchorage

Birchwood ABC ES 300/K-6
17010 Birchtree St 99567 907-742-3450
Lynn Mayberry-Burke, prin. Fax 742-3495
Chugiak ES 500/PK-5
19932 Old Glenn Hwy 99567 907-742-3400
Sarah Alvarez, prin. Fax 742-3411
Mirror Lake MS 700/6-8
22901 Lake Hill Dr 99567 907-742-3500
Alexandra Hagler, prin. Fax 742-3545

Birchwood Christian S 100/PK-12
22208 Birchwood Loop Rd 99567 907-688-2228
Todd Clark, prin. Fax 688-2159

Circle, Yukon-Koyukuk, Pop. 98
Yukon Flats SD
Supt. — See Fort Yukon
Circle S 50/PK-12
PO Box 49 99733 907-773-1250
Carmen Russo, lead tchr. Fax 773-1259

Coffman Cove, Prince of Wales-Outer Ketchikan, Pop. 173
Southeast Island SD
Supt. — See Thorne Bay
Valentine S 50/K-12
PO Box 18002 99918 907-329-2244
Colter Barnes, lead tchr. Fax 329-2210

Cooper Landing, Kenai Peninsula, Pop. 282
Kenai Peninsula Borough SD
Supt. — See Soldotna
Cooper Landing S 50/K-12
19030 Bean Creek Rd 99572 907-595-1244
Douglas Hayman, prin. Fax 595-1461

Copper Center, Valdez-Cordova, Pop. 312
Copper River SD
Supt. — See Glennallen
Kenny Lake S 100/1-12
HC 60 Box 224 99573 907-822-3870
Shawna Goodwin, lead tchr. Fax 822-3794

Cordova, Valdez-Cordova, Pop. 2,067
Cordova CSD 300/PK-12
PO Box 1330 99574 907-424-3265
Alex Russin, supt. Fax 424-3271
cordovasd.org
Mount Eccles ES 200/PK-6
PO Box 1330 99574 907-424-3236
Gayle Groff, prin. Fax 424-3117

Craig, Prince of Wales-Outer Ketchikan, Pop. 1,047
Craig CSD 300/K-12
PO Box 800 99921 907-826-3274
Jack Walsh, supt. Fax 826-3322
www.ccsd.k12.ak.us
Craig ES 100/K-5
PO Box 800 99921 907-826-3274
Jackie Hanson, prin. Fax 826-3322
Craig MS 100/6-8
PO Box 800 99921 907-826-3274
Jackie Hanson, prin. Fax 826-3309

Southeast Island SD
Supt. — See Thorne Bay
Hollis S 50/PK-12
PO Box 803 99921 907-530-7108
Julie Vasquez, lead tchr. Fax 530-7111

Crooked Creek, Bethel, Pop. 96
Kuspuk SD
Supt. — See Aniak
John Sr. S 50/PK-12
PO Box 20 99575 907-432-2205
Steven Porter, prin. Fax 675-4305

Deering, Northwest Arctic, Pop. 117
Northwest Arctic Borough SD
Supt. — See Kotzebue
Deering S 50/PK-12
PO Box 36009 99736 907-363-2121
Deidre Jenson, prin. Fax 363-2128

Delta Junction, Southeast Fairbanks, Pop. 919
Delta-Greely SD 600/PK-12
PO Box 527 99737 907-895-4657
Laural Jackson, supt. Fax 895-4781
www.dgsd.k12.ak.us
Delta Junction ES 200/PK-5
PO Box 647 99737 907-895-4696
Bill Johnson, prin. Fax 895-4051
Gerstle River S 50/PK-12
PO Box 309 99737 907 895 1043
Jeff Lansing, prin. Fax 895 5198

Dillingham, Dillingham, Pop. 2,086
Dillingham CSD 500/PK-12
PO Box 170 99576 907-842-5223
Danny Frazier, supt. Fax 530-8877
www.dlgsd.org
Dillingham ES 300/PK-5
PO Box 170 99576 907-842-5642
Nick Schollmeier, prin. Fax 842-1313

Southwest Region SD 600/PK-12
PO Box 90 99576 907-842-5287
David Piazza, supt. Fax 842-5428
www.swrsd.org
Other Schools – See Aleknagik, Ekwok, Koliganek, Manokotak, New Stuyahok, Togiak, Twin Hills

Dillingham Adventist S 50/PK-8
PO Box 182 99576 907-842-2496
Sueal Cunningham, lead tchr.

Diomede, Nome, Pop. 111
Bering Strait SD
Supt. — See Unalakleet

Diomede S 50/PK-12
PO Box 7099 99762 907-686-3021
Frank Stanek, prin. Fax 686-3022

Dot Lake, Southeast Fairbanks, Pop. 12
Alaska Gateway SD
Supt. — See Tok
Dot Lake S 50/PK-12
PO Box 2280 99737 907-882-2663
Julie Selves, prin. Fax 882-2112

Eagle, Southeast Fairbanks, Pop. 85
Alaska Gateway SD
Supt. — See Tok
Eagle Community S 50/K-12
PO Box 168 99738 907-547-2210
Kristy Robbins, prin. Fax 547-2302

Eagle River, See Anchorage
Anchorage SD
Supt. — See Anchorage
Alpenglow ES 600/PK-6
19201 Driftwood Bay Dr 99577 907-742-3300
Denise Demetree, prin. Fax 742-3348
Eagle River ES 400/PK-6
10900 Old Eagle River Rd 99577 907-742-3000
Lisa Prince, prin. Fax 742-3020
Fire Lake ES 300/PK-5
PO Box 772569 99577 907-742-3350
Christine Garbe, prin. Fax 742-3366
Gruening MS 600/7-8
9601 Lee St 99577 907-742-3600
Bobby Jefts, prin. Fax 742-3666
Homestead ES 300/K-6
18001 Baronoff Ave 99577 907-742-3550
Jane Shepherd Stuart, prin. Fax 742-3567
Ravenwood ES 400/PK-6
9500 Wren Cir 99577 907-742-3250
Kim Bautista, prin. Fax 742-3260

Eagle River Christian S 100/K-12
10336 E Eagle River Loop Rd 99577 907-694-4602
Michelle Caldwell, admin. Fax 694-4141

Eek, Bethel, Pop. 296
Lower Kuskokwim SD
Supt. — See Bethel
Eek S 100/PK-12
PO Box 50 99578 907-536-5227
Brett Stirling, prin. Fax 536-5628

Eielson AFB, Fairbanks North Star, Pop. 2,496
Fairbanks North Star Borough SD
Supt. — See Fairbanks
Anderson ES 300/PK-2
768 Kodiak St 99702 907-372-2167
Stacey Stansell, prin. Fax 372-3437
Crawford ES 300/3-6
692 Ravens Way 99702 907-372-3306
Barbara Sperl, prin. Fax 372-3199

Ekwok, Dillingham, Pop. 110
Southwest Region SD
Supt. — See Dillingham
Nelson S 50/K-8
General Delivery 99580 907-464-3344
Heath Hawkins, prin. Fax 464-3318

Elim, Nome, Pop. 322
Bering Strait SD
Supt. — See Unalakleet
Aniguiin S 100/PK-12
PO Box 29 99739 907-890-3021
Jack Kingsford, prin. Fax 890-3031

Elmendorf AFB, Anchorage
Anchorage SD
Supt. — See Anchorage
Aurora ES 400/PK-6
5085 10th St 99506 907-742-0300
Debbie Washington, prin. Fax 742-0322
Mt. Spurr ES 300/PK-6
8414 Mcguire Ave 99506 907-742-0200
Bill Schildbach, prin. Fax 742-0215
Orion ES 400/PK-6
5112 Arctic Warrior Dr 99506 907-742-0250
Brenda Cheathon, prin. Fax 742-0265

Emmonak, Wade Hampton, Pop. 759
Lower Yukon SD
Supt. — See Mountain Village
Emmonak S 200/PK-12
100 Airport Rd 99581 907-949-1248
John Brady, prin. Fax 949-1148

Fairbanks, Fairbanks North Star, Pop. 29,138
Fairbanks North Star Borough SD 13,900/PK-12
520 5th Ave 99701 907-452-2000
Dr. Karen Gaborik Ed.D., supt. Fax 451-6160
www.k12northstar.org
Badger Road ES 500/K-5
520 5th Ave 99701 907-488-0134
Joanne VanFleteren, prin. Fax 488-2045
Barnette Magnet S 400/K-8
725 10th Ave 99701 907-456-6072
Dana Evans, prin. Fax 451-9602
Brown ES 500/PK-5
785 Lakloey Dr 99705 907-488-3200
Shawna Henderson, prin. Fax 488-6208
Denali ES 400/K-6
1042 Lathrop St 99701 907-452-2456
Deborah Hall, prin. Fax 451-0792
Hunter ES 400/PK-6
1630 Gillam Way 99701 907-456-5775
Robyn Ward, prin. Fax 452-8891
Joy ES 500/PK-6
24 Margaret St 99701 907-456-5469
Lalaunie Whisenhant, prin. Fax 456-1477
Ladd ES 600/PK-6
601 F St 99701 907-451-1700
Cori Anthony, prin. Fax 451-9137
Nordale ES 300/PK-6
397 Hamilton Ave 99701 907-452-2696
Matthew Powell, prin. Fax 456-5608
North Pole ES 500/PK-6
250 Snowman Ln 99705 907-488-2286
Mark Winford, prin. Fax 488-1232
Pearl Creek ES 500/PK-6
700 Auburn Dr 99709 907-479-4234
Kate LaPlaunt, prin. Fax 479-4025
Ryan MS 400/7-8
1450 Cowles St 99701 907-452-4751
Heather Stewart, prin. Fax 451-8834
Salcha ES 100/K-6
520 5th Ave 99701 907-488-3267
Tori Brannan, prin. Fax 488-5358
Smith MS 300/7-8
1401 Bainbridge Blvd 99701 907-458-7600
Dave Dershin, prin. Fax 458-7676
Tanana MS 500/7-8
600 Trainor Gate Rd 99701 907-452-8145
Lori Swanson, prin. Fax 456-2780
Two Rivers S 100/K-8
520 5th Ave 99701 907-488-6616
Teresa Tomlinson, lead tchr. Fax 488-8487
University Park ES 500/K-6
554 Loftus Rd 99709 907-479-6963
Kyra Aizstrauts, prin. Fax 479-6219
Weller ES 500/PK-6
520 5th Ave 99701 907-457-1629
Lynn Weckesser, prin. Fax 457-2663
Wien ES 400/PK-6
1501 Hampstead Ave 99701 907-451-7500
Michael Angaiak, prin. Fax 451-7564
Woodriver ES 400/K-6
5000 Palo Verde Ave 99709 907-479-4211
Grant Guy, prin. Fax 479-5077
Other Schools – See Eielson AFB, Fort Wainwright, North Pole

Yukon-Koyukuk SD 300/PK-12
4762 Old Airport Rd 99709 907-374-9400
Kerry Boyd, supt. Fax 374-9440
www.yksd.com
Other Schools – See Allakaket, Hughes, Huslia, Kaltag, Koyukuk, Manley Hot Springs, Minto, Nulato, Ruby

---

Aurora Tutoring S 50/PK-12
201 Old Steese Hwy Ste 6 99701 907-374-8852
Baubi Jo Reid, prin. Fax 374-8853
Fairhill Christian S 100/PK-8
101 City Lights Blvd 99712 907-457-2167
Golden Heart Christian S 50/K-8
PO Box 82997 99708 907-479-2904
Immaculate Conception S 300/PK-6
PO Box 71620 99707 907-456-4574
Amanda Angaiak, prin. Fax 452-5978
Open Arms Child Development Center 200/PK-K
2980 Davis Rd 99709 907-455-9466
Maria Vilchez, dir. Fax 455-7208
Spruce Tree Montessori S 50/PK-6
1830 2nd Ave 99701 907-479-8733

False Pass, Aleutians East, Pop. 35
Aleutian East Borough SD
Supt. — See Sand Point
False Pass S 50/PK-12
PO Box 30 99583 907-548-2224
Annette Barnett, prin. Fax 548-2304

Fort Richardson, Anchorage
Anchorage SD
Supt. — See Anchorage
Ursa Major ES 500/PK-6
454 Dyea Ave 99505 907-742-1600
Ben Hardwick, prin. Fax 742-1616
Ursa Minor ES 400/PK-6
336 Hoonah Ave 99505 907-428-1311
Wendy Brons, prin. Fax 428-1346

Fort Wainwright, Fairbanks North Star
Fairbanks North Star Borough SD
Supt. — See Fairbanks
Arctic Light ES 500/PK-6
4167 Neely Rd 99703 907-356-2038
Thad Keener, prin. Fax 356-2189

Fort Yukon, Yukon-Koyukuk, Pop. 569
Yukon Flats SD 200/PK-12
PO Box 350 99740 907-662-2515
Dr. Lance Bowie Ed.D., supt. Fax 662-2519
www.yukonflats.net
Fort Yukon S 100/PK-12
PO Box 129 99740 907-662-2352
Debra Van Dyke, prin. Fax 662-2958
Other Schools – See Arctic Village, Beaver, Chalkyitsik, Circle, Venetie

Fritz Creek, Kenai Peninsula, Pop. 1,832
Kenai Peninsula Borough SD
Supt. — See Soldotna
Kachemak-Selo S 100/PK-12
PO Box 15007 99603 907-235-5552
Tim Whip, prin. Fax 235-5644
Voznesenka S 100/PK-12
PO Box 15336 99603 907-235-8549
Michael Wojciak, prin. Fax 235-6086

Galena, Yukon-Koyukuk, Pop. 441
Galena CSD 300/PK-12
PO Box 299 99741 907-656-1205
Chris Reitan, supt. Fax 656-1368
www.galenaalaska.org
Huntington ES 50/PK-6
PO Box 299 99741 907-656-1205
Ken Essex, prin. Fax 656-1368

Gambell, Nome, Pop. 678
Bering Strait SD
Supt. — See Unalakleet
Gambell S 200/PK-12
PO Box 169 99742 907-985-5515
Robert Taylor, prin. Fax 985-5435

Girdwood, See Anchorage
Anchorage SD
Supt. — See Anchorage
Girdwood S 200/PK-8
PO Box 189 99587 907-742-5300
Erik Viste, prin. Fax 742-5320

Glennallen, Valdez-Cordova, Pop. 422
Copper River SD 400/PK-12
PO Box 108 99588 907-822-3234
Tammy VanWyhe, supt. Fax 822-3949
www.crsd.us
Glennallen ES 200/K-6
PO Box 108 99588 907-822-3232
Nick Schumacher, prin. Fax 822-8500
Other Schools – See Copper Center, Slana

Golovin, Nome, Pop. 153
Bering Strait SD
Supt. — See Unalakleet
Olson S 100/PK-12
PO Box 62040 99762 907-779-3021
Steve Sammons, prin. Fax 779-3031

Goodnews Bay, Bethel, Pop. 241
Lower Kuskokwim SD
Supt. — See Bethel
Rocky Mountain S 100/PK-12
PO Box 153 99589 907-967-8213
Shannon Hutson, prin. Fax 967-8228

Grayling, Yukon-Koyukuk, Pop. 182
Iditarod Area SD
Supt. — See Mc Grath
David-Louis Memorial S 50/PK-12
PO Box 90 99590 907-453-5135
Doug Goben, prin. Fax 453-5165

Gustavus, Skagway-Hoonah-Angoon, Pop. 422
Chatham SD
Supt. — See Angoon
Gustavus S 100/K-12
PO Box 120 99826 907-697-2248
Ann Hilburn, prin. Fax 697-2378

Haines, Haines, Pop. 1,608
Chatham SD
Supt. — See Angoon
Klukwan S 50/K-12
HC 60 Box 2222 99827 907-767-5551
Katherine Carl, lead tchr. Fax 767-5573

Haines Borough SD 200/K-12
PO Box 1289 99827 907-766-6700
Fax 766-6794
www.hbsd.net
Haines ES 100/K-6
PO Box 1289 99827 907-766-6700
Rene Martin, prin. Fax 766-6791

Healy, Denali, Pop. 980
Denali Borough SD 800/PK-12
PO Box 280 99743 907-683-2278
Dan Polta, supt. Fax 683-2514
www.dbsd.org
Tri-Valley S 200/K-12
PO Box 400 99743 907-683-2267
Nathan Pitt, prin. Fax 683-2632
Other Schools – See Anderson, Cantwell

Holy Cross, Yukon-Koyukuk, Pop. 171
Iditarod Area SD
Supt. — See Mc Grath
Holy Cross S 50/PK-12
PO Box 210 99602 907-476-7131
Jeff Bader, prin. Fax 476-7161

Homer, Kenai Peninsula, Pop. 4,783
Kenai Peninsula Borough SD
Supt. — See Soldotna
Banks ES 200/PK-2
1340 E End Rd 99603 907-226-1801
Eric Pederson, prin. Fax 235-8163
Homer MS 200/7-8
500 Sterling Hwy 99603 907-235-5700
Kari Dendurent, prin. Fax 235-2513
McNeil Canyon ES 100/K-6
52188 E End Rd 99603 907-235-8181
Peter Swanson, prin. Fax 235-8183
Razdolna S 100/PK-12
PO Box 15098 99603 907-235-6870
Timothy Whip, prin. Fax 235-6485
West Homer ES 200/3-6
995 Soundview Ave Ste 1 99603 907-235-5750
Eric Waltenbaugh, prin. Fax 235-2612

Hoonah, Skagway-Hoonah-Angoon, Pop. 657
Hoonah CSD 100/PK-12
PO Box 157 99829 907-945-3611
Dr. P.J. Ford Slack Ph.D., supt. Fax 945-3492
www.hoonahschools.org
Hoonah ES 100/PK-6
PO Box 157 99829 907-945-3614
Ralph Watkins, prin. Fax 945-3730

Hooper Bay, Wade Hampton, Pop. 1,055
Lower Yukon SD
Supt. — See Mountain Village
Hooper Bay S 400/PK-12
PO Box 249 99604 907-758-1200
Hammond Gracy, prin. Fax 758-1280

Hope, Kenai Peninsula, Pop. 178
Kenai Peninsula Borough SD
Supt. — See Soldotna
Hope S 50/K-12
PO Box 47 99605 907-782-3202
Douglas Hayman, admin. Fax 782-3140

Hughes, Yukon-Koyukuk, Pop. 77
Yukon-Koyukuk SD
Supt. — See Fairbanks
Oldman S 50/K-12
PO Box 30 99745 907-889-2204
Patty White, admin. Fax 889-2220

Huslia, Yukon-Koyukuk, Pop. 272
Yukon-Koyukuk SD
Supt. — See Fairbanks
Huntington S 100/PK-12
PO Box 110 99746 907-829-2220
Casey Weter, prin. Fax 829-2270

Hydaburg, Prince of Wales-Outer Ketchikan, Pop. 342
Hydaburg CSD 100/K-12
PO Box 109 99922 907-285-3491
Lauren Burch, supt. Fax 285-3391
www.hydaburg.k12.ak.us
Hydaburg S 100/K-12
PO Box 109 99922 907-285-3591
Bart Mwarey, prin. Fax 285-3391

Hyder, Prince of Wales-Outer Ketchikan, Pop. 82
Southeast Island SD
Supt. — See Thorne Bay
Hyder S 50/K-12
PO Box 130 99923 250-636-2800
Chadwick Dillman, lead tchr. Fax 636-2880

Igiugig, Lake and Peninsula, Pop. 34
Lake & Peninsula SD
Supt. — See King Salmon
Igiugig S 50/K-12
PO Box 4010 99613 907-533-3220
Tate Gooden, lead tchr. Fax 533-3221

Iliamna, Lake and Peninsula, Pop. 96
Lake & Peninsula SD
Supt. — See King Salmon
Newhalen S 100/PK-12
PO Box 89 99606 907-571-1211
Ed Lester, prin. Fax 571-1466

Juneau, Juneau, Pop. 28,325
Juneau Borough SD 4,700/PK-12
10014 Crazy Horse Dr 99801 907-523-1700
Mark Miller, supt. Fax 523-1708
www.juneauschools.org
Auke Bay ES 300/PK-5
10014 Crazy Horse Dr 99801 907-463-1775
Lori Hoover, prin. Fax 463-1751
Dryden MS 500/6-8
10014 Crazy Horse Dr 99801 907-463-1850
Jim Thompson, prin. Fax 463-1828
Gastineau ES 300/PK-5
10014 Crazy Horse Dr 99801 907-796-5075
Brenda Edwards, prin. Fax 463-1997
Glacier Valley ES 400/PK-5
10014 Crazy Horse Dr 99801 907-780-1400
Lucy Potter, prin. Fax 780-1449
Harborview ES 500/K-5
10014 Crazy Horse Dr 99801 907-523-1850
Tom McKenna, prin. Fax 523-1899
Heeni MS 500/6-8
10014 Crazy Horse Dr 99801 907-463-1500
Molly Yerkes, prin. Fax 463-1877
Mendenhall River Community ES 400/PK-5
10014 Crazy Horse Dr 99801 907-463-1799
Kristy Dillingham, prin. Fax 463-1777
Montessori Borealis K-6
10014 Crazy Horse Dr 99801 907-523-1848
Kristen Garot, prin. Fax 523-1819
Riverbend ES 300/PK-5
10014 Crazy Horse Dr 99801 907-463-5700
Michelle Byer, prin. Fax 463-1792

Juneau Adventist Christian S 50/K-8
4890 Glacier Hwy 99801 907-780-4336

Kake, Wrangell-Petersburg, Pop. 485
Kake CSD 100/PK-12
PO Box 450 99830 907-785-3741
Richard Catahay, supt. Fax 785-6439
www.kakeschools.com
Kake S 100/PK-12
PO Box 450 99830 907-785-3741
Richard Catahay, admin. Fax 785-6439

Kaktovik, North Slope, Pop. 236
North Slope Borough SD
Supt. — See Barrow
Kaveolook S 100/PK-12
PO Box 20 99747 907-640-6626
Todd Washburn, prin. Fax 640-6718

Kalskag, Bethel, Pop. 186
Kuspuk SD
Supt. — See Aniak
Gregory ES 50/PK-2
PO Box 20 99607 907-471-2289
Severin Gardner, prin. Fax 675-4305

Kaltag, Yukon-Koyukuk, Pop. 185
Yukon-Koyukuk SD
Supt. — See Fairbanks
Kaltag S 50/PK-12
PO Box 30 99748 907-534-2204
Patty White, prin. Fax 534-2227

Karluk, Kodiak Island, Pop. 37
Kodiak Island Borough SD
Supt. — See Kodiak
Karluk S 50/PK-12
General Delivery 99608 907-241-2217
Kendra Bartz, prin. Fax 241-2207

Kasaan, Prince of Wales-Outer Ketchikan, Pop. 44
Southeast Island SD
Supt. — See Thorne Bay
Kasaan S 50/PK-12
117 Kasaan Rd 99901 907-542-2217
Shane Scamahorn, lead tchr. Fax 542-2219

Kasigluk, Bethel, Pop. 558
Lower Kuskokwim SD
Supt. — See Bethel
Akiuk Memorial S 100/PK-12
General Delivery 99609 907-477-6829
Christina Powers, prin. Fax 477-6314
Akula Elitnaurvik S 100/PK-12
PO Box 79 99609 907-477-6615
Douglas Avery, prin. Fax 477-6715

Kasilof, Kenai Peninsula, Pop. 516
Kenai Peninsula Borough SD
Supt. — See Soldotna
Tustumena ES 200/PK-6
PO Box 749 99610 907-260-1345
Douglas Hayman, prin. Fax 262-8477

Kenai, Kenai Peninsula, Pop. 6,541
Kenai Peninsula Borough SD
Supt. — See Soldotna
Kenai MS 400/6-8
201 N Tinker Ln 99611 907-283-1700
Vaughn Dosko, prin. Fax 283-3180
Mountain View ES 500/PK-5
315 Swires Rd 99611 907-283-8600
Karl Kircher, prin. Fax 283-9340

Grace Lutheran S 50/PK-8
47585 Ciechanski Rd 99611 907-283-9551
Ryan Holper, prin. Fax 283-9551

Ketchikan, Ketchikan Gateway, Pop. 7,299
Ketchikan Gateway Borough SD 2,300/PK-12
333 Schoenbar Rd 99901 907-225-2118
Robert Boyle, supt. Fax 247-3820
www.kgbsd.org
Fawn Mountain ES 300/PK-6
400 Old Homestead Rd 99901 907-228-2200
Alonso Escalante, prin. Fax 247-4741
Houghtaling ES 300/PK-6
2940 Baranof Ave 99901 907-225-4128
Sheila Klosterman, prin. Fax 225-7925
Point Higgins ES 200/PK-6
981 N Point Higgins Rd 99901 907-247-1500
Tony Sines, prin. Fax 247-1558
Schoenbar MS 300/7-8
217 Schoenbar Rd 99901 907-228-7200
Sherilinn Boehlert, prin.

Southeast Island SD
Supt. — See Thorne Bay
Naukati S 50/PK-12
PO Box NKI 99950 907-629-4121
Jessica Goldman, lead tchr. Fax 629-4122
Whale Pass S 50/PK-12
126 Bayview Rd 99950 907-846-5320
Christine Cook, lead tchr. Fax 846-5319

Clover Pass Christian S 50/PK-3
105 N Point Higgins Rd 99901 907-247-2350
Jodi Marshall, admin. Fax 247-0476
Holy Name S 100/PK-6
433 Jackson St 99901 907-225-2400
Nicole Miller, admin. Fax 247-2121

Kiana, Northwest Arctic, Pop. 351
Northwest Arctic Borough SD
Supt. — See Kotzebue
Kiana S 100/PK-12
PO Box 190 99749 907-475-2115
Rex Kilburn, prin. Fax 475-2120

King Cove, Aleutians East, Pop. 905
Aleutian East Borough SD
Supt. — See Sand Point
King Cove S 100/PK-12
PO Box 69 99612 907-497-2354
Gary Lamar, prin. Fax 497-2408

King Salmon, Bristol Bay, Pop. 341
Lake & Peninsula SD 300/PK-12
PO Box 498 99613 907-246-4280
Ty Mase, supt. Fax 246-3055
www.lpsd.com
Other Schools – See Chignik, Chignik Lagoon, Chignik Lake, Igiugig, Iliamna, Kokhanok, Levelock, Nondalton, Perryville, Pilot Point, Port Alsworth, Port Heiden

Kipnuk, Bethel, Pop. 637
Lower Kuskokwim SD
Supt. — See Bethel
Chief Paul Memorial S 200/PK-12
PO Box 19 99614 907-896-5011
LaDorothy Lightfoot, prin. Fax 896-5428

Kivalina, Northwest Arctic, Pop. 368
Northwest Arctic Borough SD
Supt. — See Kotzebue
McQueen S 100/PK-12
General Delivery 99750 907-645-2125
Dr. Zoe Theoharis, prin. Fax 645-2124

Klawock, Prince of Wales-Outer Ketchikan, Pop. 670
Klawock CSD 100/PK-12
PO Box 9 99925 907-755-2220
Jim Holien, supt. Fax 755-2320
www.klawockschool.com
Klawock City S 100/PK-12
PO Box 9 99925 907-755-2220
Kelli Larson, prin. Fax 755-2913

Kobuk, Northwest Arctic, Pop. 151
Northwest Arctic Borough SD
Supt. — See Kotzebue
Kobuk S 100/PK-12
PO Box 40 99751 907-948-2231
Jay Denton, lead tchr. Fax 948-2225

Kodiak, Kodiak Island, Pop. 5,742
Kodiak Island Borough SD 2,400/PK-12
722 Mill Bay Rd 99615 907-481-6200
Stewart McDonald, supt. Fax 481-6255
www.kibsd.org
Danger Bay S 50/K-12
722 Mill Bay Rd 99615 907-680-2357
Fax 481-6152
East ES 300/PK-5
722 Mill Bay Rd 99615 907-481-6500
Jennie Schauff, prin. Fax 481-6560
Kodiak MS 500/6-8
722 Mill Bay Rd 99615 907-481-2200
Jethro Jiones, prin. Fax 481-2201
Main ES 200/PK-5
722 Mill Bay Rd 99615 907-486-2100
Angela Chervenak, prin. Fax 486-2138
North Star ES 200/PK-5
722 Mill Bay Rd 99615 907-481-2000
Patricia Wilson, prin. Fax 481-2020
Peterson ES 300/PK-5
722 Mill Bay Rd 99615 907-481-6400
Beth Cole, prin. Fax 481-6476
Other Schools – See Akhiok, Chiniak, Karluk, Larsen Bay, Old Harbor, Ouzinkie, Port Lions

---

Kodiak Christian S 100/PK-8
3300 E Rezanof Dr 99615 907-486-4905
Katherine Baquero, prin. Fax 486-2463
St. Marys S 100/K-8
2932 Mill Bay Rd 99615 907-486-3513
Brian Cleary, prin. Fax 486-3117

Kokhanok, Lake and Peninsula, Pop. 153
Lake & Peninsula SD
Supt. — See King Salmon
Kokhanok S 50/PK-12
PO Box 1109 99606 907-282-2210
Linda Richter, prin. Fax 282-2247

Koliganek, Dillingham, Pop. 207
Southwest Region SD
Supt. — See Dillingham
Koliganek S 100/K-12
PO Box 5052 99576 907-596-3444
Michael Lee, prin. Fax 596-3484

Kongiganak, Bethel, Pop. 430
Lower Kuskokwim SD
Supt. — See Bethel
Ayagina'ar Elitnaurvik S 200/PK-12
PO Box 5109, 907-557-5551
Lewis Beaver, prin. Fax 557-5639

Kotlik, Wade Hampton, Pop. 574
Lower Yukon SD
Supt. — See Mountain Village
Kotlik S 200/PK-12
PO Box 20129 99620 907-899-4415
Corey Weiss, prin. Fax 899-4515

Kotzebue, Northwest Arctic, Pop. 2,953
Northwest Arctic Borough SD 2,100/PK-12
PO Box 51 99752 907-442-1802
Dr. Annmarie O'Brien, supt. Fax 442-2246
www.nwarctic.org
Nelson ES 400/PK-5
PO Box 264 99752 907-442-1877
John Crabb, prin. Fax 442-2142
Other Schools – See Ambler, Buckland, Deering, Kiana, Kivalina, Kobuk, Noatak, Noorvik, Selawik, Shungnak

Koyuk, Nome, Pop. 308
Bering Strait SD
Supt. — See Unalakleet
Koyuk-Malemute S 100/PK-12
PO Box 53009 99753 907-963-3021
Mary Huntington, prin. Fax 963-2428

Koyukuk, Yukon-Koyukuk, Pop. 94
Yukon-Koyukuk SD
Supt. — See Fairbanks
Vernetti S 50/PK-10
PO Box 70 99754 907-927-2212
Patty White, admin. Fax 927-2251

Kwethluk, Bethel, Pop. 696
Lower Kuskokwim SD
Supt. — See Bethel
Ket'acik and Aap'alluk Memorial S 300/PK-12
PO Box 150 99621 907-757-6014
Darrell Richard, prin. Fax 757-6013

Kwigillingok, Bethel, Pop. 316
Lower Kuskokwim SD
Supt. — See Bethel
Kwigillingok S 100/PK-12
PO Box 109 99622 907-588-8629
Megan Rosendall, prin. Fax 588-8613

Larsen Bay, Kodiak Island, Pop. 83
Kodiak Island Borough SD
Supt. — See Kodiak
Larsen Bay S 50/PK-12
PO Box 70 99624 907-847-2252
Kendra Bartz, prin. Fax 847-2260

Levelock, Lake and Peninsula, Pop. 65
Lake & Peninsula SD
Supt. — See King Salmon
Levelock S 50/K-12
PO Box 89 99625 907-287-3060
Moon McCarley, lead tchr. Fax 287-3021

Lower Kalskag, Bethel, Pop. 268
Kuspuk SD
Supt. — See Aniak

Levi ES 50/3-6
PO Box 92 99626 907-471-2318
Severin Gardner, prin. Fax 675-4305

Mc Grath, Yukon-Koyukuk, Pop. 277
Iditarod Area SD 300/PK-12
PO Box 90 99627 907-524-1200
Connie Newman, supt. Fax 524-3217
www.iditarodsd.org
Mc Grath S 100/PK-12
PO Box 290 99627 907-524-3033
Christopher Shelborne, prin. Fax 524-3751
Other Schools – See Anvik, Grayling, Holy Cross, Nikolai, Shageluk, Takotna

Manley Hot Springs, Yukon-Koyukuk, Pop. 75
Yukon-Koyukuk SD
Supt. — See Fairbanks
Dart S 50/PK-12
PO Box 29 99756 907-672-3202
Patty White, admin. Fax 672-3201

Manokotak, Dillingham, Pop. 440
Southwest Region SD
Supt. — See Dillingham
Manokotak S 100/PK-12
PO Box 30 99628 907-289-1013
Debra Forkner, prin. Fax 289-2050

Marshall, Wade Hampton, Pop. 404
Lower Yukon SD
Supt. — See Mountain Village
Marshall S 100/PK-12
PO Box 89 99585 907-679-6112
Jeff Rebitski, prin. Fax 679-6637

Mekoryuk, Bethel, Pop. 184
Lower Kuskokwim SD
Supt. — See Bethel
Nuniwarmiut S 50/PK-12
PO Box 49 99630 907-827-8415
Walt Betz, prin. Fax 827-8613

Mentasta Lake, Southeast Fairbanks, Pop. 111
Alaska Gateway SD
Supt. — See Tok
Mentasta Lake S 50/K-12
PO Box 6039 99780 907-291-2317
Craig Roach, prin. Fax 291-2327

Metlakatla, Prince of Wales-Outer Ketchikan, Pop. 1,313
Annette Islands SD 300/PK-12
PO Box 7 99926 907-886-6332
Timothy Bauer, supt. Fax 886-5130
aisdk12.org
Johnson ES 100/PK-5
PO Box 7 99926 907-886-4121
Thomas Vail, prin. Fax 886-4120
Leask MS 100/6-8
PO Box 7 99926 907-886-6095
Jason Pipkin, admin. Fax 886-4130

Minto, Yukon-Koyukuk, Pop. 200
Yukon-Koyukuk SD
Supt. — See Fairbanks
Minto S 50/PK-12
PO Box 81 99758 907-798-7212
Vicky Charlie, prin. Fax 798-7282

Moose Pass, Kenai Peninsula, Pop. 213
Kenai Peninsula Borough SD
Supt. — See Soldotna
Moose Pass S 50/K-8
PO Box 46 99631 907-288-3183
Douglas Hayman, prin. Fax 288-3607

Mountain Village, Wade Hampton, Pop. 788
Lower Yukon SD 2,000/PK-12
PO Box 32089 99632 907-591-2411
Rob Picou, supt. Fax 591-2449
www.loweryukon.org
Mountain Village S 200/PK-12
PO Box 32105 99632 907-591-2204
Platonida Kashatok, prin. Fax 591-2819
Other Schools – See Alakanuk, Emmonak, Hooper Bay, Kotlik, Marshall, Pilot Station, Russian Mission, Scammon Bay, Sheldon Point

Naknek, Bristol Bay, Pop. 421
Bristol Bay Borough SD 200/PK-12
PO Box 169 99633 907-246-4225
Bill Hill, supt. Fax 246-4447
bbbsd.net
Naknek ES 100/PK-6
PO Box 169 99633 907-246-4265
Andrew Johnson, prin. Fax 246-4447

Nanwalek, Kenai Peninsula, Pop. 231
Kenai Peninsula Borough SD
Supt. — See Soldotna
Nanwalek S 100/K-12
PO Box 8007 99603 907-281-2210
Nancy Kleine, prin. Fax 281-2211

Napakiak, Bethel, Pop. 354
Lower Kuskokwim SD
Supt. — See Bethel
Miller Memorial S 100/PK-12
PO Box 34050 99634 907-589-2420
Linda Jennings, prin. Fax 589-2515

Napaskiak, Bethel, Pop. 403
Lower Kuskokwim SD
Supt. — See Bethel
Qugcuun Memorial S 50/PK-12
PO Box 6199 99559 907-737-7214
Nick Straw, prin. Fax 737-7211
Williams Memorial S 200/PK-12
PO Box 6089 99559 907-737-7212
Talbert Bentley, prin. Fax 737-7967

Nenana, Yukon-Koyukuk, Pop. 357
Nenana CSD 1,000/K-12
PO Box 10 99760 907-832-5464
Eric Gebhart, supt. Fax 832-5625
nenanalynx.org
Nenana City S 200/K-12
PO Box 10 99760 907-832-5464
Ron Gherman, prin. Fax 832-5625

New Stuyahok, Dillingham, Pop. 495
Southwest Region SD
Supt. — See Dillingham
Chief Blunka S 100/PK-12
PO Box 29 99636 907-693-3144
Robin Jones, prin. Fax 693-3163

Newtok, Bethel, Pop. 352
Lower Kuskokwim SD
Supt. — See Bethel
Ayaprun S 200/PK-12
PO Box WWT 99559 907-237-2504
Grant Kashatok, prin. Fax 237-2506

Nightmute, Bethel, Pop. 279
Lower Kuskokwim SD
Supt. — See Bethel
Negtemiut Elitnaurviat S 100/PK-12
General Delivery 99690 907-647-6313
Rick Rohlman, prin. Fax 647-6227

Nikiski, Kenai Peninsula, Pop. 4,284
Kenai Peninsula Borough SD
Supt. — See Soldotna
Nikiski North Star ES 400/PK-5
45600 Holt Lamplight Rd, 907-776-2600
Margaret Gilman, prin. Fax 776-8423

Nikolaevsk, Kenai Peninsula, Pop. 307
Kenai Peninsula Borough SD
Supt. — See Soldotna
Nikolaevsk S 100/PK-12
PO Box 5129 99556 907-235-8972
Mike Sellers, prin. Fax 235-3617

Nikolai, Yukon-Koyukuk, Pop. 83
Iditarod Area SD
Supt. — See Mc Grath
Top of the Kuskokwim S 50/PK-12
PO Box 9190 99691 907-293-2427
Tara Wiggins, prin. Fax 293-2214

Ninilchik, Kenai Peninsula, Pop. 836
Kenai Peninsula Borough SD
Supt. — See Soldotna
Ninilchik S 100/K-12
15735 Sterling Hwy 99639 907-567-3301
Jeffrey Ambrosier, prin. Fax 567-3504

Noatak, Northwest Arctic, Pop. 502
Northwest Arctic Borough SD
Supt. — See Kotzebue
Napaaqtugmiut S 200/PK-12
PO Box 49 99761 907-485-2153
Stan VanAmburg, prin. Fax 485-2150

Nome, Nome, Pop. 3,196
Nome SD 700/PK-12
PO Box 131 99762 907-443-2231
Shawn Arnold, supt. Fax 443-5144
www.nomeschools.org
Nome ES 400/PK-6
PO Box 131 99762 907-443-8922
Kevin Theonnes, prin. Fax 443-2850

Nondalton, Lake and Peninsula, Pop. 130
Lake & Peninsula SD
Supt. — See King Salmon
Nondalton S 50/K-12
100 School Rd 99640 907-294-2210
Jerry Fisher, prin. Fax 294-2265

Noorvik, Northwest Arctic, Pop. 618
Northwest Arctic Borough SD
Supt. — See Kotzebue
Aqqaluk / Noorvik S 200/PK-12
PO Box 165 99763 907-636-2178
Faith Jurs, prin. Fax 636-2160

North Pole, Fairbanks North Star, Pop. 1,997
Fairbanks North Star Borough SD
Supt. — See Fairbanks
North Pole MS 700/6-8
300 E 8th Ave 99705 907-488-2271
Rich Smith, prin. Fax 488-9213

North Pole Christian S 100/PK-8
2936 Badger Rd 99705 907-488-0133
Chad Evans, prin. Fax 488-8248

Northway, Southeast Fairbanks, Pop. 65
Alaska Gateway SD
Supt. — See Tok
Northway S 50/PK-12
PO Box 519 99764 907-778-2287
Doug Richards, prin. Fax 778-2221

Nuiqsut, North Slope, Pop. 391
North Slope Borough SD
Supt. — See Barrow
Nuiqsut Trapper S 100/PK-12
PO Box 89167 99789 907-480-6712
Debbe Lancaster, prin. Fax 480-6621

Nulato, Yukon-Koyukuk, Pop. 263
Yukon-Koyukuk SD
Supt. — See Fairbanks
Demoski S 50/PK-12
PO Box 65029 99765 907-898-2204
Jason Johnson, prin. Fax 898-2340

Nunapitchuk, Bethel, Pop. 487
Lower Kuskokwim SD
Supt. — See Bethel

Tobeluk Memorial S 200/K-12
PO Box 150 99641 907-527-5701
Daryl Daugaard, prin. Fax 527-5610

Old Harbor, Kodiak Island, Pop. 215
Kodiak Island Borough SD
Supt. — See Kodiak
Old Harbor S 50/K-12
PO Box 49 99643 907-286-2213
Kendra Bartz, prin. Fax 286-2222

Ouzinkie, Kodiak Island, Pop. 146
Kodiak Island Borough SD
Supt. — See Kodiak
Ouzinkie S 50/K-12
PO Box 49 99644 907-680-2204
Kendra Bartz, prin. Fax 680-2288

Palmer, Matanuska-Susitna, Pop. 5,499
Matanuska-Susitna Borough SD 17,800/PK-12
501 N Gulkana St 99645 907-746-9200
Dr. Monica Goyette, supt. Fax 746-4076
www.matsuk12.us
Beryozova S 50/K-12
501 N Gulkana St 99645 907-495-2500
Carl Chamblee, prin. Fax 495-2502
Butte ES 300/PK-5
4006 S Butte Rd 99645 907-861-5200
Dan Kitchin, prin. Fax 861-5280
Colony MS 700/6-8
9250 E Bogard Rd 99645 907-761-1500
Mary McMahon, prin. Fax 761-1592
Palmer MS 600/6-8
1159 S Chugach St 99645 907-761-4300
Brad Allen, prin. Fax 761-4372
Pioneer Peak ES 400/PK-5
1959 N Trunk Rd 99645 907-861-5700
Mary Watts, prin. Fax 861-5780
Sherrod ES 400/3-5
561 N Gulkana St 99645 907-761-4100
Dan Michael, prin. Fax 761-4180
Swanson ES 400/PK-2
507 N Gulkana St 99645 907-861-5300
Mary Kate Johnston, prin. Fax 861-5380
Other Schools – See Big Lake, Sutton, Talkeetna, Trapper Creek, Wasilla, Willow

---

Amazing Grace Academy K-12
PO Box 3229 99645 907-745-2691

Pelican, Skagway-Hoonah-Angoon, Pop. 82
Pelican CSD 50/PK-12
PO Box 90 99832 907-735-2236
Larry Wilson, supt. Fax 735-2263
pelicanschool.org/
Pelican S 50/PK-12
PO Box 90 99832 907-735-2236
Larry Wilson, admin. Fax 735-2263

Perryville, Lake and Peninsula, Pop. 111
Lake & Peninsula SD
Supt. — See King Salmon
Perryville S 50/PK-12
PO Box 103 99648 907-853-2210
Joe Ward, lead tchr. Fax 853-2267

Petersburg, Wrangell-Petersburg, Pop. 2,720
Petersburg SD 400/K-12
PO Box 289 99833 907-772-4271
Erica Kludt-Painter, supt. Fax 772-4719
www.pcsd.us
Mitkof MS 100/6-8
PO Box 289 99833 907-772-3860
Rick Dormer, prin. Fax 772-3617
Stedman ES 200/K-5
PO Box 289 99833 907-772-4786
Teri Toland, prin. Fax 772-4334

Pilot Point, Lake and Peninsula, Pop. 56
Lake & Peninsula SD
Supt. — See King Salmon
Pilot Point S 50/PK-12
PO Box 467 99649 907-797-2210
Hannah Middleton, prin. Fax 797-2267

Pilot Station, Wade Hampton, Pop. 567
Lower Yukon SD
Supt. — See Mountain Village
Pilot Station S 200/PK-12
PO Box 5090 99650 907-549-3212
Cory Stringer, prin. Fax 549-3335

Platinum, Bethel, Pop. 58
Lower Kuskokwim SD
Supt. — See Bethel
Arviq S 50/PK-12
PO Box 28 99651 907-979-8111
Georgia Berry, prin. Fax 979-8308

Point Hope, North Slope, Pop. 647
North Slope Borough SD
Supt. — See Barrow
Tikigaq S 200/PK-12
PO Box 148 99766 907-368-2662
Gene Burke, prin. Fax 368-2770

Point Lay, North Slope, Pop. 187
North Slope Borough SD
Supt. — See Barrow
Kali S 100/PK-12
PO Box 59077 99759 907-833-2311
Glenn Cole, prin. Fax 833-2315

Port Alexander, Wrangell-Petersburg, Pop. 51
Southeast Island SD
Supt. — See Thorne Bay
Port Alexander S 50/PK-12
PO Box 8170 99836 907-568-2205
Laura Anania, lead tchr. Fax 568-2261

Port Alsworth, Lake and Peninsula, Pop. 150
Lake & Peninsula SD
Supt. — See King Salmon
Tanalian S 100/PK-12
1400 School Rd 99653 907-781-2210
Nathan Davis, prin. Fax 781-2254

Port Graham, Kenai Peninsula, Pop. 143
Kenai Peninsula Borough SD
Supt. — See Soldotna
Port Graham S 50/PK-12
PO Box 5550 99603 907-284-2210
Nancy Klein, prin. Fax 284-2213

Port Heiden, Lake and Peninsula, Pop. 100
Lake & Peninsula SD
Supt. — See King Salmon
Meshik S 50/PK-12
General Delivery 99549 907-837-2210
Kitza Durkop, prin. Fax 837-2265

Port Lions, Kodiak Island, Pop. 189
Kodiak Island Borough SD
Supt. — See Kodiak
Port Lions S 50/K-12
PO Box 109 99550 907-454-2237
Kendra Bartz, prin. Fax 454-2377

Quinhagak, Bethel, Pop. 642
Lower Kuskokwim SD
Supt. — See Bethel
Kuinerrarmiut Elitnaurviat S 200/PK-12
PO Box 49 99655 907-556-8628
Peggie Price, prin. Fax 556-8228

Ruby, Yukon-Koyukuk, Pop. 156
Yukon-Koyukuk SD
Supt. — See Fairbanks
Kangas S 50/PK-12
PO Box 68110 99768 907-468-4465
Anne Titus, prin. Fax 468-4444

Russian Mission, Wade Hampton, Pop. 309
Lower Yukon SD
Supt. — See Mountain Village
Russian Mission S 100/PK-12
PO Box 90 99657 907-584-5126
Mary Tierney, prin. Fax 584-5412

Saint Marys, Wade Hampton, Pop. 483
Saint Mary's SD 200/PK-12
PO Box 9 99658 907-438-2411
David Herbert, supt. Fax 438-2735
www.smcsd.us
Saint Mary's S 200/PK-12
PO Box 9 99658 907-438-2411
Dewayne Bahnsen, prin. Fax 438-2735

Saint Michael, Nome, Pop. 392
Bering Strait SD
Supt. — See Unalakleet
Andrews S 200/PK-12
100 Baker St 99659 907-923-3041
Jon Whede, prin. Fax 923-3031

Saint Paul Island, Aleutians West, Pop. 459
Pribilof SD, PO Box 207 99660 100/PK-12
Brett Agenbroad M.Ed., supt. 907-546-3300
sites.google.com/a/pribilof.org/psd
St. Paul S, PO Box 207 99660 100/PK-12
Brett Agenbroad, admin. 907-546-3300

Sand Point, Aleutians East, Pop. 929
Aleutian East Borough SD 200/PK-12
PO Box 429 99661 907-383-5222
Michael Seifert, supt. Fax 383-3496
www.aebsd.org
Sand Point S 100/PK-12
PO Box 269 99661 907-383-2393
Hilary Seifert, prin. Fax 383-3833
Other Schools – See Akutan, False Pass, King Cove

Savoonga, Nome, Pop. 668
Bering Strait SD
Supt. — See Unalakleet
Kingeekuk Memorial S 200/PK-12
PO Box 200 99769 907-984-6811
Ralph Lindquist, prin. Fax 984-6413

Scammon Bay, Wade Hampton, Pop. 473
Lower Yukon SD
Supt. — See Mountain Village
Scammon Bay S 200/PK-12
103 Askinuk St 99662 907-558-2000
Melissa Rivera, prin. Fax 558-5320

Selawik, Northwest Arctic, Pop. 742
Northwest Arctic Borough SD
Supt. — See Kotzebue
Davis-Ramoth S 300/PK-12
PO Box 29 99770 907-484-2142
Lois Ballard, prin. Fax 484-2127

Seldovia, Kenai Peninsula, Pop. 230
Kenai Peninsula Borough SD
Supt. — See Soldotna
English S 50/K-12
PO Box 171 99663 907-234-7616
Joshua Hinds, prin. Fax 234-7884

Seward, Kenai Peninsula, Pop. 2,478
Kenai Peninsula Borough SD
Supt. — See Soldotna
Seward ES 300/PK-5
PO Box 247 99664 907-224-3356
Alan Haskins, prin. Fax 224-7077
Seward MS 100/6-8
PO Box 1149 99664 907-224-9000
Jenny Martin, prin Fax 224-9001

Shageluk, Yukon-Koyukuk, Pop. 78
Iditarod Area SD
Supt. — See Mc Grath
Innoko River S 50/PK-12
PO Box 49 99665 907-473-8233
Joy Hamilton, prin. Fax 473-8268

Shaktoolik, Nome, Pop. 250
Bering Strait SD
Supt. — See Unalakleet
Shaktoolik S 100/PK-12
PO Box 40 99771 907-955-3021
Marc Jong, prin. Fax 955-3031

Sheldon Point, Wade Hampton, Pop. 121
Lower Yukon SD
Supt. — See Mountain Village
Sheldon Point S 100/PK-12
PO Box 32, Nunam Iqua AK 99666 907-498-4112
Samantha Afran, prin. Fax 498-4111

Shishmaref, Nome, Pop. 556
Bering Strait SD
Supt. — See Unalakleet
Shishmaref S 200/PK-12
1 Seaview Ln 99772 907-649-3021
Dorothy Harris, prin. Fax 649-3031

Shungnak, Northwest Arctic, Pop. 262
Northwest Arctic Borough SD
Supt. — See Kotzebue
Shungnak S 100/PK-12
PO Box 79 99773 907-437-2151
Roger Franklin, prin. Fax 437-2177

Sitka, Sitka, Pop. 8,072
Sitka SD 1,400/PK-12
300 Kostrometinoff St 99835 907-747-8622
Dr. Mary Wegner, supt. Fax 966-1260
www.sitkaschools.org
Baranof ES 300/PK-1
305 Baranof St 99835 907-747-5825
Jill Lecrone, prin. Fax 747-3049
Blatchley MS 300/6-8
601 Halibut Point Rd 99835 907-747-8672
Ben White, prin. Fax 966-1460
Keet Gooshi Heen ES 400/2-5
307 Kashevaroff St 99835 907-747-8395
Casey Demmert, prin. Fax 966-1240

Sitka Adventist S 50/1-8
1613 Halibut Point Rd 99835 907-747-8855

Skagway, Skagway-Hoonah-Angoon, Pop. 884
Skagway SD 100/PK-12
PO Box 497 99840 907-983-2960
Dr. Joshua Coughran, supt. Fax 983-2964
www.skagwayschool.org
Skagway S 100/PK-12
PO Box 497 99840 907-983-2960
Dr. Joshua Coughran, supt. Fax 983-2964

Slana, Valdez-Cordova, Pop. 142
Copper River SD
Supt. — See Glennallen
Slana S 50/PK-12
PO Box 883 99586 907-822-5868
Kathy Everett, prin. Fax 822-3850

Sleetmute, Bethel, Pop. 86
Kuspuk SD
Supt. — See Aniak
Egnaty Sr. S 50/K-12
PO Box 69 99668 907-449-4216
Steven B. Porter, prin. Fax 675-4305

Soldotna, Kenai Peninsula, Pop. 3,894
Kenai Peninsula Borough SD 8,500/PK-12
148 N Binkley St 99669 907-714-8888
Sean Dusek, supt. Fax 262-9645
www.kpbsd.k12.ak.us
Kalifornsky Beach ES 400/K-6
1049 E Poppy Ln 99669 907-260-1300
Nate Crabtree, prin. Fax 262-4096
Redoubt ES 400/PK-6
486 W Redoubt Ave 99669 907-260-4300
William Withrow, prin. Fax 262-5815
Skyview MS 400/7-8
46188 Sterling Hwy 99669 907-260-2500
Sarge Truesdell, prin. Fax 262-7036
Soldotna ES 300/PK-6
162 E Park Ave 99669 907-260-5100
Austin Stevenson, prin. Fax 262-4962
Other Schools – See Anchor Point, Cooper Landing, Fritz Creek, Homer, Hope, Kasilof, Kenai, Moose Pass, Nanwalek, Nikiski, Nikolaevsk, Ninilchik, Port Graham, Seldovia, Seward, Sterling, Tyonek

---

Cook Inlet Academy 100/PK-12
45872 Kalifornsky Beach Rd 99669 907-262-5101
Mary Rowley, prin. Fax 262-1541

Stebbins, Nome, Pop. 556
Bering Strait SD
Supt. — See Unalakleet
Tukurngailnguq S 200/K-12
General Delivery 99671 907-934-3021
John Juvinall, prin. Fax 934-3031

Sterling, Kenai Peninsula, Pop. 5,392
Kenai Peninsula Borough SD
Supt. — See Soldotna
Sterling ES 200/PK-6
PO Box 89 99672 907-262-4944
Denise Kelly, prin. Fax 262-5128

Stony River, Bethel, Pop. 49
Kuspuk SD
Supt. — See Aniak
Michael S 50/K-12
General Delivery 99557 907-537-3225
Steven B. Porter, prin. Fax 675-4305

Sutton, Matanuska-Susitna, Pop. 308
Matanuska-Susitna Borough SD
Supt. — See Palmer
Glacier View S 50/K-12
65975 S Wolverine Cir 99674 907-861-5650
Wendy Taylor, prin. Fax 861-5680
Sutton ES 50/PK-5
PO Box 216 99674 907-861-5600
Joshua Rockey, prin. Fax 861-5640

Takotna, Yukon-Koyukuk, Pop. 38
Iditarod Area SD
Supt. — See Mc Grath
Takotna S 50/PK-12
PO Box 90 99675 907-298-2115
Casey McCarty, prin. Fax 298-2316

Talkeetna, Matanuska-Susitna, Pop. 845
Matanuska-Susitna Borough SD
Supt. — See Palmer
Talkeetna ES 100/PK-6
HC 89 Box 8010 99676 907-733-9400
Lisa Shelby, prin. Fax 733-9440

Tanacross, Southeast Fairbanks, Pop. 123
Alaska Gateway SD
Supt. — See Tok
Tanacross S 50/K-8
PO Box 76030 99776 907-883-4391
Fax 883-4390

Tanana, Yukon-Koyukuk, Pop. 238
Tanana CSD 50/PK-12
PO Box 89 99777 907-366-7203
M. Therese Ashton, supt. Fax 366-7201
aktcsd.org
Sommer S 50/PK-12
PO Box 89 99777 907-366-7203
M. Therese Ashton, supt. Fax 366-7201

Tatitlek, Valdez-Cordova, Pop. 84
Chugach SD
Supt. — See Anchorage
Tatitlek Community S 50/K-12
PO Box 167 99677 907-325-2252
Jed Palmer, lead tchr. Fax 325-2299

Teller, Nome, Pop. 229
Bering Strait SD
Supt. — See Unalakleet
Isabell S 100/PK-12
100 Airport Ave 99778 907-642-3041
Susette Carroll, prin. Fax 642-3031

Tenakee Springs, Skagway-Hoonah-Angoon, Pop. 127
Chatham SD
Supt. — See Angoon
Tenakee Springs S 50/K-12
PO Box 62 99841 907-736-2204
Anne Connelly, lead tchr. Fax 736-2204

Tetlin, Southeast Fairbanks, Pop. 122
Alaska Gateway SD
Supt. — See Tok
Tetlin S 50/PK-12
100 Main St 99779 907-324-2104
Robert Litwack, prin. Fax 324-2120

Thorne Bay, Prince of Wales-Outer Ketchikan, Pop. 450
Southeast Island SD 200/PK-12
PO Box 19569 99919 907-828-8254
Lauren Burch, supt. Fax 828-8257
www.sisd.org
Thorne Bay S 100/K-12
PO Box 19005 99919 907-828-3921
Alan Schwab, prin. Fax 828-3901
Other Schools – See Coffman Cove, Craig, Hyder, Kasaan, Ketchikan, Port Alexander

Togiak, Dillingham, Pop. 691
Southwest Region SD
Supt. — See Dillingham
Togiak S 200/PK-12
PO Box 50 99678 907-493-5829
Sam Gosuk, prin. Fax 493-5933

Tok, Southeast Fairbanks, Pop. 1,157
Alaska Gateway SD 400/PK-12
PO Box 226 99780 907-883-5151
Scott MacManu, supt. Fax 883-5154
www.agsd.us/
Tok S 200/PK-12
PO Box 249 99780 907-883-5161
Scott Holmes, prin. Fax 883-5165
Other Schools – See Dot Lake, Eagle, Mentasta Lake, Northway, Tanacross, Tetlin

Toksook Bay, Bethel, Pop. 578
Lower Kuskokwim SD
Supt. — See Bethel
Nelson Island Area S 200/PK-12
101 Sunnyside Rd 99637 907-427-7815
Thomas Gobeske, prin. Fax 427-7612

Trapper Creek, Matanuska-Susitna, Pop. 456
Matanuska-Susitna Borough SD
Supt. — See Palmer
Trapper Creek ES 50/PK-6
PO Box 13108 99683 907-733-9451
Allison Wall, prin. Fax 733-9480

Tuluksak, Bethel, Pop. 370
Yupiit SD
Supt. — See Akiachak
Tuluksak S, PO Box 115 99679 100/PK-12
David Macri, prin. 907-695-5600

Tuntutuliak, Bethel, Pop. 403
Lower Kuskokwim SD
Supt. — See Bethel
Angapak Memorial S 100/PK-12
PO Box 8087 99680 907-256-2415
Zachary Bastoky, prin. Fax 256-2527

Tununak, Bethel, Pop. 322
Lower Kuskokwim SD
Supt. — See Bethel
Albert Memorial S 100/PK-12
PO Box 49 99681 907-652-6827
Gordon Tester, prin. Fax 652-6028

Twin Hills, Dillingham, Pop. 72
Southwest Region SD
Supt. — See Dillingham
Twin Hills S 50/K-8
PO Box TWA 99576 907-525-4915
Nate Preston, lead tchr. Fax 525-4216

Tyonek, Kenai Peninsula, Pop. 165
Kenai Peninsula Borough SD
Supt. — See Soldotna
Tebughna S 50/K-12
PO Box 82010 99682 907-583-2291
Pamela Potter, prin. Fax 583-2692

Unalakleet, Nome, Pop. 644
Bering Strait SD 1,900/PK-12
PO Box 225 99684 907-624-4261
Dr. Bobby Bolen, supt. Fax 624-3099
www.bssd.org
Unalakleet S 200/PK-12
PO Box 130 99684 907-624-3444
Bob Burkhart, prin. Fax 624-3388
Other Schools – See Brevig Mission, Diomede, Elim, Gambell, Golovin, Koyuk, Saint Michael, Savoonga, Shaktoolik, Shishmaref, Stebbins, Teller, Wales, White Mountain

Unalaska, Aleutians West, Pop. 4,083
Unalaska CSD 400/PK-12
PO Box 570 99685 907-581-3151
John Conwell, supt. Fax 581-3152
www.ucsd.net
Eagle's View ES 200/PK-6
PO Box 570 99685 907-581-3979
Eric Andersen, prin. Fax 581-3972

Valdez, Valdez-Cordova, Pop. 3,714
Valdez CSD 600/PK-12
PO Box 398 99686 907-835-4357
Jim Nygaard, supt. Fax 835-4964
www.valdezcityschools.org/
Gilson MS 100/6-8
PO Box 398 99686 907-835-2244
Rodney Morrison, prin. Fax 835-2540
Hutchens ES 300/PK-5
PO Box 398 99686 907-835-4728
Melissa Reese, prin. Fax 835-2047

Venetie, Yukon-Koyukuk, Pop. 159
Yukon Flats SD
Supt. — See Fort Yukon
Fredson S 100/PK-12
PO Box 81089 99781 907-849-8415
Edward Martin, lead tchr. Fax 849-8630

Wainwright, North Slope, Pop. 547
North Slope Borough SD
Supt. — See Barrow
Alak S 200/PK-12
PO Box 10 99782 907-763-2541
Bob Grimes, prin. Fax 763-2565

Wales, Nome, Pop. 132
Bering Strait SD
Supt. — See Unalakleet
Wales S 50/PK-12
PO Box 490 99783 907-664-3021
Roxanne Meneguin, prin. Fax 664-3031

Wasilla, Matanuska-Susitna, Pop. 7,351
Matanuska-Susitna Borough SD
Supt. — See Palmer
Cottonwood Creek ES 500/PK-5
800 N Seward Meridian Pkwy 99654 907-864-2100
Lisa Vrvilo, prin. Fax 864-2180
Dena'Ina ES K-8
PO Box 877469 99687 907-864-5600
Fax 864-5680
Finger Lake ES 300/PK-5
5981 Eek Street 99654 907-864-2200
Susan Steele, prin. Fax 864-2280
Goose Bay ES 500/PK-2
7362 W Parks Hwy 842, 907-352-6400
Rourka Spatz, prin. Fax 352-6480
Iditarod ES 400/PK-5
4450 E Carpenter Cir 99654 907-352-9100
Scott Nelson, prin. Fax 352-9180
Knik ES 400/3-5
PO Box 877830 99687 907-352-0300
Traci Pedersen, prin. Fax 352-0380
Larson ES 400/PK-5
2722 E Seldon Rd 99654 907-352-2300
Sheela Hull, prin. Fax 352-2345
Machetanz ES 400/PK-5
4961 E Nelson Rd 99654 907-864-2300
Jennifer Dowd, prin. Fax 864-2380
Meadow Lakes ES 400/PK-5
7362 W Parks Hwy Ste 824, 907-352-6100
Felica Pridgen, prin. Fax 352-6147
Shaw ES 400/PK-5
3750 E Paradise Ln 99654 907-352-0500
David Russell, prin. Fax 352-0580
Snowshoe ES 400/PK-5
2001 W Fairview Loop 99654 907-352-9500
Katherine Ellsworth, prin. Fax 352-9560
Tanaina ES 400/PK-5
2550 N Lucille St 99654 907-352-9400
Cheri Matson, prin. Fax 352-9481
Teeland MS 700/6-8
2788 N Seward Meridian Pkwy 99654 907-352-7500
Jason Ross, prin. Fax 352-7585
Wasilla MS 800/6-8
650 E Bogard Rd 99654 907-352-5300
Casey Hull, prin. Fax 352-5380

Our Lady of the Valley S 100/PK-8
1201 E Bogard Rd 99654 907-376-0883
Joyce Lund, prin. Fax 376-0853
Wasilla Lake Christian S 200/PK-12
2001 Palmer Wasilla Hwy 99654 907-373-6439
Cheralea Purcell, prin. Fax 373-6438

White Mountain, Nome, Pop. 178
Bering Strait SD
Supt. — See Unalakleet
White Mountain S 100/PK-12
PO Box 55 99784 907-638-3041
David Fair, prin. Fax 638-3031

Whittier, Valdez-Cordova, Pop. 187
Chugach SD
Supt. — See Anchorage
Whittier Community S 50/PK-12
PO Box 638 99693 907-472-2575
Melody Clifford, lead tchr. Fax 472-2409

Willow, Matanuska-Susitna, Pop. 2,049
Matanuska-Susitna Borough SD
Supt. — See Palmer
Willow ES 100/PK-6
PO Box 69 99688 907-495-9300
Jennifer Rinaldi, prin. Fax 495-9380

Wrangell, Wrangell-Petersburg, Pop. 2,153
Wrangell SD 300/K-12
PO Box 2319 99929 907-874-2347
Patrick Mayer, supt. Fax 874-3137
www.wpsd.us
Evergreen ES 100/K-5
PO Box 736 99929 907-874-2321
Gail Taylor, prin. Fax 874-2621
Stikine MS 100/6-8
PO Box 1935 99929 907-874-3393
William Schwan, prin. Fax 874-3149

Yakutat, Yakutat, Pop. 549
Yakutat SD 100/PK-12
PO Box 429 99689 907-784-3317
Ralph Crosslin, supt. Fax 784-3446
www.yakutatschools.org
Yakutat S 100/PK-12
PO Box 429 99689 907-784-3317
Ralph Crosslin, supt. Fax 784-3446

ARIZONA

ARIZONA DEPARTMENT OF EDUCATION
1535 W Jefferson St, Phoenix 85007-3280
Telephone 602-542-5393
Fax 602-542-5440
Website http://www.azed.gov

Superintendent of Public Instruction Diane Douglas

ARIZONA BOARD OF EDUCATION
1535 W Jefferson St, Phoenix 85007

President Vacant

COUNTY SUPERINTENDENTS OF SCHOOLS

Apache County Office of Education
R. Barry Williams, supt. 928-337-7539
PO Box 548, Saint Johns 85936 Fax 337-2033
schools.apachecounty.net

Cochise County Office of Education
Jacqui Clay, supt. 520-432-8950
PO Box 208, Bisbee 85603 Fax 432-7136
www.cochise.az.gov/schools/home

Coconino County Office of Education
Risha VanderWey, supt. 928-679-8070
2384 N Steves Blvd Fax 526-1469
Flagstaff 86004
www.coconino.az.gov/CCESA

Gila County Office of Education
Roy Sandoval, supt. 928-402-8784
1400 E Ash St, Globe 85501 Fax 402-0038
www.gilacountyaz.gov

Graham County Office of Education
Donna McGaughey, supt. 928-428-2880
921 W Thatcher Blvd Fax 428-8824
Safford 85546
www.graham.az.gov/school-superintendent

Greenlee County Office of Education
Tom Powers, supt. 928-865-2822
PO Box 1595, Clifton 85533 Fax 865-4417
www.co.greenlee.az.us/schools/

Lapaz County Office of Education
Jacquline Price, supt. 928-669-6183
1112 S Joshua Ave Ste 205 Fax 669-4406
Parker 85344
www.lapazschools.org

Maricopa County Education Service Agency
Steve Watson, supt. 602-506-3866
4041 N Central Ave Ste 1200 Fax 506-3753
Phoenix 85012
education.maricopa.gov

Mohave County Office of Education
Michael File, supt. 928-753-0747
PO Box 7000, Kingman 86402 Fax 718-4958
www.mohavecounty.us/ContentPage.aspx?id=130

Navajo County Office of Education
Jalyn Gerlich, supt. 928-524-4204
PO Box 668, Holbrook 86025 Fax 524-4209
www.navajocountyaz.gov/departments/superintendent-of-schools

Pima County Office of Education
Dustin Williams, supt. 520-724-8451
200 N Stone Ave, Tucson 85701 Fax 770-4210
www.schools.pima.gov

Pinal County Office of Education
Jill Broussard, supt. 520-866-6565
PO Box 769, Florence Fax 866-6973
www.ecrsc.org/pinalesa/

Santa Cruz County Office of Education
Alfredo Velasquez, supt. 520-375-7940
2150 N Congress Dr Fax 375-7958
Nogales 85621
www.co.santa-cruz.az.us/294/Superintendent-of-Schools

Yavapai County Office of Education
Tim Carter, supt. 928-771-3326
2970 Centerpointe East Dr Fax 771-3329
Prescott 86301
www.ycesa.com

Yuma County Office of Education
Thomas Tyree, supt 928-373-1006
210 S 1st Ave, Yuma 85364 Fax 329-2008
www.yumasupt.org

PUBLIC, PRIVATE AND CATHOLIC ELEMENTARY SCHOOLS

Aguila, Maricopa, Pop. 789
Aguila ESD 63 200/PK-8
PO Box 218 85320 928-685-2222
Andy Wannemacher, supt. Fax 685-2433
www.aguilaschool.org
Aguila ES 200/PK-8
PO Box 218 85320 928-685-2222
Andy Wannemacher, prin. Fax 685-2433

Ajo, Pima, Pop. 3,253
Ajo USD 15 400/PK-12
111 N Well Rd 85321 520-387-5618
Dr. Robert F. Dooley Ed.D., supt. Fax 387-6545
www.ajoschools.org/
Ajo ES 300/PK-8
111 N Well Rd 85321 520-387-7601
Dr. Lauren Carriere, prin. Fax 387-7603

Alpine, Apache, Pop. 142
Alpine ESD 7 100/K-8
PO Box 170 85920 928-339-4570
Shirley Brazel, admin. Fax 339-1806
alpine.az.schoolwebpages.com
Alpine ES 100/K-8
PO Box 170 85920 928-339-4570
Shirley Brazel, prin. Fax 339-1806

Amado, Pima, Pop. 290
Sahuarita USD 30
Supt. — See Sahuarita
Sopori ES 200/K-5
5000 W Arivaca Rd 85645 520-625-3502
Jim Heinzelmann, prin. Fax 398-2024

Anthem, Maricopa, Pop. 21,203
Deer Valley USD 97
Supt. — See Phoenix
Anthem S 700/K-8
41020 N Freedom Way 85086 623-376-3700
Deb Roets, prin. Fax 376-3780
Canyon Springs ES 700/K-8
42901 N 45th Ave, 623-376-5200
Tricia Graham, prin. Fax 376-5280
Diamond Canyon S 1,000/PK-8
40004 N Liberty Bell Way 85086 623-445-8000
Tara LaCount, prin. Fax 445-8080
Gavilan Peak S 800/K-8
2701 W Memorial Dr 85086 623-445-7400
Chad Segersten, prin. Fax 445-7480

Apache Junction, Pinal, Pop. 35,261
Apache Junction USD 43 3,900/K-12
1575 W Southern Ave, 480-982-1110
Dr. Krista Anderson, supt. Fax 982-6474
www.ajusd.org
Cactus Canyon JHS 800/7-8
801 W Southern Ave, 480-982-1110
Courtney Castelhano, prin. Fax 983-4913

Desert Vista ES 700/K-6
3701 E Broadway Ave, 480-982-1110
Pat Smith, prin. Fax 288-0532
Four Peaks ES 700/K-6
1785 N Idaho Rd, 480-982-1110
Karl Waggoner, prin. Fax 982-1708
Other Schools – See Gold Canyon

Arizona City, Pinal, Pop. 10,280
Toltec ESD 22
Supt. — See Eloy
Arizona City ES 500/PK-8
12115 W Benito Dr, 520-466-2360
Denise Rogers, prin. Fax 466-2466

Arlington, Maricopa, Pop. 184
Arlington ESD 47 300/PK-8
PO Box 39 85322 623-386-2031
Chad Turner, supt. Fax 386-1627
arlingtonelem.org
Arlington S 300/PK-8
PO Box 39 85322 623-386-2031
Chad Turner, admin. Fax 386-1627

Ash Fork, Yavapai, Pop. 392
Ash Fork JUSD 31 200/K-12
PO Box 247 86320 928-637-2561
Seth Staples, admin. Fax 637-2623
www.afjusd.org
Ash Fork ES 100/K-5
PO Box 247 86320 928-637-2561
Seth Staples, prin. Fax 637-2623
Ash Fork MS 100/6-8
PO Box 247 86320 928-637-2561
Seth Staples, prin. Fax 637-2623

Avondale, Maricopa, Pop. 74,219
Avondale ESD 44 5,600/PK-8
295 W Western Ave 85323 623-772-5000
Dr. Betsy Hargrove, supt. Fax 772-5001
www.avondale.k12.az.us
Anderson S 800/K-8
45 S 3rd Ave 85323 623-772-5100
Lori Goslar, prin. Fax 772-5120
Avondale MS 400/6-8
1406 N Central Ave 85323 623-772-4500
Lillian Linn, prin. Fax 772-4520
Coor S 600/PK-1
1406 N Central Ave 85323 623-772-4400
Dr. Geovanni Orozco, prin. Fax 772-4420
Other Schools – See Goodyear

Litchfield ESD 79
Supt. — See Litchfield Park
Corte Sierra ES 800/PK-5
3300 N Santa Fe Trl, 623-547-1000
Tanya Rotteger, prin. Fax 935-2108
Rancho Santa Fe ES 700/PK-5
2150 W Rancho Santa Fe Blvd, 623-535-6500
Laura Combs, prin. Fax 535-3072

Littleton ESD 65 5,500/PK-8
1600 S 107th Ave 85323 623-478-5600
Dr. Roger Freeman, supt. Fax 478-5625
www.littletonaz.org
Collier ES 900/PK-8
350 S 118th Ave 85323 623-478-5900
Bryan D'Alessio, prin. Fax 478-5920
Estrella Vista STEM Academy 900/K-8
11905 W Cocopah Cir 85323 623-478-6200
Richard Ramos, prin. Fax 478-6220
Littleton ES 900/PK-8
1252 S Avondale Blvd 85323 623-478-5700
James Verrill, prin. Fax 478-5720
Quentin ES 900/K-8
11050 W Whyman Ave 85323 623-478-6000
Eric Atuahene, prin. Fax 478-6020
Other Schools – See Tolleson

Pendergast ESD 92
Supt. — See Phoenix
Canyon Breeze S 900/K-8
11675 W Encanto Blvd, 623-772-2610
Lori Pizzo, prin. Fax 478-9912
Garden Lakes S 1,000/PK-8
10825 W Garden Lakes Pkwy, 623-772-2520
Jill Helland, prin. Fax 877-9545
Rio Vista S 800/K-8
10237 W Encanto Blvd, 623-772-2670
Siobhan McCarthy, prin. Fax 478-1972

St. Thomas Aquinas Catholic S 300/PK-8
13720 W Thomas Rd, 623-935-0945
Cynthia Scheller, prin. Fax 565-5944

Bagdad, Yavapai, Pop. 1,847
Bagdad USD 20 500/PK-12
PO Box 427 86321 928-633-4101
Bryan Bullington, supt. Fax 633-4345
bagdadschools.org
Bagdad ES 200/PK-5
PO Box 427 86321 928-633-4101
Dr. Austin Temperley, prin. Fax 633-2541
Bagdad MS 100/6-8
PO Box 427 86321 928-633-4101
Tom Finnerty, prin. Fax 633-4345

Hillside ESD 35 50/K-8
HC 1 Box 3056 86321 928-442-3416
Pamela Hampton, admin.
hillsideesd.com
Hillside ES, HC 1 Box 3056 86321 50/K-8
Pamela Hampton, prin. 928-442-3416

Bapchule, Pinal

St. Peter Indian Mission Catholic S 200/PK-8
PO Box 10840, 520-315-3835
Sr. Martha Mary Carpenter, prin. Fax 315-3963

Beaver Dam, Mohave, Pop. 1,928
Littlefield USD 9 400/PK-12
3490 E Rio Virgin Rd 86432 928-347-5486
Lael Calton, supt. Fax 347-5967
www.lusd9.com/
Beaver Dam ES 200/PK-6
3436 E Rio Virgin Rd 86432 928-347-5796
Lisa Young, prin. Fax 347-5795

Benson, Cochise, Pop. 5,014
Benson USD 9 1,100/PK-12
360 S Patagonia St 85602 520-720-6700
Micah Mortensen, supt. Fax 720-6701
www.bensonsd.k12.az.us
Benson MS 300/6-8
360 S Patagonia St 85602 520-720-6800
Thomas Webb, prin. Fax 720-6709
Benson PS 400/K-5
360 S Patagonia St 85602 520-720-6750
Jomel Jansson, prin. Fax 720-6708

Bisbee, Cochise, Pop. 5,464
Bisbee USD 2 900/PK-12
100 Old Douglas Rd 85603 520-432-5381
Tom Woody, supt. Fax 432-7622
www.busd.k12.az.us
Greenway ES 300/PK-4
100 Old Douglas Rd 85603 520-432-4361
Tad Bloss, prin. Fax 432-6121
Lowell JHS 200/5-8
100 Old Douglas Rd 85603 520-432-5391
Tari Hardy, prin. Fax 432-6106

Cochise SDA Christian S K-8
PO Box 4146 85603 520-432-9186

Black Canyon City, Yavapai, Pop. 2,790
Canon ESD 50 100/K-8
PO Box 89 85324 623-374-5588
Angela Jangula, supt. Fax 374-5045
www.canon50.org
Canon ES 100/K-8
PO Box 89 85324 623-374-5588
Trinka Hall, lead tchr. Fax 374-5045

Blue, Greenlee
Blue ESD 22 50/PK-12
PO Box 80 85922 928-339-4346
Sally Hulsey, hdmstr. Fax 339-4116
Blue S 50/PK-12
PO Box 80 85922 928-339-4346
Sally Hulsey, prin. Fax 339-4116

Bonita, Graham, Pop. 1,900
Bonita ESD 16 100/PK-8
18008 S Fort Grant Rd 85643 928-828-3363
Ed Houser, supt. Fax 828-3422
www.bonita.k12.az.us
Bonita ES 100/PK-8
18008 S Fort Grant Rd 85643 928-828-3363
Ed Houser, prin. Fax 828-3422

Bouse, LaPaz, Pop. 965
Bouse ESD 26 50/PK-8
PO Box S 85325 928-851-2213
Gregory Sackos, supt. Fax 851-2986
www.bouseschool.org
Bouse S 50/PK-8
PO Box S 85325 928-851-2213
Gregory Sackos, admin. Fax 851-2986

Bowie, Cochise, Pop. 442
Bowie USD 14 50/K-12
PO Box 157 85605 520-847-2545
Jeffry St. Clair, supt. Fax 847-2546
www.bowieschools.org
Bowie ES 50/K-8
PO Box 157 85605 520-847-2545
Wendy Conger, prin. Fax 847-2546

Buckeye, Maricopa, Pop. 49,727
Buckeye ESD 33 4,700/PK-8
25555 W Durango St 85326 623-925-3400
Dr. Kristi Sandvik, supt. Fax 386-6063
besd.k12.az.us
Bales ES 800/PK-8
25555 W Durango St 85326 623-847-8503
Fred Lugo, prin. Fax 327-0744
Buckeye ES 800/K-8
25555 W Durango St 85326 623-386-4487
Dina Cegelka, prin. Fax 386-7901
Buckeye Preschool PK-PK
25555 W Durango St 85326 623-925-3921
Brittany Tarango, dir. Fax 386-6219
Inca ES 800/K-8
25555 W Durango St 85326 623-925-3500
Veronica Griffin, prin. Fax 386-4690
Jasinski ES 900/PK-8
25555 W Durango St 85326 623-925-3100
Dr. Donna Fitzgerald, prin. Fax 327-2708
Sundance ES 800/K-8
25555 W Durango St 85326 623-847-8531
Neva Burlingame, prin. Fax 386-6049
Westpark ES 700/PK-8
25555 W Durango St 85326 623-435-3282
Kevin Bulger, prin. Fax 386-3398

Liberty ESD 25 3,300/PK-8
19871 W Fremont Rd 85326 623-474-6600
Dr. Andrew Rogers, supt. Fax 474-6629
www.liberty.k12.az.us
Freedom S 900/K-8
22150 W Sundance Pkwy 85326 623-327-2850
Toni Reynolds, prin. Fax 327-2859
Liberty S 600/PK-8
19818 W US Highway 85 85326 623-327-2810
Jennifer Gray, prin. Fax 327-2819
Rainbow Valley S 600/K-8
19716 W Narramore Rd 85326 623-327-2830
Dr. Terri Matteson, prin. Fax 327-2839
Other Schools – See Goodyear

Litchfield ESD 79
Supt. — See Litchfield Park
Verrado ES 900/PK-5
20873 W Sunrise Ln, 623-547-1600
Luke Jankee, prin. Fax 853-2314
Verrado Heritage ES 700/PK-8
20895 W Hamilton St, 623-547-3300
Kimberly Franz, prin.
Verrado MS 1,000/6-8
20880 W Main St, 623-547-1300
Karen Williams, prin. Fax 853-2358

Saddle Mountain USD 90
Supt. — See Tonopah
Tartesso ES 400/K-8
29677 W Indianola Ave, 623-474-5400
Liz Burton, prin. Fax 474-5441

Wickenburg USD 9
Supt. — See Wickenburg
Festival Foothills ES 200/K-8
26252 W Desert Vista Blvd, 928-501-6000
Julie Case, prin. Fax 501-5057

Grace Fellowship Academy 100/PK-8
1300 N Miller Rd 85326 623-393-8883
Geri Parker, prin. Fax 393-8389

Bullhead City, Mohave, Pop. 38,810
Colorado River ESD 3,000/PK-8
1004 Hancock Rd 86442 928-758-3961
Riley Frei, supt. Fax 758-4996
www.bullheadschools.com
Bullhead City JHS 500/6-8
1062 Hancock Rd 86442 928-758-3921
Pat Young, prin. Fax 758-7428
Coyote Canyon ES 500/PK-5
1820 Lakeside Dr 86442 928-758-4909
Sandra Brown, prin. Fax 758-8670
Desert Valley ES 500/PK-5
1066 Marina Blvd 86442 928-758-6606
Sandra Brown, prin. Fax 758-5726
Diamondback ES 500/K-5
2550 Tesota Way 86442 928-758-6858
Martin Muecke, prin. Fax 758-5202
Fox Creek JHS 500/6-8
3101 Desert Sky Blvd 86442 928-704-2500
Jon Jones, prin. Fax 704-2504
Sunrise ES 400/PK-5
2645 Landon Dr 86429 928-754-1815
Jennifer Lott, prin. Fax 754-1820

Bylas, Graham, Pop. 1,955
Fort Thomas USD 7
Supt. — See Fort Thomas
Mt. Turnbull ES K-3
PO Box 100 85530 928-475-2020
Marthalean Talkalai, prin. Fax 485-0117

Cameron, Coconino, Pop. 863
Tuba City USD 15
Supt. — See Tuba City
Dzil Libei ES, Highway 89 86020 100/K-5
Jerilyn Tsinigine, prin. 928-283-1080

Camp Verde, Yavapai, Pop. 10,552
Camp Verde USD 28 1,500/PK-12
410 Camp Lincoln Rd 86322 928-567-8000
Dr. Dennis Goodwin, supt. Fax 567-8004
www.campverdeschools.org
Camp Verde ES 700/PK-5
210 Camp Lincoln Rd 86322 928-567-8060
Britta Booth, prin. Fax 567-8063
Camp Verde MS 300/6-8
370 Camp Lincoln Rd 86322 928-567-8014
Danny Howe, prin. Fax 567-8022

United Christian S 100/PK-12
PO Box 3126 86322 928-567-0415
Katherine Holden, admin. Fax 567-9774

Carefree, Maricopa, Pop. 3,323

Our Lady of Joy Catholic Preschool 100/PK-PK
PO Box 1359 85377 480-595-6409
Jessica Snook, dir. Fax 437-1093

Casa Grande, Pinal, Pop. 47,575
Casa Grande ESD 4 7,000/PK-8
220 W Kortsen Rd, 520-836-2111
Dr. Joetta Gonzales, supt. Fax 426-3712
www.cgesd.org
Cactus MS 900/6-8
1220 E Kortsen Rd, 520-421-3330
Kendra Tate, prin. Fax 421-7425
Casa Grande MS 600/6-8
300 W McMurray Blvd, 520-836-7310
Jennifer Murrieta, prin. Fax 836-2399
Cholla ES 400/K-5
1180 E Kortsen Rd, 520-836-4719
Kay Brack-Steward, prin. Fax 836-1963
Cottonwood ES 500/K-5
1667 N Kadota Ave, 520-836-5601
Patricia Dee, prin. Fax 836-1437
Desert Willow ES 600/PK-5
2172 N Arizola Rd, 520-876-5397
Melissa Pieper, prin. Fax 876-0909
ECC 100/PK-PK
390 E Lakeside Pkwy, 520-876-0045
Evergreen ES 500/K-5
1000 N Amarillo St, 520-836-6694
Scott Raymond, prin. Fax 421-0423
Ironwood ES 400/K-5
1500 N Colorado St, 520-836-5086
Robin Rosales, prin. Fax 836-2203
McCartney Ranch ES 700/PK-5
2631 N Brown Ave, 520-876-4235
Robert Quinones, prin. Fax 876-4292
Mesquite ES 500/PK-5
129 N Arizola Rd, 520-836-7787
Julie Holdsworth, prin. Fax 836-3289

Palo Verde ES 500/PK-5
40 N Roosevelt Ave, 520-421-1650
Joanne Kramer, prin. Fax 421-3013
Saguaro ES 500/K-5
1501 N Center Ave, 520-836-7661
Celie Downey-Foye, prin. Fax 836-1581
Villago MS 800/6-8
574 E Lakeside Pkwy, 520-423-0176
Jeffrey Lavender, prin. Fax 423-0177

Pinal County Office of Education
Supt. — See Florence
O'Brien ES 100/K-6
PO Box 3125, 520-450-4400
Lisa Raymond, prin. Fax 450-4302

Logos Christian Academy 100/K-12
PO Box 11493, 520-421-1220
Dr. Ken Ross, admin.
St. Anthony of Padua S 200/PK-8
501 E 2nd St, 520-836-7247
Sr. Carol Seidl, prin. Fax 836-7289

Cave Creek, Maricopa, Pop. 4,956
Cave Creek USD 93
Supt. — See Scottsdale
Lone Mountain ES 600/K-6
PO Box 426 85327 480-437-3000
Robert Miller, prin. Fax 595-1312

Annunciation Catholic S 100/K-8
32648 N Cave Creek Rd 85331 480-361-8234
Dr. Sharon Pristash, prin. Fax 207-6730
Dynamite Montessori S 100/PK-6
29210 N 59th St 85331 480-563-5710
Paula Fabian-Leach, admin. Fax 515-4407
Quality Interactive Montessori S 100/PK-6
33212 N 56th St 85331 480-575-5269

Chandler, Maricopa, Pop. 229,946
Chandler USD 80 40,800/PK-12
1525 W Frye Rd 85224 480-812-7000
Dr. Camille Casteel, supt. Fax 224-9128
www.cusd80.com
Andersen ES 600/PK-5
1350 N Pennington Dr 85224 480-812-6000
Dr. Shannon Hannon, prin. Fax 812-6020
Andersen JHS 900/6-8
1255 N Dobson Rd 85224 480-883-5300
Dr. Joyce Meyer, prin. Fax 883-5320
Arizona College Prep - Oakland 500/6-8
191 W Oakland St 85225 480-224-3930
Jayson Phillips, prin. Fax 224-3940
Basha Accelerated MS 6-8
5990 S Val Vista Dr 85249 480-224-2100
David Loutzenheiser, prin. Fax 224-2120
Basha ES 800/K-6
3535 S Basha Rd 85248 480-883-4400
Jessica Edgar, prin. Fax 224-9382
Bogle JHS 1,200/7-8
1600 W Queen Creek Rd 85248 480-883-5500
Susie Avey, prin. Fax 224-9140
Bologna ES 700/K-6
1625 E Frye Rd 85225 480-883-4000
Dr. Thuy Padilla, prin. Fax 883-4020
Carlson ES 600/K-6
5400 S White Dr 85249 480-224-3800
Leo Schlueter, prin. Fax 224-9209
Conley ES 800/K-6
500 S Arrowhead Dr 85224 480-812-6200
Dr. Joe Walters, prin. Fax 812-6220
CTA - Goodman Campus 700/PK-6
2600 W Knox Rd 85224 480-812-6900
Lisa Graham, prin. Fax 224-9347
CTA - Humphrey Campus 500/PK-6
125 S 132nd St 85225 480-812-6800
Luke Hickey, prin. Fax 812-6820
CTA - Independence Campus 900/K-6
1405 W Lake Dr 85248 480-224-2700
Dr. Frank Hendricsen, prin. Fax 224-2720
CTA - Liberty Campus 700/K-6
550 N Emmett Dr 85225 480-883-4900
Dr. Beth Ann Bader, prin. Fax 883-4920
Elite Performance Academy 3-8
125 S 132nd St 85225 480-812-6800
Luke Hickey, prin. Fax 812-6820
Frye ES 700/K-6
801 E Frye Rd 85225 480-812-6400
Lisa Shore, prin. Fax 224-9339
Fulton ES 1,000/K-6
4750 S Sunland Dr 85248 480-224-3300
Dr. Amy Kramb, prin. Fax 224-3320
Galveston ES 700/K-6
661 E Galveston St 85225 480-812-6500
Annette Addair, prin. Fax 812-6520
Haley ES 700/PK-6
3401 S Layton Lakes Blvd, 480-224-3500
Pam Nephew, prin. Fax 224-3520
Hancock ES 800/K-6
2425 S Pleasant Dr, 480-883-5900
Connie Hull, prin. Fax 224-9519
Hartford Sylvia Encinas ES 700/PK-6
700 N Hartford St 85225 480-812-6700
Heather Anguiano, prin. Fax 812-6720
Hull ES 800/K-6
2424 E Maren Dr 85249 480-883-4500
Cheryl Bromich, prin. Fax 224-9388
Jacobson ES 900/K-6
1515 NW Jacaranda Pkwy 85248 480-883-4100
Liz Wolf, prin. Fax 883-4120
Knox Gifted Academy 600/K-6
700 W Orchid Ln 85225 480-812-6100
Lynn Weed, prin. Fax 224-9391
Navarrete ES 900/K-6
6490 S Sun Groves Blvd 85249 480-883-4800
Vanessa Whitlark, prin. Fax 883-4820
Ryan ES 800/K-6
4600 S Bright Angel Way 85249 480-224-3200
Diane Wells, prin. Fax 224-9362
Sanborn ES 700/K-6
700 N Superstition Blvd 85225 480-812-7300
Caryn Cole, prin. Fax 812-7320

San Marcos ES 500/K-6
451 W Frye Rd 85225 480-883-4200
Dr. Becky Henderson, prin. Fax 883-4220
Santan ES 900/K-6
1550 E Chandler Heights Rd 85249 480-883-4700
Amy O'Neal, prin. Fax 883-4648
Santan JHS 1,300/7-8
1550 E Chandler Heights Rd 85249 480-883-4600
Barbara Kowalinski, prin. Fax 883-4648
Shumway ES 500/K-6
1325 N Shumway Ave 85225 480-812-7400
Dr. Korry Brenner, prin. Fax 812-7420
Tarwater ES 800/K-6
2300 S Gardner Dr, 480-883-4300
Diane Hale, prin. Fax 883-4320
Willis JHS 900/7-8
401 S McQueen Rd 85225 480-883-5700
Jeff Delp, prin. Fax 883-5720
Other Schools – See Gilbert, Queen Creek

Kyrene ESD 28
Supt. — See Tempe
Kyrene Aprende MS 1,000/6-8
777 N Desert Breeze Blvd E 85226 480-541-6200
Renee Kory, prin. Fax 541-6210
Kyrene de la Mirada ES 500/K-5
5500 W Galveston St 85226 480-541-4200
Nancy Branch, prin. Fax 541-4210
Kyrene de la Paloma ES 500/K-5
5000 W Whitten St 85226 480-541-5000
Janet Tobias, prin. Fax 541-5010
Kyrene de las Brisas ES 800/PK-5
777 N Desert Breeze Blvd E 85226 480-541-2000
Christie Winkelmann, prin. Fax 541-2010
Kyrene del Cielo ES 800/PK-5
1350 N Lakeshore Dr 85226 480-541-2400
Kelly Alexander, prin. Fax 541-2410
Kyrene Del Pueblo MS 900/6-8
360 S Twelve Oaks Blvd 85226 480-541-6800
Kyle Ross, prin. Fax 541-6810
Kyrene Traditional Academy at Sureno ES 400/K-5
3375 W Galveston St 85226 480-541-5400
Marianne Lescher, prin. Fax 541-5410

Mesa USD 4
Supt. — See Mesa
Jordan Center Early Education 300/PK-PK
3320 N Carriage Ln 85224 480-472-3800
Allen Quie, prin. Fax 472-3888
Pomeroy ES 600/K-6
1507 W Shawnee Dr 85224 480-472-3700
Dr. James Driscoll, prin. Fax 472-3707
Sirrine ES 500/K-6
591 W Mesquite St 85225 480-472-3600
Renee Parker, prin. Fax 472-3666
Summit Academy 1,100/K-8
1560 W Summit Pl 85224 480-472-3500
Mark Andrews, prin. Fax 472-3549

Casa Del Nino Bilingual Montessori 50/PK-4
2625 W Queen Creek Rd Ste 6 85248
Shasta Payne, dir. 480-963-2550
Chandler Christian Academy 100/PK-8
19620 S McQueen Rd, 480-899-9197
Ruth Zappe, admin. Fax 899-9197
HOPE Christian Academy 100/K-8
1125 N Dobson Rd 85224 480-722-1445
Kathy Moll, prin.
Life Christian Academy K-3
11530 E Queen Creek Rd, 480-526-1521
Andy White, head sch Fax 633-5950
St. Mary-Basha Catholic S 500/PK-8
200 W Galveston St 85225 480-963-4951
Tiffany Seybert, prin. Fax 963-8959
Tri-City Christian Academy 300/K-12
2211 W Germann Rd, 480-245-7902
Lauren Brady, prin. Fax 245-7908

Chinle, Apache, Pop. 4,452
Chinle USD 24 3,500/K-12
PO Box 587 86503 928-674-9600
Quincy Natay, supt. Fax 674-9608
www.chinleusd.k12.az.us/
Canyon De Chelly ES 400/K-6
PO Box 587 86503 928-674-9200
Ronald Thompson, prin. Fax 674-9297
Chinle ES 400/K-6
PO Box 587 86503 928-674-9300
Jane Christie, prin. Fax 674-9399
Chinle JHS 400/7-8
PO Box 587 86503 928-674-9400
Tammy Smith, prin. Fax 674-9499
Mesa View ES 500/K-6
PO Box 587 86503 928-674-9000
Louise Donald, prin. Fax 674-9899
Other Schools – See Many Farms, Tsaile

Chino Valley, Yavapai, Pop. 10,639
Chino Valley USD 51 1,900/PK-12
650 E Center St 86323 928-636-2458
John Scholl, supt. Fax 636-1434
www.cvsd.k12.az.us
Del Rio ES 500/3-5
1036 N Road 1 W 86323 928-636-4414
Carolyn Reeder, prin. Fax 636-6215
Heritage MS 500/6-8
1076 N Road 1 W 86323 928-636-4464
Julie Bryce, prin. Fax 636-6214
Territorial ECC 200/PK-2
1088 Mahan Ln 86323 928-636-3842
Brandy Cox, prin. Fax 636-0267

Clarkdale, Yavapai, Pop. 4,019
Clarkdale-Jerome ESD 3 500/K-8
PO Box 248 86324 928-634-5035
Danny Brown, supt. Fax 639-0917
www.cjsd.k12.az.us
Clarkdale-Jerome S 500/K-8
PO Box 248 86324 928-634-5035
Steve Doerksen, prin. Fax 639-0917

Cochise, Cochise
Cochise ESD 26 100/K-8
PO Box 1088 85606 520-384-2540
Karl Uterhardt, supt. Fax 384-4836
www.cochiseschool.org
Cochise ES 100/K-8
PO Box 1088 85606 520-384-2540
Karl Uterhardt, admin. Fax 384-4836

Colorado City, Mohave, Pop. 4,817
Colorado City USD 14 200/PK-12
PO Box 309 86021 928-875-9000
Carol Timpson, supt. Fax 875-8068
cottonwoodk5.us
Cottonwood ES PK-5
PO Box 309 86021 928-875-9050
Carol Timpson M.A., admin. Fax 875-8068

Concho, Apache, Pop. 33
Concho ESD 6 200/PK-8
PO Box 200 85924 928-337-9356
Steven Yoder, admin. Fax 337-2455
www.conchoschool.net/
Concho S 200/PK-8
PO Box 200 85924 928-337-4665
Steven Yoder, admin. Fax 337-2455

Congress, Yavapai, Pop. 1,944
Congress ESD 100/PK-8
PO Box 68 85332 928-427-9850
Dr. Stephanie Miller, supt. Fax 427-9840
www.congressdistrict.org/
Congress ES 100/PK-8
PO Box 68 85332 928-427-9850
Dr. Stephanie Miller, admin. Fax 427-9840

Coolidge, Pinal, Pop. 11,531
Coolidge USD 21 3,700/PK-12
450 N Arizona Blvd, 520-723-2040
Charie Wallace, admin. Fax 723-2442
www.coolidgeschools.org
Coolidge JHS 500/6-8
684 W Northern Ave, 520-723-2304
Dawn Dee Hodge, prin. Fax 723-8249
Heartland Ranch ES 400/K-5
1667 W Caroline St, 520-424-2100
Jessie Arroyos, prin. Fax 424-2110
West ES 600/PK-5
460 S 7th St, 520-723-2702
Ben Armstrong, prin. Fax 723-0682

Cornville, Yavapai, Pop. 3,217
Cottonwood-Oak Creek ESD 6
Supt. — See Cottonwood
Oak Creek S 200/PK-8
11490 E Purple Sage Dr 86325 928-639-5109
Christine Griffin, prin. Fax 639-5108

Corona, Pima, Pop. 5,546
Vail USD 20
Supt. — See Vail
Copper Ridge ES K-5
17650 S Canyon Edge Trl 85641 520-879-3700
Erica Irby, prin.
Corona Foothills MS 500/6-8
16705 S Houghton Rd 85641 520-879-3500
Margaret Steuer, prin. Fax 879-3501
Sycamore ES 900/K-5
16701 S Houghton Rd 85641 520-879-2500
Ken Graff, prin. Fax 879-2501

Cottonwood, Yavapai, Pop. 11,102
Cottonwood-Oak Creek ESD 6 2,100/PK-8
1 N Willard St 86326 928-634-2288
Steve King, supt. Fax 634-2309
www.cocsd.us
Bright ES 500/PK-2
1 N Willard St 86326 928-634-7039
Nancy Erickson, prin. Fax 639-8428
Cottonwood ES 500/3-5
1 N Willard St 86326 928-634-2191
Jessica Vocca, prin. Fax 639-0467
Cottonwood MS 500/6-8
1 N Willard St 86326 928-634-2231
Mathew Schumacher, prin. Fax 634-2874
Other Schools – See Cornville

Immaculate Conception Catholic S 100/PK-8
750 N Bill Gray Rd 86326 928-649-0624
Jackie Kirkham, prin. Fax 649-1191
Verde Christian Academy 100/PK-5
102 S Willard St 86326 928-634-8113
Ben Russel, admin.
Verde Valley Adventist S 50/1-8
PO Box 1810 86326 928-634-7322

Crown King, Yavapai
Crown King ESD 41 50/PK-8
PO Box 188 86343 928-632-5207
Claudia Axton, lead tchr. Fax 632-5207
www.crownkingesd.com
Crown King S 50/PK-8
PO Box 188 86343 928-632-5207
Claudia Axton, lead tchr. Fax 632-5207

Dateland, Yuma, Pop. 414
Hyder ESD 16 100/K-8
1300 S Avenue 64 E 85333 928-454-2242
Pat Koury, supt. Fax 454-2217
www.hyderschools.org
Dateland S 100/K-8
1300 S Avenue 64 E 85333 928-454-2242
Pat Koury, admin. Fax 454-2217

Sentinel ESD 71 50/K-8
53802 W US Hwy 80 85333 928-323-3300
Christopher Maynes, supt. Fax 220-3512
sentinelesd.org
Sentinel S 50/K-8
53802 W US Hwy 80 85333 928-323-3300
Christopher Maynes, admin. Fax 220-3512

Desert Hills, Mohave, Pop. 2,216
Deer Valley USD 97
Supt. — See Phoenix

Desert Mountain S 700/PK-8
35959 N 7th Ave 85086 623-445-3500
Dr. Joann Schwarting, prin. Fax 445-3580

Dewey, Yavapai, Pop. 3,640
Humboldt USD 22
Supt. — See Prescott Valley
Bradshaw Mountain MS 300/7-8
12255 E Turquoise Cir 86327 928-759-4900
Jessica Bennett, prin. Fax 759-4920

Dolan Springs, Mohave, Pop. 1,994
Kingman USD 20
Supt. — See Kingman
Mt. Tipton S 100/K-12
PO Box 248 86441 928-767-3350
Kristina Weaver, prin. Fax 767-4330

Douglas, Cochise, Pop. 17,315
Apache ESD 42 50/PK-8
10488 E Skeleton Canyon Rd 85608 520-558-2364
Loy Guzman, admin. Fax 558-2410
www.apacheelementary.org
Apache S 50/PK-8
10488 E Skeleton Canyon Rd 85608 520-558-2364
Loy Guzman, lead tchr. Fax 558-2410

Douglas USD 27 3,700/PK-12
PO Box 1237 85608 520-364-2447
Ronald V. Aguallo, supt. Fax 224-2470
www.dusd.k12.az.us
Borane MS 400/6-8
PO Box 1237 85608 520-364-2461
Melissa Rodriguez, prin. Fax 364-5537
Carlson ES 400/PK-5
PO Box 1237 85608 520-805-4400
Geraldina Trevino, prin. Fax 364-6257
Clawson ES 300/PK-5
PO Box 1237 85608 520-364-8466
Claudia Leon, prin. Fax 805-5531
Huber MS 400/6-8
PO Box 1237 85608 520-364-2840
Randy Walker, prin. Fax 364-2421
Marley ES 300/PK-5
PO Box 1237 85608 520-364-3408
Rosella Melgoza, prin. Fax 805-5534
Stevenson ES 400/PK-5
PO Box 1237 85608 520-364-2442
Deborah Herrera, prin. Fax 364-6492
Other Schools – See Pirtleville

Loretto Catholic S 200/PK-8
1200 E 14th St 85607 520-364-5754
Sr. Mary Aloysius Marques, prin. Fax 364-5869

Duncan, Greenlee, Pop. 683
Duncan USD 2 300/K-12
PO Box 710 85534 928-359-2472
Eldon Merrell, supt. Fax 359-2807
dusdwildkats.org
Duncan ES 200/3-8
PO Box 710 85534 928-359-2471
Byron Bolen, prin. Fax 359-1105
Duncan PS 100/K-2
PO Box 710 85534 928-359-2054
Byron Bolen, prin. Fax 359-1105

Eagar, Apache, Pop. 4,784
Round Valley USD 10
Supt. — See Springerville
Round Valley ES 600/K-4
165 S Brown 85925 928-333-6600
Renita Olson, prin. Fax 333-1929
Round Valley MS 400/5-8
126 W 2nd St 85925 928-333-6700
Marcie Udall, prin. Fax 333-5252

Ehrenberg, LaPaz, Pop. 1,442
Quartzsite ESD 4 200/K-8
PO Box 130 85334 928-923-7906
Dr. Raquel Burton, supt. Fax 923-8908
www.qsd4.org
Ehrenberg ES 100/K-8
PO Box 130 85334 928-923-7900
Dr. Raquel Burton, admin. Fax 923-8908
Other Schools – See Quartzsite

Elfrida, Cochise, Pop. 454
Elfrida ESD 12 100/PK-8
PO Box 328 85610 520-642-3428
Jeremy Long, supt. Fax 642-3236
elfridaschools.org
Elfrida S 100/PK-8
PO Box 328 85610 520-642-3428
Judi King, prin. Fax 642-3236

Elgin, Santa Cruz, Pop. 160
Sonoita ESD 25 100/K-8
23 Elgin Rd 85611 520-455-5514
Dr. Christopher Bonn, supt. Fax 455-5516
www.elgink12.com
Elgin S 100/K-8
23 Elgin Rd 85611 520-455-5514
Dr. Christopher Bonn, prin. Fax 455-5516

El Mirage, Maricopa, Pop. 30,983
Dysart USD 89
Supt. — See Surprise
Dysart ES 900/K-8
12950 W Varney Rd 85335 623-876-7100
Cheryl Pete, prin. Fax 876-7137
El Mirage ES 900/K-8
13500 N El Mirage Rd 85335 623-876-7200
Fax 876-7208
Riverview S 1,000/K-8
12701 N Main St 85335 623-523-8950
Stephanie Lawrence, prin. Fax 523-8961
Surprise ES 900/K-8
12907 W Greenway Rd 85335 623-876-7400
Karie Burns, prin. Fax 876-7411
Thompson Ranch S 1,000/K-8
11800 W Thompson Ranch Rd 85335 623-523-8400
Rachel Saunders, prin. Fax 523-8411

Eloy, Pinal, Pop. 15,495
Eloy ESD 11 — 800/PK-8
1011 N Sunshine Blvd, — 520-466-2100
Ruby James, supt. — Fax 466-2101
www.eloyesd.org
Curiel PS — 400/PK-2
1011 N Sunshine Blvd, — 520-466-2120
Danny Rogers, prin. — Fax 466-2151
Eloy IS — 200/3-5
1011 N Sunshine Blvd, — 520-466-2130
Abigale Tarango, prin. — Fax 466-2114
Eloy JHS — 200/6-8
1011 N Sunshine Blvd, — 520-466-2140
Kevin Oursler, prin. — Fax 466-2150

Toltec ESD 22 — 900/PK-8
3315 N Toltec Rd 85131 — 520-466-2360
Dr. Jeff VanHandel, supt. — Fax 466-2398
www.toltecsd.org
Toltec ES — 500/PK-8
3315 N Toltec Rd, — 520-466-2350
Misty Huffman, prin. — Fax 466-2399
Other Schools – See Arizona City

Flagstaff, Coconino, Pop. 64,141
Flagstaff USD 1 — 9,700/PK-12
3285 E Sparrow Ave 86004 — 928-527-6000
Michael A. Penca, supt. — Fax 527-6015
www.fusd1.org
Cromer ES — 700/K-5
7150 Silver Saddle Rd 86004 — 928-773-4150
Traci Gordon, prin. — Fax 526-8985
DeMiguel ES — 700/K-5
3500 S Gillenwater Dr, — 928-773-4000
Ninon Wilson, prin. — Fax 773-4010
Killip ES — 500/PK-5
2300 E 6th Ave 86004 — 928-773-4080
Joseph Gutierrez, prin. — Fax 773-4086
Kinsey ES — 400/PK-5
1601 S Lone Tree Rd 86001 — 928-773-4060
Tammy Nelson, prin. — Fax 773-4070
Knoles ES — 600/K-5
4005 E Butler Ave 86004 — 928-773-4120
Pete Galvan, prin. — Fax 773-4130
Marshall ES — 600/PK-5
850 N Bonito St 86001 — 928-773-4030
John Coe, prin. — Fax 773-4035
Mount Elden MS — 800/6-8
3223 N 4th St 86004 — 928-773-8250
Tom Safranek, prin. — Fax 773-8269
Puente de Hozho Magnet S — 400/K-5
3401 N 4th St 86004 — 928-773-4090
Robert Kelty, prin. — Fax 773-4100
Sechrist ES — 500/K-5
2230 N Fort Valley Rd 86001 — 928-773-4020
John Albert, prin. — Fax 773-4025
Sinagua MS — 1,000/6-8
3950 E Butler Ave 86004 — 928-527-5500
Tari Popham, prin. — Fax 527-5561
Thomas ES — 500/K-5
3330 E Lockett Rd 86004 — 928-773-4110
Frank Garcia, prin. — Fax 773-4108
Other Schools – See Leupp

Flagstaff Community Christian S — 100/K-8
755 N Bonito St 86001 — 928-522-5968
Eric Garland, admin. — Fax 268-3571
San Francisco de Asis Catholic S — 200/PK-8
1600 E Route 66 86001 — 928-779-1337
Bill Carroll, prin. — Fax 774-1943

Florence, Pinal, Pop. 25,223
Florence USD 1 — 7,800/PK-12
PO Box 2850, — 520-866-3500
Chris Knutsen, supt. — Fax 868-2302
www.fusdaz.com
Anthem S — 900/K-8
PO Box 2850, — 520-723-6400
Leah Alisa, prin. — Fax 723-3575
Florence S — 700/K-8
PO Box 2850, — 520-866-3540
Joanne Pike, prin. — Fax 868-2312
Magma Ranch S — 700/K-8
PO Box 2850, — 520-868-7300
Janeane Candelaria, prin. — Fax 723-5370
Other Schools – See San Tan Valley

Pinal County Office of Education — 200/
PO Box 769 85132 — 520-866-6565
Jill Broussard, supt. — Fax 866-6973
www.ecrsc.org/pinalesa/
Other Schools – See Casa Grande

Fort Defiance, Apache, Pop. 3,530
Window Rock USD 8 — 1,700/K-12
PO Box 559 86504 — 928-729-6705
Lynnette Michalski, supt. — Fax 729-6841
www.wrschool.net
Tsehootsooi IS — 500/4-6
PO Box 559 86504 — 928-729-6803
William Beach, prin. — Fax 729-6801
Tsehootsooi MS — 300/7-8
PO Box 559 86504 — 928-729-6803
Elissa James, prin. — Fax 729-6814
Tsehootsooi Primary Learning Center — 50/K-3
PO Box 559 86504 — 928-729-7801
James Gordon, prin. — Fax 729-6847
Other Schools – See Window Rock

Fort Huachuca, See Sierra Vista
Fort Huachuca Accommodation SD 00 — 1,100/PK-8
PO Box 12954 85670 — 520-458-5082
Bonnie Austin, supt. — Fax 515-5972
www.fthuachuca.k12.az.us
Johnston ES — 400/PK-2
PO Box 12954 85670 — 520-459-8798
Jennifer Truitt-Lewis, prin. — Fax 452-4090
Myer ES — 300/3-5
PO Box 12954 85670 — 520-459-8986
Valerie Quarto, prin. — Fax 452-4092
Smith MS — 300/6-8
PO Box 12954 85670 — 520-459-8892
Sandy Larson, prin. — Fax 335-6803

Fort Mohave, Mohave, Pop. 14,105
Mohave Valley ESD 16
Supt. — See Mohave Valley
Camp Mohave ES — 200/3-5
1797 E La Entrada Dr 86426 — 928-704-3600
John Laurent, prin. — Fax 704-3663
Fort Mojave ES — 200/PK-2
1760 E Joy Ln 86426 — 928-768-3986
Shanon Ferguson, prin. — Fax 768-8075

Fort Thomas, Graham, Pop. 360
Fort Thomas USD 7 — 600/K-12
PO Box 300 85536 — 928-485-9423
Shane Hawkins, supt. — Fax 485-3019
www.ftusd.org/
Fort Thomas ES — 300/K-6
PO Box 55 85536 — 928-485-2433
Lonnie Lunt, prin. — Fax 485-3068
Other Schools – See Bylas

Fountain Hills, Maricopa, Pop. 22,214
Fountain Hills USD 98 — 1,800/PK-12
16000 E Palisades Blvd 85268 — 480-664-5000
Dr. Patrick Sweeney, supt. — Fax 664-5099
www.fhusd.org
Fountain Hills MS — 400/4-8
15414 N McDowell Mountain R 85268 — 480-664-5400
Linda McKeever, prin. — Fax 664-5499
McDowell Mountain ES — 500/PK-3
14825 N Fayette Dr 85268 — 480-664-5200
Valerie Dehombreux, prin. — Fax 664-5299

Fredonia, Coconino, Pop. 1,295
Fredonia-Moccasin USD 6 — 200/PK-12
PO Box 247 86022 — 928-643-7333
Joseph Wright, supt. — Fax 643-7044
www.fredonia.org
Fredonia ES — 100/PK-6
PO Box 247 86022 — 928-643-7386
Joseph Wright, supt. — Fax 643-7324

Gadsden, Yuma, Pop. 677
Gadsden ESD 32
Supt. — See San Luis
Gadsden ES — 500/K-6
18745 Gadsden St 85336 — 928-627-6970
Cecilia Arvizo, prin. — Fax 627-9771

Ganado, Apache, Pop. 1,188
Ganado USD 20 — 1,100/K-12
PO Box 1757 86505 — 928-755-1000
Dale O'Donnell, supt. — Fax 755-1012
www.ganado.k12.az.us
Ganado ES — 200/K-5
PO Box 1757 86505 — 928-755-1300
Joe Benally, prin. — Fax 755-1202
Ganado MS — 300/6-8
PO Box 1757 86505 — 928-755-1400
Leandra Begaye, prin. — Fax 755-1402

Gila Bend, Maricopa, Pop. 1,896
Gila Bend USD 24 — 300/PK-12
PO Box V 85337 — 928-683-2225
Dr. Anthony J. Perkins, supt. — Fax 683-2671
www.gbusd.org
Gila Bend ES — 200/PK-6
PO Box V 85337 — 928-683-2225
Richard Moore, prin. — Fax 683-2671

Paloma ESD 94 — 100/PK-8
38739 W I 8 85337 — 928-683-2588
Kristin Turner, supt. — Fax 683-2093
www.palomaesd.org
Kiser S — 100/PK-8
38739 W I 8 85337 — 928-683-2588
Kristin Turner, supt. — Fax 683-2093

Gilbert, Maricopa, Pop. 202,881
Chandler USD 80
Supt. — See Chandler
CTA - Freedom Campus — 900/K-6
6040 S Joslyn Ln, — 480-224-2600
Abby Druck, prin. — Fax 224-2620
Patterson ES — 900/PK-6
7520 S Adora Blvd, — 480-224-3600
Sarah Stephens, prin. — Fax 224-3620
Riggs ES — 900/K-6
6930 S Seville Blvd W, — 480-224-3400
Jan Weyenberg, prin. — Fax 224-3420
Weinberg ES — 800/K-6
5245 S Val Vista Dr, — 480-812-7500
Shirley Mathew, prin. — Fax 812-7520

Gilbert Unified SD — 37,700/PK-12
140 S Gilbert Rd 85296 — 480-497-3300
Dr. Suzanne Zentner, supt. — Fax 507-1320
www.gilbertschools.net
Ashland Ranch ES — 800/PK-6
1945 S Ashland Ranch Rd, — 480-917-9900
Suzanne Carlson, prin. — Fax 917-3400
Burk ES — 500/PK-6
545 N Burk St 85234 — 480-926-3816
Brad Paes, prin. — Fax 813-8789
Finley Farms ES — 800/K-6
375 S Columbus Dr 85296 — 480-507-1624
Aubrey Ruhser, prin. — Fax 507-1633
Gilbert ES — 600/PK-6
175 W Elliot Rd 85233 — 480-892-8624
Justin Sremba, prin. — Fax 813-7284
Greenfield ES — 700/K-6
2550 E Elliot Rd 85234 — 480-892-2801
Mary Longion, prin. — Fax 926-3673
Greenfield JHS — 1,000/7-8
101 S Greenfield Rd 85296 — 480-813-1770
Brian Yee, prin. — Fax 813-7279
Highland Park ES — 900/PK-6
230 N Cole Ct 85234 — 480-832-3034
Michelle Mowery, prin. — Fax 832-3027
Houston ES — 500/PK-6
500 E Houston Ave 85234 — 480-497-9790
Sam Valles, prin. — Fax 813-6997
Islands ES — 700/PK-6
245 S McQueen Rd 85233 — 480-497-0742
Chris Birgen, prin. — Fax 813-6809
Mesquite ES — 700/PK-6
1000 E Mesquite St 85296 — 480-813-1240
Dawn Koberstein, prin. — Fax 813-7387
Mesquite JHS — 800/7-8
130 W Mesquite St 85233 — 480-926-1433
Dan Johnson, prin. — Fax 813-9002
Neely Traditional Academy — 800/K-6
321 W Juniper Ave 85233 — 480-892-2805
Jennifer Greene, prin. — Fax 497-6953
Oak Tree ES — 600/PK-6
505 W Houston Ave 85233 — 480-632-4785
Dale Lunt, prin. — Fax 632-4794
Patterson ES — 600/PK-6
1211 E Guadalupe Rd 85234 — 480-892-2803
Lucas Blackburn, prin. — Fax 926-3674
Pioneer ES — 600/PK-6
1535 N Greenfield Rd 85234 — 480-892-2022
Mike Davis, prin. — Fax 813-9010
Playa del Rey ES — 500/PK-6
550 N Horne St 85233 — 480-892-7810
Darrin Praska Ed.D., prin. — Fax 892-8842
Quartz Hill ES — 700/K-6
3680 S Quartz St 85297 — 480-855-5732
Joan Henry, prin. — Fax 855-5797
Rae Ranch ES — 600/PK-6
3777 E Houston Ave 85234 — 480-507-1359
Thea Hansen, prin. — Fax 503-1487
Settler's Point ES — 700/PK-6
423 E Settlers Point Dr 85296 — 480-507-1481
Robert Bircher, prin. — Fax 507-1550
Sonoma Ranch ES — 500/K-6
601 N Key Biscayne Dr 85234 — 480-497-9343
Colin Kelly, prin. — Fax 497-9574
South Valley JHS — 1,300/7-8
2034 S Lindsay Rd, — 480-855-0015
Tim Cannon, prin. — Fax 855-3542
Spectrum ES — 700/PK-6
2846 S Spectrum Way, — 480-917-0117
Sharon Boomer, prin. — Fax 917-6923
Towne Meadows ES — 700/PK-6
1101 N Recker Rd 85234 — 480-854-1545
Chip Petitit, prin. — Fax 854-1641
Val Vista Lakes ES — 500/PK-6
1030 N Blue Grotto Dr 85234 — 480-926-6301
Patrick Miller, prin. — Fax 813-9011
Other Schools – See Mesa

Higley USD 60 — 11,100/PK-12
2935 S Recker Rd, — 480-279-7000
Dr. Mike Thomason, supt. — Fax 279-7500
www.husd.org
Bridges ES — K-6
5205 S Soboda, — 480-279-8700
Jeffrey Beickel, admin. — Fax 279-8705
Centennial ES — 800/K-6
3507 S Ranch House Pkwy 85297 — 480-279-8200
Rachel Broadley, prin. — Fax 279-8205
Chaparral ES — 900/K-6
3380 E Frye Rd, — 480-279-7900
Kristine Hanson, prin. — Fax 279-7905
Cooley Early Child Development Center — PK-PK
1100 S Recker Rd 85296 — 480-279-8400
Patti Gleason, dir. — Fax 279-8405
Coronado ES — 600/K-6
4333 S Deanza Blvd 85297 — 480-279-6900
Micaela Swan, prin. — Fax 279-6905
Gateway Pointe S — 700/K-6
2069 S De La Torre Dr, — 480-279-7700
Timothy Fountain, prin. — Fax 279-7705
Higley Traditional Academy — 600/K-6
3391 E Vest Ave, — 480-279-6800
Caryn Bacon, prin. — Fax 279-6805
Power Ranch S — 700/K-6
4351 S Ranch House Pkwy 85297 — 480-279-7600
Chris Reuter, prin. — Fax 279-7605
San Tan ES — 700/K-6
3443 E Calistoga Dr 85297 — 480-279-7200
Ray Mercado, prin. — Fax 279-7205
Other Schools – See Queen Creek

Christ's Greenfield Lutheran S — 300/PK-8
425 N Greenfield Rd 85234 — 480-892-8314
Tanya Calendo, prin. — Fax 503-0437
Gilbert Christian S — 600/PK-12
3632 E Jasper Dr 85296 — 480-699-1215
Jim Desmarchais, supt. — Fax 809-6677

Glendale, Maricopa, Pop. 221,458
Alhambra ESD 68
Supt. — See Phoenix
Barcelona MS — 700/4-8
6530 N 44th Ave 85301 — 623-842-8616
Amy Bradshaw, prin. — Fax 842-1384
Peck PS — 700/PK-3
5810 N 49th Ave 85301 — 623-842-3889
Melinda Schlosser, prin. — Fax 847-7151

Deer Valley USD 97
Supt. — See Phoenix
Arrowhead ES — 500/PK-6
7490 W Union Hills Dr 85308 — 623-376-4100
Vivian Hunt, prin. — Fax 376-4180
Bellair ES — 400/K-6
4701 W Grovers Ave 85308 — 602-467-5700
Jackie Deltorre, prin. — Fax 467-5780
Copper Creek ES — 700/PK-6
7071 W Hillcrest Blvd 85310 — 623-376-3900
Kathy McNeill, prin. — Fax 376-3980
Desert Sage ES — 500/K-6
4035 W Alameda Rd 85310 — 623-445-4700
Kristy Gill, prin. — Fax 445-4780
Desert Sky MS — 600/7-8
5130 W Grovers Ave 85308 — 602-467-6500
Patricia Resetar, prin. — Fax 467-6580
Greenbrier ES — 300/PK-6
6150 W Greenbriar Dr 85308 — 602-467-5500
Jody Brammer, prin. — Fax 467-5580
Highland Lakes S — 1,000/K-8
19000 N 63rd Ave 85308 — 623-376-4300
Dr. Mark Anderson, prin. — Fax 376-4380
Hillcrest MS — 1,000/7-8
22833 N 71st Ave 85310 — 623-376-3300
Matt Hreha, prin. — Fax 376-3380

Las Brisas ES 800/K-6
5805 W Alameda Rd 85310 623-445-5500
Jon Malvin, prin. Fax 445-5580
Legend Springs ES 600/PK-6
21150 N Arrowhead Loop Rd 85308 623-376-4500
Nichole Basl, prin. Fax 376-4580
Mirage ES 400/PK-6
3910 W Grovers Ave 85308 602-467-5300
Jamie Wilber, prin. Fax 467-5380
Mountain Shadows ES 500/K-6
19602 N 45th Ave 85308 623-445-4300
Janet Gilbert, prin. Fax 445-4380
Park Meadows ES 500/K-6
20012 N 35th Ave 85308 623-445-4100
Joan Wick, prin. Fax 445-4180
Sierra Verde S 900/K-8
7241 W Rose Garden Ln 85308 623-376-4800
Dr. Paula Tseunis, prin. Fax 376-4880

Dysart USD 89
Supt. — See Surprise
Luke ES 800/K-8
7300 N Dysart Rd 85307 623-876-7300
Amalia Garcia, prin. Fax 876-7305

Glendale ESD 40 13,600/PK-8
7301 N 58th Ave 85301 623-237-7100
Dr. Joe Quintana, supt. Fax 237-7291
www.gesd40.org/
Bicentennial North S 800/4-8
7237 W Missouri Ave 85303 623-237-4009
Amy Rodriguez, prin. Fax 237-4915
Bicentennial South S 600/K-3
7240 W Colter St 85303 623-237-4012
Kate Laser, prin. Fax 237-5215
Burton S 800/K-8
4801 W Maryland Ave 85301 623-237-4007
Holly Northcott, prin. Fax 237-4715
Challenger MS 700/4-8
6905 W Maryland Ave 85303 623-237-4011
Tiffany Molina, prin. Fax 237-5115
Coyote Ridge S 900/K-8
7677 W Bethany Home Rd 85303 623-237-4015
Paul Abbott, prin. Fax 237-5515
Desert Garden S 700/K-3
7020 W Ocotillo Rd 85303 623-237-4014
Joseph De La Huerta, prin. Fax 237-5415
Desert Spirit S 900/K-8
7355 W Orangewood Ave 85303 623-237-4016
Scott Winters, prin. Fax 237-5615
Discovery S 800/PK-8
7910 W Maryland Ave 85303 623-237-4013
Andrea Arellano, prin. Fax 237-5315
Glendale American S 800/K-8
8530 N 55th Ave 85302 623-237-4008
Amy Troutt, prin. Fax 237-4815
Glendale Landmark S 800/K-8
5730 W Myrtle Ave 85301 623-237-4001
Gina Schmitz, prin. Fax 237-4115
Horizon S 800/K-8
8520 N 47th Ave 85302 623-237-4010
Cheri Emerson, prin. Fax 237-5015
Imes S 500/K-8
6625 N 56th Ave 85301 623-237-4002
Shelly Hartman, prin. Fax 237-4215
Jack ES 900/PK-3
6600 W Missouri Ave 85301 623-237-4500
Denis Parcells, prin. Fax 237-4515
Mensendick IS 1,000/4-8
5535 N 67th Ave 85301 623-237-4006
Michelle Brady, prin. Fax 237-4615
Sine S 700/K-8
4932 W Myrtle Ave 85301 623-237-4004
DeAnza Baker, prin. Fax 237-4415
Smith S 900/K-8
6534 N 63rd Ave 85301 623-237-4003
Melissa Marze, prin. Fax 237-4315
Sunset Vista S 900/K-8
7775 W Orangewood Ave 85303 623-237-4017
Bryan Richman, prin. Fax 237-5708

Pendergast ESD 92
Supt. — See Phoenix
Desert Mirage S 600/PK-8
8605 W Maryland Ave 85305 623-772-2550
Matt Williams, prin. Fax 872-8401
Sonoran Sky S 700/K-8
10150 W Missouri Ave 85307 623-772-2640
Joseph Jacobo, prin. Fax 772-1005
Sunset Ridge ES 600/K-8
8490 W Missouri Ave 85305 623-772-2730
Brian Winefsky, prin. Fax 877-4935

Peoria USD 11 30,000/PK-12
6330 W Thunderbird Rd 85306 623-486-6000
Dr. Darwin Stiffler, supt. Fax 486-6009
www.peoriaud.k12.az.us
Canyon ES 400/K-8
5490 W Paradise Ln 85306 623-412-5050
Kristen Balthis, prin. Fax 412-5061
Copperwood ES 900/K-8
11232 N 65th Ave 85304 623-412-4650
Dr. Michael Crudder, prin. Fax 412-4660
Desert Palms ES 600/PK-8
11441 N 55th Ave 85304 623-412-4600
Richard Troy, prin. Fax 412-4609
Desert Valley ES 600/K-8
12901 N 63rd Ave 85304 623-412-4750
Dana Matousek, prin. Fax 412-4755
Foothills ES 600/PK-8
15808 N 63rd Ave 85306 623-412-4625
Dr. Robert Benson, prin. Fax 412-4635
Heritage ES 700/K-8
5312 W Mountain View Rd 85302 623-412-4525
Lynn Brodie, prin. Fax 412-4535
Kachina ES 500/K-8
5304 W Crocus Dr 85306 623-412-4500
Landa Tartaglio, prin. Fax 412-4509
Marshall Ranch ES 700/K-8
12995 N Marshall Ranch Dr 85304 623-486-6450
Marla Woolsey Hobbs, prin. Fax 486-6461

Pioneer ES 400/PK-8
6315 W Port Au Prince Ln 85306 623-412-4550
Brenda LoPresto, prin. Fax 412-4561
Sahuaro Ranch ES 600/K-8
10401 N 63rd Ave 85302 623-412-4775
Dr. Eric Gundrum, prin. Fax 412-4786
Other Schools – See Peoria, Sun City

Washington ESD 6 23,000/PK-8
4650 W Sweetwater Ave 85304 602-347-2600
Dr. Paul Stanton, supt. Fax 347-2720
www.wesdschools.org
Sunburst ES 600/K-6
14218 N 47th Ave 85306 602-896-6400
Rhonda Warren, prin. Fax 896-6420
Sunset ES 500/K-6
4626 W Mountain View Rd 85302 602-347-3300
Betty Paterson, prin. Fax 347-3320
Other Schools – See Phoenix

Arrowhead Christian Academy 100/K-12
4030 W Yorkshire Dr 85308 623-582-6871
Mark French, head sch Fax 581-9311
Atonement Lutheran S 200/PK-8
4001 W Beardsley Rd 85308 623-374-3019
Lynn Casselman, admin. Fax 587-8512
Grace Lutheran S 200/PK-8
5600 W Palmaire Ave 85301 623-937-2010
E. John Fredrich, prin. Fax 937-4390
Joy Christian S 600/PK-12
21000 N 75th Ave 85308 623-561-2000
Danielle Root, supt. Fax 362-3202
Our Lady of Perpetual Help Catholic S 200/PK-8
7521 N 57th Ave 85301 623-931-7288
Catherine Lucero, prin. Fax 930-0256
St. Louis the King Catholic S 200/PK-8
4331 W Maryland Ave 85301 623-939-4260
Charlene Krushinsky, prin. Fax 930-1129

Globe, Gila, Pop. 7,446
Globe USD 1 1,800/PK-12
460 N Willow St 85501 928-402-6000
Jerry Jennex, supt. Fax 425-8912
www.globeschools.org
Copper Rim ES 700/PK-4
460 N Willow St 85501 928-402-5800
Brian Peace, prin. Fax 425-8936
High Desert MS 500/5-8
460 N Willow St 85501 928-402-5900
Lori Rodriquez, prin. Fax 425-8710

Gold Canyon, Pinal, Pop. 10,017
Apache Junction USD 43
Supt. — See Apache Junction
Peralta Trail ES 500/K-6
10965 E Peralta Rd, 480-982-1110
Natalie Clement, prin. Fax 288-4490

Golden Valley, Mohave, Pop. 8,174
Kingman USD 20
Supt. — See Kingman
Black Mountain ES 600/K-8
3404 N Santa Maria Rd 86413 928-565-9111
Shelley Oestmann, prin. Fax 565-9190

Goodyear, Maricopa, Pop. 63,699
Avondale ESD 44
Supt. — See Avondale
Centerra Mirage STEM Academy 600/K-8
15151 W Centerra Dr S 85338 623-772-4800
Casey Frank, prin. Fax 772-4891
Copper Trails S 900/PK-8
16875 W Canyon Trails Blvd 85338 623-772-4100
Stacy Ellis, prin. Fax 772-4120
Desert Star S 700/K-8
2131 S 157th Ave 85338 623-772-4600
Catherine Wood, prin. Fax 772-4620
Desert Thunder S 600/K-8
16750 W Garfield St 85338 623-772-4700
Wayne Deffenbaugh, prin. Fax 772-4720
Felix S 500/2-5
540 E La Pasada Blvd 85338 623-772-4300
Monique Martinez, prin. Fax 772-4320
Wildflower S 500/K-8
325 S Wildflower Dr 85338 623-772-5200
Dr. Araceli Montoya, prin. Fax 772-5220

Liberty ESD 25
Supt. — See Buckeye
Estrella Mountain S 600/K-8
10301 S San Miguel Ave 85338 623-327-2820
Sharon Marine, prin. Fax 327-2829
Las Brisas Academy K-8
18211 W Las Brisas Dr 85338 623-327-2860
Tim Dickey, prin. Fax 327-2869
Westar S 600/K-8
17777 W Westar Dr 85338 623-327-2840
Dave Bogart, prin. Fax 327-2849

Litchfield ESD 79
Supt. — See Litchfield Park
Padgett ES 900/PK-5
15430 W Turney Ave, 623-547-3200
Gina DeCoste, prin. Fax 536-3421
Palm Valley ES 800/PK-5
2801 N 135th Ave, 623-535-6400
Jennifer Benjamin, prin. Fax 935-0058
Western Sky MS 900/6-8
4905 N 144th Ave, 623-535-6300
Tami Garrett, prin. Fax 935-9536

Montessori in the Park 100/PK-6
1832 N Litchfield Rd, 623-535-4863
Fiona Quinlan, dir. Fax 536-0313
St. John Vianney Catholic S 200/PK-8
539 E La Pasada Blvd 85338 623-932-2434
Doug Weivoda, prin. Fax 925-0094
West Valley Christian S 100/PK-8
16260 W Van Buren St 85338 623-234-2100
Nathan Wieler, prin. Fax 234-2199

Grand Canyon, Coconino
Grand Canyon USD 4 200/K-12
PO Box 519 86023 928-638-2461
Dr. Rochonne Bria Ph.D., supt. Fax 638-2045
www.grandcanyonschool.org
Grand Canyon S 200/K-12
PO Box 519 86023 928-638-2461
Tom Rowland, prin. Fax 638-2045

Green Valley, Pima, Pop. 21,276
Continental ESD 39 600/PK-8
PO Box 547 85622 520-625-4581
Roxana Rico, supt. Fax 648-2569
www.continentalesd.org
Continental S 600/PK-8
PO Box 547 85622 520-625-4581
Mary McNichols, prin. Fax 648-2569

Guadalupe, Maricopa, Pop. 5,455
Tempe ESD 3
Supt. — See Tempe
Frank ES 600/PK-5
8409 S Avenida Del Yaqui 85283 480-897-6202
Martha Jacobo-Smith, prin. Fax 777-0146

Heber, Navajo, Pop. 1,581
Heber-Overgaard USD 6 400/PK-12
PO Box 547 85928 928-535-4622
Ron Tenney, supt. Fax 535-5146
www.heberovergaardschools.org
Capps MS 100/4-6
PO Box 820 85928 928-535-4622
Tim Slade, prin. Fax 535-9044
Other Schools – See Overgaard

Hereford, Cochise
Palominas ESD 49 1,100/PK-8
PO Box 38 85615 520-366-6204
Marylotti Copeland, supt. Fax 366-5717
www.psd49.net
Palominas S 400/K-8
PO Box 38 85615 520-366-6204
Bart Nieuwenhuis, prin. Fax 366-5875
Valley View S 200/PK-PK
PO Box 38 85615 520-366-5508
Shelley Woodman, prin. Fax 366-5592
Other Schools – See Sierra Vista

Holbrook, Navajo, Pop. 4,904
Holbrook USD 3 2,100/PK-12
PO Box 640 86025 928-524-6144
Dr. Robbie Koerperich, supt. Fax 524-3073
www.holbrook.k12.az.us
Holbrook JHS 400/6-8
PO Box 640 86025 928-524-3959
Dr. Jeri McKinnon, prin. Fax 524-3766
Hulet ES 300/3-5
PO Box 640 86025 928-524-6181
Kevin Fosburgh, prin. Fax 524-2940
Indian Wells ES 400/PK-6
PO Box 640 86025 928-654-3622
Cheri Grau, prin. Fax 654-3162
Park ES 300/K-2
PO Box 640 86025 928-524-6138
Connie McPherson, prin. Fax 524-6998

Huachuca City, Cochise, Pop. 1,763
Tombstone USD 1
Supt. — See Tombstone
Huachuca City S 500/PK-8
100 School Dr 85616 520-456-9842
Kevin Beaman, prin. Fax 456-9811

Humboldt, Yavapai
Humboldt USD 22
Supt. — See Prescott Valley
Humboldt ES 400/K-6
PO Box 8 86329 928-759-4400
Stacy Brush, prin. Fax 759-4420

Joseph City, Navajo, Pop. 1,364
Joseph City USD 2 300/PK-12
PO Box 8 86032 928-288-3307
Bryan Fields, supt. Fax 288-3309
www.josephcityschools.org
Joseph City ES 200/PK-6
PO Box 8 86032 928-288-3329
Daniel Hutchens, prin. Fax 288-3317

Kayenta, Navajo, Pop. 5,074
Kayenta USD 27 1,800/K-12
PO Box 337 86033 928-697-3251
Dr. Bryce Anderson, supt. Fax 697-2160
www.kayenta.k12.az.us
Kayenta ES 600/K-4
PO Box 337 86033 928-697-3251
Dr. Jacqueline Benally, prin. Fax 697-2160
Kayenta MS 500/5-8
PO Box 337 86033 928-697-3251
James Phillips, prin. Fax 697-2160

Keams Canyon, Navajo, Pop. 299
Cedar USD 25 200/PK-8
PO Box 367 86034 928-738-2334
Duane Noggle, supt. Fax 738-2335
www.cedarusd.org
Jeddito S 200/PK-8
PO Box 367 86034 928-738-2366
Duane Noggle M.S., prin. Fax 738-5134

Kearny, Pinal, Pop. 1,932
Ray USD 3 500/PK-12
PO Box 427, 520-363-5515
Curt Cook, supt. Fax 363-5642
www.rayusd.org
Ray ES 200/PK-6
PO Box 427, 520-363-5515
Rochelle Pacheco, prin. Fax 363-5642

Kingman, Mohave, Pop. 27,434
Hackberry SD 3 50/K-6
9501 E Nellie Dr 86401 928-692-0013
Deb Warren, admin. Fax 692-1075
www.hesd.net

Cedar Hills S 50/K-6
9501 E Nellie Dr 86401 928-692-0013
Deb Warren, admin. Fax 692-1075

Kingman USD 20 6,300/PK-12
3033 McDonald Ave 86401 928-753-5678
Roger Jacks, supt. Fax 753-6910
www.kusd.org
Cerbat ES 700/K-5
2689 E Jagerson Ave, 928-757-5100
Vicki Trujillo, prin. Fax 757-4911
Desert Willow ES 500/K-5
3700 Prospector St 86401 928-753-2472
James Jones, prin. Fax 753-7895
Hualapai ES 800/K-5
350 Eastern St 86401 928-753-1919
Jerry Arave, prin. Fax 753-1418
Kingman MS 600/6-8
1969 Detroit Ave 86401 928-753-3588
Don Burton, prin. Fax 753-1336
Little Explorers Early Learning Center PK-PK
3175 E Gordon Dr, 928-753-6413
Julie Beyer, coord. Fax 753-6412
Manzanita ES 700/K-5
2601 Detroit Ave 86401 928-753-6197
Scott Taylor, prin. Fax 753-7756
White Cliffs MS 700/6-8
3550 Prospector St 86401 928-753-6216
Tonia Cobanovich, prin. Fax 753-4042
Other Schools – See Dolan Springs, Golden Valley

Emmanuel Christian Academy 50/PK-8
3120 Hualapai Mountain Rd 86401 928-681-4220
Barb Thofson, prin. Fax 681-4221

Kirkland, Yavapai
Kirkland ESD 23 100/PK-8
PO Box 210 86332 928-442-3258
Michelle Perey, supt. Fax 442-9488
www.kirklandaz.org
Kirkland ES 100/PK-8
PO Box 210 86332 928-442-3258
Michelle Perey, prin. Fax 442-9488

Lake Havasu City, Mohave, Pop. 51,709
Lake Havasu USD 1 5,400/PK-12
2200 Havasupai Blvd 86403 928-505-6900
Diana M. Asseier, supt. Fax 505-6999
www.havasu.k12.az.us/
Havasupai ES 400/K-6
880 Cashmere Dr 86404 928-505-6045
Claude Sanders, prin. Fax 505-6059
Jamaica ES 600/K-6
3437 Jamaica Blvd S 86406 928-854-7280
Andrea Helart, prin. Fax 854-7299
Nautilus ES 400/K-6
1425 Patrician Dr 86404 928-505-6061
Roger Burger, prin. Fax 505-6079
Oro Grande ES 300/K-5
1250 Pawnee Dr 86406 928-505-6080
Brett Bitterman, prin. Fax 505-6099
Smoketree ES 500/PK-6
2395 Smoketree Ave N 86403 928-505-6020
Connie Hogard, prin. Fax 505-6039
Starline ES 500/K-5
3150 Starline Dr 86406 928-505-1490
Corey Triassi, prin. Fax 505-1499
Thunderbolt MS 900/7-8
695 Thunderbolt Ave 86406 928-854-7224
Marijo Mulligan, prin. Fax 854-7482

Calvary Christian Academy 100/PK-8
1605 McCulloch Blvd S 86406 928-854-5465
Julie Morones, admin. Fax 854-4007
Our Lady of the Lake Catholic Preschool 50/PK-K
1975 Daytona Ave 86403 928-855-0154
Jeff Arner, dir. Fax 855-7172

Lakeside, Navajo, Pop. 4,210
Blue Ridge USD 32 2,200/PK-12
1200 W White Mountain Blvd 85929 928-368-6126
Michael Wright, supt. Fax 368-5570
www.brusd.org
Blue Ridge ES 600/PK-3
1200 W White Mountain Blvd 85929 928-368-6126
Dave Clark M.Ed., prin. Fax 368-6183
Blue Ridge JHS 400/7-8
1200 W White Mountain Blvd 85929 928-368-2350
Loren Webb M.Ed., prin. Fax 368-2399
Blue Ridge MS 500/4-6
1200 W White Mountain Blvd 85929 928-368-2300
Loren Webb M.Ed., prin. Fax 368-2349

Laveen, Maricopa
Laveen ESD 59 6,000/PK-8
5001 W Dobbins Rd 85339 602-237-9100
Dr. Bill Johnson, supt. Fax 237-9135
www.laveeneld.org
Cheatham ES 900/K-8
4725 W South Mountain Rd 85339 602-237-7040
Andrew Wait, prin. Fax 237-3376
Desert Meadows S 900/K-8
6855 W Meadows Loop E 85339 602-304-2020
James Ketcham, prin. Fax 304-2025
Laveen ES 900/PK-8
4141 W McNeil St 85339 602-237-9110
Dr. Robert Kaplinger, prin. Fax 237-9134
Paseo Pointe S PK-8
8800 S 55th Ave 85339 602-304-2040
Kristi Pashley, prin. Fax 304-2045
Rogers Ranch S 900/K-8
6735 S 47th Ave 85339 602-304-2030
Timothy Thomas, prin. Fax 304-2035
Trailside Point S 900/K-8
7275 W Vineyard Rd 85339 602-605-8540
Sarah Zembruski, prin. Fax 605-8545
Vista del Sur Accelerated Academy 800/K-8
3908 W South Mountain Rd 85339 602-237-3046
Jessica Epacs, prin. Fax 237-1976
Other Schools – See Phoenix

Cammack Christian Academy 50/PK-7
4950 W Southern Ave 85339 602-237-3333
Joy Pickett, head sch Fax 907-1340
Maricopa Village Christian S 50/K-8
PO Box 171 85339 520-430-6827
Larisa Quijano, prin. Fax 430-6827

Leupp, Coconino, Pop. 936
Flagstaff USD 1
Supt. — See Flagstaff
Leupp ES 86035 100/PK-5
Ryan Chee, prin. 928-686-6266
Fax 686-6246

Litchfield Park, Maricopa, Pop. 5,366
Litchfield ESD 79 11,300/PK-8
272 E Sagebrush St 85340 623-535-6000
Dr. Julianne Lein, supt. Fax 935-1448
www.lesd.k12.az.us
Dreaming Summit ES 800/PK-5
272 E Sagebrush St 85340 623-547-1200
Sarah Lewis, prin. Fax 547-4720
Heck MS 700/6-8
272 E Sagebrush St 85340 623-547-1700
Kristin Casillas, prin. Fax 536-5955
Libby ES 700/PK-5
272 E Sagebrush St 85340 623-535-6200
Rachelle Morris, prin. Fax 935-7803
Litchfield ES 800/PK-5
272 E Sagebrush St 85340 623-535-6100
Sabine Hopper, prin. Fax 935-3779
Robey ES 800/PK-5
272 E Sagebrush St 85340 623-547-1400
Sandra Flood, prin. Fax 547-1947
Wigwam Creek MS 900/6-8
272 E Sagebrush St 85340 623-547-1100
John Scudder, prin. Fax 547-0873
Other Schools – See Avondale, Buckeye, Goodyear

St. Peter's Episcopal Montessori S 50/PK-6
400 S Litchfield Rd 85340 623-935-7737
Bonnie Shearer, head sch Fax 239-3304
Trinity Lutheran S 400/PK-8
830 E Plaza Cir 85340 623-935-4690
Astraea Rohloff, head sch Fax 935-1203

Mc Nary, Apache, Pop. 517
McNary ESD 23 100/K-8
PO Box 598 85930 928-334-2293
Mary Ann Wade, supt. Fax 334-2336
www.mcnary.k12.az.us
McNary S 100/K-8
PO Box 598 85930 928-334-2293
Mary Ann Wade, admin. Fax 334-2336

Mc Neal, Cochise, Pop. 238
Double Adobe ESD 45 50/K-6
7081 N Central Hwy 85617 520-364-3041
Tammi Wilson, admin. Fax 364-6796
www.doubleadobeschool.org/
Double Adobe ES 50/K-6
7081 N Central Hwy 85617 520-364-3041
Tammi Wilson, admin. Fax 364-6796

Mc Neal ESD 55 50/K-8
PO Box 8 85617 520-642-1071
Teresa Reyna, supt. Fax 642-3356
www.mcnealesd.org
Mc Neal ES 50/K-8
PO Box 8 85617 520-642-1071
Teresa Reyna, admin. Fax 642-3356

Mammoth, Pinal, Pop. 1,411
Mammoth-San Manuel USD 8
Supt. — See San Manuel
Mammoth ES 100/PK-6
111 W Dungan Dr 85618 520-487-2242
Katy Wilkins, prin. Fax 487-9206

Many Farms, Apache, Pop. 1,325
Chinle USD 24
Supt. — See Chinle
Many Farms ES 400/K-8
US Highway 191 86538 928-674-9000
Cheryl Tsosie, prin. Fax 781-4227

Marana, Pima, Pop. 34,148
Marana USD 6 12,300/PK-12
11279 W Grier Rd Ste 106 85653 520-682-4774
Dr. Doug Wilson, supt. Fax 682-2421
www.maranausd.org
Estes ES 800/K-6
11280 W Grier Rd 85653 520-682-4738
Colleen Frederick, prin. Fax 682-9247
Gladden Farms ES PK-6
11745 W Gladden Farms Dr 85653 520-682-1180
Nancy Paddock, prin. Fax 682-1183
Marana MS 1,000/7-8
11285 W Grier Rd 85653 520-682-4730
Lerona Dickson, prin. Fax 682-4790
Roadrunner ES 400/PK-6
16651 W Calle Carmela 85653 520-616-6363
Kristina Brewer, prin. Fax 616-6383
Other Schools – See Tucson

Maricopa, Pinal, Pop. 42,031
Maricopa USD 20 5,800/PK-12
44150 W Maricopa Casa Grand,
520-568-5100
Steve Chestnut Ed.D., supt. Fax 568-5151
maricopausd.org/
Desert Wind MS 400/6-8
44150 W Maricopa Casa Grand,
520-568-7110
June Celaya, prin. Fax 568-7119
Pima Butte ES 500/K-5
44150 W Maricopa Casa Grand,
520-568-7152
Randy Lazar, prin. Fax 568-7155

Mobile ESD 86 50/K-8
42798 S 99th Ave, 520-568-2280
Dr. Kit Wood, supt. Fax 568-9361
www.mobileesd.org
Mobile S 50/K-8
42798 S 99th Ave, 520-568-2280
Dr. Kit Wood, prin. Fax 568-9361

Mayer, Yavapai, Pop. 1,462
Mayer USD 43 600/PK-12
PO Box 1059 86333 928-642-1000
Dean Slaga, supt. Fax 632-4005
www.mayerschools.org
Mayer ES 400/PK-8
PO Box 1059 86333 928-642-1101
Patti Leonard, prin. Fax 632-9610

Mesa, Maricopa, Pop. 428,892
Gilbert Unified SD
Supt. — See Gilbert
Augusta Ranch ES 1,000/K-6
9430 E Neville Ave, 480-635-2011
Michael Hansen, prin. Fax 635-2020
Boulder Creek ES 700/PK-6
8045 E Portobello Ave 85212 480-507-1404
Dr. Karen Coleman, prin. Fax 507-1666
Canyon Rim ES 1,000/PK-6
3045 S Canyon Rim 85212 480-984-3216
Dr. Kenneth Fleming, prin. Fax 380-0105
Desert Ridge JHS 1,400/7-8
10211 E Madero Ave, 480-635-2025
Jean Woods, prin. Fax 635-2044
Harris ES 500/K-6
1820 S Harris Dr 85204 480-545-7060
Bill Roth, prin. Fax 926-7160
Highland JHS 1,300/7-8
6915 E Guadalupe Rd 85212 480-632-4739
Lisa Creaser, prin. Fax 632-4729
Meridian ES 1,000/PK-6
3900 S Mountain Rd 85212 480-497-4032
Jim Leeper, prin. Fax 497-4039
Superstition Springs ES 700/K-6
7125 E Monterey Ave, 480-641-6413
Dr. Tim Moses, prin. Fax 854-8871

Mesa USD 4 63,700/PK-12
63 E Main St 85201 480-472-0000
Dr. Michael Cowan, supt. Fax 472-0204
www.mpsaz.org
Adams ES 800/K-6
738 S Longmore 85202 480-472-4300
Stephanie Montez, prin. Fax 472-4350
Brinton ES 500/K-6
11455 E Sunland Ave 85208 480-472-4075
Doreen Herrick, prin. Fax 472-4077
Bush ES 600/K-6
4925 E Ingram St 85205 480-472-8500
Tracy Olson, prin. Fax 472-8545
Carson JHS 1,000/7-8
525 N Westwood 85201 480-472-2900
Tony Elmer, prin. Fax 472-2899
Crismon ES 600/PK-6
825 W Medina Ave 85210 480-472-4000
Sandi Kuhn, prin. Fax 472-4058
Edison ES 700/K-6
545 N Horne 85203 480-472-5300
Alex MacDonald, prin. Fax 472-5281
Eisenhower Center for Innovation 500/PK-6
848 N Mesa Dr 85201 480-472-5200
Robert Meldau, prin. Fax 472-5272
Emerson ES 800/K-6
415 N Westwood 85201 480-472-4700
Christel Arbogast, prin. Fax 472-4744
Entz ES 700/K-6
4132 E Adobe St 85205 480-472-7300
William Schultz, prin. Fax 472-7373
Falcon Hill ES 500/K-6
1645 N Sterling 85207 480-472-8600
Lisa McCray-Cannon, prin. Fax 472-8597
Field ES 700/K-6
2325 E Adobe St 85213 480-472-9800
Scott Cumberledge, prin. Fax 472-9819
Franklin at Alma ES 300/K-6
1313 W Medina Ave 85202 480-472-3900
Emily Kelly, prin. Fax 472-3919
Franklin East ES 800/K-6
1753 E 8th Ave 85204 480-472-6500
Dawn Carpenter, prin. Fax 472-6488
Franklin ES at Brimhall 900/K-6
4949 E Southern Ave 85206 480-472-2600
Jeff Abrams, prin. Fax 472-2696
Franklin JHS 200/7-8
4949 E Southern Ave 85206 480-472-2600
Jeffrey Abrams, prin. Fax 472-2698
Franklin West ES 600/K-6
236 S Sirrine 85210 480-472-5400
Kelly Osburn, prin. Fax 472-5444
Fremont JHS 1,000/7-8
1001 N Power Rd 85205 480-472-8300
Todd Roberts, prin. Fax 472-8333
Guerrero ES 600/K-6
463 S Alma School Rd 85210 480-472-9200
Brian Minarcik, prin. Fax 472-9224
Hale ES 600/PK-6
1425 N 23rd St 85213 480-472-7400
Cindy Hayton, prin. Fax 472-7377
Hawthorne ES 500/PK-6
630 N Hunt Dr 85203 480-472-7500
Nicolas Parker, prin. Fax 472-7474
Hermosa Vista ES 700/K-6
2626 N 24th St 85213 480-472-7550
John Trezise, prin. Fax 472-7549
Highland Arts ES 700/K-6
3042 E Adobe St 85213 480-472-7600
Christy Cuddy, prin. Fax 472-7606
Holmes ES 600/PK-6
948 S Horne 85204 480-472-5600
Heidi Williams, prin. Fax 472-5555
Irving ES 500/PK-6
3220 E Pueblo Ave 85204 480-472-1700
Penny Briney, prin. Fax 472-1699

Ishikawa ES 800/K-6
2635 N 32nd St 85213 480-472-7700
David Shill, prin. Fax 472-7686
Jefferson ES 500/PK-6
120 S Jefferson Ave 85208 480-472-8700
Genessee Montes, prin. Fax 472-8724
Johnson ES 600/PK-6
3807 E Pueblo Ave 85206 480-472-6800
Gregory Reid, prin. Fax 472-6755
Keller ES 600/PK-6
1445 E Hilton Ave 85204 480-472-6200
Brian Hay, prin. Fax 472-6150
Kerr ES 700/PK-6
125 E McLellan Rd 85201 480-472-5100
Amy Breitenbucher, prin. Fax 472-5166
Kino JHS 1,000/7-8
848 N Horne 85203 480-472-2400
Keiko Dilbeck, prin. Fax 472-2549
Las Sendas ES 800/PK-6
3120 N Red Mountain 85207 480-472-8750
Aaron Kaczmarek, prin. Fax 472-8735
Lehi ES 400/PK-6
2555 N Stapley Dr 85203 480-472-5500
Christina Larson, prin. Fax 472-5480
Lincoln ES 800/PK-6
930 S Sirrine 85210 480-472-6400
Josh Henderson, prin. Fax 472-6390
Lindbergh ES 500/PK-6
930 S Lazona Dr 85204 480-472-6300
Thomas Heminger, prin. Fax 472-6310
Longfellow ES 700/PK-6
345 S Hall 85204 480-472-6550
Monica Mesa, prin. Fax 472-6599
Lowell ES 700/PK-6
920 E Broadway Rd 85204 480-472-1400
Charles Starkey, prin. Fax 472-1482
MacArthur ES 500/K-6
1435 E McLellan Rd 85203 480-472-7800
Mark Norris, prin. Fax 472-7824
Madison ES 400/K-6
849 S Sunnyvale 85206 480-472-8800
Sharon Webster, prin. Fax 472-8855
Mendoza ES 500/PK-6
5831 E McLellan Rd 85205 480-472-2000
Deb Lynch, prin. Fax 472-1999
Mesa Academy for Advanced Studies 400/4-8
6919 E Brown Rd 85207 480-308-7432
Nicholo Wilfort, prin. Fax 308-7428
O'Connor ES 600/PK-6
4840 E Adobe St 85205 480-472-7850
Scott Eshman, prin. Fax 472-7878
Patterson ES 700/K-6
615 S Cheshire 85208 480-472-9700
Nonie Sundve, prin. Fax 472-9788
Porter ES 400/K-6
1350 S Lindsay Rd 85204 480-472-6700
Kathy Ray, prin. Fax 472-6698
Poston JHS 1,000/7-8
2433 E Adobe St 85213 480-472-2100
Michael Rapier, prin. Fax 472-2105
Redbird ES 600/PK-6
1020 S Extension Rd 85210 480-472-1200
Terri Clark-Ringland, prin. Fax 472-1290
Red Mountain Center 300/PK-PK
950 N Sunvalley Blvd 85207 480-472-3975
Allen Quie, prin.
Red Mountain Ranch ES 500/K-6
6650 E Raftriver St 85215 480-472-7900
Sarah Collins, prin. Fax 472-7969
Rhodes JHS 1,000/7-8
1860 S Longmore 85202 480-472-2300
Patricia Christie, prin. Fax 472-2299
Robson ES 700/K-6
2122 E Pueblo Ave 85204 480-472-6600
Dr. Kent Ashton, prin. Fax 472-6660
Roosevelt ES 500/PK-6
828 S Valencia 85202 480-472-4200
Darlene Shumway, prin. Fax 472-4270
Salk ES 600/PK-6
7029 E Brown Rd 85207 480-472-8400
Vicki Hester, prin. Fax 472-8484
Shepherd JHS 700/7-8
1407 N Alta Mesa Dr 85205 480-472-1800
Renea Kennedy, prin. Fax 472-1888
Smith JHS 1,000/7-8
10100 E Adobe Rd 85207 480-472-9900
Casey Eagleburger, prin. Fax 472-9999
Sousa ES 600/PK-6
616 N Mountain Rd 85207 480-472-8900
Jen Lamanna, prin. Fax 472-8888
Stapley JHS 900/7-8
3250 E Hermosa Vista Dr 85213 480-472-2700
James Fisher, prin. Fax 472-2828
Stevenson ES 800/PK-6
638 S 96th St 85208 480-472-9000
Jessica Seaman, prin. Fax 472-9070
Taft ES 500/PK-6
9800 E Quarterline Rd 85207 480-472-9100
Russ Heath, prin. Fax 472-9090
Taylor JHS 1,100/7-8
705 S 32nd St 85204 480-472-1500
Gina Piraino, prin. Fax 472-1616
Washington ES 500/K-6
2260 W Isabella Ave 85202 480-472-4100
Michele Grimaldi, prin. Fax 472-4141
Webster ES 600/PK-6
202 N Sycamore 85201 480-472-4800
Stacey Ball, prin. Fax 472-4888
Whitman ES 700/PK-6
1829 N Grand 85201 480-472-5000
Beth Bishop, prin. Fax 472-5058
Whittier ES 600/PK-6
733 N Longmore 85201 480-472-4900
Andrea Sims, prin. Fax 472-4905
Wilson ES 700/K-6
5619 E Glade Ave 85206 480-472-9250
Shelley Heath, prin. Fax 472-9277
Zaharis ES 900/PK-6
9410 E McKellips Rd 85207 480-308-7200
Mike Oliver, prin. Fax 308-7255
Other Schools – See Chandler

Queen Creek USD 95
Supt. — See Queen Creek
Gateway Polytechnic Academy PK-8
5149 S Signal Butte 85212 480-987-7440
Allison Carmichael, prin. Fax 986-1848

Adobe SDA Christian S 50/1-8
9910 E Adobe Rd 85207 480-986-2310
Steve Shelton, prin.
Christ the King Catholic S 200/PK-8
1551 E Dana Ave 85204 480-844-4480
Shelley Conner, prin. Fax 844-4498
Faith Christian S 100/PK-12
PO Box 9086 85214 480-833-1983
Dick Buckingham, admin. Fax 325-1096
Montessori International S 100/PK-8
1230 N Gilbert Rd 85203 480-890-1580
Pilgrim Lutheran S 100/PK-8
3257 E University Dr 85213 480-830-1724
James Wade, prin. Fax 807-2921
Queen of Peace Catholic S 200/PK-8
141 N MacDonald St 85201 480-969-0226
Renee Baeza, prin. Fax 275-2097
Redeemer Christian S 100/K-12
719 N Stapley Dr 85203 480-962-5003
Dr. Denise Monroe Ed.D., prin. Fax 833-7502
St. Timothy Catholic Preschool 100/PK-PK
1730 W Guadalupe Rd 85202 480-775-5237
DeEtte Milhone, dir. Fax 820-7984
St. Timothy Catholic S 200/K-8
2520 S Alma School Rd 85210 480-775-2650
Maureen Vick, prin. Fax 775-2651
Tempe Montessori S 100/PK-6
3107 S Evergreen Rd, 480-966-7606

Miami, Gila, Pop. 1,817
Miami USD 40 1,100/K-12
PO Box 2070 85539 928-425-3271
Dr. Sherry Dorathy, supt. Fax 425-7419
www.miamiusd40.org
Bejarano ES 300/K-3
PO Box 2070 85539 928-425-3271
David Pastor, prin. Fax 425-0111
Kornegay IS 300/4-6
PO Box 2070 85539 928-425-3271
Mary Gooday, prin. Fax 425-3051

Mohave Valley, Mohave, Pop. 2,530
Mohave Valley ESD 16 600/PK-8
8450 S Olive Ave 86440 928-768-2507
Whitney Crow, supt. Fax 768-2510
www.mvesd16.org
Mohave Valley JHS 300/6-8
6565 S Girard Ave 86440 928-768-9196
Charlotte Hansen, prin. Fax 768-1129
Other Schools – See Fort Mohave

Morenci, Greenlee, Pop. 1,476
Morenci USD 18 1,500/PK-12
PO Box 1060 85540 928-865-2081
Dr. David Woodall, supt. Fax 865-3130
www.morenci.k12.az.us/
Fairbanks MS 400/5-8
PO Box 1060 85540 928-865-3501
Anna VanZile, prin. Fax 865-5980
Metcalf ES 600/K-4
PO Box 1060 85540 928-865-7290
Jennifer Morales, prin. Fax 865-7295
Morenci Early Learning Center 200/PK-PK
PO Box 1060 85540 928-865-7274
Dusty Murphy, dir.

Morristown, Maricopa
Morristown ESD 75 100/PK-8
PO Box 98 85342 623-546-5100
Fax 388-9368
www.morristowneld75.org
Morristown ES 100/PK-8
PO Box 98 85342 623-546-5100
Lucille Thompson, lead tchr. Fax 388-9368

Naco, Cochise, Pop. 1,039
Naco ESD 23 300/K-8
PO Box 397 85620 520-432-5060
Juan M. Franco, supt. Fax 432-4161
www.naco.k12.az.us
Naco ES 300/K-8
PO Box 397 85620 520-432-5060
Juan M. Franco, admin. Fax 432-4161

New River, Maricopa
Deer Valley USD 97
Supt. — See Phoenix
New River ES 300/K-6
48827 N Black Canyon Hwy 85087 623-376-3500
Dr. Stephanie Tennille, prin. Fax 376-3580

Nogales, Santa Cruz, Pop. 20,797
Nogales USD 1 5,900/K-12
PO Box 5000 85628 520-287-0800
Fernando Parra, supt. Fax 287-3586
www.nusd.k12.az.us
Bracker ES 300/K-5
121 Camino Diez Mandamiento 85621
520-377-2886
Timothy Colgate, prin. Fax 397-7251
Carpenter Middle Academy 700/6-8
595 W Kino St 85621 520-287-0820
Dr. Roman Soltero, prin. Fax 287-0817
Challenger ES 600/K-5
901 E Calle Mayer 85621 520-377-0544
Wil Arias, prin. Fax 377-2026
Desert Shadows MS 800/6-8
340 Boulevard Del Rey David 85621 520-377-2646
Dr. Joan Molera, prin. Fax 377-2674
Lincoln ES 400/K-5
652 N Tyler Ave 85621 520-287-0870
Dr. Lucina Romero, prin Fax 287-0875
Mitchell ES 400/K-5
855 N Bautista St 85621 520-287-0840
Michelle Shuman, prin. Fax 287-0847
Vasquez De Coronado ES 500/K-5
2301 N Al Harrison Rd 85621 520-377-2855
Sandra Jimenez, prin. Fax 377-0221

Welty ES 400/K-5
1050 W Cimarron St 85621 520-287-0880
Aissa Celeste Bonillas, prin. Fax 287-6955

Santa Cruz ESD 28 200/K-8
HC 2 Box 50 85621 520-287-0737
Kathy Romero, supt. Fax 287-6791
sced28.com
Santa Cruz ES - Little Red Schoolhouse 200/K-8
HC 2 Box 50 85621 520-287-0737
Kathy Romero, admin. Fax 287-6791

Lourdes S 300/PK-8
555 E Patagonia Hwy 85621 520-287-5659
Rosalinda Perez, prin. Fax 287-2910
Sacred Heart S 200/PK-8
207 W Oak St 85621 520-287-2223
Vanessa Rothstein, prin. Fax 287-3373
Sonshine Christian S 100/PK-5
PO Box 1847 85628 520-281-0356
Ana Losolla, prin. Fax 281-5154

Oracle, Pinal, Pop. 3,602
Oracle ESD 2 400/PK-8
725 N Carpenter Dr 85623 520-896-3070
Dennis Blauser, supt. Fax 896-3088
www.osd2.org
Mountain Vista S 400/PK-8
2618 W El Paseo 85623 520-896-3000
Crystle Gallegos, prin. Fax 896-3062

Oro Valley, Pima, Pop. 40,283
Amphitheater USD 10
Supt. — See Tucson
Innovation Academy K-5
825 W Desert Fairways Dr, 520-269-4610
Michael McConnell, prin. Fax 269-4620
Painted Sky ES 700/K-5
12620 N Woodburne Ave, 520-696-3800
Wendy Odell, prin. Fax 696-3888

Immaculate Heart S 300/PK-8
410 E Magee Rd 85704 520-297-6672
Sr. Veronica Loya, prin. Fax 297-9152

Overgaard, Navajo
Heber-Overgaard USD 6
Supt. — See Heber
Mountain Meadows PS 200/PK-3
PO Box 40 85933 928-535-4622
Tim Slade, prin. Fax 535-6574

Page, Coconino, Pop. 6,933
Page USD 8 2,700/K-12
PO Box 1927 86040 928-608-4100
Robert Varner, supt. Fax 645-2805
pageusd.org
Desert View IS 600/3-5
PO Box 1927 86040 928-608-4156
Rich Van Nostrand, prin. Fax 608-4169
Lake View ES 600/K-2
PO Box 1927 86040 928-608-4200
Cathy Erickson, prin. Fax 608-4291
Page MS 600/6-8
PO Box 1927 86040 928-608-4300
Alyssa Covington, prin. Fax 645-9285

Immaculate Heart Preschool 50/PK-K
PO Box 1387 86040 928-645-2301
Fr. Tom Maikowski, prin. Fax 645-2531

Palo Verde, Maricopa
Palo Verde ESD 49 400/K-8
PO Box 108 85343 623-327-3690
Robert Aldridge, supt. Fax 327-3695
www.paloverdeschools.org
Palo Verde ES 400/K-8
PO Box 108 85343 623-327-3680
Robert Aldridge, prin. Fax 386-4654

Paradise Valley, Maricopa, Pop. 12,621
Scottsdale USD 48
Supt. — See Scottsdale
Cherokee ES 600/PK-5
8801 N 56th St 85253 480-484-8700
Walter Chantler, prin. Fax 484-8701
Kiva ES 500/K-5
6911 E McDonald Dr 85253 480-484-2200
Jessica Johnston, prin. Fax 484-2201

Christ Church S 200/PK-5
4015 E Lincoln Dr 85253 602-381-9906
Kim Westfall, head sch Fax 840-4472
Phoenix Country Day S 700/PK-12
3901 E Stanford Dr 85253 602-955-8200
Andrew Rodin, head sch Fax 955-1286

Parker, LaPaz, Pop. 2,994
Parker USD 27 1,900/PK-12
PO Box 1090 85344 928-669-9244
James Lotts, supt. Fax 669-2515
www.parkerusd.org
Blake PS 500/PK-2
PO Box 1090 85344 928-669-8203
Joanna Hormoe, prin. Fax 669-8771
Le Pera ES 300/K-8
PO Box 1090 85344 928-662-4306
Brian Wedemeyer, prin. Fax 662-4308
Wallace ES 400/3-5
PO Box 1090 85344 928-669-2141
Kelly McGuire, prin. Fax 669-5352
Wallace JHS 300/6-8
PO Box 1090 85344 928-669-2141
Amanda Maxwell, prin. Fax 669-2515

Parks, Coconino, Pop. 1,159
Maine Consolidated SD 10 100/PK-8
PO Box 50010 86018 928-635-2115
Dr. Mark Williams, supt. Fax 635-5320
www.mcsd10.org
Maine Consolidated S 100/PK-8
PO Box 50010 86018 928-635-2115
Dr. Mark Williams, prin. Fax 635-5320

Patagonia, Santa Cruz, Pop. 909
Patagonia SD 200/PK-12
PO Box 254 85624 520-394-3000
Rachell Hochheim, supt. Fax 394-3001
www.patagonia.k12.az.us
Patagonia ES 100/PK-8
PO Box 295 85624 520-394-3000
Rachell Hochheim, prin. Fax 394-3001

Payson, Gila, Pop. 15,087
Payson USD 10 2,400/K-12
PO Box 919 85547 928-474-2070
Greg Wyman, supt. Fax 472-2013
www.pusd10.org
Payson ES 500/K-2
PO Box 919 85547 928-474-5882
Gail Milton, prin. Fax 472-2045
Randall ES 500/3-5
PO Box 919 85547 928-474-2353
Linda Scoville, prin. Fax 472-2041
Rim Country MS 500/6-8
PO Box 919 85547 928-474-4511
Jennifer White, prin. Fax 472-2044

Payson Christian S 100/PK-12
1000 E Frontier St 85541 928-474-8050
David Callahan M.Ed., admin. Fax 474-3252

Peach Springs, Mohave, Pop. 1,077
Peach Springs USD 8 200/K-8
PO Box 360 86434 928-769-2202
Jamie Cole, supt. Fax 769-2214
www.psusd8.org
Peach Springs ES 200/K-8
PO Box 360 86434 928-769-2613
Jamie Cole, prin. Fax 769-2676

Valentine ESD 22 100/K-8
HC 35 Box 50 86434 928-769-2310
Cliff Angle, supt. Fax 769-2389
valentineaz.net
Valentine S 100/K-8
HC 35 Box 50 86434 928-769-2310
Cliff Angle, admin. Fax 769-2389

Pearce, Cochise
Ash Creek ESD 53 50/PK-8
6460 E Highway 181 85625 520-824-3340
Sue Shepard, supt. Fax 824-3410
ashcreekschool.wordpress.com
Ash Creek ES 50/PK-8
6460 E Highway 181 85625 520-824-3340
Sue Shepard, prin. Fax 824-3410

Pearce ESD 22 100/PK-8
PO Box 979 85625 520-826-3328
Kyle Hart, supt. Fax 826-3531
www.pearceschool.org
Pearce S 100/PK-8
PO Box 979 85625 520-826-3328
Kyle Hart, prin. Fax 826-3531

Peeples Valley, Yavapai
Yarnell ESD 52 50/PK-8
18912 W Hays Ranch Rd, 928-427-3347
Fax 427-3348
www.modelcreekschool.org
Yarnell S 50/PK-8
18912 Hays Ranch Rd, 928-427-3347
Lori Bomar, lead tchr. Fax 427-3348

Peoria, Maricopa, Pop. 150,709
Deer Valley USD 97
Supt. — See Phoenix
Terramar S 800/K-8
7000 W Happy Valley Rd 85383 623-445-7600
Sharon Wieser, prin. Fax 445-7680
West Wing S 1,000/K-8
26716 N High Desert Dr 85383 623-376-5000
Dr. Linda Price-Barry, prin. Fax 376-5080

Peoria USD 11
Supt. — See Glendale
Alta Loma ES 800/PK-8
9750 N 87th Ave 85345 623-412-4575
Sherri Hedges, prin. Fax 412-4584
Apache ES 800/K-8
8633 W John Cabot Rd 85382 623-412-4875
Heidi Stillman, prin. Fax 412-4885
Cheyenne ES 800/K-8
11806 N 87th Ave 85345 623-487-5100
Dale Shough, prin. Fax 487-5110
Cotton Boll ES 900/K-8
8540 W Butler Dr 85345 623-412-4700
David Snyder, prin. Fax 412-4705
Country Meadows ES 1,100/K-8
8409 N 111th Ave 85345 623-412-5200
Danielle Skrip, prin. Fax 412-5207
Coyote Hills ES 1,100/K-8
21180 N 87th Ave 85382 623-412-5225
Terry Balliet, prin. Fax 412-5232
Desert Harbor ES 800/PK-8
15585 N 91st Ave 85382 623-486-6200
Becky Berhow, prin. Fax 486-6207
Frontier ES 1,000/K-8
21258 N 81st Ave 85382 623-412-4900
Laurie Little, prin. Fax 412-4905
Lake Pleasant ES 800/K-8
31501 N Westland Rd 85383 623-773-6575
Dustin Hamman, prin. Fax 773-6580
Murphy ES 500/K-8
7231 W North Ln 85345 623-412-4475
Alice Cushing, prin. Fax 412-4484
Oakwood ES 900/K-8
12900 N 71st Ave 85381 623-412-4725
Shawn Duguid, prin. Fax 412-4734
Oasis ES 800/K-8
7841 W Sweetwater Ave 85381 623-412-4800
Gail Miller, prin. Fax 412-4809
Parkridge ES 1,100/PK-8
9970 W Beardsley Rd 85382 623-412-5400
Janet Swarstad, prin. Fax 412-5407
Paseo Verde ES 800/K-8
7880 W Greenway Rd 85381 623-412-5075
Mark Stutesman, prin. Fax 412-5084
Peoria ES 600/K-8
11501 N 79th Ave 85345 623-412-4450
Curtis Smith, prin. Fax 412-4458
Peoria Traditional S 300/K-8
21180 N 87th Ave 85382 623-412-5350
Erik Stone, prin. Fax 412-5355
Santa Fe ES 700/K-8
9880 N 77th Ave 85345 623-486-6475
John Nitshke, prin. Fax 486-6487
Sky View ES 600/PK-8
8624 W Sweetwater Ave 85381 623-412-4850
Holly Harper, prin. Fax 412-4861
Sundance ES 700/PK-8
7051 W Cholla St 85345 623-412-4675
Jennifer Silva, prin. Fax 412-4685
Sunset Heights ES K-8
9687 W Adam Ave 85382 623-773-6650
Rae Conelley, admin. Fax 773-6655
Sun Valley ES 900/K-8
8361 N 95th Ave 85345 623-412-4825
Stephen Balliet, prin. Fax 412-4837
Vistancia ES 900/K-8
30009 N Sunrise Pt 85383 623-773-6500
Jennifer Kazmar, prin. Fax 773-6507

Cross of Glory Lutheran S 100/PK-8
10111 W Jomax Rd 85383 623-224-8841
Micah Foelske, prin.
Montessori Kingdom of Learning 100/PK-8
13111 N 94th Dr 85381 623-876-1463

Peridot, Gila, Pop. 1,346

Peridot-Our Savior's Lutheran S 100/K-8
PO Box 118 85542 928-475-7537
Benjamin Pagel, prin.

Phoenix, Maricopa, Pop. 1,416,459
Alhambra ESD 68 13,600/PK-8
4510 N 37th Ave 85019 602-336-2920
Mark Yslas, supt. Fax 336-2270
www.alhambraesd.org/
Alhambra Traditional S 700/K-8
3736 W Osborn Rd 85019 602-484-8816
Richard Stinnett, prin. Fax 484-8952
Andalucia MS 1,100/4-8
4730 W Campbell Ave 85031 623-848-8646
Raul Ruiz, prin. Fax 846-6044
Catalina Ventura S 1,100/K-8
6331 N 39th Ave 85019 602-841-7445
Alfonso Landey, prin. Fax 841-6892
Cordova ES 900/PK-8
5631 N 35th Ave 85017 602-841-0704
Dr. Sharon Spearman, prin. Fax 973-8416
Granada East MS 1,100/4-8
3022 W Campbell Ave 85017 602-589-0110
Dr. Steve Wyble, prin. Fax 589-0140
Granada PS 900/PK-3
3232 W Campbell Ave 85017 602-841-1403
Stacy O'Rourke, prin. Fax 973-8438
Montebello S 1,400/K-8
5725 N 27th Ave 85017 602-336-2000
Nicole Durazo, prin. Fax 249-7233
Rice PS 1,100/PK-3
4530 W Campbell Ave 85031 623-848-8420
Rosa Berrelleza, prin. Fax 848-1998
Sevilla PS 900/PK-3
3801 W Missouri Ave 85019 602-242-0281
Richard Holmes, prin. Fax 242-2791
Sevilla West S 1,200/4-8
3851 W Missouri Ave 85019 602-347-0232
Jennifer Bunch, prin. Fax 347-9906
Simpson MS 800/4-8
5330 N 23rd Ave 85015 602-246-0699
Alana Ragland, prin. Fax 246-4305
Westwood PS 1,000/PK-3
4711 N 23rd Ave 85015 602-242-2442
Theresa Killingsworth, prin. Fax 242-2514
Other Schools – See Glendale

Balsz ESD 31 2,700/PK-8
4825 E Roosevelt St 85008 602-629-6400
Dr. Jeffrey Smith, supt. Fax 629-6470
www.balsz.org
Balsz ES 800/K-8
4309 E Belleview St 85008 602-629-6500
Dr. Chad Smith, prin. Fax 629-6504
Brunson-Lee ES 500/K-6
1350 N 48th St 85008 602-629-6900
Dr. Ryan LoMonaco, prin. Fax 629-6904
Crockett ES 600/K-8
501 N 36th St 85008 602-629-6600
Sean Hannafin, prin. Fax 629-6604
Griffith ES 800/K-8
4505 E Palm Ln 85008 602-629-6700
Elsa Aguirre, prin. Fax 629-6704
Orangedale Early Learning Center 50/PK-PK
5048 E Oak St 85008 602-629-6800
Fax 629-6815

Cartwright ESD 83 19,100/PK-8
5220 W Indian School Rd 85031 623-691-4000
Dr. Jacob A. Chavez, supt. Fax 691-4079
www.csd83.org
Atkinson MS 1,400/6-8
4315 N Maryvale Pkwy 85031 623-691-1700
Dr. Diana Romito, prin. Fax 691-1720
Borman S 1,200/PK-8
3637 N 55th Ave 85031 623-691-5000
Derek Etheridge, prin. Fax 691-5020
Cartwright ES 900/K-8
2825 N 59th Ave 85035 623-691-4100
Robert Aguilar, prin. Fax 691-4120
Castro MS 900/6-8
2730 N 79th Ave 85035 623-691-5300
Sarah Hernandez, prin. Fax 691-5320
Davidson ES 900/K-5
6935 W Osborn Rd 85033 623-691-1500
Christine Tamayo, prin. Fax 691-1520
Desert Sands MS 1,100/6-8
6308 W Campbell Ave 85033 623-691-4900
Michael Dellisanti, prin. Fax 691-4920
Downs ES 800/K-8
3611 N 47th Ave 85031 623-691-4200
Vivian Nash, prin. Fax 691-4220
Estrella MS 1,300/6-8
3733 N 75th Ave 85033 623-691-5400
Ryan Anderson, prin. Fax 691-5420
Harris ES 1,200/K-8
2252 N 55th Ave 85035 623-691-4800
Lupe Aguirre, prin. Fax 691-4820
Heatherbrae ES 700/K-5
7070 W Heatherbrae Dr 85033 623-691-5200
Eva Stevens, prin. Fax 691-5220
Holiday Park ES 800/K-5
4417 N 66th Ave 85033 623-691-4500
Rebecca Leimkuehler, prin. Fax 691-4520
Long ES 900/K-5
4407 N 55th Ave 85031 623-691-4300
Brian Johnson, prin. Fax 691-4320
Palm Lane ES 900/PK-5
2043 N 64th Dr 85035 623-691-5500
Stephanie Ward, prin. Fax 691-5520
Pena ES 900/K-5
2550 N 79th Ave 85035 623-691-3100
Tracy Baker-Weigold, prin. Fax 691-3120
Peralta ES 900/PK-5
7125 W Encanto Blvd 85035 623-691-5600
Jennifer Botello, prin. Fax 691-5620
Spitalny ES 700/K-5
3201 N 46th Dr 85031 623-691-4400
Janet Hecht, prin. Fax 691-4420
Starlight Park ES 900/K-5
7960 W Osborn Rd 85033 623-691-4700
Dr. Felicia Durden, prin. Fax 691-4720
Sunset ES 700/K-5
6602 W Osborn Rd 85033 623-691-4600
Kristi Langley-Wells, prin. Fax 691-4620
Tarver ES 1,000/K-5
4308 N 51st Ave Ste 102 85031 623-691-1900
Dr. Joy Weiss, prin. Fax 691-1920
Tomahawk ES 1,000/K-5
7820 W Turney Ave 85033 623-691-5800
Marilyn Bond, prin. Fax 691-5820

Cave Creek USD 93
Supt. — See Scottsdale
Desert Willow ES 700/PK-6
4322 E Desert Willow Pkwy 85044 480-575-2800
Dr. Rodney Egan, prin. Fax 419-7265
Horseshoe Trails ES 700/PK-6
5405 E Pinnacle Vista Dr 85085 480-272-8500
Dr. Matt Schenk, prin. Fax 907-6643
Sonoran Trails MS 800/7-8
5555 E Pinnacle Vista Dr 85085 480-272-8600
Bill Dolezal, prin. Fax 272-8699

Creighton ESD 14 6,600/K-8
2702 E Flower St 85016 602-381-6000
Dr. Donna W. Lewis, supt. Fax 381-6019
www.creightonschools.org/
Biltmore Preparatory Academy 500/K-8
4601 N 34th St 85018 602-381-6160
Dr. Stephanie DeMar, prin. Fax 381-6170
Creighton S 800/K-8
2802 E McDowell Rd 85008 602-381-6060
Ivan Carvajal, prin. Fax 381-6047
Excelencia S 900/K-8
2181 E McDowell Rd 85006 602-381-4670
Michelle Berg, prin. Fax 381-4668
Gateway S 800/K-8
1100 N 35th St 85008 602-381-4665
Ellen Heller, prin. Fax 381-4662
Kennedy S 700/K-8
2702 E Osborn Rd 85016 602-381-6180
Andy Gutierrez, prin. Fax 381-6192
Loma Linda S 600/K-8
2002 E Clarendon Ave 85016 602-381-6080
Tracey Pastor, prin. Fax 381-6094
Machan S 500/K-8
2140 E Virginia Ave 85006 602-381-6120
Julie Frost, prin. Fax 381-6125
Monte Vista S 800/K-8
3501 E Osborn Rd 85018 602-381-6140
Joel Laurin, prin. Fax 381-6159
Papago S 900/K-8
2013 N 36th St 85008 602-381-6100
Jeffrey Geyer, prin. Fax 381-6118

Deer Valley USD 97 32,700/PK-12
20402 N 15th Ave 85027 623-445-5000
Dr. Curtis Finch, supt. Fax 445-5086
www.dvusd.org
Constitution ES 600/K-6
18440 N 15th Ave 85023 602-467-6100
Cheyana Leiva, prin. Fax 467-6180
Deer Valley MS 700/7-8
21100 N 27th Ave 85027 623-445-3300
Nikki Powell, prin. Fax 445-3380
Esperanza ES 300/K-6
251 W Mohawk Ln 85027 623-445-3700
Melissa Sepuka, prin. Fax 445-3780
Norterra Canyon S 1,100/K-8
2200 W Maya Way 85085 623-445-8200
Tish Mineer, prin. Fax 445-8280
Paseo Hills S 1,000/PK-8
3302 W Louise Dr 85027 623-445-4500
Dawn Pace, prin. Fax 445-4580
Sonoran Foothills S PK-8
32150 N North Foothills Dr 85085 623-445-8400
Sharon Matt, prin. Fax 445-8480
Stetson Hills S 1,000/K-8
25475 N Stetson Hills Loop, 623-445-5300
Carrie Mabee, prin. Fax 445-5380
Sunrise ES 500/K-6
17624 N 31st Ave 85053 602-467-5900
Karen Dial, prin. Fax 467-5980
Sunset Ridge S 1,000/PK-8
35707 N 33rd Ln 85086 623-445-7800
Lynnette Byrn, prin. Fax 445-7880

Village Meadows ES 400/K-6
2020 W Morningside Dr 85023 602-467-6300
Melissa Weinman, prin. Fax 467-6380
Other Schools – See Anthem, Desert Hills, Glendale, New River, Peoria

Fowler ESD 45 4,600/PK-8
1617 S 67th Ave 85043 623-707-4500
Dr. Marvene Lobato, supt. Fax 707-4560
www.fesd.org
Fowler ES 600/PK-5
6707 W Van Buren St 85043 623-707-2500
Robert Altavilla, prin. Fax 707-4680
Santa Maria MS 700/6-8
7250 W Lower Buckeye Rd 85043 623-707-1100
Dr. Desiree Castillo, prin. Fax 707-1110
Sun Canyon ES 600/PK-5
8150 W Durango St 85043 623-707-2000
Angela Krenkel, prin. Fax 707-2015
Sunridge ES 600/PK-5
6244 W Roosevelt St 85043 623-707-4600
Chad Ostrom, prin. Fax 707-4630
Tuscano ES 700/PK-5
3850 S 79th Ave 85043 623-707-2300
Rebecca Osorio, prin. Fax 707-2304
Western Valley ES 700/PK-5
6250 W Durango St 85043 623-707-2100
Marco Ruiz, prin. Fax 707-2104
Western Valley MS 800/6-8
6250 W Durango St 85043 623-707-2200
Marco Ruiz, prin. Fax 707-2204

Isaac ESD 5 7,200/PK-8
3348 W McDowell Rd 85009 602-455-6700
Dr. Mario Ventura, supt. Fax 278-1693
www.isaacschools.org
Butler ES 800/K-5
3843 W Roosevelt St 85009 602-442-2300
Nathan Dettmar, prin. Fax 442-2399
Coe ES 800/K-5
3801 W Roanoke Ave 85009 602-442-2400
Chelsia Stallworth, prin. Fax 442-2499
Esperanza ES 400/K-5
3025 W McDowell Rd 85009 602-442-2800
Dr. Kristen Robertson, prin. Fax 442-2899
Isaac MS 800/6-8
3402 W McDowell Rd 85009 602-455-6800
Dr. Robyn Mondragon, prin. Fax 455-6899
Mitchell ES 600/K-5
1700 N 41st Ave 85009 602-442-2600
Sylvia Carrizoza, prin. Fax 442-2699
Moya ES 500/K-5
406 N 41st Ave 85009 602-442-3100
Cindy Sanchez, prin. Fax 442-3199
Pueblo Del Sol S 1,000/K-8
3449 N 39th Ave 85019 602-455-6900
Armando Chavez, prin. Fax 484-4118
Sutton ES 800/K-5
1001 N 31st Ave 85009 602-442-3200
Dr. Randy Martinez, prin. Fax 442-3299
Tarver Preschool 100/PK-PK
3101 W McDowell Rd 85009 602-442-2900
Linda Washington, dir. Fax 442-2999
Udall MS 700/6-8
3715 W Roosevelt St 85009 602-442-2700
Rafael Sanchez, prin. Fax 442-2799
Zito ES 700/K-5
4525 W Encanto Blvd 85035 602-442-2500
Gerard Hernandez, prin. Fax 442-2599

Kyrene ESD 28
Supt. — See Tempe
Kyrene Akimel A-al MS 1,100/6-8
2720 E Liberty Ln 85048 480-541-5800
Stephanie Phillips, prin. Fax 541-5810
Kyrene Altadena MS 1,100/6-8
14620 S Desert Foothills 85048 480-541-6000
James Martin, prin. Fax 541-6010
Kyrene Centennial MS 1,000/6-8
13808 S 36th St 85044 480-541-6400
Michelle Anderson, prin. Fax 541-6410
Kyrene de la Colina ES 600/K-5
13612 S 36th St 85044 480-541-2600
Kelley Brunner, prin. Fax 541-2610
Kyrene de la Esperanza ES 600/K-5
14841 S 41st Pl 85044 480-541-2800
Cheryl Greene, prin. Fax 541-2810
Kyrene de la Estrella ES 400/K-5
2620 E Liberty Ln 85048 480-541-3000
Michael Lamp, prin. Fax 541-3010
Kyrene de la Sierra ES 600/K-5
1122 E Liberty Ln 85048 480-541-5200
Lisa Connor, prin. Fax 541-5210
Kyrene de las Lomas ES 700/PK-5
11820 S Warner Elliot Loop 85044 480-541-3400
Brian Gibson, prin. Fax 541-3410
Kyrene del Milenio ES 700/K-5
4630 E Frye Rd 85048 480-541-4000
Jaimie Weinberger, prin. Fax 541-4010
Kyrene de los Cerritos ES 500/PK-5
14620 S Desert Foothills 85048 480-541-2200
Darcy DiCosmo, prin. Fax 541-2210
Kyrene de los Lagos ES 500/K-5
17001 S 34th Way 85048 480-541-3200
Ana Gomez Del Castillo, prin. Fax 541-3210
Kyrene Monte Vista ES 500/K-5
15221 S Ray Rd 85048 480-541-4400
Suzanne Ramundo, prin. Fax 541-4410

Laveen ESD 59
Supt. — See Laveen
Cash ES 600/PK-8
3851 W Roeser Rd 85041 602-237-9120
Lisa Sandomir, prin. Fax 237-9133

Madison ESD 38 5,900/PK-8
5601 N 16th St 85016 602-664-7900
Quinn Kellis Ed.D., supt. Fax 664-7999
www.madisonaz.org
Madison # 1 MS 900/5-8
5525 N 16th St 85016 602-664-7100
Pam Warren, prin. Fax 664-7199
Madison Camelview ES 700/PK-4
2002 E Campbell Ave 85016 602-664-7200
Hilary O'Brien, prin. Fax 664-7299
Madison Heights ES 500/PK-4
7150 N 22nd St 85020 602-664-7800
Priscilla Gossett, prin. Fax 664-7899
Madison Meadows MS 800/5-8
225 W Ocotillo Rd 85013 602-664-7600
Pat Carney, prin. Fax 664-7699
Madison Park MS 400/5-8
1431 E Campbell Ave 85014 602-664-7500
Sandy Kennedy, prin. Fax 664-7599
Madison Rose Lane ES 800/PK-4
1155 E Rose Ln 85014 602-664-7400
Dr. Peter Morkert, prin. Fax 664-7499
Madison Simis ES 1,000/PK-4
7302 N 10th St 85020 602-664-7300
Dr. Joyce Flowers, prin. Fax 664-7399
Madison Traditional Academy 700/PK-8
925 E Maryland Ave 85014 602-745-4000
Mike Duff, prin.

Murphy ESD 21 1,900/K-8
2615 W Buckeye Rd 85009 602-353-5004
Jose Diaz M.A., supt. Fax 353-5081
www.msdaz.org
Garcia S 600/K-8
1441 S 27th Ave 85009 602-353-5117
Takesha Turner M.A., prin. Fax 353-5189
Hamilton S 400/K-8
2020 W Durango St 85009 602-353-5323
Erik Haarstad M.A., prin. Fax 353-5388
Kuban S 400/K-8
3201 W Sherman St 85009 602-353-5448
Jose Trevizo M.A., prin. Fax 353-5479
Sullivan S 600/K-8
2 N 31st Ave 85009 602-353-5221
Ruben Ruiz M.A., prin. Fax 353-5284

Osborn ESD 8 3,000/PK-8
1226 W Osborn Rd 85013 602-707-2000
Michael Robert, supt. Fax 707-2040
www.osbornnet.org
Clarendon ES 400/4-6
1225 W Clarendon Ave 85013 602-707-2200
Theresa Nickolich, prin. Fax 707-2240
Encanto PS 700/PK-3
1420 W Osborn Rd 85013 602-707-2300
Felipe Carranza, prin. Fax 707-2340
Longview ES 700/PK-6
1209 E Indian School Rd 85014 602-707-2700
Benjamin Smith, prin. Fax 707-2740
Osborn MS 600/7-8
1102 W Highland Ave 85013 602-707-2400
Shannon Mann, prin. Fax 707-2440
Solano ES 600/PK-6
1526 W Missouri Ave 85015 602-707-2600
Renee Hamill, prin. Fax 707-2640

Paradise Valley USD 32,000/PK-12
15002 N 32nd St 85032 602-449-2000
James P. Lee Ed.D., supt. Fax 449-2005
www.pvschools.net
Aire Libre ES 400/K-6
16428 N 21st St 85022 602-449-5400
Janice Moore, prin. Fax 449-5405
Arrowhead ES 500/K-6
3820 E Nisbet Rd 85032 602-449-2700
Kristi Williams, prin. Fax 449-2705
Boulder Creek ES 700/K-6
22801 N 22nd St 85024 602-449-4500
Melissa Molzhon, prin. Fax 449-4505
Cactus View ES 700/PK-6
17602 N Central Ave 85022 602-449-2500
Shannon Sherwood, prin. Fax 449-2505
Campo Bello ES 500/K-6
2650 E Contention Mine Rd 85032 602-449-5200
Jerry Withers, prin. Fax 449-5205
Desert Trails ES 500/K-6
4315 E Cashman Dr 85050 602-449-4100
Sheri Duggan, prin. Fax 449-4105
Eagle Ridge ES 600/K-6
19801 N 13th St 85024 602-449-5700
Allison Barbor, prin. Fax 449-5705
Echo Mountain IS 400/4-6
1811 E Michigan Ave Ste 6 85022 602-449-5600
Elizabeth Schrey, prin. Fax 449-5605
Echo Mountain PS 600/K-3
1750 E Grovers Ave 85022 602-449-5500
Natalie Wilcox, prin. Fax 449-5505
Explorer MS 800/7-8
22401 N 40th St 85050 602-449-4200
Kyle Shappee, prin. Fax 449-4205
Greenway MS 500/7-8
3002 E Nisbet Rd 85032 602-449-2400
Dr. Ibi Haghighat, prin. Fax 449-2405
Hidden Hills ES 500/K-6
1919 E Sharon Dr 85022 602-449-3100
Elaine Murray, prin. Fax 449-3105
Indian Bend ES 600/K-6
3633 E Thunderbird Rd 85032 602-449-3200
Jan Stevens, prin. Fax 449-3205
Mercury Mine ES 600/K-6
9640 N 28th St 85028 602-449-3700
Donna Alley, prin. Fax 449-3705
Mountain Trail MS 800/7-8
2323 E Mountain Gate Pass 85024 602-449-4600
Craig Lahlum, prin. Fax 449-4605
Palomino IS 500/4-6
15815 N 29th St 85032 602-449-2900
Jenny Robles, prin. Fax 449-2905
Palomino PS 700/K-3
15833 N 29th St 85032 602-449-2800
Stephen Lee, prin. Fax 449-2805
Shea MS 600/7-8
2728 E Shea Blvd 85028 602-449-3500
Dan Knak, prin. Fax 449-3505
Sunset Canyon ES 500/PK-6
2727 E Siesta Ln 85050 602-449-5100
David Franks, prin. Fax 449-5105
Vista Verde MS 700/7-8
2826 E Grovers Ave 85032 602-449-5300
Andrea Hoffler, prin. Fax 449-5305
Wildfire ES 700/K-6
3997 E Lockwood Dr 85050 602-449-4300
Erin Vranesh, prin. Fax 449-4305
Other Schools – See Scottsdale

Pendergast ESD 92 9,800/PK-8
3802 N 91st Ave 85037 623-772-2200
Dr. Lily Matos DeBlieux, supt. Fax 877-8188
www.pesd92.org/
Amberlea ES 700/K-8
8455 W Virginia Ave 85037 623-772-2900
Marisol Silva, prin. Fax 594-2786
Copper King S 800/K-8
10730 W Campbell Ave 85037 623-772-2580
Janine Ambrose, prin. Fax 872-7769
Desert Horizon S 1,000/PK-8
8525 W Osborn Rd 85037 623-772-2430
Debby Cruz, prin. Fax 873-4691
Pendergast S 800/K-8
3800 N 91st Ave 85037 623-772-2400
Mike Woolsey, prin. Fax 877-9591
Villa De Paz S 700/PK-8
4940 N 103rd Ave 85037 623-772-2490
Belinda Quezada, prin. Fax 877-8977
Westwind ES 1,100/PK-8
9040 W Campbell Ave 85037 623-772-2700
Rod Henkel, prin. Fax 772-8464
Other Schools – See Avondale, Glendale

Phoenix ESD 1 7,800/PK-8
1817 N 7th St 85006 602-257-3755
Larry Weeks, admin. Fax 257-3783
www.phxschools.org
Bethune S 500/PK-8
1310 S 15th Ave 85007 602-257-3830
Dr. Ronnie Pitre, prin. Fax 257-2915
Capitol S 600/PK-8
330 N 16th Ave 85007 602-257-3835
Russell Sanders, prin. Fax 257-6397
Dunbar S 300/PK-8
707 W Grant St 85007 602-257-3844
Gina Millsaps, prin. Fax 257-3874
Edison S 600/PK-8
804 N 18th St 85006 602-257-3848
Fred Graef, prin. Fax 257-3704
Emerson ES 500/PK-6
915 E Palm Ln 85006 602-257-3853
Lucia Raz, prin. Fax 257-3937
Faith North Montessori S 300/PK-PK
910 E Washington St 85034 602-257-3901
Garthanne DeOcampo, prin. Fax 257-3926
Garfield S 400/PK-8
811 N 13th St 85006 602-257-3863
Sylvia Bernal, prin. Fax 257-4866
Heard S 700/PK-8
2301 W Thomas Rd 85015 602-257-3880
Zariffe Magana, prin. Fax 257-3881
Herrera S 700/K-8
1350 S 11th St 85034 602-257-3885
Kevin Sotomayor, prin. Fax 257-3952
Kenilworth S 600/PK-8
1210 N 5th Ave 85003 602-257-3889
Anthony Pietrangeli, prin. Fax 257-3923
Lowell S 600/PK-8
1121 S 3rd Ave 85003 602-257-3902
Tyson Kelly, prin. Fax 257-6396
Magnet Traditional S 500/K-8
2602 N 23rd Ave 85009 602-257-6281
Adrian Walker, prin. Fax 257-6287
Shaw S 400/PK-8
123 N 13th St 85034 602-257-3914
Susan Engdall, prin. Fax 257-2954
Whittier S 500/PK-8
2000 N 16th St 85006 602-257-3925
Clare Okyere, prin. Fax 257-3924

Riverside ESD 2 900/PK-8
1414 S 51st Ave 85043 602-477-8900
Jaime Rivera Ed.D., supt. Fax 272-8378
resdonline.org
Kings Ridge Preparatory Academy 400/5-8
3650 S 64th Ln 85043 602-477-8960
Barbara Bagwill, prin. Fax 936-5531
Riverside Traditional ES 500/PK-4
1414 S 51st Ave 85043 602-272-1339
Marcus Pina, prin. Fax 477-8921

Roosevelt ESD 66 9,700/PK-8
6000 S 7th St 85042 602-243-4800
Dr. Dino Coronado, supt. Fax 243-2637
roosevelt66.schoolwires.net
Barr S 500/K-8
2041 E Vineyard Rd 85042 602-232-4900
Milinda Crawford, prin. Fax 243-2116
Black S 900/K-8
6550 S 27th Ave 85041 602-304-3180
Audra Gibson, prin. Fax 304-3185
Bush S 400/K-8
602 E Siesta Dr 85042 602-232-4260
Lisa Norwood, prin. Fax 243-4932
Campbell S 600/K-8
2624 E South Mountain Ave 85042 602-304-3170
William Collins, prin. Fax 304-3182
Chavez Community S 400/K-8
4001 S 3rd St 85040 602-232-4940
Andrea Groeninger, prin. Fax 305-4678
Conchos S 400/K-8
1718 W Vineyard Rd 85041 602-232-4250
Dr. Benjamin Roat, prin. Fax 243-4969
Davis S 500/K-8
6209 S 15th Ave 85041 602-232-4930
Evelyn Garcia, prin. Fax 232-4280
Greenfield MS 600/4-8
7009 S 10th St 85042 602-232-4240
Stuart Starky, prin. Fax 243-4973
Jorgensen S 500/PK-8
1701 W Roeser Rd 85041 602-232-4990
Dr. Joyce Luckie, prin. Fax 243-4989
Julian S 800/K-8
2149 E Carver Dr 85040 602-232-4950
Nicole Shamblin, prin. Fax 243-4906

Kennedy ES 500/K-3
6825 S 10th St 85042 602-232-4220
Lindsay Gaynier, prin. Fax 243-4939
King ECC, 4615 S 22nd St 85040 100/PK-PK
Jack Day, prin. 602-232-4910
Lassen S 500/K-8
909 W Vineyard Rd 85041 602-232-4210
Aida Frietz, prin. Fax 232-4291
Lopez S 500/K-8
4610 S 12th St 85040 602-232-4920
Megan Gestson, prin. Fax 243-4961
Pastor S 700/K-8
2101 W Alta Vista Rd 85041 602-304-3160
Stephanie Acosta, prin. Fax 304-3169
Southwest S 500/K-8
1111 W Dobbins Rd 85041 602-232-4270
Juan Sierra, prin. Fax 243-4933
Sunland S 600/K-8
5401 S 7th Ave 85041 602-232-4960
Raymond Gardea, prin. Fax 243-2125
Valley View S 600/K-8
8220 S 7th Ave 85041 602-232-4980
Bryce McClellan, prin. Fax 243-4926

Scottsdale USD 48
Supt. — See Scottsdale
Hopi ES 900/K-5
5110 E Lafayette Blvd 85018 480-484-2000
Tamara Jagodzinski, prin. Fax 484-2001
Ingleside MS 700/6-8
5402 E Osborn Rd 85018 480-484-4900
Dr. Christopher Thuman, prin. Fax 484-4901
Tavan ES 700/K-5
4610 E Osborn Rd 85018 480-484-3500
Margaret Serna, prin. Fax 484-3501

Tempe ESD 3
Supt. — See Tempe
Nevitt ES 700/PK-5
4525 E Saint Anne Ave 85042 602-431-6640
Vernice Sharpe, prin. Fax 431-6887

Tolleson ESD 17
Supt. — See Tolleson
Desert Oasis ES 800/PK-8
8802 W McDowell Rd 85037 623-533-3901
Claudia Espinoza, prin. Fax 533-3902
Sheely Farms ES 800/PK-8
9450 W Encanto Blvd 85037 623-907-5270
Christina Boston, prin. Fax 907-5271

Washington ESD 6
Supt. — See Glendale
Acacia ES 800/PK-6
3021 W Evans Dr 85053 602-896-5000
Christine Hollingsworth, prin. Fax 896-5020
Alta Vista ES 600/K-6
8710 N 31st Ave 85051 602-347-2000
Cody Riding, prin. Fax 347-2020
Cactus Wren ES 500/PK-6
9650 N 39th Ave 85051 602-347-2100
Kaylene Ashbridge, prin. Fax 347-2120
Chaparral ES 500/PK-6
3808 W Joan De Arc Ave 85029 602-896-5300
Jaclyn Farrer, prin. Fax 896-5320
Cholla MS 700/7-8
3120 W Cholla St 85029 602-896-5400
Phil Garitson, prin. Fax 896-5420
Desert Foothills JHS 700/7-8
3333 W Banff Ln 85053 602-896-5500
Susan Smith, prin. Fax 896-5520
Desert View ES 500/PK-5
8621 N 3rd St 85020 602-347-4000
Maria Farmer, prin. Fax 347-4020
Ironwood ES 600/PK-6
14850 N 39th Ave 85053 602-896-5600
Polly Schultz, prin. Fax 896-5620
Jacobs ES 600/K-6
14421 N 23rd Ave 85023 602-896-5700
Pam Wright, prin. Fax 896-5720
Lakeview ES 500/K-6
3040 W Yucca St 85029 602-896-5800
Tim Woodward, prin. Fax 896-5820
Lookout Mountain ES 900/K-6
15 W Coral Gables Dr 85023 602-896-5900
Tricia Heller-Johnson, prin. Fax 896-5920
Manzanita ES 800/K-6
8430 N 39th Ave 85051 602-347-2200
Darcy Estrada, prin. Fax 347-2220
Maryland S 900/K-8
6503 N 21st Ave 85015 602-347-2300
Nick Gupton, prin. Fax 347-2320
Miller ES 600/K-5
2021 W Alice Ave 85021 602-347-3000
Amanda Wilber, prin. Fax 347-3020
Moon Mountain ES 800/PK-6
13425 N 19th Ave 85029 602-896-6000
Sue Brown, prin. Fax 896-6020
Mountain Sky JHS 700/7-8
16225 N 7th Ave 85023 602-896-6100
Perry Mason, prin. Fax 896-6120
Mountain View S 1,500/K-8
801 W Peoria Ave 85029 602-347-4100
Jill Sarraino, prin. Fax 347-4120
Ocotillo ES 800/K-6
3225 W Ocotillo Rd 85017 602-347-2400
Dr. Steve Murosky, prin. Fax 347-2420
Palo Verde MS 900/7-8
7502 N 39th Ave 85051 602-347-2500
Mark Culbertson, prin. Fax 347-2520
Roadrunner ES 800/K-6
7702 N 39th Ave 85051 602-347-3100
Paula McWhirter, prin. Fax 347-3120
Sahuaro ES 600/PK-6
12835 N 33rd Ave 85029 602-896-6200
Deborah Menendez, prin. Fax 896-6220
Shaw Butte ES 1,100/PK-6
12202 N 21st Ave 85029 602-347-4200
Tracy Maynard, prin. Fax 347-4220
Sunnyslope S 800/K-8
245 E Mountain View Rd 85020 602-347-4300
Chance Whiteman, prin. Fax 347-4320

Tumbleweed ES 500/PK-6
4001 W Laurel Ln 85029 602-896-6600
Heather Vasquez, prin. Fax 896-6620
Washington ES 1,000/PK-6
8033 N 27th Ave 85051 602-347-3400
Sean Carney, prin. Fax 347-3420

Wilson ESD 7 1,300/PK-8
3025 E Fillmore St 85008 602-681-2200
Antonio Sanchez, supt. Fax 275-7517
www.wsd.k12.az.us
Wilson MS 600/4-8
2929 E Fillmore St 85008 602-683-2400
Cindy Campton, prin. Fax 275-8677
Wilson PS 600/PK-3
415 N 30th St 85008 602-683-2500
Nick Attridge, prin. Fax 231-0567

All Saints' Episcopal Day S 500/PK-8
6300 N Central Ave 85012 602-274-4866
Leo Dressel, head sch Fax 274-0365
Arizona Cultural Academy & College Prep 300/PK-12
7810 S 42nd Pl 85042 602-454-1222
Christ Lutheran S 500/PK-8
3901 E Indian School Rd 85018 602-957-7010
Jonathan Doyle, prin. Fax 955-8073
Emmaus Lutheran S 100/PK-8
3841 W Sweetwater Ave 85029 602-843-3853
Andy Plocher, prin. Fax 942-4924
Family of Christ Lutheran S 100/PK-K
3501 E Chandler Blvd 85048 480-759-4047
Sue Nelson, dir. Fax 759-9004
Gateway Academy 50/K-12
3939 E Shea Blvd 85028 480-998-1071
Glenview Adventist Academy 100/PK-8
6801 N 43rd Ave 85019 623-931-1846
Brian Allison, prin. Fax 209-0334
Most Holy Trinity Catholic S 100/PK-8
535 E Alice Ave 85020 602-943-9058
Maggie MacCleary, prin. Fax 943-3188
91st Psalm Christian S 100/PK-12
2020 E Baseline Rd 85042 602-243-1900
Rob Arthurs, prin. Fax 243-5919
North Valley Christian Academy 100/PK-12
33655 N 27th Dr 85085 623-551-3454
Nate Kretzmann M.Ed., dir. Fax 551-4067
Northwest Christian S 1,300/PK-12
16401 N 43rd Ave 85053 602-978-5134
Geoffrey Brown, supt. Fax 978-5804
Paradise Valley Christian College Prep S 300/PK-12
11875 N 24th St 85028 602-992-8140
Sheryl Temple M.A., hdmstr. Fax 992-8152
Phoenix Christian Preparatory S 300/PK-12
1751 W Indian School Rd 85015 602-265-4707
Joe Bradley, pres. Fax 277-7170
Phoenix Christian S Pre K-8 100/PK-8
2425 N 26th St 85008 602-956-9330
Sue Vander Ploeg M.Ed., prin. Fax 956-4207
Phoenix Hebrew Academy 200/PK-8
515 E Bethany Home Rd 85012 602-277-7479
St. Agnes Catholic S 200/PK-8
2311 E Palm Ln 85006 602-244-1451
Christine Tax, prin. Fax 286-0250
St. Catherine of Siena Catholic S 200/PK-8
6413 S Central Ave 85042 602-276-2241
Patrick Reardon, prin. Fax 268-7886
St. Francis Xavier Catholic S 600/PK-8
4715 N Central Ave 85012 602-266-5364
Kimberly Cavnar, prin. Fax 279-0423
St. Gregory Catholic S 300/PK-8
3440 N 18th Ave 85015 602-266-9527
Maureen DeGrose, prin. Fax 266-4055
St. Jerome Catholic S 300/PK-8
10815 N 35th Ave 85029 602-942-5644
Javier Bravo, prin. Fax 467-4929
St. Joan of Arc Catholic Preschool 100/PK-PK
3801 E Greenway Rd 85032 602-867-9179
Debbie Hilliard, dir. Fax 482-7930
St. John Bosco Catholic S 500/PK-8
16035 S 48th St 85048 480-219-4848
Anita Petitti, prin. Fax 219-5767
St. Matthew Catholic S 200/K-8
320 N 20th Dr 85009 602-254-0611
Michael Guerra, prin. Fax 393-7813
St. Theresa Catholic S 500/PK-8
5001 E Thomas Rd 85018 602-840-0010
Dr. Thomas Dertinger, prin. Fax 840-8323
St. Thomas the Apostle Catholic S 500/PK-8
4510 N 24th St 85016 602-954-9088
Mary Coffman, prin. Fax 381-3256
St. Vincent De Paul Catholic S 500/PK-8
3130 N 51st Ave 85031 623-247-8595
Enrique Diaz, prin. Fax 245-0132
Scottsdale Christian Academy 800/PK-12
14400 N Tatum Blvd 85032 602-992-5100
Brent Hodges, supt. Fax 992-0575
SS. Simon and Jude Cathedral Catholic S 500/PK-8
6351 N 27th Ave 85017 602-242-1299
Sr. Raphael Quinn, prin. Fax 433-7608
Summit S of Ahwatukee 300/PK-8
4515 E Muirwood Dr 85048 480-403-9500
Mark Bistricky, head sch Fax 403-9599
Torah Day S of Phoenix 200/PK-8
1118 W Glendale Ave 85021 602-374-3062
Rabbi Shmuel Field, prin. Fax 374-3110

Picacho, Pinal, Pop. 463
Picacho ESD 33 200/K-8
17865 S Vail Rd, 520-466-7942
Allen Rogers, supt. Fax 466-7165
www.picacho.k12.az.us
Picacho S 200/K-8
17865 S Vail Rd, 520-466-7942
Allen Rogers, prin. Fax 466-7165

Pima, Graham, Pop. 2,335
Pima USD 6 800/K-12
PO Box 429 85543 928-387-8000
Sean Rickert, supt. Fax 387-8020
www.pimaschools.org
Pima ES 400/K-6
PO Box 429 85543 928-387-8050
Eddy Carlton, prin. Fax 387-8022
Pima JHS 100/7-8
PO Box 429 85543 928-387-8100
Mark Squires, prin. Fax 387-8020

Pine, Gila, Pop. 1,936
Pine Strawberry ESD 12 100/PK-8
PO Box 1150 85544 928-476-3283
Kathlene Thomson, supt. Fax 476-2506
www.pineesd.org
Pine Strawberry S 100/PK-8
PO Box 1150 85544 928-476-3283
Kathlene Thomson, admin. Fax 476-2506

Pinon, Navajo, Pop. 897
Pinon USD 4 1,300/PK-12
PO Box 839 86510 928-725-3450
Chris Ostgaard, supt. Fax 725-2123
www.pusdatsa.org
Pinon ES 600/K-5
PO Box 839 86510 928-725-2201
Dr. Connie WIlliams, prin. Fax 725-2270
Pinon MS 300/6-8
PO Box 839 86510 928-725-2300
Lori Chee, prin. Fax 725-2370

Pirtleville, Cochise, Pop. 1,741
Douglas USD 27
Supt. — See Douglas
Faras ES 200/PK-5
410 W Fir Ave 85626 520-364-8461
Fernando Morales, prin. Fax 805-4148

Pomerene, Cochise
Pomerene ESD 64 100/K-8
PO Box 7 85627 520-586-2407
Michael Sherman, supt. Fax 586-7724
www.pomereneschool.org/
Pomerene S 100/K-8
PO Box 7 85627 520-586-2407
Michael Sherman, prin. Fax 586-7724

Prescott, Yavapai, Pop. 39,213
Prescott USD 1 3,400/PK-12
146 S Granite St 86303 928-445-5400
Joe Howard, supt. Fax 776-0243
www.prescottschools.com
Discovery Gardens ECC 50/PK-PK
300 E Gurley St 86301 928-442-1283
Stacy Williams, dir. Fax 442-9268
Granite Mountain MS 200/5-6
1800 N Williamson Valley Rd 86305 928-717-3253
Teresa Bruso, prin. Fax 717-3284
Hicks ES 400/K-4
1845 Campbell Ave 86301 928-717-3276
Brian Moore, prin. Fax 717-3275
Judd ES 400/K-4
1749 N Williamson Valley Rd 86305 928-717-3263
Clark Tenney, prin. Fax 717-3262
Lincoln S 300/K-4
201 Park Ave 86303 928-717-3249
Karen Hughes, prin. Fax 717-3248
Prescott Mile High MS 400/7-8
300 S Granite St 86303 928-717-3241
Mark Goligoski, prin. Fax 717-3298

Christian Academy of Prescott 100/PK-8
148 S Marina St 86303 928-445-2565
Susan B. Neil, head sch Fax 445-2563
Prescott Adventist Christian S 50/K-8
2980 Willow Creek Rd 86301 928-445-3663
Shannon Kaneshiro, prin. Fax 776-0650
Sacred Heart Catholic S 200/PK-8
131 N Summit Ave 86301 928-445-2621
Pamela Dickerson, prin. Fax 445-0966
Trinity Christian S 200/K-12
1077 Mogollon Rd 86301 928-445-6306
Kyle Maestri, hdmstr. Fax 445-7210

Prescott Valley, Yavapai, Pop. 38,121
Humboldt USD 22 5,800/PK-12
6411 N Robert Rd 86314 928-759-4000
Daniel Streeter, supt. Fax 759-4020
www.humboldtunified.com
Bright Futures Preschool 100/PK-PK
6411 N Robert Rd 86314 928-759-5130
Stephanie Rowe, prin. Fax 759-5132
Coyote Springs ES 600/K-6
6625 N Cattletrack Rd 86314 928-759-4300
Candice Blakely Stump, prin. Fax 759-4320
Glassford Hill MS 400/7-8
6901 Panther Path 86314 928-759-4600
Melissa Tannehill, prin. Fax 759-4620
Granville ES 600/K-6
5250 N Stover Dr 86314 928-759-4800
Sara Schnoor, prin. Fax 759-4820
Lake Valley ES 500/K-6
3900 N Starlight Dr 86314 928-759-4200
Aimee Fleming, prin. Fax 759-4220
Liberty Traditional S 800/K-8
3300 N Lake Valley Rd 86314 928-759-4500
Danette Derickson, prin. Fax 759-4520
Mountain View ES 600/K-6
8601 E Loos Dr 86314 928-759-4700
JoAnne Bindell, prin. Fax 759-4720
Other Schools – See Dewey, Humboldt

Quartzsite, LaPaz, Pop. 3,625
Quartzsite ESD 4
Supt. — See Ehrenberg
Quartzsite ES 100/3-8
930 Quail Trail 85359 928-927-5500
Dr. Raquel Burton, admin. Fax 927-7227

Queen Creek, Maricopa, Pop. 25,755
Chandler USD 80
Supt. — See Chandler
Auxier ES K-6
22700 S Power Rd, 480-424-8400
Tony Smith, prin. Fax 424-8420
Payne JHS 1,400/7-8
7655 S Higley Rd, 480-224-2400
Paul Bollard, prin. Fax 224-2420

Higley USD 60
Supt. — See Gilbert
Cortina ES 900/K-6
19680 S 188th St, 480-279-7800
Dan Cover, prin. Fax 279-7805
Sossaman Early Child Development Center 100/PK-PK
18655 E Jacaranda Blvd, 480-279-8600
Patti Gleason, dir. Fax 279-8605
Sossaman MS 900/7-8
18655 E Jacaranda Blvd, 480-279-8500
John Dolan, prin. Fax 279-8505

Queen Creek USD 95 4,700/PK-12
20217 E Chandler Heights Rd 85142 480-987-5935
Dr. Perry Berry, supt. Fax 987-9714
www.qcusd.org/
Barnes ES 400/K-5
20750 S 214th St, 480-987-7400
Laura Valenciano, prin. Fax 987-7415
Barney MS 800/6-8
24937 S Sossaman Rd, 480-474-6700
Denise Johnson, prin. Fax 882-3181
Brandon-Pickett ES 500/K-5
22076 Village Loop, 480-987-7420
Sherry Towns, prin. Fax 987-7439
Desert Mountain ES 400/K-5
22301 S Hawes Rd, 480-987-5912
James Richardson, prin. Fax 987-5914
Queen Creek ES 500/PK-5
23636 S 204th St, 480-987-5920
Julie Oster, prin. Fax 987-0612
Queen Creek MS 300/6-8
20435 S Old Ellsworth Rd, 480-987-5940
Joseph McKnight, prin. Fax 987-5947
Other Schools – See Mesa

Ambassador Christian Academy 100/K-12
19248 E San Tan Blvd, 480-387-0902
Amy Crislip, admin. Fax 452-0316
Freedom Christian Academy 100/PK-12
39731 N Kennedy Dr, 480-987-5488
Ben Koshtaka, admin. Fax 987-9344

Red Rock, Pinal, Pop. 165
Red Rock ESD 5 300/PK-8
PO Box 1010, 520-682-3331
Peter Dwyer, admin. Fax 917-7310
redrockschools.com
Red Rock S 300/PK-8
PO Box 1010, 520-682-3331
Peter Dwyer, admin. Fax 917-7310

Rimrock, Yavapai
Beaver Creek ESD 26 300/PK-8
4810 E Beaver Creek Rd 86335 928-567-4631
Karin Ward, supt. Fax 567-5347
www.bcs.k12.az.us
Beaver Creek S 300/PK-8
4810 E Beaver Creek Rd 86335 928-567-4631
Katrina Sacco, prin. Fax 567-5347

Rio Rico, Santa Cruz, Pop. 18,904
Santa Cruz Valley USD 35 3,000/PK-12
1374 W Frontage Rd 85648 520-281-8282
David Verdugo, supt. Fax 281-7093
www.scv35.org
Calabasas S 500/PK-8
1374 W Frontage Rd 85648 520-375-8600
John Fanning, prin. Fax 375-8690
Coatimundi MS 400/6-8
1374 W Frontage Rd 85648 520-375-8800
Rebekah Cabrera, prin. Fax 761-4669
Mountain View ES 500/K-5
1374 W Frontage Rd 85648 520-375-8400
Chris Jackson, prin. Fax 281-7990
San Cayetano ES 600/K-5
1374 W Frontage Rd 85648 520-375-8300
Mimi Renteria, prin. Fax 281-7973

Roll, Yuma
Mohawk Valley ESD 17 200/K-8
5151 S Avenue 39 E 85347 928-785-4942
Shanna Johnson, supt. Fax 785-4946
www.mohawkvalleyschool.org
Mohawk Valley S 200/K-8
5151 S Avenue 39 E 85347 928-785-4942
Shanna Johnson, admin. Fax 785-9496

Round Rock, Apache, Pop. 784
Red Mesa USD 27
Supt. — See Teec Nos Pos
Round Rock S 100/K-8
PO Box CC 86547 928-787-4530
Wanda Burton, prin. Fax 787-4500

Sacaton, Pinal, Pop. 2,641
Sacaton ESD 18 400/PK-8
PO Box 98, 520-562-8600
Cherryl Paul, supt. Fax 763-4410
www.sacatonschools.org
Sacaton ES 300/PK-4
PO Box 98, 520-562-8600
Leslie Rychel, prin. Fax 763-4430
Sacaton MS 200/5-8
PO Box 98, 520-562-8600
Philip Bonds, prin. Fax 763-4420

Safford, Graham, Pop. 9,405
Safford USD 1 3,300/PK-12
734 W 11th St 85546 928-348-7000
Ken VanWinkle, supt. Fax 348-7001
www.saffordusd.com
Nelson ES 600/K-6
1100 S 10th Ave 85546 928-348-7020
D'Anna O'Mera, prin. Fax 348-7021
Powell ES 600/K-6
1041 S 14th Ave 85546 928-348-7030
Naomi Lowery, prin. Fax 348-7031
Safford MS 500/7-8
612 W 11th St 85546 928-348-7040
Clay Emery, prin. Fax 348-7041
Stinson ES 700/PK-6
2013 S 8th Ave 85546 928-348-7010
Michael Moreno, prin. Fax 348-7011

Sahuarita, Pima, Pop. 24,638
Sahuarita USD 30 5,700/PK-12
350 W Sahuarita Rd 85629 520-625-3502
Dr. Manuel Valenzuela, supt. Fax 625-4609
www.susd30.us
Anza Trail S 1,300/K-8
350 W Sahuarita Rd 85629 520-625-3502
Darlene Robinson, prin. Fax 398-7121
Copper View ES 500/K-5
350 W Sahuarita Rd 85629 520-625-3502
Desi Raulston, prin. Fax 625-5380
ECC PK-PK
350 W Sahuarita Rd 85629 520-625-3502
Cheryl McGlothen, dir. Fax 393-7035
Sahuarita IS 600/3-5
350 W Sahuarita Rd 85629 520-625-3502
Clarisa Nido, prin. Fax 648-6181
Sahuarita MS 600/6-8
350 W Sahuarita Rd 85629 520-625-3502
Stephanie Silman, prin. Fax 620-9761
Sahuarita PS 700/PK-2
350 W Sahuarita Rd 85629 520-625-3502
Tina Anderson, prin. Fax 393-7036
Other Schools – See Amado

Saint David, Cochise, Pop. 1,668
Saint David USD 21 400/PK-12
PO Box 70 85630 520-720-4781
Mark Goodman, supt. Fax 720-4783
www.stdavidschools.org/
Saint David S 300/PK-8
PO Box 70 85630 520-720-4781
Andrew Brogan, prin. Fax 720-4783

Saint Johns, Apache, Pop. 3,399
Saint Johns USD 1 800/K-12
PO Box 3030 85936 928-337-2255
Ed Burgoyne, supt. Fax 337-2263
www.sjusd.net
Coronado ES 200/K-3
PO Box 609 85936 928-337-4435
Bryan Hollembeak, prin. Fax 337-4930
Saint Johns MS 300/4-8
PO Box 3060 85936 928-337-2132
Tim Raban, prin. Fax 337-3147

Saint Michaels, Apache, Pop. 1,404

St. Michael Indian S 300/PK-12
PO Box 650 86511 505-979-5590
Tom Sorci, prin. Fax 979-5590

Salome, LaPaz, Pop. 1,511
Salome Consolidated ESD 30 100/PK-8
PO Box 339 85348 928-859-3339
George Dean, admin. Fax 859-3085
www.salomek8.org
Salome ES 100/PK-8
PO Box 339 85348 928-859-3339
George Dean, admin. Fax 859-3085

San Carlos, Gila, Pop. 4,011
San Carlos USD 20 1,400/PK-12
PO Box 207 85550 928-475-2315
Debroah Dennison Ph.D., supt. Fax 475-2301
www.sancarlosbraves.org
Rice ES 900/PK-6
PO Box 207 85550 928-475-2315
Durena Thompson, prin. Fax 475-5944

St. Charles S 100/K-6
PO Box 339 85550 928-475-2449
Ina Salter, prin. Fax 475-2050

Sanders, Apache, Pop. 600
Sanders USD 18 800/K-12
PO Box 250 86512 928-688-4750
Dan Hute, supt. Fax 688-4723
www.sandersusd.net
Sanders ES 300/K-5
PO Box 250 86512 928-688-3850
Gregory Lelvis, prin. Fax 688-3888
Sanders MS 200/6-8
PO Box 250 86512 928-688-4770
Sheryl Soderstrom, prin. Fax 688-4776

San Luis, Yuma, Pop. 25,496
Gadsden ESD 32 5,300/PK-8
PO Box 6870 85349 928-627-6540
Dr. Raymond Aguilera, supt. Fax 627-3635
www.gesd32.org/
Arizona Desert ES 700/K-6
PO Box 6870 85349 928-627-6940
Lizette Esparza, prin. Fax 627-4692
Chavez ES 800/K-6
PO Box 6870 85349 928-627-6958
Bethany Loucks, prin. Fax 627-4480
Desert View ES 800/K-6
PO Box 6870 85349 928-627-6915
Meredith Nelson, prin. Fax 627-1190
Pastor ES 300/K-6
PO Box 6870 85349 928-627-6980
Maria Camacho, prin. Fax 722-0086
Rio Colorado ES 700/K-6
PO Box 6870 85349 928-627-6902
Alma Castillo, prin. Fax 627-9717
San Luis MS 700/7-8
PO Box 6870 85349 928-627-6920
Norma Sanchez, prin. Fax 627-9339
San Luis Preschool 100/PK-PK
PO Box 6870 85349 928-627-4774
Maria DeLaFuente, dir. Fax 627-9339
Southwest JHS 700/7-8
PO Box 6870 85349 928-627-6580
Omar Duron, prin. Fax 627-9266
Other Schools – See Gadsden

San Manuel, Pinal, Pop. 3,491
Mammoth-San Manuel USD 8 700/PK-12
PO Box 406 85631 520-385-2337
Julie Dale-Scott, supt. Fax 385-2621
www.msmusd.org
First Avenue ES 400/PK-6
PO Box 406 85631 520-385-4341
Katy Wilkins, prin. Fax 385-2118
Other Schools – See Mammoth

San Simon, Cochise, Pop. 160
San Simon USD 18 100/K-12
PO Box 38 85632 520-845-2275
Jonathan Truschke, supt. Fax 845-2480
www.sansimon.org
San Simon S 100/K-12
PO Box 38 85632 520-845-2275
Jonathan Truschke, admin. Fax 845-2480

San Tan Valley, Pinal, Pop. 79,014
Florence USD 1
Supt. — See Florence
Circle Cross Ranch S 800/K-8
35900 N Charbray Dr, 480-987-7600
Rebecca Hendry, prin. Fax 888-0349
Copper Basin S 700/PK-8
28682 N Main St, 480-888-7500
Scott Johnson, prin. Fax 888-2134
San Tan Heights S 700/PK-8
2500 W San Tan Heights Blvd, 480-888-7555
Greg Bellemare, prin. Fax 888-2932
Skyline Ranch S 700/K-8
1084 San Tan Hills Dr, 480-888-7520
Toby Haugen, prin. Fax 655-6136
Walker Butte S 900/K-8
29697 N Desert Willow Blvd, 480-987-5360
Rebeca Hendry, prin. Fax 987-5369

J.O. Combs USD 44 4,500/PK-12
301 E Combs Rd, 480-987-5300
Dr. Gayle A. Blanchard, supt. Fax 987-3487
www.jocombs.org
Combs MS 700/7-8
301 E Combs Rd, 480-882-3510
Laura Ridge, prin. Fax 888-8049
Combs Traditional Academy 200/K-6
301 E Combs Rd, 480-987-5320
Jeff Green, prin. Fax 987-5009
Ellsworth ES 700/PK-6
301 E Combs Rd, 480-882-3520
Santa Dunker, prin. Fax 987-8250
Harmon ES 600/K-6
301 E Combs Rd, 480-882-3500
Angie Beauchene, prin. Fax 888-9143
Ranch ES 500/PK-6
301 E Combs Rd, 480-882-3530
Sue Kruse, prin. Fax 655-6412
Simonton ES 600/PK-6
301 E Combs Rd, 480-987-5330
Chastity Cruz, prin. Fax 987-5281

Sasabe, Pima
San Fernando ESD 35 50/K-8
PO Box 80 85633 520-823-4243
Linda Arzoumanian, supt. Fax 823-4273
www.sanfernando35.org
San Fernando ES 50/K-8
PO Box 80 85633 520-823-4243
Tracy Banker-Murtadza, head sch Fax 823-4273

Scottsdale, Maricopa, Pop. 213,310
Cave Creek USD 93 5,400/PK-12
33016 N 60th St 85266 480-575-2000
Dr. Debbi Burdick, supt. Fax 488-7055
www.ccusd93.org
Black Mountain ES 500/PK-6
33606 N 60th St 85266 480-575-2100
Matthew Owsley, prin. Fax 488-6708
Desert Sun Academy 400/K-6
27880 N 64th Street 85262 480-575-2900
Aaron Bagwell, prin. Fax 502-2364
Other Schools – See Cave Creek, Phoenix

Paradise Valley USD
Supt. — See Phoenix
Copper Canyon ES 700/K-6
17650 N 54th St 85254 602-449-7200
Ann Furnish, prin. Fax 449-7205
Desert Shadows ES 500/PK-6
5902 E Sweetwater Ave 85254 602-449-6900
Chad Caudle, prin. Fax 449-6905
Desert Shadows MS 800/7-8
5858 E Sweetwater Ave 85254 602-449-6800
Derek Hummert, prin. Fax 449-6805
Grayhawk ES 700/K-6
7525 E Grayhawk Dr 85255 602-449-6600
Michelle Pavlik, prin. Fax 449-6605
Liberty ES 600/K-6
5125 E Marilyn Rd 85254 602-449-6200
Darlene Baumgartner, prin. Fax 449-6205
North Ranch ES 500/K-6
16406 N 61st Pl 85254 602-449-6400
Kenneth Spranger, prin. Fax 449-6405
Sunrise MS 600/7-8
4960 E Acoma Dr 85254 602-449-6100
Gregory Martin, prin. Fax 449-6105

Scottsdale USD 48 24,800/PK-12
8500 E Jackrabbit Rd 85250 480-484-6100
Dr. A. Denise Birdwell, supt. Fax 484-6287
www.susd.org
Anasazi ES 600/K-5
12121 N 124th St 85259 480-484-7300
Christopher Barnes, prin. Fax 484-7301
Cheyenne Traditional S 1,000/PK-8
13636 N 100th St 85260 480-484-5600
Grace Stombres, prin. Fax 484-5601
Cochise ES 600/PK-5
9451 N 84th St 85258 480-484-1100
Sheila Miller, prin. Fax 484-1101
Cocopah MS 900/6-8
6615 E Cholla St 85254 480-484-4400
Nick Noonan, prin. Fax 484-4401
Copper Ridge S 1,200/K-8
10101 E Thompson Peak Pkwy 85255 480-484-1500
Lindsay Stollar-Slover, prin. Fax 484-1501
Desert Canyon ES 500/K-5
10203 E McDowell Mtn Ranch 85255 480-484-1700
Kristin Kinghorn, prin. Fax 484-4602

Desert Canyon MS 600/6-8
10203 E McDowell Mtn Ranch 85255 480-484-4600
Dale Link, prin. Fax 484-4601
Echo Canyon ES 500/PK-8
4330 N 62nd St 85251 480-484-7500
Kathleen Hughes, prin. Fax 484-7501
Hohokam Traditional S 400/K-6
8451 E Oak St 85257 480-484-1800
Chuck Rantala, prin. Fax 484-1801
Laguna ES 600/PK-5
10475 E Lakeview Dr 85258 480-484-2400
Dr. Katie Root, prin. Fax 484-2401
Mohave MS 800/6-8
8490 E Jackrabbit Rd 85250 480-484-5200
Chris Asmussen, prin. Fax 484-5201
Mountainside MS 800/6-8
11256 N 128th St 85259 480-484-5500
Terri Kellen, prin. Fax 484-5501
Navajo ES 400/PK-5
4525 N Granite Reef Rd 85251 480-484-2600
Matthew Patzlaff, prin. Fax 484-2601
Pima ES 600/PK-5
8330 E Osborn Rd 85251 480-484-2800
Akexis Cruz-Freeman, prin. Fax 484-2801
Pueblo ES 500/PK-5
6320 N 82nd St 85250 480-484-3100
Shelley Hummon, prin. Fax 484-3101
Redfield ES 600/PK-5
9181 E Redfield Rd 85260 480-484-4000
Christine Bonow, prin. Fax 484-4001
Sequoya ES 500/PK-5
11808 N 64th St 85254 480-484-3200
Veronica Leiper, prin. Fax 484-3201
Tonalea ES 400/K-8
6720 E Continental 85257 480-484-5800
David Priniski, prin. Fax 484-3601
Yavapai ES 400/PK-5
701 N Miller Rd 85257 480-484-3800
Julio Martinez, prin. Fax 484-3801
Other Schools – See Paradise Valley, Phoenix

Bella Vista College Preparatory S 50/K-12
PO Box 28096 85255 480-575-6001
Blessed Sacrament Catholic Preschool 100/PK-K
11300 N 64th St 85254 480-998-9466
Heather Fraher, dir. Fax 951-3844
Camelback Desert S 200/PK-5
9606 E Kalil Dr 85260 877-959-4188
International S of Arizona 300/PK-8
9522 E San Salvador Dr 85258 480-874-2326
Gail Gold, head sch Fax 663-6894
Our Lady of Perpetual Help Catholic S 500/K-8
3801 N Miller Rd 85251 480-874-3720
Donna Lauro, prin. Fax 874-3767
Pardes Jewish Day S 300/K-8
12753 N Scottsdale Rd 85254 480-991-9141
Rancho Solano Preparatory S 600/PK-12
9180 E Via de Ventura 85258 480-646-8200
St. John XXIII Catholic S 600/K-8
16235 N 60th St 85254 480-905-0939
Preston Colao, prin. Fax 905-0955
St. Maria Goretti Catholic Preschool 100/PK-K
6261 N Granite Reef Rd 85250 480-948-3606
Kate Strohmeyer, dir. Fax 948-8815
Shepherd of the Desert Lutheran S 500/PK-8
9590 E Shea Blvd 85260 480-860-1188
Lisa Straight, admin. Fax 860-4152
Thunderbird Christian ES 100/K-8
7440 E Sutton Dr 85260 480-991-6705

Sedona, Coconino, Pop. 9,090
Sedona-Oak Creek JUSD 9 1,200/K-12
221 Brewer Rd Ste 100 86336 928-204-6800
David Lykins, supt. Fax 282-0232
www.sedona.k12.az.us
Big Park Community S 300/K-6
25 W Saddlehorn Rd 86351 928-204-6500
Deborah Jones, prin. Fax 284-9796
West Sedona S 400/K-6
570 Posse Ground Rd 86336 928-204-6600
Scott Keller, prin. Fax 282-1012

Seligman, Yavapai, Pop. 428
Seligman USD 40 100/K-12
PO Box 650 86337 928-422-3233
Diane Pritchett, supt. Fax 422-3642
www.seligmanschools.org/
Seligman ES 100/K-8
PO Box 650 86337 928-216-4123
Diane Pritchett, admin. Fax 422-3642

Sells, Pima, Pop. 2,459
Baboquivari USD 40 900/K-12
PO Box 248 85634 520-719-1200
Dr. Edna Morris, supt. Fax 383-5441
busd40.org
Indian Oasis ES 400/K-3
PO Box 248 85634 520-719-1230
Caitlin Schaefer, prin. Fax 383-5441
Indian Oasis IS 300/4-6
PO Box 248 85634 520-719-1240
Michelle Karp, prin. Fax 383-5930

Show Low, Navajo, Pop. 10,473
Show Low USD 10 2,100/K-12
500 W Old Linden Rd 85901 928-537-6000
Shad Housley, supt. Fax 537-6004
www.show-low.k12.az.us
Homestead ES 200/3-5
500 W Old Linden Rd 85901 928-537-6150
Kevin Hall, prin. Fax 537-6199
Linden ES 200/K-5
500 W Old Linden Rd 85901 928-537-6017
Jami Ramsey, prin. Fax 537-6018
Show Low JHS 600/6-8
500 W Old Linden Rd 85901 928-537-6100
Meghan Dorsett, prin. Fax 537-6149
Whipple Ranch ES 300/K-3
500 W Old Linden Rd 85901 928-537-6050
Suzanne Jaramillo, prin. Fax 537-6099

American Indian Christian S 50/3-8
924 Mission Ln Lot 1 85901 928-537-5912
Leslie Solliday, dir. Fax 537-5620
Mountain Christian S 100/K-8
3171 E Show Low Lake Rd 85901 928-537-1050
Michael Granillo, admin. Fax 537-1104
St. Anthony S 100/PK-8
PO Box 789 85902 928-537-4497
Brian Yorksmith, prin. Fax 537-4507

Sierra Vista, Cochise, Pop. 41,754
Palominas ESD 49
Supt. — See Hereford
Coronado S 400/K-8
5148 S Coronado School Dr 85650 520-378-0616
Mary Kay Ponder, prin. Fax 378-4195

Sierra Vista USD 68 5,700/PK-12
3555 E Fry Blvd 85635 520-515-2701
Kriss Hagerl, supt. Fax 515-2744
www.svusd68.org
Bella Vista ES 400/K-6
3555 E Fry Blvd 85635 520-515-2940
Heather Rodda, prin. Fax 515-2948
Carmichael ES 300/PK-6
3555 E Fry Blvd 85635 520-515-2950
Michelle Wambach, prin. Fax 515-2951
Clark MS 800/7-8
3555 E Fry Blvd 85635 520-515-2930
Roger Hill, prin. Fax 515-2941
Roadrunner Preschool PK-PK
3555 E Fry Blvd 85635 520-515-2701
Fax 515-2744
Town & Country ES 400/PK-6
3555 E Fry Blvd 85635 520-515-2980
Brenda Bland, prin. Fax 515-2985
Village Meadows ES 400/K-6
3555 E Fry Blvd 85635 520-515-2990
Scot Roppe, prin. Fax 515-2994

All Saints Catholic S 100/PK-8
1425 E Yaqui St 85650 520-378-7012
Carmen Rosado Serrano, prin. Fax 378-2726
First Baptist Christian Academy 100/PK-8
1447 S 7th St 85635 520-458-2983
Jim Carter, prin. Fax 458-8399
Veritas Christian Community S 100/K-12
215 Taylor Dr 85635 520-417-1113
Jason Tinney, head sch

Skull Valley, Yavapai
Skull Valley ESD 15 50/K-6
PO Box 127 86338 928-442-3322
Vicki Hilliker, admin. Fax 442-9198
www.skullvalleyschool.org
Skull Valley ES 50/K-6
PO Box 127 86338 928-442-3322
Vicki Hilliker, lead tchr. Fax 442-9198

Snowflake, Navajo, Pop. 5,508
Snowflake USD 5 2,500/K-12
682 W School Bus Ln 85937 928-536-4156
Hollis Merrell, supt. Fax 536-2634
home.susd5.org
Highland PS 500/K-3
682 W School Bus Ln 85937 928-536-4156
Roy Owens, prin. Fax 536-3006
Snowflake IS 400/4-6
682 W School Bus Ln 85937 928-536-4156
Kim Lewis, prin. Fax 536-2995
Snowflake JHS 400/7-8
682 W School Bus Ln 85937 928-536-4156
Brian Hoopes, prin. Fax 536-3007
Other Schools – See Taylor

Solomon, Graham, Pop. 419
Solomon ESD 5 200/PK-8
PO Box 167 85551 928-428-0477
Kevin England, supt. Fax 428-0398
solomon.k12.az.us/
Solomon S 200/PK-8
PO Box 167 85551 928-428-0477
Kevin England, supt. Fax 428-0398

Somerton, Yuma, Pop. 14,249
Somerton ESD 11 2,800/PK-8
PO Box 3200 85350 928-341-6000
Dr. Laura Noel, supt. Fax 341-6090
www.ssd11.org
Desert Sonora ES 400/PK-5
PO Box 3200 85350 928-341-6300
Maria P. Vasquez, prin. Fax 341-6390
Encanto Learning Center 300/PK-5
PO Box 3200 85350 928-341-6700
Luciano O. Munoz, prin. Fax 341-6090
Orange Grove ES 400/PK-5
PO Box 3200 85350 928-341-6200
Kim Seh, prin. Fax 341-6290
Somerton MS 900/6-8
PO Box 3200 85350 928-341-6100
Elizabeth Garza, prin. Fax 341-6190
Tierra Del Sol ES 900/PK-5
PO Box 3200 85350 928-341-6400
Maria Elena Paredes, prin. Fax 341-6490

Springerville, Apache, Pop. 1,931
Round Valley USD 10 1,300/K-12
PO Box 610 85938 928-333-6580
Travis Udall, supt. Fax 333-2823
www.elks.net
Other Schools – See Eagar

Stanfield, Pinal, Pop. 722
Stanfield ESD 24 500/PK-8
515 S Stanfield Rd, 520-424-3353
Dr. Melissa Sadorf, supt. Fax 424-3798
www.roadrunners24.net
Stanfield S 500/PK-8
515 S Stanfield Rd, 520-424-0222
Christopher Lineberry, prin. Fax 424-0300

Sun City, Maricopa, Pop. 37,274
Peoria USD 11
Supt. — See Glendale

Zuni Hills ES 700/K-8
10851 W Williams Rd 85373 623-412-5275
Fritz Maynes, prin. Fax 412-5282

Sun Valley, Navajo, Pop. 299

Native American Christian Academy 50/K-9
PO Box 4013 86029 928-524-6211
Kristopher Miller, admin. Fax 524-3230

Superior, Pinal, Pop. 2,804
Superior USD 15 400/PK-12
1500 W Panther Dr, 520-689-3000
Stephen Estatico, supt. Fax 689-3009
www.superiorusd.org
Kennedy ES 200/PK-6
1500 W Panther Dr, 520-689-3050
Manuel Ramirez, prin. Fax 689-3170
Superior JHS 100/7-8
100 W Panther Dr, 520-689-3002
William Duarte, prin. Fax 689-3197

Surprise, Maricopa, Pop. 114,476
Dysart USD 89 25,700/K-12
15802 N Parkview Pl 85374 623-876-7000
Dr. Gail Pletnick, supt. Fax 876-7042
www.dysart.org
Ashton Ranch ES 1,100/K-8
14898 W Acoma Dr 85379 623-523-8300
Emily Dean, prin. Fax 523-8311
Canyon Ridge S 900/K-8
17359 W Surprise Farms Loop, 623-523-8450
Jill Hoppe, prin. Fax 523-8461
Cimarron Springs ES 900/K-8
17032 W Surprise Farms Loop, 623-523-8600
Ginger Richards, prin. Fax 523-8611
Countryside S 900/K-8
15034 N Parkview Pl 85379 623-876-7800
Marcianne Hessler, prin. Fax 876-7811
Kingswood ES 800/K-8
15150 W Mondell Rd 85374 623-876-7600
Jeremy St. Germain, prin. Fax 876-7605
Marley Park ES 1,100/K-8
15042 W Sweetwater Ave 85379 623-523-8200
Carin Garton, prin. Fax 523-8211
Parkview ES 800/K-8
16066 N Parkview Pl 85374 623-523-8650
Dr. Rosalind Fisher, prin. Fax 523-8661
Rancho Gabriela ES 1,200/K-8
15272 W Gabriela Dr 85379 623-523-8500
Scott Kerr, prin. Fax 523-8511
Sonoran Heights S 900/K-8
11405 N Greer Ranch Pkwy 85379 623-523-8550
Andrew Frazier, prin. Fax 523-8561
Sunset Hills S 1,200/K-8
17825 W Sierra Montana Loop, 623-523-8700
Josephine Tokhi, prin. Fax 523-8711
Western Peaks ES 800/K-8
18063 W Surprise Farms Loop, 623-523-8750
Stacie Brown, prin. Fax 523-8761
West Point S 800/K-8
13700 W Greenway Rd 85374 623-876-7750
Marilee Timbrooks, prin. Fax 876-7711
Other Schools – See El Mirage, Glendale, Waddell

Nadaburg USD 81
Supt. — See Wittmann
Desert Oasis S 500/K-8
17161 W Bajada Rd 85387 623-556-5880
Angie Mason, prin. Fax 556-5898

Palms Christian S 100/K-5
17475 W Bell Rd 85374 623-544-3498
Andrew Bailey, prin. Fax 374-3896

Taylor, Navajo, Pop. 4,051
Snowflake USD 5
Supt. — See Snowflake
Taylor ES 300/K-3
300 E 29 S 85939 928-536-4156
Jeremy Hatch, prin. Fax 536-6887
Taylor IS 200/4-6
207 N 500 W 85939 928-536-4156
Debbie Muder, prin. Fax 536-7225

Teec Nos Pos, Apache, Pop. 721
Red Mesa USD 27 600/K-12
HC 61 Box 40 86514 928-656-4108
Kim Pearce, supt. Fax 656-4302
www.rmusd.net
Red Mesa ES 200/K-8
HC 61 Box 40 86514 928-656-4250
Wanda Burton, prin. Fax 656-4251
Other Schools – See Round Rock

Immanuel Mission S 100/K-12
PO Box 1080 86514 830-200-0351
John Bloom, prin. Fax 435-7041

Tempe, Maricopa, Pop. 156,729
Kyrene ESD 28 17,300/PK-8
8700 S Kyrene Rd 85284 480-541-1000
Dr. Jan Vesely, supt. Fax 541-1860
www.kyrene.org
Kyrene de la Mariposa ES 600/K-5
50 E Knox Rd 85284 480-541-3800
Spencer Fallgatter, prin. Fax 541-3810
Kyrene de las Manitas ES 600/PK-5
1201 W Courtney Ln 85284 480-541-3600
Dan Langston, prin. Fax 541-3610
Kyrene del Norte ES 500/K-5
1331 E Redfield Rd 85283 480-541-4800
Jaime Soto, prin. Fax 541-4810
Kyrene de los Ninos ES 700/PK-5
1330 E Dava Dr 85283 480-541-4600
Tonja Yalung, prin. Fax 541-4610
Kyrene MS 1,100/6-8
1050 E Carver Rd 85284 480-541-6600
Sheryl Houston, prin. Fax 541-6610
Waggoner ES 600/K-5
1050 E Carver Rd 85284 480-541-5600
Lisa Gibson, prin. Fax 541-5610
Other Schools – See Chandler, Phoenix

Tempe ESD 3 11,800/PK-8
3205 S Rural Rd 85282 480-730-7100
Christine Busch, supt. Fax 730-7177
www.tempeschools.org
Aguilar ES 500/PK-5
5800 S Forest Ave 85283 480-897-2544
Jessica Larsen, prin. Fax 838-1179
Arredondo ES 300/K-5
1330 E Carson Dr 85282 480-897-2744
Alison Bruening-Hamati, prin. Fax 839-7325
Broadmor ES 700/K-5
311 E Aepli Dr 85282 480-967-6599
Barry Fritch, prin. Fax 921-0814
Carminati ES 400/PK-5
4001 S Mcallister Ave 85282 480-784-4484
Wendy Reeck, prin. Fax 968-0626
Connolly MS 1,000/6-8
2002 E Concorda Dr 85282 480-967-8933
Katherine Mullery, prin. Fax 929-9695
Curry ES 500/PK-5
1974 E Meadow Dr 85282 480-967-8336
Ken White, prin. Fax 894-4008
Fees College Preparatory Academy 1,000/6-8
1600 E Watson Dr 85283 480-897-6063
Kacy Baxter, prin. Fax 838-0853
Fuller ES 600/K-5
1975 E Cornell Dr 85283 480-897-6228
Andrew Lebowitz, prin. Fax 820-7308
Gililland MS 1,000/6-8
1025 S Beck Ave 85281 480-966-7114
JoLyn Gibbons, prin. Fax 829-6178
Holdeman ES 600/PK-5
1326 W 18th St 85281 480-966-9934
Eric Kadel, prin. Fax 968-3165
Hudson ES 400/K-5
1325 E Malibu Dr 85282 480-897-6608
Dr. Jeffrey Shores, prin. Fax 820-7335
Laird S 500/K-8
1500 N Scovel St 85281 480-941-2440
Dr. Nancy Uxa, prin. Fax 970-4231
Meyer Montessori S PK-6
2615 S Dorsey Ln 85282 480-584-6339
Jennifer Whittington, admin.
Rover ES 500/K-5
1300 E Watson Dr 85283 480-897-7122
Dr. Mark Eley, prin. Fax 820-8503
Scales Technology Academy 600/K-5
1115 W 5th St 85281 480-929-9909
Stephen Wolf, prin. Fax 804-0384
Tempe Academy of International Studies 100/6-8
2250 S College Ave 85282 480-459-5048
David Owen, prin. Fax 621-6577
Thew ES 600/K-5
2130 E Howe Ave 85281 480-894-5574
Marissa Schneckloth, prin. Fax 894-2755
Ward Traditional Academy 500/K-8
1965 E Hermosa Dr 85282 480-491-8871
Dr. Taime Bengochea, prin. Fax 491-1710
Wood ES 600/K-5
727 W Cornell Dr 85283 480-838-0711
Marilyn Jackson, prin. Fax 838-0832
Other Schools – See Guadalupe, Phoenix

Bethany Christian S 200/K-8
6304 S Price Rd 85283 480-752-8993
Kary Sterkowitz, admin. Fax 752-7913
Emmanuel Evangelical Lutheran S 200/PK-8
715 W Southern Ave 85282 480-967-3991
John Campbell, prin. Fax 967-2809
Gethsemane Lutheran S 200/PK-8
1035 E Guadalupe Rd 85283 480-839-0906
Claire Fugit, admin. Fax 839-8876
Grace Christian Academy 300/PK-8
1200 E Southern Ave 85282 480-966-5022
Kevin Inouye, admin. Fax 968-4166
Noor Academy of Arizona 100/PK-8
1130 W 23rd St 85282 480-829-1443
Our Lady of Mt. Carmel Catholic S 400/PK-8
2117 S Rural Rd 85282 480-967-5567
Bruce Hermie, prin. Fax 967-6038

Thatcher, Graham, Pop. 4,760
Thatcher USD 4 1,500/K-12
PO Box 610 85552 928-348-7200
Dr. Kevin Spiller, supt. Fax 348-7220
www.thatcherud.org
Daley PS 500/K-2
3500 W 2nd St 85552 928-348-7240
Tracy Allred, prin. Fax 348-7243
Thatcher ES 400/3-6
1386 N 4th Ave 85552 928-348-7250
Hal Mullenaux, prin. Fax 348-7253
Thatcher MS 200/7-8
1130 N 4th Ave 85552 928-348-7260
Tye Stewart, prin. Fax 348-7263

Tolleson, Maricopa, Pop. 6,455
Littleton ESD 65
Supt. — See Avondale
Country Place ES 1,000/K-8
10207 W Country Place Blvd 85353 623-478-6100
Dr. Michael Cagle, prin. Fax 478-6120
Fine Arts Academy K-7
1700 S 103rd Ave 85353 623-478-6400
Susan Gibson, prin.
Tres Rios ES 900/K-8
5025 S 103rd Ave 85353 623-478-6300
Dr. Karen Grose, prin. Fax 478-6320

Tolleson ESD 17 2,800/PK-8
9261 W Van Buren St 85353 623-533-3900
Dr. Lupita Hightower, supt. Fax 533-3925
www.tollesonschools.com
Arizona Desert ES 400/K-6
8803 W Van Buren St 85353 623-907-5260
Brenda Catlett, prin. Fax 907-5261
Gonzales ES 800/PK-8
9401 W Garfield St 85353 623-907-5181
Cynthia Mills, prin. Fax 936-0649
Other Schools – See Phoenix

Union ESD 62 1,400/K-8
3834 S 91st Ave 85353 623-478-5005
Lorah Neville M.Ed., supt. Fax 478-5006
unionesd.org
Dos Rios S 900/K-8
2150 S 87th Ave 85353 623-474-7000
Annamarie Dowling-Garrot M.A., prin. Fax 936-9253
Hurley Ranch S 500/3-8
8950 W Illini Rd 85353 623-478-5100
Dr. Randy Watkins Ed.D., prin. Fax 742-9625
Union ES, 3834 S 91st Ave 85353 50/K-2
Michael Welsh M.Ed., prin. 623-478-5000

Tombstone, Cochise, Pop. 1,359
Tombstone USD 1 1,000/PK-12
PO Box 1000 85638 520-457-2217
Robert Devere, supt. Fax 457-3270
www.tombstoneschools.org
Meyer ES 100/K-8
PO Box 1000 85638 520-457-3371
Brent DeRoest, prin. Fax 457-3685
Other Schools – See Huachuca City

Tonopah, Maricopa, Pop. 60
Saddle Mountain USD 90 1,400/PK-12
38201 W Indian School Rd 85354 623-474-5115
Dr. Paul Tighe, supt. Fax 474-5190
www.smusd90.org
Fisher ES 700/PK-8
38201 W Indian School Rd 85354 623-474-5500
Rene Molina, prin. Fax 474-5540
Other Schools – See Buckeye

Tonto Basin, Gila, Pop. 1,414
Tonto Basin ESD 33 100/PK-8
PO Box 337 85553 928-479-2277
Chad Greer, supt. Fax 479-2720
www.tontobasinschool.org
Tonto Basin S 100/PK-8
PO Box 337 85553 928-479-2277
Chad Greer, prin. Fax 479-2720

Topock, Mohave, Pop. 10
Topock ESD 12 100/PK-6
PO Box 370 86436 928-768-3344
John Warren, supt. Fax 768-9253
www.topockschool.com
Topock ES 100/PK-6
PO Box 370 86436 928-768-3344
John Warren, prin. Fax 768-9253

Tsaile, Apache, Pop. 1,179
Chinle USD 24
Supt. — See Chinle
Tsaile ES 400/K-8
Navajo Rt 12 & Jct Hwy 86556 928-674-9100
Dr. Stephen Sorden, prin. Fax 724-3234

Tuba City, Coconino, Pop. 8,486
Tuba City USD 15 1,600/PK-12
PO Box 67 86045 928-283-1000
Dr. Harold Begay, supt. Fax 283-1200
www.tcusd.org
Tsinaabaas Habitiin ES K-4
PO Box 67 86045 928-283-1090
Sophia Begody, prin. Fax 283-1244
Tuba City JHS 200/6-8
PO Box 67 86045 928-283-1040
Dr. Melissa Bilagody, prin. Fax 283-1218
Tuba City PS 300/PK-5
PO Box 67 86045 928-283-1020
Dr. Justin Roberson, prin. Fax 283-1222
Other Schools – See Cameron

Tucson, Pima, Pop. 507,980
Altar Valley ESD 51 600/PK-8
10105 S Sasabe Rd 85736 520-822-1484
Dr. David Dumon, supt. Fax 822-1798
altarvalleyschools.org
Altar Valley MS 300/5-8
10105 S Sasabe Rd 85736 520-822-9343
Joshua Peebles, prin. Fax 822-5801
Robles ES 400/PK-4
10105 S Sasabe Rd 85736 520-822-9418
Rosalinda Rodriguez, prin. Fax 822-9428

Amphitheater USD 10 14,300/PK-12
701 W Wetmore Rd 85705 520-696-5000
Todd Jaeger, supt. Fax 696-5015
www.amphi.com
Amphitheater MS 600/6-8
315 E Prince Rd 85705 520-696-6230
Abel Morado, prin. Fax 696-6236
Copper Creek ES 500/K-5
11620 N Copper Spring Trl 85737 520-696-6800
Kristjan Laumoto, prin. Fax 696-6808
Coronado S 1,000/K-8
3401 E Wilds Rd 85739 520-696-6610
Gerad Ball, prin. Fax 696-6701
Cross MS 700/6-8
1000 W Chapala Dr 85704 520-696-5920
Andy Heinemann, prin. Fax 696-5996
Donaldson ES 400/PK-5
2040 W Omar Dr 85704 520-696-6160
Dawn Tinsley, prin. Fax 696-6204
Harelson ES 500/K-6
826 W Chapala Dr 85704 520-696-6020
Jason Weaver, prin. Fax 696-6070
Holaway ES 300/K-5
3500 N Cherry Ave 85719 520-696-6880
Chris Gutierrez, prin. Fax 696-6924
Keeling ES 400/PK-5
2837 N Los Altos Ave 85705 520-696-6940
Annette Orelup, prin. Fax 696-6977
La Cima MS 500/6-8
5600 N La Canada Dr 85704 520-696-6730
Julie Valenzuela, prin. Fax 696-6793
Mesa Verde ES 400/K-5
1661 W Sage St 85704 520-696-6090
Carol Tracy, prin. Fax 696-6107
Nash ES 500/K-5
515 W Kelso St 85705 520-696-6440
Bob Hehli, prin. Fax 696-6490

Prince ES 700/PK-5
125 E Prince Rd 85705 520-696-6350
Laurie Sheber, prin. Fax 696-6413
Rio Vista ES 500/K-5
1351 E Limberlost Dr 85719 520-696-5250
Dianna Kuhn, prin. Fax 696-5260
Walker ES 500/K-5
1750 W Roller Coaster Rd 85704 520-696-6518
Erika Vasas, prin. Fax 696-6555
Wilson S 1,300/K-8
2330 W Glover Rd 85742 520-696-5800
Christine Sullivan, prin. Fax 696-5900
Other Schools – See Oro Valley

Catalina Foothills USD 16 5,000/PK-12
2101 E River Rd 85718 520-209-7500
Dr. Mary Kamerzell, supt. Fax 209-7570
www.cfsd16.org/
Canyon View ES 400/PK-5
5725 N Sabino Canyon Rd 85750 520-209-7700
Rob Henikman, prin. Fax 209-7770
Esperero Canyon MS 600/6-8
5801 N Sabino Canyon Rd 85750 520-209-8100
Mary Setliff, prin. Fax 209-8170
Manzanita ES 700/PK-5
3000 E Manzanita Ave 85718 520-209-7800
Kim Boling, prin. Fax 209-7870
Orange Grove MS 600/6-8
1911 E Orange Grove Rd 85718 520-209-8200
Mark Rubin-Toles, prin. Fax 209-8275
Sunrise Drive ES 600/PK-5
5301 E Sunrise Dr 85718 520-209-7900
Andrea Davidson, prin. Fax 209-7970
Valley View Early Learning Center 50/PK-K
3435 E Sunrise Dr 85718 520-209-7650
Marisol Kenman, dir. Fax 209-7664
Ventana Vista ES 500/PK-5
6085 N Kolb Rd 85750 520-209-8000
Dana Mulay, prin. Fax 209-8070

Flowing Wells USD 8 5,700/PK-12
1556 W Prince Rd 85705 520-696-8800
Dr. David Baker, supt. Fax 690-2400
www.flowingwellsschools.org
Centennial ES 500/K-6
2200 W Wetmore Rd 85705 520-696-8200
Kristy Dale, prin. Fax 690-5613
Davis ES 500/K-6
4250 N Romero Rd 85705 520-696-8250
Lyle Dunbar, prin. Fax 690-5614
Douglas ES 600/K-6
3302 N Flowing Wells Rd 85705 520-696-8300
Tamara McAllister, prin. Fax 690-5615
Flowing Wells JHS 900/7-8
4545 N La Cholla Blvd 85705 520-696-8550
Chad Miller, prin. Fax 690-2420
Hendricks ES 500/K-6
3400 W Orange Grove Rd 85741 520-696-8400
Alan Schmidt, prin. Fax 690-5612
Laguna ES 400/K-6
5001 N Shannon Rd 85705 520-696-8450
Jacqueline Camacho, prin. Fax 690-5616
Meschter ECC 100/PK-PK
4605 N La Cholla Blvd 85705 520-696-8909
Susan Shinn, dir. Fax 888-1651
Richardson ES 400/K-6
6901 N Camino De La Tierra 85741 520-696-8500
Henry Linker, prin. Fax 690-5617

Marana USD 6
Supt. — See Marana
Butterfield ES 600/K-6
3400 W Massingale Rd 85741 520-579-5000
Joshua Bayne, prin. Fax 579-5029
Coyote Trail ES 600/K-6
8000 N Silverbell Rd 85743 520-579-5105
Dan Johnson, prin. Fax 579-5098
DeGrazia ES 500/K-6
5051 W Overton Rd 85742 520-579-4800
Michael Bauschka, prin. Fax 579-4840
Ironwood ES 800/K-6
3300 W Freer Dr 85742 520-579-5150
Aaron Johnson, prin. Fax 579-5164
Picture Rocks ES 300/PK-6
5875 N Sanders Rd 85743 520-616-3700
Mary O'Hara-Perkins, prin. Fax 616-3749
Quail Run ES 600/K-6
4600 W Cortaro Farms Rd 85742 520-579-4700
Andrea Divijak, prin. Fax 744-3693
Rattlesnake Ridge ES 600/K-6
8500 N Continental Reserve 85743 520-352-7000
Matt Abney, prin. Fax 744-3274
Thornydale ES 400/PK-6
7651 N Oldfather Dr 85741 520-579-4900
Zach Singer, prin. Fax 579-4909
Tortolita MS 900/7-8
4101 W Hardy Rd 85742 520-579-4600
Rex Scott, prin. Fax 579-4646
Twin Peaks ES 500/PK-6
7995 W Twin Peaks Rd 85743 520-579-4750
Dondi Luce, prin. Fax 579-4785

Sunnyside USD 12 15,600/PK-12
2238 E Ginter Rd 85706 520-545-2000
Steve Holmes, supt. Fax 545-2120
www.susd12.org
Apollo MS 500/6-8
265 W Nebraska St 85706 520-545-4500
Roy Massani, prin. Fax 545-4510
Challenger MS 700/6-8
100 E Elvira Rd, 520-545-4600
Angelica Duddleston, prin. Fax 545-4616
Craycroft ES 800/K-4
5455 E Littletown Rd, 520-545-2600
James Ridge, prin. Fax 545-2616
Drexel ES 600/PK-6
801 E Drexel Rd 85706 520-545-2700
Eneida Ortiz, prin. Fax 545-2716
Elvira ES 600/K-6
250 W Elvira Rd, 520-545-2800
Andy Townsend, prin. Fax 545-2890

Esperanza ES 600/K-6
2238 E Ginter Rd 85706 520-545-2000
Emma Carrillo, prin. Fax 545-2916
Gallego IS 4-8
3700 E Alvord Rd 85706 520-545-4700
Anna Warmbrand, prin. Fax 545-4716
Gallego PS 500/K-5
6200 S Hemisphere Pl 85706 520-545-3000
Rhonda Moore, prin. Fax 545-3016
Lauffer MS 900/5-8
5385 E Littletown Rd, 520-545-4900
Thom Luedemann, prin. Fax 545-4916
Liberty Gifted and Talented ES 800/K-6
5495 S Liberty Ave 85706 520-545-3100
Claudia Gaxiola, prin. Fax 545-3116
Los Amigos Technology Academy 700/K-6
2200 E Drexel Rd 85706 520-545-3200
Valerie Lopez-Miranda, prin. Fax 545-3216
Los Ninos ES 600/PK-6
5445 S Alvernon Way 85706 520-545-3300
Dedee Krause, prin. Fax 545-3316
Mission Manor ES 600/K-6
600 W Santa Rosa St 85706 520-545-3500
Bryan Huie, prin. Fax 545-3516
Ocotillo Early Learning Center 100/PK-1
5702 S Campbell Ave 85706 520-545-3600
Paul Ohm, coord. Fax 545-3616
Rivera ES 700/K-6
5102 S Cherry Ave 85706 520-545-3900
Patricia Gamez, prin. Fax 545-3916
Santa Clara ES 700/K-6
6910 S Santa Clara Ave, 520-545-3700
Ernesto Badilla, prin. Fax 545-3716
Sierra S 1,000/2-8
5801 S Del Moral Blvd 85706 520-545-4800
Tiffany Emerson, prin. Fax 545-4816
Summit View ES 500/K-6
1900 E Summit St, 520-545-3800
Maria Montano, prin. Fax 545-3816

Tanque Verde USD 13 2,000/PK-12
2300 N Tanque Verde Loop Rd 85749 520-749-5751
Dr. Scott Hagerman, supt. Fax 749-5400
www.tanqueverdeschools.org
Agua Caliente ES 500/PK-6
11420 E Limberlost Rd 85749 520-749-2235
Sherri Rosalik, prin. Fax 749-0338
Gray JHS 400/7-8
11150 E Tanque Verde Rd 85749 520-749-3838
Greg Miller, prin. Fax 749-9668
Tanque Verde ES 600/K-6
2600 N Fennimore Ave 85749 520-749-4244
Kim Hubbard, prin. Fax 749-4292

Tucson USD 1 48,500/PK-12
1010 E 10th St 85719 520-225-6000
Dr. Gabriel Trujillo, supt. Fax 225-6174
tusd1.schooldesk.net
Banks ES 400/K-5
3200 S Lead Flower Ave 85735 520-908-5700
Sean Wilken, prin. Fax 908-5701
Blenman ES 500/K-5
1695 N Country Club Rd 85716 520-232-6500
Kelly Mack, prin. Fax 232-6501
Bloom ES 400/PK-5
8310 E Pima St 85715 520-731-3700
Lucinda Brunenkant, prin. Fax 731-3701
Bonillas Magnet ES 400/K-5
4757 E Winsett St 85711 520-232-6600
Jennifer Ambrosio, prin. Fax 232-6601
Booth-Fickett Math Science Magnet S 1,300/K-8
450 S Montego Dr 85710 520-731-3800
Norma Flores, prin. Fax 731-3801
Borman ES 500/K-8
6630 E Lightning Dr 85708 520-584-4600
Katherine Sisler, prin. Fax 584-4601
Borton Magnet PS 200/PK-2
700 E 22nd St 85713 520-225-1000
Denice Contreras, prin. Fax 225-1001
Carrillo Magnet ES 300/K-5
440 S Main Ave 85701 520-225-1200
Lori Connor, prin. Fax 225-1201
Cavett ES 300/K-5
2120 E Naco Vis 85713 520-225-1300
Carol Leeson, prin. Fax 225-1301
Collier ES 200/K-5
3900 N Bear Canyon Rd 85749 520-584-4800
Lisa Langford, prin. Fax 584-4801
Cragin Performing Arts Magnet ES 300/K-5
2945 N Tucson Blvd 85716 520-232-6700
Mary Kolsrud, prin. Fax 232-6701
Davidson ES 300/K-5
3950 E Paradise Falls Dr 85712 520-232-6800
Sarah Andricopoulos, prin. Fax 232-6801
Davis Bilingual Magnet ES 300/K-5
500 W Saint Marys Rd 85701 520-225-1400
Carmen Campuzano, prin. Fax 225-1401
Dietz K-8 S 400/K-8
7575 E Palma St 85710 520-731-4000
Jesus Vaquez, prin. Fax 731-4001
Dodge Magnet MS 400/6-8
5831 E Pima St 85712 520-731-4100
Daniel Schulter, prin. Fax 731-4101
Doolen MS 800/6-8
2400 N Country Club Rd 85716 520-232-6900
Venessa Morales, prin. Fax 232-6901
Drachman Montessori Magnet ES 300/PK-8
1085 S 10th Ave 85701 520-225-1500
Jesus Celaya, prin. Fax 225-1501
Dunham ES 200/K-5
9850 E 29th St 85748 520-731-4200
Helen Grijalva, prin. Fax 731-4201
Erickson ES 600/PK-5
6750 E Stella Rd 85730 520-584-5000
Marie Daranyi, prin. Fax 584-5001
Ford ES 400/K-5
8001 E Stella Rd 85730 520-731-4300
Diana Johnston, prin. Fax 731-4301
Fruchthendler ES 400/K-5
7470 E Cloud Rd 85750 520-731-4400
Mary Anderson, prin. Fax 731-4401

Gale ES 400/PK-5
678 S Gollob Rd 85710 520-731-4500
Kathy Osollo, prin. Fax 731-4501
Gridley MS 700/6-8
350 S Harrison Rd 85748 520-731-4600
Kamren Taravati, prin. Fax 731-4601
Grijalva ES 700/K-5
1795 W Drexel Rd 85746 520-908-3600
Timothy Grivois-Shah, prin. Fax 908-3601
Henry ES 400/PK-5
650 N Igo Way 85710 520-731-4700
John Bellisario, prin. Fax 731-4701
Holladay Intermediate Magnet S 100/3-5
1110 E 33rd St 85713 520-225-1600
Tonya Strozier, prin. Fax 225-1601
Hollinger K-8 S 500/K-8
150 W Ajo Way 85713 520-225-1700
Brian Lambert, prin. Fax 225-1701
Howell ES 300/K-5
401 N Irving Ave 85711 520-232-7200
Jaquetta Alexander, prin. Fax 232-7201
Hudlow ES 300/K-5
502 N Caribe Ave 85710 520-731-4800
Cheri LaRochelle, prin. Fax 731-4801
Hughes ES 400/K-5
700 N Wilson Ave 85719 520-232-7400
Kathryn Bolasky, prin. Fax 232-7401
Johnson PS 300/PK-2
6060 S Joseph Ave, 520-908-3800
Rose Cota, prin. Fax 908-3801
Kellond ES 600/K-6
6606 E Lehigh Dr 85710 520-584-5100
Brenda Meneguin, prin. Fax 584-5101
Lawrence IS 400/3-8
4850 W Jeffrey Rd, 520-908-3900
Ann Kobritz, prin. Fax 908-3901
Lineweaver ES 600/K-5
461 S Bryant Ave 85711 520-232-7700
Emily Walls, prin. Fax 232-7701
Lynn/Urquides ES 600/PK-5
1573 W Ajo Way 85713 520-908-4000
Marisa Salcido, prin. Fax 908-4001
Magee MS 600/6-8
8300 E Speedway Blvd 85710 520-731-5000
Jason Lindsay, prin. Fax 731-5001
Maldonado ES 400/K-5
3535 W Messala Way 85746 520-908-4100
Eva Almonte, prin. Fax 908-4101
Mansfeld MS 800/6-8
1300 E 6th St 85719 520-225-1800
Richard Sanchez, prin. Fax 225-1801
Manzo ES 300/K-5
855 N Melrose Ave 85745 520-225-1900
Steve LaTurco, prin. Fax 225-1901
Marshall ES 300/PK-5
9066 E 29th St 85710 520-731-4900
Christopher Loya, prin. Fax 731-4901
Maxwell K-8 S 400/K-8
2802 W Anklam Rd 85745 520-225-2000
Rosanna Ortiz-Montoya, prin. Fax 225-2001
McCorkle Academy 800/PK-8
4455 S Mission Rd 85746 520-877-2000
Sandra Thiffault, prin. Fax 889-5147
Miles Exploratory Learning Center 300/PK-8
1400 E Broadway Blvd 85719 520-225-2200
Patricia Ross, prin. Fax 225-2201
Miller ES 600/PK-6
6951 S Camino De La Tierra 85746 520-908-4200
Maricella Carranza, prin. Fax 908-4201
Mission View ES 200/K-5
2600 S 8th Ave 85713 520-225-2300
Sandra Calkins, prin. Fax 225-2301
Myers/Ganoung ES 400/PK-5
5000 E Andrew St 85711 520-584-6700
Olga Gomez, prin. Fax 584-6701
Ochoa Magnet ES 200/K-5
101 W 25th St 85713 520-225-2400
Rosamaria Raub, prin. Fax 225-2401
Oyama ES 400/K-5
2700 S La Cholla Blvd 85713 520-225-5700
Tamara Christopherson, prin. Fax 225-5701
Pistor MS 1,000/6-8
5455 S Cardinal Ave 85746 520-908-5400
Angela Wichers, prin. Fax 908-5411
Pueblo Gardens K-8 S 400/PK-8
2210 E 33rd St 85713 520-225-2700
Seth Aleshire, prin. Fax 225-2701
Roberts-Naylor K-8 S 600/K-8
1701 S Columbus Blvd 85711 520-584-6800
Connie Zepeda, prin. Fax 584-6801
Robins K-8 S 600/K-8
3939 N Magnetite Ln 85745 520-908-4300
Chandra Thomas, prin. Fax 908-4301
Robison Magnet ES 400/K-5
2745 E 18th St 85716 520-232-7800
Julie Laird Ph.D., prin. Fax 232-7801
Rose K-8 S 700/K-8
710 W Michigan St 85714 520-908-4400
Alma Carmona-Alday, prin. Fax 908-4401
Roskruge Bilingual Magnet S 700/K-8
501 E 6th St 85705 520-225-2900
Yvonne Torres, prin. Fax 225-2901
Safford Magnet S 900/PK-8
200 E 13th St 85701 520-225-3000
Steven Gabaldon, prin. Fax 225-3001
Secrist MS 600/6-8
3400 S Houghton Rd 85730 520-731-5300
Deborah Garcia, prin. Fax 731-5301
Sewell ES 300/K-5
425 N Sahuara Ave 85711 520-584-7200
Robert Jewett, prin. Fax 584-7201
Soleng Tom ES 500/K-5
10520 E Camino Quince 85748 520-731-5400
Oscar Dotson M.Ed., prin. Fax 731-5401
Steele ES 300/K-6
700 S Sarnoff Dr 85710 520-731-6800
Lisa Thomas, prin. Fax 731-6801
Tolson ES 400/K-5
1000 S Greasewood Rd 85745 520-225-3300
Ryan Wilson, prin. Fax 225-3301

Tully Accelerated Magnet ES 400/K-6
1701 W El Rio Dr 85745 520-225-3400
Mary Morse, prin. Fax 225-3401
Utterback Magnet MS 700/6-8
3233 S Pinal Vis 85713 520-225-3500
Robin Dunbar, prin. Fax 225-3501
Vail MS 700/6-8
5350 E 16th St 85711 520-584-5400
Larissa Filler, prin. Fax 584-5401
Valencia MS 1,000/6-8
4400 W Irvington Rd 85746 520-908-4500
Stacey Gist, prin. Fax 908-4501
Van Buskirk ES 400/PK-5
725 E Fair St 85714 520-225-3700
Victoria Barajas, prin. Fax 225-3701
Vesey ES 600/K-5
5005 S Butts Rd, 520-908-4600
Jeffrey Uhrig, prin. Fax 908-4601
Warren ES 200/K-5
3505 W Milton Rd 85746 520-908-4700
Marco Ruiz, prin. Fax 908-4701
Wheeler ES 400/K-5
1818 S Avenida Del Sol 85710 520-584-5500
Dora Saldamando Ph.D., prin. Fax 584-5501
White ES 700/K-5
2315 W Canada St 85746 520-908-5300
Cris Lugo, prin. Fax 908-5301
Whitmore ES 400/K-5
5330 E Glenn St 85712 520-232-8000
Jennifer Figueroa, prin. Fax 232-8001
Wright ES 400/K-5
4311 E Linden St 85712 520-232-8100
Deanna Campos, prin. Fax 232-8101

Vail USD 20
Supt. — See Vail
Cottonwood ES 700/K-5
9950 E Rees Loop 85747 520-879-2600
Sarah Bates, prin. Fax 879-2601
Desert Sky MS 700/6-8
9850 E Rankin Loop 85747 520-879-2700
Katie Dabney, prin. Fax 879-2701
Desert Willow ES 800/K-5
9400 E Esmond Loop 85747 520-879-2300
Kendra Forgacs, prin. Fax 879-2301
Esmond Station K-8 K-8
9400 S Atterbury Wash Way 85747 520-879-3402
Jerry Wood, prin. Fax 879-3401
Senita Valley ES 600/K-5
10750 E Bilby Rd 85747 520-879-3100
Connie Erickson, prin. Fax 879-3101

Ascension Lutheran S 100/PK-K
1220 W Magee Rd 85704 520-742-6229
Callie Baker, admin. Fax 742-4781
Beautiful Savior Academy 100/PK-K
7570 N Thornydale Rd 85741 520-579-1453
Rhonda Karrer M.Ed., dir. Fax 572-2068
Calvary Chapel Christian S 100/K-12
8725 E Speedway Blvd 85710 520-731-2100
Catherine Swearingen, admin.
Carden Christian Academy Central 100/PK-8
2727 N Swan Rd 85712 520-318-3824
Fred Lawson, admin. Fax 318-0071
Casa Ninos S of Montessori 100/PK-4
8655 E Broadway Blvd 85710 520-751-1454
Jenny Ruth, dir. Fax 751-1479
Casas Christian S 300/K-8
10801 N La Cholla Blvd 85742 520-297-0922
Eric Dowdle, prin. Fax 878-1212
Desert Christian ES 200/PK-8
9415 E Wrightstown Rd 85715 520-885-4800
Ron Smith, prin. Fax 885-4265
Desert Valley Christian S 50/K-8
PO Box 13868 85732 520-795-0161
Faith Community Academy 100/PK-6
2551 W Orange Grove Rd 85741 520-742-4189
Royce Nelsestuen, prin. Fax 297-2073
Faith Lutheran S 50/PK-6
3925 E 5th St 85711 520-881-0670
Esther Nicholas M.A., prin. Fax 325-5625
Family Life Academy 100/K-8
530 S Pantano Rd 85710 520-296-8989
Christopher Taylor, dir. Fax 298-8916
First Southern Christian S 100/PK-6
445 E Speedway Blvd 85705 520-624-9797
Carolyn Burger, admin. Fax 624-7770
GracePointe Christian Academy 100/PK-5
5455 S Westover Ave 85746 520-883-3281
Evelia Salcido, dir. Fax 883-3289
Green Fields S 200/K-12
6000 N Camino De La Tierra 85741 520-297-2288
Rebecca Cordier M.Ed., head sch Fax 618-2599
Imago Dei MS, PO Box 3056 85702 100/5-8
Cameron Taylor, head sch 520-882-4008
Lamb's Gate Christian S 100/PK-2
4700 N Swan Rd 85718 520-299-2151
Kristen Kaveloh, dir.
Northminster Christian S 100/PK-3
2450 E Fort Lowell Rd 85719 520-327-2321
Amy Baum, head sch Fax 327-1839
Our Mother of Sorrows S 400/PK-8
1800 S Kolb Rd 85710 520-747-1027
Erin Vu, prin. Fax 747-0797
Pusch Ridge Christian Academy 200/K-5
6450 N Camino Miraval 85718 520-529-7080
Mandy Rhodes, prin. Fax 529-7140
Redeemer Lutheran S 100/PK-8
8845 N Silverbell Rd 85743 520-572-8136
Michael Peek, prin. Fax 572-8141
Saguaro Hills Adventist Christian S 50/K-8
4280 W Irvington Rd 85746 520-325-1454
St. Ambrose S 300/PK-8
300 S Tucson Blvd 85716 520-882-8678
Roseanne Villanueva, prin. Fax 617-4860
St. Cyril of Alexandria S 400/K-8
4725 E Pima St 85712 520-881-4240
Ann Zeches, prin. Fax 795-0325
St. Elizabeth Ann Seton S 500/PK-8
8650 N Shannon Rd 85742 520-219-7650
Theresa Dolan-Dixon, prin. Fax 297-1033

St. John the Evangelist S 100/PK-8
600 W Ajo Way 85713 520-624-3865
Minh Solorzano, prin. Fax 622-3193
St. Joseph S 300/PK-8
215 S Craycroft Rd 85711 520-747-3060
Holly Limon, prin. Fax 747-2024
St. Michael's S 300/K-8
602 N Wilmot Rd 85711 520-722-8478
Margaret Delk Moore, head sch Fax 886-0851
St. Thomas the Apostle S 100/PK-PK
5150 N Valley View Rd 85718 520-577-0503
Michelle Garmon, dir. Fax 577-0441
Santa Cruz S 200/PK-8
29 W 22nd St 85713 520-624-2093
Angelina Schmidt, prin. Fax 624-2833
San Xavier Mission S 100/K-8
1980 W San Xavier Rd 85746 520-294-0628
Shirley Kalinowski, prin. Fax 294-3465
SS. Peter & Paul S 400/K-8
1436 N Campbell Ave 85719 520-325-2431
Charlene Roll, prin. Fax 881-4690
Tucson Hebrew Academy 200/K-8
3888 E River Rd 85718 520-529-3888
Jon Ben-Asher, head sch Fax 529-0646
Tucson Waldorf S 100/PK-8
3605 E River Rd 85718 520-529-1032
Veritas Academy of Tucson 100/K-11
PO Box 35263 85740 520-576-0427
Rev. Christopher Barnes, head sch

Vail, Pima, Pop. 9,882
Vail USD 20 11,400/PK-12
PO Box 800 85641 520-879-2000
Calvin Baker, supt. Fax 879-2001
www.vailschooldistrict.org
Ocotillo Ridge ES 700/K-5
10170 S White Lightning Ln 85641 520-879-3600
Kate Robold, prin. Fax 879-3601
Vail Inclusive Preschool PK-PK
12775 E Mary Ann Cleveland 85641 520-879-1754
Heather Nordbrock, prin.
Other Schools – See Corona, Tucson

Vernon, Apache, Pop. 118
Vernon ESD 9 100/K-8
PO Box 89 85940 928-537-5463
Dr. Monica Barajas, supt. Fax 537-1820
www.vernon.k12.az.us
Vernon ES 100/K-8
PO Box 89 85940 928-537-5463
Dr. Monica Barajas, prin. Fax 537-1820

Waddell, Maricopa
Dysart USD 89
Supt. — See Surprise
Mountain View ES 1,300/K-8
18302 W Burton Ave 85355 623-876-7450
Gail Miller, prin. Fax 876-7461

Wellton, Yuma, Pop. 2,851
Wellton ESD 24 300/PK-8
PO Box 517 85356 928-785-3311
Lisa Jameson, admin. Fax 785-4323
www.welltonschool.org
Wellton S 300/PK-8
PO Box 517 85356 928-785-3311
Lisa Jameson, admin. Fax 785-4323

Wenden, LaPaz, Pop. 716
Wenden ESD 19 100/PK-8
PO Box 8 85357 928-859-3806
Gloria Dean, supt. Fax 859-3958
www.wendenk8.org
Wenden ES 100/PK-8
PO Box 8 85357 928-859-3806
Gloria Dean M.Ed., admin. Fax 859-3958

Whiteriver, Navajo, Pop. 4,055
Whiteriver USD 20 2,300/PK-12
PO Box 190 85941 928-358-5800
Dr. Hea Goklish, supt. Fax 358-5801
www.wusd.us
Canyon Day JHS 400/6-8
PO Box 190 85941 928-358-5680
Justin Flowers, prin. Fax 358-5681
Cradleboard ES 300/PK-5
PO Box 190 85941 928-358-5650
Virginia Warwick, prin. Fax 358-5651
Riley Seven Mile ES 500/PK-5
PO Box 190 85941 928-358-5670
Florena Kloss, prin. Fax 358-5671
Whiteriver ES 600/PK-5
PO Box 190 85941 928-358-5660
Bonnie Kasey, prin. Fax 358-5661

East Fork Lutheran S 100/K-10
PO Box 489 85941 928-338-4455
Darrell Dobberpuhl, prin. Fax 338-1575

Wickenburg, Maricopa, Pop. 6,301
Wickenburg USD 9 1,500/K-12
40 W Yavapai St 85390 928-668-5350
Dr. Howard Carlson, supt. Fax 668-5390
www.wickenburgschools.org
Hassayampa ES 400/K-5
251 S Tegner St 85390 928-684-6750
Carissa Hershkowitz, prin. Fax 684-6791
Vulture Peak MS 200/6-8
920 S Vulture Mine Rd 85390 928-684-6700
Jennifer Appleby, prin. Fax 684-6746
Other Schools – See Buckeye

Gospel Outreach Christian S 50/PK-12
515 W Wickenburg Way 85390 928-684-5227
Victor Bedoian, supt. Fax 684-2878
Wickenburg Christian Academy 100/PK-12
260 W Yavapai St 85390 928-684-5916
Kevin Armstrong, admin. Fax 684-6104

Wikieup, Mohave, Pop. 130
Owens-Whitney ESD 6 50/K-8
PO Box 38 85360 928-765-2311
Fax 765-2335
www.owens-whitney.org
Owens S 50/K-8
PO Box 38 85360 928-765-2311
Mikaela Gist, lead tchr. Fax 765-2335

Willcox, Cochise, Pop. 3,704
Willcox USD 13 1,200/PK-12
480 N Bisbee Ave 85643 520-384-8600
Kevin Davis, supt. Fax 384-4401
www.wusd13.org
Willcox ES 500/PK-4
501 W Delos St 85643 520-384-8603
Valerie Simon, prin. Fax 384-6039
Willcox MS 400/5-8
360 N Bisbee Ave 85643 520-384-8602
Mike Patterson, prin. Fax 384-6322

Williams, Coconino, Pop. 2,960
Williams USD 2 600/K-12
PO Box 427 86046 928-635-4473
Rick Honsinger, supt. Fax 635-4767
www.wusd2.org
Williams ES 400/K-8
PO Box 427 86046 928-635-4428
Dr. Carissa Morrison, prin. Fax 635-1213

Window Rock, Apache, Pop. 2,663
Window Rock USD 8
Supt. — See Fort Defiance
Tsehootsooi Dine Bi'olta Immersion S 200/K-6
Chee Dodge Dr 86515 928-810-7733
Dr. Audra Platero, prin. Fax 729-6841

Winkelman, Gila, Pop. 352
Hayden-Winkelman USD 41 200/K-12
PO Box 409, 520-356-7876
Jeff Gregorich, supt. Fax 356-7303
www.hwusd.org
Hambly S 100/K-8
PO Box 409, 520-356-7876
Pam Gonzalez, prin. Fax 356-7303

Winslow, Navajo, Pop. 9,382
Winslow USD 1 1,000/PK-12
PO Box 580 86047 928-288-8101
Cyndie Mattox, supt. Fax 288-8292
www.wusd1.org
Brennan ES 300/PK-K, 3-4
PO Box 580 86047 928-288-8400
Troy McReynolds, prin. Fax 288-8492
Jefferson ES 300/1-2
PO Box 580 86047 928-288-8500
Jodie Garner, prin. Fax 288-8592
Washington ES 200/5-6
PO Box 580 86047 928-288-8600
John Summerville, prin. Fax 288-8692
Winslow JHS 300/7-8
PO Box 580 86047 928-288-8300
Darlene McCauley, prin. Fax 288-8393

Red Sands Christian S 50/K-8
PO Box 579 86047 928-289-9221
Brian Snyder, admin. Fax 585-1053

Wittmann, Maricopa, Pop. 749
Nadaburg USD 81 700/PK-8
32919 N Center St 85361 623-388-2100
Rick Stephen, supt. Fax 388-2915
www.nadaburgsd.org
Nadaburg ES 300/PK-8
21419 W Dove Valley Rd 85361 623-388-2321
Curtis McCandlish, prin. Fax 388-2204
Other Schools – See Surprise

Young, Gila, Pop. 657
Young ESD 5 50/PK-12
PO Box 390 85554 928-462-3244
Cliff Bendau, supt. Fax 462-3283
www.youngschool.org
Young S 50/PK-12
PO Box 390 85554 928-462-3244
Cliff Bendau, admin. Fax 462-3283

Yucca, Mohave, Pop. 126
Yucca ESD 13 50/K-8
PO Box 128 86438 928-766-2581
Debbie Vincent, lead tchr. Fax 766-2509
www.yuccaschool.com
Yucca ES 50/K-8
PO Box 128 86438 928-766-2581
Debbie Vincent, lead tchr. Fax 766-2509

Yuma, Yuma, Pop. 91,424
Crane ESD 13 6,100/PK-8
4250 W 16th St 85364 928-373-3400
Laurie Doering, supt. Fax 782-6831
www.craneschools.org
Centennial MS 700/7-8
2650 W 20th St 85364 928-373-3300
Helen Coffeen, prin. Fax 376-7742
Crane MS 800/7-8
4450 W 32nd St 85364 928-373-3200
Ryan Tyree, prin. Fax 344-6821
Gowan Science Academy 200/K-6
1590 S Avenue C 85364 928-539-1200
Jamie Haines, prin. Fax 539-1299
Knox ES 700/K-6
2926 S 21st Dr 85364 928-373-5500
Laura Hurt, prin. Fax 373-5599
Mesquite ES 600/K-6
4451 W 28th St 85364 928-373-4100
Karen Burns, prin. Fax 373-4199
Pueblo ES 700/K-6
2803 W 20th St 85364 928-373-3600
Bobbie Henry, prin. Fax 373-3699
Rancho Viejo ES 400/4-6
1020 S Avenue C 85364 928-373-3800
Cindy Hookstra, prin. Fax 373-3899
Reagan Fundamental ES 700/K-6
3200 W 16th St 85364 928-373-3700
Tom Fletcher, prin. Fax 783-2635
Salida del Sol ES 500/PK-3
910 S Avenue C 85364 928-373-5600
Sheila Mendoza, prin. Fax 373-5699
Suverkrup ES 400/K-6
1590 S Avenue C 85364 928-373-3500
Trish Schoenborn, prin. Fax 782-3132
Valley Horizon ES 600/K-6
4501 W 20th St 85364 928-373-4000
Ana Noriega, prin. Fax 329-0504

Yuma ESD 1 8,900/PK-8
450 W 6th St 85364 928-502-4300
James Sheldahl, supt. Fax 502-4442
www.yuma.org
Byrne ES 300/K-5
811 W 16th St 85364 928-502-7500
Juli Peach, prin. Fax 782-1942
Carver ES 500/K-6
1341 W 5th St 85364 928-502-7600
Debra Drysdale, prin. Fax 782-4094
Castle Dome MS 800/6-8
2353 S Otondo Dr 85365 928-502-7300
Lori Sheffield, prin. Fax 502-7395
Desert Mesa ES 700/K-5
2350 S Avenue 7 1/2 E 85365 928-502-8600
Eula Baumgarner, prin. Fax 502-8675
Fourth Avenue JHS 400/6-8
450 S 4th Ave 85364 928-502-7000
Jose Cazares, prin. Fax 502-7065
Gila Vista JHS 500/6-8
2245 S Arizona Ave 85364 928-502-7100
Thad Dugan, prin. Fax 502-7190
Johnson ES 500/K-5
1201 W 12th St 85364 928-502-7900
Angela Logan, prin. Fax 502-7879
McGraw ES 600/K-5
2345 S Arizona Ave 85364 928-502-7700
Adar Garcia, prin. Fax 502-7715
Otondo ES 700/K-5
2251 S Otondo Dr 85365 928-502-8500
Chris Clayton, prin. Fax 502-8575
Palmcroft ES 600/K-5
901 W Palmcroft Dr 85364 928-502-8000
Jennette Arviso, prin. Fax 502-8048
Pecan Grove ES 400/PK-6
600 S 21st Ave 85364 928-502-8050
Matthew Kaste, prin. Fax 502-8082
Price ES 100/K-5
1010 Barranca Rd 85365 928-502-7730
Suzette Whelchel, prin. Fax 502-7748
Rolle ES 600/K-5
2711 S Engler Ave 85365 928-502-8200
LeeAnne Lagunas, prin. Fax 502-8289
Roosevelt ES 400/K-5
550 W 5th St 85364 928-502-8150
Sophia Ramirez, prin. Fax 502-8228
Sunrise ES 700/K-5
9943 E 28th St 85365 928-502-8800
Rob Monson, prin. Fax 502-8787
Watson MS 400/6-8
9851 E 28th St 85365 928-502-7400
Donna Franklin, prin. Fax 502-7403
Woodard JHS 700/6-8
2250 S 8th Ave 85364 928-502-7200
Daniel Acosta, prin. Fax 782-4596

Immaculate Conception S 200/K-8
501 S Avenue B 85364 928-783-5225
Lydia Mendoza, prin. Fax 343-0172
St. Francis of Assisi S 200/PK-8
700 W 18th St 85364 928-782-1539
Veronica Lopez, prin. Fax 782-0403
Southwestern Christian S 200/K-8
3261 S Avenue 6 E 85365 928-726-3086
Deborah Stewart, prin. Fax 217-2172
Yuma Lutheran S 300/PK-8
2555 S Engler Ave 85365 928-726-8410
Angela Schiller, prin. Fax 726-5330
Yuma SDA Christian S 50/K-8
1681 S 6th Ave 85364 928-783-0457

ARKANSAS

ARKANSAS DEPARTMENT OF EDUCATION
4 State Capitol Rm 304A, Little Rock 72201
Telephone 501-682-4475
Fax 501-682-1079
Website http://www.arkansased.org/

Commissioner of Education Johnny Key

ARKANSAS BOARD OF EDUCATION
4 State Capitol, Little Rock 72201

Chairperson Dr. Jay Barth

EDUCATION SERVICE COOPERATIVES (ESC)

Arch Ford ESC
Phillip Young, dir. 501-354-2269
101 Bulldog Dr, Plumerville 72127 Fax 354-0167
www.afsc.k12.ar.us/

Arkansas River ESC
Cathi Swan, dir. 870-531-6129
912 W 6th Ave, Pine Bluff 71601 Fax 534-2847
www.aresc.k12.ar.us

Crowley's Ridge ESC
John Manning, dir. 870-578-5426
1606 Pine Grove Ln Fax 578-5896
Harrisburg 72432
crowleys.crsc.k12.ar.us/

Dawson ESC
Darin Beckwith, dir. 870-246-3077
711 Clinton St Ste 201 Fax 246-5892
Arkadelphia 71923
dawsonesc.com

De Queen/Mena ESC
John Ponder, dir. 870-386-2251
PO Box 110, Gillham 71841 Fax 386-7731
www.dmesc.net

Great Rivers ESC
Suzann McCommon, dir. 870-338-6461
PO Box 2837, West Helena 72390 Fax 338-7905
www.greatrivers.net

Guy Fenter ESC
Roy Hester, dir. 479-965-2191
3010 Highway 22 E Ste A Fax 965-2723
Branch 72928
www.gfesc.us/

Northcentral Arkansas ESC
Gerald Cooper, dir. 870-581-3600
PO Box 739, Melbourne 72556 Fax 368-4920
www.naesc.k12.ar.us

Northeast Arkansas ESC
Donna Harris, dir., 211 W Hickory St 870-886-7717
Walnut Ridge 72476 Fax 886-7719
nea.k12.ar.us

Northwest Arkansas ESC
Dr. Charles Cudney, dir. 479-267-7450
4 N Double Springs Rd Fax 267-7456
Farmington 72730
www.starfishnw.org

Ozarks Unlimited Resource Cooperative
Rick Nance, dir. 870-429-9100
5823 Resource Dr, Harrison 72601 Fax 429-9099
www.oursc.k12.ar.us

South Central ESC
Marsha Daniels, dir. 870-836-1600
2235 California Ave SW Fax 836-1629
Camden 71701
www.scscoop.org

Southeast Arkansas ESC
Karen Eoff, dir. 870-367-6848
1022 Scogin Dr, Monticello 71655 Fax 367-9877
se.sesc.k12.ar.us/

Southwest Arkansas ESC
Phoebe Bailey, dir. 870-777-3076
2502 S Main St, Hope 71801 Fax 777-5793
www.swaec.org

Wilbur D. Mills ESC
Jeff Williams, dir. 501-882-5467
PO Box 850, Beebe 72012 Fax 882-2155
www.wilbur.k12.ar.us

PUBLIC, PRIVATE AND CATHOLIC ELEMENTARY SCHOOLS

Alexander, Saline, Pop. 2,843
Bryant SD
Supt. — See Bryant
Bethel MS 900/6-8
5415 Northlake Rd 72002 501-316-0937
Todd Sellers, prin. Fax 653-5830
Davis ES 500/K-5
12001 County Line Rd 72002 501-455-5672
Michele Lewis, prin. Fax 455-2751
Springhill ES 600/K-5
2716 Northlake Rd 72002 501-847-5675
Russ Sherrill, prin. Fax 847-5677

Avilla Christian Academy 100/PK-12
302 Avilla E 72002 501-408-4631
Rich Meyers, prin.

Alma, Crawford, Pop. 5,279
Alma SD 3,300/K-12
PO Box 2359 72921 479-632-4791
David Woolly, supt. Fax 632-4793
www.almasd.net
Alma IS 700/3-5
PO Box 2259 72921 479-632-2166
James Warnock, prin. Fax 632-2167
Alma MS 800/6-8
PO Box 2229 72921 479-632-2168
Bob Wolfe, prin. Fax 632-2160
Alma PS 700/K-2
PO Box 2299 72921 479-632-5100
Shawn Bullard, prin. Fax 632-5102

Alpena, Boone, Pop. 380
Alpena SD 500/K-12
PO Box 270 72611 870-437-2220
Andrea Martin, supt. Fax 437-2133
alpenaschools.k12.ar.us/
Alpena ES 300/K-6
PO Box 270 72611 870-437-2229
Janalee Olhausen-Kaylo, prin. Fax 437-2133

Altus, Franklin, Pop. 753
Ozark SD
Supt. — See Ozark
Ozark MS 300/6-7
PO Box 339 72821 479-468-6111
Ronald Hill, prin. Fax 468-3440

Amity, Clark, Pop. 719
Centerpoint SD 1,000/PK-12
755 Highway 8 E 71921 870-356-2912
Dan Breshears, supt. Fax 356-4637
www.goknights.us
Centerpoint ES 300/PK-5
637 Highway 8 E 71921 870-356-2912
Penny Smothers, prin. Fax 223-4296
Centerpoint MS 200/6-8
755 Highway 8 E 71921 870-356-2101
Penny Smothers, prin. Fax 356-2737

Arkadelphia, Clark, Pop. 10,545
Arkadelphia SD 2,000/K-12
235 N 11th St 71923 870 246 5564
Dr. Donnie Whitten, supt. Fax 246-1144
www.arkadelphiaschools.org
Central PS 300/2-3
233 N 11th St 71923 870-246-2872
Shannon Prince, prin. Fax 246-5523
Goza MS 400/6-8
1305 Caddo St 71923 870-246-4291
Angela Garner, prin. Fax 246-1153
Peake ES 300/4-5
1609 Pine St 71923 870-246-2361
Mary Snowden, prin. Fax 246-1135
Perritt PS 300/K-1
1900 Walnut St 71923 870-246-2260
Callie Hunley, prin. Fax 246-1138

Armorel, Mississippi
Armorel SD 400/PK-12
PO Box 99 72310 870-763-6639
Jennifer Barbaree, supt. Fax 763-0028
armoreltigers.org
Armorel ES 200/PK-6
PO Box 99 72310 870-763-5600
Joey Carr, prin. Fax 763-4108

Ashdown, Little River, Pop. 4,622
Ashdown SD 1,200/K-12
751 Rankin St 71822 870-898-3208
Jason Sanders, supt. Fax 898-3709
www.ashdownschools.org
Ashdown ES 200/K-2
1323 Foster Dr 71822 870-898-3711
Teresa Wake, prin. Fax 898-4431
Ashdown JHS 300/6-8
600 S Ellen Dr 71822 870-898-5138
James Jones, prin. Fax 898-4472
Henderson IS 200/3-5
410 Burke St 71822 870-898-3561
Keith Fricks, prin. Fax 898-4447

Atkins, Pope, Pop. 2,978
Atkins SD 1,000/K-12
307 N Church St 72823 479-641-7871
Joe Fisher, supt. Fax 641-7569
www.atkinsschools.org
Atkins ES 400/K-4
611 NW 4th St 72823 479-641-7085
Stacey Webb, prin. Fax 641-7569
Atkins MS 300/5-8
611 NW 4th St 72823 479-641-1008
Darrell Webb, prin. Fax 641-5504

Augusta, Woodruff, Pop. 2,163
Augusta SD 500/PK-12
10 Red Devil Dr 72006 870-347-2241
Cathy Tanner, supt. Fax 347-5423
www.augustasd.org
Augusta ES 300/PK-6
10 Red Devil Dr 72006 870-347-2432
Richard Greer, prin. Fax 347-1036

Bald Knob, White, Pop. 2,847
Bald Knob SD 1,200/K-12
103 W Park Ave 72010 501-724-3273
Melissa Gipson, supt. Fax 724-6621
baldknobschools.org
Bald Knob MS 300/5-8
601 N Hickory St 72010 501-724-5652
Lori Finley, prin. Fax 724-2062
Lubker ES 500/K-4
103 W Park Ave 72010 501-724-3714
Tammie Cloyes, prin. Fax 724-6253

Barling, Sebastian, Pop. 4,515
Fort Smith SD
Supt. — See Fort Smith
Barling ES 400/PK-6
1400 D St 72923 479-452-0211
Carl Hill, prin. Fax 478-3152

Batesville, Independence, Pop. 10,067
Batesville SD 3,000/K-12
955 Water St 72501 870-793-6831
Dr. Michael Hester, supt. Fax 793-6760
www.batesvilleschools.com
Central Magnet ES 300/K-6
650 Vine St 72501 870-793-7498
Byron Difani, prin. Fax 698-9829
Eagle Mountain Magnet ES 500/K-6
600 Eagle Mountain Blvd 72501 870-698-9141
Pat Rutherford, prin. Fax 793-0608
West Magnet ES 600/K-6
850 N Hill St 72501 870-793-9878
Sonya Crafton, prin. Fax 612-8017
Other Schools – See Sulphur Rock

Southside SD 1,700/PK-12
70 Scott Dr 72501 870-251-2341
Roger Rich, supt. Fax 251-3316
southsideschools.org
Southside JHS 200/7-8
70 Scott Dr 72501 870-251-4003
George Sitkowski, prin. Fax 251-4011
Southside MS 300/4-6
70 Scott Dr 72501 870-251-2332
Dion Stevens, prin. Fax 251-3316
Southside PS 700/PK-3
70 Scott Dr 72501 870-251-2661
Kimberly Poole, prin. Fax 251-3316

Bauxite, Saline, Pop. 486
Bauxite SD 1,500/PK-12
800 School St 72011 501-557-5453
Matt Donaghy, supt. Fax 557-2235
www.edline.net/pages/Bauxite_SD
Bauxite MS 400/6-8
6725 Benton Rd 72011 501-557-5491
Kim Arnold, prin. Fax 557-5509
Pine Haven ES 600/PK-5
500 Pine Haven Rd 72011 501-557-5361
Michael Driggers, prin. Fax 557-5874

Bay, Craighead, Pop. 1,780
Bay SD 600/K-12
PO Box 39 72411 870-781-3296
Oliver Layne, supt. Fax 781-3712
www.edline.net/pages/bay
Bay ES 300/K-6
PO Box 39 72411 870-781-3300
Bobby Hutchison, prin. Fax 781-3837

Bearden, Ouachita, Pop. 942
Bearden SD 600/K-12
100 Oak Ave 71720 870-687-2236
Denny Rozenberg, supt. Fax 687-3683
www.beardenschools.org
Bearden ES 300/K-6
100 Oak Ave 71720 870-687-2237
Sonya Launius, prin. Fax 687-3683

Beebe, White, Pop. 7,140
Beebe SD 3,000/PK-12
1201 W Center St 72012 501-882-5463
Dr. Belinda Shook, supt. Fax 882-5465
beebebadgers.org
Beebe ECC 600/K-1
1201 W Center St 72012 501-882-5463
Michelle Jenkins, prin. Fax 882-8406
Beebe ES 500/PK-PK, 2-
1201 W Center St 72012 501-882-5463
Karla Tarkington, prin. Fax 882-8419
Beebe JHS 500/7-8
1201 W Center St 72012 501-882-5463
Travis Barrentine, prin. Fax 882-8416
Other Schools – See Mc Rae

Bee Branch, Van Buren
South Side SD 500/PK-12
334 Southside Rd 72013 501-654-2633
Billy Jackson, supt. Fax 654-2336
www.ssbb.k12.ar.us
South Side ES 300/PK-6
334 Southside Rd 72013 501-654-2200
Julie Permenter, prin. Fax 654-2326

Bella Vista, Benton, Pop. 26,118
Bentonville SD
Supt. — See Bentonville
Cooper ES 600/K-4
2 Blowing Springs Rd 72714 479-696-3700
Chad Mims, prin. Fax 855-5942

Belleville, Yell, Pop. 432
Western Yell County SD
Supt. — See Havana
Western Yell County ES 200/K-6
300 N Grand Ave 72824 479-493-4100
Keith Jones, prin. Fax 493-4117

Benton, Saline, Pop. 30,248
Benton SD 4,900/K-12
PO Box 939 72018 501-778-4861
Dr. Mike Skelton, supt. Fax 776-5777
ww2.bentonschools.org
Benton MS 800/5-7
204 N Cox St 72015 501-776-5740
Steve Quinn, prin. Fax 776-5749
Caldwell ES 600/K-4
1800 W Sevier St, 501-778-4444
Diane Lovell, prin. Fax 776-5711
Grant ES 600/K-4
1124 Hoover St 72015 501-778-3300
Lori Bacon, prin. Fax 776-5712
Perrin ES 600/K-4
1201 Smithers 72015 501-778-7411
Stacye Shelnut, prin. Fax 776-5713
Ringgold ES 500/K-4
536 River St 72015 501-778-3500
Beverly Mayfield, prin. Fax 776-5714

Bryant SD
Supt. — See Bryant
Hurricane Creek ES 500/K-5
6001 Alcoa Rd 72015 501-653-1012
Tammie Reitenger, prin. Fax 778-7463
Salem ES 600/K-5
2701 Salem Rd, 501-316-0263
Donaven Sims, prin. Fax 794-9043

Harmony Grove SD 800/K-12
2621 N Highway 229 72015 501-778-6271
Daniel Henley, supt. Fax 778-6271
www.harmonygrovesd.org
Harmony Grove MS 100/4-6
2621 N Highway 229 72015 501-860-6796
Kevin Taylor, prin. Fax 860-6796
Westbrook ES 400/K-3
2621 N Highway 229 72015 501-778-7331
Meghann Donaldson, prin. Fax 778-7331

Our Lady of Fatima S 100/PK-8
818 W Cross St 72015 501-315-3398
Jan Cash, prin. Fax 315-1479

Bentonville, Benton, Pop. 34,453
Bentonville SD 15,100/PK-12
500 Tiger Blvd 72712 479-254-5000
Dr. Deborah Jones, supt. Fax 271-1159
district.bentonvillek12.org
Ann MS 600/5-6
3400 Highway 72 W 72712 479-254-5510
Marilyn Gilchrist, prin. Fax 271-1185
Apple Glen ES 500/K-4
1801 Brave Ln 72712 479-254-5580
Tracey Wood, prin. Fax 271-1137
Baker ES 600/K-4
301 NW 3rd St 72712 479-254-5720
Dr. Josh Draper, prin. Fax 271-1115
Barker MS 600/5-6
500 SE 18th St 72712 479-696-3300
Eric Hipp, prin. Fax 271-1161
Bright Field MS 700/5-6
5101 SW Bright Rd 72712 479-418-7200
Aaron Gaffigan, prin.
Central Park ES 800/K-4
1400 SW Liberty Ave 72712 479-696-3200
Stacee Freeman, prin. Fax 271-1148
Creekside MS 500/5-6
2901 SW 28th St 72712 479-286-9600
Jeff Wasem, prin. Fax 286-9572
Elm Tree ES 600/K-4
101 NW Elm Tree Rd 72712 479-254-5650
Amy Simpson, prin. Fax 271-1175
Fulbright JHS 700/7-8
5303 SW Bright Rd 72712 479-802-7000
Bradley Webber, prin.
Jefferson ES 500/K-4
810 Bella Vista Rd 72712 479-254-5860
Karrie Arbuckle, prin. Fax 271-1195
Jones ES 600/K-4
500 SE 14th St 72712 479-254-5930
Ashley Williams, prin. Fax 271-1139
Lincoln JHS 800/7-8
1206 Leopard Ln 72712 479-254-5250
Don Hoover, prin. Fax 271-1128
Old High MS 600/5-6
406 NW 2nd St 72712 479-254-5440
Leslie Lyons, prin. Fax 271-1111
Osage Creek ES 500/K-4
3001 SW Featherston Rd 72712 479-286-9500
Lisa St. John, prin. Fax 286-9572
Russell PS PK-PK
1110 Bella Vista Rd 72712 479-696-3775
Lori Passmore, prin. Fax 271-1177
Sugar Creek ES 500/K-4
1102 Bella Vista Rd 72712 479-254-5790
Matt Cook, prin. Fax 271-1134
Washington JHS 800/7-8
1501 NE Wildcat Way 72712 479-254-5345
Tim Sparacino, prin. Fax 271-1191
Willowbrook ES 800/K-4
1800 SW Gator Blvd 72712 479-418-7300
Cynthia Dewey, prin.
Other Schools – See Bella Vista, Centerton

Ambassadors For Christ Academy 100/PK-12
PO Box 924 72712 479-273-5635
Bentonville Christian Academy 100/PK-6
904 N Walton Blvd 72712 479-616-4880
Clay Hendrix, hdmstr. Fax 316-3429
Bentonville Seventh-Day Adventist S 50/PK-8
2522 SE 14th St 72712 479-271-8887
Elizabeth Fresse, prin. Fax 271-8887
Walnut Farm Montessori S 100/PK-3
4208 E Central Ave 72712 479-271-9424
Heather Incao, head sch Fax 271-8766

Bergman, Boone, Pop. 427
Bergman SD 1,100/K-12
PO Box 1 72615 870-741-5213
Joe Couch, supt. Fax 741-6701
bergman.k12.ar.us
Bergman ES 400/K-4
PO Box 1 72615 870-741-6404
Debbie Atkinson, prin. Fax 741-6017
Bergman MS 300/5-8
PO Box 1 72615 870-741-8557
Sarah Alexander, prin. Fax 741-3490

Berryville, Carroll, Pop. 5,283
Berryville SD 2,000/K-12
902 W Trimble Ave 72616 870-423-7065
Owen Powell, supt. Fax 423-6824
bobcat.k12.ar.us
Berryville ES 500/K-2
902 W Trimble Ave 72616 870-480-4640
Kelly Swofford, prin. Fax 480-4649
Berryville IS 500/3-5
902 W Trimble Ave 72616 870-480-4647
Lisa Geren, prin. Fax 480-4648
Berryville MS 500/6-8
902 W Trimble Ave 72616 870-480-4633
John McClellan, prin. Fax 480-4634

Bigelow, Perry, Pop. 315
East End SD 600/K-12
114 W Panther Dr 72016 501-759-2808
Dr. Doug Harris, supt. Fax 759-2667
eastendpanthers.com
Watson ES 300/K-6
114 W Panther Dr 72016 501-759-2638
Heidi Wilson, prin. Fax 759-3036

Bismarck, Hot Spring
Bismarck SD 1,000/K-12
11636 Highway 84 71929 501-865-4888
Susan Stewart, supt. Fax 865-3626
www.bismarcklions.net/
Bismarck ES 400/K-4
11636 Highway 84 71929 501-865-3616
Lana Hughes, prin. Fax 865-3947
Bismarck MS 300/5-8
11636 Highway 84 71929 501-865-4543
Michael Spraggins, prin. Fax 865-4505

Blevins, Hempstead, Pop. 310
Blevins SD 500/K-12
PO Box 98 71825 870-874-2801
Billy Lee, supt. Fax 874-2889
blevinshornets.weebly.com/
Blevins ES 300/K-6
PO Box 98 71825 870-874-2283
Lisa Doss, prin. Fax 874-2300

Blytheville, Mississippi, Pop. 15,417
Blytheville SD 2,500/PK-12
PO Box 1169 72316 870-762-2053
Richard Atwill, supt. Fax 762-0168
www.blythevilleschools.com
Blytheville ES 400/3-5
216 E Moultrie Dr 72315 870-763-5924
Chanda Walker, prin. Fax 762-0173
Blytheville MS 500/6-8
700 Chickasawba St 72315 870-762-2983
Mike Wallace, prin. Fax 762-0174
Blytheville PS 700/PK-2
1103 Byrum Rd 72315 870-763-6916
Jana Wilson, prin. Fax 762-0171

Bonnerdale, Hot Spring, Pop. 50

Ewing Jr Academy 50/K-10
709 Adventist Church Rd 71933 870-356-2780

Booneville, Logan, Pop. 3,888
Booneville SD 1,300/K-12
381 W 7th St 72927 479-675-3504
John Parrish, supt. Fax 675-3186
www.booneville.k12.ar.us/
Booneville ES 700/K-6
386 W 7th St 72927 479-675-2604
Barbette Smithson, prin. Fax 675-2625

Bradford, White, Pop. 744
Bradford SD 500/K-12
PO Box 60 72020 501-344-2707
Arthur Dunn, supt. Fax 344-2706
bradford.k12.ar.us
Bradford ES 200/K-6
PO Box 60 72020 501-344-8245
Patti Stevens, prin. Fax 344-8245

Bradley, Lafayette, Pop. 627
Emerson-Taylor-Bradley SD
Supt. — See Taylor
Bradley ES 200/PK-6
521 School Dr 71826 870-894-3477
Vickie Spruell, prin. Fax 894-3474

Branch, Franklin, Pop. 358
County Line SD 500/PK-12
12092 W State Highway 22 72928 479-635-2222
Taylor Gattis, supt. Fax 635-2087
indians.wsc.k12.ar.us
County Line ES 200/PK-6
12092 W State Highway 22 72928 479-635-4701
Linda Teague, prin. Fax 635-2102

Brinkley, Monroe, Pop. 3,151
Brinkley SD 500/K-12
200 Tigers Dr 72021 870-734-5000
Dr. Winnie Wilson, supt. Fax 734-5187
www.brinkleyschools.com
Partee ES 300/K-6
400 W Lynn St 72021 870-734-5010
Karl Brown, prin. Fax 734-5014

Brockwell, Izard
Izard County Consolidated SD 500/K-12
PO Box 115 72517 870-258-7700
Fred Walker, supt. Fax 258-3140
icc.k12.ar.us/
Izard County Consolidated MS 100/5-8
PO Box 115 72517 870-258-7788
William McBride, prin. Fax 258-3140
Other Schools – See Violet Hill

Brookland, Craighead, Pop. 1,612
Brookland SD 1,700/PK-12
200 W School St 72417 870-932-2080
Keith McDaniel, supt. Fax 932-2088
www.brooklandbearcats.org
Brookland ES 700/PK-2
220 N Oak St 72417 870-932-9382
Sandy McCall, prin. Fax 974-9760
Brookland MS 200/3-6
310 N Oak St 72417 870-932-2080
Randy Oxford, prin. Fax 974-9762

Bryant, Saline, Pop. 16,446
Bryant SD 8,900/PK-12
200 NW 4th St 72022 501-847-5600
Dr. Tom W. Kimbrell, supt. Fax 847-5695
www.bryantschools.org
Bryant ES 700/PK-5
200 NW 4th St 72022 501-847-5642
Mark Scarlett, prin. Fax 847-0674
Bryant MS 1,100/6-8
200 NW 4th St 72022 501-847-5651
Todd Sellers, prin. Fax 847-5654
Collegeville ES 600/K-5
200 NW 4th St 72022 501-847-5670
Katie Thomas, prin. Fax 847-5672
Hill Farm ES 600/K-5
200 NW 4th St 72022 501-653-5950
Karen Metcalf, prin. Fax 653-5951
Other Schools – See Alexander, Benton

Arkansas Christian Academy 200/PK-12
21815 Interstate 30 S 72022 501-847-0112
Tina Goddard, admin. Fax 847-0177

Cabot, Lonoke, Pop. 23,349
Cabot SD 9,600/PK-12
602 N Lincoln St 72023 501-843-3363
Dr. Tony Thurman, supt. Fax 843-0576
www.cabotschools.org
Cabot JHS North 800/7-8
38 Spirit Dr 72023 501-743-3572
Charlotte Sandage, prin. Fax 605-8472
Cabot JHS South 800/7-8
38 Panther Trl 72023 501-743-3573
John West, prin. Fax 941-7746
Cabot MS North 900/5-6
1900 N Lincoln St 72023 501-743-3571
Dawn Peeples, prin. Fax 605-0413
Cabot MS South 800/5-6
2555 Kerr Station Rd 72023 501-743-3570
Casey Hanna, prin. Fax 941-7432
Central ES 400/PK-4
36 Pond St 72023 501-743-3564
Bethany Hill, prin. Fax 843-4503
Eastside ES 400/K-4
17 Bellamy St 72023 501-743-3563
Jill Fletcher, prin. Fax 843-5619
Magness Creek ES 400/PK-4
16150 Highway 5 72023 501-743-3565
Kelly Bankston, prin. Fax 843-7567
Mountain Springs ES 500/K-4
3620 Mountain Springs Rd 72023 501-743-3575
Mandy Watkins, prin. Fax 605-1300
Northside ES 400/K-4
814 W Locust St 72023 501-743-3568
Suzie Kelly, prin. Fax 843-6032
Southside ES 500/K-4
2600 S Pine St 72023 501-743-3567
Stacy Allen, prin. Fax 843-6229
Stagecoach ES 500/K-4
850 S Stagecoach Rd 72023 501-743-3574
Pamela Waymack-Wilson, prin. Fax 605-1221
Westside ES 400/PK-4
1701 S 2nd St 72023 501-743-3566
Sherri Jennings, prin. Fax 843-5802
Other Schools – See Ward

Calico Rock, Izard, Pop. 1,531
Calico Rock SD 400/K-12
PO Box 220 72519 870-297-8339
Jerry Skidmore, supt. Fax 297-4233
pirates.k12.ar.us/
Calico Rock ES 200/K-6
PO Box 220 72519 870-297-8533
Kimberly Thomas, prin. Fax 297-4233

Camden, Ouachita, Pop. 11,970
Camden Fairview SD 2,400/K-12
625 Clifton St 71701 870-836-4193
Mark Keith, supt. Fax 836-6039
cfsd.k12.ar.us
Camden Fairview IS 300/4-5
255 Pope Ave 71701 870-836-6876
Amy Sanchez, prin. Fax 836-8581
Camden Fairview MS 500/6-8
647 J A Dooley Womack Dr 71701 870-836-9361
Cara Bowie, prin. Fax 836-3717
Fairview ES 500/K-1
735 Robin St 71701 870-231-5434
Treasa Thrower, prin. Fax 231-4652
Ivory PS 400/2-3
575 J A Dooley Womack Dr 71701 870-836-7381
Wayne Bradshaw, prin. Fax 836-5035

Harmony Grove SD 1,000/K-12
401 Ouachita 88 71701 870-574-0971
Walton Pigott, supt. Fax 574-2765
www.hgsd1.com
Harmony Grove ES 400/K-6
401 Ouachita 88 71701 870-574-0960
Jerri Courville, prin. Fax 574-2765
Other Schools – See Sparkman

Victory Christian S K-12
1244 Maul Rd 71701 870-836-6300

Caraway, Craighead, Pop. 1,274
Riverside SD
Supt. — See Lake City
Riverside East ES 200/K-6
502 W State St 72419 870-482-3351
Steven Sanders, prin. Fax 482-3352

Carlisle, Lonoke, Pop. 2,193
Carlisle SD 800/PK-12
520 Center St 72024 870-552-3931
Jason Clark, supt. Fax 552-7967
bison.wmsc.k12.ar.us
Carlisle ES 400/PK-6
707 E 5th St 72024 870-552-3931
Jason Stewart, prin. Fax 552-3017

Cave City, Sharp, Pop. 1,876
Cave City SD 1,000/K-12
PO Box 600 72521 870-283-5391
Steven Green, supt. Fax 283-6887
www.cavecity.k12.ar.us
Cave City ES 400/K-5
PO Box 600 72521 870-283-5393
Vicki Musick, prin. Fax 283-3257
Cave City MS 200/6-8
PO Box 600 72521 870-283-5392
Mark Smith, prin. Fax 266-3258

Cedarville, Crawford, Pop. 1,339
Cedarville SD 900/K-12
PO Box 97 72932 479-474-7220
Dr. Kerry Schneider, supt. Fax 410-1804
www.cedarvilleschools.org
Cedarville ES 300/K-4
PO Box 97 72932 479-474-5073
Rebecca Reed, prin. Fax 410-2223
Cedarville MS 300/5-8
PO Box 97 72932 479-474-5847
Sarah McPhate, prin. Fax 471-7036

Center Ridge, Conway, Pop. 385
Nemo Vista SD 500/PK-12
5690 Highway 9 72027 501-893-2925
Cody Beene, supt. Fax 893-2367
socs.nemo.k12.ar.us
Nemo Vista ES 200/PK-5
5690 Highway 9 72027 501-893-2435
Tresa Virden, prin. Fax 893-6477
Nemo Vista MS 100/6-8
5690 Highway 9 72027 501-893-6494
Tresa Virden, prin. Fax 893-6494

Centerton, Benton, Pop. 9,305
Bentonville SD
Supt. — See Bentonville
Centerton Gamble ES 700/K-4
1550 Gamble Rd 72719 479-696-3400
Cathy Hancock, prin. Fax 795-0526

Life Way Christian S 500/PK-12
PO Box 220 72719 479-795-9322
Dr. Luke Bowers, admin. Fax 795-9399

Charleston, Franklin, Pop. 2,451
Charleston SD 800/PK-12
PO Box 188 72933 479-965-7160
Jeff Stubblefield, supt. Fax 965-9989
tigers.wsc.k12.ar.us/
Charleston ES 400/PK-4
PO Box 188 72933 479-965-2460
Bruce Womack, prin. Fax 965-9989
Charleston MS 100/5-8
PO Box 188 72933 479-965-7170
Melissa Moore, prin. Fax 965-7949

Charlotte, Independence
Cedar Ridge SD
Supt. — See Newark
Cord-Charlotte ES 100/PK-5
225 School Rd 72522 870-201-2577
Kathy Magness, prin. Fax 799-3702

Cherokee Village, Sharp, Pop. 4,624
Highland SD
Supt. — See Highland
Cherokee ES 600/K-4
Highway 175 Spur 72529 870-257-3118
Meg Barnes, prin. Fax 257-3937

Clarendon, Monroe, Pop. 1,643
Clarendon SD 600/K-12
316 N 6th St 72029 870-747-3351
Lee Vent, supt. Fax 747-1527
www.clarendonlions.org
Clarendon ES 300/K-6
1115 Eason Rd 72029 870-747-3383
Linda Hamilton, prin. Fax 747-5963

Clarksville, Johnson, Pop. 9,041
Clarksville SD 2,600/K-12
1701 W Clark Rd 72830 479-705-3200
Dr. David Hopkins, supt. Fax 754-3748
www.csdar.org/
Clarksville PS 400/K-1
2023 W Clark Rd 72830 479-979-6000
Steve Ziegler, prin. Fax 979-6001
Kraus MS 400/5-6
1901 W Clark Rd 72830 479-705-3240
Janice Price, prin. Fax 705-0072
Pyron ES 600/2-4
1903 W Clark Rd 72830 479-705-3256
Christel Thompson, prin. Fax 754-3756

Clinton, Van Buren, Pop. 2,548
Clinton SD 1,300/K-12
765 Yellowjacket Ln 72031 501-508-2030
Andrew Vining, supt. Fax 745-2475
www.clintonsd.org
Clinton ES 400/K-3
852 Yellowjacket Ln 72031 501-508-2046
April Hagans, prin. Fax 745-6083
Clinton IS 300/4-5
852 Yellowjacket Ln 72031 501-508-2043
Kathryn Treadaway, prin. Fax 745-6083
Clinton JHS 300/6-8
443 Yellowjacket Ln 72031 501-508-2020
Michael Wells, prin. Fax 745-6065

College Station, Pulaski, Pop. 592
Pulaski County Special SD
Supt. — See Little Rock
College Station ES 300/PK-5
4710 Frasier Pike 72053 501-490-5750
Yolanda Harris, prin. Fax 490-5756

Conway, Faulkner, Pop. 57,689
Conway SD 10,000/PK-12
2220 Prince St 72034 501-450-4800
Dr. Greg Murry, supt. Fax 450-4898
www.conwayschools.org
Burns ES 400/K-4
1201 Donaghey Ave 72034 501-450-4825
Cynthia Thacker, prin. Fax 450-4857
Cone Pre-School Center 300/PK-PK
1629 South Blvd 72034 501-450-6693
Brenda Mason, head sch Fax 450-4856
Courtway MS 500/5-7
1200 Bob Courtway Dr 72032 501-450-4832
Amy Jordan, prin. Fax 450-4839
Cummins ES 500/K-4
1400 Padgett Rd 72034 501-513-4417
Dayna Lewis, prin. Fax 513-0155
Doyle MS 500/5-7
800 Padgett Rd 72034 501-450-6675
Debi Avra, prin. Fax 450-6669
Jones ES 400/K-4
1800 Freyaldenhoven Ln 72032 501-450-6645
Dr. Tammy Woosley, prin. Fax 450-6649
Lewis ES 500/K-4
1805 Old Military Rd 72034 501-450-4835
Dr. Tina Antley, prin. Fax 450-4896
Mattison ES 400/K-4
2001 Florence Mattison Dr 72032 501-450-4820
Stacy Defoor, prin. Fax 450-6601
Moore ES 300/K-4
1301 Country Club Rd 72034 501-450-4830
Kenny Clark, prin. Fax 450-6605
Simon MS 400/5-7
1601 E Siebenmorgan Rd 72032 501-513-6120
Christi Parrish, prin. Fax 513-6127
Smith ES 500/K-4
1601 S Donaghey Ave 72034 501-450-4815
Delanna Lacy, prin. Fax 450-6621
Stone ES 400/K-4
4255 College Ave 72034 501-450-4808
Mark Lewis, prin. Fax 450-4807
Stuart MS 800/5-7
2745 Carl Stuart St 72034 501-329-2782
Harvey Benton, prin. Fax 450-4848
Vann ES 500/K-4
2845 Carl Stuart St 72034 501-450-4870
Bobby Walker, prin. Fax 450-6659

Conway Christian S 500/PK-12
500 E German Ln 72032 501-336-9067
Jason Carson, pres. Fax 336-9251
St. Joseph S 500/K-12
502 Front St 72032 501-329-5741
Diane Wolfe, prin. Fax 513-6805

Corning, Clay, Pop. 3,348
Corning SD 1,000/K-12
PO Box 479 72422 870-857-6818
Kellee Smith, supt. Fax 857-5086
www.corningschools.k12.ar.us/
Central ES 300/3-6
PO Box 479 72422 870-857-6491
Heather Clifton, prin. Fax 857-1455
Park ES 200/K-2
PO Box 479 72422 870-857-3748
Chad Hovis, prin. Fax 857-6982

Cotter, Baxter, Pop. 947
Cotter SD 700/K-12
PO Box 70 72626 870-435-6171
Shane Lively, supt. Fax 435-1300
www.cotterschools.net
Gist ES 400/K-6
PO Box 70 72626 870-435-6655
Airl Cheek, prin. Fax 435-1300

Crossett, Ashley, Pop. 5,460
Crossett SD 1,900/PK-12
219 Main St 71635 870-364-3112
Gary Williams, supt. Fax 304-2525
www.crossettschools.org
Crossett ES 800/PK-4
1100 Camp Rd 71635 870-364-6521
Veronica Robinson, prin. Fax 364-1725
Crossett MS 500/5-8
100 Petersburg Rd 71635 870-364-4712
Lou Gregorio, prin. Fax 364-3771

Danville, Yell, Pop. 2,373
Danville SD 800/K-12
PO Box 939 72833 479-495-4800
Gregg Grant, supt. Fax 495-4803
www.dps-littlejohns.net
Danville MS 200/5-8
PO Box 939 72833 479-495-4827
Teddy Qualls, prin. Fax 495-4831
Tucker ES 400/K-4
PO Box 939 72833 479-495-4820
Nancy Barrick, prin. Fax 495-4819

Dardanelle, Yell, Pop. 4,680
Dardanelle SD 1,900/K-12
102 S Front St 72834 479-229-4111
John Thompson, supt. Fax 229-1387
www.dardanellepublicschools.org
Dardanelle IS 300/4-5
900 N 4th St 72834 479-229-3707
Terry Laughinghouse, prin. Fax 229-4686
Dardanelle MS 300/6-8
2306 State Highway 7 N 72834 479-229-4550
John Keeling, prin. Fax 229-1697
Dardanelle PS 700/K-3
1376 N Liberty Rd 72834 479-229-4185
Sue Ann Jernigan, prin. Fax 229-5036

Decatur, Benton, Pop. 1,637
Decatur SD 600/PK-12
1498 Stadium Ave 72722 479-752-3986
Jeff Gravette, supt. Fax 752-2490
www.decatursd.com
Decatur Northside ES 400/PK-6
9083 Mount Olive Rd 72722 479-752-3981
Cary Stamps, prin. Fax 752-3982

Deer, Newton
Deer / Mt. Judea SD 400/K-12
PO Box 56 72628 870-428-5433
Andrew Curry, supt. Fax 428-5901
deermtjudea.k12.ar.us
Deer S 100/K-12
PO Box 56 72628 870-428-8109
Elvis Middleton, admin. Fax 428-5901
Other Schools – See Mount Judea

Delight, Pike, Pop. 278
South Pike County SD
Supt. — See Murfreesboro
Delight ES 100/K-6
621 E Cherry St 71940 870-379-2214
Pam Bonner, prin. Fax 379-2448

De Queen, Sevier, Pop. 6,482
De Queen SD 2,300/K-12
101 N 9th St 71832 870-584-4312
Bruce Hill, supt. Fax 642-8881
www.dequeenleopards.org
De Queen ES 500/3-5
233 S Treating Plant Rd 71832 870-584-4311
Terriann Phillips, prin. Fax 642-8582
De Queen MS 400/6-7
1803 W Coulter Ave 71832 870-642-2428
Brenda Leeper, prin. Fax 642-3355
De Queen PS 600/K-2
235 S Treating Plant Rd 71832 870-642-3100
Terri Hill, prin. Fax 642-7360

Legacy Academy 50/PK-10
314 W Gilson Ave 71832 870-642-8937
Jessica Gallagher, admin. Fax 925-6893

Dermott, Chicot, Pop. 2,294
Dermott SD 400/K-12
PO Box 380 71638 870-538-1000
Kristi Ridgell, supt. Fax 538-1005
www.dermott.k12.ar.us
Dermott ES 200/K-6
PO Box 380 71638 870-538-1010
Shakelia Atkins, prin. Fax 538-1070

Des Arc, Prairie, Pop. 1,696
Des Arc SD 600/PK-12
600 Main St 72040 870-256-4164
Nicholas Hill, supt. Fax 256-3701
www.desarc.wmsc.k12.ar.us
Des Arc ES 300/PK-6
2100 Hickory St 72040 870-256-4128
Dena Rooks, prin. Fax 256-4499

De Witt, Arkansas, Pop. 3,250
De Witt SD 1,300/PK-12
PO Box 700 72042 870-946-3576
Lynne Dardenne, supt. Fax 946-1491
www.dewittschooldistrict.net
De Witt ES 500/K-5
1718 S Grandview Dr 72042 870-946-4651
Julie Amstutz, prin. Fax 946-4652
De Witt MS 300/6-8
1209 W 16th St 72042 870-946-3708
Justin Russell, prin. Fax 946-1301
Other Schools – See Gillett

Dierks, Howard, Pop. 1,118
Dierks SD 600/K-12
PO Box 124 71833 870-286-2191
Holly Cothron, supt. Fax 286-2450
www.dierksschools.org
Walters ES 300/K-6
PO Box 70 71833 870-286-2015
Karla Byrne, prin. Fax 286-3232

Donaldson, Hot Spring, Pop. 298
Ouachita SD 500/K-12
166 Schoolhouse Rd 71941 501-384-2318
Ronnie Kissire, supt. Fax 384-5615
www.ouachitasd.org
Ouachita ES 300/K-6
332 Schoolhouse Rd 71941 501-384-2341
Lyn McDade, prin. Fax 384-5616

Dover, Pope, Pop. 1,350
Dover SD 1,300/K-12
PO Box 325 72837 479-331-2916
Jerry Owens, supt. Fax 331-2205
www.doverschools.net
Dover ES 500/K-4
PO Box 325 72837 479-331-2702
Josh Daniels, prin. Fax 331-2106
Dover MS 300/5-8
203 College St 72837 479-331-4814
Donald Forehand, prin. Fax 331-4965

Dumas, Desha, Pop. 4,687
Dumas SD 1,500/PK-12
213 Adams St 71639 870-382-4571
Kelvin Gragg, supt. Fax 382-4874
dpsd.k12.ar.us
Central ES 400/PK-2
101 Court St 71639 870-382-4954
Tammy Healey, prin. Fax 382-6897
Reed ES 400/3-6
710 S Cherry St 71639 870-382-5363
Nancy Chapman, prin. Fax 382-3104

Earle, Crittenden, Pop. 2,397
Earle SD 600/K-12
PO Box 637 72331 870-792-8406
Vaughn Sanders, supt. Fax 792-8897
www.earle.crsc.k12.ar.us/
Earle ES 300/K-6
PO Box 637 72331 870-792-8732
Carloss Guess, prin. Fax 792-1011

El Dorado, Union, Pop. 18,658
El Dorado SD 4,700/K-12
200 W Oak St 71730 870-864-5001
Jim Tucker, supt. Fax 864-5015
www.eldoradopublicschools.com
Barton JHS 700/7-8
400 W Faulkner St 71730 870-864-5051
Sherry Hill, prin. Fax 864-5064
Brown ES 300/K-4
505 Dixie Dr 71730 870-864-5081
Bethanie Hale, prin. Fax 864-5080
Goodwin ES 500/K-4
201 E 5th St 71730 870-864-5071
Connie Reed, prin. Fax 864-5137
Northwest ES 500/K-4
1600 N College Ave 71730 870-864-5078
Sherry Floss, prin. Fax 864-5077
Washington MS 700/5-6
601 Martin Luther King Ave 71730 870-864-5032
Jody Vines, prin. Fax 864-5041
Yocum ES 600/K-4
308 S College Ave 71730 870-864-5096
Michelle Henry, prin. Fax 864-5095

Parkers Chapel SD 800/PK-12
401 Parkers Chapel Rd 71730 870-862-4641
Michael White, supt. Fax 881-5092
www.parkerschapelschool.com
Parkers Chapel ES 500/PK-6
401 Parkers Chapel Rd 71730 870-862-9767
Carrie Burson, prin. Fax 881-5094

West Side Christian S 100/PK-12
2400 W Hillsboro St 71730 870-863-5636
Robin Colley, admin. Fax 863-3529

Elkins, Washington, Pop. 2,568
Elkins SD 1,100/K-12
349 N Center St 72727 479-643-2172
Dan Jordan, supt. Fax 643-3605
www.elkinsdistrict.org
Elkins ES 200/3-5
349 N Center St 72727 479-643-3382
Amy Evans, prin. Fax 643-4111
Elkins MS 300/6-8
349 N Center St 72727 479-643-2552
Steve Denzer, prin. Fax 643-4272
Elkins PS 200/K-2
349 N Center St 72727 479-643-3380
Dean Rowland, prin. Fax 643-4151

Emerson, Columbia, Pop. 368
Emerson-Taylor-Bradley SD
Supt. — See Taylor
Emerson ES 200/PK-6
508 W Main St 71740 870-547-2218
Jennifer Kyle, prin. Fax 547-2077

England, Lonoke, Pop. 2,789
England SD 800/PK-12
501 Pine Bluff Hwy 72046 501-842-2996
Tyler Scott, supt. Fax 842-3698
www.englandlions.net
England ES 400/PK-6
400 E Dewitt St 72046 501-842-2041
Jeff Adams, prin. Fax 842-2986

Enola, Faulkner, Pop. 335
Mount Vernon-Enola SD
Supt. — See Mount Vernon
Mount Vernon-Enola ES 300/K-6
17 Mount Vernon Rd 72047 501-849-2211
Rob Rollins, prin. Fax 849-3270

Eudora, Chicot, Pop. 2,265
Lakeside SD
Supt. — See Lake Village
Eudora ES 200/PK-3
566 S Mabry St 71640 870-355-6040
James Maiden, prin. Fax 355-6045

Eureka Springs, Carroll, Pop. 2,008
Eureka Springs SD 600/K-12
147 Greenwood Hollow Rd 72632 479-253-5999
Bryan Pruitt, supt. Fax 253-5955
eurekaspringsschools.k12.ar.us
Eureka Springs ES 300/K-4
156 Greenwood Hollow Rd 72632 479-253-8704
Clare Lesieur, prin. Fax 253-7983
Eureka Springs MS 200/5-8
142 Greenwood Hollow Rd 72632 479-253-7716
Cindy Holt, prin. Fax 253-7809

Clear Spring S 100/PK-12
PO Box 511 72632 479-253-7888
Phyllis Poe, head sch Fax 253-0768

Everton, Marion, Pop. 128
Ozark Mountain SD
Supt. — See Saint Joe
Bruno-Pyatt S 100/K-12
4754 Highway 125 S 72633 870-427-5227
Nichole Cunningham, prin. Fax 427-5255

Farmington, Washington, Pop. 5,772
Farmington SD 2,100/K-12
42 S Double Springs Rd 72730 479-266-1800
Bryan Law, supt. Fax 267-6030
www.farmcards.org/
Folsom ES 300/K-3
230 S Grace Ln 72730 479-267-6024
Shannon Cantrell, prin. Fax 267-6033
Ledbetter ES 400/4-5
8 N Double Springs Rd 72730 479-266-1810
Julia Williams, prin. Fax 267-6045
Lynch MS 500/6-8
359 Rheas Mill Rd 72730 479-266-1840
Terry Lakey, prin. Fax 267-6051
Williams ES 400/K-3
322 Broyles St 72730 479-267-6013
Kara Gardenhire, prin. Fax 267-4506

Fayetteville, Washington, Pop. 71,413
Fayetteville SD 9,400/K-12
1000 W Bulldog Blvd 72701 479-444-3000
Dr. Matthew Wendt, supt. Fax 973-8670
www.fayar.net
Asbell ES 400/K-4
1500 N Sang Ave 72703 479-444-3080
Tracy Bratton, prin. Fax 444-3032
Butterfield Trail ES 600/K-4
3050 N Old Missouri Rd 72703 479-444-3081
Joette Folsom, prin. Fax 444-3029
Happy Hollow ES 500/K-4
2175 E Peppervine Dr 72701 479-444-3085
Dondi Frisinger, prin. Fax 444-3031
Holcomb ES 600/K-4
2900 N Salem Rd 72704 479-527-3610
Tracy Mulvenon, prin. Fax 527-3613
Holt MS 600/5-6
2365 N Rupple Rd 72704 479-527-3670
Matt Morningstar, prin. Fax 527-3677
Leverett ES 300/K-4
1124 W Cleveland St 72701 479-444-3077
Cheryl Putnam, prin. Fax 444-3079
McNair MS 700/5-6
3030 E Mission Blvd 72703 479-527-3660
Melissa Hayward, prin. Fax 527-3667
Owl Creek S 800/K-6
375 N Rupple Rd 72704 479-718-0200
Stephanie Davis, prin. Fax 718-0201
Ramay JHS 600/7-8
401 S Sang Ave 72701 479-444-3064
David Watkins, prin. Fax 444-3013
Root ES 500/K-4
1529 E Mission Blvd 72701 479-444-3075
Kristen Scott, prin. Fax 444-3033
Vandergriff ES 700/K-4
2200 Vandergriff Ln 72703 479-527-3600
Andrea Sego, prin. Fax 527-3603
Washington ES 400/K-4
425 N Highland Ave 72701 479-444-3073
Ashley McLarty, prin. Fax 527-3617

Fayetteville Christian S 200/PK-12
2006 E Mission Blvd 72703 479-442-2565
New S 200/PK-10
2514 N New School Pl 72703 479-521-7037
Dennis Chapman, head sch Fax 571-1173
Prism Education Center 200/K-12
2855 E Joyce Blvd 72703 479-249-6113
St. Joseph S 300/PK-8
1722 N Starr Dr 72701 479-442-4554
Jason Pohlmeier, prin. Fax 442-7887

Flippin, Marion, Pop. 1,337
Flippin SD 800/K-12
210 Alford St 72634 870-453-2270
Kelvin Hudson, supt. Fax 453-5059
www.flippinschools.com
Flippin ES 400/K-5
144 School Ln 72634 870-453-8860
Tracie Luttrell, prin. Fax 453-8877
Flippin MS 200/6-8
146 School Ln 72634 870-453-6464
Gregg Yarbrough, prin. Fax 453-6465

Floral, Independence
Midland SD
Supt. — See Pleasant Plains
Midland ES 300/K-6
PO Box 119 72534 501-345-2413
Bani Meharg, prin. Fax 345-2273

Fordyce, Dallas, Pop. 4,245
Fordyce SD 900/PK-12
PO Box 706 71742 870-352-3005
Dr. Albert Snow, supt. Fax 352-7187
www.fordyceschools.org
Fordyce ES 500/PK-6
PO Box 706 71742 870-352-2816
Barbara Bennett, prin. Fax 352-8693

Foreman, Little River, Pop. 984
Foreman SD 500/K-12
PO Box 480 71836 870-542-7211
George Kennedy, supt. Fax 542-7225
www.foremanschools.org
Hamilton ES 300/K-6
PO Box 480 71836 870-542-7214
Patricia Tankersley, prin. Fax 542-6369

Forrest City, Saint Francis, Pop. 15,183
Forrest City SD 3,100/PK-12
625 Irving St 72335 870-633-1485
Tiffany Hardrick Ph.D., supt. Fax 633-1415
mustang.grsc.k12.ar.us/
ABC Preschool PK-PK
1000 N Division St, 870-261-1807
Vivian Ryan, dir. Fax 261-1834
Central ES 1,000/PK-2
801 Deadrick Rd 72335 870-633-2141
Sharon Council, prin. Fax 633-1415
Forrest City JHS 400/6-8
1133 N Division St 72335 870-633-3230
Carlos Fuller, prin. Fax 633-6066
Stewart ES 400/3-5
400 Dawson Rd 72335 870-633-3248
Hazel Wallace, prin. Fax 633-1415

Calvary Christian S 100/PK-12
1611 N Washington St 72335 870-633-5333

Fort Smith, Sebastian, Pop. 83,397
Fort Smith SD 14,500/PK-12
PO Box 1948 72902 479-785-2501
Douglas Brubaker Ed.D., supt. Fax 785-1722
www.fortsmithschools.org
Ballman ES 300/PK-6
2601 S Q St 72901 479-783-1280
Lori Griffin, prin. Fax 785-1513
Beard ES 300/K-6
1600 Cavanaugh Rd 72908 479-646-0834
Pam Siebenmorgen, prin. Fax 648-8262
Bonneville ES 400/K-6
2500 S Waldron Rd 72903 479-478-3161
Sharla Whitson, prin. Fax 452-7654
Carnall ES 300/PK-6
2524 Tulsa St 72901 479-646-3612
Leslie Sharp, prin. Fax 648-8263
Cavanaugh ES 300/PK-6
1025 School St 72908 479-646-1131
Hank Needham, prin. Fax 648-8297

Cook ES 500/PK-6
3517 Brooken Hill Dr 72908 479-646-8880
Billy Spicer, prin. Fax 648-8292
Euper Lane ES 500/PK-6
6601 Euper Ln 72903 479-452-2601
Melissa Braddy, prin. Fax 478-3118
Fairview ES 700/PK-6
2400 Dallas St 72901 479-783-3214
Peggy Walter, prin. Fax 784-8127
Howard ES 400/PK-6
1301 N 8th St 72901 479-783-7382
Velmar Greene, prin. Fax 784-8180
Morrison ES 300/PK-6
3415 Newlon Rd 72904 479-782-7045
Britney Ballin, prin. Fax 784-8192
Orr ES 400/PK-6
3609 Phoenix Ave 72903 479-646-3711
Pat Cagle, prin. Fax 648-8266
Pike ES 500/K-6
4111 Park Ave 72903 479-783-4506
Monica Wilhelm Austin, prin. Fax 784-8128
Spradling ES 400/PK-6
4949 Spradling Ave 72904 479-783-8048
Robyn Dawson, prin. Fax 784-8172
Sunnymede ES 600/K-6
4201 N O St 72904 479-783-6327
Krystle Smith, prin. Fax 784-8173
Sutton ES 500/PK-6
5001 Kelley Hwy 72904 479-785-1778
Jennie Mathews, prin. Fax 784-8174
Tilles ES 400/PK-6
815 N 16th St 72901 479-785-5606
Regina Thompson, prin. Fax 784-8152
Trusty ES 400/K-6
3300 Harris Ave 72904 479-783-7720
Shantelle Edwards Ed.D., prin. Fax 784-8171
Woods ES 500/PK-6
3201 Massard Rd 72903 479-452-5808
Andrea Schwartz, prin. Fax 452-0021
Other Schools – See Barling

Christ the King S 300/PK-6
1918 S Greenwood Ave 72901 479-782-0614
Jeff Plake, prin. Fax 782-1098
First Lutheran S 200/PK-6
2407 Massard Rd 72903 479-452-5330
Dr. Philip Frusti, prin. Fax 452-3553
Fort Smith Montessori S 100/PK-6
3908 Jenny Lind Rd 72901 479-646-7225
Harvest Time Academy 100/PK-6
3300 Briarcliff Ave 72908 479-646-6003
Michelle Sloan, dir. Fax 434-3411
Immaculate Conception S 300/PK-6
223 S 14th St 72901 479-783-6798
Sharon Blentlinger, prin. Fax 783-0510
St. Boniface S 200/PK-6
201 N 19th St 72901 479-783-6601
Rebecca Kaelin, prin. Fax 783-6605
Union Christian Academy 200/PK-12
4201 Windsor Dr 72904 479-783-7327
Dennis Queen, supt. Fax 783-9342

Fouke, Miller, Pop. 849
Fouke SD 1,100/PK-12
PO Box 20 71837 870-653-4311
Dr. Jim Buie, supt. Fax 653-2856
fouke.schoolfusion.us
Fouke ES 500/PK-5
PO Box 20 71865 870-653-4165
Ken Endris, prin. Fax 653-7885
Smith MS 200/6-8
PO Box 20 71837 870-653-2304
Amanda Whitehead, prin. Fax 653-7840

Fox, Stone
Mountain View SD
Supt. — See Mountain View
Rural Special ES 100/K-6
13237 Highway 263 72051 870-363-4365
Shelia Mitchell, prin. Fax 363-4222

Garfield, Benton, Pop. 485
Rogers SD
Supt. — See Rogers
Garfield ES 100/K-5
PO Box 69 72732 479-359-3263
Stephen Bowman, prin. Fax 359-2236

Gentry, Benton, Pop. 3,064
Gentry SD 1,400/K-12
201 S Giles Ave 72734 479-736-2253
Terrie Metz, supt. Fax 736-2245
www.gentrypioneers.com
Gentry IS 300/3-5
201 S Giles Ave 72734 479-736-2252
Keeta Neal, prin. Fax 736-5308
Gentry MS 400/6-8
201 S Giles Ave 72734 479-736-2251
Larry Cozens, prin. Fax 736-3414
Gentry PS 300/K-2
201 S Giles Ave 72734 479-736-2380
Gayla Wilmoth, prin. Fax 736-0316

Ozark Adventist S 100/PK-8
21150 Dawn Hill East Rd 72734 479-736-8592

Gillett, Arkansas, Pop. 687
De Witt SD
Supt. — See De Witt
Gillett ES 100/PK-5
316 S 6th 72055 870-548-2466
Rachel Mitchell, prin. Fax 548-2281

Gosnell, Mississippi, Pop. 3,483
Gosnell SD 1,300/K-12
600 N State Highway 181 72315 870-532-4000
Bonard Mace, supt. Fax 532-4002
www.gosnellschool.net
Gosnell ES 700/K-6
600 N State Highway 181 72315 870-532-4003
Tiffany Kennemore, prin. Fax 532-4033

Gravette, Benton, Pop. 2,243
Gravette SD 1,900/PK-12
609 Birmingham St SE 72736 479-787-4100
Dr. Richard Page Ed.D., supt. Fax 787-4108
gravetteschools.net
Duffy ES 500/PK-2
601 El Paso St SE 72736 479-787-4120
Zane Vanderpool, prin. Fax 787-4128
Gravette MS 500/6-8
607 Dallas St SE 72736 479-787-4160
Duane Thomas, prin. Fax 787-4178
Gravette Upper ES 400/3-5
500 8th Ave SE 72736 479-787-4140
Dr. Mandy Barrett, prin. Fax 787-4148

Greenbrier, Faulkner, Pop. 4,616
Greenbrier SD 3,400/PK-12
4 School Dr 72058 501-679-4808
Scott Spainhour, supt. Fax 679-1024
www.greenbrierschools.org
Greenbrier Eastside ES 600/PK-5
61 Glenn Ln 72058 501-679-2111
Mandi Dunlap, prin. Fax 679-1016
Greenbrier MS 500/6-7
13 School Dr 72058 501-679-2113
Bryce Bennett, prin. Fax 679-1072
Greenbrier Springhill ES K-5
91 Elliott Rd 72058 501-679-4808
Stephanie Worthey, prin.
Greenbrier Westside ES 500/PK-5
65 Garrett Rd 72058 501-679-1029
Angie Betancourt, prin. Fax 679-1049
Greenbrier Wooster ES 500/K-5
9 Church Cir 72058 501-679-3334
Amber Brantley, prin. Fax 679-1049

Green Forest, Carroll, Pop. 2,720
Green Forest SD 1,200/K-12
PO Box 1950 72638 870-438-5201
Matt Summers, supt. Fax 438-6214
www.gf.k12.ar.us
Green Forest ES 400/K-3
PO Box 1950 72638 870-438-5205
Danette Chaney, prin. Fax 438-4380
Green Forest IS 200/4-5
PO Box 1950 72638 870-438-5129
Chandra Anderson, prin. Fax 438-5017
Green Forest MS 300/6-8
PO Box 1950 72638 870-438-5242
Tim Booth, prin. Fax 438-6343

Greenland, Washington, Pop. 1,236
Greenland SD 800/PK-12
PO Box 57 72737 479-521-2366
Dr. Andrea Martin, supt. Fax 521-1480
www.greenlandsd.com
Greenland ES 300/PK-4
PO Box 57 72737 479-521-2366
Alan Barton, prin. Fax 582-8722
Greenland MS 300/5-8
PO Box 57 72737 479-521-2366
Heather Cheevers, prin. Fax 251-1203

Greenwood, Sebastian, Pop. 8,785
Greenwood SD 3,600/K-12
420 N Main St 72936 479-996-4142
John Ciesla, supt. Fax 996-4143
www.greenwoodk12.com/
East Hills MS 600/5-6
1211 Raymond E Wells Dr 72936 479-996-0504
Beth Dixon-Fincher, prin. Fax 996-6614
East Pointe ES 800/K-4
700 Mount Harmony Rd 72936 479-996-4249
Michael Dean, prin. Fax 996-6111
Greenwood JHS 600/7-8
300 E Gary St 72936 479-996-7440
Aaron Gamble, prin. Fax 996-7469
Westwood ES 800/K-4
300 Westwood Ave 72936 479-996-7748
Jamie Foster, prin. Fax 996-7846

Greers Ferry, Cleburne, Pop. 887
West Side SD 400/PK-12
7295 Greers Ferry Rd 72067 501-825-6258
Andy Chisum, supt. Fax 825-6258
www.westsideeagles.org
West Side ES 200/PK-6
7295 Greers Ferry Rd 72067 501-825-7744
John Long, prin. Fax 825-7744

Gurdon, Clark, Pop. 2,184
Gurdon SD 800/K-12
1 Go Devil Dr 71743 870-353-4454
Allen Blackwell, supt. Fax 353-4455
www.go-devils.net
Cabe MS 200/5-8
7780 Highway 67 S 71743 870-353-4454
Amanda Jones, prin. Fax 353-5149
Gurdon PS 300/K-4
401 N 10th St 71743 870-353-4321
Rusty Manning, prin. Fax 353-5146

Guy, Faulkner, Pop. 699
Guy-Perkins SD 400/K-12
492 Highway 25 N 72061 501-679-7224
Shade Gilbert, supt. Fax 679-3508
www.gptbirds.org
Guy-Perkins ES 200/K-6
492 Highway 25 N 72061 501-679-3509
Karen Hoskins, prin. Fax 679-3508

Hackett, Sebastian, Pop. 782
Hackett SD 1,000/PK-12
102 N Oak St 72937 479-638-8822
Edward Ray, supt. Fax 638-7106
www.hackettschools.org
Hackett ES 300/PK-6
102 N Oak St 72937 479-638-8606
Tura Bailey, prin. Fax 638-8607
Other Schools – See Hartford

Hamburg, Ashley, Pop. 2,843
Hamburg SD 2,000/PK-12
202 E Parker St 71646 870-853-9851
Tracy Streeter, supt. Fax 853-2842
www.hsdlions.org
Hamburg MS 500/6-8
1109 Cub Dr 71646 870-853-2811
Penny Woods, prin. Fax 853-2835
Noble/Albritton ES 800/PK-5
206 S Bartlett St 71646 870-853-2836
Tricia Johnson, prin. Fax 853-2838
Other Schools – See Portland

Hampton, Calhoun, Pop. 1,315
Hampton SD 500/K-12
PO Box 1176 71744 870-798-2742
Jimmy Cunningham, supt. Fax 798-2239
www.edline.net/pages/Hampton_Public_Schools
Hampton ES 300/K-6
PO Box 1176 71744 870-798-2304
Thomas Sawyer, prin. Fax 798-2070

Harrisburg, Poinsett, Pop. 2,253
Harrisburg SD 1,300/K-12
207 W Estes St 72432 870-578-2416
Danny Sample, supt. Fax 578-9366
www.hbgsd.org/
Harrisburg ES 400/K-4
1003 S Illinois St 72432 870-578-2413
Cathy J. Spiegel, prin. Fax 578-9630
Harrisburg MS 400/5-8
401 W South St 72432 870-578-2410
Cindy Armstrong, prin. Fax 578-6201
Other Schools – See Weiner

Harrison, Boone, Pop. 12,739
Harrison SD 2,800/PK-12
110 S Cherry St 72601 870-741-7600
Dr. Aaron Hosman, supt. Fax 741-4520
www.harrisongoblins.org
Eagle Heights ES 200/K-4
500 N Chestnut St 72601 870-741-5043
Linda Pledger, prin. Fax 741-0057
Forest Heights ES 400/K-4
1124 Tamarind St 72601 870-741-5837
Ryan Oswalt, prin. Fax 741-8599
Harrison MS 400/5-6
1125 Goblin Dr 72601 870-741-9764
Fred Wilson, prin. Fax 741-3339
Skyline Heights ES 400/K-4
1120 W Holt Ave 72601 870-741-5821
Jeffrey Winkle, prin. Fax 741-0335
Woodland Heights ES 100/PK-4
520 E Womack St 72601 870-741-0581
Debbie Wilson, prin. Fax 741-8883

Harrison SDA S 50/K-8
4877 Highway 392 W 72601 870-741-0169

Hartford, Sebastian, Pop. 634
Hackett SD
Supt. — See Hackett
Hartford ES 200/PK-6
512 Ludlow St 72938 479-639-2831
David Lee, prin. Fax 639-2158

Hartman, Johnson, Pop. 516
Westside SD 600/K-12
1535 Rabbit Hill Rd 72840 479-497-1991
Shane Gordon, supt. Fax 497-9037
www.westsiderebels.net
Westside ES 400/K-6
193 School St 72840 479-497-1088
John Elms, prin. Fax 497-1938

Hattieville, Conway
Wonderview SD 400/PK-12
2436 Highway 95 72063 501-354-0211
Jamie Stacks, supt. Fax 354-6071
www.wonderviewschools.org
Wonderview ES 200/PK-6
2436 Highway 95 72063 501-354-4736
Brian Cossey, prin. Fax 354-8487

Havana, Yell, Pop. 375
Western Yell County SD 400/K-12
PO Box 214 72842 479-476-4116
Joe Staton, supt. Fax 476-4115
wolverines.k12.ar.us
Other Schools – See Belleville

Hazen, Prairie, Pop. 1,454
Hazen SD 700/PK-12
305 N Hazen Ave 72064 870-255-4549
William Crowder, supt. Fax 255-4508
www.hazen.k12.ar.us
Hazen ES 500/PK-8
305 N Hazen Ave 72064 870-255-4547
Tiffany Glover, prin. Fax 255-1233

Heber Springs, Cleburne, Pop. 7,068
Heber Springs SD 1,800/K-12
1100 W Pine St 72543 501-362-6712
Dr. Alan Stauffacher, supt. Fax 362-0613
hssd.k12.ar.us
Heber Springs ES 800/K-5
1100 W Pine St 72543 501-362-8155
Roxanne Riddle, prin. Fax 362-2599
Heber Springs MS 400/6-8
1100 W Pine St 72543 501-362-2488
Rita Watkins, prin. Fax 362-2193

Hector, Pope, Pop. 441
Hector SD 600/K-12
11520 SR 27 72843 479-284-2021
Mark Taylor, supt. Fax 284-2350
hectorschools.net
Hector ES 300/K-6
104 Sycamore St 72843 479-284-3586
Kathy Freeman, prin. Fax 284-4010

Helena, Phillips, Pop. 5,687
Helena/West Helena SD 1,700/PK-12
305 Valley Dr 72342 870-338-4425
John Hoy, supt. Fax 338-4411
www.hwhschools.org
Wahl PS 600/PK-3
125 Hickory Hills Dr 72342 870-338-4404
Jewell Hamilton, prin. Fax 338-4421
Other Schools – See West Helena

Hermitage, Bradley, Pop. 823
Hermitage SD 500/PK-12
PO Box 38 71647 870-463-2246
Dr. Tracy Tucker, supt. Fax 463-8520
www.hermitageschools.org
Hermitage ES 300/PK-6
PO Box 38 71647 870-463-8500
Mistie McGhee, prin. Fax 463-2034

Highland, Sharp, Pop. 1,030
Highland SD 1,600/K-12
1627 Highway 62 412 72542 870-856-3275
Don Sharp, supt. Fax 856-2765
highlandrebels.k12.ar.us
Highland MS 400/5-8
1627 Highway 62 412, 870-856-3284
Paulette Crouthers, prin. Fax 856-3288
Other Schools – See Cherokee Village

Hope, Hempstead, Pop. 9,935
Hope SD 2,800/K-12
117 E 2nd St 71801 870-722-2700
Bobby Hart, supt. Fax 777-4087
www.hpsdistrict.org
Clinton PS 1,100/K-4
601 Lakeshore Dr 71801 870-722-2723
Ashlea Stewart, prin. Fax 722-2765
Henry ES 300/5-6
2000 S Main St 71801 870-777-6222
Dr. Roy Turner, prin. Fax 722-2751
Yerger MS 400/7-8
400 E 9th St 71801 870-722-2770
Josclyn Wiley, prin. Fax 722-2707

Spring Hill SD 600/K-12
633 Highway 355 W 71801 870-777-8236
Angela Raney, supt. Fax 777-9200
www.springhill.k12.ar.us
Spring Hill ES 300/K-6
633 Highway 355 W 71801 870-722-7420
Audrey Chandler, prin. Fax 722-7440

Horatio, Sevier, Pop. 1,021
Horatio SD 900/PK-12
204 Lawson Ln 71842 870-832-1940
Lee Smith, supt. Fax 832-4465
www.horatioschools.org
Horatio ES 500/PK-6
PO Box 435 71842 870-832-1930
Susan Nelson, prin. Fax 832-3222

Hot Springs National Park, Garland, Pop. 34,276
Cutter-Morning Star SD 600/K-12
2801 Spring St 71901 501-262-2414
Nancy Anderson, supt. Fax 262-0670
eaglesnest.dsc.k12.ar.us/
Cutter-Morning Star ES 300/K-6
2801 Spring St 71901 501-262-1883
Janis Gibson, prin. Fax 262-1884

Fountain Lake SD 1,300/K-12
4207 Park Ave 71901 501-701-1700
Michael Murphy, supt. Fax 623-6447
www.flcobras.net
Fountain Lake ES 400/K-4
4207 Park Ave 71901 501-701-1707
Allyson Petty, prin. Fax 897-6413
Fountain Lake MS Cobra Digital Prep Acad 400/5-8
4207 Park Ave 71901 501-701-1730
Frank Janaskie, prin. Fax 318-6922

Hot Springs SD 3,700/PK-12
400 Linwood Ave 71913 501-624-3372
Stephanie Nehus, supt. Fax 620-7829
www.hssd.net
Gardner STEM Magnet S 500/PK-4
525 Hammond Dr 71913 501-620-7822
Cathy Johnson, prin. Fax 620-7837
Hot Springs IS 600/5-6
617 Main St 71913 501-620-7851
Becky Rosburg, prin. Fax 620-7855
Hot Springs Junior Academy 500/7-8
700 Main St 71913 501-624-5228
Natasha Lenox, prin. Fax 620-7828
Langston Aerospace & Environmental S 400/PK-4
120 Chestnut St 71901 501-620-7821
Eileen Ellars, prin. Fax 620-7836
Oaklawn Visual & Performing Arts S 600/PK-4
301 Oaklawn St 71913 501-623-2661
Jason Selig, prin. Fax 620-7834
Park Intl Baccalaureate Magnet S 300/K-4
617 Main St 71913 501-623-5661
Dr. Sarah Oatsvall, prin. Fax 620-7855

Lakeside SD 3,300/PK-12
2837 Malvern Ave 71901 501-262-1880
Shawn Cook, supt. Fax 262-2732
lakesidesd.com
Lakeside IS 700/2-4
2855 Malvern Ave 71901 501-262-2332
Sandy Hawkins, prin. Fax 262-3955
Lakeside MS 700/5-7
2923 Malvern Ave 71901 501-262-6244
Jamie Preston, prin. Fax 262-6248
Lakeside PS 600/PK-1
2841 Malvern Ave 71901 501-262-1921
Julie Burroughs, prin. Fax 262-6225

Christian Ministries Academy 100/K-12
PO Box 8500 71910 501-624-1952
David Pate, prin. Fax 318-2624
Hot Springs SDA S 50/PK-8
401 Weston Rd 71913 501-760-3336
Joan Fos, lead tchr.
St. John Catholic S 100/PK-8
583 W Grand Ave 71901 501-624-3171
Paul Guild, prin. Fax 624-3171

Hoxie, Lawrence, Pop. 2,716
Hoxie SD 900/PK-12
PO Box 240 72433 870-886-2401
Radius Baker, supt. Fax 886-4252
hoxieschools.com
Hoxie ES 500/PK-6
PO Box 240 72433 870-886-2401
Tracy Gates, prin. Fax 886-4257

Huntsville, Madison, Pop. 2,295
Huntsville SD 2,300/K-12
PO Box F 72740 479-738-2011
Clint Jones, supt. Fax 738-2563
www.huntsvilleschooldistrict.org
Huntsville IS 500/3-5
PO Box H 72740 479-738-6228
Kenena Pelfrey, prin. Fax 738-2636
Huntsville MS 500/6-8
PO Box G 72740 479-738-6520
Chip Greenwell, prin. Fax 738-6259
Watson PS 500/K-2
PO Box H 72740 479-738-2425
Candra Brasel, prin. Fax 738-6383
Other Schools – See Saint Paul

Imboden, Lawrence, Pop. 668
Sloan-Hendrix SD 600/K-12
PO Box 1080 72434 870-869-2384
Clifford Rorex, supt. Fax 869-2380
shsd.k12.ar.us
Sloan-Hendrix ES 200/K-4
PO Box 1080 72434 870-869-2101
Ligie Waddell, prin. Fax 869-2103
Sloan-Hendrix MS 100/5-7
PO Box 1080 72434 870-869-2101
Ligie Waddell, prin. Fax 869-2103

Jacksonville, Pulaski, Pop. 27,377
Jacksonville North Pulaski SD 3,800/PK-12
1414 W Main 72076 501-241-2080
Tony Wood, supt. Fax 241-2092
jnpsd.org
Arnold Drive ES 300/PK-5
4150 Arnold Dr 72076 501-988-4145
Janice Walker, prin. Fax 983-8204
Bayou Meto ES 300/PK-5
26405 Highway 107 72076 501-988-4131
Gary Beck, prin. Fax 983-8218
DuPree ES 400/K-5
700 Gregory St 72076 501-982-9541
Jamie Reed, prin. Fax 985-3800
Jacksonville MS, 718 Harris Rd 72076 600/6-8
Mike Hudgeons, prin. 501-982-9436
Pinewood ES 400/K-5
1919 Northeastern Ave 72076 501-982-7571
Karen Norton, prin. Fax 241-2054
Taylor ES 500/K-5
1401 Murrell Taylor Dr 72076 501-985-1581
Myeisha Haywood, prin. Fax 241-2069
Tolleson ES 400/PK-5
601 Harris Rd 72076 501-982-7456
Angela Srewart, prin. Fax 241-2089

Pulaski County Special SD
Supt. — See Little Rock
Adkins Pre K Center 200/PK-PK
500 Cloverdale Rd 72076 501-982-3117
Rachel Wheeler, prin. Fax 241-2004

Jasper, Newton, Pop. 462
Jasper SD 900/K-12
PO Box 446 72641 870-446-2223
Jeff Cantrell, supt. Fax 446-2305
jasper.k12.ar.us
Jasper ES 300/K-6
PO Box 446 72641 870-446-5320
David Dunlap, prin. Fax 446-5549
Other Schools – See Kingston, Oark

Jessieville, Garland
Jessieville SD 900/K-12
PO Box 4 71949 501-984-5381
Ralph Carter, supt. Fax 984-4200
www.jsdlions.net
Jessieville ES 400/K-5
PO Box 4 71949 501-984-5665
Jed Johnson, prin. Fax 984-4200
Jessieville MS 200/6-8
PO Box 4 71949 501-984-5610
Toby Packard, prin. Fax 984-4200

Jonesboro, Craighead, Pop. 66,085
Jonesboro SD 5,900/PK-12
2506 Southwest Sq 72401 870-933-5800
Dr. Kim Wilbanks, supt. Fax 933-5838
www.jonesboroschools.net
Health Wellness & Environmental Studies 600/1-6
1001 Rosemond Ave 72401 870-933-5850
Cynthia Wright, prin. Fax 933-5854
International Studies S 500/1-6
1218 Cobb St 72401 870-933-5825
Arthur Jackson, prin. Fax 933-5833
Jonesboro K 600/K-K
618 W Nettleton Ave 72401 870-933-5835
Becky Shannon, prin. Fax 933-5834
Jonesboro Preschool 200/PK-PK
1307 Flint St 72401 870-253-1674
Karen Swift, dir. Fax 253-1674
Math & Science S 600/1-6
213 E Thomas Green Rd 72401 870-933-5845
Rickey Greer, prin. Fax 933-5858
MicroSociety S 500/1-6
1110 W Washington Ave 72401 870-933-5855
Amanda Turner, prin. Fax 933-5819
Pre-K North 100/PK-PK
802 E Johnson Ave 72401 870-253-1674
Brooke Guthrie, admin.
Visual and Performing Arts S 700/1-6
1804 Hillcrest Dr 72401 870-933-5830
Dale Case, prin. Fax 933-5809

Nettleton SD 3,200/K-12
3300 One Pl 72404 870-910-7800
James Dunivan, supt. Fax 910-7854
nettletonschools.net
Fox Meadow ES 400/K-2
2305 Fox Meadow Ln 72404 870-910-7817
Amy Floyd, prin. Fax 910-7816
Fox Meadow Intermediate Center 300/3-5
2309 Fox Meadow Ln 72404 870-910-7812
Debra Johnson, prin. Fax 910-7829
Nettleton JHS 500/7-8
4208 Chieftain Ln 72401 870-910-7819
David Shipman, prin. Fax 910-6984
Nettleton MS 200/6-6
3801 Vera St 72401 870-910-7830
Brian Foster, prin. Fax 910-7834
University Heights ES 400/K-2
300 Bowling Ln 72401 870-910-7823
Julie Roark, prin. Fax 910-7824
University Heights IS 400/3-5
3801 Aggie Rd 72401 870-910-7809
Debbie Bean, prin. Fax 910-7811

Valley View SD 1,900/PK-12
2131 Valley View Dr 72404 870-935-6200
Bryan Russell, supt. Fax 972-0373
www.valleyviewschools.net
Valley View ES 700/K-2
5603 Kersey Ln 72404 870-935-1910
Pamela Clark, prin. Fax 935-6203
Valley View IS 100/PK-PK, 3-
5404 Yarbrough Dr 72404 870-935-4602
Ella Bradsher, prin. Fax 935-6204

Westside Consolidated SD 1,800/PK-12
1630 Highway 91 W 72404 870-935-7501
Scott Gaunt, supt. Fax 935-2123
www.westsideschools.org
Westside ES 700/PK-4
1834 Highway 91 W 72404 870-935-7501
Kelli Murray, prin. Fax 932-9832
Westside MS 400/5-7
1800 Highway 91 W 72404 870-935-7501
James Scott, prin. Fax 268-1157

Blessed Sacrament Catholic S 100/PK-6
1105 E Highland Dr 72401 870-932-3684
Mary Kay Jones, prin. Fax 935-4444
Concordia Christian Academy 100/PK-8
1812 Rains St 72401 870-935-2273
Kory O'Brien, prin. Fax 935-4717
Ridgefield Christian S 300/PK-12
3824 Casey Springs Rd 72404 870-932-7540

Judsonia, White, Pop. 1,987
Riverview SD
Supt. — See Searcy
Riverview-Judsonia ES 400/K-6
916 Judson Ave 72081 501-729-5196
Wes Rowland, prin. Fax 729-0018

White County Central SD 700/K-12
3259 Highway 157 72081 501-729-3947
Sheila Whitlow, supt. Fax 729-3992
wccbears.org
White County Central ES 400/K-6
3259 Highway 157 72081 501-729-4292
Beverly Froud, prin. Fax 729-4292

Junction City, Union, Pop. 576
Junction City SD 500/K-12
PO Box 790 71749 870-924-4575
William Lowe, supt. Fax 924-4565
junctioncity.k12.ar.us/
Junction City ES 300/K-6
PO Box 790 71749 870-924-4578
Teresa Matochik, prin. Fax 924-4565

Kensett, White, Pop. 1,611
Riverview SD
Supt. — See Searcy
Riverview-Kensett ES 400/K-6
701 W Dandridge St 72082 501-742-3221
Christy Bremer, prin. Fax 742-1511

Kingsland, Cleveland, Pop. 440
Cleveland County SD
Supt. — See Rison
Kingsland ES 100/K-6
16650 Highway 79 71652 870-348-5335
Danny Durey, prin. Fax 348-5781

Kingston, Madison
Jasper SD
Supt. — See Jasper
Kingston ES 100/K-6
PO Box 149 72742 479-665-2835
Marsha Shaver, prin. Fax 665-2577

Kirby, Pike, Pop. 768
Kirby SD 300/K-12
PO Box 9 71950 870-398-4212
Pike Palmer, supt. Fax 398-4442
www.kirbytrojans.net
Kirby ES 200/K-6
PO Box 9 71950 870-398-4213
Dolores Cowart, prin. Fax 398-4626

Lake City, Craighead, Pop. 2,050
Riverside SD 800/K-12
PO Box 178 72437 870-237-4329
Jeff Priest, supt. Fax 237-4867
www.riversiderebels.net
Riverside West ES 200/K-6
PO Box 178 72437 870-237-8222
Lee Ann Harrell, prin. Fax 237-4697
Other Schools – See Caraway

Lake Village, Chicot, Pop. 2,553
Lakeside SD 1,200/PK-12
1110 S Lakeshore Dr 71653 870-265-7300
Dr. Billy Adams, supt. Fax 265-5466
www.lsschool.org
Lakeside ES 500/PK-5
1110 S Lakeshore Dr 71653 870-265-2906
Cristy Stone, prin. Fax 265-7311
Lakeside MS 200/6-8
1110 S Lakeshore Dr 71653 870-265-2970
Arthur Gray, prin. Fax 265-7309
Other Schools – See Eudora

Lamar, Johnson, Pop. 1,567
Lamar SD 1,100/K-12
301 Elberta St 72846 479-885-3907
Jay Holland, supt. Fax 885-2380
lamarwarriors.org
Lamar ES 400/K-3
301 Elberta St 72846 479-885-3363
Mike McCarley, prin. Fax 885-2380
Lamar MS 300/4-7
301 Elberta St 72846 479-885-6511
Lance Spence, prin. Fax 885-3920

Lavaca, Sebastian, Pop. 2,248
Lavaca SD 900/PK-12
PO Box 8 72941 479-674-5611
Steve Rose, supt. Fax 674-2271
www.lavacaschools.com
Lavaca ES 400/PK-4
PO Box 8 72941 479-674-5613
Sam Slott, prin. Fax 674-5518
Lavaca MS 300/5-8
PO Box 8 72941 479-674-5618
Kenny Holland, prin. Fax 674-2271

Leachville, Mississippi, Pop. 1,967
Buffalo Island Central SD
Supt. — See Monette
Buffalo Island Central East ES 200/PK-6
PO Box 110 72438 870-539-6448
Nicole Stewart, prin. Fax 539-6696

Lead Hill, Boone, Pop. 266
Lead Hill SD 300/K-12
PO Box 20 72644 870-436-5250
Wanda Van Dyke, supt. Fax 436-5946
leadhillschools.net
Lead Hill ES 100/K-4
PO Box 20 72644 870-436-5677
Mark Ditmanson, prin. Fax 436-6827

Lepanto, Poinsett, Pop. 1,866
East Poinsett County SD 700/PK-12
502 McClellan St 72354 870-475-2472
Michael Pierce, supt. Fax 475-3531
epc.k12.ar.us
Lepanto ES 200/K-4
819 School St 72354 870-475-2632
Brian Weathers, prin. Fax 475-2366
Other Schools – See Tyronza

Leslie, Searcy, Pop. 431
Searcy County SD
Supt. — See Marshall
Leslie IS 100/4-6
800 Elm St 72645 870-447-2431
Bennetta Caston, prin. Fax 447-2831

Lewisville, Lafayette, Pop. 1,260
Lafayette County SD 700/K-12
PO Box 950 71845 870-921-5500
Robert Edwards, supt. Fax 921-4277
www.lcscougars.org
Lafayette County ES 400/K-6
PO Box 950 71845 870-921-4275
Harvey Sellers, prin. Fax 921-3812

South Arkansas Christian S 50/K-12
PO Box 990 71845 870-921-5050
Br. Andy Hawkins, hdmstr. Fax 921-5050

Lexa, Phillips, Pop. 285
Barton-Lexa SD 800/PK-12
9546 Highway 85 72355 870-572-7294
David Tollett, supt. Fax 572-4713
www.bartonsd.org
Barton ES 400/PK-6
9546 Highway 85 72355 870-572-3984
Bernie Winkel, prin. Fax 572-4733

Lincoln, Washington, Pop. 2,196
Lincoln Consolidated SD 48 1,100/PK-12
107 E School St 72744 479-824-7310
Mary Ann Spears, supt. Fax 824-3045
www.lincolncsd.com
Lincoln ES 400/PK-3
613 County Ave 72744 479-824-7350
Jill Jackson, prin. Fax 824-3012
Lincoln MS 400/4-7
201 E School St 72744 479-824-7400
Michele Price, prin. Fax 824-5566

Little Rock, Pulaski, Pop. 190,562
Little Rock SD 25,800/PK-12
810 W Markham St 72201 501-447-1000
Mike Poore, supt. Fax 447-1159
www.lrsd.org
Bale ES 300/PK-5
6501 W 32nd St 72204 501-447-3600
Dr. Ericka McCarroll, prin. Fax 447-3601
Baseline ES 300/PK-5
3623 Baseline Rd 72209 501-447-3700
Jonathan Crossley, prin. Fax 447-3701
Booker Arts Magnet ES 500/K-5
2016 Barber St 72206 501-447-3800
Dr. Cheryl Carson, prin. Fax 447-3801
Brady ES 400/PK-5
7915 W Markham St 72205 501-447-3900
Tyrone Harris, prin. Fax 447-3901
Carver Magnet ES 300/PK-5
2100 E 6th St 72202 501-447-4000
Romona Sawyer, prin. Fax 447-4001
Dodd ES 300/PK-5
6423 Stagecoach Rd 72204 501-447-4300
Deborah Mitchell, prin. Fax 447-4301
Dunbar Magnet MS 700/6-8
1100 Wright Ave 72206 501-447-2600
Eunice Thrasher, prin. Fax 447-2601
Fair Park ECC 200/PK-PK
616 N Harrison St 72205 501-447-4400
Judy Milam, prin. Fax 447-4401
Forest Heights STEM Academy 600/K-8
5901 Evergreen Dr 72205 501-447-2700
Dr. Maurecia Robinson, prin. Fax 447-2701
Forest Park ES 400/PK-5
1600 N Tyler St 72207 501-447-4500
Theresa Ketcher, prin. Fax 447-4501
Franklin ES 300/PK-5
1701 S Harrison St 72204 501-447-4600
Lori Brown, prin. Fax 447-4601
Fulbright ES 600/PK-5
300 Pleasant Valley Dr 72212 501-447-4700
Sherkeyer Jackson, prin. Fax 447-4701
Geyer Springs ECC 300/PK-PK
5240 Mabelvale Pike 72209 501-447-4800
Keitha Savage, prin. Fax 447-4801
Gibbs Magnet ES 300/PK-5
1115 W 16th St 72202 501-447-4900
Dr. Felicia Hobbs, prin. Fax 447-4901
Henderson Magnet MS 700/6-8
401 John Barrow Rd 72205 501-447-2800
Frank Williams, prin. Fax 447-2801
Jefferson ES 500/PK-5
2600 N McKinley St 72207 501-447-5000
Roberta Mannon, prin. Fax 447-5001
King Magnet ES 500/PK-5
905 Dr Martin Luther King 72202 501-447-5100
Karen Carter, prin. Fax 447-5101
Mann Magnet MS 800/6-8
1000 E Roosevelt Rd 72206 501-447-3100
Keith McGee, prin. Fax 447-3101
McDermott ES 400/PK-5
1200 Reservoir Rd 72227 501-447-5500
Amy Cooper, prin. Fax 447-5501
Meadowcliff ES 400/PK-5
25 Sheraton Dr 72209 501-447-5600
Ada Keown, prin. Fax 447-5601
Otter Creek ES 600/PK-5
16000 Otter Creek Pkwy 72210 501-447-5800
Donna Hall, prin. Fax 447-5801
Pinnacle View MS 200/6-7
5701 Ranch Dr 72223 501-447-8500
Dr. Jay Pickering, prin. Fax 447-8501
Pulaski Heights ES 400/PK-5
319 N Pine St 72205 501-447-5900
Lillie Carter, prin. Fax 447-5901
Pulaski Heights MS 800/6-8
401 N Pine St 72205 501-447-3200
Darryl Powell, prin. Fax 447-3201
Roberts ES 900/PK-5
16601 LaMarche Dr 72223 501-447-8300
Barbara Anderson, prin. Fax 447-8301
Rockefeller Magnet ES 400/PK-5
700 E 17th St 72206 501-447-6200
Shoutell Richardson, prin. Fax 447-6201
Romine Interdistrict ES 400/PK-5
3400 Romine Rd 72204 501-447-6300
Beverly Jones, prin. Fax 447-6301
Stephens ES 400/PK-5
3700 W 18th St 72204 501-447-6400
Phillip Carlock, prin. Fax 447-6401
Terry ES 400/PK-5
10800 Mara Lynn Rd 72211 501-447-6500
Sandra Register, prin. Fax 447-6501
Wakefield ES 600/PK-5
75 Westminister Dr 72209 501-447-6600
Leslie Taylor, prin. Fax 447-6601
Washington Magnet ES 500/PK-5
2700 Main St 72206 501-447-6700
Katherine Snyder, prin. Fax 447-6701
Watson ES 400/K-5
7000 Valley Dr 72209 501-447-6800
Stephanie Walker, prin. Fax 447-6801
Western Hills ES 300/PK-5
4901 Western Hills Ave 72204 501-447-6900
Teresa Richardson, prin. Fax 447-6901
Williams Magnet ES 400/K-5
7301 Evergreen Dr 72207 501-447-7100
Connie Green, prin. Fax 447-7101
Wilson ES 300/PK-5
4015 Stannus St 72204 501-447-7200
Dr. Eleanor Cox-Woodley, prin. Fax 447-7201
Woodruff ECC 100/PK-PK
3010 W 7th St 72205 501-447-7300
Ann Freeman, prin. Fax 447-7301
Other Schools – See Mabelvale

Pulaski County Special SD 12,700/PK-12
925 E Dixon Rd 72206 501-234-2000
Dr. Jerry Guess, supt. Fax 490-0483
www.pcssd.org
Baker Interdistrict ES 500/K-5
15001 Kanis Rd 72223 501-228-3250
Sonya Whitfield, prin. Fax 228-3257
Bates ES 500/PK-5
14300 Dineen Dr 72206 501-897-2171
Dr. Darnell Bell, prin. Fax 897-2128
Chenal ES 500/K-5
21201 Denny Rd 72223 501-821-7450
Felecia Hamilton, prin. Fax 821-7454
Fuller MS 500/6-8
808 E Dixon Rd 72206 501-490-5730
Lisa Watson, prin. Fax 490-5736
Landmark ES 300/PK-5
16712 Arch St 72206 501-888-8790
Lou Jackson, prin. Fax 888-8798
Lawson ES 300/PK-5
19901 Lawson Rd 72210 501-821-7000
Matthew Mellor, prin. Fax 821-7012
Robinson ES 200/PK-5
21600 Highway 10 72223 501-868-2420
Pamela McCurry, prin. Fax 868-2442
Robinson MS 400/6-8
21001 Highway 10 72223 501-868-2410
Lance LeVar, prin. Fax 868-2441
Other Schools – See College Station, Jacksonville, Maumelle, North Little Rock, Sherwood

Sheridan SD
Supt. — See Sheridan
East End ES 500/PK-2
21801 Arch St 72206 501-888-4264
Vickie Easley, prin. Fax 888-4275
East End IS 600/3-6
5205 W Sawmill Rd 72206 501-888-1477
Jayme Steinbeck, prin. Fax 888-8937

Agape Academy 100/PK-5
701 Napa Valley Dr 72211 501-225-0068
Cathie Dorsch, prin. Fax 687-0470
Anthony S 400/PK-8
7700 Ohio St 72227 501-225-6629
Sharon Morgan, head sch Fax 225-2149
Arkansas Baptist S 800/PK-12
62 Pleasant Valley Dr 72212 501-227-7070
Baptist Preparatory Lower S 300/K-6
62 Pleasant Valley Dr 72212 501-227-7070
Dr. Laura Bednar, hdmstr. Fax 227-0060
Bingham Road Baptist Academy 50/PK-2
923 W Bingham Rd 72206 501-888-2541
Jeana Koch, dir. Fax 846-3664
Central AR Christian S - Pleasant Valley PK-5
10900 Rodney Parham 72212 501-227-4963
Chenal Valley Montessori S 100/PK-8
14929 Cantrell Rd 72223 501-868-6030
Children's House Montessori S 100/PK-K
4023 Lee Ave 72205 501-664-5993
Christ Lutheran S 100/PK-8
315 S Hughes St 72205 501-663-5212
Heidi Jerry, prin. Fax 663-9542
Christ the King S 700/PK-8
4002 N Rodney Parham Rd 72212 501-225-7883
Kathy House, prin. Fax 225-1315
Episcopal Collegiate S 700/PK-12
1701 Cantrell Rd 72201 501-372-1194
Dr. David Perkinson, head sch Fax 372-2160
Grace Christian Academy 50/1-6
2505 Brown St 72204 501-414-8707
Dr. Cheryl Washington, admin.
Hebrew Academy 50/K-6
11905 Fairview Rd 72212 501-217-0053
Huda Academy 100/PK-7
3221 Anna St 72211 501-565-3555
Little Rock Adventist Academy 50/K-10
8708 N Rodney Parham Rd 72205 501-225-6183
Little Rock Christian Academy 1,300/PK-12
19010 Cantrell Rd 72223 501-868-9822
Dr. Gary Arnold, head sch Fax 868-8766
Miss Selma's Schools 400/PK-6
7814 T St 72227 501-225-0123
Our Lady the Holy Souls S 500/PK-8
1001 N Tyler St 72205 501-663-4513
Ileana Dobbins, prin. Fax 663-1014
Pinnacle Classical Academy 50/PK-11
PO Box 241822 72223 501-240-9080
Pulaski Academy 1,400/PK-12
12701 Hinson Rd 72212 501-604-1910
Matthew Walsh, head sch Fax 225-1974
St. Edward Catholic S 200/PK-8
805 Sherman St 72202 501-374-9166
LaTonya White, prin. Fax 907-9078
St. Theresa S 200/PK-8
6311 Baseline Rd 72209 501-565-3855
Kristy Dunn, prin. Fax 565-9522
Shiloh SDA S 50/PK-8
2400 S Maple St 72204 501-663-3256
Southwest Christian Academy 500/PK-12
11301 Geyer Springs Rd 72209 501-565-3276

London, Pope, Pop. 1,012
Russellville SD
Supt. — See Russellville
London ES 200/PK-4
154 School St 72847 479-293-4241
Krista Malin, prin. Fax 293-5141

Lonoke, Lonoke, Pop. 4,204
Lonoke SD 1,800/K-12
401 W Holly St 72086 501-676-2042
Dr. Suzanne Bailey, supt. Fax 676-7074
lonokeschools.org/

Lonoke ES 400/3-5
900 W Palm St 72086 501-676-6740
Karen Gibbs, prin. Fax 676-7088
Lonoke MS 400/6-8
1100 W Palm St 72086 501-676-6670
Jeannie Holt, prin. Fax 676-7013
Lonoke PS 400/K-2
800 Lincoln St 72086 501-676-3839
Amanda Rather, prin. Fax 676-3726

Lowell, Benton, Pop. 7,180
Rogers SD
Supt. — See Rogers
Lowell ES 400/K-5
202 McClure Ave 72745 479-631-3610
Shannon Passmore, prin. Fax 631-3611
Tucker ES 600/K-5
121 N School Ave 72745 479-631-3561
Dr. Cindy Viala, prin. Fax 631-3581

Lynn, Lawrence, Pop. 288
Hillcrest SD
Supt. — See Strawberry
Hillcrest ES 200/K-6
PO Box 70 72440 870-528-3462
Shawn Rose, prin. Fax 528-3766

Mabelvale, Pulaski
Little Rock SD
Supt. — See Little Rock
Chicot PS 800/PK-5
11100 Chicot Rd 72103 501-447-7000
Sherry Chambers, prin. Fax 447-7001
Mabelvale ES 500/PK-5
9401 Mabelvale Cut Off Rd 72103 501-447-5400
Darian Smith, prin. Fax 447-5401
Mabelvale Magnet MS 600/6-8
10811 Mabelvale West Rd 72103 501-447-3000
Rhonda Hall, prin. Fax 447-3001

Mc Crory, Woodruff, Pop. 1,707
Mc Crory SD 600/PK-12
PO Box 930 72101 870-731-2535
Bob Casteel, supt. Fax 731-2536
mccroryschools.org
Mc Crory ES 400/PK-6
PO Box 930 72101 870-731-2921
Patty Hernandez, prin. Fax 731-2160

Mc Gehee, Desha, Pop. 4,181
McGehee SD 1,200/K-12
PO Box 767 71654 870-222-3670
Thomas Gathen, supt. Fax 222-6957
www.mcgeheeschools.org
McGehee ES 700/K-6
PO Box 767 71654 870-222-5400
Twilla Hardin, prin. Fax 222-6532

Mc Rae, White, Pop. 675
Beebe SD
Supt. — See Beebe
Beebe MS 500/5-6
306 N Wilks St 72102 501-882-5463
Brandy Dillin, prin. Fax 726-4433

Magazine, Logan, Pop. 835
Magazine SD 600/PK-12
485 E Priddy St 72943 479-969-2566
Brett Bunch, supt. Fax 969-8740
magazinek12.com
Magazine ES 400/PK-6
351 E Priddy St 72943 479-969-2565
Karen Gipson, prin. Fax 969-8033

Magnolia, Columbia, Pop. 11,431
Magnolia SD 2,900/PK-12
PO Box 649 71754 870-234-4933
John D. Ward, supt. Fax 901-2508
www.magnoliaschools.net
Central ES 600/4-6
PO Box 649 71754 870-234-4911
Angie Waters, prin. Fax 234-8634
East Side ES 600/1-3
PO Box 649 71754 870-234-5611
Jill Rader, prin. Fax 234-8362
Kindergarten Center at East Side ES 200/K-K
PO Box 649 71754 870-234-3511
Jill Rader, prin. Fax 234-0229
Walker Preschool 100/PK-PK
PO Box 649 71754 870-234-5654
Lynnetta Roberts, prin. Fax 234-3557

Columbia Christian S 300/PK-12
250 Warnock Springs Rd 71753 870-234-2831
Ted Waller, supt. Fax 234-1497

Malvern, Hot Spring, Pop. 10,082
Glen Rose SD 1,000/PK-12
14334 Highway 67 72104 501-332-3694
Tim Holicer, supt. Fax 332-3031
www.grbeavers.org
Glen Rose ES 400/PK-4
14334 Highway 67 72104 501-332-3694
Lance Robinson, prin. Fax 332-0065
Glen Rose MS 300/5-8
14334 Highway 67 72104 501-332-3694
Shawn Pilgrim, prin. Fax 332-3799

Magnet Cove SD 600/K-12
472 Magnet School Rd 72104 501-332-5468
Danny Thomas, supt. Fax 337-4119
magnetcove.k12.ar.us
Magnet Cove ES 300/K-6
22083 Highway 51 72104 501-337-9131
Brian Nivens, prin. Fax 332-5747

Malvern SD 2,200/K-12
1620 S Main St 72104 501-332-7500
Brian Golden, supt. Fax 332-7501
malvernleopards.org
Malvern ES 900/K-4
1807 W Moline St 72104 501-467-3166
Meredith McCormack, prin. Fax 467-3161
Malvern MS 300/7-8
339 E Donnelly St 72104 501-332-7530
Velda Keeney, prin. Fax 332-7532
Wilson IS 300/5-6
614 E Moline St 72104 501-332-6452
LaQuita Jones, prin. Fax 332-7551

Mammoth Spring, Fulton, Pop. 962
Mammoth Spring SD 500/K-12
410 Goldsmith Ave 72554 870-625-3612
Wilma Rogers, supt. Fax 625-3609
www.mammothspringschools.com
Mammoth Spring ES 200/K-6
410 Goldsmith Ave 72554 870-625-7213
Wade Powell, prin. Fax 625-3609

Manila, Mississippi, Pop. 3,321
Manila SD 1,100/PK-12
PO Box 670 72442 870-561-4419
Pamela Castor, supt. Fax 561-4410
mps.crsc.k12.ar.us
Manila ES 500/PK-4
PO Box 670 72442 870-561-3145
Jason Evers, prin. Fax 561-8119
Manila MS 300/5-8
PO Box 670 72442 870-561-4815
LeAnn Helms, prin. Fax 561-4828

Mansfield, Scott, Pop. 1,119
Mansfield SD 900/K-12
402 Grove St 72944 479-928-4006
Robert Ross, supt. Fax 928-4482
mansfieldtigers.org
Mansfield ES 300/K-4
100 N Walnut Ave 72944 479-928-4866
Kim Arnold, prin. Fax 928-1617
Mansfield MS 300/5-8
400 Grove St 72944 479-928-4451
Floyd Fisher, prin. Fax 928-4323

Marianna, Lee, Pop. 4,065
Lee County SD 1,000/PK-12
175 Walnut St 72360 870-295-7100
Antony Hobbs, supt. Fax 295-7125
lcsd1.grsc.k12.ar.us
Strong Learning Academy 300/2-6
214 S Alabama St 72360 870-295-7140
Mary Hayden, prin. Fax 295-7314
Whitten ES 200/PK-1
175 Walnut St 72360 870-295-7100
Mary Hayden, prin. Fax 295-7125

Lee Academy 200/PK-12
973 Highway 243 72360 870-295-3444

Marion, Crittenden, Pop. 12,214
Marion SD 4,200/K-12
200 Manor St 72364 870-739-5100
Glen Fenter, supt. Fax 739-5156
www.msd3.org
Marion ES 600/2-3
133 Military Rd 72364 870-739-5120
Adam O'Neal, prin. Fax 739-5123
Marion IS 700/4-5
100 L H Polk Dr 72364 870-739-5180
Julie Molloy, prin. Fax 739-5183
Marion MS 600/6-7
10 Patriot Dr 72364 870-739-5173
Carissa Lacy, prin. Fax 739-5156
Other Schools – See West Memphis

New Life Christian Academy K-8
1093 State Highway 77 72364 870-732-8814

Marked Tree, Poinsett, Pop. 2,530
Marked Tree SD 500/PK-12
406 Saint Francis St 72365 870-358-2913
Annesa Thompson, supt. Fax 358-3953
mtree.k12.ar.us
Marked Tree ES 300/PK-6
703 Normandy St 72365 870-358-2214
Lisa Gray, prin. Fax 358-3953

Marmaduke, Greene, Pop. 1,093
Marmaduke SD 700/K-12
1010 Greyhound Dr 72443 870-597-2723
Tim Gardner, supt. Fax 597-4693
www.mhs.nesc.k12.ar.us
Marmaduke ES 400/K-6
2020 Greyhound Dr 72443 870-597-2711
Audrea King, prin. Fax 597-4324

Marshall, Searcy, Pop. 1,315
Searcy County SD 900/K-12
952 Highway 65 N 72650 870-448-3011
Alan Yarbrough, supt. Fax 448-3012
scsd.info
Marshall ES 300/K-3
201 W College St 72650 870-448-3333
Heather Bohannon, prin. Fax 448-2510
Other Schools – See Leslie

Marvell, Phillips, Pop. 1,170
Marvell-Elaine SD 400/PK-12
PO Box 1870 72366 870-829-2101
Dr. Joyce Cottoms Ph.D., supt. Fax 829-2044
marvellschools.org
Marvell-Elaine ES 200/PK-6
PO Box 1870 72366 870-829-1341
Sylvia Moore M.S., prin. Fax 829-1349

Marvell Academy 200/PK-12
PO Box 277 72366 870-829-2931
Dr. Susan Lgion, hdmstr. Fax 829-3601

Maumelle, Pulaski, Pop. 16,888
Pulaski County Special SD
Supt. — See Little Rock
Maumelle MS 900/6-8
1000 Carnahan Dr 72113 501-851-8990
Ryan Burgess, prin. Fax 851-8988
Pine Forest ES 600/K-5
400 Pine Forest Dr 72113 501-851-5380
Yolanda Thomas, prin. Fax 851-5386

Mayflower, Faulkner, Pop. 2,195
Mayflower SD 1,200/PK-12
7 Ashmore Dr 72106 501-470-0506
John Gray, supt. Fax 470-1343
www.mayflowerschools.org
Mayflower ES 400/PK-4
4 Grove St 72106 501-470-0387
Candi Watts, prin. Fax 470-2107
Mayflower MS 400/5-8
18 Eagle Circle 72106 501-470-2111
John Pipkins, prin. Fax 470-2116

Maynard, Randolph, Pop. 421
Maynard SD 500/K-12
74 Campus Dr 72444 870-647-3500
Patricia Rawlings, supt. Fax 647-2301
maynard.nesc.k12.ar.us/
Maynard ES 200/K-6
74 Campus Dr 72444 870-647-3500
Scott James, prin. Fax 647-3385

Melbourne, Izard, Pop. 1,832
Melbourne SD 800/K-12
PO Box 250 72556 870-368-7070
Dennis Sublett, supt. Fax 368-7071
bearkatz.k12.ar.us/
Melbourne ES 400/K-6
PO Box 250 72556 870-368-4365
Lori Loggains, prin. Fax 368-7071

Mena, Polk, Pop. 5,622
Mena SD 1,800/K-12
501 Hickory Ave 71953 479-394-1710
Benny Weston, supt. Fax 394-1713
www.menaschools.org
Durham ES 400/K-2
106 Reine St N 71953 479-394-2943
Jimma Holder, prin. Fax 394-2979
Harshman ES 400/3-5
1000 Geyer Dr 71953 479-394-3151
Tamara Smart, prin. Fax 394-3153
Mena MS 400/6-8
700 Morrow St S 71953 479-394-2572
Clifton Sherrer, prin. Fax 394-0258

Ouachita River SD 700/K-12
143 Polk Road 96 71953 479-394-2348
Jerrall Strasner, supt. Fax 394-6687
www.ouachitariversd.org
Acorn ES 300/K-5
143 Polk Road 96 71953 479-394-4833
Donna Reyer, prin. Fax 394-5213
Other Schools – See Oden

Mineral Springs, Howard, Pop. 1,190
Mineral Springs SD 400/K-12
PO Box 189 71851 870-287-4748
Thelma Forte, supt. Fax 287-5301
mssd2.k12.ar.us/
Mineral Springs ES 200/K-6
PO Box 189 71851 870-287-4746
Stacey Gauldin, prin. Fax 287-4743

Monette, Craighead, Pop. 1,489
Buffalo Island Central SD 800/PK-12
PO Box 730 72447 870-486-5411
Gaylon Taylor, supt. Fax 486-2657
www.bicschools.net
Buffalo Island Central West ES 200/PK-4
PO Box 730 72447 870-486-2212
Dr. Kima Stewart, prin. Fax 486-2657
Other Schools – See Leachville

Monticello, Drew, Pop. 9,357
Drew Central SD 900/K-12
250 University Dr 71655 870-367-5369
Billy Williams, supt. Fax 367-1932
www.drewcentral.org/
Drew Central ES 300/K-4
250 University Dr 71655 870-367-6893
Trudy Jackson, prin. Fax 460-5500
Drew Central MS 300/5-8
250 University Dr 71655 870-367-5235
Patti Smith, prin. Fax 460-5502

Monticello SD 2,100/K-12
935 Scogin Dr 71655 870-367-4000
Sandra Lanehart, supt. Fax 367-1531
www.billies.org
Monticello ES 500/K-2
1037 Scogin Dr 71655 870-367-4010
Cindy Hilburn, prin. Fax 367-2105
Monticello IS 400/3-5
280 Clyde Ross Dr 71655 870-367-4030
Julie Workman, prin. Fax 367-6482
Monticello MS 500/6-8
180 Clyde Ross Dr 71655 870-367-4040
Kevin Hancock, prin. Fax 367-5437

Morrilton, Conway, Pop. 6,618
South Conway County SD 2,200/K-12
100 Baramore St 72110 501-354-9400
Shawn Halbrook, supt. Fax 354-9464
www.sccsd.org
Morrilton ES 300/2-3
1203 N Saint Joseph St 72110 501-354-9443
Lori Stidham, prin. Fax 354-9474

Morrilton IS 500/4-6
1907 Poor Farm Rd 72110 501-354-9476
Karey Livingston, prin. Fax 354-9487
Morrilton JHS 400/7-8
1400 Poor Farm Rd 72110 501-354-9437
Robert Hogan, prin. Fax 354-9429
Morrilton PS 400/K-1
410 S Bridge St 72110 501-354-9423
Sharon Wilson, prin. Fax 354-9424

Sacred Heart S 200/PK-12
106 N Saint Joseph St 72110 501-354-8113
Buddy Greeson, prin. Fax 354-2001

Mountainburg, Crawford, Pop. 624
Mountainburg SD 700/PK-12
129 Highway 71 SW 72946 479-369-2121
Dennis Copeland, supt. Fax 369-2138
www.mountainburg.org
Mountainburg ES 200/PK-6
2015 Lake Fort Smith Rd 72946 479-369-2762
Tandi Jones, prin. Fax 369-4302

Mountain Home, Baxter, Pop. 12,291
Mountain Home SD 3,900/K-12
2465 Rodeo Dr 72653 870-425-1201
Dr. Jake Long, supt. Fax 425-1316
mhbombers.com
Hackler IS 900/3-5
965 West Rd 72653 870-425-1288
Sondra Monger, prin. Fax 425-1290
Mountain Home JHS 300/8-8
2301 Rodeo Dr 72653 870-425-1231
Ron Czanstkowski, prin. Fax 424-4797
Mountain Home K 300/K-K
1310 Post Oak Rd 72653 870-425-1256
Vanessa Thomas-Jones, prin. Fax 425-1090
Nelson-Wilks-Herron ES 600/1-2
618 N College St 72653 870-425-1251
Rita Persons, prin. Fax 425-1264
Pinkston MS 600/6-7
1301 S College St 72653 870-425-1236
Allyson Dewey, prin. Fax 425-1741

Mountain Home Christian Academy 100/PK-12
1989 Glenbriar Dr 72653 870-424-6622
Lori Mathis, admin. Fax 424-6622

Mountain Pine, Garland, Pop. 749
Mountain Pine SD 600/PK-12
PO Box 1 71956 501-767-1540
Bobby Applegate, supt. Fax 767-1589
www.mpsdrd.com
Mountain Pine ES 400/PK-6
PO Box 1 71956 501-767-2421
Toby Crosby, prin. Fax 767-1549

Mountain View, Stone, Pop. 2,714
Mountain View SD 1,600/PK-12
210 High School Rd 72560 870-269-3443
Rowdy Ross, supt. Fax 269-3446
mountainviewschooldistrict.k12.ar.us/
Mountain View ES 600/PK-4
201 Elementary St 72560 870-269-3104
Kay Shipman, prin. Fax 269-2840
Mountain View MS 400/5-8
210 High School Rd 72560 870-269-4335
Robert Ross, prin. Fax 269-4447
Other Schools – See Fox, Timbo

Mount Ida, Montgomery, Pop. 1,049
Mount Ida SD 500/K-12
PO Box 1230 71957 870-867-2771
Hal Landrith, supt. Fax 867-3734
www.mountidaschools.com
Barrett ES 300/K-6
PO Box 1230 71957 870-867-2661
Stehpanie Dixon, prin. Fax 867-4552

Mount Judea, Newton
Deer / Mt. Judea SD
Supt. — See Deer
Mount Judea S, PO Box 40 72655 100/K-12
Brenda Napier, admin. 870-434-5350

Mount Vernon, Faulkner, Pop. 139
Mount Vernon-Enola SD 500/K-12
38 Garland Springs Rd 72111 501-849-2220
Larry Walters, supt. Fax 849-3076
www.mve.k12.ar.us
Other Schools - See Enola

Mulberry, Crawford, Pop. 1,638
Mulberry/Pleasant View Bi-County SD 300/K-12
424 Alma Ave 72947 479-997-1715
Lonnie Myers Ed.D., supt. Fax 997-1897
www.mpvschools.com
Marvin PS 100/K-4
424 Alma Ave 72947 479-997-1495
Toni Hopkins, prin. Fax 997-1367
Other Schools – See Ozark

Murfreesboro, Pike, Pop. 1,612
South Pike County SD 700/K-12
PO Box 339 71958 870-285-2189
Roger Featherston, supt. Fax 285-2276
www.rattlers.org
Murfreesboro ES 300/K-6
PO Box 339 71958 870-285-2193
Pam Bonner, prin. Fax 285-2928
Other Schools – See Delight

Nashville, Howard, Pop. 4,566
Nashville SD 1,900/K-12
600 N 4th St 71852 870-845-3425
Douglas Graham, supt. Fax 845-7344
www.nashvillesd.com
Nashville ES 400/4-6
200 Immanual St 71852 870-845-3262
Latito Williams, prin. Fax 845-3026
Nashville PS 700/K-3
1201 N 8th St 71852 870-845-3510
Shirley Wright, prin. Fax 845-7311

Newark, Independence, Pop. 1,165
Cedar Ridge SD 800/PK-12
1502 N Hill St 72562 870-201-2577
Andy Ashley, supt. Fax 799-8647
www.cedarwolves.org
Newark ES 200/K-5
3549 Cord Rd 72562 870-201-2577
Kathy Magness, prin. Fax 799-3689
Other Schools – See Charlotte

Newport, Jackson, Pop. 7,757
Newport SD 1,200/PK-12
406 Wilkerson Dr 72112 870-523-1311
Dr. Larry Bennett, supt. Fax 523-1388
www.newportschools.org
Newport ES 800/PK-6
1700 Commerce Blvd 72112 870-523-1311
Amy Thaxton, prin. Fax 523-1374

Norfork, Baxter, Pop. 502
Norfork SD 400/K-12
44 Fireball Ln 72658 870-499-5228
Mike Seay, supt. Fax 499-5109
norfork.k12.ar.us
Goforth ES 200/K-6
161 Mildred Simpson Dr 72658 870-499-7192
Deanna Klaus, prin. Fax 499-7196

Norman, Montgomery, Pop. 367
Caddo Hills SD 600/PK-12
2268 Highway 8 E 71960 870-356-5700
Deric Owens, supt. Fax 356-3426
www.caddohills.gabbarthost.com
Caddo Hills ES 300/PK-6
2268 Highway 8 E 71960 870-356-3331
Deborah Stephens, prin. Fax 356-5740

Norphlet, Union, Pop. 829
Smackover-Norphlet SD
Supt. — See Smackover
Norphlet ES 200/K-5
301 McMillan Dr 71759 870-546-2751
Bernadette O'Guinn, prin. Fax 546-2345
Norphlet MS 100/6-8
600 School St 71759 870-546-2781
Keith Coleman, prin. Fax 546-9554

North Little Rock, Pulaski, Pop. 61,111
North Little Rock SD 7,200/PK-12
PO Box 687 72115 501-771-8000
Kelly Rodgers, supt. Fax 771-8069
www.nlrsd.org
Amboy ES 400/K-5
101 Auburn Dr 72118 501-771-8185
Allen Pennington, prin. Fax 771-8187
Boone Park ES 300/K-5
1400 Crutcher St 72114 501-340-5160
Abigail Stone, prin. Fax 907-9429
Crestwood ES 500/K-5
1901 Crestwood Rd 72116 501-771-8190
Lori Smith, prin. Fax 771-8193
Glenview ES 200/K-5
4901 E 19th St 72117 501-955-3630
Carol Thornton, prin. Fax 975-1716
Indian Hills ES 600/K-5
6800 Indian Hills Dr 72116 501-835-5622
Shanda Coleman, prin. Fax 835-9580
Lakewood ES 400/K-5
1800 Fairway Ave 72116 501-771-8270
Sara Logan, prin. Fax 907-6332
Meadow Park ES 200/K-5
801 E Bethany Rd 72117 501-955-3620
April McKinley, prin. Fax 537-0566
North Little Rock MS 1,100/6-8
2400 Lakeview Rd 72116 501-771-8200
Lee Tackett, prin. Fax 771-8206
Pike View ECC 50/PK-PK
441 McCain Blvd 72116 501-771-8170
Jody Edrington, prin. Fax 771-8172
Ridgeroad ES 600/PK-5
4601 Ridge Rd 72116 501-771-8155
Matthew How, prin. Fax 771-8159
Seventh Street ES 300/K-5
1200 Bishop Lindsey Ave 72114 501-340-5170
Kim Starr, prin. Fax 340-5173

Pulaski County Special SD
Supt. — See Little Rock
Cato ES 400/PK-5
9906 Jacksonville Cato Rd 72120 501-833-1160
Shyrel Lee, prin. Fax 833-1167
Crystal Hill Magnet ES 700/PK-5
5001 Northshore Dr 72118 501-791-8000
Stacy Donaghy, prin. Fax 791-8008
Harris ES 200/PK-5
4424 Highway 161 72117 501-955-3550
Dr. Taniesa Moore, prin. Fax 955-3555
Oak Grove ES 300/PK-5
5703 Oak Grove Rd 72118 501-851-5370
Yvette Dillingham, prin. Fax 851-5376

Central AR Christian S - N Little Rock PK-5
6101 John F Kennedy Blvd 72116 501-835-5924
Immaculate Conception S 400/PK-8
7000 John F Kennedy Blvd 72116 501-835-0771
Marcia Brucks, prin. Fax 487-6097
Immaculate Heart of Mary S 200/PK-8
7025 Jasna Gora Dr 72118 501-851-2760
Daniel Smith, prin. Fax 851-2864
North Little Rock Catholic Academy 200/PK-8
1518 Parker St 72114 501-374-5237
Denise Troutman, prin. Fax 374-4292

Oark, Johnson
Jasper SD
Supt. — See Jasper
Oark ES 100/K-6
370 Highway 215 72852 479-292-3337
David Westenhover, prin. Fax 292-3435

Oden, Montgomery, Pop. 227
Ouachita River SD
Supt. — See Mena
Maddox ES 100/K-6
135 School Dr 71961 870-326-4311
Davelynn Lane, prin. Fax 326-5552

Ola, Yell, Pop. 1,269
Two Rivers SD 800/K-12
17727 E State Highway 28 72853 479-272-3113
Nathan Morris, supt. Fax 272-3125
www.trgators.org
Two Rivers ES 300/K-4
17721 E State Highway 28 72853 479-272-3160
Mary Lawrence, prin. Fax 272-3166

Omaha, Boone, Pop. 159
Omaha SD 400/K-12
522 College Rd 72662 870-426-3366
Dr. Jacob Sherwood, supt. Fax 426-3355
omahaschool.weebly.com
Omaha ES 200/K-6
522 College Rd 72662 870-426-3372
Amanda Green, prin. Fax 436-4159

Osceola, Mississippi, Pop. 7,648
Osceola SD 1,400/PK-12
2750 W Semmes Ave 72370 870-563-2561
Michael Cox, supt. Fax 563-2181
www.osd1.org/
North K 200/PK-K
1230 W Semmes Ave 72370 870-563-1155
Sandra Landry, prin. Fax 622-1040
Smith ES 500/1-4
500 Grandview St 72370 870-563-2371
Stefanie Smithey, prin. Fax 622-1035

Ozark, Franklin, Pop. 3,615
Mulberry/Pleasant View Bi-County SD
Supt. — See Mulberry
Millsap IS 100/5-6
5750 Hornet Ln 72949 479-997-8469
Dennis Fisher, prin. Fax 997-1667
Pleasant View Campus 50/7-8
5750 Hornet Ln 72949 479-997-8469
Dennis Fisher, prin. Fax 997-1667

Ozark SD 1,400/PK-12
PO Box 135 72949 479-667-4118
James Ford, supt. Fax 667-4092
www.ozarkhillbillies.org/
Ozark Kindergarten 200/PK-K
700 N 12th St 72949 479-667-3021
Jennifer King, prin. Fax 667-0171
Ozark Lower ES 1-3
1601 Walden Dr 72949 479-667-4745
Kelly Burns, prin. Fax 667-3936
Ozark Upper ES 300/4-5
1601 Walden Dr 72949 479-667-3464
Shane Vincent, prin. Fax 667-5096
Other Schools – See Altus

Palestine, Saint Francis, Pop. 671
Palestine-Wheatley SD 600/PK-12
PO Box 790 72372 870-581-2646
Jon Estes, supt. Fax 581-4420
www.edline.net/pages/Palestine-Wheatley_School_Dist/
Palestine-Wheatley ES 300/PK-6
PO Box 790 72372 870-581-2588
Patty Hernandez, prin. Fax 581-2481
Palestine-Wheatley JHS 200/7-8
PO Box 790 72372 870-581-2246
Zenna Smith, prin.

Pangburn, White, Pop. 587
Pangburn SD 800/K-12
1100 Short St 72121 501-728-4511
David Rolland, supt. Fax 728-4514
www.pangburnschools.org
Pangburn ES 400/K-6
1100 Short St 72121 501-728-4912
Chad Ramsey, prin. Fax 728-3825

Paragould, Greene, Pop. 25,788
Greene County Technical SD 3,700/PK-12
5413 W Kingshighway 72450 870-236-2762
Gene Weeks, supt. Fax 236-7333
www.gctsd.k12.ar.us/
Greene County Technical ES 600/2-3
5203 W Kingshighway 72450 870-215-4430
Vonnie Greer, prin. Fax 239-6975
Greene County Technical IS 500/4-5
5205 W Kingshighway 72450 870-215-4440
Amie Cole, prin. Fax 239-6974
Greene County Technical MS 500/6-7
5207 W Kingshighway 72450 870-215-4480
Lisa Horton, prin. Fax 236-8087
Greene County Technical PS 500/K-1
1300 S Rockingchair Rd 72450 870-215-4420
Letha Clark, prin. Fax 239-0680
Greene County Tech Preschool 200/PK-PK
1300 S Rockingchair Rd 72450 870-215-4470
Teresa Hurt, prin. Fax 215-5231

Paragould SD 3,100/PK-12
1501 W Court St 72450 870-240-2291
Debbie Smith, supt. Fax 240-2293
paragould.k12.ar.us
Baldwin ES 200/2-4
612 W Mueller 72450 870-240-2211
Caroline Schenk, prin. Fax 240-2213
Oak Grove ES 300/2-4
5027 Highway 135 N 72450 870-240-2221
Tammy Edwards, prin. Fax 240-2223

Oak Grove MS 500/5-6
5097 Highway 135 N 72450 870-240-2241
Donna Singleton, prin. Fax 240-2243
Paragould JHS 500/7-8
1713 W Court St 72450 870-240-2261
Laurel Taylor, prin. Fax 240-2263
Paragould PS 600/PK-1
1600 Country Club Rd 72450 870-240-2201
Jerry Dickson, prin. Fax 240-2203
School of the 21st Century PK-PK
427 E Poplar St 72450 870-240-2281
Amanda Baldwin, dir. Fax 240-2283
Wilson ES 200/2-4
900 W Emerson St 72450 870-240-2231
Jon Fulkerson, prin. Fax 240-2233

Crowleys Ridge Academy 300/PK-12
606 Academy Dr 72450 870-236-6909
Raymond Lasley, admin. Fax 236-6988
St. Mary Catholic S 100/PK-6
310 N 2nd St 72450 870-236-3681
Sharon Warren, prin. Fax 393-9690

Paris, Logan, Pop. 3,477
Paris SD 1,200/PK-12
602 N 10th St 72855 844-963-3243
Wayne Fawcett, supt. Fax 208-7554
www.parisschools.org
Paris ES 500/PK-4
401 N School St 72855 844-963-3243
Alan Anderson, prin. Fax 208-5898
Paris MS 300/5-8
602 N 10th St 72855 844-963-3243
Casey Mainer, prin. Fax 208-7482

St. Joseph S 100/PK-8
25 S Spruce St 72855 479-963-2119
Christy Koprovic, prin. Fax 963-8039

Pearcy, Garland
Lake Hamilton SD 4,500/K-12
205 Wolf St 71964 501-767-2306
Steve Anderson, supt. Fax 767-5573
www.lhwolves.net
Lake Hamilton ES 700/2-3
240 Wolf St 71964 501-767-8725
Kevin Catlett, prin. Fax 767-8779
Lake Hamilton IS 700/4-5
104 Wolf St 71964 501-767-4111
Stacy Howell, prin. Fax 760-6531
Lake Hamilton MS 700/6-7
120 Wolf St 71964 501-767-3355
Brian Bales, prin. Fax 767-4202
Lake Hamilton PS 700/K-1
136 Oakbrook St 71964 501-767-9351
Heath Miller, prin. Fax 767-7909

Pea Ridge, Benton, Pop. 4,709
Pea Ridge SD 1,800/K-12
781 W Pickens Rd 72751 800-451-0032
Rick Neal, supt. Fax 431-6095
www.pearidgek12.com
Pea Ridge IS 400/3-5
1442 N Davis St 72751 800-451-4882
Sarah Stokes, prin. Fax 431-6090
Pea Ridge MS 400/6-8
1391 Weston St 72751 800-451-0692
Leslie Moline, prin. Fax 431-6169
Pea Ridge PS 400/K-2
1411 Weston St 72751 800-451-5395
Keith Martin, prin. Fax 431-6168

Perryville, Perry, Pop. 1,437
Perryville SD 1,000/K-12
614 S Fourche Ave 72126 501-889-2327
Dr. Walt Davis, supt. Fax 889-5191
www.perryvilleschool.org
Perryville ES 500/K-6
625 N Cedar St 72126 501-889-5146
Jeffrey Magie, prin. Fax 889-2153

Piggott, Clay, Pop. 3,820
Piggott SD 900/K-12
PO Box 387 72454 870-598-2572
Charnelsa Powell, supt. Fax 598-5283
www.piggottschools.net
Piggott ES 500/K-6
PO Box 387 72454 870-598-2546
Anthony Dowdy, prin. Fax 598-3360

Pine Bluff, Jefferson, Pop. 48,534
Dollarway SD 1,400/PK-12
4000 Dollarway Rd 71602 870-534-7003
Barbara Warren, supt. Fax 534-7859
www.dollarwayschools.org
Matthews ES 400/PK-5
4501 Dollarway Rd 71602 870-534-0726
Ernestine Roberts, prin. Fax 534-4515
Morehead MS 300/6-8
2601 W Fluker Ave 71601 870-534-5243
Diane Boyd-Emelife, prin. Fax 535-1215

Pine Bluff SD 3,100/PK-12
PO Box 7678 71611 870-543-4200
Dr. Michael Robinson, supt. Fax 543-4208
www.pinebluffschools.org
Belair MS 100/5-6
1301 Commerce Rd 71601 870-543-4365
Dr. Suzette Bloodman, prin. Fax 850-2003
Broadmoor ES 300/K-4
1106 S Wisconsin St 71601 870-543-4368
Clintontine Fitz, prin. Fax 543-4254
Cheney ES 300/K-4
2206 Ridgway Rd 71603 870-543-4382
Kimberly West, prin. Fax 535-8689
Greenville/Forrest Park Preschool 300/PK-PK
2501 W 10th Ave 71603 870-543-4378
Marcenia Peoples, prin. Fax 543-2004

Robey JHS 300/7-8
4101 S Olive St 71603 870-543-4290
Donald Booth, prin. Fax 850-2027
Southwood ES 400/K-4
4200 S Fir St 71603 870-543-4390
Alfred Carroll, prin. Fax 850-2006
Thirty-Fourth Avenue ES 400/K-4
801 E 34th Ave 71601 870-543-4392
Linder Anderson, prin. Fax 543-4253

Watson Chapel SD 2,900/K-12
4100 Camden Rd 71603 870-879-0220
Dr. Connie Hathorn, supt. Fax 879-0588
wc-web.k12.ar.us
Coleman IS 600/4-6
4600 W 13th Ave 71603 870-879-3630
Dr. Ronnie Johnson, prin. Fax 870-3151
Edgewood ES 500/K-1
4100 W 32nd Ave 71603 870-879-1252
Rose Martin, prin. Fax 879-7202
Owen ES 400/2-3
3605 Oakwood Rd 71603 870-879-3741
Annie Shaw, prin. Fax 879-3570

Ridgway Christian S 300/K-12
3201 Ridgway Rd 71603 870-879-6264

Pleasant Plains, Independence, Pop. 344
Midland SD 500/K-12
PO Box 630 72568 501-345-8844
Dewayne Wammack, supt. Fax 345-2086
www.midlandschools.org
Other Schools – See Floral

Pocahontas, Randolph, Pop. 6,538
Pocahontas SD 1,800/K-12
2300 N Park St 72455 870-892-4573
Tracy Ingram, supt. Fax 892-8857
www.pocahontaspsd.com
Spikes ES 400/K-2
1707 Highland Blvd 72455 870-892-4573
L. Shawn Carter, prin. Fax 892-8857
Williams IS 600/3-6
2301 N Park St 72455 870-892-4573
Fax 892-2892

St. Paul Catholic S 100/PK-6
311 Cedar St 72455 870-892-5639
Maria Dickson, prin. Fax 892-1869

Portland, Ashley, Pop. 425
Hamburg SD
Supt. — See Hamburg
Portland ES 200/PK-5
PO Box 8 71663 870-737-4333
Cristy West, prin. Fax 737-4334

Pottsville, Pope, Pop. 2,781
Pottsville SD 1,600/K-12
976 Pine Ridge Rd 72858 479-968-8101
Larry Dugger, supt. Fax 968-6339
www.pottsvilleschools.org
Pottsville ES 500/K-3
87 S B St 72858 479-968-2133
Shannon Davis, prin. Fax 968-7672
Pottsville MS 400/4-6
6926 SR 247 72858 479-890-6631
Houston Townsend, prin. Fax 968-6446

Poyen, Grant, Pop. 289
Poyen SD 600/PK-12
PO Box 209 72128 501-332-8884
Jerry Newton, supt. Fax 332-8886
www.poyenschool.com
Poyen ES 300/PK-6
PO Box 209 72128 501-332-5529
Jamie Webb, prin. Fax 332-8886

Prairie Grove, Washington, Pop. 4,291
Prairie Grove SD 1,400/PK-12
300 Ed Staggs Dr 72753 479-846-4242
Dr. Allen Williams, supt. Fax 846-2015
pgtigers.org
Prairie Grove ES 300/PK-4
801 Viney Grove Rd 72753 479-846-4211
Jonathan Warren, prin. Fax 846-4206
Prairie Grove MS 600/5-8
806 N Mock St 72753 479-846-4221
Reba Holmes, prin. Fax 846-4275

Prescott, Nevada, Pop. 3,248
Prescott SD 900/K-12
762 Martin St 71857 870-887-3016
Robert Poole, supt. Fax 887-5021
www.curleywolves.org
Prescott ES 400/K-6
335 School St 71857 870-887-2514
Kimberly Grimes, prin. Fax 887-3398

Quitman, Cleburne, Pop. 754
Quitman SD 700/PK-12
PO Box 178 72131 501-589-3156
Dennis Truxler, supt. Fax 589-3523
www.quitmansd.org
Quitman ES 400/PK-6
PO Box 178 72131 501-589-2807
Mary Rieck, prin. Fax 589-3526

Rector, Clay, Pop. 1,960
Rector SD 600/K-12
PO Box 367 72461 870-595-3151
Johnny Fowler, supt. Fax 595-9067
www.rector.k12.ar.us
Rector ES 300/K-6
PO Box 367 72461 870-595-3358
Nathan Henderson, prin. Fax 595-3141

Redfield, Jefferson, Pop. 1,264
White Hall SD
Supt. — See White Hall

Hardin ES 200/K-5
700 Schoolwood Dr 72132 501-397-2450
Jeff Glover, prin. Fax 397-5037

Rison, Cleveland, Pop. 1,329
Cleveland County SD 800/K-12
PO Box 600 71665 870-325-6344
Johnnie Johnson, supt. Fax 325-7094
www.rison.k12.ar.us
Rison ES 300/K-6
PO Box 600 71665 870-325-6894
Jeff McKinney, prin. Fax 325-7095
Other Schools – See Kingsland

Woodlawn SD 600/K-12
6760 Highway 63 71665 870-357-8108
Dudley Hume, supt. Fax 357-8718
bears.k12.ar.us
Woodlawn ES 300/K-6
6760 Highway 63 71665 870-357-2211
Genell Davis, prin. Fax 357-2180

Rogers, Benton, Pop. 54,921
Rogers SD 14,800/K-12
500 W Walnut St 72756 479-636-3910
Dr. Marlin Berry, supt. Fax 631-3504
www.rogersschools.net
Bellview ES 500/K-5
5400 S Bellview Rd 72758 479-631-3605
Dan Cox, prin. Fax 631-3584
Darr ES 300/K-5
6505 S Mount Hebron Rd 72758 479-248-2008
Sharla Osbourn, prin. Fax 633-8184
Eastside ES 500/K-5
505 E New Hope Rd 72758 479-631-3630
Robin Wilkerson, prin. Fax 531-3632
Elmwood MS 800/6-8
1610 S 13th St 72758 479-631-3600
Molly Davis, prin. Fax 631-3603
Grace Hill ES 500/K-5
901 N Dixieland Rd 72756 479-631-3670
Jennifer Little, prin. Fax 631-3672
Grimes ES 500/K-5
1801 S 13th St 72758 479-631-3660
Susan Bush, prin. Fax 631-3661
Jones ES 500/K-5
2929 S 1st St 72758 479-631-3535
Pam Camper, prin. Fax 631-3533
Kirksey MS 1,000/6-8
2930 S 1st St 72758 479-631-3625
Mel Ahart, prin. Fax 631-3624
Lingle MS 900/6-8
901 N 13th St 72756 479-631-3590
Mary Elmore, prin. Fax 631-3594
Mathias ES 500/K-5
1609 N 24th St 72756 479-631-3530
Betsy Kinkade, prin. Fax 631-3532
Northside ES 500/K-5
807 N 6th St 72756 479-631-3650
Anita Turner, prin. Fax 631-3651
Oakdale MS 700/6-8
511 N Dixieland Rd 72756 479-631-3615
Jeffery Hernandez, prin. Fax 631-3617
Old Wire ES 500/K-5
3001 S Old Wire Rd 72758 479-631-3510
Shana Maxey, prin. Fax 631-3512
Reagan ES 400/K-5
3904 W Olive St 72756 479-631-3680
Laura Quillen, prin. Fax 631-3682
Tillery ES 600/K-5
211 S 7th St 72756 479-631-3520
Kathryn Mays, prin. Fax 631-3522
Westside ES 400/K-5
2200 W Oak St 72758 479-631-3640
Amy Putnam, prin. Fax 631-3642
Other Schools – See Garfield, Lowell

First Baptist Christian S 200/PK-6
3364 W Pleasant Grove Rd 72758 479-878-1052
Jo Lynn Burke, prin. Fax 621-8665
Providence Classical Christian Academy 200/K-12
4911 W Pleasant Grove Rd 72758 479-263-8861
Jason Ross M.Ed., hdmstr. Fax 439-8130
St. Vincent De Paul S 300/PK-8
1315 W Cypress St 72758 479-636-4421
Alice Stauntzenberger, prin. Fax 636-5812
Shiloh Christian S 100/PK-2
5413 Pinnacle Point Dr 72758 479-715-8480
Greg Jones, pres.

Rose Bud, White, Pop. 462
Rose Bud SD 900/PK-12
124 School Rd 72137 501-556-5815
Christopher Nail, supt. Fax 556-6000
www.rosebudschools.com
Rose Bud ES 500/PK-6
124 School Rd 72137 501-556-5152
Melissa Kirkpatrick, prin. Fax 556-6001

Rosston, Nevada, Pop. 259
Nevada SD 400/K-12
PO Box 50 71858 870-871-2418
Richard Mcafee, supt. Fax 871-2419
www.nevadaschooldistrict.net/
Nevada ES 200/K-6
PO Box 50 71858 870-871-2475
Michael Odom, prin. Fax 871-2419

Russellville, Pope, Pop. 27,404
Russellville SD 5,200/PK-12
PO Box 928 72811 479-968-1306
Dr. Mark Gotcher, supt. Fax 968-6381
www.russellvilleschools.net/
Center Valley ES 500/PK-4
5401 SR 124 72802 479-968-4540
Tami Chandler, prin. Fax 968-4603
Crawford ES 500/PK-4
1116 N Parker Rd 72801 479-968-4677
Ginny Huckaba, prin. Fax 890-4910

Dwight ES 200/K-4
1300 W 2nd Pl 72801 479-968-3967
Laura Binz, prin. Fax 890-4958
Oakland Heights ES 500/PK-4
1501 S Detroit Ave 72801 479-968-2084
Sheri Shirley, prin. Fax 890-5956
Russellville MS 800/6-7
1203 W 4th Pl 72801 479-968-2557
Lori Edgin, prin. Fax 967-5574
Russellville Upper ES 300/5-5
1201 W 4th Pl 72801 479-968-2650
Cathy Koch, prin. Fax 967-5538
Sequoyah ES 400/PK-4
1601 W 12th St 72801 479-968-2134
Barbara McShane, prin. Fax 968-7973
Other Schools – See London

Community Christian S 50/K-12
PO Box 1786 72811 479-968-1429
Rebecca Partain, admin. Fax 968-1436
St. John Catholic S 100/PK-5
1912 W Main St 72801 479-967-4644
Mark Tyler, prin. Fax 967-4645

Saint Joe, Searcy, Pop. 132
Ozark Mountain SD 600/K-12
250 S Highway 65 72675 870-439-2218
James Jones, supt. Fax 439-2604
www.omsd.k12.ar.us
Saint Joe S 100/K-12
250 S Highway 65 72675 870-439-2213
Jess Knapp, prin. Fax 439-2604
Other Schools – See Everton, Western Grove

Saint Paul, Madison, Pop. 113
Huntsville SD
Supt. — See Huntsville
Saint Paul ES 100/K-6
PO Box 125 72760 479-677-2711
Audra Kimball, prin. Fax 677-3369

Salem, Fulton, Pop. 1,613
Salem SD 800/K-12
313 Highway 62 E Ste 1 72576 870-895-2516
Wayne Guiltner, supt. Fax 895-4062
www.salemschools.net/
Salem ES 400/K-6
313 Highway 62 E Ste 4 72576 870-895-2456
Corey Johnson, prin. Fax 895-5623

Scranton, Logan, Pop. 220
Scranton SD 400/K-12
103 N 10th St 72863 479-938-7121
Dr. James Bridges, supt. Fax 938-7564
www.scrantonrockets.net
Scranton ES 200/K-6
103 N 10th St 72863 479-938-7278
Gary Rhinehart, prin. Fax 938-1538

Searcy, White, Pop. 22,441
Riverview SD 1,400/K-12
800 Raider Dr 72143 501-279-0540
David Rutledge, supt. Fax 279-0737
www.riverviewsd.org
Riverview JHS 200/7-8
820 Raider Dr 72143 501-279-7111
Stuart Hill, prin. Fax 279-7166
Other Schools – See Judsonia, Kensett

Searcy SD 4,200/K-12
801 N Elm St 72143 501-268-3517
Diane Barrett, supt. Fax 278-2220
www.searcyschools.org/
Ahlf JHS 700/7-8
308 W Vine Ave 72143 501-268-3158
Chris Eubanks, prin. Fax 278-2212
Deener ES 400/K-3
163 Cloverdale Blvd 72143 501-268-3850
Caroline Nail, prin. Fax 278-2232
McRae ES 500/K-3
609 W McRae Ave 72143 501-268-3936
James Gurchiek, prin. Fax 278-2283
Southwest MS 900/4-6
1000 W Beebe Capps Expy 72143 501-268-3125
Carrie Parsley, prin. Fax 278-2263
Westside ES 500/K-3
512 Country Club Rd 72143 501-268-0111
Kyle Hunt, prin. Fax 278-2292

Harding Academy 700/PK-12
PO Box 10775 72149 501-279-7200
James Simmons, supt. Fax 279-7213

Sheridan, Grant, Pop. 4,558
Sheridan SD 3,700/PK-12
400 N Rock St 72150 870-942-3135
Jerrod Williams, supt. Fax 942-2931
www.sheridanschools.org
Sheridan ES 600/PK-2
707 Ridge Dr 72150 870-942-3131
Lindsey Bohler, prin. Fax 942-7477
Sheridan IS 500/3-6
708 Ridge Dr 72150 870-942-7488
Annette Neely, prin. Fax 942-3190
Other Schools – See Little Rock

Sherwood, Pulaski, Pop. 28,899
Pulaski County Special SD
Supt. — See Little Rock
Clinton Interdistrict Magnet ES 700/PK-5
142 Hollywood Ave 72120 501-833-1200
Jackye Parker, prin. Fax 833-1210
Oakbrooke ES 600/PK-5
2200 Thornhill Dr 72120 501-833-1190
Dr. Kim Truslow, prin. Fax 833-1198
Sherwood ES 400/PK-5
307 Verona Ave 72120 501-833-1150
Josie Brazil, prin. Fax 833-1155

Sylvan Hills ES 500/PK-5
402 Dee Jay Hudson Dr 72120 501-833-1140
Jason Young, prin. Fax 833-1149
Sylvan Hills MS 900/6-8
10001 Johnson Dr 72120 501-833-1120
Jo Wilcox, prin. Fax 833-1137

Abundant Life S 300/K-12
9200 Highway 107 72120 501-835-3120
Justin Moseley, supt. Fax 835-4428

Shirley, Van Buren, Pop. 283
Shirley SD 400/K-12
199 School Dr 72153 501-723-8191
Tyrene Gardner, supt. Fax 723-4020
www.shirleybluedevils.org
Shirley ES 200/K-6
1302 Highway 9 E 72153 501-723-8193
Michael Bramlett, prin. Fax 723-8422

Siloam Springs, Benton, Pop. 14,431
Siloam Springs SD 4,200/PK-12
PO Box 798 72761 479-524-3191
Kendall Ramey, supt. Fax 524-8002
www.siloamschools.com
Allen ES 600/1-2
1900 N Mount Olive St 72761 479-524-0358
Tanya Johnson, prin. Fax 524-0385
Northside K 500/PK-K
501 W Elgin St 72761 479-524-4126
Michelle Paden, prin. Fax 524-4561
Siloam Springs IS 600/5-6
1500 N Mount Olive St 72761 479-524-8152
Tim Hornbuckle, prin. Fax 524-8052
Siloam Springs MS 600/7-8
600 S Dogwood St 72761 479-524-6184
Teresa Morgan, prin. Fax 524-3228
Southside ES 600/3-4
200 W Tulsa St 72761 479-524-3183
Dan Siemens, prin. Fax 549-3812

Smackover, Union, Pop. 1,823
Smackover-Norphlet SD 900/K-12
112 E 8th St 71762 870-725-3132
Dave Wilcox, supt. Fax 725-1250
www.smackover.net
Smackover ES 400/K-5
701 Magnolia 71762 870-725-3601
Holly Strickland, prin. Fax 725-2580
Other Schools – See Norphlet

Sparkman, Dallas, Pop. 421
Harmony Grove SD
Supt. — See Camden
Sparkman ES 100/K-6
PO Box 37 71763 870-678-9312
Larry Knight, prin. Fax 678-2917

Springdale, Washington, Pop. 64,520
Springdale SD 20,500/PK-12
PO Box 8 72765 479-750-8800
Dr. Jim Rollins, supt. Fax 750-8812
www.sdale.org
Bayyari ES 600/K-5
2199 Scottsdale Ave 72764 479-750-8760
Martha Walker, prin. Fax 750-8762
Childers-Knapp ES PK-5
2634 Oriole St 72764 479-750-8850
Cindy Covington, prin. Fax 750-8846
Elmdale ES 500/K-5
420 N West End St 72764 479-750-8859
Michele Hutton, prin. Fax 750-8861
George ES 600/K-5
2878 Powell St 72764 479-750-8710
Annette Freeman, prin. Fax 750-8810
Harp ES 600/K-5
2700 Butterfield Coach Rd 72764 479-750-8740
Allison Strange, prin. Fax 750-8742
Hellstern MS 900/6-7
7771 Har Ber Ave 72762 479-750-8725
Todd Loftin, prin. Fax 306-4260
Hunt ES 600/K-5
3511 Silent Grove Rd 72762 479-750-8775
Michelle Doshier, prin. Fax 750-8774
Jones ES 600/K-5
900 Powell St 72764 479-750-8865
Melissa Fink, prin. Fax 750-8867
Kelly MS 700/6-7
1879 E Robinson Ave 72764 479-750-8730
Sara Ford, prin. Fax 750-8733
Lee ES 500/K-5
400 Quandt Ave 72764 479-750-8868
Justin Swope, prin. Fax 750-8870
Monitor ES 700/K-5
3955 E Monitor Rd 72764 479-750-8749
Maribel Childress, prin. Fax 750-8794
Parson Hills ES 500/K-5
2326 Cardinal Dr 72764 479-750-8877
Heather Cooper, prin. Fax 756-8262
Shaw ES 600/K-5
4337 Grimsley Rd 72762 479-750-8898
Cynthia Voss, prin. Fax 333-0101
Smith ES 600/K-5
3600 Falcon Rd 72762 479-750-8846
Kim Simco, prin. Fax 750-8716
Sonora ES 700/K-5
20200 Sonora Rd 72764 479-750-8820
Regina Stewman, prin. Fax 750-8779
Sonora MS 800/6-8
17051 E Highway 412 72764 479-750-8821
Martha Dodson, prin. Fax 750-8823
Springdale Pre-K PK-PK
409 N Thompson St 72764 479-750-8889
Darlene Fleeman, prin. Fax 750-8799
Turnbow ES 800/K-5
3390 Habberton Rd 72764 479-750-8785
Stacey Ferguson, prin. Fax 750-8728

Tyson ES 600/K-5
1967 Chapman Ave 72762 479-750-8862
Shelly Poage, prin. Fax 750-8864
Tyson MS 700/6-7
3304 S 40th St 72762 479-750-8720
Stephanie Anderson, prin. Fax 750-8724
Walker ES 500/K-5
1701 S 40th St 72762 479-750-8874
Lynn Ryan, prin. Fax 750-8717
Westwood ES 500/K-5
1850 McRay Ave 72762 479-750-8871
Dr. Allison Byford, prin. Fax 750-8873
Young ES 500/K-5
301 Pippin Apple Cir 72762 479-750-8770
Debbie Flora, prin. Fax 306-2002

Grace Lutheran Academy 100/PK-9
1466 Wensworth Ave 72762 479-305-0985
George Kellermann, prin. Fax 305-0985
Shiloh Christian S 900/PK-12
1707 Johnson Rd 72762 479-756-1140
Greg Jones, pres. Fax 756-7229
Springdale Adventist S 50/K-8
4001 W Don Tyson Pkwy 72762 479-750-4156

Star City, Lincoln, Pop. 2,243
Star City SD 1,600/K-12
400 E Arkansas St 71667 870-628-4237
Jon Laffoon, supt. Fax 628-4228
www.starcityschools.com
Brown ES 700/K-5
400 E Arkansas St 71667 870-628-5111
Jacob Lanehart, prin. Fax 628-5715
Star City MS 400/6-8
400 E Arkansas St 71667 870-628-5125
Gina Richard, prin. Fax 628-1393

Strawberry, Lawrence, Pop. 295
Hillcrest SD 400/K-12
PO Box 50 72469 870-528-3856
Greg Crabtree, supt. Fax 528-3383
hillcrest.k12.ar.us
Other Schools – See Lynn

Strong, Union, Pop. 548
Strong-Huttig SD 400/K-12
PO Box 735 71765 870-797-3040
Jeff Alphin, supt. Fax 797-3012
strong.k12.ar.us
Gardner-Strong ES 200/K-6
PO Box 736 71765 870-797-2321
Wendell Colen, prin. Fax 797-7633

Stuttgart, Arkansas, Pop. 9,196
Stuttgart SD 1,700/PK-12
2501 S Main St 72160 870-673-8701
Rick Gales, supt. Fax 673-7337
www.stuttgartschools.org
Meekins MS 300/5-6
2501 S Main St 72160 870-673-3565
Sharon Konency, prin. Fax 673-7337
Park Avenue ES 700/PK-4
2501 S Main St 72160 870-673-3563
Pam Dean, prin. Fax 673-7337
Stuttgart JHS 200/7-8
2501 S Main St 72160 870-673-3562
Amy Marek, prin. Fax 673-7337

Holy Rosary S 100/PK-6
920 W 19th St 72160 870-673-3211
Kathy Lorince, prin. Fax 673-3211
St. John Lutheran S 100/PK-6
2019 S Buerkle St 72160 870-673-7096
Fax 673-1583

Sulphur Rock, Independence, Pop. 448
Batesville SD
Supt. — See Batesville
Sulphur Rock Magnet ES 300/K-6
480 N Main St 72579 870-799-3149
Stacey Lindsey, prin. Fax 799-8099

Swifton, Jackson, Pop. 788
Jackson County SD
Supt. — See Tuckerman
Swifton MS 200/5-7
PO Box 556 72471 870-485-2336
Kristy Metzger, prin. Fax 485-2711

Taylor, Columbia, Pop. 562
Emerson-Taylor-Bradley SD 1,000/PK-12
506 E Pine St 71861 870-694-2251
Gary Hines, supt. Fax 694-1261
www.etbsd.org
Taylor ES 200/PK-6
506 E Pine St 71861 870-694-5811
Robby Frizzell, prin. Fax 694-7041
Other Schools – See Bradley, Emerson

Texarkana, Miller, Pop. 29,379
Genoa Central SD 1,100/PK-12
12472 Highway 196 71854 870-653-4343
Angie Bryant, supt. Fax 653-2624
www.dragons1.k12.ar.us
Cobb MS 300/5-8
11986 Highway 196 71854 870-653-2132
Deloris Coe, prin. Fax 653-6944
Genoa Central ES 400/PK-4
12018 Highway 196 71854 870-653-2248
Cathy Reeves, prin. Fax 653-6922

Texarkana Arkansas SD 4,300/K-12
3435 Jefferson Ave 71854 870-772-3371
Dr. Becky Kesler, supt. Fax 773-2602
www.tasd7.net
College Hill ES 300/K-4
3512 Grand Ave 71854 870-774-9111
Carol Miller, prin. Fax 773-0643

College Hill MS 600/5-6
3512 Grand Ave 71854 870-772-0281
J.R. Arnold, prin. Fax 773-0068
Fairview Magnet ES 300/K-4
3512 Grand Ave 71854 870-774-9241
Kevin Hamilton, prin. Fax 774-0236
Kilpatrick Magnet ES 400/K-4
3512 Grand Ave 71854 870-774-9691
Demarcus Green, prin. Fax 772-4386
North Heights Magnet JHS 600/7-8
3512 Grand Ave 71854 870-773-1091
Theresa Cowling, prin. Fax 772-2722
Trice Magnet ES 600/K-4
3512 Grand Ave 71854 870-772-8431
Tracy Boyles, prin. Fax 773-1492
Union Magnet ES 300/K-4
3512 Grand Ave 71854 870-772-7341
Lekia Jones, prin. Fax 772-8017

Trinity Christian S 300/PK-12
3107 Trinity Blvd 71854 870-779-1009
Veritas Academy 50/PK-12
2101 E 50th St 71854 870-772-0646
Ben House, hdmstr.

Timbo, Stone
Mountain View SD
Supt. — See Mountain View
Timbo S 100/PK-12
23747 Highway 263 72680 870-746-4303
Dustin Mitchell, prin. Fax 746-4844

Trumann, Poinsett, Pop. 7,174
Trumann SD 1,400/K-12
221 N Pine Ave 72472 870-483-6444
Myra Graham, supt. Fax 483-2602
www.trumannwildcat.com
Trumann ES 700/K-4
401 N Willow Ave 72472 870-483-5314
Michael Allen, prin. Fax 483-6700
Trumann MS 200/5-8
221 N Pine Ave 72472 870-483-5356
Josh Byard, prin. Fax 483-2602

Tuckerman, Jackson, Pop. 1,848
Jackson County SD 900/K-12
PO Box 1070 72473 870-349-2232
Chester Shannon, supt. Fax 349-2355
bulldogs.k12.ar.us/
Tuckerman ES 400/K-4
PO Box 1070 72473 870-349-2312
Pharis Smith, prin. Fax 349-2355
Other Schools – See Swifton

Tyronza, Poinsett, Pop. 751
East Poinsett County SD
Supt. — See Lepanto
Tyronza ES 200/PK-6
412 S Main St 72386 870-487-2259
Sandi Carroll, prin. Fax 487-2823

Umpire, Howard
Cossatot River SD
Supt. — See Wickes
Umpire ES 100/PK-6
PO Box 60 71971 870-583-2141
Carla Golden, prin. Fax 583-6264

Umpire Christian S K-8
164 School St 71971 870-583-6138

Valley Springs, Boone, Pop. 182
Valley Springs SD 900/K-12
PO Box 640 72682 870-429-9200
Judith Green, supt. Fax 429-5551
valley.k12.ar.us
Valley Springs ES 400/K-4
PO Box 640 72682 870-429-9200
L. Sherrill, prin. Fax 429-8110
Valley Springs MS 300/5-8
PO Box 640 72682 870-429-9200
Tony Mincer, prin. Fax 429-8121

Van Buren, Crawford, Pop. 22,172
Van Buren SD 5,500/K-12
2221 E Pointer Trl 72956 479-474-7942
Dr. Harold Jeffcoat, supt. Fax 471-3146
www.vbsd.us
Butterfield Trail MS 700/6-8
310 N 11th St 72956 479-474-6838
Dr. Karen Endel, prin. Fax 471-3101
Central ES 200/K-5
913 N 24th St 72956 479-474-7059
Cindy Mizell, prin. Fax 471-3159
City Heights ES 400/K-5
301 Mount Vista Blvd 72956 479-474-6918
Mary McCutchen, prin. Fax 471-3139
King ES 500/K-5
411 N 20th St 72956 479-474-2661
Carolyn Risley, prin. Fax 471-3185
Northridge MS 700/6-8
120 Northridge Dr 72956 479-471-3126
Lonnie Mitchell, prin. Fax 471-3129
Parkview ES 500/K-5
605 Parkview St 72956 479-474-8730
Stacie Wood, prin. Fax 471-3149
Rena ES 500/K-5
720 Rena Rd 72956 479-471-3190
Joyce Sanders, prin. Fax 471-3193

Tate ES 400/K-5
406 Catcher Rd 72956 479-471-3130
Robert Childers, prin. Fax 471-3134

Vandervoort, Polk, Pop. 87
Cossatot River SD
Supt. — See Wickes
Vandervoort ES 200/PK-6
122 E Adair 71972 870-387-6923
Judy Joiner, prin. Fax 387-7468

Vilonia, Faulkner, Pop. 3,760
Vilonia SD 2,100/K-12
PO Box 160 72173 501-796-2113
David Stephens, supt. Fax 796-3134
www.viloniaschools.org
Mitchell IS 4-6
98 S Mount Olive Rd 72173 501-796-4643
Andy Pennington, admin. Fax 796-4893
Vilonia ES 500/K-3
15 Eagle St 72173 501-796-2112
Kelly Walters, prin. Fax 796-2445
Vilonia MS 300/7-8
49 Eagle St 72173 501-796-2940
Lori Lombardi, prin. Fax 796-4697
Vilonia PS 400/K-3
4 Bane Ln 72173 501-796-2018
Susan Loyd, prin. Fax 796-2445

Viola, Fulton, Pop. 326
Viola SD 400/K-12
PO Box 380 72583 870-458-2323
John May, supt. Fax 458-2214
violaschool.k12.ar.us
Viola ES 200/K-6
PO Box 380 72583 870-458-2511
Andy Burden, prin. Fax 458-2214

Violet Hill, Izard
Izard County Consolidated SD
Supt. — See Brockwell
Izard County Consolidated ES 200/K-4
5555 E Arkansas Highway 56 72584 870-322-7229
Eve Hatman, prin. Fax 322-7231

Waldron, Scott, Pop. 3,541
Waldron SD 1,500/PK-12
1560 W 6th St 72958 479-637-3179
Roy Wayman, supt. Fax 637-3177
waldron.k12.ar.us
Waldron ABC ECC PK-PK
453 W 6th St 72958 479-637-2720
Ryan Walker, prin. Fax 637-0008
Waldron ES 600/K-4
1895 Rice St 72958 479-637-2454
Ryan Walker, prin. Fax 637-3173
Waldron MS 500/5-8
2075 Rice St 72958 479-637-4549
Kimberly Solomon, prin. Fax 637-3165

Walnut Ridge, Lawrence, Pop. 4,854
Lawrence County SD 800/K-12
508 E Free St 72476 870-886-6634
Terry Belcher, supt. Fax 886-6635
www.bobcats.k12.ar.us
Walnut Ridge ES 400/K-6
508 E Free St 72476 870-886-3482
LeeAnn Cheadle, prin. Fax 819-0401

Ward, Lonoke, Pop. 3,966
Cabot SD
Supt. — See Cabot
Ward Central ES 600/PK-4
1570 Wilson Loop 72176 501-743-3569
Andy Sullivan, prin. Fax 843-9744

Weiner, Poinsett, Pop. 712
Harrisburg SD
Supt. — See Harrisburg
Weiner ES 100/K-6
313 N Garfield St 72479 870-684-2252
Pamela Hogue, prin. Fax 684-2684

Western Grove, Newton, Pop. 373
Ozark Mountain SD
Supt. — See Saint Joe
Western Grove S 100/K-12
300 School St 72685 870-429-5215
William Carter, prin. Fax 429-5276

West Fork, Washington, Pop. 2,246
West Fork SD 1,200/K-12
359 School Ave 72774 479-839-2231
John Karnes, supt. Fax 839-8412
www.westforkschools.org
West Fork ES 400/K-4
245 School Ave 72774 479-839-2236
Patrick Thaler, prin. Fax 839-8412
West Fork MS 400/5-8
333 School Ave 72774 479-839-3342
Becky Ramsey, prin. Fax 839-8412

West Helena, Phillips, Pop. 7,876
Helena/West Helena SD
Supt. — See Helena
Miller ES 300/4-6
106 Miller Loop 72390 870-572-3705
Becky Alexander, prin. Fax 572-4521

De Soto S 300/PK-12
PO Box 2807 72390 870-572-6717

West Memphis, Crittenden, Pop. 26,012
Marion SD
Supt. — See Marion
Avondale ES 700/K-1
1402 Crestmere St 72301 870-735-4588
Ali Weimer, prin. Fax 735-4672

West Memphis SD 5,600/K-12
301 S Avalon St 72301 870-735-1915
Jon Collins, supt. Fax 732-8643
www.wmsd.net
Bragg ES 400/K-6
309 W Barton Ave 72301 870-735-4196
Cassie Adams, prin. Fax 732-8647
Faulk ES 600/K-6
908 Vanderbilt Ave 72301 870-735-5252
Janice Donald, prin. Fax 732-8563
Jackson ES 300/K-6
2395 SL Henry St 72301 870-735-7303
Annette Frazier, prin. Fax 732-8569
Maddux ES 500/K-6
2100 E Barton Ave 72301 870-735-4242
Sheri Lowe, prin. Fax 732-8603
Richland ES 600/K-6
1011 W Barton Ave 72301 870-735-6443
Gwen Looney, prin. Fax 732-8564
Weaver ES 400/K-6
1280 E Barton Ave 72301 870-735-7670
Shelia Grissom, prin. Fax 732-8612
Wonder ES 400/K-6
801 S 16th St 72301 870-735-4219
Leeman Brown, prin. Fax 732-8648

St. Michael S 100/PK-6
405 N Missouri St 72301 870-735-1730
Elizabeth Haney, prin. Fax 735-3017
West Memphis Christian S 200/PK-12
PO Box 996 72303 870-400-4000

White Hall, Jefferson, Pop. 5,470
White Hall SD 3,000/K-12
1020 W Holland Ave 71602 870-247-2002
Dr. Larry Smith, supt. Fax 247-3707
www.whitehallsd.org/
Gandy ES 400/K-5
400 Gandy Ave 71602 870-247-4054
Tim Taylor, prin. Fax 247-4059
Moody ES 300/K-5
700 Moody Dr 71602 870-247-4363
Beth Joslin, prin. Fax 247-4372
Taylor ES 300/K-5
805 West St 71602 870-247-1988
Tammie Canada, prin. Fax 247-2169
White Hall MS 700/6-8
8106 Dollarway Rd 71602 870-247-2711
Douglas Dorris, prin. Fax 247-4879
Other Schools – See Redfield

Wickes, Polk, Pop. 743
Cossatot River SD 1,100/PK-12
130 School Dr 71973 870-385-7101
Dewayne Taylor, supt. Fax 385-2238
www.cossatot.us
Wickes ES 300/PK-6
130 School Dr 71973 870-385-2346
Jana Richardson, prin. Fax 385-2242
Other Schools – See Umpire, Vandervoort

Wilson, Mississippi, Pop. 888
Rivercrest SD 1,000/PK-12
1700-A W State Highway 14 72395 870-655-8633
Sally Bennett, supt. Fax 655-8841
www.rivercrestcolts.org
Rivercrest ES 500/PK-6
1704 W State Highway 14 72395 870-655-8621
Gloria Phillips, prin. Fax 655-8710
Rivercrest JHS 200/7-8
1702 W State Highway 14 72395 870-655-8421
William Burfield, prin. Fax 655-9980

Delta S, PO Box 264 72395 100/PK-12
Jenifer Fox, head sch 870-655-0200

Wynne, Cross, Pop. 8,285
Wynne SD 2,700/K-12
PO Box 69 72396 870-238-5020
Carl Easley, supt. Fax 238-5011
www.wynneschools.org
Wynne IS 600/3-5
PO Box 69 72396 870-238-5060
Sandra Hollaway, prin. Fax 238-5063
Wynne JHS 600/6-8
PO Box 69 72396 870-238-5040
David Stepp, prin. Fax 238-5043
Wynne PS 600/K-2
PO Box 69 72396 870-238-5050
Debra Heath, prin. Fax 238-5053

Yellville, Marion, Pop. 1,190
Yellville-Summit SD 500/K-12
1124 N Panther Ave 72687 870-449-4061
Wes Henderson, supt. Fax 449-5003
www.yellvillesummitschools.com
Yellville-Summit ES 300/K-6
1124 N Panther Ave 72687 870-449-4244
Calvin Mallett, prin. Fax 449-2214

CALIFORNIA

CALIFORNIA DEPARTMENT OF EDUCATION
1430 N St, Sacramento 95814-5901
Telephone 916-319-0800
Fax 916-319-0100
Website http://www.cde.ca.gov

Superintendent of Public Instruction Tom Torlakson

CALIFORNIA BOARD OF EDUCATION
1430 N St, Sacramento 95814-5901

President Dr. Michael Kirst

COUNTY SUPERINTENDENTS OF SCHOOLS

Alameda County Office of Education
Karen Monroe, supt. 510-887-0152
313 W Winton Ave, Hayward 94544 Fax 670-4146
www.acoe.org

Alpine County Office of Education
Patrick Traynor, supt. 530-694-2230
43 Hawkside Dr Fax 694-2379
Markleeville 96120
www.alpinecoe.k12.ca.us

Amador County Office of Education
Dick Glock, supt. 209-257-5353
217 Rex Ave, Jackson 95642 Fax 257-5360
www.amadorcoe.org/

Butte County Office of Education
Tim Taylor, supt. 530-532-5650
1859 Bird St, Oroville 95965 Fax 532-5762
www.bcoe.org

Calaveras County Office of Education
Kathy Northington, supt. 209-736-4662
PO Box 760, Angels Camp 95221 Fax 736-2138
www.ccoe.k12.ca.us

Colusa County Office of Education
Michael West, supt. 530-458-0350
345 5th St Ste A, Colusa 95932 Fax 458-8054
www.ccoe.net

Contra Costa County Office of Education
Dr. Karen Sakata, supt. 925-942-3388
77 Santa Barbara Rd Fax 472-0875
Pleasant Hill 94523
www.cccoe.k12.ca.us

Del Norte County Office of Education
Jeff Harris, supt. 707-464-0200
301 W Washington Blvd Fax 464-0238
Crescent City 95531
www.delnortecoe.org

El Dorado County Office of Education
Ed Manansala, supt. 530-622-7130
6767 Green Valley Rd Fax 621-2543
Placerville 95667
www.edcoe.org

Fresno County Office of Education
Jim Yovino, supt. 559-265-3000
1111 Van Ness Ave, Fresno 93721 Fax 265-4005
www.fcoe.org

Glenn County Office of Education
Tracey Quarne, supt. 530-934-6575
311 S Villa Ave, Willows 95988 Fax 934-6576
www.glenncoe.org

Humboldt County Office of Education
Dr. Chris Hartley, supt. 707-445-7000
901 Myrtle Ave, Eureka 95501 Fax 445-7143
www.humboldt.k12.ca.us

Imperial County Office of Education
Jonathan Finnell, supt. 760-312-6464
1398 Sperber Rd, El Centro Fax 312-6568
www.icoe.org

Inyo County Office of Education
Dr. Lisa Fontana, supt. 760-878-2426
PO Box G, Independence 93526 Fax 878-2279
www.inyo.k12.ca.us

Kern County Office of Education
Mary Barlow, supt. 661-636-4000
1300 17th St, Bakersfield 93301 Fax 636-4130
www.kern.org/

Kings County Office of Education
Tim Bowers, supt. 559-584-1441
1144 W Lacey Blvd, Hanford 93230 Fax 589-7000
www.kings.k12.ca.us

Lake County Office of Education
Brock Falkenberg, supt. 707-262-4100
1152 S Main St, Lakeport 95453 Fax 263-0197
www.lakecoe.org

Lassen County Office of Education
Patricia Gunderson, supt. 530-257-2196
472-013 Johnstonville Rd Fax 257-2518
Susanville 96130
www.lcoe.org

Los Angeles County Office of Education
Dr. Debra Duardo, supt. 562-922-6111
9300 Imperial Hwy, Downey 90242 Fax 922-6768
www.lacoe.edu

Madera County Office of Education
Cecilia Massetti Ed.D., supt. 559-673-6051
1105 S Madera Ave, Madera 93637 Fax 673-5569
www.maderacoe.k12.ca.us

Marin County Office of Education
Mike Grant, supt. 415-472-4110
PO Box 4925, San Rafael 94913 Fax 491-6625
www.marinschools.org/

Mariposa County Office of Education
Robin Hopper, supt. 209-742-0250
PO Box 8, Mariposa 95338 Fax 966-4549
www.mariposa.k12.ca.us

Mendocino County Office of Education
Warren Galletti, supt. 707-467-5000
2240 Old River Rd, Ukiah 95482 Fax 462-0379
www.mcoe.us

Merced County Office of Education
Steve Tietjen Ed.D., supt. 209-381-6600
632 W 13th St, Merced 95341 Fax 381-6767
www.mcoe.org

Modoc County Office of Education
Mike Martin, supt. 530-233-7100
139 Henderson St, Alturas 96101 Fax 233-5531
www.modoccoe.k12.ca.us

Mono County Office of Education
Stacey Adler, supt. 760-932-7311
PO Box 477, Bridgeport 93517 Fax 932-7278
www.monocoe.org

Monterey County Office of Education
Dr. Nancy Kotowski, supt. 831-755-0300
PO Box 80851, Salinas 93912 Fax 753-6473
www.montereycoe.org

Napa County Office of Education
Barbara Nemko, supt. 707-253-6800
2121 Imola Ave, Napa 94559 Fax 253-6841
www.napacoe.org

Nevada County Office of Education
Scott Lay, supt. 530-478-6400
380 Crown Point Circle Fax 478-6410
Grass Valley 95945
www.nevco.org

Orange County Office of Education
Al Mijares, supt. 714-966-4000
PO Box 9050, Costa Mesa 92628 Fax 662-3570
www.ocde.us

Placer County Office of Education
Gayle Garbolino-Mojica, supt. 530-889-8020
360 Nevada St, Auburn 95603 Fax 888-1367
www.placercoe.k12.ca.us

Plumas County Office of Education
Terry Oestreich, admin. 530-283-6500
1446 E Main St, Quincy 95971 Fax 283-6530
www.pcoe.k12.ca.us

Riverside County Office of Education
Judy White, supt. 951-826-6530
PO Box 868, Riverside 92502 Fax 826-6199
www.rcoe.us

Sacramento County Office of Education
David Gordon, supt. 916-228-2500
10474 Mather Blvd, Mather 95655 Fax 228-2403
www.scoe.net

San Benito County Office of Education
Lorna Gilbert, supt. 831-637-5393
460 5th St, Hollister 95023 Fax 637-0140
www.sbcoe.org

San Bernardino Co. Office of Education
Ted Alejandre, supt. 909-386-2704
601 N E St, San Bernardino 92415 Fax 386-2478
www.sbcss.k12.ca.us

San Diego County Office of Education
Paul Gothold, supt. 858-292-3500
6401 Linda Vista Rd Fax 292-3653
San Diego 92111
www.sdcoe.net

San Francisco County Office of Education
Vincent Matthews, supt. 415-241-6000
555 Franklin St Fax 241-6012
San Francisco 94102
www.sfusd.edu

San Joaquin County Office of Education
Dr. James Mousalimas, supt. 209-468-4800
PO Box 213030, Stockton 95213 Fax 468-4819
www.sjcoe.org

San Luis Obispo Co. Office of Education
James Brescia, supt. 805-543-7732
3350 Education Dr Fax 541-1105
San Luis Obispo 93405
www.slocoe.org

San Mateo County Office of Education
Anne Campbell, supt. 650-802-5300
101 Twin Dolphin Dr Fax 802-5564
Redwood City 94065
www.smcoe.org

Santa Barbara County Office of Education
Susan Salcido, supt. 805-964-4711
PO Box 6307, Santa Barbara 93160 Fax 964-4712
sbceo.org

Santa Clara County Office of Education
Dr. Jon Gundry, supt. 408-453-6500
1290 Ridder Park Dr Fax 453-6601
San Jose 95131
www.sccoe.org

Santa Cruz County Office of Education
Michael Watkins, supt. 831-466-5600
400 Encinal St, Santa Cruz 95060 Fax 466-5607
www.santacruz.k12.ca.us

Shasta County Office of Education
Judy Flores, supt. 530-225-0200
1644 Magnolia Ave Fax 225-0329
Redding 96001
www.shastacoe.org

Sierra County Office of Education
Merrill Grant, supt. 530-993-1660
PO Box 955, Loyalton 96118 Fax 993-0828
www.sierracountyofficeofeducation.org/

Siskiyou County Office of Education
Kermith Walters, dir. 530-842-8400
609 S Gold St, Yreka 96097 Fax 842-8436
www.siskiyoucoe.net/

Solano County Office of Education
Lisette Estrella-Henders, supt. 707-399-4400
5100 Business Center Dr Fax 863-4174
Fairfield
www.solanocoe.net/

Sonoma County Office of Education
Steven D. Herrington Ph.D., supt. 707-524-2600
5340 Skylane Blvd Fax 578-0220
Santa Rosa 95403
www.scoe.org/

Stanislaus County Office of Education
Tom Changnon, supt. 209-238-1700
1100 H St, Modesto 95354 Fax 238-4201
www.stancoe.org/

Sutter County Office of Education
Baljinder Dhillon, supt. 530-822-2900
970 Klamath Ln, Yuba City 95993 Fax 671-3422
www.sutter.k12.ca.us

Tehama County Department of Education
Richard DuVarney, supt. 530-527-5811
1135 Lincoln St, Red Bluff 96080 Fax 529-4120
www.tehamaschools.org/

Trinity County Office of Education
Sarah Supahan, supt. 530-623-2861
PO Box 1256, Weaverville 96093 Fax 623-4489
www.tcoek12.org/

Tulare County Office of Education
Jim Vidak, supt. 559-733-6300
PO Box 5091, Visalia 93278 Fax 737-4378
www.tcoe.org/

Tuolumne County Office of Education
Marguerite Bulkin, supt. 209-536-2000
175 Fairview Ln, Sonora 95370 Fax 536-2003
www.tcsos.us

Ventura County Office of Education
Stan Mantooth, supt. 805-383-1900
5189 Verdugo Way Fax 383-1908
Camarillo 93012
www.vcoe.org

Yolo County Office of Education
Jesse Ortiz, supt. 530-668-6700
1280 Santa Anita Ct Ste 100 Fax 668-3848
Woodland 95776
www.ycoe.org

Yuba County Office of Education
Francisco Reveles, supt. 530-749-4900
935 14th St, Marysville 95901 Fax 741-6500
www.yuba.net/

PUBLIC, PRIVATE AND CATHOLIC ELEMENTARY SCHOOLS

Acampo, San Joaquin, Pop. 315
Lodi USD
Supt. — See Lodi
Houston S 200/K-8
4600 E Acampo Rd 95220 209-331-7475
Allison Gerrity, prin. Fax 331-7405

Oak View UNESD 400/K-8
7474 E Collier Rd 95220 209-368-0636
Beverly Boone, supt. Fax 368-9319
www.myoakview.com
Oak View ES 400/K-8
7474 E Collier Rd 95220 209-368-0636
Beverly Boone, supt. Fax 368-9319

Acton, Los Angeles, Pop. 7,398
Acton-Agua Dulce USD 1,300/K-12
32248 Crown Valley Rd 93510 661-269-5999
Lawrence King, supt. Fax 269-0849
www.aadusd.k12.ca.us
High Desert MS 300/6-8
3620 Antelope Woods Rd 93510 661-269-0310
Lynn David, prin. Fax 269-9336
Meadowlark ES 400/K-5
3015 Sacramento Ave 93510 661-269-8140
Cassandra Coleman, prin. Fax 269-9538

Adelanto, San Bernardino, Pop. 30,727
Adelanto ESD 8,300/K-8
PO Box 70 92301 760-246-8691
Dr. Amy Nguyen-Hernandez, supt. Fax 246-8259
www.aesd.net
Adelanto ES 500/K-5
PO Box 70 92301 760-246-5892
Ramon Rizo, prin. Fax 246-4880
Bradach ES 800/K-5
15550 Bellflower St 92301 760-246-5016
Julie Hirst, prin. Fax 246-7896
Columbia MS 400/6-8
PO Box 70 92301 760-530-1950
Richard Upshaw, prin. Fax 530-1953
El Mirage ES 100/K-8
PO Box 70 92301 760-530-7676
Dora Saldivar-Juarez, dean Fax 388-4732
Franklin STEM Academy K-6
13125 Hopland St 92301 760-530-7640
Mina Blazy, prin.
George Magnet S 700/K-8
PO Box 70 92301 760-246-8231
Carol Coburn, prin. Fax 246-5821
Magathan ES 600/K-5
11411 Holly Rd 92301 760-246-8872
Sandra Loudermilk, prin. Fax 246-7983
Vick ES 800/K-5
PO Box 70 92301 760-530-1750
Victoria Chavez, prin. Fax 530-1761
Westside Park ES 600/K-5
18270 Casaba Rd 92301 760-246-4118
Sherelle Crawford, prin. Fax 246-5446
Other Schools – See Victorville

Agoura, Los Angeles

Ramon Day S 100/PK-5
27400 Canwood St 91301 818-707-2365

Agoura Hills, Los Angeles, Pop. 19,692
Las Virgenes USD
Supt. — See Calabasas
Buttercup Preschool PK-PK
6098 Reyes Adobe Rd 91301 818-597-2153
Ruth Shaw, admin.
Lindero Canyon MS 1,000/6-8
5844 Larboard Ln 91301 818-889-2134
Jeremy Janton, prin. Fax 889-9432
Sumac ES 400/K-5
6050 Calmfield Ave 91301 818-991-4940
Liberty Logan, prin. Fax 889-6729
Willow ES 500/K-5
29026 Laro Dr 91301 818-889-0677
Laura Kintz, prin. Fax 706-0159
Yerba Buena ES 500/K-5
6098 Reyes Adobe Rd 91301 818-889-0040
Dr. Erin Roderick, prin. Fax 889-4732

Aguanga, Riverside, Pop. 1,104
Hemet USD
Supt. — See Hemet
Cottonwood S 200/K-8
44260 Sage Rd 92536 951-767-3870
John Wilder, prin. Fax 767-3877

Ahwahnee, Madera, Pop. 2,174
Bass Lake JUNESD
Supt. — See Oakhurst
Wasuma S 300/K-8
43109 Highway 49 93601 559-642-1585
Heather Archer, prin. Fax 642-1594

Alameda, Alameda, Pop. 69,145
Alameda City USD 10,600/PK-12
2060 Challenger Dr 94501 510-337-7000
Sean McPhetridge Ed.D., supt. Fax 522-6926
www.alameda.k12.ca.us
Bay Farm ES 600/K-8
200 Aughinbaugh Way 94502 510-748-4010
Babs Freitas, prin. Fax 865-2194
Bridges ES 600/K-5
351 Jack London Ave 94501 510-748-4006
Cheryl Wilson, prin. Fax 523-8862
Earhart ES 600/PK-5
400 Packet Landing Rd 94502 510-748-4003
Joy Dean, prin. Fax 523-5837
Edison ES 500/K-5
2700 Buena Vista Ave 94501 510-748-4002
Robert Slauson, prin. Fax 523-6131
Franklin ES 300/K-5
1433 San Antonio Ave 94501 510-748-4004
Jo Fetterly, prin. Fax 337-2439
Haight ES 400/PK-5
2025 Santa Clara Ave 94501 510-748-4005
Tracy Lewis, prin. Fax 523-6178
Lincoln MS 1,000/6-8
1250 Fernside Blvd 94501 510-748-4018
Michael Hans, prin. Fax 523-6217
Lin S 300/K-5
825 Taylor Ave 94501 510-748-4007
Judith Goodwin, prin. Fax 523-8798
Otis ES 600/K-5
3010 Fillmore St 94501 510-748-4013
Dr. Tanya Harris, prin. Fax 523-6880
Paden S 300/PK-5
444 Central Ave 94501 510-748-4014
Katherine Barr, prin. Fax 865-9427
Wood MS 400/6-8
420 Grand St 94501 510-748-4015
Cammie Harris, prin. Fax 523-8829
Woodstock Child Development Center PK-PK
500 Pacific Ave 94501 510-748-4001
Virginia Hunt, dir. Fax 865-9089

Alameda Christian S 50/PK-8
2226 Pacific Ave 94501 510-523-1000
Suzanne Di Lillo M.A., prin. Fax 523-4022
Chinese Christian S 200/K-8
1801 N Loop Rd 94502 510-522-0200
Edward Yue, prin. Fax 522-0204
Rising Star Montessori S 100/PK-5
1421 High St 94501 510-865-4536
Katrina Ross, dir. Fax 865-4538
St. Joseph S 300/K-8
1910 San Antonio Ave 94501 510-522-4456
Dr. Marquita Yriarte, prin. Fax 522-2890
St. Philip Neri S 300/K-8
1335 High St 94501 510-521-0787
Jessica Murray, prin. Fax 521-2418

Alamo, Contra Costa, Pop. 14,161
San Ramon Valley USD
Supt. — See Danville
Alamo ES 300/K-5
100 Wilson Rd 94507 925-855-4800
Stan Hitomi, prin. Fax 938-0454
Rancho Romero ES 500/K-5
180 Hemme Ave 94507 925-855-5700
Sandy Kontilis, prin. Fax 837-9030
Stone Valley MS 600/6-8
3001 Miranda Ave 94507 925-855-5800
Jon Campopiano, prin. Fax 838-5680

Albany, Alameda, Pop. 17,446
Albany City USD 3,800/PK-12
1051 Monroe St 94706 510-558-3750
Valerie Williams, supt. Fax 559-6560
www.ausdk12.org
Albany Childrens Center PK-PK
720 Jackson St 94706 510-559-6590
Susan Stevenson, dir. Fax 559-6593
Albany MS 900/6-8
1259 Brighton Ave 94706 510-558-3600
Deborah Brill, prin. Fax 559-6547
Cornell ES 600/K-5
920 Talbot Ave 94706 510-558-3700
Heather Duncan, prin. Fax 559-6516
Marin ES 500/K-5
1001 Santa Fe Ave 94706 510-559-4700
Melisa Pfohl, prin. Fax 559-6509
Ocean View ES 600/K-5
1000 Jackson St 94706 510-558-4800
Terry Georgeson, prin. Fax 528-6486

Albion, Mendocino, Pop. 160
Mendocino USD
Supt. — See Mendocino
Albion ES 50/K-3
30400 Albion Ridge Rd 95410 707-937-2968
Kim Humrichouse, prin. Fax 937-0714

Alhambra, Los Angeles, Pop. 81,736
Alhambra USD 17,700/K-12
1515 W Mission Rd 91803 626-943-3000
Denise Jaramillo, supt. Fax 943-8050
www.ausd.us
Baldwin S 1,100/K-8
900 S Almansor St 91801 626-943-3300
Amy Rush, prin. Fax 308-2674
Emery Park S 500/K-8
2821 W Commonwealth Ave 91803 626-943-3341
Jeremy Infranca, prin. Fax 308-3769
Fremont S 600/K-8
2001 Elm St 91803 626-943-3360
Dr. Ignacio Muniz, prin. Fax 308-2413
Garfield S 700/K-8
110 W Mclean St 91801 626-943-3380
Dr. Stephanie Richardson, prin. Fax 308-2418
Granada S 500/K-8
100 S Granada Ave 91801 626-943-3600
Chris Ng, prin. Fax 308-2421
Marguerita S 600/K-8
1603 S Marguerita Ave 91803 626-943-3620
Florence Goh, prin. Fax 308-2425
Northrup S 700/K-8
409 S Atlantic Blvd 91801 626-943-6620
Rosa Northcott, prin. Fax 281-4899
Park S 700/K-8
301 N Marengo Ave 91801 626-943-3640
Lesette Solis, prin. Fax 308-2633
Ramona S 800/K-8
509 W Norwood Pl 91803 626-943-3660
Dr. Steven Suttle, prin. Fax 308-2522
Other Schools – See Monterey Park

All Souls Parish S K-8
29 S Electric Ave 91801 626-282-5605
Carrie Fuller, prin. Fax 282-2260
Emmaus Lutheran S 200/PK-8
840 S Almansor St 91801 626-289-3664
Fax 576-0476
Oneonta Montessori S 200/PK-6
2221 Poplar Blvd 91801 626-284-0840
St. Therese S 200/K-8
1106 E Alhambra Rd 91801 626-289-3364
Alma Cornejo, prin. Fax 284-6700
St. Thomas More S 200/PK-8
2510 S Fremont Ave 91803 626-284-5778
Judith Jones, prin. Fax 284-3303

Aliso Viejo, Orange, Pop. 45,578
Capistrano USD
Supt. — See San Juan Capistrano
Aliso Viejo MS 1,100/6-8
111 Park Ave 92656 949-831-2622
Cynthia Steinert, prin. Fax 643-2784
Avila ES 800/K-5
26278 Wood Canyon Dr 92656 949-349-9452
Krystal Allen, prin. Fax 362-9108
Avila MS 1,200/6-8
26278 Wood Canyon Dr 92656 949-362-0348
Josh Wellikson, prin. Fax 362-9076
Canyon Vista ES 700/K-5
27800 Oak View Dr 92656 949-234-5941
Jeanna Dagley, prin. Fax 360-6273
Oak Grove ES 800/K-5
22705 Sanborn 92656 949-360-9001
Jill O'Connell-Bogle, prin. Fax 360-7372
Wood Canyon ES 500/K-5
23431 Knollwood 92656 949-448-0012
Paul Foucart, prin. Fax 448-0017

Aliso Viejo Christian S 400/PK-8
1 Orion 92656 949-389-0300
Kalyn Peterson, prin. Fax 389-0383
St. Mary's S 700/PK-8
7 Pursuit 92656 949-448-9027
Sharon Taylor, head sch Fax 448-0605
VanDamme Academy 100/K-8
2A Liberty 92656 949-510-4861
Lisa VanDamme, dir.

Allensworth, Tulare, Pop. 468
Allensworth ESD 100/K-8
3320 Young Rd 93219 661-849-2401
Roel Marroquin, supt. Fax 849-6634
www.allensworthesd.org
Other Schools – See Earlimart

Alpaugh, Tulare, Pop. 1,021
Alpaugh USD 600/PK-12
PO Box 9 93201 559-949-8413
Dr. Gary Mekeel, supt. Fax 949-8173
www.tcoe.org/districts/alpaugh.shtm
Alpaugh ES 200/PK-6
PO Box 9 93201 559-949-8413
Nancy Ruble, prin. Fax 949-8173

Alpine, San Diego, Pop. 13,892
Alpine UNESD 1,800/PK-8
2001 Tavern Rd 91901 619-445-3236
Dr. Richard Newman, supt. Fax 445-7045
www.alpineschools.net
Alpine ES 400/1-5
1850 Alpine Blvd 91901 619-445-2625
Travis Wall, prin. Fax 445-0484
Boulder Oaks ES 300/1-5
2320 Tavern Rd 91901 619-445-8676
Jenna Weinert, prin. Fax 445-1420
Creekside Early Learning Center 200/PK-K
8818 Harbison Canyon Rd 91901 619-659-8250
Yvette Maier, prin. Fax 659-8240
MacQueen MS 600/6-8
2001 Tavern Rd 91901 619-445-3245
Karen Hohimer, prin. Fax 445-6503
Shadow Hills ES 300/1-5
8770 Harbison Canyon Rd 91901 619-445-2977
Yvette Maier, prin. Fax 445-2157

Alta, Placer, Pop. 604
Alta-Dutch Flat UNESD 100/K-8
PO Box 958 95701 530-389-8283
Lisa Graham, supt. Fax 389-2664
www.alta.k12.ca.us
Alta-Dutch Flat ES 100/K-8
PO Box 958 95701 530-389-8283
Lisa Graham, prin. Fax 389-2664

Altadena, Los Angeles, Pop. 40,865
Pasadena USD
Supt. — See Pasadena
Altadena ES 300/K-5
743 E Calaveras St 91001 626-396-5650
Benita Scheckel, prin. Fax 296-8509
Eliot MS 600/6-8
2184 Lake Ave 91001 626-396-5680
Lori Touloumian, prin. Fax 794-7238
Franklin ES 300/K-6
527 Ventura St 91001 626-396-5640
Dr. Merian Stewart, prin. Fax 791-3421
Jackson ES 400/K-6
593 W Woodbury Rd 91001 626-396-5700
Rita Exposito, prin. Fax 794-5278

Oak Knoll Montessori S 100/PK-9
3544 Canon Blvd 91001 626-345-9929
Michel Capobianco, head sch Fax 345-9939
Pasadena Waldorf S 200/PK-12
209 E Mariposa St 91001 626-794-9564
Douglas Garrett, admin. Fax 794-4704
Renaissance Academy 100/K-12
119 W Palm St 91001 626-765-9358
Sandra Staffer, dir. Fax 765-9360
Sahag-Mesrob Armenian Christian S 200/PK-8
2501 Maiden Ln 91001 626-798-5020
Maral Boyadjian, prin. Fax 798-0082
St. Elizabeth S 300/K-8
1840 Lake Ave 91001 626-797-7727
Richard Gruttadaurio, prin. Fax 797-6541

St. Mark's S 300/PK-6
1050 E Altadena Dr 91001 626-798-8858
Jennifer Tolbert, head sch Fax 798-4180
Stratford S - Altadena Allen PK-6
2046 Allen Ave 91001 626-794-1000
Judy Burbank, head sch

Alta Loma, San Bernardino
Alta Loma ESD 6,000/K-8
9390 Baseline Rd 91701 909-484-5151
James Moore, supt. Fax 484-5155
www.alsd.k12.ca.us
Alta Loma ES 400/K-6
7085 Amethyst Ave 91701 909-484-5000
Suzanne Chrismer, prin. Fax 484-5005
Alta Loma JHS 700/7-8
9000 Lemon Ave 91701 909-484-5100
Susanne Melton, prin. Fax 484-5105
Banyan ES 600/K-6
10900 Mirador Dr 91737 909-484-5080
Alison Benson, prin. Fax 484-5085
Carnelian ES 500/K-6
7105 Carnelian St 91701 909-484-5010
Phil Suttner, prin. Fax 484-5015
Deer Canyon ES 600/K-6
10225 Hamilton St 91701 909-484-5030
Donna Carlson, prin. Fax 484-5035
Groves ES 600/K-6
10950 Emerson St 91701 909-484-5070
Lynda Hoppe, prin. Fax 484-5075
Hermosa ES 500/K-6
10133 Wilson Ave 91737 909-484-5040
Valerie Bires, prin. Fax 484-5045
Jasper ES 500/K-6
6881 Jasper St 91701 909-484-5050
Sue Geddes, prin. Fax 484-5055
Stork ES 700/K-6
5646 Jasper St 91701 909-484-5060
Michele Rachielles, prin. Fax 484-5065
Vineyard JHS 800/7-8
6440 Mayberry Ave 91737 909-484-5120
Sandy Rose, prin. Fax 484-5125

Etiwanda SD
Supt. — See Etiwanda
Caryn ES 500/K-5
6290 Sierra Crestview Loop 91737 909-941-9551
Dino Tavolazzi, prin. Fax 989-3997
Lightfoot ES 600/K-5
6989 Kenyon Way 91701 909-989-6120
Rosann Marlen, prin. Fax 941-0519

Alta Loma Christian S 200/PK-8
PO Box 8698 91701 909-989-2804
Dr. Vance Nichols, head sch Fax 466-4579
St. Peter & St. Paul S 100/PK-6
9135 Banyan St 91737 909-987-7908
Kelly Burt, prin. Fax 987-6779

Alturas, Modoc, Pop. 2,746
Modoc JUSD 800/K-12
906 W 4th St 96101 530-233-7201
Tom O'Malley, supt. Fax 233-4362
www.modoc.k12.ca.us
Alturas ES 400/K-5
809 W 8th St 96101 530-233-7201
Todd Hughes, prin. Fax 233-7607
Modoc MS 200/6-8
906 W 4th St 96101 530-233-7201
Noelle Knight, prin. Fax 233-7503

Alviso, See San Jose
Santa Clara USD
Supt. — See Santa Clara
Mayne ES 500/K-5
PO Box 187 95002 408-423-1700
Socorro Olmos, prin. Fax 423-1780

American Canyon, Napa, Pop. 18,364
Napa Valley USD
Supt. — See Napa
American Canyon MS 1,000/6-8
300 Benton Way 94503 707-259-8592
Dan Scudero, prin. Fax 259-8800
Canyon Oaks ES 700/K-5
475 Silver Oak Trl 94503 707-265-2363
Kay Vang, prin. Fax 265-2817
Donaldson Way ES 600/K-5
430 Donaldson Way 94503 707-253-3524
Marilyn Abelon, prin. Fax 253-6290
Napa Junction Magnet ES 500/K-5
300 Napa Junction Rd 94503 707-253-3461
Donna Drago, prin. Fax 253-6255

Anaheim, Orange, Pop. 327,991
Anaheim CSD 19,300/PK-6
1001 S East St 92805 714-517-7500
Dr. Linda Kimble Ed.D., supt. Fax 517-8538
anaheimelementary.org
Barton ES 700/K-6
1926 W Clearbrook Ln 92804 714-517-8900
Shawnna Derache, prin. Fax 517-9228
Edison ES 1,000/K-6
1526 E Romneya Dr 92805 714-517-8902
Greg Smet Ed.D., prin. Fax 517-9229
Franklin ES 900/K-6
521 W Water St 92805 714-517-8905
Bernadette Gzechowiak, prin. Fax 517-9230
Gauer ES 700/K-6
2000 W Ball Rd 92804 714-517-8908
Kim Hadley, prin. Fax 517-9232
Guinn ES 800/K-6
1051 S Sunkist St 92806 714-517-8911
Aleta Peters Ed.D., prin. Fax 517-9270
Henry ES 700/K-6
1123 W Romneya Dr 92801 714-517-8914
Beatriz Garcia, prin. Fax 517-9233
Jefferson ES 700/K-6
504 E South St 92805 714-517-8917
Kosal Chea, prin. Fax 517-9234
Juarez ES 800/K-6
841 S Sunkist St 92806 714-517-8923
Cecilia Roman, prin. Fax 517-9235
Lincoln ES 900/K-6
1413 E Broadway 92805 714-517-8929
Tammie Ledesma, prin. Fax 517-9237
Loara ES 600/K-6
1601 W Broadway 92802 714-517-8932
Maggie Barry Ed.D., prin. Fax 517-9238
Madison ES 600/K-6
1510 S Nutwood St 92804 714-517-8935
Diane Eatherly, prin. Fax 517-9239
Mann ES 1,100/K-6
600 W La Palma Ave 92801 714-517-8938
Carlos Perez Ed.D., prin. Fax 517-9240
Marshall ES 700/K-6
2066 W Falmouth Ave 92801 714-517-8941
Lupe Hubbard, prin. Fax 517-9241
Olive Street ES 600/K-6
890 S Olive St 92805 714-517-8920
Michael Heiner, prin. Fax 517-8779
Orange Grove ES 700/K-6
1000 S Harbor Blvd 92805 714-517-8968
Alejandro Ramirez, prin. Fax 956-2894
Palm Lane ES 800/K-6
1646 W Palm Ln 92802 714-517-8944
Tracey Golden, prin. Fax 517-9242
Ponderosa ES 1,100/K-6
2135 S Mountain View Ave 92802 714-517-8926
Yadira Moreno, prin. Fax 517-9236
Price ES 800/K-6
1516 W North St 92801 714-517-8947
Jesse Chavarria, prin. Fax 517-9243
Revere ES 1,000/K-6
140 W Guinida Ln 92805 714-517-8950
Lety Chacon, prin. Fax 517-9244
Roosevelt ES 600/K-6
1600 E Vermont Ave 92805 714-517-8953
Deanna Pelasky, prin. Fax 517-9245
Ross ES 1,000/K-6
535 S Walnut St 92802 714-517-8956
Trisha Graper, prin. Fax 517-9246
Stoddard ES 700/K-6
1841 S Ninth St 92802 714-517-8959
Dale Hillyer Ed.D., prin. Fax 517-9247
Sunkist ES 900/K-6
500 N Sunkist St 92806 714-517-8962
Maria Bolado, prin. Fax 517-9248
Westmont ES 1,000/K-6
1525 W Westmont Dr 92801 714-517-8965
Emma Robles, prin. Fax 517-9189

Anaheim UNHSD 31,600/7-12
501 N Crescent Way 92801 714-999-3511
Michael B. Matsuda, supt. Fax 535-1706
www.auhsd.us
Ball JHS 1,100/7-8
1500 W Ball Rd 92802 714-999-3663
Dr. Karen Dabney-Lieras, prin. Fax 563-9214
Brookhurst JHS 1,200/7-8
601 N Brookhurst St 92801 714-999-3613
Sam Joo, prin. Fax 999-1764
Dale JHS 1,200/7-8
900 S Dale Ave 92804 714-220-4210
Lorena Moreno, prin. Fax 220-4076
Orangeview JHS 900/7-8
3715 W Orange Ave 92804 714-220-4205
Refugio Gracian, prin. Fax 220-3023
South JHS 1,600/7-8
2320 E South St 92806 714-999-3667
Enrique Romero, prin. Fax 999-3721
Sycamore JHS 1,500/7-8
1801 E Sycamore St 92805 714-999-3616
Gary Brown, prin. Fax 776-3879
Other Schools – See Cypress, La Palma

Centralia ESD
Supt. — See Buena Park
Centralia ES 600/K-6
195 N Western Ave 92801 714-228-3210
Tia Belt Brown, prin. Fax 228-3213
Danbrook ES 700/K-6
320 S Danbrook Dr 92804 714-228-3230
Erasmo Garcia, prin. Fax 821-0328

Magnolia ESD 6,400/K-6
2705 W Orange Ave 92804 714-761-5533
Frank Donavan, supt. Fax 761-2771
www.magnoliasd.org
Disney ES 700/K-6
2323 W Orange Ave 92804 714-535-1183
Regina Ford, prin. Fax 635-7925
Lord Baden-Powell ES 700/K-6
2911 W Stonybrook Dr 92804 714-761-5442
Rudy Aguila, prin. Fax 952-3675
Low ES 700/K-6
215 N Ventura St 92801 714-533-2673
Dr. Debra Von Sprecken, prin. Fax 533-6099
Marshall ES 600/K-6
2627 W Crescent Ave 92801 714-527-8821
Sylvia Cons, prin. Fax 229-0310
Maxwell ES 800/K-6
2613 W Orange Ave 92804 714-527-2217
Steve Pescetti, prin. Fax 229-0439
Salk ES 800/K-6
1411 S Gilbert St 92804 714-527-5143
Katie Brown, prin. Fax 229-5836
Schweitzer ES 700/K-6
229 S Dale Ave 92804 714-527-7761
Marcy Chant, prin. Fax 229-5839
Walter ES 600/K-6
10802 Rustic Ln 92804 714-761-5997
Roger Nguyen, prin. Fax 229-5845
Other Schools – See Stanton

Orange USD
Supt. — See Orange
Anaheim Hills ES 500/K-6
6450 E Serrano Ave 92807 714-997-6169
Fayroze Mostafa, prin. Fax 921-0584
Canyon Rim ES 700/K-6
1090 S The Highlands 92808 714-532-7027
Erika Krohn, prin. Fax 281-0418
Crescent ES 800/K-6
5001 E Gerda Dr 92807 714-997-6371
Shele Tamaki, prin. Fax 997-6260
Imperial ES 500/K-6
400 S Imperial Hwy 92807 714-997-6282
Ginette Kelley, prin. Fax 921-9098
Nohl Canyon ES 600/K-6
4100 E Nohl Ranch Rd 92807 714-997-6203
Heather Bosworth, prin. Fax 637-2946
Parkside Pre-Kindergarten 50/PK-K
5125 E Gerda Dr 92807 714-997-6202
Bree Tippets, coord. Fax 997-6270
Running Springs ES 700/K-6
8670 E Running Springs Dr 92808 714-281-4512
Mark McLaughlin, prin. Fax 281-5048

Placentia-Yorba Linda USD
Supt. — See Placentia
Glenview ES 400/K-6
1775 N Glenview Ave 92807 714-986-7150
Alondra Ramos, prin. Fax 779-2633
Rio Vista ES 900/K-5
310 N Rio Vista St 92806 714-630-7680
Jose Cabrera, prin. Fax 666-0310
Woodsboro ES 500/K-6
7575 E Woodsboro Ave 92807 714-986-7040
Douglas Slonkosky, prin. Fax 970-6597

Savanna ESD 2,400/PK-6
1330 S Knott Ave 92804 714-236-3800
Sue Johnson Ed.D., supt. Fax 821-5073
www.savsd.k12.ca.us/
Cerritos ES 500/PK-6
3731 W Cerritos Ave 92804 714-236-3830
Briana Schnitzer, prin. Fax 821-3479
Hansen ES 800/PK-6
1300 S Knott Ave 92804 714-236-3835
Tracy Goodspeed, prin. Fax 952-1156
Reid ES 700/PK-6
720 S Western Ave 92804 714-236-3845
Erin Helenihi, prin. Fax 821-3490
Other Schools – See Buena Park

Acaciawood S 100/1-12
2530 W La Palma Ave 92801 714-995-1800
James Miller, prin. Fax 876-0723
Calvary Chapel Anaheim S 100/PK-8
270 E Palais Rd 92805 714-563-9620
John Hernandez, prin. Fax 563-9520
Fairmont Private S Anaheim Hills Campus 600/PK-8
5310 E La Palma Ave 92807 714-693-3812
Dr. Kevin Rafferty, dir. Fax 693-5078
Fairmont Private S - Historic Anaheim 400/K-8
1557 W Mable St 92802 714-563-4050
Carole Calabria, dir. Fax 774-8312
Hephatha Lutheran S 200/PK-8
5900 E Santa Ana Canyon Rd 92807 714-637-0887
Eric Deyke, prin. Fax 637-0872
Independence Christian S 200/PK-8
4905 E La Palma Ave 92807 714-970-7009
Ron Cushing, prin. Fax 970-0733
Minaret Academy 100/PK-8
1220 N State College Blvd 92806 714-533-6273
Shabnum Saeeda Husain, prin.
Orange County Christian S 300/PK-12
641 S Western Ave 92804 714-821-6227
David Lewis, admin. Fax 284-0857
Prince of Peace Lutheran S 100/PK-8
1421 W Ball Rd 92802 714-774-0993
Raymond Steinert, admin. Fax 774-0183
St. Catherines Academy 200/K-8
215 N Harbor Blvd 92805 714-772-1363
Sr. Johnellen Turner, prin. Fax 772-3004
St. Justin Martyr S 200/K-8
2030 W Ball Rd 92804 714-772-4902
Jan Balsis, prin. Fax 772-2092
Trinity Lutheran Christian S 200/PK-8
4101 E Nohl Ranch Rd 92807 714-637-8370
Rosemarie Fisher, prin. Fax 637-6534
Vineyard Christian S 400/PK-8
5340 E La Palma Ave 92807 714-777-5462
Jim Wilkinson, prin. Fax 777-5422
Zion Lutheran S 200/PK-8
1244 E Cypress St 92805 714-535-3600
Julie Kangas, prin. Fax 254-7013

Anderson, Shasta, Pop. 9,521
Cascade UNESD 1,200/PK-8
1645 Mill St 96007 530-378-7000
Jason Provence, supt. Fax 378-7001
www.cuesd.com
Anderson Heights ES 200/3-5
1530 Spruce St 96007 530-378-7050
Ramona Fletcher, prin. Fax 378-7051
Anderson MS 500/5-8
1646 Ferry St 96007 530-378-7060
Eleanor Hysell, prin. Fax 378-7061
Meadow Lane ES 400/PK-2
2770 Balls Ferry Rd 96007 530-378-7030
Rita Mitchell, prin. Fax 378-7031

Happy Valley UNESD 500/K-8
17480 Palm Ave 96007 530-357-2134
Rich Gifford, supt. Fax 357-4143
www.hvesd.org
Happy Valley MS 200/5-8
17480 Palm Ave 96007 530-357-2111
Steve Westaby, prin. Fax 357-4193
Happy Valley PS 200/K-4
16300 Cloverdale Rd 96007 530-357-2131
Shelly Craig, prin. Fax 357-2138

Pacheco UNESD
Supt. — See Redding
Prairie ES 300/K-3
20981 Dersch Rd 96007 530-365-1801
Lora Fox, prin. Fax 365-7190

Angels Camp, Calaveras, Pop. 2,997
Mark Twain UNESD 800/K-8
PO Box 1359 95222 209-736-1855
Julia Tidball, supt. Fax 736-6888
www.mtwain.k12.ca.us
Twain ES 600/K-8
PO Box 1239 95222 209-736-6533
Wendy DeSimone, prin. Fax 736-6537
Other Schools – See Copperopolis

Christian Family Learning Center 100/K-8
PO Box 880 95222 209-736-1175
Larry Smith, prin. Fax 736-1158

Angwin, Napa, Pop. 2,912
Howell Mountain ESD 100/K-8
525 White Cottage Rd N 94508 707-965-2423
Janet Tufts, supt. Fax 965-0834
www.hmesd.k12.ca.us
Howell Mountain ES 100/K-8
525 White Cottage Rd N 94508 707-965-2423
Dr. Janet Tufts, admin. Fax 965-0834

Pacific Union College ES 100/K-8
135 Neilsen Ct 94508 707-965-2459
Dr. James Dick Ed.D., prin. Fax 965-2480

Annapolis, Sonoma
Horicon ESD 100/K-8
35555 Annapolis Rd 95412 707-886-5322
Jeffrey McFarland, supt. Fax 886-5422
horiconesd.org/
Horicon ES 100/K-8
35555 Annapolis Rd 95412 707-886-5322
Jeffrey McFarland, prin. Fax 886-5422

Antelope, Sacramento, Pop. 42,966
Center JUSD 4,600/K-12
8408 Watt Ave 95843 916-338-6400
Scott Loehr, supt. Fax 338-6411
www.centerusd.org
Dudley ES 700/K-6
8000 Aztec Way 95843 916-338-6470
Lisa Coronado, prin. Fax 338-6472
North Country ES 600/K-6
3901 Little Rock Dr 95843 916-338-6480
Kathy Lord, prin. Fax 338-6488
Oak Hill ES 800/K-6
3909 N Loop Blvd 95843 916-338-6460
Patricia Spore, prin. Fax 338-6538
Spinelli ES 300/K-6
3401 Scotland Dr 95843 916-338-6490
Kristen Schmieder, prin. Fax 338-6386
Other Schools – See Roseville

Dry Creek JESD
Supt. — See Roseville
Antelope Crossing MS 1,000/6-8
9200 Palmerson Dr 95843 916-745-2100
Jon Smith, prin. Fax 745-2135
Antelope Meadows ES 800/K-5
8343 Palmerson Dr 95843 916-770-8816
Robert Garcia, prin. Fax 727-0373
Barrett Ranch ES 500/K-5
7720 Ocean Park Dr 95843 916-770-8839
Dr. Don Vu, prin. Fax 727-1336
Olive Grove ES 500/K-5
7926 Firestone Way 95843 916-727-7400
Andrew Giannini, prin. Fax 727-7410

Antelope Christian Academy 100/PK-8
4533 Antelope Rd 95843 916-727-1197
Karen Clements, prin. Fax 757-1318

Antioch, Contra Costa, Pop. 96,748
Antioch USD 17,900/K-12
510 G St 94509 925-779-7500
Stephanie Anello Ed.D., supt. Fax 779-7509
www.antioch.k12.ca.us
Antioch MS 800/6-8
1500 D St 94509 925-779-7400
Lindsay Wisely, prin. Fax 779-7414
Belshaw ES 600/K-5
2801 Roosevelt Ln 94509 925-779-7945
Casey Lewis, prin. Fax 757-7725
Black Diamond MS 700/6-8
4730 Sterling Hill Dr 94531 925-776-5500
Phyllis James, prin. Fax 779-2600
Dallas Ranch MS 1,300/6-8
1401 Mount Hamilton Dr 94531 925-779-7485
Bridget Spires, prin. Fax 706-1933
Diablo Vista ES 600/K-5
4791 Prewett Ranch Dr 94531 925-779-7470
Bonny Bausola, prin. Fax 754-0589
Dragon ES 500/K-6
4721 Vista Grande Dr 94531 925-779-7475
Mark Hemauer, prin. Fax 754-7514
Fremont ES 600/K-5
1413 F St 94509 925-779-7405
Heather Ogden, prin. Fax 779-7406
Kimball ES 500/K-5
1310 August Way 94509 925-779-7415
Theresa Romo, prin. Fax 779-7416
London ES 500/K-6
4550 Country Hills Dr 94531 925-779-7455
Dolores Williams, prin. Fax 778-7512
Lone Tree ES 800/K-5
1931 Mokelumne Dr 94531 925-779-7480
Sonja Bell, prin. Fax 706-9853
Marsh ES 500/K-5
2304 G St 94509 925-779-7410
Crystal Berry, prin. Fax 779-7411
Mission ES 700/K-5
1711 Mission Dr 94509 925-779-7435
Monte Gregg, prin. Fax 779-7436
Mno Grant ES 500/K-6
4325 Spaulding St 94531 925-779-7465
Janeen Zuniga, prin. Fax 756-6068
Muir ES 600/K-5
615 Greystone Dr 94509 925-779-7450
Zhenus Wahidi, prin. Fax 779-7451
Park MS 1,000/6-8
1 Spartan Way 94509 925-779-7420
John Jimno, prin. Fax 779-7421
Sutter ES 600/K-5
3410 Longview Rd 94509 925-779-7425
Debra Harrington, prin. Fax 779-7426
Turner ES 600/K-5
4207 Delta Fair Blvd 94509 925-779-7430
Deborah Meylan, prin. Fax 779-7431
Other Schools – See Oakley

Cornerstone Christian S 500/PK-12
1745 E 18th St 94509 925-779-2010
Logan Heyer, prin. Fax 754-1294
Heritage Baptist Academy 100/K-12
5200 Heidorn Ranch Rd 94531 925-778-2234
Hilltop Christian S 100/K-8
2200 Country Hills Dr 94509 925-778-0214
Mekey Lepulu, prin. Fax 778-7418
Holy Rosary S 600/PK-8
25 E 15th St 94509 925-757-1270
Fely Fajardo, prin. Fax 757-9309

Anza, Riverside, Pop. 2,927
Hemet USD
Supt. — See Hemet
Hamilton S 400/K-8
57550 Mitchell Rd 92539 951-763-1840
Carol Robilotta, prin. Fax 763-1845

Apple Valley, San Bernardino, Pop. 66,794
Apple Valley USD 14,400/PK-12
12555 Navajo Rd 92308 760-247-8001
Thomas Hoegerman, supt. Fax 247-4103
www.avusd.org
Desert Knolls ES 600/PK-6
18213 Symeron Rd 92307 760-242-3441
Crystal Schinhoffen, prin. Fax 242-7242
Mariana Academy 600/PK-8
10601 Manhasset Rd 92308 760-247-7258
Kristin Dupree, prin. Fax 247-4406
Phoenix Academy 1,100/PK-8
20700 Thunderbird Rd 92307 760-242-7011
Dee Castellano, prin. Fax 242-7005
Rancho Verde ES 700/PK-6
14334 Pioneer Rd 92307 760-247-2663
Joe Cranston, prin. Fax 247-4947
Rio Vista S of Applied Learning 1,000/K-6
13590 Havasu Rd 92308 760-240-0280
Larra Parr, prin. Fax 240-0899
Sandia ES 900/PK-8
21331 Sandia Rd 92308 760-240-5125
Deborah Sarkesian, prin. Fax 240-0515
Sitting Bull Academy 1,400/PK-8
19445 Sitting Bull Rd 92308 760-961-8479
Phyllis Carnahan, prin. Fax 240-8763
Sycamore Rocks ES 600/PK-6
23450 South Rd 92307 760-240-3332
Shanelle Benitez, prin. Fax 240-3440
Vanguard Preparatory S 1,200/PK-8
12951 Mesquite Rd 92308 760-961-1066
Brian Goodrow, prin. Fax 961-1069
Yucca Loma ES 700/PK-6
21351 Yucca Loma Rd 92307 760-247-2623
Marcos Clark, prin. Fax 247-4300

Apple Valley Christian S 200/PK-12
22230 Ottawa Rd 92308 760-995-3516
Alan Giles, admin. Fax 995-3524

Aptos, Santa Cruz, Pop. 6,003
Pajaro Valley USD
Supt. — See Watsonville
Aptos JHS 700/7-8
1001 Huntington Dr 95003 831-688-3234
Rich Moran, prin. Fax 728-8139
Mar Vista ES 400/K-5
6860 Soquel Dr 95003 831-688-5211
Richard Determan, prin. Fax 728-6491
Rio Del Mar ES 600/K-6
819 Pinehurst Dr 95003 831-688-2053
Deborah Dorney, prin. Fax 728-6467
Valencia ES 500/K-6
250 Aptos School Rd 95003 831-728-6376
Caryn Lane, prin. Fax 728-6489

St. Abraham's Classical Christian Acad 100/K-12
1940 Bonita Dr 95003 831-239-4657
Corey McEachran, head sch
Santa Cruz Montessori S 300/PK-9
6230 Soquel Dr 95003 831-476-1646
Kim Saxton, head sch Fax 476-5855
Twin Lakes Christian S 200/K-8
2701 Cabrillo College Dr 95003 831-465-3301
Meg Imel, prin. Fax 465-3389

Arbuckle, Colusa, Pop. 2,990
Pierce JUSD 1,400/K-12
PO Box 239 95912 530-476-2892
Carol Geyer, supt. Fax 476-2289
pierce.k12.ca.us
Arbuckle ES 600/K-5
PO Box 100 95912 530-476-2522
Summer Shadley, prin. Fax 476-2234
Johnson JHS 300/6-8
938 Wildwood Rd 95912 530-476-3261
Ron Fisher, prin. Fax 476-2017
Other Schools – See Grimes

Arcadia, Los Angeles, Pop. 55,191
Arcadia USD 9,700/PK-12
150 S 3rd Ave 91006 626-821-8300
Dr. David Vannasdall Ed.D., supt. Fax 821-8647
site.ausd.net
Camino Grove ES 600/PK-5
700 Camino Grove Ave 91006 626-821-8353
Danae Popovich, prin. Fax 294-0911
Dana MS 800/6-8
1401 S 1st Ave 91006 626-821-8361
Dr. Daniel Hacking Ed.D., prin. Fax 447-1965
First Avenue MS 800/6-8
301 S 1st Ave 91006 626-821-8362
Semeen Issa Ed.D., prin. Fax 446-1660
Foothills MS 800/6-8
171 E Sycamore Ave 91006 626-821-8363
Ben Acker, prin. Fax 303-7983
Highland Oaks ES 700/PK-5
10 Virginia Rd 91006 626-821-8354
Patricia Mattera, prin. Fax 821-4680
Holly Avenue ES 800/PK-5
360 W Duarte Rd 91007 626-821-8355
Teresa Oakland, prin. Fax 574-3809
Longley Way ES 500/PK-5
2601 Longley Way 91007 626-821-8357
Travis Long, prin. Fax 574-3812
Reid ES 600/PK-5
1000 Hugo Reid Dr 91007 626-821-8356
Laureen Leahy, prin. Fax 574-1341
Stocker ES 700/PK-5
422 W Lemon Ave 91007 626-821-8351
Jayne Nickles, prin. Fax 574-3807

El Monte City SD
Supt. — See El Monte
Rio Hondo S 900/K-8
11425 Wildflower Rd 91006 626-575-2308
Darrice Wallace, prin. Fax 443-3508

Arcadia Christian S 300/PK-8
1900 S Santa Anita Ave 91006 626-574-8229
Cindy Harmon, prin. Fax 574-1224
Barnhart S 200/K-8
240 W Colorado Blvd 91007 626-446-5588
Tonya Beilstein, head sch Fax 574-3316
Holy Angels S 300/PK-8
360 Campus Dr 91007 626-447-6312
Ted Carroll, prin. Fax 447-2843

Arcata, Humboldt, Pop. 16,233
Arcata ESD 1,000/K-9
1435 Buttermilk Ln 95521 707-822-0351
Dr. Barbara Short Ed.D., supt. Fax 822-6589
arcataschooldistrict.org
Arcata ES 300/K-5
2400 Baldwin St 95521 707-822-4858
Victoria Parker, prin. Fax 822-6419
Sunny Brae MS 200/6-8
1430 Buttermilk Ln 95521 707-822-5988
Lynda Yeoman, prin. Fax 822-7002

Pacific UNESD 600/PK-8
3001 Janes Rd 95521 707-822-4619
Karla K. Darnall, supt. Fax 822-0129
www.pacificunionschool.org
Pacific Union S 500/PK-8
3001 Janes Rd 95521 707-822-4619
Karla K. Darnall, prin. Fax 822-0129

Arcata Christian S 100/PK-8
1700 Union St 95521 707-822-5986
Ronald Wunner, admin. Fax 822-2591

Arleta, See Los Angeles
Los Angeles USD
Supt. — See Los Angeles
Beachy Avenue ES 600/K-5
9757 Beachy Ave 91331 818-899-0241
Lisa Dachs-Ornelas, prin. Fax 890-5532
Canterbury ES 1,100/K-5
13670 Montague St 91331 818-892-1104
Clara Pena, prin. Fax 895-2653
Sharp ES 800/K-5
13800 Pierce St 91331 818-896-9573
Kyla Hinson, prin. Fax 896-8403
Vena Avenue ES 500/K-5
9377 Vena Ave 91331 818-896-9551
Sonia Baron, prin. Fax 890-7189

Armona, Kings, Pop. 4,080
Armona UNESD 1,100/PK-12
PO Box 368 93202 559-583-5000
Dr. Xavier Pena Ed.D., supt. Fax 583-5004
www.auesd.com
Armona ES 600/PK-4
PO Box 368 93202 559-583-5010
Shawn Beck, prin. Fax 583-5027
Parkview MS 400/5-8
PO Box 368 93202 559-583-5020
James McDonald, prin. Fax 583-5030

Armona Union Academy 100/K-12
PO Box 397 93202 559-582-4468
Randall Bovee, prin. Fax 582-6609

Arnold, Calaveras, Pop. 3,768
Vallecito UNSD
Supt. — See Avery
Fischer ES 100/PK-5
1605 Blagen Rd 95223 209-795-8030
Brett Loring, prin. Fax 795-8033

Aromas, Monterey, Pop. 2,560
Aromas/San Juan USD
Supt. — See San Juan Bautista
Aromas S 400/K-8
365 Vega Rd 95004 831-726-5100
Heather Howell, prin. Fax 726-3040

Arroyo Grande, San Luis Obispo, Pop. 16,717
Lucia Mar USD 10,600/PK-12
602 Orchard Ave 93420 805-474-3000
Dr. Raynee Daley, supt. Fax 481-1398
www.luciamarschools.org
Branch ES 300/K-6
970 School Rd 93420 805-474-3720
Hillery Dixon, prin. Fax 473-4184
Harloe ES 600/K-6
901 Fair Oaks Ave 93420 805-474-3710
Peter Ponomaroff, prin. Fax 473-5520
Mesa MS 500/7-8
2555 S Halcyon Rd 93420 805-474-3400
Brett Gimlin, prin. Fax 473-4396

Ocean View ES 600/K-6
1208 Linda Dr 93420 805-474-3730
Sarah Butler, prin. Fax 473-5526
Paulding MS 700/7-8
600 Crown Hill St 93420 805-474-3500
Edward Arrigoni, prin. Fax 473-5525
Other Schools – See Grover Beach, Nipomo, Oceano, Pismo Beach

---

St. Patrick S 300/PK-8
900 W Branch St 93420 805-489-1210
Maureen Halderman, prin. Fax 489-7662
Valley View Adventist Academy 100/K-10
230 Vernon St 93420 805-489-2687
Kris Phillips, prin. Fax 489-2704

Artesia, Los Angeles, Pop. 16,099
ABC USD
Supt. — See Cerritos
Burbank ES 600/K-6
17711 Roseton Ave 90701 562-229-7835
Laura Makely, prin. Fax 402-9856
Elliott ES 500/K-6
18415 Cortner Ave 90703 562-229-7850
Fran Barron, prin. Fax 924-8216
Kennedy ES 500/K-6
17500 Belshire Ave 90701 562-229-7875
Melissa Valentine, prin. Fax 402-9851
Niemes ES 700/K-6
16715 Jersey Ave 90701 562-229-7890
Meg Jimenez, prin. Fax 402-8927
Ross MS 600/7-8
17707 Elaine Ave 90701 562-229-7785
Ricardo Brown, prin. Fax 402-6145

Our Lady of Fatima S 200/PK-8
18626 Clarkdale Ave 90701 562-865-1621
Luis Hayes, prin. Fax 403-0409

Arvin, Kern, Pop. 19,155
Arvin UNSD 3,100/PK-8
737 Bear Mountain Blvd 93203 661-854-6500
Michelle McLean Ed.D., supt. Fax 854-2362
www.arvinschools.com
Bear Mountain ES 800/PK-6
737 Bear Mountain Blvd 93203 661-854-6590
Candi Huizar, prin. Fax 854-6599
El Camino Real ES 900/PK-6
737 Bear Mountain Blvd 93203 661-854-6661
Betty Guyton, prin. Fax 854-2474
Haven Drive MS 700/7-8
737 Bear Mountain Blvd 93203 661-854-6540
Calletano Gutierrez Ed.D., prin. Fax 854-1440
Sierra Vista ES 800/PK-6
737 Bear Mountain Blvd 93203 661-854-6560
Rosemarie Borquez, prin. Fax 854-7523

Di Giorgio ESD 200/K-8
19405 Buena Vista Blvd 93203 661-854-2604
Terry Hallum, supt. Fax 854-8746
www.digiorgio.k12.ca.us
Di Giorgio ES 200/K-8
19405 Buena Vista Blvd 93203 661-854-2604
Fax 854-8746

Atascadero, San Luis Obispo, Pop. 27,543
Atascadero USD 4,700/K-12
5601 West Mall 93422 805-462-4200
Thomas Butler, supt. Fax 462-4421
www.atasusd.org/
Atascadero Fine Arts Academy 200/4-8
6100 Olmeda Ave 93422 805-460-2500
Kibbe Rubin, prin. Fax 460-2522
Atascadero MS 700/6-8
6501 Lewis Ave 93422 805-462-4360
Jessica Lloyd, prin. Fax 462-4373
Monterey Road ES 400/K-5
3355 Monterey Rd 93422 805-462-4270
Julie Ann Davis, prin. Fax 462-4288
San Benito ES 500/K-5
4300 San Benito Rd 93422 805-462-4330
Kathryn Holmes, prin. Fax 462-4278
San Gabriel ES 600/K-5
8500 San Gabriel Rd 93422 805-462-4340
Shauna Ames, prin. Fax 462-4268
Santa Rosa Academic Academy 400/K-5
8655 Santa Rosa Rd 93422 805-462-4290
Tim Sobraske, prin. Fax 462-4358
Other Schools – See Creston, Santa Margarita

North County Christian S 200/PK-12
PO Box 6017 93423 805-466-4457
Dr. Robert McLaughlin, admin. Fax 466-7948

Atherton, San Mateo, Pop. 6,660
Las Lomitas ESD
Supt. — See Menlo Park
Las Lomitas ES 600/K-3
299 Alameda De Las Pulgas 94027 650-854-5900
Alain Camou, prin. Fax 854-4493

Menlo Park City ESD 2,900/K-8
181 Encinal Ave 94027 650-321-7140
Erik Burmeister, supt. Fax 321-7184
www.mpcsd.org
Encinal ES 800/K-5
195 Encinal Ave 94027 650-326-5164
Sharon Burns, prin. Fax 327-0854
Laurel ES 500/K-5
95 Edge Rd 94027 650-324-0186
Linda Creighton, prin. Fax 323-0374
Other Schools – See Menlo Park

Redwood City ESD
Supt. — See Redwood City
Selby Lane ES 700/K-8
170 Selby Ln 94027 650-482-2415
Warren Sedar, prin. Fax 367-4366

Sacred Heart Lower and Middle S 500/1-8
150 Valparaiso Ave 94027 650-322-9931
Richard Dioli, dir. Fax 475-9088

Atwater, Merced, Pop. 27,459
Atwater ESD 4,600/K-8
1401 Broadway Ave 95301 209-357-6100
Dr. Sandra Schiber, supt. Fax 357-6163
www.aesd.edu
Bellevue ES 700/K-8
1020 E Bellevue Rd 95301 209-357-6140
Linda Lamerson, prin. Fax 357-6141
Colburn ES 500/K-6
2201 Heller Ave 95301 209-357-6136
Tiffani Gong, prin. Fax 357-6169
Heller ES 600/K-6
201 Lake View Dr 95301 209-357-6517
Lyndsay Olds, prin. Fax 357-6528
Mitchell ES 500/K-6
1761 Grove Ave 95301 209-357-6112
Christy Loboa, prin. Fax 357-6505
Mitchell Senior ES 800/7-8
1753 5th St 95301 209-357-6124
Aaron Delworth, prin. Fax 357-6506
Olaeta ES 500/K-6
2266 High St 95301 209-357-6148
Brandi Bailey, prin. Fax 357-6167
Shaffer ES 500/K-6
1434 California St 95301 209-357-6145
Michele McCabe, prin. Fax 357-6146
Wood ES 500/K-6
1271 Bellevue Rd 95301 209-357-6143
Kelli Parreira, prin. Fax 357-6509

St. Anthony S 100/PK-8
1801 Winton Way 95301 209-358-3341
Marianne Flynn, prin. Fax 357-0186

Auberry, Fresno, Pop. 2,272
Pine Ridge ESD 100/K-8
45828 Auberry Rd 93602 559-841-2444
Christine Skinner, supt. Fax 841-2771
www.pineridge.k12.ca.us
Pine Ridge S 100/K-8
45828 Auberry Rd 93602 559-841-2444
Christine Skinner, prin. Fax 841-2771

Auburn, Placer, Pop. 12,869
Auburn UNESD 2,100/PK-8
255 Epperle Ln 95603 530-885-7242
Wendy Frederickson, supt. Fax 885-5170
www.auburn.k12.ca.us
Auburn ES 500/PK-5
11400 Lariat Ranch Rd 95603 530-887-1958
Aurora Thompson, prin. Fax 887-1241
Rock Creek ES 300/PK-5
3050 Bell Rd 95603 530-885-5189
Amy Westberg, prin. Fax 885-5196
Skyridge ES 500/PK-5
800 Perkins Way 95603 530-885-7019
Angelika Brown, prin. Fax 885-4213

Forest Lake Christian S 400/K-12
12515 Combie Rd 95602 530-269-1540
Andrew Ricabal, supt. Fax 269-3014
Pine Hills Adventist Academy 100/K-12
13500 Richards Ln 95603 530-885-9447
Victor Anderson, prin. Fax 885-5237
St. Joseph S 200/PK-8
11610 Atwood Rd 95603 530-885-4490
Jenny Oliver, prin. Fax 885-0182

Avalon, Los Angeles, Pop. 3,671
Long Beach USD
Supt. — See Long Beach
Avalon S 600/K-12
PO Box 557 90704 310-510-0790
Christopher Lounsbery, prin. Fax 510-2986

Avenal, Kings, Pop. 15,241
Reef-Sunset USD 2,600/PK-12
205 N Park Ave 93204 559-386-9083
Dr. David East, supt. Fax 386-5303
www.rsusd.org
Avenal ES 700/PK-5
500 S 1st Ave 93204 559-386-5173
Blanca Price, prin. Fax 386-5287
Reef-Sunset MS 400/6-8
608 N 1st Ave 93204 559-386-4128
Fred Guerrero, prin. Fax 386-4918
Tamarack ES 600/PK-5
1000 S Union Ave 93204 559-386-4051
Judy Horn, prin. Fax 386-4074
Other Schools – See Kettleman City

Avery, Calaveras, Pop. 622
Vallecito UNSD 600/PK-8
PO Box 329 95224 209-795-8500
Jim Frost, supt. Fax 795-8505
vallecito-ca.schoolloop.com
Avery MS 200/6-8
PO Box 329 95224 209-795-8520
Scott Nicotero, prin. Fax 795-8539
Other Schools – See Arnold, Murphys

Azusa, Los Angeles, Pop. 45,586
Azusa USD 9,400/PK-12
PO Box 500 91702 626-967-6211
Linda Kaminski, supt. Fax 858-6137
www.azusa.org
Center MS 600/6-8
PO Box 500 91702 626-815-5184
Saida Valdez, prin. Fax 815-2601
Dalton ES 400/K-5
PO Box 500 91702 626-815-5245
Laura Clarke, prin. Fax 815-5248
Foothill MS 600/6-8
PO Box 500 91702 626-815-6600
Sam Perdomo, prin. Fax 815-1027
Gladstone Street ES 300/K-5
PO Box 500 91702 626-815-6700
Art Hinojosa, prin. Fax 815-6785
Hodge ES 700/K-5
PO Box 500 91702 626-815-4800
Victoria Velasquez, prin. Fax 815-5531
Lee ES 400/K-5
PO Box 500 91702 626-815-5269
Karen Aristizabal, prin. Fax 815-5268
Longfellow S, PO Box 500 91702 200/PK-K
Leslie Ford, prin. 626-858-4700
Magnolia ES 300/PK-5
PO Box 500 91702 626-815-5800
Alexis Norman, prin. Fax 815-2650
Mountain View ES 400/K-5
PO Box 500 91702 626-815-2900
Jenny Le, prin. Fax 815-7951
Murray ES 500/K-5
PO Box 500 91702 626-633-8700
Norma Camacho, prin. Fax 334-2918
Paramount ES 400/K-5
PO Box 500 91702 626-815-5104
Hector Alegria, prin. Fax 815-5109
Powell ES 300/K-5
PO Box 500 91702 626-633-8500
Jennifer Wiebe, prin. Fax 633-8585
Slauson MS 800/6-8
PO Box 500 91702 626-815-5144
Yvette Walker, prin. Fax 815-5147
Valleydale ES 300/K-5
PO Box 500 91702 626-633-8600
Adriana Garcia-Medina, prin. Fax 815-5199
Other Schools – See Covina

Christbridge Academy 100/K-12
405 S Azusa Ave 91702 626-969-7400
St. Frances of Rome S 200/K-8
734 N Pasadena Ave 91702 626-334-2018
Dr. Brian Wagner, prin. Fax 815-2760

Baker, San Bernardino, Pop. 711
Baker Valley USD 200/K-12
PO Box 460 92309 760-733-4567
Ronda Tremblay, supt. Fax 733-4605
www.baker.k12.ca.us
Baker ES 100/K-5
PO Box 460 92309 760-733-4567
Ronda Tremblay, supt. Fax 733-4605
Baker JHS 50/6-8
PO Box 460 92309 760-733-4567
Ronda Tremblay, supt. Fax 733-4605

Bakersfield, Kern, Pop. 338,954
Bakersfield CSD 29,700/PK-8
1300 Baker St 93305 661-631-4600
Doc Ervin Ed.D., supt. Fax 631-4623
www.bcsd.com
Casa Loma ES 800/K-5
525 E Casa Loma Dr 93307 661-631-5200
Lemuel Kwon, prin. Fax 834-7858
Cato MS, 4115 Vineland Rd 93306 6-8
Brooke Smothers-Strizic, prin. 661-631-5245
Chavez ES 800/K-6
4201 Mesa Marin Dr 93306 661-631-5870
Dawn Slaybaugh, prin. Fax 631-3264
Chipman JHS 900/7-8
2905 Eissler St 93306 661-631-5210
Russell Taylor, prin. Fax 631-3229
College Heights ES 900/K-6
2551 Sunny Ln 93305 661-631-5220
Lynn McEntire, prin. Fax 631-4510
Compton JHS 700/7-8
3211 Pico Ave 93306 661-631-5230
Jennifer Payne, prin. Fax 631-3166
Curran MS 900/6-8
1116 Lymric Way 93309 661-631-5240
Marilyn Strongin, prin. Fax 631-4538
Downtown S 300/K-8
2021 M St 93301 661-631-5920
Noreen Barthelmes, prin. Fax 631-3276
Eissler ES 600/K-6
2901 Eissler St 93306 661-631-5250
Christina Norris, prin. Fax 631-4504
Emerson MS 900/6-8
801 4th St 93304 661-631-5260
Polo Marquez, prin. Fax 327-8505
Evergreen ES 600/K-5
2600 Rose Marie Dr 93304 661-631-5930
Jason Brannen, prin. Fax 631-3190
Fletcher ES PK-5
1300 Baker St 93305 661-631-5960
Nancy Olcott, prin. Fax 366-6006
Franklin ES 500/K-6
2400 Truxtun Ave 93301 661-631-5270
Carla Tafoya, prin. Fax 631-3210
Fremont ES 900/K-6
607 Texas St 93307 661-631-5280
Teresa Arambula, prin. Fax 631-4527
Garza ES 1,000/K-5
2901 Center St 93306 661-631-5290
Julie Segura-Padilla, prin. Fax 631-3110
Harding ES 600/K-6
3201 Pico Ave 93306 661-631-5300
Bridget Fitch, prin. Fax 631-4587
Harris ES 500/K-5
4110 Garnsey Ln 93309 661-631-5310
Anne Lopez, prin. Fax 631-3178
Hills ES 500/K-5
3800 Jewett Ave 93301 661-631-5320
Steve Robinson, prin. Fax 631-3119
Hort ES 800/K-5
2301 Park Dr 93306 661-631-5330
Diana O'Neal, prin. Fax 631-3208
Jefferson ES 500/K-5
816 Lincoln St 93305 661-631-5340
Russell Gayer, prin. Fax 631-3104
Longfellow ES 800/K-6
1900 Stockton St 93305 661-631-5350
Michael Barella, prin. Fax 631-3151

Mann ES 900/K-5
2710 Niles St 93306 661-631-5360
Renee Ashley, prin. Fax 631-3256
McKinley ES 800/K-5
601 4th St 93304 661-631-5370
Rona Chacon-Mellon, prin. Fax 631-4553
Mt. Vernon ES 800/K-6
2161 Potomac Ave 93307 661-631-5380
Alfonso Ceja, prin. Fax 631-3126
Munsey ES 700/K-5
3801 Brave Ave 93309 661-631-5390
Dayna Gardner, prin. Fax 631-3222
Nichols ES 700/K-6
3401 Renegade Ave 93306 661-631-5400
Debra Craig, prin. Fax 631-4902
Noble ES 900/K-5
1015 Noble Ave 93305 661-631-5410
Jalina Baker, prin. Fax 631-3248
Owens IS 600/4-6
815 Eureka St 93305 661-631-5950
Dr. Addonica Stanley, prin. Fax 631-3269
Owens PS 700/K-3
815 Potomac Ave 93307 661-631-5420
Sarita Arredondo, prin. Fax 631-3134
Pauly ES 800/K-5
313 Planz Rd 93304 661-631-5430
Jennifer Santillan, prin. Fax 631-3215
Penn ES 300/K-5
2201 San Emidio St 93304 661-631-5440
Marshall Dillard, prin. Fax 631-3279
Pioneer Drive ES 800/K-6
4404 Pioneer Dr 93306 661-631-5450
Traci Hicks, prin. Fax 631-3196
Roosevelt ES 400/K-5
2324 Verde St 93304 661-631-5460
Warren Ramay, prin. Fax 631-4912
Sequoia MS 1,000/6-8
900 Belle Terrace 93304 661-631-5940
Gary McCloskey, prin. Fax 631-3236
Sierra MS 800/6-8
3017 Center St 93306 661-631-5470
Tomas Prieto, prin. Fax 631-4541
Stiern MS 1,400/6-8
2551 Morning Dr 93306 661-631-5480
Julie Short, prin. Fax 631-3241
Thorner ES 900/K-6
5501 Thorner St 93306 661-631-5490
Brandon Johnson, prin Fax 631-4567
Voorhies ES 1,000/K-6
6001 Pioneer Dr 93306 661-631-5800
Erick Casallas, prin. Fax 631-4579
Washington MS 700/6-8
1101 Noble Ave 93305 661-631-5810
Abraham Rivera, prin. Fax 631-3172
Wayside ES 700/K-5
1000 Ming Ave 93307 661-631-5820
Dylan Capilla, prin. Fax 631-4593
West ES 700/K-5
2400 Benton St 93304 661-631-5830
Ruscel Reader, prin. Fax 631-4519
Williams ES 500/K-5
1201 Williams St 93305 661-631-5840
David Tapia, prin. Fax 631-4560

Beardsley ESD 1,800/K-8
1001 Roberts Ln 93308 661-393-8550
Paul Miller, supt. Fax 393-5965
www.beardsleyschool.org/
Beardsley ES 400/K-6
1001 Roberts Ln 93308 661-392-1417
Tammy Barrera, prin. Fax 387-1587
Beardsley JHS 300/7-8
1001 Roberts Ln 93308 661-392-9254
David Hilton, prin. Fax 399-3925
North Beardsley ES 600/K-6
900 Sanford Dr 93308 661-392-0878
Aimee Williamson, prin. Fax 392-1399
San Lauren ES 500/K-6
5210 Victor St 93308 661-393-5511
Terri Chamberlin, prin. Fax 393-9064

Edison ESD 1,100/K-8
11518 School St 93307 661-363-5394
Erica Andrews, supt. Fax 363-4631
www.edline.net/pages/Edison_Elementary
Edison MS 500/5-8
721 S Edison Rd 93307 661-366-8216
Duane Grumling, prin. Fax 366-0922
Orangewood ES 600/K-4
9600 Eucalyptus Dr 93306 661-366-8440
Jennifer Allen, prin. Fax 366-0159

Fairfax ESD 2,100/K-8
1500 S Fairfax Rd 93307 661-366-7221
Michael Coleman, supt. Fax 366-1901
www.fairfax.k12.ca.us
Fairfax JHS 500/7-8
1500 S Fairfax Rd 93307 661-366-4461
Wendy Burkhead, prin. Fax 366-5831
Shirley Lane ES 800/K-6
6714 Shirley Ln 93307 661-363-7684
David Mack, prin. Fax 363-7552
Virginia Avenue ES 800/K-6
3301 Virginia Ave 93307 661-366-3223
Lora Brown, prin. Fax 366-2043
Zephyr Lane ES K-6
6327 Zephyr Ln 93307 661-336-0024
Charley Clark, prin. Fax 336-0266

Fruitvale SD 3,300/K-8
7311 Rosedale Hwy 93308 661-589-3830
Dr. Mary Westendorf, supt. Fax 589-3674
www.fruitvale.k12.ca.us
Columbia ES 600/K-6
703 Mondavi Way 93312 661-588-3540
Angie Summers, prin. Fax 589-5264
Discovery ES 900/K-6
7500 Vaquero Ave 93308 661-589-7336
Danyel Kelly, prin. Fax 587-9413

Endeavour ES 800/K-6
9300 Meacham Rd 93312 661-588-3550
Matt Diggle, prin. Fax 587-9318
Fruitvale JHS 700/7-8
2114 Calloway Dr 93312 661-589-3933
Leslie Garrison, prin. Fax 588-3259
Quailwood ES 400/K-6
7301 Remington Ave 93309 661-832-6415
Kim Carlson, prin. Fax 831-7391

General Shafter ESD 100/K-8
1825 Shafter Rd 93313 661-837-1931
Chris Salyards, supt. Fax 837-8261
www.generalshafter.org
Shafter ES 100/K-8
1825 Shafter Rd 93313 661-837-1931
Sandra Johnson, admin. Fax 837-8261

Greenfield UNESD 9,200/K-8
1624 Fairview Rd 93307 661-837-6000
Ramon Hendrix, supt. Fax 832-2873
www.gfusd.net
Fairview ES 500/K-5
425 E Fairview Rd 93307 661-837-6050
Valerie Duncan, prin. Fax 837-6056
Granite Pointe ES 1,000/K-5
2900 Berkshire Rd 93313 661-837-6040
Greg Adkins, prin. Fax 837-3491
Greenfield MS 900/6-8
1109 Pacheco Rd 93307 661-837-6110
Sandra Welch, prin. Fax 832-7431
Horizon ES 800/K-5
7901 Monitor St 93307 661-837-3730
Brenda Cassell, prin. Fax 837-3734
Kendrick ES 700/K-5
2200 Faith Ave 93304 661-837-6190
Hana Suleiman, prin. Fax 397-0226
McKee MS 900/6-8
205 McKee Rd 93307 661-837-6060
Brandon Duncan, prin. Fax 834-7566
Ollivier MS 1,000/6-8
7310 Monitor St 93307 661-837-6120
Sheila Johnson, prin. Fax 396-0963
Palla ES 900/K-5
800 Fairview Rd 93307 661-837-6100
Margie Berumen, prin. Fax 837-6106
Plantation ES 700/K-5
901 Plantation Ave 93304 661-837-6070
Deloris Sill, prin. Fax 837-6077
Planz ES 700/K-5
2400 E Planz Rd 93307 661-837-6080
Sarah Dawson, prin. Fax 831 5467
Valle Verde ES 900/K-5
400 Berkshire Rd 93307 661-837-6150
Nicole Zandes, prin. Fax 837-6159

Lakeside UNSD 1,300/K-8
14535 Old River Rd 93311 661-836-6658
Ty Bryson M.A., supt. Fax 836-8059
www.lakesideusd.org
Lakeside S 600/K-8
14535 Old River Rd 93311 661-831-3503
Mike McGrath M.A., prin. Fax 831-7709
Suburu ES 700/K-5
7315 Harris Rd 93313 661-665-8190
Valerie Garcia M.A., prin. Fax 665-8282

Lamont ESD
Supt. — See Lamont
Mountain View MS 600/7-8
8001 Weedpatch Hwy 93307 661-845-2291
Jonathan Martinez, prin. Fax 845-1839

Norris SD 3,900/K-8
6940 Calloway Dr 93312 661-387-7000
Kelly Miller, supt. Fax 399-9750
www.norris.k12.ca.us/
Bimat ES 500/K-6
8600 Northshore Dr 93312 661-387-7080
Michele Bryant, prin. Fax 589-7849
Norris ES 1,000/K-6
7110 Old Farm Rd 93312 661-387-7020
Erin Hudson, prin. Fax 587-9043
Norris MS 900/6-8
6940 Calloway Dr 93312 661-387-7060
Ryan Carr, prin. Fax 399-9356
Olive Drive ES 600/K-6
7800 Darrin Ave 93308 661-387-7040
Lisa Limpias, prin. Fax 399-3149
Veterans ES 1,000/K-6
6301 Old Farm Rd 93312 661-387-7050
Russelyn Sullivan, prin. Fax 589-5758

Panama-Buena Vista UNSD 17,500/K-8
4200 Ashe Rd 93313 661-831-8331
Dr. Kevin Silberberg, supt. Fax 398-2141
www.pbvusd.k12.ca.us
Actis JHS 600/7-8
2400 Westholme Blvd 93309 661-833-1250
Patrick Spears, prin. Fax 833-9656
Berkshire ES 1,100/K-6
3900 Berkshire Rd 93313 661-834-9472
Amy Mensing, prin. Fax 834-7876
Buena Vista ES 900/K-6
6547 Buena Vista Rd 93311 661-831-0818
Daniel Hansford, prin. Fax 831-4842
Castle ES 700/K-6
6001 Edgemont Dr 93309 661-834-5311
Katrina Wilson, prin. Fax 834-9422
Hart ES 600/K-6
9501 Ridge Oak Dr 93311 661-664-1296
Daryl Newton, prin. Fax 664-0176
Laurelglen ES 600/K-6
2601 El Portal Dr 93309 661-831-4444
Robert Machado, prin. Fax 831-6689
Loudon ES 800/K-6
4000 Loudon St 93313 661-398-3210
Sharon Dunn, prin. Fax 398-6233
Lum ES 800/K-6
4600 Chaney Ln 93311 661-664-1611
Shawna Manning, prin. Fax 664 1852

McAuliffe ES 600/K-6
8900 Westwold Dr 93311 661-665-9471
Dan Pokett, prin. Fax 665-9821
Miller ES 900/K-6
7345 Mountain Ridge Dr 93313 661-836-6689
Daniel Bickham, prin. Fax 836-8452
Old River ES 1,000/K-6
9815 Campus Park Dr 93311 661-664-7009
Michael Boles, prin. Fax 664-8247
Panama ES 700/K-6
9400 Stine Rd 93313 661-831-1741
Brian Malavar, prin. Fax 831-6662
Reagan ES 900/K-6
10800 Rosslyn Ln 93311 661-665-8099
Dr. Pamela Somes, prin. Fax 665-8311
Sandrini ES 600/K-6
4100 Alum Ave 93309 661-397-1515
Marsha Ketchell, prin. Fax 397-3817
Seibert ES 700/K-6
2800 Agate St 93304 661-832-4141
Rebekah Stambook, prin. Fax 832-3734
Stine ES 800/K-6
4300 Wilson Rd 93309 661-831-1022
Monica Hicks, prin. Fax 831-6610
Stockdale ES 500/K-6
7801 Kroll Way 93309 661-831-7835
Matthew Merickel, prin. Fax 831-7701
Stonecreek JHS 900/7-8
8000 Akers Rd 93313 661-834-4521
Matthew Kennedy, prin. Fax 834-6908
Tevis JHS 700/7-8
3901 Pin Oak Park Blvd 93311 661-664-7211
Paul Coon, prin. Fax 664-9659
Thompson JHS 800/7-8
4200 Planz Rd 93309 661-832-8011
Darryl Pope, prin. Fax 832-5165
Van Horn ES 600/K-6
5501 Kleinpell Ave 93309 661-324-6538
James Lopez, prin. Fax 324-2007
Warren JHS 900/7-8
4615 Mountain Vista Dr 93311 661-665-9210
George Thornburgh, prin. Fax 665-9507
Williams ES 700/K-6
5601 Harris Rd 93313 661-837-8070
Dion Lovio, prin. Fax 837-4459

Rio Bravo-Greeley UNESD 1,000/K-8
6521 Enos Ln, 661-589-2696
Jennifer Hedge, supt Fax 589-2218
www.rbgusd.k12.ca.us
Rio Bravo ES 600/K-4
22725 Elementary Ln, 661-588-6313
Christina Bussman, prin. Fax 588-6318
Rio Bravo-Greeley MS 400/5-8
6601 Enos Ln, 661-589-2505
Becky Macquarrie, prin. Fax 588-7204

Rosedale UNESD 5,400/K-8
2553 Old Farm Rd 93312 661-588-6000
John Mendiburu Ed.D., supt. Fax 588-6009
www.ruesd.net
Almondale ES 600/K-6
10510 Chippewa St 93312 661-588-6060
Janet Bianco, prin. Fax 588-6063
American ES 700/K-6
800 Verdugo Ln 93312 661-587-2277
Robert Bray, prin. Fax 829-2591
Centennial ES 500/K-6
15200 Westdale Dr, 661-588-6020
Bruce Carlile, prin. Fax 588-6023
Del Rio ES 400/K-6
600 Hidalgo Dr, 661-588-6050
Lisa Boles, prin. Fax 588 6053
Freedom MS 600/7-8
11445 Noriega Rd 93312 661-588-6044
Russell Sentes, prin. Fax 588-6048
Independence ES 600/K-6
2345 Old Farm Rd 93312 661-588-6011
Brook Webb, prin. Fax 588-6018
Patriot ES 800/K-6
4410 Old Farm Rd 93312 661-588-6065
Norm Richards, prin. Fax 587-2272
Rosedale MS 700/7-8
12463 Rosedale Hwy 93312 661-588-6030
Becky Devahl, prin. Fax 588-6039
Rosedale-North ES 500/K-6
11500 Meacham Rd 93312 661-588-6040
Wendy Camara, prin. Fax 588-6043

Standard ESD 2,900/K-8
1200 N Chester Ave 93308 661-392-2110
Paul Meyers Ed.D., supt. Fax 392-0681
www.standardschools.net
Highland ES 800/K-5
2900 Barnett St 93308 661-392-2115
Tonny Gisbertz, prin. Fax 392-2142
Standard ES 500/K-5
115 E Minner Ave 93308 661-392-2120
Susan Denton, prin. Fax 392-2137
Standard MS 900/6-8
1222 N Chester Ave 93308 661-392-2130
Vicki Albitre, prin. Fax 392-2134
Wingland ES 700/K-5
701 Douglas St 93308 661-392-2125
Robert Sheldon, prin. Fax 392-2139

Vineland ESD 800/K-8
14713 Weedpatch Hwy 93307 661-845-3713
Matthew Ross, supt. Fax 845-8449
vineland.k12.ca.us
Sunset S 300/5-8
8301 Sunset Blvd 93307 661-845-1320
Erin Gayer, prin. Fax 845-3952
Vineland ES 500/K-4
14327 S Vineland Rd 93307 661-845-3719
Erin Gayer, prin. Fax 845-1599

Bakersfield Adventist Academy 100/K-12
3333 Bernard St 93306 661-871-1591
Michael Schwartz, prin. Fax 871-1594

Bethel Apostolic Academy 100/K-12
1418 W Columbus St 93301 661-323-2851
Chad Bradley, prin.
Bethel Christian S 100/K-12
2236 E California Ave 93307 661-325-2661
Michael Kennedy, prin.
Country Christian S 200/K-8
2416 Dean Ave 93312 661-589-4703
Rose Merriman, admin. Fax 588-5944
Heritage Christian Schools 200/PK-8
2401 Bernard St 93306 661-871-4545
Daniel Barrett, admin. Fax 871-5627
Olive Knolls Christian S 300/PK-8
6201 Fruitvale Ave 93308 661-393-3566
Rusty Rhodes, admin. Fax 393-3467
Our Lady of Guadalupe S 100/PK-8
609 E California Ave 93307 661-323-6059
Sr. Susana Del Toro, prin. Fax 323-6058
Our Lady of Perpetual Help S 400/PK-8
124 Columbus St 93305 661-327-7741
Kelli Michaud, prin. Fax 325-7067
St. Francis S 600/PK-8
2516 Palm St 93304 661-326-7955
Kelli Gruszka, prin. Fax 327-0395
St. John Lutheran S 400/PK-8
4500 Buena Vista Rd 93311 661-664-8090
Spencer Peregoy, supt. Fax 661-1327
Stockdale Christian S 800/PK-8
4901 California Ave 93309 661-327-3927
Doug Pike, supt. Fax 327-9802
Valley S 300/PK-8
2300 E Brundage Ln 93307 661-325-5084
Gina Black M.Ed., prin. Fax 325-5087

Baldwin Park, Los Angeles, Pop. 74,883
Baldwin Park USD 14,500/PK-12
3699 Holly Ave 91706 626-962-3311
Dr. Froilan N. Mendoza, supt. Fax 856-4901
www.bpusd.net
Bursch ES 600/PK-6
4245 Merced Ave 91706 626-338-4319
Russhell M. Ortega, prin. Fax 856-4086
Central ES 500/PK-6
14741 Central Ave 91706 626-962-7915
Esther V. Garcia, prin. Fax 962-0676
DeAnza ES 600/PK-6
12820 Bess Ave 91706 626-338-4019
Monica Ozuna, prin. Fax 856-4495
Elwin ES 500/PK-6
13010 Waco St 91706 626-962-8015
Patricia CubillodeRomero, prin. Fax 856-4444
Foster ES 700/PK-6
13900 Foster Ave 91706 626-962-8111
Carmen Caballero, prin. Fax 856-4286
Geddes ES 700/PK-5
14600 Cavette Pl 91706 626-962-8114
Irene Garcia, prin. Fax 856-4966
Heath ES 500/PK-6
14321 School St 91706 626-338-4013
Dr. Maria Alonso, prin. Fax 856-4967
Holland MS 500/6-8
4733 Landis Ave 91706 626-962-8412
James Michael Rust, prin. Fax 813-6148
Holliday Childrens Center PK-PK
13529 Francisquito Ave 91706 626-337-2711
Debra Staveley, prin. Fax 814-4635
Jones JHS 500/7-8
14250 Merced Ave 91706 626-962-8312
Eric Lopez, prin. Fax 856-4291
Kenmore ES 600/PK-6
3823 Kenmore Ave 91706 626-962-8316
Jane Sattari, prin. Fax 856-4968
Olive MS 500/6-8
13701 Olive St 91706 626-962-8416
Blanca Risco, prin. Fax 856-4568
Pleasant View ES 400/PK-6
14900 Nubia St 91706 626-962-8512
Linda Heredia, prin. Fax 856-4369
Santa Fe S 400/3-8
4650 Baldwin Park Blvd 91706 626-856-1525
Margie Clark, prin. Fax 813-0614
Sierra Vista JHS 800/7-8
13400 Foster Ave 91706 626-962-1300
Lorena Chavira, prin. Fax 856-4577
Tracy ES 700/PK-6
13350 Tracy St 91706 626-962-9718
Erika Valenzuela, prin. Fax 856-4213
Vineland ES 800/PK-6
3609 Vineland Ave 91706 626-962-9719
Dr. Laura Rodriguez, prin. Fax 856-4929
Walnut ES 600/PK-5
4701 Walnut St 91706 626-939-4368
Leslie Peregrina, prin. Fax 856-4373

East Valley Adventist S 50/K-8
3554 Maine Ave 91706 626-960-4751
Ivanelle Perez, prin. Fax 960-4752
St. John the Baptist S 400/K-8
3870 Stewart Ave 91706 626-337-1421
Sr. Rosario Mediavilla, prin. Fax 337-3733

Ballico, Merced, Pop. 398
Ballico-Cressey ESD 400/PK-8
11818 Gregg Ave 95303 209-394-9600
Bryan Ballenger, supt. Fax 632-8929
www.ballicocressey.com
Ballico MS 200/3-8
11818 Gregg Ave 95303 209-394-9400
Bryan Ballenger, supt. Fax 632-8929
Other Schools – See Cressey

Bangor, Butte, Pop. 605
Bangor UNESD 100/K-8
PO Box 340 95914 530-679-2434
Jason Bramson, supt. Fax 679-1018
www.bangorunion.org
Bangor Union ES 100/K-8
PO Box 340 95914 530-679-2434
Jason Bramson, admin. Fax 679-1018

Banning, Riverside, Pop. 28,937
Banning USD 4,500/K-12
161 W Williams St 92220 951-922-0200
Robert Guillen, supt. Fax 922-0227
www.banning.k12.ca.us
Central ES 800/K-5
295 N San Gorgonio Ave 92220 951-922-0264
Marcia Cole Anderson, prin. Fax 922-2718
Hemmerling ES 500/K-5
1928 W Nicolet St 92220 951-922-0254
Alisha Morff, prin. Fax 922-0294
Hoffer ES 600/K-5
1115 E Hoffer St 92220 951-922-0257
Janet Gray, prin. Fax 922-0260
Nicolet MS 1,000/6-8
101 E Nicolet St 92220 951-922-0280
Albert Evinger, prin. Fax 922-2748
Other Schools – See Cabazon

Calvary Christian S 100/PK-12
1325 Mountain Ave 92220 951-849-1877
Phil Niederer, prin. Fax 849-9847

Barstow, San Bernardino, Pop. 21,497
Barstow USD 5,800/K-12
551 S Avenue H 92311 760-255-6000
Jeff Malan, supt. Fax 255-8965
www.barstow.k12.ca.us
Barstow JHS 800/7-8
551 S Avenue H 92311 760-255-6200
Jorge Gutierrez, prin. Fax 255-6205
Barstow STEM Academy 6-8
551 S Avenue H 92311 760-255-6150
Vinney Williams, prin. Fax 255-6104
Cameron ES 600/K-6
551 S Avenue H 92311 760-255-6260
Deborah Hayes, prin. Fax 255-6261
Crestline ES 500/K-6
551 S Avenue H 92311 760-252-5121
Cari Mauldin, prin. Fax 252-5152
Henderson ES 700/K-6
551 S Avenue H 92311 760-255-6250
Michele Enriquez, prin. Fax 255-6253
Lenwood ES 500/K-6
551 S Avenue H 92311 760-253-7713
Heather Reid, prin. Fax 253-7708
Montara ES 700/K-6
551 S Avenue H 92311 760-252-5150
Keith Acedo, prin. Fax 252-5185
Skyline North ES 500/K-6
551 S Avenue H 92311 760-255-6090
Kim Barilone, prin. Fax 255-6095

Barstow Christian S 100/PK-8
800 Yucca Ave 92311 760-256-3556
Heather Bradford, prin. Fax 256-1326

Bay Point, Contra Costa, Pop. 20,582
Mount Diablo USD
Supt. — See Concord
Rio Vista ES 500/K-5
611 Pacifica Ave 94565 925-458-6101
Lourdes Beleche, prin. Fax 458-8765
Riverview MS 700/6-8
205 Pacifica Ave 94565 925-458-3216
Eric Wood, prin. Fax 458-0875

Bayside, Humboldt

Humboldt Bay Christian S 50/K-8
70 Stephens Ln 95524 707-822-1738
Ruthanne Altsman, prin. Fax 822-1739

Beale AFB, Yuba, Pop. 1,225
Wheatland SD
Supt. — See Wheatland
Lone Tree ES 300/PK-5
123 Beale Hwy 95903 530-788-0248
Jodie Jacklett, prin. Fax 788-0518

Beaumont, Riverside, Pop. 35,877
Beaumont USD 9,000/K-12
PO Box 187 92223 951-845-1631
Terrence Davis, supt. Fax 845-2039
www.beaumont-ca.schoolloop.com
Brookside ES 600/K-5
PO Box 187 92223 951-845-3473
Michael Griffin M.Ed., prin. Fax 845-3714
Hause ES 800/K-5
PO Box 187 92223 951-769-1674
Dr. Christina Boursaw, prin. Fax 845-8538
Mountain View MS 1,000/6-8
PO Box 187 92223 951-845-1627
Michael Breyer, prin. Fax 845-8679
Palm ES 600/K-5
PO Box 187 92223 951-845-9579
Lora Roman M.A., prin. Fax 845-5604
San Gorgonio MS 1,000/6-8
PO Box 187 92223 951-769-4391
Drew Scherrer, prin. Fax 769-8750
Sundance ES 800/K-5
PO Box 187 92223 951-845-2621
Lauren Kinney, prin. Fax 769-8752
Three Rings Ranch ES 700/K-5
PO Box 187 92223 951-845-5052
Sean Dickinson, prin. Fax 769-3528
Tournament Hills ES 800/K-5
PO Box 187 92223 951-769-0711
Callie Beitler, prin. Fax 769-0592

Bell, Los Angeles, Pop. 35,263
Los Angeles USD
Supt. — See Los Angeles
Corona ES 1,000/K-5
3825 Bell Ave 90201 323-560-1323
Rachel Saldana, prin. Fax 560-8166
Escutia Primary Center 300/K-K
6401 Bear Ave 90201 323-585-8237
Janis Shinmei, prin. Fax 585-3797
Nueva Vista ES 1,000/K-5
4412 Randolph St 90201 323-562-3015
Bruce Clark, prin. Fax 560-3507
Orchard Academy #2B 500/6-8
6411 Orchard Ave 90201 323-826-3900
Cristopher Ziegel, prin. Fax 583-1106
Orchard Academy #2C 500/6-8
6411 Orchard Ave 90201 323-826-3900
Rosa Guerrero, prin. Fax 583-1106
Woodlawn Avenue ES 800/K-5
6314 Woodlawn Ave 90201 323-560-1445
Carolina Brockway, prin. Fax 560-7049

Bella Vista, Shasta, Pop. 2,707
Bella Vista ESD 300/K-8
22661 Old Alturas Rd 96008 530-549-4415
Charlie Hoffman, supt. Fax 549-4506
www.bveagles.com
Bella Vista S 300/K-8
22661 Old Alturas Rd 96008 530-549-4415
Bev Armelino, prin. Fax 549-4506

Bellflower, Los Angeles, Pop. 74,379
Bellflower USD 13,300/K-12
16703 Clark Ave 90706 562-866-9011
Brian Jacobs Ed.D., supt. Fax 866-7713
www.busd.k12.ca.us/
Baxter ES 500/K-6
14929 Cerritos Ave 90706 562-531-1602
Susan Curtiss, prin. Fax 531-4073
Jefferson ES 600/K-6
10027 Rose St 90706 562-804-6521
Tiffany Dominguez, prin. Fax 804-6577
Pyle ES 600/K-6
14500 Woodruff Ave 90706 562-804-6528
Lisa Paioni, prin. Fax 804-6530
Ramona ES 700/K-6
9351 Laurel St 90706 562-804-6532
Dierdre Reyes, prin. Fax 804-6562
Washington ES 800/K-6
9725 Jefferson St 90706 562-804-6535
Angelica Montelongo, prin. Fax 804-6539
Woodruff ES 700/K-6
15332 Eucalyptus Ave 90706 562-804-6545
Beverly Swanson, prin. Fax 804-6583
Other Schools – See Lakewood

Adventist Union S 50/PK-8
15548 Santa Ana Ave 90706 562-867-0718
St. Bernard S 200/PK-8
9626 Park St 90706 562-867-9410
James Cordero, prin. Fax 866-2310
St. Dominic Savio S 400/PK-8
9750 Foster Rd 90706 562-866-3617
Sr. Ignacia Carrillo, prin. Fax 804-6638
Southland Christian Academy 100/K-6
16400 Woodruff Ave 90706 562-867-8594
Deborah Metcalf, prin. Fax 867-8594
Valley Christian ES 400/PK-6
17408 Grand Ave 90706 562-920-9902
Rhonda Van Kampen, prin. Fax 920-9778

Bell Gardens, Los Angeles, Pop. 41,928
Montebello USD
Supt. — See Montebello
Bell Gardens ES 1,100/K-5
5620 Quinn St 90201 562-927-1223
James Sams, prin. Fax 806-5134
Bell Gardens IS 1,200/6-8
5841 Live Oak St 90201 562-927-1319
Jose Cuevas, prin. Fax 806-5131
Chavez ES 1,000/K-5
6139 Loveland St 90201 323-773-1804
Deanna Plascencia, prin. Fax 826-5164
Garfield ES 800/K-5
7425 Garfield Ave 90201 562-927-1915
David Hernandez, prin. Fax 806-5135
Suva ES 1,000/K-5
6740 Suva St 90201 562-927-1827
Janice Riddle, prin. Fax 806-5137
Suva IS 900/6-8
6660 Suva St 90201 562-927-2679
Miguel Miranda, prin. Fax 806-5132

St. Gertrude S 100/PK-8
6824 Toler Ave 90201 562-927-1216
Mary Flock, prin. Fax 928-9099

Belmont, San Mateo, Pop. 24,354
Belmont-Redwood Shores ESD 3,700/K-8
2960 Hallmark Dr 94002 650-637-4800
Michael Milliken Ph.D., supt. Fax 637-4811
www.brssd.org
Central ES 500/K-5
525 Middle Rd 94002 650-637-4820
Chris Marchetti, prin. Fax 637-4827
Cipriani ES 400/K-5
2525 Buena Vista Ave 94002 650-637-4840
Jennifer Gaboury, prin. Fax 637-4839
Fox ES 400/K-5
3100 Saint James Rd 94002 650-637-4850
Michael Pappas, prin. Fax 637-4858
Nesbit ES 400/K-8
500 Biddulph Way 94002 650-637-4860
Robin Pang-Maganaris, prin. Fax 637-4867
Ralston IS 1,100/6-8
2675 Ralston Ave 94002 650-637-4880
Michael Dougherty, prin. Fax 637-4888
Other Schools – See Redwood City

Armstrong S 200/2-8
1405 Solana Dr 94002 650-592-7570
Jessica Miller, head sch Fax 591-3114
Belmont Oaks Academy 400/PK-5
2200 Carlmont Dr 94002 650-593-6175
Kelly Corteway, prin. Fax 593-7937
Gloria Dei Lutheran S 50/PK-6
2600 Ralston Ave 94002 650-593-3361
Richard De Frain, prin.

Immaculate Heart of Mary S 300/PK-8
1000 Alameda De Las Pulgas 94002 650-593-4265
Teri Grosey, prin. Fax 593-4342
Notre Dame ES 200/K-8
1200 Notre Dame Ave 94002 650-591-2209
Sr. Kathryn Keenan, prin. Fax 591-4798
Serendipity S 100/K-5
2820 Ponce Ave 94002 650-596-9100

Benicia, Solano, Pop. 25,504
Benicia USD 4,900/K-12
350 E K St 94510 707-747-8300
Dr. Charles Young, supt. Fax 748-0146
www.beniciaunified.org
Benicia MS 1,200/6-8
1100 Southampton Rd 94510 707-747-8340
Damian Scott, prin. Fax 747-8349
Farmar ES 500/K-5
901 Military W 94510 707-747-8350
Wendy Smith, prin. Fax 747-8359
Henderson ES 500/K-5
650 Hastings Dr 94510 707-747-8370
Melanie Buck, prin. Fax 747-8379
Semple ES 500/K-5
2015 E 3rd St 94510 707-747-8360
Christina Moore, prin. Fax 747-8369
Turner ES 500/K-5
540 Rose Dr 94510 707-747-8390
Stephen Slater, prin. Fax 747-8399

St. Dominic S 300/PK-8
935 E 5th St 94510 707-745-1266
Katie Perata, prin. Fax 745-1841

Ben Lomond, Santa Cruz, Pop. 6,022
San Lorenzo Valley USD 4,500/PK-12
325 Marion Ave 95005 831-336-5194
Dr. Laurie Bruton, supt. Fax 336-9531
www.slvusd.org
Other Schools – See Boulder Creek, Felton

Benton, Mono, Pop. 276
Eastern Sierra USD
Supt. — See Bridgeport
Beaman ES 50/K-5
PO Box 947 93512 760-933-2397
Don Clark, prin. Fax 933-2355

Berkeley, Alameda, Pop. 106,371
Berkeley USD 10,100/PK-12
2020 Bonar St 94702 510-644-4500
Donald Evans, supt. Fax 540-5358
www.berkeleyschools.net
Berkeley Arts Magnet S at Whittier 400/K-5
2015 Virginia St 94709 510-644-6225
Rene Molina, prin. Fax 644-0265
Cragmont ES 400/K-5
830 Regal Rd 94708 510-644-8810
Michelle Sinclair, prin. Fax 644-7717
Emerson ES 300/K-5
2800 Forest Ave 94705 510-644-6890
Susan Hodge, prin. Fax 644-7758
Franklin Preschool PK-PK
1460 8th St 94710 510-644-6339
Maria Carriedo, prin. Fax 644-7711
Hopkins ECC PK-PK
1810 Hopkins St 94707 510-644-8939
Maria Carriedo, prin. Fax 644-7711
Jefferson ES 300/K-5
1400 Ada St 94702 510-644-6298
Mary Cazden, prin. Fax 644-6984
King Child Development Center PK-PK
1939 Ward St 94703 510-644-6358
Maria Carriedo, prin. Fax 644-7711
King MS 900/6-8
1781 Rose St 94703 510-644-6280
Janet Levenson, prin. Fax 644-8783
LeConte ES 300/K-5
2241 Russell St 94705 510-644-6290
Veronica Valerio, prin. Fax 644-7767
Longfellow Arts & Technology MS 500/6-8
1500 Derby St 94703 510-644-6360
Marcos Garcia, prin. Fax 644-8707
Malcolm X ES 500/K-5
1731 Prince St 94703 510-644-6313
Alexander Hunt, prin. Fax 644-6297
Muir ES 300/K-5
2955 Claremont Ave 94705 510-644-6410
Audrey Amos, prin. Fax 644-8643
Oxford ES 300/K-5
1130 Oxford St 94707 510-644-6300
Beth Rhine, prin. Fax 644-4869
Parks Magnet ES 500/K-5
920 Allston Way 94710 510-644-8812
Paco Furlan, prin. Fax 883-6986
Thousand Oaks ES 500/K-5
840 Colusa Ave 94707 510-644-6368
Jennnifer Corn, prin. Fax 644-4825
Washington ES 500/K-5
2300 Mrtn Lther King Jr Way 94704 510-644-6310
Mel Stenger, prin. Fax 644-7718
Willard MS 500/6-8
2425 Stuart St 94705 510-644-6330
Debbie Dean, prin. Fax 548-4219

Academy 100/K-8
2722 Benvenue Ave 94705 510-549-0605
Buzz Heinrich, head sch Fax 549-9119
American International Montessori S 100/K-6
3339 Martin Luther King Jr 94703 510-868-1815
Ernest Mahr, dir. Fax 610-1511
Berkeley Rose Waldorf S PK-5
1442A Walnut St #395 94709 510-859-7679
Megan Coleman, admin.
Berkeley S 300/PK-8
1310 University Ave 94702 510-665-8800
Mitch Bostian, hdmstr. Fax 665-8700
Berkwood Hedge S 100/K-5
1809 Bancroft Way 94703 510-883-6990
Love Weinstock, head sch
Black Pine Circle S 300/K-8
2027 7th St 94710 510-845-0876
John Carlstroem, hdmstr. Fax 845-9354
East Bay S for Boys 100/6-8
2340 Durant Ave 94704 510-621-3272
Jason Baeten, prin.
Ecole Bilingue De Berkeley 500/PK-8
1009 Heinz Ave 94710 510-549-3867
Dr. Mehdi Lazar, head sch Fax 845-3209
Global Montessori International S 100/PK-K
2830 9th St 94710 510-845-6969
Vivi Teng, dir. Fax 845-6699
School of the Madeleine 300/K-8
1225 Milvia St 94709 510-526-4744
Ken Willers, prin. Fax 526-5152
Shu Ren International S 100/PK-8
2125 Jefferson Ave 94703 510-841-8899
Rebecca Zipprich, head sch

Bermuda Dunes, Riverside, Pop. 7,164
Desert Sands USD
Supt. — See La Quinta
Monroe ES 600/K-5
42100 Yucca Ln, 760-772-4130
Mike Kint, prin. Fax 772-4135

Desert Christian Academy 500/PK-12
40700 Yucca Ln, 760-345-2848
Debbee Scott, head sch Fax 345-8173

Berry Creek, Butte, Pop. 1,348
Pioneer UNESD 100/K-8
286 Rockerfeller Rd 95916 530-589-1633
Patsy Oxford, supt. Fax 589-5021
www.puesd.org
Berry Creek ES 100/K-8
286 Rockerfeller Rd 95916 530-589-1633
Patsy Oxford, admin. Fax 589-5021

Beverly Hills, Los Angeles, Pop. 32,498
Beverly Hills USD 4,300/PK-12
255 S Lasky Dr 90212 310-551-5100
Dr. Michael Bregy, supt. Fax 286-2138
www.bhusd.org
Beverly Vista S 700/PK-8
200 S Elm Dr 90212 310-229-3669
Christian Fuhrer, prin. Fax 275-3532
El Rodeo S 700/PK-8
605 N Whittier Dr 90210 310-229-3670
Kevin Allen, prin. Fax 275-3185
Hawthorne S 600/PK-8
624 N Rexford Dr 90210 310-229-3675
Michelle Dar, prin. Fax 276-5023
Mann S 600/K-8
8701 Charleville Blvd 90211 310-229-3680
Juliet Fine, prin. Fax 652-8841

Good Shepherd S 200/PK-8
148 S Linden Dr 90212 310-275-8601
Danielle Colvert, prin. Fax 275-0366
Harkham Hillel Hebrew Academy 500/PK-8
9120 W Olympic Blvd 90212 310-276-6135
Jason Ablin, prin. Fax 276-6134
Kabbalah Children's Academy 100/PK-8
9250 W Olympic Blvd 90212 310-385-1187
Linda Bratcher, head sch Fax 385-8218
Page Private S of Beverly Hills 100/PK-6
419 S Robertson Blvd 90211 323-272-3429
Kristin Dickson, head sch

Bieber, Lassen, Pop. 307
Big Valley JUSD 200/K-12
PO Box 157 96009 530-294-5266
Paula Silva, supt. Fax 294-5396
www.bigvalleyschool.org
Big Valley ES 100/K-6
PO Box 157 96009 530-294-5214
Paula Silva, prin. Fax 294-5109

Big Bar, Trinity
Trinity Alps USD
Supt. — See Weaverville
Cox Bar ES 50/K-8
304 Corral Bottom Rd 96010 530-623-6316
Tom Barnett, supt. Fax 623-6316

Big Bear Lake, San Bernardino, Pop. 4,883
Bear Valley USD 2,600/PK-12
PO Box 1529 92315 909-866-4631
Mary Suzuki Ed.D., supt. Fax 866-2040
www.bearvalleyusd.org
Big Bear ES 300/PK-6
PO Box 1627 92315 909-866-4638
Christina San Nicolas, prin. Fax 866-1113
Big Bear MS 400/7-8
PO Box 1607 92315 909-866-4634
Dena Arbaugh, prin. Fax 866-5679
North Shore ES 500/K-6
PO Box 1887 92315 909-866-7501
Manny Marquez, prin. Fax 866-7510
Other Schools – See Forest Falls, Sugarloaf

Big Bend, Shasta, Pop. 96
Indian Springs ESD 50/K-8
PO Box 70 96011 530-337-6219
Ed Traverso, supt. Fax 337-6456
www.indianspringsesd.org
Indian Springs S 50/K-8
PO Box 70 96011 530-337-6219
Ed Traverso, prin. Fax 337-6456

Big Creek, Fresno, Pop. 175
Big Creek ESD 100/K-8
PO Box 98 93605 559-893-3314
Toby Wait, supt. Fax 893-3315
www.bigcreekschool.com
Big Creek ES 100/K-8
PO Box 98 93605 559-893-3314
Toby Wait, prin. Fax 893-3315

Biggs, Butte, Pop. 1,654
Biggs USD 500/PK-12
300 B St 95917 530-868-1281
Dr. Doug Kaelin, supt. Fax 868-1615
www.biggs.org/
Biggs ES 300/PK-8
300 B St 95917 530-868-5870
Minden King, prin. Fax 868-5137
Other Schools – See Richvale

Big Pine, Inyo, Pop. 1,716
Big Pine USD 200/PK-12
PO Box 908 93513 760-938-2005
Pamela Jones, supt. Fax 938-2310
www.bigpineschools.org
Big Pine ES 100/PK-8
PO Box 908 93513 760-938-2222
Ed Dardenne-Ankringa, prin. Fax 938-2310

Big Sur, Monterey
Big Sur USD 100/PK-12
69325 Highway 1 93920 805-927-4507
Gordon Piffero, supt. Fax 927-8123
www.bigsurunified.org
Pacific Valley S 50/PK-12
69325 Highway 1 93920 805-927-4507
Gordon Piffero, supt. Fax 927-8123

Carmel USD
Supt. — See Carmel
Cooper ES 100/K-5
PO Box 250 93920 831-667-2452
Julie Kolofer, prin. Fax 667-2760

Bishop, Inyo, Pop. 3,811
Bishop USD 1,500/K-12
301 N Fowler St 93514 760-872-3680
Barry Simpson, supt. Fax 872-6016
www.bishopschools.org
Bishop ES 400/K-5
800 W Elm St 93514 760-872-1278
Betsy McDonald, prin. Fax 872-5113
Home Street MS 400/6-8
201 Home St 93514 760-872-1381
Patrick Twomey, prin. Fax 872-1877

Round Valley JESD 100/K-8
300 N Round Valley Rd 93514 760-387-2525
Karen Marshall, supt. Fax 387-2330
www.roundvalley.us
Round Valley ES 100/K-8
300 N Round Valley Rd 93514 760-387-2525
Karen Marshall, admin. Fax 387-2330

Bishop SDA S 50/K-8
730 Home St 93514 760-872-1036
Erin Rodriguez, head sch Fax 872-1036

Blocksburg, Humboldt
Southern Humbolt JUSD
Supt. — See Miranda
Casterlin S 50/PK-8
24790 Alderpoint Rd 95514 707-926-5402
Don Boyd, prin. Fax 926-5150

Bloomington, San Bernardino, Pop. 23,603
Colton JUSD
Supt. — See Colton
Baca MS 900/7-8
1640 S Lilac Ave 92316 909-580-5014
Mike Williford, prin. Fax 876-4195
Crestmore ES 800/K-6
18870 Jurupa Ave 92316 909-580-5010
Patricia Frost, prin. Fax 872-6408
Grimes ES 600/K-6
1609 Spruce Ave 92316 909-580-5030
Wendy Moore, prin. Fax 876-4213
Harris MS 800/7-8
11150 Alder Ave 92316 909-580-5020
Cynthia Aguilar-Munoz Ed.D., prin. Fax 820-2238
Lewis ES 700/K-6
18040 San Bernardino Ave 92316 909-580-5025
Patrick McGinn, prin. Fax 430-2832
Smith ES 800/K-6
9551 Linden Ave 92316 909-580-5033
Sheila Brower, prin. Fax 430-2835
Zimmerman ES 800/K-6
11050 Linden Ave 92316 909-580-5019
Cynthia Coello, prin. Fax 872-6481

Bloomington Christian S 900/PK-12
955 Bloomington Ave 92316 909-877-1239
Stephane Bracken, prin. Fax 873-3160

Blue Jay, San Bernardino
Rim of the World USD 3,300/K-12
27315 N Bay Rd 92317 909-336-2031
Michelle Murphy, supt. Fax 337-4527
www.rimsd.k12.ca.us
Other Schools – See Crestline, Lake Arrowhead, Running Springs

Blue Lake, Humboldt, Pop. 1,210
Blue Lake UNESD 200/K-8
PO Box 268 95525 707-668-5674
DeAnn Waldvogel, supt. Fax 668-5619
www.humboldt.k12.ca.us/bluelake
Blue Lake ES 200/K-8
PO Box 268 95525 707-668-5674
DeAnn Waldvogel, prin. Fax 668-5619

Green Point ESD 50/K-8
180 Valkensar Ln 95525 707-668-5921
Scotty Appleford, supt. Fax 668-1986
www.humboldt.k12.ca.us/greenpoint_sd
Green Point ES 50/K-8
180 Valkensar Ln 95525 707-668-5921
Scotty Appleford, supt. Fax 668-1986

Blythe, Riverside, Pop. 20,420
Palo Verde USD 2,800/PK-12
295 N 1st St 92225 760-922-4164
Charles Bush, supt. Fax 922-5942
www.pvusd.us
Appleby ES 600/PK-8
10321 E Vernon Ave 92225 760-922-7174
Karina De La Pena, prin. Fax 922-0504
Brown ES 600/PK-8
241 N 7th St 92225 760-922-7164
Cintia Robsinson, prin. Fax 922-0636
White ES 600/PK-8
610 N Broadway 92225 760-922-5159
April Smith, prin. Fax 922-1367

Desert Preparatory Academy PK-8
721 E Chanslor Way 92225 760-544-7236
Sue Fisher, contact Fax 544-7238

Bodega Bay, Sonoma, Pop. 1,039
Shoreline USD
Supt. — See Tomales
Bodega Bay ES 50/K-5
PO Box 155 94923 707-875-2724
Amanda Mattea, prin. Fax 875-2182

Bolinas, Marin, Pop. 1,544
Bolinas-Stinson UNSD 100/K-8
125 Olema Bolinas Rd 94924 415-868-1603
John Carroll, supt. Fax 868-9406
www.bolinas-stinson.org
Bolinas-Stinson ES 100/K-8
125 Olema Bolinas Rd 94924 415-868-1603
Jason Richardson, prin. Fax 868-9406

Bonita, San Diego, Pop. 12,128
Chula Vista ESD
Supt. — See Chula Vista
Allen ES 400/K-6
4300 Allen School Ln 91902 619-479-3662
Sisi Garcia, prin. Fax 267-6237
Daly Academy 200/K-6
4300 Allen School Ln 91902 619-479-3665
Joseph Prosapio, prin. Fax 479-0133
Sunnyside ES 400/K-6
5430 San Miguel Rd 91902 619-479-0571
Robert Cochran, prin. Fax 479-7297
Valley Vista ES 600/K-6
3724 Valley Vista Way 91902 619-479-7171
Carmen Emery, prin. Fax 479-7024

Bonsall, San Diego, Pop. 3,866
Bonsall USD 2,300/K-12
31505 Old River Rd 92003 760-631-5200
David Jones, supt. Fax 941-4409
www.bonsallusd.com
Bonsall ES 1,000/K-5
31555 Old River Rd 92003 760-631-5205
Dr. Karla Groth, prin. Fax 758-3193
Sullivan MS 500/6-8
7350 W Lilac Rd 92003 760-631-5210
Joseph Clevenger, prin. Fax 631-5230
Other Schools – See Oceanside

Boonville, Mendocino, Pop. 1,016
Anderson Valley USD 500/PK-12
PO Box 457 95415 707-895-3774
Michelle Hutchins, supt. Fax 895-2665
www.avusd.k12.ca.us
Anderson Valley ES 300/PK-6
PO Box 830 95415 707-895-3010
Tracy Anderson, prin. Fax 895-2197

Boron, Kern, Pop. 2,180
Muroc JUSD
Supt. — See North Edwards
West Boron ES 300/PK-6
12300 Del Oro St 93516 760-762-5430
Robert Kostopoulos, prin. Fax 762-5019

Borrego Springs, San Diego, Pop. 3,399
Borrego Springs USD 500/PK-12
1315 Palm Canyon Dr 92004 760-767-5357
Mark Stevens, supt. Fax 767-0494
www.bsusd.com
Borrego Springs ES 200/PK-5
1315 Palm Canyon Dr 92004 760-767-5333
Martha Deichler, prin. Fax 767-7438
Borrego Springs MS 100/6-8
1315 Palm Canyon Dr 92004 760-767-5335
Katherine Girvin, prin. Fax 767-5999

Boulder Creek, Santa Cruz, Pop. 4,741
San Lorenzo Valley USD
Supt. — See Ben Lomond
Boulder Creek ES 500/PK-5
400 W Lomond St 95006 831-338-6413
Denise Fosburgh, prin. Fax 338-6118

Boulevard, San Diego, Pop. 306
Mountain Empire USD
Supt. — See Pine Valley
Clover Flat ES 100/PK-5
39639 Old Highway 80 91905 619-766-4655
Christi Martelli, prin. Fax 766-4537

Bradley, Monterey, Pop. 92
Bradley UNESD 100/K-8
PO Box 60 93426 805-472-2310
Ian Trejo, supt. Fax 472-2339
bradleyusd-ca.schoolloop.com
Bradley ES 100/K-8
PO Box 60 93426 805-472-2310
Ian Trejo, supt. Fax 472-2339

Brawley, Imperial, Pop. 24,758
Brawley ESD 3,300/K-8
261 D St 92227 760-344-2330
Jaime Silva, supt. Fax 344-8928
www.besd.org
Hildalgo ES 500/K-6
615 S Cesar Chavez St 92227 760-344-0431
David Ramos, prin. Fax 344-2423
Oakley ES 900/K-3
1401 B St 92227 760-344-4620
Craig Casey, prin. Fax 344-2019
Swing ES 700/K-6
245 W A St 92227 760-344-3350
Elizabeth Casey, prin. Fax 344-2613
Witter ES 800/K-3
150 K St 92227 760-344-0750
Debra Hale, prin. Fax 351-3097
Worth JHS 500/7-8
385 W D St 92227 760-344-2153
Andy Burnett, prin. Fax 351-5043

Magnolia UNESD 100/K-8
4502 Casey Rd 92227 760-344-2494
Blaine Smith, supt. Fax 344-8584
www.magnoliatigers.com
Magnolia ES 100/K-8
4502 Casey Rd 92227 760-344-2494
Blaine Smith, admin. Fax 344-8584

Mulberry ESD 100/K-8
1391 Rutherford Rd 92227 760-344-8600
Chelsey Galindo, supt. Fax 351-1769
www.mulberrymustangs.org
Mulberry ES 100/K-8
1391 Rutherford Rd 92227 760-344-8600
Chelsey Galindo, prin. Fax 351-1769

Brawley Christian Academy 100/K-12
430 N 2nd St 92227 760-344-3911
Tony Flores, prin. Fax 344-5864
Sacred Heart S 100/PK-8
428 S Imperial Ave 92227 760-344-2662
Annalisa Burgos, prin. Fax 344-1910

Brea, Orange, Pop. 38,164
Brea-Olinda USD 6,000/K-12
PO Box 300 92822 714-990-7800
Dr. Brad Mason, supt. Fax 529-2137
www.bousd.us
Arovista ES 600/K-6
900 Eadington Dr 92821 714-529-2185
Karen VanDine, prin. Fax 990-7899
Brea Country Hills ES 600/K-6
150 N Associated Rd 92821 714-990-3221
Patricia Walsh, prin. Fax 990-3222
Brea JHS 900/7-8
400 N Brea Blvd 92821 714-990-7500
Kelly Kennedy, prin. Fax 990-7585
Fanning ES 400/K-6
650 N Apricot Ave 92821 714-529-3908
Theresa Stevens, prin. Fax 529-3909
Laurel Elementary Magnet S 300/K-6
200 S Flower Ave 92821 714-529-2520
Heather Bojorquez, prin. Fax 529-7542
Mariposa ES 500/K-6
1111 Mariposa Dr 92821 714-529-4916
Daryn Coburn, prin. Fax 990-7552
Olinda ES 500/K-6
3145 E Birch St 92821 714-528-7475
Robert Rendon, prin. Fax 528-7481

Christ Lutheran S 100/PK-8
820 W Imperial Hwy 92821 714-529-0892
Jackson Thiesfeldt, prin. Fax 529-2157
Heights Christian S Brea Friends Campus 200/PK-4
200 S Associated Rd 92821 714-990-8780
Jodie Whittemore, prin. Fax 990-4879
St. Angela Merici S 300/K-8
575 S Walnut Ave 92821 714-529-6372
Nancy Windisch, prin. Fax 529-7755

Brentwood, Contra Costa, Pop. 49,001
Brentwood UNESD 8,500/PK-8
255 Guthrie Ln 94513 925-513-6300
Dr. Dana Eaton, supt. Fax 634-8583
www.brentwood.k12.ca.us
Adams MS 1,000/6-8
401 American Ave 94513 925-513-6450
Mike Wood, prin. Fax 513-3470
Black ES 500/PK-5
480 Farmington Dr 94513 925-513-6430
Liz Ybarra, prin. Fax 240-9971
Brentwood ES 600/PK-5
200 Griffith Ln 94513 925-513-6360
Guy Rohlfs, prin. Fax 513-0697
Bristow MS 1,100/6-8
855 Minnesota Ave 94513 925-513-6460
Jon Ovick, prin. Fax 516-8725
Garin ES 600/PK-5
250 1st St 94513 925-513-6370
Matt Dailey, prin. Fax 513-0698
Hill MS 900/6-8
140 Birch St 94513 925-513-6440
Kirsten Jobb, prin. Fax 513-0696
Krey ES 900/PK-5
190 Crawford Dr 94513 925-513-6400
Brian Jones, prin. Fax 240-1628
Loma Vista ES 600/PK-5
2110 San Jose Ave 94513 925-513-6390
Julie Croy, prin. Fax 240-5456
Marsh Creek ES 600/PK-5
601 Grant St 94513 925-513-6420
Teresa D'Alfonsi, prin. Fax 240-5382
Nunn ES 600/PK-5
1755 Central Blvd 94513 925-513-6380
Amy Wallace, prin. Fax 513-0995
Pioneer ES 900/PK-5
2010 Shady Willow Ln 94513 925-513-6410
Casey McClure, prin. Fax 513-6419

Knightsen ESD
Supt. — See Knightsen
Old River S K-8
30 Learning Ln 94513 925-626-3330
Ray Witte, prin. Fax 626-3330

Dainty Center/Willow Wood S 200/PK-8
1265 Dainty Ave 94513 925-634-4539
Shawn Guinn, dir.
Golden Hills Christian S 200/PK-8
2401 Shady Willow Ln 94513 925-634-0493
Kathy Zamora, prin. Fax 634-0402

Bridgeport, Mono, Pop. 560
Eastern Sierra USD 400/K-12
PO Box 575 93517 760-932-7443
Don Clark, supt. Fax 932-7140
www.esusd.org
Bridgeport ES 100/K-8
PO Box 577 93517 760-932-7441
Don Clark, prin. Fax 932-1188
Other Schools – See Benton, Coleville, Lee Vining

Mono County Office of Education 200/
PO Box 477 93517 760-932-7311
Stacey Adler, supt. Fax 932-7278
www.monocoe.org
Other Schools – See Mammoth Lakes

Bridgeville, Humboldt
Bridgeville ESD 50/K-8
PO Box 98 95526 707-777-3311
Beth Anderson, supt. Fax 777-3023
www.humboldt.k12.ca.us/bridgeville_sd
Bridgeville ES 50/K-8
PO Box 98 95526 707-777-3311
Beth Anderson, prin. Fax 777-3023

Brisbane, San Mateo, Pop. 4,026
Brisbane ESD 500/K-8
1 Solano St 94005 415-467-0550
Ronan Collver, supt. Fax 467-2914
www.brisbanesd.org
Brisbane ES 200/K-5
500 San Bruno Ave 94005 415-467-0120
Andrea Katotakis, prin. Fax 468-8257
Lipman MS 200/6-8
1 Solano St 94005 415-467-9541
Jolene Heckerman, prin. Fax 467-5073
Other Schools – See Daly City

Browns Valley, Yuba
Marysville JUSD
Supt. — See Marysville
Browns Valley ES 100/K-5
9555 Browns Valley Rd 95918 530-741-6107
Ashley Vette, prin. Fax 741-7831

Buellton, Santa Barbara, Pop. 4,686
Buellton UNESD 600/PK-8
595 2nd St 93427 805-686-2767
Randal Haggard, supt. Fax 686-2719
www.buelltonusd.org
Jonata MS 200/6-8
301 2nd St 93427 805-688-4222
Hans Rheinschild, prin. Fax 688-6611
Oak Valley ES 500/PK-5
595 2nd St 93427 805-688-6992
Hans Rheinschild, prin. Fax 688-1364

Buena Park, Orange, Pop. 78,169
Buena Park ESD 5,200/K-8
6885 Orangethorpe Ave 90620 714-522-8412
Greg Magnuson, supt. Fax 994-1506
www.bpsd.k12.ca.us/
Beatty ES 900/K-6
8201 Country Club Dr 90621 714-523-1160
Seri Hwang, prin. Fax 670-7628
Buena Park JHS 1,100/7-8
6931 Orangethorpe Ave 90620 714-522-8491
Erik Bagger, prin. Fax 523-1602
Corey ES 600/K-6
7351 Holder St 90620 714-522-8389
Valerie Connolly, prin. Fax 739-4058
Emery ES 700/K-6
8600 Somerset St 90621 714-521-5134
Julie Linnecke, prin. Fax 562-0541
Gilbert ES 800/K-6
7255 8th St 90621 714-522-7281
Russell Harrison, prin. Fax 670-7748
Pendleton ES 500/K-6
7101 Stanton Ave 90621 714-521-8568
Richard Rodriguez, prin. Fax 670-9391
Whitaker ES 600/K-6
8401 Montana Ave 90621 714-521-9770
Jose Alarcon, prin. Fax 521-3487

Centralia ESD 4,500/K-6
6625 La Palma Ave 90620 714-228-3100
Norma E. Martinez, supt. Fax 228-3100
www.cesd.us
Buena Terra ES 500/K-6
8299 Holder St 90620 714-228-3220
Dr. Dominic Nguyen, prin. Fax 821-3716
Dysinger ES 500/K-6
7770 Camellia Dr 90620 714-228-3240
Shawn Stuht, prin. Fax 228-3246
San Marino ES 600/K-6
6215 San Rolando Way 90620 714-228-3280
Dr. Omaira Lee, prin. Fax 220-0521
Temple ES 500/K-6
7800 Holder St 90620 714-228-3290
Dr. Estela Salas-Sarmiento, prin. Fax 228-3290
Other Schools – See Anaheim, La Palma

Savanna ESD
Supt. — See Anaheim
Holder ES 500/PK-6
9550 Holder St 90620 714-236-3840
Dr. Jerry Friedman, prin. Fax 220-1741

Bethel Baptist Academy 200/K-12
8251 La Palma Ave 90620 714-521-5586
Dr. Dan Davidson, head sch
St. Pius V S 400/K-8
7681 Orangethorpe Ave 90621 714-522-5313
Dr. Joan Bravo, prin. Fax 522-1767

Burbank, Los Angeles, Pop. 99,967
Burbank USD 15,200/PK-12
1900 W Olive Ave 91506 818-729-4400
Matt Hill, supt. Fax 729-4483
www.burbankusd.org
Burbank MS 1,100/6-8
3700 W Jeffries Ave 91505 818-558-4646
Dr. Oscar Macias, prin. Fax 842-3727
Disney ES 400/K-5
1220 W Orange Grove Ave 91506 818-558-5385
Molly Hwang, prin. Fax 558-4664
Edison ES 500/K-5
2110 Chestnut St 91506 818-558-4644
Laura Flosi, prin. Fax 558-5566
Emerson ES 600/K-5
720 E Cypress Ave 91501 818-558-5419
Jennifer Kaitz, prin. Fax 843-2359
Harte ES 700/K-5
3200 W Jeffries Ave 91505 818-558-5533
Martha Walter, prin. Fax 955-7630
Jefferson ES 700/K-5
1900 N 6th St 91504 818-558-4635
Sandra DeBarros, prin. Fax 558-4666
Jordan MS 1,100/6-8
420 S Mariposa St 91506 818-558-4622
Stacy Cashman, prin. Fax 843-3509
Mann Childrens Center PK-PK
3401 Scott Rd 91504 818-558-5540
Elizabeth Gallion, prin. Fax 845-7906
McKinley ES 400/K-5
349 W Valencia Ave 91506 818-558-5477
Liz Costella, prin. Fax 558-5485
Miller ES 700/K-5
720 E Providencia Ave 91501 818-558-5460
Judy Hession, prin. Fax 843-6077
Muir MS 1,300/6-8
1111 N Kenneth Rd 91504 818-558-5320
Dr. Greg Miller, prin. Fax 841-4637
Providencia ES 400/K-5
1919 N Ontario St 91505 818-558-5470
Jennifer Culbertson, prin. Fax 558-5475
Roosevelt ES 700/K-5
850 N Cordova St 91505 818-558-4668
Dr. Jennifer Meglemre, prin. Fax 955-7648
Stevenson ES 600/K-5
3333 W Oak St 91505 818-558-5522
Christina Desiderio, prin. Fax 841-3435
Washington ES 500/K-5
2322 N Lincoln St 91504 818-558-5550
Brandi Young, prin. Fax 558-5556

St. Finbar S 300/K-8
2120 W Olive Ave 91506 818-848-0191
Michael Marasco, prin. Fax 848-4315
St. Francis Xavier S 300/K-8
3601 Scott Rd 91504 818-504-4422
Dr. Paul Sullivan, prin. Fax 504-4424
St. Robert Bellarmine S 200/K-8
154 N 5th St 91501 818-842-5033
Annette Riggio, prin. Fax 842-3246

Burlingame, San Mateo, Pop. 27,534
Burlingame ESD 3,200/K-8
1825 Trousdale Dr 94010 650-259-3800
Maggie MacIsaac Ed.D., supt. Fax 259-3820
www.burlingameschools.org
Burlingame IS 1,000/6-8
1715 Quesada Way 94010 650-259-3830
Pamela Scott, prin. Fax 259-3843
Franklin ES 600/K-5
2385 Trousdale Dr 94010 650-259-3850
Anne Cildir, prin. Fax 259-3854
Hoover ES, 2220 Summit Dr 94010 K-5
Lisa Booth, prin. 650-259-3900
Lincoln ES 500/K-5
1801 Devereux Dr 94010 650-259-3860
Lori Guidi, prin. Fax 259-3868
McKinley ES 500/K-5
701 Paloma Ave 94010 650-259-3870
Dr. Carla Torres, prin. Fax 259-3879
Roosevelt ES 300/K-5
1151 Vancouver Ave 94010 650-259-3890
Matthew Pavao, prin. Fax 259-0111
Washington ES 300/K-5
801 Howard Ave 94010 650-259-3880
Julie Eastman, prin. Fax 259-3884

Our Lady of Angels S 300/PK-8
1328 Cabrillo Ave 94010 650-343-9200
Amy Costa, prin. Fax 343-5620
St. Catherine of Siena S 300/K-8
1300 Bayswater Ave 94010 650-344-7176
Sr. Antonella Manca, prin. Fax 344-7426

Burney, Shasta, Pop. 3,044
Fall River JUSD 1,200/K-12
20375 Tamarack Ave 96013 530-335-4538
Greg Hawkins, supt. Fax 335-3115
www.frjusd.org
Burney ES 400/K-6
37403 Toronto Ave 96013 530-335-2279
Marcy Schmidt, prin. Fax 335-2360
Other Schools – See Fall River Mills

Burnt Ranch, Trinity, Pop. 269
Burnt Ranch ESD 100/PK-8
PO Box 39 95527 530-629-2543
Kathleen Graham, supt. Fax 629-2479
www.bresd.org
Burnt Ranch ES 100/PK-8
PO Box 39 95527 530-629-2543
Kathleen Graham, prin. Fax 629-2479

Buttonwillow, Kern, Pop. 1,487
Buttonwillow UNESD 300/PK-8
42600 Highway 58 93206 661-764-5166
Stuart Packard, supt. Fax 764-5165
www.buttonwillow.k12.ca.us
Buttonwillow ES 300/PK-8
42600 Highway 58 93206 661-764-5248
Hiedi Witcher, prin. Fax 764-5805

Byron, Contra Costa, Pop. 1,236
Byron UNESD 1,600/PK-8
14301 Byron Hwy 94514 925-809-7500
Debbie Gold Ed.D., supt. Fax 634-9421
www.byronunionschooldistrict.us
Excelsior MS 600/6-8
14301 Byron Hwy 94514 925-809-7530
Paul Gengler, prin. Fax 634-5120
Other Schools – See Discovery Bay

Mountain House ESD 50/K-8
3950 Mountain House Rd 94514 209-835-2283
Marianne Griffith, admin. Fax 832-0284
www.mtnhouse.k12.ca.us
Mountain House ES 50/K-8
3950 Mountain House Rd 94514 209-835-2283
Marianne Griffith, admin. Fax 832-0284

Cabazon, Riverside, Pop. 2,434
Banning USD
Supt. — See Banning
Cabazon ES 300/K-5
50575 Carmen Ave 92230 951-922-0252
Alisha Norman, prin. Fax 922-2763

Calabasas, Los Angeles, Pop. 22,176
Las Virgenes USD 11,200/PK-12
4111 Las Virgenes Rd 91302 818-880-4000
Dan Stepenosky Ed.D., supt. Fax 880-4200
www.lvusd.org
Bay Laurel ES 600/K-5
24740 Paseo Primario 91302 818-222-9022
Elisa Cortina, prin. Fax 222-0231
Chaparral ES 600/K-5
22601 Liberty Bell Rd 91302 818-591-2428
Stephanie Brazell, prin. Fax 591-7056
Lupin Hill ES 600/K-5
26210 Adamor Rd 91302 818-880-4434
Scott Foli, prin. Fax 880-2201
Round Meadow ES 600/K-5
5151 Round Meadow Rd 91302 818-883-6750
George Hees, admin. Fax 883-7121
Stelle MS 800/6-8
22450 Mulholland Hwy 91302 818-224-4107
Ryan Emery, prin. Fax 224-4989
Wright MS 800/6-8
4029 Las Virgenes Rd 91302 818-880-4614
Elias Miles, prin. Fax 878-0453
Other Schools – See Agoura Hills, Westlake Village

MUSE ES PK-5
1666 Las Virgenes Canyon Rd 91302 818-880-5437
Jeff King, head sch Fax 880-5430
Viewpoint S 1,200/K-12
23620 Mulholland Hwy 91302 818-591-6500
Mark McKee, head sch Fax 591-0834

Calexico, Imperial, Pop. 38,495
Calexico USD 9,100/K-12
901 Andrade Ave 92231 760-768-3888
Maria Ambriz, supt. Fax 768-3856
www2.cusdk12.org/nsite/
Camarena JHS 700/7-8
800 E Rivera Ave 92231 760-768-3808
Diego Romero, prin. Fax 768-3807
Charles ES 500/K-6
1201 Kloke Rd 92231 760-768-3910
Siria Hurtado, prin. Fax 768-9640
Chavez ES 1,000/K-6
1251 E Zapata St 92231 760-768-6400
Jaime Santos, prin. Fax 357-8587
Dool ES 600/K-6
800 Encinas Ave 92231 760-768-3820
Joan Hanson, prin. Fax 357-8909
Jefferson ES 700/K-6
1120 E 7th St 92231 760-768-3812
Alejandro Avina, prin. Fax 768-1827
Kennedy Gardens ES 600/K-6
2300 Rockwood Ave 92231 760-768-3842
Gabriela Flores, prin. Fax 768-1670
Mains ES 500/K-6
655 Sheridan St 92231 760-768-3900
Bertha Noriega, prin. Fax 768-1446
Moreno JHS 800/7-8
1202 Kloke Ave 92231 760-768-3960
Mariano Velez, prin. Fax 768-1905
Rockwood ES 600/K-6
1000 Rockwood Ave 92231 760-768-3832
Dr. Ernesto Valenzuela, prin. Fax 768-1893

Calexico Mission S 300/K-12
601 E 1st St 92231 760-357-3711
Oscar Olivarria, prin. Fax 357-3713
Our Lady of Guadalupe Academy 600/PK-8
535 Rockwood Ave 92231 760-357-1986
Sr. Maria Elvia Gonzalez, prin. Fax 357-3282

Caliente, Kern
Caliente UNESD 100/PK-8
12400 Caliente Creek Rd 93518 661-867-2301
Kathleen S. Hansen, supt. Fax 867-6902
www.calienteschooldistrict.org
Piute Mountain ES 100/PK-8
12400 Caliente Creek Rd 93518 661-867-2301
Kathleen S. Hansen, admin. Fax 867-6902

California City, Kern, Pop. 13,467
Mojave USD
Supt. — See Mojave
California City MS 300/7-8
9736 Redwood Blvd 93505 760-373-3241
Jennifer Blake, prin. Fax 373-1355
Hacienda ES 500/4-6
19950 Hacienda Blvd 93505 760-373-5824
Shawnee Moore, prin. Fax 373-5787
Ulrich ES 700/K-3
9124 Catalpa Ave 93505 760-373-4824
Cheryl Bailey, prin. Fax 373-3309

California Hot Springs, Tulare, Pop. 35
Hot Springs ESD 50/K-8
PO Box 38 93207 661-548-6544
Tom Byars, supt. Fax 548-6254
www.tcoe.org/Districts/HotSprings.shtm
Hot Springs ES 50/K-8
PO Box 38 93207 661-548-6544
Tom Byars, admin. Fax 548-6254

Calimesa, Riverside, Pop. 7,727
Yucaipa-Calimesa JUSD
Supt. — See Yucaipa
Mesa View MS 800/6-8
800 Mustang Way 92320 909-790-8008
John Moore, prin. Fax 795-6810

Mesa Grande Academy 300/PK-12
975 Fremont St 92320 909-795-1112
Alfred Riddle, prin. Fax 795-1653

Calipatria, Imperial, Pop. 7,613
Calipatria USD 1,200/K-12
501 W Main St 92233 760-348-2892
Douglas Kline, supt. Fax 344-8926
www.calipatriahornets.org
Fremont PS 400/K-4
401 W Main St 92233 760-348-5025
Kelley Marmolejo, prin. Fax 348-2125
Young MS 400/5-8
220 S International Blvd 92233 760-348-2842
Virginia Calsada-Medina, prin. Fax 348-2848
Other Schools – See Niland

Calistoga, Napa, Pop. 5,085
Calistoga JUSD 800/K-12
1520 Lake St 94515 707-942-4703
Dr. Erin Smith-Hagberg, supt. Fax 942-6589
www.calistogaschools.org
Calistoga ES 500/K-6
1327 Berry St 94515 707-942-4398
Nicole Lamare, prin. Fax 942-0970

Calpella, Mendocino, Pop. 657

Waldorf S of Mendocino County 200/PK-8
PO Box 349 95418 707-485-8719

Camarillo, Ventura, Pop. 63,018
Pleasant Valley SD 7,000/PK-8
600 Temple Ave 93010 805-482-2763
Angelica Ramsey, supt. Fax 987-5511
www.pvsd.k12.ca.us
Camarillo Heights STEM Academy 400/PK-5
35 Catalina Dr 93010 805-482-9838
Claudia Stepan, prin. Fax 987-7189
Dos Caminos ES 300/PK-5
3635 Appian Way 93010 805-482-9894
Mark Asher, prin. Fax 482-7478
La Mariposa ES 700/K-5
4800 Corte Olivas 93012 805-987-8333
Justine Wienken, prin. Fax 383-8977
Las Colinas MS 900/6-8
5750 Fieldcrest Dr 93012 805-484-0461
Erik Goldman, prin. Fax 482-2443
Las Posas ES 500/PK-5
75 E Calle La Guerra 93010 805-482-4606
Vanessa Walker, prin. Fax 388-5431
Monte Vista MS 900/6-8
888 Lantana St 93010 805-482-8891
Katie Burchell, prin. Fax 987-8951
Pleasant Valley S of Engineering & Arts 400/PK-7
1099 Bedford Dr 93010 805-482-1954
Thomas Holtke, prin. Fax 388-8593
Rancho Rosal ES 600/PK-5
3535 Village at the Park Dr 93012 805-445-1147
John Reilley, prin. Fax 445-1244
Tierra Linda ES 700/K-5
1201 Woodcreek Rd 93012 805-445-8800
Robert Waggoner, prin. Fax 445-8804
Other Schools – See Santa Rosa Vlly

Beacon Hill Classical Academy 100/K-11
2304 Antonio Ave 93010 805-389-6581
Dennis Deutsch, head sch
Cornerstone Christian S 300/PK-8
1777 Arneill Rd 93010 805-987-8621
Colleen Brewer, prin. Fax 987-8208
Pleasant Valley Christian S 200/PK-8
1101 E Ponderosa Dr 93010 805-383-2672
Susan Wilson, prin. Fax 384-9328
St. Mary Magdalen S 200/K-8
2534 Ventura Blvd 93010 805-482-2611
Michael Ronan, prin. Fax 987-8211

Cambria, San Luis Obispo, Pop. 5,934
Coast USD 700/K-12
1350 Main St 93428 805-927-3880
Victoria Schumacher, supt. Fax 927-0312
www.coastusd.org
Cambria ES 300/K-5
3223 Main St 93428 805-927-4400
Jill Southern, prin. Fax 927-6753
Santa Lucia MS 200/6-8
2850 Schoolhouse Ln 93428 805-927-3693
John Calandro, prin. Fax 927-4015

Cameron Park, El Dorado, Pop. 17,664
Buckeye UNESD
Supt. — See El Dorado Hills
Blue Oak ES 600/K-5
2391 Merrychase Dr 95682 530-676-0164
Rachelle Ball, prin. Fax 676-0758
Camerado Springs MS 600/6-8
2480 Merrychase Dr 95682 530-677-1658
Doug Shupe, prin. Fax 677-9537

Camino, El Dorado, Pop. 1,712
Camino UNESD 500/K-8
3060 Snows Rd 95709 530-644-4552
Matthew Smith, supt. Fax 644-5412
www.caminoschool.org

Camino ES 400/K-8
3060 Snows Rd 95709 530-644-4552
Matthew Smith, prin. Fax 644-5412

Campbell, Santa Clara, Pop. 37,545
Campbell UNESD 7,600/K-8
155 N 3rd St 95008 408-364-4200
Dr. Shelly Viramontez, supt. Fax 341-7280
www.campbellusd.org
Campbell MS 700/5-8
295 Cherry Ln 95008 408-364-4222
Norma Jeanne Ready, prin. Fax 341-7150
Capri ES 700/K-5
850 Chapman Dr 95008 408-364-4260
David Wilce, prin. Fax 341-7120
Castlemont ES 700/K-5
3040 Payne Ave 95008 408-364-4233
Ivy Sarratt, prin. Fax 341-7050
Rosemary ES 500/K-4
401 W Hamilton Ave 95008 408-364-4254
Brian Schmaedick, prin. Fax 341-7010
Village S 300/K-5
825 W Parr Ave 95008 408-341-7042
Stephanie Lykam, prin. Fax 341-7040
Other Schools – See Los Gatos, San Jose, Saratoga

Campbell Christian S 200/PK-8
1075 W Campbell Ave 95008 408-370-4900
Shawn Stuart, supt. Fax 213-5640
Canyon Heights Academy 200/PK-8
775 Waldo Rd 95008 408-370-6727
Dr. Margaret Richardson, prin. Fax 370-7147
Casa Di Mir Montessori S 100/PK-8
90 E Latimer Ave 95008 408-370-3073
Wanda Whitehead, head sch Fax 370-3153
Delphi Academy of Campbell 100/K-8
1 W Campbell Ave Ste A110 95008 408-370-7400
Marcy Green, hdmstr.
St. Lucy S 300/PK-8
76 Kennedy Ave 95008 408-871-8023
Susan Grover, prin. Fax 378-4945
San Jose Christian S 300/PK-8
1300 Sheffield Ave 95008 408-371-7741
Jennifer Thompson, head sch Fax 371-5596
Springbridge International S 100/K-5
771 Waldo Rd 95008 408-370-7600
Robert Regan, head sch
West Valley Christian S 50/K-8
95 Dot Ave 95008 408-378-4327
Ennaoj Hawthorne, prin. Fax 378-4371

Campo, San Diego, Pop. 2,617
Mountain Empire USD
Supt. — See Pine Valley
Camp Lockett MS 100/6-8
31360 Hwy 94 91906 619-766-4464
Fax 766-4532
Campo S 400/PK-8
1654 Buckman Springs Rd 91906 619-478-5583
Mona Noren, prin. Fax 478-5982

Camptonville, Yuba, Pop. 138
Camptonville UNESD 500/K-12
PO Box 278 95922 530-288-3277
Sandra Ross M.Ed., supt. Fax 288-0805
www.cville.k12.ca.us
Camptonville ES 100/K-8
PO Box 278 95922 530-288-3277
Sandra Ross M.Ed., admin. Fax 288-0805

Canoga Park, See Los Angeles
Los Angeles USD
Supt. — See Los Angeles
Canoga Park Early Education Center PK-PK
7355 Vassar Ave 91303 818-348-2814
Sara Vasquez, prin. Fax 888-5736
Canoga Park ES 800/K-5
7438 Topanga Canyon Blvd 91303 818-340-3591
Roger Avila, prin. Fax 592-0845
Columbus MS 800/6-8
22250 Elkwood St 91304 818-702-1200
Debra McIntyre-Sciarrino, prin. Fax 348-2894
Fullbright Avenue ES 500/K-5
6940 Fullbright Ave 91306 818-340-6677
Michael Payne, prin. Fax 340-1052
Hart Street ES 900/K-5
21040 Hart St 91303 818-340-6222
Curtis Johnson, prin. Fax 340-8149
Limerick Avenue ES 800/K-5
8530 Limerick Ave 91306 818-341-1730
Betsy Garvin, prin. Fax 998-4912
Mosk ES 500/K-5
7335 Lubao Ave 91306 818-700-2020
Jodi Harrison, prin. Fax 882-1490
Sutter MS 1,100/6-8
7330 Winnetka Ave 91306 818-773-5800
Kelly Welsh, prin. Fax 341-3039
Winnetka Avenue ES 500/K-5
8240 Winnetka Ave 91306 818-341-5422
Annette Star, prin. Fax 998-1871

AGBU Manoogian-Demirdjian S 800/PK-12
6844 Oakdale Ave 91306 818-883-2428
Arpi Avanesian, prin. Fax 883-8353
Faith Baptist S 1,200/PK-12
7644 Farralone Ave 91304 818-340-6131
Roland Rasmussen, dir. Fax 592-0279
Our Lady of the Valley S 200/K-8
22041 Gault St 91303 818-592-2894
Dr. Lisa Zamora, prin. Fax 592-2896

Cantua Creek, Fresno, Pop. 466
Golden Plains USD
Supt. — See San Joaquin
Cantua S 200/K-8
PO Box 369 93608 559-829-3331
Ana Bustos-Ponce, prin. Fax 829-6783

Canyon, Contra Costa
Canyon ESD 100/K-8
PO Box 187 94516 925-376-4671
Gloria Faircloth, supt. Fax 376-2343
www.canyon.k12.ca.us
Canyon ES 100/K-8
PO Box 187 94516 925-376-4671
Gloria Faircloth, prin. Fax 376-2343

Canyon Country, See Santa Clarita
Saugus UNESD
Supt. — See Santa Clarita
Cedarcreek ES 600/K-6
27792 Camp Plenty Rd 91351 661-294-5310
Robin Payre, prin. Fax 298-3255
Rio Vista ES 700/K-6
20417 Cedarcreek St 91351 661-294-5330
Gina Nolte, prin. Fax 251-7466
Skyblue Mesa ES 500/K-6
28040 Hardesty Ave 91351 661-294-5350
Kimberly Humphries, prin. Fax 298-3256

Sulphur Springs UNESD 5,500/K-6
27000 Weyerhauser Way 91351 661-252-5131
Dr. Catherine Kawaguchi, supt. Fax 252-3589
www.sssd.k12.ca.us
Canyon Springs Community ES 500/K-6
19059 Vicci St 91351 661-252-4322
Julie Martinez, prin. Fax 252-0974
Cox Community ES 500/K-6
18643 Oakmoor St 91351 661-252-2100
Heather Drew, prin. Fax 299-4916
Mint Canyon Community ES 500/K-6
16400 Sierra Hwy 91351 661-252-2570
Roni Andrus, prin. Fax 298-3383
Mitchell Community ES 600/K-6
16821 Goodvale Rd 91387 661-252-9110
Marie Dacumos, prin. Fax 252-6537
Pinetree Community ES 600/K-6
29156 Lotusgarden Dr 91387 661-298-2280
Deb Stilson, prin. Fax 298-0331
Sulphur Springs Community ES 600/K-6
16628 Lost Canyon Rd 91387 661-252-2725
Eric Guerrero, prin. Fax 252-5403
Other Schools – See Newhall, Santa Clarita

William S. Hart UNHSD
Supt. — See Santa Clarita
Sierra Vista JHS 1,200/7-8
19425 Stillmore St 91351 661-252-3113
Carolyn Hoffman, prin. Fax 252-2790

Capistrano Beach, See Dana Point
Capistrano USD
Supt. — See San Juan Capistrano
Palisades ES 500/K-5
26462 Via Sacramento 92624 949-496-5942
Curt Visca, prin. Fax 496-7290

San Clemente Christian S 100/PK-10
25975 Domingo Ave 92624 949-496-3513
Rebecca Romo, prin. Fax 496-2138

Capitola, Santa Cruz, Pop. 9,578
Soquel UNESD 2,000/PK-8
620 Monterey Ave 95010 831-464-5633
Scott Turnbull, supt. Fax 479-7182
www.soqueldo.santacruz.k12.ca.us/
New Brighton MS 700/6-8
250 Washburn Ave 95010 831-464-5660
Craig Broadhurst, prin. Fax 464-5515
Opal Cliffs S PK-PK
620 Monterey Ave 95010 831-464-5670
Kerry le Roux, prin. Fax 476-5827
Other Schools – See Santa Cruz, Soquel

Cardiff by the Sea, See Encinitas
Cardiff SD 700/K-6
1888 Montgomery Ave 92007 760-632-5890
Jill Vinson, supt. Fax 942-5831
www.cardiffschools.com
Cardiff ES 400/K-3
1888 Montgomery Ave 92007 760-632-5892
Julie Parker, prin. Fax 632-5375
Harris S 400/3-6
1888 Montgomery Ave 92007 760-632-5894
Janelle Scheftner, prin. Fax 632-0585

Carlotta, Humboldt
Cuddeback UNESD 100/K-8
PO Box 7 95528 707-768-3372
Blaine Sigler, supt. Fax 768-3211
www.humboldt.k12.ca.us/cuddeback_sd
Cuddeback ES 100/K-8
PO Box 7 95528 707-768-3372
Blaine Sigler, prin. Fax 768-3211

Carlsbad, San Diego, Pop. 101,706
Carlsbad USD 11,000/K-12
6225 El Camino Real 92009 760-331-5000
Benjamin Churchill Ed.D., supt. Fax 431-6707
www.carlsbadusd.k12.ca.us
Aviara Oaks ES 700/K-5
6225 El Camino Real 92009 760-331-6000
James Hines, prin. Fax 438-4576
Aviara Oaks MS 1,100/6-8
6225 El Camino Real 92009 760-331-6100
Bryan Brockett, prin. Fax 729-3040
Buena Vista ES 300/K-5
6225 El Camino Real 92009 760-331-5400
Tina Howard, prin. Fax 720-0741
Calavera Hills ES 500/K-5
6225 El Camino Real 92009 760-331-6300
Kimberly Fuentes, prin. Fax 729-3040
Calavera Hills MS 500/6-8
6225 El Camino Real 92009 760-331-6400
Michael Ecker, prin. Fax 729-3040
Hope ES 600/K-5
6225 El Camino Real 92009 760-331-5900
Richard Tubbs, prin. Fax 729-4758
Jefferson ES 500/K-5
6225 El Camino Real 92009 760-331-5500
Chad Lund, prin. Fax 720-3809
Kelly ES 400/K-5
6225 El Camino Real 92009 760-331-5800
Tressie Armstrong, prin. Fax 720-0635
Magnolia ES 500/K-5
6225 El Camino Real 92009 760-331-5600
Aaron Nelson, prin. Fax 720-3879
Pacific Rim ES 900/K-5
6225 El Camino Real 92009 760-331-6200
Robert Devich, prin. Fax 929-1778
Poinsettia ES 500/K-5
6225 El Camino Real 92009 760-331-6500
Marjorie Giordani, prin. Fax 930-6005
Valley MS 1,000/6-8
6225 El Camino Real 92009 760-331-5300
Nicole Johnston, prin. Fax 720-2326

Encinitas UNESD
Supt. — See Encinitas
El Camino Creek ES 700/K-6
7885 Paseo Aliso 92009 760-943-2051
Jodi Greenberger, prin. Fax 943-2052
La Costa Heights ES 700/K-6
3035 Levante St 92009 760-944-4375
Christie Kay, prin. Fax 632-7627
Mission Estancia ES 600/K-6
3330 Calle Barcelona 92009 760-943-2004
Lisa McColl, prin. Fax 943-2008
Olivenhain Pioneer ES 700/K-6
8000 Calle Acervo 92009 760-943-2000
Beth Cameron, prin. Fax 943-2028

San Marcos USD
Supt. — See San Marcos
Carrillo ES 1,100/K-5
2875 Poinsettia Ln 92009 760-290-2900
Elizabeth Kannenberg, prin. Fax 736-2203
La Costa Meadows ES 1,000/K-5
6889 El Fuerte St 92009 760-290-2121
Adam Klimas, prin. Fax 290-2120

Beautiful Saviour Lutheran S 50/PK-8
3030 Valley St 92008 760-729-6272
Dave Nuejahr, prin. Fax 729-6573
St. Patrick's S 500/K-8
3820 Pio Pico Dr 92008 760-729-1333
Denise Nelson, prin. Fax 729-5174

Carmel, Monterey, Pop. 3,645
Carmel USD 2,500/PK-12
PO Box 222700 93922 831-624-1546
Barbara Dill-Varga, supt. Fax 626-4052
www.carmelunified.org
Carmel Child Development Center PK-PK
8460 Carmel Valley Rd 93923 831-624-8047
Laura Dunn, dir.
Carmel MS 600/6-8
PO Box 222740 93922 831-624-2785
Dan Morgan, prin. Fax 624-0839
Carmel River ES 500/K-5
PO Box 222700 93922 831-624-4609
Jay Marden, prin. Fax 624-6633
Other Schools – See Big Sur, Carmel Valley

All Saints' Day S 200/PK-8
8060 Carmel Valley Rd 93923 831-624-9171
Hugh Jebson, head sch Fax 624-3960
Junipero Serra S 200/K-8
3090 Rio Rd 93923 831-624-8322
Bruce Street, prin. Fax 624-8311
Stevenson S 200/PK-8
PO Box AP 93921 831-574-4600
Molly Bozzo, hdmstr. Fax 624-9044

Carmel Valley, Monterey, Pop. 980
Carmel USD
Supt. — See Carmel
Tularcitos ES 500/K-5
PO Box 966 93924 831-659-2276
Ryan Peterson, prin. Fax 659-1049

Carmichael, Sacramento, Pop. 58,920
San Juan USD 45,400/PK-12
PO Box 477 95609 916-971-7700
Kent Kern, supt. Fax 971-7758
www.sanjuan.edu
Barrett MS 700/6-8
4243 Barrett Rd 95608 916-971-7842
Brent Givens, prin. Fax 971-7839
Cameron Ranch ES 400/K-6
4333 Hackberry Ln 95608 916-575-2302
Tanya Reaves, prin. Fax 575-2305
Carmichael ES 400/K-5
6141 Sutter Ave 95608 916-971-5727
Brandei Smith, prin. Fax 971-5728
Churchill MS 1,000/6-8
4900 Whitney Ave 95608 916-971-7324
Michael Dolan, prin. Fax 971-7856
Coyle Avenue ES 400/K-5
6330 Coyle Ave 95608 916-867-2012
Holly Cybulski, prin. Fax 867-2019
Del Dayo ES 600/K-6
1301 McClaren Dr 95608 916-575-2323
Gianfranco Tornatore, prin. Fax 575-2328
Deterding ES 600/K-6
6000 Stanley Ave 95608 916-575-2338
Melanie Allen, prin. Fax 575-2341
Kelly ES 400/K-5
6301 Moraga Dr 95608 916-867-2041
Josh Costa, prin. Fax 867-2045
Marshall Children's Center 50/PK-PK
5309 Kenneth Ave 95608 916-971-7375
Jim Walters, admin. Fax 482-8389
Mission Avenue Open ES 500/K-6
2925 Mission Ave 95608 916-575-2362
Amberlee Townsend-Snider, prin. Fax 575-2413
Peck ES 400/K-5
6230 Rutland Dr 95608 916-867-2071
Mary Cardoso, prin. Fax 867-2075

Schweitzer ES 400/K-5
4350 Glenridge Dr 95608 916-867-2094
Rebecca Loper, prin. Fax 867-2092
Starr King S 600/K-8
4848 Cottage Way 95608 916-971-7318
Greta Scholtes, prin. Fax 971-7316
Other Schools – See Citrus Heights, Fair Oaks, Gold River, Orangevale, Sacramento

Our Lady of Assumption S 300/PK-8
2141 Walnut Ave 95608 916-489-8958
Robert Love, prin. Fax 489-3237
Sacramento Adventist Academy 200/PK-12
5601 Winding Way 95608 916-481-2300
Matthew Jakobsons M.A., prin. Fax 481-7426
St. John the Evangelist S 200/PK-8
5701 Locust Ave 95608 916-481-8845
Valerie Spangenberg, prin. Fax 481-1319
St. Michael's Episcopal Day S 200/PK-8
2140 Mission Ave 95608 916-485-3418
Mary Heise, head sch Fax 485-9084
Victory Christian S 200/K-12
3045 Garfield Ave 95608 916-488-5601
John Huffman, supt. Fax 488-2589

Carpinteria, Santa Barbara, Pop. 12,835
Carpinteria USD 2,300/K-12
1400 Linden Ave 93013 805-684-4511
Diana F. Rigby, supt. Fax 684-0218
www.cusd.net
Aliso ES 400/K-5
4545 Carpinteria Ave 93013 805-684-4539
Michelle Fox, prin. Fax 566-4759
Canalino ES 500/K-5
1480 Linden Ave 93013 805-684-4141
Jamie Persoon, prin. Fax 684-3384
Carpinteria MS 500/6-8
5351 Carpinteria Ave 93013 805-684-4544
Ron Briggs, prin. Fax 566-3839
Other Schools – See Summerland

Carson, Los Angeles, Pop. 87,081
Compton USD
Supt. — See Compton
Bunche ES 400/K-6
16223 Haskins Ln 90746 310-898-6120
Laronda Ortega, prin. Fax 329-6056

Los Angeles USD
Supt. — See Los Angeles
Ambler ES 500/K-5
319 E Sherman Dr 90746 310-532-4090
Gregory Hooker, prin. Fax 719-9881
Annalee Avenue ES 300/K-6
19410 Annalee Ave 90746 310-537-4740
Lachance Thompson, prin. Fax 764-4729
Bonita Street ES 500/K-5
21929 Bonita St 90745 310-834-8588
Jill Bradford, prin. Fax 834-8033
Broadacres Avenue ES 300/K-5
19424 Broadacres Ave 90746 310-537-1980
Ursula Martin, prin. Fax 639-4240
Carnegie MS 900/6-8
21820 Bonita St 90745 310-952-5700
Cheryl Nakata, prin. Fax 830-9015
Caroldale Avenue Learning Community 1,000/K-8
22424 Caroldale Ave 90745 310-320-8570
Hoff Brooks, prin. Fax 320-6803
Carson Street ES 700/K-5
161 E Carson St 90745 310-834-4508
Martin Leon, prin. Fax 549-9660
Catskill Avenue ES 600/K-5
23536 Catskill Ave 90745 310-834-7241
Suzanne Zopatti, prin. Fax 549-3742
Curtiss MS 700/6-8
1254 E Helmick St 90746 310-661-4500
Gina Russell-Williams, prin. Fax 537-2115
Del Amo ES 400/K-5
21228 Water St 90745 310-830-5351
Linda Sakurai, prin. Fax 830-6466
Dolores Street Early Education Center PK-PK
22309 Catskill Ave 90745 310-830-6987
Mercy Udeochu, prin. Fax 518-7842
Dolores Street ES 600/K-5
22526 Dolores St 90745 310-834-2565
Carolyn Battle, prin. Fax 830-6730
Dominguez ES 600/K-5
21250 S Santa Fe Ave 90810 310-835-7137
Rosalia McKay, prin. Fax 835-6071
Leapwood Avenue ES 300/K-5
19302 Leapwood Ave 90746 310-327-8245
Camellia Hudley, prin. Fax 527-7240
Towne Avenue ES 300/K-5
18924 Towne Ave 90746 310-329-3505
Mark Hirata, prin. Fax 329-3467
232nd Place ES 500/K-5
23240 Archibald Ave 90745 310-830-8710
Afia Hemphill, prin. Fax 835-1946
White MS 1,700/6-8
22102 Figueroa St 90745 310-783-4900
Adaina Brown, prin. Fax 782-8954

Carson Christian S 100/K-12
17705 Central Ave 90746 310-609-2300
Marian Alexander, prin.
St. Philomena S 300/K-8
21832 Main St 90745 310-835-4827
Sr. Mary Schik, prin. Fax 835-1655

Caruthers, Fresno, Pop. 2,460
Caruthers USD 1,400/K-12
PO Box 127 93609 559-864-6500
Orin Hirschkorn, supt. Fax 864-8857
www.caruthers.k12.ca.us
Caruthers ES 800/K-8
PO Box 7 93609 559-864-6500
Marla Dominguez, prin. Fax 864-0610

Castaic, Los Angeles, Pop. 18,337
Castaic UNSD
Supt. — See Valencia
Castaic ES 500/K-5
30455 Park Vista Dr 91384 661-257-4530
Stephanie Beach, prin. Fax 294-7854
Castaic MS 900/6-8
28900 Hillcrest Pkwy 91384 661-257-4550
Bob Brauneisen, prin. Fax 294-9714
Live Oak ES 600/K-5
27715 Saddleridge Way 91384 661-295-4540
Cynthia Seamands, prin. Fax 257-6384
Northlake Hills ES 600/K-7
32545 Ridge Route Rd 91384 661-257-4560
Erin Augusta, prin. Fax 295-3924

Castella, Shasta
Castle Rock UNESD 100/K-8
PO Box 180 96017 530-235-0101
Autumn Funk, supt. Fax 235-0257
www.castlerockschool.net
Castle Rock S 100/K-8
PO Box 180 96017 530-235-0101
Autumn Funk, prin. Fax 235-0257

Castro Valley, Alameda, Pop. 58,286
Castro Valley USD 9,300/PK-12
PO Box 2146 94546 510-537-3000
Parvin Ahmadi, supt. Fax 886-8962
www.cv.k12.ca.us
Alma Preschool PK-PK
4400 Alma Ave 94546 510-537-3000
Suzy Williams, dir. Fax 537-1403
Canyon MS 1,400/6-8
19600 Cull Canyon Rd 94552 510-538-8833
Matthew Steinecke, prin. Fax 247-9439
Castro Valley ES 500/K-5
20185 San Miguel Ave 94546 510-537-1919
Affie Sklut, prin. Fax 537-9892
Chabot ES 400/K-5
19104 Lake Chabot Rd 94546 510-537-2342
Vivienne Paratore, prin. Fax 537-9418
Creekside MS 800/6-8
19722 Center St 94546 510-247-0665
Jaliza Eagles, prin. Fax 581-6617
Independent ES 600/K-5
21201 Independent School Rd 94552 510-537-9558
Patrick Hansen-Schmitt, prin. Fax 537-9591
Jensen Ranch ES 400/K-5
20001 Carson Ln 94552 510-537-6365
Dustin Gacherieu, prin. Fax 728-9853
Marshall ES 500/K-5
20111 Marshall St 94546 510-537-2431
Tracie Christmas, prin. Fax 247-9826
Palomares ES 200/K-5
6395 Paloverde Rd 94552 510-582-4207
Jennifer Tomita, prin. Fax 582-3948
Proctor ES 500/K-5
17520 Redwood Rd 94546 510-537-0030
Lisa Garcia, prin. Fax 537-6752
Stanton ES 400/K-5
2644 Somerset Ave 94546 510-727-9192
Robin Ormsby, prin. Fax 247-9610
Vannoy ES 400/K-5
5100 Vannoy Ave 94546 510-537-1832
Greg Ko, prin. Fax 582-8599

Hayward USD
Supt. — See Hayward
Strobridge ES 700/K-6
21400 Bedford Dr 94546 510-723-3915
Charles Hill, prin. Fax 582-8566

Our Lady of Grace S 200/K-8
19920 Anita Ave 94546 510-581-3155
Susan Anderson, prin. Fax 581-1059
Redwood Christian ES 200/K-5
19300 Redwood Rd 94546 510-537-4288
Dale Huemoeller M.Ed., prin. Fax 728-4383

Castroville, Monterey, Pop. 6,411
North Monterey County USD
Supt. — See Moss Landing
Castroville ES 600/K-6
11161 Merritt St 95012 831-633-2570
Kyle Griffith, prin. Fax 633-0642
Elkhorn ES 600/K-6
2235 Elkhorn Rd 95012 831-633-2405
Sandra Cuevas, prin. Fax 633-0863
North Monterey County MS 600/7-8
10301 Seymour St 95012 831-633-3391
Marisa Martinez, prin. Fax 633-3680

Cathedral City, Riverside, Pop. 50,401
Palm Springs USD
Supt. — See Palm Springs
Agua Caliente ES 600/K-5
30800 San Luis Rey Dr 92234 760-416-8235
Ingrid Lin, prin. Fax 416-8245
Cathedral City ES 800/K-5
69300 Converse Rd 92234 760-770-8583
Jessica Whiteman, prin. Fax 770-4703
Coffman MS 1,100/6-8
34603 Plumley Rd 92234 760-770-8617
Carlos Flores, prin. Fax 770-8623
Landau ES 700/K-5
30310 Landau Blvd 92234 760-770-8600
Wendy Meka, prin. Fax 770-8607
Rio Vista ES 700/K-5
67700 Verona Rd 92234 760-416-0032
Dr. Steve Marlatt Ed.D., prin. Fax 416-0087
Sunny Sands ES 1,000/K-5
69310 McCallum Way 92234 760-770-8635
Pam Horton, prin. Fax 770-8641
Workman MS 1,400/6-8
69300 30th Ave 92234 760-770-8540
Brad Sauer, prin. Fax 770-8545

Cayucos, San Luis Obispo, Pop. 2,521
Cayucos ESD 200/K-8
301 Cayucos Dr 93430 805-995-3694
Scott Smith, supt. Fax 995-2876
www.cayucosschool.org
Cayucos ES 200/K-8
301 Cayucos Dr 93430 805-995-3694
Scott Smith, admin. Fax 995-2876

Cazadero, Sonoma, Pop. 340
Fort Ross ESD 50/K-8
30600 Seaview Rd 95421 707-847-3390
John Markatos, supt. Fax 847-3312
www.fortrossschool.org
Fort Ross ES 50/K-8
30600 Seaview Rd 95421 707-847-3390
John Markatos, prin. Fax 847-3312

Montgomery ESD 50/K-8
PO Box 286 95421 707-632-5221
John Quinn, supt. Fax 632-5749
www.scoe.org/pub/district/64
Montgomery ES 50/K-8
PO Box 286 95421 707-632-5221
Judy Mercieca, prin. Fax 632-5749

Cedarville, Modoc, Pop. 502
Surprise Valley JUSD 100/K-12
PO Box 100 96104 530-279-6141
Janelle Anderson, supt. Fax 279-2210
www.svjusd.org
Surprise Valley S 100/K-8
PO Box 100 96104 530-279-6161
Brian Marquardt, prin. Fax 279-6154

Ceres, Stanislaus, Pop. 43,964
Ceres USD 12,300/PK-12
PO Box 307 95307 209-556-1500
Scott Siegel, supt. Fax 556-1090
www.ceres.k12.ca.us
Beaver ES 100/K-6
PO Box 307 95307 209-556-1730
Libby Holmes, prin. Fax 541-3831
Blaker-Kinser JHS 600/7-8
PO Box 307 95307 209-556-1810
Paul Rutishauser, prin. Fax 541-0174
Caswell ES 500/PK-6
PO Box 307 95307 209-556-1620
Alfonso Navarro, prin. Fax 538-1536
Chavez JHS 600/7-8
PO Box 307 95307 209-556-1830
Rosemarie Kloepfer, prin. Fax 538-3970
Don Pedro ES 600/PK-6
PO Box 307 95307 209-556-1630
Tami Garcia, prin. Fax 538-2856
Fowler ES 700/K-6
PO Box 307 95307 209-556-1640
Bruce Clifton, prin. Fax 538-7822
Hensley JHS 600/7-8
PO Box 307 95307 209-556-1820
Carol Lubinsky, prin. Fax 538-9428
Hidahl ES 500/K-6
PO Box 307 95307 209-556-1650
Vaughn Williams, prin. Fax 581-9761
La Rosa ES 600/K-6
PO Box 307 95307 209-556-1660
Lori Mariani, prin. Fax 538-7346
Lucas ES 200/K-6
PO Box 307 95307 209-556-1720
Israel Gonzalez, prin. Fax 541-0498
Sinclear ES 700/K-6
PO Box 307 95307 209-556-1680
Connie Stark, prin. Fax 538-3910
Vaughn ES 600/K-6
PO Box 307 95307 209-556-1690
Jesse Campbell, prin. Fax 541-1363
White ES 700/K-6
PO Box 307 95307 209-556-1710
Edith Narayan, prin. Fax 538-0276
Other Schools – See Modesto

Central Valley Christian Academy 200/PK-12
2020 Academy Pl 95307 209-537-4521
John Soule, prin. Fax 538-0706

Cerritos, Los Angeles, Pop. 47,521
ABC USD 20,700/K-12
16700 Norwalk Blvd 90703 562-926-5566
Mary Sieu, supt. Fax 404-1092
www.abcusd.k12.ca.us
Bragg ES 600/K-6
11501 Bos St 90703 562-229-7830
Annette Janeway, prin. Fax 402-2580
Carmenita MS 700/7-8
13435 166th St 90703 562-229-7775
Robert Castillo, prin. Fax 404-7807
Carver ES 600/K-6
19200 Ely Ave 90703 562-229-7840
Deborah Berlyn, prin. Fax 402-8678
Cerritos ES 700/K-6
13600 183rd St 90703 562-229-7845
Kevin Amburgey, prin. Fax 404-4635
Gonsalves ES 600/K-6
13650 Park St 90703 562-229-7860
Robert Benko, prin. Fax 802-0483
Haskell MS 500/7-8
11525 Del Amo Blvd 90703 562-229-7815
Camille Lewis, prin. Fax 809-7250
Juarez ES 300/K-6
11939 Aclare St 90703 562-229-7870
Christine Balbuena, prin. Fax 809-3093
Leal ES 800/K-6
12920 Droxford St 90703 562-229-7880
Paul Andre White, prin. Fax 402-5950
Nixon ES 800/K-6
19600 Jacob Ave 90703 562-229-7895
Melinda Ortiz, prin. Fax 865-1249
Stowers ES 600/K-6
13350 Beach St 90703 562-229-7905
Dr. Tom Tracy, prin. Fax 404-9017
Tetzlaff MS 600/7-8
12351 Del Amo Blvd 90703 562-229-7795
Kester Song, prin. Fax 402-6412
Wittmann ES 600/K-6
16801 Yvette Ave 90703 562-229-7915
Miguel Marco, prin. Fax 921-3940

Other Schools – See Artesia, Hawaiian Gardens, Lakewood

Valley Christian MS 300/7-8
18100 Dumont Ave 90703 562-865-6519
Brian Petteys, prin. Fax 403-3159

Challenge, Yuba, Pop. 1,096
Marysville JUSD
Supt. — See Marysville
Yuba Feather ES 100/K-6
PO Box 398 95925 530-740-4040
Duane Triplett, prin. Fax 675-2618

Chatsworth, See Los Angeles
Los Angeles USD
Supt. — See Los Angeles
Chatsworth Park ES 400/K-5
22005 Devonshire St 91311 818-341-1371
Rachelle Ratner, prin. Fax 882-3540
Lawrence MS 1,500/6-8
10100 Variel Ave 91311 818-678-7900
Maria Pigliapoco, prin. Fax 349-4539
Superior ES 600/K-5
9756 Oso Ave 91311 818-349-1410
Claudette Williamson, prin. Fax 886-8748

Al-Falaq/Meraj Academy 100/PK-8
11070 Old Santa Susana Pass 91311 818-886-5831
Nazmuddin Mohammed, dir. Fax 886-2896
Chaminade College Prep MS 700/6-8
19800 Devonshire St 91311 818-363-8127
Michael Valentine, prin. Fax 363-1219
Chatsworth Hills Academy 200/PK-8
PO Box 5077 91313 818-998-4037
Adrian Allan, head sch Fax 998-4062
Egremont S 100/PK-5
19850 Devonshire St 91311 818-363-7803
Monarch Christian S 100/PK-5
22280 Devonshire St 91311 818-882-3621
Amanda Diaz, head sch Fax 349-2027
St. John Eudes S 300/K-8
9925 Mason Ave 91311 818-341-1454
Barbara Danowitz, prin. Fax 341-3093
Sierra Canyon S 400/PK-6
11052 Independence Ave 91311 818-882-8121
James Skrumbis, hdmstr. Fax 882-8218

Chester, Plumas, Pop. 2,075
Plumas USD
Supt. — See Quincy
Chester ES 200/K-6
PO Box 826 96020 530-258-3194
Erin Mongiello, prin. Fax 258-3195

Chico, Butte, Pop. 82,892
Chico USD 12,400/PK-12
1163 E 7th St 95928 530-891-3000
Kelly Staley, supt. Fax 891-3220
www.chicousd.org
Bidwell JHS 600/6-8
2376 North Ave 95926 530-891-3080
David McKay, prin. Fax 891-3082
Chapman ES 300/PK-5
1071 E 16th St 95928 530-891-3100
Mike Allen, prin. Fax 891-3294
Chico JHS 600/6-8
280 Memorial Way 95926 530-891-3066
Pedro Caldera, prin. Fax 891-3264
Citrus Avenue ES 300/PK-5
1350 Citrus Ave 95926 530-891-3107
Rachel Tadeo, prin. Fax 891-3180
Dow ES 300/K-5
1420 Neal Dow Ave 95926 530-891-3110
Dave Murgia, prin. Fax 891-3184
Hooker Oak Open ES 300/K-5
1238 Arbutus Ave 95926 530-891-3119
Brian Holderman, prin. Fax 891-3120
Little Chico Creek ES 500/K-5
2090 Amanda Way 95928 530-891-3285
Kristin Schrock, prin. Fax 891-3288
Marigold ES 500/K-5
2446 Marigold Ave 95926 530-891-3121
Shawneese Heath, prin. Fax 891-3242
Marsh JHS 600/6-8
2253 Humboldt Rd 95928 530-895-4110
Jessica Kamph, prin. Fax 895-4111
McManus ES 400/PK-5
988 East Ave 95926 530-891-3128
Tina Keene, prin. Fax 891-3130
Parkview ES 300/K-5
1770 E 8th St 95928 530-891-3114
Heather Sufuentes, prin. Fax 891-3230
Rosedale ES 500/K-5
100 Oak St 95928 530-891-3104
JoAnn Bettencourt, prin. Fax 891-3169
Shasta ES 600/K-5
169 Leora Ct 95973 530-891-3141
Bruce Besnard, prin. Fax 891-3239
Sierra View ES 600/K-5
1598 Hooker Oak Ave 95926 530-891-3117
Mele Benz, prin. Fax 891-3186
Wilson ES 500/K-5
1530 W 8th Ave 95926 530-891-3297
Kim Rodgers, prin. Fax 891-4097

Chico Oaks Adventist S 100/K-8
1859 Hooker Oak Ave 95926 530-342-5043
Rick Nelson, prin. Fax 342-8402
Notre Dame S 200/K-8
435 Hazel St 95928 530-342-2502
Teresa Schwabauer, prin. Fax 342-6292

Chinese Camp, Tuolumne, Pop. 120
Jamestown ESD
Supt. — See Jamestown
Chinese Camp ES 50/2-5
13444 Red Hills Rd 95309 209-984-5217
Contessa Pelfrey, prin. Fax 984-0434

Chino, San Bernardino, Pop. 76,369
Chino Valley USD 29,100/K-12
5130 Riverside Dr 91710 909-628-1201
Wayne Joseph, supt. Fax 548-6096
www.chino.k12.ca.us
Borba Fundamental ES 600/K-6
4980 Riverside Dr 91710 909-627-9638
Gerson Renderos, prin. Fax 548-6086
Briggs Fundamental S 900/K-8
11880 Roswell Ave 91710 909-628-6497
Debra Letcher-Boeve, prin. Fax 548-6085
Cal Aero Preserve Academy 1,000/K-8
15850 Main St 91708 909-606-8531
Shawna Petit-Dinkins, prin. Fax 548-6023
Cattle ES 700/K-6
13590 Cypress Ave 91710 909-591-2755
Sara Peckham, prin. Fax 465-9414
Cortez ES 800/K-6
12750 Carissa Ave 91710 909-627-9438
Yvette Farley, prin. Fax 548-6069
Dickson ES 600/K-6
3930 Pamela Dr 91710 909-591-2653
Randal Buencristiani, prin. Fax 548-6070
Magnolia JHS 800/7-8
13150 Mountain Ave 91710 909-627-9263
John Miller, prin. Fax 627-2165
Marshall ES 500/K-6
12045 Telephone Ave 91710 909-627-9741
Diane Escalante, prin. Fax 364-1283
Newman ES 700/K-6
4150 Walnut Ave 91710 909-627-9758
Luke Hackney, prin. Fax 548-6064
Ramona JHS 600/7-8
4575 Walnut Ave 91710 909-627-9144
Gabriela Rivas-Lopez, prin. Fax 548-6055
Rhodes ES 800/K-6
6655 Schaefer Ave 91710 909-364-0683
Dr. Tracy Freed, prin. Fax 548-4399
Walnut Avenue ES 800/K-6
5550 Walnut Ave 91710 909-627-9817
Karen Morales, prin. Fax 548-0205
Other Schools – See Chino Hills, Ontario

St. Margaret Mary S 300/PK-8
12664 Central Ave 91710 909-591-8419
Waylynn Senn, prin. Fax 591-6960
St. Paul the Apostle Preschool 50/PK-PK
3683 Chino Ave 91710 909-325-8950
Christina Stutzman, dir.

Chino Hills, San Bernardino, Pop. 72,538
Chino Valley USD
Supt. — See Chino
Butterfield Ranch ES 700/K-6
6350 Mystic Canyon Dr 91709 909-591-0766
Patti Jewell, prin. Fax 548-6078
Canyon Hills JHS 1,100/7-8
2500 Madrugada Dr 91709 909-464-9938
Todd Finkbiner, prin. Fax 548-6058
Chaparral ES 600/K-6
4849 Bird Farm Rd 91709 909-606-4871
Brandon Davis, prin.
Country Springs ES 500/K-6
14145 Village Center Dr 91709 909-590-8212
Tom Mackessy, prin. Fax 548-6079
Eagle Canyon ES 600/K-6
13435 Eagle Canyon Dr 91709 909-590-2707
Laurie Warner, prin. Fax 548-6073
Glenmeade ES 600/K-6
15000 Whirlaway Ln 91709 909-393-4087
Denise Sunderland, prin. Fax 393-3285
Hidden Trails ES 500/K-6
2250 Ridgeview Dr 91709 909-597-0288
Lisa Sura, prin. Fax 548-6081
Litel ES 500/K-6
3425 Eucalyptus Ave 91709 909-591-1336
Joseph Durkin, prin. Fax 548-6072
Oak Ridge ES 700/K-6
15452 Valle Vista Dr 91709 909-591-1239
Christine Hinkle, prin. Fax 393-0792
Rolling Ridge ES 500/K-6
13677 Calle San Marcos 91709 909-628-9375
Paula Thomas, prin. Fax 591-1435
Townsend JHS 1,100/7-8
15359 Ilex Dr 91709 909-591-2161
Robert Nelson, prin. Fax 548-6057
Wickman ES 900/K-6
16250 Pinehurst Dr 91709 909-393-3774
Tom Rummell, prin. Fax 597-2726

Heights Christian S Chino Hills Campus 200/K-6
2549 Madrugada Dr 91709 909-465-9905
Randy Long, prin. Fax 902-0556
Loving Savior Lutheran S 300/PK-8
14816 Peyton Dr 91709 909-597-2948
Valorie Wend, prin. Fax 393-4659
Montessori S of Chino Hills 100/K-6
14635 Pipeline Ave 91709 909-393-1982
Ranjanie Searasinghe, dir.

Chowchilla, Madera, Pop. 17,893
Alview-Dairyland UNESD 400/K-8
12861 Avenue 18 1/2 93610 559-665-2394
Loren York M.A., supt. Fax 665-7347
www.adusd.k12.ca.us
Alview S 200/K-3
20513 Road 4 93610 559-665-2275
Loren York M.A., prin. Fax 665-8510
Dairyland S 200/4-8
12861 Avenue 18 1/2 93610 559-665-2394
Loren York M.A., prin. Fax 665-7347

Chowchilla ESD 2,200/PK-8
PO Box 910 93610 559-665-8000
Dr. Charles Martin, supt. Fax 665-5134
www.chowchillaelem.k12.ca.us
Fairmead ES 500/5-6
PO Box 910 93610 559-665-8040
Terry Barnes, prin. Fax 665-8003
Fuller ES 500/1-2
PO Box 910 93610 559-665-8050
Michelle Worrell, prin. Fax 665-8026
Reagan ES 500/3-4
PO Box 910 93610 559-665-8080
Melissa Esquivel, prin. Fax 665-8083
Stephens S 300/PK-K
PO Box 910 93610 559-665-8060
Eric Griffin, prin. Fax 665-0219
Wilson MS 500/7-8
PO Box 910 93610 559-665-8070
Zach White, prin. Fax 665-8004

Chowchilla Seventh-Day Adventist S 50/K-8
22308 Road 13 93610 559-665-1853
Erin Messinger, prin. Fax 665-0612

Chualar, Monterey, Pop. 1,183
Chualar UNESD 300/K-8
PO Box 188 93925 831-679-2504
Roberto Rios, supt. Fax 679-2071
chualarusd.org
Chualar S 300/K-8
PO Box 188 93925 831-679-2313
Roberto Rios, prin. Fax 679-2071

Chula Vista, San Diego, Pop. 235,860
Chula Vista ESD 29,600/PK-12
84 E J St 91910 619-425-9600
Francisco Escobedo Ed.D., supt. Fax 427-0463
www.cvesd.org
Camarena ES 900/K-6
1650 Exploration Falls Dr 91915 619-591-5500
Jonathan Strout, prin. Fax 421-5003
Casillas ES 600/K-6
1130 E J St 91910 619-421-7555
Chris Vickers, prin. Fax 421-3008
Castle Park ES 400/K-6
25 Emerson St 91911 619-422-5301
Alicia Moreno, prin. Fax 422-4452
Chula Vista Hills ES 600/K-6
980 Buena Vista Way 91910 619-482-7066
Jacob Ruth, prin. Fax 482-6823
Clear View ES 500/K-6
455 Windrose Way 91910 619-498-3000
Erin Thiessen, prin. Fax 498-3007
Cook ES 400/K-6
875 Cuyamaca Ave 91911 619-422-8381
Gabriela Llamas, prin. Fax 427-3407
Eastlake ES 600/K-6
1955 Hillside Dr 91913 619-421-4798
Dr. Eric Banatao, prin. Fax 421-4516
Halecrest ES 500/K-6
475 E J St 91910 619-421-0771
Amber MacDonald, prin. Fax 421-8746
Harborside ES 600/K-6
681 Naples St 91911 619-422-8369
Dr. Olivia Amador-Valerio, prin. Fax 422-7361
Hedenkamp ES 1,100/K-6
930 E Palomar St 91913 619-397-5828
Gina Mazeau, prin. Fax 397-7174
Heritage ES 900/K-6
1450 Santa Lucia Rd 91913 619-421-7080
Ruth Diaz de Leon, prin. Fax 421-8525
Hilltop Drive ES 600/K-6
30 Murray St 91910 619-422-8323
Bill Willis, prin. Fax 691-1375
Kellogg ES 300/K-6
229 E Naples St 91911 619-420-4151
Sylvia Echevarria, prin. Fax 408-1433
Lauderbach ES 800/K-6
390 Palomar St 91911 619-422-1127
Melody Belcher, prin. Fax 426-5875
Liberty ES 700/K-6
2175 Proctor Valley Rd 91914 619-397-5225
Charles Grisier, prin. Fax 397-2833
Loma Verde ES 500/K-6
1450 Loma Ln 91911 619-420-3940
Sobeida Velazquez, prin. Fax 422-2667
Marshall ES 700/K-6
2295 MacKenzie Creek Rd 91914 619-656-6252
Monica Loyce, prin. Fax 656-4248
McMillin ES 900/K-6
1201 Santa Cora Ave 91913 619-397-0103
Cynthia Orr, prin. Fax 397-0122
Montgomery ES 400/K-6
1601 4th Ave 91911 619-422-6131
Monica Ruiz, prin. Fax 426-6836
Muraoka ES K-6
1644 Santa Alexia Ave 91913 619-216-5599
Erin Dare, prin. Fax 216-3377
Muraoka ES K-5
1644 Santa Alexia Ave 91913 619-409-6639
Erin Dare, prin. Fax 216-3377
Olympic View ES 800/K-6
1220 S Greensview Dr 91915 619-656-2030
Gloria McKearney, prin. Fax 656-8752
Otay ES 600/K-6
1651 Albany Ave 91911 619-425-4311
Monica Castillo, prin. Fax 425-2018
Palomar ES 400/K-6
300 E Palomar St 91911 619-420-0134
David Munoz, prin. Fax 420-8416
Parkview ES 400/K-6
575 Juniper St 91911 619-421-5483
Mathew Shy, prin. Fax 421-2119
Rice ES 700/K-6
915 4th Ave 91911 619-420-7071
Veronica Konkoly, prin. Fax 420-6124
Rogers ES 500/K-6
510 E Naples St 91911 619-656-2082
Erika Taylor, prin. Fax 421-1423
Rohr ES 400/K-6
1540 Malta Ave 91911 619-420-5533
Michael Perez, prin. Fax 476-0850
Rosebank ES 600/K-6
80 Flower St 91910 619-422-8329
Neil MacGaffey, prin. Fax 422-5014
Salt Creek ES 1,000/K-6
1055 Hunte Pkwy 91914 619-397-5494
Lalaine Perez, prin. Fax 397-4669

Tiffany ES 600/K-6
1691 Elmhurst St 91913 619-421-6300
Christopher Carroll, prin. Fax 482-3115

Valle Lindo ES 500/K-6
1515 Oleander Ave 91911 619-421-5151
Erik Latoni, prin. Fax 421-1802

Veterans ES 900/K-6
1550 Magdalena Ave 91913 619-216-1226
Froylan Villanueva, prin. Fax 216-9226

Vista Square ES 600/K-6
540 G St 91910 619-422-8374
Marissa Allan, prin. Fax 691-1086

Wolf Canyon ES 600/K-6
1950 Wolf Canyon Loop 91913 619-482-8877
Debra McLaren, prin. Fax 482-7766

Other Schools – See Bonita, San Diego

Sweetwater UNHSD 40,100/K-12
1130 5th Ave 91911 619-691-5500
Dr. Karen Janney, supt. Fax 498-1997
www.sweetwaterschools.org

Bonita Vista MS 1,100/7-8
650 Otay Lakes Rd 91910 619-397-2200
Eduardo Reyes, prin. Fax 482-9356

Castle Park MS 800/7-8
160 Quintard St 91911 619-498-6000
Gina Galvez-Mallari, prin. Fax 427-8045

Chula Vista MS 1,000/7-8
415 5th Ave 91910 619-498-6800
Julissa Gracias, prin. Fax 427-5723

Eastlake MS 1,700/7-8
900 Duncan Ranch Rd 91914 619-591-4000
Ricardo Cooke, prin. Fax 482-0553

Hilltop MS 1,200/7-8
44 E J St 91910 619-498-2700
Griselda Delgado, prin. Fax 585-3576

Rancho del Rey MS 1,700/7-8
1174 E J St 91910 619-397-2500
Juan Ulloa, prin. Fax 656-3810

Other Schools – See National City, San Diego

Calvary Christian Academy 400/PK-12
1771 E Palomar St 91913 619-591-2260
Dr. Richard Andujo, hdmstr. Fax 591-2261

Christian ES South 200/PK-8
482 L St 91911 619-422-5850
Brenda Sniff, admin. Fax 422-5012

Juan Diego Academy K-4
1615 Mater Dei Dr 91913 619-421-2121
Leticia Oseguera, prin.

Pilgrim Lutheran S 200/PK-8
497 E St 91910 619-420-6233
Bonnie Sanchez, admin. Fax 422-2740

St. Pius X S 300/PK-8
37 E Emerson St 91911 619-422-2015
John Turskey, prin. Fax 422-0048

St. Rose of Lima S 400/PK-8
278 Alvarado St Unit 2 91910 619-422-1121
Jeff Saavedra, prin. Fax 422-8007

Citrus Heights, Sacramento, Pop. 79,798

San Juan USD
Supt. — See Carmichael

Arlington Heights ES 300/K-5
6401 Trenton Way 95621 916-971-5234
Rafael Martinez, prin. Fax 725-4599

Cambridge Heights ES 400/K-5
5555 Fleetwood Dr 95621 916-867-2000
Michele Flagler, prin. Fax 867-2004

Carriage Drive ES 500/K-6
7519 Carriage Dr 95621 916-971-5241
Brooke Thomas, prin. Fax 971-5326

Grand Oaks ES 300/K-5
7901 Rosswood Dr 95621 916-971-5208
Suzanne Landuyt, prin. Fax 722-3897

Kingswood ES 600/K-8
5700 Primrose Dr 95610 916-867-2046
Vera Morris, prin. Fax 867-2053

Lichen S 600/K-8
8319 Lichen Dr 95621 916-971-5237
Heidi Garner, prin. Fax 729-4578

Mariposa Avenue ES 400/K-5
7940 Mariposa Ave 95610 916-971-5212
Candice Flint, prin. Fax 725-8793

Skycrest ES 500/K-5
5641 Mariposa Ave 95610 916-867-2098
Sandra Rangel, prin. Fax 867-2083

Sylvan MS 500/7-8
7085 Auburn Blvd 95621 916-971-7873
Kirk Bebout, prin. Fax 971-7896

Woodside S 600/K-8
8248 Villa Oak Dr 95610 916-971-5216
Marianne Williams, prin. Fax 726-7169

Faith Christian Academy 100/PK-8
7737 Highland Ave 95610 916-725-5707
Doyle Champlain, admin.

Holy Family S 300/PK-8
7817 Old Auburn Rd 95610 916-722-7788
Joshua Rucker, prin. Fax 722-5297

St. Mark's Lutheran S 100/PK-8
7869 Kingswood Dr 95610 916-961-7891
Matthew Bauer, prin. Fax 961-5034

City of Industry, Los Angeles, Pop. 217

Bassett USD
Supt. — See La Puente

Torch MS 800/6-8
751 Vineland Ave 91746 626-931-2700
Dr. Monica Murray Ed.D., prin. Fax 931-2702

Hacienda La Puente USD 19,900/K-12
PO Box 60002 91716 626-933-1000
Cynthia Parulan-Colfer, supt. Fax 855-3505
www.hlpschools.org

Other Schools – See Hacienda Heights, La Puente, Valinda

Claremont, Los Angeles, Pop. 33,627

Claremont USD 7,000/PK-12
170 W San Jose Ave 91711 909-398-0609
James Elsasser Ed.D., supt. Fax 398-0690
www.cusd.claremont.edu

Chaparral ES 700/K-6
451 Chaparral Dr 91711 909-398-0305
Lisa Yamashita, prin. Fax 398-0306

Condit ES 700/K-6
1750 N Mountain Ave 91711 909-398-0300
Dr. Christine Malally, prin. Fax 398-0479

El Roble IS 1,100/7-8
665 N Mountain Ave 91711 909-398-0343
Scott Martinez, prin. Fax 398-0399

Mountain View ES 500/K-6
851 Santa Clara Ave 91711 909-398-0308
Ralph Patterson, prin. Fax 624-0289

Oakmont ES 300/PK-6
120 W Green St 91711 909-398-0313
Jennifer Adams, prin. Fax 625-8463

Sumner ES 600/PK-6
1770 Sumner Ave 91711 909-398-0320
Brenda Hamlett, prin. Fax 398-0380

Sycamore ES 400/K-6
225 W 8th St 91711 909-398-0324
Amy Stanger, prin. Fax 625-6004

Vista Del Valle ES 300/PK-6
550 Vista Dr 91711 909-398-0331
Brad Cuff, prin. Fax 398-0017

Foothill Country Day S 300/PK-8
1035 Harrison Ave 91711 909-626-5681
Michael Silva, head sch Fax 625-4251

Our Lady of the Assumption S 400/K-8
611 W Bonita Ave 91711 909-626-7135
Bernadette Boyle, prin. Fax 398-1395

Western Christian S 400/PK-8
3105 Padua Ave 91711 909-624-8291
Blair Bryant, supt. Fax 621-4506

Clayton, Contra Costa, Pop. 10,503

Mount Diablo USD
Supt. — See Concord

Diablo View MS 600/6-8
300 Diablo View Ln 94517 925-672-0898
Patti Bannister, prin. Fax 672-4327

Mount Diablo ES 800/K-5
5880 Mt Zion Dr 94517 925-672-4840
Dawn Edwards, prin. Fax 673-9723

Clearlake, Lake, Pop. 14,540

Konocti USD
Supt. — See Lower Lake

Burns Valley S 500/K-7
PO Box 7090 95422 707-994-2272
Chris Schoeneman, prin. Fax 994-7349

Pomo S 600/K-7
3350 Acacia St 95422 707-994-6744
Joseph Madrid, prin. Fax 994-4558

Clearlake SDA Christian S 50/1-8
PO Box 5686 95422 707-994-6356
Dolly Milholland, prin. Fax 994-6356

Clearlake Oaks, Lake, Pop. 2,265

Konocti USD
Supt. — See Lower Lake

East Lake ES 100/K-6
PO Box 577 95423 707-998-3387
Thad Owens, prin. Fax 998-4936

Cloverdale, Sonoma, Pop. 8,447

Cloverdale USD 1,400/PK-12
97 School St 95425 707-894-1920
Jeremy Decker, supt. Fax 894-1922
www.cusd.org/

Jefferson ES 600/PK-4
315 North St 95425 707-894-1930
Dr. Susan Yakich Ed.D., prin. Fax 894-1906

Washington MS 400/5-8
129 S Washington St 95425 707-894-1940
Mark Lucchetti, prin. Fax 894-1946

Clovis, Fresno, Pop. 92,614

Clovis USD 38,200/K-12
1450 Herndon Ave 93611 559-327-9000
Eimear O'Farrell Ed.D., supt. Fax 327-9109
www.cusd.com

Alta Sierra IS 1,400/7-8
380 W Teague Ave, 559-327-3500
Steve Pagani, prin. Fax 327-3590

Cedarwood ES 800/K-6
2851 Palo Alto Ave 93611 559-327-6000
Matthew Lucas, prin. Fax 327-6090

Century ES 700/K-6
965 N Sunnyside Ave 93611 559-327-8400
Brion Warren, prin. Fax 327-8490

Clark IS 1,500/7-8
902 5th St 93612 559-327-1500
Teresa Barber, prin. Fax 327-1556

Clovis ES 600/K-6
1100 Armstrong Ave 93611 559-327-6100
Isabel Facio, prin. Fax 327-6190

Cole ES 800/K-6
615 W Stuart Ave 93612 559-327-6200
Marshall Hamm, prin. Fax 327-6290

Cox ES 600/K-6
2191 Sierra Ave 93611 559-327-6400
Cheryl Floth, prin. Fax 327-6490

Dry Creek ES 800/K-6
1273 N Armstrong Ave, 559-327-6500
Aaron Cook, prin. Fax 327-6590

Freedom ES 800/K-6
2955 Gettysburg Ave 93611 559-327-4800
Kristen Belknap, prin. Fax 327-4890

Garfield ES 700/K-6
1315 N Peach Ave, 559-327-6800
Jennifer Bump, prin. Fax 327-6890

Gettysburg ES 600/K-6
2100 Gettysburg Ave 93611 559-327-6900
Nick Mele, prin. Fax 327-6990

Jefferson ES 600/K-6
1880 Fowler Ave 93611 559-327-7000
Geoffrey Tiftick, prin. Fax 327-7090

Miramonte ES 600/K-6
1590 Bellaire Ave 93611 559-327-7400
Laura Hart, prin. Fax 327-7490

Rank ES 800/K-6
3650 Powers Ave, 559-327-4900
Ryan Gettman, prin. Fax 327-4990

Reagan ES 600/K-6
3701 Ashlan Ave, 559-327-8900
Kacey Gibson, prin. Fax 327-8901

Red Bank ES 800/K-6
1454 Locan Ave, 559-327-7800
Pa Vue, prin. Fax 327-7890

Sierra Vista ES 500/K-6
510 Barstow Ave 93612 559-327-7900
Cathy Dodd, prin. Fax 327-7990

Tarpey ES 700/K-6
2700 Minnewawa Ave 93612 559-327-8000
Tachua Vue, prin. Fax 327-8090

Weldon ES 700/K-6
150 Dewitt Ave 93612 559-327-8300
Ray Lozano, prin. Fax 327-8390

Woods ES 800/K-6
700 Teague Ave, 559-327-8800
Darrin Holtermann, prin. Fax 327-8801

Other Schools – See Fresno, Pinedale

Clovis Christian S 200/PK-8
3105 Locan Ave, 559-291-6302
Kim Bonjorni, supt. Fax 291-6278

Keyan Armenian Community S 100/PK-6
108 N Villa Ave 93612 559-323-1955
Nora Kassajikian, prin. Fax 323-1959

Our Lady of Perpetual Help S 200/PK-8
836 Dewitt Ave 93612 559-299-7504
Patrick Dodd, prin. Fax 299-4627

Valley Crescent S 100/K-8
547 W Nees Ave 93611 559-298-0023
Dr. Gharib Khalil, prin. Fax 298-0014

Coachella, Riverside, Pop. 40,549

Coachella Valley USD
Supt. — See Thermal

Cahuilla Desert Academy 900/7-8
82489 Avenue 52 92236 760-398-0097
Michael Reule, prin. Fax 398-0088

Chavez ES 900/K-6
49601 Avenida De Oro 92236 760-398-2004
Robert Hughes, prin. Fax 398-6713

Coral Mountain Academy 1,100/K-6
51375 Van Buren St 92236 760-398-3525
Humberto Alvarez, prin. Fax 393-0591

Duke MS 700/7-8
85358 Bagdad Ave 92236 760-398-0139
Encarnacion Becerra, prin. Fax 398-5399

Palm View ES 600/K-6
1390 7th St 92236 760-398-2861
George Zavala, prin. Fax 398-2592

Pendleton ES 600/K-6
84750 Calle Rojo 92236 760-398-0178
Armando Rivera, prin. Fax 398-0628

Valle Del Sol ES 800/K-6
51433 Education Way 92236 760-398-1025
Dr. Sean McQuown, prin. Fax 398-1746

Valley View ES 800/K-6
85270 Valley Rd 92236 760-398-4651
Norma Rodriguez, prin. Fax 398-5931

Coalinga, Fresno, Pop. 13,188

Coalinga-Huron USD 4,400/K-12
657 Sunset St 93210 559-935-7500
Dr. Lori Villanueva, supt. Fax 935-5329
www.chusd.org

Bishop ES 300/K-1
1501 Sunset St 93210 559-935-7570
Jennifer Pinto, prin. Fax 935-7573

Cheney K 100/K-K
149 Adams St 93210 559-935-7515
Jennifer Pinto, prin. Fax 935-2950

Coalinga MS 600/6-8
265 Cambridge Ave 93210 559-935-7550
Rhianna Giffin, prin. Fax 934-1311

Dawson ES 400/1-3
1303 Sunset St 93210 559-935-7580
Cari Carlson, prin. Fax 935-7588

Sunset ES 400/4-5
985 Sunset Ave 93210 559-935-7590
Cari Carlson, prin. Fax 935-7509

Other Schools – See Huron

Faith Christian Academy 100/PK-12
450 W Elm Ave 93210 559-935-9209
Rebecca Buckner, prin. Fax 935-0745

Coarsegold, Madera, Pop. 1,773

Yosemite USD
Supt. — See Oakhurst

Coarsegold S 400/K-8
45426 Road 415 93614 559-683-4842
Jared Pierce, prin. Fax 683-2625

Rivergold S 500/K-8
31800 Road 400 93614 559-658-7566
Bob Rose, prin. Fax 658-7244

Coleville, Mono, Pop. 479

Eastern Sierra USD
Supt. — See Bridgeport

Antelope ES 200/K-8
111527 US Highway 395 96107 530-495-2231
Steven Childs, prin. Fax 495-1831

Colfax, Placer, Pop. 1,892

Colfax ESD 600/K-12
24825 Ben Taylor Rd 95713 530-346-2202
John Baggett, supt. Fax 346-2205
www.colfax.k12.ca.us

Colfax ES 400/K-8
24825 Ben Taylor Rd 95713 530-346-2202
John Baggett, prin. Fax 346-2205

Colma, San Mateo, Pop. 1,713
Jefferson ESD
Supt. — See Daly City
Franklin IS 500/7-8
700 Stewart Ave, Daly City CA 94015 650-991-1200
James Parrish, prin. Fax 756-5475
Garden Village ES 400/K-5
208 Garden Ln, Daly City CA 94015 650-991-1233
Carolyn Casey, prin. Fax 755-1916

Holy Angels S 200/K-8
20 Reiner St 94014 650-755-0220
Sr. Leonarda Montealto, prin. Fax 755-0258

Colton, San Bernardino, Pop. 51,046
Colton JUSD 23,300/PK-12
1212 Valencia Dr 92324 909-580-5000
Jerry Almendarez, supt. Fax 433-9471
www.cjusd.net
Birney ES 800/K-6
1050 E Olive St 92324 909-580-5017
Jessica Gomez, prin. Fax 433-9474
Colton MS 1,000/7-8
670 W Laurel St 92324 909-580-5009
Yvette Roman, prin. Fax 876-4095
Cooley Ranch ES 700/K-6
1000 S Cooley Dr 92324 909-580-5023
Judy Scates, prin. Fax 430-2834
Grant ES 700/K-6
550 W Olive St 92324 909-580-5024
Kathy Houle-Jackson, prin. Fax 876-6325
Lincoln ES 700/K-6
444 E Olive St 92324 909-580-5026
Patricia Horton, prin. Fax 876-6348
McKinley ES 700/K-6
600 Johnston St 92324 909-580-5028
Judith Servin, prin. Fax 876-6305
Reche Canyon ES 600/K-6
3101 Canyon Vista Dr 92324 909-580-5012
Cecilia Smith, prin. Fax 876-6336
Rogers ES 800/K-6
955 W Laurel St 92324 909-580-5027
Laurie Carlton, prin. Fax 876-4252
San Salvador Preschool PK-PK
471 Agua Mansa Rd 92324 909-580-5031
Melissa Williamson, dir. Fax 433-9463
Wilson ES 700/K-6
750 S 8th St 92324 909-580-5015
Ginna Slocum, prin. Fax 872-6480
Other Schools – See Bloomington, Fontana, Grand Terrace

Rialto USD
Supt. — See Rialto
Garcia ES 700/K-5
1390 W Randall Ave 92324 909-421-7620
Ramona Rodriguez, prin. Fax 421-7624
Jehue MS 1,500/6-8
1500 N Eucalyptus Ave 92324 909-421-7377
Armando Urteaga, prin. Fax 421-7376
Morris ES 600/K-5
1900 W Randall Ave 92324 909-820-6864
Sylvia Braggs, prin. Fax 820-7944

Columbia, Tuolumne, Pop. 2,199
Columbia UNSD 600/K-8
22540 Parrotts Ferry Rd 95310 209-533-7700
Joseph Aldridge, supt. Fax 533-7709
www.columbia49er.k12.ca.us
Columbia ES 600/K-8
22540 Parrotts Ferry Rd 95310 209-533-7700
Joseph Aldridge, prin. Fax 533-4998

Colusa, Colusa, Pop. 5,849
Colusa USD 1,400/K-12
745 10th St 95932 530-458-7791
Dwayne Newman, supt. Fax 458-4030
www.colusa.k12.ca.us
Burchfield PS 500/K-3
400 Fremont St 95932 530-458-5853
Jesse Rodriguez, prin. Fax 458-8874
Egling MS 500/4-8
813 Webster St 95932 530-458-7631
Jody Johnston, prin. Fax 458-8107

Our Lady of Lourdes S 100/PK-8
741 Ware Ave 95932 530-458-8208
Barbara Genera, prin. Fax 458-8657

Commerce, Los Angeles, Pop. 12,764
Montebello USD
Supt. — See Montebello
Bandini ES 500/K-5
2318 Couts Ave 90040 323-261-8782
Benedetta Kennedy, prin. Fax 887-5856
Rosewood Park S 1,000/K-8
2353 Commerce Way 90040 323-887-7862
Jose Avila, prin. Fax 887-7863

Comptche, Mendocino, Pop. 156
Mendocino USD
Supt. — See Mendocino
Comptche ES 50/K-3
PO Box 144 95427 707-937-5945
Kim Humrichouse, prin. Fax 937-0714

Compton, Los Angeles, Pop. 94,840
Compton USD 22,400/PK-12
501 S Santa Fe Ave 90221 310-639-4321
Dr. Carmella Franco, supt. Fax 632-3014
www.compton.k12.ca.us
Anderson ES 400/PK-8
2210 E 130th St 90222 310-898-6110
Martha Funes, prin. Fax 604-4314
Bunche MS 600/6-8
12338 S Mona Blvd 90222 310-898-6010
Gipson Lyles, prin. Fax 638-4935
Bursch ES 500/PK-5
2505 W 156th St 90220 310-898-6130
Frank Lozier, prin. Fax 638-6716
Clinton ES 900/PK-6
6500 E Compton Blvd 90221 562-630-7912
Dr. Kanika White, prin. Fax 630-7914
Davis MS 900/6-8
621 W Poplar St 90220 310-898-6020
Lakeyshua Washington, prin. Fax 631-5725
Dickison ES 700/K-5
905 N Aranbe Ave 90220 310-898-6160
Pamela Neal-Robinson, prin. Fax 631-5675
Emerson ES 500/PK-8
1011 E Caldwell St 90221 310-898-6170
Sydney Ritchey-Burnett, prin. Fax 632-8316
Enterprise MS 500/6-8
2600 W Compton Blvd 90220 310-898-6030
David Herrera, prin. Fax 632-4183
Foster ES 700/PK-5
1620 N Pannes Ave 90221 310-898-6180
Jessicka Mears Ed.D., prin. Fax 638-4553
Jefferson ES 600/K-6
2508 E 133rd St 90222 310-898-6190
Diana Phillips, prin. Fax 537-3421
Kelly ES 800/K-8
2320 E Alondra Blvd 90221 310-898-6410
Ronald Keaton, prin. Fax 632-0583
Kennedy ES 600/K-8
1305 S Oleander Ave 90220 310-898-6420
Cecilia Madrid, prin. Fax 762-9847
King ES 500/PK-5
2270 E 122nd St 90222 310-898-6430
Cowana Emile, prin. Fax 631-9208
Laurel Street ES 500/PK-8
1321 W Laurel St 90220 310-898-6440
Dr. Francisa Owoaje, prin. Fax 639-8409
Longfellow ES 500/PK-5
1101 S Dwight Ave 90220 310-898-6460
Joanne Davidson, prin. Fax 632-5406
Mayo ES 600/K-5
915 N Mayo Ave 90221 310-898-6310
Fleming Robinson, prin. Fax 638-5660
McKinley ES 400/PK-5
14431 S Stanford Ave 90220 310-898-6320
Dr. Jennifer Kang-Moon, prin. Fax 516-1322
McNair ES 500/K-5
1450 W El Segundo Blvd 90222 310-898-6330
Rachel Collins, prin. Fax 898-6098
Roosevelt ES 700/PK-8
700 N Bradfield Ave 90221 310-898-6350
Salvador Aqino, prin. Fax 632-0338
Roosevelt MS 1,000/6-8
1200 E Alondra Blvd 90221 310-898-6040
Dr. Kevin Curry, prin. Fax 631-3298
Rosecrans ES 500/PK-5
1301 N Acacia Ave 90222 310-898-6360
Nabeehah Brumfield, prin. Fax 639-2224
Tibby ES 300/PK-8
1400 W Poplar St 90220 310-898-6370
Ontrece Ellerbe, prin. Fax 638-7015
Walton MS 500/6-8
900 W Greenleaf Dr 90220 310-898-6060
Dr. Bobby Walker, prin. Fax 631-3409
Washington ES 400/K-5
1421 N Wilmington Ave 90222 310-898-6390
Dr. Keisha Robinson, prin. Fax 898-6038
Whaley MS 800/6-8
14401 S Gibson Ave 90221 310-898-6070
Dr. Candice Waters, prin. Fax 638-7079
Willowbrook MS 400/6-8
2601 N Wilmington Ave 90222 310-898-6080
David Brutus, prin. Fax 537-2932
Other Schools – See Carson, Los Angeles

Optimal Christian Academy 200/K-8
1300 E Palmer St 90221 310-603-0378
Mark Mosby, admin. Fax 603-0604
Our Lady of Victory S 100/K-8
601 E Palmer St 90221 310-631-1320
Arturo Jordan-Gonzalez M.Ed., prin. Fax 631-4280
St. Albert the Great MS 100/6-8
823 E Compton Blvd 90220 310-515-3891
Tina Johnson, prin. Fax 515-1413

Concord, Contra Costa, Pop. 116,303
Mount Diablo USD 31,700/PK-12
1936 Carlotta Dr 94519 925-682-8000
Dr. Nellie Meyer, supt. Fax 689-1649
www.mdusd.org
Ayers ES 400/K-5
5120 Myrtle Dr 94521 925-682-7686
Laura Casdia, prin. Fax 827-2521
Cambridge ES 700/K-5
1135 Lacey Ln 94520 925-686-4749
Dr. Garry Galvan, prin. Fax 798-5068
El Dorado MS 1,100/6-8
1750 West St 94521 925-682-5700
Christopher Clausen, prin. Fax 685-1460
El Monte ES 500/K-5
1400 Dina Dr 94518 925-685-3113
Jennifer Molino, prin. Fax 827-5471
Highlands ES 700/K-5
1326 Pennsylvania Blvd 94521 925-672-5252
Ryan Sheehy, prin. Fax 672-6910
Holbrook Language Academy K-5
3333 Ronald Way 94519 925-685-6446
Marga Marshall, prin. Fax 827-1138
Meadow Homes ES 900/K-5
1371 Detroit Ave 94520 925-685-8760
Sandra Wilbanks, prin. Fax 689-7217
Monte Gardens ES 600/K-5
3841 Larkspur Dr 94519 925-685-3834
Erin Fairholm, prin. Fax 689-8291
Mountain View ES 400/K-5
1705 Thornwood Dr 94521 925-689-6450
Brent Brinkerhoff, prin. Fax 687-8622
Oak Grove MS 700/6-8
2050 Minert Rd 94518 925-682-1843
Christina Filios, prin. Fax 682-2083
Pine Hollow MS 700/6-8
5522 Pine Hollow Rd 94521 925-672-5444
Shelley Bain, prin. Fax 672-9751
Shadelands Preschool PK-PK
1860 Silverwood Dr 94519 925-685-3533
Jennifer Vargas, prin. Fax 603-1494
Silverwood ES 500/K-5
1649 Claycord Ave 94521 925-687-1150
Julie Johnson, prin. Fax 689-8199
Sun Terrace ES 600/K-5
2448 Floyd Ln 94520 925-682-4861
Kristan Martin-Meyer, prin. Fax 798-7476
Westwood ES 400/K-5
1748 West St 94521 925-685-4202
Nancy Klinkner, prin. Fax 680-0431
Woodside ES 400/K-5
761 San Simeon Dr 94518 925-689-7671
Cindy Matteoni, prin. Fax 689-4974
Wren Avenue ES 500/K-5
3339 Wren Ave 94519 925-685-7002
Aline Lee, prin. Fax 609-9506
Ygnacio Valley ES 500/K-5
2217 Chalomar Rd 94518 925-682-9336
Linn Kissinger, prin. Fax 609-7759
Other Schools – See Bay Point, Clayton, Martinez, Pittsburg, Pleasant Hill, Walnut Creek

---

Calvary Temple Christian S 200/PK-8
4725 Evora Rd 94520 925-458-9870
John Jackson, prin. Fax 458-9001
Concordia S 100/PK-6
2353 5th Ave 94518 925-689-6910
King's Valley Christian S 300/PK-8
4255 Clayton Rd 94521 925-687-2020
Dan Prescott, prin. Fax 687-7829
Queen of All Saints S 200/K-8
2391 Grant St 94520 925-685-8700
Lucia Prince, prin. Fax 685-2034
St. Agnes S 400/K-8
3886 Chestnut Ave 94519 925-689-3990
Jill Lucia, prin. Fax 689-3455
St. Francis of Assisi S 300/K-8
866 Oak Grove Rd 94518 925-682-5414
Sr. Patti Calton, prin. Fax 682-5480
Tabernacle Christian S 500/PK-8
4380 Concord Blvd 94521 925-685-9169
Vern Taylor, prin. Fax 685-9176
Wood Rose Academy 100/K-8
4347 Cowell Rd 94518 925-825-4644
Ygnacio Valley Christian S 100/PK-8
4977 Concord Blvd 94521 925-798-3131
Dennis Snyder, prin. Fax 798-6150

Cool, El Dorado
Black Oak Mine USD
Supt. — See Georgetown
Northside ES 300/K-6
860 Cave Valley Rd 95614 530-333-8355
Carrie Arnett, prin. Fax 333-8356

Copperopolis, Calaveras, Pop. 3,569
Mark Twain UNESD
Supt. — See Angels Camp
Copperopolis ES 300/K-6
217 School St 95228 209-785-2236
Paul Gehres, prin. Fax 785-4309

Corcoran, Kings, Pop. 24,292
Corcoran JUSD 3,300/PK-12
1520 Patterson Ave 93212 559-992-8888
Rich Merlo, supt. Fax 992-3957
www.corcoranunified.com/
Fremont ES 600/2-3
1520 Patterson Ave 93212 559-992-8883
Elizabeth Mendoza, prin. Fax 992-5105
Harte ES 600/PK-1
1520 Patterson Ave 93212 559-992-8881
Laurene Haas, prin. Fax 992-3299
Muir MS 700/6-8
1520 Patterson Ave 93212 559-992-8886
David Whitmore, prin. Fax 992-4423
Twain ES 500/4-5
1520 Patterson Ave 93212 559-992-8882
Mike Anderson, prin. Fax 992-1018

Corning, Tehama, Pop. 7,468
Corning UNESD 2,000/K-8
1590 South St 96021 530-824-7700
Richard Fitzpatrick, supt. Fax 824-2493
www.corningelementary.org
Maywood MS 300/7-8
1666 Marguerite Ave 96021 530-824-7730
Tiffany Dietz, prin. Fax 824-7742
Olive View ES 600/K-6
1402 Fig St 96021 530-824-7715
Joe Lodigiani, prin. Fax 824-7740
Rancho Tehama ES 100/K-6
PO Box 5775 96021 530-585-2800
Fax 585-2802
West Street ES 300/K-6
900 West St 96021 530-824-7705
Fax 824-7741
Woodson ES 600/K-8
150 N Toomes Ave 96021 530-824-7720
Merry Catron, prin. Fax 824-7745

Kirkwood ESD 100/PK-8
2049 Kirkwood Rd 96021 530-824-7773
John Burch, supt. Fax 824-6995
www.kirkwoodschoolca.org
Kirkwood ES 100/PK-8
2049 Kirkwood Rd 96021 530-824-7773
John Burch, supt. Fax 824-6995

Richfield ESD 200/PK-8
23875 River Rd 96021 530-824-3354
Jeff Scheele, supt. Fax 824-0569
www.richfieldschool.org
Richfield ES 200/PK-8
23875 River Rd 96021 530-824-3354
Jeff Scheele, admin. Fax 824-0569

Corona, Riverside, Pop. 147,939
Alvord USD 19,400/K-12
9 KPC Pkwy 92879 951-509-5070
Dr. Sid Salazar, supt. Fax 509-6070
alvordschools.org
Promenade ES 600/K-5
550 Hamilton Dr 92879 951-358-1650
Francisco Gonzalez, prin. Fax 358-1651
Other Schools – See Riverside

Corona-Norco USD
Supt. — See Norco
Adams ES 800/K-6
2350 Border Ave 92882 951-736-3313
Elizabeth Moore, prin. Fax 736-7130
Anthony ES 900/K-6
2665 Gilbert Ave 92881 951-739-5655
Ryan Reider, prin. Fax 739-5662
Auburndale IS 600/7-8
1255 River Rd 92880 951-736-3231
Ben Sanchez, prin. Fax 736-3360
Chavez Academy 900/K-8
1150 Paseo Grande 92882 951-736-4640
Dr. Stuart Payne, prin. Fax 736-4648
Citrus Hills IS 1,100/7-8
3211 S Main St 92882 951-736-4600
Andrew Roberts, prin. Fax 736-4623
Corona Fundamental IS 1,200/7-8
1230 S Main St 92882 951-736-3321
Kelli Jakubik, prin. Fax 736-3417
Corona Ranch ES 1,100/K-6
785 Village Loop Dr 92879 951-736-4626
Jean Trevino, prin. Fax 736-4633
Coronita ES 600/K-6
1757 Via Del Rio 92882 951-736-3389
Kevin Kazala, prin. Fax 736-3485
Eisenhower ES 900/K-6
3355 Mountain Gate Dr 92882 951-739-5960
Kelley Gelzleichter, prin. Fax 739-5968
El Cerrito MS 1,300/6-8
7610 El Cerrito Rd 92881 951-736-3216
Dr. Shelly Yarbrough, prin. Fax 736-3286
Foothill ES 1,000/K-6
2601 S Buena Vista Ave 92882 951-736-3441
Dr. Joni Howard, prin. Fax 736-3251
Franklin ES 800/K-6
2650 Oak Ave 92882 951-739-5645
Lara Gruebel, prin. Fax 739-5650
Garretson ES 1,100/K-6
1650 Garretson Ave 92879 951-736-3345
Ana Luna, prin. Fax 736-3347
Home Gardens Academy 700/K-6
13550 Tolton Ave 92879 951-736-3219
Sabrina Kaspar, prin. Fax 736-7151
Jefferson ES 800/K-6
1040 S Vicentia Ave 92882 951-736-3226
Alejandro Vasquez, prin. Fax 736-3270
Lincoln Alternative S 1,000/K-6
1041 Fullerton Ave 92879 951-736-3336
Brian Leedy, prin. Fax 736-3302
McKinley ES 800/K-6
2050 Aztec Ln 92879 951-736-7190
Dr. Trevor Dietrich, prin. Fax 736-7192
Orange ES 800/K-6
1350 Valencia Rd 92881 951-736-3455
Kelly Williams, prin. Fax 736-3490
Parkridge ES 800/K-6
750 Corona Ave 92879 951-736-3236
Ed Clement, prin. Fax 736-3478
Prado View ES 800/K-6
2800 Ridgeline Dr 92882 951-736-3474
Ginger Prewitt, prin. Fax 739-5810
Raney IS 800/6-8
1010 W Citron St 92882 951-736-3221
Michele Sanchez, prin. Fax 736-3439
Stallings ES 600/K-6
1980 Fullerton Ave 92881 951-736-3249
Dr. Tammy Strawser, prin. Fax 739-5811
Temescal Valley ES 900/K-6
22950 Claystone Ave 92883 951-736-7110
Beth Feaster, prin. Fax 736-7178
Todd Academy 800/K-6
25105 Mayhew Canyon Rd 92883 951-736-7035
Cecilia Arzaga-Chester, prin. Fax 736-7060
Vicentia ES 700/K-6
2005 S Vicentia Ave 92882 951-736-3228
Jennifer Morgan, prin. Fax 736-7140
Wilson ES 1,000/K-6
1750 Spyglass Dr 92883 951-739-5820
Fax 739-5827

Lake Elsinore USD
Supt. — See Lake Elsinore
Luiseno ES 1,000/K-8
13500 Mountain Rd 92883 951-253-7480
Ericka Restad, prin. Fax 253-7492

Calvary Chapel Christian Academy 50/K-6
130 W Chase Dr 92882 951-818-3744
Pete Lang, prin. Fax 284-1686
Christian Heritage S 300/K-12
PO Box 1780 92878 951-736-3033
Arleen Morris, admin.
Crossroads Christian S 1,000/PK-12
2380 Fullerton Ave 92881 951-278-3199
Phil Lewis, supt. Fax 493-2169
Grace Christian Academy 100/PK-12
2781 S Lincoln Ave 92882 951-736-7466
Grace Lutheran Preschool & K 50/PK-K
1114 W Ontario Ave 92882 951-737-2187
Lisa Hatton, dir.
Montessori S of Corona 100/K-8
260 W Ontario Ave 92882 951-371-6731
Olive Branch Christian Academy 100/PK-8
7702 El Cerrito Rd 92881 951-279-9977
Mandy Logan, admin. Fax 520-9797
St. Edward S 300/PK-8
500 S Merrill St 92882 951-737-2530
Nathan Arnold, prin. Fax 737-1074

Corona del Mar, Orange
Newport - Mesa USD
Supt. — See Costa Mesa
Harbor View ES 500/K-6
900 Goldenrod Ave 92625 949-515-6940
Todd Schmidt, prin. Fax 515-6811
Lincoln ES 700/K-6
3101 Pacific View Dr 92625 949-515-6955
Carrie Gammel, prin. Fax 515-6806

Harbor Day S 400/K-8
3443 Pacific View Dr 92625 949-640-1410
Angi Evans, head sch Fax 640-0908

Coronado, San Diego, Pop. 18,310
Coronado USD 3,100/PK-12
201 6th St 92118 619-522-8900
Karl Mueller, supt. Fax 437-6570
coronadousd.net
Coronado MS 700/6-8
550 F Ave 92118 619-522-8921
Karin Mellina, prin. Fax 522-6948
Silver Strand ES 300/PK-5
1350 Leyte Rd 92118 619-522-8934
Tammy Marble, prin. Fax 437-8041
Village ES 900/PK-5
600 6th St 92118 619-522-8915
Whitney DeSantis, prin. Fax 522-8988

Christ Church Day S 100/K-6
1114 9th St 92118 619-435-6393
Nancy Funk, head sch Fax 435-4574
Sacred Heart S 200/K-8
706 C Ave 92118 619-437-4431
Peter Harris, prin. Fax 437-1473

Corralitos, Santa Cruz, Pop. 2,264

Salesian S 200/K-8
605 Enos Ln 95076 831-728-5518
Sr. Ignacia Carrillo, prin. Fax 728-0273

Corte Madera, Marin, Pop. 8,835
Larkspur-Corte Madera SD
Supt. — See Larkspur
Cove S 300/K-5
330 Golden Hind Passage 94925 415-945-9046
Michelle Walker, prin.
Cummins ES 800/K-4
58 Mohawk Ave 94925 415-927-6965
Patty Elliot, prin. Fax 927-6967

Marin Country Day S 600/K-8
5221 Paradise Dr 94925 415-927-5900
Lucinda Lee Katz, head sch Fax 924-1082
Marin Montessori S 200/PK-9
5200 Paradise Dr 94925 415-924-5388

Costa Mesa, Orange, Pop. 106,497
Newport - Mesa USD 22,000/K-12
2985 Bear St 92626 714-424-5000
Frederick Navarro Ed.D., supt. Fax 424-5018
www.nmusd.us
Adams ES 400/K-6
2850 Club House Rd 92626 714-424-7935
Gabriel Del Real, prin. Fax 424-4701
California ES 400/K-6
3232 California St 92626 714-424-7940
Jacob Topete, prin. Fax 424-4711
College Park ES 600/K-6
2380 Notre Dame Rd 92626 714-424-7960
Rich Rodriguez, prin Fax 424-4721
Davis ES 600/K-6
1050 Arlington Dr 92626 714-424-7930
Christy Flores, prin. Fax 424-4711
Kaiser ES 700/3-6
2130 Santa Ana Ave 92627 949-515-6950
Deborah Granger, prin Fax 515-6851
Killybrooke ES 400/K-6
3155 Killybrooke Ln 92626 714-424-7945
Lorie Hoggard, prin. Fax 424-4731
Paularino ES 400/K-6
1060 Paularino Ave 92626 714-424-7950
Amy Nagy, prin. Fax 424-4741
Pomona ES 500/K-6
2051 Pomona Ave 92627 949-515-6980
Megan Elston-Brown, prin. Fax 515-6891
Rea ES 500/K-6
661 Hamilton St 92627 949-515-6905
Duane Cox, prin. Fax 515-6835
Sonora ES 500/K-6
966 Sonora Rd 92626 949-424-7955
Christine Anderson, prin. Fax 424-4751
TeWinkle MS 700/7-8
3224 California St 92626 714-424-7965
Kira Hurst, prin. Fax 424-5680
Victoria ES 400/K-6
1025 Victoria St 92627 949-515-6985
Aaron Peralta, prin. Fax 515-6841
Whittier ES 700/K-6
1800 Whittier Ave 92627 949-515-6990
Scott Wilcox, prin. Fax 515-6815
Wilson ES 500/K-6
801 W Wilson St 92627 949-515-6995
Mia King, prin. Fax 515-6825
Woodland ES 500/K-2
2025 Garden Ln 92627 949-515-6945
Tiffany Lewis, prin. Fax 515-6861
Other Schools – See Corona del Mar, Newport Beach, Newport Coast

---

Christ Lutheran S 200/PK-8
760 Victoria St 92627 949-548-6866
Caleb McFerran M.Ed., prin. Fax 631-6224
International Christian Montessori Acad 100/PK-6
2950 McClintock Way 92626 714-966-0303
Cecile Maida, dir. Fax 966-0360
Mariners Christian S 700/K-8
300 Fischer Ave 92626 714-437-1700
Troy Moore, head sch Fax 437-7976

Page Private S of Costa Mesa 100/PK-8
657 Victoria St 92627 949-642-0411
Kristin Dickson, head sch
St. Joachim S 300/PK-8
1964 Orange Ave 92627 949-574-7411
Sr. Kathleen Marie Pughe, prin. Fax 646-8948
St. John the Baptist S 600/K-8
1021 Baker St 92626 714-557-5060
Paula Viles, prin. Fax 557-9263
Waldorf S of Orange County 300/PK-12
2350 Canyon Dr 92627 949-574-7775

Cotati, Sonoma, Pop. 6,950
Cotati-Rohnert Park USD
Supt. — See Rohnert Park
Page Academy 500/K-8
1075 Madrone Ave 94931 707-792-4860
Teresa Peterson, prin. Fax 792-4514

Cottonwood, Shasta, Pop. 3,202
Cottonwood UNESD 1,100/PK-8
20512 1st St 96022 530-347-3165
Doug Geren Ed.D., supt. Fax 347-0247
cwusd.com
North Cottonwood ES 500/PK-4
20512 1st St 96022 530-347-1698
Don Ray, prin. Fax 347-7233
West Cottonwood JHS 400/5-8
20512 1st St 96022 530-347-3123
Terri Wright, prin. Fax 347-0247

Evergreen UNSD 1,000/PK-12
19500 Learning Way 96022 530-347-3411
Brad Mendenhall, supt. Fax 347-7954
www.evergreenusd.com
Evergreen ES 500/PK-4
19500 Learning Way 96022 530-347-3411
Kristen Nobles, prin. Fax 347-4639
Evergreen MS 400/5-8
19500 Learning Way 96022 530-347-3411
Felicia Ross, prin. Fax 347-7953
Evergreen State Preschool PK-PK
19500 Learning Way 96022 530-347-3411
Karen Provence, prin. Fax 347-4639
Other Schools – See Red Bluff

Coulterville, Mariposa, Pop. 195
Mariposa County USD
Supt. — See Mariposa
Greeley Hill ES K-8
10326 Fiske Rd 95311 209-878-3028
Tracie Baughn, prin. Fax 878-3067

Courtland, Sacramento, Pop. 350
River Delta USD
Supt. — See Rio Vista
Bates ES 200/K-6
PO Box 308 95615 916-775-1771
Maria Elena Becerra, prin. Fax 775-1702

Covelo, Mendocino, Pop. 1,175
Round Valley USD 400/K-12
PO Box 276 95428 707-983-6171
Mike Gorman, supt. Fax 983-6655
www.roundvalleyschools.org/
Round Valley ES 200/K-8
PO Box 276 95428 707-983-6171
Cheryl Tuttle, prin. Fax 983-6377

Covina, Los Angeles, Pop. 46,744
Azusa USD
Supt. — See Azusa
Ellington ES 400/K-7
5034 N Clydebank Ave 91722 626-858-6800
Shanti Molina, prin. Fax 974-8232

Charter Oak USD 5,300/K-12
20240 E Cienega Ave 91724 626-966-8331
Dr. Michael Hendricks Ed.D., supt. Fax 967-9580
www.cousd.net
Badillo ES 500/K-6
1771 E Old Badillo St 91724 626-966-1753
Lori Drake, prin. Fax 859-5765
Cedargrove ES 800/K-6
1209 N Glendora Ave 91724 626-966-8675
David Young, prin. Fax 966-6773
Glen Oak ES 500/K-6
1000 N Sunflower Ave 91724 626-331-5341
Sharon Greaves, prin. Fax 331-5312
Royal Oak MS 800/7-8
303 S Glendora Ave 91724 626-967-6354
Maria Thompson, prin. Fax 331-2074
Other Schools – See Glendora

Covina-Valley USD 12,600/K-12
519 E Badillo St 91723 626-974-7000
Dr. Richard Sheehan, supt. Fax 974-7032
www.c-vusd.org
Barranca ES 600/K-5
727 S Barranca Ave 91723 626-974-4000
Kim Sheehan, prin. Fax 974-4015
Ben Lomond ES 500/K-5
621 E Covina Blvd 91722 626-974-4100
Tanya Martin, prin. Fax 974-4115
Cypress ES 600/K-5
351 W Cypress St 91723 626-974-4300
Shannon Wyatt, prin. Fax 974-4315
Las Palmas MS 900/6-8
641 N Lark Ellen Ave 91722 626-974-7200
Nicole Higuera, prin. Fax 974-7215
Manzanita ES 300/K-5
4131 N Nora Ave 91722 626-472-7640
Beth Mossman, prin. Fax 472-7655
Sierra Vista MS 1,000/6-8
777 E Puente St 91723 626-974-7300
Danielle Travieso, prin. Fax 974-7315
Other Schools – See Irwindale, West Covina

Sacred Heart S 300/K-8
360 W Workman St 91723 626-332-7222
April Luchonok, prin. Fax 967-8836

St. Louise De Marillac S 300/K-8
1728 E Covina Blvd 91724 626-966-2317
Dr. Denise Valadez, prin. Fax 332-4431
Sonrise Christian S 500/PK-8
1220 E Ruddock St 91724 626-331-0559
Manish Patel, head sch Fax 339-8029

Crescent City, Del Norte, Pop. 7,317
Del Norte County USD 3,900/K-12
301 W Washington Blvd 95531 707-464-6141
Jeff Harris, supt. Fax 464-0238
www.delnorte.k12.ca.us
Crescent Elk MS 500/6-8
994 G St 95531 707-464-0320
Paige Swan, prin. Fax 464-7920
Hamilton ES 300/K-5
1050 E St 95531 707-464-0330
Denise Harnden, prin. Fax 465-4844
Maxwell ES 300/K-5
1124 El Dorado St 95531 707-464-0310
Dan Cartwright, prin. Fax 465-5024
Peacock ES 400/K-5
1720 Arlington Dr 95531 707-464-0301
Lara Hirt, prin. Fax 464-3399
Pine Grove ES 200/K-5
900 Pine Grove Rd 95531 707-464-0350
Bill Hartwick, prin. Fax 465-4775
Other Schools – See Fort Dick, Gasquet, Klamath, Smith River

Crescent City SDA S 50/1-8
PO Box 1905 95531 707-464-2738
Fax 464-2738
Foursquare Christian S 100/PK-2
144 Butte St 95531 707-464-9501
Maria Guy, prin. Fax 465-3254

Cressey, Merced, Pop. 386
Ballico-Cressey ESD
Supt. — See Ballico
Cressey ES 100/PK-2
9921 W Crocker Ave 95312 209-394-9600
Bliss Boesch, supt. Fax 394-3031

Crestline, San Bernardino, Pop. 10,356
Rim of the World USD
Supt. — See Blue Jay
Valley of Enchantment ES 500/K-5
22836 Fir Ln 92325 909-589-0396
Lauren Tovar, prin. Fax 589-0412

Creston, San Luis Obispo, Pop. 93
Atascadero USD
Supt. — See Atascadero
Creston ES 100/K-5
PO Box 238 93432 805-238-4771
Sarah Betz, prin. Fax 238-4185

Crockett, Contra Costa, Pop. 2,949
John Swett USD
Supt. — See Rodeo
Carquinez MS 400/6-8
1099 Pomona St 94525 510-787-1081
Annie Flores-Aikey, prin. Fax 787-2359

Crowley Lake, Mono, Pop. 853

Eastern Sierra Christian Academy 50/K-10
384 S Landing Rd 93546 760-935-4272
Rena Davis, dir. Fax 935-4273

Crows Landing, Stanislaus, Pop. 352
Chatom UNESD
Supt. — See Turlock
Mountain View MS 200/6-8
10001 Crows Landing Rd 95313 209-664-8515
Steve Lewis, prin. Fax 669-1733

Newman-Crows Landing USD
Supt. — See Newman
Bonita ES 200/K-5
425 Fink Rd 95313 209-837-4401
Brandi Johnson, prin. Fax 837-0431

Cudahy, Los Angeles, Pop. 23,704
Los Angeles USD
Supt. — See Los Angeles
Elizabeth Learning Center 1,800/K-12
4811 Elizabeth St 90201 323-271-3600
Nora Gonzalez, prin. Fax 560-8412
Escalante Early Education Center PK-PK
7221 Atlantic Ave 90201 323-890-2380
Ernestine Lara, prin. Fax 890-2381
Escalante ES 600/K-6
4443 Live Oak St 90201 323-890-2340
Lisseett Hernandez, prin. Fax 771-2427
Hughes ES 900/K-6
4242 Clara St 90201 323-560-4422
Adriana Cortez, prin. Fax 773-7568
Ochoa Learning Center 1,500/K-8
5027 Live Oak St 90201 323-869-1300
Marcos Hernandez, prin. Fax 562-8015
Park Avenue ES 600/K-6
8020 Park Ave 90201 323-832-1860
Christina Garcia, prin. Fax 560-9912

Culver City, Los Angeles, Pop. 36,982
Culver City USD 6,700/K-12
4034 Irving Pl 90232 310-842-4220
Leslie Lockhart, supt. Fax 842-4205
www.ccusd.org
Culver City MS 1,500/6-8
4601 Elenda St 90230 310-842-4200
Elsy Villafranca, prin. Fax 842-4304
El Marino ES 800/K-5
11450 Port Rd 90230 310-842-4241
Mina Shiratori, prin. Fax 572-9420
El Rincon ES 600/K-5
11177 Overland Ave 90230 310-842-4340
Dr. Cassandra Ziskind, prin. Fax 842-4317
Farragut ES 600/K-5
10820 Farragut Dr 90230 310-842-4323
Rebecca Ngo, prin. Fax 842-4320
Howe ES 500/K-5
4100 Irving Pl 90232 310-842-4338
Dr. Kim Indelicato, prin. Fax 842-4330
La Ballona ES 600/K-5
10915 Washington Blvd 90232 310-842-4334
Jennifer Slabbinck, prin. Fax 842-4298

Los Angeles USD
Supt. — See Los Angeles
Braddock Drive ES 400/K-5
4711 Inglewood Blvd 90230 310-391-6707
Eva Lopez, prin. Fax 390-5134
Playa Del Rey ES 200/K-5
12221 Juniette St 90230 310-827-3560
Valencia Blue, prin. Fax 301-9541
Stoner ES 300/K-5
11735 Braddock Dr 90230 310-390-3396
Maria Garcia-Haro, prin. Fax 397-6946

St. Augustine S 300/PK-8
3819 Clarington Ave 90232 310-838-3144
Beate Nguyen, prin. Fax 838-7479
Turning Point S 300/PK-8
8780 National Blvd 90232 310-841-2505
Dr. Laura Konigsberg, head sch Fax 841-5420
Willows Community S 400/PK-8
8509 Higuera St 90232 310-815-0411
Lisa Rosenstein, head sch Fax 815-0425

Cupertino, Santa Clara, Pop. 56,415
Cupertino UNSD
Supt. — See Sunnyvale
Collins ES 700/K-5
10300 N Blaney Ave 95014 408-252-6002
Steve Woo, prin. Fax 253-3142
Eaton ES 600/K-5
20220 Suisun Dr 95014 408-255-2848
Louis Barocio, prin. Fax 255-0610
Garden Gate ES 700/K-5
10500 Ann Arbor Ave 95014 408-252-5414
Brandi Hucko, prin. Fax 996-9725
Hyde MS 1,000/6-8
19325 Bollinger Rd 95014 408-252-6290
Lisa Taormina, prin. Fax 255-3288
Kennedy MS 1,500/6-8
821 Bubb Rd 95014 408-253-1525
Steven Hamm, prin. Fax 257-5777
Lawson MS 1,100/6-8
10401 Vista Dr 95014 408-255-7500
Kit Bragg, prin. Fax 446-4987
Lincoln ES 700/K-5
21710 McClellan Rd 95014 408-252-4798
Ann Kropp, prin. Fax 865-0813
Regnart ES 600/K-5
1170 Yorkshire Dr 95014 408-253-5250
Thien Hua, prin. Fax 253-2604
Sedgwick ES 600/PK-5
19200 Phil Ln 95014 408-252-3103
Daric Jackson, prin. Fax 253-2213
Stevens Creek ES 600/K-5
10300 Ainsworth Dr 95014 408-245-3312
Diane Prystas, prin. Fax 245-7484

Bethel Lutheran S 100/PK-5
10181 Finch Ave 95014 408-252-8512
Dawn De Bois-Weber, prin. Fax 252-8465
St. Joseph of Cupertino S 300/PK-8
10120 N De Anza Blvd 95014 408-252-6441
Michael Lee, prin. Fax 252-9771

Cutler, Tulare, Pop. 4,971
Cutler-Orosi JUSD
Supt. — See Orosi
Cutler ES 700/K-5
40532 Road 128 93615 559-528-6931
Leanne Cerda, prin. Fax 528-0932

Cypress, Orange, Pop. 46,012
Anaheim UNHSD
Supt. — See Anaheim
Lexington JHS 1,300/7-8
4351 Orange Ave 90630 714-220-4201
Amber Houston, prin. Fax 761-4989

Cypress SD 3,900/K-6
9470 Moody St 90630 714-220-6900
Anne Silavs, supt. Fax 828-6652
www.cypsd.org
Arnold ES 700/K-6
9281 Denni St 90630 714-220-6965
Carol Erbe, prin. Fax 220-6968
King ES 600/K-6
8710 Moody St 90630 714-220-6980
Jacki Teschke, prin. Fax 220-6983
Landell ES 700/K-6
9739 Denni St 90630 714-220-6960
Dr. Rena Gibbs Ed.D., prin. Fax 229-7720
Morris ES 800/K-6
9952 Graham St 90630 714-220-6995
Lori Hernandez, prin. Fax 821-9412
Vessels ES 700/K-6
5900 Cathy Ave 90630 714-220-6990
Helen Chung-Lu, prin. Fax 220-6993
Other Schools – See La Palma

Calvary Chapel Christian S 200/PK-6
PO Box 769 90630 714-236-1293
Rene Hill, prin. Fax 821-0929
Grace Christian S 400/PK-8
4545 Myra Ave 90630 714-761-5200
Don Pettinger Ed.D., supt. Fax 761-1200
St. Irenaeus Catholic S 300/K-8
9201 Grindlay St 90630 714-827-4500
Monica Hayden, prin. Fax 827-2930
Wisdom Mission S K-12
5851 Newman St 90630 714-995-1900

Daly City, San Mateo, Pop. 97,070
Bayshore ESD 400/PK-8
155 Oriente St 94014 415-467-5443
Dr. Audra Pittman, supt. Fax 467-1542
www.thebayshoreschool.org
Bayshore ES 200/PK-8
155 Oriente St 94014 415-467-5443
Khanh Yeargin, prin. Fax 467-1542

Brisbane ESD
Supt. — See Brisbane
Panorama ES 100/K-5
25 Bellevue Ave 94014 415-586-6595
Sarah Neidhart, prin. Fax 586-0782

Jefferson ESD 6,200/K-8
101 Lincoln Ave 94015 650-991-1000
Bernardo Vidales, supt. Fax 992-2265
www.jsd.k12.ca.us/
Anthony ES 600/K-5
575 Abbot Ave 94014 650-997-7880
Charlie Rohrbach, prin. Fax 755-8303
Brown ES 400/K-6
305 Eastmoor Ave 94015 650-991-1243
Beth Gough, prin. Fax 997-0351
Edison ES 400/K-6
1267 Southgate Ave 94015 650-991-1250
Riza Bell, prin. Fax 755-3040
Kennedy ES 500/K-5
785 Price St 94014 650-991-1239
Matthew Harris, prin. Fax 755-1937
Pollicita MS 700/6-8
550 E Market St 94014 650-991-1216
Benjamin Turner, prin. Fax 755-2170
Rivera IS 400/7-8
1255 Southgate Ave 94015 650-991-1225
Dina Conti, prin. Fax 755-6273
Roosevelt ES 300/K-8
1200 Skyline Dr 94015 650-991-1230
Sean Higgins, prin. Fax 755-5046
Tobias ES 400/K-6
725 Southgate Ave 94015 650-991-1246
Cathy Macay, prin. Fax 755-1599
Washington ES 400/K-5
251 Whittier St 94014 650-991-1236
Rochelle Pimentel-Yuen, prin. Fax 991-1326
Webster ES 500/K-6
425 El Dorado Dr 94015 650-991-1222
Jennifer Knopf, prin. Fax 755-8214
Westlake ES 400/K-6
80 Fieldcrest Dr 94015 650-991-1252
Annabelle Kloezeman, prin. Fax 994-6137
Wilson ES 400/K-6
43 Miriam St 94014 650-991-1255
Brian Allen, prin. Fax 994-5946
Other Schools – See Colma

South San Francisco USD
Supt. — See South San Francisco
Junipero Serra ES 400/K-5
151 Victoria St 94015 650-877-8853
Dalton Miranda, prin. Fax 878-4743
Skyline ES 400/K-5
55 Christen Ave 94015 650-877-8941
Monica Nagy, prin. Fax 754-1746

Hilldale S, 79 Florence St 94014 100/K-8
Sasha Clayton, admin. 650-756-4737
Our Lady of Mercy S 400/K-8
7 Elmwood Dr 94015 650-756-3395
Jeffrey Burgos, prin. Fax 756-5872
Our Lady of Perpetual Help S 200/K-8
80 Wellington Ave 94014 650-755-4438
Katie Franco, prin. Fax 755-7366

Dana Point, Orange, Pop. 32,532
Capistrano USD
Supt. — See San Juan Capistrano
Dana ES 300/K-5
24242 La Cresta Dr 92629 949-496-5784
Christina Portillo, prin. Fax 488-3867

Monarch Bay Montessori Academy PK-6
32920 Pacific Coast Hwy 92629 949-240-3344
Fax 429-3103
Parish S @ St. Edward the Confessor 800/PK-8
33866 Calle La Primavera 92629 949-496-1241
Dr. Catherine Muzzy Ed.D., prin. Fax 496-1819

Danville, Contra Costa, Pop. 40,475
San Ramon Valley USD 31,300/PK-12
699 Old Orchard Dr 94526 925-552-5500
Rick Schmitt, supt. Fax 838-3147
www.srvusd.net
Baldwin ES 500/PK-5
741 Brookside Dr 94526 925-855-5200
Joe Romagna, prin. Fax 820-8307
Creekside ES 700/K-5
6011 Massara St 94506 925-314-2000
Aaron Tarzian, prin. Fax 314-2097
Diablo Vista MS 900/6-8
4100 Camino Tassajara 94506 925-855-7600
Becky Ingram, prin. Fax 648-7167
Greenbrook ES 600/K-5
1475 Harlan Dr 94526 925-855-5300
Rhea Murphy, prin. Fax 837-8727
Green Valley ES 600/K-5
1001 Diablo Rd 94526 925-855-5400
Donna Grim, prin. Fax 837-3807
Los Cerros MS 700/6-8
968 Blemer Rd 94526 925-855-6800
Evan Powell, prin. Fax 837-3512
Montair ES 600/PK-5
300 Quinterra Ln 94526 925-855-5100
Ondi Tricasso, prin. Fax 820-6713
Sycamore Valley ES 700/K-5
2200 Holbrook Dr 94506 925-855-2800
Cher Situm, prin. Fax 736-0224
Tassajara Hills ES 600/K-5
4675 Camino Tassajara 94506 925-855-7800
Ann Dodson, prin. Fax 648-3190

Vista Grande ES 700/PK-5
667 Diablo Rd 94526 925-314-1000
Patricia Hansen, prin. Fax 837-5918
Wood MS 1,100/6-8
600 El Capitan Dr 94526 925-855-4400
Christopher George, prin. Fax 820-1857
Other Schools – See Alamo, San Ramon

Legacy Christian Academy 50/K-7
2615 Camino Tassajara 94506 800-496-0012
Courtney Bellig, head sch Fax 496-0012
St. Isidore S 600/K-8
435 La Gonda Way 94526 925-837-2977
Maria Ward, prin. Fax 837-2407
San Ramon Valley Christian Academy 300/K-8
220 W El Pintado 94526 925-838-9622
Jamie Westgate, prin. Fax 838-8934
Stratford S - Danville Blackhawk 100/PK-K
3201 Camino Tassajara 94506 925-648-4900
Zhila Larijani, dir.
Stratford S - Danville Sycamore Valley 100/PK-K
2615 Camino Tassajara 94506 925-648-0500
Zhila Larijani, dir. Fax 309-4677

Davenport, Santa Cruz, Pop. 394
Pacific ESD, PO Box H 95017 100/PK-6
Eric Gross M.Ed., supt. 831-425-7002
www.pacificesd.org
Pacific ES, PO Box H 95017 100/PK-6
Eric Gross M.Ed., admin. 831-425-7002

Davis, Yolo, Pop. 62,607
Davis JUSD 8,500/K-12
526 B St 95616 530-757-5300
Dr. John Bowes, supt. Fax 757-5323
www.djusd.net
Birch Lane ES 600/K-6
1600 Birch Ln 95618 530-757-5395
Jim Knight, prin. Fax 757-5413
Chavez ES 600/K-6
1221 Anderson Rd 95616 530-757-5490
Denise Beck, prin. Fax 757-5427
Fairfield ES 100/K-6
26960 County Road 96 95616 530-757-5370
Gay Bourguignon, prin. Fax 757-5412
Korematsu ES 600/K-6
3100 Loyola Dr 95618 530-757-5358
Mary Ponce, prin. Fax 757-5362
Montgomery ES 400/K-6
1441 Danbury St 95618 530-759-2100
Jennifer McNeil, prin. Fax 759-2103
North Davis ES 600/K-6
555 E 14th St 95616 530-757-5475
Sarah Roseen, prin. Fax 757-5477
Patwin ES 400/K-6
2222 Shasta Dr 95616 530-757-5383
Gay Bourguignon, prin. Fax 757-5417
Pioneer ES 500/K-6
5215 Hamel St 95618 530-757-5480
Matthew Duffy, prin. Fax 757-5482
Willett ES 500/K-6
1207 Sycamore Ln 95616 530-757-5460
Heidi Perry, prin. Fax 757-5428

Davis Waldorf S 200/PK-8
3100 Sycamore Ln 95616 530-753-1651
Tina Rheault, admin. Fax 753-0944
Grace Valley Christian Academy 100/K-8
27173 County Road 98 95616 530-758-6590
Sharon Broderick, prin. Fax 758-2406
St. James S 300/K-8
1215 B St 95616 530-756-3946
Heather Church, prin. Fax 753-9765

Delano, Kern, Pop. 52,490
Columbine ESD 200/K-8
2240 Road 160 93215 661-725-8501
Timothy Jones, supt. Fax 725-6006
www.tcoe.org/Districts/Columbine.shtm
Columbine ES 200/K-8
2240 Road 160 93215 661-725-8501
Timothy Jones, prin. Fax 725-6006

Delano UNESD 7,700/PK-8
1405 12th Ave 93215 661-721-5000
Rosalina Rivera, supt. Fax 725-2201
www.duesd.org
Albany Park ES 500/PK-5
235 W 20th Ave 93215 661-721-5020
Karina Oropeza-Gonzalez, prin. Fax 720-2833
Almond Tree MS 700/6-8
200 W 15th Ave 93215 661-721-3641
Rodney Del Rio, prin. Fax 721-3649
Fremont ES 600/PK-5
1318 Clinton St 93215 661-721-5050
Teresa Cushnyr, prin. Fax 721-5058
Harvest ES 600/K-5
1320 Vassar Dr 93215 661-720-2725
Christine Chapman, prin. Fax 720-2715
La Vina MS 700/6-8
1331 Browning Rd 93215 661-721-3601
Jennifer Townson, prin. Fax 721-3662
Morningside ES 700/K-5
2100 Summer Dr 93215 661-720-2700
Rick Chavez, prin. Fax 720-2838
Pioneer S 700/K-8
1001 Hiett Ave 93215 661-474-4911
Anna Wyatt, prin. Fax 721-7725
Princeton Street ES 700/PK-5
1959 Princeton St 93215 661-721-5080
Mark Ruiz, prin. Fax 721-5084
Terrace ES 500/PK-5
1999 Norwalk St 93215 661-721-5060
Darrell Hennessee, prin. Fax 721-5074

Delhi, Merced, Pop. 10,554
Delhi USD 2,400/K-12
9716 Hinton Ave 95315 209-656-2000
Adolfo Melara, supt. Fax 656-2000
www.delhi.k12.ca.us
Delhi MS 200/7-8
9716 Hinton Ave 95315 209-656-2050
Brett Nickelson, prin. Fax 669-3168
El Capitan ES 400/K-6
9716 Hinton Ave 95315 209-656-2030
Gena Buchanan, prin. Fax 668-6146
Harmony S 600/K-6
9716 Hinton Ave 95315 209-656-2010
Nathan Rose, prin. Fax 669-3164
Schendel S 500/K-6
9716 Hinton Ave 95315 209-656-2040
Regina Diaz, prin. Fax 668-6124

Del Mar, San Diego, Pop. 4,073
Del Mar UNESD
Supt. — See San Diego
Del Mar Heights ES 500/K-6
13555 Boquita Dr 92014 858-755-9367
Wendy Wardlow, prin. Fax 509-1412
Del Mar Hills ES 300/K-6
14085 Mango Dr 92014 858-755-9763
Carrie Gammel, prin. Fax 755-6107

Del Rey, Fresno, Pop. 1,631
Sanger USD
Supt. — See Sanger
Del Rey ES 300/K-6
PO Box 70 93616 559-524-6060
Pete Munoz, prin. Fax 888-0901

Denair, Stanislaus, Pop. 4,321
Denair USD 1,400/PK-12
3460 Lester Rd 95316 209-632-7514
Aaron Rosander, supt. Fax 632-9194
dusd.k12.ca.us
Denair ES 300/PK-5
3460 Lester Rd 95316 209-632-8887
Kelly Beard, prin. Fax 632-8442
Denair MS 300/6-8
3460 Lester Rd 95316 209-632-2510
Brian LaFountain, prin. Fax 634-0269

Descanso, San Diego, Pop. 1,393
Mountain Empire USD
Supt. — See Pine Valley
Descanso ES 200/PK-5
24842 Viejas Blvd 91916 619-445-2126
Donna Burton, prin. Fax 445-2292

Desert Center, Riverside, Pop. 197
Desert Center USD 50/K-8
PO Box 6 92239 760-392-7604
Susan Scott, supt. Fax 502-6593
www.dcusd-ca.schoolloop.com/
Eagle Mountain S 50/K-8
PO Box 6 92239 760-392-7604
Susan Scott, prin. Fax 502-6593

Desert Hot Springs, Riverside, Pop. 25,289
Palm Springs USD
Supt. — See Palm Springs
Bella Vista ES 700/K-5
65750 Avenida Jalisco 92240 760-251-7244
Lisa Arseo, prin. Fax 251-7255
Bubbling Wells ES 800/K-5
67501 Camino Campanero 92240 760-251-7230
Omar Tinoco, prin. Fax 251-7237
Cabot Yerxa ES 800/K-5
67067 Desert View Ave 92240 760-251-2223
Amber Gascoigne, prin. Fax 251-3110
Corsini ES 500/K-5
68750 Hacienda Ave 92240 760-251-7260
Elizabeth Ramirez, prin. Fax 251-7263
Desert Springs MS 900/6-8
66755 Two Bunch Palms Trl 92240 760-251-7200
Kiela Snider Ed.D., prin. Fax 251-7206
Painted Hills MS 800/6-8
9250 Sonora Dr 92240 760-251-1551
Michael Grainger Ed.D., prin. Fax 251-5330
Two Bunch Palms ES 900/K-5
14250 West Dr 92240 760-251-7220
Joe Scudder, prin. Fax 251-7272

Diamond Bar, Los Angeles, Pop. 54,094
Pomona USD
Supt. — See Pomona
Armstrong ES 400/PK-6
22750 Beaverhead Dr 91765 909-397-4563
Cynthia Sanchez, prin. Fax 397-4565
Diamond Point ES 400/PK-6
24150 Sunset Crossing Rd 91765 909-397-4587
Karen Brisley, prin. Fax 396-4017
Golden Springs ES 400/PK-6
245 Ballena Dr 91765 909-397-4596
Deanna Glenn Ed.D., prin. Fax 860-0780
Lorbeer MS 700/7-8
501 S Diamond Bar Blvd 91765 909-397-4527
Angelique Butler, prin. Fax 396-9022
Pantera ES 400/K-6
801 Pantera Dr 91765 909-397-4475
Albert Tan, prin. Fax 396-8568

Walnut Valley USD
Supt. — See Walnut
Castle Rock ES 600/K-5
2975 Castle Rock Rd 91765 909-598-5006
Reema Byrne, prin. Fax 598-5960
Chaparral MS 1,300/6-8
1405 Spruce Tree Dr 91765 909-861-6227
Ronald Thibodeaux, prin. Fax 396-0749
Evergreen ES 500/K-5
2450 Evergreen Springs Dr 91765 909-594-1041
Carolyn Wills, prin. Fax 468-5217
Maple Hill ES 500/K-5
1350 Maple Hill Rd 91765 909-861-6224
Kelly Morris, prin. Fax 861-9825
Quail Summit ES 600/K-5
23330 Quail Summit Dr 91765 909-861-3004
Dr. Jeanette Koh, prin. Fax 444-4476

Institute of Knowledge 200/K-10
1009 Via Sorella, 909-595-2401
Abdulrahman Hachache, dir. Fax 594-1472
Mt. Calvary Lutheran S 100/PK-8
23300 Golden Springs Dr 91765 909-861-2740
Dr. Steven Christopher, prin. Fax 861-5481

Dinuba, Tulare, Pop. 21,288
Dinuba USD 6,500/K-12
1327 E El Monte Way 93618 559-595-7200
Joe Hernandez Ed.D., supt. Fax 591-3334
www.dinuba.k12.ca.us
Grand View ES 400/K-6
1327 E El Monte Way 93618 559-595-7275
Kevin Thomas, prin. Fax 595-8189
Jefferson ES 700/K-6
1327 E El Monte Way 93618 559-595-7266
Lisa Benslay, prin. Fax 595-7269
Kennedy ES 500/K-6
1327 E El Monte Way 93618 559-595-7300
Cindy James, prin. Fax 596-2050
Lincoln ES 600/K-6
1327 E El Monte Way 93618 559-595-7260
Gina Ramshaw, prin. Fax 595-7287
Roosevelt ES 700/K-6
1327 E El Monte Way 93618 559-595-7290
Elizabeth Gonzalez, prin. Fax 595-9628
Washington IS 900/7-8
1327 E El Monte Way 93618 559-595-7252
Jonathan Torres, prin. Fax 595-8158
Wilson ES 600/K-6
1327 E El Monte Way 93618 559-595-7370
Jesse Sanchez, prin. Fax 595-7279

Monson-Sultana JUNESD 400/K-8
10643 Avenue 416 93618 559-591-1634
Chris Meyer, supt. Fax 591-0717
www.msschool.org/
Monson-Sultana ES 400/K-8
10643 Avenue 416 93618 559-591-1634
Chris Meyer, admin. Fax 591-0717

Dinuba Jr. Academy 50/K-8
218 S Crawford Ave 93618 559-591-0194
Evan Hendrix, prin. Fax 591-4835

Discovery Bay, Contra Costa, Pop. 12,839
Byron UNESD
Supt. — See Byron
Discovery Bay ES 500/PK-5
1700 Willow Lake Rd, 925-809-7540
Pierre Laleau, prin. Fax 634-2106
Timber Point ES 500/PK-5
40 Newberry Ln, 925-809-7550
David Croy, prin. Fax 516-9318

Dixon, Solano, Pop. 17,699
Dixon USD 3,400/K-12
180 S 1st St 95620 707-693-6300
Brian Dolan, supt. Fax 678-0726
www.dixonusd.org
Anderson ES 500/K-6
415 E C St 95620 707-678-5508
Danielle Sharp, prin. Fax 678-2073
Higgins ES 500/K-6
1525 Pembroke Way 95620 707-678-6271
Shawntel McCammon, prin. Fax 693-1960
Jacobs IS 600/7-8
200 N Lincoln St 95620 707-678-9222
Dan Bledsoe, prin. Fax 678-1245
Tremont ES 600/K-6
355 Pheasant Run Dr 95620 707-678-9533
Tori Halcon, prin. Fax 678-0298

Neighborhood Christian S 100/PK-8
655 S 1st St Ste C 95620 707-678-9336
Rick Vidmar, prin. Fax 678-6640

Dobbins, Yuba, Pop. 595
Marysville JUSD
Supt. — See Marysville
Dobbins ES 100/K-6
PO Box 129 95935 530-692-1665
Duane Triplett, prin. Fax 692-2410

Dorris, Siskiyou, Pop. 895
Butte Valley USD 300/K-12
PO Box 709 96023 530-397-4000
Heidi Gerig, supt. Fax 397-3999
www.bvalusd.org/
Butte Valley ES 200/K-8
PO Box 709 96023 530-397-3900
Heidi Gerig, prin. Fax 397-4000

Dos Palos, Merced, Pop. 4,873
Dos Palos Oro Loma JUSD 2,400/K-12
2041 Almond St 93620 209-392-0200
William Spalding, supt. Fax 392-3347
www.dpol.net
Bryant MS 500/6-8
16695 Bryant Ave 93620 209-392-0240
Laura Andrews, prin. Fax 392-2636
Dos Palos ES 600/K-2
2149 Almond St 93620 209-392-0260
Dannette Bryson, prin. Fax 392-1006
Marks ES 500/3-5
1717 Valeria St 93620 209-392-0250
Manuel Cavazos, prin. Fax 392-4115

Douglas City, Trinity, Pop. 688
Douglas City ESD 200/K-8
PO Box 280 96024 530-623-6350
Shannon Ross, supt. Fax 623-3412
dcesd.org
Douglas City ES 200/K-8
PO Box 280 96024 530-623-6350
Shannon Ross, prin. Fax 623-3412

Downey, Los Angeles, Pop. 110,312
Downey USD 22,800/K-12
PO Box 7017 90241 562-469-6500
Dr. John Garcia Ph.D., supt. Fax 469-6515
www.dusd.net
Alameda ES 700/K-3
8613 Alameda St 90242 562-904-3589
Charlene Shimada, prin. Fax 469-7100
Carpenter ES 500/4-5
9439 Foster Rd 90242 562-904-3588
Dr. Mercedes Gomez Ed.D., prin. Fax 469-7110
Doty MS 1,400/6-8
10301 Woodruff Ave 90241 562-904-3586
Brent Shubin, prin. Fax 469-7240
Gallatin ES 700/K-5
9513 Brookshire Ave 90240 562-904-3583
Dr. Kathy Estevez Ed.D., prin. Fax 469-7120
Gauldin ES 600/K-5
9724 Spry St 90242 562-904-3582
Dolores Goble, prin. Fax 469-7130
Griffiths MS 1,400/6-8
9633 Tweedy Ln 90240 562-904-3580
Dr. Rani Bertsch Ed.D., prin. Fax 469-7260
Imperial ES 600/K-3
8133 Imperial Hwy 90242 562-904-3578
Margaret Meehan, prin. Fax 469-7140
Lewis ES 800/K-5
13220 Bellflower Blvd 90242 562-904-3590
Allison Box, prin. Fax 469-7150
Old River ES 700/4-5
11995 Old River School Rd 90242 562-904-3561
Caryn Jasich, prin. Fax 469-7160
Price ES 900/K-5
9525 Tweedy Ln 90240 562-904-3575
Mary Weyers, prin. Fax 469-7180
Rio Hondo ES 900/K-5
7731 Muller St 90241 562-904-3568
Lisa Rawlings, prin. Fax 469-7190
Rio San Gabriel ES 800/K-5
9338 Gotham St 90241 562-904-3567
David Cid, prin. Fax 469-7200
Stauffer MS 1,500/6-8
11985 Old River School Rd 90242 562-904-3565
Alyda Mir, prin. Fax 469-7300
Sussman MS 1,200/6-8
12500 Birchdale Ave 90242 562-904-3572
Dr. Robert Jagielski Ed.D., prin. Fax 469-7280
Unsworth ES 600/K-5
9001 Lindsey Ave 90240 562-904-3576
Kelley Rush-Becker, prin. Fax 469-7210
Ward ES 400/K-3
8851 Adoree St 90242 562-904-3591
Karen Trejo, prin. Fax 469-7220
Williams ES 700/K-3
7530 Arnett St 90241 562-904-3564
Teresa Medina, prin. Fax 469-7230

Calvary Chapel Christian S 1,000/PK-12
12808 Woodruff Ave 90242 562-803-4076
Roger Stahlhut B.S., admin. Fax 803-1292
Kirkwood Christian S 200/PK-5
11115 Pangborn Ave 90241 562-904-6911
Jennifer Hartl M.A., prin. Fax 904-6912
Our Lady of Perpetual Help S 300/K-8
10441 Downey Ave 90241 562-869-9969
Theresa Voeltz, prin. Fax 923-0659
St. Mark's Episcopal S 100/PK-8
10354 Downey Ave 90241 562-869-7213
Glenda Roberts, head sch Fax 861-9523
St. Raymond S 300/K-8
12320 Paramount Blvd 90242 562-862-3210
Claudia Rodarte, prin. Fax 862-6328

Downieville, Sierra, Pop. 276
Sierra-Plumas JUSD
Supt. — See Loyalton
Downieville ES 50/K-6
PO Box B 95936 530-289-3473
Merrill Grant Ed.D., supt. Fax 289-3693

Duarte, Los Angeles, Pop. 20,755
Duarte USD 3,700/K-12
1620 Huntington Dr 91010 626-599-5000
Dr. Allan Mucerino, supt. Fax 599-5069
www.duarte.k12.ca.us
Beardslee Academy 400/K-8
1212 Kellwill Way 91010 626-599-5200
Jennifer Romero, prin. Fax 599-5284
Duarte Arts Academy 400/K-8
1433 Crestfield Dr 91010 626-599-5100
Erin Villaverde, prin. Fax 599-5184
Maxwell Academy 400/K-8
733 Euclid Ave 91010 626-599-5302
Kelly Buckley, prin. Fax 599-5384
Northview 8th Grade Village 500/8-8
1565 E Central Ave 91010 626-599-5600
Mark Newell, prin. Fax 599-5684
Royal Oaks STEAM Academy 500/K-8
2499 Royal Oaks Dr 91010 626-599-5400
Janice Kolodinski, prin. Fax 599-5484
Valley View ES 400/K-6
237 Mel Canyon Rd 91010 626-599-5500
Margaret Rasmussen, prin. Fax 599-5584

Foothill Oaks Academy 100/PK-8
822 Bradbourne Ave 91010 626-301-9809
Nancy Lopez, prin. Fax 301-1342

Dublin, Alameda, Pop. 43,591
Dublin USD 8,300/K-12
7471 Larkdale Ave 94568 925-828-2551
Dr. Leslie Boozer, supt. Fax 829-6532
www.dublin.k12.ca.us
Amador ES K-5
2100 E Cantara Dr 94568 925-307-1950
Holly Scroggins, prin. Fax 828-4003
Dougherty ES 800/K-5
5301 Hibernia Dr 94568 925-803-4444
Brett Nelson, prin. Fax 556-3488
Dublin ES 700/K-5
7997 Vomac Rd 94568 925-833-1204
Lauren McGovern, prin. Fax 833-3362
Fredericksen ES 700/K-5
7243 Tamarack Dr 94568 925-828-1037
Claire Mognaga, prin. Fax 829-2562
Green ES 900/K-5
3300 Antone Way 94568 925-833-4200
Lorianne Ventura, prin. Fax 829-1076
Kolb ES 1,000/K-5
3150 Palermo Way 94568 925-551-4000
Joyce Gibson, prin. Fax 479-0124
Murray ES 400/K-5
8435 Davona Dr 94568 925-828-2568
Carrie Nerheim, prin. Fax 803-1367
Wells MS 800/6-8
6800 Penn Dr 94568 925-828-6227
Ean Ainsworth, prin. Fax 829-8851

Quarry Lane S 800/PK-12
6363 Tassajara Rd, 925-829-8000
Sabri Arac Ph.D., hdmstr. Fax 829-4928
St. Philip Lutheran S 200/PK-8
8850 Davona Dr 94568 925-829-3857
Raymond Zinnel, prin. Fax 829-6672
St. Raymond S 300/K-8
11557 Shannon Ave 94568 925-828-4064
Catherine Deehan, prin. Fax 828-2454
Valley Christian S 800/PK-12
7500 Inspiration Dr 94568 925-560-6240
Angela Bruggeman, head sch Fax 828-5658

Ducor, Tulare, Pop. 604
Ducor UNESD 200/K-8
PO Box 249 93218 559-534-2261
Isidro Rodriguez, supt. Fax 534-2271
www.ducorschool.com/
Ducor Union ES 200/K-8
PO Box 249 93218 559-534-2261
Isidro Rodriguez, supt. Fax 534-2271

Dunlap, Fresno
Kings Canyon JUSD
Supt. — See Reedley
Dunlap ES 300/PK-8
PO Box 635 93621 559-305-7310
Keith Merrihew, prin. Fax 338-2026

Dunsmuir, Siskiyou, Pop. 1,565
Dunsmuir ESD 100/PK-8
4760 Siskiyou Ave 96025 530-235-4828
Helen Herd, supt. Fax 235-0145
des-desd-ca.schoolloop.com
Dunsmuir ES 100/PK-8
4760 Siskiyou Ave 96025 530-235-4828
Helen Herd, admin. Fax 235-0145

Durham, Butte, Pop. 5,377
Durham USD 1,000/K-12
PO Box 300 95938 530-895-4675
Lloyd Webb, supt. Fax 895-4692
www.durhamunified.org/
Durham ES 400/K-5
PO Box 700 95938 530-895-4695
Shirley Williams, prin. Fax 895-4665
Durham IS 200/6-8
PO Box 310 95938 530-895-4690
Jason Bramson, prin. Fax 895-4305

Earlimart, Tulare, Pop. 8,499
Allensworth ESD
Supt. — See Allensworth
Allensworth S 100/K-8
HC 1 Box 136 93219 661-849-2401
Roel Marroquin, prin. Fax 849-6634

Earlimart ESD 2,000/PK-8
PO Box 11970 93219 661-849-3386
Philip Nystrom, supt. Fax 849-2352
www.earlimart.org
Alila ES 700/PK-5
PO Box 11970 93219 661-849-4202
Melissa Ruiz, prin. Fax 849-4206
Earlimart ES 700/PK-5
PO Box 11970 93219 661-849-2651
Stephanie Mendes, prin. Fax 849-1533
Earlimart MS 600/6-8
PO Box 11970 93219 661-849-2611
Scott Staton, prin. Fax 849-4214

East Nicolaus, Sutter, Pop. 219
Marcum-Illinois UNESD 2,300/K-12
2452 El Centro Blvd 95659 530-656-2407
Jimmie Eggers, supt. Fax 755-4302
www.marcum-illinois.org
Marcum-Illinois Union ES 200/K-8
2452 El Centro Blvd 95659 530-656-2407
Jimmie Eggers, admin. Fax 755-4302

East Palo Alto, San Mateo, Pop. 25,414
Ravenswood City ESD 3,700/PK-12
2120 Euclid Ave 94303 650-329-2800
Dr. Gloria Hernandez-Goff, supt. Fax 323-1072
www.ravenswoodschools.org
Brentwood Academy 500/K-5
2086 Clarke Ave 94303 650-329-2881
Jennifer Gravem, prin. Fax 329-2877
Chavez Academy 200/6-8
2450 Ralmar Ave 94303 650-329-6700
Nancy Bui, prin. Fax 326-8902
Costano S 600/K-8
2695 Fordham St 94303 650-329-2800
Viviana Espinosa, prin. Fax 328-3214
Green Oaks Academy 300/K-5
2450 Ralmar Ave 94303 650-329-6536
Nancy Bui, prin. Fax 325-8312
McNair Academy 200/6-8
2033 Pulgas Ave 94303 650-329-2888
Amanda Kemp, prin. Fax 473-9247
Ravenswood Child Development Center PK-PK
951 OConnor St 94303 650-838-3460
Glenda Savage, dir. Fax 326-9638
Ravenswood Comprehensive MS 6-8
2450 Ralmar St 94303 650-329-2800
Douglas Garriss, prin.
Other Schools – See Menlo Park, Palo Alto

Eastvale, Riverside, Pop. 51,943
Corona-Norco USD
Supt. — See Norco
Barton ES 1,700/K-6
7437 Corona Valley Ave, 951-736-4545
Dr. Manny Gonzalez, prin. Fax 736-4538
Eastvale ES 1,400/K-6
13031 Orange St, 951-738-2180
Michele Derus, prin. Fax 738-2186
Harada ES 1,300/K-6
12884 Oakdale St, 951-739-6820
Keith Adams, prin. Fax 739-6825
Parks ES 1,500/K-6
13830 Whispering Hills Dr, 951-736-7305
Cecilia Verduzco, prin. Fax 736-7308
Ramirez IS 1,100/7-8
6905 Harrison Ave, 951-736-8241
Dr. Kim Seheult, prin. Fax 273-3145
Reagan ES K-6
8300 Fieldmaster St, 951-736-7737
Susan Helms, prin. Fax 736-8250
River Heights IS 1,100/7-8
7227 Scholar Way, 951-738-2155
Teri Dudley, prin. Fax 738-2175

Edgewood, Siskiyou, Pop. 42
Butteville UNESD 200/K-8
24512 Edgewood Rd 96094 530-938-2255
Fax 938-3976
www.butteville.k12.ca.us
Butteville Union ES 200/K-8
24512 Edgewood Rd 96094 530-938-2255
Fax 938-3976

Edwards, Kern
Muroc JUSD
Supt. — See North Edwards
Branch ES 800/PK-6
1595 Bailey Ave 93523 661-258-4418
John Siercks, prin. Fax 258-9304

El Cajon, San Diego, Pop. 94,267
Cajon Valley UNESD 16,200/K-8
PO Box 1007 92022 619-588-3000
David Miyashiro Ed.D., supt. Fax 588-7653
www.cajonvalley.net
Anza ES 600/K-5
1005 S Anza St 92020 619-588-3116
Cindy Knight, prin. Fax 579-4815
Blossom Valley ES 500/K-5
9863 Oakmont Ter 92021 619-588-3678
Kirk Hoeben, prin. Fax 588-3022
Bostonia Language Academy 600/K-5
1390 Broadway 92021 619-588-3121
Izela Jacobo, prin. Fax 579-4849
Cajon Valley MS 900/6-8
550 E Park Ave 92020 619-588-3092
Justin Goodrich, prin. Fax 579-4817
Chase Ave ES 700/K-5
195 E Chase Ave 92020 619-588-3123
Brian Handley, prin. Fax 588-3184
Crest ES 100/K-5
2000 Suncrest Blvd 92021 619-588-3128
Carmen Restrepo, prin. Fax 579-4855
Emerald MS 600/6-8
1221 Emerald Ave 92020 619-588-3097
Amanda Silva, prin. Fax 588-3225
Flying Hills ES 500/K-6
1251 Finch St 92020 619-588-3132
Mike Kuhfal, prin. Fax 579-4877
Fuerte ES 600/K-5
11625 Fuerte Dr 92020 619-588-3134
Kristen Goodrich, prin. Fax 579-4825
Greenfield MS 600/6-8
1495 Greenfield Dr 92021 619-588-3103
Greg Calvert, prin. Fax 588-3648
Hall ES 500/K-5
1376 Pepper Dr 92021 619-588-3136
Stibaly Johnson, prin. Fax 579-4887
Hillsdale MS 1,500/6-8
1301 Brabham St 92019 619-441-6156
Jacob Launder, prin. Fax 441-6185
Jamacha ES 500/K-5
2962 Jamul Dr 92019 619-441-6150
Dr. Colleen Newman, prin. Fax 588-3682
Johnson ES 600/K-5
500 W Madison Ave 92020 619-588-3139
Christine Sphar, prin. Fax 579-4852
Lexington ES 800/K-5
1145 Redwood Ave 92019 619-588-3075
Sapper Karen, prin. Fax 588-3675
Los Coches Creek MS 700/6-8
9669 Dunbar Ln 92021 619-441-5741
Scott Goergens, prin. Fax 938-1850
Madison Avenue ES 500/K-5
1615 E Madison Ave 92019 619-588-3077
Stephanie Dodds, prin. Fax 441-6183
Magnolia ES 600/K-5
650 Greenfield Dr 92021 619-588-3080
Sarah Robinson, prin. Fax 579-4854
Meridian ES 700/K-5
651 S 3rd St 92019 619-588-3083
Ryan Satterfield, prin. Fax 579-4824
Montgomery MS 800/6-8
1570 Melody Ln 92019 619-588-3107
Bryan Schultz, prin. Fax 441-6122
Naranca ES 800/K-5
1030 Naranca Ave 92021 619-588-3087
Michael Serban, prin. Fax 441-6176
Rancho San Diego ES 600/K-5
12151 Calle Albara 92019 619-588-3211
Cherie Wall, prin. Fax 579-4858
Rios ES 300/K-5
14314 Rios Canyon Rd 92021 619-588-3090
Maria Kehoe, prin. Fax 579-4842

Vista Grande ES 600/K-5
1908 Vista Grande Rd 92019 619-588-3170
Tita Cordero-Bautista, prin. Fax 579-4822
Other Schools – See La Mesa

Dehesa ESD 2,200/PK-12
4612 Dehesa Rd 92019 619-444-2161
Nancy Hauer, supt. Fax 444-2105
dehesasd.sdcoe.net
Dehesa ES 200/PK-8
4612 Dehesa Rd 92019 619-444-2161
Nancy Hauer, supt. Fax 444-2105

La Mesa-Spring Valley SD
Supt. — See La Mesa
Fletcher Hills ES 700/K-6
2330 Center Pl 92020 619-668-5820
Eileen Cotter, prin. Fax 668-8353

Santee ESD
Supt. — See Santee
Pepper Drive ES 800/K-8
1935 Marlinda Way 92021 619-956-5100
Ted Hooks, prin. Fax 956-5114

Christian ES East Campus 100/K-6
2100 Greenfield Dr 92019 619-201-8900
Terri Clark, prin. Fax 201-8923
Christian ES West Campus 100/K-6
211 S 3rd St 92019 619-201-8925
Marla Hester, prin.
El Cajon SDA Christian S 50/K-8
1640 E Madison Ave 92019 619-442-6544
Rachel Romero B.S., prin. Fax 442-0490
Foothills Christian MS 100/6-8
350 Cypress Ln Ste C 92020 619-303-1641
Holy Trinity S 300/PK-8
509 Ballard St 92019 619-444-7529
Frances Wright, prin. Fax 444-3721
Our Lady of Grace S 300/K-8
2766 Navajo Rd 92020 619-466-0055
Susan Hause, prin. Fax 466-8994
St. Kieran S 100/PK-8
1347 Camillo Way 92021 619-588-6398
Patricia Provo, prin. Fax 588-6382

El Centro, Imperial, Pop. 42,253
El Centro ESD 6,000/K-8
1256 Broadway Ave, 760-352-5712
Jon LeDoux, supt. Fax 312-9522
www.ecesd.com
De Anza S 500/K-8
1530 S Waterman Ave, 760-352-9811
Richard Sanchez, prin. Fax 352-0920
Desert Garden ES 300/K-6
1900 S 6th St, 760-352-2051
Cecilia Heraz, prin. Fax 352-3802
Harding ES 500/K-6
950 S 7th St, 760-352-4791
Juan Aguilera, prin. Fax 353-7204
Hedrick ES 500/K-6
550 S Waterman Ave, 760-352-4750
Joy Ceasar, prin. Fax 353-6832
Kennedy MS 400/7-8
900 N 6th St, 760-352-0444
Michael Castillo, prin. Fax 353-0325
King ES 400/K-6
1950 Villa Ave, 760-337-6555
Terri Ponce, prin. Fax 353-6714
Lincoln ES 400/K-6
200 N 12th St, 760-352-3060
Olga Criman, prin. Fax 352-4477
McKinley ES 400/K-6
1177 N 8th St, 760-352-3225
Karla Sigmond, prin. Fax 353-2858
Sunflower ES 400/K-6
2450 W Main St, 760-337-4890
Jeannette Quiroz, prin. Fax 337-4894
Washington ES 400/K-6
223 S 1st St, 760-352-6611
Norberto Nunez, prin. Fax 370-3089
Wilson JHS 700/7-8
600 S Wilson St, 760-352-5341
Rauna Fox, prin. Fax 337-3800

McCabe UNESD 1,400/K-8
701 W McCabe Rd, 760-335-5200
Laura Dubbe, supt. Fax 352-4398
www.mccabeschool.net
McCabe ES 1,400/K-8
701 W McCabe Rd, 760-352-5443
Armando Lopez, prin. Fax 352-6812

Meadows UNESD 500/K-8
2059 Bowker Rd, 760-352-7512
Matt Phillips, supt. Fax 337-1275
www.meadowsunion.org
Meadows ES 500/K-8
2059 Bowker Rd, 760-352-7512
Summer Herza, prin. Fax 337-1275

St. Mary S 200/PK-8
700 S Waterman Ave, 760-352-7285
Sr. Katia Chavez, prin. Fax 352-9727

El Cerrito, Contra Costa, Pop. 22,213
West Contra Costa USD
Supt. — See Richmond
Cameron ES 300/PK-PK
7140 Gladys Ave 94530 510-233-1955
Susan Moehlenbrock, admin. Fax 233-2178
Fairmont ES 600/K-6
724 Kearney St 94530 510-231-1448
Lynn Bernhardt, prin. Fax 528-9206
Harding ES 400/K-6
7230 Fairmount Ave 94530 510-231-1413
Linda Takimoto, prin. Fax 559-1365
Korematsu MS 500/6-8
1021 Navellier St 94530 510-524-0405
Matthew Burnham, prin. Fax 559-8784

Madera ES 500/K-6
8500 Madera Dr 94530 510-231-1412
Alison Makela, prin. Fax 235-8003

Montessori Family S 100/PK-8
7075 Cutting Blvd 94530 510-236-8802
Alissa Stolz, head sch Fax 236-8805
Prospect Sierra ES 200/K-4
2060 Tapscott Ave 94530 510-809-9036
Katherine Dinh, head sch Fax 232-7615
Prospect Sierra MS 300/5-8
960 Avis Dr 94530 510-809-9000
Katherine Dinh, head sch Fax 527-3728
St. Jerome S 200/K-8
320 San Carlos Ave 94530 510-525-9484
Alison Wilkie, prin. Fax 525-5227
St. John the Baptist S 200/K-8
11156 San Pablo Ave 94530 510-234-2244
Mike Gutierrez, prin. Fax 234-3726
Tehiyah Day S 200/K-8
2603 Tassajara Ave 94530 510-233-3013
Deb Massey, head sch Fax 233-0171

El Dorado Hills, El Dorado, Pop. 40,513
Buckeye UNSD 4,700/PK-8
PO Box 4768 95762 916-985-2183
Dr. David Roth, supt. Fax 934-0920
www.buckeyeusd.org/
Brooks ES 500/K-5
3610 Park Dr 95762 916-933-6618
Kevin Cadden, prin. Fax 933-3910
Oak Meadow ES 800/K-5
7701 Silva Valley Pkwy 95762 916-933-9746
Tracy Linyard, prin. Fax 933-9784
Rolling Hills MS 1,000/6-8
7141 Silva Valley Pkwy 95762 916-933-9290
Debra Bowers, prin. Fax 939-7454
Silva Valley ES 600/K-5
3001 Golden Eagle Ln 95762 916-933-3767
Kathy Holliman, prin. Fax 933-6389
Other Schools – See Cameron Park, Shingle Springs

Rescue UNESD
Supt. — See Rescue
Jackson ES 400/K-5
2561 Francisco Dr 95762 916-933-1828
Michele Miller, prin. Fax 933-5569
Lake Forest ES 400/K-5
2240 Sailsbury Dr 95762 916-933-0652
Bruce Peters, prin. Fax 933-0654
Lakeview ES 600/K-5
3371 Brittany Way 95762 916-941-2600
Kathy Miracle, prin. Fax 941-3826
Marina Village MS 800/6-8
1901 Francisco Dr 95762 916-933-3993
George Tapanes, prin. Fax 933-3995

Golden Hills School 200/PK-8
1060 Suncast Ln 95762 916-933-0100
Armaghan Mirhaj, head sch
Guiding Hands S 100/PK-12
4900 Windplay Dr 95762 916-939-0553
Starranne Meyers, prin. Fax 939-0563
Holy Trinity S 300/K-8
3115 Tierra de Dios Dr 95762 530-677-3234
Chris Nelson, prin. Fax 677-3570

El Granada, San Mateo, Pop. 5,264

Wilkinson S K-8
PO Box 1059 94018 650-726-4582

Elk Creek, Glenn, Pop. 158
Stony Creek JUSD 100/K-12
3430 County Road 309 95939 530-968-5361
Laurel Hill-Ward, supt. Fax 968-5102
www.scjusd.org
Elk Creek ES 50/K-3
3430 County Road 309 95939 530-968-5288
Laurel Hill-Ward, prin. Fax 968-5535
Other Schools – See Stonyford

Elk Grove, Sacramento, Pop. 142,334
Elk Grove USD 61,500/PK-12
9510 Elk Grove Florin Rd 95624 916-686-5085
Christopher Hoffman, supt. Fax 686-7787
www.egusd.net
Albiani MS 1,400/7-8
9140 Bradshaw Rd 95624 916-686-5210
Gabrielle Bajar, prin. Fax 686-5538
Batey ES 1,000/K-6
9421 Stonebrook Dr 95624 916-714-5520
Robert Pasley, prin. Fax 714-5588
Butler ES 1,000/K-6
9180 Brown Rd 95624 916-681-7595
Christine Baeta, prin. Fax 681-7599
Carroll ES 1,200/K-6
10325 Stathos Dr, 916-714-0106
Carrie Pearson Ed.D., prin. Fax 714-0828
Case ES 800/K-6
8565 Shasta Lily Dr 95624 916-681-8820
John Santin, prin. Fax 681-8807
Castello ES 900/K-6
9850 Fire Poppy Dr, 916-686-1725
Janet Anderson, prin. Fax 686-3082
Donner ES 900/K-6
9461 Soaring Oaks Dr 95758 916-683-3073
Michelle Jenkins, prin. Fax 683-3136
Eddy MS 1,000/7-8
9329 Soaring Oaks Dr 95758 916-683-1302
Mark Benson, prin. Fax 684-6142
Ehrhardt ES 1,000/K-6
8900 Old Creek Dr 95758 916-684-7259
William Aydlett, prin. Fax 684-0351
Elk Grove ES 900/K-6
9373 Crowell Dr 95624 916-686-3766
Dave Neves, prin. Fax 686-1299
Elliott Ranch ES 900/K-6
10000 E Taron Dr, 916-683-3877
Tierra Crothers, prin. Fax 683-3862

Feickert ES 600/K-6
9351 Feickert Dr 95624 916-686-7716
Eric Murchison, prin. Fax 686-8921
Foulks Ranch ES 900/K-6
6211 Laguna Park Dr 95758 916-684-8177
Joe Donovan, prin. Fax 684-0533
Franklin ES 700/K-6
4011 Hood Franklin Rd, 916-684-6518
Larry Quismondo, prin. Fax 684-6039
Harris MS 1,200/7-8
8691 Power Inn Rd 95624 916-688-0080
Charles Amey, prin. Fax 688-0084
Hein ES 1,200/K-6
6820 Bellaterra Dr, 916-714-0654
Lynne Mayer, prin. Fax 714-0216
Herburger ES 900/K-6
8670 Maranello Way 95624 916-681-1390
Jennifer Wilbanks, prin. Fax 682-5477
Johnson MS 1,300/7-8
10099 Franklin High Rd, 916-714-8181
Patrick McDougall, prin. Fax 714-8177
Kerr MS 900/7-8
8865 Elk Grove Blvd 95624 916-686-7728
Zachary Cheney, prin. Fax 685-2952
Markofer ES 700/K-6
9759 Tralee Way 95624 916-686-7714
Gordon Blackwood, prin. Fax 685-7653
McKee ES 500/PK-6
8701 Halverson Dr 95624 916-686-3715
Steve Looper, prin. Fax 685-9614
Mix ES K-6
4730 Laguna Park Dr 95758 916-683-7445
Tracey Panuschka, prin. Fax 683-6313
Pinkerton MS 1,000/7-8
8365 Whitelock Pkwy, 916-683-7680
Chandra Victor, prin. Fax 685-5703
Pleasant Grove ES 500/K-6
10160 Pleasant Grove Sch Rd 95624 916-685-9630
Deidra Wood, prin. Fax 685-7910
Sims ES 1,100/K-6
3033 Buckminster Dr 95758 916-683-7445
Carrie Pearson Ed.D., prin. Fax 683-6313
Stone Lake ES 800/K-6
9673 Lakepoint Dr 95758 916-683-4096
Mark Beard, prin. Fax 683-4098
West ES 1,100/K-6
8625 Serio Way 95758 916-683-4362
Brian MacNeill, prin. Fax 683-4363
Zehnder Ranch ES K-6
9330 Denali Cir, 916-793-3300
Mechale Murphy, prin.
Other Schools – See Rancho Cordova, Sacramento, Sloughhouse, Wilton

---

St. Elizabeth Ann Seton S 300/PK-8
9539 Racquet Ct 95758 916-684-7903
Trina Koontz, prin. Fax 691-4064
St. Peter's Lutheran S 200/PK-8
8701 Elk Grove Florin Rd 95624 916-689-3050
LaVonne Monroe, prin. Fax 689-3462

El Monte, Los Angeles, Pop. 112,772
El Monte City SD 9,200/K-8
3540 Lexington Ave 91731 626-453-3700
Dr. Maribel Garcia, supt. Fax 442-1063
www.emcsd.org
Cherrylee ES 500/K-6
5025 Buffington Rd 91732 626-575-2326
Doris Tran, prin. Fax 279-7059
Columbia S 900/K-8
3400 California Ave 91731 626-575-2306
Jaime Ortega, prin. Fax 279-1603
Cortada ES 500/K-6
3111 Potrero Ave 91733 626-575-2391
Brenda Ruiz, prin. Fax 442-2038
Durfee/Thompson S 1,100/K-8
12233 Star St 91732 626-443-3900
Juan Munoz, prin. Fax 579-0451
Gidley S 600/K-8
10226 Lower Azusa Rd 91731 626-575-2323
Alba Zamora-Day, prin. Fax 455-0538
Legore ES 500/K-6
11121 Bryant Rd 91731 626-575-2329
Adriana Garcia, prin. Fax 448-6921
New Lexington ES 400/K-6
10410 Bodger St 91733 626-575-2320
Cynthia Flores, prin. Fax 575-2228
Potrero S 1,000/K-8
2611 Potrero Ave 91733 626-350-9386
Teresa Pinedo, prin. Fax 443-8707
Rio Vista ES 400/K-6
4300 Esto Ave 91731 626-575-2310
Joella Richenberger, prin. Fax 579-3729
Shirpser ES 500/K-6
4020 Gibson Rd 91731 626-575-2393
Lorraine Torres, prin. Fax 443-2140
Wilkerson ES 600/K-6
2700 Doreen Ave 91733 626-575-2331
Maricela Borja, prin. Fax 443-8659
Wright S 1,000/K-8
11317 McGirk Ave 91732 626-575-2333
Dr. Monica Munoz, prin. Fax 443-8711
Other Schools – See Arcadia, Temple City

Mountain View ESD 7,500/K-8
3320 Gilman Rd 91732 626-652-4000
Lillian Maldonado French, supt. Fax 652-4052
www.mtviewschools.com/
Baker ES 700/K-5
12043 Exline St 91732 626-652-4700
Sylvia Rivera, prin. Fax 652-4715
Cogswell ES 500/K-6
11050 Fineview St 91733 626-652-4100
Gerardo Yepez, prin. Fax 652-4115
Kranz IS 800/7-8
12460 Fineview St 91732 626-652-4200
Sean Gryeel, prin. Fax 652-4216
La Primaria ES 300/K-5
4220 Gilman Rd 91732 626-652-4150
Tony Lugo, prin. Fax 652-4165

Madrid MS 900/6-8
3300 Gilman Rd 91732 626-652-4300
Cesar Flores, prin. Fax 652-4315
Maxson ES 600/K-6
12380 Felipe St 91732 626-652-4500
Dr. Veronica Godinez, prin. Fax 652-4515
Miramonte ES 500/K-6
10620 Schmidt Rd 91733 626-652-4600
Bruce Rhodes, prin. Fax 652-4615
Monte Vista ES 800/K-8
11111 Thienes Ave 91733 626-652-4650
Glenda Giron, prin. Fax 652-4665
Parkview ES 900/K-6
12044 Elliott Ave 91732 626-652-4800
Donelle Soto, prin. Fax 652-4815
Payne ES 600/K-6
2850 Mountain View Rd 91732 626-652-4900
Dr. Hugo Moreno, prin. Fax 652-4915
Twin Lakes ES 400/K-5
3900 Gilman Rd 91732 626-652-4400
Michelle Torres, prin. Fax 652-4415
Voorhis ES 500/K-5
3501 Durfee Ave 91732 626-652-4450
Carolina Galaviz, prin. Fax 652-4465

Nativity S 200/K-8
10907 Saint Louis Dr 91731 626-448-2414
Sr. Stacy Reineman, prin. Fax 448-2763

El Nido, Merced, Pop. 326
El Nido ESD 200/K-8
161 E El Nido Rd 95317 209-385-8420
Rae Ann Jimenez, supt. Fax 723-9169
www.elnidoschool.org
El Nido ES 200/K-8
161 E El Nido Rd 95317 209-385-8420
Rae Jimenez, prin. Fax 723-9169

El Portal, Mariposa, Pop. 456
Mariposa County USD
Supt. — See Mariposa
El Portal ES 100/K-8
PO Box 190 95318 209-379-2382
Sean Jacobs, prin. Fax 379-9138

El Segundo, Los Angeles, Pop. 15,912
El Segundo USD 3,400/K-12
641 Sheldon St 90245 310-615-2650
Dr. Melissa Moore, supt.
www.elsegundousd.net
Center Street ES 800/K-5
641 Sheldon St 90245 310-615-2676
Martha Monahan, prin. Fax 640-9105
El Segundo MS 800/6-8
332 Center St 90245 310-615-2690
Dr. Melissa Gooden, prin. Fax 640-9634
Richmond Street ES 600/K-5
615 Richmond St 90245 310-606-6831
Dr. Alice Lee, prin. Fax 322-8512

St. Anthony S 200/K-8
233 Lomita St 90245 310-322-4218
Patrick Kelly, prin. Fax 322-2659

El Sobrante, Contra Costa, Pop. 11,868
West Contra Costa USD
Supt. — See Richmond
Crespi MS 600/7-8
1121 Allview Ave 94803 510-231-1447
Guthrie Fleischman, prin. Fax 243-2090
Olinda ES 400/K-6
5855 Olinda Rd 94803 510-231-1452
Amandeep Randhawa, prin. Fax 223-4514

East Bay Waldorf S 100/PK-8
3800 Clark Rd 94803 510-223-3297
Kelly Chappie, admin. Fax 222-3141
El Sobrante Christian ES 200/K-6
5100 Argyle Rd 94803 510-223-2242
Jeannine Manguiat M.Ed., prin. Fax 223-8453

Elverta, Sacramento, Pop. 5,268
Elverta JESD 300/K-12
7900 Eloise Ave 95626 916-991-2244
Michael Borgaard, supt. Fax 991-0271
www.ejesd.net
Alpha Technology MS 100/6-8
7900 Eloise Ave 95626 916-991-4726
Michael Borgaard, prin.
Elverta ES 200/K-5
7900 Eloise Ave 95626 916-991-2244
Michael Borgaard, prin. Fax 991-0271

Emeryville, Alameda, Pop. 9,492
Emery USD 700/K-12
4727 San Pablo Ave 94608 510-601-4906
Dr. John Rubio, supt. Fax 601-4913
www.emeryusd.org/
Yates ES 500/K-8
1125 53rd St 94608 510-601-4916
Diane Lang, prin. Fax 601-4988

Escuela Bilingue Internacional 200/PK-8
4550 San Pablo 94608 510-652-7094
Jon Fulk, head sch Fax 652-7056

Empire, Stanislaus, Pop. 4,054
Empire UNESD
Supt. — See Modesto
Empire ES 400/K-6
PO Box 1269 95319 209-521-2970
Nancy Fox, prin. Fax 527-5620

Encinitas, San Diego, Pop. 57,785
Encinitas UNESD 5,400/K-6
101 S Rancho Santa Fe Rd 92024 760-944-4300
Dr. Timothy Baird, supt. Fax 942-7094
www.eusd.net
Capri ES 700/K-6
941 Capri Rd 92024 760-944-4360
Carrie Lancon, prin. Fax 944-4364
Ecke-Central ES 600/K-6
185 Union St 92024 760-944-4323
Adriana Chavarin, prin. Fax 944-4370
Flora Vista ES 400/K-6
1690 Wandering Rd 92024 760-944-4329
Chris Juarez, prin. Fax 944-4385
Ocean Knoll ES 600/K-6
910 Melba Rd 92024 760-944-4351
Jennifer Bond, prin. Fax 944-4353
Park Dale Lane ES 500/K-6
2050 Park Dale Ln 92024 760-944-4344
Erin Terry, prin. Fax 632-1692
Other Schools – See Carlsbad

San Dieguito UNHSD 12,400/7-12
710 Encinitas Blvd 92024 760-753-6491
Eric Dill, supt. Fax 943-3501
www.sduhsd.net
Diegueno MS 900/7-8
710 Encinitas Blvd 92024 760-944-1892
Jeffrey Copeland, prin. Fax 944-3717
Oak Crest MS 900/7-8
710 Encinitas Blvd 92024 760-753-6241
Brieahna Weatherford, prin. Fax 942-0520
Other Schools – See San Diego, Solana Beach

Encinitas Country Day 300/K-12
3616 Manchester Ave 92024 760-942-1111
Graeg Lehmunn, prin.
Pacific Academy 50/K-12
679 Encinitas Blvd Ste 211 92024 760-634-1188
Rhoades S 300/K-8
141 S Rancho Santa Fe Rd 92024 760-436-1102
St. John S 500/K-8
1003 Encinitas Blvd 92024 760-944-8227
Daniel Schuh, prin. Fax 944-8939

Encino, See Los Angeles
Los Angeles USD
Supt. — See Los Angeles
Academy for Enriched Science 300/K-5
17551 Miranda St 91316 818-609-8421
Renee Christian-Cofield, prin. Fax 609-8424
Lanai Road ES 600/K-5
4241 Lanai Rd 91436 818-788-1590
Lisa Elan, prin. Fax 788-4263

Los Encinos S 100/K-6
17100 Ventura Blvd 91316 818-990-1006
Ilene Reinfeld, head sch Fax 990-0142
Our Lady of Grace S 200/PK-8
17720 Ventura Blvd 91316 818-344-4126
Joyce Cluess, prin. Fax 344-1736
St. Cyril of Jerusalem S 300/PK-8
4548 Haskell Ave 91436 818-501-4155
Ryan Halverson, prin. Fax 501-8480
Valley Beth Shalom Harold M. Schulweis S 300/K-6
15739 Ventura Blvd 91436 818-788-2199
Westmark S 200/1-12
5461 Louise Ave 91316 818-986-5045
Claudia Koochek, head sch Fax 986-2605

Escalon, San Joaquin, Pop. 7,002
Escalon USD 2,800/K-12
1520 Yosemite Ave 95320 209-838-3591
Ron Costa, supt. Fax 838-6703
www.escalonusd.org/
Dent ES 600/K-5
1998 Yosemite Ave 95320 209-838-7031
Matthew Loretelli, prin. Fax 838-8916
El Portal MS 600/6-8
805 1st St 95320 209-838-7095
Mark Vos, prin. Fax 838-3017
Van Allen ES 300/K-5
21051 State Highway 120 95320 209-838-2931
Julio Zambrano, prin. Fax 838-1832
Other Schools – See Farmington, Stockton

Escondido, San Diego, Pop. 140,582
Escondido Union SD 19,900/PK-8
2310 Aldergrove Ave 92029 760-432-2400
Luis Rankins-Ibarra Ed.D., supt. Fax 735-2874
www.eusd.org
Bear Valley MS 1,100/6-8
3003 Bear Valley Pkwy S 92025 760-432-4060
Susan Freeman, prin. Fax 504-0158
Bernardo ES 600/K-5
1122 Mountain Heights Dr 92029 760-432-2700
Lisa Clark-DuKet, prin. Fax 432-2720
Central ES 700/K-5
122 W 4th Ave 92025 760-432-2431
Stephanie Rosson-Niess, prin. Fax 735-2862
Conway ES 700/K-5
1325 Conway Dr 92027 760-432-2435
Christina Meglich, prin. Fax 480-4312
Del Dios Academy of Arts and Sciences 800/6-8
1400 W 9th Ave 92029 760-432-2439
Albert Ngo, prin. Fax 432-0728
Farr Avenue ES 700/K-5
933 Farr Ave 92026 760-735-3049
Lizeth Lopez, prin. Fax 504-0170
Felicita ES 800/K-5
737 W 13th Ave 92025 760-432-2444
Kathy Morris, prin. Fax 745-1462
Glen View ES 700/K-5
2201 E Mission Ave 92027 760-432-2448
Cesar Carrasco, prin. Fax 480-8302
Green ES 700/K-5
3115 Las Palmas Ave 92025 760-432-2260
Randy Garcia, prin. Fax 745-9173
Hidden Valley MS 1,200/6-8
2700 Reed Rd 92027 760-432-2457
Trent Smith, prin. Fax 480-0845
Juniper ES 700/K-5
1809 S Juniper St 92025 760-432-2462
Jason Wrzeski, prin. Fax 746-2041
Lincoln ES 700/K-5
1029 N Broadway 92026 760-432-2466
Angel Gotay, prin. Fax 745-3402
Miller ES 500/K-5
1975 Miller Ave 92025 760-432-2470
Martin Hranek, prin. Fax 745-2766
Mission MS 1,000/6-8
939 E Mission Ave 92025 760-432-2452
Dr. Carlos Ulloa, prin. Fax 737-9085
North Broadway ES 600/K-5
2301 N Broadway 92026 760-432-2479
Jason Hoff, prin. Fax 745-5230
Oak Hill ES 900/K-5
1820 Oak Hill Dr 92027 760-432-2483
Rick Ausby, prin. Fax 745-5067
Orange Glen ES 800/K-5
2861 E Valley Pkwy 92027 760-432-2487
Beth Crooks, prin. Fax 735-2840
Pioneer ES 800/K-5
980 N Ash St 92027 760-432-2412
Melina Quon, prin. Fax 745-7536
Preschool PK-PK
835 W 15th Ave 92025 760-489-4131
Marcia Karadashian, prin. Fax 489-6431
Quantum Academy at the Nicolaysen Center 200/4-8
420 Falconer Rd 92027 760-432-2220
Tek Kirkbride, prin.
Reidy Creek ES 700/K-5
2869 N Broadway 92026 760-739-5800
Kelly Mussatti, prin. Fax 739-5813
Rincon MS 1,300/6-8
925 Lehner Ave 92026 760-432-2491
Tim Biland, prin. Fax 743-6713
Rock Springs ES 700/K-5
1155 Deodar Rd 92026 760-432-2284
Audrey Frank, prin. Fax 745-3549
Rose ES 600/K-5
906 N Rose St 92027 760-432-2495
Lisa Pitard, prin. Fax 745-3251

San Pasqual UNESD 500/PK-8
15305 Rockwood Rd 92027 760-745-4931
Shannon Hargrave, supt. Fax 745-2473
www.sanpasqualunion.net
San Pasqual Union S 500/PK-8
15305 Rockwood Rd 92027 760-745-4931
Shannon Hargrave, prin. Fax 745-2473

Balboa S 100/1-12
130 Woodward Ave 92025 760-294-4490
Zachary Jones, dir. Fax 294-4209
Calvin Christian ES 200/PK-5
1868 N Broadway 92026 760-489-1159
Paul Lapka, prin. Fax 489-0335
Escondido Adventist Academy 200/K-12
1301 Deodar Rd 92026 760-746-1800
Larry Rich M.Ed., prin. Fax 743-3499
Escondido Christian S 400/PK-12
PO Box 300157 92030 760-745-2071
Joel Phillips, supt. Fax 745-1905
Grace Christian S 300/PK-8
643 W 13th Ave 92025 760-747-3029
Ben Elliott, prin. Fax 745-1612
St. Mary S 200/K-8
130 E 13th Ave 92025 760-743-3431
Amanda Johnston, prin. Fax 743-6808

Esparto, Yolo, Pop. 3,053
Esparto USD 1,200/PK-12
26675 Plainfield St 95627 530-787-3446
Diego Ochoa, supt. Fax 787-3033
www.espartok12.org
Esparto ES 700/PK-5
26675 Plainfield St 95627 530-787-3417
Erika St. Andre, prin. Fax 787-4844
Esparto MS 200/6-8
26675 Plainfield St 95627 530-787-4151
Sherrie Vann, prin. Fax 787-3890

Etiwanda, See Rancho Cucamonga
Etiwanda SD 13,600/K-8
6061 East Ave 91739 909-899-2451
Shawn Judson Ed.D., supt. Fax 899-1235
www.etiwanda.k12.ca.us
Day Creek IS 1,200/6-8
12345 Coyote Dr 91739 909-803-3300
David Apodaca, prin. Fax 803-3309
Etiwanda Colony ES 900/K-5
13144 Banyan St 91739 909-803-3911
Sandra Fleming, prin. Fax 803-3917
Etiwanda IS 1,300/6-8
6925 Etiwanda Ave 91739 909-899-1701
Justin Kooyman, prin. Fax 899-5676
Golden ES 900/K-5
12400 Banyan St 91739 909-463-9105
Lisa Wildes, prin. Fax 463-9124
Grapeland ES 700/K-5
7171 Etiwanda Ave 91739 909-463-7026
Joseph Shaw, prin. Fax 463-4838
Perdew ES 800/K-5
13051 Miller Ave 91739 909-803-3316
Kelly Bray, prin. Fax 803-3941
Summit IS 1,100/6-8
5959 East Ave 91739 909-899-1704
Kristin Ledesma, prin. Fax 899-7596
Windrows ES 600/K-5
6855 Victoria Park Ln 91739 909-899-2641
Josh Lautenslager, prin. Fax 899-3197
Other Schools – See Alta Loma, Fontana, Rancho Cucamonga

Etna, Siskiyou, Pop. 666
Scott Valley USD
Supt. — See Fort Jones
Etna ES 200/K-5
220 Collier Way 96027 530-467-3320
Garren Hanon, prin. Fax 467-3465

Eureka, Humboldt, Pop. 25,748
Cutten ESD 600/K-6
4182 Walnut Dr 95503 707-441-3900
Susan Ivey, supt. Fax 441-3906
www.cuttensd.org

Cutten ES 300/3-6
4182 Walnut Dr 95503 707-441-3900
Julie Osborne, prin. Fax 441-3906
Ridgewood ES 300/K-2
2060 Ridgewood Dr 95503 707-441-3930
Susan Ivey, prin. Fax 441-3933

Eureka City SD 3,700/K-12
2100 J St 95501 707-441-2400
Fred Van Vleck Ed.D., supt. Fax 441-3326
www.eurekacityschools.org
Birney ES 500/K-5
717 South Ave 95503 707-441-2495
Beth Holcomb, prin. Fax 444-3524
Grant ES 300/K-5
3901 G St 95503 707-441-2552
Kristi Puzz, prin. Fax 441-3321
LaFayette ES 300/K-5
3100 Park St 95501 707-441-2482
Tammi Wagner, prin. Fax 441-3320
Washington ES 500/K-5
3322 Dolbeer St 95503 707-441-2547
Sheri Jensen, prin. Fax 441-3323
Winship MS, 2500 Cypress Ave 95503 300/6-8
Teri Waterhouse, prin. 707-441-2488
Zane MS 600/6-8
2155 S St 95501 707-441-2470
Randall Simms, prin. Fax 441-0286

Freshwater ESD 300/PK-8
75 Greenwood Heights Dr 95503 707-442-2969
Si Talty, supt. Fax 442-9527
www.freshwatersd.org
Freshwater ES 300/PK-6
75 Greenwood Heights Dr 95503 707-442-2969
Si Talty, admin. Fax 442-9527

Garfield ESD 100/K-6
2200 Freshwater Rd 95503 707-442-5471
Michael Quinlan, supt. Fax 442-1932
www.humboldt.k12.ca.us/garfield_sd
Garfield ES 100/K-6
2200 Freshwater Rd 95503 707-442-5471
Michael Quinlan, prin. Fax 442-1932

South Bay UNSD 800/K-12
6077 Loma Ave 95503 707-476-8549
Gary Storts, supt. Fax 476-8968
www.southbaydistrict.org
Pine Hill ES 300/K-3
5230 Vance St 95503 707-443-4596
Tami Beall, prin. Fax 443-1312
South Bay ES 200/4-6
6077 Loma Ave 95503 707-443-4828
Gary Storts, prin. Fax 444-3690

Gospel Outreach S 50/K-12
2845 Saint James Pl 95503 707-445-2214
David Sczepanski, prin. Fax 445-2212
Redwood Christian S 100/K-8
2039 E St 95501 707-442-4625
Greg Morse, head sch Fax 442-4685

Exeter, Tulare, Pop. 10,133
Exeter USD 2,900/PK-12
215 N Crespi Ave 93221 559-592-9421
Tim Hire, supt. Fax 592-9445
www.exeter.k12.ca.us/
Lincoln ES 600/PK-5
333 S D St 93221 559-592-2141
Veronica Raigoza, prin. Fax 592-5249
Rocky Hill ES 600/K-5
313 Sequoia Dr 93221 559-592-5490
Linda Montemayor, prin. Fax 592-3715
Wilson MS 700/6-8
710 W Maple St 93221 559-592-2144
Sonia Wilson, prin. Fax 592-5536

Sierra View Junior Academy 100/K-10
19933 Avenue 256 93221 559-592-3689

Fairfax, Marin, Pop. 7,179
Ross Valley SD
Supt. — See San Anselmo
Manor ES 400/K-5
150 Oak Manor Dr 94930 415-453-1544
Peg Minicozzi, prin. Fax 453-0680
White Hill MS 700/6-8
101 Glen Dr 94930 415-454-8390
David Finnane, prin. Fax 454-3980

Fairfield, Solano, Pop. 97,586
Fairfield-Suisun USD 21,300/PK-12
2490 Hilborn Rd, 707-399-5000
Kris Corey, supt. Fax 399-5160
www.fsusd.org
Bird ECC 100/PK-PK
420 E Tabor Ave 94533 707-438-6384
Stephanie Wheeler, prin. Fax 428-1536
Cordelia Hills ES 700/K-6
4770 Canyon Hills Dr, 707-864-1905
Steve Trotter, prin. Fax 864-1778
Dover Academy for International Studies K-8
301 E Alaska Ave 94533 707-435-3704
Kathy Hatzke, prin.
Fairview ES 600/K-5
830 1st St 94533 707-421-4165
George Porter, prin. Fax 427-3348
Gordon ES 700/K-5
1950 Dover Ave 94533 707-421-4125
Megan Thole, prin. Fax 421-4262
Grange MS 1,200/6-8
1975 Blossom Ave 94533 707-421-4175
Constance Hunnington, prin. Fax 422-4004
Green Valley MS 800/6-8
1350 Gold Hill Rd, 707-646-7000
Kristen Cherry, prin. Fax 864-1503
Jones ES 700/K-5
2001 Winston Dr, 707-421-4195
David Marianno, prin. Fax 421-3909

Kyle ES 700/K-5
1600 Kidder Ave 94533 707-421-4105
Steve Phillips, prin. Fax 421-3932
Laurel Creek ES 1,000/K-6
2900 Gulf Dr 94533 707-421-4291
Todd Bennett, prin. Fax 421-4305
Mundy ES 700/K-5
570 Vintage Valley Dr, 707-863-7920
Jeff Kubiak, prin. Fax 863-7927
Oakbrook ES 500/K-8
700 Oakbrook Dr, 707-863-7930
Justine Turner, prin. Fax 863-7931
Rolling Hills ES 600/K-5
2025 Fieldcrest Ave, 707-399-9566
Danny Gentry, prin. Fax 399-8452
Sheldon Academy of Innovative Learning 600/K-8
1901 Woolner Ave 94533 707-421-4150
Robin Stewart, prin. Fax 421-3203
Tolenas ES 600/K-5
4500 Tolenas Rd 94533 707-421-4350
Cara Mendoza, prin. Fax 421-3220
Weir Preparatory Academy 700/K-8
1975 Pennsylvania Ave 94533 707-399-3300
Martha Lacy-Meeks, prin. Fax 399-3370
Wilson S 900/K-8
3301 Cherry Hills Ct, 707-421-4225
Rebecca Dinwiddie, prin. Fax 421-3937
Other Schools – See Suisun City

Travis USD 5,500/K-12
2751 De Ronde Dr 94533 707-437-4604
Pam Conklin, supt. Fax 437-8122
travisusd.org
Center ES 500/K-6
3101 Markeley Ln 94533 707-437-4621
Saundra Rushford, prin. Fax 437-1226
Golden West MS 900/7-8
2651 De Ronde Dr 94533 707-437-8240
Jackie Tretten, prin. Fax 437-3416
Other Schools – See Travis AFB, Vacaville

Fairfield Christian S 100/PK-12
PO Box 2172 94533 707-427-2665
Shawn Fortney, head sch Fax 237-2307
Holy Spirit S 300/K-8
1050 N Texas St 94533 707-422-5016
Julie Thompson, prin. Fax 422-0874
Solano Christian Academy 100/PK-9
2200 Fairfield Ave 94533 707-425-7715
John Reed, head sch Fax 429-2999

Fair Oaks, Sacramento, Pop. 29,764
San Juan USD
Supt. — See Carmichael
Dewey Fundamental ES 600/K-6
7025 Falcon Rd 95628 916-867-2020
Carol Stephens-Klipp, prin. Fax 867-2023
LeGette ES 600/K-6
4623 Kenneth Ave 95628 916-867-2054
Greg Barge, prin. Fax 867-2058
Northridge ES 400/K-6
5150 Cocoa Palm Way 95628 916-867-2066
Petra Luhrsen, prin. Fax 867-2070
Orangevale Open S 700/K-8
5630 Illinois Ave 95628 916-867-2067
Rick Boster, prin. Fax 867-2077
Rogers MS 700/6-8
4924 Dewey Dr 95628 916-971-7889
Aaron Wurtzer, prin. Fax 971-7903

Freedom Christian S 100/PK-12
7736 Sunset Ave 95628 916-962-3247
Annette Coller, admin. Fax 962-0783
Sacramento Waldorf S 400/K-12
3750 Bannister Rd 95628 916-961-3900
Marcela Iglesias, admin. Fax 961-3970
St. Mel S 200/K-8
4745 Pennsylvania Ave 95628 916-967-2814
Janet Nagel, prin. Fax 967-0705
Summit Christian S 100/PK-8
5010 Hazel Ave 95628 916-536-9307
David Couchman M.Ed., prin. Fax 536-9308

Fallbrook, San Diego, Pop. 29,874
Fallbrook UNESD 5,400/PK-8
321 Iowa St 92028 760-731-5420
Stephanie Weaver, supt. Fax 723-3895
www.fuesd.k12.ca.us
Choate ECC PK-PK
407 S Mission Rd 92028 760-760-7959
Leonard Rodriguez, prin. Fax 451-9130
Ellis ES, 400 W Elder St 92028 300/K-6
Edith Powers, prin. 760-731-4132
Fallbrook Street ES 700/K-6
405 W Fallbrook St 92028 760-731-4000
Joe Knisley, prin. Fax 723-4871
Frazier ES 700/K-6
1835 Gum Tree Ln 92028 760-731-4340
Arica Rainey, prin. Fax 731-2707
La Paloma ES 700/K-6
300 Heald Ln 92028 760-731-4220
Julie Schlueter, prin. Fax 731-3202
Live Oak ES 700/K-6
1978 Reche Rd 92028 760-731-4430
Wendy Kerr, prin. Fax 731-0446
Potter IS 800/7-8
1743 Reche Rd 92028 760-731-4150
Brian Frost, prin. Fax 723-5740
Other Schools – See Oceanside, San Clemente

Vallecitos ESD
Supt. — See Rainbow
Vallecitos ES 200/PK-8
5211 5th St 92028 760-728-7092
Gary Wilson, prin. Fax 728-7712

St. Peter's S 100/K-8
450 S Stage Coach Ln 92028 760-728-6961
Linda McCotter, prin. Fax 723-8973

Zion Christian S 100/PK-5
1405 E Fallbrook St 92028 760-723-3500
Karen Robertson, prin. Fax 723-3951

Fall River Mills, Shasta, Pop. 553
Fall River JUSD
Supt. — See Burney
Fall River ES 300/K-6
24977 Curve St 96028 530-336-5551
Christine Knoch, prin. Fax 336-6892

Farmersville, Tulare, Pop. 10,466
Farmersville USD 2,600/K-12
571 E Citrus Dr 93223 559-592-2010
Randy DeGraw, supt. Fax 592-2203
www.farmersville.k12.ca.us
Farmersville JHS 400/7-8
650 N Virginia Ave 93223 559-747-0764
Manuel Mendez, prin. Fax 747-2704
Freedom ES 600/4-6
575 E Citrus Dr 93223 559-592-2662
Dr. Emily Rodriguez, prin. Fax 592-4841
Hester ES 400/K-1
477 E Ash St 93223 559-594-5801
Lupe Perez, prin. Fax 594-4022
Snowden ES 400/2-3
301 S Farmersville Blvd 93223 559-747-0781
Melinda Canning, prin. Fax 747-2709

Farmington, San Joaquin, Pop. 201
Escalon USD
Supt. — See Escalon
Farmington ES 100/K-5
25233 E Highway 4 95230 209-886-5344
Dawn Webster, prin. Fax 886-5014

Fellows, Kern, Pop. 102
Midway ESD 100/K-8
PO Box 39 93224 661-768-4344
Al Quezada, supt. Fax 768-4746
www.midwayschooldistrict.org
Midway ES 100/K-8
PO Box 39 93224 661-768-4344
Al Quezada, prin. Fax 768-4746

Felton, Santa Cruz, Pop. 3,909
San Lorenzo Valley USD
Supt. — See Ben Lomond
San Lorenzo Valley ES 600/K-5
7155 Highway 9 95018 831-335-4475
Jen Lahey, prin. Fax 335-4768
San Lorenzo Valley MS 500/6-8
7179 Hacienda Way 95018 831-335-4452
Shannon Calden, prin. Fax 335-3812

St. Lawrence Academy 50/K-8
6184 Highway 9 95018 831-335-0328
Patrick Macy, head sch Fax 335-0353

Ferndale, Humboldt, Pop. 1,343
Ferndale USD 500/PK-12
1231 Main St 95536 707-786-5900
Beth Anderson, supt. Fax 786-4865
www.ferndalek12.org
Ferndale ES 400/PK-8
164 Shaw Ave 95536 707-786-5300
Renee Henderson, prin. Fax 786-4284

Fieldbrook, Humboldt, Pop. 810
Fieldbrook ESD 100/K-8
4070 Fieldbrook Rd, 707-839-3201
Daria Lowery, supt. Fax 839-8832
Fieldbrook S 100/K-8
4070 Fieldbrook Rd, 707-839-3201
Daria Lowery, prin. Fax 839-8832

Fillmore, Ventura, Pop. 14,823
Fillmore USD 3,800/PK-12
PO Box 697 93016 805-524-6000
Adrian Palazuelos, supt. Fax 524-6060
www.fillmore.k12.ca.us
Fillmore MS 900/6-8
PO Box 697 93016 805-524-6055
John Wilber, prin. Fax 524-6063
Mountain Vista ES 600/K-5
PO Box 697 93016 805-524-6781
Sandra Cano, prin. Fax 524-6785
Rio Vista ES, PO Box 697 93016 500/K-5
Beverly Garnica, prin. 805-524-4210
San Cayetano ES 500/K-5
PO Box 697 93016 805-524-6040
Tricia Gradias, prin. Fax 524-6185
Sespe Preschool PK-PK
PO Box 697 93016 805-524-6161
Tricia Gradias, prin. Fax 524-6178
Other Schools – See Piru

Fillmore Christian Academy 100/K-8
461 Central Ave 93015 805-524-1572
Tracy Hackney, admin. Fax 524-1139

Firebaugh, Fresno, Pop. 7,529
Firebaugh-Las Deltas JUSD 2,200/PK-12
1976 Morris Kyle Dr 93622 559-659-1476
Russell Freitas, supt. Fax 659-2355
www.fldusd.org/
Bailey PS 600/PK-2
1976 Morris Kyle Dr 93622 559-659-1421
Sarah Marshall, prin. Fax 659-3929
Firebaugh MS 500/6-8
1976 Morris Kyle Dr 93622 559-659-1481
Marc Sosa, prin. Fax 659-7106
Mills IS 400/3-5
1976 Morris Kyle Dr 93622 559-659-2317
Marla Sansom, prin. Fax 659-3927

Five Points, See San Diego
Westside ESD 200/PK-8
PO Box 398 93624 559-884-2492
Baldomero Hernandez, supt. Fax 884-2206
www.westside-elem.com

Westside S 200/PK-8
PO Box 398 93624 559-884-2492
Baldomero Hernandez, prin. Fax 884-2206

Flournoy, Tehama, Pop. 98
Flournoy UNESD 50/K-8
PO Box 2260 96029 530-833-5331
Lane Bates, supt. Fax 833-5332
www.flournoyschool.org
Flournoy ES 50/K-8
PO Box 2260 96029 530-833-5331
Lane Bates, admin. Fax 833-5332

Folsom, Sacramento, Pop. 69,359
Folsom-Cordova USD
Supt. — See Rancho Cordova
Empire Oaks ES 600/K-5
1830 Bonhill Dr 95630 916-294-9130
Richard Tapia, prin. Fax 294-2484
Folsom Hills ES 600/K-5
106 Manseau Dr 95630 916-294-9135
Shawn Lundberg, prin. Fax 294-2485
Folsom MS 1,300/6-8
500 Blue Ravine Rd 95630 916-294-9040
John Bliss, prin. Fax 983-3462
Gallardo ES 700/K-5
775 Russi Rd 95630 916-294-9170
Patricia Graham, prin. Fax 294-9077
Gold Ridge ES 600/K-5
735 Halidon Way 95630 916-294-9140
David Frankel, prin. Fax 984-5353
Judah ES 500/K-6
101 Dean Way 95630 916-294-9175
Canen Peterson, prin. Fax 983-0381
Natoma Station ES 400/PK-5
500 Turn Pike Dr 95630 916-294-9145
Vickie Boudouris, prin. Fax 351-9209
Oak Chan ES 500/K-5
101 Prewett Dr 95630 916-294-9155
Kat Bahry, prin. Fax 983-0225
Russell Ranch ES 600/K-5
375 Dry Creek Rd 95630 916-294-2430
Joanie Cunningham, prin. Fax 294-2431
Sprentz ES 400/K-5
249 Flower Dr 95630 916-294-9110
Andy Smith, prin. Fax 985-7748
Sundahl ES 400/K-5
9932 Inwood Rd 95630 916-294-2425
Monika Himmrich, prin. Fax 989-2510
Sutter MS 1,400/6-8
715 Riley St 95630 916-985-3644
Keri Phillips, prin. Fax 985-7044

Brighton S 100/PK-5
405 Natoma Station Dr 95630 916-985-2222
Diane Wineland, dir. Fax 985-6145
Phoenix S 200/K-8
650 Willard Dr 95630 916-353-0185
Brian Clyne, head sch Fax 353-0637
St. John's Notre Dame S 300/K-8
309 Montrose Dr 95630 916-985-4129
Susan Halfman, prin. Fax 985-7958

Fontana, San Bernardino, Pop. 192,303
Colton JUSD
Supt. — See Colton
D'Arcy ES 500/K-6
11645 Elm Ave 92337 909-580-5018
Penny Rubin, prin. Fax 350-9637
Jurupa Vista ES 600/K-6
15920 Village Dr 92337 909-580-5021
Natasha Jones Ed.D., prin. Fax 876-4056
Sycamore Hills ES 900/K-6
11036 Mahogany Dr 92337 909-580-5029
Lisa Mannes, prin. Fax 349-2393

Etiwanda SD
Supt. — See Etiwanda
East Heritage ES 600/K-5
14250 E Constitution Way 92336 909-823-5696
Damita Walton, prin. Fax 823-2517
Falcon Ridge ES K-5
5470 Lytle Creek Rd 92336 909-463-6111
Alicia Lyon, prin. Fax 463-0229
Heritage IS 1,300/6-8
13766 S Heritage Cir 92336 909-357-1345
Jonathan Carson, prin. Fax 357-8945
Long ES 800/K-5
5383 N Bridlepath Dr 92336 909-463-1626
Eugene Yarrobino, prin. Fax 463-0810
Solorio ES 900/K-5
15172 Walnut St 92336 909-357-8691
Carol Bidwell-Pilgren Ed.D., prin. Fax 357-7329
West Heritage ES 600/K-5
13690 W Constitution Way 92336 909-899-1199
Ben Lautenslager, prin. Fax 899-2297

Fontana USD 40,000/PK-12
9680 Citrus Ave 92335 909-357-7600
Randal Bassett, supt. Fax 357-5012
www.fusd.net
Alder MS 1,200/6-8
7555 Alder Ave 92336 909-357-5330
Rosario Gomez, prin. Fax 357-5348
Almeria MS 900/6-8
7723 Almeria Ave 92336 909-357-5350
Kim Bentley, prin. Fax 357-5360
Almond ES 600/PK-6
8172 Almond Ave 92335 909-357-5130
Kathy Crowe, prin. Fax 357-5139
Beech Avenue ES 900/PK-6
9206 Beech Ave 92335 909-357-5060
Michele Mower, prin. Fax 357-7675
Binks ES 600/PK-6
7358 Cypress Ave 92336 909-357-5030
Lorena Huizar-Rodriguez, prin. Fax 357-7678
Canyon Crest ES 600/PK-5
11851 Cherry Ave 92337 909-357-5440
Kelly Wilbert, prin. Fax 357-5449
Chaparrel ES 400/PK-5
14000 Shadow Dr 92337 909-357-5450
Andrea McClain, prin. Fax 357-5459
Citrus ES 800/PK-6
16041 Randall Ave 92335 909-357-5140
Michael McGirr, prin. Fax 357-5149
Cypress ES 800/PK-5
9751 Cypress Ave 92335 909-357-5460
Adam Anderson, prin. Fax 357-5469
Date ES 700/PK-5
9011 Oleander Ave 92335 909-357-5240
Valerie Rogers, prin. Fax 357-5249
Fontana MS 1,100/6-8
8425 Mango Ave 92335 909-357-5370
Sergio Chavez, prin. Fax 357-5391
Grant ES 700/PK-5
7069 Isabel Ln 92336 909-357-5540
Anne-Marie Cabrales, prin. Fax 357-5549
Hemlock ES 400/PK-5
PO Box 5090 92334 909-357-5470
Kelly Arena, prin. Fax 357-5479
Huerta International Academy K-5
17777 Merrill Ave 92335 909-357-5070
Maribel Lopez-Tyus, prin.
Juniper ES 600/PK-5
7655 Juniper Ave 92336 909-357-5480
Tammy Fleming, prin. Fax 357-5483
Live Oak ES 600/PK-6
9522 Live Oak Ave 92335 909-357-5640
Patricia Corral, prin. Fax 357-5648
Locust ES 500/PK-6
7420 Locust Ave 92336 909-357-5650
Edmund Barker, prin. Fax 357-5659
Mango ES 600/PK-5
7450 Mango Ave 92336 909-357-5660
Michelle Avila, prin. Fax 357-5669
Maple ES 700/PK-5
751 S Maple Ave 92335 909-357-5670
Elena Zerbel, prin. Fax 357-5679
North Tamarind ES 600/PK-6
7961 Tamarind Ave 92336 909-357-5680
Sheri Cole, prin. Fax 357-5683
Oak Park ES 500/PK-5
14200 Live Oak Ave 92337 909-357-5690
Antonio Viramontes, prin. Fax 357-5699
Oleander ES 900/PK-5
8650 Oleander Ave 92335 909-357-5700
Maria Ceja, prin. Fax 357-5707
Palmetto ES 1,000/PK-5
9325 Palmetto Ave 92335 909-357-5710
Adele Thomas, prin. Fax 357-5718
Poplar ES 700/PK-6
9937 Poplar Ave 92335 909-357-5720
Darlene Meyers, prin. Fax 357-5729
Porter ES 800/PK-5
8330 Locust Ave 92335 909-357-5320
Jesus Luna, prin. Fax 357-5329
Primrose ES 600/PK-5
751 N Maple Ave 92336 909-357-5790
Alejandro Lopez, prin. Fax 357-5796
Randall-Pepper ES 700/PK-5
16613 Randall Ave 92335 909-357-5730
Randi Carbajal-Cuccia, prin. Fax 357-5736
Redwood ES 600/K-6
8570 Redwood Ave 92335 909-357-5740
Eduardo Gomez, prin. Fax 357-5749
Ruble MS 1,200/6-8
6762 Juniper Ave 92336 909-357-5530
Caroline Labonte, prin. Fax 357-5539
Sequoia MS 1,100/7-8
9452 Hemlock Ave 92335 909-357-5400
Antonio Viramontes, prin. Fax 357-5419
Shadow Hills ES 600/PK-5
14300 Shadow Dr 92337 909-357-5750
Joel Avina-Sanchez, prin. Fax 357-5759
Sierra Lakes ES 700/K-5
5740 Avenal Pl 92336 909-357-5270
James Raymond, prin. Fax 357-5279
Southridge MS 1,100/6-8
14500 Live Oak Ave 92337 909-357-5420
Gerald Mullins, prin. Fax 822-4609
South Tamarind ES 800/PK-5
8561 Tamarind Ave 92335 909-357-5760
Rita Bayne, prin. Fax 357-5769
Tokay ES 600/PK-5
7846 Tokay Ave 92336 909-357-5770
Rebecca Hinojosa, prin. Fax 357-5779
Truman MS 1,200/6-8
16224 Mallory Dr 92335 909-357-5190
Kim Hall, prin. Fax 357-5199
West Randall ES 500/PK-6
15620 Randall Ave 92335 909-357-5780
Tammy Stringer, prin. Fax 357-5789

Rialto USD
Supt. — See Rialto
Kordyak ES 500/K-5
4580 Mango Ave 92336 909-421-4203
Karen Good, prin. Fax 574-2941

Resurrection Academy 200/PK-8
17434 Miller Ave 92336 909-822-4431
Madeleine Thomas, prin. Fax 822-0617
Water of Life Christian S 400/PK-8
7625 East Ave 92336 909-463-3915
Dorothy Semanovich, prin. Fax 875-8346

Foothill Ranch, Orange
Saddleback Valley USD
Supt. — See Mission Viejo
Foothill Ranch ES 1,100/K-6
1 Torino Dr 92610 949-470-4885
Ed MacNevin, prin. Fax 586-9982

Forest Falls, San Bernardino
Bear Valley USD
Supt. — See Big Bear Lake
Fallsvale S 100/K-6
PO Box 100 92339 909-794-8630
Dottie Jaeger, admin. Fax 794-2975

Foresthill, Placer, Pop. 1,441
Foresthill UNESD 400/K-8
22888 Foresthill Rd 95631 530-367-2966
Shannon Jacinto, supt. Fax 367-2470
www.fusd.org
Foresthill Divide ES 400/K-8
24750 Main St 95631 530-367-2211
Rebecca Kattenhorn, prin. Fax 367-4568

Forestville, Sonoma, Pop. 3,212
Forestville UNESD 400/PK-6
6321 Hwy 116 95436 707-887-9767
Phyllis Parisi, supt. Fax 887-2185
www.forestvilleusd.org
Forestville ES 100/PK-1
6321 Hwy 116 95436 707-887-2279
Jennifer Hegenbart, prin. Fax 887-2185

Forks of Salmon, Siskiyou
Forks of Salmon ESD 50/K-8
15616 Salmon River Rd 96031 530-462-4762
Christina Cafferata, supt. Fax 462-4735
Forks of Salmon ES 50/K-8
15616 Salmon River Rd 96031 530-462-4762
Christina Cafferata, admin. Fax 462-4735

Fort Bragg, Mendocino, Pop. 7,053
Fort Bragg USD 1,900/PK-12
312 S Lincoln St 95437 707-961-2850
Rebecca Walker, supt. Fax 964-5002
www.fbusd.us
Fort Bragg MS 400/6-8
500 N Harold St 95437 707-961-2870
Lura Vieira, prin. Fax 964-9416
Gray ES 400/3-5
1197 E Chestnut St 95437 707-961-2865
Richard Kale, prin. Fax 961-2887
Redwood ES 400/PK-2
324 S Lincoln St 95437 707-961-2860
Linda Reece, prin. Fax 961-4231

Fort Dick, Del Norte
Del Norte County USD
Supt. — See Crescent City
Redwood S 500/K-8
6900 Lake Earl Dr, 707-464-0360
Theresa Slayton, prin. Fax 487-9051

Fort Irwin, San Bernardino, Pop. 8,282
Silver Valley USD
Supt. — See Yermo
Fort Irwin MS 400/6-8
1700 Pork Chop Hill St 92310 760-386-1133
Heidi Chavez, prin. Fax 386-2448
Lewis ES 600/PK-2
1800 Blackhawk Dr 92310 760-386-1900
Taryn Lameroux, prin. Fax 386-1956
Powell Preschool PK-PK
37041 Rhineland Dr 92310 760-386-7940
Janette Rivera, prin. Fax 386-7980
Tiefort View IS 500/3-5
8700 Anzio St 92310 760-386-3123
Aubrey Zucco, prin. Fax 386-4353

Fort Jones, Siskiyou, Pop. 789
Scott Valley USD 600/K-12
PO Box 687 96032 530-468-2727
Dr. Marie Caldwell, supt. Fax 468-2729
www.svusd.us/
Fort Jones ES 100/K-5
PO Box 249 96032 530-468-2412
Joy Isbell, prin. Fax 468-2742
Other Schools – See Etna

Fortuna, Humboldt, Pop. 11,506
Fortuna ESD 1,300/PK-8
500 9th St 95540 707-725-2293
Jeff Northern M.A., supt. Fax 725-2228
fesd-ca.schoolloop.com
Ambrosini ES 300/PK-4
3850 Rohnerville Rd 95540 707-725-4688
Amy Betts M.A., prin. Fax 725-4941
Fortuna MS 300/5-8
843 L St 95540 707-725-3415
Julie Johansen M.A., prin. Fax 725-6240
South Fortuna ES 400/PK-4
2089 Newburg Rd 95540 707-725-2519
Tim Grimmett B.A., prin. Fax 725-2085
Thomas MS 300/5-8
2800 Thomas St 95540 707-725-5197
Vince Zinselmeir B.A., prin. Fax 725-8637

Fortuna Junior Academy 50/K-8
1200 Ross Hill Rd 95540 707-725-2988
Kim Bowlby, prin. Fax 725-3986
New Life Christian S 100/PK-12
PO Box 404 95540 707-725-9136
Karen Johnson, prin. Fax 725-1638

Foster City, San Mateo, Pop. 29,077
San Mateo-Foster City ESD 11,700/K-8
1170 Chess Dr 94404 650-312-7700
Dr. Joan Rosas Ph.D., supt. Fax 312-7348
www.smfcsd.net
Audubon ES 700/K-5
841 Gull Ave 94404 650-312-7500
Maria Brady, prin. Fax 312-7506
Bowditch MS 1,000/6-8
1450 Tarpon St 94404 650-312-7680
Heather Gomez, prin. Fax 312-7639
Brewer Island ES 700/K-5
1151 Polynesia Dr 94404 650-312-7532
Alexis O'Flaherty, prin. Fax 638-7044
Foster City ES 900/K-5
461 Beach Park Blvd 94404 650-312-7522
Patrick Hurley, prin. Fax 312-7640
Other Schools – See San Mateo

Kids Connection S 200/K-5
1998 Beach Park Blvd 94404 650-578-6691
Diane Marcum, head sch Fax 372-0583

Wornick Jewish Day S 200/K-8
800 Foster City Blvd 94404 650-378-2600
Dr. Barbara Gereboff, head sch Fax 378-2669

Fountain Valley, Orange, Pop. 53,408

Fountain Valley ESD 6,300/K-8
10055 Slater Ave 92708 714-843-3200
Mark Johnson Ed.D., supt. Fax 841-0356
www.fvsd.us

Courreges ES 700/K-5
18313 Santa Carlotta St 92708 714-378-4280
Chris Christensen, prin. Fax 378-4289

Cox ES 700/K-5
17615 Los Jardines E 92708 714-378-4241
Patrick Ham, prin. Fax 378-4249

Fulton MS 800/6-8
8778 El Lago Cir 92708 714-375-2816
Kevin Johnson, prin. Fax 375-2825

Gisler ES 500/K-5
18720 Las Flores St 92708 714-378-4210
Erin Bains, prin. Fax 378-4219

Masuda MS 800/6-8
17415 Los Jardines W 92708 714-378-4250
Jay Adams, prin. Fax 378-4259

Plavan ES 500/K-5
9675 Warner Ave 92708 714-378-4230
Julie Ballesteros, prin. Fax 378-4239

Tamura ES 600/K-5
17340 Santa Suzanne St 92708 714-375-6226
Kathy Davis, prin. Fax 375-6235

Other Schools – See Huntington Beach

Garden Grove USD
Supt. — See Garden Grove

Allen ES 800/K-6
16200 Bushard St 92708 714-663-6228
Dr. Andrew Heughins, prin. Fax 663-6201

Monroe ES 50/K-6
11303 Sandstone Ave 92708 714-663-6264
Cesar Loya, prin. Fax 663-6213

Northcutt ES 700/K-6
11303 Sandstone Ave 92708 714-663-6537
Dr. Gary Gerstner, prin. Fax 663-6027

Ocean View SD
Supt. — See Huntington Beach

Vista View MS 700/6-8
16250 Hickory St 92708 714-842-0626
Scott Mooney, prin. Fax 843-9156

LePort S Fountain Valley 100/PK-8
9790 Finch Ave 92708 714-436-1441
Colleen Hazard, head sch

Shoreline Christian S 200/PK-8
10350 Ellis Ave 92708 714-962-6886
Dr. Fred Mabie, prin. Fax 968-6195

Fowler, Fresno, Pop. 5,491

Fowler USD 2,400/PK-12
658 E Adams Ave 93625 559-834-6080
Eric Cederquist, supt. Fax 834-3390
www.fowler.k12.ca.us

Fremont ES 500/3-5
306 E Tuolumne St 93625 559-834-6130
Monica Sigala, prin. Fax 834-3241

Marshall ES 400/PK-2
142 N Armstrong Ave 93625 559-834-6120
Kathleen Denton, prin. Fax 834-9125

Sutter MS 600/6-8
701 E Walter Ave 93625 559-834-6180
Gary Geringer, prin. Fax 834-4739

Other Schools – See Fresno

Freedom, Santa Cruz, Pop. 3,026

Pajaro Valley USD
Supt. — See Watsonville

Freedom ES 600/K-6
25 Holly Dr 95019 831-728-6260
Gloria Puga, prin. Fax 761-6196

Fremont, Alameda, Pop. 203,344

Fremont USD 33,700/K-12
PO Box 5008 94537 510-657-2350
Dr. Kimberly Wallace, supt. Fax 659-2597
www.fremont.k12.ca.us

Ardenwood ES 900/K-6
33955 Emilia Ln 94555 510-794-0392
Jennifer Casey, prin. Fax 794-8261

Azevada ES 600/K-6
39450 Royal Palm Dr 94538 510-657-3900
Carole Diamond, prin. Fax 657-2749

Blacow ES 500/K-6
40404 Sundale Dr 94538 510-656-5121
Jose Hernandez, prin. Fax 651-6933

Brier ES 700/K-6
39201 Sundale Dr 94538 510-657-5020
Julie Williams, prin. Fax 651-4367

Brookvale ES 600/K-6
3400 Nicolet Ave 94536 510-797-5940
Cindy Hicks, prin. Fax 797-0151

Cabrillo ES 400/K-6
36700 San Pedro Dr 94536 510-792-3232
David Thornley, prin. Fax 792-0245

Centerville JHS 900/7-8
37720 Fremont Blvd 94536 510-797-2072
Weste Petersen, prin. Fax 794-7588

Chadbourne ES 800/K-6
801 Plymouth Ave 94539 510-656-5242
Kimberley Pedrotti, prin. Fax 656-6026

Durham ES 500/K-6
40292 Leslie St 94538 510-657-7080
Teresa Bonaccorsi, prin. Fax 656-3092

Forest Park ES 1,000/K-6
34400 Maybird Cir 94555 510-713-0141
Dana Graham, prin. Fax 713-7866

Glenmoor ES 600/K-6
4620 Mattos Dr 94536 510-797-0740
Brian Benavidez, prin. Fax 797-0203

Gomes ES 800/K-6
555 Lemos Ln 94539 510-656-3414
Doug Whipple, prin. Fax 656-6817

Green ES 400/K-6
42875 Gatewood St 94538 510-656-6438
Clara Lee, prin. Fax 656-2833

Grimmer ES 400/K-6
43030 Newport Dr 94538 510-656-1250
Judy Nye, prin. Fax 656-2804

Hirsch ES 500/K-6
41399 Chapel Way 94538 510-657-3537
Murriel Evans, prin. Fax 657-9574

Hopkins JHS 1,000/7-8
600 Driscoll Rd 94539 510-656-3500
Corey Brown, prin. Fax 656-3731

Horner JHS 1,100/7-8
41365 Chapel Way 94538 510-656-4000
Jana Holmes, prin. Fax 656-2793

Leitch ES 800/K-2
47100 Fernald St 94539 510-657-6100
Tammy Pachote, prin. Fax 659-9298

Maloney ES 600/K-6
38700 Logan Dr 94536 510-797-4422
Chris Wood, prin. Fax 797-1972

Mattos ES 600/K-6
37944 Farwell Dr 94536 510-793-1359
Susan Guerrero, prin. Fax 793-8642

Millard ES 600/K-6
5200 Valpey Park Ave 94538 510-657-0344
Carri Cassidy, prin. Fax 657-8720

Mission San Jose ES 600/K-6
43545 Bryant St 94539 510-656-1200
Chuck Graves, prin. Fax 651-4211

Mission Valley ES 700/K-6
41700 Denise St 94539 510-656-2000
Denise Mapelli, prin. Fax 226-7056

Niles ES 600/K-6
37141 2nd St 94536 510-793-1141
Diana Brumbaugh, prin. Fax 793-3742

Oliveira ES 700/K-6
4180 Alder Ave 94536 510-797-1132
Ian Squibb, prin. Fax 797-0861

Parkmont ES 900/K-6
2601 Parkside Dr 94536 510-793-7492
Johanna Cho, prin. Fax 793-1476

Patterson ES 600/K-6
35521 Cabrillo Dr 94536 510-793-0420
Marlene Davis, prin. Fax 793-6581

Thornton JHS 1,100/7-8
4357 Thornton Ave 94536 510-793-9090
Stan Hicks, prin. Fax 793-9756

Vallejo Mill ES 500/K-6
38569 Canyon Heights Dr 94536 510-793-1441
Mary Lou Ulloa, prin. Fax 793-0564

Walters JHS 800/7-8
39600 Logan Dr 94538 510-656-7211
Brian Weems, prin. Fax 656-4056

Warm Springs ES 1,000/3-6
47370 Warm Springs Blvd 94539 510-656-1611
Scott Iwata, prin. Fax 656-7682

Warwick ES 900/K-6
3375 Warwick Rd 94555 510-793-8660
Barbara Ochoa, prin. Fax 793-6041

Weibel ES 800/K-6
45135 S Grimmer Blvd 94539 510-651-6958
Annie Lee, prin. Fax 651-6653

Fremont Christian S 800/PK-12
4760 Thornton Ave 94536 510-744-2241
Dr. Tricia Meyer, head sch Fax 744-2255

Holy Spirit S 300/PK-8
3930 Parish Ave 94536 510-793-3553
Holly Marsh, prin. Fax 793-2694

Kimber Hills Academy 400/PK-5
39700 Mission Blvd 94539 510-651-5437
Aaron Wall, prin. Fax 656-8793

Montessori S of Centerville 100/PK-3
4209 Baine Ave 94536 510-797-3634
Lysa Matichak, dir. Fax 797-3634

Montessori S of Fremont 300/PK-6
155 Washington Blvd 94539 510-490-0919
Lindsay Neumiller, dir. Fax 226-1248

New Horizons S 200/K-8
2550 Peralta Blvd 94536 510-791-5683
Victor Dawson, prin.

Our Lady of Guadalupe S 200/K-8
40374 Fremont Blvd 94538 510-657-1674
Sr. Janice Wellington, prin. Fax 657-3659

Peace Terrace Academy 100/K-8
33330 Peace Ter 94555 510-477-9946

Prince of Peace Lutheran S 400/PK-8
38451 Fremont Blvd 94536 510-797-8186
Dan Dueck, hdmstr. Fax 793-6993

St. Joseph S 300/K-8
PO Box 3246 94539 510-656-6525
Kelly Mendoza, prin. Fax 656-3608

Scribbles Montessori S 100/PK-3
38660 Lexington St 94536 510-797-9944
Elizabeth Thurairatnam, dir. Fax 797-9945

Stratford S - Fremont Boulevard 100/PK-K
38495 Fremont Blvd 94536 510-713-8900
Jasbir Rattan, dir. Fax 713-8989

Stratford S - Fremont Curtis 600/PK-8
5301 Curtis St 94538 510-438-9745
Nick Maramba, prin. Fax 438-9749

Stratford S - Fremont Osgood PK-8
43077 Osgood Rd 94539 510-438-9745

French Camp, San Joaquin, Pop. 3,281

Manteca USD
Supt. — See Manteca

French Camp S 700/K-8
241 E 4th St 95231 209-938-6370
Suzanne McCreath, prin. Fax 938-6381

French Gulch, Shasta, Pop. 330

French Gulch-Whiskeytown ESD 50/K-8
PO Box 368 96033 530-359-2151
Moira Casey, supt. Fax 359-2010
fgws-fgws-ca.schoolloop.com

French Gulch-Whiskeytown ES 50/K-8
PO Box 368 96033 530-359-2151
Moira Casey, prin. Fax 359-2010

Fresno, Fresno, Pop. 482,604

Central USD 15,500/K-12
4605 N Polk Ave 93722 559-274-4700
Mark G. Sutton, supt. Fax 271-8200
www.centralunified.org

Biola-Pershing ES 200/K-6
4885 N Biola Ave, 559-276-5235
Michael Ota, prin. Fax 276-2151

El Capitan MS 600/7-8
4443 W Weldon Ave 93722 559-276-5270
Jeff Wimp, prin. Fax 276-3121

Glacier Point MS 900/7-8
4055 N Bryan Ave, 559-276-3105
Heather Kuyper-McKeithen, prin. Fax 276-3152

Harvest ES 700/K-6
6514 W Gettysburg Ave, 559-271-0420
Julie Shafer, prin. Fax 271-0767

Herndon-Barstow ES 600/K-6
6265 N Grantland Ave, 559-276-5250
Sandra Morehead, prin. Fax 276-3111

Houghton-Kearney S 300/K-8
8905 W Kearney Blvd 93706 559-276-5285
Marcela Lopez Brekke, prin. Fax 264-9557

Liddell ES 700/K-6
5455 W Alluvial Ave 93722 559-276-3176
Charlene Graham, prin. Fax 276-3181

Madison ES 700/K-6
330 S Brawley Ave 93706 559-276-5280
Christine Pennington, prin. Fax 276-3103

McKinley ES 900/K-6
4444 W McKinley Ave 93722 559-276-5232
Colette Bolger, prin. Fax 276-8383

Polk ES 900/K-6
2195 N Polk Ave 93722 559-274-9780
Geoff Garratt, prin. Fax 274-9487

Rio Vista MS 800/7-8
6240 W Palo Alto Ave 93722 559-276-3185
Joe Bracamonte, prin. Fax 276-3199

River Bluff ES 900/K-6
6150 W Palo Alto Ave 93722 559-276-6001
Michelle Bergmann, prin. Fax 276-6006

Roosevelt ES 500/K-6
2600 N Garfield Ave, 559-276-5257
Brandi Fleming, prin. Fax 277-1847

Saroyan ES 700/K-6
5650 W Escalon Ave 93722 559-276-3131
Patricia McCurley, prin. Fax 276-3135

Steinbeck ES 800/K-6
3550 N Milburn Ave 93722 559-276-3141
Esther Kaercher, prin. Fax 276-3145

Teague ES 800/K-6
4725 N Polk Ave 93722 559-276-5260
Ruben Diaz, prin. Fax 275-9116

Tilley ES K-6
2280 N Valentine Ave 93722 559-276-3100
Karen Davis, prin. Fax 276-5066

Clovis USD
Supt. — See Clovis

Boris ES, 7071 E Clinton, K-6
Erin Gage, prin. 559-327-3800

Copper Hills ES 500/K-6
1881 E Plymouth Way 93720 559-327-6300
Todd Deck, prin. Fax 327-6390

Fancher Creek ES 800/K-6
5948 E Tulare Ave 93727 559-327-6700
Erin Parker, prin. Fax 327-6790

Fort Washington ES 600/K-6
960 E Teague Ave 93720 559-327-6600
Melanie Hashimoto, prin. Fax 327-6690

Fugman ES 800/K-6
10825 N Cedar Ave, 559-327-8700
Jennifer Thomas, prin. Fax 327-8750

Kastner IS 1,100/7-8
7676 N 1st St 93720 559-327-2500
Ryan Eisele, prin. Fax 327-2790

Liberty ES 600/K-6
1250 E Liberty Hill Rd 93720 559-327-7100
George Petersen, prin. Fax 327-7190

Lincoln ES 700/K-6
774 E Alluvial Ave 93720 559-327-7200
Matt Verhalen, prin. Fax 327-7290

Maple Creek ES 700/K-6
2025 E Teague Ave 93720 559-327-7300
Gina Kismet, prin. Fax 327-7390

Mountain View ES 700/K-6
2002 E Alluvial Ave 93720 559-327-7500
Monica Everson, prin. Fax 327-7590

Oraze ES 700/K-6
3468 N Armstrong Ave 93727 559-327-1700
Robyn Pellouso-Snyder, prin. Fax 327-1790

Riverview ES 800/K-6
2401 E Bohymor Ave, 559-327-8600
Marci Panoo, prin. Fax 327-8660

Temperance-Kutner ES 700/K-6
1448 N Armstrong Ave 93727 559-327-8100
Kathy Blackburn, prin. Fax 327-8190

Valley Oak ES 500/K-6
465 E Champlain Dr, 559-327-8200
Julie Duwe, prin. Fax 327-8290

Fowler USD
Supt. — See Fowler

Malaga ES 200/K-5
3910 S Ward Ave 93725 559-834-6140
Luisa Custodio Lopes, prin. Fax 264-1904

Fresno County Office of Education 1,900/
1111 Van Ness Ave 93721 559-265-3000
Jim Yovino, supt. Fax 265-4005
www.fcoe.org

Fresno COE District Wide Preschool 100/PK-PK
1111 Van Ness Ave 93721 559-265-3010
Trina Frazier, prin. Fax 265-3076

Fresno USD 72,600/PK-12
2309 Tulare St 93721 559-457-3000
Bob Nelson, supt. Fax 457-3786
www.fresnounified.org
Addams ES 800/K-6
2117 W McKinley Ave 93728 559-457-2510
Angelica Espinosa, prin. Fax 495-0311
Ahwahnee MS 700/7-8
1127 E Escalon Ave 93710 559-451-4300
Jose Guzman, prin. Fax 439-1808
Anthony ES 400/K-6
1542 E Webster Ave 93728 559-457-2520
Joy Nunes, prin. Fax 485-1177
Ayer ES 600/K-6
5272 E Lowe Ave 93727 559-253-6400
Lynn Rocha-Salazar, prin. Fax 452-0553
Aynesworth ES 700/K-6
4765 E Burns Ave 93725 559-253-6410
Jane Keeler, prin. Fax 253-6413
Baird MS 600/5-8
5500 N Maroa Ave 93704 559-451-4310
Janetta McGensy, prin. Fax 432-4075
Bakman ES, 580 N Helm Ave 93727 800/K-6
Melissa Jones, prin. 559-253-6610
Balderas ES 700/K-6
4625 E Florence Ave 93725 559-253-6420
Marilyn Lopez Cuevas, prin. Fax 253-6424
Birney ES 800/K-6
3034 E Cornell Ave 93703 559-248-7000
Kristina Montez, prin. Fax 244-0433
Bullard Talent S 800/K-8
4950 N Harrison Ave 93704 559-248-7030
Orlando Bellomo, prin. Fax 248-7032
Burroughs ES 800/K-6
166 N Sierra Vista Ave 93702 559-253-6430
Carlos Castillo, prin. Fax 253-6431
Calwa ES 700/K-6
4303 E Jensen Ave 93725 559-457-2610
Angela Brunzell, prin. Fax 266-2021
Centennial ES 800/K-6
3830 E Saginaw Way 93726 559-248-7040
Monica Alvarez, prin. Fax 248-7043
Columbia ES 600/K-6
1025 S Trinity St 93706 559-457-2630
Kimberly Hendricks-Brown, prin. Fax 495-1210
Computech MS 800/7-8
555 E Belgravia Ave 93706 559-457-2640
Andrew Scherrer, prin. Fax 457-2643
Cooper MS 500/7-8
2277 W Bellaire Way 93705 559-248-7050
Sandra Auble, prin. Fax 224-7255
Del Mar ES 600/K-6
4122 N Del Mar Ave 93704 559-248-7070
Nicole Woods, prin. Fax 225-3850
Easterby ES 700/K-6
5211 E Tulare Ave 93727 559-253-6440
Pamela Pflepsen, prin. Fax 253-6442
Eaton ES 400/K-6
1451 E Sierra Ave 93710 559-451-4470
Lisa Harrington, prin. Fax 261-2170
Ericson ES 700/K-6
4774 E Yale Ave 93703 559-253-6450
Tina Rodriguez, prin. Fax 452-8834
Ewing ES 700/K-6
4873 E Olive Ave 93727 559-253-6460
Sandra Toscano, prin. Fax 252-7533
Figarden ES 700/K-6
6235 N Brawley Ave 93722 559-451-4480
Stephen Zoller, prin. Fax 437-9411
Forkner ES 600/K-6
7120 N Valentine Ave 93711 559-451-4490
Kay Davies, prin. Fax 457-4492
Ft. Miller MS 900/7-8
1302 E Dakota Ave 93704 559-248-7100
Mike Jones, prin. Fax 221-7548
Fremont ES 600/K-6
1005 W Weldon Ave 93705 559-457-2910
Mark Mather, prin. Fax 266-1264
Gaston MS, 1100 E Church Ave 93706 6-8
Felicia Treadwell, prin. 559-457-3400
Gibson ES 600/K-6
1266 W Barstow Ave 93711 559-451-4500
Antonio Sanchez, prin. Fax 451-4503
Greenberg ES 600/K-6
5081 E Lane Ave 93727 559-253-6550
Linda Ramirez, prin. Fax 253-6555
Hamilton S 800/K-8
102 E Clinton Ave 93704 559-248-7370
Deborah Marquez, prin. Fax 228-1509
Heaton ES 600/K-6
1533 N San Pablo Ave 93728 559-457-2920
Laura Gemetti, prin. Fax 495-0422
Hidalgo ES 700/K-6
3550 E Thomas Ave 93702 559-457-2930
Reynaldo Villalobos, prin. Fax 457-2931
Holland ES 500/K-6
4676 N Fresno St 93726 559-248-7140
Adele Stewart, prin. Fax 224-2594
Homan ES 600/K-6
1602 W Harvard Ave 93705 559-457-2940
Ja Sittre-Price, prin. Fax 266-1079
Jackson ES 400/K-6
3750 E Platt Ave 93702 559-457-2950
Karina Stenfort, prin. Fax 498-0335
Jefferson ES 500/K-6
202 N Mariposa St 93701 559-457-2960
Kali Isom-Acosta, prin. Fax 457-2963
King ES 400/K-6
1001 E Florence Ave 93706 559-457-2970
Faith Medina, prin. Fax 497-6442
Kings Canyon MS 800/7-8
5117 E Tulare Ave 93727 559-253-6470
Clark Mello, prin. Fax 253-1005
Kirk ES 300/K-6
2000 E Belgravia Ave 93706 559-457-2980
Carla Manning, prin. Fax 497-8511
Kratt ES 500/K-6
650 W Sierra Ave 93704 559-451-4510
Ryan Duff, prin. Fax 436-8577

Lane ES 700/K-6
4730 E Lowe Ave 93702 559-253-6480
Rosemary Baiz, prin. Fax 456-2916
Lawless S 600/K-8
5255 N Reese Ave 93722 559-451-4520
Deborah Schueter, prin. Fax 271-1885
Leavenworth ES 800/K-6
4420 E Thomas Ave 93702 559-253-6490
Erica Piedra, prin. Fax 253-6491
Lincoln ES 500/K-6
1100 Mono St 93706 559-457-3010
Marisa Favila, prin. Fax 495-1134
Lowell ES 500/K-6
171 N Poplar Ave 93701 559-457-3020
Miguel Naranjo, prin. Fax 498-8614
Malloch ES 400/K-6
2251 W Morris Ave 93711 559-451-4530
Michiko English, prin. Fax 451-4533
Manchester GATE ES 800/2-6
2307 E Dakota Ave 93726 559-248-7220
Janet Gengozian, prin. Fax 222-8854
Mayfair ES 700/K-6
3305 E Home Ave 93703 559-457-3140
Bill Serns, prin. Fax 268-0134
McCardle ES 500/K-6
577 E Sierra Ave 93710 559-451-4540
Linda McLaughlin, prin. Fax 447-1125
Muir ES 500/K-6
410 E Dennett Ave 93728 559-457-3150
Wendy Yocum, prin. Fax 443-5172
Norseman ES 700/K-6
4636 E Weldon Ave 93703 559-253-6500
Kimberly Collins, prin. Fax 253-1778
Olmos ES 800/K-6
550 S Garden Ave 93727 559-253-6620
Sherry Tharpe, prin. Fax 253-6622
Pao ES K-6
4100 E Heaton Ave 93702 559-457-3380
Teresa Calderon, prin. Fax 457-3385
Powers/Ginsberg ES 500/PK-6
110 E Swift Ave 93704 559-248-7230
Angela Balliet, prin. Fax 225-7316
Pyle ES 700/K-6
4140 N Augusta St 93726 559-248-7240
Lisa Shipman, prin. Fax 248-7246
Robinson ES 500/K-6
555 E Browning Ave 93710 559-451-4550
Brian Wulf, prin. Fax 435-2711
Roeding ES 700/K-6
1225 W Dakota Ave 93705 559-248-7250
Rob Gaertig, prin. Fax 225-3234
Rowell ES 700/K-6
3460 E McKenzie Ave 93702 559-457-3200
Alice McClintock, prin. Fax 498-6315
Scandinavian MS 800/7-8
3216 N Sierra Vista Ave 93726 559-253-6510
Julie Goorabian-Ellis, prin. Fax 252-7608
Sequoia MS 800/7-8
4050 E Hamilton Ave 93702 559-457-3210
Matt Ward, prin. Fax 497-1745
Slater ES 700/K-6
4472 N Emerson Ave 93705 559-248-7260
Kelli Wilkins, prin. Fax 244-0432
Southeast ES 700/K-5
5090 E Church Ave 93725 559-253-6528
Teresa Calderon, prin. Fax 253-6520
Starr ES 400/K-6
1780 W Sierra Ave 93711 559-451-4560
Charles Reynolds, prin. Fax 446-0421
Storey ES 900/K-6
5250 E Church Ave 93725 559-253-6530
Gayle Frediani, prin. Fax 253-6535
Sunset ES 200/K-6
1755 S Crystal Ave 93706 559-457-3310
Anna Leon, prin. Fax 495-1334
Tehipite MS 400/7-8
630 N Augusta St 93701 559-457-3420
David Peters, prin. Fax 457-3423
Tenaya MS 900/7-8
1239 W Mesa Ave 93711 559-451-4570
Heather Garcia, prin. Fax 431-0771
Terronez MS 700/7-8
2300 S Willow Ave 93725 559-253-6570
Zerina Hargrove-Brown, prin. Fax 253-6572
Thomas ES 800/K-6
4444 N Millbrook Ave 93726 559-248-7270
Matthew Phanco, prin. Fax 228-1933
Tioga MS 800/7-8
3232 E Fairmont Ave 93726 559-248-7280
Kevin Evangilinos, prin. Fax 226-1296
Turner ES 600/K-6
5218 E Clay Ave 93727 559-253-6540
Steve Gettman, prin. Fax 253-1303
Viking ES 700/K-6
4251 N Winery Ave 93726 559-248-7290
Christie Yang, prin. Fax 291-1960
Vinland ES 600/K-6
4666 N Maple Ave 93726 559-248-7300
Jeanarta Coe, prin. Fax 294-7331
Wawona MS 600/7-8
4524 N Thorne Ave 93704 559-248-7310
Kimberly Villescaz, prin. Fax 227-5206
Webster ES 400/K-6
2600 E Tyler Ave 93701 559-457-3430
Jennifer Stacy-Alcantara, prin. Fax 266-2277
Williams ES 600/K-6
525 W Saginaw Way 93705 559-248-7540
Bonifacio Sanchez, prin.
Wilson ES 800/K-6
2131 W Ashlan Ave 93705 559-248-7320
Kelley Auston, prin. Fax 221-8373
Winchell ES 700/K-6
3722 E Lowe Ave 93702 559-457-3440
Felicia Treadwell, prin. Fax 266-5755
Wishon ES 700/K-6
3857 E Harvard Ave 93703 559-248-7330
Dr. Annarita Howell, prin. Fax 248-7331
Wolters ES 400/K-6
5174 N 1st St 93710 559-248-7340
Xee Moua, prin. Fax 225-2235

Yokomi ES 900/K-6
2323 E McKenzie Ave 93701 559-457-6140
Bruce Thele, prin. Fax 457-6142
Yosemite MS 600/7-8
1292 N 9th St 93703 559-457-3450
Nichole Horn, prin. Fax 264-0933

Monroe ESD 200/K-8
11842 S Chestnut Ave 93725 559-834-2895
Shelley Manser, supt. Fax 834-1085
www.monroe.k12.ca.us
Monroe ES 200/K-8
11842 S Chestnut Ave 93725 559-834-2895
Shelley Manser, prin. Fax 834-1085

Orange Center ESD 300/K-8
3530 S Cherry Ave 93706 559-237-0437
Terry Hirschfield, supt. Fax 237-9380
orangecenter.org
Orange Center ES 300/K-8
3530 S Cherry Ave 93706 559-237-0437
Terry Hirschfield, admin. Fax 237-9380

Pacific UNESD 400/K-8
2065 E Bowles Ave 93725 559-834-2533
Annette Machado, supt. Fax 834-6433
www.pacificunion.k12.ca.us
Pacific Union ES 400/K-8
2065 E Bowles Ave 93725 559-834-2533
Annette Machado, admin. Fax 834-6433

Sanger USD
Supt. — See Sanger
Lone Star ES 400/K-6
2617 S Fowler Ave 93725 559-524-6430
Lori Welch, prin. Fax 268-8452
Sequoia ES 500/PK-6
1820 S Armstrong Ave 93727 559-524-7500
Nichole Rosales, prin. Fax 264-7610
Wash ES 500/PK-6
6350 E Lane Ave 93727 559-524-6320
Yolanda Shahbazian, prin. Fax 251-2643

Washington Colony ESD 400/PK-8
130 E Lincoln Ave 93706 559-233-0706
Jesus Cruz, supt. Fax 233-9583
www.washingtoncolony.k12.ca.us
Washington Colony ES 400/PK-8
130 E Lincoln Ave 93706 559-233-0706
Jesus Cruz, supt. Fax 233-9583

Washington USD 2,900/PK-12
7950 S Elm Ave 93706 559-495-5600
Joey Campbell, supt.
www.washingtonunified.org
American Union ES 300/PK-8
2801 W Adams Ave 93706 559-495-5650
Heather Gomez, prin. Fax 268-5708
West Fresno ES 800/PK-5
2910 S Ivy Ave 93706 559-495-5615
Toshia Blunt, prin. Fax 233-6446
West Fresno MS 300/6-8
2888 S Ivy Ave 93706 559-495-5607
Lucio Cortez, prin. Fax 485-3006

West Park ESD 600/PK-12
2695 S Valentine Ave 93706 559-233-6501
Ralph Vigil, supt. Fax 497-1944
www.westpark.k12.ca.us
West Park ES 300/PK-8
2695 S Valentine Ave 93706 559-233-6501
Ralph Vigil, prin. Fax 497-1944

Carden S of Fresno 100/PK-8
6901 N Maple Ave Ste 101 93710 559-323-0126
Jim Blanks, hdmstr. Fax 323-0980
First Church Christian Academy 200/PK-8
3920 N 1st St 93726 559-227-3222
Monique Ouwinga, prin. Fax 227-0723
Fresno Adventist Academy 200/PK-12
5397 E Olive Ave 93727 559-251-5548
Chandra Young, prin. Fax 456-1735
Fresno Christian S 300/K-12
7280 N Cedar Ave 93720 559-299-1695
Jeremy Brown, supt. Fax 299-1051
Our Lady of Victory S 200/PK-8
1626 W Princeton Ave 93705 559-229-0205
Deborah Nettell, prin. Fax 229-3230
St. Anthony S 600/K-8
5680 N Maroa Ave 93704 559-435-0700
Susannah Nelson, prin. Fax 435-6749
St. Helen S 300/PK-8
4888 E Belmont Ave 93727 559-251-5855
Jason Garza, prin. Fax 251-5948

Fullerton, Orange, Pop. 131,685

Fullerton SD 13,800/K-8
1401 W Valencia Dr 92833 714-447-7400
Dr. Bob Pletka Ed.D., supt. Fax 447-7414
www.fullertonsd.org
Acacia ES 700/K-6
1200 N Acacia Ave 92831 714-447-7700
Elizabeth Leon, prin. Fax 447-7595
Beechwood ES 900/K-8
780 Beechwood Ave 92835 714-447-2850
Julie Graham, prin. Fax 447-2853
Commonwealth ES 400/K-6
2200 E Commonwealth Ave 92831 714-447-7705
Anita Lomeli, prin. Fax 447-7777
Fern Drive ES 600/K-6
1400 W Fern Dr 92833 714-447-7710
Julie Brandon, prin. Fax 447-7452
Fisler ES 1,000/K-8
1350 Starbuck St 92833 714-447-2890
Julienne Lee, prin. Fax 447-2893
Golden Hill ES 800/K-6
732 Barris Dr 92832 714-447-7715
JaimeAnn Hopton, prin. Fax 447-2881
Hermosa Drive ES 500/K-6
400 E Hermosa Dr 92835 714-447-7720
Danielle Ramirez, prin. Fax 447-7723

Ladera Vista JHS 900/7-8
1700 E Wilshire Ave 92831 714-447-7765
Randa Schmalfeld, prin. Fax 447-7554
Laguna Road ES 700/K-6
300 Laguna Rd 92835 714-447-7725
Ryan Weiss-Wright, prin. Fax 447-7432
Maple ES 400/K-6
244 E Valencia Dr 92832 714-447-7590
Anthony Abney, prin. Fax 447-7546
Nicolas JHS 800/7-8
1100 W Olive Ave 92833 714-447-7775
Robyn Clemente, prin. Fax 447-7586
Orangethorpe ES 700/K-6
1400 S Brookhurst Rd 92833 714-447-7730
Dr. Erlinda Soltero Ruiz Ed.D., prin. Fax 447-7527
Pacific Drive ES 600/K-6
1501 W Valencia Dr 92833 714-447-7735
Kelly Castillo, prin. Fax 447-7585
Parks JHS 1,000/7-8
1710 Rosecrans Ave 92833 714-447-7785
Laura Makely, prin. Fax 447-7753
Raymond ES 500/K-6
517 N Raymond Ave 92831 714-447-7740
Yolanda McComb, prin. Fax 447-2802
Richman ES 800/K-6
700 S Richman Ave 92832 714-447-7745
Kristen Holm, prin. Fax 447-7769
Rolling Hills ES 800/K-6
1460 Rolling Hills Dr 92835 714-447-7795
Juleen Faur, prin. Fax 447-7704
Sunset Lane ES 700/K-6
2030 Sunset Ln 92833 714-447-7750
Tracy Gyurina Ed.D., prin. Fax 447-7768
Valencia Park ES 700/K-6
3441 W Valencia Dr 92833 714-447-7755
Cindy Bak, prin. Fax 447-2868
Woodcrest ES 500/K-6
455 W Baker Ave 92832 714-447-7760
Rochelle Wolf, prin. Fax 447-7724

Placentia-Yorba Linda USD
Supt. — See Placentia
Topaz ES 600/K-6
3232 Topaz Ln 92831 714-993-9977
Christa Borgese, prin. Fax 993-1284

Arborland Montessori - Hughes Campus 100/PK-6
2121 Hughes Dr 92833 714-871-3111
Dr. Sueling Chen, prin. Fax 525-9925
Eastside Christian S 200/K-12
1701 W Valencia Dr 92833 714-525-7200
Kim Van Geloof, head sch Fax 525-7200
Grace Christian Academy 200/K-12
1619 W Louise Pl 92833 714-315-1619
Suzanne Christy, admin.
St. Juliana Falconieri S 300/K-8
1320 N Acacia Ave 92831 714-871-2829
Manuel Gonzales, prin. Fax 526-6673
Veritas Classical Academy 100/K-12
1601 W Malvern Ave 92833 949-557-1311
Dr. David Kim, hdmstr.

Galt, Sacramento, Pop. 22,880
Galt JUNESD 3,800/K-8
1018 C St Ste 210 95632 209-744-4545
Karen Schauer, supt. Fax 744-4553
www.galt.k12.ca.us
Greer ES 500/K-6
248 W A St 95632 209-745-2641
Christina Homdus, prin. Fax 745-9202
Lake Canyon ES 500/K-6
800 Lake Canyon Ave 95632 209-744-5200
Judith Hayes, prin. Fax 745-5014
Marengo Ranch ES 600/K-6
1000 Elk Hills Dr 95632 209-745-5470
Jennifer Porter, prin. Fax 745-5474
McCaffrey MS 900/7-8
997 Park Terrace Dr 95632 209-745-5462
Julie Grandinetti, prin. Fax 745-5465
River Oaks ES 600/K-6
905 Vintage Oak Ave 95632 209-745-4614
Donna Gill, prin. Fax 745-7817
Valley Oaks ES 700/K-6
21 C St 95632 209-745-1564
David Nelson, prin. Fax 744-4565

Galt Adventist Christian S 50/K-8
619 Myrtle Ave 95632 209-745-3577
Janice Deibel, prin. Fax 745-1971
Galt Christian S 50/K-8
801 Church St 95632 209-745-3316
Aaron Graves, admin. Fax 745-1357

Gardena, Los Angeles, Pop. 56,918
Los Angeles USD
Supt. — See Los Angeles
Amestoy ES 800/K-5
1048 W 149th St 90247 310-327-5592
Hugh Ryan, prin. Fax 719-8710
Chapman ES 400/K-5
1947 Marine Ave 90249 310-324-2275
Sheronda Dowdell, prin. Fax 327-3898
Denker ES 800/K-5
1620 W 162nd St 90247 310-327-9420
Judy Manyweather, prin. Fax 324-6949
Gardena Early Education Center PK-PK
1350 W 177th St 90248 310-354-5091
Candie Childress, prin.
Gardena ES 500/K-5
647 W Gardena Blvd 90247 310-324-6967
Blanca Cantu, prin. Fax 217-1876
186th Street ES 800/K-5
1581 W 186th St 90248 310-324-1153
Marcia Reed, prin. Fax 323-0388
156th Street ES 400/K-6
2100 W 156th St 90249 310-324-6639
Sidra Dudley, prin. Fax 532-2306
153rd Street ES 400/K-5
1605 W 153rd St 90247 310-323-1029
John Samaniego, prin. Fax 769-5742
135th Street ES 800/K-5
801 W 135th St 90247 310-324-4454
Pablo Osorio, prin. Fax 538-4976
Peary MS 1,400/6-8
1415 W Gardena Blvd 90247 310-225-4200
Marva Patton, prin. Fax 329-3957
Purche Avenue ES 500/K-5
13210 Purche Ave 90249 310-323-3184
David Bell, prin. Fax 532-0967

Maria Regina S 200/K-8
13510 Van Ness Ave 90249 310-327-9133
Lynnette Lino, prin. Fax 327-2636
St. Anthony of Padua S 200/PK-8
1003 W 163rd St 90247 310-329-7170
Angela Grey, prin. Fax 329-9843

Garden Grove, Orange, Pop. 166,793
Garden Grove USD 46,700/PK-12
10331 Stanford Ave 92840 714-663-6000
Gabriela Mafi, supt. Fax 663-6100
www.ggusd.us/
Alamitos IS 800/7-8
12381 Dale St 92841 714-663-6101
Christina Pflughoft, prin. Fax 663-6277
Barker ES 400/K-6
12565 Springdale St 92845 714-663-6164
Wayne Kelley, prin. Fax 663-6016
Bell IS 700/7-8
11852 Knott St 92841 714-663-6466
M'Liss Patterson, prin. Fax 663-6238
Brookhurst ES 500/K-6
9821 William Dalton Way 92841 714-663-6556
Dianna Rangel, prin. Fax 663-6019
Bryant ES 600/K-6
8371 Orangewood Ave 92841 714-663-6451
Tanya De Leon, prin. Fax 663-6014
Clinton-Mendenhall ES 800/K-6
13641 Clinton St 92843 714-663-6146
Jason Shabet, prin. Fax 663-6481
Cook ES 400/K-6
9802 Woodbury Ave 92844 714-663-6251
Sandi Ishii, prin. Fax 663-6087
Crosby ES 500/K-6
12181 West St 92840 714-663-6346
Kristine Levenson, prin. Fax 663-6553
Doig IS 900/7-8
12752 Trask Ave 92843 714-663-6241
Louie Gomez, prin. Fax 663-6845
Eisenhower ES, 13221 Lilly St 92843 900/K-6
Beth Cusimano, prin. 714-663-6401
Enders ES 500/K-6
12302 Springdale St 92845 714-663-6205
Michelle Askew, prin. Fax 663-6220
Evans ES 500/K-6
12281 Nelson St 92840 714-663-6558
Lynn Hardin, prin. Fax 663-6496
Excelsior ES 500/K-6
10421 Woodbury Rd 92843 714-663-6106
Sarah Mershon, prin. Fax 663-6069
Faylane ES 600/K-6
11731 Morrie Ln 92840 714-663-6253
Mike Ingalls, prin. Fax 663-6429
Garden Park ES 200/K-6
6861 Santa Rita Ave 92845 714-663-6074
Michelle Morales, prin. Fax 663-6076
Gilbert ES 600/K-6
9551 Orangewood Ave 92841 714-663-6318
Charise Santana, prin. Fax 663-6067
Hill ES 400/K-6
9681 11th St 92844 714-663-6561
Tricia Chinn, prin. Fax 663-6499
Irvine IS 900/7-8
10552 Hazard Ave 92843 714-663-6551
Bill Gates, prin. Fax 663-6013
Jordan IS 800/7-8
9821 Woodbury Ave 92844 714-663-6124
Tracy Conway, prin. Fax 663-6123
Lake IS 600/7-8
10801 Orangewood Ave 92840 714-663-6506
Margaret Feliciani, prin. Fax 663-6065
Lawrence ES 600/K-6
12521 Monroe St 92841 714-663-6255
Marie Kennedy, prin. Fax 663-6262
Mitchell ES 500/K-6
13451 Taft St 92843 714-663-6131
Chris Francis, prin. Fax 663-6025
Morningside ES 500/K-6
10521 Morningside Dr 92843 714-663-6328
Nathan Bellamy, prin. Fax 663-6033
Murdy ES 400/K-6
14851 Donegal Dr 92844 714-663-6405
Marcie Griffith, prin. Fax 663-6517
Paine ES 500/K-6
15792 Ward St 92843 714-663-6118
George Martinez, prin. Fax 663-6035
Parkview ES 500/K-6
12272 Wilken Way 92840 714-663-6266
Ryan Baker, prin. Fax 663-6066
Patton ES 1,000/K-6
6861 Santa Rita Ave 92845 714-663-6584
Jennifer Carter, prin. Fax 663-6034
Peters 4-6 ES 500/4-6
13200 Newhope St 92843 714-663-6070
Gurprit Dhillon, prin. Fax 663-6072
Peters K-3 ES 700/K-3
13162 Newhope St 92843 714-663-6085
Gurprit Dhillon, prin. Fax 663-6570
Ralston IS 700/7-8
10851 Lampson Ave 92840 714-663-6366
Ruth Dietze, prin. Fax 638-7155
Riverdale ES 600/K-6
13222 Lewis St 92843 714-663-6563
Chris Ash, prin. Fax 663-6568
Simmons ES 400/K-6
11602 Steele Dr 92840 714-663-6096
Jaomio Rivoro, prin. Fax 663-6018
Stanford ES 600/K-6
12721 Magnolia St 92841 714-663-6458
Melanie Mathovich, prin. Fax 663-6460
Stanley ES 400/K-6
12201 Elmwood St 92840 714-663-6484
Jamie Shippee, prin. Fax 663-6073
Sunnyside ES 700/K-6
9972 Russell Ave 92844 714-663-6158
Susie Dollbaum, prin. Fax 663-6068
Violette ES 600/K-6
12091 Lampson Ave 92840 714-663-6203
Erin Lara, prin. Fax 663-6023
Wakeham ES 400/K-6
7772 Chapman Ave 92841 714-663-6407
Dr. Michelle Rushall, prin. Fax 897-7214
Walton IS 600/7-8
12181 Buaro St 92840 714-663-6040
Janis Cody, prin. Fax 534-4814
Warren ES 500/K-6
12871 Estock Dr 92840 714-663-6331
Eileen Young, prin. Fax 663-6012
Woodbury ES 400/K-6
11362 Woodbury Rd 92843 714-663-6461
Rose Jansz, prin. Fax 663-6463
Zeyen ES 300/K-6
12081 Magnolia St 92841 714-663-6535
Sarah Van Dam, prin. Fax 663-6039
Other Schools – See Fountain Valley, Santa Ana, Stanton, Westminster

Orange USD
Supt. — See Orange
Lampson ES 800/K-5
13321 Lampson Ave 92840 714-997-6153
Heriberto Angel, prin. Fax 971-8516

Westminster SD
Supt. — See Westminster
Anderson ES 700/PK-6
8902 Hewitt Pl 92844 714-894-7201
Kim Breckenridge, prin. Fax 895-7804
Meairs ES 700/PK-5
8441 Trask Ave 92844 714-372-8800
Katherine Kane, prin. Fax 372-8809

Christ Cathedral Academy 300/PK-8
13280 Chapman Ave 92840 714-663-2330
Debbie Vallas, prin.
King of Kings Lutheran S 100/PK-8
13431 Newhope St 92843 714-530-2152
Peter Buege, prin.
Montessori Greenhouse S 100/PK-6
PO Box 5116 92846 714-897-3833
Marci Turner, admin. Fax 892-8595
Orange Crescent S 300/K-8
1 Al Rahman Plz 92844 714-531-1451
Dr. Parisa Popalzai, prin.
Orangewood Academy 200/PK-12
13732 Clinton St 92843 714-534-4694
Elizabeth Beard, prin. Fax 534-5931
St. Columban S 200/K-8
10855 Stanford Ave 92840 714-534-3947
Barbara Barreda, prin. Fax 590-9153
St. Paul Lutheran S 200/PK-8
13082 Bowen St 92843 714-534-6320
Dr. Deborah Aarhus, prin. Fax 741-8353
Trinity Christian S K-12
12761 Euclid St 92840 714-971-4159
Dr. Charles Trout, prin.

Gasquet, Del Norte, Pop. 637
Del Norte County USD
Supt. — See Crescent City
Mountain ES 50/K-8
PO Box 25 95543 707-457-3211
Rae Fearing, admin. Fax 457-3902

Gaviota, Santa Barbara, Pop. 70
Vista del Mar UNESD 100/K-8
9467 San Julian Rd 93117 805-686-1880
Dr. Emilio Handall, supt. Fax 686-8536
vista-vdm-ca.schoolloop.com
Vista de Las Cruces S 100/K-8
9467 San Julian Rd 93117 805-686-1880
Dr. Emilio Handall, prin. Fax 686-8536

Gazelle, Siskiyou, Pop. 70
Gazelle UNESD 50/K-8
PO Box 6 96034 530-435-2321
Robert Bray, lead tchr. Fax 435-2298
gazelleuesd.cyberschool.com
Gazelle ES 50/K-8
PO Box 6 96034 530-435-2321
Robert Bray, lead tchr. Fax 435-2298

Georgetown, El Dorado, Pop. 2,308
Black Oak Mine USD 1,400/K-12
6540 Wentworth Springs Rd 95634 530-333-8300
Jeremy Meyers Ed.D., supt. Fax 333-8303
www.bomusd.org/
Georgetown ES 300/K-6
6530 Wentworth Springs Rd 95634 530-333-8320
Wendy Westsmith, prin. Fax 333-8324
Otter Creek ES 50/K-5
6530 Wentworth Springs Rd 95634 530-333-8347
Wendy Westsmith, prin. Fax 333-8347
Other Schools – See Cool

Gerber, Tehama, Pop. 1,047
Gerber UNESD 400/K-8
23014 Chard Ave 96035 530-385-1041
Jenny Montoya, supt. Fax 385-1451
www.gerberschool.org
Gerber ES 400/K-8
23014 Chard Ave 96035 530-385-1041
Jenny Montoya, prin. Fax 385-1451

Geyserville, Sonoma, Pop. 841
Geyserville USD 300/K-12
1300 Moody Ln 95441 707-857-3592
Deborah Bertolucci, supt. Fax 857-3071
www.gusd.com
Geyserville ES 100/K-5
21485 Geyserville Ave 95441 707-857-3410
Denise McCullough, prin. Fax 857-3072

Gilroy, Santa Clara, Pop. 47,703
Gilroy USD 11,500/PK-12
7810 Arroyo Cir 95020 669-205-4000
Dr. Deborah A. Flores, supt. Fax 847-4717
www.gilroyunified.org
Aprea Fundamental ES 700/K-5
9225 Calle del Rey 95020 408-842-3135
Tami Espinosa, prin. Fax 846-7541
Brownell MS 1,000/6-8
7800 Carmel St 95020 408-847-3377
David Laboranti, prin. Fax 846-7521
Del Buono ES 600/PK-5
9300 Wren Ave 95020 408-848-5161
Velia Codiga, prin. Fax 846-6833
Eliot ES 500/K-5
475 Old Gilroy St 95020 408-847-5333
Patricia Pelino, prin. Fax 846-8966
El Roble ES 600/PK-5
930 3rd St 95020 408-842-8234
Scott Otteson, prin. Fax 842-3874
Glen View ES 600/K-5
600 W 8th St 95020 408-842-8292
Corina Sapien, prin. Fax 842-1237
Kelley ES 800/K-5
8755 Kern Ave 95020 408-847-1932
Maritza Salcedo, prin. Fax 847-5562
Las Animas ES 700/K-5
6550 Cimino St 95020 408-842-6414
Silvia Reyes, prin. Fax 842-3374
Rucker ES 500/K-5
325 Santa Clara Ave 95020 408-842-6471
Christine Anderson, prin. Fax 842-3563
Solorsano MS 900/6-8
7121 Grenache Way 95020 408-848-4121
Maria Walker, prin. Fax 848-7121
South Valley MS 800/6-8
385 I O O F Ave 95020 408-847-2828
Patricia Mondragon, prin. Fax 847-5708

Pacific Point Christian S 300/PK-5
1575 Mantelli Dr Ste A 95020 408-847-7922
Amanda Riley, prin. Fax 847-3003
St. Mary S 300/PK-8
7900 Church St 95020 408-842-2827
Pam Greteman, prin. Fax 847-7679

Glendale, Los Angeles, Pop. 184,933
Glendale USD 25,900/PK-12
223 N Jackson St 91206 818-241-3111
Winfred Roberson, supt. Fax 548-9041
www.gusd.net
Balboa ES 700/K-6
1844 Bel Aire Dr 91201 818-241-1801
Dr. Sonia Arakelyan, prin. Fax 241-5557
Cerritos ES 400/K-6
120 E Cerritos Ave 91205 818-244-7207
Perla Chavez-Fritz, prin. Fax 247-2532
Columbus ES 600/K-5
425 Milford St 91203 818-242-7722
Dr. Elena Rojas Ed.D., prin. Fax 247-2542
Edison ES 900/K-6
435 S Pacific Ave 91204 818-241-1807
Carmen Labrecque, prin. Fax 241-8028
Franklin ES 600/K-6
1610 Lake St 91201 818-243-1809
Vickie Atikian, prin. Fax 552-5097
Fremont ES 700/K-6
3320 Las Palmas Ave 91208 818-249-3241
Dr. Christin Molano Ed.D., prin. Fax 249-7921
Glenoaks ES 600/K-6
2015 E Glenoaks Blvd 91206 818-242-3747
Daniel DiMundo, prin. Fax 247-4423
Jefferson ES 600/K-6
1540 5th St 91201 818-243-4279
Armineh Alexan, prin. Fax 551-1069
Keppel ES 1,000/K-5
730 Glenwood Rd 91202 818-244-2113
Kristine Siegal, prin. Fax 507-6542
Mann ES 700/K-5
501 E Acacia Ave 91205 818-246-2421
Rosa Alonso, prin. Fax 507-6238
Marshall ES 500/K-5
1201 E Broadway 91205 818-242-6834
Carla Walker, prin. Fax 242-1761
Muir ES 800/K-6
912 S Chevy Chase Dr 91205 818-241-4848
Juanita Shahijanian, prin. Fax 241-1058
Roosevelt MS 800/6-8
1017 S Glendale Ave 91205 818-242-6845
Dr. Kyle Bruich Ed.D., prin. Fax 552-5188
Toll MS 1,100/6-8
700 Glenwood Rd 91202 818-244-8414
Dr. Thomas Crowther Ed.D., prin. Fax 500-1487
Verdugo Woodlands ES 800/K-6
1751 N Verdugo Rd 91208 818-241-2433
Kristina Provost, prin. Fax 548-4173
White ES 900/K-5
744 E Doran St 91206 818-241-2164
Dr. Narek Kassabian Ed.D., prin. Fax 409-8974
Wilson MS 1,300/6-8
1221 Monterey Rd 91206 818-244-8145
Dr. Chris Coulter Ed.D., prin. Fax 244-2050
Other Schools – See La Crescenta

Chamlian Armenian S 500/1-8
4444 Lowell Ave 91214 818-957-3398
Dr. Talin Kargodorian, prin. Fax 957-1827
First Lutheran S 100/PK-8
1300 E Colorado St 91205 818-244-7319
Michelle Goetsch, prin. Fax 244-7319
Glendale Adventist Academy 600/K-12
700 Kimlin Dr 91206 818-244-8671
Dr. Nancy Garcilazo, prin. Fax 546-1180
Holy Family S 300/K-8
400 S Louise St 91205 818-243-9239
Fidela Suelto, prin. Fax 243-0976
Incarnation S 300/K-8
123 W Glenoaks Blvd 91202 818-241-2269
Dr. Colby Boysen, prin. Fax 241-4734
Salem Lutheran S 200/K-8
1211 N Brand Blvd 91202 818-243-8264
Pamela Perry, prin. Fax 243-4491

Glendora, Los Angeles, Pop. 48,747
Charter Oak USD
Supt. — See Covina
Washington ES 500/K-6
325 W Gladstone St 91740 626-914-2704
Beverly Gonzalez, prin. Fax 852-7690
Willow ES 400/K-6
1427 Willow Ave 91740 626-914-5839
Michelle Lee, prin. Fax 852-7689

Glendora USD 7,600/PK-12
500 N Loraine Ave 91741 626-963-1611
Dr. Ann Keyes, supt. Fax 335-2196
www.glendora.k12.ca.us
Cullen ES 700/PK-5
440 N Live Oak Ave 91741 626-852-4593
Dr. Cheryl Bonner, prin. Fax 852-4570
Goddard MS 900/6-8
859 E Sierra Madre Ave 91741 626-852-4500
Jennifer Prince, prin. Fax 852-4520
La Fetra ES 800/K-5
547 W Bennett Ave 91741 626-852-4566
Marie Porcell, prin. Fax 852-4650
Sandburg MS 900/6-8
819 W Bennett Ave 91741 626-852-4530
Eric Osborne, prin. Fax 852-4521
Sellers ES 600/K-5
500 N Loraine Ave 91741 626-852-4574
Steve Bishop, prin. Fax 852-4572
Stanton ES 600/PK-5
725 S Vecino Dr 91740 626-852-4604
Dr. Sara Najarro, prin. Fax 852-4573
Sutherland ES 600/PK-5
1330 Amelia Ave 91740 626-852-4614
Carren Acevedo, prin. Fax 852-4660

Foothill Christian S 400/K-8
242 W Baseline Rd 91740 626-914-1849
Robert Gutzwiller, supt. Fax 914-5940
Hope Lutheran S 200/PK-8
1041 E Foothill Blvd 91741 626-335-5315
Scott Ferguson, prin. Fax 852-0836
St. Dorothy S 200/K-8
215 S Valley Center Ave 91741 626-335-0772
Adrienne Ferguson, prin. Fax 335-0059

Glen Ellen, Sonoma, Pop. 747
Sonoma Valley USD
Supt. — See Sonoma
Dunbar ES 300/K-5
11700 Dunbar Rd 95442 707-935-6070
Jillian Beall, prin. Fax 935-4268

Glennville, Kern
Linns Valley-Poso Flat UNSD 50/K-8
PO Box 399 93226 661-536-8811
Tammy Pritchard, supt. Fax 536-8878
linnsvalleyschooldistrict.org
Linns Valley-Poso Flat Union ES 50/K-8
PO Box 399 93226 661-536-8811
Tammy Pritchard, prin. Fax 536-8878

Gold River, Sacramento, Pop. 7,625
San Juan USD
Supt. — See Carmichael
Gold River Discovery Center 800/K-8
2200 Roaring Camp Dr 95670 916-867-2109
Teresa Cummings, prin. Fax 867-2040

Goleta, Santa Barbara, Pop. 29,028
Goleta UNESD 3,600/PK-6
401 N Fairview Ave 93117 805-681-1200
Dr. Donna Lewis, supt. Fax 692-0857
www.goleta.k12.ca.us
Brandon ES 400/K-6
195 Brandon Dr 93117 805-571-3770
Ryan Sparre, prin. Fax 571-3771
Ellwood ES 400/PK-6
7686 Hollister Ave 93117 805-571-3774
Ned Schoenwetter, prin. Fax 571-3775
Isla Vista ES 500/K-6
6875 El Colegio Rd 93117 805-685-4418
Mary Kahn, prin. Fax 968-1338
Kellogg ES 400/K-6
475 Cambridge Dr 93117 805-681-1277
Kim Bruzzese, prin. Fax 681-4823
La Patera ES 400/K-6
555 N La Patera Ln 93117 805-681-1280
Sonia Arnold-DeHay, prin. Fax 964-7402
Other Schools – See Santa Barbara

Santa Barbara USD
Supt. — See Santa Barbara
Goleta Valley JHS 900/7-8
6100 Stow Canyon Rd 93117 805-967-3486
Mauricio Ortega, prin. Fax 967-8176

Coastline Christian Academy 100/K-8
5950 Cathedral Oaks Rd 93117 805-967-5834
Deedee Underwood, prin.
Montessori Center S 300/PK-6
401 N Fairview Ave Ste 1 93117 805-683-9383
Melanie Jacobs, head sch Fax 683-9384
Waldorf S of Santa Barbara 100/PK-8
PO Box 788 93116 805-967-6656

Gonzales, Monterey, Pop. 8,098
Gonzales USD 2,500/K-12
PO Box G 93926 831-675-0100
Candice McFarland, supt. Fax 675-2763
www.gonzalesusd.net
Fairview MS 700/5-8
PO Box G 93926 831-675-3704
Joni Madolora, prin. Fax 675-3274
La Gloria ES 1,000/K-4
PO Box G 93926 831-675-3663
Yolanda Barba, prin. Fax 675-3260

Gorman, Los Angeles
Gorman ESD 1,900/PK-8
PO Box 104 93243 661-248-6441
Joe Andrews, supt. Fax 248-6849
gorman.k12.ca.us
Gorman ES 100/PK-8
PO Box 104 93243 661-248-6441
Joe Andrews, prin. Fax 248-0604

Granada Hills, See Los Angeles
Los Angeles USD
Supt. — See Los Angeles
Danube Avenue ES 500/K-5
11220 Danube Ave 91344 818-366-6463
Danika Free, prin. Fax 363-4047
Frost MS 1,500/6-8
12314 Bradford Pl 91344 818-332-6900
Jose Ayala, prin. Fax 360-9584
Granada Community Charter S 400/K-5
17170 Tribune St 91344 818-363-3188
Cynthia Van Houten, prin. Fax 368-0821
Haskell STEAM ES 600/K-5
15850 Tulsa St 91344 818-366-6431
Connie Covert, prin. Fax 360-4627
Henry MS 1,000/6-8
17340 San Jose St 91344 818-832-3870
Sandra Cruz, prin. Fax 368-7333
Knollwood Preparatory Academy 400/K-5
11822 Gerald Ave 91344 818-363-9558
Cecilia Salazar, prin. Fax 832-9276
Porter MS 1,700/6-8
15960 Kingsbury St 91344 818-920-2050
Suzanne Blake, prin. Fax 891-7826
Tulsa ES 500/K-5
10900 Hayvenhurst Ave 91344 818-363-5061
Lester Powell, prin. Fax 831-6935

Concordia S 100/PK-8
16603 San Fernando Mssn Bl 91344 818-368-0892
Katherine Moore, prin. Fax 831-9222
Heritage Christian S North Campus 300/PK-5
17531 Rinaldi St 91344 818-368-7071
Martin Frendt, prin. Fax 363-4455
St. Euphrasia S 200/K-8
17637 Mayerling St 91344 818-363-5515
Mary Blair, prin. Fax 832-6678
St. John Baptist De La Salle S 500/K-8
16535 Chatsworth St 91344 818-363-2270
Monica Castaneda, prin. Fax 832-8950

Grand Terrace, San Bernardino, Pop. 11,712
Colton JUSD
Supt. — See Colton
Grand Terrace ES 700/K-6
12066 Vivienda Ave 92313 909-580-5032
Neera Kohli, prin. Fax 876-4059
Terrace Hills MS 1,000/7-8
22579 De Berry St 92313 909-580-5022
Scott Boggs, prin. Fax 783-3836
Terrace View ES 800/K-6
22731 Grand Terrace Rd 92313 909-580-5016
Joseph Adeyemo Ed.D., prin. Fax 876-6366

Granite Bay, Placer, Pop. 19,714
Eureka UNSD 3,400/PK-8
5455 Eureka Rd 95746 916-791-4939
Tom Janis, supt. Fax 791-5527
www.eurekausd.org
Cavitt JHS 400/7-8
7200 Fuller Dr 95746 916-791-4152
Jennifer Platt, prin. Fax 791-7414
Greenhills ES 400/PK-3
8200 Greenhills Way 95746 916-791-4230
Peter Towne, prin. Fax 791-4212
Oakhills ES 500/PK-3
9233 Twin School Rd 95746 916-791-5391
Sarah O'Brien, prin. Fax 791-6484
Ridgeview ES 600/4-6
9177 Twin School Rd 95746 916-791-3477
Patrice McCallum, prin. Fax 774-2707
Other Schools – See Roseville

Grass Valley, Nevada, Pop. 12,474
Chicago Park ESD 200/K-8
15725 Mount Olive Rd 95945 530-346-2153
Dan Zeisler, supt. Fax 346-8559
www.chicagoparkschool.org/
Chicago Park S 100/K-8
15725 Mount Olive Rd 95945 530-346-2153
Katie Kohler, prin. Fax 346-8559

Clear Creek ESD 200/K-8
17700 McCourtney Rd 95949 530-273-3664
Dan Zeisler, supt. Fax 273-4168
www.clearcreekschool.org
Clear Creek ES 200/K-8
17700 McCourtney Rd 95949 530-273-3664
Carolyn Cramer, prin. Fax 273-4168

Grass Valley ESD 1,700/PK-8
10840 Gilmore Way 95945 530-273-4483
Eric Fredrickson, supt. Fax 273-0248
www.gvsd.us
Bell Hill Academy 200/K-4
342 S School St 95945 530-273-2281
Heather Graham, prin. Fax 273-3219
Gilmore MS 500/5-8
10837 Rough and Ready Hwy 95945 530-273-8479
Christopher Roberts, prin. Fax 273-1675
Grass Valley Preschool PK-PK
10840 Gilmore Way 95945 530-274-9106
Carol Viola, dir.
Scotten ES 500/K-4
10821 Squirrel Creek Rd 95945 530-273-6472
Carrie Roberts, prin. Fax 273-6233

Pleasant Ridge UNESD 1,300/K-8
22580 Kingston Ln 95949 530-268-2800
Rusty Clark, supt. Fax 268-2804
www.prsd.us

Alta Sierra ES 300/K-5
16607 Annie Dr 95949 530-272-2319
Thomas Bivens, prin. Fax 274-8761

Cottage Hill ES 500/K-5
22600 Kingston Ln 95949 530-268-2808
Karen Montero, prin. Fax 268-2810

Magnolia IS 500/6-8
22431 Kingston Ln 95949 530-268-2815
Gene Morgan, prin. Fax 268-2819

Union Hill ESD 600/K-8
10879 Bartlett Dr 95945 530-273-0647
David Curry, supt. Fax 273-5626
www.uhsd.k12.ca.us

Union Hill ES 500/K-6
11638 Colfax Hwy 95945 530-273-8456
Joseph Limov, prin. Fax 273-0152

Union Hill MS 100/7-8
11638 Colfax Hwy 95945 530-273-8456
Joe Limov, prin. Fax 273-0152

Mt. St. Mary S 100/K-8
400 S Church St 95945 530-273-4694
Edee Wood, prin. Fax 273-1724

Graton, Sonoma, Pop. 1,648

Pacific Christian Academy 50/K-12
PO Box 369 95444 707-823-2880

Greenfield, Monterey, Pop. 16,188

Greenfield UNESD 2,800/K-8
493 El Camino Real 93927 831-674-2840
Zandra Galvan, supt. Fax 674-3712
www.greenfield.k12.ca.us

Cesar Chavez ES 800/K-5
250 Apple Ave 93927 831-674-2412
Sarah Amezcua, prin. Fax 674-2469

Chapa Literacy & Tech Academy 500/K-2
490 El Camino Real 93927 831-674-5586
Rosalinda Silva, prin. Fax 674-3510

Oak Avenue ES 800/K-5
1239 Oak Ave 93927 831-674-5916
Sonia Aramburo, prin. Fax 674-3682

Vista Verde MS 800/6-8
1199 Elm Ave 93927 831-674-1420
Paddy Douglas, prin. Fax 674-1425

Greenville, Plumas, Pop. 1,068

Plumas USD
Supt. — See Quincy

Indian Valley ES 100/K-6
225 Grand St 95947 530-284-7195
Traci Cockerill, prin. Fax 284-6720

Grenada, Siskiyou, Pop. 348

Grenada ESD 200/K-8
PO Box 10 96038 530-436-2233
GingerLee Charles, supt. Fax 436-2235
www.grenada.k12.ca.us

Grenada ES 200/K-8
PO Box 10 96038 530-436-2233
GingerLee Charles, supt. Fax 436-2235

Gridley, Butte, Pop. 6,408

Gridley USD 2,100/K-12
429 Magnolia St 95948 530-846-4721
Jordan Reeves, supt. Fax 846-4595
www.gusd.org

McKinley ES 300/K-1
1045 Sycamore St 95948 530-846-5686
Chris McIntire, prin. Fax 846-3283

Sycamore MS 400/6-8
1125 Sycamore St 95948 530-846-3636
Clint Johnson, prin. Fax 846-6796

Wilson ES 600/2-5
409 Magnolia St 95948 530-846-3675
Tracey Allen, prin. Fax 846-3872

Manzanita ESD 300/PK-8
627 E Evans Reimer Rd 95948 530-846-5594
Minden King, supt. Fax 846-4084
www.manzanitaelementaryschool.com

Manzanita S 300/PK-8
627 E Evans Reimer Rd 95948 530-846-5594
Minden King, prin. Fax 846-4084

Grimes, Colusa, Pop. 373

Pierce JUSD
Supt. — See Arbuckle

Grand Island ES 100/K-5
PO Box 30 95950 530-437-2416
Summer Shadley, prin. Fax 437-2296

Grizzly Flats, El Dorado, Pop. 1,013

Pioneer UNESD
Supt. — See Somerset

Tyler ES 50/K-2
6801 Tyler Rd 95636 530-622-2995
John Sanguinetti, prin. Fax 622-2896

Groveland, Tuolumne, Pop. 585

Big Oak Flat-Groveland USD 400/K-12
PO Box 1397 95321 209-962-5765
Dave Urquhart, supt. Fax 962-6108
www.bigoakflatgrovelandusd.org

Tenaya ES 200/K-8
19177 State Highway 120 95321 209-962-7846
Wynette Hilton, prin. Fax 962-5076

Grover Beach, San Luis Obispo, Pop. 12,742

Lucia Mar USD
Supt. — See Arroyo Grande

Fairgrove ES 500/K-6
2101 The Pike 93433 805-474-3740
Carol Littlefield-Halfma, prin. Fax 473-4109

Grover Beach ES 500/K-6
365 S 10th St 93433 805-474-3770
James Snyder, prin. Fax 473-5502

Grover Heights ES 500/K-6
770 N 8th St 93433 805-474-3700
Susan Kesselring, prin. Fax 473-4323

Guadalupe, Santa Barbara, Pop. 6,975

Guadalupe UNESD 1,200/K-8
PO Box 788 93434 805-343-2114
Ed Cora, supt. Fax 343-6155
www.guadusd.org

Buren ES 900/K-5
PO Box 788 93434 805-343-2411
Jesely Alvarez-Masencup Ph.D., prin. Fax 343-2512

McKenzie JHS 400/6-8
PO Box 788 93434 805-343-1951
Gabriel Solorio, prin. Fax 343-6931

Guerneville, Sonoma, Pop. 4,341

Guerneville SD 300/K-8
14630 Armstrong Woods Rd 95446 707-869-2864
Dana Pedersen, supt. Fax 869-3149
www.guernevilleschool.org

Guerneville ES 300/K-8
14630 Armstrong Woods Rd 95446 707-869-2864
Amber Stringfellow, prin. Fax 869-3149

Gustine, Merced, Pop. 5,420

Gustine USD 1,800/K-12
1500 Meredith Ave 95322 209-854-3784
Bill Morones, supt. Fax 854-9164
www.gustineusd.org

Gustine ES 600/K-5
2806 Grove Ave 95322 209-854-6496
Lisa Filippini, prin. Fax 854-9165

Gustine MS 400/6-8
28075 Sullivan Rd 95322 209-854-5030
Peter Duenas, prin. Fax 854-9592

Other Schools – See Santa Nella

Our Lady of Miracles S 100/PK-8
370 Linden Ave 95322 209-854-3180
Chandra Brace, prin. Fax 854-3961

Hacienda Heights, Los Angeles, Pop. 53,234

Hacienda La Puente USD
Supt. — See City of Industry

Bixby ES 300/K-5
16446 Wedgeworth Dr 91745 626-933-8201
Dr. Robert Kimble, prin. Fax 855-3506

Cedarlane Academy 600/K-8
16333 Cedarlane Dr 91745 626-933-8001
Ellen Park, prin. Fax 855-3819

Grazide ES 600/K-5
2850 Leopold Ave 91745 626-933-6101
Amy Moss, prin. Fax 369-0653

Kwis ES 400/K-5
1925 Kwis Ave 91745 626-933-2101
Erika Terrazas, prin. Fax 855-3198

Los Altos ES 400/K-5
15565 Los Altos Dr 91745 626-933-2301
Rosalie Sinapi, prin. Fax 855-3735

Los Molinos ES 300/K-5
3112 Las Marias Ave 91745 626-933-2201
Tamara McElroy, prin. Fax 855-3746

Los Robles Academy 400/K-5
1530 Ridley Ave 91745 626-933-7201
Vivienne Thomas, prin. Fax 855-3157

Mesa Robles S 1,100/K-8
16060 Mesa Robles Dr 91745 626-933-6001
Carmel Horseman, prin. Fax 855-3827

Newton MS 600/6-8
15616 Newton St 91745 626-933-2401
Dan Ma, prin. Fax 855-3832

Orange Grove MS 600/6-8
14505 Orange Grove Ave 91745 626-933-7001
Maria Elena Navarro, prin. Fax 855-3837

Palm ES 400/K-5
14740 Palm Ave 91745 626-933-7401
Kevin Maldonado, prin. Fax 855-3761

Wedgeworth ES 400/K-5
16949 Wedgeworth Dr 91745 626-933-8101
Dr. Paulina Cho, prin. Fax 855-3790

St. Mark's Lutheran S 700/PK-8
2323 Las Lomitas Dr 91745 626-968-0428
Barbara Clark, prin. Fax 333-4998

Half Moon Bay, San Mateo, Pop. 11,097

Cabrillo USD 3,300/K-12
498 Kelly Ave 94019 650-712-7100
Jane Yuster, supt. Fax 726-0279
www.cabrillo.k12.ca.us/

Cunha IS 700/6-8
600 Church St 94019 650-712-7190
Seth Feldman, prin. Fax 712-7195

El Granada ES 500/K-5
400 Santiago St, 650-712-7150
Martha Ladd, prin. Fax 712-0126

Hatch ES 700/K-5
490 Miramontes Ave 94019 650-712-7160
David Percel, prin. Fax 712-1623

Other Schools – See Montara, Woodside

Sea Crest S 200/K-8
901 Arnold Way 94019 650-712-9892
Dr. T.M. Pernambuco-Wise, head sch Fax 458-4459

Hamilton City, Glenn, Pop. 1,746

Hamilton USD 700/K-12
PO Box 488 95951 530-826-3261
Charles Tracy, supt. Fax 826-0440
www.husdschools.org

Hamilton ES 400/K-8
277 Capay Ave 95951 530-826-3474
Darcy Pollak, prin. Fax 826-0419

Hanford, Kings, Pop. 52,527

Hanford ESD 5,800/K-8
PO Box 1067 93232 559-585-3601
Joy Gabler, supt. Fax 584-7833
www.hesd.k12.ca.us/

Hamilton ES 600/K-6
PO Box 1067 93232 559-585-3820
Ramiro Flores, prin. Fax 583-7295

Jefferson ES 200/K-6
PO Box 1067 93232 559-585-3700
Javier Espindola, prin. Fax 583-0723

Kennedy JHS 500/7-8
PO Box 1067 93232 559-585-3850
Rick Johnston, prin. Fax 585-2374

King ES 600/K-6
PO Box 1067 93232 559-585-3715
Cruz Sanchez, prin. Fax 585-2363

Lincoln ES 500/K-6
PO Box 1067 93232 559-585-3730
Jennifer Pitkin, prin. Fax 585-2282

Monroe ES 700/K-6
PO Box 1067 93232 559-585-3745
Julie Pulis, prin. Fax 585-2288

Richmond ES 500/K-6
PO Box 1067 93232 559-585-3760
Lindsey Calvillo, prin. Fax 585-2302

Roosevelt ES 500/K-6
PO Box 1067 93232 559-585-3775
Anthony Carrillo, prin. Fax 585-2317

Simas ES 600/K-6
PO Box 1067 93232 559-585-3790
Kristina Baldwin, prin. Fax 585-2386

Washington ES 600/K-6
PO Box 1067 93232 559-585-3805
Matthew Gamble, prin. Fax 585-2325

Wilson JHS 600/7-8
PO Box 1067 93232 559-585-3870
Kenny Eggert, prin. Fax 585-2336

Kit Carson UNESD 400/K-8
9895 7th Ave 93230 559-582-2843
Todd Barlow, supt. Fax 582-7565
kitcarson.ca.schoolwebpages.com

Kit Carson Union ES 400/K-8
9895 7th Ave 93230 559-582-2843
Todd Barlow, prin. Fax 582-7565

Lakeside UNESD 300/K-8
9100 Jersey Ave 93230 559-582-2868
Cynthia Marshall, supt. Fax 582-7638
www.lakeside.k12.ca.us/

Lakeside ES 300/K-8
9100 Jersey Ave 93230 559-582-2868
Cynthia Marshall, admin. Fax 582-7638

Hanford Christian S 100/PK-8
11948 Flint Ave 93230 559-584-9207
Diana Schmidt, prin. Fax 584-2602

St. Rose-McCarthy S 100/PK-8
1000 N Harris St 93230 559-584-5218
Jamie Perkins, prin. Fax 584-0899

Happy Camp, Siskiyou, Pop. 1,130

Happy Camp UNESD 100/K-8
PO Box 467 96039 530-493-2267
Kevin Triance, supt. Fax 493-2734
hces-ca.schoolloop.com/

Happy Camp Union ES 100/K-8
PO Box 467 96039 530-493-2267
Kevin Triance, prin. Fax 493-2734

Harbor City, See Los Angeles

Los Angeles USD
Supt. — See Los Angeles

Harbor City ES 600/K-5
1508 254th St 90710 310-326-5075
Kimberly Reems, prin. Fax 326-8914

Normont Early Education Center PK-PK
25028 Petroleum Ave 90710 310-326-3344
Deborah Aguet, prin. Fax 784-0441

Normont ES 500/K-5
1001 253rd St 90710 310-326-5261
Veronica McKenrick, prin. Fax 326-8034

President ES 400/K-6
1465 243rd St 90710 310-326-7400
Charity Weber, prin. Fax 326-4936

Hawaiian Gardens, Los Angeles, Pop. 14,073

ABC USD
Supt. — See Cerritos

Fedde MS 400/7-8
21409 Elaine Ave 90716 562-229-7805
Ricardo Lois, prin. Fax 809-6895

Furgeson ES 400/K-6
22215 Elaine Ave 90716 562-229-7855
Alejandro Gutierrez, prin. Fax 421-5345

Hawaiian ES 400/K-6
12350 226th St 90716 562-229-7865
Mayra Lozano, prin. Fax 431-9547

Hawthorne, Los Angeles, Pop. 81,457

Hawthorne SD 8,900/PK-12
14120 S Hawthorne Blvd 90250 310-676-2276
Dr. Helen Morgan Ed.D., supt. Fax 675-9464
www.hawthorne.k12.ca.us

Carson MS 800/6-8
13838 S Yukon Ave 90250 310-676-1908
Mark Silva, prin. Fax 676-0634

Davis ES 1,300/PK-5
13435 Yukon Ave 90250 310-679-1771
Kathy Carbajal, prin. Fax 675-4962

Eucalyptus ES 1,100/PK-5
12044 Eucalyptus Ave 90250 310-675-3369
Mike Goldstein, prin. Fax 675-5628

Hawthorne MS 900/6-8
4366 W 129th St 90250 310-676-0167
Rudy Salas, prin. Fax 675-0924

Jefferson ES 600/K-5
4091 W 139th St 90250 310 676 9423
Josh Godin, prin. Fax 676-4234

Kornblum ES 600/K-5
3620 W El Segundo Blvd 90250 310-970-4294
LaTima Jones, prin. Fax 970-4298

Prairie Vista MS 1,000/6-8
13600 Prairie Ave 90250 310-679-1003
Wendy Ostensen, prin. Fax 679-1142

Ramona ES 800/K-5
4617 W 136th St 90250 310-675-7189
Dr. Patricia Ray, prin. Fax 675-6593
Washington ES 800/K-5
4339 W 129th St 90250 310-676-3422
Maritza Cruz-Brown, prin. Fax 644-4824
York ES 600/K-5
11838 York Ave 90250 310-675-1189
Jennifer Beekman, prin. Fax 675-4892

Los Angeles USD
Supt. — See Los Angeles
Cimarron Avenue ES 300/K-5
11559 Cimarron Ave 90250 323-757-1226
Dana Rivers, prin. Fax 756-1686

Wiseburn USD 3,900/K-12
13530 Aviation Blvd 90250 310-643-3025
Dr. Tom Johnstone, supt. Fax 643-7659
www.wiseburn.k12.ca.us
Burnett ES 400/3-5
5403 W 138th St 90250 310-725-2151
Kim Jones, prin. Fax 643-4306
Cabrillo ES 500/K-2
5309 W 135th St 90250 310-725-5400
Lisa Baggio, prin. Fax 643-5141
Dana MS 1,000/6-8
5504 W 135th St 90250 310-725-4700
Dr. Blake Silvers, prin. Fax 536-9091
De Anza ES 700/K-5
12110 Hindry Ave 90250 310-725-2100
Alberto Paredes, prin. Fax 643-0383

Al -Huda Islamic S 200/PK-8
12227 Hawthorne Way 90250 310-973-0500
Sr. Rima Mekdashi, prin. Fax 978-4036
St. Joseph S 400/PK-8
11886 Acacia Ave 90250 310-679-1014
Kevin Donohue, prin. Fax 679-1310
Trinity Lutheran S 100/K-8
4783 W 130th St 90250 310-675-4493
Fran Sanders, admin. Fax 675-9523

Hayfork, Trinity, Pop. 2,231
Mountain Valley USD 300/PK-12
PO Box 339 96041 530-628-5265
Debbie Miller, supt. Fax 628-5267
www.mvusd.us
Hayfork ES 200/PK-8
PO Box 70 96041 530-628-5294
Wendy Platt, prin. Fax 628-5344
Other Schools – See Hyampom

Hayward, Alameda, Pop. 133,787
Alameda County Office of Education 2,200/
313 W Winton Ave 94544 510-887-0152
Karen Monroe, supt. Fax 670-4146
www.acoe.org
Alameda County Community S 300/K-12
313 W Winton Ave 94544 510-670-6619
Carolyn Hobbs, prin. Fax 293-9201

Hayward USD 21,500/K-12
PO Box 5000 94540 510-784-2600
Dr. Matt Wayne, supt. Fax 784-2641
www.husd.us
Bowman ES 500/K-6
PO Box 5000 94540 510-723-3800
Heidi Andrews, prin. Fax 582-7178
Burbank ES 800/K-6
PO Box 5000 94540 510-723-3805
Irma Torres-Fitzsimons, prin. Fax 582-7142
Chavez MS 500/7-8
PO Box 5000 94540 510-723-3110
Sean Moffatt, prin. Fax 538-8478
Cherryland ES 800/K-6
PO Box 5000 94540 510-723-3810
Mathew Clark, prin. Fax 582-7133
East Avenue ES 600/K-6
PO Box 5000 94540 510-723-3815
Peter Wilson, prin. Fax 781-6151
Eden ES 500/K-6
PO Box 5000 94540 510-723-3855
Leigh Woodmansee, prin. Fax 783-2839
Eden Gardens ES 600/K-6
PO Box 5000 94540 510-723-3820
Craig McKinley, prin. Fax 783-4069
Eldridge ES 500/K-6
PO Box 5000 94540 510-723-3825
Enrique Pin, prin. Fax 783-3922
Fairview ES 500/K-6
PO Box 5000 94540 510-723-3830
Patrick Brose, prin. Fax 781-6134
Glassbrook ES 500/K-6
PO Box 5000 94540 510-723-3835
Guadalupe Berzunza, prin. Fax 782-8796
Harder ES 600/K-6
PO Box 5000 94540 510-723-3840
Cynthia Ortiz, prin. Fax 733-0951
Harte MS 700/7-8
PO Box 5000 94540 510-723-3100
Seana Condit-Gordon, prin. Fax 886-5926
King MS 800/7-8
PO Box 5000 94540 510-723-3120
Alvaro Franco, prin. Fax 781-6129
Longwood ES 700/K-6
PO Box 5000 94540 510-723-3850
Luis Garcia, prin. Fax 781-6138
Ochoa MS 600/7-8
PO Box 5000 94540 510-723-3130
Ariel Dolowich, prin. Fax 786-0559
Palma Ceia ES 600/K-6
PO Box 5000 94540 510-723-3870
Monica Manriquez, prin. Fax 783-2839
Park ES 600/K-6
PO Box 5000 94540 510-723-3875
Pia Macchiavello, prin. Fax 781-6106
Ringgold S 100/K-6
PO Box 5000 94540 510-723-3865
Gabriel Morales, prin. Fax 781-6147
Ruus ES 600/K-6
PO Box 5000 94540 510-723-3855
Evelyn Ocasio, prin. Fax 783-2536
Schafer Park ES 700/K-6
PO Box 5000 94540 510-723-3895
Rafael Flores, prin. Fax 781-6149
Southgate ES 700/K-6
PO Box 5000 94540 510-723-3905
Brian White, prin. Fax 781-0840
Stonebrae ES 800/K-6
PO Box 5000 94540 510-723-3910
Lisa Nolting, prin. Fax 733-1437
Treeview ES 400/2-6
PO Box 5000 94540 510-723-3925
Guillermo Morales, prin. Fax 489-1211
Treeview ES Bidwell K-1
PO Box 5000 94540 510-723-3930
Guillermo Morales, prin. Fax 471-5783
Tyrrell ES 800/K-6
PO Box 5000 94540 510-723-3935
Stacey Vidal, prin. Fax 781-6113
Winton MS 500/7-8
PO Box 5000 94540 510-723-3140
Lisa Tess, prin. Fax 733-9043
Other Schools – See Castro Valley

New Haven USD
Supt. — See Union City
Hillview Crest ES 700/PK-5
31410 Wheelon Ave 94544 510-471-5720
Jessica Lange-Brar, prin. Fax 471-1436

San Lorenzo USD
Supt. — See San Lorenzo
Colonial Acres ES 700/K-5
17115 Meekland Ave 94541 510-317-4500
Ruben Olivares, prin. Fax 481-1423
Lorenzo Manor ES 600/K-5
18250 Bengal Ave 94541 510-317-5400
John Shimko, prin. Fax 481-1312
San Lorenzo Preschool PK-PK
20450 Royal Ave 94541 510-317-4400
Abigail Kotzin, prin. Fax 784-1083

All Saints S 200/K-8
22870 2nd St 94541 510-582-1910
Jennifer Diaz, prin. Fax 582-0866
Bayside Adventist Christian S 50/K-8
26400 Gading Rd 94544 510-785-1313
Robert Robinson, prin. Fax 785-3302
Northstar S 100/K-8
22502 Woodroe Ave 94541 510-397-1501
Salwa Abed, prin. Fax 740-4432
St. Bede S 200/K-8
26910 Patrick Ave 94544 510-782-3444
Jocelyn Pierre-Antoine, prin. Fax 782-2243
St. Clement S 300/K-8
790 Calhoun St 94544 510-538-5885
Anne Crowthers, prin. Fax 538-1643
St. Joachim S 400/PK-8
21250 Hesperian Blvd 94541 510-783-3177
Armond Seishas, prin. Fax 783-2161

Healdsburg, Sonoma, Pop. 11,079
Alexander Valley Union ESD 100/K-6
8511 Highway 128 95448 707-433-1375
Matt Reno, supt. Fax 431-0102
www.alexandervalleyusd.org
Alexander Valley ES 100/K-6
8511 Highway 128 95448 707-433-1375
Matt Reno, prin. Fax 431 0102

Healdsburg USD 2,300/K-12
1028 Prince Ave 95448 707-431-3488
Chris Vanden Heuvel, supt. Fax 433-8403
www.husd.com
Healdsburg ES - Fitch Mountain Campus 800/3-5
520 Monte Vista Ave 95448 707-473-4449
Erika McGuire, prin. Fax 473-4483
Healdsburg ES - HES Campus 300/K-2
400 1st St 95448 707-431-3440
Stephanie Feith, prin. Fax 431-3592
Healdsburg JHS 400/6-8
315 Grant St 95448 707-431-3410
Michael DeFrancesco, prin. Fax 431-3593

West Side UNESD 700/K-12
1201 Felta Rd 95448 707-433-3923
Rhonda Bellmer, supt. Fax 433-7341
www.westsideusd.org/
West Side ES 200/K-6
1201 Felta Rd 95448 707-433-3923
Rhonda Bellmer, prin. Fax 433-7341

Healdsburg S 200/K-8
33 Healdsburg Ave Ste H 95448 707-433-4847
Dr. Nicholas Egan, head sch Fax 433-4846
St. John the Baptist S 200/PK-8
217 Fitch St 95448 707-433-2758
James Brandt, prin. Fax 433-0353

Heber, Imperial, Pop. 4,270
Heber ESD 1,300/K-8
1052 Heber Ave 92249 760-337-6530
Juan Cruz, supt. Fax 353-3421
www.hesdk8.org
Dogwood ES 600/K-3
44 E Correll Rd 92249 760-337-6530
Jeralyn Shaw, prin. Fax 482-5731
Heber ES 700/4-8
1052 Heber Ave 92249 760-337-6530
Cynthia Silva, prin. Fax 353-3421

Helendale, San Bernardino
Helendale ESD 1,500/K-12
PO Box 249 92342 760-952-1180
Ross Swearingen, supt. Fax 952-1178
www.helendalesd.org
Helendale ES 400/K-6
PO Box 249 92342 760-952-1204
Cynthia Espinoza, prin. Fax 952-1762
Riverview MS 100/7-8
PO Box 249 92342 760-952-1266
Chet Richards, prin. Fax 952-1178

Helm, Fresno
Golden Plains USD
Supt. — See San Joaquin
Helm S 100/K-8
13883 S Lassen Ave 93627 559-866-5683
Guillermo Jimenez, prin. Fax 866-5209

Hemet, Riverside, Pop. 76,330
Hemet USD 21,300/K-12
1791 W Acacia Ave 92545 951-765-5100
Christi Barrett, supt. Fax 765-5115
www.hemetusd.org
Acacia MS 700/6-8
1200 E Acacia Ave 92543 951-765-1620
Dr. Jeff Franks, prin. Fax 765-5149
Bautista Creek ES 900/K-5
441 N Lake St 92544 951-927-0822
Greg Giroux, prin. Fax 927-0821
Cawston ES 800/K-5
4000 W Menlo Ave 92545 951-765-0277
Dr. Colleen Flavin, prin. Fax 929-2496
Dartmouth MS 900/6-8
41535 Mayberry Ave 92544 951-765-2550
Dr. Jennifer Martin, prin. Fax 765-2559
Diamond Valley MS 1,100/6-8
291 W Chambers Ave 92543 951-925-2899
Robert Dominguez, prin. Fax 925-6297
Fruitvale ES 900/K-5
2800 W Fruitvale Ave 92545 951-765-1680
Karen Brooks, prin. Fax 765-1685
Harmony ES 900/K-5
1500 S Cawston Ave 92545 951-791-1830
Teresa McFarland, prin. Fax 791-1876
Hemet ES 800/K-5
633 E Kimball Ave 92543 951-765-1630
Dr. Kristi Watson, prin. Fax 765-1631
Little Lake ES 900/K-5
26091 Meridian St 92544 951-765-1660
Robert Broecker, prin. Fax 765-1696
McSweeny ES 800/K-5
451 W Chambers Ave 92543 951-925-4366
Ekko DePriest, prin. Fax 925-8321
Ramona ES 700/K-5
41051 Whittier Ave 92544 951-765-1670
Stacy Sorenson, prin. Fax 765-1677
Rancho Viejo MS 1,200/6-8
985 N Cawston Ave 92545 951-765-6287
Jon Workman, prin. Fax 925-5244
Valle Vista ES 600/K-5
43900 Mayberry Ave 92544 951-927-0800
Dr. Christine Ramirez-Shows, prin. Fax 927-0808
Whittier ES 1,100/K-5
400 W Whittier Ave 92543 951-765-1650
Jeffrey Keeney, prin. Fax 765-1654
Wiens ES 800/K-5
935 E Campus Way 92543 951-929-3734
Dana Childs-Mazzei, prin. Fax 929-4425
Other Schools – See Aguanga, Anza, Idyllwild, Winchester

Hemet Adventist Christian S 50/K-8
26312 Hemet St 92544 951-927-3972
Melody Wuttke, prin. Fax 927-3972
St. John's Lutheran S 100/PK-8
26410 Columbia St 92544 951-925-7756
Stephanie Lynch, prin. Fax 925-6136

Herald, Sacramento, Pop. 1,157
Arcohe UNESD 400/K-8
PO Box 93 95638 209-748-2313
Troy Miller, supt. Fax 748-5798
www.arcohe.net
Arcohe ES 400/K-8
PO Box 93 95638 209-748-2313
Troy Miller, prin. Fax 748-5798

Hercules, Contra Costa, Pop. 22,834
West Contra Costa USD
Supt. — See Richmond
Hanna Ranch ES 500/K-5
2480 Refugio Valley Rd 94547 510-231-1441
Greg Santiago, prin. Fax 799-5795
Hercules MS 700/6-8
1900 Refugio Valley Rd 94547 510-231-1429
Renee Lama, prin. Fax 245-1089
Lupine Hills ES 400/K-5
1919 Lupine Rd 94547 510-231-1411
Heather Best, prin. Fax 799-1587
Ohlone ES 400/K-5
1616 Pheasant Dr 94547 510-231-1443
Stephanie Serrano, prin. Fax 799-1556

Herlong, Lassen, Pop. 264
Fort Sage USD 200/K-12
PO Box 35 96113 530-827-2129
Michael Altenburg, supt. Fax 827-2019
www.fortsage.org
Fort Sage MS 50/7-8
PO Box 35 96113 530-827-2101
Michael Altenburg, prin. Fax 827-3362
Sierra ES 100/K-6
PO Box 6 96113 530-827-2126
Michael Altenburg, prin. Fax 827-3239

Hermosa Beach, Los Angeles, Pop. 18,753
Hermosa Beach City ESD 1,400/K-8
1645 Valley Dr 90254 310-937-5877
Patricia Escalante, supt. Fax 376-4974
www.hbcsd.org
Hermosa Valley ES 900/3-8
1645 Valley Dr 90254 310-937-5888
Kimberly Taylor, prin. Fax 798-4365
Hermosa View ES 500/K-2
1800 Prospect Ave 90254 310-798-1680
Sylvia Gluck, prin. Fax 798-4681

Our Lady of Guadalupe S 200/K-8
340 Massey St 90254 310-372-7486
April Beuder, prin. Fax 798-4051

Hesperia, San Bernardino, Pop. 88,087
Hesperia USD 23,400/K-12
15576 Main St 92345 760-244-4411
David Olney, supt. Fax 244-2806
www.hesperiausd.org
Carmel ES 700/K-6
9321 Glendale Ave 92345 760-947-3188
Craig Gunter, prin. Fax 947-6545
Cedar MS 1,100/7-8
13565 Cedar St, 760-244-6093
Kelly Maxwell, prin. Fax 244-5439
Cottonwood ES 800/K-6
8850 Cottonwood Ave 92345 760-949-1390
Chris Mauger, prin. Fax 949-6172
Cypress S of the Arts 900/K-6
10365 Cypress Ave 92345 760-949-2596
Pamela Seeger, prin. Fax 949-3179
Eucalyptus ES 700/K-6
11224 10th Ave 92345 760-949-0815
Stephanie Poindexter, prin. Fax 949-2886
Hesperia JHS 900/7-8
10275 Cypress Ave 92345 760-244-9386
Lisa Kelly, prin. Fax 244-0595
Joshua Circle ES 800/K-6
10140 8th Ave 92345 760-244-6133
James Elgan, prin. Fax 244-3564
Juniper ES 600/K-6
9400 I Ave 92345 760-244-6161
Theresa Kallenberger, prin. Fax 244-1931
Kingston ES 600/K-6
7473 Kingston Ave 92345 760-244-8869
Benjamin Skinner, prin. Fax 947-2719
Krystal S of Science Math and Technology 800/K-6
17160 Krystal Dr 92345 760-948-3611
Amanda Arceo, prin. Fax 948-3822
Lime Street ES 700/K-6
16852 Lime St 92345 760-244-0512
Eric Land, prin. Fax 244-2326
Maple ES 700/K-6
10616 Maple Ave 92345 760-244-3096
Alex Cristales, prin. Fax 244-0337
Mesa Grande ES 600/K-6
9172 3rd Ave 92345 760-244-3709
Tom Kirk, prin. Fax 244-5259
Mesquite Trails ES 900/K-6
13884 Mesquite St, 760-949-3149
Matt Sheffield, prin. Fax 949-3602
Mission Crest ES 1,000/K-6
13065 Muscatel St, 760-949-8265
Ryan Plescia, prin. Fax 949-8202
Ranchero MS 1,000/7-8
17607 Ranchero Rd 92345 760-948-0175
Isaac Newman-Gomez, prin. Fax 948-0381
Topaz Preparatory Academy 600/K-6
14110 Beech St 92345 760-244-4622
Karen Prestwood, prin. Fax 244-2511
Other Schools – See Victorville

Hesperia Christian S 300/PK-12
16775 Olive St 92345 760-244-6164
Sharon Romero, admin. Fax 244-9756
New Life Christian Academy 100/PK-6
15975 Hercules St 92345 760-244-1283
Debbie Lund, prin. Fax 244-3403

Highland, San Bernardino, Pop. 51,532
Redlands USD
Supt. — See Redlands
Arroyo Verde ES 600/K-5
7701 Church St 92346 909-307-5590
Rachel Malatesta, prin. Fax 307-5594
Beattie MS 1,200/6-8
7800 Orange St 92346 909-307-2400
Angela Neuhaus, prin. Fax 307-2416
Cram ES 600/K-5
29700 Water St 92346 909-425-9300
Jean Joye, prin. Fax 425-9393
Highland Grove ES 500/K-5
7700 Orange St 92346 909-307-2420
Luanna Bamsch, prin. Fax 307-2429

San Bernardino City USD
Supt. — See San Bernardino
Belvedere ES 700/K-6
2501 Marshall Blvd 92346 909-862-7111
Ann Pearson, prin. Fax 862-6575
Cole ES 400/K-6
1331 Cole Ave 92346 909-388-6510
Keishia Handy, prin. Fax 862-8453
Cypress ES 600/K-6
26825 Cypress St 92346 909-388-6514
Ryan Rubio, prin. Fax 862-5783
Highland-Pacific ES 400/K-6
3340 Pacific St 92346 909-388-6518
Evette Peters, prin. Fax 864-9853
Lankershim ES 800/K-6
7499 Lankershim Ave 92346 909-862-4213
Crecia Sims, prin. Fax 862-1899
Oehl ES 600/K-6
2525 Palm Ave 92346 909-862-2261
Robert Morales, prin. Fax 862-3306
Serrano MS 800/7-8
3131 Piedmont Dr 92346 909-388-6530
Michelle Cleveland, prin. Fax 864-6232
Thompson ES 600/K-6
7401 Church Ave 92346 909-388-6512
Howanda Lundy, prin. Fax 862-4729

St. Adelaide Academy 200/PK-8
27487 Baseline St 92346 909-862-5851
Barbara Malouf, prin. Fax 862-2877

Hillsborough, San Mateo, Pop. 10,401
Hillsborough CSD 1,500/K-8
300 El Cerrito Ave 94010 650-342-5193
Louann Carlomagno, supt. Fax 342-6964
www.hcsd.k12.ca.us
Crocker MS 500/6-8
2600 Ralston Ave 94010 650-342-6331
Jamie Adams, prin. Fax 579-5943
North Hillsborough ES 400/K-5
545 Eucalyptus Ave 94010 650-347-4175
Aleyda Barrera-Cruz, prin. Fax 347-2832
South Hillsborough ES 300/K-5
303 El Cerrito Ave 94010 650-344-0303
Elizabeth Veal, prin. Fax 548-9443
West Hillsborough ES 400/K-5
376 Barbara Way 94010 650-344-9870
Matthew Lindner, prin. Fax 340-1630

Nueva S 400/PK-8
6565 Skyline Blvd 94010 650-350-4600
Diane Rosenberg, head sch Fax 348-3642

Hilmar, Merced, Pop. 3,392
Hilmar USD 2,200/K-12
7807 Lander Ave 95324 209-667-5701
Isabel Cabral-Johnson, supt. Fax 667-1721
www.hilmar.k12.ca.us
Elim ES 900/K-5
7807 Lander Ave 95324 209-667-1082
Lisa Marques, prin. Fax 667-9066
Hilmar MS 500/6-8
7807 Lander Ave 95324 209-632-8847
Amy Fitzgerald, prin. Fax 667-7018
Other Schools – See Stevinson

Hollister, San Benito, Pop. 34,317
Cienega UNESD 50/K-8
11936 Cienega Rd 95023 831-637-3821
Nancy MacLean, supt. Fax 637-3961
www.sbcoe.k12.ca.us/cienega.html
Cienega S 50/K-8
11936 Cienega Rd 95023 831-637-3821
Nancy MacLean, prin. Fax 637-3961

Hollister SD 5,000/PK-8
2690 Cienega Rd 95023 831-630-6300
Dr. Lisa Andrew, supt. Fax 634-2080
www.hesd.org
Accelerated Achievement Academy 100/4-8
1151 Buena Vista Rd 95023 831-636-4460
Dr. Scott Wilbur, admin. Fax 634-4970
Calaveras ES 600/PK-8
1151 Buena Vista Rd 95023 831-636-4460
Ken Woods, prin. Fax 634-4960
Cerra Vista ES 600/PK-5
2151 Cerra Vista Dr 95023 831-636-4470
Gabriella Armenta, prin. Fax 634-4970
Gabilan Hills S 400/K-5
921 Santa Ana Rd Ste 100 95023 831-636-4430
Monique Ruiz, prin. Fax 636-3908
Hardin ES 500/PK-5
881 Line St 95023 831-636-4440
Elena Hatchett, prin. Fax 636-7537
Hollister Dual Language Academy 400/PK-8
873 Santa Ana Rd Ste 200 95023 831-634-4930
Monique Ruiz, prin. Fax 634-4934
Ladd Lane ES 600/PK-5
161 Ladd Ln 95023 831-636-4490
Kip Ward, prin. Fax 634-4992
Maze MS 600/6-8
900 Meridian St 95023 831-636-4480
Hugo Galvan, prin. Fax 636-4488
Rancho San Justo MS 600/6-8
1201 Rancho Dr 95023 831-636-4450
Lisa Jelinek, prin. Fax 634-4952
Sunnyslope ES 700/PK-5
1475 Memorial Dr 95023 831-636-4420
Joe Rivas, prin. Fax 634-4920

North County JUNESD 800/PK-8
500 Spring Grove Rd 95023 831-637-5574
Jennifer Bernosky, supt. Fax 637-0682
www.ncjusd.k12.ca.us
Spring Grove ES 800/PK-8
500 Spring Grove Rd 95023 831-637-3745
Jennifer Bernosky, prin. Fax 637-0682

Southside ESD 300/K-8
4991 Southside Rd 95023 831-637-4439
John Schilling, supt. Fax 634-0156
www.southsideschool.net
Southside ES 300/K-8
4991 Southside Rd 95023 831-637-4439
John Schilling, prin. Fax 634-0156

Hollister SDA Christian S 50/PK-8
400 Isabel Ln 95023 831-637-5570
Sacred Heart Parish S 300/PK-8
670 College St 95023 831-637-4157
Dr. Rachel McKenna, prin. Fax 637-4164

Hollywood, See Los Angeles
Los Angeles USD
Supt. — See Los Angeles
Le Conte MS 900/6-8
1316 N Bronson Ave 90028 323-308-1700
Rosemary Hindinger, prin. Fax 856-3053

Holtville, Imperial, Pop. 5,905
Holtville USD 1,600/PK-12
621 E 6th St 92250 760-356-2974
Celso Ruiz, supt. Fax 356-4936
www.husd.net
Finley ES 500/PK-5
627 E 6th St 92250 760-356-2929
Lupita Perez, prin. Fax 356-2052
Holtville JHS 300/6-8
800 Beale Ave 92250 760-356-2811
Fawn Nielsen, prin. Fax 356-5741
Pine ES 200/K-8
3295 Holt Rd 92250 760-356-2615
Mitchell Drye, prin. Fax 356-2957

Homeland, Riverside, Pop. 5,870
Romoland ESD 3,000/K-8
25900 Leon Rd 92548 951-926-9244
Dr. Julie A. Vitale, supt. Fax 926-2170
www.romoland.net
Other Schools – See Menifee, Romoland

Honeydew, Humboldt
Mattole USD
Supt. — See Petrolia
Honeydew ES 50/K-8
1 Wilder Ridge Rd 95545 707-629-3230
Karen Ashmore, prin. Fax 629-3239

Hoopa, Humboldt
Klamath-Trinity JUSD 1,000/PK-12
PO Box 1308 95546 530-625-5600
Jon Ray, supt. Fax 625-5611
www.ktjusd.k12.ca.us
Hoopa Valley ES 500/K-8
PO Box 1308 95546 530-625-5600
Paula Wyant, prin. Fax 625-1949
Norton ES 50/K-8
PO Box 1308 95546 707-625-5600
Jeff Landry, prin. Fax 625-5611
Weitchpec ES, PO Box 1308 95546 50/K-8
Jeff Landry, prin. 530-625-5600
Other Schools – See Orleans, Willow Creek

Hornbrook, Siskiyou, Pop. 223
Hornbrook ESD 50/PK-8
PO Box 169 96044 530-475-3598
Kelly Bear, supt. Fax 475-0929
www.hornbrookschool.org
Hornbrook S 50/PK-8
PO Box 169 96044 530-475-3598
Kelly Bear, admin. Fax 475-0929

Horse Creek, Siskiyou
Klamath River UNESD 50/K-8
30438 Walker Rd 96050 530-496-3406
Mark Greenfield, supt. Fax 496-3426
Klamath River ES 50/K-8
30438 Walker Rd 96050 530-496-3406
Mark Greenfield, supt. Fax 496-3426

Hughson, Stanislaus, Pop. 6,490
Hughson USD 2,100/K-12
PO Box 189 95326 209-883-4428
Brian Beck, supt. Fax 883-4639
www.hughson.k12.ca.us
Fox Road ES 300/4-5
7668 Fox Rd 95326 209-883-2256
Carrie Duckart, prin. Fax 883-2279
Hughson ES 600/K-3
PO Box 189 95326 209-883-4412
Eric Peterson, prin. Fax 883-4704
Ross MS 500/6-8
7448 Fox Rd 95326 209-883-4425
Ryan Smith, prin. Fax 883-2017

Keyes UNESD
Supt. — See Keyes
Spratling MS 200/6-8
5277 Washington Rd 95326 209-664-3833
John Stuart, prin. Fax 656-2384

Hughson Christian S 50/PK-5
1519 Tully Rd 95326 209-883-2874
Sheila Parnell, prin. Fax 883-0840

Huntington Beach, Orange, Pop. 183,010
Fountain Valley ESD
Supt. — See Fountain Valley
Newland ES 400/K-5
8787 Dolphin Dr, 714-378-4200
Chris Mullin, prin. Fax 378-4209
Oka ES 400/K-5
9800 Yorktown Ave, 714-378-4260
Erik Miller, prin. Fax 378-4269
Talbert MS 700/6-8
9101 Brabham Dr, 714-378-4220
Jennifer Morgan, prin. Fax 378-4229

Huntington Beach City ESD 7,000/PK-8
17011 Beach Blvd Ste 560, 714-964-8888
Gregg Haulk, supt. Fax 963-9565
www.hbcsd.us
Dwyer MS 1,300/6-8
1502 Palm Ave, 714-536-7507
Christa Glembocki, prin. Fax 960-0955
Eader ES 600/K-5
9291 Banning Ave, 714-962-2451
Debbi Randall, prin. Fax 378-3601
Hawes ES 700/K-5
9002 Yellowstone Dr, 714-963-8302
Julie Jennings, prin. Fax 378-3603
Huntington Seacliff ES 700/K-5
6701 Garfield Ave, 714-841-7081
Dr. Monique Huibregste, prin. Fax 841-4593
Moffett ES 600/K-5
8800 Burlcrest Dr, 714-963-8985
Mike Andrzejewski, prin. Fax 378-3602
Perry ES 500/PK-5
19231 Harding Ln, 714-962-3348
Renee Johnson, prin. Fax 962-3347
Peterson ES 700/K-5
20661 Farnsworth Ln, 714-378-1515
Dr. Constance Polhemus, prin. Fax 378-1520
Smith ES 800/K-5
770 17th St, 714-536-1469
Carolyn Beck, prin. Fax 536-7484
Sowers MS 1,200/6-8
9300 Indianapolis Ave, 714-962-7738
Dr. John Ashby, prin. Fax 968-5580

Ocean View SD 9,200/PK-8
17200 Pinehurst Ln 92647 714-847-2551
Dr. Carol Hansen, supt. Fax 847-1430
www.ovsd.org
Circle View ES 700/K-5
6261 Hooker Dr, 714-893-5035
Kristi Hickman, prin. Fax 898-6495

College View ES 500/K-5
6582 Lennox Dr, 714-847-3505
Kathy Smith, prin. Fax 847-8615
Golden View ES 500/K-5
17251 Golden View Ln, 714-847-2516
Brett Hardy, prin. Fax 375-0736
Harbour View ES 800/K-5
4343 Pickwick Cir, 714-846-6602
Cindy Osterhout, prin. Fax 377-0952
Hope View ES 700/K-5
17622 Flintstone Ln, 714-847-8571
Paul Kraft, prin. Fax 841-1591
Lake View ES, 17451 Zeider Ln, 300/K-5
Jamie Goodwyn, prin. 714-842-2589
Marine View MS 800/6-8
5682 Tilburg Dr, 714-846-0624
Bill Lynch, prin. Fax 846-2074
Mesa View MS 800/6-8
17601 Avilla Ln, 714-842-6608
Randy Lempert, prin. Fax 842-8798
Oak View ES 700/K-5
17241 Oak Ln, 714-842-4459
Rosa Guerra, prin. Fax 842-4769
Oak View Preschool PK-PK
17131 Emerald Ln, 714-843-6938
Nicole Baitx-Kennedy, dir. Fax 375-6354
Pleasant View Preschool/OVPP PK-PK
16692 Landau Ln, 714-845-5000
Paul James, prin. Fax 845-5881
Spring View MS 800/6-8
16662 Trudy Ln, 714-846-2891
Jason Blade, prin. Fax 377-9821
Sun View ES 300/K-5
7721 Juliette Low Dr, 714-847-9643
Elaine Burney, prin. Fax 847-4173
Village View ES 600/K-5
5361 Sisson Dr, 714-846-2801
Francesca Ligman, prin. Fax 846-1631
Other Schools – See Fountain Valley, Midway City, Westminster

Westminster SD
Supt. — See Westminster
Clegg ES 600/K-5
6311 Larchwood Dr, 714-894-7218
John Staggs, prin. Fax 898-6176
Schroeder ES 600/PK-6
15151 Columbia Ln, 714-894-7268
Carrie Hernandez, prin. Fax 379-5861
Stacey MS 900/6-8
6311 Larchwood Dr, 714-894-7212
Heidi DeBritton, prin. Fax 372-8810

Grace Lutheran S 400/PK-8
5172 McFadden Ave, 714-899-1600
Elizabeth Lind, admin. Fax 899-1615
Hebrew Academy 300/PK-12
14401 Willow Ln, 714-898-0051
Dr. Bryn Harari, prin. Fax 898-0051
Heritage Montessori S 100/PK-4
15881 Goldenwest St, 714-891-9921
Shalane Seymour, dir.
Huntington Christian S 600/K-8
9700 Levee Dr, 714-378-9932
Josh Aaron, prin. Fax 378-9973
Liberty Christian S 200/PK-12
7661 Warner Ave, 714-842-5992
David Whitmire, prin. Fax 848-7484
Pegasus S 600/PK-8
19692 Lexington Ln, 714-964-1224
Jason Lopez, head sch Fax 962-6047
St. Bonaventure S 600/K-8
16377 Bradbury Ln, 714-846-2472
Jan Callender, prin. Fax 840-0498
SS. Simon & Jude S 500/PK-8
20400 Magnolia St, 714-962-4451
Crystal Pinkofsky, prin. Fax 968-1329

Huntington Park, Los Angeles, Pop. 57,940
Los Angeles USD
Supt. — See Los Angeles
Gage MS 1,900/6-8
2880 E Gage Ave 90255 323-826-1500
Cesar Quezada, prin. Fax 589-6925
Hope ES 600/K-5
7560 State St 90255 323-586-5700
Pamella Lemuiex, prin. Fax 585-6885
Huntington Park ES 500/K-5
6055 Corona Ave 90255 323-869-5920
David Ocampo, prin. Fax 560-1615
Middleton ES 1,100/K-6
6537 Malabar St 90255 323-582-6387
Edgardo Soberanes, prin. Fax 587-7006
Middleton Primary Center 200/K-1
2410 Zoe Ave 90255 323-826-9533
Lorena Avalos, prin. Fax 826-9556
Miles Avenue ES 1,000/K-5
6720 Miles Ave 90255 323-588-8296
Cora Watkins, prin. Fax 581-4567
Miles Early Education Center PK-PK
2855 Saturn Ave 90255 323-581-2410
Ana Vidal, prin. Fax 589-0672
Nimitz MS 2,000/6-8
6021 Carmelita Ave 90255 323-887-5400
Lorenzo Garcia, prin. Fax 773-5201
Pacific Boulevard ES 500/K-5
2660 E 57th St 90255 323-586-8640
Fabiola Hernandez, prin. Fax 586-8677
Roybal-Allard ES 600/K-6
3232 Saturn Ave 90255 323-826-1650
Reina Schaffer, prin. Fax 586-9920
San Antonio ES 700/K-5
6222 State St 90255 323-582-1250
Evangelina Cantu, prin. Fax 582-1710
State Early Education Center PK-PK
3210 Broadway 90255 323-589-3718
Ernestine Lara, prin. Fax 581-3339
Walnut Park ES 900/K-5
2642 Olive St 90255 323-588-3145
Saraid Luna, prin. Fax 588-5965

St. Matthias S 200/PK-8
7130 Cedar St 90255 323-588-7253
Joe Gallardo, prin. Fax 588-1136

Huron, Fresno, Pop. 6,708
Coalinga-Huron USD
Supt. — See Coalinga
Huron ES 900/K-5
PO Box 370 93234 559-945-2236
Johnny Garza, prin. Fax 945-1215
Huron MS 400/6-8
PO Box 99 93234 559-945-2926
Javier Gonzalez, prin. Fax 945-8482

Hyampom, Trinity, Pop. 228
Mountain Valley USD
Supt. — See Hayfork
Hyampom Arts Magnet S 50/PK-3
PO Box 140 96046 530-628-5912
Wendy Platt, prin. Fax 628-5902

Hydesville, Humboldt, Pop. 1,191
Hydesville ESD 200/K-8
PO Box 551 95547 707-768-3610
Lisa Jager, supt. Fax 768-3612
www.hydesvilleschool.org
Hydesville ES 200/K-8
PO Box 551 95547 707-768-3610
Lisa Jager, prin. Fax 768-3612

Idyllwild, Riverside, Pop. 2,853
Hemet USD
Supt. — See Hemet
Idyllwild S 300/K-8
PO Box 97 92549 951-659-0750
Matt Kraemer, prin. Fax 659-0757

Igo, Shasta
Igo-Ono-Platina UNESD
Supt. — See Redding
Igo-Ono S 100/K-8
PO Box 250 96047 530-396-2841
Kim Miller, prin. Fax 396-2848

Imperial, Imperial, Pop. 14,611
Imperial USD 3,800/K-12
219 N E St 92251 760-355-3200
Bryan Thomason, supt. Fax 355-4511
www.imperialusd.org
Hulse ES 900/K-5
303 S D St 92251 760-355-3210
Traci Gibbs, prin. Fax 355-3248
Waggoner ES 800/K-5
627 Joshua Tree St 92251 760-355-3266
Javier Ramos, prin. Fax 355-3180
Wright MS 900/6-8
885 N Imperial Ave 92251 760-355-3240
Diego Lopez, prin. Fax 355-3256

Imperial Beach, San Diego, Pop. 25,203
South Bay UNSD 7,800/PK-8
601 Elm Ave 91932 619-628-1600
Katie McNamara, supt. Fax 628-1608
www.sbusd.org
Bayside STEAM Academy 500/K-6
490 Emory St 91932 619-628-2500
Kevin Coordt, prin. Fax 628-2580
Central ES 600/K-6
1290 Ebony Ave 91932 619-628-5000
Cori Herbst-Loehr, prin. Fax 628-5080
Oneonta ES 600/K-6
1311 10th St 91932 619-628-8600
Marla Fernandez, prin. Fax 628-8680
VIP Village Preschool 100/PK-PK
1001 Fern Ave 91932 619-628-8690
David Sheppard, dir. Fax 628-8691
Other Schools – See San Diego, San Ysidro

Independence, Inyo, Pop. 646
Owens Valley USD 100/K-12
PO Box E 93526 760-878-2405
Dan Moore M.Ed., supt. Fax 878-2405
www.ovusd.org
Owens Valley ES 50/K-8
PO Box E 93526 760-878-2405
Dan Moore M.Ed., prin. Fax 878-2626

Indian Wells, Riverside, Pop. 4,909
Desert Sands USD
Supt. — See La Quinta
Ford ES 800/K-5
44210 Warner Trl 92210 760-772-4120
Fax 772-4125

Indio, Riverside, Pop. 75,249
Coachella Valley USD
Supt. — See Thermal
Mountain Vista ES 1,000/K-6
49750 Hjorth St 92201 760-775-6888
Valerie Perez, prin. Fax 775-6568

Desert Sands USD
Supt. — See La Quinta
Carreon Academy 700/K-5
47368 Monroe ST 92201 760-863-1544
Tiffany Norton, prin. Fax 863-1540
Carrillo Ranch ES 700/K-5
43775 Madison St 92201 760-238-9700
John Waybrant, prin. Fax 347-0489
Desert Ridge Academy 1,100/6-8
79767 Avenue 39 92203 760-393-5500
Bradley Fisher, prin. Fax 393-5502
Earhart ES of Intl Studies 900/K-5
45250 Dune Palms Rd 92201 760-200-3720
Ann Morales, prin. Fax 200-3729
Eisenhower ES 500/K-5
83391 Dillon Ave 92201 760-775-3810
Theresa Kramer, prin. Fax 775-3598
Glenn MS of International Studies 1,400/6-8
79655 Miles Ave 92201 760-200-3700
Scott Davis, prin. Fax 200-3709

Hoover ES 500/K-5
44300 Monroe St 92201 760-775-3820
Todd Biggert, prin. Fax 775-3863
Indio MS 800/6-8
81195 Miles Ave 92201 760-775-3800
Jesus Jimenez, prin. Fax 775-3807
Jackson ES 700/K-5
82850 Kenner Ave 92201 760-775-3830
Vicki Barber, prin. Fax 775-3836
Jefferson MS 600/6-8
83089 US Highway 111 92201 760-863-3660
Margo McCormick, prin. Fax 775-3597
Johnson ES 500/K-5
44640 Clinton St 92201 760-863-3680
Patrick Moon, prin. Fax 863-3684
Kennedy ES 600/K-5
45100 Clinton St 92201 760-775-3840
Patricia Rice, prin. Fax 347-5187
Madison ES 500/K-5
80845 Avenue 46 92201 760-775-3850
David Karlquist, prin. Fax 775-3855
Roosevelt ES 600/K-5
83200 Doctor Carreon Blvd 92201 760-775-3860
Daniel Martinez, prin. Fax 775-3856
Van Buren ES 600/K-5
47733 Van Buren St 92201 760-775-3870
Dr. Melissa Pizano-Grunnet, prin. Fax 775-3846

Our Lady of Perpetual Help S 200/PK-8
82470 Bliss Ave 92201 760-347-3786
Diane Arias, prin. Fax 347-7207

Inglewood, Los Angeles, Pop. 107,237
Inglewood USD 12,200/K-12
401 S Inglewood Ave 90301 310-419-2700
Dr. Thelma Melendez, admin. Fax 680-5144
myiusd.net/
Bennett/Kew ES 600/K-6
11710 Cherry Ave 90303 310-680-5400
Marzella Brown, prin. Fax 680-5409
Centinela ES 800/K-6
1123 Marlborough Ave 90302 310-680-5440
Oscar Rodriguez, prin. Fax 680-5347
Crozier MS 700/7-8
1210 W Regent St 90301 310-680-5280
La Royce Murphy, prin. Fax 680-5299
Highland ES 700/K-6
430 Venice Way 90302 310-680-5460
Annette Beasley, prin. Fax 680-5478
Hudnall ES 400/K-6
331 W Olive St 90301 310-680-5420
Dawnyelle Goolsby, prin. Fax 680-5428
Kelso ES 700/K-6
809 E Kelso St 90301 310-680-5480
Brian Coffey, prin. Fax 680-5489
Lane ES 300/K-6
2602 W 79th St 90305 310-680-5330
Eboni Kemp, prin. Fax 680-5336
Monroe MS 500/6-8
10711 S 10th Ave 90303 310-680-5310
Franklin Tilley, prin. Fax 680-5317
Oak Street ES 700/K-6
633 S Oak St 90301 310-680-5340
Richard Barter, prin. Fax 680-5347
Parent ES 600/K-8
5354 W 64th St 90302 310-680-5430
Garry Gregory, prin. Fax 680-5436
Payne ES 700/K-5
215 W 94th St 90301 310-680-5410
Karen Horowitz, prin. Fax 680-5418
Woodworth ES 500/K-6
3200 W 104th St 90303 310-680-5360
Alberto Paredes, prin. Fax 680-5377
Worthington ES 600/K-6
11101 Yukon Ave 90303 310-680-5350
Fax 680-5359

Los Angeles USD
Supt. — See Los Angeles
Century Park ES 400/K-5
10935 Spinning Ave 90303 323-757-8231
Kim Pavageau, prin. Fax 757-7449

Anthony's S 100/K-6
8420 Crenshaw Blvd 90305 323-758-1187
Margaret Johnson, head sch
St. John Chrysostom S 300/PK-8
530 E Florence Ave 90301 310-677-5868
Jae Kim, prin. Fax 677-3429

Inverness, Marin, Pop. 1,282
Shoreline USD
Supt. — See Tomales
Inverness ES 50/K-1
1 Forres Way 94937 415-663-1014
Matthew Nagle, prin. Fax 663-8558

Inyokern, Kern, Pop. 1,057
Sierra Sands USD
Supt. — See Ridgecrest
Inyokern ES 200/K-5
PO Box 1597 93527 760-499-1683
Beverly Ewbank, prin. Fax 499-1687

Ione, Amador, Pop. 7,650
Amador County USD
Supt. — See Jackson
Ione ES 500/K-6
415 S Ione St 95640 209-257-7000
Jeni DeWalt, prin. Fax 274-2167
Ione JHS 300/6-8
450 S Mill St 95640 209-257-5500
Dr. Jessica Dorris, prin. Fax 274-0671

Irvine, Orange, Pop. 201,858
Irvine USD 30,100/PK-12
5050 Barranca Pkwy 92604 949-936-5000
Terry L. Walker, supt. Fax 936-5259
www.iusd.org

Alderwood ES 800/K-6
2005 Knollcrest 92603 949-936-5400
Kelli Cheshire, prin. Fax 936-5409
Beacon Park ES, 200 Cultivate 92618 K-8
Bob Curley, prin. 949-936-8400
Bonita Canyon ES 500/K-6
1 Sundance 92603 949-936-5450
Corey Pace, prin. Fax 936-5459
Brywood ES 600/K-6
1 Westwood 92620 949-936-5500
Astrid Ramirez, prin. Fax 936-5509
Canyon View ES 900/K-6
12025 Yale Ct 92620 949-936-6900
Christina Giguiere, prin. Fax 936-6909
College Park ES 800/K-6
3700 Chaparral Ave 92606 949-936-5550
Meg Gwyn, prin. Fax 936-5559
Culverdale ES 700/K-6
2 Paseo Westpark 92614 949-936-5600
Aaron Jetzer, prin. Fax 936-5609
Cypress Village ES K-6
355 Rush Lily 92620 949-936-8900
Carla Beal, prin. Fax 936-8909
Deerfield ES 700/K-6
2 Deerfield Ave 92604 949-936-5650
Julie Hatchel, prin. Fax 936-5659
Early Childhood Learning Center 50/PK-PK
1 Smoketree 92604 949-936-5857
Robin Hunter, admin. Fax 936-5809
Eastshore ES 600/K-6
155 Eastshore 92604 949-936-5700
Lisa Kadam, prin. Fax 936-5709
Eastwood ES K-6
99 Meander 92620 949-936-8100
Aaron Jetzer, prin. Fax 936-8109
Greentree ES 600/K-6
4200 Manzanita 92604 949-936-5800
Tamara Brown, prin. Fax 936-5809
Jeffrey Trail MS 700/7-8
155 Visions 92620 949-936-8700
Michael Georgino, prin. Fax 936-8709
Lakeside MS 700/7-8
3 Lemongrass 92604 949-559-1601
Gina Cuneo, prin. Fax 936-6109
Meadow Park ES 700/K-6
50 Blue Lk S 92614 949-936-5900
Thomas Potwora, prin. Fax 936-5909
Northwood ES 700/K-6
28 Carson 92620 949-936-5950
Janelle Kellar, prin. Fax 936-5959
Oak Creek ES 900/K-6
1 Dovecreek 92618 949-936-8550
Carlo Grasso, prin. Fax 936-8559
Plaza Vista S 900/K-8
670 Paseo Westpark 92606 949-936-6955
James Parker, prin. Fax 936-6959
Portola Springs ES K-6
12100 Portola Springs Pkwy 92618
Heather Phillips, prin.
Rancho San Joaquin MS 900/7-8
4861 Michelson Dr 92612 949-936-6500
Mike Modeer, prin. Fax 936-6509
Santiago Hills ES 700/K-6
29 Christamon W 92620 949-936-6000
Michele Ogden, prin. Fax 936-6009
Sierra Vista MS 800/7-8
2 Liberty 92620 949-936-6600
Lynn Matassarin, prin. Fax 936-6609
South Lake MS 700/7-8
655 W Yale Loop 92614 949-936-6700
Belinda Averill, prin. Fax 936-6709
Springbrook ES 700/K-6
655 Springbrook N 92614 949-936-6050
Sunny Shen, prin. Fax 936-6059
Stone Creek ES, 2 Stone Crk S 92604 600/K-6
Jenna Berumen, prin. 949-551-1201
Stonegate ES 1,100/K-6
100 Honors 92620 949-936-6450
Harmony Briscoe, prin. Fax 936-6451
Turtle Rock ES 900/K-6
5151 Amalfi Dr 92603 949-936-6250
Karen Catabijan, prin. Fax 936-6259
University Park ES 600/K-6
4572 Sandburg Way 92612 949-936-6300
Christine Amoroso, prin. Fax 936-6309
Venado MS 600/7-8
4 Deerfield Ave 92604 949-936-6800
Luis Torrez, prin. Fax 936-6809
Vista Verde S 1,000/K-8
6 Federation Way 92603 949-936-6350
Jerry Vlasic, prin. Fax 936-6359
Westpark ES 700/K-6
25 San Carlo 92614 949-936-6400
Deanna Rutter, prin. Fax 936-6409
Woodbury ES 1,100/K-6
125 Great Lawn 92620 949-936-5750
Alan Battenfield, prin. Fax 936-5759

Tustin USD
Supt. — See Tustin
Hicks Canyon ES 1,000/K-4
3817 View Park 92602 714-734-1878
Deena Vela, prin. Fax 669-0564
Myford ES 800/K-5
3181 Trevino Dr 92602 714-734-1875
Rena Fairchild, prin. Fax 731-7614
Orchard Hills S 1,100/4-8
11555 Culver Dr 92602 714-430-2078
Cindy Agopian, prin. Fax 430-2278

LePort S 200/PK-8
1 Technology Dr Bldg A 92618 949-427-3968
New Horizon S - Irvine 200/PK-6
1 Truman St 92620 949-552-5411
Dr. Dina Eletreby, head sch Fax 552-5945
Tarbut V'Torah Community Day S 300/PK-5
5200 Bonita Canyon Dr 92603 949-509-9500
Dr. Jeffrey Davis, head sch Fax 856-2400

Irwindale, Los Angeles, Pop. 1,410
Covina-Valley USD
Supt. — See Covina
Merwin ES 400/K-5
16125 Cypress St 91706 626-472-7660
Stephanie Kearns, prin. Fax 472-7675

Isleton, Sacramento, Pop. 770
River Delta USD
Supt. — See Rio Vista
Isleton ES 200/K-6
PO Box 728 95641 916-777-6515
Antonia Slagle, prin. Fax 777-6525

Ivanhoe, Tulare, Pop. 4,457
Visalia USD
Supt. — See Visalia
Ivanhoe ES 600/PK-8
16030 Avenue 332 93235 559-730-7849
George Rodriguez, prin. Fax 730-7848

Jackson, Amador, Pop. 4,513
Amador County USD 3,700/K-12
217 Rex Ave 95642 209-223-1750
Amy Slavensky Ph.D., supt. Fax 296-3133
www.amadorcoe.org
Jackson ES 400/K-6
220 Church St 95642 209-257-5600
Barbara Magpusao, prin. Fax 223-2366
Jackson JHS 200/6-8
747 Sutter St 95642 209-257-5700
Janet DeLeo, prin. Fax 257-5757
Pine Grove ES 300/K-6
20101 State Highway 88 95642 209-296-2800
Amanda Avila, prin. Fax 296-3133
Other Schools – See Ione, Pioneer, Plymouth, Sutter Creek

Jamestown, Tuolumne, Pop. 3,305
Jamestown ESD 300/K-8
18299 5th Ave 95327 209-984-4058
Contessa Polfrey, supt. Fax 984-0434
www.jamestown.k12.ca.us
Jamestown ES 300/K-8
18299 5th Ave 95327 209-984-5217
Bart Taylor, prin. Fax 984-2069
Other Schools – See Chinese Camp

Sierra Waldorf S 200/PK-8
19234 Hawhide Rd 95327 209-984-0454
Kimberly Pendleton, dir. Fax 984-4125

Jamul, San Diego, Pop. 5,990
Jamul-Dulzura UNSD 1,000/K-12
14581 Lyons Valley Rd 91935 619-669-7700
Nadine Bennett, supt. Fax 669-0254
www.jdusd.net
Jamul IS 100/4-5
14545 Lyons Valley Rd 91935 619-669-7900
Yesenia Robinson, prin. Fax 669-5324
Jamul PS 200/K-3
14567 Lyons Valley Rd 91935 619-669-7800
Yesenia Robinson, prin. Fax 669-0438
Oak Grove MS 200/6-8
14344 Olive Vista Dr 91935 619-669-2700
Dr. Minerva Salas, prin. Fax 669-7632

Janesville, Lassen, Pop. 1,372
Janesville UNESD 300/K-8
PO Box 280 96114 530-253-3660
Edward Brown, supt. Fax 253-3891
www.janesvilleschool.org
Janesville ES 300/K-8
PO Box 280 96114 530-253-3551
Edward Brown, prin. Fax 253-3891

Joshua Tree, San Bernardino, Pop. 7,144
Morongo USD
Supt. — See Twentynine Palms
Friendly Hills ES 400/K-6
7252 Sunny Vista Rd 92252 760-366-3812
Deanna Skinta, prin. Fax 366-1061
Joshua Tree ES 300/K-6
4950 Sunburst St 92252 760-366-8459
Daniele Snider, prin. Fax 366-5364

Julian, San Diego, Pop. 1,474
Julian UNESD 3,500/PK-12
PO Box 337 92036 760-765-0661
Brian Duffy, supt. Fax 765-0220
www.juesd.net
Julian ES 200/PK-5
PO Box 337 92036 760-765-0661
Scot Copeland, prin. Fax 765-0220
Julian JHS 100/6-8
PO Box 337 92036 760-765-0575
Brian Duffy, prin. Fax 765-3340

Junction City, Trinity, Pop. 646
Junction City ESD 100/K-8
430 Red Hill Rd 96048 530-623-6381
Christine Camara, supt. Fax 623-5652
www.jcesd.org
Junction City ES 100/K-8
430 Red Hill Rd 96048 530-623-6381
Christine Camara, prin. Fax 623-5652

Jurupa Valley, Riverside
Jurupa USD 19,400/PK-12
4850 Pedley Rd, 951-360-4100
Elliott Duchon, supt. Fax 360-4194
www.jusd.k12.ca.us
Arbuckle ES 500/K-6
3600 Packard St, 951-222-7788
James Wandrie, prin. Fax 369-3913
Camino Real ES 800/K-6
4655 Camino Real, 951-360-2714
Erika Pham, prin. Fax 360-2819
Glen Avon ES 700/K-6
4352 Pyrite St, 951-360-2764
Sylvia Bottom, prin. Fax 685-6938
Granite Hill ES 800/K-6
9371 Granite Hill Dr, 951-360-2725
Denise Hernandez, prin. Fax 685-6568
Indian Hills ES 600/K-6
7750 Linares Ave, 951-360-2724
Victoria Jobe, prin. Fax 681-4742
Jurupa MS 1,200/7-8
8700 Galena St, 951-360-2846
Damien Hernandez, prin. Fax 360-8928
Mira Loma MS 900/7-8
5051 Steve Ave, 951-360-2883
Mary Boules, prin. Fax 685-7405
Mission Bell ES 500/K-6
4020 Conning St, 951-360-2748
Joan Lauritzen, prin. Fax 681-7714
Mission MS 800/7-8
5961 Mustang Ln, 951-222-7842
Nicholas Blake, prin. Fax 369-1407
Pacific Avenue Academy of Music 400/K-6
6110 45th St, 951-222-7877
Maureen Dalimot, prin. Fax 684-4540
Pedley ES 600/K-6
5871 Hudson St, 951-360-2793
Monica Leon, prin. Fax 360-2791
Peralta ES 700/K-6
6450 Peralta Pl, 951-222-7701
Robert Cmelak, prin. Fax 779-9143
Rustic Lane ES 600/K-6
6420 Rustic Ln, 951-222-7837
Krisit Batchelder, prin. Fax 788-6401
School Readiness Center PK-PK
5960 Mustang Ln, 951-222-7850
Maricela Tafoya, coord. Fax 222-7853
Sky Country ES 500/K-6
5520 Lucretia Ave, 951-360-2816
Ann Marie Farias, prin. Fax 681-5197
Stone Avenue ES 800/K-6
5111 Stone Ave, 951-360-2859
Dr. Marian Gutterud, prin. Fax 681-5933
Sunnyslope ES 800/K-6
7050 38th St, 951-360-2781
Olga Alferez, prin. Fax 360-5462
Troth Street ES 800/K-6
5565 Troth St, 951-360-2866
Dr. Ilsa Crocker, prin. Fax 360-5342
Van Buren ES 600/K-6
9501 Jurupa Rd, 951-360-2865
Ronald Zahnd, prin. Fax 685-3314
West Riverside ES 700/K-6
3972 Riverview Dr, 951-222-7759
Marcy Hale, prin. Fax 781-6873

Life Christian Academy 100/PK-4
3270 Rubidoux Blvd, 951-684-3639
Elizabeth Flores, prin. Fax 684-7093

Kelseyville, Lake, Pop. 3,286
Kelseyville USD 1,700/K-12
4410 Konocti Rd 95451 707-279-1511
Dave McQueen, supt. Fax 279-9221
www.kvusd.org
Kelseyville ES 500/K-5
5065 Konocti Rd 95451 707-279-4232
Barbara Gleason, prin. Fax 279-8748
Mountain Vista MS 400/6-8
5081 Konocti Rd 95451 707-279-4060
Heather Thomas, prin. Fax 279-8835
Riviera ES 300/K-5
10505 Fairway Dr 95451 707-277-6050
Tavis Perkins, prin. Fax 277-6060

Kensington, Contra Costa, Pop. 4,793
West Contra Costa USD
Supt. — See Richmond
Kensington ES 500/K-6
90 Highland Blvd 94708 510-231-1415
Judith Sanders, prin. Fax 526-3189

Kentfield, Marin, Pop. 6,290
Kentfield ESD 1,200/K-8
750 College Ave 94904 415-458-5130
Elizabeth Schott, supt. Fax 458-5137
www.kentfieldschools.org/
Bacich ES 700/K-4
699 Sir Francis Drake Blvd 94904 415-925-2220
Sally Peck, prin. Fax 925-2226
Kent MS 500/5-8
800 College Ave 94904 415-458-5970
Skip Kniesche, prin. Fax 458-5973

Kenwood, Sonoma, Pop. 1,007
Kenwood ESD 200/PK-6
PO Box 220 95452 707-833-2500
Robert Bales, supt. Fax 833-2181
www.kenwoodschool.org/
Kenwood ES 200/PK-6
PO Box 220 95452 707-833-2500
Robert Bales, prin. Fax 833-2181

Kerman, Fresno, Pop. 13,348
Kerman USD 4,900/PK-12
151 S 1st St 93630 559-843-9000
Robert Frausto, supt. Fax 840-4283
www.kermanusd.com
Goldenrod ES 900/K-6
445 S Goldenrod Ave 93630 559-843-9500
Mandi Guizar, prin. Fax 840-4289
Kerman-Floyd ES 700/PK-6
14655 W F St 93630 559-843-9400
Kathy Goodlad, prin. Fax 840-3707
Kerman MS 800/7-8
601 S 1st St 93630 559-843-9600
Margaret Nichols, prin. Fax 840-4291
Liberty ES 700/K-6
16001 W E St 93630 559-843-9300
Melissa Andresen, prin. Fax 478-2992
Sun Empire ES 500/K-6
2649 N Modoc Ave 93630 559-843-9200
Albert de Leon, prin. Fax 840-4352

Kerman Christian S 100/PK-6
15495 W Whitesbridge Ave 93630 559-846-7200
Suzanne Ocampo, prin. Fax 842-7491

Kernville, Kern, Pop. 1,326
Kernville UNESD
Supt. — See Lake Isabella
Kernville ES 100/K-3
13550 Sierra Way 93238 760-376-2249
Brian Polston, prin. Fax 376-1935

Kettleman City, Kings, Pop. 1,426
Reef-Sunset USD
Supt. — See Avenal
Kettleman City S 300/K-8
PO Box 599 93239 559-386-5702
Kristi Castillo, prin. Fax 386-0207

Keyes, Stanislaus, Pop. 5,468
Keyes UNESD 1,100/PK-12
PO Box 310 95328 209-669-2921
Dr. Helio Brasil, supt. Fax 669-2923
www.keyes.k12.ca.us/
Keyes ES 500/PK-5
PO Box 549 95328 209-667-1660
Timothy Torres, prin. Fax 668-8714
Other Schools – See Hughson

King City, Monterey, Pop. 12,778
Bitterwater-Tully UNESD 50/PK-8
45980 Airline Hwy 93930 831-385-5339
Candace Brewen, supt. Fax 385-9105
www.sbcoe.org/District/1272-Untitled.html
Bitterwater-Tully S 50/PK-8
45980 Airline Hwy 93930 831-385-5339
Candace Brewen, prin. Fax 385-9105

King City UNSD 2,600/PK-8
104 S Vanderhurst St 93930 831-385-2940
Rory Livingston, supt. Fax 386-0372
www.kcusd.org
Chalone Peaks MS 800/6-8
667 Meyer St 93930 831-385-4400
Matt Daniels, prin. Fax 385-4422
Del Rey ES 800/PK-5
502 King St 93930 831-385-4884
Charlynn Davidson, prin. Fax 385-1045
King City Arts Magnet S 300/K-5
415 Pearl St 93930 831-385-5473
Brad Smith, prin. Fax 385-1016
Phoenix Academy Community Day S 5-8
667 Meyer St 93930 831-385-2940
Matt Daniels, prin. Fax 386-0372
Santa Lucia ES 700/K-5
502 Collins St 93930 831-385-3246
Brinet Greenlee, prin. Fax 385-6310

Kings Beach, Placer, Pop. 3,765
Tahoe Truckee USD
Supt. — See Truckee
Kings Beach ES 400/K-4
PO Box 1177 96143 530-582-3730
Kyle Mohagen, prin. Fax 546-5066

Tahoe Expedition Academy 100/PK-12
8651 Speckled Ave 96143 530-546-5253
Fax 579-3206

Kingsburg, Fresno, Pop. 11,129
Clay JESD 300/K-8
12449 S Smith Ave 93631 559-897-4185
Brenda Sylvia, supt. Fax 897-2280
www.clayschool.k12.ca.us
Clay ES 300/K-8
12449 S Smith Ave 93631 559-897-4185
Brenda Sylvia, prin. Fax 897-2280

Kings River UNESD 500/K-8
3961 Avenue 400 93631 559-897-7209
Sherry Martin, supt. Fax 897-0320
www.kingsriverelementary.org
Kings River ES 500/K-8
3961 Avenue 400 93631 559-897-7209
Sherry Martin, supt. Fax 897-0320

Kingvale, Nevada, Pop. 140
Tahoe Truckee USD
Supt. — See Truckee
Donner Trail ES 100/K-5
52755 Donner Pass Rd, 530-582-2720
Susan Phebus, prin. Fax 426-0530

Klamath, Del Norte, Pop. 722
Del Norte County USD
Supt. — See Crescent City
Keating ES 100/K-6
300 Minot Creek Rd 95548 707-464-0340
Jake Williams, prin. Fax 482-0404

Kneeland, Humboldt
Kneeland ESD 50/K-8
9313 Kneeland Rd 95549 707-442-5472
Justin Wallace, supt. Fax 442-7784
www.humboldt.k12.ca.us/kneeland_sd/
Kneeland S 50/K-8
9313 Kneeland Rd 95549 707-442-5472
Justin Wallace, admin. Fax 442-7784

Knightsen, Contra Costa, Pop. 1,521
Knightsen ESD 500/K-8
PO Box 265 94548 925-625-0073
Theresa Estrada, supt. Fax 625-8766
www.knightsen.k12.ca.us
Knightsen ES 500/K-8
PO Box 265 94548 925-625-0073
Leanne Sarmento, prin. Fax 625-8766
Other Schools – See Brentwood

Knights Ferry, Stanislaus
Knights Ferry ESD 100/K-8
PO Box 840 95361 209-881-3382
Dr. Janet Skulina, supt. Fax 881-3525
www.knightsferryesd.org
Knights Ferry ES 100/K-8
PO Box 840 95361 209-881-3382
Dr. Anita Ivaschenko, prin. Fax 881-3525

Korbel, Humboldt
Maple Creek ESD 50/PK-8
15933 Maple Creek Rd 95550 707-668-5596
Wendy Orlandi, supt. Fax 668-4132
apps.humboldt.k12.ca.us/sites/mapleck_sd/
Maple Creek S 50/PK-8
15933 Maple Creek Rd 95550 707-668-5596
Wendy Orlandi, admin. Fax 668-4132

Kyburz, El Dorado
Silver Fork ESD
Supt. — See Pollock Pines
Silver Fork S 50/K-8
1325 Sugarloaf Ave 95720 530-293-3163
Pat Atkins, prin. Fax 293-3193

La Canada, Los Angeles

Learning Castle S & La Canada Prep 400/PK-8
4490 Cornishon Ave 91011 818-952-8008
Terry Villanueva, dir. Fax 952-5101

La Canada Flintridge, Los Angeles, Pop. 19,647
La Canada USD 4,000/K-12
4490 Cornishon Ave 91011 818-952-8300
Wendy Sinnette, supt. Fax 952-8309
www.lcusd.net
La Canada ES 600/K-6
4540 Encinas Dr 91011 818-952-8350
Emily Blaney, prin. Fax 952-8355
Palm Crest ES 600/K-6
5025 Palm Dr 91011 818-952-8360
Karen Hurley, prin. Fax 952-8365
Paradise Canyon ES 700/K-6
471 Knight Way 91011 818-952-8340
Debra Cradduck, prin. Fax 952-8337

Crestview Preparatory S 200/K-6
140 Foothill Blvd 91011 818-952-0925
Baudelia Taylor, head sch Fax 952-8470
St. Bede the Venerable S 300/K-8
4524 Crown Ave 91011 818-790-7884
Ralph Valente, prin. Fax 790-0699

La Crescenta, Los Angeles, Pop. 19,112
Glendale USD
Supt. — See Glendale
Cloud Pre-School 50/PK-PK
4444 Cloud Ave 91214 818-249-1414
Dr. Rebeca Andrade Ed.D., admin. Fax 249-5855
Dunsmore ES 400/K-6
4717 Dunsmore Ave 91214 818-248-1758
Karen Stegman, prin. Fax 249-7918
La Crescenta ES 500/K-6
4343 La Crescenta Ave 91214 818-249-3187
Dr. Josephine Bixler Ed.D., prin. Fax 248-3168
Lincoln ES 500/K-6
4310 New York Ave 91214 818-249-1863
Stephen Williams, prin. Fax 249-7876
Monte Vista ES 700/K-6
2620 Orange Ave 91214 818-248-2617
Suzanne Risse, prin. Fax 248-5263
Mountain Avenue ES 500/K-6
2307 Mountain Ave 91214 818-248-7766
Jaclyn Scott, prin. Fax 248-6352
Rosemont MS 1,200/7-8
4725 Rosemont Ave 91214 818-248-4224
Dr. Scott Anderle Ed.D., prin. Fax 248-3790
Valley View ES 400/K-6
4900 Maryland Ave 91214 818-236-3771
Dr. Brook Reynolds Ed.D., prin. Fax 542-6480

St. James - Holy Redeemer S 100/K-8
4635 Dunsmore Ave 91214 818-248-7778
Susan Romero, prin. Fax 248-5242

Ladera Ranch, Orange, Pop. 21,970
Capistrano USD
Supt. — See San Juan Capistrano
Chaparral ES 900/K-5
29001 Sienna Pkwy 92694 949-234-5349
Melissa Schaefer, prin. Fax 364-3952
Ladera Ranch ES 900/K-5
29551 Sienna Pkwy 92694 949-234-5915
Sandy Miller, prin. Fax 364-1149
Ladera Ranch MS 1,400/6-8
29551 Sienna Pkwy 92694 949-234-5922
George Duarte, prin. Fax 364-1149
Oso Grande ES 1,200/K-5
30251 Sienna Pkwy 92694 949-234-5966
Jayne Martin, prin. Fax 365-1716

Montessori of Ladera Ranch 100/PK-3
2101 Corporate Dr 92694 949-218-6990

Lafayette, Contra Costa, Pop. 22,962
Lafayette SD 3,500/PK-8
3477 School St 94549 925-927-3500
Rachel Zinn, supt. Fax 284-1525
www.lafsd.org
Burton Valley ES 700/PK-5
561 Merriewood Dr 94549 925-927-3550
Meredith Dolley, prin. Fax 284-5891
Happy Valley ES 500/K-5
3855 Happy Valley Rd 94549 925-927-3560
Shayna Peeff, prin. Fax 284-5973
Lafayette ES 600/K-5
950 Moraga Rd 94549 925-927-3570
Ann Kim, prin. Fax 283-4091
Springhill ES 500/K-5
3301 Springhill Rd 94549 925-927-3580
Mette Thallaug, prin. Fax 283-3675
Stanley MS 1,200/6-8
3455 School St 94549 925-927-3530
Betsy Balmat, prin. Fax 283-1797

Contra Costa Jewish Day S 200/PK-8
955 Risa Rd 94549 925-284-8288
Dean Goldfein, head sch Fax 284-8289
Meher S 200/PK-5
999 Leland Dr 94549 925-938-9958
Dr. Wendy Ritchey, pres. Fax 938-9184
St. Perpetua S 300/K-8
3445 Hamlin Rd 94549 925-284-1640
Karen Goodshaw, prin. Fax 284-5676

La Grange, Stanislaus
Mariposa County USD
Supt. — See Mariposa
Lake Don Pedro S 200/K-8
2411 Hidalgo St 95329 209-852-2144
Reed Yancey, prin. Fax 852-2184

Laguna Beach, Orange, Pop. 22,111
Laguna Beach USD 2,800/PK-12
550 Blumont St 92651 949-497-7700
Jason Viloria Ed.D., supt. Fax 497-6021
www.lbusd.org
El Morro ES 600/PK-5
8681 N Coast Hwy 92651 949-497-7780
Christopher Duddy, prin. Fax 497-7784
Thurston MS 800/6-8
2100 Park Ave 92651 949-497-7785
Jennifer Salberg, prin. Fax 497-7798
Top of the World ES 700/PK-5
21601 Tree Top Ln 92651 949-497-7790
Mike Conlon, prin. Fax 497-5397

Anneliese's S 400/PK-6
20062 Laguna Canyon Rd 92651 949-497-8310
Maria Onesi, dir.
St. Catherine of Siena S 200/K-8
30516 S Coast Hwy 92651 949-494-7339
Michael Letourneau, prin. Fax 376-5752

Laguna Hills, Orange, Pop. 29,183
Saddleback Valley USD
Supt. — See Mission Viejo
Lomarena ES 500/K-6
25100 Earhart Rd 92653 949-581-1370
Brendon Morrow, prin. Fax 581-8520
San Joaquin ES 500/K-6
22182 Barbera 92653 949-581-3450
Karen Schibler, prin. Fax 598-3779
Valencia ES 700/K-6
25661 Paseo De Valencia 92653 949-830-3650
Wendie Hauschild, prin. Fax 830-1868

Laguna Niguel, Orange, Pop. 60,641
Capistrano USD
Supt. — See San Juan Capistrano
Bergeson ES 600/K-5
25302 Rancho Niguel Rd 92677 949-643-1540
Greg Hauser, prin. Fax 643-7931
Hidden Hills ES 400/K-5
25142 Hidden Hills Rd 92677 949-495-0050
Pam Sawyer, prin. Fax 495-6920
Laguna Niguel ES 600/K-5
27922 Niguel Heights Blvd 92677 949-234-5308
Michelle Moore, prin. Fax 360-4407
Malcom ES 700/K-5
32261 Charles Rd 92677 949-248-0542
Peggy Baerst, prin. Fax 248-7697
Moulton ES 600/K-5
29851 Highlands Ave 92677 949-234-5980
Jackie Campbell, prin. Fax 495-5233
Niguel Hills MS 1,300/6-8
29070 Paseo De La Escuela 92677 949-234-5360
Tim Reece, prin. Fax 249-2069
White ES 700/K-5
25422 Chapparosa Park Rd 92677 949-249-3875
Andrew Klinenberg, prin. Fax 249-5316

Grace Classical Academy 100/K-8
24600 La Plata Dr 92677 949-558-5065
Laguna Niguel Jr. Academy 100/K-10
29702 Kensington Dr 92677 949-495-3428
David Tripp, prin. Fax 495-3438
McDowell S 200/PK-5
29028 Aloma Ave 92677 949-495-5162
Chris Lincoln M.Ed., head sch Fax 495-6733
St. Anne S 800/PK-8
32451 Bear Brand Rd 92677 949-276-6700
Steven Cunningham, head sch Fax 276-6706

La Habra, Orange, Pop. 59,112
La Habra City ESD 5,100/K-8
PO Box 307 90633 562-690-2305
Dr. Joanne Culverhouse, supt. Fax 690-4154
www.lahabraschools.org
Arbolita ES 400/K-3
PO Box 307 90633 562-690-2352
Rosa Maria Murillo, prin. Fax 697-8862
El Cerrito ES 500/K-2
PO Box 307 90633 562-690-2340
Emily Szary, prin. Fax 690-2342
Imperial MS 900/6-8
PO Box 307 90633 562-690-2344
Cathy Seighman, prin. Fax 526-3678
Ladera Palma ES 500/K-2
PO Box 307 90633 562-690-2348
Jennifer Rodriguez, prin. Fax 697-9734
Las Lomas ES 500/K-2
PO Box 307 90633 562-690-2353
Pam Cunningham, prin. Fax 870-9049
Las Positas ES 600/3-5
PO Box 307 90633 562-690-2356
Sharon Hensley, prin. Fax 871-2073
Sierra Vista ES 600/3-5
PO Box 307 90633 562-690-2359
Anna Dorado, prin. Fax 690-2093
Walnut ES 500/3-5
PO Box 307 90633 562-690-2369
Susan Goellrich, prin. Fax 697-3621

Washington MS 900/6-8
PO Box 307 90633 562-690-2374
Dr. George Lopez, prin. Fax 690-7834

Lowell JSD
Supt. — See Whittier
El Portal ES 500/K-6
200 Nada St 90631 562-902-4211
Rhonda Esparza, prin. Fax 694-0022
Macy ES 600/K-6
2301 Russell St 90631 562-902-4231
David Shun, prin. Fax 690-8989
Olita ES 500/K-6
950 Briercliff Dr 90631 562-902-4251
Krista Van Hoogmoed, prin. Fax 690-0273

Our Lady of Guadalupe S 200/K-8
920 W La Habra Blvd 90631 562-697-9726
Francine Kubasek, prin. Fax 905-0095

La Honda, San Mateo, Pop. 874
La Honda-Pescadero USD
Supt. — See Pescadero
La Honda ES 100/PK-5
PO Box 87 94020 650-747-0051
Elizabeth Morgan, prin. Fax 747-0617

La Jolla, See San Diego
San Diego USD
Supt. — See San Diego
Bird Rock ES 500/K-5
5371 La Jolla Hermosa Ave 92037 858-488-0537
Dr. Amanda Hale, prin. Fax 539-0541
La Jolla ES 600/K-5
1111 Marine St 92037 858-454-7196
Donna Tripi, prin. Fax 459-6918
Muirlands MS 1,000/6-8
1056 Nautilus St 92037 858-459-4211
Harlan Klein, prin. Fax 459-8075
Torrey Pines ES 500/K-5
8350 Cliffridge Ave 92037 858-453-2323
Sarah Ott, prin. Fax 452-6923

All Hallows Academy 200/K-8
2390 Nautilus St 92037 858-459-6074
Mary Skeen, prin. Fax 459-4602
Childrens S 300/PK-8
2225 Torrey Pines Ln 92037 858-454-0184
John Fowler, head sch Fax 454-0186
Evans S 100/K-6
6510 La Jolla Scenic Dr S 92037 858-459-2066
Gillispie S 300/PK-6
7380 Girard Ave 92037 858-459-3773
Alison Fleming, head sch Fax 459-3834
La Jolla Country Day S 1,200/PK-12
9490 Genesee Ave 92037 858-453-3440
Dr. Gary Krahn, head sch Fax 453-8210
San Diego French-American S 400/PK-8
6550 Soledad Mountain Rd 92037 858-456-2807
Mark Rosenblum, hdmstr. Fax 459-2670
Stella Maris Academy 200/K-8
7654 Herschel Ave 92037 858-454-2461
Patricia Lowell, prin. Fax 454-4913

Lake Almanor, Plumas, Pop. 353

Lake Almanor Christian S 50/K-8
2610 State Route A13 96137 530-596-4100
Jeri Kendrick, prin. Fax 596-4682

Lake Arrowhead, San Bernardino, Pop. 12,063
Rim of the World USD
Supt. — See Blue Jay
Henck IS 900/6-8
PO Box 430 92352 909-336-0360
Jennifer Whiteside, prin. Fax 336-3449
Lake Arrowhead ES 400/K-5
PO Box 430 92352 909-336-0387
Veronica McGilvery, prin. Fax 336-3440

Lake Elsinore, Riverside, Pop. 50,250
Lake Elsinore USD 21,900/PK-12
545 Chaney St 92530 951-253-7000
Doug Kimberly Ed.D., supt. Fax 253-7084
www.leusd.k12.ca.us
Canyon Lake MS 1,300/6-8
33005 Canyon Hills Rd 92532 951-244-2123
Nick Powers, prin. Fax 244-2103
Cottonwood Canyon ES 900/K-5
32100 Lost Rd 92532 951-244-2585
Elizabeth Atkinson, prin. Fax 244-2549
Elsinore ES 600/K-5
512 W Sumner Ave 92530 951-253-7615
Lorraine Pelaez, prin. Fax 253-7620
Elsinore MS 700/6-8
1203 W Graham Ave 92530 951-674-2118
Greg Stanley, prin. Fax 674-6302
Lakeland Village S 1,000/K-8
18730 Grand Ave 92530 951-253-7400
Dr. Preston Perez, prin. Fax 253-7424
Machado ES 700/K-5
15150 Joy St 92530 951-253-7500
Sandra Valles Metzger, prin. Fax 253-7501
Preschool PK-PK
565 Chaney St 92530 951-253-7091
Frieda Brands Ed.D., prin. Fax 253-7187
Railroad Canyon ES 600/K-5
1300 Mill St 92530 951-253-7510
Lori Recatto, prin. Fax 253-7520
Rice Canyon ES 900/K-5
29535 Westwind Dr 92530 951-471-2184
Robert Recatto, prin. Fax 471-2186
Terra Cotta MS 1,200/6-8
29291 Lake St 92530 951-253-7380
Kathy Nash Ed.D., prin. Fax 253-7424
Tuscany Hills ES 800/K-5
23 Ponte Russo 92532 951-253-7530
Jeff Marks, prin. Fax 253-7535
Warren ES 900/K-5
41221 Rosetta Canyon Dr 92532 951-253-7810
Scott Poncy, prin. Fax 253-7817

Withrow ES 700/K-5
30100 Audelo St 92530 951-253-7570
Ahmet Baskent, prin. Fax 253-7584
Other Schools – See Corona, Wildomar

Menifee UNESD
Supt. — See Menifee
Bouris ES 700/K-5
34257 Kalanchoe Rd 92532 951-244-7657
David Mobley, prin. Fax 244-8406

Lake Forest, Orange, Pop. 74,539
Saddleback Valley USD
Supt. — See Mission Viejo
Lake Forest ES 900/K-6
21801 Pittsford 92630 949-830-9945
Audra Bailey, prin. Fax 830-6478
La Madera ES 600/K-6
25350 Serrano Rd 92630 949-770-1415
Heather Ramsey, prin. Fax 770-0257
Olivewood ES 500/K-6
23391 Dune Mear Rd 92630 949-837-6682
Eva Neuer, prin. Fax 586-8014
Rancho Canada ES 700/K-6
21801 Winding Way 92630 949-768-5252
Larry Hausner, prin. Fax 768-5741
Santiago ES 500/K-6
24982 Rivendell Dr 92630 949-586-2820
Howard Johnston, prin. Fax 586-4232
Serrano IS 1,200/7-8
24642 Jeronimo Rd 92630 949-586-3221
Robert Sherlock, prin. Fax 586-3773

Abiding Savior Lutheran S 300/PK-8
23262 El Toro Rd 92630 949-830-1461
Donna Lucas, prin. Fax 830-7921
Arbor Christian S 50/PK-K
23302 El Toro Rd 92630 949-855-4599
Rev. Faye Martnick, dir. Fax 855-3891
Grace Christian S 500/PK-6
26052 Trabuco Rd 92630 949-951-8683
Danielle Boldt, prin. Fax 247-4737
Montessori on the Lake S 100/K-8
23311 Muirlands Blvd 92630 949-855-5630
Therese Barto, dir. Fax 855-5633

Lake Hughes, Los Angeles, Pop. 635
Hughes-Elizabeth Lakes UNESD 300/K-8
PO Box 530 93532 661-724-2395
Jean Cummings, admin. Fax 724-0967
www.heluesd.org
Hughes-Elizabeth Lakes S 300/K-8
PO Box 530 93532 661-724-1231
Dr. Lori Slaven, prin. Fax 724-1485

Lake Isabella, Kern, Pop. 3,311
Kernville UNESD 800/K-8
3240 Erskine Creek Rd 93240 760-379-3651
Robin Shive, supt. Fax 379-3812
www.kernvilleusd.org
Wallace ES 400/K-4
3240 Erskine Creek Rd 93240 760-379-2621
Brian Polston, prin. Fax 379-1324
Wallace MS 300/5-8
3240 Erskine Creek Rd 93240 760-379-4646
Jill Shaw, prin. Fax 379-1322
Other Schools – See Kernville

Lakeport, Lake, Pop. 4,650
Lakeport USD 1,500/K-12
2508 Howard Ave 95453 707-262-3000
April Leiferman, supt. Fax 263-7332
www.lakeport.k12.ca.us
Lakeport ES 500/K-3
2508 Howard Ave 95453 707-262-3005
Aaron Carter, prin. Fax 262-5531
Terrace MS 500/4-8
2508 Howard Ave 95453 707-262-3007
Rachel Paarsch, prin. Fax 262-5532

Konocti Christian Academy 100/K-8
PO Box 1515 95453 707-262-1522
Becky Madison, prin. Fax 263-4466
Westlake Seventh-Day S 50/1-8
6585 Westlake Rd 95453 707-263-4607
Vicky Rosales-Wery, prin. Fax 263-7160

Lakeside, San Diego, Pop. 20,041
Lakeside UNSD 5,100/PK-12
12335 Woodside Ave 92040 619-390-2600
David Lorden, supt. Fax 561-7929
www.lsusd.net
Eucalyptus Hills ES K-K
11838 Valle Vista Rd 92040 619-390-2634
Robert Brown, prin. Fax 390-2575
Lakeside Farms ES 700/K-5
11915 Lakeside Ave 92040 619-390-2646
Matt Thompson, prin. Fax 390-2648
Lakeside MS 900/6-8
11833 Woodside Ave 92040 619-390-2636
Stephen Mull, prin. Fax 390-2643
Lakeview ES 700/K-5
9205 Lakeview Rd 92040 619-390-2652
Staci Arnold, prin. Fax 390-2693
LEAPP, 9745 Marilla Dr 92040 PK-PK
Robyn Bowman, prin. 619-390-2391
Lemon Crest ES 600/K-5
12463 Lemon Crest Dr 92040 619-390-2527
Veronica Maxwell, prin. Fax 390-2563
Lindo Park ES 600/K-5
12824 Lakeshore Dr 92040 619-390-2656
Nina Drammissi, prin. Fax 390-2551
Riverview ES 500/2-5
9308 Winter Gardens Blvd 92040 619-390-2662
Brian Thurman, prin. Fax 390-2668
Tierra Del Sol MS 500/6-8
9611 Petite Ln 92040 619-390-2670
Scott Goergens, prin. Fax 390-2518
Winter Gardens ES 200/K-1
8501 Pueblo Rd 92040 619-390-2687
Steven Will, prin. Fax 390-2695

Foothills Christian ES 100/K-5
PO Box 2029 92040 619-561-2295
Regina Hoffman, prin. Fax 561-0238

Lakewood, Los Angeles, Pop. 76,583
ABC USD
Supt. — See Cerritos
Aloha Health Medical Academy 400/K-6
11737 214th St 90715 562-229-7825
Linda Dohm, prin. Fax 809-3297
Melbourne ES 500/K-6
21314 Claretta Ave 90715 562-229-7885
Karina Martir, prin. Fax 402-2764
Palms ES 600/K-6
12445 207th St 90715 562-229-7900
Julie Yabumoto, prin. Fax 924-9439
Willow ES 500/K-6
11733 205th St 90715 562-229-7910
Eveline Huh, prin. Fax 402-9837

Bellflower USD
Supt. — See Bellflower
Foster ES 700/K-6
5223 Bigelow St 90712 562-804-6518
Confidence Johnson, prin. Fax 804-6520
Intensive Learning Center 600/K-6
4718 Michelson St 90712 562-804-6513
Mike Remland, prin. Fax 633-3957
Lindstrom ES 900/K-6
5900 Canehill Ave 90713 562-804-6525
Lisa Luna, prin. Fax 804-6579
Williams ES 900/K-6
6144 Clark Ave 90712 562-804-6540
Stacey Williams, prin. Fax 804-6543

Long Beach USD
Supt. — See Long Beach
Cleveland ES 600/K-5
4760 Hackett Ave 90713 562-420-7552
Ellen Ryan, prin. Fax 420-7820
Gompers S 800/K-8
5206 Briercrest Ave 90713 562-925-2285
Kelly Ludden, prin. Fax 920-0053
Holmes ES 500/K-5
5020 Barlin Ave 90712 562-633-4427
Luana Wesley, prin. Fax 633-3083
Hoover MS 900/6-8
3501 Country Club Dr 90712 562-421-1213
Stephanie Cooper, prin. Fax 421-0003
MacArthur ES 400/K-5
6011 Centralia St 90713 562-420-3588
Scott Fleming, prin. Fax 420-7883
Madison ES 500/K-5
2801 Bomberry St 90712 562-420-7731
Kimberly Carpenter, prin. Fax 420-7819
Riley ES 400/K-5
3319 Sandwood St 90712 562-420-9595
LaShell Diggs, prin. Fax 420-7708

St. Pancratius S 200/K-8
3601 Saint Pancratius Pl 90712 562-634-6310
Kimberly French, prin. Fax 633-0731

La Mesa, San Diego, Pop. 54,494
Cajon Valley UNESD
Supt. — See El Cajon
Avocado ES 500/K-5
3845 Avocado School Rd 91941 619-588-3100
Keith Himaka, prin. Fax 579-4872

La Mesa-Spring Valley SD 12,000/K-8
4750 Date Ave 91942 619-668-5700
Brian Marshall, supt. Fax 668-5809
www.lmsvsd.org
La Mesa Arts Academy 600/4-8
4200 Parks Ave 91941 619-668-5730
Beth Thomas, prin. Fax 668-8303
La Mesa Dale ES 400/K-6
4370 Parks Ave 91941 619-668-5740
Kelley Rabasco, prin. Fax 668-8352
Lemon Avenue ES 600/K-6
8787 Lemon Ave 91941 619-668-5835
Natalie Martinez, prin. Fax 668-8354
Maryland Avenue ES 400/K-6
5400 Maryland Ave 91942 619-668-5744
Kelli Maringer, prin. Fax 668-5746
Murdock ES 800/K-6
4354 Conrad Dr 91941 619-668-5775
Jennifer Luibel, prin. Fax 668-8343
Murray Manor ES 800/K-6
8305 El Paso St 91942 619-668-5865
Gina Miller, prin. Fax 668-8318
Northmont ES 500/K-6
9405 Gregory St 91942 619-668-5830
Laura Hollis, prin. Fax 668-8340
Parkway MS 800/7-8
9009 Park Plaza Dr 91942 619-668-5810
Mary Beason, prin. Fax 668-5779
Rolando ES 600/K-6
6925 Tower St 91942 619-688-5800
Noelle Suffield, prin. Fax 668-5805
Other Schools – See El Cajon, Spring Valley

Lemon Grove SD
Supt. — See Lemon Grove
Vista La Mesa ES 700/PK-8
3900 Violet St 91941 619-825-5645
Bonita DeAmicis, prin. Fax 825-5783

Christ Lutheran S 200/PK-8
7921 La Mesa Blvd 91942 619-462-5211
Xavria Schwarz, admin. Fax 462-5275
Mt. Helix Academy 200/PK-8
5955 Severin Dr 91942 619-243-1400
St. Martin of Tours Academy 300/PK-8
7708 El Cajon Blvd 91942 619-466-3241
Antoinette Dimuzio, prin. Fax 466-0285
Shepherd of the Hills Lutheran S 50/K-8
9191 Fletcher Pkwy 91942 619-469-9443
Timothy Vogel, prin. Fax 469-9443

Warren-Walker S La Mesa 300/PK-5
5150 Wilson St 91942 619-460-3663
Raymond Volker, hdmstr. Fax 460-6951

La Mirada, Los Angeles, Pop. 47,368
Norwalk-La Mirada USD
Supt. — See Norwalk
Benton MS 600/6-8
15709 Olive Branch Dr 90638 562-210-2500
Benjamin Webster, prin. Fax 947-3861
Dulles ES 300/K-5
12726 Meadow Green Rd 90638 562-210-2610
Shanti Gallegos, prin. Fax 902-0438
Eastwood ES 500/K-5
15730 Pescados Dr 90638 714-210-2650
Yvette Cantu, prin. Fax 521-6485
Escalona ES 500/K-5
15135 Escalona Rd 90638 714-210-2745
Bonnie Lytle, prin. Fax 521-1173
Foster Road ES 400/K-5
13930 Foster Rd 90638 562-210-2790
Salvador Villagomez, prin. Fax 404-3952
Gardenhill ES 800/K-5
14607 Gardenhill Dr 90638 562-210-2840
Sarah Gilbert, prin. Fax 944-8188
Hutchinson MS 500/6-8
13900 Estero Rd 90638 562-210-2945
Robin Padget, prin. Fax 944-3269
La Pluma ES 500/K-5
14420 La Pluma Dr 90638 562-210-3205
Terry Pace, prin. Fax 943-6884
Los Coyotes MS 600/6-8
14640 Mercado Ave 90638 714-210-3595
Jacob Muniz, prin. Fax 739-2368

Beatitudes of Our Lord S 300/PK-8
13021 Santa Gertrudes Ave 90638 562-943-3218
Maria Watson, prin. Fax 943-9718
Heights Christian JHS 300/5-8
12900 Bluefield Ave 90638 562-947-3309
Rebecca Neal, prin. Fax 947-1001
Heights Christian S - La Mirada Campus 300/PK-4
12200 Oxford Dr 90638 562-902-1779
Andrea Taylor, prin. Fax 902-1769
St. Paul of the Cross S 200/K-8
14030 Foster Rd 90638 562-921-2118
Sandra Hernandez, prin. Fax 802-2048

Lamont, Kern, Pop. 15,088
Lamont ESD 2,900/K-8
7915 Burgundy Ave 93241 661-845-0751
Dr. Miguel Guerrero, supt. Fax 845-0689
www.lamontschooldistrict.org
Alicante Avenue ES 1,300/K-6
7915 Burgundy Ave 93241 661-845-1452
Frod Molina, prin. Fax 845-5114
Lamont ES 700/K-3
7915 Burgundy Ave 93241 661-845-4404
Brandy Charles, prin. Fax 845-5837
Myrtle Avenue ES 500/4-6
7915 Burgundy Ave 93241 661-845-2217
Maria Ozuna, prin. Fax 845-4816
Other Schools – See Bakersfield

Lancaster, Los Angeles, Pop. 151,168
Eastside UNSD 3,300/K-8
45006 30th St E 93535 661-952-1200
Melinda Jaggi Ed.D., supt. Fax 952-1220
www.eastsideusd.org
Cole MS 800/6-8
3126 E Avenue I 93535 661-946-1041
Francisco Pinto, prin. Fax 946-0166
Columbia ES 900/K-5
2640 E Avenue J4 93535 661-946-5656
Ed Beleno, prin. Fax 946-6002
Eastside ES 800/K-6
6742 E Avenue H 93535 661-946-3907
Marisa Rissling, prin. Fax 946-5431
Enterprise ES, 3730 E Ave J4 93535 K-5
Mary Kruppe, prin. 661-946-6277
Tierra Bonita ES 700/K-6
44820 27th St E 93535 661-946-3038
Christa Waldvogel, prin. Fax 946-3198

Lancaster ESD 15,000/PK-8
44711 Cedar Ave 93534 661-948-4661
Dr. Michele Bowers Ed.D., supt. Fax 942-9452
www.lancsd.org
Amargosa Creek MS 1,000/6-8
44333 27th St W 93536 661-729-6064
Richelle Pulos, prin. Fax 729-6858
Cory ES 600/K-6
3540 W Avenue K4 93536 661-722-1010
David Denning, prin. Fax 722-0625
Desert View ES 800/K-6
1555 W Avenue H10 93534 661-942-9521
Eric George, prin. Fax 942-4321
Discovery ES 900/K-5
44910 17th St E 93535 661-949-3175
Kathy Lee, admin. Fax 949-8107
El Dorado ES 700/K-5
361 E Pondera St 93535 661-942-8487
Todd Coleman, prin. Fax 942-2267
Endeavour MS 800/6-8
43755 45th St W 93536 661-723-0351
Cheri Newlander, prin. Fax 723-1362
Fulton & Alsbury Acad Arts & Engineering 6-8
831 E Avenue K2 93535 661-206-0120
Dr. Andrew Glatfelter, prin.
Joshua ES 700/K-5
43926 2nd St E 93535 661-948-0743
Lorraine Zapata, prin. Fax 940-6671
Lancaster Early Childhood Education 700/PK-PK
808 W Avenue J 93534 661-723-0351
Kelly Fountain, dir. Fax 723-1362
Lincoln ES 800/K-5
44021 15th St E 93535 661-726-9913
Ardrella Hamilton, prin. Fax 726-4353
Linda Verde ES 600/K-5
44924 5th St E 93535 661-942-0431
Storm Lydon, prin. Fax 942-7621

Mariposa ES 700/K-6
737 W Avenue H6 93534 661-942-0437
Michael Choate, prin. Fax 949-1324
Miller ES 600/K-6
43420 22nd St W 93536 661-726-1826
Elaine Darby, prin. Fax 726-2683
Monte Vista ES 800/K-6
1235 W Kettering St 93534 661-942-1477
Darlene Anderson, prin. Fax 949-1328
New Vista MS 1,000/6-8
753 E Avenue K2 93535 661-726-4271
Kymberlee Cochran, prin. Fax 726-4278
Northrop ES 700/K-5
835 E Avenue K4 93535 661-949-0435
Sherry Peterson, prin. Fax 945-3463
Piute MS 800/6-8
425 E Avenue H11 93535 661-942-9508
Michael Davis, prin. Fax 940-6676
Sierra ES 700/K-5
747 W Avenue J12 93534 661-942-9536
Janice Forte-Watson, prin. Fax 942-0682
Sunnydale ES 600/K-6
1233 W Avenue J8 93534 661-948-2636
Paulette Volmer, prin. Fax 940-6670
West Wind ES 900/K-5
44044 36th St W 93536 661-948-0192
Nancy Volkenant, prin. Fax 940-8388

Westside UNESD
Supt. — See Quartz Hill
Del Sur S 800/K-8
9023 W Avenue H 93536 661-942-0488
Jessica Kott, prin. Fax 722-0747
Sundown ES 1,000/K-6
6151 W Avenue J8 93536 661-722-3026
Timothy Barker, prin. Fax 722-0196
Valley View ES 800/K-6
3310 W Avenue L8 93536 661-943-2451
Rebecca Davis, prin. Fax 943-9103

Wilsona SD
Supt. — See Palmdale
Challenger MS 600/5-8
41725 170th St E 93535 661-264-1790
Janice Stowers, prin. Fax 264-1793

Antelope Valley Adventist S 100/K-8
45002 Fern Ave 93534 661-942-6552
Lisa Ruebush, prin. Fax 942-5699
Bethel Christian S 400/PK-12
3100 W Avenue K 93536 661-943-2224
Dr. Mathias Konnerth, prin. Fax 943-6574
Desert Christian ES 400/K-5
44662 15th St W 93534 661-948-5071
Dave Pratt, admin. Fax 948-0858
Desert Christian MS 200/6-8
44662 15th St W 93534 661-723-0665
Lisa Costello, prin. Fax 723-6774
Grace Lutheran Christian S 100/PK-8
856 W Newgrove St 93534 661-948-1018
David Ingwersen, prin. Fax 948-2731
Lancaster Baptist S 400/K-12
4020 E Lancaster Blvd 93535 661-946-4668
Jim Lee, admin. Fax 946-7374
Sacred Heart S 300/K-8
625 W Kettering St 93534 661-948-3613
David Schatz, prin. Fax 948-4486
Vineyard Christian S 200/PK-8
1011 E Avenue I 93535 661-948-3766
Kimberly Moakley M.A., prin. Fax 942-2908

Landers, San Bernardino
Morongo USD
Supt. — See Twentynine Palms
Landers ES 100/K-6
56450 Reche Rd 92285 760-364-2382
Terrie Panzarella, prin. Fax 364-1397

La Palma, Orange, Pop. 15,047
Anaheim UNHSD
Supt. — See Anaheim
Walker JHS 1,100/7-8
8132 Walker St 90623 714-220-4051
Jennifer Gladysz-Brown, prin. Fax 220-2237

Centralia ESD
Supt. — See Buena Park
Los Coyotes ES 600/K-6
8122 Moody St 90623 714-228-3260
Robyn Yarbrough, prin. Fax 228-3260
Miller ES 600/K-6
7751 Furman Rd 90623 714-228-3270
Dr. Stacy Chang, prin. Fax 522-7978

Cypress SD
Supt. — See Cypress
Luther ES 500/K-6
4631 La Palma Ave 90623 714-220-6918
Denine Kelly, prin. Fax 229-7738

La Puente, Los Angeles, Pop. 39,527
Bassett USD, 904 Willow Ave 91746 4,100/K-12
Debra French, supt. 626-931-3000
www.bassettusd.org
Edgewood Academy 700/K-8
904 Willow Ave 91746 626-931-7800
Rhonda Lentz, prin. Fax 931-7810
Julian ES 500/K-5
904 Willow Ave 91746 626-931-2900
Martha Arceo, prin. Fax 931-2951
Sunkist ES 500/K-5
904 Willow Ave 91746 626-931-7700
Jason Tveit, prin. Fax 931-7710
Vanwig ES 500/K-5
904 Willow Ave 91746 626-931-8000
Andrew Candelaria, prin. Fax 931-8010
Other Schools – See City of Industry

Hacienda La Puente USD
Supt. — See City of Industry
Baldwin Academy 700/K-6
1616 Griffith Ave 91744 626-933-3701
Lilia Picado, prin. Fax 855-3700
California ES 400/K-6
1111 N California Ave 91744 626-933-5201
Kim Lee, prin. Fax 855-3712
Del Valle ES 500/K-6
801 Del Valle Ave 91744 626-933-4101
Shawn Harrington, prin. Fax 855-3158
Fairgrove Academy 900/K-8
15540 Fairgrove Ave 91744 626-933-8501
Sherri Franson, prin. Fax 333-5794
Lassalette S 700/K-8
14333 Lassalette St 91744 626-933-3001
Joseph Zepeda, prin. Fax 855-3536
Nelson ES 400/K-6
330 N California Ave 91744 626-933-8401
Cristina McCall, prin. Fax 855-3537
Sierra Vista MS 300/7-8
15801 Sierra Vista Ct 91744 626-933-4001
Lisa Carrera, prin. Fax 855-3817
Sparks ES 500/K-6
15151 Temple Ave 91744 626-933-5105
Alma Noche, prin. Fax 855-3770
Sparks MS 500/7-8
15100 Giordano St 91744 626-933-5001
Collin Miller, prin. Fax 855-3848
Sunset ES 200/K-6
800 Tonopah Ave 91744 626-933-3201
Rosette Holmes, prin. Fax 918-9531
Temple Academy 300/K-6
635 N California Ave 91744 626-933-3101
Mary Castner, prin. Fax 855-3782
Valinda S of Academics 600/K-8
1030 Indian Summer Ave 91744 626-933-4701
Elizabeth Bermejo, prin. Fax 855-3787
Workman ES 500/K-6
16000 Workman St 91744 626-933-4201
Julia Gavilanes, prin. Fax 855-3799

Rowland USD
Supt. — See Rowland Heights
Hurley ES 600/K-6
535 Dora Guzman Ave 91744 626-965-2429
Yesenia Alvarez, prin. Fax 965-1499
Northam ES 500/K-6
17800 Renault St 91744 626-965-2404
Celia Munguia, prin. Fax 965-3014
Rorimer ES 600/K-6
18750 Rorimer St 91744 626-965-3333
Joyce Garcia, prin. Fax 965-8983
Villacorta ES 500/K-6
17840 Villa Corta St 91744 626-964-2385
George Herrera, prin. Fax 964-8701
Yorbita ES 600/K-6
520 Vidalia Ave 91744 626-964-3486
Sylvia Cadena, prin. Fax 964-3736

St. Joseph S 200/PK-8
15650 Temple Ave 91744 626-336-2821
Diana Rosas, prin. Fax 369-8921
St. Louis of France S 200/K-8
13901 Temple Ave 91746 626-918-6210
Vaughn Bernardez, prin. Fax 918-9549
St. Martha S 200/1-8
440 N Azusa Ave 91744 626-964-1093
Sr. Carmen Fernandez, prin. Fax 912-2014

La Quinta, Riverside, Pop. 36,785
Desert Sands USD 28,700/K-12
47950 Dune Palms Rd 92253 760-777-4200
Dr. Scott Bailey, supt. Fax 771-8505
www.dsusd.us
Franklin ES 500/K-5
77800 Calle Tampico 92253 760-238-9424
Elvira Gutzwiller, prin. Fax 238-9433
La Quinta MS 500/6-8
78900 Avenue 50 92253 760-777-4220
Dan Borgen, prin. Fax 777-4216
Paige MS 900/6-8
43495 Palm Royale Dr 92253 760-238-9710
Janet Seto, prin. Fax 345-1202
Truman ES 500/K-5
78870 Avenue 50 92253 760-777-4240
Carol Bishop, prin. Fax 777-4237
Other Schools – See Bermuda Dunes, Indian Wells, Indio, Palm Desert

Larkspur, Marin, Pop. 11,461
Larkspur-Corte Madera SD 1,800/K-8
230 Doherty Dr 94939 415-927-6960
Brett Geithman, supt. Fax 927-6964
www.lcmschools.org
Hall MS 600/5-8
200 Doherty Dr 94939 415-927-6978
Eric Saibel, prin. Fax 927-6985
Other Schools – See Corte Madera

Marin Primary & MS 400/PK-8
20 Magnolia Ave 94939 415-924-2608
Andrew Slater, head sch Fax 924-9351
St. Patrick S 200/K-8
120 King St 94939 415-924-0501
Linda Kinkade, prin. Fax 924-3544

Lathrop, San Joaquin, Pop. 17,283
Manteca USD
Supt. — See Manteca
Lathrop S 900/K-8
15851 5th St 95330 209-858-7250
David Silveira, prin. Fax 858-7520
Mossdale S 900/K-8
455 Brookhurst Blvd 95330 209-938-6285
Susan Sanders, prin. Fax 938-6392
Widmer S 900/K-8
751 Stonebridge Ave 95330 209-938-6340
Kathy Brown-Snyder, prin. Fax 982-5331

Laton, Fresno, Pop. 1,814
Laton USD 700/K-12
PO Box 248 93242 559-922-4015
Victor Villar, supt. Fax 923-4791
latonunified.org
Conejo MS 200/6-8
PO Box 7 93242 559-922-4030
Lori Montejano, prin. Fax 923-9651
Laton ES 400/K-5
PO Box 7 93242 559-922-4030
Lori Montejano, prin. Fax 923-9651

La Verne, Los Angeles, Pop. 30,232
Bonita USD
Supt. — See San Dimas
LaVerne Heights ES 500/K-5
1550 Baseline Rd 91750 909-971-8205
Patrick McKee, prin. Fax 971-8255
Miller ES 400/K-5
1629 Holly Oak St 91750 909-971-8206
Tomeika Carter, prin. Fax 971-8256
Oak Mesa ES 600/K-5
5200 Wheeler Ave 91750 909-971-8209
Steven Patterson, prin. Fax 971-8259
Ramona MS 1,300/6-8
3490 Ramona Ave 91750 909-971-8260
James Ellis, prin. Fax 971-8269
Roynon ES 700/K-5
2715 E St 91750 909-971-8207
Tammi DiGrazia, prin. Fax 971-8257

Calvary Baptist S 100/PK-12
2990 Damien Ave 91750 909-593-4672
Taylora Dial, prin. Fax 392-9533

Lawndale, Los Angeles, Pop. 31,604
Lawndale ESD 5,900/K-12
4161 W 147th St 90260 310-973-1300
Betsy Hamilton Ed.D., supt. Fax 675-6462
www.lawndalesd.net
Addams MS 900/6-8
4161 W 147th St 90260 310-676-4806
Dennis Perry, prin. Fax 676-8621
Anderson ES 800/K-5
4161 W 147th St 90260 310-676-0197
Adam Jaquette, prin. Fax 676-8053
Green ES 800/K-5
4161 W 147th St 90260 310-370-3585
Jonny Padilla, prin. Fax 370-0522
Mitchell ES 600/K-5
4161 W 147th St 90260 310-676-6140
Courtney Gillette, prin. Fax 676-7616
Rogers MS 900/6-8
4161 W 147th St 90260 310-676-1197
Dr. Maurita De La Torre Ed.D., prin. Fax 675-0489
Roosevelt ES 400/K-5
4161 W 147th St 90260 310-675-1121
Dr. Denise Appell Ed.D., prin. Fax 219-3180
Smith ES 500/K-5
4161 W 147th St 90260 310-970-2915
Dr. Rosa Isiah Ed.D., prin. Fax 675-7584
Twain ES 500/K-5
4161 W 147th St 90260 310-675-9134
Thelma Gonzalez, prin. Fax 675-6367

Laytonville, Mendocino, Pop. 1,182
Laytonville USD 400/K-12
PO Box 868 95454 707-984-6414
Joan Potter, supt. Fax 984-8223
layt.k12.ca.us
Branscomb ES, PO Box 325 95454 50/K-2
Lorre Stange, prin. 707-984-8568
Laytonville ES 300/K-8
PO Box 325 95454 707-984-6123
Lorre Stange, prin. Fax 984-8761
Spy Rock ES 50/K-3
PO Box 325 95454 707-984-6172
Lorre Stange, prin. Fax 984-8761

Lebec, Kern, Pop. 1,432
El Tejon USD 800/K-12
PO Box 876 93243 661-248-6247
Rodney Wallace, supt. Fax 248-6714
www.el-tejon.k12.ca.us
El Tejon MS 200/5-8
PO Box 876 93243 661-248-6680
Rosalie Jimenez, prin. Fax 248-5203
Frazier Park ES 300/K-4
PO Box 876 93243 661-245-3312
Patrick Gross, prin. Fax 245-3424

Lee Vining, Mono, Pop. 220
Eastern Sierra USD
Supt. — See Bridgeport
Lee Vining ES 100/K-8
PO Box 270 93541 760-647-6460
Roger Yost, prin. Fax 647-6489

Leggett, Mendocino, Pop. 105
Leggett Valley USD 100/PK-12
PO Box 186 95585 707-925-6230
Anthony Loumena, supt. Fax 925-6396
www.leggett.k12.ca.us
Leggett Valley ES 100/PK-8
PO Box 186 95585 707-925-6285
Anthony Loumena, prin. Fax 925-6396
Other Schools – See Whitethorn

Le Grand, Merced, Pop. 1,644
Le Grand UNESD 400/K-8
PO Box 27 95333 209-389-4515
Rosina Hurtado, supt. Fax 389-4041
www.legrand.k12.ca.us
Le Grand ES 400/K-8
PO Box 27 95333 209-389-4515
Rosina Hurtado, prin. Fax 389-4041

Lemon Grove, San Diego, Pop. 24,153
Lemon Grove SD 3,900/PK-8
8025 Lincoln St 91945 619-825-5600
Dr. Kimberly Berman, supt. Fax 462-7959
www.lgsd.k12.ca.us
Lemon Grove Academy ES 600/PK-6
7885 Golden Ave 91945 619-825-5637
Richard Oser, prin. Fax 825-5782
Lemon Grove Academy MS 700/7-8
7866 Lincoln St 91945 619-825-5628
Rick Oser, prin. Fax 825-5781
Monterey Heights ES 400/PK-6
7550 Canton Dr 91945 619-825-5633
Donna Willson, prin. Fax 825-5784
Mt. Vernon ES 500/PK-8
8350 Mount Vernon St 91945 619-825-5613
Russell Little, prin. Fax 825-5788
San Altos ES 500/PK-6
1750 Madera St 91945 619-825-5621
Larry Buchanan, prin. Fax 825-5787
San Miguel ES 600/PK-6
7059 San Miguel Ave 91945 619-825-5619
Dr. Norma Sandoval, prin. Fax 825-5785
Other Schools – See La Mesa

St. John of the Cross S 600/PK-8
8175 Lemon Grove Way 91945 619-466-8624
Gregory Krumm, prin. Fax 466-0034

Lemoore, Kings, Pop. 23,462
Central UNESD 1,800/PK-8
15783 18th Ave 93245 559-924-3405
Thomas Addington, supt. Fax 924-1153
www.central.k12.ca.us/
Akers ES 700/PK-8
15783 18th Ave 93245 559-998-5707
Heiko Sweeney, prin. Fax 998-7517
Central ES 300/PK-8
15783 18th Ave 93245 559-924-7797
Nancy Davis, prin. Fax 924-0919
Neutra ES 500/K-5
15783 18th Ave 93245 559-998-6823
Courtney Kirchman, prin. Fax 998-7521
Other Schools – See Stratford

Lemoore ESD 3,200/K-8
100 Vine St 93245 559-924-6800
Cheryl Hunt, supt. Fax 924-6809
www.luesd.k12.ca.us
Cinnamon ES 600/K-6
100 Vine St 93245 559-924-6870
Loretta Black, prin. Fax 924-6879
Engvall ES 700/K-6
100 Vine St 93245 559-924-6850
Renea Fagundes, prin. Fax 924-6879
Lemoore ES 600/K-6
100 Vine St 93245 559-924-6820
Amy Garcia, prin. Fax 924-6829
Liberty MS 600/7-8
100 Vine St 93245 559-924-6860
Bon Luis, prin. Fax 924-6869
Meadow Lane ES 500/K-6
100 Vine St 93245 559-924-6840
Rhett Kenney, prin. Fax 924-6849

Kings Christian S 300/PK-12
900 E D St 93245 559-924-8301
Kevin Dalafu, admin. Fax 924-0607
Mary Immaculate Queen S 200/PK-8
884 N Lemoore Ave 93245 559-924-3424
Roxie Martin, prin. Fax 924-7848

Lennox, Los Angeles, Pop. 22,462
Lennox ESD 7,000/K-12
10319 Firmona Ave 90304 310-695-4000
Kent Taylor, supt. Fax 677-3817
www.lennox.k12.ca.us
Buford ES, 10319 Firmona Ave 90304 700/K-5
Farnoosh Aguila, prin. 310-680-8900
Felton ES 600/K-5
10319 Firmona Ave 90304 310-680-8950
Norma Martinez, prin. Fax 673-6101
Huerta ES 600/K-5
10319 Firmona Ave 90304 310-677-7050
Maria Castellanos, prin. Fax 330-4574
Jefferson ES 800/K-5
10319 Firmona Ave 90304 310-680-5650
Robert Estrada, prin. Fax 672-5031
Lennox MS 1,600/6-8
11033 Buford Ave 90304 310-419-1800
Raul Roman Ed.D., prin. Fax 677-4635
Moffett ES 800/K-5
10319 Firmona Ave 90304 310-680-6200
Oscar Cisneros, prin. Fax 412-3275

Leona Valley, Los Angeles, Pop. 1,564
Westside UNESD
Supt. — See Quartz Hill
Leona Valley ES 100/K-6
9063 Leona Ave 93551 661-948-9010
Cathy Bennett, prin. Fax 270-9758

Lewiston, Trinity, Pop. 1,148
Lewiston ESD 100/K-8
685 Lewiston Rd 96052 530-778-3984
Allan Carver, supt. Fax 778-3103
www.lewistonesd.com
Lewiston ES 100/K-8
685 Lewiston Rd 96052 530-778-3984
Allan Carver, prin. Fax 778-3103

Lincoln, Placer, Pop. 41,451
Western Placer USD 8,000/PK-12
600 6th St Ste 400 95648 916-645-6350
Scott Leaman, supt. Fax 645-6356
www.wpusd.k12.ca.us
Coppin ES 400/PK-5
150 E 12th St 95648 916-645-6390
Shamryn Coyle, prin. Fax 645-6363
Creekside Oaks ES 600/PK-5
2030 1st St 95648 916-645-6380
Reno Penders, prin. Fax 645-6383
Edwards MS 700/6-8
204 L St 95648 916-645-6370
Stacey Brown, prin. Fax 645-6379
First Street ES 500/K-5
1400 1st St 95648 916-645-6330
Ruben Ayala, prin. Fax 645-6284
Foskett Ranch ES 500/K-5
1561 Joiner Pkwy 95648 916-434-5220
Kelly Castillo, prin. Fax 434-5240
Lincoln Crossing ES 700/K-5
635 Groveland Ln 95648 916-434-5292
Jennifer Hladun, prin. Fax 434-5261
Twelve Bridges ES 700/PK-5
2450 Eastridge Dr 95648 916-434-5220
Rey Cubias, prin. Fax 434-5201
Twelve Bridges MS 800/6-8
770 Westview Dr 95648 916-434-5270
Randy Woods, prin. Fax 434-5240
Other Schools – See Sheridan

Community Christian S 100/PK-8
PO Box 870 95648 916-645-6280
Jenny Tandy, head sch Fax 645-1345

Linden, San Joaquin, Pop. 1,741
Linden USD 2,300/K-12
18527 E Highway 26 95236 209-887-3894
Rick Hall, supt. Fax 887-2250
www.lindenusd.com
Linden ES 400/K-4
18100 E Front St 95236 209-887-3600
Mary Evans, prin. Fax 887-2252
Other Schools – See Stockton

Lindsay, Tulare, Pop. 11,716
Lindsay USD 4,200/PK-12
371 E Hermosa St 93247 559-562-5111
Thomas L. Rooney, supt. Fax 562-4637
www.lindsay.k12.ca.us
Jefferson ES 500/K-8
333 N Westwood Ave 93247 559-562-6303
Gina Wise, prin. Fax 562-8529
Kennedy ES, 1701 E Tulare Rd 93247 500/PK-8
Chirs McJunkin, prin. 559-562-5466
Lincoln ES 400/K-8
851 N Stanford Ave 93247 559-562-2571
Tammy Milligan, prin. Fax 562-8555
Reagan ES, 340 N Harvard Ave 93247 400/PK-8
Cindy Alonzo, prin. 559-562-1311
Roosevelt ES, 461 Hickory St 93247 500/PK-8
Debbie Warner, prin. 559-562-7208
Washington ES 700/K-8
451 E Samoa St 93247 559-562-5916
Cinnamon Scheufele, prin. Fax 562-8518

Litchfield, Lassen, Pop. 190
Shaffer UNESD 200/K-8
PO Box 320 96117 530-254-6577
Terri Daniels, supt. Fax 254-6126
www.shafferschool.com
Shaffer ES 200/K-8
PO Box 320 96117 530-254-6577
Jeff Baker, prin. Fax 254-6126

Littlerock, Los Angeles, Pop. 1,327
Keppel UNESD
Supt. — See Pearblossom
Alpine ES 500/K-8
8244 Pearblossom Hwy 93543 661-944-3221
Nesha Prather, prin. Fax 944-0597
Antelope ES 400/K-8
37237 100th St E 93543 661-944-2148
Dimas Molina, prin. Fax 944-0683
Keppel Academy 400/5-8
9330 E Avenue U 93543 661-944-2152
Gary Schatz, prin. Fax 944-0694

Live Oak, Sutter, Pop. 8,180
Live Oak USD 1,700/K-12
2201 Pennington Rd 95953 530-695-5400
Mathew Gulbrandsen, supt. Fax 695-5460
www.lousd.k12.ca.us
Encinal ES 100/K-8
6484 Larkin Rd 95953 530-695-5458
Michelle Smith A.M., prin. Fax 695-5459
Live Oak MS 500/5-8
2082 Pennington Rd 95953 530-695-5435
Parm Virk, prin. Fax 695-5443
Luther ES 600/K-4
10123 Connecticut Ave 95953 530-695-5450
Parveen Bains, prin. Fax 695-5429

Nuestro ESD 100/PK-8
3934 Broadway 95953 530-822-5100
Joe Hendrix, supt. Fax 822-5178
www.nuestroschool.org
Nuestro ES 100/PK-8
3934 Broadway 95953 530-822-5100
Joe Hendrix, admin. Fax 822-5178

Livermore, Alameda, Pop. 77,773
Livermore Valley JUSD 14,000/PK-12
685 E Jack London Blvd 94551 925-606-3200
Kelly Bowers, supt. Fax 606-3329
www.livermoreschools.com
Altamont Creek ES 600/K-5
6600 Garavonta Ranch Rd 94551 925-454-5575
Tara Aderman, prin. Fax 454-5591
Arroyo Seco ES 700/K-5
5280 Irene Way 94550 925-606-4700
Gatee Esmat, prin. Fax 606-3427
Christensen MS 700/6-8
5757 Haggin Oaks Ave 94551 925-606-4702
Pat Avilla, prin. Fax 606-4705
Croce ES 600/K-5
5650 Scenic Ave 94551 925-606-4706
Kendra Helsley, prin. Fax 606-4708
East Avenue MS 600/6-8
3951 East Ave 94550 925-606-4711
Mistee Guzman, prin. Fax 606-4763
Jackson Avenue ES 500/K-5
554 Jackson Ave 94550 925-606-4717
Shari Johnston, prin. Fax 606-4766

Junction Avenue S 800/K-8
298 Junction Ave 94551 925-606-4720
Dayna Taylor, prin. Fax 606-3318
Lawrence ES PK-5
2451 Portola Ave 94551 925-960-2923
Kristie Starkovich, prin. Fax 449-2008
Marylin Avenue ES 500/K-5
800 Marylin Ave 94551 925-606-4724
Denise Nathanson, prin. Fax 454-5504
Mendenhall MS 1,000/6-8
1701 El Padro Dr 94550 925-606-4731
Susan Sambuceti, prin. Fax 606-4737
Michell S 500/K-8
1001 Elaine Ave 94550 925-606-4738
Laura Lembo, prin. Fax 606-3349
Rancho Las Positas ES 500/K-5
401 E Jack London Blvd 94551 925-606-4748
Chris Calabrese, prin. Fax 606-3346
Smith ES 700/K-5
391 Ontario Dr 94550 925-606-4750
Tammy Rankin, prin. Fax 606-3330
Sunset ES 800/K-5
1671 Frankfurt Way 94550 925-606-5230
Tom Jones, prin. Fax 606-4753

Our Savior Lutheran S 300/PK-8
1385 S Livermore Ave 94550 925-447-1246
Evan Anwyl, prin. Fax 447-0201
St. Michael S 200/K-8
345 Church St 94550 925-447-1888
Alison Wilkie, prin. Fax 447-6720
TriValley Classical Christian S 100/K-12
945 Concannon Blvd 94550 925-961-4664
Valley Montessori S 400/PK-8
1273 N Livermore Ave 94551 925-455-8021
Ann Clark, head sch Fax 455-8002

Livingston, Merced, Pop. 12,876
Livingston UNSD 2,600/K-8
922 B St 95334 209-394-5400
Andres Zamora, supt. Fax 394-5401
www.livingstonusd.org
Campus Park ES 600/K-5
1845 H St 95334 209-394-5460
Jorge Arteaga, prin. Fax 394-5461
Herndon ES 600/K-5
714 Prusso St 95334 209-394-5480
Stella Montanez, prin. Fax 394-5481
Livingston MS 900/6-8
101 F St 95334 209-394-5450
Victoria Bradshaw, prin. Fax 394-5451
Yamato Colony ES 500/K-5
800 N Main St 95334 209-394-5470
Alma De Luna, prin. Fax 394-5471

Lockeford, San Joaquin, Pop. 3,135
Lodi USD
Supt. — See Lodi
Lockeford S 400/K-7
19456 N Tully Rd 95237 209-331-7214
Michael Rogers, prin. Fax 727-5802

Lockwood, Monterey, Pop. 367
San Antonio UNESD 200/K-8
PO Box 5000 93932 831-385-3051
Pam Hernandez, supt. Fax 385-4240
www.sanantoniousd.org
San Antonio S 200/K-8
PO Box 5000 93932 831-385-3051
Pam Gildersleeve-Hernand, supt. Fax 385-4240

Lodi, San Joaquin, Pop. 60,610
Lodi USD 28,600/PK-12
1305 E Vine St 95240 209-331-7000
Dr. Cathy Nichols-Washer Ed.D., supt. Fax 331-7256
www.lodiusd.net
Beckman ES 700/K-6
2201 Scarborough Dr 95240 209-331-7411
Erin Church, prin. Fax 331-8301
Borchardt ES 800/K-6
375 Culbertson Dr 95240 209-331-8212
Julie Vaz, prin. Fax 331-8241
Heritage ES 500/PK-6
509 Eden St 95240 209-331-7334
Alberto Lopez-Velarde, prin. Fax 331-7341
Lakewood ES 600/K-6
1100 N Ham Ln 95242 209-331-7348
Bruce Spaulding, prin. Fax 331-7351
Larson ES 600/K-6
2375 Giannoni Way 95242 209-331-8391
Leslie Maldonado, prin. Fax 331-8375
Lawrence ES 500/PK-6
721 Calaveras St 95240 209-331-7356
Juan Carlos Villafana, prin. Fax 331-7357
Live Oak ES 300/K-6
5099 Bear Creek Rd 95240 209-331-7370
Dr. Rafael Ceja Ed.D., prin. Fax 331-7302
Lodi MS 800/7-8
945 S Ham Ln 95242 209-331-7540
Scott McGregor, prin. Fax 331-7550
Millswood MS 900/7-8
233 N Mills Ave 95242 209-331-8332
Erin Lenzi, prin. Fax 331-8347
Needham ES 300/K-6
420 S Pleasant Ave 95240 209-331-7375
Ruth Barajas, prin. Fax 331-7483
Nichols ES 400/K-6
1301 S Crescent Ave 95240 209-331-7378
Susan Petersen, prin. Fax 331-7380
Reese ES 600/K-6
1800 W Elm St 95242 209-331-7424
Gary Odell, prin. Fax 331-7431
Vinewood ES 500/K-6
1600 W Tokay St 95242 209-331-7445
Norm Tanaka, prin. Fax 331-7447
Washington ES 400/K-6
831 W Lockeford St 95240 209-331-7451
Dan Faith, prin. Fax 331-7320
Woodbridge ES 400/K-6
1290 Lilac St 95242 209-331-8160
Neil Young, prin. Fax 331-7580
Other Schools – See Acampo, Lockeford, Stockton, Victor

Life Training Academy 100/K-12
11451 North West Ln 95242 209-339-7373
Jeff Craig, dir.
Lodi Christian S 200/PK-8
751 S Lower Sacramento Rd 95242 209-368-7627
Ron Hittle, prin. Fax 368-7600
Lodi SDA ES 200/K-8
1240 S Central Ave 95240 209-368-5341
Ally Emmerson, prin. Fax 368-5370
St. Anne S 200/K-8
200 S Pleasant Ave 95240 209-333-7580
Rose Herold, prin. Fax 369-1971
St. Peter Lutheran S 200/PK-8
2400 Oxford Way 95242 209-333-2225
David Warmbier, prin. Fax 334-4633
Vineyard Christian MS 100/6-8
2301 W Lodi Ave 95242 209-333-8300
Randal Oliver, prin. Fax 339-4327

Loleta, Humboldt, Pop. 757
Loleta UNESD 200/K-8
PO Box 547 95551 707-733-5705
John Sutter, supt. Fax 733-5367
www.loletaschool.com
Loleta ES 100/K-8
PO Box 547 95551 707-733-5705
John Sutter, prin. Fax 733-5367

Loma Linda, San Bernardino, Pop. 22,264
Redlands USD
Supt. — See Redlands
Bryn Mawr ES 700/K-5
11680 Whittier Ave 92354 909-478-5650
Richard Aleksak, prin. Fax 478-5654

Loma Linda Academy 1,300/K-12
10656 Anderson St 92354 909-796-0161
Dr. Douglas Herrmann, hdmstr. Fax 478-6829

Lomita, Los Angeles, Pop. 19,339
Los Angeles USD
Supt. — See Los Angeles
Eshelman Avenue ES 600/K-5
25902 Eshelman Ave 90717 310-326-1576
Rhonda Pannell, prin. Fax 326-2749
Fleming MS 1,600/6-8
25425 Walnut St 90717 310-257-4500
Peter Hastings, prin. Fax 326-9071
Lomita Math/Science/Technology Magnet S 1,000/K-5
2211 247th St 90717 310-784-6700
Monica Friedman, prin. Fax 326-0632

Harbor Church S 100/K-8
1716 254th St 90717 310-534-8278
Lee Ann Bowman, prin. Fax 325-1890
Nishiyamato Academy 100/PK-9
2458 Lomita Blvd 90717 310-325-7040
Katsuyuki Nishikawa, prin. Fax 325-7621
St. Margaret Mary Alacoque S 300/K-8
25515 Eshelman Ave 90717 310-326-9494
Elisa Zimmerman, prin. Fax 326-2712

Lompoc, Santa Barbara, Pop. 41,015
Lompoc USD 9,900/K-12
PO Box 8000 93438 805-742-3300
Trevor McDonald, supt. Fax 735-8452
www.lusd.org
Buena Vista ES 600/K-6
PO Box 8000 93438 805-742-2020
Dr. Vicki Murray, prin. Fax 742-2021
Fillmore ES 700/K-6
PO Box 8000 93438 805-742-2100
Colleen Million, prin. Fax 742-2135
Hapgood ES 500/K-6
PO Box 8000 93438 805-742-2200
Susan Insch, prin. Fax 742-3309
La Canada ES 700/K-6
PO Box 8000 93438 805-742-2250
Lisa Wilson, prin. Fax 742-2217
La Honda STEAM Academy 500/K-6
PO Box 8000 93438 805-742-2300
Noelle Barthel, prin. Fax 742-2307
Lompoc Valley MS 600/7-8
PO Box 8000 93438 805-742-2600
Schel Brown, prin. Fax 737-9480
Los Berros ES 400/K-6
PO Box 8000 93438 805-742-2350
Heather Anderson, prin. Fax 742-2352
Miguelito ES 600/K-6
PO Box 8000 93438 805-742-2440
Becky Sausker, prin. Fax 742-2450
Ruth ES 600/K-6
PO Box 8000 93438 805-742-2500
Judi Denton, prin. Fax 742-2504
Other Schools – See Vandenberg AFB

Children's Montessori S 50/PK-6
PO Box 3510 93438 805-733-2290
James Murphy, dir. Fax 733-2290
La Purisima Concepcion S 100/K-8
219 W Olive Ave 93436 805-736-6210
Orlando Leon, prin. Fax 735-7649

Lone Pine, Inyo, Pop. 1,990
Lone Pine USD 400/K-12
PO Box 159 93545 760-876-5579
Heidi Torix, supt. Fax 876-5438
lpusd-ca.schoolloop.com
Lo-Inyo ES 300/K-8
PO Box 159 93545 760-876-5581
Heidi Torix, prin. Fax 876-5584

Long Beach, Los Angeles, Pop. 443,652
Long Beach USD 79,700/PK-12
1515 Hughes Way 90810 562-997-8000
Christopher Steinhauser, supt. Fax 997-8280
www.lbschools.net
Addams ES 1,000/K-5
5320 Pine Ave 90805 562-428-0202
Armando Duenas, prin. Fax 428-4322
Bancroft MS 1,000/6-8
5301 E Centralia St 90808 562-425-7461
Pilar Perossio, prin. Fax 425-9741
Barton ES 600/K-5
1100 E Del Amo Blvd 90807 562-428-0555
Richard Littlejohn, prin. Fax 984-8509
Birney ES 700/K-5
710 W Spring St 90806 562-427-8512
Athena Uribe, prin. Fax 424-9417
Bixby ES 500/K-5
5251 E Stearns St 90815 562-498-3794
Sam Platis, prin. Fax 498-1711
Bryant ES 400/K-5
4101 E Fountain St 90804 562-498-3802
Matthew Hammond, prin. Fax 494-6952
Burbank ES 800/K-5
501 Junipero Ave 90814 562-439-0997
Vanesha Davis, prin. Fax 434-8285
Burcham ES 600/K-5
5610 E Monlaco Rd 90808 562-420-2685
Christopher Eckert, prin. Fax 420-7865
Burnett ES 700/K-5
565 E Hill St 90806 562-595-9466
Juan Gonzalez, prin. Fax 424-8796
Carver ES 500/K-5
5335 E Pavo St 90808 562-420-2697
Matthew Monaghan, prin. Fax 420-7868
Chavez ES 500/K-5
730 W 3rd St 90802 562-590-0904
Hugo Figueroa, prin. Fax 590-6538
Cubberley S 1,000/K-8
3200 Monogram Ave 90808 562-420-8810
Cathleen Imbroane, prin. Fax 420-7821
Dooley ES 1,100/K-5
5075 Long Beach Blvd 90805 562-428-7274
Nicole Howton-Chiles, prin. Fax 428-6010
Edison ES 700/K-5
625 Maine Ave 90802 562-590-8481
Edward Garcia, prin. Fax 435-2605
Franklin Classical MS 1,100/6-8
540 Cerritos Ave 90802 562-435-4952
Wendy Sowinski, prin. Fax 432-6308
Fremont ES 500/K-5
4000 E 4th St 90814 562-439-6873
Cassandra Richards, prin. Fax 433-1826
Gant ES 600/K-5
1854 N Britton Dr 90815 562-430-3384
Cassandra Fanton, prin. Fax 431-6091
Garfield ES 800/K-5
2240 Baltic Ave 90810 562-424-8167
Claire Alvarez, prin. Fax 595-8823
Grant ES 1,100/K-5
1225 E 64th St 90805 562-428-4616
Kimberley Baril, prin. Fax 428-0926
Hamilton MS 900/6-8
1060 E 70th St 90805 562-602-0302
Kathleen Cruz, prin. Fax 602-1354
Harte ES 1,000/K-5
1671 E Phillips St 90805 562-428-0333
Lisa Worsham, prin. Fax 428-7985
Henry ES 800/K-8
3720 Canehill Ave 90808 562-421-3754
Veronica Madrigal, prin. Fax 420-7849
Herrera ES 1,000/K-5
1620 Temple Ave 90804 562-494-5101
Christi Granado, prin. Fax 494-5198
Hudson S 800/K-8
2335 Webster Ave 90810 562-426-0470
Lisa Colburn, prin. Fax 424-1569
Hughes MS 1,600/6-8
3846 California Ave 90807 562-595-0831
Edward Samuels, prin. Fax 595-9221
Jefferson Leadership Academies 1,000/6-8
750 Euclid Ave 90804 562-438-9904
Connie Magee, prin. Fax 439-3718
Keller Dual Immersion MS 6-8
7020 Brittain St 90808 562-421-8851
Thomas Espinoza, prin.
Kettering ES 400/K-5
550 Silvera Ave 90803 562-598-9486
Juan Gutierrez, prin. Fax 594-9359
King ES 800/K-5
145 E Artesia Blvd 90805 562-428-1232
Osvaldo Ocampo, prin. Fax 422-1481
LaFayette ES 1,000/K-5
2445 Chestnut Ave 90806 562-426-7075
David Komatz, prin. Fax 490-7318
Lincoln ES 1,100/K-5
1175 E 11th St 90813 562-599-5005
Caroline Nemec, prin. Fax 591-5375
Lindbergh STEM Academy 600/6-8
1022 E Market St 90805 562-422-2845
Dawn Lomeli, prin. Fax 423-8176
Lindsey Academy 900/6-8
5075 Daisy Ave 90805 562-423-6451
Renny Chu, prin. Fax 422-3800
Longfellow ES 1,100/K-5
3800 Olive Ave 90807 562-595-0308
Edward Sigur, prin. Fax 424-3991
Los Cerritos ES 600/K-5
515 W San Antonio Dr 90807 562-595-6337
Alissa Gamboa, prin. Fax 595-7994
Lowell ES 700/K-5
5201 E Broadway 90803 562-433-6757
Lester Lawson, prin. Fax 438-3264
Mann ES 300/K-5
257 Coronado Ave 90803 562-439-6897
Tracy Fiala, prin. Fax 439-8046
Marshall Academy of the Arts 900/6-8
5870 E Wardlow Rd 90808 562-429-7013
Marie Hatwan, prin. Fax 429-6973
McKinley ES 700/K-5
6822 N Paramount Blvd 90805 562-630-6200
Scott Tardibuono, prin. Fax 633-2891
Muir Academy 1,100/K-8
3038 Delta Ave 90810 562-426-5571
Sophia Griffieth, prin. Fax 426-0828

Naples Bayside Academy 400/K-5
5537 E The Toledo 90803 562-433-0489
Jeffrey Wood, prin. Fax 434-9016
Newcomb Academy 1,000/K-8
3351 Val Verde Ave 90808 562-421-8851
Donna Ryono, prin. Fax 420-2759
Oropeza ES 800/PK-5
700 Locust Ave 90813 562-436-4420
Mona Cook, prin. Fax 437-0690
Powell Academy for Success 1,300/K-8
150 W Victoria St 90805 310-631-8794
Wendy Claflin, prin. Fax 631-8983
Prisk ES 600/K-5
2375 Fanwood Ave 90815 562-598-9601
Damon Jespersen, prin. Fax 431-8718
Robinson Academy 1,000/K-8
2750 Pine Ave 90806 562-492-6003
Damita Myers-Miller, prin. Fax 492-6013
Rogers MS 900/6-8
365 Monrovia Ave 90803 562-434-7411
Douglas Jordan, prin. Fax 434-0581
Roosevelt ES 1,000/K-5
1574 Linden Ave 90806 562-591-7477
Clarissa Tolentino, prin. Fax 218-3667
Stanford MS 1,300/6-8
5871 E Los Arcos St 90815 562-594-9793
David Costa, prin. Fax 594-8591
Stephens MS 800/6-8
1830 W Columbia St 90810 562-595-0841
Salvador Madrigal, prin. Fax 426-5631
Stevenson ES 800/K-5
515 Lime Ave 90802 562-437-0407
Kevin Maddox, prin. Fax 435-2862
Tincher Prep S 900/K-8
1701 Petaluma Ave 90815 562-493-2636
Rosemary Sissons, prin. Fax 594-0818
Twain ES 600/K-5
5021 E Centralia St 90808 562-421-8421
Jacqueline Williams, prin. Fax 420-7654
Washington MS 1,100/6-8
1450 Cedar Ave 90813 562-591-2434
Megan Traver, prin. Fax 591-6888
Webster ES 600/K-5
1755 W 32nd Way 90810 562-595-6568
Sarah Forrester, prin. Fax 595-5710
Whittier ES 900/K-5
1761 Walnut Ave 90813 562-599-6263
Lori Grady, prin. Fax 591-4046
Willard ES 800/K-5
1055 Freeman Ave 90804 562-438-9934
Jennifer Rodarte, prin. Fax 439-8156
Other Schools – See Avalon, Lakewood, Signal Hill

Paramount USD
Supt. — See Paramount
Collins ES 600/K-5
6125 Coke Ave 90805 562-602-8008
Theresa Diaz, prin. Fax 602-8009

Bethany Lutheran S 200/PK-8
5100 E Arbor Rd 90808 562-420-7783
Dr. Mary Fink, prin. Fax 429-1693
Bethany S 400/PK-8
2244 Clark Ave 90815 562-597-2814
Rev. Bill Cook, prin. Fax 597-1396
Holy Innocents S 200/K-8
2500 Pacific Ave 90806 562-424-1018
Sr. Caridad Sandoval, prin. Fax 492-9250
Lakewood Christian S 400/PK-8
5336 E Arbor Rd 90808 562-425-3358
Brenda Barton, prin. Fax 420-9140
Los Altos Brethren S 200/PK-6
6565 E Stearns St 90815 562-430-6983
Debbie Martin, admin. Fax 431-7013
Maple Village Waldorf S PK-8
4017 E 6th St 90814 562-434-8200
Our Lady of Refuge S 100/PK-8
5210 E Los Coyotes Diagonal 90815 562-597-0819
Patricia Holmquist, prin. Fax 597-1419
Pacific Baptist S 200/PK-12
3332 Magnolia Ave 90806 562-426-5214
St. Anthony S 200/K-8
855 E 5th St 90802 562-432-5946
Allison Kargas, prin. Fax 435-8606
St. Athanasius S 200/K-8
5377 Linden Ave 90805 562-428-7422
Stacey Brown, prin. Fax 422-0306
St. Barnabas S 300/PK-8
3980 Marron Ave 90807 562-424-7476
Jennifer Kellam, prin. Fax 981-3351
St. Cornelius S 300/K-8
3330 N Bellflower Blvd 90808 562-425-7813
Nancy Hayes, prin. Fax 425-2743
St. Cyprian S 200/K-8
5133 E Arbor Rd 90808 562-425-7341
Rachelle Riemersma, prin. Fax 421-1642
St. Joseph S 300/K-8
6200 E Willow St 90815 562-596-6115
Margaret Alvarez, prin. Fax 596-6725
St. Lucy S 200/PK-8
2320 Cota Ave 90810 562-424-9062
Fax 424-8572
St. Maria Goretti S 100/K-8
3950 Palo Verde Ave 90808 562-425-5112
Kathleen Hernandez, prin. Fax 425-5672
Westerly S 100/K-8
2950 E 29th St 90806 562-981-3151
Patrick Brown, head sch Fax 981-3153

Loomis, Placer, Pop. 6,199
Loomis UNSD 2,700/K-12
3290 Humphrey Rd 95650 916-652-1800
Gordon Medd, supt. Fax 652-1809
www.loomis-usd.k12.ca.us
Franklin ES 500/K-8
7050 Franklin School Rd 95650 916-652-1818
Brittaney Meyer, prin. Fax 652-1821
Loomis ES 500/K-8
3505 Taylor Rd 95650 916-652-1824
Angie Borgwardt, prin. Fax 652-1826
Placer ES 400/K-8
8650 Horseshoe Bar Rd 95650 916-652-1830
Rick Judd, prin. Fax 652-1832
Powers ES 500/K-8
3296 Humphrey Rd 95650 916-652-2635
Cara Kopecky, prin. Fax 652-2679
Other Schools – See Newcastle, Penryn

Los Alamitos, Orange, Pop. 10,908
Los Alamitos USD 9,900/PK-12
10293 Bloomfield St 90720 562-799-4700
Dr. Sherry Kropp Ed.D., supt. Fax 799-4730
www.losal.org
Hopkinson ES 700/PK-5
12582 Kensington Rd 90720 562-799-4500
Evelyn Garcia, prin. Fax 799-4510
Lee ES 700/PK-5
11481 Foster Rd 90720 562-799-4540
Amy Laughlin, prin. Fax 799-4550
Los Alamitos ES 700/PK-5
10862 Bloomfield St 90720 714-816-3300
Gary Willems, prin. Fax 816-3315
McAuliffe MS 1,300/6-8
4112 Cerritos Ave 90720 714-816-3320
Ann Allen, prin. Fax 816-3362
Oak MS 1,100/6-8
10821 Oak St 90720 562-799-4740
Erin Kominsky, prin. Fax 799-4773
Rossmoor ES 700/PK-5
3272 Shakespeare Dr 90720 562-799-4520
Amy Belsha, prin. Fax 799-4530
Weaver ES 700/PK-5
11872 Wembley Rd 90720 562-799-4580
Dr. Robert Briggerman Ed.D., prin. Fax 799-4589
Other Schools – See Seal Beach

St. Hedwig S 500/K-8
3591 Orangewood Ave 90720 562-296-9060
Erin Rucker, prin. Fax 296-9089

Los Alamos, Santa Barbara, Pop. 1,869
Orcutt UNESD
Supt. — See Orcutt
Reed S 200/K-8
PO Box 318 93440 805-344-2401
Linda Denton, prin. Fax 344-2321

Los Altos, Santa Clara, Pop. 27,727
Cupertino UNSD
Supt. — See Sunnyvale
Montclaire ES 500/K-5
1160 Saint Joseph Ave 94024 650-967-9388
Alison Luvara, prin. Fax 938-0342

Los Altos ESD 4,500/K-8
201 Covington Rd 94024 650-947-1150
Jeffrey Baier, supt. Fax 947-0118
www.lasdschools.org/
Almond ES 500/K-6
550 Almond Ave 94022 650-917-5400
Erika Benadom, prin. Fax 948-7338
Blach IS 500/7-8
1120 Covington Rd 94024 650-934-3800
Bhavna Narula, prin. Fax 968-3918
Covington ES 500/K-6
205 Covington Rd 94024 650-947-1100
Wade Spenader, prin. Fax 941-8175
Egan IS 600/7-8
100 W Portola Ave 94022 650-917-2200
Keith Rocha, prin. Fax 949-3748
Loyola ES 500/K-6
770 Berry Ave 94024 650-254-2400
Kimberly Attell, prin. Fax 967-7531
Oak Avenue ES 500/K-6
1501 Oak Ave 94024 650-237-3900
Amy Romem, prin. Fax 964-9634
Santa Rita ES 600/K-6
700 Los Altos Ave 94022 650-559-1600
Gregory Land, prin. Fax 941-5316
Other Schools – See Los Altos Hills, Mountain View

Canterbury Christian S 100/K-6
101 N El Monte Ave 94022 650-949-0909
Rev. Ron Johnson, admin. Fax 949-0909
Heritage Academy 100/K-6
858 University Ave 94024 650-641-0280
Marilyn Davidson, prin. Fax 641-3168
Los Altos Christian S 200/PK-8
625 Magdalena Ave 94024 650-948-3738
Gabe Pethtel M.Ed., prin. Fax 949-6092
Miramonte Christian S 200/PK-8
1175 Altamead Dr 94024 650-967-2783
Pinewood S Lower Campus 100/K-2
477 Fremont Ave 94024 650-209-3050
Scott Riches, pres. Fax 209-3051
Pinewood S Middle Campus 200/3-6
327 Fremont Ave 94024 650-209-3030
Scott Riches, pres. Fax 209-3031
St. Simon S 500/PK-8
1840 Grant Rd 94024 650-968-9952
Ryan Roth, prin. Fax 988-9308
Waldorf S of the Peninsula 200/PK-5
11311 Mora Dr 94024 650-209-9400

Los Altos Hills, Santa Clara, Pop. 7,599
Los Altos ESD
Supt. — See Los Altos
Gardner Bullis ES 300/K-6
25890 W Fremont Rd 94022 650-559-3200
Nadia Oskolkoff, prin. Fax 949-1312

St. Nicholas S 200/K-8
12816 El Monte Rd 94022 650-941-4056
Jan Popolizo, prin. Fax 917-9872

Los Angeles, Los Angeles, Pop. 3,699,911
Compton USD
Supt. — See Compton
Carver ES 300/PK-6
1425 E 120th St 90059 310-898-6150
Dr. Damian Kessler, prin. Fax 569-7133

Los Angeles USD 617,100/PK-12
333 S Beaudry Ave 90017 213-241-1000
Michelle King, supt. Fax 241-8442
www.lausd.net
Adams MS 1,000/6-8
151 W 30th St 90007 213-745-3700
Carlos Gonzalez, prin. Fax 749-8542
Albion Early Education Center PK-PK
348 S Avenue 18 90031 323-221-1798
Scarlett Holguin, prin. Fax 342-0094
Albion Street ES 300/K-6
322 S Avenue 18 90031 323-221-3108
Sarah Garcia, prin. Fax 223-4077
Aldama ES 600/K-5
632 N Avenue 50 90042 323-255-1434
Sergio Corral, prin. Fax 254-2159
Alexandria Early Education Center PK-PK
4304 Rosewood Ave 90004 323-662-8127
Euna Anderson, prin. Fax 953-9485
Alexandria ES 700/K-5
4211 Oakwood Ave 90004 323-660-1936
Manuel Ponce, prin. Fax 666-3977
Allesandro ES 500/K-6
2210 Riverside Dr 90039 323-666-7162
Mark Raia, prin. Fax 669-8096
Alta Loma ES 700/K-5
1745 Vineyard Ave 90019 323-939-2113
Sean Leyva, prin. Fax 965-9233
Amanecer Primary Center 200/K-2
832 S Eastman Ave 90023 323-264-6494
Heidi Acosta Morteo, prin. Fax 264-6505
Ambassador School of Global Education 400/K-5
3201 W 8th St 90005 213-480-4520
Youmee Oh, prin. Fax 480-4539
Angeles Mesa ES 400/K-5
2611 W 52nd St 90043 323-294-5103
Emily Williams, prin. Fax 294-0930
Annandale ES 300/K-5
6125 Poppy Peak Dr 90042 323-254-9168
Veronica Vega, prin. Fax 254-3023
Ann ES 100/K-6
126 Bloom St 90012 323-221-3194
Frances Sanchez, prin. Fax 225-6079
Anton Early Education Center PK-PK
831 N Bonnie Beach Pl 90063 323-981-3670
Irene Santillan, prin. Fax 981-3673
Anton ES 900/K-6
831 N Bonnie Beach Pl 90063 323-981-3640
Patricia Castro, prin. Fax 415-9010
Aragon Avenue ES 400/K-5
1118 Aragon Ave 90065 323-221-5173
Forrest Baird, prin. Fax 221-6708
Arlington Heights ES 600/K-5
1717 7th Ave 90019 323-735-1021
Jose Macias, prin. Fax 732-6061
Arroyo Seco Museum Science S 500/K-8
4805 Sycamore Ter 90042 323-254-5141
Robin Polito Shuffer, prin. Fax 344-0235
Ascot ES 900/K-5
1447 E 45th St 90011 323-235-3178
Elvira Juarez, prin. Fax 231-1486
Atwater ES 400/K-6
3271 Silver Lake Blvd 90039 323-665-5941
Jorge Rios, prin. Fax 665-5708
Audubon MS 700/6-8
4120 11th Ave 90008 323-290-6300
Harold Boger, prin. Fax 296-2433
Aurora ES 500/K-5
1050 E 52nd Pl 90011 323-238-1500
Jennifer Gage, prin. Fax 233-5228
Avalon Gardens ES 300/K-6
13940 S San Pedro St 90061 310-532-8540
Gina Barnett, prin. Fax 217-1586
Baca Arts Academy 700/K-6
1536 E 89th St 90002 323-826-3560
Tracye McWhorter, prin. Fax 589-1068
Bakewell Primary Center 200/K-K
8621 Baring Cross St 90044 323-751-3887
Karen Ward, prin. Fax 751-5990
Baldwin Hills ES 400/K-5
5421 Rodeo Rd 90016 323-937-7223
Letitia Johnson-Davis, prin. Fax 937-6529
Bancroft MS 900/6-8
929 N Las Palmas Ave 90038 323-993-3400
Maria Rico, prin. Fax 461-8246
Barrett ES 1,000/K-5
419 W 98th St 90003 323-756-1419
Jera Turner, prin. Fax 418-0227
Beethoven Street ES 300/K-5
3711 Beethoven St 90066 310-398-6286
Cara Fields, prin. Fax 390-7587
Belvedere ES 900/K-5
3724 E 1st St 90063 323-269-0345
Beatriz Bogan, prin. Fax 269-5581
Belvedere MS 1,400/6-8
312 N Record Ave 90063 323-266-5400
Helen Carrillo, prin. Fax 269-6769
Berendo MS 1,000/6-8
1157 S Berendo St 90006 213-739-5600
Rosa Trujillo, prin. Fax 382-8599
Bethune MS 1,400/6-8
155 W 69th St 90003 323-541-1800
L.G. Garrett, prin. Fax 759-1271
Boys Academic Leadership Academy 6-7
10860 S Denker Ave 90047
Donald Moorer, prin.
Bradley Early Education Center PK-PK
10925 S Central Ave 90059 323-357-7790
Alice Reed, prin. Fax 563-1478
Bradley Global Awareness S 400/K-5
3875 Dublin Ave 90008 323-292-8195
Monique Bell, prin. Fax 292-2413
Breed ES 500/K-6
2226 E 3rd St 90033 323-269-4343
Patricia Romero, prin. Fax 269-0733
Brentwood Science ES 1,100/K-5
740 S Gretna Green Way 90049 310-826-5631
Jean Pennicooke, prin. Fax 826-1021

Bridge ES 300/K-5
605 N Boyle Ave 90033 323-222-0165
Roberto Salazar, prin. Fax 226-0494

Bright ES 700/K-5
1771 W 36th St 90018 323-733-1178
Madeleine Gygli, prin. Fax 735-5103

Brockton ES 300/K-5
1309 Armacost Ave 90025 310-479-6090
Ruth Kim, prin. Fax 996-1168

Brooklyn Avenue ES 600/K-8
4620 E Cesar E Chavez Ave 90022 323-269-8161
Ricardo Tapanes, prin. Fax 264-6144

Brooklyn Early Education Center PK-PK
329 N Arizona Ave 90022 323-269-4085
Karla Corona, prin. Fax 268-8691

Buchanan Street ES 500/K-6
5024 Buchanan St 90042 323-255-7118
Nancy Haig, prin. Fax 254-9363

Budlong Avenue ES 900/K-5
5940 S Budlong Ave 90044 323-750-6955
Cheri Hodo, prin. Fax 778-3811

Burbank MS 900/6-8
6460 N Figueroa St 90042 323-340-4400
Christine Moore, prin. Fax 257-7420

Burroughs MS 1,900/6-8
600 S McCadden Pl 90005 323-549-5000
Steve Martinez, prin. Fax 934-9051

Bushnell Way ES 400/K-6
5507 Bushnell Way 90042 323-255-6511
Liliana Narvaez, prin. Fax 255-6343

Business and Technology S 6-8
1420 E Adams Blvd 90011 323-846-2235
Maria Ozaeta, prin.

Cahuenga ES 600/K-5
220 S Hobart Blvd 90004 213-386-6303
Helen Yu, prin. Fax 387-7010

Canfield ES 400/K-5
9233 Airdrome St 90035 310-552-2525
Tamara Gullatt, prin. Fax 551-3012

Carson-Gore Academy 700/K-5
3200 W Washington Blvd 90018 323-766-5500
Gema Guardado, prin. Fax 735-1039

Carthay Center ES 300/K-6
6351 W Olympic Blvd 90048 323-935-8173
Sharon Hall Johnson, prin. Fax 933-2698

Carver MS 1,100/6-8
4410 McKinley Ave 90011 323-846-2900
Latasha Buck, prin. Fax 232-5344

Castelar Early Education Center PK-PK
840 Yale St 90012 213-624-6740
Ana Oregel, prin. Fax 617-1439

Castelar ES 600/K-5
840 Yale St 90012 213-626-3674
Wing Fung, prin. Fax 680-1894

Castle Heights ES 600/K-5
9755 Cattaraugus Ave 90034 310-839-4528
Sean Kearney, prin. Fax 839-3097

Castro MS 500/6-8
1575 W 2nd St 90026 213-241-4415
Erick Mitchell, prin. Fax 241-4418

Charnock Road ES 300/K-6
11133 Charnock Rd 90034 310-838-6110
Mark Duncan, prin. Fax 838-2950

Chavez ES 300/K-6
5243 Oakland St 90032 323-276-1440
Armando Ramirez, prin. Fax 276-1232

Cheremoya ES 300/K-6
6017 Franklin Ave 90028 323-464-1722
Stephen Salva, prin. Fax 463-2928

Cienega ES 700/K-5
2611 S Orange Dr 90016 323-939-1138
Kimberly Wright, prin. Fax 933-5316

City Terrace ES 400/K-5
4350 City Terrace Dr 90063 323-269-0581
Sonia Vargas, prin. Fax 267-9959

Clifford ES 100/K-6
2150 Duane St 90039 323-663-0474
Consuelo Garcia, prin. Fax 663-6822

Clinton MS 900/6-8
3500 S Hill St 90007 323-235-7200
Andres Favela, prin. Fax 846-0054

Clover Avenue ES 600/K-5
11020 Clover Ave 90034 310-479-7739
Sharon Fabian, prin. Fax 444-9744

Cochran MS 1,000/6-8
4066 W Johnnie Cochran Vst 90019 323-730-4300
Gilberto Samuel, prin. Fax 733-9106

Coliseum Street ES 300/K-5
4400 Coliseum St 90016 323-294-5244
Jacob Smith, prin. Fax 292-9490

Commonwealth Avenue ES 800/K-5
215 S Commonwealth Ave 90004 213-384-2546
Elizabeth Arellano, prin. Fax 386-3652

Compton ES 400/K-5
1515 E 104th St 90002 323-564-5767
Lashon Sanford, prin. Fax 563-6311

Cowan Avenue ES 300/K-6
7615 Cowan Ave 90045 310-645-1973
Richard DaSylveira, prin. Fax 645-6273

Crescent Heights Boulevard ES 400/K-5
1661 S Crescent Hts Blvd 90035 323-931-2761
Kimberly Mitchell, prin. Fax 939-7560

Crescent Heights Early Education Center PK-PK
1700 Alvira St 90035 323-939-1224
Michael Haggood, prin. Fax 937-1668

Cruz Early Education Center PK-PK
1020 Valencia St 90015 213-388-6485
Constance Majors, prin. Fax 388-6193

Dacotah Early Education Center PK-PK
3142 Lydia Dr 90023 323-268-9868
Elizabeth Mares, prin. Fax 263-7418

Dahlia Heights ES 400/K-6
5063 Floristan Ave 90041 323-255-1419
Kristin Phelps-Shaw, prin. Fax 344-9129

Dayton Early Education Center PK-PK
3917 Clinton St 90004 323-664-1024
Jay Rallion, prin. Fax 953-6076

Dayton Heights ES 600/K-5
607 N Westmoreland Ave 90004 323-661-3308
Diane Rodriguez, prin. Fax 662-5278

Delevan Drive ES 500/K-6
4168 W Avenue 42 90065 323-255-0571
Angie Woo, prin. Fax 254-8368

Del Olmo ES 800/K-6
100 N New Hampshire Ave 90004 213-427-7200
Ricardo Romero, prin. Fax 487-0788

Dena ES 500/K-6
1314 S Dacotah St 90023 323-269-9222
Jose Hernandez, prin. Fax 263-2371

Dorris Place ES 300/K-6
2225 Dorris Pl 90031 323-222-9185
John Han, prin. Fax 222-3686

Drew MS 1,000/6-8
8511 Compton Ave 90001 323-826-1700
Maisha James McIntosh, prin. Fax 583-6030

Eagle Rock ES 800/K-6
2057 Fair Park Ave 90041 323-254-6851
Stephanie Leach, prin. Fax 344-9720

Eastman Early Education Center PK-PK
1266 S Gage Ave 90023 323-268-7408
Elizabeth Mares, prin. Fax 260-7249

Eastman ES 1,000/K-5
4112 E Olympic Blvd 90023 323-269-0456
Teresa Armas, prin. Fax 269-3625

Edison MS 1,200/6-8
6500 Hooper Ave 90001 323-826-2500
Salvador Velasco, prin. Fax 581-8389

El Sereno Early Education Ctr PK-PK
3802 Pueblo Ave 90032 323-221-2121
Josefina Navarro, prin. Fax 225-9227

El Sereno ES 400/K-6
3838 Rosemead Ave 90032 323-222-3389
Helen Kim, prin. Fax 226-0200

El Sereno MS 1,300/6-8
2839 N Eastern Ave 90032 323-224-4700
Joyce Dara, prin. Fax 223-9024

Elysian Heights ES 200/K-6
1562 Baxter St 90026 323-665-6315
Emilio Garza, prin. Fax 661-5961

Esperanza ES 800/K-5
680 Little St 90017 213-484-0326
Bradley Rumble, prin. Fax 484-1137

Estrella ES 600/PK-5
120 E 57th St 90011 323-846-4880
Gabriel Arreguin, prin. Fax 235-4147

Euclid Avenue ES 900/K-5
806 Euclid Ave 90023 323-263-6792
Cristina Munoz, prin. Fax 780-7992

Evergreen Early Education Center PK-PK
1027 N Evergreen Ave 90033 323-269-0406
Karla Corona, prin. Fax 267-8146

Evergreen ES 900/K-6
2730 Ganahl St 90033 323-269-0415
Maricela Sanchez Robles, prin. Fax 261-1128

Fairburn Avenue ES 500/K-5
1403 Fairburn Ave 90024 310-470-1344
Pamela Marton, prin. Fax 470-3981

Farmdale ES 500/K-5
2660 Ruth Swiggett Dr 90032 323-222-6659
Oscar Sandoval, prin. Fax 222-9693

54th Street ES 300/K-5
5501 Eileen Ave 90043 323-294-5275
Haywood Thompson, prin. Fax 298-0820

59th Street ES 400/K-5
5939 2nd Ave 90043 323-294-5118
Renee Rawles, prin. Fax 291-9424

52nd Street ES 800/K-5
816 W 51st St 90037 323-753-3175
Osbaldo Jimenez, prin. Fax 750-9542

Figueroa ES 500/K-5
510 W 111th St 90044 323-756-9268
Daniel Carrillo, prin. Fax 754-1905

1st Street ES 700/K-6
2820 E 1st St 90033 323-269-0138
Luis Cuevas, prin. Fax 269-8776

Fletcher Drive ES 400/K-6
3350 Fletcher Dr 90065 323-254-5246
Jim Canelas, prin. Fax 258-8014

Florence ES 800/K-6
7211 Bell Ave 90001 323-582-0758
Consuelo Acosta, prin. Fax 582-7804

Flournoy ES 600/K-5
1630 E 111th St 90059 323-564-2545
Patricia Scates, prin. Fax 567-0816

Ford Boulevard ES 1,300/K-6
1112 S Ford Blvd 90022 323-268-8508
Ana Vega, prin. Fax 264-6953

49th Street ES 800/K-5
750 E 49th St 90011 323-234-9045
Maria Rosas, prin. Fax 234-3824

42nd Street ES 300/K-5
4231 4th Ave 90008 323-296-7550
Eve Sherman, prin. Fax 292-7680

4th Street ES 1,000/K-5
420 Amalia Ave 90022 323-266-0182
Maria Freese, prin. Fax 264-4071

4th Street Primary Center 200/PK-1
469 Amalia Ave 90022 323-268-8775
Danny Balderrama, prin. Fax 268-8755

Franklin ES 500/K-6
1910 N Commonwealth Ave 90027 323-663-0320
Veronica Sasso, prin. Fax 663-1684

Gardner ES 400/K-5
7450 Hawthorn Ave 90046 323-876-4710
Michael Rosner, prin. Fax 878-0954

Garvanza ES 400/K-6
317 N Avenue 62 90042 323-254-7328
Sarah Gilman, prin. Fax 256-6351

Garza Primary Center 200/K-2
2750 Hostetter St 90023 323-981-0270
Juan Gonzalez Marin, prin. Fax 981-0951

Gates Early Education Center PK-PK
2306 Thomas St 90031 323-222-0277
Scarlett Holguin, prin. Fax 225-0473

Gates ES 700/K-5
3333 Manitou Ave 90031 323-225-9574
Omar Malaszczuk, prin. Fax 225-8562

Glassell Park Early Education Center PK-PK
3003 Carlyle St 90065 323-221-1008
Jorge Reyes, prin. Fax 221-1003

Glassell Park ES 500/K-6
2211 W Avenue 30 90065 323-223-2277
Lillian Sugahara, prin. Fax 227-6391

Glen Alta ES 200/K-8
3410 Sierra St 90031 323-223-1195
Lupe Buenrostro, prin. Fax 223-3573

Glenfeliz Boulevard ES 400/K-6
3955 Glenfeliz Blvd 90039 323-666-1431
Karen Sulahian, prin. Fax 666-5735

Glenfeliz Early Education Center PK-PK
3745 Dover Pl 90039 323-665-4165
Jay Rallion, prin. Fax 953-0240

Gompers MS 800/6-8
234 E 112th St 90061 323-241-4000
Blanca Esquivel, prin. Fax 418-0778

Graham Early Education Center PK-PK
8332 S Elm St 90001 323-582-1222
Alice Reed, prin. Fax 581-0936

Graham ES 800/K-6
8407 S Fir Ave 90001 323-583-1263
Elsa Bolado, prin. Fax 583-5367

Grand View Boulevard ES 600/K-5
3951 Grand View Blvd 90066 310-390-3618
Mary Collier, prin. Fax 390-5836

Grant Early Education Center PK-PK
1559 N St Andrews Pl 90028 323-463-4112
Ade Hernandez, prin. Fax 466-7989

Grant ES 600/K-6
1530 N Wilton Pl 90028 323-469-4046
Christopher Ikeanyi, prin. Fax 469-4861

Grape ES 700/K-5
1940 E 111th St 90059 323-564-5941
Keith Nakano, prin. Fax 564-7168

Gratts Early Education Center PK-PK
1415 W 5th St 90017 213-481-3230
Ana Oregel, prin. Fax 481-3238

Gratts Learning Academy 600/K-6
309 Lucas Ave 90017 213-250-2932
Andra Estrada, prin. Fax 250-3648

Griffin Avenue ES 600/K-5
2025 Griffin Ave 90031 323-222-8131
Leonel Angulo, prin. Fax 222-0837

Griffith Joyner ES 600/K-5
1963 E 103rd St 90002 323-569-8141
Melanie Edmond, prin. Fax 249-0939

Griffith MS 1,400/6-8
4765 E 4th St 90022 323-266-7400
Rose Anne Ruiz, prin. Fax 268-6375

Hamasaki ES 400/K-6
4865 E 1st St 90022 323-263-3869
Michelle Hernandez, prin. Fax 268-8830

Hancock Park ES 800/K-5
408 S Fairfax Ave 90036 323-935-5272
Ashley Parker, prin. Fax 857-1795

Harmony ES 700/K-5
899 E 42nd Pl 90011 323-238-0791
Sylvia Salazar, prin. Fax 238-0793

Harrison S 500/K-6
3529 City Terrace Dr 90063 323-263-9191
Carlos Madrigal, prin. Fax 263-7708

Harte Prep MS 900/6-8
9301 S Hoover St 90044 323-242-5400
Sonia Leffall, prin. Fax 757-0408

Harvard ES 500/K-5
330 N Harvard Blvd 90004 323-953-4540
Mark Paz, prin. Fax 669-2833

Hillcrest Drive ES 700/K-5
4041 Hillcrest Dr 90008 323-296-6867
Anthony Jackson, prin. Fax 292-9180

Hillside ES 300/K-5
120 E Avenue 35 90031 323-222-2665
Richard Ycaza, prin. Fax 222-6033

Hobart Boulevard ES 700/K-5
980 S Hobart Blvd 90006 213-386-8661
Sylvia Valles, prin. Fax 382-2859

Hobart Early Education Center PK-PK
982 S Serrano Ave 90006 213-380-0411
Carol Hampar, prin. Fax 365-9458

Hollenbeck MS 1,300/6-8
2510 E 6th St 90023 323-780-3000
Randy Romero, prin. Fax 269-8137

Hollywood Primary Center 200/K-3
1115 Tamarind Ave 90038 323-464-0331
Mary Hall, prin. Fax 464-4206

Holmes Avenue ES 300/K-6
5108 Holmes Ave 90058 323-582-7238
Rene Baez, prin. Fax 582-0723

Hooper Early Education Center PK-PK
1224 E 52nd St 90011 323-232-3801
Lynn Stanford, prin. Fax 232-4055

Hooper ES 900/1-5
1225 E 52nd St 90011 323-232-3571
Gustavo Ortiz, prin. Fax 235-0847

Hooper Primary Center 200/K-K
1280 E 52nd St 90011 323-233-5866
Roslyn Simpson, prin. Fax 233-3188

Hoover ES 800/K-5
2726 Francis Ave 90005 213-387-3296
Martha Avelar, prin. Fax 387-9054

Huerta ES 500/K-5
260 E 31st St 90011 323-846-4820
Estela Lopez, prin. Fax 234-1202

Humphreys Avenue ES 800/K-5
500 S Humphreys Ave 90022 323-263-6958
Alejandro Almaguer, prin. Fax 780-2978

Huntington Drive ES 400/K-6
4435 Huntington Dr N 90032 323-223-1336
Lupe Hernandez, prin. Fax 223-7931

Hyde Park Early Education Center PK-PK
6428 11th Ave 90043 323-751-4147
Carol Collins, prin. Fax 759-3996

Irving Magnet MS 600/6-8
3010 Estara Ave 90065 323-259-3700
Kirk Roskam, prin. Fax 254-6447

Ivanhoe ES 500/K-5
2828 Herkimer St 90039 323-664-0051
Lynda Rescia, prin. Fax 666-7417

Jones ES 100/K-5
900 E 33rd St 90011 323-235-7940
Luis Gadea, prin. Fax 521-1083

Jones Primary Center 200/K-2
1017 W 47th St 90037 323-235-8911
Susan Montano, prin. Fax 235-1887

Kennedy ES 400/K-6
4010 Ramboz Dr 90063 323-263-9627
Robert Martinez, prin. Fax 263-6871

Kentwood ES 400/K-5
8401 Emerson Ave 90045 310-670-8977
Adil Khan, prin. Fax 670-6957

Kim Academy 800/6-8
615 Shatto Pl 90005 213-739-6500
Edward Colacion, prin. Fax 384-3083

Kim ES 700/K-5
225 S Oxford Ave 90004 213-368-5600
Jonathan Paek, prin. Fax 739-2550

King ES 500/K-5
3989 S Hobart Blvd 90062 323-294-0031
Eva Carpenter, prin. Fax 294-0277

King MS 1,700/6-8
4201 Fountain Ave 90029 323-644-6700
Mark Naulls, prin. Fax 913-3594

Kingsley ES 500/K-5
5200 Virginia Ave 90029 323-644-7700
Karina Salazar, prin. Fax 913-3360

Knox ES 1,000/K-6
8919 S Main St 90003 323-565-2960
Keisha Bennett-Moton, prin. Fax 758-6001

Lafayette Park Primary Center 100/K-K
310 S La Fayette Park Pl 90057 213-380-5039
Irma Cobian, prin. Fax 380-5196

Lake Street PS 200/K-1
135 N Lake St 90026 213-413-3305
Bruce Onodera, prin. Fax 413-3827

La Salle Avenue ES 500/K-5
8715 La Salle Ave 90047 323-759-1161
Aleta Taylor, prin. Fax 751-5591

Latona ES 200/K-6
4312 Berenice Ave 90031 323-221-5148
Ramona Garcia, prin. Fax 225-6417

Laurel ES 400/K-8
925 N Hayworth Ave 90046 323-654-1930
Amy Diaz, prin. Fax 656-5801

Lawson Academy of the Arts K-6
929 W 69th St 90044 323-565-3650
Pamela Gray, prin. Fax 778-2494

Lee Medical and Health Science ES 400/K-5
3600 W Council St 90004 323-368-8775
Kerry Kehrley, prin. Fax 241-8482

Lexington Ave Primary Center 200/K-2
4564 Lexington Ave 90029 323-644-2884
Berta Cochario, prin. Fax 644-8115

Liechty MS 1,200/6-8
650 S Union Ave 90017 213-989-1200
Adalberto Vega, prin. Fax 484-2700

Lillian Street ES 600/K-6
5909 Lillian St 90001 323-582-0705
William Downing, prin. Fax 582-8873

Lizarraga ES 700/K-5
401 E 40th Pl 90011 323-235-6960
Martin Sandoval, prin. Fax 846-9824

Locke Early Education Center PK-PK
320 E 111th St 90061 323-755-0721
Tracey Washington, prin. Fax 242-8621

Lockwood Avenue ES 500/K-6
4345 Lockwood Ave 90029 323-662-2101
Paula Kurilich, prin. Fax 663-3136

Logan Academy of Global Ecology 500/K-8
1711 Montana St 90026 213-413-6353
Mojgan Moazzez, prin. Fax 413-1261

Logan Early Education Ctr PK-PK
1712 Montana St 90026 213-989-1909
Jorge Reyes, prin. Fax 989-1908

Lorena Street ES 600/K-5
1015 S Lorena St 90023 323-268-1128
Patricia Gonzalez, prin. Fax 264-9437

Loreto ES 400/K-5
3408 Arroyo Seco Ave 90065 323-222-5176
Maria Arciniega, prin. Fax 222-6370

Los Angeles Academy 1,600/6-8
644 E 56th St 90011 323-238-1800
Ruben Hernandez, prin. Fax 231-0136

Los Angeles ES 800/K-5
1211 S Hobart Blvd 90006 323-734-8233
Rafael Alvarez, prin. Fax 734-8639

Los Feliz STEM ES 400/K-6
1740 N New Hampshire Ave 90027 323-663-0674
Katherine Pilkinton, prin. Fax 664-6045

Loyola Village ES 400/K-5
8821 Villanova Ave 90045 310-670-0480
Krishnay Smith, prin. Fax 216-9529

MacArthur Park ES VAPA 500/K-5
2300 W 7th St 90057 213-381-7217
Luis Velasco, prin. Fax 381-1872

Mack ES 400/K-5
3020 S Catalina St 90007 323-730-7620
Ana Guzman, prin. Fax 373-9655

Magnolia ES 1,100/K-6
1626 Orchard Ave 90006 213-748-6281
Juan Reyes, prin. Fax 748-3722

Main Street ES 800/K-5
129 E 53rd St 90011 323-232-4856
Eva Rodriguez Chavez, prin. Fax 231-1260

Malabar Street ES 700/K-6
3200 Malabar St 90063 323-261-1103
Margarita Gutierrez, prin. Fax 261-3252

Manchester ES 800/1-6
661 W 87th St 90044 323-778-3472
Veronica Brown, prin. Fax 751-5321

Manhattan Place ES 400/K-5
1850 W 96th St 90047 323-756-1308
Evelyn Samos, prin. Fax 756-9685

Mann JHS 500/6-8
7001 S St Andrews Pl 90047 323-541-1900
Orlando Johnson, prin. Fax 758-8203

Maple Primary Center 200/K-1
3601 Maple Ave 90011 323-232-0984
Sharyn Clark, prin. Fax 238-0780

Marianna ES 400/K-6
4215 Gleason St 90063 323-262-6382
Rafael Escobar, prin. Fax 780-0971

Marina Del Rey MS 700/6-8
12500 Braddock Dr 90066 310-578-2700
Lorraine Machado, prin. Fax 821-3248

Marina Early Education Center PK-PK
4908 Westlawn Ave 90066 310-822-8436
Nicola Boykin, prin. Fax 305-8220

Mariposa-Nabi PS 300/K-2
987 S Mariposa Ave 90006 213-385-0241
Brenda Grady, prin. Fax 385-0257

Markham MS 1,200/6-8
1650 E 104th St 90002 323-568-5500
Alex Kim, prin. Fax 569-6066

Marvin Early Education Center PK-PK
2341 S Curson Ave 90016 323-933-5882
Michael Haggood, prin. Fax 939-8392

Marvin ES 900/K-5
2411 S Marvin Ave 90016 323-938-3608
Elizabeth Banuelos, prin. Fax 938-0411

Mar Vista ES 600/K-5
3330 Granville Ave 90066 310-391-1175
Katherine Choe, prin. Fax 398-0924

Mayberry Street ES 300/K-6
2414 Mayberry St 90026 213-413-3420
Jessica Niessen, prin. Fax 413-5975

McKinley Avenue ES 800/K-6
7812 McKinley Ave 90001 323-582-7481
Tanya Stokes Mack, prin. Fax 588-1858

Melrose ES 300/K-6
731 N Detroit St 90046 323-938-6275
Mathew Needleman, prin. Fax 938-4981

Menlo Avenue ES 600/K-5
4156 Menlo Ave 90037 323-232-4291
Vive Jones, prin. Fax 232-0696

Meridian Early Education Center PK-PK
6124 Ruby Pl 90042 323-254-6749
Barbara George, prin. Fax 258-2865

Micheltorena Street ES 300/K-6
1511 Micheltorena St 90026 323-661-2125
Nichole Sakellarion, prin. Fax 661-2086

Mid-City Magnet S 300/K-8
3150 W Adams Blvd 90018 323-731-9346
Christian Panes, prin. Fax 730-1976

Mikes Early Education Center PK-PK
7720 S Vermont Ave 90044 323-758-1136
Ayanna Davis, prin. Fax 753-5379

Miller ES 800/K-6
830 W 77th St 90044 323-753-4445
Linda Arnold Funches, prin. Fax 758-5081

Miramonte Early Education Center PK-PK
1341 E 70th St 90001 323-581-6223
Catherine Ikediashi, prin. Fax 582-7827

Miramonte ES 900/K-6
1400 E 68th St 90001 323-583-1257
Veronica Herrarte, prin. Fax 582-6736

Monte Vista Early Education Center PK-PK
5509 Ash St 90042 323-258-3842
Barbara George, prin. Fax 257-6414

Monte Vista Street ES 500/2-6
5423 Monte Vista St 90042 323-254-7261
Megan Guerrero, prin. Fax 259-9757

Moore MST Academy 800/K-6
1321 E 61st St 90001 323-277-2310
Isabel Perez, prin. Fax 583-5886

Mt. Washington ES 400/K-6
3981 San Rafael Ave 90065 323-225-8320
Georgina Gravino, prin. Fax 223-2514

Muir MS 1,100/6-8
5929 S Vermont Ave 90044 323-565-2200
Aminika Readeux, prin. Fax 778-9824

Multnomah ES 500/K-5
2101 N Indiana Ave 90032 323-225-6005
Narajphan Asavasopon, prin. Fax 226-0220

Murchison Early Education Center PK-PK
1537 Murchison St 90033 323-225-2787
Josefina Navarro, prin. Fax 223-1748

Murchison Street ES 500/K-6
1501 Murchison St 90033 323-222-0148
Jeremiah Gonzalez, prin. Fax 225-2418

Nevin ES 600/K-5
1569 E 32nd St 90011 323-232-2236
Rachael Perkins, prin. Fax 232-5648

New MS Pathway 6-7
8701 Park Hill Dr 90045 323-673-1230
Kyle Hunsberger, prin.

New Open World Academy 1,100/K-12
3201 W 8th St 90005 213-480-3700
Charles Smith, prin. Fax 389-1559

Nightingale MS 800/6-8
3311 N Figueroa St 90065 323-224-4800
Rafael Gaeta, prin. Fax 222-4506

95th Street Early Education Center PK-PK
1027 W 96th St 90044 323-777-0920
Candie Childress, prin. Fax 242-7905

95th Street ES 900/K-5
1109 W 96th St 90044 323-756-1466
Manuel Nava, prin. Fax 754-8339

99th Street ES 600/K-6
9900 Wadsworth Ave 90002 323-564-2677
Courtney Sawyer, prin. Fax 249-9354

92nd Street ES 900/K-6
9211 Grape St 90002 323-564-7946
Priscilla Currie, prin. Fax 249-9417

97th Street Early Education Center PK-PK
430 W Colden Ave 90003 323-777-1233
Obiome Uchi, prin. Fax 242-7911

96th Street ES 900/K-6
1471 E 96th St 90002 323-567-8871
Lisa Smith, prin. Fax 567-3491

93rd Street ES 1,100/K-6
330 E 93rd St 90003 323-754-2869
Victor Sanchez, prin. Fax 756-8345

Ninth Street ES 200/K-5
835 Stanford Ave 90021 213-896-2700
Dean Simpson, prin. Fax 533-8001

Normandie Early Education Center PK-PK
4407 S Raymond Ave 90037 323-292-0266
Gregory Johnson, prin. Fax 294-9571

Normandie ES 900/K-5
4505 S Raymond Ave 90037 323-294-5171
Sandra Sklarsh, prin. Fax 294-7061

Norwood Street ES 700/K-5
2020 Oak St 90007 213-748-3733
Irene Worrell, prin. Fax 747-3380

Obama Global Preparation Academy 900/6-8
1700 W 46th St 90062 323-421-1700
David Devereaux, prin. Fax 293-2003

Olympic Primary Center 200/K-K
950 Albany St 90015 213-739-2753
Debra Rodriguez, prin. Fax 739-0048

118th Street ES 600/K-5
144 E 118th St 90061 323-757-1717
Grace Lee, prin. Fax 757-9916

109th Street ES 500/K-5
10915 McKinley Ave 90059 323-756-9206
Chrystal Brown, prin. Fax 755-2307

102nd Street Early Education Center PK-PK
1925 E 102nd St 90002 323-569-8159
Tracey Washington, prin. Fax 569-0446

107th Street ES 900/K-5
147 E 107th St 90003 323-756-8137
Katherine Nelson, prin. Fax 779-6942

116th Street ES 500/K-5
11610 Stanford Ave 90059 323-754-3121
Tyra Brookins-Henderson, prin. Fax 777-5977

112th Street Early Education Center PK-PK
1319 E 112th St 90059 323-567-9631
Obioma Uche, prin. Fax 567-7946

112th Street ES 500/K-5
1265 E 112th St 90059 323-567-2108
Agustin Garcia, prin. Fax 567-2611

122nd Street ES 700/K-5
405 E 122nd St 90061 323-757-8117
Christine Sanders, prin. Fax 757-0689

Overland ES 500/K-5
10650 Ashby Ave 90064 310-838-7308
Anna Born, prin. Fax 842-9392

Palms ES 400/K-5
3520 Motor Ave 90034 310-838-7337
William Lamb, prin. Fax 841-0814

Palms MS 1,500/6-8
10860 Woodbine St 90034 310-253-7600
Derek Moriuchi, prin. Fax 559-0397

Parks/Huerta Early Education Center 100/PK-PK
1020 W 58th Pl 90044 323-759-0667
Iadrana Williams, prin. Fax 759-1369

Parmelee ES 900/K-6
1338 E 76th Pl 90001 323-587-4235
Elizabeth Kane, prin. Fax 587-0257

Pio Pico MS 600/6-8
1512 Arlington Ave 90019 323-733-8801
Miranda Conston-Ra, prin. Fax 735-2665

Plasencia ES 700/K-6
1321 Cortez St 90026 213-250-7450
Ana Escobedo, prin. Fax 482-1815

Playa Vista ES 300/K-5
13150 Bluff Creek Dr 90094 424-228-1800
Rebecca Johnson, prin. Fax 862-9310

Poindexter LaMotte ES K-5
4410 Orchard Ave 90037 323-235-8350
Doramanda Higuchi, prin. Fax 846-9864

Politi ES 700/K-5
2481 W 11th St 90006 213-480-1244
Luis Ochoa, prin. Fax 736-0486

Queen Anne Place ES 400/K-5
1212 Queen Anne Pl 90019 323-939-7322
Phyllis Bradford, prin. Fax 939-6605

Ramona ES 700/K-6
1133 N Mariposa Ave 90029 323-663-2158
Guillermo George, prin. Fax 665-4934

Raymond Avenue ES 500/K-5
7511 Raymond Ave 90044 323-759-1183
Christian Perez, prin. Fax 778-2569

Richland Avenue ES 200/K-6
11562 Richland Ave 90064 310-473-0467
Gerard Granade, prin. Fax 268-7948

Ride ES A SMArT Academy 500/K-5
1041 E 46th St 90011 323-235-7117
Catherine Daley, prin. Fax 232-2405

Riordan PS 300/K-1
5531 Monte Vista St 90042 323-551-6822
Marilee Wood, prin. Fax 551-6944

Ritter ES 400/K-5
11108 Watts Ave 90059 323-564-2478
Michelle Rappino, prin. Fax 564-0230

Roberti Early Education Center PK-PK
1156 E Vernon Ave 90011 323-234-1428
Celestine Pearman, prin. Fax 234-2528

Rockdale Visual & Performing Arts S 300/K-6
1303 Yosemite Dr 90041 323-255-6793
Stefani Williams, prin. Fax 255-2906

Roscomare Road ES 500/K-5
2425 Roscomare Rd 90077 310-472-9829
Denise Collier, prin. Fax 476-7970

Rosemont Avenue ES 500/2-5
421 Rosemont Ave 90026 213-413-5310
William Estrada, prin. Fax 483-4341

Rosemont Early Education Center PK-PK, 1-
430 Rosemont Ave 90026 213-413-2999
Carol Hampar, prin. Fax 413-9680

Rosewood ES 300/K-6
503 N Croft Ave 90048 323-651-0166
Linda Kaye-Crowder, prin. Fax 852-9653

Rowan Avenue ES 1,000/K-5
600 S Rowan Ave 90023 323-261-7191
Guadalupe Carrandi, prin. Fax 261-0610

Russell ES 900/K-6
1263 Firestone Blvd 90001 323-582-7247
John Sayers, prin. Fax 582-3751

San Pascual Avenue STEAM ES 200/K-6
815 San Pascual Ave 90042 323-255-8354
Paula Cordoba, prin. Fax 255-5663

San Pedro Street ES 700/K-5
1635 S San Pedro St 90015 213-747-9538
Rigoberto Rodriguez, prin. Fax 747-6332

Saturn Street ES 400/K-5
5360 Saturn St 90019 323-931-1688
Tracie Bryant, prin. Fax 933-6370

School of Arts and Culture 6-8
1420 E Adams Blvd 90011 323-846-2245
Anita Maxon, prin.

2nd Street ES 400/K-6
1942 E 2nd St 90033 323-269-9401
Laura Naulls, prin. Fax 780-2912
Selma Avenue ES 200/K-6
6611 Selma Ave 90028 323-461-9418
Glendy Marin, prin. Fax 962-9258
75th Street Early Edcuation Center PK-PK
242 W 75th St 90003 323-753-1177
Ayanna Davis, prin. Fax 971-8306
75th Street ES 1,100/K-6
142 W 75th St 90003 323-971-8885
Miguel Campa, prin. Fax 778-0783
74th Street ES 600/K-5
2112 W 74th St 90047 323-753-2338
Barbara Lake, prin. Fax 778-2347
Shenandoah Early Education Center PK-PK
8861 Beverlywood St 90034 310-838-7328
Carol Collins, prin. Fax 838-8778
Shenandoah Street ES 500/K-5
2450 S Shenandoah St 90034 310-838-3142
Joy Naval, prin. Fax 842-9892
Sheridan Street ES 1,100/K-6
416 Cornwell St 90033 323-263-9818
Antonio Amparan, prin. Fax 261-4710
Short ES 300/K-6
12814 Maxella Ave 90066 310-397-4234
Karen Reynolds, prin. Fax 390-8940
Sierra Park ES 500/K-6
3170 Budau Ave 90032 323-223-1081
Richard Quijano, prin. Fax 222-1661
Sierra Vista ES 300/K-6
4342 Alpha St 90032 323-222-2530
Maria DeLaTorre, prin. Fax 222-4347
6th Avenue ES 700/K-5
3109 6th Ave 90018 323-733-9107
Jaime Miranda, prin. Fax 732-4001
68th Street ES 900/K-6
612 W 68th St 90044 323-753-2133
Brenda Cortez, prin. Fax 752-9909
61st Street ES 600/K-6
6020 S Figueroa St 90003 323-759-1138
Gonzalo Bayardo, prin. Fax 750-9685
66th Street Early Education Center PK-PK
405 E 67th St 90003 323-750-7861
Catherine Ikediashi, prin. Fax 758-7392
66th Street ES 800/K-5
6600 S San Pedro St 90003 323-753-1589
Renee Dolberry, prin. Fax 758-6505
Solano Avenue ES 300/K-6
615 Solano Ave 90012 323-223-4291
William Bertrand, prin. Fax 343-1975
Soto Street ES 200/K-6
1020 S Soto St 90023 323-262-6513
Eric Medina, prin. Fax 268-7453
South Park ES 1,000/K-6
8510 Towne Ave 90003 323-753-4591
Dennis Schaffer, prin. Fax 753-7256
Sterry ES 300/K-5
1730 Corinth Ave 90025 310-473-2172
Sara Lasnover, prin. Fax 444-1988
Stevenson MS 1,800/6-8
725 S Indiana St 90023 323-780-6400
Leo Gonzalez, prin. Fax 265-3952
Studio S 6-8
2050 San Fernando Rd 90065 323-225-4542
Leah Raphael, prin. Fax 276-5444
Sunrise ES 500/K-6
2821 E 7th St 90023 323-263-6744
Luis Barraza, prin. Fax 780-3985
Tenth Street ES 700/K-5
1000 Grattan St 90015 213-380-8990
William Otto, prin. Fax 480-6732
Third Street ES 700/K-5
201 S June St 90004 323-939-8337
Daniel Kim, prin. Fax 939-3098
32nd Street / USC MaST S 1,100/K-12
822 W 32nd St 90007 213-748-0126
Ezequiel Gonzalez, prin. Fax 744-1608
37th Street Early Education Center PK-PK
1204 W 36th Pl 90007 213-733-2133
Elizabeth Blackwell, prin. Fax 732-9134
36th Street Early Education Center PK-PK
3556 S St Andrews Pl 90018 323-734-3644
Gregory Johnson, prin. Fax 735-3973
Toland Way ES 400/K-6
4545 Toland Way 90041 323-255-3142
Nery Paiz, prin. Fax 255-0555
Trinity Early Education Center PK-PK
3816 Trinity St 90011 323-232-4017
Wendy Peel, prin. Fax 234-0841
Trinity Street ES 400/K-5
3736 Trinity St 90011 323-232-2358
Jorge Villalobos, prin. Fax 231-2441
Twain MS 700/6-8
2224 Walgrove Ave 90066 310-305-3100
Althea Ford, prin. Fax 398-1627
20th Street ES 600/K-5
1353 E 20th St 90011 213-747-7151
Mario Garcielita, prin. Fax 745-7606
28th Street Early Education Center PK-PK
747 E 28th St 90011 323-231-6921
Wendy Peel, prin. Fax 234-4679
28th Street ES 800/K-5
2807 Stanford Ave 90011 323-232-3496
Christina Beltrocco, prin. Fax 232-3029
24th Street Early Ed Center PK-PK
2101 W 24th St 90018 323-733-2164
Constance Majors, prin. Fax 733-6354
24th Street ES 600/K-5
2055 W 24th St 90018 323-735-0278
Marry Sullivan, prin. Fax 730-1865
UCLA Community S 1,000/K-12
700 S Mariposa Ave 90005 213-480-3750
Leyda Garcia, prin. Fax 480-3759
Union ES 1,100/K-5
150 S Burlington Ave 90057 213-483-1345
Veronica Herrera, prin. Fax 483-8109
Utah ES 500/K-8
255 Gabriel Garcia Marquez 90033 323-261-1171
Deborah Gayle, prin. Fax 265-2090

Valley View ES 200/K-6
6921 Woodrow Wilson Dr 90068 323-851-0020
Susan Kim, prin. Fax 851-6185
Van Ness Avenue ES 300/K-5
501 N Van Ness Ave 90004 323-469-0992
Jung Hong, prin. Fax 469-8376
Vermont ES 800/K-5
1435 W 27th St 90007 323-733-2195
Patricia Ferguson, prin. Fax 766-0577
Vine Early Education Center PK-PK
6312 Eleanor Ave 90038 323-465-1167
Euna Anderson, prin. Fax 469-9168
Vine Street ES 600/K-6
955 Vine St 90038 323-469-0877
Kurt Lowry, prin. Fax 461-7536
Virgil MS 1,000/6-8
152 N Vermont Ave 90004 213-368-2800
William Gurr, prin. Fax 383-8774
Virginia Road ES 400/K-5
2925 Virginia Rd 90016 323-735-0570
Davita McCauley, prin. Fax 735-8224
Wadsworth Early Education Center PK-PK
1047 E 41st St 90011 323-232-0581
Lynn Stanford, prin. Fax 231-8932
Wadsworth ES 700/K-5
981 E 41st St 90011 323-232-5234
Hector Carreno, prin. Fax 233-9612
Walgrove Avenue ES 300/K-5
1630 Walgrove Ave 90066 310-391-7104
Olivia Adams, prin. Fax 391-9809
Warner ES 700/K-5
615 Holmby Ave 90024 310-475-5893
Agnes Kamau, prin. Fax 470-5840
Washington Primary Center 200/K-1
860 W 112th St 90044 323-779-7550
TaJuanna Starks, prin. Fax 779-7473
Webster MS 500/6-8
11330 Graham Pl 90064 310-235-4600
Peter Benefiel, prin. Fax 477-0146
Weemes ES 800/K-5
1260 W 36th Pl 90007 323-733-9186
Elizabeth Bernal, prin. Fax 732-3973
Weigand Avenue ES 400/K-5
10401 Weigand Ave 90002 323-567-9606
Tamara Honegan, prin. Fax 564-2916
West Athens ES 800/K-5
1110 W 119th St 90044 323-756-9114
Ruth Castillo, prin. Fax 418-8467
Western ES 500/K-5
1724 W 53rd St 90062 323-295-3261
Shilby Sims, prin. Fax 295-4809
Westport Heights ES 400/K-5
6011 W 79th St 90045 310-645-5611
Jacqueline Hughes, prin. Fax 645-4258
West Vernon ES 800/K-5
4312 S Grand Ave 90037 323-232-4218
Frances Valadez, prin. Fax 232-7801
White ES 300/1-5
2401 Wilshire Blvd 90057 213-487-9172
Alfredo Juarez, prin. Fax 487-9177
Wilshire Crest ES 200/K-5
5241 W Olympic Blvd 90036 323-938-5291
Harold Klein, prin. Fax 933-1481
Wilshire Park ES 600/K-5
4063 Ingraham St 90005 213-739-4760
Leighanne Creary, prin. Fax 381-6178
Wilton Place Early Education Center PK-PK
4030 Leeward Ave 90005 213-383-4971
Curtis Johnson, prin. Fax 382-7094
Wilton Place ES 900/K-5
745 S Wilton Pl 90005 213-389-1181
Jung Kim, prin. Fax 387-5192
Windsor Hills Math Science ES 600/K-5
5215 Overdale Dr 90043 323-293-6251
Aresa Allen, prin. Fax 293-2021
Wisdom ES 900/K-6
1125 E 74th St 90001 323-586-5760
Connie Brandstetter, prin. Fax 589-8699
Wonderland Avenue ES 500/K-5
8510 Wonderland Ave 90046 323-654-4401
Sean Teer, prin. Fax 656-3228
Woodcrest ES 900/K-5
1151 W 109th St 90044 323-756-1371
Tina Choyce, prin. Fax 756-1432
Wright Magnet MS 600/6-8
6550 W 80th St 90045 310-258-6600
Christina Wantz, prin. Fax 568-8942
YES Academy 600/K-5
3140 Hyde Park Blvd 90043 323-778-4992
Robin Willis, prin. Fax 753-2280
Yorkdale ES 300/K-6
5657 Meridian St 90042 323-255-0587
Brian Grass, prin. Fax 255-1348
Other Schools – See Arleta, Bell, Canoga Park, Carson, Chatsworth, Cudahy, Culver City, Encino, Gardena, Granada Hills, Harbor City, Hawthorne, Hollywood, Huntington Park, Inglewood, Lomita, Marina del Rey, Maywood, Mission Hills, Monterey Park, North Hills, North Hollywood, Northridge, Pacoima, Panorama City, Playa Del Rey, Porter Ranch, Rancho Palos Verdes, Reseda, San Fernando, San Pedro, Sherman Oaks, South Gate, Sunland, Sun Valley, Sylmar, Tarzana, Torrance, Tujunga, Van Nuys, Venice, Vernon, Walnut Park, West Hills, West Hollywood, Wilmington, Winnetka, Woodland Hills

Montebello USD
Supt. — See Montebello
Gascon ES 900/K-5
630 Leonard Ave 90022 323-721-2025
Miguel Valencia, prin. Fax 887-3034
Montebello Park ES 700/K-5
6300 Northside Dr 90022 323-721-3305
Gina Andujo, prin. Fax 887-3073
Winter Gardens ES 700/K-5
1277 Clela Ave 90022 323-268-0477
Leticia Garcia, prin. Fax 887-7894

All Saints S 100/K-8
3420 Portola Ave 90032 323-225-7264
Maria Palermo, prin. Fax 225-1240
Ascension S 200/PK-8
500 W 111th Pl 90044 323-756-4064
Marina De La Rosa, prin. Fax 756-1060
Assumption S 100/PK-8
3016 Winter St 90063 323-269-4319
Carolina Gomez, prin. Fax 269-2434
Bais Chaya Mushka S 300/PK-8
9051 W Pico Blvd 90035 310-859-8840
Rabbi Danny Yiftach, dir. Fax 859-9824
Bais Tzivia Girls' S 300/K-8
7269 Beverly Blvd 90036 323-935-9274
Berkeley Hall S 300/PK-8
16000 Mulholland Dr 90049 310-476-6421
Dr. Lisle Staley, head sch Fax 476-5748
Blessed Sacrament S 100/PK-8
6641 W Sunset Blvd 90028 323-467-4177
Danina Uy, prin. Fax 467-6099
Brawerman ES 300/K-6
11661 W Olympic Blvd 90064 424-208-8934
Brandon Cohen, head sch Fax 689-4569
Brentwood ES 300/K-6
12001 W Sunset Blvd 90049 310-471-1041
Dr. Michael Riera, head sch Fax 440-1989
Cathedral Chapel S 300/K-8
755 S Cochran Ave 90036 323-938-9976
Tina Kipp, prin. Fax 938-9930
Cheder Menachem 300/PK-8
1606 S La Cienega Blvd 90035 323-623-1470
Rabbi Mendel Greenbaum, prin. Fax 623-1462
Christ the King S 200/K-8
617 N Arden Blvd 90004 323-462-4753
Patty Hager, prin. Fax 462-8475
Culver City Christian S 200/PK-5
11312 W Washington Blvd 90066 310-391-6963
Angela Gonzalez, admin. Fax 397-8031
Curtis S 500/PK-6
15871 Mulholland Dr 90049 310-476-1251
Meera Ratnesar, head sch Fax 476-1542
Divine Savior S 100/K-8
624 Cypress Ave 90065 323-222-6077
Norma Ceballos, prin. Fax 222-6994
Dolores Mission S 200/PK-8
170 S Gless St 90033 323-881-0001
Melissa Jara, prin. Fax 881-0034
Dye S 300/K-6
11414 Chalon Rd 90049 310-476-2811
Rose Helm, head sch Fax 476-8675
Gindi Maimonides Academy 500/PK-8
8511 Beverly Pl 90048 310-659-2456
Rabbi Aharon Wilk, head sch Fax 659-2865
Good Shepherd Lutheran S 50/PK-6
6338 N Figueroa St 90042 323-255-2786
Diana Springfield, prin. Fax 255-8452
Hollywood Schoolhouse 200/PK-6
1233 N McCadden Pl 90038 323-465-1320
Ilise Faye, head sch Fax 465-1720
Holy Name of Jesus S 200/K-8
1955 W Jefferson Blvd 90018 323-731-2255
Marva Belisle, prin. Fax 730-0321
Holy Spirit S 100/K-4
1418 S Burnside Ave 90019 323-933-7775
Nuria Gordillo, prin. Fax 933-7453
Holy Trinity S 100/PK-8
3716 Boyce Ave 90039 323-663-2064
Karen Lloyd, prin. Fax 664-2581
Immaculate Conception S 300/PK-8
830 Green Ave 90017 213-382-5931
Mary Murphy, prin. Fax 382-4563
Immaculate Heart of Mary S 200/K-8
1055 N Alexandria Ave 90029 323-663-4611
Allyson Alberto, prin. Fax 663-6216
Intl S of Los Angeles - Los Feliz 300/PK-5
4155 Russell Ave 90027 323-655-4526
Nordine Bouriche, dir. Fax 665-2607
Lanier S of Sinai Temple 500/PK-8
10400 Wilshire Blvd 90024 310-475-6401
Dr. Sarah Shulkind, head sch Fax 234-9184
Le Lycee Francais de Los Angeles PK-K
3261 Overland Ave 90034 310-839-1055
Frederique Haustete, head sch Fax 558-8069
Le Lycee Francais de Los Angeles 100/K-1
3261 Overland Ave 90034 310-553-7444
Michel Zala, head sch Fax 558-8069
Le Lycee Francais de Los Angeles 300/1-8
3261 Overland Ave 90034 310-836-3464
Josette Cole, head sch Fax 558-8069
Los Angeles Adventist Academy 200/PK-12
846 E El Segundo Blvd 90059 323-743-8818
Dr. Lilly Nelson, prin. Fax 324-3207
Los Angeles Cheder 400/PK-8
801 N La Brea Ave 90038 323-932-6347
Barry Weiss, dir. Fax 932-6335
Los Angeles Christian S 100/K-8
1620 W 20th St 90007 323-735-2867
Sara Marroquin, prin. Fax 735-2576
Mirman S 400/K-8
16180 Mulholland Dr 90049 310-476-2868
Dan Vorenberg, head sch Fax 471-1532
Mother of Sorrows S 200/PK-8
100 W 87th Pl 90003 323-758-6204
Griselda Villarreal, prin. Fax 758-6203
Nativity S 300/K-8
944 W 56th St 90037 323-752-0720
Antonio Felix, prin. Fax 752-1945
New Covenant Academy 100/K-12
3119 W 6th St 90020 213-487-5437
Dr. Jason Song, prin. Fax 487-5430
New Horizon S Westside 100/PK-5
1819 Sawtelle Blvd 90025 310-231-6092
Dalal Antabli, head sch Fax 231-6096
New World Montessori S 100/PK-6
10520 Regent St 90034 310-838-4044
Normandie Christian S 100/K-6
6306 S Normandie Ave 90044 323-752-3122
Teresa Wilson, prin. Fax 750-5180

Notre Dame Academy 300/K-8
2911 Overland Ave 90064 310-287-3895
Lilliam Paetzold, prin. Fax 838-8983
Oaks S 200/K-6
6817 Franklin Ave 90028 323-850-3755
Ted Hamory, head sch Fax 850-3758
Our Lady of Guadalupe S 200/K-8
436 N Hazard Ave 90063 323-269-4998
Teresa Villarreal, prin. Fax 780-7001
Our Lady of Guadalupe S - Rose Hill 200/K-8
4522 Browne Ave 90032 323-221-8187
Evangelina Lopez, prin. Fax 221-8197
Our Lady of Loretto S 200/K-8
258 N Union Ave 90026 213-483-5251
Nivia Aldrete-Brito, prin. Fax 483-6709
Our Lady of Lourdes S 100/PK-8
315 S Eastman Ave 90063 323-526-3813
Margaret Fabrizius, prin. Fax 526-3814
Our Lady of the Rosary S of Talpa 200/PK-8
411 S Evergreen Ave 90033 323-261-0583
Sr. Adella Armentrout, prin. Fax 261-0352
Our Mother of Good Counsel S 100/K-8
4622 Ambrose Ave 90027 323-664-2131
Rev. Allison Essman, prin. Fax 664-1906
Page Private S of Hancock Park 100/PK-8
565 N Larchmont Blvd 90004 323-463-5118
Kristin Dickson, head sch
Pilgrim S 300/PK-12
540 S Commonwealth Ave 90020 213-385-7351
Paul Barsky, head sch Fax 386-7264
Pilibos Armenian S 700/K-12
1615 N Alexandria Ave 90027 323-668-2661
Dr. Alina Dorian, prin. Fax 662-0332
Precious Blood S 200/PK-8
307 S Occidental Blvd 90057 213-382-3345
Maria Cunanan, prin. Fax 382-2078
Pressman Academy 300/K-8
1055 S La Cienega Blvd 90035 310-652-2002
Dr. Erica Rothblum, head sch Fax 360-0850
Price III Christian S 200/PK-12
7901 S Vermont Ave 90044 323-565-4199
Madeline Butler, prin. Fax 753-6770
Redeemer Baptist S 100/PK-8
10792 National Blvd 90064 310-475-4598
ReJOYce in Jesus Christian S 50/K-8
PO Box 47775 90047 323-934-5962
Dr. Vondalier Pipkin, dir. Fax 954-9936
Resurrection S 200/PK-8
3360 Opal St 90023 323-261-5750
Catalina Saenz, prin. Fax 268-1141
Ribet Academy 400/PK-12
2911 N San Fernando Rd 90065 323-344-4330
Sacred Heart S 200/PK-8
2109 Sichel St 90031 323-225-4177
Sr. Maria Gutierrez, prin. Fax 225-2615
St. Agnes S 300/K-8
1428 W Adams Blvd 90007 323-734-6441
Kevin Dempsey, prin. Fax 735-7719
St. Aloysius Gonzaga S 200/PK-8
2023 Nadeau St 90001 323-582-4965
Nicole Johnson, prin. Fax 585-4938
St. Alphonsus S 200/PK-8
552 Amalia Ave 90022 323-268-5165
Minerva Munguia-Sanchez, prin. Fax 264-4858
St. Anastasia S 300/K-8
8631 Stanmoor Dr 90045 310-645-8816
Mike Muir, prin. Fax 645-6923
St. Bernard S 200/K-8
3254 Verdugo Rd 90065 323-256-4989
Philip McCreary, prin. Fax 256-4963
St. Brendan S 300/K-8
238 S Manhattan Pl 90004 213-382-7401
Sr. Maureen O'Connor, prin. Fax 382-8918
St. Cecilia S 200/K-8
4224 S Normandie Ave 90037 323-293-4266
Norma Guzman, prin. Fax 293-5556
St. Columbkille S 300/K-8
145 W 64th St 90003 323-758-2284
Dr. Karen Holyk-Casey, prin. Fax 750-7141
St. Dominic S 200/K-8
2005 Merton Ave 90041 323-255-5803
Emily Diaz, prin. Fax 255-2817
St. Eugene S 200/K-8
9521 Haas Ave 90047 323-754-9536
Leona Sorrell M.A., prin. Fax 754-0913
St. Frances Xavier Cabrini S 200/K-8
1428 W Imperial Hwy 90047 323-756-1354
Carmen Hart, prin. Fax 756-1157
St. Francis of Assisi S 100/K-8
1550 Maltman Ave 90026 323-665-3601
Leslie De Leonardis, prin. Fax 665-4143
St. Gregory Nazianzen S 100/K-8
911 S Norton Ave 90019 323-936-2542
Linda Guzman, prin. Fax 936-1600
St. Ignatius of Loyola S 200/K-8
6025 Monte Vista St 90042 323-255-6456
Ileana Wade, prin. Fax 255-0959
St. James' Episcopal S 300/PK-6
625 S St Andrews Pl 90005 213-382-2315
Deborah David, hdmstr. Fax 382-2436
St. Jerome S 200/PK-8
5580 Thornburn St 90045 310-670-1678
Priscilla Doorbar, prin. Fax 670-1678
St. Lawrence of Brindisi S 300/K-8
10044 Compton Ave 90002 323-564-3051
Paula Anderson, prin. Fax 564-4050
St. Malachy S 200/K-8
1200 E 81st St 90001 323-582-3112
Rosio Orozco, prin. Fax 582-9340
St. Martin of Tours S 200/K-8
11955 W Sunset Blvd 90049 310-472-7419
Dr. Gavin Colvert, prin. Fax 440-2298
St. Mary Magdalen S 100/5-8
1223 S Corning St 90035 310-652-4723
Nuria Gordillo, prin. Fax 933-7453
St. Mary S 200/PK-8
416 S St Louis St 90033 323-262-3395
Sr. Jonathan Medina, prin. Fax 300-6039
St. Michael S 200/K-8
1027 W 87th St 90044 323-752-6101
Anabel Rodriguez, prin. Fax 752-6785

St. Odilia S 300/K-8
5300 Hooper Ave 90011 323-232-5449
Sima Saravia-Perez, prin. Fax 231-9714
St. Paul S 200/K-8
1908 S Bronson Ave 90018 323-734-4022
Diane Gehner, prin. Fax 734-5057
St. Paul the Apostle S 500/K-8
1536 Selby Ave 90024 310-474-1588
Richard Billups, prin.
St. Raphael S 300/PK-8
924 W 70th St 90044 323-751-2774
Allison Hurtt, prin. Fax 751-1244
St. Sebastian S 200/PK-8
1430 Federal Ave 90025 310-473-3337
Patricia Harty, prin. Fax 473-3178
St. Teresa of Avila S 200/K-8
2215 Fargo St 90039 323-662-3777
Christina Fernandez, prin. Fax 662-3420
St. Thomas the Apostle S 300/K-8
2632 W 15th St 90006 323-737-4730
Michael Santa Maria M.Ed., prin. Fax 737-6348
St. Timothy S 200/PK-8
10479 W Pico Blvd 90064 310-474-1811
Lena Randle, prin. Fax 470-1391
St. Turibius S 200/K-8
1524 Essex St 90021 213-749-8894
Victor Serna, prin. Fax 749-0424
St. Vincent S 300/K-8
2333 S Figueroa St 90007 213-748-5367
Erika Avila-Auzenne, prin. Fax 748-5347
San Miguel S 200/PK-8
2270 E 108th St 90059 323-567-6892
Maryanne Reynoso M.Ed., prin. Fax 567-1850
Santa Isabel S 200/K-8
2424 Whittier Blvd 90023 323-263-3716
Hilda Orozco, prin. Fax 263-3763
Santa Teresita S 200/K-8
2646 Zonal Ave 90033 323-221-1129
Sr. Mary Antczak, prin. Fax 221-6339
Star Christian S 100/PK-6
2120 Estrella Ave 90007 213-746-6900
Silvia Santis, prin. Fax 748-5301
Stratford S - Los Angeles Melrose PK-8
1200 N Cahuenga Blvd 90038 323-962-3075
Jamie Patrick, dir.
Tashbar Sephardic Yeshiva Ketana 200/PK-8
1210 S La Cienega Blvd 90035 310-652-2626
Rabbi David Miller, dir. Fax 652-6979
Temple Israel of Hollywood S 200/K-6
7300 Hollywood Blvd 90046 323-876-8330
Rachel Lewin, head sch Fax 876-8193
Transfiguration S 200/PK-8
4020 Roxton Ave 90008 323-292-3011
Evelyn Rickenbacker, prin. Fax 292-1527
Visitation S 300/PK-8
8740 Emerson Ave 90045 310-645-6620
Christopher Watson, prin. Fax 645-4407
Westchester Lutheran S 300/PK-8
7831 S Sepulveda Blvd 90045 310-670-5422
Sandra Masted, head sch Fax 670-1476
Westland S 100/K-6
16200 Mulholland Dr 90049 310-472-5544
Melinda Tsapatsaris, head sch Fax 472-5807
Westside Neighborhood S 400/PK-8
5401 Beethoven St 90066 310-574-8650
Bradley Zacuto, head sch Fax 574-8657
White Memorial Adventist S 100/K-8
1605 New Jersey St 90033 323-268-7159
David Olivares, admin. Fax 268-7033
Wildwood S 300/K-12
11811 W Olympic Blvd 90064 310-478-7189
Landis Green, head sch
Wilshire Private S 100/K-6
4900 Wilshire Blvd 90010 323-939-3800
Edward Shin, head sch Fax 937-0013
Wise S 500/PK-6
15500 Stephen S Wise Dr 90077 310-889-2300
Norma Guzman, prin.
Woodcrest Nazarene Christian S 100/PK-6
10936 S Normandie Ave 90044 323-754-4933
Vanessa Beverly, prin. Fax 754-1642
Yavneh Academy 400/PK-8
5353 W 3rd St 90020 323-931-5808
Rabbi Moshe Dear, hdmstr. Fax 931-5818
Yeshiva Aharon Yaakov Ohr Eliyahu 300/PK-8
241 S Detroit St 90036 323-556-6900
Rabbi Shlomo Goldberg, prin. Fax 556-6901
Yeshiva Rav Isacsohn Girls' S 900/PK-8
555 N La Brea Ave 90036 323-549-3188
Yeshiva Rav Isacsohn/Torah Emeth Academy 400/PK-8
540 N La Brea Ave 90036 323-549-3170
Rabbi Jacob Krause, dir. Fax 938-5232

Los Banos, Merced, Pop. 35,167
Los Banos USD 10,000/K-12
1717 S 11th St 93635 209-826-3801
Dr. Mark Marshall, supt. Fax 826-6810
www.losbanosusd.k12.ca.us
Charleston ES 400/K-6
18463 Charleston Rd 93635 209-826-5270
Lou Ruiz, prin. Fax 826-5288
Creekside JHS 7-8
1401 Prairie Springs Dr 93635 209-826-1005
Carolina Moreno, prin. Fax 826-1051
Falasco ES 900/K-6
310 Overland Rd 93635 209-827-5834
Jane Brittell, prin. Fax 827-6009
Los Banos ES 800/K-6
1260 7th St 93635 209-826-4981
Renee Leonard, prin. Fax 826-5551
Los Banos JHS 1,600/7-8
1750 San Luis St 93635 209-826-0867
Deolinda Brasil, prin. Fax 826-8532
Mercey Springs ES 300/K-6
1717 S 11th St 93635 209-826-3601
Eric Sowersby, prin.
Miano ES 1,000/K-6
1129 E B St 93635 209-826-3877
Antonio Rosales, prin. Fax 826-9201
Miller ES 900/K-6
545 W L St 93635 209-826-3816
Jason Waltman, prin. Fax 826-9772

Volta ES 400/K-6
24307 Ingomar Grade 93635 209-826-2912
Jan Whitehurst, prin. Fax 826-0855
Westside Union ES 700/K-6
659 K St 93635 209-827-9390
Joe McColloch, prin. Fax 827-6003

Los Banos Adventist S 100/1-8
404 Overland Rd 93635 209-827-4624
Lea Gilbert, prin. Fax 827-4625
Our Lady of Fatima S 200/PK-8
1625 Center Ave 93635 209-826-2709
Kendyl Darnell, prin. Fax 826-7320

Los Gatos, Santa Clara, Pop. 28,259
Campbell UNESD
Supt. — See Campbell
Rolling Hills MS 1,000/5-8
1585 More Ave 95032 408-364-4235
Cynthia Dodd, prin. Fax 341-7070

Lakeside JESD 100/K-5
19621 Black Rd 95033 408-354-2372
Shameram Karim, supt. Fax 354-8819
www.lakesidelosgatos.org
Lakeside ES 100/K-5
19621 Black Rd 95033 408-354-2372
Shameram Karim, prin. Fax 354-8819

Loma Prieta JUNESD 500/PK-8
23800 Summit Rd 95033 408-353-1101
Corey Kidwell, supt. Fax 353-8051
www.loma.k12.ca.us
English MS 200/6-8
23800 Summit Rd 95033 408-353-1123
Denee Signorelli, prin. Fax 353-5024
Loma Prieta ES 300/PK-5
23800 Summit Rd 95033 408-353-1106
Denee Signorelli, prin. Fax 353-3274

Los Gatos UNESD 3,300/K-8
17010 Roberts Rd 95032 408-335-2000
Diana Abbati, supt. Fax 395-6481
www.lgusd.org
Blossom Hill ES 700/K-5
16400 Blossom Hill Rd 95032 408-335-2100
Lisa Reynolds, prin. Fax 358-6438
Fisher MS 1,200/6-8
19195 Fisher Ave 95032 408-335-2300
Lisa Fraser, prin. Fax 356-7616
Lexington ES 200/K-5
19700 Old Santa Cruz Hwy 95033 408-335-2150
Lauren Honda, prin. Fax 354-2014
Van Meter ES 700/K-5
16445 Los Gatos Blvd 95032 408-335-2250
Rick Rauscher, prin. Fax 356-9487
Other Schools – See Monte Sereno

Union ESD
Supt. — See San Jose
Alta Vista ES 600/K-5
200 Blossom Valley Dr 95032 408-356-6146
Larry Thomas, prin. Fax 356-6706

Eitz Chaim Academy 50/PK-8
16555 Shannon Rd 95032 408-402-0264
Hillbrook S 300/PK-8
300 Marchmont Dr 95032 408-356-6116
Dr. Mark Silver, hdmstr. Fax 358-1286
Los Gatos Christian S 400/PK-8
16845 Hicks Rd 95032 408-997-4681
Stephen Torode, head sch Fax 997-4659
Mulberry S 200/PK-8
220 Belgatos Rd 95032 408-358-9080
Kara Riordan, head sch Fax 358-9082
St. Mary of the Immaculate Conception S 300/K-8
30 Lyndon Ave 95030 408-354-3944
James Johnston, prin. Fax 395-9151
Stratford S - Los Gatos 400/PK-5
220 Kensington Way 95032 408-371-3020
Poonam Majmudar, prin.
Yavneh Day S 200/K-8
14855 Oka Rd Ste 100 95032 408-984-6700

Los Molinos, Tehama, Pop. 1,963
Lassen View UNESD 300/PK-8
10818 State Highway 99E 96055 530-527-5162
Jerry Walker, supt. Fax 527-2331
www.lassenview.org
Lassen View ES 300/PK-8
10818 State Highway 99E 96055 530-527-5162
Jerry Walker, admin. Fax 527-2331

Los Molinos USD 600/K-12
7851 State Highway 99E 96055 530-384-7826
Joey Adame, supt. Fax 384-7832
www.lmusd.net
Los Molinos ES 300/K-8
PO Box 7 96055 530-384-7903
Jennie Bachmeyer, prin. Fax 384-7918
Other Schools – See Vina

Los Nietos, Los Angeles, Pop. 24,164
Los Nietos ESD 1,800/PK-8
8324 Westman Ave 90606 562-692-0271
Jonathan Vasquez, supt. Fax 699-0082
www.losnietos.k12.ca.us
Los Nietos MS 400/7-8
11425 Rivera Rd 90606 562-695-0637
Shanonn Brann Zelaya, prin. Fax 695-3805
Other Schools – See Santa Fe Springs, Whittier

Los Olivos, Santa Barbara, Pop. 1,116
Los Olivos ESD 200/K-8
PO Box 208 93441 805-688-4025
Bridget Baublits, supt. Fax 688-4885
www.sbceoportal.org/losolivos/
Los Olivos ES 200/K-8
PO Box 208 93441 805-688-4025
Bridget Baublits, prin. Fax 688-4885

Los Osos, San Luis Obispo, Pop. 13,912
San Luis Coastal USD
Supt. — See San Luis Obispo
Baywood ES 400/PK-5
1330 9th St 93402 805-534-2856
Jennifer Dinielli, prin. Fax 528-8065
Los Osos MS 600/6-8
1555 El Morro Ave 93402 805-534-2835
Andre Illig, prin. Fax 528-5133
Monarch Grove ES 300/K-5
348 Los Osos Valley Rd 93402 805-534-2844
Lara Storm, prin. Fax 528-5374

Lost Hills, Kern, Pop. 2,409
Lost Hills Union ESD 600/K-8
21109 Highway 46 93249 661-797-2626
Harrison Favereaux, supt. Fax 797-2580
www.losthills.k12.ca.us
Lost Hills ES 400/K-5
14821 Primary Ct 93249 661-797-2626
Veronica Sanchez-Gregory, prin. Fax 797-3015
Thomas MS 200/6-8
20979 Lobos Ct 93249 661-797-2626
Veronica Sanchez-Gregory, prin. Fax 797-3015

Lower Lake, Lake, Pop. 1,225
Konocti USD 2,800/K-12
PO Box 759 95457 707-994-6475
Donna Becnel, supt. Fax 994-0210
www.konoctiusd.org
Lower Lake ES 600/K-7
9240 Lake St 95457 707-994-5787
Tarin Benson, prin. Fax 994-7707
Other Schools – See Clearlake, Clearlake Oaks

Loyalton, Sierra, Pop. 752
Sierra-Plumas JUSD 400/K-12
PO Box 955 96118 530-993-1660
Merrill Grant Ed.D., supt. Fax 993-0828
www.sierracountyofficeofeducation.org
Loyalton ES 200/K-8
PO Box 127 96118 530-993-4482
Andrea White, prin. Fax 993-1007
Other Schools – See Downieville

Lucerne, Lake, Pop. 2,932
Lucerne ESD 300/K-8
PO Box 1083 95458 707-274-5578
Mike Brown, supt. Fax 274-9865
www.lucerne.k12.ca.us
Lucerne ES 300/K-8
PO Box 1083 95458 707-274-5578
Mike Brown, prin. Fax 274-9865

Lucerne Valley, San Bernardino, Pop. 5,647
Lucerne Valley USD 2,700/PK-12
8560 Aliento Rd 92356 760-248-6108
Peter Livingston, supt. Fax 248-6677
lucernevalleyusd.org
Lucerne Valley ES 400/PK-6
8560 Aliento Rd 92356 760-248-7659
Burt Umstead, prin. Fax 248-2806

Lynwood, Los Angeles, Pop. 69,209
Lynwood USD 14,200/K-12
11321 Bullis Rd 90262 310-886-1600
Gudiel Crosthwaite, supt. Fax 763-0959
www.lynwood.k12.ca.us
Abbott ES 800/K-6
5260 Clark St 90262 310-603-1498
Adolfo Herrera, prin. Fax 639-8074
Chavez MS 700/6-8
3898 Abbott Rd 90262 310-886-7300
Dr. Maria Pimienta, prin. Fax 603-2048
Hosler MS 700/7-8
11300 Spruce St 90262 310-603-1447
Hector Marquez, prin. Fax 764-4124
Keller ES 700/K-6
3521 Palm Ave 90262 310-886-5700
Luz Castillo, prin. Fax 637-8033
Lincoln ES 600/K-5
11031 State St 90262 310-603-1518
Geraldine Rescinito, prin. Fax 632-5673
Lindbergh ES 800/K-5
3300 Cedar Ave 90262 310-603-1521
Flavio Gallarzo, prin. Fax 632-8242
Lugo ES 400/K-6
4345 Pendleton Ave 90262 310-603-1493
Dionne Garner, prin. Fax 639-3682
Marshall ES 700/K-5
3593 Martin Luther King Jr 90262 310-886-5900
Deette Clay, prin. Fax 604-3000
Parks ES 600/K-6
3900 Agnes Ave 90262 310-603-1401
Dawn Green, prin. Fax 603-2013
Rogers ES 700/K-6
11220 Duncan Ave 90262 310-603-1542
Matthew Skoll, prin. Fax 631-3923
Roosevelt ES 600/K-6
10835 Mallison Ave 90262 310-603-1511
Sandra Verduzco, prin. Fax 669-8631
Twain ES 700/K-6
12315 Thorson Ave 90262 310-603-1500
Edward Espino, prin. Fax 632-8269
Washington ES 800/K-6
4225 Sanborn Ave 90262 310-603-1513
Shamell Wilson, prin. Fax 608-2694
Wilson ES 700/K-6
11700 School St 90262 310-603-1525
Raymond Schmidt, prin. Fax 635-5237

St. Emydius S 200/K-8
10990 California Ave 90262 310-635-7184
Rev. Rigoberto Rodriguez, admin. Fax 605-3041
St. Philip Neri S 100/K-8
12522 Stoneacre Ave 90262 310-638-0341
Elvia Villasenor, prin. Fax 638-9805

Mc Clellan, Sacramento
Twin Rivers USD 26,300/PK-12
5115 Dudley Blvd Bay A 95652 916-566-1600
Dr. Steven Martinez, supt. Fax 566-1784
www.twinriversusd.org
Other Schools – See North Highlands, Rio Linda, Sacramento

Mc Cloud, Siskiyou, Pop. 1,075
McCloud UNESD 100/K-8
PO Box 700 96057 530-964-2133
Shelley Cain, supt. Fax 964-2153
mccloudelementary.webs.com
McCloud ES 100/K-8
PO Box 700 96057 530-964-2133
Shelley Cain, prin. Fax 964-2153

Mc Farland, Kern, Pop. 12,620
McFarland USD 3,400/K-12
601 2nd St 93250 661-792-3081
Victor Hopper, supt. Fax 792-2447
www.mcfarlandusd.com
Browning Road ES 600/K-5
410 E Perkins Ave 93250 661-792-2113
Dario Diaz, prin. Fax 792-5423
Horizon ES K-5
800 S Garzoli Ave 93250 661-792-3081
Matthew Roderick, prin. Fax 792-2447
Kern Avenue ES 1,100/K-5
356 W Kern Ave 93250 661-792-3033
Francisco Flores, prin. Fax 792-6036
Mc Farland MS 700/6-8
405 Mast Ave 93250 661-792-3340
Manuel Cantu, prin. Fax 792-5681

Mc Kinleyville, Humboldt, Pop. 14,503
McKinleyville UNESD 1,200/K-8
2275 Central Ave 95519 707-839-1549
Jan Schmidt, supt. Fax 839-1540
Dows Prairie ES 500/K-2
3940 Dows Prairie Rd 95519 707-839-1558
Kevin Scheffler, prin. Fax 839-5652
McKinleyville MS 400/6-8
2285 Central Ave 95519 707-839-1508
Julie Giannini-Previde, prin. Fax 839-2548
Morris ES 300/3-5
2395 McKinleyville Ave 95519 707-839-1529
Teri Waterhouse, prin. Fax 839-4754

Mc Kittrick, Kern, Pop. 110
Belridge ESD 50/K-8
19447 Wagon Wheel Rd 93251 661-762-7381
Tammy Reynolds, supt. Fax 762-9751
belridgeschool.org/
Belridge ES 50/K-8
19447 Wagon Wheel Rd 93251 661-762-7381
Tammy Reynolds, prin. Fax 762-9751

Mc Kittrick ESD 100/K-8
PO Box 277 93251 661-762-7303
Barry Koerner, supt. Fax 762-7283
mckittrickschool.org
Mc Kittrick ES 100/K-8
PO Box 277 93251 661-762-7303
Barry Koerner, prin. Fax 762-7283

Madera, Madera, Pop. 60,700
Golden Valley USD 2,000/PK-12
37479 Avenue 12 559-645-7500
Andrew Alvarado, supt. Fax 645-7144
www.gvusd.k12.ca.us
Ranchos MS 300/7-8
12455 Road 35 1/2, 559-645-3550
Felipe Piedra, prin. Fax 645-3565
Sierra View ES 400/PK-6
16436 Paula Rd, 559-645-3560
Chris Imperatrice, prin. Fax 645-5161
Webster ES 600/K-6
36477 Ruth Ave, 559-645-3540
Lalo Lopez, prin. Fax 276-1921

Madera USD 20,200/K-12
1902 Howard Rd 93637 559-675-4500
Todd Lile, supt. Fax 661-7764
www.madera.k12.ca.us
Adams ES 800/K-6
1822 National Ave 93637 559-674-4631
Melissa Murray, prin. Fax 674-3867
Alpha ES 700/K-6
900 Stadium Rd 93637 559-661-4101
Tom Chagoya, prin. Fax 673-0931
Berenda ES 800/K-6
26820 Club Dr 93638 559-674-3325
Carsten Christiansen, prin. Fax 674-5617
Chavez ES 800/K-6
2600 E Pecan 93638 559-664-9701
Stephanie McPherson, prin. Fax 664-9716
Desmond MS 800/7-8
26490 Martin St 93638 559-664-1775
Prince Marshall, prin. Fax 664-1308
Dixieland ES 300/K-8
18440 Road 19 93637 559-673-9119
Ana Carrillo, prin. Fax 673-8232
Eastin Arcola ES 100/K-8
29551 Avenue 8 93637 559-674-8841
Danene Guglielmana, prin. Fax 674-2566
Howard ES 600/K-8
13878 Road 21 1/2 93637 559-674-8568
Judy Szpor, prin. Fax 673-5882
Jefferson MS 1,100/7-8
1407 Sunset Ave 93637 559-673-9286
Jesse Carrasco, prin. Fax 673-6930
King MS 700/7-8
601 Lilly St 93638 559-674-4681
Sabrina Rodriquez, prin. Fax 674-4261
La Vina ES 400/K-8
8594 Road 23 93637 559-673-5194
Jesus Navarro, prin. Fax 673-9091
Lincoln ES 800/K-6
650 Liberty Ln 93637 559-675-4600
Linda Monreal, prin. Fax 674-3061
Madison ES 600/K-6
109 Stadium Rd 93637 559-675-4630
Mercedes Ochoa, prin. Fax 661-8397
Millview ES 900/K-6
1609 Clinton St 93638 559-674-8509
Rosalinda Galvez, prin. Fax 674-9683
Monroe ES 800/K-6
1819 N Lake St 93638 559-674-5679
Kimberly Bitter, prin. Fax 674-3008
Nishimoto ES 800/K-6
26460 Martin St 93638 559-664-8110
Isabel Guzman, prin. Fax 664-8343
Parkwood ES 900/K-6
1150 E Pecan Ave 93637 559-673-2500
Omar Jeronimo, prin. Fax 673-9822
Pershing ES 900/K-6
1505 E Ellis St 93638 559-664-9741
Andy Beakes, prin. Fax 664-9756
Rose ES, 1001 Lilly St 93638 K-6
Lisa Fernandez, prin. 559-662-2662
Sierra Vista ES 800/K-6
917 E Olive Ave 93638 559-674-8579
Kathleen Nekumanesh, prin. Fax 674-1503
Washington ES 800/K-6
509 E South St 93638 559-674-6705
Adalberto Hernandez, prin. Fax 674-7386

Crossroads Christian S 100/PK-8
17755 Road 26 93638 559-662-1624
Rev. Jim Wallace M.Ed., prin. Fax 662-1625
St. Joachim S 300/PK-8
310 N I St 93637 559-674-7628
Darlene Lopez, prin. Fax 674-8770

Mad River, Trinity, Pop. 402
Southern Trinity JUSD 100/K-12
680 Van Duzen Rd, 707-574-6237
Peggy Canale, supt. Fax 574-6538
stjusd.org
Van Duzen S 100/K-8
680 Van Duzen Rd, 707-574-6237
Peggy Canale, prin. Fax 574-6538
Other Schools – See Zenia

Magalia, Butte, Pop. 10,902
Paradise USD
Supt. — See Paradise
Cedarwood ES 300/PK-5
6400 Columbine Rd 95954 530-873-3785
Lori Kerns, prin. Fax 873-1017
Pine Ridge S 500/K-8
13878 Compton Dr 95954 530-873-3800
Carrie Dawes, prin. Fax 873-2828

Magalia Adventist S 1-8
PO Box 998 95954 530-873-9168
Tom Hunt, prin. Fax 873-9168

Malibu, Los Angeles, Pop. 12,292
Santa Monica-Malibu USD
Supt. — See Santa Monica
Cabrillo ES 200/K-5
30237 Morning View Dr 90265 310-457-0360
Dr. Pamela Herkner, prin. Fax 457-0367
Point Dume ES 200/K-5
6955 Fernhill Dr 90265 310-457-9370
Mark Demick, prin. Fax 457-8064
Webster ES 300/K-5
3602 Winter Canyon Rd 90265 310-456-6494
Dr. Patrick Miller, prin. Fax 456-9304

Our Lady of Malibu S 100/K-8
3625 Winter Canyon Rd 90265 310-456-8071
Michael Smith, prin. Fax 456-7767

Mammoth Lakes, Mono, Pop. 8,104
Mammoth USD 1,200/K-12
PO Box 3509 93546 760-934-6802
Lois Klein, supt. Fax 934-6803
www.mammothusd.org
Mammoth ES 600/K-5
PO Box 3209 93546 760-934-7545
Rosanne Lampariello, prin. Fax 934-7341
Mammoth MS 300/6-8
PO Box 2429 93546 760-934-7072
Annie Rinaldi, prin. Fax 934-7073

Mono County Office of Education
Supt. — See Bridgeport
Sierra Early Education PK-PK
1500 Meridian Blvd 93546 760-934-0031
Jenni Huh, admin. Fax 934-1443

Manchester, Mendocino, Pop. 186
Manchester UNESD 100/K-8
PO Box 98 95459 707-882-2374
Cynthia Gonzalez, supt. Fax 882-3106
Manchester S 100/K-8
PO Box 98 95459 707-882-2374
Cynthia Gonzalez, prin. Fax 882-3106

Manhattan Beach, Los Angeles, Pop. 33,631
Manhattan Beach USD 6,900/PK-12
325 S Peck Ave 90266 310-318-7345
Dr. Michael Matthews, supt. Fax 303-3822
www.mbusd.org
Grand View ES 700/K-5
325 S Peck Ave 90266 310-546-8022
Nancy Doyle, prin. Fax 303-3817
Manhattan Beach MS 1,500/6-8
325 S Peck Ave 90266 310-545-4878
Kim Linz, prin. Fax 303-3829
Manhattan Beach Preschool 50/PK-PK
325 S Peck Ave 90266 310-546-7655
Kim Johnson, prin. Fax 303-3831
Meadows Avenue ES 500/K-5
325 S Peck Ave 90266 310-546-8033
Katherine Whittaker Stop, prin. Fax 303-3819
Pacific ES 700/K-5
325 S Peck Ave 90266 310-546-8044
Rhonda Steinberg, prin. Fax 303-3806

Pennekamp ES 600/K-5
325 S Peck Ave 90266 310-798-6223
Dr. Toni Brown, prin. Fax 303-3839
Robinson ES 400/K-5
325 S Peck Ave 90266 310-318-5120
John Jackson, prin. Fax 303-3813

American Martyrs S 700/PK-8
1701 Laurel Ave 90266 310-545-8559
Dr. Camryn Friel, prin. Fax 546-7219

Manteca, San Joaquin, Pop. 64,370
Manteca USD 22,800/K-12
PO Box 32 95336 209-825-3200
Jason Messer, supt. Fax 858-7570
www.mantecausd.net
Brockman S 800/K-8
763 Silverado Dr 95337 209-858-7200
Candace Espinola, prin. Fax 858-7554
Cowell S 500/K-8
740 Pestana Ave 95336 209-858-7310
Christie Newman, prin. Fax 858-7516
Elliott S 800/K-8
1110 Stonum Ln 95337 209-858-7260
Debbie Ruger, prin. Fax 858-7503
Golden West S 700/K-8
1031 N Main St 95336 209-858-7300
Sherie Gates, prin. Fax 825-3343
Hafley S 800/K-8
849 Northgate Dr 95336 209-858-7215
Lori Guzman-Alvarez, prin. Fax 858-7542
Lincoln S 600/K-8
750 E Yosemite Ave 95336 209-858-7320
Steve Anderson, prin. Fax 858-7522
McParland S 700/3-8
1601 Northgate Dr 95336 209-858-7290
Dale Borgeson, prin. Fax 858-7510
New Haven S 600/K-8
14600 S Austin Rd 95336 209-858-7360
David O'Leary, prin. Fax 858-7544
Nile Garden S 500/K-8
5700 Nile Rd 95337 209-858-7370
Deborah Noceti-Ward, prin. Fax 858-7546
Sequoia S 800/K-8
710 Martha St 95337 209-858-7440
Lisa Herrin, prin. Fax 858-7549
Shasta S 800/K-8
751 E Edison St 95336 209-858-7400
Audrey Greene, prin. Fax 858-7563
Veritas S 600/K-8
1600 Pagola Ave 95337 209-858-7390
Tracie Crawford, prin. Fax 858-7559
Woodward S 1,000/K-8
575 Tannehill Dr 95337 209-858-7430
Sherrie Jamero, prin. Fax 858-7560
Other Schools – See French Camp, Lathrop, Stockton

Cornerstone Christian S 100/PK-6
17900 Comconex Rd 95336 209-825-1422
Douglas Scott, admin. Fax 825-1222
Manteca Adventist Christian S 50/1-8
PO Box 2548 95336 209-239-3140
Heidi Jorgenson, prin. Fax 239-3140
St. Anthony S 300/PK-8
323 N Fremont St 95336 209-823-4513
Susie Dickert, prin. Fax 825-7447

Manton, Tehama, Pop. 340
Antelope ESD
Supt. — See Red Bluff
Manton S 50/PK-5
PO Box 410 96059 530-474-3167
Richard Hassay, admin. Fax 474-5550

Maricopa, Kern, Pop. 1,126
Maricopa USD 1,000/K-12
955 Stanislaus St 93252 661-769-8231
Scott Meier, supt. Fax 769-8168
maricopaschools.org
Maricopa ES 200/K-5
955 Stanislaus St 93252 661-769-8231
Scott Meier, prin. Fax 769-8168
Maricopa MS 100/6-8
955 Stanislaus St 93252 661-769-8231
Fax 769-8168

Marina, Monterey, Pop. 17,783
Monterey Peninsula USD
Supt. — See Monterey
Crumpton ES 400/K-5
460 Carmel Ave 93933 831-392-3520
Sarah Hudson, prin. Fax 384-6952
Los Arboles MS 600/6-8
294 Hillcrest Ave 93933 831-384-3550
Stephanie Herrera, prin. Fax 384-6353
Marina Child Development Center PK-PK
3066 Lake Dr 93933 831-384-0255
Nattaya Robinson, admin. Fax 384-7451
Marina Vista ES 400/K-5
390 Carmel Ave 93933 831-392-3580
Cristy Campanaro, prin. Fax 384-1785
Olson ES 400/K-5
261 Beach Rd 93933 831-392-3590
Frances Malloway, prin. Fax 384-2369

Marina del Rey, Los Angeles, Pop. 8,515
Los Angeles USD
Supt. — See Los Angeles
Westside Global Awareness Magnet S 400/K-8
104 Anchorage St 90292 310-821-2039
Cyril Baird, prin. Fax 306-9730

Mariposa, Mariposa, Pop. 2,123
Mariposa County USD 1,800/K-12
PO Box 8 95338 209-742-0250
Robin Hopper, supt. Fax 966-4549
www.mariposa.k12.ca.us/
Mariposa ES 400/K-8
PO Box 5002 95338 209-742-0340
Erin Vereschagin, prin. Fax 742-0383

Woodland ES 400/K-8
3394 Woodland Dr 95338 209-742-0310
Lydia Lower, prin. Fax 742-0313
Other Schools – See Coulterville, El Portal, La Grange, Yosemite National Park

Markleeville, Alpine, Pop. 204
Alpine County USD 100/K-12
43 Hawkside Dr 96120 530-694-2230
Patrick Traynor, admin. Fax 694-2379
www.alpinecoe.k12.ca.us
Diamond Valley ES 100/K-8
35 Hawkside Dr 96120 530-694-2238
Dr. Patrick Traynor, admin. Fax 694-2386

Martinez, Contra Costa, Pop. 34,098
Martinez USD 4,100/K-12
921 Susana St 94553 925-335-5800
C.J. Cammack, supt. Fax 335-5961
www.martinezusd.net
Las Juntas ES 500/K-5
4105 Pacheco Blvd 94553 925-335-5830
Crystal Castaneda, prin. Fax 335-5891
Martinez JHS 900/6-8
1600 Court St 94553 925-335-5820
Katie Martin, prin. Fax 335-5829
Morello Park ES 500/K-5
1200 Morello Park Dr 94553 925-335-5840
Stacy Joslin, prin. Fax 335-5842
Muir ES 400/K-5
205 Vista Way 94553 925-335-5850
Kathy Frazer, prin. Fax 335-5859
Swett ES 500/K-5
4955 Alhambra Valley Rd 94553 925-335-5860
Mike Cannon, prin. Fax 335-5869

Mount Diablo USD
Supt. — See Concord
Hidden Valley ES 800/K-5
500 Glacier Dr 94553 925-228-9530
Nina Crossland, prin. Fax 313-8938

St. Catherine of Siena S 200/PK-8
604 Mellus St 94553 925-228-4140
Pamela Seto, prin. Fax 228-0697

Marysville, Yuba, Pop. 11,483
Marysville JUSD 9,200/K-12
1919 B St 95901 530-741-6000
Gay Todd Ed.D., supt. Fax 741-7894
www.mjusd.com
Cordua ES 100/K-5
2830 State Highway 20 95901 530-741-6115
Ashley Vette, prin. Fax 741-6031
Covillaud ES 500/K-5
628 F St 95901 530-741-6121
Doug Escheman, prin. Fax 741-7868
Edgewater ES 400/K-6
5715 Oakwood Dr 95901 530-741-0866
Lori Guy, prin. Fax 741-1332
Foothill IS 100/6-8
5351 Fruitland Rd 95901 530-741-6130
Kathleen Hansen, prin. Fax 741-6017
Kynoch ES 600/K-5
1905 Ahern St 95901 530-741-6141
Angela Huerta, prin. Fax 741-6020
Linda ES 700/K-6
6180 Dunning Ave 95901 530-741-6196
Judy Hart, prin. Fax 741-7849
Loma Rica ES 100/K-5
5150 Fruitland Rd 95901 530-741-6144
Kathleen Hansen, prin. Fax 741-6098
McKenney IS 500/6-8
1904 Huston St 95901 530-741-6187
Tom Reusser, prin. Fax 741-6004
Other Schools – See Browns Valley, Challenge, Dobbins, Olivehurst

Mather, Sacramento, Pop. 4,082
Folsom-Cordova USD
Supt. — See Rancho Cordova
Mather Heights ES 500/K-6
4370 Mather School Rd 95655 916-294-2440
Sara Parenzin, prin. Fax 294-2486

Maxwell, Colusa, Pop. 1,095
Maxwell USD 300/K-12
PO Box 788 95955 530-438-2291
Zach Thurman, supt. Fax 438-2693
www.maxwell.k12.ca.us
Maxwell S 200/K-6
PO Box 788 95955 530-438-2401
Staci DeWit, prin. Fax 438-2460

Maywood, Los Angeles, Pop. 27,328
Los Angeles USD
Supt. — See Los Angeles
Fishburn Avenue ES 600/K-5
5701 Fishburn Ave 90270 323-560-0878
Patricia Ponce, prin. Fax 560-6391
Heliotrope ES 800/K-5
5911 Woodlawn Ave 90270 323-560-1230
Gabriela Rodriguez, prin. Fax 562-4415
Loma Vista ES 900/K-5
3629 E 58th St 90270 323-582-6153
Carmen Hernandez, prin. Fax 585-2130
Maywood ES 500/K-5
5200 Cudahy Ave 90270 323-890-2440
Ana Garcia, prin. Fax 560-2889

St. Rose of Lima S 200/K-8
4422 E 60th St 90270 323-560-3376
Veronica Macias, prin. Fax 560-8539

Meadow Vista, Placer, Pop. 3,116
Placer Hills UNESD 500/K-8
16801 Placer Hills Rd 95722 530-878-2606
Cindy Uptain, supt. Fax 878-2663
www.phusd.org
Sierra Hills ES 300/K-3
16505 Placer Hills Rd 95722 530-878-9473
David Figuly, prin. Fax 878-9475

Other Schools – See Weimar

Live Oak Waldorf S 200/PK-8
410 Crother Rd 95722 530-878-8720

Mecca, Riverside, Pop. 8,553
Coachella Valley USD
Supt. — See Thermal
Martinez ES 1,100/K-6
65705 Johnson St 92254 760-396-1935
Delia Alvarez, prin. Fax 396-2103
Mecca ES 800/K-6
65250 Coahuilla St 92254 760-396-2143
Gracie Avalos, prin. Fax 396-0463

Mendocino, Mendocino, Pop. 866
Mendocino USD 500/K-12
PO Box 1154 95460 707-937-5868
Jason Morse, supt. Fax 937-0714
www.mendocinousd.org/
Mendocino K-8 S 300/K-8
PO Box 226 95460 707-937-0515
Kim Humrichouse, prin. Fax 937-1538
Other Schools – See Albion, Comptche

Mendota, Fresno, Pop. 10,983
Mendota USD 3,000/K-12
115 McCabe Ave 93640 559-655-4942
Paul Lopez, supt. Fax 655-4944
www.musdaztecs.com
McCabe ES 900/3-6
250 Derrick Ave 93640 559-655-4262
Richard Garcia, prin. Fax 655-1220
Mendota ES K-6
605 Bass Ave 93640 559-655-2014
Juanita Villar, prin. Fax 655-2023
Mendota JHS 400/7-8
1258 Belmont Ave 93640 559-655-4301
Randy Jarrett, prin. Fax 655-1229
Washington ES 900/K-2
1599 5th St 93640 559-655-4365
Rhyanna Cervantes, prin. Fax 655-7007

Menifee, Riverside, Pop. 75,080
Menifee UNESD 10,600/PK-12
29775 Haun Rd 92586 951-672-1851
Steve Kennedy Ed.D., supt. Fax 672-1385
www.menifeeusd.org
Bell Mountain MS 1,200/6-8
28525 La Piedra Rd 92584 951-301-8496
Kat Marshall, prin. Fax 301-5286
Christensen MS 800/6-8
27625 Sherman Rd, 951-679-8356
Kristina Lyman, prin. Fax 679-4090
Evans Ranch ES 600/K-5
30465 Evans Rd 92584 951-246-7690
Michael Reyes, prin. Fax 246-7805
Freedom Crest ES 800/K-5
29282 Menifee Rd 92584 951-679-5285
Christine Rich, prin. Fax 672-2651
Kirkpatrick ES 600/K-5
28800 Reviere Dr 92584 951-672-6420
Lynn Hanke, prin. Fax 672-6423
Menifee Preschool PK-PK
26350 La Piedra Rd 92584 951-672-6478
Jennifer Adcock, admin. Fax 672-6479
Menifee Valley MS 1,000/6-8
26255 Garbani Rd 92584 951-672-6400
Ed Resnick, prin. Fax 672-6415
Morrison ES 400/K-5
30250 Bradley Rd 92584 951-679-7076
Manuel Valdes, prin. Fax 672-6436
Quail Valley ES 600/K-5
23757 Canyon Heights Dr, 951-244-1937
Lily Pena, prin. Fax 244-6842
Ridgemoor ES 700/K-5
25455 Ridgemoor Rd, 951-672-6450
Mike Walsh, prin. Fax 672-6456
Southshore ES 900/K-5
30975 Southshore Dr 92584 951-672-0013
Sandy Vilas, prin. Fax 723-1230
Other Schools – See Lake Elsinore, Murrieta, Winchester

Romoland ESD
Supt. — See Homeland
Chase MS 700/6-8
28100 Calm Horizon Dr, 951-566-4400
Chris Hernandez, prin. Fax 639-5943

Menlo Park, San Mateo, Pop. 30,400
Las Lomitas ESD 1,400/K-8
1011 Altschul Ave 94025 650-854-2880
Lisa Cesario, supt. Fax 854-0882
llesd-ca.schoolloop.com
La Entrada MS 800/4-8
2200 Sharon Rd 94025 650-854-3962
Mark Jones, prin. Fax 854-5947
Other Schools – See Atherton

Menlo Park City ESD
Supt. — See Atherton
Hillview MS 900/6-8
1100 Elder Ave 94025 650-326-4341
Willy Haug, prin. Fax 325-3861
Oak Knoll ES 800/K-5
1895 Oak Knoll Ln 94025 650-854-4433
Kristen Gracia, prin. Fax 854-0179

Ravenswood City ESD
Supt. — See East Palo Alto
Belle Haven ES 600/K-8
415 Ivy Dr 94025 650-329-2898
Todd Gaviglio, prin. Fax 566-9386
Willow Oaks ES 700/K-8
620 Willow Rd 94025 650-329-2850
Cynthia Chin, prin. Fax 327-2684

Redwood City ESD
Supt. — See Redwood City
Garfield ES 700/K-8
3600 Middlefield Rd 94025 650-369-3759
Michelle Griffith, prin. Fax 367-4358

Alto International S 200/PK-12
475 Pope St 94025 650-324-8617
Sally Thorogood, head sch
Beechwood S 200/K-8
50 Terminal Ave 94025 650-327-5052
David Laurance, prin. Fax 327-5066
Nativity S 300/K-8
1250 Laurel St 94025 650-325-7304
Maureen Huntington, prin. Fax 325-3841
Peninsula S 200/PK-8
920 Peninsula Way 94025 650-325-1584
Jim Benz, head sch Fax 325-1313
Phillips Brooks S 300/PK-5
2245 Avy Ave 94025 650-854-4545
Dr. Scott Erickson, head sch Fax 854-6532
St. Raymond S 200/PK-8
1211 Arbor Rd 94025 650-322-2312
Kellie Mullin, prin. Fax 322-2910
Synapse S 200/K-8
3375 Edison Way 94025 650-294-4570
Jim Eagen, head sch Fax 294-4579
Trinity S 100/PK-5
2650 Sand Hill Rd 94025 650-854-0288
Mary Menacho, head sch Fax 854-1374

Mentone, San Bernardino, Pop. 8,447
Redlands USD
Supt. — See Redlands
Mentone ES 500/K-5
1320 Crafton Ave 92359 909-794-8610
Sonya Balingit, prin. Fax 794-8614

Merced, Merced, Pop. 76,840
McSwain UNESD 900/K-8
926 Scott Rd 95341 209-354-2700
Steve Rosa, supt. Fax 723-2267
www.mcswain.k12.ca.us
McSwain S 900/K-8
922 Scott Rd 95341 209-354-2700
Laurie Havel, prin. Fax 723-2630

Merced City ESD 10,100/K-8
444 W 23rd St 95340 209-385-6600
Rosemary Parga Duran Ed.D., supt. Fax 385-6316
www.mcsd.k12.ca.us
Burbank ES 600/K-6
609 E Alexander Ave 95340 209-385-6674
Jill Settera, prin. Fax 385-6377
Chenoweth ES 800/K-6
3200 N Parsons Ave 95340 209-385-6620
Vance d'Escoto, prin. Fax 385-6386
Cruickshank MS 500/7-8
601 Mercy Ave 95340 209-385-6330
Jerod Garst, prin. Fax 385-6338
Franklin ES 500/K-3
2736 Franklin Rd 95348 209-385-6623
Cesar Hernandez, prin. Fax 385-6303
Fremont ES 400/K-6
1120 W 22nd St 95340 209-385-6627
Dawn Walker, prin. Fax 385-6301
Givens ES 500/K-6
2900 Green St 95340 209-385-6610
Tara Bright, prin. Fax 385-6388
Gracey ES 600/K-6
945 N West Ave 95341 209-385-6710
Jose Munoz, prin. Fax 385-6748
Hoover MS 500/7-8
800 E 26th St 95340 209-385-6631
Julie Rivard, prin. Fax 385-6799
Muir ES 500/K-6
300 W 26th St 95340 209-385-6667
Michelle Colburn, prin. Fax 385-6320
Peterson ES 700/K-6
848 E Donna Dr 95340 209-385-6700
Suzanne Silva-Fagundes, prin. Fax 385-6379
Reyes ES 500/K-6
123 S N St 95341 209-385-6761
Aaron Alexander, prin. Fax 385-6775
Rivera ES 600/K-6
945 Buena Vista Dr 95348 209-724-2550
Catherine Puckett, prin. Fax 724-2551
Rivera MS 600/7-8
945 Buena Vista Dr 95348 209-385-6680
Sergio Mendez, prin. Fax 385-6702
Sheehy ES 500/K-6
1240 W 6th St 95341 209-385-6676
Rojelio Gutierrez, prin. Fax 385-6389
Stefani ES 500/3-6
2768 Ranchero Ln 95348 209-724-2500
Rick Her, prin. Fax 724-2501
Stowell ES 500/K-6
251 E 11th St 95341 209-381-2803
Dalinda Saich, prin. Fax 381-2807
Tenaya MS 600/7-8
760 W 8th St 95341 209-385-6687
Anthony Arista, prin. Fax 385-6365
Wright ES 500/K-6
900 E 20th St 95340 209-385-6615
Ken Cooper, prin. Fax 385-6302

Plainsburg UNESD 100/K-8
3708 Plainsburg Rd 95341 209-389-4707
Kristi Kingston, supt. Fax 389-4817
sites.google.com/a/plainsburg.k12.ca.us/web
Plainsburg Union ES 100/K-8
3708 Plainsburg Rd 95341 209-389-4707
Marsha Griffin, prin. Fax 389-4817

Weaver UNSD 2,900/PK-8
3076 E Childs Ave 95341 209-723-7606
John Curry M.A., supt. Fax 725-7128
www.weaverusd.org
Farmdale ES 900/K-5
100 Winder Ave 95341 209-725-7170
Kathy Moser, prin. Fax 725-7175
Pioneer ES 1,000/K-5
2950 E Gerard Ave 95341 209-725-7111
Michal Lomeli M.A., prin. Fax 725-7117
Weaver MS 900/6-8
3076 E Childs Ave 95341 209-723-2174
Elias Villa M.A., prin. Fax 725-7116
Weaver Preschool 100/PK-PK
3076 E Childs Ave 95341 209-725-7125
Mike Weber M.A., dir. Fax 725-7128

Our Lady of Mercy S 400/PK-8
1400 E 27th St 95340 209-722-7496
Judy Blackburn, prin. Fax 722-7532
Providence Christian S 200/PK-6
2142 E Yosemite Ave 95340 209-383-4727
Dr. Christopher Busch, prin. Fax 384-1343
St. Paul Lutheran S 100/PK-6
2916 McKee Rd 95340 209-383-3302
Amy Mello, prin. Fax 383-3642

Meridian, Sutter, Pop. 343
Meridian ESD 100/K-12
15898 Central St 95957 530-696-2604
Javier Lopez, supt. Fax 696-0406
www.meridiantigers.com
Meridian ES 100/K-8
15898 Central St 95957 530-696-2604
Javier Lopez, prin. Fax 696-0406

Winship-Robbins ESD 200/K-12
4305 S Meridian Rd 95957 530-696-2451
Dr. Laurie Goodman, supt. Fax 696-2262
winship-robbins.sutter.k12.ca.us
Winship S 50/K-8
4305 S Meridian Rd 95957 626-932-1802
Laurie Goodman, supt. Fax 932-1804
Other Schools – See Robbins

Middletown, Lake, Pop. 1,281
Middletown USD 1,600/K-12
20932 Big Canyon Rd 95461 707-987-4100
Catherine Stone, supt. Fax 987-4105
www.middletownusd.org
Cannon ES 200/K-6
20932 Big Canyon Rd 95461 707-987-4130
Brandy Fischer, prin. Fax 987-4136
Cobb Mountain ES 200/K-6
20932 Big Canyon Rd 95461 707-928-5229
David Leonard, prin. Fax 928-5414
Coyote Valley ES 500/K-6
20932 Big Canyon Rd 95461 707-987-3357
Shane Lee, prin. Fax 987-4111
Middletown MS 200/7-8
20932 Big Canyon Rd 95461 707-987-4160
Mitch Tucker, prin. Fax 987-4162

Middletown Adventist S 50/K-8
PO Box 1664 95461 707-987-9147
Cyndee Westernrider, prin. Fax 987-3546
Middletown Christian S 100/PK-12
PO Box 989 95461 707-987-2556
Anna Mayfield, admin. Fax 987-2126

Midway City, Orange, Pop. 8,289
Ocean View SD
Supt. — See Huntington Beach
Star View ES 600/K-5
8411 Worthy Dr 92655 714-897-1009
Carrie Haskin, prin. Fax 373-0769

Westminster SD
Supt. — See Westminster
DeMille ES 500/PK-6
15400 Van Buren St 92655 714-894-7224
Shannon Villanueva, prin. Fax 372-8806
Hayden ES 900/PK-5
14782 Eden St 92655 714-894-7261
Mark Murphy, prin. Fax 379-1774

Millbrae, San Mateo, Pop. 20,615
Millbrae ESD 2,400/K-8
555 Richmond Dr 94030 650-697-5693
Vahn Phayprasert, supt. Fax 697-6865
www.millbraeschooldistrict.org
Green Hills ES 400/K-5
401 Ludeman Ln 94030 650-588-6485
Peter Fong, prin. Fax 583-8052
Meadows ES 400/K-5
1101 Helen Dr 94030 650-583-7590
Daina Lujan, prin. Fax 588-5461
Spring Valley ES 400/K-5
817 Murchison Dr 94030 650-697-5681
Kathleen D'or-Reid, prin. Fax 697-2931
Taylor MS 900/6-8
850 Taylor Blvd 94030 650-697-4096
Phillip Hophan, prin. Fax 697-8435
Other Schools – See San Bruno

St. Dunstan S 300/K-8
1150 Magnolia Ave 94030 650-697-8119
James Spray, prin. Fax 697-9295

Mill Valley, Marin, Pop. 13,420
Mill Valley ESD 3,300/K-8
411 Sycamore Ave 94941 415-389-7700
Paul Johnson, supt. Fax 389-7773
www.mvschools.org
Maguire ES 600/K-5
80 Lomita Dr 94941 415-389-7733
Leo Kostelnik, prin. Fax 389-7776
Mill Valley MS 1,000/6-8
425 Sycamore Ave 94941 415-389-7711
Anna Lazzarini, prin. Fax 389-7780
Old Mill ES 300/K-5
352 Throckmorton Ave 94941 415-389-7727
Jason Deppong, prin. Fax 389-7778
Park ES 400/K-5
360 E Blithedale Ave 94941 415-389-7735
Kim Kirley, prin. Fax 389-7779
Strawberry Point ES 400/K-5
117 E Strawberry Dr 94941 415-389-7660
Leslie Cohl, prin. Fax 380-2499
Tamalpais Valley ES 500/K-5
350 Bell Ln 94941 415-389-7731
Laura Myers, prin. Fax 389-7781

Greenwood S 100/K-8
17 Buena Vista Ave 94941 415-388-0495
Shaheer Faltas, head sch Fax 388-6895
Marin Horizon S 300/PK-8
305 Montford Ave 94941 415-388-8408
Cathy Hunter, head sch Fax 388-7831
Mt. Tamalpais S 200/K-8
100 Harvard Ave 94941 415-383-9434
Andrew Davis, dir. Fax 383-7519
Ring Mountain Day S 100/K-8
70 Lomita Dr 94941 415-381-8183

Millville, Shasta, Pop. 710
Millville ESD 200/K-8
8570 Brookdale Rd 96062 530-547-4471
Mindy DeSantis, supt. Fax 547-3760
www.millvilleschool.net
Millville ES 200/K-8
8570 Brookdale Rd 96062 530-547-4471
Mindy DeSantis, prin. Fax 547-3760

Milpitas, Santa Clara, Pop. 64,272
Milpitas USD 10,200/PK-12
1331 E Calaveras Blvd 95035 408-635-2600
Cheryl Jordan, supt. Fax 635-2616
www.musd.org
Burnett ES 700/K-6
400 Fanyon St 95035 408-635-2650
Richard Julian, prin. Fax 635-2655
Curtner ES 700/K-6
275 Redwood Ave 95035 408-635-2852
Jackie Vo Felbinger, prin. Fax 635-2857
Pomeroy ES 700/K-6
1505 Escuela Pkwy 95035 408-635-2858
Nichol Klein, prin. Fax 635-2863
Rancho Milpitas MS 700/7-8
1915 Yellowstone Ave 95035 408-635-2656
Casey McMurray, prin. Fax 635-2661
Randall ES 400/K-6
1300 Edsel Dr 95035 408-635-2662
Carlos Salcido, prin. Fax 635-2667
Rose Child Development Center 100/PK-PK
250A Roswell Dr 95035 408-635-2686
Gerardo Lopez, coord. Fax 635-9503
Rose ES 500/K-6
250 Roswell Dr 95035 408-635-2668
Nanci Pass, prin. Fax 635-2673
Russell MS 800/7-8
1500 Escuela Pkwy 95035 408-635-2864
Damon James, prin. Fax 635-2869
Sinnott ES 800/K-6
2025 Yellowstone Ave 95035 408-635-2674
Laurie Armino, prin. Fax 635-2679
Spangler ES 500/K-6
140 N Abbott Ave 95035 408-635-2870
Catherine Waslif, prin. Fax 635-2875
Sunnyhills Child Development Center 100/PK-PK
356 Dixon Rd 95035 408-945-5577
Gerardo Lopez, coord. Fax 945-2779
Weller ES 500/K-6
345 Boulder St 95035 408-635-2876
Alicia Padilla, prin. Fax 635-2880
Zanker ES 700/K-6
1585 Fallen Leaf Dr 95035 408-635-2882
Trisha Lee, prin. Fax 635-2887

Foothill Adventist ES 100/PK-8
1991 Landess Ave 95035 408-263-2568
Patricia Carpio, prin. Fax 263-1994
Merryhill ES, 1500 Yosemite Dr 95035 500/PK-8
Quinn Letan, prin. 408-945-9090
Monarch Christian S 50/K-5
136 Piedmont Rd 95035 408-263-4842
Asunta Reinman, admin. Fax 263-4840
St. John the Baptist S 200/PK-8
360 S Abel St 95035 408-262-8110
Christopher Brazil, prin. Fax 262-0814
Stratford S - Milpitas PK-8
341 Great Mall Pkwy 95035 408-262-6200
Philip Dolan M.A., head sch

Mira Loma, Riverside, Pop. 21,582
Corona-Norco USD
Supt. — See Norco
VanderMolen Fundamental ES 1,100/K-6
6744 Carnelian St 91752 951-739-7120
Jeremy Barnes, prin. Fax 739-7128

Miranda, Humboldt, Pop. 496
Southern Humbolt JUSD 800/PK-12
PO Box 650 95553 707-943-1789
Don Boyd, supt. Fax 943-1921
Miranda JHS 100/7-8
PO Box 188 95553 707-943-3144
Don Boyd, prin. Fax 943-3129
Other Schools – See Blocksburg, Redway, Weott, Whitethorn

Mission Hills, Los Angeles, Pop. 3,460
Los Angeles USD
Supt. — See Los Angeles
San Jose ES 700/K-5
14928 Clymer St 91345 818-365-3218
Catherine Estrada, prin. Fax 365-5067

Mission Viejo, Orange, Pop. 89,770
Capistrano USD
Supt. — See San Juan Capistrano
Bathgate ES 700/K-5
27642 Napoli Way 92692 949-348-0451
Shelly Kurtz, prin. Fax 348-0426
Castille ES 600/K-5
24042 Via La Coruna 92691 949-234-5976
Laura Lyon, prin. Fax 586-6739
Hankey S 400/K-8
27252 Nubles 92692 949-234-5315
Dana Aguilera, prin. Fax 347-0536
Newhart MS 1,300/6-8
25001 Veterans Way 92692 949-855-0162
Jeff Jones, prin. Fax 770-1262

Reilly ES 500/K-5
24171 Pavion 92692 949-454-1590
Sharla Pitzen, prin. Fax 588-6315
Viejo ES 400/K-5
26782 Via Grande 92691 949-582-2424
Jesus Becerra, prin. Fax 348-2499

Saddleback Valley USD 29,800/PK-12
25631 Peter A Hartman Way 92691 949-586-1234
Crystal Turner, supt. Fax 951-0994
www.svusd.org
Cordillera ES 700/K-6
25952 Cordillera Dr 92691 949-830-3400
Deborah Shaver, prin. Fax 830-7673
Del Cerro ES 500/K-6
24382 Regina St 92691 949-830-5430
Larry Callison, prin. Fax 830-5151
Del Lago ES 700/K-6
27181 Entidad 92691 949-855-1125
Jennifer Televik, prin. Fax 829-6733
De Portola ES 600/K-6
27031 Preciados Dr 92691 949-586-5830
Michael Gomez, prin. Fax 586-5876
Glen Yermo ES 400/K-6
26400 Trabuco Rd 92691 949-586-6766
Lisa Graham, prin. Fax 837-3528
La Paz IS 1,000/7-8
25151 Pradera Dr 92691 949-830-1720
Jean Walker, prin. Fax 830-3320
La Tierra ECC 100/PK-PK
24150 Lindley St 92691 949-707-5276
Marion Springett, prin. Fax 598-3755
Linda Vista ES 400/K-6
25222 Pericia Dr 92691 949-830-0970
Suzanne McMasters, prin. Fax 830-9237
Los Alisos IS 900/7-8
25171 Moor Ave 92691 949-830-9700
Rich Freda, prin. Fax 472-3968
Montevideo ES 500/K-6
24071 Carrillo Dr 92691 949-586-8050
Mona Montgomery, prin. Fax 586-4633
Other Schools – See Foothill Ranch, Laguna Hills, Lake Forest, Rancho Santa Margarita, Trabuco Canyon

---

Carden Academy 200/K-8
24741 Chrisanta Dr 92691 949-458-1776
P.L. de Avila, dir. Fax 458-5071
Heritage Christian S 200/PK-11
22081 Hidalgo 92691 949-598-9166
George Gay M.A., prin. Fax 598-1892
Mission Viejo Christian S 200/K-8
24701 San Doval Ln 92691 949-465-1950
Bob Sladek, prin. Fax 465-1949
Stratford S - Mission Viejo PK-8
24741 Chrisanta Dr 92691 949-458-1776
P.L. de Avila, dir.

Modesto, Stanislaus, Pop. 192,307
Ceres USD
Supt. — See Ceres
Adkison ES 600/K-6
1824 Nadine Ave 95351 209-556-1600
Antony Little, prin. Fax 531-0216
Parks ES 700/PK-6
1021 Moffett Rd 95351 209-556-1670
Jennifer Backman, prin. Fax 531-0619
Westport ES 500/K-6
5218 S Carpenter Rd 95358 209-556-1700
Jennifer Cervantes, prin. Fax 537-9589

Empire UNESD 3,000/PK-8
116 N McClure Rd 95357 209-521-2800
David Garcia, supt. Fax 526-6421
www.empire.k12.ca.us
Capistrano ES 500/PK-6
400 Capistrano Dr 95354 209-521-8664
James Jensen, prin. Fax 575-0734
Glick MS 600/7-8
400 Frazine Rd 95357 209-577-3945
Isaias Rumayor, prin. Fax 577-3975
Hughes ES 500/PK-6
512 N McClure Rd 95357 209-527-1330
Jeri Hamera, prin. Fax 550-0537
Sipherd ES 500/K-6
3420 E Orangeburg Ave 95355 209-524-4844
Tiffany Davenport, prin. Fax 569-0913
Stroud ES 400/PK-6
815 Frazine Rd 95357 209-491-0754
Scott Borba, prin. Fax 529-3738
Other Schools – See Empire

Hart-Ransom UNESD 1,100/PK-12
3920 Shoemake Ave 95358 209-523-9996
Matthew Shipley, supt. Fax 523-9997
www.hartransom.org
Hart-Ransom ES 800/K-8
3930 Shoemake Ave 95358 209-523-9979
Jerrianna Boer, prin. Fax 523-0588

Modesto CSD 29,900/K-12
426 Locust St 95351 209-574-1500
Pamela Able, supt. Fax 576-4184
www.monet.k12.ca.us
Beard ES 400/K-6
915 Bowen Ave 95350 209-574-1942
Beth Weston, prin. Fax 569-2757
Bret Harte ES 900/K-6
909 Glenn Ave 95358 209-576-4673
Marla Conteh, prin. Fax 576-4288
Burbank ES 700/K-6
1135 Paradise Rd 95351 209-574-1962
James Mendonca, prin. Fax 576-4859
El Vista ES 400/K-6
450 El Vista Ave 95354 209-576-4665
Don Jackson, prin. Fax 576-4567
Enslen ES 400/K-6
515 Coldwell Ave 95354 209-574-1982
Sarah Cox, prin. Fax 569-2731
Everett ES 400/K-6
1530 Mount Vernon Dr 95350 209-574-1992
Gretchen Griffin, prin. Fax 576-4069

Fairview ES 900/K-6
1937 W Whitmore Ave 95358 209-574-8102
Paulo Pimentel, prin. Fax 576-4696
Franklin ES 900/K-6
120 S Emerald Ave 95351 209-574-8112
Scott Genzmer, prin. Fax 576-4853
Fremont ES 600/K-6
1220 W Orangeburg Ave 95350 209-574-8122
Lori Jonas, prin. Fax 569-2754
Garrison ES 300/K-6
1811 Teresa St 95350 209-574-8132
Chanthon Phe, prin. Fax 576-4640
Hanshaw MS 800/7-8
1725 Las Vegas St 95358 209-574-1794
Jesika Farhadi, prin. Fax 576-4723
Kirschen ES 700/K-6
1900 Kirschen Dr 95351 209-576-4611
Millie Griggs, prin. Fax 576-4270
Lakewood ES 400/K-6
2920 Middleboro Pl 95355 209-574-8152
Denise Powell, prin. Fax 576-4980
La Loma JHS 700/7-8
1800 Encina Ave 95354 209-574-1906
Dan Iverson, prin. Fax 576-4631
Marshall ES 800/K-6
515 Sutter Ave 95351 209-576-4697
Francisco Guerrero, prin. Fax 576-4699
Martone ES 700/K-6
1413 Poust Rd 95358 209-574-8172
Heidi Nunes, prin. Fax 569-2753
Muir ES 500/K-6
1215 Lucern Ave 95350 209-574-8182
Megan Reisz, prin. Fax 569-2755
Robertson Road ES 400/K-6
1821 Robertson Rd 95351 209-574-8402
Kathryne Pound, prin. Fax 576-4642
Roosevelt JHS 800/7-8
1330 College Ave 95350 209-576-4871
David Sanchez, prin. Fax 569-2713
Rose Avenue ES 600/K-6
1120 Rose Ave 95355 209-574-8412
Heather Herbst, prin. Fax 569-2752
Shackelford ES 600/K-6
100 School Ave 95351 209-574-8422
Ignacio Cantu, prin. Fax 576-4860
Sonoma ES 500/K-6
1325 Sonoma Ave 95355 209-574-8432
Darin Willett, prin. Fax 576-2725
Tuolumne ES 700/K-6
707 Herndon Rd 95351 209-574-8442
Linda Diaz, prin. Fax 576-4663
Twain JHS 800/7-8
707 S Emerald Ave 95351 209-576-4814
Sherri Louthan, prin. Fax 576-4843
Wilson ES 300/K-6
201 Wilson Ave 95354 209-574-8452
Sue McHann, prin. Fax 569-2756
Wright ES 400/K-6
1602 Monterey Ave 95354 209-574-8462
Ernesto Calderon, prin. Fax 576-4824

Paradise ESD 200/K-8
3361 California Ave 95358 209-524-0184
Heath Thomason, supt. Fax 524-0363
www.paradiseesd.org
Paradise ES 100/K-8
3361 California Ave 95358 209-524-0184
Heath Thomason, prin. Fax 524-0363

Salida UNESD
Supt. — See Salida
Perkins ES 400/K-5
3920 Blue Bird Dr 95356 209-545-4415
Agustin Mireles, prin. Fax 545-4248

Shiloh ESD 200/K-12
6633 Paradise Rd 95358 209-522-2261
Seth Ehrler, supt. Fax 522-0188
www.shiloh.k12.ca.us
Shiloh ES 100/K-8
6633 Paradise Rd 95358 209-522-2261
Seth Ehrler, prin. Fax 522-0188

Stanislaus UNESD 3,200/K-8
2410 Janna Ave 95350 209-529-9546
Britta Skavdahl, supt. Fax 529-0243
www.stanunion.k12.ca.us
Baptist ES 600/K-6
1825 Cheyenne Way 95356 209-527-0450
Jim Schuller, prin. Fax 527-6351
Chrysler ES 600/K-6
2818 Conant Ave 95350 209-529-5430
Miguel Espinoza, prin. Fax 529-4401
Dieterich ES 600/K-6
2412 Warm Springs Dr 95356 209-550-8400
Sarah Gillum, prin. Fax 578-1520
Eisenhut ES 500/K-6
1809 Sheldon Dr 95350 209-527-7867
Trish Anderson, prin. Fax 527-3438
Prescott JHS 700/7-8
2243 W Rumble Rd 95350 209-529-9892
Harjinder Mattu, prin. Fax 529-4406
Stanislaus ES 300/K-6
1931 Kiernan Ave 95356 209-545-0718
Kimberly West, prin. Fax 543-7909

Sylvan Union ESD 8,200/K-8
605 Sylvan Ave 95350 209-574-5000
Debra M. Hendricks, supt. Fax 524-2672
www.sylvan.k12.ca.us
Brown ES 400/K-5
2024 Vera Cruz Dr 95355 209-574-5100
Katie Bennett, prin. Fax 524-6278
Coffee ES 500/K-5
3900 Northview Dr 95355 209-574-5500
Lauric Hulin, prin. Fax 521-5601
Freedom ES 700/K-5
2101 Fine Ave 95355 209-552-3400
Audry Garza, prin. Fax 552-3405
Orchard ES 500/K-5
1800 Wisdom Way 95355 209-552-3100
Travis Manley, prin. Fax 552-3105

Sanders ES 600/K-5
3101 Fine Ave 95355 209-552-3200
Carrie Albert, prin. Fax 552-3205
Savage MS 1,000/6-8
1900 Maid Mariane Ln 95355 209-552-3300
Michael Stagnaro, prin. Fax 552-3305
Sherwood ES 500/K-5
819 E Rumble Rd 95350 209-574-5200
Scott Ferriera, prin. Fax 574-5202
Somerset MS 900/6-8
1037 Floyd Ave 95350 209-574-5300
Lisa Ferguson, prin. Fax 529-1110
Standiford ES 500/K-5
605 Tokay Ave 95350 209-574-5400
Amber Wethern, prin. Fax 524-7405
Sylvan ES 300/K-5
2908 Coffee Rd 95355 209-574-5600
Tedde' Vaupel, prin. Fax 527-6259
Ustach MS 1,000/6-8
2701 Kodiak Dr 95355 209-552-3000
Gary Miller, prin. Fax 552-3010
Woodrow ES 400/K-5
800 Woodrow Ave 95350 209-574-5700
Nancee Davis, prin. Fax 574-5010
Other Schools – See Riverbank

Big Valley Christian S 700/PK-12
4040 Tully Rd Ste D 95356 209-527-3481
Michelle Mott, supt. Fax 529-1748
Brethren Heritage S 100/K-12
3549 Dakota Ave 95358 209-543-7860
John Fall, prin. Fax 543-7862
Modesto Christian S 300/PK-12
5755 Sisk Rd 95356 209-529-5510
Dr. Jonathan Burton, supt.
Our Lady of Fatima S 200/K-8
501 W Granger Ave 95350 209-524-4170
Melissa Neder, prin. Fax 524-7713
St. Stanislaus S 200/PK-8
1416 Maze Blvd 95351 209-524-9036
Mercedes Hollcraft, prin. Fax 524-4344

Mojave, Kern, Pop. 4,110
Mojave USD 2,700/PK-12
3500 Douglas Ave 93501 661-824-4001
Dr. Aaron Haughton, supt. Fax 824-2686
www.mojave.k12.ca.us/
Mojave ES 500/PK-5
15800 O St 93501 661-824-2456
Daniel Sexton, prin. Fax 824-2461
Other Schools – See California City

Mokelumne Hill, Calaveras, Pop. 628
Calaveras USD
Supt. — See San Andreas
Mokelumne Hill ES 100/K-6
8350 Highway 26 95245 209-754-2140
Michelle Besmer, prin. Fax 286-1038

Monrovia, Los Angeles, Pop. 35,498
Monrovia USD 6,000/PK-12
325 E Huntington Dr 91016 626-471-2000
Dr. Katherine Thorossian, supt. Fax 471-2077
www.monroviaschools.net
Bradoaks ES 600/K-5
930 E Lemon Ave 91016 626-471-2100
Aimee Dyrek, prin. Fax 471-2110
Canyon Early Learning Center PK-PK
1000 S Canyon Blvd 91016 626-471-2001
Mariana Sanchez, dir. Fax 471-2086
Clifton MS 700/6-8
226 S Ivy Ave 91016 626-471-2600
Jennifer Jackson, prin. Fax 471-2610
Mayflower ES 600/K-5
210 N Mayflower Ave 91016 626-471-2200
Michelle Costarella, prin. Fax 471-2210
Monroe ES 500/K-5
402 W Colorado Blvd 91016 626-471-2300
Dr. Lily Jarvis, prin. Fax 471-2310
Plymouth ES 400/K-5
1300 Boley St 91016 626-471-2400
Greg Gero, prin. Fax 471-2410
Santa Fe Computer Science Magnet S 700/6-8
148 W Duarte Rd 91016 626-471-2700
Geoff Zamarripa, prin. Fax 471-2710
Wild Rose ES 500/K-5
232 Jasmine Ave 91016 626-471-2500
Dr. Leslie Miller, prin. Fax 471-2510

Immaculate Conception/Annunciation S 200/K-8
726 S Shamrock Ave 91016 626-358-5129
Carmela Lovano, prin. Fax 358-3933

Montague, Siskiyou, Pop. 1,370
Big Springs UNESD 100/K-8
7405 County Highway A12 96064 530-459-3189
Gilbert Pimentel, supt. Fax 459-3201
www.bgsp.k12.ca.us
Big Springs ES 100/K-8
7405 County Highway A12 96064 530-459-3189
Janet Thomsen, prin. Fax 459-3201

Bogus ESD 50/K-7
13735 Ager Beswick Rd 96064 530-459-3163
Kermith Walters, supt. Fax 459-0706
sites.google.com/a/sisnet.ssku.k12.ca.us/bogus-elementary
Bogus ES 50/K-7
13735 Ager Beswick Rd 96064 530-459-3163
Marilee Dalton, prin. Fax 459-0706

Delphic ESD 100/K-8
1420 Delphic Rd 96064 530-842-3653
Jami Thomas, supt. Fax 842-0249
Delphic ES 100/K-8
1420 Delphic Rd 96064 530-842-3653
Jami Thomas, prin. Fax 842-0249

Little Shasta ESD 50/K-6
8409 Lower Little Shasta Rd 96064 530-459-3269
Todd Clark, supt. Fax 459-1619
lse-lsesd-ca.schoolloop.com/
Little Shasta ES 50/K-6
8409 Lower Little Shasta Rd 96064 530-459-3269
Todd Clark, prin. Fax 459-1619

Montague ESD 200/PK-8
PO Box 308 96064 530-459-3001
Marni Posl, supt. Fax 459-3788
www.montague.k12.ca.us
Montague S 200/PK-8
PO Box 308 96064 530-459-3001
Marni Posl, prin. Fax 459-3788

Willow Creek ESD 50/K-8
5321 York Rd 96064 530-459-3313
Ron Ferrando, supt. Fax 459-1537
www.willowcreek.k12.ca.us
Willow Creek ES 50/K-8
5321 York Rd 96064 530-459-3313
Ron Ferrando, supt. Fax 459-1537

Montara, San Mateo, Pop. 2,798
Cabrillo USD
Supt. — See Half Moon Bay
Farallone View ES 400/K-5
1100 LeConte Ave 94037 650-712-7170
Cesar Gaytan, prin. Fax 728-3352

Montclair, San Bernardino, Pop. 36,107
Ontario-Montclair SD
Supt. — See Ontario
Buena Vista Arts-Integrated S 400/K-6
5685 San Bernardino St 91763 909-984-9556
Nick Zajicek, prin. Fax 459-2602
Howard ES 700/PK-6
4650 Howard St 91763 909-591-2339
Kelly Guillen, prin. Fax 517-3943
Kingsley ES 800/PK-6
5625 Kingsley St 91763 909-984-3634
Hugo Lopez, prin. Fax 459-2848
Lehigh ES 700/PK-6
10200 Lehigh Ave 91763 909-624-5697
Christiane Ayoub-Garcia, prin. Fax 445-1613
Montera ES 600/PK-6
4825 Bandera St 91763 909-445-1062
Rudy Sandoval, prin. Fax 445-1493
Monte Vista ES 700/PK-6
4900 Orchard St 91763 909-626-5046
Sultana Dixon, prin. Fax 445-1650
Moreno ES 500/PK-6
4825 Moreno St 91763 909-445-1661
Amy D'Andrea, prin. Fax 445-1662
Ramona ES 800/PK-6
4225 Howard St 91763 909-627-3411
Ricky Ramirez, prin. Fax 517-3987
Serrano MS 800/7-8
4725 San Jose St 91763 909-624-0029
Mauricio Gormaz, prin. Fax 445-1687
Vernon MS 800/7-8
9775 Vernon Ave 91763 909-624-5036
Kim Tovar, prin. Fax 445-1720

Our Lady of Lourdes S 200/K-8
5303 Orchard St 91763 909-621-4418
Beverly Diaz DeLeon, prin. Fax 625-5034

Montebello, Los Angeles, Pop. 62,028
Montebello USD 29,900/K-12
123 S Montebello Blvd 90640 323-887-7900
Dr. Anthony Martinez Ph.D., supt. Fax 887-5890
www.montebello.k12.ca.us
Eastmont IS 1,000/6-8
400 Bradshawe St 90640 323-721-5133
Cecilia Ramirez, prin. Fax 887-3058
Fremont ES 500/K-5
200 W Madison Ave 90640 323-721-2435
Dr. Norma Lopez-Reid, prin. Fax 887-3139
Greenwood ES 1,100/K-5
900 S Greenwood Ave 90640 323-721-4605
Maria Valenzuela, prin. Fax 887-5882
La Merced ES 800/K-5
724 N Poplar Ave 90640 323-721-5043
Rebecca Castro, prin. Fax 887-5806
La Merced IS 1,300/6-8
215 E Avenida De La Merced 90640 323-722-7262
Constantino Duarte, prin. Fax 887-5816
Montebello IS 1,200/6-8
1600 W Whittier Blvd 90640 323-721-5111
Sterling Schubert, prin. Fax 887-3192
Washington ES 1,000/K-5
1400 W Madison Ave 90640 323-721-3621
Elizabeth Rodarte, prin. Fax 887-5891
Wilcox ES 700/K-5
816 Donna Way 90640 323-728-1833
Leo Gallegos, prin. Fax 887-3096
Other Schools – See Bell Gardens, Commerce, Los Angeles, Monterey Park, Pico Rivera, South San Gabriel

---

Montebello Christian S 100/K-8
136 S 7th St 90640 323-728-4119
Victoria Martinez, admin. Fax 728-8396
Our Lady of The Miraculous Medal S 500/PK-8
840 N Garfield Ave 90640 323-728-5435
Analisa Moreno, prin. Fax 728-8038
St. Benedict S 600/K-8
217 N 10th St 90640 323-721-3348
Frank Loya, prin. Fax 721-8698

Monterey, Monterey, Pop. 26,593
Monterey Peninsula USD 10,800/PK-12
PO Box 1031 93942 831-645-1200
Dr. Daniel Diffenbaugh, supt. Fax 649-4175
www.mpusd.k12.ca.us
Colton MS 700/6-8
100 Toda Vis 93940 831-649-1951
Joshua Phillips, prin. Fax 649-4692
Foothill ES 400/K-5
1700 Via Casoli 93940 831-649-1744
Lauren Park, prin. Fax 649-3428
La Mesa ES 400/K-5
1 La Mesa Way 93940 831-649-1872
Phillip Menchaca, prin. Fax 649-3942
Monte Vista ES 400/K-5
251 Soledad Dr 93940 831-392-3890
Joseph Ashby, prin. Fax 392-3894
Other Schools – See Marina, Seaside

San Carlos S 300/K-8
450 Church St 93940 831-375-1324
Teresa Bennett, prin. Fax 375-9736
Santa Catalina S 500/PK-12
1500 Mark Thomas Dr 93940 831-655-9300
Margaret Bradley, head sch Fax 649-3056

Monterey Park, Los Angeles, Pop. 59,435
Alhambra USD
Supt. — See Alhambra
Brightwood S 1,000/K-8
1701 Brightwood St 91754 626-570-6200
Natalie Tee Gaither, prin. Fax 308-2407
Monterey Highlands S 1,000/K-8
400 Casuda Canyon Dr 91754 626-570-6220
Dr. Debbie Kotani, prin. Fax 308-2429
Repetto S 800/K-8
650 S Grandridge Ave 91754 626-570-6240
Carin Gasca, prin. Fax 572-2233
Ynez S 900/K-8
120 S Ynez Ave 91754 626-570-6260
Stacie Colman-Hsu, prin. Fax 571-8265

Garvey ESD
Supt. — See Rosemead
Hillcrest ES 400/K-6
795 Pepper St 91755 626-307-3371
Robin Libby, prin. Fax 572-4225
Monterey Vista ES 500/K-6
901 E Graves Ave 91755 626-307-3300
Hing Chow, prin. Fax 307-3490

Los Angeles USD
Supt. — See Los Angeles
Lane ES 400/K-6
1500 Avenida Cesar Chavez 91754 323-263-3877
Josefina Flores, prin. Fax 263-7600

Montebello USD
Supt. — See Montebello
Bella Vista ES 700/K-5
2410 Findlay Ave 91754 323-721-4335
Stephanie Hardaway, prin. Fax 887-3077
Macy IS 900/6-8
2101 Lupine Ave 91755 323-722-0260
Jacinto Zavala, prin. Fax 887-3068

Meher Montessori S 50/PK-8
2009 S Garfield Ave 91754 323-724-0683
Adela Munoz, dir. Fax 724-0028
St. Stephen Martyr S 100/PK-8
119 S Ramona Ave 91754 626-573-1716
Christina Arellano, prin. Fax 573-3251
St. Thomas Aquinas S 200/K-8
1501 S Atlantic Blvd 91754 323-261-6583
Gloria Castillo, prin. Fax 261-5972

Monte Rio, Sonoma, Pop. 1,101
Monte Rio UNESD 100/K-8
20700 Foothill Dr 95462 707-865-2200
Ross Bickford, supt. Fax 865-9356
www.monterioschool.org/
Monte Rio S 100/K-8
20700 Foothill Dr 95462 707-865-2266
Ross Bickford, admin. Fax 865-9356

Monte Sereno, Santa Clara, Pop. 3,221
Los Gatos UNESD
Supt. — See Los Gatos
Daves Avenue ES 600/K-5
17770 Daves Ave 95030 408-335-2200
Iqbal Chadda, prin. Fax 395-6314

Montgomery Creek, Shasta, Pop. 149
Mountain UNESD 100/PK-8
PO Box 368 96065 530-337-6214
Wendy Platt, supt. Fax 337-6215
mcs-shastacoe-ca.schoolloop.com
Montgomery Creek ES 100/PK-8
PO Box 368 96065 530-337-6214
Wendy Platt, admin. Fax 337-6215

Montrose, See La Crescenta

Armenian Sisters' Academy PK-8
2361 Florencita Ave 91020 818-249-8783
Armenian Sisters Academy 300/PK-8
2361 Florencita Ave 91020 818-249-8783
Sr. Jeanette Taslakian, prin. Fax 249-7288
Montrose Christian Montessori S 100/K-6
2545 Honolulu Ave 91020 818-249-2319
Scott Lee, dir. Fax 249-6290
St. Monica Academy 200/1-12
2361 Del Mar Rd 91020 818-369-7310
Marguerite Grimm, hdmstr. Fax 369-7305

Moorpark, Ventura, Pop. 33,338
Moorpark USD 6,800/K-12
5297 Maureen Ln 93021 805-378-6300
Dr. Kelli Hays, supt. Fax 529-8592
www.mrpk.org
Arroyo West ES 400/K-5
4117 Country Hill Rd 93021 805-378-6308
Angela Ryals, prin. Fax 531-6611
Campus Canyon ES 600/K-8
15300 Monroe Ave 93021 805-378-6301
Susan Rossiter, prin. Fax 531-6612
Chaparral MS 600/6-8
280 Poindexter Ave 93021 805-378-6302
Scott Carroll, prin. Fax 378-6324
Flory Academy of Sciences and Technology 500/K-5
240 Flory Ave 93021 805-378-6303
Scott Mastroianni, prin. Fax 531-6609
Mesa Verde MS 700/6-8
14000 Peach Hill Rd 93021 805-378-6309
Adam Rauch, prin. Fax 531-6622
Mountain Meadows ES 500/K-5
4200 Mountain Meadow Dr 93021 805-378-6306
Marcia Hamilton, prin. Fax 531-6624
Peach Hill Academy 500/K-5
13400 Christian Barrett Dr 93021 805-378-6307
Vicky Yasenchok, prin. Fax 531-6450
Walnut Canyon ES 500/K-5
280 Casey Rd 93021 805-517-1722
Theresa Garner, prin. Fax 517-1726

Moraga, Contra Costa, Pop. 15,277
Moraga ESD 1,800/PK-8
1540 School St 94556 925-376-5943
Bruce K. Burns, supt. Fax 376-8132
www.moraga.k12.ca.us
Camino Pablo ES 400/PK-5
1111 Camino Pablo 94556 925-376-4435
Chris Reddam, prin. Fax 376-6749
Los Perales ES 400/PK-5
22 Wakefield Dr 94556 925-631-0105
Stephanie Richards, prin. Fax 376-7452
Moraga IS 600/6-8
1010 Camino Pablo 94556 925-376-7206
Joan Danilson, prin. Fax 376-6836
Rheem ES 400/K-5
90 Laird Dr 94556 925-376-4441
Brian Sullivan, prin. Fax 376-3248

Saklan S 100/PK-8
1678 School St 94556 925-376-7900
Hans Peter Metzger, head sch Fax 376-1156

Moreno Valley, Riverside, Pop. 186,933
Moreno Valley USD 34,200/K-12
25634 Alessandro Blvd 92553 951-571-7500
Martinrex Kedziora Ed.D., supt. Fax 571-7550
www.mvusd.net
Armada ES 700/K-5
25201 John F Kennedy Dr 92551 951-571-4500
Mario Perez, prin. Fax 571-4505
Badger Springs MS 1,200/6-8
24750 Delphinium Ave 92553 951-571-4200
Jason Barney, prin. Fax 571-4205
Bear Valley ES 900/K-5
26125 Fir Ave 92555 951-571-4520
Sam Stager, prin. Fax 571-4525
Box Springs ES 400/K-5
11900 Athens Dr 92557 951-571-4530
Wade Hamilton, prin. Fax 571-4535
Butterfield ES 800/K-5
13400 Kitching St 92553 951-571-4540
Esmerelda Chalfant, prin. Fax 571-4545
Chaparral Hills ES 800/K-5
24850 Delphinium Ave 92553 951-571-4730
Gregory White, prin. Fax 571-4735
Cloverdale ES 700/K-5
12050 Kitching St 92557 951-571-4550
Genaro Garcia, prin. Fax 571-4555
Creekside ES 700/K-5
13563 Heacock St 92553 951-571-4560
Nadakia Neal, prin. Fax 571-4565
Edgemont ES 700/K-5
21790 Eucalyptus Ave 92553 951-571-4570
Dr. Smiley Villavicencio, prin. Fax 571-4575
Hendrick Ranch ES 700/K-5
25570 Brodiaea Ave 92553 951-571-4580
Marie White, prin. Fax 571-4585
Hidden Springs ES 600/K-5
9801 Hidden Springs Dr 92557 951-571-4590
Latrice Thomas, prin. Fax 571-4595
Honey Hollow ES 600/K-5
11765 Honey Hollow 92557 951-571-4600
Joshua Jackson, prin. Fax 571-4605
La Jolla ES 800/K-5
14745 Willow Grove Pl 92555 951-571-4740
Tia May, prin. Fax 571-4745
Landmark MS 1,300/6-8
15261 Legendary Dr 92555 951-571-4220
Scott Walker, prin. Fax 571-4225
Midland ES 700/K-5
11440 Davis St 92557 951-571-4610
Alycia Benson, prin. Fax 571-4615
Moreno ES 600/K-5
26700 Cottonwood Ave 92555 951-571-4620
Penny Macon, prin. Fax 571-4625
Mountain View MS 1,200/6-8
13130 Morrison St 92555 951-571-4240
Jon Black, prin. Fax 571-4245
North Ridge ES 800/K-5
25101 Kalmia Ave 92557 951-571-4630
Dr. Casaundra McNair, prin. Fax 571-4635
Palm MS 1,300/6-8
11900 Slawson Ave 92557 951-571-4260
Mallanie Avinger, prin. Fax 571-4265
Ramona ES 800/K-5
24801 Bay Ave 92553 951-571-4720
Jeff Jones, prin. Fax 571-4725
Ridge Crest ES 600/K-5
28500 John F Kennedy Dr 92555 951-571-4640
Misty Kelley, prin. Fax 571-4645
Seneca ES 500/K-5
11615 Wordsworth Rd 92557 951-571-4650
Emilio Gallegos, prin. Fax 571-4655
Serrano ES 600/K-5
24100 Delphinium Ave 92553 951-571-4660
Maria Arreola, prin. Fax 571-4665
Sugar Hill ES 500/K-5
24455 Old Country Rd 92557 951-571-4670
Gwendolyn Green, prin. Fax 571-4675
Sunnymead ES 800/K-5
24050 Dracaea Ave 92553 951-571-4680
Marisa Brough, prin. Fax 571-4685
Sunnymead MS 1,500/6-8
23996 Eucalyptus Ave 92553 951-571-4280
Jennifer Castillo, prin. Fax 571-4285

Sunnymeadows ES 700/K-5
23200 Eucalyptus Ave 92553 951-571-4690
Vicky Dudek, prin. Fax 571-4695
TownGate ES 900/K-5
22480 Dracaea Ave 92553 951-571-4700
Paula Rynders, prin. Fax 571-4705
Vista Heights MS 1,400/6-8
23049 Old Lake Dr 92557 951-571-4300
Mark Hasson, prin. Fax 571-4305

Val Verde USD
Supt. — See Perris
Bethune ES 700/K-5
25390 Krameria St 92551 951-490-0380
Katrina Piche, prin. Fax 490-0385
El Potrero Preschool PK-PK
16820 Via Pamplona 92551 951-940-8530
Julie Singletary, prin. Fax 940-8535
Lasselle ES 800/K-5
26446 Krameria Ave 92555 951-490-0350
Tom Gronotte, prin. Fax 490-0355
March MS 800/6-8
15800 Indian St 92551 951-490-0430
Jim Owen, prin. Fax 490-0435
Rainbow Ridge ES 800/K-5
15950 Indian St 92551 951-490-0420
Laura Pulido, prin. Fax 490-0425
Victoriano ES 700/K-5
25650 Los Cabos Dr 92551 951-490-0390
Molly Large, prin. Fax 490-0395
Vista Verde MS 1,000/6-8
25777 Krameria St 92551 951-485-6270
Esperanza Arce, prin. Fax 485-6278

Calvary Chapel Christian S 300/K-12
28010 Ironwood Ave 92555 951-485-6088
Tim Hamilton, prin. Fax 485-6718
St. Christopher Preschool 50/PK-PK
25075 Cottonwood Ave 92553 951-571-8347
Eleanor Manucal, dir. Fax 571-8348
Valley Adventist Christian S 50/K-8
12649 Indian St Ste 100 92553 951-242-3012
Kimberly Matthews, prin. Fax 247-1245
Valley Christian Academy 200/PK-8
26755 Alessandro Blvd 92555 951-242-5683
Patrick Peacock, admin. Fax 242-6185

Morgan Hill, Santa Clara, Pop. 36,440
Morgan Hill USD 8,600/PK-12
15600 Concord Cir 95037 408-201-6000
Steve Betando, supt. Fax 201-6007
www.mhusd.org
Barrett ES 500/K-5
895 Barrett Ave 95037 408-201-6340
Mary Alice Callahan, prin. Fax 201-6350
Britton MS 600/6-8
80 W Central Ave 95037 408-201-6160
Chris Moore, prin. Fax 201-6175
El Toro Health Science Academy 400/PK-5
455 E Main Ave 95037 408-201-6380
Darren McDonald, prin. Fax 201-6390
Jackson Academy of Music and Math 600/K-8
2700 Fountain Oaks Dr 95037 408-201-6400
Patrick Buchser, prin. Fax 776-8065
Nordstrom ES 600/K-5
1425 E Dunne Ave 95037 408-201-6440
Debbie Grove, prin. Fax 201-6450
Paradise Valley/Machado ES 600/PK-5
1400 La Crosse Dr 95037 408-201-6460
Swati Dagar, prin. Fax 201-6470
Walsh ES 500/PK-5
353 W Main Ave 95037 408-201-6500
Teresa Sermersheim, prin. Fax 201-6510
Other Schools – See San Jose, San Martin

Crossroads Christian S 100/PK-5
145 Wright Ave 95037 408-779-8850
Marsha Anguiano, prin. Fax 779-0444
Oakwood S 400/PK-12
105 John Wilson Way 95037 408-782-7177
Patty Crone, prin. Fax 782-7138
St. Catherine S 300/K-8
17500 Peak Ave 95037 408-779-9950
Fabienne Esparza, prin. Fax 779-9928
Stratford S - Morgan Hill 100/PK-5
410 Llagas Rd 95037 408-776-8801
Cheryl Damato, prin. Fax 776-8804

Morongo Valley, San Bernardino, Pop. 3,458
Morongo USD
Supt. — See Twentynine Palms
Morongo Valley ES 200/K-6
10951 Hess Blvd 92256 760-363-6216
Georgianne Pope, prin. Fax 363-8185

Morro Bay, San Luis Obispo, Pop. 10,002
San Luis Coastal USD
Supt. — See San Luis Obispo
Del Mar ES 500/PK-5
501 Sequoia St 93442 805-771-1858
Janet Gould, prin. Fax 772-0859

Moss Landing, Monterey, Pop. 194
North Monterey County USD 4,400/K-12
8142 Moss Landing Rd 95039 831-633-3343
Kari Yeater, supt. Fax 633-2937
www.nmcusd.org
Other Schools – See Castroville, Salinas

Mountain House, San Joaquin, Pop. 9,039
Lammersville USD 3,800/PK-10
111 S De Anza Blvd 95391 209-836-7400
Dr. Kirk Nicholas, supt. Fax 836-7402
www.lammersvilleschooldistrict.net
Altamont ES 700/PK-8
452 W Saint Francis Ave 95391 209-836-7240
James Yeager, admin. Fax 836-7242
Bethany ES 800/K-8
570 S Escuela Dr 95391 209-836-7250
Deborah Wingo, prin. Fax 836-7252
Sebastian Questa ES 900/K-8
685 N Montebello St 95391 209-836-7230
Heather Sharp, prin. Fax 836-7232
Wicklund ES 700/K-8
300 E Legacy Dr 95391 209-836-7200
Ryan Gonzales, prin. Fax 836-7202
Other Schools – See Tracy

Mountain View, Santa Clara, Pop. 70,771
Los Altos ESD
Supt. — See Los Altos
Springer ES 500/K-6
1120 Rose Ave 94040 650-943-4200
Lynn Boskie, prin. Fax 965-9683

Mountain View Whisman SD 5,000/K-8
750A San Pierre Way 94043 650-526-3500
Dr. Ayindo Rudolph, supt. Fax 964-8907
www.mvwsd.org
Bubb ES 500/K-5
525 Hans Ave 94040 650-526-3480
Cyndee Nguyen, prin. Fax 428-1556
Castro ES 700/K-5
505 Escuela Ave 94040 650-526-3590
Terri Lambert, prin. Fax 964-9013
Crittenden MS 600/6-8
1701 Rock St 94043 650-903-6945
Angie Dillman, prin. Fax 967-1707
Graham MS 800/6-8
1175 Castro St 94040 650-526-3570
Kim Thompson, prin. Fax 965-9278
Huff ES 600/K-5
253 Martens Ave 94040 650-526-3490
Geoff Chang, prin. Fax 564-9046
Landels ES 500/K-5
115 W Dana St 94041 650-526-3520
Stephen Chesley, prin. Fax 969-7036
Mistral ES K-5
505 Escuela Ave 94040 650-526-3575
Dr. Marcela de Carvalho Ed.D., prin. Fax 526-3576
Monta Loma ES 500/K-5
460 Thompson Ave 94043 650-903-6915
Gloria Higgins, prin. Fax 903-6921
Stevenson ES 400/K-5
750 San Pierre Way Ste B 94043 650-526-3500
Rebecca Westover, prin. Fax 903-6951
Theuerkauf ES 500/K-5
1625 San Luis Ave 94043 650-903-6925
Ryan Santiago, prin. Fax 903-6931

German International S of Silicon Valley 400/PK-12
310 Easy St 94043 650-254-0748
Michael Koops, head sch Fax 254-0749
St. Joseph S 200/PK-8
1120 Miramonte Ave 94040 650-967-1839
Anne Nowell, prin. Fax 691-1630
Torah Academy 6-7
2015 Latham St 94040 650-424-9800
Yew Chung International S of Silicon Vly 200/PK-7
310 Easy St 94043 650-903-0986
Annette Hanson M.Ed., prin. Fax 903-0976

Mount Baldy, Los Angeles
Mount Baldy JESD 100/PK-8
PO Box 489 91759 909-985-0991
Dr. Mitch Hovey Ed.D., supt. Fax 982-8009
www.mtbaldy.k12.ca.us
Mount Baldy S 100/PK-8
PO Box 489 91759 909-985-0991
Nancy Sirski M.A., prin. Fax 982-8009

Mount Madonna, Santa Cruz

Mount Madonna S 200/PK-12
491 Summit Rd 408-847-2717
Mary McDonald, head sch Fax 847-5633

Mount Shasta, Siskiyou, Pop. 3,264
Mount Shasta UNSD 500/K-8
595 E Alma St 96067 530-926-6007
Barry Barnhart, supt. Fax 926-6103
www.mountshastausd.com
Mount Shasta ES 200/K-3
501 Cedar St 96067 530-926-3434
Barry Barnhart, prin. Fax 926-2827
Sisson S 300/4-8
601 E Alma St 96067 530-926-3846
Kale Riccomini, prin. Fax 926-2152

Murphys, Calaveras, Pop. 2,171
Vallecito UNSD
Supt. — See Avery
Michelson ES 200/PK-5
196 Pennsylvania Gulch Rd 95247 209-728-3441
Louise Simson, prin. Fax 795-2510

Murrieta, Riverside, Pop. 99,237
Menifee UNESD
Supt. — See Menifee
Oak Meadows ES 1,000/K-5
28600 Poinsettia St 92563 951-246-4210
Daphne Donoho, prin. Fax 679-4637

Murrieta Valley USD 22,900/K-12
41870 McAlby Ct 92562 951-696-1600
Patrick Kelley, supt. Fax 304-1523
www.murrieta.k12.ca.us
Alta Murrieta ES 700/K-5
39475 Whitewood Rd 92563 951-696-1403
Brent Coley, prin. Fax 304-1766
Antelope Hills ES 900/K-5
36105 Murrieta Oaks Ave 92562 951-445-4110
Preston Fairchild, prin. Fax 304-1871
Avaxat ES 700/K-5
24300 Las Brisas Rd 92562 951-696-1402
David Ciabattini, prin. Fax 304-1629
Buchanan ES 1,000/K-5
40121 Torrey Pines Rd 92563 951-696-1428
Jennifer Randel, prin. Fax 304-1851
Cole Canyon ES 1,200/K-5
23750 Via Alisol 92562 951-696-1421
Kimberly Ciabattini, prin. Fax 304-1861
Curran ES 600/K-5
40855 Chaco Canyon Rd 92562 951-696-1405
Pamela Rodden, prin. Fax 304-1726
Mails ES 1,000/K-5
35185 Briggs Rd 92563 951-304-1880
Joshua Fogal, prin. Fax 304-1726
McElhinney MS 1,300/6-8
35125 Briggs Rd 92563 951-304-1885
Thomas Patane, prin. Fax 304-1889
Monte Vista ES 1,000/K-5
37420 Via Mira Mosa 92563 951-894-5085
Pamela Picchiottino, prin. Fax 304-1842
Murrieta ES 900/K-5
24725 Adams Ave 92562 951-696-1401
Rob Lurkins, prin. Fax 304-1705
Rail Ranch ES 600/K-5
25030 Via Santee 92563 951-696-1404
Tammy Hunter-Wethers, prin. Fax 304-1745
Shivela MS 1,500/6-8
24515 Lincoln Ave 92562 951-696-1406
Michael Marble, prin. Fax 304-1643
Thompson MS 1,700/6-8
24040 Hayes Ave 92562 951-696-1410
John Fox, prin. Fax 304-1691
Tovashal ES 800/K-5
23801 Saint Raphael Dr 92562 951-696-1411
Kathy Dixon, prin. Fax 304-1783
Warm Springs MS 900/6-8
39245 Calle de Fortuna 92563 951-696-3503
Terry Picchiottino, prin. Fax 304-1611

Temecula Valley USD
Supt. — See Temecula
Alamos ES 800/K-5
38200 Pacific Park Dr 92563 951-294-6760
Jenniffer Aynesworth, prin. Fax 294-6770
Bella Vista MS 1,200/6-8
31650 Browning St 92563 951-294-6600
Tina Miller, prin. Fax 294-6624

Calvary Murrieta Christian S 700/PK-12
24225 Monroe Ave 92562 951-834-9190
Desmond Starr, supt. Fax 698-4896
Murrieta Springs Adventist Christian Acd 100/K-8
32477 Starbuck Cir 92562 951-461-2243
Daneil Olmedo, prin. Fax 461-9565

Napa, Napa, Pop. 75,253
Napa County Office of Education 100/
2121 Imola Ave 94559 707-253-6800
Barbara Nemko, supt. Fax 253-6841
www.napacoe.org
Napa County Opportunity S 50/K-8
2121 Imola Ave 94559 707-253-6817
Caroline Wilson, dir. Fax 253-6983

Napa Valley USD 18,400/K-12
2425 Jefferson St 94558 707-253-3511
Patrick J. Sweeney Ed.D., supt. Fax 253-3855
www.nvusd.k12.ca.us
Alta Heights Magnet ES 400/K-5
15 Montecito Blvd 94559 707-253-3671
Kirstin Gerhardt, prin. Fax 253-6291
Bel Aire Park Magnet ES 500/K-5
3580 Beckworth Dr 94558 707-253-3775
Janine Burt, prin. Fax 259-8420
Browns Valley ES 600/K-5
1001 Buhman Ave 94558 707-253-3761
Frank Silva, prin. Fax 259-8421
El Centro ES 300/K-5
1480 El Centro Ave 94558 707-253-3771
Pam Perkins, prin. Fax 259-8422
Harvest Magnet MS 700/6-8
2449 Old Sonoma Rd 94558 707-259-8866
Monica Ready, prin. Fax 253-4013
McPherson ES 600/K-5
2670 Yajome St 94558 707-253-3488
Troy Knox, prin. Fax 259-8423
Mt. George ES 300/K-5
1019 2nd Ave 94558 707-253-3766
Julie Tyler, prin. Fax 253-3624
Northwood ES 400/K-5
2214 Berks St 94558 707-253-3471
Sarah Knox, prin. Fax 259-8424
Phillips ES 600/K-6
1210 Shetler Ave 94559 707-253-3481
Matt Manning, prin. Fax 259-8425
Pueblo Vista Magnet ES 200/K-5
1600 Barbara Rd 94558 707-253-3491
Helen Rocca, prin. Fax 253-6239
Redwood MS 1,000/6-8
3600 Oxford St 94558 707-253-3415
Maryanne Christoffersen, prin. Fax 259-0718
Salvador Magnet ES 200/K-5
1850 Salvador Ave 94558 707-253-3476
Pamela Perkins, prin. Fax 253-6293
Shearer ES 600/K-5
1590 Elm St 94559 707-253-3508
Elizabeth Gonzalez, prin. Fax 253-3847
Silverado MS 800/6-8
1133 Coombsville Rd 94558 707-253-3688
Jen Kohl, prin. Fax 253-3830
Snow ES 500/K-5
1130 Foster Rd 94558 707-253-3666
Olivia McCormick, prin. Fax 253-6241
West Park ES 300/K-5
2315 W Park Ave 94558 707-253-3516
Amye Scott, prin. Fax 253-6244
Other Schools – See American Canyon, Yountville

Blue Oak S 200/K-8
1436 Polk St 94559 707-261-4500
Dan Schwartz, head sch Fax 261-4509
First Christian S 200/PK-8
2659 1st St 94558 707-253-7226
Dawnelle Ellis, admin. Fax 253-1261
Kolbe Academy Trinity Prep 100/PK-12
2055 Redwood Rd 94558 707-258-9030
John Bertolini, hdmstr. Fax 258-9031

Napa Christian S 100/K-12
2201 Pine St 94559 707-255-5233
Justine Leonie, prin. Fax 255-8530
St. Apollinaris S 300/K-8
3700 Lassen St 94558 707-224-6525
Connie Howard, prin. Fax 224-5400
St. John's Lutheran S 300/PK-8
3521 Linda Vista Ave 94558 707-226-7970
Joel Wahlers, prin. Fax 226-7974
St. John the Baptist S 200/K-8
983 Napa St 94559 707-224-8388
Nancy Jordan, prin. Fax 224-0236
Sunrise Montessori of Napa Valley 100/PK-6
PO Box 4077 94558 707-253-1105
Janice Tres, dir. Fax 409-6242

National City, San Diego, Pop. 57,012

National SD 5,900/PK-8
1500 N Ave 91950 619-336-7500
Leighangela Brady, supt. Fax 336-7551
www.nsd.us
Central ES 700/K-6
933 E Ave 91950 619-336-7400
Vanessa Lerma, prin. Fax 336-7455
El Toyon ES 500/K-6
2000 E Division St 91950 619-336-8000
William Mellman, prin. Fax 336-8055
Harbison ES 600/K-6
3235 E 8th St 91950 619-336-8200
Isabel Silva, prin. Fax 336-8255
Kimball ES 400/K-6
302 W 18th St 91950 619-336-8300
Sonia Ruan, prin. Fax 336-8355
Las Palmas ES 700/K-6
1900 E 18th St 91950 619-336-8500
Steve Sanchez, prin. Fax 336-8555
Lincoln Acres ES 600/K-6
2200 S Lanoitan Ave 91950 619-336-8600
Luz Vicario, prin. Fax 336-8655
National School District Preschool PK-PK
2401 E 24th St 91950 619-336-8670
Charmaine Lawson, prin. Fax 336-8673
Olivewood ES 600/K-6
2505 F Ave 91950 619-336-8700
Beverly Hayes, prin. Fax 336-8755
Otis ES 500/K-6
621 E 18th St 91950 619-336-8800
Felipe DeLaPena, prin. Fax 336-8855
Palmer Way ES 600/K-6
2900 Palmer St 91950 619-336-8900
Alfonso Denegri, prin. Fax 336-8955
Rancho de la Nacion S 500/K-6
1830 E Division St 91950 619-336-8100
Katherine Melanese, prin. Fax 336-8155

Sweetwater UNHSD
Supt. — See Chula Vista
National City MS 800/7-8
1701 D Ave 91950 619-336-2600
Juan Gonzalez, prin. Fax 474-1756

Kuyper Preparatory S 100/K-12
2400 Euclid Ave 91950 877-458-9737
Gabriela Lozoya, admin. Fax 458-9737
San Diego Academy 300/K-12
2800 E 4th St 91950 619-267-9550
Nicholas Lindquist, prin. Fax 267-8662

Needles, San Bernardino, Pop. 4,672

Needles USD 900/K-12
1900 Erin Dr 92363 760-326-3891
Mary McNeil, supt. Fax 326-4218
www.needlesusd.org
Chemehuevi Valley ES 50/K-5
1900 Erin Dr 92363 760-858-4222
Jim Rolls, prin. Fax 858-4224
Needles MS 200/6-8
1900 Erin Dr 92363 760-326-3894
Amy Avila, prin. Fax 326-4052
Vista Colorado ES 400/K-5
1900 Erin Dr 92363 760-326-2167
Marie Armijo, prin. Fax 326-6565

Needles Adventist Christian S 50/1-8
PO Box 306 92363 760-326-4406
Norma Howard M.A., prin. Fax 326-4406

Nevada City, Nevada, Pop. 2,983

Nevada City ESD 900/K-8
800 Hoover Ln 95959 530-265-1820
Trisha Dellis, supt. Fax 265-1822
www.ncsd.k12.ca.us
Deer Creek ES 400/K-4
805 Lindley Ave 95959 530-265-1870
Monica Daugherty, prin. Fax 265-1876
Seven Hills IS 400/5-8
700 Hoover Ln 95959 530-265-1840
Sam Schug, prin. Fax 265-1846

Twin Ridges ESD 100/K-8
16661 Old Mill Rd 95959 530-265-9052
James Berardi, supt. Fax 265-3049
twinridgeselementary.com
Grizzly Hill S 100/K-8
16661 Old Mill Rd 95959 530-265-9052
James Berardi, prin. Fax 265-3049
Other Schools – See Washington

Ananda Living Wisdom S 100/PK-12
14618 Tyler Foote Rd 95959 530-478-7640
Diane Atwell, dir. Fax 478-7646
Echo Ridge Christian S 50/K-8
15504 Liberty Cir 95959 530-265-2057

Newark, Alameda, Pop. 40,127

Newark USD 6,300/PK-12
5715 Musick Ave 94560 510-818-4112
Dr. Partick Sanchez, supt. Fax 794-2199
www.newarkunified.org
Birch Grove IS 400/3-6
37490 Birch St 94560 510-818-3600
Cathreene Ingham-Watters, prin. Fax 793-2437
Birch Grove PS 500/PK-2
6071 Smith Ave 94560 510-818-3100
Elie Wasser, prin. Fax 792-5624
Graham ES 400/K-6
36270 Cherry St 94560 510-818-3300
Akilah Byrd, prin. Fax 494-0582
Kennedy ES 400/K-6
35430 Blackburn Dr 94560 510-818-3400
Pam Hughes, prin. Fax 793-1579
Lincoln ES 400/K-6
36111 Bettencourt St 94560 510-818-3500
Angela Ehrlich, prin. Fax 793-3446
Musick ES 300/K-6
5735 Musick Ave 94560 510-818-4000
Amanda Golliher, prin. Fax 791-5792
Newark JHS 900/7-8
6201 Lafayette Ave 94560 510-818-3050
Mark Neal, prin. Fax 794-2079
Schilling ES 500/K-6
36901 Spruce St 94560 510-818-3800
Nicole Paredes, prin. Fax 791-9203
Snow ES 400/K-6
6580 Mirabeau Dr 94560 510-818-3900
Robin Sehrt, prin. Fax 791-8942

Challenger S 800/PK-8
35487 Dumbarton Ct 94560 510-739-0300
Daisy Salazar, hdmstr. Fax 739-1796
St. Edward S 300/K-8
5788 Thornton Ave 94560 510-793-7242
Sr. Carolyn Monahan, prin. Fax 793-3189

Newberry Springs, San Bernardino

Silver Valley USD
Supt. — See Yermo
Newberry Springs ES 100/PK-5
33713 Newberry Rd 92365 760-257-3211
Jeff Koenig, prin. Fax 257-4838

Newbury Park, See Thousand Oaks

Conejo Valley USD
Supt. — See Thousand Oaks
Banyan ES 500/K-5
1120 Knollwood Dr 91320 805-498-6641
Allison Kennedy, prin. Fax 375-6626
Cypress ES 400/K-5
4200 Kimber Dr 91320 805-498-6683
Carey Bartlow, prin. Fax 375-5600
Environmental Academy of Research Tech 500/K-5
2626 Michael Dr 91320 805-498-3686
Jeff Rickert, prin. Fax 375-5602
Maple ES 300/K-5
3501 Kimber Dr 91320 805-498-6748
Patty Lewis, prin. Fax 375-5603
Sequoia MS 1,100/6-8
2855 Borchard Rd 91320 805-498-3617
Hallie Chambers, prin. Fax 375-5605
Sycamore Canyon S 1,400/K-8
4601 Via Rio 91320 805-498-1573
Doug Hedin, prin. Fax 498-0385
Walnut ES 400/K-5
581 Dena Dr 91320 805-498-3608
Aileen Wall, prin. Fax 375-5604

Conejo Adventist ES 100/K-8
1250 Academy Dr 91320 805-498-2391
Jennifer Lew, prin. Fax 498-1816

Newcastle, Placer, Pop. 1,197

Loomis UNSD
Supt. — See Loomis
Ophir ES 200/K-8
1373 Lozanos Rd 95658 530-885-3495
Kevin Roche, prin. Fax 823-9101

Newcastle ESD 1,700/PK-12
PO Box 1028 95658 916-259-2832
Denny Rush, supt. Fax 259-2835
www.newcastle.k12.ca.us
Newcastle ES 200/PK-8
8951 Valley View Dr 95658 916-663-3307
David Cory, prin. Fax 663-3524

New Cuyama, Santa Barbara, Pop. 510

Cuyama JUSD 200/PK-12
2300 Highway 166 93254 661-766-2482
Dr. Les Imel, supt. Fax 766-2255
www.cuyamaunified.org
Cuyama ES 200/PK-8
2300 Highway 166 93254 661-766-2642
Dr. Rachel Leyland, admin. Fax 766-2255

Newhall, See Santa Clarita

Newhall ESD
Supt. — See Valencia
McGrath ES 700/K-6
21501 Deputy Jake Dr 91321 661-291-4090
Carla Hicks, prin. Fax 291-4091
Newhall ES 700/K-6
24607 Walnut St 91321 661-291-4010
Jane D'Anna, prin. Fax 291-4011
Peachland Avenue ES 500/K-6
24800 Peachland Ave 91321 661-291-4020
Kate Peattie, prin. Fax 291-4021
Wiley Canyon ES 700/K-6
24240 La Glorita Cir 91321 661-291-4030
Timothy Lankford, prin. Fax 291-4031

Sulphur Springs UNESD
Supt. — See Canyon Country
Valley View Community ES 600/K-6
19414 Sierra Estates Dr 91321 661-251-2000
Rick Drew, prin. Fax 298-5428

William S. Hart UNHSD
Supt. — See Santa Clarita
Placerita JHS 1,100/7-8
25015 Newhall Ave 91321 661-259-1551
Jan Hayes-Rennels, prin. Fax 287-9748

Newman, Stanislaus, Pop. 10,029

Newman-Crows Landing USD 2,900/PK-12
1223 Main St 95360 209-862-2933
Randy Fillpot, supt. Fax 862-0113
www.nclusd.org
Hunt ES 400/PK-5
907 R St 95360 209-862-1020
Lupe Robles, prin. Fax 862-0579
Hurd Barrington ES 500/PK-5
838 Eucalyptus Ave 95360 209-862-2585
Janette Springer, prin. Fax 862-3028
Von Renner ES 400/K-5
1388 Patchett Dr 95360 209-862-2868
Heather Vargas, prin. Fax 862-3639
Yolo MS 600/6-8
901 Hoyer Rd 95360 209-862-2984
Eva Luna, prin. Fax 862-3734
Other Schools – See Crows Landing

Newport Beach, Orange, Pop. 82,964

Newport - Mesa USD
Supt. — See Costa Mesa
Andersen ES 400/K-6
1900 Port Seabourne Way 92660 949-515-6935
Shannon Bray, prin. Fax 515-6821
Eastbluff ES 400/K-6
2627 Vista Del Oro 92660 949-515-5920
Cheryl Beck, prin. Fax 515-6848
Ensign IS 1,100/7-8
2000 Cliff Dr 92663 949-515-6910
Michael Sciacca, prin. Fax 515-3370
Mariners ES 800/K-6
2100 Mariners Dr 92660 949-515-6960
Matthew Broesamle, prin. Fax 515-6801
Newport ES 500/K-6
1327 W Balboa Blvd 92661 949-515-6965
Amanda Estrada, prin. Fax 515-6831
Newport Heights ES 700/K-6
300 E 15th St 92663 949-515-6970
Somer Harding, prin. Fax 515-6871

Carden Hall 400/PK-8
1541 Monrovia Ave 92663 949-645-1773
Kim Dablow, dir. Fax 645-3782
Newport Christian S 100/K-11
1000 Bison Ave 92660 949-760-5485
Kevin Cyprian, prin. Fax 760-5071
Our Lady Queen of Angels S 500/PK-8
750 Domingo Dr 92660 949-644-1166
Eileen Ryan, prin. Fax 644-6213

Newport Coast, Orange

Newport - Mesa USD
Supt. — See Costa Mesa
Newport Coast ES 600/K-6
6655 Ridge Park Rd 92657 949-515-6975
Julie McCormick, prin. Fax 515-6881

Nicasio, Marin, Pop. 96

Nicasio ESD 100/K-8
PO Box 711 94946 415-662-2184
Nancy Neu, supt. Fax 662-2250
www.nicasioschool.org
Nicasio S 100/K-8
PO Box 711 94946 415-662-2184
Nancy Neu, admin. Fax 662-2250

Niland, Imperial, Pop. 983

Calipatria USD
Supt. — See Calipatria
Smith ES 100/K-4
PO Box 1005 92257 760-359-0636
Douglas Kline, prin. Fax 359-3612

Nipomo, San Luis Obispo, Pop. 16,314

Lucia Mar USD
Supt. — See Arroyo Grande
Dana ES 600/K-6
920 W Tefft St 93444 805-474-3790
Stacey Russell, prin. Fax 473-5521
Lange ES 600/K-6
1661 Via Alta Mesa 93444 805-474-3670
Michael Flushman, prin. Fax 473-4303
Nipomo ES 400/K-6
190 E Price St 93444 805-474-3780
Julia Bowles, prin. Fax 473-4229

Norco, Riverside, Pop. 26,516

Corona-Norco USD 53,500/K-12
2820 Clark Ave 92860 951-736-5000
Michael H. Lin Ed.D., supt. Fax 736-5015
www.cnusd.k12.ca.us
Highland ES 700/K-6
2301 Alhambra St 92860 951-736-3308
Jason Scott, prin. Fax 736-3488
Norco ES 600/K-6
1700 Temescal Ave 92860 951-736-3348
Russ Schriver, prin. Fax 736-7145
Norco IS 800/7-8
2711 Temescal Ave 92860 951-736-3206
Amy Shainman, prin. Fax 736-3208
Riverview ES 300/K-6
4600 Pedley Ave 92860 951-736-3245
Brenda Pearson, prin. Fax 736-3341
Sierra Vista ES 500/K-6
3560 Corona Ave 92860 951-736-3311
Lori Clays, prin. Fax 736-7154
Washington ES 900/K-6
1220 Parkridge Ave 92860 951-736-3326
Veronica Rodriguez, prin. Fax 736-3479
Other Schools – See Corona, Eastvale, Mira Loma

Turning Point Christian S 100/K-8
2000 Norco Dr 92860 951-735-4480
Jennifer Booth, prin.

North Edwards, Kern, Pop. 1,016

Muroc JUSD 2,000/PK-12
17100 Foothill Ave 93523 760-769-4821
Dr. Michael McCoy Ph.D., supt. Fax 769-4241
www.muroc.k12.ca.us
Other Schools – See Boron, Edwards

North Fork, Madera
Chawanakee USD 1,100/K-12
PO Box 400 93643 559-877-6209
Darren Sylvia, supt. Fax 877-2065
www.chawanakee.k12.ca.us
North Fork ES 300/K-8
33087 Road 228 93643 559-877-2215
Gayle Fain, prin. Fax 877-2377
Other Schools – See O Neals

North Highlands, Sacramento, Pop. 40,275
Twin Rivers USD
Supt. — See Mc Clellan
Allison ES 400/PK-6
4315 Don Julio Blvd 95660 916-566-1810
Jacqueline DeWitt, prin. Fax 566-1811
Hillsdale ES 400/K-6
6469 Guthrie St 95660 916-566-1860
Renee Scott-Femenella, prin. Fax 566-1861
Joyce ES 500/PK-8
6050 Watt Ave 95660 916-556-1880
Jim Davis, prin. Fax 556-1881
Kohler S 500/PK-8
4004 Bruce Way 95660 916-566-1850
Will Pope, prin. Fax 566-3557
Madison ES 700/PK-6
5241 Harrison St 95660 916-566-1900
Yvette Streeter, prin. Fax 566-3564
Oakdale S 500/PK-8
3708 Myrtle Ave 95660 916-566-1910
Debra Chandler, prin. Fax 566-1911
Sierra View ES 400/PK-6
3638 Bainbridge Dr 95660 916-566-1960
Stephanie Tarrell, prin. Fax 566-1961
Village S 600/K-8
6845 Larchmont Dr 95660 916-566-1970
Jordan Alvarado, prin. Fax 566-3567

Grace Family Christian S 50/K-6
7031 Watt Ave 95660 916-239-2239
Liliya Olesenko, prin.

North Hills, Los Angeles
Los Angeles USD
Supt. — See Los Angeles
Gledhill Early Education Center PK-PK
16058 Gledhill St 91343 818-895-2491
Carolina Gomez, prin. Fax 892-7731
Gledhill Street ES 500/K-5
16030 Gledhill St 91343 818-894-1151
Linda Bueno, prin. Fax 894-2462
Langdon Avenue ES 600/K-5
8817 Langdon Ave 91343 818-892-0779
Alfredo Montes, prin. Fax 830-7532
Lassen ES 500/K-5
15017 Superior St 91343 818-892-8618
Lance Moore, prin. Fax 892-5731
Mayall Street ES 400/K-5
16701 Mayall St 91343 818-363-5058
Linda Kim, prin. Fax 831-3379
Noble Avenue ES 900/K-5
8329 Noble Ave 91343 818-892-1151
Maria Loon, prin. Fax 830-1898
Noble Early Education Center PK-PK
8315 Noble Ave 91343 818-894-2716
Carolina Gomez, prin. Fax 892-5469
Parks Learning Center 700/K-5
8855 Noble Ave 91343 818-895-9620
Mariam King, prin. Fax 894-4711
Parthenia ES 700/K-5
16825 Napa St 91343 818-891-6955
Phillip Hollis, prin. Fax 892-7467
Plummer ES 1,000/K-6
9340 Noble Ave 91343 818-895-2481
Ibia Gomez, prin. Fax 891-1594
Santana Arts Academy 600/K-5
9301 Columbus Ave 91343 818-920-4060
Leah Bayliss, prin. Fax 894-4515
Sepulveda MS 1,600/6-8
15330 Plummer St 91343 818-920-2130
Gabriel Ortega, prin. Fax 891-5754
Vintage Math/Science/Technology Magnet S 800/K-5
15848 Stare St 91343 818-892-8661
Nancy Williams-Mourao, prin. Fax 830-9456

Centers of Learning 100/PK-12
PO Box 2037 91393 818-894-3213
Christa Eadson, prin. Fax 893-8074
Holy Martyrs Armenian S 300/PK-5
16617 Parthenia St 91343 818-892-7991
John Kossakian, prin. Fax 892-5044
Our Lady of Peace S 200/PK-8
9022 Langdon Ave 91343 818-894-4059
Lourdes Jasso, prin. Fax 894-6759
Valley Presbyterian S 100/PK-6
9240 Haskell Ave 91343 818-894-3674
Claudia Moreland, prin. Fax 893-3754

North Hollywood, See Los Angeles
Los Angeles USD
Supt. — See Los Angeles
Arminta Early Education Center PK-PK
7911 Goll Ave 91605 818-765-4312
Viken Kazarian, prin. Fax 982-7767
Arminta ES 500/K-5
11530 Strathern St 91605 818-765-5911
Rene Ramirez, prin. Fax 764-9648
Bellingham ES 600/K-5
6728 Bellingham Ave 91606 818-759-0119
John Graham, prin. Fax 759-0181
Burbank ES 400/K-5
12215 Albers St 91607 818-763-6497
Paula Grace, prin. Fax 763-1431
Camellia Avenue ES 800/K-5
7451 Camellia Ave 91605 818-765-5255
Piedad Sanchez, prin. Fax 765-4909
Coldwater Canyon Avenue ES 800/K-5
6850 Coldwater Canyon Ave 91605 818-765-6634
Cynthia Braley, prin. Fax 982-1387
Fair Avenue ES 1,000/K-5
6501 Fair Ave 91606 818-761-5444
Alma Flores, prin. Fax 762-5316
Fair Early Education Center PK-PK
11300 Kittridge St 91606 818-985-1790
Viken Kazarian, prin. Fax 505-0365
Korenstein ES 600/K-5
7650 Ben Ave 91605 818-255-4140
Sonia Mendoza, prin. Fax 765-5381
Lankershim ES 500/K-5
5250 Bakman Ave 91601 818-769-3130
Christopher Clarke, prin. Fax 769-2802
Madison MS 1,700/6-8
13000 Hart St 91605 818-255-5200
Estelle Baptiste, prin. Fax 765-4692
Monlux ES 700/K-5
6051 Bellaire Ave 91606 818-763-4693
Daniel Mulia, prin. Fax 762-7509
Oxnard Street ES 500/K-5
10912 Oxnard St 91606 818-762-3397
Kenny Yau, prin. Fax 753-4935
Reed MS 1,700/6-8
4525 Irvine Ave 91602 818-487-7600
Jeanne Gamba, prin. Fax 766-9069
Rio Vista ES 400/K-5
4243 Satsuma Ave 91602 818-761-6147
Pia Sadaqatmal, prin. Fax 508-8158
Romer MS 1,200/6-8
6501 Laurel Canyon Blvd 91606 818-505-2200
Luis Rodriguez, prin. Fax 761-9343
Saticoy ES 600/K-5
7850 Ethel Ave 91605 818-765-0783
Anait Vardoumian, prin. Fax 503-4781
Sendak ES 600/K-5
11414 Tiara St 91601 818-509-3400
George Khatchadourian, prin. Fax 487-3727
Strathern ES 700/K-5
7939 Saint Clair Ave 91605 818-765-4234
Cynthia Diaz, prin. Fax 764-5912
Toluca Lake Early Education Center PK-PK
4915 Strohm Ave 91601 818-980-0925
Ade Hernandez, prin. Fax 752-6704
Toluca Lake ES 500/K-5
4840 Cahuenga Blvd 91601 818-761-3339
Joseph Prendez, prin. Fax 761-7197
Victory ES 600/K-5
6315 Radford Ave 91606 818-761-4676
Michelle Diamond, prin. Fax 769-2729

Campbell Hall S 1,100/K-12
4533 Laurel Canyon Blvd 91607 818-980-7280
Rev. Julian Bull, hdmstr. Fax 505-5319
Laurel Hall S 500/PK-8
11919 Oxnard St 91606 818-763-5434
Jay Guidetti, prin. Fax 509-6979
Oakwood S 300/K-6
11230 Moorpark St 91602 818-732-3500
Dr. James Astman, hdmstr.
Or Hachaim Academy 300/K-8
6021 Laurel Canyon Blvd 91606 818-766-2417
Debbie Raskin, prin. Fax 505-1636
St. Charles Borromeo S 300/K-8
10850 Moorpark St 91602 818-508-5359
John Genova, prin. Fax 508-4511
St. Jane Frances De Chantal S 300/PK-8
12950 Hamlin St 91606 818-766-1714
Gabrielle Benson, prin. Fax 766-5372
St. Patrick S 200/PK-8
10626 Erwin St 91606 818-761-7363
Raquel Shin, prin. Fax 761-6349
St. Paul's First Lutheran S 100/PK-8
11330 McCormick St 91601 818-763-2892
Rendy Koeppel, prin.
Wesley S 200/K-8
4832 Tujunga Ave 91601 818-508-4542
H. John Walter M.A., head sch Fax 508-4570

Northridge, See Los Angeles
Los Angeles USD
Supt. — See Los Angeles
Andasol ES 400/K-5
10126 Encino Ave 91325 818-349-8631
Paula Denen, prin. Fax 886-7156
Balboa Gifted High Ability Magnet ES 700/1-5
17020 Labrador St 91325 818-349-4801
Jana Davenport, prin. Fax 993-3470
Castlebay Lane Charter S 800/K-5
19010 Castlebay Ln 91326 818-360-1908
Ruth Gamboa Brooks, prin. Fax 831-5492
Holmes MS 1,600/6-8
9351 Paso Robles Ave 91325 818-678-4100
Hanh Aloisio, prin. Fax 886-3358
Lorne Street ES 600/K-5
17440 Lorne St 91325 818-342-3123
Patricia Newman, prin. Fax 705-0860
Napa Street ES 500/K-5
19010 Napa St 91324 818-885-1441
Brenda Fernandez, prin. Fax 993-4824
Northridge Early Education Center PK-PK
17960 Chase St 91325 818-678-5190
Terri Winbush, prin. Fax 885-1461
Northridge MS 800/6-8
17960 Chase St 91325 818-678-5100
Richard Ramos, prin. Fax 885-1461

Casa Montessori 50/PK-6
17633 Lassen St 91325 818-886-7922
First Presbyterian Preparatory S 200/PK-5
10400 Zelzah Ave 91326 818-368-7254
Marylou Pennington, prin. Fax 832-0295
Heschel Day S 400/PK-8
17701 Devonshire St 91325 818-368-5781
Larry Kligman, head sch Fax 360-6162
Highland Hall Waldorf S 300/PK-12
17100 Superior St 91325 818-349-1394
Lynn Kern, admin. Fax 349-2390
Northridge Community S 50/K-8
8212 Louise Ave 91325 818-360-1111
Christine Gutierrez, prin.
Our Lady of Lourdes S 300/PK-8
18437 Superior St 91325 818-349-0245
Kris Brough, prin. Fax 349-4156
St. Mary S 50/PK-5
17431 Roscoe Blvd 91325 818-345-3500
David Elias, prin. Fax 345-3593
St. Nicholas S 200/PK-8
9501 Balboa Blvd 91325 818-886-6751
San Fernando Valley Academy 100/PK-12
17601 Lassen St 91325 818-349-1373
Jerlene Johnson-Thorne, prin. Fax 773-6353

North Tustin, Santa Ana

Fairmont Private S - North Tustin 300/PK-8
12421 Newport Ave, 714-832-4867
Kristen Jansen, dir. Fax 832-8336

Norwalk, Los Angeles, Pop. 103,851
Little Lake City SD
Supt. — See Santa Fe Springs
Cresson ES 300/K-5
11650 Cresson St 90650 562-868-6620
Linda Rigg, prin. Fax 868-2454
Lakeland ES 300/K-5
11224 Bombardier Ave 90650 562-868-8887
Janet Alonso, prin. Fax 868-0247
Lakeside MS 700/6-8
11000 Kenney St 90650 562-868-9422
Ana Gutierrez, prin. Fax 863-9252
Orr ES 400/K-5
12130 Jersey Ave 90650 562-868-7988
Rebecca Casillas, prin. Fax 863-2518
Paddison ES 400/K-5
12100 Crewe St 90650 562-868-7741
Dr. Lorena Martinez-Vargas, prin. Fax 864-1591
Studebaker ES 500/K-5
11800 Halcourt Ave 90650 562-868-7882
Paula Rode, prin. Fax 929-0092

Norwalk-La Mirada USD 19,300/PK-12
12820 Pioneer Blvd 90650 562-210-2000
Dr. Hasmik Danielian Ed.D., supt. Fax 864-9857
www.nlmusd.org
Chavez ES 400/K-5
12110 Walnut St 90650 562-210-4490
Gabriela Galvez-Reyna, prin. Fax 863-8193
Corvallis MS 800/6-8
11032 Leffingwell Rd 90650 562-210-4125
Bob Easton, prin. Fax 863-4755
Dolland ES 600/K-5
15021 Bloomfield Ave 90650 562-210-2560
Lorena Sierra, prin. Fax 404-4302
Edmondson ES 500/K-5
15121 Grayland Ave 90650 562-210-4440
Sharon Stewart, prin. Fax 929-4861
Glazier ES 500/K-5
10932 Excelsior Dr 90650 562-210-2890
Adriano Nakano, prin. Fax 863-8797
Johnston ES 400/K-5
13421 Fairford Ave 90650 562-210-3120
Angela Togia, prin. Fax 868-5799
Lampton ES 700/K-5
14716 Elmcroft Ave 90650 562-210-3255
Cindy Rayburn, prin. Fax 484-0223
Los Alisos MS 1,200/6-8
14800 Jersey Ave 90650 562-210-3495
Majid Salehi, prin. Fax 864-2967
Moffitt ES 500/K-5
13323 Goller Ave 90650 562-210-3650
Rachel Garcia, prin. Fax 864-0471
Morrison ES 800/K-5
13510 Maidstone Ave 90650 562-210-3710
Rodolfo Gonzalez, prin. Fax 868-9879
New River ES 500/K-5
13432 Halcourt Ave 90650 562-210-3770
David Hoffman, prin. Fax 868-0726
Nuffer ES 400/K-5
14821 Jersey Ave 90650 562-210-4060
Makara Sar, prin. Fax 868-5167
Ramona Preschool PK-PK
14616 Dinard Ave 90650 562-210-4205
Laurel Parker, dir. Fax 921-1605
Sanchez ES 400/K-5
11960 162nd St 90650 562-210-4315
Alicia Rubio, prin. Fax 926-2366
Waite MS 700/6-8
14320 Norwalk Blvd 90650 562-210-4370
Dr. Susan Newcomb, prin. Fax 921-8114
Other Schools – See La Mirada

New Harvest Christian S 100/K-12
11364 Imperial Hwy 90650 562-929-6034
Robert Romero, admin. Fax 484-3260
Norwalk Christian S 50/PK-6
11129 Pioneer Blvd 90650 562-863-5751
Anna Hernandez, prin. Fax 863-5245
St. John of God S 200/PK-8
13817 Pioneer Blvd 90650 562-863-5722
Elizabeth Mendez, prin. Fax 406-3928
St. Linus S 300/PK-8
13913 Shoemaker Ave 90650 562-921-0336
Greg Climaco, prin. Fax 926-9077
Trinity Christian S 200/PK-8
11507 Studebaker Rd 90650 562-864-3712
Jeff Jepsen M.A., prin. Fax 864-1877

Novato, Marin, Pop. 49,983
Novato USD 8,000/K-12
1015 7th St 94945 415-897-4201
Jim Hogeboom, supt. Fax 898-5790
www.nusd.org
Hamilton S 700/K-8
5530 Nave Dr 94949 415-883-4691
Stephen Hospodar, prin. Fax 883-2249
Loma Verde ES 400/K-5
399 Alameda De La Loma 94949 415-883-4681
Tehniat Cheema, prin. Fax 883-0834
Lu Sutton ES 400/K-5
1800 Center Rd 94947 415-897-3196
Bonnie Barron, prin. Fax 897-7016

Lynwood ES 400/K-5
1320 Lynwood Dr 94947 415-897-4161
Andy Cline, prin. Fax 897-3322
Olive ES 400/K-5
629 Plum St 94945 415-897-2131
Elizabeth Sesma-Olynik, prin. Fax 897-0931
Pleasant Valley ES 500/K-5
755 Sutro Ave 94947 415-897-5104
Dana Sadan, prin. Fax 897-5704
Rancho ES 500/K-5
1430 Johnson St 94947 415-897-3101
Angela Kriesler, prin. Fax 897-7492
San Jose MS 700/6-8
1000 Sunset Pkwy 94949 415-883-7831
Justin Mori, prin. Fax 883-0624
San Ramon ES 500/K-5
45 San Ramon Way 94945 415-897-1196
Amanda Langford, prin. Fax 897-2326
Sinaloa MS 900/6-8
2045 Vineyard Rd 94947 415-897-2111
Jim Larson, prin. Fax 892-1201

Good Shepherd Lutheran S 300/PK-8
1180 Lynwood Dr 94947 415-897-2510
Mimi Latno, prin. Fax 892-0663
Marin Christian Academy 200/PK-12
1370 S Novato Blvd 94947 415-892-5713
Christopher Mychajluk, supt. Fax 892-4719
Our Lady of Loretto S 200/K-8
1811 Virginia Ave 94945 415-892-8621
Kathleen Kraft, prin. Fax 892-9631

Nuevo, Riverside, Pop. 6,326
Nuview UNESD 2,700/K-12
29780 Lakeview Ave 92567 951-928-0066
David Pyle, supt. Fax 928-0324
www.nuview.k12.ca.us
Mountain Shadows MS 400/7-8
30401 Reservoir Ave 92567 951-928-3836
Debra Orona, prin. Fax 928-3015
Nuview ES 600/K-6
29680 Lakeview Ave 92567 951-928-0201
Fax 928-9171
Valley View ES 600/K-6
21220 Maurice St 92567 951-928-1841
Erica Williams, prin. Fax 928-9581

Oakdale, Stanislaus, Pop. 20,174
Oakdale JUSD 5,300/PK-12
168 S 3rd Ave 95361 209-848-4884
Marc Malone, supt. Fax 847-0155
www.ojusd.org
Cloverland ES 500/PK-6
201 Johnson Ave 95361 209-847-4276
Larry Bonds, prin. Fax 847-9059
Fair Oaks ES 800/PK-6
151 N Lee Ave 95361 209-847-0391
Kathy Pinol, prin. Fax 847-9067
Magnolia ES 600/PK-6
739 Magnolia St 95361 209-847-3056
Janet Hamby, prin. Fax 848-0815
Oakdale JHS 800/7-8
400 S Maag Ave 95361 209-847-2294
Jon Webb, prin. Fax 847-8521
Sierra View ES 700/PK-6
1323 E J St 95361 209-848-4200
David Kindred, prin. Fax 848-4203

Riverbank USD
Supt. — See Riverbank
Mesa Verde ES 500/K-5
4850 Mesa Dr 95361 209-869-7320
Kimberly Ott, prin. Fax 869-7326

Oakhurst, Madera, Pop. 2,743
Bass Lake JUNESD 900/K-8
40096 Indian Springs Rd 93644 559-642-1555
Randall Seals, supt. Fax 642-1556
www.basslakeschooldistrict.com/
Oak Creek IS 200/6-8
40094 Indian Springs Rd 93644 559-642-1570
Brad Barcus, prin. Fax 683-7279
Oakhurst ES 400/K-5
49495 Road 427 93644 559-642-1580
Kathleen Murphy, prin. Fax 642-1584
Other Schools – See Ahwahnee

Yosemite USD 2,000/K-12
50200 Road 427 93644 559-683-8801
Dr. Cecelia Lynn Greenberg, supt. Fax 683-4160
www.yosemiteusd.com
Other Schools – See Coarsegold

Oakhurst Adventist Christian S 50/K-8
50690 Road 426 93644 559-683-7020
Diana Pleitez, prin.

Oakland, Alameda, Pop. 373,354
Oakland USD 42,400/PK-12
1000 Broadway Ste 680 94607 510-879-8200
Kyla Johnson-Trammell, supt.
www.ousd.org
ACORN Woodland ES 300/K-5
1025 81st Ave 94621 510-639-3344
Leroy Gaines, prin. Fax 639-3346
Allendale ES 400/K-5
3670 Penniman Ave 94619 510-535-2812
Charles Miller, prin. Fax 535-2815
Alliance Academy 400/6-8
1800 98th Ave 94603 510-639-2893
Stacey Wyatt, prin. Fax 639-3387
Arroyo Viejo CDC 100/PK-PK
1895 78th Ave 94621 510-879-0802
Ofelia Mendoza, prin.
ASCEND S 400/K-8
3709 E 12th St 94601 510-879-3140
Morgan Alconcher, prin. Fax 534-7222
Bella Vista CDC, 2410 10th Ave 94606 100/PK-PK
Anna Mansker, prin. 510-535-2808
Bella Vista ES 500/K-5
1025 E 28th St 94610 510-436-4900
Linda Flynn, prin. Fax 436-4925
Brewer MS 800/6-8
3748 13th Ave 94610 510-531-6600
Aubrey Lane, prin. Fax 531-6626
Bridges Academy 400/K-5
1325 53rd Ave 94601 510-535-3876
Anita Iverson-Comelo, prin. Fax 535-3875
Brookfield Village ES 400/K-5
401 Jones Ave 94603 510-639-3310
Marie Roberts, prin. Fax 639-3313
Burbank Preschool PK-PK
3550 64th Ave 94605 510-729-7771
Christie Anderson, prin.
Burckhalter ES 300/K-5
3994 Burckhalter Ave 94605 510-729-7700
Carin Geathers, prin. Fax 729-7703
Centro Infantil CDC Annex 100/PK-PK
314 E 10th St 94606 510-874-7748
Caroline Jones, prin.
Chabot ES 600/K-5
6686 Chabot Rd 94618 510-654-4884
Jessica Cannon, prin. Fax 654-4135
Claremont MS 400/6-8
5750 College Ave 94618 510-654-7337
Jonathan Mayer, prin. Fax 654-7341
Cleveland ES 400/K-5
745 Cleveland St 94606 510-874-3600
Peter Van Tassel, prin. Fax 874-3603
Community United ES 400/K-5
6701 International Blvd 94621 510-639-2850
Humphrey Kiuruwi, prin. Fax 639-2853
Cox ECE Center PK-PK
9860 Sunnyside St 94603 510-729-7771
Crocker Highlands ES 400/K-5
525 Midcrest Rd 94610 510-451-5900
Jocelyn Kelleher, prin. Fax 451-5905
East Oakland Pride ES 500/K-5
8000 Birch St 94621 510-636-8217
Michelle Grant, prin. Fax 636-8220
Elmhurst Community Prep S 400/6-8
1800 98th Ave 94603 510-639-2888
Kilian Betlach, prin. Fax 639-2891
Emerson CDC 100/PK-PK
4801 Lawton Ave 94609 510-654-7760
Anna Mansker, prin.
Emerson ES 300/K-5
4803 Lawton Ave 94609 510-654-7373
Heather Palin, prin. Fax 654-7360
Encompass Academy 300/K-5
1025 81st Ave 94621 510-639-3350
Minh-Tram Nguyen, prin. Fax 639-3352
Esperanza ES 300/K-5
10315 E St 94603 510-639-3367
Kathleen Arnold, prin. Fax 639-3370
Franklin ES 800/K-5
915 Foothill Blvd 94606 510-874-3354
Ingrid Seyer-Ochi, prin. Fax 874-3358
Frick MS 300/6-8
2845 64th Ave 94605 510-729-7736
Ruby DeTie, prin. Fax 729-7739
Fruitvale ES 400/PK-5
3200 Boston Ave 94602 510-535-2840
Patricia Ceja, prin. Fax 535-2843
Futures ES 300/K-5
6701 International Blvd 94621 510-636-0520
Shelley McCray, prin. Fax 636-9075
Garfield ES 600/K-5
1640 22nd Ave 94606 510-535-2857
Alicia Arenas, prin. Fax 535-2801
Glenview ES 500/K-5
4215 La Cresta Ave 94602 510-531-6677
Chelsea Toller, prin. Fax 531-6668
Global Family ES 400/K-5
2035 40th Ave 94601 510-879-1280
Dante Ruiz, prin. Fax 536-5883
Grass Valley ES 300/K-5
4720 Dunkirk Ave 94605 510-636-4653
Brandee Stewart, prin. Fax 636-4655
Greenleaf ES 500/PK-8
6328 E 17th St 94621 510-636-1400
Romy Trigg-Smith, prin. Fax 636-1411
Harte MS 500/6-8
3700 Coolidge Ave 94602 510-531-6400
Bianca D'Allesandro, prin. Fax 482-7272
Hillcrest ES 300/K-8
30 Marguerite Dr 94618 510-654-6590
Sherry Segura, prin. Fax 874-3354
Hintil Kuu Ka CDC 100/PK-PK
11850 Campus Dr 94619 510-531-8400
Ofelia Mendoza, prin.
Hoover ES 300/K-5
890 Brockhurst St 94608 510-879-1700
Ashley Martin, prin. Fax 654-4816
Howard ES 200/K-5
8755 Fontaine St 94605 510-639-3244
Nikki Williams, prin. Fax 639-3246
International Community S 300/K-5
2825 International Blvd 94601 510-532-5400
Eleanor Alderman, prin. Fax 261-2040
Jefferson CDC PK-PK
1975 40th Ave 94601 510-535-3871
Caroline Jones, prin. Fax 879-1723
Kaiser ES 300/K-5
25 S Hill Ct 94618 510-549-4900
Dennis Guikema, prin. Fax 549-4904
King ES 300/PK-3
960 10th St 94607 510-874-3381
Roma Groves-Waters, prin. Fax 874-3388
Korematsu Discovery Academy 400/K-5
10315 E St 94603 510-639-3377
Amie LaMontagne, prin. Fax 639-3380
La Escuelita ES 300/K-5
1100 3rd Ave 94606 510-874-7762
Jeffrey Franey, prin. Fax 874-7764
Lafayette ES 300/4-5
991 14th St 94607 510-874-7774
Roma Groves-Waters, prin. Fax 874-7742
Laurel CDC PK-PK
3825 California St 94619 510-531-6226
Caroline Jones, prin. Fax 531-6270
Laurel ES 600/K-5
3750 Brown Ave 94619 510-531-6868
John Stangl, prin. Fax 531-6725
Learning Without Limits ES 400/K-5
2035 40th Ave 94601 510-879-1282
Leo Fuchs, prin. Fax 536-4470
Lincoln ES 700/K-5
225 11th St 94607 510-874-3372
Ivanna Huthman, prin. Fax 872-3375
Madison Park Academy 200/K-5
470 El Paseo Dr 94603 510-636-7919
Lucinda Taylor, prin. Fax 636-7920
Mann ES 400/K-5
5222 Ygnacio Ave 94601 510-879-1360
Patricia Sheehan, prin. Fax 535-1355
Manzanita CDC PK-PK
2618 Grande Vista Ave 94601 510-535-2804
Caroline Jones, prin. Fax 535-2807
Manzanita Community S 400/K-5
2409 E 27th St 94601 510-535-2822
Eyana Spencer, prin. Fax 535-2825
Manzanita SEED ES 400/K-5
2409 E 27th St 94601 510-535-2832
Beatrice Martinez, prin. Fax 535-2834
Markham ES 300/K-5
7220 Krause Ave 94605 510-639-3202
Alana Whitt-Smith, prin. Fax 639-3206
Melrose Leadership Academy 400/K-8
4730 Fleming Ave 94619 510-535-3832
Moyra Contreras, prin. Fax 535-3834
Miller ES 400/K-5
5525 Ascot Dr 94611 510-531-6688
Sara Green, prin. Fax 532-5464
Montclair ES 500/K-5
1757 Mountain Blvd 94611 510-339-6100
Elizabeth Austin, prin. Fax 339-6105
Montera MS 900/6-8
5555 Ascot Dr 94611 510-531-6070
Darren Avent, prin. Fax 531-6354
Munck ES 300/K-5
11900 Campus Dr 94619 510-531-4900
Denise Burroughs, prin. Fax 531-4920
New Highland Academy 300/K-5
8521 A St 94621 510-729-7723
Yolanda Cater, prin. Fax 729-7725
Parker ES 200/K-5
7929 Ney Ave 94605 510-879-1440
Koy Hill, prin. Fax 879-1449
Peralta ES 300/K-5
460 63rd St 94609 510-654-7365
Rosette Costello, prin. Fax 654-7452
Piedmont Avenue ES 400/K-5
4314 Piedmont Ave 94611 510-654-7377
Zarina Ahmad, prin. Fax 654-7309
Prep Literary Acad Cultural Excellence 200/K-5
920 Campbell St 94607 510-874-3332
Enomwoyi Booker, prin. Fax 874-3337
Reach Academy 400/K-5
9860 Sunnyside St 94603 510-879-1100
Natasha Flint-Moore, prin. Fax 879-1109
Redwood Heights ES 400/K-5
4401 39th Ave 94619 510-531-6644
Cynthia Bagby, prin. Fax 531-6616
Rise Community ES 300/K-5
8521 A St 94621 510-729-7732
Samantha Keller, prin. Fax 729-7734
Roosevelt MS 600/6-8
1926 E 19th St 94606 510-535-2877
Clifford Hong, prin. Fax 535-2883
ROOTS International Academy 300/6-8
1390 66th Ave 94621 510-639-3226
Geoff Vu, prin. Fax 639-3214
Sankofa Academy 300/PK-8
581 61st St 94609 510-654-7787
Deitra Atkins, prin. Fax 654-7715
Sequoia ES 400/K-5
3730 Lincoln Ave 94602 510-531-6696
Donald Bertolo, prin. Fax 531-6611
Stonehurst CDC, 10315 E St 94603 PK-PK
Caroline Jones, prin. 510-639-3382
Think College Now ES 300/K-5
2825 International Blvd 94601 510-532-5500
Allison Henkel, prin. Fax 532-5551
Thornhill ES 400/K-5
5880 Thornhill Dr 94611 510-339-6800
Steven Daubenspeck, prin. Fax 339-6801
Tubman Preschool PK-PK
800 33rd St 94608 510-654-7890
Anna Mansker, prin. Fax 654-7896
United for Success Academy 400/6-8
2101 35th Ave 94601 510-535-3880
Nicole Pierce, prin. Fax 535-7139
Urban Promise Academy 300/6-8
3031 E 18th St 94601 510-436-3636
Claire Fisher, prin. Fax 436-3638
Westlake MS 600/6-8
2629 Harrison St 94612 510-879-2130
Johnathan Ferrer, prin. Fax 835-7170
West Oakland MS 200/6-8
991 14th St 94607 510-874-6788
Neha Ummat, prin. Fax 874-6790
Yuk Yau CDC PK-PK
291 10th St 94607 510-874-7759
Anna Mansker, prin. Fax 874-7761

ACTS Christian Academy 100/K-8
1034 66th Ave 94621 510-568-3333
Dr. Doris Limbrick, prin. Fax 568-4125
Aurora S 100/K-5
40 Dulwich Rd 94618 510-428-2606
Abbie Koss, dir. Fax 428-9183
Bentley Lower S - Hiller Campus 300/K-8
1 Hiller Dr 94618 510-843-2512
Arlene Hogan, head sch Fax 845-6516
Guice Christian Academy PK-8
6925 International Blvd 94621 510-729-0330
Adria Angelo, dir.

Head-Royce S 800/K-12
4315 Lincoln Ave 94602 510-531-1300
Crystal Land, head sch Fax 531-2649
Morgan S for Girls 200/6-8
PO Box 9966 94613 510-632-6000
Sandra Luna, head sch Fax 632-6301
Northern Light S 100/PK-8
3710 Dorisa Ave 94605 510-957-0570
Michelle Lewis, dir. Fax 957-0559
Oakland Hebrew Day S 200/PK-8
5500 Redwood Rd 94619 510-531-8600
Tania Schweig, head sch
Park Day S 300/K-8
360 42nd St 94609 510-653-0317
Roel Mason-Vivit, head sch Fax 653-0637
Patten Academy of Christian Education 100/K-12
2430 Coolidge Ave 94601 510-533-3121
Dr. Sharon Anderson, prin.
Raskob Day S 100/2-8
3520 Mountain Blvd 94619 510-436-1275
Edith Ben Ari, dir. Fax 436-1106
Redwood Day S 400/K-8
3245 Sheffield Ave 94602 510-534-0800
John Loeser, head sch Fax 534-0806
St. Anthony S 200/K-8
1500 E 15th St 94606 510-534-3334
Marisol Preciado, prin. Fax 534-3378
St. Elizabeth S 300/PK-8
1516 33rd Ave 94601 510-532-7392
Deline Easterday, prin. Fax 532-0321
St. Lawrence O'Toole S 200/K-8
3695 High St 94619 510-530-0266
Ruby Williams, prin. Fax 530-7568
St. Leo the Great S 200/PK-8
4238 Howe St 94611 510-654-7828
Sonya Simril, prin. Fax 654-4057
St. Paul's Episcopal S 400/K-8
116 Montecito Ave 94610 510-285-9600
Josh Stern, head sch Fax 899-7299
St. Theresa S 300/K-8
4850 Clarewood Dr 94618 510-547-3146
Judith Koneffklatt, prin. Fax 547-3253

Oakley, Contra Costa, Pop. 33,914
Antioch USD
Supt. — See Antioch
Orchard Park S 700/K-8
5150 Live Oak Ave 94561 925-779-7445
Ed Dacus, prin. Fax 679-2630

Oakley UNESD 4,900/K-8
91 Mercedes Ln 94561 925-625-0700
Greg Hetrick Ed.D., supt. Fax 625-1863
www.ouesd.k12.ca.us
Almond Grove ES K-5
5000 Amaryllis Dr 94561 925-625-6270
Christina Karg-Edwards, prin. Fax 625-6719
Delta Vista MS 800/6-8
4901 Frank Hengel Way 94561 925-625-6840
Harvey Yurkovich, prin. Fax 625-6850
Gehringer ES 800/K-5
100 Simoni Ranch Rd 94561 925-625-7070
Tawney Leonard, prin. Fax 625-6356
Iron House ES 800/K-5
4801 Frank Hengel Way 94561 925-625-6825
Rusty Ehrlich, prin. Fax 625-6866
Laurel ES 600/K-5
1141 Laurel Rd 94561 925-625-7090
Anne Heaney, prin. Fax 625-8300
Oakley ES 500/K-5
501 Norcross Ln 94561 925-625-7050
Kaylene Merrill, prin. Fax 625-7068
O'Hara Park MS 900/6-8
1100 OHara Ave 94561 925-625-5060
Colleen Creswell, prin. Fax 625-5096
Vintage Parkway ES 500/K-5
1000 Vintage Pkwy 94561 925-625-6800
Erin Roberts, prin. Fax 625-6813

Oak Park, Ventura, Pop. 13,435
Oak Park USD 4,700/PK-12
5801 Conifer St 91377 818-735-3200
Dr. Anthony Knight, supt. Fax 879-0372
www.opusd.org
Brookside ES 600/PK-5
165 Satinwood Ave 91377 818-597-4200
Sara Ahl, prin. Fax 889-0725
Medea Creek MS 1,100/6-8
1002 Doubletree Rd 91377 818-707-7922
Brad Benioff, prin. Fax 865-8641
Oak Hills ES 500/PK-5
1010 Kanan Rd 91377 818-707-4224
Erik Warren, prin. Fax 707-4232
Oak Park Neighborhood S PK-PK
1010 Kanan Rd 91377 818-707-7742
Kim Gregorchuk, dir.
Red Oak ES 600/K-5
4857 Rockfield St 91377 818-707-7972
Dr. Jon Duim, prin. Fax 597-4244

Oak Run, Shasta
Oak Run ESD 50/PK-8
PO Box 48 96069 530-472-3241
Sue Cooper, supt. Fax 472-1087
www.oakrunschool.org
Oak Run ES 50/PK-8
PO Box 48 96069 530-472-3241
Sue Cooper, prin. Fax 472-1087

Oak View, Ventura, Pop. 3,992
Ventura USD
Supt. — See Ventura
Sunset S 400/K-8
400 Sunset Ave 93022 805-649-6600
Kelsie Sims, prin. Fax 649-8745

Occidental, Sonoma, Pop. 1,073
Harmony UNSD 700/PK-12
1935 Bohemian Hwy 95465 707-874-1205
Rene McBride, supt. Fax 874-1226
www.harmonyusd.org
Harmony ES 100/PK-1
1935 Bohemian Hwy 95465 707-874-1205
Rene McBride, prin. Fax 874-1226

Oceano, San Luis Obispo, Pop. 7,137
Lucia Mar USD
Supt. — See Arroyo Grande
Oceano ES 400/PK-6
1551 17th St 93445 805-474-3800
Michelle Johnson, prin. Fax 473-5519

Oceanside, San Diego, Pop. 159,148
Bonsall USD
Supt. — See Bonsall
Bonsall West ES 600/K-6
5050 El Mirlo Dr 92057 760-721-8001
Tina Calabrese, prin. Fax 721-8117

Fallbrook UNESD
Supt. — See Fallbrook
Pendleton S 900/K-8
110 Marine Dr 92058 760-731-4050
Chad McGough, prin. Fax 385-4254

Oceanside USD 21,200/K-12
2111 Mission Ave 92058 760-966-4000
Dr. Duane Coleman, supt. Fax 433-8620
ousd.ca.schoolloop.com
Chavez MS 700/6-8
202 Oleander Dr 92057 760-966-4900
Jenny Morgan, prin. Fax 945-4665
Del Rio ES 500/K-5
5200 N River Rd 92057 760-901-7300
Kimo Marquardt, prin. Fax 433-3240
Foussat ES 800/K-5
3800 Pala Rd 92058 760-721-2200
Sam Glassford, prin. Fax 754-1567
Garrison ES, 333 Garrison St 92054 500/K-5
Dr. Leah Dardis, prin. 760-901-7600
Ivey Ranch ES 800/K-5
4275 Via Rancho Rd 92057 760-966-4800
Dieter Swank, prin. Fax 967-4077
Jefferson MS 700/6-8
823 Acacia Ave 92058 760-966-4700
Frank Balanon, prin. Fax 757-5791
King MS 1,500/6-8
1290 Ivey Ranch Rd 92057 760-901-8800
Dr. Greg Smedley, prin. Fax 967-4154
Laurel ES 500/K-5
1410 Laurel St 92058 760-966-4200
Freddie Chavarria, prin. Fax 966-4202
Libby ES 600/K-5
423 W Redondo Dr 92057 760-901-7000
Cesar Mora, prin. Fax 967-0623
Lincoln MS 900/6-8
2000 California St 92054 760-901-8900
Steve Bessant, prin. Fax 433-2035
McAuliffe ES 800/K-5
3701 Kelton Dr 92056 760-722-8357
Bob Rowe, prin. Fax 722-1576
Mission ES 600/K-5
2100 Mission Ave 92058 760-966-8700
Glenda Cuevas, prin. Fax 757-6492
Nichols ES 800/K-5
4250 Old Grove Rd 92057 760-435-7400
Traci Galloway, prin. Fax 435-7402
North Terrace ES 800/K-7
141 Santa Rosa Dr 92058 760-901-7500
Art Carrasco, prin. Fax 430-7147
Palmquist ES 700/K-5
1999 California St 92054 760-901-8500
Mandy Bell, prin. Fax 433-6795
Reynolds ES 600/K-5
4575 Douglas Dr 92057 760-901-7200
Juanita Hernandez, prin. Fax 433-5329
San Luis Rey ES 400/K-5
3535 Hacienda Dr 92054 760-757-2360
Dominic Camacho, prin. Fax 757-3945
Santa Margarita ES 800/K-7
1 Carnes Rd 92058 760-901-7900
Brad Hamby, prin. Fax 430-1415
South Oceanside ES 800/K-5
1806 S Horne St 92054 760-435-2100
David Morrow, prin. Fax 439-9954
Stuart Mesa ES 600/K-7
100 Yamanaka Way 92058 760-430-3331
Emily Parra, prin. Fax 430-8288

Vista USD
Supt. — See Vista
Alamosa Park ES 600/K-5
5130 Alamosa Park Dr 92057 760-940-0700
Cindy Anderson, prin. Fax 940-0522
Empresa ES 800/K-5
4850 Avenida Empresa 92056 760-940-8454
Dr. Cheree McKean, prin. Fax 940-1578
Lake ES 900/K-5
4950 Lake Blvd 92056 760-945-5300
Krista Berntsen, prin. Fax 945-7102
Madison MS 1,200/6-8
4930 Lake Blvd 92056 760-940-0176
Steven Bailey, prin. Fax 940-2081
Mission Meadows ES 500/K-5
5657 Spur Ave 92057 760-630-7884
Dr. William Porter, prin. Fax 630-8598
Roosevelt MS 1,100/6-8
850 Sagewood Dr 92057 760-726-8003
Heather Golly, prin. Fax 726-8596
Temple Heights ES 700/K-5
1550 Temple Heights Dr 92056 760-631-6242
Kim Morton, prin. Fax 631-6240

Oceanside Adventist ES 100/K-8
1943 California St 92054 760-722-6894
St. Mary Star of the Sea S 400/PK-8
515 Wisconsin Ave 92054 760-722-7259
Angie Willburn, prin. Fax 722-0862

Ojai, Ventura, Pop. 7,310
Ojai USD 2,800/PK-12
PO Box 878 93024 805-640-4300
Andrew Cantwell, supt. Fax 640-4419
www.ojaiusd.org
A Place to Grow Preschool PK-PK
PO Box 878 93024 805-640-4300
Rebecca Kirkland, dir.
Matilija JHS 400/7-8
703 El Paseo Rd 93023 805-640-4355
Javier Ramirez, prin. Fax 640-4398
Meiners Oaks ES 300/K-6
400 S Lomita Ave 93023 805-640-4378
Theresa Dutter, prin. Fax 640-4380
Mira Monte ES 400/K-6
1216 Loma Dr 93023 805-640-4384
Katherine White, prin. Fax 640-9362
San Antonio ES 100/K-6
650 Carne Rd 93023 805-640-4373
Robin Monson, prin. Fax 640-4376
Summit ES 100/K-6
12525 Ojai Santa Paula Rd 93023 805-640-4391
Marilyn Smith, prin. Fax 525-0698
Topa Topa ES 500/K-6
916 Mountain View Ave 93023 805-640-4366
Dawn Damianos, prin. Fax 640-4369

Laurel Springs S 1,600/K-12
302 El Paseo Rd 93023 805-646-2473
Darby Carr, head sch Fax 646-0186
Oak Grove S 200/PK-12
220 W Lomita Ave 93023 805-646-8236
Jodi Grass, head sch Fax 646-6509
Ojai Valley S 300/PK-12
723 El Paseo Rd 93023 805-646-1423
Michael Hall-Mounsey, pres. Fax 646-0362

Olivehurst, Yuba, Pop. 13,017
Marysville JUSD
Supt. — See Marysville
Arboga ES 500/K-6
1686 Broadway St 95961 530-741-6101
Eric Preston, prin. Fax 741-7836
Cedar Lane ES 500/K-6
841 Cedar Ln 95961 530-741-6112
Jill Segner, prin. Fax 741-7860
Ella ES 500/K-6
4850 Olivehurst Ave 95961 530-741-6124
Rob Gregor, prin. Fax 741-7806
Johnson Park ES 400/K-6
4364 Lever Ave 95961 530-741-6133
John Kovach, prin. Fax 741-7864
Olivehurst ES 500/K-6
1778 Mcgowan Pkwy 95961 530-741-6191
Richard Sullivan, prin. Fax 741-7827
Yuba Gardens IS 700/7-8
1964 11th Ave 95961 530-741-6194
Kari Ylst, prin. Fax 741-7847

O Neals, Madera
Chawanakee USD
Supt. — See North Fork
Spring Valley ES 200/K-8
PO Box 9 93645 559-868-3343
Jessica Fairbanks, prin. Fax 868-3407

Ontario, San Bernardino, Pop. 161,020
Chino Valley USD
Supt. — See Chino
Dickey ES 600/K-6
2840 S Parco Ave 91761 909-947-6693
Patricia Custodio, prin. Fax 548-6071
Liberty ES 600/K-6
2730 S Bon View Ave 91761 909-947-9749
Deborah Hutchinson, prin. Fax 673-1348
Woodcrest JHS 400/7-8
2725 S Campus Ave 91761 909-923-3455
Donald Jones, prin. Fax 548-6059

Cucamonga ESD
Supt. — See Rancho Cucamonga
Ontario Center S 700/K-5
835 N Center Ave 91764 909-948-3044
Stu Schlappi, prin. Fax 948-1712

Mountain View ESD 2,700/K-8
2585 S Archibald Ave 91761 909-947-2205
Dr. Douglass Moss, supt. Fax 947-2291
www.mtnview.k12.ca.us
Creek View ES 600/K-5
3742 Lytle Creek Loop 91761 909-947-8385
Curtis Schibye, prin.
Mountain View ES 500/K-5
2825 E Walnut St 91761 909-947-3516
Julie Alba, prin.
Ranch View ES 600/K-5
3300 Old Archibald Ranch Rd 91761
Adrena Edmonds, prin. 909-947-5545
Yokley MS, 2947 S Turner Ave 91761 900/6-8
Kristie Jackson, prin. 909-947-6774

Ontario-Montclair SD 22,700/PK-8
950 W D St 91762 909-459-2500
Dr. James Hammond, supt. Fax 459-2542
www.omsd.net
Arroyo ES 400/K-5
1700 E 7th St 91764 909-985-1012
Kristie Bennett, prin. Fax 608-7385
Berlyn ES 700/K-6
1320 N Berlyn Ave 91764 909-986-8995
Patti Hobbs, prin. Fax 459-2586
Bon View ES 700/PK-6
2121 S Bon View Ave 91761 909-947-3932
Cristina Raskovic, prin. Fax 930-6751
Central Language Academy 600/K-8
415 E G St 91764 909-983-8522
Arlene Rodriguez, prin. Fax 459-2611
Corona ES 600/PK-5
1140 N Corona Ave 91764 909-984-6411
Sal Flores, prin. Fax 459-2632

Danks MS 900/7-8
1020 N Vine Ave 91762 909-983-2691
Yesenia Arvizu, prin. Fax 459-2959
De Anza MS 600/7-8
1450 S Sultana Ave 91761 909-986-8577
Adriana Gonzalez, prin. Fax 459-2673
Del Norte ES 600/K-5
850 N Del Norte Ave 91764 909-986-9515
Carmen Mejico, prin. Fax 459-2662
Edison ES 900/K-8
515 E 6th St 91764 909-984-5618
Jennifer Berry, prin. Fax 459-2698
El Camino ES 500/PK-6
1525 W 5th St 91762 909-986-6402
Gianna Roca, prin. Fax 459-2716
Elderberry ES 800/K-6
950 N Elderberry Ave 91762 909-986-0108
Alicia Acala-Mateus, prin. Fax 459-2741
Euclid ES 600/K-6
1120 S Euclid Ave 91762 909-984-5119
Monica Ayala, prin. Fax 459-2769
Hawthorne ES 800/K-6
705 W Hawthorne St 91762 909-986-6582
Eileen La Turno, prin. Fax 459-2808
Haynes ES 900/PK-6
715 W Francis St 91762 909-984-1759
Jamemy Barnett, prin. Fax 459-2775
Lincoln ES 700/PK-6
440 N Allyn Ave 91764 909-983-9803
William Corrette, prin. Fax 459-2865
Mariposa ES 700/K-5
1605 E D St 91764 909-983-4116
Camille Johnson, prin. Fax 459-2906
Mission ES 800/K-6
5555 Howard St 91762 909-627-3010
Rhonda O'Neil, prin. Fax 517-3971
Oaks MS 900/7-8
1221 S Oaks Ave 91762 909-988-2050
Dave Foley, prin. Fax 988-2081
Sultana ES 800/K-6
1845 S Sultana Ave 91761 909-986-1215
Cara Molina, prin. Fax 459-2916
Vineyard S 800/PK-8
1500 E 6th St 91764 909-984-2306
Alec Hobbs, prin. Fax 459-2965
Vista Grande ES 600/K-6
1390 W Francis St 91762 909-988-2234
Amanda Colon, prin. Fax 986-6609
Wiltsey MS 1,000/6-8
1450 E G St 91764 909-986-5838
Henry Romero, prin. Fax 459-2834
Other Schools – See Montclair

Ontario Christian S 800/PK-8
1907 S Euclid Ave 91762 909-983-1010
Len Fakkema, prin. Fax 984-3270
Redeemer Lutheran Christian S 100/PK-8
920 W 6th St 91762 909-986-6510
Beth Borke, prin. Fax 986-0757
St. George S 300/K-8
322 W D St 91762 909-984-9123
Peter Horton, prin. Fax 984-0921
San Antonio Christian S 100/K-10
1722 E 8th St 91764 909-982-2301
Catherine Killebrew, prin. Fax 982-0921

Orange, Orange, Pop. 133,187
Orange USD 29,500/PK-12
PO Box 11022 92856 714-628-4001
Fax 628-4041
www.orangeusd.org/
California ES 700/K-6
1080 N California St 92867 714-997-6104
Dr. John Albert Ed.D., prin. Fax 532-4753
Cambridge ES 500/K-6
425 N Cambridge St 92866 714-997-6103
Diane Lew, prin. Fax 532-4754
Chapman Hills ES 500/K-6
170 Aspen 92869 714-532-8043
Jana Saenz, prin. Fax 289-0302
Esplanade ES 500/K-6
381 N Esplanade St 92869 714-997-6157
Christina Yokoyama, prin. Fax 532-6369
Fletcher ES 300/K-6
515 W Fletcher Ave 92865 714-997-6181
Sara Pelly, prin. Fax 921-9155
Handy ES 600/K-6
860 N Handy St 92867 714-997-6183
Dr. Michelle Owen Ed.D., prin. Fax 532-6368
Jordan ES 500/K-6
4319 E Jordan Ave 92869 714-997-6187
Lorena Rubio, prin. Fax 532-6360
LaVeta ES 800/K-6
2800 E La Veta Ave 92869 714-997-6155
Lydia Roach, prin. Fax 639-5990
Linda Vista ES 500/K-6
1200 N Cannon St 92869 714-997-6201
Robert Johnson, prin. Fax 532-5705
McPherson Magnet S 900/K-8
333 S Prospect St 92869 714-997-6384
Joe Erven, prin. Fax 628-4321
Olive ES 500/K-6
3038 N Magnolia Ave 92865 714-637-8218
Heather Darrow, prin. Fax 637-8237
Palmyra ES 500/K-6
1325 E Palmyra Ave 92866 714-997-6207
Brenna Godsey, prin. Fax 532-5704
Portola MS 800/6-8
270 N Palm Dr 92868 714-997-6361
Jill Katevas, prin. Fax 978-0274
Prospect ES 500/K-6
379 N Virage St 92869 714-997-6271
Sally Hughson, prin. Fax 532-4092
Sycamore ES 400/K-6
340 N Main St 92868 714-997-6277
Renee Ybarra, prin. Fax 532-5896
Taft ES 600/K-6
1829 N Cambridge St 92865 714-997-6254
Connie Smith, prin. Fax 997-6259
West Orange ES 500/K-5
243 S Bush St 92868 714-997-6283
Sandra Preciado-Martin, prin. Fax 532-5894
Yorba MS 500/7-8
935 N Cambridge St 92867 714-997-6161
Tracy Knibb, prin. Fax 532-4759
Other Schools – See Anaheim, Garden Grove, Santa Ana, Villa Park

---

Camelot Academy of Arts Science & Tech PK-12
815 S Esplanade St 92869 714-602-7797
Rose Cheung, dir.
Covenant Christian S 100/PK-8
1855 N Orange Olive Rd 92865 714-998-4852
Patty Thoma Lundberg, prin. Fax 998-5425
Holy Family S 500/PK-8
530 S Glassell St 92866 714-538-6012
Margaret Harlow, prin. Fax 633-5892
Intl S of Los Angeles - Orange County 100/PK-8
1838 N Shaffer St 92865 714-771-4710
Franck Reynaud, dir. Fax 771-7110
La Purisima S 200/PK-8
11712 Hewes St 92869 714-633-5411
Rosaura Ramirez, prin. Fax 633-1588
Oakridge Private S 200/PK-8
19111 Villa Park Rd 92869 714-288-1432
St. John's Lutheran S 800/PK-8
154 S Shaffer St 92866 714-288-4406
Dr. Jacob Hollatz, prin. Fax 997-4521
St. Norbert S 300/K-8
300 E Taft Ave 92865 714-637-6822
Joseph Ciccioanni, prin. Fax 637-1604
St. Paul's Lutheran S 600/PK-8
901 E Heim Ave 92865 714-921-3188
James Beaudoin, prin. Fax 921-0131
Salem Lutheran S 500/PK-8
6500 E Santiago Canyon Rd 92869 714-639-1946
Meredith Arldt, prin. Fax 639-6484

Orange Cove, Fresno, Pop. 9,005
Kings Canyon JUSD
Supt. — See Reedley
Citrus MS 600/6-8
1400 Anchor Ave 93646 559-305-7370
Patricia Ledesma, prin. Fax 626-7255
Connor ES 400/PK-5
222 4th St 93646 559-305-7200
Robert Areyano, prin. Fax 626-3008
McCord ES 500/PK-5
333 Center St 93646 559-305-7250
Oscar Villasenor, prin. Fax 626-3332
Sheridan ES 500/K-5
1001 9th St 93646 559-305-7260
Linda Klein, prin. Fax 626-3137

Orangevale, Sacramento, Pop. 32,766
San Juan USD
Supt. — See Carmichael
Carnegie MS 1,000/6-8
5820 Illinois Ave 95662 916-971-7853
Suzanne Bender, prin. Fax 971-7849
Green Oaks Fundamental ES 500/K-6
7145 Filbert Ave 95662 916-986-2209
Rob Reynolds, prin. Fax 986-2214
Oakview Community ES 400/K-5
7229 Beech Ave 95662 916-986-2215
Shana Walters, prin. Fax 986-2219
Ottomon Way ES 300/K-5
9460 Ottomon Way 95662 916-986-2228
Cassidy Butler, prin. Fax 986-2235
Pasteur MS 700/6-8
8935 Elm Ave 95662 916-971-7891
Janet Deal, prin. Fax 971-7893
Pershing ES 600/K-6
9010 Pershing Ave 95662 916-867-2076
Kendra Shelton, prin. Fax 867-2081
Trajan ES 500/K-5
6601 Trajan Dr 95662 916-971-5200
Monica Curiel, prin. Fax 726-4137
Twin Lakes ES 600/K-6
5515 Main Ave 95662 916-986-2243
Jennifer Lawson, prin. Fax 986-2249

Orangevale Christian Academy 50/K-8
5948 Pecan Ave 95662 916-273-2735
Leonid Morgun, admin.
Orangevale SDA S 100/K-8
5810 Pecan Ave 95662 916-988-4310
Brad Davis, prin. Fax 988-8026

Orcutt, Santa Barbara, Pop. 28,086
Orcutt UNESD 5,100/K-12
500 Dyer St 93455 805-938-8900
Deborah Blow, supt. Fax 938-8919
www.orcutt-schools.net
Orcutt JHS 500/7-8
608 Pinal Ave 93455 805-938-8700
Kelly Osborne, prin. Fax 938-8749
Other Schools – See Los Alamos, Santa Maria

Orick, Humboldt, Pop. 332
Orick ESD 50/PK-8
PO Box 128 95555 707-488-2821
William Hawkins, supt. Fax 488-2831
orickschool.org
Orick ES 50/PK-8
PO Box 128 95555 707-488-2821
William Hawkins, admin. Fax 488-2831

Orinda, Contra Costa, Pop. 16,885
Orinda UNESD 2,500/K-8
8 Altarinda Rd 94563 925-254-4901
Carolyn Seaton Ed.D., supt. Fax 254-5261
www.orindaschools.org/
Del Rey ES 400/K-5
25 El Camino Moraga 94563 925-258-3099
Kirsten Theurer, prin. Fax 376-1832
Glorietta ES 400/K-5
15 Martha Rd 94563 925-254-8770
Ron Langer, prin. Fax 254-4856
Orinda IS 900/6-8
80 Ivy Dr 94563 925-258-3090
Michael Randall, prin. Fax 631-7985
Sleepy Hollow ES 400/K-5
20 Washington Ln 94563 925-254-8711
Dr. Ken Gallegos, prin. Fax 253-8320
Wagner Ranch ES 400/K-5
350 Camino Pablo 94563 925-258-0016
Jim Manheimer, prin. Fax 258-0351

Orland, Glenn, Pop. 7,173
Capay JUNESD 200/K-8
7504 Cutting Ave 95963 530-865-1222
Jim Scribner, supt. Fax 865-1214
www.cjuesd.org
Capay Joint Union ES 200/K-8
7504 Cutting Ave 95963 530-865-1222
Jim Scribner, prin. Fax 865-1214

Lake ESD 200/K-8
4672 County Road N 95963 530-865-1255
Nikol Baker, supt. Fax 865-1203
www.lakeschool.org
Lake ES 200/K-8
4672 County Road N 95963 530-865-1255
Nikol Baker, prin. Fax 865-1203

Orland JUSD 2,200/PK-12
903 South St 95963 530-865-1200
Dr. Ken Geisick, supt. Fax 865-1202
www.orlandusd.net
Fairview ES 500/3-5
903 South St 95963 530-865-1235
Tracy Sailsbery, prin. Fax 865-1238
Mill Street ES 500/PK-2
903 South St 95963 530-865-1240
Lisa Ramirez, prin. Fax 865-1129
Price IS 500/6-8
903 South St 95963 530-865-1225
Ryan Bentz, prin. Fax 865-1227

Plaza ESD 100/K-8
7322 County Road 24 95963 530-865-1250
Patrick Conklin, supt. Fax 865-1252
www.plazaschool.org
Plaza ES 100/K-8
7322 County Road 24 95963 530-865-1250
Patrick Conklin, prin. Fax 865-1252

Providence Christian S 100/PK-12
1148 E Walker St 95963 530-865-4924
Gordon Wiens, supt. Fax 865-4926

Orleans, Humboldt
Klamath-Trinity JUSD
Supt. — See Hoopa
Orleans ES 100/PK-8
PO Box 130 95556 530-625-5600
Jeff Landry, prin. Fax 627-3332

Oro Grande, San Bernardino
Oro Grande ESD 3,800/K-12
PO Box 386 92368 760-243-5884
Dr. Heather Griggs, supt. Fax 245-1339
www.orogrande.net
Oro Grande ES 100/K-6
PO Box 386 92368 760-245-9260
Eugene Titus, prin. Fax 245-1339

Orosi, Tulare, Pop. 8,702
Cutler-Orosi JUSD 4,100/K-12
12623 Avenue 416 93647 559-528-4763
Yolanda Valdez, supt. Fax 528-3132
www.cojusd.org
El Monte MS 900/6-8
12623 Avenue 416 93647 559-528-3017
Michelle Kettle, prin. Fax 528-2822
Golden Valley ES 600/K-5
12623 Avenue 416 93647 559-528-9004
Leticia Trevino, prin. Fax 528-9137
Palm ES 800/K-5
12623 Avenue 416 93647 559-528-4751
Jayboy Camaquin, prin. Fax 528-9260
Other Schools – See Cutler

Oroville, Butte, Pop. 14,775
Feather Falls UNESD 50/K-12
2651 Lumpkin Rd 95966 530-589-1810
Ted Fredenburg, supt. Fax 589-1446
www.bcoe.org/cms/one.aspx?portalId=757608&pageId=1279916
Feather Falls ES 50/K-8
2651 Lumpkin Rd 95966 530-589-1810
Ted Fredenburg, prin. Fax 589-1446

Golden Feather UNESD 200/K-12
11679 Nelson Bar Rd 95965 530-533-3833
Joshua Peete, supt. Fax 533-3887
gfusd.org
Concow S 100/K-8
11679 Nelson Bar Rd 95965 530-533-6033
Joshua Peete, prin. Fax 533-3887

Oroville City ESD 2,600/PK-8
2795 Yard St 95966 530-532-3000
Penny Chennell-Carter, supt. Fax 532-3050
www.ocesd.org
Bird Street ES 200/K-5
1421 Bird St 95965 530-532-3001
Patrick O'Brien, prin. Fax 532-3041
Central MS 400/7-8
2565 Mesa Ave 95966 530-532-3002
Mikeial Williamson, prin. Fax 532-3042
Ishi Hills MS 300/6-8
1 Ishi Hills Way 95966 530-532-3078
Chris Renzullo, prin. Fax 532-3040
Oakdale Heights ES 400/K-6
2255 Las Plumas Ave 95966 530-532-3004
John Bettencourt, prin. Fax 532-3044
Ophir ES 500/K-6
210 Oakvale Ave 95966 530-532-3005
Teresa Lightle, prin. Fax 532-3045

Sierra Del Oro Preschool PK-PK
2900 Wyandotte Ave 95966 530-532-5690
Teresa Lightle, prin. Fax 532-5691
Stanford Avenue ES 500/K-6
1801 Stanford Ave 95966 530-532-3006
Shannon Capshew, prin. Fax 532-3046
Wyandotte Avenue ES 300/K-6
2800 Wyandotte Ave 95966 530-532-3007
Jonathan Dowell, prin. Fax 532-3047

Palermo UNESD
Supt. — See Palermo
Golden Hills ES 300/4-5
2400 Via Canela 95966 530-532-6000
Carol Brown, prin. Fax 534-7982
Honcut ES 50/K-2
68 School St 95966 530-742-5284
Heather Scott, prin. Fax 742-2955
Wilcox ES 600/K-3
5737 Autrey Ln 95966 530-533-7627
Heather Scott, prin. Fax 533-6949

Thermalito UNESD 1,400/K-8
400 Grand Ave 95965 530-538-2900
Gregory Blake, supt. Fax 538-2908
www.thermalito.org
Nelson Avenue MS 400/6-8
2255 6th St 95965 530-538-2940
Rochelle Simmons, prin. Fax 538-2949
Plumas Avenue ES 300/K-5
440 Plumas Ave 95965 530-538-2930
Stacie Schuman, prin. Fax 538-2939
Poplar Avenue ES 200/K-5
2075 Poplar St 95965 530-538-2910
William Harrington, prin. Fax 538-2919
Sierra Avenue ES 400/K-5
1050 Sierra Ave 95965 530-538-2920
Ed Gregorio, prin. Fax 538-2929

Feather River Adventist S 50/K-8
27 Cox Ln 95965 530-533-8848
Dana VanHook, prin. Fax 533-6496
Oroville Christian S 100/PK-8
3785 Olive Hwy 95966 530-533-2888
Debra Ward, prin. Fax 533-4155
St. Thomas the Apostle S 100/K-8
1380 Bird St 95965 530-534-6969
Kasia Heinert, prin. Fax 534-9374

Oxnard, Ventura, Pop. 194,223

Hueneme ESD
Supt. — See Port Hueneme
Blackstock JHS 1,200/6-8
701 E Bard Rd 93033 805-488-3644
Tom Beneke, prin. Fax 488-1250
Green JHS 1,000/6-8
3739 S C St 93033 805-986-8750
Heidi Haines, prin. Fax 986-8756
Hathaway ES 600/K-5
405 E Dollie St 93033 805-488-2217
Felicitas Perez, prin. Fax 488-1304
Haycox ES 1,000/K-5
5400 Perkins Rd 93033 805-488-3578
Julianne Pena, prin. Fax 488-2459
Hollywood Beach ES 400/K-6
4000 Sunset Ln 93035 805-986-8720
Tracy Lipsett, prin. Fax 986-8719
Larsen ES 800/K-5
550 E Thomas Ave 93033 805-986-8740
Dr. Maria Natalia Torres, prin. Fax 986-8781
Williams ES 700/K-5
4300 Anchorage St 93033 805-488-3541
Dr. Sue Parsons, prin. Fax 986-1184

Ocean View ESD 2,600/PK-8
4200 Olds Rd 93033 805-488-4441
Dr. Craig Helmstedter Ed.D., supt. Fax 986-6797
www.oceanviewsd.org
Laguna Vista ES 500/PK-5
5084 Etting Rd 93033 805-488-3638
Antoinette Dodge, prin. Fax 986-6759
Mar Vista ES 600/K-5
2382 Etting Rd 93033 805-488-3659
Alison McCormick, prin. Fax 986-6754
Ocean View Early Education Center PK-PK
4600 Olds Rd 93033 805-488-5277
Denise Adams, dir. Fax 488-5669
Ocean View JHS 800/6-8
4300 Olds Rd 93033 805-488-6421
Heather Hendrix, prin. Fax 488-4132
Ocean Vista Early Education S PK-PK
5191 Squires Dr 93033 805-986-3186
Shahida Chaudry, admin. Fax 986-6857
Tierra Vista ES 700/PK-5
2001 Sanford St 93033 805-986-6764
Javier Bolivar, prin. Fax 986-6792

Oxnard SD 15,700/K-8
1051 S A St 93030 805-385-1501
Dr. Cesar Morales, supt. Fax 483-7426
www.oxnardsd.org
Brekke ES 600/K-5
1400 Martin Luther King Jr 93030 805-385-1521
Dr. Bertha Anguiano, prin. Fax 485-4467
Chavez ES 900/K-8
301 N Marquita St 93030 805-385-1524
Brasilia Perez, prin. Fax 483-4799
Curren ES 800/K-8
1101 N F St 93030 805-385-1527
Christine McDaniels, prin. Fax 485-7593
Driffill ES 1,000/K-8
910 S E St 93030 805-385-1530
Carol Flores-Beck, prin. Fax 487-7723
Elm Street ES 700/K-5
450 E Elm St 93033 805-385-1533
Leticia Ramos, prin. Fax 487-0061
Frank MS 1,300/6-8
701 N Juanita Ave 93030 805-385-1536
Dr. Richard Caldwell, prin. Fax 981-1754
Fremont MS 1,100/6-8
1130 N M St 93030 805-385-1539
Chantal Witherspoon, prin. Fax 485-2486
Harrington ES 500/K-5
451 E Olive St 93033 805-385-1542
Luis Ramirez, prin. Fax 486-8364
Haydock Academy of Arts & Sciences 800/6-8
647 Hill St 93033 805-385-1545
Dr. Greg Brisbine, prin. Fax 487-7159
Kamala ES 1,000/K-8
634 W Kamala St 93033 805-385-1548
Jodi Nocero, prin. Fax 486-2893
Lemonwood ES 900/K-8
2200 Carnegie Ct 93033 805-385-1551
Sally Wennes, prin. Fax 487-7293
Marina West ES 600/K-5
2501 Carob St 93035 805-385-1544
Jorge Mares, prin. Fax 984-5494
Marshall ES 600/K-5
2900 Thurgood Marshall Dr, 805-385-1557
Dr. Marlene Breitenbach, prin. Fax 983-7215
McAuliffe ES 800/K-5
3300 Via Marina Ave 93035 805-385-1560
Dr. Mary Elisondo, prin. Fax 985-4690
McKinna ES 600/K-5
1611 S J St 93033 805-385-1563
Wendy Garner, prin. Fax 487-2231
Ramona ES 500/K-5
804 Cooper Rd 93030 805-385-1569
Andres Duran, prin. Fax 486-7049
Ritchen ES 700/K-5
2200 Cabrillo Way 93030 805-385-1572
Andrs Santamara, prin. Fax 981-4685
Rose Avenue ES 700/K-5
220 S Driskill St 93030 805-385-1575
Pablo Ordaz, prin. Fax 485-8061
Sierra Linda ES 500/K-5
2201 Jasmine St, 805-385-1581
Carmen Serrano, prin. Fax 485-5796
Soria ES 1,100/K-8
3101 Dunkirk Dr 93035 805-385-1584
Aracely Fox, prin. Fax 815-4216

Rio SD 4,800/PK-8
2500 E Vineyard Ave, 805-485-3111
Dr. John Puglisi Ph.D., supt. Fax 981-7736
rioschools.org
Rio del Mar ES 500/K-5
3150 Thames River Dr, 805-485-0560
Dr. Scott Barlow, prin. Fax 485-6634
Rio del Norte ES 500/K-5
2500 Lobelia Dr, 805-604-1412
Jake Waltrip, prin. Fax 604-1792
Rio Del Valle MS 700/6-8
3100 N Rose Ave, 805-485-3119
Dr. Adrienne Peralta Ed.D., prin. Fax 981-7737
Rio Lindo ES 400/K-5
2131 Snow Ave, 805-485-3113
Veronica Rauschenb, prin. Fax 981-7738
Rio Plaza ES 500/K-5
600 Simon Way, 805-485-3121
Robert Guynn, prin. Fax 981-7740
Rio Real ES 800/K-8
1140 Kenny St, 805-485-3117
Dr. Maria Hernandez Ed.D., prin. Fax 981-7739
Rio Rosales ES 600/PK-5
1001 Kohala St 93030 805-983-0277
Ryan Howatt, prin. Fax 983-0617
Rio Vista MS 700/6-8
3050 Thames River Dr, 805-981-1507
Matt Klinefelter, prin. Fax 981-6791

Linda Vista Adventist ES 100/PK-8
5050 Perry Way, 805-647-2220
New Harvest Christian S 100/PK-8
723 S D St 93030 805-486-4656
Carol Ford, admin. Fax 201-6687
Our Lady of Guadalupe S 300/PK-8
530 N Juanita Ave 93030 805-483-5116
Dr. Julio Tellez, prin. Fax 385-7242
Our Redeemer Preschool & Kindergarten 200/PK-K
721 Doris Ave 93030 805-983-0619
Amy Vega, dir. Fax 983-0443
St. Anthony S 200/PK-8
2421 S C St 93033 805-487-5317
Henry Barajas, prin. Fax 486-1537
St. John's Lutheran S 200/K-8
1500 N C St 93030 805-983-0330
J. Gynther, prin. Fax 983-2171
Santa Clara S 200/PK-8
324 S E St 93030 805-483-6935
Dotty Massa, prin. Fax 487-6686

Pacifica, San Mateo, Pop. 35,016

Pacifica SD 3,200/PK-8
375 Reina Del Mar Ave 94044 650-738-6600
Dr. Wendy Tukloff, supt. Fax 557-9672
www.pacificasd.org/
Cabrillo S 600/K-8
601 Crespi Dr 94044 650-738-6660
Tom Stafford, prin. Fax 738-2870
Lacy MS 600/6-8
1427 Palmetto Ave 94044 650-738-6665
Daniel Lyttle, prin. Fax 738-6669
Linda Mar Educational Center 50/PK-PK
830 Rosita Rd 94044 650-738-6615
Ray Avila, dir. Fax 738-3799
Ocean Shore S 400/K-8
411 Oceana Blvd 94044 650-738-6650
Joseph Funk, prin. Fax 355-0660
Ortega ES 500/K-5
1283 Terra Nova Blvd 94044 650-738-6670
Debbie Skiles, prin. Fax 738-6672
Sunset Ridge ES 600/K-5
340 Inverness Dr 94044 650-738-6687
Ellie Cundiff, prin. Fax 355-4042
Vallemar S 500/K-8
377 Reina Del Mar Ave 94044 650-738-6655
Monica Lobao, prin. Fax 359-2476

Alma Heights Christian S 300/K-12
1295 Seville Dr 94044 650-359-0555
Dr. David Gross, dir. Fax 898-1730
Good Shepherd S 200/K-8
909 Oceana Blvd 94044 650-359-4544
Andreina Gualco, prin. Fax 359-4558

Pacific Grove, Monterey, Pop. 14,485

Pacific Grove USD 2,100/K-12
435 Hillcrest Ave 93950 831-646-6520
Ralph Porras, supt. Fax 646-6500
pgusd.org
Down ES 500/K-5
485 Pine Ave 93950 831-646-6540
Linda Williams, prin. Fax 648-8414
Forest Grove ES 500/K-5
1065 Congress Ave 93950 831-646-6560
Buck Roggeman, prin. Fax 648-8415
Pacific Grove MS 500/6-8
835 Forest Ave 93950 831-646-6568
Sean Roach, prin. Fax 646-6652

St. Angela's Children's Center 100/PK-PK
136 8th St 93950 831-372-3555
Heather Diaz, dir. Fax 372-5026

Pacific Palisades, See Los Angeles

Calvary Christian S 400/PK-8
701 Palisades Dr 90272 310-573-0082
Vince Downey, head sch Fax 230-9268
Corpus Christi S 300/K-8
890 Toyopa Dr 90272 310-454-9411
Ryan Bushore, prin. Fax 454-3776
Le Lycee Francais de Los Angeles 50/PK-2
16720 Marquez Ave 90272 310-454-9395
Catherine Leloup, head sch
St. Matthew's Parish S 400/PK-8
1031 Bienveneda Ave 90272 310-454-1350
Stuart Work, head sch Fax 573-7423
Seven Arrows ES 100/K-6
15240 La Cruz Dr 90272 310-230-0257
Margarita Pagliai, head sch Fax 230-7725
Village S 300/PK-6
780 Swarthmore Ave 90272 310-459-8411
Nora Malone, head sch Fax 459-3285
Westside Waldorf S 200/PK-8
17310 W Sunset Blvd 90272 310-454-7064
Ellie Jenkins, admin. Fax 454-7084

Pacoima, See Los Angeles

Los Angeles USD
Supt. — See Los Angeles
Broadous Early Education Center PK-PK
11736 Bromont Ave 91331 818-897-2009
Rachel Mermell, prin. Fax 890-3250
Broadous ES 700/K-5
12561 Filmore St 91331 818-896-5236
Victoria Littlejohn, prin. Fax 834-4961
Coughlin ES 700/K-5
11035 Borden Ave 91331 818-686-6428
Leticia Sanchez, prin. Fax 686-6509
Haddon Avenue ES 800/K-5
10115 Haddon Ave 91331 818-899-0244
Deborah Plat, prin. Fax 834-6024
Haddon Early Education Center PK-PK
10085 Haddon Ave 91331 818-896-5501
Claudia Araujo, prin. Fax 834-1127
MacLay MS 900/6-8
12540 Pierce St 91331 818-686-3800
Carlos Tobar, prin. Fax 834-1012
Pacoima Early Education Center PK-PK
11059 Herrick Ave 91331 818-896-3722
Susan Han, prin. Fax 897-6442
Pacoima MS 1,500/6-8
9919 Laurel Canyon Blvd 91331 818-686-4200
Simerjit Garcha, prin. Fax 834-2021
Telfair Avenue ES 800/K-5
10975 Telfair Ave 91331 818-896-7411
Jose Razo, prin. Fax 834-9582
Telfair Early Education Center PK-PK
10915 Telfair Ave 91331 818-896-2118
Sheila Hardy, prin. Fax 896-2088
Vaughn Early Education Center PK-PK
11480 Herrick Ave 91331 818-899-2278
Sheila Hardy, prin. Fax 834-0229

Guardian Angel S 200/K-8
10919 Norris Ave 91331 818-896-1113
Mario Landeros, prin. Fax 834-4014
Mary Immaculate S 300/PK-8
10390 Remick Ave 91331 818-834-8551
Federina Gullano, prin. Fax 896-7996

Paicines, San Benito

Jefferson ESD 50/K-8
221 Old Hernandez Rd 95043 831-389-4593
Carole Greenwald, supt. Fax 389-4593
Jefferson ES 50/K-8
221 Old Hernandez Rd 95043 831-389-4593
Carole Greenwald, prin. Fax 389-4593

Panoche ESD 50/K-8
31441 Panoche Rd 95043 831-628-3438
Panoche ES 50/K-8
31441 Panoche Rd 95043 831-628-3438
Sharon Prather, prin.

Willow Grove UNSD 50/K-8
PO Box 46 95043 831-628-3256
Linda Smith, admin. Fax 628-3458
www.sbcoe.org/District/1252-Untitled.html
Willow Grove ES 50/K-8
PO Box 46 95043 831-628-3256
Linda Smith, prin. Fax 628-3458

Palermo, Butte, Pop. 5,130

Palermo UNESD 1,300/K-8
7390 Bulldog Way 95968 530-533-4842
Dr. Bryan Caples, supt. Fax 532-1047
www.palermoschools.org

Palermo MS 400/6-8
7350 Bulldog Way 95968 530-533-4708
Kathleen Andoe, prin. Fax 532-7801
Other Schools – See Oroville

Palmdale, Los Angeles, Pop. 148,782
Keppel UNESD
Supt. — See Pearblossom
Gibson ES 600/PK-8
9650 E Palmdale Blvd 93591 661-944-6590
Dr. Vishna Herrity, prin. Fax 944-0656
Lake Los Angeles S 500/K-8
16310 E Avenue Q 93591 661-264-3700
Tangie Schatz, prin. Fax 264-4570

Palmdale ESD 21,500/K-12
39139 10th St E 93550 661-947-7191
Raul Maldonado, supt. Fax 273-5137
www.palmdalesd.org
Barrel Springs ES 800/K-5
3636 Ponderosa Way 93550 661-285-9270
Kim Wright, prin. Fax 456-2929
Buena Vista ES 600/K-5
37005 Hillcrest Dr 93552 661-285-4158
Alusine Conteh, prin. Fax 285-0240
Cactus IS 900/6-8
3243 E Avenue R8 93550 661-273-0847
Danny Kanga, prin. Fax 273-5514
Chaparral ES 900/K-5
37500 50th St E 93552 661-285-9777
Tom Pitts, prin. Fax 285-3702
Cimarron ES 900/K-5
36940 45th St E 93552 661-285-9780
Chris O'Neill, prin. Fax 285-9185
Desert Rose ES 1,200/K-5
37730 27th St E 93550 661-272-0584
Melanie Pagliaro, prin. Fax 224-1329
Desert Willow IS 500/7-8
36555 Sunny Ln 93550 661-285-5866
Timothy Howell, prin. Fax 456-1145
Dos Caminos ES 400/K-6
39066 Palm Tree Way 93551 661-947-1849
Laura Cervantes, prin. Fax 947-3768
Golden Poppy ES 800/K-5
37802 Rockie Ln 93552 661-285-3683
Melanie Culver, prin. Fax 456-1540
Joshua Hills ES 900/K-6
3030 Fairfield Ave 93550 661-265-9992
Michelle White, prin. Fax 265-7211
Los Amigos S 1,000/K-8
6640 E Avenue R8 93552 661-285-1546
Sonia Salcedo, prin. Fax 456-2959
Manzanita ES 700/K-5
38620 33rd St E 93550 661-947-3128
Roberto Lopez, prin. Fax 947-2980
Mesquite ES 900/K-5
37622 43rd St E 93552 661-285-8376
Ken Young, prin. Fax 285-2530
Millen IS 500/6-8
39221 22nd St W 93551 661-947-3075
Ryan Beardsley, prin. Fax 538-9035
Ocotillo ES 1,000/K-5
38737 Ocotillo Dr 93551 661-947-9987
Larry Lueck, prin. Fax 267-2186
Palmdale Learning Plaza 800/K-8
38043 Division Ln 93551 661-538-9034
Michael McNelis, prin. Fax 947-3916
Palm Tree ES 800/K-5
326 E Avenue R 93550 661-265-9357
Gerald Luke, prin. Fax 266-3790
Quail Valley ES 700/K-5
37236 58th St E 93552 661-533-7100
Kathy Moshier, prin. Fax 533-7155
SAGE Academy 6-8
38060 20th St E 93550 661-537-6101
Dr. Susan McDougal, prin.
Shadow Hills IS 900/6-8
37315 60th St E 93552 661-533-7400
Dr. Donna Campbell, prin. Fax 533-7445
Summerwind S 900/K-5
39360 Summerwind Dr 93551 661-947-3863
Linda Brandts, prin. Fax 947-4692
Tamarisk ES 800/K-5
1843 E Avenue Q5 93550 661-225-9647
Martin Herrera, prin. Fax 273-7245
Tumbleweed ES 1,200/K-5
1100 E Avenue R4 93550 661-273-4166
Dr. Regina Tillman, prin. Fax 273-9384
Yucca ES 900/K-5
38440 2nd St E 93550 661-273-5052
Terrie Dowling, prin. Fax 273-1995

Westside UNESD
Supt. — See Quartz Hill
Anaverde Hills S 500/K-8
2902 Greenbrier St 93551 661-575-9923
Dr. Kristin Kruizinga, prin. Fax 575-0946
Anderson Academy 900/K-6
5151 W Avenue N8 93551 661-206-3750
Shelly Dearinger, prin. Fax 206-3751
Cottonwood ES 500/K-6
2740 W Avenue P8 93551 661-267-2825
Laura Duran, prin. Fax 267-1847
Esperanza ES 1,000/K-6
40521 35th St W 93551 661-575-0420
Nicole Hernandez, prin. Fax 942-2576
Hillview MS 1,000/6-8
40525 Peonza Ln 93551 661-722-9993
Rodney Lots, prin. Fax 722-9483
Rancho Vista ES 700/K-6
40641 Peonza Ln 93551 661-722-0148
Cathy Bennett, prin. Fax 722-9962

Wilsona SD 1,300/K-8
18050 E Avenue O 93591 661-264-1111
Teresa Grey, supt. Fax 261-3259
www.wilsonasd.net
Vista San Gabriel ES 700/K-4
18020 E Avenue O 93591 661-264-1155
Debbie Lopez, prin. Fax 261-9348
Other Schools – See Lancaster

St. Mary S 300/K-8
1600 E Avenue R4 93550 661-273-5555
Anna-Maria Rios, prin. Fax 273-3845
Westside Christian S 200/K-8
40021 11th St W 93551 661-947-7000
Mrs Curry, prin. Fax 947-3417

Palm Desert, Riverside, Pop. 47,665
Desert Sands USD
Supt. — See La Quinta
Carter ES 700/K-5
74251 Hovley Ln E 92260 760-862-4370
Jeff Hisgen, prin. Fax 862-4375
Lincoln ES 700/K-5
74100 Rutledge Way 92260 760-862-4340
Maryalice Owings, prin. Fax 862-4344
Reagan ES 900/K-5
39800 Liberty Dr 92211 760-772-0456
Mark Baldwin, prin. Fax 360-4304

Desert Adventist Academy 100/K-8
74200 Country Club Dr Ste 2 92260 760-779-1799
William Bartlett, prin. Fax 779-0179
Palm Desert Learning Tree Center 200/PK-5
42675 Washington St 92211 760-345-8100
Angela Morway, dir. Fax 360-1909
Sacred Heart S 600/PK-8
43775 Deep Canyon Rd 92260 760-346-3513
Alan Bruzzio, prin. Fax 773-0673

Palm Springs, Riverside, Pop. 43,639
Palm Springs USD 23,300/K-12
980 E Tahquitz Canyon Way 92262 760-416-6000
Sandra Lyon Ed.D., supt. Fax 416-6015
www.psusd.us
Cahuilla ES 600/K-5
833 E Mesquite Ave 92264 760-416-8161
Ryan Saunders, prin. Fax 416-8164
Cree MS 1,000/6-8
1011 E Vista Chino 92262 760-416-8283
Bernie Marez, prin. Fax 416-8287
Finchy ES 600/K-5
777 E Tachevah Dr 92262 760-416-8190
Arlan Anderson, prin. Fax 416-8201
Vista Del Monte ES 400/K-5
2744 N Via Miraleste 92262 760-416-8176
Blanca Luna, prin. Fax 416-8178
Other Schools – See Cathedral City, Desert Hot Springs, Rancho Mirage, Thousand Palms

---

Desert Chapel Christian S 200/K-12
710 S Sunrise Way 92264 760-327-2772
Frank Marshall, prin. Fax 325-7048
King's S 200/PK-8
67675 Bolero Rd 92264 760-324-5464
Don DeLair, hdmstr. Fax 321-0266
St. Theresa S 300/PK-8
455 S Compadre Rd 92262 760-327-4919
Mike Keno, prin. Fax 327-4429

Palo Alto, Santa Clara, Pop. 61,626
Palo Alto USD 12,300/PK-12
25 Churchill Ave 94306 650-329-3700
Glenn McGee Ph.D., supt. Fax 329-3803
www.pausd.org
Addison ES 500/K-5
650 Addison Ave 94301 650-322-5935
Amanda Boyce, prin. Fax 322-3306
Barron Park ES 300/K-5
800 Barron Ave 94306 650-858-0508
Anne Brown, prin. Fax 813-1031
Briones ES 400/K-5
4100 Orme St 94306 650-856-0877
Tom Jacoubowsky, prin. Fax 856-3750
Duveneck ES 500/K-5
705 Alester Ave 94303 650-322-5946
Christopher Grierson, prin. Fax 322-4387
El Carmelo ES 400/K-5
3024 Bryant St 94306 650-856-0960
Danae Reynolds, prin. Fax 856-4817
Escondido ES 600/K-5
890 Escondido Rd 94305 650-856-1337
Chuck Merritt, prin. Fax 424-1079
Fairmeadow ES 600/K-5
500 E Meadow Dr 94306 650-856-0845
Grant Althouse, prin. Fax 852-9436
Greendell Preschool 50/PK-PK
4120 Middlefield Rd 94303 650-856-0833
Shannon Coleman, prin. Fax 493-8371
Hays ES 500/K-5
1525 Middlefield Rd 94301 650-322-5956
Mary Bussmann, prin. Fax 329-8713
Hoover ES 400/K-5
445 E Charleston Rd 94306 650-320-8106
Katy Bimpson, prin. Fax 493-8130
Jordan MS 1,000/6-8
750 N California Ave 94303 650-494-8120
Valerie Royaltey-Quandt, prin. Fax 858-1310
Nixon ES 500/K-5
1711 Stanford Ave 94305 650-856-1622
Mary Pat O'Connell, prin. Fax 813-1417
Ohlone ES 600/K-5
950 Amarillo Ave 94303 650-856-1726
Dawn Yoshinaga, prin. Fax 852-9447
Palo Verde ES 400/K-5
3450 Louis Rd 94303 650-856-1672
Hillary Miller, prin. Fax 856-6316
Stanford MS 1,000/6-8
480 E Meadow Dr 94306 650-856-5188
Lisa Hickey, prin. Fax 856-3248
Terman MS 700/6-8
655 Arastradero Rd 94306 650-856-9810
Melissa Howell, prin. Fax 856-9878

Ravenswood City ESD
Supt. — See East Palo Alto
Los Robles Magnet Academy 300/K-8
2450 Ralmar Ave 94303 650-329-6536
Keith Bookwalter, prin.

Bowman S 200/K-8
4000 Terman Dr 94306 650-813-9131
Mary Beth Ricks, head sch Fax 813-9132
Challenger S 400/PK-8
3880 Middlefield Rd 94303 650-213-8245
Neena Bhave, hdmstr.
Emerson S 50/PK-8
2800 W Bayshore Rd 94303 650-424-1267
Linda Paz, dir. Fax 856-2778
Girls' MS 200/6-8
3400 W Bayshore Rd 94303 650-968-8338
Jennifer Ayer, head sch Fax 968-4775
Hausner Jewish Day S 400/K-8
450 San Antonio Rd 94306 650-494-8200
David Zimand, head sch Fax 424-0714
Hope Technology S 100/K-10
2525 E Bayshore Rd 94303 650-565-8391
International S of the Peninsula 600/PK-8
151 Laura Ln 94303 650-251-8500
Philippe Dietz, head sch Fax 251-8501
International S of the Peninsula 500/K-8
151 Laura Ln 94306 650-251-8500
Philippe Dietz, head sch
Keys S 300/K-8
2890 Middlefield Rd 94306 650-328-1711
Alona Scott, head sch Fax 328-4506
St. Elizabeth Seton S 300/PK-8
1095 Channing Ave 94301 650-326-9004
Evelyn Rosa, prin. Fax 326-2949
Stratford S - Palo Alto 300/PK-5
870 N California Ave 94303 650-493-1151
Neena Bhave, head sch Fax 493-1161

Palo Cedro, Shasta, Pop. 1,232
Junction ESD 200/K-8
9087 Deschutes Rd 96073 530-547-3274
Richard Gifford, supt. Fax 547-4080
www.junctionesd.net
Junction ES 200/K-8
9087 Deschutes Rd 96073 530-547-3274
Shawn Martinez, prin. Fax 547-4080

North Cow Creek ESD 200/K-8
10619 Swede Creek Rd 96073 530-549-4488
Kevin Kurtz, supt. Fax 549-4490
www.northcowcreek.org
North Cow Creek ES 200/K-8
10619 Swede Creek Rd 96073 530-549-4488
Kevin Kurtz, prin. Fax 549-4490

Redding Christian S 500/PK-12
21945 Old 44 Dr 96073 530-547-5600
Erika Piper, prin. Fax 547-5655

Palos Verdes Estates, Los Angeles, Pop. 12,975
Palos Verdes Peninsula USD 11,700/PK-12
375 Via Almar 90274 310-378-9966
Don Austin Ed.D., supt. Fax 378-0732
www.pvpusd.net
Lunada Bay ES 300/K-5
520 Paseo Lunado 90274 310-377-3005
Julie Tarango, prin. Fax 544-1265
Montemalaga ES 400/K-5
1121 Via Nogales 90274 310-378-5228
Jody Pastell, prin. Fax 375-7484
Palos Verdes IS 1,000/6-8
2161 Via Olivera 90274 310-544-4816
Frank Califano, prin. Fax 265-5944
Sunrise Preschool PK-PK
3801 Via La Selva 90274 310 701 5078
Codean Reed, prin.
Valmonte Early Learning Academy 50/PK-PK
3801 Via La Selva 90274 310-791-5078
Codean Reed, coord. Fax 378-1971
Other Schools – See Rancho Palos Verdes, Rolling Hills

Palos Verdes Peninsula, See Rolling Hills Estates

Chadwick S 800/K-12
26800 Academy Dr 90274 310-377-1543
Dr. John Creeden, head sch Fax 377-0380

Panorama City, See Los Angeles
Los Angeles USD
Supt. — See Los Angeles
Alta California ES 900/K-5
14859 Rayen St 91402 818-830-4400
Jose Benitez, prin. Fax 891-3414
Burton ES 500/K-5
8111 Calhoun Ave 91402 818-908-1287
Jorge Rios, prin. Fax 785-6680
Chase Early Education Center PK-PK
8635 Colbath Ave 91402 818-830-4455
Terri Winbush, prin. Fax 892-7472
Chase Street ES 700/K-5
14041 Chase St 91402 818-830-4440
Connie Gervasoni, prin. Fax 892-8136
Liggett ES 800/K-5
9373 Moonbeam Ave 91402 818-892-4388
Nancy Vallens, prin. Fax 830-0880
Obama ES 800/K-5
8150 Cedros Ave 91402 818-778-5425
Carmen Dominguez, prin. Fax 782-2249
Panorama City ES 500/K-5
8600 Kester Ave 91402 818-895-4230
Olivia Flores-Torres, prin. Fax 895-2884
Primary Academy for Success 300/K-2
9075 Willis Ave 91402 818-920-2932
Phyllis Scadron, prin. Fax 893-5718
Ranchito Avenue ES 600/K-5
7940 Ranchito Ave 91402 818-988-1710
Giovanna Foschetti, prin. Fax 988-4238

St. Genevieve S 600/K-8
14024 Community St 91402 818-892-3802
Amanda Allen, head sch Fax 893-8143

Paradise, Butte, Pop. 25,494
Paradise USD 4,300/PK-12
6696 Clark Rd 95969 530-872-6400
Donna Colosky, supt. Fax 872-6409
www.pusdk12.org
Paradise ES 600/PK-5
588 Pearson Rd 95969 530-872-6415
Debbi Davis, prin. Fax 872-6419
Paradise IS 400/6-8
5657 Recreation Dr 95969 530-872-6465
Reiner Light, prin. Fax 876-1852
Ponderosa ES 500/PK-5
6593 Pentz Rd 95969 530-872-6470
Betsy Amis, prin. Fax 872-6474
Other Schools – See Magalia

Paradise Adventist Academy 200/K-12
PO Box 2169 95967 530-877-6540

Paramount, Los Angeles, Pop. 53,159
Paramount USD 15,900/K-12
15110 California Ave 90723 562-602-6000
Ruth Perez Ed.D., supt. Fax 602-8123
www.paramount.k12.ca.us
Alondra MS 900/6-8
16200 Downey Ave 90723 562-602-8004
Lynn Butler, prin. Fax 602-8005
Gaines ES 500/K-3
7340 Jackson St 90723 562-602-8012
Michael Naruko, prin. Fax 602-8013
Jackson MS 800/4-8
7220 Jackson St 90723 562-602-8020
Kelly Anderson, prin. Fax 602-8021
Jefferson ES 500/K-5
8600 Jefferson St 90723 562-602-8024
Kelly Williams, prin. Fax 602-8025
Keppel ES 500/K-5
6630 Mark Keppel St 90723 562-602-8028
Darren Platt, prin. Fax 602-8029
Lincoln ES 600/K-5
15324 California Ave 90723 562-602-8036
Topekia Jones, prin. Fax 602-8037
Los Cerritos ES 600/K-5
14626 Gundry Ave 90723 562-602-8040
Hilda Verdugo, prin. Fax 602-8041
Mokler ES 700/K-5
8571 Flower Ave 90723 562-602-8044
Linh Roberts, prin. Fax 602-8045
Paramount Park MS 800/6-8
14608 Paramount Blvd 90723 562-602-8052
Kevin Longworth, prin. Fax 602-8053
Roosevelt ES 800/K-5
13451 Merkel Ave 90723 562-602-8056
Margie Domino, prin. Fax 602-8057
Tanner ES 600/K-5
7210 Rosecrans Ave 90723 562-602-8060
Holly Hennessy, prin. Fax 602-8061
Wirtz ES 700/K-5
8535 Contreras St 90723 562-602-8068
Connie Toscano, prin. Fax 602-8069
Zamboni MS 1,000/6-8
15733 Orange Ave 90723 562-602-8048
Sue Saikaly, prin. Fax 602-8049
Other Schools – See Long Beach, South Gate

Our Lady of the Rosary S 200/K-8
14813 Paramount Blvd 90723 562-633-6360
Vanessa Rivas, prin. Fax 633-2641

Shandon JUSD
Supt. — See Shandon
Parkfield ES 50/K-6
70585 Parkfield Coalinga Rd 93451 805-463-2331
Teresa Taylor, supt.

Parlier, Fresno, Pop. 14,454
Kings Canyon JUSD
Supt. — See Reedley
Riverview ES 400/K-8
8662 S Lac Jac Ave 93648 559-305-7290
Josh Darnell, prin. Fax 637-1279

Parlier USD 3,400/K-12
900 S Newmark Ave 93648 559-646-2731
Mike Berg, supt. Fax 888-0210
www.parlierunified.org
Benavidez ES 500/K-6
13900 Tuolumne St 93648 559-646-2963
Courtney Jimenez, prin. Fax 646-2975
Brletic ES 500/K-6
601 3rd St 93648 559-646-3551
Alan Macedo, prin. Fax 646-2850
Chavez ES 500/K-6
500 Tuolumne St 93648 559-646-3595
Sylvia Gomez, prin. Fax 646-0782
Martinez ES 500/K-6
13174 E Parlier Ave 93648 559-646-3527
Dr. George Alvarado, prin. Fax 646-2025
Parlier JHS 500/7-8
1200 E Parlier Ave 93648 559-646-1660
Julissa Alvarado, prin. Fax 646-1633

Pasadena, Los Angeles, Pop. 132,725
Pasadena USD 18,400/K-12
351 S Hudson Ave 91101 626-396-3600
Dr. Brian McDonald, supt. Fax 795-5309
www.pusd.us/
Cleveland ES 200/K-6
524 Palisade St 91103 626-396-5670
Debra Lucas, prin. Fax 794-2556
Don Benito Fundamental ES 600/K-5
3700 Denair St 91107 626-396-5870
Linda Chang, prin. Fax 351-8892
Field ES 500/K-6
3600 E Sierra Madre Blvd 91107 626-396-5860
Daniel Bagby, prin. Fax 351-4202
Hamilton ES 600/K-6
2089 Rose Villa St 91107 626-396-5730
Erika Cooper, prin. Fax 793-7581
Jefferson ES 500/K-5
1500 E Villa St 91106 626-396-5710
Amin Oria, prin. Fax 793-6994
Longfellow ES 500/K-6
1065 E Washington Blvd 91104 626-396-5720
Erica Ingber, prin. Fax 398-6340
Madison ES 500/K-5
515 E Ashtabula St 91104 626-396-5780
Noemi Montano, prin. Fax 793-6868
McKinley S 1,100/K-8
325 S Oak Knoll Ave 91101 626-396-5630
Dr. Nicole Duchette, prin. Fax 844-7888
Roosevelt ES 300/K-5
315 N Pasadena Ave 91103 626-396-5770
Dr. Merle Bugarin, prin. Fax 795-5180
San Rafael ES 400/K-6
1090 Nithsdale Rd 91105 626-396-5790
Rodolfo Ramirez, prin. Fax 683-7429
Washington Accelerated ES 600/K-5
1520 N Raymond Ave 91103 626-396-5840
Karrone Meeks, prin. Fax 296-2693
Washington MS 500/6-8
1505 N Marengo Ave 91103 626-396-5830
Dr. Shannon Malone, prin. Fax 798-2844
Webster ES 500/K-5
2101 E Washington Blvd 91104 626-396-5740
Dr. Jeffrey Bauer, prin. Fax 798-8216
Willard ES 600/K-5
301 Madre St 91107 626-396-5690
Angela Baxter, prin. Fax 744-3375
Wilson MS 600/6-8
300 Madre St 91107 626-396-5800
Sarah Rudchenko, prin. Fax 584-9895
Other Schools – See Altadena, Sierra Madre

Assumption of the Blessed Virgin Mary S 300/K-8
2660 E Orange Grove Blvd 91107 626-793-2089
Joanne Testacross, prin. Fax 793-4070
Chandler S 500/K-8
1005 Armada Dr 91103 626-795-9314
John Finch, head sch Fax 795-6508
Harambee Preparatory S 50/PK-6
1609 Navarro Ave 91103 626-798-7431
Harlan Redmond, prin. Fax 798-1865
High Point Academy 400/K-8
1720 Kinneloa Canyon Rd 91107 626-798-8989
Gary Stern, head sch Fax 798-8751
Intl S of Los Angeles - Pasadena 100/PK-5
30 Marion Ave 91106 626-793-0943
Phillippe Detzen, dir. Fax 793-7043
Judson International S 100/K-12
1610 E Elizabeth St 91104 626-398-2476
Diana Bjoraker, prin. Fax 398-2222
Mayfield Junior S 500/PK-8
405 S Euclid Ave 91101 626-796-2774
Joseph Gill, hdmstr. Fax 796-5753
New Horizon S 100/PK-8
651 N Orange Grove Blvd 91103 626-795-5186
Amira Al-Sarraf, prin. Fax 395-9519
Pasadena Christian S 500/PK-8
1515 N Los Robles Ave 91104 626-791-1214
Dr. Steven Gray, supt. Fax 791-1256
Polytechnic S 900/K-12
1030 E California Blvd 91106 626-396-6300
John Bracker, head sch Fax 796-2249
St. Andrew S 200/K-8
42 Chestnut St 91103 626-796-7697
Raphael Domingo, prin. Fax 796-1931
St. Gregory's A & M Hovsepian S 100/PK-8
2215 E Colorado Blvd 91107 626-578-1343
Shahe Mankerian, prin. Fax 578-7378
St. Philip the Apostle S 500/K-8
1363 Cordova St 91106 626-795-9691
Jennifer Ramirez, prin. Fax 795-9946
San Marino Montessori S 100/K-8
444 S Sierra Madre Blvd 91107 626-577-8007
Hilda Koorn, dir. Fax 577-4566
Sequoyah S 200/K-8
535 S Pasadena Ave 91105 626-795-4351
Josh Brody, head sch Fax 795-8773
Walden S 200/PK-6
74 S San Gabriel Blvd 91107 626-792-6166
Terra Toscano, head sch Fax 792-1335
Waverly S 100/PK-12
67 W Bellevue Dr 91105 626-792-5940
Heidi Johnson, head sch Fax 683-5460
Weizmann Day S 100/K-8
1434 N Altadena Dr 91107 626-797-0204
Lisa Feldman, head sch Fax 797-0389

Paskenta, Tehama, Pop. 106
Elkins ESD 50/K-8
PO Box 407 96074 530-833-5582
Marla Katzler, supt. Fax 833-9859
www.elkinsschoolca.org
Elkins S 50/K-8
PO Box 407 96074 530-833-5582
Marla Katzler, prin. Fax 833-9859

Paso Robles, San Luis Obispo, Pop. 20,187
Paso Robles JUSD 6,500/K-12
PO Box 7010 93447 805-769-1000
Chris Williams, supt. Fax 237-3339
www.pasoschools.org
Arts Academy ar Bauer Speck ES 500/K-5
PO Box 7010 93447 805-769-1350
Dorothy Halic, prin. Fax 237-3498
Brown ES 500/K-5
PO Box 7010 93447 805-769-1200
Dr. Michele Tesauro, prin. Fax 237-3426
Butler ES 500/K-5
PO Box 7010 93447 805-769-1750
Damien Capalare, prin. Fax 237-3496
Flamson MS 700/6-8
PO Box 7010 93447 805-769-1400
Dr. Gene Miller, prin. Fax 237-3427
Kermit King ES 500/K-5
PO Box 7010 93447 805-769-1700
Kelly Ward, prin. Fax 237-6169
Lewis MS 800/6-8
PO Box 7010 93447 805-769-1450
Erin Haley, prin. Fax 237-3458
Peterson ES 500/K-5
PO Box 7010 93447 805-769-1250
Melanie Crawford, prin. Fax 237-3497
Pifer ES 500/K-5
PO Box 7010 93447 805-769-1300
Carol Stoner, prin. Fax 237-3398

San Miguel JUNESD
Supt. — See San Miguel
Culver ES 200/K-8
11011 Heritage Ranch Loop 93446 805-227-1040
Stephanie Schofield, prin. Fax 227-1045

St. Rose of Lima S 200/PK-8
900 Tucker Ave 93446 805-238-0304
Sr. Rebeca Munoz, prin. Fax 238-7393
Trinity Lutheran S 300/PK-8
940 Creston Rd 93446 805-238-0335
Jane Fairbank, prin. Fax 238-0892

Patterson, Stanislaus, Pop. 19,584
Patterson JUSD 6,000/PK-12
510 Keystone Blvd 95363 209-895-7700
Dr. Philip Alfano Ed.D., supt. Fax 892-5803
www.patterson.k12.ca.us
Apricot Valley ES 900/K-5
1320 Henley Pkwy 95363 209-892-4700
Toney Henry, prin. Fax 892-4310
Creekside MS 1,200/6-8
535 Peregrine Dr 95363 209-892-4710
Catherine Aumoeualogo, prin. Fax 892-7101
Las Palmas ES 600/K-5
624 W Las Palmas Ave 95363 209-892-4730
Sandra Villasenor, prin. Fax 892-7769
Northmead ES 600/PK-5
625 L St 95363 209-892-4740
Joseph Silveira, prin. Fax 892-7770
Walnut Grove S 700/K-8
775 N Hartley St 95363 209-892-4770
Alma Romo, prin. Fax 892-5333
Other Schools – See Westley

Sacred Heart S 300/PK-8
505 M St 95363 209-892-3544
Heidi Kuliga, prin. Fax 892-3214

Pauma Valley, San Diego
Valley Center-Pauma USD
Supt. — See Valley Center
Pauma ES 300/K-8
33158 Cole Grade Rd 92061 760-742-3741
Leiani Osugi, prin. Fax 742-1214

Paynes Creek, Tehama, Pop. 57
Antelope ESD
Supt. — See Red Bluff
Plum Valley ES 50/PK-5
29950 Plum Creek Rd 96075 530-597-2248
Richard Hassay, admin. Fax 597-2890

Pearblossom, Los Angeles
Keppel UNESD 2,700/PK-8
PO Box 186 93553 661-944-2155
Dr. Ruben Zepeda, supt. Fax 944-2933
www.keppel.k12.ca.us
Pearblossom ES 400/K-8
PO Box 205 93553 661-944-6019
Dr. Santos DeCasas, prin. Fax 944-0733
Other Schools – See Littlerock, Palmdale

Penn Valley, Nevada, Pop. 1,545
Penn Valley Union ESD 700/K-12
14806 Pleasant Valley Rd 95946 530-432-7311
Torie England Ed.D., supt. Fax 432-7314
www.pennvalleyschools.k12.ca.us/pages/Penn_Valley_Union_Elem_SD
Ready Springs S 200/K-8
10862 Spenceville Rd 95946 530-432-1118
Teena Corker, prin. Fax 432-9473
Williams Ranch ES 200/K-5
14804 Pleasant Valley Rd 95946 530-432-7300
Melissa Conley, lead tchr. Fax 432-7305

Penryn, Placer, Pop. 803
Loomis UNSD
Supt. — See Loomis
Penryn ES 200/K-8
6885 English Colony Way 95663 916-663-3993
Cara Alfonso, prin. Fax 663-2127

Perris, Riverside, Pop. 66,780
Perris ESD 6,200/PK-8
143 E 1st St 92570 951-657-3118
Vincent Ponce, supt. Fax 940-5115
www.perris.k12.ca.us
Clearwater ES 800/K-6
1640 Murrieta Rd 92571 951-423-2016
Claudia Velez, admin.
Enchanted Hills ES 500/K-6
1357 Mount Baldy St 92570 951-443-4790
Michelle Miller, prin. Fax 443-1692
Good Hope ES 700/K-6
24050 Theda St 92570 951-657-5181
Jennifer Lujano, prin. Fax 657-9961
Palms ES 900/K-6
255 E Jarvis St 92571 951-940-5112
Kathleen Rittikaidachar, prin. Fax 940-5179
Perris ES 600/K-6
500 S A St 92570 951-657-2124
Eric Rivera, prin. Fax 657-0854
Railway ES 900/K-6
555 Alpine Dr 92570 951-943-3259
Jewel Desosa, prin. Fax 943-8517
Reiner Children & Families Center PK-PK
2221 South A St 92570 951-657-1441
Carol Jimenez, dir.
Sky View ES 1,000/K-6
625 Mildred St 92571 951-657-4214
Teresa Flynn-Everett, prin. Fax 940-5816

Perris UNHSD 10,400/5-12
155 E 4th St 92570 951-943-6369
Grant Bennett, supt. Fax 940-5378
www.puhsd.org
Pinacate MS 1,100/7-8
1990 S A St 92570 951-943-6441
Rebecca Brown, prin. Fax 940-5344

Val Verde USD 19,000/PK-12
975 Morgan St 92571 951-940-6100
Michael McCormick, supt. Fax 940-6121
www.valverde.edu
Avalon ES 800/K-5
1815 E Rider St 92571 951-490-0360
Tammy Roughton, prin. Fax 490-0365
Columbia ES 700/K-5
21350 Rider St 92570 951-443-2460
Thelma Almuena, prin. Fax 443-2465
Lakeside MS 1,200/7-8
27720 Walnut St 92571 951-443-2440
John Parker, prin. Fax 443-2445
May Ranch ES 900/K-5
900 E Morgan St 92571 951-490-4670
Aimee Breton, prin. Fax 490-4675
Mead Valley ES 600/K-5
21100 Oleander Ave 92570 951-940-8540
Fax 940-8545
Real ES 700/K-5
19150 Clark St 92570 951-940-8520
Dr. Fernando Betanzos, prin. Fax 940-8525
Rivera MS 1,000/6-8
21675 Martin St 92570 951-940-8570
Nicky Smith, prin. Fax 940-6133
Sierra Vista ES 700/K-6
20300 Sherman Rd 92571 951-443-2430
Corby Warren, prin. Fax 443-2435
Triple Crown ES 900/K-5
530 Orange Ave 92571 951-490-0440
Deni Seagrave, prin. Fax 490-0445
Val Verde ES 700/K-6
2656 Indian Ave 92571 951-940-8550
Tim Tanner, prin. Fax 940-8555
Other Schools – See Moreno Valley

St. James S 200/K-8
250 W 3rd St 92570 951-657-5226
Camile Lara, prin. Fax 657-1793
Temple Christian S 100/PK-6
745 N Perris Blvd 92571 951-657-7326
Nancy Elliott, prin. Fax 657-5838

Pescadero, San Mateo, Pop. 633
La Honda-Pescadero USD 300/PK-12
360 Butano Cut Off 94060 650-879-0286
Amy Woollever, supt. Fax 879-0816
www.lhpusd.com
Pescadero ES 100/PK-5
620 North St 94060 650-879-0332
Erica Hays, prin. Fax 879-1066
Other Schools – See La Honda

Petaluma, Sonoma, Pop. 56,146
Dunham ESD 200/PK-6
4111 Roblar Rd 94952 707-795-5050
Christin Barkas, supt. Fax 795-5166
www.dunhamsd.org
Dunham ES 50/PK-6
4111 Roblar Rd 94952 707-795-5050
Christin Barkas, prin. Fax 795-5166

Laguna JESD 50/K-6
2657 Chileno Valley Rd 94952 707-762-6051
Luke McCann, supt. Fax 762-6051
lagunaschool.org
Laguna ES 50/K-6
2657 Chileno Valley Rd 94952 707-762-6051
Cindy Demchuk, prin. Fax 762-6051

Lincoln ESD 50/K-6
1300 Hicks Valley Rd 94952 707-763-0045
Luke McCann, supt. Fax 763-1255
Lincoln ES 50/K-6
1300 Hicks Valley Rd 94952 707-763-0045
Sharon Jeffrey, prin. Fax 763-1255

Old Adobe UNESD 1,800/K-6
845 Crinella Dr 94954 707-765-4322
Craig Conte, supt. Fax 765-4343
www.oldadobe.org
La Tercera ES 300/K-6
1600 Albin Way 94954 707-765-4303
Michele Crncich-Hodge, prin. Fax 765-4333

Petaluma SD 7,800/PK-12
200 Douglas St 94952 707-778-4604
Gary Callahan, supt. Fax 778-4736
www.petalumacityschools.org
Grant ES 400/K-6
200 Grant Ave 94952 707-778-4742
Emily Todd, prin. Fax 778-4852
Kenilworth JHS 900/7-8
800 Riesling Rd 94954 707-778-4710
Bennett Holley, prin. Fax 766-8231
McDowell ES 300/PK-4
421 S McDowell Blvd 94954 707-778-4745
Lauren Anderson, prin. Fax 778-4789
McKinley ES 200/PK-K, 4-6
110 Ellis St 94952 707-778-4750
Matthew Harris, prin. Fax 766-8337
McNear ES 400/PK-6
605 Sunnyslope Ave 94952 707-778-4752
Sheila Garvey, prin. Fax 778-4859
Petaluma JHS 700/7-8
700 Bantam Way 94952 707-778-4724
Renee Semik, prin. Fax 778-4600
Valley Vista ES 400/PK-6
730 N Webster St 94952 707-778-4762
Catina Haugen, prin. Fax 778-4840

Two Rock UNESD 200/K-6
5001 Spring Hill Rd 94952 707-762-6617
Toni Beal, supt. Fax 762-1923
www.trusd.org/
Two Rock ES 200/K-6
5001 Spring Hill Rd 94952 707-762-6617
Toni Beal, prin. Fax 762-1923

Waugh ESD 900/K-6
1851 Hartman Ln 94954 707-765-3331
Rebecca Rosales, supt. Fax 782-9666
www.waughsd.org
Corona Creek ES 500/K-6
1851 Hartman Ln 94954 707-765-3331
Rebecca Rosales, prin. Fax 782-9666
Meadow ES 500/K-6
880 Maria Dr 94954 707-762-4905
Melissa Becker, prin. Fax 762-5751

Wilmar UNESD 200/PK-6
3775 Bodega Ave 94952 707-765-4340
Eric Hoppes, supt. Fax 765-4342
www.wilsonschoolpetaluma.org/
Wilson ES 200/PK-6
3775 Bodega Ave 94952 707-765-4340
Eric Hoppes, supt. Fax 765-4342

Harvest Christian S 100/PK-8
3700 Lakeville Hwy Ste 210 94954 707-763-2954
Jonathan Wraith, prin. Fax 763-0159
St. Vincent de Paul S 300/K-8
100 Union St 94952 707-762-6426
Katie Salmassian, prin. Fax 762-6791
Spring Hill S PK-8
825 Middlefield Dr 94952 707-763-9222
Shaharazad Hamidi, head sch Fax 763-7331

Petrolia, Humboldt
Mattole USD 700/PK-12
PO Box 211 95558 707-629-3311
Shari Lovett, supt. Fax 629-3575
www.humboldt.k12.ca.us/mattole_usd
Mattole S 50/K-8
PO Box 211 95558 707-629-3311
Karen Ashmore, prin. Fax 629-3575
Other Schools – See Honeydew

Phelan, San Bernardino, Pop. 13,933
Snowline JUSD 7,800/K-12
PO Box 296000 92329 760-868-5817
Dr. Ryan Holman, supt. Fax 868-5309
www.snowlineschools.com/
Baldy Mesa ES 900/K-5
PO Box 296000 92329 760-949-1232
Dan MacDonald, prin. Fax 949-2770
Heritage S 500/K-8
PO Box 296000 92329 760-868-2422
Dale Levine, prin. Fax 868-0589
Phelan ES 500/K-5
PO Box 296000 92329 760-868-3252
Tony Buckley, prin. Fax 868-1044
Pinon Mesa MS 700/6-8
PO Box 296000 92329 760-868-3126
Burt Umstead, prin. Fax 868-3033
Quail Valley MS 1,000/6-8
PO Box 296000 92329 760-949-4888
Dennis Zimmerman, prin. Fax 949-3663
Other Schools – See Pinon Hills, Victorville, Wrightwood

Pico Rivera, Los Angeles, Pop. 62,624
El Rancho USD 9,300/PK-12
9333 Loch Lomond Dr 90660 562-942-1500
Karling Aguilera-Fort, supt. Fax 949-2821
erusd.org
Birney Tech Academy 500/K-5
8501 Orange Ave 90660 562-801-5153
Kendall Goyenaga, prin. Fax 801-9354
Durfee ES 500/K-5
4220 Durfee Ave 90660 562-801-5070
Melissa Garcia, prin. Fax 692-8922
Early Learning Program PK-PK
9515 Haney St 90660 562-801-5365
Roberta Gonzalez, prin. Fax 801-0164
Magee ES 500/K-5
8200 Serapis Ave 90660 562-801-5000
Gisela Castanon, prin. Fax 801-5004
North Park Academy of the Arts 800/6-8
4450 Durfee Ave 90660 562-801-5137
Rosalio Medrano, prin. Fax 801-5143
North Ranchito ES 500/K-5
8837 Olympic Blvd 90660 562-801-5031
Rachel Aguirre, prin. Fax 699-0216
Rio Vista ES 400/K-5
8809 Coffman Pico Rd 90660 562-801-5049
Janet Alonso, prin. Fax 942-7989
Rivera ES 700/K-5
7250 Citronell Ave 90660 562-801-5095
Roxane Fuentes, prin. Fax 801-0383
Rivera MS 800/6-8
7200 Citronell Ave 90660 562-801-5088
Yvette Ventura-Rincon, prin. Fax 801-9158
South Ranchito Dual Language Academy 600/K-5
5241 Passons Blvd 90660 562-801-5177
Maria Morales-Thomas, prin. Fax 942-8927
STEAM Academy @ Burke 500/6-8
8101 Orange Ave 90660 562-801-5059
Edna Tristan, prin. Fax 801-5067
Valencia Academy of the Arts 400/K-5
9241 Cosgrove St 90660 562-801-5079
Tarcio Lara, prin. Fax 801-0146

Montebello USD
Supt. — See Montebello
Montebello Gardens ES 400/K-5
4700 Pine St 90660 562-463-5191
Robert Cornejo J.D., prin. Fax 463-5196

Armenian Mesrobian S 200/PK-12
8420 Beverly Rd 90660 562-699-2057
David Ghoogasian, prin. Fax 699-0757

St. Hilary S 200/K-8
5401 Citronell Ave 90660 562-942-7361
Louis Johnston, prin. Fax 801-9131
St. Marianne De Paredes S 200/K-8
7911 Buhman Ave 90660 562-949-1234
Dr. Laura Lukens, pres. Fax 948-3855

Piedmont, Alameda, Pop. 10,117
Piedmont City USD 2,600/K-12
760 Magnolia Ave 94611 510-594-2600
Randall Booker, supt. Fax 654-7374
www.piedmont.k12.ca.us
Beach ES 400/K-5
100 Lake Ave 94611 510-594-2666
Michael Corritone, prin. Fax 655-6751
Havens ES 500/K-5
323 Highland Ave 94611 510-594-2680
Anne Dolid, prin. Fax 428-2079
Piedmont MS 600/6-8
740 Magnolia Ave 94611 510-594-2660
Ryan Fletcher, prin. Fax 595-3523
Wildwood ES 300/K-5
301 Wildwood Ave 94611 510-594-2710
Carol Cramer, prin. Fax 451-8134

Corpus Christi S 300/K-8
1 Estates Dr 94611 510-530-4056
Kathleen Murphy, prin. Fax 530-5926

Pinedale, Fresno
Clovis USD
Supt. — See Clovis
Nelson ES 600/K-6
1336 W Spruce Ave 93650 559-327-7600
Kendra Matson, prin. Fax 327-7690
Pinedale ES 500/K-6
7171 N Sugar Pine Ave 93650 559-327-7700
Debra Bolls, prin. Fax 327-7790

Pine Valley, San Diego, Pop. 1,469
Mountain Empire USD 2,200/PK-12
3291 Buckman Springs Rd 91962 619-473-9022
Dr. Kathy Granger, supt. Fax 473-9728
www.meusd.k12.ca.us
Pine Valley MS 100/6-8
PO Box 571 91962 619-473-8693
Gary Brannon, prin. Fax 473-8026
Other Schools – See Boulevard, Campo, Descanso, Potrero

Pinole, Contra Costa, Pop. 17,432
West Contra Costa USD
Supt. — See Richmond
Collins ES 400/K-6
1224 Pinole Valley Rd 94564 510-231-1446
Pinney Denise, prin. Fax 741-1268
Ellerhorst ES 400/K-6
3501 Pinole Valley Rd 94564 510-231-1426
Jeff Carr, prin. Fax 243-6754
Pinole MS 600/7-8
1575 Mann Dr 94564 510-231-1436
Denise Van Hook, prin. Fax 724-9583
Shannon ES 400/K-6
685 Marlesta Rd 94564 510-231-1454
Daniel MacDonald, prin. Fax 741-8690
Stewart ES 500/K-8
2040 Hoke Dr 94564 510-231-1410
Peter Aloo, prin. Fax 758-1639

St. Joseph S 300/K-8
1961 Plum St 94564 510-724-0242
Arlene Marseille, prin. Fax 724-9886

Pinon Hills, San Bernardino, Pop. 7,119
Snowline JUSD
Supt. — See Phelan
Pinon Hills ES 400/K-5
878 Mono Rd 92372 760-868-4424
Shawn Premo, prin. Fax 868-1028

Pioneer, Amador, Pop. 1,065
Amador County USD
Supt. — See Jackson
Pioneer Magnet S Visual Performing Arts 200/K-6
24625 State Highway 88 95666 209-295-6500
Laurie Carson, prin. Fax 295-1660

Piru, Ventura, Pop. 2,040
Fillmore USD
Supt. — See Fillmore
Piru ES 300/K-6
PO Box 215 93040 805-521-1709
Diana Vides, prin. Fax 521-1044

Pismo Beach, San Luis Obispo, Pop. 7,494
Lucia Mar USD
Supt. — See Arroyo Grande
Judkins MS 500/7-8
680 Wadsworth Ave 93449 805-474-3600
Ian Penton, prin. Fax 473-4376
Shell Beach ES 400/K-6
2100 Shell Beach Rd 93449 805-474-3760
Sammie Cervantez, prin. Fax 473-5517

Coastal Christian S 200/K-12
1005 Oak Park Blvd 93449 805-489-1213
Tom Olmstead, head sch Fax 489-5394

Pittsburg, Contra Costa, Pop. 60,137
Mount Diablo USD
Supt. — See Concord
Bel Air ES 500/K-5
663 Canal Rd 94565 925-458-2606
Robert Humphrey, prin. Fax 458-2065
Delta View ES 700/K-5
2916 Rio Verde 94565 925-261-0240
Cheryl Champion, prin. Fax 261-0246
Shore Acres ES 500/K-5
351 Marina Rd 94565 925-458-3261
Suleyma Moss, prin. Fax 458-6465

Pittsburg USD 10,700/PK-12
2000 Railroad Ave 94565 925-473-2300
Janet Schulze Ed.D., supt. Fax 473-4274
www.pittsburg.k12.ca.us
Foothill ES 500/PK-5
1200 Jensen Dr 94565 925-473-2450
Fax 473-4305
Heights ES 600/PK-5
40 Seeno St 94565 925-473-2410
Laura Francis, prin. Fax 473-4315
Highlands ES 600/PK-5
4141 Harbor St 94565 925-473-2440
Julie Blackburn, prin. Fax 473-4311
Hillview JHS 900/6-8
333 Yosemite Dr 94565 925-473-2380
Heidi Leber, prin. Fax 473-4406
King JHS, 2012 Carion Ct 94565 700/6-8
Angela Stevenson, prin. 925-473-2500
Los Medanos ES 800/PK-5
610 Crowley Ave 94565 925-473-2460
Joanne Rovner-Curtis, prin. Fax 473-4335
Marina Vista ES 700/PK-5
50 E 8th St 94565 925-473-2490
Kirsten Wollenweber, prin. Fax 473-9039
Parkside ES 600/PK-5
985 W 17th St 94565 925-473-2420
Jeff Varner, prin. Fax 473-4343
Rancho Medanos JHS 900/6-8
2301 Range Rd 94565 925-473-2490
Eric Peyko, prin. Fax 473-1060
Stoneman ES 600/PK-5
2929 Loveridge Rd 94565 925-473-2430
Terry Dunn, prin. Fax 473-4355
Willow Cove ES 700/PK-5
1880 Hanlon Way 94565 925-473-2470
Catherine Bojorquez, prin. Fax 709-2005

Legacy Christian S 100/K-7
1210 Stoneman Ave 94565 925-439-2552
Amber Urias, prin. Fax 439-2555
St. Peter Martyr S 300/PK-8
425 W 4th St 94565 925-439-1014
Joseph Siino, prin. Fax 439-1506

Pixley, Tulare, Pop. 3,289
Pixley UNSD 1,100/PK-8
300 N School St 93256 559-757-5207
Heather Elick, supt. Fax 757-0705
www.pixley.k12.ca.us/
Pixley ES 800/PK-5
300 N School St 93256 559-757-3131
Lisa Hoover, prin. Fax 757-1701
Pixley MS 300/6-8
1520 E Court Ave 93256 559-757-3018
Erika Cortez, prin. Fax 757-3507

Placentia, Orange, Pop. 49,404
Placentia-Yorba Linda USD 25,600/K-12
1301 E Orangethorpe Ave 92870 714-986-7000
Gregory S.Plutko Ed.D., supt. Fax 524-3034
www.pylusd.org/
Brookhaven ES 600/K-6
1851 Brookhaven Ave 92870 714-996-7110
Julie Lucas, prin. Fax 996-4308
Golden Ave ES 800/K-6
740 Golden Ave 92870 714-986-7160
Roann Turk, prin. Fax 996-7690
Kraemer MS 1,000/6-8
645 N Angelina Dr 92870 714-996-1551
Keith Carmona, prin. Fax 996-8407
Melrose ES 600/K-6
974 S Melrose St 92870 714-630-4992
Cynthia Alvarez, prin. Fax 630-6742
Morse Ave ES 400/K-6
431 Morse Ave 92870 714-524-6300
Tonia Gordilla, prin. Fax 524-3260
Ruby Drive ES 400/K-6
601 Ruby Dr 92870 714-996-1921
Diana McKibben, prin. Fax 996-2143
Sierra Vista ES 500/K-6
1811 N Placentia Ave 92870 714-986-7270
Shirley Fargo, prin. Fax 572-9506
Tuffree MS 700/7-8
2151 N Kraemer Blvd 92870 714-986-7480
Cindy Freeman, prin. Fax 993-6359
Tynes ES 800/K-6
735 Stanford Dr 92870 714-986-7290
Debra Silverman, prin. Fax 996-7931
Valadez MS Academy 700/6-8
161 E La Jolla St 92870 714-986-7410
James Hardin, prin. Fax 238-9159
Van Buren ES 700/K-6
1245 N Van Buren St 92870 714-986-7290
Connie Roe, prin. Fax 996-5133
Wagner ES 500/K-6
717 E Yorba Linda Blvd 92870 714-986-7180
Janice Weber, prin. Fax 792-0852
Other Schools – See Anaheim, Fullerton, Yorba Linda

St. Joseph S 300/PK-8
801 N Bradford Ave 92870 714-528-1794
JoAnn Telles, prin. Fax 528-0668

Placerville, El Dorado, Pop. 10,089
Gold Oak UNESD 500/PK-8
3171 Pleasant Valley Rd 95667 530-626-3150
Meg Enns, supt. Fax 626-3145
www.gousd.org
Gold Oak ES 300/PK-5
3171 Pleasant Valley Rd 95667 530-626-3160
Shirleen Hernandez, prin. Fax 626-3144
Pleasant Valley MS 200/6-8
4120 Pleasant Valley Rd 95667 530-644-9620
Meg Enns, prin. Fax 644-9622

Gold Trail UNESD 600/K-8
1575 Old Ranch Rd 95667 530-626-3194
Scott Lyons, supt. Fax 626-3199
www.gtusd.org
Gold Trail MS 300/4-8
889 Cold Springs Rd 95667 530-626-2595
Boyd Holler, head sch Fax 626-3289
Sutter's Mill ES 300/K-3
4801 Luneman Rd 95667 530-626-2591
Scott Lyons, prin. Fax 626-3199

Mother Lode UNESD 1,100/K-8
3783 Forni Rd 95667 530-622-6464
Marcy Guthrie, supt. Fax 622-6163
www.mlusd.net
Green MS 500/5-8
3781 Forni Rd 95667 530-622-4668
Leslie Redkey, prin. Fax 622-4680
Indian Creek ES 600/K-4
6701 Green Valley Rd 95667 530-626-0765
Rhonda White, prin. Fax 626-9695

Placerville UNSD 1,300/K-8
1032 Thompson Way 95667 530-622-7216
Eric Bonniksen, supt. Fax 622-0336
www.pusdk8.us/
Louisiana Schnell S 400/K-5
2871 Schnell School Rd 95667 530-622-6244
Patrick Paturel, prin. Fax 622-2309
Markham MS 400/6-8
2800 Moulton Dr 95667 530-622-0403
Terry Edinger, prin. Fax 622-5584
Sierra S 500/K-5
1100 Thompson Way 95667 530-622-0814
Patricia Horn, prin. Fax 622-0532

Cedar Springs Waldorf S 200/PK-8
6029 Gold Meadows Rd 95667 530-642-9903
Jennifer Bumgarner, contact Fax 642-1904
El Dorado Adventist S 200/K-12
1900 Broadway 95667 530-622-3560
Hector Alvarez, prin. Fax 622-2604

Planada, Merced, Pop. 4,571
Planada ESD 800/PK-8
PO Box 236 95365 209-382-0756
Jose L. Gonzalez, supt. Fax 382-1750
www.planada.org
Chavez MS 200/6-8
PO Box 236 95365 209-382-0768
Diana Jimenez, prin. Fax 382-0775
Planada ES 500/PK-5
PO Box 236 95365 209-382-0351
Ildefonso Nava, prin. Fax 382-0113

Playa Del Rey, See Los Angeles
Los Angeles USD
Supt. — See Los Angeles
Paseo Del Rey Fundamental ES 500/K-5
7751 Paseo Del Rey 90293 310-823-2356
Jennifer Theodore-Sulliv, prin. Fax 305-0251

Pleasant Grove, Sutter
Pleasant Grove Joint Union SD 200/K-8
3075 Howsley Rd 95668 916-655-3235
Dave Tarr, supt. Fax 655-3501
www.pgroveschool.org
Pleasant Grove S 200/K-8
3075 Howsley Rd 95668 916-655-3235
Dave Tarr, prin. Fax 655-3501

Pleasant Hill, Contra Costa, Pop. 31,678
Mount Diablo USD
Supt. — See Concord
Fair Oaks ES 400/K-5
2400 Lisa Ln 94523 925-685-4494
Jon Pierce, prin. Fax 687-3170
Gregory Gardens ES 400/K-5
1 Corritone Ct 94523 925-827-3770
Cheryl Kolano, prin. Fax 687-8677
Pleasant Hill ES 700/K-5
2097 Oak Park Blvd 94523 925-934-3341
Aurelia Buscemi, prin. Fax 935-3748
Pleasant Hill MS 1,000/6-8
1 Santa Barbara Rd 94523 925-256-0791
Terry McCormick, prin. Fax 937-6271
Sequoia ES 600/K-5
277 Boyd Rd 94523 925-935-5721
Glendaly Gascot Reyes, prin. Fax 988-8049
Sequoia MS 900/6-8
265 Boyd Rd 94523 925-934-8174
Kevin Honey, prin. Fax 946-9063
Shearer Preschool PK-PK
1 Corritone Ct 94523 925-685-1960
Cheryl Kolano, prin. Fax 685-1901
Strandwood ES 700/K-5
416 Gladys Dr 94523 925-685-3212
Cheri Scripter, prin. Fax 798-4582
Valhalla S 600/K-8
530 Kiki Dr 94523 925-687-1700
Marji Calbeck, prin. Fax 687-3083
Valley View MS 900/6-8
181 Viking Dr 94523 925-686-6136
Ean Ainsworth, prin. Fax 687-5381

Christ the King S 300/K-8
195 Brandon Rd 94523 925-685-1109
Christopher Caban, prin. Fax 685-1289
Pleasant Hill Adventist Academy 200/K-12
796 Grayson Rd 94523 925-934-9261
Dr. Lisa Bissell Paulson, prin. Fax 934-5871

Pleasanton, Alameda, Pop. 67,470
Pleasanton USD 14,700/K-12
4665 Bernal Ave 94566 925-462-5500
David Haglund, supt. Fax 484-3591
pleasantonusd.net
Alisal ES 600/K-5
1454 Santa Rita Rd 94566 925-426-4201
Karen Johnson, prin. Fax 426-9852

Apperson Hearst ES 700/K-5
5301 Case Ave 94566 925-426-3772
Elias Rodriguez, prin. Fax 846-2841
Donlon ES 800/K-5
4150 Dorman Rd 94588 925-426-4221
Janet Gates, prin. Fax 484-5423
Fairlands ES 700/K-5
4151 W Las Positas Blvd 94588 925-426-4211
Shay Galletti, prin. Fax 417-1245
Hart MS 1,100/6-8
4433 Willow Rd 94588 925-426-3102
Leslie Heller, prin. Fax 460-0799
Harvest Park MS 1,200/6-8
4900 Valley Ave 94566 925-426-4444
Robin Munsell, prin. Fax 426-9613
Lydiksen ES 700/K-5
7700 Highland Oaks Dr 94588 925-426-4421
Jacob Berg, prin. Fax 417-8987
Mohr ES 700/K-5
3300 Dennis Dr 94588 925-426-4256
Julie Berglin, prin. Fax 484-9430
Pleasanton MS 1,200/6-8
5001 Case Ave 94566 925-426-4390
Jill Butler, prin. Fax 426-1382
Valley View ES 700/K-5
480 Adams Way 94566 925-426-4230
Soraya Villasenor, prin. Fax 426-0731
Vintage Hills ES 600/K-5
1125 Concord St 94566 925-426-4240
Ann Jayne, prin. Fax 417-7388
Walnut Grove ES 700/K-5
1999 Harvest Rd 94566 925-426-4250
Christopher Connor, prin. Fax 462-6382

Hacienda S 100/1-8
3800 Stoneridge Dr 94588 925-485-5750
JoAnne Camara M.Ed., dir. Fax 485-5757
Stratford S - Pleasanton 200/PK-7
4576 Willow Rd 94588 925-737-0001
Adam Brown, prin. Fax 737-0076

Plumas Lake, Yuba, Pop. 5,494
Plumas Lake ESD 1,100/PK-8
2743 Plumas School Rd, 530-743-4428
Jeff Roberts, supt. Fax 743-1408
www.plusd.org
Cobblestone ES 400/PK-5
1718 Churchill Way, 530-634-9723
Marcie Nichols, prin. Fax 749-9765
Rio Del Oro ES 500/PK-5
1220 Zanes Dr, 530-749-0690
Tiffany Steele, prin. Fax 749-0689
Riverside Meadows IS 300/6-8
1751 Cimarron Dr, 530-743-1271
Julie Rojo, prin. Fax 743-8970

Plymouth, Amador, Pop. 952
Amador County USD
Supt. — See Jackson
Plymouth ES 200/K-6
18601 Sherwood St 95669 209-257-7800
Donna Custodio, prin. Fax 245-6376

Point Arena, Mendocino, Pop. 438
Point Arena SD 500/K-12
PO Box 87 95468 707-882-2803
Brent Cushenbery Ed.D., supt. Fax 882-2848
www.pointarenaschools.org
Arena ES 300/K-8
PO Box 45 95468 707-882-2131
Scott Carson, prin. Fax 882-3076

Point Reyes Station, Marin, Pop. 829
Shoreline USD
Supt. — See Tomales
West Marin S 100/2-8
PO Box 300 94956 415-663-1014
Matthew Nagle, prin. Fax 663-8558

Pollock Pines, El Dorado, Pop. 6,676
Pollock Pines ESD 700/PK-8
2701 Amber Trl 95726 530-644-5416
Pat Atkins, supt. Fax 644-5483
www.ppesd.org
Pinewood ES 400/PK-4
6181 Pine St 95726 530-644-2384
Kevin Potter, prin. Fax 644-6215
Sierra Ridge MS 300/5-8
2700 Amber Trl 95726 530-644-2031
Kim Little, prin. Fax 644-0198

Silver Fork ESD 50/K-8
2701 Amber Trl 95726 530-644-5416
Pat Atkins, supt. Fax 644-5483
Other Schools – See Kyburz

Pomona, Los Angeles, Pop. 146,537
Pomona USD 26,000/PK-12
PO Box 2900 91769 909-397-4800
Richard Martinez, supt. Fax 397-4881
www.pusd.org
Alcott ES 900/PK-6
1600 S Towne Ave 91766 909-397-4552
Juan Arretche, prin. Fax 623-4601
Allison ES 400/PK-6
1011 Russell Pl 91767 909-397-4556
Elizabeth Valenzuela, prin. Fax 622-3760
Arroyo ES 700/PK-6
1605 Arroyo Ave 91768 909-397-4568
Miguel Hurtado, prin. Fax 865-0440
Barfield ES 400/PK-6
2181 N San Antonio Ave 91767 909-397-4575
Rosario Ambriz, prin. Fax 623-5479
Cortez Math/Science Magnet S 800/PK-8
1300 N Dudley St 91768 909-397-4750
Lacey Lemus, prin. Fax 623-8473
Decker ES 500/PK-6
20 Village Loop Rd 91766 909-397-4581
Rebecca Norwood, prin. Fax 397-4585
Emerson MS 700/6-8
635 Lincoln Ave 91767 909-397-4516
Jesus Altamirano, prin. Fax 397-5280

Harrison S — 400/PK-8
425 E Harrison Ave 91767 — 909-397-4600
Shandria Roberts, prin. — Fax 626-2135
Kellogg Polytechnic ES — 400/PK-6
610 Medina St 91768 — 909-397-4604
Rabia Minhas, prin. — Fax 444-9782
Kingsley ES — 700/PK-5
1170 Washington Ave 91767 — 909-397-4608
Krista Fairley, prin. — Fax 620-3910
Lexington ES — 700/PK-8
550 W Lexington Ave 91766 — 909-397-4616
Anna Rico, prin. — Fax 865-3138
Lincoln ES — 400/PK-6
1200 N Gordon St 91768 — 909-397-4624
Alicia McMullin, prin. — Fax 620-0982
Lopez ES — 700/PK-6
701 S White Ave 91766 — 909-397-4438
Janet Fults, prin. — Fax 397-7751
Madison ES — 600/PK-6
351 W Phillips Blvd 91766 — 909-397-4643
Jesus Peralta, prin. — Fax 629-4351
Marshall MS — 500/6-8
1921 Arroyo Ave 91768 — 909-397-4532
Juan Ortiz, prin. — Fax 629-8275
Montvue ES — 300/PK-6
1440 San Bernardino Ave 91767 — 909-397-4655
Samuel Padilla, prin. — Fax 397-4658
Philadelphia ES — 900/PK-6
600 Philadelphia St 91766 — 909-397-4660
Alicia Castaneda, prin. — Fax 397-4607
Ranch Hills ES — 500/PK-6
2 Trabuco Rd 91766 — 909-397-4978
Todd Riffell, prin. — Fax 623-3628
Roosevelt ES — 700/PK-5
701 N Huntington Blvd 91768 — 909-397-4666
Alejandro Villa, prin. — Fax 623-2720
San Antonio ES — 600/PK-5
855 E Kingsley Ave 91767 — 909-397-4981
Selene Amancio, prin. — Fax 623-9789
San Jose S — 500/PK-8
2015 Cadillac Dr 91767 — 909-397-4670
Jorge Amancio, prin. — Fax 469-9890
Simons MS — 800/6-8
900 E Franklin Ave 91766 — 909-397-4544
Cristine Goens, prin. — Fax 623-4691
Vejar S — 900/PK-8
950 W Grand Ave 91766 — 909-397-4985
Madelene Brooks, prin. — Fax 865-3627
Washington ES — 700/PK-5
975 E 9th St 91766 — 909-397-4675
Alan Pantanini, prin. — Fax 397-4653
Westmont ES — 400/PK-6
1780 W 9th St 91766 — 909-397-4680
Cynthia Badillo, prin. — Fax 620-1686
Other Schools – See Diamond Bar

City of Knowledge S — 200/PK-12
3285 N Garey Ave 91767 — 909-392-0251
Dr. Haleema Shaikley, prin. — Fax 392-0295
ICC Community S — 100/K-8
3619 N Garey Ave 91767 — 909-392-9692
Fax 392-9652
St. Joseph S — 200/PK-8
1200 W Holt Ave 91768 — 909-622-3365
Diane Gehner, prin. — Fax 469-5146
St. Madeleine S — 100/K-8
935 E Kingsley Ave 91767 — 909-623-9602
Maria Jimenez, prin. — Fax 620-5766

Pond, Kern
Pond UNESD — 200/K-8
29585 Pond Rd 93280 — 661-792-2545
Frank Ohnesorgen, supt. — Fax 792-2303
www.pond.k12.ca.us
Pond ES — 200/K-8
29585 Pond Rd 93280 — 661-792-2545
Frank Ohnesorgen, prin. — Fax 792-2303

Pope Valley, Napa
Pope Valley UNSD — 50/K-8
PO Box 167 94567 — 707-965-2402
Kenneth Burkhart, supt. — Fax 965-0946
www.pvk8.org
Pope Valley ES — 50/K-8
PO Box 167 94567 — 707-965-2402
Kenneth Burkhart, prin. — Fax 965-0946

Porter Ranch, Los Angeles
Los Angeles USD
Supt. — See Los Angeles
Porter Ranch Community S — 900/K-8
12450 Mason Ave 91326 — 818-709-7100
Mary Paulino Melvin, prin. — Fax 993-1363

Porterville, Tulare, Pop. 53,236
Alta Vista ESD — 600/PK-8
2293 E Crabtree Ave 93257 — 559-782-5700
Robert M. Hudson Ed.D., supt. — Fax 782-5715
www.altavistaesd.org
Alta Vista ES — 600/PK-8
2293 E Crabtree Ave 93257 — 559-782-5700
Cliff Cantrell, prin. — Fax 788-2320

Burton ESD — 4,600/K-12
264 N Westwood St 93257 — 559-781-8020
Sharon Kamberg Ed.D., supt. — Fax 781-1403
www.burtonschools.org
Buckley ES — 500/K-5
2573 W Westfield Ave 93257 — 559-788-6412
Matt Baxter, prin. — Fax 788-6417
Burton ES — 500/K-5
2375 W Morton Ave 93257 — 559-784-2401
Jean Miller, prin. — Fax 793-1686
Burton MS — 500/7-8
1155 N Elderwood St 93257 — 559-781-2671
Chastity Lollis Ed.D., prin. — Fax 788-6424
Maples Academy — 600/K-6
252 N Westwood St 93257 — 559-781-1658
Mitzie Styles, prin. — Fax 781-8574
Oak Grove ES — 500/K-5
1873 W Mulberry Ave 93257 — 559-784-0310
Troy Hayes, prin. — Fax 788-6411

Hope ESD — 200/PK-8
613 W Teapot Dome Ave 93257 — 559-784-1064
Deborah McCaskill, supt. — Fax 784-1905
Hope ES — 200/PK-8
613 W Teapot Dome Ave 93257 — 559-784-1064
Deborah McCaskill, prin. — Fax 784-1905

Pleasant View ESD — 600/PK-8
14004 Road 184 93257 — 559-784-6769
Mark Odsather, supt. — Fax 784-6819
www.pleasant-view.org
Pleasant View ES — 400/PK-4
14004 Road 184 93257 — 559-788-2002
Richard Thornberry, supt. — Fax 788-2030
Pleasant View West S — 200/5-8
14004 Road 184 93257 — 559-784-6769
Mark Odsather, supt. — Fax 784-6819

Porterville USD — 13,800/K-12
600 W Grand Ave 93257 — 559-793-2400
Ken Gibbs Ed.D., supt. — Fax 793-1088
www.portervilleschools.org
Bartlett MS — 500/7-8
600 W Grand Ave 93257 — 559-782-7100
Mike Tsuboi, prin. — Fax 784-3432
Belleview ES — 500/K-6
600 W Grand Ave 93257 — 559-782-7110
Crystal Milinich, prin. — Fax 788-0216
Doyle ES — 700/K-6
600 W Grand Ave 93257 — 559-782-7140
Ubaldo Ortiz, prin. — Fax 788-0214
Los Robles ES — 500/K-6
600 W Grand Ave 93257 — 559-782-7011
Carla Crocker, prin. — Fax 788-0139
Monte Vista ES — 500/K-6
600 W Grand Ave 93257 — 559-782-7350
Andrew Woodley, prin. — Fax 793-0150
Olive Street ES — 700/K-6
600 W Grand Ave 93257 — 559-782-7190
Isaac Nunez, prin. — Fax 783-9233
Pioneer MS — 600/6-8
600 W Grand Ave 93257 — 559-782-7200
Angel Valdez, prin. — Fax 784-3507
Roche Avenue ES — 400/K-6
600 W Grand Ave 93257 — 559-782-7250
Patricia Jorgensen, prin. — Fax 783-8356
Santa Fe ES — 800/K-5
600 W Grand Ave 93257 — 559-782-6614
Julissa Leyva Ed.D., prin. — Fax 782-6613
Sequoia MS — 600/7-8
600 W Grand Ave 93257 — 559-788-0925
Joe Santos Ed.D., prin. — Fax 788-0927
Vandalia ES — 600/K-5
600 W Grand Ave 93257 — 559-782-7260
Laura Vera, prin. — Fax 782-7268
Westfield ES — 600/K-6
600 W Grand Ave 93257 — 559-782-7270
Cindy Ervin, prin. — Fax 783-8219
West Putnam ES — 600/K-6
600 W Grand Ave 93257 — 559-782-7280
Lissa Lambie, prin. — Fax 783-2969

Rockford ESD — 400/K-8
14983 Road 208 93257 — 559-784-5406
Caron Borba, supt. — Fax 784-8608
rockfordschooldistrict.org
Rockford ES — 400/K-8
14983 Road 208 93257 — 559-784-5406
Caron Borba, prin. — Fax 784-8608

Woodville Union ESD — 500/K-8
16541 Road 168 93257 — 559-686-9712
Jesse Navarro, supt. — Fax 685-0875
www.woodville.k12.ca.us
Woodville Union ES — 500/K-8
16541 Road 168 93257 — 559-686-9713
Jesse Navarro, admin. — Fax 685-0875

St. Anne S — 200/PK-8
385 N F St 93257 — 559-784-4096
Kayla Trueblood, prin. — Fax 784-4338

Port Hueneme, Ventura, Pop. 20,969
Hueneme ESD — 8,400/K-8
205 N Ventura Rd 93041 — 805-488-3588
Dr. Christine Walker, supt. — Fax 986-8755
www.huensd.k12.ca.us
Bard ES — 700/K-5
622 E Pleasant Valley Rd 93041 — 805-488-3583
David Castellano, prin. — Fax 488-1303
Hueneme ES — 500/K-5
354 N 3rd St 93041 — 805-488-3569
Dr. Martha S. Romero, prin. — Fax 986-8765
Parkview ES — 700/K-5
1416 N 6th Pl 93041 — 805-986-8730
Cara Comstock, prin. — Fax 986-8734
Sunkist ES — 800/K-5
1400 Teakwood St 93041 — 805-986-8722
Cynthia Delgado, prin. — Fax 486-8753
Other Schools – See Oxnard

Hueneme Christian S — 200/PK-5
328 N Ventura Rd 93041 — 805-488-8781
Patricia Hernandez, prin. — Fax 488-2891

Portola, Plumas, Pop. 2,059
Plumas USD
Supt. — See Quincy
Carmichael ES — 300/K-6
895 West St 96122 — 530-832-0211
Melissa Leal, prin. — Fax 832-0667

Portola Valley, San Mateo, Pop. 4,271
Portola Valley ESD — 700/K-8
4575 Alpine Rd 94028 — 650-851-1777
Dr. Lisa Gonzales, supt. — Fax 851-3700
www.pvsd.net
Corte Madera MS — 400/4-8
4575 Alpine Rd 94028 — 650-851-1777
Cyndi Maijala, prin. — Fax 529-8553

Ormondale ES — 300/K-3
200 Shawnee Pass 94028 — 650-851-1777
Lynette Hovland, prin. — Fax 529-2086

Woodland S — 200/PK-8
360 La Cuesta Dr 94028 — 650-854-9065
Marja Brandon, head sch — Fax 854-6006

Potrero, San Diego, Pop. 643
Mountain Empire USD
Supt. — See Pine Valley
Potrero S — 300/PK-8
24875 Potrero Valley Rd 91963 — 619-478-5930
Cheryl Lugo, prin. — Fax 478-5821

Potter Valley, Mendocino, Pop. 628
Potter Valley Community USD — 200/PK-12
PO Box 219 95469 — 707-743-2101
Holly McLaughlin, supt. — Fax 743-1930
www.pottervalleyschools.us
Potter Valley ES — 100/PK-6
PO Box 219 95469 — 707-743-1115
Lori Candelaria, prin. — Fax 743-1483

Poway, San Diego, Pop. 46,170
Poway USD
Supt. — See San Diego
Chaparral ES — 900/K-5
17250 Tannin Dr 92064 — 858-485-0042
Rhiannon Buhr, prin. — Fax 673-8579
Garden Road ES — 400/K-5
14614 Garden Rd 92064 — 858-748-0230
Jeannie Dickinson, prin. — Fax 748-2961
Meadowbrook MS — 1,300/6-8
12320 Meadowbrook Ln 92064 — 858-748-0802
Miguel Carrillo, prin. — Fax 679-0149
Midland ES — 600/K-5
13910 Midland Rd 92064 — 858-748-0047
Sidia Martinez, prin. — Fax 748-8934
Painted Rock ES — 700/K-5
16711 Martincoit Rd 92064 — 858-487-1180
Denise Davis, prin. — Fax 673-8254
Pomerado ES — 500/K-5
12321 9th St 92064 — 858-748-1320
Luis Ortiz, prin. — Fax 748-8695
Tierra Bonita ES — 500/K-5
14678 Tierra Bonita Rd 92064 — 858-748-8540
Mandy Bedard, prin. — Fax 748-8864
Twin Peaks MS — 1,200/6-8
14640 Tierra Bonita Rd 92064 — 858-748-5131
Kelly Burke, prin. — Fax 679-6823
Valley ES — 800/K-5
13000 Bowron Rd 92064 — 858-748-2007
Ricardo Cecena, prin. — Fax 748-6587

Country Montessori S of Poway — 200/PK-5
12642 Monte Vista Rd 92064 — 858-673-1756
Adela Corrales, head sch — Fax 673-8379
St. Michael's S — 500/K-8
15542 Pomerado Rd 92064 — 858-485-1303
Kathleen Mock, prin. — Fax 485-5059

Prather, Fresno, Pop. 30
Sierra USD — 1,300/K-12
29143 Auberry Rd 93651 — 559-855-3662
Melissa Ireland Ed.D., supt. — Fax 855-3585
www.sierrausd.org
Foothill S — 600/K-6
29147 Auberry Rd 93651 — 559-855-3551
Dr. Alan Harris, prin. — Fax 855-5350
Other Schools – See Tollhouse

Princeton, Colusa, Pop. 299
Princeton JUSD — 200/K-12
PO Box 8 95970 — 530-439-2261
Randy Wise, supt. — Fax 439-2113
www.pjusd.org
Princeton ES — 100/K-6
PO Box 8 95970 — 530-439-2501
Cody Walker, prin. — Fax 439-2512

Prunedale, Monterey, Pop. 16,965

Prunedale Christian Academy — 100/PK-12
8145 Prunedale North Rd 93907 — 831-663-2211
Rev. Betty Moon, prin. — Fax 663-1663

Quartz Hill, Los Angeles, Pop. 10,599
Westside UNESD — 8,900/K-8
41914 50th St W 93536 — 661-722-0716
Regina Rossall, supt. — Fax 206-3645
www.westside.k12.ca.us
Quartz Hill ES — 800/K-6
41820 50th St W 93536 — 661-943-3236
Andrea Paxton, prin. — Fax 943-1496
Walker MS — 900/6-8
5632 W Avenue L8 93536 — 661-943-3258
Steve Wood, prin. — Fax 943-2969
Other Schools – See Lancaster, Leona Valley, Palmdale

Quincy, Plumas, Pop. 1,652
Plumas USD — 2,100/K-12
1446 E Main St 95971 — 530-283-6500
Terry Oestreich, supt. — Fax 283-6530
www.pcoe.k12.ca.us
Quincy ES — 400/K-6
246 Alder St 95971 — 530-283-6550
Lara Hollister, prin. — Fax 283-6508
Other Schools – See Chester, Greenville, Portola

Plumas Christian S — 100/K-6
49 S Lindan Ave 95971 — 530-283-0415
Shannon Little, prin. — Fax 283-2933

Rail Road Flat, Calaveras, Pop. 453
Calaveras USD
Supt. — See San Andreas
Rail Road Flat ES — 50/K-6
PO Box 217 95248 — 209-754-2275
Mark Campbell, prin. — Fax 293-7709

Rainbow, San Diego, Pop. 1,796
Vallecitos ESD 200/PK-12
5211 5th St 92028 760-728-7092
Gary Wilson, supt. Fax 728-7712
www.vallecitossd.net
Other Schools – See Fallbrook

Raisin City, Fresno, Pop. 378
Raisin City ESD 300/K-8
PO Box 69 93652 559-233-0128
Juan Sandoval, supt. Fax 486-0891
www.raisincity.k12.ca.us
Raisin City ES 300/K-8
PO Box 69 93652 559-233-0128
Juan Sandoval, prin. Fax 486-0891

Ramona, San Diego, Pop. 19,844
Ramona USD 5,700/K-12
720 9th St 92065 760-787-2000
Dr. Anne Staffieri Ed.D., supt. Fax 789-9168
www.ramonausd.net
Barnett ES 500/K-6
23925 Couna Way 92065 760-787-3500
Linda Marthis, prin. Fax 788-5358
Dukes ES 500/K-6
24908 Abalar Way 92065 760-788-5060
Joy Harris, prin. Fax 788-6170
Hanson ES 500/K-6
2520 Boundary Ave 92065 760-787-2100
Christopher Gunnett, prin. Fax 788-5363
Mt. Woodson ES 500/K-6
17427 Archie Moore Rd 92065 760-788-5120
Robin Arend, prin. Fax 788-5353
Peirce MS 800/7-8
1521 Hanson Ln 92065 760-787-2400
Pauline Leavitt, prin. Fax 788-5014
Ramona ES 500/K-6
415 8th St 92065 760-787-4400
Pixie Sulser, prin. Fax 788-5110

Ramona Lutheran Christian S 100/PK-6
520 16th St 92065 760-789-4804
Elaine Crary, admin. Fax 789-8110

Rancho Cordova, Sacramento, Pop. 60,932
Elk Grove USD
Supt. — See Elk Grove
McGarvey ES K-6
4350 Sophistry Dr 95742 916-793-3400
Michael Gulden, prin.
Sunrise ES 1,000/K-6
11821 Cobble Brook Dr 95742 916-985-4350
Martin Hock, prin. Fax 985-8927

Folsom-Cordova USD 19,300/PK-12
1965 Birkmont Dr 95742 916-294-9000
Sarah Koligian, supt. Fax 294-9020
www.fcusd.org
Cordova Gardens ES 300/K-6
2400 Dawes St 95670 916-294-9115
Dr. Karen Redfield, prin. Fax 363-5359
Cordova Lane Center Preschool 100/PK-PK
2460 Cordova Ln 95670 916-294-9090
Jacqueline Wyse, prin.
Cordova Meadows ES 400/K-5
2550 La Loma Dr 95670 916-294-9120
Marie Pawlek, prin. Fax 294-2482
Cordova Villa ES 500/K-5
10359 S White Rock Rd 95670 916-294-9425
Jessica Hutchinson, prin. Fax 294-2483
Mills MS 800/6-8
10439 Coloma Rd 95670 916-294-9045
Peter Maroon, prin. Fax 294-2476
Mitchell MS 700/6-8
2100 Zinfandel Dr 95670 916-294-9050
Jim Huber, prin. Fax 294-2477
Navigator ES 400/K-5
10679 Bear Hollow Dr 95670 916-294-2420
Carole Vargas, prin. Fax 859-0740
Rancho Cordova ES 400/K-5
2562 Chassella Way 95670 916-294-9165
Larry Mahoney, prin. Fax 294-2489
Riverview STEM Academy K-5
10700 Ambassador Dr 95670 916-294-2435
Tony Peterson, prin. Fax 294-2436
Shields ES 400/K-5
10434 Georgetown Dr 95670 916-294-9160
Tod Bosque, prin. Fax 294-2488
White Rock ES 500/K-6
10487 White Rock Rd 95670 916-294-9180
Sandra Spaulding, prin. Fax 294-9072
Williamson ES 600/K-5
2275 Benita Dr 95670 916-294-9185
Angi Carlomagno, prin. Fax 294-9073
Other Schools – See Folsom, Mather

St. John Vianney S 200/K-8
10499 Coloma Rd 95670 916-363-4610
Ada Bauman, prin. Fax 363-3243

Rancho Cucamonga, San Bernardino, Pop. 159,896
Central ESD 4,700/K-8
10601 Church St Ste 112 91730 909-989-8541
Donna Libutti, supt. Fax 941-1732
www.csd-ca.schoolloop.com
Bear Gulch ES 500/K-5
8355 Bear Gulch Pl 91730 909-989-9396
Keri Applegate, prin. Fax 484-2730
Central ES 500/K-5
7955 Archibald Ave 91730 909-987-2541
Renee Barnett, prin. Fax 484-2740
Coyote Canyon ES 800/K-4
7889 Elm Ave 91730 909-980-4743
Michelle Dynes, prin. Fax 980-1596
Cucamonga MS 800/6-8
7611 Hellman Ave 91730 909-987-1788
Allan Morales, prin. Fax 483-3201
Dona Merced ES 600/K-5
10333 Palo Alto St 91730 909-980-1600
Pam Schlappi, prin. Fax 980-0066
Musser MS 1,000/5-8
10789 Terra Vista Pkwy 91730 909-980-1230
Mary Kate Perez, prin. Fax 980-3042
Valle Vista ES 500/K-5
7727 Valle Vista Dr 91730 909-981-8697
Luanne Weaver, prin. Fax 981-9718

Cucamonga ESD 2,500/K-8
8776 Archibald Ave 91730 909-987-8942
Janet Temkin, supt. Fax 980-3628
www.cucamonga-ca.schoolloop.com
Cucamonga ES 500/K-5
8776 Archibald Ave 91730 909-980-1318
Joyce Kozyra, prin. Fax 980-4040
Los Amigos ES 500/K-5
8776 Archibald Ave 91730 909-982-8387
Amber Arrequin, prin. Fax 982-8679
Rancho Cucamonga MS 800/6-8
8776 Archibald Ave 91730 909-980-0969
Bruce LaVallee, prin. Fax 481-5381
Other Schools – See Ontario

Etiwanda SD
Supt. — See Etiwanda
Terra Vista ES 800/K-5
7497 Mountain View Dr 91730 909-945-5715
Jeannie Tavolazzi, prin. Fax 945-3373

Sacred Heart S 300/K-8
12676 Foothill Blvd 91739 909-899-1049
Trenna Meins, prin. Fax 899-0413
Upland Christian Academy 400/K-12
10900 Civic Center Dr 91730 909-758-8747
Tim Hoy, supt. Fax 204-4555

Rancho Dminguez, Los Angeles

St. Albert the Great S 200/PK-5
804 E Compton Blvd, 310-323-4559
Tina Johnson, prin. Fax 323-4825

Rancho Mirage, Riverside, Pop. 16,964
Palm Springs USD
Supt. — See Palm Springs
Rancho Mirage ES 400/K-5
42985 Indian Trl 92270 760-836-3680
LaTrice Johnson Ed.D., prin. Fax 836-3684

Palm Valley S 400/PK-12
35525 Da Vall Dr 92270 760-328-0861
Susan Rice, head sch Fax 770-4541

Rancho Palos Verdes, Los Angeles, Pop. 39,919
Los Angeles USD
Supt. — See Los Angeles
Crestwood Street ES 500/K-6
1946 W Crestwood St 90275 310-832-8130
Ron Tanimura, prin. Fax 832-7458
Dodson MS 1,900/6-8
28014 S Montereina Dr 90275 310-241-1900
John Vladovic, prin. Fax 832-4709

Palos Verdes Peninsula USD
Supt. — See Palos Verdes Estates
Cornerstone at Pedregal ES 400/K-5
6069 Groveoak Pl 90275 310-378-0324
Michele Marcus, prin. Fax 378-1484
Mira Catalina ES 400/K-5
30511 Lucania Dr 90275 310-377-6731
Brett Egan, prin. Fax 541-4220
Miraleste Early Learning Academy 50/PK-PK
6245 Via Canada 90275 310-732-0922
Mary Ellen Haworth, lead tchr. Fax 732-5660
Miraleste IS 900/6-8
29323 Palos Verdes Dr E 90275 310-732-0900
Brent Kuykendall, prin. Fax 521-8915
Point Vicente ES 400/K-5
30540 Rue De La Pierre 90275 310-377-6972
Beth Hadley, prin. Fax 377-7692
Ridgecrest IS 900/6-8
28915 Northbay Rd 90275 310-544-2747
Kelli Keller, prin. Fax 265-1716
Silver Spur ES 500/K-5
5500 Ironwood St 90275 310-378-5011
Marta Jevenois, prin. Fax 378-7674
Soleado ES 400/K-5
27800 Longhill Dr 90275 310-377-6854
Gina Stutzel, prin. Fax 544-0916
Vista Grande ES 500/K-5
7032 Purple Ridge Dr 90275 310-377-6066
Jeri Delatorre, prin. Fax 541-4692

Christ Lutheran S 200/PK-8
28850 S Western Ave 90275 310-831-0848
Dennis Jacobson, prin. Fax 831-0090
Peninsula Montessori S 200/PK-6
31100 Hawthorne Blvd 90275 310-544-3099
St. John Fisher S 300/PK-8
5446 Crest Rd 90275 310-377-2800
Anne-Marie Hudani, prin. Fax 377-3863

Rancho Santa Fe, San Diego, Pop. 3,061
Rancho Sante Fe ESD 700/K-8
PO Box 809 92067 858-756-1141
David Jaffe, supt. Fax 756-0912
rsfschool.net
Rowe ES 400/K-5
PO Box 809 92067 858-756-1141
Kim Pinkerton, prin. Fax 756-0712
Rowe MS 300/6-8
PO Box 809 92067 858-756-1141
Garrett Corduan, prin. Fax 759-0712

Solana Beach ESD
Supt. — See Solana Beach
Solana Santa Fe ES 400/K-6
PO Box 8940 92067 858-794-4700
Becky Gauthier, prin. Fax 794-4750

Horizon Prep 500/PK-12
PO Box 9070 92067 858-756-5599
Dr. Erik Konsmo, head sch Fax 759-5827
Nativity S 200/K-8
PO Box 9180 92067 858-756-6763
Paul Parker, prin. Fax 756-9128

Rancho Santa Margarita, Orange, Pop. 46,094
Capistrano USD
Supt. — See San Juan Capistrano
Arroyo Vista S 600/K-8
23371 Arroyo Vis 92688 949-234-5951
Joe McGann, prin. Fax 589-6924
Las Flores ES 600/K-5
25862 Antonio Pkwy 92688 949-589-6935
Holly Wiseman, prin. Fax 589-9286
Las Flores MS 1,100/6-8
25862 Antonio Pkwy 92688 949-589-6543
Sean McNamara, prin. Fax 589-9286
Tijeras Creek ES 400/K-5
23072 Avenida Empresa 92688 949-234-5300
Diann Buckingham, prin. Fax 858-3862

Saddleback Valley USD
Supt. — See Mission Viejo
Cielo Vista ES 900/K-6
21811 Avnida De Los Fundado 92688 949-589-7456
Beth Ewing Ed.D., prin. Fax 589-8671
Melinda Heights ES 1,100/K-6
21001 Rancho Trabuco 92688 949-888-7311
Kathy Martin, prin. Fax 888-7429
Rancho Santa Margarita IS 1,400/7-8
21931 Alma Aldea 92688 949-459-8253
Brian Ferguson, prin. Fax 459-8258
Trabuco Mesa ES 600/K-6
21301 Avenida De Las Flores 92688 949-858-3339
Caryn McGrew, prin. Fax 858-5476

Kingdom Life Academy 100/K-8
30615 Avenida De Las Flores 92688 949-329-8620
Renee Rose, prin.
Mission Hills Christian S 500/PK-8
29582 Aventura 92688 949-589-4504
Larry Ahl, prin. Fax 589-7566
St. John's Episcopal S 600/PK-8
30382 Via Con Dios 92688 949-858-5144
Dr. Michael Pratt Ph.D., head sch Fax 858-1403
St. Junipero Serra Catholic S 1,100/PK-8
23652 Antonio Pkwy 92688 949-888-1990
Angeline Trudell, pres. Fax 888-1994

Ravendale, Lassen
Ravendale-Termo ESD 400/PK-12
709-855 Termo-Grasshopper 96123 530-251-8938
Jason Waddell, supt. Fax 251-8940
www.juniperridge.org
Juniper Ridge S 50/PK-8
709-855 Termo-Grasshopper 96123 530-251-8938
Jason Waddell, prin. Fax 251-8940

Raymond, Madera
Raymond Knowles UNESD 100/K-8
PO Box 47 93653 559-689-3336
Michelle Townsend, supt. Fax 689-3203
www.rkusd.k12.ca.us
Raymond-Knowles ES 100/K-8
PO Box 47 93653 559-689-3336
Michelle Townsend, prin. Fax 689-3203

Red Bluff, Tehama, Pop. 13,607
Antelope ESD 700/PK-8
22630 Antelope Blvd 96080 530-527-1272
Richard Hassay, supt. Fax 527-0656
www.antelopeschools.org
Antelope ES 400/PK-5
22630 Antelope Blvd 96080 530-527-1272
Barney Thomas, prin. Fax 527-2931
Berrendos MS 200/6-8
401 Chestnut Ave 96080 530-527-6700
Jim Weber, prin. Fax 527-2506
Other Schools – See Manton, Paynes Creek

Evergreen UNSD
Supt. — See Cottonwood
Bend ES 100/PK-8
22270 Bend Ferry Rd 96080 530-527-4648
Nancy Veatch, prin. Fax 527-4670

Red Bluff UNESD 2,100/K-8
1755 Airport Blvd 96080 530-527-7200
Cliff Curry, supt. Fax 527-9308
www.rbuesd.org
Bidwell ES 500/K-5
1256 Walnut St 96080 530-527-7171
Suzanne Adkins, prin. Fax 527-8439
Jackson Heights ES 500/K-5
225 Jackson St 96080 530-527-7150
Will Barnett, prin. Fax 527-1172
Metteer S 500/K-5
695 Kimball Rd 96080 530-527-9015
Jennifer Brockman, prin. Fax 527-7240
Vista Preparatory Academy 600/6-8
1770 S Jackson St 96080 530-527-7840
Shane Humphreys, prin. Fax 527-9374

Reeds Creek ESD 100/PK-8
18335 Johnson Rd 96080 530-527-6006
Cindy Haase, supt. Fax 527-6849
www.reedscreek.org
Reeds Creek S 100/PK-8
18335 Johnson Rd 96080 530-527-6006
Cindy Haase, prin. Fax 527-6849

Adventist Christian ES 1-8
720 S Jackson St 96080 530-527-1846
Deborah Judson, prin.
Sacred Heart S 100/K-8
2255 Monroe Ave 96080 530-527-6727
Bill Koppes, prin. Fax 527-5026

Redding, Shasta, Pop. 86,489
Columbia ESD 800/PK-8
10140 Old Oregon Trl 96003 530-223-1915
Clay Ross, supt. Fax 223-4168
www.columbiasd.com
Columbia ES 500/K-4
10142 Old Oregon Trl 96003 530-223-4070
Cortney Pratt, prin. Fax 223-5245
Columbia Preschool PK-PK
10142 Old Oregon Trl 96003 530-223-4070
Shelley Anstine, dir. Fax 223-5245
Mountain View MS 400/5-8
675 Shasta View Dr 96003 530-221-5224
Shannon Angstadt, prin. Fax 221-5620

Enterprise ESD 3,800/PK-12
1155 Mistletoe Ln 96002 530-224-4100
Brian Winstead Ed.D., supt. Fax 224-4101
www.eesd.net/
Alta Mesa ES 300/PK-5
2301 Saturn Skwy 96002 530-224-4130
Darin Pust, prin. Fax 224-4131
Boulder Creek S 1,000/PK-8
505 Springer Dr 96003 530-224-4140
Tina Croes, prin. Fax 224-4141
Lassen View ES 400/PK-5
705 Loma Vista Dr 96002 530-224-4150
Caryn Emerson, prin. Fax 224-4151
Mistletoe S 600/PK-8
1225 Mistletoe Ln 96002 530-224-4160
Heather Armelino, prin. Fax 224-4161
Parsons JHS 600/6-8
750 Hartnell Ave 96002 530-224-4190
Tony Moebes, prin. Fax 224-4191
Rother ES 400/PK-5
795 Hartnell Ave 96002 530-224-4170
Robert Shaw, prin. Fax 224-4171
Shasta Meadows ES 300/PK-5
2825 Yana Ave 96002 530-224-4180
Scotti Gleason, prin. Fax 224-4181

Gateway USD 3,600/PK-12
4411 Mountain Lakes Blvd 96003 530-245-7900
James Harrell, supt. Fax 245-7920
www.gateway-schools.org
Buckeye S of the Arts 600/PK-8
3407 Hiatt Dr 96003 530-225-0420
Terri Daniels, prin. Fax 225-0402
Other Schools – See Shasta Lake

Grant ESD 600/K-8
8835 Swasey Dr 96001 530-243-0561
Mike Freeman, supt. Fax 243-7631
grantschoolcougars.com
Grant S 600/K-8
8835 Swasey Dr 96001 530-243-0561
Michael Freeman, supt. Fax 243-7631

Igo-Ono-Platina UNESD 100/K-8
5885 E Bonnyview Rd 96001 530-225-0011
Robert Adams, supt. Fax 225-0015
igo.reddingschools.net
Other Schools – See Igo

Pacheco UNESD 600/K-8
7424 Pacheco School Rd 96002 530-224-4599
Kathryn Pearce Ed.D., supt. Fax 224-4591
www.pacheco.k12.ca.us
Pacheco S 300/4-8
7430 Pacheco School Rd 96002 530-224-4585
Kathryn Pearce, prin. Fax 224-4588
Other Schools – See Anderson

Redding ESD 3,400/K-12
5885 E Bonnyview Rd 96001 530-225-0011
Robert Adams, supt. Fax 225-0015
www.reddingschools.net/
Bonny View ES 300/K-5
5885 E Bonnyview Rd 96001 530-225-0030
Jennifer Mosier, prin. Fax 225-0034
Cypress ES 200/K-5
5885 E Bonnyview Rd 96001 530-225-0040
Rich Hall, prin. Fax 225-0044
Juniper S 300/K-8
5885 E Bonnyview Rd 96001 530-225-0045
Molly Stimpel, prin. Fax 225-0049
Manzanita ES 600/K-5
5885 E Bonnyview Rd 96001 530-225-0050
Kellie Dunham, prin. Fax 225-0054
Sequoia MS 800/4-8
5885 E Bonnyview Rd 96001 530-225-0020
John Moser, prin. Fax 225-0029
Sycamore ES 200/K-5
5885 E Bonnyview Rd 96001 530-225-0055
Susanna Winstead, prin. Fax 225-0059
Turtle Bay S 800/K-8
5885 E Bonnyview Rd 96001 530-225-0035
AJ Anderson, prin. Fax 225-0039

Shasta UNESD 100/K-8
5885 E Bonnyview Rd 96001 530-225-0011
Robert Adams, supt. Fax 241-5193
www.shastaunionschool.net/
Other Schools – See Shasta

Bethel Christian S 300/PK-8
933 College View Dr 96003 530-246-6010
H. Don Mayer M.Ed., prin. Fax 246-6020
Country Christian S 200/PK-8
873 Canby Rd 96003 530-222-0675
Jeff Wilson, admin. Fax 222-2631
Liberty Christian S 200/PK-10
2970 Hartnell Ave 96002 530-222-2232
Tom Adams, admin. Fax 222-1784
Mt. Calvary Lutheran S 50/PK-8
3961 Alta Mesa Dr 96002 530-221-2451
Jacob Rothe, prin. Fax 222-1403
Redding Adventist Academy 100/K-8
1356 E Cypress Ave 96002 530-222-1018
Wayne Gungl, prin. Fax 222-4260
St. Joseph S 200/K-8
2460 Gold St 96001 530-243-2302
Bill Koppes, prin. Fax 243-2747

Redlands, San Bernardino, Pop. 66,575
Redlands USD 21,000/K-12
PO Box 3008 92373 909-307-5300
Mauricio Arellano, supt. Fax 748-6711
www.redlandsusd.net
Clement MS 1,000/6-8
501 E Pennsylvania Ave 92374 909-307-5400
Robert Clarey, prin. Fax 307-5414
Cope MS 1,400/6-8
1000 W Cypress Ave 92373 909-307-5420
Lisa Bruich, prin. Fax 307-5436
Crafton ES 600/K-5
311 N Wabash Ave 92374 909-794-8600
Patricia Buchmiller, prin. Fax 794-8605
Franklin ES 600/K-5
850 E Colton Ave 92374 909-307-5530
Heidi Vazquez, prin. Fax 307-5539
Judson & Brown ES 600/K-5
1401 E Pennsylvania Ave 92374 909-307-2430
Jennifer Hosch, prin. Fax 307-2438
Kimberly ES 600/K-5
301 W South Ave 92373 909-307-5540
Matthew Osmond, prin. Fax 307-5545
Kingsbury ES 400/K-5
600 Cajon St 92373 909-307-5550
Todd Flowers, prin. Fax 307-5555
Lugonia ES 600/K-5
202 E Pennsylvania Ave 92374 909-307-5560
Kimberly Lium, prin. Fax 307-5566
Mariposa ES 600/K-5
30800 Palo Alto Dr 92373 909-794-8620
Scott Bohlender, prin. Fax 794-8624
McKinley ES 400/K-5
645 W Olive Ave 92373 909-307-5570
Marc Aponte, prin. Fax 307-5579
Mission ES 600/K-5
10568 California St 92373 909-307-2480
Denise Fee, prin. Fax 307-2481
Moore MS 1,100/6-8
1550 E Highland Ave 92374 909-307-5440
Maisie McCue, prin. Fax 307-5453
Smiley ES 600/K-5
1210 W Cypress Ave 92373 909-307-5580
Jennifer Sherman, prin. Fax 307-5339
Other Schools – See Highland, Loma Linda, Mentone, San Bernardino

---

Montessori in Redlands 300/PK-6
1890 Orange Ave 92373 909-793-6989
Jenny Davidson, head sch Fax 335-2749
Packinghouse Christian Academy 200/K-12
27165 San Bernardino Ave 92374 909-793-4984
Jeff Lindeman, prin. Fax 307-1852
Redlands Adventist Academy 500/K-12
130 Tennessee St 92373 909-793-1000
Redlands Christian S 500/PK-5
1145 Church St 92374 909-793-5172
Daniel Cole, head sch Fax 335-9593
Sacred Heart Academy 300/PK-8
215 S Eureka St 92373 909-792-3958
Angela Williams, prin. Fax 792-7292
Valley Preparatory S 200/PK-8
1605 Ford St 92373 909-793-3063
John Black, head sch Fax 798-5963

Redondo Beach, Los Angeles, Pop. 63,466
Redondo Beach Unified SD 9,100/K-12
1401 Inglewood Ave 90278 310-379-5449
Steven Keller Ed.D., supt. Fax 798-8610
www.rbusd.org
Adams MS 900/6-8
2600 Ripley Ave 90278 310-798-8636
Anthony Taranto, prin. Fax 318-3064
Alta Vista ES 600/K-5
815 Knob Hill Ave 90277 310-798-8650
Susan Wildes, prin. Fax 798-8662
Beryl Heights ES 500/K-5
920 Beryl St 90277 310-798-8611
Karen Mohr, prin. Fax 937-6513
Birney ES 400/K-5
1600 Green Ln 90278 310-798-8626
Fax 937-6511
Jefferson ES 600/K-5
600 Harkness Ln 90278 310-798-8631
Fax 937-6506
Lincoln ES 600/K-5
2223 Plant Ave 90278 310-798-8646
Jason Johnson, prin. Fax 793-6786
Madison ES 400/K-5
2200 MacKay Ln 90278 310-798-8623
Drew Gamet, prin. Fax 798-3923
Parras MS 1,100/6-8
200 N Lucia Ave 90277 310-798-8616
Dr. Lars Nygren, prin. Fax 798-8620
Tulita ES 500/K-5
1520 S Prospect Ave 90277 310-798-8628
Dr. Tanaz Bruna, prin. Fax 798-8698
Washington ES 700/K-5
1100 Lilienthal Ln 90278 310-798-8641
Andrea Bittick, prin. Fax 798-8302

Riviera Hall Lutheran S 200/PK-8
330 Palos Verdes Blvd 90277 310-375-5528
Kelly McCabe, prin. Fax 791-8939
St. Lawrence Martyr S 300/K-8
1950 S Prospect Ave 90277 310-316-3049
Diane Kaiser, prin. Fax 316-0888
Valor Christian Academy 200/PK-8
525 Earle Ln 90278 310-798-5181
Jon Fast, prin. Fax 798-1575

Redway, Humboldt, Pop. 1,171
Southern Humboldt JUSD
Supt. — See Miranda
Redway ES 300/PK-6
PO Box 369 95560 707-923-2526
Stephanie Steffano-Davis, prin. Fax 923-3289

Redwood City, San Mateo, Pop. 73,481
Belmont-Redwood Shores ESD
Supt. — See Belmont
Redwood Shores ES 400/K-5
225 Shearwater Pkwy 94065 650-802-8060
Annie Cahoon, prin. Fax 802-8903
Sandpiper ES 500/K-6
801 Redwood Shores Pkwy 94065 650-631-5510
Tamara Moore, prin. Fax 631-5515

Redwood City ESD 9,100/PK-8
750 Bradford St 94063 650-423-2200
Dr. John R. Baker, supt. Fax 423-2204
www.rcsdk8.net
Adelante Spanish Immersion S 500/K-5
3150 Granger Way 94061 650-482-2401
Christine Hiltbran, prin. Fax 482-5984
Clifford ES 700/K-8
225 Clifford Ave 94062 650-482-2402
Joshua Swerdlow, prin. Fax 367-4354
Cloud ES 800/K-8
3790 Red Oak Way 94061 650-482-2414
Dana Hardester, prin. Fax 367-4355
Fair Oaks ES 400/K-5
2950 Fair Oaks Ave 94063 650-482-2403
Joshua Griffith, prin. Fax 367-4356
Ford ES 400/K-5
2498 Massachusetts Ave 94061 650-482-2404
Lynne Griffiths, prin. Fax 367-4357
Gill ES 500/K-5
555 Avenue Del Ora 94062 650-482-2406
Katherine Rivera, prin. Fax 367-4359
Hawes ES 400/K-5
909 Roosevelt Ave 94061 650-482-2407
Al Rosell, prin. Fax 367-4360
Hoover ES 800/K-8
701 Charter St 94063 650-482-2408
Tina Mercer, prin. Fax 367-4361
Kennedy MS 800/6-8
2521 Goodwin Ave 94061 650-482-2409
Stephen Brady, prin. Fax 367-4362
McKinley Institute of Technology 400/6-8
400 Duane St 94062 650-482-2410
Nick Fanourgiakis, prin. Fax 367-4363
North Star Academy 500/3-8
400 Duane St 94062 650-482-2411
Sara Shackel, prin. Fax 482-5980
Rocketship Redwood City Prep S PK-4
701 Charter St 94063 650-482-2429
Esther Lin, prin.
Roosevelt ES 600/K-8
2223 Vera Ave 94061 650-482-2413
Tracy DaCosta, prin. Fax 367-4365
Taft ES 500/K-5
903 10th Ave 94063 650-482-2589
Grady Wright, prin. Fax 367-4367
Other Schools – See Atherton, Menlo Park

Our Lady of Mt. Carmel S 300/PK-8
301 Grand St 94062 650-366-6127
Teresa Anthony, prin. Fax 366-0902
Redeemer Lutheran S 200/K-8
468 Grand St 94062 650-366-3466
Michael Mancini, prin. Fax 366-5897
St. Pius S 300/PK-8
1100 Woodside Rd 94061 650-368-8327
Rita Carroll, prin. Fax 368-7031

Redwood Valley, Mendocino, Pop. 1,695
Ukiah USD
Supt. — See Ukiah
Eagle Peak MS 400/5-8
8601 West Rd 95470 707-472-5250
Dan Stearns, prin. Fax 485-9542

Deep Valley Christian S 100/PK-12
PO Box 9 95470 707-485-8778
Sandra Peters, head sch Fax 485-9362

Reedley, Fresno, Pop. 23,944
Kings Canyon JUSD 9,900/PK-12
1801 10th St 93654 559-305-7010
John Campbell, supt. Fax 637-1292
www.kcusd.com
Alta ES 400/K-5
21771 E Parlier Ave 93654 559-305-7210
Vickie Nishida, prin. Fax 637-1277
Bartsch S 700/PK-8
2225 E North Ave 93654 559-305-7360
Rodney Cisneros, prin. Fax 638-5308
Grant MS 500/6-8
360 N East Ave 93654 559-305-7330
Sharon Matsuzaki, prin. Fax 638-6772
Great Western ES 300/PK-5
5051 S Frankwood Ave 93654 559-305-7220
Lori Botkin, prin. Fax 637-1348
Jefferson ES 400/PK-5
1037 E Duff Ave 93654 559-305-7230
Agustin Villarreal, prin. Fax 638-2486
KC Kids Preschool PK-PK
1220 E Washington Ave 93654 559-305-7270
Freda Kaprielian, prin. Fax 638-0026
Lincoln ES 400/PK-5
374 E North Ave 93654 559-305-7240
Gabriela Cazares, prin. Fax 638-3064
Navelencia MS 300/6-8
22620 Wahtoke Ave 93654 559-305-7350
Jennifer McConnon, prin. Fax 637-1316
Reed ES 600/K-8
1400 N Frankwood Ave 93654 559-305-7300
Rick McCollum, prin. Fax 637-9486
Washington ES 400/PK-5
1250 K St 93654 559-305-7270
Mary Stanley, prin. Fax 637-1223
Other Schools – See Dunlap, Orange Cove, Parlier

Immanuel S 400/K-12
1128 S Reed Ave 93654 559-638-2529
Phil Goertzen, prin. Fax 638-7030

St. La Salle S 300/PK-8
404 E Manning Ave 93654 559-638-2621
Sr. Lucy Cassarino, prin. Fax 638-5542

Rescue, El Dorado
Rescue UNESD 3,800/K-8
2390 Bass Lake Rd 95672 530-677-4461
David Swart, supt. Fax 677-0719
www.rescueusd.org
Green Valley ES 600/K-5
2380 Bass Lake Rd 95672 530-677-3686
Michelle Winberg, prin. Fax 677-6532
Pleasant Grove MS 600/6-8
2540 Green Valley Rd 95672 530-672-4400
Hope Migliaccio, prin. Fax 677-5829
Rescue ES 400/K-5
3880 Green Valley Rd 95672 530-677-2720
Dustin Haley, prin. Fax 677-9705
Other Schools – See El Dorado Hills

Reseda, See Los Angeles
Los Angeles USD
Supt. — See Los Angeles
Bertrand Avenue ES 400/K-5
7021 Bertrand Ave 91335 818-342-1103
Sylvia Guzman, prin. Fax 609-8761
Blythe Street ES 500/K-5
18730 Blythe St 91335 818-345-4066
Dustin Merritt, prin. Fax 344-1637
Cantara Street ES 600/K-5
17950 Cantara St 91335 818-342-5191
Meline Karabedian, prin. Fax 344-1214
Cleveland Early Education Center PK-PK
19031 Strathern St 91335 818-885-3677
Sara Vasquez, prin. Fax 727-0964
Garden Grove ES 400/K-5
18141 Valerio St 91335 818-343-4762
Connie Hershelman, prin. Fax 343-4793
Melvin Avenue ES 500/K-5
7700 Melvin Ave 91335 818-886-7171
Danny Dixon, prin. Fax 886-3658
Newcastle ES 400/K-5
6520 Newcastle Ave 91335 818-343-8795
Luis Rojas, prin. Fax 343-8864
Reseda ES 400/K-5
7265 Amigo Ave 91335 818-343-1312
Rosemarie Kubena, prin. Fax 705-7346
Shirley ES 600/K-5
19452 Hart St 91335 818-342-6183
Wing Kwan Leung, prin. Fax 774-9051
Vanalden ES 400/K-5
19019 Delano St 91335 818-342-5131
Yoshim Yang, prin. Fax 996-5109

Kirk O' the Valley S 200/PK-5
19620 Vanowen St 91335 818-344-1242
Hillary Felder, dir. Fax 881-4217
Masoret Yehudit 50/PK-K
7350 Reseda Blvd 91335 818-457-4041
St. Catherine of Siena S 300/PK-8
18125 Sherman Way 91335 818-343-9880
Liliana Rivas, prin. Fax 343-6851

Rialto, San Bernardino, Pop. 97,244
Rialto USD 26,400/K-12
182 E Walnut Ave 92376 909-820-7700
Dr. Cuauhtemoc Avila, supt. Fax 873-0448
www.rialto.k12.ca.us
Bemis ES 700/K-5
774 E Etiwanda Ave 92376 909-820-7916
Danielle Osonduagw, prin. Fax 873 8557
Boyd ES 600/K-5
310 E Merrill Ave 92376 909-820-7929
Owen Ross, prin. Fax 820-6889
Casey ES 900/K-5
219 N Eucalyptus Ave 92376 909-820-7904
Cuellar Johanna, prin. Fax 820-7957
Curtis ES 600/K-5
451 S Lilac Ave 92376 909-421-7366
Vince Rollins, prin. Fax 421-7369
Dollahan ES 700/K-5
1060 W Etiwanda Ave 92376 909-820-7943
Daniel Husbands, prin. Fax 421-7644
Dunn ES 700/K-5
830 N Lilac Ave 92376 909-820-7873
Alberto Gutierrez, prin. Fax 421-3462
Fitzgerald ES 500/K-5
2568 W Terra Vista Dr 92377 909-421-7625
Yolanda Jackson, prin. Fax 421-7633
Frisbie MS 1,300/6-8
1442 N Eucalyptus Ave 92376 909-820-7887
Akinlana Osonduagwuike, prin. Fax 820-7885
Henry ES 500/K-5
470 E Etiwanda Ave 92376 909-820-7910
Mitzi Moreland, prin. Fax 820-7947
Hughbanks ES 700/K-5
2241 N Apple Ave 92377 909-820-7970
Monte Stewart, prin. Fax 421-7607
Kelley ES 700/K-5
380 S Meridian Ave 92376 909-820-7924
Raymond Delgado, prin. Fax 820-6880
Kolb MS 1,000/6-8
2351 N Spruce Ave 92377 909-820-7849
Carolyn Eide, prin. Fax 875-0374
Kucera MS 1,200/6-8
2140 W Buena Vista Dr 92377 909-421-7662
Monique Conway, prin. Fax 421-7681
Morgan ES 500/K-5
1571 N Sycamore Ave 92376 909-820-7884
Alejandro Vara, prin. Fax 421-3472
Myers ES 600/K-5
975 N Meridian Ave 92376 909-820-7921
Alberto Camarena, prin. Fax 421-7532
Preston ES 600/K-5
1750 N Willow Ave 92376 909-820-7932
Robin McMillon, prin. Fax 421-7697
Rialto MS 1,200/6-8
1262 W Rialto Ave 92376 909-879-7308
Adam Waggonner, prin. Fax 877-4893

Simpson ES 700/K-5
1050 S Lilac Ave 92376 909-820-7954
Connie Richardson, prin. Fax 421-3456
Trapp ES 500/K-5
2750 N Riverside Ave 92377 909-820-7911
Roxanne Ulivarri, prin. Fax 421-7643
Werner ES 900/K-5
1050 W Rialto Ave 92376 909-820-6830
Andrea Roman, prin. Fax 562-0078
Other Schools – See Colton, Fontana

St. Catherine of Siena S 200/PK-8
335 N Sycamore Ave 92376 909-875-7821
Beverly Winn, prin. Fax 875-7948

Richgrove, Tulare, Pop. 2,871
Richgrove ESD 700/K-8
PO Box 540 93261 661-725-2424
Mario Millan, supt. Fax 725-5772
www.richgrove.org
Richgrove ES 700/K-8
PO Box 540 93261 661-725-2424
Mario Millan, prin. Fax 725-5772

Richmond, Contra Costa, Pop. 99,595
West Contra Costa USD 30,400/PK-12
1108 Bissell Ave 94801 510-231-1100
Matt Duffy, supt. Fax 236-6784
www.wccusd.net
Chavez ES 700/K-6
960 17th St 94801 510-231-1418
Alison Evert, prin. Fax 412-3353
Coronado ES 500/K-6
2100 Maine Ave 94804 510-231-1419
Keilan Hunter, prin. Fax 215-4181
DeJean MS 600/7-8
3400 MacDonald Ave 94805 510-231-1430
William McGee, prin. Fax 236-6680
Ford ES 500/K-6
2711 Maricopa Ave 94804 510-231-1421
Teresa Barrera, prin. Fax 234-3243
Grant ES 600/K-6
2400 Downer Ave 94804 510-231-1422
Farmaz Heydari, prin. Fax 412-5005
Highland ES 500/K-6
2829 Moyers Rd 94806 510-231-1424
David Ranch, prin. Fax 758-4445
King ES 500/K-6
4022 Florida Ave 94804 510-231-1403
Joanne Sundberg, prin. Fax 235-7206
Lincoln ES 500/K-6
29 6th St 94801 510-231-1404
Megan Burnham, prin. Fax 235-7205
Mira Vista ES 500/K-8
6397 Hazel Ave 94805 510-231-1416
Gabriel Chilcott, prin. Fax 234-8739
Murphy ES 500/K-6
4350 Valley View Rd 94803 510-231-1427
Chelsea LaForest, prin. Fax 223-4111
Nystrom ES 500/K-6
230 Harbour Way S 94804 510-231-1406
James Allardice, prin. Fax 215-8165
Peres ES 600/K-6
719 5th St 94801 510-231-1407
Jawan Eldridge, prin. Fax 215-8103
Sheldon ES 400/K-6
2601 May Rd 94803 510-231-1414
Melissa Sigars, prin. Fax 243-2093
Stege ES 300/K-6
4949 Cypress Ave 94804 510-231-1425
Kim Moses, prin. Fax 235-7239
Valley View ES 300/K-6
3416 Maywood Dr 94803 510 231 1455
Ann Marie Marinakis, prin. Fax 222-8896
Verde ES 300/K-6
2000 Giaramita St 94801 510-231-1408
Eric Acosta-Verprauskus, prin. Fax 215-9485
Washington ES 500/K-6
565 Wine St 94801 510-231 1417
Lisa Levi, prin. Fax 236-1642
West County Mandarin S 100/K-5
6028 Ralston Ave 94805 510-231-1529
Eric Peterson, prin. Fax 215-0530
Wilson ES 500/K-6
629 42nd St 94805 510-231-1456
Claudia Velez, prin. Fax 412-5011
Other Schools – See El Cerrito, El Sobrante, Hercules, Kensington, Pinole, San Pablo

---

New Direction Christian Academy 50/K-8
2800 Rheem Ave 94804 510-890-9740
Christine Jones, prin.
St. Cornelius S 200/K-8
201 28th St 94804 510-232-3326
Shervin Moradi, prin. Fax 232-4071
St. David S 200/PK-8
871 Sonoma St 94805 510-232-2283
Jojo de Guzman, prin. Fax 231-0484
Williams - Brown Academy 50/K-6
2225 Gaynor Ave 94801 510-236-9101
Mary Brown, prin. Fax 236-9101

Richvale, Butte, Pop. 244
Biggs USD
Supt. — See Biggs
Richvale ES, 5236 Church St 95974 50/1-6
Minden King, prin. 530-882-4273

Ridgecrest, Kern, Pop. 26,434
Sierra Sands USD 4,900/K-12
113 W Felspar Ave 93555 760-499-1600
Ernest Bell, supt. Fax 375-3338
www.ssusdschools.org
Faller ES 400/K-5
1500 W Upjohn Ave 93555 760-499-1690
Melissa Christman, prin. Fax 499-1695
Gateway ES 400/K-5
501 S Gateway Blvd 93555 760-499-1850
Margaret Bergens, prin. Fax 384-2608

Las Flores ES 500/K-5
720 W Las Flores Ave 93555 760-499-1860
Susan Marvin, prin. Fax 375-8432
Monroe MS 500/6-8
340 W Church Ave 93555 760-499-1830
Bonny Porter, prin. Fax 375-8781
Murray MS 600/6-8
200 E Drummond Ave 93555 760-499-1820
Kirsti Smith, prin.
Pierce ES 300/K-5
674 N Gold Canyon St 93555 760-499-1670
Traci Freese, prin. Fax 499-1678
Richmond ES 500/K-5
1206 Kearsarge Ave 93555 760-499-1840
Michael Yancey, prin. Fax 446-3302
Other Schools – See Inyokern

Adventist Christian S 50/K-8
555 W Las Flores Ave 93555 760-375-8673
Bethany Rubino, prin. Fax 375-8402
Immanuel Christian S 200/K-12
201 W Graaf Ave 93555 760-446-6114
Lisa Waddill, prin. Fax 284-8320
St. Ann S 100/K-8
446 W Church Ave 93555 760-375-4713
Asteria Galacio, prin. Fax 375-6345

Rio Dell, Humboldt, Pop. 3,219
Rio Dell ESD 300/K-8
95 Center St 95562 707-764-5694
Kevin Trone, supt. Fax 764-2656
riodellschools.net
Eagle Prairie ES 200/K-5
95 Center St 95562 707-764-5694
Angela Johnson, supt. Fax 764-2656
Monument MS 100/6-8
95 Center St 95562 707-764-3783
Angela Johnson, supt. Fax 764-2656

Rio Linda, Sacramento, Pop. 14,536
Twin Rivers USD
Supt. — See Mc Clellan
Dry Creek ES 400/PK-4
1230 G St 95673 916-566-1820
Amanda Forde, prin. Fax 991-1821
Orchard S 600/PK-8
1040 Q St 95673 916-566-1930
Paula Roach, prin. Fax 566-3566
Rio Linda Preparatory Academy 400/5-8
1101 G St 95673 916-566-2720
Cindy Harrison, prin. Fax 566-3578
Vineland Preschool 50/PK-K
6450 20th St 95673 916-566-1980
Shaen Hosie, coord. Fax 566-1790
Westside ES 400/K-6
6537 W 2nd St 95673 916-566-1990
Laura Lofgren, prin. Fax 566-1991

Rio Oso, Sutter, Pop. 349
Browns ESD 200/PK-8
1248 Pacific Ave 95674 530-633-2523
Mike Scully, supt. Fax 633-0345
www.brownsschool.org
Browns ES 200/PK-8
1248 Pacific Ave 95674 530-633-2523
Mike Scully, admin. Fax 633-0345

Rio Vista, Solano, Pop. 7,140
River Delta USD 2,300/K-12
445 Montezuma St 94571 707-374-1700
Don Beno, supt. Fax 374-2995
www.riverdelta.org
Riverview MS 200/6-8
525 S 2nd St 94571 707-374-2345
Sonia Rambo, prin. Fax 374-5623
White ES 400/K-5
500 Elm Way 94571 707-374-5335
Nicholas Casey, prin. Fax 374-4364
Other Schools – See Courtland, Isleton, Walnut Grove

Ripon, San Joaquin, Pop. 13,864
Ripon USD 3,000/PK-12
304 N Acacia Ave 95366 209-599-2131
Dr. Ziggy Robeson Ed.D., supt. Fax 599-6271
www.riponusd.net
Colony Oak ES 400/K-8
22241 S Murphy Rd 95366 209-599-7145
Cheryl Griffiths, prin. Fax 599-2772
Park View ES 400/K-8
751 Cindy Dr 95366 209-599-1882
Eva Matthews, prin. Fax 599-1886
Ripona ES 400/K-8
415 Oregon St 95366 209-599-4104
Greggory Elliott, prin. Fax 599-1886
Ripon ES 400/PK-8
509 W Main St 95366 209-599-4225
Mike Larson, prin. Fax 599-8725
Weston ES 400/K-8
1660 Stanley Dr 95366 209-599-7113
Lisa Fereria, prin. Fax 599-4063

Ripon Christian ES 500/PK-8
217 Maple Ave 95366 209-599-2155
Kevin Schenk, prin. Fax 599-9487

Riverbank, Stanislaus, Pop. 22,068
Riverbank USD 2,800/K-12
6715 7th St 95367 209-869-2538
Dr. Daryl Camp, supt. Fax 869-1487
www.riverbank.k12.ca.us
California Avenue ES 600/K-5
3800 California Ave 95367 209-869-2597
Kathy Briggs, prin. Fax 869-7375
Cardozo MS 500/6-8
0525 Santa Fe St 95367 209-869-2591
Kevin Bizzini, prin. Fax 869-2714
Other Schools – See Oakdale

Sylvan Union ESD
Supt. — See Modesto
Crossroads ES 900/K-5
5800 Saxon Way 95367 209-869-2100
Rebecca Harms, prin. Fax 869-7425

Riverdale, Fresno, Pop. 3,092
Burrel UNESD 100/K-8
16704 S Jameson Ave 93656 559-866-5634
Steve Rosa, supt. Fax 866-5280
www.burrel.k12.ca.us
Burrel ES 100/K-8
16704 S Jameson Ave 93656 559-866-5634
Steve Rosa, admin. Fax 866-5280

Riverdale JUSD 1,600/K-12
PO Box 1058 93656 559-867-8200
Jeff Percell, supt. Fax 867-6722
www.rjusd.org
Fipps PS 500/K-3
PO Box 338 93656 559-867-3353
Gina Daniels, prin. Fax 867-4949
Riverdale ES 600/4-8
PO Box 338 93656 559-867-3589
Chris Stilson, prin. Fax 867-3393

Riverside, Riverside, Pop. 295,499
Alvord USD
Supt. — See Corona
Arizona MS 1,100/6-8
11045 Arizona Ave 92503 951-358-1675
Jason Jones, prin. Fax 358-1676
Arlanza ES 600/K-5
5891 Rutland Ave 92503 951-358-1600
Michelle Pierce, prin. Fax 358-1601
Collett ES 700/K-5
10850 Collett Ave 92505 951-358-1605
Ricardo Chaparro, prin. Fax 358-1606
Foothill ES 600/K-5
8230 Wells Ave 92503 951-358-1610
Israel Avila, prin. Fax 358-1611
Kennedy ES 600/K-5
6411 Mitchell Ave 92505 951-358-1655
Jason Burns, prin. Fax 358-1656
La Granada ES 700/K-5
10346 Keller Ave 92505 951-358-1615
Carrie Mondt, prin. Fax 358-1616
Lake Hills ES 800/K-5
16345 Village Meadow Dr 92503 951-358-1620
Gonzalo Avila, prin. Fax 358-1621
Linn ES 600/K-5
10435 Branigan Way 92505 951-358-1630
Theresa Steele, prin. Fax 358-1631
Loma Vista MS 1,100/6-8
11050 Arlington Ave 92505 951-358-1685
Diane Kammeyer, prin. Fax 358-1686
McAuliffe ES 800/K-5
4100 Golden Ave 92505 951-358-1625
Gerardo Aguilar, prin. Fax 358-1626
Orrenmaa ES 600/K-5
3350 Fillmore St 92503 951-358-1635
Jeffrey Fanning, prin. Fax 358-1636
Stokoe ES 800/K-5
4501 Ambs Dr 92505 951-358-1640
Debra Johnson, prin. Fax 358-1641
Terrace ES 700/K-5
6601 Rutland Ave 92503 951-358-1660
Emily Devor, prin. Fax 358-1661
Twinhill ES 600/K-5
11000 Campbell Ave 92505 951-358-1665
Mary Parsons, prin Fax 358-1666
Valley View ES 400/K-5
11750 Gramercy Pl 92505 951-358-1670
Traci Vaughn, prin. Fax 358-1671
Villegas MS 1,300/6-8
3754 Harvill Ln 92503 951-358-1695
David Ferguson, prin. Fax 358-1696
Wells MS 1,000/6-8
10000 Wells Ave 92503 951-358-1705
Karin Ribaudo, prin. Fax 358-1706

Riverside USD 42,100/PK-12
PO Box 2800 92516 951-788-7135
David Hansen Ed.D., supt. Fax 778-5668
www.rusdlink.org
Adams ES 500/K-6
8362 Colorado Ave 92504 951-352-6709
Carolina Michel, prin. Fax 328-2547
Alcott ES 800/K-6
2433 Central Ave 92506 951-788-7451
Patrisha Tran, prin. Fax 328-5480
Beatty ES 700/K-6
4261 Latham St 92501 951-276-2070
Jacqueline Hall, prin. Fax 274-4231
Bryant ES 500/K-6
4324 3rd St 92501 951-788-7453
Lari Nelson, prin. Fax 328-4080
Castle View ES 600/K-6
6201 Shaker Dr 92506 951-788-7460
Tiffany Farris, prin. Fax 778-5780
Central MS 700/7-8
4795 Magnolia Ave 92506 951-788-7282
Lynn McCown, prin. Fax 328-2580
Chemawa MS 1,000/7-8
8830 Magnolia Ave 92503 951-352-8244
Raul Ayala, prin. Fax 328-2980
Earhart MS 1,000/7-8
20202 Aptos St 92508 951-697-5700
Sean Curtin, prin. Fax 328-7580
Emerson ES 800/K-6
4660 Ottawa Ave 92507 951-788-7462
Russ Bouton, prin. Fax 274-4221
Franklin ES 900/K-6
19661 Orange Terrace Pkwy 92508 951-571-6502
Dawn Smith, prin. Fax 328-7280
Fremont ES 600/K-6
1925 N Orange St 92501 951-788-7466
Shani Dahl, prin. Fax 778-5380
Gage MS 1,000/7-8
6400 Lincoln Ave 92506 951-788-7350
Dr. Gary Reller, prin. Fax 328-5680
Harrison ES 600/K-6
2901 Harrison St 92503 951-352-6712
Jamelia Oliver, prin. Fax 274-4227
Hawthorne ES 700/K-6
2700 Irving St 92504 951-352-6716
Carrie Brown, prin. Fax 778-5180
Highgrove ES 700/K-6
690 Center St 92507 951-788-7296
Elizabeth Gosnell, prin. Fax 274-4291
Highland ES 800/K-6
700 Highlander Dr 92507 951-788-7292
Donna Dorsey, prin. Fax 778-5280
Jackson ES 800/K-6
4585 Jackson St 92503 951-352-8211
JoLynn Barnes, prin. Fax 328-2509
Jefferson ES 900/K-6
4285 Jefferson St 92504 951-352-8218
Maria Ortega, prin. Fax 274-4296
Kennedy ES 1,100/K-6
19125 Schoolhouse Ln 92508 951-789-7570
Lisa Betts, prin. Fax 328-7380
Lake Mathews ES 900/K-6
12252 Blackburn Rd 92503 951-352-5520
Pamela Williams, prin. Fax 328-7180
Liberty ES 800/K-6
9631 Hayes St 92503 951-352-8225
Esther Garcia, prin. Fax 328-5580
Longfellow ES 800/K-6
3610 Eucalyptus Ave 92507 951-788-7335
Geri Castro, prin. Fax 328-5080
Madison ES 700/K-6
3635 Madison St 92504 951-352-8236
John McCombs, prin. Fax 328-2516
Magnolia ES 700/K-6
3975 Maplewood Pl 92506 951-788-7274
Annette Raspudic, prin. Fax 328-2556
Miller MS 1,000/7-8
17925 Krameria Ave 92504 951-789-8181
Chuck Hiroto, prin. Fax 328-2912
Monroe ES 700/K-6
8535 Garfield St 92504 951-352-8241
Tasceaie Churchwell, prin. Fax 328-2505
Mountain View ES 800/K-6
6180 Streeter Ave 92504 951-788-7433
Kathleen Doubravsky, prin. Fax 778-5580
Pachappa ES 800/K-6
6200 Riverside Ave 92506 951-788-7355
Erica Square, prin. Fax 328-2501
Rivera ES 700/K-6
20440 Red Poppy Ln 92508 951-697-5757
Wilson Cuellar, prin. Fax 328-7480
Sierra MS 900/7-8
4950 Central Ave 92504 951-788-7501
Ratmony Yee, prin. Fax 328-2552
Taft ES 700/K-6
959 Mission Grove Pkwy N 92506 951-776-3018
Bernardo Torres, prin. Fax 328-2921
Twain ES 1,100/K-6
19411 Krameria Ave 92508 951-789-8170
Paula Allbeck, prin. Fax 274-4280
University Heights MS 800/7-8
1155 Massachusetts Ave 92507 951-788-7388
Coleman Kells, prin. Fax 328-2566
Victoria ES 600/K-6
2910 Arlington Ave 92506 951-788-7441
Linda Daltrey, prin. Fax 274-4223
Washington ES 800/K-6
2760 Jane St 92506 951-788-7305
Michele Lenertz, prin. Fax 328-4011
Woodcrest ES 700/K-6
16940 Krameria Ave 92504 951-776-4122
Jeanette Prescott, prin. Fax 328-7080

Bethel Christian S 200/PK-12
2425 Van Buren Blvd 92503 951-359-1123
Dr. Mike Crites, supt. Fax 359-1719
Carnegie S - Riverside 600/PK-12
8775 Magnolia Ave 92503 951-687-0077
Dr. Tiffany Edwards, supt. Fax 687-3340
Harvest Christian S 400/K-6
6115 Arlington Ave 92504 951-359-3932
Forrest Rickard, prin. Fax 637-1217
Immanuel Lutheran S 300/PK-6
5455 Alessandro Blvd 92506 951-682-4211
Carl Boburka, prin. Fax 682-9403
Islamic Academy of Riverside 100/PK-7
1038 W Linden St Ste B 92507 951-682-1202
Reham Shaath, prin.
La Sierra Academy 700/K-12
4900 Golden Ave 92505 951-351-1445
Walter Lancaster, prin. Fax 689-3708
Our Lady of Perpetual Help S 300/PK-8
6686 Streeter Ave 92504 951-689-2125
Ann Meier, prin. Fax 689-9354
St. Catherine of Alexandria S 300/K-8
7025 Brockton Ave 92506 951-684-1091
Enrique Landin, prin. Fax 684-4936
St. Francis De Sales S 200/PK-8
4205 Mulberry St 92501 951-683-5083
Kathy Kothlow, prin. Fax 683-0249
St. Thomas the Apostle S 200/K-8
9136 Magnolia Ave 92503 951-689-1981
Dr. Dian Pizurie, admin. Fax 689-1985
Woodcrest Christian Day S 400/K-6
3612 Arlington Ave 92506 951-686-1818
Laurie Leach, prin. Fax 686-4041

Robbins, Sutter, Pop. 318
Winship-Robbins ESD
Supt. — See Meridian
Robbins S 200/K-8
PO Box 237 95676 530-738-4386
Laurie Goodman, prin. Fax 738-4291

Rocklin, Placer, Pop. 54,666
Rocklin USD 12,800/PK-12
2615 Sierra Meadows Dr 95677 916-624-2428
Roger Stock, supt. Fax 630-2229
www.rocklinusd.org
Antelope Creek ES 500/PK-6
6185 Springview Dr 95677 916-632-1095
Brian Arcuri, prin. Fax 632-2381
Breen ES 600/K-6
2751 Breen Dr 95765 916-632-1155
Jennifer Palmer, prin. Fax 632-9471
Cobblestone ES 400/PK-6
5740 Cobblestone Dr 95765 916-632-0140
Kathleen Goddard, prin. Fax 632-9732
Granite Oaks MS 900/7-8
2600 Wyckford Blvd 95765 916-315-9009
Jay Holmes, prin. Fax 315-9885
Parker Whitney ES 400/PK-6
5145 Topaz Ave 95677 916-624-2491
Melody Thorson, prin.
Rock Creek ES 500/PK-6
2140 Collet Quarry Dr 95765 916-788-4282
Mark Williams, prin. Fax 788-8161
Rocklin ES 600/PK-6
5025 Meyers St 95677 916-624-3311
Amanda Makis, prin. Fax 624-5908
Ruhkala ES 400/K-6
6530 Turnstone Way 95765 916-632-6560
Lara Kikosicki, prin. Fax 797-2062
Sierra ES 500/K-6
6811 Camborne Way 95677 916-788-7141
Hannah Anderson, prin. Fax 788-7161
Spring View MS 800/7-8
5040 5th St 95677 916-624-3381
Beth Davidson, prin. Fax 624-5737
Sunset Ranch ES 800/K-6
2500 Bridlewood Dr 95765 916-624-2048
Bill MacDonald, prin. Fax 624-2351
Twin Oaks ES 400/K-6
2835 Club Dr 95765 916-624-4101
Sarah James, prin. Fax 624-4124
Valley View ES 500/K-6
3000 Crest Dr 95765 916-435-4844
Shari Anderson, prin. Fax 435-4944

Rodeo, Contra Costa, Pop. 8,152
John Swett USD 1,700/K-12
400 Parker Ave 94572 510-245-4300
Dr. Charles Miller, supt. Fax 245-4312
www.jsusd.org
Rodeo Hills ES 700/K-5
545 Garretson Ave 94572 510-799-4431
Krishna Fenney, prin. Fax 799-5230
Other Schools – See Crockett

St. Patrick S 300/PK-8
907 7th St 94572 510-799-2506
Kelly Stevens, prin. Fax 799-6781

Rohnert Park, Sonoma, Pop. 39,217
Cotati-Rohnert Park USD 5,800/PK-12
7165 Burton Ave 94928 707-792-4722
Robert Haley, supt. Fax 792-4537
www.crpusd.org
Crane ES 100/PK-5
1290 Southwest Blvd 94928 707-285-3150
Teresa Ruffoni, prin. Fax 795-7434
Evergreen ES 600/K-5
1125 Emily Ave 94928 707-588-5715
Jennifer Hansen, prin. Fax 588-5720
Hahn ES 500/K-5
825 Hudis St 94928 707-588-5675
Ashley Tatman, prin. Fax 588-5680
Jones MS 900/6-8
5154 Snyder Ln 94928 707-588-5600
Scott Johnson, prin. Fax 588-5607
Monte Vista ES 600/K-5
1400 Magnolia Ave 94928 707-792-4531
Sarah Fountain, prin. Fax 792-4513
Reed ES 300/K-2
390 Arlen Dr 94928 707-792-4845
Susan Lopez, prin. Fax 792-4517
Rohnert ES 300/3-5
550 Bonnie Ave 94928 707-792-4830
Susan Lopez, prin. Fax 792-4519
Technology MS 300/6-8
7165 Burton Ave 94928 707-792-4800
Sara McKenna-McKee, prin. Fax 792-4516
University ES at La Fiesta 50/K-3
8511 Liman Way 94928 707-792-4840
Charlotte Straub, prin.
Other Schools – See Cotati

Cross & Crown Lutheran S 100/PK-5
5475 Snyder Ln 94928 707-795-7863
Jean Bashi, admin. Fax 795-0509

Rolling Hills, Los Angeles, Pop. 1,810
Palos Verdes Peninsula USD
Supt. — See Palos Verdes Estates
Dapplegray ES 600/K-5
3011 Palos Verdes Dr N 90274 310-541-3706
Nancy Parsons, prin. Fax 541-8265
Rancho Vista ES 500/K-5
4323 Palos Verdes Dr N 90274 310-378-8388
Salvatrice Kuykendall, prin. Fax 378-4980

Peninsula Heritage S 100/K-8
26944 Rolling Hills Rd 90274 310-541-4795
Patricia Cailler, head sch Fax 541-8264
Rolling Hills Country S 400/K-8
26444 Crenshaw Blvd 90274 310-377-4848
Karen Shipherd, dir. Fax 377-9651

Romoland, Riverside, Pop. 1,639
Romoland ESD
Supt. — See Homeland
Boulder Ridge ES 600/K-5
27327 Junipero Rd 92585 951-723-8931
Jon Mitchem, prin. Fax 723-8929
Harvest Valley ES 600/K-5
29955 Watson Rd 92585 951-928-2915
Michelle Giroux, prin. Fax 928-2920

Mesa View ES 600/K-5
27227 Heritage Lake Dr 92585 951-723-1284
Jawad Pearson, prin. Fax 723-1325
Romoland ES 500/K-5
25890 Antelope Rd 92585 951-928-2910
Michelle Echiverri, prin. Fax 928-2918

Rosamond, Kern, Pop. 17,416
Southern Kern USD 3,000/PK-12
PO Box CC 93560 661-256-5000
Jeffrey Weinstein, supt. Fax 256-1247
www.skusd.k12.ca.us
Rosamond ES 700/PK-5
PO Box CC 93560 661-256-5050
Nino Torres, prin. Fax 256-6248
Tropico MS 600/6-8
PO Box CC 93560 661-256-5040
Nat Adams, prin. Fax 256-0630
Westpark ES 700/K-5
PO Box CC 93560 661-256-5030
Kathy Wilson, prin. Fax 256-8300

Rosemead, Los Angeles, Pop. 53,367
Garvey ESD 5,200/K-8
2730 Del Mar Ave 91770 626-307-3400
Anita Chu, supt. Fax 307-1964
www.garvey.k12.ca.us
Bitely ES 600/K-6
7501 Fern Ave 91770 626-307-3318
Rudy Torres, prin. Fax 307-8156
Emerson ES 600/K-6
7544 Emerson Pl 91770 626-307-3333
Anna Marie Knight, prin. Fax 312-3566
Garvey IS 800/7-8
2720 Jackson Ave 91770 626-307-3385
Gema Macias, prin. Fax 307-3443
Rice ES 500/K-6
2150 Angelus Ave 91770 626-307-3348
Christina HIrales, prin. Fax 307-8163
Sanchez ES 500/K-6
8470 Fern Ave 91770 626-307-3368
Gabriela Benitez, prin. Fax 312-2035
Temple IS 500/7-8
8470 Fern Ave 91770 626-307-3360
Dr. Robert Boyd, prin. Fax 307-8162
Willard ES 500/K-6
3152 Willard Ave 91770 626-307-3375
Michelle Collaso, prin. Fax 312-3571
Other Schools – See Monterey Park, San Gabriel

Rosemead ESD 2,700/PK-8
3907 Rosemead Blvd 91770 626-312-2900
Dr. Amy Enomoto-Perez Ed.D., supt. Fax 312-2906
www.rosemead.k12.ca.us
Encinita ES 400/PK-6
4515 Encinita Ave 91770 626-286-3155
Dr. Jennifer Fang, prin. Fax 285-8584
Janson ES 600/PK-6
8628 Marshall St 91770 626-288-3150
Gabriel Cardenas, prin. Fax 307-6184
Muscatel MS 600/7-8
4201 Ivar Ave 91770 626-287-1139
Jessica Ancona, prin. Fax 307-6185
Savannah ES 500/PK-6
3720 Rio Hondo Ave 91770 626-443-4015
Ruth Soto, prin. Fax 442-5478
Shuey ES 500/PK-6
8472 Wells St 91770 626-287-5221
Jan Brydle, prin. Fax 307-6187

Roseville, Placer, Pop. 114,218
Center JUSD
Supt. — See Antelope
Riles MS 700/7-8
4747 PFE Rd 95747 916-787-8100
Joyce Frisch, prin. Fax 773-4131

Dry Creek JESD 6,400/K-8
9707 Cook Riolo Rd 95747 916-770-8800
Brad Tooker, supt. Fax 771-0650
www.drycreekschools.us
Coyote Ridge ES 900/K-5
1751 Morningstar Dr 95747 916-774-8282
Julie Herrmann, prin. Fax 774-8292
Creekview Ranch S 500/K-8
8779 Cook Riolo Rd 95747 916-770-8845
Marty Alberti, prin. Fax 772-4145
Heritage Oak ES 500/K-5
2271 Americana Dr 95747 916-773-3960
Richard Knox, prin. Fax 773-3955
Quail Glen ES 500/K-5
1250 Canevari Dr 95747 916-789-7100
Greg O'Meara, prin. Fax 789-7113
Silverado MS 1,100/6-8
2525 Country Club Dr 95747 916-780-2620
Priscilla Rasanen, prin. Fax 780-2635
Other Schools – See Antelope

Eureka UNSD
Supt. — See Granite Bay
Excelsior ES 600/4-6
2701 Eureka Rd 95661 916-780-2701
Heidi Williams, prin. Fax 780-4314
Maidu ES 400/PK-3
1950 Johnson Ranch Dr 95661 916-789-7910
Stephanie Groat, prin. Fax 789-7914
Olympus JHS 600/7-8
2625 La Croix Dr 95661 916-782-1667
Sean Healy, prin. Fax 782-1339

Roseville City ESD 10,100/PK-8
1050 Main St 95678 916-771-1600
Derk Garcia, supt. Fax 771-1620
www.rcsdk8.org
Blue Oaks ES 600/K-5
8150 Horncastle Ave 95747 916-771-1700
Erin Peterson, prin. Fax 772-7839
Brown ES 500/K-5
250 Trestle Rd 95678 916-771-1710
Pam Kissick, prin. Fax 773-1808

Buljan MS 1,100/6-8
100 Hallissy Dr 95678 916-771-1720
Ryan Hartsoch, prin. Fax 773-2696
Chilton MS 300/6-8
4501 Bob Doyle Dr 95747 916-771-1870
Jeff Ancker, prin. Fax 771-1871
Cirby ES 400/K-5
814 Darling Way 95678 916-771-1730
Karen Quinlan, prin. Fax 783-1020
Cooley MS 1,000/6-8
9300 Prairie Woods Way 95747 916-771-1740
Karen Calkins, prin. Fax 786-3003
Crestmont ES 500/K-5
1501 Sheridan Ave 95661 916-771-1750
Jeri Farmer, prin. Fax 781-2042
Diamond Creek ES 700/K-5
3151 Hopscotch Way 95747 916-771-1760
Angela Turry, prin. Fax 626-2014
Eich MS 700/6-8
1509 Sierra Gardens Dr 95661 916-771-1770
Darren Brown, prin. Fax 783-7292
Fiddyment Farm ES 300/K-5
4001 Brick Mason Cir 95747 916-771-1880
Ryam Poulsen, prin.
Gates ES 600/K-5
1051 Trehowell Dr 95678 916-771-1780
Mary Patrick, prin. Fax 786-2060
Jefferson ES 600/K-5
750 Central Park Dr 95678 916-771-1840
Kirsten Thomas-Acke, prin. Fax 772-7195
Junction ES 700/K-5
2150 Ellison Dr 95747 916-771-1860
Susan Fridly, prin. Fax 771-1861
Kaseberg ES 400/K-5
1040 Main St 95678 916-771-1790
Marc Welty, prin. Fax 782-4090
Orchard Ranch ES PK-4
4375 Brookstone Dr 95747 916-771-1600
Josh Joseph, prin.
Sargeant ES 500/K-5
1200 Ridgecrest Way 95661 916-771-1800
Rachael Peck, prin. Fax 782-1090
Spanger ES 500/K-5
699 Shasta St 95678 916-771-1820
Manny Villalpando, prin. Fax 773-2404
Stoneridge ES 500/K-5
2501 Alexandra Dr 95661 916-771-1830
Jennifer Kloczko, prin. Fax 786-5898
Woodbridge ES 300/K-5
515 Niles Ave 95678 916-771-1850
Martha Paso, prin. Fax 782-4363

Adventure Christian S 600/PK-8
6401 Stanford Ranch Rd 95678 916-781-2986
Renee Flores, prin. Fax 771-8005
Christian Life Academy 50/K-12
1301 Coloma Way 95661 916-956-4662
Gary Gubitz, prin. Fax 786-7916
Granite Bay Montessori S 200/PK-8
9330 Sierra College Blvd 95661 916-791-7849
Merryhill S 100/PK-5
1115 Orlando Ave 95661 916-783-3010
St. Albans Country Day S 200/PK-8
2312 Vernon St 95678 916-782-3557
Laura Bernauer, head sch Fax 782-3505
St. Rose S 300/K-8
633 Vine Ave 95678 916-782-1161
Suzanne Smoley, prin. Fax 782-7862
Valley Christian Academy 300/PK-12
301 W Whyte Ave 95678 916-728-5500
Dr. Brad Gunter, admin. Fax 721-3305

Ross, Marin, Pop. 2,341
Ross ESD 400/K-8
PO Box 1058 94957 415-457-2705
Michael McDowell Ed.D., supt. Fax 457-8923
www.rossbears.org
Ross ES 400/K-8
PO Box 1058 94957 415-457-2705
Stacy Marshall, prin. Fax 457-8923

Rowland Heights, Los Angeles, Pop. 48,135
Rowland USD 15,100/K-12
1830 Nogales St 91748 626-965-2541
Julie Mitchell Ed.D., supt. Fax 854-8302
www.rowlandschools.org
Alvarado IS 800/7-8
1901 Desire Ave 91748 626-964-2358
Scott Cavanias, prin. Fax 810-5579
Blandford ES 700/K-6
2601 Blandford Dr 91748 626-965-3410
Ryan Bourke, prin. Fax 965-2360
Jellick ES 500/K-6
1400 Jellick Ave 91748 626-964-1275
John Staumont, prin. Fax 964-8345
Killian ES 600/K-6
19100 Killian Ave 91748 626-964-6409
Karen Magana, prin. Fax 965-7729
Rowland ES 500/K-6
2036 Fullerton Rd 91748 626-964-3441
John Martinez, prin. Fax 964-0931
Shelyn ES 400/K-6
19500 Nacora St 91748 909-444-0584
Sarah Opatkiewicz, prin. Fax 444-0582
Other Schools – See La Puente, Walnut, West Covina

Southlands Christian S 400/PK-12
18550 Farjardo St 91748 909-598-9733
Glenn Duncan, pres. Fax 468-9943

Running Springs, San Bernardino, Pop. 4,676
Rim of the World USD
Supt. — See Blue Jay
Hoffman ES 300/K-5
2851 Running Springs School 92382 909-939-0006
Marlynn Humphries, prin. Fax 939-0153

Sacramento, Sacramento, Pop. 437,732
Elk Grove USD
Supt. — See Elk Grove
Adreani ES 800/K-6
9927 Wildhawk West Dr 95829 916-525-0630
Mark Vierra, prin. Fax 525-0725
Beitzel ES 900/K-6
8140 Caymus Dr 95829 916-688-8484
Yvonne Wright, prin. Fax 688-5371
Fite ES 700/K-6
9561 Fite School Rd 95829 916-689-2854
Melissa Chin, prin. Fax 689-2917
Florin ES 700/K-6
7300 Kara Dr 95828 916-383-0530
Paul Cordero, prin. Fax 383-6404
Jackman MS 900/7-8
7925 Kentwall Dr 95823 916-393-2352
Michael Anderson, prin. Fax 393-4053
Jackson ES 900/K-6
8351 Cutler Way 95828 916-689-2115
Martin Fine, prin. Fax 689-2091
Kennedy ES 900/K-6
7037 Briggs Dr 95828 916-383-3311
Wendy Thompson, prin. Fax 383-0242
Kirchgater ES 900/K-6
8141 Stevenson Ave 95828 916-689-9150
Cheryl Sanchez, prin. Fax 689-7938
Leimbach ES 600/K-6
8101 Grandstaff Dr 95823 916-689-2120
Abelardo Cordova, prin. Fax 689-8400
Mack ES 900/K-6
4701 Brookfield Dr 95823 916-422-5524
Omar Field-Ridley, prin. Fax 422-2673
Morse ES 800/K-6
7000 Cranleigh Ave 95823 916-688-8586
Kilolo Umi, prin. Fax 682-5098
Prairie ES 1,100/K-6
5251 Valley Hi Dr 95823 916-422-1843
Robin Riley, prin. Fax 422-4722
Reese ES 900/K-6
7600 Lindale Dr 95828 916-422-2450
LaTyia Rolle, prin. Fax 422-4790
Reith ES 600/K-6
8401 Valley Lark Dr 95823 916-399-0110
Louise Roachford-Gould, prin. Fax 391-6763
Rutter MS 900/7-8
7350 Palmer House Dr 95828 916-422-7590
Kenneth Smith, prin. Fax 422-8354
Sierra-Enterprise ES 500/K-6
9115 Fruitridge Rd 95826 916-381-2767
Patricia Hecht, prin. Fax 381-0572
Smedberg MS 1,100/7-8
8239 Kingsbridge Dr 95829 916-681-7525
Richard Wall, prin. Fax 681-7530
Tsukamoto ES 900/K-6
8737 Brittany Park Dr 95828 916-689-7580
Elizabeth Rueda, prin. Fax 682-7955
Union House ES 900/K-6
7850 Deer Creek Dr 95823 916-424-9201
Dorothy Stoppelman, prin. Fax 424-3510

Natomas USD 12,800/PK-12
1901 Arena Blvd 95834 916-567-5400
Chris Evans, supt. Fax 567-5405
natomasunified.org
American Lakes ES 500/K-6
2800 Stonecreek Dr 95833 916-567-5500
Ann Veu, prin. Fax 567-5509
Bannon Creek ES 600/K-6
2755 Millcreek Dr 95833 916-567-5600
Oscar Garcia, prin. Fax 567-5609
Heron S 1,000/K-8
5151 Banfield Dr 95835 916-567-5680
Amy Whitten, prin. Fax 567-5689
Hight ES 700/K-6
3200 N Park Dr 95835 916-567-5700
Talin Tamzarian, prin. Fax 567-5709
Jefferson ES 500/K-6
2001 Pebblewood Dr 95833 916-567-5580
Danisha Keeler, prin. Fax 567-5589
Natomas Gateways MS 7-8
3301 Fong Ranch Rd 95834 916-567-5430
Suzen Holtemann, prin.
Natomas MS 700/7-8
3200 N Park Dr 95835 916-567-5540
Shea Borges Ed.D., prin. Fax 567-5549
Natomas Park ES 900/K-6
4700 Crest Dr 95835 916-925-5234
Nou Vang, prin. Fax 928-5219
Paso Verde S K-8
3800 Del Paso Rd 95835
Tonja Jarrell, prin.
Two Rivers ES 600/K-6
3201 W River Dr 95833 916-567-5520
Colleen Perry, prin. Fax 567-5529
Witter Ranch ES 900/K-6
3790 Poppy Hill Way 95834 916-567-5620
Patrick Birdsong, prin. Fax 567-5629

Robla ESD 2,200/PK-12
5248 Rose St 95838 916-649-5248
Ruben Reyes, supt. Fax 992-0308
www.robla.k12.ca.us
Bell Avenue ES 500/K-6
1900 Bell Ave 95838 916-922-0202
Lisa Hall, prin. Fax 568-7774
Glenwood ES 500/K-6
201 Jessie Ave 95838 916-922-2767
David Gutierrez, prin. Fax 922-5035
Main Avenue ES 300/K-6
1400 Main Ave 95838 916-929-9559
Sarah Neuhaus, prin. Fax 929-4253
Robla ES 500/K-6
5200 Marysville Blvd 95838 916-649-5200
Mario Penman, prin. Fax 991-8643
Robla Preschool PK-PK
4351 Pinell St 95838 916-927-0136
Laura Lystrup, prin. Fax 568-7808

Taylor Street ES 500/K-6
4350 Taylor St 95838 916-927-5340
Ben Torrecampo, prin. Fax 927-6396

Sacramento City USD 45,500/PK-12
PO Box 246870 95824 916-643-9000
Jorge Aguilar, supt. Fax 643-9480
www.scusd.edu
Anthony ES 300/K-6
7864 Detroit Blvd 95832 916-433-5353
Bao Moua, prin. Fax 433-5578
Bacon MS 700/7-8
4140 Cuny Ave 95823 916-395-5340
Mary Coronado, prin. Fax 433-5166
Baker ES 700/K-6
5717 Laurine Way 95824 916-395-4560
Amber Carter, prin. Fax 433-5533
Bancroft ES 500/K-6
2929 Belmar St 95826 916-395-4595
Lorena Carrillo, prin. Fax 382-5943
Bidwell ES 400/K-6
1730 65th Ave 95822 916-433-5047
Shannon Henry, prin. Fax 433-5557
Birney Waldorf Inspired S 600/K-8
6251 13th St 95831 916-395-4510
Mechelle Horning, prin. Fax 433-5589
Brannan MS 700/7-8
5301 Elmer Way 95822 916-395-5360
Enrique Flores, prin. Fax 264-4481
Burnett ES 700/K-6
6032 36th Ave 95824 916-277-6685
Manuel Huezo, prin. Fax 277-6442
Cabrillo ES 400/K-6
1141 Seamas Ave 95822 916-395-4615
Samantha Holmes, prin. Fax 264-4005
California MS 700/7-8
1600 Vallejo Way 95818 916-395-5302
Andrea Egan, prin. Fax 264-4477
Camellia ES 500/K-6
6600 Cougar Dr 95828 916-395-4520
Suzanne McKelvey, prin. Fax 382-5918
Chavez IS 400/4-6
7500 32nd St 95822 916-395-4530
Eracelo Guevara, prin. Fax 433-7396
Cohen ES 300/K-6
9025 Salmon Falls Dr 95826 916-228-5840
Belinda Bridgewater, prin. Fax 228-5818
Crocker/Riverside ES 600/K-6
2970 Riverside Blvd 95818 916-395-4535
Daniel McCord, prin. Fax 264-4705
DaVinci S 800/K-8
4701 Joaquin Way 95822 916-395-4635
Devon Davis, prin. Fax 277-6806
Didion S 600/K-8
6490 Harmon Dr 95831 916-433-5039
Norman Policar, prin. Fax 433-5189
Einstein MS 700/7-8
9325 Mirandy Dr 95826 916-395-5310
Garrett Kirkland, prin. Fax 228-5813
Elder Creek ES 800/K-6
7934 Lemon Hill Ave 95824 916-382-5970
Thu Le-Doan, prin. Fax 382-5959
Erlewine ES 400/K-6
2441 Stansberry Way 95826 916-395-4660
Terry Smith, prin. Fax 228-5872
Floyd ES 300/K-6
401 McClatchy Way 95818 916-395-4630
Eric Chapman, prin. Fax 264-4182
Golden Empire ES 600/K-6
9045 Canberra Dr 95826 916-395-4580
Dr. Irene Eister, prin. Fax 228-5838
Greenwood S 400/K-8
5457 Carlson Dr 95819 916-277-6266
Erin Hanson, prin. Fax 277-6591
Harkness ES 400/K-6
2147 54th Ave 95822 916-433-5042
Isabel Govea, prin. Fax 433-5346
Harte ES 400/K-6
2751 9th Ave 95818 916-277-6261
James Tucker, prin. Fax 277-6456
Hearst ES 600/1-6
1410 60th St 95819 916-277-6690
Nathan McGill, prin. Fax 277-6739
Hollywood Park ES 400/K-6
4915 Harte Way 95822 916-395-4590
Tenley Luke, prin. Fax 277-6292
Judah ES 600/K-6
3919 McKinley Blvd 95819 916-395-4790
Troy Holding, prin. Fax 277-6388
Kemble ES 500/K-3
7495 29th St 95822 916-395-4550
Mary Alvarez-Jett, prin. Fax 433-5579
King S 500/K-8
480 Little River Way 95831 916-395-4645
Denise Lambert, prin. Fax 433-5179
Land ES 400/K-6
2120 12th St 95818 916-264-4166
Ellen Carlson, prin. Fax 264-4357
Lincoln ES 500/K-6
3324 Glenmoor Dr 95827 916-228-5830
Laura Butler, prin. Fax 228-5834
Lubin ES 600/K-6
3535 M St 95816 916-277-6271
Richard Dixon, prin. Fax 277-6526
Marshall ES 400/K-6
9525 Goethe Rd 95827 916-395-4605
Marla Van Laningha, prin. Fax 228-5819
Matsuyama ES 600/K-6
7680 Windbridge Dr 95831 916-395-4650
Judy Montgomery, prin. Fax 433-5556
Nicholas ES 700/K-6
6601 Steiner Dr 95823 916-433-5076
Rachel Lane, prin. Fax 433-5560
Oak Ridge ES 500/K-6
4501 M L King Blvd 95820 916-395-4665
Daniel Rolleri, prin. Fax 277-6849
Pacific ES 700/K-6
6201 41st St 95824 916-433-5089
Tara Lampkins, prin. Fax 433-5439
Parks ES 800/K-8
2250 68th Ave 95822 916-395-5327
Robert Sullivan, prin. Fax 433-5518
Parkway ES 600/K-6
4720 Forest Pkwy 95823 916-433-5082
Doyal Martin, prin. Fax 433-5572
Phillips ES 600/K-6
2930 21st Ave 95820 916-277-6277
Daniel Hernandez, prin. Fax 277-6762
Pony Express ES 400/K-6
1250 56th Ave 95831 916-395-4690
Herbert Walls, prin. Fax 433-5267
Sequoia ES 500/K-6
3333 Rosemont Dr 95826 916-228-5850
Cindy Hollander, prin. Fax 228-5853
Sloat ES 300/K-6
7525 Candlewood Way 95822 916-433-5051
Angela Novotny-Katzakis, prin. Fax 433-5272
Still ES 900/K-8
2200 John Still Dr 95832 916-433-5191
Reginald Brown, prin. Fax 433-5212
Sutter MS 1,100/7-8
3150 I St 95816 916-395-5370
Cristin Tahara-Martin, prin. Fax 264-3436
Sutterville ES 600/K-6
4967 Monterey Way 95822 916-277-6693
Lori Aoun, prin. Fax 277-6590
Tahoe ES 300/K-6
3110 60th St 95820 916-277-6360
Aprille Shafto, prin. Fax 277-6419
Twain ES 400/K-6
4914 58th St 95820 916-395-4640
Rosario Jovel, prin. Fax 277-6486
Warren ES 600/K-6
5420 Lowell St 95820 916-395-4545
Cory Jones, prin. Fax 382-5977
Washington ES 300/K-6
520 18th St, 916-264-4160
Gema Godina, prin. Fax 264-4360
Wenzel ES 400/K-6
6870 Greenhaven Dr 95831 916-433-5432
Yee Yang, prin. Fax 433-5285
Winn ES 400/K-8
3351 Explorer Dr 95827 916-228-5880
Nisha Turturici, prin. Fax 228-5820
Woodbine ES 300/K-6
2500 52nd Ave 95822 916-433-5358
Chase Tafoya, prin. Fax 433-5094
Wood MS 700/7-8
6201 Lemon Hill Ave 95824 916-395-5380
Tuan Duong, prin. Fax 382-5914

San Juan USD
Supt. — See Carmichael
Arcade Fundamental MS 500/6-8
3500 Edison Ave 95821 916-971-7300
LeeAnn Hopton, prin. Fax 971-7821
Arden MS 900/6-8
1640 Watt Ave 95864 916-971-7306
Jeff Banks, prin. Fax 971-7830
Cottage ES 300/K-5
2221 Morse Ave 95825 916-575-2306
Karen Mix, prin. Fax 575-2311
Cowan Fundamental ES 500/K-6
3350 Becerra Way 95821 916-575-2312
Millie Happoldt, prin. Fax 575-2316
Del Paso Manor ES 600/K-6
2700 Maryal Dr 95821 916-575-2330
Damon Smith, prin. Fax 575-2335
Dyer-Kelly ES 400/K-5
2236 Edison Ave 95821 916-566-2150
Cassandra Bennett Porter, prin. Fax 566-2156
Edison Language Institute 600/K-6
2950 Hurley Way 95864 916-575-2342
Danielle Storey, prin. Fax 575-2348
General Davie Primary Center PK-PK
1500 Dom Way 95864 916-575-2416
Debbie McMannis, coord. Fax 575-2438
Greer ES 500/K-5
2301 Hurley Way 95825 916-566-2157
Arthur Estrada, prin. Fax 566-2161
Howe Avenue ES 600/K-5
2404 Howe Ave 95825 916-566-2165
Kathryn Ferreira, prin. Fax 566-2180
Mariemont ES 600/K-6
1401 Corta Way 95864 916-575-2360
Beth Wahl, prin. Fax 575-2353
Pasadena Avenue ES 300/K-5
4330 Pasadena Ave 95821 916-575-2373
Mirna Pelayo, prin. Fax 575-2376
Sierra Oaks S 700/K-8
171 Mills Rd 95864 916-575-2390
Matt English, prin. Fax 575-2395
Whitney Avenue ES 400/K-5
4248 Whitney Ave 95821 916-575-2407
Vincent Arias, prin. Fax 575-2412

Twin Rivers USD
Supt. — See Mc Clellan
Babcock ES 400/PK-6
2400 Cormorant Way 95815 916-566-3415
Mark Vigario, prin. Fax 566-3579
Castori ES 700/PK-6
1801 South Ave 95838 916-566-3420
Martin Powers, prin. Fax 566-3580
Del Paso Heights ES 500/PK-6
590 Morey Ave 95838 916-566-3425
Javier Macias, prin. Fax 566-3535
Fairbanks ES 400/PK-6
227 Fairbanks Ave 95838 916-566-3435
Janis Wade, prin. Fax 566-3581
Foothill Oaks ES 500/K-6
5520 Lancelot Dr 95842 916-566-1830
Carolyn Cowles, prin. Fax 566-3569
Foothill Ranch MS 600/5-8
5001 Diablo Dr 95842 916-566-3440
Rob Myers, prin. Fax 566-3574
Frontier ES 500/K-6
6691 Silverthorne Cir 95842 916-566-1840
Ellen Giffin, prin. Fax 566-1841
Garden Valley ES 400/PK-6
3601 Larchwood Dr 95834 916-566-3460
Michele Williams, prin. Fax 566-3545
Hagginwood ES 500/PK-6
1418 Palo Verde Ave 95815 916-566-3475
Gina Pasquini, prin. Fax 566-3582
Johnson ES 600/3-6
577 Las Palmas Ave 95815 916-566-3480
David Nevarez, prin. Fax 566-3552
King Technology Academy 400/7-8
3051 Fairfield St 95815 916-566-3490
Shana Henry, prin. Fax 566-7815
Morey Avenue Early Childhood Development 100/PK-K
155 Morey Ave 95838 916-566-3485
Tabitha Thompson, prin. Fax 566-3486
Noralto ES 500/PK-2
477 Las Palmas Ave 95815 916-566-2700
Brad Allen, prin. Fax 566-3576
Northwood ES 500/PK-6
2630 Taft St 95815 916-566-2705
Kelly Grashoff, prin. Fax 566-3583
Norwood JHS 800/6-8
4601 Norwood Ave 95838 916-566-2710
Diedre Barlow, prin. Fax 566-3529
Pioneer S 700/K-8
5816 Pioneer Way 95841 916-566-1940
K.J. Rhoads, prin. Fax 566-3554
Regency Park ES 900/PK-5
5901 Bridgecross Dr 95835 916-566-1660
Timothy Hammons, prin. Fax 566-3570
Ridgepoint S 700/K-8
4680 Monument Dr 95842 916-566-1950
Jim McLaughlin, prin. Fax 566-1951
Rio Tierra JHS 600/6-8
3201 Northstead Dr 95833 916-566-2730
Micah Simmons, prin. Fax 566-3533
Strauch ES 600/PK-5
3141 Northstead Dr 95833 916-566-2745
Marlisa Rodriguez, prin. Fax 566-3546
Woodlake ES 500/PK-6
700 Southgate Rd 95815 916-566-2755
Jennifer Ekelund, prin. Fax 566-3577
Woodridge ES 500/PK-4
5761 Brett Dr 95842 916-566-1650
Roberta Raymond, prin. Fax 566-7820

Al-Arqam Islamic S 300/PK-12
6990 65th St 95823 916-391-3333
Dr. Lula Abusalih, prin. Fax 391-3334
Bergamo Montessori S 200/PK-6
8144 Pocket Rd 95831 916-399-1900
Bradshaw Christian S 1,200/PK-12
8324 Bradshaw Rd 95829 916-688-0521
Carl Eastvold, admin. Fax 688-0502
Brookfield S 200/PK-8
6115 Riverside Blvd 95831 916-442-1255
Dr. Jo Gonsalves, prin. Fax 443-5477
Camellia Waldorf S 100/PK-8
7450 Pocket Rd 95831 916-427-5022
Fax 427-8287
Capital Christian S 1,100/PK-12
9470 Micron Ave 95827 916-856-5600
Todd W. Jacobs, supt. Fax 856-5951
Cornerstone Christian S 200/K-12
5073 Andrea Blvd 95842 916-334-6236
Richard Batista, hdmstr. Fax 334-6200
Holy Spirit S 300/K-8
3920 W Land Park Dr 95822 916-448-5663
Patrick McIntosh, prin. Fax 448-1465
Merryhill ES 200/PK-5
2565 Millcreek Dr 95833 877-959-4187
Merryhill S, 2600 V St 95818 400/PK-8
Elaine Westphal, head sch 916-429-6055
Natomas Christian S 100/K-12
1921 Arena Blvd Ste 100 95834 916-246-3320
Kelvin Jackson, prin. Fax 928-9007
Presentation S 300/PK-8
3100 Norris Ave 95821 916-482-0351
Sr. Carrie Donahue, prin. Fax 482-0377
Sacramento Country Day S 500/PK-12
2636 Latham Dr 95864 916-481-8811
Lee Thomsen, head sch Fax 481-6016
Sacred Heart S 300/K-8
856 39th St 95816 916-456-1576
Theresa Sparks, prin. Fax 456-4773
St. Charles Borromeo S 200/PK-8
7580 Center Pkwy 95823 916-421-6189
Antoinette Perez, prin. Fax 421-3954
St. Francis S 300/K-8
5700 13th Ave 95820 916-442-5494
Ivan Hrga, prin. Fax 442-1390
St. Ignatius S 400/PK-8
3245 Arden Way 95825 916-488-3907
Patty Kochis, prin. Fax 488-0569
St. Mary S 400/K-8
1351 58th St 95819 916-452-1100
Laura Allen, prin. Fax 453-2750
St. Patrick Academy 200/PK-8
5945 Franklin Blvd 95824 916-421-4963
Leslie M. Lastra M.A., prin. Fax 421-1379
St. Philomene S 100/K-8
2320 El Camino Ave 95821 916-489-1506
Ann Marie Faires, prin. Fax 489-2642
St. Robert S 200/K-8
2251 Irvin Way 95822 916-452-2111
Dr. Jennifer Havey, prin. Fax 452-5765
Shalom Day S 200/PK-6
2320 Sierra Blvd 95825 916-485-4151
Nancy Leaderman, head sch Fax 485-3970
Trinity Christian S 100/PK-9
5225 Hillsdale Blvd 95842 916-331-7377
George Muntean, prin. Fax 331-3152

Saint Helena, Napa, Pop. 5,723
St. Helena USD 1,300/PK-12
465 Main St 94574 707-967-2708
Dr. Marylou Wilson Ed.D., supt. Fax 963-1335
www.sthelena.k12.ca.us

St. Helena ES 300/3-5
1325 Adams St 94574 707-967-2712
Tanya Pearson, prin. Fax 967-2756
St. Helena PS 200/PK-2
1701 Grayson Ave 94574 707-967-2772
Tamara Sanguinetti, prin. Fax 963-2959
Stevenson MS 300/6-8
1316 Hillview Pl 94574 707-967-2725
Karin Cox, prin. Fax 967-2734

Foothills Adventist S 50/PK-8
711 Sunnyside Rd 94574 707-963-3546
Katie Richmond, prin. Fax 963-7651
St. Helena Montessori 100/PK-9
880 College Ave 94574 707-963-1527
Elena Heil, head sch Fax 967-3392
St. Helena S 100/K-8
1255 Oak Ave 94574 707-963-4677
Mary Herboth, prin. Fax 963-4659

Salida, Stanislaus, Pop. 13,232
Salida UNESD 3,000/K-8
4801 Sisk Rd 95368 209-545-0339
Twila Tosh, supt. Fax 545-2682
www.salida.k12.ca.us/
Boer ES 600/K-5
4801 Gold Valley Rd 95368 209-543-8163
Katie Kline, prin. Fax 543-0669
Salida ES 500/K-5
4519 Finney Rd 95368 209-545-9394
Ana Garcia, prin. Fax 545-3711
Salida MS - Vella Campus 900/6-8
5041 Toomes Rd 95368 209-545-1633
Dean Way, prin. Fax 545-0831
Sisk ES 600/K-5
5337 Sugar Creek Ln 95368 209-545-1671
Jeri Passalaqua, prin. Fax 545-1624
Other Schools – See Modesto

Salinas, Monterey, Pop. 147,570
Alisal UNSD 8,800/K-6
1205 E Market St 93905 831-753-5700
Dr. Hector Rico, supt. Fax 753-5709
www.alisal.org
Alisal Community ES 700/K-6
1437 Del Monte Ave 93905 831-753-5720
Dr. Elizabeth Armenta, prin. Fax 753-5725
Bardin ES 700/K-6
425 Bardin Rd 93905 831-753-5730
Jairo Arrellano, prin. Fax 753-5758
Chavez ES 900/K-6
1225 Towt St 93905 831-753-5224
Petra Martinez-Diaz, prin. Fax 753-5230
Creekside ES 700/K-6
1770 Kittery St 93906 831-753-5252
Jose Juan Urquizo, prin. Fax 753-5256
Fremont ES 900/K-6
1255 E Market St 93905 831-753-5750
John Jimenez, prin. Fax 753-5754
King Academy 400/4-6
925 N Sanborn Rd 93905 831-796-3916
Abel DeLeon, prin. Fax 796-3921
Loya ES 800/K-6
1505 Cougar Dr 93905 831-751-1945
Diana Garcia, prin. Fax 751-1953
Monte Bella ES 500/K-6
1300 Tuscany Blvd 93905 831-770-6000
Dr. Roberto Nunez, prin. Fax 754-5520
Paul ES 900/K-6
1300 Rider Ave 93905 831-753-5740
Yolanda McIntosh, prin. Fax 753-5268
Rocca Barton ES 700/K-6
680 Las Casitas Dr 93905 831-753-5770
Alberto Jaramillo, prin. Fax 753-5797
Sanchez ES 800/K-6
901 N Sanborn Rd 93905 831-753-5760
Roberto Rodriguez, prin. Fax 753-5764
Steinbeck ES 700/K-6
1714 Burlington Dr 93906 831-753-5780
Dr. Christina Palmer, prin. Fax 443-0977

Graves ESD 50/K-8
15 McFadden Rd 93908 831-422-6392
Rosemarie Grounds, supt. Fax 422-3211
gravESelementary.com
Graves ES 50/K-8
15 McFadden Rd 93908 831-422-6392
Rosemarie Grounds, prin. Fax 422-3211

Lagunita ESD 100/K-8
975 San Juan Grade Rd 93907 831-449-2800
Daniel Stonebloom, supt. Fax 449-9671
www.sites.google.com/site/lagunitaschooldistrict/hom
e
Lagunita ES 100/K-8
975 San Juan Grade Rd 93907 831-449-2800
Daniel Stonebloom, supt. Fax 449-9671

North Monterey County USD
Supt. — See Moss Landing
Echo Valley ES 600/K-6
147 Echo Valley Rd 93907 831-663-2308
Kathryn Singh, prin. Fax 663-1006
N Monterey Co. Ctr for Independent Study 100/K-12
17500 Pesante Rd 93907 831-663-7050
Aida Ramirez, prin. Fax 663-6184
Prunedale ES 700/K-6
17719 Pesante Rd 93907 831-663-3963
Melissa Lewington, prin. Fax 663-5295

Salinas City ESD 8,900/PK-6
840 S Main St 93901 831-753-5600
Dr. Martha Martinez, supt. Fax 753-5610
www.salinascity.k12.ca.us
Boronda Dual Immersion Academy PK-1
1114 Fontes Ln 93907 831-753-5615
Mary Pritchard, admin. Fax 751-0253
Boronda Meadows ES 800/K-6
915 Larkin St 93907 831-784-5400
Susana Mancera, prin. Fax 770-1987
El Gabilan ES 700/K-6
1256 Linwood Dr 93906 831-753-5660
Esabel Cervantes, prin. Fax 442-9860
Kammann ES 900/K-6
521 Rochex Ave 93906 831-753-5665
Leticia Garcia, prin. Fax 753-5223
Laurel Wood ES 500/K-6
645 Larkin St 93907 831-753-5620
Albert Velasquez, prin. Fax 783-3050
Lincoln ES 500/PK-6
705 California St 93901 831-753-5625
Juan Chaidez, prin. Fax 753-5699
Loma Vista ES 600/K-6
757 Sausal Dr 93906 831-753-5670
Katie Venza-Balesteri, prin. Fax 443-2181
Los Padres ES 800/K-6
1130 John St 93905 831-753-5630
Gabriel Ramirez, prin. Fax 751-3564
Mission Park ES 700/K-6
403 W Acacia St 93901 831-753-5635
Jennifer Zanzot, prin. Fax 753-4191
Monterey Park ES 600/K-6
410 San Miguel Ave 93901 831-753-5640
Brian Hays, prin. Fax 751-3626
Natividad ES 700/K-6
1465 Modoc Ave 93906 831-753-5675
Elizabeth Lopez, prin. Fax 753-5218
Roosevelt ES 600/K-6
120 Capitol St 93901 831-753-5645
Linda Barrera, prin. Fax 769-0956
Sherwood ES 900/K-6
110 S Wood St 93905 831-753-5650
Everardo Marquez Ph.D., prin. Fax 751-3616
University Park ES 600/K-6
833 W Acacia St 93901 831-753-5655
Daniel Lee, prin. Fax 751-3622

Salinas UNHSD 13,800/7-12
431 W Alisal St 93901 831-796-7000
Dan Burns, supt. Fax 796-7005
www.salinas.k12.ca.us
El Sausal MS 900/7-8
1155 E Alisal St 93905 831-796-7200
Francisco Huerta, prin. Fax 796-7205
Harden MS 1,200/7-8
1561 McKinnon St 93906 831-796-7300
Kimberly McCullick, prin. Fax 796-7305
La Paz MS 900/7-8
1300 N Sanborn Rd 93905 831-796-7900
Irelia Dominguez, prin. Fax 796-7905
Washington MS 1,100/7-8
560 Iverson St 93901 831-796-7100
Anthony Hinton, prin. Fax 796-7105

Santa Rita UNSD 3,200/K-8
57 Russell Rd 93906 831-443-7200
Dr. Shelly Morr, supt. Fax 442-1729
www.santaritaschools.org
Bolsa Knolls MS 500/6-8
1031 Rogge Rd 93906 831-443-3300
John Gutierrez, prin. Fax 443-4766
Gavilan View MS 500/6-8
18250 Van Buren Ave 93906 831-443-7212
Donna Koenig, prin. Fax 443-0908
La Joya ES 500/K-5
55 Rogge Rd 93906 831-443-7216
Donna Smith, prin. Fax 443-9539
McKinnon ES 500/K-5
2100 McKinnon St 93906 831-443-7224
Leslie Patronik, prin. Fax 443-7240
New Republic ES 500/K-5
636 Arcadia Way 93906 831-443-7246
RaeAnn Madrid, prin. Fax 443-7256
Santa Rita ES 600/K-5
2014 Santa Rita St 93906 831-443-7221
Ana Cuevas, prin. Fax 443-7228

Spreckels UNESD
Supt. — See Spreckels
Buena Vista MS 400/6-8
18250 Tara Dr 93908 831-455-8936
Eric Tarallo, prin. Fax 455-8832

Washington UNESD 900/K-8
43 San Benancio Rd 93908 831-484-2166
Gina Uccelli, supt. Fax 484-2828
www.washingtonusd.org
San Benancio MS 300/6-8
43 San Benancio Rd 93908 831-484-1172
Joe Carnazzo, prin. Fax 484-6509
Toro Park ES 400/K-3
43 San Benancio Rd 93908 831-484-9691
Carissa Edeza, prin. Fax 484-5666
Washington Union S 200/4-5
43 San Benancio Rd 93908 831-484-1331
Whitney Meyer, prin. Fax 484-5736

Anthem Christian S 100/K-8
345 E Alvin Dr 93906 831-449-0140
Robin Young, prin. Fax 449-7161
Madonna Del Sasso S 300/PK-8
20 Santa Teresa Way 93906 831-424-7813
Angel Rivera, prin. Fax 424-3359
Montessori Learning Center 100/PK-5
PO Box 2387 93902 831-455-1546
Fax 769-9410
Sacred Heart S 300/K-8
123 W Market St 93901 831-771-1310
Connie Rains, prin. Fax 771-1314

Salton City, Imperial, Pop. 3,695
Coachella Valley USD
Supt. — See Thermal
Sea View ES 500/K-6
2467 Sea Shore Ave, 760-848-1565
Tim Steele, prin. Fax 394-0916

Samoa, Humboldt, Pop. 237
Peninsula UNESD 50/K-8
PO Box 175 95564 707-443-2731
Lark Doolan, supt. Fax 443-3685
www.humboldt.k12.ca.us/peninsula_sd
Peninsula Union ES 50/K-8
PO Box 175 95564 707-443-2731
Lark Doolan, admin. Fax 443-3685

San Andreas, Calaveras, Pop. 2,665
Calaveras USD 3,100/K-12
PO Box 788 95249 209-754-2300
Mark Campbell, supt. Fax 754-2215
www.calaveras.k12.ca.us
San Andreas ES 300/K-6
PO Box 67 95249 209-754-2365
Dan Mayers, prin. Fax 754-9387
Other Schools – See Mokelumne Hill, Rail Road Flat, Valley Springs, West Point

San Anselmo, Marin, Pop. 11,931
Ross Valley SD 2,200/PK-8
110 Shaw Dr 94960 415-454-2162
Dr. Rick E. Bagley Ed.D., supt. Fax 454-6840
rossvalleyschools.org
Brookside ES 300/PK-5
116 Butterfield Rd 94960 415-453-2948
Judith Barry, prin. Fax 453-0243
Hidden Valley ES 400/PK-5
46 Green Valley Ct 94960 415-454-7409
Kristi Fish, prin. Fax 454-3782
Thomas ES 400/K-5
150 Ross Ave 94960 415-454-4603
Donna Faulkner, prin. Fax 485-5506
Other Schools – See Fairfax

St. Anselm S 300/K-8
40 Belle Ave 94960 415-454-8667
Kim Orendorff, prin. Fax 454-4730
San Domenico Lower S 200/PK-5
1500 Butterfield Rd 94960 415-258-1900
LeaAnne Parlette, prin. Fax 258-1901
San Domenico MS 200/6-8
1500 Butterfield Rd 94960 415-258-1900
Carrie Robley, prin. Fax 258-1901

San Ardo, Monterey, Pop. 511
San Ardo UNESD 100/K-8
PO Box 170 93450 831-627-2520
Catherine Reimer, supt. Fax 627-2078
sausd-k12-pt.schoolloop.com
San Ardo ES 100/K-8
PO Box 170 93450 831-627-2520
Catherine Reimer, prin. Fax 627-2078

San Bernardino, San Bernardino, Pop. 204,762
Redlands USD
Supt. — See Redlands
Victoria ES 500/K-5
1505 Richardson St 92408 909-478-5670
Larry Elwell, prin. Fax 478-5676

San Bernardino City USD 51,500/PK-12
777 N F St 92410 909-381-1100
Dr. Dale Marsden, supt. Fax 885-6392
www.sbcusd.k12.ca.us/
Anton ES 600/K-5
1501 Anton Ct 92404 909-386-2000
Toni Woods, prin. Fax 891-1922
Arrowhead ES 300/K-5
3825 N Mountain View Ave 92405 909-881-8100
Tina Murray, prin. Fax 881-8104
Arrowview MS 700/7-8
2299 N G St 92405 909-881-8109
Berenice Rios, prin. Fax 881-8119
Barton ES 400/K-5
2214 Pumalo St 92404 909-388-6534
Janice Gordon-Ellis, prin. Fax 862-3583
Bradley ES 600/K-6
1300 Valencia Ave 92404 909-388-6317
Amy Coker, prin. Fax 888-9716
Brown ES 600/K-6
2525 N G St 92405 909-881-5010
Maria Martinez, prin. Fax 881-5064
Chavez MS 1,300/6-8
6650 Magnolia Ave 92407 909-386-2050
Ernestine Hopwood, prin. Fax 473-8443
Curtis MS 900/6-8
1050 Del Rosa Ave 92410 909-388-6332
Marlene Bicondova, prin. Fax 388-6339
Davidson ES 500/K-6
2844 Davidson Ave 92405 909-881-8153
Stacy Martinez, prin. Fax 881-5633
Del Rosa ES 700/K-6
3395 Mountain Ave 92404 909-881-8160
Patricia King, prin. Fax 881-2926
Del Vallejo MS 200/6-8
1885 E Lynwood Dr 92404 909-881-8280
Toni Woods, prin. Fax 881-8285
Dominguez ES, 135 S Allen St 92408 K-5
Alejandro Hernandez, prin. 909-888-8020
Emmerton ES 600/K-6
1888 Arden Ave 92404 909-862-6400
Tasha Lindsay-Doizan, prin. Fax 862-4353
Fairfax ES 400/K-6
1362 Pacific St 92404 909-381-1283
Ruth Curry, prin. Fax 384-0582
Golden Valley MS 800/6-8
3800 N Waterman Ave 92404 909-881-8168
Kristen Vicondova, prin. Fax 881-5196
Gomez ES 600/K-6
1480 W 11th St 92411 909-383-8159
Alicia Paz, prin. Fax 383-8091
Henry ES 400/K-6
1250 W 14th St 92411 909-888-2353
Dr. Grace Monroe, prin. Fax 888-2403
Hillside ES 700/K-6
4975 N Mayfield Ave 92407 909-881-8264
Tommie Archuleta, prin. Fax 881-4270
Holcomb ES K-6
1345 W 48th St 92407 909-887-2505
Luis Chavez-Andere, prin. Fax 887-4890
Hunt ES 600/K-5
1342 Pumalo St 92404 909-881-8178
Kristin Kolling, prin. Fax 881-8175

Inghram ES 300/K-5
1695 W 19th St 92411 909-880-6633
Joan West, prin. Fax 880-6638
Jones ES 500/K-6
700 N F St 92410 909-386-2020
Ramon Belasco, prin. Fax 885-8181
Kendall ES 400/K-5
4951 N State St 92407 909-880-6626
Alicia Fields, prin. Fax 880-6629
Kimbark ES 500/K-6
18021 W Kenwood Ave 92407 909-880-6641
Mario Jacquez, prin. Fax 880-9341
King MS 700/6-8
1250 Medical Center Dr 92411 909-388-6350
Maria Jauregui, prin. Fax 388-6361
Lincoln ES 900/K-6
255 W 13th St 92405 909-388-6370
Kevin Goodly, prin. Fax 388-6379
Lytle Creek ES 700/K-6
275 S K St 92410 909-388-6382
Alvina Pawlik, prin. Fax 381-0483
Marshall ES 400/K-6
3288 N G St 92405 909-881-8185
Denise Martinez, prin. Fax 882-6705
Monterey ES 500/K-5
794 E Monterey Ave 92410 909-388-6391
Diane Silva, prin. Fax 381-5031
Mt. Vernon ES 500/K-5
1271 W 10th St 92411 909-388-6400
Sylvette Del Llano, prin. Fax 889-9797
Muscoy ES 800/K-6
2119 Blake St 92407 909-880-6649
Dana Jamison, prin. Fax 880-6654
Newmark ES 400/K-5
4121 N 3rd Ave 92407 909-881-8192
Santosh Trikha, prin. Fax 881-9563
North Park ES 500/K-6
5378 N H St 92407 909-881-8202
Yadira Downing, prin. Fax 882-7142
North Verdemont ES 500/K-6
3555 W Meyers Rd 92407 909-880-6730
Dan Durst, prin. Fax 880-6734
Norton ES 700/K-6
747 N Mountain View Ave 92401 909-888-6369
Liz Cochrane-Benoit, prin. Fax 888-7232
Paakuma K-8 S PK-8
17825 Sycamore Creek Loop 92407 909-355-3137
V. Morales-Roberson, prin. Fax 355-3150
Palm Avenue ES 700/K-6
6565 Palm Ave 92407 909-880-6753
Kathy Wade, prin. Fax 880-6759
Parkside ES 600/K-6
3775 N Waterman Ave 92404 909-881-8209
Cynthia Nicolaisen, prin. Fax 881-1359
Ramona-Alessandro ES 600/K-5
670 Ramona Ave 92411 909-388-6300
David Juarez, prin. Fax 381-1993
Richardson Prep MS 600/6-8
455 S K St 92410 909-388-6438
Keith Keiper, prin. Fax 383-0368
Riley ES 700/K-6
1266 N G St 92405 909-388-6460
Jaime Esteves, prin. Fax 388-6467
Rio Vista ES 400/K-5
1451 N California St 92411 909-388-6450
Bradley McDuffee, prin. Fax 884-9518
Roberts ES 600/K-6
494 E 9th St 92410 909-388-6409
Laura Ramos, prin. Fax 885-0536
Rodriguez Prep MS 500/6-8
1985 Guthrie St 92404 909-884-6030
Randy Clyde, prin. Fax 863-7869
Roosevelt ES 600/K-3
1554 Garner Ave 92411 909-388-6470
Martha Servin, prin. Fax 889-1378
Salinas ES 600/K-5
2699 N California St 92407 909-880-6600
Heather Regalado, prin. Fax 880-9607
Shandin Hills MS 800/6-8
4301 Little Mountain Dr 92407 909-880-6666
Victoria Flores, prin. Fax 880-6672
Urbita ES 400/K-6
771 S J St 92410 909-388-6488
Sarah McCain, prin. Fax 388-7488
Vermont ES 700/K-6
3695 Vermont St 92407 909-880-6658
Ana Perez, prin. Fax 880-1348
Warm Springs ES 600/K-6
7497 Sterling Ave 92410 909-388-6500
Houn Hib, prin. Fax 888-6045
Wilson ES 400/K-6
2894 Belle St 92404 909-881-8253
Dennis Wolbert, prin. Fax 886-6943
Wong ES 800/K-6
1250 E 9th St 92410 909-888-1500
Ryan Rainbolt, prin. Fax 889-8929
Other Schools – See Highland

Del Rosa Christian S 100/K-8
1333 E 39th St 92404 909-882-3004
Lorna McWells, prin. Fax 886-8630
Dikaios Christian Academy 200/K-12
PO Box 9067 92427 909-881-8310
Jerry Sommerville, dir. Fax 881-8315
Holy Rosary Academy 200/PK-8
2620 N Arrowhead Ave 92405 909-886-1088
Cheryll Austin, prin. Fax 475-5263
Our Lady of the Assumption S 200/PK-8
796 W 48th St 92407 909-881-2416
Sue Long, prin. Fax 886-7892
Rock Christian S 100/PK-12
2345 S Waterman Ave 92408 909-825-8887

San Bruno, San Mateo, Pop. 37,955
Millbrae ESD
Supt. — See Millbrae
Lomita Park ES 300/K-5
200 Santa Helena Ave 94066 650-588-5852
Christina Spicker, prin. Fax 873-8014

San Bruno Park ESD 2,800/K-8
500 Acacia Ave 94066 650-624-3100
Cheryl Olson, supt. Fax 266-9626
sbpsd.k12.ca.us
Allen ES 400/K-5
875 Angus Ave W 94066 650-624-3140
Kathleen Cosgriff, prin. Fax 875-7490
Belle Air ES 300/K-5
450 3rd Ave 94066 650-624-3155
Leo Alvarez, prin. Fax 875-7596
El Crystal ES 300/K-5
201 Balboa Way 94066 650-624-3150
Jeanne Elliott, prin. Fax 875-9308
Muir ES 300/K-5
130 Cambridge Ln 94066 650-624-3160
Fran Dunleavy, prin. Fax 875-9462
Parkside MS 900/6-8
1801 Niles Ave 94066 650-624-3180
Kerry Dees, prin. Fax 877-8195
Portola ES 300/K-5
300 Amador Ave 94066 650-624-3175
Barbara Alford, prin. Fax 738-6697
Rollingwood ES 300/K-5
2500 Cottonwood Dr 94066 650-624-3165
Colleen Hennessy, prin. Fax 877-8298

South San Francisco USD
Supt. — See South San Francisco
Monte Verde ES 600/K-5
2551 Saint Cloud Dr 94066 650-877-8838
Deborah Mirt, prin. Fax 952-0904

Highlands Christian S 600/PK-8
1900 Monterey Dr 94066 650-873-4090
Dr. David Johnston, supt. Fax 742-6228
St. Robert S 300/K-8
345 Oak Ave 94066 650-583-5065
Margo Wright, prin. Fax 583-1418
Stratford S - Crestmoor Canyon PK-5
2322 Crestmoor Dr 94066 650-837-9222
Teresa Wertman, prin.

San Carlos, San Mateo, Pop. 27,121
San Carlos ESD 3,000/PK-8
1200 Industrial Rd Ste 9 94070 650-508-7333
Dr. Craig Baker, supt. Fax 508-7340
www.scsdk8.org
Arroyo S 4-5
1710 Arroyo Ave 94070 650-632-8300
Marie Crawford, prin. Fax 632-8339
Central MS 500/6-8
757 Cedar St 94070 650-508-7321
Tom Domer, prin. Fax 508-7342

St. Charles S 300/K-8
850 Tamarack Ave 94070 650-593-1629
Megan Armando, prin. Fax 593-9723

San Clemente, Orange, Pop. 61,767
Capistrano USD
Supt. — See San Juan Capistrano
Ayer MS 900/6-8
1271 Calle Sarmentoso 92673 949-366-9607
Nick Stever, prin. Fax 366-1519
Benedict ES 700/K-5
1251 Calle Sarmentoso 92673 949-498-6617
Heidi Harvey, prin. Fax 361-8462
Concordia ES 700/K-5
3120 Avenida Del Presidente 92672 949-492-3060
Robert McKane, prin. Fax 361-8652
Las Palmas ES 800/K-5
1101 Calle Puente 92672 949-234-5333
Kristen Nelson, prin. Fax 369-1427
Lobo ES 400/K-5
200 Avenida Vista Montana 92672 949-366-6740
Cheryl Sampson, prin. Fax 366-0764
Marblehead ES 400/K-5
2410 Via Turqueza 92673 949-234-5339
Faith Morris, prin. Fax 361-0712
Shorecliffs MS 1,000/6-8
240 Via Socorro 92672 949-498-1660
Brad Baker, prin. Fax 498-0826
Vista Del Mar ES 1,200/K-5
1130 Avenida Talega 92673 949-234-5950
Troy Hunt, prin. Fax 940-0262
Vista del Mar MS 600/6-8
1130 Avenida Talega 92673 949-234-5955
Michelle Benham, prin. Fax 940-0262

Fallbrook UNESD
Supt. — See Fallbrook
San Onofre S 700/K-8
200 Pate Dr 92672 949-492-3372
Lillian Perez, prin. Fax 492-1368

Our Lady of Fatima S 200/PK-8
105 N La Esperanza 92672 949-492-7320
Joanne Williams, prin. Fax 492-3793
Our Savior's Lutheran S 300/PK-5
200 Avenida San Pablo 92672 949-492-6165
Kathleen Schmitt, prin. Fax 492-6132
St. Michael's Academy 100/K-8
107 W Marquita 92672 949-366-9468
Phillip Johnson, prin. Fax 492-7238

San Diego, San Diego, Pop. 1,256,111
Chula Vista ESD
Supt. — See Chula Vista
Finney ES 400/K-6
3950 Byrd St 92154 619-690-1334
Dr. Beverly Prange, prin. Fax 428-4138
Juarez-Lincoln ES 600/K-6
849 Twining Ave 92154 619-690-9222
Toni Faddis, prin. Fax 662-9679
Los Altos ES 400/K-6
1332 Kenalan Dr 92154 619-690-5880
Santos Gonzalez, prin. Fax 428-4712
Silver Wing ES 400/K-6
3730 Arey Dr 92154 619-423-3950
Theresa Corona, prin. Fax 423-7438

Del Mar UNESD 4,400/K-6
11232 El Camino Real 92130 858-755-9301
Holly McClurg, supt. Fax 755-4361
www.dmusd.org
Ashley Falls ES 400/K-6
13030 Ashley Falls Dr 92130 858-259-7812
Abby Farricker, prin. Fax 259-1828
Carmel Del Mar ES 500/K-6
12345 Carmel Park Dr 92130 858-481-6789
Jessica Morales, prin. Fax 481-7418
Ocean Air S 800/K-6
11444 Canter Heights Dr 92130 858-481-4040
Ryan Stanley, prin. Fax 481-6657
Sage Canyon S 700/K-6
5290 Harvest Run Dr 92130 858-481-7844
William Cameron, prin. Fax 481-7949
Sycamore Ridge S 500/K-6
5333 Old Carmel Valley Rd 92130 858-755-1060
Emily Morris, prin. Fax 755-1258
Torrey Hills S 600/K-6
10830 Calle Mar De Mariposa 92130 858-481-4266
Monica Sorenson, prin. Fax 481-0344
Other Schools – See Del Mar

Poway USD 35,200/K-12
15250 Avenue of Science 92128 858-521-2800
Marian Kim-Phelps, supt.
www.powayusd.com
Adobe Bluffs ES 400/K-5
8707 Adobe Bluffs Dr 92129 858-538-8403
Edward Park, prin. Fax 538-2749
Bernardo Heights MS 1,400/6-8
12990 Paseo Lucido 92128 858-485-4850
Marie Galaz, prin. Fax 485-4865
Black Mountain MS 1,300/6-8
9353 Oviedo St 92129 858-484-1300
Scott Corso, prin. Fax 538-9440
Canyon View ES 500/K-5
9225 Adolphia St 92129 858-484-0981
Jill Halsey, prin. Fax 538-9441
Creekside ES 600/K-5
12362 Springhurst Dr 92128 858-391-1514
Christine Donnelly, prin. Fax 391-1511
Deer Canyon ES 500/K-5
13455 Russet Leaf Ln 92129 858-484-6064
Terry Worthington, prin. Fax 538-9453
Del Sur ES 700/K-5
15665 Paseo Del Sur 92127 858-674-6200
Eric Takeshita, prin. Fax 759-6915
Design 39 Campus K-7
17050 Del Sur Ridge Rd 92127 858-679-6639
Joe Erpelding, prin.
Highland Ranch ES 700/K-5
14840 Waverly Downs Way 92128 858-674-4707
Cindy Venolia, prin. Fax 485-7642
Los Penasquitos ES 600/K-5
14125 Cuca St 92129 858-672-3600
Deanne McLaughlin, prin. Fax 672-4390
Mesa Verde MS 1,300/6-8
8375 Entreken Way 92129 858-538-5478
Cliff Mitchell, prin. Fax 538-8636
Monterey Ridge ES 1,100/K-5
17117 4S Ranch Pkwy 92127 858-487-6887
Sal Embry, prin. Fax 487-2050
Morning Creek ES 800/K-5
10925 Morning Creek Dr S 92128 858-748-4334
Rhonda Taylor, prin. Fax 748-8672
Oak Valley MS 1,400/6-8
16055 Winecreek Rd 92127 858-487-2939
Casey Currigan, prin. Fax 457-0991
Park Village ES 700/K-5
7930 Park Village Rd 92129 858-484-5621
Mke Mosgrove, prin. Fax 484-5138
Rolling Hills ES 400/K-5
15255 Penasquitos Dr 92129 858-672-3400
Libby Keller, prin. Fax 672-4324
Shoal Creek ES 600/K-5
11775 Shoal Creek Dr 92128 858-613-9080
Mark Atkins, prin. Fax 613-0375
Stone Ranch ES 1,200/K-5
16150 4S Ranch Pkwy 92127 858-487-8474
Lisa Danzer, prin. Fax 487-6225
Sundance ES 500/K-5
8944 Twin Trails Dr 92129 858-484-2950
Bob Rodrigo, prin. Fax 538-9452
Sunset Hills ES 400/K-5
9291 Oviedo St 92129 858-484-1600
Lisa Wilken, prin. Fax 538-9451
Turtleback ES 600/K-5
15855 Turtleback Rd 92127 858-673-5514
Ann Auten, prin. Fax 673-8884
Westwood ES 800/K-5
17449 Matinal Rd 92127 858-487-2026
Kaleb Rashad, prin. Fax 673-9103
Willow Grove ES 900/K-5
14727 Via Azul 92127 858-674-6300
Amy Huff, prin. Fax 759-8511
Other Schools – See Poway

San Diego County Office of Education 2,000/
6401 Linda Vista Rd 92111 858-292-3500
Paul Gothold, supt. Fax 292-3653
www.sdcoe.net
Monarch S 300/K-12
1625 Newton Ave 92113 858-652-4100
Fax 652-4107
Other Schools – See San Marcos

San Diego USD 127,200/PK-12
4100 Normal St 92103 619-725-8000
Cindy Marten, supt. Fax 291-7182
www.sandiegounified.org
Adams ES 300/K-5
4672 35th St 92116 619-362-4200
Sylvia Ferrer-McGrade, prin. Fax 563-7532
Alcott ES 200/K-5
4680 Hidalgo Ave 92117 858-273-3415
Michelle Riley, prin. Fax 581-6429
Angier ES 600/K-5
8450 Hurlbut St 92123 858-496-8295
Andrew Gergurich, prin. Fax 277-9279

Audubon S 500/K-8
8111 San Vicente St 92114 619-344-5800
Tim Suanico, prin. Fax 344-5849
Baker ES 500/K-6
4041 T St 92113 619-344-4800
Kathleen Gallagher, prin. Fax 344-4849
Balboa ES 600/K-5
1844 S 40th St 92113 619-362-4100
Hector Bravo, prin. Fax 362-4149
Barnard Asian Pacific Language Academy 400/K-6
2445 Fogg St 92109 858-800-5700
Edward Park, prin. Fax 800-5749
Bay Park ES 400/K-5
2433 Denver St 92110 619-276-1471
Leslie Barnes, prin. Fax 276-3243
Bell MS 900/6-8
620 Briarwood Rd 92139 619-430-1000
Precious Hubbard-Jackson, prin. Fax 470-6054
Benchley/Weinberger ES 500/K-5
6269 Twin Lake Dr 92119 619-463-9271
Mariclaret Patton, prin. Fax 697-8617
Bethune S 700/K-8
6835 Benjamin Holt Rd 92114 619-267-2271
Valerie Jurado, prin. Fax 475-5068
Birney ES 600/K-5
4345 Campus Ave 92103 619-497-3500
Amanda Hammond-Williams, prin. Fax 688-3017
Boone ES 600/K-5
7330 Brookhaven Rd 92114 619-344-6000
Juan Nunez, prin. Fax 344-6049
Burbank ES 400/K-5
2146 Julian Ave 92113 619-652-4500
Carolina Flores-Wittman, prin. Fax 231-4106
Cabrillo ES 200/K-4
3120 Talbot St 92106 619-223-7154
Irene Hightower, prin. Fax 221-9051
Cadman ES 200/K-5
4370 Kamloop Ave 92117 858-397-6500
Linda Trousdale, prin.
Carson ES 500/K-5
6905 Kramer St 92111 858-397-6900
Courtney Young, prin. Fax 397-6949
Carver ES 200/K-5
3251 Juanita St 92105 619-344-6600
Maria Vera, prin. Fax 344-6649
Central ES 800/K-5
4063 Polk Ave 92105 619-344-6100
Cynthia Marten, prin. Fax 344-6149
Challenger MS 1,000/6-8
10810 Parkdale Ave 92126 858-586-7001
Kathrynn Dominique, prin. Fax 271-5203
Chavez ES 500/K-5
1404 S 40th St 92113 619-362-3600
Francisco Santos, prin. Fax 362-3249
Cherokee Point ES 500/K-5
3735 38th St 92105 619-641-3400
Quyen Corral, prin. Fax 282-2665
Chesterton ES 500/K-5
7335 Wheatley St 92111 858-496-8070
Heriberto Delute, prin. Fax 571-5766
Chollas/Mead ES 600/K-5
401 N 45th St 92102 619-362-3300
Julia Bridi, prin. Fax 262-7526
Clark MS 1,100/6-8
4388 Thorn St 92105 619-344-4200
Thomas Liberto, prin. Fax 344-4274
Clay ES, 6506 Solita Ave 92115 300/K-5
Lindsey Duncan, prin. 619-344-5700
Correia MS 800/7-8
4302 Valeta St 92107 619-222-0476
Jonathan McDade, prin. Fax 221-0147
Creative Performing & Media Arts S 900/6-8
5050 Conrad Ave 92117 858-800-5550
Scott Thomason, prin.
Crown Point ES 400/K-5
4033 Ingraham St 92109 858-273-9830
Armando Lopez, prin. Fax 274-5165
Cubberley ES 200/K-5
3201 Marathon Dr 92123 858-496-8075
Magdalena Ruvalcaba, prin. Fax 496-8325
Curie ES 600/K-5
4080 Governor Dr 92122 858-453-4184
Cara Ramsey, prin. Fax 546-3972
Dailard ES 600/K-5
6425 Cibola Rd 92120 619-286-1550
Beverly Fitzpatric, prin. Fax 286-8395
Dana S 900/5-6
1775 Chatsworth Blvd 92107 619-225-3897
Scott Irwin, prin. Fax 225-3878
De Portola MS 1,000/6-8
11010 Clairemont Mesa Blvd 92124 858-496-8080
Ryan Brock, prin. Fax 576-4419
Dewey ES 400/K-4
3251 Rosecrans St 92110 619-430-1800
Tanya McMillan, prin. Fax 523-9338
Dingeman ES 900/K-5
11840 Scripps Creek Dr 92131 858-549-4437
Tamara Lewis, prin. Fax 635-8948
Doyle ES 900/K-5
3950 Berino Ct 92122 858-455-6230
Kimberly Moore, prin. Fax 455-9486
Edison ES 600/K-5
4077 35th St 92104 619-344-5400
Eileen Moreno, prin. Fax 344-5449
Emerson/Bandini ES 600/K-6
3510 Newton Ave 92113 619-344-6200
Juan Romo, prin. Fax 344-6249
Encanto ES, 822 65th St 92114 500/K-5
Audra Mandler, prin. 619-344-6700
Ericson ES 700/K-5
11174 Westonhill Dr 92126 858-271-0505
Darius Ashton, prin. Fax 566-6614
Euclid ES, 4166 Euclid Ave 92105 600/K-5
Jose Valdez, prin. 619-344-5600
Farb MS 500/6-8
4880 La Cuenta Dr 92124 858-697-6750
Courtney Rizzo, prin. Fax 697-6790
Fay ES, 4080 52nd St 92105 700/K-5
Armando Tovar, prin. 619-624-2600

Field ES 300/K-6
4375 Bannock Ave 92117 858-800-5900
Amy Griffiths, prin. Fax 800-5949
Fletcher ES 300/K-5
7666 Bobolink Way 92123 858-496-8100
Gina Camacho-McGrath, prin. Fax 496-8045
Florence ES, 3914 1st Ave 92103 300/K-5
Alexis Conerty, prin. 619-344-5900
Foster ES 400/K-5
6550 51st St 92120 619-582-2728
Karla Shiminski, prin. Fax 583-6812
Franklin ES 300/K-5
4481 Copeland Ave 92116 619-344-3000
Don Whisman, prin. Fax 344-3040
Freese ES 300/K-5
8140 Greenlawn Dr 92114 619-344-3100
Shannon Lewis, prin. Fax 344-3140
Fulton S 400/K-8
7055 Skyline Dr 92114 619-344-3200
Emmitt Dodd, prin. Fax 527-4172
Gage ES 400/K-5
6811 Bisby Lake Ave 92119 619-463-0202
Kathy Burns, prin. Fax 463-0534
Garfield ES 300/K-5
4487 Oregon St 92116 619-362-4300
Lali Barhoumi, prin. Fax 284-2096
Golden Hill S 500/K-8
1240 33rd St 92102 619-236-5600
Steve Elizondo, prin. Fax 236-5690
Grant S 700/K-8
1425 Washington Pl 92103 619-293-4420
Kathy Lorden, prin. Fax 297-8404
Green ES 500/K-5
7030 Wandermere Dr 92119 619-460-5755
Sandra McClure, prin. Fax 465-8814
Hage ES 600/K-5
9750 Galvin Ave 92126 858-566-0273
James Lee, prin. Fax 693-7942
Hamilton ES 500/K-5
2807 Fairmount Ave 92105 619-344-6800
Tavga Bustani, prin. Fax 344-6849
Hancock ES 600/K-5
3303 Taussig St 92124 858-496-8310
Nona Richard, prin. Fax 278-6549
Hardy ES 400/K-5
5420 Montezuma Rd 92115 619-582-0136
Laura Alluin, prin. Fax 286-2016
Hawthorne ES 300/K-6
4750 Lehrer Dr 92117 858-273-3341
Stanley Anjan, prin. Fax 274-6379
Hearst ES 500/K-5
6230 Del Cerro Blvd 92120 619-583-5704
Jamie Jorgensen, prin. Fax 287-9921
Hickman ES 600/K-5
10850 Montongo St 92126 858-271-5210
Tobie Pace, prin. Fax 566-0010
Holmes ES 500/K-6
4902 Mount Ararat Dr 92111 858-496-8110
Jonathan Saipe, prin. Fax 496-8734
Horton ES 500/K-5
5050 Guymon St 92102 619-264-0171
Staci Dent, prin. Fax 262-8023
Ibarra ES, 4877 Orange Ave 92115 500/K-5
Susie Sovereign, prin. 619-641-5400
Innovation MS 500/7-8
5095 Arvinels Ave 92117 858-278-5948
Nicola Labas, prin.
Jefferson ES 400/K-5
3770 Utah St 92104 619-344-3300
Francisco Morga, prin. Fax 344-3340
Jerabek ES 700/K-5
10050 Avenida Magnifica 92131 858-578-5330
Kristie Joiner, prin. Fax 578-7367
Johnson ES 500/K-5
1355 Kelton Rd 92114 619-344-4900
Tracey Jenkins-Martin, prin. Fax 344-4949
Jones ES 400/K-5
2751 Greyling Dr 92123 858-496-8140
Allison Buell, prin. Fax 571-2877
Joyner ES 700/K-5
4271 Myrtle Ave 92105 619-640-4000
Rebecca Penh, prin. Fax 640-4090
Juarez ES 200/K-5
2633 Melbourne Dr 92123 858-496-8145
Skye Oluwa, prin. Fax 627-7410
Kimbrough ES 500/K-5
321 Hoitt St 92102 619-525-2010
Hernan Baeza, prin. Fax 525-2018
Knox S 600/K-8
1098 S 49th St 92113 619-344-5500
Heather Potter, prin. Fax 344-5549
Kumeyaay ES 500/K-5
6475 Antigua Blvd 92124 858-279-1022
Angela Zarzosa, prin. Fax 569-7418
Lafayette ES 300/K-6
6125 Printwood Way 92117 858-496-8160
Anne McCarty, prin. Fax 576-9739
Language Academy 1,000/K-8
4961 64th St 92115 619-287-1182
Rosario Villarreal, prin. Fax 582-1769
Lewis MS 1,000/6-8
5170 Greenbrier Ave 92120 619-583-3233
Brad Callahan, prin. Fax 229-1338
Linda Vista ES 500/K-5
2772 Ulric St 92111 858-800-5450
Michael Beraud, prin. Fax 800-5499
Lindbergh/Schweitzer ES 600/K-6
4133 Mount Albertine Ave 92111 858-496-8400
Victoria Peterson, prin. Fax 292-0746
Logan S 700/K-8
2875 Ocean View Blvd 92113 619-525-7440
Antonio Villar, prin. Fax 237-1004
Loma Portal ES 400/K-4
3341 Browning St 92106 619-223-1683
Marc Morici, prin. Fax 224-1352
Longfellow S 800/K-8
5055 July St 92110 619-276-4206
Diana Sanchez, prin. Fax 276-7008
Mann MS 800/6-8
4345 54th St 92115 619-582-8990
Allen Teng, prin. Fax 583-2637

Marshall ES 500/K-5
3550 Altadena Ave 92105 619-344-5100
Staci Monreal, prin. Fax 344-5149
Marshall MS 1,500/6-8
9700 Avenue of Nations 92131 858-549-5400
Michelle Irwin, prin. Fax 549-5490
Marston MS 800/6-8
3799 Clairemont Dr 92117 858-273-2030
Dr. John Gollias, prin. Fax 272-3460
Marvin ES 400/K-5
5720 Brunswick Ave 92120 619-583-1355
Nate Sachdeva, prin. Fax 582-7853
Mason ES 900/K-5
10340 San Ramon Dr 92126 858-271-0410
Dawn Powell, prin. Fax 578-6822
McKinley ES 500/K-5
3045 Felton St 92104 619-282-7694
Deb Ganderton, prin. Fax 281-3478
Memorial Prep for Scholars & Athletes 500/6-8
2850 Logan Ave 92113 619-344-4350
Mirna Estrada, prin. Fax 344-4424
Millennial Tech MS 600/6-8
1110 Carolina Ln 92102 619-527-6933
William Neil, prin.
Miller ES 700/K-5
4343 Shields St 92124 858-496-8319
Jennifer O'Connor, prin. Fax 278-1649
Miramar Ranch ES 700/K-5
10770 Red Cedar Dr 92131 858-271-0470
Peggy Crane, prin. Fax 549-6817
Montgomery MS 500/6-8
2470 Ulric St 92111 858-397-6600
Stephanie Brown, prin. Fax 397-6642
Normal Heights ES 300/K-5
3750 Ward Rd 92116 619-584-6000
John Aguilar, prin.
Nye ES 600/K-5
981 Valencia Pkwy 92114 619-430-1200
Pamela Thompson, prin. Fax 527-0472
Oak Park ES 600/K-5
2606 54th St 92105 619-344-5000
Reashon Villery, prin. Fax 344-5049
Ocean Beach ES 500/K-4
4741 Santa Monica Ave 92107 619-223-1631
Marco Drapeau, prin. Fax 224-0141
Pacific Beach ES 400/K-5
1234 Tourmaline St 92109 858-488-8316
Sherry Turner, prin. Fax 488-7852
Pacific Beach MS 600/6-8
4676 Ingraham St 92109 858-273-9070
Kimberly Meng, prin. Fax 270-8063
Pacific View ES 400/K-5
6196 Childs Ave 92139 619-430-1600
Silvia Martinez, prin. Fax 475-2091
Paradise Hills ES 300/K-5
5816 Alleghany St 92139 619-344-5200
Marisol Marin, prin. Fax 344-5249
Parks ES 900/K-5
4510 Landis St 92105 619-282-6803
Carolanne Buguey, prin. Fax 282-5895
Penn ES 400/K-5
2797 Utica Dr 92139 619-479-5638
Maria Gomez, prin. Fax 479-2225
Perkins S 400/K-8
1770 Main St 92113 619-344-5300
Fernando Hernandez, prin. Fax 344-5349
Perry ES 500/K-5
6290 Oriskany Rd 92139 619-479-4040
Micheline Morales, prin. Fax 267-6172
Pershing MS 800/6-8
8204 San Carlos Dr 92119 619-465-3234
Susan Levy, prin. Fax 461-5447
Porter North ES 600/2-5
445 S 47th St 92113 619-266-7700
Lillie McMillan, prin. Fax 266-7790
Porter South ES 400/K-1
4800 T St 92113 619-266-4500
Lillie McMillan, prin. Fax 266-4590
Rodriguez ES 600/K-5
825 S 31st St 92113 619-699-4500
Claudia Jordan, prin. Fax 699-4590
Rolando Park ES 200/K-5
6620 Marlowe Dr 92115 619-344-3600
Anthony DeLuca, prin. Fax 344-3620
Roosevelt International MS 900/6-8
3366 Park Blvd 92103 619-293-4450
Dr. Christina Casillas, prin. Fax 497-0918
Ross ES 300/K-5
7470 Bagdad St 92111 858-800-5800
Rosemary Cruz, prin. Fax 800-5849
Rowan ES 300/K-5
1755 Rowan St 92105 619-344-3400
Jennifer Carpenter, prin. Fax 344-3440
Salk ES, 7825 Flanders Dr 92126 K-5
Deidre Hardson, prin. 858-935-2100
Sandburg ES 700/K-5
11230 Avenida Del Gato 92126 858-566-0510
Geoffrey Martin, prin. Fax 693-3896
Scripps ES 800/K-5
11778 Cypress Canyon Rd 92131 858-693-8593
Gregory Collamer, prin. Fax 536-2364
Sequoia ES 200/K-6
4690 Limerick Ave 92117 858-496-8240
Ryan Kissel, prin. Fax 496-8329
Sessions ES 500/K-5
2150 Beryl St 92109 858-273-3111
Adam Carlin, prin. Fax 272-0260
Sherman ES, 301 22nd St 92102 700/K-5
Nicole Enriquez, prin. 619-615-7000
Silver Gate ES 600/K-4
1499 Venice St 92107 619-222-1139
Sandra McClure, prin. Fax 226-3058
Spreckels ES 700/K-5
6033 Stadium St 92122 858-453-5377
Dr. Michel Cazary, prin. Fax 546-1269
Standley MS 1,000/6-8
6298 Radcliffe Dr 92122 858-455-0550
William Pearson, prin. Fax 546-7627
Sunset View ES 500/K-4
4365 Hill St 92107 619-223-7156
Jamey Jaramillo, prin. Fax 224-6920

Taft MS 500/6-8
9191 Gramercy Dr 92123 858-935-2650
Michael George, prin. Fax 496-8138
Tierrasanta ES 500/K-5
5450 La Cuenta Dr 92124 858-496-8255
Sally Viavada, prin. Fax 627-9753
Toler ES 300/K-5
3350 Baker St 92117 858-273-0294
Peggy Lewis, prin. Fax 483-3832
Valencia Park ES 500/K-5
5880 Skyline Dr 92114 619-344-3500
Lori Moore, prin. Fax 344-3540
Vista Grande ES 400/K-5
5606 Antigua Blvd 92124 858-496-8290
Nikki Mitchell, prin. Fax 569-7647
Walker ES 600/K-5
9225 Hillery Dr 92126 858-271-8050
Justin Phillips, prin. Fax 578-8364
Wangenheim MS 1,000/6-8
9230 Gold Coast Dr 92126 858-578-1400
Matthew Fallon, prin. Fax 578-9481
Washington ES 300/K-5
1789 State St 92101 619-344-6300
David Crum, prin. Fax 344-6349
Webster ES 300/K-6
4801 Elm St 92102 619-362-3000
Carmi Strom, prin. Fax 362-3049
Wegeforth ES 200/K-5
3443 Ediwhar Ave 92123 858-496-8274
Linda Williams, prin. Fax 496-8109
Whitman ES 300/K-6
4050 Appleton St 92117 858-273-2700
Carly Romero, prin. Fax 483-8946
Wilson MS 600/6-8
3838 Orange Ave 92105 619-362-3400
David Downey, prin. Fax 362-3474
Zamorano ES 1,300/K-5
2655 Casey St 92139 619-430-1400
Derek Murchison, prin. Fax 475-9748
Other Schools – See La Jolla

San Dieguito UNHSD
Supt. — See Encinitas
Carmel Valley MS 1,500/7-8
3800 Mykonos Ln 92130 858-481-8221
Cara Dolnik, prin. Fax 481-8256
Pacific Trails MS 7-8
5975 Village Center Loop Rd 92130 760-509-1000
Mary Anne Nuskin, prin. Fax 509-1005

San Ysidro ESD
Supt. — See San Ysidro
Ocean View Hills S 700/PK-6
4919 Del Sol Blvd 92154 619-661-0457
Nadia Aviles, prin. Fax 710-0280
Vista Del Mar MS 600/7-8
4885 Del Sol Blvd 92154 619-661-6753
Maria Rodriguez, prin. Fax 690-7556

Solana Beach ESD
Supt. — See Solana Beach
Carmel Creek ES 500/K-3
4210 Carmel Center Rd 92130 858-794-4400
Lisa Ryder, prin. Fax 794-4450
Solana Highlands ES 400/K-3
3520 Long Run Dr 92130 858-794-4300
Matthew Frumovitz, prin. Fax 794-4350
Solana Pacific ES 500/4-6
3901 Townsgate Dr 92130 858-794-4500
Elisa Fregoso, prin. Fax 794-4550
Solana Ranch ES K-6
13605 Pacific Highlands Rnc 92130 858-350-6600
Jerry Jones, prin.

South Bay UNSD
Supt. — See Imperial Beach
Berry ES 500/K-6
2001 Rimbey Ave 92154 619-628-3500
Gil Luna, prin. Fax 628-3580
Emory ES 600/K-6
1915 Coronado Ave 92154 619-628-5300
Jennifer Grondek, prin. Fax 628-5380
Mendoza ES 1,000/K-6
2050 Coronado Ave 92154 619-424-0100
Jil Palmer, prin. Fax 424-0180
Pence ES 700/K-6
877 Via Tonga Ct 92154 619-662-8100
Bob Daily, prin. Fax 662-8180
Sunnyslope ES 500/K-6
2500 Elm Ave 92154 619-628-8800
Cynthia Smith-Ough, prin. Fax 628-8880

Sweetwater UNHSD
Supt. — See Chula Vista
Montgomery MS 800/7-8
1051 Picador Blvd 92154 619-662-8200
Louie Zumstein, prin. Fax 428-6517
Southwest MS 700/7-8
2710 Iris Ave 92154 619-628-4000
Oscar Medina, prin. Fax 423-1151

Blessed Sacrament S 200/PK-8
4551 56th St 92115 619-582-3862
Anne Egan, prin. Fax 265-9310
Cambridge S 100/PK-12
12855 Black Mountain Rd 92129 858-484-3488
Jean Kim, head sch Fax 484-3458
Chabad Hebrew Academy 400/PK-8
10785 Pomerado Rd 92131 858-566-1996
Rabbi Josef Fradkin, head sch Fax 547-8078
Childrens Creative/Performing Arts Acad 200/PK-12
3051 El Cajon Blvd 92104 619-584-2454
Janet Cherif, dir. Fax 584-2422
Christ the Cornerstone Academy 200/PK-5
9028 Westmore Rd 92126 858-566-1741
Karen Dusi, prin. Fax 566-1965
City Tree Christian S 200/PK-8
320 Date St 92101 619-232-3794
Sue Kennedy, prin. Fax 232-2447
Coastal Christian Academy 50/PK-12
4633 Doliva Dr 92117 858-598-6846
Matthew Chavez, head sch
Del Mar Pines S 200/K-6
3975 Torrington St 92130 858-481-5615
Marci McCord, dir. Fax 481-0942
Good Shepherd S 200/K-8
8180 Gold Coast Dr 92126 858-693-1522
Ladonna Lambert, prin. Fax 693-3439
Holy Family S 200/PK-8
1945 Coolidge St 92111 858-277-0222
Erica Stevens, prin. Fax 277-0224
Islamic S of San Diego 200/K-8
PO Box 407 92111 858-278-7970
Cemil Gulseven, prin. Fax 278-7995
La Petite Ecole 100/K-7
3219 Clairemont Mesa Blvd 92117 858-274-2890
Thierry Pasquet, dir.
Maranatha Christian S 500/PK-12
9050 Maranatha Dr 92127 858-759-9737
Jess Hetherington, supt. Fax 759-4001
Maria Montessori S 100/PK-8
4544 Pocahontas Ave 92117 858-270-9350
Dena Stoneman, dir. Fax 273-4254
Mission Bay Montessori Academy 400/PK-6
2640 Soderblom Ave 92122 858-457-5895
Kristie Miller, prin. Fax 457-3081
Nativity Prep Academy 6-8
2755 55th St 92105 619-544-9455
Brendan Sullivan, prin. Fax 501-1734
Nazareth S 300/PK-8
10728 San Diego Mission Rd 92108 619-641-7987
Dr. Colleen Mauricio, prin.
Notre Dame Academy 400/PK-8
4345 Del Mar Trails Rd 92130 858-509-2300
Sr. Marie Pascale, prin. Fax 509-5915
Ocean View Christian Academy 300/PK-12
2460 Palm Ave 92154 619-424-7875
Stephen Johnson, prin. Fax 621-5274
Our Lady of the Sacred Heart S 200/PK-8
4106 42nd St 92105 619-284-1715
Christina Alton, prin. Fax 284-8332
Our Lady's S 300/PK-8
650 24th St 92102 619-233-8888
Noel Bishop, prin. Fax 501-2951
Parker S 800/PK-12
6501 Linda Vista Rd 92111 858-569-7900
Kevin Yaley, head sch Fax 569-0621
Reformation Lutheran S 100/PK-8
4670 Mount Abernathy Ave 92117 858-279-3311
Michael Homan, prin. Fax 627-9898
Rock Academy 400/K-12
2277 Rosecrans St 92106 619-764-5200
Kristen Cherry, prin. Fax 764-5201
St. Charles Borromeo S 200/PK-8
2808 Cadiz St 92110 619-223-8271
Chris Moeller, prin. Fax 223-2695
St. Charles S 200/K-8
929 18th St 92154 619-423-3701
Sylvia Benning, prin. Fax 423-5331
St. Columba S 200/PK-8
3327 Glencolum Dr 92123 858-279-1882
Rose Navarro, prin. Fax 279-1653
St. Didacus S 300/PK-8
4630 34th St 92116 619-284-8730
Maria Tollefson, prin. Fax 284-1764
St. Gregory the Great S K-8
15315 Stonebridge Pkwy 92131 858-397-1290
Maeve O'Connell, prin. Fax 397-1294
St. Michael Academy 200/PK-8
2637 Homedale St 92139 619-470-4880
Mary Johnson, prin. Fax 470-1050
St. Patricks S 200/K-8
3014 Capps St 92104 619-297-1314
Daniel O'Neal, prin. Fax 297-3346
St. Paul's Lutheran S 200/PK-8
1376 Felspar St 92109 858-272-6282
Meredith Binnie, prin. Fax 272-4397
St. Rita's S 200/PK-8
5165 Imperial Ave 92114 619-264-0109
Gina Olsen, prin. Fax 269-4316
St. Therese Academy 300/PK-8
6046 Camino Rico 92120 619-583-6270
Mark Sperrazzo, prin. Fax 583-5721
St. Vincent de Paul S 200/PK-8
4077 Ibis St 92103 619-296-2222
Sr. Kathleen Walsh, prin. Fax 296-2763
San Diego Jewish Academy 600/PK-12
11860 Carmel Creek Rd 92130 858-704-3700
Chaim Heller, head sch Fax 704-3850
School of the Madeleine 600/PK-8
1875 Illion St 92110 619-276-6545
Donna Wittouck, prin. Fax 276-5359
Scripps Montessori S 100/PK-6
9939 Old Grove Rd 92131 858-566-3632
Soille San Diego Hebrew Day S 300/PK-8
3630 Afton Rd 92123 858-279-3300
Rabbi Simcha Weiser, head sch Fax 279-3389
Waldorf S of San Diego 300/PK-12
3547 Altadena Ave 92105 619-280-8016
Warren-Walker MS 100/6-8
2231 Camino Del Rio S 92108 619-260-3663
Raymond Volker, hdmstr. Fax 260-3573
Warren-Walker S 200/PK-5
4605 Point Loma Ave 92107 619-223-3663
Raymond Volker, hdmstr. Fax 223-5567

San Dimas, Los Angeles, Pop. 32,412
Bonita USD 9,900/K-12
115 W Allen Ave 91773 909-971-8200
Christina Goennier, supt. Fax 971-8329
www.bonita.k12.ca.us
Allen Avenue ES 400/K-5
115 W Allen Ave 91773 909-971-8202
Debbie Grenier, prin. Fax 971-8252
Ekstrand ES 500/K-5
115 W Allen Ave 91773 909-971-8203
Lucinda Newton, prin. Fax 971-8253
Gladstone ES 500/K-5
115 W Allen Ave 91773 909-971-8204
Jon Blickenstaff, prin. Fax 971-8254
Lone Hill MS 900/6-8
115 W Allen Ave 91773 909-971-8270
Jason Coss, prin. Fax 971-8279
Shull ES 600/K-5
115 W Allen Ave 91773 909-971-8208
Jennifer Powell, prin. Fax 971-8258
Other Schools – See La Verne

Holy Name of Mary S 300/PK-8
124 S San Dimas Canyon Rd 91773 909-542-0449
Deborah Marquez, prin. Fax 592-3884

San Fernando, Los Angeles, Pop. 23,530
Los Angeles USD
Supt. — See Los Angeles
Gridley ES 700/K-5
1907 8th St 91340 818-361-1243
Jill Imperiale, prin. Fax 361-5959
Morningside ES 700/K-5
576 N Maclay Ave 91340 818-365-7181
Oliver Ramirez, prin. Fax 365-8359
O'Melveny ES 600/K-5
728 Woodworth St 91340 818-365-5621
Henry Vidrio, prin. Fax 837-7974
San Fernando Early Education Center PK-PK
1204 Woodworth St 91340 818-365-9105
Susan Han, prin. Fax 898-1410
San Fernando ES 700/K-5
1130 Mott St 91340 818-365-3201
Mari Awakian, prin. Fax 365-3632
San Fernando Institute of Applied Media 400/6-8
130 N Brand Blvd 91340 818-837-5455
Pearl Arredondo, prin. Fax 365-8911
San Fernando MS 800/6-8
130 N Brand Blvd 91340 818-837-5400
Freddy Ortiz, prin. Fax 365-8911
Vista del Valle Dual Language Academy 500/K-5
12441 Bromont Ave 91340 818-838-3860
Mary Mendoza, prin. Fax 837-1827

St. Ferdinand S 200/PK-8
1012 Coronel St 91340 818-361-3264
Thomas Ambriz, prin. Fax 361-5894
Santa Rosa De Lima S 200/PK-8
1309 Mott St 91340 818-361-5096
Sr. Socorro Cuevas, prin. Fax 361-2259

San Francisco, San Francisco, Pop. 773,534
San Francisco USD 55,500/PK-12
555 Franklin St 94102 415-241-6000
Vincent Matthews, supt. Fax 241-6012
www.sfusd.edu
Alamo ES 500/K-5
250 23rd Ave 94121 415-750-8456
Rosa Fong, prin. Fax 750-8434
Alvarado ES 500/K-5
625 Douglass St 94114 415-695-5695
Sarah Shenkan-Rich, prin. Fax 695-5447
Aptos MS 1,100/6-8
105 Aptos Ave 94127 415-469-4520
Doug Dent, prin. Fax 333-9038
Argonne Early Education S PK-PK
750 16th Ave 94118 415-750-8617
Nkechi Nwankwo, prin. Fax 750-8619
Brown MS 6-8
2055 Silver Ave 94124 415-642-8901
Bill Kappenhagen, prin. Fax 641-1120
Bryant ES 300/K-5
2641 25th St 94110 415-695-5780
Christina Velasco, prin. Fax 206-0538
Buena Vista/Horace Mann S 600/K-8
3351 23rd St 94110 415-695-5881
Richard Zapien, prin. Fax 282-7869
Carmichael ES / FEC 600/PK-8
375 7th St 94103 415-355-6916
Tina Lagdamen, prin. Fax 355-7683
Carver ES 200/K-5
1360 Oakdale Ave 94124 415-330-1540
Emmanuel Stewart, prin. Fax 467-7217
Chavez ES 500/PK-5
825 Shotwell St 94110 415-695-5765
Catherine Rico, prin. Fax 695-5843
Chin ES 300/K-5
350 Broadway 94133 415-291-7946
Allen Lee, prin. Fax 291-7943
Chinese Immersion S 400/K-5
1250 Waller St 94117 415-241-6325
Wendy Cheong, prin. Fax 241-6540
Cleveland ES 300/K-5
455 Athens St 94112 415-469-4709
Mark Sanchez, prin. Fax 469-4051
Cobb ES 200/K-5
2725 California St 94115 415-749-3505
Chad Slife, prin. Fax 749-3436
Cooper Child Development Center PK-PK
940 Filbert St 94133 415-749-3550
Ivy Sw Ng, prin. Fax 749-3466
Denman MS 600/6-8
241 Oneida Ave 94112 415-469-4535
Teresa Kohler, prin. Fax 585-8402
Drew College Prep Academy 300/K-5
50 Pomona St 94124 415-330-1526
Marian Currell, prin. Fax 822-9210
El Dorado ES 300/K-5
70 Delta St 94134 415-330-1537
Silvia Cordero, prin. Fax 467-2435
Everett MS 400/6-8
450 Church St 94114 415-241-6344
Richard Curci, prin. Fax 241-6361
Excelxior CDC at Guadalupe PK-PK
859 Prague St 94112 415-469-4753
Gene Barresi, prin. Fax 469-4578
Fairmount ES 400/K-5
65 Chenery St 94131 415-695-5669
Luis Rodriguez, prin. Fax 695-5343
Feinstein ES 500/K-5
2550 25th Ave 94116 415-615-8460
Michelle Chang, prin. Fax 242-2532

Flynn ES 500/K-5
3125 Cesar Chavez 94110 415-695-5770
Ricky Mendoza, prin. Fax 695-5837
Francisco MS 600/6-8
2190 Powell St 94133 415-291-7900
Patricia Theel, prin. Fax 291-7910
Garfield ES 200/K-5
420 Filbert St 94133 415-291-7924
Jennifer Sethasang, prin. Fax 291-7916
Giannini MS 1,200/6-8
3151 Ortega St 94122 415-759-2770
Tai-Sun Schoeman, prin. Fax 664-8541
Glen Park ES 300/K-5
151 Lippard Ave 94131 415-469-4713
Jean Robertson, prin. Fax 337-6942
Grattan ES 400/K-5
165 Grattan St 94117 415-759-2815
Catherine Walter, prin. Fax 759-2803
Guadalupe ES 500/K-5
859 Prague St 94112 415-469-4718
Maria Luz Agudelo, prin. Fax 469-4066
Harte ES 200/K-5
1035 Gilman Ave 94124 415-330-1520
Jeremy Hilinski, prin. Fax 330-1555
Harvard Early Education S PK-PK
1520 Oakdale Ave 94124 415-695-5660
Eli Horn, prin. Fax 695-5421
Hillcrest ES 400/K-5
810 Silver Ave 94134 415-469-4722
Katerina Palomares, prin. Fax 469-4067
Hoover MS 1,000/6-8
2290 14th Ave 94116 415-759-2783
Thomas Graven, prin. Fax 759-2881
Jefferson ES 500/K-5
1725 Irving St 94122 415-759-2821
Kim Adams, prin. Fax 759-2806
Jefferson Preschool PK-PK
1350 25th Ave 94122 415-759-2852
Candace Lee, prin. Fax 759-2872
Key ES 500/K-5
1530 43rd Ave 94122 415-759-2811
Mimi Kasner, prin. Fax 759-2810
King Academic MS 500/6-8
350 Girard St 94134 415-330-1500
Michael Essien, prin. Fax 468-7295
King ES 400/K-5
1215 Carolina St 94107 415-695-5797
Darlene Martin, prin. Fax 695-5338
Lafayette ES 500/K-5
4545 Anza St 94121 415-750-8483
Heath Caceres, prin. Fax 750-8472
Las Americas Child Development Center PK-PK
801 Treat Ave 94110 415-695-5746
David Hollands, prin. Fax 695-5415
Lau ES 700/K-5
950 Clay St 94108 415-291-7921
Dennis Chew, prin. Fax 291-7952
Lick MS 600/6-8
1220 Noe St 94114 415-695-5675
Bita Nazarian, prin. Fax 695-5360
Longfellow ES 600/K-5
755 Morse St 94112 415-469-4730
Alicia Aleman, prin. Fax 469-4068
Mahler Child Development Center PK-PK
990 Church St 94114 415-695-5871
Ugonma Uwakah, prin. Fax 695-5443
Malcom X Academy 100/K-5
350 Harbor Rd 94124 415-695-5950
Elena Rosen, prin. Fax 647-1647
Marina MS 800/6-8
3500 Fillmore St 94123 415-749-3495
Joanna Fong, prin. Fax 921-7539
Marshall ES 300/K-5
1575 15th St 94103 415-241-6280
Peter Avila, prin. Fax 241-6547
McCoppin ES 300/K-5
651 6th Ave 94118 415-750-8475
Bennett Lee, prin. Fax 750-8474
McKinley ES 400/K-5
1025 14th St 94114 415-241-6300
Molly Pope, prin. Fax 241-6548
McLaren Child Development Center PK-PK
2055 Sunnydale Ave 94134 415-469-4519
Ugonma Uwakah, prin. Fax 469-4577
Milk Civil Rights Academy 200/K-5
4235 19th St 94114 415-241-6276
Ronnie Machado, prin. Fax 241-6545
Miraloma ES 400/K-5
175 Omar Way 94127 415-469-4734
Noah Ingber, prin. Fax 469-4069
Monroe ES 500/K-5
260 Madrid St 94112 415-469-4736
Benjamin Salas-Velasco, prin. Fax 469-4070
Moscone ES 400/K-5
2576 Harrison St 94110 415-695-5736
Valerie Hoshino, prin. Fax 695-5341
Muir ES 300/PK-5
380 Webster St 94117 415-241-6335
Shawn Mansager, prin. Fax 431-9938
New Traditions ES 300/K-5
2049 Grove St 94117 415-750-8490
Jacob Hodgson, prin. Fax 750-8479
Noriega Early Education S PK-PK
1775 44th Ave 94122 415-759-2853
Ivy Sw Ng, prin. Fax 759-2873
Ortega ES 300/K-5
400 Sargent St 94132 415-469-4726
Benjamin Klaus, prin. Fax 584-7972
Parker ES 300/K-5
840 Broadway 94133 415-291-7990
Wesley Tang, prin. Fax 291-7996
Parks ES 400/K-5
1501 Ofarrell St 94115 415-749-3519
Paul Jacobsen, prin. Fax 749-3610
Peabody ES 300/K-5
251 6th Ave 94118 415-750-8480
Willem Vroegh, prin. Fax 750-8487
Presidio Early Education PK-PK
387 Moraga Ave 94129 415-561-5822
Carolyne Cook, prin. Fax 561-5711

Presidio MS 1,100/6-8
450 30th Ave 94121 415-750-8435
Thomas Ekno, prin. Fax 750-8445
Redding ES 300/K-5
1421 Pine St 94109 415-749-3525
Jeanne Dowd, prin. Fax 749-3527
Revere ES 400/K-8
555 Tompkins Ave 94110 415-695-5656
Rebecca Padilla, prin. Fax 647-0878
Roosevelt MS 700/6-8
460 Arguello Blvd 94118 415-750-8446
Michael Stachon, prin. Fax 750-8455
Sanchez ES 200/K-5
325 Sanchez St 94114 415-241-6380
Ann Marin, prin. Fax 522-6729
San Francisco Montessori S 100/K-5
2340 Jackson St 94115 415-749-3544
Sharon Richardon, prin. Fax 749-3494
San Miguel Early Education S PK-PK
300 Seneca Ave 94112 415-469-4756
Eli Horn, prin. Fax 469-4576
Serra Early Education Annex PK-K
155 Appleton Ave 94110 415-920-5138
Caroline Asis, prin. Fax 920-5128
Serra ES 300/K-5
625 Holly Park Cir 94110 415-695-5685
Eve Cheung, prin. Fax 920-5194
Sheridan ES 200/K-5
431 Capitol Ave 94112 415-469-4743
Dina Edwards, prin. Fax 469-4089
Sherman ES 400/K-5
1651 Union St 94123 415-749-3530
Lisa Levin, prin. Fax 749-3433
Sloat ES 400/K-5
50 Darien Way 94127 415-759-2807
Fowzigiah Abdolcader, prin. Fax 759-2843
Spring Valley ES 400/K-5
1451 Jackson St 94109 415-749-3535
Marlene Callejas, prin. Fax 749-3555
Stevenson ES 500/K-5
2051 34th Ave 94116 415-759-2837
Diane Lau-Yee, prin. Fax 759-2844
Stockton Child Developmnt Ctr PK-PK
1 Trenton St 94108 415-291-7932
Ivy Ng, prin. Fax 291-7961
Sunnyside ES 400/K-5
250 Foerster St 94112 415-469-4746
Renee Marcy, prin. Fax 334-3569
Sunset ES 400/K-5
1920 41st Ave 94116 415-759-2760
Sophie Lee, prin. Fax 759-2729
Sutro ES 300/K-5
235 12th Ave 94118 415-750-8525
Myra Quadros, prin. Fax 750-8498
Taylor ES 700/K-5
423 Burrows St 94134 415-330-1530
Barbara Berman, prin. Fax 468-1742
Tenderloin Community S 400/K-5
627 Turk St 94102 415-749-3567
Anastasia Shattner, prin. Fax 749-3643
Tule Elk Park Child Development Center PK-PK
2110 Greenwich St 94123 415-749-3551
E'leva Gibson, prin. Fax 749-3467
Ulloa ES 500/K-5
2650 42nd Ave 94116 415-759-2841
Carol Fong, prin. Fax 759-2845
Visitacion Valley ES 500/K-5
55 Schwerin St 94134 415-469-4796
Johnnie Spearman, prin. Fax 469-4099
Visitacion Valley MS 500/6-8
450 Raymond Ave 94134 415-469-4590
Joe Truss, prin. Fax 469-4703
Webster ES 300/K-5
465 Missouri St 94107 415-695-5787
Carrie Betti, prin. Fax 826-6813
Weill Child Development Center PK-PK
1501 OFarrell St 94115 415-749-3548
David Hollands, prin. Fax 749-3493
West Portal ES 600/K-5
5 Lenox Way 94127 415-759-2846
William Lucey, prin. Fax 242-2526
Yick Wo ES 300/K-5
2245 Jones St 94133 415-749-3540
Sarah Van Velsor, prin. Fax 749-3543

Alta Vista ES, 450 Somerset St 94134 200/K-8
Ed Walters, head sch 415-467-3700
Brandeis S of San Francisco 600/K-8
655 Brotherhood Way 94132 415-406-1035
Dr. Dan Glass, head sch Fax 584-1099
Burke S 400/K-8
7070 California St 94121 415-751-0177
Michele Williams, head sch Fax 666-0535
Cathedral S for Boys 300/K-8
1275 Sacramento St 94108 415-771-6600
Burns Jones, hdmstr. Fax 771-2547
Children's Day S 400/PK-8
333 Dolores St 94110 415-861-5432
Molly Huffman, head sch Fax 861-5419
Chinese American International S 500/PK-8
150 Oak St 94102 415-865-6000
Jeff Bissell, head sch Fax 865-6006
Clevenger S, 180 Fair Oaks St 94110 200/K-8
Benjamin Harrison, dir. 415-824-2240
Convent of the Sacred Heart ES 400/K-8
2222 Broadway St 94115 415-563-2900
Angela Taylor, prin. Fax 563-3005
Cornerstone Academy Cambridge Campus 300/6-8
501 Cambridge St 94134 415-585-5183
Derrick Wong, head sch Fax 469-9600
Cornerstone Academy Silver Campus 800/PK-5
801 Silver Ave 94134 415-587-7256
Derrick Wong, head sch Fax 333-6923
De Marillac Academy 100/4-8
175 Golden Gate Ave 94102 415-552-5220
Chellsea Rivera, prin. Fax 520-6969
Ecole Notre Dame des Victoires S 300/K-8
659 Pine St 94108 415-421-0069
Mary Ghisolfo, prin. Fax 421-1440

French-American International S 1,100/PK-12
150 Oak St 94102 415-558-2000
Dr. Melinda Bihn, head sch Fax 558-2024
Hamlin S 400/K-8
2120 Broadway St 94115 415-922-0300
Wanda Holland Greene, head sch Fax 674-5409
Holy Name S 400/PK-8
1560 40th Ave 94122 415-731-4077
Natalie Cirigliano, prin. Fax 731-3328
Kampner Hebrew Academy 100/1-12
3145 Geary Blvd Ste 280 94118 415-533-1830
Katheryn Schopp, prin.
KZV Armenian S 100/PK-8
825 Brotherhood Way 94132 415-586-8686
Grace Andonian, prin. Fax 586-8689
La Scuola Italian International S 200/PK-8
735 Fell St 94117 415-551-0000
Valentina Imbeni, head sch Fax 390-9006
Live Oak S 300/K-8
1555 Mariposa St 94107 415-861-8840
Virginia Paik, head sch Fax 861-7153
Lycee Francais de San Francisco 500/PK-5
755 Ashbury St 94117 415-661-5232
Patrice Possenti, dir. Fax 661-0945
Marin Preparatory S 100/PK-8
117 Diamond St 94114 415-865-0899
Jeff Escabar, head sch Fax 241-7831
Mission Dolores Academy 200/K-8
3371 16th St 94114 415-346-9500
Meredith Essalat, prin. Fax 346-8001
Our Lady of the Visitacion S 300/K-8
785 Sunnydale Ave 94134 415-239-7840
Hannah Everhart, prin. Fax 239-2559
Presidio Hill S 200/PK-8
3839 Washington St 94118 415-751-9318
Kevin Jacobson, head sch Fax 751-9334
Presidio Knolls S 100/PK-5
250 10th St 94103 415-202-0770
St. Anne S 400/K-8
1320 14th Ave 94122 415-664-7977
Thomas C. White, prin. Fax 661-6904
St. Anthony-Immaculate Conception S 200/K-8
299 Precita Ave 94110 415-648-2008
Barbara Moodie, prin. Fax 648-1825
St. Brendan S 300/K-8
940 Laguna Honda Blvd 94127 415-731-2665
Dianne Lakatta, prin. Fax 731-7207
St. Brigid S 300/K-8
2250 Franklin St 94109 415-673-4523
Sr. Angeles Marin, prin. Fax 674-4187
St. Cecilia S 600/K-8
660 Vicente St 94116 415-731-8400
Marian Connelly, prin. Fax 731-5686
St. Finn Barr S 200/K-8
419 Hearst Ave 94112 415-333-1800
Mele Mortonson, prin. Fax 333-9307
St. Gabriel S 500/K-8
2550 41st Ave 94116 415-566-0314
Sr. Gina Deal, prin. Fax 566-3223
St. James S 100/K-8
321 Fair Oaks St 94110 415-647-8972
Alex Endo, prin. Fax 647-0166
St. John of San Fran Orthodox Academy 100/PK-12
6210 Geary Blvd 94121 415-221-3484
St. John S 300/K-8
925 Chenery St 94131 415-584-8383
Sr. Shirley Ann Garibaldi, prin. Fax 584-8359
St. Monica S 200/K-8
5950 Geary Blvd 94121 415-751-9564
Vincent Sweeters, prin. Fax 751-0781
St. Paul S 200/K-8
1690 Church St 94131 415-648-2055
Katie Kiss, prin. Fax 648-1920
St. Peter S 400/K-8
1266 Florida St 94110 415-647-8662
Sandra Jimenez, prin. Fax 647-4618
St. Philip S 200/K-8
665 Elizabeth St 94114 415-824-8467
Tony LesCallett, prin. Fax 282-0121
St. Stephen S 300/K-8
401 Eucalyptus Dr 94132 415-664-8331
Sharon McCarthy Allen, prin. Fax 242-5608
St. Thomas More S 300/K-8
50 Thomas More Way 94132 415-337-0100
Marie Fitzpatrick, prin. Fax 333-2564
St. Thomas the Apostle S 300/K-8
3801 Balboa St 94121 415-221-2711
Judith Borelli, prin. Fax 221-8611
St. Vincent de Paul S 300/K-8
2350 Green St 94123 415-346-5505
Marguerite Pini, prin. Fax 346-0970
San Francisco Adventist S 50/K-8
66 Geneva Ave 94112 415-585-5550
Lizbeth Caraballo, prin.
San Francisco Christian S 200/K-12
25 Whittier St 94112 415-802-2851
Mike Allen, admin. Fax 841-0833
San Francisco City Academy 100/K-8
PO Box 16217 94116 415-345-0924
Pushpa Samuel, prin. Fax 345-0925
San Francisco Day S 400/K-8
350 Masonic Ave 94118 415-931-2422
Dr. Mike Walker, head sch Fax 931-1753
San Francisco Friends S 400/K-8
250 Valencia St 94103 415-565-0400
Mike Hanas, hdmstr. Fax 565-0401
San Francisco Pacific Academy K-9
3301 Balboa St 94121 415-800-0730
Eleonora Nayberg, head sch
San Francisco S 300/PK-8
300 Gaven St 94134 415-239-5065
Steve Morris, head sch Fax 239-4833
San Francisco Schoolhouse 50/K-6
301 14th Ave 94118 415-221-3435
Aimee Giles, head sch
San Francisco Waldorf ES 500/PK-8
2938 Washington St 94115 415-931-2750
Gerhard Engels, admin. Fax 931-0590
School of the Epiphany 500/K-8
600 Italy Ave 94112 415-337-4030
Diane Elkins, prin. Fax 337-8583

SS. Peter & Paul S 200/PK-8
660 Filbert St 94133 415-421-5219
Dr. Lisa Harris, prin. Fax 421-1831
Star of the Sea S 300/K-8
360 9th Ave 94118 415-221-8558
Theresa Poon, prin. Fax 221-7118
Stratford MS - San Francisco 6-8
75 Francis St 94112 415-333-3134
Stratford S - San Francisco 200/PK-8
301 De Montfort Ave 94112 415-333-3134
Terry Britt, prin.
Stuart Hall for Boys S 300/K-8
2222 Broadway St 94115 415-292-3144
Jaime Dominguez, prin. Fax 292-3165
Synergy S 200/K-8
1387 Valencia St 94110 415-567-6177
Tanya Baker, admin. Fax 567-0607
Town S for Boys 400/K-8
2750 Jackson St 94115 415-921-3747
Lorri Hamilton Durbin, head sch Fax 921-1126
West Portal Lutheran S 500/K-8
200 Sloat Blvd 94132 415-665-6330
Les Morris, prin. Fax 242-8876
Zion Lutheran S, 495 9th Ave 94118 100/K-8
Jennifer Lee, prin. 415-221-7500

San Gabriel, Los Angeles, Pop. 39,114
Garvey ESD
Supt. — See Rosemead
Dewey Avenue ES 400/K-6
525 Dewey Ave 91776 626-307-3341
Fax 307-3473

San Gabriel USD 5,300/K-12
408 Junipero Serra Dr 91776 626-451-5400
John Pappalardo Ed.D., supt. Fax 451-5494
www.sgusd.k12.ca.us
Coolidge ES 400/K-5
421 N Mission Dr 91775 626-282-6952
William Wong, prin. Fax 308-0354
Jefferson MS 1,200/6-8
1372 E Las Tunas Dr 91776 626-287-5260
Dr. Matthew Arnold, prin. Fax 285-5387
McKinley ES 600/K-5
1425 Manley Dr 91776 626-288-6681
Jim Symonds, prin. Fax 288-3021
Roosevelt ES 400/K-5
401 S Walnut Grove Ave 91776 626-287-0512
Claudia De La Torre, prin. Fax 287-4604
Washington ES 500/K-5
300 N San Marino Ave 91775 626-282-3926
Thomas Chen, prin. Fax 282-9970
Wilson ES 400/K-5
8317 Sheffield Rd 91775 626-287-0497
Jeannine McGuigan, prin. Fax 285-4247

Temple City USD
Supt. — See Temple City
Emperor ES 700/K-6
6415 N Muscatel Ave 91775 626-548-5084
Bob Westgate, prin. Fax 548-5090

Clairbourn S 300/PK-8
8400 Huntington Dr 91775 626-286-3108
Dr. Robert Nafie, head sch Fax 286-1528
St. Anthony S 200/PK-8
1905 S San Gabriel Blvd 91776 626-280-7255
Lauren Doherty, prin. Fax 280-3870
San Gabriel Academy 500/PK-12
8827 E Broadway 91776 626-292-1156
Paul Negrete, prin Fax 285-4949
San Gabriel Christian S 500/PK-8
117 N Pine St 91775 626-656-1000
Joel Staggers, prin. Fax 656-1001
San Gabriel Mission S 200/K-8
416 S Mission Dr 91776 626-281-2454
Eva Garcia, prin. Fax 281-4817

Sanger, Fresno, Pop. 24,008
Sanger USD 11,100/PK-12
1905 7th St 93657 559-524-6521
Matt Navo, supt. Fax 875-0311
www.sanger.k12.ca.us/
Centerville ES 300/K-6
48 S Smith Ave 93657 559-524-6000
Cristina Hernandez, prin. Fax 787-3101
Fairmont S 500/K-8
3095 N Greenwood Ave 93657 559-524-6120
Jared Savage, prin. Fax 875-1365
Jackson ES 400/PK-5
1810 3rd St 93657 559-524-6180
Debra Santos, prin. Fax 875-1363
Jefferson ES 400/K-5
1110 Tucker Ave 93657 559-524-6250
Sam Polanco, prin. Fax 875-1352
Lincoln ES 400/K-5
1700 14th St 93657 559-524-6370
Johnny Gonzalez, prin. Fax 875-1332
Madison ES 500/PK-5
2324 Cherry Ave 93657 559-524-7430
Stephanie Rodriguez, prin. Fax 875-1219
Reagan ES 400/PK-5
1586 S Indianola Ave 93657 559-524-6780
John Hannigan, prin. Fax 876-0170
Washington Academic MS 1,700/6-8
1705 10th St 93657 559-524-7015
Leo Castillo, prin. Fax 875-6365
Wilson ES 500/PK-5
610 Faller Ave 93657 559-524-6900
Ken Garcia, prin. Fax 875-1328
Other Schools – See Del Rey, Fresno

San Geronimo, Marin, Pop. 433
Lagunitas ESD 300/K-8
PO Box 308 94963 415-488-4118
John A. Carroll, supt. Fax 488-9617
www.lagunitas.org
Lagunitas S 200/K-8
PO Box 308 94963 415-488-9437
Laura Shain, prin. Fax 488-9617
San Geronimo Valley ES 100/K-6
PO Box 308 94963 415-488-9421
Laura Shain, prin. Fax 488-1011

San Jacinto, Riverside, Pop. 42,978
San Jacinto USD 10,100/PK-12
2045 S San Jacinto Ave 92583 951-929-7700
Diane Perez, supt. Fax 658-3574
www.sanjacinto.k12.ca.us/
Cope ES 800/K-5
2550 Via La Sierra Ln 92582 951-654-6069
Bridget Heeren, prin. Fax 929-1434
De Anza ES 600/PK-5
1089 De Anza Dr 92582 951-654-4777
Lauren Armijo, prin. Fax 654-7720
Estudillo ES 600/K-5
900 Las Rosas Dr 92583 951-654-1003
Dr. Sonya Scott, prin. Fax 654-1101
Hyatt ES 500/PK-5
400 E Shaver St 92583 951-654-9391
Inelda Luna, prin. Fax 654-8034
Monte Vista MS 900/6-8
181 N Ramona Blvd 92583 951-654-9361
Janet Covacevich, prin. Fax 654-0173
North Mountain MS 1,000/6-8
1202 E 7th St 92583 951-487-7797
Gilbert Rodriguez, prin. Fax 487-7799
Park Hill ES 800/K-5
1157 E Commonwealth Ave 92583 951-654-6651
Dulce Noriega, prin. Fax 487-7756
Record ES 500/K-5
1600 Malaga Dr 92583 951-487-6644
Shelley Mendez, prin. Fax 487-6557
San Jacinto ES 600/K-5
136 N Ramona Blvd 92583 951-654-7349
Juan Penaloza, prin. Fax 487-7721
San Jacinto Leadership Academy 200/6-8
1599 Malaga Dr 92583 951-929-1954
Col. Francis Sick, prin.
San Jacinto Preschool PK-PK
257 Grand Army 92583 951-654-1531
Elizabeth Zaragoza, prin.

St. Hyacinth Academy 300/PK-8
275 S Victoria Ave 92583 951-654-2013
Tami Jimenez, prin. Fax 654-5644
St. Jude Mission S 50/K-5
PO Box 399 92581 951-213-1276
Fax 487-8822

San Joaquin, Fresno, Pop. 3,985
Golden Plains USD 1,900/K-12
PO Box 937 93660 559-693-1115
Martin Macias, supt. Fax 693-2526
www.gpusd.org
San Joaquin S 800/K-8
PO Box 408 93660 559-693-4321
Joel Ramirez, prin. Fax 693-2369
Other Schools – See Cantua Creek, Helm, Tranquillity

San Jose, Santa Clara, Pop. 914,803
Alum Rock UNESD 12,300/PK-8
2930 Gay Ave 95127 408-928-6800
Dr. Hilaria Bauer Ph.D., supt. Fax 928-6400
www.arusd.org
Adelante Dual Language Academy II PK-3
1970 Cinderella Ln 95116 408-928-7100
Edith Gonzales, prin.
Adelante I Dual Language Academy 500/PK-8
2999 Ridgemont Dr 95127 408-928-1900
Nuria Bravo Sanz, admin. Fax 928-1901
Arbuckle ES 400/PK-5
1970 Cinderella Ln 95116 408-928-7100
Olga Martinez, prin. Fax 928-7101
Cassell ES 500/PK-5
1300 Tallahassee Dr 95122 408-928-7200
Dr. Sandra Sarmiento Ed.D., prin. Fax 928-7201
Chavez ES 500/PK-5
2000 Kammerer Ave 95116 408-928-7300
Dr. Julio Villalobos Ed.D., prin. Fax 928-7301
Cureton ES 600/PK-5
3720 E Hills Dr 95127 408-928-7350
Le Tran, prin. Fax 928-7351
Dorsa ES 500/PK-5
1290 Bal Harbor Way 95122 408-928-7400
Viviana Cabrales-Garcia, prin. Fax 928-7401
Fischer MS of Business and Communication 500/6-8
1720 Hopkins Dr 95122 408-928-7500
Dr. Imee Almazan Ed.D., prin. Fax 928-7501
George MS 600/6-8
277 Mahoney Dr 95127 408-928-7600
Tara Bickford, prin. Fax 928-7601
Hubbard Media Arts Academy 500/PK-7
1680 Foley Ave 95122 408-928-7700
Jonathan Natividad, prin. Fax 928-7701
Linda Vista ES 600/PK-5
100 Kirk Ave 95127 408-928-7800
Ted Henderson, prin. Fax 928-7801
L.U.C.H.A. 200/PK-5
1711 E San Antonio St 95116 408-928-8300
Kristin Burt, prin. Fax 928-8301
Lyndale ES 500/PK-5
13901 Nordyke Dr 95127 408-928-7900
Paula Alli, prin. Fax 928-7901
Mathson Institute of Technology 500/6-8
2050 Kammerer Ave 95116 408-928-7950
Vince Iwasaki, prin. Fax 928-7951
McCollam ES 400/PK-5
3311 Lucian Ave 95127 408-928-8000
Pablo Fiene, prin. Fax 928-8001
Meyer ES 600/PK-5
1824 Daytona Dr 95122 408-928-8200
Anacelia Rocha, prin. Fax 928-8201
Ocala STEAM Academy 600/6-8
2800 Ocala Ave 95148 408-928-8350
Tracy Leathers, prin. Fax 928-8351
Painter ES 500/PK-5
500 Rough and Ready Rd 95133 408-928-8400
George Kleidon, prin. Fax 928-8401
Renaissance Academy at Fischer 300/6-8
1720 Hopkins Dr 95122 408-928-1950
Doug Kleinhenz, prin. Fax 928-1951
Renaissance Academy at Mathson 200/6-8
2050 Kammerer Ave 95116 408-928-8500
Doug Kleinhenz, prin. Fax 928-8501
Russo/McEntee Academy 300/PK-5
2851 Gay Ave 95127 408-928-8900
Tereasa Smith, prin. Fax 928-8901
Ryan ES 500/PK-5
1241 McGinness Ave 95127 408-928-8650
Raquel Katz, prin. Fax 928-8651
San Antonio ES 500/PK-5
1721 E San Antonio St 95116 408-928-8700
Lyssa Perry, prin. Fax 928-8701
Sheppard MS 700/6-8
480 Rough and Ready Rd 95133 408-928-8800
Jackie Montejano, prin. Fax 928-8801

Berryessa UNESD 7,900/PK-8
1376 Piedmont Rd 95132 408-923-1800
Will Ector, supt. Fax 923-0623
www.berryessa.k12.ca.us
Brooktree ES 500/PK-5
1781 Olivetree Dr 95131 408-923-1910
Mya Duong, prin. Fax 923-1635
Cherrywood ES 500/PK-5
2550 Greengate Dr 95132 408-923-1915
Tina Tong Choy, prin. Fax 258-8356
Laneview ES 500/K-5
2095 Warmwood Ln 95132 408-923-1920
Carol Mar, prin. Fax 262-5804
Majestic Way ES 600/K-5
1855 Majestic Way 95132 408-923-1925
Lakeisha Blackshire, prin. Fax 254-1315
Morrill MS 800/6-8
1970 Morrill Ave 95132 408-923-1930
Joann Vaars, prin. Fax 946-0776
Noble ES 600/K-5
3466 Grossmont Dr 95132 408-923-1935
Andrea Ortiz, prin. Fax 937-5006
Northwood ES 500/PK-5
2760 E Trimble Rd 95132 408-923-1940
Andrew Derrick, prin. Fax 942-9032
Piedmont MS 800/6-8
955 Piedmont Rd 95132 408-923-1945
Stefani Garino, prin. Fax 251-2392
Ruskin ES 700/K-5
1401 Turlock Ln 95132 408-923-1950
Virginia Pender, prin. Fax 937-4846
Sierramont MS 1,100/6-8
3155 Kimlee Dr 95132 408-923-1955
Chris Mosley, prin. Fax 729-5840
Summerdale ES 500/K-5
1100 Summerdale Dr 95132 408-923-1960
Patty McDonald, prin. Fax 937-4923
Toyon ES 300/PK-5
995 Bard St 95127 408-923-1965
Maria Smith, prin. Fax 937-4908
Vinci Park ES 600/PK-5
1311 Vinci Park Way 95131 408-923-1970
Parisa Nunez, prin. Fax 254-3790

Cambrian ESD 3,300/K-8
4115 Jacksol Dr 95124 408-377-2103
Dr. Carrie Andrews, supt. Fax 377-5944
www.cambriansd.org
Bagby ES 700/K-5
1840 Harris Ave 95124 408-377-3882
Allison White, prin. Fax 377-8648
Steindorf STEAM K-8 S K-8
3001 Ross Ave 95124 408-377-3022
Kristi Schwiebert, prin. Fax 377-3093

Campbell UNESD
Supt. — See Campbell
Blackford ES 600/K-5
1970 Willow St 95125 408-978-4675
Katie Middlebrook, prin. Fax 341-7110
Forest Hill ES 600/K-5
4450 McCoy Ave 95130 408-364-4279
Denise Khalid, prin. Fax 341-7140
Lynhaven ES 600/K-5
881 Cypress Ave 95117 408-556-0368
Sarah Jellin, prin. Fax 341-7170
Monroe MS 900/5-8
1055 S Monroe St 95128 408-556-0360
Dawnel Sonntag, prin. Fax 341-7020
Sherman Oaks Community Charter S 500/K-6
1800 Fruitdale Ave Ste C 95128 408-795-1140
Donna Tonry, prin. Fax 341-7180

Cupertino UNSD
Supt. — See Sunnyvale
De Vargas ES 500/K-5
5050 Moorpark Ave 95129 408-252-0303
Nick Prychodko, prin. Fax 253-4962
Dilworth ES 500/K-5
1101 Strayer Dr 95129 408-253-2850
Kerstin Johnson, prin. Fax 366-0743
Meyerholtz ES 800/K-5
6990 Melvin Dr 95129 408-252-7450
Drew Coleman, prin. Fax 446-2597
Miller MS 1,300/6-8
6151 Rainbow Dr 95129 408-252-3755
Amy Steele, prin. Fax 255-5269
Muir ES 600/K-5
6560 Hanover Dr 95129 408-252-5265
Adrienne Van Gorden, prin. Fax 253-3116

Evergreen ESD 13,200/K-8
3188 Quimby Rd 95148 408-270-6800
Kathy Gomez, supt. Fax 274-3894
www.eesd.org/
Cadwallader ES 400/K-6
3799 Cadwallader Ave 95121 408-270-4950
Maureen McClintock, prin. Fax 223-4839
Cedar Grove ES 700/K-6
2702 Sugarplum Dr 95148 408-270-4958
Bob Pruitt, prin. Fax 223-4852

Chaboya MS 1,200/7-8
3276 Fowler Rd 95135 408-270-6900
Derrick Watkins, prin. Fax 270-6916
Clark ES 800/K-6
3701 Rue Mirassou 95148 408-223-4560
Gina Juarez, prin. Fax 223-4567
Dove Hill ES 600/K-6
1460 Colt Way 95121 408-270-4964
Linda Mora, prin. Fax 223-4536
Evergreen ES 700/K-6
3010 Fowler Rd 95135 408-270-4966
Steve Sweeney, prin. Fax 270-4968
Holly Oak ES 700/K-6
2995 Rossmore Way 95148 408-270-4975
Kyle Sanchez, prin. Fax 223-4513
Laurelwood ES 400/K-6
4280 Partridge Dr 95121 408-270-4983
Hong Nguyen, prin. Fax 270-6922
LeyVa IS 1,000/7-8
1865 Monrovia Dr 95122 408-270-4993
James Sherman, prin. Fax 270-5462
Matsumoto ES 800/K-6
4121 Mackin Woods Ln 95135 408-223-4873
Julie Page, prin. Fax 223-4883
Millbrook ES 700/K-6
3200 Millbrook Dr 95148 408-270-6767
Dolores Garcia, prin. Fax 223-4887
Montgomery ES 700/K-6
2010 Daniel Maloney Dr 95121 408-270-6718
Guillermo Ramos, prin. Fax 223-4848
Norwood Creek ES 700/K-6
3241 Remington Way 95148 408-270-6727
Nanette Donohue, prin. Fax 223-9266
Quimby Oak MS 1,000/7-8
3190 Quimby Rd 95148 408-270-6735
Phil Bond, prin. Fax 223-4533
Silver Oak ES 700/K-6
5000 Farnsworth Dr 95138 408-223-4515
Howard Greenfield, prin. Fax 223-4540
Smith ES 800/K-6
2220 Woodbury Ln 95121 408-532-2150
Roberta Ortega, prin. Fax 223-2165
Smith ES 600/K-6
2025 Clarice Dr 95122 408-270-6751
Aaron Brengard, prin. Fax 270-6877
Whaley ES 600/K-6
2655 Alvin Ave 95121 408-270-6759
Tonya Trim, prin. Fax 223-4537

Franklin-McKinley ESD 11,100/PK-8
645 Wool Creek Dr 95112 408-283-6006
Juan Cruz, supt. Fax 283-6022
www.fmsd.org
Dahl ES 700/PK-6
3200 Water St 95111 408-363-5650
Elizabeth Herbstreith, prin. Fax 363-5669
Franklin ES 800/K-6
420 Tully Rd 95111 408-283-6375
Jose Jacinto, prin. Fax 283-6060
Hellyer ES 400/K-6
725 Hellyer Ave 95111 408-363-5750
Laura Franks, prin. Fax 363-5761
Kennedy ES 600/PK-6
1602 Lucretia Ave 95122 408-283-6325
Mariana Alvarez, prin. Fax 283-6337
Lairon College Preparatory Academy 500/4-8
3975 Mira Loma Way 95111 408-363-5775
Jennifer Laxton, prin. Fax 363-5642
Los Arboles Literacy & Tech Academy 500/PK-3
455 Los Arboles St 95111 408-363-5675
Tina Ybarra, prin. Fax 363-5641
McKinley ES 500/K-6
651 Macredes Ave 95116 408-283-6350
Julie Aguirre, prin. Fax 283-6355
Meadows ES 500/PK-6
1250 Taper Ln 95122 408-283-6300
Magdalena Moore, prin. Fax 283-6061
Ramblewood ES 400/K-6
1351 Lightland Rd 95121 408-283-6275
Victoria Fernandez, prin. Fax 283-6217
Santee ES 500/PK-6
1313 Audubon Dr 95122 408-283-6450
Maria Reyes, prin. Fax 283-6062
Shirakawa S 900/K-8
665 Wool Creek Dr 95112 408-938-3200
Yvonne Sugimura, prin. Fax 938-3206
Stonegate ES 600/PK-8
2605 Gassmann Dr 95121 408-363-5625
Kim Sheffield, prin. Fax 363-5631
Sylvandale MS 800/7-8
653 Sylvandale Ave 95111 408-363-5700
Amber Andrade, prin. Fax 363-5649
Windmill Springs ES 600/PK-8
2880 Aetna Way 95121 408-363-5600
Zarpana Rietman, prin. Fax 363-5606

Luther Burbank ESD 600/PK-8
4 Wabash Ave 95128 408-295-2450
Dr. Christopher Ortiz, supt. Fax 295-3168
www.lbsd.k12.ca.us
Burbank ES 600/PK-8
4 Wabash Ave 95128 408-295-1814
Christopher Ortiz, prin. Fax 295-3168

Moreland SD 5,200/K-8
4711 Campbell Ave 95130 408-874-2900
Mary Kay Going, supt. Fax 374-8863
www.moreland.org
Anderson ES 500/K-5
4000 Rhoda Dr 95117 408-874-3100
Tasha Quinonez, prin. Fax 243-4312
Baker ES 800/K-5
4845 Bucknall Rd 95130 408-874-3200
Christopher Barbara, prin. Fax 379-3726
Country Lane ES 800/K-5
5140 Country Ln 95129 408-874-3400
Kori Billings, prin. Fax 252-4576
Easterbrook Discovery S 1,000/K-8
4835 Doyle Rd 95129 408-874-3500
Sherri Vasquez, prin. Fax 253-7321

Latimer ES 500/K-8
4250 Latimer Ave 95130 408-874-3600
Nancy Cisler, prin. Fax 379-2436
Moreland MS 1,000/6-8
4600 Student Ln 95130 408-875-3300
Ann Doumanian, prin. Fax 379-3622
Payne ES 600/K-5
3750 Gleason Ave 95130 408-874-3700
Cathy Bailey, prin. Fax 241-4932

Morgan Hill USD
Supt. — See Morgan Hill
Los Paseos ES 500/PK-5
121 Avenida Grande 95139 408-201-6420
Jenna Mittleman, prin. Fax 201-6430
Murphy MS 500/6-8
141 Avenida Espana 95139 408-201-6260
Heather Nursement, prin. Fax 201-6270

Mount Pleasant ESD 2,500/PK-8
3434 Marten Ave 95148 408-223-3700
Mariann Engle, supt. Fax 223-3715
www.mountpleasant.k12.ca.us
Boeger MS 600/6-8
1944 Flint Ave 95148 408-223-3770
Mia Cruz, prin. Fax 223-6959
Mount Pleasant STEAM Academy 400/PK-5
14275 Candler Ave 95127 408-258-6451
Dr. Jose Gonzalez, prin. Fax 272-9705
Sanders ES 500/PK-5
3411 Rocky Mountain Dr 95127 408-258-7288
Julie Howard, prin. Fax 272-9646
Valle Vista ES 500/K-5
2400 Flint Ave 95148 408-238-3525
Andrew Donati, prin. Fax 223-7465

Oak Grove ESD 11,100/K-8
6578 Santa Teresa Blvd 95119 408-227-8300
Jose Manzo, supt. Fax 629-7183
www.ogsd.net
Anderson ES 500/K-6
5800 Calpine Dr 95123 408-225-6556
Christy Flores, prin. Fax 224-6964
Baldwin ES 400/K-6
280 Martinvale Ln 95119 408-226-3370
Tonya Bailey, prin. Fax 224-8506
Bernal IS 800/7-8
6610 San Ignacio Ave 95119 408-578-5731
Jamal Splane, prin. Fax 578-7367
Christopher ES 500/K-6
565 Coyote Rd 95111 408-227-8550
Bill Abraham, prin. Fax 224-8265
Davis IS 700/7-8
5035 Edenview Dr 95111 408-227-0616
Kim Kianidehkian, prin. Fax 224-8957
Del Roble ES 500/K-6
5345 Avenida Almendros 95123 408-225-5675
Yolanda Ross, prin. Fax 224-8748
Edenvale ES 600/K-6
285 Azucar Ave 95111 408-227-7060
Ryan Haven, prin. Fax 224-8732
Frost ES 700/K-8
530 Gettysburg Dr 95123 408-225-1881
Genvieve Dorsey, prin. Fax 224-8932
Glider ES 700/K-6
511 Cozy Dr 95123 408-227-1505
Vivian Martin, prin. Fax 224-8386
Hayes ES 500/K-6
5035 Poston Dr 95136 408-227-0424
Tracy Cochran, prin. Fax 224-7191
Herman IS 900/5-8
5955 Blossom Ave 95123 408-226-1886
Laura Meusel, prin. Fax 226-1897
Ledesma ES 500/K-6
1001 Schoolhouse Rd 95138 408-224-2191
Tammy Unck, prin. Fax 224-1566
Miner ES 500/K-6
5629 Lean Ave 95123 408-225-2144
Lisa Barlesi, prin. Fax 224-5891
Oak Ridge ES 500/K-6
5920 Bufkin Dr 95123 408-578-5900
Sheetal Singh, prin. Fax 224-3960
Parkview ES 600/K-6
330 Bluefield Dr 95136 408-226-4655
Susan Kind, prin. Fax 224-9105
Sakamoto ES 600/K-6
6280 Shadelands Dr 95123 408-227-3411
Jenay Enna, prin. Fax 224 8784
Santa Teresa ES 600/K-6
6200 Encinal Dr 95119 408-227-3303
Mark Lepori, prin. Fax 226-3379
Stipe ES 400/K-6
5000 Lyng Dr 95111 408-227-7332
Virgilio Caruz, prin. Fax 224-2231
Taylor ES 700/K-6
410 Sautner Dr 95123 408-226-0462
Lauryce Haney, prin. Fax 224-3279

Orchard ESD 900/K-8
921 Fox Ln 95131 408-944-0397
Michelle Quilantang, supt. Fax 944-0394
www.orchardsd.org
Orchard ES 900/K-8
921 Fox Ln 95131 408-944-0388
Michelle Quilantang, prin. Fax 944-0394

San Jose USD 32,900/K-12
855 Lenzen Ave 95126 408-535-6000
Dr. Vincent Matthews, supt. Fax 535-2362
www.sjusd.org
Allen S @ Steinbeck 800/K-8
820 Steinbeck Dr 95123 408-535-6205
Janice Samuels, prin. Fax 578-6059
Almaden ES 400/K-5
1295 Dentwood Dr 95118 408-535-6207
Lisa Montes, prin. Fax 535-2328
Booksin ES 800/K-5
1590 Dry Creek Rd 95125 408-535-6213
Peter Park, prin. Fax 448-2507
Burnett Academy 900/6-8
850 N 2nd St 95112 408-535-6267
Fax 298-1675
Canoas ES 400/K-5
880 Wren Dr 95125 408-535-6391
Barbara Keesaw, prin. Fax 265-4126
Carson ES 400/K-5
4245 Meg Dr 95136 408-535-6287
Neil Aratin, prin. Fax 264-6743
Castillero MS 1,200/6-8
6384 Leyland Park Dr 95120 408-535-6385
Darbi O'Connell, prin. Fax 268-4489
Darling ES 500/K-5
333 N 33rd St 95133 408-535-6209
Ronald Hammond, prin. Fax 535-6334
Empire Gardens ES 500/K-5
1060 E Empire St 95112 408-535-6221
Barbara Friedenbach, prin. Fax 297-6914
Galarza ES 500/K-5
1610 Bird Ave 95125 408-535-6671
Angela Guzman, prin. Fax 265-3495
Gardner Academy 500/K-5
502 Illinois Ave 95125 408-535-6225
Daisy Rojas, prin. Fax 535-2358
Grant ES 600/K-5
470 Jackson St 95112 408-535-6227
Paulette Zades, prin. Fax 535-6061
Graystone ES 700/K-5
6982 Shearwater Dr 95120 408-535-6317
Amy Shumway, prin. Fax 323-1034
Hacienda Science/Environmental Magnet ES 700/K-5
1290 Kimberly Dr 95118 408-535-6259
Carmen Loy, prin. Fax 723-8225
Hammer Montessori ES 300/K-5
1610 Bird Ave 95125 408-535-6470
Lynn Belmonte, prin. Fax 445-0134
Harte MS 1,200/6-8
7050 Bret Harte Dr 95120 408-535-6270
Tina VanLaarhoven, prin. Fax 927-0698
Hoover MS 1,100/6-8
1635 Park Ave 95126 408-535-6274
Don McCloskey, prin. Fax 286-4864
Los Alamitos ES 700/K-5
6130 Silberman Dr 95120 408-535-6297
Thom Rousseau, prin. Fax 268-8929
Lowell ES 400/K-5
625 S 7th St 95112 408-535-6243
Melitta Nerhood, prin. Fax 298-3708
Mann ES 600/K-5
55 N 7th St 95112 408-535-6237
Loretta Gustafson, prin. Fax 535-2315
Muir MS 1,200/6-8
1260 Branham Ln 95118 408-535-6281
Jeannette Harding, prin. Fax 535-2319
Olinder ES 500/K-5
890 E William St 95116 408-535-6245
Jesus Radillo, prin. Fax 535-2313
Reed ES 500/K-5
1524 Jacob Ave 95118 408-535-6247
Melody Mendoza, prin. Fax 978-0842
River Glen S 500/K-8
1088 Broadway Ave 95125 408-535-6240
Tracy Young, prin. Fax 298-8377
Schallenberger ES 600/K-5
1280 Koch Ln 95125 408-535-6253
Ryan Chamberlin, prin. Fax 445-9638
Simonds ES 700/K-5
6515 Grapevine Way 95120 408-535-6251
Stephanie Monroe, prin. Fax 268-6868
Terrell ES 500/K-5
3925 Pearl Ave 95136 408-535-6255
Michelle Reghitto, prin. Fax 265-2917
Trace ES 1,000/K-5
651 Dana Ave 95126 408-535-6257
Maria Rodriguez, prin. Fax 535 2304
Washington ES 500/K-5
100 Oak St 95110 408-535-6261
Stephanie Palmeri Farias, prin. Fax 535-2369
Williams ES 700/K-5
1150 Rajkovich Way 95120 408-535-6196
Devin Blizzard, prin. Fax 535-6525
Willow Glen ES 800/K-5
1425 Lincoln Ave 95125 408-535-6265
Kelli Knapp Rahn, prin. Fax 297-0946
Willow Glen MS 1,200/6-8
2105 Cottle Ave 95125 408-535-6277
Paul Slayton, prin. Fax 535-2353

Union ESD 5,300/K-8
5175 Union Ave 95124 408-377-8010
Denise Clay Ed.D., supt. Fax 377-7182
www.unionsd.org
Carlton ES 700/K-5
2421 Carlton Ave 95124 408-356-1141
Bitsey Stark, prin. Fax 356-5993
Dartmouth MS 800/6-8
5575 Dartmouth Dr 95118 408-264-1122
Randy Martino, prin. Fax 264-9332
Guadalupe ES 600/K-5
6044 Vera Cruz Dr 95120 408-268-1030
Chris Izor, prin. Fax 268-6914
Lietz ES 500/K-5
5300 Carter Ave 95118 408-264-8314
Sandya Lopez, prin. Fax 264-9615
Noddin ES 700/K-5
1755 Gilda Way 95124 408-356-2126
Eric Scharer, prin. Fax 358-9807
Oster ES 500/K-5
1855 Lencar Way 95124 408-266-8121
Dianne McEntee, prin. Fax 266-3751
Union MS 900/6-8
2130 Los Gatos Almaden Rd 95124 408-371-0366
Todd Feinberg, prin. Fax 371-1217
Other Schools – See Los Gatos

Achiever Christian S 300/PK-6
540 Sands Dr 95125 408-264-6789
Elliot Sands, prin. Fax 264-2001
Apostles Lutheran S 200/PK-12
5828 Santa Teresa Blvd 95123 408-578-4800
Joel Walker M.Ed., prin. Fax 225-0720

Calvary Chapel Christian S 100/PK-12
1175 Hillsdale Ave 95118 408-269-2222
Mike McClure, head sch Fax 269-8342
Carden Day S of San Jose 200/PK-8
1980 Hamilton Ave 95125 408-626-8008
Elizabeth Asadi, dir. Fax 626-8044
Challenger S 700/PK-8
711 E Gish Rd 95112 408-998-2860
Sheela Vijay, hdmstr. Fax 998-1852
Challenger S 200/PK-8
19950 McKean Rd 95120 408-927-5771
Sandip Panesar, hdmstr.
Challenger S, 500 Shawnee Ln 95123 400/PK-8
Joseph Morrison, hdmstr. 408-365-9298
Challenger S 200/PK-8
4949 Harwood Rd 95124 408-723-0111
Sara Kolb, hdmstr.
Challenger S 600/PK-8
730 Camina Escuela 95129 408-213-0083
Aaron Schiffner, head sch Fax 973-8787
Champion S 100/K-9
5670 Camden Ave 95124 408-976-8696
Muna Khanna, pres.
East Valley Christian S 200/K-8
2833 Dayo Ct 95148 408-270-2500
Jennifer Schmedding, prin. Fax 270-2521
Grace Christian S 50/K-5
2350 Leigh Ave 95124 408-377-2387
Jan Starke, lead tchr. Fax 377-2332
Harker Lower S 600/K-5
4300 Bucknall Rd 95130 408-871-4600
Brian yager, head sch Fax 871-4320
Harker MS 400/6-8
3800 Blackford Ave 95117 408-248-2510
Brian Yager, head sch Fax 248-2502
Holy Family S 500/PK-8
4850 Pearl Ave 95136 408-978-1355
Maeve Hannon, prin. Fax 978-0290
Holy Spirit S 600/PK-8
1198 Redmond Ave 95120 408-268-0794
Peggy Krewson, prin. Fax 268-5281
Legacy Christian S 200/PK-8
420 Allegan Cir 95123 408-225-5976
Debbie Hudson, prin. Fax 854-8589
Liberty Baptist S 200/PK-12
2790 S King Rd 95122 408-274-5613
Milpitas Christian S 400/PK-8
3435 Birchwood Ln 95132 408-945-6530
Robyn Ritsema, prin. Fax 945-3124
Most Holy Trinity S 300/PK-8
1940 Cunningham Ave 95122 408-729-3431
Jamie McIntyre, prin. Fax 272-4945
Primary Plus ES 300/PK-8
3500 Amber Dr 95117 408-248-2464
Michelle O'Hara, prin. Fax 248-9447
Queen of Apostles S 300/PK-8
4950 Mitty Way 95129 408-252-3659
Martin Chargin, prin. Fax 873-2645
SABA Academy PK-9
4415 Fortran Ct 95134 408-946-5900
Br. Sami Hijazi, prin.
Sacred Heart Nativity Schools 100/6-8
310 Edwards Ave 95110 408-993-1293
Lorraine Shepherd, prin. Fax 993-0675
St. Christopher S 600/K-8
2278 Booksin Ave 95125 408-723-7223
Sally Douthit, prin. Fax 978-5458
St. Frances Cabrini S 600/PK-8
15325 Woodard Rd 95124 408-377-6545
Jane Daigle, prin. Fax 377-8491
St. John Vianney S 500/K-8
4601 Hyland Ave 95127 408-258-7677
Anthony Barajas, prin. Fax 258-5997
St. Leo the Great S 300/PK-8
1051 W San Fernando St 95126 408-293-4846
Matt Komar, prin. Fax 293-3516
St. Martin of Tours S 300/PK-8
300 OConnor Dr 95128 408-287-3630
Deborah Gisi-Rodriguez, prin. Fax 287-4313
St. Patrick S 200/PK-8
51 N 9th St 95112 408-283-5858
Olga Islas, prin. Fax 283-5852
St. Timothy Lutheran S 100/PK-5
5100 Camden Ave 95124 408-265-0244
Gayle Renken, prin. Fax 265-0275
St. Victor S 300/K-8
3150 Sierra Rd 95132 408-251-1740
Patricia Wolf, prin. Fax 251-1492
Stratford MS, 1718 Andover Ln 95124 200/6-8
Maggie Schwartz, prin. 408-626-0001
Stratford S - San Jose 400/PK-5
6670 San Anselmo Way 95119 408-363-2130
Beth Ann Zuvella, prin. Fax 363-2131
Valley Christian ES 400/K-5
1450 Leigh Ave 95125 408-559-4400
Gabriel Guven, prin. Fax 559-4022
Valley Christian JHS 500/6-8
100 Skyway Dr Ste 140 95111 408-513-2460
Lisa Arnett, prin. Fax 513-2472

San Juan Bautista, San Benito, Pop. 1,810
Aromas/San Juan USD 1,100/PK-12
2300 San Juan Hwy 95045 831-623-4500
Michele Huntoon, supt. Fax 623-4907
www.asjusd.k12.ca.us
San Juan S 400/PK-8
100 Nyland Dr 95045 831-623-4538
Elizabeth Cord, prin. Fax 623-0614
Other Schools – See Aromas

San Juan Capistrano, Orange, Pop. 33,954
Capistrano USD 52,500/K-12
33122 Valle Rd 92675 949-234-9200
Kirsten Vital, supt. Fax 493-8729
capousd.ca.schoolloop.com
Ambuehl ES 400/K-5
28001 San Juan Creek Rd 92675 949-661-0400
Tony Bogle, prin. Fax 488-3158
Del Obispo ES 400/K-5
25591 Camino Del Avion 92675 949-234-5905
Suzanne Heck, prin. Fax 488-3062
Forster MS 1,400/6-8
25601 Camino Del Avion 92675 949-234-5907
Carrie Bertini, prin. Fax 488-3567
Kinoshita ES 700/K-5
2 Via Positiva 92675 949-489-2131
Jose Pedraza, prin. Fax 234-0405
San Juan ES 800/K-5
31642 El Camino Real 92675 949-493-4533
Silvia Pule, prin. Fax 240-9174
Other Schools – See Aliso Viejo, Capistrano Beach, Dana Point, Ladera Ranch, Laguna Niguel, Mission Viejo, Rancho Santa Margarita, San Clemente, Trabuco Canyon

---

Capistrano Valley Christian S 400/PK-12
32032 Del Obispo St 92675 949-493-5683
Christopher Rutz, head sch Fax 493-6057
Mission Basilica S 300/K-8
31641 El Camino Real 92675 949-234-1385
Alycia Beresford, prin. Fax 234-1397
Saddleback Valley Christian S 900/PK-12
26333 Oso Rd 92675 949-443-4050
Erick Streelman, head sch Fax 443-3941
St. Margaret Episcopal S 1,100/PK-12
31641 La Novia Ave 92675 949-661-0108
William Moseley, head sch Fax 661-8637
Stoneybrooke Christian S 400/PK-8
26300 Via Escolar 92692 949-364-4407
Sherry Worel, supt. Fax 364-6303

San Leandro, Alameda, Pop. 81,465
San Leandro USD 8,600/K-12
835 E 14th St 94577 510-667-3500
Dr. Mike McLaughlin, supt. Fax 667-3569
www.sanleandro.k12.ca.us
Bancroft MS 900/6-8
1150 Bancroft Ave 94577 510-618-4380
Valentin Del Rio, prin. Fax 895-4113
Garfield ES 400/K-5
13050 Aurora Dr 94577 510-618-4300
Lynda Hornada, prin. Fax 352-5399
Jefferson ES 600/K-5
14300 Bancroft Ave 94578 510-618-4310
Nicole Seaberg, prin. Fax 895-4161
Madison ES 400/K-5
14751 Juniper St 94579 510-895-7944
Garry Grotke, prin. Fax 895-7959
McKinley ES 500/K-5
2150 E 14th St 94577 510-618-4320
Grozelia Ward, prin. Fax 895-7457
Monroe ES 400/K-5
3750 Monterey Blvd 94578 510-618-4340
Jeanette McNeil, prin. Fax 614-0298
Muir MS 1,000/6-8
1444 Williams St 94577 510-618-4400
Vernon Walton, prin. Fax 667-3545
Roosevelt ES 500/K-5
951 Dowling Blvd 94577 510-618-4350
David Kumamoto, prin. Fax 639-0832
Washington ES 400/K-5
250 Dutton Ave 94577 510-618-4360
Elisa Alvarez, prin. Fax 895-4112
Wilson ES 800/K-5
1300 Williams St 94577 510-618-4370
Sally Lewis, prin. Fax 895-4179

San Lorenzo USD
Supt. — See San Lorenzo
Corvallis ES 600/K-5
14790 Corvallis St 94579 510-317-4900
Bryan Dunn-Ruiz, prin. Fax 317-4925
Dayton ES 500/K-5
1500 Dayton Ave 94579 510-317-3600
Kevin Moore, prin. Fax 317-3690
Hillside ES 500/K-5
15980 Marcella St 94578 510-317-5300
Moraima Machado, prin. Fax 317-5322
Washington Manor MS 800/6-8
1170 Fargo Ave 94579 510-317-5500
Theresa Armada, prin. Fax 317-5597

Assumption S 300/K-8
1851 136th Ave 94578 510-357-8772
Joseph Petersen, prin. Fax 357-7018
Montessori S of San Leandro 100/PK-K
16492 Foothill Blvd 94578 510-278-0288
Dr. Pamela Rigg, admin. Fax 278-1118
Principled Academy 100/PK-8
2305 Washington Ave Ste A 94577 510-351-6400
St. Felicitas S 300/K-8
1650 Manor Blvd 94579 510-357-2530
Meghan Jorgensen, prin. Fax 357-5358
St. Leander S 200/PK-8
451 Davis St 94577 510-351-4144
Fax 483-6060

San Lorenzo, Alameda, Pop. 22,527
San Lorenzo USD 12,200/PK-12
15510 Usher St 94580 510-317-4600
Dr. Fred Brill, supt. Fax 278-4344
www.slzusd.org
Bay ES 600/K-5
2001 Bockman Rd 94580 510-317-4300
Kimberly Yearns, prin. Fax 317-4350
Bohannon MS 900/6-8
800 Bockman Rd 94580 510-317-3800
Gwendolyn Rehling, prin. Fax 278-7794
Del Rey ES 600/K-5
1510 Via Sonya 94580 510-317-5000
Donald Carpenter, prin. Fax 481-1422
Edendale MS 700/6-8
16160 Ashland Ave 94580 510-317-5100
Evelyn Baffico, prin. Fax 317-5190
Grant ES 400/K-5
879 Grant Ave 94580 510-317-3700
Joshua Jackson, prin. Fax 317-3720
Hesperian ES 700/K-5
620 Drew St 94580 510-317-5200
Brian McComb, prin. Fax 317-5230
Other Schools – See Hayward, San Leandro

Lea's Christian S 100/PK-4
17200 Via Magdalena 94580 510-785-0334
St. John S 300/PK-8
270 E Lewelling Blvd 94580 510-276-6632
Paige Child, prin. Fax 276-5645

San Lucas, Monterey, Pop. 254
San Lucas UNESD 100/K-8
PO Box 310 93954 831-382-4426
Nicole Hester, supt. Fax 382-4088
sanlucasusd-ca.schoolloop.com
San Lucas ES 100/K-8
PO Box 310 93954 831-382-4426
Nicole Hester, admin. Fax 382-4088

San Luis Obispo, San Luis Obispo, Pop. 43,697
San Luis Coastal USD 7,500/PK-12
1500 Lizzie St 93401 805-549-1200
Dr. Eric Prater, supt. Fax 549-9074
www.slcusd.org
Bishop's Peak ES 400/K-6
451 Jaycee Dr 93405 805-596-4030
Dan Block, prin. Fax 544-9308
Hawthorne ES 300/PK-6
2125 Story St 93401 805-596-4070
James McMillen, prin. Fax 544-5759
Laguna MS 700/7-8
11050 Los Osos Valley Rd 93405 805-596-4055
John Calandro, prin. Fax 544-2449
Los Ranchos ES 500/K-6
5785 Los Ranchos Rd 93401 805-596-4075
Marlie Schmidt, prin. Fax 543-2366
Pacheco ES 500/PK-6
261 Cuesta Dr 93405 805-596-4081
Rick Mayfield, prin. Fax 782-0597
Sinsheimer ES 400/K-6
2755 Augusta St 93401 805-596-4088
Jeffrey Martin, prin. Fax 544-9634
Smith ES 400/PK-6
1375 Balboa St 93405 805-596-4094
Joyce Hansen, prin. Fax 544-0703
Teach ES 100/4-6
145 Grand Ave 93405 805-596-4100
Darla Batistic, prin. Fax 596-4020
Other Schools – See Los Osos, Morro Bay

Christ Classical S K-6
880 Laureate Ln 93405 805-453-6161
Old Mission S 400/PK-8
761 Broad St 93401 805-543-6019
Stefani Higuera, admin. Fax 543-6246
San Luis Obispo Christian S 50/PK-6
2075 Johnson Ave 93401 805-543-1146
Jonell Griffith, prin. Fax 548-0546
San Luis Obispo Classical Academy 300/PK-12
PO Box 3601 93405 805-548-8700
Susan Theule Ph.D., dir.

San Marcos, San Diego, Pop. 80,807
San Diego County Office of Education
Supt. — See San Diego
North Coastal Consortium S 100/PK-12
255 Pico Ave 92069 760-761-5110
Theresa Kurtz, prin.

San Marcos USD 20,100/K-12
255 Pico Ave Ste 250 92069 760-752-1299
Melissa Hunt, supt.
www.smusd.org
Discovery ES 1,000/K-5
730 Applewilde Dr 92078 760-290-2077
Carrie Geldard, prin. Fax 744-8847
Double Peak S K-8
111 San Elijo Rd 92078 760-290-2340
Steve Baum, prin. Fax 736-8398
Dunn ES 700/K-6
3697 La Mirada Dr 92078 760-290-2000
Jennifer Carter, prin. Fax 598-5727
Knob Hill ES 900/K-5
1825 Knob Hill Rd 92069 760-290-2080
Daniel Trujillo, prin. Fax 741-7843
Paloma ES 1,000/K-5
660 Camino Magnifico 92069 760-290-2199
Dana Spencer, prin. Fax 736-2212
Richland ES 800/K-5
910 Borden Rd 92069 760-290-2400
Julie Barbara, prin. Fax 290-2412
San Elijo ES 1,400/K-5
1615 Schoolhouse Way 92078 760-290-2600
Carolyn Kalicki, prin. Fax 290-2807
San Elijo MS 1,700/6-8
1600 Schoolhouse Way 92078 760-290-2800
Gary DeBora, prin. Fax 290-2828
San Marcos ES 900/K-5
1 Tiger Way 92069 760-290-2430
Stephanie Wallace, prin. Fax 736-2213
San Marcos MS 1,300/6-8
650 W Mission Rd 92069 760-290-2500
Spencer Wavra, prin. Fax 744-0893
Twin Oaks ES 700/K-5
1 Cassou Rd 92069 760-290-2588
Silvia Ventura-Jacobsen, prin. Fax 752-3155
Woodland Park MS 1,300/6-8
1270 Rock Springs Rd 92069 760-290-2455
Josh Way, prin. Fax 741-6178
Other Schools – See Carlsbad, Vista

St. Joseph Academy K-12
500 Las Flores Dr 92078 760-305-8505
Anthony Biese, prin. Fax 305-8466
Valley Christian S 200/K-8
1350 Discovery St 92078 760-744-0207
Melissa Johnson, prin. Fax 744-6231

San Marino, Los Angeles, Pop. 12,791
San Marino USD 3,100/K-12
1665 West Dr 91108 626-299-7000
Alex Cherniss, supt. Fax 299-7010
www.smusd.us

Carver ES 600/K-5
3100 Huntington Dr 91108 626-299-7080
Michael Lin, prin. Fax 299-7086
Huntington MS 800/6-8
1700 Huntington Dr 91108 626-299-7060
Jason Kurtenbach, prin. Fax 299-7064
Valentine ES 600/K-5
1650 Huntington Dr 91108 626-299-7090
Colleen Shields, prin. Fax 299-7094

SS. Felicitas & Perpetua S 200/PK-8
2955 Huntington Dr 91108 626-796-8223
Stella Costello, prin. Fax 683-8129

San Martin, Santa Clara, Pop. 6,857
Morgan Hill USD
Supt. — See Morgan Hill
San Martin/Gwinn ES 500/PK-8
13745 Llagas Ave 95046 408-201-6480
Claudia Olaciregui, prin. Fax 201-6490

San Mateo, San Mateo, Pop. 91,447
San Mateo-Foster City ESD
Supt. — See Foster City
Abbott MS 800/6-8
600 36th Ave 94403 650-312-7600
Joe Hadley, prin. Fax 312-7605
Bayside Academy 600/6-8
2025 Kehoe Ave 94403 650-312-7660
John Cosmos, prin. Fax 312-7634
Baywood ES 700/K-5
600 Alameda De Las Pulgas 94402 650-312-7511
Maria Majka, prin. Fax 312-7508
Beresford ES 300/K-5
300 28th Ave 94403 650-312-7551
Amy Snow, prin. Fax 312-1970
Borel MS 900/6-8
425 Barneson Ave 94402 650-312-7670
Kenyetta Cook, prin. Fax 312-7644
College Park ES 400/K-5
715 Indian Ave 94401 650-312-7691
Steven Chuang, prin. Fax 312-7729
Fiesta Gardens International ES 500/K-5
1001 Bermuda Dr 94403 650-312-7737
Jeanette Ramirez, prin. Fax 312-7697
Hall ES 500/K-5
130 San Miguel Way 94403 650-312-7533
Kristen Ugrin, prin. Fax 312-7637
Highlands ES 600/K-5
2320 Newport St 94402 650-312-7544
Lana Fenech, prin. Fax 312-7635
Horrall/LEAD ES 500/K-5
949 Ocean View Ave 94401 650-312-7550
Patti Dullea, prin. Fax 312-7641
Laurel ES 500/K-5
316 36th Ave 94403 650-312-7555
Lori Fukumoto, prin. Fax 312-7636
Meadow Heights ES 300/K-5
2619 Dolores St 94403 650-312-7566
Stephanie Fraumeni, prin. Fax 312-7560
North Shoreview Montessori 400/K-8
1301 Cypress Ave 94401 650-312-7588
Melinda Fore, prin. Fax 312-7642
Park ES 500/K-5
161 Clark Dr 94402 650-312-7577
Cristina Haley, prin. Fax 312-7643
Parkside Montessori 400/K-5
1685 Eisenhower St 94403 650-312-7575
Abbie Wishart, prin. Fax 312-7638
Sunnybrae ES 500/K-5
1031 S Delaware St 94402 650-312-7599
Robin May, prin. Fax 312-7596

Carey S 300/PK-5
1 Carey School Ln 94403 650-345-8205
Duncan Lyon, head sch Fax 345-2528
Dawn Christian Academy 100/K-12
525 42nd Ave 94403 650-212-4222
Chris Chu, prin.
Grace Lutheran S 100/PK-8
2825 Alameda De Las Pulgas 94403 650-345-9082
Fred Brauer, prin. Fax 377-4831
Pacific Rim International S 100/PK-12
454 Peninsula Ave 94401 650-685-1881
Christinia Cheung, head sch Fax 685-1820
St. Gregory S 300/K-8
2701 Hacienda St 94403 650-573-0111
Laura Miller, prin. Fax 573-6548
St. Matthew S 600/K-8
910 S El Camino Real 94402 650-343-1373
Adrian Peterson, prin. Fax 343-2046
St. Matthew's Episcopal Day S 200/PK-8
16 Baldwin Ave 94401 650-274-0700
Julie Galles, head sch
St. Timothy S 200/K-8
1515 Dolan Ave 94401 650-342-6567
Michelle Basile, prin. Fax 342-5913

San Miguel, San Luis Obispo, Pop. 2,293
Pleasant Valley JUNESD 100/K-6
2025 Ranchita Canyon Rd 93451 805-467-3453
Wendy Nielsen, supt. Fax 467-2306
www.pleasant-valley-school.org
Pleasant Valley ES 100/K-6
2025 Ranchita Canyon Rd 93451 805-467-3453
Wendy Nielsen, admin. Fax 467-2306

San Miguel JUNESD, 1601 L St 93451 800/K-8
Dr. Curt Dubost, supt. 805-467-3216
sanmiguelschools.org
Larsen ES 400/K-8
1601 L St 93451 805-467-3216
Curt Dubost, prin. Fax 467-3410
Other Schools – See Paso Robles

San Pablo, Contra Costa, Pop. 28,206
West Contra Costa USD
Supt. — See Richmond
Bayview ES 700/K-6
3001 16th St 94806 510-231-1401
Armando Torres, prin. Fax 215-6681
Dover ES 800/K-6
1871 21st St 94806 510-231-1420
Ruby Gonzalez, prin. Fax 236-5483
Downer ES 700/K-6
1231 18th St 94806 510-234-3851
Marco Gonzales, prin. Fax 233-8961
Helms MS 1,000/7-8
2500 Road 20 94806 510-233-3988
Jessica Petrilli, prin. Fax 234-5977
Lake ES 400/K-6
2700 11th St 94806 510-231-1451
Wendy Gonzalez, prin. Fax 215-8948
Montalvin Manor ES 400/K-6
300 Christine Dr 94806 510-231-1405
Katherine Verprauskus, prin. Fax 758-8742
Riverside ES 400/K-6
1300 Amador St 94806 510-231-1409
Christine Hatcher, prin. Fax 237-6991
Tara Hills ES 600/K-6
2300 Dolan Way 94806 510-231-1428
Robert Mendoza, prin. Fax 724-3224

St. Paul S 200/K-8
1825 Church Ln 94806 510-233-3080
Natalie Lenz-Acuna, prin. Fax 231-8776

San Pedro, See Los Angeles
Los Angeles USD
Supt. — See Los Angeles
Bandini Street ES 400/K-6
425 N Bandini St 90731 310-832-4593
Robert Fenton, prin. Fax 547-3300
Barton Hill ES 700/K-6
423 N Pacific Ave 90731 310-547-2471
Michael Pile, prin. Fax 832-4531
Cabrillo Avenue ES 400/K-5
732 S Cabrillo Ave 90731 310-832-6446
Jason South, prin. Fax 833-2699
Cabrillo Early Education Center PK-PK
741 W 8th St 90731 310-832-2809
Josemie Dill, prin. Fax 833-5956
Dana MS 1,500/6-8
1501 S Cabrillo Ave 90731 310-241-1100
Steven Gebhart, prin. Fax 514-9925
15th Street ES 500/K-5
1527 S Mesa St 90731 310-547-3323
Jennifer Mak, prin. Fax 547-1156
Leland Street ES 600/K-6
2120 S Leland St 90731 310-832-0505
Lora Caudill, prin. Fax 831-0837
Park Western Early Education Center PK-PK
1220 Park Western Pl 90732 310-833-2875
Josemie Dill, prin. Fax 548-0177
Park Western Place ES 700/K-5
1214 Park Western Pl 90732 310-833-3591
Noelle Wakasa-Manzano, prin. Fax 833-6413
Point Fermin Marine Science Magnet S 300/K-5
3333 S Kerckhoff Ave 90731 310-832-2649
Dayna Wells, prin. Fax 833-4307
7th Street ES 500/K-5
1570 W 7th St 90732 310-832-1538
Wendy Sanchez, prin. Fax 548-7004
South Shores Visual Performing Arts S 500/K-5
2060 W 35th St 90732 310-832-6596
Paul Suzuki, prin. Fax 832-4994
Taper Avenue ES 600/K-5
1824 N Taper Ave 90731 310-832-3056
Steven Skrumbis, prin. Fax 548-4485
White Point ES 400/K-5
1410 Silvius Ave 90731 310-833-5232
Lisa O'Brien, prin. Fax 514-8726

Holy Trinity S 600/PK-8
1226 W Santa Cruz St 90732 310-833-0703
Linda Wiley M.A., prin. Fax 833-5219
Mary Star of the Sea S 300/PK-8
717 S Cabrillo Ave 90731 310-831-0875
Noreen Maricich, prin. Fax 831-0877

San Rafael, Marin, Pop. 55,927
Dixie ESD 1,900/PK-8
380 Nova Albion Way 94903 415-492-3700
Dr. Jason L. Yamashiro, supt. Fax 492-3707
dixieschooldistrict.org
Dixie ES 400/PK-5
1175 Idylberry Rd 94903 415-492-3730
Jason Manviller, prin. Fax 492-3736
Miller Creek MS 600/6-8
2255 Las Gallinas Ave 94903 415-492-3760
Kristy Treewater, prin. Fax 492-3765
Silveira ES 500/K-5
375 Blackstone Dr 94903 415-492-3741
Will Anderson, prin. Fax 507-9783
Vallecito ES 500/K-5
50 Nova Albion Way 94903 415-492-3750
Tracy Smith, prin. Fax 492-3757

San Rafael CSD 6,700/PK-12
310 Nova Albion Way 94903 415-492-3233
Dr. Michael Watenpaugh, supt. Fax 492-3245
www.srcs.org
Bahia Vista ES 600/K-5
125 Bahia Way 94901 415-485-2415
Cecilia Perez, prin. Fax 485-2474
Coleman ES 400/K-5
800 Belle Ave 94901 415-485-2420
Mike Taylor, prin. Fax 485-2494
Davidson MS 1,000/6-8
280 Woodland Ave 94901 415-485-2400
Robert Marcucci, prin. Fax 485-2476
Gallinas ES PK-1
251 N San Pedro Rd 94903 415-492-3205
Glenwood ES 400/K-5
25 W Castlewood Dr 94901 415-485-2430
Kim Goodhope, prin. Fax 485-2434
Laurel Dell ES 200/K-5
225 Woodland Ave 94901 415-485-2317
Pepe Gonzalez, prin. Fax 485-2361
San Pedro ES 500/K-5
498 Point San Pedro Rd 94901 415-485-2450
Mimi Melodia, prin. Fax 485-2454
Short ES 200/K-5
35 Marin St 94901 415-485-3793
Vanessa Flynn, prin. Fax 721-1055
Sun Valley ES 500/K-5
75 Happy Ln 94901 415-485-2440
Julie Harris, prin. Fax 485-2443
Venetia Valley K-8 S 700/K-8
177 N San Pedro Rd 94903 415-492-3150
Juan Rodriguez, prin. Fax 492-3160

Brandeis Marin 200/K-8
180 N San Pedro Rd 94903 415-472-1833
Dr. Peg Sandel, hdmstr.
Marin Waldorf S 200/PK-8
755 Idylberry Rd 94903 415-479-8190
Steve Bennett, dir. Fax 479-9921
Mark Day S 400/K-8
39 Trellis Dr 94903 415-472-8000
Joseph Harvey, head sch Fax 472-0722
Montessori De Terra Linda 100/PK-6
610 Del Ganado Rd 94903 415-479-7373
Jaye Flynn, head sch Fax 479-5394
St. Isabella S 200/K-8
PO Box 6188 94903 415-479-3727
Susan Naretto, prin. Fax 479-9961
St. Raphael S 200/K-8
1100 5th Ave 94901 415-454-4455
Lydia Collins, prin. Fax 454-5927

San Ramon, Contra Costa, Pop. 68,811
San Ramon Valley USD
Supt. — See Danville
Armstrong ES 600/K-5
2849 Calais Dr 94583 925-479-1600
Lorna Monteith, prin. Fax 828-8473
Bella Vista ES K-5
1050 Trumpet Vine Ln, 925-552-2960
Jen Torres, prin. Fax 328-0560
Bollinger Canyon ES 600/K-5
2300 Talavera Dr 94583 925-242-3200
Shawn Wells, prin. Fax 830-9595
Country Club ES 500/PK-5
7534 Blue Fox Way 94583 925-479-6000
Christy Glaser, prin. Fax 803-9827
Coyote Creek ES 1,100/PK-5
8700 Northgale Ridge Rd, 925-855-7300
Bill Alpert, prin. Fax 735-1197
Disney ES 500/PK-5
3250 Pine Valley Rd 94583 925-479-3900
Curtis Haar, prin. Fax 829-8957
Gale Ranch MS 1,000/6-8
6400 Main Branch Rd, 925-479-1500
Susan Goldman, prin. Fax 479-1595
Golden View ES 600/PK-5
5025 Canyon Crest Dr, 925-855-2700
Christine Huajardo, prin. Fax 735-2104
Hidden Hills ES 1,100/K-5
12995 Harcourt Way, 925-479-3800
Melodie Huynh, prin. Fax 803-9792
Iron Horse MS 1,000/6-8
12601 Alcosta Blvd 94583 925-790-2500
Joe Nguyen, prin. Fax 824-2830
Live Oak ES 1,100/K-5
5151 Sherwood Way, 925-803-3100
Nadine Rosenzweig, prin. Fax 803-3197
Montevideo ES 700/K-5
13000 Broadmoor Dr 94583 925-479-6100
Katie Cavanaugh, prin. Fax 828-1727
Pine Valley MS 1,000/6-8
3000 Pine Valley Rd 94583 925-479-7700
Jason Law, prin. Fax 828-1972
Quail Run ES 1,100/K-5
4000 Goldenbay Ave, 925-560-4000
Mimi Quan, prin. Fax 560-4059
Twin Creeks ES 500/K-5
2785 Marsh Dr 94583 925-855-2900
Shelli Kravtiz, prin. Fax 838-8431
Windemere Ranch MS 1,200/6-8
11611 E Branch Pkwy, 925-479-7400
David Bolin, prin. Fax 479-7469

Dorris-Eaton S, 1 Annabel Ln 94583 300/PK-8
Gerald Ludden, head sch 925-930-9000

Santa Ana, Orange, Pop. 321,180
Garden Grove USD
Supt. — See Garden Grove
Fitz IS 700/7-8
4600 W McFadden Ave 92704 714-663-6351
Mischelle Repsher, prin. Fax 663-6527
Hazard ES 700/K-6
4218 W Hazard Ave 92703 714-663-6403
Melissa Sais, prin. Fax 663-6261
Heritage ES 600/K-6
426 S Andres Pl 92704 714-663-6108
Michelle Pinchot, prin. Fax 663-6032
Newhope ES 500/K-6
4419 W Regent Dr 92704 714-663-6581
Adam Bernstein, prin. Fax 663-6022
Rosita ES 600/K-6
4726 W Hazard Ave 92703 714-663-6418
Don Terreri, prin. Fax 663-6015
Russell ES 700/K-6
600 S Jackson St 92704 714-663-6151
Kai Chang, prin. Fax 663-6026

Orange USD
Supt. — See Orange
Fairhaven ES 600/K-6
1415 Fairhaven Ave 92705 714-997-6178
Karen Sanders, prin. Fax 532-8073
Panorama ES 400/K-6
10512 Crawford Canyon Rd 92705 714-997-6265
Jeremy Mortensen, prin. Fax 771-3402

Santa Ana USD 57,500/PK-12
1601 E Chestnut Ave 92701 714-558-5501
Stefanie Phillips Ed.D., supt. Fax 558-5610
www.sausd.us
Adams ES 500/K-5
2130 S Raitt St 92704 714-967-3100
Sara Shorey, prin. Fax 967-3199
Carr IS 1,600/6-8
2120 W Edinger Ave 92704 714-480-4100
Jose Luis Pedroza, prin. Fax 957-8766
Carver ES 600/K-3
1401 W Santa Ana Blvd 92703 714-564-2000
Kimberly Kempa, prin. Fax 564-2099
Davis ES 700/K-5
1405 French St 92701 714-564-2200
Robert Anguiano Ed.D., prin. Fax 564-2299
Diamond ES 600/K-5
1450 S Center St 92704 714-480-8100
Denise Bertrand Ed.D., prin. Fax 480-8199
Edison ES 600/K-5
2063 Orange Ave 92707 714-479-6900
Gina Zyburt, prin. Fax 479-6999
Esqueda ES 1,200/K-8
2240 S Main St 92707 714-431-1500
Kevin Tonai Ed.D., prin. Fax 431-1599
Franklin ES 500/K-5
210 W Cubbon St 92701 714-564-2900
Rita Pereira, prin. Fax 564-2999
Fremont ES 800/K-5
1930 W 10th St 92703 714-972-4300
Maricela Roque, prin. Fax 972-4399
Garfield ES 700/K-5
850 Brown St 92701 714-972-5300
Kasey Klappenback, prin. Fax 972-5399
Greenville Fundamental ES 1,100/K-5
3600 S Raitt St 92704 714-558-3400
Felisa Gear, prin. Fax 431-3299
Harvey ES 500/K-5
1635 S Center St 92704 714-479-4200
Robert McDonald, prin. Fax 479-4299
Heninger ES 1,100/K-7
417 W Walnut St 92701 714-953-3800
William Skelly, prin. Fax 953-3899
Heroes ES 700/K-5
1111 W Civic Center Dr 92703 714-568-9600
Diana Torres, prin. Fax 568-9699
Hoover Academy 400/K-5
408 E Santa Clara Ave 92706 714-564-2100
Armando Gutierrez, prin. Fax 564-2199
Jackson ES 1,100/K-5
1143 S Nakoma Dr 92704 714-569-3500
Marisela Longacre, prin. Fax 569-3599
Jefferson ES 900/K-6
1522 W Adams St 92704 714-285-3700
Fernando Duran, prin. Fax 285-3799
Kennedy ES 800/K-5
1300 E McFadden Ave 92705 714-972-5700
Steve Kotsubo, prin. Fax 972-5799
King ES 800/K-5
1001 Graham Ln 92703 714-972-6000
Eleanor Rodriguez, prin. Fax 972-6099
Lathrop IS 1,100/6-8
1111 S Broadway 92707 714-567-3300
Julie Infante, prin. Fax 567-3399
Lincoln ES 1,000/K-5
425 S Sullivan St 92704 714-972-6200
Edna Velado, prin. Fax 972-6299
Lowell ES 900/K-5
700 S Flower St 92703 714-972-6300
Miriam Perez, prin. Fax 972-6399
MacArthur Fundamental IS 1,300/6-8
600 W Alton Ave 92707 714-568-7700
David Casper, prin. Fax 568-7799
Madison ES 1,100/K-6
1124 Hobart St 92707 714-972-6400
Lisa Gonzalez-Solomon, prin. Fax 972-6499
Martin ES 800/K-5
939 W Wilshire Ave 92707 714-480-8000
Peter Richardson, prin. Fax 480-8099
McFadden IS 1,500/6-8
2701 S Raitt St 92704 714-479-4000
Ignacio Muniz, prin. Fax 479-4099
Mendez Fundamental IS 1,400/6-8
2000 N Bristol St 92706 714-972-7800
Gabriel Moreno, prin. Fax 972-7899
Mitchell Child Development Center PK-PK
3001 W Harvard St 92704 714-430-5600
Mark Bello, prin. Fax 430-5699
Monroe ES 500/K-5
417 E Central Ave 92707 714-569-9700
Betty Tamara-Rios, prin. Fax 569-9799
Monte Vista ES 700/K-5
2116 W Monta Vista Ave 92704 714-564-8500
Meg Greene, prin. Fax 564-8599
Muir Fundamental ES 1,100/K-5
1951 Mabury St 92705 714-972-6700
Laura Martin, prin. Fax 972-6799
Pio Pico ES 600/K-5
931 Highland St 92703 714-972-7500
Lupe Lopez, prin. Fax 972-7599
Romero-Cruz ES 300/4-5
2701 W Fifth St 92703 714-564-8000
Erica Graves, prin. Fax 564-8099
Roosevelt ES 800/K-5
501 S Halladay St 92701 714-564-1200
Jaime Ramirez, prin. Fax 564-1299
Santiago ES 1,200/K-8
2212 N Baker St 92706 714-564-8400
Norris Perez, prin. Fax 564-8799
Sepulveda ES 500/K-5
1801 S Poplar St 92704 714-433-6500
Ana Gonzalez, prin. Fax 433-6599
Sierra Preparatory Academy 1,000/6-8
2021 N Grand Ave 92705 714-567-3500
Elisa Younger, prin. Fax 567-3591
Spurgeon IS 900/6-8
2701 W 5th St 92703 714-480-2200
Stuart Caldwell, prin. Fax 480-2215

Taft ES 600/PK-6
500 Keller Ave 92707 714-550-1400
Herminio Bautista, prin. Fax 550-1499
Thorpe Fundamental ES 1,100/K-5
2450 W Alton Ave 92704 714-430-5800
Cindy Landsiedel, prin. Fax 430-5899
Villa Fundamental IS 1,400/6-8
1441 E Chestnut Ave 92701 714-558-5100
Anissa Sequeida, prin. Fax 558-5199
Walker ES 500/K-5
811 E Bishop St 92701 714-647-2800
Mariana Garate, prin. Fax 647-2899
Washington ES 1,000/K-5
910 W Anahurst Pl 92707 714-445-5100
Jose Montano Ph.D., prin. Fax 445-5199
Willard IS 900/6-8
1342 N Ross St 92706 714-480-4800
Amy Scruton, prin. Fax 480-4899
Wilson ES 700/K-5
1317 N Baker St 92706 714-564-8100
Ligia Halstrom, prin. Fax 564-8199

Tustin USD
Supt. — See Tustin
Arroyo ES 600/K-5
11112 Coronel Rd 92705 714-730-7381
Amy Jones, prin. Fax 734-9462
Foss ES 400/K-5
18492 Vanderlip Ave 92705 714-730-7552
Kelly Fresch, prin. Fax 838-5287
Hewes MS 900/6-8
13232 Hewes Ave 92705 714-730-7348
Eric Kilian, prin. Fax 730-7315
Loma Vista ES 500/K-5
13822 Prospect Ave 92705 714-730-7528
Katie Sheyka, prin. Fax 730-7550
Red Hill ES 500/K-5
11911 Red Hill Ave 92705 714-730-7543
Will Neddersen, prin. Fax 730-1306
Tustin Memorial Academy 700/K-5
12712 Browning Ave 92705 714-730-7546
Sharon Maeda, prin. Fax 730-7524

Bethel Baptist S 200/PK-12
901 S Euclid St 92704 714-839-3600
Dr. Terry Cantrell, admin. Fax 839-4953
Calvary Chapel S 1,500/K-12
3800 S Fairview St 92704 714-662-7485
Jay Henry, supt. Fax 979-3515
Calvary Christian S 400/K-8
1010 N Tustin Ave 92705 714-973-2056
Leah Hess, head sch Fax 558-8043
Minassian Armenian S 100/PK-6
5315 W McFadden Ave 92704 714-839-7831
Sanan Shirinian, prin. Fax 839-1036
St. Anne S 200/PK-8
1324 S Main St 92707 714-542-9328
Sr. Teresa Lynch, prin. Fax 542-3431
St. Barbara S 400/K-8
5306 W McFadden Ave 92704 714-775-9477
Melissa Baroldi, prin. Fax 775-9468
St. Joseph S 200/K-8
608 E Civic Center Dr 92701 714-542-2704
Dr. Brad Snyder, prin. Fax 542-2132
School of our Lady 200/K-8
2204 W McFadden Ave 92704 714-545-8185
Adela Solis, prin. Fax 545-2362
Storybook S, 1032 N Ross St 92701 100/PK-6
Michelle Rubalcaba, dir. 714-541-9378

Santa Barbara, Santa Barbara, Pop. 86,425

Cold Spring ESD 200/K-6
2243 Sycamore Canyon Rd 93108 805-969-2678
Dr. Amy Alzina, supt. Fax 969-0787
www.coldspringschool.net
Cold Spring ES 200/K-6
2243 Sycamore Canyon Rd 93108 805-969-2678
Dr. Amy Alzina, admin. Fax 969-0787

Goleta UNESD
Supt. — See Goleta
El Camino ES 200/PK-6
5020 San Simeon Dr 93111 805-692-5574
Sarah Bautista, prin. Fax 692-5578
Foothill ES 400/K-6
711 Ribera Dr 93111 805-681-1268
Felicia Roggero, prin. Fax 681-0700
Hollister ES 500/K-6
4950 Anita Ln 93111 805-681-1271
Pam Rennick, prin. Fax 681-0331
Mountain View ES 300/K-6
5465 Queen Ann Ln 93111 805-681-1284
Abby Vasquez, prin. Fax 681-4814

Hope ESD 1,000/K-6
3970 La Colina Rd Ste 14 93110 805-682-2564
Anne Hubbard, supt. Fax 687-7954
www.hopeschooldistrict.org
Hope ES 300/K-6
3970-A La Colina Rd 93110 805-563-2974
Barbara LaCorte, prin. Fax 563-4906
Monte Vista ES 300/K-6
730 N Hope Ave 93110 805-687-5333
Nancy Lorenzen, prin. Fax 687-0457
Vieja Valley ES 300/K-6
434 Nogal Dr 93110 805-967-1239
Juan Ricoy, prin. Fax 967-5947

Montecito UNESD 500/K-6
385 San Ysidro Rd 93108 805-969-3249
Anthony Ranii, supt. Fax 969-9714
www.montecitou.org
Montecito Union S 500/K-6
385 San Ysidro Rd 93108 805-969-3249
Nicholas Bruski, prin. Fax 969-9714

Santa Barbara USD 15,500/PK-12
720 Santa Barbara St 93101 805-963-4338
Cary Matsuoka, supt. Fax 962-3146
www.sbunified.org
Adams ES 600/PK-6
2701 Las Positas Rd 93105 805-563-2515
Kelly Fresch, prin. Fax 563-4365
Cleveland ES 400/PK-6
123 Alameda Padre Serra 93103 805-963-8873
Gabriel Sandoval, prin. Fax 965-3523
Franklin ES 600/PK-6
1111 E Mason St 93103 805-963-4283
Casie Killgore, prin. Fax 962-6846
Harding ES 400/PK-6
1625 Robbins St 93101 805-965-8994
Veronica Binkley, prin. Fax 962-1846
La Colina JHS 800/7-8
4025 Foothill Rd 93110 805-967-4506
David Ortiz, prin. Fax 967-3056
La Cumbre JHS 500/7-8
2255 Modoc Rd 93101 805-687-0761
Jo Ann Caines, prin. Fax 563-4636
McKinley ES 400/PK-6
350 Loma Alta Dr 93109 805-966-9926
Rachel Gonzalez, prin. Fax 899-3286
Monroe ES 500/PK-6
431 Flora Vista Dr 93109 805-966-7023
Brian Naughton, prin. Fax 963-4198
Roosevelt ES 600/PK-6
1990 Laguna St 93101 805-563-2062
Christy Bazemore, prin. Fax 563-6092
Santa Barbara Community Academy 300/PK-6
850 Portesuello Ave 93101 805-687-2081
Alicia Saballa-Santana, prin. Fax 687-6530
Santa Barbara JHS 900/7-8
721 E Cota St 93103 805-963-7751
Lito Garcia, prin. Fax 962-7196
Santa Barbara Unified ECC PK-PK
1030 East Yanonali St 93103 805-963-8685
Michelle Robertson, prin. Fax 965-8431
Washington ES 600/K-6
290 Lighthouse Rd 93109 805-965-6653
Sierra Loughridge, prin. Fax 962-5328
Other Schools – See Goleta

Crane Country Day S 300/K-8
1795 San Leandro Ln 93108 805-969-7732
Joel Weiss, head sch Fax 969-3635
El Montecito S 100/PK-6
3225 Calle Pinon 93105 805-962-3091
Timothy Loomer, head sch Fax 962-3092
Garden Street Academy 100/K-12
2300 Garden St 93105 805-687-3717
Angela Jevons, admin. Fax 456-1897
Laguna Blanca S 300/PK-12
4125 Paloma Dr 93110 805-687-2461
Robert Hereford, head sch Fax 682-2553
Marymount S 200/PK-8
2130 Mission Ridge Rd 93103 805-569-1811
Andrew Wooden, head sch Fax 569-0573
Notre Dame S 200/PK-8
33 E Micheltorena St 93101 805-965-1033
Christina Stefanec, prin. Fax 965-1034
Our Lady of Mt. Carmel S 200/PK-8
530 Hot Springs Rd 93108 805-969-5965
Tracie Simolon, prin. Fax 565-9841
Providence A Santa Barbara Christian S 100/PK-6
3723 Modoc Rd 93105 805-563-4770
St. Raphael S 300/PK-8
160 Saint Josephs St 93111 805-967-2115
Michelle Limb, prin. Fax 683-9765
Santa Barbara Montessori S 100/PK-9
7421 Mirano Dr 93117 805-685-7600
Jim Fitzpatrick, head sch Fax 685-7660

Santa Clara, Santa Clara, Pop. 111,315

Cupertino UNSD
Supt. — See Sunnyvale
Eisenhower ES 700/K-5
277 Rodonovan Dr 95051 408-248-4313
Joanne Connor, prin. Fax 248-2063

Santa Clara USD 15,400/K-12
PO Box 397 95052 408-423-2000
Dr. Stanley Rose, supt. Fax 423-2285
www.santaclarausd.org
Bowers ES 400/K-5
2755 Barkley Ave 95051 408-423-1100
Lisa Blanc, prin. Fax 423-1180
Bracher ES 400/K-5
2700 Chromite Dr 95051 408-423-1200
Wayne Leach, prin. Fax 423-1280
Briarwood ES 400/K-5
1930 Townsend Ave 95051 408-423-1300
Susan Jezyk, prin. Fax 423-1380
Buchser MS 1,000/6-8
1111 Bellomy St 95050 408-423-3000
Monica Stoffal, prin. Fax 423-3080
Cabrillo MS 800/6-8
2550 Cabrillo Ave 95051 408-423-3700
Stan Garber, prin. Fax 423-3780
Callejon S 1,000/K-8
4176 Lick Mill Blvd 95054 408-423-3300
Mary Martinez, prin. Fax 423-3380
Central Park ES K-5
2720 Sonoma Pl 95051 408-423-4400
Miakje Kamstra, prin. Fax 423-4403
Haman ES 400/K-5
865 Los Padres Blvd 95050 408-423-1400
Kimberly Wakefield, prin. Fax 423-1480
Hughes ES 500/K-5
4949 Calle De Escuela 95054 408-423-1500
Dr. Teri Morrow, prin. Fax 423-1580
Laurelwood ES 700/K-5
955 Teal Dr 95051 408-423-1600
Dr. Lori Rogers, prin. Fax 423-1680
Millikin Basics+ ES 500/K-5
615 Hobart Ter 95051 408-423-1800
Bob Moss, prin. Fax 423-1880

Montague ES 400/K-5
750 Laurie Ave 95054 408-423-1900
Ramis Ahrary, prin. Fax 423-1980
Pomeroy ES 500/K-5
1250 Pomeroy Ave 95051 408-423-3800
Tricia Ringel, prin. Fax 423-3880
Scott Lane ES 500/K-5
1925 Scott Blvd 95050 408-423-4100
Priscilla Reza, prin. Fax 423-4180
Sutter ES 500/K-5
3200 Forbes Ave 95051 408-423-4200
Michael Fong, prin. Fax 423-4280
Washington Open ES 400/K-5
270 Washington St 95050 408-423-3900
Barbara Berman, prin. Fax 423-3980
Westwood ES 500/K-5
435 Saratoga Ave 95050 408-423-4300
Cori Ghaffari, prin. Fax 423-4380
Other Schools – See Alviso, Sunnyvale

Granada Islamic S 400/PK-10
3003 Scott Blvd 95054 408-980-1161
Rania El-Sioufi, prin. Fax 980-1120
Monticello Academy 400/PK-8
3345 Lochinvar Ave 95051 408-615-9416
Trinh Trinh, prin. Fax 615-0894
St. Clare S 300/K-8
725 Washington St 95050 408-246-6797
Madeline Rader, prin. Fax 246-6726
St. Justin S 300/PK-8
2655 Homestead Rd 95051 408-248-1094
Karen Suty, prin. Fax 246-0691
St. Lawrence the Martyr S 300/PK-8
1977 Saint Lawrence Dr 95051 408-296-2260
Marty Proccacio, prin. Fax 296-1068
Santa Clara Christian S 100/PK-5
3421 Monroe St 95051 408-246-5423
Stuart Nice, prin. Fax 246-4883
Sierra S 100/K-12
220 Blake Ave 95051 408-247-4740
Carolyn Grundt, dir. Fax 247-0996
Stratford S - Santa Clara Pomeroy 300/PK-5
890 Pomeroy Ave 95051 408-244-4073
Susan Morrissey, prin. Fax 244-2332
Stratford S - Santa Clara Winchester 50/PK-K
400 N Winchester Blvd 95050 408-244-2121
Pam Elkhechen, prin.

Santa Clarita, Los Angeles, Pop. 171,060

Saugus UNESD 10,000/K-6
24930 Avenue Stanford 91355 661-294-5300
Dr. Joan M. Lucid, supt. Fax 294-3111
www.saugususd.org
Bridgeport ES 1,000/K-6
23670 Newhall Ranch Rd 91355 661-294-5375
Carin Fractor, prin. Fax 286-1598
Other Schools – See Canyon Country, Saugus, Valencia

Sulphur Springs UNESD
Supt. — See Canyon Country
Fair Oaks Ranch Community ES 900/K-6
26933 Silverbell Ln 91387 661-299-1790
Julie McBride, prin. Fax 299-1879
Golden Oak Community ES 500/K-6
25201 Via Princessa 91387 661-251-8929
Gretchen Lupica, prin. Fax 251-8727

William S. Hart UNHSD 23,700/7-12
21380 Centre Pointe Pkwy 91350 661-259-0033
Vicki Engbrecht, supt. Fax 254-8653
www.hartdistrict.org
La Mesa JHS 1,100/7-8
26623 May Way 91351 661-250-0022
Michele Krantz, prin. Fax 252-3326
Rio Norte JHS 1,200/7-8
28771 Rio Norte Dr 91354 661-295-3700
Audrey Asplund, prin. Fax 257-1413
Other Schools – See Canyon Country, Newhall, Stevenson Ranch, Valencia

---

Our Lady of Perpetual Help S 300/K-8
23225 Lyons Ave 91321 661-259-1141
Sharon Krahl, prin. Fax 259-8254
Santa Clarita Christian S 500/K-12
27249 Luther Dr 91351 661-252-7371
Kirk Huckabone, admin. Fax 252-4354

Santa Cruz, Santa Cruz, Pop. 57,302

Bonny Doon UNESD 100/PK-6
1492 Pine Flat Rd 95060 831-427-2300
Stephanie Siddens M.A., supt. Fax 427-2800
www.bduesd.org
Bonny Doon ES 100/PK-6
1492 Pine Flat Rd 95060 831-427-2300
Stephanie Siddens M.A., prin. Fax 427-2800

Happy Valley ESD 100/K-6
3125 Branciforte Dr 95065 831-429-1456
Michelle McKinny, supt. Fax 429-6205
www.hvesd.com
Happy Valley ES 100/K-6
3125 Branciforte Dr 95065 831-429-1456
Michelle McKinny, prin. Fax 429-6205

Live Oak SD 2,100/PK-12
984 Bostwick Ln Ste 1 95062 831-475-6333
Tamra Taylor, supt. Fax 475-2638
www.losd.ca
Del Mar ES 400/PK-5
1959 Merrill St 95062 831-477-2063
Marilyn Rockey, prin. Fax 477-9555
Green Acres ES 400/PK-5
966 Bostwick Ln 95062 831-475-0111
Nancy Krueger, prin. Fax 475-4813
Live Oak ES 400/PK-5
1916 Capitola Rd 95062 831-475-2000
Greg Stein, prin. Fax 475-0458
Shoreline MS 500/6-8
855 17th Ave 95062 831-475-6565
Colleen Martin, prin. Fax 462-1653

Santa Cruz CSD
Supt. — See Soquel
Bay View ES 500/K-5
1231 Bay St 95060 831-429-3991
Yvette Garcia, prin. Fax 429-3513
Branciforte MS 400/6-8
315 Poplar Ave 95062 831-429-3883
Kristin Pfotenhauer, prin. Fax 429-3962
De Laveaga ES 700/K-5
1145 Morrissey Blvd 95065 831-429-3807
Robert Greenlee, prin. Fax 429-3999
Gault ES 400/K-5
1320 Seabright Ave 95062 831-429-3856
Amariah Hernandez, prin. Fax 427-4812
Mission Hill MS 700/6-8
425 King St 95060 831-429-3860
Ann Mekis, prin. Fax 427-4846
Westlake ES 600/K-5
1000 High St 95060 831-429-3878
Clyde Curley, prin. Fax 429-3835

Scotts Valley USD
Supt. — See Scotts Valley
Brook Knoll ES 600/PK-5
151 Brook Knoll Dr 95060 831-423-2454
Josh Wahl, prin. Fax 429-8508

Soquel UNESD
Supt. — See Capitola
Santa Cruz Gardens ES 300/K-5
8005 Winkle Ave 95065 831-464-5670
Kerry le Roux, prin. Fax 476-5827

Gateway S 200/K-8
126 Eucalyptus Ave 95060 831-423-0341
Dr. Zachary Roberts, head sch Fax 454-0843
Good Shepherd S 200/PK-8
2727 Mattison Ln 95065 831-476-4000
Diane Rabago, prin. Fax 476-0948
Holy Cross S 200/PK-8
150 Emmett St 95060 831-423-4447
Patricia Patano, prin. Fax 423-0752
Santa Cruz Waldorf S 200/PK-8
2190 Empire Grade 95060 831-425-0519
Tori Milburn, admin. Fax 425-1326
Spring Hill S 100/K-6
250 California St 95060 831-427-2641
Cindy Jaconette, prin. Fax 427-2958
VHM Christian S 100/PK-8
427 Capitola Road Ext 95062 831-475-4762
Philip Ermshar, prin. Fax 475-4845

Santa Fe Springs, Los Angeles, Pop. 16,058

Little Lake City SD 4,600/K-8
10515 Pioneer Blvd 90670 562-868-8241
Dr. William Crean Ed.D., supt. Fax 868-1192
www.llcsd.net
Jersey Avenue ES 500/K-5
9400 Jersey Ave 90670 562-948-3772
Dr. Michael Trimmell, prin. Fax 942-7902
Lake Center MS 900/6-8
10503 Pioneer Blvd 90670 562-868-4977
Jack Sokoloff, prin. Fax 929-4527
Lakeview ES 600/K-5
11500 Joslin St 90670 562-868-8655
Lauren Hernandez, prin. Fax 868-1647
Other Schools – See Norwalk

Los Nietos ESD
Supt. — See Los Nietos
Rancho Santa Gertrudes ES 400/K-6
11233 Charlesworth Rd 90670 562-692-0841
Octavio Perez, prin. Fax 699-6955

St. Pius X S 200/PK-8
10855 Pioneer Blvd 90670 562-864-4818
Christine Soler, prin. Fax 864-7120
Santa Fe Springs Christian S 200/K-8
11434 Otto St 90670 562-868-2263
Cindy Jarvis M.A., prin. Fax 868-8398

Santa Margarita, San Luis Obispo, Pop. 1,216

Atascadero USD
Supt. — See Atascadero
Carrisa Plains ES 50/K-5
9640 Carrisa Hwy 93453 805-475-2244
Sarah Betz, prin. Fax 475-2046
Santa Margarita ES 300/K-5
PO Box 380 93453 805-438-5633
Marshawn Porter, prin. Fax 438-3323

Santa Maria, Santa Barbara, Pop. 97,930

Blochman UNESD 900/K-12
4949 Foxen Canyon Rd 93454 805-937-1148
Doug Brown, supt. Fax 937-2291
www.sbceoportal.org/blochman/
Foxen S 100/K-8
4949 Foxen Canyon Rd 93454 805-937-1148
Doug Brown, supt. Fax 937-2291

Orcutt UNESD
Supt. — See Orcutt
Dunlap ES 600/K-6
1220 Oak Knoll Rd 93455 805-938-8500
Joe Schmidt, prin. Fax 938-8549
Lakeview JHS 500/7-8
3700 Orcutt Rd 93455 805-938-8600
Ted Lyon, prin. Fax 938-8649
Nightingale ES 800/K-6
255 Winter Rd 93455 805-938-8650
Kate McInerney, prin. Fax 938-8699
Patterson Road ES 600/K-6
400 Patterson Rd 93455 805-938-8750
Julie Kozel, prin. Fax 938-8799
Pine Grove ES 600/K-6
1050 E Rice Ranch Rd 93455 805-938-8800
Denee Signorelli, prin. Fax 938 8849
Shaw ES 600/K-6
759 Dahlia Pl 93455 805-938-8850
Jenee Severance, prin. Fax 938-8899

Santa Maria-Bonita ESD 15,500/K-8
708 S Miller St 93454 805-928-1783
Luke Ontiveros, supt. Fax 928-7874
www.smbsd.org
Adam ES 1,000/K-6
500 Windsor St 93458 805-361-6700
Laurie Graack, prin. Fax 352-9104
Alvin ES 1,000/K-6
301 E Alvin Ave 93454 805-361-6760
Ann McDaniel, prin. Fax 349-2737
Arellanes ES 300/K-6
1890 Sandalwood Dr 93455 805-361-6860
Ronald Smith, prin. Fax 346-8540
Arellanes JHS 600/7-8
1890 Sandalwood Dr 93455 805-361-6820
Genevieve Beaird, prin. Fax 346-8535
Battles ES 1,000/K-6
605 E Battles Rd 93454 805-361-6880
Carlee Gruver, prin. Fax 346-1836
Bonita ES 600/K-6
2715 W Main St 93458 805-361-8280
Rosalie Jones, prin. Fax 925-1179
Bruce ES 900/K-6
601 W Alvin Ave 93458 805-361-6940
Lisa Caruso, prin. Fax 346-1838
El Camino JHS 700/7-8
219 W El Camino St 93458 805-361-7800
Betty Romero, prin. Fax 346-1851
Fairlawn ES 800/K-6
120 Mary Dr 93458 805-361-7500
Kathleen Carlson-Bryant, prin. Fax 346-1839
Fesler JHS 900/7-8
1100 E Fesler St 93454 805-361-7880
Anjanette Winckler, prin. Fax 346-1849
Jimenez ES, 1970 Biscayne St 93458 K-6
Richard Ruiz, prin. 805-361-4340
Kunst JHS 800/7-8
930 Hidden Pines Way 93458 805-361-5800
Carmen Rivera, prin. Fax 925-8239
Liberty ES 800/K-6
1300 Sonya Ln 93458 805-361-4530
Cindy Duncan, prin. Fax 925-2165
Miller ES 900/K-6
410 E Camino Colegio 93454 805-361-7560
Jim Bissin, prin. Fax 346-1840
Oakley ES 900/K-6
1120 W Harding Ave 93458 805-361-7620
Cristina Ortega, prin. Fax 346-1841
Ontiveros ES 1,000/K-6
930 Rancho Verde 93458 805-361-7680
Gayle Vyenielo, prin. Fax 346-1846
Rice ES 900/K-6
700 Vickie Ave 93454 805-361-7740
Colleen Lathery, prin. Fax 346-1842
Sanchez ES 900/K-6
804 Liberty St 93458 805-361-4625
Kathleen Lester, prin. Fax 925-8410
Taylor ES 900/K-6
1921 Carlotti Dr 93454 805-361-6250
Jennifer Loftus, prin. Fax 346-2683
Tunnell ES 800/K-6
1248 Dena Way 93454 805-361-7940
Linda Muranaka, prin. Fax 349-2017

Pacific Christian S 300/PK-8
3435 Santa Maria Way 93455 805-934-1253
Lynne Plunkett, prin. Fax 934-3445
St. Louis De Montfort S 300/K-8
5095 Harp Rd 93455 805-937-5571
Kathy Crow, prin. Fax 937-3181
St. Mary of the Assumption S 200/PK-8
424 E Cypress St 93454 805-925-6713
Michelle Cox, prin. Fax 925-3815
Valley Christian Academy 300/PK-12
2970 Santa Maria Way 93455 805-937-6317
Charles Mason, prin. Fax 934-2563

Santa Monica, Los Angeles, Pop. 86,130

Santa Monica-Malibu USD 11,300/PK-12
1651 16th St 90404 310-450-8338
Dr. Ben Drati, supt. Fax 450-1667
www.smmusd.org
Adams MS 1,000/6-8
2425 16th St 90405 310-452-2326
Steven Richardson, prin. Fax 452-5352
Edison Language Academy 500/K-5
2402 Virginia Ave 90404 310-828-0335
Lori Orum, prin. Fax 449-1250
Franklin ES 800/K-5
2400 Montana Ave 90403 310-828-2814
Deanna Sinfield, prin. Fax 449-1252
Grant ES 700/K-5
2368 Pearl St 90405 310-450-7651
Jezelle Fullwood, prin. Fax 452-4350
Lincoln MS 1,000/6-8
1501 California Ave 90403 310-393-9227
Dr. Florence Culpepper, prin. Fax 393-4297
McKinley ES 500/K-5
2401 Santa Monica Blvd 90404 310-828-5011
Ashley Benjamin, prin. Fax 449-1251
Muir ES 300/K-5
2526 6th St 90405 310-399-7721
Paula Lytz, prin. Fax 452-4351
Rogers ES 500/K-5
2401 14th St 90405 310-452-2364
Elizabeth Cochran, prin. Fax 452-9035
Roosevelt ES 800/K-5
801 Montana Ave 90403 310-395-0941
Lynda Holeva, prin. Fax 587-1169
Santa Monica-Malibu Preschool PK-PK
1651 16th St 90404 310-450-8338
Pam Kazee, prin. Fax 396-6149
Other Schools – See Malibu

Carlthorp S 300/K-6
438 San Vicente Blvd 90402 310-451-1332
Tim Kusserow, head sch Fax 451-8559
Crossroads S for Arts & Sciences 1,100/K-12
1714 21st St 90404 310-829-7391
Bob Riddle, head sch Fax 828-5636

Lighthouse Church S 100/PK-12
1220 20th St 90404 310-829-1741
Josh Scribner, prin. Fax 829-1743
New Roads ES 100/K-4
3131 Olympic Blvd 90401 310-828-5582
Luthern Williams, head sch Fax 828-2582
PS1 Pluralistic S 200/K-6
1225 Broadway 90404 310-394-1313
Joel Pelcyger, head sch Fax 395-1093
St. Anne S 200/K-8
2015 Colorado Ave 90404 310-829-2775
Michael Browning, prin. Fax 829-3945
St. Monica S 300/K-8
1039 7th St 90403 310-451-9801
Dr. Neil Quinly, prin. Fax 394-6001

Santa Nella, Merced, Pop. 1,366
Gustine USD
Supt. — See Gustine
Romero ES 200/K-5
13500 Luis Ave 95322 209-854-6177
Terry Souza, prin. Fax 826-6858

Santa Paula, Ventura, Pop. 29,121
Briggs ESD 600/PK-8
12465 Foothill Rd 93060 805-525-7540
Deborah Cuevas, supt. Fax 933-1111
www.briggsesd.org
Briggs MS 300/5-8
14438 W Telegraph Rd 93060 805-525-7151
Samuel Pacheco, prin. Fax 933-3565
Olivelands ES 300/PK-4
12465 Foothill Rd 93060 805-933-2254
Lindsay Winegar, prin. Fax 933-1111

Mupu ESD 100/K-8
4410 Ojai Rd 93060 805-525-6111
Dr. Sheryl Barnd, supt. Fax 525-2871
www.mupu.k12.ca.us
Mupu ES 100/K-8
4410 Ojai Rd 93060 805-525-6111
Dr. Sheryl Barnd, supt. Fax 525-2871

Santa Clara ESD 100/K-6
20030 E Telegraph Rd 93060 805-525-4573
Kari Skidmore, supt. Fax 525-4985
www.scesd.k12.ca.us
Santa Clara ES 100/K-6
20030 E Telegraph Rd 93060 805-525-4573
Kari Skidmore, prin. Fax 525-4985

Santa Paula USD 5,400/K-12
201 S Steckel Dr 93060 805-933-8800
Alfonso Gamino, supt. Fax 933-8026
www.santapaulaunified.org
Bedell ES 300/K-5
1305 Laurel Rd 93060 805-933-8950
Jeff Robinson, prin. Fax 933-9735
Blanchard ES 500/K-5
115 N Peck Rd 93060 805-933-8866
Ana Rodriguez, prin. Fax 933-4409
Glen City ES 600/K-5
141 S Steckel Dr 93060 805-933-8850
Alice Pacheco, prin. Fax 525-2821
Isbell MS 1,100/6-8
221 S 4th St 93060 805-933-8880
Dr. Ricardo Araiza, prin. Fax 933-5582
McKevett ES 400/K-5
955 E Pleasant St 93060 805-933-8910
Lydia Olivio, prin. Fax 933-0542
Thille ES 400/K-5
1144 E Ventura St 93060 805-933-8920
Mary Doane, prin. Fax 933-0192
Webster ES 400/K-5
1150 Saticoy St 93060 805-933-8930
Jeff Madrigal, prin. Fax 933-5588

St. Sebastian S 200/PK-8
325 E Santa Barbara St 93060 805-525-1575
Ninette Reyes Slinger, prin. Fax 525-1576

Santa Rosa, Sonoma, Pop. 161,788
Bellevue UNESD 1,800/PK-10
3150 Education Dr 95407 707-542-5197
David Alexander Ed.D., supt. Fax 542-6127
www.busd.org
Bellevue ES 400/PK-6
3223 Primrose Ave 95407 707-542-5195
Nina Craig, prin. Fax 542-6083
Meadow View ES 400/PK-6
2665 Dutton Mdw 95407 707-541-3715
Daniel Hoffman, prin. Fax 541-3717
Taylor Mountain ES 500/PK-6
1210 E Bellevue Ave 95407 707-542-3671
Tawny Fernandez, prin. Fax 542-3904

Bennett Valley UNESD 1,000/PK-6
2250 Mesquite Dr 95405 707-542-2201
Sue Field Ed.D., supt. Fax 544-6629
www.bvusd.org
Strawberry ES 400/4-6
2311 Horseshoe Dr 95405 707-526-4433
Josh Wilson, prin. Fax 526-0906
Yulupa ES 600/PK-3
2250 Mesquite Dr 95405 707-542-6272
John Eberly Ed.D., prin. Fax 544-0360

Mark West UNESD 1,500/K-8
305 Mark West Springs Rd 95404 707-524-2970
Ron Calloway, supt. Fax 524-2976
www.mwusd.k12.ca.us/
West ES 400/K-6
4600 Lavell Rd 95403 707-524-2990
Tracy Lavin-Kendall, prin. Fax 524-2999

Piner-Olivet UNESD 1,500/K-12
3450 Coffey Ln 95403 707-522-3000
Carmen Diaz-French, supt. Fax 522-3007
www.pousd.org
London ES 300/K-6
2707 Francisco Ave 95403 707-522-3030
Betha MacClain, prin. Fax 522-3317

Rincon Valley UNESD 3,400/PK-8
1000 Yulupa Ave 95405 707-542-7375
Dr. Tony Roehrick, supt. Fax 542-9802
www.rvusd.org
Austin Creek ES 400/K-6
1480 Snowy Egret Dr 95409 707-538-2122
Jenny Lynch, prin. Fax 538-1774
Madrone ES 400/PK-6
4550 Rinconada Dr 95409 707-539-9665
Mike Herfurth, prin. Fax 539-1362
Sequoia ES 400/K-6
5305 Dupont Dr 95409 707-539-3410
Brooklynn Clark, prin. Fax 537-1791
Whited ES 500/K-6
4995 Sonoma Hwy 95409 707-539-2400
Beth Acosta, prin. Fax 539-9253

Roseland SD 2,400/K-12
1691 Burbank Ave 95407 707-545-0102
Amy Jones-Kerr, supt. Fax 545-5096
www.roselandsd.org
Roseland Creek ES 400/K-6
1683 Burbank Ave 95407 707-543-2800
William Nilsen, prin. Fax 527-1588
Roseland ES 700/K-6
950 Sebastopol Rd 95407 707-545-0100
Michelle Leisen, prin. Fax 542-2111
Sheppard Accelerated ES 600/K-6
1777 West Ave 95407 707-546-7050
Jenny Young, prin. Fax 546-0434

Santa Rosa CSD 16,100/K-12
211 Ridgway Ave 95401 707-528-5388
Diann Kitamura, supt. Fax 528-5440
www.srcs.k12.ca.us
Biella ES 400/K-6
2140 Jennings Ave 95401 707-522-3110
Aida Diaz, prin. Fax 522-3109
Brook Hill ES 500/K-6
1850 Vallejo St 95404 707-522-3120
Guadalupe Perez-Cook, prin. Fax 522-3127
Burbank ES 400/K-6
203 S A St 95401 707-522-3140
Julian Szot, prin. Fax 522-3149
Comstock MS 400/7-8
2750 W Steele Ln 95403 707-528-5266
Laura Hendrickson, prin. Fax 528-5480
Cook MS 400/7-8
2480 Sebastopol Rd 95407 707-528-5156
Matthew Pollack, prin. Fax 528-5163
Hidden Valley ES K-6
3435 Bonita Vista Ln 95404 707-522-3180
Jacqui Parker, prin. Fax 522-3181
Hidden Valley ES Satellite 700/K-6
3555 Parker Hill Rd 95404 707-522-3190
Jacqui Parker, prin. Fax 522-3193
Lehman ES 500/K-6
1700 Jennings Ave 95401 707-522-3200
Alisa Haley, prin. Fax 522-3195
Lincoln ES 400/K-6
850 W 9th St 95401 707-522-3210
Jeanine Wilson, prin. Fax 522-3213
Monroe ES 400/K-6
2567 Marlow Rd 95403 707-522-3230
Michelle Smith, prin. Fax 522-3229
Proctor Terrace ES 500/K-6
1711 Bryden Ln 95404 707-522-3240
Kathy Olmsted, prin. Fax 522-3249
Rincon Valley MS 800/7-8
4650 Badger Rd 95409 707-528-5255
Ed Navarro, prin. Fax 528-5644
Santa Rosa MS 700/7-8
500 E St 95404 707-528-5281
Tom Fierro, prin. Fax 528-5283
Slater MS 700/7-8
3500 Sonoma Ave 95405 707-528-5241
Rachele Cunningham, prin. Fax 528-5733
Steele Lane ES 400/K-6
301 Steele Ln 95403 707-522-3260
Dan Noble, prin. Fax 522-3256

Windsor USD
Supt. — See Windsor
Washburn ES 500/PK-1
75 Pleasant Ave 95403 707-837-7727
Benita Jones, prin. Fax 837-7732

Wright ESD 1,600/PK-8
4385 Price Ave 95407 707-542-0550
Adam Schaible, supt. Fax 577-7962
www.wrightesd.org
Stevens ES 500/K-6
2345 Giffen Ave 95407 707-575-8883
Lori Pola Hoard, prin. Fax 573-0317
Wilson ES 600/K-6
246 Brittain Ln 95401 707-525-8350
Corina Rice, prin. Fax 525-0116
Wright Start Preschool PK-PK
950 S Wright Rd 95407 707-542-1940
Talia Casci Noethig Ph.D., dir. Fax 542-1975

Brush Creek Montessori S 100/PK-6
1569 Brush Creek Rd 95404 707-539-7980
Jed Burchett, head sch Fax 539-7549
Redwood Adventist Academy 100/K-12
385 Mark West Springs Rd 95404 707-545-1697
Rincon Valley Christian S 400/PK-12
4585 Badger Rd 95409 707-539-1486
Paul Eggenberger, admin. Fax 539-1493
St. Eugene Cathedral S 400/PK-8
300 Farmers Ln 95405 707-545-7252
Barbara Gasparini, prin. Fax 545-2594
St. Rose S 400/PK-8
4300 Old Redwood Hwy 95403 707-545-0379
Kathy Ryan, prin. Fax 545-7150
Sonoma Country Day S 200/PK-8
4400 Day School Pl 95403 707-284-3200
Dr. Brad Weaver, head sch Fax 284-3254
Summerfield Waldorf S 400/PK-12
655 Willowside Rd 95401 707-575-7194
Fax 575-3217

Santa Rosa Vly, Ventura
Pleasant Valley SD
Supt. — See Camarillo
Santa Rosa Technology Magnet S 600/K-8
13282 Santa Rosa Rd, 805-491-3822
Kelly Borchard, prin. Fax 491-2702

Santa Ynez, Santa Barbara, Pop. 4,319
College ESD 400/K-8
3525 Pine St 93460 805-686-7300
James Brown, supt. Fax 686-7305
www.collegeschooldistrict.org
College ES 50/K-1
3525 Pine St 93460 805-686-7300
Maurene Donner, lead tchr. Fax 686-7305
Santa Ynez ES 200/2-8
3325 Pine St 93460 805-686-7310
Maurene Donner, lead tchr. Fax 686-7340

Santa Ysabel, San Diego
Spencer Valley ESD 50/K-8
PO Box 159 92070 760-765-0336
Julie Weaver, supt. Fax 765-3135
svesd.net
Spencer Valley S 50/K-8
PO Box 159 92070 760-765-0336
Julie Weaver, prin. Fax 765-3135

Santee, San Diego, Pop. 51,246
Santee ESD 6,400/K-8
9625 Cuyamaca St 92071 619-258-2300
Kristin Baranski, supt. Fax 258-2305
www.santeesd.net
Cajon Park ES 1,000/K-8
10300 N Magnolia Ave 92071 619-956-2400
Mike Olander, prin. Fax 956-2408
Carlton Hills ES 500/K-8
9353 Pike Rd 92071 619-258-3400
Stephanie Southcott, prin. Fax 258-3414
Carlton Oaks ES 900/K-8
9353 Wethersfield Rd 92071 619-956-4500
Andrew Johnston, prin. Fax 956-4509
Harritt ES 500/K-8
8120 Arlette St 92071 619-258-4800
Tylene Hicks, prin. Fax 258-4816
Hill Creek ES 700/K-8
9665 Jeremy St 92071 619-956-5000
Suzie Martin, prin. Fax 956-5014
PRIDE Academy at Prospect Avenue ES 600/K-8
9303 Prospect Ave 92071 619-956-5200
Terry Heck, prin. Fax 956-5212
Rio Seco ES 1,000/K-8
9545 Cuyamaca St 92071 619-956-5500
Debra Simpson, prin. Fax 956-5514
Sycamore Canyon ES 300/K-6
10201 Settle Rd 92071 619-956-5400
Jeri Billick, prin. Fax 956-5412
Other Schools – See El Cajon

San Ysidro, See San Diego
San Ysidro ESD 5,100/PK-8
4350 Otay Mesa Rd 92173 619-428-4476
Dr. Julio Fonseca Ed.D., supt. Fax 428-1505
www.sysd.k12.ca.us
La Mirada S 500/K-6
222 Avenida De La Madrid 92173 619-428-4424
Luis Ramos, prin. Fax 428-0858
San Ysidro MS 600/7-8
4345 Otay Mesa Rd 92173 619-428-5551
Roberto Carrillo, prin. Fax 690-2837
Smythe S 800/K-6
1880 Smythe Ave 92173 619-428-4447
Joel Tapia, prin. Fax 428-0041
Sunset S 900/PK-6
3825 Sunset Ln 92173 619-428-1148
Efrain Burciaga, prin. Fax 428-0065
Willow S 1,100/K-6
226 Willow Rd 92173 619-428-2231
Manuel Bojorquez, prin. Fax 428-4932
Other Schools – See San Diego

South Bay UNSD
Supt. — See Imperial Beach
Nicoloff ES 900/K-6
1777 Howard Ave 92173 619-428-7000
Rigoberto Lara, prin. Fax 428-7080

Our Lady of Mt. Carmel S 300/K-8
4141 Beyer Blvd 92173 619-428-2091
Sr. Eva Lujano, prin. Fax 428-8324

Saratoga, Santa Clara, Pop. 28,911
Campbell UNESD
Supt. — See Campbell
Marshall Lane ES 600/K-5
14114 Marilyn Ln 95070 408-364-4259
Carrie Andrews Ph.D., prin. Fax 341-7080

Cupertino UNSD
Supt. — See Sunnyvale
Blue Hills ES 500/K-5
12300 De Sanka Ave 95070 408-257-9282
Audrey Prouse, prin. Fax 366-0611

Saratoga UNESD 2,100/K-8
20460 Forrest Hills Dr 95070 408-867-3424
Nancy Johnson, supt. Fax 867-2312
www.saratogausd.org
Argonaut ES 400/K-5
13200 Shadow Mountain Dr 95070 408-867-4773
Karen Van Putten, prin. Fax 867-5737
Foothill ES 400/K-5
13919 Lynde Ave 95070 408-867-4036
Joe Bosco, prin. Fax 867-7959
Redwood MS 900/6-8
13925 Fruitvale Ave 95070 408-867-3042
Barbara Neal, prin. Fax 867-3195
Saratoga ES 400/K-5
14592 Oak St 95070 408-867-3476
Brian White, prin. Fax 867-0538

Sacred Heart S 200/PK-8
13718 Saratoga Ave 95070 408-867-9241
Thomas Pulchny, prin. Fax 867-9242
St. Andrew's Episcopal S 400/PK-8
13601 Saratoga Ave 95070 408-867-3785
David Davies, head sch Fax 741-1852

Saugus, See Santa Clarita
Saugus UNESD
Supt. — See Santa Clarita
Emblem Academy 600/K-6
22635 Espuella Dr 91350 661-294-5315
Jon Baker, prin. Fax 296-3265
Foster ES 600/K-6
22500 Pamplico Dr 91350 661-294-5355
Dr. Deborah Bohn, prin. Fax 297-8844
Highlands ES 500/K-6
27332 Catala Ave 91350 661-294-5320
Susan Bender, prin. Fax 297-8632
Mountainview ES 900/K-6
22201 Cypress Pl 91390 661-294-5325
Katie Demsher, prin. Fax 297-8637
Plum Canyon ES 700/K-6
28360 N Alfreds Way 91350 661-294-5365
Mary Mann, prin. Fax 297-8625
Rosedell ES 800/K-6
27853 Urbandale Ave 91350 661-294-5335
Kathy Stendel, prin. Fax 297-8619
Santa Clarita ES 400/K-6
27177 Seco Canyon Rd 91350 661-294-5340
Theophane Korie, prin. Fax 297-8631

Sausalito, Marin, Pop. 6,877
Sausalito Marin CSD 400/PK-8
3030 Bridgeway 94965 415-332-3190
William McCoy, supt. Fax 332-9643
smcsd.org
Bayside King Jr Academy 100/PK-8
200 Phillips Dr 94965 415-332-3573
David Finnane, prin. Fax 332-2492

Lycee Francais de San Francisco 200/PK-5
610 Coloma St 94965 415-661-5232
Elsa Rodriguez, dir. Fax 289-0995

Scotia, Humboldt, Pop. 806
Scotia UNESD 200/K-8
PO Box 217 95565 707-764-2212
Chris Cox, supt. Fax 764-5111
www.humboldt.k12.ca.us/scotia_sd
Murphy ES 200/K-8
PO Box 217 95565 707-764-2212
Chris Cox, prin. Fax 764-5111

Scotts Valley, Santa Cruz, Pop. 11,122
Scotts Valley USD 2,500/PK-12
4444 Scotts Valley Dr # 5B 95066 831-438-1820
Tanya Krause, supt. Fax 438-2314
www.scottsvalleyusd.org
Scotts Valley MS 600/6-8
8 Bean Creek Rd 95066 831-438-0610
Mary Lonhart, prin. Fax 439-8935
Vine Hill ES 500/PK-5
151 Vine Hill School Rd 95066 831-438-1090
Julie Ebert, prin. Fax 438-4087
Other Schools – See Santa Cruz

Baymonte Christian S 400/PK-8
5000B Granite Creek Rd 95066 831-438-0100
Steve Patterson, prin. Fax 438-0715

Seal Beach, Orange, Pop. 23,477
Los Alamitos USD
Supt. — See Los Alamitos
McGaugh ES 800/PK-5
1698 Bolsa Ave 90740 562-799-4560
Roni Ellis, prin. Fax 799-4570

Seaside, Monterey, Pop. 30,879
Monterey Peninsula USD
Supt. — See Monterey
Del Rey Woods ES 500/K-5
1281 Plumas Ave 93955 831-392-3907
Lynn Ebora, prin. Fax 394-8207
Dual Language Academy Monterey Peninsula 300/K-8
225 Normandy Rd 93955 831-899-1100
Rita Burks, prin.
Highland ES 400/K-5
1650 Sonoma Ave 93955 831-583-2024
Julie Rosewood, prin. Fax 899-3857
King ES 500/K-5
1713 Broadway Ave 93955 831-392-3970
Samuel Humphrey, prin. Fax 394-0859
Marshall ES 500/2-5
300 Normandy Rd 93955 831-899-7052
Cathleen Main, prin. Fax 899-4773
Ord Terrace ES 500/K-5
1755 La Salle Ave 93955 831-392-3922
Joe Sampson, prin. Fax 899-7826
Seaside Childen's Center PK-PK
1450 Elm Ave 93955 831-392-3456
Nittaya Robinson, dir.
Seaside MS 800/6-8
999 Coe Ave 93955 831-899-7080
Manuel Nunez, prin. Fax 899-0663

Chartwell S 100/2-12
2511 Numa Watson Rd 93955 831-394-3468
Kate Mulligan, head sch Fax 394-6809
Monterey Bay Christian S 200/PK-8
1184 Hilby Ave 93955 831-899-2060
Jacob Voyce, prin. Fax 899-1250
Peninsula Adventist S 50/K-8
1025 Mescal St 93955 831 394-5578
Yvonne Ford, prin.

Sebastopol, Sonoma, Pop. 7,156
Gravenstein UNESD 700/K-8
3840 Twig Ave 95472 707-823-7008
Jennifer Schwinn, supt. Fax 823-2108
www.grav.k12.ca.us/
Gravenstein ES 400/K-5
3840 Twig Ave 95472 707-823-5361
Keri Pugno, prin. Fax 823-0478
Hillcrest MS 300/6-8
725 Bloomfield Rd 95472 707-823-7653
David Fichera, prin. Fax 823-4630

Sebastopol UNESD 800/PK-8
7611 Huntley St 95472 707-829-4570
Linda Irving, supt. Fax 829-7427
www.sebastopolschools.org
Brook Haven MS 200/5-8
7905 Valentine Ave 95472 707-829-4590
Deborah Hanks, prin. Fax 829-6285
Park Side ES 200/PK-4
7450 Bodega Ave 95472 707-829-7400
Linda Irving, prin. Fax 829-7409

Twin Hills UNESD 1,200/K-12
700 Watertrough Rd 95472 707-823-0871
Barbara Bickford, supt. Fax 823-5832
www.twinhillsusd.org
Apple Blossom ES 400/K-5
700 Watertrough Rd 95472 707-823-1041
Jill Rosenquist, prin. Fax 823-8946

Pleasant Hill Christian S 50/PK-6
1782 Pleasant Hill Rd 95472 707-823-5868
Beth See, prin. Fax 823-7092

Seeley, Imperial, Pop. 1,711
Seeley UNESD 300/PK-8
PO Box 868 92273 760-352-3571
Cecilia Dial, supt. Fax 352-1629
www.seeleyusd.org
Seeley ES 300/PK-8
PO Box 868 92273 760-352-3571
Toni Dickerson, admin. Fax 352-1629

Seiad Valley, Siskiyou
Seiad ESD 50/K-8
PO Box 647 96086 530-496-3308
Marsha Jackson, supt. Fax 496-3310
Seiad ES 50/K-8
PO Box 647 96086 530-496-3308
Marsha Jackson, supt. Fax 496-3310

Selma, Fresno, Pop. 22,943
Selma USD 6,300/PK-12
3036 Thompson Ave 93662 559-898-6500
Dr. Tanya A. Fisher Ed.D., supt. Fax 896-7147
www.selmausd.org
Garfield ES 200/K-6
2535 B St 93662 559-898-6740
Monica Chapa, prin. Fax 896-6084
Indianola ES 500/K-6
11524 E Dinuba Ave 93662 559-898-6680
Shane Pinkard, prin. Fax 896-0120
Jackson ES 700/K-6
2220 Huntsman Ave 93662 559-898-6690
Victoria Cuevas, prin. Fax 891-8618
Lincoln MS 1,000/7-8
1239 Nelson Blvd 93662 559-898-6600
Charles Coleman, prin. Fax 896-0733
Roosevelt ES 700/K-6
1802 Floral Ave 93662 559-898-6700
Linda Turpin, prin. Fax 896-4655
Terry ES 200/K-6
12906 S Fowler Ave 93662 559-898-6710
Rosa Baly, prin. Fax 891-7889
Washington ES 200/K-1
1420 2nd St 93662 559-898-6720
Raquel Hammond, prin. Fax 891-8626
White ES 500/PK-PK, 2-
2001 Mitchell Ave 93662 559-898-6650
Sandra Aguilera, prin. Fax 891-0633
Wilson ES 400/K-6
1325 Stillman St 93662 559-898-6730
Alicia Gonzalez, prin. Fax 896-0711

Shafter, Kern, Pop. 16,846
Maple ESD 300/K-8
29161 Fresno Ave 93263 661-746-4439
Julie Boesch, supt. Fax 746-4765
www.maple.k12.ca.us
Maple ES 300/K-8
29161 Fresno Ave 93263 661-746-4439
Julie Boesch, prin. Fax 746-4765

Richland UNESD 3,500/PK-8
331 N Shafter Ave 93263 661-746-8600
Dr. Dagoberto Garcia, supt. Fax 746-8614
www.rsdshafter.org
Golden Oak ES 1,000/PK-6
331 N Shafter Ave 93263 661 746 8670
Annette Blacklock, prin. Fax 746-8614
Redwood ES 1,000/PK-6
331 N Shafter Ave 93263 661 746-8650
Monica Garza, prin. Fax 746-8614
Richland JHS 700/7-8
331 N Shafter Ave 93263 661-746-8630
Kenneth Wright, prin. Fax 746-8614
Sequoia ES 800/PK-6
331 N Shafter Ave 93263 661-746-8740
Luis Rodriguez, prin. Fax 746 8614

Shandon, San Luis Obispo, Pop. 1,278
Shandon JUSD 300/K-12
PO Box 79 93461 805-238-0286
Teresa Taylor, supt. Fax 238-0777
www.shandonschools.org
Shandon ES 200/K-8
PO Box 49 93461 805-238-1782
Shannon Kepins, prin. Fax 238-6314
Other Schools – See

Shasta, Shasta, Pop. 1,703
Shasta UNESD
Supt. — See Redding
Shasta Union ES 100/K-8
PO Box 1125 96087 530-243-1110
Kim Miller, prin. Fax 241-5193

Shasta Lake, Shasta, Pop. 9,765
Gateway USD
Supt. — See Redding
Grand Oaks ES 300/PK-5
5309 Grand Ave 96019 530-275-7040
Robert Effa, prin. Fax 275-7045
Shasta Lake S 700/PK-8
4620 Vallecito St 96019 530-275-7020
Melanie Sanderson, prin. Fax 275-7025

Sheridan, Placer, Pop. 1,199
Western Placer USD
Supt. — See Lincoln
Sheridan ES 100/PK-5
4730 H St 95681 530-633-2591
Emily Ortiz, prin. Fax 633-9565

Sherman Oaks, See Los Angeles
Los Angeles USD
Supt. — See Los Angeles
Kester Avenue ES 900/K-5
5353 Kester Ave 91411 818-787-6751
Victoria Christie, prin. Fax 787-5480
Millikan MS 2,200/6-8
5041 Sunnyslope Ave 91423 818-528-1600
John Plevack, prin. Fax 990-7651
Millikan STEM Magnet S 6-8
5041 Sunnyslope Ave 91423 818-528-1662
Carlos Lauchu, prin. Fax 528-1665

Buckley S 800/K-12
3900 Stansbury Ave 91423 818-783-1610
Dr. James Busby, head sch Fax 461-6714
Emek Hebrew Acad/Teichman Family Torah 400/PK-8
15365 Magnolia Blvd 91403 818-783-3663
Rabbi Mordechai Shifman, head sch Fax 783-3739
Merdinian Armenian Evangelical S 200/PK-8
13330 Riverside Dr 91423 818-907-8149
Lina Arslanian, prin. Fax 907-6147
St. Francis De Sales S 300/PK-8
13368 Valleyheart Dr 91423 818-784-9573
Dr. Elizabeth Gregg, prin. Fax 784-9649

Shingle Springs, El Dorado, Pop. 4,277
Buckeye UNSD
Supt. — See El Dorado Hills
Buckeye ES 400/K-5
4561 Buckeye Rd 95682 530-677-2277
Deedra Devine, prin. Fax 672-1483

Latrobe SD 100/K-8
7900 S Shingle Rd 95682 530-677-0260
Natalie Miller, supt. Fax 672-0463
www.latrobeschool.com
Latrobe ES 50/K-3
7900 S Shingle Rd 95682 530-677-0260
Natalie Miller, admin. Fax 672-0463
Miller's Hill S 100/4-8
7900 S Shingle Rd 95682 530-677-0260
Natalie Miller, admin. Fax 672-0463

Providence Christian S 100/PK-8
PO Box 719 95682 530-672-6657
Gail Gilbertson, prin. Fax 672-6189

Shingletown, Shasta, Pop. 2,210
Black Butte UNESD 200/PK-8
7752 Ponderosa Way 96088 530-474-3125
Don Aust, supt. Fax 474-3118
www.blackbutteschool.org
Black Butte ES 100/PK-5
7752 Ponderosa Way 96088 530-474-3125
Don Aust, admin. Fax 474-3118
Black Butte JHS 100/6-8
7946 Ponderosa Way 96088 530-474-3441
Don Aust, admin. Fax 474-1361

Shoshone, Inyo, Pop. 30
Death Valley USD 50/K-12
PO Box 217 92384 760-852-4303
James Copeland, supt. Fax 852-4395
www.deathvalleyschools.org
Shoshone ES 50/K-6
PO Box 217 92384 760-852-4303
Craig Hill, prin. Fax 852-4395
Other Schools – See Tecopa

Sierra Madre, Los Angeles, Pop. 10,555
Pasadena USD
Supt. — See Pasadena
Sierra Madre ES 700/K-5
141 W Highland Ave 91024 626-396-5890
Lindsay Lewis, prin. Fax 355-0388
Sierra Madre MS 400/6-8
160 N Canon Ave 91024 626-836-2947
Garret Newson, prin. Fax 836-2964

Bethany Christian S 200/PK-8
93 N Baldwin Ave 91024 626-355-3527
Dr. William Walner, prin. Fax 921-1285
Gooden S 200/K-8
192 N Baldwin Ave 91024 626-355-2410
Dr. Marianne Ryan, admin. Fax 355-4212
St. Rita S 300/K-8
322 N Baldwin Ave 91024 626-355-6114
Joanne Harabedian, prin. Fax 355-0713

Signal Hill, Los Angeles, Pop. 10,477
Long Beach USD
Supt. — See Long Beach
Alvarado ES 400/K-5
1900 E 21st St, 562-985-0019
Lucy Salazar, prin. Fax 986-9451
Nelson Academy 800/6-8
1951 Cherry Ave, 562-591-6041
Sparkle Peterson, prin. Fax 591-8690
Signal Hill ES 700/K-5
2285 Walnut Ave, 562-426-8170
Tammy LaVelle, prin. Fax 426-6072

Simi Valley, Ventura, Pop. 120,233

Simi Valley USD 17,600/K-12
875 Cochran St 93065 805-520-6500
Dr. Jason Peplinski, supt. Fax 520-6504
www.simivalleyusd.org

Arroyo ES 300/K-6
225 Ulysses St 93065 805-306-4420
Aldo Calcagno, prin. Fax 520-6763

Atherwood ES 600/K-6
2350 Greensward St 93065 805-520-6730
Sean Platt, prin. Fax 520-6738

Berylwood ES 500/K-6
2300 Heywood St 93065 805-520-6705
Robin Hunter, prin. Fax 520-6102

Big Springs ES 700/K-6
3401 Big Springs Ave 93063 805-520-6710
Lori Rangel, prin. Fax 520-6103

Crestview ES 400/K-6
900 Crosby Ave 93065 805-520-6715
Nora Kuntz, prin. Fax 520-6104

Garden Grove ES 500/K-6
2250 Tracy Ave 93063 805-520-6700
Martha Feinstein, prin. Fax 520-6105

Hillside MS 700/6-8
2222 Fitzgerald Rd 93065 805-520-6810
Timothy Bednar, prin. Fax 520-6156

Hollow Hills ES 700/K-6
828 Gibson Ave 93065 805-520-6720
Shawn Rumble, prin. Fax 520-6106

Katherine ES 400/K-6
5455 Katherine St 93063 805-520-6780
Shay Lundstrom, prin. Fax 520-6108

Knolls ES 400/K-6
6334 Katherine Rd 93063 805-520-6735
Shanda Weaver, prin. Fax 520-6109

Madera ES 500/K-6
250 Royal Ave 93065 805-520-6740
Melody Dennert, prin. Fax 520-6742

Mountain View ES 200/K-6
2925 Fletcher St 93065 805-520-6775
Jennifer Goldman, prin. Fax 520-6110

Park View ES 300/K-6
1500 Alexander St 93065 805-520-6755
Erin Taggert, prin. Fax 520-6120

Santa Susana ES 300/K-6
4300 Apricot Rd 93063 805-520-6765
Stacy Walker, prin. Fax 520-6121

Sinaloa MS 1,000/6-8
601 Royal Ave 93065 805-520-6830
Diana Janke, prin. Fax 520-6835

Sycamore ES 400/K-6
2100 Ravenna St 93065 805-520-6745
Michelle McManigal, prin. Fax 520-6123

Township ES 500/K-6
4101 Township Ave 93063 805-520-6770
Lori Neiman, prin. Fax 520-6124

Valley View MS 1,400/6-8
3347 Tapo St 93063 805-520-6820
Michael Hall, prin. Fax 520-6157

Vista ES 700/K-6
2175 Wisteria St 93065 805-520-6750
Julie Ellis, prin. Fax 520-6752

White Oak ES 600/K-6
2201 Alscot Ave 93063 805-520-6617
Nicole Perryman, prin. Fax 520-6126

Wood Ranch ES 600/K-6
455 Circle Knoll Dr 93065 805-520-6370
Kate Snowden, prin. Fax 579-6373

Good Shepherd Lutheran S 100/K-6
2949 Alamo St 93063 805-526-2482
Catherine Barker, prin. Fax 526-4857

Grace Brethren ES 400/K-6
1717 Arcane St 93065 805-527-0101
Karen Simeri, prin. Fax 527-4011

Phoenix Ranch S 200/K-8
1845 Oak Rd 93063 805-526-0136
Evan Levi, pres. Fax 526-5002

St. Peter Claver S PK-K
5670 Cochran St 93063 805-526-2244
Angela Meyer, prin.

St. Rose of Lima S 200/K-8
1325 Royal Ave 93065 805-526-5304
Dr. Jayne Quinn, prin. Fax 526-0939

Simi Valley SDA S 50/PK-8
1636 Sinaloa Rd 93065 805-583-1866

Sloughhouse, Sacramento

Elk Grove USD
Supt. — See Elk Grove

Cosumnes River ES 500/K-6
13580 Jackson Rd 95683 916-682-2653
Sheila Caruthers, prin. Fax 682-5320

Smith River, Del Norte, Pop. 838

Del Norte County USD
Supt. — See Crescent City

Smith River S 200/K-8
564 W First St 95567 707-464-0370
Diane Cochran-Wiese, prin. Fax 487-8932

Snelling, Merced, Pop. 229

Snelling-Merced Falls UNESD 100/K-8
PO Box 189 95369 209-563-6414
Alison Kahl, supt. Fax 563-6672
www.snelling.k12.ca.us

Snelling-Merced Falls S 100/K-8
PO Box 189 95369 209-563-6414
Alison Kahl, supt. Fax 563-6672

Solana Beach, San Diego, Pop. 12,580

San Dieguito UNHSD
Supt. — See Encinitas

Warren MS 700/7-8
155 Stevens Ave 92075 858-755-1558
Reno Medina, prin. Fax 755-0891

Solana Beach ESD 2,700/K-6
309 N Rios Ave 92075 858-794-7100
Terry Decker, supt. Fax 794-7105
www.sbsd.net

Skyline ES 400/4-6
606 Lomas Santa Fe Dr 92075 858-794-3600
Lisa Denham, prin. Fax 755-3650

Solana Vista ES 500/K-3
780 Santa Victoria 92075 858-794-3700
Katie Zimmer, prin. Fax 794-3750

Other Schools – See Rancho Santa Fe, San Diego

St. James Academy 200/K-8
623 S Nardo Ave 92075 858-755-1777
Kathryn Dunn, prin. Fax 755-3124

Santa Fe Christian S 1,000/PK-12
838 Academy Dr 92075 858-755-8900
Matt Hannan, prin. Fax 755-2480

Soledad, Monterey, Pop. 25,398

Mission UNESD 100/K-8
36825 Foothill Rd 93960 831-678-3524
Dr. Jinane Annous, supt. Fax 678-0491
www.missionusd.org

Mission S 100/K-8
36825 Foothill Rd 93960 831-678-3524
Dr. Jinane Annous, supt. Fax 678-0491

Soledad USD 4,800/PK-12
1261 Metz Rd 93960 831-678-3987
Timothy J. Vanoli, supt. Fax 678-2866
www.soledadusd.org

Ferrero ES 600/PK-6
400 Entrada Dr 93960 831-678-6480
Tommy Frank, prin. Fax 678-4241

Franscion ES 600/K-6
779 Orchard Ln 93960 831-678-6340
Leslie Davis, prin. Fax 678-3442

Gabilan ES 400/PK-6
330 N Walker Dr 93960 831-678-6440
Abbie Madsen, prin. Fax 678-3467

Ledesma ES 600/K-6
973 Vista de Soledad 93960 831-678-6320
Richard Radtke, prin. Fax 678-8029

Main Street MS 700/7-8
441 Main St 93960 831-678-6460
Eric Olsen, prin. Fax 678-0797

San Vincente ES 500/PK-6
1300 Metz Rd 93960 831-678-6420
Jaime Calderon, prin. Fax 678-2786

Solvang, Santa Barbara, Pop. 5,164

Ballard ESD 100/K-6
2425 School St 93463 805-688-4812
Allan Pelletier, supt. Fax 688-7325
www.ballardschool.org

Ballard ES 100/K-6
2425 School St 93463 805-688-4812
Allan Pelletier, prin. Fax 688-7325

Solvang ESD 600/K-8
565 Atterdag Rd 93463 805-688-4810
Dr. Steve Seaford Ed.D., supt. Fax 688-6410
www.solvangschool.org

Solvang ES, 565 Atterdag Rd 93463 600/K-8
Dare Holdren, prin. 805-697-4453

Somerset, El Dorado

Indian Diggings ESD 50/K-8
6020 Omo Ranch Rd 95684 530-620-6546
Grant Coffin, supt. Fax 620-8690
www.indiandiggingsschool.com

Indian Diggings ES 50/K-8
6020 Omo Ranch Rd 95684 530-620-6546
Grant Coffin, admin. Fax 620-8690

Pioneer UNESD 300/K-8
6862 Mount Aukum Rd 95684 530-620-3556
Annette Lane, supt. Fax 620-4932
www.pioneerusd.org

Mountain Creek MS 100/5-8
6862 Mount Aukum Rd 95684 530-620-4393
John Sanguinetti, prin. Fax 620-6509

Pioneer ES 200/K-4
6862 Mount Aukum Rd 95684 530-620-7210
John Sanguinetti, prin. Fax 620-9509

Other Schools – See Grizzly Flats

Somesbar, Siskiyou

Junction ESD 50/K-8
98821 State Highway 96 95568 530-469-3373
Alan Merrill, supt. Fax 469-3390

Junction S 50/K-8
98821 State Highway 96 95568 530-469-3373
Andrea Butler-Crosby, prin. Fax 469-3390

Somis, Ventura

Mesa UNESD 1,400/K-12
3901 Mesa School Rd 93066 805-485-1411
Jeff Turner, supt. Fax 485-4387
www.mesaschool.org/

Mesa S 700/K-8
3901 Mesa School Rd 93066 805-485-1411
Stephen Bluestein, prin. Fax 485-4387

Somis UNESD 300/PK-8
5268 North St 93066 805-386-8258
Dr. Colleen Robertson Ed.D., supt. Fax 386-2324
www.somisusd.org

Somis Union ES 300/PK-8
5268 North St 93066 805-386-5711
Dr. Colleen Robertson Ed.D., prin. Fax 386-4596

Sonoma, Sonoma, Pop. 10,444

Sonoma Valley USD 4,600/K-12
17850 Railroad Ave 95476 707-935-6000
Charles Young Ph.D., supt. Fax 939-2235
svusdca.org

Altimira MS 500/6-8
17805 Arnold Dr 95476 707-935-6020
William Deeths, prin. Fax 935-6027

El Verano ES 400/K-5
18606 Riverside Dr 95476 707-935-6050
Maite Iturri, prin. Fax 935-4256

Flowery ES 300/K-5
17600 Highway 12 95476 707-935-6060
Esmeralda Moseley, prin. Fax 935-4256

Harrison MS 400/6-8
1150 Broadway 95476 707-935-6080
Mary Ann Spitzer, prin. Fax 935-6083

Prestwood ES 400/K-5
343 E MacArthur St 95476 707-935-6030
Jason Sutter, prin. Fax 935-4262

Sassarini ES 400/K-5
652 5th St W 95476 707-935-6040
Andrew Ryan, prin. Fax 935-6049

Other Schools – See Glen Ellen

Crescent Montessori S 50/PK-8
276 E Napa St 95476 707-996-2456
Karin Niehoff, head sch Fax 938-4792

Presentation S 200/K-8
20872 Broadway 95476 707-935-0122
Scott Parker, head sch Fax 996-2598

St. Francis Solano S 300/K-8
342 W Napa St 95476 707-996-4994
Deborah Picard, prin. Fax 996-2662

Sonora, Tuolumne, Pop. 4,736

Belleview ESD 100/K-8
22736 Kuien Mill Rd 95370 209-586-5510
Carla Haakma, supt. Fax 586-5516
mybelleview.org

Belleview ES 100/K-8
22736 Kuien Mill Rd 95370 209-586-5510
Carla Haakma, prin. Fax 586-5516

Curtis Creek ESD 500/K-8
18755 Standard Rd 95370 209-533-1083
Sharon Johnson, supt. Fax 532-6080
www.curtiscreekschool.com

Curtis Creek ES 500/K-8
18755 Standard Rd 95370 209-532-1428
Sharon Johnson, prin. Fax 588-9593

Sonora ESD 700/K-8
830 Greenley Rd 95370 209-532-5491
Leigh Shampain, supt. Fax 532-4828
www.ses.k12.ca.us

Sonora ES 700/K-8
830 Greenley Rd 95370 209-532-3159
Christopher Boyles, prin. Fax 532-7244

Mother Lode Adventist Junior Academy 100/K-10
80 N Forest Rd 95370 209-532-2855
Patrice Osborne, prin. Fax 532-7757

Soquel, Santa Cruz, Pop. 9,255

Mountain ESD 100/K-6
3042 Old San Jose Rd 95073 831-475-6812
Diane Morgenstern, supt. Fax 464-7200
www.mountainesd.org

Mountain ES 100/K-6
3042 Old San Jose Rd 95073 831-475-6812
Diane Morgenstern, prin. Fax 464-7200

Santa Cruz CSD 7,000/K-12
405 Old San Jose Rd 95073 831-429-3410
Kris Munro, supt. Fax 429-3439
sccs.net

Other Schools – See Santa Cruz

Soquel UNESD
Supt. — See Capitola

Main Street ES 500/K-5
3400 N Main St 95073 831-464-5650
Annette Bitter, prin. Fax 462-6295

Soquel ES 500/K-5
2700 Porter St 95073 831-464-5655
Gerri Fippin, prin. Fax 475-4678

Soulsbyville, Tuolumne, Pop. 2,151

Soulsbyville ESD 500/K-8
20300 Soulsbyville Rd 95372 209-532-1419
Jeff Winfield, supt. Fax 532-4371
www.soulsbyville.k12.ca.us

Soulsbyville S 500/K-8
20300 Soulsbyville Rd 95372 209-532-1419
Jeff Winfield, admin. Fax 533-2922

South El Monte, Los Angeles, Pop. 19,998

Valle Lindo ESD 1,200/K-8
1431 Central Ave 91733 626-580-0610
Dr. Mary Labrucherie, supt. Fax 575-1534
www.vallelindo.k12.ca.us

New Temple ES 700/K-4
11033 Central Ave 91733 626-580-0692
John Gannon, prin. Fax 580-0691

Shively MS 600/5-8
1431 Central Ave 91733 626-580-0610
Lynn Bulgin, prin. Fax 575-1534

Epiphany S 100/K-8
10915 Michael Hunt Dr 91733 626-442-6264
Gabriela Negrete, prin. Fax 442-6074

South Gate, Los Angeles, Pop. 94,017

Los Angeles USD
Supt. — See Los Angeles

Bryson ES 800/K-5
4470 Missouri Ave 90280 323-569-7141
April Diedrich, prin. Fax 567-5386

Independence ES 800/K-5
8435 Victoria Ave 90280 323-249-9559
Milday Quito, prin. Fax 564-9165

Liberty Boulevard ES 600/K-5
2728 Liberty Blvd 90280 323-583-4196
Reuben Rios, prin. Fax 589-5680

Madison ES 600/K-5
9820 Madison Ave 90280 323-568-3900
Gretchen Young, prin. Fax 357-0301

Montara Avenue ES 800/K-6
10018 Montara Ave 90280 323-567-1451
Juana Cortez, prin. Fax 249-7394
San Gabriel Avenue ES 600/K-5
8628 San Gabriel Ave 90280 323-567-1488
Elizabeth Martinez, prin. Fax 563-3762
San Miguel Avenue ES 1,100/K-5
9801 San Miguel Ave 90280 323-567-0511
Marcelino Diaz, prin. Fax 249-0997
Southeast MS 1,200/6-8
2560 Tweedy Blvd 90280 323-568-3100
Wanda Sequeira, prin. Fax 564-9398
South Gate MS 2,300/6-8
4100 Firestone Blvd 90280 323-568-4000
Salvador Torress, prin. Fax 564-7434
Stanford ES 600/K-5
2833 Illinois Ave 90280 323-569-8117
Mark Reiland, prin. Fax 569-1786
Stanford Primary Center 200/K-K
3020 Kansas Ave 90280 323-563-9208
Maria Tovares, prin. Fax 563-9225
State ES 600/K-5
3211 Santa Ana St 90280 323-582-7358
Susanne Fisher, prin. Fax 582-5981
Tweedy ES 700/K-5
9724 Pinehurst Ave 90280 323-568-2828
Angelina Ines, prin. Fax 249-1788
Victoria ES 500/K-5
3320 Missouri Ave 90280 323-567-1261
Laura Bazan, prin. Fax 563-2056
Willow ES 600/K-5
2777 Willow Pl 90280 323-568-5760
Gloria Buenrostro, prin. Fax 567-2369

Paramount USD
Supt. — See Paramount
Hollydale S 1,100/K-8
5511 Century Blvd 90280 562-602-8016
Lisa Nunley-Macon, prin. Fax 602-8017

Redeemer Lutheran S 100/PK-8
2626 Liberty Blvd 90280 323-588-0934
Elizabeth Payan, prin. Fax 588-0990
St. Helen S 200/PK-8
9329 Madison Ave 90280 323-566-5491
Kurt Spanel, prin. Fax 566-2810

South Lake Tahoe, El Dorado, Pop. 20,898
Lake Tahoe USD 3,900/PK-12
1021 Al Tahoe Blvd 96150 530-541-2850
Dr. James Tarwater, supt. Fax 541-5930
www.ltusd.org/
Bijou Community S 600/K-5
3501 Spruce Ave 96150 530-543-2337
Cindy Martinez, prin. Fax 543-2342
Lake Tahoe Environmental Sci Magnet S 400/K-5
1095 E San Bernardino Ave 96150 530-543-2371
Joel Damoral, prin. Fax 543-2375
Sierra House ES 500/K-5
1709 Remington Trl 96150 530-543-2327
Karin Holmes, prin. Fax 543-2330
South Tahoe MS 800/6-8
2940 Lake Tahoe Blvd 96150 530-541-6404
John Simons, prin. Fax 541-4624
Tahoe Valley ES 400/PK-5
943 Tahoe Island Dr 96150 530-543-2350
Christina Grubbs, prin. Fax 543-2362

South Pasadena, Los Angeles, Pop. 24,612
South Pasadena USD 4,700/PK-12
1020 El Centro St 91030 626-441-5810
Dr. Geoff Yantz, supt. Fax 441-5815
www.spusd.net
Arroyo Vista ES 700/PK-5
335 El Centro St 91030 626-441-5840
Cheryl Busick, prin. Fax 441-5845
Marengo ES 800/PK-5
1400 Marengo Ave 91030 626-441-5850
Patricia Cheadle, prin. Fax 441-5855
Monterey Hills ES 600/PK-5
1624 Via Del Rey 91030 626-441-5860
Dr. Laurie Narro, prin. Fax 441-5865
South Pasadena MS 1,100/6-8
1500 Fair Oaks Ave 91030 626-441-5830
Dave Kubela, prin. Fax 441-5835

Holy Family S 300/PK-8
1301 Rollin St 91030 626-799-4354
Dr. Frank Montejano, prin. Fax 403-6180

South San Francisco, San Mateo, Pop. 60,202
South San Francisco USD 9,200/K-12
398 B St 94080 650-877-8700
Shawnterra Moore, supt. Fax 583-4717
www.ssfusd.org
Alta Loma MS 800/6-8
116 Romney Ave 94080 650-877-8797
Lou Delorio, prin. Fax 877-8824
Buri Buri ES 600/K-5
325 Del Monte Ave 94080 650-877-8776
Victoria Dye, prin. Fax 583-5742
Los Cerritos ES 300/K-5
210 W Orange Ave 94080 650-877-8841
Kennelyn Celeste, prin. Fax 589-8093
Martin ES 400/K-5
35 School St 94080 650-877-3955
Jonathan Covacha, prin. Fax 877-3957
Parkway Heights MS 600/6-8
650 Sunset Ave 94080 650-877-8788
Marco Lopez, prin. Fax 225-9427
Ponderosa ES 400/K-5
295 Ponderosa Rd 94080 650-877-8825
Julie Erskine, prin. Fax 583-8275
Spruce ES 700/K-5
501 Spruce Ave 94080 650-877-8780
Israel Castillo, prin. Fax 589-9376
Sunshine Gardens ES 400/K-5
1200 Miller Ave 94080 650-877-8784
Shelby Biddy, prin. Fax 877-5285

Westborough MS 700/6-8
2570 Westborough Blvd 94080 650-877-8848
April Holland, prin. Fax 871-5356
Other Schools – See Daly City, San Bruno

All Souls S 300/PK-8
479 Miller Ave 94080 650-583-3562
Vincent Riener, prin. Fax 952-1167
Hillside Christian Academy 100/PK-8
1415 Hillside Blvd 94080 650-588-6860
Helen Yoo-Lee, prin. Fax 588-6827
St. Veronica S 300/K-8
434 Alida Way 94080 650-589-3909
Mary Boland, prin. Fax 589-2826

South San Gabriel, Los Angeles, Pop. 7,960
Montebello USD
Supt. — See Montebello
Potrero Heights ES 500/K-5
8026 Hill Dr, Rosemead CA 91770 626-307-7010
Lili Atoyan, prin. Fax 307-7013

Spreckels, Monterey, Pop. 663
Spreckels UNESD 1,000/K-8
PO Box 7362 93962 831-455-2550
Eric Tarallo Ed.D., supt. Fax 455-1871
www.spreckelsunionsd.org
Spreckels ES 600/K-5
PO Box 7308 93962 831-455-1831
Teresa Scherpinski Ed.D., prin. Fax 455-0786
Other Schools – See Salinas

Spring Valley, San Diego, Pop. 26,795
La Mesa-Spring Valley SD
Supt. — See La Mesa
Avondale ES 600/K-6
8401 Stansbury St 91977 619-668-5880
John Ashley, prin. Fax 668-8330
Bancroft ES 500/K-5
8805 Tyler St 91977 619-668-5890
Kimberly Libenguth, prin. Fax 668-8335
Casa De Oro ES 300/K-6
10227 Ramona Dr 91977 619-668-5715
Dana James, prin. Fax 668-8337
Highlands ES 500/K-6
3131 S Barcelona St 91977 619-668-5780
Jon McEvoy, prin. Fax 668-8320
Kempton Street Literacy Academy 700/K-3
740 Kempton St 91977 619-668-5870
Wendy Newmark, prin. Fax 668-8317
La Presa ES 500/K-6
519 La Presa Ave 91977 619-668-5790
Peter Dean, prin. Fax 668-8795
Loma ES 500/K-6
10355 Loma Ln 91978 619-668-5862
Elizabeth Rackliffe, prin. Fax 670-6830
Quest Academy 6-8
8805 Tyler St 91977 619-668-5890
Kimberly Libenguth, prin. Fax 668-8335
Rancho ES 500/K-6
8845 Noeline Ave 91977 619-668-5885
Dana Siegel, prin. Fax 668-8339
Spring Valley Academy 500/4-8
3900 Conrad Dr 91977 619-668-5750
Margaret Jacobsen, prin. Fax 668-8302
STEAM Academy @ La Presa 500/4-8
1001 Leland St 91977 619-668-5720
Mike Allmann, prin. Fax 668-8305
Sweetwater Springs Community ES 600/K-6
10129 Austin Dr 91977 619-668-5895
Monica Robinson, prin. Fax 668-8324

Santa Sophia Academy 200/PK-8
9806 San Juan St 91977 619-463-0488
Karen Laaperi, prin. Fax 668-5469
Trinity Christian S 100/PK-8
3902 Kenwood Dr 91977 619-462-6440
Sharon Axe, prin. Fax 462-4011

Springville, Tulare, Pop. 912
Springville UNESD 300/PK-8
PO Box 349 93265 559-539-2605
Connie Owens, supt. Fax 539-5616
www.springvilleschool.org/
Springville S 300/PK-8
PO Box 349 93265 559-539-2605
Connie Owens, supt. Fax 539-5616

Stanton, Orange, Pop. 37,275
Garden Grove USD
Supt. — See Garden Grove
ECC - Carver Campus PK-PK
11150 Santa Rosalia St 90680 714-663-6177
Sharla Staab, prin.

Magnolia ESD
Supt. — See Anaheim
Pyles STEM Academy 800/K-6
10411 Dale Ave 90680 714-761-6324
Dawn Breese, prin. Fax 229-5832

St. Polycarp S 200/K-8
8182 Chapman Ave 90680 714-893-8882
Alison Daley, prin. Fax 897-3357

Stevenson Ranch, Los Angeles, Pop. 16,902
Newhall ESD
Supt. — See Valencia
Pico Canyon ES 1,000/K-6
25255 Pico Canyon Rd 91381 661-291-4080
Tammi Rainville, prin. Fax 291-4081
Stevenson Ranch ES 800/K-6
25820 Carroll Ln 91381 661-291-4070
Chad Rose, prin. Fax 291-4071

William S. Hart UNHSD
Supt. — See Santa Clarita
Rancho Pico JHS 1,000/7-8
26250 Valencia Blvd 91381 661-284-3260
Erum Jones, prin. Fax 255-7523

Stevinson, Merced, Pop. 308
Hilmar USD
Supt. — See Hilmar
Merquin ES 200/K-5
20316 3rd Ave 95374 209-634-4938
Veronica Valdez Garcia, admin. Fax 634-1542

Stewarts Point, Sonoma
Kashia ESD 50/K-8
PO Box 129 95480 707-785-9682
Frances Johnson, supt. Fax 785-2802
kashiaelementaryschool.weebly.com
Kashia ES 50/K-8
PO Box 129 95480 707-785-9682
Frances Johnson, admin. Fax 785-2802

Stockton, San Joaquin, Pop. 279,493
Escalon USD
Supt. — See Escalon
Collegeville ES 100/K-5
6701 S Jack Tone Rd 95215 209-941-2007
Dawn Webster, prin. Fax 462-7126

Lincoln USD 9,200/PK-12
2010 W Swain Rd 95207 209-953-8700
Thomas Uslan, supt. Fax 474-7817
www.lusd.net
Barron S, 6835 Cumberland Pl 95219 800/K-8
Ellen Wehrs, prin. 209-953-8795
Brookside S 800/K-8
2962 Brookside Rd 95219 209-953-8642
Shane Conklin, prin. Fax 953-8640
Colonial Heights S 600/PK-8
8135 Balboa Ave 95209 209-953-8783
Nicole Merolla, prin. Fax 953-8785
Knoles S, 6511 Clarksburg Pl 95207 800/PK-8
Christina Pappas-Boettge, prin. 209-953-8776
Landeen S 600/K-8
4128 Feather River Dr 95219 209-953-8660
Veronica Tigert, prin. Fax 953-8821
Lincoln ES 700/PK-6
6910 Gettysburg Pl 95207 209-953-8652
Logan Williams, prin. Fax 953-8651
Riggio S 700/K-8
3110 Brookside Rd 95219 209-953-8753
Joan Calonico, prin. Fax 953-8823
Sierra MS 600/7-8
6768 Alexandria Pl 95207 209-953-8749
Scott Tatum, prin. Fax 953-8747
Williams ES 600/PK-6
2450 Meadow Ave 95207 209-953-8767
Nancy Martin, prin. Fax 952-4642

Linden USD
Supt. — See Linden
Glenwood ES 400/K-8
2005 N Alpine Rd 95215 209-931-3229
Wendy Heinze, prin. Fax 931-2612
Waterloo MS 400/5-8
7007 Pezzi Rd 95215 209-931-0818
Shannon Roberson, prin. Fax 931-2915
Waverly ES 300/K-8
3507 Wilmarth Rd 95215 209-931-0735
Jessica Riley, prin. Fax 931-3509

Lodi USD
Supt. — See Lodi
Adams ES 800/K-6
9275 Glacier Point Dr 95212 209-953-9601
Michael Coughlin, prin. Fax 953-9603
Clairmont ES 500/K-6
8282 Le Mans Ave 95210 209-953-8267
Annette Roberts, prin. Fax 953-8276
Creekside ES 500/PK-6
2515 Estate Dr 95209 209-953-8285
Yvette Shields, prin. Fax 953-8296
Davis ES 300/K-6
5224 E Morada Ln 95212 209-953-8301
Damon Auchard, prin. Fax 953-8304
Delta Sierra MS 400/7-8
2255 Wagner Heights Rd 95209 209-953-8510
Brad Watson, prin. Fax 953-8139
Elkhorn S 300/4-8
10505 Davis Rd 95209 209-953-8312
Pat White, prin. Fax 953-8319
McAuliffe MS 1,000/7-8
3880 Iron Canyon Cir 95209 209-953-9431
Pierre Kirby, prin. Fax 953-9430
Morada MS 700/7-8
5001 Eastview Dr 95212 209-953-8490
Janet Godina Perez, prin. Fax 953-8502
Morgan ES 600/K-6
3777 A G Spanos Blvd 95209 209-953-8453
Ruth McMaster, prin. Fax 953-8090
Mosher ES 600/K-6
3220 Buddy Holly Dr 95212 209-953-9298
Patti Cuenin, prin. Fax 953-3218
Muir ES 600/K-6
2303 Whistler Way 95209 209-953-8106
Eric Collins, prin. Fax 953-8110
Oakwood ES 500/PK-6
1315 Woodcreek Way 95209 209-953-8392
Richard Perez, prin. Fax 953-8004
Parklane ES 500/K-3
8405 Tam O Shanter Dr 95210 209-953-8410
Dara Chhun, prin. Fax 953-8084
Podesta Ranch ES 500/K-6
9950 Windmill Park Dr 95209 209-953-8543
Jann Lyall, prin. Fax 953-8547
Silva ES 900/K-6
6250 Scotts Creek Dr 95219 209-953-9302
Ben Koh, prin. Fax 953-9309
Sutherland ES 300/4-6
550 Spring River Cir 95210 209-953-8999
Harold Brown, prin. Fax 953-8031
Wagner-Holt ES 500/PK-6
8778 Brattle Pl 95209 209-953-8407
Jennifer Huiras, prin. Fax 953-8403
Westwood ES 600/PK-6
9444 Caywood Dr 95210 209-953-8333
Tim Shepherd, prin. Fax 953-8337

Manteca USD
Supt. — See Manteca
Great Valley Annex S 500/7-8
4550 Star Way 95206 209-938-6310
Patricia Boutte, prin. Fax 938-6383
Great Valley ES 900/K-6
4223 McDougald Blvd 95206 209-938-6300
Patricia Boutte, prin. Fax 938-6385
Knodt S 800/K-8
3939 Ews Woods Blvd 95206 209-938-6200
Sherryl Price, prin. Fax 938-6235
Komure S 1,000/K-8
2121 Henry Long Blvd 95206 209-938-6320
Jeff Podesto, prin. Fax 938-6398

Stockton USD 36,300/PK-12
701 N Madison St 95202 209-933-7000
Eliseo Davalos Ph.D., supt. Fax 933-7071
www.stocktonusd.net
Adams S 500/K-8
6402 Inglewood Ave 95207 209-933-7155
Sharon Womble, prin. Fax 952-9208
August S 700/K-8
2101 Sutro Ave 95205 209-933-7160
Lori Risso, prin. Fax 463-1179
Bush S 900/K-8
5420 Fred Russo Dr 95212 209-933-7350
Youlin Aissa, prin. Fax 473-9792
Cleveland S 700/K-8
20 E Fulton St 95204 209-933-7165
Heidi Mohammadkhan, prin. Fax 943-6592
El Dorado S 600/K-8
1540 N Lincoln St 95204 209-933-7175
Kristin Buckenham, prin. Fax 465-4358
Elmwood S 800/K-8
840 S Cardinal Ave 95215 209-933-7180
John Semillo, prin. Fax 465-1042
Fillmore S 800/K-8
2644 E Poplar St 95205 209-933-7185
Tamara Pronoitis, prin. Fax 467-3672
Fremont S 900/K-8
2021 E Flora St 95205 209-933-7385
Joseph Martinez, prin. Fax 462-3542
Grunsky S 600/K-8
1550 N School Ave 95205 209-933-7200
Michael Sousa, prin. Fax 467-3190
Hamilton S 900/K-8
2245 E 11th St 95206 209-933-7395
Dr. Mary Pedraza, prin. Fax 464-4851
Harrison S 600/K-8
3203 Sanguinetti Ln 95205 209-933-7205
Yanik Ruley, prin. Fax 948-3345
Hazelton S 600/K-6
535 W Jefferson St 95206 209-933-7210
Victor Zamora, prin. Fax 465-5925
Henry S 900/K-8
1107 S Wagner Ave 95215 209-933-7490
Kraig Jorgensen, prin. Fax 467-4640
Hong Kingston / Valenzuela S 900/K-8
6324 N Alturas Ave 95207 209-933-7493
Silvia Martinez, prin. Fax 478-3256
Hoover S 600/K-8
2900 Kirk St 95204 209-933-7215
Charlene Mah, prin. Fax 463-3094
Huerta S 500/K-8
1644 S Lincoln St 95206 209-933-7220
Valerie Standridge, prin. Fax 933-7221
Kennedy S 500/K-8
630 Ponce De Leon Ave 95210 209-933-7225
Chris Goodwin, prin. Fax 474-6449
King S 900/K-8
2640 E Lafayette St 95205 209-933-7230
Connie Fabian, prin. Fax 466-4528
Madison S 800/K-8
2939 Mission Rd 95204 209-933-7240
Essa Allred, prin. Fax 942-0426
Marshall S 600/K-8
1141 Lever Blvd 95206 209-933-7405
Eduardo Martir, prin. Fax 466-4962
McKinley S 800/K-8
30 W 9th St 95206 209-933-7245
Sonia Ambriz, prin. Fax 948-2260
Monroe S 500/K-8
2236 E 11th St 95206 209-933-7250
Mary Lou Rios, prin. Fax 948-2648
Montezuma S 700/K-8
2843 Farmington Rd 95205 209-933-7255
James Cowan, prin. Fax 465-4036
Peyton S 900/K-8
2525 Goldbrook Dr 95212 209-933-7420
Carla Gonzales, prin. Fax 476-0711
Primary Years Academy 300/K-5
1540 N Lincoln St 95204 209-933-7355
Shelly Spessard, prin. Fax 941-4580
Pulliam S 700/K-8
230 Presidio Way 95207 209-933-7265
Brittony Billingslea, prin. Fax 473-3540
Rio Calaveras S 1,000/K-8
1819 E Bianchi Rd 95210 209-933-7270
Gina Hall, prin. Fax 957-1769
Roosevelt S 500/K-8
776 S Broadway Ave 95205 209-933-7275
Ruben Garza, prin. Fax 946-0657
San Joaquin S 900/K-8
2020 S Fresno Ave 95206 209-933-7280
Vendetta Brown, prin. Fax 467-7057
Spanos S 500/K-8
536 S California St 95203 209-933-7335
Danielle Valtierra, prin. Fax 948-3122
Stockton Skills S 1,100/K-8
2725 Michigan Ave 95204 209-933-7170
Gina Lopez, prin. Fax 466-3711
Taft S 400/K-8
419 Downing Ave 95206 209-933-7285
Jana Brooks, prin. Fax 982-4257
Taylor S 500/K-8
1101 Lever Blvd 95206 209-933-7290
Conner Sloan, prin. Fax 462-7143
Tyler S 500/K-8
3830 Webster Ave 95204 209-933-7295
Henry Phillips, prin. Fax 943-7631
Van Buren S 600/K-8
1628 E 10th St 95206 209-933-7305
Keri Van De Star, prin. Fax 466-3705
Victory S 500/K-8
1838 W Rose St 95203 209-933-7310
Nancy Lane, prin. Fax 948-2559
Washington S 200/K-8
1735 W Sonora St 95203 209-933-7320
Shanna Laney, prin. Fax 943-6209
Wilson S 400/K-8
150 E Mendocino Ave 95204 209-933-7325
Suzanne Agbulos-Loera, prin. Fax 948-3480

Annunciation S 300/PK-8
1110 N Lincoln St 95203 209-444-4000
Beverly Fondacabe, prin. Fax 444-4013
Brookside Christian S 200/K-12
915 Rosemarie Ln 95207 209-954-7650
Jessica Carter, prin. Fax 954-7670
First Baptist Christian S 100/PK-8
3535 N El Dorado St 95204 209-466-1577
Stephanie Bulleri, prin. Fax 466-4337
Presentation S 300/PK-8
1635 W Benjamin Holt Dr 95207 209-472-2140
Maria Amen, prin. Fax 320-1515
St. George S 100/K-8
144 W 5th St 95206 209-463-1540
Deborah Fox, prin. Fax 463-2707
St. Luke S 200/PK-8
4005 N Sutter St 95204 209-464-0801
John Rieschick, prin. Fax 466-1150
Stockton Christian S 200/K-12
9021 West Ln 95210 209-957-3043
Tim Miller, prin. Fax 957-4120

Stonyford, Colusa, Pop. 144
Stony Creek JUSD
Supt. — See Elk Creek
Indian Valley ES 50/4-6
5180 Lodoga Stonyford Rd 95979 530-963-3210
Laurel Hill-Ward, prin. Fax 963-3047

Stratford, Kings, Pop. 1,272
Central UNESD
Supt. — See Lemoore
Stratford ES 300/PK-8
20227 1st St 93266 559-947-3391
Bill Bilbo, prin. Fax 947-3840

Strathmore, Tulare, Pop. 2,793
Strathmore UNESD 900/K-8
PO Box 247 93267 559-568-1283
Shelly Long Ed.D., supt. Fax 568-1262
www.suesd.k12.ca.us
Strathmore ES 500/K-4
PO Box 247 93267 559-568-2118
Joanie Stone, prin. Fax 568-1280
Strathmore MS 300/5-8
PO Box 247 93267 559-568-9293
Joanie Stone, prin. Fax 568-2944

Sunnyside UNESD 400/K-8
21644 Avenue 196 93267 559-568-1741
Steve Tsuboi, supt. Fax 568-0291
www.sunnysideunion.com
Sunnyside ES 400/K-8
21644 Avenue 196 93267 559-568-1741
Steve Tsuboi, prin. Fax 568-0291

Sugarloaf, San Bernardino
Bear Valley USD
Supt. — See Big Bear Lake
Baldwin Lane ES 500/PK-6
44500 Baldwin Ln 92386 909-585-7766
Melinda Peterson, prin. Fax 585-8135

Suisun City, Solano, Pop. 25,805
Fairfield-Suisun USD
Supt. — See Fairfield
Crescent ES 700/K-5
1001 Anderson Dr 94585 707-435-2771
Jodie Phan, prin. Fax 428-1536
Crystal MS 900/6-8
400 Whispering Bay Ln 94585 707-435-5800
Jay Dowd, prin. Fax 435-5806
Root ES 600/K-5
820 Harrier Dr 94585 707-421-4240
Julie Reece, prin. Fax 421-4298
Suisun ES 600/K-5
725 Golden Eye Way 94585 707-421-4210
Ann Marie Neubert, prin. Fax 421-3981
Suisun Valley S 500/K-8
4985 Lambert Rd, 707-421-4338
Jas Wright, prin. Fax 422-5710

Summerland, Santa Barbara, Pop. 1,412
Carpinteria USD
Supt. — See Carpinteria
Summerland ES 100/K-5
PO Box 460 93067 805-969-1011
Michelle Fox, prin. Fax 969-1524

Sunland, See Los Angeles
Los Angeles USD
Supt. — See Los Angeles
Apperson ES 400/K-5
10233 Woodward Ave 91040 818-353-5544
Rene Chavez, prin. Fax 951-6682
Mt. Gleason MS 1,000/6-8
10965 Mount Gleason Ave 91040 818-951-2580
Deborah Acosta, prin. Fax 352-6209
Sunland ES 500/K-5
8350 Hillrose St 91040 818-353-1631
Eduardo Carrillo, prin. Fax 951-3814

Sunnyvale, Santa Clara, Pop. 134,677
Cupertino UNSD 19,200/PK-8
1309 S Mary Ave 94087 408-252-3000
Dr. Craig Baker, supt. Fax 343-2801
www.cusdk8.org
Cupertino MS 1,400/6-8
1650 S Bernardo Ave 94087 408-245-0303
Mike Cellini, prin. Fax 732-4152
Nimitz ES 700/K-5
545 Cheyenne Dr 94087 408-736-2180
Kari Ito, prin. Fax 737-7182
Stocklmeir ES 1,200/K-5
592 Dunholme Way 94087 408-732-3363
Eric Witter, prin. Fax 738-5904
West Valley ES 600/K-5
1635 Belleville Way 94087 408-245-0148
Robin Robinson, prin. Fax 736-7543
Other Schools – See Cupertino, Los Altos, San Jose, Santa Clara, Saratoga

Santa Clara USD
Supt. — See Santa Clara
Braly ES 500/K-5
675 Gail Ave 94086 408-423-1000
Ryan Lee, prin. Fax 423-1080
Peterson MS 900/6-8
1380 Rosalia Ave 94087 408-423-2800
Susan Harris, prin. Fax 423-2880
Ponderosa ES 600/K-5
804 Ponderosa Ave 94086 408-423-4000
Alissa Meltzer, prin. Fax 423-4080

Sunnyvale ESD 6,800/K-8
PO Box 3217 94088 408-522-8200
Benjamin Picard Ed.D., supt. Fax 522-8221
www.sesd.org
Bishop ES 600/K-5
450 N Sunnyvale Ave 94085 408-522-8229
Suzanne Cicala, prin. Fax 522-8238
Cherry Chase ES 900/K-5
1138 Heatherstone Way 94087 408-522-8241
Allison White, prin. Fax 522-4679
Columbia MS 700/6-8
739 Morse Ave 94085 408-522-8247
Mary Beth Allmann, prin. Fax 522-8254
Cumberland ES 700/K-5
824 Cumberland Dr 94087 408-522-8255
Edith Mourtos, prin. Fax 522-8314
Ellis ES 800/K-5
550 E Olive Ave 94086 408-522-8260
Eric Panosian, prin. Fax 522-8232
Fairwood ES 400/K-5
1110 Fairwood Ave 94089 408-523-4870
Rachelle Romander, prin. Fax 523-4873
Lakewood ES 500/K-5
750 Lakechime Dr 94089 408-522-8272
Pamela Cheng, prin. Fax 522-8276
San Miguel ES 400/K-5
777 San Miguel Ave 94085 408-522-8279
Brenda Guy, prin. Fax 522-8328
Sunnyvale MS 1,200/6-8
1080 Mango Ave 94087 408-522-8288
Nabil Shahin, prin. Fax 522-8296
Vargas ES 500/K-5
1054 Carson Dr 94086 408-522-8267
Kathryn Armstrong, prin. Fax 522-8308

Challenger S 500/PK-8
1185 Hollenbeck Ave 94087 408-245-7170
Deepali Deshmukh, hdmstr.
French American S of Silicon Valley 100/K-5
1522 Lewiston Dr 94087 408-746-0460
Helios S 100/K-8
597 Central Ave 94086 408-475-1024
Patti Wilczek Ph.D., head sch Fax 618-8527
Rainbow Montessori S 400/PK-6
790 E Duane Ave 94085 408-738-3261
Spyroula Rodenborn, prin. Fax 738-0239
Resurrection S 200/PK-8
1395 Hollenbeck Ave 94087 408-245-4571
Jacque Wright, prin. Fax 733-7301
South Penninsula Hebrew S 200/PK-8
1030 Astoria Dr 94087 408-738-3060
Stratford S - Sunnyvale De Anza 500/PK-5
1196 Lime Dr 94087 408-732-4424
Laura Morgan, head sch
Stratford S - Sunnyvale Raynor MS 6-8
1500 Partridge Ave 94087 408-247-4400
Becky Turner, prin.
Stratford S - Washington Park 400/PK-5
820 W Mc Kinley Ave 94086 408-737-1500
Laura Morgan, head sch Fax 737-1511
Sunnyvale Christian S 100/PK-5
445 S Mary Ave 94086 408-736-3286
Leanna Christie, prin. Fax 736-3549

Sunol, Alameda, Pop. 862
Sunol Glen USD 300/K-8
11601 Main St 94586 925-862-2026
Molleen Barnes, supt. Fax 862-0127
www.sunol.k12.ca.us
Sunol Glen ES 300/K-8
11601 Main St 94586 925-862-2026
Molleen Barnes, prin. Fax 862-0127

Sun Valley, See Los Angeles
Los Angeles USD
Supt. — See Los Angeles
Byrd MS 1,700/6-8
8501 Arleta Ave 91352 818-394-4300
Deborah Wiltz, prin. Fax 768-1837
Fernangeles ES 700/K-5
12001 Art St 91352 818-767-0380
Anna Martinez, prin. Fax 504-9905
Glenwood ES 500/K-5
8001 Ledge Ave 91352 818-767-6406
Claudia Ruiz, prin. Fax 504-8081
Roscoe ES 700/K-5
10765 Strathern St 91352 818-767-3018
Beatriz Smissen, prin. Fax 504-1597
Stonehurst Avenue ES 300/K-5
9851 Stonehurst Ave 91352 818-767-8014
John Dargahi, prin. Fax 768-7564
Sun Valley MS 1,000/6-8
7330 Bakman Ave 91352 818-255-5100
Roberto Lee, prin. Fax 503-9846
Vinedale ES 200/K-5
10150 La Tuna Canyon Rd 91352 818-767-0106
Aurora Arreola, prin. Fax 768-2452

Our Lady of the Holy Rosary S 200/PK-8
7802 Vineland Ave 91352 818-765-4897
Sr. Maria Aguilar, prin. Fax 765-5791
Village Christian ES 300/PK-5
8930 Village Ave 91352 818-767-8382
Village Christian MS 200/6-8
8930 Village Ave 91352 818-767-8382

Susanville, Lassen, Pop. 17,110
Johnstonville ESD 200/K-8
704-795 Bangham Ln 96130 530-257-2471
Dr. Danny Whetton, supt. Fax 251-5557
www.johnstonville.org
Johnstonville ES 200/K-8
704-795 Bangham Ln 96130 530-257-2471
Dr. Danny Whetton, admin. Fax 251-5557

Richmond ESD 200/K-8
700-585 Richmond Rd E 96130 530-257-2338
Vicky Leitaker, supt. Fax 257-6398
www.richmondelementary.com
Richmond ES 200/K-8
700-585 Richmond Rd E 96130 530-257-2338
Vicky Leitaker, prin. Fax 257-6398

Susanville ESD 1,000/K-8
109 S Gilman St 96130 530-257-8200
Jason Waddell, supt. Fax 257-8246
www.susanvillesd.org
Diamond View MS 300/6-8
850 Richmond Rd 96130 530-257-5144
Jamie Huber, prin. Fax 257-7232
McKinley ES 400/K-2
2005 4th St 96130 530-257-5161
Lynn Parker, prin. Fax 257-4967
Meadow View ES 400/3-5
1200 Paiute Ln 96130 530-257-3000
Charlotte Klinock, prin. Fax 257-2631

Susanville Adventist Christian S 50/K-8
455 Cedar St 96130 530-257-5045
Dona Dunbar, head sch

Sutter, Sutter, Pop. 2,803
Brittan ESD 400/PK-8
2340 Pepper St 95982 530-822-5155
Staci Kaelin, supt. Fax 822-5143
www.brittan.k12.ca.us/
Brittan S 400/PK-8
2340 Pepper St 95982 530-822-5155
Staci Kaelin, supt. Fax 822-5143

Sutter Creek, Amador, Pop. 2,442
Amador County USD
Supt. — See Jackson
Sutter Creek ES 200/4-6
340 Spanish St 95685 209-257-7200
Sean Snider, prin. Fax 267-1231
Sutter Creek PS 200/K-3
110 Broad St 95685 209-257-7100
Sean Snider, prin. Fax 267-9210

Sylmar, See Los Angeles
Los Angeles USD
Supt. — See Los Angeles
Brainard ES 200/K-5
11407 Brainard Ave 91342 818-899-5241
Jacqueline Shehab, prin. Fax 890-9991
Dyer Street ES 800/K-5
14500 Dyer St 91342 818-367-1932
Ernestina Gandera, prin. Fax 364-1913
El Dorado Avenue ES 600/K-5
12749 El Dorado Ave 91342 818-367-5816
Adan Martinez, prin. Fax 362-6576
Harding Street ES 500/K-5
13060 Harding St 91342 818-365-9237
Laura Fuentes, prin. Fax 365-0759
Herrick Avenue ES 600/K-5
13350 Herrick Ave 91342 818-367-1864
Jose Dorado, prin. Fax 364-9304
Hubbard Street ES 700/K-5
13325 Hubbard St 91342 818-367-1944
Joseph Casas, prin. Fax 362-7495
Olive Vista MS 1,200/6-8
14600 Tyler St 91342 818-833-3900
Rodney Wright, prin. Fax 367-8273
Osceola Street ES 300/K-5
14940 Osceola St 91342 818-362-1556
Joseph Velasquez, prin. Fax 362-8456
Sylmar ES 600/K-5
13291 Phillippi Ave 91342 818-367-1078
Julie Maravilla, prin. Fax 362-4844
Sylmar Leadership Academy 1,000/K-8
14550 Bledsoe St 91342 818-367-1300
Suellen Helm Torres, prin. Fax 367-8603

Delphi Academy of Los Angeles 200/PK-12
11341 Brainard Ave 91342 818-583-1070
Karen Dale, head sch Fax 583-1082
St. Didacus S 200/PK-8
14325 Astoria St 91342 818-367-5886
Krishana Gonzales, prin. Fax 364-5486

Taft, Kern, Pop. 9,099
Taft CSD 2,000/K-8
820 6th St 93268 661-763-1521
Julie Graves, supt. Fax 763-1495
www.taftcityschools.org
Conley ES 200/K-3
623 Rose Ave 93268 661-765-4117
Lisa Kindred, prin. Fax 765-2065
Jefferson ES 200/K-3
318 Taylor St 93268 661-763-4236
Heather Ward, prin. Fax 763-3054
Lincoln JHS 600/6-8
810 6th St 93268 661-765-2127
Brandi Swearengin, prin. Fax 763-3970
Parkview ES 000/K-3
520 A St 93268 661-763-4164
Lisa Kindred, prin. Fax 763-3020
Roosevelt ES 400/2-5
811 6th St 93268 661-763-3113
Lavona Callaghan, prin. Fax 763-3732
Taft PS 200/K-3
212 Lucard St 93268 661-765-4151
Heather Ward, prin. Fax 763-3783

Tahoe City, Placer, Pop. 1,643
Tahoe Truckee USD
Supt. — See Truckee
North Tahoe S 400/5-8
PO Box 794 96145 530-581-7050
Chad Lindeen, prin. Fax 581-1237
Tahoe Lake ES 300/K-4
PO Box 856 96145 530-582-2700
Stephanie Welsh-Foucek, prin. Fax 583-7623

Tarzana, See Los Angeles
Los Angeles USD
Supt. — See Los Angeles
Portola MS 1,800/6-8
18720 Linnet St 91356 818-654-3300
Jungun Yoo, prin. Fax 996-0292
Tarzana ES 500/K-5
5726 Topeka Dr 91356 818-881-1424
Vicki Lee, prin. Fax 343-4418
Vanalden Early Education Center PK-PK
6212 Vanalden Ave 91335 818-343-5595
Johanna Curd, prin. Fax 996-0353

Intl S of Los Angeles - West Valley 100/PK-5
5933 Lindley Ave 91356 818-345-0155
Sebastien Pelletier, dir. Fax 345-7355
Woodcrest S 200/K-8
6043 Tampa Ave Ste 101A 91356 818-345-3002
Luanne Paglione, prin. Fax 345-7880

Tecate, San Diego

Tecate Christian S 100/1-6
PO Box 1000 91980 619-468-3355
Diane Lyles, prin. Fax 478-5910

Tecopa, Inyo, Pop. 134
Death Valley USD
Supt. — See Shoshone
Tecopa-Francis ES 50/K-6
1555 Old Spanish Trail Hwy 92389 760-852-4303
Craig Hill, prin. Fax 852-4395

Tehachapi, Kern, Pop. 14,166
Tehachapi USD 4,200/K-12
300 S Robinson St 93561 661-822-2100
Susan Andreas-Bervel, supt. Fax 822-2159
www.teh.k12.ca.us
Cummings Valley ES 600/K-5
24220 Bear Valley Rd 93561 661-822-2190
Traci Minjares, prin. Fax 822-2128
Golden Hills ES 600/K-5
20215 Park Rd 93561 661-822-2180
Kendra Bailey, prin. Fax 822-2185
Jacobsen MS 900/6-8
711 Anita Dr 93561 661-822-2150
Paul Kaminski, prin. Fax 822-2156
Tompkins ES 700/K-5
1120 S Curry St 93561 661-822-2170
Cheri Belcoe, prin. Fax 822-2198

Heritage Oak S 100/K-12
20915 Schout Rd 93561 661-823-0885
Amy Walker, head sch Fax 823-0863

Temecula, Riverside, Pop. 95,946
Temecula Valley USD 29,900/K-12
31350 Rancho Vista Rd 92592 951-676-2661
Timothy Ritter, supt. Fax 695-7121
www.tvusd.k12.ca.us
Barnett ES 900/K-5
39925 Harveston Dr 92591 951-296-5579
Dr. Amber Lane, prin. Fax 296-9029
Crowne Hill ES 700/K-5
33535 Old Kent Rd 92592 951-294-6370
Kathi Eiseler, prin. Fax 294-6373
Day MS 1,000/6-8
40775 Camino Campos Verde 92591 951-699-8138
Rob Sousa, prin. Fax 699-4198
Gardner MS 1,100/6-8
45125 Via Del Coronado 92592 951-699-0080
Michael McTasney, prin. Fax 699-0081
Jackson ES 400/K-5
32400 Camino San Dimas 92592 951-302-5199
James Evans, prin. Fax 302-6643
Margarita MS 900/6-8
30600 Margarita Rd 92591 951-695-7370
Duane Legg, prin. Fax 695-7378
Nicolas Valley ES 800/K-5
39600 N General Kearny Rd 92591 951-695-7180
Chrissy Lansing, prin. Fax 695-7186
Paloma ES 600/K-5
42940 Via Rami 92592 951-302-5165
Kelly Gradstein, prin. Fax 302-5176
Pauba Valley ES 600/K-5
33125 Regina Dr 92592 951-302-5140
Shelley Maxwell, prin. Fax 302-5146
Rancho ES 500/K-5
31530 La Serena Way 92591 951-695-7150
Pam May, prin. Fax 695-7154
Red Hawk ES 500/K-5
32045 Camino San Jose 92592 951-302-5125
Leilani Russi, prin. Fax 302-5133
Reinke ES 900/K-5
43799 Sunny Meadows Dr 92592 951-302-6610
Jon Cole, prin. Fax 302-6616
Temecula ES 600/K-5
41951 Moraga Rd 92591 951-695-7130
Sandra McKay, prin. Fax 695-7137
Temecula Luiseno ES 1,000/K-5
45754 Wolf Creek Dr N 92592 951-294-6340
Tim Dignan, prin. Fax 294-6343
Temecula MS 1,000/6-8
42075 Meadows Pkwy 92592 951-302-5151
Marvin Morton, prin. Fax 302-5160
Tobin ES 900/K-5
45200 Morgan Hl 92592 951-294-6355
Kristin Larson, prin. Fax 294-6358
Vail ES 600/K-5
29835 Mira Loma Dr 92592 951-695-7140
Jona Hazlett, prin. Fax 695-7148
Vail Ranch MS 1,300/6-8
33340 Camino Piedra Rojo 92592 951-302-5188
Kevin Groepper, prin. Fax 302-5195
Vintage Hills ES 700/K-5
42240 Camino Romo 92592 951-695-4260
Kelli Sunderland, prin. Fax 695-4268
Other Schools – See Murrieta, Winchester

Concord Lutheran Academy 50/K-8
29581 N General Kearny Rd 92591 951-699-8463
Patrick Walker M.S., prin.
Linfield Christian S 700/PK-12
31950 Pauba Rd 92592 951-676-8111
Drake Charles, head sch Fax 695-1291
Oakhill Academy PK-8
29275 Santiago Rd 92592 951-506-0944
Maria Sweeney, head sch
Rancho Christian S 500/PK-12
31300 Rancho Community Way 92592 951-303-1408
Betsy Kunau, dir. Fax 302-1580
St. Jeanne de Lestonnac S 500/PK-8
32650 Avenida Lestonnac 92592 951-587-2505
Annette Zaleski, prin. Fax 587-2515
Van Avery Preparatory S 400/K-8
29851 Santiago Rd 92592 951-506-3123
Angela Pena, prin.

Temple City, Los Angeles, Pop. 34,921
El Monte City SD
Supt. — See El Monte
Cloninson ES 400/K-6
5213 Daleview Ave 91780 626-575-2327
Dr. Carlos Salcedo, prin. Fax 443-8661

Temple City USD 5,900/K-12
9700 Las Tunas Dr 91780 626-548-5000
Kathryn Perini, supt. Fax 548-5022
www.tcusd.net
Cloverly ES 500/4-6
5476 Cloverly Ave 91780 626-548-5092
Stephen Edo, prin. Fax 548-5095
La Rosa ES 600/K-3
9301 La Rosa Dr 91780 626-548-5076
Jason Rose, prin. Fax 548-5081
Longden ES 1,000/K-6
9501 Wendon St 91780 626-548-5068
Nancy Hong, prin. Fax 548-5175
Oak Avenue IS 1,000/7-8
6623 Oak Ave 91780 626-548-5060
Lawton Gray, prin. Fax 548-5170
Other Schools – See San Gabriel

St. Luke S 200/K-8
5521 Cloverly Ave 91780 626-291-5959
Yvette Jefferys, prin. Fax 865-5367

Templeton, San Luis Obispo, Pop. 7,486
Templeton USD 2,400/PK-12
960 Old County Rd 93465 805-434-5800
Joe Koski, supt. Fax 434-5879
tusd.ca.schoolloop.com/
Templeton ES 600/PK-2
215 8th St 93465 805-434-5820
Renee Argain, prin. Fax 434-5811
Templeton MS 500/6-8
925 Old County Rd 93465 805-434-5813
Kristina Benson, prin. Fax 434-5812
Vineyard ES 500/3-5
2121 Vineyard Dr 93465 805-434-5840
Laura Brooks, prin. Fax 434-3105

Templeton Hills Christian S 50/K-8
PO Box 70 93465 805-434-1638
Steven Champion, prin. Fax 434-1638

Terra Bella, Tulare, Pop. 3,287
Saucelito ESD 100/K-8
17615 Avenue 104 93270 559-784-2164
Cynthia Lamb, supt. Fax 784-7109
www.tcoe.org/Districts/Saucelito.shtm
Saucelito ES 100/K-8
17615 Avenue 104 93270 559-784-2164
Cynthia Lamb, prin. Fax 784-7109

Terra Bella UNESD 900/PK-8
9121 Road 240 93270 559-535-4451
Guadalupe Roman, supt. Fax 535-0314
www.tbuesd.org
Smith MS 300/6-8
23825 Avenue 92 93270 559-535-4451
Guadalupe Roman, prin. Fax 535-0829
Terra Bella ES 600/PK-5
9364 Road 238 93270 559-535-4451
Juan Flores, prin. Fax 535-4457

Zion Lutheran S 50/K-8
10368 Road 256 93270 559-535-4346
Stephanie Bamsch, head sch

Thermal, Riverside, Pop. 2,856
Coachella Valley USD 18,700/K-12
PO Box 847 92274 760-399-5137
Dr. Edwin Gomez, supt. Fax 399-1052
www.cvusd.us
Kelley ES 600/K-6
87163 Center St 92274 760-399-5101
Mary Lou Padilla, prin. Fax 399-1427
Las Palmitas ES 700/K-6
86150 Avenue 66 92274 760-397-2200
Michael Williams, prin. Fax 397-8790

Oasis ES 700/K-6
88175 74th Ave 92274 760-397-4112
Dora Flores, prin. Fax 397-0192
Toro Canyon MS 1,100/7-8
86150 Avenue 66 92274 760-397-2244
Charles Housewright, prin. Fax 397-8760
Westside ES 600/K-6
82225 Airport Blvd 92274 760-399-5171
Rosemary Hyder, prin. Fax 399-1284
Other Schools – See Coachella, Indio, Mecca, Salton City

Thornton, San Joaquin, Pop. 1,115
New Hope ESD 200/K-8
PO Box 238 95686 209-794-2376
Janet Stemler, supt. Fax 794-2230
nhesd-ca.schoolloop.com
New Hope ES 200/K-8
PO Box 238 95686 209-794-2376
Janet Stemler, admin. Fax 794-2230

Thousand Oaks, Ventura, Pop. 122,978
Conejo Valley USD 20,200/PK-12
1400 E Janss Rd 91362 805-497-9511
Mark McLaughlin Ed.D., supt. Fax 371-9170
www.conejousd.org
Acacia ES 400/K-5
55 W Norman Ave 91360 805-495-5550
Kirsten Walker, prin. Fax 374-1156
Aspen ES 400/K-5
1870 Oberlin Ave 91360 805-495-2810
Paula Golem, prin. Fax 374-1157
Colina MS 1,100/6-8
1500 E Hillcrest Dr 91362 805-495-7429
Shane Frank, prin. Fax 374-1163
Conejo ES 400/K-5
280 N Conejo School Rd 91362 805-495-7058
Kari Taketa, prin. Fax 374-1158
Glenwood ES 400/K-5
1135 Windsor Dr 91360 805-495-2118
Vivian Vina, prin. Fax 374-1159
Ladera ES 300/K-5
1211 Calle Almendro 91360 805-492-3565
Lori Wall, prin. Fax 493-8851
Lang Ranch ES 700/K-5
2450 Whitechapel Pl 91362 805-241-4417
Dena Sellers, prin. Fax 241-4617
Los Cerritos MS 900/6-8
2100 E Ave De Las Flores 91362 805-492-3538
Jason Klinger, prin. Fax 493-8854
Madrona ES 500/K-5
612 Camino Manzanas 91360 805-498-6102
Amy Simmons-Folkes, prin. Fax 375-5601
Redwood MS 1,000/6-8
233 W Gainsborough Rd 91360 805-497-7264
Shauna Ashmore, prin. Fax 497-3734
Weathersfield ES 400/K-5
3151 Darlington Dr 91360 805-492-3563
Laurie Davis, prin. Fax 492-4452
Wildwood ES 400/K-5
620 Velarde Dr 91360 805-492-3531
Donna Vollmer, prin. Fax 493-8855
Wonder Preschool 100/PK-PK
2801 Atlas Ave 91360 805-492-3567
Tobey Shaw, prin.
Other Schools – See Newbury Park, Westlake Village

Ascension Lutheran S 200/PK-8
1600 E Hillcrest Dr 91362 805-496-2419
Karen Jonas, prin. Fax 495-7249
Bethany Christian S 200/PK-8
200 Bethany Ct 91360 805-497-7072
Tara Morrow, prin. Fax 494-4879
Conejo Jewish Day S 100/K-8
1080 E Janss Rd 91360 805-494-7217
Hillcrest Christian S 300/PK-12
384 Erbes Rd 91362 805-497-7501
Kathy Horan J.D., prin. Fax 494-9355
Honey Tree ECC 200/PK-K
1 W Avenida De Los Arboles 91360 805-492-1232
Sherri Schuler, dir. Fax 493-5390
St. Paschal Baylon S 300/K-8
154 E Janss Rd 91360 805-495-9340
Suzanne Duffy, prin. Fax 778-1509
St. Patrick's Day S 100/K-6
1 Church Rd 91362 805-497-1416
Nancy Whitson, head sch Fax 496-8331
Trinity Pacific Christian S 400/K-12
3389 Camino Calandria 91360 805-492-0863
Barbara Richert, admin.

Thousand Palms, Riverside, Pop. 7,606
Palm Springs USD
Supt. — See Palm Springs
Lindley ES 600/K-5
31495 Robert Rd 92276 760-343-7570
Denise Fenton, prin. Fax 343-7576

Three Rivers, Tulare, Pop. 2,120
Three Rivers UNESD 200/K-8
PO Box 99 93271 559-561-4466
Susan Sherwood, supt. Fax 561-4468
www.3rusd.org
Three Rivers ES 200/K-8
PO Box 99 93271 559-561-4466
Susan Sherwood, prin. Fax 561-4468

Tiburon, Marin, Pop. 8,606
Reed UNESD 1,600/K-8
277 Karen Way Ste A 94920 415-381-1112
Nancy Lynch Ed.D., supt. Fax 384-0890
www.reedschools.org
Bel Aire ES 500/3-5
277 Karen Way 94920 415-388-7100
Alexis Cala, prin. Fax 388-7176
Del Mar MS 500/6-8
105 Avenida Miraflores 94920 415-435-1468
Brian Lynch, prin. Fax 435-6190
Reed ES 500/K-2
1199 Tiburon Blvd 94920 415-435-7840
Dr. Mary Niesyn, prin. Fax 435-7853

St. Hilary S 200/K-8
765 Hilary Dr 94920 415-435-2224
Marie Bordeleau, prin. Fax 435-5895

Tipton, Tulare, Pop. 2,533
Tipton ESD 600/K-8
PO Box 787 93272 559-752-4213
Anthony Hernandez, supt. Fax 752-1230
www.tiptonschool.org
Tipton ES 600/K-8
PO Box 787 93272 559-752-4213
Stacey Bettencourt, prin. Fax 687-2221

Tollhouse, Fresno
Sierra USD
Supt. — See Prather
Sierra JHS 200/7-8
33326 Lodge Rd 93667 559-855-8311
Sean Osterberg, prin. Fax 855-2162

Tomales, Marin, Pop. 200
Shoreline USD 600/K-12
PO Box 198 94971 707-878-2266
Bob Raines, supt. Fax 878-2554
www.shorelineunified.org
Tomales ES 200/K-8
PO Box 14 94971 707-878-2214
Amanda Mattea, prin. Fax 878-2467
Other Schools – See Bodega Bay, Inverness, Point Reyes Station

Torrance, Los Angeles, Pop. 138,782
Los Angeles USD
Supt. — See Los Angeles
Halldale ES 600/K-5
21514 Halldale Ave 90501 310-328-3100
Deborah Evers Allen, prin. Fax 328-7928
Meyler ES 800/K-5
1123 W 223rd St 90502 310-328-3910
Elizabeth Pratt, prin. Fax 787-9116
Van Deene ES 400/K-6
826 Javelin St 90502 310-320-8680
Jennifer Cheng, prin. Fax 782-6537

Torrance USD 24,100/PK-12
2335 Plaza Del Amo 90501 310-972-6500
Dr. George Mannon Ed.D., supt. Fax 972-6012
www.tusd.org
Adams ES 500/K-5
2121 W 238th St 90501 310-533-4480
Shayla Smith-Taranto, prin. Fax 972-6385
Anza ES 700/K-5
21400 Ellinwood Dr 90503 310-533-4559
Barbara Marks, prin. Fax 972-6386
Arlington ES 600/K-5
17800 Van Ness Ave 90504 310-533-4510
Dr. Vicki Hath, prin. Fax 972-6387
Arnold ES 700/K-5
4100 W 227th St 90505 310-533-4524
Justine Lang, prin. Fax 972-6388
Calle Mayor MS 800/6-8
4800 Calle Mayor 90505 310-533-4548
David Mosley, prin. Fax 972-6389
Carr ES 400/K-5
3404 W 168th St 90504 310-533-4467
Katherine Schenkelberg, prin. Fax 972-6390
Casimir MS 700/6-8
17220 Casimir Ave 90504 310-533-4498
Susan Holmes, prin. Fax 972-6391
Edison ES 500/K-5
3800 W 182nd St 90504 310-533-4513
Jayne Okazaki, prin. Fax 972-6392
Fern ES 600/K-5
1314 Fern Ave 90503 310-533-4506
Debbie Mabry, prin. Fax 972-6393
Hickory ES 900/K-5
2800 W 227th St 90505 310-533-4672
Edna Schumacher, prin. Fax 972-6396
Hull MS 700/6-8
2080 W 231st St 90501 310-533-4516
Patty Girgis, prin. Fax 972-6397
Jefferson MS 600/6-8
21717 Talisman St 90503 310-533-4794
Yvonne Marin, prin. Fax 972-6398
Launch Preschool 100/PK-PK
4000 W 227th St 90505 310-533-4769
Dr. Teresa Lanphere, prin. Fax 381-1330
Lincoln ES 400/K-5
2418 W 166th St 90504 310-533-4464
Katherine Castleberry, prin. Fax 972-6400
Lynn MS 700/6-8
5038 Halison St 90503 310-533-4495
Leroy Jackson, prin. Fax 972-6401
Madrona MS 700/6-8
21364 Madrona Ave 90503 310-533-4562
Chris Lipsey, prin. Fax 972-6402
Magruder MS 600/6-8
4100 W 185th St 90504 310-533-4527
Lisa Nunes, prin. Fax 972-6403
Richardson MS 700/6-8
23751 Nancylee Ln 90505 310-533-4790
Ian Drummond, prin. Fax 972-6405
Riviera ES 700/K-5
365 Paseo De Arena 90505 310-533-4460
Christie Forshey, prin. Fax 972-6406
Seaside ES 600/K-5
4651 Sharynne Ln 90505 310-533-4532
Michele Bauer, prin. Fax 972-6407
Torrance ES 500/K-5
2125 Lincoln Ave 90501 310-533-4500
Dr. Kelly Joseph, prin. Fax 972-6453
Towers ES 600/K-5
5600 Towers St 90503 310-533-4535
Sandra Skora, prin. Fax 972-6456
Victor ES 1,000/K-5
4820 Spencer St 90503 310-533-4542
William Baker, prin. Fax 972-6457
Walteria ES 600/K-5
24456 Madison St 90505 310-533-4487
Efren Ponce, prin. Fax 972-6458
Wood ES 400/K-5
2250 W 235th St 90501 310-533-4484
Dr. Shawn Johnson, prin. Fax 972-6484
Yukon ES 300/K-5
17815 Yukon Ave 90504 310-533-4477
Elaine Wassil, prin. Fax 972-6485

Ascension Lutheran S 100/PK-8
17910 Prairie Ave 90504 310-371-3531
Paul Brege, prin. Fax 214-4657
First Lutheran S 400/PK-8
2900 W Carson St 90503 310-320-9920
Tammy Kirkpatrick, prin. Fax 320-1963
Hickory Tree S 100/K-5
21720 Madrona Ave 90503 310-533-4830
Jennifer Walla, dir.
Nativity S 200/PK-8
2371 W Carson St 90501 310-328-5387
Dr. Michelle Wechsler, prin. Fax 328-5365
St. Catherine Laboure S 400/PK-8
3846 Redondo Beach Blvd 90504 310-324-8732
Jennifer Bagheri, prin. Fax 324-2471
St. James S 300/K-8
4625 Garnet St 90503 310-371-0416
Sr. Mary Margaret Krueper, prin. Fax 371-8377
South Bay Junior Academy 200/PK-10
4400 Del Amo Blvd 90503 310-370-6215
Susan Vlach, prin. Fax 793-8665

Trabuco Canyon, Orange
Capistrano USD
Supt. — See San Juan Capistrano
Wagon Wheel ES 600/K-5
30912 Bridle Path 92679 949-589-1953
Jean Grabowski, prin. Fax 589-2813

Saddleback Valley USD
Supt. — See Mission Viejo
Portola Hills ES 800/K-6
19422 Saddleback Ranch Rd 92679 949-459-9370
Joe Ledoux, prin. Fax 459-9376
Robinson ES 600/K-6
21400 Lindsay Dr 92679 949-589-2446
Jonathan Kaplan, prin. Fax 589-1374
Trabuco ES 100/K-6
31052 Trabuco Canyon Rd 92678 949-858-0343
Lisa Paisley, prin. Fax 858-9188

Tracy, San Joaquin, Pop. 78,298
Banta ESD 700/K-8
22375 El Rancho Rd 95304 209-229-4651
Albert Garibaldi, supt. Fax 835-9851
bantaesd.net
Banta ES 300/K-8
22345 El Rancho Rd 95304 209-229-4650
Rechelle Pearlman, prin. Fax 835-0319

Jefferson ESD 2,400/K-8
1219 Whispering Wind Dr 95377 209-836-3388
James W. Bridges Ed.D., supt. Fax 836-2930
www.jeffersonschooldistrict.com
Hawkins ES 800/K-8
475 Darlene Ln 95377 209-839-2380
Christina Orsi, prin. Fax 839-2384
Jefferson S 400/5-8
7500 W Linne Rd 95304 209-835-3053
Alyssa Wooten, prin. Fax 835-4419
Monticello ES 400/K-4
1001 Cambridge Ln 95377 209-833-9300
Emily Stroup, prin. Fax 833-9317
Traina ES 800/K-8
4256 Windsong Dr 95377 209-839-2379
Ken Silman, prin. Fax 839-2314

Lammersville USD
Supt. — See Mountain House
Lammersville ES 200/K-8
16555 Von Sosten Rd 95304 209-836-7220
Irene Busuttil, prin. Fax 836-7222

Tracy JUSD 17,300/K-12
1875 W Lowell Ave 95376 209-830-3200
Brian Stephens, supt. Fax 830-3204
www.tracy.k12.ca.us
Bohn ES 500/K-5
350 E Mount Diablo Ave 95376 209-830-3300
Lemuel Vergara, prin. Fax 830-3301
Central ES 500/K-5
1370 Parker Ave 95376 209-830-3303
Nancy Link, prin. Fax 830-3304
Freiler S 1,000/K-8
2421 W Lowell Ave 95377 209-830-3309
Karen Alcorn, prin. Fax 830-3310
Hirsch ES 600/K-5
1280 Dove Dr 95376 209-830-3312
Cindy Sasser, prin. Fax 830-3313
Jacobson ES 600/K-5
1750 W Kavanagh Ave 95376 209-830-3315
Tania Salinas, prin. Fax 830-3316
Kelly S 1,100/K-8
535 Mabel Josephine Dr 95377 209-830-3390
Jeanine Wilson, prin. Fax 830-3391
McKinley ES 400/K-5
800 W Carlton Way 95376 209-830-3319
Carla Washington, prin. Fax 830-3320
Monte Vista MS 900/6-8
751 W Lowell Ave 95376 209-830-3340
Barbara Silver, prin. Fax 830-3341
North S 800/K-8
2875 Holly Dr 95376 209-830-3350
Mayte Ramirez, prin. Fax 830-3351
Poet-Christian S 600/K-8
1701 S Central Ave 95376 209-830-3325
William Masylar, prin. Fax 830-3326
South/West Park ES 900/K-5
501 Mount Oso Ave 95376 209-830-3335
Ramona Soto, prin. Fax 830-3336
Villalovoz ES 600/K-5
1550 Cypress Dr 95376 209-830-3331
Shameram Karim, prin. Fax 830-3332

Williams MS 1,100/6-8
1600 Tennis Ln 95376 209-830-3345
Barbara Montgomery, prin. Fax 830-3346

Bella Vista Christian Academy 300/PK-8
1635 Chester Dr 95376 209-835-7438
Jonathan Heinemann M.Ed., prin. Fax 835-7951

Montessori S of Tracy 300/PK-6
100 S Tracy Blvd 95376 209-833-3458

St. Bernard S 300/PK-8
165 W Eaton Ave 95376 209-835-8018
Patricia Paredes, prin. Fax 835-2496

Tracy SDA Christian ES 50/K-8
126 W 21st St 95376 209-835-6607
Jim Beierle, prin. Fax 835-3036

West Valley Christian Academy 200/PK-8
1790 Sequoia Blvd 95376 209-832-4072
Teresa Smith, prin. Fax 832-4073

Tranquillity, Fresno, Pop. 794

Golden Plains USD
Supt. — See San Joaquin

Tranquillity S 200/K-8
PO Box 337 93668 559-698-5517
Matthew Kinnunen, prin. Fax 698-5546

Traver, Tulare, Pop. 708

Traver JESD 200/K-8
PO Box 69 93673 559-897-2755
Steve Ramirez, supt. Fax 897-0239
www.travermustangs.com/

Traver ES 200/K-8
PO Box 69 93673 559-897-0236
Steve Ramirez, admin. Fax 897-0239

Travis AFB, See Fairfield

Travis USD
Supt. — See Fairfield

Scandia ES 600/K-6
100 Broadway St 94535 707-437-4691
Mark Pennington, prin. Fax 437-9234

Travis ES 500/K-6
100 Fairfield Ave 94535 707-437-2070
Deanna Yasaki, prin. Fax 437-2687

Tres Pinos, San Benito, Pop. 474

Tres Pinos UNESD 100/PK-8
PO Box 188 95075 831-637-0503
Bronson Mendes-LoBue, supt. Fax 637-9423
www.trespinosschool.org/

Tres Pinos ES 100/PK-8
PO Box 188 95075 831-637-0503
Bronson Mendes-LoBue, prin. Fax 637-9423

Trinidad, Humboldt, Pop. 353

Big Lagoon UNESD 100/PK-8
269 Big Lagoon Park Rd 95570 707-677-3688
Jennifer Glueck, supt. Fax 677-3642
www.humboldt.k12.ca.us/blagoon_sd

Big Lagoon ES 100/PK-8
269 Big Lagoon Park Rd 95570 707-677-3688
Jennifer Glueck, prin. Fax 677-3642

Trinidad UNSD 200/K-8
PO Box 3030 95570 707-677-3631
Matthew Malkus, supt. Fax 677-0954
www.humboldt.k12.ca.us/trinidad_sd

Trinidad Union S 200/K-8
PO Box 3030 95570 707-677-3631
Matthew Malkus, prin. Fax 677-0954

Trinity Center, Trinity, Pop. 261

Coffee Creek ESD 50/K-8
HC 2 Box 4740 96091 530-266-3344
Ed Traverso, supt. Fax 266-3344
www.coffeecreekesd.org/

Coffee Creek S 50/K-8
HC 2 Box 4740 96091 530-266-3344
Ed Traverso, prin. Fax 266-3344

Trinity Center ESD 50/K-8
PO Box 127 96091 530-266-3342
Carole Havens, supt. Fax 266-3381
www.trinitycenterschool.org

Trinity Center ES 50/K-8
PO Box 127 96091 530-266-3342
Carole Havens, prin. Fax 266-3381

Trona, San Bernardino, Pop. 18

Trona JUSD 200/K-12
83600 Trona Rd 93562 760-372-2861
Keith Tomes, supt. Fax 372-4534
www.trona.k12.ca.us

Trona ES 100/K-6
83600 Trona Rd 93562 760-372-2868
Alan Tsubota, prin. Fax 372-5519

Truckee, Nevada, Pop. 15,914

Tahoe Truckee USD 3,900/K-12
11603 Donner Pass Rd 96161 530-582-2500
Robert Leri Ed.D., supt. Fax 582-7606
www.ttusd.org

Alder Creek MS 500/6-8
10931 Alder Dr 96161 530-582-2750
Hein Larson, prin. Fax 582-7640

Glenshire ES 500/K-5
10990 Dorchester Dr 96161 530-582-3720
Kerstin Kramer, prin. Fax 582-7676

Truckee ES 500/K-5
11911 Donner Pass Rd 96161 530-582-2650
Valerie Simpson, prin. Fax 582-7696

Other Schools – See Kings Beach, Kingvale, Tahoe City

Tujunga, See Los Angeles

Los Angeles USD
Supt. — See Los Angeles

Mountain View ES 400/K-5
6410 Olcott St 91042 818-352-1616
Richard Guillen, prin. Fax 951-9286

Pinewood Early Education Center PK-PK
7051 Valmont St 91042 818-352-4469
Rachel Mermell, prin. Fax 353-2753

Pinewood ES 300/K-5
10111 Silverton Ave 91042 818-353-2515
Patrizia Puccio, prin. Fax 353-3179

Our Lady of Lourdes S 200/K-8
7324 Apperson St 91042 818-353-1106
Jennifer Reynaga, prin. Fax 951-4276

Tulare, Tulare, Pop. 58,086

Buena Vista ESD 200/K-8
21660 Road 60 93274 559-686-2015
Carole Mederos, supt. Fax 684-0932
buenavistaeagles.org

Buena Vista ES 200/K-8
21660 Road 60 93274 559-686-2015
Carole Mederos, prin. Fax 684-0932

Liberty ESD 400/K-8
1771 E Pacific Ave 93274 559-686-1675
Keri Montoya, supt. Fax 686-2879
www.liberty.k12.ca.us

Liberty ES 400/K-8
1771 E Pacific Ave 93274 559-686-1675
Keri Montoya, prin. Fax 686-2879

Oak Valley UNESD 500/K-8
24500 Road 68 93274 559-688-2908
Fernie Marroquin M.A., supt. Fax 688-8023
www.oakvalleyschool.org/

Oak Valley Union S 500/K-8
24500 Road 68 93274 559-688-2908
Kelli Ruby M.Ed., prin. Fax 688-8023

Palo Verde UNESD 500/PK-8
9637 Avenue 196 93274 559-688-0648
Ernie Flores, supt. Fax 688-0640
pvuesd-ca.schoolloop.com

Palo Verde Union S 500/PK-8
9637 Avenue 196 93274 559-688-0648
Ernie Flores, prin. Fax 688-0640

Sundale UNESD 800/K-8
13990 Avenue 240 93274 559-688-7451
Terri Rufert, supt. Fax 688-5905
suesd-ca.schoolloop.com

Sundale ES 800/K-8
13990 Avenue 240 93274 559-688-7451
Cindy Gist, prin. Fax 688-5905

Tulare CSD 9,500/K-8
600 N Cherry St 93274 559-685-7200
Clare Gist Ed.D., supt. Fax 685-7287
www.tcsdk8.org/

Alpine Vista S 700/K-8
2975 E Alpine Ave 93274 559-687-3135
Terri Martindale, prin.

Cherry Avenue MS 700/6-8
540 N Cherry St 93274 559-685-7320
Greg Anderson, prin. Fax 685-5621

Cypress ES 500/K-5
1870 S Laspina St 93274 559-685-7290
Gary Bates, prin. Fax 685-7299

Garden ES 700/K-6
640 E Pleasant Ave 93274 559-685-7330
Debbie Portillo, prin. Fax 685-7336

Heritage ES 600/K-6
895 W Gail Ave 93274 559-685-7360
Elaine Sewell, prin. Fax 685-7369

Kohn ES 600/K-6
500 S Laspina St 93274 559-685-7340
Whitney Gallegos, prin. Fax 685-7344

Lincoln ES 300/K-6
909 E Cedar Ave 93274 559-685-7350
Don Dargo, prin. Fax 685-7355

Live Oak MS 600/7-8
980 N Laspina St 93274 559-685-7310
Michelle McPhetridge, prin. Fax 685-7313

Los Tules MS 600/6-8
801 W Gail Ave 93274 559-687-3156
Mark Thompson, prin. Fax 685-7374

Maple ES 800/K-5
640 W Cross Ave 93274 559-685-7270
Valerie Brown, prin. Fax 685-7337

Mission Valley ES 900/K-6
1695 Bella Oaks Dr 93274 559-685-7396
Gary Yentes, prin. Fax 685-7392

Mulcahy MS 700/5-8
1001 W Sonora Ave 93274 559-685-7250
Tracey Jenkins, prin. Fax 687-6412

Pleasant ES 700/K-5
1855 W Pleasant Ave 93274 559-685-7300
Tara Houston, prin. Fax 687-6413

Roosevelt ES 600/K-4
1046 W Sonora Ave 93274 559-685-7280
Anthony Felix, prin. Fax 685-7386

Wilson ES 400/K-5
955 E Tulare Ave 93274 559-685-7260
John Pendleton, prin. Fax 687-6414

Waukena JUNESD 300/K-8
19113 Road 28 93274 559-686-3328
Terri Lancaster, supt. Fax 686-8136
www.tcoe.org/Districts/Waukena.shtm

Waukena Joint Union ES 300/K-8
19113 Road 28 93274 559-686-3328
Terri Lancaster, supt. Fax 686-8136

St. Aloysius S 200/K-8
627 N Beatrice Dr 93274 559-686-6250
Luan Sozinho, prin. Fax 686-0479

Tulelake, Siskiyou, Pop. 985

Tulelake Basin JUSD 500/K-12
PO Box 640 96134 530-667-2295
Bryce Brin, supt. Fax 667-4298
www.tulelake.k12.ca.us

Tulelake Basin ES 300/K-6
PO Box 610 96134 530-667-2294
Dennis Butler, prin. Fax 667-3448

Tuolumne, Tuolumne

Summerville ESD 400/PK-8
18451 Carter St 95379 209-928-4291
Leigh Shampain, supt. Fax 928-1602
www.sumel.k12.ca.us

Summerville ES 400/PK-8
18451 Carter St 95379 209-928-4291
Mitch Heldstab, prin. Fax 928-1602

Mother Lode Christian S 100/PK-8
18393 Gardner Ave 95379 209-928-4126
Rachel Talavera-Dean, prin. Fax 928-4613

Tupman, Kern, Pop. 151

Elk Hills ESD 200/K-8
PO Box 129 93276 661-765-7431
Jeff Tensley, supt. Fax 765-4583
www.elkhills.k12.ca.us

Elk Hills S 200/K-8
PO Box 129 93276 661-765-7431
Jeff Tensley, prin. Fax 765-4583

Turlock, Stanislaus, Pop. 66,239

Chatom UNESD 600/PK-8
7201 Clayton Rd 95380 209-664-8505
Cherise Olvera, supt. Fax 664-8508
www.chatom.k12.ca.us

Chatom ES 400/PK-5
7221 Clayton Rd 95380 209-664-8500
Chanda Rowley, prin. Fax 664-8520

Other Schools – See Crows Landing

Turlock USD 13,900/K-12
PO Box 819013 95381 209-667-0632
Dana Trevethan Ed.D., supt. Fax 667-6520
www.turlock.k12.ca.us

Brown ES 600/K-6
1400 Georgetown Ave 95382 209-634-7231
Nicole Aviles, prin. Fax 668-3584

Crowell ES 800/K-6
118 North Ave 95382 209-667-0885
Margaret Osmer, prin. Fax 668-3631

Cunningham ES 800/K-6
324 W Linwood Ave 95380 209-667-0794
Tami Truax, prin. Fax 668-3730

Dutcher MS 700/7-8
1441 Colorado Ave 95380 209-667-8817
Scott Lucas, prin. Fax 667-1332

Earl ES 900/K-6
4091 N Olive Ave 95382 209-634-1090
Laura Fong, prin. Fax 634-6750

Julien ES 800/K-6
1924 E Canal Dr 95380 209-667-0891
Angela Freeman, prin. Fax 668-3782

Medeiros ES 800/K-6
651 W Springer Dr 95382 209-668-9600
Dr. Anna Epperson, prin. Fax 668-4669

Osborn Two-Way Immersion Academy 900/K-6
201 N Soderquist Rd 95380 209-667-0893
Ed Ewing, prin. Fax 668-3910

Turlock JHS 1,300/7-8
3951 N Walnut Rd 95382 209-667-0881
Robert Ruiz, prin. Fax 668-3985

Wakefield ES 700/K-6
400 South Ave 95380 209-667-0895
Luisa Salinas, prin. Fax 668-3945

Walnut Elementary Education Center 900/K-6
4219 N Walnut Rd 95382 209-664-9907
Sumeet Singh, prin. Fax 664-9970

Sacred Heart S - Turlock 200/PK-8
1225 Cooper Ave 95380 209-634-7787
Linda Murphy-Lopes, prin. Fax 634-0156

Turlock Christian ES 200/K-6
PO Box 1540 95381 209-632-6250
Pamela Hanson, prin. Fax 632-5721

Tustin, Orange, Pop. 73,165

Tustin USD 23,400/K-12
300 S C St 92780 714-730-7305
Dr. Gregory Franklin Ed.D., supt. Fax 730-7436
www.tustin.k12.ca.us

Benson ES 300/K-5
12712 Elizabeth Way 92780 714-730-7531
Jackie Christy, prin. Fax 730-7368

Beswick ES 700/K-5
1362 Mitchell Ave 92780 714-730-7385
Ryan Bollenbach, prin. Fax 730-7387

Columbus Tustin MS 900/6-8
17952 Beneta Way 92780 714-730-7352
Maggie Burdette, prin. Fax 730-7512

Currie MS 700/6-8
1402 Sycamore Ave 92780 714-730-7360
Erick Fineberg, prin. Fax 730-7603

Estock ES 400/K-5
14741 N B St 92780 714-730-7390
Wendy Hudson, prin. Fax 730-7562

Heideman ES 600/K-5
15571 Williams St 92780 714-730-7521
Sean Lindsay, prin. Fax 558-3820

Heritage ES K-5
15400 Lansdowne Rd 92782 714-430-2066
Beth Blackman, prin.

Ladera ES 400/K-5
2515 Rawlings Way 92782 714-730-7505
Dr. Jennifer Harrison Ed.D., prin. Fax 734-0193

Nelson ES 600/K-5
14392 Browning Ave 92780 714-730-7536
Melinda Smith, prin. Fax 730-7557

Peters Canyon ES 500/K-5
26900 Peters Canyon Rd 92782 714-730-7540
Brooke Carreras, prin. Fax 838-3385

Pioneer MS 1,300/6-8
2700 Pioneer Rd 92782 714-730-7534
Tracey Vander Hayden, prin. Fax 730-5405

Thorman ES 600/K-5
1402 Sycamore Ave 92780 714-730-7364
Deanna Parks, prin. Fax 730-7593

Tustin Ranch ES 700/K-5
12950 Robinson Dr 92782 714-730-7580
Tracy Barquer, prin. Fax 508-1654

Utt MS 1,000/6-8
13601 Browning Ave 92780 714-730-7573
Dr. C.K. Green Ed.D., prin. Fax 750-7576
Veeh ES 500/K-5
1701 San Juan St 92780 714-730-7544
Rafael Plascencia, prin. Fax 505-4615
Other Schools – See Irvine, Santa Ana

Grace Harbor ES 100/PK-6
12881 Newport Ave 92780 714-544-4431
Kathleen DeSantis, prin. Fax 544-5738
Red Hill Lutheran S 500/PK-8
13200 Red Hill Ave 92780 714-544-3132
Paul Marquardt, prin. Fax 544-8176
St. Cecilia S 300/PK-8
1311 Sycamore Ave 92780 714-544-1533
Mary Alvarado, prin. Fax 544-0643
St. Jeanne De Lestonnac S 500/PK-8
16791 E Main St 92780 714-542-4271
Sr. Cecilia Duran, prin. Fax 542-0644
Spirit Christian Academy 200/K-12
1372 Irvine Blvd 92780 714-731-2630

Twain Harte, Tuolumne, Pop. 2,173
Twain Harte SD 100/PK-8
22974 Twain Harte Dr 95383 209-586-3772
Rick Hennes, supt. Fax 586-9938
www.thsd.k12.ca.us
Twain Harte S 100/PK-8
18815 Manzanita Dr 95383 209-586-3266
Dan Mayers, prin. Fax 586-3975

Twentynine Palms, San Bernardino, Pop. 23,540
Morongo USD 8,500/K-12
PO Box 1209 92277 760-367-9191
Tom Baumgarten, supt. Fax 367-7189
www.morongousd.com
Condor ES 600/K-6
2551 Condor Rd 92277 760-367-0750
Paul Gattuso, prin. Fax 368-1144
Oasis ES 600/K-6
73175 El Paseo Dr 92277 760-367-3595
Cheryl Koeller-Hopton, prin. Fax 367-2103
Palm Vista ES 300/K-6
74350 Baseline Rd 92277 760-367-7538
Dr. Cynthia Dunn, prin. Fax 367-6766
Twentynine Palms ES 600/K-6
74350 Playa Vista Dr 92277 760-367-3545
Megan Pfau, prin. Fax 367-9801
Twentynine Palms JHS 500/7-8
5798 Utah Trl 92277 760-367-9507
Stacy Smalling, prin. Fax 367-0742
Other Schools – See Joshua Tree, Landers, Morongo Valley, Yucca Valley

Twin Peaks, San Bernardino

Lake Arrowhead Christian S 100/K-12
PO Box 870 92391 909-337-3739
Linda Huffman M.Ed., prin. Fax 337-4550

Ukiah, Mendocino, Pop. 15,561
Ukiah USD 6,400/PK-12
511 S Orchard Ave 95482 707-472-5000
Debra Kubin, supt. Fax 463-2120
www.uusd.net
Calpella ES 500/K-4
151 W Moore St 95482 707-472-5630
Tina Burrell, prin. Fax 485-0965
Hudson ES 500/K-5
251 Jefferson Ln 95482 707-472-5460
Kara Mikesell, prin. Fax 463-3814
Nokomis ES 400/K-5
495 Washington Ave 95482 707-472-5550
John McCann, prin. Fax 468-3305
Oak Manor ES 400/K-6
400 Oak Manor Dr 95482 707-472-5180
Rachel Prosser, prin. Fax 462-6223
Pomolita MS 800/6-8
740 N Spring St 95482 707-472-5350
Bryan Barrett, prin. Fax 463-5203
Yokayo ES 500/K-6
790 S Dora St 95482 707-463-5236
Dana Milani, prin. Fax 472-5690
Zeek ES 400/K-6
1060 N Bush St 95482 707-472-5100
Dara Brown, prin. Fax 468-3421
Other Schools – See Redwood Valley

Instilling Goodness Developing Virtue S 100/K-12
2001 Talmage Rd 95482 707-468-3896
Jin Jr Shi, prin.
St. Mary of the Angels S 200/K-8
991 S Dora St 95482 707-462-3888
Mary Thomas, prin. Fax 462-6014
Ukiah Junior Academy 100/K-10
180 Stipp Ln 95482 707-462-6350
Eric Stubbert, prin. Fax 462-4026

Union City, Alameda, Pop. 65,266
New Haven USD 12,400/PK-12
34200 Alvarado Niles Rd 94587 510-471-1100
Dr. Arlando Smith, supt. Fax 471-7108
www.mynhusd.org
Alvarado ES 900/PK-5
31100 Fredi St 94587 510-471-1039
Marcus Lam, prin. Fax 471-9414
Chavez MS 1,300/6-8
2801 Hop Ranch Rd 94587 510-487-1700
Ramon Camacho, prin. Fax 475-3938
Eastin ES 900/PK-5
34901 Eastin Dr 94587 510-475-9630
Carla Victor, prin. Fax 475-9638
Emanuele ES 700/PK-5
100 Decoto Rd 94587 510-471-2461
Clinton Puckett, prin. Fax 471-8799
Itliong-Vera Cruz MS 1,400/6-8
31604 Alvarado Blvd 94587 510-489-0700
Heather Thorner, prin. Fax 475-3936
Kitayama ES 900/PK-5
1959 Sunsprite Dr 94587 510-475-3982
Mikey McKelvey, prin. Fax 475-3989
Pioneer ES 900/PK-5
32737 Bel Aire St 94587 510-487-4530
Jeanette Alday, prin. Fax 487-0313
Searles ES 700/PK-5
33629 15th St 94587 510-471-2772
Raquel Bocage, prin. Fax 471-8420
Other Schools – See Hayward

Upland, San Bernardino, Pop. 71,871
Upland USD 11,700/PK-12
390 N Euclid Ave 91786 909-985-1864
Nancy Kelly Ed.D., supt. Fax 949-7872
www.upland.k12.ca.us
Baldy View ES 700/K-6
979 W 11th St 91786 909-982-2564
Albert Cahueque, prin. Fax 949-7712
Cabrillo ES 800/K-6
1562 W 11th St 91786 909-985-2619
Whitnee Verdi, prin. Fax 982-5511
Citrus ES 700/K-6
925 W 7th St 91786 909-949-7731
Mario Carranza, prin. Fax 949-7733
Foothill Knolls STEM Acad of Innovation 400/PK-8
1245 Veterans Ct 91786 909-949-7740
Michelle Wavering, prin. Fax 949-7744
Magnolia ES 600/K-6
465 W 15th St 91786 909-949-7750
Deborah Davis, prin. Fax 949-7752
Pepper Tree ES 800/K-6
1045 W 18th St 91784 909-949-9635
Dionthe Cusimano, prin. Fax 949-7763
Pioneer JHS 900/7-8
245 W 18th St 91784 909-949-7770
Aaron Dover, prin. Fax 949-7778
Sierra Vista ES 400/K-6
253 E 14th St 91786 909-949-7780
Stacey Wickum, prin. Fax 982-2659
Sycamore ES 500/K-6
1075 W 13th St 91786 909-982-0347
Ji Wang, prin. Fax 949-7792
Upland ES 600/K-6
601 5th Ave 91786 909-949-7800
Glenda Levesque, prin. Fax 946-9764
Upland JHS 900/7-8
444 E 11th St 91786 909-949-7810
Richie Vega, prin. Fax 949-7817
Valencia ES 600/K-6
541 W 22nd St 91784 909-949-7830
Heather Smith, prin. Fax 949-7837

Carden Arbor View S 200/K-8
1530 N San Antonio Ave 91786 909-982-9919
Cathy Edwards, hdmstr. Fax 981-3221
St. Joseph S 300/K-8
905 N Campus Ave 91786 909-920-5185
Sandra Alamo-Ng, prin. Fax 920-5190
St. Mark's Episcopal S 200/PK-8
330 E 16th St 91784 909-920-5565
Mark Ravelli, head sch Fax 920-5569

Upper Lake, Lake, Pop. 1,026
Upper Lake USD 800/K-12
675 Clover Valley Rd 95485 707-275-2655
Dr. Giovanni H. Annous, supt. Fax 275-9750
www.ulusd.org
Upper Lake MS 200/6-8
725 Old Lucorno Rd 95485 707-275-0223
Don Boyd, prin. Fax 275-2911
Upper Lake Union ES 400/K-5
679 2nd St 95485 707-275-2357
Stephanie Wayment, prin. Fax 275-2205

Vacaville, Solano, Pop. 87,007
Travis USD
Supt. — See Fairfield
Cambridge ES 600/K-6
100 Cambridge Dr 95687 707-446-9494
Susan Nader, prin. Fax 448-4942
Foxboro ES 700/K-6
600 Morning Glory Dr 95687 707-447-7883
Samantha Chizauskie, prin. Fax 447-6055

Vacaville USD 12,900/K-12
401 Nut Tree Rd 95687 707-453-6100
Jane Shamieh, supt. Fax 453-7114
www.vacavilleusd.org
Alamo ES 700/K-6
500 S Orchard Ave 95688 707-453-6200
Derek Wickliff, prin. Fax 446-2834
Browns Valley ES 1,000/K-6
333 Wrentham Dr 95688 707-453-6205
Jennifer Austin, prin. Fax 447-5307
Callison ES 1,000/K-6
6261 Vanden Rd 95687 707-453-6250
Jeff Crane, prin. Fax 446-3729
Cooper ES 900/K-6
750 Christine Dr 95687 707-453-6210
Tina Ahn, prin. Fax 447-5041
Hemlock ES 300/K-6
400 Hemlock St 95688 707-453-6245
Jennifer Buzolich, prin. Fax 448-7933
Jepson MS 900/7-8
580 Elder St 95688 707-453-6280
Adam Wight, prin. Fax 447-7128
Markham ES 800/K-6
101 Markham Ave 95688 707-453-6230
Rafael Soler, prin. Fax 453-0668
Orchard ES 400/K-6
805 N Orchard Ave 95688 707-453-6255
Ken Ratti, prin. Fax 453-7169
Padan ES 600/K-6
200 Padan School Rd 95687 707-453-6235
Ramiro Barron, prin. Fax 448-3748
Sierra Vista ES 400/K-8
301 Bel Air Dr 95687 707-453-6260
Catherine Bozzini, prin. Fax 449-1810
Vaca Pena MS 900/7-8
200 Keith Way 95687 707-453-6270
Ramon Cusi, prin. Fax 451-9501

Bethany Lutheran S 200/PK-8
1011 Ulatis Dr 95687 707-451-6683
Dr. Chris Smith, prin. Fax 359-2230
Notre Dame S 300/K-8
1781 Marshall Rd 95687 707-447-1460
Susan Walls, prin. Fax 447-1498
Vacaville Adventist Christian S 50/1-8
4740 Allendale Rd 95688 707-448-2842
Nancy Matthews B.A., prin. Fax 448-9717
Vacaville Christian S 1,000/PK-12
1117 Davis St 95687 707-446-1776
Paul Harrell, head sch Fax 446-1538

Valencia, See Santa Clarita
Castaic UNSD 2,700/K-8
28131 Livingston Ave 91355 661-257-4500
Steven Doyle, supt. Fax 257-3596
castaicusd.com
Other Schools – See Castaic

Newhall ESD 6,800/K-6
25375 Orchard Village Rd 91355 661-291-4000
Paul Cordeiro, supt. Fax 291-4001
www.newhallschooldistrict.net
Meadows ES 600/K-6
25577 Fedala Rd 91355 661-291-4050
Kim Sorenson, prin. Fax 291-4051
Oak Hills ES 600/K-6
26730 Old Rock Rd, 661-291-4100
Luis Gamarra, prin. Fax 291-4102
Old Orchard ES 500/K-6
25141 Avenida Rondel 91355 661-291-4040
Ken Hintz, prin. Fax 291-4041
Valencia Valley ES 700/K-6
23601 Carrizo Dr 91355 661-291-4060
Amanda Montemayor, prin. Fax 291-4061
Other Schools – See Newhall, Stevenson Ranch

Saugus UNESD
Supt. — See Santa Clarita
Helmers ES 800/K-6
27300 Grandview Dr 91354 661-294-5345
Pete Bland, prin. Fax 286-4391
North Park ES 800/K-6
23335 W Sunset Hills Dr 91354 661-294-5370
Vicki Kubasak, prin. Fax 297-1480
Tesoro del Valle ES 600/K-6
29171 N Bernardo Way 91354 661-294-5380
Paul Martinsen, prin. Fax 294-1461
West Creek Academy 700/K-6
28767 N West Hills Dr 91354 661-294-5385
Susan Bett, prin. Fax 294-1932

William S. Hart UNHSD
Supt. — See Santa Clarita
Arroyo Seco JHS 1,300/7-8
27171 Vista Delgado Dr 91354 661-296-0991
Andy Keyne, prin. Fax 296-3436

Legacy Christian Academy 400/K-8
27680 Dickason Dr 91355 661-257-7377
Matthew Millett, head sch Fax 257-7370
Trinity Classical Academy 200/PK-12
28310 Kelly Johnson Pkwy 91355 661-296-2601
Liz Caddow, head sch Fax 607-0664

Valinda, Los Angeles, Pop. 22,597
Hacienda La Puente USD
Supt. — See City of Industry
Grandview College Preparatory Academy 700/K-8
795 Grandview Ln, La Puente CA 91744
626-933-5801
Cynthia Herrera, prin. Fax 855-3824
Wing Lane ES 300/K-5
16605 Wing Ln, La Puente CA 91744 626-933-5901
Tabitha Blanton, prin. Fax 855-3797

Vallejo, Solano, Pop. 108,826
Vallejo City USD 14,600/K-12
665 Walnut Ave 94592 707-556-8921
Dr. Adam Clark, supt. Fax 649-3907
www.vallejo.k12.ca.us
Beverly Hills ES 300/K-5
1450 Coronel Ave 94591 707-556-8400
Tamara Madson, prin. Fax 638-0438
Cave Dual Language Academy 200/K-5
770 Tregaskis Ave 94591 707-556-8410
Lorena Hernandez, prin. Fax 638-0491
Cooper ES 600/K-5
612 Del Mar Ave 94589 707-556-8420
Tony Gross, prin. Fax 638-0459
Federal Terrace ES 400/K-5
415 Daniels Ave 94590 707-556-8460
Marisa Carbonell, prin. Fax 638-0406
Franklin MS, 501 Starr Ave 94590 700/6-8
Dr. Michelle Jordan-Faucett, prin. 707-556-8470
Glen Cove ES 500/K-5
501 Glen Cove Pkwy 94591 707-556-8491
Roxanne Tuggle, prin. Fax 638-3585
Highland ES 600/K-5
1309 Ensign Ave 94590 707-556-8500
Amy Parangan, prin. Fax 638-3514
Hogan MS 1,100/6-8
850 Rosewood Ave 94591 707-556-8510
Rosalind Hines, prin. Fax 638-3504
Lincoln ES 200/K-5
620 Carolina St 94590 707-556-8540
Sandra Nahal, prin. Fax 638-0348
Loma Vista Environmental Science Academy 500/K-8
146 Rainier Ave 94589 707-556-8550
Britt Hammon, prin. Fax 638-3589
Mare Island Health & Fitness Academy 400/K-6
400 Rickover St 94592 707-556-8560
Rhonda Coyle, prin. Fax 638-3557
Mini ES, 1530 Lorenzo Dr 94589 500/K-5
Heather Topacio, prin. 707-556-8570

Patterson ES, 1080 Porter St 94590 400/K-5
Megan De La Mater, prin. 707-556-8580
Pennycook ES 600/K-5
3620 Fernwood St 94591 707-556-8590
Kim Mitchell-Lewis, prin. Fax 638-0386
Solano MS 700/6-8
1025 Corcoran Ave 94589 707-556-8600
Shayla Bowman, prin. Fax 638-0379
Steffan Manor ES, 815 Cedar St 94591 700/K-5
Roland Davis, prin. 707-556-8640
Wardlaw ES 900/K-5
1698 Oakwood Ave 94591 707-556-8730
Juli Robbins, prin. Fax 556-8739
Widenmann ES 500/K-5
100 Whitney Ave 94589 707-556-8740
Pamela Hatter, prin. Fax 638-3596

North Hills Christian S 300/PK-12
200 Admiral Callaghan Ln 94591 707-644-5284
Florence Wright, supt. Fax 644-5295
St. Basil S 400/PK-8
1230 Nebraska St 94590 707-642-7629
Julia Boen, prin. Fax 642-8635
St. Catherine of Sienna S 300/K-8
3460 Tennessee St 94591 707-643-6691
Christine Walsh, prin. Fax 647-4441
St. Vincent Ferrer S 300/PK-8
411 Kentucky St 94590 707-642-4311
Jessica Dare, prin. Fax 642-1329

Valley Center, San Diego, Pop. 9,007
Valley Center-Pauma USD 4,200/K-12
28751 Cole Grade Rd 92082 760-749-0464
Mary Gorsuch, supt. Fax 749-1208
www.vcpusd.net
Lilac ES 600/K-5
28751 Cole Grade Rd 92082 760-751-1042
Maria Cordero, prin. Fax 751-7407
Valley Center ES 600/3-5
28751 Cole Grade Rd 92082 760-749-1631
Stephanie McEntire, prin. Fax 749-5501
Valley Center MS 800/6-8
28751 Cole Grade Rd 92082 760-751-4295
Rose Flowers, prin. Fax 751-4259
Valley Center PS 600/K-2
28751 Cole Grade Rd 92082 760-749-8282
Michael Schanze, prin. Fax 751-2654
Other Schools – See Pauma Valley

Valley Glen, Los Angeles

Laurence S 300/K-6
13639 Victory Blvd, 818-782-4001
Lauren Wolke, head sch Fax 782-4004

Valley Home, Stanislaus, Pop. 218
Valley Home Joint SD 200/K-8
13231 Pioneer Ave 95361 209-847-0117
Tom Price, supt. Fax 848-9456
www.vhjsd.org
Valley Home S 200/K-8
13231 Pioneer Ave 95361 209-847-0117
Tom Price, prin. Fax 848-9456

Valley Springs, Calaveras, Pop. 3,427
Calaveras USD
Supt. — See San Andreas
Lind ES 600/K-6
5100 Driver Rd 95252 209-754-2350
Richard Gorton, prin. Fax 772-2566
Toyon MS 500/7-8
PO Box 1510 95252 209-754-2137
Amy Hasselwander, prin. Fax 754-5327
Valley Springs ES 500/K-6
240 Pine St 95252 209-754-2141
Angela Koch, prin. Fax 772-1013

Valley Village, See Los Angeles

Adat Ari El Day S 200/PK-6
12020 Burbank Blvd 91607 818-766-4992
Shara Peters, head sch Fax 766-1436
Beth Hillel Day S 100/PK-6
12326 Riverside Dr 91607 818-763-8308
Kathryn Jensen, head sch
Country S 100/PK-8
5243 Laurel Canyon Blvd 91607 818-769-2473
Holly Novick, head sch Fax 752-3097

Vandenberg AFB, Santa Barbara, Pop. 3,111
Lompoc USD
Supt. — See Lompoc
Crestview ES 600/K-6
Utah Ave 93437 805-742-2050
Dr. Candice Grossi, prin. Fax 742-2083
Vandenberg MS 800/7-8
Mountain View Blvd 93437 805-742-2700
Joel Jory, prin. Fax 742-2759

Van Nuys, See Los Angeles
Los Angeles USD
Supt. — See Los Angeles
Anatola Avenue ES 400/K-5
7364 Anatola Ave 91406 818-343-8733
Maria Gonzalez, prin. Fax 344-1550
Bassett Street ES 900/K-5
15756 Bassett St 91406 818-782-1340
Carl Christoff, prin. Fax 782-8681
Cardenas ES 600/K-5
6900 Calhoun Ave 91405 818-908-6700
Ada Yslas, prin. Fax 374-1327
Chandler Learning Academy 600/K-5
14030 Weddington St 91401 818-789-6173
Kristine McIntire, prin. Fax 995-7095
Cohasset ES 600/K-5
15810 Saticoy St 91406 818-787-2113
Andrea Yahudian, prin. Fax 782-3522
Columbus Avenue ES 600/K-5
6700 Columbus Ave 91405 818-779-5440
Kathie Galan-Jaramillo, prin. Fax 779-7947
Erwin Street ES 700/K-5
13400 Erwin St 91401 818-988-6292
Kevin McClay, prin. Fax 785-2674
Gault Street ES 400/K-5
17000 Gault St 91406 818-343-1933
Jerilyn Schubert, prin. Fax 776-0237
Hazeltine Avenue ES 800/K-5
7150 Hazeltine Ave 91405 818-781-1040
Seth Avery, prin. Fax 781-8613
Kittridge Street ES 800/K-5
13619 Kittridge St 91401 818-786-7926
Alfonso Jimenez, prin. Fax 988-0692
Lemay Early Education Center PK-PK
17553 Lemay St 91406 818-345-0731
Johanna Curd, prin. Fax 343-0911
LeMay ES 400/K-5
17520 Vanowen St 91406 818-343-4696
Long Nguyen, prin. Fax 708-0549
Mulholland MS 1,300/6-8
17120 Vanowen St 91406 818-609-2500
Gregory Vallone, prin. Fax 345-1933
Stagg ES 500/K-5
7839 Amestoy Ave 91406 818-881-9850
Angel Barrett, prin. Fax 609-8537
Sylvan Park Early Education Center PK-PK
15011 Delano St 91411 818-997-8972
Claudia Araujo, prin. Fax 994-5163
Sylvan Park ES 900/K-5
6238 Noble Ave 91411 818-988-4020
Lawrence Kraft Orozco, prin. Fax 997-7630
Valerio Street ES 1,000/K-5
15035 Valerio St 91405 818-785-8683
Susan Tandberg, prin. Fax 786-8749
Van Nuys ES 600/K-5
6464 Sylmar Ave 91401 818-785-2195
Franne Goldstein, prin. Fax 782-4173
Van Nuys MS 1,300/6-8
5435 Vesper Ave 91411 818-267-5900
Cristina Serrano, prin. Fax 909-7274
Vista MS 1,400/6-8
15040 Roscoe Blvd 91402 818-901-2727
Guiseppe Nardulli, prin. Fax 901-2740

Children's Community S 100/K-6
14702 Sylvan St 91411 818-780-6226
Neal Wrightson, head sch Fax 780-5834
St. Bridget of Sweden S 200/K-8
7120 Whitaker Ave 91406 818-785-4422
Fax 785-0490
St. Elisabeth S 200/PK-8
6635 Tobias Ave 91405 818-779-1766
Marita Olango, prin. Fax 779-1768
Valley S 200/PK-8
15700 Sherman Way 91406 818-786-4720
James Haddad, prin. Fax 786-2688

Venice, See Los Angeles
Los Angeles USD
Supt. — See Los Angeles
Broadway ES 500/K-6
1015 Lincoln Blvd 90291 310-392-4944
Susan Wang, prin. Fax 314-7349
Coeur D'Alene Avenue ES 500/K-5
810 Coeur D Alene Ave 90291 310-821-7813
Andrew Jenkins, prin. Fax 823-4486
Westminster Early Education Center PK-PK
1010 Main St 90291 310-392-4581
Nicola Boykin, prin. Fax 450-0738
Westminster ES 300/K-5
1010 Abbot Kinney Blvd 90291 310-392-3041
Barry Cohen, prin. Fax 392-6506

St. Mark S 200/K-8
912 Coeur D Alene Ave 90291 310-821-6612
Mary McQueen, prin. Fax 822-6101
Venice Lutheran S 100/K-8
815 Venice Blvd 90291 310-823-9367
Nancy Gill, prin. Fax 823-4822

Ventura, Ventura, Pop. 103,287
Ventura USD 17,400/K-12
255 W Stanley Ave Ste 100 93001 805-641-5000
David Creswell, supt. Fax 653-7855
www.venturausd.org
Anacapa MS 800/6-8
100 S Mills Rd 93003 805-289-7900
Barbara Boggio, prin. Fax 289-7909
ATLAS @ Saticoy ES 300/K-5
760 Jazmin Ave 93004 805-672-2701
Jennifer Duston, prin. Fax 672-0296
Balboa MS 1,200/6-8
247 S Hill Rd 93003 805-289-1800
Wes Wade, prin. Fax 289-1806
Cabrillo MS 1,000/6-8
1426 E Santa Clara St 93001 805-641-5155
Lorelle Dawes, prin. Fax 641-5377
Citrus Glen ES 600/K-5
9655 Darling Rd 93004 805-672-0220
Susan Martinez, prin. Fax 672-0224
De Anza Academy 900/6-8
2060 Cameron St 93001 805-641-5165
Hector Guerrero, prin. Fax 641-5282
Elmhurst ES 600/K-5
5080 Elmhurst St 93003 805-289-1860
Fax 289-1865
Foster ES 500/K-5
20 Pleasant Pl 93001 805-641-5420
Carlos Covarrubias, prin. Fax 641-5390
Juanamaria ES 500/K-5
100 S Crocker Ave 93004 805-672-0291
Gina Wolowicz, prin. Fax 659-3078
Junipero Serra ES 600/K-5
8880 Halifax St 93004 805-672-2717
Karen Senesac, prin. Fax 672-2716
Lincoln ES 300/K-5
1107 E Santa Clara St 93001 805-641-5438
Rob Lewis, prin. Fax 641-5398
Loma Vista ES 400/K-5
300 Lynn Dr 93003 805-641-5443
Marlene McMullen, prin. Fax 641-5334
Montalvo ES 400/K-5
2050 Grand Ave 93003 805-289-1872
Claudia Caudill, prin. Fax 289-1871
Mound ES 600/K-5
455 S Hill Rd 93003 805-289-1886
Todd Tyner, prin. Fax 289-1883
Pierpont ES 300/K-5
1254 Marthas Vineyard Ct 93001 805-641-5470
Jim Sather, prin. Fax 641-5283
Poinsettia ES 500/K-5
350 N Victoria Ave 93003 805-289-7971
Elisabeth Harris, prin. Fax 289-7970
Portola ES 600/K-5
6700 Eagle St 93003 805-289-1734
Robert Ruiz, prin. Fax 289-9987
Reynolds ES 400/K-8
450 Valmore Ave 93003 805-289-1817
Kelly Hatton, prin. Fax 289-1814
Rogers ES 500/K-5
316 Howard St 93003 805-641-5496
Fax 653-0625
Sheridan Way ES 500/K-5
573 Sheridan Way 93001 805-641-5491
Maria Elizarraras, prin. Fax 641-5276
Other Schools – See Oak View

City Christian S 100/K-8
6360 Telephone Rd 93003 805-658-2900
Jay Smith, prin. Fax 642-3402
Holy Cross S 100/PK-8
211 E Main St 93001 805-643-1500
Edie Lanphar, prin. Fax 643-7831
Our Lady of the Assumption S 300/PK-8
3169 Telegraph Rd 93003 805-642-7198
Patricia Groff, prin. Fax 642-7110
Sacred Heart S 200/PK-8
10770 Henderson Rd 93004 805-647-6174
Christine Benner, prin. Fax 647-2291
St. Augustine Academy 100/K-12
PO Box 4506 93007 805-672-0411
Michael Van Hecke, hdmstr. Fax 672-0177
Ventura County Christian S 50/K-12
96 MacMillan Ave 93001 805-641-0187
Tanja Geue, admin. Fax 641-0252
Ventura Missionary S 400/PK-8
500 High Point Dr 93003 805-644-9515
Dr. Tammy Ennis, dean Fax 642-5197

Vernon, Los Angeles, Pop. 112
Los Angeles USD
Supt. — See Los Angeles
Holmes Early Education Center PK-PK
1810 E 52nd St 90058 323-589-6427
Iadrana Williams, prin. Fax 584-8576
Vernon City ES 300/K-7
2360 E Vernon Ave 90058 323-582-3727
Diane Espino, prin. Fax 585-9957

Victor, San Joaquin, Pop. 289
Lodi USD
Supt. — See Lodi
Victor ES 200/K-6
PO Box L 95253 209-331-7441
Allison Gerrity, prin. Fax 331-7530

Victorville, San Bernardino, Pop. 111,837
Adelanto ESD
Supt. — See Adelanto
Davis Academy of Excellence 6-8
15831 Diamond Rd 92394 760-530-7650
Kathy Youskievicz, prin.
Eagle Ranch ES 800/K-5
12545 Eagle Ranch Pkwy 92392 760-949-2100
Laura Ramos, prin. Fax 949-2558
Mesa Linda MS 800/6-8
13001 Mesa Linda Ave 92392 760-246-6363
Alicia Tuttle, prin. Fax 956-7456
Morgan/Kincaid Prep S 1,000/K-5
13257 Mesa Linda Ave 92392 760-956-9006
Kristen Cooper, prin. Fax 956-2734
West Creek ES 700/K-5
15763 Cobalt Rd 92394 760-951-3628
Deborah Bowers, prin. Fax 955-7862

Hesperia USD
Supt. — See Hesperia
Hollyvale ES 400/K-6
11645 Hollyvale Ave 92392 760-947-3484
Shannon Erath, prin. Fax 947-2048

Snowline JUSD
Supt. — See Phelan
Vista Verde ES 700/K-5
13403 Vista Verde St 92392 760-662-5650
Maria Hughes, prin. Fax 662-5659

Victor ESD 11,500/K-6
12219 Second Ave, 760-245-1691
Jan Gonzales M.Ed., supt. Fax 245-6245
www.vesd.net
Brentwood S of Environmental Studies 900/K-6
12219 Second Ave, 760-243-2301
Lori Billig, prin. Fax 243-4675
Challenger S of Sports and Fitness 1,000/K-6
12219 Second Ave, 760-843-6866
Matthew Alsbury, prin. Fax 843-5854
Del Rey AVID ES 600/K-6
12219 Second Ave, 760-245-7941
Douglas Bergquist, prin. Fax 245-1627
Discovery S of the Arts 1,000/K-6
12219 Second Ave, 760-843-3577
Linda Rueter, prin. Fax 843-1078
Endeavour S of Exploration 800/K-6
12219 Second Ave, 760-843-7303
Shannon Hansen, prin. Fax 843-7348
Galileo S of Gifted & Talented Education 400/K-6
12219 Second Ave, 760-241-1753
Conor Devlin, prin. Fax 245-2524
Green Tree East Leadership Academy 700/K-6
12219 Second Ave, 760-955-7600
Brian Bettger, prin. Fax 955-7550

Irwin Academy of Performing Arts 300/K-6
12219 Second Ave, 760-245-7691
Patricia Frederick, prin. Fax 245-2139
Liberty S of Creativity & Innovation 900/K-6
12219 Second Ave, 760-241-1520
Kimberly Verduzco, prin. Fax 241-7674
Lomitas Institute of Technology 700/K-6
12219 Second Ave, 760-243-2012
Kenisha Williams, prin. Fax 243-1291
Mojave Vista S of Cultural Arts 1,000/K-6
12219 Second Ave, 760-241-2474
Gayle LaBrosse, prin. Fax 241-3606
Park View ES 800/K-6
12219 Second Ave, 760-241-7731
Fortune Barles, prin. Fax 241-7269
Puesta Del Sol No Excuses ES 500/K-6
12219 Second Ave, 760-243-2028
Nicole Anderson, prin. Fax 243-4140
Village ES 800/K-6
12219 Second Ave, 760-243-1160
Barbara Lord, prin. Fax 243-5752
West Palms Conservatory 700/K-6
12219 Second Ave, 760-245-3525
Jackie Lester, prin. Fax 245-3683

Victor Valley UNHSD 11,400/7-12
16350 Mojave Dr, 760-955-3200
Ron Williams Ed.D., supt. Fax 245-4634
www.vvuhsd.org
Hook JHS 900/7-8
15000 Hook Blvd 92394 760-955-3360
Carlos Cerna, prin. Fax 245-5839

Victor Valley Christian S 300/PK-12
15260 Nisqualli Rd, 760-241-8827
Deb Clarkson, admin. Fax 243-0654
Victor Valley Seventh-day Adventist S 50/K-8
17137 Crestview Dr, 760-243-4176
Janet Lopez, prin. Fax 245-5606
Zion Lutheran S 50/PK-8
15342 Jeraldo Dr 92394 760-243-3074
Michael Glowinski, dir. Fax 245-5945

Villa Park, Orange, Pop. 5,691
Orange USD
Supt. — See Orange
Cerro Villa MS 1,100/7-8
17852 Serrano Ave 92861 714-997-6251
Lisa Ogan Ed.D., prin. Fax 921-9331
Serrano ES 600/K-6
17741 Serrano Ave 92861 714-997-6275
Katherine Rizzo, prin. Fax 637-2051
Villa Park ES 700/K-6
10551 Center Dr 92861 714-997-6281
RaeAnne Little, prin. Fax 532-5895

Vina, Tehama, Pop. 227
Los Molinos USD
Supt. — See Los Molinos
Vina ES 100/K-8
PO Box 230 96092 530-839-2182
Debra Burgett, prin. Fax 839-2743

Visalia, Tulare, Pop. 121,741
Outside Creek ESD 100/K-8
26452 Road 164 93292 559-747-0710
Derrick Bravo, supt. Fax 747-0398
www.tcoe.org/Districts/OutsideCreek.shtm
Outside Creek ES 100/K-8
26452 Road 164 93292 559-747-0710
Derrick Bravo, prin. Fax 747-0398

Stone Corral ESD 500/K-12
15590 Avenue 383 93292 559-528-4455
Christopher Kemper, supt. Fax 528-3808
www.tcoe.org/Districts/StoneCorral.shtm
Stone Corral S 100/K-8
15590 Avenue 383 93292 559-528-4455
Christopher Kemper, supt. Fax 528-3808

Visalia USD 28,100/PK-12
5000 W Cypress Ave 93277 559-730-7300
Todd Oto Ed.D., supt. Fax 730-7508
www.vusd.org
Conyer ES 400/K-6
814 S Sowell St 93277 559-730-7751
Tara Sharp, prin. Fax 730-7380
Cottonwood Creek ES 700/K-6
4222 S Dans St 93277 559-735-3539
Cristin Ochoa, prin. Fax 735-3541
Crestwood ES 600/K-6
3001 W Whitendale Ave 93277 559-730-7754
Debbie Peterson, prin. Fax 730-7744
Crowley ES 600/PK-6
214 E Ferguson Ave 93291 559-730-7758
Claudia Ardon-Diaz, prin. Fax 730-7945
Divisadero MS 900/7-8
1200 S Divisadero St 93277 559-730-7661
Robert Aguilar, prin. Fax 730-7908
Elbow Creek ES 500/PK-6
32747 Road 138 93292 559-730-7766
Alma Navarro, prin. Fax 730-7878
Four Creeks ES 700/PK-6
1844 N Burke St 93292 559-622-3115
Rosa Mota-Montoya, prin. Fax 622-3118
Golden Oak ES 500/K-6
1700 N Lovers Ln 93292 559-730-7851
Kimberly Leon, prin. Fax 730-7840
Goshen ES 700/PK-6
6505 Avenue 308 93291 559-730-7847
Rachel Mendez, prin. Fax 730-7972
Green Acres MS 1,300/7-8
1147 N Mooney Blvd 93291 559-730-7671
Andy Di Meo, prin. Fax 730-7918
Hernandez ES 800/K-6
2133 N Leila St 93291 559-622-3199
Andres Gomez, prin. Fax 622-3201
Highland ES 500/PK-6
701 N Stevenson St 93291 559-730-7769
Cheryl LaVerne, prin. Fax 730-7980
Houston ES 600/PK-6
1200 N Giddings St 93291 559-730-7772
Adrian Leal, prin. Fax 730-7721
Hurley ES 600/K-6
6600 W Hurley Ave 93291 559-730-7905
Stephanie Gendron, prin. Fax 730-7458
La Joya MS 1,000/7-8
4711 W La Vida Ave 93277 559-730-7921
Travis Hambleton, prin. Fax 730-7505
Linwood ES 700/K-6
3129 S Linwood St 93277 559-730-7776
Natalie Taylor, prin. Fax 730-7461
Mineral King ES 700/PK-6
3333 E Kaweah Ave 93292 559-730-7779
Silvia Duvall, prin. Fax 730-7781
Mitchell ES 700/K-6
2121 E Laura Ave 93292 559-622-3195
Loretta Bryant, prin. Fax 622-3197
Mountain View ES 600/K-8
2021 S Encina St 93277 559-730-7783
John Alvarez, prin. Fax 730-7407
Oak Grove ES 600/K-8
4445 W Ferguson Ave 93291 559-622-3105
John Davis, prin. Fax 622-3108
Pinkham ES 500/K-6
2200 E Tulare Ave 93292 559-730-7853
Dori Bingaman, prin. Fax 730-7982
Ridgeview MS 300/7-7
3315 N Akers St 93291 559-622-3308
Michal Yates, prin. Fax 622-3313
Riverway ES 600/K-6
1341 Glendale Ave 93291 559-931-8020
Monica Saenz, admin. Fax 931-8029
Royal Oaks ES 600/K-6
1323 S Clover St 93277 559-730-7787
Lisa Majarian, prin. Fax 730-7844
Shannon Ranch ES 700/K-6
3637 N Ranch St 93291 559-622-3258
Susan Wallace-Sims, prin. Fax 622-3259
Valley Oak MS 900/7-8
2000 N Lovers Ln 93292 559-730-7681
Michael Hernandez, prin. Fax 730-7822
Veva Blunt ES 600/K-7
1119 S Chinowth St 93277 559-730-7793
Natali Matta, prin. Fax 730-7893
Washington ES 300/PK-6
500 S Garden St 93277 559-730-7795
Elizabeth Serrato, prin. Fax 730-7484
Willow Glen ES 600/PK-8
310 N Akers St 93291 559-730-7798
Blanca Martinez-Ramirez, prin. Fax 730-7788
Other Schools – See Ivanhoe

Catholic S of Visalia 300/PK-8
200 E Race Ave 93291 559-732-5831
Sheila Rast, prin. Fax 741-1562
Central Valley Christian S 900/PK-12
5600 W Tulare Ave 93277 559-734-9481
Larry Baker, supt. Fax 734-7963
Grace Christian S 200/PK-8
1111 S Conyer St 93277 559-734-7694
Sandra Eitel, prin. Fax 734-0146
St. Paul's S 300/PK-8
6101 W Goshen Ave 93291 559-739-1619
Cathy Guadagni, dir. Fax 739-0950

Vista, San Diego, Pop. 90,562
San Marcos USD
Supt. — See San Marcos
Leichtag ES 900/K-5
653 Poinsettia Ave, 760-290-2888
Andrea Holmes, prin. Fax 290-2855

Vista USD 25,500/K-12
1234 Arcadia Ave 92084 760-726-2170
Dr. Matt Doyle, supt. Fax 758-7838
www.vistausd.org
Beaumont ES 600/K-5
550 Beaumont Dr 92084 760-726-4040
Sochie Schmitz, prin. Fax 726-7961
Bobier ES 700/K-5
220 W Bobier Dr 92083 760-724-8501
Jenifer Golden, prin. Fax 940-8695
Breeze Hill ES 900/K-5
1111 Melrose Way, 760-945-2373
Lori Higley, prin. Fax 945-8259
Casita Center for Science/Math & Tech 600/K-5
260 Cedar Rd 92083 760-724-8442
Laura Smith, prin. Fax 758-4697
Foothill-Oak ES 700/K-5
1370 Oak Dr 92084 760-631-3458
Dr. Erin English, prin. Fax 631-3464
Grapevine ES 600/K-5
630 Grapevine Rd 92083 760-724-8329
Rafael Olavide, prin. Fax 724-1821
Hannalei ES 700/K-5
120 Hannalei Dr 92083 760-631-6248
Tracy Zachry, prin. Fax 631-6254
Maryland ES 600/K-5
700 North Ave 92083 760-631-6675
Carol Lebreche, prin. Fax 643-2668
Monte Vista ES 700/K-5
1720 Monte Vista Dr 92084 760-726-0410
Charlene Manuto, prin. Fax 726-0423
Olive ES 400/K-5
740 Olive Ave 92083 760-724-7129
Stephanie Vasquez, prin. Fax 724-3820
Rancho Minerva MS 900/6-8
2245 Foothill Dr 92084 760-631-4500
Juan Ayala, prin. Fax 643-2490
Vista Academy of Arts 700/K-5
600 N Santa Fe Ave 92083 760-941-0880
Catina Hancock, prin. Fax 945-3201
Vista Innovation & Design Academy 700/6-8
740 Olive Ave 92083 760-724-7115
Dr. Eric Chagala, prin. Fax 941-6912
Vista Magnet MS 800/6-8
151 Civic Center Dr 92084 760-726-5766
Steve Post, prin. Fax 945-4273
Other Schools – See Oceanside

St. Francis of Assisi S 300/PK-8
525 W Vista Way 92083 760-630-7960
Elizabeth Joseph, prin. Fax 726-2910
Sanderling Waldorf S 200/PK-8
2585 Business Park Dr, 760-635-3747
Brian Wolff, admin. Fax 635-1037
Tri City Christian S 600/PK-12
302 N Emerald Dr 92083 760-630-8227
Rod King, prin. Fax 724-6643
Vista Christian S 200/K-8
290 N Melrose Dr 92083 760-724-7353
Therese Ramirez, prin. Fax 724-9887

Walnut, Los Angeles, Pop. 28,480
Rowland USD
Supt. — See Rowland Heights
Oswalt Academy 1,000/K-8
19501 Shadow Oak Dr 91789 626-810-4109
Kevin Despard, prin. Fax 964-1372
Ybarra Academy of Arts and Technology 600/K-8
1300 Brea Canyon Cut Off Rd 91789 909-598-3744
Annette Ramirez, prin. Fax 598-9264

Walnut Valley USD 14,600/K-12
880 S Lemon Ave 91789 909-595-1261
Dr. Robert Taylor, supt. Fax 444-3435
www.wvusd.k12.ca.us
Collegewood ES 600/K-5
20725 Collegewood Dr 91789 909-598-5308
Mary Wendland, prin. Fax 598-2838
Morris ES 500/K-5
19875 Calle Baja 91789 909-594-0053
Shehzad Bhojani, prin. Fax 595-9438
South Pointe MS 1,100/6-8
20671 Larkstone Dr 91789 909-595-8171
Susan Arzola, prin. Fax 468-5201
Suzanne MS 1,400/6-8
525 Suzanne Rd 91789 909-594-1657
Lester Ojeda, prin. Fax 598-6741
Vejar ES 600/K-5
20222 Vejar Rd 91789 909-594-1434
Jennifer DeAnda, prin. Fax 594-7164
Walnut ES 500/K-5
841 Glenwick Ave 91789 909-594-1820
Robert Chang, prin. Fax 595-4680
Westhoff ES 600/K-5
20151 Amar Rd 91789 909-594-6483
Denise Rendon, prin. Fax 594-1393
Other Schools – See Diamond Bar

Walnut Creek, Contra Costa, Pop. 61,759
Mount Diablo USD
Supt. — See Concord
Bancroft ES 500/K-5
2200 Parish Dr 94598 925-933-3405
Linda Schuler, prin. Fax 943-1587
Foothill MS 1,100/6-8
2775 Cedro Ln 94598 925-939-8600
April Bush, prin. Fax 256-4281
Valle Verde ES 500/K-5
3275 Peachwillow Ln 94598 925-939-5700
Beverly Tom, prin. Fax 930-7508
Walnut Acres ES 600/K-5
180 Cerezo Dr 94598 925-939-1333
Colleen Dowd, prin. Fax 939-1155

Walnut Creek ESD 3,600/K-8
960 Ygnacio Valley Rd 94596 925-944-6850
Marie Morgan, supt. Fax 944-1768
www.walnutcreeksd.org
Buena Vista ES 500/K-5
2355 San Juan Ave 94597 925-944-6822
Kelly Eagan, prin. Fax 934-8907
Indian Valley ES 500/K-5
551 Marshall Dr 94598 925-944-6828
Milissa Banister, prin. Fax 935-1091
Murwood ES 400/K-5
2050 Vanderslice Ave 94596 925-943-2462
Carol Nenni, prin. Fax 934-0356
Parkmead ES 500/K-5
1920 Magnolia Way 94595 925-944-6858
Alison Gomez, prin. Fax 939-2849
Tice Creek ES K-8
1847 Newell Ave 94595 925-746-5515
Connie McCarley, prin. Fax 295-0781
Walnut Creek IS 1,200/6-8
2425 Walnut Blvd 94597 925-944-6840
Brandy Byers, prin. Fax 933-1922
Walnut Heights ES 400/K-5
4064 Walnut Blvd 94596 925-944-6834
Joy Inouye, prin. Fax 934-0648

Contra Costa Christian S 300/PK-12
2721 Larkey Ln 94597 925-934-4964
Chris Winters, head sch Fax 934-4966
NorthCreek Academy 600/PK-8
2303 Ygnacio Valley Rd # A 94598 925-954-6322
Greg Steele, prin. Fax 954-6396
Palmer S for Boys & Girls 300/K-8
2740 Jones Rd 94597 925-934-4888
Samuel Mendes, hdmstr. Fax 932-4888
St. Mary S 300/PK-8
1158 Bont Ln 94596 925-935-5054
Tracey Schmidt, prin. Fax 935-5063
Seven Hills S 400/PK-8
975 N San Carlos Dr 94598 925-933-0666
Kathleen McNamara, head sch Fax 933-6271
Walnut Creek Christian Academy 300/PK-8
2336 Buena Vista Ave 94597 925-935-1587
Kristi McComas, prin. Fax 934-1518

Walnut Grove, Sacramento, Pop. 1,517
River Delta USD
Supt. — See Rio Vista
Walnut Grove ES 200/K-6
PO Box 145 95690 916-776-1844
Carrie Norris, prin. Fax 776-2074

Walnut Park, Los Angeles, Pop. 15,927
Los Angeles USD
Supt. — See Los Angeles

Science Tech Engineering & Math Academy 6-8
7500 Marbrisa Ave 90255 323-277-2600
Joseph Dileva, prin. Fax 589-1529
S of Social Justice and Service Learning 6-8
7500 Marbrisa Ave 90255 323-277-2600
Aida Coronado-Delon, prin. Fax 589-1529

Warner Springs, San Diego
Warner USD 300/PK-12
PO Box 8 92086 760-782-3517
David MacLeod, supt. Fax 782-9117
www.warnerusd.net
Warner ES 100/PK-6
PO Box 8 92086 760-782-3517
David MacLeod, prin. Fax 782-9117
Warner Preschool PK-PK
PO Box 8 92086 760-782-3517
David MacLeod, prin. Fax 782-9117

Wasco, Kern, Pop. 25,343
Semitropic ESD 300/K-8
25300 Highway 46 93280 661-758-6412
Bethany Ferguson, supt. Fax 758-4134
www.semitropicschool.org
Semitropic ES 300/K-8
25300 Highway 46 93280 661-758-6412
Bethany Ferguson, prin. Fax 758-4134

Wasco UNESD 3,500/PK-8
1102 5th St 93280 661-758-7100
Kelly Richers, supt. Fax 758-7110
www.wuesd.org
Burke ES 800/PK-6
1301 Filburn St 93280 661-758-7480
Sam Torres, prin. Fax 758-3024
Clemens ES 600/PK-6
523 Broadway St 93280 661-758-7120
Danny Arellano, prin. Fax 758-9200
Jefferson MS 800/7-8
305 Griffith Ave 93280 661-758-7140
Steve Davis, prin. Fax 758-9366
Palm Avenue ES 600/PK-6
1017 Palm Ave 93280 661-758-7130
Steffanie Pemberton, prin. Fax 758-9369
Prueitt ES 800/PK-6
3501 7th St 93280 661-758-7180
Rosalinda Chairez, prin. Fax 758-9361

North Kern Christian S 100/PK-8
710 Peters St 93280 661-758-5997
Kendall Funk, prin. Fax 758-4370

Washington, Nevada, Pop. 177
Twin Ridges ESD
Supt. — See Nevada City
Washington ES 50/K-8
16661 Old Mill Rd 95986 530-265-2880
Patricia Gardiner, lead tchr. Fax 265-6588

Waterford, Stanislaus, Pop. 8,248
Roberts Ferry UNESD 100/K-8
101 Roberts Ferry Rd 95386 209-874-2331
Bob Loretelli, supt. Fax 874-4625
www.robertsferry.k12.ca.us
Roberts Ferry Union ES 100/K-8
101 Roberts Ferry Rd 95386 209-874-2331
Bob Loretelli, prin. Fax 874-4625

Waterford USD 4,000/K-12
219 N Reinway Ave 95386 209-874-1809
Donald J. Davis Ed.D., supt. Fax 874-3109
www.waterford.k12.ca.us
Moon PS 500/K-3
319 N Reinway Ave 95386 209-874-2371
Steven Kuykendall, prin. Fax 874-5910
Waterford JHS 200/7-8
12916 Bentley St 95386 209-874-2382
Yvette Fagundes-Hall, prin. Fax 874-3652
Whitehead IS 400/4-6
119 N Reinway Ave 95386 209-874-1080
Lorinda Ferguson, prin. Fax 874-9018

Watsonville, Santa Cruz, Pop. 50,582
Pajaro Valley USD 20,200/K-12
294 Green Valley Rd 95076 831-786-2100
Dr. Michelle Rodriguez, supt. Fax 728-4288
www.pvusd.net
Amesti ES 700/K-5
25 Amesti Rd 95076 831-728-6250
Erin Haley, prin. Fax 728-6276
Bradley ES 500/K-6
321 Corralitos Rd 95076 831-728-6366
Brian Saxton, prin. Fax 728-6946
Calabasas ES 600/K-6
202 Calabasas Rd 95076 831-728-6368
Todd Westfall, prin. Fax 761-6053
Chavez MS 600/6-8
440 Arthur Rd 95076 831-761-7699
Benjamin Benavidez, prin. Fax 728-6477
Hall District ES 600/K-5
300 Sill Rd 95076 831-728-6371
Claudia Monasterio, prin. Fax 761-6174
Hall MS 600/6-8
201 Brewington Ave 95076 831-728-6270
Adelina Cervero, prin. Fax 761-6150
Hyde ES 600/K-5
125 Alta Vista St 95076 831-728-6243
Michael Berman, prin. Fax 728-6211
Lakeview MS 700/6-8
2350 E Lake Ave 95076 831-728-6454
Dr. Rosa Hernandez, prin. Fax 728-6480
Landmark ES 700/K-5
235 Ohlone Pkwy 95076 831-761-7940
Roberto Torres, prin. Fax 761-6100
MacQuiddy ES 700/K-5
330 Martinelli St 95076 831-728-6315
Tom Hiltz, prin. Fax 728-6466
Ohlone ES 500/K-5
21 Bay Farms Rd 95076 831-728-6977
Brett Knupfer, prin. Fax 761-6144
Pajaro MS 400/6-8
250 Salinas Rd 95076 831-728-6238
Dr. Victoria Sorensen, prin. Fax 728-6219
Radcliff ES 500/K-6
550 Rodriguez St 95076 831-728-6469
Ulli Kummerow, prin. Fax 728-8171
Rolling Hills MS 600/6-8
130 Herman Ave 95076 831-728-6341
Rick Ito, prin. Fax 724-7323
Soldo ES 700/K-5
1140 Menasco Dr 95076 831-786-1310
Elaine Parker, prin. Fax 786-1314
Starlight ES 700/K-5
225 Hammer Dr 95076 831-728-6979
Dr. Jaclynne Medina, prin. Fax 761-6102
White ES 700/K-5
515 Palm Ave 95076 831-728-6321
Vicki Hallof, prin. Fax 728-6450
Other Schools – See Aptos, Freedom

Green Valley Christian S 200/K-8
376 S Green Valley Rd 95076 831-724-6505
James Stewart, prin. Fax 288-0214
Moreland Notre Dame S 200/K-8
133 Brennan St 95076 831-728-2051
Cathy Mottau, prin. Fax 728-2052

Weaverville, Trinity, Pop. 3,455
Trinity Alps USD 700/PK-12
PO Box 1227 96093 530-623-6104
Tom Barnett, supt. Fax 623-3418
www.tausd.org
Weaverville ES 300/PK-8
PO Box 1000 96093 530-623-5533
Katie Poburko, prin. Fax 623-5548
Other Schools – See Big Bar

Weed, Siskiyou, Pop. 2,802
Weed UNESD 200/K-8
575 White Ave 96094 530-938-2715
Amanda Bonivert, supt. Fax 938-2715
www.weedelementaryschool.com
Weed ES 200/K-8
575 White Ave 96094 530-938-2715
Alisa Cummings, prin. Fax 938-2973

Siskiyou Christian S 50/K-8
750 S Weed Blvd 96094 530-938-1706
Michelle McGee, admin. Fax 938-1706

Weimar, Placer, Pop. 1,300
Placer Hills UNESD
Supt. — See Meadow Vista
Weimar Hills MS 200/4-8
PO Box 255 95736 530-637-4121
Rebecca Evers, prin. Fax 637-4054

Weldon, Kern, Pop. 2,564
South Fork UNSD 100/PK-8
5225 S Kelso Valley Rd 93283 760-378-4000
Kim Villani, supt. Fax 378-3046
www.southforkschool.org
South Fork ES 100/PK-8
5225 S Kelso Valley Rd 93283 760-378-1130
Kim Villani, supt. Fax 378-4369

Weott, Humboldt, Pop. 272
Southern Humbolt JUSD
Supt. — See Miranda
Johnson ES 100/PK-6
PO Box 280 95571 707-946-2347
Don Boyd, prin. Fax 946-2507

West Covina, Los Angeles, Pop. 103,993
Covina-Valley USD
Supt. — See Covina
Grovecenter ES 500/K-5
775 N Lark Ellen Ave 91791 626-974-4400
Autumn Williams, prin. Fax 974-4415
Mesa ES 600/K-5
409 S Barranca St 91791 626-974-4600
Dr. Chris Hert, prin. Fax 974-4615
Rowland Avenue ES 500/K-5
1355 E Rowland Ave 91790 626-974-4700
Page Christensen, prin. Fax 974-4715
Traweek MS 900/6-8
1941 E Rowland Ave 91791 626-974-7400
Dr. Mathew Kodama, prin. Fax 974-7415
Workman Avenue ES 500/K-5
1941 E Workman Ave 91791 626-974-4900
Chris Deegan, prin. Fax 974-4915

Rowland USD
Supt. — See Rowland Heights
Giano IS 700/7-8
3223 S Giano Ave 91792 626-965-2461
Carlos Ochoa, prin. Fax 854-2212
Hollingworth ES 500/K-6
3003 E Hollingworth St 91792 909-598-3661
Dr. Michael Hoon, prin. Fax 468-9581
Telesis Academy of Science & Math 800/K-8
2800 E Hollingworth St 91792 626-965-1696
Johan Schmitz, prin. Fax 810-4916

West Covina USD 10,500/K-12
1717 W Merced Ave 91790 626-939-4600
Dr. Charles Hinman Ed.D., supt. Fax 939-4701
www.wcusd.org
California ES 400/3-6
1125 W Bainbridge Ave 91790 626-939-4800
Lori Wilds, prin. Fax 939-4805
Cameron ES 500/K-5
1225 E Cameron Ave 91790 626-931-1740
Karla Contreras, prin. Fax 931-1745
Edgewood MS 600/6-8
1625 W Durness St 91790 626-939-4900
Veronica Maddox, prin. Fax 939-4999
Hollencrest MS 800/6-8
2101 E Merced Ave 91791 626-931-1760
Devon Rose, prin. Fax 931-1762
Merced ES 500/K-5
1545 E Merced Ave 91791 626-931-1700
Damian Kessler, prin. Fax 931-1704
Merlinda ES 600/K-6
1120 S Valinda Ave 91790 626-931-1720
Rochelle Johnson Evans, prin. Fax 931-1726
Monte Vista ES 600/K-6
1615 W Eldred Ave 91790 626-939-4830
Lilia Gonzalez-Gomez, prin. Fax 939-4835
Orangewood ES 500/K-5
1440 S Orange Ave 91790 626-939-4820
Janet Shirley, prin. Fax 939-4825
Vine ES 600/K-5
1901 E Vine Ave 91791 626-931-1790
Valerie Jaramillo, prin. Fax 931-1795
Walnut Grove IS 500/7-8
614 W Vine Ave 91790 626-919-7018
Rich Nambu, prin. Fax 919-7207
Wescove ES 400/K-2
1010 W Vine Ave 91790 626-939-4870
Richard Ortega, prin. Fax 939-4875

Christ Lutheran S 300/PK-8
311 S Citrus St 91791 626-967-7531
Christopher Andrade, prin. Fax 967-8513
Jubilee Christian S 200/PK-8
1211 E Badillo St 91790 626-732-1500
Yvette Taylor, prin. Fax 858-8412
St. Christopher S 200/PK-8
900 W Christopher St 91790 626-960-3079
Lucia Saborio, prin. Fax 338-7910
South Hills Academy 300/PK-12
1600 E Francisquito Ave 91791 626-919-2000
Dr. Gabriel Ramirez, head sch Fax 918-7730
West Covina Christian S 300/PK-8
763 N Sunset Ave 91790 626-962-7080
Christine Petersen, prin. Fax 962-1589
West Covina Hills Adventist S 100/K-8
3528 E Temple Way 91791 626-859-5005

West Hills, Los Angeles
Los Angeles USD
Supt. — See Los Angeles
Capistrano Avenue ES 400/K-5
8118 Capistrano Ave 91304 818-883-8981
Sonja Cao Garcia, prin. Fax 340-2187
Nevada ES 500/K-5
22120 Chase St 91304 818-348-2169
Sosie Kralian, prin. Fax 592-0894

Kadima Day S 200/PK-8
7011 Shoup Ave 91307 818-346-0849
Shepherd of the Valley Lutheran S 100/PK-6
23838 Kittridge St 91307 818-347-6784
Jennifer Farrell, prin. Fax 347-9944
West Valley Christian S 200/PK-8
22450 Sherman Way 91307 818-884-4710
Derek Swales, admin. Fax 884-4749

West Hollywood, Los Angeles, Pop. 33,330
Los Angeles USD
Supt. — See Los Angeles
Laurel Early Education Center PK-PK
8023 Willoughby Ave 90046 323-654-0812
Curtis Johnson, prin. Fax 650-6319
West Hollywood ES 400/K-6
970 Hammond St 90069 310-274-5313
Peter Pannell, prin. Fax 858-8139

Center for Early Education S 500/PK-6
563 N Alfred St 90048 323-651-0707
Mark Brooks, head sch Fax 651-0860
West Hollywood College Preparatory S 100/PK-12
1317 N Crescent Heights Blv 90046 323-822-7900
Dr. Elina Dvorskaya, dir. Fax 822-7999

Westlake Village, Los Angeles, Pop. 8,064
Conejo Valley USD
Supt. — See Thousand Oaks
Westlake ES 500/K-5
1571 E Potrero Rd 91361 805-374-2150
Megan Triplett, prin. Fax 496-4006
Westlake Hills ES 500/K-5
3333 Medicine Bow Ct 91362 805-497-9339
James Marshall, prin. Fax 374-1162

Las Virgenes USD
Supt. — See Calabasas
White Oak ES 400/K-5
31761 Village School Rd 91361 818-889-1450
Mary-Allyn Garcia, prin. Fax 889-5904

Carden Conejo S 200/PK-6
975 Evenstar Ave 91361 805-497-7005
Holly Fleming Ed.D., head sch Fax 496-5628
St. Jude the Apostle S 200/K-8
32036 Lindero Canyon Rd 91361 818-889-9483
Michele Schulte, prin. Fax 889-1536

Westley, Stanislaus, Pop. 602
Patterson JUSD
Supt. — See Patterson
Grayson ES 300/K-5
PO Box 7 95387 209-892-4725
Arturo Duran, prin. Fax 894-3393

Westminster, Orange, Pop. 87,394
Garden Grove USD
Supt. — See Garden Grove
Anthony ES 500/K-6
15320 Pickford St 92683 714-663-6104
Tyleen Perez, prin. Fax 663-6017
Carrillo ES 600/K-6
15270 Bushard St 92683 714-663-6230
Kim Kroyer, prin. Fax 663-6169
Marshall ES 500/K-6
15791 Bushard St 92683 714-663-6528
Lorrie Klevos, prin. Fax 663-6036
McGarvin IS 800/7-8
9802 Bishop Pl 92683 714-663-6218
Thanh Phan, prin. Fax 663-6163

Post ES 600/K-6
14641 Ward St 92683 714-663-6354
Joy Ellsworth Ed.D., prin. Fax 663-6337

Ocean View SD
Supt. — See Huntington Beach
Westmont ES 400/K-5
8251 Heil Ave 92683 714-847-3561
Sue Broderson Ed.D., prin. Fax 842-6051

Westminster SD 9,700/PK-8
14121 Cedarwood St 92683 714-894-7311
Dr. Gary Rutherford, supt. Fax 899-2781
www.wsdk8.us
Eastwood ES 500/PK-6
13552 University St 92683 714-894-7227
Dr. Jason Kuncewicki, prin. Fax 901-9104
Finley ES 400/PK-5
13521 Edwards St 92683 714-895-7764
Raul Olivas, prin. Fax 901-7184
Fryberger ES 400/PK-5
6952 Hood Dr 92683 714-894-7237
Dr. Dena Kiouses, prin. Fax 896-8471
Johnson MS 800/6-8
13603 Edwards St 92683 714-894-7244
Daniel Owens, prin. Fax 372-8807
Land S PK-PK
15151 Temple St 92683 714-898-8389
Reagan Lopez, prin. Fax 895-6525
Schmitt ES 500/PK-5
7200 Trask Ave 92683 714-894-7264
Orchid Rocha, prin. Fax 890-9255
Sequoia ES 400/PK-6
5900 Iroquois Rd 92683 714-894-7271
Michelle Watkins, prin. Fax 891-9164
Warner MS 1,100/6-8
14171 Newland St 92683 714-894-7281
Amy Kwon, prin. Fax 895-2378
Webber ES 400/PK-6
14142 Hoover St 92683 714-894-7288
Kevin Whitney, prin. Fax 894-7301
Willmore ES 400/PK-5
7122 Maple St 92683 714-895-3765
Dr. Nicole Jacoboson, prin. Fax 372-8811
Other Schools – See Garden Grove, Huntington Beach, Midway City

---

Bethany Christian Academy 100/K-8
13431 Edwards St 92683 714-891-9783
Patricia Harnish, prin. Fax 892-5379
Blessed Sacrament S 300/PK-8
14146 Olive St 92683 714-893-7701
Roisin McAree, prin. Fax 891-7186
Covenant Christian Academy 50/K-8
10101 Cunningham Ave 92683 714-531-9950
Joe LoGiudice, prin. Fax 531-9936

Westmorland, Imperial, Pop. 2,208
Westmorland UNESD 400/K-8
PO Box 88 92281 760-344-4364
Nancy Johnson, supt. Fax 344-7294
www.wued.org
Westmorland ES 400/K-8
PO Box 88 92281 760-344-4364
Nancy Johnson, prin. Fax 344-7294

West Point, Calaveras, Pop. 646
Calaveras USD
Supt. — See San Andreas
West Point S 100/K-6
PO Box 96 95255 209-754-2255
Katie Hood, prin. Fax 293-4727

West Sacramento, Yolo, Pop. 45,910
Washington USD 7,800/PK-12
930 Westacre Rd 95691 916-375-7600
Linda Luna Ed.D., supt. Fax 375-7619
www.wusd.k12.ca.us
Bridgeway Island ES 1,000/K-8
3255 Half Moon Bay Cir 95691 916-375-7778
Grace Chin, prin. Fax 375-7794
Elkhorn Village ES 600/K-8
750 Cummins Way 95605 916-375-7670
Sal Garcia, prin. Fax 375-7879
Riverbank ES 900/PK-8
1100 Carrie St 95605 916-375-7700
Hortencia Phifer, prin. Fax 375-7709
Southport ES 800/PK-8
2747 Linden Rd 95691 916-375-7890
Matt Ainsworth, prin. Fax 375-7894
Stonegate ES 800/K-8
2500 La Jolla St 95691 916-375-0960
Ben Kingsbury, prin. Fax 372-6057
Westfield Village ES 400/PK-5
508 Poplar Ave 95691 916-375-7720
Roxanna Villasenor, prin. Fax 375-7729
Westmore Oaks ES 800/K-8
1100 Clarendon St 95691 916-375-7730
Stacey Falconer, prin. Fax 375-0963

Bryte Christian Academy 50/PK-7
1000 Sacramento Ave 95605 916-233-2503
Sergiy Pronin, prin. Fax 233-2504
Our Lady of Grace S 300/K-8
1990 Linden Rd 95691 916-371-9416
Laura MacDonald, prin. Fax 371-1319

Westwood, Lassen, Pop. 1,610
Westwood USD 300/K-12
PO Box 1225 96137 530-256-2311
Randy Bobby, supt. Fax 256-3539
www.westwoodusd.org
Walker ES 100/K-5
PO Box 1490 96137 530-256-3295
Marci Johnson, prin. Fax 256-2949

Wheatland, Yuba, Pop. 3,292
Wheatland SD 1,300/PK-8
111 Main St 95692 530-633-3130
Craig Guensler, supt. Fax 633-4807
www.wheatlandsd.com
Bear River S 500/4-8
100 Wheatland Park Dr 95692 530-633-3135
Angela Gouker, prin. Fax 633-3142
Wheatland ES 300/PK-3
111 Hooper St 95692 530-633-3140
Jim Evans, prin. Fax 633-2367
Other Schools – See Beale AFB

Whitethorn, Humboldt
Leggett Valley USD
Supt. — See Leggett
Whale Gulch ES 50/K-8
76811 Usal Rd 95589 707-986-7131
Anthony Loumena, prin. Fax 986-1355

Southern Humbolt JUSD
Supt. — See Miranda
Whitethorn S 100/PK-6
16851 Briceland Thorn Rd 95589 707-986-7420
Don Boyd, prin. Fax 986-1676

Whitmore, Shasta
Whitmore UNESD 300/K-12
PO Box 10 96096 530-472-3243
Dr. Larry Robins, supt. Fax 472-1127
www.wujesd.org
Whitmore ES 50/K-8
PO Box 10 96096 530-472-3243
Dr. Larry Robins, admin. Fax 472-1127

Whittier, Los Angeles, Pop. 84,209
East Whittier City ESD 9,200/PK-8
14535 Whittier Blvd 90605 562-907-5959
Marc Patterson, supt. Fax 696-9256
www.ewcsd.org/
Ceres ES 400/K-5
10601 Ceres Ave 90604 562-464-2200
Julie Gonzalez, prin. Fax 946-0971
East Whittier MS 1,300/6-8
14421 Whittier Blvd 90605 562-789-7220
Gabriela Aldana, prin. Fax 945-3542
Evergreen ES 500/PK-5
12915 Helmer Dr 90602 562-464-2300
Skarlette Torres, prin. Fax 698-6951
Granada MS 1,100/6-8
15337 Lemon Dr 90604 562-464-2330
Justin Mayernik, prin. Fax 943-5413
Hillview MS 700/6-8
10931 Stamy Rd 90604 562-789-2000
David Herrera, prin. Fax 946-3066
La Colima ES 600/K-5
11225 Miller Rd 90604 562-789-7200
Elisa Clarke, prin. Fax 944-0062
Laurel ES 800/K-5
13550 Lambert Rd 90605 562-789-2100
Daniel Ruiz, prin. Fax 945-3698
Leffingwell ES 600/K-5
10625 Santa Gertrudes Ave 90603 562-907-6300
Dr. Scott Blackwell, prin. Fax 943-2445
Mulberry ES 600/PK-5
14029 Mulberry Dr 90605 562-789-7100
Virginia Salamanca, prin. Fax 693-2324
Murphy Ranch ES 600/K-5
16021 Janine Dr 90603 562-789-2150
Nick Damico, prin. Fax 902-0267
Ocean View ES 900/K-5
14359 2nd St 90605 562-907-6400
Tim Strand, prin. Fax 693-7424
Orchard Dale ES 600/PK-5
10625 Cole Rd 90604 562-789-7000
Renee Mackay, prin. Fax 941-5197
Scott Avenue ES 700/K-5
11701 Scott Ave 90604 562-907-6440
Hal Eldred, prin. Fax 943-0454

Los Nietos ESD
Supt. — See Los Nietos
Aeolian ES 500/K-6
11600 Aeolian St 90606 562-699-0913
Rebecca Speh, prin. Fax 699-2545
Nelson ES 500/PK-6
8140 Vicki Dr 90606 562-692-0615
Marla Duncan, prin. Fax 695-0484

Lowell JSD 3,200/PK-8
11019 Valley Home Ave 90603 562-943-0211
Dr. Jim Coombs, supt. Fax 947-7874
www.ljsd.org
Jordan ES 400/K-6
10654 Jordan Rd 90603 562-902-4221
Marikate Wissman, prin. Fax 947-9984
Meadow Green ES 500/PK-6
12025 Grovedale Dr 90604 562-902-4241
Tara Ryan, prin. Fax 902-9208
Rancho-Starbuck IS 800/7-8
16430 Woodbrier Dr 90604 562-902-4261
Linda Takacs, prin. Fax 947-9911
Other Schools – See La Habra

South Whittier ESD 3,200/K-8
11200 Telechron Ave 90605 562-944-6231
Dr. Gary Gonzales, supt. Fax 944-9659
www.swhittier.k12.ca.us
Carmela ES 500/K-6
13300 Lakeland Rd 90605 562-941-2132
Dr. Trena Salcedo Gonzalez, prin. Fax 941-5443
Graves MS 800/7-8
13243 Los Nietos Rd 90605 562-944-0135
Dr. Matthew Fraijo, prin. Fax 944-9433
Lake Marie ES 300/K-6
10001 Carmenita Rd 90605 562-944-0208
Lisa Palomino, prin. Fax 944-6784
Loma Vista ES 500/K-6
13463 Meyer Rd 90605 562-941-4712
Kristine Carreon, prin. Fax 941-5472
Los Altos ES 400/K-3
12001 Bonavista Ln 90604 562-941-3711
Dr. Marti Ayala, prin. Fax 941-5281
McKibben ES 400/K-6
10550 Mills Ave 90604 562-944-9878
Sandra Gallegos, prin. Fax 944-4288
Monte Vista MS 300/3-6
12000 Loma Dr 90604 562-946-1494
Andrea Larios, prin. Fax 946-0914

Whittier City ESD 6,200/K-8
7211 Whittier Ave 90602 562-789-3075
Dr. Ron Carruth, supt. Fax 698-6534
www.whittiercity.net
Andrews ES 500/K-7
1010 Caraway Dr 90601 562-789-3140
Chris Quirarte, prin. Fax 789-3145
Dexter MS 1,100/6-8
11532 Floral Dr 90601 562-789-3090
Robert Allard Ed.D., prin. Fax 789-3095
Edwards MS 800/6-8
6812 Norwalk Blvd 90606 562-789-3120
Andrew Alvidrez, prin. Fax 789-3133
Hoover ES 500/K-5
6302 Alta Ave 90601 562-789-3150
Kay Oborn, prin. Fax 789-3155
Jackson ES 500/K-5
8015 Painter Ave 90602 562-789-3160
Maria Ruiz, prin. Fax 789-3165
Longfellow ES 600/K-5
6005 Magnolia Ave 90601 562-789-3180
Melissa Garcia, prin. Fax 789-3185
Mill S and Terchnology Academy 400/K-5
4030 Workman Mill Rd 90601 562-789-3190
Reanna Mendoza, prin. Fax 789-3195
Orange Grove ES 400/K-5
10626 Orange Grove Ave 90601 562-789-3200
Lisa El Sabbagh, prin. Fax 789-3205
Phelan ES 500/K-5
7150 Cully Ave 90606 562-789-3210
Rebecca Rodriguez, prin. Fax 789-3215
Sorensen ES 500/K-5
11493 Rose Hedge Dr 90606 562-789-3220
Lilia Vargas Ed.D., prin. Fax 789-3225
West Whittier ES 400/K-5
6411 Norwalk Blvd 90606 562-789-3240
Michelle Aceves, prin. Fax 789-3245

Broadoaks Children S of Whittier College 300/PK-8
PO Box 634 90608 562-907-4250
Dr. Judith Wagner, dir. Fax 907-4960
Carden Whittier Private S 300/PK-8
11537 Grovedale Dr 90604 562-694-1879
Heights Christian ES - Maybrook 300/K-6
11700 Maybrook Ave 90604 562-947-3757
Michael Stovall, prin. Fax 902-9137
Plymouth Christian S 200/PK-6
12058 Beverly Blvd 90601 562-695-0745
Sandra Johnson, prin. Fax 699-3038
Primanti Montessori S - Whittier 100/K-8
10947 Valley Home Ave 90603 562-943-0246
Ann Desilva, dir.
St. Bruno S 300/K-8
15700 Citrustree Rd 90603 562-943-8812
Catherine Carvalho, prin. Fax 943-2172
St. Gregory the Great S 200/PK-8
13925 Telegraph Rd 90604 562-941-0750
Paulette Clagon, prin. Fax 903-7325
St. Mary of the Assumption S 200/K-8
7218 Pickering Ave 90602 562-698-0253
Maria Ortiz-Lopez, prin. Fax 698-0206
Whittier Friends S 50/PK-6
6726 Washington Ave 90601 562-945-1654
Cassie Caringella, lead tchr.

Wildomar, Riverside, Pop. 31,160
Lake Elsinore USD
Supt. — See Lake Elsinore
Brown MS 1,000/6-8
21861 Grand Ave 92595 951-253-7430
Karen Gaither, prin. Fax 253-7437
Collier ES 600/K-5
20150 Mayhall Dr 92595 951-253-7630
Dorri Neal, prin. Fax 253-7631
Graham ES 500/K-6
35450 Frederick St 92595 951-253-7590
Laura Konecni, prin. Fax 253-7589
Reagan ES 700/K-6
35445 Porras Rd 92595 951-253-7650
Nori Chandler, prin. Fax 253-7655
Wildomar ES 700/K-5
21575 Palomar St 92595 951-253-7555
Michael Hoffman Ed.D., prin. Fax 253-7563

Bundy Canyon Christian S 100/PK-8
23411 Bundy Canyon Rd 92595 951-674-1254
Rev. Phillip Walker, admin. Fax 674-2444
Cornerstone Christian S 200/PK-12
34570 Monte Vista Dr 92595 951-674-9381
Sharon Privett, head sch Fax 674-8462
St. Frances of Rome Preschool 50/PK-PK
21591 Lemon St 92595 951-471-5144
Susy Olivera, dir. Fax 674-6443

Williams, Colusa, Pop. 5,073
Williams USD 1,300/PK-12
PO Box 7 95987 530-473-2550
Edgar Lampkin, supt. Fax 473-5894
www.williamsusd.net
Williams ES 500/PK-3
PO Box 7 95987 530-473-2885
Fax 473-3780
Williams Upper ES 300/4-6
PO Box 7 95987 530-473-5304
Denise Conrado, prin. Fax 473-5928

Willits, Mendocino, Pop. 4,738
Willits USD 1,600/K-12
1277 Blosser Ln 95490 707-459-5314
Mark Westerburg, supt. Fax 459-7862
www.willitsunified.com
Baechtel Grove MS 300/6-8
1150 Magnolia St 95490 707-459-2417
Maria Mungia, prin. Fax 459-7881
Blosser Lane ES 200/3-5
1275 Blosser Ln 95490 707-459-3232
Nancy Runberg, prin. Fax 459-7621

Brookside ES 300/K-2
20 Spruce St 95490 707-459-5385
Kathleen Crossman, prin. Fax 459-7857
Sherwood ES, 1277 Blosser Ln 95490 50/K-8
Mark Westerburg, prin. 707-984-6769

Adventist Christian S of Willits 50/1-8
22751 Bray Rd 95490 707-459-4333

Willow Creek, Humboldt, Pop. 1,610
Klamath-Trinity JUSD
Supt. — See Hoopa
Trinity Valley ES 200/PK-8
PO Box 1229 95573 530-625-5600
Elizabeth Franklin, prin. Fax 629-2452

Willows, Glenn, Pop. 6,043
Willows USD 1,400/PK-12
823 W Laurel St 95988 530-934-6600
Dr. Mort Geivett, supt. Fax 934-6609
www.willowsunified.org
Murdock ES 600/PK-5
655 French St 95988 530-934-6640
Stephen Montana, prin. Fax 934-6557
Willows IS 300/6-8
1145 W Cedar St 95988 530-934-6633
Steve Sailsbery, prin. Fax 934-6697

Wilmington, See Los Angeles
Los Angeles USD
Supt. — See Los Angeles
Bridges Span S 1,200/K-8
1235 Broad Ave 90744 310-522-5400
Louie Mardesich, prin. Fax 835-1575
Broad Avenue ES 800/K-5
24815 Broad Ave 90744 310-835-3118
Angela Tenette, prin. Fax 835-6012
De La Torre ES 200/K-5
500 Island Ave 90744 310-847-1400
Katherine Durke, prin. Fax 834-9171
Fries Avenue ES 600/K-5
1301 N Fries Ave 90744 310-834-6431
Tracy Joseph, prin. Fax 834-9238
Gulf ES 800/K-5
828 W L St 90744 310-835-3157
David Kooper, prin. Fax 549-7986
Hawaiian Avenue ES 700/K-5
540 Hawaiian Ave 90744 310-830-1151
Luis Rivera, prin. Fax 835-0028
Hawaiian Early Education Center PK-PK
501 Hawaiian Ave 90744 310-834-7186
Deborah Aguet, prin. Fax 834-3391
Wilmington Early Education Center PK-PK
1419 E Young St 90744 310-518-3207
Mercy Udeochu, prin. Fax 834-2718
Wilmington Park ES 900/K-5
1140 Mahar Ave 90744 310-518-7460
Lowell Bernstein, prin. Fax 830-8716
Wilmington STEAM MS 1,500/6-8
1700 Gulf Ave 90744 310-847-1500
Karen Mercado, prin. Fax 549-5307

Pacific Harbor Christian S 200/PK-12
1530 N Wilmington Blvd 90744 310-835-5665
Kathy Gutierrez, head sch Fax 835-6316
SS. Peter & Paul S 200/K-8
706 Bay View Ave 90744 310-834-5574
Nancy Kuria, prin. Fax 834-1601

Wilton, Sacramento, Pop. 5,148
Elk Grove USD
Supt. — See Elk Grove
Dillard ES 400/K-6
9721 Dillard Rd 95693 916-687-6121
Sandra Wiest, prin. Fax 687-8183

Wilton Christian S 100/PK-12
9697 Dillard Rd 95693 916-687-7693
Rev. John Schmidt, admin. Fax 687-6587

Winchester, Riverside, Pop. 2,466
Hemet USD
Supt. — See Hemet
Winchester ES 600/K-5
28751 Winchester Rd 92596 951-926-0700
Mark Delano, prin. Fax 926-0706

Menifee UNESD
Supt. — See Menifee
Harvest Hill STEAM Academy K-5
31600 Pat Rd 92596 951-325-6000
Brian Martes, prin. Fax 325-6997

Temecula Valley USD
Supt. — See Temecula
French Valley ES 900/K-5
36680 Cady Rd 92596 951-926-3643
Kim Mazelin, prin. Fax 926-3683
LaVorgna ES 800/K-5
31777 Algarve Ave 92596 951-294-6385
Lisa Brown, prin. Fax 294-6388

Windsor, Sonoma, Pop. 26,016
Windsor USD 5,400/PK-12
9291 Old Redwood Hwy 95492 707-837-7700
Brandon Krueger, supt. Fax 838-4031
www.wusd.org
Brooks ES 500/4-5
750 Natalie Dr 95492 707-837-7717
Kimberlee Kimes, prin. Fax 837-7722
Windsor Creek ES 400/2-3
8955 Conde Ln 95492 707-837-7757
Julie Stearn, prin. Fax 837-7760
Windsor MS 900/6-8
9500 Brooks Rd S 95492 707-837-7737
Brian Williams, prin. Fax 837-7743
Other Schools – See Santa Rosa

Windsor Christian Academy 300/PK-8
PO Box 1880 95492 707-838-3757
Tad Theiss, prin. Fax 838-3542

Winnetka, See Los Angeles
Los Angeles USD
Supt. — See Los Angeles
Sunny Brae ES 600/K-5
20620 Arminta St 91306 818-341-0931
Olivia Tamayo Minjares, prin. Fax 709-1232

St. Joseph the Worker S 300/PK-8
19812 Cantlay St 91306 818-341-6616
Sr. C.J. Kruska, prin. Fax 341-3875
St. Martin-in-the-Fields S 100/PK-8
7136 Winnetka Ave 91306 818-340-5144
Wendy Byrnes, head sch Fax 340-5882

Winterhaven, Imperial, Pop. 381
San Pasqual Valley USD 800/K-12
676 Base Line Rd 92283 760-572-0222
Dr. Rauna Fox, supt. Fax 572-0711
www.spvusd.org/
San Pasqual Valley ES 400/K-5
676 Base Line Rd 92283 760-572-0222
Gabriel Sandoval, prin. Fax 572-5600
San Pasqual Valley MS 200/6-8
676 Base Line Rd 92283 760-572-0222
Mary Kay Monson, prin. Fax 572-0829

Winters, Yolo, Pop. 6,490
Winters JUSD 1,500/K-12
909 Grant Ave 95694 530-795-6100
Dr. Todd Cutler, supt. Fax 795-6114
www.wintersjusd.org
Rominger IS 200/4-5
502 Niemann St 95694 530-795-6320
Gregory Moffitt, prin. Fax 795-6123
Waggoner ES 400/K-3
500 Edwards St 95694 530-795-6121
Gregory Moffitt, prin. Fax 795-6120
Winters MS 400/6-8
425 Anderson Ave 95694 530-795-6130
John Barsotti, prin. Fax 795-6137

Winton, Merced, Pop. 10,450
Merced River UNESD 100/K-8
4402 Oakdale Rd 95388 209-358-5679
Richard Lopez, supt. Fax 358-2855
www.mrusd.us
Washington S 200/K-8
4402 Oakdale Rd 95388 209-358-5679
Richard Lopez, supt. Fax 358-2855

Winton SD 1,900/PK-8
PO Box 8 95388 209-357-6175
Randall Heller, supt. Fax 357-1994
www.winton.k12.ca.us
Crookham ES 400/PK-5
PO Box 130 95388 209-357-6182
Kim Cuthriell, prin. Fax 357-6185
Sparkes ES 400/PK-5
PO Box 1477 95388 209-357-6180
Ka Vang, prin. Fax 357-6580
Winfield ES 400/PK-5
PO Box 1839 95388 209-357-6891
Kim Sherman, prin. Fax 357-6893
Winton MS 600/6-8
PO Box 1299 95388 209-357-6189
Craig Perry, prin. Fax 358-5889

Woodlake, Tulare, Pop. 7,217
Woodlake USD 2,300/K-12
300 W Whitney Ave 93286 559-564-8081
Drew Sorensen, supt. Fax 564-3831
www.w-usd.org
Castle Rock ES 500/3-5
360 N Castle Rock St 93286 559-564-8001
Jason Trevino, prin. Fax 564-8030
White Learning Center 500/K-2
700 N Cypress St 93286 559-564-8021
Nancy Stidman, prin. Fax 564-0901
Woodlake Valley MS 500/6-8
497 N Palm St 93286 559-564-8061
Antonio Rivera, prin. Fax 564-0702

Woodland, Yolo, Pop. 54,082
Woodland JUSD 9,900/K-12
435 6th St 95695 530-662-0201
Dr. Thomas Pritchard, supt. Fax 662-6956
www.wjusd.org
Beamer Park ES 500/K-6
525 Beamer St 95695 530-662-1769
Georgina Llamas-Cruz, prin. Fax 668-5653
Dingle ES 400/K-6
625 Elm St 95695 530-662-7084
Silvia Tovar, prin. Fax 669-7101
Douglass MS 800/7-8
525 Granada Dr 95695 530-666-2191
Derek Cooper, prin. Fax 668-9217
Freeman ES 500/K-6
126 N West St 95695 530-662-1758
Dr. Eduardo Gonzalez, prin. Fax 662-9395
Gibson ES 700/K-6
312 Gibson Rd 95695 530-662-3944
Parveen Saenz, prin. Fax 662-0945
Lee MS 700/7-8
520 West St 95695 530-662-0251
Sandra Garcia, prin. Fax 662-9423
Maxwell ES 500/K-6
50 Ashley Ave 95695 530-662-1784
Bradley Clagg, prin. Fax 662-1526
Plainfield ES 300/K-6
20450 County Road 97 95695 530-662-9301
Jacob Holt, prin. Fax 662-5043
Tafoya ES 800/K-6
720 Homestead Way 95776 530-666-4324
Alison Kasta, prin. Fax 666-3702
Whitehead ES 400/K-6
624 W Southwood Dr 95695 530-662-2824
Maria Sevilla, prin. Fax 662-7551
Woodland Prairie ES 600/K-6
1444 Stetson St 95776 530-662-2898
Scott Clary, prin. Fax 666-3549

Zamora ES 500/K-6
1716 Cottonwood St 95695 530-666-3641
Dr. Felicia Rodoni-Wilson, prin. Fax 668-0985

Community Christian Academy 50/K-8
434 Cleveland St 95695 530-383-1246
Val Kampf, prin. Fax 662-1621
Holy Rosary S 200/K-8
505 California St 95695 530-662-3494
Natalie McCullough, prin. Fax 668-2442
Woodland Christian S 300/PK-12
1787 Matmor Rd 95776 530-406-8800
Justin Smith, admin. Fax 406-0900
Woodland Montessori S 100/PK-6
1738 Cottonwood St 95695 530-662-1900
Sylvia Flood, dir.

Woodland Hills, See Los Angeles
Los Angeles USD
Supt. — See Los Angeles
Calabash Charter Academy 400/K-5
23055 Eugene St 91364 818-224-4430
Esther Gillis, prin. Fax 225-9385
Woodland Hills Academy 1,100/6-8
20800 Burbank Blvd 91367 818-226-2900
Ted Yamane, prin. Fax 716-0649

St. Bernardine of Siena S 300/PK-8
6061 Valley Circle Blvd 91367 818-340-2130
Katy Kruska, prin. Fax 340-3417
St. Mel S 600/K-8
20874 Ventura Blvd 91364 818-340-1924
Mary Beth Lutz, prin. Fax 347-4426
Woodland Hills Private S 100/PK-5
22555 Oxnard St 91367 818-348-6563

Woodside, San Mateo, Pop. 5,153
Cabrillo USD
Supt. — See Half Moon Bay
Kings Mountain ES 100/K-5
211 Swett Rd 94062 650-712-7180
Dinae Siegal, prin. Fax 851-9370

Woodside ESD 500/K-8
3195 Woodside Rd 94062 650-851-1571
Beth Polito, supt. Fax 851-5577
www.woodside.k12.ca.us
Woodside ES 500/K-8
3195 Woodside Rd 94062 650-851-1571
Pamela Duarte, prin. Fax 851-5577

Woody, Kern
Blake ESD 50/K-8
PO Box 40 93287 661-536-8559
Gary Bray, supt. Fax 536-9389
blakesd.org
Blake S 50/K-8
PO Box 40 93287 661-536-8559
Dawn Carver, prin. Fax 536-9389

Wrightwood, San Bernardino, Pop. 4,412
Snowline JUSD
Supt. — See Phelan
Wrightwood ES 300/K-5
1175 State Hwy 2 92397 760-249-5828
John Garner, prin. Fax 249-5820

Yermo, San Bernardino
Silver Valley USD 2,400/PK-12
PO Box 847 92398 760-254-2916
Jill Kemock, supt. Fax 254-2091
www.svusdk12.net
Yermo S 300/PK-8
PO Box 847 92398 760-254-2931
Kate Henson, prin. Fax 254-2932
Other Schools – See Fort Irwin, Newberry Springs

Yorba Linda, Orange, Pop. 62,269
Placentia-Yorba Linda USD
Supt. — See Placentia
Bryant Ranch ES 600/K-5
24695 Paseo De Toronto 92887 714-986-7120
Dominque Polchow, prin. Fax 694-0569
Fairmont ES 900/K-6
5241 Fairmont Blvd 92886 714-986-7130
Cindy Rex, prin. Fax 970-7983
Glenknoll ES 500/K-6
6361 Glenknoll Dr 92886 714-970-0720
David Cammarato, prin. Fax 970-0721
Lakeview ES 500/K-5
17510 Lakeview Ave 92886 714-986-7190
Katherine Dailey, prin. Fax 223-7509
Linda Vista ES 500/K-5
5600 Ohio St 92886 714-986-7200
Kristen Petrovacki, prin. Fax 779-2138
Paine ES 400/K-5
4444 Plumosa Dr 92886 714-986-7210
Melanie Carmona, prin. Fax 777-4398
Rose Drive ES 400/K-5
4700 Rose Dr 92886 714-986-7250
Dr. Katherine Dailey, prin. Fax 528-9406
Travis Ranch S 1,400/K-8
5200 Via De La Escuela 92887 714-986-7460
Susan Metcalf, prin. Fax 777-8312
Yorba Linda MS 900/6-8
4777 Casa Loma Ave 92886 714-986-7080
Tamar Kataroyan, prin. Fax 996-2752
Yorba MS 700/7-8
5350 Fairmont Blvd 92886 714-986-7400
Ken Valburg, prin. Fax 970-1647

Calvary Chapel of Yorba Linda Academy 200/PK-8
18821 Yorba linda Blvd 92886 714-777-7131
Beth Holiday, prin. Fax 777-1766
Discovery Depot Child Care Center 200/PK-K
16800 Imperial Hwy 92886 714-572-0522
Michele Nelson, dir. Fax 572-1687
Friends Christian ES 500/K-4
5151 Lakeview Ave 92886 714-777-3009
Becki Crandall, prin. Fax 777-4028

Friends Christian MS 400/5-8
4231 Rose Dr 92886 714-524-5240
Joy Swift, prin. Fax 524-5784
Heritage Oak Private Education 600/PK-8
16971 Imperial Hwy 92886 714-524-1350
Phyllis Cygan, dir. Fax 524-1352
St. Francis of Assisi S 400/PK-8
5330 Eastside Cir 92887 714-695-3700
Thomas Waszak, prin. Fax 695-3704

Yosemite National Park, Mariposa
Mariposa County USD
Supt. — See Mariposa
Yosemite Valley ES 50/K-8
PO Box 485 95389 209-372-4791
Sean Jacobs, prin. Fax 372-8791

Yountville, Napa, Pop. 2,856
Napa Valley USD
Supt. — See Napa
Yountville ES 100/K-5
6554 Yount St 94599 707-253-3485
Tara Bianchi, prin. Fax 253-6209

Yreka, Siskiyou, Pop. 7,387
Yreka UNSD 1,000/K-8
309 Jackson St 96097 530-842-1168
Dave Parsons, supt. Fax 842-4576
www.yrekausd.net
Evergreen ES 500/K-3
416 Evergreen Ln 96097 530-842-4912
Amy Dunlap, prin. Fax 842-9438
Jackson Street ES 500/4-8
405 Jackson St 96097 530-842-3561
Chris Harris, prin. Fax 842-1716

Yreka Adventist Christian S 50/K-8
346 Payne Ln 96097 530-842-7071
Mary Korcek, prin. Fax 842-7463

Yuba City, Sutter, Pop. 62,225
Franklin ESD 500/K-8
332 N Township Rd 95993 530-822-5151
Lisa Shelton, supt. Fax 822-5177
www.franklin.k12.ca.us
Franklin ES 500/K-8
332 N Township Rd 95993 530-822-5151
Lisa Shelton, prin. Fax 822-5177

Yuba City USD 13,400/PK-12
750 N Palora Ave 95991 530-822-5200
Doreen Osumi, supt. Fax 671-2454
www.ycusd.org
April Lane ES 500/PK-5
800 April Ln 95991 530-822-5215
Valerie Bradley, prin. Fax 822-5028
Barry S 600/PK-8
1255 Barry Rd 95991 530-822-5220
Ben Moss, prin. Fax 822-7262
Bridge Street ES 500/PK-5
500 Bridge St 95991 530-822-5225
Melissa McIntyre, prin. Fax 822-5002
Butte Vista ES 1,000/PK-8
2195 Blevin Rd 95993 530-822-5034
Jaswindar Peterson, prin. Fax 822-5008
Central-Gaither ES 200/K-8
8403 Bailey Rd 95993 530-822-5230
Mary Reinhardt, prin. Fax 822-5004
Gray Avenue MS 700/6-8
808 Gray Ave 95991 530-822-5240
Brian Gault, prin. Fax 822-5057
Karperos S 1,400/PK-8
1700 Camino De Flores 95993 530-822-4440
Clint Johnson, prin. Fax 671-5356
King Avenue ES 400/K-5
630 King Ave 95991 530-822-5250
Frank Alvarez, prin. Fax 822-5031
Lincoln ES 600/PK-5
1582 Lincoln Rd 95993 530-822-5255
Ron Taylor, prin. Fax 822-5303
Lincrest ES 700/PK-5
1400 Phillips Rd 95991 530-822-5260
Sara Nowinski, prin. Fax 674-9430
Park Avenue ES 600/PK-5
100 Morton St 95991 530-822-5265
Clark Bryant, prin. Fax 822-5279
Riverbend ES 1,200/PK-8
301 Stewart Rd 95991 530-822-3100
Tom Walters, prin. Fax 822-2520
Tierra Buena ES 800/K-8
1794 Villa Ave 95993 530-822-5280
Brian Brown, prin. Fax 822-5024

Adventist Christian S 50/K-8
369 Harding Rd 95993 530-673-7645
Tamra Clemons, prin. Fax 673-3458
Faith Christian ES 200/K-6
PO Box 1690 95992 530-674-3922
Bill Hannold, supt. Fax 674-0192
St. Isidore S 200/PK-8
200 Clark Ave 95991 530-673-2217
Laura Clark, prin. Fax 673-3673

Yucaipa, San Bernardino, Pop. 50,145
Yucaipa-Calimesa JUSD 9,700/K-12
12797 3rd St 92399 909-797-0174
Cali Binks, supt. Fax 797-5751
www.yucaipaschools.com
Calimesa ES 500/K-6
13523 2nd St 92399 909-790-8570
Leslie Burghardt, prin. Fax 790-8576
Chapman Heights ES 800/K-6
33692 Cramer Rd 92399 909-790-8080
Andy Anderson, prin. Fax 797-3755
Dunlap ES 500/K-6
32870 Avenue E 92399 909-797-5171
Lindy Ward, prin. Fax 790-6177
Park View MS 600/7-8
34875 Tahoe Dr 92399 909-790-3285
Frank Tucci, prin. Fax 790-3295
Ridgeview ES 800/K-6
11021 Sunnyside Dr 92399 909-790-3270
Giovanni Bernier, prin. Fax 790-3278
Valley ES 600/K-6
12333 8th St 92399 909-797-1125
Kathlene Miller, prin. Fax 790-8560
Wildwood ES 700/K-6
35972 Susan St 92399 909-790-8521
Lucia Hudec, prin. Fax 790-8525
Other Schools – See Calimesa

Wildwood Christian Academy 100/K-6
35145 Oak Glen Rd 92399 909-790-5356
Reid Isaac, prin.

Yucca Valley, San Bernardino, Pop. 20,139
Morongo USD
Supt. — See Twentynine Palms
La Contenta MS 800/7-8
7050 La Contenta Rd 92284 760-228-1802
Garrett Gruwell, prin. Fax 369-6324
Onaga ES 700/K-6
58001 Onaga Trl 92284 760-369-6333
Kristen Mery, prin. Fax 369-6329
Yucca Mesa ES 400/K-6
3380 Avalon Ave 92284 760-228-1777
Matt Gay, prin. Fax 365-2467
Yucca Valley ES 600/K-6
7601 Hopi Trl 92284 760-365-3381
Kurt McLachlan, prin. Fax 369-6303

Joshua Springs Christian S 200/PK-12
57373 Joshua Ln 92284 760-365-3599
Fem Ontiveros, admin. Fax 369-0315

Zenia, Trinity
Southern Trinity JUSD
Supt. — See Mad River
Hoaglin-Zenia S 50/K-8
HC 62 Box 54 95595 707-923-9670
Robin Drechsler, lead tchr. Fax 923-4294

COLORADO

COLORADO DEPARTMENT OF EDUCATION
201 E Colfax Ave, Denver 80203-1799
Telephone 303-866-6646
Fax 303-830-0793
Website http://www.cde.state.co.us

Commissioner of Education Dr. Katy Anthes

COLORADO BOARD OF EDUCATION
201 E Colfax Ave, Denver 80203-1704

Chairperson Angelika Schroeder

BOARDS OF COOPERATIVE EDUCATIONAL SERVICES (BOCES)

Adams County BOCES
Eric Wiant, dir. 303-286-7294
1400 W 122nd Ave Ste 110 Fax 286-9078
Denver 80234
www.aboces.org

Centennial BOCES
Dr. Randy Zila, dir. 970-352-7404
2020 Clubhouse Dr, Greeley 80634 Fax 352-7350
www.cboces.org

Colorado Digital BOCES
Kindra Whitmyre, dir., 4035 Tutt Blvd 719-418-5276
Colorado Springs 80922
www.cdboces.org

East Central BOCES
Don Anderson, dir. 719-775-2342
PO Box 910, Limon 80828 Fax 775-9714
www.ecboces.org

Expeditionary BOCES
Chad Burns, dir. 303-759-2076
1700 S Holly St, Denver 80222 Fax 757-7442
www.rmsel.org

Front Range BOCES
Hi Howard, dir. 720-561-5096
6500 Arapahoe Rd, Boulder 80303
www.frboces.org

Grand Valley BOCES
, 2508 Blichman Ave 970-255-2700
Grand Junction 81505 Fax 255-2626
grandvalleyboces.org/

Mountain BOCES
Allan Ward, dir. 719-486-2603
1713 Mount Lincoln Dr W Fax 486-2109
Leadville 80461
www.mtnboces.org/

Mount Evans BOCES
Terri Jones, dir. 303-567-3878
PO Box 3399, Idaho Springs 80452 Fax 567-3880
mtevansboces.com

Northeast Colorado BOCES
Bret Miles, dir. 970-774-6152
PO Box 98, Haxtun 80731 Fax 774-6157
www.neboces.org

Northwest Colorado BOCES
Tina Goar, dir., PO Box 773390 970-879-0391
Steamboat Springs 80477 Fax 879-0442
www.nwboces.org

Pikes Peak BOCES
Pat Bershinsky, dir. 719-570-7474
2883 S Circle Dr Fax 380-9685
Colorado Springs 80906
www.ppboces.org

Rio Blanco BOCES
Teresa Schott, dir. 970-675-2064
402 W Main St Ste 219 Fax 675-5738
Rangely 81648
www.rioblancoboces.org

San Juan BOCES
Adrea Bogle, dir. 970-247-3261
162 Stewart St, Durango 81303 Fax 247-8333
www.sjboces.org

San Luis Valley BOCES
Nita McAuliffe, dir. 719-589-5851
2261 Enterprise Dr, Alamosa 81101 Fax 589-5007
www.slvboces.org

Santa Fe Trail BOCES
Sandy Malouff, dir. 719-383-2623
PO Box 980, La Junta 81050 Fax 383-2627
www.sftboces.org

South Central BOCES
Dr. Henry Roman, dir. 719-647-0023
323 S Purcell Blvd, Pueblo 81007 Fax 647-0136
www.sc-boces.org

Southeastern BOCES
Loraine Saffer, dir. 719-336-9046
PO Box 1137, Lamar 81052 Fax 336-9679
www.seboces.org

Uncompahgre BOCES
Tammy Johnson, dir. 970-626-2977
PO Box 728, Ridgway 81432 Fax 626-2978
www.unboces.org/

Ute Pass BOCES
Marcy Palmer, dir., 405 El Monte Pl 719-685-2640
Manitou Springs 80829 Fax 685-4536
www.upboces.org

PUBLIC, PRIVATE AND CATHOLIC ELEMENTARY SCHOOLS

Agate, Elbert, Pop. 100
Agate SD 300 50/K-5
PO Box 118 80101 719-764-2741
Kendra Ewing, supt. Fax 764-2751
www.agateschools.net
Agate ES 50/K-5
PO Box 118 80101 719-764-2741
Kendra Ewing, admin. Fax 764-2751

Aguilar, Las Animas, Pop. 527
Aguilar RSD 6 100/PK-12
PO Box 567 81020 719-941-4188
Dr. Stacy Houser, supt. Fax 941-4279
www.aguilarschools.com
Aguilar ES 100/PK-6
PO Box 567 81020 719-941-4188
Dr. Stacy Houser, supt. Fax 941-4279

Akron, Washington, Pop. 1,685
Akron SD R-1 300/PK-12
PO Box 429 80720 970-345-2053
Brian Christensen, supt. Fax 345-6508
akronrams.schoolwires.net
Akron ES 200/PK-6
600 Elm Ave 80720 970-345-2266
Ed Lundquist, prin. Fax 345-2827

Alamosa, Alamosa, Pop. 8,620
Alamosa SD RE-11J 2,000/K-12
209 Victoria Ave 81101 719-587-1600
Rob Alejo, supt. Fax 587-1712
dist.alamosa.k12.co.us
Alamosa ES 1,000/K-5
1707 W 10th St 81101 719-587-6650
Christy McBee, prin. Fax 587-2685
Ortega MS 500/6-8
401 Victoria Ave 81101 719-587-1650
Amy Ortega, prin. Fax 587-1721

Sunshine Christian S 50/PK-8
313 Craft Dr 81101 719-589-2557
Trinity Lutheran S, PO Box 787 81101 50/PK-1
Mary Conner, dir. 719-589-3271

Anton, Washington, Pop. 40
Arickaree SD R-2 100/PK-12
12155 County Road NN 80801 970-383-2202
S. Shane Walkinshaw, supt. Fax 383-2205
www.arickaree.org
Arickaree ES 100/PK-5
12155 County Road NN 80801 970-383-2202
S. Shane Walkinshaw, supt. Fax 383-2205

Antonito, Conejos, Pop. 772
South Conejos SD RE-10 200/K-12
PO Box 398 81120 719-376-5512
Dr. Emma Martinez, supt. Fax 376-5425
southconejos.com
Antonito MS 50/7-8
PO Box 398 81120 719-376-7000
Angela Montoya, prin. Fax 376-5425
Guadalupe ES 100/K-6
PO Box 398 81120 719-376-5407
Angela Montoya, prin. Fax 376-5425

Arvada, Jefferson, Pop. 104,595
Jefferson County SD R-1
Supt. — See Golden
Allendale ES 200/PK-6
5900 Oak St 80004 303-982-1165
Rob Malling, prin. Fax 982-1164
Arvada S 600/K-8
5751 Balsam St 80002 303-982-1240
Scott Simon, prin. Fax 982-1241
Campbell ES 300/K-6
6500 Oak St 80004 303-982-1440
Ryan Stadler, prin. Fax 982-1441
Drake MS 700/7-8
12550 W 52nd Ave 80002 303-982-1510
Rod Pugnetti, prin. Fax 982-1511
Fitzmorris ES 300/PK-6
6250 Independence St 80004 303-982-1640
Pamela Bartholomay, prin. Fax 982-1639
Foster ES 500/PK-6
5300 Saulsbury Ct 80002 303-982-1680
Leigh Hiester, prin. Fax 982-1679
Fremont ES 400/K-6
6420 Urban St 80004 303-982-1699
David Alex, prin. Fax 982-1698
Hackberry Hill ES 500/K-6
7300 W 76th Ave 80003 303-982-0260
Don Klene, prin. Fax 982-0261
Lawrence ES 400/PK-6
5611 Zephyr St 80002 303-982-1825
Christopher Benisch, prin. Fax 982-1826
Little ES 400/K-6
8448 Otis Dr 80003 303-982-0310
Robert Lopez, prin. Fax 982-0309
Meiklejohn ES 800/PK-6
13405 W 83rd Pl 80005 303-982-5695
Carrie Cornejo, prin. Fax 982-5696
Moore MS 500/7-8
8455 W 88th Ave 80005 303-982-0400
Brenda Fletcher, prin. Fax 982-0462
North Arvada MS 400/7-8
7285 Pierce St 80003 303-982-0528
Sohne Van Selus, prin. Fax 982-0529
Oberon MS 600/7-8
7300 Quail St 80005 303-982-2020
Tara Pena, prin. Fax 982-2021
Parr ES 400/PK-6
5800 W 84th Ave 80003 303-982-9890
Scott Thompson, prin. Fax 982-9891
Peck ES 300/K-6
6495 Carr St 80004 303-982-0590
Deborah Pearce, prin. Fax 982-0591
Secrest ES 400/PK-6
6875 W 64th Ave 80003 303-982-0760
Franziska Zenhaeusern, prin. Fax 982-0759
Sierra ES 500/K-6
7771 Oak St 80005 303-982-0821
Robert Brickley, prin. Fax 982-0822
Stott ES 400/PK-6
6600 Yank Way 80004 303-982-2638
Caryn Jehn-McCormick, prin. Fax 982-2639
Swanson ES 400/K-6
6055 W 68th Ave 80003 303-982-0891
Kristina Carothers, prin. Fax 982-0892
Thompson ES 400/K-6
7750 Harlan St 80003 303-982-9935
Natalie Berges-Tucker, prin. Fax 982-9936
Three Creeks ES K-6
19486 W 94th Ave 80003 303-982-1140
Laura Wilson, prin.

Van Arsdale ES 400/K-6
7535 Alkire St 80005 303-982-1080
Susan Chapla, prin. Fax 982-1081
Vanderhoof ES 500/K-6
5875 Routt St 80004 303-982-2744
Zachary Martin, prin. Fax 982-2743
Warder ES 300/K-6
7840 Carr Dr 80005 303-982-0950
Matthew Hilbert, prin. Fax 982-0949
Weber ES 500/K-6
8725 W 81st Pl 80005 303-982-1012
Lisa Malloy, prin. Fax 982-1013
West Woods ES 600/K-6
16650 W 72nd Ave 80007 303-982-5649
Patti Katsampes, prin. Fax 982-5650

Westminster SD
Supt. — See Westminster
Tennyson Knolls ES 400/PK-5
6330 Tennyson St 80003 303-429-4090
Heather McGuire, prin. Fax 657-3877

Faith Christian Academy ES 400/K-8
6210 Ward Rd 80004 303-424-7310
Bryan Thompson, prin. Fax 403-2710
St. Joan of Arc ELC PK-K
12735 W 58th Ave 80002 303-422-4949
Diane Murray, prin. Fax 420-0126
Shrine of St. Anne S 400/K-8
7320 Grant Pl 80002 303-422-1800
Patricia Hershwitzky, prin. Fax 422-1011

Aspen, Pitkin, Pop. 6,573
Aspen SD 1 1,700/PK-12
235 High School Rd 81611 970-925-3760
Dr. John Maloy, supt. Fax 925-5721
www.aspenk12.net/
Aspen ES 500/K-4
235 High School Rd 81611 970-925-3760
Christopher Basten, prin. Fax 925-6878
Aspen MS 500/5-8
235 High School Rd 81611 970-925-3760
Craig Rogers, prin. Fax 925-8374
Cottage Preschool 100/PK-PK
235 High School Rd 81611 970-925-3760
Emily Anderson, dir.

Aspen Country Day S 200/PK-8
85 Country Day Way 81611 970-925-1909
Josh Wolman, head sch Fax 925-7074

Ault, Weld, Pop. 1,488
Weld County SD RE-9 800/K-12
PO Box 1390 80610 970-834-1345
Robert Ring, supt. Fax 834-1347
www.weldre9.k12.co.us
Highland MS 200/6-8
PO Box 1390 80610 970-834-2829
Clay Naughton, prin. Fax 834-2663
Other Schools – See Pierce

Aurora, Arapahoe, Pop. 313,203
Aurora SD 40,300/PK-12
15701 E 1st Ave 80011 303-365-7800
Rico Munn, supt. Fax 326-1280
aurorak12.org
Altura ES 600/PK-5
1650 Altura Blvd 80011 303-340-3500
Jennifer Harrington, prin. Fax 326-1204
APS Early Beginnings PK-PK
812 N Jamaica St 80010 303-326-1018
Debra McCammond, dir. Fax 326-1289
Arkansas ES 500/PK-5
17301 E Arkansas Ave 80017 303-755-0323
Lori Petersen, prin. Fax 326-1205
Aurora Frontier S 700/PK-8
3200 S Jericho Way 80013 303-693-1995
Cari Roberts, prin. Fax 326-1208
Aurora Hills MS 900/6-8
1009 S Uvalda St 80012 303-341-7450
Marcella Garcia, prin. Fax 326-1250
Aurora Quest Academy 600/K-8
17315 E 2nd Ave 80011 303-343-3664
Dave Schoenhals, prin. Fax 326-1237
Boston S 500/K-8
1365 Boston St 80010 303-364-6878
Ruth Baldivia, prin. Fax 326-1206
Century ES 400/PK-5
2500 S Granby Way 80014 303-745-4424
Anthony Lawson, prin. Fax 326-1207
Columbia MS 700/6-8
17600 E Columbia Ave 80013 303-690-6570
Steve Hamilton, prin. Fax 326-1251
Court ES 600/PK-5
395 S Troy St 80012 303-366-9594
Kim Pippenger, prin. Fax 326-1244
Crawford ES 800/PK-5
1600 Florence St 80010 303-340-3290
Jennifer Passchier, prin. Fax 326-1210
Dalton ES 500/PK-5
17401 E Dartmouth Ave 80013 303-693-7561
Bonnie Hargrove, prin. Fax 326-1211
Dartmouth ES 400/PK-5
3050 S Laredo St 80013 303-690-1155
Jeanne Ulrich, prin. Fax 326-1212
East MS 1,000/6-8
1275 Fraser St 80011 303-340-0660
Biaze Houston, prin. Fax 326-1252
Elkhart ES 800/K-5
1020 Eagle St 80011 303-340-3050
Ronald Schumacher, prin. Fax 326-1214
Fletcher Community ES 500/PK-5
10455 E 25th Ave 80010 303-343-1707
Heather Stewart, prin. Fax 326-1219
Fulton Academy of Excellence 500/PK-5
755 Fulton St 80010 303-364-8078
Dawn McWilliams, dir. Fax 326-1216
Iowa ES 500/K-5
16701 E Iowa Ave 80017 303-751-3660
Bonnie Estrada, prin. Fax 326-1217
Jamaica Child Development Center 300/PK-PK
800 Jamaica St 80010 303-364-8126
Anita Walker, prin. Fax 326-1218
Jewell ES 500/PK-5
14601 E Jewell Ave 80012 303-751-8862
Nadine Ritchotte, prin. Fax 326-1220
Kenton ES 500/K-5
1255 Kenton St 80010 303-364-0947
Heather Woodward, prin. Fax 326-1222
Knoll ES 300/K-5
12445 E 2nd Ave 80011 303-364-8455
Andrea Tucker, prin. Fax 326-1228
Lansing ES 400/K-5
551 Lansing St 80010 303-364-8297
Jennifer Murtha, prin. Fax 326-1224
Laredo Child Development Center 300/PK-PK
1420 Laredo St 80011 303-363-0484
Cindy Andrews, coord. Fax 326-1215
Laredo ES 500/K-5
1350 Laredo St 80011 303-366-0314
Sandy Fenley, prin. Fax 326-1226
Meadowood Child Development Center 300/PK-PK
3333 S Norfolk Way 80013 303-400-0863
Marsha Haxby, prin. Fax 326-1231
Miller S 600/PK-8
1701 Espana St 80011 303-364-7918
Ashlee Saddler, prin. Fax 326-1209
Montview ES 500/PK-5
2055 Moline St 80010 303-364-8549
Mia Robinson, prin. Fax 326-1232
Mosley S PK-8
55 N Salida Way 80011 303-366-2807
Carrie Clark, prin. Fax 326-1233
Mrachek MS 900/6-8
1955 S Telluride St 80013 303-750-2836
Michelle Davis, prin. Fax 326-1254
Murphy Creek S 700/PK-8
1400 S Old Tom Morris Rd 80018 303-366-0579
Lisa Grosz, prin. Fax 326-1227
North MS 900/6-8
12095 Montview Blvd 80010 303-364-7411
Rachel Langberg, prin. Fax 326-1256
Paris ES 500/K-5
1635 Paris St 80010 303-341-1702
Tammy Stewart, prin. Fax 326-1234
Park Lane ES 400/PK-5
13001 E 30th Ave 80011 303-343-8313
Mary Duran, prin. Fax 326-1236
Peoria ES 600/PK-5
875 Peoria St 80011 303-340-0770
Lisa Toner, prin. Fax 326-1235
Sable ES 500/PK-5
2601 Sable Blvd 80011 303-340-3140
Jennifer Dichter, prin. Fax 326-1238
Side Creek ES 700/K-5
19191 E Iliff Ave 80013 303-755-1785
Susan Gariepy, prin. Fax 326-1239
Sixth Avenue ES 600/K-5
560 Vaughn St 80011 303-366-6019
Vanessa Valencia, prin. Fax 326-1240
South MS 700/6-8
12310 E Parkview Dr 80011 303-364-7623
Courtney Goertz, prin. Fax 326-1258
Tollgate ES 700/K-5
701 S Kalispell Way 80017 303-696-0944
Joseph Longbottom, prin. Fax 326-1221
Vassar ES 500/K-5
18101 E Vassar Pl 80013 303-752-3772
Stacey Stuart, prin. Fax 326-1241
Vaughn ES 600/PK-5
1155 Vaughn St 80011 303-366-8430
Sangita Patel, prin. Fax 326-1242
Vista PEAK Exploratory S 1,100/PK-8
24551 E 1st Pl 80018 303-364-3757
Yolanda Greer, dir. Fax 326-1230
Wheeling IB World ES 600/PK-5
472 S Wheeling St 80012 303-344-8670
Ramone Carson, prin. Fax 326-1246
Yale ES 500/PK-5
16001 E Yale Ave 80013 303-751-7470
Andrew Bruckner, prin. Fax 326-1248

Cherry Creek SD 5
Supt. — See Greenwood Village
Antelope Ridge ES 600/PK-5
5455 S Tempe St 80015 720-886-3300
Chris Powell, prin. Fax 886-3388
Arrowhead ES 600/PK-5
19100 E Bates Ave 80013 720-886-2800
Roberta Ballard, prin. Fax 886-2888
Aspen Crossing ES 600/PK-5
4655 S Himalaya St 80015 720-886-3700
Karen Puga, prin. Fax 886-3788
Black Forest Hills ES 600/PK-5
25233 E Glasgow Dr 80016 720-886-8900
Ty Muma, prin. Fax 886-8988
Buffalo Trail ES 600/PK-5
24300 E Progress Dr 80016 720-886-4000
Tamara Speidel, prin. Fax 886-4088
Canyon Creek ES 600/K-5
6070 S Versailles Pkwy 80015 720-886-3600
Darryl Sigman, prin. Fax 886-3687
Cimarron ES 600/PK-5
17373 E Lehigh Pl 80013 720-886-8100
La Toyua Tolbert, prin. Fax 886-8188
Coyote Hills ES 700/PK-5
24605 E Davies Way 80016 720-886-3900
Amber Sorg, prin. Fax 886-3988
Dakota Valley ES 800/K-5
3950 S Kirk Way 80013 720-886-3000
Aisha Johnson, prin. Fax 886-3088
Eastridge ES 900/PK-5
11777 E Wesley Ave 80014 720-747-2200
Amy Cribbs, prin. Fax 747-2288
Falcon Creek MS 1,000/6-8
6100 S Genoa St 80016 720-886-7700
Lisa Ruiz, prin. Fax 886-7788
Fox Hollow ES 700/PK-5
6363 S Waco St 80016 720-886-8700
Dominique Jones, prin. Fax 886-8788
Fox Ridge MS 1,100/6-8
26301 E Arapahoe Rd 80016 720-886-4400
Joleta Gallozzi, prin. Fax 886-4488
Highline Community ES 600/PK-5
11000 E Exposition Ave 80012 720-747-2300
Darla Thompson, prin. Fax 747-2388
Horizon Community MS 1,000/6-8
3981 S Reservoir Rd 80013 720-886-6100
Nickie Bell, prin. Fax 886-6253
Independence ES 500/PK-5
4700 S Memphis St 80015 720-886-8200
Lisa Morris, prin. Fax 886-8288
Indian Ridge ES 600/PK-5
16501 E Progress Dr 80015 720-886-8400
Matthew McDonald, prin. Fax 886-8488
Laredo MS 1,100/6-8
5000 S Laredo St 80015 720-886-5000
Edie Alvarez, prin. Fax 886-5298
Liberty MS 1,100/6-8
21500 E Dry Creek Rd 80016 720-886-2400
Kevin Doherty, prin. Fax 886-2688
Meadow Point ES 500/PK-5
17901 E Grand Ave 80015 720-886-8600
Thomas McDowell, prin. Fax 886-8688
Mission Viejo ES 700/PK-5
3855 S Alicia Pkwy 80013 720-886-8000
Andre Pearson, prin. Fax 886-8088
Pine Ridge ES 800/PK-5
6525 S Wheatlands Pkwy 80016 720-886-8800
Diana Roybal, prin. Fax 886-8888
Polton ES 500/PK-5
2985 S Oakland St 80014 720-747-2600
Michael Chipman, prin. Fax 747-2688
Ponderosa ES 800/PK-5
1885 S Lima St 80012 720-747-2800
Elizabeth Sloan, prin. Fax 747-2888
Prairie MS 1,700/6-8
12600 E Jewell Ave 80012 720-747-3000
David Gonzales, prin. Fax 747-3097
Red Hawk Ridge ES 800/PK-5
16251 E Geddes Ave 80016 720-886-3800
Kait Whitaker, prin. Fax 886-3888
Rolling Hills ES 600/PK-5
5756 S Biscay St 80015 720-886-3400
Ashley Gehrke, prin. Fax 886-3488
Sagebrush ES 600/PK-5
14700 E Temple Pl 80015 720-886-8300
Chris Tolliver, prin. Fax 886-8388
Sky Vista MS 900/6-8
4500 S Himalaya St 80015 720-886-4710
Michelle McCourt, prin. Fax 886-4714
Summit ES 400/K-5
18201 E Quincy Ave 80015 720-886-6400
Rachel Rubio, prin. Fax 886-6488
Sunrise ES 700/PK-5
4050 S Genoa Way 80013 720-886-2900
Chris Hardy, prin. Fax 886-2988
Village East ES 800/PK-5
1433 S Oakland St 80012 720-747-2000
John Cramer, prin. Fax 747-2088

CedarWood Christian Academy 100/K-12
PO Box 111389 80042 303-361-6456
Gene Oborny, admin. Fax 340-0971
Christ our Redeemer Lutheran S 100/PK-8
17700 E Iliff Ave 80013 303-337-3108
Phillip Scriver, prin. Fax 671-9807
Crescent View Academy 200/PK-8
10958 E Bethany Dr 80014 303-745-2245
Peace with Christ Christian S 200/PK-8
3290 S Tower Rd 80013 303-766-7116
David Robinson, prin. Fax 643-5858
St. Michael the Archangel Preschool PK-PK
19099 E Floyd Ave 80013 303-690-6797
Dee Ann Toby, dir. Fax 690-6932
St. Pius X S 300/PK-8
13680 E 14th Pl 80011 303-364-6515
Eileen Michalczyk, prin. Fax 364-1822
St. Therese S 200/PK-8
1200 Kenton St 80010 303-364-7494
Toni Vaeth, prin. Fax 364-1340

Avon, Eagle, Pop. 6,405
Eagle County SD RE-50
Supt. — See Eagle
Avon ES 300/PK-5
PO Box 7567 81620 970-328-2950
Leroy Getchel, prin. Fax 328-2955
Homestake Peak S 600/PK-8
PO Box 5810 81620 970-328-2940
Bobby Young, prin. Fax 328-2945

Avondale, Pueblo, Pop. 662
Pueblo County SD 70
Supt. — See Pueblo
Avondale ES 200/PK-5
213 E US Highway 50 81022 719-947-3484
Carmen Avalos, prin. Fax 947-3403

Bailey, Park, Pop. 150
Platte Canyon SD 1 1,000/PK-12
PO Box 1069 80421 303-838-7666
Dr. Brenda Krage Ed.D., supt. Fax 679-7504
www.plattecanyonschools.org
Deer Creek ES 500/PK-5
PO Box 1069 80421 303-838-7666
Jeff Lubansky, prin. Fax 816-0162
Fitzsimmons MS 200/6-8
PO Box 1069 80421 303-838-7666
Ginger Slocum, prin. Fax 679-7506

Basalt, Pitkin, Pop. 3,792
Roaring Fork SD RE-1
Supt. — See Glenwood Springs
Basalt ES 700/PK-4
151 Cottonwood Dr 81621 970-384-5800
Suzanne Wheeler, prin. Fax 385-5805
Basalt MS 500/5-8
51 School St 81621 970-384-5900
Jennifer Ellsperman, prin. Fax 384-5905

Cornerstone Classical S 50/PK-12
20449 Highway 82 81621 970-927-9106
Steve Marshall, hdmstr.

Bayfield, LaPlata, Pop. 2,294
Bayfield SD 10 JT-R 1,300/K-12
24 S Clover Dr 81122 970-884-2496
Amy Lyons, supt. Fax 884-4284
www.bayfield.k12.co.us
Bayfield ES 400/2-5
24 S Clover Dr 81122 970-884-9571
Diane Sallinger, prin. Fax 884-9572
Bayfield MS 300/6-8
24 S Clover Dr 81122 970-884-9592
Tod Lokey, prin. Fax 884-4110
Bayfield PS 200/K-1
24 S Clover Dr 81122 970-884-0881
Diane Sallinger, prin. Fax 884-3126

Bellvue, Larimer, Pop. 300
Poudre SD R-1
Supt. — See Fort Collins
Stove Prairie ES 50/PK-5
3891 Stove Prairie Rd 80512 970-488-6575
Tom Schachet, prin. Fax 488-6577

Bennett, Adams, Pop. 2,268
Bennett SD 29J 1,000/PK-12
610 7th St 80102 303-644-3234
Robin Purdy, supt. Fax 644-4121
www.bennett29j.k12.co.us
Bennett ES 400/K-5
462 8th St 80102 303-644-3234
Sharon Hebert, prin. Fax 644-4679
Bennett MS 300/6-8
455 8th St 80102 303-644-3234
JaLee Kitzman, prin. Fax 644-4398
Bennett Preschool 100/PK-PK
805 Washington Way 80102 303-644-3234
Patricia Kopang, dir. Fax 644-4679

Berthoud, Larimer, Pop. 5,034
Thompson SD R-2J
Supt. — See Loveland
Berthoud ES 400/K-5
560 Bunyan Ave 80513 970-613-7500
Melanie Patterson, prin. Fax 613-7520
Stockwell ES 300/K-5
175 S 5th St 80513 970-613-6100
Rick Bowles, prin. Fax 613-6120
Turner MS 500/6-8
950 Massachusetts Ave 80513 970-613-7400
Brandy Grieves, prin. Fax 613-7420

Bethune, Kit Carson, Pop. 236
Bethune SD R-5 100/PK-12
PO Box 127 80805 719-346-7513
Shila Adolf, supt. Fax 346-5048
bethuneschool.com
Bethune ES 100/PK-6
PO Box 127 80805 719-346-7513
Shila Adolf, prin. Fax 346-5048

Beulah, Pueblo, Pop. 600
Pueblo County SD 70
Supt. — See Pueblo
Beulah S 100/PK-8
8734 School House Ln W 81023 719-485-3127
Perry Rogers, prin. Fax 485-3701

Black Hawk, Gilpin, Pop. 118
Gilpin County SD RE-1 400/PK-12
10595 Highway 119 80422 303-582-3444
Dr. David MacKenzie, supt. Fax 582-3346
www.gilpin.k12.co.us
Gilpin County ES 300/PK-5
10595 Highway 119 80422 303-582-3444
Heather Huntoon, prin. Fax 582-3346

Blanca, Costilla, Pop. 380
Sierra Grande SD R-30 300/K-12
17523 E Highway 160 81123 719-379-3259
Darren Edgar, supt. Fax 379-2572
www.sierragrandeschool.net
Sierra Grande ES 100/K-5
17523 E Highway 160 81123 719-379-3257
Manuel Montano, prin. Fax 379-2572
Sierra Grande MS 100/6-8
17523 E Highway 160 81123 719-379-3257
Brandon Mizokami, prin. Fax 379-2572

Boulder, Boulder, Pop. 95,063
Boulder Valley SD RE-2 30,100/PK-12
PO Box 9011 80301 303-447-1010
Dr. Cynthia Stevenson, supt. Fax 561-5134
www.bvsd.org
BCSIS @ Aurora 7 300/PK-5
3995 Aurora Ave 80303 720-561-6500
Phil Katsampes, prin. Fax 561-6501
Bear Creek ES 400/K-5
2500 Table Mesa Dr 80305 720-561-3500
Kent Cruger, prin. Fax 561-3501
Casey MS 600/6-8
1301 High St 80304 720-561-2700
Justin McMillan, prin. Fax 561-2701
Centennial MS 600/6-8
2205 Norwood Ave 80304 720-561-5441
John McCluskey, prin. Fax 561-2090
Columbine ES 500/PK-5
3130 Repplier St 80304 720-561-2500
Bianca Gallegos, prin. Fax 561-2501
Community Montessori ES 300/PK-5
805 Gillaspie Dr 80305 720-561-3700
Shannon Minch, prin. Fax 561-3701
Creekside ES 300/K-5
3740 Martin Dr 80305 720-561-3800
Francine Eufemia, prin. Fax 561-3801
Crest View ES 600/K-5
1897 Sumac Ave 80304 720-561-5461
Hollene Davis, prin. Fax 561-2855
Douglass ES 500/K-5
840 75th St 80303 720-561-5541
Jon Wolfer, prin. Fax 561-6699
Eisenhower ES 400/K-5
1220 Eisenhower Dr 80303 720-561-6700
Brady Stroup, prin. Fax 561-6701
Flatirons ES 300/K-5
1150 7th St 80302 720-561-4600
Scott Boesel, prin. Fax 561-4601
Foothill ES 600/K-5
1001 Hawthorn Ave 80304 720-561-2600
Lisa Schuba, prin. Fax 561-2601
Heatherwood ES 400/K-5
7750 Concord Dr 80301 720-561-6900
Genna Jaramillo, prin. Fax 561-6965
High Peaks ES 300/PK-5
3995 Aurora Ave 80303 720-561-6500
Jeannie Tynecki, prin. Fax 561-6501
Manhattan S of Arts and Academics 500/6-8
290 Manhattan Dr 80303 720-561-6300
John Riggs, prin. Fax 561-6301
Mapleton ECC 100/PK-PK
840 Mapleton Ave 80304 720-561-6200
Theresa Clements, admin.
Mesa ES 300/K-5
1575 Lehigh St 80305 720-561-3000
Josh Baldner, prin. Fax 561-3001
Platt MS 500/6-8
6096 Baseline Rd 80303 720-561-5536
Theo Robison, prin. Fax 561-6898
Southern Hills MS 600/6-8
1500 Knox Dr 80305 720-561-3400
Chavonne Gloster, prin. Fax 561-3401
University Hill ES 400/K-5
956 16th St 80302 720-561-5416
Ina Rodriguez-Meyer, prin. Fax 561-2900
Whittier ES 400/K-5
2008 Pine St 80302 720-561-5431
Sarah Oswick, prin. Fax 561-2480
Other Schools – See Broomfield, Erie, Gold Hill, Jamestown, Lafayette, Louisville, Nederland, Superior

---

Bixby S 100/PK-5
4760 Table Mesa Dr 80305 303-494-7508
Beth Heller Suitor, head sch Fax 494-7510
Boulder Country Day S 300/PK-8
4820 Nautilus Ct N 80301 303-527-4931
John Suitor, head sch Fax 527-4944
Friends S 200/PK-7
5465 Pennsylvania Ave 80303 303-499-1999
Steve de Beer, hdmstr. Fax 499-1365
Jarrow Montessori S 200/PK-6
3900 Orange Ct 80304 303-443-0511
Mackintosh Academy K-8
6717 S Boulder Rd 80303 303-554-2011
Mountain Shadows Montessori S 100/PK-6
4154 63rd St 80301 303-530-5353
Sacred Heart of Jesus S 400/PK-8
1317 Mapleton Ave 80304 303-447-2362
Roonie Leittem-Murrell, prin. Fax 443-2466
Shining Mountain Waldorf S 300/PK-12
999 Violet Ave 80304 303-444-7697
Jane M. Zeender, dir. Fax 444-7701

Breckenridge, Summit, Pop. 4,489
Summit SD RE-1
Supt. — See Frisco
Breckenridge ES 200/K-5
PO Box 1213 80424 970-368-1300
Khristian Brace, prin. Fax 368-1399
Upper Blue ES 300/PK-5
PO Box 1255 80424 970-368-1800
Robyn Sutherland, prin. Fax 368-1899

Briggsdale, Weld, Pop. 225
Briggsdale SD RE-10 200/PK-12
PO Box 129 80611 970-656-3417
Rick Mondt, supt. Fax 656-3479
www.briggsdaleschool.org
Briggsdale ES 100/PK-5
PO Box 129 80611 970-656-3417
Cathi Fulton, prin. Fax 656-3479

Brighton, Adams, Pop. 32,801
Adams 12 Five Star SD
Supt. — See Thornton
Glacier Peak ES 500/K-5
12060 Jasmine St 80602 720-972-5940
Tim Griffin, prin. Fax 972-5999

SD 27J 16,500/PK-12
18551 E 160th Ave 80601 303-655-2900
Chris Fiedler Ed.D., supt. Fax 655-2870
www.sd27j.org/
Northeast ES 600/PK-5
1605 Longs Peak St 80601 303-655-2550
Toby Karr, prin. Fax 655-2575
North ES 400/PK-5
89 N 6th Ave 80601 303-655-2500
Carmella Schroeder, prin. Fax 655-2548
Overland Trail MS 700/6-8
455 N 19th Ave 80601 303-655-4000
Eric Lambright, prin. Fax 655-2880
Pennock ES 700/K-5
3707 Estrella St 80601 720-685-7500
Valerie Ortega, prin. Fax 685-7504
Southeast ES 600/K-6
1595 E Southern St 80601 303-655-2650
Heath Wilson, prin. Fax 655-2893
South ES 500/K-5
305 S 5th Ave 80601 303-655-2600
Kay Collins, prin. Fax 655-2649
Vikan MS 600/6-8
879 Jessup St 80601 303-655-4050
Trina Norris-Buck, prin. Fax 655-2881
Other Schools – See Commerce City, Henderson, Thornton

Brighton Adventist Academy 100/K-10
820 S 5th Ave 80601 303-659-1223
Elmwood Baptist Academy 100/PK-12
13100 E 144th Ave 80601 303-659-3818
Zion Lutheran S 200/PK-8
1400 Skeel St 80601 303-659-3443
Zach Brewer, prin. Fax 659-2342

Broomfield, Boulder, Pop. 54,716
Adams 12 Five Star SD
Supt. — See Thornton
Centennial ES 400/PK-5
13200 Westlake Dr 80020 720-972-5280
Christine Parkes, prin. Fax 972-5299
Coyote Ridge ES 500/K-5
13770 Broadlands Dr, 720-972-5780
Michael Keppler, prin. Fax 972-5799
Meridian ES 700/K-5
14256 McKay Park Cir, 720-972-7880
Matt Haviland, prin. Fax 972-7886
Mountain View ES 600/K-5
12401 Perry St 80020 720-972-5520
Peggy Heath, prin. Fax 972-5539
Westlake MS 1,100/6-8
2800 W 135th Ave 80020 720-972-5200
Rachel Heide, prin. Fax 972-5239

Boulder Valley SD RE-2
Supt. — See Boulder
Aspen Creek PK-8 S 900/PK-8
5500 Aspen Creek Dr 80020 720-561-8000
Tracy Stegall, prin. Fax 561-8001
Birch ES 300/K-5
1035 Birch St 80020 720-561-8800
Tanya Santee, prin. Fax 561-8801
Broomfield Heights MS 600/6-8
1555 Daphne St 80020 720-561-8400
Chris Meyer, prin. Fax 561-8401
Emerald ES 300/K-5
257 Emerald St 80020 720-561-8500
Samara Williams, prin. Fax 561-8501
Kohl ES 500/PK-5
1000 W 10th Ave 80020 720-561-8600
Mike Lowe, prin. Fax 561-8601

Beautiful Savior Lutheran S 200/PK-5
PO Box 8 80038 303-469-2049
James Woodburn, prin. Fax 469-6999
Broomfield Academy 100/PK-8
7203 W 120th Ave 80020 303-469-6449
Nativity of Our Lord S 400/K-8
900 W Midway Blvd 80020 303-466-4177
Kathy Shadel, prin. Fax 460-0391

Brush, Morgan, Pop. 5,401
Brush SD RE-2(J) 1,400/PK-12
527 Industrial Park Rd 80723 970-842-5176
Dr. Bill Wilson, supt. Fax 842-4481
www.brushschools.org
Beaver Valley ES 300/3-5
527 Industrial Park Rd 80723 970-842-4794
Jennifer Kral, prin. Fax 842-3924
Brush MS 200/6-8
527 Industrial Park Rd 80723 970-842-5035
Connie Droitz, prin. Fax 842-3009
Thomson PS 400/PK-2
527 Industrial Park Rd 80723 970-842-5139
Joseph Hermocillo, prin. Fax 842-2808

Buena Vista, Chaffee, Pop. 2,579
Buena Vista SD R-31 1,000/PK-12
PO Box 2027 81211 719-395-7000
Lisa Yates, supt. Fax 395-7007
www.bvschools.org
Avery/Parsons ES 500/PK-5
PO Box 2027 81211 719-395-7020
Tim Scott, prin. Fax 395-7015
McGinnis MS 200/6-8
PO Box 2027 81211 719-395-7060
John Emilsson, prin. Fax 395-7090

Patterson Christian Academy 100/PK-12
PO Box 1243 81211 719-395-6046
Ashley Blazer, dir. Fax 395-2055

Burlington, Kit Carson, Pop. 4,206
Burlington SD RE-6J 800/PK-12
PO Box 369 80807 719-346-8737
Tom Satterly, supt. Fax 346-8541
www.burlingtonk12.org/
Burlington ES 400/PK-4
450 11th St 80807 719-346-8166
Kandy Davis, prin. Fax 346-8165
Burlington MS 200/5-8
2600 Rose Ave 80807 719-346-5440
Pam Pekarek, prin. Fax 346-7900

Byers, Arapahoe, Pop. 1,139
Byers SD 32J 600/PK-12
444 E Front St 80103 303-822-5292
Tom Turrell, supt. Fax 822-9592
www.byers32j.k12.co.us
Byers ES 300/PK-6
444 E Front St 80103 303-822-5292
Gloria Mitchell, prin. Fax 822-9511

Calhan, El Paso, Pop. 759
Calhan SD RJ-1 500/PK-12
800 Bulldog Dr 80808 719-347-2766
David Slothower, supt. Fax 347-2108
calhanschool.org
Calhan ES 200/PK-5
800 Bulldog Dr 80808 719-347-2766
Jen Hart, prin. Fax 347-2108
Calhan MS 100/6-8
800 Bulldog Dr 80808 719-347-2766
David Slothower, prin. Fax 347-2108

Campo, Baca, Pop. 109
Campo SD RE-6 50/PK-12
PO Box 70 81029 719-787-2226
Nikki Johnson, supt. Fax 787-0140
www.campok12.org
Campo ES 50/PK-5
PO Box 70 81029 719-787-2226
Nikki Johnson, admin. Fax 787-0140

Canon City, Fremont, Pop. 16,140
Canon City SD RE-1 3,700/K-12
101 N 14th St 81212 719-276-5700
George Welsh, supt. Fax 276-5739
www.canoncityschools.org
Canon City MS 400/6-8
1215 Main St 81212 719-276-5740
Tim Renn, prin. Fax 276-5795
Canon Exploratory S 300/K-6
2855 N 9th St 81212 719-276-6050
Kelly Albrecht, prin. Fax 276-6080
Harrison S 700/K-8
920 Field Ave 81212 719-276-5970
Marne Autobee, prin. Fax 275-2414
Lincoln S of Science & Tech 300/K-5
420 Myrtle Ave 81212 719-276-5830
Tammy DeWolfe, prin. Fax 276-5865
McKinley ES 300/K-5
1240 McKinley St 81212 719-276-6010
Scott Morton, prin. Fax 276-6045
Washington ES 400/K-5
606 N 9th St 81212 719-276-6090
Brian Zamarripa, prin. Fax 276-6130

Four Mile Adventist S 50/PK-8
3180 E Main St 81212 719-275-6111

Carbondale, Garfield, Pop. 6,354
Roaring Fork SD RE-1
Supt. — See Glenwood Springs
Carbondale MS 400/5-8
180 Snowmass Dr 81623 970-384-5700
Jennifer Lamont, prin. Fax 384-5705
Crystal River ES 500/PK-4
160 Snowmass Dr 81623 970-384-5620
Matt Koenigsknecht, prin. Fax 384-5625

Waldorf S on the Roaring Fork 200/PK-8
16543 Highway 82 81623 970-963-1960

Castle Pines, Douglas, Pop. 3,571
Douglas County SD RE-1
Supt. — See Castle Rock
Buffalo Ridge ES 500/K-5
7075 Shoreham Dr, 303-387-5575
John Veit, prin. Fax 387-5576

Castle Rock, Douglas, Pop. 47,126
Douglas County SD RE-1 61,200/PK-12
620 Wilcox St 80104 303-387-0100
Erin Kane, supt. Fax 387-0107
www.dcsdk12.org
Castle Rock ES 400/K-6
1103 Canyon Dr 80104 303-387-5000
Deborah Warr, prin. Fax 387-5001
Castle Rock MS 900/7-8
2575 Meadows Pkwy, 303-387-1300
LeeAnn Hayen, prin. Fax 387-1301
Clear Sky ES 800/K-6
1470 Clear Sky Way, 303-387-5900
Kellie Roe, prin. Fax 387-5901
Flagstone ES 600/K-6
104 Lovington St 80104 303-387-5225
Kelli Smith, prin. Fax 387-5226
Meadow View ES 500/PK-6
3700 Butterfield Crossing, 303-387-5425
Lacey Dahl, prin. Fax 387-5426
Mesa MS 1,000/7-8
365 N Mitchell St 80104 303-387-4750
Anthony Jackowski, prin. Fax 387-4751
Renaissance Expeditionary S 400/K-6
3960 Trail Boss Ln 80104 303-387-8000
Deborah Lemmer, prin. Fax 387-8001
Rock Ridge ES 700/K-6
400 Heritage Ave 80104 303-387-5150
Peter Mosby, prin. Fax 387-5151
Sage Canyon ES 600/K-6
2420 Autumn Sage St, 303-433-0110
Mandy Hill, prin. Fax 433-0111
Soaring Hawk ES 600/K-6
4665 Tanglevine Dr, 303-387-5825
Christopher Neville, prin. Fax 387-5826
South Ridge ES 500/K-6
1100 South St 80104 303-387-5075
Erin Carlson, prin. Fax 387-5076
Timber Trail ES 600/K-5
690 W Castle Pines Pkwy, 303-387-5700
Michele Radke, prin. Fax 387-5701
Other Schools – See Castle Pines, Franktown, Highlands Ranch, Larkspur, Littleton, Lonetree, Parker, Sedalia

---

Castle Rock Christian Academy 100/PK-8
4881 Cherokee Dr, 720-598-2722
Sally Baier, prin. Fax 688-0854

Cedaredge, Delta, Pop. 2,222
Delta County SD 50(J)
Supt. — See Delta
Cedaredge ES 400/K-5
380 N Grand Mesa Dr 81413 970-856-3885
Daniel Renfrow, prin. Fax 856-3934
Cedaredge MS 200/6-8
845 SE Deer Creek Dr 81413 970-856-3118
Delaine Hudson, prin. Fax 856-3235

Centennial, Arapahoe, Pop. 97,891
Cherry Creek SD 5
Supt. — See Greenwood Village
Creekside ES 700/PK-5
19993 E Long Ave 80016 720-886-3500
Kelly Sommerfeld, prin. Fax 886-3588
Dry Creek ES 400/PK-5
7686 E Hinsdale Ave 80112 720-554-3300
Heidi Schriver, prin. Fax 554-3388
Heritage ES 300/PK-5
6867 E Heritage Pl S 80111 720-554-3500
Ryan Langdon, prin. Fax 554-3588
Homestead ES 500/PK-5
7451 S Homestead Pkwy 80112 720-554-3700
Kyle Sworg, prin. Fax 554-3788
Mountain Vista ES K-5
22200 E Radcliff Pkwy 80015 720-886-2700
Toby Arritola, prin. Fax 886-2788
Peakview ES 700/PK-5
19451 E Progress Cir 80015 720-886-3100
Scott May, prin. Fax 886-3188
Thunder Ridge MS 1,300/6-8
5250 S Picadilly St 80015 720-886-1500
Angie Zehner, prin. Fax 886-1582
Timberline ES 600/PK-5
5500 S Killarney St 80015 720-886-3200
Todd Wynne, prin. Fax 886-3288
Trails West ES 600/PK-5
5400 S Waco St 80015 720-886-8500
Cheryl Fullmer, prin. Fax 886-8588
Walnut Hills Community ES 400/PK-5
8195 E Costilla Blvd 80112 720-554-3800
Teolyn Bourbonnie, prin. Fax 554-3888
Willow Creek ES 500/PK-5
7855 S Willow Way 80112 720-554-3900
Diana Price, prin. Fax 554-3988

Littleton SD
Supt. — See Littleton
Franklin ES 500/K-5
1603 E Euclid Ave 80121 303-347-4500
John Melkonian, prin. Fax 347-4524
Highland ES 400/PK-5
711 E Euclid Ave 80121 303-347-4525
Kirsten McCabe, prin. Fax 347-4240
Hopkins ES 400/PK-5
7171 S Pennsylvania St 80122 303-347-4550
Lyndsey Case, prin. Fax 347-4570
Lenski ES 600/K-5
6350 S Fairfax Way 80121 303-347-4575
Dr. Barbara DeSpain, prin. Fax 347-4580
Newton MS 600/6-8
4001 E Arapahoe Rd 80122 303-347-7900
James O'Tremba, prin. Fax 347-3945
Peabody ES 400/PK-5
3128 E Maplewood Ave 80121 303-347-4625
Linda Jones, prin. Fax 347-4630
Sandburg ES 500/K-5
6900 S Elizabeth St 80122 303-347-4675
Karen Tarbell, prin. Fax 347-4680
Twain ES 400/K-5
6901 S Franklin St 80122 303-347-4700
Teresa Burden, prin. Fax 347-4720
Village @ Ames 100/PK-PK
7300 S Clermont Dr 80122 303-347-4400
Tracey Hansen, prin. Fax 347-4420

Montessori S of Aurora 100/PK-K
18585 E Smoky Hill Rd 80015 303-617-0611
St. Thomas More S 700/PK-8
7071 E Otero Ave 80112 303-770-0441
Jan Altevogt, prin. Fax 267-1899
Shepherd of the Hills Christian S 200/PK-8
7691 S University Blvd 80122 303-798-0711
Lisa Jennings, prin. Fax 798-0718

Center, Saguache, Pop. 2,207
Center Consolidated SD 26JT 700/PK-12
550 S Sylvester Ave 81125 719-754-3442
Chris Vance, supt. Fax 754-3952
www.center.k12.co.us
Haskin ES 300/PK-5
550 S Sylvester Ave 81125 719-754-3982
Sarah Vance, prin. Fax 754-2857
Skoglund MS 100/6-8
550 S Sylvester Ave 81125 719-754-2232
Luis Murillo, prin. Fax 754-2856

Cheraw, Otero, Pop. 245
Cheraw SD 31 200/PK-12
PO Box 160 81030 719-853-6655
Tonya Rodwell, supt. Fax 853-6322
cheraw.k12.co.us
Cheraw ES 100/PK-5
PO Box 160 81030 719-853-6655
Todd Werner, prin. Fax 853-6322
Cheraw MS 100/6-8
PO Box 160 81030 719-853-6655
Todd Werner, prin. Fax 853-6322

Cheyenne Wells, Cheyenne, Pop. 839
Cheyenne County SD RE-5 200/PK-12
PO Box 577 80810 719-767-5866
Glen Bradshaw M.A., supt. Fax 767-8773
www.cheyennesd.net/
Cheyenne Wells ES 100/PK-6
PO Box 577 80810 719-767-5656
Glen Bradshaw M.A., prin. Fax 767-5136
Cheyenne Wells MS 50/7-8
PO Box 577 80810 719-767-5656
Mike Miller, prin. Fax 767-5136

Chipita Park, El Paso, Pop. 1,479
Manitou Springs SD 14
Supt. — See Manitou Springs
Ute Pass ES 100/K-5
9230 Chipita Park Rd 80809 719-685-2227
Chris Briggs-Hale, prin. Fax 685-2220

Clifton, Mesa, Pop. 19,453
Mesa County Valley SD 51
Supt. — See Grand Junction
Clifton ES 500/PK-5
3276 F Rd 81520 970-254-4760
Yogi Cherp, prin. Fax 434-9725
Mt. Garfield MS 600/6-8
3475 Front St 81520 970-254-4720
Rocio Roybal, prin. Fax 464-0536
Rocky Mountain ES 500/PK-5
3260 D 1/2 Rd 81520 970-254-4900
Patti Virden, prin. Fax 434-2804

Collbran, Mesa, Pop. 699
Plateau Valley SD 50 500/PK-12
56600 Highway 330 81624 970-487-3547
Mike Page, supt. Fax 487-3876
www.pvsd50.org
Plateau Valley ES 200/PK-5
56600 Highway 330 81624 970-487-3547
Leroy Gutierrez, prin. Fax 487-3876
Plateau Valley MS 100/6-8
56600 Highway 330 81624 970-487-3547
Leroy Gutierrez, prin. Fax 487-3876

Colorado City, Pueblo, Pop. 2,165
Pueblo County SD 70
Supt. — See Pueblo
Craver MS 200/6-8
PO Box 19369 81019 719-676-3030
Gene Padilla, prin. Fax 676-3511

Colorado Springs, El Paso, Pop. 400,464
Academy SD 20 26,400/PK-12
1110 Chapel Hills Dr 80920 719-234-1200
Dr. Mark Hatchell, supt. Fax 234-1299
www.asd20.org/
Academy Endeavour ES 600/K-5
3475 Hampton Park Dr 80920 719-234-5600
Bobbi Harper, prin. Fax 234-5699
Academy International ES 600/K-5
8550 Charity Dr 80920 719-234-4000
Laura McNally, prin. Fax 234-4099
Antelope Trails ES 500/K-5
15280 Jessie Dr 80921 719-234-4100
Laura Cresap, prin. Fax 234-4199
Challenger MS 800/6-8
10215 Lexington Dr 80920 719-234-3000
Tony Scott, prin. Fax 234-3199
Chinook Trail ES 700/K-5
11795 Grand Lawn Cir, 719-234-5700
Patrick Schumaker, prin. Fax 234-5799
da Vinci Academy 400/K-5
1335 Bridle Oaks Ln 80921 719-234-5400
Cindy Fesgen, prin. Fax 234-5499
Discovery Canyon Campus 2,500/PK-12
1810 N Gate Blvd 80921 719-234-1800
Jim Bailey, prin. Fax 234-1899
Eagleview MS 1,000/6-8
1325 Vindicator Dr 80919 719-234-3400
John Jamison, prin. Fax 234-3599
Explorer ES 500/PK-5
4190 Bardot Dr 80920 719-234-4400
Kay Lynn Waddell, prin. Fax 234-4499
Foothills ES 400/K-5
825 Allegheny Dr 80919 719-234-4500
Brandan Comfort, prin. Fax 234-4599
Frontier ES 400/K-5
3755 Meadow Ridge Dr 80920 719-234-4600
Kelly Garnhart, prin. Fax 234-4699
High Plains ES 300/K-5
2248 Vintage Dr 80920 719-234-4700
Tom Andrew, prin. Fax 234-4799
Mountain Ridge MS 1,100/6-8
9150 Lexington Dr 80920 719-234-3200
Jeff Sterk, prin. Fax 234-3399
Mountain View ES 600/K-5
10095 Lexington Dr 80920 719-234-4800
Jill Hooper, prin. Fax 234-4899
Pioneer ES 400/K-5
3663 Woodland Hills Dr 80918 719-234-5000
Diane Naghi, prin. Fax 234-5099
Prairie Hills ES 500/K-5
8025 Telegraph Dr 80920 719-234-5100
Vicki Axford, prin. Fax 234-5199
Ranch Creek ES 500/K-5
9155 Tutt Blvd, 719-234-5500
Susan Paulson, prin. Fax 234-5599
Rockrimmon ES 400/K-5
195 Mikado Dr W 80919 719-234-5200
Carre Bonilla, prin. Fax 234-5299
Timberview MS 1,100/6-8
8680 Scarborough Dr 80920 719-234-3600
Brett Smith, prin. Fax 234-3799
Wolford ES 400/K-5
13710 Black Forest Rd 80908 719-234-4300
Bob Wedel, prin. Fax 234-4399
Woodmen-Roberts ES 400/PK-5
8365 Orchard Path Rd 80919 719-234-5300
Jenny Sterk, prin. Fax 234-5399
Other Schools – See USAF Academy

Cheyenne Mountain SD 12 4,700/PK-12
1775 LaClede St 80905 719-475-6100
Dr. Walter Cooper, supt. Fax 475-6106
www.cmsd.k12.co.us
Broadmoor ES 300/K-6
440 W Cheyenne Mountain Blv 80906 719-475-6130
Lynda Henderson, prin. Fax 475-6126

Canon S 100/PK-PK
1201 W Cheyenne Rd 80906 719-475-6140
Linda Knight, coord. Fax 475-6143
Cheyenne Mountain ES 300/K-6
5250 Farthing Dr 80906 719-576-3080
Eric Paugh, prin. Fax 576-6834
Cheyenne Mountain JHS 600/7-8
1200 W Cheyenne Rd 80906 719-475-6120
Greg Watkins, prin. Fax 475-6123
Gold Camp ES 500/PK-6
1805 Preserve Dr 80906 719-327-2820
Becki Royall, prin. Fax 327-2825
Pinon Valley ES 300/PK-6
6205 Farthing Dr 80906 719-527-0300
Robin Reintsema, prin. Fax 527-8018
Skyway ES 300/K-6
1100 Mercury Dr 80905 719-475-6150
Stacy Aldridge, prin. Fax 630-4114

Colorado Springs SD 11 27,700/PK-12
1115 N El Paso St 80903 719-520-2000
Dr. Nicholas Gledich, supt. Fax 577-4546
www.d11.org
Adams ES 300/K-5
2101 Manitoba Dr 80910 719-328-2900
Nate Hansen, prin. Fax 630-2245
Audubon ES 300/PK-5
2400 E Van Buren St 80909 719-328-2600
Nancy Smith, prin. Fax 630-0178
Bristol ES 200/K-5
890 N Walnut St 80905 719-328-4000
Manuel Ramsey, prin. Fax 630-0182
Buena Vista ES 300/PK-6
924 W Pikes Peak Ave 80905 719-328-4100
Sharon Gateley, prin. Fax 630-3672
Carver ES 300/PK-5
4740 Artistic Cir 80917 719-328-7100
Michelle Hollenbeck, prin. Fax 596-3614
Chipeta ES 500/PK-5
2340 Ramsgate Ter 80919 719-328-5500
Sarah Scott, prin. Fax 260-8825
Columbia ES 300/PK-5
835 E Saint Vrain St 80903 719-328-2700
Karen Shaw, prin. Fax 630-0235
Edison ES 300/PK-5
3125 N Hancock Ave 80907 719-328-2800
Kevin Willis, prin. Fax 630-0238
Freedom ES 500/K-5
5280 Butterfield Dr, 719-228-0800
Sandra Park, prin. Fax 593-1749
Fremont ES 400/PK-5
5110 El Camino Dr 80918 719-328-5600
Brian Leatham, prin. Fax 260-8811
Galileo S of Math & Science 500/6-8
1600 N Union Blvd 80909 719-328-2200
Richard Law, prin. Fax 448-0498
Grant ES 500/PK-5
3215 Westwood Blvd 80918 719-328-5700
Ryan Miller, prin. Fax 260-8822
Henry ES 400/PK-5
1310 Lehmberg Blvd 80915 719-328-7200
Brian Casebeer, prin. Fax 596-0922
Holmes MS 700/6-8
2455 Mesa Rd 80904 719-328-3800
Robert Utter, prin. Fax 448-0358
Howbert ES 300/PK-5
1023 N 31st St 80904 719-328-4200
Bryan Relich, prin. Fax 630-0187
Jackson ES 400/PK-5
4340 Edwinstowe Ave 80907 719-328-5800
Sara Miller, prin. Fax 260-8813
Jenkins MS 1,000/6-8
6410 Austin Bluffs Pkwy, 719-328-5300
Darren Joiner, prin. Fax 266-5276
Keller ES 500/PK-5
3730 Montebello Dr W 80918 719-328-5900
Stacy Brisben, prin. Fax 260-8819
King ES 400/PK-5
6110 Sapporo Dr 80918 719-328-6000
Chris Lehman, prin. Fax 260-8816
Madison ES 400/PK-5
4120 Constitution Ave 80909 719-328-7300
Dorion Latimer, prin. Fax 596-4323
Mann MS 500/6-8
1001 E Van Buren St 80907 719-328-2300
Shawn Limberg, prin. Fax 448-0354
Martinez ES 600/PK-5
6460 Vickers Dr 80918 719-328-6100
Bobbie Long, prin. Fax 260-8806
McAuliffe ES 600/PK-5
830 Hathaway Dr 80915 719-228-0900
Carla Auld, prin. Fax 574-8372
Midland International ES 200/PK-5
2110 Broadway Ave 80904 719-328-4500
Jennifer Breeding, prin. Fax 630-0247
Monroe ES 500/PK-5
15 S Chelton Rd 80910 719-328-7400
Carole Wilson, prin. Fax 596-4465
North MS 700/6-8
612 E Yampa St 80903 719-328-2400
Christopher Kilroy, prin. Fax 448-0268
Palmer ES 200/PK-5
1921 E Yampa St 80909 719-328-3200
Julie Fahey, prin Fax 630-7806
Penrose ES 400/PK-5
4285 S Nonchalant Cir 80917 719-328-7500
Tamara Sobin, prin. Fax 596-0883
Rogers ES 300/PK-5
110 S Circle Dr 80910 719-328-3300
Linda Slothower, prin. Fax 630-7809
Rudy ES 400/PK-5
5370 Cracker Barrel Cir 80917 719-328-7600
Deb Coomes, prin. Fax 596-0005
Russell MS 700/6-8
3825 Montebello Dr W 80918 719-328-5200
Julie Johnson, prin. Fax 531-5520

Sabin MS 900/6-8
3605 N Carefree Cir 80917 719-328-7000
Jared Welch, prin. Fax 573-4960
Scott ES 700/PK-5
6175 Whetstone Dr, 719-328-6200
Jennifer Radford, prin. Fax 260-9587
Steele ES 300/K-5
1720 N Weber St 80907 719-328-4700
Ryan Capp, prin. Fax 630-0232
Stratton ES 400/PK-5
2460 Paseo Rd 80907 719-328-3400
Julie Edner, prin. Fax 630-3382
Swigert Aerospace Academy 500/6-8
4220 E Pikes Peak Ave 80909 719-328-6900
James Nason, prin. Fax 573-5295
Taylor ES 300/K-5
900 E Buena Ventura St 80907 719-328-3500
Kimberly Gilbert, prin. Fax 630-3397
Trailblazer ES 300/PK-6
2015 Wickes Rd 80919 719-328-6300
Denise Rubio-Gurnett, prin. Fax 260-1049
Twain ES 500/PK-5
3402 E San Miguel St 80909 719-328-7700
Cynthia Martinez, prin. Fax 596-6889
West ES 300/K-5
25 N 20th St 80904 719-328-3900
Karen Newton, prin. Fax 328-4901
West MS 300/6-8
1920 W Pikes Peak Ave 80904 719-328-3900
Shalah Sims, prin. Fax 448-0141
Wilson ES 400/PK-5
1409 De Reamer Cir 80915 719-328-7800
Stephanie Atencio, prin. Fax 596-7452

Falcon SD 49
Supt. — See Falcon
Evans International ES 600/K-5
1675 Winnebago Rd 80915 719-495-5299
Michelle Slyter, prin. Fax 495-5298
Horizon MS 600/6-8
1750 Piros Dr 80915 719-495-5210
Dustin Horras, prin. Fax 495-5209
Odyssey ES 600/K-5
6275 Bridle Spur Ave 80922 719-494-8622
Sarah McAfee, prin. Fax 495-8623
Remington ES 500/K-5
2825 Pony Tracks Dr 80922 719-495-5266
Lisa Fillo, prin. Fax 495-5267
Ridgeview ES 700/K-5
6573 Shimmering Creek Dr, 719-494-8700
Theresa Ritz, prin. Fax 494-8708
Skyview MS 1,000/6-8
6350 Windom Peak Blvd, 719-495-5566
Catherine Tinucci, prin. Fax 495-5569
Springs Ranch ES 600/PK-5
4350 Centerville Dr 80922 719-494-8600
Jim Kyner, prin. Fax 494-8612
Stetson ES 600/K-5
4910 Jedediah Smith Rd 80922 719-495-5252
Jeff Moulton, prin. Fax 495-5253

Fountain-Fort Carson SD 8
Supt. — See Fountain
Abrams ES 500/K-5
600 Chiles Ave, 719-382-1490
Lois Skaggs, prin. Fax 382-8572
Carson MS 700/6-8
6200 Prussman Blvd, 719-382-1610
Josh Hobgood, prin. Fax 382-8526
Mountainside ES 500/K-5
5506 Harr Ave, 719-382-1430
Eric Owen, prin. Fax 527-9273
Patriot ES 700/K-5
7010 Harr Ave, 719-382-1460
Rosa Saenz-Aragon, prin. Fax 576-4237
Weikel ES 800/PK-5
6565 Lindstrom St, 719-358-4320
Misty DeHerrera, prin. Fax 538-8888

Hanover SD 28 200/PK-12
17050 S Peyton Hwy 80928 719-683-2247
Dr. Grant Schmidt, supt. Fax 683-2299
www.hanoverhornets.org
Other Schools – See Fountain

Harrison SD 2 11,100/PK-12
1060 Harrison Rd 80905 719-579-2000
Andre Spencer Ed.D., supt. Fax 579-2019
www.hsd2.org
Bricker ES 400/PK-5
4880 Dover Dr 80916 719-579-2150
Tracy Jarboe, prin. Fax 579-2808
Carmel MS 400/6-8
1740 Pepperwood Dr 80910 719-579-3210
Lorna Breske, prin. Fax 579-2695
Centennial ES 500/PK-5
1860 S Chelton Rd 80910 719-579-2155
Kim Noyes, prin. Fax 538-1383
Fox Meadow MS 500/6-8
1450 Cheyenne Meadows Rd 80906 719-527-7100
John Rogerson, prin. Fax 576-0918
Giberson ES 300/PK-5
2880 Ferber Dr 80916 719-579-2166
Angelina Ramirez, prin. Fax 579-4994
Monterey ES 400/K-5
2311 Monterey Rd 80910 719-579-2170
Kellie Moore, prin. Fax 574-3301
Mountain Vista Community S 700/K-8
2550 Dorset Dr 80910 719-527-3400
Britney Gandhi, prin. Fax 473-1134
Oak Creek ES 300/PK-5
3333 Oak Creek Dr W 80906 719-579-2175
Linda Donaldson, prin. Fax 579-2991
Otero ES 400/PK-5
1650 Charmwood Dr 80906 719-579-2110
Amy Karbowski, prin. Fax 579-2002
Panorama MS 500/6-8
2145 S Chelton Rd 80916 719-579-3220
Elizabeth Domangue, prin. Fax 579-2756

Pikes Peak ES 400/K-5
1520 Verde Dr 80910 719-579-2180
Mike Roth, prin. Fax 579-3565
Sand Creek ES 500/K-5
550 Sand Creek Dr 80916 719-579-3760
Rachel Laufer, prin. Fax 579-4943
Soaring Eagles ES 600/PK-5
4710 Harrier Ridge Dr 80916 719-540-4000
Kimberly Easdon, prin. Fax 540-4020
Stratmoor Hills ES 300/K-5
200 Loomis Ave 80906 719-579-2185
Pamela Robinson, prin.
Stratton Meadows ES 400/K-5
610 Brookshire Ave 80905 719-579-2190
Dr. Christina Clayton, prin. Fax 538-1400
Turman ES 300/K-5
3245 Springnite Dr 80916 719-579-2195
Wendy Smith-Koceski, prin. Fax 579-3699
Wildflower ES 500/K-5
1160 Keith Dr 80916 719-579-2115
Wendy Godwin, prin. Fax 579-3757

Lewis-Palmer SD 38
Supt. — See Monument
Kilmer ES 400/PK-6
4285 Walker Rd 80908 719-488-4740
Drew Francis, prin. Fax 488-4744

Widefield SD 3 9,400/PK-12
1820 Main St 80911 719-391-3000
Scott Campbell, supt. Fax 390-4372
www.wsd3.org
French ES 600/K-5
5225 Alturas Dr 80911 719-391-3495
Michelle Blasko, prin. Fax 391-9141
King ES 500/K-5
6910 Defoe Ave 80911 719-391-3455
Tricia Bentley, prin. Fax 391-9324
North Preschool 500/PK-PK
209 Leta Dr 80911 719-391-3375
Andrea Waltermire, prin. Fax 391-9425
Pinello ES 300/K-5
2515 Cody Dr 80911 719-391-3395
Annette Butala, prin. Fax 392-1605
Sproul JHS 600/6-8
235 Sumac Dr 80911 719-391-3215
Maureen di Stasio, prin. Fax 391-3215
Sunrise ES 600/K-5
7070 Grand Valley Dr 80911 719-391-3415
Amy Roden, prin. Fax 391-9104
Talbott STEAM Innovation S 400/K-5
401 Dean Dr 80911 719-391-3475
Tracey Vsetecka, prin. Fax 391-9414
Venetucci ES 400/K-5
405 Willis Dr 80911 719-391-3355
Rebecca Harris, prin. Fax 391-7706
Watson JHS 700/6-8
136 Fontaine Blvd 80911 719-391-3255
Justin Lee, prin. Fax 392-3419
Webster ES 700/K-5
445 Jersey Ln 80911 719-391-3435
Jennifer Bonds, prin. Fax 391-9166
Widefield ES 400/K-5
509 Widefield Dr 80911 719-391-3335
Dawn Hunke, prin. Fax 391-9416
Other Schools – See Fountain

Colorado Springs Christian S 800/K-12
4855 Mallow Rd 80907 719-599-3553
Dr. Roland DeRenzo, supt. Fax 268-2184
Colorado Springs S 300/PK-12
21 Broadmoor Ave 80906 719-475-9747
Aaron Schubach, head sch Fax 475-9864
Corpus Christi Catholic S 200/PK-8
2410 N Cascade Ave 80907 719-632-5092
John Kraus, prin. Fax 578-9124
Divine Redeemer S 200/PK-8
901 N Logan Ave 80909 719-471-7771
David Brilliant, prin. Fax 234-0300
Evangelical Christian Academy 200/PK-6
2511 N Logan Ave 80907 719-634-7024
Darla Blue, prin. Fax 328-1554
Holy Apostles Preschool 100/PK-PK
4925 N Carefree Cir 80917 719-591-1566
McKenna Anderson, dir. Fax 591-1816
Hope Montessori Academy 50/PK-K
2041 Chuckwagon Rd 80919 719-388-8818
Hope Montessori Academy PK-K
6353 Stetson Hills Blvd, 719-573-5300
Pikes Peak Christian S 400/PK-12
5905 Flintridge Dr 80918 719-598-8610
St. Paul Catholic S - Pauline Memorial 200/PK-8
1601 Mesa Ave 80906 719-632-1846
James Welte, prin. Fax 632-0231
Springs Adventist Academy 50/K-8
5410 Palmer Park Blvd 80915 719-597-0155
University S 100/PK-12
2713 W Cucharras St 80904 719-302-3751
Jeff Cooper, admin. Fax 377-3903
Valley Christian S 50/K-2
9355 Peaceful Valley Rd 80925 719-465-3932
Renee Green, dir.

Commerce City, Adams, Pop. 45,019

Adams County SD 14 7,600/PK-12
5291 E 60th Ave 80022 303-853-3333
Dr. Javier Abrego, supt. Fax 853-3329
www.adams14.org
Adams City MS 800/6-8
4451 E 72nd Ave 80022 303-289-5881
Martin Pearson, prin. Fax 288-8574
Alsup ES 500/K-5
7101 Birch St 80022 303-288-6865
Michael Abdale, prin. Fax 288-6866
Central ES 600/PK-5
6450 Holly St 80022 303-287-0327
Deana Valadez, prin. Fax 287-0328

Dupont ES 700/K-5
7970 Kimberly St 80022 303-287-0189
Pat Almeida, prin. Fax 287-0180
Hanson ES 500/PK-5
7133 E 73rd Ave 80022 303-853-5800
Diego Romero, prin. Fax 288-5578
Kearney MS 800/6-8
6160 Kearney St 80022 303-287-0261
Veronica Jeffers, prin. Fax 287-0432
Kemp ES 600/PK-5
6775 Oneida St 80022 303-288-6633
Robert Savage, prin. Fax 288-6634
Monaco ES 500/K-5
7631 Monaco St 80022 303-287-0307
Dr. Mary Helen Lechuga, prin. Fax 287-0308
Rose Hill ES 500/PK-5
6900 E 58th Ave 80022 303-287-0163
Bonnie Martinez, prin. Fax 322-8167
Sanville Preschool 100/PK-PK
5941 E 64th Ave 80022 303-853-5675
Karen Weaver, prin. Fax 287-2473
STARS Early Learning Center 100/PK-K
5650 Bowen Ct 80022 303-853-5000
Karen Weaver, prin. Fax 853-5013

SD 27J
Supt. — See Brighton
Reunion ES PK-5
11021 Landmark Dr 80022 720-685-8501
David Felten, prin.
Second Creek ES 700/PK-5
9950 Laredo Dr 80022 720-685-7550
Evoice Sims, prin. Fax 685-7554
Stuart MS 600/6-8
15955 E 101st Way 80022 720-685-5500
Fabricio Velez, prin. Fax 685-5506
Turnberry ES 900/PK-5
13069 E 106th Pl 80022 720-685-5350
Kate Pelton, prin. Fax 685-5354

Conifer, Jefferson, Pop. 600
Jefferson County SD R-1
Supt. — See Golden
West Jefferson ES 400/PK-5
26501 Barkley Rd 80433 303-982-2975
Wendy Woodland, prin. Fax 982-2976
West Jefferson MS 600/6-8
9449 Barnes Ave 80433 303-982-3056
Rebecca Brown, prin. Fax 982-3057

Cortez, Montezuma, Pop. 8,328
Montezuma-Cortez SD RE-1 2,800/PK-12
PO Box R 81321 970-565-7522
Lori Haukeness, supt. Fax 565-2161
www.cortez.k12.co.us
Beech Street Preschool 100/PK-PK
510 N Beech St 81321 970-565-7491
Dan Porter, prin.
Cortez MS 600/6-8
450 W 2nd St 81321 970-565-7824
Katherine Ott, prin. Fax 565-5120
Kemper ES 400/K-5
620 E Montezuma Ave 81321 970-565-3737
Jamie Haukeness, prin. Fax 565-5158
Lewis-Arriola ES 100/K-5
21434 Road U 81321 970-882-4494
Jim Parr, prin. Fax 882-7617
Manaugh ES 300/K-5
300 E 4th St 81321 970-565-7691
Donotta Jonoo, prin. Fax 565-5142
Mesa ES 400/K-5
703 W 7th St 81321 970-565-3858
K.D. Umbarger, prin. Fax 565-5137
Other Schools – See Pleasant View

Cortez Adventist Christian S 50/K-8
540 W 4th St 81321 970-565-8257
Deirdre Franklin, prin. Fax 565-7171

Cotopaxi, Fremont, Pop. 45
Cotopaxi SD RE-3 100/PK-12
PO Box 385 81223 719-942-4131
Randy Bohlander, supt. Fax 942-4134
www.cotopaxire3.org/
Cotopaxi S 100/PK-12
PO Box 385 81223 719-942-4131
Jackie Crabtree, prin. Fax 942-4134

Craig, Moffat, Pop. 9,327
Moffat County SD RE-1 2,200/PK-12
775 Yampa Ave 81625 970-824-3268
David Ulrich Ed.D., supt. Fax 824-6655
moffatsd.org
Craig MS 500/6-8
915 Yampa Ave 81625 970-824-3289
Dave Grabowski, prin. Fax 824-3858
East ES 300/PK-5
600 Texas Ave 81625 970-824-6042
Sarah Hepworth, prin. Fax 824-3513
Maybell ES, 775 Yampa Ave 81625 K-5
Sarah Hepworth, prin. 970-272-3266
Ridgeview ES 300/PK-5
600 Westridge Rd 81625 970-824-7018
John Haddan, prin. Fax 824-7010
Sandrock ES 300/PK-5
201 E 9th St 81625 970-824-3287
Kamisha Siminoe, prin. Fax 824-5278
Sunset ES 300/PK-5
800 W 7th St 81625 970-824-5762
Jill Hafey, prin. Fax 824-2816

Crawford, Delta, Pop. 423
Delta County SD 50(J)
Supt. — See Delta
North Fork Montessori @ Crawford 100/PK-6
PO Box 98 81415 970-921-4935
Bill Eyler, admin. Fax 921-3671

Creede, Mineral, Pop. 412
Creede SD 100/K-12
PO Box 429 81130 719-658-2220
Elisabeth Richard, supt. Fax 658-2942
www.creedek12.net
Creede S 50/K-12
PO Box 429 81130 719-658-2220
John Goss, prin. Fax 658-2942

Crested Butte, Gunnison, Pop. 1,477
Gunnison Watershed SD RE 1J
Supt. — See Gunnison
Crested Butte Community S 600/K-12
PO Box 339 81224 970-641-7720
Stephanie Niemi, prin. Fax 641-7729

Cripple Creek, Teller, Pop. 1,167
Cripple Creek-Victor SD RE-1 400/PK-12
PO Box 897 80813 719-689-2685
Leslie Lindauer, supt. Fax 689-2256
www.ccvschools.org
Cresson ES 200/PK-5
PO Box 897 80813 719-689-9230
Miriam Mondragon, prin. Fax 689-9236

De Beque, Mesa, Pop. 499
De Beque SD 49JT 100/PK-12
PO Box 70 81630 970-283-5596
Alan Dillon, supt. Fax 283-5598
www.dbschools.org
De Beque ES 100/PK-6
PO Box 70 81630 970-283-5418
Becky Graham, prin. Fax 283-5598

Deer Trail, Arapahoe, Pop. 538
Deer Trail SD 26J 200/PK-12
PO Box 129 80105 303-769-4421
Kevin Schott, supt. Fax 769-4600
www.dt26j.org
Deer Trail ES 100/PK-5
PO Box 129 80105 303-769-4421
Dave Casey, prin. Fax 769-4600

Del Norte, Rio Grande, Pop. 1,670
Del Norte SD C-7 400/K-12
770 11th St 81132 719-657-4040
Chris Burr, supt. Fax 657-2546
delnorte.schoolfusion.us
Del Norte ES 100/K-8
770 11th St 81132 719-657-4030
Amy Duda, prin. Fax 657-9087

Delta, Delta, Pop. 8,798
Delta County SD 50(J) 4,600/PK-12
7655 2075 Rd 81416 970-874-4438
Caryn Gibson, supt. Fax 874-5744
www.deltaschools.com
Delta MS 500/6-8
910 Grand Ave 81416 970-874-8046
Sheryl Yeager, prin. Fax 874-8049
Garnet Mesa ES 600/K-5
600 A St 81416 970-874-8003
Joseph Mock, prin. Fax 874-8303
Lincoln ES 500/K-5
1050 Hastings St 81416 970-874-3700
Jennifer Magner, prin. Fax 874-4714
Other Schools – See Cedaredge, Crawford, Hotchkiss, Paonia

Delta SDA S 50/K-8
PO Box 91 81416 970-874-9482

Denver, Denver, Pop. 585,815
Cherry Creek SD 5
Supt. — See Greenwood Village
Challenge S 500/K-8
9659 E Mississippi Ave, 720-747-2100
Linda Maccagnan, prin. Fax 747-2183
Holly Hills ES 300/3-5
6161 E Cornell Ave 80222 720-747-2500
Chad Gerity, prin. Fax 747-2588
Holly Ridge PS PK-2
3301 S Monaco Pkwy 80222 720-747-2400
Chad Gerity, prin. Fax 747-2488

Denver County SD 1 83,600/PK-12
1860 N Lincoln St 80203 720-423-3200
Tom Boasberg, supt. Fax 423-3413
www.dpsk12.org
Academia Ana Marie Sandoval Montessori 400/PK-6
3655 Wyandot St 80211 720-424-4370
Araceli O'Clair, prin. Fax 424-4395
Amesse ES 600/PK-5
5440 Scranton St 80239 720-424-9988
Charmaine Keeton, prin. Fax 424-9914
Archuleta ES 600/PK-5
16000 Maxwell Pl 80239 720-424-9888
Yolanda Ortega, prin. Fax 424-9834
Asbury ES 300/K-5
1320 E Asbury Ave 80210 720-424-9750
Pam Kirk, prin. Fax 424-9775
Ashley ES 300/PK-5
1914 Syracuse St 80220 720-424-9748
Zachary Rahn, prin. Fax 424-9694
Barnum ES 500/PK-5
85 Hooker St 80219 720-424-9590
Elizabeth Vinson, prin. Fax 424-9615
Beach Court ES 300/PK-5
4950 Beach Ct 80221 720-424-9470
Leah Schultz-Bartlett, prin. Fax 424-9495
Bear Valley International S 6-8
3005 S Golden Way 80227 720-423-9600
Lindsay Meier, prin.
Bird Community S 100/PK-5
2701 Lima St 80238 720-423-9900
Brian Ricker, prin. Fax 423-9918
Bradley International S 500/PK-5
3051 S Elm St 80222 720-424-9468
Stephen Wera, prin. Fax 424-9414

Bromwell ES 300/PK-5
2500 E 4th Ave 80206 720-424-9330
Andrew Hodges, prin. Fax 424-9355
Brown International Academy 600/PK-5
2550 Lowell Blvd 80211 720-424-9250
Susan Williams, prin. Fax 424-9275
Bryant-Webster Dual Language S 400/PK-8
3635 Quivas St 80211 720-424-9170
Jose Martinez, prin. Fax 424-9195
Carson ES 400/PK-5
5420 E 1st Ave 80220 720-424-9090
Anne Larkin, prin. Fax 424-9115
Castro ES 600/PK-5
845 S Lowell Blvd 80219 720-424-8990
Dr. Bob Villarreal, prin. Fax 424-9015
Centennial ES 400/PK-5
4665 N Raleigh St 80212 720-424-8900
Laura Munro, prin. Fax 424-8925
Cheltenham ES 500/PK-5
1580 Julian St 80204 720-424-8810
Felicia Manzanares, prin. Fax 424-8836
CMS Community S 500/PK-5
1300 S Lowell Blvd 80219 720-424-4300
Alejandra Sotiros, prin. Fax 424-4325
Cole Arts and Science Academy 500/PK-5
3240 N Humboldt St 80205 720-423-9120
Jennifer Jackson, prin. Fax 423-9123
Colfax ES 400/PK-5
1526 Tennyson St 80204 720-424-8740
Sandra Beruman, prin. Fax 424-8765
College View ES 500/PK-5
2675 S Decatur St 80219 720-424-8660
Shelley Boberschmidt, prin. Fax 424-8685
Columbian ES 300/PK-5
2925 W 40th Ave 80211 720-424-8580
Jenifer Rouse, prin. Fax 424-8605
Columbine ES 200/PK-5
2540 E 29th Ave 80205 720-424-8510
Jason Krause, prin. Fax 424-8535
Cory ES 400/1-5
1550 S Steele St 80210 720-424-8380
Liz Tencate, prin. Fax 424-8405
Cowell ES 500/PK-5
4540 W 10th Ave 80204 720-424-8300
Shayley Levensalor, prin. Fax 424-8325
Creativity Challenge Community 200/K-5
1551 S Monroe St 80210 720-424-0630
Julia Shepherd, prin.
DCIS at Fairmont 300/PK-5
520 W 3rd Ave 80223 720-424-7620
Vanessa Acevedo, prin. Fax 424-7645
DCIS at Ford 600/PK-5
14500 Maxwell Pl 80239 720-424-7300
Ginger Conroy, prin. Fax 424-7345
Denison Montessori 400/PK-6
1821 S Yates St 80219 720-424-8080
Kathryn Mattis, prin. Fax 424-8105
Denver Discovery S 6-8
3480 Syracuse St 80238 720-424-4790
Kristen Atwood, prin. Fax 424-4791
Denver Green S 500/PK-8
6700 E Virginia Ave 80224 720-424-7480
Frank Coyne, prin. Fax 424-7537
Doull ES 500/PK-5
2520 S Utica St 80219 720-424-8000
Jodie Carrigan, prin. Fax 424-8025
Eagleton ES 500/PK-5
880 Hooker St 80204 720-424-7930
Lee Thomas, prin. Fax 424-7955
Edison ES 600/PK-5
3350 Quitman St 80212 720-424-7780
Sally Whitelock, prin. Fax 424-7805
Ellis ES 500/PK-5
1651 S Dahlia St 80222 720-424-7700
Nichole Whiteman, prin. Fax 424-7725
Escalante Biggs Academy 400/PK-K
5300 Crown Blvd 80239 720-424-4620
Eric Love, prin. Fax 424-4630
Fairview ES 300/PK-5
2715 W 11th Ave 80204 720-424-7540
Antoinette Hudson, prin. Fax 424-7565
Force ES 600/PK-5
1550 S Wolff St 80219 720-424-7400
Valerie Burke, prin. Fax 424-7425
Garden Place ES 400/PK-6
4425 Lincoln St 80216 720-424-7220
Rebecca Salomon, prin. Fax 424-7245
Godsman ES 600/PK-5
2120 W Arkansas Ave 80223 720-424-7060
Priscilla Hopkins, prin. Fax 424-7085
Goldrick ES 600/PK-5
1050 S Zuni St 80223 720-424-6980
Jessica Ridgway, prin. Fax 424-7005
Grant Beacon MS 400/6-8
1751 S Washington St 80210 720-423-9360
Alex Magana, prin. Fax 423-9385
Grant Ranch S 800/PK-8
5400 S Jay Cir 80123 720-424-6880
Patricia Hurietta, prin. Fax 424-6905
Greenlee ES 400/PK-5
1150 Lipan St 80204 720-424-6800
Sheldon Reynolds, prin. Fax 424-6825
Green Valley ES 700/PK-5
4100 Jericho St 80249 720-424-6710
Blake Hammond, prin. Fax 424-6735
Greenwood Academy 700/PK-8
5130 Durham Ct 80239 720-424-6630
Rachel Payne, prin. Fax 424-6655
Gust ES 800/PK-5
3440 W Yale Ave 80219 720-424-6560
Joanne Lander, prin. Fax 424-6585
Hallett Fundamental Academy 400/PK-5
2950 Jasmine St 80207 720-424-6070
Dominique Jefferson, prin. Fax 424-6095
Hamilton MS 900/6-8
8600 E Dartmouth Ave 80231 720-423-9500
Christian Sawyer, prin. Fax 423-9445

Henry World MS 800/6-8
3005 S Golden Way 80227 720-423-9560
Lani Nobles, prin. Fax 423-9585
High Tech ES, 8499 Stoll Pl 80238 PK-5
Amy Gile, prin. 720-424-2100
Hill MS Campus of Arts & Sciences 800/6-8
451 Clermont St 80220 720-423-9680
Sean Kavanaugh, prin. Fax 423-9709
Holm ES 600/PK-5
3185 S Willow St 80231 720-424-6350
James Metcalfe, prin. Fax 424-6375
Howell S 800/PK-8
14250 Albrook Dr 80239 720-424-2740
Rachel Massey, prin. Fax 424-2765
Inspire ES K-5
5500 Central Park Blvd 80238 720-424-4850
Marisol Enriquez, prin.
International Academy at Harrington 400/PK-5
2401 E 37th Ave 80205 720-424-6420
Karin Johnson, prin. Fax 424-6445
Johnson ES 400/PK-5
1850 S Irving St 80219 720-424-6290
Elliot Lepert, prin. Fax 424-6315
Kaiser ES 300/PK-5
4500 S Quitman St 80236 720-424-6210
Mike Rowley, prin. Fax 424-6235
Kepner Beacon MS 6-8
911 S Hazel Ct 80219 720-424-0027
Alex Magana, prin.
Kepner MS 800/6-8
911 S Hazel Ct 80219 720-424-0000
Elza Guajardo, prin. Fax 424-0023
Knapp ES 700/PK-5
500 S Utica St 80219 720-424-6130
Shane Knight, prin. Fax 424-6155
Knight Center for Early Education 300/PK-K
3245 E Exposition Ave 80209 720-424-6500
Shelia Deacon, prin. Fax 424-6526
Kunsmiller Creative Arts Academy 900/K-12
2250 S Quitman Way 80219 720-424-0200
Dan Villesces, prin. Fax 424-0145
Lake International MS 400/6-8
1820 Lowell Blvd 80204 720-424-0260
Rebecca Marques-Guerrero, prin. Fax 424-0380
LeDoux Academy PK-PK
1055 S Hazel Ct 80219 720-423-9240
Leticia Jara-Leake, prin.
Lincoln ES 400/PK-5
710 S Pennsylvania St 80209 720-424-5990
Janice Spearman, prin. Fax 424-6015
Lowry ES 500/PK-5
8001 E Cedar Ave 80230 720-424-5910
Ben Cooper, prin. Fax 424-5935
Marrama ES 600/PK-5
19100 E 40th Ave 80249 720-424-5820
Merida Fraguada, prin. Fax 424-5845
Math and Science Leadership Academy 300/K-5
451 S Tejon St 80223 720-424-1310
Rebecca Lane, prin. Fax 424-1326
Maxwell ES 500/PK-5
14390 Bolling Dr 80239 720-424-5740
Nivan Khosravi, prin. Fax 424-5765
McAuliffe International MS 400/6-8
2540 Holly St 80207 720-424-1540
Kurt Dennis, prin. Fax 424-1565
McAuliffe Manual MS 6-8
1700 E 28th Ave 80205 720-423-6550
Jessica Long, prin.
McGlone Academy 700/PK-8
4500 Crown Blvd 80239 720-424-5660
Sara Goodall, prin. Fax 424-5685
McKinley-Thatcher ES 200/PK-5
1230 S Grant St 80210 720-424-5600
Sonia Geerdes, prin. Fax 424-5625
McMeen ES 600/PK-5
1000 S Holly St 80246 720-424-5520
David Adams, prin. Fax 424-5545
Merrill MS 500/6-8
1551 S Monroe St 80210 720-424-0600
Christina Sylvester, prin. Fax 424-0625
Montclair S of Academics/Enrichment 500/PK-5
1151 Newport St 80220 720-424-5380
Ryan Kockler, prin. Fax 424-5405
Moore S 500/K-8
846 N Corona St 80218 720-424-5300
Karen Barker, prin. Fax 424-5325
Morey MS 600/6-8
840 E 14th Ave 80218 720-424-0700
Noah Tonk, prin. Fax 424-0727
Munroe ES 600/PK-5
3440 W Virginia Ave 80219 720-424-5230
Abigail Brown, prin. Fax 424-5255
Newlon ES 500/PK-5
361 Vrain St 80219 720-424-5150
Rob Beam, prin. Fax 424-5175
Oakland ES PK-5
4580 Dearborn St 80239 720-424-5070
Lisa Mahannah, prin. Fax 424-5080
Palmer ES 300/PK-5
995 Grape St 80220 720-424-5000
LuAnn Tallman, prin. Fax 424-5025
Park Hill ES 600/PK-5
5050 E 19th Ave 80220 720-424-4910
Ken Burdette, prin. Fax 424-4935
Pitt-Waller S 900/PK-8
21601 E 51st Pl 80249 720-424-2840
Kayla Grayson-Yizar, prin. Fax 424-2866
Place Bridge Academy 1,100/PK-8
7125 Cherry Creek North Dr 80224 720-424-0960
Brenda Kazin, prin. Fax 424-0985
Polaris S at Ebert 300/1-5
410 Park Ave W 80205 720-424-7860
Anne Sterrett, prin. Fax 424-7885
Roberts S 800/PK-8
2100 Akron Way 80238 720-424-2640
Patricia Lea, prin. Fax 424-2665

Sabin World ES 700/PK-5
3050 S Vrain St 80236 720-424-4520
Kirsten Frassanito, prin. Fax 424-4545
Samuels ES 600/PK-5
3985 S Vincennes Ct 80237 720-424-4450
Cesar Rivera, prin. Fax 424-4475
Schmitt ES 400/PK-5
1820 S Vallejo St 80223 720-424-4230
Jesse Tang, prin. Fax 424-4255
Shoemaker ES PK-5
3333 S Havana St 80231 720-423-9333
Christine Fleming, prin.
Skinner MS 500/6-8
3435 W 40th Ave 80211 720-424-1420
Michelle Koyama, prin. Fax 424-1446
Slavens S 600/PK-8
3000 S Clayton St 80210 720-424-4150
Kurt Siebold, prin. Fax 424-4175
Smith ES 400/PK-5
3590 Jasmine St 80207 720-424-4000
Emily El Moudaffar, prin. Fax 424-4025
Southmoor ES 500/PK-5
3755 S Magnolia Way 80237 720-424-3930
Sarina Compoz, prin. Fax 424-3955
Steck ES 400/PK-5
450 Albion St 80220 720-424-3870
Robert Kline, prin. Fax 424-3895
Stedman ES 400/PK-5
2940 Dexter St 80207 720-424-3800
Melissa Peterson, prin. Fax 424-3825
Steele ES 400/K-5
320 S Marion Pkwy 80209 720-424-3720
Cindy Kapeller, prin. Fax 424-3745
Swansea ES 600/PK-5
4650 Columbine St 80216 720-424-3630
Gilberto Munoz, prin. Fax 424-3655
Swigert International ES 600/PK-5
3480 Syracuse St 80238 720-424-4800
Shelby Dennis, prin. Fax 424-4825
Teller ES 500/PK-5
1150 Garfield St 80206 720-424-3560
Sabrina Bates, prin. Fax 424-3585
Todd-Williams Academy PK-PK
4909 Cathay St 80249 720-424-8240
Leslie Harvey, prin. Fax 424-8249
Traylor Academy 600/PK-5
2900 S Ivan Way 80227 720-424-3480
Dawn Carrico, prin. Fax 424-3505
Trevista S at Horace Mann 500/PK-8
4130 Navajo St 80211 720-423-9800
Jesus Rodriguez, prin. Fax 423-9850
University Park ES 400/K-5
2300 S Saint Paul St 80210 720-424-3410
Grant Varveris, prin. Fax 424-3435
Valdez ES 400/PK-5
2525 W 29th Ave 80211 720-424-3310
Jessica Buckley, prin. Fax 424-3335
Valverde ES 400/PK-5
2030 W Alameda Ave 80223 720-424-3250
Andrew Schutz, prin. Fax 424-3275
Westerly Creek ES 700/PK-5
8800 E 28th Ave 80238 720-424-3160
Jill Corcoran, prin. Fax 424-3185
Whittier S 300/PK-8
2480 N Downing St 80205 720-424-3040
Jai Palmer, prin. Fax 424-3065

Mapleton SD 1 8,500/PK-12
7350 N Broadway 80221 303-853-1000
Charlotte Ciancio, supt. Fax 853-1087
www.mapleton.us
Adventure ES 400/PK-6
7700 Delta St 80221 303-853-1410
Laura Nelson, dir. Fax 853-1426
Global Intermediate Academy 4-8
7480 N Broadway 80221 303-853-1930
Tiffany Dragoo, dir. Fax 853-1956
Global Primary Academy 200/PK-3
7480 N Broadway 80221 303-853-1930
A.J. Staniszewski, dir. Fax 853-1956
Monterey Community S 500/PK-8
2201 McElwain Blvd 80229 303-853-1360
Sarah Kopperud, dir. Fax 853-1396
Valley View S 500/K-8
660 W 70th Ave 80221 303-853-1560
Toni Booth, dir. Fax 853-1596
Welby Community S 300/PK-6
1200 E 78th Ave 80229 303-853-1700
Candace Hyatt, dir. Fax 853-1726
Other Schools – See Thornton

Sheridan SD 2
Supt. — See Sheridan
Early Childhood Education Center 200/PK-PK
4107 S Federal Blvd 80236 720-833-6600
Aimee Chapman, prin. Fax 833-6649
Ft. Logan Northgate S 300/3-8
4000 S Lowell Blvd 80236 720-833-6853
Nelson Van Vranken, prin. Fax 833-6746

Westminster SD
Supt. — See Westminster
Carpenter MS 600/6-8
7001 Lipan St 80221 303-428-8583
Tige Asnicar, prin. Fax 657-3962
Day ES 400/PK-5
1740 Jordan Dr 80221 303-428-1330
Rick Bucher, prin. Fax 657-3835
Early Learning Center PK-PK
7125 Mariposa St 80221 303-650-7657
Kelly Altizer, coord.
Fairview ES 300/PK-5
7826 Fairview Ave 80221 303-428-1405
Camile Carlson, prin. Fax 487-2063
Hodgkins ES 700/PK-5
3475 W 67th Ave 80221 303-428-1121
Amber Swieckowski, prin. Fax 657-3820

Metz ES 400/PK-5
2341 Sherrelwood Dr 80221 303-428-1884
Claudette Trujillo, prin. Fax 657-3865
Ranum MS 800/6-8
2401 W 80th Ave 80221 303-428-9577
Shannon Willy, prin. Fax 657-3952
Sherrelwood ES 300/PK-5
8095 Kalamath St 80221 303-428-5353
Cindy Davis, prin. Fax 657-3868
Skyline Vista ES 400/PK-5
7395 Zuni St 80221 303-428-2300
Zack White, prin. Fax 657-3871

Accelerated Schools 50/K-12
2160 S Cook St 80210 303-758-2003
Annunciation S 200/K-8
3536 N Lafayette St 80205 303-295-2515
Deb Roberts, prin. Fax 295-2516
Assumption S 100/PK-8
2341 E 78th Ave 80229 303-288-2159
Sarah Grey, prin. Fax 288-4716
Blessed Sacrament S 500/PK-8
1973 Elm St 80220 303-377-8835
Dr. Carla Capstick, prin. Fax 321-7765
Christ the King S 200/PK-8
860 Elm St 80220 303-321-2123
Bernadette Hensen, prin. Fax 321-2191
Colorado Academy 900/PK-12
3800 S Pierce St 80235 303-986-1501
Michael Davis Ph.D., hdmstr. Fax 914-2583
Denver Academy 400/1-12
4400 E Iliff Ave 80222 303-777-5870
Mark Twarogowski, hdmstr. Fax 777-5893
Denver Academy of Torah 100/PK-12
6825 E Alameda Ave 80224 720-859-6806
Denver Jewish Day School 400/K-12
2450 S Wabash St 80231 303-369-0663
Avi Halzel, head sch Fax 369-0664
Denver Waldorf S 300/PK-12
2100 S Pennsylvania St 80210 303-777-0531
Kelly Church, admin. Fax 744-1216
Escuela de Guadalupe PK-8
660 Julian St 80204 303-964-8456
Excel Institute 100/PK-8
3050 Richard Allen Ct 80205 303-355-0667
Good Shepherd S 400/PK-8
620 Elizabeth St 80206 303-321-6231
Mark Strawbridge, prin. Fax 261-1059
Graland Country Day S 600/PK-8
55 Clermont St 80220 303-399-0390
Josh Cobb, head sch Fax 388-2803
Guardian Angels S 200/PK-8
1843 W 52nd Ave 80221 303-480-9005
Mary Gold, prin. Fax 480-3527
Hillel Academy 200/PK-8
450 S Hudson St 80246 303-333-1511
Inner-City S 50/PK-6
3560 Josephine St 80205 303-316-4533
Jacquelyn Graham, prin. Fax 316-4535
International S of Denver 400/PK-8
7701 E 1st Pl Ste C 80230 303-340-3647
David Magill, head sch Fax 360-9426
Logan S for Creative Learning 300/K-8
1005 Yosemite St 80230 303-340-2444
Markus Hunt, head sch Fax 340-2041
Montessori Academy of Colorado 200/PK-5
2500 Curtis St 80205 303-623-2609
Nancy James, head sch
Montessori Children's House of Denver 100/PK-6
1467 Birch St 80220 303-322-8324
Montessori S of Denver 300/PK-8
1460 S Holly St 80222 303-756-9441
Stephanie Flanigan, hdmstr. Fax 757-6145
Most Precious Blood S 400/K-8
3959 E Iliff Ave 80210 303-757-1279
Colleen McManamon, prin. Fax 757-1270
Notre Dame S 300/PK-8
2165 S Zenobia St 80219 303-935-3549
Charlene Molis, prin. Fax 937-4868
Our Lady of Lourdes S 100/PK-8
2256 S Logan St 80210 303-722-7525
Rosemary Anderson, prin. Fax 765-5305
Redeemer Learning Center 100/1-8
3400 W Nevada Pl 80219 303-934-0422
Fax 935-9256
Ricks Center for Gifted Children 200/PK-8
2040 S York St 80210 303-871-2982
Anne Sweet, dir. Fax 871-3197
St. Anne's Episcopal S 400/PK-8
2701 S York St 80210 303-756-9481
Alan Smiley, admin. Fax 756-5512
St. Catherine of Siena S 100/PK-8
4200 Federal Blvd 80211 303-477-8035
Douglas Sandusky, prin. Fax 477-0110
St. Elizabeth's S 100/K-8
2350 N Gaylord St 80205 303-322-4209
Ramsay Stabler, head sch Fax 322-4210
St. Francis de Sales S 200/PK-8
235 S Sherman St 80209 303-744-7231
Sr. Mary Rose Lieb, prin. Fax 744-1028
St. James S 200/PK-8
1250 Newport St 80220 303-333-8275
Carol Hovell-Genth, prin. Fax 780-0137
St. John's Lutheran S 300/PK-8
700 S Franklin St 80209 303-733-3777
Loren Otte, prin. Fax 778-6070
St. Rose of Lima S 300/PK-8
1345 W Dakota Ave 80223 303-733-5806
Elias Moo, prin. Fax 733-0125
St. Vincent De Paul S 500/PK-8
1164 S Josephine St 80210 303-777-3812
Fax 733-9528
Stanley British PS 400/K-8
350 Quebec Ct 80230 303-360-0803
Tim Barrier, head sch Fax 360-0353

Trinity Lutheran Early Child Lrng Center 100/PK-K
4225 W Yale Ave 80219 303-359-7633
Gwen Marshall, dir. Fax 936-1515
Zion Evangelical Lutheran S 100/PK-8
2600 S Wadsworth Blvd 80227 303-985-2334
Philip Adickes B.A., prin.

Dillon, Summit, Pop. 888
Summit SD RE-1
Supt. — See Frisco
Dillon Valley ES 400/PK-5
PO Box 4788 80435 970-368-1400
Kendra Carpenter, prin. Fax 368-1499
Summit Cove ES 300/PK-5
727 Cove Blvd 80435 970-368-1700
Crystal Miller, prin. Fax 368-1799

Divide, Teller, Pop. 126
Woodland Park SD RE-2
Supt. — See Woodland Park
Summit ES 300/PK-5
PO Box 339 80814 719-686-2401
Katie Rexford, prin. Fax 687-8469

Dolores, Montezuma, Pop. 903
Dolores SD RE-4A 700/PK-12
PO Box 727 81323 970-882-7255
Dr. Scott Cooper, supt. Fax 882-7685
www.doloresschools.org
Dolores ES 300/K-6
PO Box 727 81323 970-882-4688
Gary Livick, prin. Fax 882-7669
Dolores MS 100/7-8
PO Box 727 81323 970-882-7288
Jenifer Hufman, admin. Fax 882-7289
Teddy Bear Preschool 100/PK-PK
PO Box 727 81323 970-882-7277
Valiena Rosenkrance, dir. Fax 882-7922

Dove Creek, Dolores, Pop. 714
Dolores County SD RE-2J 300/PK-12
PO Box 459 81324 970-677-2522
Bruce Hankins, supt. Fax 677-2712
www.dc2j.org
Seventh Street ES 100/PK-5
PO Box 459 81324 970-677-2296
Bruce Hankins, admin. Fax 677-2712
Other Schools – See Rico

Durango, LaPlata, Pop. 16,541
Durango SD 9-R 4,900/PK-12
201 E 12th St 81301 970-247-5411
Dan Snowberger, supt. Fax 247-9581
www.durangoschools.org
Animas Valley ES 300/PK-5
373 Hermosa Meadows Rd 81301 970-247-0124
Michol Brammer, prin. Fax 385-1183
Escalante MS 500/6-8
141 Baker Ln 81303 970-247-9490
Jeremy Voss, prin. Fax 385-1194
Florida Mesa ES 300/PK-5
216 Highway 172 81303 970-247-4250
Vanessa Fisher, prin. Fax 385-7453
Miller MS 400/6-8
2608 Junction St 81301 970-247-1418
Vicki Trousdale, prin. Fax 385-1191
Needham ES 500/PK-5
2425 W 3rd Ave 81301 970-247-4791
Jennifer McKenna, prin. Fax 247-3388
Park ES 500/PK-5
510 E 6th Ave 81301 970-247-3718
Marie Patterson, prin. Fax 385-1492
Riverview ES 600/PK-5
2900 Mesa Ave 81301 970-247-3862
Doug Geygan, prin. Fax 247-4761
Sunnyside ES 200/PK-5
75 County Road 218 81303 970-259-5249
Patrick Hyatt, prin. Fax 382-2953
Other Schools – See Hesperus

Columbine Christian S 100/PK-8
1775 Florida Rd 81301 970-259-1189
St. Columba S 200/PK-8
1801 E 3rd Ave 81301 970-247-5527
Kevin Chick, prin. Fax 382-9355

Eads, Kiowa, Pop. 605
Kiowa County SD RE-1 200/PK-12
210 W 10th St 81036 719-438-2218
Glenn Smith, supt. Fax 438-2272
www.eadseagles.org
Eads ES 100/PK-5
900 Maine St 81036 719-438-2216
Glenn Smith, prin. Fax 438-2272
Eads MS 50/6-8
900 Maine St 81036 719-438-2216
Betsy Barnett, prin. Fax 438-2272

Eagle, Eagle, Pop. 6,436
Eagle County SD RE-50 6,500/PK-12
PO Box 740 81631 970-328-6321
Dr. Margarita Lopez, supt. Fax 328-1024
www.eagleschools.net
Brush Creek ES 500/PK-5
PO Box 4630 81631 970-328-8930
Brooke Cole, prin. Fax 328-8935
Eagle Valley ES 300/K-5
PO Box 780 81631 970-328-6981
Tiffany Dougherty, prin. Fax 328-8925
Eagle Valley MS 300/6-8
PO Box 1019 81631 970-328-6224
Katie Jarnot, prin. Fax 328-8915
Other Schools – See Avon, Edwards, Gypsum, Vail

Eaton, Weld, Pop. 4,298
Eaton SD RE-2 1,800/K-12
211 1st St 80615 970-454-3402
Randy Miller Ed.D., supt. Fax 454-5193
www.eaton.k12.co.us
Eaton ES 400/K-2
25 Cheyenne Ave 80615 970-454-3331
Rebecca Benedict, prin. Fax 454-5123
Eaton ES 400/3-5
100 S Mountain View Dr 80615 970-454-5200
Kenny Gartrell, prin. Fax 462-9241
Eaton MS 400/6-8
225 Juniper Ave 80615 970-454-3358
Jim Orth, prin. Fax 454-1337
Other Schools – See Galeton

Edgewater, Jefferson, Pop. 5,086
Jefferson County SD R-1
Supt. — See Golden
Edgewater ES 500/PK-6
5570 W 24th Ave 80214 303-982-6050
Katherine Chumacero, prin. Fax 982-6044
Lumberg ES 500/PK-6
6705 W 22nd Ave 80214 303-982-6182
Rhonda Hatch-Rivera, prin. Fax 982-6183

Edwards, Eagle, Pop. 10,187
Eagle County SD RE-50
Supt. — See Eagle
Berry Creek MS 400/6-8
PO Box 1416 81632 970-328-2960
Amy Vanwel, prin. Fax 926-4137
Edwards ES 300/K-5
22 Meile Ln 81632 970-328-2970
Matthew Abramowitz, prin. Fax 328-2975
June Creek ES 300/PK-5
1121 Miller Ranch Rd 81632 970-328-2980
Dr. Erika Donahue, prin. Fax 328-2985

St. Clare of Assisi S 200/K-8
31622 Highway 6 81632 970-926-8980
Sr. Marirose Rudek, prin. Fax 926-8973
Vail Christian Academy 100/K-8
31621 Highway 6 81632 970-306-0076
Beth Raitt, hdmstr. Fax 306-0618

Elbert, Elbert, Pop. 225
Elbert SD 200 200/PK-12
PO Box 38 80106 303-648-3030
Kelli Thompson, supt. Fax 648-3652
www.elbertschool.org
Elbert ES 100/PK-5
PO Box 38 80106 303-648-3030
Kelli Thompson, prin. Fax 648-3652

Elizabeth, Elbert, Pop. 1,335
Elizabeth SD C-1 2,500/PK-12
PO Box 610 80107 303-646-1836
Douglas Bissonette, supt. Fax 646-0337
www.elizabethschooldistrict.org
Elizabeth MS 500/6-8
PO Box 660 80107 303-646-4520
Pamela Eschief, prin. Fax 646-0980
Running Creek ES 300/PK-5
PO Box 550 80107 303-646-4620
Tammy Krueger, prin. Fax 648-5305
Other Schools – See Parker

Ellicott, El Paso, Pop. 1,094
Ellicott SD 22 1,000/PK-12
322 S Ellicott Hwy 80808 719-683-2700
Chris Smith, supt. Fax 941-7500
www.ellicottschools.org
Ellicott ES 500/PK-5
399 S Ellicott Hwy 80808 719-683-2700
Miranda Smith, prin. Fax 683-5432
Ellicott MS 200/6-8
350 S Ellicott Hwy 80808 719-683-2700
Diane Garduno, prin. Fax 683-5430

Englewood, Arapahoe, Pop. 29,512
Cherry Creek SD 5
Supt. — See Greenwood Village
Campus MS 1,400/6-8
4785 S Dayton St 80111 720-554-2677
Greg Connellan, prin. Fax 554-2795
Cherry Hills Village ES 600/PK-5
2400 E Quincy Ave, 720-747-2700
Molly Drvenkar, prin. Fax 747-2788
Cottonwood Creek ES 600/K-5
11200 E Orchard Rd 80111 720-554-3200
Julie Jaeger, prin. Fax 554-3288
High Plains ES 500/PK-5
6100 S Fulton St 80111 720-554-3600
Derek Mullner, prin. Fax 554-3688

Englewood SD 1 2,800/PK-12
4101 S Bannock St 80110 303-761-7050
Wendy Rubin Ed.D., supt. Fax 806-2064
www.englewoodschools.net
Bishop ES 300/K-6
3100 S Elati St 80110 303-761-1496
Shanna Martin, prin. Fax 761-5994
Cherrelyn ES 200/K-6
4500 S Lincoln St, 303-761-2102
Eva Pasiewicz, prin. Fax 806-2064
Clayton ES 500/K-6
4600 S Fox St 80110 303-781-7831
Jenny Buster, prin. Fax 806-2500
Englewood Early Childhood Education 200/PK-PK
700 W Mansfield Ave 80110 303-781-7585
Leigh Pytlinkski, prin.
Englewood Leadership Academy 100/6-8
3800 S Logan St, 303-781-7817
Ryan West, prin. Fax 806-2399
Englewood MS 300/7-8
3800 S Logan St, 303-781-7817
Ryan West, prin. Fax 806-2399
Hay World ES 400/K-6
3195 S Lafayette St, 303-761-2433
Ryan Cowell, prin. Fax 761-8156

All Souls S 500/PK-8
4951 S Pennsylvania St, 303-789-2155
Tracy Alarcon, prin. Fax 833-2778
St. Mary's Academy 700/PK-12
4545 S University Blvd, 303-762-8300
Bill Barrett, pres. Fax 783-6201

Erie, Weld, Pop. 17,723
Boulder Valley SD RE-2
Supt. — See Boulder
Meadowlark PK-8 S PK-8
2300 Meadow Sweet Ln 80516 720-561-5533
Brent Caldwell, prin. Fax 561-3001

St. Vrain Valley SD RE-1J
Supt. — See Longmont
Black Rock ES 700/PK-5
2000 Mountain View Blvd 80516 720-890-3995
Cathy O'Donnell, prin. Fax 652-8195
Erie ES 400/PK-5
4137 NE County Line Rd 80516 303-828-3395
Lauren Eker, prin. Fax 652-7896
Erie MS 700/6-8
650 Main St 80516 303-828-3391
Kim Watry, prin. Fax 652-8293
Red Hawk ES 700/PK-5
1500 Telleen Ave 80516 303-774-2700
Tim Garcia, prin. Fax 774-2719

Vista Ridge Academy 100/PK-8
3100 Ridgeview Dr 80516 303-828-4944
Sandy Hodgson, prin. Fax 828-1525

Estes Park, Larimer, Pop. 5,792
Estes Park SD R-3 1,100/PK-12
1605 Brodie Ave 80517 970-586-2361
Sheldon Rosenkrance, supt. Fax 586-1108
www.psdr3.k12.co.us
Estes Park ES 500/PK-5
1505 Brodie Ave 80517 970-586-7406
John Bryant, prin. Fax 586-7407
Estes Park MS 200/6-8
1500 Manford Ave 80517 970-586-4439
Janet Bielmaier, prin. Fax 586-1100

Evans, Weld, Pop. 18,255
Weld County SD 6
Supt. — See Greeley
Centennial ES 600/K-5
1400 37th St 80620 970-348-1100
Anthony Asmus, prin. Fax 348-1130
Chappelow Arts & Literacy Magnet S 700/K-8
2001 34th St 80620 970-348-1200
Christopher Kieffer, prin. Fax 348-1230
Dos Rios ES 400/K-5
2201 34th St 80620 970-348-1300
Matthew Thompson, prin. Fax 348-1330
Heiman ES 700/K-5
3500 Palermo Ave 80620 970-348-2400
Anne Ramirez, prin. Fax 348-2430
Prairie Heights MS 6-8
3737 65th Ave, 970-348-3600
Dr. Dawn Hillman Ed.D., admin. Fax 348-3632

Evergreen, Jefferson, Pop. 8,923
Clear Creek SD RE-1
Supt. — See Idaho Springs
Clear Creek MS 100/7-8
185 Beaver Brook Canyon Rd 80439 303-670-4600
Jeff Miller, prin. Fax 670-4690
King-Murphy ES 200/PK-6
425 Circle K Ranch Rd 80439 303-670-0005
Anthony Pascoe, prin. Fax 674-6735

Jefferson County SD R-1
Supt. — See Golden
Bergen Meadow PS 300/PK-2
1928 Hiwan Dr 80439 303-982-4890
Peggy Miller, prin. Fax 982-4891
Bergen Valley IS 300/3-5
1422 Sugarbush Dr 80439 303-982-4964
Peggy Miller, prin. Fax 982-4965
Evergreen MS 700/6-8
2059 Hiwan Dr 80439 303-982-5020
Timothy Vialpando, prin. Fax 982-5021
Marshdale ES 300/K-5
26663 N Turkey Creek Rd 80439 303-982-5188
Christian Kingsbury, prin. Fax 982-5187
Wilmot ES 400/PK-5
5124 S Hatch Dr 80439 303-982-5370
Matt Cormier, prin. Fax 982-5371

Evergreen Country Day S 200/PK-8
1036 El Rancho Rd 80439 303-674-3400
Brad Davies, head sch Fax 670-7957
Montessori School of Evergreen 300/PK-8
PO Box 2468 80437 303-674-0093
Bill Schuver, head sch Fax 670-6993

Fairplay, Park, Pop. 659
Park County SD RE-2 600/PK-12
PO Box 189 80440 719-836-3111
Joe Torrez, supt. Fax 836-2275
www.parkcountyre2.org/
South Park MS 100/6-8
PO Box 189 80440 719-836-4406
Alan Nall, prin. Fax 836-4429
Teter ES 200/PK-5
PO Box 189 80440 719-836-2949
Cindy Bear, prin. Fax 836-2275

Falcon, El Paso, Pop. 200
Falcon SD 49 17,600/PK-12
10850 E Woodmen Rd 80831 719-495-1100
Peter Hilts, admin. Fax 494-8900
www.d49.org
Other Schools – See Colorado Springs, Peyton

Federal Heights, Adams, Pop. 11,293
Adams 12 Five Star SD
Supt. — See Thornton
Federal Heights ES 600/K-5
2500 W 96th Ave 80260 720-972-5360
Erica Garcia, prin. Fax 972-5379

Firestone, Weld, Pop. 9,981
St. Vrain Valley SD RE-1J
Supt. — See Longmont
Centennial ES 600/K-5
10290 Neighbors Pkwy 80504 720-652-8240
Dr. Shirley Jirik, prin. Fax 652-8255
Coal Ridge MS 800/6-8
6201 Booth Dr 80504 303-833-4176
Liza Nybo, prin. Fax 494-3813
Prairie Ridge ES 400/K-5
6632 St Vrain Ranch Blvd 80504 720-494-3641
Jill Lliteras, prin. Fax 494-3642

Flagler, Kit Carson, Pop. 558
Arriba-Flagler SD C-20 100/PK-12
PO Box 218 80815 719-765-4684
Valorie McCleary, supt. Fax 765-4418
www.colorado.gov/af20
Flagler S 100/PK-12
PO Box 218 80815 719-765-4684
Valorie McCleary, admin. Fax 765-4418

Fleming, Logan, Pop. 408
Frenchman SD RE-3 200/PK-12
506 N Fremont Ave 80728 970-265-2111
Steve McCracken, supt. Fax 265-2815
www.flemingschools.org
Fleming ES 100/PK-6
506 N Fremont Ave 80728 970-265-2111
Stacy McDaniel, prin. Fax 265-2815

Florence, Fremont, Pop. 3,816
Fremont SD RE-2 1,500/K-12
403 W 5th St 81226 719-784-6312
Rhonda Roberts, supt. Fax 784-4140
www.re-2.org/
Fremont ES 400/K-5
500 W 5th St 81226 719-784-6303
Jan Draper, prin. Fax 784-4060
Fremont MS 300/6-8
215 Maple St 81226 719-784-4856
Andy Fieth, prin. Fax 784-3821
Other Schools – See Penrose

Fort Collins, Larimer, Pop. 140,582
Poudre SD R-1 27,800/PK-12
2407 Laporte Ave 80521 970-482-7420
Dr. Sandra Smysor, supt. Fax 490-3514
www.psdschools.org
Bacon ES 500/K-5
5844 S Timberline Rd 80528 970-488-5300
Joe Horky, prin. Fax 488-5306
Bauder ES 600/PK-5
2345 W Prospect Rd 80526 970-488-4150
Brian Carpenter, prin. Fax 488-4152
Beattie ES 300/PK-5
3000 Meadowlark Ave 80526 970-488-4225
Dave Patterson, prin. Fax 488-4227
Bennett ES 500/K-5
1125 Bennett Rd 80521 970-488-4750
Amy Smythe, prin. Fax 488-4752
Blevins MS 500/6-8
2101 S Taft Hill Rd 80526 970-488-4000
David Linehan, prin. Fax 488-4011
Boltz MS 600/6-8
720 Boltz Dr 80525 970-472-3700
Brett Larsen, prin. Fax 472-3730
Dunn ES 400/K-5
501 S Washington Ave 80521 970-488-4825
Deb Ellis, prin. Fax 488-4827
Fullana Learning Center PK-PK
220 N Grant Ave 80521 970-490-3160
Carolyn Martin, dir. Fax 490-3134
Harris Bilingual ES 300/K-5
501 E Elizabeth St 80524 970-488-5200
Luis Camas, prin. Fax 488-5203
Irish ES 400/PK-5
515 Irish Dr 80521 970-488-6900
Lindsey Walton, prin. Fax 488-6902
Johnson ES 400/K-5
4101 Seneca St 80526 970-488-5000
Georgianna Dawson, prin. Fax 488-5007
Kinard Core Knowledge MS 800/6-8
3002 E Trilby Rd 80528 970-488-5400
Jesse Morrill, prin. Fax 488-5402
Kruse ES 500/K-5
4400 McMurry Ave 80525 970-488-5625
Kirk Samples, prin. Fax 488-5627
Laurel ES 500/PK-5
1000 Locust St 80524 970-488-5925
Tommi Sue Cox, prin. Fax 488-5927
Lesher MS 700/6-8
1400 Stover St 80524 970-472-3800
Thomas Dodd, prin. Fax 472-3880
Lincoln MS 500/6-8
1600 Lancer Dr 80521 970-488-5700
Penny Stires, prin. Fax 488-5752
Linton ES 400/K-5
4100 Caribou Dr 80525 970-488-5850
Kristin Stolte, prin. Fax 488-5852
Lopez ES 400/K-5
637 Wabash St 80526 970-488-8800
Dr. Traci Gile, prin. Fax 488-8802
McGraw ES 500/PK-5
4800 Hinsdale Dr 80526 970-488-8335
Amy Smith, prin. Fax 488-8337
O'Dea Core Knowledge ES 400/K-5
312 Princeton Rd 80525 970-488-4450
Laurie Corso, prin. Fax 488-4452
Olander ES 400/K-5
3401 Auntie Stone St 80526 970-488-8410
Mark Strasberg, prin. Fax 488-8412
Polaris Expeditionary Learning S 300/K-12
1905 Orchard Pl 80521 970-488-8260
Joe Gawronski, prin. Fax 488-8262
Preston MS 1,100/6-8
4901 Corbett Dr 80528 970-488-7300
Amy Schmer, prin. Fax 488-7307
Putnam ES 400/PK-5
1400 Maple St 80521 970-488-7700
Steve Apodaca, prin. Fax 488-7702
Riffenburgh ES 400/K-5
1320 E Stuart St 80525 970-488-7935
Melanie Mierzwa, prin. Fax 488-7937
Shepardson STEM S 400/K-5
1501 Springwood Dr 80525 970-488-4525
Alissa Poduska, prin. Fax 488-4527
Tavelli ES 600/K-5
1118 Miramont Dr 80524 970-488-6725
Christine Hendricks, prin. Fax 488-6727
Traut Core Knowledge ES 400/K-5
2515 Timberwood Dr 80528 970-488-7500
Alissa McEachern, prin. Fax 488-7504
Webber MS 800/6-8
4201 Seneca St 80526 970-488-7800
Bryan Davis, prin. Fax 488-7811
Werner ES 600/K-5
5400 Mail Creek Ln 80525 970-488-5550
Hayden Camp, prin. Fax 488-5552
Zach Core Knowledge ES 600/K-5
3715 Kechter Rd 80528 970-488-5100
Aisha Thomas, prin. Fax 488-5106
Other Schools – See Bellvue, Laporte, Livermore, Red Feather Lakes, Timnath, Wellington

Thompson SD R-2J
Supt. — See Loveland
Cottonwood Plains ES 400/K-5
525 Turman Dr 80525 970-613-5900
Eric Harting, prin. Fax 613-5920
Coyote Ridge ES 400/K-5
7115 Avondale Rd 80525 970-679-9400
Deon Davis, prin. Fax 679-9420

Beebe Christian S 50/PK-8
502 E Pitkin St 80524 970-482-4409
Front Range Baptist Academy 100/PK-12
625 E Harmony Rd 80525 970-223-2173
Heritage Christian Academy 200/PK-12
2506 Zurich Dr 80524 970-494-1022
Mike Cuckler, admin. Fax 494-1025
Rivendell S of Northern Colorado 200/PK-5
1800 E Prospect Rd 80525 970-493-9052
Holly Warren, prin. Fax 704-5108
St. Joseph S 200/PK-8
127 N Howes St 80521 970-484-1171
Chuck Hubbeling, prin. Fax 482-5291

Fort Lupton, Weld, Pop. 7,284
Weld County SD RE-8 2,600/PK-12
301 Reynolds St 80621 303-857-3200
Alan Kaylor, supt. Fax 857-3219
www.weld8.org
Butler ES 700/PK-5
411 S McKinley Ave 80621 303-857-7300
Nativity Miller, prin. Fax 857-7340
Fort Lupton MS 500/6-8
201 S McKinley Ave 80621 303-857-7200
Candace Kensinger, prin. Fax 857-7287
Twombly ES 600/PK-5
1600 9th St 80621 303-857-7400
Julie Baker, prin. Fax 857-7497

Fort Morgan, Morgan, Pop. 11,188
Ft. Morgan SD RE-3 3,000/PK-12
715 W Platte Ave 80701 970-867-5633
Ron Echols, supt. Fax 867-0262
www.morgan.k12.co.us
Baker Central ES 200/1-5
300 Lake St 80701 970-867-8422
Daniel Cooper, prin. Fax 867-8498
Columbine ES 300/1-5
815 West St 80701 970-867-7418
Nick Ng, prin. Fax 867-2369
Fort Morgan MS 500/6-8
605 Education Ave 80701 970-867-8253
Jason Frasco, prin. Fax 867-4876
Green Acres ES 300/1-5
930 Sherman St 80701 970-867-5460
Sandra Bills, prin. Fax 867-9408
Pioneer ES 300/1-5
415 Spruce St 80701 970-867-2080
Rod Link, prin. Fax 867-9365
Sherman ECC 500/PK-K
300 Sherman St 80701 970-867-2998
Debra Lee, prin. Fax 867-2702

Lighthouse SDA Christian S 1-8
PO Box 860 80701 970-867-8840
Trinity Lutheran S 100/PK-8
1215 W 7th Ave 80701 970-867-4931
Kevin Rhode, prin. Fax 229-9085

Fountain, El Paso, Pop. 24,314
Fountain-Fort Carson SD 8 8,100/PK-12
10665 Jimmy Camp Rd 80817 719-382-1300
Dr. Keith Owen, supt. Fax 382-7338
www.ffc8.org
Aragon ES 500/PK-5
211 S Main St 80817 719-382-1340
Tracey Landrum, prin. Fax 382-8594
Conrad Early Learning Center PK-K
10605 Jimmy Camp Rd 80817 719-304-3500
Laurie Noblitt, prin. Fax 382-1067
Eagleside ES 600/K-5
9750 Sentry Dr 80817 719-382-1520
Jason Crow, prin. Fax 382-7656
Fountain MS 900/6-8
515 N Santa Fe Ave 80817 719-382-1580
Dr. William Dallas, prin. Fax 382-9065
Jordahl ES 500/PK-5
800 Progress Dr 80817 719-382-1400
Donnell Potter, prin. Fax 382-3556
Mesa ES 400/PK-5
400 Camino Del Rey 80817 719-382-1370
Megan Oleson, prin. Fax 382-8520
Other Schools – See Colorado Springs

Hanover SD 28
Supt. — See Colorado Springs
Prairie Heights ES 100/PK-5
7930 Indian Village Hts 80817 719-382-1260
Dr. Grant Schmidt, prin. Fax 382-9589

Widefield SD 3
Supt. — See Colorado Springs
Janitell JHS 800/6-8
7635 Fountain Mesa Rd 80817 719-391-3295
David Gish, prin. Fax 390-7869

Fowler, Otero, Pop. 1,170
Fowler SD R-4J 400/K-12
PO Box 218 81039 719-263-4224
Alfie Lotrich, supt. Fax 263-4625
www.fowler.k12.co.us
Fowler ES 200/K-6
PO Box 218 81039 719-263-4364
Alfie Lotrich, prin. Fax 263-4625
Fowler JHS 100/7-8
PO Box 218 81039 719-263-4224
Russell Bates, prin. Fax 263-4625

Foxfield, Arapahoe

Our Lady of Loreto S K-8
18000 E Arapahoe Rd 80016 303-951-8330
Sr. Julia Balu, prin. Fax 951-8340

Franktown, Douglas, Pop. 392
Douglas County SD RE-1
Supt. — See Castle Rock
Cherry Valley ES 50/K-6
9244 S State Highway 83 80116 303-387-8800
Nancy Wortmann, prin. Fax 688-8096
Franktown ES 300/K-5
PO Box 308 80116 303-387-5300
Mark Harrell, prin. Fax 387-5301

Trinity Lutheran S 100/PK-8
4740 N State Highway 83 80116 303-841-4660
Deanna Ayers, prin. Fax 841-2761

Fraser, Grand, Pop. 1,207
East Grand SD 2
Supt. — See Granby
Fraser Valley ES 300/PK-5
PO Box 128 80442 970-726-8033
Dr. James Chamberlin, prin. Fax 726-8340

Frederick, Weld, Pop. 8,509
St. Vrain Valley SD RE-1J
Supt. — See Longmont
Legacy ES 600/K-5
7701 Eagle Blvd 80504 720-652-8160
Sean Corey, prin. Fax 652-8161
Spark Discovery Preschool 200/PK-PK
555 8th St 80530 720-652-7906
Paige Gordon, head sch Fax 652-7910
Thunder Valley K-8 S 700/K-8
600 5th St 80530 303-833-2456
Dr. Karen Musick, prin. Fax 494-3883

Frisco, Summit, Pop. 2,654
Summit SD RE-1 3,300/PK-12
PO Box 7 80443 970-368-1000
Kerry Buhler, supt. Fax 368-1049
www.summit.k12.co.us
Frisco ES 200/PK-5
PO Box 4820 80443 970-368-1500
Laura Rupert, prin. Fax 368-1599
Summit MS 700/6-8
PO Box 7 80443 970-368-1200
Greg Guevara, prin. Fax 368-1299
Other Schools – See Breckenridge, Dillon, Silverthorne

Fruita, Mesa, Pop. 12,442
Mesa County Valley SD 51
Supt. — See Grand Junction
Fruita MS 600/6-7
239 N Maple St 81521 970-254-6570
Brigham Leane, prin. Fax 858-0486
Rim Rock ES 600/PK-5
1810 J 6/10 Rd 81521 970-254-6770
Sharon Kallus, prin. Fax 858-7654
Shelledy ES 500/PK-5
353 N Mesa St 81521 970-254-6460
Deborah Lamb, prin. Fax 858-9693

Galeton, Weld, Pop. 200
Eaton SD RE-2
Supt. — See Eaton
Galeton ES 100/K-5
PO Box 759 80622 970-454-3421
Kathryn Friesen, prin. Fax 454-2926

Gardner, Huerfano, Pop. 200
Huerfano SD RE-1
Supt. — See Walsenburg
Gardner S 100/PK-8
PO Box 191 81040 719-746-2446
Pam Levie, lead tchr. Fax 746-2066

Gateway, Mesa, Pop. 7,510
Mesa County Valley SD 51
Supt. — See Grand Junction
Gateway S 50/K-12
PO Box 240 81522 970-254-7080
Mark Allen, prin. Fax 931-2883

Gilcrest, Weld, Pop. 1,023
Weld County SD RE-1 1,900/PK-12
PO Box 157 80623 970-737-2403
Don Rangel, supt. Fax 737-2516
www.weld-re1.k12.co.us
Gilcrest ES 200/PK-5
PO Box 158 80623 970-737-2409
Tad McDonald, prin. Fax 737-2400
Other Schools – See La Salle, Platteville

Glenwood Springs, Garfield, Pop. 9,485
Roaring Fork SD RE-1 5,600/PK-12
1405 Grand Ave 81601 970-384-6000
Dr. Rob Stein, supt. Fax 384-6005
www.rfschools.com
Glenwood Springs ES 600/PK-5
915 School St 81601 970-384-5450
Audrey Hazleton, prin. Fax 384-5455
Glenwood Springs MS 600/6-8
120 Soccerfield Rd 81601 970-384-5500
Joel Hathaway, prin. Fax 384-5505
Riverview S - Escuela de Riverview 400/PK-8
228 Flying M Ranch Rd 81601 970-928-0240
Adam Volek M.Ed., admin. Fax 384-6165
Sopris ES 700/PK-5
1150 Mount Sopris Dr 81601 970-384-5400
Dave Lindenberg, prin. Fax 384-5405
Other Schools – See Basalt, Carbondale

Columbine Christian S 50/K-8
2314 Blake Ave 81601 970-945-7630
St. Stephen S 200/PK-8
414 Hyland Park Dr 81601 970-945-7746
Glenda Oliver, prin. Fax 945-1208

Golden, Jefferson, Pop. 18,494
Jefferson County SD R-1 82,600/PK-12
PO Box 4001 80402 303-982-6500
Dr. Jason Glass, supt. Fax 982-6814
www.jeffcopublicschools.org
Bell MS 600/6-8
1001 Ulysses St 80401 303-982-4280
Michele DeAndrea-Austin, prin. Fax 982-4281
Coal Creek Canyon S 200/K-8
11719 Ranch Elsie Rd 80403 303-982-3409
Jennifer Livingston, prin. Fax 982-3408
Fairmount ES 600/K-6
15975 W 50th Ave 80403 303-982-5422
Sally Mills, prin. Fax 982-5423
Kyffin ES 600/K-6
205 Flora Way 80401 303-982-5760
James Havens, prin. Fax 982-5761
Litz Preschool 100/PK-PK
13950 W 20th Ave 80401 303-982-5928
Bernadette Marquez, dir. Fax 982-5966
Maple Grove ES 400/K-6
3085 Alkire St 80401 303-982-5808
Ian Stone, prin. Fax 982-5815
Mitchell ES 500/K-5
201 Rubey Dr 80403 303-982-5875
Samantha Hollman, prin. Fax 982-5874
Ralston ES 400/K-6
25856 Columbine Glen Ave 80401 303-982-4386
Donna Neill, prin. Fax 982-4387
Shelton ES 500/K-6
420 Crawford St 80401 303-982-5686
Karen Brown, prin. Fax 982-5685
Welchester ES 300/PK-6
13000 W 10th Ave 80401 303-982-7450
Bethany Robinson, prin. Fax 982-7451
Other Schools – See Arvada, Conifer, Edgewater, Evergreen, Indian Hills, Lakewood, Littleton, Morrison, Pine, Westminster, Wheat Ridge

Gold Hill, Boulder, Pop. 226
Boulder Valley SD RE-2
Supt. — See Boulder
Gold Hill ES 50/K-5
890 Main St, Boulder CO 80302 720-561-5940
Josh Baldner, prin. Fax 449-2043

Granada, Prowers, Pop. 515
Granada SD RE-1 200/PK-12
PO Box 259 81041 719-734-5492
Ty Kemp, supt. Fax 734-5495
www.granadaschools.org
Granada ES 100/PK-6
PO Box 259 81041 719-734-5492
Ty Kemp, admin. Fax 734-5495

Granby, Grand, Pop. 1,839
East Grand SD 2 1,300/PK-12
PO Box 125 80446 970-887-2581
Frank Reeves, supt. Fax 887-2635
www.egsd.org
East Grand MS 300/6-8
PO Box 2210 80446 970-887-3382
Jenny Rothboeck, prin. Fax 887-9234
Granby ES 400/PK-5
PO Box 2240 80446 970-887-3312
Kelly Martin, prin. Fax 887-9565
Other Schools – See Fraser

Grand Junction, Mesa, Pop. 57,510
Mesa County Valley SD 51 21,300/PK-12
2115 Grand Ave 81501 970-254-5100
Dr. Ken Haptonstall, supt. Fax 245-2714
www.d51schools.org
Appleton ES 400/PK-5
2358 H Rd 81505 970-254-6400
Corey Hafey, prin. Fax 243-6604
Bookcliff MS 600/6-8
540 29 1/4 Rd 81504 970-254-6220
Jim Butterfield, prin. Fax 245-7812
Broadway ES 200/PK-5
2248 Broadway, 970-254-6430
Scot Bingham, prin. Fax 242-6292
Chatfield ES 400/PK-5
3188 D 1/2 Rd 81504 970-254-4930
Dave McCall, prin. Fax 434-1856
Chipeta ES 400/K-5
950 Chipeta Ave 81501 970-254-6825
Jayme Chiaro, prin. Fax 242-6386
Dos Rios ES 400/PK-5
265 Linden Ave 81503 970-254-7910
Vernann Raney, prin. Fax 255-8504
East MS 500/6-8
830 Gunnison Ave 81501 970-254-5020
Leah Gonyeau, prin. Fax 242-0513
Fruitvale ES 500/PK-5
585 30 Rd 81504 970-254-5930
Angela Galyon, prin. Fax 245-9143
Grand Mesa MS 600/6-8
585 31 1/2 Rd 81504 970-254-6270
Jennifer Marsh, prin. Fax 523-5938
Hawthorne Preschool 100/PK-PK
410 Hill Ave 81501 970-254-5429
Kim Self, prin. Fax 245-0825
Lincoln Orchard Mesa ES 400/PK-5
2888 B 1/2 Rd 81503 970-254-7940
Leia Kraeuter, prin. Fax 243-8341
Mesa View ES 400/PK-5
2967 B Rd 81503 970-254-7970
Stacey Morton-Cohen, prin. Fax 243-1449
New Emerson ES 100/K-5
2660 Unaweep Ave 81503 970-254-6500
Terry Schmalz, prin. Fax 256-9868
Nisley ES 500/PK-5
543 28 3/4 Rd 81501 970-254-5900
Crystal Stephenson, prin. Fax 243-3065
Orchard Avenue ES 500/PK-5
1800 Orchard Ave 81501 970-254-7560
Vicki Woods, prin. Fax 244-8650
Orchard Mesa MS 500/6-8
2736 C Rd 81503 970-254-6320
Cheryl Vana, prin. Fax 245-7343
Pear Park ES 500/PK-5
432 30 1/4 Rd 81504 970-254-5960
Dan Bunnell, prin. Fax 434-7415
Pomona ES 400/K-5
588 25 1/2 Rd 81505 970-254-4990
Emma-Leigh Larsen, prin. Fax 242-2613
Redlands MS 600/6-8
2200 Broadway, 970-254-7000
Jory Sorensen, prin. Fax 245-1985
Scenic ES 300/K-5
451 W Scenic Dr, 970-254-6370
Ben Alexander, prin. Fax 245-8605
Thunder Mountain ES 600/PK-5
3063 F 1/2 Rd 81504 970-254-5870
Diane Carver, prin. Fax 434-4457
Tope ES 400/PK-5
2220 N 7th St 81501 970-254-7070
Carrie Bollinger, prin. Fax 241-0687
West MS 400/6-8
123 W Orchard Ave 81505 970-254-5090
Vernon Walker, prin. Fax 243-0574
Wingate ES 500/K-5
351 S Camp Rd, 970-254-4960
Amie Landman, prin. Fax 245-0748
Other Schools – See Clifton, Fruita, Gateway, Loma, Palisade

Bookcliff Christian S 100/PK-5
2702 Patterson Rd 81506 970-243-2999
Kristin Pingleton, prin. Fax 263-4028
Holy Family S 400/PK-8
786 26 1/2 Rd 81506 970-242-6168
Jake Aubert, prin. Fax 242-4244
Intermountain Adventist Academy 50/K-8
1704 N 8th St 81501 970-242-5116
Messiah Lutheran S 100/PK-8
840 N 11th St 81501 970-245-2838
Tessa Miller, dir. Fax 245-8145

Greeley, Weld, Pop. 91,409
Weld County SD 6 19,000/PK-12
1025 9th Ave 80631 970-348-6000
Dr. Deirdre Pilch Ed.D., supt. Fax 348-6231
www.greeleyschools.org
Brentwood MS 600/6-8
2600 24th Avenue Ct 80634 970-348-3000
Nicole Petersen, prin. Fax 348-3030
Early Childhood University PK-PK
2651 11th St Rd 80634 970-888-1552
Franklin MS 800/6-8
818 35th Ave 80634 970-348-3200
Chris Joseph, prin. Fax 348-3230
Heath MS 700/6-8
2223 16th St 80631 970-348-3400
Dr. Blakley Wallace, prin. Fax 348-3430
Jackson ES 500/K-5
2002 25th St 80631 970-348-1500
Ingrid Dillehay, prin. Fax 348-1530
Madison ES 500/K-5
500 24th Ave 80634 970-348-1700
Val Smythe, prin. Fax 348-1730
Maplewood ES 700/K-5
1201 21st Ave 80631 970-348-3800
Dr. Mark Thompson, prin. Fax 348-3830
Martinez ES 600/K-5
341 14th Ave 80631 970-348-1800
Monica Draper, prin. Fax 348-1830
McAuliffe ES 500/PK-8
600 51st Ave 80634 970-348-1900
Jeff Petersen, prin. Fax 348-1930
Meeker ES 400/PK-5
2221 28th Ave 80634 970-348-2000
Cathy Nelson, prin. Fax 348-2030
Monfort ES 500/K-6
2101 47th Ave 80634 970-348-2100
Justin Ungeheuer, prin. Fax 348-2130
Romero Academy 700/K-8
1400 E 20th St 80631 970-348-2500
Jonathan Cooney, prin. Fax 348-2530
Scott ES 400/PK-5
3000 W 13th St 80634 970-348-2200
Ryan McDougal, prin. Fax 348-2230
Shawsheen ES 400/K-5
4020 W 7th St 80634 970-348-2300
Jill Barnes, prin. Fax 348-2330
Winograd S 600/K-8
320 N 71st Ave 80634 970-348-2600
Holly Bressler, prin. Fax 348-2630
Other Schools – See Evans

Dayspring Christian Academy 300/PK-12
3734 W 20th St 80634 970-330-1151
Weston Kurz, dir. Fax 330-0565
Greeley Adventist Christian S 50/K-8
612 23rd Ave 80634 970-353-2770
St. Mary S 200/PK-8
2351 22nd Ave 80631 970-353-8100
Donna Bornhoft, prin. Fax 353-8700
Trinity Lutheran S 50/PK-8
3000 35th Ave 80634 970-330-2485
Fax 330-2844

Greenwood Village, Arapahoe, Pop. 13,663
Cherry Creek SD 5 52,700/PK-12
4700 S Yosemite St 80111 303-773-1184
Dr. Harry Bull, supt. Fax 773-9370
www.cherrycreekschools.org
Belleview ES 600/K-5
4851 S Dayton St 80111 720-554-3100
Tiffany Kophs, prin. Fax 554-3109
Greenwood ES 400/PK-5
5550 S Holly St 80111 720-554-3400
Darik Williams, prin. Fax 554-3488
West MS 1,200/6-8
5151 S Holly St 80121 720-554-5180
Kate Bergles, prin. Fax 554-5181
Other Schools – See Aurora, Centennial, Denver, Englewood

Aspen Academy 400/PK-8
5859 S University Blvd 80121 303-346-3500
Kristina Scala, head sch Fax 379-7744
Beacon Country Day S 100/PK-8
6100 E Belleview Ave 80111 303-771-3990

Grover, Weld, Pop. 137
Pawnee SD RE-12 50/PK-12
PO Box 220 80729 970-895-2222
Bret Robinson, supt. Fax 895-2221
www.pawneeschool.org
Pawnee S 50/PK-12
PO Box 220 80729 970-895-2222
Bret Robinson, prin. Fax 895-2221

Gunnison, Gunnison, Pop. 5,730
Gunnison Watershed SD RE 1J 1,900/PK-12
800 N Boulevard St 81230 970-641-7770
Doug Tredway, supt. Fax 641-7777
www.gunnisonschools.net
Gunnison ES 400/1-5
1099 N 11th St 81230 970-641-7710
Jim Woytek, prin. Fax 641-7739
Gunnison MS 300/6-8
1099 N 11th St 81230 970-641-7710
Todd Witzel, prin. Fax 641-7739
Lake S 200/PK-K
800 N Boulevard St 81230 970-641-7770
Jennifer Kennedy, dir. Fax 641-7777
Other Schools – See Crested Butte

Gypsum, Eagle, Pop. 6,422
Eagle County SD RE-50
Supt. — See Eagle
Gypsum Creek MS 400/6-8
PO Box 5129 81637 970-328-8980
David Russell, prin. Fax 328-8985
Gypsum ES 400/PK-5
PO Box 570 81637 970-328-8940
Mitch Forsberg, prin. Fax 524-7054
Red Hill ES 400/K-5
PO Box 1009 81637 970-328-8970
Eric Olsen, prin. Fax 328-8975

Haxtun, Phillips, Pop. 937
Haxtun SD RE-2J 300/PK-12
201 W Powell St 80731 970-774-6111
Darcy Garretson, supt. Fax 774-7568
www.haxtunschools.com
Haxtun ES 200/PK-8
201 W Powell St 80731 970-774-6161
Becky Heinz, admin. Fax 774-3260

Hayden, Routt, Pop. 1,785
Hayden SD RE-1 400/PK-12
PO Box 70 81639 970-276-3864
Christy Sinner, supt. Fax 276-4217
haydenschools.org
Hayden MS 100/6-8
PO Box 70 81639 970-276-3762
Gina Zabel, prin. Fax 276-7235
Hayden Valley ES 200/PK-5
PO Box 70 81639 970-276-3756
Rhonda Sweetser, prin. Fax 276-4468

Henderson, Adams, Pop. 500
SD 27J
Supt. — See Brighton
Henderson ES 500/PK-5
12301 E 124th Ave 80640 303-655-2700
Natalie Rooney, prin. Fax 655-2704
Prairie View MS 800/6-8
12915 E 120th Ave 80640 720-685-5400
Cristina Costas-Bissell, prin. Fax 685-5404

Thimmig ES 600/PK-5
11453 Oswego St 80640 303-655-2750
Candice Reese, prin. Fax 655-2754

Hesperus, LaPlata
Durango SD 9-R
Supt. — See Durango
Ft. Lewis Mesa ES 200/PK-5
11274 Highway 140 81326 970-588-3331
Karen Gray, prin. Fax 588-3629

Highlands Ranch, Douglas, Pop. 94,597
Douglas County SD RE-1
Supt. — See Castle Rock
Arrowwood ES 400/K-6
10345 Arrowwood Dr 80130 303-387-6875
Linda Chadrick, prin. Fax 387-6876
Bear Canyon ES 600/K-6
9660 Salford Ln 80126 303-387-6475
Kelly Ursetta, prin. Fax 387-6476
Copper Mesa ES 700/K-6
3501 Poston Pkwy 80126 303-387-7377
Steve Getchell, prin. Fax 387-7376
Cougar Run ES 500/K-6
8780 Venneford Ranch Rd 80126 303-387-6675
John Gutierrez, prin. Fax 387-6676
Coyote Creek ES 400/K-6
2861 Baneberry Ct 80129 303-387-6175
Gigi Whalen, prin. Fax 387-6176
Cresthill MS 900/7-8
9195 Cresthill Ln 80130 303-387-2800
Sid Rundle, prin. Fax 387-2801
Eldorado ES 600/K-6
1305 Timbervale Trl 80129 303-387-6325
Katy Kollasch, prin. Fax 387-6326
Fox Creek ES 600/K-6
6585 Collegiate Dr 80130 303-387-7000
Brian Rodda, prin. Fax 387-7001
Heritage ES 600/K-6
3350 Summit View Pkwy 80126 303-387-6725
Alisa Pauley, prin. Fax 387-6726
Mountain Ridge MS 1,100/7-8
10590 Mountain Vista Rdg 80126 303-387-1800
Shannon Clarke, prin. Fax 387-1801
Northridge ES 700/K-6
555 Southpark Rd 80126 303-387-6525
Katie Lynch, prin. Fax 387-6526
Ranch View MS 1,000/7-8
1731 W Wildcat Reserve Pkwy 80129 303-387-2300
Tanner Fitch, prin. Fax 387-2301
Redstone ES 700/K-5
9970 Glenstone Cir 80130 303-387-7300
Amy Moyle, prin. Fax 387-7301
Saddle Ranch ES 600/K-6
805 English Sparrow Trl 80129 303-387-6400
Jennifer Malouff, prin. Fax 387-6401
Sand Creek ES 600/K-6
8898 Maplewood Dr 80126 303-387-6600
Philip Ranford, prin. Fax 387-6601
Stone Mountain ES 600/K-6
10635 Weathersfield Way 80129 303-387-7525
Michelle Framci, prin. Fax 387-7526
Summit View ES 600/K-6
10200 Piedmont Dr 80126 303-387-6800
George Boser, prin. Fax 387-6801
Trailblazer ES 500/K-6
9760 S Hackberry St 80129 303-387-6250
Dr. Deanne Kirby, prin. Fax 387-6251

Arma Dei Academy 100/K-8
345 E Wildcat Reserve Pky 80126 303-346-4523
Cherry Hills Christian S 1,000/PK-8
3900 Grace Blvd 80126 303-791-5500
Robert Bignell, supt. Fax 683-5252
Mile High Academy 100/PK-12
1733 Dad Clark Dr 80126 303-744-1069

Hoehne, Las Animas, Pop. 111
Hoehne RSD 3 200/K-12
PO Box 91 81046 719-846-4457
Joe Deangelis, supt. Fax 846-2208
www.hoehnesd.org
Hoehne S 200/K-12
PO Box 91 81046 719-846-4457
Yvonne Wiening, prin. Fax 846-2208

Holly, Prowers, Pop. 799
Holly SD RE-3 200/PK-12
PO Box 608 81047 719-537-6616
Corey Doss, supt. Fax 537-0315
www.hollyschool.org
Shanner ES 200/PK-8
PO Box 608 81047 719-537-6662
Heather Flint, prin. Fax 537-0822

Holyoke, Phillips, Pop. 2,299
Holyoke SD RE-1J 600/K-12
435 S Morlan Ave 80734 970-854-3634
John McCleary, supt. Fax 854-4049
www.hcosd.org
Holyoke ES 300/K-6
326 E Kellogg St 80734 970-854-3411
Kyle Stumpf, prin. Fax 854-2703

Hotchkiss, Delta, Pop. 933
Delta County SD 50(J)
Supt. — See Delta
Hotchkiss S 400/PK-8
465 Lorah Ln 81419 970-872-3325
John Marchino, prin. Fax 872-3808

Hudson, Weld, Pop. 2,293
Weld County SD RE-3J
Supt. — See Keenesburg
Hudson Academy of Arts & Sciences 300/PK-5
300 Beech St 80642 303-536-2200
Gregory Dent, prin. Fax 536-2210

Hugo, Lincoln, Pop. 718
Genoa-Hugo SD C113 200/PK-12
PO Box 247 80821 719-743-2428
Randy Holmen, supt. Fax 743-2194
www.genoahugo.org
Genoa-Hugo ES 100/PK-5
PO Box 247 80821 719-743-2428
Shari Humphrey, prin. Fax 743-2194
Genoa-Hugo MS 50/6-8
PO Box 247 80821 719-743-2428
Shari Humphrey, prin. Fax 743-2194

Idaho Springs, Clear Creek, Pop. 1,695
Clear Creek SD RE-1 900/PK-12
PO Box 3399 80452 303-567-3850
Roslin Marshall, supt. Fax 567-3861
www.ccsdre1.org/
Carlson ES 200/PK-6
PO Box 3339 80452 303-567-4431
Marcia Jochim, prin. Fax 567-9135
Other Schools – See Evergreen

Idalia, Yuma, Pop. 88
Idalia SD RJ-3 200/PK-12
PO Box 40 80735 970-354-7298
Tim Krause, supt. Fax 354-7416
www.idaliaco.us
Idalia ES 100/PK-5
PO Box 40 80735 970-354-7298
Myles Johnson, prin. Fax 354-7416

Ignacio, LaPlata, Pop. 652
Ignacio SD 11 JT 600/K-12
PO Box 460 81137 970-563-0500
Rocco Fuschetto Ed.D., supt. Fax 563-4524
www.ignacioschools.org
Ignacio ES 200/K-5
PO Box 460 81137 970-563-0675
Kathy Herrera, prin. Fax 563-4208
Ignacio MS 200/6-8
PO Box 460 81137 970-563-0600
Chris deKay, prin. Fax 563-0234

Southern Ute Indian Montessori Academy 100/PK-6
PO Box 737 81137 970-563-0253

Iliff, Logan, Pop. 261
Valley SD RE-1
Supt. — See Sterling
Caliche ES 200/PK-6
26308 County Road 65 80736 970-522-8330
Doug Stutzman, prin. Fax 522-8331

Indian Hills, Jefferson, Pop. 1,262
Jefferson County SD R-1
Supt. — See Golden
Parmalee ES 300/K-5
4460 Parmalee Gulch Rd 80454 303-982-8014
Ingrid Mielke, prin. Fax 982-8013

Jamestown, Boulder, Pop. 268
Boulder Valley SD RE-2
Supt. — See Boulder
Jamestown ES 50/K-5
PO Box 309 80455 720-561-6020
Scott Boesel, prin. Fax 447-0459

Joes, Yuma, Pop. 78
Liberty SD J-4 50/PK-12
PO Box 112 80822 970-358-4288
Richard Walter, supt. Fax 358-4282
www.libertyschoolj4.com
Liberty S 50/PK-12
PO Box 112 80822 970-358-4288
Richard Walter, admin. Fax 358-4282

Johnstown, Weld, Pop. 9,738
Weld County SD RE-5J
Supt. — See Milliken
Letford ES 500/PK-5
2 Jay Ave 80534 970-587-6150
Kerry Boren, prin. Fax 587-0115
Pioneer Ridge ES 600/K-5
2300 Cinnamon Teal Ave 80534 970-587-8100
Tami Kramer, prin. Fax 587-8169

Julesburg, Sedgwick, Pop. 1,216
Julesburg SD RE-1 300/PK-12
102 W 6th St 80737 970-474-3365
Shawn Ehnes, supt. Fax 474-3742
www.julesburg.org
Julesburg ES 200/PK-6
525 Spruce St 80737 970-474-3365
Rhonda Palic, prin. Fax 474-3319

Karval, Lincoln, Pop. 50
Karval SD RE-23 100/PK-12
PO Box 5 80823 719-446-5311
Chris Whetzel, supt. Fax 446-5332
www.karvalschool.org
Karval ES 50/PK-6
PO Box 5 80823 719-446-5311
Chris Whetzel, admin. Fax 446-5332

Keenesburg, Weld, Pop. 1,112
Weld County SD RE-3J 2,300/PK-12
PO Box 269 80643 303-536-2000
Greg Rabenhorst Ed.D., supt. Fax 536-2010
www.re3j.com
Hoff ES 300/PK-5
7558 County Road 59 80643 303-536-2300
Ronda Soliz, prin. Fax 536-2310
Weld Central MS 500/6-8
4977 County Road 59 80643 303-536-2700
Jamie Jeffery, prin. Fax 536-2710
Other Schools – See Hudson, Lochbuie

Kersey, Weld, Pop. 1,432
Platte Valley School District 1,100/PK-12
PO Box 485 80644 970-336-8500
Dr. E. Glenn McClain Ed.D., supt. Fax 336-8511
www.plattevalley.k12.co.us
Platte Valley ES 500/PK-5
PO Box 486 80644 970-336-8520
Jason McNair, prin. Fax 336-8538
Platte Valley MS 300/6-8
PO Box 515 80644 970-336-8610
Jason Taylor, prin. Fax 336-8635

Kim, Las Animas, Pop. 73
Kim RSD 88 50/PK-12
PO Box 100 81049 719-643-5295
Blake Byall, supt. Fax 643-5299
www.kimk12.org
Kim ES 50/PK-5
PO Box 100 81049 719-643-5295
Blake Byall, prin. Fax 643-5299

Kiowa, Elbert, Pop. 708
Kiowa SD C-2 300/PK-12
PO Box 128 80117 303-621-2220
Jason Westfall, supt. Fax 621-2239
www.kiowaschool.org
Kiowa ES 200/PK-5
PO Box 128 80117 303-621-2042
Amy Smith, prin. Fax 867-8417
Kiowa MS 100/6-8
PO Box 128 80117 303-621-2785
Amy Smith, prin. Fax 621-2239

Kit Carson, Cheyenne, Pop. 230
Kit Carson SD R-1 100/PK-12
PO Box 185 80825 719-962-3219
Robert Framel, supt. Fax 962-3317
www.kcsdr1.org
Carson ES 100/PK-5
PO Box 185 80825 719-962-3219
James T. Hogan, prin. Fax 962-3317

Kremmling, Grand, Pop. 1,417
West Grand SD 1-JT 200/K-12
PO Box 515 80459 970-724-3217
Dr. Darrin Peppard, supt. Fax 724-9373
www.wgsd.us
West Grand ES and MS 100/K-8
PO Box 515 80459 970-724-1000
Jess Buller, prin. Fax 724-9052

Lafayette, Boulder, Pop. 23,902
Boulder Valley SD RE-2
Supt. — See Boulder
Angevine MS 600/6-8
1150 W South Boulder Rd 80026 720-561-7100
Mike Medina, prin. Fax 561-7101
Escuela Bilingue Pioneer 500/PK-5
101 E Baseline Rd 80026 720-561-7800
Guillermo Medina, prin. Fax 561-7801
Lafayette ES 600/PK-5
101 N Bermont Ave 80026 720-561-8900
Stephanie Jackman, prin. Fax 561-8901
Ryan ES 400/K-5
1405 Centaur Village Dr 80026 720-561-7000
Toby Bassoff, prin. Fax 561-7001
Sanchez ES 300/PK-5
655 Sir Galahad Dr 80026 720-561-7300
Becky Escamilla, prin. Fax 561-7301

Adventure Montessori Learning Center 100/PK-5
250 S Cherrywood Dr 80026 303-665-6789
Dawson S 500/K-12
10455 Dawson Dr 80026 303-665-6679
George Moore, head sch Fax 665-0757
Flatirons Academy 100/K-3
355 W South Boulder Rd 80026 303-284-1402
Teresa Fraser, prin. Fax 926-0431

La Jara, Conejos, Pop. 805
North Conejos SD RE-1J 1,000/PK-12
PO Box 72 81140 719-274-5174
Curt Wilson, supt. Fax 274-5621
www.northconejos.com
Centauri MS 200/6-8
17891 US Highway 285 81140 719-274-4301
Tyler Huffaker, prin. Fax 274-4306
La Jara ES 200/PK-5
PO Box 470 81140 719-274-5791
Ricky Salazar, prin. Fax 274-5794
Other Schools – See Manassa

La Junta, Otero, Pop. 6,961
East Otero SD R-1 1,300/K-12
301 Raton Ave 81050 719-384-6900
Rick Lovato, supt. Fax 384-6910
www.lajuntaschools.org
La Junta IS 400/3-6
901 Smithland Ave 81050 719-384-9151
Brenda Woodyard, prin. Fax 384-8203
La Junta PS 300/K-2
601 Topeka Ave 81050 719-384-2991
Cindy Haberman, prin. Fax 384-4295

Lake City, Hinsdale, Pop. 393
Hinsdale County SD RE 1 100/PK-12
PO Box 39 81235 970-944-2314
Dr. Leslie Nichols, supt. Fax 944-2662
www.lakecityschool.org
Lake City Community S 100/PK-12
PO Box 39 81235 970-944-2314
Dr. Leslie Nichols, prin. Fax 944-2662

Lakewood, Jefferson, Pop. 140,229
Jefferson County SD R-1
Supt. — See Golden
Bear Creek S 1,100/K-8
9601 W Dartmouth Pl 80227 303-982-8714
Jason Smith, prin. Fax 982-8715

Belmar ES 300/K-6
885 S Garrison St 80226 303-982-8220
Meredith Leighty, prin. Fax 982-8221
Carmody MS 600/7-8
2050 S Kipling St 80227 303-982-8930
Wendy Doran, prin. Fax 982-8931
Creighton MS 700/7-8
50 S Kipling St 80226 303-982-6282
Nick Kemmer, prin. Fax 982-6283
Deane ES 500/K-6
580 S Harlan St 80226 303-982-9655
Melinda Feir, prin. Fax 982-9660
Dennison ES 600/K-6
401 Independence St 80226 303-982-6382
Pamela Yoder, prin. Fax 982-6383
Devinny ES 500/K-6
1725 S Wright St 80228 303-982-9200
Patty DeLorenzo, prin. Fax 982-9201
Dunstan MS 600/7-8
1855 S Wright St 80228 303-982-9270
Jennifer Kirksey, prin. Fax 982-9269
Eiber ES 400/K-6
1385 Independence St 80215 303-982-6406
Stacy Bedell, prin. Fax 982-6407
Emory ES K-6
1275 S Teller St 80232 303-982-7407
Samantha Salazar, prin. Fax 982-7408
Foothills ES 400/PK-6
13165 W Ohio Ave 80228 303-982-9324
Josh Shapiro, prin. Fax 982-9325
Glennon Heights ES 200/K-6
11025 W Glennon Dr 80226 303-982-8240
Bill Stidham, prin. Fax 982-8241
Great Work Montessori S PK-3
5300 W Center Ave 80226
Amy Malik, prin.
Green Gables ES 300/K-6
8701 W Woodard Dr 80227 303-982-8314
Suanne Hawley, prin. Fax 982-8315
Green Mountain ES 400/K-6
12250 W Kentucky Dr 80228 303-982-9380
Thomas Gardner, prin. Fax 982-9381
Hutchinson ES 400/K-6
12900 W Utah Ave 80228 303-982-9561
Melissa Karp, prin. Fax 982-9562
Irwin Preschool PK-PK
1505 S Pierson St 80232 303-982-9550
Lorraine Bricker, dir. Fax 982-9546
Jefferson County Open S 300/PK-12
7655 W 10th Ave 80214 303-982-7045
Scott Bain, prin. Fax 982-7046
Kendrick Lakes ES 400/K-6
1350 S Hoyt St 80232 303-982-8324
David Singh, prin. Fax 982-8325
Lasley ES 600/K-6
1401 S Kendall St 80232 303-982-9720
Lisa Nolan, prin. Fax 982-9721
Molholm ES 500/PK-6
6000 W 9th Ave 80214 303-982-6240
John D'Orazio, prin. Fax 982-6238
Patterson ES 600/PK-6
1263 S Dudley St 80232 303-982-8470
Valerie Pollitt, prin. Fax 982-8467
Rooney Ranch ES 500/K-6
2200 S Coors St 80228 303-982-9620
Beth Larson, prin. Fax 982-9619
Slater ES 300/K-6
8605 W 23rd Ave 80215 303-982-7575
Andy Schrant, prin. Fax 982-7574
South Lakewood ES 500/K-6
8425 W 1st Ave 80226 303-982-7325
Loren Huwa, prin. Fax 982-7324
Stein International ES 100/PK-6
80 S Teller St 80226 303-982-9144
Esther Valdez, dir. Fax 982-9153
Stober ES 300/K-6
2300 Urban St 80215 303-982-7610
Anne Dicola, prin. Fax 982-7609
Vivian ES 200/PK-6
10500 W 25th Ave 80215 303-982-7670
Sherry Carter, prin. Fax 982-7666
Westgate ES 600/K-6
8550 W Vassar Dr 80227 303-982-9130
David Weiss, prin. Fax 982-9131

Augustine Classical Academy 100/PK-12
480 S Kipling St 80226 720-446-6286
Bethlehem Lutheran S 300/PK-8
2100 Wadsworth Blvd 80214 303-233-0401
Nathan Richter, prin. Fax 237-4011
Concordia Lutheran S 100/PK-K
13371 W Alameda Pkwy 80228 303-989-5260
Emily M. Pees, dir. Fax 988-3136
Denver Christian S 200/PK-12
3898 S Teller St 80235 303-733-2421
Todd Lanting, dir. Fax 733-7734
Our Lady of Fatima S 300/PK-8
10530 W 20th Ave 80215 303-233-2500
Lisa Taylor, prin. Fax 205-1567
St. Bernadette S 100/PK-8
1100 Upham St 80214 303-237-0401
Laura Dement, prin. Fax 237-0608

Lamar, Prowers, Pop. 7,721
Lamar SD RE-2 1,700/PK-12
210 W Pearl St 81052 719-336-3251
Dave Tecklenburg, supt. Fax 336-2817
www.lamarschools.org
Hendrickson Development Center 100/PK-PK
510 Savage Ave 81052 719-336-2022
Denise Gallegos, dir. Fax 336-4725
Lamar MS 400/6-8
104 W Park St 81052 719-336-7436
Matt Snyder, prin. Fax 336-5457
Parkview ES 300/3-5
1105 Parkview Ave 81052 719-336-7413
Aron Jones, prin. Fax 336-0183
Washington ES 300/K-2
510 S 9th St 81052 719-336-7764
Kenny Davis, prin. Fax 336-4458

Laporte, Larimer, Pop. 2,391
Poudre SD R-1
Supt. — See Fort Collins
Cache La Poudre ES 300/PK-5
3511 W County Road 54G 80535 970-488-7600
Landus Boucher, prin. Fax 488-7676
Cache La Poudre MS 300/6-8
3515 W County Road 54G 80535 970-488-7400
Alicia Bono, prin. Fax 488-7433

Larkspur, Douglas, Pop. 179
Douglas County SD RE-1
Supt. — See Castle Rock
Larkspur ES 300/K-6
1103 Perry Park Ave 80118 303-387-5375
Jen Oldham, prin. Fax 387-5376

La Salle, Weld, Pop. 1,932
Weld County SD RE-1
Supt. — See Gilcrest
Mirich ES 400/PK-5
300 1st Ave 80645 970-284-5513
Mike Andrews, prin. Fax 284-6913
North Valley MS 300/6-8
300 2nd Ave 80645 970-284-4310
Mark Avery, prin. Fax 284-6595

Las Animas, Bent, Pop. 2,388
Las Animas SD RE-1 500/PK-12
1021 2nd St 81054 719-456-0161
Elsie Goines, supt. Fax 456-1117
la-schools.com
Jump Start Learning Center 50/PK-PK
530 Poplar Ave 81054 719-456-1990
Amy Deatherage, dir. Fax 456-1201
Las Animas ES 300/K-6
530 Poplar Ave 81054 719-456-1862
Lana Gardner, prin. Fax 456-1201
Las Animas JHS 100/7-8
1021 2nd St 81054 719-456-0228
Tom Meardon, prin. Fax 456-0241

La Veta, Huerfano, Pop. 774
La Veta SD RE-2 200/PK-12
PO Box 85 81055 719-742-3662
Bree Lessar, supt. Fax 742-5799
lvk12.org
La Veta ES 100/PK-5
PO Box 85 81055 719-742-3621
Suzanne Pierce, prin. Fax 742-3959

Leadville, Lake, Pop. 2,564
Lake County SD R-1 700/PK-12
107 Spruce St 80461 719-486-6800
Wendy Wyman, supt. Fax 486-2048
www.lakecountyschools.net/
Lake County IS 200/3-6
1000 W 6th St 80461 719-486-6830
Stephanie Gallegos, prin. Fax 486-8172
Pitts ES 100/PK-PK
315 W 6th St 80461 719-486-6920
Tanya Lenhard, coord. Fax 486-8174
Westpark ES 200/K-2
130 W 12th St 80461 719-486-6890
Kathleen Fitzsimmons, prin. Fax 486-3421

Limon, Lincoln, Pop. 1,854
Limon SD RE-4J 500/K-12
PO Box 249 80828 719-775-2350
Dave Marx, supt. Fax 775-9052
www.limonbadgers.com
Limon ES 200/K-5
PO Box 249 80828 719-775-2350
Joel Albers, prin. Fax 775-9052

Littleton, Arapahoe, Pop. 40,946
Douglas County SD RE-1
Supt. — See Castle Rock
Acres Green ES 700/PK-6
13524 Acres Green Dr 80124 303-387-7125
Gina Smith, prin. Fax 387-7126
Rocky Heights MS 1,400/6-8
11033 Monarch Blvd 80124 303-387-3300
Celine Wicks, prin. Fax 387-3301
Roxborough IS 500/3-6
7370 E Village Cir 80125 303-387-7600
Meghan Ofer, prin. Fax 387-7601
Roxborough PS 400/K-2
8000 Village Cir W 80125 303-387-6000
Rick Kendall, prin. Fax 387-6001
Wildcat Mountain ES 600/K-5
6585 Lionshead Pkwy 80124 303-387-6925
Molly Milley, prin. Fax 387-6926

Jefferson County SD R-1
Supt. — See Golden
Blue Heron ES 500/PK-6
5987 W Dorado Dr 80123 303-982-2770
Sandy Burch, prin. Fax 982-2771
Bradford IS 400/4-8
2 Woodruff Dr 80127 303-982-4882
Sam Palamara, prin. Fax 982-4883
Bradford PS 400/K-3
1 White Oak Dr 80127 303-982-3480
Eugene Lewis, prin. Fax 982-3481
Colorow ES 300/K-6
6317 S Estes St 80123 303-982-5480
Lori Young, prin. Fax 982-5479
Columbine Hills ES 400/PK-6
6005 W Canyon Ave 80128 303-982-5540
Christa Wilson, prin. Fax 982-5541
Coronado ES 600/PK-5
7922 S Carr St 80128 303-982-3737
Amanda Pierorazio, prin. Fax 982-3738
Deer Creek MS 500/6-8
9201 W Columbine Dr 80128 303-982-3820
Rob Hoover, prin. Fax 982-3821
Dutch Creek ES 300/K-6
7304 W Roxbury Pl 80128 303-982-4565
Jennifer Pennell, prin. Fax 982-4566
Falcon Bluffs MS 600/6-8
8449 S Garrison St 80128 303-982-9900
Thomas Burns, prin. Fax 982-9901
Governor's Ranch ES 400/K-6
5354 S Field St 80123 303-982-4625
Mary Keyes, prin. Fax 982-4626
Ken Caryl MS 700/6-8
6509 W Ken Caryl Ave 80128 303-982-4710
Christie Hurt, prin. Fax 982-4711
Leawood ES 400/PK-6
6155 W Leawood Dr 80123 303-982-7860
Martha Shehan, prin. Fax 982-7861
Mortensen ES 400/PK-6
8006 S Iris Way 80128 303-982-0022
Karla Hankins, prin. Fax 982-0021
Mount Carbon ES 500/PK-6
12776 W Cross Ave 80127 303-982-7900
Tracy Jett, prin. Fax 982-7901
Normandy ES 600/K-6
6750 S Kendall Blvd 80128 303-982-4766
Andrea Cosens, prin. Fax 982-4767
Peiffer ES 400/PK-6
4997 S Miller Way 80127 303-982-4800
Molly Touher, prin. Fax 982-4801
Powderhorn ES 700/K-6
12109 W Coal Mine Ave 80127 303-982-0074
Denein Cusack, prin. Fax 982-0066
Shaffer ES 600/PK-5
7961 Sangre De Cristo Rd 80127 303-982-3901
Jeremy Brasher, prin. Fax 982-3899
Stony Creek ES 500/PK-6
7203 S Everett St 80128 303-982-4120
Stephanie Cavallaro, prin. Fax 982-4121
Summit Ridge MS 800/7-8
11809 W Coal Mine Ave 80127 303-982-9013
Andrea Schulz, prin. Fax 982-8998
Ute Meadows ES 400/K-5
11050 W Meadows Dr 80127 303-982-4044
Susan Borzych, prin. Fax 982-4045
Westridge ES 500/PK-6
10785 W Alamo Pl 80127 303-982-3975
Cheryl Borst, prin. Fax 982-3976

Littleton SD 15,900/PK-12
5776 S Crocker St 80120 303-347-3300
Brian Ewert, supt. Fax 347-4350
www.littletonpublicschools.net
Centennial Academy of Fine Arts 500/K-5
3306 W Berry Ave 80123 303-347-4425
Karla Gruenwald, prin. Fax 347-4430
East ES 300/K-5
5933 S Fairfield St 80120 303-347-4450
Kelly Card, prin. Fax 347-4470
Euclid MS 700/6-8
777 W Euclid Ave 80120 303-347-7800
Cindy Corlett, prin. Fax 347-7830
Field ES 400/K-5
5402 S Sherman Way 80121 303-347-4475
Lyn Bajaj, prin. Fax 347-4490
Goddard MS 700/6-8
3800 W Berry Ave 80123 303-347-7850
Bryan Breuer, prin. Fax 347-7880
Moody ES 400/PK-5
6390 S Windermere St 80120 303-347-4600
Dr. Allyson Mallory, prin. Fax 347-4620
Powell MS 900/6-8
8000 S Corona Way 80122 303-347-7950
Steve Wolf, prin. Fax 347-3975
Runyon ES 500/K-5
7455 S Elati St 80120 303-347-4650
Trudy Meisinger, prin. Fax 347-4670
Village at North 300/PK-PK
1907 W Powers Ave 80120 303-347-6985
Marnie Yanacheak, dir. Fax 347-6981
Wilder ES 700/PK-5
4300 W Ponds Cir 80123 303-347-4750
Susan Dalton, prin. Fax 347-4755
Other Schools – See Centennial

Abiding Hope Preschool and K 100/PK-K
6337 S Robb Way 80127 303-932-9160
Erin Fisher, dir. Fax 972-0424
Front Range Christian S 400/PK-12
6657 W Ottawa Ave Ste A17 80128 720-922-3269
David Cooper, head sch Fax 922-3296
Hope Christian Academy 100/PK-8
7462 S Everett St 80128 303-979-6839
Nancy Thurston, prin. Fax 979-6907
Mackintosh Academy 100/PK-8
7018 S Prince St 80120 303-794-6222
St. Katharine Drexel Catholic Preschool PK-PK
5761 McArthur Ranch Rd 80124 303-799-1036
Cynthia Vigil, dir. Fax 799-1072
St. Mary S 500/PK-8
6833 S Prince St 80120 303-798-2375
Jim Baker, prin. Fax 283-4756
Truth Christian Academy 50/PK-12
PO Box 621961 80162 303-670-3360
Stanley Silverman, admin. Fax 978-0770

Livermore, Larimer, Pop. 200
Poudre SD R-1
Supt. — See Fort Collins
Livermore ES 50/K-5
360 Red Feather Lakes Rd 80536 970-488-6520
Tom Schachet, prin. Fax 488-6522

Lochbuie, Weld, Pop. 4,644
Weld County SD RE-3J
Supt. — See Keenesburg
Lochbuie ES 500/PK-5
201 Bonanza Blvd 80603 303-536-2400
Jennifer Forbes, prin. Fax 536-2410

Loma, Mesa, Pop. 1,279
Mesa County Valley SD 51
Supt. — See Grand Junction
Loma ES 300/PK-5
PO Box 43 81524 970-254-6520
Margaret Hofer, prin. Fax 858-7909

Lonetree, See Littleton
Douglas County SD RE-1
Supt. — See Castle Rock
Eagle Ridge ES 600/K-6
7716 Timberline Rd 80124 303-387-7075
Doug Humphreys, prin. Fax 387-7076
Lonetree ES 500/K-6
9375 Heritage Hills Cir 80124 303-387-7450
Mindy Persichina, prin. Fax 387-7451

Longmont, Boulder, Pop. 84,733
St. Vrain Valley SD RE-1J 29,700/PK-12
395 S Pratt Pkwy 80501 303-776-6200
Don Haddad Ed.D., supt. Fax 682-7396
www.svvsd.org
Alpine ES 500/PK-5
2005 Alpine St 80504 720-652-8140
Amber Marsolek, prin. Fax 652-8141
Altona MS 800/6-8
4600 Clover Basin Dr 80503 720-494-3980
Jeremy LaCrosse, prin. Fax 494-3989
Blue Mountain ES 600/PK-5
1260 Mountain Dr 80503 720-652-8220
Stephen Hoel, prin. Fax 652-8235
Burlington ES 400/PK-5
1051 S Pratt Pkwy 80501 303-776-8861
Kerin McClure, prin. Fax 652-7805
Central ES 400/PK-5
1020 4th Ave 80501 303-776-3236
Jim Hecocks, prin. Fax 652-7823
Columbine ES 400/PK-5
111 Longs Peak Ave 80501 303-776-2840
Audrey Seybold, prin. Fax 652-7846
Eagle Crest ES 600/PK-5
4444 Clover Basin Dr 80503 303-485-6073
Ryan Ball, prin. Fax 652-7872
Fall River ES 600/PK-5
1400 Deerwood Dr 80504 720-652-7920
Dr. Jennifer Guthals, prin. Fax 652-7931
Hygiene ES 300/PK-5
11968 N 75th St 80503 720-652-8021
Renee Collier, prin. Fax 652-8025
Indian Peaks ES 400/PK-5
1335 S Judson St 80501 303-772-7240
Kathi Jo Walder, prin. Fax 652-7945
Longmont Estates ES 500/PK-5
1601 Northwestern Rd 80503 720-652-8101
Traci Haley, prin. Fax 652-8100
Longs Peak MS 400/5-8
1500 14th Ave 80501 303-776-5611
Ann Reed, prin. Fax 494-3663
Mountain View ES 400/PK-4
1415 14th Ave 80501 720-652-8261
Jennifer Ryan, prin. Fax 652-8267
Northridge ES 400/PK-5
1200 19th Ave 80501 303-772-3040
Lorynda Sampson, prin. Fax 652-8085
Rocky Mountain ES 400/PK-5
800 E 5th Ave 80504 303-772-6750
Jill Fuller, prin. Fax 652-7987
Sanborn ES 400/PK-5
2235 Vivian St 80501 303-772-3838
John Wahler, prin. Fax 652-8128
Sunset MS 600/6-8
1300 S Sunset St 80501 303-776-3963
Dr. Dawn Macy, prin. Fax 494-3703
Timberline PK-8 S 1,000/PK-8
233 E Mountain View Ave 80504 303-772-7900
Karrie Borski, prin. Fax 494-3624
Trail Ridge MS 700/6-8
1000 Button Rock Dr 80504 720-494-3820
Eddie Cloke, prin. Fax 494-3829
Westview MS 700/6-8
1651 Airport Rd 80503 303-772-3134
Mark Spencer, prin. Fax 494-3786
Other Schools – See Erie, Firestone, Frederick, Lyons, Mead, Niwot

---

Longmont Christian S 300/PK-12
1440 Collyer St 80501 303-776-3254
Dave Stoecker, dir. Fax 485-6937
St. John the Baptist S 400/PK-8
350 Emery St 80501 303-776-8760
Kimmery Hill, prin. Fax 532-2741

Louisville, Boulder, Pop. 17,982
Boulder Valley SD RE-2
Supt. — See Boulder
Coal Creek ES 400/K-5
801 W Tamarisk St 80027 720-561-4500
John Kiemele, prin. Fax 561-4501
Fireside ES 500/PK-5
845 W Dahlia St 80027 720-561-7900
Christa Keppler, prin. Fax 561-7901
Louisville ES 600/K-5
400 Hutchinson St 80027 720-561-7200
Jeff Miller, prin. Fax 561-7201
Louisville MS 600/6-8
1341 Main St 80027 720-561-7400
Ginny Vidulich, prin. Fax 561-7401
Monarch K-8 S 800/PK-8
263 Campus Dr 80027 720-561-4000
Robin Techmanski, prin. Fax 561-4001
Superior ES 600/K-5
1800 S Indiana St 80027 720-561-4100
Jennifer Bedford, prin. Fax 561-4101

Louisville Montessori S 50/PK-K
461 Tyler Ave 80027 303-665-2002
St. Louis S 200/PK-8
925 Grant Ave 80027 303-666-6220
Kathleen Byrnes, prin. Fax 666-5244

Loveland, Larimer, Pop. 65,828
Thompson SD R-2J 16,100/PK-12
800 S Taft Ave 80537 970-613-5000
Dr. Stan Scheer, supt. Fax 613-5095
www.thompsonschools.org
Ball MS 700/6-8
2660 Monroe Ave 80538 970-613-7300
Tiffany Miller, prin. Fax 613-7341
Big Thompson ES 200/K-5
7702 W US Highway 34 80537 970-613-5600
Sarah Walgast, prin. Fax 613-5620
Blair ES 400/K-5
860 E 29th St 80538 970-613-6400
Valerie Lara-Black, prin. Fax 613-6420
Centennial ES 500/K-5
1555 W 37th St 80538 970-613-5800
Fax 613-5820
Clark MS 500/6-8
2605 Carlisle Dr 80537 970-613-5400
Christine Smith, prin. Fax 613-5420
Edmondson ES 300/K-5
307 W 49th St 80538 970-613-6300
Trish Malik, prin. Fax 613-6320
Erwin MS 900/6-8
4700 Lucerne Ave 80538 970-613-7600
Tim Ridder, prin. Fax 613-7619
Garfield ES 300/K-5
720 Colorado Ave 80537 970-613-6000
John Kleiber, prin. Fax 613-6020
High Plains S K-8
4255 Buffalo Mountain Dr 80538 970-679-9800
Danielle Feeney, prin. Fax 679-9820
Kitchen ES 200/K-5
915 Deborah Dr 80537 970-613-5500
Justin Blick, prin. Fax 613-5520
Lincoln ES 200/K-5
3312 Douglas Ave 80538 970-613-6200
Michelle Malvey, prin. Fax 613-6220
Martin ES 200/K-5
4129 Joni Ln 80537 970-613-5700
Alex Martin, prin. Fax 613-5720
Milner ES 300/K-5
743 Jocelyn Dr 80537 970-613-6700
Dale Bryant, prin. Fax 613-6720
Monroe ES 300/K-5
1500 Monroe Ave 80538 970-613-6500
Kathy Sather, prin. Fax 613-6520
Namaqua ES 400/K-5
209 N Namaqua Ave 80537 970-613-6600
Dan Cox, prin. Fax 613-6620
Ponderosa ES 500/K-5
4550 Florence Dr 80538 970-679-9500
Kandi Smith, prin. Fax 679-9520
Reed MS 700/6-8
370 W 4th St 80537 970-613-7200
Arnold Jahnke, prin. Fax 613-7287
Stansberry ES 200/K-5
407 E 42nd St 80538 970-613-6800
Angie Geraghty, prin. Fax 613-6820
Thompson ECC 600/PK-PK
800 S Taft Ave 80537 970-613-5052
Lamb Caro, prin. Fax 613-5766
Truscott ES 300/K-5
211 W 6th St 80537 970-613-6900
Karen Hanford, prin. Fax 613-6920
Van Buren ES 200/K-5
1811 W 15th St 80538 970-613-7000
Nichole Randazzo, prin. Fax 613-7020
Winona ES 500/K-5
201 S Boise Ave 80537 970-613-7100
Kim Tymkowych, prin. Fax 613-7120
Other Schools – See Berthoud, Fort Collins

HMS Richards SDA S 100/PK-8
342 42nd St SW 80537 970-667-2427
Immanuel Lutheran S 300/PK-8
4650 Sunview Dr 80538 970-667-7606
Fax 624-3422
Resurrection Christian S 800/PK-12
6508 E Crossroads Blvd 80538 970-612-0674
Rev. Allen Howlett M.A., supt. Fax 612-0975
St. John the Evangelist S 200/PK-8
1730 W 12th St 80537 970-635-5830
Lois Schmitt, prin. Fax 667-9298

Lyons, Boulder, Pop. 2,004
St. Vrain Valley SD RE-1J
Supt. — See Longmont
Lyons ES 300/PK-5
PO Box 559 80540 303-823-6915
Andrew Moore, prin. Fax 652-8007

Mc Clave, Bent, Pop. 150
McClave SD RE-2 300/PK-12
PO Box 1 81057 719-829-4517
Terry Weber, supt. Fax 829-4430
www.mcclaveschool.org
Mc Clave ES 100/PK-6
PO Box 1 81057 719-829-4517
Rachel Dunning, prin. Fax 829-4430

Manassa, Conejos, Pop. 979
North Conejos SD RE-1J
Supt. — See La Jara
Manassa ES 200/K-5
PO Box 430 81141 719-843-5277
Denny Fringer, prin. Fax 843-5080

Mancos, Montezuma, Pop. 1,302
Mancos SD RE-6 400/PK-12
395 W Grand Ave 81328 970-533-7748
Brian Hanson, supt. Fax 533-7954
www.mancosre6.edu
Mancos Early Learning Center PK-PK
1331 S Walnut St 81328 970-533-1587
Grace Kennedy, dir. Fax 533-9010
Mancos ES 200/K-5
301 W Grand Ave 81328 970-533-7744
Cathy Epps, prin. Fax 533-1165
Mancos MS 100/6-8
100 S Beech St 81328 970-533-9143
Adam Priestley, prin. Fax 533-2003

Manitou Springs, El Paso, Pop. 4,882
Manitou Springs SD 14 1,500/PK-12
405 El Monte Pl 80829 719-685-2024
Ed Longfield, supt. Fax 685-4536
www.mssd14.org
Manitou Springs ES 500/PK-5
110 Pawnee Ave 80829 719-685-2195
Russ Vogel, prin. Fax 685-2185
Manitou Springs MS 400/6-8
415 El Monte Pl 80829 719-685-2127
Ron Hamilton, prin. Fax 685-4552
Other Schools – See Chipita Park

Manzanola, Otero, Pop. 429
Manzanola SD 3J 100/K-12
PO Box 148 81058 719-462-5527
Tom Wilke, supt. Fax 462-5708
www.manzanola.k12.co.us/
Manzanola ES 100/K-5
PO Box 148 81058 719-462-5578
Tom Wilke, admin. Fax 462-5708

Mead, Weld, Pop. 3,346
St. Vrain Valley SD RE-1J
Supt. — See Longmont
Mead ES 500/PK-5
520 Welker Ave 80542 970-535-4488
Betsy Ball, prin. Fax 652-8053
Mead MS 400/6-8
620 Welker Ave 80542 970-535-4446
Joshua Barnett, prin. Fax 494-3686

Meeker, Rio Blanco, Pop. 2,417
Meeker SD RE-1 700/PK-12
PO Box 1089 81641 970-878-9040
Chris Selle, supt. Fax 878-3682
www.meeker.k12.co.us
Barone MS 200/6-8
PO Box 690 81641 970-878-9060
Jim Hanks, prin. Fax 878-4291
Meeker ES 400/PK-5
PO Box 988 81641 970-878-9050
Kathy Collins, prin. Fax 878-0016

Merino, Logan, Pop. 281
Buffalo SD RE-4J 300/K-12
PO Box 198 80741 970-522-7424
Robert Sanders, supt. Fax 522-1541
merino.k12.co.us
Merino ES 200/K-6
PO Box 198 80741 970-522-7229
Courtney Rank, prin. Fax 522-2547

Milliken, Weld, Pop. 5,520
Weld County SD RE-5J 3,500/PK-12
110 Centennial Dr Ste A 80543 970-587-6050
Dr. Martin Foster, supt. Fax 587-2607
www.weldre5j.k12.co.us
Milliken ES 500/PK-5
100 Broad St 80543 970-587-6200
Tucker Willard, prin. Fax 587-2855
Milliken MS 700/6-8
PO Box 339 80543 970-587-6300
Ron Hruby, prin. Fax 587-5749
Other Schools – See Johnstown

Moffat, Saguache, Pop. 116
Moffat SD 2, PO Box 428 81143 200/PK-12
Christina Larson, supt. 719-745-0500
www.moffatschools.org
Moffat S, PO Box 428 81143 100/PK-12
Christina Larson, admin. 719-745-0500

Monte Vista, Rio Grande, Pop. 4,392
Monte Vista SD C-8 1,000/PK-12
349 E Prospect Ave 81144 719-852-5996
Robert Webb, supt. Fax 852-6184
www.monte.k12.co.us
Marsh ES 100/PK-K
215 Lyell St 81144 719-852-3231
Stacey Plane, prin. Fax 852-5870
Metz ES 400/1-5
545 2nd Ave 81144 719-852-4041
Gabriel Futrell, prin. Fax 852-6196
Monte Vista MS 200/6-8
3720 Sherman Ave 81144 719-852-5984
Thomas Tichy, prin. Fax 852-6199

Sargent SD RE-33J 400/K-12
7090 N County Road 2 E 81144 719-852-4023
Greg Slover, supt. Fax 852-9890
www.sargent.k12.co.us
Sargent ES 200/K-6
7090 N County Road 2 E 81144 719-852-4024
Joni Hemmerling, prin. Fax 852-0399

St. Peter Lutheran S 50/K-8
330 Faraday St 81144 719-852-5449
Kristen Lipke, lead tchr.

Montrose, Montrose, Pop. 18,812
Montrose County SD RE-1J 6,200/PK-12
PO Box 10000 81402 970-249-7726
Steve Schiell, supt. Fax 249-7173
www.mcsd.org
Centennial MS 600/6-8
PO Box 10000 81402 970-249-2576
Joe Simo, prin. Fax 240-6461
Columbine MS 500/6-8
PO Box 10000 81402 970-249-2581
Ben Stephenson, prin. Fax 240-6404

Cottonwood ES 500/K-5
PO Box 10000 81402 970-249-2539
Sandra Steele, prin. Fax 240-6407
ECC 300/PK-PK
PO Box 10000 81402 970-249-5858
Penny Harris, dir. Fax 249-7537
Johnson ES 500/PK-5
PO Box 10000 81402 970-249-2584
Cheryl Gomez, prin. Fax 240-6408
Northside ES 400/K-5
PO Box 10000 81402 970-249-2554
Carrie Clark, prin. Fax 240-6403
Oak Grove ES 400/K-5
PO Box 10000 81402 970-249-6867
Dana Burwell, prin. Fax 240-6409
Pomona ES 400/K-5
PO Box 10000 81402 970-249-2514
Chris Braaten, prin. Fax 240-6406
Other Schools – See Olathe

Colorado West Christian S 100/PK-12
2705 Sunnyside Rd 81401 970-249-1094

Monument, El Paso, Pop. 5,337
Lewis-Palmer SD 38 6,300/PK-12
PO Box 40 80132 719-488-4700
Karen Brofft, supt. Fax 488-4704
www.lewispalmer.org
Bear Creek ES 900/PK-6
1330 Creekside Dr 80132 719-488-4770
Peggy Parsley, prin. Fax 481-9447
Lewis-Palmer ES 400/PK-6
1315 Lake Woodmoor Dr 80132 719-488-4750
Jenny Day, prin. Fax 488-4752
Lewis-Palmer MS 800/7-8
1776 Woodmoor Dr 80132 719-488-4776
Seann O'Connor, prin. Fax 488-4780
Prairie Winds ES 400/PK-6
790 E Kings Deer Pt 80132 719-559-0800
Aileen Finnegan, prin. Fax 559-0805
Other Schools – See Colorado Springs, Palmer Lake

Hope Montessori Academy 100/PK-K
18075 Minglewood Trl 80132 719-488-8723
Fax 488-1310
St. Peters Catholic S 100/PK-8
124 1st St 80132 719-481-1855
Sheila Whalen, prin. Fax 266-3402

Morrison, Jefferson, Pop. 426
Jefferson County SD R-1
Supt. — See Golden
Kendallvue ES 500/PK-6
13658 W Marlowe Ave 80465 303-982-7990
Christina Austin, prin. Fax 982-7991
Red Rocks ES 300/K-6
17199 Highway 74 80465 303-982-8063
Gregory Isaac, prin. Fax 982-8064

Mosca, Alamosa, Pop. 180
Sangre De Cristo SD RE-22J 300/PK-12
8751 Lane 7 N 81146 719-378-2321
Brady Stagner, supt. Fax 378-2327
sdc.schooldesk.net
Sangre De Cristo ES 200/PK-6
8751 Lane 7 N 81146 719-378-2321
John Stephens, prin. Fax 378-2327

Naturita, Montrose, Pop. 539
West End SD RE-2
Supt. — See Nucla
Naturita ES 200/PK-6
PO Box 400 81422 970-865-2204
Michael Epright, supt. Fax 865-2850

Nederland, Boulder, Pop. 1,417
Boulder Valley SD RE-2
Supt. — See Boulder
Nederland ES 300/PK-5
1 Sundown Trl 80466 720-561-4800
Laurel Reckert, prin. Fax 561-4801

New Castle, Garfield, Pop. 4,478
Garfield SD RE-2
Supt. — See Rifle
Elk Creek ES 300/PK-4
804 Main Dr 81647 970-665-6900
Lisa Pierce, prin. Fax 665-6901
Riverside MS 700/5-8
215 Alder Ave 81647 970-665-7800
Karen Satter, prin. Fax 665-7846
Senor ES 300/PK-4
101 Alder Ave 81647 970-665-7700
Jana Price, prin. Fax 665-7722

New Raymer, Weld, Pop. 95
Prairie SD RE-11 200/PK-12
PO Box 68 80742 970-437-5351
Joe Kimmel, supt. Fax 437-5732
www.prairieschool.org
Prairie ES 100/PK-5
PO Box 68 80742 970-437-5351
Tabitha Piel, prin. Fax 437-5732

Niwot, Boulder, Pop. 3,929
St. Vrain Valley SD RE-1J
Supt. — See Longmont
Niwot ES 500/PK-5
8778 Morton Rd 80503 303-652-2828
Nancy Pitz, prin. Fax 652-8075

Boulder Valley Waldorf S 100/PK-8
6500 Dry Creek Pkwy 80503 303-652-0130
Rocky Mountain Christian Academy 300/PK-8
9447 Niwot Rd 80503 303-652-9162
Brandon Byrd, prin. Fax 301-7999

Northglenn, Adams, Pop. 35,024
Adams 12 Five Star SD
Supt. — See Thornton
Hillcrest ES 500/K-5
10335 Croke Dr 80260 720-972-5380
Stephanie Taylor, prin. Fax 972-5399
Hulstrom K-8 S 700/K-8
11551 Wyco Dr 80233 720-972-5400
Judi Madsen, prin. Fax 972-5419
Leroy ES 400/K-5
1451 Leroy Dr 80233 720-972-5460
Tracie Stauffer, prin. Fax 972-5479
Malley Drive ES 400/K-5
1300 Malley Dr 80233 720-972-5480
Francesca Craver, prin. Fax 972-5499
Northglenn MS 800/6-8
1123 Muriel Dr 80233 720-972-5080
Jami Miller, prin. Fax 972-5119
North Mor ES 400/K-5
9580 Damon Dr 80260 720-972-5540
Amy Herrman, prin. Fax 972-5559
STEM Magnet Lab S 500/K-8
11700 Irma Dr 80233 720-972-3340
Tracy Tellinger, prin. Fax 972-3371
Studio S 300/K-5
10604 Grant Dr 80233 720-972-3620
Sharla Kaczar, prin. Fax 972-3719
Stukey ES 300/K-5
11080 Grant Dr 80233 720-972-5420
Lori Bailey, prin. Fax 972-5439
Westview ES 400/K-5
1300 Roseanna Dr 80234 720-972-5680
Leslie Burke-Dominick, prin. Fax 972-5699

Gethsemane Lutheran S 200/PK-8
10675 Washington St 80233 303-451-6908
Sarah Glover, admin. Fax 451-1067

Norwood, San Miguel, Pop. 505
Norwood SD R-2J 300/PK-12
PO Box 448 81423 970-327-4336
David Crews, supt. Fax 327-4116
norwoodk12.org
Norwood ES 100/PK-5
PO Box 448 81423 970-327-4336
Sara Rasmussen, prin. Fax 327-4116

Nucla, Montrose, Pop. 704
West End SD RE-2 300/PK-12
PO Box 570 81424 970-864-7350
Michael Epright, supt. Fax 864-7269
www.westendschools.org
Other Schools – See Naturita

Oak Creek, Routt, Pop. 865
South Routt SD RE-3 400/PK-12
PO Box 158 80467 970-736-2313
Rim Watson, supt. Fax 736-2458
www.southroutt.k12.co.us
Soroco MS 100/6-8
PO Box 158 80467 970-736-8531
George Purnell, prin. Fax 870-3791
Other Schools – See Yampa

Olathe, Montrose, Pop. 1,821
Montrose County SD RE-1J
Supt. — See Montrose
Olathe ES 400/K-5
211 North Roberts 81425 970-252-7940
Joe Drummitt, prin. Fax 323-6339
Olathe MS 300/6-8
410 Highway 50 81425 970-252-7950
Scot Brown, prin. Fax 323-5947

Ordway, Crowley, Pop. 1,058
Crowley County SD RE-1-J 200/K-12
1001 Main St 81063 719-267-3117
Scott Cuckow, supt. Fax 267-3130
www.cck12.net
Crowley County IS 100/4-5
1001 Main St 81063 719-267-9880
Deanna Brewer, prin. Fax 267-3130
Crowley County PS K-3
630 Main St 81063 719-267-3558
Deanna Brewer, prin. Fax 267-4195

Otis, Washington, Pop. 462
Lone Star SD 101 100/K-12
44940 County Road 54 80743 970-848-2778
Susan Sonnenberg, supt. Fax 848-0340
www.lonestarschool.net
Lone Star ES 100/K-5
44940 County Road 54 80743 970-848-2778
Susan Sonnenberg, supt. Fax 848-0340

Otis SD R-3 200/PK-12
518 Dungan St 80743 970-246-3486
Kendra Anderson, supt. Fax 246-0518
www.otisr3.com
Otis ES 100/PK-6
518 Dungan St 80743 970-246-3366
Michelle Patterson, prin. Fax 246-0518

Ouray, Ouray, Pop. 990
Ouray SD R-1 200/PK-12
PO Box N 81427 970-325-4505
Scott Pankow, supt. Fax 325-7343
www.ouray.k12.co.us
Ouray ES 100/PK-6
PO Box N 81427 970-325-4505
Scott Pankow, admin. Fax 325-7343
Ouray MS 50/7-8
PO Box N 81427 970-325-4505
Scott Pankow, admin. Fax 325-7343

Ovid, Sedgwick, Pop. 314
Revere SD 100/PK-12
500 Main St 80744 970-463-5477
Sharon Green, supt. Fax 503-2318
www.revereschool.com

Revere ES 100/PK-6
500 Main St 80744 970-463-5477
Sharon Green, prin. Fax 503-2318

Pagosa Springs, Archuleta, Pop. 1,685
Archuleta SD 50 JT 1,300/K-12
PO Box 1498 81147 970-264-2228
Linda Reed, supt. Fax 264-4631
www.mypagosaschools.com
Pagosa Springs ES 500/K-4
PO Box 1498 81147 970-264-2229
Justin Cowan, prin. Fax 264-4871
Pagosa Springs MS 400/5-8
PO Box 1498 81147 970-264-2794
Chris Hinger, prin. Fax 264-6112

Our Savior Lutheran S 50/PK-3
56 Meadows Dr 81147 970-731-3512
Anette McInnis, dir. Fax 731-4668

Palisade, Mesa, Pop. 2,644
Mesa County Valley SD 51
Supt. — See Grand Junction
Taylor ES 400/PK-5
689 Brentwood Dr 81526 970-254-4870
Jennifer Morrell, prin. Fax 464-7503

Palmer Lake, El Paso, Pop. 2,341
Lewis-Palmer SD 38
Supt. — See Monument
Palmer Lake ES 400/PK-6
PO Box 10 80133 719-488-4760
Peggy Griebenow, prin. Fax 488-4764

Paonia, Delta, Pop. 1,427
Delta County SD 50(J)
Supt. — See Delta
Paonia ES 200/K-6
PO Box 1179 81428 970-527-3639
Sam Cox, prin. Fax 527-3339

Parachute, Garfield, Pop. 1,062
Garfield County SD 16 1,100/PK-12
PO Box 68 81635 970-285-5701
Brad Ray, supt. Fax 285-5711
www.garfield16.org
Grand Valley Center for Family Learning 200/PK-1
PO Box 68 81635 970-285-5702
Meri Nofzinger, prin. Fax 864-6754
Grand Valley MS 200/6-8
PO Box 68 81635 970-285-5707
Kelly McCormick, prin. Fax 285-5717
Underwood ES 300/2-5
PO Box 68 81635 970-285-5703
Amber Clark, prin. Fax 593-9228

Parker, Douglas, Pop. 44,230
Douglas County SD RE-1
Supt. — See Castle Rock
Cherokee Trail ES 500/K-6
17302 Clarke Farms Dr 80134 303-387-8125
Josh Miller, prin. Fax 387-8126
Cimarron MS 1,000/7-8
12130 Canterberry Pkwy 80138 303-433-0120
Christopher Zimmerman, prin. Fax 433-0121
Frontier Valley ES 700/K-5
23919 Canterberry Pkwy 80138 303-387-8475
Kimberly Seefried, prin. Fax 387-8476
Gold Rush ES 700/K-6
12021 S Swift Fox Way 80134 303-387-7700
Jenny Brown, prin. Fax 387-7701
Iron Horse ES 500/K-5
20151 Tallman Dr 80138 303-387-8525
Kirsten Bloomfield, prin. Fax 387-8526
Legacy Point ES 500/K-5
12736 Red Rosa Cir 80134 303-387-8725
Patti Magby, prin. Fax 387-8726
Mammoth Heights ES 800/K-6
9500 Stonegate Pkwy 80134 303-387-8925
Nick Holtvluwer, prin. Fax 387-8926
Mountain View ES 300/K-2
8502 E Pinery Pkwy 80134 303-387-8675
Mildred Grotts, prin. Fax 387-8676
Northeast ES 400/3-5
6598 N Highway 83 80134 303-387-8600
Kara Tidemann, prin. Fax 387-8601
Pine Grove ES 600/K-6
10450 Stonegate Pkwy 80134 303-387-8075
Kelly Coonts, prin. Fax 387-8076
Pine Lane IS 400/4-6
6485 Ponderosa Dr 80138 303-387-8275
Jason Starkey, prin. Fax 387-8276
Pine Lane PS 500/PK-3
6475 Ponderosa Dr 80138 303-387-8325
Jason Starkey, prin. Fax 387-8326
Pioneer ES 600/K-5
10881 Riva Ridge St 80138 303-387-8400
Kelli Bainbridge, prin. Fax 387-8401
Prairie Crossing ES 500/K-6
11605 Bradbury Ranch Dr 80134 303-387-8200
Carrie Rotherham, prin. Fax 387-8201
Sagewood MS 1,000/6-8
4725 Fox Sparrow Rd 80134 303-387-4300
Daniel Winsor, prin. Fax 387-4301
Sierra MS 1,100/7-8
6651 E Pine Ln 80138 303-387-3800
Darrell Meredith, prin. Fax 387-3801

Elizabeth SD C-1
Supt. — See Elizabeth
Singing Hills ES 400/PK-5
41012 Madrid Dr 80138 303-646-1858
Regina Montera, prin. Fax 841-9732

Ave Maria Catholic S 500/PK-8
9056 E Parker Rd 80138 720-842-5400
Terri Loiselle, prin. Fax 842-5402

Parker Montessori S 100/PK-K
10750 Victorian Dr 80138 303-841-4325
Anitha Harshan, dir. Fax 841-5878
Southeast Christian S 600/PK-8
9650 Jordan Rd 80134 303-841-5988
Michelle Thompson-Davis, head sch Fax 831-9594

Peetz, Logan, Pop. 237
Peetz Plateau SD RE-5 200/PK-12
PO Box 39 80747 970-334-2361
Mark Collard, supt. Fax 334-2360
www.peetzschool.org
Peetz ES 100/PK-6
311 Coleman Ave 80747 970-334-2361
Lori Heller, prin. Fax 334-2360

Penrose, Fremont, Pop. 3,520
Fremont SD RE-2
Supt. — See Florence
Penrose ES 200/K-5
100 Illinois St 81240 719-372-6777
Michelle Lesser, prin. Fax 372-0719

Peyton, El Paso, Pop. 247
Falcon SD 49
Supt. — See Falcon
Falcon ES 300/K-5
12050 Falcon Hwy 80831 719-495-5272
Michael Roth, prin. Fax 495-5282
Falcon MS 900/6-8
9755 Towner Ave 80831 719-495-5232
Brian Smith, prin. Fax 495-5237
Meridian Ranch International ES 700/K-5
10480 Rainbow Bridge Dr 80831 719-494-2909
Sheehan Freeman-Todd, prin. Fax 494-2912
Woodmen Hills ES 700/K-5
8308 Del Rio Rd 80831 719-495-5500
Dr. Kathy Pickering, prin. Fax 495-5501

Peyton SD 23 JT 500/PK-12
18320 Main St 80831 719-749-2330
Tim Kistler, supt. Fax 749-2368
www.peyton.k12.co.us
Peyton ES 300/PK-6
13550 Bradshaw Rd 80831 719-749-0170
Janette Watts, prin. Fax 749-0060

Pierce, Weld, Pop. 823
Weld County SD RE-9
Supt. — See Ault
Highland ES 300/K-5
PO Box 39 80650 970-834-2853
Bev Scheer, prin. Fax 834-1294

Pine, Jefferson, Pop. 600
Jefferson County SD R-1
Supt. — See Golden
Elk Creek ES 300/PK-5
13304 US Highway 285 80470 303-982-2900
Ryan Lucas, prin. Fax 982-2901

Platteville, Weld, Pop. 2,448
Weld County SD RE-1
Supt. — See Gilcrest
Platteville ES 400/PK-5
PO Box 427 80651 970-785-2271
Darron Diemert, prin. Fax 785-6468
South Valley MS 200/6-8
1004 Main St 80651 970-785-4347
Jeff Angus, prin. Fax 785-2182

Pleasant View, Montezuma
Montezuma-Cortez SD RE-1
Supt. — See Cortez
Pleasant View ES 50/K-5
15328 Road CC 81331 970-562-4286
Jim Parr, prin. Fax 562-4287

Pritchett, Baca, Pop. 140
Pritchett SD RE-3 100/PK-12
PO Box 7 81064 719-523-4045
William Carwin, supt. Fax 523-6991
www.pritchettre3.org
Pritchett ES 50/PK-5
PO Box 7 81064 719-523-4045
William Carwin, prin. Fax 523-6991
Pritchett JHS 50/6-8
PO Box 7 81064 719-523-4045
William Carwin, prin. Fax 523-6991

Pueblo, Pueblo, Pop. 104,988
Pueblo CSD 60 17,700/PK-12
315 W 11th St 81003 719-549-7100
Charlotte Macaluso, supt. Fax 549-7112
www.pueblocityschools.us
Baca ES 300/PK-5
2800 E 17th St 81001 719-549-7530
Julie Griego, prin. Fax 253-5240
Belmont ES 500/PK-5
31 MacNaughton Rd 81001 719-549-7500
Stephanie Smith, prin. Fax 253-5241
Bessemer Academy 500/PK-5
1125 E Routt Ave 81004 719-549-7505
Angela Flores, prin. Fax 253-5242
Beulah Heights ES 400/PK-5
2670 Delphinium St 81005 719-549-7510
Jonathan Dehn, prin. Fax 253-5243
Bradford ES 500/PK-5
107 S La Crosse Ave 81001 719-549-7515
Sandra Alvarez, prin. Fax 253-5244
Carlile ES 300/PK-5
736 W Evans Ave 81004 719-549-7520
Erika Slaughter, prin. Fax 549-7990
Columbian ES 400/PK-6
1203 Palmer Ave 81004 719-549-7525
Michelle Alcon-Montoya, prin. Fax 253-5245
Corwin International Magnet MS 600/4-8
1500 Lakeview Ave 81004 719-549-7400
Ryan Masciotra, prin. Fax 253-5264
Fountain International Magnet ES 400/K-3
925 N Glendale Ave 81001 719-549-7535
Charlotte Martinez, prin. Fax 253-5250
Franklin ES 500/PK-5
1315 Horseshoe Dr 81001 719-549-7540
Cary Palumbo, prin. Fax 562-0428
Goodnight S 700/PK-8
624 Windy Way 81005 719-549-7545
Andrea Glaeser, prin. Fax 253-5253
Haaff ES 400/PK-5
15 Chinook Ln 81001 719-549-7550
Betsy DeCesaro, prin. Fax 253-5254
Heaton MS 700/6-8
6 Adair Rd 81001 719-549-7420
Jayme Stangier, prin. Fax 549-7838
Heritage ES 400/PK-5
625 Brown Ave 81004 719-549-7575
Kim Cura, prin. Fax 253-5256
Heroes K-8 Academy 300/K-8
715 W 20th St 81003 719-549-7410
Julie Shue, prin. Fax 253-5262
Highland Park ES 600/PK-5
2701 Vinewood Ln 81005 719-549-7560
Crystal Gallegos, prin. Fax 564-3282
Irving ES 400/PK-5
1629 W 21st St 81003 719-549-7570
Valarie Davis, prin. Fax 543-5329
Minnequa ES 400/PK-5
1708 E Orman Ave 81004 719-549-7580
Melissa Patterson, prin. Fax 253-5259
Morton ES 600/PK-5
1900 W 31st St 81008 719-549-7585
Susan Sanchez, prin. Fax 253-5260
Park View ES 500/PK-5
1327 E 9th St 81001 719-549-7590
Floyd Gallegos, prin. Fax 562-0673
Pueblo Academy of Arts 400/6-8
29 Lehigh Ave 81005 719-549-7430
Rhonda Holcomb, prin. Fax 549-7878
Risley International Academy 400/6-8
625 N Monument Ave 81001 719-549-7440
Dawn Johnson, prin. Fax 549-7926
Roncalli STEM Academy 500/6-8
4202 W State Highway 78 81005 719-549-7450
Marci Imes, prin. Fax 549-7469
South Park ES 300/PK-5
3100 Hollywood Dr 81005 719-549-7600
Lynne Brunjak, prin. Fax 253-5263
Sunset Park ES 500/PK-5
110 University Cir 81005 719-549-7610
John Hull, prin. Fax 253-5265

Pueblo County SD 70 9,100/PK-12
24951 E US Highway 50 81006 719-542-0220
C. Edward Smith, supt. Fax 542-0225
www.district70.org
North Mesa ES 400/PK-5
28881 Gale Rd 81006 719-948-3303
Jeff Howes, prin. Fax 948-0178
Pleasant View MS 400/6-8
23600 Everett Rd 81006 719-542-7813
Ronda Rein, prin. Fax 545-6291
Sierra Vista ES 500/PK-5
500 S Spaulding Ave 81007 719-547-2878
Tammy Neal, prin. Fax 547-2920
South Mesa ES 400/PK-5
23701 Preston Rd 81006 719-543-6444
Shad Glenn, prin. Fax 545-6191
Vineland ES 300/PK-5
35777 Iris Rd 81006 719-948-3331
Angie Fillmore, prin. Fax 948-0179
Vineland MS 300/6-8
1132 36th Ln 81006 719-948-3336
Sandy Gibbs, prin. Fax 948-2323
Other Schools – See Avondale, Beulah, Colorado City, Pueblo West, Rye

---

Daystar Christian S 50/1-8
3912 Oneal Ave 81005 719-561-9120
Park Hill Christian Academy 100/K-9
PO Box 8147 81008 719-544-6154
Douglas Cox, head sch Fax 544-6175
St. John Neuman Catholic S 100/PK-8
2415 E Orman Ave 81004 719-561-9419
Joyce Anderson, admin. Fax 561-4718
St. Therese Catholic S 200/PK-12
320 Goodnight Ave 81004 719-561-1121
Nadine Montoya, prin. Fax 561-2252
Trinity Evangelical Lutheran S 100/PK-8
701 W Evans Ave 81004 719-542-1864
Randy Daberkow, prin. Fax 542-1864

Pueblo West, Pueblo, Pop. 29,092
Pueblo County SD 70
Supt. — See Pueblo
Cedar Ridge ES 500/PK-5
1267 W Oro Grande Dr 81007 719-547-8268
Ted Shepard, prin. Fax 547-8310
Desert Sage ES 400/PK-5
935 S Palomar Dr 81007 719-647-8878
Eva Chamberlin, prin. Fax 647-9034
Liberty Point ES 300/PK-5
386 E Hahns Peak Ave 81007 719-547-2191
Cheryl Vincent, admin. Fax 547-0677
Liberty Point International S 500/6-8
484 S Maher Dr 81007 719-547-3752
Chris Slobodnik, prin. Fax 547-0499
Prairie Winds ES 500/PK-5
579 E Earl Dr 81007 719-647-9732
Stephanie Russell, prin. Fax 647-9730
Skyview MS 600/6-8
1047 S Camino De Bravo 81007 719-547-1175
Robert DiPietro, prin. Fax 647-9667

Rangely, Rio Blanco, Pop. 2,325
Rangely SD RE-4 600/PK-12
402 W Main St 81648 970-675-2207
Matthew Scoggins, supt. Fax 675-5023
www.rangelyk12.org
Parkview ES 300/PK-5
550 River Rd 81648 970-675-2267
Mike Kruger, prin. Fax 675-5032

Red Feather Lakes, Larimer, Pop. 343
Poudre SD R-1
Supt. — See Fort Collins
Red Feather Lakes ES 50/PK-5
505 N County Road 73C 80545 970-488-6550
Tom Schachet, prin. Fax 488-6552

Rico, Dolores, Pop. 265
Dolores County SD RE-2J
Supt. — See Dove Creek
Rico ES, PO Box 250 81332 50/PK-5
Bruce Hankins, admin. 970-967-3450

Ridgway, Ouray, Pop. 910
Ridgway SD R-2 300/PK-12
1115 Clinton St 81432 970-626-4320
Steve Smith, supt. Fax 626-4337
www.ridgway.k12.co.us
Ridgway ES 100/PK-5
1115 Clinton St 81432 970-626-5468
Trish Greenwood, prin. Fax 626-5597
Ridgway MS 100/6-8
1200 Green St 81432 970-626-5788
Jeremy Voytko, prin. Fax 626-3249

Rifle, Garfield, Pop. 9,029
Garfield SD RE-2 4,800/PK-12
839 Whiteriver Ave 81650 970-665-7600
Brent Curtice, supt. Fax 665-7623
www.garfieldre2.org
Graham Mesa ES 400/PK-4
1575 Farmstead Pkwy 81650 970-665-7500
Brian Sprenger, prin. Fax 665-7501
Highland ES 400/PK-4
1500 E 7th St 81650 970-665-6800
Rich Hills, prin. Fax 665-6801
Rifle MS 800/5-8
753 Railroad Ave 81650 970-665-7600
Jenny Nipper, prin. Fax 665-7930
Wamsley ES 300/PK-4
225 E 30th St 81650 970-665-7950
Kathi Senor, prin. Fax 665-7985
Other Schools – See New Castle, Silt

Rocky Ford, Otero, Pop. 3,914
Rocky Ford SD R-2 800/PK-12
601 S 8th St 81067 719-254-7423
Kermit Snyder, supt. Fax 254-7425
www.rockyfordk12.org
Jefferson IS 300/3-6
901 S 11th St 81067 719-254-7669
Patti Aldea, prin. Fax 254-4307
Washington PS 200/PK-2
709 S 11th St 81067 719-254-7681
Ellen Froman, prin. Fax 254-7889

Rush, El Paso, Pop. 100
Miami-Yoder SD 60 JT 200/PK-12
420 S Rush Rd 80833 719-478-2186
Dwight Barnes, supt. Fax 478-5380
www.miamiyoder.com
Miami-Yoder ES 100/PK-5
420 S Rush Rd 80833 719-478-2186
Sheila Hartley, prin. Fax 478-5380

Rye, Pueblo, Pop. 153
Pueblo County SD 70
Supt. — See Pueblo
Rye ES 300/PK-5
PO Box 220 81069 719-489-2272
Sue Moore, prin. Fax 489-2275

Saguache, Saguache, Pop. 479
Mountain Valley SD RE-1 100/PK-12
PO Box 127 81149 719-655-0268
Travis Garoutte, supt. Fax 655-2875
www.mountainvalleyschool.org
Mountain Valley ES 100/PK-5
PO Box 127 81149 719-655-2578
Kathy Hill, prin. Fax 655-2875
Mountain Valley MS 50/6-8
PO Box 127 81149 719-655-2578
Kathy Hill, prin. Fax 655-2875

Salida, Chaffee, Pop. 5,163
Salida SD R-32 1,200/PK-12
349 E 9th St 81201 719-530-5200
David Blackburn, supt. Fax 539-6220
salidaschools.com
Longfellow ES 400/K-4
425 W 7th St 81201 719-530-5260
Chuck McKenna, prin. Fax 539-5072
Salida ECC 100/PK-PK
516 Teller St 81201 719-530-5360
Ilona Witty, dir. Fax 539-1844
Salida MS 300/5-8
520 Milford St 81201 719-530-5300
Will Wooddell, prin. Fax 530-5364

Sanford, Conejos, Pop. 874
Sanford SD 6J 400/PK-12
PO Box 39 81151 719-274-5167
Kevin Edgar M.Ed., supt. Fax 274-5830
www.sanfordschools.org
Sanford ES 200/PK-6
PO Box 39 81151 719-274-5167
Luella Crowther, prin. Fax 274-5830

San Luis, Costilla, Pop. 618
Centennial SD R-1 200/PK-12
PO Box 350 81152 719-672-3322
Lance Northey, supt. Fax 672-3345
www.centennialschool.net
Centennial S 100/PK-12
PO Box 350 81152 719-672-3322
Gilbert Apodaca, prin. Fax 672-3345

Sedalia, Douglas, Pop. 201
Douglas County SD RE-1
Supt. — See Castle Rock
Sedalia ES 300/K-6
5449 Huxtable St 80135 303-387-5500
Jeff Johnson, prin. Fax 387-5501

Seibert, Kit Carson, Pop. 178
Hi-Plains SD R-23 100/PK-12
PO Box 238 80834 970-664-2636
Michael Warren, supt. Fax 664-2283
www.hp-patriots.com/
Hi-Plains ES 100/PK-6
PO Box 238 80834 970-664-2636
Michael Clark, prin. Fax 664-2283

Severance, Weld, Pop. 3,116
Weld County SD RE-4
Supt. — See Windsor
Range View ES 600/PK-5
700 Ponderosa Dr, 970-833-7300
Kelly Johnson, prin. Fax 833-7301

Sheridan, Arapahoe, Pop. 5,532
Sheridan SD 2 1,300/PK-12
4150 S Hazel Ct 80110 720-833-6616
Michael Clough, supt. Fax 833-6650
www.ssd2.org
Terry ES 300/K-2
4485 S Irving St 80110 720-833-6990
Joe Hayes, prin. Fax 833-6698
Other Schools – See Denver

Sheridan Lake, Kiowa, Pop. 88
Kiowa County SD RE-2 100/PK-12
13997 County Road 71 81071 719-729-3331
Lance Mosness, supt. Fax 729-3451
www.plainviewhawks.org
Plainview ES 50/PK-5
13997 County Road 71 81071 719-729-3331
Lance Mosness, admin. Fax 729-3451

Silt, Garfield, Pop. 2,889
Garfield SD RE-2
Supt. — See Rifle
Cactus Valley ES 400/PK-4
222 Grand Ave 81652 970-665-7850
Kelly Detlefsen, prin. Fax 665-7884

Silverthorne, Summit, Pop. 3,826
Summit SD RE-1
Supt. — See Frisco
Silverthorne ES 300/PK-5
PO Box 1039 80498 970-368-1600
Joel Rivera, prin. Fax 368-1699

Silverton, San Juan, Pop. 625
Silverton SD 1 100/K-12
PO Box 128 81433 970-387-5543
Kim White, supt. Fax 387-5791
www.silvertonschool.org
Silverton ES 50/K-5
PO Box 128 81433 970-387-5543
Kim White, prin. Fax 387-5791
Silverton MS 50/6-8
PO Box 128 81433 970-387-5543
Kim White, prin. Fax 387-5791

Simla, Elbert, Pop. 614
Big Sandy SD 100J 200/PK-12
PO Box 68 80835 719-541-2292
Steve Wilson, supt. Fax 541-2186
bigsandy100j.com
Simla ES 100/PK-5
PO Box 68 80835 719-541-2291
Kathy Tucker, prin. Fax 541-2443

Springfield, Baca, Pop. 1,423
Springfield SD RE-4 300/PK-12
389 Tipton St 81073 719-523-6654
Richard Hargrove, supt. Fax 523-4192
www.spre4.org
Springfield ES 100/K-6
389 Tipton St 81073 719-523-4391
Richard Hargrove, prin. Fax 523-4192
Springfield JHS 50/7-8
389 Tipton St 81073 719-523-6522
Kyle Lasley, prin. Fax 523-4361
Springfield Preschool PK-PK
389 Tipton St 81073 719-523-6920
Debbie Sharpe, dir.

Steamboat Springs, Routt, Pop. 11,946
Steamboat Springs SD RE-2 2,400/PK-12
325 7th St 80487 970-871-3199
Dr. Brad Meeks, supt. Fax 879-3943
www.sssd.k12.co.us
Soda Creek ES 600/K-5
220 Park Ave 80487 970-879-0652
Michelle Miller, prin. Fax 879-7834
Steamboat Springs ECC PK-PK
325 7th St 80487 970-871-3177
Meaghan Franges, prin.
Steamboat Springs MS 500/6-8
39610 Amethyst St 80487 970-879-1058
Heidi Chapman-Hoy, prin. Fax 870-0368
Strawberry Park ES 500/K-5
39620 Amethyst Dr 80487 970-879-7550
Tracy Stoddard, prin. Fax 879-6217

Emerald Mountain S 100/K-8
PO Box 770723 80477 970-879-8081
Samantha Donnel, head sch Fax 879-9332

Sterling, Logan, Pop. 14,616
Valley SD RE-1 2,300/PK-12
301 Hagen St 80751 970-522-0792
Dr. Jan DeLay Ph.D., supt. Fax 522-0525
www.re1valleyschools.org
Ayres ES 400/K-2
1812 Robin Rd 80751 970-522-1409
Joe Skerjanec, prin. Fax 522-5908
Campbell ES 400/3-5
902 Clark St 80751 970-522-2514
Dennis Klein, prin. Fax 522-2516
Hagen Early Education Center 200/PK-PK
301 Hagen St 80751 970-522-0432
Georgia Sanders, coord. Fax 522-5439
Sterling MS 400/6-8
1177 Pawnee Ave 80751 970-522-1041
Robert Hall, prin. Fax 522-0209
Other Schools – See Iliff

Strasburg, Adams, Pop. 2,413
Strasburg SD 31J 1,100/PK-12
56729 Colorado Ave 80136 303-622-9211
Monica Johnson, supt. Fax 622-9224
www.strasburg31j.com
Hemphill MS 200/6-8
2100 Wagner St 80136 303-622-9213
Sara Turrell, prin. Fax 622-2613
Strasburg ES 500/PK-5
56729 Colorado Ave 80136 303-622-9215
Carol Wethington, prin. Fax 622-4891

Stratton, Kit Carson, Pop. 658
Stratton SD R-4 200/PK-12
219 Illinois Ave 80836 719-348-5369
Jeff Durbin, supt. Fax 348-5555
www.strattonschools.org
Stratton ES 100/PK-5
6 Main St 80836 719-348-5521
Jennifer Witzel, prin. Fax 348-5555
Stratton MS 50/6-8
219 Illinois Ave 80836 719-348-5369
Jennifer Witzel, prin. Fax 348-5555

Superior, Boulder, Pop. 12,074
Boulder Valley SD RE-2
Supt. — See Boulder
Eldorado K-8 S 1,000/K-8
3351 S Indiana St 80027 720-561-4400
Robyn Hamasaki, prin. Fax 561-4401

Swink, Otero, Pop. 607
Swink SD 33 300/K-12
PO Box 487 81077 719-384-8103
Kyle Hebberd, supt. Fax 384-5471
www.swinkk12.net
Swink ES 200/K-6
PO Box 487 81077 719-384-8103
Lauren Votruba, prin. Fax 384-5471

Tabernash, Grand, Pop. 408

Winter Park Christian S 100/K-12
PO Box 518 80478 970-887-9784

Telluride, San Miguel, Pop. 2,291
Telluride SD R-1 600/PK-12
725 W Colorado Ave 81435 970-728-6617
Michael Gass, supt. Fax 728-9490
www.tellurideschool.org
Telluride ES 300/PK-3
447 W Columbia Ave 81435 970-728-6615
Susan Altman, prin. Fax 728-5035
Telluride IS 100/4-6
717 W Colorado Ave 81435 970-369-4719
Chad Terry, prin. Fax 369-4883

Telluride Mountain S 100/PK-12
200 San Miguel River Dr 81435 970-728-1969
Karen Walker, head sch Fax 369-4412

Thornton, Adams, Pop. 116,276
Adams 12 Five Star SD 36,800/PK-12
1500 E 128th Ave 80241 720-972-4000
Chris Gdowski, supt. Fax 972-4008
www.adams12.org
Century MS 1,100/6-8
13000 Lafayette St 80241 720-972-5240
Howard Holbrook, prin. Fax 972-5279
Cherry Drive ES 400/K-5
11500 Cherry Dr 80233 720-972-5300
Tina Hepp, prin. Fax 972-5319
Coronado Hills ES 500/PK-5
8300 Downing Dr 80229 720-972-5320
Donald Beuke, prin. Fax 972-5339
Eagleview ES 600/K-5
4601 Summit Grove Pkwy 80241 720-972-5760
Bianca Porter, prin. Fax 972-5779
Hunters Glen ES 500/K-5
13222 Corona St 80241 720-972-5440
Christopher Blados, prin. Fax 972-5459
International S 800/6-8
9451 Hoffman Way 80229 720-972-5160
Jessica Fiedler, prin. Fax 972-5199
McElwain ES 400/K-5
1020 Dawson Dr 80229 720-972-5500
Justina Carney, prin. Fax 972-5519
North Star ES 500/K-5
8740 Northstar Dr 80260 720-972-5560
Grace Taylor, prin. Fax 972-5579
Prairie Hills ES 500/K-5
13801 Garfield Pl 80602 720-972-8780
Kathy Hastings, prin. Fax 972-8800
Riverdale ES 400/K-5
10724 Elm Dr 80233 720-972-5580
Kristin Golden, prin. Fax 972-5599
Rocky Top MS 1,200/6-8
14150 York St 80602 720-972-2200
Chelsea Behana, prin. Fax 972-2303
Shadow Ridge MS 1,000/6-8
12551 Holly St 80241 720-972-5040
Susie Wickham, prin. Fax 972-5079
Silver Creek ES 700/K-5
15101 Fillmore St 80602 720-972-3940
Darren Oliver, prin. Fax 972-3999
Skyview ES 500/K-5
5021 E 123rd Ave 80241 720-972-5620
Stephanie Auday, prin. Fax 972-5639
Stellar ES 600/K-5
3901 E 124th Ave 80241 720-972-2340
Jennifer Buck, prin. Fax 972-2399
STEM Launch 800/K-8
9450 Pecos St 80260 720-972-5120
Martin McCarthy, prin. Fax 972-6062
Tarver ES 500/K-5
3500 Summit Grove Pkwy 80241 720-972-5640
Chris Trujillo, prin. Fax 972-5659
Thornton ES 400/K-5
991 Eppinger Blvd 80229 720-972-5660
Betsy Miller, prin. Fax 972-5679
Woodglen ES 400/K-5
11717 Madison St 80233 720-972-5700
Brett Drobney, prin. Fax 972-5719
Other Schools – See Brighton, Broomfield, Federal Heights, Northglenn, Westminster

Mapleton SD 1
Supt. — See Denver
Achieve Academy 500/PK-8
9100 Poze Blvd 80229 303-853-1300
Ron Salazar, dir. Fax 853-1356
Clayton Partnership S 500/K-8
8970 York St 80229 303-853-1460
Janice Phelps, dir. Fax 853-1496
Explore ES 400/PK-6
2410 Poze Blvd 80229 303-853-1170
Annaleah Bloom, dir. Fax 853-1169
Meadow Community S 500/PK-8
9150 Monroe St 80229 303-853-1500
Esmeralda Orrin, dir. Fax 853-1556
York International S 700/K-12
9200 York St 80229 303-853-1600
James Long, dir. Fax 853-1656

SD 27J
Supt. — See Brighton
Brantner ES 300/PK-5
7800 E 133rd Ave 80602 720-685-5050
Michele Saller, prin. Fax 685-5054
West Ridge ES 700/PK-5
13102 Monaco St 80602 720-685-5300
Amy Bruce, prin. Fax 685-5304

Lord of Life Lutheran S 100/PK-8
12021 Northaven Cir 80241 303-457-2408
Joshua Glowicki, prin.
Thorncreek Christian S 200/PK-12
12505 Colorado Blvd 80241 303-452-7514
Joseph Davis, admin.

Timnath, Larimer, Pop. 615
Poudre SD R-1
Supt. — See Fort Collins
Bethke ES 500/K-5
5100 School House Dr 80547 970-488-4300
Ann Alfonso, prin. Fax 488-4302
Timnath ES 300/K-5
3909 Main St 80547 970-488-6825
Lori Sander, prin. Fax 488-6827

Trinidad, Las Animas, Pop. 8,973
Trinidad SD 1 1,100/PK-12
PO Box 760 81082 719-846-3324
Scott Mader, supt. Fax 846-2957
www.tsd1.org
Eckhart ES 200/PK-1
PO Box 760 81082 719-846-6995
Olivia Bachicha, prin. Fax 846-2775
Fisher's Peak ES 300/2-5
PO Box 760 81082 719-846-2513
Shonie Pachelli, prin. Fax 846-2519
Trinidad MS 300/6-8
PO Box 760 81082 719-846-4411
Deana Pachelli, prin. Fax 846-4740

Grace Christian Center 50/K-12
1001 Obregon St 81082 719-846-6133
Fax 846-6133
Heritage Christian S 50/K-12
PO Box 801 81082 719-859-3508
Jean Griffis, admin.

USAF Academy, El Paso, Pop. 9,062
Academy SD 20
Supt. — See Colorado Springs
Douglass Valley ES 400/PK-5
4610 E Douglass Dr, 719-234-4200
Kelly Farmer, prin. Fax 234-4299

Vail, Eagle, Pop. 5,245
Eagle County SD RE-50
Supt. — See Eagle
Red Sandstone ES 300/PK-5
551 N Frontage Rd 81657 970-328-2910
Marcelle Laidman, prin. Fax 328-2915

Vail Mountain S 300/K-12
3000 Booth Falls Rd 81657 970-476-3850
Michael Imperi, head sch Fax 476-3860

Vilas, Baca, Pop. 112
Vilas SD RE-5 100/PK-12
PO Box 727 81087 719-523-6738
Samantha Yocum, supt. Fax 523-4818
www.vilasre5.us

Vilas ES 50/PK-6
PO Box 727 81087 719-523-6738
Samantha Yocum, admin. Fax 523-4818

Walden, Jackson, Pop. 599
North Park SD R-1 200/PK-12
PO Box 798 80480 970-723-3300
Robert Fulton, supt. Fax 723-8486
npk12.org
Walden ES 100/PK-5
PO Box 798 80480 970-723-3300
Chrissy Carlstrom, prin. Fax 723-4417

Walsenburg, Huerfano, Pop. 3,036
Huerfano SD RE-1 500/PK-12
201 E 5th St 81089 719-738-1520
Michael Moore, supt. Fax 738-3148
huerfano.k12.co.us
Peakview S 300/PK-8
375 W Pine St 81089 719-738-2190
Brenda Duran, prin. Fax 738-5746
Other Schools – See Gardner

Walsh, Baca, Pop. 543
Walsh SD RE-1 200/PK-12
PO Box 68 81090 719-324-5632
Stephanie Hund, supt. Fax 324-5426
www.walsheagles.com
Walsh ES 100/PK-6
PO Box 68 81090 719-324-5400
Stephanie Hund, supt. Fax 324-5426

Weldona, Morgan, Pop. 139
Weldon Valley SD RE-20(J) 200/PK-12
911 North Ave 80653 970-645-2411
Doug Pfau M.S., supt. Fax 645-2377
www.weldonvalley.org/
Weldon Valley ES 100/PK-6
911 North Ave 80653 970-645-2411
Jeff Sparrow, prin. Fax 645-2377
Weldon Valley JHS 50/7-8
911 North Ave 80653 970-645-2411
Jeff Sparrow, prin. Fax 645-2377

Wellington, Larimer, Pop. 6,177
Poudre SD R-1
Supt. — See Fort Collins
Eyestone ES 500/PK-5
PO Box 69 80549 970-488-8600
David Sobson, prin. Fax 488-8602
Rice ES 400/K-5
7000 3rd St 80549 970-488-8700
Karen Koehn, prin. Fax 488-8702
Wellington MS 400/6-8
4001 Wilson Ave 80549 970-488-6600
Alicia Durand, prin. Fax 488-6602

Westcliffe, Custer, Pop. 555
Custer County SD C-1 400/PK-12
PO Box 730 81252 719-783-2357
Mark Payler, supt. Fax 783-2334
www.custercountyschools.org
Custer County ES 200/PK-5
PO Box 730 81252 719-783-2291
Jack Christensen, prin. Fax 783-4944
Custer County JHS 100/6-8
PO Box 730 81252 719-783-2291
Jack Christensen, prin. Fax 783-4944

Westminster, Adams, Pop. 103,933
Adams 12 Five Star SD
Supt. — See Thornton
Arapahoe Ridge ES 600/K-5
13095 Pecos St 80234 720-972-5740
Kate Vogel, prin. Fax 972-5759
Cotton Creek ES 600/K-5
11100 Vrain St 80031 720-972-5340
Bill Kempsell, prin. Fax 972-5355
Rocky Mountain ES 500/K-5
3350 W 99th Ave 80031 720-972-5600
Steve Isenhour, prin. Fax 972-5619
Silver Hills MS 1,100/6-8
12400 Huron St 80234 720-972-5000
Julie Evans, prin. Fax 972-5039

Jefferson County SD R-1
Supt. — See Golden
Adams ES 500/PK-6
6450 W 95th Pl 80021 303-982-9790
Brendan Feely, prin. Fax 982-9791
Carle MS 400/7-8
10200 W 100th Ave 80021 303-982-9070
John White, prin. Fax 982-9071
Lukas ES 500/K-6
9650 W 97th Ave 80021 303-982-0368
Renee Williams, prin. Fax 982-0369
Mandalay MS 400/7-8
9651 Pierce St 80021 303-982-9802
John Schalk, prin. Fax 982-9813
Ryan ES 500/K-6
5851 W 115th Ave 80020 303-982-3105
Kristi Shaner, prin. Fax 982-3106
Semper ES 400/PK-6
7575 W 96th Ave 80021 303-982-0400
Kim Schlarbaum, prin. Fax 982-6461
Sheridan Green ES 300/PK-6
10951 Harlan St 80020 303-982-3182
Kurt Freeman, prin. Fax 982-3183

Witt ES 400/PK-6
10255 W 104th Dr 80021 303-982-3380
Chalee McDougal, prin. Fax 982-3381

Westminster SD 10,100/PK-12
6933 Raleigh St 80030 303-428-3511
Dr. Pamela Swanson, supt. Fax 428-2810
www.westminsterpublicschools.org
Colorado STEM Academy 200/K-8
7281 Irving St 80030 303-429-7836
Brenda Martin, prin.
ECC 300/PK-PK
8030 Irving St 80031 303-428-1560
Mathieu Aubuchon, dir. Fax 657-3846
Flynn ES 300/PK-5
8731 Lowell Blvd 80031 303-428-2161
Brian Kosena, dir. Fax 657-3843
Harris Park ES 400/PK-5
4300 W 75th Ave 80030 303-428-1721
Nancy Richey, prin. Fax 657-3849
Mesa ES 400/PK-5
9100 Lowell Blvd 80031 303-428-2891
Janelle Stastny, prin. Fax 657-3856
Shaw Heights MS 600/6-8
8780 Circle Dr 80031 303-428-9533
Mike Carlson, prin. Fax 657-3973
Sunset Ridge ES 400/PK-5
9451 Hooker St 80031 303-426-8907
Roger Vadeen, prin. Fax 657-3874
Westminster Academy 300/PK-7
7482 Irving St 80030 303-428-2494
Russell Warwick, prin. Fax 657-3883
Other Schools – See Arvada, Denver

Belleview Christian S 300/PK-12
3455 W 83rd Ave 80031 303-427-5459
Dr. Peggy Polson, prin. Fax 426-6768
Cornerstone Christian Academy 200/PK-12
12000 Zuni St 80234 303-451-1421
Larry Zimbelman, prin.
Holy Trinity S 200/PK-8
3050 W 76th Ave 80030 303-427-5632
Joseph Skerjanec, prin. Fax 427-4125
Hyland Christian S 100/K-12
5255 W 98th Ave 80020 303-466-1673
LIFE Christian Academy 200/PK-12
11500 Sheridan Blvd 80020 303-438-1260
Cheri Strong, admin. Fax 438-1866
Shepherd of the Lutheran Valley S 100/PK-8
8997 W 88th Ave 80021 303-424-1306
Jeffrey Falck, prin. Fax 996-2995

Weston, Las Animas, Pop. 54
Primero RSD RE-2 200/PK-12
20200 State Highway 12 81091 719-868-2715
Bill Naccarato, supt. Fax 868-2241
www.primeroschool.org
Primero ES 100/PK-5
20200 State Highway 12 81091 719-868-2715
Bill Naccarato, supt. Fax 868-2241

Wheat Ridge, Jefferson, Pop. 29,601
Jefferson County SD R-1
Supt. — See Golden
Anderson Preschool 200/PK-PK
10801 W 44th Ave 80033 303-982-1740
Heather Hall, dir. Fax 982-1742
Everitt MS 400/7-8
3900 Kipling St 80033 303-982-1580
Jeff Gomez, prin. Fax 982-1581
Kullerstrand ES 200/K-6
12225 W 38th Ave 80033 303-982-1780
Cheryl Clay, prin. Fax 982-1782
Pennington ES 300/PK-6
4617 Independence St 80033 303-982-2083
Sandy Craig, prin. Fax 982-2082
Prospect Valley ES 500/K-6
3400 Pierson St 80033 303-982-7535
Mike Collins, prin. Fax 982-7536
Stevens ES 400/PK-6
7101 W 38th Ave 80033 303-982-2198
Trina McManus, prin. Fax 982-2163
Wilmore-Davis ES 300/K-6
7975 W 41st Ave 80033 303-982-2890
Janace Fischer, prin. Fax 982-2891

Beth Eden Baptist S 200/K-12
2600 Wadsworth Blvd 80033 303-232-2313
SS. Peter & Paul S 300/PK-8
3920 Pierce St 80033 303-424-0402
Sr. Mary Matamoros, prin. Fax 456-1888

Wiggins, Morgan, Pop. 888
Wiggins SD RE-50(J) 500/PK-12
320 Chapman St 80654 970-483-7762
Trent Kerr, supt. Fax 483-6205
www.wiggins50.k12.co.us
Wiggins ES 300/PK-5
415 Main St 80654 970-483-7784
Tara Boyer, prin. Fax 483-7227

Wiley, Prowers, Pop. 402
Wiley SD RE-13 JT 100/PK-12
PO Box 247 81092 719-829-4806
Dave Eastin, supt. Fax 829-4808
www.wileyschool.org

Wiley S 100/PK-12
PO Box 247 81092 719-829-4806
Michelle Wallace, prin. Fax 829-4808

Windsor, Weld, Pop. 18,391
Weld County SD RE-4 4,800/PK-12
PO Box 609 80550 970-686-8000
Dan Seegmiller, supt. Fax 686-8001
www.weldre4.org
Grandview ES 400/PK-5
1583 Grand Ave 80550 970-686-8600
David Grubbs, prin. Fax 686-8601
Mountain View ES 300/3-5
810 3rd St 80550 970-686-8300
Shelly Prenger, prin. Fax 686-5262
Severance MS 400/6-8
1801 Avery Plaza St 80550 970-833-7200
Carmen Williams, prin. Fax 833-7201
Skyview ES 400/PK-5
1000 Stone Mountain Ct 80550 970-686-8500
Tammy Seib, prin. Fax 686-5232
Tozer PS 400/PK-2
501 Oak St 80550 970-686-8400
Shelly Butcher, prin. Fax 686-0866
Windsor MS 600/6-8
900 Main St 80550 970-686-8200
Eric Johnson, prin. Fax 686-7122
Other Schools – See Severance

Woodland Park, Teller, Pop. 7,047
Woodland Park SD RE-2 2,600/PK-12
PO Box 99 80866 719-686-2000
Jed Bowman Ph.D., supt. Fax 687-8408
www.wpsdk12.org
Columbine ES 400/PK-5
PO Box 6700 80866 719-686-2300
Veronica Wolken, prin. Fax 687-8473
Gateway ES 400/PK-5
PO Box 6670 80866 719-686-2051
Ashley Lawson, prin. Fax 687-8475
Woodland Park MS 600/6-8
PO Box 6790 80866 719-686-2200
Yvonne Goings, prin. Fax 687-8458
Other Schools – See Divide

Colorado Springs Christian ES 100/K-5
1003 Tamarac Pkwy 80863 719-686-0706
Miko Aragon, prin. Fax 686-0081

Woodrow, Washington, Pop. 20
Woodlin SD R-104 100/PK-12
15400 County Road L 80757 970-386-2223
Rose Cronk, supt. Fax 386-2241
www.woodlinschool.com
Woodlin ES 50/PK-5
15400 County Road L 80757 970-386-2223
Debbie Atwater, prin. Fax 386-2241

Wray, Yuma, Pop. 2,328
Wray SD RD-2 700/PK-12
30222 County Road 35 80758 970-332-5764
Levi Kramer, admin. Fax 506-2912
www.wrayschools.org
Buchanan MS 200/5-8
620 W 7th St 80758 970-332-3600
Laurie Unger, prin. Fax 332-3356
Wray ES 300/PK-4
30204 County Road 35 80758 970-332-3729
Andrea Kammer, prin. Fax 332-5408

Yampa, Routt, Pop. 424
South Routt SD RE-3
Supt. — See Oak Creek
Soroco Preschool @ Yampa 50/PK-PK
PO Box 97 80483 970-638-1065
Cindy Ashley, dir.
South Routt ES 200/K-5
PO Box 97 80483 970-638-4558
Randall Foster, prin. Fax 870-2689

Yoder, El Paso, Pop. 40
Edison SD 54 JT 200/PK-12
14550 Edison Rd 80864 719-478-2125
Paul Frank, supt. Fax 478-3000
www.edison54jt.schoolfusion.us
Edison ES 100/PK-5
14550 Edison Rd 80864 719-478-2125
Paul Frank, prin. Fax 478-3000

Yuma, Yuma, Pop. 3,498
Yuma SD-1 800/PK-12
PO Box 327 80759 970-848-5831
Dianna Chrisman, supt. Fax 848-2256
www.yumaschools.org
Little Indians Preschool 50/PK-PK
709 W 3rd Ave 80759 970-848-4572
Ana Arvizo, dir. Fax 848-4291
Morris ES 300/K-4
416 S Elm St 80759 970-848-5738
Keri Chapman, prin. Fax 848-5400
Yuma MS 200/5-8
500 S Elm St 80759 970-848-2000
Brenda Kloberdanz, prin. Fax 848-4261

CONNECTICUT

CONNECTICUT DEPARTMENT OF EDUCATION
165 Capitol Ave, Hartford 06106-1659
Telephone 860-713-6500
Fax 860-713-7001
Website http://www.sde.ct.gov

Commissioner of Education Dianna Wentzell

CONNECTICUT BOARD OF EDUCATION
165 Capitol Ave, Hartford 06106-1659

Chairperson Allan Taylor

REGIONAL EDUCATIONAL SERVICE CENTERS

Area Coop. Educational Services RESC
Thomas Danehy Ed.D., dir. 203-498-6800
350 State St, North Haven 06473 Fax 498-6890
www.aces.org

Capitol Region Education Council RESC
Dina Crowl, supt. 860-247-2732
111 Charter Oak Ave
Hartford 06106
www.crec.org

Cooperative Educational Services RESC
Dr. Evan Pitkoff, dir. 203-365-8800
40 Lindeman Dr, Trumbull 06611 Fax 365-8804
www.ces.k12.ct.us

Eastconn RESC
Paula Colen, dir. 860-455-0707
376 Hartford Tpke, Hampton 06247 Fax 455-8026
www.eastconn.org

Ed Advance RESC
Dr. Jeffrey Kitching, dir. 860-567-0863
PO Box 909, Litchfield 06759 Fax 567-3381
www.educationconnection.org

Learn RESC
Dr. Eileen Howley, dir. 860-434-4800
44 Hatchetts Hill Rd Fax 434-4837
Old Lyme 06371
www.learn.k12.ct.us

PUBLIC, PRIVATE AND CATHOLIC ELEMENTARY SCHOOLS

Andover, Tolland
Andover SD 300/PK-6
35 School Rd 06232 860-742-7339
Dr. Sally Doyen, supt. Fax 742-8288
www.andoverelementaryct.org
Andover ES 300/PK-6
35 School Rd 06232 860-742-7339
John Briody, prin. Fax 742-8288

Ansonia, New Haven, Pop. 18,821
Ansonia SD 2,200/PK-12
42 Grove St 06401 203-736-5095
Carol Merlone Ed.D., supt. Fax 736-5098
www.ansonia.org
Ansonia MS 400/7-8
115 Howard Ave 06401 203-736-5070
Michael Marotto Ph.D., prin. Fax 736-1044
Mead ES 600/PK-6
75 Ford St 06401 203-736-5090
Amy O'Brien, prin. Fax 736-1042
Prendergast ES 700/K-6
60 Finney St 06401 203-736-5080
Elizabeth Nimons, prin. Fax 736-1045

Assumption S 200/PK-8
51 N Cliff St 06401 203-734-0855
Kathleen Molner, prin. Fax 734-5521

Ashford, Windham
Ashford SD 400/PK-8
440 Westford Rd 06278 860-429-1927
Dr. James Longo, supt. Fax 429-3651
www.ashfordct.org
Ashford S 400/PK-8
440 Westford Rd 06278 860-429-6419
Troy Hopkins, prin. Fax 429-3651

Avon, Hartford
Avon SD 3,300/PK-12
34 Simsbury Rd 06001 860-404-4700
JeanAnn Paddyfote, supt. Fax 404-4702
www.avon.k12.ct.us
Avon MS 600/7-8
375 W Avon Rd 06001 860-404-4770
Dave Kimball, prin. Fax 404-4773
Pine Grove ES 600/K-4
151 Scoville Rd 06001 860-404-4790
Jess Giannini, prin. Fax 404-4793
Roaring Brook ES 600/PK-4
30 Old Wheeler Ln 06001 860-404-4810
Noam Sturm, prin. Fax 404-4813
Thompson Brook S 600/5-6
150 Thompson Rd 06001 860-404-4870
Mike Renkawitz, prin. Fax 404-4873

Capitol Region Education Council RESC
Supt. — See Hartford
Grace Academy of the Arts Magnet S PK-4
20 Security Dr 06001 860-677-0380
Patricia Phelan, prin. Fax 677-0408
Reggio Magnet School of the Arts 400/PK-5
59 Waterville Rd 06001 860-674-8549
Josephine Smith, prin. Fax 674-9004

Farmington Valley Academy Montessori 100/PK-8
150 Fisher Dr 06001 860-677-2403

Baltic, New London, Pop. 1,192
Sprague SD 400/PK-8
25 Scotland Rd 06330 860-822-8264
Christopher Eichner, supt. Fax 822-8667
www.saylesschool.org
Sayles S 400/PK-8
25 Scotland Rd 06330 860-822-8264
Diana Burns, prin. Fax 822-8667

St. Joseph S 100/PK-8
10 School Hill Rd 06330 860-822-6141
Sr. M. Patrick Mulready, prin. Fax 822-1479

Barkhamsted, Litchfield
Barkhamsted SD 300/PK-6
65 Ripley Hill Rd 06063 860-738-4016
Jeffrey Linton, supt. Fax 738-3642
www.barkhamstedschool.org
Barkhamsted ES 300/PK-6
65 Ripley Hill Rd 06063 860-379-2729
Kristen Plocki, prin. Fax 379-4412

Beacon Falls, New Haven
Regional SD 16
Supt. — See Prospect
Laurel Ledge ES 400/PK-5
30 Highland Ave 06403 203-729-5355
Regina Murzak, prin. Fax 729-7349

Berlin, Hartford
Berlin SD 3,000/PK-12
238 Kensington Rd 06037 860-828-6581
David B. Erwin, supt. Fax 829-0832
www.berlinschools.org
McGee MS 700/6-8
899 Norton Rd 06037 860-828-0323
Salvatore Urso, prin. Fax 828-0676
Willard ES 500/PK-5
1088 Norton Rd 06037 860-828-4151
Matthew Correia Ed.D., prin. Fax 828-4178
Other Schools – See East Berlin, Kensington

Bethany, New Haven
Bethany SD 400/PK-6
44 Peck Rd 06524 203-393-1170
Colleen Murray, supt. Fax 393-0239
www.bethany-ed.org
Bethany Community ES 400/PK-6
44 Peck Rd 06524 203-393-3350
Robert Davis, prin. Fax 393-3849

Regional SD 5
Supt. — See Woodbridge
Amity Regional MS 400/7-8
190 Luke Hill Rd 06524 203-393-3102
Richard Dellinger, prin. Fax 393-0583

Bethel, Fairfield, Pop. 9,266
Bethel SD 3,000/PK-12
PO Box 253 06801 203-794-8601
Dr. Christine Carver, supt. Fax 794-8723
www.bethel.k12.ct.us
Berry ES 600/PK-3
200 Whittlesey Dr 06801 203-794-8680
Danielle Legnard, prin. Fax 794-8783
Bethel MS 700/6-8
600 Whittlesey Dr 06801 203-794-8670
Nicholas DaPonte, prin. Fax 830-7318
Johnson ES 400/4-5
500 Whittlesey Dr 06801 203-794-8700
Alison Salerno, prin. Fax 794-8716
Rockwell ES 400/K-3
400 Whittlesey Dr 06801 203-794-8688
Trisha Soucy, prin. Fax 794-8687

St. Mary S 200/PK-8
24 Dodgingtown Rd 06801 203-744-2922
Greg Viceroy, prin. Fax 798-8803

Bethlehem, Litchfield
Regional SD 14
Supt. — See Woodbury
Bethlehem ES 300/PK-5
92 East St 06751 203-266-7506
Susan Ruddock, prin. Fax 266-7876

Bloomfield, Hartford, Pop. 7,200
Bloomfield SD 2,100/PK-12
1133 Blue Hills Ave 06002 860-769-4200
Dr. James Thompson, supt. Fax 769-4215
www.bloomfieldschools.org
Arace IS 200/5-6
390 Park Ave 06002 860-286-2622
Sarah Williams, prin. Fax 242-8939
Arace MS 200/7-8
390 Park Ave 06002 860-286-2622
Trevor Ellis, prin. Fax 242-0347
Laurel ES 300/K-2
1 Filley St 06002 860-286-2675
Paul Guzzo, prin. Fax 769-5517
Metacomet ES 200/3-4
185 School St 06002 860-286-2660
Jesse White, prin. Fax 769-5296
Wintonbury Early Childhood Magnet School 300/PK-K
44 Brown St 06002 860-769-5510
Lisa Eells, prin. Fax 769-5525

Sigel Hebrew Academy 100/PK-8
53 Gabb Rd 06002 860-243-8333

Bolton, Tolland
Bolton SD 900/PK-12
72 Brandy St 06043 860-643-1569
Kristin B. Heckt, supt. Fax 647-8452
www.boltonpublicschools.com/
Bolton Center S 500/PK-8
108 Notch Rd 06043 860-643-2411
Mary Grande, prin. Fax 646-4860

Bozrah, New London, Pop. 2,297
Bozrah SD 200/PK-8
PO Box 185 06334 860-887-2561
John Welch Ed.D., supt. Fax 889-2715
www.fmsbozrah.org
Fields Memorial S 200/PK-8
PO Box 185 06334 860-887-2561
Mark Westkott, prin. Fax 889-2715

Branford, New Haven, Pop. 27,603
Branford SD, 1111 Main St 06405 3,200/PK-12
Hamlet Hernandez, supt. 203-488-7276
www.branfordschools.org/
Chipkin Early Years Center 50/PK-PK
12 Melrose Ave 06405 203-315-3540
Dr. Dianibel Aviles, prin. Fax 315-4143
Murphy ES 400/PK-4
14 Brushy Plain Rd 06405 203-483-1832
Raeanne Reynolds, prin. Fax 483-5189
Sliney ES 400/PK-4
23 Eades St 06405 203-481-5386
Margaret-Mary Gethings, prin. Fax 483-0749
Tisko ES 400/PK-4
118 Damascus Rd 06405 203-483-1826
James O'Connor, prin. Fax 483-7528
Walsh IS 900/5-8
185 Damascus Rd 06405 203-488-8317
Robin Goeler, prin. Fax 481-2785

St. Mary S 100/PK-8
62 Cedar St 06405 203-488-8386
Sr. Annette D'Antonio, prin. Fax 488-2347

Bridgeport, Fairfield, Pop. 139,433
Bridgeport SD 20,000/PK-12
45 Lyon Ter Rm 203 06604 203-275-1001
Dr. Aresta Johnson, supt. Fax 576-8488
www.bridgeportedu.com
Barnum S 600/PK-8
495 Waterview Ave 06608 203-275-2301
Amy Marshall, prin. Fax 337-0144
Batalla S 1,200/PK-8
606 Howard Ave 06605 203-579-8500
Hector Sanchez, prin. Fax 337-0196
Beardsley ES 400/PK-6
500 Huntington Rd 06610 203-275-3828
Sharon Pivirotto, prin. Fax 337-1069
Blackham S 1,100/PK-8
425 Thorme St 06606 203-275-4118
Marcie Julian-Branca, prin. Fax 337-0138
Black Rock ES 400/K-8
545 Brewster St 06605 203-275-3872
Stephen Cassidy, prin. Fax 337-0170
Bryant ES 400/PK-6
230 Poplar St 06605 203-275-4501
Vicki Egri, prin. Fax 330-2442
Classical Studies Magnet Academy 300/3-8
240 Linwood Ave 06604 203-275-4200
Helen Giles, prin. Fax 337-0195
Classical Studies Magnet Academy Annex PK-2
659 Beechwood Ave 06605 203-275-4250
Helen Giles, prin.
Claytor Magnet Academy PK-6
240 Ocean Ter 06605 203-275-4816
Steve Douglas, prin. Fax 337-0142
Columbus S 900/PK-8
275 George St 06604 203-275-1901
John Scalice, prin. Fax 337-0104
Cross S 400/PK-8
1775 Reservoir Ave 06606 203-275-2600
Deborah Tisdale, prin. Fax 337-0136
Curiale S 700/K-8
300 Laurel Ave 06605 203-576-8437
Brett Gustafson, prin. Fax 337-0110
Discovery Interdistrict Magnet S 500/PK-8
4510 Park Ave 06604 203-275-1801
Sangeeta Bella, prin. Fax 337-0097
Dunbar S 300/K-8
445 Union Ave 06607 203-275-3631
Alyshia Perrin, prin. Fax 337-0112
Edison ES 300/K-6
115 Boston Ter 06610 203-275-2253
Gladys Walker Jones, prin. Fax 337-2534
Hall ES 300/K-6
290 Clermont Ave 06610 203-275-3222
Cynthia Fernandes, prin. Fax 337-0166
Hallen ES 300/PK-6
68 Omega Ave 06606 203-275-3783
Dyrene Newton, prin. Fax 337-0126
High Horizons Magnet S 400/K-8
700 Palisade Ave 06610 203-275-4550
Francine Carbone, prin. Fax 337-0178
Hooker S 400/K-8
138 Roger Williams Rd 06610 203-275-3723
Shaun Smith, prin. Fax 337-0156
Johnson S 800/PK-8
474 Lexington Ave 06604 203-275-2501
Luisa Wolfe, prin. Fax 337-0191
Madison ES 500/K-6
386 Wayne St 06606 203-275-3812
Rebecca Cabrera, prin. Fax 337-0180
Marin S 900/PK-8
479 Helen St 06608 203-275-4404
Olga Leiva, prin. Fax 337-0183
Multicultural Magnet S 400/K-8
700 Palisade Ave 06610 203-275-4601
Dr. Luis Planas, prin. Fax 337-0184
Park City Magnet S 500/PK-8
1526 Chopsey Hill Rd 06606 203-275-2677
Terese Maguire, prin. Fax 337-0186
Read S 800/PK-8
130 Ezra St 06606 203-576-8030
Sarhanna Smith, prin. Fax 337-0187
Roosevelt S 600/PK-8
680 Park Ave 06604 203-275-2102
Jacqueline Simmons, prin. Fax 337-0120
Tisdale S 700/PK-8
250 Hollister Ave 06607 203-275-2010
Dr. Charmaine Worthy, prin. Fax 337-0108
Waltersville S 500/PK-8
150 Hallett St 06608 203-275-2401
Carmen Ortiz, prin. Fax 337-0106
Winthrop S 700/K-8
85 Eckart St 06606 203-275-3000
Selena Morgan, prin. Fax 337-0101

Fairfield County SDA S 100/K-8
827 Trumbull Ave 06606 203-374-3203
Joycelyn Sargeant, prin. Fax 374-3203
St. Andrew Academy 300/PK-8
395 Anton St 06606 203-373-1552
Lori Wilson, prin. Fax 396-0378
St. Ann Academy 200/PK-8
521 Brewster St 06605 203-334-5856
Patricia Griffin, prin. Fax 333-8263
St. Augustine Academy 100/4-8
63 Pequonnock St 06604 203-366-6500
Dr. Deborah Boccanfuso, prin. Fax 362-2934
St. Raphael Academy 100/PK-3
324 Frank St 06604 203-333-6818
Sr. Christine Hoffner, prin. Fax 336-9205

Bridgewater, Litchfield
Regional SD 12
Supt. — See Washington Depot
Burnham S 100/K-5
80 Main St S 06752 860-354-5559
Cathy Colella, prin. Fax 350-1597

Bristol, Hartford, Pop. 59,288
Bristol SD 8,200/PK-12
PO Box 450 06011 860-584-7000
Ellen Solek Ed.D., supt. Fax 584-7611
www.bristol.k12.ct.us
Chippins Hill MS 700/6-8
551 Peacedale St 06010 860-584-3881
Matthew Harnett, prin. Fax 584-4833
Edgewood ES 400/K-5
345 Mix St 06010 860-584-7828
Margaret Giordano, prin. Fax 584-7991
Greene-Hills S 900/PK-8
718 Pine St 06010 860-584-7822
Scott Gaudet, prin. Fax 314-4632
Hubbell ES 400/PK-5
90 W Washington St 06010 860-584-7842
Rochelle Schwartz, prin. Fax 584-3886
Ivy Drive ES 400/K-5
160 Ivy Dr 06010 860-584-7844
Dr. RoseAnn Vojtek, prin. Fax 584-3876
Mountain View ES 400/PK-5
71 Vera Rd 06010 860-584-7726
Mary Hawk, prin. Fax 314-4629
Northeast MS 500/6-8
530 Stevens St 06010 860-584-7839
Mary Hawk, prin. Fax 584-7837
South Side ES 500/PK-5
21 Tuttle Rd 06010 860-584-7812
Dr. David Huber, prin. Fax 584-7810
Stafford ES 500/PK-5
212 Louisiana Ave 06010 860-584-7824
Kristin Irvine, prin. Fax 314-4631
West Bristol S 900/PK-8
500 Clark Ave 06010 860-584-7815
Michelle LeVasseur, prin. Fax 584-7814

Immanuel Lutheran S 100/PK-8
154 Meadow St 06010 860-583-5631
James Krupski, prin. Fax 585-4785
St. Joseph S 300/PK-8
335 Center St 06010 860-582-8696
Eric Frenette, prin. Fax 584-9907

Broad Brook, Hartford, Pop. 3,997
East Windsor SD
Supt. — See East Windsor
Broad Brook ES 500/PK-4
14 Rye St 06016 860-623-2433
Laura Foxx, prin. Fax 623-0717
East Windsor MS 300/5-8
38 Main St 06016 860-623-4488
Kimberly Hellerich, prin. Fax 654-1915

Brookfield, Fairfield
Brookfield SD 2,800/PK-12
PO Box 5194 06804 203-775-7620
John Barile, supt. Fax 740-3195
www.brookfieldps.org
Center ES 400/PK-1
8 Obtuse Hill Rd 06804 203-775-7650
Dr. Krys Salon, prin. Fax 775-7672
Huckleberry Hill ES 600/2-4
100 Candlewood Lake Rd 06804 203-775-7675
Mary Rose Dymond, prin. Fax 775-7684
Whisconier MS 900/5-8
17 W Whisconier Rd 06804 203-775-7710
Deane Renda, prin. Fax 775-7615

Christian Life Academy 100/PK-8
133 Junction Rd 06804 203-775-5191
Joan Freeman, prin. Fax 775-5567
St. Joseph S 200/PK-8
5 Obtuse Hill Rd 06804 203-775-2774
Scott Bannon, prin. Fax 775-5810

Brooklyn, Windham, Pop. 976
Brooklyn SD 900/PK-8
119 Gorman Rd 06234 860-774-9153
Patricia Buell, supt. Fax 774-6938
www.brooklynschools.org
Brooklyn ES 500/PK-4
119 Gorman Rd 06234 860-774-7577
Shelley Michaud, prin. Fax 779-1162
Brooklyn MS 400/5-8
119 Gorman Rd 06234 860-774-9153
Alan Yanku, prin. Fax 774-6938

Burlington, Hartford
Regional SD 10 2,600/PK-12
24 Lyon Rd 06013 860-673-2538
Alan Beitman, supt. Fax 673-4976
www.region10ct.org
Har-Bur MS 800/5-8
24 Lyon Rd 06013 860-673-6163
Kenneth Smith, prin. Fax 673-3481
Lake Garda ES 500/PK-4
61 Monce Rd 06013 860-673-2511
Stefanie Carbone, prin. Fax 673-3721
Other Schools – See Harwinton

Canaan, Litchfield, Pop. 1,201
North Canaan SD
Supt. — See Falls Village
North Canaan ES 300/PK-8
PO Box 758 06018 860-824-5149
Rosemary Keilty, prin. Fax 824-4879

Canterbury, Windham
Canterbury SD 500/PK-8
45 Westminster Rd 06331 860-546-6950
Dr. Lois DaSilva-Knapton, supt. Fax 546-6423
www.canterburypublicschools.org/
Baldwin MS 200/5-8
45 Westminster Rd 06331 860-546-9421
Ryan Earley, prin. Fax 546-6289
Canterbury ES 200/PK-4
67 Kitt Rd 06331 860-546-6744
Sarah Cary, prin. Fax 546-6742

Canton, Hartford
Canton SD 1,700/PK-12
4 Market St Ste 100 06019 860-693-7704
Kevin Case, supt. Fax 693-7706
www.cantonschools.org
Canton IS 400/4-6
39 Dyer Ave 06019 860-693-7717
Kevin Hanlon, prin. Fax 693-7814
Canton MS 300/7-8
76 Simonds Ave 06019 860-693-7712
Pamela Hamad, prin. Fax 693-7812
Cherry Brook PS 500/PK-3
4 Barbourtown Rd 06019 860-693-7721
Andrew Robbin, prin. Fax 693-7647

Centerbrook, Middlesex
Essex SD
Supt. — See Deep River
Essex ES 500/PK-6
108 Main St 06409 860-767-8215
Jennifer Tousignant, prin. Fax 767-1476

Chaplin, Windham
Chaplin SD 200/PK-6
304 Parish Hill Rd 06235 860-455-9306
Kenneth Henrici, supt. Fax 455-1263
www.chaplinschool.org
Chaplin ES 200/PK-6
240 Palmer Rd 06235 860-455-9593
Patricia King, prin. Fax 455-0742

Cheshire, New Haven, Pop. 25,684
Cheshire SD 4,600/PK-12
29 Main St 06410 203-250-2400
Jeffrey Solan, supt. Fax 250-2453
www.cheshire.k12.ct.us
Chapman ES 300/K-6
38 Country Club Rd 06410 203-272-3591
Marlene Silano, prin. Fax 271-9833
Darcey K 300/PK-K
1686 Waterbury Rd 06410 203-272-3343
Ann Donnery, prin. Fax 271-2554
Dodd MS 700/7-8
100 Park Pl 06410 203-272-3249
Michael Woods, prin. Fax 250-7614
Doolittle ES 500/1-6
735 Cornwall Ave 06410 203-272-3549
Russell Hinckley, prin. Fax 272-0546
Highland ES 700/K-6
490 Highland Ave 06410 203-272-0335
Scott Jeffrey, prin. Fax 272-9003
Norton ES 400/K-6
414 N Brooksvale Rd 06410 203-272-7283
Kelly Grillo, prin. Fax 250-0654

St. Bridget S 400/PK-8
171 Main St 06410 203-272-5860
V. Jennifer Furlong, prin. Fax 271-7031

Chester, Middlesex, Pop. 1,538
Chester SD
Supt. — See Deep River
Chester ES 200/PK-6
23 Ridge Rd 06412 860-526-5797
Dr. Joanne Beekley, prin. Fax 526-3570

Clinton, Middlesex, Pop. 3,326
Clinton SD 2,000/PK-12
137B Glenwood Rd 06413 860-664-6500
Maryann O'Donnell, supt. Fax 664-6580
www.clintonpublic.net
Eliot MS 500/6-8
69 Fairy Dell Rd 06413 860-664-6503
Linda Tucker, prin. Fax 664-6583
Joel ES 600/PK-3
137 Glenwood Rd 06413 860-664-6501
Claudia Norman, prin. Fax 664-6581
Pierson ES 300/4-5
75 E Main St 06413 860-664-6502
Angela Guarascio, prin. Fax 664-6582

Colchester, New London, Pop. 4,696
Colchester SD 2,700/PK-12
127 Norwich Ave Ste 202 06415 860-537-7260
Karen Goodwin, supt. Fax 537-1252
www.colchesterct.org/
Colchester ES 600/PK-2
315 Halls Hill Rd 06415 860-537-0717
Judy O'Meara, prin. Fax 537-6573
Jackter IS 600/3-5
215 Halls Hill Rd 06415 860-537-9421
Elise Butson, prin. Fax 537-0349
Johnston MS 700/6-8
360 Norwich Ave 06415 860-537-2313
Christopher Bennett, prin. Fax 537-6258

Colebrook, Litchfield
Colebrook SD 100/K-6
PO Box 9 06021 860-379-2179
Dr. Danuta Thibodeau, supt. Fax 379-9506
www.colebrookschool.org/
Colebrook Consolidated S 100/K-6
PO Box 9 06021 860-379-2179
Elizabeth Driscoll, prin. Fax 379-9506

Columbia, Tolland
Columbia SD 500/PK-8
PO Box 166 06237 860-228-8590
Laurence Fearon, supt. Fax 228-8592
columbiaschoolsystem.webs.com/
Porter S 500/PK-8
PO Box 166 06237 860-228-9493
Alyssa Gwinnell, prin. Fax 228-8592

Cos Cob, Fairfield, Pop. 6,608
Greenwich SD
Supt. — See Greenwich
Cos Cob ES 400/K-5
300 E Putnam Ave 06807 203-869-4670
Gene Schmidt, prin. Fax 869-7640

Coventry, Tolland, Pop. 10,063
Coventry SD 1,700/PK-12
1700 Main St 06238 860-742-7317
David Petrone, supt. Fax 742-4567
www.coventrypublicschools.org/
Coventry Grammar S 400/K-2
3453 Main St 06238 860-742-7313
Marybeth Moyer, prin. Fax 742-4555
Hale ECC 50/PK-PK
1776 Main St 06238 860-742-4550
Jill Miner, dir. Fax 742-5736

Hale MS 400/6-8
1776 Main St 06238 860-742-7334
Dena DeJulius, prin. Fax 742-4565
Robertson IS 400/3-5
227 Cross St 06238 860-742-7341
Dr. Beth Giller, prin. Fax 742-4582

Cromwell, Middlesex
Cromwell SD 1,900/PK-12
9 Mann Memorial Dr 06416 860-632-4830
Dr. Paula Talty, supt. Fax 632-4865
www.cromwell.k12.ct.us/
Cromwell MS 500/6-8
9 Mann Memorial Dr 06416 860-632-4853
Ann Cocchiola, prin. Fax 632-4855
Stevens ES 500/PK-2
25 Court St 06416 860-632-4866
Lucille DiTunno, prin. Fax 632-4881
Woodside IS 500/3-5
30 Woodside Rd 06416 860-632-3564
Christopher Butwill, prin. Fax 613-3970

Danbury, Fairfield, Pop. 77,029
Danbury SD 10,500/PK-12
63 Beaver Brook Rd 06810 203-797-4701
Dr. Sal Pascarella Ed.D., supt. Fax 830-6562
www.danbury.k12.ct.us
Broadview MS 1,100/6-8
72 Hospital Ave 06810 203-797-4861
Edie Thomas, prin. Fax 790-2856
Ellsworth Avenue ES 400/K-5
53 Ellsworth Ave 06810 203-797-4741
Dr. Anna Rocco, prin. Fax 830-6527
Great Plain ES 300/K-5
10 Stadley Rough Rd 06811 203-797-4749
Keshia Smith, prin. Fax 830-6581
Hayestown Avenue ES 400/K-5
42 Tamarack Ave 06811 203-797-4771
Stephanie Furman, prin. Fax 830-6505
King Street IS 400/4-5
151 S King St 06811 203-797-4761
Tina Hislop, prin. Fax 830-6515
King Street PS 400/PK-3
151 S King St 06811 203-797-4744
Tina Hislop, prin. Fax 830-6596
Mill Ridge PS 400/K-3
49A High Ridge Rd 06811 203-797-4781
Dr. Mary Cronin, prin. Fax 830-6583
Morris Street ES 400/K-5
28 Morris St 06810 203-797-4809
William Santarsiero, prin. Fax 830-6514
Park Avenue ES 400/K-5
82 Park Ave 06810 203-797-4763
David Krafick, prin. Fax 790-2608
Pembroke ES 400/K-5
34 1/2 Pembroke Rd 06811 203-797-4751
Sharon Epple, prin. Fax 830-6585
Rogers Park MS 1,200/6-8
21 Memorial Dr 06810 203-797-4880
Patricia Joaquim, prin. Fax 790-2829
Shelter Rock ES 400/K-5
2 Crows Nest Ln 06810 203-797-4778
Jamal Gibson, prin. Fax 830-6586
South Street ES 400/K-5
129 South St 06810 203-797-4787
Carmen Vargas-Guevera, prin. Fax 830-6587
Stadley Rough ES 400/K-5
25 Karen Rd 06811 203-797-4773
Lenny Cerlich, prin. Fax 830-6520
Western CT Acad of International Studies 400/K-5
201 University Blvd 06811 203-778-7462
Christopher Roche, prin. Fax 778-7467
Westside MS Academy 6-8
1 School Ridge Rd 06811 203-329-6700
Dr. Frank LaBanca, prin. Fax 797-4722

Hudson Country Montessori S 200/PK-8
44A Shelter Rock Rd 06810 203-744-8088
Immanuel Lutheran S 100/PK-8
18 Clapboard Ridge Rd 06811 203-748-7823
Victoria Baker, prin. Fax 748-5022
St. Gregory the Great S 300/PK-8
85 Great Plain Rd 06811 203-748-1217
Suzanne Curra, prin. Fax 778-0414
St. Joseph S 300/PK-8
370 Main St 06810 203-748-6615
Lisa Lanni, prin. Fax 748-6508
St. Peter S 100/PK-8
98 Main St 06810 203-748-2895
Mary McCormack, prin. Fax 748-5684
Wooster S 300/PK-12
91 Miry Brook Rd 06810 203-830-3900
Matt Byrnes, head sch Fax 790-7147

Danielson, Windham, Pop. 3,941
Killingly SD
Supt. — See Killingly
Killingly Memorial S 300/2-4
339 Main St 06239 860-779-6680
Tina Chahanovich, prin. Fax 774-6028

St. James S 200/PK-8
120 Water St 06239 860-774-3281
Linda Marie Joyal, prin. Fax 779-2137

Darien, Fairfield, Pop. 20,500
Darien SD 4,900/PK-12
PO Box 1167 06820 203-656-7400
Dr. Dan Brenner, supt. Fax 656-3052
www.darienps.org
Hindley ES 600/PK-5
10 Nearwater Ln 06820 203-655-1323
D.J Colella, prin. Fax 655-7024
Holmes ES 500/PK-5
18 Hoyt St 06820 203-353-4371
Paula Bleakley, prin. Fax 359-2533
Middlesex MS 1,100/6-8
204 Hollow Tree Ridge Rd 06820 203-655-2518
Shelley Somers, prin. Fax 655-1627
Ox Ridge ES 500/K-5
395 Mansfield Ave 06820 203-655-2579
Dr. Luke Forshaw, prin. Fax 655-9012
Royle ES 400/K-5
133 Mansfield Ave 06820 203-655-0044
Dean Ketchum, prin. Fax 655-9920
Tokeneke ES 500/PK-5
7 Old Farm Rd 06820 203-655-9666
Mary Michelson, prin. Fax 655-7084

Pear Tree Point S 200/PK-6
90 Pear Tree Point Rd 06820 203-655-0030
David Trigaux, hdmstr. Fax 655-3164

Dayville, Windham
Killingly SD
Supt. — See Killingly
Killingly Central S 200/PK-1
60 Soap St 06241 860-779-6750
Emily Caviggia, prin. Fax 774-3299
Killingly IS 800/5-8
1599 Upper Maple St 06241 860-779-6700
Heather Taylor, prin. Fax 779-9639

Deep River, Middlesex, Pop. 2,444
Chester SD 200/PK-6
PO Box 187 06417 860-526-2417
Dr. Ruth Levy, supt. Fax 526-5469
www.reg4.k12.ct.us
Other Schools – See Chester

Deep River SD 300/PK-6
PO Box 187 06417 860-526-2417
Dr. Ruth Levy, supt. Fax 526-5469
www.reg4.k12.ct.us
Deep River ES 300/PK-6
12 River St 06417 860-526-5319
Christian Strickland, prin. Fax 526-4208

Essex SD 500/PK-6
PO Box 187 06417 860-526-2417
Dr. Ruth Levy, supt. Fax 526-5469
www.reg4.k12.ct.us
Other Schools – See Centerbrook

Regional SD 4 1,000/7-12
PO Box 187 06417 860-526-2417
Dr. Ruth Levy, supt. Fax 526-5469
www.reg4.k12.ct.us
Winthrop MS 400/7-8
1 Winthrop Rd 06417 860-526-9546
William Duffy, prin. Fax 526-3721

Derby, New Haven, Pop. 12,664
Derby SD 1,500/PK-12
PO Box 373 06418 203-736-5027
Dr. Matthew Conway, supt. Fax 736-5031
www.derbyps.org/
Bradley ES 400/PK-5
155 David Humphrey Rd 06418 203-736-5040
Mario Ciccarini, prin. Fax 736-5041
Derby MS 400/6-8
73 Chatfield St 06418 203-736-1426
William Vitelli, prin. Fax 736-3234
Irving ES 400/PK-5
9 Garden Pl 06418 203-736-5043
Jennifer Olson, prin. Fax 736-5045

St. Mary - St. Michael S 100/PK-8
14 Seymour Ave 06418 203-735-6471
Grace Torres, prin. Fax 732-9009

Durham, Middlesex, Pop. 2,900
Regional SD 13 1,700/PK-12
135A Pickett Ln 06422 860-349-7200
Kathryn Veronesi Ed.D., supt. Fax 349-7203
www.rsd13ct.org/
Brewster ES 200/PK-3
126 Tuttle Rd 06422 860-349-7227
Nancy Heckler, prin. Fax 349-7232
Strong MS 300/7-8
191 Main St 06422 860-349-7222
Scott Sadinsky, prin. Fax 349-7225
Other Schools – See Middlefield

East Berlin, Hartford
Berlin SD
Supt. — See Berlin
Hubbard ES 300/K-5
139 Grove St 06023 860-828-4119
Alfred Souza, prin. Fax 828-6324

Eastford, Windham
Eastford SD 200/PK-8
PO Box 158 06242 860-974-1130
Linda Loretz, supt. Fax 974-0837
www.eastfordct.org
Eastford ES 200/PK-8
PO Box 158 06242 860-974-1130
Heather Tamsin, prin. Fax 974-0837

East Granby, Hartford
East Granby SD 900/PK-12
PO Box 674 06026 860-653-6486
Dr. Christine Mahoney Ed.D., supt. Fax 413-9075
www.eastgranby.k12.ct.us
Allgrove ES 200/PK-2
33 Turkey Hills Rd 06026 860-653-2505
Maylah Uhlinger, prin. Fax 413-9080
East Granby MS 200/6-8
95 S Main St 06026 860-653-7113
Melissa Bavaro-Grande, prin. Fax 413-9126
Seymour ES 200/3-5
185 Hartford Ave 06026 860-653-7214
Robert McGrath, prin. Fax 413-9084

East Hampton, Middlesex, Pop. 2,637
East Hampton SD 1,900/PK-12
94 Main St 06424 860-365-4000
Paul Smith, supt. Fax 365-4004
www.easthamptonps.org
Center ES 300/4-5
7 Summit St 06424 860-365-4050
Christopher Sullivan, prin. Fax 365-4054
East Hampton MS 400/6-8
19 Childs Rd 06424 860-365-4060
Jason Lehmann, prin. Fax 365-4064
Memorial ES 600/PK-3
20 Smith St 06424 860-365-4020
Andrew Gonzalez, prin. Fax 365-4024

East Hartford, Hartford, Pop. 50,077
Capitol Region Education Council RESC
Supt. — See Hartford
Two Rivers Magnet MS 700/6-8
337 E River Dr 06108 860-290-5320
Jill Wnuk, prin. Fax 509-3609

East Hartford SD 6,600/PK-12
1110 Main St 06108 860-622-5000
Nathan Quesnel M.A., supt. Fax 622-5119
www.easthartford.org
Early Childhood Learning Center 300/PK-PK
191 Main St 06118 860-622-5440
Lisa Beauchamp, prin. Fax 622-5459
East Hartford MS 1,100/6-8
777 Burnside Ave 06108 860-622-5600
Anthony Menard, prin. Fax 622-5619
Goodwin ES 300/K-5
1235 Forbes St 06118 860-622-5420
Daniel Brodeur, prin. Fax 622-5439
Langford ES 400/K-5
61 Alps Dr 06108 860-622-5701
Cynthia Callahan, prin. Fax 622-5719
Mayberry ES 400/K-5
101 Great Hill Rd 06108 860-622-5720
Anne Axton-Jones, prin. Fax 622-5739
Norris ES 300/K-5
40 Remington Rd 06108 860-622-5740
Edward Orszulak Ed.D., prin. Fax 622-5759
O'Brien STEM Academy 500/K-6
56 Farm Dr 06108 860-622-5761
Lesley Morgan-Thompson Ed.D., prin. Fax 622-5779
Pitkin ES 300/K-5
330 Hills St 06118 860-622-5481
Jennifer Hills-Papetti, prin. Fax 568-7657
Silver Lane ES 300/K-5
15 Mercer Ave 06118 860-622-5501
Joseph LaBarbera, prin. Fax 622-5519
Sunset Ridge MS 100/6-8
450 Forbes St 06118 860-622-5800
Dan Catlin, prin. Fax 622-5819
Other Schools – See Hartford

Learn RESC
Supt. — See Old Lyme
Riverside Magnet S 200/PK-K
29 Willowbrook Rd 06118 860-709-6800
Jasdeep Singh, prin.

New Testament Baptist S 100/PK-12
111 Ash St 06108 860-290-6696
Michael Parker, prin. Fax 290-6698
St. Christopher S 200/PK-8
570 Brewer St 06118 860-568-4100
Kathleen Welch, prin. Fax 568-1070

East Hartland, Hartford
Hartland SD 200/PK-8
30 South Rd 06027 860-653-7207
Dr. Anthony Distasio, supt. Fax 844-8528
www.hartlandschool.com
Hartland S 200/PK-8
30 South Rd 06027 860-653-7207
Laura Hollingsworth, prin. Fax 844-8528

East Haven, New Haven, Pop. 28,923
East Haven SD 2,800/PK-12
35 Wheelbarrow Ln 06513 203-468-3261
Erica Forti, supt. Fax 468-3918
www.east-haven.k12.ct.us
Deer Run ES 300/K-2
311 Foxon Rd 06513 203-468-3324
Phyllis Savo, prin. Fax 468-3246
East Haven Academy 300/1-8
67 Hudson St 06512 203-468-3219
Marianne Johnson, prin. Fax 468-3961
Ferrara ES 200/3-5
22 Maynard Rd 06513 203-468-3318
Paul DeBernardo, prin. Fax 468-3875
Melillo MS 600/6-8
67 Hudson St 06512 203-468-3227
Laura Lynn, prin. Fax 468-3866
Momauguin ES 200/K-5
99 Cosey Beach Rd 06512 203-468-3321
Diane MacKinnon, prin. Fax 468-3313
Overbrook ES 200/PK-PK
54 Gerrish Ave 06512 203-468-3305
Erica Forti, admin. Fax 468-3306
Tuttle ES 200/K-5
108 Prospect Rd 06512 203-467-3315
Matthew Espinosa, prin. Fax 467-8861

East Lyme, New London
East Lyme SD 2,800/PK-12
PO Box 220 06333 860-739-3966
Jeffrey Newton, supt. Fax 739-1215
www.eastlymeschools.org
Flanders ES 400/K-4
167 Boston Post Rd 06333 860-739-8475
Linda Anania, prin. Fax 739-1242
Other Schools – See Niantic

Easton, Fairfield
Easton SD 1,000/PK-8
PO Box 500 06612 203-261-2513
Thomas McMorran Ed.D., supt. Fax 261-7936
www.er9.org
Keller MS 400/6-8
360 Sport Hill Rd 06612 203-268-8651
Susan Kaplan, prin. Fax 268-6105
Staples ES 600/PK-5
515 Morehouse Rd 06612 203-261-3607
Kimberly Fox Santora, prin. Fax 452-8403

Redding SD 1,000/K-8
PO Box 500 06612 203-261-2513
Thomas McMorran, supt. Fax 261-7936
www.er9.org
Other Schools – See Redding

Easton Country Day S 200/PK-12
660 Morehouse Rd 06612 203-268-5530
Jody Smith, dir. Fax 268-5863

East Windsor, Hartford
East Windsor SD 1,200/PK-12
70 S Main St 06088 860-623-3346
Dr. Theresa Kane, supt. Fax 292-6817
www.eastwindsork12.org
Other Schools – See Broad Brook

Ellington, Tolland
Ellington SD 2,200/PK-12
PO Box 179 06029 860-896-2300
Dr. Scott Nicol, supt. Fax 896-2312
www.ellingtonpublicschools.org
Center ES 400/K-6
PO Box 220 06029 860-896-2315
Trudie Luck Roberts, prin. Fax 896-2321
Crystal Lake ES 200/K-6
59 South Rd 06029 860-896-2322
Michael Larkin, prin. Fax 896-2328
Ellington MS 400/7-8
46 Middle Butcher Rd 06029 860-896-2339
David Pearson, prin. Fax 896-2351
Windermere ES 400/PK-6
PO Box 259 06029 860-896-2329
David Welch, prin. Fax 896-2338

Enfield, Hartford, Pop. 45,500
Enfield SD 4,100/PK-12
1010 Enfield St 06082 860-253-6531
Christopher Drezek, supt. Fax 253-6515
www.enfieldschools.org
Barnard ES 300/K-2
27 Shaker Rd 06082 860-253-6540
James Graham, prin. Fax 253-6545
Crandall ES 400/3-5
150 Brainard Rd 06082 860-253-6464
Jennifer Miller, prin. Fax 253-6467
Enfield Street ES 300/K-2
1318 Enfield St 06082 860-253-6565
Katherine Reeves, prin. Fax 253-6568
Hazardville Memorial ES 300/K-2
68 N Maple St 06082 860-763-7500
Lisa Hunter, prin. Fax 763-7507
Kennedy MS 1,100/6-8
155 Raffia Rd 06082 860-763-8855
Steve Sargalski, prin. Fax 763-8888
Parkman ES 300/3-5
165 Weymouth Rd 06082 860-253-6570
Irene Roman, prin. Fax 253-6577
Preschool STEAM Academy 50/PK-PK
27 Shaker Rd 06082 860-253-4741
Jacklyn Valley, admin. Fax 253-6510
Whitney ES 400/3-5
94 Middle Rd 06082 860-763-7540
Anthony Brooks, prin. Fax 763-7547

Enfield Montessori S 100/PK-6
1370 Enfield St 06082 860-745-5847
Cliona Beaulieu, head sch Fax 745-2010
Little Angels Preschool PK-PK
424 Hazard Ave 06082 860-745-6135
Charlene Mongillo, prin. Fax 741-7358
St. Bernard S 200/K-8
232 Pearl St 06082 860-745-5275
Charlene Mongillo, prin. Fax 745-0167
St. Martha S 200/K-8
214 Brainard Rd 06082 860-745-3833
Dr. Ann Southworth, prin. Fax 745-3329

Fairfield, Fairfield, Pop. 54,400
Fairfield SD 10,300/PK-12
PO Box 320189, 203-255-8371
Dr. Toni Jones Ed.D., supt. Fax 255-8245
fairfieldschools.org
Burr ES 500/PK-5
1960 Burr St, 203-255-7385
Jason Bluestein, prin. Fax 255-8244
Dwight ES 300/PK-5
1600 Redding Rd, 203-255-8312
Mimi Maniscalco, prin. Fax 255-8201
Early Childhood Education Center 100/PK-PK
755 Melville Ave, 203-255-8380
Kristen Bruno, prin. Fax 255-8247
Fairfield Woods MS 900/6-8
1115 Fairfield Woods Rd, 203-255-8334
Dr. Gary Rosato, prin. Fax 255-8210
Holland Hill ES 400/K-5
105 Meadowcroft Rd, 203-255-8314
Laura Cretella, prin. Fax 255-8202
Jennings ES 300/K-5
31 Palm Dr, 203-255-8316
Anthony Vuolo, prin. Fax 255-8203
Ludlowe MS 900/6-8
689 Unquowa Rd, 203-255-8345
Meg Tiley, prin. Fax 255-8214
McKinley ES 500/K-5
60 Thompson St, 203-255-8318
Leslie Pearson, prin. Fax 255-8204
North Stratfield ES 400/K-5
190 Putting Green Rd, 203-255-8322
Deborah Jackson, prin. Fax 255-8206
Osborn Hill ES 500/K-5
760 Stillson Rd, 203-255-8340
Frank Arnone, prin. Fax 255-8213
Riverfield ES 400/K-5
1625 Mill Plain Rd, 203-255-8328
Brenda Anziano, prin. Fax 255-8207
Sherman ES 500/K-5
250 Fern St, 203-255-8330
Eileen Roxbee, prin. Fax 255-8208
Stratfield ES 500/K-5
1407 Melville Ave, 203-255-8332
Elizabeth McGoey, prin. Fax 255-8209
Tomlinson MS 700/6-8
200 Unquowa Rd, 203-255-8336
Anthony Formato, prin. Fax 255-8211
Other Schools – See Southport

Assumption Catholic S 200/PK-8
605 Stratfield Rd, 203-334-6271
Steven Santoli, prin. Fax 382-0399
Fairfield Country Day S 200/PK-9
2970 Bronson Rd, 203-259-2723
John Munro, hdmstr. Fax 259-3249
Great Beginnings Montessori S PK-6
148 Beach Rd, 203-254-8208
Hillel Academy 50/PK-8
1571 Stratfield Rd, 203-374-6147
St. Thomas Aquinas S 400/PK-8
1719 Post Rd, 203-255-0556
Patricia Brady, prin. Fax 255-0596
Unquowa S 200/PK-8
981 Stratfield Rd, 203-336-3801
Sharon Lauer, head sch Fax 336-3479

Falls Village, Litchfield, Pop. 534
Canaan SD 100/K-8
246 Warren Tpke 06031 860-824-0855
Pamela Vogel, supt. Fax 824-1271
www.region1schools.org
Kellogg S 100/K-8
47 Main St 06031 860-824-7791
Alexandra Juch, prin. Fax 824-7892

Cornwall SD 100/K-8
246 Warren Tpke 06031 860-824-0855
Pamela Vogel, supt. Fax 824-1271
www.region1schools.org
Other Schools – See West Cornwall

North Canaan SD 300/PK-8
246 Warren Tpke 06031 860-824-0855
Pamela Vogel, supt. Fax 824-1271
www.region1schools.org
Other Schools – See Canaan

Salisbury SD 300/PK-8
246 Warren Tpke 06031 860-824-0855
Pamela Vogel, supt. Fax 824-1271
www.region1schools.org
Other Schools – See Lakeville

Sharon SD 200/PK-8
246 Warren Tpke 06031 860-824-0855
Pamela Vogel, supt. Fax 824-1271
www.region1schools.org
Other Schools – See Sharon

Farmington, Hartford, Pop. 2,500
Farmington SD 3,900/PK-12
1 Monteith Dr 06032 860-673-8268
Kathleen Greider, supt. Fax 673-8224
www.fpsct.org
East Farms ES 400/PK-4
25 Wolf Pit Rd 06032 860-674-9519
Renee St. Hilaire, prin. Fax 677-7915
Robbins MS 600/7-8
20 Wolf Pit Rd 06032 860-677-2683
Ted Donahue, prin. Fax 676-0697
Wallace ES 300/K-4
2 School St 06032 860-677-1659
Kelly Sanders, prin. Fax 677-8024
West Woods Upper ES 600/5-6
50 Judson Ln 06032 860-284-1230
Alicia Bowman, prin. Fax 284-1240
Other Schools – See Unionville

Forestville, See Bristol

St. Matthew S 300/PK-8
33 Welch Dr 06010 860-583-5214
Helen Treacy, prin. Fax 314-1541

Gales Ferry, New London, Pop. 1,137
Ledyard SD
Supt. — See Ledyard
Gales Ferry ES 200/PK-2
1858 Route 12 06335 860-464-7664
Anne Hogsten, prin. Fax 464-5138
Ledyard MS 300/7-8
1860 Route 12 06335 860-464-3188
Christopher Pomroy, prin. Fax 464-2155
Long ES 300/3-6
1854 Route 12 06335 860-464-2780
Anne Hogsten, prin. Fax 464-5139

Glastonbury, Hartford, Pop. 27,901
Capitol Region Education Council RESC
Supt. — See Hartford
Glastonbury East Hartford Magnet ES 400/PK-5
95 Oak St 06033 860-633-4455
Ryan Donlon, prin. Fax 657-8427

Glastonbury SD 6,400/PK-12
PO Box 191 06033 860-652-7951
Dr. Alan Bookman, supt. Fax 652-7982
www.glastonburyus.org
Buttonball Lane ES 500/K-5
376 Buttonball Ln 06033 860-652-7276
Kent Hurlburt, prin. Fax 652-7285
Eastbury ES 300/PK-5
1389 Neipsic Rd 06033 860-652-7858
Janet Balthazar, prin. Fax 652-7866
Hebron Avenue ES 400/K-5
1363 Hebron Ave 06033 860-652-7875
Dr. Linda Provost, prin. Fax 652-7887
Naubuc ES 400/K-5
84 Griswold St 06033 860-652-7918
Michael Litke, prin. Fax 652-7630
Smith MS 1,000/7-8
216 Addison Rd 06033 860-652-7040
Scott Hurwitz, prin. Fax 652-4450
Welles S 500/6-6
1029 Neipsic Rd 06033 860-652-7800
James Gregorski, prin. Fax 652-7825
Other Schools – See South Glastonbury

Goshen, Litchfield
Regional SD 6
Supt. — See Litchfield
Goshen Center ES 200/PK-6
50 North St 06756 860-491-6020
Tracy Keilty, prin. Fax 491-6025

Granby, Hartford
Granby SD 1,600/PK-12
15B N Granby Rd 06035 860-844-5250
Dr. Alan Addley, supt. Fax 844-6081
www.granby.k12.ct.us
Granby Memorial MS 300/6-8
321 Salmon Brook St 06035 860-844-3029
Sue Henneberry, prin. Fax 844-3039
Kelly Lane PS 300/PK-2
60 Kelly Ln 06035 860-844-3041
Kimberly Dessert, prin. Fax 413-9295
Wells Road IS 200/3-5
134 Wells Rd 06035 860-844-3048
Dr. Anna Fortenza-Bailey, prin. Fax 844-6180

Greens Farms, Fairfield

Greens Farms Academy 700/PK-12
PO Box 998, 203-256-0717
Janet Hartwell, head sch Fax 256-7501

Greenwich, Fairfield, Pop. 12,646
Greenwich SD 8,800/PK-12
290 Greenwich Ave 06830 203-625-7400
Dr. Jill Gildea, supt. Fax 618-9379
www.greenwich.k12.ct.us
Central MS 600/6-8
9 Indian Rock Ln 06830 203-661-8500
Thomas Healy, prin. Fax 661-2576
Curtiss ES 300/K-5
180 E Elm St 06830 203-869-1896
Patricia McGuire, prin. Fax 869-5101
Glenville ES 400/K-5
33 Riversville Rd 06831 203-531-9287
Marc D'Amico, prin. Fax 531-9285
Hamilton Avenue ES 300/PK-5
184 Hamilton Ave 06830 203-869-1685
John Grasso, prin. Fax 869-1702
New Lebanon ES 300/K-5
25 Mead Ave 06830 203-531-9139
Barbara Riccio, prin. Fax 531-3457
North Street ES 400/PK-5
381 North St 06830 203-869-6756
Jill Flood, prin. Fax 869-1052
Parkway ES 200/PK-5
141 Lower Cross Rd 06831 203-869-7466
Mary Grandville, prin. Fax 869-9352
Western MS 500/6-8
1 Western Junior Hwy 06830 203-531-5700
Gordon Beinstein, prin. Fax 531-5220
Other Schools – See Cos Cob, Old Greenwich, Riverside

Brunswick S 900/PK-12
100 Maher Ave 06830 203-625-5800
Daniel Griffin, dir. Fax 625-5889
Convent of Sacred Heart S 700/PK-12
1177 King St 06831 203-531-6500
Pamela Hayes, head sch Fax 531-5206
Greenwich Academy 900/PK-12
200 N Maple Ave 06830 203-625-8900
Molly King, head sch Fax 869-4921
Greenwich Country Day S 800/PK-9
PO Box 623, 203-863-5600
Adam Rohdie, hdmstr. Fax 622-6046
Greenwich S 500/PK-8
471 North St 06830 203-869-4000
Patrice Kopas, prin. Fax 869-3405
Stanwich S 400/PK-12
257 Stanwich Rd 06830 203-542-0000
Charlie Sachs, head sch Fax 542-0025
Whitby S 400/PK-8
969 Lake Ave 06831 203-869-8464
Jason Anklowitz, head sch Fax 869-2215

Griswold, See Jewett City
Griswold SD 2,000/PK-12
211 Slater Ave 06351 860-376-7600
Sean McKenna, supt. Fax 376-7607
www.griswold.k12.ct.us
Griswold ES 800/PK-4
303 Slater Ave 06351 860-376-7610
Joseph Bordeau, prin. Fax 376-7612
Griswold MS 600/5-8
211 Slater Ave 06351 860-376-7630
Glenn LaBossiere, prin. Fax 376-7631

Groton, New London, Pop. 9,886
Groton SD
Supt. — See Mystic
Barnum ES 400/K-5
68 Briar Hill Rd 06340 860-449-5640
Seth Danner, prin. Fax 449-5642
Chester ES 400/PK-5
1 Harry Day Dr 06340 860-449-5636
Jamie Giordano, prin. Fax 449-5638
Kolnaski STEAM Magnet S 400/PK-5
500 Poquonnock Rd 06340 860-449-5612
Christine Dauphinais, prin. Fax 449-5616
Morrisson ES 400/PK-5
154 Toll Gate Rd 06340 860-449-5655
Kathleen Miner, prin. Fax 449-5654
West Side MS 500/6-8
250 Brandegee Ave 06340 860-449-5630
Jeffrey Kotecki, prin. Fax 449-5628

Sacred Heart S 200/PK-8
50 Sacred Heart Dr 06340 860-445-0611
Gail Kingston, prin. Fax 448-4999

Guilford, New Haven, Pop. 19,848
Guilford SD 3,500/PK-12
PO Box 367 06437 203-453-8200
Dr. Paul Freeman Ed.D., supt. Fax 453-8211
www.guilfordschools.org
Adams MS 600/7-8
233 Church St 06437 203-453-2755
Catherine Walker, prin. Fax 453-8446

Baldwin MS 600/5-6
68 Bullard Dr 06437 203-457-0222
Douglas Hammel, prin. Fax 457-9502
Cox ES 300/K-4
143 Three Mile Crse 06437 203-453-5291
Peter Fragola, prin. Fax 453-8552
Guilford Lakes ES 300/PK-4
40 Maupas Rd 06437 203-453-5201
Mandy Ryan, prin. Fax 453-9507
Jones ES 300/K-4
181 Ledge Hill Rd 06437 203-457-0773
Paula McCarthy, prin. Fax 457-9263
Leete ES 300/K-4
280 S Union St 06437 203-453-2726
William Grimm, prin. Fax 458-2468

Hamden, New Haven, Pop. 52,600
Area Coop. Educational Services RESC
Supt. — See North Haven
Wintergreen Magnet S 600/K-8
670 Wintergreen Ave 06514 203-281-9668
Suzanne Duran-Crelin, prin. Fax 281-7946

Hamden SD 5,800/PK-12
60 Putnam Ave 06517 203-407-2000
Jody Ian Goeler, supt. Fax 407-2001
www.hamden.org
Bear Path ES 400/K-6
10 Kirk Rd 06514 203-407-2015
Scott Trauner, prin. Fax 407-5102
Church Street ES 400/PK-6
95 Church St 06514 203-407-2020
Stacie D'Antonio, prin. Fax 407-5860
Dunbar Hill ES 300/PK-6
315 Lane St 06514 203-407-2025
Erin Bailey, prin. Fax 407-2027
Hamden MS 900/7-8
2623 Dixwell Ave 06518 203-407-3140
Dan Levy, prin. Fax 407-3141
Helen Street ES 300/PK-6
285 Helen St 06514 203-407-2030
Michael Lorenzo, prin. Fax 407-2052
Peck ES 100/PK-5
35 Hillfield Rd 06518 203-407-2010
Judith Antignani, admin. Fax 407-5861
Ridge Hill ES 300/K-6
120 Carew Rd 06517 203-407-2035
Karen Butler, prin. Fax 407-2012
Shepherd Glen ES 300/K-6
1 Skiff Street Ext 06514 203-407-2070
Joseph DiBacco, prin. Fax 407-2072
Spring Glen ES 400/K-6
1908 Whitney Ave 06517 203-407-2045
Howard Hornreich, prin. Fax 407-2048
West Woods ES 500/K-6
350 W Todd St 06518 203-407-2050
Michelle Coogan, prin. Fax 407-5179

New Haven SD
Supt. — See New Haven
East Rock Global Studies Magnet S 500/PK-8
133 Nash St, 475-220-5900
Margaret Pelley, prin. Fax 503-5905

Hamden Hall Country Day S 600/PK-12
1108 Whitney Ave 06517 203-752-2600
Robert Izzo, head sch Fax 752-2651
Laurel Oaks SDA S 50/PK-8
14 W Shepard Ave 06514 203-248-3251
St. Rita S 400/PK-8
1601 Whitney Ave 06517 203-248-3114
Patricia Tiezzi, prin. Fax 248-1016
West Woods Christian Academy 100/K-12
2105 State St 06517 203-562-9922
William Kane, prin. Fax 786-4730

Hampton, Windham
Hampton SD 100/PK-6
380 Main St 06247 860-455-9409
Dr. Frank Olah, supt. Fax 455-9397
www.hamptonschool.org
Hampton ES 100/PK-6
380 Main St 06247 860-455-9409
Sam Roberson, prin. Fax 455-9397

Hartford, Hartford, Pop. 121,829
Capitol Region Education Council RESC 5,300/
111 Charter Oak Ave 06106 860-247-2732
Dina Crowl, supt.
www.crec.org
Greater Hartford Academy of the Arts MS 6-8
75 Van Dyke Ave 06106 860-724-0685
Bo Ryan, prin.
Montessori Magnet S 300/PK-6
1460 Broad St 06106 860-757-6100
Antonio Napoleone, prin. Fax 757-6117
University of Hartford Magnet S 400/PK-5
196 Bloomfield Ave 06117 860-236-2899
Timothy Barber, prin. Fax 236-2062
Other Schools – See Avon, East Hartford, Glastonbury, Rocky Hill, South Windsor, Wethersfield, Windsor

East Hartford SD
Supt. — See East Hartford
O'Connell ES 500/K-5
301 May Rd 06118 860-622-5461
Greg Fox, prin. Fax 622-5479

Hartford SD 21,500/PK-12
960 Main St 06103 860-695-8000
Fax 722-6161
www.hartfordschools.org
Asian Studies Academy 600/PK-8
215 South St 06114 860-695-2400
Anthony Davila, prin. Fax 722-8070
Batchelder S 500/PK-8
757 New Britain Ave 06106 860-695-2720
Paul Casey, prin. Fax 953-4604
Betances Early Reading Lab ES 300/PK-3
42 Charter Oak Ave 06106 860-695-2840
Corinne Clark-Barney, prin. Fax 278-0126
Betances STEM Magnet S 4-8
585 Wethersfield Ave 06114 860-695-2970
Ventine Richardson, prin.

Breakthrough II Magnet ES 200/PK-6
395 Lyme St 06112 860-695-6380
Katherine Leonard, prin. Fax 524-5395
Breakthrough Magnet S 400/PK-8
290 Brookfield St 06106 860-695-5700
Julie Goldstein, prin. Fax 722-6817
Burns Latino Studies Academy 500/PK-8
195 Putnam St 06106 860-695-2980
Victor Cristofaro, prin. Fax 722-8469
Burr S 700/PK-8
400 Wethersfield Ave 06114 860-695-3080
Fabienne Pierre-Maxwell, prin. Fax 296-0717
Capital Preparatory Magnet S 700/PK-12
1304 Main St 06103 860-695-9800
Kitsia Ferguson, prin. Fax 722-8520
Environmental Sciences S at Hooker 600/PK-8
440 Broadview Ter 06106 860-695-3760
Lindsey Thompson, prin. Fax 522-7590
Expeditionary Learning Academy 600/PK-5
101 Catherine St 06106 860-695-4500
Christine McCarthy, prin. Fax 722-8133
Fox S 600/PK-8
470 Maple Ave 06114 860-695-7725
Kenneasha Sloley, prin. Fax 724-5855
Global Communications Academy 500/K-12
85 Edwards St 06120 860-695-6020
Kimberly Stone, prin.
Hartford PreKindergarten Magnet S 100/PK-PK
121 Cornwall St 06112 860-695-5820
Valerie Fenn, prin.
Kennelly S 700/PK-8
180 White St 06114 860-695-3860
Marylou Duffy, prin. Fax 522-9372
King S 300/PK-8
25 Ridgefield St 06112 860-695-3980
Doreen Crawford, prin. Fax 722-8342
Kinsella Sch of Performing Arts 800/PK-12
65 Van Block Ave 06106 860-695-4140
Kenneth O'Brien, prin. Fax 522-0004
McDonough Expeditionary Learning S 300/6-8
111 Hillside Ave 06106 860-695-4260
Bethany Sullivan, prin. Fax 722-8825
Montessori Magnet at Moylan S 200/PK-6
101 Catherine St 06106 860-695-2600
Carolyn Havrda, prin. Fax 951-7074
Montessori Magnet S at Annie Fisher 300/PK-6
280 Plainfield St 06112 860-695-3560
Vivian Novo-MacDonald, prin. Fax 722-8443
Naylor Academy 700/PK-8
639 Franklin Ave 06114 860-695-4620
Fax 296-2595
Parkville Community ES 500/PK-5
47 New Park Ave 06106 860-695-4720
Dirk Olmstead, prin. Fax 232-7350
Rawson ES 500/PK-8
260 Holcomb St 06112 860-695-4840
Tayarisha Stone, prin. Fax 242-3238
Renzulli Gifted & Talented Academy 100/4-8
110 Washington St 06106 860-695-2140
Tina Jeter, prin. Fax 722-8529
Sanchez ES 300/PK-5
176 Babcock St 06106 860-695-4940
Azra Redzic, prin. Fax 560-3493
SAND S 500/K-8
1750 Main St 06120 860-695-5040
Gerardo Heredia, prin. Fax 722-8377
Simpson-Waverly S 300/PK-8
55 Waverly St 06112 860-695-5160
Leoanardo Watson, prin. Fax 724-3548
STEM Magnet S at Annie Fisher 400/K-8
280 Plainfield St 06112 860-695-3500
Sherri Tanner, prin.
Webster MicroSociety S 700/PK-8
5 Cone St 06105 860-695-5380
Jay Mihalko, prin. Fax 722-8786
West Middle ES, 44 Niles St 06112 400/PK-8
Lynn Estey, prin. 860-695-5484
Wish Museum S 400/PK-8
350 Barbour St 06120 860-695-5600
Kesha Ryan, prin. Fax 722-8326

Covenant Preparatory S 5-8
135 Broad St 06105 860-547-0289
Glenn Winfree, head sch
Hartford Area SDA S 100/PK-9
474 Woodland St 06112 860-724-5777
Trinity Academy 2-4
120 Sigourney St 06105 860-251-8337
Karen Connal, head sch Fax 527-2863

Harwinton, Litchfield, Pop. 5,228
Regional SD 10
Supt. — See Burlington
Harwinton Consolidated ES 400/PK-4
115 Litchfield Rd 06791 860-485-9029
Megan Mazzei, prin. Fax 485-9237

Hebron, Tolland
Hebron SD 900/PK-6
580 Gilead St 06248 860-228-2577
Timothy Van Tasel, supt. Fax 228-2235
www.hebron.k12.ct.us
Gilead Hill ES 300/PK-2
580 Gilead St 06248 860-228-9458
Katie Uriano, prin. Fax 228-1106
Hebron ES 500/3-6
92 Church St 06248 860-228-9465
Eric Brody, prin. Fax 228-1378

Regional SD 8 1,700/7-12
PO Box 1438 06248 860-228-2115
Dr. Patricia Law Ed.D., supt. Fax 228-4346
www.reg8.k12.ct.us
RHAM MS 600/7-8
25 RHAM Rd 06248 860-228-9423
Dr. Michael Seroussi, prin. Fax 228-5316

Higganum, Middlesex, Pop. 1,666
Regional SD 17 2,300/PK-12
57 Little City Rd 06441 860-345-4534
Howard Thiery, supt. Fax 345-2817
rsd17.org

Burr District ES 300/PK-4
792 Killingworth Rd 06441 860-345-4584
Eric Larson, prin. Fax 345-7963
Haddam ES 300/K-4
272 Saybrook Rd 06441 860-345-4551
Brienne Whidden, prin. Fax 345-8709
Other Schools – See Killingworth

Kensington, Hartford, Pop. 8,382
Berlin SD
Supt. — See Berlin
Griswold ES 600/K-5
133 Heather Ln 06037 860-828-6336
David Kitzman, prin. Fax 829-2923

St. Paul S 200/PK-8
461 Alling St 06037 860-828-4343
Fayne Molloy, prin. Fax 828-1226

Kent, Litchfield
Kent SD 300/PK-8
PO Box 219 06757 860-824-0855
Pamela Vogel, supt. Fax 824-1271
www.region1schools.org/
Kent Center S 300/PK-8
PO Box 219 06757 860-927-3537
Florence Budge, prin. Fax 927-3925

Killingly, Windham
Killingly SD 2,100/PK-12
PO Box 210 06239 860-779-6600
Lynne Pierson, supt. Fax 779-3798
www.killinglyschools.org
Other Schools – See Danielson, Dayville, Rogers

Killingworth, Middlesex
Regional SD 17
Supt. — See Higganum
Haddam-Killingworth MS 800/5-8
451 Route 81 06419 860-663-1241
Dr. Jennifer Olsen, prin. Fax 663-2071
Killingworth ES 300/K-4
340 Route 81 06419 860-663-1121
Dennis Reed, prin. Fax 663-3827

Lakeville, Litchfield, Pop. 909
Salisbury SD
Supt. — See Falls Village
Salisbury Central S 300/PK-8
PO Box 1808 06039 860-435-9871
Stephanie Magyar, prin. Fax 435-3925

Indian Mountain S 200/PK-9
211 Indian Mountain Rd 06039 860-435-0871
Jody Soja, head sch Fax 435-0641

Lebanon, New London
Lebanon SD 1,100/PK-12
891 Exeter Rd 06249 860-642-7795
Robert Angeli, supt. Fax 642-4589
www.lebanonct.org
Lebanon ES 400/PK-4
479 Exeter Rd 06249 860-642-7593
Rita Quiles-Glover, prin. Fax 642-3548
Lebanon MS 400/5-8
891 Exeter Rd 06249 860-642-4702
Robert Laskarzewski, prin. Fax 642-3534

Ledyard, New London
Ledyard SD 2,600/PK-12
4 Blonders Blvd 06339 860-464-9255
Jason Hartling, supt. Fax 464-8589
www.ledyard.net
Gallup Hill ES 400/K-6
169 Gallup Hill Rd 06339 860-536-9477
Dr. Pam Austen, prin. Fax 572-2788
Ledyard Center ES 400/K-6
740 Colonel Ledyard Hwy 06339 860-464-8080
Dr. Susan Nash-Ditzel, prin. Fax 464-5140
Other Schools – See Gales Ferry

Lisbon, New London, Pop. 3,790
Lisbon SD 400/PK-8
15 Newent Rd 06351 860-376-2403
Sally Keating, supt. Fax 376-1102
www.lisbonschool.org/
Lisbon Central S 400/PK-8
15 Newent Rd 06351 860-376-2403
Brian Apperson, prin. Fax 376-1102

Litchfield, Litchfield, Pop. 1,239
Litchfield SD 1,000/PK-12
PO Box 110 06759 860-567-7500
Sherri Turner, supt. Fax 567-7508
www.litchfieldschools.org
Center ES 300/PK-3
PO Box 110 06759 860-567-7510
Abe Ammary, prin. Fax 567-7518
Litchfield IS 200/4-6
PO Box 110 06759 860-567-7520
Jennifer Murphy, prin. Fax 567-7528
Litchfield MS 200/7-8
PO Box 110 06759 860-567-7540
Stephanie Kubisek, admin. Fax 567-7544

Regional SD 6 900/PK-12
98 Wamogo Rd 06759 860-567-7400
Christopher Leone, supt. Fax 567-6652
www.rsd6.org
Other Schools – See Goshen, Morris, Warren

Lyme, New London
Regional SD 18
Supt. — See Old Lyme
Lyme Consolidated ES 200/K-5
478 Hamburg Rd 06371 860-434-1233
James Cavalieri, prin. Fax 434-5735

Madison, New Haven, Pop. 15,485
Madison SD 3,300/K-12
PO Box 71 06443 203-245-6300
Thomas Scarice, supt. Fax 245-6336
www.madison.k12.ct.us

Brown MS 500/5-6
980 Durham Rd 06443 203-245-6400
Julianne Phelps, prin. Fax 245-6425
Island Avenue ES 300/K-4
20 Island Ave 06443 203-245-6450
Doreen O'Leary, prin. Fax 245-6456
Jeffrey ES 300/K-4
331 Copse Rd 06443 203-245-6460
Kathryn Hart, prin. Fax 245-6466
Polson MS 600/7-8
302 Green Hill Rd 06443 203-245-6480
Frank Henderson, prin. Fax 245-6494
Ryerson ES 200/K-4
982 Durham Rd 06443 203-245-6440
Kelly Spooner, prin. Fax 245-6446

Country S 200/PK-8
341 Opening Hill Rd 06443 203-421-3113
John Fixx, head sch Fax 421-4390
Our Lady of Mercy S 200/PK-8
149 Neck Rd 06443 203-245-4393
Cheryl Panzo, prin. Fax 245-3498

Manchester, Hartford, Pop. 29,743
Manchester SD 6,200/PK-12
45 N School St, 860-647-3441
Matt Geary, supt. Fax 647-5042
publicschools.manchesterct.gov
Bennet Academy 400/6-6
1151 Main St 06040 860-647-3571
Joseph Chella, prin. Fax 647-3577
Bowers ES 400/K-5
141 Princeton St, 860-647-3313
Mary Lou Ruggiero, prin. Fax 647-5001
Buckley ES 400/PK-5
250 Vernon St, 860-647-3302
Matt Daly, prin. Fax 647-5007
Highland Park ES 300/K-5
397 Porter St 06040 860-647-3430
Hassan Robinson, prin. Fax 647-6376
Illing MS 800/7-8
227 Middle Tpke E 06040 860-647-3400
Fax 647-5008
Keeney ES 300/PK-5
179 Keeney St 06040 860-647-3354
Julie Martin-Beauleau, prin. Fax 647-5043
Manchester Preschool 200/PK-PK
60 Washington St, 860-647-3502
Sinthia Sone-Moyano, prin. Fax 647-5046
Martin ES 300/K-5
140 Dartmouth Rd 06040 860-647-3367
Sophia Krisch, prin. Fax 647-3492
Robertson ES 400/K-5
65 N School St, 860-647-3372
Stuart Wolf, prin. Fax 647-6378
Verplanck ES 400/PK-5
126 Olcott St 06040 860-647-3383
Nicolas Jones, prin. Fax 647-5029
Waddell ES 300/K-5
163 Broad St, 860-647-3392
Kimberly Loveland, prin. Fax 647-6377
Washington ES 400/PK-5
94 Cedar St 06040 860-647-3332
Dr. Jim Collin, prin. Fax 647-5026

Cornerstone Christian S 200/PK-12
236 Main St, 860-643-0792
Tonya Snyder, head sch Fax 647-9291
St. Bridget S 200/PK-8
74 Main St, 860-649-7731
Mary Alice Nadaskay, prin. Fax 646-6936
St. James S 400/PK-8
73 Park St 06040 860-643-5088
Bridget Zorger, prin. Fax 649-6462

Mansfield Center, Tolland, Pop. 921
Mansfield SD
Supt. — See Storrs
Southeast ES 200/PK-4
134 Warrenville Rd 06250 860-423-2793
Lauren Rodriguez, prin. Fax 423-0610
Vinton ES 300/PK-4
306 Stafford Rd 06250 860-423-3086
Mike Seal, prin. Fax 456-4694

Oak Grove Montessori S 100/PK-6
132 Pleasant Valley Rd 06250 860-456-1031

Marlborough, Hartford
Marlborough SD 600/PK-6
25 School Dr 06447 860-295-6236
Dr. David Sklarz, supt. Fax 295-6153
www.marlborough.k12.ct.us
Thienes-Hall ES 600/PK-6
25 School Dr 06447 860-295-6220
Dan White, prin. Fax 295-6223

Meriden, New Haven, Pop. 59,747
Area Coop. Educational Services RESC
Supt. — See North Haven
Edison MS 700/6-8
1355 N Broad St 06450 203-639-8403
Karen Habegger, prin. Fax 639-8323

Meriden SD 8,100/PK-12
22 Liberty St 06450 203-630-4171
Mark Benigni Ed.D., supt. Fax 630-0110
www.meridenk12.org
Barry ES 500/K-5
124 Columbia St 06451 203-237-8831
Daniel Crispino, prin. Fax 630-4212
Franklin ES 400/K-5
426 W Main St 06451 203-235-7997
Joanne Conte, prin. Fax 630-4055
Hale ES 600/K-5
277 Atkins Street Ext 06450 203-237-7486
Karen Dahn, prin. Fax 630-4216
Hanover ES 600/K-5
208 Main St 06451 203-235-6359
Jennifer Kelley, prin. Fax 630-4099
Hooker ES 400/K-5
70 Overlook Dr 06450 203-237-8839
Louise Moss, prin. Fax 630-4114

Lincoln MS 800/6-8
164 Centennial Ave 06451 203-238-2381
Dianne Vumback, prin. Fax 238-7258
Pulaski ES 600/1-5
100 Clearview Ave 06450 203-238-1273
Daniel Coffey, prin. Fax 630-4144
Putnam ES 600/K-5
133 Parker Ave 06450 203-237-8493
Enza Adamcewicz, prin. Fax 630-4189
Sherman ES 500/PK-5
64 N Pearl St 06450 203-238-1286
Dr. Lysette Torres, prin. Fax 630-4199
Washington MS 800/6-8
1225 N Broad St 06450 203-235-6606
Raymond Southland, prin. Fax 235-6040

Our Lady of Mt. Carmel S 200/PK-8
115 Lewis Ave 06451 203-235-2959
Christa Chodkowski, prin. Fax 238-3629

Middlebury, New Haven, Pop. 4,100
Regional SD 15 4,000/PK-12
PO Box 395 06762 203-758-8259
Regina Botsford, supt. Fax 758-1908
www.region15.org
Long Meadow ES 600/PK-5
65 N Benson Rd 06762 203-758-1144
Christopher Wermuth, prin. Fax 758-1934
Memorial MS 500/6-8
PO Box 903 06762 203-758-2496
Jennifer Murphy, prin. Fax 758-9594
Middlebury ES 400/K-5
PO Box 1093 06762 203-758-2401
Heather Pellicone, prin. Fax 758-9918
Other Schools – See Southbury

Middlefield, Middlesex
Regional SD 13
Supt. — See Durham
Lyman ES 300/K-4
106 Way Rd 06455 860-349-7240
Thomas Ford, prin. Fax 349-7242
Middlefield Memorial MS 300/4-6
PO Box 446 06455 860-349-7235
Debra Stone, prin. Fax 349-7246

Independent Day S 200/PK-8
PO Box 451 06455 860-347-7235
Dr. Marijke Kehrhahn, head sch Fax 347-8852

Middletown, Middlesex, Pop. 46,173
Middletown SD 4,800/PK-12
311 Hunting Hill Ave 06457 860-638-1401
Patricia Charles Ed.D., supt. Fax 638-1495
www.middletownschools.org
Bielefield ES 300/K-5
70 Maynard St 06457 860-347-4124
Jeff Fournier, prin. Fax 347-4284
Farm Hill ES 400/K-5
390 Ridge Rd 06457 860-346-1225
Jennifer Calabrese, prin. Fax 343-0918
Keigwin MS 300/6-6
99 Spruce St 06457 860-632-2433
Silvia Mayo Molina, prin. Fax 632-2032
Lawrence ES 300/K-5
Kaplan Dr 06457 860-632-2158
James Gaudreau, prin. Fax 632-0738
Macdonough ES 200/K-5
66 Spring St 06457 860-347-8553
Damian Reardon, prin. Fax 346-7684
Moody ES 300/K-5
300 Country Club Rd 06457 860-347-2561
Yolande Eldridge, prin. Fax 347-5688
Snow ES 400/PK-5
299 Wadsworth St 06457 860-347-2579
Jennifer Cannata, prin. Fax 638-3748
Spencer ES 300/K-5
207 Westfield St 06457 860-344-0711
Richard Henderson, prin. Fax 344-0490
Wesley ES 300/K-5
10 Wesleyan Hills Rd 06457 860-344-0381
Thomas Cannata, prin. Fax 346-5653
Wilson MS 700/7-8
370 Hunting Hill Ave 06457 860-347-8594
Cheryl Gonzales, prin. Fax 347-2158

St. John Paul II Regional S 200/PK-8
87 S Main St 06457 860-347-2978
Dr. Larry Fitzgerald, prin. Fax 347-7767

Milford, New Haven, Pop. 50,507
Milford SD 6,500/PK-12
70 W River St 06460 203-783-3400
Dr. Elizabeth E. Feser, supt. Fax 783-3475
www.milforded.org
Calf Pen Meadow ES 300/K-5
395 Welchs Point Rd 06460 203-783-3521
Amy Fedigan, prin. Fax 783-3680
East Shore MS 500/6-8
240 Chapel St 06460 203-783-3559
Catherine Williams, prin. Fax 301-5060
Harborside MS 600/6-8
175 High St 06460 203-783-3523
Steve Gottlieb, prin. Fax 783-3687
Kennedy ES 400/PK-5
404 West Ave, 203-783-3568
Sean Smyth, prin. Fax 783-3688
Live Oaks ES 300/PK-5
575 Merwin Ave 06460 203-783-3564
Rose Marzinotto, prin. Fax 783-3616
Mathewson ES 400/K-5
466 W River St, 203-783-3527
Melissa Currier, prin. Fax 783-3563
Meadowside ES 500/K-5
80 Seemans Ln 06460 203-783-3555
Gail Krois, prin. Fax 783-4826
Orange Avenue ES 400/PK-5
260 Orange Ave, 203-783-3537
Joe Apicella, prin. Fax 783-3619
Orchard Hills ES 300/PK-5
185 Marino Dr 06460 203-783-3566
Clifford Dudley, prin. Fax 783-3716

Pumpkin Delight ES 400/K-5
24 Art St 06460 203-783-3531
Carrie Keramis, prin. Fax 783-3696
West Shore MS 500/6-8
70 Kay Ave 06460 203-783-3553
Paul Cavanna, prin. Fax 783-4827

New England S of Montessori 100/PK-6
40 Quirk Rd 06460 203-878-9822
St. Mary S 300/PK-8
72 Gulf St 06460 203-878-6539
Frank Lacerenza, prin. Fax 878-1866

Monroe, Fairfield
Monroe SD 3,400/PK-12
375 Monroe Tpke 06468 203-452-2860
John Battista, supt. Fax 452-5818
www.monroeps.org
Fawn Hollow ES 500/K-5
345 Fan Hill Rd 06468 203-452-2923
Rebecca Kosisko, prin. Fax 452-2444
Jockey Hollow S 800/6-8
365 Fan Hill Rd 06468 203-452-2905
John Ceccolini, prin. Fax 452-2444
Monroe ES 400/PK-5
375 Monroe Tpke 06468 203-452-2870
Debra Kovachi, prin. Fax 452-5868
Stepney ES 500/K-5
180 Old Newtown Rd 06468 203-452-2885
Bruce Lazar, prin. Fax 452-5873

Moodus, Middlesex, Pop. 1,397
East Haddam SD 1,200/PK-12
26 Plains Rd 06469 860-873-5090
Brian Reas, supt. Fax 873-5092
www.easthaddamschools.org
East Haddam ES 300/PK-3
PO Box 425 06469 860-873-5076
Joanne Collins, prin. Fax 873-5155
Hale-Ray MS 500/4-8
PO Box 363 06469 860-873-5081
Jason Peacock, prin. Fax 873 5086

Moosup, Windham, Pop. 3,159
Plainfield SD
Supt. — See Plainfield
Moosup ES 300/PK-3
35 Church St 06354 860-564-6430
Colleen Lugauskas, prin. Fax 564-6175

Morris, Litchfield
Regional SD 6
Supt. — See Litchfield
Morris ES 100/PK-6
10 East St 06763 860-567-7420
KC Chapman, prin. Fax 567-7425

Mystic, New London, Pop. 4,136
Groton SD 4,700/PK-12
1300 Flanders Rd 06355 860-572-2100
Dr. Michael Graner Ph.D., supt. Fax 572-2107
www.groton.k12.ct.us
Butler ES 300/PK-5
155 Ocean View Ave 06355 860-572-5825
Steven Wheeler, prin. Fax 572-5827
Cutler MS 400/6-8
160 Fishtown Rd 06355 860-572-5830
Peter Bass, prin. Fax 572-5834
Northeast Academy Arts Magnet S 400/K-5
115 Oslo St 06355 860-572-5852
Paul Esposito, prin. Fax 572-5869
Other Schools – See Groton

Stonington SD
Supt. — See Old Mystic
Mystic MS 400/5-8
204 Mistuxet Ave 06355 860-536-9613
Gregory Keith, prin. Fax 536-4508

Naugatuck, New Haven, Pop. 31,134
Naugatuck SD 4,200/PK-12
497 Rubber Ave 06770 203-720-5265
Sharon Locke, supt. Fax 720-5434
www.naugy.net
Andrew Avenue ES 200/K-4
140 Andrew Ave 06770 203-720-5221
Taran Gruber, prin. Fax 720-5213
Central Avenue Preschool 50/PK-PK
28 Central Ave 06770 203-720-5224
Jackie Bacon, prin. Fax 720-5214
City Hill MS 700/7-8
441 City Hill St 06770 203-720-5250
Eileen Mezzo, prin. Fax 720-5256
Cross Street IS 300/5-6
120 Cross St 06770 203-720-5227
Melissa Cooney, prin. Fax 720-5215
Hillside IS 400/5-6
51 Hillside Ave 06770 203-720-5260
Johnna Hunt, prin. Fax 720-5209
Hop Brook ES 300/K-4
75 Crown St 06770 203-720-5232
Kathryn Taylor, prin. Fax 720-5234
Maple Hill ES 500/PK-4
641 Maple Hill Rd 06770 203-720-5236
Cheryl Kane, prin. Fax 720-5217
Salem ES 300/K-4
124 Meadow St 06770 203-720-5242
Jennifer Kruge, prin. Fax 720-5219
Western ES 300/K-4
100 Pine St 06770 203-720-5244
Brenda Goodrich, prin. Fax 720-5220

St. Francis - St. Hedwig S 300/PK-8
294 Church St 06770 203-729-2247
Dr. John Alfone, prin. Fax 729-0512

New Britain, Hartford, Pop. 71,606
New Britain SD 9,500/PK-12
PO Box 1960 06050 860-827-2200
Nancy Sarra, supt. Fax 612-1533
www.csdnb.org
Chamberlain ES 500/K-5
120 Newington Ave 06051 860-832-5691
Jane Perez, prin. Fax 224-1597

DiLoreto Elementary & MS 800/PK-8
732 Slater Rd 06053 860-223-2885
Alejandro Ortiz, prin. Fax 832-5685
Gaffney ES 600/PK-5
322 Slater Rd 06053 860-225-6247
Anita Fazio, prin. Fax 225-1128
HALS Academy 200/6-8
40 Goodwin St 06051 860-826-1866
Elizabeth Crooks, prin. Fax 826-1867
Holmes ES 500/PK-5
2150 Stanley St 06053 860-223-8294
Mitchell Page, prin. Fax 832-9666
Jefferson ES 400/K-5
140 Horseplain Rd 06053 860-223-8007
Wanda Lickwar, prin. Fax 225-1646
Lincoln ES 700/PK-5
145 Steele St 06052 860-229-2564
Lisa Torres, prin. Fax 225-1638
Northend ES 300/K-5
160 Bassett St 06051 860-223-3819
Talisha Foy, prin. Fax 225-1660
Pulaski MS 600/6-8
755 Farmington Ave 06053 860-225-7665
Mark Fernandes, prin. Fax 223-3840
Roosevelt Early Learning Center PK-PK
40 Goodwin St 06051 860-827-2017
Terry Turcotte, prin.
Slade MS 600/6-8
183 Steele St 06052 860-225-6395
Todd Verdi, prin. Fax 826-7894
Smalley Academy 700/K-5
221 Farmington Ave 06051 860-225-8647
Elsa Saavedra, prin. Fax 225-8044
Smith ES 600/K-5
142 Rutherford St 06051 860-223-1574
Karen Falvey, prin. Fax 832-5682
Vance ES 500/K-5
183 Vance St 06052 860-225-8731
Sarah Harris, prin. Fax 225-1019

Sacred Heart S 200/PK-8
35 Orange St 06053 860-229-7663
Katherine Muller, prin. Fax 832-6098
St. Matthew Lutheran S 50/K-8
87 Franklin Sq 06051 860-223-7829
Martin Boettner, admin. Fax 223-7829

New Canaan, Fairfield, Pop. 17,864

New Canaan SD 4,200/PK-12
39 Locust Ave 06840 203-594-4000
Dr. Bryan D. Luizzi, supt. Fax 594-4035
www.newcanaan.k12.ct.us
East ES 500/K-4
54 Little Brook Rd 06840 203-594-4200
Kristine Woleck, prin. Fax 594-4215
Saxe MS 1,300/5-8
468 South Ave 06840 203-594-4500
Greg Macedo, prin. Fax 594-4565
South ES 500/K-4
8 Farm Rd 06840 203-594-4300
Joanne Rocco, prin. Fax 594-4314
West ES 500/PK-4
769 Ponus Rdg 06840 203-594-4400
Jan Murphy, prin. Fax 594-4412

New Canaan Country S 600/PK-9
635 Frogtown Rd 06840 203-972-0771
Dr. Robert P. Macrae, head sch Fax 966-5924
St. Aloysius S 200/K-8
33 South Ave 06840 203-966-0786
Bardhyl Gjoka, prin. Fax 972-6960

New Fairfield, Fairfield, Pop. 12,911

New Fairfield SD 2,700/PK-12
3 Brush Hill Rd 06812 203-312-5770
Dr. Alicia Roy, supt. Fax 312-5609
www.newfairfieldschools.org
Consolidated ES 500/PK-2
12 Gillotti Rd 06812 203-312-5940
Rob Spino, prin. Fax 312-5942
Meeting House Hill ES 600/3-5
24 Gillotti Rd 06812 203-312-5905
James Mandracchia, prin. Fax 312-5907
New Fairfield MS 600/6-8
56 Gillotti Rd 06812 203-312-5885
Christine Baldelli, prin. Fax 312-5887

New Hartford, Litchfield, Pop. 5,769

New Hartford SD 500/PK-6
PO Box 315 06057 860-379-8546
Brian Murphy, supt. Fax 738-1766
www.newhtfd.org
Antolini ES 300/3-6
30 Antolini Rd 06057 860-489-4169
Amanda Shaw, prin. Fax 489-0392
Bakerville Consolidated ES 100/K-2
51 Cedar Ln 06057 860-482-0288
Dr. Roxanne Pangallo, prin. Fax 482-1905
New Hartford ES 100/PK-2
PO Box 367 06057 860-379-0713
Dr. Roxanne Pangallo, prin. Fax 379-6762

New Haven, New Haven, Pop. 126,396

New Haven SD 20,300/PK-12
54 Meadow St 06519 475-220-1000
Dr. Reginald Mayo, supt. Fax 946-7300
www.nhps.net
Barnard Envioronmental Studies Magnet S 600/PK-8
170 Derby Ave 06511 475-220-3500
Dr. Belinda Carberry, prin. Fax 936-5235
Beecher Museum S of Arts & Sciences 500/PK-8
100 Jewell St 06515 475-220-3800
Kathy Russell-Beck, prin. Fax 220-3805
Bishop Woods S 500/PK-8
1481 Quinnipiac Ave 06513 475-220-7300
Rosalind Garcia, prin. Fax 220-7305
Brennan/Rogers S of Arts and Sciences 200/PK-2
199 Wilmot Rd 06515 475-220-2250
Dr. Gail DeBlasio, prin. Fax 946-5404
Brennan/Rogers S of Arts and Sciences 200/3-8
200 Wilmot Rd 06515 475-220-2200
Dr. Gail DeBlasio, prin. Fax 946-7516
Celentano Biotech Health Magnet S 400/PK-8
400 Canner St 06511 475-220-3400
Keisha Hannans, prin. Fax 946-5064
Clemente Leadership Academy 500/PK-8
360 Columbus Ave 06519 475-220-7600
Pamela Franco, prin. Fax 220-7605
Clinton Avenue S 600/K-8
293 Clinton Ave 06513 475-220-3300
Kristina DeNegre, prin. Fax 946-5034
Columbus Family Academy 400/PK-8
255 Blatchley Ave 06513 475-220-2500
Roy Araujo, prin. Fax 220-2505
Conte/West Hills Magnet S 600/PK-8
511 Chapel St 06511 475-220-5400
Dianne Spence, prin. Fax 946-8802
Daniels S of Intl Communication 500/PK-8
569 Congress Ave 06519 475-220-3600
Daniel Bonet-Ojeda, prin. Fax 220-3605
Davis Street Arts and Academics S 500/PK-8
35 Davis St 06515 475-220-7800
Sequella Coleman, prin. Fax 220-7805
Edgewood Magnet S 400/K-8
737 Edgewood Ave 06515 475-220-8000
Shanta Smith, prin. Fax 946-8957
Fair Haven S 800/PK-8
164 Grand Ave 06513 475-220-2600
Heriberto Cordero, prin. Fax 220-2697
Hale S 600/PK-8
480 Townsend Ave 06512 475-220-4200
Tara Cass, prin. Fax 946-7331
Hill Central Music Academy 200/PK-8
140 Dewitt St 06519 475-220-6100
Jaime Ramos, prin. Fax 220-6106
Hooker ES 200/K-2
180 Canner St 06511 475-220-3700
Dr. Evelyn Robles-Rivas, prin. Fax 220-3705
Hooker MS 300/3-8
691 Whitney Ave 06511 475-220-7200
Dr. Evelyn Robles-Rivas, prin. Fax 220-7205
Jepson Magnet S 500/PK-8
15 Lexington Ave 06513 475-220-2900
Lesley Stancarone, prin. Fax 220-2905
King/Robinson Magnet S 600/PK-8
150 Fournier St 06511 475-220-2700
Dr. Joseph Johnson, prin. Fax 220-2786
Lincoln-Bassett S 300/PK-6
130 Bassett St 06511 475-220-8500
Jenny Clarino, prin. Fax 492-5607
Martinez S 500/PK-8
100 James St 06513 475-220-2000
Luis Menacho, prin. Fax 220-2095
Mauro-Sheridan Sci Tech & Comm Magnet S 500/PK-8
191 Fountain St 06515 475-220-2800
Sandra Kalizewski, prin. Fax 220-2805
Quinnipiac Real World Math STEM S 300/K-4
460 Lexington Ave 06513 475-220-4700
Grace Nathman, prin. Fax 946-5525
Ross Arts Magnet S 500/5-8
150 Kimberly Ave 06519 475-220-5300
Shawn True, prin. Fax 946-5824
Ross/Woodward S 700/PK-8
185 Barnes Ave 06513 475-220-3100
Cheryl Brown, prin. Fax 220-3170
Strong 21st Century Communications S 500/K-4
130 Orchard St 06519 475-220-4800
Susan DeNicola, prin. Fax 946-2322
Troup S 500/PK-8
259 Edgewood Ave 06511 475-220-3000
Monica Joyner, prin. Fax 220-3005
Truman S 500/PK-8
114 Truman St 06519 475-220-2100
Kathleen Mattern, prin. Fax 220-2193
West Rock STREAM Academy 200/PK-4
311 Valley St 06515 475-220-4900
Rosalyn Bannon, prin. Fax 946-5794
Wexler/Grant S 400/PK-8
55 Foote St 06511 475-220-5600
David Diah, prin. Fax 220-5605
Other Schools – See Hamden

Cold Spring S 100/PK-6
263 Chapel St 06513 203-787-1584
Arati Pandit, dir. Fax 787-9444
Foote S 500/K-9
50 Loomis Pl 06511 203-777-3464
Carol Maoz, head sch Fax 777-2809
St. Aedan and St. Brendan S 200/PK-8
351 McKinley Ave 06515 203-387-5693
Michael Votto, prin. Fax 387-1609
St. Bernadette S 100/PK-8
20 Burr St 06512 203-469-2271
Edward Goad, prin. Fax 469-4615
St. Francis & St. Rose of Lima S 200/PK-8
423 Ferry St 06513 203-777-5352
Taryn Duncan, prin. Fax 865-1271
St. Martin de Porres Academy 100/5-8
208 Columbus Ave 06519 203-772-2424
Dr. Kelly O'Leary, prin. Fax 772-2425
St. Thomas's Day S 100/K-6
830 Whitney Ave 06511 203-776-2123
Gina Panza, head sch Fax 776-3467
Yeshiva ES 50/PK-8
765 Elm St 06511 203-777-2200

Newington, Hartford, Pop. 30,076

Newington SD 4,200/PK-12
131 Cedar St 06111 860-665-8610
Dr. William C. Collins, supt. Fax 665-8616
www.npsct.org
Chaffee ES 400/K-4
160 Superior Ave 06111 860-666-4687
Beverly Lawrence, prin. Fax 667-5847
Green ES 300/PK-4
30 Thomas St 06111 860-666-3394
James Marciano, prin. Fax 667-5843
Kellogg MS 600/5-8
155 Harding Ave 06111 860-666-5418
Jason Lambert, prin. Fax 666-5925
Paterson ES 400/PK-4
120 Church St 06111 860-666-4657
Michael Gaydos, prin. Fax 667-5853
Reynolds ES 500/PK-4
85 Reservoir Rd 06111 860-521-7830
Jason Smith, prin. Fax 561-9725
Wallace MS 700/5-8
71 Halleran Dr 06111 860-667-5888
David Milardo, prin. Fax 667-5893

New London, New London, Pop. 26,373

Learn RESC
Supt. — See Old Lyme
Regional Multicultural Magnet S 500/K-5
1 Bulkeley Pl 06320 860-437-7775
Susan Iwanicki, prin. Fax 437-1475

New London SD 3,200/PK-12
134 Williams St 06320 860-447-6000
Dr. Stephen Tracy, supt. Fax 447-6017
www.newlondon.org
Hale Arts Magnet S 500/PK-5
37 Beech Dr 06320 860-447-6060
Carlos Leal, prin. Fax 447-6066
Harbor S 100/PK-5
432 Montauk Ave 06320 860-447-6040
Jason Foster, coord. Fax 447-6046
Jackson MS 600/6-8
36 Waller St 06320 860-437-6480
Dr. Alison Burdick, dir. Fax 437-6494
Jennings ES 600/PK-5
50 Mercer St 06320 860-447-6050
Jose Ortiz, prin. Fax 437-6267
Winthrop STEM Magnet ES 500/PK-5
74 Grove St 06320 860-447-6070
Michele Han, prin. Fax 447-6076

St. Joseph S 200/K-8
25 Squire St 06320 860-442-1720
Marianne Cote, prin. Fax 443-5247

New Milford, Litchfield, Pop. 6,408

New Milford SD 3,500/PK-12
50 East St 06776 860-355-8406
Joshua Smith, supt. Fax 210-4132
www.newmilfordps.org
Hill & Plain ES 400/PK-2
60 Old Town Park Rd 06776 860-354-5430
Paula Kelleher, prin. Fax 355-3568
Noble IS 700/3-5
25 Sunny Valley Rd 06776 860-210-4020
Anne Bilko, prin. Fax 210-4030
Northville ES 300/PK-2
22 Hipp Rd 06776 860-355-3713
Susan Murray, prin. Fax 350-4234
Schaghticoke MS 700/6-8
23 Hipp Rd 06776 860-354-2204
Dr. Christopher Longo, prin. Fax 210-2216

Faith Preparatory S 100/K-12
600 Danbury Rd Ste 2 06776 860-210-3677
Jaclyn Mattison, prin. Fax 210-3685

New Preston, Litchfield, Pop. 1,162

Washington Montessori S 200/PK-8
240 Litchfield Tpke 06777 860-868-0551
Patricia Werner, head sch Fax 868-1362

Newtown, Fairfield, Pop. 1,929

Newtown SD 4,500/PK-12
3 Primrose St 06470 203-426-7600
Dr. Joseph Erardi Ed.D., supt. Fax 270-6199
www.newtown.k12.ct.us
Hawley ES 300/K-4
29 Church Hill Rd 06470 203-426-7666
Christopher Moretti, prin. Fax 270-6543
Head O'Meadow ES 300/K-4
94 Boggs Hill Rd 06470 203-426-7670
Barbara Gasparine, prin. Fax 270-4559
Middle Gate ES 400/K-4
7 Cold Spring Rd 06470 203-426-7662
Christopher Geissler, prin. Fax 426-7896
Newtown MS 900/7-8
11 Queen St 06470 203-426-7642
Thomas Einhorn, prin. Fax 270-6102
Reed IS 800/5-6
3 Trades Ln 06470 203-270-4880
Anne Uberti, prin. Fax 270-4899
Other Schools – See Sandy Hook

Fraser-Woods Montessori S 200/PK-8
173 S Main St 06470 203-426-3390
Chris Robertson, head sch Fax 426-0692
Housatonic Valley Waldorf S 100/PK-8
40 Dodgingtown Rd 06470 203-364-1113
Alex Exley, admin. Fax 364-0630
St. Rose of Lima S 500/PK-8
40 Church Hill Rd 06470 203-426-5102
Sr. Colleen Smith, prin. Fax 426-5374

Niantic, New London, Pop. 3,074

East Lyme SD
Supt. — See East Lyme
East Lyme MS 900/5-8
31 Society Rd 06357 860-739-4491
Dr. Judy DeLeeuw, prin. Fax 691-5400
Haynes ES 300/PK-4
29 Society Rd 06357 860-739-2922
Melissa DeLoreto, prin. Fax 739-1527
Niantic Center ES 200/K-4
7 W Main St 06357 860-739-3961
Jeffrey Provost, prin. Fax 739-1258

Norfolk, Litchfield, Pop. 546

Norfolk SD 100/PK-6
128 Greenwoods Rd E 06058 860-542-5286
Dr. Mary Beth Iacobelli, supt. Fax 542-5770
www.botelleschool.org
Botelle ES 100/PK-6
128 Greenwoods Rd E 06058 860-542-5286
Lauren Valentino, prin. Fax 542-5770

North Branford, New Haven, Pop. 12,996

North Branford SD
Supt. — See Northford

Harrison ES 400/K-2
335 Foxon Rd 06471 203-484-1235
Elizabeth Parker, prin. Fax 484-1237
North Branford IS 500/6-8
654 Foxon Rd 06471 203-484-1500
Keith O'Rourke, prin. Fax 484-1505

Northfield, Litchfield

Litchfield Montessori S 100/PK-6
5 Knife Shop Rd 06778 860-283-5920

Northford, New Haven, Pop. 3,200
North Branford SD 2,000/K-12
PO Box 129 06472 203-484-1440
Scott Schoonmaker, supt. Fax 484-1445
www.northbranfordschools.org
Totoket Valley ES 500/3-5
1388 Middletown Ave 06472 203-484-1455
Dr. Carter Welch, prin. Fax 484-6090
Other Schools – See North Branford

North Franklin, New London
Franklin SD 200/PK-8
206 Pond Rd 06254 860-642-6113
Dr. Larry Fenn, supt. Fax 642-7256
www.franklinschoolct.org
Franklin S 200/PK-8
206 Pond Rd 06254 860-642-7063
Dr. KellyAnn Graves, prin. Fax 642-7241

North Grosvenordale, Windham, Pop. 1,481
Thompson SD 1,100/PK-12
785 Riverside Dr 06255 860-923-9581
Melinda Smith M.Ed., supt. Fax 923-9638
www.thompsonk12.org
Fisher ES 400/PK-4
785 Riverside Dr 06255 860-923-9142
Noveline Beltram, prin. Fax 923-2062
Thompson MS 300/5-8
785 Riverside Dr 06255 860-923-9380
Christopher Scott, prin. Fax 923-9638

St. Joseph S 100/PK-8
PO Box 137 06255 860-923-2090
Sharon Briere, prin. Fax 923-3609

North Haven, New Haven, Pop. 23,822
Area Coop. Educational Services RESC 2,100/
350 State St 06473 203-498-6800
Thomas Danehy Ed.D., dir. Fax 498-6890
www.aces.org
Other Schools – See Hamden, Meriden

North Haven SD 3,400/PK-12
5 Linsley St 06473 203-239-2581
Robert Cronin Ph.D., supt. Fax 234-9811
www.north-haven.k12.ct.us/
Clintonville ES 300/K-5
456 Clintonville Rd 06473 203-239-5865
Lauretta Dowling, prin. Fax 239-4009
Green Acres ES 400/PK-5
146 Upper State St 06473 203-239-5387
Laurie Bankowski, prin. Fax 239-4773
Montowese ES 300/K-5
145 Fitch St 06473 203-239-2564
Kathryn Russo, prin. Fax 234-7205
North Haven MS 800/6-8
55 Bailey Rd 06473 203-239-1683
Philip Piazza, prin. Fax 234-2846
Ridge Road ES 400/K-5
1341 Ridge Rd 06473 203-248-4050
Patrick Stirk, prin. Fax 407-1816

North Stonington, New London
North Stonington SD 800/PK-12
297 Norwich Westerly Rd 06359 860-535-2800
Peter Nero, supt. Fax 535-1470
www.northstonington.k12.ct.us
North Stonington ES 400/PK-5
311 Norwich Westerly Rd 06359 860-535-2805
Veronica Wilkison, prin. Fax 535-4641
Wheeler MS 200/6-8
298 Norwich Westerly Rd 06359 860-535-0377
Kristen St. Germain, prin. Fax 535-2536

North Stonington Christian Academy 100/PK-12
12 Stillman Rd 06359 860-599-5071
Pamela Wilkinson, dir. Fax 599-2815

North Windham, Windham
Windham SD
Supt. — See Willimantic
North Windham ES 500/K-5
112 Jordan Ln 06256 860-465-2400
Elizabeth Bumgardner, prin. Fax 465-2403
STEM Academy 300/K-8
141 Tuckie Rd 06256 860-465-2610
Alan Cox, prin. Fax 942-8736

Norwalk, Fairfield, Pop. 84,099
Norwalk SD 10,900/PK-12
PO Box 6001 06852 203-854-4000
Dr. Steven Adamowski, supt. Fax 838-3299
www.norwalkps.org
Brookside ES 400/K-5
382 Highland Ave 06854 203-899-2830
Sandra Faioes, prin. Fax 899-2834
Columbus ES 300/K-5
46 Concord St 06854 203-899-2840
Medard Thomas, prin. Fax 899-2844
Cranbury ES 500/PK-5
10 Knowalot Ln 06851 203-846-3600
Kristin Goldstein, prin. Fax 899-2854
Fox Run ES 400/PK-5
228 Fillow St 06850 203-899-2860
James Martinez, prin. Fax 899-2864
Hale MS 600/6-8
170 Strawberry Hill Ave 06851 203-899-2910
Dr. Albert Sackey, prin. Fax 899-2914
Jefferson Science Magnet ES 600/K-5
75 Van Buren Ave 06850 203-899-2870
Nicholas Brophy, prin. Fax 899-2874

Kendall ES 600/PK-5
57 Fillow St 06850 203-899-2880
Zakiyyah Baker, prin. Fax 899-2884
Marvin ES 500/PK-5
15 Calf Pasture Beach Rd 06855 203-899-2890
Sue O'Shea, prin. Fax 899-2894
Naramake ES 400/K-5
16 King St 06851 203-899-2900
Jane Wilkins, prin. Fax 899-2904
Ponus Ridge MS 600/6-8
21 Hunters Ln 06850 203-847-3557
Dr. Damon Lewis, prin. Fax 899-2924
Roton MS 400/6-8
201 Highland Ave 06853 203-899-2930
Joseph Vellucci, prin. Fax 899-2934
Rowayton ES 500/K-5
1 Roton Ave 06853 203-899-2940
Sara Reilly, prin. Fax 899-2944
Silvermine ES 500/K-5
157 Perry Ave 06850 203-899-2950
Ivette Ellis, prin. Fax 899-2954
Tracey ES 400/K-5
20 Camp St 06851 203-899-2960
Theresa Rangel, prin. Fax 899-2964
West Rocks MS 700/6-8
81 W Rocks Rd 06851 203-899-2970
Dr. Lynne Moore, prin. Fax 899-2974
Wolfpit ES 300/PK-5
1 Starlight Dr 06851 203-899-2980
Jennnifer Masone, prin. Fax 899-2984

All Saints S 500/PK-8
139 W Rocks Rd 06851 203-847-3881
Linda Dunn, prin. Fax 847-8055

Norwich, New London, Pop. 38,601
Norwich SD 3,200/PK-8
90 Town St 06360 860-823-4245
Abby I. Dolliver, supt. Fax 823-1880
www.norwichpublicschools.org
Bishop Early Learning Center 200/PK-PK
526 E Main St 06360 860-823-4201
Lynn DePina, dir. Fax 823-4220
Case Street Early Learning Center 100/PK-PK
30 Case St 06360 860-892-4354
Lynn DePina, dir.
Huntington ES 400/K-5
80 W Town St 06360 860-823-4204
Siobhan O'Connor, prin. Fax 823-4241
Kelly MS 400/7-8
25 Mahan Dr 06360 860-823-4211
William Peckrul, prin. Fax 892-4302
Mahan ES 300/PK-5
94 Salem Tpke 06360 860-823-4205
Donna Funk, prin. Fax 823-4235
Moriarty ES 400/K-5
20 Lawler Ln 06360 860-823-4206
Rebecca Pellerin, prin. Fax 823-4246
Stanton ES 400/K-5
386 New London Tpke 06360 860-823-4207
Billie Shea, prin. Fax 823-4250
Teachers Memorial MS 200/6-6
15 Teachers Dr 06360 860-823-4212
Alexandria Lazzari, prin. Fax 823-4277
Uncas ES 300/K-5
280 Elizabeth Street Ext 06360 860-823-4208
Peter Camp, prin. Fax 823-4251
Veterans Memorial ES 300/K-5
80 Crouch Ave 06360 860-823-4209
Adam Rosenberg, prin. Fax 823-4252
Other Schools – See Taftville

Montessori Discovery S 100/PK-6
218 Dudley St 06360 860-889-0340
St. Patrick Cathedral S 200/K-8
211 Broadway 06360 860-889-4174
Catherine Reed, prin. Fax 889-0040
Wildwood Christian S 100/PK-8
35 Wawecus Hill Rd 06360 860-887-7830
Katherine Anderson, prin. Fax 885-1835

Oakdale, New London
Montville SD 2,400/PK-12
800 Old Colchester Rd 06370 860-848-1228
Brian Levesque, supt. Fax 848-0589
www.montvilleschools.org
Murphy ES 400/K-5
500 Chesterfield Rd 06370 860-848-9241
Amy Espinoza, prin. Fax 848-1703
Oakdale ES 400/PK-5
30 Indiana Cir 06370 860-859-1800
Jill Mazzalupo, prin. Fax 859-2170
Tyl MS 600/6-8
166 Chesterfield Rd 06370 860-848-2822
Mary Jane Dix, prin. Fax 848-8854
Other Schools – See Uncasville

Oakville, Litchfield, Pop. 8,924
Watertown SD
Supt. — See Watertown
Polk ES 300/3-5
435 Buckingham St 06779 860-945-4840
Lisa Fekete, prin. Fax 945-7113
Swift MS 700/6-8
250 Colonial St 06779 860-945-4830
Marylu Lerz, prin. Fax 945-6449
Trumbull PS 700/PK-2
779 Buckingham St 06779 860-945-2776
Laura Meka, prin. Fax 945-2781

St. Mary Magdalen S 300/PK-8
140 Buckingham St 06779 860-945-0621
Deborah Mulhall, prin. Fax 945-6162

Old Greenwich, Fairfield, Pop. 6,474
Greenwich SD
Supt. — See Greenwich
Old Greenwich ES 400/PK-5
285 Sound Beach Ave 06870 203-637-0150
Jennifer Bencivengo, prin. Fax 637-4666

Old Lyme, New London
Learn RESC 2,100/
44 Hatchetts Hill Rd 06371 860-434-4800
Dr. Eileen Howley, dir. Fax 434-4837
www.learn.k12.ct.us
Other Schools – See East Hartford, New London, Waterford

Regional SD 18 1,200/K-12
49 Lyme St 06371 860-434-7238
Ian Neviaser, supt. Fax 434-9959
www.region18.org
Lyme-Old Lyme MS 400/6-8
53 Lyme St 06371 860-434-2568
Mark Ambruso, prin. Fax 434-0717
Mile Creek ES 200/K-5
205 Mile Creek Rd 06371 860-434-2209
Patricia Downes, prin. Fax 434-8347
Other Schools – See Lyme

Old Mystic, New London, Pop. 3,422
Stonington SD 2,300/K-12
PO Box 479 06372 860-572-0506
Dr. Van Riley, supt. Fax 572-8155
www.stoningtonschools.org
Other Schools – See Mystic, Pawcatuck, Stonington

Old Saybrook, Middlesex, Pop. 9,552
Old Saybrook SD 1,400/PK-12
50 Sheffield St 06475 860-395-3157
Jan Perruccio, supt. Fax 395-3162
www.oldsaybrookschools.org
Goodwin ES 400/PK-3
80 Old Boston Post Rd 06475 860-395-3165
Heston Sutman, prin. Fax 395-3360
Old Saybrook MS 600/4-8
60 Sheffield St 06475 860-395-3168
Mandy Ryan, prin. Fax 395-3350

Children's Tree Montessori S 100/PK-6
96 Essex Rd 06475 860-388-3536
St. John S 200/PK-8
42 Maynard Rd 06475 860-388-0849
Sr. Elaine Moorcraft, prin. Fax 388-6265

Orange, New Haven, Pop. 13,774
Orange SD 1,200/PK-6
637 Orange Center Rd 06477 203-891-8020
Dr. Vince Scarpetti, supt. Fax 891-8025
www.oess.org/
Peck Place ES 400/1-6
500 Peck Ln 06477 203-891-8034
Eric E. Carbone, prin. Fax 891-8038
Race Brook ES 400/1-6
107 Grannis Rd 06477 203-891-8030
Michael Gray, prin. Fax 891-8044
Tracy S 100/PK-K
650 Schoolhouse Ln 06477 203-891-8028
Kai Byrd, prin. Fax 795-2119
Turkey Hill ES 300/1-6
441 Turkey Hill Rd 06477 203-891-8040
Denise Arterbery, prin. Fax 891-8043

Regional SD 5
Supt. — See Woodbridge
Amity Regional MS 400/7-8
100 Ohman Ave 06477 203-392-3200
Kathleen Fuller-Cutler, prin. Fax 387-7603

Southern Connecticut Hebrew Academy 100/PK-8
261 Derby Ave 06477 203-795-5261

Oxford, New Haven
Oxford SD 2,000/PK-12
1 Great Hill Rd 06478 203-888-7754
Anna Ortiz, supt. Fax 888-5955
www.oxfordpublicschools.org
Great Oak MS 500/6-8
50 Great Oak Rd 06478 203-888-5418
Anthony Hibbert, prin. Fax 888-7798
Oxford Center S 500/3-5
462 Oxford Rd 06478 203-888-6492
Heath Hendershot, prin. Fax 881-5212
Quaker Farms ES 400/PK-2
30 Great Oak Rd 06478 203-888-5842
Rachael Cacace, prin. Fax 888-6813

Pawcatuck, New London, Pop. 5,474
Stonington SD
Supt. — See Old Mystic
Pawcatuck MS 300/5-8
40 Field St 06379 860-599-5696
Tim Smith, prin. Fax 599-8948
West Broad Street ES 100/3-4
131 W Broad St 06379 860-599-5633
Alicia Dawe, prin. Fax 599-0611
West Vine Street ES 200/K-2
17 W Vine St 06379 860-599-5832
Alicia Dawe, prin. Fax 599-1560

St. Michael S 200/K-8
63 Liberty St 06379 860-599-1084
Doris Messina, prin. Fax 599-8079

Plainfield, Windham, Pop. 14,363
Plainfield SD 2,400/PK-12
651 Norwich Rd 06374 860-564-6403
Kenneth DiPietro, supt. Fax 564-6412
www.plainfieldschools.org
Plainfield Central S 600/6-8
75 Canterbury Rd 06374 860-564-6437
Scott Gagnon, prin. Fax 564-1147
Plainfield Memorial S 400/4-5
95 Canterbury Rd 06374 860-564-6440
Natasha Hutchinson, prin. Fax 564-6076
Shepard Hill ES 400/PK-3
234 Shepard Hill Rd 06374 860-564-6432
William Nagel, prin. Fax 564-6060
Other Schools – See Moosup

Plainville, Hartford, Pop. 17,932
Plainville SD 2,300/PK-12
1 Central Sq 06062 860-793-3210
Dr. Maureen Brummett, supt. Fax 747-6790
www.plainvilleschools.org
Linden Street ES 400/PK-5
69 Linden St 06062 860-793-3270
Paula Eshoo, prin. Fax 793-3269
MS of Plainville 500/6-8
150 Northwest Dr 06062 860-793-3250
Matthew Guarino, prin. Fax 793-3265
Toffolon ES 400/K-5
145 Northwest Dr 06062 860-793-3280
Lynn Logoyke, prin. Fax 793-6302
Wheeler ES 300/K-5
15 Cleveland Memorial Dr 06062 860-793-3290
Andrew Batchelder, prin. Fax 793-3288

Plantsville, Hartford, Pop. 7,000
Southington SD
Supt. — See Southington
Kennedy MS 800/6-8
1071 S Main St 06479 860-628-3275
Richard Terino, prin. Fax 628-3404
Plantsville ES 300/K-5
70 Church St 06479 860-628-3450
Stephen Bergin, prin. Fax 620-1620
South End ES 200/K-5
10 Maxwell Noble Dr 06479 860-628-3320
Erin Nattrass, prin. Fax 620-1667
Strong ES 300/K-5
820 Marion Ave 06479 860-628-3314
Melissa Barbuto, prin. Fax 628-3322

Plymouth, Litchfield
Plymouth SD
Supt. — See Terryville
Plymouth Center ES 400/PK-5
107 North St 06782 860-283-6321
Chrystal Collins, prin. Fax 283-6981

Pomfret, Windham

Rectory S 300/K-9
PO Box 68 06258 860-963-6740
Fred Williams, hdmstr. Fax 963-2355

Pomfret Center, Windham
Pomfret SD 400/PK-8
20 Pomfret St 06259 860-928-2718
Stephen Cullinan, supt. Fax 928-3839
www.pomfret.ctschool.net
Pomfret Community S 400/PK-8
20 Pomfret St 06259 860-928-2718
Susan Imschweiler, prin. Fax 928-3839

Portland, Middlesex, Pop. 5,757
Portland SD 1,300/PK-12
33 E Main St 06480 860-342-6790
Dr. Philip O'Reilly, supt. Fax 342-6791
www.portlandctschools.org
Brownstone IS 200/5-6
314 Main St 06480 860-342-6765
Allison Hine, prin. Fax 342-6766
Gildersleeve ES 200/2-4
575 1/2 Main St 06480 860-342-0411
Ryan Walstrom, prin. Fax 342-3194
Portland MS 300/7-8
93 High St 06480 860-342-1880
Scott Giegerich, prin. Fax 342-3934
Valley View ES 200/PK-1
81 High St 06480 860-342-3131
Jessica Bruenn, prin. Fax 342-3138

Preston, New London
Preston SD 400/PK-8
325 Shetucket Tpke 06365 860-889-6098
Dr. Roy Seitsinger, supt. Fax 889-8685
www.prestonschools.org/
Preston Plains MS 200/6-8
1 Route 164 06365 860-889-3831
Ivy Davis-Tomczuk, prin. Fax 204-0126
Preston Veteran's Memorial S 300/PK-5
325 Shetucket Tpke 06365 860-887-3113
Raymond Bernier, prin. Fax 889-5478

Prospect, New Haven, Pop. 7,775
Regional SD 16 1,700/PK-12
PO Box 7038 06712 203-758-6671
Michael Yamin, supt. Fax 758-5797
www.region16ct.org
Long River MS 600/6-8
38 Columbia Ave 06712 203-758-4421
Derek Muharem, prin. Fax 758-6948
Prospect ES PK-5
75 New Haven Rd 06712 203-578-3300
Dr. Rima McGeehan, prin. Fax 758-7505
Other Schools – See Beacon Falls

Putnam, Windham, Pop. 7,034
Putnam SD 1,200/PK-12
152 Woodstock Ave 06260 860-963-6900
William Hull, supt. Fax 963-6903
www.putnam.k12.ct.us/
Putnam ES 700/PK-5
33 Wicker St 06260 860-963-6925
Catherine Colavecchio, prin. Fax 963-5364
Putnam MS 300/6-8
35 Wicker St 06260 860-963-6920
Teri Bruce, prin. Fax 963-6921

Crossway Christian Academy 50/K-8
250 E Putnam Rd 06260 860-963-3787
Linda Filteau, prin. Fax 963-0623

Quaker Hill, New London
Waterford SD
Supt. — See Waterford
Quaker Hill ES 400/K-5
285 Bloomingdale Rd 06375 860-442-1095
Chris Discordia, prin. Fax 447-6267

Redding, Fairfield
Redding SD
Supt. — See Easton
Read MS 500/5-8
486 Redding Rd 06896 203-938-2533
Diane Martin, prin. Fax 938-8667
Redding ES 500/K-4
33 Lonetown Rd 06896 203-938-2519
Fax 938-3251

Ridgefield, Fairfield, Pop. 7,542
Ridgefield SD 5,300/PK-12
70 Prospect St 06877 203-894-5550
Dr. Karen Baldwin, supt. Fax 431-2811
www.ridgefield.org
Barlow Mountain ES 400/PK-5
115 Barlow Mountain Rd 06877 203-894-5800
Rebecca Pembrook, prin. Fax 894-7701
Branchville ES 400/K-5
40 Florida Rd 06877 203-894-5850
Keith Margolus, prin. Fax 544-7984
East Ridge MS 800/6-8
10 E Ridge Rd 06877 203-894-5500
Patricia Raneri, prin. Fax 431-2843
Farmingville ES 400/K-5
324 Farmingville Rd 06877 203-894-5570
Susan Gately, prin. Fax 431-2835
Ridgebury ES 400/K-5
112 Bennetts Farm Rd 06877 203-894-5875
Jamie Palladino, prin. Fax 431-2854
Scotland ES 400/K-5
111 Barlow Mountain Rd 06877 203-894-5825
Joanna Genovese, prin. Fax 431-2861
Scotts Ridge MS 500/6-8
750 N Salem Rd 06877 203-894-5725
Tim Salem, prin. Fax 894-3411
Veterans Park ES 300/K-5
8 Governor St 06877 203-894-5525
Lisa Singer, prin. Fax 431-2875

Ridgefield Academy 300/PK-8
223 W Mountain Rd 06877 203-894-1800
James P. Heus, head sch Fax 894-1810
St. Mary S 300/PK-8
183 High Ridge Ave 06877 203-438-7288
Anna O'Rourke, prin. Fax 431-8742
St. Padre Pio S 50/K-8
209 Tackora Trl 06877 203-431-0201
Fax 431-0202

Riverside, Fairfield, Pop. 8,283
Greenwich SD
Supt. — See Greenwich
Eastern MS 800/6-8
51 Hendrie Ave 06878 203-637-1744
Ralph Mayo, prin. Fax 637-3567
International S at Dundee 400/K-5
55 Florence Rd 06878 203-637-3800
Terri Ricci, prin. Fax 637-5423
North Mianus ES 400/K-5
309 Palmer Hill Rd 06878 203-637-9730
Angela Schmidt, prin. Fax 637-9387
Riverside ES 500/K-5
90 Hendrie Ave 06878 203-637-1440
Christopher Weiss, prin. Fax 637-1004

Rocky Hill, Hartford, Pop. 16,554
Capitol Region Education Council RESC
Supt. — See Hartford
Academy of Aerospace & Engineering ES PK-5
525 Brook St 06067 860-529-1652
Gayle Hills, prin. Fax 529-1743

Rocky Hill SD 2,400/PK-12
PO Box 627 06067 860-258-7701
Dr. Mark Zito, supt. Fax 258-7710
www.rockyhillps.com
Griswold MS 600/5-8
144 Bailey Rd 06067 860-258-7741
Richard Watson, prin. Fax 258-7746
Stevens ES 500/K-5
322 Orchard St 06067 860-258-7751
Jason Maziarz, prin. Fax 258-7753
West Hill ES 600/PK-5
95 Cronin Dr 06067 860-258-7761
Scott Nozik, prin. Fax 258-7764

Rogers, Windham
Killingly SD
Supt. — See Killingly
Goodyear ECC 100/PK-PK
22 Williamsville Rd 06263 860-779-6770
Sally Sherman, dir. Fax 774-6772

Roxbury, Litchfield
Regional SD 12
Supt. — See Washington Depot
Booth Free S 100/K-5
14 South St 06783 860-354-9391
Cathy Colella, prin. Fax 350-6563

Salem, New London, Pop. 3,310
Salem SD 400/PK-8
200 Hartford Rd 06420 860-892-1223
Joseph Onofrio, supt. Fax 859-2130
www.salemschools.org
Salem S 400/PK-8
200 Hartford Rd 06420 860-859-0267
Joan Phillips, prin. Fax 859-2130

Sandy Hook, Fairfield
Newtown SD
Supt. — See Newtown
Newtown Preschool 100/PK-PK
12 Dickinson Dr 06482 203-426-7683
Deborah Petersen, dir. Fax 270-4899

Scotland, Windham
Scotland SD 100/PK-6
PO Box 97 06264 860-423-0064
Dr. Francis Baran, supt. Fax 423-0390
www.scotlandelementaryct.com
Scotland ES 100/PK-6
PO Box 97 06264 860-423-0064
Dr. C. Pinsonneault, prin. Fax 423-0390

Seymour, New Haven, Pop. 14,288
Seymour SD 2,000/PK-12
98 Bank St 06483 203-888-4564
Michael Wilson, supt. Fax 888-1704
www.seymourschools.org
Bungay ES 500/PK-5
35 Bungay Rd 06483 203-881-7500
Mary Sue Feige, prin. Fax 881-7506
Chatfield-LoPresti ES 300/PK-5
51 Skokorat St 06483 203-888-4640
David Olechna, prin. Fax 888-5492
Seymour MS 600/6-8
211 Mountain Rd 06483 203-888-4513
Bernadette Hamad, prin. Fax 881-7535

Sharon, Litchfield, Pop. 722
Sharon SD
Supt. — See Falls Village
Sharon Center S 200/PK-8
80 Hilltop Rd 06069 860-364-5153
Karen Manning, prin. Fax 364-5473

Shelton, Fairfield, Pop. 39,118
Shelton SD 4,900/PK-12
382 Long Hill Ave 06484 203-924-1023
Dr. Christopher Clouet, supt. Fax 924-5894
www.sheltonpublicschools.org
Booth Hill ES 300/K-4
544 Booth Hill Rd 06484 203-929-5625
Dr. James Zavodjancik, prin. Fax 225-1587
Long Hill ES 400/K-4
565 Long Hill Ave 06484 203-929-4077
Andrea D'Aiuto, prin. Fax 929-8250
Mohegan ES 300/PK-4
47 Mohegan Rd 06484 203-929-4121
Kristen Santilli, prin. Fax 929-8246
Perry Hill S 800/5-6
60 Perry Hill Rd 06484 203-924-4002
Lorraine Williams, prin. Fax 922-0160
Shelton ES 400/K-4
138 Willoughby Rd 06484 203-929-1330
Beverly Belden, prin. Fax 225-1574
Shelton IS 800/7-8
675 Constitution Blvd N 06484 203-926-2000
Kenneth Saranich, hdmstr. Fax 926-2017
Sunnyside ES 200/K-4
418 River Rd 06484 203-922-3021
Amy Yost, prin. Fax 924-7581

Holy Trinity Catholic Academy 300/PK-8
503 Shelton Ave 06484 203-929-4422
Laura Varrone, prin. Fax 929-3669

Sherman, Fairfield
Sherman SD 400/PK-8
2 Route 37 E 06784 860-355-3793
Dr. Jeff Melendez, supt. Fax 355-9023
www.shermanschool.com
Sherman S 400/PK-8
2 Route 37 E 06784 860-355-3793
Dr. Jeff Melendez, prin. Fax 355-9023

Simsbury, Hartford, Pop. 22,023
Simsbury SD 4,300/PK-12
933 Hopmeadow St 06070 860-651-3361
Matthew Curtis, supt. Fax 651-4343
www.simsbury.k12.ct.us
Central ES 400/PK-6
29 Massaco St 06070 860-658-4732
Beth Hennessy, prin. Fax 658-3620
James Memorial MS 700/7-8
155 Firetown Rd 06070 860-651-3341
Brian White, prin. Fax 658-3629
Squadron Line ES 600/K-6
44 Squadron Line Rd 06070 860-658-2251
Meg Evans, prin. Fax 658-3627
Other Schools – See Tariffville, Weatogue, West Simsbury

Cobb S Montessori 100/PK-6
112 Sand Hill Rd 06070 860-658-1144
St. Mary S 200/PK-8
946 Hopmeadow St 06070 860-658-9412
Margaret Williamson, prin. Fax 658-1737

Somers, Tolland, Pop. 1,774
Somers SD 1,500/PK-12
1 Vision Blvd 06071 860-749-2270
Brian Czapla, supt. Fax 763-0748
www.somers.k12.ct.us
Avery MS 400/6-8
1 Vision Blvd 06071 860-749-2270
Clay Krevolin, prin. Fax 763-2073
Somers ES 600/PK-5
4 Vision Blvd 06071 860-749-2270
Jennifer Oliver, prin. Fax 763-0620

Southbury, New Haven, Pop. 15,818
Regional SD 15
Supt. — See Middlebury
Gainfield ES 400/K-5
307 Old Field Rd 06488 203-264-5312
Jon Romeo, prin. Fax 264-6439
Pomperaug ES 400/K-5
607 Main St S 06488 203-264-8283
Theresa Forish, prin. Fax 264-7387
Rochambeau MS 500/6-8
100 Peter Rd 06488 203-264-2711
Michael Bernardi, prin. Fax 264-6638

South Glastonbury, Hartford
Glastonbury SD
Supt. — See Glastonbury
Hopewell ES 400/K-5
1068 Chestnut Hill Rd 06073 860-652-7897
Kathleen Murphy, prin. Fax 652-7904
Nayaug ES 600/PK-5
222 Old Maids Ln 06073 860-652-4949
Kristine Garofalo, prin. Fax 652-4950

Southington, Hartford, Pop. 39,200
Southington SD 6,700/PK-12
200 N Main St 06489 860-628-3200
Timothy J. Connellan, supt. Fax 821-8056
www.southingtonschools.org
DePaolo MS 800/6-8
385 Pleasant St 06489 860-628-3260
Frank Pepe, prin. Fax 628-3403
Derynoski ES 600/K-5
240 Main St 06489 860-628-3286
Jan Verderame, prin. Fax 628-3381
Flanders ES 300/K-5
100 Victoria Dr 06489 860-628-3372
Katie Guerrette, prin. Fax 628-3253
Hatton ES 500/PK-5
50 Spring Lake Rd 06489 860-628-3377
Robert Garry, prin. Fax 628-3210
Kelley ES 400/K-5
501 Ridgewood Rd 06489 860-628-3310
Marilyn Kahl, prin. Fax 628-3335
Thalberg ES 400/K-5
145 Dunham St 06489 860-628-3370
Megan Bennett, prin. Fax 628-3308
Other Schools – See Plantsville

Southington Catholic S 200/PK-8
133 Bristol St 06489 860-628-2485
Eileen Sampiere, prin. Fax 628-7341

Southport, Fairfield, Pop. 1,565
Fairfield SD
Supt. — See Fairfield
Mill Hill ES 400/K-5
635 Mill Hill Ter, 203-255-8320
Kevin Chase, prin. Fax 255-8205

South Windsor, Hartford, Pop. 22,090
Capitol Region Education Council RESC
Supt. — See Hartford
International S for Global Citizenship PK-5
625 Chapel Rd 06074 860-291-6001
Nguyet Tinh, prin. Fax 289-0383

South Windsor SD 4,200/PK-12
1737 Main St 06074 860-291-1200
Kate Carter Ed.D., supt. Fax 291-1291
www.southwindsorschools.org
Edwards MS 1,000/6-8
100 Arnold Way 06074 860-648-5030
Nancy Larson, prin. Fax 648-5029
Orchard Hill ES 400/K-5
350 Foster St 06074 860-648-5015
Michael Tortora, prin. Fax 648-0141
Pleasant Valley ES 300/K-5
591 Ellington Rd 06074 860-610-0291
Tiffany Caouette, prin. Fax 282-2287
Smith ES 400/K-5
949 Avery St 06074 860-648-5025
Michelle Dixon, prin. Fax 648-5014
Terry ES 400/PK-5
569 Griffin Rd 06074 860-648-5020
Vincent Federici, prin. Fax 648-0142
Wapping ES 300/K-5
91 Ayers Rd 06074 860-648-5010
Laura Hickson, prin. Fax 648-5802

Stafford Springs, Tolland, Pop. 4,869
Stafford SD 1,600/PK-12
16 Levinthal Run 06076 860-684-2208
Dr. Patricia Collin, supt. Fax 684-5172
www.stafford.k12.ct.us
Stafford ES 500/2-5
11 Levinthal Run 06076 860-684-6677
Steve Montgomery, prin. Fax 684-3925
Stafford MS 300/6-8
21 Levinthal Run 06076 860-684-2785
Paul Muska, prin. Fax 684-4671
Staffordville ES 200/PK-1
21 Lyons Rd 06076 860-684-3298
Peggy Falcetta, prin. Fax 684-7088
West Stafford ES 200/PK-1
153 W Stafford Rd 06076 860-684-3181
Anna Gagnon, prin. Fax 684-0328

St. Edward S 100/PK-8
25 Church St 06076 860-684-2600
MaryAnne Pelletier, prin. Fax 684-4030

Stamford, Fairfield, Pop. 120,428
Stamford SD 15,700/PK-12
888 Washington Blvd Fl 5 06901 203-977-4105
Earl Kim, supt. Fax 977-5964
www.stamfordpublicschools.org/
Cloonan MS 600/6-8
11 W North St 06902 203-977-4544
David Tate, prin. Fax 977-4867
Davenport Ridge ES 600/K-5
1300 Newfield Ave 06905 203-977-4291
Michael Pisseri, prin. Fax 977-5116
Dolan MS 600/6-8
51 Toms Rd 06906 203-977-4441
Charmaine Tourse, prin. Fax 977-4880
Hart Magnet ES 600/K-5
61 Adams Ave 06902 203-977-5082
Linda Darling, prin. Fax 977-5084
Murphy ES 500/K-5
19 Horton St 06902 203-977-4516
Sherri Prendergast, prin. Fax 977-5103
Newfield ES 700/K-5
345 Pepper Ridge Rd 06905 203-977-4282
Lisa Saba-Price, prin. Fax 977-4818
New S @ Strawberry Hill K-1
200 Strawberry Hill Ave 06902 203-977-6600
Frank Rodriguez, prin. Fax 977-6607
Northeast ES 700/K-5
82 Scofieldtown Rd 06903 203-977-4469
Hubert Gordon, prin. Fax 977-4312
Rippowam MS 700/5-8
381 High Ridge Rd 06905 203-977-5255
Jason Martin, prin. Fax 977-5154
Rogers International S 800/K-8
202 Blachley Rd 06902 203-977-4560
Cathy Cummings, prin. Fax 977-5732
Roxbury ES 600/K-5
751 W Hill Rd 06902 203-977-4287
Mark Bonasera, prin. Fax 977-4615
Scofield Magnet MS 600/5-8
641 Scofieldtown Rd 06903 203-977-2750
Scott Clayton, prin. Fax 977-2766
Springdale ES 700/K-5
1127 Hope St 06907 203-977-4575
Gloria Manna, prin. Fax 977-4058
Stark ES 600/PK-5
398 Glenbrook Rd 06906 203-977-4583
Edith Presley, prin. Fax 977-5426
Stillmeadow ES 700/K-5
800 Stillwater Rd 06902 203-977-4507
Dr. Michael Sanders, prin. Fax 977-4506
Toquam Magnet ES 700/K-5
123 Ridgewood Ave 06907 203-977-4556
Amy Beldotti, prin. Fax 977-5055
Turn of River MS 500/6-8
117 Vine Rd 06905 203-977-4284
Brendan Fox, prin. Fax 977-5037
Westover Magnet ES 700/PK-5
412 Stillwater Ave 06902 203-977-4572
Kathy Wunder, prin. Fax 977-5180

Bi-Cultural Day S 400/PK-8
2186 High Ridge Rd 06903 203-329-2186
Catholic Academy of Stamford 300/PK-5
1186 Newfield Ave 06905 203-322-6505
Patricia Brady, head sch Fax 322-6835
Catholic Academy of Stamford 200/6-8
948 Newfield Ave 06905 203-322-7383
Patricia Brady, head sch Fax 324-4435
Children's S 100/PK-2
118 Scofieldtown Rd 06903 203-329-8815
Maureen Murphy, head sch Fax 329-9443
King S 700/PK-12
1450 Newfield Ave 06905 203-322-3496
Thomas Main, hdmstr. Fax 461-9988
Long Ridge S 100/PK-5
478 Erskine Rd 06903 203-322-7693
John Ora, head sch Fax 322-0406
Mead S 100/PK-8
1095 Riverbank Rd 06903 203-595-9500
Stephanie Whitney, head sch Fax 595-0735
Waterside S 100/PK-5
770 Pacific St 06902 203-975-8579
Jody Visage, head sch Fax 975-9655

Sterling, Windham
Sterling SD 500/PK-8
251 Sterling Rd 06377 860-564-4219
Gail Lanza, supt. Fax 564-1989
www.sterlingschool.org
Sterling Community S 500/PK-8
251 Sterling Rd 06377 860-564-2728
Sharon Ternowchek, prin. Fax 564-1989

Stonington, New London, Pop. 920
Stonington SD
Supt. — See Old Mystic
Deans Mill ES 400/K-4
35 Deans Mill Rd 06378 860-535-2235
Jennifer McCurdy, prin. Fax 535-1417

Pine Point S 200/PK-9
89 Barnes Rd 06378 860-535-0606
Diana Owen, head sch Fax 535-8033

Storrs, Tolland, Pop. 14,985
Mansfield SD 1,200/PK-8
4 S Eagleville Rd 06268 860-429-3350
Kelly Lyman, supt. Fax 429-3379
www.mansfieldct.gov/content/11150/default.aspx
Goodwin ES 200/PK-4
321 Hunting Lodge Rd 06268 860-429-6316
Susan Muirhead, prin. Fax 487-5641
Mansfield MS 500/5-8
205 Spring Hill Rd 06268 860-429-3941
Candace Morell, prin. Fax 429-1020
Other Schools – See Mansfield Center

Stratford, Fairfield, Pop. 50,391
Stratford SD 6,900/PK-12
1000 E Broadway 06615 203-385-4210
Dr. Janet Robinson, supt. Fax 381-2012
stratfordk12.org
Chapel ES 600/K-6
380 Chapel St 06614 203-385-4192
Dr. Carla Armistead, prin. Fax 381-6964
Flood MS 600/7-8
490 Chapel St 06614 203-385-4280
Lea Ann Bradford, prin. Fax 381-2033
Franklin ES 300/K-6
1895 Barnum Ave 06614 203-385-4190
Sherrod McNeill, prin. Fax 385-4116
Lordship ES 200/K-6
254 Crown St 06615 203-385-4170
Kate Murphy, prin. Fax 385-4118
Nichols ES 400/K-6
396 Nichols Ave 06614 203-385-4294
Diana Dilorio, prin. Fax 381-6913
Second Hill Lane ES 700/PK-6
65 2nd Hill Ln 06614 203-385-4292
James Noga, prin. Fax 385-4291
Stratford Academy - Johnson House 500/PK-PK, 3-
719 Birdseye St 06615 203-385-4180
Maureen DiDomenico, prin. Fax 385-4185
Stratford Academy - Victoria Soto S PK-2
699 Birdseye St 06615 203-375-2206
Dr. Koren Paul, prin. Fax 375-1174
Whitney ES 500/K-6
1130 Huntington Rd 06614 203-385-4198
Victoria Horek, prin. Fax 381-6950
Wilcoxson ES 400/K-6
600 Wilcoxson Ave 06614 203-385-4196
Noelle Guerini, prin. Fax 381-6912
Wooster MS 500/7-8
150 Lincoln St 06614 203-385-4275
Bryan Darcy, prin. Fax 381-6918

St. James S 400/PK-8
50 Harvey Pl 06615 203-375-5994
Jack Lynch, prin. Fax 380-0749
St. Mark S 200/PK-8
500 Wigwam Ln 06614 203-375-4291
Donna Wuhrer, prin. Fax 375-4833

Suffield, Hartford
Suffield SD 2,400/PK-12
350 Mountain Rd 06078 860-668-3800
Karen Berasi, supt. Fax 668-3805
www.suffield.org
McAlister IS 500/3-5
260 Mountain Rd 06078 860-668-3830
Karen Carpenter-Snow, prin. Fax 668-3809
Suffield MS 600/6-8
350 Mountain Rd 06078 860-668-3820
Damon Pearce, prin. Fax 668-3088
Other Schools – See West Suffield

Taftville, See Norwich
Norwich SD
Supt. — See Norwich
Wequonnoc ES 200/K-5
155 Providence St 06380 860-823-4210
Scott Fain, prin. Fax 823-4253

Sacred Heart S 200/K-8
15 Hunters Ave 06380 860-887-1757
Sr. Christina Van Beck, prin. Fax 889-7276

Tariffville, Hartford, Pop. 1,289
Simsbury SD
Supt. — See Simsbury
Tariffville ES 200/1-6
42 Winthrop St 06081 860-658-5825
Scott Baker, prin. Fax 658-3626

Terryville, Litchfield, Pop. 5,299
Plymouth SD 1,500/PK-12
77 Main St 06786 860-314-8005
Dr. Martin Semmel, supt. Fax 314-2766
www.plymouth.k12.ct.us
Fisher ES 300/PK-5
79 N Main St 06786 860-314-2777
Phyllis Worhunsky, prin. Fax 314-8008
Terry MS 400/6-8
21 N Main St 06786 860-314-2790
Angela Suffridgo, prin. Fax 314-2768
Other Schools – See Plymouth

Thomaston, Litchfield, Pop. 1,888
Thomaston SD 900/PK-12
PO Box 166 06787 860-283-4796
Francine Coss, supt. Fax 283-6708
www.thomastonschools.net/
Black Rock ES 300/PK-3
57 Branch Rd 06787 860-283-3040
Jonathan Kozlak, prin. Fax 283-3043
Thomaston Center S 200/4-6
1 Thomas Ave 06787 860-283-3036
Kristin Bernier, prin. Fax 283-3048

Tolland, Tolland
Tolland SD 2,700/PK-12
51 Tolland Grn 06084 860-870-6850
Walter Willett Ph.D., supt. Fax 870-7737
www.tolland.k12.ct.us
Birch Grove PS 600/PK-2
247 Rhodes Rd 06084 860-870-6750
Thomas Swanson, prin. Fax 870-6754
Tolland IS 600/3-5
96 Old Post Rd 06084 860-870-6885
James Dineen, prin. Fax 872-7126
Tolland MS 700/6-8
1 Falcon Way 06084 860-870-6860
Daniel Uriano, prin. Fax 870-5737

St. Matthew Preschool PK-PK
111 Tolland Grn 06084 860-872-0200
Eveline Siebesma, dir. Fax 875-4413

Torrington, Litchfield, Pop. 35,694
Torrington SD 4,300/PK-12
355 Migeon Ave 06790 860-489-2327
Denise Clemons, supt. Fax 489-0726
www.torrington.org
East ES 400/PK-5
215 Hogan Dr 06790 860-489-2303
Susan Fergusson, prin. Fax 489-2308
Forbes ES 400/K-5
500 Migeon Ave 06790 860-489-2500
Joanne Creedon, prin. Fax 489-2555
Southwest ES 300/K-5
340 Litchfield St 06790 860-489-2311
Judith Theeb, prin. Fax 489-2324
Torringford ES 600/K-5
800 Charles St 06790 860-489-2300
Cathleen Todor, prin. Fax 489-2325
Torrington MS 1,000/6-8
200 Middle School Dr 06790 860-496-4050
Mary Ann Buchanan, prin. Fax 496-1089
Vogel-Wetmore ES 500/K-5
68 Church St 06790 860-489-2570
Andrew Tripaldi, prin. Fax 489-2577

St. Peter / St. Francis of Assisi S 200/PK-8
360 Prospect St 06790 860-489-4177
Jo-Anne Gauger, prin. Fax 489-1590

Trumbull, Fairfield, Pop. 35,588
Trumbull SD 6,800/PK-12
6254 Main St 06611 203-452-4300
Gary Cialfi, supt. Fax 452-4305
www.trumbullps.org
Booth Hill ES 500/K-5
545 Booth Hill Rd 06611 203-452-4377
Dana Pierce, prin. Fax 452-4375
Daniels Farm ES 500/K-5
710 Daniels Farm Rd 06611 203-452-4388
Gary Kunschaft, prin. Fax 452-4387

Frenchtown ES 700/K-5
30 Frenchtown Rd 06611 203-452-4227
Jacqueline Norcel, prin. Fax 452-4226
Hillcrest MS 800/6-8
530 Daniels Farm Rd 06611 203-452-4466
Stafford Thomas, prin. Fax 452-4479
Madison MS 800/6-8
4630 Madison Ave 06611 203-452-4499
Peter Sullivan, prin. Fax 452-4490
Middlebrook ES 500/K-5
220 Middlebrooks Ave 06611 203-452-4411
Patricia Frillici, prin. Fax 452-4426
Ryan ES 400/K-5
190 Park Ln 06611 203-452-4400
Mary Ellen Bolton, prin. Fax 452-4409
Tashua ES 400/K-5
401 Stonehouse Rd 06611 203-452-4433
Jennifer Neumeyer, prin. Fax 452-4432
Trumbull ECC 200/PK-PK
240 Middlebrooks Ave 06611 203-452-4422
Dr. Matthew Wheeler, prin. Fax 452-4419

Christian Heritage S 500/K-12
575 White Plains Rd 06611 203-261-6230
Dr. Brian Modarelli, head sch Fax 452-1531
St. Catherine of Siena S 200/PK-8
190 Shelton Rd 06611 203-375-1947
Eunice Giaquinto, prin. Fax 378-3935
St. Theresa S 300/PK-8
55 Rosemond Ter 06611 203-268-3236
Salvatore Vittoria, prin. Fax 268-7966

Uncasville, New London, Pop. 2,975
Montville SD
Supt. — See Oakdale
Mohegan ES 400/K-5
49 Golden Rd 06382 860-848-9261
William Klinefelter, prin. Fax 848-1603

Union, Tolland
Union SD 100/K-8
18 Kinney Hollow Rd 06076 860-684-3146
Joe Reardon, supt. Fax 684-9385
www.union.k12.ct.us
Union ES 100/K-8
18 Kinney Hollow Rd 06076 860-684-3146
Steven Jackopsic, prin. Fax 684-9385

Unionville, Hartford, Pop. 3,500
Farmington SD
Supt. — See Farmington
Union ES 300/K-4
173 School St 06085 860-673-2575
Caitlin Eckler, prin. Fax 675-4264
West District ES 300/K-4
114 W District Rd 06085 860-673-2579
Peter Michelson, prin. Fax 675-4103

Vernon Rockville, Tolland, Pop. 28,900
Vernon SD 3,300/PK-12
PO Box 600 06066 860-870-6000
Dr. Joseph Macary, supt. Fax 870-6005
vernonpublicschools.org
Center Road ES 500/PK-5
20 Center Rd 06066 860-870-6300
Jocelyn Poglitsch, prin. Fax 870-6309
Lake Street ES 300/PK-5
210 Lake St 06066 860-870-6085
Terese Duenzl, prin. Fax 870-6084
Maple Street ES 300/PK-5
20 Maple St 06066 860-870-6175
Melissa Trantolo, prin. Fax 870-6181
Northeast ES 300/K-5
69 East St 06066 860-870-6080
Brenda Greene, prin. Fax 870-6095
Skinner Road ES 300/PK-5
90 Skinner Rd 06066 860-870-6180
Bryan Kerachsky, prin. Fax 870-6187
Vernon Center MS 700/6-8
777 Hartford Tpke 06066 860-870-6070
James Harrison, prin. Fax 870-6318

St. Bernard Preschool 50/PK-PK
25 Saint Bernard Terr 06066 860-875-0753
Sherry Yarusewicz, dir.

Voluntown, New London
Voluntown SD 300/PK-8
PO Box 129 06384 860-376-9167
Adam S. Burrows, supt. Fax 376-3185
www.voluntownct.org
Voluntown ES 300/PK-8
PO Box 129 06384 860-376-2325
Alicia M. Trakas, prin. Fax 376-6690

Wallingford, New Haven, Pop. 41,700
Wallingford SD 6,000/PK-12
100 S Turnpike Rd 06492 203-949-6500
Dr. Salvatore Menzo, supt. Fax 949-6550
www.wallingford.k12.ct.us
Beach ES 300/PK-2
340 N Main St 06492 203-294-3940
Robert Arciero, prin. Fax 294-3969
Cook Hill ES 300/PK-2
57 Hall Rd 06492 203-284-5400
Kristine Friend, prin. Fax 284-5439
Hammarskjold MS 700/6-8
106 Pond Hill Rd 06492 203-294-3700
Todd Snyder, prin. Fax 294-3749
Highland ES 300/K-2
200 Highland Ave 06492 203-294-3970
Victoria Reed, prin. Fax 294-3999
Moran MS 700/6-8
141 Hope Hill Rd 06492 203-741-2900
Joseph Piacentini, prin. Fax 741-2939
Parker Farms ES 300/3-5
30 Parker Farms Rd 06492 203-294-6200
Christina Sagnella, prin. Fax 294-6229
Pond Hill ES 400/3-5
299 Pond Hill Rd 06492 203-294-6230
Danielle Bellizzi, prin. Fax 294-6259
Rock Hill ES 300/3-5
910 Old Rock Hill Rd 06492 203-294-6260
Carrie LaTorre, prin. Fax 294-6289
Stevens ES 400/PK-2
18 Kondracki Ln 06492 203-284-3750
Kristina Kiely, prin. Fax 294-3779
Yalesville ES 400/3-5
415 Church St 06492 203-284-6900
Mary Poisson, prin. Fax 284-6929

Holy Trinity S 200/K-8
11 N Whittlesey Ave 06492 203-269-4477
Sr. Kathleen Kelly, prin. Fax 294-4983

Warren, Litchfield
Regional SD 6
Supt. — See Litchfield
Warren ES 100/PK-6
21 Sackett Hill Rd 06754 860-868-2223
Angela Rossbach, prin. Fax 868-7375

Washington Depot, Litchfield
Regional SD 12 600/PK-12
PO Box 386 06794 860-868-6100
Patricia Cosentino Ed.D., supt. Fax 868-6103
www.region-12.org
Washington PS 200/PK-5
11 School St 06793 860-868-7331
Emily Judd, prin. Fax 868-2975
Other Schools – See Bridgewater, Roxbury

Rumsey Hall S 300/K-9
201 Romford Rd 06794 860-868-0535
Matthew Hoeniger, hdmstr. Fax 868-7907

Waterbury, New Haven, Pop. 106,427
Waterbury SD 18,300/PK-12
236 Grand St 06702 203-574-8000
Dr. Kathleen Ouellette, supt. Fax 574-8010
www.waterbury.k12.ct.us
Bucks Hill ES 500/PK-5
330 Bucks Hill Rd 06704 203-574-8182
Dr. Delia Bello-DaVila, prin. Fax 573-6643
Bunker Hill ES 500/PK-5
170 Bunker Hill Ave 06708 203-574-8183
Celia Piccochi, prin. Fax 574-8007
Carrington ES 400/PK-8
24 Kenmore Ave 06708 203-574-8184
Karen Renna, prin. Fax 574-6728
Chase ES 800/K-5
40 Woodtick Rd 06705 203-574-8188
Matthew Calabrese, prin. Fax 573-6652
Cross ES 400/PK-5
1255 Hamilton Ave 06706 203-574-8171
Joseph Amato, prin. Fax 574-0719
Driggs ES 500/PK-5
77 Woodlawn Ter 06710 203-574-8160
Michael Theriault, prin. Fax 574-8299
Duggan ES 500/PK-8
38 W Porter St 06708 203-574-8875
Dr. Patricia Frageau, prin. Fax 574-8877
Generali ES 600/K-5
3196 E Main St 06705 203-574-8174
Kathy Stamp, prin. Fax 574-6719
Gilmartin ES 500/PK-8
94 Spring Lake Rd 06706 203-574-8175
Jennifer Dwyer, prin. Fax 573-6649
Hopeville ES 500/PK-5
2 Cypress St 06706 203-574-8173
Debra Ponte, prin. Fax 597-3419
Kingsbury ES 500/K-5
220 Columbia Blvd 06710 203-574-8172
Erik Brown, prin. Fax 573-6644
Maloney Magnet ES 600/PK-5
233 S Elm St 06706 203-574-8162
Donna Cullen, prin. Fax 574-8389
North End MS 1,100/6-8
534 Bucks Hill Rd 06704 203-574-8097
Jacquelyn Gilmore, prin. Fax 574-8203
Reed ES 400/PK-8
33 Griggs St 06704 203-574-8180
Juan Mendoza, prin. Fax 574-6884
Regan ES 300/K-5
2780 N Main St 06704 203-574-8187
Angela Razza, prin. Fax 573-6647
Rotella Interdistict Magnet ES 600/PK-5
380 Pierpont Rd 06705 203-574-8168
Robin Henry, prin. Fax 574-8045
Sprague ES 500/PK-5
1443 Thomaston Ave 06704 203-574-8189
Diane Bakewell, prin. Fax 573-6622
Tinker ES 600/K-5
809 Highland Ave 06708 203-574-8186
Darlene Lerz, prin. Fax 597-3440
Wallace MS 1,200/6-8
3465 E Main St 06705 203-574-8140
Michael LoRusso, prin. Fax 574-8141
Walsh ES 500/PK-5
55 Dikeman St 06704 203-574-8164
Ellen Paolino, prin. Fax 597-3488
Washington ES 300/K-5
685 Baldwin St 06706 203-574-8177
Lori Eldridge, prin. Fax 573-6645
West Side MS 1,000/6-8
483 Chase Pkwy 06708 203-574-8120
Maria Burns, prin. Fax 574-8130
Wilson ES 400/PK-5
235 Birch St 06704 203-573-6660
Jennifer Rosser, prin. Fax 573-6663

Blessed Sacrament S 200/PK-8
386 Robinwood Rd 06708 203-756-5313
Michele Banach, prin. Fax 756-5313
Chase Collegiate S 500/PK-12
565 Chase Pkwy 06708 203-236-9500
Dr. Polly Peterson Ph.D., head sch Fax 236-9539
Children's Community S 100/PK-5
PO Box 1746 06721 203-575-0659
Our Lady of Mt. Carmel S 300/PK-8
645 Congress Ave 06708 203-755-6809
Joaquim Tavares, prin. Fax 755-5850
St. Mary S 300/PK-8
43 Cole St 06706 203-753-2574
Jonathan DeRosa, prin. Fax 596-2498
SS. Peter & Paul S 300/PK-8
116 Beecher Ave 06705 203-755-0881
James Gambardella, prin. Fax 755-3535
Yeshiva Ketana of Waterbury 300/PK-8
32 Hillside Ave 06710 203-528-4147
Rabbi Yehuda Brecher, prin.

Waterford, New London, Pop. 2,818
Learn RESC
Supt. — See Old Lyme
Dual Language & Arts Magnet MS 100/6-8
51 Daniels Ave 06385 860-443-0461
Christina Chamberlain, dir. Fax 443-0468
Friendship S 500/PK-K
24 Rope Ferry Rd 06385 860-447-4049
Andrea Simmons, prin. Fax 447-4056

Waterford SD 2,500/K-12
15 Rope Ferry Rd 06385 860-444-5801
Thomas Giard, supt. Fax 444-5870
www.waterfordschools.org
Clark Lane MS 700/6-8
105 Clark Ln 06385 860-443-2837
James Sachs, prin. Fax 437-6985
Great Neck ES 300/K-5
165 Great Neck Rd 06385 860-442-2593
Patricia Fedor, prin. Fax 437-6996
Oswegatchie ES 400/K-5
470 Boston Post Rd 06385 860-442-4331
Chris Ozmun, prin. Fax 447-6261
Other Schools – See Quaker Hill

Solomon Schecter Academy 50/PK-5
29B Dayton Rd 06385 860-443-5589
Barbara Wolfe, head sch Fax 443-5589

Watertown, Litchfield, Pop. 6,000
Watertown SD 2,900/PK-12
10 Deforest St 06795 860-945-4801
Dr. B. Heston Carnemolla, supt. Fax 945-2775
www.watertownps.org/
Judson ES 300/3-5
124 Hamilton Ln 06795 860-945-4850
Kathleen Scully, prin. Fax 945-2711
Other Schools – See Oakville

St. John the Evangelist S 200/PK-8
760 Main St 06795 860-274-9208
John Petto, prin. Fax 945-1082

Weatogue, Hartford, Pop. 2,719
Simsbury SD
Supt. — See Simsbury
Latimer Lane ES 400/K-6
33 Mountain View Dr 06089 860-658-4774
Michael Luzietti, prin. Fax 658-3618

Westbrook, Middlesex, Pop. 2,342
Westbrook SD 800/PK-12
158 McVeagh Rd 06498 860-399-6432
Patricia A. Ciccone, supt. Fax 399-8817
www.westbrookctschools.org/
Ingraham ES 300/PK-4
105 Goodspeed Dr 06498 860-399-7925
Ruth Rose, prin. Fax 399-2002
Westbrook MS 300/5-8
154 McVeagh Rd 06498 860-399-2010
Sharon Weirsman, prin. Fax 399-2006

West Cornwall, Litchfield
Cornwall SD
Supt. — See Falls Village
Cornwall Consolidated S 100/K-8
5 Cream Hill Rd 06796 860-672-6617
Michael Croft, prin. Fax 672-4879

West Hartford, Hartford, Pop. 61,804
West Hartford SD 9,800/PK-12
50 S Main St, 860-561-6600
Thomas Moore, supt. Fax 561-6910
www.whps.org
Aiken ES 500/PK-5
212 King Philip Dr, 860-233-6994
Shannon Mlodzinski, prin. Fax 236-9184
Braeburn ES 400/K-5
45 Braeburn Rd, 860-561-2200
Jeffrey Sousa, prin. Fax 521-8416
Bristow MS 400/6-8
34 Highland St, 860-231-2100
Steven Cook, prin. Fax 231-2107
Bugbee ES 500/K-5
1943 Asylum Ave, 860-929-5500
Kelly Brouse, prin. Fax 236-2486
Charter Oak International Academy 300/PK-5
425 Oakwood Ave, 860-233-8506
Juan Melian, prin. Fax 231-9654
Duffy ES 500/K-5
95 Westminster Dr, 860-521-0110
Kristi Laverty, prin. Fax 561-1492
King Philip MS 900/6-8
100 King Philip Dr, 860-233-8236
Joy Wright, prin. Fax 233-0812
Morley ES 300/K-5
77 Bretton Rd, 860-233-8535
Ryan Cleary, prin. Fax 233-7705
Norfeldt ES 400/K-5
35 Barksdale Rd, 860-233-4421
Jennifer Derick, prin. Fax 232-4732
Sedgwick MS 800/6-8
128 Sedgwick Rd, 860-521-0610
Andrew Clapsaddle, prin. Fax 521-7502
Smith STEM 400/PK-5
64 Saint James St, 860-236-3315
Teresa Giolito, prin. Fax 236-3342
Webster Hill ES 500/PK-5
125 Webster Hill Blvd, 860-521-0320
Jeffrey Wallowitz, prin. Fax 561-1230
Whiting Lane ES 500/PK-5
47 Whiting Ln, 860-233-8541
Karen Kukish, prin. Fax 236-9367

Wolcott ES 500/K-5
71 Wolcott Rd, 860-561-2300
Scott Dunn, prin. Fax 521-7545

Montessori S of Greater Hartford 200/PK-8
141 N Main St, 860-236-4565
Kathy Aldridge, head sch Fax 586-7420
Renbrook S 500/PK-8
2865 Albany Ave, 860-236-1661
Scott Hutchinson, head sch Fax 231-8206
St. Brigid - St. Augustine S 200/PK-8
100 Mayflower St, 860-561-2130
John Mirabito, prin. Fax 561-0011
St. Thomas the Apostle S 200/PK-5
25 Dover Rd, 860-236-6257
Colleen DiSanto, prin. Fax 236-8865
St. Timothy MS 100/6-8
225 King Philip Dr, 860-236-0614
Tara Bellefleur M.Ed., prin. Fax 920-0293
Solomon Schechter Day S 100/PK-8
26 Buena Vista Rd, 860-561-0700

West Haven, New Haven, Pop. 54,140
West Haven SD 5,900/PK-12
PO Box 26010 06516 203-937-4300
Neil Cavallaro, supt. Fax 937-4315
www.whschools.org
Bailey MS 900/7-8
106 Morgan Ln 06516 203-937-4380
Anthony Cordone Ed.D., prin. Fax 937-4385
Carrigan IS 900/5-6
2 Tetlow St 06516 203-937-4390
Frank Paolino, prin. Fax 937-4393
Forest ES 400/K-4
95 Burwell Rd 06516 203-931-6800
Thomas Hunt, prin. Fax 931-6803
Haley ES 500/PK-4
148 South St 06516 203-931-6810
Amy Jo Palermo, prin. Fax 931-6813
Mackrille ES 400/PK-4
806 Jones Hill Rd 06516 203-931-6820
Judith Drenzek, prin. Fax 931-6823
Pagels ES 400/PK-4
26 Benham Hill Rd 06516 203-931-6840
Gary Palermo, prin. Fax 931-6844
Savin Rock Community ES 500/PK-4
50 Park St 06516 203-931-6850
Taryn Driend, prin. Fax 931-6853
Washington ES 500/PK-4
369 Washington Ave 06516 203-931-6880
Steven Lopes, prin. Fax 931-6883

Our Lady of Victory S 200/PK-8
620 Jones Hill Rd 06516 203-932-6457
Ardell Bartolotta, prin. Fax 932-6456
St. Lawrence S 200/PK-8
231 Main St 06516 203-933-2518
Paul DeFonzo, prin. Fax 933-2058

Weston, Fairfield
Weston SD 2,400/PK-12
24 School Rd 06883 203-291-1400
Dr. William McKersie Ph.D., supt. Fax 291-1415
www.westonps.org
Hurlbutt ES, 9 School Rd 06883 500/PK-2
Laura Kaddis, prin. 203-557-5900
Weston IS 600/3-5
95 School Rd 06883 203-291-2701
Patricia Falber, prin. Fax 291-2707
Weston MS 600/6-8
135 School Rd 06883 203-291-1500
Dan Doak, prin. Fax 291-1516

Westport, Fairfield, Pop. 25,982
Westport SD 5,800/PK-12
110 Myrtle Ave 06880 203-341-1025
Colleen Palmer, supt. Fax 341-1029
www.westport.k12.ct.us/
Bedford MS 900/6-8
88 North Ave 06880 203-341-1500
Adam Rosen, prin. Fax 341-1508
Coleytown ES 500/PK-5
65 Easton Rd 06880 203-341-1700
Janna Sirowich, prin. Fax 341-1702
Coleytown MS 500/6-8
255 North Ave 06880 203-341-1600
Kris Szabo, prin. Fax 341-1614
Green's Farms ES 400/K-5
17 Morningside Dr S 06880 203-222-3600
Kevin Cazzetta, prin. Fax 222-3668
Kings Highway ES 500/K-5
125 Post Rd W 06880 203-341-1800
Mary Lou DiBella, prin. Fax 341-1804
Long Lots ES 600/K-5
13 Hyde Ln 06880 203-341-1900
Jeffrey Golubchick, prin. Fax 341-1905
Saugatuck ES 500/K-5
170 Riverside Ave 06880 203-221-2900
Elizabeth Messler, prin. Fax 221-2952
Stepping Stones Preschool 50/PK-PK
65 Easton Rd 06880 203-341-1712
Lynda Codeghini, dir. Fax 341-1714

Pierrepont S, 1 Sylvan Rd N 06880 100/K-12
Sarah Marchoci, hoad sch 203 226 1801

West Simsbury, Hartford, Pop. 2,411
Simsbury SD
Supt. — See Simsbury
Tootin Hills ES 400/PK-6
25 Nimrod Rd 06092 860-658-7629
Maggie Seidel, prin. Fax 658-3624

Master's S 300/PK-12
36 Westledge Rd 06092 860-651-9361
Ray Lagan, head sch Fax 651-9363

West Suffield, Hartford
Suffield SD
Supt. — See Suffield

Spaulding ES 500/PK-2
945 Mountain Rd 06093 860-668-3826
Dr. Roxanne Pangallo, prin. Fax 668-3087

Wethersfield, Hartford, Pop. 26,301
Capitol Region Education Council RESC
Supt. — See Hartford
Discovery Academy 300/PK-5
176 Cumberland Ave 06109 860-296-2090
Kurt Stanco, prin. Fax 296-2087

Wethersfield SD 3,600/PK-12
127 Hartford Ave 06109 860-571-8100
Michael Emmett, supt. Fax 571-8130
www.wethersfield.k12.ct.us
Deane MS 600/7-8
551 Silas Deane Hwy 06109 860-571-8300
Susan Czapla, prin. Fax 563-0563
Emerson-Williams ES 400/K-6
461 Wells Rd 06109 860-571-8360
Neela Thakur, prin. Fax 721-0044
Hanmer ES 400/K-6
50 Francis St 06109 860-571-8370
Pauline Greer, prin. Fax 257-1629
Highcrest ES 400/K-6
95 Highcrest Rd 06109 860-571-8380
Siobhan O'Connor, prin. Fax 563-9193
Webb ES 300/PK-6
51 Willow St 06109 860-571-8340
Michael Verderame, prin. Fax 257-1668
Wright ES 300/K-6
186 Nott St 06109 860-571-8350
Glenn Horter, prin. Fax 563-2198

Corpus Christi S 400/PK-8
581 Silas Deane Hwy 06109 860-529-5487
Ann Sarpu, prin. Fax 257-9106

Willimantic, Windham, Pop. 17,404
Windham SD 3,200/PK-12
322 Prospect St 06226 860-465-2300
Patricia Garcia Ph.D., supt. Fax 456-2311
www.windham.k12.ct.us/
Natchaug ES 300/K-5
123 Jackson St 06226 860-465-2380
Robert Kallajian, prin. Fax 465-2383
Sweeney ES 300/K-5
60 Oak Hill Dr 06226 860-465-2420
Angela Kiss, prin. Fax 465-2423
Windham ECC 200/PK-PK
322 Prospect St 06226 860-465-2627
Aliki Caraganis, dir. Fax 465-2605
Windham MS 700/6-8
123 Quarry St 06226 860-465-2350
Brett Fiore, prin. Fax 465-2353
Other Schools – See North Windham, Windham

SS. Mary & Joseph S 200/PK-8
35 Valley St 06226 860-423-0479
Abby Demars, prin. Fax 423-8365

Willington, Tolland
Willington SD 500/PK-8
40 Old Farms Rd Ste A 06279
David Harding, supt.
www.willingtonpublicschools.org
Center ES 200/PK-3
12 Old Farms Rd 06279 860-429-9367
Phil Stevens, prin. Fax 429-8768
Hall Memorial MS 300/4-8
111 River Rd 06279 860-429-9391
Kenneth Craig, prin. Fax 429-5682

Wilton, Fairfield, Pop. 7,200
Wilton SD 4,300/PK-12
PO Box 277 06897 203-762-3381
Dr. Kevin Smith, supt. Fax 762-2177
www.wilton.k12.ct.us
Cider Mill ES 1,000/3-5
240 School Rd 06897 203-762-3351
Dr. Jennifer Mitchell, prin. Fax 761-0382
Middlebrook MS 1,100/6-8
131 School Rd 06897 203-762-8388
Lauren Feltz, prin. Fax 762-1716
Miller-Driscoll ES 900/PK-2
217 Wolfpit Rd 06897 203-762-8678
Kathryn Coon, prin. Fax 761-1570

Montessori S 300/PK-6
34 Whipple Rd 06897 203-834-0440
Lisa Potter, head sch Fax 761-9386
Our Lady of Fatima S 200/PK-8
225 Danbury Rd 06897 203-762-8100
Stan Steele, prin. Fax 834-0614

Windham, Windham
Windham SD
Supt. — See Willimantic
Windham Center ES 300/K-5
45 North Rd 06280 860-465-2440
Kathleen Goodwin, prin. Fax 465-2343

Windsor, Hartford, Pop. 27,817
Capitol Region Education Council RESC
Supt. — See Hartford
Museum Academy 400/PK-5
10 Targeting Ctr 06095 860-231-7800
Shandra Brown M.Ed., prin. Fax 231-7236

Windsor SD 3,200/PK-12
601 Matianuck Ave 06095 860-687-2000
Dr. Craig Cooke, supt. Fax 687-2009
www.windsorct.org
Clover Street S 300/3-5
57 Clover St 06095 860-687-2050
Michelle Williams, prin. Fax 687-2059
Ellsworth S 500/PK-2
730 Kennedy Rd 06095 860-687-2070
Ronda Lezberg, prin. Fax 687-2079
Kennedy S 400/3-5
530 Park Ave 06095 860-687-2060
Mary Kay Ravenola, prin. Fax 687-2069

Poquonock S 200/K-2
1760 Poquonock Ave 06095 860-687-2080
Tracie Peterson, prin. Fax 687-2089
Sage Park MS 700/6-8
25 Sage Park Rd 06095 860-687-2030
Paul Cavaliere, prin. Fax 687-2039

Madina Academy 200/PK-12
519 Palisado Ave 06095 860-219-0569
Praise Power & Prayer Christian S 100/K-12
PO Box 474 06095 860-285-8898
Rev. Raymond McMahon, prin.
St. Gabriel S 200/PK-8
77 Bloomfield Ave 06095 860-688-6401
Patricia Martin, prin. Fax 298-8668
Trinity Christian S 200/PK-6
180 Park Ave 06095 860-688-2008
Kasinda Bristol, head sch Fax 687-9737
Windsor Montessori S 50/PK-K
114 Palisado Ave 06095 860-285-1400

Windsor Locks, Hartford, Pop. 12,219
Windsor Locks SD 1,700/PK-12
58 S Elm St 06096 860-292-5000
Susan Bell, supt. Fax 292-5003
www.wlps.org
North Street ES 400/PK-2
325 North St 06096 860-292-5027
Jeff Ferreira, prin. Fax 292-8191
South ES 400/3-5
87 South St 06096 860-292-5021
Monica Briggs, prin. Fax 292-5026
Windsor Locks MS 400/6-8
7 Center St 06096 860-292-5012
David Prinstein, prin. Fax 292-5017

Winsted, Litchfield, Pop. 7,586
Regional SD 7 1,100/7-12
PO Box 656 06098 860-379-8525
Dr. Judith Palmer, supt. Fax 379-6059
www.nwr7.com
Northwestern Regional MS 400/7-8
100 Battistoni Rd 06098 860-379-7243
Francis Amara, prin. Fax 738-6205

Winchester SD 400/PK-6
PO Box 648 06098 860-379-0706
Melony Brady-Shanley, supt. Fax 738-0638
www.winchesterschools.org
Batcheller ECC 200/PK-2
201 Pratt St 06098 860-379-5423
Debra Grainsky, prin. Fax 379-1301
Pearson MS 200/3-6
2 Wetmore Ave 06098 860-379-7588
Barbara Silverio, prin. Fax 379-0406

St. Anthony S 200/PK-8
55 Oak St 06098 860-379-7521
Louis Howe, prin. Fax 379-7522

Wolcott, New Haven, Pop. 13,700
Wolcott SD 2,500/PK-12
1488 Woodtick Rd 06716 203-879-8183
Dr. Tony Gasper, supt. Fax 879-8182
www.wolcottps.org
Alcott ES 300/PK-5
1490 Woodtick Rd 06716 203-879-8160
Shawn Simpson, prin. Fax 879-8163
Frisbie ES 300/K-5
24 Todd Rd 06716 203-879-8146
Joseph Norcross, prin. Fax 879-8148
Tyrrell MS 700/6-8
500 Todd Rd 06716 203-879-8151
Arline Tansley, prin. Fax 879-8419
Wakelee ES 400/K-5
12 Hemple Dr 06716 203-879-8154
Debra Osvald, prin. Fax 879-8035

Woodbridge, New Haven, Pop. 7,924
Regional SD 5 2,400/7-12
25 Newton Rd 06525 203-392-2106
Charles Dumais, supt. Fax 397-4864
www.amityregion5.org
Other Schools – See Bethany, Orange

Woodbridge SD 400/PK-6
40 Beecher Rd 06525 203-387-6631
Robert F. Gilbert, supt. Fax 397-0724
www.woodbridge.k12.ct.us
Beecher Road ES 400/PK-6
40 Beecher Rd 06525 203-389-2195
Gina Prisco, prin. Fax 389-2196

Ezra Academy 100/K-8
75 Rimmon Rd 06525 203-389-5500

Woodbury, Litchfield, Pop. 8,131
Regional SD 14 1,900/PK-12
PO Box 469 06798 203-263-4330
Dr. Anna Cutaia-Leonard, supt. Fax 263-0372
www.ctreg14.org
Mitchell ES 400/PK-5
14 School St 06798 203-263-4314
Jodie Roden, prin. Fax 263-4244
Woodbury MS 400/6-8
67 Washington Ave 06798 203-263-4306
Eric Bergeron, prin. Fax 263-0825
Other Schools – See Bethlehem

Woodstock, Windham
Woodstock SD 900/PK-8
147A Route 169 06281 860-928-7453
Viktor Toth, supt. Fax 928-0206
www.woodstockschools.net
Woodstock ES 500/PK-4
24 Frog Pond Rd 06281 860-928-0471
Jenna Demers, prin. Fax 928-1220
Woodstock MS 400/5-8
147B Route 169 06281 860-963-6575
Wendy Durand, prin. Fax 963-6577

DELAWARE

DELAWARE DEPARTMENT OF EDUCATION
401 Federal St Ste 2, Dover 19901-3639
Telephone 302-735-4000
Fax 302-739-4654
Website http://www.doe.k12.de.us

Secretary of Education Susan Bunting

DELAWARE BOARD OF EDUCATION
1006 Tulip Tree Ln, Newark 19713

President Teri Quinn Gray

PUBLIC, PRIVATE AND CATHOLIC ELEMENTARY SCHOOLS

Bear, New Castle, Pop. 18,842
Appoquinimink SD
Supt. — See Odessa
Loss ES 600/1-5
200 Brennan Blvd 19701 302-832-1343
Jenine Thomas, prin. Fax 832-3213

Christina SD
Supt. — See Wilmington
Oberle ES 700/K-5
500 Caledonia Way 19701 302-834-5910
Marilyn Dollard, prin. Fax 834-5916

Colonial SD
Supt. — See New Castle
Wilbur ES 1,100/K-5
4050 Wrangle Hill Rd 19701 302-832-6330
Beth Howell, prin. Fax 832-6335

Aquinas Academy 100/PK-12
2370 Red Lion Rd 19701 302-838-9601
John Moore, prin. Fax 838-9602
Caravel Academy 1,200/PK-12
2801 Del Laws Rd 19701 302-834-8938
Donald Keister, hdmstr. Fax 834-3658
Fairwinds Christian S 200/PK-12
801 Seymour Rd 19701 302-328-7404
Red Lion Christian Academy 700/PK-12
1390 Red Lion Rd 19701 302-834-2526
Sam Osbourn, prin. Fax 836-6346
St. Elizabeth Ann Seton Preschool PK-PK
345 Bear-Christiana Rd 19701 302-322-2631
Janet Gargani, prin. Fax 322-6297
Tall Oaks Classical S 200/K-12
1390 Red Lion Rd 19701 302-730-3337

Blades, Sussex, Pop. 1,195
Seaford SD
Supt. — See Seaford
Blades ES 300/K-2
900 S Arch St 19973 302-628-4416
Kirsten Jennette, prin. Fax 628-4480

Bridgeville, Sussex, Pop. 1,988
Woodbridge SD 1,700/PK-12
16359 Sussex Hwy 19933 302-337-7990
Heath Chasanov, supt. Fax 337-7998
www.woodbridgeraiders.net
Wheatley ES 3-5
48 Church St 19933 302-337-3469
Lynn Brown, prin. Fax 337-6016
Woodbridge MS 600/6-8
307 S Laws St 19933 302-337-8289
Tina Morroni, prin. Fax 337-0631
Other Schools – See Greenwood

Camden, Kent, Pop. 3,311
Caesar Rodney SD
Supt. — See Wyoming
Fifer MS 800/6-8
109 E Camden Wyoming Ave 19934 302-698-8400
Brian Smith, prin. Fax 698-8409
Frear ES 700/1-5
238 Sorghum Mill Rd 19934 302-697-3279
Julie Lavender, prin. Fax 697-4056
Postlethwait MS 800/6-8
2841 S State St 19934 302-698-8410
Derek Prillaman, prin. Fax 698-8419

Claymont, New Castle, Pop. 8,108
Brandywine SD
Supt. — See Wilmington
Claymont ES 800/K-5
3401 Green St 19703 302-792-3880
Tamara Grimes-Stewart, prin. Fax 792-3877
Maple Lane ES 400/K-5
100 Maple Ln 19703 302-792-3906
Yulonda Murray, prin. Fax 792-3941

Clayton, Kent, Pop. 2,835
Smyrna SD
Supt. — See Smyrna
Clayton ES 500/K-4
510 Main St 19938 302-653-8587
Stephanie McGuire, prin. Fax 653-3421
Clayton IS 400/5-6
86 Sorrento Dr 19938 302-653-4512
David Paltrineri, prin. Fax 653-3271

Dagsboro, Sussex, Pop. 782

Lighthouse Christian S 100/PK-8
28157 Lighthouse Xing 19939 302-732-3309
Terri Menoche, dir. Fax 732-6974

Delmar, Sussex, Pop. 1,524
Delmar SD 1,300/5-12
200 N 8th St 19940 302-846-9544
Charity Phillips, supt. Fax 846-2793
www.delmar.k12.de.us
Delmar MS 700/5-8
200 N 8th St 19940 302-846-9544
Andy O'Neal, prin. Fax 846-5056

Dover, Kent, Pop. 34,742
Caesar Rodney SD
Supt. — See Wyoming
Brown ES 400/1-5
360 Webbs Ln 19904 302-697-2101
Susan Frampton Ed.D., prin. Fax 697-4973
Dover AFB MS 200/6-8
3100 Hawthorne Dr 19901 302-674-3284
David Santore Ed.D., prin. Fax 730-4283
Star Hill ES 500/1-5
594 Voshells Mill Star Hill 19901 302-697-6117
Nicole McDowell, prin. Fax 697-4983
Stokes ES 500/1-5
3874 Upper King Rd 19904 302-697-3205
Nicole Jones, prin. Fax 697-4029
Welch ES 400/K-5
3100 Hawthorne Dr 19901 302-674-9080
Jason Payne, prin. Fax 674-0682

Capital SD 6,400/PK-12
198 Commerce Way 19904 302-672-1500
Dr. Dan Shelton, supt. Fax 672-1714
www.capital.k12.de.us
Central MS 900/7-8
211 Delaware Ave 19901 302-672-1772
Shan Green, prin. Fax 672-1733
East Dover ES 300/PK-4
852 S Little Creek Rd 19901 302-672-1655
Julie Giangiulio, prin. Fax 672-1663
Fairview ES 400/PK-4
700 Walker Rd 19904 302-672-1645
Melissa White, prin. Fax 672-1654
Henry MS 900/5-6
65 Carver Rd 19904 302-672-1622
Charles Sheppard, prin. Fax 672-1633
North Dover ES 400/K-4
855 College Rd 19904 302-672-1980
Kelly Green, prin. Fax 672-1985
South Dover ES 500/K-4
955 S State St 19901 302-672-1690
Jeffrey Sheehan, prin. Fax 672-1697
Towne Point ES 300/K-4
629 Buckson Dr 19901 302-672-1590
Tori Giddens, prin. Fax 672-1595
Washington ES 300/K-4
901 Forest St 19904 302-672-1900
Paige Morgan, prin. Fax 672-1902
Other Schools – See Hartly

Calvary Christian Academy 300/PK-12
1143 E Lebanon Rd 19901 302-697-7860
Aaron Coon, head sch Fax 697-0284
Dover First Christian S 50/PK-9
655 Wyoming Ave 19904 302-526-4998
Holy Cross S 600/PK-8
631 S State St 19901 302-674-5787
Linda Pollitt, prin. Fax 674-5782
St. John Lutheran S 100/PK-8
1156 Walker Rd 19904 302-734-3767
Dr. Dina Vendetti, prin. Fax 734-8809

Felton, Kent, Pop. 1,251
Lake Forest SD 3,700/PK-12
5423 Killens Pond Rd 19943 302-284-3020
Dr. Brenda Wynder, supt. Fax 284-4491
www.lf.k12.de.us
Lake Forest Central ES 600/4-5
5424 Killens Pond Rd 19943 302-284-5810
Michele Martel, prin. Fax 284-5819
Lake Forest North ES 500/PK-3
319 E Main St 19943 302-284-9611
Alexis Ray, prin. Fax 284-5820
Other Schools – See Frederica, Harrington

Frankford, Sussex, Pop. 835
Indian River SD
Supt. — See Selbyville
Clayton ES 600/PK-5
252 Clayton Ave 19945 302-732-3808
Allisa Booth, prin. Fax 732-3811

Frederica, Kent, Pop. 739
Lake Forest SD
Supt. — See Felton
Lake Forest East ES 300/PK-3
124 W Front St 19946 302-335-5261
Douglas Brown, prin. Fax 335-5273

Georgetown, Sussex, Pop. 6,322
Indian River SD
Supt. — See Selbyville
District K Center K-K
301 W Market St Ste A 19947 302-856-1946
Janet Hickman, prin. Fax 855-2149
Georgetown ES 800/1-5
301 W Market St Ste A 19947 302-856-1940
Neil Stong, prin. Fax 856-1915
Georgetown MS 600/6-8
301 W Market St 19947 302-856-1900
David Hudson, prin. Fax 856-1915
North Georgetown ES 700/1-5
664 N Bedford St 19947 302-855-2430
Heather Cramer, prin. Fax 855-2439

Jefferson S 100/PK-8
22051 Wilson Rd 19947 302-856-3300
Constance Hendricks M.Ed., hdmstr. Fax 856-1750

Greenwood, Sussex, Pop. 943
Woodbridge SD
Supt. — See Bridgeville
Woodbridge ECC 600/PK-2
400 Governors Ave 19950 302-349-4010
Kimberly Mitchell, prin. Fax 349-1413

Greenwood Mennonite S 200/PK-12
12802 Mennonite School Rd 19950 302-349-4131
Duane Miller, admin. Fax 349-5076

Harrington, Kent, Pop. 3,428
Lake Forest SD
Supt. — See Felton
Chipman MS 1,000/6-8
101 W Center St 19952 302-398-8197
Eric Stancell, prin. Fax 398-8375
Delaware ECC PK-PK
100 W Mispillion St 19952 302-398-8945
Dr. Tanya Robinson, dir. Fax 398-8983
Lake Forest South ES 400/PK-3
301 Dorman St 19952 302-398-8011
Clifford Owens, prin. Fax 398-8492

Hartly, Kent, Pop. 73
Capital SD
Supt. — See Dover
Hartly ES 400/PK-4
PO Box 25 19953 302-492-1870
Tammy Augustus, prin. Fax 492-1883

Hockessin, New Castle, Pop. 13,327
Red Clay Consolidated SD
Supt. — See Wilmington
Cooke ES K-5
2025 Graves Rd 19707 302-235-6600
Linda Ennis, prin. Fax 235-6635
DuPont MS 800/6-8
735 Meeting House Rd 19707 302-239-3420
Jason Bastianelli, prin. Fax 239-3450
North Star ES 700/K-5
1340 Little Baltimore Rd 19707 302-234-7200
Jenine Thomas, prin. Fax 234-7212

CACC Montessori S 100/PK-K
1313 Little Baltimore Rd 19707 302-239-2917
Hockessin Montessori S 100/PK-8
1000 Old Lancaster Pike 19707 302-234-1240
St. Mary's Early Education Program PK-PK
7200 Lancaster Pike 19707 302-239-7100
Karen Rombach, dir. Fax 239-8219
Sanford S 600/PK-12
6900 Lancaster Pike 19707 302-235-6500
Mark Anderson, head sch Fax 239-5389
Wilmington Christian S 500/PK-12
825 Loveville Rd 19707 302-239-2121
Dr. Roger Erdvig, head sch Fax 239-2778

Laurel, Sussex, Pop. 3,540
Laurel SD 1,800/PK-12
1160 S Central Ave 19956 302-875-6100
Shawn Larrimore, supt. Fax 875-6106
www.laurelschooldistrict.org
Dunbar ES 500/PK-1
1110 W 6th St 19956 302-875-6140
Brandon Snyder, prin. Fax 875-6143
Laurel MS 300/5-8
1131 S Central Ave 19956 302-875-6110
Dr. Richard Evans, prin. Fax 875-6109
North Laurel ES 600/2-4
600 Wilson St 19956 302-875-6130
David Hudson, prin. Fax 875-6133

Epworth Christian S 100/PK-8
14511 Sycamore Rd 19956 302-875-4488
Clint Moore, prin. Fax 875-7207

Lewes, Sussex, Pop. 2,714
Cape Henlopen SD 5,000/K-12
1270 Kings Hwy 19958 302-645-6686
Robert S. Fulton M.Ed., supt. Fax 645-6684
www.capehenlopenschools.com/
Beacon MS 600/6-8
19483 John J Williams Hwy 19958 302-645-6288
David Frederick, prin. Fax 644-6118
Love Creek ES K-5
19488 John J Williams Hwy 19958 302-703-3456
Patricia Mumford, prin.
Shields ES 700/K-5
910 Shields Ave 19958 302-645-7748
Jennifer Nauman, prin. Fax 644-7924
Other Schools – See Milton, Rehoboth Beach

Lincoln, Sussex
Milford SD
Supt. — See Milford
Morris ECC 400/PK-K
8609 3rd St 19960 302-422-1650
Jennifer Hallman, prin. Fax 424-5447

Geneva Academy 50/K-12
11146 Ponder Rd 19960 302-422-2130

Magnolia, Kent, Pop. 218
Caesar Rodney SD
Supt. — See Wyoming
McIlvaine ECC 500/K-K
11 E Walnut St 19962 302-335-5039
Brook Castillo, prin. Fax 335-3705

Middletown, New Castle, Pop. 18,350
Appoquinimink SD
Supt. — See Odessa
Appoquinimink Preschool Center 200/PK-PK
502 S Broad St 19709 302-376-4400
Dr. Kimberly Brancato, prin. Fax 378-5696
Brick Mill ES 500/1-5
378 Brick Mill Rd 19709 302-378-5288
Dr. Rebecca Feathers, prin. Fax 378-5299
Bunker Hill ES 600/1-5
1070 Bunker Hill Rd 19709 302-378-5135
Dr. Edward Gurdo, prin. Fax 378-5139
Cedar Lane ECC 200/K-K
1221 Cedar Lane Rd 19709 302-449-5873
Gina Robinson, prin. Fax 449-5877
Cedar Lane ES 600/1-5
1259 Cedar Lane Rd 19709 302-378-5045
Melisa Stilwell, prin. Fax 378-5091
Meredith MS 700/6-8
504 S Broad St 19709 302-378-5001
Nick Hoover, prin. Fax 378-5008
Redding MS 800/6-8
201 New St 19709 302-378-5030
Dr. Edward Small, prin. Fax 378-5080
Silver Lake ES 500/1-5
200 E Cochran St 19709 302-378-5023
Cynthia Clay, prin. Fax 378-5092
Waters MS 900/6-8
1235 Cedar Lane Rd 19709 302-449-3490
Thomas Poehlmann, prin. Fax 449-3496

St. Anne's Episcopal S 300/PK-8
211 Silver Lake Rd 19709 302-378-3179
Peter Thayer, head sch Fax 449-0957

Milford, Sussex, Pop. 9,349
Milford SD 4,000/PK-12
906 Lakeview Ave 19963 302-422-1600
Dr. Kevin Dickerson, supt. Fax 422-1608
www.milfordschooldistrict.org/
Banneker ES 500/1-5
449 North St 19963 302-422-1630
Dr. Bobbie Kilgore, prin. Fax 424-5487
Milford Central Academy 1,000/6-8
1021 N Walnut St 19963 302-424-7900
Dr. Nancy Carnevale, prin. Fax 424-4163
Mispillion ES 600/1-5
311 Lovers Ln 19963 302-424-5800
Teresa Wallace, prin. Fax 422-3469
Ross ES 400/1-5
310 Lovers Ln 19963 302-422-1640
Cynthia McKenzie, prin. Fax 424-5453

Other Schools – See Lincoln

Millsboro, Sussex, Pop. 3,755
Indian River SD
Supt. — See Selbyville
East Millsboro ES 700/PK-5
29346 Iron Branch Rd 19966 302-934-3222
Kelly Dorman, prin. Fax 934-3227
Long Neck ES 700/PK-5
26064 School Ln 19966 302-945-6200
Clara Conn, prin. Fax 945-6203
Millsboro MS 700/6-8
302 E State St 19966 302-934-3200
Renee Jerns Ed.D., prin. Fax 934-3215

Milton, Sussex, Pop. 2,504
Cape Henlopen SD
Supt. — See Lewes
Brittingham ES 600/K-5
400 Mulberry St 19968 302-684-8522
Ned Gladfelter, prin. Fax 684-2043
Mariner MS 500/6-8
16391 Harbeson Rd 19968 302-684-8516
Fred Best, prin. Fax 684-5606
Milton ES 600/K-5
512 Federal St 19968 302-684-2516
Dr. Beth Conaway, prin. Fax 684-8565

Delmarva Christian S Milton Campus 300/PK-8
PO Box 129 19968 302-684-4983
John Sadler, prin. Fax 684-2905

Newark, New Castle, Pop. 30,774
Christina SD
Supt. — See Wilmington
Brader ES 500/K-5
350 Four Seasons Pkwy 19702 302-454-5959
Dr. Jeanette Ganc, prin. Fax 454-5459
Brookside ES 300/K-5
800 Marrows Rd 19713 302-454-5454
Eric Stephens, prin. Fax 454-3480
Christina Early Education Center 300/PK-PK
620 E Chestnut Hill Rd 19713 302-454-2720
Rebecca Ryan, prin. Fax 454-2010
Downes ES 500/K-5
220 Casho Mill Rd 19711 302-454-2133
Patricia Prettyman, prin. Fax 454-3483
Gallaher ES 500/K-5
800 N Brownleaf Rd 19713 302-454-2464
Jacqueline Lee, prin. Fax 454-3484
Gauger-Cobbs MS 1,100/6-8
50 Gender Rd 19713 302-454-2358
Sean Mulrine, prin. Fax 454-3482
Jones ES 400/K-5
35 W Main St 19702 302-454-2131
Shevena Cale, prin. Fax 454-3481
Keene ES 700/K-5
200 LaGrange Ave 19702 302-454-2018
Mariellen Taraboletti, prin. Fax 454-5969
Kirk MS 800/6-8
140 Brennen Dr 19713 302-451-7021
Norman Kennedy, prin. Fax 454-3491
Leasure ES 600/K-5
1015 Church Rd 19702 302-454-2103
Deirdra Aikens, prin. Fax 454-2109
MacLary ES 400/K-5
300 Saint Regis Dr 19711 302-454-2142
Bartley Dryden, prin. Fax 454-3485
Marshall ES 600/K-5
101 Barrett Run Dr 19702 302-454-4700
Amy Selheimer, prin. Fax 454-4701
McVey ES 400/K-5
908 Janice Dr 19713 302-454-2145
David Wilkie, prin. Fax 454-3486
Shue-Medill MS 1,000/6-8
1500 Capitol Trl 19711 302-454-2171
Michele Savage, prin. Fax 454-3492
Smith ES 500/K-5
142 Brennen Dr 19713 302-454-2174
Dr. Mae Gaskins, prin. Fax 454-3487
West Park Place ES 400/K-5
193 W Park Pl 19711 302-454-2290
Ledonnis Hernandez, prin. Fax 454-3488
Wilson ES 500/K-5
14 Forge Rd 19711 302-454-2180
Natalie Birch, prin. Fax 454-3489

Red Clay Consolidated SD
Supt. — See Wilmington
Forest Oak ES 500/K-5
55 S Meadowood Dr 19711 302-454-3420
Erin McNulty, prin. Fax 454-3423

Christ the Teacher Catholic S 600/PK-8
2451 Frazer Rd 19702 302-838-8850
Sr. LaVerne King, prin. Fax 838-8854
Delaware Tarbiyah S 100/PK-8
698 Old Baltimore Pike 19702 302-533-8114
Holy Angels S 400/PK-8
82 Possum Park Rd 19711 302-731-2210
Barbara Snively, prin. Fax 731-2211
Independence S 800/PK-8
1300 Paper Mill Rd 19711 302-239-0330
Victoria Yatzus, head sch Fax 239-3696
Islamic Academy of Delaware 100/PK-8
28 Salem Church Rd 19713 302-455-9988
Learning Express Academy 100/K-8
302 Darling St 19702 302-737-8260

New Castle, New Castle, Pop. 5,184
Colonial SD 9,700/K-12
318 E Basin Rd 19720 302-323-2700
Dolon Blakey Ed.D., supt. Fax 323-2748
www.colonialschooldistrict.org
Bedford MS 1,000/6-8
801 Cox Neck Rd 19720 302-832-6280
Andrew Moffett, prin. Fax 834-6729
Castle Hills ES 700/K-5
502 Moores Ln 19720 302-323-2915
Janissa Nuneville, prin. Fax 323-2921
Downie ES 400/K-5
1201 Delaware St 19720 302-323-2926
Douglas Timm, prin. Fax 323-2929
Eisenberg ES 600/K-5
27 Landers Ln 19720 302-429-4074
David Distler, prin. Fax 429-4081
McCullough MS 800/6-8
20 Chase Ave 19720 302-429-4000
Ige Purnell, prin. Fax 429-4005
New Castle ES 600/K-5
903 Delaware St 19720 302-323-2880
Nneka Jones, prin. Fax 323-2897
Pleasantville ES 500/K-5
16 Pleasant Pl 19720 302-323-2935
Jennifer Alexander, prin. Fax 323-2943
Read MS 700/6-8
314 E Basin Rd 19720 302-323-2760
Holly Sage, prin. Fax 323-2763
Southern ES 900/K-5
795 Cox Neck Rd 19720 302-832-6300
Jeffory Gibeault, prin. Fax 832-6305
Wilmington Manor ES 300/K-5
200 E Roosevelt Ave 19720 302-323-2901
Stacie Ruiz, prin. Fax 323-2908
Other Schools – See Bear

St. Peter the Apostle S 200/PK-8
515 Harmony St 19720 302-328-1191
Mark Zitz, prin. Fax 328-8049
Serviam Girls Academy 50/5-8
14 Halcyon Dr 19720 302-651-9700
Kate Lucyk, prin. Fax 651-9703

Ocean View, Sussex, Pop. 1,869
Indian River SD
Supt. — See Selbyville
Baltimore ES 700/PK-5
PO Box 21 19970 302-537-2700
Pam Webb, prin. Fax 537-2708

Odessa, New Castle, Pop. 353
Appoquinimink SD 10,200/PK-12
PO Box 4010 19730 302-376-4128
Dr. Matthew Burrows, supt. Fax 378-5007
www.apposchooldistrict.com
Other Schools – See Bear, Middletown, Townsend

Rehoboth Beach, Sussex, Pop. 1,324
Cape Henlopen SD
Supt. — See Lewes
Rehoboth ES 600/K-5
500 Stockley St 19971 302-227-2571
Susan Donahue, prin. Fax 227-5178

Seaford, Sussex, Pop. 6,739
Seaford SD 2,400/K-12
390 N Market Street Ext 19973 302-629-4587
David Perrington, supt. Fax 629-2619
www.seafordbluejays.org
Douglass ES 200/3-5
1 Swain Rd 19973 302-628-4413
Carol Leveillee, prin. Fax 628-4486
Seaford Central ES 200/3-5
1 Delaware Pl 19973 302-629-4587
Becky Neubert, prin. Fax 628-4380
Seaford MS 800/6-8
500 E Stein Hwy 19973 302-629-4587
Jason Cameron, prin. Fax 628-4485
West Seaford ES 200/K-2
511 Sussex Ave 19973 302-628-4414
Laura Schneider, prin. Fax 628-4487
Other Schools – See Blades

Child Craft Company S 100/PK-8
26396 Seaford Rd 19973 302-628-1231
Cross Christian Academy 50/K-12
110 Holly St 19973 302-629-7161
Donald Porter, dir. Fax 629-7726

Selbyville, Sussex, Pop. 2,147
Indian River SD 9,100/PK-12
31 Hosier St 19975 302-436-1000
Mark Steele, supt. Fax 436-1034
www.irsd.net
Selbyville MS 700/6-8
80 Bethany Rd 19975 302-436-1020
Jason Macrides, prin. Fax 436-1035
Showell ES 400/PK-5
41 Bethany Rd 19975 302-436-1040
Karen Clausen, prin. Fax 436-1053
Southern Delaware S of the Arts 400/K-8
27 Hosier St 19975 302-436-1066
Barkley Heck, prin. Fax 436-1068
Other Schools – See Frankford, Georgetown, Millsboro, Ocean View

Smyrna, Kent, Pop. 9,689
Smyrna SD 5,200/PK-12
82 Monrovia Ave 19977 302-653-8585
Patrik Williams, supt. Fax 653-3149
www.smyrna.k12.de.us
Moore IS 400/5-8
20 W Frazier St 19977 302-659-6297
Elyse Baerga, prin. Fax 659-6299
North Smyrna ES 500/PK-4
365 N Main St 19977 302-653-8589
Kelly Holt, prin. Fax 653-3146
Smyrna ES 500/PK-4
121 S School Ln 19977 302-653-8588
David Morrison, prin. Fax 653-3411
Smyrna MS 800/5-8
700 Duck Creek Pkwy 19977 302-653-8584
Steven Gull, prin. Fax 653-3424
Sunnyside ES 600/K-4
123 Rabbit Chase Ln 19977 302-653-8580
Deborah Judy, prin. Fax 653-5402

Other Schools – See Clayton

Academy at St. Polycarp PK-PK
499 E South St 19977 302-653-1496
Nancy Koska, dir. Fax 653-3509
Smyrna Christian S 50/PK-6
1630 Joe Goldsborough Rd 19977 302-653-4556
Jim Marr, admin. Fax 653-4556

Townsend, New Castle, Pop. 1,994
Appoquinimink SD
Supt. — See Odessa
Old State ES 800/1-5
580 Tony Marchio Dr 19734 302-378-6720
Rene Nolan, admin. Fax 378-4265
Spring Meadow ECC 200/K-K
611 Campus Dr 19734 302-376-6760
Dr. Gayle Rutter, admin. Fax 378-4615
Townsend ECC 100/K-K
10 Brook Ramble Ln 19734 302-378-9960
Carolyn Joynt, prin. Fax 378-5128
Townsend ES 400/1-5
126 Main St 19734 302-378-5020
Don Davis, prin. Fax 378-5088

Wilmington, New Castle, Pop. 69,534
Brandywine SD 10,800/K-12
1311 Brandywine Blvd 19809 302-793-5000
Dr. Mark Holodick, supt. Fax 792-3823
www.brandywineschools.org
Carrcroft ES 500/K-5
503 Crest Rd 19803 302-762-7165
Mark Overly, prin. Fax 762-7106
duPont MS 1,000/6-8
701 W 34th St 19802 302-762-7146
Delethia McIntire, prin. Fax 762-7196
Forwood ES 500/K-5
1900 Westminster Dr 19810 302-475-3956
Holly Van Such, prin. Fax 529-3092
Hanby ES 600/K-5
2523 Berwyn Rd 19810 302-479-2220
Veronica Wilkie, prin. Fax 479-2216
Harlan ES 400/K-5
3601 N Jefferson St 19802 302-762-7156
Hekima Wicker, prin. Fax 762-7117
Lancashire ES 500/K-5
2000 Naamans Rd 19810 302-475-3990
Lavina Davis, prin. Fax 475-3999
Lombardy ES 600/K-5
412 Foulk Rd 19803 302-762-7190
Lynn Sharps, prin. Fax 762-7108
Mt. Pleasant ES 800/K-5
500 Duncan Rd 19809 302-762-7120
Matt Auerbach, prin. Fax 762-7040
Springer MS 900/6-8
2220 Shipley Rd 19803 302-479-1621
Dr. Tracy Woodson, prin. Fax 479-1628
Talley MS 700/6-8
1110 Cypress Rd 19810 302-475-3976
Mark Mayer, prin. Fax 475-3998
Other Schools – See Claymont

Christina SD 15,900/PK-12
600 N Lombard St 19801 302-552-2600
Richard Gregg, supt. Fax 429-5857
www.christina.k12.de.us
Bancroft ES 400/PK-5
700 N Lombard St 19801 302-429-4102
Harold Ingram, prin. Fax 429-3956
Bayard MS 500/6-8
200 S Dupont St 19805 302-429-4118
Victoir Cahoon, prin. Fax 429-4153
Elbert-Palmer ES 200/PK-5
1210 Lobdell St 19801 302-429-4188
Dr. Gina Moody, prin. Fax 429-3957
Pulaski ES 400/K-5
1300 Cedar St 19805 302-429-4136
Raushann Austin, prin. Fax 429-3955
Stubbs ES 300/PK-5
1100 N Pine St 19801 302-429-4175
Jeffers Brown, prin. Fax 429-3958
Other Schools – See Bear, Newark

Red Clay Consolidated SD 18,400/PK-12
1502 Spruce Ave 19805 302-552-3700
Dr. Mervin Daugherty, supt. Fax 992-7820
redclay.schoolwires.net
Baltz ES 600/PK-5
1500 Spruce Ave 19805 302-992-5560
Amy O'Neill, prin. Fax 992-5518
Brandywine Springs S 1,100/K-8
2916 Duncan Rd 19808 302-636-5681
Fax 636-5683
DuPont MS 500/6-8
3130 Kennett Pike 19807 302-651-2690
Susan Huffman, prin. Fax 425-4585
Heritage ES 600/K-5
2815 Highlands Ln 19808 302-454-3424
Alice Conlin, prin. Fax 454-3427
Highlands ES 400/K-5
2100 Gilpin Ave 19806 302-651-2715
Barbara Land, prin. Fax 425-4599
Lewis ES 500/PK-5
920 N Van Buren St 19806 302-651-2695
Ariadna Castaneda, prin. Fax 651-2759
Linden Hill ES 900/K-5
3415 Skyline Dr 19808 302-454-3406
Thomas Glennon, prin. Fax 454-3549
Marbrook ES 600/K-5
2101 Centerville Rd 19808 302-992-5555
Melissa Phillips, prin. Fax 892-3253
Mote ES 600/PK-5
2110 Edwards Ave 19808 302-992-5565
Anthony Gray-Bolden, prin. Fax 892-3251
Richardson Park ES 500/K-5
16 Idella Ave 19804 302-992-5570
Alice Mason, prin. Fax 892-3255
Richey ES 400/K-5
105 E Highland Ave 19804 302-992-5535
Dorothy Johnson, prin. Fax 892-3242
Shortlidge Academy 200/PK-2
100 W 18th St 19802 302-651-2710
Maribeth Courtney, prin. Fax 425-3385
Skyline MS 800/6-8
2900 Skyline Dr 19808 302-454-3410
Frank Rumford, prin. Fax 454-3541
Stanton MS 700/6-8
1800 Limestone Rd 19804 302-992-5540
Tawanda Bond, prin. Fax 992-5586

Warner ES 400/PK-K, 3-5
801 W 18th St 19802 302-651-2740
Dr. Chrishaun Fitzgerald, prin. Fax 651-2661
Other Schools – See Hockessin, Newark

All Saints Catholic S 500/PK-8
907 New Rd 19805 302-995-2231
Dr. Mary Elizabeth Muir, prin. Fax 993-0767
Concord Christian Academy 200/PK-12
2510 Marsh Rd 19810 302-475-3247
Einstein Academy 50/K-5
101 Garden of Eden Rd 19803 302-478-5026
Rabbi Jeremy Winaker, head sch Fax 478-0664
Harvest Christian Academy 100/PK-8
2205 Lancaster Ave 19805 302-654-2613
Dr. Raymond Williams, hdmstr. Fax 654-2614
Immaculate Heart of Mary S 500/PK-8
1000 Shipley Rd 19803 302-764-0977
John Mitchell, prin. Fax 764-0375
Nativity Preparatory S 50/5-8
1515 Linden St 19805 302-777-1015
Paul Webster, prin. Fax 777-1225
Pilot School 200/K-8
208 Woodlawn Rd 19803 302-478-1740
Alexandra Kokkoris, dir. Fax 478-1746
St. Ann S 300/PK-8
2006 Shallcross Ave 19806 302-652-6567
Stacy Solomon, prin. Fax 652-4156
St. Anthony of Padua S 300/PK-8
1715 W 9th St 19805 302-421-3743
Judith White, prin. Fax 421-3796
St. Edmond's Academy 200/PK-8
2120 Veale Rd 19810 302-475-5370
Brian Ray, hdmstr. Fax 475-2256
St. Elizabeth S 300/PK-6
1500 Cedar St 19805 302-655-8208
Christina Wecht, prin. Fax 655-5457
St. John the Beloved S 600/PK-8
905 Milltown Rd 19808 302-998-5525
Richard Hart, prin. Fax 998-1923
St. Mary Magdalen S 500/PK-8
9 Sharpley Rd 19803 302-656-2745
Kathy O'Toole, prin. Fax 656-7889
St. Peter Cathedral S 200/PK-8
310 6th Ave 19805 302-656-5234
Sr. Donna Smith, prin. Fax 658-6489
Sharon Temple Adventist S 50/K-8
2001 N Washington St 19802 302-428-0216
Tatnall S 700/PK-12
1501 Barley Mill Rd 19807 302-998-2292
Christopher Tompkins, head sch Fax 892-4389
Tower Hill S 800/PK-12
2813 W 17th St 19806 302-575-0550
Elizabeth C. Speers, head sch Fax 657-8366
Ursuline Academy 500/PK-12
1106 Pennsylvania Ave 19806 302-658-7158
Cathie Field-Lloyd, pres. Fax 658-4297
Wilmington Friends S 800/PK-12
101 School Rd 19803 302-576-2900
Ken Aldridge, head sch Fax 576-2939
Wilmington Junior Academy 50/K-8
3001 Mill Creek Rd 19808 302-998-0530
Wilmington Montessori S 300/PK-8
1400 Harvey Rd 19810 302-475-0555
Lisa Lalama, head sch Fax 529-7004

Wyoming, Kent, Pop. 1,263
Caesar Rodney SD 7,600/K-12
7 Front St 19934 302-698-4800
Kevin Fitzgerald Ed.D., supt. Fax 697-3406
www.cr.k12.de.us
Simpson ES 500/1-5
5 Old North Rd 19934 302-697-3207
Michael Kijowski, prin. Fax 697-4963
Other Schools – See Camden, Dover, Magnolia

DISTRICT OF COLUMBIA

DISTRICT OF COLUMBIA PUBLIC SCHOOLS
1200 1st St NE, Washington 20002
Telephone 202-442-5885
Fax 202-442-5026
Website dcps.dc.gov/

Chancellor Amanda Alexander

DISTRICT OF COLUMBIA BOARD OF EDUCATION
441 4th St NW Ste 723N, Washington 20001

President Karen Williams

PUBLIC, PRIVATE AND CATHOLIC ELEMENTARY SCHOOLS

Washington, District of Columbia, Pop. 587,406

District of Columbia SD 45,700/PK-12
1200 1st St NE 20002 202-442-5885
Antwan Wilson, chncllr. Fax 442-5026
dcps.dc.gov

Aiton ES 200/PK-5
533 48th Pl NE 20019 202-671-6060
Malaika Golden, prin. Fax 724-4630

Amidon-Bowen ES 300/PK-5
401 I St SW 20024 202-724-4867
TaMikka Sykes, prin. Fax 724-4868

Bancroft ES 500/PK-5
4300 13th St NW 20011 202-673-7280
Arthur Mola, prin. Fax 673-6991

Barnard ES 600/PK-5
430 Decatur St NW 20011 202-576-1100
Grace Reid, prin. Fax 541-6010

Beers ES 400/PK-5
3600 Alabama Ave SE 20020 202-939-4800
Gwendolyn Payton, prin. Fax 645-3225

Brent ES 400/PK-5
301 N Carolina Ave SE 20003 202-698-3363
Norah Lycknell, prin. Fax 698-3369

Brightwood Education Campus 600/PK-8
1300 Nicholson St NW 20011 202-722-5670
Maurice Kennard, prin. Fax 576-6168

Brookland MS 6-8
1150 Michigan Ave NE 20017 202-759-1999
Kerry Richardson, prin. Fax 671-6251

Browne Education Campus 300/PK-8
850 26th St NE 20002 202-671-6210
Dwight Davis, prin. Fax 671-2305

Bruce-Monroe ES 500/PK-5
3560 Warder St NW 20010 202-576-6222
Alethea Bustillo, prin. Fax 576-6225

Bunker Hill ES PK-5
1401 Michigan Ave NE 20017 202-576-6095
Kara Kuchemba, prin. Fax 576-4632

Burroughs ES 200/PK-5
1820 Monroe St NE 20018 202-576-6150
LeVar Jenkins, prin. Fax 576-6819

Burrville ES 400/PK-5
801 Division Ave NE 20019 202-671-6020
Tui Roper, prin. Fax 724-5578

Capitol Hill Montessori S 300/PK-8
215 G St NE 20002 202-698-4467
Brandon Eatman, prin. Fax 698-4533

Cleveland ES 300/PK-5
1825 8th St NW 20001 202-939-4380
Anna Krughoff, prin. Fax 673-6461

Cooke ES 400/PK-5
2525 17th St NW 20009 202-939-5390
Katie Larkin, prin. Fax 671-2757

Deal MS 1,200/6-8
3815 Fort Dr NW 20016 202-939-2010
Diedre Neal, prin. Fax 282-1116

Drew ES 200/PK-5
5600 Eads St NE 20019 202-671-6040
Naimah Salahuddin, prin. Fax 724-4924

Eaton ES 500/PK-5
3301 Lowell St NW 20008 202-282-0103
Dale Mann, prin. Fax 282-0074

Eliot-Hine MS 300/6-8
1830 Constitution Ave NE 20002 202-939-5380
Eugenia Young, prin. Fax 673-8063

Garfield ES 300/PK-5
2435 Alabama Ave SE 20020 202-671-6140
Kennard Branch, prin. Fax 698-1614

Garrison ES 300/PK-5
1200 S St NW 20009 202-673-7263
Brigham Kiplinger, prin. Fax 673-6828

Hardy MS 400/6-8
1819 35th St NW 20007 202-729-4350
Lucas Cooke, prin. Fax 576-9443

Harris ES 300/PK-5
301 53rd St SE 20019 202-645-3188
Heather Hairston, prin. Fax 645-3190

Hart MS 600/6-8
601 Mississippi Ave SE 20032 202-671-6426
Charlette Butler, prin. Fax 645-3426

Hearst ES 300/PK-5
3950 37th St NW 20008 202-282-0106
Jennifer Thomas, prin. Fax 282-2303

Height ES PK-5
1300 Allison St NW 20011 202-723-4100
Masi Preston, prin. Fax 723-6867

Hendley ES 500/PK-5
425 Chesapeake St SE 20032 202-645-3450
Sundai Riggins, prin. Fax 645-7098

Houston ES 300/PK-5
1100 50th Pl NE 20019 202-671-6170
Rembert Seaward, prin. Fax 724-4625

Hyde-Addison ES 300/PK-5
2501 11th St NW 20001 202-282-0170
Elizabeth Namba, prin. Fax 282-0087

Janney ES 600/PK-5
4130 Albemarle St NW 20016 202-282-0110
Alysia Lutz, prin. Fax 282-0112

Jefferson MS Academy 300/6-8
801 7th St SW 20024 202-729-3270
Greg Dohmann, prin. Fax 724-2459

Johnson MS 300/6-8
1400 Bruce Pl SE 20020 202-939-3140
Courtney Taylor, prin. Fax 645-5882

Ketcham ES 300/PK-5
1919 15th St SE 20020 202-698-1122
Maisha Riddlesprigger, prin. Fax 698-1113

Key ES 400/PK-5
5001 Dana Pl NW 20016 202-729-3280
David Landeryou, prin. Fax 282-0188

Kimball ES 300/PK-5
4430 H St SE 20019 202-671-6260
Johann Lee, prin. Fax 645-3147

King ES 400/PK-5
3200 6th St SE 20032 202-939-4900
Angel Hunter, prin. Fax 645-7308

Kramer MS 400/6-8
1700 Q St SE 20020 202-939-3150
Roman Smith, prin. Fax 698-1169

LaFayette ES 700/PK-5
5701 Broad Branch Rd NW 20015 202-282-0116
Carrie Broquard, prin. Fax 282-1126

Langdon ES 300/PK-5
1900 Evarts St NE 20018 202-576-6048
Kemi Husbands, prin. Fax 576-7976

Langley ES 300/PK-5
101 T St NE 20002 202-724-4223
Vanessa Drumm, prin. Fax 832-1377

LaSalle-Backus Education Campus 300/PK-8
501 Riggs Rd NE 20011 202-671-6340
Justin Ralstom, prin. Fax 541-3859

Leckie ES 400/PK-8
4201 Martin Luther King Jr 20032 202-645-3330
Niyeka Wilson, prin. Fax 645-3331

Ludlow-Taylor ES 300/PK-5
659 G St NE 20002 202-698-3244
Andrew Smith, prin. Fax 698-3250

MacFarland MS 6-7
4400 Iowa Ave NW 20011 202-671-6033
Mark Sanders, prin. Fax 671-6036

Malcolm X ES 200/PK-5
1500 Mississippi Ave SE 20032 202-645-3409
Zara Berry-Young, prin. Fax 645-7219

Mann ES 300/PK-5
4430 Newark St NW 20016 202-282-0126
Elizabeth Whisnant, prin. Fax 282-0128

Maury ES 300/PK-5
1250 Constitution Ave NE 20002 202-698-3838
Carolyne Albert-Garvey, prin. Fax 698-3844

McKinley MS 200/6-8
151 T St NE 20002 202-281-3950
Mary Louise Jones, prin. Fax 832-1293

Miller MS 500/6-8
301 49th St NE 20019 202-388-6870
Kortni Stafford, prin. Fax 727-8330

Miner ES 400/PK-5
601 15th St NE 20002 202-397-3960
Bruce Jackson, prin. Fax 724-4957

Moten ES 400/PK-5
1565 Morris Rd SE 20020 202-698-1111
Akeia Dogbe, prin. Fax 698-1112

Murch ES 600/PK-5
3373 Van Ness St NW 20008 202-282-0130
Chris Cebrzynski, prin. Fax 282-0132

Nalle ES 400/PK-5
219 50th St SE 20019 202-671-6280
Kim Adutwum, prin. Fax 645-3196

Noyes ES 200/PK-5
2725 10th St NE 20018 202-281-2580
Kermit Burks, prin. Fax 576-7397

Orr ES 400/PK-5
2200 Minnesota Ave SE 20020 202-671-6240
Carolyn Jackson-King, prin. Fax 645-3292

Oyster-Adams Bilingual ES 300/PK-3
2801 Calvert St NW 20008 202-671-6130
Mayra Canizales, prin. Fax 671-3087

Oyster-Adams Bilingual MS 300/4-8
2020 19th St NW 20009 202-673-7311
Mayra Canizales, prin. Fax 673-6500

Patterson ES 400/PK-5
4399 S Capitol Ter SW 20032 202-939-5280
Victorie Thomas, prin. Fax 645-3851

Payne ES 300/PK-5
1445 C St SE 20003 202-698-3262
Stephanie Byrd, prin. Fax 698-3263

Peabody ECC 200/PK-K
425 C St NE 20002 202-698-3277
Elena Bell, prin. Fax 698-3275

Plummer ES 400/PK-5
4601 Texas Ave SE 20019 202-939-4360
Terri Fuller, prin. Fax 645-3176

Powell ES 400/PK-5
1350 Upshur St NW 20011 202-671-6270
O'kiyyah Lyons-Lucas, prin. Fax 576-7155

Randle Highlands ES 300/PK-5
1650 30th St SE 20020 202-729-3250
Kristie Edwards, prin. Fax 645-3911

Raymond Education Campus 500/PK-8
915 Spring Rd NW 20010 202-576-6236
Natalie Hubbard, prin. Fax 576-7275

Reed ES 400/PK-5
2201 18th St NW 20011 202-673-7308
Katie Lundgren, prin. Fax 671-5042

Ross ES 200/PK-5
1730 R St NW 20009 202-673-7200
Holly Searl, prin. Fax 673-6644

Savoy ES 400/PK-5
2400 Shannon Pl SE 20020 202-939-2000
Lisa Rosado, prin. Fax 535-1415

School Within School 200/PK-5
920 F St NE 20002 202-727-7377
John Burst, lead tchr. Fax 727-9276

School Without Walls 300/PK-8
2425 N St NW 20037 202-724-4841
Richard Trogisch, prin. Fax 724-3957

Seaton ES 300/PK-5
1503 10th St NW 20001 202-673-7215
Kim Jackson, prin. Fax 671-5014

Shepherd ES 300/PK-5
7800 14th St NW 20012 202-576-6140
Jade Brawley, prin. Fax 576-7578

Simon ES 300/PK-5
401 Mississippi Ave SE 20032 202-645-3360
Sharon Holmes, prin. Fax 645-3359

Smothers ES 300/PK-5
4400 Brooks St NE 20019 202-939-3600
Kiana Williams, prin. Fax 724-2377

Sousa MS 300/6-8
3650 Ely Pl SE 20019 202-729-3260
Courtney Wilkerson, prin. Fax 645-0456

Stanton ES 600/PK-5
2701 Naylor Rd SE 20020 202-671-6180
Caroline Fisherow, prin. Fax 645-3264

Stoddert ES 400/PK-5
4001 Calvert St NW 20007 202-671-6030
Donald Bryant, prin. Fax 282-0145

Stuart-Hobson MS 400/6-8
410 E St NE 20002 202-671-6010
Kristofer Comeforo, prin. Fax 698-4720

Takoma Education Campus 400/PK-8
7010 Piney Branch Rd NW 20012 202-671-6050
Loren Brody, prin. Fax 576-7592

Thomas ES 400/PK-5
650 Anacostia Ave NE 20019 202-724-4593
Davia Walker, prin. Fax 724-5053

Thomson ES 300/PK-5
1200 L St NW 20005 202-898-4660
Carmen Shepherd, prin. Fax 442-8706

Truesdale Education Campus 500/PK-8
800 Ingraham St NW 20011 202-576-6202
Mary Ann Stinson, prin. Fax 576-6205

Tubman ES 500/PK-5
3101 13th St NW 20010 202-673-7285
Amanda Delabar, prin. Fax 673-2172
Turner ES 400/PK-5
3264 Stanton Rd SE 20020 202-645-3470
Eric Bethel, prin. Fax 610-9515
Tyler ES 500/PK-5
1001 G St SE 20003 202-939-4810
Mitchell Brunson, prin. Fax 698-3848
Van Ness ES PK-2
1150 5th St SE 20003 202-727-4314
Cynthia Robinson-Rivers, prin. Fax 727-6781
Walker-Jones Education Campus 500/PK-8
1125 New Jersey Ave NW 20001 202-939-5934
Clinton Turner, prin. Fax 535-1307
Watkins ES 500/1-5
420 12th St SE 20003 202-698-3355
Elena Bell, prin. Fax 698-3340
West Education Campus 300/PK-8
1338 Farragut St NW 20011 202-576-6226
Megan Vroman, prin. Fax 541-6087
Wheatley Education Campus 400/PK-8
1299 Neal St NE 20002 202-939-5970
Shenora Plenty, prin. Fax 724-9088
Whittier Education Campus 400/PK-8
6201 5th St NW 20011 202-576-6156
Tenia Pritchard, prin. Fax 576-6158
Wilson ES 400/PK-5
660 K St NE 20002 202-698-4733
Heidi Haggerty, prin. Fax 698-4727

Academia de la Recta Porta Christian S 100/K-12
7614 Georgia Ave NW 20012 202-726-8737
Annette Miles, admin. Fax 726-8759
Aidan Montessori S 200/PK-6
2700 27th St NW 20008 202-387-2700
Kevin Clark, head sch Fax 387-1777
Annunciation S 100/PK-8
3810 Massachusetts Ave 20016 202-362-1408
Nathaniel Juarez, prin. Fax 363-4057
Beauvoir S 400/PK-3
3500 Woodley Rd NW 20016 202-537-6485
Michael Eanes, head sch Fax 537-6512
Blessed Sacrament S 500/K-8
5841 Chevy Chase Pkwy NW 20015 202-966-6682
Christopher Kelly, prin. Fax 966-4938
British S of Washington 400/PK-12
2001 Wisconsin Ave NW 20007 202-829-3700
Ian Piper, prin. Fax 829-6522
Calvary Christian Academy 200/PK-8
806 Rhode Island Ave NE 20018 202-526-5176
Bernard Perry, prin. Fax 354-5423
Capitol Hill Day S 200/PK-8
210 S Carolina Ave SE 20003 202-547-2244
Jason Gray, head sch Fax 543-4597
Cornerstone S of Washington DC 100/PK-12
3742 Ely Pl SE 20019 202-575-0027
Derrick Max, prin. Fax 575-0669
Dupont Park Adventist S 200/PK-8
3942 Alabama Ave SE 20020 202-583-8500
Dr. George Thornton, prin. Fax 583-0650
Georgetown Day S 600/PK-8
4530 MacArthur Blvd NW 20007 202-295-6200
Russell Shaw, head sch Fax 364-9603
Holy Trinity S 300/PK-8
1325 36th St NW 20007 202-337-2339
Charles Hennessey, prin. Fax 337-0368
Jewish Primary Day S of Nations Capital 300/PK-8
6045 16th St NW 20011 202-291-5737
Naomi Reem, head sch Fax 291-4686
Lab S of Washington 200/1-12
4759 Reservoir Rd NW 20007 202-965-6600
Katherine Schantz, head sch Fax 965-5015
Lowell S 300/PK-8
1640 Kalmia Rd NW 20012 202-577-2000
Debbie Gibbs, head sch Fax 577-2001
Maret S 600/K-12
3000 Cathedral Ave NW 20008 202-939-8800
Marjo Talbott, head sch Fax 939-8845
National Presbyterian S 300/PK-6
4121 Nebraska Ave NW 20016 202-537-7500
Malcolm Lester, head sch Fax 537-7568
Our Lady of Victory S 200/PK-8
4755 Whitehaven Pkwy NW 20007 202-337-1421
Sheila Martinez, prin. Fax 337-2068
Preparatory S of the DC 100/PK-12
4501 16th St NW 20011 202-722-5080
Betty North, prin. Fax 722-5060
River S 200/PK-3
4880 MacArthur Blvd NW 20007 202-337-3554
Nancy Mellon, head sch Fax 337-3534
Sacred Heart S 200/PK-8
1625 Park Rd NW 20010 202-265-4828
Elise Heil, prin. Fax 265-0595
St. Anthony S 200/PK-8
3400 12th St NE 20017 202-526-4657
Michael Thomasian, prin. Fax 832-5567
St. Augustine S 200/PK-8
1421 V St NW 20009 202-667-2608
Sr. Gloriamary Agumagu, prin. Fax 667-2610
St. Francis Xavier Academy 200/PK-8
2700 O St SE 20020 202-581-2010
Harold Thomas, prin. Fax 581-1142
St. Patrick's Episcopal Day S 500/PK-8
4700 Whitehaven Pkwy NW 20007 202-342-2805
Peter Barrett, head sch Fax 342-7001
St. Peters S 200/PK-8
422 3rd St SE 20003 202-544-1618
Karen Clay, prin. Fax 547-5101
St. Thomas More Academy 200/PK-8
4265 4th St SE 20032 202-561-1189
Bridget Coates, prin. Fax 562-2336
San Miguel MS 100/6-8
7705 Georgia Ave NW 20012 202-232-8345
Dave Palank, prin. Fax 232-3987
Sheridan S 200/K-8
4400 36th St NW 20008 202-362-7900
Jessica Donovan, head sch Fax 244-9696
Sidwell Friends S 1,100/PK-12
3825 Wisconsin Ave NW 20016 202-537-8100
Bryan Garman, head sch Fax 537-8138
Walker S for Boys 100/K-6
3640 MLK Jr Ave SE 20032 202-678-1515
James Woody, dir. Fax 591-3061
Washington International S Primary Cmps 500/PK-5
1690 36th St NW 20007 202-243-1700
Clayton Lewis, head sch Fax 243-1797
Washington Jesuit Academy 100/5-8
900 Varnum St NE 20017 202-832-7679
Marcus Washington, hdmstr. Fax 832-8098
Washington S for Girls 100/3-8
1901 Mississippi Ave SE 20020 202-678-1113
Brianne Wetzel M.A., head sch Fax 678-1114

FLORIDA

FLORIDA DEPARTMENT OF EDUCATION
325 W Gaines St, Tallahassee 32399-0400
Telephone 850-245-0505
Fax 850-245-9667
Website http://www.fldoe.org/

Commissioner of Education Pam Stewart

FLORIDA BOARD OF EDUCATION
325 W Gaines St, Tallahassee 32399-0400

Chairperson Marva Johnson

PUBLIC, PRIVATE AND CATHOLIC ELEMENTARY SCHOOLS

Alachua, Alachua, Pop. 8,873
Alachua County SD
Supt. — See Gainesville
Alachua ES 400/3-5
13800 NW 152nd Pl 32615 386-462-1841
Heather Harbour, prin. Fax 273-4585
Irby ES 500/PK-2
13505 NW 140th St 32615 386-462-5002
Valdenora Fortner, prin. Fax 527-8215
Mebane MS 400/6-8
16401 NW 140th St 32615 386-462-1648
Manda Bessner, prin. Fax 273-4632

Forest Grove Christian Academy 100/PK-12
22575 NW 94th Ave 32615 386-462-3921

Altamonte Springs, Seminole, Pop. 40,483
Seminole County SD
Supt. — See Sanford
Altamonte ES 800/PK-5
525 Pineview St 32701 407-746-2950
Pam Gamble, prin. Fax 746-2999
Forest City ES 900/PK-5
1010 Sand Lake Rd 32714 407-746-1060
Paul Senko, prin. Fax 746-1099
Lake Orienta ES 700/PK-5
612 Newport Ave 32701 407-746-2650
Donna Weaver, prin. Fax 746-2699
Spring Lake ES 700/PK-5
695 Orange Ave 32714 407-746-1650
Nomie Kuniak, prin. Fax 746-1695
Teague MS 1,400/6-8
1350 Mcneil Rd 32714 407-320-1550
Debra Abbott, prin. Fax 320-1545

Altamonte Christian S 300/K-12
601 Palm Springs Dr 32701 407-831-0950
Annunciation Academy 600/PK-8
593 Jamestown Blvd 32714 407-774-2801
Patricia Kahle, prin. Fax 774-2826
St. Mary Magdalen S 500/PK-8
869 Maitland Ave 32701 407-339-7301
Lorianne Rotz, prin. Fax 339-9556

Altha, Calhoun, Pop. 529
Calhoun County SD
Supt. — See Blountstown
Altha S 600/PK-12
25793 N Main St 32421 850-762-3121
Sue Price, prin. Fax 762-9502

Alturas, Polk, Pop. 4,117
Polk County SD
Supt. — See Bartow
Alturas ES 300/PK-5
PO Box 97 33820 863-519-3917
Charles Pemberton, prin. Fax 519-3923

Alva, Lee, Pop. 2,582
Lee County SD
Supt. — See Fort Myers
Alva ES 400/PK-8
17500 Church Ave 33920 239-728-2494
Dale Houchin, prin. Fax 728-3259
River Hall ES 1,000/PK-5
2800 River Hall Pkwy 33920 239-693-0349
Alice Barfield, prin. Fax 693-5307

Anthony, Marion
Marion County SD
Supt. — See Ocala
Anthony ES 300/PK-5
9501 NE Jacksonville Rd 32617 352-671-6000
Lisa Coy, prin. Fax 671-6001
Sparr ES 400/PK-5
2525 NE County Road 329 32617 352-671-6060
Gay Street, prin. Fax 671-6061

Apollo Beach, Hillsborough, Pop. 13,822
Hillsborough County SD
Supt. — See Tampa
Apollo Beach ES 600/K-5
501 Apollo Beach Blvd 33572 813-671-5172
Kelly McMillan, prin. Fax 672-5075
Doby ES 800/PK-5
6720 Covington Garden Dr 33572 813-672-5388
Catherine Ferguson, prin. Fax 672-5392

Apopka, Orange, Pop. 40,626
Orange County SD
Supt. — See Orlando
Apopka ES 700/PK-5
311 Vick Rd 32712 407-884-2200
Lukeshia Miller, prin. Fax 884-2296
Apopka MS 1,100/6-8
425 N Park Ave 32712 407-884-2208
Kelly Pelletier, prin. Fax 884-2217
Clay Springs ES 800/PK-5
555 N Wekiwa Springs Rd 32712 407-884-2275
Patricia Weisbach, prin. Fax 884-2289
Dream Lake ES 800/PK-5
500 N Park Ave 32712 407-884-2227
Carol-Ann Clenton-Martin, prin. Fax 884-2298
Lakeville ES 900/K-5
2015 Lakeville Rd 32703 407-814-6110
Cynthia Swanson, prin. Fax 814-6120
Lovell ES 700/PK-5
815 Roger Williams Rd 32703 407-884-2235
Oscar Aguirre, prin. Fax 884-5270
Piedmont Lakes MS 1,200/6-8
2601 Lakeville Rd 32703 407-884-2265
Edward Thompson, prin. Fax 884-2287
Rock Springs ES 700/PK-5
2400 Rock Springs Rd 32712 407-884-2242
Nathan Hay, prin. Fax 884-6225
Wheatley ES 300/PK-5
1475 Marvin C Zanders Ave 32703 407-884-2250
Linton Atkinson, prin. Fax 884-3102
Wolf Lake ES 1,200/PK-5
1771 W Ponkan Rd 32712 407-464-3342
Caroll Grimando, prin. Fax 464-3366
Wolf Lake MS 1,200/6-8
1725 W Ponkan Rd 32712 407-464-3317
Caroll Grimando, prin. Fax 464-3336

Seminole County SD
Supt. — See Sanford
Bear Lake ES 1,000/K-5
3399 Gleaves Ct 32703 407-746-5550
Virginia Brouillard, prin. Fax 746-5599

Books Christian Academy 50/PK-8
1001 Roger Williams Rd 32703 407-884-0031
Sue Book, admin. Fax 884-0566
Champion Preparatory Academy 300/PK-12
1935 S Orange Blossom Trl 32703 407-788-0018
Community Christian Learning Center 100/K-12
PO Box 2347 32704 407-410-0049
StarChild Academy 400/PK-5
1550 N Wekiwa Springs Rd 32712 407-880-6060
Cindy Zimmerman, admin. Fax 880-7688
Trinity Christian S 200/PK-8
1022 S Orange Blossom Trl 32703 407-886-0212
Shawn Weeks, admin. Fax 886-3052

Arcadia, DeSoto, Pop. 7,533
De Soto County SD 4,600/PK-12
PO Box 2000 34265 863-494-4222
Dr. Karyn Gary, supt. Fax 494-0389
www.desotoschools.com
Desoto ECC 100/PK-PK
318 N Wilson Ave 34266 863-494-9303
Phyllis Clemons, prin. Fax 494-9030
DeSoto MS 1,100/6-8
420 E Gibson St 34266 863-494-4133
Dr. Christina Britton, prin. Fax 494-6263
Memorial ES 900/K-5
851 E Hickory St 34266 863-494-2736
Tracey White, prin. Fax 993-2202
West ES 800/K-5
304 W Imogene St 34266 863-494-3155
Bradley Warren, prin. Fax 494-3689
Other Schools – See Nocatee

Archer, Alachua, Pop. 1,106
Alachua County SD
Supt. — See Gainesville
Archer Community ES 500/PK-5
14533 SW 170th St 32618 352-495-2111
Stella Arduser, prin. Fax 495-1796

Jordan Glen S 100/PK-8
12425 SW 154th St 32618 352-495-2728

Astatula, Lake, Pop. 1,779
Lake County SD
Supt. — See Tavares
Astatula ES 600/PK-5
13925 Florida Ave 34705 352-343-1334
Robert Sherman, prin. Fax 343-1457

Astatula Christian S 100/K-12
13239 Florida Ave 34705 352-742-2221

Atlantic Beach, Duval, Pop. 12,332
Duval County SD
Supt. — See Jacksonville
Atlantic Beach ES 500/PK-5
298 Sherry Dr 32233 904-247-5924
Kimberly Gallagher, prin. Fax 270-1894
Finegan ES 400/K-5
555 Wonderwood Dr 32233 904-247-5996
Shameka Brown, prin. Fax 270-1858
Mayport ES 400/PK-5
2753 Shangri La Dr 32233 904-247-5988
Amy Cline, prin. Fax 247-5990
Mayport MS 900/6-8
2600 Mayport Rd 32233 904-247-5977
Katrina McCray, prin. Fax 247-5987

Auburndale, Polk, Pop. 13,305
Polk County SD
Supt. — See Bartow
Auburndale Central ES 400/PK-5
320 Lemon St 33823 863-965-5450
Octavia May, prin. Fax 965-6390
Boswell ES 400/K-5
2820 K Ville Ave 33823 863-499-2990
Martin Young, prin. Fax 284-4251
Caldwell ES 600/K-5
141 Dairy Rd 33823 863-965-5470
Cheryl Hill, prin. Fax 965-5473
Lena Vista ES 800/PK-5
925 Berkley Rd 33823 863-965-5464
Deneece Sharp, prin. Fax 965-6274
Stambaugh MS 800/6-8
226 N Main St 33823 863-965-5494
Trish Butler, prin. Fax 965-5496

Kingdom Preparatory S 100/K-12
301 Charlotte Rd 33823 863-551-8184

Ave Maria, Collier

Donahue Academy 300/K-12
4955 Seton Way, 239-280-2450
Dr. Dan Guernsey, prin. Fax 304-7033

Aventura, Miami-Dade, Pop. 35,370

Cheder Yesod Hadas PK-1
2956 Aventura Blvd 33180 305-933-1177
Lamb Athletic & Art Academy 200/K-12
1704 Buchanan St 33180 305-527-1997

Avon Park, Highlands, Pop. 8,676
Highlands County SD
Supt. — See Sebring
Avon ES 500/PK-5
705 Winthrop St 33825 863-452-4355
Carla Ball, prin. Fax 452-4372
Avon Park MS 700/6-8
401 S Lake Ave 33825 863-452-4333
Seth Lambert, prin. Fax 452-4341
Memorial ES 600/PK-5
867 Memorial Dr 33825 863-784-0200
Courtney Floyd, prin. Fax 784-0211
Park ES 600/PK-5
327 E Palmetto St 33825 863-452-4373
Carey Conner, prin. Fax 452-4382

Community Christian Academy 100/PK-12
1400 County Road 17A N 33825 863-452-0644
Hannah Okwengu, admin.

Cornerstone Christian Academy 50/K-10
2600 N Highlands Blvd 33825 863-453-0894
George Hall, admin.
Parkview Prep Academy 200/PK-10
107 A Miracle Ave 33825 863-453-8687
Brittany McGuire, dir. Fax 453-7454
Walker Memorial Academy 200/K-12
1525 W Avon Blvd 33825 863-453-3131

Baker, Okaloosa
Okaloosa County SD
Supt. — See Fort Walton Beach
Baker S 1,400/K-12
1369 14th St 32531 850-689-7279
Michael Martello, prin. Fax 689-7416

Baldwin, Duval, Pop. 1,376
Duval County SD
Supt. — See Jacksonville
Jones ES 400/K-5
700 Orange Ave 32234 904-266-1214
Angela Jordan, prin. Fax 266-1222

Bartow, Polk, Pop. 17,008
Polk County SD 97,500/PK-12
PO Box 391 33831 863-534-0500
Jacqueline Byrd, supt. Fax 519-8231
www.polk-fl.net
Bartow ES 500/K-5
590 S Wilson Ave 33830 863-534-7410
Tracy Nelson, prin. Fax 534-7218
Bartow MS 800/6-8
550 E Clower St 33830 863-534-7415
Christopher Roberts, prin. Fax 534-7418
Floral Avenue ES 500/PK-5
1530 S Floral Ave 33830 863-534-7420
Rebekah Eckman, prin. Fax 534-5003
Gibbons Street ES 300/PK-5
1860 E Gibbons St 33830 863-534-7430
Chabre Timmons, prin. Fax 534-7472
Holland ES 800/K-5
2342 EF Griffin Rd 33830 863-648-3031
Melody Butler, prin. Fax 648-3033
Stephens ES 400/PK-5
1350 N Maple Ave 33830 863-534-7455
Chandra Hall, prin. Fax 534-0438
Union Academy 400/6-8
1795 E Wabash St 33830 863-534-7435
Stephen Scheloske, prin. Fax 534-7487
Other Schools – See Alturas, Auburndale, Davenport, Dundee, Eagle Lake, Fort Meade, Frostproof, Haines City, Highland City, Lake Alfred, Lakeland, Lake Wales, Mulberry, Poinciana, Polk City, Winter Haven

First Methodist S 100/PK-8
455 S Broadway Ave 33830 863-533-0905

Bay Harbor Islands, Miami-Dade, Pop. 5,550
Miami-Dade County SD
Supt. — See Miami
Broad/Bay Harbor K-8 Center 1,300/PK-8
1155 93rd St 33154 305-865-7912
Scott Saperstein, prin. Fax 864-1396

Bell, Gilchrist, Pop. 455
Gilchrist County SD
Supt. — See Trenton
Bell ES 500/PK-5
2771 E Bell Ave 32619 352-463-3275
Suzanne Mathe, prin. Fax 463-3456

Belle Glade, Palm Beach, Pop. 17,323
Palm Beach County SD
Supt. — See West Palm Beach
Belle Glade ES 500/K-5
500 NW Avenue L 33430 561-829-4800
Robera Walker-Thompson, prin. Fax 829-4850
Glade View ES 300/K-5
1100 SW Avenue G 33430 561-993-8800
Linda Edgecomb, prin. Fax 993-8851
Gove ES 900/K-6
1000 SE Avenue G 33430 561-993-8700
Kim Thomasson, prin. Fax 993-8750
Lake Shore MS 700/6-8
425 W Canal St N 33430 561-829-1100
Carl Gibbons, prin. Fax 829-1130
Pioneer Park ES 400/K-5
39500 Pioneer Park Rd 33430 561-993-8600
Pamela Buckman, prin. Fax 993-8650

Glades Day S 300/PK-12
400 Gator Blvd 33430 561-996-6769
Amie Pitts, admin. Fax 992-9274

Belleview, Marion, Pop. 4,408
Marion County SD
Supt. — See Ocala
Belleview ES 700/PK-5
5556 SE County Highway 484 34420 352-671-6100
Dr. Stacey Varner, prin. Fax 671-6105
Belleview MS 1,000/6-8
10500 SE 36th Ave 34420 352-671-6235
Dr. Dion Gary, prin. Fax 671-6239
Belleview-Santos ES 500/K-5
9600 SE US Highway 441 34420 352-671-6260
Brian Greene, prin. Fax 671-6261

Belleview Christian Academy 200/PK-10
6107 SE Agnew Rd 34420 352-245-6151
Mike LaCrone, admin. Fax 245-3717
Souls Harbor Christian Academy 200/PK-12
12650 SE County Highway 484 34420 352-245-6252

Beverly Hills, Citrus, Pop. 8,274

St. Paul's Lutheran S 100/PK-8
6150 N Lecanto Hwy 34465 352-489-3027
Kyle Bender, prin. Fax 489-1062

Blountstown, Calhoun, Pop. 2,466
Calhoun County SD 2,200/PK-12
20859 Central Ave E Ste G20 32424 850-674-5927
Ralph Yoder, supt. Fax 674-5814
www.calhounflschools.org
Blountstown ES 700/PK-5
20883 NE Fuller Warren Dr 32424 850-674-8169
Pam Bozeman, prin. Fax 674-8844
Blountstown MS 300/6-8
17586 Main St N 32424 850-674-8234
Neva Miller, prin. Fax 674-6480
Other Schools – See Altha, Clarksville

Boca Raton, Palm Beach, Pop. 83,145
Palm Beach County SD
Supt. — See West Palm Beach
Boca Raton Community MS 1,400/6-8
1251 NW 8th St 33486 561-416-8700
Peter Slack, prin. Fax 416-8777
Boca Raton ES 300/K-5
103 SW 1st Ave 33432 561-544-1700
Renee Elfe, prin. Fax 544-1750
Calusa ES 900/K-5
2051 Clint Moore Rd 33496 561-989-7500
Dianne Rivelli-Schreiber, prin. Fax 989-7550
Coral Sunset ES 600/K-5
22400 Hammock St 33428 561-477-2100
Danielle Garcia, prin. Fax 477-2150
Del Prado ES 900/K-5
7900 Del Prado Cir N 33433 561-544-1800
Kathryn Morem, prin. Fax 544-1850
Eagles Landing MS 1,300/6-8
19500 Coral Ridge Dr 33498 561-470-7000
Joe Peccia, prin. Fax 470-7030
Estridge High Tech MS 1,200/6-8
1798 NW Spanish River Blvd 33431 561-989-7800
Rachel Capitano, prin. Fax 989-7810
Hammock Pointe ES 900/K-5
8400 SW 8th St 33433 561-477-2200
Stephanie Cook, prin. Fax 477-2250
Loggers Run Community MS 1,000/6-8
11584 W Palmetto Park Rd 33428 561-883-8000
Edmund Capitano, prin. Fax 883-8027
Mitchell ES 800/K-5
2470 NW 5th Ave 33431 561-750-4900
Joan Pierre-Jerome, prin. Fax 750-4906
Mizner ES 900/K-5
199 SW 12th Ave 33486 561-362-3100
Kelly Burke, prin. Fax 362-3150
Omni MS 1,400/6-8
5775 Jog Rd 33496 561-989-2800
Gerald Riopelle, prin. Fax 981-9651
Sandpiper Shores ES 800/K-5
11201 Glades Rd 33498 561-883-4000
Stephanie Coletto, prin. Fax 883-4050
Sunrise Park ES 900/K-5
19400 Coral Ridge Dr 33498 561-477-4300
Alicia Steiger, prin. Fax 477-4350
Verde ES 800/K-5
6590 Verde Trl 33433 561-218-6800
Seth Moldovan, prin. Fax 218-6850
Waters Edge ES 800/K-5
21601 Shorewind Dr 33428 561-852-2400
Joshua Davidow, prin. Fax 852-2450
Whispering Pines ES 800/K-5
9090 Spanish Isles Blvd 33496 561-672-2700
Barbara Riemer, prin. Fax 672-2750

Advent Lutheran S 200/PK-8
300 Yamato Rd 33431 561 306 3631
Laura Bluhm, admin. Fax 750-3632
Boca Raton Christian S 500/PK-12
315 NW 4th St 33432 561-391-2727
Robert Tennies Ed.D., hdmstr. Fax 226-0617
Boca Raton Prep International S 200/PK-12
10333 Diego Dr S 33428 561-852-1410
Emerging Minds Montessori Academy PK-8
9087 Glades Rd 33434 561-487-3535
Garden of the Sahaba Academy 300/PK-11
3100 NW 5th Ave 33431 561-395-3011
Grandview Preparatory S 200/PK-12
336 NW Spanish River Blvd 33431 561-416-9737
Hillel S of Boca Raton 500/PK-8
21011 95th Ave S 33428 561-470-5000
Klein Jewish Academy 700/K-12
9701 Donna Klein Blvd 33428 561-852-3300
Pine Crest S at Boca Raton 900/PK-8
2700 Saint Andrews Blvd 33434 561-852-2800
David Clark, head sch Fax 852-2832
St. Andrew's S 1,300/PK-12
3900 Jog Rd 33434 561-210-2000
Ethan Shapiro, head sch Fax 210-2007
St. Joan of Arc S 600/PK-8
501 SW 3rd Ave 33432 561-392-7974
Caroline Roberts, prin. Fax 368-6671
St. Jude Catholic S 300/PK-8
21689 Toledo Rd 33433 561-392-9160
Deborah Armstrong, prin. Fax 392-5815
St. Paul Lutheran S 400/PK-8
701 W Palmetto Park Rd 33486 561-395-8548
Dr. Jeffery Krempler, prin. Fax 395-2902
Sea Star S PK-8
2450 NW 5th Ave 33431 561-452-3618
Spanish River Christian S 600/PK-8
2400 Yamato Rd 33431 561-994-5006
Torah Academy of Boca Raton 200/PK-7
447 NW Spanish River Blvd 33431 561-347-1821

Bokeelia, Lee, Pop. 1,766
Lee County SD
Supt. — See Fort Myers
Pine Island ES 200/PK-5
5360 Ridgewood Dr 33922 239-283-0505
Steven Hook, prin. Fax 283-1748

Bonifay, Holmes, Pop. 2,723
Holmes County SD 3,300/PK-12
701 E Pennsylvania Ave 32425 850-547-9341
Terry Mears, supt. Fax 547-0381
www.hdsb.org
Bethlehem S 500/PK-12
2767 Highway 160 32425 850-547-3621
Brent Jones, prin. Fax 547-4856
Bonifay ES 800/PK-4
307 W North Ave 32425 850-547-3631
Rodd Jones, prin. Fax 547-4026
Bonifay MS 500/5-8
401 Mclaughlin Ave 32425 850-547-2754
Donald Etheridge, prin. Fax 547-3685
Other Schools – See Graceville, Ponce de Leon

Bonita Springs, Lee, Pop. 43,637
Lee County SD
Supt. — See Fort Myers
Bonita Springs ES 500/PK-5
10701 Dean St 34135 239-992-0801
Susan Caputo, prin. Fax 992-9118
Bonita Springs MS for the Arts 800/6-8
10141 W Terry St 34135 239-992-4422
Melissa Layner, prin. Fax 992-9157
Spring Creek ES 700/PK-5
25571 Elementary Way 34135 239-947-0001
Diane Sherman, prin. Fax 947-4690

Bowling Green, Hardee, Pop. 2,888
Hardee County SD
Supt. — See Wauchula
Bowling Green ES 400/K-5
4530 Church Ave 33834 863-375-2288
Kathy Clark, prin. Fax 375-3501

Boynton Beach, Palm Beach, Pop. 66,992
Palm Beach County SD
Supt. — See West Palm Beach
Citrus Cove ES 900/K-5
8400 Lawrence Rd 33436 561-292-7000
Laura Green, prin. Fax 292-7050
Congress MS 1,000/6-8
101 S Congress Ave 33426 561-374-5600
Denise O'Conner, prin. Fax 374-5642
Crosspointe ES 700/K-5
3015 S Congress Ave 33426 561-292-4100
Annmarie Dilbert, prin. Fax 292-4150
Crystal Lakes ES 600/PK-5
6050 Gateway Blvd, 561-292-6600
Diane Curcio-Greaves, prin. Fax 292-6650
Forest Park ES 600/K-5
1201 SW 3rd St 33435 561-292-6900
Nancy Robinson, prin. Fax 292-6950
Freedom Shores ES 900/K-5
3400 Hypoluxo Rd 33436 561-804-3100
Daniel Smith, prin. Fax 804-3150
Galaxy E3 ES 600/PK-5
550 NW 4th Ave 33435 561-739-5600
Lisa Steele, prin. Fax 739-5650
Hagen Road ES 700/K-5
10565 Hagen Ranch Rd 33437 561-292-6700
Robyn Saltzman, prin. Fax 292-6750
McAuliffe MS 1,100/6-8
6500 Le Chalet Blvd, 561-374-6600
Jeff Silverman, prin. Fax 374-6636
Odyssey MS 900/6-8
6161 W Woolbright Rd 33437 561-752-1300
Bonnie Fox, prin. Fax 752-1305
Poinciana ES 500/K-5
1203 N Seacrest Blvd 33435 561-739-5700
Kathleen DePuma, prin. Fax 739-5750
Rolling Green ES 800/K-5
550 Miner Rd 33435 561-202-9500
Allyson Manning, prin. Fax 202-9550
Sunset Palms ES 1,000/K-5
8650 Boynton Beach Blvd, 561-752-1100
Karen Riddle, prin. Fax 752-1150

Lake Worth Christian S 500/PK-12
7592 High Ridge Rd 33426 561-586-8216
Jim Harwood, supt. Fax 586-4382
St. Joseph's Episcopal S 200/PK-8
3300B S Seacrest Blvd 33435 561-732-2045
Kyle Aubrey M.A., prin. Fax 732-1315
St. Thomas More Academy 100/PK-PK
10935 S Military Trl 33436 561-737-3770
Fax 737-8128

Bradenton, Manatee, Pop. 48,642
Manatee County SD 44,600/PK-12
PO Box 9069 34206 941-708-8770
Dr. Diana Greene, supt. Fax 708-8686
www.manateeschools.net
Ballard ES 500/K-5
912 18th St W 34205 941-708-8400
Mike Masiello, prin. Fax 708-8408
Bashaw ES 600/PK-5
3515 Morgan Johnson Rd 34208 941-741-3307
Josh Bennett, prin. Fax 741-3559
Bayshore ES 700/PK-5
6120 26th St W 34207 941-751-7000
Jackie West, prin. Fax 753-0802
Braden River ES 600/K-5
6125 River Club Blvd 34202 941-751-7012
Hayley Rio, prin. Fax 753-0911
Braden River MS 1,000/6-8
6215 River Club Blvd 34202 941-751-7080
Randy Petrilla, prin. Fax 751-7085
Daughtrey ES 800/PK-5
515 63rd Ave E 34203 941-751-7023
Ruby Zickafoose, prin. Fax 753-0849
Freedom ES 800/PK-5
9515 E State Road 64 34212 941-708-4990
Guy Grimes, prin. Fax 708-4919
Gullett ES 600/PK-5
12125 44th Ave E 34211 941-727-2067
Todd Richardson, prin. Fax 727-2094
Haile MS 1,100/6-8
9501 E State Road 64 34212 941-714-7240
Kate Collis, prin. Fax 714-7245
Harllee MS 500/6-8
6423 9th St E 34203 941-751-7027
Verdya Bradley, prin. Fax 751-7030

Johnson MS 500/6-8
2121 26th Ave E 34208 941-741-3344
Angela Lindsey, prin. Fax 741-3345
King MS 1,100/6-8
600 75th St NW 34209 941-798-6820
Michele Romeo, prin. Fax 798-6835
Lee MS 1,000/6-8
4000 53rd Ave W 34210 941-727-6500
Scott Cooper, prin. Fax 727-6513
Manatee ES 500/K-5
1609 6th Ave E 34208 941-741-3319
Tami VanOverbeke, prin. Fax 741-3507
McNeal ES 700/PK-5
6325 Lorraine Rd 34202 941-751-8165
Cheryl McGrew, prin. Fax 751-8155
Miller ES 800/PK-5
601 43rd St W 34209 941-741-3300
Scott Boyes, prin. Fax 741-3415
Moody ES 600/K-5
5425 38th Ave W 34209 941-741-3170
Tina Stancil, prin. Fax 741-3555
Nolan MS 1,100/6-8
6615 Greenbrook Blvd 34202 941-751-8200
Scot Boice, prin. Fax 751-8210
Oneco ES 500/PK-5
5214 22nd Street Ct E 34203 941-751-7018
Ronnie King, prin. Fax 753-0926
Palma Sola ES 600/PK-5
6806 5th Ave NW 34209 941-741-3179
Jennie Grimes, prin. Fax 741-3181
Prine ES 900/PK-5
3801 Southern Pkwy W 34205 941-751-7006
Lynne Menard, prin. Fax 753-0924
Rogers Garden-Bullock ES 200/PK-5
515 13th Ave W 34205 941-209-7540
Pat Stream, prin. Fax 209-7550
Samoset ES 600/PK-5
3300 19th St E 34208 941-708-6400
Maribeth Mason, prin. Fax 708-6408
Sea Breeze ES 600/K-5
3601 71st St W 34209 941-741-3190
Greg Sanders, prin. Fax 741-3614
Stewart ES 400/K-5
7905 15th Ave NW 34209 941-741-3176
Joe Hougland, prin. Fax 741-3467
Sugg MS 800/6-8
3801 59th St W 34209 941-741-3157
Ann McDonald, prin. Fax 741-3514
Tara ES 600/K-5
6950 Linger Lodge Rd E 34203 941-751-7660
Laura Campbell, prin. Fax 753-0975
Wakeland ES 600/PK-5
1812 27th St E 34208 941-741-3358
Mario Mendoza, prin. Fax 741-3549
Willis ES 700/PK-5
14705 the Masters Ave 34202 941-316-8245
Bill Stenger, prin. Fax 316-8259
Witt ES 700/PK-5
200 Rye Rd E 34212 941-741-3028
David Marshall, prin. Fax 741-3630
Other Schools – See Holmes Beach, Myakka City, Palmetto, Parrish, Sarasota

---

Bradenton Christian S 500/PK-12
3304 43rd St W 34209 941-792-5454
Dan Vande Pol, supt. Fax 795-7190
Center for Education Montessori S 200/PK-8
6024 26th St W 34207 941-753-4987
Mara Fulk, admin. Fax 756-4985
Community Christian S 200/PK-12
5500 18th St E 34203 941-756-8748
Gulfcoast Christian Academy 50/K-12
1700 51st Ave E 34203 941-755-0332
Carol Pope, admin. Fax 981-1564
IMG Academy 600/PK-12
5650 Bollettieri Blvd 34210 941-757-8258
Fax 752-2630
Manatee Learning Academy 200/PK-10
6210 17th Ave W 34209 941-794-0088
Peace Lutheran S 50/3-8
1611 30th Ave W 34205 941-747-6753
Rev. John Maasch, prin. Fax 747-6753
St. Joseph Catholic S 300/PK-8
2990 26th St W 34205 941-755-2611
Deborah Suddarth, prin. Fax 753-6339
St. Stephen's Episcopal S 600/PK-12
315 41st St W 34209 941-746-2121
Dr. Janet Pullen, head sch Fax 746-5699
Shepherd's Heart Christian S 50/1-10
6502 44th Ave E 34203 941-782-8929
Liza Shedelbower, head sch
West Coast Christian Academy 50/PK-8
1112 49th Ave E 34203 941-755-9667

Brandon, Hillsborough, Pop. 100,869
Hillsborough County SD
Supt. — See Tampa
Brooker ES 900/PK-5
812 Dewolf Rd 33511 813-744-8184
Julie Kelly, prin. Fax 740-3621
Burns MS 1,300/6-8
615 Brooker Rd 33511 813-744-8383
Matthew DiPrima, prin. Fax 740-3623
Kingswood ES 600/K-5
3102 S Kings Ave 33511 813-744-8234
Lisa Amos, prin. Fax 744-8150
Limona ES 500/K-5
1115 Telfair Rd 33510 813-744-8200
Robin Johnson-Hewitt, prin. Fax 744-8147
Mann MS 1,100/6-8
409 E Jersey Ave 33510 813-744-8400
Barbara Fillhart, prin. Fax 744-6707
McLane MS 900/6-8
306 N Knights Ave 33510 813-744-8100
Dina Langston, prin. Fax 744-8135
Mintz ES 800/PK-5
1510 Heather Lakes Blvd 33511 813-744-8353
Deborah Moltisanti, prin. Fax 744-6755
Schmidt ES 600/PK-5
1250 Williams Rd 33510 813-651-2110
Janet Kelly, prin. Fax 651-2114
Yates ES 700/K-5
301 Kingsway Rd 33510 813-744-8177
Richard Shields, prin. Fax 744-8179

Bell Shoals Baptist Academy 500/PK-8
2102 Bell Shoals Rd 33511 813-689-9183
Sandra Carnley, prin. Fax 643-1649
Brandon Academy 200/PK-11
801 Limona Rd 33510 813-689-1952
Nicholas Rodriguez, head sch Fax 651-4278
Central Baptist Christian S 300/PK-12
402 E Windhorst Rd 33510 813-689-6133
First Baptist Brandon Christian Academy 300/PK-8
216 N Parsons Ave 33510 813-689-9435
Rev. Paul Pucciarelli, prin. Fax 685-3853
Freedom Academy 100/K-12
1118 N Parsons Ave 33510 813-654-0836
Immanuel Lutheran S 200/PK-8
2913 John Moore Rd 33511 813-685-1978
Lisa Talbott, prin. Fax 681-6852
Nativity S 700/PK-8
705 E Brandon Blvd 33511 813-689-3395
Robert Yevich, prin. Fax 681-5406

Branford, Suwannee, Pop. 686
Suwannee County SD
Supt. — See Live Oak
Branford ES 700/PK-5
26801 State Road 247 32008 386-935-5700
Jennifer Barrs, prin. Fax 935-6311

Bristol, Liberty, Pop. 982
Liberty County SD 1,400/PK-12
PO Box 429 32321 850-643-2275
David Summers, supt. Fax 643-2533
www.lcsb.org
Tolar S 600/K-8
PO Box 609 32321 850-643-2426
Steve Benton, prin. Fax 643-4168
Other Schools – See Hosford

Bronson, Levy, Pop. 1,084
Levy County SD 4,900/PK-12
480 Marshburn Dr 32621 352-486-5231
Jeffery Edison, supt. Fax 486-5237
www.levy.k12.fl.us
Bronson ES 600/PK-5
400 Ishie Ave 32621 352-486-5281
Cheryl Beachamp, prin. Fax 486-5285
Other Schools – See Cedar Key, Chiefland, Williston, Yankeetown

Brooker, Bradford, Pop. 337
Bradford County SD
Supt. — See Starke
Brooker ES 100/PK-5
PO Box 7 32622 352-485-1812
Deborah Parmenter, prin. Fax 485-2036

Brooksville, Hernando, Pop. 7,591
Hernando County SD 21,600/PK-12
919 N Broad St 34601 352-797-7000
Dr. Lori Romano Ph.D., supt. Fax 797-7101
www.hernandoschools.org
Brooksville ES 800/PK-5
885 N Broad St 34601 352-797-7014
Jill Renihan, prin. Fax 797-7114
Chocachatti ES 800/PK-5
4135 California St 34604 352-797-7067
Lara Silva, prin. Fax 797-7167
Eastside ES 400/PK-5
27151 Roper Rd 34602 352-797-7045
Mary Ledoux, prin. Fax 797-7145
Moton ES 600/PK-5
7175 Emerson Rd 34601 352-797-7065
Joe Franna, prin. Fax 797-7165
Parrott MS 800/6-8
19220 Youth Dr 34601 352-797-7075
Brent Gaustad, prin. Fax 797-7175
Pine Grove ES 600/PK-5
14411 Ken Austin Pkwy 34613 352-797-7090
Nancy Johnson, prin. Fax 797-7190
Powell MS 800/6-8
4100 Barclay Ave 34609 352-797-7095
Thomas Dye, prin. Fax 797-7195
West Hernando MS 700/6-8
14325 Ken Austin Pkwy 34613 352-797-7035
Lori Lessley, prin. Fax 797-7135
Other Schools – See Spring Hill, Weeki Wachee

Hernando Christian Academy 200/PK-12
7200 Emerson Rd 34601 352-796-0616
Dr. Anthony Bryan, supt. Fax 799-3400
Methodist S Center 100/PK-8
109 S Broad St 34601 352-796-3496

Bryceville, Nassau
Nassau County SD
Supt. — See Fernandina Beach
Bryceville ES 200/K-5
6504 Church Ave 32009 904-491-7932
Amber Nicholas Bovinette, prin. Fax 266-2155

Bunnell, Flagler, Pop. 2,615
Flagler County SD 12,700/PK-12
1769 E Moody Blvd 32110 386-437-7526
James Tager, supt. Fax 586-2641
www.flaglerschools.com
Bunnell ES 1,200/PK-6
305 N Palmetto St 32110 386-437-7533
Marcus Sanfilippo, prin. Fax 437-7591
Other Schools – See Flagler Beach, Palm Coast

First Baptist Christian Academy 200/PK-12
201 E Moody Blvd 32110 386-446-0094

Bushnell, Sumter, Pop. 2,367
Sumter County SD 7,500/PK-12
2680 W C 476 33513 352-793-2315
Richard Shirley, supt. Fax 793-4180
www.sumter.k12.fl.us
Bushnell ES 700/K-5
218 W Flannery Ave 33513 352-793-3501
Kelly Goodwin, prin. Fax 793-1336
Other Schools – See Lake Panasoffkee, Webster, Wildwood

Callahan, Nassau, Pop. 1,111
Nassau County SD
Supt. — See Fernandina Beach
Callahan ES 600/PK-2
449618 US Highway 301 32011 904-491-7933
Sabrina Faircloth, prin. Fax 879-5560
Callahan IS 600/3-5
34586 Ball Park Rd 32011 904-491-7934
Rhonda Devereaux, prin. Fax 879-5288
Callahan MS 800/6-8
450121 Old Dixie Hwy 32011 904-491-7935
Kimberly Harrison, prin. Fax 879-2860

Sonshine Christian Academy 300/PK-12
PO Box 5026 32011 904-879-1260
Lorie Johnson, prin. Fax 879-2640

Canal Point, Palm Beach, Pop. 361
Palm Beach County SD
Supt. — See West Palm Beach
Cunningham/Canal Point ES 300/PK-5
37000 Main St 33438 561-924-9800
Derrick Hibler, prin. Fax 924-9850

Cantonment, Escambia, Pop. 4,500
Escambia County SD
Supt. — See Pensacola
Allen ES 600/K-5
1051 N Highway 95A 32533 850-937-2260
Rachel Watts, prin. Fax 937-2269
Ransom MS 1,400/6-8
1000 W Kingsfield Rd 32533 850-937-2220
Brent Brummet, prin. Fax 937-2232

Cape Canaveral, Brevard, Pop. 9,755
Brevard County SD
Supt. — See Melbourne
Cape View ES 400/PK-6
8440 Rosalind Ave 32920 321-784-0284
Jill Keane, prin. Fax 868-6690

Cape Coral, Lee, Pop. 151,800
Lee County SD
Supt. — See Fort Myers
Cafferata ES 700/K-5
250 Santa Barbara Blvd N 33993 239-458-7391
James Moreland, prin. Fax 772-0749
Caloosa ES 900/PK-5
620 Del Prado Blvd S 33990 239-574-3113
Shelley Markgraf, prin. Fax 574-1449
Caloosa MS 900/6-8
610 Del Prado Blvd S 33990 239-574-3232
Dr. Ann Cole, prin. Fax 574-2660
Cape ES 700/K-5
4519 Vincennes Blvd 33904 239-542-3551
Nicole Osterholm, prin. Fax 542-3264
Challenger MS 1,100/6-8
624 SW Trafalgar Pkwy 33991 239-242-4341
Teri Cannady, prin. Fax 242-7217
Diplomat ES 900/PK-5
1115 NE 16th Ter 33909 239-458-0033
Mara Vertrees, prin. Fax 458-1697
Diplomat MS 800/6-8
1039 NE 16th Ter 33909 239-574-5257
Maura Bennington, prin. Fax 574-4008
Gulf ES 1,000/K-5
3400 SW 17th Pl 33914 239-549-2726
Kim Verblaauw, prin. Fax 549-2117
Gulf MS 800/6-8
1809 SW 36th Ter 33914 239-549-0606
Dr. Michelle Cort-Mora, prin. Fax 549-2806
Mariner MS 900/6-8
425 Chiquita Blvd N 33993 239-772-1848
Rachel Gould, prin. Fax 242-1256
Patriot ES 700/K-5
711 SW 18th St 33991 239-242-1023
Jami Browder, prin. Fax 242-1238
Pelican ES 900/K-5
3525 SW 3rd Ave 33914 239-549-4966
Edwin Carter, prin. Fax 549-4973
Skyline ES 900/PK-5
620 SW 19th St 33991 239-772-3223
Laura Trombetti, prin. Fax 772-8934
Trafalgar ES 800/PK-5
1850 SW 20th Ave 33991 239-283-3043
Lisa Murphy, prin. Fax 282-5595
Trafalgar MS 900/6-8
2120 SW Trafalgar Pkwy 33991 239-283-2001
Dr. Michael Galbreath, prin. Fax 283-5620

Cape Coral Christian S 100/PK-12
PO Box 150129 33915 239-574-3707
Providence Christian S 100/PK-8
701 Mohawk Pkwy 33914 239-549-8024
Jami Hommerbocker, head sch Fax 549-4465
St. Andrew Catholic S 300/PK-8
1509 SE 27th St 33904 239-772-3922
Dr. Judi Hughes, prin. Fax 772-7182

Casselberry, Seminole, Pop. 25,625
Seminole County SD
Supt. — See Sanford
Casselberry ES 700/PK-5
1075 Crystal Bowl Cir 32707 407-746-2550
Mallory Holliday, prin. Fax 746-2599
Red Bug ES 800/PK-5
4000 Red Bug Lake Rd 32707 407-746-8350
Christine Watson, prin. Fax 746-8399

South Seminole MS 1,300/6-8
101 S Winter Park Dr 32707 407-746-1350
Dr. Mia Coleman-Baker, prin. Fax 746-1420
Sterling Park ES 800/PK-5
905 Eagle Cir S 32707 407-746-8250
Dumari Dillard, prin. Fax 746-8299

Socrates Preparatory S 100/1-12
3955 Red Bug Lake Rd 32707 407-422-0825

Cedar Key, Levy, Pop. 698
Levy County SD
Supt. — See Bronson
Cedar Key S 300/PK-12
951 Whiddon Ave 32625 352-543-5223
Josh Slemp, prin. Fax 543-5988

Celebration, Osceola, Pop. 7,281
Osceola County SD
Supt. — See Kissimmee
Celebration S 1,300/K-8
510 Campus St 34747 407-566-2300
Kim Manion, prin. Fax 566-2354

Montessori S of Celebration 100/PK-10
901 Begonia Rd 34747 407-566-1561
Karen Simon, head sch Fax 566-1544

Century, Escambia, Pop. 1,651
Escambia County SD
Supt. — See Pensacola
Bratt ES 500/PK-5
5721 Highway 99 32535 850-327-6137
Karen Hall, prin. Fax 327-4879

Chattahoochee, Gadsden, Pop. 3,611
Gadsden County SD
Supt. — See Quincy
Chattahoochee ES 200/PK-5
335 Maple St 32324 850-662-2080
Valencia Denson, prin. Fax 663-2236

Chiefland, Levy, Pop. 2,173
Levy County SD
Supt. — See Bronson
Chiefland ES 800/PK-5
1205 NW 4th Ave 32626 352-493-6040
Lacy Redd, prin. Fax 493-6042

Chipley, Washington, Pop. 3,525
Washington County SD 3,100/PK-12
652 3rd St 32428 850-638-6222
Joseph Taylor, supt. Fax 638-6226
www.wcsdschools.com
Roulhac MS 400/6-8
1535 Brickyard Rd 32428 850-638-6170
Nancy Holley, prin. Fax 638-6319
Smith ES 800/PK-5
1447 South Blvd 32428 850-638-6220
Lesa Burdeshaw, prin. Fax 638-6279
Other Schools – See Vernon

Grace and Glory Christian S 200/PK-12
929 Main St 32428 850-638-3700
Washington County Christian S 100/PK-12
1405 Brickyard Rd 32428 850-638-9227
Jason Haddock, admin. Fax 638-9234

Chuluota, Seminole, Pop. 2,431
Seminole County SD
Supt. — See Sanford
Walker ES 700/K-5
3101 Snow Hill Rd 32766 407-871-7350
Debbie Jose, prin. Fax 871-7399

Double R Private S 100/PK-8
725 Country School Rd 32766 407-365-6856

Citra, Marion
Marion County SD
Supt. — See Ocala
North Marion MS 800/6-8
2085 W Highway 329 32113 352-671-6035
Dawn Mobley, prin. Fax 671-6044

Citrus Springs, Citrus, Pop. 8,462
Citrus County SD
Supt. — See Inverness
Central Ridge ES 800/PK-5
185 W Citrus Springs Blvd 34434 352-344-3833
Nancy Simon, prin. Fax 249-2103
Citrus Springs ES 700/PK-5
3570 W Century Blvd 34433 352-344-4079
Brendan Bonomo, prin. Fax 249-2110
Citrus Springs MS 800/6-8
150 W Citrus Springs Blvd 34434 352-344-2244
John Weed, prin. Fax 249-2111

Clarksville, Calhoun
Calhoun County SD
Supt. — See Blountstown
Carr S 300/PK-8
PO Box 110A 32430 850-674-5395
Darryl Taylor, prin. Fax 674-5421

Clearwater, Pinellas, Pop. 105,537
Pinellas County SD
Supt. — See Largo
Belcher ES 600/K-5
2215 Lancaster Dr 33764 727-538-7437
Lisa Roth, prin. Fax 538-7255
Belleair ES 600/PK-5
1156 Lakeview Rd 33756 727-469-5983
Tabitha Griffin, prin. Fax 469-5972
Clearwater Fundamental MS 800/6-8
1660 Palmetto St 33755 727-298-1609
Linda Burris, prin. Fax 298-1614
Davis ES 700/K-5
2630 Landmark Dr 33761 727-725-7972
William Durst, prin. Fax 725-7975
De Leon ES 600/PK-5
1301 Ponce De Leon Blvd 33756 727-588-3573
Stephanie Blackman, prin. Fax 588-3700
Eisenhower ES 800/PK-5
2800 Drew St 33759 727-725-7978
Antonette Wilson, prin. Fax 725-7981
Frontier ES 700/PK-5
6995 Hopedale Ln 33764 727-538-7335
Tracie Bergman, prin. Fax 538-7444
High Point ES 700/K-5
5921 150th Ave N 33760 727-538-7440
Michael Feeney, prin. Fax 538-7442
Kings Highway ES 400/K-5
1715 Kings Hwy 33755 727-223-8949
Garyn Boyd, prin. Fax 754-8650
McMullen-Booth ES 700/PK-5
3025 Union St 33759 727-669-1800
Susan Manche, prin. Fax 669-1803
Oak Grove MS 1,100/6-8
1370 S Belcher Rd 33764 727-524-4430
Barry Brown, prin. Fax 524-4416
Plumb ES 800/PK-5
1920 Lakeview Rd 33764 727-469-5976
Sandra Kemp, prin. Fax 469-5728
Sandy Lane ES 500/K-5
1360 Sandy Ln 33755 727-469-5974
Kristina Bauman, prin. Fax 469-5986
Skycrest ES 700/K-5
10 N Corona Ave 33765 727-469-5987
Angelean Bing, prin. Fax 469-4186

Allendale Academy 800/K-12
2655 Ulmerton Rd Ste 402 33762 727-531-2481
Clearwater Academy International 200/PK-12
801 Drew St 33755 727-446-1722
Countryside Christian Academy 200/PK-8
1850 N McMullen Booth Rd 33759 727-799-1618
Crystal Mascaro M.Ed., admin. Fax 499-1841
First Lutheran S 100/PK-8
1644 Nursery Rd 33756 727-462-8000
Elaine Popp, prin. Fax 442-7473
Guardian Angels S 300/K-8
2270 Evans Rd 33763 727-799-6724
Mary Stalzer, prin. Fax 724-9018
Iva Christian S 100/K-12
1430 Bellair Rd 33756 727-442-2424
Lakeside Christian S 300/K-12
1897 Sunset Point Rd 33765 727-461-3311
Jim Jensen, head sch Fax 445-1835
Light of Christ ECC 100/PK-PK
2176 Marilyn St 33765 727-442-4797
Becky Daschbach, dir. Fax 441-8771
NorthBay Christian Academy 100/PK-8
2525 N McMullen Booth Rd 33761 727-462-0134
Robbin Isham, dir. Fax 724-1191
Safety Harbor Montessori Academy 200/PK-8
2669 N McMullen Booth Rd 33761 727-724-1767
St. Cecelia S 500/PK-8
1350 Court St 33756 727-461-1200
Valerie Wostbrock, prin. Fax 446-9140
St. Paul's S 300/PK-8
1600 Saint Pauls Dr 33764 727-536-2756
Samantha Campbell, head sch Fax 531-2276
Skycrest Christian S 400/PK-8
129 N Belcher Rd 33765 727-797-1186
Steven Clagg, prin. Fax 797-8516
Washburn Academy 100/PK-12
222 S Lincoln Ave 33756 727-647-1668

Clermont, Lake, Pop. 27,603
Lake County SD
Supt. — See Tavares
Clermont ES 600/PK-5
680 E Highland Ave 34711 352-394-2706
Jeffrey Williams, prin. Fax 394-5081
Clermont MS 700/6-8
301 East Ave 34711 352-243-2460
Robert McCue, prin. Fax 243-1407
Cypress Ridge ES 600/K-5
350 East Ave 34711 352-394-6633
Dale Delpit, prin. Fax 394-1170
East Ridge MS 1,100/6-8
13201 Excalibur Rd 34711 352-536-8020
Stephanie Mayuski, prin. Fax 536-8039
Lost Lake ES 1,000/PK-5
1901 Johns Lake Rd 34711 352-243-2433
Susan Pegram, prin. Fax 243-3541
Pine Ridge ES 900/PK-5
10245 County Road 561 34711 352-242-2223
Laine Obando, prin. Fax 242-2818
Sawgrass Bay ES 1,200/PK-5
16325 Superior Blvd, 352-243-1845
Andrea Steenken, prin. Fax 394-5732
Windy Hill MS 1,300/6-8
3575 Hancock Rd 34711 352-394-2123
William Roberts, prin. Fax 394-7901

Family Christian S of Clermont 200/K-12
2500 S Hwy 27 34711 352-241-0323
Real Life Christian Academy 300/PK-12
1501 Steves Rd 34711 352-394-5575
Michael Fernandes, admin. Fax 394-7860
South Lake Montessori S 50/PK-5
983 W Desoto St 34711 352-365-7212
Wesley Christian Academy 50/K-2
950 7th St 34711 352-394-0191
Beth Reed, prin. Fax 394-4899

Clewiston, Hendry, Pop. 7,087
Hendry County SD
Supt. — See LaBelle
Central ES 600/PK-5
1000 S Deane Duff Ave 33440 863-983-1550
Melissa Carter, prin. Fax 983-1558
Clewiston MS 700/6-8
601 W Pasadena Ave 33440 863-983-1530
Kristi Durance, prin. Fax 983-1541
Eastside ES 600/PK-5
201 Arroyo Ave 33440 863-983-1560
Sarah Sanchez, prin. Fax 983-1564
Westside ES 600/PK-5
205 Arroyo Ave 33440 863-983-1570
Anthony Busin, prin. Fax 902-4232

Clewiston Christian S 200/PK-12
PO Box 129 33440 863-983-5388
George Duckstein, admin. Fax 983-5027
Harvest Academy Christian S 100/K-12
370 Holiday Isles Blvd 33440 863-805-0485

Cocoa, Brevard, Pop. 16,719
Brevard County SD
Supt. — See Melbourne
Atlantis ES 600/PK-6
7300 Briggs Ave 32927 321-633-6143
Cynthia Adams, prin. Fax 633-6038
Cambridge ES 600/PK-6
2000 Cambridge Dr 32922 321-633-3550
Dr. Wendy Smith, prin. Fax 633-3420
Challenger 7 ES 500/PK-6
6135 Rena Ave 32927 321-636-5801
Magali Rassel, prin. Fax 631-3208
Endeavour ES 800/PK-6
905 Pineda St 32922 321-633-3545
Christopher Reed, prin. Fax 633-3546
Enterprise ES 600/K-6
7000 Enterprise Rd 32927 321-633-3434
Jean Bartleson, prin. Fax 633-3438
Fairglen ES 700/PK-6
201 Indian Trl 32927 321-631-1993
Dr. Richard Dunkel, prin. Fax 631-3011
Saturn ES 700/K-6
880 N Range Rd 32926 321-633-3535
Janice Rutherford, prin. Fax 633-3539

Brevard Adventist Christian Academy 50/PK-8
1500 Cox Rd 32926 321-636-2551
St. Mark's Episcopal Academy 100/PK-6
2 Church St 32922 321-639-5771
Joi Robertson M.Ed., head sch Fax 639-5774
Space Coast Christian Academy 100/PK-12
1950 Michigan Ave 32922 321-636-0883

Cocoa Beach, Brevard, Pop. 11,096
Brevard County SD
Supt. — See Melbourne
Freedom 7 ES of International Studies 400/K-6
400 S 4th St 32931 321-868-6610
Dorine Zimmerman, prin. Fax 868-6615
Roosevelt ES 400/K-6
1400 Minutemen Cswy 32931 321-868-6660
Kimberly Humphrey, prin. Fax 783-2331

Our Saviour S 200/PK-8
5301 N Atlantic Ave 32931 321-783-2330
Kenn Hitchcock, prin. Fax 784-6330

Coconut Creek, Broward, Pop. 51,291
Broward County SD
Supt. — See Fort Lauderdale
Coconut Creek ES 800/K-5
500 NW 45th Ave 33066 754-322-5800
Katherine Good, prin. Fax 322-5840
Lyons Creek MS 1,800/6-8
4333 Sol Press Blvd 33073 754-322-3700
Horace Hamm, prin. Fax 322-3785
Tradewinds ES 1,200/PK-5
5400 Johnson Rd 33073 754-322-8700
Michael Breslaw, prin. Fax 322-8740
Winston Park ES 1,100/K-5
4000 Winston Park Blvd 33073 754-322-9000
Carolyn Eggelletion, prin. Fax 322-9040

North Broward Preparatory S 1,400/PK-12
7600 Lyons Rd 33073 954-247-0011
Elise Ecoff, head sch Fax 247-0012

Coconut Grove, See Miami

Carrollton S of the Sacred Heart 800/PK-12
3747 Main Hwy 33133 305-446-5673
Olen Kalkus, hdmstr. Fax 592-6533
St. Hugh S 300/PK-8
3460 Royal Rd 33133 305-448-5602
Mary Fernandez, prin. Fax 444-4299
St. Stephen's Episcopal S 300/PK-5
3439 Main Hwy 33133 305-445-2606
Silvia Larrauri, head sch Fax 445-7320

Cooper City, Broward, Pop. 28,003
Broward County SD
Supt. — See Fort Lauderdale
Cooper City ES 800/PK-5
5080 SW 92nd Ave 33328 754-323-5200
Monica Schlosser, prin. Fax 323-5240
Embassy Creek ES 1,000/K-5
10905 SE Lake Blvd 33026 754-323-5550
Robert Becker, prin. Fax 323-5590
Griffin ES 500/K-5
5050 SW 116th Ave 33330 754-323-5900
Gail Silig, prin. Fax 323-5940
Pioneer MS 1,300/6-8
5350 SW 90th Ave 33328 754-323-4100
Michael Consaul, prin. Fax 323-4185

Beth Emet ES 100/K-5
4807 S Flamingo Rd 33330 954-680-1882
Cooper City Christian Academy 100/K-12
5201 S Flamingo Rd 33330 954-779-6221
Lycee Franco-Americain International S 100/PK-5
8900 Stirling Rd 33024 954-237-0356
Nur Ul-Islam Academy 300/PK-12
10600 SW 59th St 33328 954-434-3288
Potential Christian Academy 200/PK-8
12401 Stirling Rd 33330 954-434-1550
Dr. Julia Elliott, head sch Fax 318-0077

Westlake Preparatory S & Academy 100/K-12
8950 Stirling Rd 33024 954-236-2300

Coral Gables, Miami-Dade, Pop. 46,270
Miami-Dade County SD
Supt. — See Miami
Carver ES 500/PK-5
238 Grand Ave 33133 305-443-5286
Patricia Fairclough, prin. Fax 567-3531
Carver MS 1,000/6-8
4901 Lincoln Dr 33133 305-444-7388
Shelley Stroleny, prin. Fax 529-5148
Coral Gables Preparatory Academy 800/PK-8
105 Minorca Ave 33134 305-448-1731
Graciela Cerra, prin. Fax 442-2075
De Leon MS 1,100/6-8
5801 Augusto St 33146 305-661-1611
Hebert Penton, prin. Fax 666-3140
West Laboratory ES 300/K-8
5300 Carillo St 33146 305-661-7661
Barbara Pujadas, prin. Fax 662-2935

French American S of Miami 200/PK-5
6565 S Red Rd 33143 786-268-1914
Lena McLorin Salvant, dir. Fax 268-1941
Gulliver Acad - Marian Krutulis Campus 1,000/PK-8
12595 Red Rd 33156 305-665-3593
Clifton Kling, pres. Fax 669-1569
Riviera Day S and Riviera Preparatory S 600/PK-12
6800 Nervia St 33146 305-666-1856
St. Philip's Episcopal S 200/PK-5
1121 Andalusia Ave 33134 305-444-6366
Dr. Greg Blackburn, head sch Fax 442-0236
St. Theresa S 900/PK-8
2701 Indian Mound Trl 33134 305-446-1738
Sr. Caridad Sandoval, prin. Fax 446-2877
St. Thomas Episcopal Parish S 400/PK-5
5692 N Kendall Dr 33156 305-665-4851
Lillian Issa, head sch

Coral Springs, Broward, Pop. 117,909
Broward County SD
Supt. — See Fort Lauderdale
Coral Park ES 600/K-5
8401 Westview Dr 33067 754-322-5850
Camille Pontillo, prin. Fax 322-5890
Coral Springs ES 600/PK-8
3601 NW 110th Ave 33065 754-322-5900
Vonda Oliver, prin. Fax 322-5940
Coral Springs MS 1,300/6-8
10300 Wiles Rd 33076 754-322-3000
Ian Murray, prin. Fax 322-3085
Country Hills ES 900/PK-5
10550 Westview Dr 33076 754-322-5950
Kellee Stroup, prin. Fax 322-5990
Eagle Ridge ES 800/PK-5
11500 Westview Dr 33076 754-322-6300
Thomas Redshaw, prin. Fax 322-6340
Forest Glen MS 1,400/6-8
6501 Turtle Run Blvd 33067 754-322-3400
Ronald Foresman, prin. Fax 322-3485
Forest Hills ES 600/PK-5
3100 NW 85th Ave 33065 754-322-6400
Barbara Rothman, prin. Fax 322-6440
Hunt ES 800/K-5
7800 NW 35th Ct 33065 754-322-6500
Ernie Lozano, prin. Fax 322-6540
Maplewood ES 700/PK-5
9850 Ramblewood Dr 33071 754-322-6850
Leena Itty, prin. Fax 322-6890
Parkside ES 700/K-5
10257 NW 29th St 33065 754-322-7850
Laneia Hall, prin. Fax 322-7890
Park Springs ES 900/PK-5
5800 NW 66th Ter 33067 754-322-7750
Katherine Policastro, prin. Fax 322-7790
Ramblewood ES 800/K-5
8950 Shadow Wood Blvd 33071 754-322-8150
Maria Perez, prin. Fax 322-8190
Ramblewood MS 1,200/6-8
8505 W Atlantic Blvd 33071 754-322-4300
Cory Smith, prin. Fax 322-4385
Riverside ES 700/K-5
11450 Riverside Dr 33071 754-322-8250
Merideth Schnur, prin. Fax 322-8290
Sawgrass Springs MS 1,200/6-8
12500 W Sample Rd 33065 754-322-4500
James Cecil, prin. Fax 322-4585
Westchester ES 1,200/PK-5
12405 Royal Palm Blvd 33065 754-322-8900
Melissa Frame-Geraine, prin. Fax 322-8940

Coral Springs Christian Academy 900/PK-12
2251 Riverside Dr 33065 954-752-2870
Joseph E. Sanelli, head sch Fax 346-1112
Parkridge Christian Academy 100/PK-8
5600 Coral Ridge Dr 33076 954-346-0236
Joshua Halulko, prin. Fax 346-0013
St. Andrew S 200/PK-8
9990 NW 29th St 33065 954-753-1280
Kristen Hughes, prin. Fax 753-1933

Cottondale, Jackson, Pop. 899
Jackson County SD
Supt. — See Marianna
Cottondale ES 400/PK-5
2766 Levy St 32431 850-482-9820
Jessica Craven, prin. Fax 482-9825

Crawfordville, Wakulla, Pop. 3,618
Wakulla County SD 4,800/PK-12
PO Box 100 32326 850-926-0065
Robert Pearce, supt. Fax 926-0123
wakulla.schooldesk.net
Crawfordville ES 600/K-5
379 Arran Rd 32327 850-926-3641
Belinda McElroy, prin. Fax 926-4303
Medart ES 500/K-5
2558 Coastal Hwy 32327 850-962-4881
Stanley Ward, prin. Fax 962-3953
Riversink ES 500/K-5
530 Lonnie Raker Ln 32327 850-926-2664
Simeon Nelson, prin. Fax 926-9462
Riversprings MS 600/6-8
800 Spring Creek Hwy 32327 850-926-2300
Michele Yeomans, prin. Fax 926-2111
Shadeville ES 600/K-5
45 Warrior Way 32327 850-926-7155
Nicholas Weaver, prin. Fax 926-5044
Wakulla MS 600/6-8
22 Jean Dr 32327 850-926-7143
Tolar Griffin, prin. Fax 926-3752
Wakulla Preschool 100/PK-PK
87 Andrew J Hargrett Sr Rd 32327 850-926-8111
Laura Kelly, prin. Fax 926-1694

Crescent City, Putnam, Pop. 1,539
Putnam County SD
Supt. — See Palatka
Middleton-Burney ES 700/PK-5
1020 Huntington Rd 32112 386-698-1238
Joseph Theobold, prin. Fax 698-4364
Miller IS 400/6-8
101 S Prospect St 32112 386-698-1360
Tim Adams, prin. Fax 698-1973

Crestview, Okaloosa, Pop. 20,112
Okaloosa County SD
Supt. — See Fort Walton Beach
Antioch ES 900/K-5
4700 Whitehurst Ln 32536 850-683-7540
Kelli Sanders, prin. Fax 683-7561
Davidson MS 900/6-8
6261 Old Bethel Rd 32536 850-683-7500
Jay Sanders, prin. Fax 683-7523
Northwood ES 700/K-5
501 4th Ave 32536 850-689-7252
Dr. Donna Goode, prin. Fax 689-7488
Riverside ES 900/K-5
3400 E Redstone Ave 32539 850-689-7203
Tammy Matz, prin. Fax 689-7401
Shoal River MS 900/6-8
3200 E Redstone Ave 32539 850-689-7229
Gary Massey, prin. Fax 689-7245
Sikes ES 900/K-5
425 Adams Dr 32536 850-689-7268
Vicki Hayden, prin. Fax 689-7263
Southside PS 200/PK-2
650 S Pearl St 32539 850-689-7211
Debbie Haan, prin. Fax 689-7999
Walker ES 700/K-5
2988 Stillwell Blvd 32539 850-689-7220
Lorna Carnley, prin. Fax 689-7654

Rocky Bayou Christian S K-6
951 S Ferdon Blvd 32536 850-279-3729
Denise Bowers, prin.

Cross City, Dixie, Pop. 1,899
Dixie County SD 2,000/PK-12
16077 NE Highway 19 32628 352-498-6131
Mike Thomas, supt. Fax 498-1308
www.dixie.k12.fl.us/
Anderson ES 500/PK-5
815 SE Highway 351 32628 352-498-1333
Kristen McCaskill, prin. Fax 498-1342
Rains MS 400/6-8
981 SE Highway 351 32628 352-498-1346
Chris Lord, prin. Fax 498-1283
Other Schools – See Old Town

Crystal River, Citrus, Pop. 3,056
Citrus County SD
Supt. — See Inverness
Crystal River MS 800/6-8
344 NE Crystal St 34428 352-795-2116
Inge Frederick, prin. Fax 249-2107
Crystal River PS 600/PK-5
8624 W Crystal St 34428 352-795-2211
Donnie Brown, prin. Fax 249-2109

Cutler Bay, Miami-Dade, Pop. 39,453
Miami-Dade County SD
Supt. — See Miami
Bel-Aire ES 400/PK-5
10205 SW 194th St, 305-233-5401
Prudence Hill, prin. Fax 256-3101
Cutler Bay MS 1,100/6-8
19400 Gulfstream Rd, 305-235-4761
Ignacio Rodriguez, prin. Fax 254-3746
Cutler Ridge ES 800/PK-5
20210 Coral Sea Rd, 305-235-4611
Adrienne Wright-Mullings, prin. Fax 232-6740
Gulfstream ES 700/PK-5
20900 SW 97th Ave, 305-235-6811
Marybel Baldessari, prin. Fax 254-1721
Whigham ES 800/PK-5
21545 SW 87th Ave, 305-234-4840
Kathryn Guerra, prin. Fax 234-4837
Whispering Pines ES 600/PK-5
18929 SW 89th Rd, 305-238-7382
Tamela Brown, prin. Fax 251-3615

OLO the Holy Rosary - St. Richard S 400/PK-8
18455 Franjo Rd, 305-235-5442
Ilma Lozano, prin. Fax 235-5670

Dade City, Pasco, Pop. 6,339
Pasco County SD
Supt. — See Land O Lakes
Centennial ES 600/K-5
38501 Centennial Rd 33525 352-524-5000
Gretchen Rudolph, prin. Fax 524-5091
Centennial MS 600/6-8
38505 Centennial Rd 33525 352-524-9700
Rick Saylor, prin. Fax 524-9791
Cox ES 400/PK-5
37615 Martin Luther King 33523 352-524-5100
Claudia Steinacker, prin. Fax 524-5191
Lacoochee ES 400/PK-5
38815 Cummer Rd 33523 352-524-5600
Latoya Jordan, prin. Fax 524-5691
Pasco ES 700/PK-5
37350 Florida Ave 33525 352-524-5200
Nena Green, prin. Fax 524-5291
Pasco MS 900/6-8
13925 14th St 33525 352-524-8400
Jeffrey Wolff, prin. Fax 524-8491
San Antonio ES 700/PK-5
32416 Darby Rd 33525 352-524-5300
Kimberly Anderson, prin. Fax 524-5391

East Pasco Adventist Academy 100/PK-10
38434 Centennial Rd 33525 352-567-3646
Sacred Heart ECC 200/PK-PK
32245 Saint Joe Rd 33525 352-588-4060
Lucinda O'Quinn, dir. Fax 588-4871

Dania Beach, Broward, Pop. 29,112
Broward County SD
Supt. — See Fort Lauderdale
Collins ES 300/PK-5
1050 NW 2nd St 33004 754-323-5150
Tracy Jackson, prin. Fax 323-5175
Dania ES 500/PK-5
300 SE 2nd Ave 33004 754-323-5350
Lewis Jackson, prin. Fax 323-5390
Olsen MS 900/6-8
330 SE 11th Ter 33004 754-323-3800
Valerie Harris, prin. Fax 323-3885

Davenport, Polk, Pop. 2,854
Polk County SD
Supt. — See Bartow
Citrus Ridge: A Civics Academy K-8
1775 Sand Mine Rd 33897 863-259-4001
Russell Donnelly, prin. Fax 424-2242
Davenport S of the Arts 1,000/PK-8
4751 County Road 547 N 33837 863-420-2557
Brian Kier, prin. Fax 424-3611
Horizons ES 900/K-5
1700 Forest Lake Dr 33837 863-419-3430
Amy Heiser-Meyers, prin. Fax 419-3432
Loughman Oaks ES 1,100/PK-5
4600 US Highway 17 92 N 33837 863-421-3309
Wanda Aponte, prin. Fax 421-3333

Ridge Christian Academy 200/PK-12
41219 Highway 27 33837 863-420-2885

Davie, Broward, Pop. 90,050
Broward County SD
Supt. — See Fort Lauderdale
Davie ES 800/PK-5
7025 SW 39th St 33314 754-323-5400
Robert Schneider, prin. Fax 323-5440
Flamingo ES 700/PK-5
1130 SW 133rd Ave 33325 754-323-5700
Janice Crosby, prin. Fax 323-5740
Fox Trail ES 1,200/K-5
1250 S Nob Hill Rd 33324 754-323-5800
Lynn Burgess, prin. Fax 323-5840
Hawkes Bluff ES 800/PK-5
5900 SW 160th Ave 33331 754-323-6100
Melinda Cunningham, prin. Fax 323-6140
Indian Ridge MS 1,800/6-8
1355 S Nob Hill Rd 33324 754-323-3300
Frank Zagari, prin. Fax 323-3385
Nova Blanche Forman ES 800/K-5
3521 Davie Rd 33314 754-323-6600
Russell Schwartz, prin. Fax 323-6640
Nova Dwight Eisenhower ES 800/K-5
6501 SW 39th St 33314 754-323-6650
Carol Lesser, prin. Fax 323-6690
Nova MS 1,200/6-8
3602 College Ave 33314 754-323-3700
Rayner Garranchan, prin. Fax 323-3785
Silver Ridge ES 900/PK-5
9100 SW 36th St 33328 754-323-7500
Wendy Borowski, prin. Fax 323-7540

American Preparatory Academy 100/K-12
4850 S Pine Island Rd 33328 954-434-8936
Gloria Dei Lutheran Academy 200/PK-6
7601 SW 39th St 33328 954-475-8584
Sharon Vonada, prin. Fax 475-2232
Montessori Institute of Broward 100/PK-5
12425 Orange Dr 33330 954-357-0369
Parkway Christian S 300/PK-8
1200 S Flamingo Rd 33325 954-424-6425
Nicole Koski, admin. Fax 424-6761
Posnack Jewish Day S 500/K-12
5810 S Pine Island Rd 33328 954-583-6100
St. Bonaventure S 600/PK-8
1301 SW 136th Ave 33325 954-476-5200
Lisa Kempinski, prin. Fax 476-5203
St. David S 500/PK-8
3900 S University Dr 33328 954-472-7086
Jane Broder, prin. Fax 452-8243
Summit-Questa Montessori S 300/PK-8
5451 SW 64th Ave 33314 954-584-3466

Daytona Beach, Volusia, Pop. 59,727
Volusia County SD
Supt. — See De Land
Campbell MS, 625 S Keech St 32114 900/6-8
Dr. Jerry Picott, prin. 386-258-4661
Champion ES 600/K-5
921 Tournament Dr 32124 386-258-4664
Leslie McLean, prin. Fax 506-5072
Hinson MS 900/6-8
1860 N Clyde Morris Blvd 32117 386-258-4682
Robert Ouellette, prin. Fax 506-5064
Longstreet ES 400/K-5
2745 S Peninsula Dr 32118 386-322-6172
Judith Watson, prin. Fax 756-7281
Ortona ES 200/K-5
1265 N Grandview Ave 32118 386-258-4668
Shantell Adkins, prin. Fax 239-6386

Palm Terrace ES 600/PK-5
1825 Dunn Ave 32114 386-258-4670
Dr. Lloyd Haynes, prin. Fax 274-3448
Small ES 500/K-5
800 South St 32114 386-258-4675
Cameron Robinson, prin. Fax 239-6346
Westside ES 500/K-5
1210 Jimmy Ann Dr 32117 386-258-4678
Willie Williams, prin. Fax 274-3417

Basilica S of St. Paul 200/PK-8
317 Mullally St 32114 386-252-7915
Ronald Pagano, prin. Fax 238-7903
Indigo Christian Academy 50/PK-8
401 N Williamson Blvd 32114 386-255-5917
Living Faith Academy 100/PK-8
950 Derbyshire Rd 32117 386-258-1258
Lourdes Academy 300/PK-8
1014 N Halifax Ave 32118 386-252-0391
Stephen Dole, prin. Fax 259-1201
Mt. Calvary Academy 100/PK-6
700 Bellevue Ave 32114 386-255-8654

De Bary, Volusia, Pop. 19,046
Volusia County SD
Supt. — See De Land
De Bary ES 800/K-5
88 W Highbanks Rd 32713 386-575-4230
Alisa Fedigan, prin. Fax 668-3538

Deerfield Beach, Broward, Pop. 72,542
Broward County SD
Supt. — See Fort Lauderdale
Deerfield Beach ES 700/PK-5
650 NE 1st St 33441 754-322-6100
Andrew Gerlach, prin. Fax 322-6140
Deerfield Beach MS 1,200/6-8
701 SE 6th Ave 33441 754-322-3300
Francine Baugh, prin. Fax 322-3385
Deerfield Park ES 600/PK-5
650 SW 3rd Ave 33441 754-322-6150
Jocelyn Reid, prin. Fax 322-6190
Park Ridge ES 500/PK-5
5200 NE 9th Ave 33064 754-322-7700
Joseph Balchunas, prin. Fax 322-7740
Quiet Waters ES 1,400/PK-5
4150 W Hillsboro Blvd 33442 754-322-8100
Geoffrey Henning, prin. Fax 322-8140
Tedder ES 700/PK-5
4157 NE 1st Ter 33064 754-322-8650
Shinita Coachman-Beavers, prin. Fax 322-8690

St. Ambrose S 200/PK-8
363 SE 12th Ave 33441 954-427-2226
Lisa Dodge, prin. Fax 427-2293

De Funiak Springs, Walton, Pop. 5,054
Walton County SD 8,000/PK-12
145 S Park St Ste 2 32435 850-892-1100
Russell Hughes, supt. Fax 892-1191
www.walton.k12.fl.us
Mossy Head ES 300/K-5
13270 US Highway 90 W 32433 850-892-1290
Ronita Hinote, prin. Fax 892-1299
Saunders ES 600/K-5
416 John Baldwin Rd 32433 850-892-1260
Pam Jones, prin. Fax 892-1269
Walton MS 700/6-8
605 Bruce Ave 32435 850-892-1281
Jason Campbell, prin. Fax 892-1289
West DeFuniak ES 700/PK-5
815 Lincoln Ave 32435 850-892-1250
Darlene Paul, prin. Fax 892-1259
Wise PK at Saunders PK-PK
416 John Baldwin Rd 32433 850-892-1111
Tracey Dickey, prin. Fax 892-1198
Other Schools – See Freeport, Paxton, Santa Rosa Beach

First Christian Academy 50/PK-6
216 Live Oak Ave E 32435 850-520-4604
Cherelle Weeks, prin. Fax 892-2381

De Land, Volusia, Pop. 26,549
Volusia County SD 60,500/PK-12
PO Box 2118 32721 386-734-7190
James Russell, supt. Fax 822-6790
myvolusiaschools.org
Blue Lake ES 700/PK-5
282 N Blue Lake Ave 32724 386-822-4070
Jasmine Hinson, prin. Fax 822-4070
Citrus Grove ES, 729 Hazen Rd 32720 800/K-5
Jennifer Williams, prin. 386-626-0053
DeLand MS 1,100/6-8
1400 Aquarius Ave 32724 386-822-5678
William Dunnigan, prin. Fax 822-6583
Freedom ES 700/K-5
1395 S Blue Lake Ave 32724 386-943-4375
Michael Leader, prin. Fax 943-7680
Marks ES 600/K-5
1000 N Garfield Ave 32724 386-822-6986
Julie Roseboom, prin. Fax 822-6636
Southwestern MS 700/6-8
605 W New Hampshire Ave 32720 386-822-6815
Jacquese Slocum, prin. Fax 822-6708
Starke ES 400/K-5
730 S Parsons Ave 32720 386-943-9651
Dwayne Copeland, prin. Fax 943-7957
Woodward Avenue ES 600/PK-5
1201 S Woodward Ave 32720 386-740-7910
Kate Godbee, prin. Fax 943-7921
Other Schools – See Daytona Beach, De Bary, De Leon Springs, Deltona, Edgewater, Enterprise, Holly Hill, Lake Helen, New Smyrna Beach, Orange City, Ormond Beach, Osteen, Pierson, Port Orange, South Daytona

---

Childrens House Montessori S 200/PK-9
509 E Pennsylvania Ave 32724 386-736-3632
Sherri Holzman, admin. Fax 736-3667
Lighthouse Christian Prep Academy 200/K-12
126 S Ridgewood Ave 32720 386-734-5380
St. Barnabas Episcopal S 400/PK-8
322 W Michigan Ave 32720 386-734-3005
Paul Garcia, head sch Fax 822-9417
St. Peter S 300/PK-8
421 W New York Ave 32720 386-822-6010
Peter Randlov, prin. Fax 822-6013
Stetson Baptist Christian S 300/PK-8
1025 W Minnesota Ave 32720 386-734-7791

De Leon Springs, Volusia, Pop. 2,583
Volusia County SD
Supt. — See De Land
McInnis ES 400/K-5
5175 US Highway 17 32130 386-943-6384
Maite Porter, prin. Fax 985-6710

Delray Beach, Palm Beach, Pop. 59,547
Palm Beach County SD
Supt. — See West Palm Beach
Banyan Creek ES 1,000/PK-5
4243 Sabal Lakes Rd 33445 561-894-7100
Allison Castellano, prin. Fax 894-7150
Carver Community MS 900/6-8
101 Barwick Rd 33445 561-638-2100
Kiwana Prophete, prin. Fax 638-2181
Morikami Park ES 800/K-5
6201 Morikami Park Rd 33484 561-894-7300
Stacey Quinones, prin. Fax 894-7350
Orchard View ES 600/K-5
4050 Germantown Rd 33445 561-894-7400
Lisa Lee, prin. Fax 894-7450
Pine Grove ES 400/K-5
400 SW 10th St 33444 561-266-1100
Shauntay King, prin. Fax 266-1150
Plumosa S of the Arts 600/K-5
2501 Seacrest Blvd 33444 561-330-3900
Catherine Reynolds, prin. Fax 330-3950
Spady ES 600/PK-5
901 NW 3rd St 33444 561-454-7800
Rona Tata, prin. Fax 454-7801
Village Academy 800/K-12
400 SW 12th Ave 33444 561-243-6100
Latoya Dixon, prin. Fax 243-6150

American Heritage S of Boca/Delray 1,200/PK-12
6200 Linton Blvd 33484 561-495-7272
Daughter of Zion Junior Academy 100/PK-8
250 NW 3rd Ave 33444 561-243-0715
St. Vincent Ferrer S 200/PK-8
810 George Bush Blvd 33483 561-278-3868
Vikki Delgado, prin. Fax 279-9508
Trinity Lutheran S 400/PK-8
400 N Swinton Ave 33444 561-276-8458
Jamie Wagner, prin. Fax 272-3215
Unity S 300/PK-8
101 NW 22nd St 33444 561-276-4414
Louis St-Laurent, head sch Fax 265-0990

Deltona, Volusia, Pop. 83,518
Volusia County SD
Supt. — See De Land
Deltona Lakes ES 700/PK-5
2022 Adelia Blvd 32725 386-575-4115
Ramonita Ortiz, prin. Fax 789-7018
Deltona MS 1,100/6-8
250 Enterprise Rd 32725 386-575-4150
Dr. Rick Inge, prin. Fax 968-0015
Discovery ES 700/K-5
975 Abagail Dr 32725 386-575-4133
Kimberly Feltner, prin. Fax 860-3316
Forest Lake ES, 1600 Doyle Rd 32725 700/K-5
Dr. Paul Nehrig, prin. 386-575-4166
Friendship ES 400/PK-5
2746 Fulford St 32738 386-575-4130
Cristina Raimundo, prin. Fax 789-7032
Galaxy MS 1,100/6-8
2400 Eustace Ave 32725 386-575-4144
Patricia Corr, prin. Fax 968-0016
Heritage MS 1,200/6-8
1001 Parnell Ct 32738 386-575-4113
Thomas Vaughan, prin. Fax 708-0020
Pride ES, 1100 Learning Ln 32738 500/K-5
Carrie Korkus, prin. 386-968-0010
Spirit ES, 1500 Meadowlark Dr 32725 700/K-5
Shannon Young, prin. 386-575-4080
Sunrise ES, 3155 Phonetia Dr 32738 500/K-5
Efrain Alejandro, prin. 386-575-4103
Timbercrest ES 700/K-5
2401 Eustace Ave 32725 386-575-4221
Kimberly McKinney, prin. Fax 775-5412

Deltona Adventist S 100/PK-8
1725 Catalina Blvd 32738 386-532-9333
Deltona Christian S 200/PK-12
1200 Providence Blvd 32725 386-574-1971
Good Shepherd Academy 100/PK-8
750 Howland Blvd 32738 407-324-2274
Jared Rathje, prin. Fax 936-2635
Trinity Christian Academy 600/PK-12
875 Elkcam Blvd 32725 386-789-4515

Destin, Okaloosa, Pop. 11,900
Okaloosa County SD
Supt. — See Fort Walton Beach
Destin ES 800/PK-4
630 Kelly St 32541 850-833-4360
Al Gardner, prin. Fax 833-4370
Destin MS 700/5-8
4608 Legendary Marina Dr 32541 850-833-7655
Grant Meyer, prin. Fax 833-7677

Rocky Bayou Christian S 50/K-6
201 Beach Dr 32541 850-837-7247
Joe Quilit M.Ed., prin. Fax 654-6090

Doral, Miami-Dade, Pop. 45,331
Miami-Dade County SD
Supt. — See Miami
Bilbao Preparatory Academy 600/PK-8
8905 NW 114 Ave, 305-863-5750
Tracy Crews, prin. Fax 883-5530
Espinosa K-8 Center 1,600/K-8
11250 NW 86th St, 305-889-5757
Matha Munoz, prin. Fax 889-5758
Smith K-8 Center 1,400/PK-8
10415 NW 52nd St, 305-406-0220
Genaro Navarro, prin. Fax 406-0225
Thomas K-8 Center 1,600/PK-8
5950 NW 114th Ave, 305-592-7914
Debbie Saumell, prin. Fax 463-7241

Divine Savior Lutheran Academy 400/PK-12
10311 NW 58th St, 305-597-4545
Timothy Biesterfeld, head sch Fax 597-4077
Shelton Academy 200/K-8
11300 NW 41st St, 305-599-9967
World of Kids Academy 200/PK-2
8130 NW 56th St, 305-593-7010

Dover, Hillsborough, Pop. 3,664
Hillsborough County SD
Supt. — See Tampa
Bailey ES 700/K-5
4630 Gallagher Rd 33527 813-707-7531
Jarrod Haneline, prin. Fax 707-7535
Dover ES 700/PK-5
3035 Nelson Ave 33527 813-757-9457
Kayla Forcucci, prin. Fax 707-7161
Nelson ES 800/K-5
5413 Durant Rd 33527 813-651-2120
Mary Hewett, prin. Fax 651-2124

Dundee, Polk, Pop. 3,628
Polk County SD
Supt. — See Bartow
Dundee Academy 400/PK-4
415 E Frederick Ave 33838 863-421-3316
Lana Tatom, prin. Fax 421-3317
Dundee Ridge Middle Academy 1,000/6-8
5555 Lake Trask Rd 33838 863-419-3088
Stacy Gideons, prin. Fax 419-3157

Dunedin, Pinellas, Pop. 34,705
Pinellas County SD
Supt. — See Largo
Curtis Fundamental ES 500/K-5
531 Beltrees St 34698 727-738-6483
Richard Knight, prin. Fax 738-6488
Dunedin ES 600/K-5
900 Union St 34698 727-738-2990
Kerry Wyatt, prin. Fax 738-2004
Dunedin Highland MS 1,100/6-8
70 Patricia Ave 34698 727-469-4112
Michael Vasallo, prin. Fax 469-4115
Garrison-Jones ES 700/PK-5
3133 Garrison Rd 34698 727-469-5716
Karen Buckles, prin. Fax 469-5725
San Jose ES 500/PK-5
1670 San Helen Dr 34698 727-469-5956
Lisa Brown, prin. Fax 469-5960

Cornerstone Christian S 100/PK-8
317 Milwaukee Ave 34698 727-733-1438
Dunedin Academy 200/PK-12
1408 County Road 1 34698 727-733-9148
Our Lady of Lourdes S 200/PK-8
730 San Salvador Dr 34698 727-733-3776
Darrell Fulford, prin. Fax 733-4333

Dunnellon, Marion, Pop. 1,711
Marion County SD
Supt. — See Ocala
Dunnellon ES 700/PK-5
10235 SW 180th Avenue Rd 34432 352-465-6710
Karen English, prin. Fax 465-6711
Dunnellon MS 600/6-8
21005 Chestnut St 34431 352-465-6720
Delbert Smallridge, prin. Fax 465-6721
Romeo ES 700/K-5
19550 SW 36th St 34431 352-465-6700
Cathy Balius, prin. Fax 465-6701

Dunnellon Christian Academy 200/PK-12
20831 Powell Rd 34431 352-489-7716

Eagle Lake, Polk, Pop. 2,207
Polk County SD
Supt. — See Bartow
Eagle Lake ES 500/PK-5
400 W Crystal Beach Rd 33839 863-291-5357
Connie Loutenhiser, prin. Fax 291-5360
Pinewood ES 700/K-5
1400 Gilbert St 33839 863-298-7977
April Campbell, prin. Fax 298-7978

Bethel's Christian Academy 50/K-8
75 Don Polston Dr 33839 863-280-2080
Frank O'Harroll, prin. Fax 875-5574
Jordan Christian Preparatory S 100/K-12
1770 Gilbert St 33839 863-430-5431

Eastpoint, Franklin, Pop. 2,298
Franklin County SD 1,200/K-12
85 School Rd Ste 1 32328 850-670-2810
Traci Moses, supt. Fax 670-8579
www.franklincountyschools.org
Franklin County S 900/K-12
1250 US Highway 98 32328 850-670-2800
Chip Clatto, prin. Fax 670-2801

Edgewater, Volusia, Pop. 20,442
Volusia County SD
Supt. — See De Land

Edgewater ES 600/K-5
801 S Old County Rd 32132 386-424-2573
Rebecca Porter, prin. Fax 426-7349
Indian River ES 700/PK-5
650 Roberts Rd 32141 386-424-2650
Carrie Crkvenac, prin.

Discovery Days Institute of Learning 100/PK-8
227 N Ridgewood Ave 32132 386-428-0860

Eglin AFB, Okaloosa, Pop. 2,119
Okaloosa County SD
Supt. — See Fort Walton Beach
Eglin ES 500/K-4
200 Gaffney Rd 32542 850-833-4320
Dennis Samac, prin. Fax 833-3671

Elkton, Saint Johns
St. Johns County SD
Supt. — See Saint Augustine
South Woods ES 600/PK-5
4750 State Road 206 W 32033 904-547-8610
Randy Kelley, prin. Fax 547-8615

Englewood, Sarasota, Pop. 14,723
Sarasota County SD
Supt. — See Sarasota
Englewood ES 500/K-5
150 N Mccall Rd 34223 941-474-3247
Mark Grossenbacher, prin. Fax 474-0872

Enterprise, Volusia
Volusia County SD
Supt. — See De Land
Enterprise ES 600/PK-5
211 Main St 32725 386-575-4135
Sharilou McConnell, prin. Fax 668-3513

Estero, Lee, Pop. 22,447
Lee County SD
Supt. — See Fort Myers
Pinewoods ES 1,000/PK-5
11900 Stoneybrook Golf Dr 33928 239-947-7500
Leslie Gunderson, prin. Fax 947-0834

Eustis, Lake, Pop. 18,227
Lake County SD
Supt. — See Tavares
Eustis ES 500/K-5
714 E Citrus Ave 32726 352-357-2779
Kay Sawchuk, prin. Fax 357-4179
Eustis Heights ES 600/PK-5
250 W Atwater Ave 32726 352-357-2447
Chad Frazier, prin. Fax 357-3602
Eustis MS 1,000/6-8
18725 Bates Ave 32736 352-357-3366
Bill Miller, prin. Fax 357-5963
Seminole Springs ES 600/PK-5
26200 W Huff Rd 32736 352-589-1117
Leah Fischer, prin. Fax 589-1749

Faith Lutheran S 200/PK-8
2727 S Grove St 32726 352-589-5683
Steve Hoffschneider, admin. Fax 589-1328
Learning Curve Academy 100/PK-12
480 CR 44 32726 352-357-5500

Everglades City, Collier
Collier County SD
Supt. — See Naples
Everglades City S 200/PK-12
PO Box 170 34139 239-377-9800
James Ragusa, prin. Fax 377-9801

Fellsmere, Indian River, Pop. 5,172
Indian River County SD
Supt. — See Vero Beach
Fellsmere ES 700/PK-5
50 N Cypress St 32948 772-564-5970
Ramon Echeverria, prin. Fax 564-6020

Fernandina Beach, Nassau, Pop. 11,315
Nassau County SD 11,200/PK-12
1201 Atlantic Ave 32034 904-491-9900
Kathy Burns, supt. Fax 277-9042
www.nassau.k12.fl.us
Fernandina Beach MS 600/6-8
315 Citrona Dr 32034 904-491-7938
Dr. John Mazzella, prin. Fax 261-8919
Hardee ES 600/3-5
2200 Susan Dr 32034 904-491-7936
Rebecca Smith, prin. Fax 321-5890
Southside ES 600/PK-2
1112 Jasmine St 32034 904-491-7941
Marlena Palmer, prin. Fax 321-5073
Other Schools – See Bryceville, Callahan, Hilliard, Yulee

Amelia Island Montessori S 100/PK-8
1423 Julia St 32034 904-261-6610
Faith Christian Academy 100/PK-8
96282 Brady Point Rd 32034 904-321-2137
Bryan Alvare, hdmstr. Fax 321-1707
St. Michael Academy 200/PK-8
228 N 4th St 32034 904-321-2102
Christopher Hampton Ed.D., prin. Fax 321-2330

Fern Park, Seminole, Pop. 7,563
Seminole County SD
Supt. — See Sanford
English Estates ES 800/PK-5
299 Oxford Rd 32730 407-746-2850
Shannon Akerson, prin. Fax 746-2858

Flagler Beach, Flagler, Pop. 4,438
Flagler County SD
Supt. — See Bunnell
Old Kings ES 1,100/K-6
301 Old Kings Rd S 32136 386-517-2060
Benjamin Osypian, prin. Fax 517-2074

Floral City, Citrus, Pop. 5,163
Citrus County SD
Supt. — See Inverness
Floral City ES 400/PK-5
PO Box 340 34436 352-726-1554
Dr. Tara Wells, prin. Fax 249-2127

Florida City, Miami-Dade, Pop. 11,104
Miami-Dade County SD
Supt. — See Miami
Florida City ES 800/PK-5
364 NW 6th Ave 33034 305-247-4676
Rachelle Surrancy, prin. Fax 245-7106

Bethel SDA ES 50/K-8
32900 SW 187th Ave 33034 305-248-4973

Fort Lauderdale, Broward, Pop. 162,648
Broward County SD 251,700/PK-12
600 SE 3rd Ave 33301 754-321-0000
Robert Runcie, supt. Fax 321-2701
www.browardschools.com
Bayview ES 600/K-5
1175 Middle River Dr 33304 754-322-5400
Tonya Frost, prin. Fax 322-5440
Bennett ES 400/PK-5
1755 NE 14th St 33304 754-322-5450
Danielle Smith, prin. Fax 322-5490
Croissant Park ES 700/PK-5
1800 SW 4th Ave 33315 754-323-5300
Michelle Ann Allison, prin. Fax 323-5340
Dandy MS 1,100/6-8
2400 NW 26th St 33311 754-322-3200
Shernette Grant, prin. Fax 322-3285
Dillard ES 800/PK-5
2330 NW 12th Ct 33311 754-322-6200
Gretchen Atkins-Brown, prin. Fax 322-6240
Floranada ES 700/K-5
5251 NE 14th Way 33334 754-322-6350
John Vetter, prin. Fax 322-6390
Foster ES 700/PK-5
3471 SW 22nd St 33312 754-323-5750
Ricardo Grimaldo, prin. Fax 323-5790
Harbordale ES 400/PK-5
900 SE 15th St 33316 754-323-6050
Theresa Bucolo, prin. Fax 323-6090
Marshall ES 500/PK-5
800 NW 13th St 33311 754-322-7000
Michael Billins, prin. Fax 322-7040
Meadowbrook ES 700/PK-5
2300 SW 46th Ave 33317 754-323-6500
Matthew Whaley, prin. Fax 323-6540
New River MS 1,400/6-8
3100 Riverland Rd 33312 754-323-3600
Melinda Wessinger, prin. Fax 323-3685
North Fork ES 600/PK-5
101 NW 15th Ave 33311 754-322-7350
Rendolyn Amaker, prin. Fax 322-7390
North Side ES 500/PK-5
120 NE 11th St 33304 754-322-7450
Heilange Porcena, prin. Fax 322-7490
Riverland ES 600/PK-5
2600 SW 11th Ct 33312 754-323-7200
Oslay Gil, prin. Fax 323-7240
Rock Island ES 600/PK-5
2350 NW 19th St 33311 754-322-8300
Cormic Priester, prin. Fax 322-8340
Sunland Park ES 400/PK-3
919 NW 13th Ter 33311 754-322-8550
Sharonda Bailey, prin. Fax 322-8590
Sunrise MS 1,300/6-8
1750 NE 14th St 33304 754-322-4700
Michael Walker, prin. Fax 322-4785
Walker ES 600/K-5
1001 NW 4th St 33311 754-322-8800
Philip Bullock, prin. Fax 322-8840
Westwood Heights ES 600/PK-5
2861 SW 9th St 33312 754-323-7900
Jodi Washington, prin. Fax 323-7940
Young ES 700/PK-5
101 NE 11th Ave 33301 754-322-9050
Cynthia Felton, prin. Fax 322-9090
Other Schools – See Coconut Creek, Cooper City, Coral Springs, Dania Beach, Davie, Deerfield Beach, Hallandale Beach, Hollywood, Lauderdale Lakes, Lauderhill, Margate, Miramar, North Lauderdale, Oakland Park, Parkland, Pembroke Park, Pembroke Pines, Plantation, Pompano Beach, Sunrise, Tamarac, Weston, Wilton Manors

Alternative Education Foundation Prep S 200/PK-12
4650 SW 61st Ave 33314 954-581-8222
Bethany Christian S 200/PK-8
615 SE 9th St 33316 954-522-2554
Sam Kastensmidt, head sch Fax 522-3406
Brauser Maimonides Academy 400/PK-8
5300 SW 40th Ave 33314 954-989-6886
Calvary Christian Academy 1,700/PK-12
2401 W Cypress Creek Rd 33309 954-905-5100
Dr. Jason Rachels, head sch Fax 653-2991
Christ Church S 300/PK-5
4845 NE 25th Ave 33308 954-771-7700
Tarie Bonham, prin. Fax 776-4553
Fort Lauderdale Preparatory S 200/PK-12
3275 W Oakland Park Blvd 33311 954-485-7500
Gateway Christian Academy 100/PK-5
2130 NW 26th St 33311 954-485-7012
Holy Temple Christian Academy 200/PK-12
1800 NW 9th Ave 33311 954-467-0758
Master's Academy 200/PK-8
13900 Griffin Rd 33330 954-434-2960
Mt. Bethel Christian Academy 100/PK-8
901 NW 11th Ave 33311 954-462-0255
Mt. Olivet SDA Junior Academy 100/PK-8
3013 NW 11th St 33311 954-792-6010
Cynthia Murray, prin. Fax 792-2248
New Hope Christian S 100/PK-5
6400 NW 31st Ave 33309 954-973-1129
Brandy Andrews, head sch Fax 984-1935

New Hope SDA S 50/K-6
545 E Campus Cir 33312 954-587-3842
NSU University S 1,900/PK-12
3375 SW 75th Ave 33314 954-262-4506
Dr. William Kopas, head sch
Our Lady Queen of Martyrs S 200/PK-8
2785 SW 11th Ct 33312 954-583-8112
Althea Mossop, prin. Fax 797-4984
Pine Crest S 2,500/PK-12
1501 NE 162nd St 33334 954-492-4100
David Clark, prin. Fax 492-4188
Redeeming Word Christian Academy 100/PK-8
2800 W Prospect Rd 33309 954-485-1435
Lashaon Brooks, dir. Fax 485-6023
St. Anthony S 400/PK-8
820 NE 3rd St 33301 954-467-7747
Terry Maus, prin. Fax 467-9908
St. Helen S 200/PK-8
3340 W Oakland Park Blvd 33311 954-739-7094
Stephanie Tascillo, prin. Fax 739-0797
St. Jerome S 300/PK-8
2601 SW 9th Ave 33315 954-524-1990
David Revezzo, prin. Fax 524-7439
St. Mark's Episcopal S 400/PK-8
1750 E Oakland Park Blvd 33334 954-563-4508
Kathleen Rotella Ed.D., prin. Fax 563-0487
Shepherd of the Coast Christian S 100/PK-8
1901 E Commercial Blvd 33308 954-772-5468
Larry Ueltzen, prin. Fax 772-2232
Trinity Lutheran Academy 50/K-8
110 SW 11th St 33315 954-463-7471
Candace Church, prin. Fax 463-3928
Westminster Academy 900/PK-12
5601 N Federal Hwy 33308 954-771-4600

Fort Mc Coy, Marion
Marion County SD
Supt. — See Ocala
Fort Mc Coy S 1,000/PK-8
16160 NE Highway 315 32134 352-671-6325
Mike Hearn, prin. Fax 671-6326

Fort Meade, Polk, Pop. 5,552
Polk County SD
Supt. — See Bartow
Woodbury ES - Lewis Campus 400/PK-3
115 S Oak Ave 33841 863-285-1150
Alexandra Wise, prin. Fax 285-1155
Woodbury ES - Woodbury Campus 200/4-5
610 S Charleston Ave 33841 863-285-1133
Alexandra Wise, prin. Fax 285-1138

Fort Myers, Lee, Pop. 60,807
Lee County SD 84,300/PK-12
2855 Colonial Blvd 33966 239-334-1102
Gregory Adkins Ed.D., supt. Fax 337-8301
www.leeschools.net
Allen Park ES 900/PK-5
3345 Canelo Dr 33901 239-936-1459
Lisa Estridge, prin. Fax 936-3470
Colonial ES 800/PK-5
3800 Schoolhouse Rd E 33916 239-939-2242
Dr. Marsha Bur, prin. Fax 939-5143
Cypress Lake MS 800/6-8
8901 Cypress Lake Dr 33919 239-481-1533
Kelly Maniscalco, prin. Fax 481-3121
Dunbar MS 1,000/6-8
4750 Winkler Ave, 239-334-1357
Dr. Nathan Shaker, prin. Fax 334-7633
Edgewood Academy 500/PK-5
3464 Edgewood Ave 33916 239-334-6205
Robert Mazzoli, prin. Fax 334-6776
Edison Park Creative/Expressive Arts ES 400/K-5
2401 Euclid Ave 33901 239-334-6232
Cherise Trent, prin. Fax 332-3474
Fort Myers Middle Academy 400/6-8
3050 Central Ave 33901 239-936-1759
Lynn Edwards, prin. Fax 936-4350
Franklin Park ES 400/PK-5
2323 Ford St 33916 239-332-1969
Dr. Bethany Quisenberry, prin. Fax 337-1127
Gateway ES 700/K-5
13280 Griffin Dr 33913 239-768-3737
Christine Siebenaler, prin. Fax 768-2967
Heights ES 1,100/K-5
15200 Alexandria Ct 33908 239-481-1761
Douglas Palow, prin. Fax 481-3154
Lexington MS 1,000/6-8
16351 Summerlin Rd 33908 239-454-6130
Linda Berry, prin. Fax 489-3419
Manatee ES 800/K-5
5301 Tice St 33905 239-694-2097
Ashley LaMar, prin. Fax 694-4282
Oak Hammock MS 1,100/6-8
5321 Tice St 33905 239-693-0469
Jennifer Sneddon, prin. Fax 694-4089
Orange River ES 800/PK-5
4501 Underwood Dr 33905 239-694-1258
Karen Manzi, prin. Fax 694-8680
Orangewood ES 600/PK-5
4001 Deleon St 33901 239-936-2950
Angela Nader, prin. Fax 936-2134
Page ES 800/K-5
17000 S Tamiami Trl 33908 239-432-2737
Valerie Sheckler, prin. Fax 432-2749
Pottorf ES 700/K-5
4600 Challenger Blvd, 239-274-3932
Dorothy Whittaker, prin. Fax 275-3381
San Carlos Park ES 800/PK-5
17282 Lee Rd, 239-267-7177
Christy Kutz, prin. Fax 267-0057
Stephens International Academy 700/K-5
1333 Marsh Ave 33905 239-337-1333
Kenneth Savage, prin. Fax 334-4144
Tanglewood ES 700/PK-5
1620 Manchester Blvd 33919 239-936-0891
Linda Buckley, prin. Fax 939-0411
Three Oaks ES 800/PK-5
19600 Cypress View Dr, 239-267-8020
Jody Moorhead, prin. Fax 267-9559

Three Oaks MS 1,000/6-8
18500 3 Oaks Pkwy, 239-267-5757
Mike Carson, prin. Fax 267-4007
Tice ES 500/PK-5
4524 Tice St 33905 239-694-1257
Ronda Amaya, prin. Fax 694-8745
Treeline ES 1,000/K-5
10900 Treeline Ave 33913 239-768-5208
Kelly Thornton, prin. Fax 768-5415
Villas ES 800/PK-5
8385 Beacon Blvd 33907 239-936-3776
Shane Musich, prin. Fax 936-6884
Other Schools – See Alva, Bokeelia, Bonita Springs, Cape Coral, Estero, Fort Myers Beach, Lehigh Acres, North Fort Myers, Sanibel

---

Canterbury S 600/PK-12
8141 College Pkwy 33919 239-481-4323
Rick Kirschner, head sch Fax 481-8339
Crestwell S 200/PK-8
1901 Park Meadows Dr 33907 239-481-4478
Crown of Life Christian Academy 50/PK-5
5820 Daniels Pkwy 33912 239-482-7315
Rebecca Rixe, dir. Fax 482-5694
Evangelical Christian S 800/PK-12
8237 Beacon Blvd 33907 239-936-3319
Fort Myers Christian S 200/PK-8
1550 Colonial Blvd 33907 239-939-4642
Mel Mitchell, prin. Fax 936-5016
Millennium Christian Academy 100/PK-5
13235 Palm Beach Blvd 33905 239-208-9852
Lucy Feliciano, prin. Fax 895-3006
Renaissance Montessori S 50/PK-6
37 Barkley Cir 33907 239-275-2022
Kathleen Leitch, head sch Fax 275-8638
St. Francis Xavier Catholic S 600/PK-8
2055 Heitman St 33901 239-334-7707
John Gulley, prin. Fax 334-8605
St. Michael Lutheran S 400/PK-8
3595 Broadway 33901 239-939-1218
Kati Miser, prin. Fax 939-1839
Sonshine Christian Academy 200/PK-12
12925 Palm Beach Blvd 33905 239-694-8882
Dr. Bob Calvert, admin. Fax 694-8885
Southwest Florida Christian Academy 500/K-12
3750 Colonial Blvd, 239-936-8865
Lisa Kleinmann, hdmstr. Fax 936-7095
Summit Christian S 100/PK-8
9065 Ligon Ct 33908 239-482-7007
Kyle Mast, head sch Fax 481-9617

Fort Myers Beach, Lee, Pop. 6,234
Lee County SD
Supt. — See Fort Myers
Fort Myers Beach ES 100/K-5
2751 Oak St 33931 239-463-6356
Jeff Dobbins, prin. Fax 463-3592

Fort Pierce, Saint Lucie, Pop. 40,874
St. Lucie County SD 40,600/PK-12
4204 Okeechobee Rd 34947 772-429-3600
E. Wayne Gent, supt. Fax 429-3916
www.stlucie.k12.fl.us
Fairlawn ES 600/K-5
3203 Rhode Island Ave 34947 772-468-5345
Pamela Holmes, prin. Fax 465-5377
Forest Grove MS 900/6-8
3201 S 25th St 34981 772-468-5885
Monarae Miller-Buchanan, prin. Fax 595-1187
Fort Pierce Magnet S of the Arts 400/K-8
1200 Delaware Ave 34950 772-467-4278
Lori Reid, prin. Fax 460-3094
Gaines Academy 1,200/PK-8
2250 S Jenkins Rd 34947 772-462-8888
Roberto Bonsenor, prin. Fax 468-5004
Lakewood Park ES 700/PK-5
7800 Indrio Rd 34951 772-468-5830
Dianne Young, prin. Fax 468-5833
Lawnwood ES 700/PK-5
1900 S 23rd St 34950 772-468-5740
Traci Wilke, prin. Fax 468-5204
McCarty MS 600/6-8
1201 Mississippi Ave 34950 772-468-5700
Lisa Sullivan, prin. Fax 468-5737
Moore ES 700/PK-5
827 N 29th St 34947 772-468-5315
Ucola Barrett-Baxter, prin. Fax 468-5896
Parkway ES 600/PK-5
7000 NW Selvitz Rd 34983 772-340-4800
Carolyn Wilkins, prin. Fax 340-4807
St. Lucie ES 800/PK-5
2020 S 13th St 34950 772-468-5213
Michelle Herrington, prin. Fax 468-5823
Sweet ES 600/K-5
1400 Avenue Q 34950 772-468-5330
Juanita Wright, prin. Fax 468-5334
Weatherbee ES 700/PK-5
800 E Weatherbee Rd 34982 772-468-5300
Michael Hitsman, prin. Fax 467-4033
White City ES 600/PK-5
905 W 2nd St 34982 772-468-5840
Felicia Nixon, prin. Fax 467-4067
Other Schools – See Port Saint Lucie

Liberty Baptist Academy 500/PK-12
3660 W Midway Rd 34981 772-461-2731
Katherine Johnson, admin. Fax 461-2542
St. Anastasia S 500/PK-8
401 S 33rd St 34947 772-461-2232
Dr. Kevin Hoeffner, prin. Fax 468-2037
St. Andrew's Episcopal Academy 200/PK-12
210 S Indian River Dr 34950 772-461-7689
Suzanne D. Barry, head sch Fax 461-4683
St James Christian Academy 100/PK-12
4100 Okeechobee Rd 34947 772-466-2000
Sampson Memorial SDA S 50/PK-8
3201 Memory Ln 34981 772-465-8386
Sun Grove Montessori S 100/PK-8
5610 Oleander Ave 34982 772-464-5436

Fort Walton Beach, Okaloosa, Pop. 18,836
Okaloosa County SD 29,800/PK-12
120 Lowery Pl SE 32548 850-833-3100
Mary Beth Jackson, supt. Fax 833-3436
www.okaloosaschools.com
Bruner MS 800/6-8
322 Holmes Blvd NW 32548 850-833-3266
Dr. Cynthia Hudson, prin. Fax 833-3434
Edwins Fine & Performing Arts S 400/PK-5
7 Wright Pkwy SW 32548 850-833-3333
Gwen Morris, prin. Fax 833-3480
Elliott Point ES 600/PK-5
301 Hughes St NE 32548 850-833-3355
Kathy Ard, prin. Fax 833-3473
Kenwood ES 600/PK-5
15 Eagle St NE 32547 850-833-3570
Joan Pickard, prin. Fax 833-3597
Pryor MS 600/6-8
201 Racetrack Rd NW 32547 850-833-3613
Brooke Barron, prin. Fax 833-4276
Wright ES 600/PK-5
305 Lang Rd 32547 850-833-3580
Dr. Anita Choice, prin. Fax 833-3584
Other Schools – See Baker, Crestview, Destin, Eglin AFB, Laurel Hill, Mary Esther, Niceville, Shalimar, Valparaiso

---

Beulah Christian Academy 50/PK-6
109 McGriff St NE 32548
Calvary Christian Academy 200/PK-12
535 Clifford St 32547 850-862-1414
Cinco Baptist S 200/PK-8
26 Yacht Club Dr NE 32548 850-243-7515
Emerald Coast Christian S 50/1-8
119 Saint Mary Ave SW 32548 850-243-1910
St. Mary S 400/PK-8
110 Robinwood Dr SW 32548 850-243-8913
Amy Akins, prin. Fax 243-7895

Fort White, Columbia, Pop. 554
Columbia County SD
Supt. — See Lake City
Fort White ES 700/PK-5
18119 SW State Road 47 32038 386-497-2301
Tom Lashley, prin. Fax 497-4684

Freeport, Walton, Pop. 1,743
Walton County SD
Supt. — See De Funiak Springs
Freeport ES 600/PK-4
15381 331 Business 32439 850-892-1211
Kristen Lewis, prin. Fax 892-1219
Freeport MS 400/5-8
360 Kylea Laird Dr 32439 850-892-1221
Josh Harrison, prin. Fax 892-1229

Frostproof, Polk, Pop. 2,965
Polk County SD
Supt. — See Bartow
Frostproof ES 400/PK-2
118 W 3rd St 33843 863-635-7802
Dart Meyers, prin. Fax 635-8501
Griffin ES 400/3-5
501 McCloud Rd 33843 863-635-7820
Patti McGill, prin. Fax 635-8500

Fruitland Park, Lake, Pop. 3,984
Lake County SD
Supt. — See Tavares
Fruitland Park ES 600/K-5
304 W Fountain St 34731 352-787-2693
Tammy Langley, prin. Fax 787-9402

Gainesville, Alachua, Pop. 121,031
Alachua County SD 26,800/PK-12
620 E University Ave 32601 352-955-7300
Karen Clarke, supt. Fax 955-6700
www.sbac.edu
Bishop MS 700/6-8
1901 NE 9th St 32609 352-955-6701
Mike Gamble, prin. Fax 316-7370
Chiles ES 700/PK-5
2525 School House Rd 32608 352-333-2825
Cory Tomlinson, prin. Fax 585-9512
Duval Early Learning Academy 300/PK-K
2106 NE 8th Ave 32641 352-955-6703
Judy Black, prin. Fax 955-6967
Fearnside Family Services Center 100/PK-PK
3600 NE 15th St 32609 352-955-6875
Natalie Strappy, prin. Fax 955-6955
Finley ES 600/K-5
1912 NW 5th Ave 32603 352-955-6705
Kathleen Valdes, prin. Fax 955-7128
Ft. Clarke MS 800/6-8
9301 NW 23rd Ave 32606 352-333-2800
Kelly Brill Jones, prin. Fax 333-2806
Foster ES 500/K-5
3800 NW 6th St 32609 352-955-6706
Lisa Peterson, prin. Fax 955-6746
Glen Springs ES 500/K-5
2826 NW 31st Ave 32605 352-955-6708
Kelly Armstrong, prin. Fax 955-7304
Hidden Oak ES 700/PK-5
2100 Fort Clarke Blvd 32606 352-333-2801
Jim Kuhn, prin. Fax 506-5805
Idylwild ES 700/K-5
4601 SW 20th Ter 32608 352-955-6709
Wanza Wakeley, prin. Fax 955-7123
Kanapaha MS 1,000/6-8
5005 SW 75th St 32608 352-955-6960
Sherry Estes, prin. Fax 955-6858
Lake Forest ES 300/PK-5
4401 SE 4th Ave 32641 352-955-6710
Karla Hutchinson, prin. Fax 955-6750
Lincoln MS 700/6-8
1001 SE 12th St 32641 352-955-6711
Latroy Strappy, prin. Fax 955-7133
Littlewood ES 600/PK-5
812 NW 34th St 32605 352-955-6712
Justin Russell, prin. Fax 955-7149
Meadowbrook ES 700/K-5
11525 NW 39th Ave 32606 352-333-2828
Brad Burklew, prin. Fax 333-2862
Metcalfe ES 300/1-5
1250 NE 18th Ave 32609 352-955-6713
Elena Mayo, prin. Fax 955-6753
Norton ES 700/K-5
2200 NW 45th Ave 32605 352-955-6765
Kim Neal, prin. Fax 955-7126
Rawlings ES 200/1-5
3500 NE 15th St 32609 352-955-6715
Daniel Burney, prin. Fax 955-7137
Talbot ES 700/PK-5
5701 NW 43rd St 32653 352-955-6716
Nannette Dell, prin. Fax 955-7132
Terwilliger ES 700/PK-5
301 NW 62nd St 32607 352-955-6717
Ashlea Zeller, prin. Fax 955-7134
Westwood MS 1,000/6-8
3215 NW 15th Ave 32605 352-955-6718
James TenBieg, prin. Fax 955-6897
Wiles ES 800/K-5
4601 SW 75th St 32608 352-955-6955
Dr. Barbara Buys, prin. Fax 955-7124
Williams ES 600/K-5
1245 SE 7th Ave 32641 352-955-6719
Jacquatte Rolle, prin. Fax 955-6759
Other Schools – See Alachua, Archer, Hawthorne, High Springs, Newberry

---

Brentwood S 200/PK-5
1111 NW 55th St 32605 352-373-3222
Christian Life Academy 100/K-12
12000 SW Archer Rd 32608 352-495-3040
Cornerstone Academy 200/PK-12
PO Box 357430 32635 352-378-9337
Doug Lawson, hdmstr. Fax 378-7708
Countryside Christian S 100/PK-12
10926 NW 39th Ave 32606 352-332-1493
Gainesville Country Day S 300/PK-5
6801 SW 24th Ave 32607 352-332-7783
Heart Pine Waldorf S 100/1-5
1000 NE 16th Ave Bldg C 32601 352-219-5829
Tamara Bish, admin.
Millhopper Montessori S 200/PK-8
8505 NW 39th Ave 32606 352-375-6773
Oak Hall Lower S 400/PK-5
7715 SW 14th Ave 32607 352-332-1452
Dr. James Hutchins, head sch Fax 332-4945
Queen of Peace Academy 400/PK-8
10900 SW 24th Ave 32607 352-332-8808
Tammie Vassou, prin. Fax 331-7347
Rock S 300/PK-12
9818 SW 24th Ave 32607 352-331-7625
St. Patrick Interparish S 300/PK-8
550 NE 16th Ave 32601 352-376-9878
Frank Mackritis, prin. Fax 371-6177
Star Christian Academy 100/PK-8
6702 NW 28th Terr 32653 352-336-5300
Phyllis Thomas-Dykes, prin. Fax 372-2994
Sung SDA S 50/1-10
2115 NW 39th Ave 32605 352-376-6040

Geneva, Seminole, Pop. 2,879
Seminole County SD
Supt. — See Sanford
Geneva ES 500/PK-5
275 1st St 32732 407-320-4950
Rod Dunaye, prin. Fax 320-4981

Gibsonton, Hillsborough, Pop. 13,940
Hillsborough County SD
Supt. — See Tampa
Corr ES 700/K-5
13020 Kings Lake Dr 33534 813-672-5345
Kristi-Lyn Ricketts, prin. Fax 672-5349
Eisenhower MS 1,200/6-8
7620 Old Big Bend Rd 33534 813-671-5121
Johan Von Ancken, prin. Fax 671-5039
Gibsonton ES 600/PK-5
7723 Gibsonton Dr 33534 813-671-5100
Cindy Guy, prin. Fax 672-5003

Glen Saint Mary, Baker, Pop. 430
Baker County SD
Supt. — See Macclenny
Westside ES 600/1-3
1 Panther Cir 32040 904-259-2216
Kelly Horne, prin. Fax 259-5172

Gotha, Orange, Pop. 1,873

Central Florida Preparatory S 200/PK-12
1450 Citrus Oaks Ave 34734 407-290-8073
Crenshaw S 50/PK-12
2342 Hempel Ave 34734 407-757-2241

Graceville, Jackson, Pop. 2,229
Holmes County SD
Supt. — See Bonifay
Poplar Springs S 400/PK-12
3726 Atomic Dr 32440 850-263-6260
Gordon Wells, prin. Fax 263-1252

Jackson County SD
Supt. — See Marianna
Graceville ES 400/PK-5
5331 Alabama St 32440 850-263-4402
Laurence Pender, prin. Fax 263-3304

Grand Ridge, Jackson, Pop. 874
Jackson County SD
Supt. — See Marianna
Grand Ridge S 600/PK-8
6925 Florida St 32442 850-482-9835
Laura Cullifer Kent, prin. Fax 482-9834

Greenacres, Palm Beach, Pop. 36,906
Palm Beach County SD
Supt. — See West Palm Beach

Cholee Lake ES 1,000/K-5
6680 Dillman Rd 33413 561-383-9600
Dr. Marline Campbell, prin. Fax 383-9650
Diamond View ES 900/K-5
5300 S Haverhill Rd 33463 561-304-4200
Carolyn Seal, prin. Fax 304-4210
Greenacres ES 700/K-5
405 Jackson Ave 33463 561-649-7200
Deborah McNichols, prin. Fax 649-7250
Heritage ES 900/K-5
5100 Melaleuca Ln 33463 561-804-3200
Nina Lant, prin. Fax 804-3250
Liberty Park ES 1,000/K-5
6601 Constitution Way 33413 561-804-3400
Joseph Schneider, prin. Fax 804-3450
Okeeheelee MS 1,500/6-8
2200 Pinehurst Dr 33413 561-434-3200
David Samore, prin. Fax 434-3244
Swain MS 1,200/6-8
5332 Lake Worth Rd 33463 561-649-6900
James Thomas, prin. Fax 649-6906
Tradewinds MS 1,200/6-8
5090 S Haverhill Rd 33463 561-493-6400
Rebecca Subin, prin. Fax 493-6410

Greenacres Christian Academy 100/PK-12
4982 Cambridge St 33463 561-965-0363

Green Cove Springs, Clay, Pop. 6,779
Clay County SD 34,800/PK-12
900 Walnut St 32043 904-284-6500
Addison Davis, supt. Fax 284-6525
www.oneclay.net
Bennett ES 800/PK-6
1 S Oakridge Ave 32043 904-336-0475
Sarah Lawson, prin. Fax 336-0477
Green Cove Springs JHS 800/7-8
1220 Bonaventure Ave 32043 904-336-5175
Jen Halter, prin. Fax 336-6563
Lake Asbury ES 800/K-6
2901 Sandridge Rd 32043 904-336-1525
Tiffany Outman, prin. Fax 336-1527
Lake Asbury JHS 1,100/7-8
2851 Sandridge Rd 32043 904-336-5375
Becky Murphy, prin. Fax 336-5377
Shadowlawn ES 700/PK-6
2945 County Road 218 32043 904-336-3375
Nancy Crowder, prin. Fax 336-3377
Other Schools – See Jacksonville, Keystone Heights, Middleburg, Orange Park

Greenville, Madison, Pop. 828
Madison County SD
Supt. — See Madison
Greenville ES 200/PK-5
729 SW Overstreet Ave 32331 850-973-5033
Barbara Pettiford, prin. Fax 973-5040

Groveland, Lake, Pop. 8,373
Lake County SD
Supt. — See Tavares
Gray MS 1,000/6-8
205 E Magnolia St 34736 352-429-3322
Pam Chateauneuf, prin. Fax 429-0133
Groveland ES 800/PK-5
930 Parkwood Ave 34736 352-429-2472
Kimberly Sneed, prin. Fax 429-2516

H.O.P.E. Academy 100/K-12
13806 State Rd 33 34736 352-557-8306
Integrity Christian Academy 100/K-12
7432 State Rd 50 34736 352-429-4402

Gulf Breeze, Santa Rosa, Pop. 5,682
Santa Rosa County SD
Supt. — See Milton
Gulf Breeze ES 700/K-5
549 Gulf Breeze Pkwy 32561 850-934-5185
Warren Stevens, prin. Fax 934-5189
Gulf Breeze MS 900/6-8
649 Gulf Breeze Pkwy 32561 850-934-4080
Michael Brandon, prin. Fax 934-4085
Oriole Beach ES 800/PK-5
1260 Oriole Beach Rd 32563 850-934-5160
Josh McGrew, prin. Fax 934-5166
Woodlawn Beach MS 1,000/6-8
1500 Woodlawn Way 32563 850-934-4010
Victor Lowrimore, prin. Fax 934-4015

Good Shepherd Lutheran S 100/PK-2
4257 Gulf Breeze Pkwy 32563 850-932-9127
Fax 344-9684
Gulf Pointe Academy 100/K-5
6464 Gulf Breeze Pkwy 32563 850-547-6729

Gulfport, Pinellas, Pop. 11,800
Pinellas County SD
Supt. — See Largo
Gulfport ES 600/PK-5
2014 52nd St S 33707 727-893-2643
Jesley Hathaway, prin. Fax 552-1574

Gulf Stream, Palm Beach, Pop. 781

Gulf Stream S 300/PK-8
3600 Gulfstream Rd 33483 561-276-5225
Joseph Zaluski, hdmstr. Fax 276-7115

Haines City, Polk, Pop. 20,261
Polk County SD
Supt. — See Bartow
Alta Vista ES 900/PK-5
801 Scenic Hwy 33844 863-421-3235
Nikeshia Leatherwood, prin. Fax 421-3344
Bethune Academy 500/K-5
900 Avenue F 33844 863-421-3334
Sharon Knowles, prin. Fax 421-3243
Boone MS 800/6-8
225 S 22nd St 33844 863-421-3302
Sharon Chipman, prin. Fax 421-3305
Eastside ES 1,200/PK-5
1820 E Johnson Ave 33844 863-421-3254
Johna Jozwiak, prin. Fax 421-3256
Jenkins Academy of Technology 500/6-8
701 Ledwith Ave 33844 863-421-3267
Brad Tarver, prin. Fax 421-3269
Sandhill ES 800/PK-5
1801 Tyner Rd 33844 863-419-3166
Kathleen Conely, prin. Fax 419-3167

Landmark Christian S 200/PK-12
2020 E Hinson Ave 33844 863-422-2037

Hallandale Beach, Broward, Pop. 36,609
Broward County SD
Supt. — See Fort Lauderdale
Gulfstream Academy of Hallandale Beach 1,100/K-8
1000 SW 3rd St, 754-323-5950
Robert Pappas, prin. Fax 323-5990

Masoret Yehudit Academy 200/PK-6
680 E Hallandale Beach Blvd, 954-457-3899

Hampton, Bradford, Pop. 488
Bradford County SD
Supt. — See Starke
Hampton ES 200/PK-5
PO Box 200 32044 352-468-1212
Brenda Donaldson, prin. Fax 468-1659

Havana, Gadsden, Pop. 1,746
Gadsden County SD
Supt. — See Quincy
Havana Magnet S 200/PK-8
1210 Kemp Rd 32333 850-662-2750
Delshauna Jackson, prin. Fax 539-2866

Tallavana Christian S 200/PK-12
5840 Havana Hwy 32333 850-539-5300

Hawthorne, Alachua, Pop. 1,398
Alachua County SD
Supt. — See Gainesville
Shell ES 200/K-5
21633 SE 65th Ave 32640 352-481-1901
Holly Burton, prin. Fax 481-1911

Putnam County SD
Supt. — See Palatka
Ochwilla ES 400/PK-5
299 N State Road 21 32640 352-481-0204
Evelyn Langston, prin. Fax 481-5541

Hernando, Citrus, Pop. 8,946
Citrus County SD
Supt. — See Inverness
Forest Ridge ES 700/PK-5
2927 N Forest Ridge Blvd 34442 352-527-1808
Laura Windham, prin. Fax 249-2128
Hernando ES 600/PK-5
2975 E Trailblazer Ln 34442 352-726-1833
Chris Bosse, prin. Fax 249-2130

Hialeah, Miami-Dade, Pop. 224,295
Miami-Dade County SD
Supt. — See Miami
Bright/Johnson ES 700/PK-5
2530 W 10th Ave 33010 305-885-1683
Claudine Winsor, prin. Fax 888-7059
Dupuis ES 700/PK-5
1150 W 59th Pl 33012 305-821-6361
Lourdes Nunez, prin. Fax 825-2433
Earhart ES 500/PK-5
5987 E 7th Ave 33013 305-688-9619
Lisa Wiggins, prin. Fax 769-9038
Filer MS 1,100/6-8
531 W 29th St 33012 305-822-6601
John Donohue, prin. Fax 822-2063
Flamingo ES 700/PK-5
701 E 33rd St 33013 305-691-5531
Eleana Sotolongo, prin. Fax 835-8525
Graham K-8 Academy 1,500/PK-8
7330 W 32nd Ave 33018 305-825-2122
Mayra Alfaro, prin. Fax 557-5739
Hialeah ES 700/PK-5
550 E 8th St 33010 305-888-6709
Rosa Iglesias, prin. Fax 884-6503
Hialeah Gardens Primary Learning Center PK-K
9749 NW 127th St 33018 305-818-7976
Fax 818-7978
Hialeah MS 900/6-8
6027 E 7th Ave 33013 305-681-3527
Nelson Gonzalez, prin. Fax 681-6225
Meadowlane ES 1,000/PK-5
4280 W 8th Ave 33012 305-822-0660
Maritza Garcia, prin. Fax 362-9904
Milam K-8 Center 1,000/PK-8
6020 W 16th Ave 33012 305-822-0301
Anna Hernandez, prin. Fax 556-1388
North Hialeah ES 600/PK-5
4251 E 5th Ave 33013 305-681-4611
Carlos Salcedo, prin. Fax 688-6652
North Twin Lakes ES 600/PK-5
625 W 74th Pl 33014 305-822-0721
Jose Fernandez, prin. Fax 558-1697
Palm Lakes ES 800/PK-5
7450 W 16th Ave 33014 305-823-6970
Alina Iglesias, prin. Fax 828-6136
Palm Springs ES 700/PK-5
6304 E 1st Ave 33013 305-822-0911
Roxana Herrera, prin. Fax 828-5802
Palm Springs MS 1,200/6-8
1025 W 56th St 33012 305-821-2460
Leonard Torres, prin. Fax 828-3987
Palm Springs North ES 1,000/PK-5
17615 NW 82nd Ave 33015 305-821-4631
Maribel Dotres, prin. Fax 825-0422
Sheppard ES 900/K-5
5700 W 24th Ave 33016 305-556-2204
Dr. Eduardo Tagle, prin. Fax 822-0558
Sheppard Primary Learning Center PK-K
5601 W 24th Ave 33016 305-818-7984
Fax 818-7986
South Hialeah ES 1,200/PK-5
265 E 5th St 33010 305-885-4556
Linette Tellez, prin. Fax 888-7730
Twin Lakes ES 600/PK-5
6735 W 5th Pl 33012 305-822-0770
Ivette Bernal-Pino, prin. Fax 824-0915
Walters ES 700/PK-5
650 W 33rd St 33012 305-822-4600
Milko Brito, prin. Fax 827-4465
West Lakes Preparatory Academy 400/PK-8
13835 NW 97th Ave 33018 305-826-6104
Richelle Thomas, prin. Fax 826-6105

American Christian S 100/PK-12
5888 W 20th Ave 33016 305-827-6544
Asbury Christian S 100/PK-6
5559 Palm Ave 33012 305-823-5313
Cinderella S 200/PK-5
2335 W 12th Ave 33010 305-885-8556
Edison Private S 400/PK-12
3720 E 4th Ave 33013 305-824-0303
Faith Lutheran S 100/PK-8
293 Hialeah Dr 33010 305-885-2845
Ruth Wessling, prin. Fax 885-2845
Growing Treasures Learning Center 100/PK-1
8318 NW 103rd St 33016 305-558-0133
Horeb Christian S 200/PK-12
795 W 68th St 33014 305-557-6811
Kevin Macki M.Ed., prin. Fax 821-5048
Immaculate Conception S 700/PK-8
125 W 45th St 33012 305-822-6461
Victoria Leon, prin. Fax 822-0289
Kids Learning Center 200/PK-3
1265 W 66th St 33012 305-362-4009
Lincoln-Marti S 300/1-12
1750 E 4th Ave 33010 305-884-1570
Lincoln-Marti S 500/PK-8
7675 W 32nd Ave 33018 305-826-4214
Masters Preparatory S 300/PK-8
1395 E 4th Ave 33010 305-887-4233
Miss Carusi Learning Center 100/PK-5
1905 W 35th St 33012 305-823-8884
Nuestra Senora De Lourdes S 200/PK-4
1164 W 71st St 33014 305-822-2645
Our Lady of Charity S 300/PK-9
1900 W 44th Pl 33012 305-556-5494
St. John the Apostle S 300/PK-8
479 E 4th St 33010 305-888-6819
Robert Hernandez, prin. Fax 887-1256
Snow White the Seven Dwarfs S 300/PK-6
2400 W 56th St 33016 305-825-1477
Thumbelina Learning Center S 300/PK-8
1395 E 4th Ave 33010 305-887-4233
Trinity Christian Academy 100/PK-12
1408 W 84th St 33014 305-819-8999
World Children's Academy 100/PK-5
930 E 9th St 33010 305-887-5437
Agnes Gonzalez, prin. Fax 524-3257

Hialeah Gardens, Miami-Dade, Pop. 21,719
Miami-Dade County SD
Supt. — See Miami
Hialeah Gardens ES 900/PK-5
9702 NW 130th St 33018 305-827-8830
Rachel Autler, prin. Fax 818-7970
Hialeah Gardens MS 1,800/6-8
11690 NW 92nd Ave 33018 305-817-0017
Maritza Jimenez, prin. Fax 817-0018
West Hialeah Gardens ES 1,200/PK-5
11990 NW 92nd Ave 33018 305-818-4000
Sharon Gonzalez, prin. Fax 818-4001

Royal Kids Academy 100/PK-5
12503 W Okeechobee Rd 33018 305-557-5437

Highland City, Polk, Pop. 10,661
Polk County SD
Supt. — See Bartow
Highland City ES 400/K-5
PO Box 1327 33846 863-648-3540
Amy Weingarth, prin. Fax 648-3542

High Springs, Alachua, Pop. 5,260
Alachua County SD
Supt. — See Gainesville
High Springs Community S 900/K-8
1015 N Main St 32643 386-454-1958
Lynn McNeill, prin. Fax 454-2298

First Christian Academy 200/PK-12
24530 NW 199th Ln 32643 386-454-1641
Rev. Stanford Stone, hdmstr. Fax 454-9727
Living Springs Academy 50/K-8
PO Box 537 32655 386-454-2777

Hilliard, Nassau, Pop. 3,050
Nassau County SD
Supt. — See Fernandina Beach
Hilliard ES 700/PK-5
27568 Ohio St 32046 904-491-7939
Dr. LeeAnn Jackson, prin. Fax 845-7427

Hobe Sound, Martin, Pop. 11,387
Martin County SD
Supt. — See Stuart
Hobe Sound ES 700/K-5
11555 SE Gomez Ave 33455 772-219-1540
Dr. Dianne Memmer-Novak, prin. Fax 219-1546
SeaWind ES 700/K-5
3700 SE Seabranch Blvd 33455 772-219-1625
Birgit Ager, prin. Fax 219-1631

Hobe Sound Christian Academy 200/PK-12
PO Box 1065 33475 772-545-1455

Pine S 200/K-12
12350 SE Federal Hwy 33455 772-675-7005
Binney Caffrey, head sch Fax 675-7006

Holiday, Pasco, Pop. 21,981
Pasco County SD
Supt. — See Land O Lakes
Gulfside ES 500/K-5
2329 Anclote Blvd 34691 727-774-6000
Jeanne Krapfl, prin. Fax 774-6091
Gulf Trace ES 600/K-5
3303 Gulf Trace Blvd 34691 727-246-3600
Hope Schooler, prin. Fax 246-3691
Smith MS 1,100/6-8
1410 Sweetbriar Dr 34691 727-246-3200
Joel DiVincent, prin. Fax 246-3291
Sunray ES 500/K-5
4815 Sunray Dr 34690 727-774-9100
Debra Viggiano, prin. Fax 774-9191

World of Knowledge A Montessori S 100/PK-8
1935 Abacus Rd 34690 727-934-3028

Holly Hill, Volusia, Pop. 11,392
Volusia County SD
Supt. — See De Land
Holly Hill ES 900/K-8
1500 Center Ave 32117 386-258-4662
Jason Watson, prin. Fax 239-6336

Hollywood, Broward, Pop. 137,985
Broward County SD
Supt. — See Fort Lauderdale
Apollo MS 1,200/6-8
6800 Arthur St 33024 754-323-2900
Shawn Aycock, prin. Fax 323-2985
Attucks MS 700/6-8
3500 N 22nd Ave 33020 754-323-3000
Errol Evans, prin. Fax 323-3085
Beachside Montessori Village 800/PK-8
2230 Lincoln St 33020 754-323-8050
Vered Roberts, prin. Fax 323-8090
Bethune ES 700/PK-5
2400 Meade St 33020 754-323-4900
Michelle Alvarez, prin. Fax 323-4940
Boulevard Heights ES 700/K-5
7201 Johnson St 33024 754-323-4950
Juan Alejo, prin. Fax 323-4990
Colbert Museum Magnet S 600/PK-5
2702 Funston St 33020 754-323-5100
Marisa Fishlock, prin. Fax 323-5140
Driftwood ES 600/PK-5
2700 NW 69th Ave 33024 754-323-5450
Marina Rashid, prin. Fax 323-5490
Driftwood MS 1,500/6-8
2751 NW 70th Ter 33024 754-323-3100
Steven Williams, prin. Fax 323-3160
Hollywood Central ES 600/K-5
1700 Monroe St 33020 754-323-6150
Delicia Decembert, prin. Fax 323-6190
Hollywood Hills ES 700/K-5
3501 Taft St 33021 754-323-6200
John Fossas, prin. Fax 323-6240
Hollywood Park ES 500/PK-5
901 N 69th Way 33024 754-323-6250
Maria Menendez, prin. Fax 323-6290
McNicol MS 900/6-8
1602 S 27th Ave 33020 754-323-3400
Melissa Gurreonero, prin. Fax 323-3485
Oakridge ES 600/PK-5
1507 N 28th Ave 33020 754-323-6700
Eduardo Aguilar, prin. Fax 323-6740
Orange Brook ES 900/K-5
715 S 46th Ave 33021 754-323-6750
Devon O'Neal, prin. Fax 323-6790
Sheridan Hills ES 600/K-5
5001 Thomas St 33021 754-323-7300
Josetta Campbell, prin. Fax 323-7340
Sheridan Park ES 700/PK-5
2310 NW 70th Ter 33024 754-323-7350
Jacqueline Carro, prin. Fax 323-7390
Stirling ES 700/K-5
5500 Stirling Rd 33021 754-323-7600
Tamara Zaslow, prin. Fax 323-7640
West Hollywood ES 700/PK-5
6301 Hollywood Blvd 33024 754-323-7850
Lina Palacios, prin. Fax 323-7890

Beacon Hill S 100/PK-8
7600 Davie Road Ext 33024 954-963-2600
Andrew Liss, dir. Fax 963-2878
First Baptist Academy 100/K-12
2700 N Palm Ave 33026 954-404-7706
Hollywood Christian S 300/PK-12
1708 N 60th Ave 33021 954-322-4375
Dr. Mike Hill, head sch Fax 322-4383
Lamb Athletic and Art Academy 100/K-12
1704 Buchanan St 33020 954-935-5023
Little Flower S 300/PK-8
1843 Pierce St 33020 954-922-1217
Maureen McNulty, prin. Fax 927-8962
Marblue Montessori Academy 100/PK-6
2230 Hollywood Blvd 33020 954-923-7100
Nativity S 900/PK-8
5200 Johnson St 33021 954-987-3300
Elena Ortiz, prin. Fax 987-6368
St. Bernadette S 300/PK-8
7450 Stirling Rd 33024 954-432-7022
Maria Wagner, prin. Fax 443-8030
Sheridan Hills Christian S 500/PK-12
3751 Sheridan St 33021 954-966-7995
Eric Spee, head sch Fax 961-1359

Holmes Beach, Manatee, Pop. 3,810
Manatee County SD
Supt. — See Bradenton
Anna Maria ES 300/K-5
4700 Gulf Dr 34217 941-708-5525
Jackie Featherston, prin. Fax 708-5529

Homestead, Miami-Dade, Pop. 59,655
Miami-Dade County SD
Supt. — See Miami
Air Base K-8 Center 800/PK-8
12829 SW 272nd St 33032 305-258-3676
Raul Calzadilla, prin. Fax 258-7241
Avocado ES 600/PK-3
16969 SW 294th St 33030 305-247-4942
Jacqua Little, prin. Fax 246-9603
Campbell Drive K-8 Center 900/PK-8
15790 SW 307th St 33033 305-245-0270
Thelma Fornell, prin. Fax 247-7903
Chapman Partnership ECC South PK-PK
28205 SW 124th Pl 33033 305-416-7189
Dr. Rita Mallett, admin. Fax 416-7114
Coconut Palm K-8 Academy 1,300/PK-8
24400 SW 124th Ave 33032 305-257-0500
Dr. Carmen Jones-Carey, prin. Fax 257-0501
Gateway Environmental K-8 Learning Ctr 1,700/K-8
955 SE 18th Ave 33035 305-257-6000
Tiffany Anderson, prin. Fax 257-6001
Homestead MS 500/6-8
650 NW 2nd Ave 33030 305-247-4221
Dr. Contessa Bryant, prin. Fax 247-1098
Leisure City K-8 Center 900/K-8
14950 SW 288th St 33033 305-247-5431
Kenneth Williams, prin. Fax 247-5179
Mandarin Lakes K-8 Academy 1,100/K-8
12225 SW 280th St 33032 305-257-0377
Cadian Collman, prin. Fax 257-0378
Peskoe K-8 Center 700/PK-8
29035 SW 144th Ave 33033 305-242-8340
Madelyn Sierra-Hernandez, prin. Fax 242-8351
Redland ES 900/K-5
24501 SW 162nd Ave 33031 305-247-8141
Adrian Montes, prin. Fax 242-4698
Redland MS 500/6-8
16001 SW 248th St 33031 305-247-6112
Gregory Beckford, prin. Fax 248-0628
Redondo ES 700/PK-3
18480 SW 304th St 33030 305-247-5943
Keith Anderson, prin. Fax 242-0318
Saunders ES 700/PK-5
505 SW 8th St 33030 305-247-3933
Barbara Levielle-Brown, prin. Fax 247-8522
South Dade MS 1,200/4-8
29100 SW 194th Ave 33030 305-224-5200
John Galardi, prin. Fax 224-5201
West Homestead K-8 Center 700/K-8
1550 SW 6th St 33030 305-248-0812
Dr. Earl Burth, prin. Fax 247-3205

Atala Montessori S 100/PK-8
240 N Krome Ave 33030 786-738-1210
Colonial Christian S 200/PK-12
17105 SW 296th St 33030 305-246-8608
Faith Fellowship S 50/PK-12
28945 SW 187th Ave 33030 305-246-5534
Monica Upegui B.A., prin. Fax 246-5586
First United Methodist Christian S 300/PK-8
622A N Krome Ave 33030 305-248-7992
Windy Parker, prin. Fax 243-2512
Kingswood Montessori S 100/PK-8
20130 SW 304th St 33030 305-248-2308
Redland Christian Academy 300/PK-12
17700 SW 280th St 33031 305-247-7399
St. John's Episcopal S 200/PK-8
145 NE 10th St 33030 305-247-5445
Lakshmi Nair, prin. Fax 245-4063
Thinking Child Christian Academy 100/PK-8
155 NW 4th St 33030 305-247-3036
Villa Preparatory Academy 200/PK-12
14112 SW 288th St 33033 305-247-5858

Homosassa, Citrus, Pop. 2,549
Citrus County SD
Supt. — See Inverness
Homosassa ES 300/PK-5
10935 W Yulee Dr 34448 352-628-2953
Alice Harrell, prin. Fax 249-2131
Rock Crusher ES 600/PK-5
814 S Rock Crusher Rd 34448 352-795-2010
Rene Johnson, prin. Fax 249-2143

Hosford, Liberty, Pop. 641
Liberty County SD
Supt. — See Bristol
Hosford S 400/PK-8
16864 NE State Road 65 32334 850-379-8480
Jessica Bennett, prin. Fax 379-8703

Hudson, Pasco, Pop. 12,006
Pasco County SD
Supt. — See Land O Lakes
Hudson ES 700/PK-5
7229 Hudson Ave 34667 727-774-4000
Dawn Scilex, prin. Fax 774-4091
Hudson MS 800/6-8
14540 Cobra Way 34669 727-774-8200
Joseph Musselman, prin. Fax 774-8291
Northwest ES 700/PK-5
14302 Cobra Way 34669 727-774-4700
Nicole Reynolds, prin. Fax 774-4791

Grace Christian S 100/K-12
9403 Scot St 34669 727-863-1825
Glenwood Pratt, prin. Fax 862-4484

Immokalee, Collier, Pop. 23,830
Collier County SD
Supt. — See Naples
Eden Park ES 600/K-5
3650 Westclox St 34142 239-377-9200
Linda Salazar, prin. Fax 377-9201
Highlands ES 600/K-5
1101 Lake Trafford Rd 34142 239-377-7100
Laura Mendicino, prin. Fax 377-7101
Immokalee MS 800/6-8
401 N 9th St 34142 239-377-4200
Ryan Nemeth, prin. Fax 377-4201
Lake Trafford ES 600/PK-5
3500 Lake Trafford Rd 34142 239-377-7300
Elizabeth Alvarez, prin. Fax 377-7301
Pinecrest ES 700/K-6
313 S 9th St 34142 239-377-8000
Dr. Susan Jordan, prin. Fax 377-8001
Village Oaks ES 500/PK-6
1601 State Road 29 S 34142 239-377-8600
Renee Hanson, prin. Fax 377-8601

Indialantic, Brevard, Pop. 2,676
Brevard County SD
Supt. — See Melbourne
Hoover MS 600/7-8
2000 Hawk Haven Dr 32903 321-727-1611
Bradley Merrill, prin. Fax 725-0076
Indialantic ES 700/K-6
1050 N Palm Ave 32903 321-723-2811
Lori Braga, prin. Fax 952-5848

Holy Name Jesus S 300/PK-8
3060 N Highway A1A 32903 321-773-1630
Mary Ann Irwin, prin. Fax 773-7148

Indian Harbor Beach, Brevard, Pop. 8,072
Brevard County SD
Supt. — See Melbourne
Ocean Breeze ES 500/K-6
1101 Cheyenne Dr 32937 321-779-2040
Laurie Hering, prin. Fax 779-2045

Indian Harbour Montessori 100/PK-6
1230 Banana River Dr 32937 321-777-1480

Indiantown, Martin, Pop. 6,057
Martin County SD
Supt. — See Stuart
Indiantown MS 500/5-8
16303 SW Farm Rd 34956 772-597-2146
Jeff Raimann, prin. Fax 597-5854
Warfield ES 700/K-4
15260 SW 150th St 34956 772-597-2551
Ivy Menken, prin. Fax 597-2119

Hope Rural S 100/PK-5
15929 SW 150th St 34956 772-597-2203
Sr. Martha Rohde, prin. Fax 597-2259

Interlachen, Putnam, Pop. 1,381
Putnam County SD
Supt. — See Palatka
Interlachen ES 800/PK-5
251 S County Road 315 32148 386-684-2130
Beth Nelson, prin. Fax 684-3909
Price MS 600/6-8
140 N County Road 315 32148 386-684-2113
Mechele Higginbotham, prin. Fax 684-3908

Inverness, Citrus, Pop. 7,057
Citrus County SD 15,000/PK-12
1007 W Main St 34450 352-726-1931
Sandra Himmel, supt. Fax 726-4418
www.citrus.k12.fl.us
Inverness MS 1,000/6-8
1950 Highway 41 N 34450 352-726-1471
Ernest Hopper, prin. Fax 249-2133
Inverness PS 700/PK-5
206 S Line Ave 34452 352-726-2632
Kay Harper, prin. Fax 249-2134
Pleasant Grove ES 700/PK-5
630 Pleasant Grove Rd 34452 352-637-4400
Janet Tuggle, prin. Fax 249-2141
Other Schools – See Citrus Springs, Crystal River, Floral City, Hernando, Homosassa, Lecanto

---

Inverness Christian Academy 200/PK-12
4222 S Florida Ave 34450 352-726-3759
Solid Rock Christian Academy 100/PK-8
972 N Christy Way 34453 352-726-9788

Islamorada, Monroe, Pop. 1,220

Island Christian S 200/PK-12
83400 Overseas Hwy 33036 305-664-4933

Jacksonville, Duval, Pop. 800,944
Clay County SD
Supt. — See Green Cove Springs
Clay Hill ES 400/K-6
6345 County Road 218 32234 904-336-0775
Adele Reed, prin. Fax 336-0777

Duval County SD 121,600/PK-12
1701 Prudential Dr 32207 904-390-2000
Dr. Patricia Willis, supt. Fax 390-2586
www.duvalschools.org
Abess Park ES 700/PK-5
12731 Abess Blvd 32225 904-220-1260
Kristin Shore, prin. Fax 220-1264
Alimacani ES 800/PK-5
2051 San Pablo Rd S 32224 904-221-7101
Kathy Stalls, prin. Fax 221-8823
Arlington ES 300/K-5
1201 University Blvd N 32211 904-745-4900
Kimberly Brown, prin. Fax 745-4946
Arlington Heights ES 500/K-5
1520 Sprinkle Dr 32211 904-745-4923
Charlene McEarl, prin. Fax 745-4944
Arlington MS 700/6-8
8141 Lone Star Rd 32211 904-720-1680
Maysha Shelton, prin. Fax 720-1702
Axson ES 600/PK-5
4763 Sutton Park Ct 32224 904-992-3600
Cecilia Robinson-Vanhoy, prin. Fax 992-3605
Bartram Springs ES 900/PK-5
14799 Bartram Springs Pkwy 32258 904-260-5860
Kimberly Wright, prin. Fax 260-5868
Bayview ES 400/PK-5
3257 Lake Shore Blvd 32210 904-381-3920
Lindsey Connor, prin. Fax 381-3919

Beauclerc ES 1,100/K-5
4555 Craven Rd W 32257 904-739-5226
Mariah Spassoff, prin. Fax 739-5317

Biltmore ES 400/PK-5
2101 W Palm Ave 32254 904-693-7569
Sabrina Session-Jones, prin. Fax 693-7574

Biscayne ES 600/PK-5
12230 Biscayne Blvd 32218 904-714-4650
DeShune Bush, prin. Fax 714-4655

Brentwood ES 300/K-5
3750 Springfield Blvd 32206 904-630-6630
Jackie Jones, prin. Fax 630-6638

Brewer ES 500/3-5
3385 Hartsfield Rd 32277 904-745-4990
Jennifer Gray, prin. Fax 745-4986

Brookview ES 700/K-5
10450 Theresa Dr 32246 904-565-2720
Katie O'Connell, prin. Fax 565-2734

Brown ES 500/K-5
1535 Milnor Ave 32206 904-630-6570
Tammy Haberman, prin. Fax 630-6576

Butler MS 600/6-8
900 Acorn St 32209 904-630-6900
Truitte Moreland, prin. Fax 630-6913

Carver ES 400/PK-5
2854 W 45th St 32209 904-924-3122
Tangia Anderson, prin. Fax 924-3280

Cedar Hills ES 500/PK-5
6534 Ish Brant Rd 32210 904-573-1050
Marva McKinney, prin. Fax 573-1051

Central Riverside ES 400/K-5
2555 Gilmore St 32204 904-381-7495
Dinah Stewart, prin. Fax 381-7423

Chaffee Trail ES 700/PK-5
11400 Sam Caruso Way 32221 904-693-7510
Casie Doyle, prin. Fax 693-7932

Chet's Creek ES 1,300/K-5
13200 Chets Creek Blvd 32224 904-992-6390
Susan Phillips, prin. Fax 992-6398

Chimney Lakes ES 1,100/K-5
9353 Staples Mill Dr 32244 904-573-1100
Melissa Metz, prin. Fax 573-1109

Crown Point ES 1,000/PK-5
3800 Crown Point Rd 32257 904-260-5808
Brett Hartley, prin. Fax 260-5839

Crystal Springs ES 1,000/PK-5
1200 Hammond Blvd 32221 904-693-7645
Leshawn Russ, prin. Fax 693-7658

Daniels ES 300/K-2
1951 W 15th St 32209 904-630-6872
Lashawn Caldwell, prin. Fax 630-6875

Davis MS 1,100/6-8
7050 Melvin Rd 32210 904-573-1060
Marshana Bush, prin. Fax 573-3220

Dinsmore ES 500/K-5
7126 Civic Club Dr 32219 904-924-3126
Wanda Reese, prin. Fax 924-3142

DuPont MS 800/6-8
2710 Dupont Ave 32217 904-739-5200
Marilyn Barnwell, prin. Fax 739-5321

Englewood ES 400/K-5
4359 Spring Park Rd 32207 904-739-5280
Dino Mullin, prin. Fax 739-5316

Enterprise Learning Academy 700/PK-5
8085 Old Middleburg Rd S 32222 904-573-3260
Sylvia Embry, prin. Fax 573-3270

Fishweir ES 400/PK-5
3977 Herschel St 32205 904-381-3910
Kimberly Dennis, prin. Fax 381-3916

Ford S 700/PK-8
1137 Cleveland St 32209 904-630-6540
Tina Bennett, prin. Fax 630-6548

Ft. Caroline ES 500/K-5
3925 Athore Dr 32277 904-745-4904
Violet Stovall, prin. Fax 745-4945

Ft. Caroline MS 700/6-8
3787 University Club Blvd 32277 904-745-4927
Meghan Green, prin. Fax 745-4937

Garden City ES 500/K-5
2814 Dunn Ave 32218 904-924-3130
Mychelle Grover, prin. Fax 924-3178

Gilbert MS 500/6-8
1424 Franklin St 32206 904-630-6700
Jamelle Goodwin, prin. Fax 630-6713

Greenfield ES 500/PK-5
6343 Knights Ln N 32216 904-739-5249
Todd Simpson, prin. Fax 739-5299

Greenland Pines ES 900/PK-5
5050 Greenland Rd 32258 904-260-5450
Jacquelyn Sneddon, prin. Fax 260-5455

Gregory Drive ES 800/K-5
7800 Gregory Dr 32210 904-573-1190
Andrea Schletter, prin. Fax 573-3210

Hendricks Avenue ES 700/K-5
3400 Hendricks Ave 32207 904-346-5610
Mindy McLendon, prin. Fax 346-5616

Highlands ES 400/PK-5
1000 Depaul Dr 32218 904-696-8754
Jeffrey Collins, prin. Fax 696-8787

Highlands MS 900/6-8
10913 Pine Estates Rd E 32218 904-696-8771
Jessica Guthrie, prin. Fax 696-8782

Hogan-Spring Glen ES 400/K-5
6736 Beach Blvd 32216 904-720-1640
Charlene James, prin. Fax 720-1706

Holiday Hill ES 600/K-5
6900 Altama Rd 32216 904-720-1676
Linda Pratt, prin. Fax 720-1731

Hull ES 300/PK-5
7528 Hull St 32219 904-924-3136
Angela Lott, prin. Fax 924-3139

Hyde Grove ES 500/PK-5
2056 Lane Ave S 32210 904-693-7562
Augena Sapp, prin. Fax 693-7565

Hyde Park ES 400/K-5
5300 Park St 32205 904-381-3950
Tarsha Mitchell, prin. Fax 381-3954

Jackson ES 300/K-5
6127 Cedar Hills Blvd 32210 904-573-1020
Erica Starling, prin. Fax 573-1059

Jacksonville Heights ES 700/K-5
7750 Tempest St S 32244 904-573-1120
Michelle Walsh, prin. Fax 573-1043

Jefferson ES 600/K-5
8233 Nevada St 32220 904-693-7500
Lori Turner, prin. Fax 693-7507

Johnson College Prep MS 1,100/6-8
3276 Norman E Thagard Blvd 32254 904-693-7600
Tamara Feagins, prin. Fax 693-7661

Kernan MS 1,200/6-8
2271 Kernan Blvd S 32246 904-220-1350
Julie Hemphill, prin. Fax 220-1355

Kernan Trail ES 700/PK-5
2281 Kernan Blvd S 32246 904-220-1310
Suzanne Shall, prin. Fax 220-1315

King ES 400/K-5
8801 Lake Placid Dr E 32208 904-924-3027
Cindy Gentry, prin. Fax 766-9031

Kings Trail ES 500/K-5
7401 Old Kings Rd S 32217 904-739-5254
Sanethette Shubert, prin. Fax 739-5326

Kirby-Smith MS 1,000/6-8
2034 Hubbard St 32206 904-630-6600
Kenya Griffin, prin. Fax 630-6605

Kite ES 300/PK-5
9430 Lem Turner Rd 32208 904-924-3031
Bianca Hill, prin. Fax 924-3473

Lake Forest ES 500/PK-5
901 Kennard St 32208 904-924-3024
Cassandra Thomas, prin. Fax 924-3194

Lake Lucina ES 400/K-5
6527 Merrill Rd 32277 904-745-4916
Shirley Winfrey, prin. Fax 745-4917

Lake Shore MS 1,200/6-8
2519 Bayview Rd 32210 904-381-7440
Caleb Gottberg, prin. Fax 381-7437

Landmark MS 1,200/6-8
101 Kernan Blvd N 32225 904-221-7125
David Gilmore, prin. Fax 221-8847

Landon MS 700/6-8
1819 Thacker Ave 32207 904-346-5650
Timothy Feagins, prin. Fax 346-5657

LaVilla S of the Arts 1,100/6-8
501 N Davis St 32202 904-633-6069
Lianna Knight, prin. Fax 633-8089

Livingston ES 300/PK-2
1128 Barber St 32209 904-630-6580
Robert Gresham, prin. Fax 630-6587

Lone Star ES 700/K-5
10400 Lone Star Rd 32225 904-565-2711
Cheryl Quarles-Gaston, prin. Fax 565-2733

Long Branch ES 200/PK-5
3723 Franklin St 32206 904-630-6620
Alecia Clayton, prin. Fax 630-6639

Loretto ES 1,100/PK-5
3900 Loretto Rd 32223 904-260-5800
Kristie Kemp, prin. Fax 260-5835

Love ES 100/PK-2
1531 Winthrop St 32206 904-630-6790
Niketah Johnson, prin. Fax 630-6793

Love Grove ES 500/PK-5
2446 University Blvd S 32216 904-720-1645
Tiffany Emanuel-Wright, prin. Fax 720-1742

Mandarin MS 1,300/6-8
5100 Hood Rd 32257 904-292-0555
Moses Williams, prin. Fax 260-5415

Mandarin Oaks ES 1,100/PK-5
10600 Hornets Nest Rd 32257 904-260-5820
Leigh Butterfield, prin. Fax 260-5846

Mathis ES 400/PK-5
3501 Winton Dr 32208 904-924-3086
Kathleen Adkins, prin. Fax 924-3193

Merrill Road ES 700/PK-2
8239 Merrill Rd 32277 904-745-4919
Peggy Sue Heybruch, prin. Fax 745-4943

Morgan ES 400/PK-5
964 Saint Clair St 32254 904-381-3970
LaShawn Streater, prin. Fax 381-3998

New Berlin ES 1,200/PK-5
3613 New Berlin Rd 32226 904-714-4601
Crystal Lewis, prin. Fax 714-4610

Normandy Village ES 400/K-5
8257 Herlong Rd 32210 904-693-7548
Helen Dunbar, prin. Fax 693-7553

North Shore Magnet ES 700/PK-5
5701 Silver Plz 32208 904-924-3081
Felicia Hardaway, prin. Fax 924-3191

Northwestern MS 400/6-8
2100 W 45th St 32209 904-924-3100
Shawn Platts, prin. Fax 924-3284

Oak Hill ES 600/PK-5
6910 Daughtry Blvd S 32210 904-573-1030
Stephanie Smith, prin. Fax 573-3214

Oceanway ES 600/K-5
12555 Gillespie Ave 32218 904-696-8762
Michelle Hinkley, prin. Fax 696-8788

Oceanway MS 1,200/6-8
143 Oceanway Ave 32218 904-714-4680
Emily Kristansen, prin. Fax 714-4685

Ortega ES 400/K-5
4010 Baltic St 32210 904-381-7460
Shannon Rose-Hammond, prin. Fax 381-7484

Parkwood Heights ES 400/K-5
1709 Lansdowne Dr 32211 904-720-1670
Ashton Price, prin. Fax 720-1674

Payne ES 400/PK-5
6725 Hema Rd 32209 904-924-3020
Weisha Day-Killette, prin. Fax 924-3181

Pearson ES 300/PK-6
4346 Roanoke Blvd 32208 904-924-3077
Erica Little, prin. Fax 924-3160

Pickett ES 200/K-6
6305 Old Kings Rd 32254 904-693-7555
Carlene Smith, prin. Fax 693-7558

Pinedale ES 400/PK-5
4229 Edison Ave 32254 904-381-7490
Alicia Hinson, prin. Fax 381-7466

Pine Estates ES 300/K-5
10741 Pine Estates Rd E 32218 904-696-8767
Michelle Quarles, prin. Fax 696-8745

Pine Forest ES of the Arts 500/K-5
3929 Grant Rd 32207 904-346-5600
Stephanie Jackson, prin. Fax 346-5632

Ramona Boulevard ES 400/K-5
5540 Ramona Blvd 32205 904-693-7576
Detra Demps, prin. Fax 693-7582

Reynolds Lane ES 300/PK-5
840 Reynolds Ln 32254 904-381-3960
Marianne Simon, prin. Fax 381-3964

Ribault MS 600/6-8
3610 Ribault Scenic Dr 32208 904-924-3062
Angela Maxey, prin. Fax 924-3167

Robinson ES 700/PK-5
101 W 12th St 32206 904-630-6550
Latrice Fann, prin. Fax 630-6555

Sabal Palm ES 1,100/PK-5
1201 Kernan Blvd N 32225 904-221-7169
Linda Graham, prin. Fax 221-8811

Saint Clair Evans Academy 500/PK-5
5443 Moncrief Rd 32209 904-924-3035
Lawanda Polydore, prin. Fax 924-3038

San Jose ES 800/K-5
5805 Saint Augustine Rd 32207 904-739-5260
Paula Smith, prin. Fax 739-5327

San Mateo ES 800/K-5
600 Baisden Rd 32218 904-696-8750
Caroline Wells, prin. Fax 696-8748

Sheffield ES 800/K-5
13333 Lanier Rd 32226 904-696-8758
Cassandra Delay, prin. Fax 696-8791

Southside Estates ES 500/PK-5
9775 Ivey Rd 32246 904-565-2706
Anastasia Washington, prin. Fax 565-2737

Southside MS 700/6-8
2948 Knights Ln E 32216 904-739-5238
Jennifer Crady, prin. Fax 739-5244

Spring Park ES 400/PK-5
2250 Spring Park Rd 32207 904-346-5640
Davina Parker, prin. Fax 346-5646

Stilwell MS 900/6-8
7840 Burma Rd 32221 904-693-7523
Jennifer Campese, prin. Fax 693-7539

Stockton ES 500/K-5
4827 Carlisle Rd 32210 904-381-3955
Stephanie Brannan, prin. Fax 381-7408

Stuart MS 900/6-8
4815 Wesconnett Blvd 32210 904-573-1000
Sadie Milliner-Smith, prin. Fax 573-3213

Tillis ES 600/K-5
6084 Morse Ave 32244 904-573-1090
Marianne Lee, prin. Fax 573-1169

Timucuan ES 500/K-5
5429 110th St 32244 904-573-1130
Darrell Perry, prin. Fax 573-1136

Tolbert ES 300/3-5
1925 W 13th St 32209 904-630-6860
Andrea Williams-Scott, prin. Fax 630-6868

Twin Lakes Academy ES 900/K-5
8000 Point Meadows Dr 32256 904-538-0238
Denise Robertson, prin. Fax 538-0241

Twin Lakes Academy MS 1,300/6-8
8050 Point Meadows Dr 32256 904-538-0825
Tamara Tuschhoff, prin. Fax 538-0840

Upson ES 500/PK-5
1090 Dancy St 32205 904-381-7485
Yvonne Spinner, prin. Fax 381-3976

Venetia ES 400/K-5
4300 Timuquana Rd 32210 904-381-3990
Monique Worthen, prin. Fax 381-7451

Waterleaf ES 700/K-5
450 Kernan Blvd N 32225 904-565-8000
Lisa Brady, prin. Fax 565-8027

West Riverside ES 300/PK-5
2801 Herschel St 32205 904-381-3900
Shawna White, prin. Fax 381-3905

Westview S 1,200/PK-8
5270 Connie Jean Rd 32210 904-573-1082
Claire St. Amand, prin. Fax 573-1087

Whitehouse ES 400/K-5
11160 General Ave 32220 904-693-7542
Bill Gilley, prin. Fax 693-7544

Windy Hill ES 700/K-5
3831 Forest Blvd 32246 904-565-2700
Calvin Reddick, prin. Fax 565-2702

Woodland Acres ES 800/PK-5
328 Bowlan St N 32211 904-720-1663
Tiffany Fullwood, prin. Fax 720-1730

Woodson ES 600/PK-5
2334 Butler Ave 32209 904-924-3004
Brandon Clayton, prin. Fax 924-3442

Other Schools – See Atlantic Beach, Baldwin, Jacksonville Beach, Neptune Beach

---

Academie De Montessori 100/PK-5
1216 LaSalle St 32207 904-398-3830

Al-Furqan Academy 100/PK-8
2333 Saint Johns Bluff Rd S 32246 904-645-0810

Arlington Country Day S 400/PK-12
5725 Fort Caroline Rd 32277 904-762-0123

Assumption S 600/PK-8
2431 Atlantic Blvd 32207 904-398-1774
Maryann Jimenez, prin. Fax 398-6712

Baymeadows Baptist Day S 200/PK-7
4826 Baymeadows Rd 32217 904-733-3400

Blessed Trinity S 300/PK-8
10472 Beach Blvd 32246 904-641-6458
Marie Davis, prin. Fax 645-3762

Bolles S - Bartram Campus 400/6-8
2264 Bartram Rd 32207 904-724-8850
David Farace, pres. Fax 724-8862

Bolles S - Whitehurst Campus PK-5
7400 San Jose Blvd 32217 904-733-9292
David Farace, pres.

Cedar Creek Christian S 300/PK-12
1372 Lane Ave S 32205 904-781-9151
Cedar Hills Baptist Christian S 200/PK-8
4200 Jammes Rd 32210 904-772-0812
Chatman's Early Learning Christian Acad 200/PK-6
1614 Leonid Rd 32218 904-751-9803
Christian Heritage Academy 100/K-8
3930 University Blvd S 32216 904-733-4722
Jim Stephens, admin. Fax 338-9977
Christ's Church Academy 400/K-12
10850 Old Saint Augustine 32257 904-268-8667
Dr. Madison Nichols, head sch Fax 880-3251
Christ the King S 300/PK-8
6822 Larkin Rd 32211 904-724-2954
Stephanie Engelhardt, prin. Fax 721-8004
Cornerstone Christian S 300/PK-12
9039 Beach Blvd 32216 904-730-5500
Donna Stables, prin. Fax 730-5502
Eagle's View Academy 400/K-12
7788 Ramona Blvd W 32221 904-786-1411
Ephesus SDA Jr. Academy 100/K-8
2760 Edgewood Ave W 32209 904-765-3225
Esprit De Corps Center for Learning 200/K-12
9840 Wagner Rd 32219 904-924-2000
Dr. Jeannette Holmes-Vann, supt. Fax 766-8870
First Baptist Academy of Jacksonville 200/K-8
124 W Ashley St 32202 904-265-7474
Susan Johnson, head sch Fax 265-7470
First Coast Christian S 600/PK-12
7587 Blanding Blvd 32244 904-777-3040
Richard Spain, admin. Fax 777-3045
Foundation Academy 200/K-12
3675 San Pablo Rd S 32224 904-493-7300
Gottlieb Day S 100/K-8
3662 Crown Point Rd 32257 904-268-4200
Grace Lutheran S 200/PK-8
12200 Mccormick Rd 32225 904-928-9136
Jennifer Tanner, prin. Fax 928-0181
Harvest Community S 200/PK-12
2360 Saint Johns Bluff Rd S 32246 904-997-1882
Patty Wilcox, admin. Fax 997-1862
Heart to Heart Christian Academy 100/PK-12
8247 W Ramona Blvd 32221 904-783-8638
Holy Family S 400/PK-8
9800 Baymeadows Rd Ste 3 32256 904-645-9875
Marcel DeMaio, prin. Fax 899-6060
Holy Rosary S 200/PK-8
4920 Brentwood Ave 32206 904-765-6522
Sr. Cynthia Shaffer, prin. Fax 765-9486
Holy Spirit S 300/PK-8
11665 Fort Caroline Rd 32225 904-642-9165
Dr. John Luciano, prin. Fax 642-1047
Impact Christian Academy 100/PK-12
8985 Lone Star Rd 32211 904-652-1441
Jacksonville Adventist Academy 100/PK-8
4298 Livingston Rd 32257 904-268-2433
Jacksonville Country Day S 500/PK-6
10063 Baymeadows Rd 32256 904-641-6644
Pat Walker, head sch Fax 641-1494
Millennial Christian S 100/K-12
2000 Lane Ave S 32210 904-772-6400
North Florida Educational Institute 100/K-8
6803 Arques Rd 32205 904-574-8059
Old Plank Christian Academy 200/PK-12
8964 Old Plank Rd 32220 904-783-4888
Gary Griffis, prin. Fax 786-9809
Parsons Christian Academy 200/PK-12
5705 Fort Caroline Rd 32277 904-745-4588
Potters House Christian Academy 200/PK-8
5732 Normandy Blvd 32205 904-786-0028
Promise Land Academy 100/K-5
3990 Loretto Rd 32223 904-268-2422
Robbin Jackson, prin. Fax 268-5321
Providence S 1,400/PK-12
2701 Hodges Blvd 32224 904-223-5270
Don Barfield, head sch Fax 223-7837
Resurrection S 200/PK-8
5710 Jack Rd 32277 904-744-1266
Patricia Donahue, prin. Fax 744-5800
Riverside Presbyterian Day S 500/PK-6
830 Oak St 32204 904-353-5511
Ben Ketchum, head sch Fax 634-1739
Sacred Heart S 400/PK-8
5752 Blanding Blvd 32244 904-771-5800
Jason Acosta, prin. Fax 771-5323
St. Joseph S 500/PK-8
11600 Old St Augustine Rd 32258 904-268-6688
Rhonda Rose, prin. Fax 268-8989
St. Mark's Episcopal Day S 400/PK-6
4114 Oxford Ave 32210 904-388-2632
Kevin Conklin, head sch Fax 387-5647
St. Matthew S 300/PK-8
1773 Blanding Blvd 32210 904-387-4401
Katherine Tuerk, prin. Fax 388-4404
St. Patrick S 200/PK-8
601 Airport Center Dr E 32218 904-768-6323
Mary Martin, prin. Fax 768-2144
St. Paul S 200/PK-8
2609 Park St 32204 904-387-2841
Kim Repper, prin. Fax 388-1781
St. Pius V S 200/PK-8
1470 W 13th St 32209 904-354-2613
Lauren May, prin. Fax 356-4522
San Jose Episcopal S 300/PK-6
7423 San Jose Blvd 32217 904-733-0352
Lori Menger, head sch Fax 733-2582
San Jose S 400/PK-8
3619 Toledo Rd 32217 904-733-2313
Brian Wheeler, prin. Fax 731-7169
Shepherd of the Woods Lutheran S 100/K-9
6595 Columbia Park Ct 32258 904-641-3393
Dr. Madelyn Speagle, prin. Fax 641-0919
Temple Christian Academy 200/K-12
4200 Georgetown Rd 32210 904-778-8655
Torah Academy of Jacksonville 100/PK-8
10167 San Jose Blvd 32257 904-268-7719
Trinity Christian Academy 1,500/PK-12
800 Hammond Blvd 32221 904-596-2400
University Christian S 500/PK-12
5520 University Blvd W 32216 904-737-6330
Heath Nivens, head sch Fax 737-7403
Victory Christian Academy 200/PK-12
10613 Lem Turner Rd 32218 904-764-7781
West Meadows Baptist Academy 100/K-12
11711 Normandy Blvd 32221 904-786-2711

Jacksonville Beach, Duval, Pop. 20,925
Duval County SD
Supt. — See Jacksonville
Fletcher MS 1,100/6-8
2000 3rd St N 32250 904-247-5929
Teresa Mowbray, prin. Fax 247-5940
Jacksonville Beach ES 600/K-5
315 10th St S 32250 904-247-5942
Cameron Mattingly, prin. Fax 270-1825
San Pablo ES 600/K-5
801 18th Ave N 32250 904-247-5947
Stephanie Manabat, prin. Fax 270-1860
Seabreeze ES 600/K-5
1400 Seabreeze Ave 32250 904-247-5900
Aimee Kimball, prin. Fax 270-1850

Beaches Episcopal S 200/PK-6
450 11th Ave N 32250 904-246-2466
Martha Milton, head sch Fax 246-1626
Discovery S 100/PK-6
102 15th St S 32250 904-247-4577
Kim Bednarek, head sch Fax 247-5626
St. Paul S 600/PK-8
428 2nd Ave N 32250 904-249-5934
Krissy Thompson, prin. Fax 241-2911

Jasper, Hamilton, Pop. 4,513
Hamilton County SD 1,700/PK-12
5683 US Highway 129 S # 1 32052 386-792-1228
Thomas Moffses, supt. Fax 792-3681
www.hamiltonfl.com
Hamilton County ES PK-6
5686 US Highway 129 S 32052 386-792-8000
Peggy Hasty, prin.

Corinth Christian Academy 100/K-12
7042 SW 41st Ave 32052 386-938-2270

Jay, Santa Rosa, Pop. 529
Santa Rosa County SD
Supt. — See Milton
Chumuckla ES 300/K-6
2312 Highway 182 32565 850-995-3690
Danny Carnley, prin. Fax 995-3695
Jay ES 500/K-6
13833 Alabama St 32565 850-675-4554
Kelly Short, prin. Fax 675-3362

Jensen Beach, Martin, Pop. 11,571
Martin County SD
Supt. — See Stuart
Jensen Beach ES 600/K-5
2525 NE Savannah Rd 34957 772-219-1555
Joan Gibbons, prin. Fax 219-1558

Jupiter, Palm Beach, Pop. 54,490
Palm Beach County SD
Supt. — See West Palm Beach
Beacon Cove IS 900/3-5
150 Schoolhouse Rd 33458 561-366-6400
Leslie Bolte, prin. Fax 366-6450
Independence MS 1,300/6-8
4001 Greenway Dr 33458 561-799-7500
Kathy Koerner, prin. Fax 799-7505
Jupiter ES 800/K-5
200 S Loxahatchee Dr 33458 561-741-5300
Patricia Trejo, prin. Fax 741-5350
Jupiter Farms ES 500/K-5
17400 Haynie Ln 33478 561-741-5400
Suzanne Matuella, prin. Fax 741-5450
Jupiter MS 1,200/6-8
15245 Military Trl 33458 561-745-7200
Lisa Hastey, prin. Fax 745-7242
Lighthouse ES 700/K-2
4750 Dakota Dr 33458 561-741-9400
Julie Hopkins, prin. Fax 741-9450
Limestone Creek ES 900/K-5
6701 Church St 33458 561-741-9200
Maria Lloyd, prin. Fax 741-9250
Thomas ES 900/K-5
800 Maplewood Dr 33458 561-741-9100
Jeff Eassa, prin. Fax 741-9155

All Saints Catholic S 400/PK-8
1759 Indian Creek Pkwy 33458 561-748-8994
Jill Broz, prin. Fax 748-8979
Jupiter Christian S 600/PK-12
700 S Delaware Blvd 33458 561-746-7800
Daniel Steinfield, pres. Fax 746-1955
Turtle River Montessori S 200/PK-8
926 Maplewood Dr 33458 561-745-1995
Lisa Cuomo, dir. Fax 745-1313

Key Biscayne, Miami-Dade, Pop. 12,269
Miami-Dade County SD
Supt. — See Miami
Key Biscayne K-8 Center 1,400/PK-8
150 W McIntyre St 33149 305-361-5418
Silvia Tarafa, prin. Fax 361-8120

St. Agnes Academy 500/PK-8
122 Harbor Dr 33149 305-361-3245
Susana Rivera-Cabrera, prin. Fax 361-6329
St. Christophers By-the-Sea Episcopal S 100/PK-6
95 Harbor Dr 33149 305-361-5080
Leslie Lasseville, prin. Fax 361-0355

Key Largo, Monroe, Pop. 10,273
Monroe County SD
Supt. — See Key West
Key Largo S 900/PK-8
104801 Overseas Hwy 33037 305-453-1255
Laura Lietaert, prin. Fax 453-1248

Academy at Ocean Reef 50/PK-8
395 S Harbor Dr 33037 305-367-2409
Christina Simonds, head sch Fax 367-2055

Keystone Heights, Clay, Pop. 1,326
Clay County SD
Supt. — See Green Cove Springs
Keystone Heights ES 800/PK-6
335 SW Pecan St, 904-336-1375
Melanie Sanders, prin. Fax 336-1377
McRae ES 500/PK-6
6770 County Road 315-C, 904-336-2125
Tammy Winkler, prin. Fax 336-2139

Key West, Monroe, Pop. 24,199
Monroe County SD 8,200/PK-12
241 Trumbo Rd 33040 305-293-1400
Mark Porter, supt. Fax 293-1408
keysschools.schoolfusion.us/
Adams ES 500/PK-5
5855 College Rd 33040 305-293-1609
Dr. Frannie Herrin, prin. Fax 293-1608
O'Bryant S 900/PK-8
1105 Leon St 33040 305-296-5628
Christina McPherson, prin. Fax 293-1644
Poinciana ES 700/PK-5
1407 Kennedy Dr 33040 305-293-1630
Dr. Larry Schmiegel, prin. Fax 293-1667
Other Schools – See Key Largo, Marathon, Sugarloaf Key, Tavernier

Basilica S of St. Mary Star of the Sea 200/PK-8
700 Truman Ave 33040 305-294-1031
Robert Wright, prin. Fax 294-2095
Grace Lutheran S 100/PK-8
2713 Flagler Ave 33040 305-296-8262
Melinda Emert, prin. Fax 296-0622

Kissimmee, Osceola, Pop. 58,578
Osceola County SD 56,300/PK-12
817 Bill Beck Blvd 34744 407-870-4600
Dr. Debra Pace, supt. Fax 870-4010
www.osceolaschools.net
Boggy Creek ES 800/PK-5
810 Florida Pkwy 34743 407-344-5060
Rhonda McMahan, prin. Fax 344-5070
Central Avenue ES 700/K-5
500 W Columbia Ave 34741 407-343-7330
Sharon Hahn, prin. Fax 343-7332
Chestnut ES 700/PK-5
4300 Chestnut St 34759 407-870-4862
Audie Confessor, prin. Fax 870-4864
Cypress ES 700/PK-5
2251 Lakeside Dr 34743 407-344-5000
Libby Raymond, prin. Fax 344-5006
Deerwood ES 600/K-5
3701 Marigold Ave 34758 407-870-2400
Jason Hayes, prin. Fax 870-2648
Denn John MS 1,100/6-8
2001 Denn John Ln 34744 407-935-3560
Hank Hoyle, prin. Fax 935-3572
Discovery IS 1,200/6-8
5350 San Miguel Rd 34758 407-343-7300
Henry Santiago, prin. Fax 343-7310
East Lake ES 900/K-5
4001 Boggy Creek Rd 34744 407-943-8450
Hilary Deluca, prin. Fax 943-7255
Flora Ridge ES 1,000/PK-5
2900 Dyer Blvd 34741 407-933-3999
Peter Hodges, prin. Fax 933-3998
Highlands ES 1,000/PK-5
800 W Donegan Ave 34741 407-935-3620
Allison Doe, prin. Fax 935-3629
Horizon MS 1,200/6-8
2020 Ham Brown Rd 34746 407-943-7240
Michael Ballone, prin. Fax 943-7250
Kissimmee ES 1,000/PK-5
3700 W Donegan Ave 34741 407-935-3640
David Noyes, prin. Fax 935-3651
Kissimmee MS 1,300/6-8
2410 Dyer Blvd 34741 407-870-0857
Gary Weeden, prin. Fax 870-5669
Koa ES 800/K-5
5000 Koa St 34758 407-518-1161
Virginia Scott, prin. Fax 518-2012
Mill Creek ES 900/PK-5
1700 Mill Slough Rd 34744 407-935-3660
Susan Cavinee, prin. Fax 935-3667
Neptune MS 1,400/6-8
2727 Neptune Rd 34744 407-935-3500
Joumana Moukaddam, prin. Fax 935-3519
Parkway MS 1,000/6-8
857 Florida Pkwy 34743 407-344-7000
Megan Gould, prin. Fax 348-2797
Partin Settlement ES 800/K-5
2434 Remington Blvd 34744 407-518-2000
Karen Corbett, prin. Fax 518-2019
Pleasant Hill ES 1,000/PK-5
1253 Pleasant Hill Rd 34741 407-935-3700
Gary Bressler, prin. Fax 935-3705
Poinciana Academy of Fine Arts 700/K-5
4201 Rhododendron Ave 34758 407-343-4500
Sheri Turchi, prin. Fax 343-4519
Reedy Creek ES 900/PK-5
5100 Eagles Trl 34758 407-935-3580
Timi Godin, prin. Fax 935-3590
Sunrise ES 1,000/PK-5
1925 Ham Brown Rd 34746 407-870-4866
Wendy Honeycutt, prin. Fax 870-4868
Thacker Avenue ES 900/PK-5
301 N Thacker Ave 34741 407-935-3540
Yara Tavarez-DeLaFuentes, prin. Fax 935-3549
Ventura ES 1,000/PK-5
275 Waters Edge Dr 34743 407-344-5040
Ashley Condo, prin. Fax 344-5046

Westside S 1,300/K-8
2551 Westside Blvd 34747 407-390-1748
Nadia Winston, prin. Fax 518-2010
Other Schools – See Celebration, Saint Cloud

Central Pointe Academy 100/PK-12
2031 Simpson Rd 34744 407-433-2276
Central Pointe Christian Academy 100/K-12
4925 Old Pleasant Hill Rd 34759 407-433-2276
Chosen Generation Christian Academy 100/1-12
4906 Old Pleasant Hill Rd 34759 407-870-2839
City of Life Christian Academy 400/PK-12
2874 E Irlo Bronson Mem Hwy 34744 407-847-5184
Dr. Kathy Harkema, prin. Fax 870-2679
First United Methodist S 200/PK-8
122 W Sproule Ave 34741 407-847-8805
Dennis Foley, prin. Fax 847-7997
Freedomland Christian Academy PK-12
1210 N Main St 34744 407-935-9088
Heritage Christian S 500/K-12
1500 E Vine St 34744 407-847-4087
Holy Redeemer S 300/PK-8
1800 W Columbia Ave 34741 407-870-9055
Gloria Del Orbe, prin. Fax 870-2214
Life Christian Academy 300/PK-12
2269 Partin Settlement Rd 34744 407-847-8222
North Kissimmee Christian S 100/PK-12
425 W Donegan Ave 34741 407-847-2877
Richard Johnson, prin. Fax 847-5372
Osceola Adventist Christian Academy 100/PK-8
2395 Fortune Rd 34744 407-348-2226
Osceola Christian Preparatory S 100/K-12
1515 Michigan Ave 34744 407-729-5974
Peace Lutheran S 100/PK-9
3249 Windmill Point Blvd 34746 407-870-5965
Adam Pavelchik, prin.
PHA Preparatory S 200/PK-12
1820 Armstrong Blvd 34741 407-944-1378
Poinciana Christian Preparatory S 100/K-12
2525 Trafalger Blvd 34758 407-749-2078
Southland Christian S 400/PK-12
2440 Fortune Rd 34744 407-201-7999
Rob Ennis, prin. Fax 350-5929
Trinity Lutheran S 100/PK-10
3016 W Vine St 34741 407-847-5377
Sheila Miles M.Ed., prin. Fax 944-0805

LaBelle, Hendry, Pop. 4,611
Glades County SD
Supt. — See Moore Haven
West Glades S 500/PK-8
2586 County Road 731 33935 863-675-3490
Doreen Backes, prin. Fax 675-3890

Hendry County SD 6,800/PK-12
PO Box 1980 33975 863-674-4642
Paul K. Puletti, supt. Fax 674-4090
www.hendry-schools.org
Country Oaks ES 800/K-5
2052 NW Eucalyptus Blvd 33935 863-674-4140
Robin Jones, prin. Fax 674-4129
La Belle ES 500/PK-5
150 W Cowboy Way 33935 863-674-4150
Sandra Taylor, prin. Fax 674-4155
La Belle MS 700/6-8
8000 E Cowboy Way 33935 863-674-4646
Kenneth Pickles, prin. Fax 674-4645
Upthegrove ES 400/K-5
280 N Main St 33935 863-612-0750
Richard Talada, prin. Fax 612-0753
Other Schools – See Clewiston

Lady Lake, Lake, Pop. 13,751
Lake County SD
Supt. — See Tavares
Villages ES 800/PK-5
695 Rolling Acres Rd 32159 352-751-0111
David Bordenkircher, prin. Fax 751-0117

Lake Alfred, Polk, Pop. 4,919
Polk County SD
Supt. — See Bartow
Lake Alfred ES 600/PK-5
550 E Cummings St 33850 863-295-5985
Matt Burkett, prin. Fax 295-5987
Lake Alfred Polytech Academy 800/6-8
925 N Buena Vista Dr 33850 863-295-5988
Julie Grice, prin. Fax 295-5992

Lake Butler, Union, Pop. 1,869
Union County SD 2,300/PK-12
55 SW 6th St 32054 386-496-2045
Carlton Faulk, supt. Fax 496-4819
www.union.k12.fl.us
Lake Butler ES 1,000/PK-4
800 SW 6th St 32054 386-496-3047
Marcie Tucker, prin. Fax 496-4395
Lake Butler MS 700/5-8
150 SW 6th St 32054 386-496-3046
Carolyn Parrish, prin. Fax 496-4352

Lake City, Columbia, Pop. 11,774
Columbia County SD 9,900/PK-12
372 W Duval St 32055 386-755-8000
Alex Carswell, supt. Fax 755-8008
www.columbiak12.com
Columbia City ES 600/PK-5
7438 SW State Road 47 32024 386-758-4850
Hope Jernigan, prin. Fax 758-4857
Eastside ES 600/PK-5
256 SE Beech St 32025 386-755-8220
Roger Little, prin. Fax 758-4885
Five Points ES 400/PK-5
303 NW Johnson St 32055 386-755-8230
Lisa Lee, prin. Fax 755-8240
Lake City MS 1,000/7-8
843 SW Arlington Blvd 32025 386-758-4800
Robert Cooper, prin. Fax 758-4839
Melrose Park ES 500/PK-5
820 SE Putnam St 32025 386-755-8260
Syreeta Jackson-Lee, prin. Fax 755-8276
Niblack ES 300/PK-5
837 NE Broadway Ave 32055 386-755-8200
Nakitha Ivery, prin. Fax 755-8218
Pinemount ES 500/PK-5
324 SW Gabriel Pl 32024 386-755-8179
Donna Darby, prin. Fax 755-8172
Richardson Sixth Grade Academy 600/6-6
646 SE Pennsylvania St 32025 386-755-8130
Sonya Judkins, prin. Fax 755-8154
Summers ES 700/PK-5
1388 SW McFarlane Ave 32025 386-755-8250
Jennifer Saucer, prin. Fax 758-4916
Westside ES 700/PK-5
1956 SW County Road 252B 32024 386-755-8280
Dennis Dotson, prin. Fax 755-8285
Other Schools – See Fort White

Epiphany S 100/K-8
1937 SW Epiphany Ct 32025 386-752-2320
Rita Klenk, prin. Fax 752-2364
Lake City Christian Academy 100/PK-12
3035 SW Pinemount Rd 32024 386-758-0055
New Generation Christian S 200/K-12
608 SW Marvin Burnett Rd 32025 386-758-4710

Lake Helen, Volusia, Pop. 2,576
Volusia County SD
Supt. — See De Land
Volusia Pines ES 600/K-5
500 E Kicklighter Rd 32744 386-575-4125
Julie Cusack-Gordon, prin. Fax 228-1144

Lakeland, Polk, Pop. 95,497
Polk County SD
Supt. — See Bartow
Blake Academy 700/PK-8
510 Hartsell Ave 33815 863-499-2870
Sybille Oldham-Jackson, prin. Fax 284-4521
Chiles Middle Academy 700/6-8
400 N Florida Ave 33801 863-499-2742
Brian Andrews, prin. Fax 499-2774
Churchwell ES 600/PK-5
8201 Park Byrd Rd 33810 863-853-6011
Jacqueline Agard, prin. Fax 815-6538
Cleveland Court ES 400/K-5
328 E Edgewood Dr 33803 863-499-2929
Cheryl Rutenbar, prin. Fax 499-2625
Combee Academy 700/PK-5
2805 Morgan Combee Rd 33801 863-499-2960
Tammy Farrens, prin. Fax 284-4421
Crystal Lake ES 600/PK-5
700 Galvin Dr 33801 863-499-2966
Bryan Kim, prin. Fax 603-6329
Crystal Lake MS 1,100/6-8
2410 N Crystal Lake Dr 33801 863-499-2970
Ronda Cotter, prin. Fax 603-6267
Dixieland ES 500/K-5
416 Ariana St 33803 863-499-2930
Dawn Mulder, prin. Fax 499-2932
Griffin ES 500/PK-5
3315 Kathleen Rd 33810 863-853-6020
Melissa Durrance, prin. Fax 853-6189
Highlands Grove ES 700/K-5
4510 Lakeland Highlands Rd 33813 863-648-3002
Benjamin Henry, prin. Fax 648-3005
Kathleen ES 500/PK-5
3515 Sherertz Rd 33810 863-853-6030
Nadia Lewis, prin. Fax 853-6033
Kathleen MS 800/6-8
3627 Kathleen Pnes 33810 863-853-6040
Sheila Gregory, prin. Fax 853-6037
Keen ES 700/PK-5
815 Plateau Ave 33815 863-499-2880
Joseph Griffin, prin. Fax 413-2506
Lake Gibson MS 1,100/6-8
6901 N Socrum Loop Rd 33809 863-853-6151
Alain Douge, prin. Fax 853-6171
Lakeland Highlands MS 1,300/6-8
740 Lake Miriam Dr 33813 863-648-3500
Telay Kendrick, prin. Fax 648-3580
Lincoln Avenue Academy 600/K-5
1330 N Lincoln Ave 33805 863-499-2955
Evelyn Hollen, prin. Fax 499-2959
Medulla ES 600/PK-5
850 Schoolhouse Rd 33813 863-648-3515
Myra Richardson, prin. Fax 648-3214
North Lakeland ES 700/PK-5
410 W Robson St 33805 863-499-2850
Kimberly Sealey, prin. Fax 499-2760
O'Brien ES 600/K-5
1225 E Lime St 33801 863-499-2950
Merri Crawford, prin. Fax 688-8774
Padgett ES 500/PK-5
110 Leelon Rd 33809 863-853-6044
Antionette Kirby, prin. Fax 853-6092
Palmore ES 500/PK-5
3725 Cleveland Heights Blvd 33803 863-648-3510
Badonna Dardis, prin. Fax 648-3122
Pope ES 500/PK-5
2730 Maine Ave 33801 863-499-2992
Carol Griffin, prin. Fax 499-2996
Roberts ES 700/PK-5
6600 Green Rd 33810 863-815-6633
Timothy Warren, prin. Fax 815-6640
Rochelle S of the Arts 800/PK-8
1501 Martin L King Jr Ave 33805 863-499-2810
Julie Ward, prin. Fax 499-2797
Scott Lake ES 700/K-5
1140 E County Road 540A 33813 863-648-3520
Ruth Reimer, prin. Fax 701-1076
Sikes ES 900/K-5
2727 Shepherd Rd 33811 863-648-3525
Kerry Chapman, prin. Fax 648-3187
Sleepy Hill ES 700/PK-5
2205 Sleepy Hill Rd 33810 863-815-6768
Gregory Deal, prin. Fax 815-6775
Sleepy Hill MS 800/6-8
2215 Sleepy Hill Rd 33810 863-815-6577
Kathryn Blackburn, prin. Fax 815-6586
Socrum ES 600/PK-5
9400 Old Dade City Rd 33810 863-853-6050
Kenyetta Feacher, prin. Fax 853-6059
Southwest ES 400/K-5
2650 Southwest Ave 33803 863-499-2830
Julie Sloan, prin. Fax 499-2943
Southwest MS 900/6-8
2815 Eden Pkwy 33803 863-499-2840
Tye Bruno, prin. Fax 499-2762
Valleyview ES 700/PK-5
2900 E County Road 540A 33813 863-648-3535
Katherine Riley, prin. Fax 648-3598
Wagner ES 900/PK-5
5500 Yates Rd 33811 863-701-1450
Ryan Foster, prin. Fax 701-1457
Watson ES 800/K-5
6800 Walt Williams Rd 33809 863-853-6060
Kelly Burgess, prin. Fax 853-6056
Winston Academy of Engineering 600/PK-5
3415 Swindell Rd 33810 863-499-2890
Ava Brown, prin. Fax 499-2894

Excel Christian Academy 200/PK-12
6505 Odom Rd 33809 863-853-9235
Faith Celebration Christian Prep S 100/K-8
1736 New Jersey RD 33803 863-797-4877
Geneva Classical Academy 100/PK-12
4204 Lakeland Highlands Rd 33813 863-644-1408
Lakeland Christian S 1,000/PK-12
1111 Forest Park St 33803 863-688-2771
Dr. Michael Sligh, hdmstr. Fax 682-5637
Resurrection Catholic S 400/PK-8
3720 Old Highway 37 33813 863-644-3931
Deborah Schwope, prin. Fax 648-0625
St. Anthony S 200/PK-8
924 Marcum Rd 33809 863-858-0671
Janet Peddecord, prin. Fax 858-0876
St. Joseph Academy 200/PK-8
310 Frank Lloyd Wright Way 33803 863-686-6415
Jessica Bruchey, prin. Fax 687 8074
St. Paul Lutheran S 300/PK-8
4450 Harden Blvd 33813 863-644-7710
Robert Boyd, prin. Fax 644-7491
Victory Christian Academy 300/PK-12
1401 Griffin Rd 33810 863-858-5614
Whitestone Academy 100/PK-12
3151 Hardin Combee Rd 33801 863-665-4187

Lake Mary, Seminole, Pop. 13,545
Seminole County SD
Supt. — See Sanford
Crystal Lake ES 700/K-5
231 Rinehart Rd 32746 407-871-8150
Kristina Marshall, prin. Fax 871-8199
Greenwood Lakes MS 1,000/6-8
601 Lake Park Dr 32746 407-320-7650
Breezi Erickson, prin. Fax 320-7699
Heathrow ES 900/PK-5
5715 Markham Woods Rd 32746 407-320-6850
Brett White, prin. Fax 320-6890
Lake Mary ES 1,000/PK-5
132 S Country Club Rd 32746 407-320-5650
Christine Peacock, prin. Fax 320-5699
Markham Woods MS 1,100/6-8
6003 Markham Woods Rd 32746 407-871-1750
Linda Mumey, prin. Fax 871-1799

Lake Mary Montessori Academy 100/PK-6
3551 W Lake Mary Blvd 32746 407-324-2304
Lake Mary Preparatory S 700/PK-12
650 Rantoul Ln 32746 407-805-0095
Jack Delman, hdmstr. Fax 322-3872
Starchild Academy Lake Mary 400/PK-5
200 Longwood Lake Mary Rd 32746 407-333-8901

Lake Panasoffkee, Sumter, Pop. 3,500
Sumter County SD
Supt. — See Bushnell
Lake Panasoffkee ES 600/PK-5
790 CR 482N 33538 352-793-1093
Nicole Wade, prin. Fax 568-8080

Lake Park, Palm Beach, Pop. 7,949
Palm Beach County SD
Supt. — See West Palm Beach
Lake Park ES 300/K-5
410 3rd St 33403 561-494-1300
Michelle Fleming, prin. Fax 494-1350

Lake Park Baptist S 200/PK-8
625 Park Ave 33403 561-844-2747

Lake Placid, Highlands, Pop. 2,195
Highlands County SD
Supt. — See Sebring
Lake Country ES 600/PK-5
516 County Road 29 33852 863-699-5050
Erica Ashley, prin. Fax 699-5058
Lake Placid ES 900/PK-5
101 Green Dragon Dr 33852 863-699-5070
Andrea Summers, prin. Fax 699-5079
Lake Placid MS 600/6-8
201 S Tangerine Ave 33852 863-699-5030
Jennifer Sanchez, prin. Fax 699-5029

Lake Wales, Polk, Pop. 13,989
Polk County SD
Supt. — See Bartow
McLaughlin MS and Fine Arts Academy 700/6-8
800 4th St S 33853 863-678-4233
Donna Drisdom, prin. Fax 678-4033
Spook Hill ES 600/K-5
321 Dr J A Wiltshire Ave E 33853 863-678-4262
Michelle Browning, prin. Fax 678-4210

Canaan Christian Academy 50/K-8
640 S Scenic Hwy 33853 863-676-5356
Sherol Larkin, admin. Fax 589-5211

Candlelight Christian Academy 200/K-12
209 E Sessoms Ave 33853 863-676-0049
Endtime Christian S of Excellence 50/PK-12
200 S 3rd St 33853 863-676-8299
Betty Hill, prin. Fax 678-1193

Lake Worth, Palm Beach, Pop. 34,358
Palm Beach County SD
Supt. — See West Palm Beach
Barton ES 800/K-5
1700 Barton Rd 33460 561-540-9100
Denise Sanon, prin. Fax 540-9128
Coral Reef ES 900/K-5
6151 Hagen Ranch Rd 33467 561-804-3700
Bobbi Moretto, prin. Fax 804-3750
Discovery Key ES 800/K-5
3550 Lyons Rd 33467 561-491-8200
Catherine Lewis, prin. Fax 491-8250
Hidden Oaks ES 800/K-5
7685 S Military Trl 33463 561-804-3800
Sari Myers, prin. Fax 804-3850
Highland ES 900/K-5
500 Highland Ave 33460 561-202-0500
Ellizabeth Morales, prin. Fax 202-0550
Indian Pines ES 800/K-5
6000 Oak Royal Dr 33463 561-804-3300
Jill Robinson, prin. Fax 804-3350
Lake Worth MS 1,000/6-8
1300 Barnett Dr 33461 561-540-5500
Mike Williams, prin. Fax 540-5559
Manatee ES 1,000/K-5
7001 Charleston Shores Blvd 33467 561-357-1800
Mary Churchill-Jones, prin. Fax 357-1850
North Grade ES 800/K-5
824 N K St 33460 561-202-9300
Nicole Patterson, prin. Fax 202-9350
Palm Springs ES 900/K-5
101 Davis Rd 33461 561-804-3000
Dawn Lewis, prin. Fax 804-3050
Panther Run ES 600/K-5
10775 Lake Worth Rd, 561-804-3900
Edilia DeLaVega, prin. Fax 804-3950
South Grade ES 600/K-5
716 S K St 33460 561-202-9400
Ana Arce-Gonzalez, prin. Fax 202-9450
Woodlands MS 1,200/6-8
5200 Lyons Rd 33467 561-357-0300
Enrique Vela, prin. Fax 357-0307

Sacred Heart S 200/PK-8
410 N M St 33460 561-582-2242
Candace Tamposi, prin. Fax 547-9699
Suncoast Christian Academy 100/PK-5
5561 Hypoluxo Rd 33463 561-641-1446
Trinity Christian Academy 600/PK-12
7259 S Military Trl 33463 561-967-1900
Tobi Manke, prin. Fax 965-4347
Wellington Preparatory S 50/K-5
9135 Lake Worth Rd 33467 561-649-7900
Sandy Montoya, prin.

Land O Lakes, Pasco, Pop. 31,370
Pasco County SD 68,500/PK-12
7227 Land O Lakes Blvd 34638 813-794-2000
Kurt Browning, supt. Fax 794-2716
www.pasco.k12.fl.us
Bexley ES K-5
4380 Ballantrae Blvd, 813-346-4300
Vicki Wolin, prin. Fax 346-4391
Connerton ES 800/K-5
9300 Flourish Dr, 813-346-1800
Edward Abernathy, prin. Fax 346-1891
Lake Myrtle ES 700/K-5
22844 Weeks Blvd 34639 813-794-1000
Megan Hermansen, prin. Fax 794-1091
Oakstead ES 1,100/K-5
19925 Lake Patience Rd, 813-346-1500
Tammy Kimpland, prin. Fax 346-1591
Pine View ES 700/K-5
5333 Parkway Blvd 34639 813-794-0600
Kathryn Moore, prin. Fax 794-0691
Pine View MS 900/6-8
5334 Parkway Blvd 34639 813-794-4800
Jennifer Warren, prin. Fax 794-4891
Rushe MS 1,300/6-8
18654 Mentmore Blvd, 813-346-1200
David Salerno, prin. Fax 346-1291
Sanders Memorial ES 1,000/PK-5
5126 School Rd, 813-794-1500
Jason Petry, prin. Fax 794-1591
Other Schools – See Dade City, Holiday, Hudson, Lutz, New Port Richey, Port Richey, Spring Hill, Wesley Chapel, Zephyrhills

---

Academy at the Lakes - Wendlek 100/PK-4
2220 Collier Pkwy 34639 813-948-2133
Mark Heller, head sch Fax 948-2943
Land O' Lakes Christian S 200/PK-12
5105 School Rd, 813-995-9040
Mary's House ECC PK-PK
2348 Collier Pkwy 34639 813-948-5999
Corrine Ertl, dir. Fax 948-5998

Lantana, Palm Beach, Pop. 10,206
Palm Beach County SD
Supt. — See West Palm Beach
Lantana Community MS 800/6-8
1225 W Drew St 33462 561-540-3400
Edward Burke, prin. Fax 540-3435
Lantana ES 500/K-5
710 W Ocean Ave 33462 561-202-0300
Janyn Robinson, prin. Fax 202-0350
Starlight Cove ES 900/K-5
6300 Seminole Dr 33462 561-804-3600
Cara Hayden, prin. Fax 804-3650

Kentwood Preparatory S 200/1-12
6210 S Congress Ave 33462 561-649-6141

Paolo Preparatory Academy 50/PK-12
125 Hypoluxo Rd 33462 561-299-4792

Largo, Pinellas, Pop. 76,001
Pinellas County SD 101,500/PK-12
301 4th St SW 33770 727-588-6000
Dr. Michael Grego, supt. Fax 588-6200
www.pcsb.org
Anona ES 400/K-5
12301 Indian Rocks Rd 33774 727-588-4730
Michael Rebman, prin. Fax 588-4733
Fitzgerald MS 1,200/6-8
6410 118th Ave 33773 727-547-4526
Anthony Francois, prin. Fax 549-6631
Fuguitt ES 600/PK-5
13010 101st St 33773 727-588-3576
Dr. Kathlene Bentley, prin. Fax 588-4630
Helms ES 600/PK-5
561 Clearwater Largo Rd S 33770 727-588-3569
Shannon Brennan, prin. Fax 588-3603
Largo MS 800/6-8
155 8th Ave SE 33771 727-588-4600
Stephanie Joyner, prin. Fax 588-3720
Oakhurst ES 700/K-5
10535 137th St N 33774 727-588-6801
Kelly Kennedy, prin. Fax 588-6811
Ridgecrest ES 800/PK-5
1901 119th St 33778 727-588-3580
Michael Moss, prin. Fax 588-4608
Southern Oak ES 700/PK-5
9101 Walsingham Rd 33773 727-588-4654
Susan Taylor, prin. Fax 588-4656
Walsingham ES 600/PK-5
9099 Walsingham Rd 33773 727-588-3519
Quinn Williams, prin. Fax 588-6990
Other Schools – See Clearwater, Dunedin, Gulfport, Madeira Beach, Oldsmar, Palm Harbor, Pinellas Park, Safety Harbor, Saint Petersburg, Saint Petersburg Beach, Seminole, Tarpon Springs

---

Country Day S 300/PK-8
11499 131st St 33774 727-596-1902
Indian Rocks Christian S 800/PK-12
12685 Ulmerton Rd 33774 727-596-4342
Walter Weller, supt. Fax 593-8778
St. Jerome ECC 100/PK-PK
10895 Hamlin Blvd 33774 727-596-9491
Denise Roach, dir. Fax 596-8953
St. Patrick S 200/PK-8
1501 Trotter Rd 33770 727-581-4865
Keith Galley, prin. Fax 581-7842

Lauderdale Lakes, Broward, Pop. 31,785
Broward County SD
Supt. — See Fort Lauderdale
Lauderdale Lakes MS 1,000/6-8
3911 NW 30th Ave 33309 754-322-3500
James Griffin, prin. Fax 322-3585
Oriole ES 700/PK-5
3081 NW 39th St 33309 754-322-7550
Sheneka Blue, prin. Fax 322-7590
Park Lakes ES 1,100/K-5
3925 N State Road 7 33319 754-322-7650
Orinthia Dias, prin. Fax 322-7690

Lauderhill, Broward, Pop. 65,234
Broward County SD
Supt. — See Fort Lauderdale
Broward Estates ES 500/PK-5
441 NW 35th Ave 33311 754-322-5550
Cyntheria Hunt, prin. Fax 322-5590
Castle Hill ES 600/PK-5
2640 NW 46th Ave 33313 754-322-5600
Letitia Ingram, prin. Fax 322-5640
Endeavour Primary Learning Center 400/PK-3
2701 NW 56th Ave 33313 754-321-6600
Denise Lawrence, prin. Fax 321-6640
King Montessori Acad 500/PK-5
591 NW 31st Ave 33311 754-322-6550
Mitshuca Moreau, prin. Fax 322-6590
Larkdale ES 400/PK-5
3250 NW 12th Pl 33311 754-322-6600
Carla Hart, prin. Fax 322-6640
Lauderhill Paul Turner ES 700/PK-5
1500 NW 49th Ave 33313 754-322-6700
Richard Garrick, prin. Fax 322-6740
Parkway MS 1,600/6-8
3600 NW 5th Ct 33311 754-322-4000
Bradford Mattair, prin. Fax 322-4085
Royal Palm STEM S 700/PK-5
1951 NW 56th Ave 33313 754-322-8350
Ducarmel Augustin, prin. Fax 322-8390

Piney Grove Boys Academy 100/K-10
4699 W Oakland Park Blvd 33313 954-735-1470
Upperroom Christian Academy 200/K-12
850 NW 36th Ave 33311 754-281-2118
Upperroom Christian Academy 200/K-12
404 NW 7th Terrace 33313 754-306-8696

Laurel Hill, Okaloosa, Pop. 532
Okaloosa County SD
Supt. — See Fort Walton Beach
Laurel Hill S 400/PK-12
8078 4th St 32567 850-652-4111
Lee Martello, prin. Fax 652-4659

Lawtey, Bradford, Pop. 715
Bradford County SD
Supt. — See Starke
Lawtey S 200/PK-8
22703 Park St 32058 904-966-6795
Jennifer Vaughan, prin. Fax 966-6748

Lecanto, Citrus, Pop. 5,799
Citrus County SD
Supt. — See Inverness
Lecanto MS 700/6-8
3800 W Educational Path 34461 352-746-2050
Brian Lancaster, prin. Fax 249-2138

Lecanto PS 800/PK-5
3790 W Educational Path 34461 352-746-2220
Victoria Lofton, prin. Fax 249-2139

St. John Paul II Catholic S 200/PK-8
4341 W Homosassa Trl 34461 352-746-2020
John Larkin, prin. Fax 746-3448
Seven Rivers Christian S 300/PK-12
4221 W Gulf to Lake Hwy 34461 352-746-5696

Lee, Madison, Pop. 344
Madison County SD
Supt. — See Madison
Lee ES 200/PK-5
7731 E US Highway 90 32059 850-973-5030
Amanda Brown, prin. Fax 973-5032

Leesburg, Lake, Pop. 19,677
Lake County SD
Supt. — See Tavares
Beverly Shores ES 600/K-5
1108 Griffin Rd 34748 352-787-4175
Monica Gordon, prin. Fax 787-1760
Carver MS 800/6-8
1200 Beecher St 34748 352-787-7868
Kinetrai Kelley-Truitt, prin. Fax 787-1339
Leesburg ES 800/K-5
2229 South St 34748 352-365-6308
Heather Gelb, prin. Fax 365-9018
Oak Park MS 600/6-8
2101 South St 34748 352-787-3232
Barbara Longo, prin. Fax 326-2177
Rimes Early Learning Center 200/PK-3
3101 Schoolview St 34748 352-787-5757
Greggory Dudley, admin. Fax 787-5615
Treadway ES 900/PK-5
10619 Treadway School Rd 34788 352-742-2291
Cindy Christidis, prin. Fax 742-8343

First Academy-Leesburg 300/PK-12
219 N 13th St 34748 352-787-7762
Gregory Frescoln, admin. Fax 323-1773
Lake Montessori and Learning Institute 100/PK-5
415 Lee St 34748 352-787-5333
St. Paul S 200/PK-8
1320 Sunshine Ave 34748 352-787-4657
Jacquelyn Gehrsitz, prin. Fax 787-0324

Lehigh Acres, Lee, Pop. 85,066
Lee County SD
Supt. — See Fort Myers
Harns Marsh ES 900/K-5
1800 Unice Ave N 33971 239-690-1249
Tracey Zenoniani, prin. Fax 694-1325
Harns Marsh MS 1,100/6-8
1820 Unice Ave N 33971 239-690-2025
Linda Maere, prin. Fax 690-2028
Hipps ES 700/K-5
1200 Homestead Rd N 33936 239-368-7042
Aida Saldivar, prin. Fax 369-0469
Lehigh Acres MS 1,100/6-8
104 Arthur Ave 33936 239-369-6108
Neketa Watson, prin. Fax 369-8808
Lehigh ES 1,100/PK-5
200 Schoolside Ct 33936 239-369-2477
Sherri Wipf, prin. Fax 369-4506
Mirror Lakes ES 1,100/PK-5
525 Charwood Ave S, 239-369-2200
Robert Cooper, prin Fax 369-0542
Sunshine ES 1,200/PK-5
601 Sara Ave N 33971 239-369-5836
Cherry Gibson, prin. Fax 369-1455
Tortuga Preserve ES 900/K-5
1711 Gunnery Rd N 33971 239-693-5023
Dr. Scott LeMaster, prin. Fax 693-5033
Varsity Lakes MS 1,000/6-8
801 Gunnery Rd N 33971 239-694-3464
Matthew Mederios, prin. Fax 694-7093
Veterans Park Academy for the Arts 1,500/K-8
49 Homestead Rd S 33936 239-303-3003
Laura Stanford, prin. Fax 303-3075

Lighthouse Point, Broward, Pop. 10,186

Trinity Christian S 100/K-5
3901 NE 22nd Ave, 954-941-8033
Debbie Galup, prin. Fax 941-3240

Lithia, Hillsborough
Hillsborough County SD
Supt. — See Tampa
Barrington MS 1,200/6-8
5925 Village Center Dr 33547 813-657-7266
Amy Rappleyea, prin. Fax 657-7369
Bevis ES 800/K-5
5720 Osprey Ridge Dr 33547 813-740-4000
Melanie Cochrane, prin. Fax 740-4004
Fishhawk Creek ES 1,000/PK-5
16815 Dorman Rd 33547 813-651-2150
Pamela Bush, prin. Fax 651-2154
Pinecrest ES 600/PK-5
7950 Lithia Pinecrest Rd 33547 813-744-8164
Denise Mobley, prin. Fax 740-4456
Randall MS 1,300/6-8
16510 Fishhawk Blvd 33547 813-740-3900
Claire Mawhinney, prin. Fax 740-3910
Stowers ES 900/K-5
13915 Barrington Stowers Dr 33547 813-657-7431
Catherine Lennard, prin. Fax 657-7435

Live Oak, Suwannee, Pop. 6,744
Suwannee County SD 5,900/PK-12
702 2nd St NW 32064 386-647-4600
Ted Roush, supt. Fax 364-2635
www.suwannee.k12.fl.us
Suwannee ES 800/2-3
1748 Ohio Ave S 32064 386-647-4400
Amy Boggus, prin. Fax 330-1215

Suwannee IS 600/4-5
1419 Walker Ave SW 32064 386-647-4700
Gary Caldwell, prin. Fax 364-2680
Suwannee MS 1,000/6-8
1730 Walker Ave SW 32064 386-647-4500
Jimmy Wilkerson, prin. Fax 208-1474
Suwannee PS 900/PK-1
1625 Walker Ave SW 32064 386-647-4300
Marsha Tedder, prin. Fax 364-2667
Other Schools – See Branford

Melody Christian Academy 200/PK-12
PO Box 100 32064 386-364-4800
Westwood Christian S 100/PK-12
920 11th St SW 32064 386-362-3735

Longwood, Seminole, Pop. 13,382
Seminole County SD
Supt. — See Sanford
Longwood ES 600/PK-5
840 Orange Ave 32750 407-746-3350
Brian Emmans, prin. Fax 746-3349
Milwee MS 1,200/6-8
1341 S Ronald Reagan Blvd 32750 407-746-3850
James Kubis, prin. Fax 746-3899
Rock Lake MS 900/6-8
250 Slade Dr 32750 407-746-9350
Jordan Rodriguez, prin. Fax 746-9399
Sabal Point ES 900/PK-5
960 Wekiva Springs Rd 32779 407-746-3050
Dr. Tina Benitez, prin. Fax 746-3098
Wekiva ES 700/PK-5
1450 E Wekiva Trl 32779 407-746-3150
Marjorie Adamczyk, prin. Fax 746-3163
Woodlands ES 800/PK-5
1420 EE Williamson Rd 32750 407-746-2750
Patricia May, prin. Fax 746-2799

Forest Lake Education Center 500/PK-8
1275 Learning Loop 32779 407-862-7688
Longwood Christian Academy 100/K-3
891 SR 434 E 32750 407-767-8823
Kathy Stear, prin. Fax 767-9725
One S of the Arts 100/PK-12
1675 Dixon Rd 32779 407-774-0168
Sweetwater Episcopal Academy 200/PK-7
251 E Lake Brantley Dr 32779 407-862-1882

Loxahatchee, Palm Beach
Palm Beach County SD
Supt. — See West Palm Beach
Acreage Pines ES 400/K-5
14200 Orange Blvd 33470 561-904-9500
Darline Karbowski, prin. Fax 904-9550
Frontier ES 600/K-5
6701 180th Ave N 33470 561-904-9900
Susan Groth, prin. Fax 904-9950
Loxahatchee Groves ES 500/K-5
16020 Okeechobee Blvd 33470 561-904-9200
Richard Myerson, prin. Fax 904-9250
Osceola Creek MS 600/6-8
6775 180th Ave N 33470 561-422-2500
Nicole Daly, prin. Fax 422-2510
Pierce Hammock ES 600/K-5
14255 Hamlin Blvd 33470 561-633-4500
Ariel Alejo, prin. Fax 633-4550

Lutz, Hillsborough, Pop. 19,035
Hillsborough County SD
Supt. — See Tampa
Lutz ES 600/PK-5
202 5th Ave SE 33549 813-949-1452
Lori Branhan, prin. Fax 909-9908
Maniscalco ES 500/PK-5
939 Debuel Rd 33549 813-949-0337
Tammy Reale, prin. Fax 948-3270
Martinez MS 1,100/6-8
5601 W Lutz Lake Fern Rd 33558 813-558-1190
Brent McBrien, prin. Fax 558-1226
McKitrick ES 1,000/K-5
5503 W Lutz Lake Fern Rd 33558 813-558-5427
Allison Cline, prin. Fax 558-5431
Schwarzkopf ES 600/K-5
18333 Calusa Trace Blvd 33558 813-975-6945
Cheryl Holley, prin. Fax 975-6948

Pasco County SD
Supt. — See Land O Lakes
Denham Oaks ES 700/K-5
1422 Oak Grove Blvd 33559 813-794-1600
Mardee Powers, prin. Fax 794-1691

Mother Teresa Catholic S 200/K-8
17534 Lakeshore Rd 33558 813-933-4750
Johnnathan Combs, prin. Fax 933-3181
St. Timothy ECC 100/PK-PK
17512 Lakeshore Rd 33558 813-960-4857
Daisy Cintron, dir. Fax 961-9429
Tampa Christian Community S 100/PK-12
960 W Lutz Lake Fern Rd 33548 813-949-2144
Melissa Walker, prin. Fax 877-3111

Lynn Haven, Bay, Pop. 18,004
Bay County SD
Supt. — See Panama City
Lynn Haven ES 800/PK-5
301 W 9th St 32444 850-767-1454
Debra Spradley, prin. Fax 271-3685
Mowat MS 1,000/6-8
1903 W Highway 390 32444 850-767-4040
Ed Sheffield, prin. Fax 265-2179

Macclenny, Baker, Pop. 6,242
Baker County SD 5,000/PK-12
392 South Blvd E 32063 904-259-6251
Sherrie Raulerson, supt. Fax 259-1387
www.bakerk12.org
Baker County MS 1,100/6-8
211 E Jonathan St 32063 904-259-2226
Debbie Fraser, prin. Fax 259-7955
Baker County PK/K Center 600/PK-K
362 South Blvd E 32063 904-259-0405
Bonnie Jones, prin. Fax 259-0379
Keller IS 800/4-5
420 S 8th St 32063 904-259-4244
David Davis, prin. Fax 259-3771
Macclenny ES 600/1-3
1 Wild Kitten Dr 32063 904-259-2551
Sherry Barrett, prin. Fax 259-1103
Other Schools – See Glen Saint Mary

MacDill AFB, See Tampa
Hillsborough County SD
Supt. — See Tampa
Tinker ES 600/K-8
8207 Tinker St 33621 813-840-2043
Nancy Mooy, prin. Fax 233-3664

Madeira Beach, Pinellas, Pop. 4,207
Pinellas County SD
Supt. — See Largo
Madeira Beach Fundamental S 1,400/K-8
591 Tom Stuart Cswy 33708 727-547-7838
Christopher Ateek, prin. Fax 545-6432

Madison, Madison, Pop. 2,801
Madison County SD 2,400/PK-12
210 NE Duval Ave 32340 850-973-5022
Dr. Karen Pickles, supt. Fax 973-5027
www.madison.k12.fl.us
Madison County Central S 1,200/PK-8
2093 W US 90 32340 850-973-5192
David Chambers, prin. Fax 973-5194
Other Schools – See Greenville, Lee, Pinetta

Maitland, Orange, Pop. 15,449
Orange County SD
Supt. — See Orlando
Dommerich ES 600/PK-5
601 N Thistle Ln 32751 407-623-1407
Karen Verano, prin. Fax 623-5738
Hungerford ES 300/PK-5
230 S College Ave 32751 407-623-1430
Letecia Foster, prin. Fax 623-1498
Lake Sybelia ES 600/PK-5
600 Sandspur Rd 32751 407-623-1445
John Dobbs, prin. Fax 623-1452
Maitland MS 900/6-8
701 N Thistle Ln 32751 407-623-1462
Andrew Leftakis, prin. Fax 623-1474

Jewish Academy of Orlando 200/K-5
851 N Maitland Ave Ste 100 32751 407-647-0713
Alan Rusonik, head sch Fax 647-1223
King of Kings Lutheran S 50/PK-8
1101 N Wymore Rd 32751 407-628-5230
Randy Cochran, prin. Fax 628-5230
Lake Forrest Preparatory S 200/PK-8
866 Lake Howell Rd 32751 407-331-5144
Maitland Montessori S 100/PK-8
236 N Swoope Ave 32751 407-628-0019
Orangewood Christian S 100/PK-4
1221 Trinity Woods Ln 32751 888-479-9510
Allyn Williams, head sch Fax 339-5479
Park Maitland S 600/PK-6
PO Box 941095 32794 407-647-3038

Malone, Jackson, Pop. 2,054
Jackson County SD
Supt. — See Marianna
Malone S 500/PK-12
5361 9th St 32445 850-482-9950
Doug Powell, prin. Fax 482-9901

Marathon, Monroe, Pop. 8,204
Monroe County SD
Supt. — See Key West
Switlik ES 500/PK-5
3400 Overseas Hwy 33050 305-289-2490
Brett Unke, prin. Fax 289-2496

Marco Island, Collier, Pop. 16,302
Collier County SD
Supt. — See Naples
Barfield ES 600/K-5
101 Kirkwood St 34145 239-377-8500
Kathryn Maya, prin. Fax 377-8501

Island Montessori Academy 50/PK-3
PO Box 224 34146 239-642-2020

Margate, Broward, Pop. 51,792
Broward County SD
Supt. — See Fort Lauderdale
Atlantic West ES 600/K-5
301 NW 69th Ter 33063 754-322-5300
Diane Eagan, prin. Fax 322-5340
Liberty ES 1,000/K-5
2450 Banks Rd 33063 754-322-6750
David Levine, prin. Fax 322-6790
Margate ES 900/K-5
6300 NW 18th St 33063 754-322-6900
Thomas Schroeder, prin. Fax 322-6940
Margate MS 1,400/6-8
500 NW 65th Ave 33063 754-322-3800
Ernest Toliver, prin. Fax 322-3885

Abundant Life Christian Academy 400/PK-8
1494 Banks Rd 33063 954-979-2665
Hebrew Academy Community S 400/PK-8
1500 N State Road 7 33063 954-978-6341
Rivka Denburg, head sch Fax 333-3913
Phyl's Academy K-6
7205 Royal Palm Blvd 33063 954-731-7524

Marianna, Jackson, Pop. 5,957
Jackson County SD 6,600/PK-12
PO Box 5050 32447 850-482-1200
Steve Benton, supt. Fax 482-1299
www.jcsb.org
Golson ES 800/K-2
4258 2nd Ave 32446 850-482-9607
Dr. Jennifer Hawthorne, prin. Fax 482-1203
Marianna MS 700/6-8
4144 South St 32448 850-482-9609
Eddie Ellis, prin. Fax 482-9795
Riverside ES 600/3-5
2958 Cherokee St 32446 850-482-9611
Christopher Franklin, prin. Fax 482-9300
Other Schools – See Cottondale, Graceville, Grand Ridge, Malone, Sneads

---

Dayspring Christian Academy 200/PK-12
4685 Meadowview Rd 32446 850-526-4919

Mary Esther, Okaloosa, Pop. 3,705
Okaloosa County SD
Supt. — See Fort Walton Beach
Florosa ES 600/PK-5
1700 W Highway 98 32569 850-833-4381
Dawn Massey, prin. Fax 833-4391
Mary Esther ES 600/PK-5
320 E Miracle Strip Pkwy 32569 850-833-3371
Jason McClelland, prin. Fax 833-3474

Mayo, Lafayette, Pop. 1,208
LaFayette County SD 1,200/PK-12
363 NE Crawford St 32066 386-294-1351
Robert Edwards, supt. Fax 294-3072
lafayette.schooldesk.net
LaFayette ES 600/PK-5
811 E Main St 32066 386-294-4112
Stephen Clark, prin. Fax 294-4320

Lighthouse Christian Academy 100/PK-12
772 N State Road 51 32066 386-294-2994
Lisa Walker, admin. Fax 294-3449

Melbourne, Brevard, Pop. 74,011
Brevard County SD 68,900/PK-12
2700 Judge Fran Jamieson 32940 321-633-1000
Dr. Desmond Blackburn, supt. Fax 633-3432
www.edline.net/pages/Brevard_County_Schools
Allen ES 600/K-6
2601 Fountainhead Blvd 32935 321-242-6450
Lori Migliore, prin. Fax 242-6453
Creel ES 900/PK-6
2000 Glenwood Dr 32935 321-259-3233
Kathryn Eward, prin. Fax 259-3044
Croton ES 700/PK-6
1449 Croton Rd 32935 321-259-3818
Roseann Bennett, prin. Fax 242-6477
Harbor City ES 500/PK-6
1377 Sarno Rd 32935 321-254-5534
Joy Salamone, prin. Fax 242-6468
Johnson MS 800/7-8
2155 Croton Rd 32935 321-242-6430
Marina Middleton, prin. Fax 242-6436
Longleaf ES 600/PK-6
4290 N Wickham Rd 32935 321-242-4700
Kimberly Bias, prin. Fax 242-4708
Quest ES 700/K-6
8751 Trafford Dr 32940 321-242-1411
Christine Boyd, prin. Fax 242-1719
Sabal ES 600/PK-6
1401 N Wickham Rd 32935 321-254-7261
Stephanie Hall, prin. Fax 242-6475
Sherwood ES 500/K-6
2541 Post Rd 32935 321-254-6424
Karen Ivery, prin. Fax 242-6478
Stone MS 800/7-8
1101 E University Blvd 32901 321-723-0741
Mary Bland, prin. Fax 951-1497
Suntree ES 600/K-6
900 Jordan Blass Dr 32940 321-242-6480
Shari Tressler, prin. Fax 242-6485
University Park ES 700/PK-6
500 W University Blvd 32901 321-723-2566
Ana Diaz, prin. Fax 952-5971
Other Schools – See Cape Canaveral, Cocoa, Cocoa Beach, Indialantic, Indian Harbor Beach, Melbourne Beach, Merritt Island, Mims, Palm Bay, Rockledge, Satellite Beach, Titusville, Viera, West Melbourne

---

Ascension Catholic S 500/PK-8
2950 N Harbor City Blvd 32935 321-254-1595
Anita Brady, prin. Fax 259-0993
Community Christian S 100/K-12
1616 Ferndale Ave 32935 321-259-1590
Laurel Earls, prin. Fax 259-5301
Holy Trinity Episcopal Academy 300/PK-6
50 W Strawbridge Ave 32901 321-723-8323
Dr. Katherine Cobb, head sch Fax 723-2553
Our Lady of Lourdes S 200/PK-8
420 E Fee Ave 32901 321-723-3631
Donna Witherspoon, prin. Fax 723-7408
Shiloh Christian Academy 100/PK-12
155 E University Blvd 32901 321-956-1404
West Melbourne Christian Academy 100/K-12
3150 Milwaukee Ave 32904 321-725-3743

Melbourne Beach, Brevard, Pop. 3,072
Brevard County SD
Supt. — See Melbourne
Gemini ES 500/K-6
2100 Oak St 32951 321-727-3090
Jennifer Julian, prin. Fax 725-7481

Melrose, Putnam
Putnam County SD
Supt. — See Palatka
Melrose ES 400/PK-5
401 State Road 26 32666 352-475-2060
Leah Lundy, prin. Fax 475-1049

Merritt Island, Brevard, Pop. 33,904
Brevard County SD
Supt. — See Melbourne

Audubon ES 700/PK-6
1201 N Banana River Dr 32952 321-452-2085
Elia Lea, prin. Fax 454-1055
Carroll ES 600/K-6
1 Skyline Blvd 32953 321-452-1234
Jenifer Born, prin. Fax 454-1064
Jefferson MS 600/7-8
1275 S Courtenay Pkwy 32952 321-453-5154
Meara Trine, prin. Fax 459-2854
MILA ES 500/PK-6
288 W Merritt Ave 32953 321-454-1070
Kelli Dufresne, prin. Fax 454-1071
Stevenson S of the Arts 500/K-6
1450 Martin Blvd 32952 321-454-3550
Michael Corneau, prin. Fax 454-3553
Tropical ES 700/K-6
885 S Courtenay Pkwy 32952 321-454-1080
Kristin Sorokin, prin. Fax 454-1087

Ambassador Christian Academy 100/K-12
175 Cone Rd 32952 321-305-6931
Divine Mercy Catholic S 200/PK-8
1940 N Courtenay Pkwy 32953 321-452-0263
Julie Harris, prin. Fax 453-7573
Merritt Island Christian S 500/PK-12
140 Magnolia Ave 32952 321-453-2710
Dr. Nanci Dettra, supt. Fax 452-6580

Miami, Miami-Dade, Pop. 396,081
Miami-Dade County SD 338,900/PK-12
1450 NE 2nd Ave 33132 305-995-1000
Alberto Carvalho, supt. Fax 995-1488
www.dadeschools.net/
Ammons MS 1,200/6-8
17990 SW 142nd Ave 33177 305-971-0158
Maria Costa, prin. Fax 971-0179
Angelou ES 700/PK-5
1850 NW 32nd St 33142 305-636-3480
Adrena Williams, prin. Fax 636-3486
Arcola Lake ES 500/PK-5
1037 NW 81st St 33150 305-836-2820
Dr. Cynthia Hannah, prin. Fax 694-2340
Arvida MS 1,300/6-8
10900 SW 127th Ave 33186 305-385-7144
Nancy Aragon, prin. Fax 383-9472
Ashe/Doolin K-8 Academy 1,300/PK-8
6601 SW 152nd Ave 33193 305-386-6667
Lisset Vazquez-Rios, prin. Fax 385-6408
Ashe Primary Learning Center PK-K
16251 SW 72nd St 33193 305-380-1927
Fax 380-1930
Auburndale ES 900/PK-5
3255 SW 6th St 33135 305-445-3587
Ania Marti, prin. Fax 446-4709
Aventura Waterways K-8 Center 1,900/K-8
21101 NE 26th Ave 33180 305-933-5200
Luis Bello, prin. Fax 933-5201
Banyan ES 300/PK-5
3060 SW 85th Ave 33155 305-221-4011
Cheri Davis, prin. Fax 225-4602
Barreiro ES 800/K-5
5125 SW 162nd Ave 33185 305-229-4800
Maritza Correa, prin. Fax 229-4801
Beckford/Richmond ES 300/PK-5
16929 SW 104th Ave 33157 305-238-5194
Crystal Coffey, prin. Fax 238-0397
Beckham ES 800/PK-5
4702 SW 143rd Ct 33175 305-222-8161
Cecilia Sanchez, prin. Fax 222-4900
Bell MS 500/6-8
11800 NW 2nd St 33182 305-220-2075
Ingrid Soto, prin. Fax 229-0798
Bent Tree ES 500/K-5
4861 SW 140th Ave 33175 305-221-0461
Victoria Bourland, prin. Fax 551-2661
Biscayne Gardens ES 600/PK-5
560 NW 151st St 33169 305-681-5721
Deborah Riera, prin. Fax 685-8036
Blanton ES 600/PK-5
10327 NW 11th Ave 33150 305-696-9241
Pedro Cedeno, prin. Fax 693-5375
Blue Lakes ES 500/PK-6
9250 SW 52nd Ter 33165 305-271-7411
Aida Marrero, prin. Fax 279-5103
Boone/Highland Oaks ES 800/PK-5
20500 NE 24th Ave 33180 305-931-1770
Julio Fong, prin. Fax 936-5722
Bossard ES 1,300/K-5
15950 SW 144th St 33196 305-254-5200
Concepcion Santana, prin. Fax 254-5201
Broadmoor ES 400/PK-5
3401 NW 83rd St 33147 305-691-0861
Dr. Omar Riaz, prin. Fax 696-7908
Brownsville MS 500/6-8
4899 NW 24th Ave 33142 305-633-1481
Marcus Miller, prin. Fax 635-8702
Calusa ES 900/PK-5
9580 W Calusa Club Dr 33186 305-385-0589
Carmen Fuentes, prin. Fax 383-3829
Canosa MS 2,000/6-8
15735 SW 144th St 33196 305-252-5900
Elio Falcon, prin. Fax 252-5901
Caribbean K-8 Center 600/PK-8
11990 SW 200th St 33177 305-233-7131
Maria Calvet-Cuba, prin. Fax 238-7082
Chapman ES 500/PK-5
27190 SW 140th Ave, 305-245-1055
Carzell Morris, prin. Fax 245-1187
Chapman Partnership ECC North PK-PK
1550 N Miami Ave 33136 305-329-3057
Dr. Rita Mallett, admin. Fax 995-7650
Chiles MS 600/6-8
8190 NW 197th St 33015 305-816-9101
Nelson Izquierdo, prin. Fax 816-9248
Citrus Grove ES 800/PK-5
2121 NW 5th St 33125 305-642-4141
Sharon Johnson, prin. Fax 649-3789

Citrus Grove MS 900/6-8
2153 NW 3rd St 33125 305-642-5055
Dr. Cory Rodriguez, prin. Fax 642-9349
Coconut Grove ES 300/PK-5
3351 Matilda St 33133 305-445-7876
Julissa Pina, prin. Fax 443-6748
Colonial Drive ES 300/PK-5
10755 SW 160th St 33157 305-238-2392
Laura Tennant, prin. Fax 232-4674
Comstock ES 600/PK-5
2420 NW 18th Ave 33142 305-635-7341
Dorothy Mindingall, prin. Fax 636-1740
Coral Park ES 1,000/K-5
1225 SW 97th Ave 33174 305-221-5632
Aileen Vega, prin. Fax 227-5734
Coral Terrace ES 500/PK-5
6801 SW 24th St 33155 305-262-8300
Eva Ravelo, prin. Fax 267-1526
Coral Way K-8 Center 1,500/PK-8
1950 SW 13th Ave 33145 305-854-0515
Barbara Martin, prin. Fax 285-9632
Country Club MS 1,200/6-8
18305 NW 75th Pl 33015 305-820-8800
Cynthia Prado, prin. Fax 820-8801
Curry MS 1,100/6-8
15750 SW 47th St 33185 305-222-2775
Jean Baril, prin. Fax 229-1521
Cypress K-8 Center 300/PK-8
5400 SW 112th Ct 33165 305-271-1611
Eduardo Alonso, prin. Fax 279-3622
Dario MS 600/6-8
350 NW 97th Ave 33172 305-226-0179
Dr. Verona McCarthy, prin. Fax 559-0919
De Diego MS 600/6-8
3100 NW 5th Ave 33127 305-573-7229
Dr. April Williams, prin. Fax 573-6415
Devon Aire K-8 Center 1,500/PK-8
10501 SW 122nd Ave 33186 305-274-7100
Brian Hamilton, prin. Fax 270-1826
Douglas ES 1,000/PK-5
11901 SW 2nd St 33184 305-226-4356
Moraima Perez, prin. Fax 553-0001
Douglas Primary Learning Ctr PK-K
650 NW 132nd Ave 33182 305-222-4822
Fax 227-3602
Douglass ES 300/PK-5
314 NW 12th St 33136 305-371-4687
Yolanda Ellis, prin. Fax 350-7590
Drew K-8 Center 400/PK-8
1775 NW 60th St 33142 305-691-8021
Raymond Sands, prin. Fax 691-3960
Dunbar K-8 Center 400/PK-8
505 NW 20th St 33127 305-573-2344
Maria Dearmas, prin. Fax 573-8482
Earlington Heights ES 500/PK-5
4750 NW 22nd Ave 33142 305-635-7505
Jackson Nicolas, prin. Fax 634-4973
Edelman / Sabal Palm ES 600/K-5
17101 NE 7th Ave 33162 305-651-2411
Alicia Costa-Devito, prin. Fax 654-7219
Edison Park K-8 Center 500/PK-8
500 NW 67th St 33150 305-758-3658
Carla Patrick, prin. Fax 758-5732
Emerson ES 400/PK-5
8001 SW 36th St 33155 305-264-5757
Leonardo Mourino, prin. Fax 267-2476
Evans K-8 Center 500/PK-8
1895 NW 75th St 33147 305-691-4973
Bridgette Tate-Wyche, prin. Fax 691-4867
Eve ES 700/PK-5
16251 SW 99th St 33196 305-383-9392
Lidia Gonzalez, prin. Fax 380-1919
Everglades K-8 Center 1,200/PK-8
8375 SW 16th St 33155 305-264-4154
Ramon Garrigo, prin. Fax 261-8179
Fairchild ES 700/PK-5
5757 SW 45th St 33155 305-665-5483
Lucy Amengual, prin. Fax 669-5401
Fairlawn ES 700/PK-5
444 SW 60th Ave 33144 305-261-8880
Heather Tyler, prin. Fax 267-9174
Fascell ES 500/PK-5
15625 SW 80th St 33193 305-380-1901
Margaret Ferrarone, prin. Fax 380-1912
Finlay ES 500/PK-5
851 SW 117th Ave 33184 305-552-7122
Marie Orth-Sanchez, prin. Fax 480-7652
Flagami ES 500/PK-5
920 SW 76th Ave 33144 305-261-2031
Maria Mason, prin. Fax 267-2980
Flagler ES 800/PK-5
5222 NW 1st St 33126 305-443-2529
Dr. Zulema Lamazares, prin. Fax 448-8508
Floyd ES 600/PK-5
12650 SW 109th Ave 33176 305-255-3934
Mayte Dovale, prin. Fax 234-0484
Glades MS 1,100/6-8
9451 SW 64th Ter 33173 305-271-3342
Cynthia Valdes-Garcia, prin. Fax 271-0402
Good ES 1,000/PK-5
6350 NW 188th Ter 33015 305-625-2008
Lizette O'Halloran, prin. Fax 628-0460
Gordon ES 1,100/PK-5
14600 Country Walk Dr 33186 305-234-4805
Maileen Ferrer, prin. Fax 234-4815
Goulds ES 600/PK-5
23555 SW 112th Ave, 305-257-4400
Alonza Pendergrass, prin. Fax 257-4401
Gratigny ES 700/PK-5
11905 N Miami Ave 33168 305-681-6685
Bisleixis Tejeiro, prin. Fax 687-3321
Greenglade ES 500/PK-5
3060 SW 127th Ave 33175 305-223-5330
Dr. Maria Tercilla, prin. Fax 222-8141
Hadley ES 1,000/PK-5
8400 NW 7th St 33126 305-261-3719
Maria Menchero, prin. Fax 267-2984

Hall ES 600/PK-5
1901 SW 134th Ave 33175 305-223-9823
Cathay Abreu, prin. Fax 220-9758
Hammocks MS 1,100/6-8
9889 Hammocks Blvd 33196 305-385-0896
Deborah Leal, prin. Fax 382-0861
Hartner ES 600/PK-5
401 NW 29th St 33127 305-573-8181
Dr. Derick McKoy, prin. Fax 571-2511
Hibiscus ES 500/K-5
18701 NW 1st Ave 33169 305-652-3018
Valerie Gilchrist, prin. Fax 654-5700
Highland Oaks MS 1,200/6-8
2375 NE 203rd St 33180 305-932-3810
Cheryl Kushi, prin. Fax 932-0676
Holmes ES 600/PK-5
1175 NW 67th St 33150 305-836-3421
Dr. Yvonne Perry, prin. Fax 696-4517
Hoover ES 800/PK-5
9050 Hammocks Blvd 33196 305-385-4382
Mercy Aguilar, prin. Fax 380-9609
Hoover Preschool PK-PK
15700 SW 96th St 33196 305-383-0915
Fax 385-2717
Hurston ES 800/PK-5
13137 SW 26th St 33175 305-222-8152
Isabel Valenzano, prin. Fax 222-4923
IPreparatory Academy 200/PK-12
1500 Biscayne Blvd 33132 305-995-1929
Alberto Carvalho, prin. Fax 523-8405
Ives K-8 Preparatory Academy 500/K-8
20770 NE 14th Ave 33179 305-651-3155
Deborah Johnson-Brinson, prin. Fax 770-3740
Jefferson MS 300/6-8
525 NW 147th St 33168 305-681-7481
Alexander Santoyo, prin. Fax 688-5912
Jones-Ayers MS 500/6-8
1331 NW 46th St 33142 305-634-9787
Bernard Edwards, prin. Fax 638-8254
Kendale ES 500/PK-5
10693 SW 93rd St 33176 305-274-2735
Aryam Alvarez-Garcia, prin. Fax 274-4792
Kendale Lakes ES 700/PK-5
8000 SW 142nd Ave 33183 305-385-2575
Martha Jaureguizar, prin. Fax 386-2718
Kensington Park ES 1,200/PK-5
711 NW 30th Ave 33125 305-649-2811
Susana Suarez, prin. Fax 642-9346
Kensington Park Primary Learning Center PK-K
1025 NW 30th Ave 33125 305-649-4301
Fax 649-2316
Kenwood K-8 Center 1,100/PK-8
9300 SW 79th Ave 33156 305-271-5061
Rodolfo Rodriguez, prin. Fax 273-2132
King Primary Learning Ctr PK-PK
7124 NW 12th Ave 33150 305-836-0928
Orna Duneus, prin. Fax 691-0638
Kinloch Park ES 800/PK-5
4275 NW 1st St 33126 305-445-1351
Kisa Humphrey, prin. Fax 567-3530
Kinloch Park MS 1,200/6-8
4340 NW 3rd St 33126 305-445-5467
Scott Weiner, prin. Fax 445-3110
Lakeview ES 400/PK-5
1290 NW 115th St 33167 305-757-1535
Sandra Banky, prin. Fax 754-0657
Leewood K-8 Center 800/PK-8
10343 SW 124th St 33176 305-233-7430
Bart Christie, prin. Fax 256-3104
Lehman ES 700/PK-5
10990 SW 113th Pl 33176 305-273-2140
Maria Cruz, prin. Fax 273-2228
Liberty City ES 400/PK-5
1855 NW 71st St 33147 305-691-8532
Adrian Rogers, prin. Fax 696-7842
Lorah Park ES 400/PK-5
5160 NW 31st Ave 33142 305-633-1424
Atunya Walker, prin. Fax 636-3075
L'Ouverture ES 500/PK-5
120 NE 59th St 33137 305-758-2600
Lilia Dobao, prin. Fax 751-6764
Mack/West Little River K-8 Center 500/PK-8
2450 NW 84th St 33147 305-691-6491
Dr. Kimula Oce, prin. Fax 693-1960
Madison MS 500/6-8
3400 NW 87th St 33147 305-836-2610
David Ladd, prin. Fax 696-5249
Mann MS 800/6-8
8950 NW 2nd Ave 33150 305-757-9537
Kevin Lawrence, prin. Fax 754-0724
Martin K-8 Center 1,100/PK-8
14250 Boggs Dr 33176 305-238-3688
Felicia Joseph, prin. Fax 232-4068
Matthews ES 500/PK-5
12345 SW 18th Ter 33175 305-222-8150
Alina Gonzalez, prin. Fax 222-8168
McCrary ES 600/PK-5
514 NW 77th St 33150 305-754-7531
Trellany Parrish-Gay, prin. Fax 756-8768
McMillan MS 900/6-8
13100 SW 59th St 33183 305-385-6877
Hilca Thomas, prin. Fax 387-9641
Meek/Westview K-8 Center 600/PK-8
2101 NW 127th St 33167 305-688-9641
Marchel Woods, prin. Fax 769-0166
Melrose ES 700/PK-5
3050 NW 35th St 33142 305-635-8676
Sergio Munoz, prin. Fax 635-4006
Merritt K-8 Center 700/PK-8
660 SW 3rd St 33130 305-326-0791
Carmen Garcia, prin. Fax 326-0749
Miami Heights ES 1,200/PK-5
17661 SW 117th Ave 33177 305-238-3602
Renita Lee, prin. Fax 233-0991
Miami Park ES 400/PK-5
2225 NW 103rd St 33147 305-691-6361
Dr. Philippe Napoleon, prin. Fax 694-8328

Miller ES 700/PK-5
840 NE 87th St 33138 305-756-3800
Donna Lewis, prin. Fax 756-3804
Morningside K-8 Academy 500/PK-8
6620 NE 5th Ave 33138 305-758-6741
Jordana Schneider, prin. Fax 751-2980
Moton ES 400/PK-5
18050 Homestead Ave 33157 305-235-3612
Eric Wright, prin. Fax 256-3128
Ojus ES 1,000/PK-5
18600 W Dixie Hwy 33180 305-931-4881
Dr. Marta Mejia, prin. Fax 933-8592
Olympia Heights ES 500/PK-5
9797 SW 40th St 33165 305-221-3821
Francisca Nobregas, prin. Fax 221-5195
Orchard Villa ES 400/PK-5
5720 NW 13th Ave 33142 305-754-0607
Tony Ullivarri, prin. Fax 754-0929
Paschal/Olinda ES 400/PK-5
5536 NW 21st Ave 33142 305-633-0308
Jennifer Savigne, prin. Fax 635-8919
Pepper ES 700/PK-5
14550 SW 96th St 33186 305-386-5244
Dr. Annette Diaz, prin. Fax 382-7150
Pharr ES 200/PK-5
2000 NW 46th St 33142 305-633-0429
Dr. Carol Sampson, prin. Fax 634-8487
Pine Lake ES 400/PK-5
16700 SW 109th Ave 33157 305-233-7018
Crystal Coffey, prin. Fax 233-4042
Pine Villa ES 400/PK-5
21799 SW 117th Ct 33170 305-258-5366
Elianeys Basulto, prin. Fax 258-5848
Poinciana Park ES 500/PK-5
6745 NW 23rd Ave 33147 305-691-5640
Tania Jones, prin. Fax 696-8624
Porter ES 800/PK-5
15851 SW 112th St 33196 305-382-0792
Raul Gutierrez, prin. Fax 383-2761
Reeves ES 800/K-5
2005 NW 111th St 33167 305-953-7243
Julian Gibbs, prin. Fax 953-7251
Richmond Heights MS 600/6-8
15015 SW 103rd Ave 33176 305-238-2316
Larhonda Donaldson, prin. Fax 251-3712
Riverside ES 1,200/PK-5
1190 SW 2nd St 33130 305-547-1520
Dr. Erica Paramore-Respress, prin. Fax 547-4102
Riviera MS 800/6-8
10301 SW 48th St 33165 305-226-4286
Jorge Rivas, prin. Fax 226-1025
Roberts K-8 Center 900/PK-8
14850 Cottonwood Cir 33185 305-220-8254
Milagro Arango, prin. Fax 226-8345
Rockway ES 400/PK-5
2790 SW 93rd Ct 33165 305-221-1192
Denise Vigoa, prin. Fax 223-5794
Rockway MS 1,000/6-8
9393 SW 29th Ter 33165 305-221-8212
Melanie Megias, prin. Fax 221-5940
Royal Green ES 600/PK-5
13047 SW 47th St 33175 305-221-4452
Alba Misas, prin. Fax 220-6238
Royal Palm ES 500/K-5
4200 SW 112th Ct 33165 305-221-7961
Marta Garcia, prin. Fax 222-8145
Santa Clara ES 600/PK-5
1051 NW 29th Ter 33127 305-635-1417
Stephen Papp, prin. Fax 637-1705
Seminole ES 600/PK-5
121 SW 78th Pl 33144 305-261-7071
Mayra DeLeon, prin. Fax 262-8740
Shadowlawn ES 300/PK-5
149 NW 49th St 33127 305-758-3673
Gwendolyn Haynes, prin. Fax 759-9352
Shenandoah ES 1,000/PK-5
1023 SW 21st Ave 33135 305-643-4433
Michelle Coto, prin. Fax 643-3745
Shenandoah MS 1,100/6-8
1950 SW 19th St 33145 305-856-8282
Bianca Calzadilla, prin. Fax 856-7049
Sibley K-8 Academy 900/PK-8
255 NW 115th St 33168 305-953-3737
Michael Charlot, prin. Fax 953-5447
Silver Bluff ES 600/PK-5
2609 SW 25th Ave 33133 305-856-5197
Mayra Barreira, prin. Fax 854-9671
Smith ES 400/PK-5
4700 NW 12th Ave 33127 305-635-0873
Shawntai Dalton, prin. Fax 637-1124
Snapper Creek ES 500/PK-5
10151 SW 64th St 33173 305-271-2111
Dr. Mirta Segredo, prin. Fax 596-2475
South Miami Heights ES 700/PK-5
12231 SW 190th Ter 33177 305-238-6610
Suzet Hernandez, prin. Fax 233-7632
Southside ES 900/PK-5
45 SW 13th St 33130 305-371-3311
Annette Degoti, prin. Fax 381-6237
Spanish Lake ES 1,700/K-5
7940 NW 194th St 33015 305-816-0300
Jacqueline Gonzalez, prin. Fax 816-0301
Stirrup ES 900/PK-5
330 NW 97th Ave 33172 305-226-7001
Dr. Maria Hernandez, prin. Fax 220-6737
Sunset Park ES 700/PK-5
10235 SW 84th St 33173 305-279-3222
Wendy Hernandez, prin. Fax 273-2130
Sweetwater ES 800/PK-5
10655 SW 4th St 33174 305-559-1101
Janet Olivera, prin. Fax 485-9396
Sylvania Heights ES 500/PK-5
5901 SW 16th St 33155 305-266-3511
Amor Reyes, prin. Fax 266-4435
Thomas MS 1,100/6-8
13001 SW 26th St 33175 305-995-3800
Wendy Barnett, prin. Fax 995-3537

Tropical ES 500/PK-5
4545 SW 104th Ave 33165 305-221-0284
Viviana Debs, prin. Fax 220-4902
Tucker ES 400/PK-5
3500 S Douglas Rd 33133 305-567-3533
Fredrelette Pickett, prin. Fax 529-0409
Village Green ES 400/PK-5
12265 SW 34th St 33175 305-226-0441
Henry Fernandez, prin. Fax 222-8140
Vineland K-8 Center 900/PK-8
8455 SW 119th St 33156 305-238-7931
Catherine Krtausch, prin. Fax 378-0776
West Miami MS 900/6-8
7525 SW 24th St 33155 305-261-8383
Katyna Lopez-Martin, prin. Fax 267-8204
Westview MS 400/6-8
1901 NW 127th St 33167 305-681-6647
Valtena Brown, prin. Fax 685-3192
Wheatley ES 300/PK-5
1801 NW 1st Pl 33136 305-573-2638
Cathy Williams, prin. Fax 573-2423
Winston Park K-8 Center 1,300/PK-8
13200 SW 79th St 33183 305-386-7622
Raquel Pelletier, prin. Fax 386-5684
Wyche ES 700/K-5
5241 NW 195th Dr 33055 305-628-5776
Dr. Barbara Johnson, prin. Fax 628-5775
Other Schools – See Bay Harbor Islands, Coral Gables, Cutler Bay, Doral, Florida City, Hialeah, Hialeah Gardens, Homestead, Key Biscayne, Miami Beach, Miami Gardens, Miami Lakes, Miami Shores, Miami Springs, North Bay Village, North Miami, North Miami Beach, Opa Locka, Palmetto Bay, Pinecrest, South Miami, Sunny Isles Beach

---

Academy for Young Learners 100/PK-5
18191 NW 68th Ave 33015 305-698-0202
Biltmore S 100/PK-8
1600 S Red Rd 33155 305-266-4666
Brito Miami Private S 300/PK-12
2732 SW 32nd Ave 33133 305-448-1463
Calusa Preparatory S 200/PK-12
12515 SW 72nd St 33183 305-596-3787
Cattoria Montessori S 100/PK-5
9385 SW 79th Ave 33156 305-274-6509
Center of Life Academy 100/2-12
4850 NW 17th Ave 33127 305-571-9191
Children's Rainbow Day S /Christian Acad 300/PK-8
22940 Old Dixie Hwy 33170 305-258-0194
Coconut Grove Montessori S 100/PK-3
2850 SW 27th Ave 33133 305-444-4484
Coral Park Christian Academy 200/PK-7
8755 SW 16th St 33165 305-559-9409
Jesus Perez, prin. Fax 559-0237
Cushman S 500/PK-8
592 NE 60th St 33137 305-757-1966
Arvi Balseiro, head sch Fax 757-1632
Cutler Ridge Christian Academy 100/PK-8
10301 Caribbean Blvd 33189 305-251-1534
Dade Christian S 900/PK-12
6601 NW 167th St 33015 305-822-7690
Douglas Flores, prin. Fax 826-4072
Epiphany S 1,000/PK-8
5557 SW 84th St 33143 305-667-5251
Sr. Margaret Fagan, prin. Fax 667-6828
Espinosa Academy 700/PK-8
12975 SW 6th St 33184 305-227-1149
Florida Christian S 1,400/PK-12
4200 SW 89th Ave 33165 305-226-8152
Dr. Robert Andrews, hdmstr. Fax 226-8166
Future Leaders Academy 100/PK-2
16237 SW 88th St 33196 305-380-7280
Gladeview Christian S 200/PK-8
12201 SW 26th St 33175 305-551-6143
Good Shepherd S 200/PK-8
14187 SW 72nd St 33183 305-385-7002
Clara Cabrera, prin. Fax 385-7026
Gordon Day S of Beth David Congregation 100/K-5
2625 SW 3rd Ave 33129 305-854-3282
Grace Christian Preparatory S 100/K-12
11000 SW 216th St 33170 305-259-1929
Greater Miami Adventist Academy 300/PK-12
500 NW 122nd Ave 33182 305-220-5955
Highpoint Academy 200/PK-8
12101 SW 34th St 33175 305-552-0202
Key Point Christian Academy 100/PK-8
609 Brickell Ave 33131 305-755-9258
Kids Learning Center of South Dade 200/PK-5
11500 Quail Roost Dr 33157 786-573-3017
Killian Oaks Academy 100/PK-12
10545 SW 97th Ave 33176 305-274-2221
Kings Christian S 100/PK-8
8951 SW 44th St 33165 305-221-2008
Debbie Hew, prin. Fax 223-3823
La Progressiva Presbyterian S 400/PK-12
2480 NW 7th St 33125 305-642-8600
Lincoln-Marti S 1,100/PK-12
931 SW 1st St 33130 305-324-4060
Lincoln-Marti S 400/PK-8
1001 SW 1st St 33130 305-324-7322
Lincoln-Marti S 300/PK-6
904 SW 23rd Ave 33135 305-643-6443
Marti S 100/PK-4
2660 SW 17th St 33145 305-856-9044
Marti S 100/4-8
1685 SW 32nd Ave 33145 305-441-0565
Edith Ysada, prin. Fax 443-9359
Mckinney Christian Academy 100/K-6
2300 NW 135th St 33167 786-318-3818
Miami Arts Montessori Academy 100/PK-6
1999 1st St SW 33135 305-814-5588
Miami Christian S 300/PK-12
200 NW 109th Ave 33172 305-221-7754
Dr. Lorena Morrison Ed.D., head sch Fax 221-7783
Miami Country Day S 1,000/PK-12
601 NE 107th St 33161 305-779-7200
Dr. John Davies, head sch Fax 397-0370

Mother of Christ S 200/PK-8
14141 SW 26th St 33175 786-497-6111
Rita Rodriguez, prin. Fax 497-6113
Mother of Our Redeemer S 200/PK-8
8445 NW 186th St 33015 305-829-3988
Ana Casariego, prin. Fax 829-3019
New Jerusalem Christian Academy 100/K-5
777 NW 85th St 33150 305-691-1291
Northwest Christian Academy 300/PK-12
951 NW 136th St 33168 305-685-8734
Jerry Nelson, admin. Fax 685-5341
Our Lady of Lourdes S 600/PK-8
14000 SW 112th St 33186 305-386-8446
Thomas Halfaker, prin. Fax 386-6694
Our Lady of the Rosary S 200/PK-5
10701 SW 95th St 33176 305-598-9123
Pentab Academy 200/PK-8
18415 NW 7th Ave 33169 305-405-0088
Perrine SDA S 50/PK-8
9750 W Datura St 33157 786-228-9549
Revelation S of Florida 500/PK-12
10658 SW 186th St 33157 305-969-9448
Rosemont Academy 100/K-8
9400 SW 87th Ave 33176 305-403-2344
St. Agatha S 500/PK-8
1125 SW 107th Ave 33174 305-222-8751
Patricia Hernandez, prin. Fax 222-1517
St. Brendan S 500/PK-8
8755 SW 32nd St 33165 305-221-2722
Maria Capote-Alonso, prin. Fax 554-6726
St. John Neumann S 300/PK-8
12115 SW 107th Ave 33176 305-255-7315
Maria Vilas, prin. Fax 255-7316
St. Kevin S 700/PK-8
4001 SW 127th Ave 33175 305-227-7571
Mayra Constantino Ed.D., prin. Fax 227-7574
St. Mary Cathedral S 400/PK-8
7485 NW 2nd Ave 33150 305-795-2000
Sr. Michelle Fernandez, prin. Fax 795-2013
St. Michael the Archangel S 400/PK-8
300 NW 28th Ave 33125 305-642-6732
Carmen Alfonso, prin. Fax 649-5867
St. Thomas the Apostle S 500/PK-8
7303 SW 64th St 33143 305-661-8591
Lisa Figueredo, prin. Fax 661-2181
St. Timothy S 600/PK-8
5400 SW 102nd Ave 33165 305-274-8229
Annie Seiglie, prin. Fax 598-7107
Sierra Norwood Calvary Child Dev Center 100/PK-3
19101 NW 5th Ave 33169 305-770-3733
Karen Smith-Williams, prin. Fax 652-7763
SS. Peter & Paul S 500/PK-8
1435 SW 12th Ave 33129 305-858-3722
Carlota Morales Ed.D., prin. Fax 856-4322
Sunflowers Academy 300/PK-8
2901 SW 7th St 33135 305-631-1284
Temple Beth Am Day S 400/PK-5
5950 N Kendall Dr 33156 305-665-6228
Town Center S 200/PK-6
10201 Hammocks Blvd Ste 149 33196 305-385-9981
Vann Academy 200/PK-5
400 NW 112th Ave 33172 305-223-3241
Village Pines S 100/PK-5
15000 SW 92nd Ave 33176 305-235-6621
Westwood Christian S 500/PK-12
5801 SW 120th Ave 33183 305-274-3380
Worshipers House of Prayer Academy 100/K-12
8350 NW 7th Ave 33150 305-200-3245

Miami Beach, Miami-Dade, Pop. 86,463
Miami-Dade County SD
Supt. — See Miami
Biscayne ES 700/PK-5
800 77th St 33141 305-868-7727
Karen Villalba-Belusic, prin. Fax 864-5543
Fienberg-Fisher K-8 Center 800/PK-8
1420 Washington Ave 33139 305-531-0419
Maria Costa, prin. Fax 534-3925
Nautilus MS 700/6-8
4301 N Michigan Ave 33140 305-532-3481
Rene Bellmas, prin. Fax 532-8906
North Beach ES 1,100/PK-5
4100 Prairie Ave 33140 305-531-7666
Dr. Alice Quarles, prin. Fax 674-8425
South Pointe ES 600/PK-5
1050 4th St 33139 305-531-5437
Melanie Fishman, prin. Fax 532-6096

Casa Dei Bambini Montessori S 100/PK-5
4025 Pine Tree Dr 33140 305-534-8911
Rachel Redington, dir. Fax 531-6667
Fisher Island Day S 100/PK-6
2 Fisher Island Dr 33109 305-531-2350
Michael Bell, head sch Fax 531-2349
Hebrew Academy (RASG) 500/PK-12
2400 Pine Tree Dr 33140 305-532-6421
Lehrman Community Day S 300/PK-5
727 77th St 33141 305-866-2771
Montessori Academy at St. John's 100/PK-5
4760 Pine Tree Dr 33140 305-534-8234
Cynthia Rodriguez, head sch Fax 534-8841
Papillon Montessori S 200/PK-8
1021 Biarritz Dr 33141 305-867-4244
Damarys Zarling, hdmstr.
St. Patrick S 200/PK-8
3700 Garden Ave 33140 305-534-4616
Bertha Moro, prin. Fax 538-5463
Yeshiva ES 300/PK-6
7902 Carlyle Ave 33141 305-867-3322

Miami Gardens, Miami-Dade, Pop. 105,806
Miami-Dade County SD
Supt. — See Miami
Andover MS 900/6-8
121 NE 207th St, 305-654-2727
Kenneth Williams, prin. Fax 654-2728
Brentwood ES 800/PK-5
3101 NW 191st St, 305-624-2657
Dr. Sharon Jackson, prin. Fax 625-4981

Bunche Park ES 300/PK-5
16001 Bunche Park School Dr, 305-621-1469
Yesenia Aponte, prin. Fax 628-1416
Carol City ES 600/PK-5
4375 NW 173rd Dr, 305-621-0509
Dr. Thalya Watkins, prin. Fax 620-5638
Carol City MS 500/6-8
3737 NW 188th St, 305-624-2652
Maria Medina, prin. Fax 623-2955
Crestview ES 500/PK-5
2201 NW 187th St, 305-624-1495
Maria Kerr, prin. Fax 628-3198
Golden Glades ES 300/PK-5
16520 NW 28th Ave, 305-624-9641
Jason Allen, prin. Fax 628-5760
Hawkins ES 400/PK-5
19010 NW 37th Ave, 305-624-2615
Rhonda Williams, prin. Fax 621-9839
Lake Stevens ES 300/PK-5
5101 NW 183rd St, 305-625-6536
Vanady Daniels, prin. Fax 624-0437
Lake Stevens MS 700/6-8
18484 NW 48th Pl, 305-620-1294
Jorge Bulnes, prin. Fax 620-1345
Miami Gardens ES 300/PK-5
4444 NW 195th St, 305-625-5321
Kathleen John-Louissaint, prin. Fax 628-5764
Myrtle Grove K-8 Center 500/PK-8
3125 NW 176th St, 305-624-8431
Dr. Apryle Kirnes, prin. Fax 624-3015
Norland ES 600/PK-5
19340 NW 8th Ct, 305-652-6074
Christina Ravelo, prin. Fax 651-4553
Norland MS 900/6-8
1235 NW 192nd Ter, 305-653-1210
Ronald Redmon, prin. Fax 654-1237
North County K-8 Center 500/PK-8
3250 NW 207th St, 305-624-9648
Melissa Mesa, prin. Fax 620-2372
North Dade MS 800/6-8
1840 NW 157th St, 305-624-8415
Kharim Armand, prin. Fax 628-2954
North Glade ES 400/PK-5
5000 NW 177th St, 305-624-3608
Ann Lewis, prin. Fax 621-3606
Norwood ES 500/PK-5
19810 NW 14th Ct, 305-653-0068
Dr. Kevin Williams, prin. Fax 654-5702
Parkview ES 400/PK-5
17631 NW 20th Ave, 305-625-1591
Dr. Crystal Spence, prin. Fax 621-5027
Parkway ES 400/PK-5
1320 NW 188th St, 305-653-0066
Maria Fernandez, prin. Fax 654-5701
Rainbow Park ES 400/PK-5
15355 NW 19th Ave, 305-688-4631
Robin Armstrong, prin. Fax 685-0693
Scott Lake ES 600/PK-5
1160 NW 175th St, 305-624-1443
Lakesha Wilson-Rochelle, prin. Fax 625-2567
Wilson/Skyway ES 400/PK-5
4555 NW 206th Ter, 305-621-5838
Dr. Linda Whye, prin. Fax 621-0919

Beacon Hill S 100/PK-8
18001 NW 22nd Ave, 305-621-3604
Kirlew Jr. Academy 100/K-8
18900 NW 32nd Ave, 305-474-4760

Miami Lakes, Miami-Dade, Pop. 29,182
Miami-Dade County SD
Supt. — See Miami
Graham Education Center 1,700/K-8
15901 NW 79th Ave 33016 305-557-3303
Yecenia Martinez, prin. Fax 826-5434
Graham Primary Learning Center PK-K
8875 NW 143rd St 33018 305-231-8778
Fax 231-9034
Miami Lakes K-8 Center 1,400/PK-8
14250 NW 67th Ave 33014 305-822-7757
Yanelys Canales, prin. Fax 557-6595
Miami Lakes MS 1,000/6-8
6425 Miami Lakeway N 33014 305-557-3900
Dr. Manuel Sanchez, prin. Fax 828-6753
Miami Lakes Primary Learning Center PK-PK
14250 NW 67th Ave 33014 305-822-7757
Fax 557-6595

Our Lady of the Lakes S 500/PK-8
6600 Miami Lakeway N 33014 305-362-5315
Ricardo Briz, prin. Fax 362-4573

Miami Shores, Miami-Dade, Pop. 10,271
Miami-Dade County SD
Supt. — See Miami
Miami Shores ES 800/PK-5
10351 NE 5th Ave 33138 305-758-5525
Brenda Swain, prin. Fax 756-3805

Miami Shores Montessori S 50/PK-1
577 NE 107th St 33161 305-756-7733
Sylvia Laurent M.Ed., dir. Fax 756-7721
Miami Shores Presbyterian Church S 100/PK-5
602 NE 96th St 33138 305-759-2548
Montessori Achievement Center 200/1-8
10832 NE 6th Ave 33161 305-893-5994
St. Rose of Lima S 500/PK-8
425 NE 105th St 33138 305-751-4257
Dr. Stephen Brown, prin. Fax 751-5034

Miami Springs, Miami-Dade, Pop. 13,739
Miami-Dade County SD
Supt. — See Miami
Miami Springs ES 500/PK-5
51 Park St 33166 305-888-4558
Naomi Simon, prin. Fax 882-0521
Miami Springs MS 1,500/6-8
150 S Royal Poinciana Blvd 33166 305-888-6457
Kimberly Emmanuel, prin. Fax 887-5281
Springview ES 500/PK-5
1122 Bluebird Ave 33166 305-885-6466
Catalina Flor, prin. Fax 883-8391

Blessed Trinity S 300/PK-8
4020 Curtiss Pkwy 33166 305-871-5766
Maria Perez, prin. Fax 876-1755
Miami Springs SDA S 100/PK-8
701 Curtiss Pkwy 33166 305-888-2244

Middleburg, Clay, Pop. 12,797
Clay County SD
Supt. — See Green Cove Springs
Coppergate ES 600/K-6
3460 Copper Colts Ct 32068 904-336-0675
Amy Dyal, prin. Fax 336-0677
Doctors Inlet ES 800/PK-6
2634 County Road 220 32068 904-336-0975
Thomas Gerds, prin. Fax 336-0977
Middleburg ES 600/K-6
3958 Main St 32068 904-336-1875
Becky Wilkerson, prin. Fax 336-1877
RideOut ES 500/PK-6
3065 Apalachicola Blvd 32068 904-336-2875
Kimberly Marks, prin. Fax 336-2877
Swimming Pen Creek ES 400/PK-6
1630 Woodpecker Ln 32068 904-336-3475
Rodney Ivey, prin. Fax 336-3601
Tynes ES 900/PK-6
1550 Tynes Blvd 32068 904-336-3850
Laura Fogarty, prin. Fax 336-3872
Wilkinson ES 700/PK-6
4965 County Road 218 32068 904-336-4075
Heather Teto, prin. Fax 336-4077
Wilkinson JHS 800/7-8
5025 County Road 218 32068 904-336-6175
Christina Cornwell, prin. Fax 336-6177

Annunciation S 400/PK-8
1610 Blanding Blvd 32068 904-282-0504
Victoria Farrington, prin. Fax 282-6808
Pinewood Christian Academy 200/PK-7
198 Knight Boxx Rd 32068 904-272-6408
Jason Borko, head sch Fax 644-0566

Milton, Santa Rosa, Pop. 8,470
Santa Rosa County SD 25,600/PK-12
5086 Canal St 32570 850-983-5000
Tim Wyrosdick, supt. Fax 983-5013
www.santarosa.k12.fl.us
Avalon MS 800/6-8
5445 King Arthurs Way 32583 850-983-5540
David Sigurnjak, prin. Fax 983-5545
Bagdad ES 400/K-5
4512 Forsyth St 32583 850-983-5680
Daniel Baxley, prin. Fax 983-5687
Berryhill ES 800/K-5
4900 Berryhill Rd 32570 850-983-5690
Roger Golden, prin. Fax 983-5694
Central S 500/K-12
6180 Central School Rd 32570 850-983-5640
Sean Twitty, prin. Fax 983-5645
East Milton ES 700/K-5
5156 Ward Basin Rd 32583 850-983-5620
Terry Paschall, prin. Fax 983-5625
Hobbs MS 700/6-8
5317 Glover Ln 32570 850-983-5630
Wesley Underwood, prin. Fax 983-5635
Jackson Preschool 200/PK-PK
4950 Susan St 32570 850-983-5720
Dawn Alt, dir. Fax 983-5722
King MS 600/6-8
5928 Stewart St 32570 850-983-5660
Darren Brock, prin. Fax 983-5665
Rhodes ES 800/K-5
5563 Byrom St 32570 850-983-5670
Michele Barlow, prin. Fax 983-5672
Russell ES 800/K-5
3740 Excalibur Way 32583 850-983-7000
Suzi Godwin, prin. Fax 983-7007
Other Schools – See Gulf Breeze, Jay, Navarre, Pace

Santa Rosa Christian S 300/PK-12
6331 Chestnut St 32570 850-623-4671
West Florida Baptist Academy 200/K-12
5621 Highway 90 32583 850-623-9307

Mims, Brevard, Pop. 6,938
Brevard County SD
Supt. — See Melbourne
Mims ES 600/PK-6
2582 US Highway 1 32754 321-264-3020
Sheryl Haskins, prin. Fax 264-3026
Pinewood ES 400/PK-6
3757 Old Dixie Hwy 32754 321-269-4530
Mitzi Robinson, prin. Fax 264-3030

Minneola, Lake, Pop. 9,082
Lake County SD
Supt. — See Tavares
Grassy Lake ES 1,000/K-5
1100 Fosgate Rd, 352-242-0313
Julie Williams, prin. Fax 242-1504

Miramar, Broward, Pop. 118,644
Broward County SD
Supt. — See Fort Lauderdale
Coconut Palm ES 900/K-5
13601 Monarch Lakes Blvd 33027 754-323-5050
Teresa Thelmas, prin. Fax 323-5090
Coral Cove ES 800/K-5
5100 SW 148th Ave 33027 754-323-7950
Stephanie Saban, prin. Fax 323-7990
Dolphin Bay ES 700/K-5
16450 Miramar Pkwy 33027 754-323-8000
Sandra Nelson, prin. Fax 323-8040
Fairway ES 700/K-5
7850 Fairway Blvd 33023 754-323-5650
Michelle Engram, prin. Fax 323-5690
Glades MS 1,500/6-8
16700 SW 48th Ct 33027 754-323-4600
Ricardo Reyes, prin. Fax 323-4685
Miramar ES 800/K-5
6831 SW 26th St 33023 754-323-6550
Joanne Schlissel, prin. Fax 323-6590
New Renaissance MS 1,100/6-8
10701 Miramar Blvd 33025 754-323-3500
Janet Morales, prin. Fax 323-3585
Perry ES 800/PK-8
6850 SW 34th St 33023 754-323-7050
Thomas Correll, prin. Fax 323-7090
Sea Castle ES 800/K-5
9600 Miramar Blvd 33025 754-323-7250
Riquelme Rodriguez, prin. Fax 323-7290
Silver Lakes ES 500/K-5
2300 SW 173rd Ave 33029 754-323-7400
Tammy Gilbert, prin. Fax 323-7440
Silver Shores ES 500/K-5
1701 SW 160th Ave 33027 754-323-7550
Jonathan Leff, prin. Fax 323-7590
Sunset Lakes ES 800/K-5
18400 SW 25th St 33029 754-323-7650
Marc Charpentier, prin. Fax 323-7690
Sunshine ES 700/PK-5
7737 Lasalle Blvd 33023 754-323-7700
Donna Aaron, prin. Fax 323-7740

St. Bartholomew S 200/PK-8
8001 Miramar Pkwy 33025 954-431-5253
Christine Gonzalez, prin. Fax 431-3385

Miramar Beach, Walton, Pop. 6,050

Gateway Academy 100/PK-8
122 Poinciana Blvd 32550 850-654-9095
Sondra Dutram, prin. Fax 654-1888

Molino, Escambia, Pop. 1,260
Escambia County SD
Supt. — See Pensacola
Molino Park ES 400/PK-5
899 Highway 97 32577 850-587-5265
Lisa Arnold, prin. Fax 587-2340

Monticello, Jefferson, Pop. 2,477
Jefferson County SD 900/PK-12
1490 W Washington St 32344 850-342-0100
Marianne Arbulu, supt. Fax 342-0108
www.jeffersonschooldistrict.org
Jefferson County ES 600/PK-5
960 Rocky Branch Rd 32344 850-342-0115
Elijah Key, prin. Fax 342-0123

Aucilla Christian Academy 300/PK-12
7803 Aucilla Rd 32344 850-997-3597

Montverde, Lake, Pop. 1,436

Montverde Academy 900/PK-12
17235 7th St 34756 407-469-2561
Dr. Kasey Kesselring, hdmstr. Fax 469-3711

Moore Haven, Glades, Pop. 1,667
Glades County SD 1,400/PK-12
PO Box 459 33471 863-946-0323
Scott Bass, supt. Fax 946-1529
www.gladesedu.org
Moore Haven ES 300/PK-5
PO Box 160 33471 863-946-0737
Jim Brickel, prin. Fax 946-1670
Other Schools – See LaBelle

Mount Dora, Lake, Pop. 12,205
Lake County SD
Supt. — See Tavares
Mount Dora MS 800/6-8
1405 Lincoln Ave 32757 352-383-6101
Jacob Stein, prin. Fax 383-4949
Triangle ES 700/PK-5
1707 Eudora Rd 32757 352-383-6176
Marlene Straughan, prin. Fax 383-6674

Gateway Christian S 100/PK-8
18440 US Highway 441 32757 352-383-9920
Montessori at Roseborough 200/PK-9
751 E 5th Ave 32757 352-735-2324
Mount Dora Christian Academy 600/PK-12
301 W 13th Ave 32757 352-383-2155
Dr. Brad Moser, head sch Fax 383-0098
Solid Rock Christian S 100/PK-12
21951 US Highway 441 32757 352-735-5777

Mulberry, Polk, Pop. 3,765
Polk County SD
Supt. — See Bartow
Kingsford ES 600/PK-5
1400 Dean St 33860 863-701-1054
Susanne Bizerra, prin. Fax 701-1059
Mulberry MS 1,000/6-8
500 Dr MLK Jr Ave 33860 863-701-1066
Cynthia Cangelose, prin. Fax 701-1068
Purcell ES 500/PK-5
305 NE 1st Ave 33860 863-701-1061
Beth Nave, prin. Fax 701-1064

Mulberry Christian Academy 50/PK-8
PO Box 1109 33860 863-425-1241

Myakka City, Manatee
Manatee County SD
Supt. — See Bradenton
Myakka City ES 200/PK-5
37205 Manatee Ave 34251 941-708-5515
Kathleen Price, prin. Fax 708-5517

Naples, Collier, Pop. 19,366
Collier County SD 43,800/PK-12
5775 Osceola Trl 34109 239-377-0001
Dr. Kamela Patton, supt. Fax 377-0181
www.collierschools.com
Avalon ES 500/PK-5
3300 Thomasson Dr 34112 239-377-6200
Jessica Campbell, prin. Fax 377-6201
Big Cypress ES 900/K-5
3250 Golden Gate Blvd W 34120 239-377-6300
Diana Little, prin. Fax 377-6387
Calusa Park ES 900/K-5
4600 Santa Barbara Blvd 34104 239-377-6400
Lynda Walcott, prin. Fax 377-6401
Corkscrew ES 700/PK-5
1065 County Road 858 34120 239-377-6500
Rebecca Merhar, prin. Fax 377-6501
Corkscrew MS 700/6-8
1165 County Road 858 34120 239-377-3400
Ronna Smith, prin. Fax 377-3401
Cypress Palm MS 800/6-8
4255 18th Ave NE 34120 239-377-5200
John Kasten, prin. Fax 377-5201
Davis ES 800/K-5
3215 Magnolia Pond Dr 34116 239-377-9000
Melanie Fike, prin. Fax 377-9001
East Naples MS 1,100/6-8
4100 Estey Ave 34104 239-377-3600
Kevin Huelsman, prin. Fax 377-3601
Estates ES 600/PK-5
5945 Everglades Blvd N 34120 239-377-6600
Jill Rexford, prin. Fax 377-6601
Golden Gate IS 400/3-5
5055 20th Pl SW 34116 239-377-6900
Kelly Bergey, prin. Fax 377-6901
Golden Gate MS 1,000/6-8
2701 48th Ter SW 34116 239-377-3800
Dr. Mason Clark, prin. Fax 377-3801
Golden Gate PS 500/PK-2
4911 20th Pl SW 34116 239-377-6900
Kelly Bergey, prin. Fax 377-6901
Golden Terrace IS 300/4-5
2965 44th Ter SW 34116 239-377-7000
Terri Lonneman, prin. Fax 377-7001
Golden Terrace PS 700/PK-3
2711 44th Ter SW 34116 239-377-7000
Terri Lonneman, prin. Fax 377-7001
Gulfview MS 700/6-8
255 6th St S 34102 239-377-4000
Kristina Lee, prin. Fax 377-4001
Lake Park ES 500/K-5
1295 14th Ave N 34102 239-377-7200
Christopher Marker, prin. Fax 377-7201
Laurel Oak ES 800/K-5
7800 Immokalee Rd 34119 239-377-7400
Marilou Andrews, prin. Fax 377-7401
Lely ES 700/PK-5
8125 Lely Cultural Pkwy 34113 239-377-7500
Christa Crehan, prin. Fax 377-7501
Manatee ES 800/PK-5
1880 Manatee Rd 34114 239-377-7600
Laurie Mearsheimer, prin. Fax 377-7601
Manatee MS 900/6-8
1920 Manatee Rd 34114 239-377-4400
Pamela Vickaryous, prin. Fax 377-4401
Naples Park ES 600/PK-5
685 111th Ave N 34108 239-377-7700
Meredith Kirby, prin. Fax 377-7701
North Naples MS 900/6-8
16165 Learning Ln 34110 239-377-4600
Margaret Jackson, prin. Fax 377-4601
Oakridge MS 1,000/6-8
14975 Collier Blvd 34119 239-377-4800
Kimberly Lonergan, prin. Fax 377-4801
Osceola ES 700/K-5
5770 Osceola Trl 34109 239-377-7800
Dr. Brian Castellani, prin. Fax 377-7801
Palmetto ES 500/K-5
3000 10th Ave SE 34117 239-377-9100
Christen Krembs, prin. Fax 377-9101
Parkside ES 700/K-5
5322 Texas Ave 34113 239-377-8900
Tamie Stewart, prin. Fax 377-8901
Pelican Marsh ES 800/PK-5
9480 Airport Pulling Rd N 34109 239-377-7900
Dr. Susan Barcellino, prin. Fax 377-7901
Pine Ridge MS 1,000/6-8
1515 Pine Ridge Rd 34109 239-377-5000
Dr. Sean Kinsley, prin. Fax 377-5001
Poinciana ES 700/PK-5
2825 Airport Rd S 34105 239-377-8100
Jessica Davis, prin. Fax 377-8101
Sabal Palm ES 600/PK-5
4095 18th Ave NE 34120 239-377-8200
Angie Torrez, prin. Fax 377-8201
Sea Gate ES 800/K-5
650 Seagate Dr 34103 239-377-8300
Beverly Budzynski, prin. Fax 377-8301
Shadowlawn ES 600/K-5
2161 Shadowlawn Dr 34112 239-377-8400
Dr. Oliver Phipps, prin. Fax 377-8401
Veterans Memorial ES 800/K-5
15960 Veterans Memorial Blv 34110 239-377-8800
Dana Franklin, prin. Fax 377-8801
Vineyards ES 800/PK-5
6225 Arbor Blvd W 34119 239-377-8700
Georgetta Elgin, prin. Fax 377-8701
Other Schools – See Everglades City, Immokalee, Marco Island

Cedar Montessori S 100/K-6
10904 Winterview Dr 34119 239-597-7190
Community S of Naples 700/PK-12
13275 Livingston Rd 34109 239-597-7575
Dr. David Watson, head sch Fax 598-2973
First Baptist Academy 500/PK-12
3000 Orange Blossom Dr 34109 239-597-2233
Dr. Ray Casey, head sch Fax 597-4187
Naples Adventist Christian S 50/K-8
2629 Horseshoe Dr S 34104 239-777-6404
Naples Christian Academy 100/PK-8
3161 Santa Barbara Blvd 34116 239-455-1080
Dr. Phillip Tingle, hdmstr. Fax 455-5225
Nicaea Academy 200/PK-12
14785 Collier Blvd 34119 239-353-9099
Royal Palm Academy 200/PK-8
16100 Livingston Rd 34110 239-594-9888
Scott Baier, head sch Fax 594-9893
St. Ann Catholic S 300/PK-8
542 8th Ave S 34102 239-262-4110
Gina Groch, prin. Fax 262-3991
St. Elizabeth Seton Catholic S 300/PK-8
2730 53rd Ter SW 34116 239-455-2262
Maria Niebuhr, prin. Fax 455-0549
Seacrest Country Day S 500/PK-12
7100 Davis Blvd 34104 239-793-1986
Erin Duffy, head sch Fax 793-1460
Village S 500/PK-10
6000 Goodlette Rd N 34109 239-593-7686
Virginia Sauter, head sch Fax 593-6599

Navarre, Santa Rosa, Pop. 30,113
Santa Rosa County SD
Supt. — See Milton
Holley-Navarre IS 800/3-5
1936 Navarre School Rd 32566 850-936-6020
Beth Mosley, prin. Fax 936-6026
Holley-Navarre MS 800/6-8
1976 Williams Creek Dr 32566 850-936-6040
Joie DeStefano, prin. Fax 936-6049
Holley-Navarre PS 800/K-2
8019 Escola St 32566 850-936-6130
Barbara Scott, prin. Fax 936-6132
West Navarre IS 1,000/PK-PK, 3-
1970 Cotton Bay Ln 32566 850-936-6060
Shana Dorsey, prin. Fax 936-6067
West Navarre PS 800/K-2
1955 Lowe Rd 32566 850-936-6000
William Price, prin. Fax 963-6010

Neptune Beach, Duval, Pop. 6,907
Duval County SD
Supt. — See Jacksonville
Neptune Beach ES 900/PK-5
1515 Florida Blvd 32266 904-247-5954
Elizabeth Kavanagh, prin. Fax 247-5969

Beaches Chapel Christian S 300/PK-12
610 Florida Blvd 32266 904-241-4211

Newberry, Alachua, Pop. 4,851
Alachua County SD
Supt. — See Gainesville
Newberry ES 500/PK-4
25705 SW 15th Ave 32669 352-472-1100
Beth Pearlman, prin. Fax 472-1120
Oak View MS 600/6-8
1203 SW 250th St 32669 352-472-1102
Katherine Munn, prin. Fax 472-1131

New Port Richey, Pasco, Pop. 14,612
Pasco County SD
Supt. — See Land O Lakes
Anclote ES 600/PK-5
3610 Madison St 34652 727-774-3200
Barbara Kleinsorge, prin. Fax 774-3291
Bayonet Point MS 700/6-8
11125 Little Rd 34654 727-774-7400
Shelley Carrino, prin. Fax 774-7491
Calusa ES 600/K-5
7520 Orchid Lake Rd 34653 727-774-3700
Kara Merlin, prin. Fax 774-3791
Cotee River ES 600/K-5
7515 Plathe Rd 34653 727-774-3000
Sharon Slusher, prin. Fax 774-3091
Cypress ES 800/K-5
10055 Sweet Bay Ct 34654 727-774-4500
Tracy Graziaplene, prin. Fax 774-4591
Deer Park ES 500/K-5
8636 Trouble Creek Rd 34653 727-774-8900
Margie Polen, prin. Fax 774-8991
Gulf MS 800/6-8
6419 Louisiana Ave 34653 727-774-8000
Jason Joens, prin. Fax 774-8091
Locke ES 600/PK-5
4339 Evans Ave 34652 727-774-3100
Adam Wolin, prin. Fax 774-3191
Longleaf ES 600/K-5
3253 Town Ave 34655 727-774-0800
Jennifer Heptig, prin. Fax 774-0891
Marlowe ES 400/K-5
5642 Cecelia Dr 34652 727-774-8600
Hilda Martin, prin. Fax 774-8691
Moon Lake ES 700/PK-5
12019 Tree Breeze Dr 34654 727-774-4600
Elise Landahl, prin. Fax 774-4691
Odessa ES 700/K-5
12810 Interlaken Rd 34655 727-246-3700
Teresa Love, prin. Fax 246-3791
Richey ES 700/PK-5
6850 Adams St 34652 727-774-3500
Keri Allen, prin. Fax 774-3591
River Ridge MS 1,100/6-8
11646 Town Center Rd 34654 727-774-7000
Angela Murphy, prin. Fax 774-7291
Schrader ES 500/PK-5
11041 Little Rd 34654 727-774-5900
Lee-Anne Yerkey, prin. Fax 774-5991
Seven Springs ES 500/K-5
8025 Mitchell Ranch Rd 34655 727-774-9600
Todd Cluff, prin. Fax 774-9691
Seven Springs MS 1,400/6-8
2441 Little Rd 34655 727-774-6700
Cortney Gantt, prin. Fax 774-6791
Trinity ES 600/K-5
2209 Duck Slough Blvd 34655 727-774-9900
Aimee Mielke, prin. Fax 774-9991
Trinity Oaks ES 700/K-5
1827 Trinity Oaks Blvd 34655 727-774-0900
Allison Hoskins, prin. Fax 774-0991

Elfers Christian S 200/PK-12
5630 Olympia St 34652 727-845-0235
Esthers S 100/K-12
5418 Madison St 34653 727-312-3760
First Christian Academy 200/PK-7
6800 Trouble Creek Rd 34653 727-943-7411
Susan Kunsman, prin. Fax 497-7891
Genesis S - East Campus 200/PK-5
8100 Mitchell Ranch Rd 34655 727-372-9333
Millennium Academy 100/K-12
10005 Ridge Rd 34654 727-845-8150
Lori Ekblad, hdmstr. Fax 844-5424
New Port Richey SDA S 100/PK-12
4416 Thys Rd 34653 727-842-8919
Keith Nelson, prin. Fax 842-1517
St. Thomas Aquinas ECC 100/PK-PK
8320 Old County Road 54 34653 727-376-2330
Alicia Mumma, admin. Fax 376-7204

New Smyrna Beach, Volusia, Pop. 22,191
Volusia County SD
Supt. — See De Land
Chisholm ES 400/K-5
557 Ronnoc Ln 32168 386-424-2540
Craig Zablo, prin. Fax 424-2500
Coronado Beach ES 300/K-5
3550 Michigan Ave 32169 386-424-2525
Tracy Buckner, prin. Fax 426-7438
New Smyrna Beach MS 1,200/6-8
1200 S Myrtle Ave 32168 386-424-2550
Elizabeth Johnson, prin. Fax 424-2504
Read-Pattilo ES 400/K-5
400 6th St 32168 386-424-2600
Kelly Lewis, prin. Fax 426-7409

Sacred Heart S 200/PK-8
1003 Turnbull St 32168 386-428-4732
Leigh Svajko, prin. Fax 428-4087

Niceville, Okaloosa, Pop. 12,288
Okaloosa County SD
Supt. — See Fort Walton Beach
Bluewater ES 900/PK-5
4545 Range Rd 32578 850-833-4240
Dr. Amy Klugh, prin. Fax 833-4232
Edge ES 600/PK-5
300 Highway 85 N 32578 850-833-4138
Dr. Samantha Dawson, prin. Fax 833-3496
Plew ES 700/PK-5
220 Pine Ave 32578 850-833-4100
Carolyn McAllister, prin. Fax 833-4103
Ruckel MS 1,000/6-8
201 Partin Dr N 32578 850-833-4142
Paul Whiddon, prin. Fax 833-3291

Rocky Bayou Christian S 600/PK-12
2101 Partin Dr N 32578 850-729-7227
Dr. Michael Mosley, supt. Fax 729-2513
St. Paul Christian S 50/PK-3
1407 John Sims Pkwy E 32578 850-678-1298
Neicy Mott, prin. Fax 678-5712

Nocatee, DeSoto, Pop. 4,377
De Soto County SD
Supt. — See Arcadia
Nocatee ES 600/K-5
PO Box 188 34268 863-494-4511
Dan Dubbert, prin. Fax 494-3264

Nokomis, Sarasota, Pop. 3,148
Sarasota County SD
Supt. — See Sarasota
Laurel Nokomis S 1,000/K-8
1900 Laurel Rd E 34275 941-486-2171
Ray Wilson, prin. Fax 486-2013

North Bay Village, Miami-Dade, Pop. 6,999
Miami-Dade County SD
Supt. — See Miami
Treasure Island ES 700/PK-5
7540 E Treasure Dr, 305-865-3141
Dalia Villar, prin. Fax 864-1729

North Fort Myers, Lee, Pop. 39,050
Lee County SD
Supt. — See Fort Myers
Bayshore ES 600/PK-5
17050 Williams Rd 33917 239-543-3663
Benjamin Ausman, prin. Fax 543-4040
English ES 400/PK-5
120 Pine Island Rd 33903 239-995-2258
Joe Williams, prin. Fax 995-5681
Hancock Creek ES 800/PK-5
1601 Skyline Dr 33903 239-995-3600
Dr. Denise Phillips-Luster, prin. Fax 995-7674
Littleton ES 500/PK-5
700 Hutto Rd 33903 239-995-3800
Monica Broughton, prin. Fax 995-6551
North Fort Myers Academy for the Arts 1,000/PK-8
1856 Arts Way 33917 239-997-2131
Thomas Millins, prin. Fax 997-6762
Tropic Isles ES 900/PK-5
5145 Orange Grove Blvd 33903 239-995-4704
Alane Adams, prin. Fax 997-2422

Good Shepherd Lutheran S 200/PK-8
4770 Orange Grove Blvd 33903 239-995-7711
Lynn Hudnall, prin. Fax 995-0473
Temple Christian S 100/PK-12
18841 State Road 31 33917 239-543-3222

North Lauderdale, Broward, Pop. 39,771
Broward County SD
Supt. — See Fort Lauderdale

Broadview ES 1,000/PK-5
1800 SW 62nd Ave 33068 754-322-5500
Joshua Kisten, prin. Fax 322-5540
Morrow ES 500/PK-5
408 SW 76th Ter 33068 754-322-7150
Laurel Crowle, prin. Fax 322-7190
North Lauderdale ES 600/PK-8
7500 Kimberly Blvd 33068 754-322-7400
Nichele Williams, prin. Fax 322-7440
Pinewood ES 600/PK-5
1600 SW 83rd Ave 33068 754-322-7950
Kicia Johnson, prin. Fax 322-7990
Silver Lakes MS 800/6-8
7600 Tam Oshanter Blvd 33068 754-322-4600
Alison Trautmann, prin. Fax 322-4685

North Miami, Miami-Dade, Pop. 57,562
Miami-Dade County SD
Supt. — See Miami
Arch Creek ES 600/K-5
702 NE 137th St 33161 305-892-4000
Dr. Marie Bazile, prin. Fax 892-4001
Bryan ES 700/PK-5
1201 NE 125th St 33161 305-891-0602
Milagros Maytin, prin. Fax 895-4708
Franklin K-8 Center 600/PK-8
13100 NW 12th Ave 33168 305-681-3547
Dr. Fabrice Laguerre, prin. Fax 769-2845
Lawrence K-8 Center 1,700/K-8
15000 Bay Vista Blvd 33181 305-354-2600
Mary Parton, prin. Fax 354-2601
Lentin K-8 Center 1,000/PK-8
14312 NE 2nd Ct 33161 305-891-4011
Monefe Young, prin. Fax 895-0545
Natural Bridge ES 600/PK-5
1650 NE 141st St 33181 305-891-8649
Frank McBride, prin. Fax 899-9695
North Miami ES 600/PK-5
655 NE 145th St 33161 305-949-6156
Debra Dubin, prin. Fax 949-3153
North Miami MS 700/6-8
700 NE 137th St 33161 305-891-5611
Miriam Walker, prin. Fax 891-4057

Holy Cross Lutheran S 300/PK-8
650 NE 135th St 33161 305-893-0851
Sherri Mackey, prin. Fax 893-3044
Holy Family S 200/PK-8
14650 NE 12th Ave 33161 305-947-6535
Doreen Roberts, prin. Fax 947-1826
Miami Union Academy 300/PK-12
12600 NW 4th Ave 33168 305-953-9907
St. James S 400/PK-8
601 NW 131st St 33168 305-681-3822
Sr. Stephanie Flynn, prin. Fax 681-6435

North Miami Beach, Miami-Dade, Pop. 40,525
Miami-Dade County SD
Supt. — See Miami
Fulford ES 600/PK-5
16140 NE 18th Ave 33162 305-949-3425
Dr. Jean Gordon, prin. Fax 949-2243
Greynolds Park ES 800/PK-5
1536 NE 179th St 33162 305-949-2129
Jorge Mazon, prin. Fax 949-0899
Greynolds Park Primary Learning Center PK-K
1575 NE 177th St 33162 305-354-3208
Fax 354-3207
Kennedy MS 1,200/6-8
1075 NE 167th St 33162 305-947-1451
Bernard Osborn, prin. Fax 949-9046
Oak Grove ES 600/PK-5
15640 NE 8th Ave 33162 305-945-1511
Joyce Jones, prin. Fax 949-4090

Aventura Learning Center 100/PK-4
2221 NE 171st St 33160 305-940-0408
Eileen Otero B.S., prin. Fax 947-7343
Hochberg Preparatory S 100/K-5
20350 NE 26th Ave, Miami FL 33180 305-933-6936
Dayna Wald, head sch Fax 279-7811
Jacobson Sinai Academy 200/PK-8
18801 NE 22nd Ave, Miami FL 33180 305-932-9011
Klurman ES 400/PK-5
1051 N Miami Beach Blvd 33162 305-947-6000
Rohr MS 6-8
1051 N Miami Beach Blvd 33162 305-947-7779
St. Lawrence S 200/K-8
2200 NE 191st St, Miami FL 33180 305-932-4912
Dian Hyatt, prin. Fax 932-7898
Scheck Hillel Community S 900/PK-12
19000 NE 25th Ave, Miami FL 33180 305-931-2831
Dr. Ezra Levy, hdmstr. Fax 932-7463

North Palm Beach, Palm Beach, Pop. 11,885
Palm Beach County SD
Supt. — See West Palm Beach
Conservatory S 400/K-8
401 Anchorage Dr 33408 561-494-1800
Teresa Stoupas, prin. Fax 494-1850

Baldwin Prep S 100/K-12
200 Castlewood Dr 33408 561-844-7700
Benjamin S 1,300/PK-8
11000 Ellison Wilson Rd 33408 561-626-3747
Robert Goldberg, head sch Fax 626-8752
St. Clare Catholic S 400/PK-8
821 Prosperity Farms Rd 33408 561-622-7171
Rita Kissel, prin. Fax 627-4426

North Port, Sarasota, Pop. 56,337
Sarasota County SD
Supt. — See Sarasota
Atwater ES 700/K-5
4701 Huntsville Ave 34288 941-257-2317
Kirk Hutchinson, prin. Fax 257-2319
Cranberry ES 800/K-5
2775 Shalimar Ter 34286 941-480-3400
Linda Daniels, prin. Fax 480-3401
Glenallen ES 700/PK-5
7050 Glenallen Blvd 34287 941-426-9517
Rebecca Drum, prin. Fax 423-8131
Heron Creek MS 900/6-8
6501 W Price Blvd, 941-480-3371
Kristine Lawrence, prin. Fax 480-3398
Lamarque ES 900/K-5
3415 Lamarque Ave 34286 941-426-6371
Ryan Bruck, prin. Fax 426-6392
Toledo Blade ES 700/K-5
1201 Geranium Ave 34288 941-426-6100
Jennifer Dolciotto, prin. Fax 426-9340
Woodland MS 800/6-8
2700 Panacea Blvd 34289 941-240-8590
Dr. Cindy Hall, prin. Fax 240-8589

Oakland Park, Broward, Pop. 40,410
Broward County SD
Supt. — See Fort Lauderdale
Lloyd Estates ES 600/PK-5
750 NW 41st St 33309 754-322-6800
Shawn Allen, prin. Fax 322-6840
North Andrews Gardens ES 800/K-5
345 NE 56th St 33334 754-322-7300
Catrice Duhart, prin. Fax 322-7340
Oakland Park ES 600/PK-5
936 NE 33rd St 33334 754-322-7500
Michelle Garcia, prin. Fax 322-7540
Rickards MS 1,000/6-8
6000 NE 9th Ave 33334 754-322-4400
Washington Collado, prin. Fax 322-4485

Ocala, Marion, Pop. 55,278
Marion County SD 41,200/PK-12
PO Box 670 34478 352-671-7700
Heidi Maier Ed.D., supt. Fax 671-7581
www.marionschools.net
Bowen ES 800/K-5
4397 SW 95th St 34476 352-291-7900
Traci Crowford, prin. Fax 291-7901
College Park ES 800/PK-5
1330 SW 33rd Ave 34474 352-291-4040
Laura Burgess, prin. Fax 291-4042
Eighth Street ES 300/K-5
513 SE 8th St 34471 352-671-7125
Treasa Buck, prin. Fax 671-7126
Emerald Shores ES 700/PK-5
404 Emerald Rd 34472 352-671-4800
Stacy Houston, prin. Fax 671-4805
Evergreen ES 600/PK-5
4000 W Anthony Rd 34475 352-671-4925
Wayne Livingston, prin. Fax 671-4931
Fessenden ES 500/PK-5
4200 NW 89th Pl 34482 352-671-4935
Valda Niznik, prin. Fax 671-4936
Fort King MS 1,100/6-8
545 NE 17th Ave 34470 352-671-4725
Gary Smallridge, prin. Fax 671-4726
Greenway ES 700/PK-5
207 Midway Rd 34472 352-671-4845
Jamie North, prin. Fax 671-4853
Horizon Academy at Marion Oaks 800/5-8
365 Marion Oaks Dr 34473 352-671-6290
Don Maier, prin. Fax 671-6291
Howard MS 1,200/6-8
1655 NW 10th St 34475 352-671-7225
Robert Hensel, prin. Fax 671-7226
Jones ES 700/PK-5
1900 SW 5th St 34471 352-671-7260
Dawana Gary, prin. Fax 671-7266
Legacy ES 600/K-5
8496 Juniper Rd 34480 352-671-0800
Dawn Prestipino, prin. Fax 671-0801
Liberty MS 1,100/6-8
4773 SW 95th St 34476 352-291-7930
Melissa Forsyth, prin. Fax 291-7931
Madison Street Academy 400/K-5
401 NW Martin Luther King 34475 352-671-7250
Ryan Bennett, prin. Fax 671-7252
Maplewood ES 700/PK-5
4751 SE 24th St 34471 352-671-6820
Lamar Rembert, prin. Fax 671-6821
Marion Oaks ES 700/K-5
280 Marion Oaks Trl 34473 352-291-7975
Shay Guynn, prin. Fax 291-7976
Oakcrest ES 700/PK-5
1112 NE 28th St 34470 352-671-6350
Diane Leinenbach, prin. Fax 671-6357
Ocala Springs ES 600/K-5
5757 NE 40th Avenue Rd 34479 352-671-6360
Cassandra Boston, prin. Fax 671-6368
Osceola MS 900/6-8
526 SE Tuscawilla Ave 34471 352-671-7100
Melissa Kinard, prin. Fax 671-7101
Saddlewood ES 900/PK-5
3700 SW 43rd Ct 34474 352-291-4075
Heather Lipira, prin. Fax 291-4079
Shady Hill ES 600/PK-5
5959 S Magnolia Ave 34471 352-291-4085
Debra Riedl, prin. Fax 291-4087
South Ocala ES 700/PK-5
1430 SE 24th Rd 34471 352-671-4750
Stephanie Callaway, prin. Fax 671-4759
Sunrise ES 800/PK-5
375 Marion Oaks Crse 34473 352-671-6200
Dr. Anna Dewese, prin. Fax 671-6206
Ward-Highlands ES 800/PK-5
537 SE 36th Ave 34471 352-671-6810
Regina Dickey, prin. Fax 671-6813
Wyomina Park ES 700/PK-5
511 NE 12th Ave 34470 352-671-6370
Charlotte Biela, prin. Fax 671-6372
Other Schools – See Anthony, Belleview, Citra, Dunnellon, Fort Mc Coy, Reddick, Silver Springs, Summerfield, Weirsdale

---

Ambleside S of Ocala 100/PK-8
507 SE Broadway St 34470 352-694-1635
Blessed Trinity S 700/PK-8
5 SE 17th St 34471 352-622-5808
Jason Halstead, prin. Fax 622-1660
Cornerstone S 200/PK-8
2313 SE Lake Weir Ave 34471 352-351-8840
Ingrid Wasserfall, dir. Fax 351-4226
First Assembly Christian S 300/PK-12
1827 NE 14th St 34470 352-351-1913
Earlene Carte, prin. Fax 351-5170
Grace Christian S 200/PK-8
4410 SE 3rd Ave 34480 352-387-3090
Bethany McKee-Alexander, head sch Fax 629-7724
GraceWay Academy 100/PK-5
2255 SE 38th St 34480 352-629-4523
Meadowbrook Academy 300/K-12
4741 SW 20th St Bldg 1 34474 352-861-0700
Tina Stelogeannis, prin. Fax 861-0533
Montessori House of Ocala S 100/PK-5
9880 SW 84th Ct 34481 352-282-0195
Montessori Preparatory S of Ocala 200/PK-6
2967 N Silver Springs Blvd 34470 352-351-3140
Ocala Christian Academy 400/PK-12
1714 SE 36th Ave 34471 352-694-4178
Dr. Andy Bloom, pres. Fax 694-7192
Redeemer Christian S 200/PK-12
155 SW 87th Pl 34476 352-854-2999
St. John Lutheran S 400/PK-12
1915 SE Lake Weir Ave 34471 352-622-7275
Tim Schmidt, prin. Fax 433-2540
Shiloh SDA S 100/PK-8
500 SW 17th Ave 34471 352-629-6857
Victory Academy Ocala 100/PK-7
3401 SE Lake Weir Ave 34471 352-622-4410
Carey Jones, hdmstr. Fax 694-1003

Ocoee, Orange, Pop. 34,484
Orange County SD
Supt. — See Orlando
Citrus ES 700/K-5
87 N Clarke Rd 34761 407-445-5475
Delaine Bender, prin. Fax 445-5499
Ocoee ES 800/PK-5
400 S Lakewood Ave 34761 407-877-5027
Dr. Ana Gonzalez, prin. Fax 877-8583
Ocoee MS 1,400/6-8
300 S Bluford Ave 34761 407-877-5035
Samuel Davis, prin. Fax 877-5045
Spring Lake ES 500/PK-5
1105 Sarah Lee Ln 34761 407-877-5047
Patty Harrelson, prin. Fax 877-5062
Thornebrooke ES 700/K-5
601 Thornebrooke Dr 34761 407-909-1301
Christopher Daniels, prin. Fax 909-1318
Westbrooke ES 700/PK-5
500 Tomyn Blvd 34761 407-656-6228
Michelle Couret, prin. Fax 656-6741

Victory Christian Academy 200/K-8
1601 A D Mims Rd 34761 407-656-1295

Odessa, Hillsborough, Pop. 7,133
Hillsborough County SD
Supt. — See Tampa
Hammond ES 700/K-5
8008 North Mobley Rd 33556 813-792-5120
Sheri Norkas, prin. Fax 792-5124
Walker MS 900/6-8
8282 North Mobley Rd 33556 813-631-4726
Anthony Jones, prin. Fax 631-4738

Odessa Christian S 200/K-12
19521 Michigan Ave 33556 813-792-1825
Erin Ciulla, head sch Fax 749-6690

Okeechobee, Okeechobee, Pop. 5,542
Okeechobee County SD 6,000/PK-12
700 SW 2nd Ave 34974 863-462-5000
Ken Kenworthy, supt. Fax 462-5151
www.okee.k12.fl.us
Central ES 500/K-5
610 SW 5th Ave 34974 863-462-5077
Joseph Stanley, prin. Fax 462-5082
Everglades ES 700/K-5
3725 SE 8th St 34974 863-462-5108
Leslie Lundy, prin. Fax 462-5113
North ES 600/K-5
3000 NW 10th Ter 34972 863-462-5100
Tuuli Robinson, prin. Fax 462-5107
Osceola MS 700/6-8
825 SW 28th St 34974 863-462-5070
Sean Downing, prin. Fax 462-5076
Seminole ES 600/K-5
2690 NW 42nd Ave 34972 863-462-5116
Dr. Thelma Jackson, prin. Fax 462-5119
South ES 400/K-5
2468 SW 7th Ave 34974 863-462-5087
Tracy Downing, prin. Fax 462-5094
Yearling MS 700/6-8
925 NW 23rd Ln 34972 863-462-5056
Jody Hays, prin. Fax 462-5062

Okeechobee Adventist Christian S 50/K-8
PO Box 2118 34973 863-763-0763
Okeechobee Christian Academy 100/PK-12
701 S Parrott Ave 34974 863-763-3072
Melissa King, prin. Fax 213-1339
Rock Solid Christian Academy 200/PK-6
401 SW 4th St 34974 863-763-0164
Latishia Alderman, dir. Fax 763-0968

Oldsmar, Pinellas, Pop. 13,296
Pinellas County SD
Supt. — See Largo
Forest Lakes ES 600/PK-5
301 Pine Ave N 34677 813-891-0785
Karen Aspen, prin. Fax 891-9178
Oldsmar ES 500/K-5
302 Dartmouth Ave W 34677 813-855-7316
Jeffrey Moss, prin. Fax 855-5136

Oldsmar Christian S 200/PK-12
650 Burbank Rd 34677 813-855-5746
Br. Eddie Preston, prin. Fax 855-4476

Old Town, Dixie
Dixie County SD
Supt. — See Cross City
Old Town ES 500/PK-5
221 SE 136th Ave 32680 352-542-7818
Karen Tillis, prin. Fax 542-8797

Dixie County Learning Academy 100/K-12
1357 NE 82nd Ave 32680 352-542-3306
Dr. Sylvia Lamenta, prin. Fax 542-7291

Opa Locka, Miami-Dade, Pop. 15,115
Miami-Dade County SD
Supt. — See Miami
Ingram ES 400/PK-5
600 Ahmad St 33054 305-688-4605
Dr. Cynthia Clay, prin. Fax 688-3971
North Dade Center for Modern Language 400/K-5
1840 NW 157th St 33054 305-625-3885
Dr. Maria Castaigne, prin. Fax 625-6069
Young ES 400/PK-5
14120 NW 24th Ave 33054 305-685-7204
Dr. Tonya Dillard, prin. Fax 688-6465

Betesda Christian S 100/K-12
PO Box 540392 33054 305-685-8255
Miriam Armas, prin. Fax 685-5338
South Florida S of Excellence 100/K-12
3400 NW 135th St 33054 754-204-3738

Orange City, Volusia, Pop. 10,438
Volusia County SD
Supt. — See De Land
Manatee Cove ES 700/PK-5
734 W Ohio Ave 32763 386-968-0004
Michelle Sojka, prin. Fax 968-0017
Orange City ES 600/K-5
555 E University Ave 32763 386-575-4215
Charles Bynum, prin. Fax 775-5227
River Springs MS 1,400/6-8
900 W Ohio Ave 32763 386-968-0011
Stacy Gotlib, prin. Fax 456-5355

Sunshine State S of Leadership 100/PK-12
2700 Enterprise Rd 32763 386-218-3906

Orange Park, Clay, Pop. 8,196
Clay County SD
Supt. — See Green Cove Springs
Argyle ES 600/K-6
2625 Spencer Plantation Blv 32073 904-336-0375
Angela Ward, prin. Fax 336-0327
Cherry ES 600/K-6
420 Edson Dr 32073 904-336-3975
Angela Whiddon, prin. Fax 336-3977
Fleming Island ES 800/PK-6
4425 Lakeshore Dr 32003 904-336-1075
Jennifer Collins, prin. Fax 336-1077
Grove Park ES 500/PK-6
1643 Miller St 32073 904-336-1275
Scott Voytko, prin. Fax 336-1277
Jennings ES 500/PK-6
215 Corona Dr 32073 904-336-3185
Elise Love, prin. Fax 336-3182
Lakeside ES 800/K-6
2752 Moody Ave 32073 904-336-1675
Jeffrey Schriver, prin. Fax 336-1677
Lakeside JHS 800/7-8
2750 Moody Ave 32073 904-336-5575
Mallory McConnell, prin. Fax 336-5577
Montclair ES 500/K-6
2398 Moody Ave 32073 904-336-1975
Bill Miller, prin. Fax 336-1977
Oakleaf JHS 900/6-8
4085 Plantation Oaks Blvd 32065 904-336-5775
Kristin Rousseau, prin. Fax 336-5777
Oakleaf Village ES 1,000/PK-5
410 Oakleaf Village Pkwy 32065 904-336-2425
Tracey Kendrick, prin. Fax 336-2477
Orange Park ES 500/K-6
1401 Plainfield Ave 32073 904-336-2275
Carole McCullough, prin. Fax 336-2277
Orange Park JHS 700/7-8
1500 Gano Ave 32073 904-336-5975
Al DeJesus, prin. Fax 336-5977
Paterson ES 900/K-6
5400 Pine Ave 32003 904-336-2575
John O'Brian, prin. Fax 336-2576
Plantation Oaks ES 1,000/K-5
4150 Plantation Oaks Blvd 32065 904-336-2775
Jennifer Roach, prin. Fax 336-2777
Ridgeview ES 600/K-6
421 Jefferson Ave 32065 904-336-3075
Tracy McLaughlin, prin. Fax 336-3077
Thunderbolt ES 1,000/PK-6
2020 Thunderbolt Rd 32003 904-336-3675
Lacy Healy, prin. Fax 336-3677

Grace Episcopal Day S 200/PK-8
156 Kingsley Ave 32073 904-269-3718
Stephanie Massey, head sch Fax 269-9183
St. Johns Country Day S 600/PK-12
3100 Doctors Lake Dr 32073 904-264-9572
Todd Zehner, hdmstr. Fax 264-0375

Orlando, Orange, Pop. 231,839
Orange County SD 183,800/PK-12
445 W Amelia St 32801 407-317-3200
Dr. Barbara Jenkins, supt. Fax 317-3401
www.ocps.net
Andover ES 800/PK-5
3100 Sanctuary Point Blvd 32825 407-658-6800
Angela Clayton, prin. Fax 658-6801
Arbor Ridge S 700/K-8
2900 Logandale Dr 32817 407-672-3110
Vanessa Demars, prin. Fax 672-1310
Audubon Park ES 1,200/PK-5
1750 Common Way Rd 32814 407-897-6400
Anna Ferratusco, prin. Fax 897-2415
Avalon ES 900/K-5
13500 Tanja King Blvd 32828 407-207-3825
Jeffrey Aldridge, prin. Fax 207-3828
Avalon MS 1,600/6-8
13914 Mailer Blvd 32828 407-207-7839
Karen Furno, prin. Fax 207-7872
Azalea Park ES 600/PK-5
1 Carol Ave 32807 407-249-6280
Sheila Burke, prin. Fax 249-4419
Bay Meadows ES 600/PK-5
9150 S Apopka Vineland Rd 32836 407-876-7500
Krista Bixler, prin. Fax 876-7509
Blankner S 1,000/K-8
2500 S Mills Ave 32806 407-245-1720
Dr. Junella Kreil, prin. Fax 245-1725
Bonneville ES 500/PK-5
14700 Sussex Dr 32826 407-249-6290
Kimrey Sheehan, prin. Fax 249-4661
Camelot ES 600/K-5
14501 Waterford Chase Pkwy 32828 407-207-3875
Dr. Yvette Irizarry, prin. Fax 207-3881
Carver MS 700/6-8
4500 Columbia St 32811 407-296-5110
Alisa Dorsett, prin. Fax 296-6407
Castle Creek ES 800/PK-5
1245 Avalon Park North Blvd 32828 407-207-7428
Monica Johnson, prin. Fax 207-7723
Catalina ES 700/PK-5
2448 29th St 32805 407-245-1735
Seth Daub, prin. Fax 245-2744
Chain of Lakes MS 1,300/6-8
8700 Conroy Windermere Rd 32835 407-909-5400
Cheron Anderson, prin. Fax 909-5410
Cheney ES 500/PK-5
2000 N Forsyth Rd 32807 407-672-3120
Tracey Gibson, prin. Fax 672-3126
Chickasaw ES 700/PK-5
6900 Autumnvale Dr 32822 407-249-6300
Janet Medina-Maestre, prin. Fax 249-4407
Chiles ES 700/K-5
11001 Bloomfield Dr 32825 407-737-1470
Dennis Gonzalez, prin. Fax 737-1471
College Park MS 1,000/6-8
1201 Maury Rd 32804 407-245-1800
Cynthia Haupt, prin. Fax 245-1809
Columbia ES 1,100/PK-5
18501 Cypress Lake Glen 32820 407-568-2921
Matthew Pritts, prin. Fax 568-7330
Conway ES 600/PK-5
4100 Lake Margaret Dr 32812 407-249-6310
Sean Maguire, prin. Fax 249-6319
Conway MS 1,000/6-8
4600 Anderson Rd 32812 407-249-6420
Margaret Nampon, prin. Fax 249-6429
Corner Lake MS 1,300/6-8
1700 Chuluota Rd 32820 407-568-0510
Luis Tousent, prin. Fax 568-0920
Cypress Park ES 300/PK-5
9601 11th Ave 32824 407-858-3100
Gloria McGarvey, prin. Fax 858-4633
Cypress Springs ES 700/K-5
10401 Cypress Springs Pkwy 32825 407-249-6950
Dr. Ruthie Haniff, prin. Fax 249-4537
Deerwood ES 500/PK-5
1356 S Econlockhatchee Trl 32825 407-249-6320
Anthony Serianni, prin. Fax 249-4422
Discovery MS 1,000/6-8
601 Woodbury Rd 32828 407-384-1555
Dr. Gloria Fernandez, prin. Fax 384-1580
Dover Shores ES 600/PK-5
1200 Gaston Foster Rd 32812 407-249-6330
Randall Hart, prin. Fax 249-4401
Eagle Creek ES PK-5
10025 Eagle Creek Sanctuary 32832 407-930-5592
Robert McCloe, prin. Fax 930-5599
Eagle's Nest ES 600/K-5
5353 Metrowest Blvd 32811 407-521-2795
Britt Despenza, prin. Fax 521-2797
East Lake ES 700/PK-5
3971 N Tanner Rd 32826 407-658-6825
Sylvia Schaffer, prin. Fax 658-6830
Eccleston ES 700/PK-5
1500 Aaron Ave 32811 407-296-6400
Julie Helton, prin. Fax 521-3321
Endeavor ES 600/K-5
13501 Balcombe Rd 32837 407-251-2560
Amanda Ellis, prin. Fax 251-2561
Engelwood ES 500/PK-5
900 Engel Dr 32807 407-249-6340
Vidal Reyes, prin. Fax 249-6344
Forsyth Woods ES 700/K-5
6651 Curtis St 32807 407-207-7495
James Leslie, prin. Fax 250-6212
Frangus ES 600/PK-5
380 Killington Way 32835 407-296-6469
DeCheryl Britton, prin. Fax 521-3323
Freedom MS 1,000/6-8
2850 W Taft Vineland Rd 32837 407-858-6130
Cheri Godek, prin. Fax 858-6132
Glenridge MS 1,400/6-8
2900 Upper Park Rd 32814 407-623-1415
Trevor Honahan, prin. Fax 623-1427
Hiawassee ES 800/PK-5
6800 Hennepin Blvd 32818 407-296-6410
Sharon Jenkins, prin. Fax 521-3340
Hidden Oaks ES 500/PK-5
9051 Suburban Dr 32829 407-249-6350
Kenisha Holmes, prin. Fax 249-4406
Hillcrest ES 500/PK-5
1121 N Ferncreek Ave 32803 407-245-1770
Ruth Ortega, prin. Fax 245-1779
Howard MS 1,000/6-8
800 E Robinson St 32801 407-245-1780
Dan Huff, prin. Fax 245-1785
Hunters Creek ES 900/PK-5
4650 W Town Center Blvd 32837 407-858-4610
Fresia Urdaneta, prin. Fax 858-4611
Hunters Creek MS 1,100/6-8
13400 Town Loop Blvd 32837 407-858-4620
Amy McHale, prin. Fax 858-4621
Innovation MS 6-8
13950 Storey Park Blvd 32832 407-730-4670
Hector Maestre Ed.D., prin. Fax 207-7213
Ivey Lane ES 400/PK-5
209 Silverton St 32811 407-296-6420
Wendy Ivory, prin. Fax 521-3324
Jackson MS 1,400/6-8
6000 Stonewall Jackson Rd 32807 407-249-6430
Dr. Jhunu Mohapatra, prin. Fax 249-6438
Kaley-Lake Como ES 200/PK-5
1600 E Kaley Ave 32806 407-897-6420
Isolda Antonio Fisher, prin. Fax 897-2407
Lake Gem ES 900/K-5
4801 Bloodhound St 32818 407-532-7900
LaTonya Brown, prin. Fax 532-7911
Lake George ES 600/K-5
4101 Gatlin Ave 32812 407-737-1430
Jessica Abrew, prin. Fax 737-1440
Lake Nona MS 1,400/6-8
13700 Narcoossee Rd 32832 407-858-5522
Stephanie Jackson, prin. Fax 858-5530
Lake Silver ES 700/PK-5
2401 N Rio Grande Ave 32804 407-245-1850
Sara Bigalke, prin. Fax 245-1865
Lake Weston ES 600/PK-5
5500 Milan Dr 32810 407-296-6430
Charles Jackson, prin. Fax 521-3341
Lancaster ES 900/PK-5
6700 Sheryl Ann Dr 32809 407-858-3130
Lisa Suggs, prin. Fax 858-2202
Laureate Park ES K-5
7800 Laureate Blvd 32827 407-730-8730
Suzanne Workum, prin.
Legacy MS 900/6-8
11398 Lake Underhill Rd 32825 407-658-5330
Hilary Buckridge, prin. Fax 658-5334
Liberty MS 1,000/6-8
3405 S Chickasaw Trl 32829 407-249-6440
James Russo, prin. Fax 249-6449
Little River ES 500/PK-5
100 Caswell Dr 32825 407-249-6360
Wilma Baez, prin. Fax 249-4409
Lockhart ES 500/PK-5
7500 Edgewater Dr 32810 407-296-6440
Ella Shanks, prin. Fax 521-3342
Lockhart MS 800/6-8
3411 Dr Love Rd 32810 407-296-5120
Lisa James, prin. Fax 296-6549
McCoy ES 800/PK-5
5225 S Semoran Blvd 32822 407-249-6370
Elaine Martinez, prin. Fax 249-4423
Meadowbrook MS 1,100/6-8
6000 North Ln 32808 407-296-5130
Robin Brown, prin. Fax 296-5139
Meadow Woods ES 600/PK-5
500 Rhode Island Woods Cir 32824 407-858-3140
Aleli Santiago, prin. Fax 858-2200
Meadow Woods MS 1,100/6-8
1800 Rhode Island Woods Cir 32824 407-850-5180
Marisol Mendez, prin. Fax 850-5190
Memorial MS 800/6-8
2220 29th St 32805 407-245-1810
Tamara Baker-Drayton, prin. Fax 245-1820
Metrowest ES 1,500/PK-5
1801 Lake Vilma Dr 32835 407-296-6450
Christine Szymanski, prin. Fax 445-5432
Millennia ES 900/K-5
5301 Cypress Creek Dr 32811 407-355-5730
Anne Lynaugh, prin. Fax 355-5711
Millennia Gardens ES PK-5
3515 Gardens Ridge Way 32839 407-845-0665
Anne Lynaugh, prin. Fax 845-0674
Moss Park ES 1,300/K-5
9301 N Shore Golf Club Blvd 32832 407-249-4747
Stephanie Osmond, prin. Fax 249-4469
Northlake Park Community ES 900/PK-5
9055 Northlake Pkwy 32827 407-852-3500
Lee Parker, prin. Fax 850-5173
Oak Hill ES 500/PK-5
11 S Hiawassee Rd 32835 407-296-6470
Dr. June Jones, prin. Fax 521-3343
Oakshire ES 600/K-5
14501 Oakshire Blvd 32824 407-251-2500
Raquel Flores, prin. Fax 251-2514
OCPS Academic Center for Excellence PK-8
701 W Livingston St 32805 407-866-1280
Dr. Andrew Rollins, prin.
Odyssey MS 900/6-8
9290 Lee Vista Blvd 32829 407-207-3850
Ann Hembrook, prin. Fax 207-3871
Orange Center ES 200/PK-5
621 S Texas Ave 32805 407-296-6480
Margarete Talbert-Irving, prin. Fax 521-3344
Orlo Vista ES 600/PK-5
3 N Hastings St 32835 407-296-6490
Tamara Baker Drayton, prin. Fax 521-3315
Palmetto ES 1,100/PK-5
2015 Duskin Ave 32839 407-858-3150
Meredith Leftakis, prin. Fax 858-3159
Palm Lake ES 600/PK-5
8000 Pin Oak Dr 32819 407-354-2610
James Weis, prin. Fax 354-2618
Pershing ES 400/PK-5
905 Waltham Ave 32809 407-858-3160
Bernadette Jaster, prin. Fax 858-2226
Phillips ES 600/PK-5
6909 Dr Phillips Blvd 32819 407-354-2600
Tiffany Smid, prin. Fax 354-2606

Pinar ES 500/PK-5
3701 Anthony Ln 32822 407-249-6380
Joscelyn Harold-Gladden, prin. Fax 249-4424
Pine Castle ES 300/PK-5
905 Waltham Ave 32809 407-858-3170
Bernadette Jaster, prin. Fax 858-2227
Pine Hills ES 700/PK-5
1006 Ferndell Rd 32808 407-296-6500
Fredrick Brooks, prin. Fax 296-6436
Pineloch ES 800/PK-5
3101 Woods St 32805 407-245-1825
Stacey Price, prin. Fax 245-1830
Pinewood ES 600/K-5
3005 N Apopka Vineland Rd 32818 407-532-7930
Kandace Goshe, prin. Fax 532-7933
Prairie Lake ES 1,100/PK-5
8723 Hackney Prairie Rd 32818 407-884-2220
Dr. Robert Strenth, prin. Fax 884-6314
Princeton ES 500/PK-5
311 W Princeton St 32804 407-245-1840
Jason Fritz, prin. Fax 245-1849
Ray ES 500/PK-5
2000 Beecher St 32808 407-296-6460
Lindsey Smestad, prin. Fax 521-3327
Ridgewood Park ES 700/PK-5
3401 Pioneer Rd 32808 407-296-6510
Deborah Coffie, prin. Fax 521-3345
Riverdale ES 700/K-5
11301 Lokanotosa Trl 32817 407-737-1400
William Charlton, prin. Fax 737-1414
Riverside ES 600/PK-5
3125 Pembrook Dr 32810 407-296-6520
Kimberly Hankerson, prin. Fax 521-3346
Robinswood MS 1,300/6-8
6305 Balboa Dr 32818 407-296-5140
Nicole Jefferson, prin. Fax 296-5148
Rock Lake ES 300/PK-5
408 N Tampa Ave 32805 407-245-1880
Robin Broner, prin. Fax 245-1885
Rolling Hills ES 700/PK-5
4903 Donovan St 32808 407-296-6530
Margarete Talbert-Irving, prin. Fax 521-3347
Rosemont ES 900/PK-5
4650 Point Look Out Rd 32808 407-522-6050
Kelly Maldonado, prin. Fax 522-6064
Sadler ES 800/PK-5
4000 W Oak Ridge Rd 32809 407-354-2620
Kahlil Ortiz, prin. Fax 354-2665
Sand Lake ES 400/PK-5
8301 Buenavista Woods Blvd 32836 407-903-7400
Laura Suprenard, prin. Fax 903-7411
Shenandoah ES 600/PK-5
4827 Conway Rd 32812 407-858-3180
Pamela Crabb, prin. Fax 858-2208
Shingle Creek ES 1,200/PK-5
5620 Harcourt Ave 32839 407-354-2650
Jennifer DeGelleke, prin. Fax 354-2657
South Creek MS 1,000/6-8
3801 Wetherbee Rd 32824 407-251-2413
Sean Brown, prin. Fax 251-2464
Southwest MS 1,200/6-8
6450 Dr Phillips Blvd 32819 407-370-7200
Raymond Yockel, prin. Fax 370-7210
Southwood ES 600/PK-5
12600 Bisted Dr 32824 407-858-2230
Stacey Merritt, prin. Fax 858-4698
Stone Lakes ES 900/PK-5
15200 Stoneybrook Blvd 32828 407-207-7793
Bryan Dolfi, prin. Fax 207-7805
Sun Blaze ES 700/PK-5
9101 Randal Park Blvd 32832 407-207-5110
Tami Turner, prin. Fax 250-6228
Sunrise ES 500/PK-5
101 Lone Palm Rd 32828 407-384-1585
Denise Bainbridge, prin. Fax 384-1599
Tangelo Park ES 400/PK-5
5115 Anzio St 32819 407-354-2630
Christina Ray, prin. Fax 354-2663
Three Points ES 700/PK-5
4001 S Goldenrod Rd 32822 407-207-3800
Charles Lindlau, prin. Fax 207-3803
Timber Lakes ES 900/K-5
2149 Crown Hill Blvd 32828 407-249-6177
Arlene Carlock, prin. Fax 249-6172
Timber Springs MS 6-8
16001 Timber Park Ln 32828 321-413-2201
Dr. Eric Cantrell, prin. Fax 207-7789
Union Park ES 500/PK-5
1600 N Dean Rd 32825 407-249-6390
Amy Klaber, prin. Fax 249-4416
Union Park MS 900/6-8
1844 Westfall Dr 32817 407-249-6309
Melanie May, prin. Fax 249-4404
Ventura ES 800/PK-5
4400 Woodgate Blvd 32822 407-249-6400
Debra Vereen, prin. Fax 249-4417
Vista Lakes ES 800/PK-5
6050 Lake Champlain Dr 32829 407-207-4991
Tiffany Griffin, prin. Fax 207-7701
Walker MS 1,000/6-8
150 Amidon Ln 32809 407-858-3210
Rebecca Watson, prin. Fax 858-3218
Washington Shores ES 500/PK-5
944 W Lake Mann Dr 32805 407-296-6540
Nathaniel Stephens, prin. Fax 521-3348
Waterbridge ES 1,100/PK-5
11100 Galvin Dr 32837 407-858-3190
John Carcera, prin. Fax 858-2205
Waterford ES 600/PK-5
12950 Lake Underhill Rd 32828 407-249-6410
Kathy Petersen, prin. Fax 249-4425
Wedgefield School K-5
3835 Bancroft Blvd 32833 321-413-2989
Natalie Stevens, prin. Fax 413-2998
West Creek ES 700/K-5
5056 Tacon Dr 32837 407-858-5920
Sheri Sico, prin. Fax 858-5922
West Oaks ES 600/K-5
905 Dorscher Rd 32818 407-532-3875
Cherie Thompson, prin. Fax 532-3878
Westpointe ES K-5
7525 WestPointe Blvd 32835 407-866-1271
Patricia Smith, prin. Fax 866-1278
Westridge MS 1,200/6-8
3800 W Oak Ridge Rd 32809 407-354-2640
Christopher Camacho, prin. Fax 354-2637
Wetherbee ES 700/K-5
701 E Wetherbee Rd 32824 407-850-5130
Sandy Sauma, prin. Fax 850-5159
Windy Ridge S 1,100/K-8
3900 Beech Tree Dr 32835 407-296-5100
Tracy Webley, prin. Fax 296-5107
Winegard ES 700/PK-5
7055 Winegard Rd 32809 407-858-3200
Meigan Rivera, prin. Fax 858-2215
Wyndham Lakes ES 800/PK-5
14360 Wyndham Lakes Blvd 32824 407-251-2347
Margarita Zizza, prin. Fax 251-2376
Young ES 700/PK-5
12550 Marsfield Ave 32837 407-858-3120
Lino Rodriguez, prin. Fax 858-2224
Other Schools – See Apopka, Maitland, Ocoee, Windermere, Winter Garden, Winter Park, Zellwood

---

Agape Christian Academy 400/PK-12
2425 N Hiawassee Rd 32818 407-298-1111
Alpha Learning Academy 100/K-5
1960 Bruton Blvd 32805 407-447-2897
Avalon S 100/K-12
5002 Andrus Ave 32804 407-297-4353
Azalea Park Baptist S 100/PK-11
5725 Dahlia Dr 32807 407-277-4056
Baldwin Oaks Academy 100/PK-K
1862 E Winter Park Rd 32803 407-647-0119
Nieves Lyman, admin. Fax 647-2590
Beryl Wisdom Adventist S 100/PK-8
4955 Rose Ave 32808 407-291-3073
Brenda Trim, prin. Fax 291-6149
Brush Arbor Christian S 200/PK-10
2304 N Goldenrod Rd 32807 407-678-2284
Central Florida Christian Academy 200/PK-12
700 Good Homes Rd 32818 407-850-2322
Pam Theobald, prin. Fax 293-6914
Christ S 400/K-8
106 E Church St 32801 407-849-1665
Aaron Farrant, head sch Fax 481-2325
Conrad Academy 200/K-12
2008 N Goldenrod Rd 32807 407-243-2211
Downey Christian S 300/K-12
10201 E Colonial Dr 32817 407-275-0340
Eastland Christian S 300/PK-12
9000 Lake Underhill Rd 32825 407-277-5858
Elite Preparatory Academy 200/PK-8
730 Sand Lake Rd 32809 407-855-5811
Faith Christian Academy 400/PK-12
9307 Curry Ford Rd 32825 407-275-8031
Family Christian Academy 100/K-10
15060 Old Cheney Hwy 32828 407-568-9837
First Academy 1,000/PK-12
2667 Bruton Blvd 32805 407-206-8600
Dr. Steve Whitaker Ph.D., head sch
Forest City Adventist S 100/K-8
7563 Forest City Rd 32810 407-299-0703
Generation of Hope Academy 100/PK-8
1131 N Goldenrod Rd 32807 407-382-6068
Glad Tidings Academy East Campus 100/PK-6
8550 Clarcona-Ocoee Rd 32818 407-292-9998
Good Shepherd S 600/PK-8
5902 Oleander Dr 32807 407-277-3973
Jayme Hartmann, prin. Fax 277-2605
Heritage Prep S 200/PK-12
6000 W Colonial Dr 32808 407-293-6000
Holy Family S 700/PK-8
5129 S Apopka Vineland Rd 32819 407-876-9344
Sr. Dorothy Sayers, prin. Fax 876-8775
Ibn Seena Academy 200/PK-8
12908 S Orange Blossom Trl 32837 407-888-1000
IEC Christian Academy 100/PK-12
2500 W Oak Ridge Rd 32809 407-581-6120
Ingrams Academy 100/PK-5
7856 Forest City Rd 32810 407-291-6556
Kingsway Christian Academy 400/PK-8
4161 N Powers Dr 32818 407-295-8901
Rev. Thomas Copeland, pres. Fax 295-9651
Lake Highland Preparatory S 2,000/PK-12
901 Highland Ave 32803 407-206-1900
Dr. David Rowe, pres.
Leaders Preparatory S 200/PK-12
1021 N Goldenrod Rd 32807 407-382-9900
Living Word Academy 100/PK-8
653 Wetherbee Rd 32824 407-851-9800
Montessori S of East Orlando 50/PK-8
2526 Percival Rd 32826 407-447-5860
Marcia Hurlbutt, dir. Fax 737-1087
Montessori S of Orlando 100/PK-8
1187 Florida Mall Ave 32809 407-601-4247
Marilou Esguerra, dir. Fax 601-4321
Montessori World S 200/PK-8
11659 Ruby Lake Rd 32836 407-239-6024
Mt. Sinai Jr Academy 100/K-10
2610 Orange Center Blvd 32805 407-298-7871
Muslim Academy of Greater Orlando 300/PK-8
11551 Ruby Lake Rd 32836 407-238-0144
One Accord Christian Academy 100/K-12
7301 Edgewater Dr 32810 407-523-3002
Orlando Christian Prep S 400/PK-12
500 S Semoran Blvd 32807 407-823-9744
Pamela Piorkowski M.Ed., admin. Fax 380-1186
Orlando Junior Academy 200/PK-8
30 E Evans St 32804 407-898-1251
Lauren Merklin, prin. Fax 894-6213
Orlando Torah Academy 100/PK-8
8561 Commodity Cir 32819 407-270-4936
Pathways Private S 200/PK-12
1877 W Oak Ridge Rd 32809 407-816-2040
Pine Castle Christian Academy 200/PK-12
7101 Lake Ellenor Dr 32809 407-313-7222
Brent DuCray, admin. Fax 313-7226
Potter's House Academy 100/PK-12
7051 Pershing Ave 32822 407-273-2683
Radiant Life Academy 100/PK-10
8151 Clarcona Ocoee Rd 32818 407-299-7460
Regency Christian Academy 100/PK-8
11513 S Orange Blossom Trl 32837 407-851-7270
Risen Savior Academy PK-2
1331 S Alafaya Trl 32828 407-207-8500
Fax 207-5115
St. Andrew S 300/PK-8
877 N Hastings St 32808 407-295-4230
Latrina Gipson, prin. Fax 290-0959
St. Charles Borromeo S 400/PK-8
4005 Edgewater Dr 32804 407-293-7691
Nathan Nadeau, prin. Fax 295-9839
St. James Cathedral S 500/PK-8
505 E Ridgewood St 32803 407-841-4432
Dawn Helwig, prin. Fax 648-4603
St. John Vianney S 600/PK-8
6200 S Orange Blossom Trl 32809 407-855-4660
Cathy Marshall, prin. Fax 857-7932
Saints Academy 100/K-12
PO Box 680487 32868 407-683-5537
South Orlando Christian Academy 200/PK-12
5815 Makoma Dr 32839 407-859-9511
Treasure of Knowledge Christian Academy 200/PK-12
13001 Landstar Blvd 32824 407-859-8755
Trinity Lutheran S 300/PK-8
123 E Livingston St 32801 407-488-1919
Dr. Kevin Brockberg, prin. Fax 488-1230
Victory Christian Academy 100/K-12
240 N Ivey Ln 32811 407-295-3332
West Oaks Academy 200/PK-12
8624 A D Mims Rd 32818 407-292-8481

Ormond Beach, Volusia, Pop. 37,607
Volusia County SD
Supt. — See De Land
Ormond Beach ES 300/K-5
100 Corbin Ave 32174 386-258-4666
Tucker Harris, prin. Fax 676-5321
Ormond Beach MS 1,100/6-8
151 Domicilio Ave 32174 386-258-4667
Matt Krajewski, prin. Fax 676-1258
Osceola ES 400/K-5
100 Osceola Ave 32176 386-258-4669
Kevin Flassig, prin. Fax 676-1233
Pathways ES 700/K-5
2100 Airport Rd 32174 386-258-4671
Greg Schwartz, prin. Fax 676-5363
Pine Trail ES 700/K-5
300 Airport Rd 32174 386-258-4672
Tami Fisher, prin. Fax 676-5308
Tomoka ES 700/K-5
999 Old Tomoka Rd 32174 386-258-4676
Susan Tuten, prin. Fax 676-1215

Calvary Christian Academy 400/PK-12
1687 W Granada Blvd 32174 386-672-2081
Riverbend Academy 300/PK-12
2080 W Granada Blvd 32174 386-615-0986
Jason Karr, hdmstr. Fax 672-7945
St. Brendan S 200/PK-8
1000 Ocean Shore Blvd 32176 386-441-1331
Philip Gorrasi, prin. Fax 441-0774
Temple Beth-El S 100/PK-5
579 N Nova Rd 32174 386-267-0952

Osprey, Sarasota, Pop. 6,031
Sarasota County SD
Supt. — See Sarasota
Pine View School 2,200/2-12
1 Python Path 34229 941-486-2001
Dr. Stephen Covert, prin. Fax 486-2042

Osteen, Volusia
Volusia County SD
Supt. — See De Land
Osteen ES 500/K-5
500 Doyle Rd 32764 386-575-4255
Jim Bambrick, prin. Fax 668-9501

Oviedo, Seminole, Pop. 32,607
Seminole County SD
Supt. — See Sanford
Carillon ES 900/PK-5
3200 Lockwood Blvd 32765 407-320-4650
Dr. Daniel Windish, prin. Fax 320-4699
Chiles MS 1,300/6-8
1240 Sanctuary Dr 32766 407-871-7050
Dr. John Antmann, prin. Fax 871-7099
Evans ES 900/PK-5
100 E Chapman Rd 32765 407-320-9850
CarolAnn Darnell, prin. Fax 320-9899
Jackson Heights MS 1,200/6-8
41 Academy Ave 32765 407-320-4550
Sarah Mansur, prin. Fax 320-4599
Lawton ES 800/PK-5
151 Graham Ave 32765 407-320-6350
Dr. Leslie Durias, prin. Fax 320-6399
Partin ES 800/PK-5
1500 Twin Rivers Blvd 32766 407-320-4850
Nancy Urban, prin. Fax 320-4899
Stenstrom ES 600/K-5
1800 Alafaya Woods Blvd 32765 407-320-2450
Dr. Janet Garzia, prin. Fax 320-2488
Tuskawilla MS 1,100/6-8
1801 Tuskawilla Rd 32765 407-746-8550
Randy Shuler, prin. Fax 746-8599

Master's Academy of Central Florida 900/PK-12
1500 Lukas Ln 32765 407-971-2221
Rev. Mike Armstrong, admin. Fax 706-0254
St. Luke's Lutheran S 700/PK-8
2025 W State Road 426 32765 407-365-3228
Rod Jackson, supt. Fax 366-9346

Starchild Academy Oviedo 100/PK-K
961 Eastbridge Dr 32765 407-977-8989
Ron Browning, prin. Fax 977-8993
Tuskawilla Montessori Academy 100/PK-8
1625 Montessori Pt 32765 407-678-3879

Pace, Santa Rosa, Pop. 19,523
Santa Rosa County SD
Supt. — See Milton
Dixon IS 700/3-5
5540 Education Dr 32571 850-995-3650
Linda Gooch, prin. Fax 995-3655
Dixon PS 700/K-2
4560 Pace Patriot Blvd 32571 850-995-3660
Nancy Haupt, prin. Fax 995-3675
Pea Ridge ES 700/K-5
4775 School Ln 32571 850-995-3680
Dana Fleming, prin. Fax 995-3688
Sims MS 900/6-8
5500 Education Dr 32571 850-995-3676
Emily Donalson, prin. Fax 995-3696

L.E.A.D. Academy Classical S 200/PK-12
4106 Berryhill Rd 32571 850-995-1900
H. Frank Lay, admin. Fax 995-1901

Pahokee, Palm Beach, Pop. 5,609
Palm Beach County SD
Supt. — See West Palm Beach
Pahokee ES 400/K-6
560 E Main Pl 33476 561-924-9700
Karen Abrams, prin. Fax 924-9751
Pahokee MS 400/6-8
850 Larrimore Rd 33476 561-924-6500
Dwayne Dennard, prin. Fax 924-6550

Palatka, Putnam, Pop. 10,395
Putnam County SD 11,100/PK-12
200 Reid St 32177 386-329-0538
Rick Surrency, supt. Fax 312-4918
www.putnamschools.org
Jenkins MS 700/7-8
1100 N 19th St 32177 386-329-0588
Randall Hedstrom, prin. Fax 329-0636
Long ES 600/PK-5
1400 Old Jacksonville Rd 32177 386-329-0575
Mary Beth Hedstrom, prin. Fax 329-0675
Mellon ES 500/PK-5
301 Mellon Rd 32177 386-329-0593
Libby Weaver, prin. Fax 329-0594
Moseley ES 400/PK-5
1100 Husson Ave 32177 386-329-0562
SaraJean McDaniel, prin. Fax 329-0563
Overturf 6th Grade Center 400/6-6
1100 S 18th St 32177 386-329-0569
Michael Tucker, prin. Fax 329-0670
Smith ES 700/PK-5
141 Kelley Smith School Rd 32177 386-329-0568
Tracy Taylor, prin. Fax 329-0629
Other Schools – See Crescent City, Hawthorne, Interlachen, Melrose, San Mateo

---

Hillcrest Academy 50/K-12
2009 President St 32177 386-328-6514
Peniel Baptist Academy 300/PK-12
110 Peniel Church Rd 32177 386-328-1707
Leigh Rion, admin. Fax 328-0950

Palm Bay, Brevard, Pop. 100,267
Brevard County SD
Supt. — See Melbourne
Columbia ES 600/PK-6
1225 Waco Blvd SE 32909 321-676-1319
Rachel Roberts, prin. Fax 952-5854
Discovery ES 700/K-6
1275 Glendale Ave NW 32907 321-951-4920
Elizabeth Evander, prin. Fax 952-5870
Jupiter ES 700/K-6
950 Tupelo Rd SW 32908 321-952-5990
Sherie Troisi, prin. Fax 952-5992
Lockmar ES 800/K-6
525 Pepper St NE 32907 321-676-3730
Norma Hostetler, prin. Fax 952-5879
McAuliffe ES 800/PK-6
155 Del Mundo St NW 32907 321-768-0465
Victoria Finsted, prin. Fax 952-5985
Palm Bay ES 800/PK-6
1200 Alamanda Rd NE 32905 321-723-1055
Michael Mahl, prin. Fax 952-5924
Port Malabar ES 700/K-6
301 Pioneer Ave NE 32907 321-725-0070
Cindy Whalin, prin. Fax 952-5949
Riviera ES 700/PK-6
351 Riviera Dr NE 32905 321-676-4237
Kori Hurst, prin. Fax 952-5957
Southwest MS 1,000/7-8
451 Eldron Blvd SE 32909 321-952-5800
Todd Scheuerer, prin. Fax 952-5819
Sunrise ES 700/K-6
1651 Mara Loma Blvd SE 32909 321-674-6145
Barry Pichard, prin. Fax 674-6147
Turner ES 700/PK-6
3175 Jupiter Blvd SE 32909 321-676-5700
Tanya Knowles, prin. Fax 952-5964
Westside ES 800/K-6
2175 Degroodt Rd SW 32908 321-956-5050
Darlene Rogers, prin. Fax 956-5053

Covenant Christian S 300/PK-12
720 Emerson Dr NE 32907 321-727-2661
Ron Fischer, head sch Fax 728-9574
St. Joseph Parish S 200/PK-8
5320 Babcock St NE 32905 321-723-8866
Claudia Stokes, prin. Fax 727-1181

Palm Beach, Palm Beach, Pop. 8,309
Palm Beach County SD
Supt. — See West Palm Beach
Palm Beach ES 400/K-5
239 Cocoanut Row 33480 561-822-0700
Christie Schwab, prin. Fax 822-0750

Palm Beach Day Academy 200/4-9
241 Seaview Ave 33480 561-655-1188
Dr. Edwin Gordon, hdmstr. Fax 655-5794

Palm Beach Gardens, Palm Beach, Pop. 47,764
Palm Beach County SD
Supt. — See West Palm Beach
Allamanda ES 600/K-5
10300 Allamanda Dr 33410 561-803-7200
Marilu Garcia, prin. Fax 803-7250
Duncan MS 1,300/6-8
5150 117th Ct N 33418 561-776-3500
Phillip D'Amico, prin. Fax 776-3550
Eisenhower ES 600/PK-5
2926 Lone Pine Rd 33410 561-366-6000
Debbie Battles, prin. Fax 366-6050
Grove Park ES 700/K-5
8330 N Military Trl 33410 561-904-7700
JoAnne Rogers, prin. Fax 904-7750
Marsh Pointe ES 900/K-5
12649 Ibiiza Dr 33418 561-366-6800
Maureen Werner, prin. Fax 366-6850
Palm Beach Gardens ES 700/K-5
10060 Riverside Dr 33410 561-366-6500
Marie Caracuzzo, prin. Fax 366-6550
Timber Trace ES 900/K-5
5200 117th Ct N 33418 561-366-6200
Kathy Pasquariello, prin. Fax 366-6250
Watkins MS 800/6-8
9480 MacArthur Blvd 33403 561-776-3600
Don Hoffman, prin. Fax 776-3603

Meyer Jewish Academy 300/K-8
5225 Hood Rd 33418 561-686-6520
St. Mark's Episcopal S 400/PK-8
3395 Burns Rd 33410 561-622-1504
Deborah Strainge M.Ed., head sch Fax 622-6801
Trinity Christian S of Palm Beach Garden 300/PK-8
9625 N Military Trl 33410 561-253-3950
Vernita Martial, prin. Fax 253-3953
Weiss S 200/PK-8
4176 Burns Rd 33410 561-627-0740

Palm City, Martin, Pop. 22,880
Martin County SD
Supt. — See Stuart
Bessey Creek ES 500/K-5
2201 SW Matheson Ave 34990 772-219-1500
Tyson Villwock, prin. Fax 219-1506
Citrus Grove ES 600/K-5
2527 SW Citrus Blvd 34990 772-223-2513
Todd Morrow, prin. Fax 223-2535
Hidden Oaks MS 1,100/6-8
2801 SW Martin Hwy 34990 772-219-1655
Jeri Eckler, prin. Fax 219-1663
Palm City ES 600/K-5
1951 SW 34th St 34990 772-219-1565
Robyn Monte, prin. Fax 219-1570

Palm Coast, Flagler, Pop. 73,538
Flagler County SD
Supt. — See Bunnell
Belle Terre ES 1,300/K-6
5545 Belle Terre Pkwy 32137 386-447-1500
Dr. Terence Culver, prin. Fax 447-1516
Indian Trails MS 800/7-8
5505 Belle Terre Pkwy 32137 386-446-6732
Paul Peacock, prin. Fax 446-7662
Rymfire ES 1,300/K-6
1425 Rymfire Dr 32164 386-206-4600
Barbara Sauvelpahkick, prin. Fax 586-2305
Taylor MS 1,000/7-8
4500 Belle Terre Pkwy 32164 386-446-6700
John Fanelli, prin. Fax 446-6711
Wadsworth ES 800/PK-6
4550 Belle Terre Pkwy 32164 386-446-6720
Anna Crawford, prin. Fax 446-7681

Christ the King S 200/PK-8
5625 N US Highway 1 32164 386-447-7979
Jeff Loberger M.Ed., admin. Fax 447-4121
St. Elizabeth Ann Seton S 200/PK-8
4600 Belle Terre Pkwy Ste B 32164 386-445-2411
Therese Majewski, prin. Fax 445-2522

Palmetto, Manatee, Pop. 12,420
Manatee County SD
Supt. — See Bradenton
Blackburn ES 500/PK-5
3904 17th St E 34221 941-723-4800
Latrina Singleton, prin. Fax 721-6647
Buffalo Creek MS 1,000/6-8
7320 69th St E 34221 941-721-2260
Dustin Dahlquist, prin. Fax 721-2275
Lincoln MS 600/6-8
305 17th St E 34221 941-721-6840
Ed Hundley, prin. Fax 721-6853
Mills ES 1,000/K-5
7200 69th St E 34221 941-721-2140
James Mennes, prin. Fax 721-2152
Palmetto ES 700/K-5
1540 10th St W 34221 941-723-4822
Michelle Mealor, prin. Fax 723-4607
Palm View ES 400/K-7
6025 Bayshore Rd 34221 941-723-4812
Angela Essig, prin. Fax 723-4532
Tillman ES 300/PK-K, 3-5
1415 29th St E 34221 941-723-4833
Marla Massi, prin. Fax 723-4530

Palmetto Bay, Miami-Dade
Miami-Dade County SD
Supt. — See Miami
Coral Reef ES 800/PK-5
7955 SW 152nd St, 305-235-1464
Christina Guerra, prin. Fax 254-3725
Howard Drive ES 600/PK-5
7750 SW 136th St, 305-235-1412
Deanna Dalby, prin. Fax 256-3105
Perrine Academy of the Arts 800/PK-5
8851 SW 168th St, 305-235-2442
Carla Rivas, prin. Fax 253-6817
Southwood MS 1,400/6-8
16301 SW 80th Ave, 305-251-5361
Raul Garcia, prin. Fax 251-7464

Alexander Montessori S - Ludlam Rd Cmps 300/1-5
14850 SW 67th Ave, 305-235-3995
Christ Fellowship Academy 300/PK-6
8900 SW 168th St, 305-238-1833
Westminster Christian S 1,000/PK-12
6855 SW 152nd St, 305-233-2030
David Medder, head sch Fax 238-2259

Palm Harbor, Pinellas, Pop. 56,551
Pinellas County SD
Supt. — See Largo
Carwise MS 1,200/6-8
3301 Bentley Dr 34684 727-724-1442
Robert Vicari, prin. Fax 724-1446
Curlew Creek ES 600/K-5
3030 Curlew Rd 34684 727-724-1423
Kathleen Brickley, prin. Fax 724-1426
Cypress Woods ES 700/PK-5
4900 Cypress Woods Blvd 34685 727-538-7325
Kimberly Hill, prin. Fax 725-7988
Highland Lakes ES 500/PK-5
1230 Highlands Blvd 34684 727-724-1429
Tijuana Baker, prin. Fax 724-1435
Lake St. George ES 500/K-5
2855 County Road 95 34684 727-669-1161
Monika Wolcott, prin. Fax 669-1165
Ozona ES 700/PK-5
601 Tampa Rd 34683 727-724-1589
Belinda Atkins, prin. Fax 724-1591
Palm Harbor MS 1,400/6-8
1800 Tampa Rd 34683 727-669-1146
Mary Athanson, prin. Fax 669-1244
Sutherland ES 600/PK-5
3150 N Belcher Rd 34683 727-724-1466
Kristy Cantu, prin. Fax 724-1469

New Horizons Country Day S 200/PK-5
2060 Nebraska Ave 34683 727-785-8591
Palm Harbor Montessori Academy 200/PK-8
2355 Nebraska Ave 34683 727-786-1854
St. Luke ECC 100/PK-PK
2757 Alderman Rd 34684 727-787-2914
Kathleen Mitchell, dir. Fax 786-8648
Suncoast Waldorf S 100/PK-5
1857 Curlew Rd 34683 727-786-8311
Amanda Tipton, admin. Fax 789-8265
Westlake Christian S 300/K-8
1551 Belcher Rd 34683 727-781-3808
Jayanne K. Roggenbaum, head sch Fax 785-2608

Palm Springs, Palm Beach, Pop. 18,607
Palm Beach County SD
Supt. — See West Palm Beach
Taylor/Kirklane ES 1,200/K-5
4200 Purdy Ln 33461 561-804-3500
Patricia Lucas, prin. Fax 804-3551

St. Luke S 200/PK-8
2896 S Congress Ave 33461 561-965-8190
Amy Lopez, prin. Fax 965-2404

Panama City, Bay, Pop. 35,536
Bay County SD 26,100/PK-12
1311 Balboa Ave 32401 850-767-4100
William Husfelt, supt.
www.bay.k12.fl.us
Bozeman S 1,100/K-12
13410 Highway 77 32409 850-767-1300
Josh Balkom, prin. Fax 265-5377
Brown MS 800/6-8
5044 Merritt Brown Way 32404 850-767-3976
Charlotte Marshall, prin. Fax 767-4008
Callaway ES 500/PK-5
7115 E Highway 22 32404 850-767-1241
Tim Keiffer, prin. Fax 871-2865
Cedar Grove ES 500/PK-5
2826 E 15th St 32405 850-767-4550
Shirley Baker, prin. Fax 767-5649
Deer Point ES 600/PK-5
4800 Highway 2321 32404 850-767-5462
Rebecca Reeder, prin. Fax 767-3669
Everitt MS 800/6-8
608 School Ave 32401 850-767-3776
Phillip Mullins, prin. Fax 872-7721
Hiland Park ES 800/PK-5
2507 E Baldwin Rd 32405 850-767-4685
Rhonda Woodward, prin. Fax 747-5307
Jinks MS 600/6-8
600 W 11th St 32401 850-767-4695
Britt Smith, prin. Fax 872-7612
Merriam Cherry Street ES 400/PK-5
1125 Cherry St 32401 850-767-1480
Blythe Carpenter, prin. Fax 747-5499
Moore ES 500/PK-5
1900 Michigan Ave 32405 850-767-1428
Lisa Jones, prin. Fax 747-5686
Northside ES 700/PK-5
2001 Northside Dr 32405 850-767-1506
Amy Harvey, prin. Fax 747-5315
Oakland Terrace S for Visual/Perfrmg Art 400/PK-5
2010 W 12th St 32401 850-767-4565
Kimberly Kirkman, prin. Fax 872-7613
Parker ES 600/PK-5
640 S Highway 22 A 32404 850-767-4570
Christopher Coan, prin. Fax 747-5197
Patronis ES 800/PK-5
7400 Patronis Dr 32408 850-767-5075
Ellie Spivey, prin. Fax 233-5077

Patterson ES 400/PK-5
1025 Redwood Ave 32401 850-767-4675
Darnita Rivers, prin. Fax 747-5478
Smith ES 700/PK-5
5044 Tommy Smith Dr 32404 850-767-1688
Clint Whitfield, prin. Fax 747-5339
Southport ES 400/PK-5
1835 Bridge St 32409 850-767-1636
Holly Buchanan, prin. Fax 265-3703
Springfield ES 500/PK-5
520 School Ave 32401 850-767-4575
Russell Brock, prin. Fax 747-5386
West Bay ES 300/K-5
14813 School Dr 32413 850-767-1850
Jerri Moss, prin. Fax 767-1851
Other Schools – See Lynn Haven, Panama City Beach, Tyndall AFB, Youngstown

---

Adventist Christian Academy 50/K-8
2700 Lisenby Ave 32405 850-769-3405
Covenant Christian S 300/PK-12
2350 Frankford Ave 32405 850-769-7448
Holy Nativity Episcopal S 200/PK-8
205 Hamilton Ave 32401 850-747-0060
Fax 747-7447
Kaleidoscope S of Discovery 100/K-12
2420 Jenks Ave 32405 850-785-7157
Panama City Advanced S 100/PK-12
3332 Token Rd 32405 850-784-2520
Rashid Karaman, prin. Fax 784-2575
St. John the Evangelist S 100/PK-8
1005 Fortune Ave 32401 850-763-1775
Wilma Wilson, prin. Fax 784-4461

Panama City Beach, Bay, Pop. 11,689
Bay County SD
Supt. — See Panama City
Breakfast Point Academy 1,400/PK-8
601 N Richard Jackson Blvd 32407 850-767-1190
Keri Weatherly, prin. Fax 230-1006
Hutchison Beach ES 700/PK-5
12900 Hutchison Blvd 32407 850-767-5195
Glenda Nouskhajian, prin. Fax 233-5178
Surfside MS 700/6-8
300 Nautilus St 32413 850-767-5180
Dr. Sue Harrell, prin. Fax 233-5193

St. Bernadette Child Development Center 100/PK-PK
1214 Moylan Rd 32407 850-230-0009
Juli Roock, dir. Fax 230-6989

Parkland, Broward, Pop. 23,535
Broward County SD
Supt. — See Fort Lauderdale
Heron Heights ES 1,000/K-5
11010 Nob Hill Rd 33076 754-322-9150
Kenneth King, prin. Fax 322-9190
Park Trails ES 1,000/K-5
10700 Trails End 33076 754-322-7800
Charles McCanna, prin. Fax 322-7840
Riverglades ES 600/K-5
7400 Parkside Dr 33067 754-322-8200
JoAnne Seltzer, prin. Fax 322-8240
Westglades MS 1,400/6-8
11000 Holmberg Rd 33076 754-322-4800
Matthew Bianchi, prin. Fax 322-4835

Mary Help of Christians S 100/PK-8
6000 N University Dr 33067 954-323-8006
Dr. Alexandra Fernandez, prin. Fax 323-8012

Parrish, Manatee
Manatee County SD
Supt. — See Bradenton
Williams ES 900/PK-5
3404 Fort Hamer Rd 34219 941-776-4040
Connie Dixon, prin. Fax 776-4080

Paxton, Walton, Pop. 626
Walton County SD
Supt. — See De Funiak Springs
Paxton S 700/PK-12
21893 US Highway 331 N 32538 850-892-1230
Cindy Neale, prin. Fax 892-1239

Pembroke Park, Broward, Pop. 5,970
Broward County SD
Supt. — See Fort Lauderdale
Lake Forest ES 800/PK-5
3550 SW 48th Ave 33023 754-323-6350
Sharon Boyd, prin. Fax 323-6390
Watkins ES 700/PK-5
3520 SW 52nd Ave 33023 754-323-7800
Lori Mendez, prin. Fax 323-7840

Pembroke Pines, Broward, Pop. 151,189
Broward County SD
Supt. — See Fort Lauderdale
Chapel Trail ES 700/K-5
19595 Taft St 33029 754-323-5000
Teresa Lipkins, prin. Fax 323-5040
Lakeside ES 700/K-5
900 NW 136 Ave 33028 754-323-6400
Kathy May, prin. Fax 323-6440
Palm Cove ES 800/K-5
11601 Washington St 33025 754-323-6800
Davida Johnson, prin. Fax 323-6840
Panther Run ES 500/K-5
801 NW 172nd Ave 33029 754-323-6850
Elaine Saef, prin. Fax 323-6890
Pasadena Lakes ES 600/PK-5
8801 Pasadena Blvd 33024 754-323-6900
Janet Phelps, prin. Fax 323-6940
Pembroke Lakes ES 500/K-5
11251 Taft St 33026 754-323-6950
Marsha Wagner, prin. Fax 323-6990
Pembroke Pines ES 600/K-5
6700 SW 9th St 33023 754-323-7000
April Schentrup, prin. Fax 323-7040

Pines Lakes ES 600/PK-5
10300 Johnson St 33026 754-323-7100
Susan Sasse, prin. Fax 323-7140
Pines MS 1,400/6-8
200 NW Douglas Rd 33024 754-323-4000
Carlton Campbell, prin. Fax 323-4085
Silver Palms ES 600/K-5
1209 NW 155th Ave 33028 754-323-7450
Irina Shearer, prin. Fax 323-7490
Silver Trail MS 1,500/6-8
18300 Sheridan St 33331 754-323-4300
Stephen Frazier, prin. Fax 323-4385
Young MS 1,200/6-8
901 NW 129th Ave 33028 754-323-4500
Harold Osborn, prin. Fax 323-4585

Montessori Academy 600/PK-8
19200 Pines Blvd 33029 954-435-4622

Pensacola, Escambia, Pop. 50,807
Escambia County SD 39,500/PK-12
75 N Pace Blvd 32505 850-432-6121
Malcolm Thomas, supt. Fax 469-6379
ecsd-fl.schoolloop.com
Bailey MS 1,500/6-8
4110 Bauer Rd 32506 850-492-6136
Janet Penrose, prin. Fax 492-9860
Bellview ES 700/K-5
4425 Bellview Ave 32526 850-941-6060
Melissa Groff, prin. Fax 941-6062
Bellview MS 1,000/6-8
6201 Mobile Hwy 32526 850-941-6080
Melia Adams, prin. Fax 941-6073
Beulah ES 900/K-5
6201 Helms Rd 32526 850-941-6180
Monica Silvers, prin. Fax 941-6183
Blue Angels ES 800/K-5
1551 Dog Track Rd 32506 850-457-6356
Karen Montgomery, prin. Fax 457-6954
Brentwood ES 600/PK-5
4820 N Palafox St 32505 850-595-6800
Jennifer Sewell, prin. Fax 595-6802
Brown-Barge MS 500/6-8
201 Hancock Ln 32503 850-494-5640
Joe Snyder, prin. Fax 494-5699
Caro ES 900/PK-5
12551 Meadson Rd 32506 850-492-0531
Sandra Moore, prin. Fax 492-3592
Cook ES 600/K-5
1310 N 12th Ave 32503 850-595-6826
Larry Knight, prin. Fax 595-6823
Cordova Park ES 700/K-5
2250 Semur Rd 32503 850-595-6830
Aggie Bauer, prin. Fax 595-6835
Ensley ES 500/PK-5
501 E Johnson Ave 32514 850-494-5600
Jayne Cecil, prin. Fax 494-5603
Ferry Pass ES 700/PK-5
8310 N Davis Hwy 32514 850-494-5605
Rhonda Shuford, prin. Fax 494-7480
Ferry Pass MS 1,000/6-8
8355 Yancey Ave 32514 850-494-5650
Sherri Mims, prin. Fax 494-5653
Global Learning Academy 800/K-5
100 N P St 32505 850-430-7560
Judy LaBounty, prin. Fax 595-0421
Holm ES 400/PK-5
6101 Lanier Dr 32504 850-494-5610
Kristin Cain, prin. Fax 494-7290
Lincoln Park PS 200/PK-3
7600 Kershaw St 32534 850-494-5620
Cassandra Smith, prin. Fax 494-7481
Lipscomb ES 900/K-5
10200 Ashton Brosnaham Rd 32534 850-494-5760
Susan Sanders, prin. Fax 494-5722
Longleaf ES 800/K-5
2600 Longleaf Dr 32526 850-941-6110
Troy Brown, prin. Fax 941-6112
McArthur ES 700/K-5
330 E Ten Mile Rd 32534 850-494-5625
Dr. Tama Vaughn, prin. Fax 494-5707
McMillan Preschool 100/PK-PK
1403 W Saint Joseph Ave 32501 850-595-6910
Dr. Patrice Moody, prin. Fax 595-6944
Montclair ES 400/PK-5
820 Massachusetts Ave 32505 850-595-6969
Hollie Wilkins, prin. Fax 595-6968
Myrtle Grove ES 700/K-5
6115 Lillian Hwy 32506 850-453-7410
Robin Maloy, prin. Fax 453-7740
Navy Point ES 500/K-5
1321 Patton Dr 32507 850-453-7415
Dr. Monica Ford-Harris, prin. Fax 453-7419
Oakcrest ES 600/PK-5
1820 Hollywood Ave 32505 850-595-6980
Linda Bonifay, prin. Fax 595-6988
Pine Meadow ES 900/PK-5
10001 Omar Ave 32534 850-494-5630
Terri Fina, prin. Fax 494-7318
Pleasant Grove ES 600/PK-5
3000 Owen Bell Ln 32507 850-492-0233
Pam Mullen, prin. Fax 492-6991
Scenic Heights ES 900/K-5
3801 Cherry Laurel Dr 32504 850-494-5635
Michelle Cox, prin. Fax 494-5624
Semmes ES 400/K-5
1250 E Texar Dr 32503 850-595-6975
Connie Farish, prin. Fax 595-6977
Sherwood ES 600/PK-5
501 Cherokee Trl 32506 850-453-7420
Kristen Danley, prin. Fax 453-7466
Suter ES 400/K-5
501 Pickens Ave 32503 850-595-6810
Russell Queen, prin. Fax 595-6819
Warrington ES 500/PK-5
220 N Navy Blvd 32507 850-453-7425
Dr. David Schmittou, prin. Fax 453-7519

Warrington MS 600/6-8
450 S Old Corry Field Rd 32507 850-453-7440
Dr. Regina Lipnick, prin. Fax 453-7572
Weis ES 600/PK-5
2701 N Q St 32505 850-595-6888
Holly Magee, prin. Fax 595-6893
West Pensacola ES 400/K-5
801 N 49th Ave 32506 850-453-7470
Christine Baker, prin. Fax 453-7717
Woodham MS 700/6-8
150 E Burgess Rd 32503 850-494-7140
Wilson Taylor, prin. Fax 494-7484
Workman MS 1,000/6-8
6299 Lanier Dr 32504 850-494-5665
Traci Ursery, prin. Fax 494-5697
Other Schools – See Cantonment, Century, Molino, Walnut Hill

Aletheia Christian Academy 200/PK-12
PO Box 10568 32524 850-969-0088
Jeffrey Caulfield-James, admin. Fax 969-0906
Carden Christian Academy 100/PK-8
3290 Bauer Rd 32506 850-898-1501
Angela Nicholas, prin. Fax 492-4877
Creative Learning Academy 200/PK-8
3151 Hyde Park Rd 32503 850-432-1768
DT Preparatory Academy 200/PK-8
8440 Ashland Ave 32534 850-418-6390
Ciequinita Vaughn, prin. Fax 471-1961
East Hill Christian S 200/PK-12
1301 E Gonzalez St 32501 850-438-7746
Glenn Dickson, hdmstr. Fax 434-7384
Episcopal Day S of Christ Church Parish 500/PK-8
223 N Palafox St 32502 850-434-6474
Ed Costello, head sch Fax 434-6560
Escambia Christian S 100/PK-8
PO Box 17449 32522 850-433-8476
Jones Christian Academy 200/PK-12
100 Boeing St 32507 850-456-2249
Jubilee Christian Academy 200/PK-8
5910 N W St 32505 850-494-2477
JaDean Stricker, head sch Fax 494-2900
Little Flower Catholic S 200/PK-8
PO Box 3009 32516 850-455-4851
Tina D'Aversa, prin. Fax 457-8982
Marcus Pointe Christian S 200/PK-5
6205 N W St 32505 850-479-1605
Montessori S of Pensacola 100/PK-K
1010 N 12th Ave Ste 138 32501 850-433-4155
Kathy Turtle, dir. Fax 433-5613
Montessori S of Pensacola 200/PK-8
4100 Montessori Dr 32504 850-469-8138
Pensacola Christian Academy 2,300/PK-12
10 Brent Ln 32503 850-478-8483
Pensacola Jr Academy 50/K-8
8751 University Pkwy 32514 850-478-8838
Redeemer Lutheran S 200/PK-8
333 Commerce St 32507 850-455-0330
John Price, prin. Fax 455-3083
Sacred Heart Cathedral S 200/PK-8
1603 N 12th Ave 32503 850-436-6440
Elizabeth Snow, prin. Fax 436-6444
St. John the Evangelist S 200/PK-8
325 S Navy Blvd 32507 850-456-5218
Ann Williams, prin. Fax 456-5956
St. Paul S 200/PK-8
3121 Hyde Park Rd 32503 850-436-6435
Lara Schuler, prin. Fax 436-6437
Trinitas Christian S 200/K-12
3301 E Johnson Ave 32514 850-484-3515

Perry, Taylor, Pop. 6,889
Taylor County SD 3,000/PK-12
318 N Clark St 32347 850-838-2500
Danny Glover, supt. Fax 838-2501
www.taylor.k12.fl.us
Perry PS 700/K-2
400 N Clark St 32347 850-838-2506
Pam Padgett, prin. Fax 838-2556
Taylor County ES 600/3-5
1600 E Green St 32347 850-838-2530
Charles Finley, prin. Fax 838-1379
Taylor County MS 600/6-8
610 E Lafayette St 32347 850-838-2516
Kiki Puhl, prin. Fax 838-2559
Taylor County Pre K 300/PK-PK
524 E Lafayette St 32347 850-838-2535
Cheryl Brantley, coord. Fax 838-2575
Other Schools – See Steinhatchee

Point of Grace Christian S 100/K-10
920 N Courtney Rd 32347 850-584-5445

Pierson, Volusia, Pop. 1,725
Volusia County SD
Supt. — See De Land
Pierson ES 600/PK-5
1 W 1st Ave 32180 386-740-0850
Kimberly Hutcherson, prin. Fax 749-6870

Pinecrest, Miami-Dade
Miami-Dade County SD
Supt. — See Miami
Palmetto ES 600/PK-5
12401 SW 74th Ave 33156 305-238-4306
Eric Torres, prin. Fax 254-7774
Palmetto MS 700/6-8
7351 SW 128th St 33156 305-238-3911
Jesus Gonzalez, prin. Fax 233-4849
Pinecrest ES 1,100/PK-5
10250 SW 57th Ave 33156 305-667-5579
Lynn Zaldua, prin. Fax 662-7163

Gulliver Academy - Montgomery Dr Campus 100/5-8
7500 SW 120th St 33156 305-238-3424
Clifton Kling, pres. Fax 675-7744
St. Louis Covenant S 400/PK-5
7270 SW 120th St 33156 305-238-7562
Edward Garcia, prin. Fax 238-4296

Pinellas Park, Pinellas, Pop. 47,904
Pinellas County SD
Supt. — See Largo
Cross Bayou ES 500/PK-5
6886 102nd Ave N 33782 727-547-7834
Katherine Wickett, prin. Fax 547-7837
Pinellas Central ES 600/PK-5
10501 58th St N 33782 727-547-7853
Cara Walsh, prin. Fax 547-7856
Pinellas Park ES 600/K-5
7520 52nd St N 33781 727-547-7888
Lisa Freeman, prin. Fax 547-7892
Pinellas Park MS 1,100/6-8
6940 70th Ave N 33781 727-545-6400
David Rosenberger, prin. Fax 547-7894
Rawlings ES 700/PK-5
6505 68th St N 33781 727-547-7828
Rebecca Moore, prin. Fax 547-7777
Skyview ES 700/PK-5
8601 60th St N 33782 727-547-7857
Suzanne Hester, prin. Fax 545-7521

Classical Christian S for the Arts 100/K-12
PO Box 1455 33780 727-547-6820
Sacred Heart S 200/PK-8
7951 46th Way N 33781 727-544-1106
Heather Boyle, prin. Fax 548-9606

Pinetta, Madison
Madison County SD
Supt. — See Madison
Pinetta ES 200/PK-5
135 NE Empress Tree Ave 32350 850-973-5028
Amy Kendrick, prin. Fax 973-5147

Plantation, Broward, Pop. 82,808
Broward County SD
Supt. — See Fort Lauderdale
Central Park ES 1,100/K-5
777 N Nob Hill Rd 33324 754-322-5700
Cherise Coleman, prin. Fax 322-5740
Mirror Lake ES 500/PK-5
1200 NW 72nd Ave 33313 754-322-7100
Marlen Veliz, prin. Fax 322-7140
Peters ES 700/PK-5
851 NW 68th Ave 33317 754-322-7900
Joyce Krzemienski, prin. Fax 322-7940
Plantation ES 600/PK-5
651 NW 42nd Ave 33317 754-322-8000
Judith Pitter, prin. Fax 322-8040
Plantation MS 1,000/6-8
6600 W Sunrise Blvd 33313 754-322-4100
Sherri Wilson, prin. Fax 322-4185
Plantation Park ES 500/K-5
875 SW 54th Ave 33317 754-323-7150
Julie Gittelman, prin. Fax 323-7190
Seminole MS 1,100/6-8
6200 SW 10th St 33317 754-323-4200
Kathryn Marlow, prin. Fax 323-4285
Tropical ES 900/K-5
1500 SW 66th Ave 33317 754-323-7750
Erik Anderson, prin. Fax 323-7790

American Heritage S 2,300/PK-12
12200 W Broward Blvd 33325 954-472-0022
Blake S PK-8
7011 W Sunrise Blvd 33313 954-584-6816
Broward Junior Academy 100/K-8
201 NW 46th Ave 33317 954-316-8301
Our Savior Lutheran S 200/PK-8
8001 NW 5th St 33324 954-370-2161
Linda Root, prin. Fax 473-0395
St. Gregory the Great S 800/PK-8
200 N University Dr 33324 954-473-8169
Caridad Canino, prin. Fax 472-1638
Sawgrass Adventist S 100/PK-8
11701 NW 4th St 33325 954-473-4622
Trinitas Academy 100/PK-7
1101 SW 49th Ave 33317 954-581-2744
Rev. Jorge del Pino M.A., supt. Fax 581-7724
Von Wedel Montessori S 100/PK-K
8250 Peters Rd 33324 954-473-4400
Johanna Tapia, dir. Fax 473-4433

Plant City, Hillsborough, Pop. 34,205
Hillsborough County SD
Supt. — See Tampa
Bryan ES 800/PK-5
2006 W Oak Ave, 813-757-9300
Jennifer McCrystal, prin. Fax 707-7075
Burney ES 300/PK-5
901 S Evers St, 813-707-7334
Donna Ippolito, prin. Fax 707-7339
Cork ES 700/K-5
3501 Cork Rd 33565 813-757-9353
Sherri Black, prin. Fax 707-7076
Jackson ES 500/K-5
502 E Gilchrist St, 813-757-9341
Michelle McClellan, prin. Fax 757-9343
Knights ES 700/PK-5
4815 Keene Rd 33565 813-757-9333
Janine Hall, prin. Fax 757-9319
Lincoln Magnet ES 400/PK-5
1207 E Renfro St, 813-757-9329
Jennifer West, prin. Fax 757-9077
Marshall MS 800/6-8
18 S Maryland Ave, 813-757-9360
Daphne Blanton, prin. Fax 707-7385
Robinson ES 500/PK-5
4801 Turkey Creek Rd 33567 813-757-9424
Alicia Wilkerson, prin. Fax 757-9074
Springhead ES 800/PK-5
3208 Nesmith Rd 33566 813-757-9321
Ann Rushing, prin. Fax 757-9500
Tomlin MS 1,600/6-8
501 N Woodrow Wilson St, 813-757-9400
Traci Durrance, prin. Fax 707-7024
Trapnell ES 600/PK-5
1605 W Trapnell Rd 33566 813-757-9313
Alan Black, prin. Fax 757-9129
Turkey Creek MS 1,000/6-8
5005 Turkey Creek Rd 33567 813-757-9442
Fredda Johnson, prin. Fax 757-9451
Walden Lake ES 900/K-5
2800 Turkey Creek Rd 33566 813-757-9433
Dina Wyatt, prin. Fax 707-7170
Wilson ES 400/PK-5
702 W English St, 813-757-9307
Gina Becker, prin. Fax 757-9310

Poinciana, Osceola, Pop. 51,604
Polk County SD
Supt. — See Bartow
Lake Marion Creek MS 800/5-8
3055 Lake Marion Creek Dr 34759 863-427-1471
Amanda Robinson, prin. Fax 427-1502
Laurel ES 700/PK-5
1851 Laurel Ave 34759 863-427-1375
Julia Allen, prin. Fax 427-1303
Palmetto ES 800/PK-5
315 Palmetto St 34759 863-427-6012
Edgar Santiago, prin. Fax 427-6013

Polk City, Polk, Pop. 1,538
Polk County SD
Supt. — See Bartow
Polk City ES 500/PK-5
125 S Bougainvillea Ave 33868 863-965-6338
Jennifer Erb-Hancock, prin. Fax 965-6340

Pompano Beach, Broward, Pop. 97,655
Broward County SD
Supt. — See Fort Lauderdale
Cresthaven ES 600/K-5
801 NE 25th St 33064 754-322-6000
Donald Lee, prin. Fax 322-6040
Crystal Lake MS 1,400/6-8
3551 NE 3rd Ave 33064 754-322-3100
Sabine Phillips, prin. Fax 322-3185
Cypress ES 900/PK-5
851 SW 3rd Ave 33060 754-322-6050
Vanessa Schnur, prin. Fax 322-6090
Drew ES 600/K-5
1000 NW 31st Ave 33069 754-322-6250
Angeline Flowers, prin. Fax 322-6290
Markham ES 600/PK-5
1501 NW 15th Ave 33069 754-322-6950
Shedrick Dukes, prin. Fax 322-6990
McNab ES 700/K-5
1350 SE 9th Ave 33060 754-322-7050
Dorys Palacio, prin. Fax 322-7090
Norcrest ES 800/K-5
3951 NE 16th Ave 33064 754-322-7250
Kyna Duarte, prin. Fax 322-7290
Palmview ES 700/PK-5
2601 NE 1st Ave 33064 754-322-7600
Robert Gibson, prin. Fax 322-7640
Pompano Beach ES 500/PK-5
700 NE 13th Ave 33060 754-322-8050
Shezette Blue-Small, prin. Fax 322-8090
Pompano Beach MS 1,100/6-8
310 NE 6th St 33060 754-322-4200
Sonja Braziel, prin. Fax 322-4285
Sanders Park ES 600/PK-5
800 NW 16th St 33060 754-322-8400
Trevor Roberts, prin. Fax 322-8440

Highlands Christian Academy 500/PK-12
501 NE 48th St 33064 954-421-1747
Lighthouse Christian S 200/K-8
2331 NE 26th Ave 33062 954-941-7501
Rita O'Leary, admin. Fax 933-4033
St. Coleman S 600/PK-8
2250 SE 12th St 33062 954-942-3500
Dr. Lori St. Thomas, prin. Fax 785-0603

Ponce de Leon, Holmes, Pop. 585
Holmes County SD
Supt. — See Bonifay
Ponce De Leon ES 300/PK-5
1473 Ammons Rd 32455 850-836-4296
Anissa Locke, prin. Fax 836-5325

Ponte Vedra Beach, Saint Johns
St. Johns County SD
Supt. — See Saint Augustine
Landrum MS 1,300/6-8
230 Landrum Ln 32082 904-547-8410
Ryan Player, prin. Fax 547-8415
Ocean Palms ES 900/PK-5
355 Landrum Ln 32082 904-547-3760
Jessica Richardson, prin. Fax 547-3775
Ponte Vedra-Palm Valley/Rawlings ES 1,300/PK-5
630 A1A N 32082 904-547-8570
Catherine Van Housen, prin. Fax 547-8575
Valley Ridge Academy K-8
105 Greenleaf Dr, 904-547-4090
Sandra McMandon, prin. Fax 547-4095

Bolles S - Ponte Vedra Beach PK-5
200 ATP Tour Blvd 32082 904-285-4658
David Farace, pres. Fax 285-1423
Christ Church Episcopal S 200/PK-K
400 San Juan Dr 32082 904-285-6371
Palmer Catholic Academy 400/K-8
4889 Palm Valley Rd 32082 904-543-8515
Linda Earp, prin. Fax 543-8750
Palmer Catholic Academy Preschool PK-PK
545 A1A N 32082 904-285-2698
Chris Saliba, dir. Fax 273-9740

Port Charlotte, Charlotte, Pop. 53,337
Charlotte County SD 15,800/PK-12
1445 Education Way 33948 941-255-0808
Steve Dionisio, supt. Fax 255-7571
yourcharlotteschools.net
Armstrong ES 800/PK-5
22100 Breezeswept Ave 33952 941-255-7450
Angie Taillon, prin. Fax 255-7456
Kingsway ES 600/PK-5
23300 Quasar Blvd 33980 941-255-7590
Ron Rogala, prin. Fax 255-7591
Liberty ES 600/PK-5
370 Atwater St 33954 941-255-7515
Sheila Brown, prin. Fax 255-7519
Meadow Park ES 800/PK-5
750 Essex Ave 33948 941-255-7470
Matthew Loge, prin. Fax 255-7477
Murdock MS 800/6-8
17325 Mariner Way 33948 941-255-7525
Demetrius Revelas, prin. Fax 255-7533
Myakka River ES 500/PK-5
12650 Willmington Blvd 33981 941-697-7111
Grace Shepard, prin. Fax 697-6326
Peace River ES 700/PK-5
4070 Beaver Ln 33952 941-255-7622
Jody Poulakis, prin. Fax 255-7626
Port Charlotte MS 800/6-8
23000 Midway Blvd 33952 941-255-7460
John LeClair, prin. Fax 255-7469
Other Schools – See Punta Gorda, Rotonda West

Charlotte Prep S 200/PK-8
365 Orlando Blvd 33954 941-764-7673
Peggy Fear, head sch Fax 764-0342
Community Christian S 300/PK-12
20035 Quesada Ave 33952 941-625-8977
Dr. Sarah Mielke, head sch Fax 625-1735
Genesis Christian S 100/PK-8
19150 Helena Ave 33948 941-627-4849
Dr. Scott Porter, prin. Fax 627-5890
Port Charlotte Adventist S 100/K-12
2100 Loveland Blvd 33980 941-625-5237
St. Charles Borromeo Catholic S 200/PK-8
21505 Augusta Ave 33952 941-625-5533
Tonya Peters, prin. Fax 625-7359

Port Orange, Volusia, Pop. 55,114
Volusia County SD
Supt. — See De Land
Creekside MS 1,100/6-8
6801 Airport Rd 32128 386-322-6155
John Cash, prin. Fax 506-0002
Cypress Creek ES 800/K-5
6100 S Williamson Blvd 32128 386-322-6101
Dr. Scott Lifvendahl, prin. Fax 506-0003
Horizon ES 700/K-5
4751 Hidden Lake Dr 32129 386-322-6150
Gary Harms, prin. Fax 756-7162
Port Orange ES 400/K-5
402 Dunlawton Ave 32127 386-322-6271
Tennille Wallace, prin. Fax 756-7117
Silver Sands MS 1,100/6-8
1300 Herbert St 32129 386-322-6175
Amanda Wiles, prin. Fax 322-7574
Spruce Creek ES 700/PK-5
642 Taylor Rd 32127 386-322-6200
Andrea Hall, prin. Fax 322-7515
Sugar Mill ES 600/PK-5
1101 Charles St 32129 386-322-6171
Dr. Mary Speidel, prin. Fax 756-7140
Sweetwater ES 600/K-5
5800 Victoria Gardens Blvd 32127 386-322-6230
Tamara Hopkins, prin. Fax 322-7526

Port Richey, Pasco, Pop. 2,626
Pasco County SD
Supt. — See Land O Lakes
Chasco ES 700/K-5
7906 Ridge Rd 34668 727-774-1200
Michele Boylan, prin. Fax 774-1291
Chasco MS 700/6-8
7702 Ridge Rd 34668 727-774-1300
Brandon Bracciale, prin. Fax 774-1391
Fox Hollow ES 600/PK-5
8309 Fox Hollow Dr 34668 727-774-7600
Karyn Kinzie, prin. Fax 774-7691
Gulf Highlands ES 500/K-5
8019 Gulf Highlands Dr 34668 727-774-7700
Judith Cosh, prin. Fax 774-7791

Bishop Larkin S 300/PK-8
8408 Monarch Dr 34668 727-862-6981
Sr. Regina Ozuzu, prin. Fax 869-9893

Port Saint Joe, Gulf, Pop. 3,399
Gulf County SD 1,900/PK-12
150 Middle School Dr 32456 850-229-8256
Jim Norton, supt. Fax 229-6089
www.gulf.k12.fl.us
Port Saint Joe ES 600/PK-6
2201 Long Ave 32456 850-227-1221
Joni Mock, admin. Fax 227-3422
Other Schools – See Wewahitchka

Port Saint Lucie, Saint Lucie, Pop. 160,756
St. Lucie County SD
Supt. — See Fort Pierce
Allapattah Flats K-8 S 900/PK-8
12051 NW Copper Creek Dr 34987 772-468-5050
Ana Rodriguez-Oronoz, prin. Fax 468-5013
Bayshore ES 700/PK-5
1661 SW Bayshore Blvd 34984 772-340-4720
Jacqueline Lynch, prin. Fax 340-4726
Floresta ES 600/K-5
1501 SE Floresta Dr 34983 772-340-4755
Jennifer Hedeen, prin. Fax 340-4756
Manatee Academy 1,400/K-8
1450 SW Heatherwood Blvd 34986 772-340-4745
Lillian Beauchamp, prin. Fax 340-4775
Mariposa ES 800/PK-5
2620 SE Mariposa Ave 34952 772-337-5960
Craig Logue, prin. Fax 337-5976
Morningside ES 600/K-5
2300 SE Gowin Dr 34952 772-337-6730
Kathleen Melrose, prin. Fax 337-6744
Northport K-8 S 1,200/PK-8
250 NW Floresta Dr 34983 772-340-4700
Glenn Rustay, prin. Fax 340-4716

Oak Hammock K-8 S 1,500/K-8
1251 SW California Blvd 34953 772-344-4490
Brooke Wigginton, prin. Fax 204-7211
Rivers Edge ES 700/K-5
5600 NE Saint James Dr 34983 772-785-5600
Kerri Walukiewicz, prin. Fax 785-5625
St. Lucie West K-8 S 1,400/K-8
1501 SW Cashmere Blvd 34986 772-785-6630
Eldrique Gardner, prin. Fax 785-6632
Savanna Ridge ES 500/PK-5
6801 SE Lennard Rd 34952 772-460-3050
D'Jion Jackson, prin. Fax 460-3003
Southern Oaks MS 1,000/6-8
5500 NE Saint James Dr 34983 772-785-5640
Bridgette Hargadine, prin. Fax 785-5660
Southport MS 800/6-8
2420 SE Morningside Blvd 34952 772-337-5900
Nicole Telese, prin. Fax 337-5903
Village Green ES 500/K-5
1700 SE Lennard Rd 34952 772-337-6750
Terrance Davis, prin. Fax 337-6764
West Gate K-8 S 1,200/K-8
1050 NW Cashmere Blvd 34986 772-807-7600
Kristi Parker, prin. Fax 807-7616
Windmill Point ES 800/K-5
700 SW Darwin Blvd 34953 772-336-6950
Nicole Ortega, prin. Fax 336-6962

Barnabas Christian Academy 100/K-12
1860 SW Fountainview Blvd 34986 772-344-1643
Bill Reed, admin. Fax 344-1443
Morningside Academy 200/PK-5
2180 SE Morningside Blvd 34952 772-335-3231

Princeton, Miami-Dade, Pop. 21,761

Princeton Christian S 300/PK-12
PO Box 924916 33092 305-257-3644

Punta Gorda, Charlotte, Pop. 16,453
Charlotte County SD
Supt. — See Port Charlotte
Baker Center 200/PK-PK
311 E Charlotte Ave 33950 941-575-5470
Nicole Hansen, coord. Fax 255-5474
Deep Creek ES 700/PK-5
26900 Harbor View Rd 33983 941-255-7535
Adrienne McElroy, prin. Fax 255-7541
East ES 700/PK-5
27050 Fairway Dr 33982 941-575-5475
Dr. Lauralee Carr, prin. Fax 575-5482
Jones ES 600/PK-5
1230 Narranja St 33950 941-575-5440
Jennie Hoke, prin. Fax 575-5444
Punta Gorda MS 1,100/6-8
1001 Education Ave 33950 941-575-5485
Justina Dionisio, prin. Fax 575-5491

Good Shepherd Episcopal S 100/PK-8
1800 Shreve St 33950 941-575-2139
Greg Summers, head sch Fax 575-2769

Quincy, Gadsden, Pop. 7,889
Gadsden County SD 5,200/PK-12
35 Martin Luther King Jr Bl 32351 850-627-9651
Reginald James, supt. Fax 627-2760
www.gcps.k12.fl.us
Gadsden Magnet Center 200/PK-8
500 W King St 32351 850-627-7557
Allysun Davis, prin. Fax 627-6695
Greensboro ES 400/PK-5
559 Greensboro Hwy 32351 850-442-6327
Stephen Pitts, prin. Fax 442-9524
Munroe ES 600/PK-5
1830 W King St 32351 850-875-8800
Rebecca Gaines, prin. Fax 875-8805
Shanks MS 600/6-8
1400 W King St 32351 850-875-8737
Juanita Ellis, prin. Fax 875-8775
Stewart Street ES 600/PK-5
749 S Stewart St 32351 850-627-3145
Lisa Robinson, prin. Fax 875-8750
Other Schools – See Chattahoochee, Havana

Munroe Day S 200/PK-12
91 Old Mt Pleasant Rd 32352 850-856-5500
Dr. Adam Gaffey, head sch Fax 856-5856

Reddick, Marion, Pop. 502
Marion County SD
Supt. — See Ocala
Reddick-Collier ES 400/PK-5
4595 W Highway 316 32686 352-671-6070
Joelene Vining, prin. Fax 671-6075

Riverview, Hillsborough, Pop. 68,857
Hillsborough County SD
Supt. — See Tampa
Boyette Springs ES 500/K-5
10141 Sedgebrook Dr 33569 813-671-5060
Tamethea Simmons, prin. Fax 672-5077
Collins ES 1,000/K-5
12424 Summerfield Blvd, 813-672-5400
Rebecca Sargable, prin. Fax 672-5404
Dawson ES K-5
12961 Boggy Creek Dr, 813-442-7396
Derrick McLaughlin, prin. Fax 559-8492
Frost ES 800/PK-5
3950 S Falkenburg Rd, 813-740-4900
Anthony Montoto, prin. Fax 740-4904
Giunta MS 1,000/6-8
4202 S Falkenburg Rd, 813-740-4888
Michael Bobo, prin. Fax 740-4892
Ippolito ES 900/K-5
6874 S Falkenburg Rd, 813-672-5180
Nicole Bennett, prin. Fax 672-5184
Riverview ES 700/PK-5
10809 Hannaway Dr, 813-671-5105
Melody Murphy, prin. Fax 671-5087

Rodgers MS 700/6-8
11910 Tucker Rd 33569 813-671-5288
Michael Miranda, prin. Fax 671-5245
Sessums ES 800/K-5
11525 Ramble Creek Dr 33569 813-672-5230
Allison Norgard, prin. Fax 672-5234
Summerfield Crossings ES 900/K-5
11050 Fairway Meadow Dr, 813-672-5621
Brian Harvey, prin. Fax 672-5625
Summerfield ES 800/PK-5
11990 Big Bend Rd, 813-671-5115
Carmine Alfano, prin. Fax 672-5221
Symmes ES 600/K-5
6280 Watson Rd, 813-740-4182
Anna Rothenbush, prin. Fax 740-4186

Ace International Academy K-12
10010 Park Place Ave, 813-769-5777
Providence Christian S 200/PK-12
5416 Providence Rd, 813-661-0588
Resurrection ECC 50/PK-PK
6819 Krycul Ave, 813-672-0077
Ivonne Roldan-Cortes, dir. Fax 671-7844
Riverview Montessori S 100/PK-1
11520 Ramble Creek Dr 33569 813-741-3300
St. Stephen S 300/PK-8
10424 Saint Stephen Cir 33569 813-741-9203
Linda Umoh, prin. Fax 741-9622

Riviera Beach, Palm Beach, Pop. 31,825
Palm Beach County SD
Supt. — See West Palm Beach
Bethune ES 400/K-5
1501 Avenue U 33404 561-882-7600
Katrina Granger, prin. Fax 882-7650
Kennedy MS 800/6-8
1901 Avenue S 33404 561-845-4500
Corey Brooks, prin. Fax 845-4537
Lincoln ES 500/PK-5
1160 W 10th St 33404 561-494-1400
Alicia Porter, prin. Fax 494-1450
Washington ES 400/K-5
1709 W 30th St 33404 561-494-1200
Sandra Edwards, prin. Fax 494-1250
West Riviera ES 700/K-5
1057 W 6th St 33404 561-494-1900
Robin Brown, prin. Fax 494-1950

Bethel Junior Academy 50/PK-8
2850 Avenue F 33404 561-881-0130
Hendley Christian Education Center 300/PK-8
2760 R J Henley Ave 33404 561-842-1349

Rockledge, Brevard, Pop. 24,317
Brevard County SD
Supt. — See Melbourne
Andersen ES 700/K-6
3011 S Fiske Blvd 32955 321-633-3610
Denise Johnson, prin. Fax 633-3619
Golfview ES 600/PK-6
1530 S Fiske Blvd 32955 321-633-3570
Katrina Hudson, prin. Fax 633-3579
Kennedy MS 600/7-8
2100 S Fiske Blvd 32955 321-633-3500
Richard Myers, prin. Fax 633-3509
McNair Magnet MS 500/7-8
1 Challenger Dr 32955 321-633-3630
Jasmine DeLaughter, prin. Fax 633-3639
Williams ES 500/K-6
1700 Clubhouse Dr 32955 321-617-7700
Wes Harold, prin. Fax 617-7703

Rockledge Christian S 100/PK-8
2175 S Fiske Blvd 32955 321-632-6966
Ric Speigner, prin. Fax 632-8951
Rockledge Montessori S 50/PK-K
3260 S Fiske Blvd 32955 321-639-2266
St. Mary S 400/PK-8
1152 Seminole Dr 32955 321-636-4208
Sandra Basinger, prin. Fax 636-0591
Trinity Lutheran S 100/PK-8
1330 S Fiske Blvd 32955 321-636-5431
Jon Wareham, prin. Fax 638-4498

Rosemary Beach, Walton

Ohana Institute 100/3-12
82 S Barret Sq 32461 850-231-1140

Rotonda West, Charlotte
Charlotte County SD
Supt. — See Port Charlotte
Ainger MS 900/6-8
245 Cougar Way 33947 941-697-5800
Jeff Harvey, prin. Fax 697-5470
Vineland ES 600/PK-5
467 Boundary Blvd 33947 941-697-6600
Laura Blunier, prin. Fax 697-5902

Royal Palm Beach, Palm Beach, Pop. 33,307
Palm Beach County SD
Supt. — See West Palm Beach
Crestwood MS 1,000/6-8
64 Sparrow Dr 33411 561-753-5000
Stephanie Nance, prin. Fax 753-5035
Cypress Trails ES 500/K-5
133 Park Rd N 33411 561-904-9000
Shari Bremekamp, prin. Fax 904-9050
Johnson ES 900/K-5
1000 Crestwood Blvd N 33411 561-904-9300
Dr. Jennifer Makowski, prin. Fax 904-9350
Royal Palm Beach ES 600/K-5
11911 Okeechobee Blvd 33411 561-633-4400
Tracy Gaugler, prin. Fax 633-4450

Ideal S of Advanced Learning 200/PK-8
400 Royal Commerce Rd 33411 561-791-2881

Ruskin, Hillsborough, Pop. 16,985
Hillsborough County SD
Supt. — See Tampa
Cypress Creek ES 1,100/K-5
4040 19th Ave NE 33573 813-671-5167
Roy Moral, prin. Fax 671-5204
Ruskin ES 1,100/PK-5
101 E College Ave 33570 813-671-5177
Rebecca Salgado, prin. Fax 671-5182
Shields MS 1,500/6-8
15732 Beth Shields Way 33573 813-672-5338
Tia Brown, prin. Fax 672-5342
Thompson ES K-5
2020 E Shell Point Rd 33570 813-938-1203
Milady Astacio, prin. Fax 938-1204

Ruskin Christian S 200/PK-12
820 W College Ave 33570 813-645-6441

Safety Harbor, Pinellas, Pop. 16,579
Pinellas County SD
Supt. — See Largo
Safety Harbor ES 600/K-5
535 5th Ave N 34695 727-724-1462
Cecelia Palmer, prin. Fax 724-1461
Safety Harbor MS 1,400/6-8
901 1st Ave N 34695 727-724-1400
Carrie Armstrong, prin. Fax 724-1407

Espiritu Santos Catholic S 500/PK-8
2405A Phillippe Pkwy 34695 727-812-4650
Margaret Penn, prin. Fax 812-4658

Saint Augustine, Saint Johns, Pop. 12,760
St. Johns County SD 33,100/PK-12
40 Orange St 32084 904-547-7500
Tim Forson, supt. Fax 547-7515
www.stjohns.k12.fl.us
Crookshank ES 700/K-5
1455 N Whitney St 32084 904-547-7840
Marquez Jackson, prin. Fax 547-7845
Hartley ES 700/K-5
260 Cacique Dr 32086 904-547-8400
Antonio Scott, prin. Fax 547-8385
Hunt ES 700/K-5
125 Magnolia Dr 32080 904-547-7960
Amanda Garman, prin. Fax 547-7955
Ketterlinus ES 500/PK-5
67 Orange St 32084 904-547-8540
Kathy Tucker, prin. Fax 547-8554
Mason ES 600/PK-5
207 Mason Manatee Way 32086 904-547-8440
Nigel Pillay, prin. Fax 547-8445
Mill Creek ES 900/K-5
3750 International Golf Pkw 32092 904-547-3720
Amanda Riedl, prin. Fax 547-3730
Murray MS 800/6-8
150 N Holmes Blvd 32084 904-547-8470
Tom Schwarm, prin. Fax 547-8475
Osceola ES 700/PK-5
1605 Osceola Elementary Rd 32084 904-547-3780
Tina Waldrop, prin. Fax 547-3795
Pacetti Bay MS 1,000/6-8
245 Meadowlark Ln 32092 904-547-8760
Jay Willets, prin. Fax 547-8765
Palencia ES 600/K-5
355 Palencia Village Dr 32095 904-547-4010
Allen Anderson, prin. Fax 547-4015
Picolata Crossing ES K-5
2675 Pacetti Rd 32092 904-547-4160
Randall Strickland, prin. Fax 547-4165
Rogers MS 800/6-8
6250 US Highway 1 S 32086 904-547-8700
Greg Bergamasco, prin. Fax 547-8705
Sebastian MS 600/6-8
2955 Lewis Speedway 32084 904-547-3840
Wayne King, prin. Fax 547-3845
Timberlin Creek ES 1,000/PK-5
555 Pine Tree Ln 32092 904-547-7400
Linda Edel, prin. Fax 547-7405
Wards Creek ES 800/PK-5
6555 State Road 16 32092 904-547-8730
Bethany Mitidieri, prin. Fax 547-8735
Webster ES 600/PK-5
420 N Orange St 32084 904-547-3860
Bethany Groves, prin. Fax 547-3865
Other Schools – See Elkton, Ponte Vedra Beach, Saint Johns

Beacon of Hope Christian S 100/K-12
1230 Kings Estate Rd 32086 904-797-6996
Cathedral Parish Early Ed Center 100/PK-PK
10 Sebastian Ave 32084 904-829-2933
Jill Valley, dir. Fax 829-9339
Cathedral Parish S 300/K-8
259 Saint George St 32084 904-824-2861
Katherine Boice, prin. Fax 829-2059
St. John's Academy 100/K-8
1533 Wildwood Dr 32086 904-824-9224
Wallis Brooks, prin. Fax 823-1145
Turning Point Christian Academy 400/PK-8
3500 State Rd 16 32092 904-829-9795
Victory Prep S, 110 Masters Dr 32084 K-12
Michelle Mauro, prin. 904-810-0535
Washington Classical Christian S PK-3
2121 US Highway 1 S Ste 28 32086 904-323-2911

Saint Cloud, Osceola, Pop. 34,423
Osceola County SD
Supt. — See Kissimmee
Harmony Community S 900/K-8
3365 Schoolhouse Rd 34773 407-892-1655
Sandra Davenport, prin. Fax 343-8745
Hickory Tree ES 700/K-5
2355 Old Hickory Tree Rd 34772 407-891-3120
Karen Vislocky, prin. Fax 891-3129
Lakeview ES 700/PK-5
2900 5th St 34769 407-891-3220
Tracy Shenuski, prin. Fax 891-3228

Michigan Avenue ES 600/PK-5
2015 Michigan Ave 34769 407-891-3140
Diane Crook-Nichols, prin. Fax 891-3149
Narcoossee ES 700/PK-5
2690 N Narcoossee Rd 34771 407-892-6858
Scott Knoebel, prin. Fax 518-2009
Narcoossee MS 1,100/6-8
2700 N Narcoossee Rd 34771 407-891-6600
Frank Telemko, prin. Fax 891-6610
Neptune ES 900/PK-5
1200 Betsy Ross Ln 34769 407-892-8387
Linda Harwood, prin. Fax 957-2684
Saint Cloud ES 900/K-5
2701 Budinger Ave 34769 407-891-3160
Megan Dierickx, prin. Fax 891-3169
Saint Cloud MS 1,100/6-8
1975 Michigan Ave 34769 407-891-3200
Cynthia Chiavini, prin. Fax 891-3206

St. Thomas Aquinas S 300/PK-8
800 Brown Chapel Rd 34769 407-957-1772
Maura Cox, prin. Fax 957-8700

Saint Johns, Saint Johns
St. Johns County SD
Supt. — See Saint Augustine
Cunningham Creek ES 800/PK-5
1205 Roberts Rd, 904-547-7860
Edie Jarrell, prin. Fax 547-7854
Durbin Creek ES 900/K-5
4100 Race Track Rd, 904-547-3880
Angie Fuller, prin. Fax 547-3885
Fruit Cove MS 1,300/6-8
3180 Race Track Rd, 904-547-7880
Kelly Jacobson, prin. Fax 547-7885
Hickory Creek ES 800/K-5
235 Hickory Creek Trl, 904-547-7450
Joy Reichenberg, prin. Fax 547-7455
Julington Creek ES 1,100/K-5
2316 Race Track Rd, 904-547-7980
Jeanette Murphy, prin. Fax 547-7985
Liberty Pines Academy 1,400/K-8
10901 Russell Sampson Rd, 904-547-7900
Traci Hemingway, prin. Fax 547-7905
Patriot Oaks Academy K-8
475 Longleaf Pine Pkwy, 904-547-4050
Allison Olson, prin. Fax 547-4055
Switzerland Point MS 1,300/6-8
777 Greenbriar Rd, 904-547-8650
Kirstie Gabaldon, prin. Fax 547-8645

San Juan Del Rio S 400/PK-8
1714 State Road 13, 904-287-8081
Ann Marie Barta, prin. Fax 287-4574

Saint Petersburg, Pinellas, Pop. 239,351
Pinellas County SD
Supt. — See Largo
Azalea ES 600/PK-5
1680 74th St N 33710 727-893-2187
Kris Sulte, prin. Fax 893-2190
Azalea MS 1,000/6-8
7855 22nd Ave N 33710 727-893-2606
Dr. Solomon Lowery, prin. Fax 893-2624
Bay Point ES 700/K-5
5800 22nd St S 33712 727-552-1449
Sara DePerro, prin. Fax 552-1455
Bay Point MS 900/6-8
2151 62nd Ave S 33712 727-893-1153
Jason Shedrick, prin. Fax 893-1181
Bay Vista Fundamental ES 600/K-5
5900 Dr Martin L King St S 33705 727-893-2335
Keila Victor, prin. Fax 893-1800
Bear Creek ES 400/PK-5
350 61st St S 33707 727-893-2332
Willette Houston, prin. Fax 893-2334
Blanton ES 500/PK-5
6400 54th Ave N 33709 727-547-7820
Cheryl Maggio, prin. Fax 545-6562
Campbell Park ES 600/PK-5
1051 7th Ave S 33705 727-893-2650
Kathleen Young-Parker, prin. Fax 893-2652
Fairmount Park ES 600/PK-5
575 41st St S 33711 727-893-2132
Kristy Moody, prin. Fax 893-5451
Hopkins MS 900/6-8
701 16th St S 33705 727-893-2400
Dr. Dallas Jackson, prin. Fax 893-1600
Jamerson ES 600/K-5
1200 37th St S 33711 727-552-1703
Brandie Williams-Macon, prin. Fax 552-1704
Lakeview Fundamental ES 300/K-5
2229 25th St S 33712 727-893-2139
Susan Garcia-Nikolova, prin. Fax 893-1359
Lakewood ES 500/PK-5
4151 6th St S 33705 727-893-2196
Daphne Miles, prin. Fax 893-9152
Lealman Avenue ES 500/PK-5
4001 58th Ave N 33714 727-570-3020
Kristen Sulte, prin. Fax 570-3300
Lynch ES 700/PK-5
1901 71st Ave N 33702 727-570-3170
Cynthia Kidd, prin. Fax 570-3186
Marshall Fundamental MS 900/6-8
3901 22nd Ave S 33711 727-552-1737
Nicole Wilson, prin. Fax 552-1741
Maximo ES 500/PK-5
4850 31st St S 33712 727-893-2191
Lakisha Falana, prin. Fax 754-8375
Meadowlawn MS 1,200/6-8
6050 16th St N 33703 727-570-3097
Ursula Parris, prin. Fax 570-3396
Melrose ES 400/K-5
1752 13th Ave S 33712 727-893-2175
Nikita Reed, prin. Fax 893-1884
Mt. Vernon ES 500/K-5
4629 13th Ave N 33713 727-893-1815
Robert Ovalle, prin. Fax 550-4149
New Heights ES 800/PK-5
3901 37th St N 33714 727-521-5350
Lisa Austin, prin. Fax 521-5355
North Shore ES 400/K-5
200 35th Ave NE 33704 727-893-2181
Cooper Dawson, prin. Fax 893-5483
Northwest ES 600/K-5
5601 22nd Ave N 33710 727-893-2147
Marie Brainard, prin. Fax 893-1888
Pasadena Fundamental ES 500/K-5
95 72nd St N 33710 727-893-2646
Donita Moody, prin. Fax 893-2408
Perkins ES 600/PK-5
2205 18th Ave S 33712 727-893-2117
Tony Pleshe, prin. Fax 893-1113
Sanderlin IB World S 600/K-8
2350 22nd Ave S 33712 727-552-1700
Dr. Denise Miller, prin. Fax 552-1701
Sawgrass Lake ES 700/PK-5
1815 77th Ave N 33702 727-570-3121
Jessica Clements, prin. Fax 217-7251
Seventy-Fourth Street ES 600/PK-5
3801 74th St N 33709 727-893-2120
Donna Gehringer, prin. Fax 893-2143
Sexton ES 700/PK-5
1997 54th Ave N 33714 727-570-3400
Suzette Burns, prin. Fax 217-7236
Shore Acres ES 700/PK-5
1800 62nd Ave NE 33702 727-570-3173
Benigna Pollauf, prin. Fax 570-3175
Tyrone MS 900/6-8
6421 22nd Ave N 33710 727-893-1819
Robin Mobley, prin. Fax 893-1946
Westgate ES 600/K-5
3560 58th St N 33710 727-893-2144
Bonita Paquette, prin. Fax 893-2146
Woodlawn ES 400/K-5
1600 16th St N 33704 727-893-1857
Tammy Keiper, prin. Fax 893-5482

Admiral Farragut Academy 400/PK-12
501 Park St N 33710 727-384-5500
Robert Fine, hdmstr. Fax 347-5160
Alegria Montessori S 100/PK-6
3200 58th Ave S 33712 727-866-1901
Canterbury S of Florida - Hough Campus 200/PK-4
1200 Snell Isle Blvd NE 33704 727-525-1419
Mac Hall, head sch Fax 521-5998
Cathedral School of St. Jude 300/PK-8
600 58th St N 33710 727-347-8622
Ross Bubolz, prin. Fax 343-0305
Elim Jr. Academy 50/K-8
4824 2nd Ave S 33711 727-289-7089
Grace Lutheran S 200/PK-8
4301 16th St N 33703 727-527-6213
Nicole Clifton, prin. Fax 522-4535
Gulfcoast Seventh Day Adventist S 50/K-8
6001 7th Ave S 33707 727-345-2141
Holy Family Catholic S 200/K-8
250 78th Ave NE 33702 727-526-8194
Christopher Meyer, prin. Fax 527-6567
Holy Family ECC PK-PK
200 78th Ave NE 33702 727-525-8489
Nina Meyers, dir. Fax 851-9913
Keswick Christian S 500/PK-12
10101 54th Ave N 33708 727-393-9100
Nick Stratis, supt. Fax 397-5378
Liberty Christian S 200/PK-5
9401 4th St N 33702 727-576-9635
Lutheran Church of the Cross Day S 400/PK-8
4400 Chancellor St NE 33703 727-522-8331
Holly Carlson, head sch Fax 527-3252
Northside Christian S 600/PK-12
7777 62nd Ave N 33709 727-541-7593
Dr. Donald James, hdmstr. Fax 546-5836
Our Savior Lutheran S 200/PK-8
5843 4th Ave S 33707 727-344-1026
Jesse Crosmer, prin. Fax 381-3980
St. Paul Catholic S 300/PK-8
1900 12th St N 33704 727-823-6144
Rose Smoot, prin. Fax 896-0609
St. Petersburg Christian S 500/K-8
2021 62nd Ave N 33702 727-522-3000
Bobby Hunter, hdmstr. Fax 525-0998
St. Raphael S 200/PK-8
1376 Snell Isle Blvd NE 33704 727-821-9663
Kathy Bogataj, prin. Fax 502-9594
School of the Immaculata 100/PK-12
4265 13th Ave N 33713 727-321-8890
Shorecrest Preparatory S 1,000/PK-12
5101 1st St NE 33703 727-522-2111
Michael Murphy, hdmstr. Fax 527-4191
Southside Christian Academy 100/PK-5
3647 18th Ave S 33711 727-327-2691
Rev. Richard Jackson, prin. Fax 321-2981

Saint Petersburg Beach, Pinellas, Pop. 9,248
Pinellas County SD
Supt. — See Largo
Gulf Beaches ES 400/K-5
8600 Boca Ciega Dr 33706 727-893-2630
Robert Kalach, prin. Fax 754-8651

Montessori by the Sea 50/PK-6
1603 Gulf Way 33706 727-360-7621
Nicole Wilson, head sch
St. John Vianney S 300/PK-8
500 84th Ave 33706 727-360-1113
Jillian Hudson, prin. Fax 367-8734

San Antonio, Pasco, Pop. 1,128

St. Anthony S 200/PK-8
PO Box 847 33576 352-588-3041
Sr. Alice Ottapurackal, prin. Fax 588-3142

Sanford, Seminole, Pop. 52,277
Seminole County SD 64,400/PK-12
400 E Lake Mary Blvd 32773 407-320-0000
Dr. Walt Griffin, supt. Fax 320-0281
www.scps.k12.fl.us
Bentley ES 1,000/PK-5
2190 S Oregon Ave 32771 407-871-9950
Martha Garcia, prin. Fax 871-9996
Goldsboro Magnet ES 700/PK-5
1300 W 20th St 32771 407-320-5850
Keaton Schreiner, prin. Fax 320-5896
Hamilton ES 700/PK-5
1501 E 8th St 32771 407-320-6050
Michael Pfeiffer, prin. Fax 320-6005
Idyllwilde ES 800/PK-5
430 Vihlen Rd 32771 407-320-3750
Robert Navarro, prin. Fax 320-3799
Midway ES 700/PK-5
2368 Brisson Ave 32771 407-320-5950
Cathy Lambert, prin. Fax 320-5961
Millennium MS 1,600/6-8
21 Lakeview Ave 32773 407-320-6550
Dr. Maggie Gunderson, prin. Fax 320-6599
Pine Crest ES 900/PK-5
405 W 27th St 32773 407-320-5450
Alex Agosto, prin. Fax 320-5499
Sanford MS 1,500/6-8
1700 S French Ave 32771 407-320-6150
Byron Durias, prin. Fax 320-6265
Wicklow ES 700/K-5
100 Placid Lake Dr 32773 407-320-1250
Martina Herndon, prin. Fax 320-1215
Wilson ES 900/PK-5
985 Orange Blvd 32771 407-320-6950
Kelly Mitchell, prin. Fax 320-6999
Other Schools – See Altamonte Springs, Apopka, Casselberry, Chuluota, Fern Park, Geneva, Lake Mary, Longwood, Oviedo, Winter Park, Winter Springs

All Souls Catholic S 300/PK-8
810 S Oak Ave 32771 407-322-7090
Dr. Kathleen Kiley, prin. Fax 321-7255
Central Florida Academy 100/PK-12
1626 W Airport Blvd 32771 407-363-0063
Holy Cross Academy 300/PK-4
5450 Holy Cross Ct 32771 407-936-3636
Rob Sinninger, prin. Fax 936-0041
Liberty Christian S 100/PK-12
2626 S Palmetto Ave 32773 407-323-1583
William Simpson, prin. Fax 323-1588

Sanibel, Lee, Pop. 6,439
Lee County SD
Supt. — See Fort Myers
Sanibel S 300/K-8
3840 Sanibel Captiva Rd 33957 239-472-1617
Charles Vilardi, prin. Fax 472-6544

San Mateo, Putnam
Putnam County SD
Supt. — See Palatka
Browning-Pearce ES 800/PK-5
100 Bear Blvd 32187 386-329-0557
Ashley McCool, prin. Fax 329-0623

Santa Rosa Beach, Walton
Walton County SD
Supt. — See De Funiak Springs
Bay ES 300/PK-4
118 Gilmore Rd 32459 850-622-5050
Meredith Spence, prin. Fax 622-5059
Butler ES 900/PK-4
6694 W County Highway 30A 32459 850-622-5040
Tammy Smith, prin. Fax 622-5048
Emerald Coast MS 700/5-8
4019 Highway 98 E 32459 850-622-5025
Jeff Infinger, prin. Fax 622-5027

St. Rita PreSchool PK-PK
137 Moll Dr 32459 850-461-5635
Lisa Brooks, dir. Fax 267-3711
South Walton Montessori Academy 50/PK-8
101 Eden Gardens Rd 32459 850-231-5955

Sarasota, Sarasota, Pop. 51,038
Manatee County SD
Supt. — See Bradenton
Abel ES 500/K-5
7100 Madonna Pl 34243 941-751-7040
James Horner, prin. Fax 753-0919
Kinnan ES 700/K-5
3415 Tallevast Rd 34243 941-358-2888
Paul Hockenbury, prin. Fax 358-2956

Sarasota County SD 40,400/PK-12
1960 Landings Blvd 34231 941-927-9000
Dr. Todd Bowden, supt.
sarasotacountyschools.net
Alta Vista ES 600/K-5
1050 S Euclid Ave 34237 941-361-6400
Dr. Barbara Shirley, prin. Fax 361-6956
Ashton ES 800/K-5
5110 Ashton Rd 34233 941-361-6440
Kristi Jarvis, prin. Fax 361-6444
Bay Haven S of Basics Plus 600/K-5
2901 W Tamiami Cir 34234 941-359-5800
Chad Erickson, prin. Fax 359-5694
Booker ES 500/K-5
2350 Dr Martin Luther King 34234 941-361-6480
Edwina Oliver, prin. Fax 361-6484
Booker MS 800/6-8
2250 Myrtle St 34234 941-359-5824
Dr. LaShawn Houston-Frost, prin. Fax 359-5898
Brentwood ES 600/K-5
2500 Vinson Ave 34232 941-361-6230
John Weida, prin. Fax 361-6381
Brookside MS 800/6-8
3636 S Shade Ave 34239 941-361-6472
Matthew Gruhl, prin. Fax 361-6508

Fruitville ES 800/PK-5
601 Honore Ave 34232 941-361-6200
Steven French, prin. Fax 361-6203
Gocio ES 700/K-5
3450 Gocio Rd 34235 941-361-6405
Steven Royce, prin. Fax 361-6793
Gulf Gate ES 700/K-5
6500 S Lockwood Ridge Rd 34231 941-361-6499
Robin Magac, prin. Fax 361-6799
Lakeview ES 600/K-5
7299 Proctor Rd 34241 941-361-6571
Lisa Wheatley, prin. Fax 361-6573
McIntosh MS 800/6-8
701 McIntosh Rd 34232 941-361-6520
Dr. Harriet Moore, prin. Fax 361-6340
Philippi Shores ES 700/K-5
4747 S Tamiami Trl 34231 941-361-6424
Dr. Allison Foster, prin. Fax 361-6814
Sarasota MS 1,200/6-8
4826 Ashton Rd 34233 941-361-6464
Janel Dorn, prin. Fax 361-6798
Southside ES 800/K-5
1901 Webber St 34239 941-361-6420
Steven Dragon, prin. Fax 361-6866
Tatum Ridge ES 700/K-5
4100 Tatum Rd 34240 941-316-8188
Barry Dunn, prin. Fax 316-8189
Tuttle ES 700/K-5
2863 8th St 34237 941-361-6433
Tomas Dinverno, prin. Fax 361-6530
Wilkinson ES 500/PK-5
3400 Wilkinson Rd 34231 941-361-6477
Susan Nations, prin. Fax 361-1877
Other Schools – See Englewood, Nokomis, North Port, Osprey, Venice

Ascension Lutheran S 100/PK-8
800 McIntosh Rd 34232 941-371-5909
Luke Beilke, prin. Fax 377-9670
Calvary Chapel S 100/PK-8
3800 27th Pkwy 34235 941-366-6522
Nicholas Sommer, prin. Fax 366-1906
Classical Academy of Sarasota 100/PK-12
8751 Fruitville Rd 34240 941-925-2153
Foundations Christian Montessori Academy 100/PK-8
4141 Desoto Rd 34235 941-907-7078
Hershorin-Schiff Community Day S 200/PK-8
1050 S Tuttle Ave 34237 941-552-2770
Incarnation Catholic S 200/PK-8
2911 Bee Ridge Rd 34239 941-924-8588
Coleen Curlett, prin. Fax 925-1248
NewGate S 100/PK-12
5237 Ashton Rd 34233 941-922-4949
Out of Door Academy 200/PK-5
444 Reid St 34242 941-349-3223
David Mahler, head sch Fax 349-8133
Potter's Wheel Academy 100/K-12
PO Box 50203 34232 941-284-4076
Providence Community S 200/PK-12
5600 Deer Dr 34240 941-727-6860
Barry Batson, admin. Fax 727-6870
St. Martha Catholic S 400/PK-8
4380 Fruitville Rd 34232 941-953-4181
Siobhan Young, prin. Fax 366-5580
Sarasota Christian S 400/PK-12
5415 Bahia Vista St 34232 941-371-6481
Ryan Lehman, head sch Fax 371-0898

Satellite Beach, Brevard, Pop. 9,911
Brevard County SD
Supt. — See Melbourne
DeLaura MS 700/7-8
300 Jackson Ave 32937 321-773-7581
Robert Pruett, prin. Fax 773-0702
Holland ES 400/K-6
50 Holland Ct 32937 321-773-7591
Samantha Alison, prin. Fax 773-6315
Sea Park ES 300/PK-6
300 Sea Park Blvd 32937 321-779-2050
Ena Leiba, prin. Fax 779-2052
Surfside ES 400/K-6
475 Cassia Blvd 32937 321-773-2818
Lori Masterson, prin. Fax 777-1841

Sebastian, Indian River, Pop. 21,634
Indian River County SD
Supt. — See Vero Beach
Pelican Island ES 500/PK-5
1355 Schumann Dr 32958 772-564-6500
Chris Kohlstedt, prin. Fax 564-6493
Sebastian ES 500/K-5
400 Sebastian Blvd 32958 772-978-8200
Letitia Whitfield, prin. Fax 978-8205
Sebastian River MS 900/6-8
9400 County Road 512 32958 772-564-5111
Jody Idlette, prin. Fax 564-5225
Treasure Coast ES 600/K-5
8955 85th St 32958 772-978-8500
Liz Tetreault, prin. Fax 978-8503

Sebring, Highlands, Pop. 10,311
Highlands County SD 12,100/PK-12
426 School St 33870 863-471-5555
Wally Cox, supt. Fax 471-5600
www.highlands.k12.fl.us
Cracker Trail ES 600/1-5
8200 Sparta Rd 33875 863-471-5777
Laura Waldon, prin. Fax 471-5785
Hill-Gustat MS 700/6-8
4700 Schumacher Rd 33872 863-471-5437
Chris Doty, prin. Fax 314-5245
Kindergarten Learning Center 400/K-K
3560 US Highway 27 S 33870 863-314-5281
Karin Doty, prin. Fax 314-5287
Sebring MS 700/6-8
500 E Center Ave 33870 863-471-5700
Kevin Tunning, prin. Fax 471-5710
Sun N Lake ES 800/PK-5
4515 Ponce De Leon Blvd 33872 863-471-5464
Dr. Linda Laye, prin. Fax 471-5466
Wild ES 500/PK-PK, 1-
3550 Youth Care Ln 33870 863-471-5400
Jeannie Inagawa, prin. Fax 471-5426
Woodlawn ES 600/PK-PK, 1-
817 Woodlawn Dr 33870 863-471-5444
Melissa Blackman, prin. Fax 471-5446
Other Schools – See Avon Park, Lake Placid

St. Catherine Catholic S 100/PK-6
747 S Franklin St 33870 863-385-7300
Jorge Rivera, prin. Fax 385-7310

Seffner, Hillsborough, Pop. 7,410
Hillsborough County SD
Supt. — See Tampa
Burnett MS 900/6-8
1010 N Kingsway Rd 33584 813-744-6745
Dante Jones, prin. Fax 744-8973
Colson ES 700/K-5
1520 Lakeview Ave 33584 813-744-8031
Orestes Mendez, prin. Fax 744-8439
Jennings MS 800/6-8
9325 Governors Run Dr 33584 813-740-4575
Richard Scionti, prin. Fax 740-4579
Lopez ES 500/PK-5
200 N Kingsway Rd 33584 813-744-8000
Michael Engle, prin. Fax 744-8005
Mango ES 800/PK-5
4220 County Road 579 33584 813-744-8208
Felicia Davis, prin. Fax 744-8211
McDonald ES 600/K-5
501 Pruett Rd 33584 813-744-8154
Jessica Hessler, prin. Fax 744-8012
Seffner ES 700/K-5
109 Cactus Rd 33584 813-744-8171
Shelly Hermann, prin. Fax 740-3984

New Jerusalem Christian Academy 100/PK-8
PO Box 1238 33583 813-684-2754
Dari Valladares, prin. Fax 684-0051
Seffner Christian Academy 700/PK-12
11605 E US Highway 92 33584 813-626-0001
Roger Duncan, admin. Fax 627-0330

Seminole, Pinellas, Pop. 17,030
Pinellas County SD
Supt. — See Largo
Bardmoor ES 600/PK-5
8900 Greenbriar Rd 33777 727-547-7824
Leigh Brown, prin. Fax 545-6593
Bauder ES 800/PK-5
12755 86th Ave 33776 727-547-7829
Lisa Bultmann, prin. Fax 547-4564
Orange Grove ES 400/K-5
10300 65th Ave 33772 727-547-7845
Christine Porter, prin. Fax 547-7505
Osceola MS 1,200/6-8
9301 98th St 33777 727-547-7689
Susan Arsenault, prin. Fax 547-7667
Seminole ES 600/K-5
10950 74th Ave 33772 727-547-7668
Nanette Grasso, prin. Fax 545-6585
Seminole MS 1,200/6-8
8701 131st St 33776 727-547-4520
Wendy Bryan, prin. Fax 547-7741
Starkey ES 600/K-5
9300 86th Ave 33777 727-547-7841
Audrey Chaffin, prin. Fax 545-7550

Bay Pines Lutheran S 100/PK-8
7589 113th Ln 33772 727-397-3204
Matt Oppermann, prin. Fax 391-6823
Blessed Sacrament S 200/K-8
11501 66th Ave 33772 727-391-4060
Rebecca Clark, prin. Fax 391-5638

Shalimar, Okaloosa, Pop. 699
Okaloosa County SD
Supt. — See Fort Walton Beach
Longwood ES 600/PK-5
50 Holly Ave 32579 850-833-4329
Yvonne Michna, prin. Fax 833-4336
Meigs MS 500/6-8
150 Richbourg Ave 32579 850-833-4301
Michelle Heck, prin. Fax 833-9392
Shalimar ES 600/K-5
1350 Joe Martin Cir 32579 850-833-4339
Kim McSparren, prin. Fax 833-4357

Silver Springs, Marion
Marion County SD
Supt. — See Ocala
East Marion ES 700/PK-5
14550 NE 14th Street Rd 34488 352-671-4810
Suzette Parker, prin. Fax 671-4811

Sneads, Jackson, Pop. 1,817
Jackson County SD
Supt. — See Marianna
Sneads ES 500/PK-5
1961 Lockey Dr 32460 850-482-9003
Melynda Howell, prin. Fax 482-9590

Sorrento, Lake, Pop. 846
Lake County SD
Supt. — See Tavares
Sorrento ES 700/PK-5
24605 Wallick Rd 32776 352-385-1140
Brenna Burkhead, prin. Fax 385-1159

South Bay, Palm Beach, Pop. 4,842
Palm Beach County SD
Supt. — See West Palm Beach
Rosenwald ES 200/K-5
1321 Martin L King Jr Blvd 33493 561-993-8900
Dionne Napier, prin. Fax 993-8938

South Daytona, Volusia, Pop. 12,013
Volusia County SD
Supt. — See De Land
South Daytona ES 800/K-5
600 Elizabeth Pl 32119 386-322-6180
Lynn Bruner, prin. Fax 756-7191

Warner Christian Academy 700/PK-12
1730 S Ridgewood Ave 32119 386-767-5451
Mark Tress, supt. Fax 760-6834

South Miami, Miami-Dade, Pop. 11,508
Miami-Dade County SD
Supt. — See Miami
Ludlam ES 400/PK-5
6639 SW 74th St 33143 305-667-5551
Dr. Georgette Menocal, prin. Fax 666-3070
South Miami K-8 Ctr 800/PK-8
6800 SW 60th St 33143 305-667-8847
Lourdes Lopez, prin. Fax 665-3217
South Miami MS 1,000/6-8
6750 SW 60th St 33143 305-661-3481
Fabiola Izaguirre, prin. Fax 665-6728
Sunset ES 1,100/PK-5
5120 Sunset Dr 33143 305-661-8527
Dr. Marlene Vidal, prin. Fax 666-2327

Southwest Ranches, Broward, Pop. 7,178

St. Mark S 700/PK-8
5601 S Flamingo Rd, 954-434-3887
Teresita Wardlow, prin. Fax 434-3595

Spring Hill, Hernando, Pop. 96,871
Hernando County SD
Supt. — See Brooksville
Challenger S of Science and Mathematics 1,600/K-8
13400 Elgin Blvd 34609 352-797-7024
Lisa Piesik, prin. Fax 797-7124
Deltona ES 800/PK-5
2055 Deltona Blvd 34606 352-797-7040
Debi Vermette, prin. Fax 797-7140
Explorer K-8 S 1,700/K-8
10252 Northcliffe Blvd 34608 352-797-7094
Lisa Braithwaite, prin. Fax 797-7194
Floyd S 700/PK-5
3139 Dumont Ave 34609 352-797-7055
Joyce Lewis, prin. Fax 797-7155
Fox Chapel MS 600/6-8
9412 Fox Chapel Ln 34606 352-797-7025
Ray Pinder, prin. Fax 797-7125
Spring Hill ES 700/PK-5
6001 Mariner Blvd 34609 352-797-7030
Michael Maine, prin. Fax 797-7130
Suncoast ES 900/PK-5
11135 Quality Dr 34609 352-797-7085
Scott Piesik, prin. Fax 797-7185
Westside ES 600/PK-5
5400 Applegate Dr 34606 352-797-7080
Kristina Stratton, prin. Fax 797-7180

Pasco County SD
Supt. — See Land O Lakes
Crews Lake MS 700/6-8
15144 Shady Hills Rd 34610 727-246-1600
David Huyck, prin. Fax 246-1691
Giella ES 700/PK-5
14710 Shady Hills Rd 34610 727-774-5800
George Papaemanuel, prin. Fax 774-5891
Shady Hills ES 500/PK-5
18000 Shady Hills Rd 34610 813-794-4100
Thomas Barker, prin. Fax 794-4191

Notre Dame S 200/PK-8
1095 Commercial Way 34606 352-683-0755
Florie Buono, prin. Fax 683-3924
Spring Hill Christian Academy 300/PK-12
3140 Mariner Blvd 34609 352-683-8485
West Hernando Christian S 300/PK-12
2250 Osowaw Blvd 34607 352-688-9918
David Hand, prin. Fax 683-1184
Wider Horizons S 100/PK-12
4060 Castle Ave 34609 352-686-1934

Starke, Bradford, Pop. 5,317
Bradford County SD 3,100/PK-12
501 W Washington St 32091 904-966-6018
Chad Farnsworth, supt. Fax 966-6030
www.bradfordschools.org
Bradford MS 700/6-8
527 N Orange St 32091 904-966-6705
Mallory McConnell, prin. Fax 966-6714
Southside ES 600/PK-5
823 Stansbury St 32091 904-966-6061
Earnest Williams, prin. Fax 964-8881
Starke ES 500/PK-5
1000 W Weldon St 32091 904-966-6045
Talitha Chestnut, prin. Fax 966-6868
Other Schools – See Brooker, Hampton, Lawtey

Hope Christian Academy 200/PK-12
3900 SE State Road 100 32091 352-473-4040
Jane Thurman, prin. Fax 473-2024
Northside Christian Academy 200/PK-12
7415 NW County Road 225 32091 904-964-7124
Toby Roehn, admin. Fax 966-2350

Steinhatchee, Taylor, Pop. 1,045
Taylor County SD
Supt. — See Perry
Steinhatchee S 100/K-5
1209 1st Ave SE 32359 352-498-3303
Marion McCray, prin. Fax 498-6050

Stuart, Martin, Pop. 15,329
Martin County SD 18,100/PK-12
500 SE Ocean Blvd 34994 772-219-1200
Laurie J. Gaylord, supt. Fax 219-1231
www.martinschools.org
Anderson MS 900/6-8
7000 SE Atlantic Ridge Dr 34997 772-221-7100
Timothy Aitken, prin. Fax 221-7149

Crystal Lake ES 600/PK-5
2095 SW 96th St 34997 772-219-1525
Brenda Watkins, prin. Fax 219-1529
Murray MS 800/6-8
4400 SE Murray St 34997 772-219-1670
Amy Laws, prin. Fax 219-1677
Parker ES 700/K-5
1010 SE 10th St 34996 772-219-1580
Dr. Chris Jones, prin. Fax 219-1583
Pinewood ES 700/K-5
5200 SE Willoughby Blvd 34997 772-219-1595
Jennifer Radcliff, prin. Fax 219-1603
Port Salerno ES 800/K-5
3260 SE Lionel Ter 34997 772-219-1610
Allysa Eberst, prin. Fax 219-1615
Stuart MS 1,000/6-8
575 SE Georgia Ave 34994 772-219-1685
David Krakoff, prin. Fax 219-1690
Williams ES 700/K-5
401 NW Baker Rd 34994 772-219-1640
Deborah Riley, prin. Fax 219-1646
Other Schools – See Hobe Sound, Indiantown, Jensen Beach, Palm City

---

Bridges Montessori S 100/PK-7
51 SE Central Pkwy 34994 772-221-9490
Community Christian Academy 300/K-12
777 SE Salerno Rd 34997 772-288-7227
First Baptist Christian S 200/PK-12
201 SW Ocean Blvd 34994 772-287-5161
Alli Blackwell, prin. Fax 287-7735
Redeemer Lutheran S 200/PK-8
2450 SE Ocean Blvd 34996 772-286-0932
James Essig, prin. Fax 287-0434
St. Joseph Catholic S 300/PK-8
1200 SE 10th St 34996 772-287-6975
Stacy McNerney, prin. Fax 287-4733

Sugarloaf Key, Monroe
Monroe County SD
Supt. — See Key West
Sugarloaf S 600/PK-8
255 Crane Blvd 33042 305-745-3282
Harry Russell, prin. Fax 745-2019

Summerfield, Marion
Marion County SD
Supt. — See Ocala
Harbour View ES 700/PK-5
8445 SE 147th Pl 34491 352-671-6110
Heather Guest, prin. Fax 671-6111
Lake Weir MS 1,300/6-8
10220 SE Sunset Harbor Rd 34491 352-671-6120
David Ellers, prin. Fax 671-6121

Sunny Isles Beach, Miami-Dade, Pop. 20,565
Miami-Dade County SD
Supt. — See Miami
Fdelcup/Sunny Isles Beach K-8 Center 1,900/K-8
201 182nd Dr 33160 305-933-6161
Dr. Adam Kosnitzky, prin. Fax 933-6162

Sunrise, Broward, Pop. 82,120
Broward County SD
Supt. — See Fort Lauderdale
Bair MS 900/6-8
9100 NW 21st Mnr 33322 754-322-2900
Keietta Givens, prin. Fax 322-2985
Banyan ES 700/K-5
8800 NW 50th St 33351 754-322-5350
Dr. Eric Miller, prin. Fax 322-5390
Discovery ES 900/K-5
8800 NW 54th Ct 33351 754-322-9100
Julie DeGreeff, prin. Fax 322-9140
Horizon ES 500/K-5
2101 N Pine Island Rd 33322 754-322-6450
Thaddeus Smith, prin. Fax 322-6490
Nob Hill ES 600/K-5
2100 NW 104th Ave 33322 754-322-7200
Jeannie Floyd, prin. Fax 322-7240
Sandpiper ES 600/K-5
3700 N Hiatus Rd 33351 754-322-8450
Camille LaChance, prin. Fax 322-8490
Sawgrass ES 900/PK-5
12655 NW 8th St 33325 754-322-8500
Stephen DeCotis, prin. Fax 322-8540
Village ES 800/PK-5
2100 NW 70th Ave 33313 754-322-8750
Wanda Haynes, prin. Fax 322-8790
Welleby ES 700/PK-5
3230 N Nob Hill Rd 33351 754-322-8850
Frances Fuce-Ollivierre, prin. Fax 322-8890
Westpine MS 1,200/6-8
9393 NW 50th St 33351 754-322-4900
Paula Meadows, prin. Fax 322-4985

All Saints S 300/PK-8
10900 W Oakland Park Blvd 33351 954-742-4842
Antoinette McNamara, prin. Fax 742-4871
Tawfik ES 200/PK-8
5455 NW 108th Ave 33351 954-741-8130

Tallahassee, Leon, Pop. 177,584
Leon County SD 32,600/PK-12
2757 W Pensacola St 32304 850-487-7100
Rocky Hanna, supt. Fax 487-7141
www.leonschools.net
Apalachee ES 600/PK-5
650 Trojan Trl 32311 850-488-7110
Iris Wilson, prin. Fax 922-0202
Astoria Park ES 600/PK-5
2465 Atlas Rd 32303 850-488-4673
Marsha Glover-Sanders, prin. Fax 922-4174
Bond ES 700/PK-5
2204 Saxon St 32310 850-488-7676
Patrick Wright, prin. Fax 922-5206
Buck Lake ES 700/PK-5
1600 Pedrick Rd 32317 850-488-6133
Billy Millard, prin. Fax 922-4161
Canopy Oaks ES 700/PK-5
3250 Point View Dr 32303 850-488-3301
Paul Lambert, prin. Fax 414-7356
Chaires ES 400/PK-5
4774 Chaires Cross Rd 32317 850-488-5977
Michelle Prescott, prin. Fax 922-6462
Cobb MS 900/6-8
915 Hillcrest Ave 32308 850-488-3364
Tonja Fitzgerald, prin. Fax 922-2452
Conley ES 900/PK-5
2400 Orange Ave E 32311 850-414-5610
Taka Mays, prin. Fax 414-8163
Deerlake MS 900/6-8
9902 Deer Lk W 32312 850-922-6545
Scotty Crowe, prin. Fax 488-3275
DeSoto Trail ES 700/PK-5
5200 Tredington Park Dr 32309 850-488-4511
Michele Keltner, prin. Fax 487-1623
Fairview MS 800/6-8
3415 Zillah St 32305 850-488-6880
Scott Hansen, prin. Fax 922-6326
Ft. Braden S 800/PK-8
15100 Blountstown Hwy 32310 850-488-9374
Jim Jackson, prin. Fax 488-5948
Gilchrist ES 1,000/PK-5
1301 Timberlane Rd 32312 850-487-4310
David Solz, prin. Fax 487-0959
Griffin MS 500/6-8
800 Alabama St 32304 850-617-5353
Gwendolyn Lynn-Thomas, prin. Fax 617-5354
Hartsfield ES 500/PK-5
1414 Chowkeebin Nene 32301 850-488-7322
Rhonda Flanagan, prin. Fax 922-2372
Hawks Rise ES 800/PK-5
205 Meadow Ridge Dr 32312 850-487-4733
Evy Friend, prin. Fax 488-6971
Killearn Lakes ES 900/PK-5
8037 Deer Lk E 32312 850-921-1265
Brenda Wagner, prin. Fax 922-2566
Montford MS 1,100/6-8
5789 Pimlico Dr 32309 850-922-6011
Lewis Blessing, prin. Fax 922-7974
Moore ES 500/PK-5
1706 Dempsey Mayo Rd 32308 850-488-2858
Kerri Anderson, prin. Fax 922-6658
Nims MS 500/6-8
723 W Orange Ave 32310 850-617-6161
Dr. Kelvin Norton, prin. Fax 922-0203
Oak Ridge ES 500/PK-5
4530 Shelfer Rd 32305 850-488-3124
Jasmine Smith, prin. Fax 922-7145
Pineview ES 400/PK-5
2230 Lake Bradford Rd 32310 850-488-2819
Marilyn Rahming, prin. Fax 487-4559
Raa MS 900/6-8
401 W Tharpe St 32303 850-488-6287
Christopher Small, prin. Fax 922-5835
Riley ES 600/PK-5
1400 Indiana St 32304 850-488-5840
Karwynn Paul, prin. Fax 922-4227
Roberts ES 800/K-5
5777 Pimlico Dr 32309 850-488-0923
Kim McFarland, prin. Fax 487-2416
Ruediger ES 500/PK-5
526 W 10th Ave 32303 850-488-1074
Sally Stephens, prin. Fax 487-0007
Sabal Palm ES 600/PK-5
2813 Ridgeway St 32310 850-488-0167
Anicia Robinson, prin. Fax 922-8481
Sealey ES 600/K-5
2815 Allen Rd 32312 850-488-5640
Demetria Clemons, prin. Fax 488-1239
Springwood ES 600/K-5
3801 Fred George Rd 32303 850-488-6225
Tina Austin, prin. Fax 922-8932
Sullivan ES 800/K-5
927 Miccosukee Rd 32308 850-487-1216
Mike Bryant, prin. Fax 487-0005
Swift Creek MS 800/6-8
2100 Pedrick Rd 32317 850-414-2670
Sue Rishell, prin. Fax 414-2650
Woodville ES 400/PK-5
9373 Woodville Hwy 32305 850-487-7043
Taita Scott, prin. Fax 921-4281

Betton Hills S 100/1-12
2205 Thomasville Rd 32308 850-656-9211
Community Christian S 300/PK-12
4859 Kerry Forest Pkwy 32309 850-893-6628
David Pinson, hdmstr. Fax 668-3966
Community Leadership Academy 100/PK-8
3210 Thomasville Rd 32308 850-597-9124
Cornerstone Learning Community 200/PK-8
2524 Hartsfield Rd 32303 850-386-5550
Jason Flom, dir. Fax 386-5421
Holy Comforter Episcopal S 600/PK-8
2001 Fleischmann Rd 32308 850-383-1007
Peter Klekamp, head sch Fax 383-1021
Maclay S 900/PK-12
3737 N Meridian Rd 32312 850-893-2138
James Milford, head sch Fax 893-7434
North Florida Christian S 800/PK-12
3000 N Meridian Rd 32312 850-386-6327
Dr. Tom Phillips, admin. Fax 386-8409
Symphony Seven S of Arts & Technology 100/PK-8
1410 E Indianhead Dr 32301 850-878-1752
Tallahassee Adventist Christian Academy 50/K-9
616 Capital Cir NE 32301 850-597-7825
Trinity Catholic S 500/PK-8
706 E Brevard St 32308 850-222-0444
James Bridges, prin. Fax 224-5067

Tamarac, Broward, Pop. 59,173
Broward County SD
Supt. — See Fort Lauderdale
Challenger ES 900/K-5
5703 NW 94th Ave 33321 754-322-5750
Tara Zdanowicz, prin. Fax 322-5790
Tamarac ES 900/K-5
7601 N University Dr 33321 754-322-8600
Roberta Ray, prin. Fax 322-8640

Alazhar S 200/PK-8
7201 W McNab Rd 33321 954-722-1555
Bethlehem Junior Academy 200/K-8
6855 W Commercial Blvd 33319 954-597-9200
Audrey Nelson, dir. Fax 597-9002
Excelsior Artz Preparatory S 100/PK-8
8197 N University Dr Ste 13 33321 954-721-3471
Minerva Rodriguez, prin. Fax 721-3872

Tampa, Hillsborough, Pop. 328,173
Hillsborough County SD 198,600/PK-12
PO Box 3408 33601 813-272-4000
Jeff Eakins, supt. Fax 272-4510
www.sdhc.k12.fl.us
Adams MS 1,100/6-8
10201 N Boulevard 33612 813-975-7665
Heath Beauregard, prin. Fax 632-6889
Alexander ES 600/PK-5
5602 N Lois Ave 33614 813-872-5395
Kristina Alvarez, prin. Fax 356-1121
Anderson ES 400/K-5
3910 W Fair Oaks Ave 33611 813-272-3075
Delia Gadson-Yarbrough, prin. Fax 276-5919
Ballast Point ES 400/K-5
2802 W Ballast Point Blvd 33611 813-272-3070
Elizabeth Hastings, prin. Fax 276-5923
Bay Crest ES 800/K-5
4925 Webb Rd 33615 813-872-5382
Lisa Maltezos, prin. Fax 356-1153
Bellamy ES 700/K-5
9720 Wilsky Blvd 33615 813-872-5387
Dr. Francine Lazarus, prin. Fax 873-4877
Benito MS 1,100/6-8
10101 Cross Creek Blvd 33647 813-631-4694
John Sanders, prin. Fax 631-4706
Bing ES 600/PK-5
6409 36th Ave S 33619 813-744-8088
Amber Cronin, prin. Fax 740-3620
Broward ES 400/K-5
400 W Osborne Ave 33603 813-276-5592
Angela Livingston, prin. Fax 276-5887
Bryant ES 1,000/K-5
13910 Nine Eagles Dr 33626 813-356-1645
Ellen Oberschall, prin. Fax 356-1649
Buchanan MS 700/6-8
1001 W Bearss Ave 33613 813-975-7600
Scott Hilgenberg, prin. Fax 975-7610
Cahoon ES 400/PK-8
2312 E Yukon St 33604 813-975-7647
Ovett Wilson, prin. Fax 975-7650
Cannella ES 700/K-5
10707 Nixon Rd 33624 813-975-6941
Matthew Hoff, prin. Fax 631-5328
Carrollwood ES 800/K-5
3516 McFarland Rd 33618 813-975-7640
Melanie Bottini, prin. Fax 631-5364
Chiaramonte ES 400/K-5
6001 S Himes Ave 33611 813-272-3066
Daniel Opila, prin. Fax 272-3284
Chiles ES 800/K-5
16541 Tampa Palms Blvd W 33647 813-558-5422
Teresa Evans, prin. Fax 558-5426
Citrus Park ES 600/PK-5
7700 Gunn Hwy 33625 813-558-5356
Christopher Fonteyn, prin. Fax 558-5111
Clair-Mel ES 600/PK-5
1025 S 78th St 33619 813-744-8080
Gloria Waite, prin. Fax 744-8083
Clark ES 800/K-5
19002 Wood Sage Dr 33647 813-631-4333
Paulette English, prin. Fax 631-4349
Claywell ES 700/K-5
4500 Northdale Blvd 33624 813-975-7300
Robert Jones, prin. Fax 631-4536
Cleveland ES 400/PK-5
723 E Hamilton Ave 33604 813-276-5583
Lynn Roberts, prin. Fax 276-5586
Coleman MS 900/6-8
1724 S Manhattan Ave 33629 813-872-5335
Michael Hoskinson, prin. Fax 872-5338
Crestwood ES 900/K-5
7824 N Manhattan Ave 33614 813-872-5374
Diane Aliakbarian, prin. Fax 871-7788
Davidsen MS 1,000/6-8
10501 Montague St 33626 813-558-5300
Stacy Arena, prin. Fax 558-5299
Davis ES 800/K-5
10907 Memorial Hwy 33615 813-854-6010
Patrick LaLone, prin. Fax 854-6014
Deer Park ES 900/K-5
11605 Citrus Park Dr 33626 813-854-6031
Shirley Porebski, prin. Fax 854-6041
DeSoto ES 200/PK-5
2618 Corrine St 33605 813-276-5779
Gilda Garcia, prin. Fax 233-2475
Dickenson ES 600/PK-5
4720 Kelly Rd 33615 813-873-4732
Ryan Moody, prin. Fax 356-1156
Dowdell MS 600/6-8
1208 Wishing Well Way 33619 813-744-8322
Roger Stanley, prin. Fax 740-3616
Dunbar Magnet ES 200/K-5
1730 W Union St 33607 813-276-5677
Frankye Bulmer, prin. Fax 272-2254
Edison ES 500/K-5
1607 E Curtis St 33610 813-276-5579
Marc Gaillard, prin. Fax 276-5582
Egypt Lake ES 500/PK-5
6707 N Glen Ave 33614 813-872-5225
Julie Scardino, prin. Fax 554-2358
Essrig ES 700/K-5
13131 Lynn Rd 33624 813-975-7307
Joshua Hodges, prin. Fax 558-5104

Farnell MS 1,400/6-8
13912 Nine Eagles Dr 33626 813-356-1640
John Cobb, prin. Fax 356-1644
Ferrell Girls Prep Academy 400/6-8
4302 N 24th St 33610 813-276-5608
Karen French, prin. Fax 276-5615
Forest Hills ES 1,000/PK-5
10112 N Ola Ave 33612 813-975-7633
Elizabeth Giles, prin. Fax 975-4812
Foster ES 400/K-5
2014 E Diana St 33610 813-276-5573
Kimberly Thompson, prin. Fax 276-5731
Franklin Boys Prep Academy 400/6-8
3915 E 21st Ave 33605 813-744-8108
John Haley, prin. Fax 744-8579
Gorrie ES 600/K-5
705 W De Leon St 33606 813-276-5673
Marjorie Sandler, prin. Fax 276-5880
Grady ES 500/PK-5
3910 W Morrison Ave 33629 813-872-5325
Kristine Dosal, prin. Fax 356-1476
Graham ES 400/PK-5
2915 N Massachusetts Ave 33602 813-276-5408
Sharron Doyle, prin. Fax 276-5534
Heritage ES 600/K-5
18201 E Meadow Rd 33647 813-740-4580
MaryJo Stover, prin. Fax 740-4584
Hill MS 900/6-8
5200 Ehrlich Rd 33624 813-975-7325
Ronald Mason, prin. Fax 975-4819
Hunter's Green ES 800/K-5
9202 Highland Oak Dr 33647 813-973-7394
Gaye Holt, prin. Fax 631-4525
James ES 600/K-5
4302 E Ellicott St 33610 813-740-4800
Debra Fitzpatrick, prin. Fax 740-4804
Just ES 700/PK-5
1315 W Spruce St 33607 813-276-5708
Ire Carolina, prin. Fax 272-2379
Kenly ES 500/PK-5
2909 N 66th St 33619 813-744-8074
Carisa Spires, prin. Fax 744-8077
Kimbell ES 600/K-5
8406 N 46th St 33617 813-983-3900
Dave McMeen, prin. Fax 983-3974
Lake Magdalene ES 800/K-5
2002 Pine Lake Dr 33612 813-975-7625
Crystal Brown, prin. Fax 644-7681
Lamb ES K-5
6274 S 78th St 33619 813-605-4950
Steven Sims, prin. Fax 605-4963
Lanier ES 400/PK-5
4704 W Montgomery Ave 33616 813-272-3060
Rachael O'Dea, prin. Fax 272-3065
Lee ES 300/K-5
305 E Columbus Dr 33602 813-276-5405
Beverly Smith, prin. Fax 272-3228
Liberty MS 1,100/6-8
17400 Commerce Park Blvd 33647 813-558-1180
James Ammirati, prin. Fax 558-1184
Lockhart ES 400/PK-5
3719 N 17th St 33610 813-276-5727
Sharon Waite, prin. Fax 233-3565
Lomax ES 400/K-5
4207 N 26th St 33610 813-276-5569
Connie Chisholm, prin. Fax 272-2803
Lowry ES 800/K-5
11505 Country Hollow Dr 33635 813-855-8178
Michelle Spagnuolo, prin. Fax 356-1597
Mabry ES 800/K-5
4201 W Estrella St 33629 813-872-5364
Sherri Frick, prin. Fax 554-2252
MacFarlane Park Magnet ES 400/K-5
1721 N MacDill Ave 33607 813-356-1760
Dr. M. Denyse Riviero, prin. Fax 356-1764
Madison MS 800/6-8
4444 W Bay Vista Ave 33611 813-272-3050
Joseph Brown, prin. Fax 233-2796
Memorial MS 700/6-8
4702 N Central Ave 33603 813-872-5230
April Gillyard, prin. Fax 872-5238
Mendenhall ES 700/K-5
5202 N Mendenhall Dr 33603 813-872-5221
Cristina Fernandez, prin. Fax 872-5224
Miles ES 800/PK-5
317 E 124th Ave 33612 813-975-7337
Greg Cannella, prin. Fax 975-7099
Mitchell ES 600/K-5
205 S Bungalow Park Ave 33609 813-872-5216
Deborah Anderson, prin. Fax 356-1662
Monroe MS 500/6-8
4716 W Montgomery Ave 33616 813-272-3020
Peter Megara, prin. Fax 272-3027
Morgan Woods ES 500/K-5
7001 Armand Dr 33634 813-872-5369
Kilsys Garcia, prin. Fax 873-4869
Mort ES 800/PK-5
1806 E Bearss Ave 33613 813-975-7373
Woodland Johnson Ed.D., prin. Fax 558-5489
MOSI Partnership S 200/K-5
4801 E Fowler Ave Ste 100 33617 813-983-3989
Renel Mathurin, prin. Fax 983-3998
Muller ES 300/K-5
13615 N 22nd St 33613 813-558-1355
Mary Booth, prin. Fax 558-1359
Northwest ES 600/K-5
16438 Hutchison Rd 33625 813-975-7315
Bryan Quigley, prin. Fax 975-7322
Oak Grove ES 900/PK-5
6315 N Armenia Ave 33604 813-356-1532
Cynthia Thro, prin. Fax 356-1536
Oak Park ES 600/PK-5
2716 N 46th St 33605 813-740-7733
Marlou Bates, prin. Fax 740-7744
Orange Grove Magnet MS 600/6-8
3415 N 16th St 33605 813-276-5717
Lydia Giglio-Sierra, prin. Fax 276-5857

Palm River ES 500/K-5
805 Maydell Dr 33619 813-744-8066
Dawn Stites, prin. Fax 744-8069
Pierce MS 1,100/6-8
5511 N Hesperides St 33614 813-872-5344
Pablo Gallego, prin. Fax 871-7978
Pizzo ES 700/K-5
11701 USF Bull Run St 33617 813-987-6500
Pamela Wilkins, prin. Fax 987-6516
Potter ES 600/PK-5
3224 E Cayuga St 33610 813-276-5564
Melanie Hill, prin. Fax 233-3693
Pride ES 900/PK-5
10310 Lions Den Dr 33647 813-558-5400
Amy Zilbar, prin. Fax 558-5404
Progress Village Magnet MS 900/6-8
8113 Zinnia Dr 33619 813-671-5110
Andrew Olson, prin. Fax 671-5240
Rampello Downtown S 800/K-8
802 E Washington St 33602 813-233-2333
Liz Uppercue, prin. Fax 233-2337
Robles ES 700/PK-5
4405 E Sligh Ave 33610 813-744-8033
Carol Brown, prin. Fax 744-8350
Roland Park S 800/K-8
1510 N Manhattan Ave 33607 813-872-5212
Scott Weaver, prin. Fax 673-4388
Roosevelt ES 700/K-5
3205 S Ferdinand Ave 33629 813-272-3090
Christina Dickens, prin. Fax 272-3577
Seminole ES 400/K-5
6201 N Central Ave 33604 813-276-5556
Jackie Masters, prin. Fax 272-2279
Shaw ES 600/K-5
11311 N 15th St 33612 813-975-7366
Rachel Walters, prin. Fax 558-5025
Sheehy ES 400/PK-5
6402 N 40th St 33610 813-233-3800
Patricia McCants, prin. Fax 233-3804
Shore ES 400/K-5
1908 E 2nd Ave 33605 813-276-5712
Cheri Bollinger, prin. Fax 272-0426
Sligh MS 600/6-8
2011 E Sligh Ave 33610 813-276-5596
Shellie Blackwood-Green, prin. Fax 276-5606
Smith MS 900/6-8
14303 Citrus Pointe Dr 33625 813-792-5125
JoAnn Johnson, prin. Fax 792-5129
Stewart MS 900/6-8
1125 W Spruce St 33607 813-276-5691
Baretta Wilson, prin. Fax 276-5698
Sullivan Partnership ES K-5
2202 N Florida Ave 33602 813-347-4160
Daphne Fourqurean, prin. Fax 347-4167
Sulphur Springs Community S 600/PK-8
8412 N 13th St 33604 813-975-7305
Chantel Angeletti, prin. Fax 975-7398
Tampa Bay Boulevard ES 700/PK-5
3111 W Tampa Bay Blvd 33607 813-872-5208
Glenda Rodriguez, prin. Fax 871-7586
Tampa Palms ES 800/K-5
6100 Tampa Palms Blvd 33647 813-975-7390
Maryann Lippek, prin. Fax 975-6654
Town and Country ES 500/PK-5
6025 Hanley Rd 33634 813-871-7500
Melissa Babanats, prin. Fax 554-2378
Turner/Bartles ES 1,100/K-8
9020 Imperial Oak Blvd 33647 813-907-6801
Cindy Land, prin. Fax 907-6805
Twin Lakes ES 700/K-5
8507 N Habana Ave 33614 813-975-7380
Edith Lefler, prin. Fax 631-4153
USF/Patel ES 200/K-5
11801 USF Bull Run St 33617 813-983-3966
Keith Laycock, prin. Fax 983-3987
Van Buren MS 600/6-8
8715 N 22nd St 33604 813-975-7652
Ovette Wilson, prin. Fax 631-4312
Washington ES 500/PK-5
1407 Estelle St 33605 813-233-3720
Jaime Gerding, prin. Fax 233-3724
Webb MS 800/6-8
6035 Hanley Rd 33634 813-872-5351
Frank Diaz, prin. Fax 872-5359
Westchase ES 900/K-5
9517 W Linebaugh Ave 33626 813-631-4600
Erik Holley, prin. Fax 631-4617
West Shore ES 300/PK-5
7110 S West Shore Blvd 33616 813-272-3080
Linda Drawdy, prin. Fax 233-2443
West Tampa ES 500/PK-5
2700 W Cherry St 33607 813-872-5200
Louis Murphy, prin. Fax 356-1452
Williams MS 800/6-8
5020 N 47th St 33610 813-744-8600
Arlene Castelli, prin. Fax 744-8665
Wilson MS 600/6-8
1005 W Swann Ave 33606 813-276-5682
Colleen Faucett, prin. Fax 233-2540
Witter ES 600/PK-5
10801 N 22nd St 33612 813-975-7383
Susan Persbacker, prin. Fax 631-4447
Woodbridge ES 600/K-5
8301 Woodbridge Blvd 33615 813-871-7460
Sarah Jocobsen Capps, prin. Fax 871-7063
Young Magnet MS 600/6-8
1807 E Dr Martin L King Jr 33610 813-276-5739
Nadine Johnson, prin. Fax 276-5893
Other Schools – See Apollo Beach, Brandon, Dover, Gibsonton, Lithia, Lutz, MacDill AFB, Odessa, Plant City, Riverview, Ruskin, Seffner, Temple Terrace, Thonotosassa, Valrico, Wimauma

---

Academy of the Holy Names S 400/PK-8
3319 Bayshore Blvd 33629 813-839-5371
Bridgid Fishman, prin. Fax 839-1486
Academy Prep Center of Tampa 100/5-8
1407 E Columbus Dr 33605 813-248-5600
American Youth Academy 400/PK-12
5905 E 130th Ave 33617 813-987-9282
Bayshore Christian S 200/PK-12
3909 S MacDill Ave 33611 813-839-4297
Melanie Humenansky, head sch Fax 835-1404
Beach Park S 100/PK-8
4200 W North A St 33609 813-289-3747
Berkeley Preparatory S 1,300/PK-12
4811 Kelly Rd 33615 813-885-1673
Joseph Seivold, hdmstr. Fax 886-6933
Cambridge Christian S 600/PK-12
6101 N Habana Ave 33614 813-872-6744
Carrollwood Day S 800/PK-12
1515 W Bearss Ave 33613 813-920-2288
Dr. Ryan Kelly, head sch Fax 960-9269
Christ the King S 500/PK-8
3809 W Morrison Ave 33629 813-876-8770
Nick Tanis, prin. Fax 879-0315
Citrus Park Christian S 400/PK-12
7705 Gunn Hwy 33625 813-920-3960
Corbett Preparatory S of IDS 500/PK-8
12015 Orange Grove Dr 33618 813-961-3087
Dr. Joyce Burick Swarzman, hdmstr. Fax 963-0846
Faith Outreach Academy 200/PK-12
7607 Sheldon Rd 33615 813-887-5546
Family of Christ Christian S 400/PK-8
16190 Bruce B Downs Blvd 33647 813-558-9343
Jennifer Snow, prin. Fax 977-0549
Gateway Christian Academy 100/PK-12
14205 N Florida Ave 33613 813-964-9800
Hebrew Academy of Tampa Bay 50/PK-8
14908 Pennington Rd 33624 813-963-0706
Hillel Academy 200/PK-8
2020 W Fletcher Ave 33612 813-963-2242
Allison Oakes, head sch Fax 264-0544
Hillsdale Christian Academy 100/PK-12
6201 Ehrlich Rd 33625 813-884-8250
Tanya B. Henry M.A., prin. Fax 886-5251
Holy Trinity Lutheran S 50/PK-2
3712 W El Prado Blvd 33629 813-839-0665
Kelly Reilly, prin. Fax 839-2706
Incarnation Catholic S 300/PK-8
5111 Webb Rd 33615 813-884-4502
Michael Zelenka, prin. Fax 885-3734
Kings Kids Christian Academy of Tampa 100/PK-K
3000 N 34th St 33605 813-248-6548
Montessori Academy of Tampa Bay 200/PK-5
1901 W Waters Ave 33604 813-933-4782
Montessori Children's House of Hyde Park 100/PK-6
2416 W Cleveland St 33609 813-354-9511
Montessori House Day S 50/PK-K
7010 Hanley Rd 33634 813-884-7220
Sally Parker, head sch Fax 886-7552
Montessori House Day S 100/PK-6
5117 Ehrlich Rd 33624 813-961-9295
Sally Parker, head sch Fax 961-8639
Mt. Calvary Junior Academy 100/K-8
3111 E Wilder Ave 33610 813-238-0433
Northdale Lutheran S 50/K-8
15709 Mapledale Dr 33624 813-961-9195
Mark Thiesfeldt, admin. Fax 961-2435
Paideia S of Tampa Bay 100/K-12
7834 N 56th St 33617 813-988-7700
Dr. Tim Bridges, hdmstr. Fax 988-7740
St. John's Episcopal Parish Day S 600/PK-8
240 S Plant Ave 33606 813-849-4200
Robert Stephens, head sch Fax 849-1026
St. Joseph S 200/PK-8
2200 N Gomez Ave 33607 813-879-7720
Brenda Budd, prin. Fax 873-0804
St. Lawrence S 600/PK-8
5223 N Himes Ave 33614 813-879-5090
Therese Hernandez, prin. Fax 879-6886
St. Mary's Episcopal Day S 400/PK-8
2101 S Hubert Ave 33629 813-258-5508
Scott Laird, hdmstr. Fax 258-5603
St. Paul Child Enrichment Center 200/PK-PK
12708 N Dale Mabry Hwy 33618 813-264-3314
Martha Aguiar, dir. Fax 962-8780
St. Peter Claver S 100/PK-8
1401 N Governor St 33602 813-224-0865
Sr. Maria Babatunde, prin. Fax 223-6726
Tampa Adventist Academy 100/PK-12
3205 N Boulevard 33603 813-228-7950
Tampa Bay Christian Academy 300/PK-12
6815 N Rome Ave 33604 813-343-0600
Natasha Sherwood, head sch Fax 343-0601
Universal Academy of Florida 400/PK-12
6801 Orient Rd 33610 813-664-0695
Villa Madonna S 400/PK-8
315 W Columbus Dr 33602 813-229-1322
Sr. Mary Jackson, prin. Fax 223-4812
West Gate Christian S 100/PK-12
5121 Kelly Rd 33615 813-884-5147

Tarpon Springs, Pinellas, Pop. 23,056
Pinellas County SD
Supt. — See Largo
Brooker Creek ES 500/K-5
3130 Forelock Rd 34688 727-943-4600
Jennifer Mekler, prin. Fax 943-4603
East Lake MS Academy of Engineering 6-8
1200 Silver Eagle Dr 34688 727-940-7624
Karen Huzar, prin. Fax 754-8653
Sunset Hills ES 500/K-5
1347 Gulf Rd 34689 727-943-5523
Johnnie Crawford, prin. Fax 943-4939
Tarpon Springs ES 600/K-5
555 Pine St 34689 727-943-5500
Arthur Steullet, prin. Fax 943-5580
Tarpon Springs Fundamental ES 300/K-5
400 E Harrison St 34689 727-943-5508
Dr. Elaine Meils, prin. Fax 942-5443
Tarpon Springs MS 1,000/6-8
501 N Florida Ave 34689 727-943-5511
Raquel Giles, prin. Fax 943-5519

St. Ignatius ECC 100/PK-PK
725 E Orange St 34689 727-937-5427
Sharon Stokely, dir. Fax 722-9000

Tavares, Lake, Pop. 13,762
Lake County SD 39,400/PK-12
201 W Burleigh Blvd 32778 352-253-6500
Diane S. Kornegay M.Ed., supt. Fax 253-6503
www.lake.k12.fl.us/
Tavares ES 900/PK-5
720 E Clifford St 32778 352-343-2861
Durenda McKinney, prin. Fax 343-6618
Tavares MS 1,000/6-8
1335 Lane Park Cutoff 32778 352-343-4545
Trella Mott, prin. Fax 343-7212
Other Schools – See Astatula, Clermont, Eustis, Fruitland Park, Groveland, Lady Lake, Leesburg, Minneola, Mount Dora, Sorrento, Umatilla

Adventure Christian Academy 100/K-12
3800 State Road 19 32778 352-742-4543
Gary Johnson, admin. Fax 343-3820
Liberty Christian Prep 200/PK-12
2451 Dora Ave 32778 352-343-0061
Jeremy Thomas, admin. Fax 343-2424

Tavernier, Monroe, Pop. 2,111
Monroe County SD
Supt. — See Key West
Plantation Key S 500/PK-8
100 Lake Rd 33070 305-853-3281
Lisa Taylor, prin. Fax 853-3279

Temple Terrace, Hillsborough, Pop. 23,889
Hillsborough County SD
Supt. — See Tampa
Greco MS 900/6-8
6925 E Fowler Ave 33617 813-987-6926
Valerie Newton, prin. Fax 987-6863
Lewis ES 800/K-5
6700 Whiteway Dr 33617 813-987-6947
Delilah Rabeiro, prin. Fax 987-6920
Riverhills ES 300/K-5
405 S Riverhills Dr 33617 813-987-6911
Todd Connolly, prin. Fax 987-6962
Temple Terrace ES 600/PK-5
124 Flotto Ave 33617 813-987-6903
Ann Marie Perez, prin. Fax 987-6406

Corpus Christi S 200/PK-8
9715 N 56th St 33617 813-988-1722
Dr. Carmen Caltagirone, prin. Fax 989-2665
Florida College Academy 200/PK-8
7032 Temple Terrace Hwy 33637 813-899-6800
Libertas Academy 50/K-8
6718 E Fowler Ave 33617 813-964-1779
Montessori Preparatory S 200/PK-5
11302 N 53rd St 33617 813-899-2345
Sonia Johnson, dir. Fax 989-9870

Tequesta, Palm Beach, Pop. 5,577

Good Shepherd Episcopal S 100/PK-5
402 Seabrook Rd 33469 561-746-5507
James Hoye, head sch Fax 746-2870

Thonotosassa, Hillsborough, Pop. 12,732
Hillsborough County SD
Supt. — See Tampa
Folsom ES 500/K-5
9855 Harney Rd 33592 813-987-6755
Krystal Lofton, prin. Fax 987-6970
Thonotosassa ES 400/PK-5
10050 Skewlee Rd 33592 813-987-6987
Lisa Varnum, prin. Fax 987-6865

Titusville, Brevard, Pop. 42,761
Brevard County SD
Supt. — See Melbourne
Apollo ES 800/K-6
3085 Knox Mcrae Dr 32780 321-267-7890
Frank O'Leary, prin. Fax 269-3838
Coquina ES 600/K-6
850 Knox Mcrae Dr 32780 321-264-3060
Blair Nave, prin. Fax 264-3062
Imperial Estates ES 600/K-6
900 Imperial Estates Ln 32780 321-267-1773
Kathryn Lott, prin. Fax 264-3038
Jackson MS 500/7-8
1515 Knox Mcrae Dr 32780 321-269-1812
Tina Susin, prin. Fax 269-7811
Madison MS 500/7-8
3375 Dairy Rd 32796 321-264-3120
Sherry Tomlinson, prin. Fax 264-3124
Oak Park ES 800/PK-6
3395 Dairy Rd 32796 321-269-3252
Jennifer Brockwell, prin. Fax 264-3080
Riverview S 50/PK-PK
3000 Jolly St 32780 321-269-2326
Terri Barlow, prin. Fax 264-3092

Childrens Montessori Academy 100/PK-2
1300 Armstrong Dr 32780 321-264-9900
Park Avenue Christian Academy 300/PK-8
2600 S Park Ave 32780 321-267-1871
Dr. Brian McKinney, admin. Fax 268-4057
St. Teresa Catholic S 200/PK-8
207 Ojibway Ave 32780 321-267-1643
Jacqueline Zackel, prin. Fax 268-5124
Temple Christian S 100/PK-12
1400 N Washington Ave 32780 321-269-2837

Trenton, Gilchrist, Pop. 1,949
Gilchrist County SD 2,600/PK-12
310 NW 11th Ave 32693 352-463-3200
Robert G. Rankin, supt. Fax 463-3276
gilchristschools.schoolfusion.us
Trenton ES 800/PK-5
1350 SW State Road 26 32693 352-463-3224
Ronda Adkins, prin. Fax 463-3299
Other Schools – See Bell

Riverside Christian S 100/PK-11
8149 SW County Rd 341 32693 352-463-1569

Tyndall AFB, Bay, Pop. 2,821
Bay County SD
Supt. — See Panama City
Tyndall ES 800/PK-5
7800 Tyndall Pkwy 32403 850-767-1714
Susan Ross, prin. Fax 286-6484

Umatilla, Lake, Pop. 3,433
Lake County SD
Supt. — See Tavares
Umatilla ES 700/PK-5
401 Lake St 32784 352-669-3181
Debra Rogers, prin. Fax 669-8740
Umatilla MS 600/6-8
305 E Lake St 32784 352-669-3171
Thomas Sanders, prin. Fax 669-5424

Valparaiso, Okaloosa, Pop. 4,829
Okaloosa County SD
Supt. — See Fort Walton Beach
Lewis S 600/K-8
281 Mississippi Ave 32580 850-833-4130
Mike Fantaski, prin. Fax 833-4197
Okaloosa STEMM Academy 100/6-8
379 Edge Ave 32580 850-833-4120
Wanda Avery, admin. Fax 833-4177

Valrico, Hillsborough, Pop. 34,795
Hillsborough County SD
Supt. — See Tampa
Alafia ES 600/K-5
3535 Culbreath Rd, 813-744-8190
Lisa Tierney-Jackson, prin. Fax 744-8207
Buckhorn ES 700/K-5
2420 Buckhorn School Ct 33594 813-744-8240
Tamara Brooks, prin. Fax 740-3622
Cimino ES 800/K-5
4329 Culbreath Rd, 813-740-4450
Joanne Griffiths, prin. Fax 740-4454
Lithia Springs ES 600/K-5
4332 Lynx Paw Trl, 813-744-8016
Kevin Martin, prin. Fax 744-4462
Mulrennan MS 1,100/6-8
4215 Durant Rd, 813-651-2100
Tim Ducker, prin. Fax 651-2104
Valrico ES 800/K-5
609 S Miller Rd 33594 813-744-6777
Tricia Simonsen, prin. Fax 740-3535

Foundation Christian Academy 200/PK-12
3955 Lithia Pinecrest Rd, 813-654-2969
Jonathan Smith, pres. Fax 655-4780
Grace Christian S 200/K-12
1425 N Valrico Rd 33594 813-689-8815

Venice, Sarasota, Pop. 20,602
Sarasota County SD
Supt. — See Sarasota
Garden ES 600/K-5
700 Center Rd 34285 941-486-2110
Amy Archer, prin. Fax 486-2610
Taylor Ranch ES 600/K-5
2500 Taylor Ranch Trl 34293 941-486-2000
Dr. William Bolander, prin. Fax 486-2129
Venice ES 600/K-5
150 Miami Ave E 34285 941-486-2111
Erin delCastillo, prin. Fax 486-2117
Venice MS 500/6-8
1900 Center Rd 34292 941-486-2100
Dr. Karin Schmidt, prin. Fax 486-2108

Epiphany Cathedral Catholic S 200/PK-8
316 Sarasota St 34285 941-488-2215
Mary Heffner, prin. Fax 480-1565
Venice Christian S 200/PK-12
1200 Center Rd 34292 941-496-4411
Jerry Frimmel, admin. Fax 408-8362

Vernon, Washington, Pop. 673
Washington County SD
Supt. — See Chipley
Vernon ES 500/PK-5
3665 Roche Ave 32462 850-535-2486
Steven Griffin, prin. Fax 535-1437
Vernon MS 300/6-8
3206 Moss Hill Rd 32462 850-535-2807
Kimberly Register, prin. Fax 535-1683

Vero Beach, Indian River, Pop. 15,009
Indian River County SD 17,000/PK-12
6500 57th St 32968 772-564-3000
Dr. Mark Rendell, supt. Fax 564-3054
www.indianriverschools.org
Beachland ES 600/K-5
3350 Indian River Dr E 32963 772-564-3300
Dr. Colleen Lord, prin. Fax 564-3350
Citrus ES 700/K-5
2771 4th St 32968 772-978-8350
Kimberly Garcia, prin. Fax 978-8351
Dodgertown ES 400/PK-5
4350 43rd Ave 32967 772-564-4100
Aretha Vernette, prin. Fax 564-4093
Gifford MS 900/6-8
4530 28th Ct 32967 772-564-3550
Mintosha Jones, prin. Fax 564-3561
Glendale ES 500/PK-5
4940 8th St 32968 772-978-8050
Adam Faust, prin. Fax 978-8098
Indian River Academy 500/K-5
500 20th St SW 32962 772-564-3390
Diane Fannin, prin. Fax 564-3443
Liberty Magnet ES 600/K-5
6850 81st St 32967 772-564-5350
Takeisha Harris, prin. Fax 564-5303
Osceola Magnet ES 500/K-5
1110 18th Ave SW 32962 772-564-5821
Scott Simpson, prin. Fax 564-5827
Oslo MS 900/6-8
480 20th Ave SW 32962 772-564-3980
Beth Hofer, prin. Fax 564-4029
Rosewood Magnet ES 500/K-5
3850 16th St 32960 772-564-3840
Casandra Flores, prin. Fax 564-3888
Storm Grove MS 900/6-8
6400 57th St 32967 772-564-6400
Anne Bieber, prin. Fax 564-6321
Vero Beach ES 700/PK-5
1770 12th St 32960 772-564-4550
Cynthia Emerson, prin. Fax 564-4552
Other Schools – See Fellsmere, Sebastian

Glendale Christian S 100/PK-12
790 27th Ave 32968 772-569-1095
Master's Academy of Vero Beach 200/PK-12
1105 58th Ave 32966 772-794-4655
Dr. Wayne Smith, head sch
St. Edward's S 500/PK-12
1895 Saint Edwards Dr 32963 772-231-4136
Michael Mersky, head sch Fax 231-2427
St. Helen Catholic S 200/K-8
2050 Vero Beach Ave 32960 772-567-5457
Joan Silo, prin. Fax 567-4823
Willow S 50/K-8
950 43rd Ave 32960 772-770-0758

Viera, Brevard
Brevard County SD
Supt. — See Melbourne
Manatee ES 800/K-6
3425 Viera Blvd 32940 321-433-0050
Carl Brown, prin. Fax 433-9927

Walnut Hill, Escambia
Escambia County SD
Supt. — See Pensacola
Ward MS 500/6-8
7650 Highway 97 32568 850-327-4283
Nancy Perry, prin. Fax 327-4991

Wauchula, Hardee, Pop. 4,954
Hardee County SD 5,100/PK-12
PO Box 1678 33873 863-773-9058
Bob Shayman, supt. Fax 773-0069
www.hardee.k12.fl.us
Hardee JHS 1,200/6-8
2405 US Highway 17 N 33873 863-773-3147
Dr. Sheryl Mosley, prin. Fax 773-3167
Hilltop ES 400/K-5
2395 US Highway 17 N 33873 863-773-2750
Beverly Cornelius, prin. Fax 773-2751
North Wauchula ES 500/K-5
1120 N Florida Ave 33873 863-773-2183
Jessica Gray, prin. Fax 773-3514
Wauchula ES 700/PK-5
400 S Florida Ave 33873 863-773-3141
Sonja Bennett, prin. Fax 773-0416
Other Schools – See Bowling Green, Zolfo Springs

Webster, Sumter, Pop. 770
Sumter County SD
Supt. — See Bushnell
South Sumter MS 800/6-8
773 NW 10th Ave 33597 352-793-2232
Allen Shirley, prin. Fax 793-3976
Webster ES 700/PK-5
349 S Market Blvd 33597 352-793-2828
Eileen Goodson, prin. Fax 793-6785

Weeki Wachee, Hernando, Pop. 12
Hernando County SD
Supt. — See Brooksville
Winding Waters S 1,200/K-8
12240 Vespa Way 34614 352-797-7092
Janet Cerro, prin. Fax 797-7192

Weirsdale, Marion
Marion County SD
Supt. — See Ocala
Stanton-Weirsdale ES 500/PK-5
16705 SE 134th Ter 32195 352-671-6150
Cynthia Broadie, prin. Fax 671-6155

Wellington, Palm Beach, Pop. 55,375
Palm Beach County SD
Supt. — See West Palm Beach
Binks Forest ES 1,000/K-5
15101 Bent Creek Rd 33414 561-904-9800
Michella Levy, prin. Fax 904-9850
Emerald Cove MS 1,200/6-8
9950 Stribling Way 33414 561-803-8000
Eugina Feaman, prin. Fax 803-8050
Equestrian Trails ES 800/K-5
9720 Stribling Way 33414 561-904-9600
Michele Johnson, prin. Fax 904-9650
Gale ES 1,000/K-5
1915 Royal Fern Dr 33414 561-422-9300
Gail Pasterczyk, prin. Fax 422-9310
New Horizons ES 600/K-5
13900 Greenbriar Blvd 33414 561-651-0500
Elizabeth Cardozo, prin. Fax 651-0550
Polo Park MS 800/6-8
11901 Lake Worth Rd, 561-333-5500
Ann Clark, prin. Fax 333-5505
Wellington ES 700/K-5
13000 Paddock Dr 33414 561-651-0600
Dr. Maria Vaughan, prin. Fax 651-0650
Wellington Landings MS 1,100/6-8
1100 Aero Club Dr 33414 561-792-8100
Blake Bennett, prin. Fax 792-8106

St. David's Episcopal S 100/PK-2
465 Forest Hill Blvd 33414 561-793-1272
Kathy Vandamas, head sch Fax 793-2301

Wesley Chapel, Pasco, Pop. 42,858
Pasco County SD
Supt. — See Land O Lakes
Double Branch ES 900/PK-5
31500 Chancey Rd 33543 813-346-0400
Vaughnette Chandler, prin. Fax 346-0491
Long MS 1,600/6-8
2025 Mansfield Blvd 33543 813-346-6200
Christine Wolff, prin. Fax 346-6291
New River ES 700/K-5
4710 River Glen Blvd, 813-346-0500
Sara Pabst, prin. Fax 346-0591
Quail Hollow ES 400/PK-5
7050 Quail Hollow Blvd 33544 813-794-1100
Kara Smucker, prin. Fax 794-1191
Sand Pine ES 600/K-5
29040 County Line Rd 33543 813-794-1900
Christina Twardosz, prin. Fax 794-1991
Seven Oaks ES 1,000/K-5
27633 Mystic Oak Blvd 33544 813-794-0700
Shirley Ray, prin. Fax 794-0791
Veterans ES 800/K-5
26940 Progress Pkwy 33544 813-346-1400
Melissa Bidgood, prin. Fax 346-1491
Watergrass ES 700/K-5
32750 Overpass Rd, 813-346-0600
Scott Mitchell, prin. Fax 346-0691
Weightman MS 1,200/6-8
30649 Wells Rd, 813-794-0200
Rachel Fowler, prin. Fax 794-0291
Wesley Chapel ES 800/PK-5
30243 Wells Rd, 813-794-0100
Stanley Mykita, prin. Fax 794-0191
Wiregrass ES K-5
29732 Wiregrass School Rd 33543 813-346-0700
Steven Williams, prin. Fax 346-0791

Saddlebrook Preparatory S 100/3-12
5700 Saddlebrook Way 33543 813-907-4500
Chris Wester, hdmstr. Fax 991-4713

West Melbourne, Brevard, Pop. 17,945
Brevard County SD
Supt. — See Melbourne
Central MS 1,300/7-8
2600 Wingate Blvd 32904 321-722-4150
Gregory Potter, prin. Fax 722-4165
Meadowlane IS 900/3-6
2700 Wingate Blvd 32904 321-722-5539
Adrienne Schwab, prin. Fax 722-4719
Meadowlane PS 800/K-2
2800 Wingate Blvd 32904 321-723-6354
Susan Schroeder, prin. Fax 952-5948
West Melbourne ES of Science 600/K-6
2255 Meadowlane Ave 32904 321-956-5040
Dr. Neleffra Marshall, prin. Fax 956-5043

Bethany Christian S 300/PK-8
1100 Dorchester Ave 32904 321-727-2038
Calvary Chapel Academy 400/PK-8
2955 Minton Rd 32904 321-729-9922
Tim Flay, head sch Fax 215-9478
Country Day For Children Montessori S 50/PK-K
1281 S Wickham Rd 32904 321-951-8005
Mustard Seed Kidz 200/PK-3
2975 Eber Blvd 32904 321-733-1733
New Hope Lutheran Academy 50/K-8
PO Box 120208 32912 321-768-1500
Harmon Krause, prin. Fax 984-0274
Palm Bay SDA ES K-5
3507 Carraige Gate Dr 32904 321-733-4551

Weston, Broward, Pop. 64,228
Broward County SD
Supt. — See Fort Lauderdale
Country Isles ES 900/K-5
2300 Country Isles Rd 33326 754-323-5250
Mindy Morgan, prin. Fax 323-5290
Eagle Point ES 1,200/K-5
100 Indian Trce 33326 754-323-5500
Christine Fernandez, prin. Fax 323-5540
Everglades ES 900/K-5
2900 Bonaventure Blvd 33331 754-323-5600
Eliot Tillinger, prin. Fax 323-5640
Falcon Cove MS 2,200/6-8
4251 Bonaventure Blvd 33332 754-323-3200
Dr. Mark Kaplan, prin. Fax 323-3285
Gator Run ES 1,200/PK-5
1101 Glades Pkwy 33327 754-323-5850
Keith Peters, prin. Fax 323-5890
Indian Trace ES 700/K-5
400 Indian Trce 33326 754-323-6300
Amy Winder, prin. Fax 323-6340
Manatee Bay ES 1,200/PK-5
19200 Manatee Isles Dr 33332 754-323-6450
Heather Hedman-DeVaughn, prin. Fax 323-6490
Tequesta Trace MS 1,400/6-8
1800 Indian Trce 33326 754-323-4400
Paul Micensky, prin. Fax 323-4485

Sagemont S - Lower Campus 300/PK-5
1570 Sagemont Way 33326 954-384-5454
Three Village Montessori S 100/PK-5
1400 Indian Trce 33326 954-384-7325
Weston Christian Academy 300/PK-8
1420 Indian Trce 33326 954-349-9224
Dr. Steve Kitchens, hdmstr. Fax 349-0678

West Palm Beach, Palm Beach, Pop. 98,081
Palm Beach County SD 176,500/PK-12
3300 Forest Hill Blvd 33406 561-434-8000
Robert Avossa Ed.D., supt. Fax 434-8571
www.palmbeachschools.org/
Bak MS of the Arts 1,300/6-8
1725 Echo Lake Dr 33407 561-882-3870
Sally Rozanski, prin. Fax 882-3879
Bear Lakes MS 800/6-8
3505 Shenandoah Rd 33409 561-615-7700
Kirk Howell, prin. Fax 615-7756
Belvedere ES 500/K-5
3000 Parker Ave 33405 561-838-5900
Diane Mahar, prin. Fax 838-5950
Benoist Farms ES 700/K-5
1765 Benoist Farms Rd 33411 561-383-9700
Ruthann Miller, prin. Fax 383-9756
Berkshire ES 1,100/K-5
1060 Kirk Rd 33406 561-304-2000
Diana Perez, prin. Fax 304-2051
Conniston Community MS 1,100/6-8
3630 Parker Ave 33405 561-802-5400
Oscar Otero, prin. Fax 802-5409
Egret Lake ES 700/K-5
5115 47th Pl N 33417 561-616-7900
Christine Rick, prin. Fax 616-7950
Everglades ES 800/K-5
407 Marginal Rd 33411 561-792-9500
Dwan Moore-Ross, prin. Fax 792-9550
Forest Hill ES 800/K-5
5555 Purdy Ln 33415 561-432-2300
Scott McNichols, prin. Fax 432-2350
Golden Grove ES 500/K-5
5959 140th Ave N 33411 561-904-9700
Adam Miller, prin. Fax 904-9750
Grassy Waters ES 700/K-5
3550 N Jog Rd 33411 561-383-9000
Jennifer Galindo, prin. Fax 383-9054
Hope-Centennial ES 700/K-5
5350 Stacy St 33417 561-640-1200
Awilda Tomas-Andres, prin. Fax 640-1250
Jeaga MS 1,200/6-8
3777 N Jog Rd 33411 561-242-8000
Anthony Allen, prin. Fax 242-8005
Kinsey/Palmview ES 600/K-5
800 11th St 33401 561-671-6500
Adrienne Howard, prin. Fax 671-6550
Meadow Park ES 600/K-5
956 Florida Mango Rd 33406 561-357-2800
Valerie Zuloaga-Haines, prin. Fax 357-2828
Melaleuca ES 800/K-5
5759 Gun Club Rd 33415 561-598-7300
Deborah Maupin, prin. Fax 598-7350
Northboro ES 800/PK-5
400 40th St 33407 561-494-1600
Gayle Harper, prin. Fax 494-1650
Northmore ES 500/K-5
4111 N Terrace Dr 33407 561-494-1700
Vonda Daniels, prin. Fax 494-1750
Palmetto ES 600/K-5
5801 Parker Ave 33405 561-202-0400
Gladys Harris, prin. Fax 202-0450
Palm Springs Community MS 1,600/6-8
1560 Kirk Rd 33406 561-434-3300
Sandra Jinks, prin. Fax 434-3303
Pine Jog ES 900/K-5
6315 Summit Blvd 33415 561-656-5400
Tarachell Thomas, prin. Fax 656-5450
Pleasant City ES 300/K-5
2222 Spruce Ave 33407 561-838-5800
Valarie Jones Ed.D., prin. Fax 838-5850
Roosevelt Community MS 1,100/6-8
1900 N Australian Ave 33407 561-822-0200
Moneek McTier, prin. Fax 822-0222
Roosevelt ES 400/K-5
1220 L A Kirksey St 33401 561-653-5100
Sharonda Alleyne, prin. Fax 653-5150
Seminole Trails ES 700/K-5
4075 Willow Pond Rd 33417 561-598-7000
Judith Garrard, prin. Fax 598-7050
South Olive ES 700/K-5
7101 S Olive Ave 33405 561-202-0200
Melinda Springman, prin. Fax 202-0250
Western Pines MS 1,100/6-8
5949 140th Ave N 33411 561-792-2500
Robert Hatcher, prin. Fax 792-2530
West Gate ES 700/K-5
1545 Loxahatchee Dr 33409 561-684-7100
Patricia Feliciano Ph.D., prin. Fax 684-7150
Westward ES 700/K-5
1101 Golf Ave 33401 561-653-5200
Bobbie Brooks, prin. Fax 653-5249
Wynnebrook ES 900/PK-5
1167 Drexel Rd 33417 561-598-7400
Suzanne Berry, prin. Fax 598-7450
Other Schools – See Belle Glade, Boca Raton, Boynton Beach, Canal Point, Delray Beach, Greenacres, Jupiter, Lake Park, Lake Worth, Lantana, Loxahatchee, North Palm Beach, Pahokee, Palm Beach, Palm Beach Gardens, Palm Springs, Riviera Beach, Royal Palm Beach, South Bay, Wellington

Atlantic Christian Academy 300/PK-12
4900 Summit Blvd 33415 561-686-8081
Jim Rozendal, hdmstr. Fax 640-7613
Berean Christian S 600/PK-12
8350 Okeechobee Blvd 33411 561-798-9300
William Dupere, hdmstr. Fax 792-3073
Ephesus Junior Academy 100/PK-8
4011 N Shore Dr 33407 561-841-0033
Greene S, 2001 S Dixie Hwy 33401 50/PK-8
Dr. Denise Spirou, prin. 561-293-2888
Holy Cross Preschool & Center 100/PK-PK
930 Southern Blvd 33405 561-366-8026
Ana Fundora, dir. Fax 366-8577
King's Academy 1,000/PK-12
8401 Belvedere Rd 33411 561-686-4244
Douglas Raines, hdmstr. Fax 686-8017
Palm Beach Christian Academy 50/PK-4
1101 S Flagler Dr 33401 561-671-5795
Christina Sosnicki, prin. Fax 671-5792
Palm Beach Day Academy 300/PK-3
1901 S Flagler Dr 33401 561-832-8815
Dr. Edwin Gordon, hdmstr. Fax 832-3343
Rosarian Academy 400/PK-8
807 N Flagler Dr 33401 561-832-5131
Stephen Rubenacker, head sch Fax 820-8750
St. Ann Catholic S 200/PK-8
324 N Olive Ave 33401 561-832-3676
Susan Demes, prin. Fax 832-1791
St. Juliana Catholic S 200/PK-8
4355 S Olive Ave 33405 561-655-1922
Katie Kervi, prin. Fax 655-8552
West Palm Beach Junior Academy 100/PK-8
6300 Summit Blvd 33415 561-689-9575
Glenn Timmons, prin. Fax 689-6183

West Park, Broward, Pop. 13,901

Annunciation S 300/PK-8
3751 SW 39th St, 954-989-8287
Jennifer Nicholson, prin. Fax 989-0660

Wewahitchka, Gulf, Pop. 1,928
Gulf County SD
Supt. — See Port Saint Joe
Wewahitchka ES 400/PK-6
514 E River Rd 32465 850-639-2476
Tracy Bowers, prin. Fax 639-3298

Wildwood, Sumter, Pop. 6,607
Sumter County SD
Supt. — See Bushnell
Wildwood ES 800/K-5
300 Huey St 34785 352-748-3353
John Temple, prin. Fax 748-4788

Williston, Levy, Pop. 2,726
Levy County SD
Supt. — See Bronson
Bullock ES 600/PK-2
130 SW 3rd St 32696 352-528-3341
Melissa Lewis, prin. Fax 528-5541
Williston ES 400/3-5
801 S Main St 32696 352-528-6030
Jaime Handlin, prin. Fax 528-5458

Williston Central Christian Academy 100/K-12
PO Box 680 32696 352-529-0900
Julie Alexander, admin. Fax 529-0901

Wilton Manors, Broward, Pop. 11,446
Broward County SD
Supt. — See Fort Lauderdale
Wilton Manors ES 600/PK-5
2401 NE 3rd Ave 33305 754-322-8950
Melissa Holtz, prin. Fax 322-8990

Wimauma, Hillsborough, Pop. 6,330
Hillsborough County SD
Supt. — See Tampa
Reddick ES 800/K-5
325 W Lake Dr 33598 813-634-0809
J. Thomas Roth, prin. Fax 634-0814
Wimauma ES 500/PK-5
5709 Hickman St 33598 813-671-5159
Ismael Lebron-Bravo, prin. Fax 672-5222

Windermere, Orange, Pop. 2,437
Orange County SD
Supt. — See Orlando
Bay Lake ES K-5
12005 Silver Lake Park Dr 34786 407-217-7960
Myrlene Jackson-Kimble, prin. Fax 217-7969
Gotha MS 1,300/6-8
9155 Gotha Rd 34786 407-521-2360
Patrice Knowles, prin. Fax 521-2361
Keenes Crossing ES 1,000/PK-5
5240 Keenes Pheasant Dr 34786 407-654-1351
Sherry Donaldson, prin. Fax 654-1829
Sunset Park ES 1,200/K-5
12050 Overstreet Rd 34786 407-905-3724
Janet Bittick, prin. Fax 905-3815
Windermere ES 800/PK-5
11125 Park Ave 34786 407-876-7520
Diana Greer, prin. Fax 876-7523

Windermere Preparatory S 1,100/PK-12
6189 Winter Garden Vineland 34786 407-905-7737
Dr. Thomas Marcy Ed.D., hdmstr. Fax 905-7710

Winter Garden, Orange, Pop. 33,427
Orange County SD
Supt. — See Orlando
Bridgewater MS 1,100/6-8
5600 Tiny Rd 34787 407-905-3710
Andrew Jackson, prin. Fax 905-3858
Dillard Street ES 800/PK-5
311 N Dillard St 34787 407-877-5000
Michelle Thomas, prin. Fax 877-5009
Independence ES PK-5
6255 New Independence Pkwy 34787 407-217-7727
Dr. Angela Murphy-Osborne, prin. Fax 217-7731
Lakeview MS 1,000/6-8
1200 W Bay St 34787 407-877-5010
Gracemarie Howland, prin. Fax 877-5019
Lake Whitney ES 600/PK-5
1351 Windermere Rd 34787 407-877-8888
Elizabeth Prince, prin. Fax 877-1181
Maxey ES 300/PK-5
1100 E Maple St 34787 407-877-5020
Carletta Davis-Wilson, prin. Fax 877-2580
Sunridge ES 700/K-5
14455 Sunridge Blvd 34787 407-656-0809
Christy Gorberg, prin. Fax 656-0830
Sunridge MS 1,200/6-8
14955 Sunridge Blvd 34787 407-656-0794
Patricia Bowen-Painter, prin. Fax 656-0806
Tildenville ES 500/PK-5
1221 Brick Rd 34787 407-877-5054
Agatha Alvarez, prin. Fax 877-5060
Whispering Oak ES 800/PK-5
15300 Stoneybrook West Pkwy 34787 407-656-7773
Lee Montgomery, prin. Fax 905-3566

Central Florida Preparatory S 100/K-12
16301 Phil Ritson Way 34787 407-290-8073
Cranium Academy 200/K-6
4068 Winter Garden Vineland 34787 407-294-6950
Family Christian S 100/PK-8
PO Box 770698 34777 407-656-7904
Terri Schneberger, prin. Fax 656-0274
Foundation Academy - North Campus 400/PK-6
125 E Plant St 34787 407-656-3677
Angel Whitehead, prin. Fax 656-0118

Winter Haven, Polk, Pop. 33,292
Polk County SD
Supt. — See Bartow
Brigham Academy 500/K-5
601 Avenue C SE 33880 863-291-5300
Lynn Boland, prin. Fax 298-7913
Chain of Lakes ES 1,000/PK-5
7001 State Road 653 33884 863-326-5388
Victor Duncan, prin. Fax 326-5391
Denison MS 800/6-8
400 Avenue A SE 33880 863-291-5353
Terri Christian, prin. Fax 291-5347
Elbert ES 600/PK-5
205 15th St NE 33881 863-291-5364
William Dawson, prin. Fax 291-5363
Garden Grove ES 600/K-5
4599 Cypress Gardens Rd 33884 863-291-5396
Deborah Compton, prin. Fax 297-3061
Garner ES 600/PK-5
2500 Havendale Blvd NW 33881 863-965-5455
Qvonda Birdsong, prin. Fax 965-5459
Inwood ES 400/K-5
2200 Avenue G NW 33880 863-291-5369
Paulette Bruno, prin. Fax 291-5342
Jewett Middle Academy 600/6-8
601 Avenue T NE 33881 863-291-5320
Jacquelyn Moore, prin. Fax 297-3049
Jewett S of the Arts 700/K-8
2250 8th St NE 33881 863-291-5373
Michael Sears, prin. Fax 295-5963
Lake Shipp ES 500/PK-5
250 Camellia Dr 33880 863-291-5384
Stacy Nelson, prin. Fax 298-7511
Snively ES 500/PK-5
848 Snively Ave 33880 863-291-5325
Diane Rosebrough, prin. Fax 297-3080
Wahneta ES 500/PK-5
205 4th Wahneta St E 33880 863-291-5392
Nildalis Caraballo, prin. Fax 295-5962
Westwood MS 800/6-8
3520 Avenue J NW 33881 863-965-5484
Todd Bennett, prin. Fax 965-5585

All Saints Academy 600/PK-12
5001 State Road 540 W 33880 863-293-5980
Carolyn Baldwin, hdmstr. Fax 294-2819
Christian Academy of Winter Haven 200/K-12
PO Box 3515 33885 863-294-8934
Curtis White, supt. Fax 299-2489
Grace Lutheran S 400/PK-8
320 Bates Ave SE 33880 863-293-9744
Michael Rottmann, prin. Fax 595-0106
Heritage Christian Academy 100/PK-11
244 Avenue D SW 33880 863-293-0012
Mark Montgomery, head sch Fax 299-4146
Oasis Christian Academy 200/PK-12
151 King Rd 33880 863-293-0930
Matthew Wiggins, admin. Fax 293-0429
St. Joseph S 400/PK-8
535 Avenue M NW 33881 863-293-3311
Tammi Haas, prin. Fax 299-7894
Winter Haven Adventist Academy 50/K-9
PO Box 7169 33883 863-299-7984
Winter Haven Christian S 200/PK-12
1700 Buckeye Loop Rd 33881 863-294-4135

Winter Park, Orange, Pop. 27,399
Orange County SD
Supt. — See Orlando
Aloma ES 500/PK-5
2949 Scarlet Rd 32792 407-672-3100
Jennifer Sanders, prin. Fax 672-0391
Brookshire ES 600/PK-5
2500 Cady Way 32792 407-623-1400
Susan Mulchrone, prin. Fax 623-5739
Killarney ES 400/PK-5
2401 Wellington Blvd 32789 407-623-1438
Kelly Steinke, prin. Fax 623-1437
Lakemont ES 700/PK-5
901 N Lakemont Ave 32792 407-623-1453
Dr. Brenda Cunningham, prin. Fax 623-5737

Seminole County SD
Supt. — See Sanford
Eastbrook ES 800/PK-5
5525 Tangerine Ave 32792 407-746-7950
Ricky Carver, prin. Fax 746-7999

Geneva S 500/PK-12
2025 State Road 436 32792 407-332-6363
International Community S 400/PK-12
4800 Howell Branch Rd 32792 407-645-2343
Robyn Terwilleger, prin. Fax 645-2366
Learning Tree S 100/PK-K
1021 N New York Ave 32789 407-628-1761
Monarch Learning Academy 100/PK-6
1600 S Orlando Ave 32789 407-478-8577
Parke House Academy 200/PK-6
1776 Minnesota Ave 32789 407-647-3624
St. Margaret Mary S 600/PK-8
142 E Swoope Ave 32789 407-644-7537
Kathleen Walsh, prin. Fax 644-7357
Walden Community S 50/K-12
4505 Howell Branch Rd 32792 407-677-8225

Winter Springs, Seminole, Pop. 32,650
Seminole County SD
Supt. — See Sanford
Highlands ES 600/PK-5
1600 Shepard Rd 32708 407-746-6650
Lenore Logsdon, prin. Fax 746-6700
Indian Trails MS 1,000/6-8
415 Tuskawilla Rd 32708 407-320-4350
Dr. Lesley Sileo Robinson, prin. Fax 320-4399
Keeth ES 600/K-5
425 Tuskawilla Rd 32708 407-320-5350
Julia Kirkner, prin. Fax 320-5399
Layer ES 600/PK-5
4201 State Road 419 32708 407-871-8050
Cheryl Nicholas, prin. Fax 871-8099
Rainbow ES 700/K-5
1412 Rainbow Trl 32708 407-320-8450
Kristen Ramkissoon, prin. Fax 320-8499
Winter Springs ES 600/PK-5
701 W State Road 434 32708 407-320-0650
Dr. Tina Erwin, prin. Fax 320-0600

Yankeetown, Levy, Pop. 491
Levy County SD
Supt. — See Bronson
Yankeetown S 200/PK-8
4500 Highway 40 W 34498 352-447-2372
Jeannine Mills, prin. Fax 447-3961

Youngstown, Bay
Bay County SD
Supt. — See Panama City
Waller ES 500/PK-5
11332 E Highway 388 32466 850-767-4341
Christopher Beard, prin. Fax 722-0988

Yulee, Nassau, Pop. 11,311
Nassau County SD
Supt. — See Fernandina Beach
Wildlight ES, 550 Curiosity Ave 32097 PK-5
Scott Hodges, prin. 904-491-9900
Yulee ES 800/3-5
86063 Felmor Rd 32097 904-491-7943
George Raysor, prin. Fax 225-9993
Yulee MS 900/6-8
85439 Miner Rd 32097 904-491-7944
Amanda Cooper, prin. Fax 225-0104
Yulee PS 900/PK-2
86426 Goodbread Rd 32097 904-491-7945
Misty Mathis, prin. Fax 225-8269

Zellwood, Orange, Pop. 2,799
Orange County SD
Supt. — See Orlando
Zellwood ES 600/PK-5
3551 N Washington St 32798 407-884-2258
Franklin Mattucci, prin. Fax 884-3100

Hampden DuBose Academy 100/K-12
PO Box 639 32798 407-880-4321

Zephyrhills, Pasco, Pop. 13,107
Pasco County SD
Supt. — See Land O Lakes
Stewart MS 1,000/6-8
38505 10th Ave, 813-794-6500
Shae Davis, prin. Fax 794-6591
Taylor ES 500/K-5
3638 Morris Bridge Rd 33543 813-794-6900
Julie Marks, prin. Fax 794-6991
West Zephyrhills ES 800/PK-5
37900 14th Ave, 813-794-6300
Scott Atkins, prin. Fax 794-6391
Woodland ES 900/PK-5
38203 Henry Dr, 813-794-6400
Shauntte Butcher, prin. Fax 794-6491

Heritage Academy 200/PK-8
35636 State Road 54 33541 813-782-7848
Zephyrhills Christian Academy 100/K-12
34927 Elland Blvd 33541 813-779-1648

Zolfo Springs, Hardee, Pop. 1,811
Hardee County SD
Supt. — See Wauchula
Zolfo Springs ES 600/K-5
3215 School House Rd 33890 863-735-1221
Tammy Pohl, prin. Fax 735-1788

GEORGIA

GEORGIA DEPARTMENT OF EDUCATION
2066 Twin Towers E, Atlanta 30334
Telephone 404-656-2800
Fax 404-651-8737
Website http://www.doe.k12.ga.us

State Superintendent of Schools Richard Woods

GEORGIA BOARD OF EDUCATION
2053 Twin Towers East, Atlanta 30334

Chairperson Mike Royal

REGIONAL EDUCATIONAL SERVICE AGENCIES (RESA)

Central Savannah River Area RESA
Gene Sullivan, dir. 706-556-6225
4683 Augusta Hwy, Dearing 30808 Fax 556-8891
www.csraresa.net
Chattahoochee-Flint RESA
Richard McCorkle, dir. 229-937-5341
PO Box 1150, Ellaville 31806 Fax 937-5754
www.cfresa.org
Coastal Plains RESA
Harold Chambers, dir. 229-546-4094
245 N Robinson St, Lenox 31637 Fax 546-4167
www.cpresa.org
First District RESA
Dr. Whit Myers, dir. 912-842-5000
PO Box 780, Brooklet 30415 Fax 842-5161
www.fdresa.org/
Griffin RESA
Dr. Stephanie Gordy, dir. 770-229-3247
440 Tilney Ave, Griffin 30224 Fax 228-7316
www.griffinresa.net/
Heart of Georgia RESA
Dr. Steven Miletto, dir. 478-353-8693
717 Smith St, Dublin 31021 Fax 353-8697
www.hgresa.org/

Metro RESA
Leigh Ann Putman, dir. 770-432-2404
1870 Teasley Dr SE, Smyrna 30080 Fax 432-6105
www.ciclt.net/mresa
Middle Georgia RESA
Carolyn Williams, dir. 478-988-7170
80 Cohen Walker Dr Fax 988-7176
Warner Robins 31088
www.mgresa.org
Northeast Georgia RESA
Dr. Keith Everson, dir. 706-742-8292
375 Winter St, Winterville 30683 Fax 742-8928
www.negaresa.org
North Georgia RESA
Dr. Samuel DePaul, dir. 706-276-1111
4731 Old Highway 5 S Fax 276-1114
Ellijay 30540
www.ngresa.org
Northwest Georgia RESA
Dexter Mills, dir. 706-295-6189
3167 Cedartown Hwy SE Fax 295-6098
Rome 30161
www.nwgaresa.com/

Oconee RESA
Dr. Hayward Cordy, dir. 478-552-5178
206 S Main St, Tennille 31089 Fax 552-6499
www.oconeeresa.org
Okefenokee RESA
Dr. Greg Jacobs, dir. 912-285-6151
1450 N Augusta Ave Fax 287-6650
Waycross 31503
www.okresa.org
Pioneer RESA
Justin Old, dir. 706-865-2141
PO Box 1789, Cleveland 30528 Fax 865-6748
www.pioneerresa.org
Southwest Georgia RESA
Tim Helms, dir. 229-207-0600
570 Martin Luther King Jr Fax 336-2888
Camilla 31730
www.swresa.org
West Georgia RESA
Rachel Spates, dir. 770-583-2528
99 Brown School Dr Fax 583-3223
Grantville 30220
www.garesa.org

PUBLIC, PRIVATE AND CATHOLIC ELEMENTARY SCHOOLS

Abbeville, Wilcox, Pop. 2,863
Wilcox County SD 1,200/PK-12
395 College St W 31001 229-467-2141
Julie Childers, supt. Fax 467-2302
www.wilcox.k12.ga.us
Other Schools – See Rochelle

Acworth, Cobb, Pop. 19,875
Bartow County SD
Supt. — See Cartersville
Allatoona ES 500/PK-5
4150 New Hope Church Rd SE 30102 770-606-5843
Jim Bishop, prin. Fax 975-4173

Cherokee County SD
Supt. — See Canton
Clark Creek ES STEM Academy 900/K-5
3219 Hunt Rd 30102 770-721-5800
Joey Moss, prin. Fax 721-5830
Oak Grove ES Fine Arts Academy 600/PK-5
6118 Woodstock Rd 30102 770-721-8550
Penny Valle, prin.

Cobb County SD
Supt. — See Marietta
Acworth ES 800/2-5
4220 Cantrell Rd NW 30101 770-975-6600
Bertha Nelson, prin. Fax 975-6602
Baker ES 700/PK-5
2361 Baker Rd NW 30101 770-975-6629
Alison Broughton, prin. Fax 975-6631
Barber MS 1,000/6-8
4222 Cantrell Rd NW 30101 770-975-6764
Tia Amlett, prin. Fax 529-0325
Durham MS 1,000/6-8
2891 Mars Hill Rd NW 30101 770-975-6641
Dr. Patricia Alford, prin. Fax 975-6643
Ford ES 700/K-5
1345 Mars Hill Rd NW 30101 678-594-8092
Dr. Jami Frost, prin. Fax 594-8094
Frey ES 700/PK-5
2865 Mars Hill Rd NW 30101 770-975-6655
Jason Cathey, prin. Fax 975-6657
McCall ES 400/K-1
4496 Dixie Ave 30101 770-975-6775
Thomas Farrell, prin. Fax 529-1580
Picketts Mill ES 700/K-5
6400 Old Stilesboro Rd NW 30101 770-975-7172
Jenny Douglas, prin. Fax 975-7121
Pitner ES 900/PK-5
4575 Wade Green Rd NW 30102 678-594-8320
Ashley Hosey, prin. Fax 594-8319

Cornerstone Preparatory Academy 400/K-12
3588 Hickory Grove Rd NW 30101 770-529-7077
Jeanne Borders, head sch Fax 529-7477

Adairsville, Bartow, Pop. 4,584
Bartow County SD
Supt. — See Cartersville
Adairsville ES 700/PK-5
122 King St 30103 770-606-5840
Melissa Zarefoss, prin. Fax 773-7755
Adairsville MS 700/6-8
485 Old Highway 41 NW 30103 770-606-5842
Dr. Tony Stanfill, prin. Fax 606-5179

Adel, Cook, Pop. 5,286
Cook County SD 3,300/PK-12
1109 N Parrish Ave 31620 229-896-2294
Dr. Jeff Shealey Ed.D., supt. Fax 896-3443
www.cook.k12.ga.us
Cook PS 1,000/PK-2
1531 Patterson St 31620 229-549-7715
Leslie Folsom, prin. Fax 549-8312
Other Schools – See Sparks

Ailey, Montgomery, Pop. 429
Montgomery County SD
Supt. — See Mount Vernon
Montgomery County ES 500/PK-5
900 Martin Luther King Dr 30410 912-583-2279
Dr. Justin Russell, prin. Fax 583-4560
Montgomery County MS 200/6-8
800 Martin Luther King Dr 30410 912-583-2351
Dr. Scott Barrow, prin. Fax 583-4469

Alamo, Wheeler, Pop. 2,788
Wheeler County SD 1,000/PK-12
18 McRae St 30411 912-568-7198
Dr. Suzanne Couey, supt. Fax 568-1985
www.wheelercountyschools.org
Wheeler County ES 600/PK-5
63 S Commerce St 30411 912-568-7159
Pat Ethredge, prin. Fax 568-1935

Albany, Dougherty, Pop. 76,579
Dougherty County SD 15,000/PK-12
200 Pine Ave 31701 229-431-1285
Kenneth Dyer, supt. Fax 431-1276
www.docoschools.org
Albany MS 700/6-8
1700 Cordell Ave 31705 229-431-3325
Frederick Polite, prin. Fax 431-3474
Coachman ES 500/K-5
1425 W Oakridge Dr 31707 229-431-3488
Melissa Brubaker, prin. Fax 431-3490

Cross MS 500/6-8
324 Lockett Station Rd, 229-431-3362
Thelma Chunn, prin. Fax 431-3476
Harvey ES, 1305 E 2nd Ave 31705 K-5
Dr. John Davis, prin. 229-431-3367
Jackson Heights ES 300/3-5
1305 E 2nd Ave 31705 229-431-3367
Dr. Brian Simon, prin. Fax 431-3355
King ES 500/K-5
3125 Mrtn Luther King Jr Dr 31701 229-438-3502
Vontressa Childs, prin. Fax 438-3504
Lake Park ES 600/PK-5
605 Meadowlark Dr 31707 229-431-3370
Kenosha Coleman, prin. Fax 431-3356
Lincoln Magnet ES 900/K-5
518 W Society Ave 31701 229-431-3373
Todd Deariso, prin. Fax 431-3357
Live Oak ES 600/K-5
4529 Gillionville Rd, 229-431-1209
Laytona Stephenson, prin. Fax 431-1237
Merry Acres MS 900/6-8
1601 Florence Dr 31707 229-431-3338
Dr. Gail Griffin, prin. Fax 431-1204
Morningside ES 200/PK-5
120 Sunset Ln 31705 229-431-3387
Christine Ford, prin. Fax 431-3383
Northside ES 400/PK-5
901 14th Ave 31701 229-431-3390
Katina Allen, prin. Fax 431-3383
Radium Springs ES 600/PK-5
2400 Roxanna Rd 31705 229-431-3395
Bruce Bowles, prin. Fax 431-3444
Radium Springs MS 700/6-8
2600 Radium Springs Rd 31705 229-431-3346
Dr. Valerie Williams, prin. Fax 431-3552
Reese ES 500/PK-5
1215 Lily Pond Rd 31701 229-431-3495
Dr. Angela Shumate, prin. Fax 431-3497
Sherwood Acres ES 800/PK-5
2201 Doncaster Dr 31707 229-431-3397
Yvette Simmons, prin. Fax 431-3446
Sylvandale Pre K Center PK-PK
1520 Cordell Ave 31705 229-431-1290
Dr. Gail Solomon, prin.
Turner ES 500/PK-5
2001 Leonard Ave 31705 229-431-3406
Dr. Deborah Jones, prin. Fax 431-3472
West Town ES 400/PK-5
1113 University St 31707 229-431-3409
Steven Dudley, prin. Fax 431-3470

Byne Christian S 100/PK-12
2832 Ledo Rd 31707 229-436-0173

Deerfield-Windsor S 800/PK-12
PO Box 71149 31708 229-435-1301
Geoffrey Sudderth, head sch Fax 888-6085
Emmanuel SDA Jr. Academy 50/K-8
1534 E Broad Ave 31705 229-420-9823
St. Teresa's Catholic S 200/PK-8
417 Edgewood Ln 31707 229-436-0134
Susie Hatcher, prin. Fax 436-0135
Sherwood Christian Academy 400/PK-12
1418 Old Pretoria Rd, 229-883-5677
Dr. Brian Dougherty, hdmstr. Fax 883-5794

Alma, Bacon, Pop. 3,400
Bacon County SD 2,100/PK-12
102 W 4th St 31510 912-632-7363
Judy M. Rowland, supt. Fax 632-2454
www.bcraiders.com
Bacon County ES 400/3-5
523 E 16th St 31510 912-632-4133
Dr. Darrell Ellis, prin. Fax 632-5414
Bacon County MS 500/6-8
1188 US Highway 1 S 31510 912-632-4662
Charlie Powell, prin. Fax 632-6603
Bacon County PS 600/PK-2
251 Cumberland Rd 31510 912-632-4765
Marcy Chancey, prin. Fax 632-6611

Alpharetta, Fulton, Pop. 56,130
Forsyth County SD
Supt. — See Cumming
Brandywine ES 1,000/K-5
175 Martin Dr 30004 770-667-2585
Todd Smith, prin. Fax 667-2586
DeSana MS 700/6-8
625 James Rd 30004 770-667-2591
Terri North, prin. Fax 667-2592
Midway ES 800/PK-5
4805 Atlanta Hwy 30004 770-475-6670
Jan Munroe, prin. Fax 521-1866

Fulton County SD
Supt. — See Atlanta
Alpharetta ES 600/PK-5
192 Mayfield Rd 30009 470-254-7015
Coretta Stewart, prin. Fax 667-2840
Creek View ES 1,000/K-5
3995 Webb Bridge Rd 30005 470-254-2932
Monica In, prin. Fax 254-2936
Haynes Bridge MS 700/6-8
10665 Haynes Bridge Rd 30022 470-254-7030
Lauren Malekebu, prin. Fax 254-2842
Holcomb Bridge MS 800/6-8
2700 Holcomb Bridge Rd 30022 470-254-5280
Christopher Shearer, prin. Fax 254-3333
Lake Windward ES 800/PK-5
11770 E Fox Ct 30005 470-254-7050
Julie Morris, prin. Fax 254-7069
Manning Oaks ES 800/PK-5
405 Cumming St 30004 470-254-2912
Deborah Pernice, prin. Fax 254-2916
New Prospect ES 600/K-5
3055 Kimball Bridge Rd 30022 470-254-2800
Amy Lemons, prin. Fax 254-2843
Webb Bridge MS 1,400/6-8
4455 Webb Bridge Rd 30005 470-254-2940
Rebecca Perkins, prin. Fax 254-2948

Alpharetta Christian Academy 300/PK-5
44 Academy St 30009 770-475-5762
Bridgeway Christian Academy 200/PK-8
4755 Kimball Bridge Rd 30005 770-751-1972
Jennifer Gastley, prin. Fax 942-1159
Crabapple Montessori S 100/PK-6
12387 Crabapple Rd 30004 770-569-5200
Fulton Science Academy 500/PK-12
3035 Fanfare Way 30009 678-366-2555
King's Ridge Christian S 700/PK-12
2765 Bethany Bnd 30004 770-754-5738
Dr. Jeff Williams, hdmstr. Fax 754-9785
McGinnis Woods Country Day S 500/PK-8
5380 Faircroft Dr 30005 770-664-7764
Mill Springs Academy 300/1-12
13660 New Providence Rd 30004 770-360-1336
Robert Moore, hdmstr. Fax 360-1341

Ambrose, Coffee, Pop. 376
Coffee County SD
Supt. — See Douglas
Ambrose ES 400/PK-5
3753 Vickers Xing 31512 912-359-5500
Dr. Mary Vickers, prin. Fax 359-5565

Americus, Sumter, Pop. 16,892
Sumter County SD 3,000/PK-12
100 Learning Ln, 229-931-8500
Dr. Torrance Choates, supt. Fax 931-8601
www.sumterschools.org
Sumter County ES 500/2-3
438 Bumphead Rd, 229-924-7835
Dr. Sharon Tullis, prin. Fax 924-8831
Sumter County IS 200/4-6
439 Bumphead Rd, 229-924-3168
Dr. Renee Mays, prin. Fax 924-2135
Sumter County MS 300/7-8
200 Industrial Blvd, 229-924-1010
Anton Anthony, prin. Fax 928-5571
Sumter County PS 500/PK-1
123 Learning Ln, 229-924-1012
Dr. Lezley Anderson, prin. Fax 931-0662

Southland Academy 600/PK-12
PO Box 1127 31709 229-924-4406

Appling, Columbia
Columbia County SD
Supt. — See Evans
North Columbia ES 300/PK-5
2874 Ray Owens Rd 30802 706-541-1158
Tonya Gambrell, prin. Fax 854-5833

Arlington, Calhoun, Pop. 1,473
Calhoun County SD
Supt. — See Morgan
Calhoun County ES 300/PK-5
18904 Morgan Rd, 229-213-0147
Robert Grimes, prin. Fax 233-7932

Armuchee, Floyd
Floyd County SD
Supt. — See Rome
Armuchee MS 500/6-8
471 Floyd Springs Rd NE 30105 706-378-7924
Jeanie Hubbard, prin. Fax 378-7983

Ashburn, Turner, Pop. 4,108
Turner County SD 1,500/PK-12
423 N Cleveland St 31714 229-567-3338
Dr. Jeff McDaniel, supt. Fax 567-3285
www.turner.k12.ga.us
Turner County ES 600/PK-5
705 Hudson Ave 31714 229-567-2461
Bernard Joiner, prin. Fax 567-2546
Turner County MS 300/6-8
330 Gilmore St 31714 229-567-4343
Bernice Martin, prin. Fax 567-2877

Athens, Clarke, Pop. 113,262
Clarke County SD 12,800/PK-12
PO Box 1708 30603 706-546-7721
Dr. Demond Means, supt. Fax 208-9124
www.clarke.k12.ga.us
Alps Road ES 300/PK-5
205 Alps Rd 30606 706-548-2261
Dr. Anita Lumpkin-Barnett, prin. Fax 227-7818
Barnett Shoals ES 500/PK-5
3220 Barnett Shoals Rd 30605 706-357-5334
Jennifer Scott, prin. Fax 208-8835
Barrow ES 600/PK-5
100 Pinecrest Dr 30605 706-543-2676
Dr. Ellen Sabatini, prin. Fax 357-5279
Burney-Harris-Lyons MS 600/6-8
1600 Tallassee Rd 30606 706-548-7208
Dr. Makeba Clark, prin. Fax 357-5263
Chase Street ES 500/PK-5
757 N Chase St 30601 706-543-1081
Dr. Adam Kurtz, prin. Fax 357-5249
Clarke MS 600/6-8
1235 Baxter St 30606 706-543-6547
Theodore MacMillan, prin. Fax 548-0257
Coile MS 600/6-8
110 Old Elberton Rd 30601 706-357-5318
tomas ramirez, prin. Fax 357-5321
Fowler Drive ES 500/PK-5
400 Fowler Dr 30601 706-357-5330
Anissa Johnson, prin. Fax 357-5329
Gaines ES 600/PK-5
900 Gaines School Rd 30605 706-357-5338
Katrina Daniel, prin. Fax 357-5297
Hilsman MS 700/6-8
870 Gaines School Rd 30605 706-548-7281
Utevia Tolbert, prin. Fax 357-5295
Oglethorpe Avenue ES 600/PK-5
1150 Oglethorpe Ave 30606 706-549-0762
Dr. Scarlett Dunne, prin. Fax 227-7813
Stroud ES 400/PK-5
715 Fourth St 30601 706-369-1893
Dr. Marsha Thomas, prin. Fax 357-5254
Timothy Road ES 600/PK-5
1900 Timothy Rd 30606 706-549-0107
Kena Worthy, prin. Fax 357-5255
Whit Davis Road ES 500/K-5
1450 Whit Davis Rd 30605 706-369-1036
Susan Tolbert, prin. Fax 357-5298
Whitehead Road ES 700/PK-5
555 Quailwood Dr 30606 706-548-7296
Luther McDaniel, prin. Fax 357-5282
Other Schools – See Bogart, Winterville

Jackson County SD
Supt. — See Jefferson
South Jackson ES 500/PK-5
1630 New Kings Bridge Rd 30607 706-543-8798
Resa Brooksher, prin. Fax 543-4032

Athens Academy 1,000/PK-12
PO Box 6548 30604 706-549-9225
John Thorsen, head sch Fax 354-3775
Athens Christian S 800/PK-12
1270 Highway 29 N 30601 706-549-7586
Steve Cummings, head sch Fax 549-2899
Downtown Academy 100/K-5
165 Pulaski St 30601 706-353-8996
Patrick Ennis, hdmstr. Fax 535-3128
St. Joseph Catholic S 300/PK-8
958 Epps Bridge Pkwy 30606 706-543-1621
Theresa Napoli, prin. Fax 543-0149

Atlanta, Fulton, Pop. 412,360
Atlanta CSD 44,700/PK-12
130 Trinity Ave SW 30303 404-802-3500
Meria Carstarphen Ed.D., supt. Fax 802-1803
www.atlantapublicschools.us
Beecher Hills ES 300/PK-5
2257 Bolling Brook Dr SW 30311 404-802-8300
Crystal Jones, prin. Fax 802-9205
Benteen ES 300/PK-5
200 Cassanova St SE 30315 404-802-7300
Dr. Andrew Lovett, prin. Fax 802-9210
Bolton Academy 700/PK-5
2268 Adams Dr NW 30318 404-802-8350
Laura Strickling, prin. Fax 350-2853
Boyd ES 500/PK-5
1891 Johnson Rd NW 30318 404-802-8150
Joi Kilpatrick, prin. Fax 792-5763
Brandon ES 700/3-5
2741 Howell Mill Rd NW 30327 404-802-7250
Kara Stimpson, prin. Fax 350-2826
Brandon PS K-2
2845 Margaret Mitchell Dr 30327 404-802-7280
Kara Stimpson, prin.
Brown MS, 765 Peeples St SW 30310 700/6-8
Tiauna Crooms, prin. 404-802-6800
Bunche MS 700/6-8
1925 Niskey Lake Rd SW 30331 404-802-6700
Mario Watkins, prin.
Burgess/Peterson ES 300/PK-5
480 Clifton St SE 30316 404-802-3400
David White, prin.
Cascade ES 400/PK-5
2326 Venetian Dr SW 30311 404-802-8100
Dr. Sylvia Hall, prin. Fax 802-8147
Cleveland Avenue ES 300/PK-5
2672 Old Hapeville Rd SW 30315 404-802-8400
Dr. Anyee Payne, prin. Fax 669-2725
Continental Colony ES 400/PK-5
3181 Hogan Rd SW 30331 404-802-8000
Kristen Vaughn, prin. Fax 802-8049
Deerwood Academy 600/PK-5
3070 Fairburn Rd SW 30331 404-802-3300
Camisha Perry, prin. Fax 349-6736
Dobbs ES 500/PK-5
2025 Jonesboro Rd SE 30315 404-802-8050
Dr. Charnita West, prin. Fax 624-2024
Dunbar ES 400/K-5
500 Whitehall Ter SW 30312 404-802-7950
Karen Brown-Collier, prin. Fax 525-2778
Fain ES 500/PK-5
101 Hemphill School Rd NW 30331 404-802-8600
Desmond Moore, prin. Fax 699-4579
Fickett ES 500/PK-5
3935 Rux Rd SW 30331 404-802-7850
Cheryl Twyman, prin. Fax 346-2358
Finch ES 500/PK-5
1114 Avon Ave SW 30310 404-802-4000
Carol Evans, prin. Fax 752-5563
Garden Hills ES 600/PK-5
285 Sheridan Dr NE 30305 404-802-7800
Stacey Abbott, prin. Fax 842-3050
Gideons ES 500/PK-5
897 Welch St SW 30310 404-802-7700
Danielle Washington, prin. Fax 752-0806
Harper-Archer MS 600/7-8
3399 Collier Dr NW 30331 404-802-6500
Marques Stewart, prin. Fax 699-4569
Heritage Academy 500/PK-5
3500 Villa Cir SE 30354 404-802-8650
Trennis Harvey, prin. Fax 608-8321
Hollis Innovation Academy PK-8
225 James P Brawley Dr NW 30314 404-802-8217
Diamond Jack, prin.
Hope-Hill ES 400/PK-5
112 Boulevard NE 30312 404-802-7450
Maureen Wheeler, prin. Fax 330-4965
Humphries ES 400/PK-5
3029 Humphries Dr SE 30354 404-802-8750
Melanie Mitchell, prin. Fax 362-2408
Hutchinson ES 400/PK-5
650 Cleveland Ave SW 30315 404-802-7650
Dr. Shuanta Broadway, prin. Fax 768-5690
Inman MS 1,000/6-8
774 Virginia Ave NE 30306 404-802-3200
Dr. Kevin Maxwell, prin. Fax 802-3299
Jackson ES 800/PK-5
1325 Mount Paran Rd NW 30327 404-802-8800
Brent McBride, prin. Fax 802-9440
Jones ES 500/PK-5
1040 Fair St SW 30314 404-802-3900
Margul Woolfolk, prin. Fax 752-5655
Kimberly ES 500/PK-5
3090 McMurray Dr SW 30311 404-802-7600
Joseph Salley, prin. Fax 802-7649
King MS 500/6-8
545 Hill St SE 30312 404-802-5400
Paul Brown, prin. Fax 802-5499
Lewis Invictus Academy 6-8
1890 D LHollowell Pkwy NW 30318 404-802-3500
Lucious Brown, prin.
Lin ES 600/K-5
586 Candler Park Dr NE 30307 404-802-8850
Sharyn Briscoe, prin. Fax 802-8899
Long MS 700/6-8
3200 Latona Dr SW 30354 404-802-4800
Lisa Hill, prin. Fax 802-4899
Miles ES 300/PK-5
4215 Bakers Ferry Rd SW 30331 404-802-8900
Thalise Perry, prin.
Morningside ES 800/PK-5
1053 E Rock Springs Rd NE 30306 404-802-8950
Audrey Sofianos, prin. Fax 853-4043
Obama Academy 200/K-5
970 Martin St SE 30315 404-802-4200
Robin Robbins, prin. Fax 635-0287
Parkside ES 600/PK-5
685 Mercer St SE 30312 404-802-4100
Tim Foster, prin. Fax 802-4199
Perkerson ES 500/PK-5
2040 Brewer Blvd SW 30310 404-802-3950
Tony Ford, prin. Fax 802-3995
Peyton Forest ES 500/PK-5
301 Peyton Rd SW 30311 404-802-7100
Cynthia Gunner, prin.
Price MS 300/6-8
1670 B W Bickers Dr SE 30315 404-802-6300
Luqman Abdur-Rahman, prin. Fax 624-5137
Rivers ES 700/PK-5
8 Peachtree Battle Ave NW 30305 404-802-7050
John Waller, prin. Fax 350-2831
Scott ES 300/PK-5
1752 Hollywood Rd NW 30318 404-802-7000
Langston Longley, prin. Fax 794-6796
Slater ES 600/PK-5
1320 Pryor Rd SW 30315 404-802-4050
Lenise Bostic, prin. Fax 624-2045

Smith ES 500/K-5
370 Old Ivy Rd NE 30342 404-802-3850
Michael Forehand, prin. Fax 842-3046
Springdale Park ES 600/K-5
1246 Ponce De Leon Ave NE 30306 404-802-6050
Terry Harness, prin. Fax 802-6047
Stanton ES 300/PK-5
1625 Martin Luther King SW 30314 404-802-7500
Dr. Phyllis Earls, prin. Fax 756-8689
Sutton MS 1,500/6-8
2875 Northside Dr NW 30305 404-802-5600
Gail Johnson, prin.
Sylvan Hills MS 600/6-8
1461 Sylvan Rd SW 30310 404-802-6200
Artesa Portee, prin. Fax 802-6299
Thomasville Heights ES 400/PK-5
1820 Henry Thomas Dr SE 30315 404-802-5750
Nicole Jones, prin. Fax 624-2048
Toomer ES 400/PK-5
65 Rogers St NE 30317 404-802-3450
Ashley Adamo, prin. Fax 687-7992
Towns ES 300/PK-5
760 Bolton Rd NW 30331 404-802-7400
Dr. Dione Simon, prin. Fax 505-6519
Tuskegee Airmen Global Academy 400/PK-5
1654 S Alvarado Ter SW 30311 404-802-8450
Lincoln Woods, prin. Fax 752-0807
Usher-Collier ES 400/PK-5
631 Harwell Rd NW 30318 404-802-5700
Jerry Parker, prin. Fax 691-6521
West Manor ES 300/K-5
570 Lynhurst Dr SW 30311 404-802-3350
Dr. Reginald Lawrence, prin. Fax 699-6784
Woodson Park Academy 400/PK-5
20 Evelyn Way NW 30318 404-802-7750
Dr. Susan McClendon, prin.
Young MS 1,000/6-8
3116 Benjamin E Mays Dr SW 30311 404-802-5900
Kevin Scott, prin. Fax 802-5999

DeKalb County SD
Supt. — See Stone Mountain
Ashford Park ES 500/PK-5
2968 Cravenridge Dr NE 30319 678-676-6702
Dr. LaShawn McMillan, prin. Fax 676-6710
Briar Vista ES 400/PK-5
1131 Briar Vista Ter NE 30324 678-874-5902
Cammie Neill, prin. Fax 874-5910
Fernbank ES 600/PK-5
157 Heaton Park Dr 30307 678-874-9302
Joan Ray, prin. Fax 874-9310
Hawthorne ES 400/PK-5
2535 Caladium Dr NE 30345 678-874-2802
Lisa Limoncelli, prin. Fax 874-2810
Henderson MS 1,500/6-8
2830 Henderson Mill Rd 30341 678-874-2902
Rochelle Patillo, prin. Fax 874-2910
Henderson Mill ES 600/PK-5
2408 Henderson Mill Rd NE 30345 678-874-3102
Mitchell Green, prin. Fax 874-3110
Kittredge Magnet ES 400/4-6
1663 E Nancy Creek Dr NE 30319 678-874-6602
Dr. Laura Neely, prin. Fax 874-6610
Lewis ES PK-5
2383 N Druid Hills Rd 30329 678-874-1502
Dr. Julie Brown, prin. Fax 874-1510
Montclair ES 1,100/PK-5
1680 Clairmont Pl NE 30329 678-874-7302
Laura Baez, prin. Fax 874-7310
Montgomery ES 700/PK-5
3995 Ashford Dunwoody Rd NE 30319
678-676-7502
Lori Bolds, prin. Fax 676-7510
Oak Grove ES 600/PK-5
1857 Oak Grove Rd NE 30345 678-874-7402
Lynda Mauborgne, prin. Fax 874-7410
Obama Magnet ES of Technology PK-5
3132 Clifton Church Rd SE 30316 678-874-4402
Angela Bethea, prin. Fax 874-4410
Sagamore Hills ES 400/PK-5
1865 Alderbrook Rd NE 30345 678-874-7502
Dr. Julie Taylor, prin. Fax 874-7510
Woodward ES 1,000/PK-5
3034 Curtis Dr NE 30319 678-874-7802
Dr. Demetria Haddock, prin. Fax 874-7810

Fulton County SD 94,500/PK-12
6201 Powers Ferry Rd 30339 470-254-3600
Dr. Jeff Rose, supt. Fax 254-1246
www.fultonschools.org
Randolph ES 600/PK-5
5320 Campbellton Rd SW 30331 470-254-6520
LaToya Miley, prin. Fax 254-6526
Sandtown MS 1,200/6-8
5400 Campbellton Rd SW 30331 470-254-6500
Estella Cook, prin. Fax 254-6510
Wolf Creek ES K-5
4440 Derrick Rd 30349 470-254-2760
Dionne Glass, prin.
Other Schools – See Alpharetta, College Park, East Point, Fairburn, Hapeville, Johns Creek, Milton, Palmetto, Roswell, Sandy Springs, Union City

---

Atlanta International S 1,000/PK-12
2890 N Fulton Dr NE 30305 404-841-3840
Kevin Glass, hdmstr. Fax 841-3896
Atlanta Jewish Academy 300/PK-8
5200 Northland Dr 30342 404-843-9900
Rabbi Ari Leubitz, head sch Fax 252-0934
Atlanta Montessori International S 100/PK-9
1970 Cliff Valley Way NE 30329 404-325-6777
Atlanta Speech S 400/PK-6
3160 Northside Pkwy NW 30327 404-233-5332
Comer Yates, dir. Fax 266-2175
Atlanta Youth Academy 100/PK-8
PO Box 18237 30316 404-370-1960

Berean Christian Junior Academy 200/K-8
401 Hamilton E Holmes Dr NW 30318 404-799-0337
Karohn Young, prin. Fax 225-7250
Children's S 400/PK-7
345 10th St NE 30309 404-873-6985
Nishant Mehta, head sch Fax 607-8565
Christ the King S 600/K-8
46 Peachtree Way NE 30305 404-233-0383
Tricia Ward, prin. Fax 266-0704
Clark Academy 100/5-8
228 Margaret St SE 30315 678-651-2100
Cliff Valley S 200/PK-8
2426 Clairmont Rd NE 30329 678-302-1302
Dr. Michael Edwards Ed.D., head sch Fax 302-1300
Dar Un Noor Academy 200/PK-11
434 14th St NW 30318 404-876-5051
Halit Erdogdu, prin. Fax 874-6740
Davis Academy 600/PK-8
8105 Roberts Dr 30350 770-671-0085
Amy Shafron, head sch Fax 671-8838
Dunwoody Christian S 50/K-2
2250 Dunwoody Club Dr 30350 770-712-2896
Bob Baima, prin.
Galloway S 700/PK-12
215 W Wieuca Rd NW 30342 404-252-8389
Suzanna Jemsby, head sch Fax 252-7770
Heritage Preparatory S 100/PK-8
1700 Piedmont Ave NE 30324 404-815-7711
Beth McCauley, head sch Fax 815-7737
Holy Innocents' Episcopal S 1,300/PK-12
805 Mount Vernon Hwy 30327 404-255-4026
Paul Barton, head sch Fax 250-0815
Holy Spirit Preparatory S 600/PK-12
4449 Northside Dr NW 30327 678-904-2811
Kyle Pietrantonio, head sch Fax 904-4983
Imhotep Academy 200/PK-8
667 Fairburn Rd NW 30331 404-586-9595
Dr. Joe Brown Ed.D., prin. Fax 586-9597
Immaculate Heart of Mary S 500/K-8
2855 Briarcliff Rd NE 30329 404-636-4488
Kellie DesOrmeaux, prin. Fax 636-1853
Intown Community S 200/K-8
2059 Lavista Rd NE 30329 404-633-8081
Lovett S 1,600/K-12
4075 Paces Ferry Rd NW 30327 404-262-3032
William Peebles, hdmstr. Fax 261-1967
Midtown International S 100/K-10
1575 Sheridan Road NE 30324 404-542-7003
Ande Noktes, head sch Fax 935-0530
Mohammed Schools of Atlanta 200/PK-12
735 Fayetteville Rd SE 30316 404-378-4219
Qur'an Shakir, prin. Fax 378-4600
Mount Nebo Christian Academy 100/PK-1
1025 McDonough Blvd SE 30315 404-622-3161
Keisha Sewell, dir. Fax 627-9065
Mt. Vernon Presbyterian S 700/PK-12
471 Mount Vernon Hwy NE 30328 404-252-3448
Dr. Brett Jacobsen, head sch Fax 252-6777
Our Lady of the Assumption S 500/PK-8
1320 Hearst Dr NE 30319 404-364-1902
Lisa Cordell, prin. Fax 364-1914
Pace Academy 1,000/K-12
966 W Paces Ferry Rd NW 30327 404-262-1345
Frederick Assaf, head sch Fax 264-9376
Paideia S 1,000/PK-12
1509 Ponce De Leon Ave NE 30307 404-377-3491
Paul Bianchi, hdmstr. Fax 377-0032
St. Anne's Day S 100/PK-K
3098 Saint Annes Ln NW 30327 404-237-7024
Kristin Watts, dir. Fax 237-9226
St. Jude the Apostle S 500/K-8
7171 Glenridge Dr 30328 770-394-2880
Patty Childs, prin. Fax 804-9248
St. Martin's Episcopal S 600/PK-8
3110 Ashford Dunwoody Rd NE 30319
404-237-4260
Luis Ottley Ed.D., hdmstr. Fax 237-9311
Southwest Atlanta Christian Academy 200/PK-12
PO Box 310750 31131 404-346-2080
Springmont S 200/PK-8
5750 Long Island Dr NW 30327 404-252-3910
Jerri King, head sch Fax 843-9815
Torah S of Atlanta 300/K-8
1985 Lavista Rd NE 30329 404-982-0800
Dr. Peshie Kasloff, head sch Fax 248-1039
Trinity S 600/PK-6
4301 Northside Pkwy NW 30327 404-231-8100
Joe Marshall, head sch Fax 231-8111
Westminster S 1,900/K-12
1424 W Paces Ferry Rd NW 30327 404-355-8673
Keith Evans, pres. Fax 355-6606

Auburn, Barrow, Pop. 6,757
Barrow County SD
Supt. — See Winder
Auburn ES 700/K-5
1334 6th Ave 30011 770-963-7887
Julia Hodges, prin. Fax 963-2923
Bramlett ES 700/PK-5
622 Freeman Brock Rd 30011 770-307-1627
Karen Dowis, prin. Fax 868-1442

Gwinnett County SD
Supt. — See Suwanee
Mulberry ES 600/PK-5
442 E Union Grove Cir 30011 678-226-7460
Jonathan Day, prin. Fax 226-7467

Old Peachtree Montessori S 100/PK-6
33 Hills Shop Rd 30011 770-963-3052

Augusta, Richmond, Pop. 193,101
Columbia County SD
Supt. — See Evans
Martinez ES 700/PK-5
213 Flowing Wells Rd 30907 706-863-8308
Wade White, prin. Fax 868-2185

Richmond County SD 30,800/PK-12
864 Broad St 30901 706-826-1000
Dr. Angela Pringle, supt. Fax 826-4612
www.rcboe.org
Barton Chapel Road ES 500/PK-5
2329 Barton Chapel Rd 30906 706-796-4955
Dr. Barbara Brown, prin. Fax 796-4774
Bayvale ES 500/PK-5
3309 Milledgeville Rd 30909 706-737-7255
Tonethia Beasley, prin. Fax 737-7256
Copeland ES 500/PK-5
1440 Jackson Rd 30909 706-737-7228
Cheryl Elder, prin. Fax 731-7656
Craig-Houghton ES 400/PK-5
1001 4th St 30901 706-823-6946
Sophia Cogle, prin. Fax 823-6988
Garrett ES 300/PK-5
1100 Eisenhower Dr 30904 706-737-7222
Stacey Walk, prin. Fax 737-1166
Glenn Hills ES 500/PK-5
2838 Glenn Hills Dr 30906 706-796-4942
Dr. Vanessa Lancaster, prin. Fax 796-4701
Glenn Hills MS 700/6-8
2941 Glenn Hills Dr 30906 706-796-4705
Dr. Bernard Chatman, prin. Fax 796-4716
Goshen ES 500/PK-5
4040 Old Waynesboro Rd 30906 706-796-4646
Cheryl Fry, prin. Fax 796-4676
Gracewood ES 400/PK-5
2032 Tobacco Rd 30906 706-796-4969
Chris Neal, prin. Fax 796-4677
Hains ES 200/PK-K, 4-5
1820 Windsor Spring Rd 30906 706-796-4918
Rachel McRae, prin. Fax 790-1368
Hornsby S 700/PK-8
310 Kentucky Ave 30901 706-823-6928
Dr. Isaac Lee, prin. Fax 823-4372
Lake Forest Hills ES 600/PK-5
3140 Lake Forest Dr 30909 706-737-7317
Dr. Emily Driggers, prin. Fax 737-7318
Lamar-Milledge ES 500/PK-5
510 Eve St 30904 706-737-7262
Raye Robinson, prin. Fax 737-7261
Langford MS 900/6-8
3019 Walton Way Ext 30909 706-737-7301
Marva Tutt, prin. Fax 737-7302
Meadowbrook ES 600/PK-5
3630 Goldfinch Dr 30906 706-796-4915
Bettina Kyler, prin. Fax 796-4681
Merry ES 400/PK-5
415 Boy Scout Rd 30909 706-737-7185
Kimberly Mungo, prin. Fax 731-7653
Monte Sano ES 300/PK-5
2164 Richmond Ave 30904 706-481-1813
Cynthia Scoggins, prin. Fax 481-1814
Reynolds ES 800/PK-5
3840 Wrightsboro Rd 30909 706-855-2540
Amy McClure, prin. Fax 855-2546
Rollins ES 500/PK-5
2160 Mura Dr 30906 706-796-4972
Dr. Sharon Ray, prin. Fax 796-4971
Southside ES 400/PK-5
3310 Old Louisville Rd 30906 706-796-4952
Dr. Tonya Bradburn, prin. Fax 772-8117
Terrace Manor ES 400/PK-5
3110 Tate Rd 30906 706-796-4910
Major Lee, prin. Fax 796-4686
Tobacco Road ES 500/PK-5
2397 Tobacco Rd 30906 706-796-4658
Ny McRae, prin. Fax 796-4663
Tutt MS 500/6-8
495 Boy Scout Rd 30909 706-737-7288
Angela Sheahan, prin. Fax 481-1620
Walker Magnet S 800/K-8
1301 Wrightsboro Rd 30901 706-823-6950
Aletha Snowberger, prin. Fax 823-6954
Warren Road ES 600/PK-5
311 Warren Rd 30907 706-868-4022
Tammy Hendley, prin. Fax 868-3647
Wilkinson Gardens ES 400/PK-5
1925 Kratha Dr 30906 706-737-7219
Dr. Brenda Taylor, prin. Fax 731-8803
Windsor Spring ES 500/PK-5
2534 Windsor Spring Rd 30906 706-796-4939
Dr. Valerie McGahee, prin. Fax 796-4702
Other Schools – See Blythe, Fort Gordon, Hephzibah

Alleluia Community S 200/K-12
2819 Peach Orchard Rd 30906 706-793-9663
Augusta First SDA S 50/PK-8
4301 Wheeler Rd 30907 706-651-0491
Curtis Baptist S 400/PK-12
1326 Broad St 30901 706-828-6624
Mark Sterling, head sch Fax 828-6627
Ebenezer SDA Christian Academy 50/K-8
1699 Olive Rd 30904 706-496-6958
Episcopal Day S 400/PK-8
2248 Walton Way 30904 706-733-1192
Dr. Ned Murray, head sch Fax 733-1388
Heritage Academy 200/K-8
333 Greene St 30901 706-821-0034
Jan Hitchcock, prin. Fax 821-0122
Hillcrest Baptist S 200/PK-8
3045 Deans Bridge Rd 30906 706-798-5600
Immaculate Conception Catholic S 100/PK-8
811 Telfair St 30901 706-722-9964
Allison Palfy, prin. Fax 722-9994
St. Mary on the Hill Catholic S 400/K-8
1220 Monte Sano Ave 30904 706-733-6193
Laura Webster, prin. Fax 737-7985
Westminster S of Augusta 500/PK-12
3067 Wheeler Rd 30909 706-731-5260
Brian Case, head sch Fax 731-5274
Whole Life Christian Academy 100/PK-5
2621 Washington Rd 30904 706-364-1439
Dr. Sabrina McTyre, admin. Fax 737-4113

Austell, Cobb, Pop. 6,416
Cobb County SD
Supt. — See Marietta
Austell ES 500/K-5
5600 Mulberry St 30106 770-819-5804
Dr. Marvin Bynes, prin. Fax 398-0041
Clarkdale ES 600/PK-5
4725 Ewing Rd 30106 770-819-2422
Dr. Liss Maynard, prin. Fax 819-2424
Cooper MS 900/6-8
4605 Ewing Rd 30106 770-819-2438
Dr. Vanessa Watkins, prin. Fax 819-2440
Garrett MS 800/6-8
5235 Austell Pwdr Sprgs Rd 30106 770-819-2466
Kimberly Jackson, prin. Fax 819-2468
Sanders ES 800/PK-5
1550 Anderson Mill Rd 30106 770-819-2568
Laura Fiedler, prin. Fax 819-2570

Connection Pointe Christian Academy 100/PK-8
888 E West Connector 30106 770-803-6475
Teresa Sigman, prin. Fax 401-3730
Cumberland Christian Academy 200/PK-5
2356 Clay Rd 30106 678-426-1600
Sherry Campbell, prin. Fax 945-0224
Destiny Christian Academy 100/PK-5
7400 Factory Shoals Rd 30168 770-948-0200
Krisandra Lee, prin. Fax 874-8280

Avondale Estates, DeKalb, Pop. 2,893
DeKalb County SD
Supt. — See Stone Mountain
Avondale ES 500/PK-5
8 Lakeshore Dr 30002 678-676-5202
Dr. Dontae Andrews, prin. Fax 676-5210
DeKalb ES of the Arts 600/PK-7
3131 Old Rockbridge Rd 30002 678-874-1302
Bianca Hamilton, prin. Fax 874-1310

Baconton, Mitchell, Pop. 898
Mitchell County SD
Supt. — See Camilla
Mitchell County ES 300/2-4
15815 GA Highway 93 31716 229-336-2118
Vickie Hicks, prin. Fax 787-5829

Bainbridge, Decatur, Pop. 12,559
Decatur County SD 5,500/PK-12
100 S West St, 229-248-2200
Tim Cochran, supt. Fax 248-2252
www.dcboe.com
Bainbridge MS 800/7-8
1301 E College St, 229-248-2206
Letitia Austin, prin. Fax 248-2817
Elcan King ES 500/PK-4
725 E Louise St, 229-248-2212
Jennifer Wilkinson, prin. Fax 248-2263
Hutto MS 800/5-6
1201 Martin Luther King Jr, 229-248-2224
Crycynthia Gardner, prin. Fax 243-5303
Johnson ES 500/PK-4
1947 S West St, 229-248-2215
Tammi Godwin, prin. Fax 248-2272
Jones-Wheat ES 500/PK-4
1401 E Shotwell St, 229-248-2218
Dr. Larry Clark, prin. Fax 248-2265
Potter Street ES 300/PK-4
725 Potter St, 229-248-2253
Jeanette Grimsley, prin. Fax 248-2255
West Bainbridge ES 600/PK-4
915 Zorn Rd, 229-248-2821
Jamie Ard, prin. Fax 248-2820

Grace Christian Academy 300/PK-12
1302 Lake Douglas Rd, 229-243-8851
Rob Starner, head sch Fax 243-0515

Baldwin, Banks, Pop. 3,231
Habersham County SD
Supt. — See Clarkesville
Baldwin ES 400/PK-5
894 Willingham Ave 30511 706-778-6435
Rodney Long, prin. Fax 776-5946

Ball Ground, Cherokee, Pop. 1,414
Cherokee County SD
Supt. — See Canton
Ball Ground ES STEM Academy 500/PK-5
321 Valley St 30107 770-721-5900
Christian Kirby, prin. Fax 735-4182

Barnesville, Lamar, Pop. 6,626
Lamar County SD 2,600/PK-12
100 Victory Ln 30204 770-358-5891
Dr. Jute Wilson, supt. Fax 358-5858
www.lamar.k12.ga.us
Lamar County ES 600/3-5
228 Roberta Dr 30204 770-358-5556
Dr. Andrea Scandrett, prin. Fax 358-5560
Lamar County MS 600/6-8
100 Burnette Rd 30204 770-358-8652
Dr. Julie Steele, prin. Fax 358-8657
Lamar County PS 700/PK-2
154 Burnette Rd 30204 770-358-8661
Jeremy Hawkins, prin. Fax 358-8666

Baxley, Appling, Pop. 4,360
Appling County SD 3,600/PK-12
249 Blackshear Hwy 31513 912-367-8600
Dr. Scarlett Copeland, supt. Fax 367-1011
www.appling.k12.ga.us
Altamaha ES 400/PK-5
344 Altamaha School Rd 31513 912-367-3713
Dr. Rhonda Hollis, prin. Fax 367-2609
Appling County ES 600/3-5
680 Blackshear Hwy 31513 912-367-8640
Debra Crosby, prin. Fax 367-8649
Appling County MS 800/6-8
2997 Blackshear Hwy 31513 912-367-8630
Cathy Campbell, prin. Fax 367-8803
Appling County PS 800/PK-2
678 Blackshear Hwy 31513 912-367-8642
Cindy Stewart, prin. Fax 367-8141
Other Schools – See Surrency

Appling Christian Academy 100/PK-12
1479 Hatch Pkwy S 31513 912-367-3004

Bellville, Evans, Pop. 123

Pinewood Christian Academy 600/PK-12
PO Box 7 30414 912-739-1272

Bethlehem, Barrow, Pop. 594
Barrow County SD
Supt. — See Winder
Bethlehem ES 800/PK-5
47 McElhannon Rd SW 30620 770-867-2238
Mindy Reid, prin. Fax 307-0529

Bethlehem Christian Academy 400/PK-12
544 Christmas Ave 30620 770-307-1574
Rhonda Whiting, head sch Fax 425-6553

Bishop, Oconee, Pop. 223
Oconee County SD
Supt. — See Watkinsville
High Shoals ES 400/K-5
401 Hopping Rd 30621 706-310-1985
Mike Eddy, prin. Fax 310-1986

Black Creek, Bryan
Bryan County SD 8,300/PK-12
8810 US Highway 280 E 31308 912-851-4000
Dr. Paul Brooksher, supt. Fax 851-4093
www.bryan.k12.ga.us/
Other Schools – See Pembroke, Richmond Hill

Blackshear, Pierce, Pop. 3,390
Pierce County SD 3,700/PK-12
PO Box 349 31516 912-449-2044
Dr. Kevin Smith, supt. Fax 449-2046
www.pierce.k12.ga.us/
Blackshear ES 900/PK-5
5217 GA Highway 121 31516 912-449-2088
Tonya Johnson, prin. Fax 449-2081
Midway ES 500/PK-5
3244 Midway Church Rd 31516 912-807-0084
Dr. Walker Todd, prin. Fax 807-0087
Pierce County MS 900/6-8
5216 County Farm Rd 31516 912-449-2077
Perry Tison, prin. Fax 449-2075
Other Schools – See Patterson

Blairsville, Union, Pop. 642
Union County SD 2,700/PK-12
124 Hughes St 30512 706-745-2322
Dr. Fred Rayfield, supt. Fax 745-5025
www.ucschools.org
Union County ES 600/3-5
165 Elementary Way 30512 706-745-9615
Trish Cook, prin. Fax 745-6081
Union County MS 600/6-8
367 Wellborn St 30512 706-745-2483
Gwen Stafford, prin. Fax 781-6200
Union County PS 600/PK-2
592 School Cir 30512 706-745-5450
Millie Owenby, prin. Fax 745-8391
Other Schools – See Suches

Blakely, Early, Pop. 5,032
Early County SD 2,200/PK-12
11927 Columbia St, 229-723-4337
Bronwyn Ragan-Martin Ed.D., supt. Fax 723-8183
www.early.k12.ga.us
Early County ES 1,000/PK-5
283 Martin Luther King Jr, 229-723-4101
Matthew Cullifer, prin. Fax 723-6072
Early County MS 500/6-8
12053 Columbia St, 229-723-3746
Angela Bell, prin. Fax 723-3942

Bloomingdale, Chatham, Pop. 2,668
Savannah-Chatham County SD
Supt. — See Savannah
Bloomingdale ES 400/PK-5
101 E Main St 31302 912-395-3680
Aysha Parks, prin. Fax 201-8696

Blue Ridge, Fannin, Pop. 1,269
Fannin County SD 3,000/PK-12
2290 E First St 30513 706-632-3771
Dr. Michael Gwatney, supt. Fax 632-7583
www.fannin.k12.ga.us
Blue Ridge ES 500/PK-5
224 E Highland St 30513 706-632-5772
April Hodges, prin. Fax 632-6069
Fannin County MS 800/6-8
4560 Old Highway 76 30513 706-632-6100
Keith Nuckolls, prin. Fax 632-0461
West Fannin ES 500/K-5
5060 Blue Ridge Dr 30513 706-492-3644
Lucas Roof, prin. Fax 492-4523
Other Schools – See Morganton

Blythe, Richmond, Pop. 706
Richmond County SD
Supt. — See Augusta
Blythe ES 300/PK-5
290 Church St 30805 706-592-4090
Pam Ward, prin. Fax 592-3708

Bogart, Clarke, Pop. 1,021
Clarke County SD
Supt. — See Athens
Cleveland Road ES 400/PK-5
1700 Cleveland Rd 30622 706-357-5333
Lindsey Chatham, prin. Fax 357-5336

Oconee County SD
Supt. — See Watkinsville
Malcom Bridge ES 500/K-5
2600 Malcom Bridge Rd 30622 706-310-1998
Susan Stancil, prin. Fax 310-1999
Malcom Bridge MS 800/6-8
2500 Malcom Bridge Rd 30622 706-310-1992
Dr. Merideth Blackburn, prin. Fax 310-1993
Rocky Branch ES 600/K-5
5250 Hog Mountain Rd 30622 706-769-3235
Laura Mason, prin. Fax 310-2000

Living Word Academy 50/PK-6
2761 Monroe Hwy 30622 678-753-0018
Sonya Rice, dir.
Prince Avenue Christian S 700/PK-12
2201 Ruth Jackson Rd 30622 678-726-2300
Seth Hathaway, head sch Fax 726-2301

Bonaire, Houston
Houston County SD
Supt. — See Perry
Bonaire ES 700/PK-5
101 Elm St 31005 478-929-7826
Dr. Catherine Gardner, prin. Fax 542-2281
Bonaire MS 1,000/6-8
125 GA Highway 96 E 31005 478-929-6235
Cindy Randall, prin. Fax 929-6245
Hilltop ES 600/PK-5
301 Robert Bryson Smith Pky 31005 478-929-6113
Dr. Ovedia Glover, prin. Fax 929-6109

Bowdon, Carroll, Pop. 1,987
Carroll County SD
Supt. — See Carrollton
Bowdon ES 700/PK-5
223 Kent Ave 30108 770-258-2161
Lorie Teal, prin. Fax 258-8204
Bowdon MS 300/6-8
129 N Jonesville Rd 30108 770-258-1778
Scott Estes, prin. Fax 258-4374

Bowersville, Hart, Pop. 450
Hart County SD
Supt. — See Hartwell
North Hart ES 600/K-5
124 Ankerich Rd 30516 706-856-7369
Brooks Mewborn, prin. Fax 856-7372

Braselton, Jackson, Pop. 7,379

Braselton Christian Academy 50/PK-12
401 Zion Church Rd 30517 706-824-9943

Bremen, Haralson, Pop. 6,130
Bremen CSD 2,100/PK-12
501 Pacific Ave 30110 770-537-5508
Dr. David Hicks, supt. Fax 537-0610
www.bremencs.com
Bremen 4/5 Academy 300/4-5
2440 Crosstown Pkwy 30110 770-537-9340
Brian Evans, prin. Fax 537-1866
Bremen MS 500/6-8
2440 Crosstown Pkwy 30110 770-537-4874
Brian Evans, prin. Fax 537-5043
Jones ES 700/PK-3
206 Lakeview Dr 30110 770-537-4352
Silas Brown, prin. Fax 537-1280

Brooklet, Bulloch, Pop. 1,369
Bulloch County SD
Supt. — See Statesboro
Brooklet ES 600/PK-5
600 W Lane St 30415 912-842-8300
Mike Yawn, prin. Fax 842-9413
Southeast Bulloch MS 700/6-8
9124 Brooklet Denmark Rd 30415 912-842-8400
Dr. Torian White, prin. Fax 842-9559
Stilson ES 400/PK-5
15569 GA Highway 119 30415 912-842-8480
Tanita McDowell, prin. Fax 823-9057

Broxton, Coffee, Pop. 1,178
Coffee County SD
Supt. — See Douglas
Broxton-Mary Hayes ES 300/PK-5
410 S Alabama St 31519 912-359-2391
Allyson Speight, prin. Fax 359-3968

Brunswick, Glynn, Pop. 15,115
Glynn County SD, PO Box 1677 31521 12,800/PK-12
Dr. Virgil Cole, supt. 912-267-4100
www.glynn.k12.ga.us
Altama ES 500/PK-5
5505 Altama Ave 31525 912-264-3563
Michelle Drew, prin. Fax 267-4111
Burroughs-Molette ES 600/PK-5
1900 Lee St 31520 912-267-4130
Mavis Jaudon, prin. Fax 267-4178
FACES Prekindergarten PK-PK
1900 Lee St 31520 912-267-4229
Stephanie Thompson, prin. Fax 267-4195
Glyndale ES 600/PK-5
1785 Old Jesup Rd 31525 912-264-8740
Fern Way-Currin, prin. Fax 280-6767
Glynn MS 800/6-8
635 Lanier Blvd 31520 912-267-4150
Robin Hunter, prin. Fax 267-4158
Golden Isles ES 800/PK-5
1350 Cate Rd 31525 912-264-6822
Kathie Matthews, prin. Fax 264-6110
Goodyear ES 600/PK-5
3000 Roxboro Rd 31520 912-267-4170
Dr. Oatanisha Dawson, prin. Fax 261-4443

Greer ES 700/PK-5
695 Harry Driggers Blvd 31525 912-267-4135
Carter Akins, prin. Fax 267-4139
Macon MS 700/6-8
201 McKenzie Dr 31523 912-265-3337
Michele Seals, prin. Fax 267-4118
Needwood MS 700/6-8
669 Harry Driggers Blvd 31525 912-261-4488
Marlowe Hinson, prin. Fax 261-4491
Risley MS 600/6-8
707 S Port Pkwy 31523 912-280-4020
Lori Joiner, prin. Fax 261-3252
Satilla Marsh ES 800/PK-5
360 S Port Pkwy 31523 912-265-3675
Tere Miller, prin. Fax 267-4197
Sterling ES 700/K-5
200 McKenzie Dr 31523 912-279-1509
Dr. Kelly Howe, prin. Fax 279-1738
Other Schools – See Saint Simons Island

Brunswick Christian Academy 200/PK-12
4231 US Highway 17 N 31525 912-264-4546
Heritage Christian Academy 200/PK-12
4265 Norwich Street Ext 31520 912-264-5491
Cindy Zangla, admin. Fax 264-0799
St. Francis Xavier Catholic S 300/PK-8
1121 Union St 31520 912-265-9470
Dr. Terry Mermann, prin. Fax 261-9950

Buchanan, Haralson, Pop. 1,089
Haralson County SD
Supt. — See Tallapoosa
Buchanan ES 300/3-5
215 College Cir 30113 770-646-5140
Ethelyn Johnson, prin. Fax 646-8893
Buchanan PS 500/PK-2
271 Van Wert St 30113 770-646-5523
Pepper Moon, prin. Fax 646-8309

Buena Vista, Marion, Pop. 2,149
Marion County SD 1,400/PK-12
1697 Pineville Rd 31803 229-649-2234
Glenn Tidwell, supt. Fax 649-7423
www.marion.k12.ga.us
Moss ES 600/PK-5
PO Box 578 31803 229-649-5567
Dr. Leigh Medders, prin. Fax 649-5565

Buford, Gwinnett, Pop. 12,025
Buford CSD 4,000/K-12
2625 Sawnee Ave 30518 770-945-5035
Dr. Geye Hamby, supt. Fax 945-4629
www.bufordcityschools.org
Buford Academy 1,200/2-5
2705 Robert Bell Pkwy 30518 678-482-6960
Kaleen Pulley, prin. Fax 482-6969
Buford ES 700/K-1
2500 Sawnee Ave 30518 770-945-5248
Tara Prince, prin. Fax 932-7579
Buford MS 1,000/6-8
2700 Robert Bell Pkwy 30518 770-904-3690
Melanie Reed, prin. Fax 904-3689

Gwinnett County SD
Supt. — See Suwanee
Harmony ES 600/K-5
3946 S Bogan Rd 30519 770-945-7272
Anne Keskonis, prin. Fax 932-7497
Ivy Creek ES 900/K-5
3443 Ridge Rd 30519 678-714-3655
Laura Callahan, prin. Fax 714-3657
Jones MS 1,300/6-8
3575 Ridge Rd 30519 770-904-5450
Memorie Reesman, prin. Fax 904-5452
Patrick ES 800/K-5
2707 Kilgore Rd 30519 678-765-5260
Stephanie Stewart, prin. Fax 765-5267
Twin Rivers MS 1,500/6-8
2300 Braselton Hwy 30519 678-407-7550
Linda Boyd, prin. Fax 407-7560

Hall County SD
Supt. — See Gainesville
Friendship ES 600/K-5
4450 Friendship Rd 30519 770-932-1223
Tracie Brack, prin. Fax 932-2162

Butler, Taylor, Pop. 1,959
Taylor County SD 1,500/PK-12
23 Mulberry St 31006 478-862-5224
Dr. Jennifer Albritton, supt. Fax 862-5818
taylor.schooldesk.net
Taylor County MS 200/7-8
PO Box 580 31006 478-862-5285
Brian Barnhill, prin. Fax 862-5368
Taylor County PS 300/K-2
PO Box 1946 31006 478-862-4855
Gwen Jenkins, prin. Fax 862-4856
Taylor County Upper ES 500/PK-PK, 3-
218 E Main St 31006 478-862-5690
Linda Ward, prin. Fax 862-9122

Byron, Peach, Pop. 4,436
Houston County SD
Supt. — See Perry
Eagle Springs ES 800/PK-5
3591 US Highway 41 N 31008 478-953-0450
Dr. Andrea McGee, prin. Fax 953-0444

Peach County SD
Supt. — See Fort Valley
Byron ES 600/K-5
202 New Dunbar Rd 31008 478-825-9650
Preston Lauritsen, prin. Fax 956-5910
Byron MS 400/6-8
201 Linda Dr 31008 478-825-9660
Dr. Jeff Bell, prin. Fax 956-3916
Kay Road ES 700/K-5
880 Kay Rd 31008 478-825-8893
Pamela Slocumb, prin. Fax 956-0618

Cairo, Grady, Pop. 9,480
Grady County SD 4,700/PK-12
122 N Broad St, 229-377-3701
Dr. Kermit V. Gilliard Ed.D., supt. Fax 377-3437
www.grady.k12.ga.us
Eastside ES 700/PK-5
1201 20th St NE, 229-377-8441
Chiquila Wright, prin. Fax 377-7816
Northside ES 400/PK-5
985 1st St NW, 229-377-2422
Dr. Cheryl Larkins, prin. Fax 378-1133
Southside ES 700/PK-5
322 4th Ave SE, 229-377-3723
Stacy Whigham, prin. Fax 377-5939
Washington MS 600/6-8
1277 Martin Luther King Jr, 229-377-2106
Tilda Brimm, prin. Fax 377-7779
Other Schools – See Pelham, Whigham

Calhoun, Gordon, Pop. 15,378
Calhoun CSD 3,700/PK-12
380 Barrett Rd 30701 706-629-2900
Dr. Michele Taylor, supt. Fax 629-3235
www.calhounschools.org
Calhoun ES 900/3-5
101 Raymond King Dr 30701 706-629-7130
Beth Holcomb, prin. Fax 602-6701
Calhoun MS 800/6-8
399 S River St 30701 706-629-3340
Peter Coombe, prin. Fax 629-0236
Calhoun Pre K PK-PK
380 Barrett Rd 30701 706-629-2900
Kelly Fuquea, coord. Fax 629-3235
Calhoun PS 900/K-2
102 Raymond King Dr 30701 706-629-8323
Beth Holcomb, prin. Fax 602-6725

Gordon County SD 6,500/PK-12
PO Box 12001 30703 706-629-7366
Dr. Susan Remillard, supt. Fax 625-5671
www.gcbe.org
Ashworth MS 700/6-8
PO Box 12001 30703 706-625-9545
Scott McClanahan, prin. Fax 879-5073
Belwood ES 500/PK-5
PO Box 12001 30703 706-629-9547
Justin Timms, prin. Fax 879-5213
Red Bud ES 600/PK-5
PO Box 12001 30703 706-625-2111
Debra Brock, prin. Fax 625-2730
Red Bud MS 600/6-8
PO Box 12001 30703 706-879-5261
Jenny Hayes, prin. Fax 879-5270
Sonoraville ES 600/PK-5
PO Box 12001 30703 706-879-5302
Amy Beason, prin. Fax 879-5303
Other Schools – See Fairmount, Plainville, Resaca

Coble SDA S 100/PK-8
450 Academy Dr SW 30701 706-629-1578

Camilla, Mitchell, Pop. 5,311
Mitchell County SD 1,700/PK-12
108 S Harney St 31730 229-336-2100
Robert Adams, supt. Fax 336-3870
www.mitchell.k12.ga.us
Mitchell County MS 400/5-7
55 Griffin Rd 31730 229-336-0980
Rodney Conine, prin. Fax 336-2139
Mitchell County PS 600/PK-1
50 Griffin Rd 31730 229-336-8250
Donna Johnson, prin. Fax 336-2135
Other Schools – See Baconton

Westwood S 400/PK-12
255 Fuller St 31730 229-336-7992

Canton, Cherokee, Pop. 22,432
Cherokee County SD 39,500/PK-12
1250 Bluffs Pkwy 30114 770-479-1871
Dr. Brian Hightower, supt. Fax 479-7758
cherokeek12.net
Avery ES 1,100/K-5
6391 E Cherokee Dr 30115 770-704-1343
Dr. Lisa Turner, prin. Fax 479-6215
Bunche Center 100/PK-PK
400 Belletta Dr 30114 770-721-5370
Donna Adams, admin. Fax 479-8506
Canton STEM Academy 800/PK-5
712 Marietta Hwy 30114 770-704-1240
Dr. Abigail May, prin. Fax 720-6328
Clayton ES 200/K-5
221 Upper Burris Rd 30114 770-721-5860
Abbey Philpot, prin.
Creekland MS 1,400/6-8
1555 Owens Store Rd 30115 770-704-4460
Dr. Sue Zinkil, prin.
Freedom MS 1,200/6-8
10550 Bells Ferry Rd 30114 770-704-1100
Sheila Grimes, prin.
Free Home ES 300/K-5
12525 Cumming Hwy 30115 770-721-5960
Kim Hagood, prin. Fax 781-8095
Hasty ES 900/PK-6
205 Brown Industrial Pkwy 30114 770-721-6555
Rodney Larrotta, prin.
Hickory Flat ES 500/K-6
2755 E Cherokee Dr 30115 770-704-1444
Whitney Nolan, prin. Fax 345-2689
Holly Springs ES 1,000/K-6
1965 Hickory Rd 30115 770-704-1420
Donna Bertram, prin. Fax 345-5913
Indian Knoll ES 1,100/K-6
3635 Univeter Rd 30115 770-721-6600
Dr. Ann Gazell, prin. Fax 721-6670
Knox ES 700/K-5
151 River Bend Way 30114 770-704-1265
Tammy Sandell, prin. Fax 345-4482

Liberty ES 1,300/K-5
10500 Bells Ferry Rd 30114 770-704-1300
Doug Knott, prin. Fax 345-6922
Macedonia ES 800/K-5
10370 E Cherokee Dr 30115 770-704-1372
Caroline Daugherty, prin. Fax 479-4026
Rusk MS, 2761 E Cherokee Dr 30115 900/7-8
Dawn Weinbaum, prin. 770-704-1135
Sixes ES, 20 Ridge Rd 30114 800/K-5
Cindy Crews, prin. 770-721-5840
Teasley MS 900/6-8
151 Hickory Log Dr 30114 770-721-5420
Dr. Benjamin Lester, prin. Fax 479-3275
Other Schools – See Acworth, Ball Ground, Waleska, Woodstock

Anchor Christian Academy 100/PK-8
6613 Hickory Flat Hwy 30115 678-880-8767
Tisha Gotte, prin. Fax 880-9564
Brenwood Academy 200/PK-5
8991 E Cherokee Dr 30115 770-704-4925

Carnesville, Franklin, Pop. 574
Franklin County SD 3,600/PK-12
280 Busha Rd 30521 706-384-4554
Wayne Randall, supt. Fax 384-7472
www.franklin.k12.ga.us
Carnesville IS 300/3-5
11555 Highway 59 30521 706-384-7326
Karen Correia, prin. Fax 384-5510
Carnesville PS 300/PK-2
825 Hull Ave 30521 706-384-4523
Karen Correia, prin. Fax 384-2226
Franklin County MS 900/6-8
485 Turkey Creek Rd 30521 706-384-4581
Kelly Akin, prin. Fax 384-2285
Other Schools – See Lavonia, Royston

Carrollton, Carroll, Pop. 23,838
Carroll County SD 14,600/PK-12
164 Independence Dr 30116 770-832-3568
Scott Cowart, supt. Fax 834-6399
www.carrollcountyschools.com/
Central ES 1,000/PK-5
633 Stripling Chapel Rd 30116 770-832-6466
Matthew Huckeba, prin. Fax 830-5017
Central MS 900/6-8
155 Whooping Creek Rd 30116 770-832-8114
Jimmy LeBlanc, prin. Fax 836-2782
Mount Zion ES 700/PK-5
260 Eureka Church Rd 30117 770-832-8588
Cindy Parker, prin. Fax 832-0326
Sand Hill ES 700/PK-5
45 Sandhill School Rd 30116 770-832-8541
Carla Meigs, prin. Fax 830-5034
Sharp Creek ES 600/PK-5
115 Old Muse Rd 30116 770-214-8848
Shelly Hester, prin. Fax 836-2734
Other Schools – See Bowdon, Mount Zion, Roopville, Temple, Villa Rica, Whitesburg

Carrollton CSD 4,800/PK-12
106 Trojan Dr 30117 770-832-9633
Dr. Mark Albertus, supt. Fax 836-9950
www.carrolltoncityschools.net
Carrollton ES 1,600/PK-3
401 Ben Scott Blvd 30117 770-832-2120
Amanda Carden, prin. Fax 214-2079
Carrollton JHS 700/7-8
510 Ben Scott Blvd 30117 770-832-6535
Travis Thomaston, prin. Fax 832-7003
Carrollton MS 1,100/4-6
151 Tom Reeves Dr 30117 770-830-0997
Stacy Lawler, prin. Fax 834-5391

Oak Grove Montessori S 100/PK-4
180 Oak Grove Rd 30117 770-214-0112
Oak Mountain Academy 200/PK-12
222 Cross Plains Rd 30116 770-834-6651
Paula Gillispie, head sch Fax 834-6785

Cartersville, Bartow, Pop. 19,341
Bartow County SD 14,200/PK-12
PO Box 200007 30120 770-606-5800
John Harper Ed.D., supt. Fax 606-5855
www.bartow.k12.ga.us
Cass MS 1,000/6-8
195 Fire Tower Rd NW 30120 770-606-5846
Dr. Kristy Arnold, prin. Fax 606-3835
Clear Creek ES 600/PK-5
50 Pleasant Valley Rd NW 30121 770-606-5886
Dr. Kelly Wade, prin. Fax 386-4450
Cloverleaf ES 800/PK-5
291 State Route 20 Spur SE 30121 770-606-5847
Dr. Evie Barge, prin. Fax 606-5176
Hamilton Crossing ES 600/PK-5
116 Hamilton Crossing Rd NW 30120 770-606-5849
Lynn Robertson, prin. Fax 606-3852
Mission Road ES 500/PK-5
1100 Mission Rd SW 30120 770-606-5863
Sherrie Hughes, prin. Fax 606-3862
Other Schools – See Acworth, Adairsville, Emerson, Euharlee, Kingston, Rydal, Taylorsville, White

Cartersville CSD 4,000/PK-12
PO Box 3310 30120 770-382-5880
Dr. J. Howard Hinesley Ed.D., supt. Fax 387-7476
www.cartersville.k12.ga.us
Cartersville ES 1,000/3-5
340 Old Mill Rd 30120 770-382-0983
Melissa White, prin. Fax 387-7497
Cartersville MS 1,000/6-8
825 Douthit Ferry Rd 30120 770-382-3666
Ken MacKenzie, prin. Fax 387-7495
Cartersville PS 900/K-2
315 Etowah Dr 30120 770-382-1733
Gina Bishop, prin. Fax 387-7493

Kids & Company Preschool PK-PK
323 S Erwin St 30120 678-535-6330
Dr. Denise Osborn, dir. Fax 535-6329

Excel Christian Academy 300/K-12
325 Old Mill Rd 30120 770-382-9488
Shelia Langford, prin. Fax 606-9884
Trinity S 100/PK-12
814 West Ave 30120 770-386-7479
Stephanie K. Dietz, head sch Fax 606-9942

Cataula, Harris
Harris County SD
Supt. — See Hamilton
Creekside S 800/5-6
8403 GA Highway 315 31804 706-596-1300
Dr. Dan Lomax, prin. Fax 596-1371
Mulberry Creek ES 500/PK-4
8405 GA Highway 315 31804 706-320-9397
Dr. Justin Finney, prin. Fax 322-4569

Cave Spring, Floyd, Pop. 1,186
Floyd County SD
Supt. — See Rome
Cave Spring ES 300/PK-5
13 Rome Rd SW 30124 706-777-3371
Trina Self, prin. Fax 777-9943

Cedartown, Polk, Pop. 9,595
Polk County SD 7,700/PK-12
612 S College St 30125 770-748-3821
Greg Teems, supt. Fax 748-5131
www.polk.k12.ga.us/
Cedartown MS 1,000/6-8
1664 Syble W Brannon Pkwy 30125 770-749-8850
Shannon Hulsey, prin. Fax 749-2795
Cherokee ES 600/PK-5
191 Evergreen Ln 30125 770-748-5614
Jonathan Kirsch, prin. Fax 748-5607
Northside ES 500/PK-5
100 N Philpot St 30125 770-748-4932
Kenneth Wallace, prin. Fax 748-8318
Westside ES 600/PK-5
51 Frank Lott Dr 30125 770-748-0831
Laura Little, prin. Fax 748-5859
Youngs Grove ES 700/PK-5
601 Wooten Rd 30125 770-901-4294
Wesley Styles, prin.
Other Schools – See Rockmart

Centerville, Houston, Pop. 6,978
Houston County SD
Supt. — See Perry
Centerville ES 700/PK-5
450 N Houston Lake Blvd 31028 478-953-0400
Ruthann Bowden, prin. Fax 953-0411
Thomson MS 800/6-8
301 Thomson St 31028 478-953-0489
Dr. Walter Stephens, prin. Fax 953-0484

Chamblee, DeKalb, Pop. 9,782
DeKalb County SD
Supt. — See Stone Mountain
Chamblee MS 900/6-8
3601 Sexton Woods Dr 30341 678-874-8202
John Martin, prin. Fax 874-8210
Dresden ES 1,100/PK-5
2449 Dresden Dr 30341 678-676-7202
Jesse Berger, prin. Fax 676-7210
Huntley Hills ES 500/PK-5
2112 Seaman Cir 30341 678-676-7402
Dr. Mia Ford, prin. Fax 676-7410

Chatsworth, Murray, Pop. 4,251
Murray County SD 7,600/PK-12
PO Box 40 30705 706-695-4531
Eric McFee Ed.D., supt. Fax 695-8425
www.murray.k12.ga.us
Bagley MS 500/7-8
4600 Highway 225 N 30705 706-695-1115
Shalina Stone, prin. Fax 695-7289
Chatsworth ES 800/PK-6
500 Green Rd 30705 706-695-2434
Fax 695-7735
Coker ES 800/PK-6
1733 Leonard Bridge Rd 30705 706-695-0888
Daphne Winkler, prin. Fax 695-0863
Eton ES 600/PK-6
829 Highway 286 30705 706-695-3207
Judy Redmond, prin. Fax 517-1414
Gladden MS 600/7-8
700 Old Dalton Ellijay Rd 30705 706-695-7448
Dr. Phillip Greeson, prin. Fax 517-2479
Northwest ES 500/PK-6
110 McEntire Cir 30705 706-695-2262
Paula Martin, prin. Fax 695-7751
Spring Place ES 700/PK-6
2795 Leonard Bridge Rd 30705 706-695-2525
Donna Standridge, prin. Fax 517-0184
Woodlawn ES 900/PK-6
4580 Highway 225 N 30705 706-517-5213
Pam Rich, prin. Fax 517-5147

Chickamauga, Walker, Pop. 3,044
Chickamauga CSD 1,400/K-12
402 Cove Rd 30707 706-382-3100
Melody Day, supt. Fax 375-5364
chickamaugacityschools.org
Chickamauga ES 600/K-5
210 Crescent Ave 30707 706-382-3100
Jeff Sikes, prin. Fax 375-7995
Lee MS 300/6-8
300 Crescent Ave 30707 706-382-3100
Benny Ashley, prin. Fax 375-1020

Walker County SD
Supt. — See La Fayette
Cherokee Ridge ES 700/PK-5
2423 Johnson Rd 30707 706-375-9831
Lori Vann, prin. Fax 375-9834

Chula, Tift

Tiftarea Academy 500/PK-12
PO Box 10 31733 229-382-0436

Clarkesville, Habersham, Pop. 1,712
Habersham County SD 7,000/PK-12
PO Box 70 30523 706-754-2118
Matthew Cooper, supt. Fax 754-1549
www.habershamschools.com/
Clarkesville ES 400/PK-5
6539 Highway 115 30523 706-754-2442
Patrick Franklin, prin. Fax 754-5964
North Habersham MS 500/6-8
1500 Wall Bridge Rd 30523 706-754-2915
Brent Tuck, prin. Fax 754-8218
Woodville ES 200/K-5
911 Historic Old Hwy 441 30523 706-754-4225
Susan Davis, prin. Fax 754-1812
Other Schools – See Baldwin, Cornelia, Demorest, Mount Airy

Clarkston, DeKalb, Pop. 7,202
DeKalb County SD
Supt. — See Stone Mountain
Indian Creek ES 1,100/PK-5
724 N Indian Creek Dr 30021 678-676-5702
Dr. Antonette Campbell, prin. Fax 676-5710
Jolly ES 800/PK-5
1070 Otello Ave 30021 678-676-5802
Judy Rosemond, prin. Fax 676-5810

Claxton, Evans, Pop. 2,710
Evans County SD 1,900/PK-12
613 W Main St 30417 912-739-3544
Martin Waters, supt. Fax 739-2492
www.evans.k12.ga.us
Claxton ES 1,100/PK-5
6463 US Highway 301 30417 912-739-2714
Myron Midgett, prin. Fax 739-0834
Claxton MS 400/6-8
600 Hendrix St 30417 912-739-3646
Dr. Diane Holland, prin. Fax 739-7217

Cleveland, White, Pop. 3,334
White County SD 3,900/PK-12
136 Warriors Path 30528 706-865-2315
Jeffrey Wilson Ed.D., supt. Fax 865-7784
www.white.k12.ga.us
Mossy Creek ES 500/K-5
128 Horace Fitzpatrick Dr 30528 706-865-5000
Jennifer King, prin. Fax 865-5001
Nix ES 500/PK-5
342 W Kytle St 30528 706-865-6935
Stacie Ward, prin. Fax 865-5569
Tesnatee Gap ES 400/K-5
2696 Tesnatee Gap Valley Rd 30528 706-865-1037
Octavius Mulligan, prin. Fax 219-3141
White County MS 900/6-8
283 Old Blairsville Rd 30528 706-865-4060
Kristi Gerrells, prin. Fax 865-1947
Other Schools – See Sautee

Bowman Hills S PK-8
300 Westview Dr NE, 423-476-6014

Cochran, Bleckley, Pop. 5,096
Bleckley County SD 2,300/PK-12
PO Box 516 31014 478-934-2821
Steve Smith, supt. Fax 934-9595
www.bleckley.k12.ga.us
Bleckley County ES 500/3-5
470 GA Highway 26 E 31014 478-934-3600
Michele Dyal, prin. Fax 934-0309
Bleckley County Learning Center PK-PK
242 E Dykes St 31014 478-934-9094
Pansy Corbett, dir. Fax 934-6713
Bleckley County MS 500/6-8
590 GA Highway 26 E 31014 478-934-7270
Carla Thrower, prin. Fax 934-6502
Bleckley County PS 600/K-2
259 E Peter St 31014 478-934-2280
Quent Floyd, prin. Fax 934-2006

Cohutta, Whitfield, Pop. 658
Whitfield County SD
Supt. — See Dalton
Cohutta ES 300/PK-5
254 Wolfe St 30710 706-694-8812
Tim Wright, prin. Fax 694-8390

Colbert, Madison, Pop. 588
Madison County SD
Supt. — See Danielsville
Colbert ES 400/K-5
255 Colbert School Rd 30628 706-788-2341
Chris Forrer, prin. Fax 788-3619

College Park, Fulton, Pop. 13,682
Clayton County SD
Supt. — See Jonesboro
King ES 1,000/PK-5
5745 W Lees Mill Rd 770-991-4651
Dr. Carl Jackson, prin. Fax 991-4079
North Clayton MS 900/6-8
5517 W Fayetteville Rd, 770-994-4025
Shakira Rice, prin. Fax 994-4028
Northcutt ES 700/PK-5
5451 W Fayetteville Rd, 770-994-4020
Dr. Wynton Walker, prin. Fax 994-4479
West Clayton ES 500/PK-5
5580 Riverdale Rd, 770-994-4005
Edward Williams, prin. Fax 994-4009

Fulton County SD
Supt. — See Atlanta
Bethune ES 700/PK-5
5925 Old Carriage Dr, 470-254-7940
Taylor Pratt, prin. Fax 254-7945
Camp Creek MS 700/6-8
4345 Welcome All Rd SW, 470-254-8030
Jarvis Adams, prin. Fax 254-8228
Cliftondale ES 900/PK-5
3340 W Stubbs Rd, 470-254-4070
Minnie Miller, prin. Fax 254-4077
College Park ES 500/PK-5
2075 Princeton Ave 30337 470-254-8040
Mari Early, prin. Fax 254-8192
Feldwood ES 800/PK-5
5790 Feldwood Rd, 470-254-2001
Racquel Harris, prin. Fax 254-2002
Heritage ES 800/PK-5
2600 Jolly Rd, 470-254-8144
Cheree Turner, prin. Fax 254-8148
Lee ES 500/PK-5
4600 Scarborough Rd, 470-254-8025
Kin'e Geathers, prin. Fax 254-8229
Lewis ES 500/PK-5
6201 Connell Rd, 470-254-3450
Ethel Lett, prin. Fax 254-3581
McNair MS 800/6-8
2800 Burdett Rd, 470-254-4160
John Madden, prin. Fax 254-4165
Nolan ES 800/PK-5
2725 Creel Rd, 470-254-7950
Evon Hewitt, prin. Fax 254-7955
Stonewall Tell ES 1,000/PK-5
3310 Stonewall Tell Rd, 470-254-3500
Philip Hammonds, prin. Fax 254-3504

Woodward Academy 2,800/PK-12
1662 Rugby Ave 30337 404-765-4000
F. Stuart Gulley Ph.D., pres. Fax 765-4009

Collins, Tattnall, Pop. 579
Tattnall County SD
Supt. — See Reidsville
Collins S 300/PK-8
720 W Main St 30421 912-693-2455
Starla Barker, prin. Fax 693-9046

Colquitt, Miller, Pop. 1,979
Miller County SD 1,100/PK-12
96 Perry St, 229-758-5592
James Phillips, supt. Fax 758-6040
www.miller.k12.ga.us
Miller County ES 600/PK-5
996 Phillipsburg Rd, 229-758-4140
Allen Martin, prin. Fax 758-3244
Miller County MS 200/6-8
996 Phillipsburg Rd, 229-758-4130
Cleve Roland, prin. Fax 758-3244

Columbus, Muscogee, Pop. 184,779
Muscogee County SD 31,100/PK-12
PO Box 2427 31902 706-748-2000
Dr. David Lewis, supt. Fax 748-2001
www.muscogee.k12.ga.us
Allen ES 400/PK-5
5201 23rd Ave 31904 706-748-2418
Karen Garner, prin. Fax 748-2415
Arnold Magnet Academy 700/6-8
2011 51st St 31904 706-748-2436
Stacy Day, prin. Fax 748-2435
Baker MS 600/6-8
1215 Benning Dr 31903 706-683-8721
Ramona Horn, prin. Fax 683-8731
Blackmon Road MS 600/6-8
7251 Blackmon Rd 31909 706-565-2998
Penny Bowen, prin. Fax 565-3006
Blanchard ES 600/PK-5
3512 Weems Rd 31909 706-748-2461
Dawn Grantham, prin. Fax 748-2466
Brewer ES 600/PK-5
2951 Martin Luther King Jr 31906 706-748-2479
Dr. Cenobia Moore, prin. Fax 748-2481
David Elementary Magnet Academy 600/K-5
5801 Armour Rd 31909 706-748-2617
Clara Davis, prin. Fax 748-2620
Davis ES 400/PK-5
1822 Shepherd Dr 31906 706-748-2638
Dr. Aetavia Williams, prin. Fax 748-2647
Dawson ES 300/PK-5
180 Northstar Dr 31907 706-683-8732
Dr. Renee Tharp, prin. Fax 683-8737
Dimon Magnet ES 500/PK-5
480 Dogwood Dr 31907 706-683-8772
Janet Sellers, prin. Fax 683-8776
Double Churches ES 400/PK-5
1213 Double Churches Rd 31904 706-748-2660
Dr. Paula Shaw-Powell, prin. Fax 748-2663
Double Churches MS 500/6-8
7611 Whitesville Rd 31904 706-748-2678
Craig Fitts, prin. Fax 748-2682
Downtown Magnet Academy 500/PK-5
1400 1st Ave 31901 706-748-2702
Dr. Tujuana Wiggins, prin. Fax 748-2708
Eagle Ridge Academy 700/PK-5
7601 Schomburg Rd 31909 706-569-3746
Amy Parker, prin. Fax 569-3753
East Columbus Magnet Academy 700/6-8
6100 Georgetown Dr 31907 706-565-3026
Tamura Magwood, prin. Fax 565-3031
Eddy MS 500/6-8
2100 S Lumpkin Rd 31903 706-683-8782
Shermaine Derrick, prin. Fax 683-8789
Forrest Road ES 400/PK-5
6400 Forrest Rd 31907 706-565-3062
Stephanie Dalton, prin. Fax 565-3066
Fort MS 600/6-8
2900 Woodruff Farm Rd 31907 706-569-3740
Sonja Coaxum, prin. Fax 569-3616
Fox ES 300/K-5
600 38th St 31904 706-748-2723
Dr. Yvette Scarborough, prin. Fax 748-2726

Gentian ES 500/PK-5
4201 Primrose Rd 31907 706-569-3625
Jessica Burnett, prin. Fax 569-3628
Georgetown ES 500/PK-5
954 High Ln 31907 706-565-2980
Dr. LaVerne Brown, prin. Fax 565-2985
Hannan Magnet Academy 400/K-5
1338 Talbotton Rd 31901 706-748-2744
Dr. Lisa Whitaker, prin. Fax 748-2749
Height ES K-5
1458 Benning Dr 31903 706-683-8871
Eddie Lindsey, prin. Fax 683-8880
Jackson Academy 400/K-5
4601 Buena Vista Rd 31907 706-565-3039
Amia Burnette, prin. Fax 565-3046
Johnson ES 400/PK-5
3700 Woodlawn Ave 31904 706-748-2795
Mark Hanner, prin. Fax 748-2799
Key ES 400/PK-5
2520 Broadmoor Dr 31903 706-683-8797
Dr. Jacqueline Flakes, prin. Fax 683-8802
King ES 700/PK-5
350 30th Ave 31903 706-683-8815
Dr. Barbara Weaver, prin. Fax 683-8819
North Columbus ES 700/K-5
2006 Old Guard Rd 31909 706-748-3183
Gayla Childs, prin. Fax 748-3189
Reese Road Leadership Academy 600/PK-5
3100 Reese Rd 31907 706-569-3684
Jeanella Pendleton, prin. Fax 569-3686
Richards MS 800/6-8
2892 Edgewood Rd 31906 706-569-3697
Lance Henderson, prin. Fax 569-3704
Rigdon Road ES 500/K-5
1320 Rigdon Rd 31906 706-565-2989
Charleen Robinson, prin. Fax 565-2994
River Road ES 400/K-5
516 Heath Dr 31904 706-748-3072
Philip Bush, prin. Fax 748-3074
Rothschild Leadership Academy 600/6-8
1136 Hunt Ave 31907 706-569-3709
Dr. Michael Forte, prin. Fax 569-3717
St. Elmo Center for Gifted Education K-5
2101 18th Ave 31901 706-748-3115
Christine Hull, dir. Fax 748-3118
St. Marys Road Magnet Academy 500/PK-5
4408 Saint Marys Rd 31907 706-683-8841
LaTonya Hamilton, prin. Fax 683-8847
South Columbus ES 400/PK-5
1964 Torch Hill Rd 31903 706-683-8833
Jessie Harper, prin. Fax 683-8838
Veterans Memorial MS 600/6-8
2008 Old Guard Rd 31909 706-748-3203
Melanie Knight, prin. Fax 748-3211
Waddell ES 500/K-5
6101 Miller Rd 31907 706-569-3722
Tonya Douglass, prin. Fax 569-3727
Wesley Heights ES 500/PK-5
1801 Amber Dr 31907 706-569-3733
Dr. Precious Evans, prin. Fax 569-3737
Other Schools – See Midland

Brookstone S 800/PK-12
440 Bradley Park Dr 31904 706-324-1392
Marty Lester, head sch Fax 571-0178
Calvary Christian S 600/PK-12
7556 Old Moon Rd 31909 706-323-0467
Jim Koan, hdmstr. Fax 323-1491
Columbus Adventist S 50/1-8
7880 Schomburg Rd 31909 706-561-7601
Grace Christian S 100/PK-12
2915 14th Ave 31904 706-323-9161
New Bethel Christian S 50/K-8
2423 Woodruff Farm Rd 31907 706-569-0004
Pinehurst Christian S 200/PK-5
4217 Saint Marys Rd 31907 706-689-8044
Dr. Beverly Law, prin. Fax 689-3027
St. Anne Pacelli Catholic S 500/PK-12
2020 Kay Cir 31907 706-561-8232
Ronie Collins, pres. Fax 563-0211
St. Luke S 600/K-8
318 11th St 31901 706-256-1301
Wynnbrook Christian S 100/K-8
500 River Knoll Way 31904 706-323-0795

Comer, Madison, Pop. 1,110
Madison County SD
Supt. — See Danielsville
Comer ES 400/PK-5
565 Gholston St 30629 706-783-2797
Dr. Christine Register, prin. Fax 783-3138
Madison County MS 1,100/6-8
3215 Highway 172 30629 706-783-2400
Chuck Colquitt, prin. Fax 783-4390

Commerce, Jackson, Pop. 6,437
Banks County SD 2,800/K-12
1989 Historic Homer Hwy 30529 706-677-2224
Stan Davis, supt. Fax 677-2223
www.banks.k12.ga.us
Other Schools – See Homer

Commerce CSD 1,500/PK-12
PO Box 29 30529 706-335-5500
Dr. Joy Tolbert, supt. Fax 335-5214
www.commercecityschools.org
Commerce ES 200/3-4
825 Lakeview Dr 30529 706-335-1801
Cara Lindsey, prin. Fax 335-1866
Commerce MS 500/5-8
7690 Jefferson Rd 30529 706-335-5594
Derrick Maxwell, prin. Fax 335-6222
Commerce PS 400/PK-2
395 Minish Dr 30529 706-335-5587
Susan Tolbert, prin. Fax 335-7382

Jackson County SD
Supt. — See Jefferson
East Jackson ES 500/PK-5
1531 Hoods Mill Rd 30529 706-336-7900
Jennifer Halley, prin. Fax 336-7919
East Jackson MS 800/6-7
1880 Hoods Mill Rd 30529 706-335-2083
Tiffany Barnett, prin. Fax 335-0935

Conley, Clayton, Pop. 6,132
Clayton County SD
Supt. — See Jonesboro
Anderson ES 600/PK-5
4199 Old Rock Cut Rd 30288 404-473-3269
Cynthia Dickerson, prin. Fax 473-3272

Conyers, Rockdale, Pop. 14,890
Rockdale County SD 16,000/PK-12
PO Box 1199 30012 770-860-4211
Shirley Chesser, supt. Fax 860-4285
www.rockdaleschools.org
Barksdale ES 600/PK-5
596 Oglesby Bridge Rd SE 30094 770-483-9514
Dr. Jill Murphy, prin. Fax 483-0665
Conyers MS 900/6-8
400 Sigman Rd NW 30012 770-483-3371
Allison Barbour, prin. Fax 483-9448
Edwards MS 1,000/6-8
2633 Stanton Rd SE 30094 770-483-3255
Fred Middleton, prin. Fax 483-3676
Flat Shoals ES 700/PK-5
1455 Flat Shoals Rd SE 30013 770-483-5136
Dr. LaSharon McClain, prin. Fax 483-3579
Hicks ES 900/PK-5
1300 Pine Log Rd NE 30012 770-483-4410
Tiwon Toney, prin. Fax 483-0592
Hightower Trail ES 700/K-5
2510 Highway 138 NE 30013 770-388-0751
Dr. Penny Mosley, prin. Fax 918-9620
Honey Creek ES 600/PK-5
700 Honey Creek Rd SE 30094 770-483-5706
Susan Norton, prin. Fax 483-9433
House ES 700/PK-5
2930 Highway 20 NE 30012 770-483-9504
Kim Melly, prin. Fax 483-0397
Memorial MS 900/6-8
3205 Underwood Rd SE 30013 770-922-0139
Michell Glover, prin. Fax 922-6192
Peeks Chapel ES 600/PK-5
2800 Avalon Pkwy 30013 770-761-1842
Brian Travis, prin. Fax 761-1843
Pine Street ES 600/PK-5
960 Pine St NE 30012 770-483-8713
Kim Vier, prin. Fax 483-0158
Shoal Creek ES 700/PK-5
1300 McWilliams Rd SW 30094 770-929-1430
Patrice Graham, prin. Fax 483-8676
Sims ES 600/PK-5
1821 Walker Rd SW 30094 770-922-0666
Dr. Chara Moore, prin. Fax 922-2499
Other Schools – See Stockbridge

Peachtree Academy Conyers 200/PK-5
1801 Ellington Rd SE 30013 770-860-8900
Young Americans Christian S 600/PK-12
1701 Honey Creek Rd SE 30013 770-760-7902
Dr. David Taylor Ed.D., admin. Fax 760-7981

Cordele, Crisp, Pop. 11,020
Crisp County SD 2,400/PK-12
PO Box 729 31010 229-276-3400
Dr. David Mims, supt. Fax 276-3406
www.crispschools.org
Crisp County ES 400/4-5
1001 W 24th Ave 31015 229-276-3420
Jennifer Abercrombie, prin. Fax 276-3421
Crisp County MS 900/6-8
1116 E 24th Ave 31015 229-276-3460
Brandon Williams Ed.D., prin. Fax 276-3466
Crisp County Pre K PK-PK
802 E 24th Ave 31015 229-276-3410
Monica Warren, dir.
Crisp County PS K-3
330 Old Hatley Rd 31015 229-276-3450
Kinney Coleman, prin. Fax 276-3456

Crisp Academy 200/PK-12
150 Crisp Academy Dr 31015 229-273-6330

Cornelia, Habersham, Pop. 4,030
Habersham County SD
Supt. — See Clarkesville
Cornelia ES 600/PK-5
375 Old Cleveland Rd 30531 706-778-6526
Amy McCurdy, prin. Fax 776-7828
Level Grove ES 600/PK-5
2525 Level Grove Rd 30531 706-778-3087
Dr. Darlene Hudson, prin. Fax 778-3731
South Habersham MS 500/6-8
237 Old Athens Hwy 30531 706-778-7121
Daphne Penick, prin. Fax 778-2110

Covington, Newton, Pop. 12,895
Newton County SD 19,200/PK-12
PO Box 1469 30015 770-787-1330
Samantha Fuhrey, supt. Fax 784-2950
www.newtoncountyschools.org
Clements MS 700/6-8
66 Jack Neely Rd 30016 770-784-2934
Joy Scavella, prin. Fax 784-2992
Cousins MS 900/6-8
8187 Carlton Trl NW 30014 770-786-7311
Terrence Martin, prin. Fax 784-2991
East Newton ES 500/PK-5
2286 Dixie Rd 30014 770-784-2973
Dr. Kim Coady, prin. Fax 784-2976
Fairview ES 700/PK-5
3324 Fairview Rd 30016 770-786-2636
Dr. Lamoyne Brunson, prin. Fax 784-2938
Heard-Mixon ES 500/PK-5
14110 Highway 36 30014 770-784-2980
Marquita Wilkins, prin. Fax 784-2984
Indian Creek MS 1,100/6-8
11051 Covington by Pass Rd 30014 770-385-6453
Dr. Swade Huff, prin. Fax 385-6456
Liberty MS 900/6-8
5225 Salem Rd 30016 678-625-6617
Keisa Taylor, prin. Fax 625-6200
Live Oak ES 1,000/PK-5
500 Kirkland Rd 30016 678-625-6654
Ericka Anderson, prin. Fax 625-6021
Livingston ES 500/PK-5
3657 Highway 81 S 30016 770-784-2930
Dr. Patrick Carter, prin. Fax 784-2996
Middle Ridge ES 700/PK-5
11649 Covington By Pass Rd 30014 770-385-6463
Rhonda Battle, prin. Fax 385-6466
Newton County Theme S at Ficquett 400/K-8
2207 Williams St NE 30014 770-784-2959
Dr. Naomi Cobb, prin. Fax 784-2963
Oak Hill ES 700/PK-5
6243 Highway 212 30016 770-385-6906
Dr. Brenda Gammans, prin. Fax 385-6909
Porterdale ES 500/PK-5
45 Ram Dr 30014 770-784-2928
Clydia Newell, prin. Fax 784-2993
Rocky Plains ES 700/PK-5
5300 Highway 162 S 30016 770-784-4987
Dr. Miranda Jones, prin. Fax 784-4988
South Salem ES 900/PK-5
5335 Salem Rd 30016 678-342-5907
Terran Newman, prin. Fax 342-5908
Veterans Memorial MS 700/6-8
13357 Brown Bridge Rd 30016 770-385-6893
Dr. Takila Curry, prin. Fax 385-6899
West Newton ES 800/K-5
13387 Brown Bridge Rd 30016 770-385-6472
Sammy Fudge, prin. Fax 385-6475
Other Schools – See Mansfield, Oxford

Walton County SD
Supt. — See Monroe
Walnut Grove ES 600/PK-5
460 Highway 81 SW 30014 678-684-2684
Dr. Cindy Callaway, prin. Fax 784-5599

First Baptist Academy 100/PK-6
1139 Usher St NW 30014 770-784-7570
Julie Harpe, dir. Fax 786-1810
Peachtree Academy 200/PK-12
14101 Highway 278 E 30014 678-729-9111

Crawford, Oglethorpe, Pop. 804
Oglethorpe County SD
Supt. — See Lexington
Oglethorpe County MS 500/6-8
270 Buddy Faust Rd 30630 706-743-8146
Mack Baldwin, prin. Fax 743-0849

Cumming, Forsyth, Pop. 5,371
Forsyth County SD 42,200/PK-12
1120 Dahlonega Hwy 30040 770-887-2461
Dr. Jeff Bearden, supt. Fax 781-6632
www.forsyth.k12.ga.us
Big Creek ES 800/K-5
1994 Peachtree Pkwy 30041 770-887-4584
Laura Webb, prin. Fax 781-2247
Brookwood ES 700/K-5
2980 Vaughan Dr 30041 678-965-5060
Tracey Smith, prin. Fax 965-5061
Chattahoochee ES 800/K-5
2800 Holtzclaw Rd 30041 770-781-2240
Barbara Vella, prin. Fax 781-2244
Coal Mountain ES 600/K-5
3455 Coal Mountain Dr 30028 770-887-7705
Kimberly Davis, prin. Fax 781-2286
Cumming ES 900/K-5
540 Dahlonega St 30040 770-887-7749
Lee Anne Rice, prin. Fax 888-1233
Daves Creek ES 1,300/K-5
3740 Melody Mizer Ln 30041 770-888-1222
Eric Ashton, prin. Fax 888-1223
Haw Creek ES 800/K-5
2555 Echols Rd 30041 678-965-5070
June Tribble, prin. Fax 965-5071
Lakeside MS 1,100/6-8
2565 Echols Rd 30041 678-965-5080
Kim Head, prin. Fax 965-5081
Liberty MS 900/6-8
7465 Wallace Tatum Rd 30028 770-781-4889
Cheryl Riddle, prin. Fax 513-3877
Little Mill MS 900/6-8
6800 Little Mill Rd 30041 678-965-5000
Connie McCrary, prin. Fax 965-5001
Mashburn ES 600/K-5
3777 Samples Rd 30041 770-889-1630
Carla Gravitt, prin. Fax 888-1202
Matt ES 1,000/K-5
7455 Wallace Tatum Rd 30028 678-455-4500
Charlley Stalder, prin. Fax 455-4514
Mill ES 1,200/K-5
1180 Chamblee Gap Rd 30040 678-965-4953
Ron McAllister, prin. Fax 965-4958
North Forsyth MS 1,000/6-8
3645 Coal Mountain Dr 30028 770-889-0743
Todd McClelland, prin. Fax 888-1210
Otwell MS 1,100/6-8
605 Tribble Gap Rd 30040 770-887-5248
Steve Miller, prin. Fax 888-1214
Piney Grove MS 1,200/6-8
8135 Majors Rd 30041 678-965-5010
Pam Pajerski, prin. Fax 965-5011

Sawnee ES 1,200/K-5
1616 Canton Hwy 30040 770-887-6161
Dr. Eileen Nix, prin. Fax 781-2254
Shiloh Point ES 1,200/K-5
8145 Majors Rd 30041 678-341-6481
Derrick Hershey, prin. Fax 341-6491
Silver City ES 1,000/K-5
6200 Dahlonega Hwy 30028 678-965-5020
Paige Andrews, prin. Fax 965-5021
South Forsyth MS 1,000/6-8
4670 Windermere Pkwy 30041 770-888-3170
Sandy Tinsley, prin. Fax 888-3175
Vickery Creek ES 1,100/K-5
6280 Post Rd 30040 770-346-0040
Kristan Riedinger, prin. Fax 346-0045
Vickery Creek MS 1,200/6-8
6240 Post Rd 30040 770-667-2580
Scott Feldkamp, prin. Fax 667-2589
Whitlow ES 1,100/K-5
3655 Castleberry Rd 30040 678-965-5090
Dr. Lynne Castleberry, prin. Fax 965-5091
Other Schools – See Alpharetta, Gainesville, Suwanee

Covenant Christian Academy 200/PK-12
6905 Post Rd 30040 770-674-2990
Johnathan Arnold, hdmstr. Fax 674-2989
Fideles Christian S 100/PK-12
1390 Weber Industrial Dr 30041 770-888-6705
Carla Rutherford, dir. Fax 888-9720
Horizon Christian Academy 300/K-12
PO Box 2715 30028 678-947-0711
Gary Bennett, head sch Fax 947-0721
Montessori Academy at Sharon Springs 200/PK-12
2830 Old Atlanta Rd 30041 770-205-6277
Montessori at Vickery 200/PK-3
6285 Post Rd 30040 770-777-9131
Montessori Kids Academy PK-6
3034 Old Atlanta Rd 30041 678-208-0774
Pinecrest Academy 800/PK-12
955 Peachtree Pkwy 30041 770-888-4477
Dr. Edward Lindekugel, head sch Fax 888-0404

Cusseta, Chattahoochee, Pop. 1,258
Chattahoochee County SD 900/PK-12
326 Broad St 31805 706-989-3774
David McCurry, supt. Fax 989-3776
www.chattco.org
Chattahoochee County Education Center 300/PK-5
140 Merrell St 31805 706-989-3648
Kenyada Heard, prin. Fax 989-3103
Chattahoochee County MS 200/6-8
360 GA Highway 26 31805 706-989-3678
Sandi Veliz, prin. Fax 989-0649

Cuthbert, Randolph, Pop. 3,851
Randolph County SD 1,100/PK-12
98 School Dr, 229-732-3601
Dr. Marvin Howard, supt. Fax 732-3840
www.sowegak12.org/
Randolph-Clay MS 200/6-8
3451 GA Highway 266, 229-732-2790
Sherrod Willaford, prin. Fax 732-5633
Randolph County ES 600/PK-5
214 Highland Ave, 229-732-3794
Robbin Temples, prin. Fax 732-6027

Dacula, Gwinnett, Pop. 4,365
Gwinnett County SD
Supt. — See Suwanee
Alcova ES 1,100/K-5
770 Ewing Chapel Rd 30019 678-376-8500
Dr. Todd Langley, prin. Fax 376-8502
Dacula ES 1,200/K-5
2500 Fence Rd 30019 770-963-7174
Holly Warren, prin. Fax 277-4448
Dacula MS 1,600/6-8
137 Dacula Rd 30019 770-963-1110
Dr. Kellye Riggins, prin. Fax 338-4632
Dyer ES 800/K-5
1707 Hurricane Shoals Rd 30019 770-963-6214
Michael DiFilippo, prin. Fax 338-4775
Fort Daniel ES 700/PK-5
1725 Auburn Rd 30019 770-932-7400
Paul Willis, prin. Fax 271-5194
Harbins ES 900/K-5
3550 New Hope Rd 30019 770-682-4270
Jennifer Chatham, prin. Fax 682-4285
Puckett's Mill ES 1,000/K-5
2442 S Pucketts Mill Rd 30019 678-765-5110
Ruth Westbrooks, prin. Fax 765-5240

Dacula Classical Academy 100/PK-12
PO Box 906 30019 678-377-0080
Hebron Christian Academy 400/K-5
775 Dacula Rd 30019 770-963-9250
Dr. Tracey Pritchard, head sch Fax 277-3581
Oak Hill Classical S 100/PK-12
2955 Old Fountain Rd 30019 770-338-7945

Dahlonega, Lumpkin, Pop. 5,151
Lumpkin County SD 3,800/PK-12
56 Indian Dr 30533 706-864-3611
Dr. Robert W. Brown, supt. Fax 864-3755
www.lumpkinschools.com
Long Branch ES 500/K-5
4518 Highway 52 E 30533 706-864-5361
Jane Mullinax, prin. Fax 864-5477
Lumpkin County ES 600/PK-5
153 School Dr 30533 706-864-3254
Stacie Gerrells, prin. Fax 864-2103
Lumpkin County MS 900/6-8
44 School Dr 30533 706-864-6109
Matt Remillard, prin. Fax 864-0199
Other Schools – See Dawsonville

Dallas, Paulding, Pop. 11,233
Paulding County SD 28,300/K-12
3236 Atlanta Hwy 30132 770-443-8000
Brian Otott, supt. Fax 443-8089
www.paulding.k12.ga.us
Abney ES 900/K-5
1186 Colbert Rd 30132 770-443-2756
Scott Brock, prin. Fax 443-2653
Allgood ES 900/K-5
312 Hart Rd 30157 770-443-8070
Donna Oldham, prin. Fax 443-8071
Burnt Hickory ES 900/K-5
80 N Paulding Dr 30132 678-363-0970
Joy Viness, prin. Fax 505-0640
Dallas ES 500/K-5
520 Hardee St 30132 770-443-8018
Blake Keown, prin. Fax 443-8020
East Paulding MS 800/6-8
2945 Hiram Acworth Hwy 30157 770-443-7000
Tom Alverson, prin. Fax 443-0116
Jones MS 700/6-8
100 Stadium Dr 30132 770-443-8024
Glen Bigham, prin. Fax 443-8026
McClure MS 1,100/6-8
315 Bob Grogan Dr 30132 770-505-3700
Jaynath Hayes, prin. Fax 505-7253
Moses MS 500/6-8
1066 Old County Farm Rd 30132 770-443-8727
Scott Viness, prin. Fax 443-8078
Nebo ES 800/K-5
2843 Nebo Rd 30157 770-443-8777
Cynthia Davies, prin. Fax 445-6465
Northside ES 400/K-5
2223 Cartersville Hwy 30132 770-443-7008
Tiffany Frachiseur, prin. Fax 443-7010
Poole ES 400/K-5
1002 Wayside Ln 30132 770-505-5541
Paul Chaffee, prin. Fax 505-5540
Ritch MS 600/6-8
60 Old Country Trl 30157 770-443-1449
Christine Carson, prin. Fax 443-4339
Roberts ES 600/K-5
1833 Mount Tabor Church Rd 30157 770-443-8060
Dee White, prin. Fax 443-2624
Russom ES 800/K-5
44 Russom Elementary School 30132 678-574-3480
Libby Bell, prin. Fax 574-5893
Scoggins MS 700/6-8
1663 Mulberry Rock Rd 30157 770-456-4188
Tammy Allen, prin. Fax 456-4189
Shelton ES 1,000/K-5
1531 Cedarcrest Rd 30132 770-443-4244
Dr. Jeff Robinson, prin. Fax 975-9172
South Paulding MS 500/6-8
592 Nebo Rd 30157 770-445-8500
Sandra Webb, prin. Fax 445-9989
Other Schools – See Douglasville, Hiram, Powder Springs, Rockmart, Temple, Villa Rica

Dalton, Whitfield, Pop. 32,710
Dalton CSD 7,700/PK-12
PO Box 1408 30722 706-876-4000
Dr. Jim Hawkins Ph.D., supt. Fax 226-4583
www.daltonpublicschools.com/
Blue Ridge ES 700/PK-5
100 Bogle St 30721 706-260-2700
Dr. Alan Martineaux, prin. Fax 260-2848
Brookwood ES 600/PK-5
501 Central Ave 30720 706-278-9202
Dr. Celeste Martin, prin. Fax 278-8224
City Park ES 800/PK-5
405 School St 30720 706-278-8859
Jason Brock, prin. Fax 226-5457
Dalton MS 1,700/6-8
1250 Cross Plains Trl 30721 706-278-3903
Dr. Phil Jones, prin. Fax 428-7852
Park Creek ES 700/PK-5
1500 Hale Bowen Dr 30721 706-428-7700
Dr. Will Wsters, prin. Fax 428-7725
Roan ES 500/PK-5
1116 Roan St 30721 706-226-3225
Cindy Parrott, prin. Fax 278-0979
Westwood ES 600/PK-5
708 Trammell St 30720 706-278-2809
Scott Ehlers, prin. Fax 278-1379

Whitfield County SD 13,400/PK-12
PO Box 2167 30722 706-217-6780
Dr. Judy Gilreath, supt. Fax 217-6755
www.whitfield.k12.ga.us
Antioch ES 600/PK-5
1819 Riverbend Rd 30721 706-270-7550
Tracie Dempsey, prin. Fax 226-9674
Beaverdale ES 400/PK-5
9196 Highway 2 30721 706-275-4414
Robb Kittle, prin. Fax 259-2562
Cedar Ridge ES 500/PK-5
285 Cedar Ridge Rd SE 30721 706-712-8400
Cindy Dobbins, prin. Fax 277-7249
Dawnville ES 500/PK-5
1380 Dawnville Rd NE 30721 706-259-3914
Beth Tuck, prin. Fax 259-7462
Dug Gap ES 400/PK-5
2032 Dug Gap Rd 30720 706-226-3919
Mandy Locke, prin. Fax 226-9753
Eastbrook MS 700/6-8
1382 Eastbrook Rd SE 30721 706-278-6135
Dr. Gregory Bailey, prin. Fax 226-9859
Eastside ES 600/PK-5
102 Hill Rd 30721 706-278-3074
Ben Hunt, prin. Fax 226-9951
New Hope ES 600/K-5
1175 New Hope Rd NW 30720 706-673-3180
Carla Maret, prin. Fax 673-3182
New Hope MS 600/6-8
1111 New Hope Rd NW 30720 706-673-2295
Belinda Sloan, prin. Fax 673-2086

North Whitfield MS 900/6-8
3264 Cleveland Hwy 30721 706-259-3381
Larry Farner, prin. Fax 259-8168
Pleasant Grove ES 500/K-5
2725 Cleveland Hwy 30721 706-259-3920
Laurie Grant, prin. Fax 259-6271
Valley Point ES 500/PK-5
3798 S Dixie Rd SE 30721 706-277-3259
Doris McLemore, prin. Fax 277-7721
Valley Point MS 500/6-8
3796 S Dixie Rd 30721 706-277-9662
Joe Barnett, prin. Fax 277-7035
Varnell ES 500/K-5
4421 Highway 2 30721 706-694-3471
Lisa Jones, prin. Fax 694-3289
Other Schools – See Cohutta, Rocky Face, Tunnel Hill

Christian Heritage S 400/K-12
PO Box 2066 30722 706-277-1198
Kent Harrison, head sch Fax 277-2300
Learning Tree ES 100/PK-8
300 S Tibbs Rd 30720 706-278-2736

Damascus, Early, Pop. 251

Southwest Georgia Academy 400/PK-12
14105 GA Highway 200, 229-725-4792

Danielsville, Madison, Pop. 548
Madison County SD 4,800/PK-12
PO Box 37 30633 706-795-2191
Dr. Allen McCannon, supt. Fax 795-5029
www.madison.k12.ga.us
Danielsville ES 500/PK-5
900 Madison St 30633 706-795-2181
Angie Waggoner, prin. Fax 795-5420
Other Schools – See Colbert, Comer, Hull, Ila

Darien, McIntosh, Pop. 1,951
McIntosh County SD 1,700/PK-12
200 Pine St SE 31305 912-437-6645
Dr. John Barge, supt. Fax 437-2140
www.mcintosh.k12.ga.us/
McIntosh County MS 400/6-8
500 Greene St 31305 912-437-6685
Melissa Williams, prin. Fax 437-5676
Todd-Grant ES 600/PK-5
1102 CA Devillars Rd 31305 912-437-6675
Cassandra Noble, prin. Fax 437-5296

Dawson, Terrell, Pop. 4,502
Terrell County SD 1,500/PK-12
PO Box 151, 229-995-4425
Robert Aaron, supt. Fax 995-4632
www.terrell.k12.ga.us
Cooper-Carver ES 400/PK-5
455 Greenwave Blvd, 229-995-2843
Latosha Peters, prin. Fax 995-4454
Terrell County MS 300/6-8
201 Greenwave Blvd, 229-995-2828
Valencia Gardner, prin. Fax 995-5418

Terrell Academy 300/K-12
602 Academy Dr SE, 229-995-4242

Dawsonville, Dawson, Pop. 2,501
Dawson County SD 3,100/PK-12
28 Main St 30534 706-265-3246
Dr. Damon Gibbs, supt. Fax 265-1226
www.dawsoncountyschools.org
Black's Mill ES 300/K-5
1860 Dawson Forest Rd E 30534 706-216-3300
Cindy Kinney, prin. Fax 216-6822
Dawson County MS 300/6-7
5126 Highway 9 S 30534 706-216-4849
Dr. Randi Sagona, prin. Fax 265-1426
Kilough ES 400/PK-5
1063 Kilough Church Rd 30534 706-216-8595
Teresa Conowal, prin. Fax 216-7424
Riverview ES 300/PK-5
370 Dawson Forest Rd W 30534 706-216-5812
Julia Mashburn, prin. Fax 216-0182
Robinson ES 600/K-5
1150 Perimeter Rd 30534 706-265-6544
Page Arnette, prin. Fax 265-1529

Lumpkin County SD
Supt. — See Dahlonega
Blackburn ES 700/K-5
45 Blackburn Rd 30534 706-864-8180
Dr. Betsy Green, prin. Fax 864-8176

Dearing, McDuffie, Pop. 543
McDuffie County SD
Supt. — See Thomson
Dearing ES 500/PK-5
500 Main St N 30808 706-986-4900
Stacey Amerson, prin. Fax 986-4901

Decatur, DeKalb, Pop. 18,866
City Schools of Decatur 4,600/PK-12
125 Electric Ave 30030 404-371-3601
Dr. David Dude, supt. Fax 371-5568
www.csdecatur.net
Clairemont ES 400/K-3
155 Erie Ave 30030 404-370-4450
Billy Heaton, prin. Fax 370-4453
College Heights ECLC 400/PK-PK
917 S McDonough St 30030 404-370-4480
Sarah Garland, prin. Fax 370-4482
4/5 Academy at Fifth Avenue 600/4-5
101 5th Ave 30030 404-371-6680
Karen Newton, prin. Fax 371-9573
Glennwood ES 300/K-3
440 E Ponce de Leon Ave 30030 404-370-4435
Dianna Watson, prin. Fax 370-4489
Oakhurst ES 400/K-3
175 Mead Rd 30030 404-370-4470
Marcia Fowler, prin. Fax 370-4467

Renfroe MS 900/6-8
220 W College Ave 30030 404-370-4440
Johnathan Clark, prin. Fax 370-4449
Westchester ES, 758 Scott Blvd 30030 200/K-3
Rochelle Lofstrand, prin. 404-370-4400
Winnona Park ES 400/K-3
510 Avery St 30030 404-370-4490
Greg Wiseman, prin. Fax 370-4493

DeKalb County SD
Supt. — See Stone Mountain
Bethune MS 900/6-8
5200 Covington Hwy 30035 678-875-0302
Myron Broome, prin. Fax 875-0310
Briarlake ES 400/PK-5
3590 Lavista Rd 30033 678-874-2502
Jamela Lewis, prin. Fax 874-2510
Canby Lane ES 700/PK-5
4150 Green Hawk Trl 30035 678-874-0602
Dr. Keshier Smikle, prin. Fax 874-0610
Cedar Grove MS 900/6-8
2300 Wildcat Rd 30034 678-874-4202
Dr. Candace Alexander, prin. Fax 874-4210
Chapel Hill ES 600/PK-5
3536 Radcliffe Blvd 30034 678-676-8402
Lawanzer Smith, prin. Fax 676-8410
Chapel Hill MS 900/6-8
3535 Dogwood Farm Rd 30034 678-676-8502
Lisa McGhee, prin. Fax 676-8510
Columbia ES 600/PK-5
3230 Columbia Woods Dr 30032 678-874-0702
Raymond Stanley, prin. Fax 874-0710
Columbia MS 1,000/6-8
3001 Columbia Dr 30034 678-875-0502
Dr. Keith Jones, prin. Fax 875-0510
Druid Hills MS 1,000/6-8
3100 Mount Olive Dr 30033 678-874-7602
Jacqueline Taylor, prin. Fax 874-7610
Flat Shoals ES 500/PK-5
3226 Flat Shoals Rd 30034 678-874-4602
Laconduas Freeman, prin. Fax 874-4610
Harris ES 900/PK-5
3981 Mcgill Dr 30034 678-676-9202
Dr. Sean Tartt, prin. Fax 676-9210
Kelley Lake ES 400/PK-5
2590 Kelly Lake Rd 30032 678-874-4802
Peggy Davis, prin. Fax 874-4810
Laurel Ridge ES 400/PK-5
1215 Balsam Dr 30033 678-874-6902
Beth Kyle, prin. Fax 874-6910
Mathis ES 400/PK-5
3505 Boring Rd 30034 678-874-5802
Dawn Blackwell, prin. Fax 874-5810
McLendon ES 400/PK-5
3169 Hollywood Dr 30033 678-676-5902
Dr. Kia Billingsley, prin. Fax 676-5910
McNair Discovery Learning Academy 800/PK-5
2162 Second Ave 30032 678-875-3402
Dr. Brian Bolden, prin. Fax 875-3410
McNair MS 700/6-8
2190 Wallingford Dr 30032 678-874-5102
Ronald Mitchell, prin. Fax 874-5110
Miller Grove MS 1,000/6-8
2215 Miller Rd 30035 678-676-8902
Marcus Kimber, prin. Fax 676-8910
Oak View ES 800/PK-5
3574 Oakvale Rd 30034 678-875-1302
Sabrina Pressley, prin. Fax 875-1310
Peachcrest ES PK-5
1530 Joy Ln 30032 678-874-1602
Dr. Sheila Nelloms, prin. Fax 874-1610
Rainbow ES 500/PK-5
2801 Kelley Chapel Rd 30034 678-874-1702
Dr. Carolyn Benson, prin. Fax 874-1710
Rockbridge ES 400/PK-5
2084 Green Forrest Dr 30032 678-676-6102
Derrick Brown, prin. Fax 676-6110
Snapfinger ES 800/PK-5
1365 Snapfinger Rd 30032 678-874-1802
Johnny Potter, prin. Fax 874-1810
Toney ES 400/PK-5
2701 Oakland Ter 30032 678-874-2102
Oliver Dean, prin. Fax 874-2110
Wadsworth Magnet S 200/4-6
3039 Santa Monica Dr 30032 678-874-2402
Dr. Cornellia Crum, prin. Fax 874-2410

Arbor Montessori S 300/PK-8
2998 Lavista Rd 30033 404-321-9304
Friends S of Atlanta 200/PK-8
862 Columbia Dr 30030 404-373-8746
Waman French, head sch Fax 990-1318
Greenforest-McCalep Christian Academy 500/PK-12
3250 Rainbow Dr 30034 404-486-6737
Dr. Millicent Black, prin. Fax 486-1127
Green Pastures Christian S 100/PK-9
5455 Flat Shoals Pkwy 30034 770-987-8121
Collette Gunby, pres. Fax 987-7078
Montessori S at Emory 200/PK-8
3021 N Decatur Rd 30033 404-634-5777
New Life Christian Academy of Achievers 100/PK-8
3592 Flat Shoals Rd 30034 404-241-0659
Justina Jenkins, dir. Fax 974-5189
St. Peter Claver Regional S 200/PK-8
2560 Tilson Rd 30032 404-241-3063
Susanne Greenwood, prin. Fax 241-4382
St. Thomas More S 500/K-8
630 W Ponce De Leon Ave 30030 404-373-8456
Jerry Raymond, prin. Fax 377-8554
Waldorf S of Atlanta 200/PK-8
827 Kirk Rd 30030 404-377-1315
Sara Walsh, admin. Fax 377-5013

Demorest, Habersham, Pop. 1,780
Habersham County SD
Supt. — See Clarkesville
Demorest ES 500/PK-5
3116 Demorest Mt Airy Hwy 30535 706-778-4126
Dr. Connie Yearwood, prin. Fax 776-6691
Fairview ES 400/PK-5
2925 Cannon Bridge Rd 30535 706-778-2030
Jennifer Chitwood, prin. Fax 778-2033
Wilbanks MS 500/6-8
3115 Demorest Mt Airy Hwy 30535 706-894-1341
Marybeth Thomas, prin. Fax 894-1342

Doerun, Colquitt, Pop. 774
Colquitt County SD
Supt. — See Moultrie
Doerun ES 300/PK-5
111 Mathis Ave 31744 229-782-5276
Charles Jones, prin. Fax 782-5945

Donalsonville, Seminole, Pop. 2,610
Seminole County SD 1,700/PK-12
800 S Woolfork Ave, 229-524-2433
Brinson Register, supt. Fax 524-2212
www.seminole.k12.ga.us
Seminole County ES 800/PK-5
800 Marianna Hwy, 229-524-5235
Dr. Renea Pierce, prin. Fax 524-8638

Doraville, DeKalb, Pop. 8,200
DeKalb County SD
Supt. — See Stone Mountain
Evansdale ES 600/PK-5
2914 Evans Woods Dr 30340 678-874-2702
Stephanie Chattman, prin. Fax 874-2710
Hightower ES 900/PK-5
4236 Tilly Mill Rd, Atlanta GA 30360 678-676-7302
Sheila George, prin. Fax 676-7310
Oakcliff ES 800/PK-5
3151 Willow Oak Way 30340 678-676-3102
Dr. Delores Paschall, prin. Fax 676-3110
Pleasantdale ES 700/PK-5
3695 Northlake Dr 30340 678-874-3502
Terri Brown, prin. Fax 874-3510
Reynolds ES 1,100/PK-5
3498 Pine St 30340 678-676-6802
Jennifer Leupold, prin. Fax 676-6810
Sequoyah MS 1,200/6-8
3456 Aztec Rd 30340 678-676-7902
Sedrick Anthony, prin. Fax 676-7910

Northwoods Montessori S 200/PK-6
3340 Chestnut Dr 30340 770-457-7261

Douglas, Coffee, Pop. 11,434
Coffee County SD 7,800/PK-12
1311 Peterson Ave S 31533 912-384-2086
Dr. Morris Leis, supt. Fax 383-5333
www.coffee.k12.ga.us
Coffee MS 1,700/6-8
901 Connector 206 N 31533 912-720-1011
Sherri Berry, prin. Fax 720-1032
Eastside ES 700/PK-5
603 Mcdonald Ave N 31533 912-384-3187
Dr. Christina Tucker, prin. Fax 383-4180
Indian Creek ES 700/PK-5
2033 GA Highway 158 W 31535 912-393-1300
Tamara Morgan, prin. Fax 393-3040
Satilla ES 700/PK-5
5325 Old Axson Rd 31535 912-384-2602
Lee Mobley, prin. Fax 383-5492
Westside ES 600/PK-5
1302 Gordon St W 31533 912-384-5506
Wendy Jowers, prin. Fax 383-7833
Other Schools – See Ambrose, Broxton, Nicholls, West Green

Citizens Christian Academy 200/PK-12
PO Box 1064 31534 912-384-8862
William Rish, hdmstr. Fax 384-8426

Douglasville, Douglas, Pop. 30,224
Douglas County SD 25,400/PK-12
PO Box 1077 30133 770-651-2000
Trent North, supt. Fax 920-4159
www.douglas.k12.ga.us
Arbor Station ES 600/PK-5
9999 Parkway S 30135 770-651-3000
Melissa Joe, prin. Fax 920-4314
Arp ES 600/PK-5
6550 Alexander Pkwy 30135 770-651-3200
Paul Spence, prin. Fax 920-4213
Beulah ES 500/PK-5
1150 S Burnt Hickory Rd 30134 770-651-3300
Susan Calderara, prin. Fax 651-3317
Bright Star ES 400/K-5
6300 John West Rd 30134 770-651-3400
Heather Stewart, prin. Fax 840-3688
Burnett ES 500/K-5
8277 Connally Dr 30134 770-651-3500
Dr. Kacia Thompson, prin. Fax 920-4348
Chapel Hill ES 800/PK-5
4433 Coursey Lake Rd 30135 770-651-3600
Robert Blevins, prin. Fax 920-4254
Chapel Hill MS 1,100/6-8
3989 Chapel Hill Rd 30135 770-651-5000
Dr. Jolene Morris, prin. Fax 920-4242
Chestnut Log MS 700/6-8
2544 Pope Rd 30135 770-651-5100
Dr. Nicole Hayes, prin. Fax 651-5103
Dorsett Shoals ES 400/PK-5
5866 Dorsett Shoals Rd 30135 770-651-3700
Cher Algarin, prin. Fax 651-3703
Eastside ES 500/PK-5
8266 Connally Dr 30134 770-651-3800
Tim Jenkins, prin. Fax 920-4086
Factory Shoals MS 800/6-8
3301 Shoals School Rd 30135 770-651-5800
Angela Carter, prin. Fax 920-4356
Fairplay MS 500/6-8
8311 Highway 166 30135 770-651-5300
Fhonda Strong, prin. Fax 651-5303
Holly Springs ES 500/K-5
4909 W Chapel Hill Rd 30135 770-651-4000
Melanie Manley, prin. Fax 947-7615
Mt. Carmel ES 500/PK-5
2356 Fairburn Rd 30135 770-651-4200
Tracey Seymour, prin. Fax 920-4471
New Manchester ES 900/K-5
2242 Old Lower River Rd 30135 770-651-4400
Alesia Stanley, prin. Fax 947-3830
North Douglas ES 600/K-5
1630 Dorris Rd 30134 770-651-4800
Fran Davis, prin. Fax 920-4590
South Douglas ES 600/PK-5
8299 Highway 166 30135 770-651-4500
Casey Duffey, prin. Fax 651-4503
Stewart MS 600/6-8
8138 Malone St 30134 770-651-5400
Robyn Scott, prin. Fax 920-4229
Yeager MS 600/6-8
4000 Kings Hwy 30135 770-651-5600
Dr. Fred Ervin, prin. Fax 947-7374
Other Schools – See Lithia Springs, Villa Rica, Winston

Paulding County SD
Supt. — See Dallas
Austin MS 900/6-8
3490 Ridge Rd 30134 770-942-0316
Greg Musgrove, prin. Fax 942-0548
Dugan ES 800/K-5
1362 Winn Rd 30134 770-949-5261
DeAnna Byers, prin. Fax 949-5423
Hutchens ES 900/K-5
586 Clonts Rd 30134 678-838-2683
Stephanie Bowen, prin. Fax 838-2783

Douglasville SDA S 50/PK-8
2836 Bright Star Rd 30134 770-949-6734
Harvester Christian Academy 300/PK-12
4241 Central Church Rd 30135 770-942-1583
Joel Slater, hdmstr. Fax 942-9332
Heirway Christian Academy 200/PK-12
6758 Spring St 30134 770-489-4392
Kings Way Christian S 300/PK-12
6456 The Kings Way 30135 770-949-0812

Dublin, Laurens, Pop. 16,025
Dublin CSD 2,200/PK-12
207 Shamrock Dr 31021 478-353-8000
Dr. Fred Williams, supt. Fax 353-8001
www.dublincityschools.us
Dasher ES 500/PK-4
911 Martin Luther King Jr 31021 478-353-8250
Lakeisha Fluker, prin. Fax 353-8251
Dublin MS 600/5-8
1501 N Jefferson St 31021 478-353-8130
Jaroy Stuckey, prin. Fax 353-8131

Laurens County SD 6,400/PK-12
467 Firetower Rd 31021 478-272-4767
Dan Brigman, supt. Fax 277-2619
www.lcboe.net
East Laurens MS 500/6-8
920 US Highway 80 E 31027 478-272-1201
Dr. Otha Hall, prin. Fax 609-2176
West Laurens MS 1,000/6-8
332 W Laurens School Rd 31021 478-272-8452
Sherri Moorman, prin. Fax 609-2202
Other Schools – See Dudley, East Dublin, Rentz

Trinity Christian S 400/PK-12
200 Trinity Rd 31021 478-272-7699

Dudley, Laurens, Pop. 567
Laurens County SD
Supt. — See Dublin
Northwest Laurens ES 1,100/PK-5
3330 US Highway 80 W 31022 478-676-3475
Dr. Amy Duke, prin. Fax 676-2246

Duluth, Gwinnett, Pop. 25,917
Gwinnett County SD
Supt. — See Suwanee
Berkeley Lake ES 1,200/PK-5
4300 S Berkeley Lake Rd NW 30096 770-446-0947
Lesley Pendleton, prin. Fax 582-7514
Chattahoochee ES 1,200/K-5
2930 Albion Farm Rd 30097 770-497-9907
Jeff Lee, prin. Fax 232-3272
Chesney ES 1,200/K-5
3878 Old Norcross Rd 30096 678-542-2300
Dr. Ricardo Quinn, prin. Fax 542-2304
Coleman MS 6-8
3057 Main St 30096 678-407-7400
J.W. Mozley, prin. Fax 407-7436
Duluth MS 2,000/6-8
3200 Pleasant Hill Rd 30096 770-476-3372
Deborah Fusi, prin. Fax 232-3295
Ferguson ES 1,000/K-5
1755 Centerview Dr 30096 678-245-5450
Angelique Mitchell, prin. Fax 245-5448
Harris ES 800/K-5
3123 Claiborne Dr 30096 770-476-2241
Erin Hahn, prin. Fax 232-3258
Hull MS 2,300/6-8
1950 Old Peachtree Rd 30097 770-232-3200
Denise Showell, prin. Fax 232-3203
Mason ES 900/PK-5
3030 Bunten Rd 30096 770-232-3370
David Jones, prin. Fax 232-3372
Radloff MS 1,800/6-8
3939 Shackleford Rd 30096 678-245-3400
Dr. Sarah Skinner, prin. Fax 245-3403

Duluth Adventist Christian S 200/PK-8
2959 Duluth Highway 120 30096 770-497-8607

Duluth Montessori S | 100/PK-8
2997 Main St 30096 | 770-476-9307
Notre Dame Academy | 500/PK-12
4635 River Green Pkwy 30096 | 678-387-9385
Debra Orr, head sch | Fax 990-9353

Dunwoody, DeKalb, Pop. 45,357
DeKalb County SD
Supt. — See Stone Mountain
Austin ES | 600/PK-5
5435 Roberts Dr 30338 | 678-874-8102
Dr. Ann Culbreath, prin. | Fax 874-8110
Dunwoody ES | 900/PK-5
1923 Womack Rd 30338 | 678-875-4002
Jennifer Sanders, prin. | Fax 875-4010
Vanderlyn ES | 800/K-5
1877 Vanderlyn Dr 30338 | 678-874-9002
Tracey Crenshaw, prin. | Fax 874-9010

Atlanta North S of Seventh-Day Adventist | 100/PK-8
5123 Chamblee Dunwoody Rd 30338 770-512-8456

Eastanollee, Stephens
Stephens County SD
Supt. — See Toccoa
Big A ES | 100/PK-K
289 Sorrells Dr 30538 | 706-886-2987
John Stith, prin. | Fax 282-4698

East Dublin, Laurens, Pop. 2,401
Laurens County SD
Supt. — See Dublin
East Laurens ES | 500/PK-5
960 US Highway 80 E 31027 | 478-272-8612
Kelly Dean, prin. | Fax 277-2641
East Laurens PS | 600/PK-2
950 US Highway 80 E 31027 | 478-272-4440
James Lawhorn, prin. | Fax 272-7815

Eastman, Dodge, Pop. 4,921
Dodge County SD | 3,100/PK-12
720 College St 31023 | 478-374-3783
Mike Hilliard, supt. | Fax 374-6697
www.dodge.k12.ga.us
Dodge County MS | 700/6-8
5911 Oak St 31023 | 478-374-6492
Dr. Elvis Davis, prin. | Fax 374-6484
North Dodge ES | 800/PK-5
167 Orphans Cemetery Rd 31023 | 478-374-6690
Cindy Screws, prin. | Fax 374-6486
South Dodge ES | 800/K-5
1118 McRae Hwy 31023 | 478-374-6691
Sonya Bundick, prin. | Fax 374-6750

East Point, Fulton, Pop. 33,152
Fulton County SD
Supt. — See Atlanta
Brookview ES | 500/PK-5
3250 Hammarskjold Dr 30344 | 470-254-8020
Jovita Wallace, prin. | Fax 254-8046
Conley Hills ES | 500/PK-5
2580 Dolowe Dr 30344 | 470-254-8170
Jami Pettway, prin. | Fax 254-8175
Hilliard ES | 700/PK-5
3353 Mount Olive Rd 30344 | 470-254-8050
Adrienne Grainger-Smith, prin. | Fax 254-8230
Holmes ES | 900/PK-5
2301 Connally Dr 30344 | 470-254-3092
Shateena Brown, prin. | Fax 254-5439
Parklane ES | 500/PK-5
2809 Blount St 30344 | 470-254-8070
Kedra Fairweather, prin. | Fax 254-8079
West MS | 800/6-8
2376 Headland Dr 30344 | 470-254-8130
Darrell Stephens, prin. | Fax 254-8121
Woodland MS | 1,100/6-8
2745 Stone Rd 30344 | 470-254-2182
Jason Stamper, prin. | Fax 254-2190

OSBY Christian Academy | 100/PK-6
2435 Ben Hill Rd 30344 | 404-767-6729
Franceska Osby, dir. | Fax 767-6790

Eatonton, Putnam, Pop. 6,410

Gatewood S | 400/PK-12
139 Phillips Dr 31024 | 706-485-8231
Jeffrey Decker, hdmstr. | Fax 485-2455

Edison, Calhoun, Pop. 1,517
Calhoun County SD
Supt. — See Morgan
Calhoun County MS | 200/6-8
PO Box 364, | 229-213-0146
Craveous Butler, prin. | Fax 213-0146

Elberton, Elbert, Pop. 4,600
Elbert County SD | 2,000/PK-12
50 Laurel Dr 30635 | 706-213-4000
Charles Bell, supt. | Fax 283-6674
www.elbert.k12.ga.us
Blackwell Learning Center | 100/PK-PK
373 Campbell St 30635 | 706-213-4400
Dr. Sonya Barnett, prin. | Fax 283-1162
Elbert County ES | 100/2-4
1150 Athens Tech Rd 30635 | 706-213-4600
Stephanie Wiles, prin. | Fax 283-1180
Elbert County MS | 900/5-8
1108 Athens Tech Rd 30635 | 706-213-4200
Sandee Drake, prin. | Fax 283-1117
Elbert County PS | 100/K-1
1019 Falling Creek Dr 30635 | 706-213-4700
Rosa Harris, prin. | Fax 283-8878

Ellaville, Schley, Pop. 1,796
Schley County SD | 1,400/PK-12
PO Box 66 31806 | 229-937-2405
Adam Hathaway, supt. | Fax 937-5180
www.schleyk12.org/
Schley County ES | 700/PK-5
1997 US Highway 19 S 31806 | 229-937-0550
Brian Hall, prin. | Fax 937-5318

Ellenwood, Clayton
Clayton County SD
Supt. — See Jonesboro
East Clayton ES | 600/PK-5
2750 Forest Pkwy 30294 | 404-362-3885
Fax 362-8895

DeKalb County SD
Supt. — See Stone Mountain
Cedar Grove ES | 600/PK-5
2330 River Rd 30294 | 678-874-3902
Dr. Bernetta Jones, prin. | Fax 874-3910

Anointed Word Christian S International | 50/PK-12
3800 Linecrest Rd 30294 | 404-241-8200
Markell Davis-Haynes, admin. | Fax 328-9801

Ellerslie, Harris
Harris County SD
Supt. — See Hamilton
Pine Ridge ES | 600/PK-4
PO Box 129 31807 | 706-568-6578
Dr. Jackie Lintner, prin. | Fax 562-9576

Ellijay, Gilmer, Pop. 1,600

Edwards Christian S | 50/1-8
12472 Highway 515 N, | 706-635-2644
North Georgia Christian Academy | 100/PK-12
191 Harold Pritchett Rd 30540 | 706-635-6422
Mary Pierce, admin. | Fax 635-6425

Emerson, Bartow, Pop. 1,449
Bartow County SD
Supt. — See Cartersville
Emerson ES | 400/PK-5
220 Old Alabama Rd SE 30137 | 770-606-5848
Tracy Mulkey, prin. | Fax 606-5181
South Central MS | 600/6-8
224 Old Alabama Rd SE 30137 | 770-606-5865
Tia Windsor, prin. | Fax 606-5168

Euharlee, Bartow, Pop. 4,058
Bartow County SD
Supt. — See Cartersville
Euharlee ES | 600/PK-5
1058 Euharlee Rd, | 770-606-5900
Dr. Sharon Collum, prin. | Fax 721-4266
Woodland MS | 800/6-8
1061 Euharlee Rd, | 770-606-5871
Michael Blankenship, prin. | Fax 606-2092

Evans, Columbia, Pop. 28,398
Columbia County SD | 24,900/PK-12
4781 Hereford Farm Rd 30809 | 706-541-0650
Dr. Sandra Carraway, supt. | Fax 541-2723
www.ccboe.net
Blue Ridge ES | 700/PK-5
550 Blue Ridge Dr 30809 | 706-868-0094
Deanne Murphy, prin. | Fax 854-5827
Evans ES | 700/PK-5
618 Gibbs Rd 30809 | 706-863-1202
Dr. Naesha Parks, prin. | Fax 854-5812
Evans MS | 900/6-8
4785 Hereford Farm Rd 30809 | 706-863-2275
Juliet King, prin. | Fax 854-5810
Greenbrier ES | 900/PK-5
5116 Riverwood Pkwy 30809 | 706-650-6060
Mary Bridges, prin. | Fax 855-3889
Greenbrier MS | 600/6-8
5120 Riverwood Pkwy 30809 | 706-650-6080
Chip Fulmer, prin. | Fax 854-5800
Lakeside MS | 700/6-8
527 Blue Ridge Dr 30809 | 706-855-6900
Felicia Turner, prin. | Fax 854-5805
Lewiston ES | 700/PK-5
5426 Hereford Farm Rd 30809 | 706-650-6064
Sherry Allen, prin. | Fax 854-5831
Parkway ES | PK-5
2660 William Few Pkwy 30809 | 706-868-2346
Michael Doolittle, prin. | Fax 854-6387
River Ridge ES | 700/K-5
4109 Mullikin Rd 30809 | 706-447-1016
Revelle Cox, prin. | Fax 854-5835
Riverside ES | 600/K-5
4431 Hardy Mcmanus Rd 30809 | 706-868-3736
Kirk Wright, prin. | Fax 854-5834
Riverside MS | 700/6-8
1095 Furys Ferry Rd 30809 | 706-868-3712
Yvette Foster, prin. | Fax 854-5824
Other Schools – See Appling, Augusta, Grovetown, Harlem, Martinez

Fairburn, Fulton, Pop. 12,742
Fulton County SD
Supt. — See Atlanta
Bear Creek MS | 1,000/6-8
7415 Herndon Rd 30213 | 470-254-6080
Anthony Newbold, prin. | Fax 254-3584
Campbell ES | 900/PK-5
91 Elder St 30213 | 470-254-3430
Leah Mackey, prin. | Fax 254-3522
Renaissance ES | 800/PK-5
7250 Hall Rd 30213 | 470-254-4320
Neill Crosslin, prin. | Fax 254-4327
Renaissance MS | 1,300/6-8
7155 Hall Rd 30213 | 470-254-4330
Creseda Hawk, prin. | Fax 254-4338
West ES | 800/PK-5
7040 Rivertown Rd 30213 | 470-254-3460
Jennifer Burton, prin. | Fax 254-3583

Arlington Christian S | 300/K-12
4500 Ridge Rd 30213 | 770-964-9871
Landmark Christian S | 800/PK-12
50 SE Broad St 30213 | 770-306-0647
Mike Titus, head sch | Fax 969-6551

Fairmount, Gordon, Pop. 714
Gordon County SD
Supt. — See Calhoun
Fairmount ES | 400/PK-5
130 Peachtree St 30139 | 706-879-5380
Deryl Dennis, prin. | Fax 337-4481

Fayetteville, Fayette, Pop. 15,530
Clayton County SD
Supt. — See Jonesboro
Rivers Edge ES | 600/PK-5
205 Northbridge Rd 30215 | 770-460-2340
Alisha Mohr, prin. | Fax 460-2343

Fayette County SD | 20,100/PK-12
PO Box 879 30214 | 770-460-3535
Dr. Joseph Barrow Ed.D., supt. | Fax 460-8191
www.fcboe.org
Bennetts Mill MS | 1,000/6-8
210 Lester Rd 30215 | 770-716-3982
Dr. Marcus Broadhead, prin. | Fax 716-3983
Cleveland ES | 500/K-5
190 Lester Rd 30215 | 770-716-3905
Angie Southers, prin. | Fax 716-3909
Fayetteville ES | 600/PK-5
490 Hood Ave 30214 | 770-460-3560
Tabatha Lawrence, prin. | Fax 460-3402
Inman ES | 500/PK-5
677 Inman Rd 30215 | 770-460-3565
Dr. Louis Robinson, prin. | Fax 460-3563
Minter ES | 700/K-5
1650 Highway 85 S 30215 | 770-716-3910
Erinn Angelo, prin. | Fax 716-3914
North Fayette ES | 600/PK-5
609 Kenwood Rd 30214 | 770-460-3570
Oatha Mann, prin. | Fax 460-3581
Peeples ES | 600/K-5
153 Panther Path 30215 | 770-486-2734
Buffy Blodgett, prin. | Fax 486-2731
Rising Starr MS | 1,000/6-8
183 Panther Path 30215 | 770-486-2721
Nancy Blair, prin. | Fax 486-2727
Spring Hill ES | 600/K-5
100 Bradford Sq 30215 | 770-460-3432
Randy Hudson, prin. | Fax 460-3433
Whitewater MS | 900/6-8
1533 Highway 85 S 30215 | 770-460-3450
Connie Baldwin, prin. | Fax 460-0362
Other Schools – See Peachtree City, Tyrone

Fayette Montessori S | 100/PK-6
190 Weatherly Dr 30214 | 770-460-6790
GRACE Christian Academy | 200/PK-12
355 McDonough Rd 30215 | 770-461-0137
Charlotte Sanders, prin. | Fax 461-1190
Journey Academy | 50/PK-5
155 Bradford Sq Ste A 30214 | 770-895-0714
Angie Hamilton, head sch
Solid Rock Academy | 200/PK-12
106 Commerce St 30214 | 770-997-9744
Sherry Moore-Wright, prin. | Fax 997-0061

Fitzgerald, Ben Hill, Pop. 8,940
Ben Hill County SD | 3,100/PK-12
509 W Palm St 31750 | 229-409-5500
Dr. J. Shawn Haralson, supt. | Fax 409-5513
benhillcounty.schoolinsites.com
Ben Hill County ES | 700/3-5
328 Lobinger Ave 31750 | 229-409-5586
Dr. Tracy McCray-Barnes, prin. | Fax 409-5590
Ben Hill County MS | 700/6-8
134 JC Hunter Rd 31750 | 229-409-5578
James Clements, prin. | Fax 409-5580
Ben Hill County Preschool | PK-PK
405 N Longstreet St 31750 | 229-409-5598
Jaquetta Brown, prin. | Fax 409-5601
Ben Hill County PS | 900/K-2
221 JC Hunter Rd 31750 | 229-409-5592
Ben Webb, prin. | Fax 409-5595

Flintstone, Walker
Walker County SD
Supt. — See La Fayette
Chattanooga Valley ES | 600/K-5
3420 Chattanooga Valley Rd 30725 | 706-820-2511
Heather Culberson, prin. | Fax 820-7921
Chattanooga Valley MS | 500/6-8
847 Allgood Rd 30725 | 706-820-0735
Wade Breeden, prin. | Fax 820-0736

Flowery Branch, Hall, Pop. 5,590
Hall County SD
Supt. — See Gainesville
Davis MS | 1,200/6-8
4450 Hog Mountain Rd 30542 | 770-965-3020
Eddie Millwood, prin. | Fax 965-3025
Flowery Branch ES | 600/K-5
5544 Radford Rd 30542 | 770-967-6621
Susan Miller, prin. | Fax 967-4880
South Hall MS | 1,200/6-8
4335 Falcon Pkwy 30542 | 770-532-4416
Paula Stubbs, prin. | Fax 967-5852

Lanier Christian Academy | 200/PK-12
5285 Strickland Rd 30542 | 678-828-8350
Al Gainey, pres. | Fax 828-8357

Folkston, Charlton, Pop. 2,443
Charlton County SD | 1,700/PK-12
1259 Third St 31537 | 912-496-2596
Dr. John Lairsey, supt. | Fax 496-2595
www.charlton.k12.ga.us
Bethune MS | 600/4-8
285 Little Phoebe Church Rd 31537 | 912-496-2360
Danny McCoy, prin. | Fax 496-3766

Folkston ES 600/PK-3
34754 Okefenokee Dr 31537 912-496-7369
Michael Walker, prin. Fax 496-4291
Other Schools – See Saint George

Forest Park, Clayton, Pop. 18,177
Clayton County SD
Supt. — See Jonesboro
Babb MS 800/6-8
5500 Reynolds Rd 30297 404-473-3248
Brenda Ross, prin. Fax 473-3252
Edmonds ES 600/PK-5
4495 Simpson Rd 30297 678-827-7932
Maurice Roberts, prin. Fax 827-7933
Forest Park MS 700/6-8
930 Finley Dr 30297 770-472-2817
Monique Drewry, prin. Fax 472-2833
Fountain ES 600/PK-5
5215 West St 30297 770-472-2462
Jamilah Hud-Kirk, prin. Fax 472-2465
Huie ES 700/PK-5
1260 Rockcut Rd 30297 678-827-7937
Roxanne Dixons, prin. Fax 827-7938

Forsyth, Monroe, Pop. 3,748
Monroe County SD 3,900/PK-12
PO Box 1308 31029 478-994-2031
Dr. Mike Hickman, supt. Fax 994-3364
www.monroe.k12.ga.us
Hubbard ES 600/PK-5
558 GA Highway 83 S 31029 478-994-7066
Jay Johnston, prin. Fax 994-7068
Monroe County MS - Banks Stephens Campus 600/7-8
66 Thornton Rd 31029 478-994-6186
Dr. Efrem Yarber, prin. Fax 994-7061
Monroe Co. MS - William Hubbard Campus 100/6-6
500 GA Highway 83 S 31029 478-994-6803
Dr. Efrem Yarber, prin. Fax 994-3061
Scott ES 900/PK-5
70 Thornton Rd 31029 478-994-3495
Dr. Richard Bazemore, prin. Fax 994-2860
Sutton ES 400/PK-5
1315 GA Highway 83 N 31029 478-994-9906
Becky Brown, prin. Fax 994-8498

Fort Gaines, Clay, Pop. 1,094
Clay County SD 300/PK-8
111 Commerce St E, 229-768-2232
Johnnie Grimsley, supt. Fax 768-3654
www.clay.k12.ga.us
Clay County ES 200/PK-5
200 Hobbs Ln, 229-768-2234
Kimberly Johnson, prin. Fax 768-2363
Clay County MS 100/6-8
200 Hobbs Ln, 229-768-0160
Michelle Oliver, prin. Fax 768-2363

Fort Gordon, Richmond, Pop. 9,140
Richmond County SD
Supt. — See Augusta
Freedom Park S 700/PK-8
345 42nd St Bldg 43400 30905 706-796-8428
Dr. Titiana Singh, prin. Fax 796-2265

Fort Oglethorpe, Catoosa, Pop. 9,051
Catoosa County SD
Supt. — See Ringgold
Battlefield ES 500/3-5
2206 Battlefield Pkwy 30742 706-866-9183
Dr. Kent McCrary, prin. Fax 861-6640
Battlefield PS 500/K-2
2204 Battlefield Pkwy 30742 706-861-5778
Geoff Rhodes, prin. Fax 861-5798

Fortson, Muscogee
Harris County SD
Supt. — See Hamilton
New Mountain Hill ES 400/PK-4
33 Mountain Hill Rd 31808 706-323-1144
Mark Gilreath, prin. Fax 324-0296

Fort Valley, Peach, Pop. 9,695
Peach County SD 3,800/K-12
523 Vineville St 31030 478-825-5933
Daryl Fineran, supt. Fax 825-9970
www.peachschools.org
Fort Valley MS 500/6-8
712 Peggy Dr 31030 478-825-2413
Damika Glover, prin. Fax 825-1332
Hunt ES 500/K-5
1750 US Highway 341 31030 478-825-5296
Anita Mathis, prin. Fax 825-1123
Other Schools – See Byron

Franklin, Heard, Pop. 969
Heard County SD 2,000/PK-12
PO Box 1330 30217 706-675-3320
Rodney Kay, supt. Fax 675-3357
www.heard.k12.ga.us
Centralhatchee ES 200/PK-5
315 Centralhatchee Pkwy 30217 770-854-4002
Dawn Bennett, prin. Fax 854-4124
Heard County ES 700/PK-5
4647 Pea Ridge Rd 30217 706-675-3687
Paul Mixon, prin. Fax 675-0999
Heard County MS 500/6-8
269 Old Field Rd 30217 706-675-9247
Brian Hadley, prin. Fax 675-9255
Other Schools – See Roopville

Gainesville, Hall, Pop. 33,306
Forsyth County SD
Supt. — See Cumming
Chestatee ES 1,000/PK-5
6945 Keith Bridge Rd 30506 770-887-2341
Polly Tennies, prin. Fax 781-2281

Gainesville CSD 7,600/PK-12
508 Oak St 30501 770-536-5275
Dr. Jeremy Williams, supt. Fax 287-2019
www.gcssk12.net
Centennial Arts Academy 900/K-5
852 Century Pl 30501 770-287-2044
Leslie Frierson, prin. Fax 287-2047
Enota Multiple Intelligences Academy 800/K-5
1340 Enota Ave NE 30501 770-532-7711
Wesley Roach, prin. Fax 287-2011
Fair Street International Academy 600/K-5
695 Fair St 30501 770-536-5295
William Campbell, prin. Fax 287-2016
Gainesville Exploration Academy 1,000/K-5
1145 McEver Rd 30504 770-287-1223
Renee Boatright, prin. Fax 535-3798
Gainesville MS 1,600/6-8
1581 Community Way 30501 770-534-4237
Dr. Rose Prejean-Harris, prin. Fax 287-2022
Mundy Hill Academy 400/K-5
4260 Millside Pkwy 30504 770-287-2016
Crystal Brown, admin. Fax 336-6170
New Holland Knowledge Academy 900/PK-5
170 Barn St 30501 770-287-1095
Pam Wood, prin. Fax 718-9935

Hall County SD 26,500/PK-12
711 Green St NW 30501 770-534-1080
Will Schofield, supt. Fax 535-7404
www.hallco.org
Chicopee Woods ES 700/K-5
2029 Calvary Church Rd 30507 770-536-2057
Jamie Hitges, prin. Fax 536-2175
Da Vinci Academy 6-8
3215 Poplar Springs Rd 30507 770-533-4004
Fax 533-4018
East Hall MS 900/6-8
4120 E Hall Rd 30507 770-531-9457
Kristin Finley, prin. Fax 531-2327
Lanier ES 600/K-5
4782 Thompson Bridge Rd 30506 770-532-8781
John Wiggins, prin. Fax 531-3017
Lyman Hall ES 800/K-5
2150 Memorial Park Dr 30504 770-534-7044
Robert Wilson, prin. Fax 531-2321
Myers ES 700/K-5
2676 Candler Rd 30507 770-536-0814
Beth Hudgins, prin. Fax 531-2323
North Hall MS 900/6-8
4856 Rilla Rd 30506 770-983-9749
Tamara Etterling, prin. Fax 983-9993
Riverbend ES 400/K-5
1742 Cleveland Hwy 30501 770-534-4141
Donna Wiggins, prin. Fax 531-3054
Sugar Hill Academy 700/K-5
3259 Athens Hwy 30507 770-503-1749
Beth Skarda, prin. Fax 503-9686
Tadmore ES 500/K-5
3278 Gillsville Hwy 30507 770-536-9929
Robin Gower, prin. Fax 531-2325
White Sulphur ES 500/K-5
2480 Old Cornelia Hwy 30507 770-532-0945
Dr. Betsy Ainsworth, prin. Fax 531-2324
Other Schools – See Buford, Flowery Branch, Lula, Oakwood

Lakeview Academy 500/PK-12
796 Lakeview Dr 30501 770-532-4383
Dr. John P. Kennedy, head sch Fax 536-6142
Montessori Children's House of N Forsyth 50/PK-3
7395 Browns Bridge Rd 30506 404-862-5437

Garden City, Chatham, Pop. 8,628
Savannah-Chatham County SD
Supt. — See Savannah
Garden City ES 800/PK-5
4037 Kessler Ave 31408 912-395-6820
Renae Miller-McCullough, prin. Fax 395-6823

Georgetown, Quitman, Pop. 912
Quitman County SD 300/PK-12
215 Kaigler Rd, 229-334-4189
Victoria Harris, supt. Fax 334-2109
www.quitman.k12.ga.us/
Quitman County ES 300/PK-8
173 Kaigler Rd, 229-334-4298
Jon-Erik Jones, prin. Fax 334-4700

Glennville, Tattnall, Pop. 3,528
Tattnall County SD
Supt. — See Reidsville
Glennville ES 800/PK-5
525 Sylvester Ashford Dr 30427 912-654-3931
Krisi Kaiser, prin. Fax 654-4998
Glennville MS 300/6-8
721 E Barnard St 30427 912-654-1467
Adam Kirby, prin. Fax 654-1300

Grantville, Coweta, Pop. 2,977
Coweta County SD
Supt. — See Newnan
Glanton ES 400/PK-5
5725 Highway 29 30220 770-583-2873
Lisa Skinner, prin. Fax 583-2268

Gray, Jones, Pop. 3,239
Jones County SD 5,500/PK-12
125 Stewart Ave 31032 478-986-3032
Chuck Gibson, supt. Fax 986-4412
jones.schooldesk.net/
Dames Ferry ES 600/PK-5
545 GA Highway 18 W 31032 478-986-2023
Leigh Ann Knowles, prin. Fax 986-2027
Gray ES 600/PK-5
365 GA Highway 18 E 31032 478-986-6295
Leslie Poythress, prin. Fax 986-3911
Gray Station MS 700/6-8
324 GA Highway 18 E 31032 478-986-2090
Wes Cavender, prin. Fax 986-2099

Jones County Pre K 50/PK-PK
273 Railroad St 31032 478-986-5384
Keisha Pitts, prin. Fax 986-5388
Turner Woods ES 700/PK-5
144 Willie L Fluellen Dr 31032 478-986-2222
Lance Rackley, prin. Fax 986-2264
Other Schools – See Macon

Grayson, Gwinnett, Pop. 2,619
Gwinnett County SD
Supt. — See Suwanee
Bay Creek MS 1,000/6-8
821 Cooper Rd 30017 678-344-7570
Dr. Maggie Fehrman, prin. Fax 736-6908
Couch MS 1,000/6-8
1777 Grayson Hwy 30017 678-407-7272
Devon Williams, prin. Fax 407-7326
Grayson ES 800/K-5
460 Grayson Pkwy 30017 770-963-7189
Christopher Brown, prin. Fax 682-4151
Starling ES 1,000/K-5
1725 Grayson Hwy 30017 678-344-6100
Rachel Ernst, prin. Fax 344-3296
Trip ES 900/K-5
841 Cooper Rd 30017 678-639-3850
Dr. Rukina Walker, prin. Fax 639-3870

Greensboro, Greene, Pop. 3,310
Greene County SD 2,100/PK-12
101 E Third St 30642 706-453-7688
Dr. Chris Houston, supt. Fax 453-9019
www.greene.k12.ga.us
Carson MS 300/6-8
1010 S Main St 30642 706-453-3308
Russell Brock, prin. Fax 453-4674
Greensboro ES 500/K-5
1441 Martin Luther King Jr 30642 706-453-2214
Dr. Jacqueline Jackson, prin. Fax 453-3316
Jackson Preschool PK-PK
103 E Third St 30642 706-454-1064
Priscilla Jones, coord. Fax 453-9019

Greenville, Meriwether, Pop. 862
Meriwether County SD 3,100/PK-12
PO Box 70 30222 706-441-0601
Dr. Tim Dixon, supt. Fax 672-1618
www.mcssga.org
Greenville MS 300/6-8
17656 Roosevelt Hwy 30222 706-672-4930
Michael Perry, prin. Fax 672-1424
Other Schools – See Luthersville, Manchester, Woodbury

Griffin, Spalding, Pop. 23,259
Griffin Spalding County School System 10,600/PK-12
PO Box N 30224 770-229-3700
Jim Smith, supt. Fax 229-3708
www.spalding.k12.ga.us
Anne Street ES 500/PK-5
802 Anne St 30224 770-229-3746
Pearla Hodo, prin. Fax 467-4636
Atkinson ES 400/PK-5
307 Atkinson Dr 30223 770-229-3715
Tiffany Campbell, prin. Fax 229-3713
Beaverbrook ES 500/PK-5
251 Birdie Rd 30223 770-229-3750
Renee Mallard, prin. Fax 467-5006
Carver Road MS 500/6-8
2185 Carver Rd 30224 770-229-3739
Tiffany Taylor, prin. Fax 229-3712
Cowan Road ES 600/PK-5
1233 Cowan Rd 30223 770-229-3790
Alsehia McCray, prin. Fax 229-3749
Cowan Road MS 600/6-8
1185 Cowan Rd 30223 770-229-3722
Laura Jordan, prin. Fax 227-8583
Crescent Road ES 400/PK-5
201 Crescent Rd 30224 770-229-3719
Natalie Wood, prin. Fax 467-4633
Jackson Road ES 500/PK-5
1233 Jackson Rd 30223 770-229-3717
Karen Oot, prin. Fax 467-6616
Jordan Hill Road ES 500/PK-5
75 Jordan Hill Rd 30223 770-229-3777
Dottie English, prin. Fax 229-1929
Kennedy Road MS 500/6-8
280 Kennedy Rd 30223 770-229-3760
Dexter Sands, prin. Fax 467-4626
Moore ES 400/PK-5
201 Cabin Creek Dr 30223 770-229-3756
Dr. Gloria Brown, prin. Fax 229-3785
Moreland Road ES 500/PK-5
455 Moreland Rd 30224 770-229-3755
Stan Mangham, prin. Fax 229-4022
Orrs ES 700/PK-5
1553 Flynt St 30223 770-229-3743
Evelyn Jones, prin. Fax 467-4629
Rehoboth Road MS 700/6-8
1500 Rehoboth Rd 30224 770-229-3727
Larry Jones, prin. Fax 229-3770

Griffin Christian Academy 200/PK-6
2000 W McIntosh Rd 30223 770-228-2711

Grovetown, Columbia, Pop. 10,773
Columbia County SD
Supt. — See Evans
Baker Place ES 1,000/PK-5
2011 Hero Way 30813 706-447-2115
Leeann Fleischauer, prin. Fax 447-2116
Brookwood ES 700/PK-5
455 S Old Belair Rd 30813 706-855-7538
Melissa Culpepper, prin. Fax 854-5828
Cedar Ridge ES 1,000/PK-5
1000 Trudeau Trl 30813 706-447-2100
Katherine LeeAnne Gregg, prin. Fax 854-5839
Columbia MS 900/6-8
2013 Raider Way 30813 706-541-1252
Eli Putnam, prin. Fax 854-5820

Euchee Creek ES 500/PK-5
795 Louisville Rd 30813 706-556-4000
Katy Yeargain, prin. Fax 854-5829
Grovetown ES 600/PK-5
300 Ford Ave 30813 706-863-0800
Stephanie Reese, prin. Fax 854-5830
Grovetown MS 900/6-8
5463 Harlem Grovetown Rd 30813 706-855-2514
Marcus Allen, prin. Fax 854-5822

Guyton, Effingham, Pop. 1,661
Effingham County SD
Supt. — See Springfield
Effingham County MS 800/6-8
1659 GA Highway 119 S 31312 912-772-7001
Timothy Hood, prin. Fax 772-7005
Guyton ES 700/PK-5
719 W Central Blvd 31312 912-772-3384
Charlotte Connelly, prin. Fax 772-5523
Marlow ES 700/PK-5
5160 GA Highway 17 S 31312 912-728-3262
Leslie Dickerson, prin. Fax 728-4477
Sand Hill ES 600/PK-5
199 Stagecoach Ave 31312 912-728-5112
Christy Brown, prin. Fax 728-5125
South Effingham ES 700/PK-5
767 Kolic Helmey Rd 31312 912-728-3801
Anna Barton, prin. Fax 728-4487
South Effingham MS 1,000/6-8
1200 Noel C Conaway Rd 31312 912-728-7500
Brigid Nesmith, prin. Fax 728-7508

Hahira, Lowndes, Pop. 2,695
Lowndes County SD
Supt. — See Valdosta
Hahira ES 800/PK-5
350 Claudia Dr 31632 229-316-8600
Iris Mathis, prin. Fax 316-8605
Hahira MS 800/6-8
101 S Nelson St 31632 229-316-8601
Stacy Dickey, prin. Fax 316-8606

Valwood S 400/PK-12
4380 Old US 41 N 31632 229-242-8491
Nan Wodarz, hdmstr. Fax 245-7894

Hamilton, Harris, Pop. 1,001
Harris County SD 5,200/PK-12
132 Barnes Mill Rd 31811 706-628-4206
Dr. James Martin, supt. Fax 628-5609
harriscounty.ga.schoolwebpages.com
Harris County - Carver MS 800/7-8
11696 US Highway 27 E 31811 706-628-4951
Stacey Carlisle, prin. Fax 628-5737
Park ES 500/PK-4
13185 US Highway 27 N 31811 706-628-4997
Janice Owen, prin. Fax 628-5413
Other Schools – See Cataula, Ellerslie, Fortson

Hampton, Henry, Pop. 6,827
Clayton County SD
Supt. — See Jonesboro
Hawthorne ES 900/PK-5
10750 English Rd 30228 770-472-7669
Cynthia James, prin. Fax 472-7663
Kemp ES 700/3-5
10990 Folsom Rd 30228 770-473-2870
Zsa Zsa Davis, prin. Fax 473-5058
Kemp PS 700/PK-2
1090 McDonough Rd 30228 678-610-4300
Dr. Brenda Cloud, prin. Fax 610-4321
White Academy 1,400/K-8
11808 Panhandle Rd 30228 770-472-2850
Angel McCrary, prin. Fax 472-2851

Henry County SD
Supt. — See Mc Donough
Dutchtown ES 600/K-5
159 Mitchell Rd 30228 770-471-0844
Dr. Sherri Edwards, prin. Fax 471-8066
Dutchtown MS 1,000/6-8
155 Mitchell Rd 30228 770-515-7500
Shawana Griffin, prin. Fax 515-7505
Hampton MS 800/6-8
799 Hampton Locust Grove Rd 30228 770-707-2130
Purvis Jackson, prin. Fax 946-3545
Mt. Carmel ES 600/K-5
2450 Mount Carmel Rd 30228 770-897-9799
Ssean Thompson, prin. Fax 897-9806
Rocky Creek ES 700/K-5
803 Hampton Locust Grove Rd 30228 770-707-1469
Jay Fowler, prin. Fax 946-4385

Bible Baptist Christian S 200/PK-12
2780 Mount Carmel Rd 30228 770-946-4700

Hapeville, Fulton, Pop. 6,258
Fulton County SD
Supt. — See Atlanta
Hapeville ES 700/PK-5
3440 N Fulton Ave 30354 470-254-8220
Thomas Garrett, prin. Fax 254-8226

St. John the Evangelist S 300/PK-8
240 Arnold St 30354 404-767-4312
Karen Votgner, prin. Fax 767-0359

Harlem, Columbia, Pop. 2,608
Columbia County SD
Supt. — See Evans
Harlem MS 500/6-8
424 Hawes Branch Pkwy 30814 706-556-5990
Carl Jackson, prin. Fax 854-5816
North Harlem ES 600/PK-5
525 Fairview Dr 30814 706-556-5995
Sonya Bailey, prin. Fax 854-5818

Hartsfield, Colquitt
Colquitt County SD
Supt. — See Moultrie
Hamilton ES 300/PK-5
5110 GA Highway 111 31756 229-941-5594
Krista Harrell, prin. Fax 941-5818

Hartwell, Hart, Pop. 4,400
Hart County SD 3,400/K-12
PO Box 696 30643 706-376-5141
Jaybez Floyd, supt. Fax 376-7046
www.hart.k12.ga.us
Hart County MS 800/6-8
176 Powell Rd 30643 706-376-5431
Bryan Edwards, prin. Fax 376-2207
Hartwell ES 500/K-5
147 S College Ave 30643 706-376-4425
Sonia Cobb, prin. Fax 856-7317
South Hart ES 500/K-5
121 EM Dairy Rd 30643 706-856-7383
Lydia Bennett, prin. Fax 856-7386
Other Schools – See Bowersville

Hawkinsville, Pulaski, Pop. 4,540
Pulaski County SD 1,300/PK-12
72 Warren St 31036 478-783-7200
Jane Williams, supt. Fax 783-7204
www.pulaski.k12.ga.us
L.I.T.T.L.E. Children Growing Preschool PK-PK
1 Academy St 31036 478-783-7205
Gini Thompson, dir. Fax 783-7494
Pulaski County ES 600/K-5
280 Broad St 31036 478-783-7275
A. Keith Green Ed.D., prin. Fax 783-4918
Pulaski County MS 300/6-8
8 Red Devil Dr 31036 478-892-7215
Natasha Kilgore, prin. Fax 783-7297

Hazlehurst, Jeff Davis, Pop. 4,181
Jeff Davis County SD 3,100/PK-12
PO Box 1780 31539 912-375-6700
Dr. Stan Rentz, supt. Fax 375-6703
www.jeff-davis.k12.ga.us
Davis ES 700/3-5
81 Pat Dixon Rd 31539 912-375-4142
Richard Stone, prin. Fax 375-7604
Davis MS 700/6-8
93 Collins St 31539 912-375-6750
Doug Alexander, prin. Fax 375-6756
Davis Pre K and Choices Learning Academy 200/PK-PK
96 W Jefferson St 31539 912-375-5048
Deidra Higgins, dir. Fax 375-1464
Davis PS 700/K-2
71 Burketts Ferry Rd 31539 912-375-6720
Ginger White, prin. Fax 375-0820

Hephzibah, Richmond, Pop. 3,910
Richmond County SD
Supt. — See Augusta
Deer Chase ES 600/PK-5
1780 Deer Chase Ln 30815 706-772-6240
Dr. Valerie Squire-Kelly, prin. Fax 772-6244
Diamond Lakes ES 600/PK-5
4153 Windsor Spring Rd 30815 706-771-2881
Dr. Cheri Ogden, prin. Fax 771-2885
Foreman ES 300/PK-5
2413 Willis Foreman Rd 30815 706-592-3991
Shaunta Payton, prin. Fax 592-3706
Hephzibah ES 500/PK-5
2542 GA Highway 88 30815 706-592-4561
Tim Jones, prin. Fax 592-3703
Hephzibah MS 500/6-8
2427 Mims Rd 30815 706-592-4534
Cameron Henry, prin. Fax 592-3979
Jamestown ES 400/PK-5
3637 Hiers Blvd 30815 706-796-4760
Vanetta Lawrence-Chapman, prin. Fax 796-4703
McBean ES 500/PK-5
1165 Hephzibah McBean Rd 30815 706-592-3723
Dr. Janina Dallas, prin. Fax 592-3729
Morgan Road MS 500/6-8
3635 Hiers Blvd 30815 706-796-4992
Dr. Shontier Barnes, prin. Fax 560-3947
Pine Hill MS 600/6-8
2147 McElmurray Rd 30815 706-592-3730
Brian Hadden, prin. Fax 592-3741
Spirit Creek MS 500/6-8
115 Dolphin Way 30815 706-592-3987
Kierstin Johnson, prin. Fax 592-3999

Hiawassee, Towns, Pop. 877
Towns County SD 1,100/PK-12
67 Lakeview Cir Ste C 30546 706-896-2279
Dr. Darren Berrong, supt. Fax 896-2632
www.towns.k12.ga.us
Towns County ES 400/PK-5
1150 Konahetah Rd 30546 706-896-4131
Dr. Sandy Page, prin. Fax 896-9872
Towns County MS 300/6-8
1400 Highway 76 E 30546 706-896-4131
Erica Chastain, prin. Fax 896-6628

Hinesville, Liberty, Pop. 31,826
Liberty County SD 9,800/PK-12
200 Bradwell St 31313 912-876-2161
Dr. Franklin Perry, supt. Fax 368-6201
www.liberty.k12.ga.us/
Frasier MS 800/6-8
910 Long Frasier Dr 31313 912-877-5367
Jermaine Williams, prin. Fax 877-3291
Gwinnett ES 600/K-5
635 Taylor Rd 31313 912-876-0146
Delores Crawford, prin. Fax 876-0256
Hall ES 500/K-5
1396 Shaw Rd 31313 912-368-3348
Jason Stickler, prin. Fax 368-3402
Liberty County Pre K PK-PK
206 Bradwell St 31313 912-876-0773
Greg McCallar, dir. Fax 876-6966
Long ES 700/K-5
920 Long Frasier Dr 31313 912-368-3595
Dr. Debra Sukaratana, prin. Fax 368-3512
Martin ES 700/K-5
1000 Joseph Martin Rd 31313 912-368-3114
Rebecca Moch, prin. Fax 368-5449
Pafford ES 700/K-5
2550 15th St 31313 912-877-4188
Valarie Lawson, prin. Fax 877-5249
Snelson-Golden MS 700/6-8
465 Coates Rd 31313 912-877-3112
Roland VanHorn, prin. Fax 368-5342
Taylors Creek ES 600/K-5
378 Airport Rd 31313 912-369-0378
Dr. Brittney Mobley, prin. Fax 369-0377
Other Schools – See Midway

First Presbyterian Christian Academy 300/PK-12
308 E Court St 31313 912-876-0441

Hiram, Paulding, Pop. 3,455
Paulding County SD
Supt. — See Dallas
Hiram ES 600/K-5
200 Seaboard Ave 30141 770-443-3392
Paul Wilder, prin. Fax 943-0636
McGarity ES 600/K-5
262 Rakestraw Mill Rd 30141 770-445-9007
Karla Dodgen, prin. Fax 445-6691
Panter ES 600/K-5
190 Panter School Rd 30141 770-443-4303
Priscilla Smith, prin. Fax 222-9775

Grace Christian Academy 300/PK-12
5790 Powder Springs/Dallas 30141 770-222-8955
Eddie Fincher, hdmstr. Fax 222-3321

Hoboken, Brantley, Pop. 527
Brantley County SD
Supt. — See Nahunta
Hoboken ES 600/PK-6
224 Church St N 31542 912-458-2135
Stephanie Boyd, prin. Fax 458-2133

Hogansville, Troup, Pop. 3,003
Troup County SD
Supt. — See LaGrange
Hogansville ES 500/PK-5
611 E Main St 30230 706-812-7990
Bret Bryant, prin. Fax 812-7996

Homer, Banks, Pop. 1,123
Banks County SD
Supt. — See Commerce
Banks County ES 600/3-5
180 Highway 51 S 30547 706-677-2308
Nancy Bentley, prin. Fax 677-4346
Banks County MS 700/6-8
712 Thompson St 30547 706-677-2277
Hank Ramey, prin. Fax 677-5227
Banks County PS 600/K-2
266 Highway 51 S 30547 706-677-2355
Janice Reiselt, prin. Fax 677-4797

Homerville, Clinch, Pop. 2,408
Clinch County SD 1,400/PK-12
46 S College St 31634 912-487-5321
Dr. Donna Ryan, supt. Fax 487-5068
www.clinchcounty.com/
Clinch County ES 600/PK-4
575 Woodlake Dr 31634 912-487-5385
Amanda James, prin. Fax 487-1732
Clinch County MS 300/5-7
575 Woodlake Dr 31634 912-487-5385
Matt Kimbrell, prin. Fax 487-1732

Hoschton, Jackson, Pop. 1,352
Gwinnett County SD
Supt. — See Suwanee
Duncan Creek ES 1,100/K-5
4500 Braselton Hwy 30548 678-714-5800
Carrie Yougel, prin. Fax 714-5804
Osborne MS 1,600/6-8
4404 Braselton Hwy 30548 770-904-5400
Kenney Wells, prin. Fax 765-5981

Jackson County SD
Supt. — See Jefferson
West Jackson ES 400/PK-5
391 E Jefferson St 30548 706-654-2044
Amity Hardegree, prin. Fax 824-9911

Hull, Madison, Pop. 197
Madison County SD
Supt. — See Danielsville
Hull-Sanford ES 500/PK-5
9193 Fortson Store Rd 30646 706-353-7888
Donna Bulla, prin. Fax 546-0303

Ila, Madison, Pop. 325
Madison County SD
Supt. — See Danielsville
Ila ES 500/PK-5
PO Box 48 30647 706-789-3445
Amanda Wommack, prin. Fax 789-2528

Irwinton, Wilkinson, Pop. 587
Wilkinson County SD 1,600/PK-12
PO Box 206 31042 478-946-5521
Dr. Aaron Geter, supt. Fax 946-5565
www.wilkinson.k12.ga.us/
Wilkinson County ES 300/3-5
PO Box 530 31042 478-946-5527
Dr. Judith Geter, prin. Fax 946-7153
Wilkinson County MS 300/6-8
PO Box 527 31042 478-946-2541
Dr. Angela Smith, prin. Fax 946-8981
Wilkinson County PS 500/PK-2
PO Box 570 31042 478-946-2161
Dr. Bonnie Green, prin. Fax 946-3678

Jackson, Butts, Pop. 4,955
Butts County SD 3,400/PK-12
181 N Mulberry St 30233 770-504-2300
Robert Costley, supt. Fax 504-2305
www.butts.k12.ga.us
Daughtry ES 500/PK-5
150 Shiloh Rd 30233 770-504-2356
Fran Dundore, prin. Fax 504-2474
Henderson MS 700/6-8
494 George Tate Dr 30233 770-504-2310
Tracey Allen, prin. Fax 504-2315
Jackson ES 500/PK-5
1105 Brownlee Rd 30233 770-775-9480
Sheila Barlow, prin. Fax 775-9488
Stark ES 700/PK-5
209 Stark Rd 30233 770-775-9470
Renee Burgdorf, prin. Fax 775-9478

Jasper, Pickens, Pop. 3,647
Pickens County SD 4,300/PK-12
100 D B Carrol St 30143 706-253-1700
Dr. Carlton Wilson, supt. Fax 253-1705
www.pickenscountyschools.org
Harmony ES 600/K-5
550 Harmony School Rd 30143 706-253-1840
Corey Thompson, prin. Fax 253-1845
Hill City ES 500/PK-5
600 Hill Cir 30143 706-253-1880
Jennifer Halko, prin. Fax 253-1885
Jasper ES 500/K-5
158 Stegall Dr 30143 706-253-1730
Dr. David Wilds, prin. Fax 253-1735
Jasper MS 500/6-8
339 W Church St 30143 706-253-1760
Anita Walker, prin. Fax 253-1765
Pickens County MS 500/6-8
1802 Refuge Rd 30143 706-253-1830
Pennie Fowler, prin. Fax 253-1835
Other Schools – See Tate

Jefferson, Jackson, Pop. 9,285
Jackson County SD 6,900/PK-12
1660 Winder Hwy 30549 706-367-5151
April Howard Ed.D., supt. Fax 367-9457
www.jackson.k12.ga.us
Gum Springs ES 800/PK-5
600 Gum Springs Church Rd 30549 706-654-5580
Alisa Hanley, prin. Fax 654-1255
West Jackson MS 900/6-8
400 Gum Springs Church Rd 30549 706-654-2775
Joe Cobb, prin. Fax 824-1969
Other Schools – See Athens, Commerce, Hoschton, Maysville, Talmo

Jefferson CSD 3,000/PK-12
345 Storey Ln 30549 706-367-2880
Dr. John Jackson, supt. Fax 367-2291
www.jeffcityschools.org/
Jefferson Academy 700/3-5
99 Dragon Dr 30549 706-367-2300
Laurie Gray, prin. Fax 367-1831
Jefferson ES 800/PK-2
415 Hoschton St 30549 706-367-8242
Annette Beckwith, prin. Fax 367-5405
Jefferson MS 700/6-8
100 Dragon Dr 30549 706-367-2882
Melanie Sigler, prin. Fax 367-5207

Jeffersonville, Twiggs, Pop. 1,016
Twiggs County SD 800/PK-12
952 Main St 31044 478-945-3127
Elgin Dixon, supt. Fax 945-3078
www.twiggs.k12.ga.us
Jeffersonville ES 400/PK-5
675 Bullard Rd 31044 478-945-3114
Jamie Paulk, prin. Fax 945-3228
Twiggs County MS 200/6-8
375 Watson Dr 31044 478-945-3113
Jason Thomas, prin. Fax 945-3140

Twiggs Academy 100/PK-12
961 Hamlin Floyd Rd 31044 478-945-3175

Jesup, Wayne, Pop. 10,029
Wayne County SD 5,500/PK-12
555 Sunset Blvd 31545 912-427-1000
Dr. Jay Brinson, supt. Fax 427-1004
www.wayne.k12.ga.us
Bacon ES 800/PK-5
1425 W Orange St 31545 912-427-1077
Kathy Carter, prin. Fax 427-1079
Jesup ES 800/PK-5
1155 S US Highway 301 31546 912-427-1033
Dr. Mark Priester, prin. Fax 427-1037
Puckett MS 600/6-8
475 Durrence Rd 31545 912-427-1061
Dr. Pam Shuman, prin. Fax 427-1069
Smith ES 600/PK-5
1206 N 4th St 31545 912-427-1044
Dr. Brian Simon, prin. Fax 427-1043
Williams MS 600/6-8
1175 S US Highway 301 31546 912-427-1025
Dr. Reggie Burgess, prin. Fax 427-1032
Other Schools – See Odum, Screven

Johns Creek, Fulton, Pop. 74,864
Fulton County SD
Supt. — See Atlanta
Abbotts Hill ES 700/K-5
5575 Abbotts Bridge Rd, 470-254-2860
Roytunda Stabler, prin. Fax 254-2864
Autrey Mill MS 1,400/6-8
4110 Old Alabama Rd, 470-254-7622
Trey Martin, prin. Fax 254-7630
Barnwell ES 800/PK-5
9425 Barnwell Rd, 470-254-4960
Martin Neuhaus, prin. Fax 254-3330
Dolvin ES 900/K-5
10495 Jones Bridge Rd, 470-254-7020
Laura Zoll, prin. Fax 254-7025
Findley Oaks ES 700/K-5
5880 Findley Chase Dr, 470-254-3800
Lacey Andrews, prin. Fax 254-3810
Medlock Bridge ES 600/PK-5
10215 Medlock Bridge Pkwy, 470-254-2980
Matthew Vance, prin. Fax 254-2988
Ocee ES 800/PK-5
4375 Kimball Bridge Rd, 470-254-2960
Ryan Moore, prin. Fax 254-2964
River Trail MS 1,400/6-8
10795 Rogers Cir, 470-254-3860
Dawn Melin, prin. Fax 254-3866
Shakerag ES 800/PK-5
10885 Rogers Cir, 470-254-3880
Christine Lemerond, prin. Fax 254-3886
State Bridge Crossing ES 800/PK-5
5530 State Bridge Rd, 470-254-3850
Bridgette Marques, prin. Fax 254-3856
Taylor Road MS 1,000/6-8
5150 Taylor Rd, 470-254-7090
Ed Williamson, prin. Fax 254-5609
Wilson Creek ES 800/K-5
6115 Wilson Rd, 470-254-3811
Andrea Cushing, prin. Fax 254-3819

Holy Redeemer S 500/K-8
3380 Old Alabama Rd, 770-410-4056
Lauren Schell, prin. Fax 410-1454
Mt. Pisgah Christian S 800/PK-12
9820 Nesbit Ferry Rd, 678-336-3443
Ruston Pierce, head sch Fax 336-3399
Perimeter Christian S 500/K-8
9500 Medlock Bridge Rd, 678-405-2300
Woodward North Academy 400/PK-6
6565 Boles Rd, 404-765-4490
Beth Marien, prin. Fax 765-4499

Jonesboro, Clayton, Pop. 4,639
Clayton County SD 52,200/PK-12
1058 5th Ave 30236 770-473-2700
Dr. Morcease Beasley, supt. Fax 473-2706
www.clayton.k12.ga.us
Arnold ES 500/K-5
216 Stockbridge Rd 30236 770-473-2800
Myron Allen, prin. Fax 473-5057
Brown ES 800/PK-5
9771 Poston Rd 30238 770-473-2785
Trina Reaves, prin. Fax 603-5799
Callaway ES 800/PK-5
120 Oriole Dr 30238 678-479-2600
Dr. Sheadric Barbra, prin. Fax 479-2613
Jackson ES 1,000/PK-5
7711 Mount Zion Blvd 30236 678-610-4401
Dr. Donna Jackson, prin. Fax 610-4422
Jonesboro MS 900/6-8
1308 Arnold St 30236 678-610-4331
Fax 610-4347
Kendrick MS 800/6-8
7971 Kendrick Rd 30238 770-472-8400
Dr. Kimberly Dugger, prin. Fax 472-8413
Kilpatrick ES 600/PK-5
7534 Tara Rd 30236 770-473-2790
Candice Jester, prin. Fax 603-5198
Lee Street ES 600/PK-5
178 Lee St 30236 770-473-2815
Rochelle Taylor, prin. Fax 603-5771
Mt. Zion ES 600/3-5
2984 Mount Zion Rd 30236 770-968-2935
Rochelle Harris, prin. Fax 968-2939
Mt. Zion PS 700/PK-2
2920 Mount Zion Rd 30236 770-472-2828
Enika Bryant, prin. Fax 472-2832
Mundy's Mill MS 800/6-8
1251 Mundys Mill Rd 30238 770-473-2880
Sharra Cunningham, prin. Fax 603-5779
Pointe South MS 800/6-8
8495 Thomas Rd 30238 770-473-2890
Sandra Nicholson, prin. Fax 477-4603
Roberts MS 800/6-8
1905 Walt Stephens Rd 30236 678-479-0100
Sara Stephens, prin. Fax 479-0114
Suder ES 700/PK-5
1400 Lake Jodeco Rd 30236 770-473-2820
Dr. Sharon Jones, prin. Fax 603-5197
Swint ES 600/K-5
500 Highway 138 W 30238 770-473-2780
Sarah Cainion, prin. Fax 603-5778
Other Schools – See College Park, Conley, Ellenwood, Fayetteville, Forest Park, Hampton, Lake City, Lovejoy, Morrow, Rex, Riverdale

---

Atlanta Adventist International S 50/K-8
9940 Dixon Industrial Blvd 30236 678-545-3656

Kathleen, Houston
Houston County SD
Supt. — See Perry
Arthur ES 800/PK-5
2500 GA Highway 127 31047 478-988-6170
Dr. VaRee Harrell, prin. Fax 988-6178
Mossy Creek MS 700/6-8
200 Danny Carpenter Dr 31047 478-988-6171
Dr. Andy Gentry, prin. Fax 218-7538

Kennesaw, Cobb, Pop. 28,907
Cobb County SD
Supt. — See Marietta
Awtrey MS 800/6-8
3601 Nowlin Rd NW 30144 770-975-6615
Jeffrey Crawford, prin. Fax 975-6617
Big Shanty ES 800/PK-5
1575 Ben King Rd NW 30144 678-594-8023
Dr. Kelly Luscre, prin. Fax 594-8026
Bullard ES 900/K-5
3656 Old Stilesboro Rd NW 30152 678-594-8720
Dr. Patrice Moore, prin. Fax 594-8727
Chalker ES 600/K-5
325 N Booth Rd NW 30144 678-494-7621
Sharon Arduino, prin. Fax 494-7623
Hayes ES 900/K-5
1501 Kennesaw Due West Rd 30152 678-594-8127
Teressa Watson, prin. Fax 594-8129
Kennesaw ES 700/PK-2
3155 Jiles Rd NW 30144 678-594-8172
Monica Howard, prin. Fax 594-8174
Lewis ES 700/PK-5
4179 Jim Owens Rd NW 30152 770-975-6673
Kristi Kee, prin. Fax 975-6675
Lost Mountain MS 900/6-8
700 Old Mountain Rd NW 30152 678-594-8224
Candace Wilkes, prin. Fax 594-8226
McClure MS 1,100/6-8
3660 Old Stilesboro Rd NW 30152 678-331-8131
Kelly Metcalfe, prin. Fax 331-8132
Palmer MS 1,000/6-8
690 N Booth Rd NW 30144 770-591-5020
Lisa Jackson, prin. Fax 591-5032
Pine Mountain MS 700/6-8
2720 Pine Mountain Cir NW 30152 678-594-8252
Dr. Jasmine Kullar, prin. Fax 594-8254

First Baptist Christian S 100/PK-5
2958 N Main St NW 30144 770-422-3254
Sue Gunderman, head sch Fax 427-2332
Foundations for the Future S 100/PK-6
1500 Stanley Rd NW 30152 770-429-4799
Lynn McKinnon, head sch Fax 794-3284
Mount Paran Christian S 1,200/PK-12
1275 Stanley Rd NW 30152 770-578-0182
Shaunda Brooks, admin. Fax 977-9284
North Cobb Christian S 800/PK-12
4500 Eagle Dr 30144 770-975-0252
Todd Clingman, head sch Fax 975-9051
St. Catherine of Siena S 400/PK-8
1618 Ben King Rd NW 30144 770-419-8601
Sr. Mary Jacinta, prin. Fax 626-0000
Shiloh Hills Christian S 300/PK-12
260 Hawkins Store Rd NE 30144 770-926-7729
Mike Gallien, admin. Fax 926-3762
TLE Christian Academy 50/K-12
2765 S Main St NW 30144 770-218-1790
Sandi Rodriguez, prin.

Kingsland, Camden, Pop. 15,425
Camden County SD 9,200/PK-12
311 S East St 31548 912-729-5687
Dr. William Hardin, supt. Fax 729-1489
www.camden.k12.ga.us
Camden MS 1,100/6-8
1300 Middle School Rd 31548 912-729-3113
James McCarter, prin. Fax 729-7489
Harris ES 500/PK-5
1100 The Lakes Blvd 31548 912-729-2940
Dr. Heath Heron, prin. Fax 729-2223
Kingsland ES 400/PK-5
900 W King Ave 31548 912-729-5246
Dr. Karon Ellis, prin. Fax 729-8431
Rainer ES 500/PK-5
850 May Creek Dr 31548 912-729-9071
Dr. Deborah Milstead, prin. Fax 576-8991
Other Schools – See Saint Marys, Woodbine

Kingston, Bartow, Pop. 626
Bartow County SD
Supt. — See Cartersville
Kingston ES 600/PK-5
240 Hardin Bridge Rd 30145 770-606-5850
Philena Johnson, prin. Fax 336-5591

La Fayette, Walker, Pop. 6,986
Walker County SD 9,200/PK-12
201 S Duke St 30728 706-638-1240
Damon Raines, supt. Fax 638-7827
www.walkerschools.org
Gilbert ES 500/PK-5
87 S Burnt Mill Rd 30728 706-638-2432
Amy Ashley, prin. Fax 638-0122
La Fayette MS 700/6-8
419 Roadrunner Blvd 30728 706-638-6440
Kelly Long, prin. Fax 638-7616
Naomi ES 400/PK-5
4038 E Highway 136 30728 706-638-2443
Debbie Ingles, prin. Fax 638-2446
North LaFayette ES 500/PK-5
610 N Duke St 30728 706-638-1869
Sandra Morrison, prin. Fax 638-7046
Other Schools – See Chickamauga, Flintstone, Lookout Mountain, Rock Spring, Rossville

LaGrange, Troup, Pop. 29,111
Troup County SD 12,300/PK-12
100 N Davis Rd 30241 706-812-7900
Dr. Cole Pugh, supt. Fax 812-7904
www.troup.org
Callaway ES 700/PK-5
2200 Hammett Rd 30241 706-845-2059
Amy Thornton, prin. Fax 812-2295
Callaway MS 700/6-8
2244 Hammett Rd 30241 706-845-2080
Melissa Trimeloni, prin. Fax 845-2081
Franklin Forest ES 700/PK-5
1 Scholar Ln 30240 706-845-7556
Lindsey Barnes Lynch, prin. Fax 845-7572
Gardner Newman MS 1,100/6-8
101 Shannon Dr 30241 706-883-1535
Derek Pitts, prin. Fax 883-1562
Hand ES 600/PK-5
641 Country Club Rd 30240 706-883-1580
Jack Morman, prin. Fax 883-1582

Hillcrest ES 400/PK-5
3116 Robert Hayes Rd 30240 706-812-7940
Carol Montgomery, prin. Fax 812-7942
Kight ES 600/PK-5
75 Gordon Rd 30240 706-812-7943
Candance McGhee, prin. Fax 812-7945
Long Cane ES 600/PK-5
238 Long Cane Rd 30240 706-812-7948
Dr. Linda Wood, prin. Fax 812-7950
Long Cane MS 1,000/6-8
326 Long Cane Rd 30240 706-845-2085
Chip Giles, prin. Fax 845-2086
Rosemont ES 600/PK-5
4679 Hamilton Rd 30241 706-812-7954
Christina Grace, prin. Fax 812-7956
Weathersbee ES 400/PK-5
1200 Forrest Ave 30240 706-883-1570
Willie Cooks, prin. Fax 883-1573
Whitesville Road ES 700/PK-5
1700 Whitesville Rd 30241 706-812-7968
Debra Brock, prin. Fax 812-7970
Other Schools – See Hogansville, West Point

Lafayette Christian S 300/PK-12
1904 Hamilton Rd 30241 706-884-6684
John Cipolla, hdmstr.
LaGrange Academy 200/PK-12
1501 Vernon Rd 30240 706-882-8097
Brian Dolinger, head sch Fax 882-8640

Lake City, Clayton, Pop. 2,550
Clayton County SD
Supt. — See Jonesboro
Lake City ES 600/PK-5
5354 Phillips Dr 30260 770-473-3229
Erica Johnson, prin. Fax 473-2931

Lakeland, Lanier, Pop. 3,308
Lanier County SD 1,800/PK-12
247 S Highway 221 31635 229-482-3966
Dr. Keith Humphrey, supt. Fax 482-3020
www.lanier.k12.ga.us/
Lanier County ES 400/3-5
92 S Valdosta Rd 31635 229-482-3870
Jennifer Whilden, prin. Fax 482-3866
Lanier County MS 400/6-8
52 W Patten Ave 31635 229-482-8247
Rhonda Rodgers, prin. Fax 482-3643
Lanier County PS 600/PK-2
28 S Valdosta Rd 31635 229-482-3580
Kevin Moore, prin. Fax 482-8339

Lake Park, Lowndes, Pop. 712
Lowndes County SD
Supt. — See Valdosta
Lake Park ES 700/PK-5
604 W Marion Ave 31636 229-316-8603
Suzanne Tanner, prin. Fax 316-8607

Lavonia, Franklin, Pop. 2,115
Franklin County SD
Supt. — See Carnesville
Lavonia ES 600/K-5
818 Hartwell Rd 30553 706-356-8209
Dr. Darrell McDowell, prin. Fax 356-2966

Lawrenceville, Gwinnett, Pop. 27,847
Gwinnett County SD
Supt. — See Suwanee
Alford ES 1,000/K-5
2625 Lawrenceville Hwy 30044 678-924-5300
Dr. Shon Davis, prin. Fax 924-5305
Baggett ES 1,100/K-5
2136 Old Norcross Rd 30044 678-518-6652
Dr. Charlotte Sadler, prin. Fax 518-6653
Benefield ES 1,300/PK-5
1221 Old Norcross Rd 30046 770-962-3771
Shonda Stevens, prin. Fax 682-4187
Bethesda ES 1,300/K-5
525 Bethesda School Rd 30044 770-921-2000
Pam Williams, prin. Fax 931-5690
Cedar Hill ES 1,400/K-5
3615 Sugarloaf Pkwy 30044 770-962-5015
Jose DeJesus, prin. Fax 377-8080
Corley ES 1,400/K-5
1331 Pleasant Hill Rd 30044 678-924-5330
Ruth Tomlinson, prin. Fax 924-5334
Craig ES 1,000/K-5
1075 Rocky Rd 30044 770-978-5560
Angie Wright, prin. Fax 978-5567
Creekland MS 2,200/6-8
170 Russell Rd 30043 770-338-4700
Dr. Eddie Maresh, prin. Fax 338-4703
Crews MS 1,300/6-8
1000 Old Snellville Hwy 30044 770-982-6940
Dr. Stacey Schepens, prin. Fax 982-6942
Five Forks MS 1,100/6-8
3250 River Dr 30044 770-972-1506
Christine Douthart, prin. Fax 736-4547
Freeman's Mill ES 900/K-5
2303 Old Peachtree Rd NE 30043 678-377-8955
Angie Pacholke, prin. Fax 377-8958
Gwin Oaks ES 1,000/K-5
400 Gwin Oaks Dr 30044 770-972-3110
Dr. Craig Barlow, prin. Fax 982-6901
Jackson ES 1,600/K-5
1970 Sever Rd 30043 770-682-4200
Kara Dutton, prin. Fax 513-6858
Jenkins ES 1,000/K-5
12 Village Way 30046 678-407-8900
Dr. Michelle Smith, prin. Fax 407-8904
Jordan MS 6-8
8 Village Way 30046 770-822-6500
Melissa Walker, prin. Fax 407-8889
Kanoheda ES 1,100/K-5
1025 Herrington Rd 30044 770-682-4221
Nicole White, prin. Fax 682-4266
Lawrenceville ES 700/K-5
122 Gwinnett Dr 30046 770-963-1813
Grelauris Calcano, prin. Fax 513-6741
Lovin ES 800/PK-5
1705 New Hope Rd 30045 678-518-6940
Dr. Janet Blanchette, prin. Fax 518-6975
McKendree ES 1,200/K-5
1600 Riverside Pkwy 30043 678-377-8933
Tyese Scott, prin. Fax 377-8915
Moore MS 1,000/6-8
1221 Lawrenceville Hwy 30046 678-226-7100
Lamont Mays, prin. Fax 226-7103
Richards MS 1,500/6-8
3555 Sugarloaf Pkwy 30044 770-995-7133
Mark McCain, prin. Fax 338-4791
Rock Springs ES 900/PK-5
888 Rock Springs Rd 30043 770-932-7474
Penny Clavijo, prin. Fax 932-7476
Simonton ES 800/K-5
275 Simonton Rd 30045 770-513-6637
Clifton Alexander, prin. Fax 682-4197
Sweetwater MS 1,900/6-8
3500 Cruse Rd 30044 770-923-4131
Jay Nebel, prin. Fax 806-8930
Taylor ES 900/K-5
600 Taylor School Dr 30043 770-338-4680
Paula Cobb, prin. Fax 338-4685
Winn-Holt ES 1,200/K-5
588 Old Snellville Hwy 30046 678-376-8600
Ellyce Cone, prin. Fax 376-8611
Woodward Mill ES 900/K-5
2020 Buford Dr 30043 678-407-7590
Mike Bender, prin. Fax 407-7827

Agape Junior Academy 50/PK-8
186 New Hope Rd 30046 678-376-0883
Bernadette Charles, prin. Fax 226-9718
Gerard Preparatory S 200/PK-12
263 Jackson St 30046 770-277-4722
Dr. J.G. Sinclair, admin. Fax 277-4365
Oak Meadow Montessori S 100/PK-6
2145 Collins Hill Rd 30043 770-963-8303
Sola Fide Lutheran S 100/PK-8
1307 Webb Gin House Rd 30045 770-972-1771
Jeremiah Schmiege, prin. Fax 972-6079
Strong Wall Academy 100/PK-12
PO Box 1647 30046 678-679-3070

Leesburg, Lee, Pop. 2,853
Lee County SD 6,100/PK-12
PO Box 399 31763 229-903-2100
Dr. Jason Miller, supt. Fax 903-2130
www.lee.k12.ga.us
Kinchafoonee PS 700/K-2
295 Leslie Hwy 31763 229-903-2200
Trina Muse, prin. Fax 903-2218
Lee County ES 700/3-5
314 Lovers Lane Rd 31763 229-903-2220
Holly Black, prin. Fax 903-2237
Lee County MS East 700/6-8
185 Firetower Rd 31763 229-903-3500
Kelli Duke, prin. Fax 903-3521
Lee County MS West 800/6-8
190 Smithville Rd N 31763 229-903-2140
John Savelle, prin. Fax 903-2160
Lee County PreK Center PK-PK
126 Starksville Ave N 31763 229-903-2136
Ashley Brim, dir. Fax 903-3997
Lee County PS 700/K-2
282 Magnolia Ave 31763 229-903-2180
Debbie DeBane, prin. Fax 903-2196
Twin Oaks ES 700/3-5
240 Smithville Rd N 31763 229-903-2240
Katie Peppers, prin. Fax 903-2257

Lexington, Oglethorpe, Pop. 225
Oglethorpe County SD 2,300/PK-12
735 Athens Rd 30648 706-743-8128
Beverley Levine, supt. Fax 743-3211
www.oglethorpe.k12.ga.us
Oglethorpe County ES 500/3-5
15 Fairground Rd 30648 706-743-8750
Dr. Katie Coyne, prin. Fax 743-3092
Oglethorpe County PS 500/PK-2
300 Comer Rd 30648 706-743-8194
Dr. Olivett James-Robinson, prin. Fax 743-5720
Other Schools – See Crawford

Lilburn, Gwinnett, Pop. 11,365
Gwinnett County SD
Supt. — See Suwanee
Arcado ES 1,200/K-5
5150 Arcado Rd SW 30047 770-925-2100
Penny Palmer-Young, prin. Fax 931-7026
Borkmar MS 1,100/6-8
4355 Lawrenceville Hwy NW 30047 770-638-2300
Nicole Mosley, prin. Fax 638-2309
Camp Creek ES 1,000/K-5
958 Cole Dr SW 30047 770-921-1626
Valerie Robinett, prin. Fax 806-3784
Head ES 500/K-5
1801 Hewatt Rd SW 30047 770-972-8050
Lisa Johnson, prin. Fax 736-4498
Hopkins ES 1,900/K-5
1315 Dickens Rd NW 30047 770-564-2661
Tamara Candis, prin. Fax 931-7010
Knight ES 700/K-5
401 N River Dr SW 30047 770-921-2400
Toni Ferguson, prin. Fax 806-3876
Lilburn ES 1,600/K-5
531 Lilburn School Rd NW 30047 770-921-7707
Guerlene Merisme, prin. Fax 931-5627
Lilburn MS 1,700/6-8
4994 Lawrenceville Hwy NW 30047 770-921-1776
Dr. Yvette Arthur, prin. Fax 806-3866
Minor ES 1,100/K-5
4129 Shady Dr NW 30047 770-925-9543
Scott Frandsen, prin. Fax 931-7056
Mountain Park ES 600/K-5
1500 Pounds Rd SW 30047 770-921-2224
Dr. Allan Gee, prin. Fax 931-7071
Trickum MS 2,000/6-8
130 Killian Hill Rd SW 30047 770-921-2705
Ryan Queen, prin. Fax 806-3742

Al-Falah Academy 300/PK-12
4805 Lawrenceville Hwy #220 30047 678-502-7211
Calvary Chapel Christian S 100/K-5
1969 McDaniels Bridge Rd SW 30047 770-736-2828
James Chapman, prin. Fax 736-2830
Killian Hill Christian S 400/K-12
151 Arcado Rd SW 30047 770-921-3224
Dr. Douglas Abels, head sch Fax 921-9395
Providence Christian Academy 600/K-12
4575 Lawrenceville Hwy NW 30047 770-279-7200
Dr. Sean Chapman, head sch Fax 279-8258
St. John Neumann Regional Catholic S 500/K-8
791 Tom Smith Rd SW 30047 770-381-0557
Julie Broom Ed.D., prin. Fax 381-0276

Lincolnton, Lincoln, Pop. 1,557
Lincoln County SD 1,200/PK-12
423 Metasville Rd 30817 706-359-3742
Dr. Samuel Light, supt. Fax 359-7938
www.lincolncountyschools.org
Lincoln County ES 600/PK-5
175 Rowland York Dr 30817 706-359-3449
Jeana Aycock, prin. Fax 359-6996
Lincoln County MS 300/6-8
200B Charles Ward Elam Dr 30817 706-359-3069
Patty Arthur, prin. Fax 359-2200

Lindale, Floyd, Pop. 4,135
Floyd County SD
Supt. — See Rome
Pepperell ES 500/3-5
270 Hughes Dairy Rd SE 30147 706-290-8527
Terri Pendley, prin. Fax 290-8530
Pepperell MS 700/6-8
200 Hughes Dairy Rd SE 30147 706-236-1849
Becky McCoy, prin. Fax 802-6776
Pepperell PS 400/PK-2
1 Dragon Dr SE 30147 706-236-1835
Carmen Jones, prin. Fax 236-1843

Lithia Springs, Douglas, Pop. 15,167
Douglas County SD
Supt. — See Douglasville
Factory Shoals ES 700/K-5
2375 Mount Vernon Rd 30122 770-651-3900
Tara Cowins, prin. Fax 651-3999
Lithia Springs ES 600/PK-5
6946 Florence Dr 30122 770-651-4100
William Marchant, prin. Fax 732-2699
Sweetwater ES 600/PK-5
2505 E County Line Rd 30122 770-651-4600
Dr. Emily Felton, prin. Fax 840-3706
Turner MS 800/6-8
7101 Turner Dr 30122 770-651-5500
Darron Franklin, prin. Fax 651-5503
Winn ES 400/PK-5
3536 Bankhead Hwy 30122 770-651-3100
Dr. Sherritta Abell, prin. Fax 651-3103

Lithonia, DeKalb, Pop. 1,901
DeKalb County SD
Supt. — See Stone Mountain
Bouie ES 800/PK-5
5100 Rock Springs Rd 30038 678-676-8202
Dr. Linda Priester, prin. Fax 676-8210
Browns Mill ES 700/PK-5
4863 Browns Mill Rd 30038 678-676-8302
Dr. Tiffany Brown, prin. Fax 676-8310
Candler ES 500/PK-5
6775 S Goddard Rd 30038 678-676-9102
Marsha Sears, prin. Fax 676-9110
Fairington ES 400/PK-2
5505 Philip Bradley Dr 30038 678-676-8702
Dr. Walter Burke, prin. Fax 676-8710
Flat Rock ES 1,000/PK-5
4603 Evans Mill Rd 30038 678-875-3202
Malik Douglas, prin. Fax 875-3210
Lithonia MS 1,200/6-8
2451 Randall Ave 30058 678-875-0702
Debra Phillips, prin. Fax 875-0710
Marbut ES 800/PK-5
5776 Marbut Rd 30058 678-676-8802
Andre Mountain, prin. Fax 676-8810
Panola Way ES 900/PK-5
2170 Panola Way Ct 30058 678-676-9302
Corey Stegall, prin. Fax 676-9310
Princeton ES 900/PK-5
1321 S Deshon Rd 30058 678-875-3002
Dr. Angela Hairston, prin. Fax 875-3010
Redan ES 500/PK-5
1914 Stone Mtn Lithonia Rd 30058 678-676-3502
Dr. Deborah Cowan-Steele, prin. Fax 676-3510
Redan MS 800/6-8
1775 Young Rd 30058 678-874-7902
Karen Davis, prin. Fax 874-7910
Rock Chapel ES 500/PK-5
1130 Rock Chapel Rd 30058 678-676-3802
Lisa Green, prin. Fax 676-3810
Salem MS 1,100/6-8
5333 Salem Rd 30038 678-676-9402
Terrence Harvey, prin. Fax 676-9410
Shadow Rock ES 600/PK-5
1040 King Way Dr 30058 678-676-3902
Viva Jones, prin. Fax 676-3910
Stoneview ES 800/PK-5
2629 Huber St 30058 678-676-3202
Cassandra Davis, prin. Fax 676-3210

Lithonia Adventist Academy 100/PK-8
3533 Ragsdale Rd 30038 770-482-0294

Lizella, Bibb
Bibb County SD
Supt. — See Macon
Skyview ES 500/PK-5
5700 Fulton Mill Rd 31052 478-779-4000
Sara Carlson, prin. Fax 779-3958

Locust Grove, Henry, Pop. 5,279
Henry County SD
Supt. — See Mc Donough
Bethlehem ES 600/K-5
1000 Academic Pkwy 30248 770-288-8571
Dr. Jessalyn Askew, prin. Fax 288-8577
Locust Grove ES 400/K-5
95 L G Griffin Rd 30248 770-957-5416
Dr. Attenya Scott, prin. Fax 957-4775
Locust Grove MS 1,000/6-8
3315 S Ola Rd 30248 770-957-6055
Kevin Van Tone, prin. Fax 957-7160
Luella ES 600/K-5
575 Walker Dr 30248 770-288-2035
Dr. Carla Montgomery, prin. Fax 288-2040
Luella MS 800/6-8
2075 Hmpton Locust Grove Rd 30248 678-583-8919
Mary Carol Stanley, prin. Fax 583-8920
New Hope ES 600/K-5
1655 New Hope Rd 30248 770-898-7362
Dr. Tim Tilley, prin. Fax 898-7370
Unity Grove ES 800/K-5
1180 LeGuin Mill Rd 30248 770-898-8886
Anne Wilson, prin. Fax 898-8834

Strong Rock Christian S 700/PK-12
4200 Strong Rock Pkwy 30248 678-833-1200
Paul McCracken, head sch Fax 833-1395

Loganville, Walton, Pop. 10,219
Gwinnett County SD
Supt. — See Suwanee
Cooper ES 1,100/K-5
555 Ozora Rd 30052 770-554-7050
Dr. Donna Bishop, prin. Fax 554-7058
Magill ES 1,200/K-5
3900 Brushy Fork Rd 30052 770-554-1030
Tonya Burnley, prin. Fax 554-1048
McConnell MS 1,600/6-8
550 Ozora Rd 30052 770-554-1000
Clent Chatham, prin. Fax 554-1003
Rosebud ES 1,000/K-5
4151 Rosebud Rd 30052 678-639-3800
Monica Ball, prin. Fax 639-3804
Snell MS 1,100/6-8
3800 Brushy Fork Rd 30052 770-554-7750
Allen Craine, prin. Fax 554-7749

Walton County SD
Supt. — See Monroe
Bay Creek ES 800/PK-5
100 Homer Moon Rd 30052 678-684-2800
Dr. Tammy Delk, prin. Fax 684-2801
Loganville ES 600/PK-5
4889 Bay Creek Church Rd 30052 678-684-2840
Camie McGaughey, prin. Fax 684-2839
Loganville MS 1,100/6-8
4869 Bay Creek Church Rd 30052 678-684-2960
Christy Bowman, prin. Fax 684-2983
Sharon ES 800/PK-5
2700 White Rd 30052 678-684-2850
Dr. Freda Doster, prin. Fax 684-2849
Youth ES 800/PK-5
4009 Center Hill Church Rd 30052 770-554-0172
Susan Enfinger, prin. Fax 466-7069
Youth MS 1,100/6-8
1804 Highway 81 30052 770-466-6849
David Todd, prin. Fax 466-8596

Covenant Christian Academy 300/PK-12
3425 Loganville Hwy 30052 770-466-7890
Emmaline McKinnon, admin. Fax 466-2833
Loganville Christian Academy 600/PK-12
2575 Highway 81 30052 770-554-9888
Christy Monda, admin. Fax 554-9881

Lookout Mountain, Walker, Pop. 1,588
Walker County SD
Supt. — See La Fayette
Fairyland ES 200/PK-5
1306 Lula Lake Rd 30750 706-820-1171
Jeremy Roerdink, prin. Fax 820-9199

Louisville, Jefferson, Pop. 2,485
Jefferson County SD 2,800/PK-12
1001 Peachtree St 30434 478-625-7626
Dr. Molly Howard, supt. Fax 625-7459
www.jefferson.k12.ga.us
Louisville Academy ES 500/PK-5
425 W 9th St 30434 478-625-7794
Tina Ethridge, prin. Fax 625-3548
Louisville MS 400/6-8
1200 School St 30434 478-625-7764
Ken Hildebrant, prin. Fax 625-3120
Other Schools – See Wadley, Wrens

Jefferson Academy 200/K-12
2264 US Highway 1 N 30434 478-625-8861

Lovejoy, Clayton, Pop. 6,281
Clayton County SD
Supt. — See Jonesboro
Lovejoy MS 700/6-8
1588 Lovejoy Rd 30250 770-473-2933
Dr. Debra Bostick-Smtih, prin. Fax 603-5777

Ludowici, Long, Pop. 1,650
Long County SD 3,000/PK-12
PO Box 428 31316 912-545-2367
Dr. Robert Waters, supt. Fax 545-2380
www.longcountyps.com
Long County MS 700/6-8
PO Box 729 31316 912-545-2069
Heath Crane, prin. Fax 545-2775
Smiley ES 1,100/K-3
1530 GA Highway 57 31316 912-545-2147
Beverly Hill, prin. Fax 545-2639
Walker ES 400/PK-PK, 4-
PO Box 769 31316 912-545-7910
Lisa Long, prin. Fax 545-7911

Lula, Hall, Pop. 2,700
Hall County SD
Supt. — See Gainesville
Lula ES 500/K-5
6130 Chattahoochee St 30554 770-869-3261
Theresa London, prin. Fax 869-1961

Lumpkin, Stewart, Pop. 2,722
Stewart County SD 500/PK-12
PO Box 547 31815 229-838-4329
Valerie Roberts, supt. Fax 838-6984
www.stewart.k12.ga.us/
Stewart County ES 300/PK-5
PO Box 37 31815 229-838-4374
Bari Geeslin, prin. Fax 838-4342
Stewart County MS 100/6-8
PO Box 547 31815 229-838-4374
Carolyn Hamilton, prin. Fax 838-4352

Luthersville, Meriwether, Pop. 854
Meriwether County SD
Supt. — See Greenville
Unity ES 500/PK-5
172 N Main St 30251 770-927-6488
Tammy Sibley, prin. Fax 927-1358

Lyerly, Chattooga, Pop. 537
Chattooga County SD
Supt. — See Summerville
Lyerly ES 400/PK-8
150 Oak Hill Rd 30730 706-895-3323
Charles Cooper, prin. Fax 895-2848

Lyons, Toombs, Pop. 4,285
Toombs County SD 3,100/PK-12
117 E Wesley Ave 30436 912-526-3141
Richard Smith, supt. Fax 526-3291
www.toombscountyschools.org
Lyons PS 600/PK-2
600 Bulldog Rd 30436 912-526-8391
Judy Hellgren, prin. Fax 526-3298
Lyons Upper ES 500/3-5
830 S State St 30436 912-526-5816
Tabatha Nobles, prin. Fax 526-4600
Toombs Central ES 500/PK-5
6287 US Highway 1 S 30436 912-565-7781
Tonawanda Irie, prin. Fax 565-9069
Toombs County MS 700/6-8
701 Bulldog Rd 30436 912-526-8363
Renee Garbutt, prin. Fax 526-0240

Toombs Christian Academy 300/PK-12
PO Box 227 30436 912-526-8938

Mableton, Cobb, Pop. 36,289
Cobb County SD
Supt. — See Marietta
Bryant ES 1,000/K-5
6800 Factory Shoals Rd SW 30126 770-819-2402
Timeka Cline, prin. Fax 819-2404
Clay ES 400/PK-5
730 Boggs Rd SW 30126 770-819-2430
Cynthia Winter, prin. Fax 819-2432
Floyd MS 1,000/6-8
4803 Floyd Rd SW 30126 770-819-2453
Dr. Teresa Hargrett, prin. Fax 819-2455
Harmony-Leland ES 700/PK-5
5891 Dodgen Rd SW 30126 770-819-2483
Angela Whitehead, prin. Fax 819-2485
Lindley 6th Grade Academy 50/6-6
1550 Pebblebrook Cir SE 30126 770-819-2414
Dr. Denise Magee, prin. Fax 819-2418
Lindley MS 1,300/7-8
50 Veterans Memorial Hwy SE 30126 770-819-2496
Dana Giles, prin. Fax 819-2498
Mableton ES 1,000/PK-5
5220 Church St SW 30126 770-819-2513
Pamela Cain, prin. Fax 819-2515
Riverside IS 1,100/2-5
285 S Gordon Rd SW 30126 770-819-2553
Dr. Barbara Swinney, prin. Fax 819-2643
Riverside PS 700/K-1
461 S Gordon Rd SW 30126 770-819-5851
Dr. Doris Billups-McClure, prin. Fax 398-0040

Cumberland Christian Academy 100/6-8
4900 Floyd Rd SW 30126 678-426-1600
Cara Micale, prin. Fax 819-9091
Whitefield Academy 700/PK-12
1 Whitefield Dr SE 30126 678-305-3000
Dr. Kevin Bracher Ph.D., hdmstr. Fax 305-3010

Mc Donough, Henry, Pop. 21,578
Henry County SD 39,700/PK-12
33 N Zack Hinton Pkwy 30253 770-957-6601
Rodney Bowler, supt. Fax 914-6178
www.henry.k12.ga.us
Eagle's Landing MS 900/6-8
295 Tunis Rd 30253 770-914-8189
Derrick Thomas, prin. Fax 914-2989
East Lake ES 700/K-5
199 E Lake Rd 30252 678-583-8947
Jennifer Laughridge, prin. Fax 583-8927
Flippen ES 700/K-5
425 Peach Dr 30253 770-954-3522
Dr. Toni Obenauf, prin. Fax 954-3525
Henry County MS 800/6-8
166 Holly Smith Dr 30253 770-957-3945
LaRita Wiggins, prin. Fax 898-4986
Oakland ES 700/PK-5
551 Highway 81 W 30253 770-954-1901
Walter Shields, prin. Fax 914-5565
Ola ES 900/K-5
278 N Ola Rd 30252 770-957-5777
Mitchell Stehens, prin. Fax 957-7031
Ola MS 1,200/6-8
353 N Ola Rd 30252 770-288-2108
Kathleen Truitt, prin. Fax 288-2114
Rock Spring ES 700/K-5
1550 Stroud Rd 30252 770-957-6851
Tracy Blackburn, prin. Fax 957-2238
Timber Ridge ES 600/K-5
2825 Highway 20 E 30252 770-288-3237
Kristen McRae, prin. Fax 288-3316
Tussahaw ES 500/PK-5
225 Coan Dr 30252 770-957-0164
Dr. Joselyn Lakani-Jones, prin. Fax 957-0546
Union Grove MS 1,100/6-8
210 E Lake Rd 30252 678-583-8978
Dr. Matt Isenberg, prin. Fax 583-8580
Walnut Creek ES 500/K-5
3535 McDonough Pkwy 30253 770-288-8561
Rita Pitner, prin. Fax 288-8566
Wesley Lakes ES 500/PK-5
685 McDonough Pkwy 30253 770-914-1889
Jodye Rowe-Callaway, prin. Fax 914-9955
Other Schools – See Hampton, Locust Grove, Stockbridge

Creekside Christian Academy 500/PK-12
175 Foster Dr 30253 770-961-9300
Rodney Knox, hdmstr. Fax 960-1875
Eagle's Landing Christian Academy 1,100/PK-12
2400 Highway 42 N 30253 770-957-2927
Chuck Gilliam, head sch Fax 957-2290

Macon, Bibb, Pop. 90,157
Bibb County SD 21,700/PK-12
484 Mulberry St 31201 478-765-8711
Dr. Curtis L. Jones, supt. Fax 765-8549
www.bcsdk12.net
Alexander II Magnet ES 600/K-5
1156 College St 31201 478-779-2700
Walsetta Miller, prin. Fax 779-2670
Appling MS 600/6-8
1210 Shurling Dr 31211 478-779-2200
Dr. Christopher Ridley, prin. Fax 779-2202
Ballard-Hudson MS 400/6-8
1070 Anthony Rd 31204 478-779-3400
Eclan David, prin. Fax 779-3396
Bernd ES 500/PK-5
4160 Ocmulgee East Blvd 31217 478-779-2750
Dr. John Thompson, prin. Fax 779-2731
Brookdale ES 500/PK-5
3600 Brookdale Ave 31204 478-779-2800
Kim Tolbert, prin. Fax 779-2770
Bruce ES 500/PK-5
3660 Houston Ave 31206 478-779-4550
Dr. Angela James, prin. Fax 779-4562
Burdell-Hunt Magnet ES 500/K-5
972 Fort Hill St 31217 478-779-2950
Tanya Allen, prin. Fax 779-2940
Carter ES 600/PK-5
5910 Zebulon Rd 31210 478-779-3350
Latricia Reeves, prin. Fax 779-3328
Hartley ES 500/PK-5
2230 Anthony Rd 31204 478-779-2500
Carmalita Dillard, prin. Fax 779-2485
Heard ES 600/PK-5
6515 Houston Rd 31216 478-779-4250
Carole Cote, prin. Fax 779-4219
Heritage ES 800/PK-5
6050 Thomaston Rd 31220 478-779-4700
Jennifer Askew, prin. Fax 779-4721
Howard MS 1,000/6-8
6600 Forsyth Rd 31210 478-779-3500
Kevin Adams, prin. Fax 779-3458
Ingram-Pye ES 700/PK-5
855 Anthony Rd 31204 478-779-3000
Danielle Howard, prin. Fax 779-2989
King Jr. ES, 1301 Shurling Dr 31211 300/K-5
Dr. Suzan Watkins, prin. 478-779-2100
Lane ES 500/PK-5
990 Newport Rd 31210 478-779-3150
Georglyn Stephens, prin. Fax 779-3151
Miller Magnet MS 900/6-8
751 Hendley St 31204 478-779-4050
Jim Montgomery, prin. Fax 779-4032
Northwoods Academy 200/PK-K
709 Pierce Ave 31204 478-779-3200
April Harriger, dir. Fax 779-3202
Porter ES 500/PK-5
5802 School Rd 31216 478-779-4350
Cami Hamlin, prin. Fax 779-4320
Riley ES 400/PK-5
3522 Greenbriar Rd 31204 478-779-2050
Sonya Coley, prin. Fax 779-2066
Rutland MS 900/6-8
6260 Skipper Rd 31216 478-779-4400
Richard Key, prin. Fax 779-4373
Southfield ES PK-5
4375 Bloomfield Drive Ext 31206 478-779-4800
Janice Sharpe, prin.
Springdale ES 700/PK-5
4965 Northside Dr 31210 478-779-3750
Dr. Constance Winds, prin. Fax 779-3742
Taylor ES 600/PK-5
2976 Crestline Dr 31204 478-779-3550
Dr. Susan Simpson, prin. Fax 779-3569
Union ES 600/PK-5
4831 Mamie Carter Dr 31210 478-779-2650
LaLisa Burston, prin. Fax 779-2631
Veterans ES K-5
4901 Faubus Ave 31204 478-779-2400
Dr. Cleveland Johnson, prin. Fax 779-2411

Vineville Academy of the Arts 600/K-5
2260 Vineville Ave 31204 478-779-3250
Kristy Graham, prin. Fax 779-3228
Weaver MS 900/6-8
2570 Heath Rd 31206 478-779-4650
Dr. Sherri Flagg, prin. Fax 779-4627
Williams ES 300/PK-5
325 Pursley St 31201 478-779-3650
Dr. Shandrina Stewart, prin. Fax 779-3661
Other Schools – See Lizella

Jones County SD
Supt. — See Gray
Clifton Ridge MS 600/6-8
169 Dusty Ln 31211 478-743-5182
Charles Lundy, prin. Fax 743-8282
Wells ES 800/PK-5
101 Mattie Wells Dr 31217 478-742-5959
Teresa McCuen, prin. Fax 742-5930

Bethany Christian Academy 50/K-8
1550 Edna Place Rd 31217 478-746-0203
Thomasa Henry, prin. Fax 746-8481
Central Fellowship Christian Academy 300/PK-12
8460 Hawkinsville Rd 31216 478-788-6909
Covenant Academy 400/PK-12
4652 Ayers Rd 31210 478-471-0285
First Presbyterian Day S 1,000/PK-12
5671 Calvin Dr 31210 478-477-6505
Gregg Thompson, hdmstr. Fax 477-2804
Montessori of Macon 100/PK-12
855 Tolliver Pl 31210 478-757-8927
St. Joseph Catholic S 300/PK-6
905 High St 31201 478-742-0636
Alex Porto, prin. Fax 746-7685
St. Peter Claver Catholic S 200/PK-8
133 Ward St 31204 478-743-3985
Sr. Cheryl Hillig, prin. Fax 743-0054
Stratford Academy 900/PK-12
6010 Peake Rd 31220 478-477-8073
Dr. Robert Veto, head sch Fax 477-0299
Tattnall Square Academy 600/PK-12
111 Trojan Trl 31210 478-477-6760
Wimbish Adventist S 50/K-8
640 Wimbish Rd 31210 478-477-4600
RuthAnn Weston, prin. Fax 477-4875
Windsor Academy 200/PK-12
4150 Jones Rd 31216 478-781-1621

Mc Rae, Telfair, Pop. 5,685
Telfair County SD 1,700/PK-12
PO Box 240 31055 229-868-5661
Lenard Harrelson, supt. Fax 868-5549
www.telfairschools.org
Telfair County ES 800/K-5
PO Box 240 31055 229-868-7483
Anthony McIver, prin. Fax 868-7578
Telfair County MS 400/6-8
PO Box 240 31055 229-868-7465
Christopher Ellis, prin. Fax 868-2616
Telfair County Preschool 100/PK-PK
PO Box 240 31055 229-868-5414
Shirley Martin, dir. Fax 868-5549

Manchester, Meriwether, Pop. 4,197
Meriwether County SD
Supt. — See Greenville
Manchester MS 400/6-8
231 W Perry St 31816 706-846-2846
Kimberly Parks, prin. Fax 846-8242
Mountain View ES 800/PK-5
2600 Judson Bulloch Rd 31816 706-655-3969
Todd McRae, prin. Fax 655-3962

Mansfield, Newton, Pop. 405
Newton County SD
Supt. — See Covington
Mansfield ES 500/PK-5
45 E Third Ave 30055 770-784-2948
Chris Haymore, prin. Fax 784-2995

Marietta, Cobb, Pop. 54,999
Cobb County SD 109,300/PK-12
514 Glover St SE 30060 770-426-3300
Chris Ragsdale, supt. Fax 426-3329
www.cobb.k12.ga.us
Addison ES 600/PK-5
3055 Ebenezer Rd 30066 770-578-2700
Susan Hallmark, prin. Fax 578-2702
Bells Ferry ES 600/PK-5
2600 Bells Ferry Rd 30066 678-594-8950
Gail May, prin. Fax 594-8952
Birney ES 700/PK-5
775 Smyrn Pdr Spgs St 30060 678-842-6824
Michael Perkins, prin. Fax 842-6826
Blackwell ES 700/PK-5
3470 Canton Rd 30066 678-494-7600
Melissa Shackelford, prin. Fax 494-7602
Brumby ES 1,000/K-5
1306 Powers Ferry Rd SE 30067 770-916-7070
Dr. Amanda Richie, prin. Fax 916-7072
Cheatham Hill ES 1,100/PK-5
1350 John Ward Rd SW 30064 678-594-8034
Keeli Bowen, prin. Fax 594-8036
Daniell MS 1,000/6-8
2900 Scott Rd 30066 678-594-8048
David Nelson, prin. Fax 594-8050
Davis ES 600/PK-5
2433 Jamerson Rd 30066 678-494-7636
Kristin Erbskorn, prin. Fax 494-7638
Dickerson MS 1,200/6-8
855 Woodlawn Dr NE 30068 770-578-2710
Dr. Carole Brink, prin. Fax 578-2712
Dodgen MS 1,200/6-8
1725 Bill Murdock Rd 30062 770-578-2726
Dr. Loralee Hill, prin. Fax 578-2728
Dowell ES 900/PK-5
2121 W Sandtown Rd SW 30064 678-594-8059
Christine Dinizio, prin. Fax 594-8061
Due West ES 600/K-5
3900 Due West Rd NW 30064 678-594-8071
Ladonna Starnes, prin. Fax 594-8073
East Cobb MS 1,300/6-8
380 Holt Rd NE 30068 770-578-2740
Leetonia Young, prin. Fax 578-2742
East Side ES 1,300/K-5
3850 Roswell Rd 30062 770-578-7200
Elizabeth Mavity, prin. Fax 578-7202
Eastvalley ES 700/K-5
2570 Lower Roswell Rd 30068 770-578-7214
Kendall Foster, prin. Fax 578-7216
Fair Oaks ES 900/PK-5
407 Barber Rd SE 30060 678-594-8080
Elizabeth Murphy, prin. Fax 594-8082
Garrison Mill ES 700/PK-5
4111 Wesley Chapel Rd 30062 770-642-5600
Kyle Giesler, prin. Fax 642-5602
Hightower Trail MS 1,000/6-8
3905 Post Oak Tritt Rd 30062 770-578-7225
Laura Montgomery, prin. Fax 578-7227
Hollydale ES 700/PK-5
2901 Bay Berry Dr SW 30008 678-594-8143
Jennifer Ridgway, prin. Fax 594-8145
Keheley ES 500/PK-5
1985 Kemp Rd 30066 678-494-7836
Tucker Smith, prin. Fax 494-7838
Kincaid ES 700/PK-5
1410 Kincaid Rd 30066 770-578-7238
Deborah Blake, prin. Fax 578-7240
LaBelle ES 600/PK-5
230 Cresson Dr SW 30060 678-842-6955
Susan Stanton, prin. Fax 842-6957
Mabry MS 900/6-8
2700 Jims Rd NE 30066 770-928-5546
Merrilee Heflin, prin. Fax 928-5548
McCleskey MS 700/6-8
4080 Maybreeze Rd 30066 770-928-5560
Andrea Jenkins-Mann, prin. Fax 928-5562
Milford ES 400/K-5
2390 Austell Rd SW 30008 678-842-6966
Hermia Deveaux, prin. Fax 842-6968
Mountain View ES 800/PK-5
3151 Sandy Plains Rd 30066 770-578-7265
Dr. Renee Ingram Garriss, prin. Fax 578-7267
Mt. Bethel ES 1,000/PK-5
1210 Johnson Ferry Rd 30068 770-578-7248
Jessica Appleyard, prin. Fax 578-7250
Murdock ES 900/PK-5
2320 Murdock Rd 30062 770-509-5071
Lynn Hamblett, prin. Fax 509-5217
Nicholson ES 500/PK-5
1599 Shallowford Rd 30066 770-928-5573
Juan Johnson, prin. Fax 928-5575
Powers Ferry ES 400/K-5
403 Powers Ferry Rd SE 30067 770-578-7936
Dr. Patrice Jones, prin. Fax 570-7938
Rocky Mount ES 600/PK-5
2400 Rocky Mountain Rd NE 30066 770-591-5050
Peggy Fleming, prin. Fax 591-5041
Shallowford Falls ES 600/K-5
3529 Lassiter Rd 30062 770-642-5610
Felicia Angelle, prin. Fax 642-5612
Simpson MS 900/6-8
3340 Trickum Rd NE 30066 770-971-4711
Ansley Daniel, prin. Fax 971-4507
Smitha MS 1,000/6-8
2025 Powder Springs Rd SW 30064 678-594-8267
Chris Salter, prin. Fax 594-8269
Sope Creek ES 1,200/PK-5
3320 Paper Mill Rd SE 30067 770-916-7085
Dr. Douglas Daugherty, prin. Fax 916-7087
Timber Ridge ES 600/PK-5
5000 Timber Ridge Rd 30068 770-642-5621
Jeffrey Castle, prin. Fax 642-5623
Tritt ES 900/PK-5
4435 Post Oak Tritt Rd 30062 770-642-5630
Tricia Patterson, prin. Fax 642-5632
Other Schools – See Acworth, Austell, Kennesaw, Mableton, Powder Springs, Smyrna

Marietta CSD 8,800/K-12
250 Howard St NE 30060 770-422-3500
Dr. Grant Rivera, supt. Fax 425-4095
www.marietta-city.org
Burruss ES 500/K-5
325 Manning Rd SW 30064 770-429-3144
Julie King, prin. Fax 429-3146
Dunleith ES 700/K-5
120 Saine Dr SW 30008 770-429-3190
Jeffery Mosley, prin. Fax 429-3193
Hickory Hills ES 500/K-5
500 Redwood Dr SW 30064 770-429-3125
Kristen Beaudin, prin. Fax 429-3126
Lockheed ES 900/K-5
1205 Merritt Rd 30062 770-429-3196
Dr. Devonne Harper, prin. Fax 429-3184
Marietta Center for Advanced Academics 300/3-5
311 Aviation Rd SE 30060 770-420-0822
Dr. Christina Wagoner, prin. Fax 420-0839
Marietta MS 1,300/7-8
121 Winn St NW 30064 770-422-0311
James Guthrie, prin. Fax 429-3162
Marietta Sixth Grade Academy 700/6-6
340 Aviation Rd SE 30060 770-429-3115
Corey Lawson, prin. Fax 429-3118
Park Street ES 600/K-5
105 Park St SE 30060 770-429-3180
Matt Freedman, prin. Fax 429-3182
West Side ES 500/K-5
344 Polk St NW 30064 770-429-3172
Dr. Daniel McGuire, prin. Fax 429-3173

Carman Adventist S 100/PK-8
1330 Cobb Pkwy N 30062 770-424-0606
Casa Montessori 200/PK-6
150 Powers Ferry Rd SE 30067 770-973-2731
Covenant Christian Ministries Academy 100/PK-12
PO Box 4065 30061 770-919-0022
Vanessa Anderson, admin. Fax 919-2098
East Cobb Christian S 100/K-8
4616 Roswell Rd 30062 770-565-0881
Teresa Staley, prin. Fax 565-0689
Eastside Christian S 300/K-8
2450 Lower Roswell Rd 30068 770-971-2332
Deb Knoblock, head sch Fax 578-7967
Faith Lutheran S 200/PK-8
2111 Lower Roswell Rd 30068 770-973-8921
Daryl Kruse, prin. Fax 971-7796
Johnson Ferry Christian Academy 300/K-12
955 Johnson Ferry Rd 30068 678-784-5231
Dr. Kimberly Maiocco, head sch Fax 795-3240
Mt. Bethel Christian Academy 500/PK-12
4385 Lower Roswell Rd 30068 770-971-0245
Jim R. Callis, head sch Fax 971-3770
Riverstone Montessori Academy 100/PK-9
455 Casteel Rd SW 30064 770-422-9194
St. Joseph Catholic S 500/K-8
81 Lacy St NW 30060 770-428-3328
Patricia Allen, prin. Fax 424-2960
Stonehaven S 100/K-8
505 Atlanta St SE 30060 770-874-8885
Walker S 1,100/PK-12
700 Cobb Pkwy N 30062 770-427-2689
Jack Hall, head sch Fax 514-8122
West Cobb Preparatory Academy 200/PK-2
270 Windy Hill Rd SE 30060 770-435-5720

Martinez, Columbia, Pop. 34,798
Columbia County SD
Supt. — See Evans
South Columbia ES 600/PK-5
325 McCormick Rd 30907 706-863-3220
Lisa Reeder, prin. Fax 854-5836
Stallings Island MS 600/6-8
3830 Blackstone Camp Rd 30907 706-447-2106
Don Putnam, prin. Fax 447-2103
Stevens Creek ES 800/PK-5
3780 Evans To Locks Rd 30907 706-868-3705
Michelle Paschal, prin. Fax 854-5837
Westmont ES 500/PK-5
4558 Oakley Pirkle Rd 30907 706-863-0992
Tami Flowers, prin. Fax 854-5838

Augusta Christian S 500/PK-12
313 Baston Rd 30907 706-863-2905
Les Walden, head sch Fax 860-6618
Augusta Preparatory Day S 500/PK-12
285 Flowing Wells Rd 30907 706-863-1906
Peter Huestis, head sch Fax 863-6198
Community Christian Academy 100/PK-10
4594 Columbia Rd 30907 706-426-8881
Beverly Neal, prin. Fax 994-1821

Maysville, Jackson, Pop. 1,762
Jackson County SD
Supt. — See Jefferson
Maysville ES 400/PK-5
9270 Highway 82 Spur 30558 706-652-2241
Michele Archibald, prin. Fax 652-3185

Menlo, Chattooga, Pop. 472
Chattooga County SD
Supt. — See Summerville
Menlo ES 400/PK-8
2430 Highway 337 30731 706-862-2323
Mark Pickle, prin. Fax 862-2360

Metter, Candler, Pop. 4,108
Candler County SD 2,000/PK-12
210 S College St 30439 912-685-5713
Dr. Bubba Longgrear, supt. Fax 685-3068
www.metter.org
Metter ES 700/PK-5
33661 GA Highway 129 S 30439 912-685-5050
Lesa Brown, prin. Fax 685-3477
Metter MS 400/6-8
33661 GA Highway 129 S 30439 912-685-5580
Ralph Carlyle, prin. Fax 685-4970

Midland, Muscogee
Muscogee County SD
Supt. — See Columbus
Cohn MS 500/6-8
7352 Garrett Rd 31820 706-569-3801
Richard Green, prin. Fax 569-3825
Mathews ES 500/K-5
7533 Lynch Rd 31820 706-569-3656
Janice Greene, prin. Fax 569-3663
Midland Academy 600/PK-5
7373 Psalmond Rd 31820 706-569-3664
Janice Miley, prin. Fax 569-3668
Midland MS 400/6-8
6990 Warm Springs Rd 31820 706-569-3673
Barrie Clarke, prin. Fax 569-3678

Midway, Liberty, Pop. 2,059
Liberty County SD
Supt. — See Hinesville
Liberty ES 800/PK-5
600 Edgewater Dr 31320 912-884-3326
Chris Anderson, prin. Fax 884-3631
Midway MS 800/6-8
425 Edgewater Dr 31320 912-884-6677
Debra Frazier, prin. Fax 884-5944

Milledgeville, Baldwin, Pop. 17,451
Baldwin County SD 5,900/PK-12
PO Box 1188 31059 478-453-4176
Dr. Noris Price, supt. Fax 457-3327
www.baldwin-county-schools.com
Early Learning Center 300/PK-PK
100 ABC Dr 31061 478-457-2461
Lori Smith, dir. Fax 457-2470
Lakeview Academy 800/3-5
220 N ABC Dr 31061 478-457-2967
Dr. Shawne Holder, prin. Fax 457-2924

Lakeview PS 900/K-2
372 Blandy Rd NW 31061 478-457-3301
Tracy Clark, prin. Fax 457-3340
Midway Hills Academy 600/3-5
101 Carl Vinson Rd SE 31061 478-457-2440
Antonio Ingram, prin. Fax 453-2680
Midway Hills PS 800/K-2
375 Blandy Rd NW 31061 478-457-2495
Pamela Shields, prin. Fax 457-2499
Oak Hill MS 1,200/6-8
356 Blandy Rd NW 31061 478-457-3370
Daymond Ray, prin. Fax 457-2422

Milledge Academy 500/PK-12
197 Log Cabin Rd NE 31061 478-452-5570
Jessica Jones, head sch Fax 452-5000

Millen, Jenkins, Pop. 3,092
Jenkins County SD 1,400/PK-12
1152 E Winthrope Ave 30442 478-982-6000
Tara Cooper, supt. Fax 982-6002
www.jchs.com/
Jenkins County ES 700/PK-5
220 Landrum Dr 30442 478-982-5503
Randy Dailey, prin. Fax 982-6027
Jenkins County MS 300/6-8
409 Barney Ave 30442 478-982-1063
Rob Gray, prin. Fax 982-6015

Milner, Lamar, Pop. 597

Rock Springs Christian Academy 200/PK-12
219 Rock Springs Rd 30257 678-692-0192
Derrell Jeffcoat, head sch Fax 692-0601
St. George's Episcopal S 100/PK-11
103 Birch St 30257 770-358-9432
Dr. Larry Collins, hdmstr. Fax 358-9495

Milton, Fulton, Pop. 31,916
Fulton County SD
Supt. — See Atlanta
Birmingham Falls ES 800/PK-5
14865 Birmingham Hwy, 470-254-2820
Don Webb, prin. Fax 254-2806
Cogburn Woods ES 900/K-5
13080 Cogburn Rd, 470-254-2845
Lisa Garosi, prin. Fax 254-2854
Crabapple Crossing ES 800/K-5
12775 Birmingham Hwy, 470-254-7055
Dr. Rachel Williams, prin. Fax 254-2841
Hopewell MS 1,300/6-8
13060 Cogburn Rd, 470-254-3240
Michael LeMoyne, prin. Fax 254-3250
Northwestern MS 1,300/6-8
12805 Birmingham Hwy, 470-254-2870
Charles Chester, prin. Fax 254-2878
Summit Hill ES 700/PK-5
13855 Providence Rd, 470-254-2830
LaToya Gray, prin. Fax 254-2834

Montessori Scholars Academy 100/PK-6
13100 Morris Rd, 770-754-0777

Monroe, Walton, Pop. 12,993
Walton County SD 13,700/PK-12
200 Double Spring Church SW 30656 770-266-4417
Dr. Nathan Franklin, supt. Fax 266-4420
www.walton.k12.ga.us
Atha Road ES 800/PK-5
821 H D Atha Rd 30655 770-266-5995
Madenna Landers, prin. Fax 266-5965
Carver MS 1,000/6-8
1095 Good Hope Rd 30655 770-207-3333
Alan Satterfield, prin. Fax 207-3332
Harmony ES 800/PK-5
934 Harmony Church Rd NE 30655 770-267-6574
Dr. Barbara Griffieth, prin. Fax 207-3300
Monroe ES 700/PK-5
140 Dillard Dr 30656 770-207-3205
Dr. Zeester Swint, prin. Fax 207-3207
Walker Park ES 700/PK-5
333 Carl Davis Rd NW 30656 770-207-3240
Dr. Seabrook Royal, prin. Fax 207-3241
Other Schools – See Covington, Loganville

Walton Academy 900/PK-12
1 Bulldog Dr 30655 770-267-7578

Monticello, Jasper, Pop. 2,623
Jasper County SD 2,300/PK-12
1411 College St 31064 706-468-6350
Dr. Mike Newton, supt. Fax 468-0045
www.jasper.k12.ga.us
Jasper County MS 500/6-8
1289 College St 31064 706-468-2227
Cheryl Marrett, prin. Fax 468-1847
Jasper County Preschool 100/PK-PK
495 GA Highway 212 W 31064 706-468-4972
Nannette Manning, dir. Fax 468-4975
Jasper County PS 500/K-2
495 GA Highway 212 W 31064 706-468-4968
Pam Edge, prin. Fax 468-4985
Washington Park ES 500/3-5
721 GA Highway 212 W 31064 706-468-6284
Susan Stone, prin. Fax 468-4984

Piedmont Academy 300/PK-12
PO Box 231 31064 706-468-8818

Moreland, Coweta, Pop. 394
Coweta County SD
Supt. — See Newnan
Moreland ES 500/PK-5
145 Railroad St 30259 770-254-2875
Melanie Perry, prin. Fax 304-5920

Morgan, Calhoun, Pop. 236
Calhoun County SD 700/PK-12
PO Box 39 39866 229-213-0189
Dr. Yolanda Turner, supt. Fax 213-3837
www.calhoun.k12.ga.us
Other Schools – See Arlington, Edison

Morganton, Union, Pop. 300
Fannin County SD
Supt. — See Blue Ridge
East Fannin ES 400/K-5
1 Elementary Cir 30560 706-374-6418
Mathew Price, prin. Fax 374-2470

Mountain Area Christian Academy 200/PK-12
14090 Old Highway 76 30560 706-374-6222
Steve Shamblin, admin. Fax 621-4940

Morrow, Clayton, Pop. 6,303
Clayton County SD
Supt. — See Jonesboro
Haynie ES 900/K-5
1169 Morrow Rd 30260 770-968-2905
Jeannie Wynne, prin. Fax 968-2904
Marshall ES 800/K-5
5885 Maddox Rd 30260 678-827-7942
Dr. Kathryn Holloman, prin. Fax 827-7943
McGarrah ES 700/PK-5
2201 Lake Harbin Rd 30260 770-968-2910
Dr. Cassandra Hopkins, prin. Fax 968-2920
Morrow ES 500/PK-5
6115 Reynolds Rd 30260 770-968-2900
Tammy Burroughs, prin. Fax 968-2903
Morrow MS 700/6-8
5934 Trammell Rd 30260 770-210-4001
Lawvigneaud Harrell, prin. Fax 210-4002
Tara ES 700/PK-5
937 Mount Zion Rd 30260 770-968-2916
Dr. Wakea Brown, prin. Fax 968-2919

Morven, Brooks, Pop. 559
Brooks County SD
Supt. — See Quitman
North Brooks ES 400/K-5
10295 Coffee Rd 31638 229-775-2414
Tara Moss, prin. Fax 775-3322

Moultrie, Colquitt, Pop. 14,082
Colquitt County SD 9,700/PK-12
PO Box 2708 31776 229-890-6200
James Howell, supt. Fax 890-6246
www.colquitt.k12.ga.us/
Cox ES 600/PK-5
1275 11th Ave SE 31768 229-890-6190
Jim Horne, prin. Fax 890-6127
Funston ES 400/PK-5
137 N Academy St 31768 229-941-2626
Ricky Reynolds, prin. Fax 941-5039
Odom ES 700/PK-5
2902 Sardis Church Rd, 229-324-3313
Patricia Lirio, prin. Fax 324-3292
Okapilco ES 500/PK-5
3300 GA Highway 33 N 31768 229-890-6191
Eric Croft, prin. Fax 890-6129
Stringfellow ES 400/PK-5
200 5th Ave SW 31768 229-890-6187
Dr. Tret Witherspoon, prin. Fax 890-5007
Sunset ES 700/PK-5
698 US Highway 319 S 31768 229-890-6184
Josh Purvis, prin. Fax 873-3306
Williams MS 1,400/6-7
950 4th St SW 31768 229-890-6183
Dr. Jamie Horne, prin. Fax 890-6258
Wright ES 600/PK-5
1812 2nd St SE 31768 229-890-6186
Summer Hall, prin. Fax 890-5002
Other Schools – See Doerun, Hartsfield, Norman Park

Colquitt Christian Academy 50/PK-12
2929 S Main St 31768 229-668-2000

Mount Airy, Habersham, Pop. 1,271
Habersham County SD
Supt. — See Clarkesville
Hazel Grove ES 200/K-5
6390 Dicks Hill Pkwy 30563 706-754-2942
Frances Blackburn, prin. Fax 754-3308

Trinity Classical S 50/PK-12
243 Hazel Creek Church Rd 30563 706-894-2404

Mount Berry, Floyd

Berry College S 100/K-8
PO Box 490247 30149 706-236-2242

Mount Vernon, Montgomery, Pop. 2,411
Montgomery County SD 1,100/PK-12
703 Dobbins St 30445 912-583-2301
Hugh Kight, supt. Fax 583-4822
www.montgomery.k12.ga.us
Other Schools – See Ailey

Mount Zion, Carroll, Pop. 1,655
Carroll County SD
Supt. — See Carrollton
Mount Zion MS 300/6-8
132 Eagle Dr 30150 770-834-3389
Connie Robison, prin. Fax 214-7794

Nahunta, Brantley, Pop. 1,033
Brantley County SD 3,500/PK-12
272 School Cir 31553 912-462-6176
Dr. Kim Morgan, supt. Fax 462-6731
www.brantley.k12.ga.us
Brantley County MS 500/7-8
10990 Highway 82 31553 912-462-7092
Dr. Christopher Harris, prin. Fax 462-6785

Nahunta ES 300/4-6
9110 Main St S 31553 912-462-5166
Dr. Kathy Stevens, prin. Fax 462-7330
Nahunta PS 500/PK-3
479 School Cir 31553 912-462-5179
Dr. Brandon Carter, prin. Fax 462-7118
Other Schools – See Hoboken, Waynesville

Nashville, Berrien, Pop. 4,886
Berrien County SD 3,200/PK-12
810 S Dogwood Dr 31639 229-686-2081
Dr. Lili Wylam Drawdy, supt. Fax 686-9002
www.berrien.k12.ga.us
Berrien ES 700/3-5
802 Middle School Cir 31639 229-686-2939
Belinda West, prin. Fax 686-5500
Berrien MS 700/6-8
800 Tifton Hwy 31639 229-686-2021
Margo Mathis, prin. Fax 686-6546
Berrien PS 900/PK-2
1427 N Davis St 31639 229-686-7438
Nicole Richbourg, prin. Fax 686-6211

Newborn, Newton, Pop. 690

Shiloh Christian Academy 50/K-12
9595 Highway 142 30056 706-468-2606

Newnan, Coweta, Pop. 32,285
Coweta County SD 22,500/PK-12
PO Box 280 30264 770-254-2800
Dr. Steve Barker, supt. Fax 254-2807
www.cowetaschools.net
Arbor Springs ES 400/PK-5
4840 Highway 29 N 30265 770-463-5903
Dr. Julie Durrance, prin. Fax 463-5937
Arnall MS 900/6-8
700 Lora Smith Rd 30265 770-254-2765
Dr. Patrick Sullivan, prin. Fax 254-2770
Arnco-Sargent ES 500/PK-5
2449 Highway 16 W 30263 770-254-2830
Vicki Vaughan, prin. Fax 304-5916
Atkinson ES 500/PK-5
14 Nimmons St 30263 770-254-2835
Latrina Gates, prin. Fax 304-5917
Brooks ES 700/PK-5
35 Genesee Pt 30263 770-683-0013
Amy Harrison, prin. Fax 423-2824
Elm Street ES 500/PK-5
46 Elm St 30263 770-254-2865
Dr. Christi Hildebrand, prin. Fax 304-5918
Evans MS 800/6-8
41 Evans Dr 30263 770-254-2780
Vera Perry-Harris, prin. Fax 254-2783
Hill ES 500/PK-5
57 Sunset Ln 30263 770-254-2895
Dr. Aaron Corley, prin. Fax 304-5923
Jefferson Parkway ES 600/PK-5
154 Millard Farmer Ind Blvd 30263 770-254-2771
Dr. Sean Dye, prin. Fax 254-2775
Madras MS 1,100/6-8
240 Edgeworth Rd 30263 770-254-2744
Lorraine Johnson, prin. Fax 304-5928
Newnan Crossing ES 900/PK-5
1267 Lower Fayetteville Rd 30265 770-254-2872
Terri Lassetter, prin. Fax 304-5921
Northside ES 400/PK-5
720 Country Club Rd 30263 770-254-2890
Dr. Dana Ballou, prin. Fax 304-5922
Smokey Road MS 700/6-8
965 Smokey Rd 30263 770-254-2840
Keafer Triplett, prin. Fax 304-5933
Welch ES 800/PK-5
240 Mary Freeman Rd 30265 770-254-2597
Janice Smith, prin. Fax 251-0986
Western ES 400/PK-5
1730 Welcome Rd 30263 770-254-2790
Jan Franks, prin. Fax 304-5925
White Oak ES 700/PK-5
770 Lora Smith Rd 30265 770-254-2860
Andy Clarke, prin. Fax 304-5927
Other Schools – See Grantville, Moreland, Senoia, Sharpsburg

Barron Montessori S 100/PK-8
195 Jackson St 30263 770-253-2135
Heritage S 400/PK-12
2093 Highway 29 N 30263 770-253-9898
Kristin Skelly, head sch Fax 253-4850

Newton, Baker, Pop. 647
Baker County SD 300/PK-12
PO Box 40, 229-734-5274
Dr. Roy Brooks, supt. Fax 734-3071
bck12.baker.k12.ga.us
Baker County S 300/PK-12
260 GA Highway 37 SW, 229-734-5274
Michael Best, prin. Fax 734-3071

Nicholls, Coffee, Pop. 2,776
Coffee County SD
Supt. — See Douglas
Nicholls ES 400/PK-5
704 Atlantic Ave 31554 912-345-2429
Lori Bratcher, prin. Fax 345-5455

Norcross, Gwinnett, Pop. 8,915
Gwinnett County SD
Supt. — See Suwanee
Baldwin ES K-5
123 Price Pl 30071 770-225-5500
Dr. Brenda Johnson, prin. Fax 226-2270
Beaver Ridge ES 1,300/PK-5
1978 Beaver Ruin Rd 30071 770-447-6307
Karen Lillard, prin. Fax 447-2688
Graves ES K-5
1700 Graves Rd 30093 770-326-8000
Clayborn Knight, prin. Fax 326-8001

Meadowcreek ES 1,200/PK-5
5025 Georgia Belle Ct 30093 770-931-5701
Laurie Gardner, prin. Fax 931-5705
Norcross ES 1,100/K-5
150 Hunt St 30071 770-448-2188
Kassia Morris-Sutton, prin. Fax 417-2492
Rockbridge ES 1,100/K-5
6066 Rockbridge School Rd 30093 770-448-9363
Kelly Scarborough, prin. Fax 417-2443
Stripling ES 1,200/K-5
6155 Atlantic Blvd 30071 770-582-7577
Elisa Brown, prin. Fax 582-7586
Summerour MS 1,400/6-8
321 Price Pl 30071 770-448-3045
Dorothy Parker-Jarrett, prin. Fax 417-2476

Country Brook Montessori S 100/PK-3
2175 N Norcross Tucker Rd 30071 770-446-2397
Greater Atlanta Christian S 1,900/PK-12
1575 Indian Trail Lilburn 30093 770-243-2000
Dr. David Fincher, pres. Fax 243-2268
Torch and the Sword Christian Academy 1-12
100 Pinnacle Way #190 30071 678-691-3164
Victory World Christian S 100/PK-5
5905 Brook Hollow Pkwy 30071 678-684-2030
Jeff LeMay Ph.D., admin. Fax 684-2031
Wesleyan S 1,100/K-12
5405 Spalding Dr 30092 770-448-7640
Chris Cleveland, hdmstr. Fax 448-3699

Norman Park, Colquitt, Pop. 956
Colquitt County SD
Supt. — See Moultrie
Norman Park ES 600/PK-5
249 W Weeks St 31771 229-769-3612
Stacey Rutledge, prin. Fax 769-5003

Oakwood, Hall, Pop. 3,904
Hall County SD
Supt. — See Gainesville
Oakwood ES 500/K-5
4500 Allen St 30566 770-532-1656
Dana Magill, prin. Fax 531-2326
West Hall MS 900/6-8
5470 McEver Rd 30566 770-967-4871
Rodney Stephens, prin. Fax 967-4874

Ocilla, Irwin, Pop. 3,380
Irwin County SD 1,800/PK-12
PO Box 225 31774 229-468-7485
Dr. Thad Clayton, supt. Fax 468-7220
www.irwin.k12.ga.us/
Irwin County ES 900/PK-5
521 Lax Hwy 31774 229-468-9476
Holly Tucker, prin Fax 468-9478
Irwin County MS 400/6-8
149 Chieftain Cir 31774 229-468-5517
Edd Cunningham, prin. Fax 468-3134

Odum, Wayne, Pop. 494
Wayne County SD
Supt. — See Jesup
Odum ES 400/PK-5
322 Walter St 31555 912-586-2225
Gena Ierardi, prin. Fax 586-6906

Oglethorpe, Macon, Pop. 1,323
Macon County SD 1,600/PK-12
31 Buck Creek Bypass Rd 31068 478-472-8188
Marc Maynor, supt. Fax 472-2042
www.macon.k12.ga.us/
Macon County ES 800/PK-5
400 GA Highway 128 31068 478-472-7221
Robert James M.S., prin. Fax 472-2591
Macon County MS 400/6-8
400 St Hwy 128 31068 478-472-7045
Taricka Russell, prin. Fax 472-2549

Oglethorpe SDA S 50/1-8
PO Box 1088 31068 478-472-2388

Omega, Tift, Pop. 1,207
Tift County SD
Supt. — See Tifton
Omega ES 400/K-5
150 College Ave 31775 229-387-2418
Dr. Victoria Melton, prin. Fax 528-6298

Oxford, Newton, Pop. 2,073
Newton County SD
Supt. — See Covington
Flint Hill ES 1,200/PK-5
1300 Airport Rd 30054 770-784-2969
Dr. Lynne DiNardo, prin. Fax 784-2994

Providence Classical Christian S 100/PK-12
252 Byrd Rd 30054 770-788-6618

Palmetto, Fulton, Pop. 4,369
Fulton County SD
Supt. — See Atlanta
Palmetto ES 600/PK-5
505 Carlton Rd 30268 470-254-6100
Jacqueline Bowens, prin. Fax 254-6105

Patterson, Pierce, Pop. 721
Pierce County SD
Supt. — See Blackshear
Patterson ES 500/PK-5
3414 Drawdy St 31557 912-647-5373
Teresa Dixon, prin. Fax 647-5523

Peachtree City, Fayette, Pop. 33,616
Fayette County SD
Supt. — See Fayetteville
Booth MS 1,200/6-8
250 S Peachtree Pkwy 30269 770-631-3240
Steve Greene, prin. Fax 631-3245
Braelinn ES 500/K-5
975 Robinson Rd 30269 770-631-5410
Wenonah Bell, prin. Fax 631-5430
Crabapple Lane ES 700/PK-5
450 Crabapple Ln 30269 770-487-5425
Margaret Davis, prin. Fax 487-6590
Huddleston ES 700/PK-5
200 Mcintosh Trl 30269 770-631-3255
Heidi Pfannensteil, prin. Fax 631-3252
Kedron ES 600/PK-5
200 Kedron Dr 30269 770-486-2700
Dr. Julie Turner, prin. Fax 486-2707
Oak Grove ES 500/PK-5
101 Crosstown Dr 30269 770-631-3260
Dr. Felecia Spicer, prin. Fax 631-5431
Peachtree City ES 500/PK-5
201 Wisdom Rd 30269 770-631-3250
Dr. Kristin Berryman, prin. Fax 631-3249

St. Paul Lutheran S 200/PK-8
700 Ardenlee Pkwy 30269 770-486-3545
Jim Richards, prin. Fax 692-6389

Peachtree Crnrs, Gwinnett
Gwinnett County SD
Supt. — See Suwanee
Peachtree ES 1,800/K-5
5995 Crooked Creek Rd, 770-448-8710
Gretchen Runaldue, prin. Fax 417-2451
Pinckneyville MS 1,300/6-8
5440 W Jones Bridge Rd, 770-263-0860
Marci Sledge, prin. Fax 447-2617
Simpson ES 700/K-5
4525 E Jones Bridge Rd, 770-417-2400
Bron Gayna Schmit, prin. Fax 417-2406

Cornerstone Christian Academy 200/K-8
5295 Triangle Pkwy, 770-441-9222

Pearson, Atkinson, Pop. 2,082
Atkinson County SD 1,800/PK-12
98 Roberts Ave E 31642 912-422-7373
Bob Brown, supt. Fax 422-7369
www.atkinson.k12.ga.us
Atkinson County MS 400/6-8
145 Rebel Ln 31642 912-422-3267
Anthony Davis, prin. Fax 422-3348
Pearson ES 700/PK-5
563 King St N 31642 912-422-3882
Jarred Morris, prin. Fax 422-7024
Other Schools – See Willacoochee

Pelham, Mitchell, Pop. 3,877
Grady County SD
Supt. — See Cairo
Shiver ES 600/PK-8
1847 GA Highway 93 N 31779 229-377-2325
Todd Jones, prin. Fax 377-4366

Pelham CSD 1,500/PK-12
203 Mathewson Ave SW 31779 229-294-8715
Floyd Fort, supt. Fax 294-2760
www.pelham-city.k12.ga.us
Pelham City ES 700/PK-5
534 Barrow Ave SW 31779 229-294-8170
Shauwan Carter, prin. Fax 294-7454
Pelham City MS 300/6-8
209 Mathewson Ave SW 31779 229-294-6063
John Hamilton, prin. Fax 294-6046

Pembroke, Bryan, Pop. 2,165
Bryan County SD
Supt. — See Black Creek
Bryan County ES 400/3-5
250 Payne Dr 31321 912-626-5033
Jeff Hodges, prin. Fax 653-4350
Bryan County MS 500/6-8
600 Payne Dr 31321 912-626-5050
Dr. Elizabeth Raeburn, prin. Fax 653-2705
Lanier PS 600/PK-2
6024 US Highway 280 E 31321 912-626-5020
Lynnie Clemens, prin. Fax 858-4350

Perry, Houston, Pop. 13,635
Houston County SD 26,900/PK-12
PO Box 1850 31069 478-988-6200
Dr. Mark Scott, supt. Fax 988-6259
www.hcbe.net
Kings Chapel ES 500/PK-5
460 Arena Rd 31069 478-988-6273
William Ray, prin. Fax 988-6346
Langston Road ES PK-5
315 Langston Rd 31069 478-988-6160
Dr. Elgin Mayfield, prin.
Morningside ES 400/PK-5
1206 Morningside Dr 31069 478-988-6261
Dr. Pat Witt, prin. Fax 988-6265
Perry MS 900/6-8
495 Perry Pkwy 31069 478-988-6285
Heath Burch, prin. Fax 988-6345
Tucker ES 400/PK-5
1300 Tucker Rd 31069 478-988-6278
Dr. Kim Halstead, prin. Fax 988-6379
Other Schools – See Bonaire, Byron, Centerville, Kathleen, Warner Robins

---

Westfield S 600/PK-12
2005 US Highway 41 S 31069 478-987-0547

Pinehurst, Dooly, Pop. 452
Dooly County SD
Supt. — See Vienna
Dooly County ES 800/PK-5
11949 US Highway 41 31070 229-645-3421
Felicia Madison, prin. Fax 645-3840
Dooly County MS 300/6-8
11949 US Highway 41 31070 229-645-3421
Dr. Kelvin Butts, prin. Fax 645-3840

Fullington Academy 300/PK-12
PO Box B 31070 229-645-3383

Plainville, Gordon, Pop. 308
Gordon County SD
Supt. — See Calhoun
Swain ES 500/PK-5
2505 Rome Rd SW 30733 706-629-0141
Dr. Elizabeth Anderson, prin. Fax 879-5291

Pooler, Chatham, Pop. 18,668
Savannah-Chatham County SD
Supt. — See Savannah
Godley Station S 1,600/K-8
2135 Benton Blvd, 912-395-6000
John King, prin. Fax 201-5688
Pooler ES 500/PK-5
308 Holly Ave 31322 912-395-3625
Stacey McPipkin, prin. Fax 395-3636
West Chatham ES 900/PK-5
820 Pine Barren Rd 31322 912-395-3600
Sharon Draeger, prin. Fax 201-5646
West Chatham MS 1,000/6-8
800 Pine Barren Rd 31322 912-395-3650
Julian Childers, prin. Fax 201-7688

Risen Savior Christian Academy 50/PK-4
1755 Quacco Rd 31322 912-925-9431
Sylvia Beahm, dir. Fax 925-9423
Savannah Adventist Christian S 100/PK-10
50 Godley Way 31322 912-748-5977

Portal, Bulloch, Pop. 637
Bulloch County SD
Supt. — See Statesboro
Portal ES 400/PK-5
328 Grady St S 30450 912-842-8340
Dr. Lori Mascolo, prin. Fax 865-9553

Port Wentworth, Chatham, Pop. 5,224
Savannah-Chatham County SD
Supt. — See Savannah
Port Wentworth ES 400/PK-2
507 S Coastal Hwy 31407 912-395-6742
Dr. Tamika Wright, prin. Fax 965-6734
Rice Creek S K-8
100 Mulberry Ave 31407 912-395-4100
Dr. Troy Brown, prin. Fax 201-5068

Powder Springs, Cobb, Pop. 13,580
Cobb County SD
Supt. — See Marietta
Compton ES 500/K-5
3450 New Macland Rd 30127 770-222-3700
Beth Lair, prin. Fax 222-3702
Hendricks ES 500/K-5
5243 Meadows Rd 30127 770-819-2387
Patrick O'Connell, prin. Fax 819-2389
Kemp ES 1,000/K-5
865 Corner Rd 30127 678-594-8158
Shea Thomas, prin. Fax 594-8160
Lovinggood MS 1,400/6-8
3825 Luther Ward Rd 30127 678-331-3015
Derrick Bailey, prin. Fax 331-3016
Powder Springs ES 800/PK-5
4570 Grady Grier Dr 30127 770-222-3746
Debbie Broadnax, prin. Fax 222-3748
Still ES 800/K-5
870 Casteel Rd 30127 678-594-8287
Michelle Pearce, prin. Fax 594-8289
Tapp MS 800/6-8
3900 Macedonia Rd 30127 770-222-3758
Dr. Tony Wilcher, prin. Fax 222-3760
Varner ES 700/PK-5
4761 Gaydon Rd 30127 770-222-3775
Althea Singletary, prin. Fax 222-3777
Vaughan ES 600/K-5
5950 Nichols Rd 30127 678-594-8298
Dr. Shannon McGill, prin. Fax 594-8300

Paulding County SD
Supt. — See Dallas
Baggett ES 700/K-5
948 Williams Lake Rd 30127 678-460-1570
Karniese Daniel, prin. Fax 943-6255
Dobbins MS 800/6-8
637 Williams Lake Rd 30127 770-443-4835
Cartess Ross, prin. Fax 439-1672

Midway Covenant Christian S 300/PK-8
4635 Dallas Hwy 30127 770-590-1866
Barbara Kline, admin. Fax 422-6416
Praise Academy 300/PK-12
4052 Hiram Lithia Springs 30127 770-943-2484
Joe White M.Ed., admin. Fax 943-9458

Preston, Webster, Pop. 438
Webster County SD 400/PK-12
7307 Washington St 31824 229-828-3315
Janie Downer, supt. Fax 828-3206
www.websterbobcats.org
Webster County S 300/PK-8
7168 Washington St 31824 229-828-3365
Janie Downer, admin. Fax 828-2014

Quitman, Brooks, Pop. 3,809
Brooks County SD 2,200/K-12
1081 Barwick Rd 31643 229-263-7531
Dr. Vickie Reed, supt. Fax 263-5206
www.brooks.k12.ga.us
Brooks County MS 500/6-8
2171 Moultrie Hwy 31643 229-263-7521
Christine Freeman, prin. Fax 263-9038
Quitman ES 700/K-5
2200 Moultrie Hwy 31643 229-263-9302
Charles Perry, prin. Fax 263-4169
Other Schools – See Morven

Rabun Gap, Rabun

Rabun Gap-Nacoochee S 300/PK-12
339 Nacoochee Dr 30568 706-746-7467
Dr. Anthony Sgro, head sch Fax 746-2594

Reidsville, Tattnall, Pop. 4,920
Tattnall County SD 3,500/PK-12
146 W Brazell St 30453 912-557-4726
Dr. Gina Williams, supt. Fax 557-3036
www.tattnallschools.org
Reidsville ES 800/PK-5
147 Chandler Ave 30453 912-557-6711
Tina Debevec, prin. Fax 557-3265
Reidsville MS 300/6-8
148 W Brazell St 30453 912-557-3993
Gwenda Johnson, prin. Fax 557-4124
Other Schools – See Collins, Glennville

Rentz, Laurens, Pop. 289
Laurens County SD
Supt. — See Dublin
Southwest Laurens ES 900/PK-5
1799 GA Highway 117 31075 478-984-4276
Aurelia Tippett, prin. Fax 984-4711

Resaca, Gordon, Pop. 530
Gordon County SD
Supt. — See Calhoun
Tolbert ES 600/PK-5
1435 Hall Memorial Rd NW 30735 706-629-4404
Kedeira Angland, prin. Fax 629-6720

Rex, Clayton
Clayton County SD
Supt. — See Jonesboro
Adamson MS 600/6-8
3187 Rex Rd 30273 770-968-2925
Chuck Wilkerson, prin. Fax 968-2949
Rex Mill MS 1,100/6-8
6380 Evans Dr 30273 770-474-0702
Dr. Caryn Turner, prin. Fax 474-5812
Smith ES 900/PK-5
6340 Highway 42 30273 770-960-5750
Dr. Scharbrenia Lockhart, prin. Fax 960-5764

Richmond Hill, Bryan, Pop. 8,989
Bryan County SD
Supt. — See Black Creek
Carver ES 1,000/4-5
476 Frances Meeks Way 31324 912-459-5111
Karen Smith, prin. Fax 756-5872
McAllister ES PK-5
224 Veterans Memorial Pkwy 31324 912-851-4040
Bivins Miller, prin. Fax 727-2071
Richmond Hill ES 900/2-3
473 Frances Meeks Way 31324 912-459-5100
Walt Barnes, prin. Fax 756-3916
Richmond Hill MS 1,500/6-8
503 Warren Hill Rd 31324 912-459-5130
Dr. William McGrath, prin. Fax 756-5369
Richmond Hill PS 1,000/PK-1
471 Frances Meeks Way 31324 912-459-5080
Nancy Highsmith, prin. Fax 756-5153

Rincon, Effingham, Pop. 8,590
Effingham County SD
Supt. — See Springfield
Blandford ES 900/PK-5
4650 McCall Rd 31326 912-826-4200
LaToya Jones, prin. Fax 826-4747
Ebenezer ES 600/PK-5
1198 Ebenezer Rd 31326 912-754-5522
Beth Kight, prin. Fax 754-5527
Ebenezer MS 800/6-8
1100 Ebenezer Rd 31326 912-754-7757
Amie Dickerson, prin. Fax 754-4012
Rincon ES 600/PK-5
501 Richland Ave 31326 912-826-5523
Dr. Paige Dickey, prin. Fax 826-4052

Ringgold, Catoosa, Pop. 3,500
Catoosa County SD 10,700/PK-12
PO Box 130 30736 706-965-2297
Denia Reese, supt. Fax 965-8913
www.catoosa.k12.ga.us
Boynton ES 600/K-5
3938 Boynton Dr 30736 706-866-1521
Jennifer Scott, prin. Fax 861-6641
Graysville ES 500/K-5
944 Graysville Rd 30736 706-937-3147
Kerri Sholl, prin. Fax 937-2812
Heritage MS 1,000/6-8
4005 Poplar Springs Rd 30736 706-937-3568
Chris Lusk, prin. Fax 937-2483
Ringgold ES 500/3-5
322 Evitt Ln 30736 706-935-2912
Kim Erwin, prin. Fax 965-8907
Ringgold MS 800/6-8
217 Tiger Trl 30736 706-935-3381
Jeff Fricks, prin. Fax 965-8908
Ringgold PS 600/PK-2
340 Evitt Ln 30736 706-937-5437
Nancy Gurganus, prin. Fax 937-8383
Other Schools – See Fort Oglethorpe, Rock Spring, Rossville, Tunnel Hill

---

Misty Meadows SDA S 50/K-8
124 Kittle St 30736 706-937-9923

Riverdale, Clayton, Pop. 14,852
Clayton County SD
Supt. — See Jonesboro
Church Street ES 900/K-5
7013 Church St 30274 770-994-4000
Samuel West, prin. Fax 994-4469
Harper ES 900/K-5
93 Valley Hill Rd SW 30274 678-479-2654
Dr. Denise Stevens, prin. Fax 479-2673
Lake Ridge ES 700/PK-5
7900 Lake Ridge Cir 30296 770-907-5170
Dr. Michael Powell, prin. Fax 907-5185
Oliver ES 600/PK-5
1725 Cheryl Leigh Dr 30296 770-994-4010
Dr. Sheneaise Ratcliff, prin. Fax 994-4014
Pointe South ES 700/PK-5
8482 Thomas Rd 30274 770-473-2900
Dr. Charlotte Shoemaker, prin. Fax 603-5774
Riverdale ES 700/PK-5
6253 Garden Walk Blvd 30274 770-994-4015
Michael Faison, prin. Fax 994-4018
Riverdale MS 700/6-8
400 Roberts Dr 30274 770-994-4045
Adrian Courtland, prin. Fax 994-4467
Sequoyah MS 900/6-8
95 Valley Hill Rd SW 30274 770-515-7524
Fax 515-7540

Roberta, Crawford, Pop. 993
Crawford County SD 1,800/PK-12
PO Box 8 31078 478-836-3131
Brent Lowe, supt. Fax 836-3114
crawfordcounty.schoolinsites.com
Crawford County ES 900/PK-5
191 Lowe Rd 31078 478-836-3171
Paris Raines, prin. Fax 836-9721
Crawford County MS 400/6-8
401 Lowe Rd 31078 478-836-3181
Chadwick Chafin, prin. Fax 836-3795

Rochelle, Wilcox, Pop. 1,171
Wilcox County SD
Supt. — See Abbeville
Wilcox County ES 600/PK-5
104 Gordon St 31079 229-365-2441
Gary Howell, prin. Fax 365-2553
Wilcox County MS 300/6-8
114 7th Ave 31079 229-365-2331
Chad Davis, prin. Fax 365-2641

Rockmart, Polk, Pop. 4,119
Paulding County SD
Supt. — See Dallas
Ragsdale ES 600/K-5
528 Holly Springs Rd 30153 770-443-2140
Ann Arnold, prin. Fax 443-2153

Polk County SD
Supt. — See Cedartown
Eastside ES 900/PK-5
425 Prospect Rd 30153 770-684-5335
Dr. Wesley Cupp, prin. Fax 684-1335
Rockmart MS 700/6-8
60 Knox Mountain Rd 30153 678-757-1479
Chris Loveless, prin. Fax 757-9868
Van Wert ES 800/PK-5
370 Atlanta Hwy 30153 770-684-6924
Tamra Walker, prin. Fax 684-9612

Rock Spring, Walker
Catoosa County SD
Supt. — See Ringgold
Woodstation ES 500/K-5
3404 Colbert Hollow Rd 30739 706-935-6700
Ernie Ellis, prin. Fax 935-3377

Walker County SD
Supt. — See La Fayette
Rock Spring ES 400/PK-5
372 Highway 95 30739 706-764-1383
Kandy Gilstrap, prin. Fax 764-2248
Saddle Ridge ES 500/PK-8
9558 N Highway 27 30739 706-375-1219
Wendy Ingram, prin. Fax 375-1210

Rocky Face, Whitfield
Whitfield County SD
Supt. — See Dalton
West Side ES 600/PK-5
1815 Utility Rd 30740 706-673-6531
Tami Dodd, prin. Fax 673-5556
Westside MS 500/6-8
580 Lafayette Rd 30740 706-673-2611
Angela Hargis, prin. Fax 673-5349

Rome, Floyd, Pop. 35,635
Floyd County SD 9,800/PK-12
600 Riverside Pkwy NE 30161 706-234-1031
Dr. John Jackson, supt. Fax 236-1824
www.floydboe.net
Alto Park ES 500/PK-5
525 Burnett Ferry Rd SW 30165 706-236-1892
Angela Brock, prin. Fax 236-1894
Armuchee ES 400/3-5
5075 Martha Berry Hwy NW 30165 706-802-6758
Rodney Stewart, prin. Fax 802-6761
Coosa MS 600/6-8
212 Eagle Dr NW 30165 706-236-1856
Vondell Ringer, prin. Fax 802-6766
Garden Lakes ES 600/PK-5
2903 Garden Lakes Blvd NW 30165 706-236-1865
Mary Alcorn, prin. Fax 802-6773
Glenwood PS 500/PK-2
75 Glenwood School Rd NE 30165 706-236-1855
Jill Shepherd, prin. Fax 290-8156
Johnson ES 600/PK-5
1839 Morrison Camp Grnd NE 30161 706-236-1830
Tanya Welchel, prin. Fax 290-8152
McHenry PS 200/PK-2
100 McHenry Dr SW 30161 706-236-1833
Brig Larry, prin. Fax 290-8166
Model ES 600/PK-5
3200 Calhoun Rd NE 30161 706-236-1827
Aimee Hays, prin. Fax 290-8162
Model MS 500/6-8
164 Barron Rd NE 30161 706-290-8150
Steve Turrentine, prin. Fax 802-6775
Other Schools – See Armuchee, Cave Spring, Lindale

Rome CSD 5,800/PK-12
508 E 2nd St 30161 706-236-5050
Louis Byars, supt. Fax 802-4311
www.rcs.rome.ga.us
Davie ES 200/PK-6
24 E Main St 30161 706-232-4913
Dr. Clifton Nicholson Ph.D., prin. Fax 295-4833
East Central ES 500/K-6
1502 Dean Ave SE 30161 706-232-8310
Kristin Teems, prin. Fax 234-5374
Elm Street ES 600/PK-6
8 S Elm St SW 30165 706-232-5313
Dr. JoAnn Moss Ph.D., prin. Fax 314-0647
North Heights ES 200/PK-6
26 Atteiram Dr NE 30161 706-295-4442
Tonya Wood, prin. Fax 234-5727
Rome MS 900/7-8
1020 Veterans Memorial NE 30161 706-235-4695
Parke Wilkinson, prin. Fax 234-5903
West Central ES 800/PK-6
409 Lavender Dr NW 30165 706-235-8836
Leslie Dixon, prin. Fax 234-5854
West End ES 800/PK-6
5 Brown Fox Dr SW 30165 706-234-9366
Buffi Murphy, prin. Fax 234-5869

Darlington S 800/PK-12
1014 Cave Spring Rd SW 30161 706-235-6051
Brent Bell, hdmstr. Fax 232-3600
St. Mary S 300/PK-8
401 E 7th St SE 30161 706-234-4953
Melissa Reder, prin. Fax 234-3030
Unity Christian S 400/PK-12
2960 New Calhoun Hwy NE 30161 706-292-0700
Eric Munn, head sch Fax 292-0772

Roopville, Carroll, Pop. 218
Carroll County SD
Supt. — See Carrollton
Roopville ES 400/PK-5
60 Old Carrollton Rd 30170 770-854-4421
Cherri LeBlanc, prin. Fax 854-3001

Heard County SD
Supt. — See Franklin
Ephesus ES 100/PK-5
24414 Georgia Highway 100 30170 770-854-4400
Melanie Brooks, prin. Fax 854-6888

Rossville, Walker, Pop. 4,039
Catoosa County SD
Supt. — See Ringgold
Cloud Springs ES 400/PK-5
163 Fernwood Dr 30741 706-866-6640
Kellie Yarbrough, prin. Fax 861-6642
Lakeview MS 700/6-8
416 Cross St 30741 706-866-1040
Steve McClure, prin. Fax 861-6644
West Side ES 400/K-5
72 Braves Ln 30741 706-866-9211
Mike Rich, prin. Fax 861-6647

Walker County SD
Supt. — See La Fayette
Rossville ES 500/PK-5
1250 Wilson Rd 30741 706-866-5901
Courtney Gadd, prin. Fax 866-6169
Rossville MS 600/6-8
316 Bull Dog Trl 30741 706-820-0638
Jason Pelham, prin. Fax 820-0696
Stone Creek ES 500/PK-5
1600 Happy Valley Rd 30741 706-866-3600
Brandon Mosgrove, prin. Fax 861-4325

Roswell, Fulton, Pop. 86,448
Fulton County SD
Supt. — See Atlanta
Crabapple MS 900/6-8
10700 Crabapple Rd 30075 470-254-4520
Rako Morrissey, prin. Fax 254-4524
Elkins Pointe MS 1,100/6-8
11290 Elkins Rd 30076 470-254-2892
Kindra Smith, prin. Fax 254-2898
Hembree Springs ES 800/PK-5
815 Hembree Rd 30076 470-254-2902
Laurie Woodruff, prin. Fax 254-2906
Hillside ES 700/PK-5
9250 Scott Rd 30076 470-254-6362
Maisha Otway, prin. Fax 254-6366
Jackson ES 600/PK-5
1400 Martin Rd 30075 470-254-5290
Jennifer Cassidy, prin. Fax 254-3332
Mimosa ES 1,100/PK-5
1550 Warsaw Rd 30076 470-254-4540
Ariane Holcombe, prin. Fax 254-6346
Mountain Park ES 800/K-5
11895 Mountain Park Rd 30075 470-254-4530
Stacy Perlman, prin. Fax 254-3331
Northwood ES 800/K-5
10200 Wooten Rd 30076 470-254-6390
Ritu Ahuja, prin. Fax 254-6397
River Eves ES 800/K-5
9000 Eves Rd 30076 470-254-4550
Neil Pinnock, prin. Fax 254-4557
Roswell North ES 1,100/PK-5
10525 Woodstock Rd 30075 470-254-6320
Maureen Lilly, prin. Fax 254-6326
Sweet Apple ES 700/K-5
12025 Etris Rd 30075 470-254-3310
Andy Allison, prin. Fax 254-3316
Vickery Mill ES PK-5
1201 Alpharetta St 30075 470-254-2400
Adam Maroney, prin. Fax 254-2401

Atlanta Academy 200/PK-8
2000 Holcomb Woods Pkwy 30076 678-461-6102
Angela Naples, hdmstr. Fax 461-6105

Cross of Life Christian Montessori S 100/PK-K
1000 Hembree Rd 30076 770-475-3812
Stefanie Graper, dir. Fax 751-5726
Eaton Academy 200/K-12
1000 old Roserll Lakes Pkwy 30076 770-645-2673
Fellowship Christian S 700/PK-12
10965 Woodstock Rd 30075 770-993-1650
Dr. Kathy Teston, head sch Fax 993-9262
High Meadows S 400/PK-8
1055 Willeo Rd 30075 770-993-2940
Jay Underwood, head sch Fax 993-8331
ILM Academy 200/PK-8
1200 Grimes Bridge Rd 30075 678-624-1157
Queen of Angels S 500/K-8
11340 Woodstock Rd 30075 770-518-1804
Jamie Arthur Ph.D., prin. Fax 518-0945
St. Francis Day S 900/1-12
9375 Willeo Rd 30075 770-641-8257
Village Montessori S 100/PK-8
1610 Woodstock Rd 30075 770-552-0834

Royston, Franklin, Pop. 2,535
Franklin County SD
Supt. — See Carnesville
Royston ES 500/K-5
660 College St 30662 706-245-9252
Dr. David Gailer, prin. Fax 245-0903

Rydal, Bartow
Bartow County SD
Supt. — See Cartersville
Pine Log ES 400/PK-5
1095 Cass Pine Log Rd 30171 770-606-5864
Dr. Lenora Nyeste, prin. Fax 721-1917

Saint George, Charlton
Charlton County SD
Supt. — See Folkston
Saint George ES 200/PK-6
13215 Florida Ave, 912-843-2383
Dr. Drew Sauls, prin. Fax 843-8287

Saint Marys, Camden, Pop. 16,595
Camden County SD
Supt. — See Kingsland
Clark ES 500/PK-5
318 Mickler Dr 31558 912-882-4373
Laurie Sutton, prin. Fax 576-5126
Crooked River ES 600/PK-5
3570 Charlie Smith Sr Hwy 31558 912-673-6995
Dr. Shawny Thorpe, prin. Fax 882-2761
Saint Marys ES 600/PK-5
600 Osborne St 31558 912-882-4839
Rhonda Lee, prin. Fax 882-9200
Saint Marys MS 1,000/6-8
205 Martha Dr 31558 912-882-8626
Dr. Angela McManigal, prin. Fax 882-5473
Sugarmill ES 600/PK-5
2885 Winding Rd 31558 912-882-8191
Terri Slattery, prin. Fax 882-8681

Saint Simons Island, Glynn, Pop. 12,646
Glynn County SD
Supt. — See Brunswick
Oglethorpe Point ES 600/PK-5
6200 Frederica Rd 31522 912-638-6200
Anna Wiles, prin. Fax 634-1289
St. Simons ES 500/PK-5
805 Ocean Blvd 31522 912-638-2851
Katy Ginn, prin. Fax 638-1783

Frederica Academy 400/PK-12
200 Murray Way 31522 912-638-9981
Ellen Flemming, head sch Fax 638-1442
Saint Simons Christian S 100/PK-8
1060 Coquina Dr 31522 912-634-8177
Mark Kok, hdmstr. Fax 634-2900

Sandersville, Washington, Pop. 5,844
Washington County SD 3,100/PK-12
PO Box 716 31082 478-552-3981
Dr. Donna Hinton, supt. Fax 552-3128
www.washington.k12.ga.us/
Elder MS 600/6-8
902 Linton Rd 31082 478-552-2007
Dr. Darryl Gilbert, prin. Fax 552-7388
Ridge Road ES 700/3-5
285 Ridge Rd 31082 478-552-2245
Leah Clark, prin. Fax 552-0870
Ridge Road PS 900/PK-2
285 Ridge Rd 31082 478-552-6047
Dexter Wansley, prin. Fax 552-9020

Brentwood S 400/PK-12
PO Box 955 31082 478-552-5136

Sandy Springs, Fulton, Pop. 91,346
Fulton County SD
Supt. — See Atlanta
Dunwoody Springs ES 700/PK-5
8100 Roberts Dr 30350 470-254-4060
Ivy Goggins, prin. Fax 254-4064
Heards Ferry ES 700/PK-5
6151 Powers Ferry Rd, 470-254-6190
Lisa Nash, prin. Fax 254-6195
High Point ES 900/PK-5
520 Greenland Rd, 470-254-7716
Carrie Pitchford, prin. Fax 254-3294
Ison Springs ES 800/PK-5
8261 Ison Rd 30350 470-254-4020
Sara White, prin. Fax 254-4021
Lake Forest ES 900/PK-5
5920 Sandy Springs Cir 30328 470-254-8740
Taylor Barton, prin. Fax 254-8746
Ridgeview Charter MS 1,100/6-8
5340 S Trimble Rd, 470-254-7710
Oliver Blackwell, prin. Fax 254-3292
Sandy Springs MS 900/6-8
8750 Pride Pl 30350 470-254-4970
Jerome Huff, prin. Fax 254-3334
Spalding Drive ES 500/PK-5
130 W Spalding Dr 30328 470-254-5880
Lynn Johnson, prin. Fax 254-4090
Woodland ES 900/PK-5
1130 Spalding Dr 30350 470-254-5890
Tara McGee, prin. Fax 254-4091

Epstein S 600/PK-8
335 Colewood Way 30328 404-250-5600

Sardis, Burke, Pop. 990
Burke County SD
Supt. — See Waynesboro
S.G.A. ES 400/PK-5
1265 Charles Perry Ave 30456 478-569-4322
Joshua Brantley, prin. Fax 569-4065

Sautee, White
White County SD
Supt. — See Cleveland
Mount Yonah ES 500/K-5
1161 Duncan Bridge Rd, 706-865-3514
Jill Baughman, prin. Fax 865-1466

Savannah, Chatham, Pop. 133,567
Savannah-Chatham County SD 37,100/PK-12
208 Bull St 31401 912-395-5600
Dr. M. Ann Levett, supt. Fax 201-9073
www.savannah.chatham.k12.ga.us/
Brock ES 600/PK-5
1804 Stratford St 31415 912-395-5300
Selina Gillans, prin. Fax 201-5302
Butler ES 700/PK-5
1909 Cynthia St 31415 912-395-2525
Lynette Ward, prin. Fax 201-7578
Coastal MS 800/6-8
4595 US Highway 80 E 31410 912-395-3950
Allison Schuster-Jones, prin. Fax 898-3951
DeRenne MS 700/6-8
1009 Clinch St 31405 912-395-5900
Carol Mobley, prin. Fax 201-5903
East Broad Street S 700/PK-8
400 E Broad St 31401 912-395-5500
Elijah West, prin. Fax 201-5503
Ellis Montessori Academy 600/PK-8
220 E 49th St 31405 912-395-5470
Tanya Melville, prin. Fax 201-5473
Gadsden ES 700/PK-5
919 May St 31415 912-395-5940
Dr. Renee Bryant-Evans, prin. Fax 201-5943
Garrison S for the Arts 700/PK-8
649 W Jones St 31401 912-395-5975
James Heater, prin. Fax 201-5978
Georgetown S 700/K-8
1516 King George Blvd 31419 912-395-3475
Kelli Hamilton, prin. Fax 961-3479
Gould ES 900/PK-5
4910 Pineland Dr 31405 912-395-5400
Jim Roszkowiak, prin. Fax 201-5403
Haven ES 400/PK-5
5111 Dillon Ave 31405 912-395-6501
Dionne Young, prin. Fax 303-6509
Heard ES 600/PK-5
414 Lee Blvd 31405 912-395-6630
Sylvia Wallis, prin. Fax 303-6637
Hesse S 1,000/PK-8
9116 Whitfield Ave 31406 912-395-6440
Kimberly Newman, prin. Fax 303-6450
Hodge ES 500/PK-5
975 Clinch St 31405 912-395-5200
Yvette Wells, prin. Fax 201-5213
Howard ES 700/K-5
115 Wilmington Island Rd 31410 912-395-3925
Tahisha Wright, prin. Fax 898-3934
Hubert MS 500/6-8
768 Grant St 31401 912-395-5235
Lesley Jordan, prin. Fax 201-5238
Isle of Hope S 700/PK-8
100 Parkersburg Rd 31406 912-395-6555
Lawrence Butler, prin. Fax 201-5489
Largo-Tibet ES 800/PK-5
430 Tibet Ave 31406 912-395-3450
Andrea Burkiett, prin. Fax 961-3460
Marshpoint ES 900/PK-5
135 Whitemarsh Island Rd 31410 912-395-4000
Lynne Phillips, prin. Fax 898-4001
Mercer MS 500/6-8
201 Rommel Ave 31408 912-395-6700
Horace Magwood, prin. Fax 201-5979
Myers MS 700/6-8
2025 E 52nd St 31404 912-395-6600
Ericka Washington, prin. Fax 303-6604
Pulaski ES 700/PK-5
1001 Tibet Ave 31419 912-395-6466
Antonio Byrd, prin. Fax 303-6473
S of Humanities at Juliette Gordon Low PK-5
15 Blue Rige Ave 31404 912-395-6380
Kathleen Taylor, prin. Fax 303-6386
Shuman ES 700/K-5
415 Goebel Ave 31404 912-395-4500
Sylvia Jenkins, prin. Fax 201-7503
Smith ES 400/K-5
210 Lamara Dr 31405 912-395-6530
Vernon Cole, prin. Fax 303-6538
Southwest ES 700/K-5
6020 Ogeechee Rd 31419 912-395-3301
Tara Fitzgerald, prin. Fax 961-3312
Southwest MS 900/6-8
6030 Ogeechee Rd 31419 912-395-3540
Craig Daughtry, prin. Fax 201-5831
Spencer ES 600/PK-5
3609 Hopkins St 31405 912-395-2500
Andrea Williams, prin. Fax 201-7528
STEM Academy 600/6-8
207 E Montgomery Xrd 31406 912-395-3500
Jimmie Cave, prin. Fax 201-4161
White Bluff ES 600/PK-5
9902 White Bluff Rd 31406 912-395-3325
Christopher Jacobs, prin. Fax 961-3334
Windsor Forest ES 700/PK-5
414 Briarcliff Cir 31419 912-395-3353
Kimsherion Reid, prin. Fax 201-4876
Other Schools – See Bloomingdale, Garden City, Pooler, Port Wentworth

---

Blessed Sacrament Catholic S 400/PK-8
1003 E Victory Dr 31405 912-356-6987
Lynn Brown, prin. Fax 356-6988
Butler Christian Academy 100/PK-12
707 Little Neck Rd 31419 912-921-0088
Calvary Day S 700/PK-12
4625 Waters Ave 31404 912-644-5080
Dr. James Taylor, hdmstr. Fax 351-2280
Habersham S 100/PK-12
505 E 54th St 31405 912-509-0540
Hancock Day S 300/PK-8
6600 Howard Foss Dr 31406 912-351-4500
Francine Wright, head sch Fax 351-4550
Memorial Day S 300/PK-12
6500 Habersham St 31405 912-352-4535
Providence Christian S 200/PK-12
401 Tibet Ave 31406 912-335-7976
Ramah SDA Junior Academy 200/K-8
PO Box 24307 31403 912-233-3101
Rambam Day S 100/PK-8
111 Atlas St 31405 912-352-7994
Ester Rabhan, prin. Fax 352-1920
St. Andrew's S 400/PK-12
601 Penn Waller Rd 31410 912-897-4941
Dr. Kelley Waldron, hdmstr. Fax 897-4943
St. Frances Cabrini Catholic S 100/PK-8
11500 Middleground Rd 31419 912-925-6249
Kelly Ryan, prin. Fax 925-5661
St. James Catholic S 300/PK-8
8412 Whitefield Ave 31406 912-355-3132
Sr. Lisa Golden, prin. Fax 355-1996
St. Peter the Apostle Catholic S 300/PK-8
PO Box 30460 31410 912-897-5224
Joe Thomas, prin. Fax 897-0801
Savannah Christian Preparatory S 1,300/PK-12
PO Box 2848 31402 912-234-1653
Savannah Country Day S 900/PK-12
824 Stillwood Dr 31419 912-925-8800
Kef Wilson, head sch Fax 920-7800
Veritas Academy 100/PK-12
PO Box 8332 31412 912-238-1222

Scottdale, DeKalb, Pop. 10,220
DeKalb County SD
Supt. — See Stone Mountain
Shaw ES 500/PK-5
385 Glendale Rd 30079 678-676-6002
Katrina Massey, prin. Fax 676-6010

Screven, Wayne, Pop. 759
Wayne County SD
Supt. — See Jesup
Screven ES 200/PK-5
PO Box 159 31560 912-579-2261
Shawn Yeomans, prin. Fax 579-2225

Senoia, Coweta, Pop. 3,245
Coweta County SD
Supt. — See Newnan
East Coweta MS 700/6-8
6291 Highway 16 30276 770-599-6607
Dr. Jeannette Hallam, prin. Fax 599-1051
Eastside ES 500/PK-5
1225 Eastside School Rd 30276 770-599-6621
Leigh Munson, prin. Fax 599-8530

Sharpsburg, Coweta, Pop. 336
Coweta County SD
Supt. — See Newnan
Canongate ES 600/PK-5
200 Pete Rd 30277 770-463-8010
Betty Robinson, prin. Fax 463-0053
Lee MS 1,000/6-8
370 Willis Rd 30277 770-251-1547
Dr. Cindy Bennett, prin. Fax 253-8381
Poplar Road ES 600/PK-5
2925 Poplar Rd 30277 770-254-2740
Lesley Goodwin, prin. Fax 304-5926
Thomas Crossroads ES 400/PK-5
3530 Highway 34 E 30277 770-254-2751
Dr. Fato Simmons, prin. Fax 304-5924
Willis Road ES 700/PK-5
430 Willis Rd 30277 770-304-7995
Dr. Charles Smith, prin. Fax 304-7999

Central Christian S 100/PK-12
3613 Highway 34 E 30277 770-252-1234
Bill Parsons, head sch Fax 304-9576
Shoal Creek Adventist S 100/K-8
4957 Highway 34 E 30277 770-251-1464
Trinity Christian S of Sharpsburg 1,000/PK-12
8817 Highway 54 W 30277 770-251-6770
Dean Demos, hdmstr. Fax 251-6714

Siloam, Greene, Pop. 278

Greene Academy 200/PK-12
PO Box 109 30665 706-467-2147

Smyrna, Cobb, Pop. 49,900
Cobb County SD
Supt. — See Marietta
Argyle ES 600/PK-5
2420 Spring Rd SE 30080 678-842-6800
Robert Babay, prin. Fax 842-6802

Belmont Hills ES 300/PK-5
605 Glendale Pl SE 30080 678-842-6810
Ashley Campoli, prin. Fax 842-6812
Campbell MS 1,300/6-8
3295 Atlanta Rd SE 30080 678-842-6873
Jonathan Tanner, prin. Fax 842-6875
Green Acres ES 800/PK-5
2000 Gober Ave SE 30080 678-842-6905
Ashley Mize, prin. Fax 842-6907
Griffin MS 1,200/6-8
4010 King Springs Rd SE 30082 678-842-6917
Paul Gillihan, prin. Fax 842-6919
King Springs IS 500/2-5
1041 Reed Rd SE 30082 678-842-6944
Cindy Szwec, prin. Fax 842-6946
King Springs PS 300/K-1
3265 Brown Rd SE 30080 678-842-6944
Cindy Szwec, prin. Fax 842-6946
Nickajack ES 1,000/K-5
4555 Mavell Rd SE 30082 678-842-5814
Adam Hill, prin. Fax 842-5832
Norton Park ES 800/PK-5
3041 Gray Rd SE 30082 678-842-5833
Michelle Curry, prin. Fax 842-5835
Russell ES 700/PK-5
3920 S Hurt Rd SW 30082 770-437-5937
Tammy Watson, prin. Fax 437-5939
Smyrna ES 800/K-5
1099 Fleming St SE 30080 678-842-6741
Brett Ward, prin. Fax 842-6749
Teasley ES 700/PK-5
3640 Spring Hill Rd SE 30080 770-437-5945
Leslie Mansfield, prin. Fax 437-5947

Covenant Christian S 200/PK-8
3130 Atlanta Rd SE 30080 770-435-1596
Covered Bridge Montessori S 100/PK-3
488 Hurt Rd SW 30082 770-801-8292
St. Benedict's Episcopal S 300/PK-8
2160 Cooper Lake Rd SE 30080 678-279-4300
Rev. Brian Sullivan, head sch Fax 279-4309

Snellville, Gwinnett, Pop. 17,762
Gwinnett County SD
Supt. — See Suwanee
Anderson-Livsey ES 800/K-5
4521 Centerville Hwy 30039 678-344-2082
Christine Knox, prin. Fax 344-2083
Annistown ES 500/K-5
3150 Spain Rd 30039 770-979-2950
Dr. Steve Frandsen, prin. Fax 736-4491
Britt ES 600/K-5
2503 Skyland Dr 30078 770-972-4500
Melissa Madsen, prin. Fax 736-4426
Brookwood ES 1,100/K-5
1330 Holly Brook Rd 30078 770-736-4360
Cheri Carter, prin. Fax 736-4410
Centerville ES 700/K-5
3115 Centerville Hwy 30039 770-972-2220
Bonita Banks, prin. Fax 639-3704
Norton ES 1,100/K-5
3050 Xavier Ray Ct 30039 770-985-1933
Melanie Lee, prin. Fax 736-2005
Partee ES 700/PK-5
4350 Campbell Rd 30039 770-982-6920
Kelli McCain, prin. Fax 344-4400
Pharr ES 700/K-5
1500 North Rd 30078 770-985-0244
Lisa Rhodes, prin. Fax 736-4510
Shiloh ES 700/K-5
2400 Ross Rd 30039 770-985-6883
Thomas Trippany, prin. Fax 736-2061
Shiloh MS 1,900/6-8
4285 Shiloh Rd 30039 770-972-3224
Dr. Eli Welch, prin. Fax 736-4563
Snellville MS 900/6-8
3155 Pate Rd 30078 770-972-1530
Katise Menchan, prin. Fax 736-4444

Social Circle, Walton, Pop. 4,199
Social Circle CSD 1,700/PK-12
147 Alcova Dr 30025 770-464-2731
Dr. Todd McGhee, supt. Fax 464-4920
www.socialcircleschools.com/
Social Circle ES 400/3-5
240 W Hightower Trl 30025 770-464-2664
Elizabeth Pridgen, prin. Fax 464-2665
Social Circle MS 400/6-8
154 Alcova Dr 30025 770-464-1932
Lottie Aziamadi, prin. Fax 464-2612
Social Circle PS 400/PK-2
439 Annie P Henderson Dr 30025 770-464-1411
Darlene Favors, prin. Fax 464-9233

Soperton, Treutlen, Pop. 3,093
Treutlen County SD 1,200/PK-12
5040 S Third St 30457 912-529-7101
Dr. Cheryl Conley, supt. Fax 529-4226
www.treutlen.k12.ga.us
Treutlen ES 600/PK-5
7892 GA Highway 29 30457 912-529-7161
Forrest Edge, prin. Fax 529-6831

Sparks, Cook, Pop. 2,024
Cook County SD
Supt. — See Adel
Cook ES 700/3-5
1512 N Elm St 31647 229-549-6250
Gabe Hammock, prin. Fax 549-8568
Cook MS 700/6-8
1601 N Elm St 31647 229-549-5999
Russell Meadows, prin. Fax 549-5986

Sparta, Hancock, Pop. 1,390
Hancock County SD 1,000/PK-12
11311 GA Highway 15 31087 706-444-5775
Dr. Charles Culver, supt. Fax 444-7026
www.hancock.k12.ga.us
Hancock Central MS 200/6-8
11311 GA Highway 15 31087 706-444-6652
Anthony Webb, prin. Fax 444-4344
Lewis ES 500/PK-5
11145 GA Highway 15 31087 706-444-7028
Norman Hart, prin. Fax 444-0380

Springfield, Effingham, Pop. 2,815
Effingham County SD 11,500/PK-12
405 N Ash St 31329 912-754-6491
Dr. Randy Shearouse, supt. Fax 754-7033
www.effinghamschools.com
Springfield ES 700/PK-5
300 Old Dixie Hwy S 31329 912-754-3326
Lisa Woods, prin. Fax 754-7172
Other Schools – See Guyton, Rincon

Statenville, Echols, Pop. 1,016
Echols County SD 800/PK-12
216 US Highway 129 N 31648 229-559-5734
Lance Heard, supt. Fax 559-0484
www.echols.k12.ga.us
Echols County S 600/PK-8
PO Box 40 31648 229-559-5413
Wade Beale, prin. Fax 559-0423

Statesboro, Bulloch, Pop. 27,883
Bulloch County SD 9,900/PK-12
150 Williams Rd Ste A 30458 912-212-8500
Charles Wilson, supt. Fax 212-8529
www.bulloch.k12.ga.us
Bryant ES 900/PK-5
421 W Main St 30458 912-212-8680
Dr. Julie Blackmar, prin. Fax 489-5867
James MS 600/6-8
18809 US Highway 80 W 30458 912-212-8820
Julie Mizell, prin. Fax 489-5916
Langston Chapel ES 800/PK-5
150 Langston Chapel Rd 30458 912-212-8700
Pam Goodman, prin. Fax 681-7802
Langston Chapel MS 700/6-8
156 Langston Chapel Rd 30458 912-212-8720
Dr. Evelyn Gamble-Hilton, prin. Fax 681-6416
Lively ES 600/PK-5
204 Debbie Dr 30458 912-212-8760
Dr. Carolyn Vasilatos, prin. Fax 489-5891
Mill Creek ES 700/PK-5
239 Beasley Rd 30461 912-212-8780
Jennifer Wade, prin. Fax 764-3842
Nevils ES 400/PK-5
8438 Nevils Groveland Rd 30458 912-842-8320
Nate Pennington, prin. Fax 839-2357
Zetterower ES 500/K-5
1200 Cawana Rd 30461 912-212-8800
Marlin Baker, prin. Fax 489-5941
Other Schools – See Brooklet, Portal

Bulloch Academy 500/PK-12
873 Westside Rd 30458 912-764-6297
Trinity Christian S 200/PK-12
571 E Main St 30461 912-489-1375
David Lattner, hdmstr. Fax 764-3136

Statham, Barrow, Pop. 2,353
Barrow County SD
Supt. — See Winder
Bear Creek MS 700/6-8
228 Jefferson St 30666 770-725-5575
Dr. Jennifer Wood, prin. Fax 725-7656
Statham ES 800/K-5
1970 Broad St 30666 770-725-7112
Dr. Shawn Williams, prin. Fax 725-1550

Stillmore, Emanuel, Pop. 530

Emanuel Academy 200/PK-12
PO Box 400 30464 912-562-4405

Stockbridge, Henry, Pop. 24,827
Henry County SD
Supt. — See Mc Donough
Austin Road ES 400/K-5
50 Austin Rd 30281 770-389-6556
Arthur Blevins, prin. Fax 389-5909
Austin Road MS 800/6-8
100 Austin Rd 30281 770-507-5407
Gabriel Wiley, prin. Fax 507-5413
Cotton Indian ES 700/K-5
1201 Old Conyers Rd 30281 770-474-9983
Lisa Travis, prin. Fax 474-6959
Fairview ES 600/PK-5
458 Fairview Rd 30281 770-474-8265
Dr. Vaneisa Benjamin, prin. Fax 474-5528
Pate's Creek ES 700/PK-5
1309 Jodeco Rd 30281 770-389-8819
Cynthia McCray, prin. Fax 507-3558
Pleasant Grove ES 400/K-5
150 Reagan Rd 30281 770-898-0176
Tracie Copper, prin. Fax 898-0185
Red Oak ES 800/K-5
175 Monarch Village Way 30281 770-389-1464
Dr. Cemond Robinzine, prin. Fax 389-1737
Smith-Barnes ES 300/4-5
147 Tye St 30281 770-474-4066
Dr. Carolyn Flemister-Bell, prin. Fax 474-0039
Stockbridge ES 600/K-3
4617 N Henry Blvd 30281 770-474-8743
Cynthia Jewell, prin. Fax 474-2357
Stockbridge MS 600/6-8
533 Old Conyers Rd 30281 770-474-5710
Julissa Forbes, prin. Fax 507-8406
Woodland ES 700/K-5
830 Moseley Dr 30281 770-506-6391
Christine Anderson, prin. Fax 506-6396
Woodland MS 700/6-8
820 Moseley Dr 30281 770-389-2774
Dr. Joycelyn Jackson, prin. Fax 389-2780

Rockdale County SD
Supt. — See Conyers
Davis MS 900/6-8
3375 E Fairview Rd SW 30281 770-388-5675
Randy Goerner, prin. Fax 388-5676
Lorraine ES 700/K-5
3343 E Fairview Rd SW 30281 770-483-0657
Dr. David Ray, prin. Fax 483-5858

Community Christian S 900/PK-12
2001 Jodeco Rd 30281 678-432-0191
North Henry Academy 100/PK-8
1093 Flat Rock Rd 30281 770-389-1591
Cynthia Temple, prin. Fax 289-6162

Stone Mountain, DeKalb, Pop. 5,717
DeKalb County SD 98,000/PK-12
1701 Mountain Industrial Bl 30083 678-676-1200
Dr. R. Stephen Green, supt. Fax 676-0785
www.dekalbschoolsga.org
Allgood ES 600/PK-5
659 Allgood Rd 30083 678-676-5102
Dr. William Carter, prin. Fax 676-5110
Champion MS 800/6-8
5265 Mimosa Dr 30083 678-875-1502
Antoine Rhodes, prin. Fax 875-1510
Dunaire ES 700/PK-5
651 S Indian Creek Dr 30083 678-676-5502
Obelia Hall, prin. Fax 676-5510
Freedom MS 1,100/6-8
505 S Hairston Rd 30088 678-874-8702
Dr. Marchell Boston, prin. Fax 874-8710
Hambrick ES 600/PK-5
1101 Hambrick Rd 30083 678-676-5602
Dr. Audrey Brooks, prin. Fax 676-5610
Miller ES 500/PK-5
919 Martin Rd 30088 678-676-3302
Mark Bryant, prin. Fax 676-3310
Pine Ridge ES 600/PK-5
750 Pine Ridge Dr 30087 678-676-3402
Annette Maclin, prin. Fax 676-3410
Rowland ES 600/PK-5
1317 S Indian Creek Dr 30083 678-676-6202
Vanessa Jones, prin. Fax 676-6210
Stephenson MS 1,000/6-8
922 Stephenson Rd 30087 678-676-4402
Rasheen Booker, prin. Fax 676-4410
Stone Mill ES 600/PK-5
4900 Sheila Ln 30083 678-676-4602
Dr. Kyia Clark, prin. Fax 676-4610
Stone Mountain ES 600/PK-5
6720 James B Rivers Dr 30083 678-676-4702
Corey Davidson, prin. Fax 676-4710
Stone Mountain MS 1,000/6-8
4301 Sarr Pkwy 30083 678-676-4802
Dr. Vincent Hinton, prin. Fax 676-4810
Woodridge ES 600/PK-5
4120 Cedar Ridge Trl 30083 678-874-0202
Brandy Jermon, prin. Fax 874-0210
Wynbrooke ES 800/PK-5
440 Wicksbury Way 30087 678-676-5002
Jermain Sumler-Faison, prin. Fax 676-5010
Other Schools – See Atlanta, Avondale Estates, Chamblee, Clarkston, Decatur, Doraville, Dunwoody, Ellenwood, Lithonia, Scottdale, Tucker

---

Berean Christian S 100/K-8
2197 Young Rd 30088 678-518-1678
Decatur Adventist Jr. Academy 100/PK-8
2584 Young Rd 30088 770-808-2188
St. Timothy S 50/PK-8
5365 Memorial Dr 30083 404-297-8913
Lora Ingram, head sch Fax 292-3396

Suches, Union
Union County SD
Supt. — See Blairsville
Woody Gap S 100/K-12
2331 State Highway 60 30572 706-747-2401
Carol Knight, prin. Fax 747-1419

Sugar Hill, Gwinnett, Pop. 18,185
Gwinnett County SD
Supt. — See Suwanee
Lanier MS 1,400/6-8
6482 Suwanee Dam Rd 30518 770-945-8419
Todd Hamilton, prin. Fax 271-5108
North Gwinnett MS 2,000/6-8
170 Peachtree Industrial Bl 30518 678-745-2300
Wanda Law, prin. Fax 745-2348
Sugar Hill ES 1,200/K-5
939 Level Creek Rd 30518 770-945-5735
Dr. Taffeta Connery, prin. Fax 932-7421
Sycamore ES 700/K-5
5695 Sycamore Rd 30518 678-714-5770
Crystal Thompson, prin. Fax 714-5790
White Oak ES 800/K-5
6442 Suwanee Dam Rd 30518 678-546-5550
Jean Loethen-Payne, prin. Fax 546-5551

Sugar Hill Christian Academy 300/PK-12
4600 Nelson Brogdon Blvd 30518 678-745-4121
Lyn Cantrell, prin. Fax 745-4205

Summerville, Chattooga, Pop. 4,440
Chattooga County SD 2,800/PK-12
33 Middle School Rd 30747 706-857-3447
Jimmy Lenderman, supt. Fax 857-3440
chattooga.schoolfusion.us
Massey ES 900/PK-5
403 Dot Johnson Way 30747 706-857-7876
Brian Beasley, prin. Fax 857-5898
Summerville MS 400/6-8
200 Middle School Rd 30747 706-857-2444
Kevin Muskett, prin. Fax 857-7769
Other Schools – See Lyerly, Menlo

Surrency, Appling, Pop. 196
Appling County SD
Supt. — See Baxley
Fourth District ES 200/PK-5
13396 Blackshear Hwy 31563 912-367-3250
Scott Kirkland, prin. Fax 367-0992

Suwanee, Gwinnett, Pop. 15,041
Forsyth County SD
Supt. — See Cumming
Johns Creek ES 900/K-5
6205 Old Atlanta Rd 30024 678-965-5041
Alyssa Degliumberto, prin. Fax 475-1725
Riverwatch MS 1,400/6-8
610 James Burgess Rd 30024 678-455-7311
Pamela Bibik, prin. Fax 455-7316
Settles Bridge ES 1,000/K-5
600 James Burgess Rd 30024 770-887-1883
Sarah Von Esh, prin. Fax 887-7383
Sharon ES 900/K-5
3595 Old Atlanta Rd 30024 770-888-7511
Amy Bartlett, prin. Fax 888-7510

Gwinnett County SD 170,400/PK-12
437 Old Peachtree Rd NW 30024 678-301-6000
J. Alvin Wilbanks, supt. Fax 301-6030
www.gwinnett.k12.ga.us
Burnette ES 700/K-5
3221 McGinnis Ferry Rd 30024 678-546-2170
Kim Reed, prin. Fax 546-2515
Level Creek ES 900/K-5
4488 Tench Rd 30024 770-904-7950
Daniel Skelton, prin. Fax 904-7952
Northbrook MS 6-8
1221 Northbrook Pkwy 30024 678-407-7140
Dr. Keith Thompson, prin. Fax 407-7157
Parsons ES 800/K-5
1615 Old Peachtree Rd NW 30024 678-957-3050
Tamara Perkins, prin. Fax 957-3055
Riverside ES 1,100/K-5
5445 Settles Bridge Rd 30024 678-482-1000
Ben Pope, prin. Fax 482-1018
Roberts ES 800/K-5
251 Buford Hwy 30024 678-745-2370
Dr. Dion Jones, prin. Fax 745-2371
Suwanee ES 700/K-5
3875 Smithtown Rd 30024 770-945-5763
Emily Keag, prin. Fax 714-5835
Walnut Grove ES 900/K-5
75 Taylor Rd 30024 770-513-6892
Dr. Dale Pugh, prin. Fax 682-4219
Other Schools – See Auburn, Buford, Dacula, Duluth, Grayson, Hoschton, Lawrenceville, Lilburn, Loganville, Norcross, Peachtree Crnrs, Snellville, Sugar Hill, Tucker

---

Friendship Christian S 200/PK-12
3160 Old Atlanta Rd 30024 678-845-0418
Dr. Rick Johnson Ph.D., head sch Fax 845-0417
Sage S 50/1-7
800 Satellite Blvd NW 30024 678-318-3588
Angela Patton, head sch Fax 945-1371

Swainsboro, Emanuel, Pop. 7,222
Emanuel County SD 4,000/PK-12
PO Box 130 30401 478-237-6674
Dr. Kevin Judy, supt. Fax 419-1102
www.emanuel.k12.ga.us
Emanuel County Early Learning Center PK-PK
308 Tiger Trl 30401 478-237-9593
Maria Daniels, dir. Fax 419-1187
Swainsboro ES 600/3-5
258 Tiger Trl 30401 478-237-7266
Valorie Watkins, prin. Fax 419-1164
Swainsboro MS 600/6-8
200 Tiger Trl 30401 478-237-8047
Dr. Willie Gibson, prin. Fax 419-1148
Swainsboro PS 800/K-2
308 Tiger Trl 30401 478-237-8302
Maribeth Clark, prin. Fax 419-1177
Other Schools – See Twin City

Sylvania, Screven, Pop. 2,925
Screven County SD 2,400/PK-12
382 Halcyondale Rd 30467 912-451-2000
William Bland, supt. Fax 451-2001
www.screven.k12.ga.us
Screven County ES 1,200/PK-5
1333 Frontage Rd E 30467 912-451-2100
Brett Warren, prin. Fax 451-2101
Screven County MS 500/6-8
126 Friendship Rd 30467 912-451-2200
Dr. Bobby Costlow, prin. Fax 451-2201

Sylvester, Worth, Pop. 6,122
Worth County SD 3,400/PK-12
103 Eldridge St 31791 229-776-8600
William Settle, supt. Fax 776-8603
www.worthschools.net
Worth County ES 700/3-5
1906 GA Highway 313 31791 229-776-8605
Dr. Steven Rouse, prin. Fax 776-8607
Worth County MS 800/6-8
1305 N Isabella St 31791 229-776-8620
Tiffany Sevier, prin. Fax 776-8624
Worth County PS 1,000/PK-2
1304 N Isabella St 31791 229-776-8660
Jared Worthy, prin. Fax 776-8665

Talbotton, Talbot, Pop. 965
Talbot County SD 500/PK-12
PO Box 308 31827 706-665-8528
Dr. James Catrett, supt. Fax 665-3620
www.talbot.k12.ga.us/
Central S 500/PK-12
PO Box 308 31827 706-665-8577
Johnathan Taylor, prin. Fax 665-3946

Tallapoosa, Haralson, Pop. 3,111
Haralson County SD 3,600/PK-12
299 Robertson Ave 30176 770-574-2500
Jerry Bell, supt. Fax 574-2225
www.haralson.k12.ga.us
Haralson County MS 800/6-8
2633 Georgia Highway 120 30176 770-646-8600
Dr. Jodi Cash, prin. Fax 646-0108
Tallapoosa PS 500/PK-2
581 Georgia Highway 120 30176 770-574-7444
Jenstie Johns, prin. Fax 574-8932
West Haralson ES 400/3-5
4552 Georgia Highway 100 N 30176 770-574-7060
Dr. Brandi Hurston, prin. Fax 574-7086
Other Schools – See Buchanan

Talmo, Jackson, Pop. 177
Jackson County SD
Supt. — See Jefferson
North Jackson ES 300/PK-5
1880 Old Gainesville Hwy 30575 706-693-2246
Teresa Strickland, prin. Fax 693-4389

Tate, Pickens
Pickens County SD
Supt. — See Jasper
Tate ES 300/K-5
PO Box 268 30177 706-253-1860
Sandy Layman, prin. Fax 253-1865

Taylorsville, Bartow, Pop. 207
Bartow County SD
Supt. — See Cartersville
Taylorsville ES 500/PK-5
1502 Old Alabama Rd 30178 770-606-5867
Dr. Bernadette Dipetta, prin. Fax 606-2056

Temple, Paulding, Pop. 4,145
Carroll County SD
Supt. — See Carrollton
Providence ES 400/PK-5
287 Rainey Rd 30179 770-537-8100
Christi McLendon, prin. Fax 562-8933
Temple ES 500/PK-5
95 Otis St 30179 770-562-3076
Tricia Langford, prin. Fax 562-0135
Temple MS 500/6-8
275 Rainey Rd 30179 770-562-6001
Gail Parmer, prin. Fax 562-6002
Villa Rica MS 500/6-8
614 Tumlin Lake Rd 30179 770-459-0407
Greta Jackson, prin. Fax 459-5496

Paulding County SD
Supt. — See Dallas
Union ES 500/K-5
206 Highway 101 S 30179 770-443-4191
Teresa Benefield, prin. Fax 459-5436

Thomaston, Upson, Pop. 9,037
Thomaston-Upson County SD 4,200/PK-12
205 Civic Center Dr 30286 706-647-9621
Dr. Marguerite Shook, supt. Fax 647-7154
www.upson.k12.ga.us
Upson-Lee ES 600/3-5
334 Knight Trl 30286 706-647-3632
Shad Seymour, prin. Fax 646-9468
Upson-Lee MS 1,100/6-8
101 Holston Dr 30286 706-647-6256
Rhonda Gulley, prin. Fax 647-0011
Upson-Lee Preschool PK-PK
216 E Lee St 30286 706-646-4729
Cristina Cunningham, dir. Fax 646-9456
Upson-Lee PS 1,300/K-2
172 Knight Trl 30286 706-647-7516
Dr. Tracy Wainwright, prin. Fax 646-7806

Westwood Christian Academy 100/PK-12
96 Pickard Rd 30286 706-647-8131

Thomasville, Thomas, Pop. 18,212
Thomas County SD 5,600/PK-12
200 N Pinetree Blvd 31792 229-225-4380
Dr. George Kornegay, supt. Fax 225-5012
www.thomas.k12.ga.us
Cross Creek ES 700/3-4
324 Clark Rd 31757 229-225-3900
Clay Stanaland, prin. Fax 225-3904
Garrison-Pilcher ES 800/1-2
277 Hall Rd 31757 229-225-4387
Sharonda Wilson, prin. Fax 227-2428
Hand-in-Hand PS 700/PK-K
4687 US Highway 84 Byp W 31792 229-225-3908
Jeanna Mayhall, prin. Fax 225-3982
Thomas County MS 1,700/5-8
4681 US Highway 84 Byp W 31792 229-225-4394
Jamie Thompson, prin. Fax 225-4378

Thomasville CSD 3,000/PK-12
404 N Broad St Fl 3 31792 229-225-2600
Dr. Laine Reichert, supt. Fax 226-6997
www.tcitys.org
Harper ES 500/PK-5
520 Fletcher St 31792 229-225-2622
Melvin Hugans, prin. Fax 225-2692
Jerger ES 800/PK-5
1006 S Broad St 31792 229-225-2625
Lawana Rayburn, prin. Fax 225-2676
MacIntyre Park MS 600/6-8
117 Glenwood Dr 31792 229-225-2628
Tina McBride, prin. Fax 225-3502
Scott ES 400/PK-5
100 N Hansell St 31792 229-225-2631
Brian Beaty, prin. Fax 225-2672

Brookwood S 500/PK-12
301 Cardinal Ridge Rd 31792 229-226-0070
Dr. Randolph Watts, hdmstr. Fax 227-0326

Thomasville Christian S 100/PK-5
1040 Glenwood Dr 31792 229-227-1515
Melissa Clark, admin. Fax 226-7744

Thomson, McDuffie, Pop. 6,688
McDuffie County SD 4,300/PK-12
716 Lee St 30824 706-986-4000
Dr. Mychele Rhodes, supt. Fax 986-4001
www.mcduffie.k12.ga.us
Maxwell ES 700/PK-1
520 Mount Pleasant Rd 30824 706-986-4800
Donna Bennett, prin. Fax 986-4801
Norris ES 400/4-5
1861 Harrison Rd 30824 706-986-4400
Shantell Crockett, prin. Fax 986-4401
Thomson ES 500/2-3
409 Guill St 30824 706-986-4700
Caroline Sowell, prin. Fax 986-4701
Thomson-McDuffie MS 1,000/6-8
1191 White Oak Rd 30824 706-986-4300
Anita Cummings, prin. Fax 986-4301
Other Schools – See Dearing

Tifton, Tift, Pop. 16,154
Tift County SD 7,500/PK-12
PO Box 389 31793 229-387-2400
Patrick Atwater, supt. Fax 386-1020
www.tiftschools.com
Bailey PS 400/K-3
1430 Newton Dr 31794 229-387-2415
Dr. Jamie Dawson, prin. Fax 386-1046
Clark PS 900/K-3
1464 Carpenter Rd S 31793 229-387-2410
Stephanie Morrow, prin. Fax 386-1044
Eighth Street MS 1,200/7-8
700 8th St W 31794 229-387-2445
Dr. Chad Stone, prin. Fax 386-1036
Lastinger PS 500/K-3
1210 Lake Dr 31794 229-387-2420
Richard Fisher, prin. Fax 386-1048
Northside PS 500/K-3
1815 Chestnut Ave 31794 229-387-2425
Kelly Pearson, prin. Fax 386-1049
Reddick ES 600/6-6
404 Martin Luther King Dr 31794 229-387-2435
Jim Torell, prin. Fax 386-1041
Spencer ES 500/4-5
65 Tifton Eldorado Rd 31794 229-387-2430
Tammy Corbin, prin. Fax 386-1040
Tift County Pre K Center 300/PK-PK
506 12th St W 31794 229-387-2455
Wanda Veazey, dir. Fax 386-1051
Wilson ES 500/4-5
510 17th St W 31794 229-387-2440
Jason Clark, prin. Fax 386-1043
Other Schools – See Omega

Tiger, Rabun, Pop. 402
Rabun County SD 2,300/PK-12
963 Tiger Connector 30576 706-212-4350
Melissa Williams, supt. Fax 782-6224
www.rabuncountyschools.org
Rabun County ES 700/3-6
1115 E Boggs Mountain Rd 30576 706-782-3116
Lisa Patterson, prin. Fax 782-2828
Rabun County MS 400/7-8
95 Wildcat Pride Way 30576 706-782-5470
Vicki Tyler, prin. Fax 782-4520
Rabun County PS 600/PK-2
801 E Boggs Mountain Rd 30576 706-782-3831
Kelly McKay, prin. Fax 782-0069

Toccoa, Stephens, Pop. 8,279
Stephens County SD 2,500/PK-12
191 Big A School Rd 30577 706-886-9415
Bryan Dorsey, supt. Fax 886-3882
www.stephens.k12.ga.us
Liberty ES 200/1-2
222 Old Liberty Hill Rd 30577 706-886-3934
Jason Swiney, prin. Fax 886-9983
Stephens County 5th Grade Academy 5-5
1315 Rose Ln 30577 706-886-2880
Sheila Pressley, prin. Fax 886-2882
Stephens County MS 900/5-8
1315 Rose Ln 30577 706-886-2880
Michael Shawler, prin. Fax 886-2882
Toccoa ES 100/3-4
304 N Pond St 30577 706-886-3194
Dr. Chris Colwell, prin. Fax 282-0559
Other Schools – See Eastanollee

Trenton, Dade, Pop. 2,264
Dade County SD 2,200/PK-12
PO Box 188 30752 706-657-4361
Dr. Jan Harris, supt. Fax 657-4572
www.dadecountyschools.org
Dade ES 800/PK-5
306 Wolverine Dr 30752 706-657-8253
Tracy Blevins, prin. Fax 657-5232
Dade MS 500/6-8
250 Pace Dr 30752 706-657-6491
Dr. Sandra Spivoy, prin. Fax 657-3055
Davis ES 300/PK-5
5491 Highway 301 30752 706-657-6300
Josh Ingle, prin. Fax 657-7932

Trion, Chattooga, Pop. 1,797
Trion CSD 1,400/PK-12
239 Simmons St 30753 706-734-2363
Dr. Phil Williams, supt. Fax 734-3397
www.trionschools.org/
Trion ES 700/PK-5
919 Allgood St Ste 1 30753 706-734-2991
Christopher Byrnes, prin. Fax 734-7549
Trion MS 300/6-8
919 Allgood St Ste 2 30753 706-734-7433
Scott Crabbe, prin. Fax 734-7517

Tucker, DeKalb, Pop. 26,961
DeKalb County SD
Supt. — See Stone Mountain
Brockett ES 400/PK-5
1855 Brockett Rd 30084 678-874-2602
Vanessa Bines-Truitt, prin. Fax 874-2610
Idlewood ES 900/PK-5
1484 Idlewood Rd 30084 678-874-3202
Rosemary Malone, prin. Fax 874-3210
Livsey ES 400/PK-5
4137 Livsey Rd 30084 678-874-3302
Dr. Jamie Wilson, prin. Fax 874-3310
Midvale ES 500/PK-5
3836 Midvale Rd 30084 678-874-3402
Deborah Satterfield, prin. Fax 874-3410
Tucker MS 1,200/6-8
2160 Idlewood Rd 30084 678-875-0902
Dr. Kathy Cunningham, prin. Fax 875-0910

Gwinnett County SD
Supt. — See Suwanee
Nesbit ES 2,000/K-5
6575 Cherokee Dr 30084 770-414-2740
Dr. Marketa Myers, prin. Fax 414-2757

Tunnel Hill, Whitfield, Pop. 854
Catoosa County SD
Supt. — See Ringgold
Tiger Creek ES 500/PK-5
134 Rhea McClanahan Dr 30755 706-935-9890
David Beard, prin. Fax 965-8906

Whitfield County SD
Supt. — See Dalton
Tunnel Hill ES 300/K-5
203 E School St 30755 706-673-4550
Connie Kopcsak, prin. Fax 673-4956

Twin City, Emanuel, Pop. 1,730
Emanuel County SD
Supt. — See Swainsboro
Twin City ES 600/PK-5
PO Box 280 30471 478-763-2253
Dr. Tremayne Hall, prin. Fax 237-3831

Tyrone, Fayette, Pop. 6,701
Fayette County SD
Supt. — See Fayetteville
Burch ES 500/PK-5
330 Jenkins Rd 30290 770-969-2820
Lisa Howe, prin. Fax 969-2824
Flat Rock MS 800/6-8
325 Jenkins Rd 30290 770-969-2830
Jade Bolton, prin. Fax 969-2835

Our Lady of Victory S 200/K-8
211 Kirkley Rd 30290 770-306-9026
George Wilkerson, prin. Fax 306-0323

Union City, Fulton, Pop. 19,078
Fulton County SD
Supt. — See Atlanta
Gullatt ES 500/PK-5
6110 Dodson Rd 30291 470-254-3425
Felipe Jackson, prin. Fax 254-3582
Liberty Point ES 700/PK-5
9000 Highpoint Rd 30291 470-254-3510
James Payne, prin. Fax 254-3516
Oakley ES 800/K-5
7220 Oakley Ter 30291 470-254-4050
Latrina Coxton, prin. Fax 254-4057

Valdosta, Lowndes, Pop. 53,506
Lowndes County SD 10,900/PK-12
1592 Norman Dr 31601 229-245-2250
Wes Taylor, supt. Fax 245-2255
www.lowndes.k12.ga.us
Clyattville ES 700/PK-5
5386 Madison Hwy 31601 229-316-8620
Tenry Berry, prin. Fax 316-8608
Dewar ES 700/PK-5
3539 Mount Zion Church Rd 31605 229-219-1370
Dr. Katie Chappuis, prin. Fax 219-1376
Lowndes MS 900/6-8
2379 Copeland Rd 31601 229-245-2280
Bill Haskin, prin. Fax 245-2470
Moulton-Branch ES 600/PK-5
5725 Inner Perimeter Rd 31601 229-245-2294
Debra Brantley, prin. Fax 259-5072
Pine Grove ES 800/PK-5
4175 River Rd 31605 229-245-2297
Mickie Jones, prin. Fax 259-5070
Pine Grove MS 700/6-8
4159 River Rd 31605 229-219-3234
Ivy Smith, prin. Fax 219-3233
Westside ES 900/PK-5
2470 James Rd 31601 229-245-2289
Beth Lind, prin. Fax 259-5068
Other Schools – See Hahira, Lake Park

Valdosta CSD 8,200/PK-12
PO Box 5407 31603 229-333-8500
Dr. William Todd Cason, supt. Fax 247-7757
www.gocats.org
Lomax ES 600/PK-5
PO Box 5407 31603 229-333-8520
Dr. LaConya McCrae, prin. Fax 671-1640
Mahone ES 1,100/PK-5
PO Box 5407 31603 229-333-8530
Gary Glover, prin. Fax 245-5652
Mason ES 900/PK-5
PO Box 5407 31603 229-333-8525
Kevin Daw, prin. Fax 245-5650
Newbern MS 800/6-8
PO Box 5407 31603 229-333-8566
Rick Thomas, prin. Fax 245-5655
Nunn ES 1,300/PK-5
PO Box 5407 31603 229-333-8575
Francisco Diaz, prin. Fax 245-5653
Pinevale ES 400/PK-5
PO Box 5407 31603 229-333-8535
Royce Thomas, prin. Fax 245-5651
Valdosta MS 900/6-8
PO Box 5407 31603 229-333-8555
Beth DeLoach, prin. Fax 245-5656

Crossroads Baptist S 200/PK-5
3001 Country Club Dr 31602 229-241-1430
Karen Barker, prin. Fax 242-7627
Georgia Christian S 200/PK-12
4359 Dasher Rd 31601 229-559-5131
Dr. Brad Lawson, pres. Fax 559-7401
Highland Christian Academy 200/K-12
4023 Pine Grove Rd 31605 229-245-8111
Ron Kooy, prin. Fax 245-8110
Open Bible Christian S 300/PK-12
3992 N Oak Street Ext 31605 229-244-6694
St. John the Evangelist S 200/K-8
800 Gornto Rd 31602 229-244-2556
Dr. Barbara Stanley, prin. Fax 244-0865
Valdosta Christian Academy K-8
PO Box 4894 31604 229-469-5090

Vidalia, Toombs, Pop. 10,364
Vidalia CSD 2,700/PK-12
301 Adams St 30474 912-537-3088
Dr. J. Garrett Wilcox, supt. Fax 538-0938
www.vidaliacity.schoolinsites.com
Dickerson PS 600/PK-1
800 North St E 30474 912-537-3421
Scott Stephens, prin. Fax 537-6282
Meadows ES 800/2-5
205 Waters Dr 30474 912-537-4755
Tammy McFadden, prin. Fax 537-1160
Trippe MS 600/6-8
2200 McIntosh St 30474 912-537-3813
Sandy Reid, prin. Fax 537-3223

Vidalia Heritage Academy 100/PK-12
101 E 1st St 30474 912-537-6679
Jeff McCormick, hdmstr. Fax 226-3495

Vienna, Dooly, Pop. 3,989
Dooly County SD 1,400/PK-12
202 E Cotton St 31092 229-268-4761
Celeta Thomas, supt. Fax 268-6148
www.dooly.k12.ga.us
Other Schools – See Pinehurst

Villa Rica, Carroll, Pop. 13,578
Carroll County SD
Supt. — See Carrollton
Bay Springs MS 800/6-8
122 Bay Springs Rd 30180 770-459-2098
Marti Stephens, prin. Fax 459-2097
Glanton-Hindsman ES 700/PK-5
118 Glanton St 30180 770-459-4491
Beth Chandler, prin. Fax 459-9716
Ithica ES 600/PK-5
75 Whitworth Rd 30180 678-840-5101
Brad Corbett, prin. Fax 840-5105
Villa Rica ES 500/PK-5
314 Peachtree St 30180 770-459-5762
Mitch Springer, prin. Fax 459-2041

Douglas County SD
Supt. — See Douglasville
Mirror Lake ES 500/K-5
2613 Tyson Rd 30180 770-651-4300
Chandell Johnson, prin. Fax 947-3842

Paulding County SD
Supt. — See Dallas
New Georgia ES 300/K-5
5800 Mulberry Rock Rd 30180 770-445-3597
Sonja Nelson, prin. Fax 443-2044

Wadley, Jefferson, Pop. 2,056
Jefferson County SD
Supt. — See Louisville
Carver ES 300/PK-5
104 Bedingfield St 30477 478-252-5762
Tiffany Pitts, prin. Fax 252-0577

Waleska, Cherokee, Pop. 623
Cherokee County SD
Supt. — See Canton
Moore ES 500/PK-5
1375 Puckett Rd 30183 770-704-1212
Jan Adamson, prin. Fax 479-4383

Warner Robins, Houston, Pop. 64,686
Houston County SD
Supt. — See Perry
Feagin Mill MS 800/6-8
1200 Feagin Mill Rd 31088 478-953-0430
Dr. Jesse Davis, prin. Fax 953-0438
Huntington MS 800/6-8
206 Wellborn Rd 31088 478-542-2240
Dr. Gwen Taylor, prin. Fax 542-2247
Lake Joy ES 600/3-5
985 Lake Joy Rd 31088 478-971-2712
Tami Godman, prin. Fax 971-2710
Lake Joy PS 600/PK-2
995 Lake Joy Rd 31088 478-953-0465
Dr. April Greene, prin. Fax 953-0473
Lindsey ES 400/PK-5
81 Tabor Dr 31093 478-929-7818
Dr. Anisa Baker-Busby, prin. Fax 542-2296
Miller ES 600/PK-5
101 Pine Valley Dr 31088 478-929-7814
Elizabeth Johnson, prin. Fax 929-7762
Northside ES 500/PK-5
305 Sullivan Rd 31093 478-929-7816
David Sams, prin. Fax 329-2233
Northside MS 700/6-8
500 Johnson Rd 31093 478-929-7845
Jan Melnick, prin. Fax 929-7124
Parkwood ES 700/PK-5
503 Parkwood Dr 31093 478-929-7822
Dr. Janet Sorrell, prin. Fax 542-2273
Perdue ES 600/3-5
115 Sutherlin Dr 31088 478-988-6350
Andy Payne, prin. Fax 988-6109
Perdue PS 700/PK-2
150 Bear Country Blvd 31088 478-218-7500
Leslie Shultz, prin. Fax 218-7508
Quail Run ES 700/PK-5
250 Smithville Church Rd 31088 478-953-0415
Dr. Cheryl Thomas, prin. Fax 953-0425
Russell ES 700/PK-5
101 Patriot Way 31088 478-929-7830
William Wilson, prin. Fax 542-2272
Shirley Hills ES 600/PK-5
300 Mary Ln 31088 478-929-7824
Dr. Traci Jackson, prin. Fax 929-7121
Stephens ES 200/3-5
420 Pearl Stephens Way 31098 478-929-7895
Gloria Smith, prin. Fax 929-7109
Warner Robins MS 800/6-8
425 Mary Ln 31088 478-929-7832
Brett Wallace, prin. Fax 929-7834
Watson PS 300/PK-2
61 Martin Luther King Jr 31088 478-929-6360
Alicia Conner, prin. Fax 929-6366
Westside ES 600/PK-5
201 N Pleasant Hill Rd 31093 478-929-7820
Dr. Cynthia Hammond, prin. Fax 929-7122

Sacred Heart Catholic S 200/K-8
300 S Davis Dr 31088 478-923-9668
Allan Chromy, prin. Fax 923-5822

Warrenton, Warren, Pop. 1,925
Warren County SD 700/PK-12
PO Box 228 30828 706-465-3383
Carole Carey, supt. Fax 465-9141
www.warren.k12.ga.us/
Freeman ES 400/PK-5
1253 Atlanta Hwy 30828 706-465-3342
Katherine Hinesley, prin. Fax 465-9256
Warren County MS 100/6-8
1253 Atlanta Hwy 30828 706-465-3742
Shauna Andrews, prin. Fax 465-0901

Briarwood Academy 300/PK-12
4859 Thomson Hwy 30828 706-595-5641

Washington, Wilkes, Pop. 4,057
Wilkes County SD 1,700/PK-12
313 N Alexander Ave Ste A 30673 706-678-2718
Dr. Rosemary Caddell, supt. Fax 678-3799
www.wilkes.k12.ga.us
Washington-Wilkes ES 400/PK-PK, 4-
109 East St 30673 706-678-7124
Angela McGill, prin. Fax 678-7826
Washington-Wilkes MS 400/6-8
1180 Tignall Rd 30673 706-678-7131
Deleki Lee, prin. Fax 678-3546
Washington-Wilkes PS 500/K-3
910 E Robert Toombs Ave 30673 706-678-2633
Janet Pharr, prin. Fax 678-2666

Watkinsville, Oconee, Pop. 2,786
Oconee County SD 6,700/K-12
PO Box 146 30677 706-769-5130
Dr. Jason Branch, supt. Fax 769-3500
www.oconeeschools.org/
Colham Ferry ES 500/K-5
191 Colham Ferry Rd 30677 706-769-7764
Tony McCullers, prin. Fax 769-3538
Oconee County ES 500/3-5
2230 Hog Mountain Rd 30677 706-769-7791
Ashley Templeton, prin. Fax 769-3541
Oconee County MS 800/6-8
1101 Mars Hill Rd 30677 706-769-3575
Keith Carter, prin. Fax 310-2001
Oconee County PS 400/K-2
2290 Hog Mountain Rd 30677 706-769-7941
Jennifer Adams, prin. Fax 769-3553
Other Schools – See Bishop, Bogart

Westminster Christian Academy 300/PK-12
PO Box 388 30677 706-769-9372

Waycross, Ware, Pop. 14,397
Ware County SD 5,700/PK-12
1301 Bailey St 31501 912-283-8656
Jim LeBrun, supt. Fax 283-8698
www.ware.k12.ga.us
Center ES 500/K-5
2114 Dorothy St 31501 912-287-2366
Tyler Bennett, prin. Fax 287-2361
DAFFODIL Preschool PK-PK
1321 Buchannon St 31501 912-287-2311
Dr. Linda Houseal, coord. Fax 287-2204
Memorial Drive ES 400/K-5
2580 Ambrose St 31503 912-287-2327
Dr. Wendy Good, prin. Fax 287-2326
Ruskin ES 400/K-5
3550 Valdosta Hwy 31503 912-287-2325
Donna Solomon, prin. Fax 287-2356
Wacona ES 700/K-5
3101 State St 31503 912-287-2362
John Chancey, prin. Fax 284-2057
Ware County MS 700/6-8
2301 Cherokee St 31503 912-287-2341
Dr. Darlene Tanner, prin. Fax 287-2353
Waresboro ES 400/K-5
3379 W Church St 31503 912-287-2393
Jenny Barnes, prin. Fax 287-2395
Waycross MS 600/6-8
700 Central Ave 31501 912-287-2333
David Hitt, prin. Fax 287-2352

Williams Heights ES 500/K-5
705 Dewey St 31501 912-287-2399
Staci Smallwood, prin. Fax 287-2350

Southside Christian S 100/PK-12
3439 Knight Ave 31503 912-285-5438
Rev. Aaron Smith, supt. Fax 285-2565

Waynesboro, Burke, Pop. 5,700
Burke County SD 4,400/PK-12
789 Burke Veterans Pkwy 30830 706-554-5101
Rudy Falana, supt. Fax 554-8051
www.burke.k12.ga.us
Blakeney ES 800/3-5
100 Olympic Dr 30830 706-554-2265
Earl Ishmal, prin. Fax 554-8075
Burke County MS 1,000/6-8
356 Southside Dr 30830 706-554-3532
Dr. Mona Reynolds, prin. Fax 554-8063
Waynesboro PS 1,100/PK-2
352 Southside Dr 30830 706-554-5125
Sam Adkins, prin. Fax 554-8064
Other Schools – See Sardis

Burke Academy 400/PK-12
PO Box 787 30830 706-554-4479
Gregg Bunn, hdmstr. Fax 554-7582
Faith Christian Academy 100/PK-12
726 GA Highway 24 S 30830 706-554-1577
Amy Grubb, prin. Fax 554-2566

Waynesville, Brantley
Brantley County SD
Supt. — See Nahunta
Atkinson ES 300/4-6
4327 Highway 110 E 31566 912-778-6098
Dr. Lori Anne Lee, prin. Fax 778-6099
Waynesville ES 400/PK-3
5726 Old Waynesville Rd 31566 912-778-3068
Dr. Adrian Thompson, prin. Fax 778-3071

West Green, Coffee
Coffee County SD
Supt. — See Douglas
West Green ES 400/PK-5
106 School Circle Rd 31567 912-384-2032
Anne Peterson, prin. Fax 383-4166

West Point, Troup, Pop. 3,435
Troup County SD
Supt. — See LaGrange
West Point ES 400/PK-5
1701 E 12th St 31833 706-812-7973
Jan Franks, prin. Fax 812-1250

Whigham, Grady, Pop. 470
Grady County SD
Supt. — See Cairo
Whigham ES 500/PK-8
211 W Broad Ave, 229-762-4167
Mark Willis, prin. Fax 762-4477

White, Bartow, Pop. 658
Bartow County SD
Supt. — See Cartersville
White ES 600/PK-5
505 Colonel Way NE 30184 770-606-5869
Amy Heater, prin. Fax 606-5177

Whitesburg, Carroll, Pop. 584
Carroll County SD
Supt. — See Carrollton
Whitesburg ES 400/PK-5
868 Main St 30185 770-832-3875
Dr. Marissa Ogando, prin. Fax 214-8824

Willacoochee, Atkinson, Pop. 1,376
Atkinson County SD
Supt. — See Pearson
Willacoochee ES 200/PK-5
430 Vickers St S 31650 912-534-5302
Susan Garrity, prin. Fax 534-5337

Williamson, Pike, Pop. 334

CrossPointe Christian Academy 100/PK-12
5224 Hollonville Rd 30292 770-412-6000

Winder, Barrow, Pop. 13,757
Barrow County SD 12,900/PK-12
179 W Athens St 30680 770-867-4527
Dr. Chris McMichael, supt. Fax 867-4540
www.barrow.k12.ga.us
County Line ES 900/PK-5
334 Rockwell Church Rd NW 30680 770-867-2902
Shawanna Stevens, prin. Fax 867-8942
Haymon-Morris MS 700/6-8
1008 Haymon Morris Rd 30680 678-963-0602
Dr. James Bowen, prin. Fax 867-1854
Holsenbeck ES 1,000/PK-5
445 Holsenbeck School Rd 30680 770-307-1540
Jackie Robinson, prin. Fax 307-1255
Kennedy ES 800/PK-5
200 Matthews School Rd 30680 770-867-3182
Ryan Butcher, prin. Fax 307-4532
Russell MS 800/6-8
364 W Candler St 30680 770-867-8181
Paul DeFoor, prin. Fax 868-1215
Westside MS 700/6-8
240 Matthews School Rd 30680 770-307-2972
Dr. Brad Bowling, prin. Fax 307-2976
Winder ES PK-5
194 McNeal Rd NW 30680 678-425-2914
Jerry Stapleton, prin. Fax 425-2915
Yargo ES 800/PK-5
1000 Haymon Morris Rd 30680 770-867-1147
Diane Bresson, prin. Fax 867-1214
Other Schools – See Auburn, Bethlehem, Statham

Winston, Douglas
Douglas County SD
Supt. — See Douglasville
Mason Creek ES 500/K-5
3400 Johnston Rd 30187 770-651-4900
Kathleen French, prin. Fax 920-4282
Mason Creek MS 800/6-8
7777 Mason Creek Rd 30187 770-651-2500
Eric Collins, prin. Fax 920-4278
Winston ES 400/PK-5
7465 Highway 78 30187 770-651-4700
Dawn Taylor, prin. Fax 651-4703

Winterville, Clarke, Pop. 1,116
Clarke County SD
Supt. — See Athens
Winterville ES 400/PK-5
305 Cherokee Rd 30683 706-357-5222
Donna Elder, prin. Fax 357-5223

Woodbine, Camden, Pop. 1,384
Camden County SD
Supt. — See Kingsland
Gross ES 500/PK-5
277 Roberts Path 31569 912-576-4800
Dr. Bruce Wilkerson, prin. Fax 510-6538
Woodbine ES 400/PK-5
495 Broadwood Dr 31569 912-576-5245
Maura Fegel, prin. Fax 576-3778

Woodbury, Meriwether, Pop. 960
Meriwether County SD
Supt. — See Greenville
Washington ES 400/PK-5
18425 Main St 30293 706-553-3951
Lashanda Acres, prin. Fax 553-2477

Flint River Academy 300/PK-12
PO Box 247 30293 706-553-2541

Woodstock, Cherokee, Pop. 23,245
Cherokee County SD
Supt. — See Canton
Arnold Mill ES 800/K-5
710 Arnold Mill Rd 30188 770-721-6470
Dan Fuller, prin.
Bascomb ES 1,100/K-5
1335 Wyngate Pkwy 30189 770-721-6630
Kathleen Chandler, prin.
Booth MS 1,600/6-8
6550 Putnam Ford Dr 30189 770-721-5500
Michael Manzella, prin.
Boston ES 600/K-5
105 Othello Dr 30189 770-704-1400
Izell McGruder, prin. Fax 924-0392
Carmel ES 1,200/K-5
2275 Bascomb Carmel Rd 30189 770-704-1184
Paula Crumbley, prin.
Johnston ES 600/PK-5
2031 E Cherokee Dr 30188 770-721-8461
Amy Graham, prin. Fax 591-0109
Little River ES 1,400/PK-5
3170 Trickum Rd 30188 770-721-5940
Karen Carl, prin.
Mill Creek MS 1,200/6-8
442 Arnold Mill Rd 30188 770-721-6400
Dr. Kerry Martin, prin. Fax 926-5439
Mountain Road ES 600/K-6
615 Mountain Rd 30188 770-721-8520
Melinda Roulier, prin.
Woodstock ES 1,100/K-5
230 Rope Mill Rd 30188 770-704-1320
Kim Montalbano, prin. Fax 924-6332
Woodstock MS 1,100/6-8
2000 Towne Lake Hills S Dr 30189 770-721-3060
David Childress, prin. Fax 591-8054

Cherokee Christian S 400/K-12
3075 Trickum Rd 30188 678-494-5464
Michael Lee, supt. Fax 592-4881
Lyndon Academy 200/K-12
485 Toonigh Rd 30188 770-926-0166

Wrens, Jefferson, Pop. 2,160
Jefferson County SD
Supt. — See Louisville
Wrens ES 600/PK-5
1711 Highway 17 N 30833 706-547-2063
Dr. Sharon Dye, prin. Fax 547-0209
Wrens MS 300/6-8
101 Griffin St 30833 706-547-6580
Julia Wells, prin. Fax 547-6224

Wrightsville, Johnson, Pop. 2,174
Johnson County SD 1,100/PK-12
PO Box 110 31096 478-864-3302
Eddie Morris, supt. Fax 864-4053
www.johnson.k12.ga.us
Johnson County ES 500/PK-5
2160 W Elm St 31096 478-864-3446
Beth Martin, prin. Fax 864-4056
Johnson County MS 300/6-8
150 Hershel Walker Dr 31096 478-864-2222
Elaine Merritt, prin. Fax 864-4054

Zebulon, Pike, Pop. 1,154
Pike County SD 3,400/PK-12
PO Box 386 30295 770-567-8489
Dr. Michael Duncan, supt. Fax 567-8349
www.pike.k12.ga.us/
Pike County ES 800/3-5
607 Pirate Dr 30295 770-567-4444
Melissa Smith, prin. Fax 567-0544
Pike County MS 800/6-8
406 Hughley Rd 30295 770-567-3353
Michael Maddox, prin. Fax 567-5054
Pike County PS 700/PK-2
7218 Highway 19 S 30295 770-567-8443
Holly Harvil, prin. Fax 567-1636

HAWAII

HAWAII DEPARTMENT OF EDUCATION
PO Box 2360, Honolulu 96804-2360
Telephone 808-586-3230
Fax 808-586-3234
Website doe.k12.hi.us

Superintendent of Education   Dr. Christina Kishimoto

HAWAII BOARD OF EDUCATION
PO Box 2360, Honolulu 96804-2360

Chairperson   Lance Mizumoto

PUBLIC, PRIVATE AND CATHOLIC ELEMENTARY SCHOOLS

Aiea, Honolulu, Pop. 7,258
Hawaii SD
Supt. — See Honolulu
Aiea ES 400/PK-6
99-370 Moanalua Rd 96701 808-483-7200
James Kau, prin. Fax 483-7201
Aiea IS 600/7-8
99-600 Kulawea St 96701 808-483-7230
Sandra Yoshimi, prin. Fax 483-7235
Pearl Ridge ES 600/K-6
98-940 Moanalua Rd 96701 808-305-9300
Blaine Takeguchi, prin. Fax 483-7255
Scott ES 500/PK-6
98-1230 Moanalua Rd 96701 808-483-7220
Sandra Watanabe, prin. Fax 483-7223
Waimalu ES 500/PK-6
98-825 Moanalua Rd 96701 808-307-4500
Glen Iwamoto, prin. Fax 483-7213
Webling ES 500/PK-6
99-370 Paihi St 96701 808-483-7240
Chad Matsuda, prin. Fax 483-7242

Calvary Chapel Christian S 100/PK-12
98-1016 Komo Mai Dr 96701 808-524-0846
Rev. Ed Arcalas, dir. Fax 275-5193
Our Savior Lutheran S 200/PK-8
98-1098 Moanalua Rd 96701 808-488-0000
George Evensen, prin. Fax 488-4515
St. Elizabeth S 200/K-8
99-310 Moanalua Rd 96701 808-488-5322
Sr. Bernarda Sindol, prin. Fax 486-0856

Captain Cook, Hawaii, Pop. 2,270
Hawaii SD
Supt. — See Honolulu
Honaunau ES 200/PK-5
83-5360 Mamalahoa Hwy 96704 808-328-2727
Noreen Kunitomo, prin. Fax 328-2729
Ho'okena ES 100/PK-5
86-4355 Mamalahoa Hwy 96704 808-328-2710
Nancy Jadallah, prin. Fax 328-2712

Kona Adventist S 50/K-8
PO Box 739 96704 808-323-2788

Eleele, Kauai, Pop. 1,815
Hawaii SD
Supt. — See Honolulu
Ele'ele ES 500/PK-5
4750 Uliuli Rd 96705 808-335-2111
Paul Zina, prin. Fax 335-8415

Ewa Beach, Honolulu, Pop. 10,071
Hawaii SD
Supt. — See Honolulu
Ewa Beach ES 800/PK-6
91-740 Papipi Rd 96706 808-689-1271
Sherry Kobayashi, prin. Fax 689-1275
Ewa ES 1,100/PK-6
91-1280 Renton Rd 96706 808-681-8202
Stanley Tamashiro, prin. Fax 681-8206
Ewa Makai MS 800/7-8
91-6291 Kapolei Pkwy 96706 808-687-9500
Kim Sanders, prin. Fax 685-2052
Holomua ES 1,400/PK-6
91-1561 Keaunui Dr 96706 808-685-9100
Gary Yasui, prin. Fax 685-9191
Ilima IS 900/7-8
91-884 Fort Weaver Rd 96706 808-687-9300
Christopher Bonilla, prin. Fax 689-1258
Iroquois Point ES 800/K-6
5553 Cormorant Ave 96706 808-499-6500
Ofelia Reed, prin. Fax 499-6508
Kaimiloa ES 700/PK-6
91-1028 Kaunolu St 96706 808-689-1280
Debra Hatada, prin. Fax 689-1284
Keone'ula ES 900/K-6
91-970 Kaileolea Dr 96706 808-689-1380
Paul Taga, prin. Fax 689-1395
Pohakea ES 600/PK-6
91-750 Fort Weaver Rd 96706 808-307-2000
Judith Wong, prin. Fax 689-1293

Friendship Christian S 300/PK-12
91-1207 Renton Rd 96706 808-681-8838
Our Lady of Perpetual Help S 200/K-8
91-1010 North Rd 96706 808-689-0474
Sr. M. Davilyn AhChick, prin. Fax 689-4847

Haiku, Maui, Pop. 4,509
Hawaii SD
Supt. — See Honolulu
Ha'iku ES 500/K-5
105 Pauwela Rd 96708 808-575-3000
Desiree Sides, prin. Fax 575-3003

Haleiwa, Honolulu, Pop. 2,653
Hawaii SD
Supt. — See Honolulu
Hale'iwa ES 200/PK-6
66-505 Haleiwa Rd 96712 808-637-8237
Malaea Wetzel, prin. Fax 637-8240
Sunset Beach ES 500/K-6
59-360 Kamehameha Hwy 96712 808-638-8777
Anela Pia, prin. Fax 638-8789

Hana, Maui, Pop. 446
Hawaii SD
Supt. — See Honolulu
Hana S 300/K-12
PO Box 128 96713 808-248-4815
Richard Paul, prin. Fax 248-4819

Hanalei, Kauai, Pop. 358
Hawaii SD
Supt. — See Honolulu
Hanalei ES 300/PK-6
5-5415 Kuhio Highway 96714 808-826-4300
Taharaa Stein, prin. Fax 826-4302

Hauula, Honolulu, Pop. 1,320
Hawaii SD
Supt. — See Honolulu
Hau'ula ES 300/K-6
54-046 Kamehameha Hwy 96717 808-293-8925
Uilani Kaitoku, prin. Fax 293-8927

Asia Pacific International S 50/K-12
54-230 Kamehameha Hwy 96717 808-670-1900
Euysung Kim Ph.D., dir. Fax 670-1911

Hawi, Hawaii, Pop. 608

Kohala Mission S 50/K-8
PO Box 99 96719 808-889-5646

Hilo, Hawaii, Pop. 26,125
Hawaii SD
Supt. — See Honolulu
DeSilva ES 400/PK-6
278 Ainako Ave 96720 808-974-4855
Dennis O'Brien, prin. Fax 974-4858
Ha'aheo ES 200/K-6
121 Haaheo Rd 96720 808-974-4111
Jennifer Sueoka, prin. Fax 974-4112
Hilo IS 500/7-8
587 Waianuenue Ave 96720 808-974-4955
Heather Dansdill, prin. Fax 974-6184
Hilo Union ES 500/PK-6
506 Waianuenue Ave 96720 808-933-0900
Bryan Arbles, prin. Fax 933-0905
Kapi'olani ES 400/PK-6
966 Kilauea Ave 96720 808-974-4160
Gregg Yonemori, prin. Fax 974-4161
Ka'umana ES 300/K-6
1710 Kaumana Dr 96720 808-974-4190
Ray Mizuba, prin. Fax 974-4197
Keaukaha ES 400/K-6
240 Desha Ave 96720 808-974-4181
Stacey Bello, prin. Fax 974-4868
Waiakea ES 900/PK-5
180 W Puainako St 96720 808-981-7215
Ken Watanabe, prin. Fax 981-7218
Waiakea IS 900/6-8
200 W Puainako St 96720 808-981-7231
Lisa Souza, prin. Fax 981-7237
Waiakeawaena ES 700/K-5
2420 Kilauea Ave 96720 808-981-7200
Kasie Kaleohano, prin. Fax 981-7205

Haili Christian S 200/PK-8
190 Ululani St 96720 808-961-5026
Kim McCarty, admin. Fax 933-1981
Mauna Loa S 50/K-8
172 Kapiolani St 96720 808-935-1545
Joey Freitas, prin. Fax 203-6942
St. Joseph ES - Hilo 200/PK-6
999 Ululani St 96720 808-935-4935
Dr. Llewellyn Young Ed.D., admin. Fax 935-6894
St. Joseph S 100/PK-12
1000 Ululani St 96720 808-935-4935
Llewellyn Young Ed.D., prin. Fax 935-6894

Holualoa, Hawaii, Pop. 6,646
Hawaii SD
Supt. — See Honolulu
Holualoa ES 500/K-5
76-5957 Mamalahoa Hwy 96725 808-322-4800
Glenn Gray, prin. Fax 322-4801

Honokaa, Hawaii, Pop. 1,529
Hawaii SD
Supt. — See Honolulu
Honoka'a ES 400/K-6
45-534 Pakalana St 96727 808-775-8820
Rory Souza, prin. Fax 775-8828

Honolulu, Honolulu, Pop. 378,155
Hawaii SD 186,100/PK-12
PO Box 2360 96804 808-586-3230
Kathryn Matayoshi, supt. Fax 586-3234
www.hawaiipublicschools.org
Aina Haina ES 600/PK-5
801 W Hind Dr 96821 808-377-2419
Brendan Burns, prin. Fax 377-2426
Ala Wai ES 500/PK-5
503 Kamoku St 96826 808-973-0070
Michelle DeBusca, prin. Fax 973-0081
Aliamanu ES 800/PK-6
3265 Salt Lake Blvd 96818 808-421-4280
Sandra Yoshimi, prin. Fax 421-4283
Aliamanu MS 700/7-8
3271 Salt Lake Blvd 96818 808-421-4100
Albert Hetrick, prin. Fax 421-4103
Ali'iolani ES 300/K-5
1240 7th Ave 96816 808-733-4750
Joseph Passantino, prin. Fax 733-4758
Central MS 400/6-8
1302 Queen Emma St 96813 808-587-4400
Anne Murphy, prin. Fax 587-4409
Dole MS 800/6-8
1803 Kamehameha IV Rd 96819 808-832-3340
Mavis Tasaka, prin. Fax 832-3349
Fern ES 500/K-5
1121 Middle St 96819 808-832-3040
Fred Yoshinaga, prin. Fax 832-3043
Haha'ione ES 500/K-5
595 Pepeekeo St 96825 808-397-5822
Shannon Goo, prin. Fax 397-5827
Hickam ES 600/PK-6
825 Manzelman Cir 96818 808-421-4148
Alisa Bender, prin. Fax 421-4157
Hokulani ES 400/K-5
2940 Kamakini St 96816 808-733-4789
Laurie Luczak, prin. Fax 733-4792
Jarrett MS 300/6-8
1903 Palolo Ave 96816 808-733-4888
Reid Kuba, prin. Fax 733-4894
Jefferson ES 500/PK-5
324 Kapahulu Ave 96815 808-971-6922
Garret Zakahi, prin. Fax 971-6915
Ka'ahumanu ES 600/K-5
1141 Kinau St 96814 808-587-4414
Cindy Yun-Kim, prin. Fax 587-4415
Ka'ewai ES 300/K-5
1929 Kamehameha IV Rd 96819 808-832-3500
Bert Carter, prin. Fax 832-3509
Kahala ES 500/K-5
4559 Kilauea Ave 96816 808-733-8455
Christine Gardner, prin. Fax 733-4669

Kaimuki MS 1,000/6-8
631 18th Ave 96816 808-733-4800
Frank Fernandes, prin. Fax 733-4810
Kai'ulani ES 400/K-5
783 N King St 96817 808-832-3160
Jill Puletasi, prin. Fax 832-3164
Kalakaua MS 1,000/6-8
821 Kalihi St 96819 808-832-3130
Lorelei Aiwohi, prin. Fax 832-3140
Kalihi ES 300/K-5
2471 Kula Kolea Dr 96819 808-832-3177
William Grindell, prin. Fax 832-3179
Kalihi Kai ES 600/PK-5
626 McNeill St 96817 808-832-3322
Laura Vines, prin. Fax 832-3327
Kalihi Uka ES 300/K-5
2411 Kalihi St 96819 808-305-6200
Laura Ahn, prin. Fax 832-3313
Kalihi Waena ES 600/PK-5
1240 Gulick Ave 96819 808-832-3210
Ronnie Victor, prin. Fax 832-3213
Kamiloiki ES 400/K-5
7788 Hawaii Kai Dr 96825 808-397-5800
Jason Yoshimoto, prin. Fax 397-5806
Kapalama ES 600/K-5
1601 N School St 96817 808-832-3290
Patricia Dang, prin. Fax 832-3302
Kauluwela ES 400/K-5
1486 Aala St 96817 808-587-4447
Christopher Daly, prin. Fax 587-4453
Kawananakoa MS 900/6-8
49 Funchal St 96813 808-307-0300
Ann Sugibayashi, prin. Fax 587-4443
Koko Head ES 400/PK-5
189 Lunalilo Home Rd 96825 808-397-5811
Jeffrey Shitaoka, prin. Fax 397-5816
Kuhio ES 300/K-5
2759 S King St 96826 808-973-0085
Lynn Kobayashi, prin. Fax 973-0088
Kula Kaiapuni O Anuenue S 400/K-12
2528 10th Ave 96816 808-733-8465
Glen Miyasato, prin. Fax 733-8467
Lanakila ES 400/PK-5
717 N Kuakini St 96817 808-587-4466
Katherine Balatico, prin. Fax 587-4468
Liholiho ES 500/PK-5
3430 Maunaloa Ave 96816 808-733-4850
Christina Small, prin. Fax 733-4856
Likelike ES 400/PK-5
1618 Palama St 96817 808-832-3370
Kelly Bart, prin. Fax 832-3374
Linapuni ES 200/PK-1
1434 Linapuni St 96819 808-305-2150
Cindy Sunahara, prin. Fax 832-3305
Lincoln ES 400/K-5
615 Auwaiolimu St 96813 808-587-4480
Jacqueline Ornellas, prin. Fax 587-4487
Lunalilo ES 500/K-5
810 Pumehana St 96826 808-973-0270
Amy Kantrowitz, prin. Fax 973-0276
Ma'ema'e ES 700/K-5
319 Wyllie St 96817 808-595-5400
Lenn Uyeda, prin. Fax 595-5405
Makalapa ES 700/PK-6
4435 Salt Lake Blvd 96818 808-421-4110
Denise Arai, prin. Fax 421-4112
Manoa ES 600/PK-6
3155 Manoa Rd 96822 808-988-1868
Kerry Higa, prin. Fax 988-1860
Moanalua ES 700/PK-6
1337 Mahiole St 96819 808-305-1200
Lynda Galera, prin. Fax 831-7877
Moanalua MS 800/7-8
1289 Mahiole St 96819 808-305-1289
Wayne Guevara, prin. Fax 831-7859
Mokulele ES 500/PK-6
250 Aupaka St 96818 808-421-4180
Shannon Tamashiro, prin. Fax 421-4182
Nimitz ES 700/PK-6
520 Main St 96818 808-307-4400
Marcy Kagami, prin. Fax 421-4170
Niu Valley MS 900/6-8
310 Halemaumau St 96821 808-377-2440
Sean Tajima, prin. Fax 377-2444
Noelani ES 500/K-5
2655 Woodlawn Dr 96822 808-988-1858
Dr. Rochelle Mahoe, prin. Fax 988-1855
Nu'uanu ES 400/K-5
3055 Puiwa Ln 96817 808-595-5422
James Toyooka, prin. Fax 595-5425
Palolo ES 300/PK-5
2106 10th Ave 96816 808-733-4700
Holly Kiyonaga, prin. Fax 733-4708
Pauoa ES 300/PK-5
2301 Pauoa Rd 96813 808-587-4500
Dale Arakaki, prin. Fax 587-4506
Pearl Harbor ES 700/PK-6
1 Moanalua Rdg 96818 808-421-4130
Wayne Guevara, prin. Fax 421-4128
Pearl Harbor Kai ES 600/PK-6
1 C Ave 96818 808-421-4245
Dean Casupang, prin. Fax 421-4248
Pu'uhale ES 300/K-5
345 Puuhale Rd 96819 808-832-3190
Arnie Kikkawa, prin. Fax 832-3195
Red Hill ES 500/K-6
1265 Ala Kula Pl 96819 808-305-1530
Rory Vierra, prin. Fax 831-7861
Royal ES 400/K-5
1519 Queen Emma St 96813 808-587-4510
Eleanor Gonsalves, prin. Fax 587-4518
Salt Lake ES 800/PK-6
1131 Ala Lilikoi St 96818 808-305-1600
Duwayne Abe, prin. Fax 831-7873
Shafter ES 500/PK-6
2 Fort Shafter 96819 808-305-1500
Alison Higa, prin. Fax 832-3562

Stevenson MS 700/6-8
1202 Prospect St 96822 808-587-4520
Linell Dilwith, prin. Fax 587-4523
Waikiki ES 500/K-6
3710 Leahi Ave 96815 808-971-6900
Bonnie Tabor, prin. Fax 971-6902
Washington MS 800/6-8
1633 S King St 96826 808-973-0177
Michael Harano, prin. Fax 973-0181
Wilson ES 600/K-5
4945 Kilauea Ave 96816 808-733-4740
Ryan Amine, prin. Fax 733-4746
Other Schools – See Aiea, Captain Cook, Eleele, Ewa Beach, Haiku, Haleiwa, Hana, Hanalei, Hauula, Hilo, Holualoa, Honokaa, Hoolehua, Kaaawa, Kahuku, Kahului, Kailua, Kailua Kona, Kalaheo, Kamuela, Kaneohe, Kapaa, Kapaau, Kapolei, Kaunakakai, Keaau, Kealakekua, Kekaha, Kihei, Kilauea, Koloa, Kula, Lahaina, Laie, Lanai City, Lihue, Makawao, Maunaloa, Mililani, Mountain View, Naalehu, Paauilo, Pahala, Pahoa, Paia, Papaikou, Pearl City, Wahiawa, Waialua, Waianae, Waikoloa, Wailuku, Waimanalo, Waimea, Waipahu

---

Assets S 400/K-12
1 Ohana Nui Way 96818 808-423-1356
Paul Singer, head sch Fax 422-1920
Blessed Marianne Cope Preschool PK-PK
2707 Pamoa Rd 96822 808-988-4111
Jocelyn Burch, prin. Fax 988-5497
Central Union Preschool & K 200/PK-K
1660 S Beretania St 96826 808-946-4025
Chaminade/L Robert Allen Montessori Ctr 50/PK-K
3140 Waialae Ave 96816 808-735-4875
Yan Yan Imamura, dir. Fax 735-4876
Christian Academy 400/PK-12
3400 Moanalua Rd 96819 808-836-0233
E. Rebecca Furuhashi, prin. Fax 836-4415
Hanahau'oli S 100/PK-6
1922 Makiki St 96822 808-949-6461
Cynthia Gibbs-Wilborn, head sch Fax 941-2216
Hawaiian Mission Academy Ka Lama Iki 100/K-8
1415 Makiki St 96814 808-949-2033
Hawaii Baptist Academy 400/K-6
420 Wyllie St 96817 808-595-5000
Ronald Shiira, pres.
Hawaii Baptist Academy 200/7-8
420 Wyllie St 96817 808-595-5000
Ronald Shiira, pres.
Holy Family Catholic Academy 500/1-8
830 Main St 96818 808-423-9611
P.J. Foehr, prin. Fax 422-3040
Holy Family Early Learning Center 100/PK-K
830 Main St 96818 808-421-1265
Allen Akiona, dir. Fax 422-5030
Holy Nativity S 100/PK-8
5286 Kalanianaole Hwy 96821 808-373-3232
Tim Spurrier, head sch Fax 377-9618
Hongwanji Mission S 300/PK-8
1728 Pali Hwy 96813 808-532-0522
Honolulu Waldorf S 200/PK-8
350 Ulua St 96821 808-377-5471
Dr. Jocelyn Demirbag, dir. Fax 373-2040
Iolani S 1,900/K-12
563 Kamoku St 96826 808-949-5355
Dr. Timothy Cottrell Ph.D., head sch Fax 943-2297
Kaimuki Christian S 300/PK-12
1117 Koko Head Ave 96816 808-732-1781
Robyn Ahn, prin. Fax 735-1354
Kamehameha S - Kapalama Campus 3,200/K-12
1887 Makuakane St 96817 808-842-8211
Dr. Taran Chun, head sch Fax 842-8411
Kawaiaha'o Church S 50/PK-5
872 Mission Ln 96813 808-585-0622
Maryknoll S 600/K-12
1526 Alexander St 96822 808-952-8400
Shana Tong, prin. Fax 952-7201
Mary Star of the Sea Early Learning Ctr 200/PK-K
4470 Aliikoa St 96821 808-734-3840
Dr. Lisa Foster Ed.D., prin. Fax 732-1738
Mary Star of the Sea S 200/1-8
4469 Malia St 96821 808-734-0208
Margaret Rufo, prin. Fax 735-9790
Mid-Pacific Institute 1,500/PK-12
2445 Kaala St 96822 808-973-5000
Dr. Paul Turnbull Ph.D., pres. Fax 973-5099
Montessori Community S 200/PK-6
1239 Nehoa St 96822 808-522-0244
Navy Hale Keiki S 200/PK-4
153 Bougainville Dr 96818 808-423-1727
Monique Raduziner, prin. Fax 423-1778
Punahou S 3,700/K-12
1601 Punahou St 96822 808-944-5711
Dr. James Scott, pres. Fax 944-5762
Sacred Hearts Academy 1,100/PK-12
3253 Waialae Ave 96816 808-734-5058
Betty White, head sch Fax 737-7867
St. Andrew's S 400/PK-12
224 Queen Emma Sq 96813 808-536-6102
Dr. Ruth Fletcher, head sch Fax 538-1035
St. Anthony S - Honolulu 100/PK-8
640 Puuhale Rd 96819 808-845-2769
Sr. Victoria Lavente, prin. Fax 853-2234
St. Clement's S 100/PK-K
1515 Wilder Ave 96822 808-949-2082
Fax 943-1049
St. Francis S 300/PK-12
2707 Pamoa Rd 96822 808-988-4111
Sr. Joan of Arc Souza, prin. Fax 988-5497
St. John the Baptist Catholic S 200/PK-8
2340 Omilo Ln 96819 808-841-5551
Carol Chong, prin. Fax 842-6104
St. Louis S 600/K-12
3142 Waialae Ave 96816 808-739-7777
Glenn Medeiros Ed.D., pres. Fax 739-4853

St. Patrick S 300/PK-8
3320 Harding Ave 96816 808-734-8979
Sr. Anne Clare DeCosta, prin. Fax 732-2851
St. Philomena Early Learning Center 200/PK-K
3300 Ala Laulani St 96818 808-833-8080
Peter Tedtaotao, dir. Fax 834-3438
St. Theresa S - Honolulu 300/PK-8
712 N School St 96817 808-536-4703
Conception Gora, prin. Fax 524-6861
Waolani-Judd Nazarene S 100/PK-8
408 N Judd St 96817 808-531-5251
Rachelle Wong, prin. Fax 586-9567

Hoolehua, Maui
Hawaii SD
Supt. — See Honolulu
Moloka'i MS 200/7-8
PO Box 443 96729 808-567-6940
Dawn Mains, prin. Fax 567-6939

Kaaawa, Honolulu, Pop. 677
Hawaii SD
Supt. — See Honolulu
Ka'a'awa ES 100/K-6
51-296 Kamehameha Hwy 96730 808-237-7751
Jennifer Luke-Payne, prin. Fax 237-7755

Kahuku, Honolulu, Pop. 995
Hawaii SD
Supt. — See Honolulu
Kahuku ES 500/PK-6
56-170 Pualalea St 96731 808-293-8980
Pauline Masaniai, prin. Fax 293-8985

Kahului, Maui, Pop. 18,567
Hawaii SD
Supt. — See Honolulu
Kahului ES 1,100/PK-5
410 Hina Ave 96732 808-873-3055
Christopher Wilhelm, prin. Fax 873-3089
Lihikai ES 900/K-5
335 S Papa Ave 96732 808-873-3033
Shannon Cabanilla, prin. Fax 873-3570
Maui Waena IS 1,100/6-8
795 Onehee Ave 96732 808-873-3070
Jacquelyn McCandless, prin. Fax 873-3066
Pomaika'i ES 600/K-5
4650 S Kamehameha Ave 96732 808-873-3410
Kim Otani, prin. Fax 873-3414

Christ the King Child Development Center 100/PK-K
211 Kaulawahine St 96732 808-877-3587
Carol Arakawa, dir. Fax 871-8101
Emmanuel Lutheran S 200/PK-8
520 One St 96732 808-873-6334
David Hobus, admin. Fax 877-6819
Maui Adventist S 50/K-8
261 S Puunene Ave 96732 808-877-7813

Kailua, Honolulu, Pop. 26,779
Hawaii SD
Supt. — See Honolulu
Aikahi ES 500/PK-6
281 Ilihau St 96734 808-254-7944
Keoki Fraser, prin. Fax 254-7962
Enchanted Lake ES 500/PK-6
770 Keolu Dr 96734 808-266-7800
Pua'ala McElhaney, prin. Fax 266-7804
Ka'elepulu ES 200/K-6
530 Keolu Dr 96734 808-266-7811
Jamie Dela-Cruz, prin. Fax 266-7813
Kailua ES 400/PK-6
315 Kuulei Rd 96734 808-266-7878
James Rippard, prin. Fax 266-7882
Kailua IS 700/7-8
145 S Kainalu Dr 96734 808-263-1500
Lisa DeLong, prin. Fax 266-7984
Kainalu ES 600/PK-6
165 Kaiholu St 96734 808-266-7835
Sheri Sunabe, prin. Fax 266-7837
Keolu ES 100/PK-6
1416 Keolu Dr 96734 808-266-7818
Gay Kong, prin. Fax 266-7892
Maunawili ES 400/PK-6
1465 Ulupii St 96734 808-266-7822
Christine Udarbe, prin. Fax 266-7834
Mokapu ES 900/PK-6
1193 Mokapu Rd 96734 808-254-7964
Charles Fradley, prin. Fax 254-7969

Hawaiian Mission Academy-Windward Campus 100/K-8
160 Mookua St 96734 808-261-0565
Le Jardin Academy 800/PK-12
917 Kalanianaole Hwy 96734 808-261-0707
D.J. Condon, head sch Fax 262-9339
St. Anthony S - Kailua 400/PK-8
148 Makawao St 96734 808-261-3331
Bridget Olsen, prin. Fax 263-3518
St. John Vianney S 200/PK-8
940 Keolu Dr 96734 808-261-4651
Caryn Demello, prin. Fax 263-0505
Trinity Christian S 300/PK-12
875 Auloa Rd 96734 808-262-8501

Kailua Kona, Hawaii, Pop. 7,780
Hawaii SD
Supt. — See Honolulu
Kahakai ES 700/PK-5
76-147 Royal Poinciana Dr 96740 808-313-6200
James Denight, prin. Fax 327-4333
Kealakehe ES 1,100/PK-5
74-5118 Kealakaa St 96740 808-327-4308
Nancy Matsukawa, prin. Fax 327-4347
Kealakehe IS 700/6-8
74-5062 Onipaa St 96740 808-327-4314
Mark Hackelberg, prin. Fax 327-4315

Makua Lani Christian Academy 100/PK-7
PO Box 1179 96745 808-329-3093
Nancy Begley, prin. Fax 329-5449

Kalaheo, Kauai, Pop. 3,504
Hawaii SD
Supt. — See Honolulu
Kalaheo ES 500/K-5
4400 Maka Rd 96741 808-332-6801
Erik Burkman, prin. Fax 332-6804

Kamuela, Hawaii, Pop. 5,972
Hawaii SD
Supt. — See Honolulu
Waimea ES 600/PK-5
67-1225 Mamalahoa Hwy 96743 808-887-7636
Scott Tamura, prin. Fax 887-7640

Hawaii Preparatory Academy 600/K-12
65-1692 Kohala Mountain Rd 96743 808-885-7321
Robert McKendry, head sch Fax 881-4003
Parker S 300/K-12
65-1224 Lindsey Rd 96743 808-885-7933
Carl Sturges Ph.D., hdmstr. Fax 885-6233
Waimea Country S 50/K-6
PO Box 399 96743 808-885-0067

Kaneohe, Honolulu, Pop. 22,238
Hawaii SD
Supt. — See Honolulu
Ahuimanu ES 300/K-6
47-470 Hui Aeko Pl 96744 808-239-3125
Kimi Ikeda, prin. Fax 239-3127
He'eia ES 500/PK-6
46-202 Haiku Rd 96744 808-233-5677
Alma Souki, prin. Fax 233-5679
Kahalu'u ES 300/K-6
47-280 Waihee Rd 96744 808-239-3101
Gary Harada, prin. Fax 239-3102
Kane'ohe ES 700/PK-6
45-495 Kamehameha Hwy 96744 808-305-0000
Derek Minakami, prin. Fax 235-9185
Kapunahala ES 600/K-6
45-828 Anoi Rd 96744 808-233-5650
Deborah Nekomoto, prin. Fax 233-5651
King IS 600/7-8
46-155 Kamehameha Hwy 96744 808-233-5727
Wendy Matsuzaki, prin. Fax 233-5747
Parker ES 300/PK-6
45-259 Waikalua Rd 96744 808-233-5686
Kathy Kahikina, prin. Fax 233-5689
Pu'ohala ES 300/PK-6
45-233 Kulauli St 96744 808-305-5900
Shawna Paakaula, prin. Fax 233-5663
Waiahole ES 100/PK-6
48-215 Waiahole Valley Rd 96744 808-239-3111
Alexandra Obra, prin. Fax 239-3113

Koolau Baptist Academy 200/K-12
45-633 Keneke St 96744 808-233-2900
St. Ann's Model Early Learning Center 200/PK-K
46-125 Haiku Rd 96744 808-247-3092
Cynthia Achong, dir. Fax 235-0717
St. Ann's Model S 200/1-8
46-125 Haiku Rd 96744 808-247-3092
Mandy Brown, prin. Fax 235-0717
St. Mark Lutheran S 200/K-8
45-725 Kamehameha Hwy 96744 808-247-5589
Dr. R. David Gaudi Ed.D., head sch Fax 235-6155
Windward Nazarene Academy 300/PK-8
PO Box 1633 96744 808-235-8787
Kay Hishinuma, prin. Fax 236-0174

Kapaa, Kauai, Pop. 7,352
Hawaii SD
Supt. — See Honolulu
Kapa'a ES 1,000/PK-5
4886 Kawaihau Rd 96746 808-821-4424
Jason Kuloloia, prin. Fax 821-4431
Kapa'a MS 600/6-8
4867 Olohena Rd 96746 808-821-4460
Nathan Aiwohi, prin. Fax 821-6967

St. Catherine S 200/PK-8
PO Box 1832 96746 808-822-4212
Britt Cocumelli, prin. Fax 823-0991

Kapaau, Hawaii, Pop. 1,135
Hawaii SD
Supt. — See Honolulu
Kohala ES 400/PK-5
PO Box 819 96755 808-889-7100
Danny Garcia, prin. Fax 889-7103
Kohala MS 200/6-8
PO Box 777 96755 808-889-7119
Alan Brown, prin. Fax 889-7121

Kapolei, Honolulu, Pop. 8,781
Hawaii SD
Supt. — See Honolulu
Barbers Point ES 700/PK-5
3001 Boxer Rd 96707 808-673-7400
Jaclyn Riel, prin. Fax 673-7403
Hookele ES 500/PK-5
511 Kunehi St 96707 808-305-8500
Laureen Dunn, prin. Fax 674-8590
Kapolei ES 1,200/K-5
91-1119 Kamaaha Loop 96707 808-693-7000
Cindy Otsu, prin. Fax 693-7011
Kapolei MS 1,500/6-8
91-5335 Kapolei Pkwy 96707 808-693-7025
Richard Fajardo, prin. Fax 693-7030
Makakilo ES 600/K-5
92-675 Anipeahi St 96707 808-672-1122
Todd Fujimori, prin. Fax 672-1128
Mauka Lani ES 700/PK-5
92-1300 Panana St 96707 808-672-1100
Sam Izumi, prin. Fax 672-1114

American Renaissance Academy 100/K-12
PO Box 75357 96707 808-682-7337
Dr. Kelly Tanizaki, head sch Fax 682-7336
Island Pacific Academy 700/K-12
909 Haumea St 96707 808-674-3523
Gerald Teramae, head sch Fax 674-3575
New Hope Christian S 200/K-8
480 Kamokila Blvd 96707 808-678-3776
CinDee Enos, prin. Fax 678-3774

Kaunakakai, Maui, Pop. 1,463
Hawaii SD
Supt. — See Honolulu
Kaunakakai ES 300/PK-6
PO Box 1950 96748 808-553-1730
Daniel Espaniola, prin. Fax 553-1737
Kilohana ES 100/K-6
HC 1 Box 334 96748 808-558-2200
Marilyn Simms, prin. Fax 558-2203

Keaau, Hawaii, Pop. 1,591
Hawaii SD
Supt. — See Honolulu
Kea'au ES 800/K-5
16-680 Keaau Pahoa Rd 96749 808-982-4210
Janice Blaber, prin. Fax 982-4217
Kea'au MS 600/6-8
16-565 Keaau Pahoa Rd 96749 808-982-4200
Elna Gomes, prin. Fax 982-4219

Christian Liberty S 300/PK-12
16-675 Milo St 96749 808-966-8445
Troy Rimel, dir. Fax 966-8866
Kamehameha S - Hawaii Campus 1,100/K-12
16-716 Volcano Rd 96749 808-982-0000
Monica Naeole-Wong, head sch Fax 982-0010
Malamalama Waldorf S 100/PK-8
HC 3 Box 13068 96749 808-982-7701

Kealakekua, Hawaii, Pop. 1,317
Hawaii SD
Supt. — See Honolulu
Konawaena ES 600/PK-5
81-901 Onouli Rd 96750 808-323-4555
Claire Yoshida, prin. Fax 323-4551
Konawaena MS 600/6-8
81-1045 Konawaena School Rd 96750
808-323-4566
Teddy Burgess, prin. Fax 323-4574

Kekaha, Kauai, Pop. 2,073
Hawaii SD
Supt. — See Honolulu
Kekaha ES 400/K-5
PO Box 580 96752 808-337-7655
Marilyn Asahi, prin. Fax 337-7657

St. Theresa S - Kekaha 100/PK-8
PO Box 277 96752 808-337-1351
Wendy Castillo, prin. Fax 337-1714

Kihei, Maui, Pop. 16,763
Hawaii SD
Supt. — See Honolulu
Kamali'i ES 600/K-5
180 Alanui Kealii Dr 96753 808-875-6840
Cynthia Rothdeutsch, prin. Fax 875-6843
Kihei ES 1,000/PK-5
250 E Lipoa St 96753 808-875-6818
Sue Forbes, prin. Fax 875-6825
Lokelani IS 600/6-8
1401 Liloa Dr 96753 808-875-6800
Francoise Wittenburg, prin. Fax 875-6835

Montessori Hale O Keiki 50/PK-8
PO Box 2348 96753 808-874-7441
Lara Gauthier, admin. Fax 874-2573

Kilauea, Kauai, Pop. 2,283
Hawaii SD
Supt. — See Honolulu
Kilauea ES 300/PK-6
2440 Kolo Rd 96754 808-828-1212
Sherry Gonsalves, prin. Fax 828-2034

Kauai Christian Academy 100/PK-12
PO Box 1121 96754 808-828-0047
Daniel Plunkett, prin. Fax 828-1850

Koloa, Kauai, Pop. 1,524
Hawaii SD
Supt. — See Honolulu
Koloa ES 400/K-5
3223 Poipu Rd 96756 808-742-8460
Linda Uyehara, prin. Fax 742-8466

Kahili Adventist S K-12
2-4035 Kaumualii Hwy 96756 808-742-9294

Kula, Maui, Pop. 5,082
Hawaii SD
Supt. — See Honolulu
Kula ES 400/K-5
5000 Kula Hwy 96790 808-876-7610
Chris Bachaus, prin. Fax 876-7616

Haleakala Waldorf S 200/PK-12
4160 Lower Kula Rd 96790 808-878-2511
Kelly Brewer, admin. Fax 878-3341

Lahaina, Maui, Pop. 8,745
Hawaii SD
Supt. — See Honolulu
Kamehameha III ES 800/K-5
611 Front St 96761 808-662-3955
Steve Franz, prin. Fax 662-3958
Lahaina IS 600/6-8
871 Lahainaluna Rd 96761 808-662-3965
Stacy Bookland, prin. Fax 662-3968
Nahi'ena'ena ES 800/PK-5
816 Niheu St 96761 808-662-4020
Rebecca Winkie, prin. Fax 662-4023

Maui Preparatory Academy 200/PK-12
4910 Honoapiilani Hwy 96761 808-665-9966
Sacred Hearts S 200/PK-8
239 Dickenson St 96761 808-661-4720
Rebecca Spitznagel, prin. Fax 667-5363

Laie, Honolulu, Pop. 2,912
Hawaii SD
Supt. — See Honolulu
La'ie ES 700/PK-6
55-109 Kulanui St 96762 808-293-8965
Loha Kaka, prin. Fax 293-8968

Lanai City, Maui, Pop. 2,317
Hawaii SD
Supt. — See Honolulu
Lanai S 600/K-12
PO Box 630630 96763 808-565-7900
Elton Kinoshita, prin. Fax 565-7904

Lihue, Kauai, Pop. 4,702
Hawaii SD
Supt. — See Honolulu
Kamakahelei MS 900/6-8
4431 Nuhou St 96766 808-241-3200
Debra Badua, prin. Fax 241-3210
Kaumuali'i ES 700/PK-5
4380 Hanamaulu Rd 96766 808-241-3150
Jason Yoshida, prin. Fax 241-3159
Wilcox ES 900/K-5
4319 Hardy St 96766 808-274-3150
Corey Nakamura, prin. Fax 274-3152

Island S 400/PK-12
3-1875 Kaumualii Hwy 96766 808-246-0233
L. Shannon Graves M.Ed., head sch Fax 245-6053

Makawao, Maui, Pop. 4,664
Hawaii SD
Supt. — See Honolulu
Kalama IS 800/6-8
120 Makani Rd 96768 808-573-8735
Timothy Shim, prin. Fax 573-8748
Makawao ES 600/PK-5
3542 Baldwin Ave 96768 808-573-8770
Robyn Honda, prin. Fax 573-8774
Pukalani ES 500/K-5
2945 Iolani St 96768 808-573-8760
Dr. Kathleen Dimino, prin. Fax 573-8766

Montessori S of Maui 200/PK-8
2933 Baldwin Ave 96768 808-573-0374
Eric Dustman Ph.D., head sch Fax 573-0389
St. Joseph Early Learning Ctr - Makawao 50/PK-K
1294 Makawao Ave 96768 808-572-6235
Helen Souza, dir. Fax 572-0748

Maunaloa, Maui, Pop. 138
Hawaii SD
Supt. — See Honolulu
Maunaloa ES 100/K-6
PO Box 128 96770 808-552-2000
Joe Yamamoto, prin. Fax 552-2004

Mililani, Honolulu, Pop. 19,872
Hawaii SD
Supt. — See Honolulu
Kipapa ES 600/PK-5
95-076 Kipapa Dr 96789 808-627-7322
Corinne Yogi, prin. Fax 627-7326
Mililani 'Ike ES 1,000/K-5
95-1330 Lehiwa Dr 96789 808-626-2980
Lynne Ajifu, prin. Fax 626-2958
Mililani Mauka ES 900/PK-5
95-1111 Makaikai St 96789 808-626-3350
Avis Nanbu, prin. Fax 626-3360
Mililani MS 1,700/6-8
95-1140 Lehiwa Dr 96789 808-626-7355
Elynne Chung, prin. Fax 626-7358
Mililani Uka ES 700/PK-5
94-380 Kuahelani Ave 96789 808-627-7303
Heather Wilhelm, prin. Fax 627-7387
Mililani Waena ES 700/PK-5
95-502 Kipapa Dr 96789 808-627-7300
Troy Tamura, prin. Fax 627-7455

Hanalani S 700/PK-12
94-294 Anania Dr 96789 808-625-0737
Mark Sugimoto, head sch Fax 625-0691
St. John's Catholic Preschool 100/PK-K
95-370 Kuahelani Ave 96789 808-623-3332
Catherine Awong, dir. Fax 623-6496

Mountain View, Hawaii, Pop. 2,280
Hawaii SD
Supt. — See Honolulu
Mountain View ES 500/K-5
PO Box 9 96771 808-313-3200
Wilma Roddy, prin. Fax 968-2305

Naalehu, Hawaii, Pop. 502
Hawaii SD
Supt. — See Honolulu
Na'alehu ES 500/PK-6
955547 Mamalahoa Hwy 96772 808-939-2413
Darlene Javar, prin. Fax 939-2419

Paauilo, Hawaii, Pop. 371
Hawaii SD
Supt. — See Honolulu

Pa'auilo S 200/K-9
PO Box 329 96776 808-776-7710
Michelle Barber, prin. Fax 776-7714

Pahala, Hawaii, Pop. 832
Hawaii SD
Supt. — See Honolulu
Ka'u HS & Pahala ES 500/K-12
963150 Pikake St 96777 808-313-4100
Sharon Beck, prin. Fax 928-2092

Pahoa, Hawaii, Pop. 606
Hawaii SD
Supt. — See Honolulu
Keonepoko ES 600/K-6
15-890 Kahakai Blvd 96778 808-313-4500
Brandon Gallagher, prin. Fax 965-2138
Pahoa ES 400/PK-6
15-3030 Puna Rd 96778 808-313-4400
Michelle Payne-Arakaki, prin. Fax 965-2180

Paia, Maui, Pop. 1,965
Hawaii SD
Supt. — See Honolulu
Pa'ia ES 400/K-5
955 Baldwin Ave 96779 808-579-2100
Kehau Luuwai, prin. Fax 579-2103

Todd Memorial Christian S 200/PK-12
519 Baldwin Ave 96779 808-579-9237
Carolyn Moore, prin. Fax 579-9449

Papaikou, Hawaii, Pop. 907
Hawaii SD
Supt. — See Honolulu
Kalanianaole S 300/K-8
27-330 Old Mamalahoa Hwy 96781 808-964-9700
David Dinkel, prin. Fax 964-9703

Pearl City, Honolulu, Pop. 36,969
Hawaii SD
Supt. — See Honolulu
Highlands IS 900/7-8
1460 Hoolaulea St 96782 808-453-6480
Amy Martinson, prin. Fax 453-6484
Lehua ES 400/PK-6
791 Lehua Ave 96782 808-307-3700
Aaron Tominaga, prin. Fax 453-6497
Manana ES 500/K-6
1147 Kumano St 96782 808-307-5300
Bryan Loo, prin. Fax 453-6437
Momilani ES 400/K-6
2130 Hookiekie St 96782 808-307-5800
Doreen Higa, prin. Fax 453-6448
Palisades ES 400/K-6
2306 Auhuhu St 96782 808-453-6550
Gavin Tsue, prin. Fax 453-5910
Pearl City ES 600/PK-6
1090 Waimano Home Rd 96782 808-453-6455
Susan Hirokane Ph.D., prin. Fax 453-6467
Pearl City Highlands ES 500/PK-6
1419 Waimano Home Rd 96782 808-453-6470
Michael Nakasato, prin. Fax 453-6472
Waiau ES 500/PK-6
98-450 Hookanike St 96782 808-453-6530
Troy Takazono, prin. Fax 453-6541

Children's House 300/PK-6
1840 Komo Mai Dr 96782 808-455-4131
Our Lady of Good Counsel S 200/PK-8
1530 Hoolana St 96782 808-455-4533
Melanie Chinen, prin. Fax 455-5587

Pukalani, Maui, Pop. 4,987

Carden Academy of Maui 100/PK-8
55 Makaena Pl, 808-573-6651
Nina Sato, dir. Fax 573-6652
Kamehameha Schools Maui 1,000/K-12
275 Aapueo Pkwy, 808-572-3100
Dr. Scott Parker, hdmstr. Fax 572-3150

Wahiawa, Honolulu, Pop. 11,315
Hawaii SD
Supt. — See Honolulu
Helemano ES 600/K-5
1001 Ihiihi Ave 96786 808-622-6336
Ernest Muh, prin. Fax 622-6340
Iliahi ES 500/K-5
2035 California Ave 96786 808-622-6411
Garett Yukumoto, prin. Fax 622-6413
Inouye ES 900/K-5
1 Ayres Ave 96786 808-305-3400
Jan Iwase, prin. Fax 622-6382
Ka'ala ES 500/K-5
130 California Ave 96786 808-622-6366
Sam Bennett, prin. Fax 622-6368
Solomon ES 1,100/PK-5
2875 Waianae Uka Ave 96786 808-305-1800
Sally Omalza, prin. Fax 624-9505
Wahiawa ES 500/PK-5
1402 Glen Ave 96786 808-622-6393
Jamie Oshiro, prin. Fax 622-6394
Wahiawa MS 800/6-8
275 Rose St 96786 808-305-3300
Ursula Kawaguchi, prin. Fax 622-6506
Wheeler ES 600/PK-5
1 Wheeler Army Airfield 96786 808-622-6400
Kendrick Kakazu, prin. Fax 622-6403
Wheeler MS 800/6-8
2 Wheeler Army Airfield 96786 808-622-6525
Brenda Vierra-Chun, prin. Fax 622-6529

Abundant Life S, 650 Kilani Ave 96786 100/PK-6
Judie Wasson M.Ed., prin. 808-621-5433
Ho'ala S 100/K-12
1067 California Ave Ste A 96786 808-621-1898
Trinity Lutheran S 200/PK-8
1611 California Ave 96786 808-621-6033
Paul Krueger, prin. Fax 621-6029

Waialua, Honolulu, Pop. 2,839
Hawaii SD
Supt. — See Honolulu
Waialua ES 600/PK-6
67-020 Waialua Beach Rd 96791 808-637-8228
Scott Moore, prin. Fax 637-8225

St. Michael S 200/PK-8
67-340 Haona St 96791 808-637-7772
Kainoa Fukumoto, prin. Fax 637-7722

Waianae, Honolulu, Pop. 4,907
Hawaii SD
Supt. — See Honolulu
Leihoku ES 900/PK-6
86-285 Leihoku St 96792 808-697-7100
Randall Miura, prin. Fax 697-7142
Ma'ili ES 1,000/PK-6
87-360 Kulaaupuni St 96792 808-697-7150
Suzie Lee, prin. Fax 697-7151
Makaha ES 600/K-6
84-200 Ala Naauao Pl 96792 808-695-7900
Nelson Shigeta, prin. Fax 695-7905
Nanaikapono ES 1,000/PK-6
89-153 Mano Ave 96792 808-668-5800
Debra Knight, prin. Fax 668-5890
Nanakuli ES 500/PK-6
89-778 Haleakala Ave 96792 808-668-5813
Lisa Ann Higa, prin. Fax 668-5817
Wai'anae ES 600/PK-6
85-220 Mcarthur St 96792 808-697-7083
Ray Pikelny, prin. Fax 697-7090
Wai'anae IS 900/7-8
85-626 Farrington Hwy 96792 808-697-7121
John Wataoka, prin. Fax 697-7124

Adventist Malama S 100/PK-8
86-072 Farrington Hwy 96792 808-696-3988

Waikoloa, Hawaii, Pop. 4,526
Hawaii SD
Supt. — See Honolulu
Waikoloa S 800/PK-8
68-1730 Hooko St 96738 808-883-6808
Kris Kosa-Correia, prin. Fax 883-6811

Wailuku, Maui, Pop. 10,085
Hawaii SD
Supt. — See Honolulu
Iao IS 900/6-8
260 S Market St 96793 808-984-5610
Matthew Dillo, prin. Fax 984-5617
Pu'u Kukui ES 500/K-5
3700 Kehalani Mauka Pkwy 96793 808-727-3000
Chad Okamoto, prin. Fax 727-3120
Waihe'e ES 800/K-5
2125 Kahekili Hwy 96793 808-984-5644
Lori Yatsushiro, prin. Fax 984-5648
Wailuku ES 700/K-5
355 S High St 96793 808-984-5622
Beverly Stanich, prin. Fax 984-5627

St. Anthony Preschool 50/PK-PK
1627 Mill St Ste B 96793 808-242-9024
Carlene Santos, dir. Fax 986-0654
St. Anthony S 200/K-12
1627 Mill St Ste A 96793 808-244-4976
Timothy Cullen, pres. Fax 244-7950

Waimanalo, Honolulu, Pop. 2,473
Hawaii SD
Supt. — See Honolulu
Pope ES 200/PK-6
41-133 Huli St 96795 808-259-0450
Aaron Okumura, prin. Fax 259-0452
Waimanalo S 500/K-8
41-1330 Kalanianaole Hwy 96795 808-259-0460
Noel Richardson, prin. Fax 259-0463

Waimea, Kauai, Pop. 1,080
Hawaii SD
Supt. — See Honolulu
Niihau S 50/K-12
PO Box 339 96796 808-338-6800
Mahina Anguay, prin. Fax 338-6807
Waimea Canyon MS 400/6-8
9555 Huakai St 96796 808-338-6830
Melissa Speetjens, prin. Fax 338-6832

Waipahu, Honolulu, Pop. 28,747
Hawaii SD
Supt. — See Honolulu
Ahrens ES 1,400/PK-6
94-1170 Waipahu St 96797 808-675-0202
Hanh Nguyen, prin. Fax 675-0216
Honowai ES 800/PK-6
94-600 Honowai St 96797 808-675-0165
Kent Matsumura, prin. Fax 675-0167
Kale'iopu'u ES 1,000/PK-6
94-665 Kaaholo St 96797 808-675-0266
Pat Anbe, prin. Fax 675-0269
Kanoelani ES 800/PK-6
94-1091 Oli Loop 96797 808-675-0195
Stacie Kunihisa, prin. Fax 675-0135
Waikele ES 700/K-6
94-1035 Kukula St 96797 808-677-6100
Sheldon Oshio, prin. Fax 677-6106
Waipahu ES 1,100/K-6
94-465 Waipahu St 96797 808-675-0150
Keith Hui, prin. Fax 675-0121
Waipahu IS 1,300/7-8
94-455 Farrington Hwy 96797 808-675-0177
Randell Dunn, prin. Fax 675-0181

Lanakila Baptist ES 100/K-6
94-1250 Waipahu St 96797 808-677-0731
Maria Pauley, prin. Fax 677-0733
Pearl Harbor Christian Academy 400/PK-8
94-1044 Waipio Uka St 96797 808-678-3997
Phebe Sumida M.Ed., prin. Fax 678-6607
Rosary Preschool 50/PK-PK
94-1249 Lumikula St Ste A 96797 808-676-1452
Sr. Oliva Fuentes, dir. Fax 677-1202
St. Joseph S - Waipahu 400/PK-8
94-651 Farrington Hwy 96797 808-677-4475
Beverly Sandobal, prin. Fax 677-8937

IDAHO

IDAHO DEPARTMENT OF EDUCATION

PO Box 83720, Boise 83720-0003
Telephone 208-332-6800
Fax 208-334-2228
Website http://www.sde.idaho.gov

Superintendent of Public Instruction Sherry Ybarra

IDAHO BOARD OF EDUCATION

PO Box 83720, Boise 83720-0003

President Emma Atchley

PUBLIC, PRIVATE AND CATHOLIC ELEMENTARY SCHOOLS

Aberdeen, Bingham, Pop. 1,945
Aberdeen SD 58 800/PK-12
PO Box 610 83210 208-397-4113
Jane Ward, supt. Fax 397-4114
aberdeen58.org/
Aberdeen ES 400/PK-5
PO Box 610 83210 208-397-4115
Robi Colton, prin. Fax 397-4117
Aberdeen MS 200/6-8
PO Box 610 83210 208-397-3280
Ann Mennear, prin. Fax 397-3281

Acequia, Minidoka, Pop. 124
Minidoka County JSD 331
Supt. — See Rupert
Acequia ES 300/K-5
360 N 350 E 83350 208-436-6985
Heather Hepworth, prin. Fax 436-4359

Albion, Cassia, Pop. 265
Cassia County JSD 151
Supt. — See Burley
Albion ES 50/K-5
PO Box 38 83311 208-673-6653
Scott Muir, prin. Fax 673-6653

Almo, Cassia
Cassia County JSD 151
Supt. — See Burley
Almo ES 50/K-3
PO Box 168 83312 208-824-5526
Eric Boden, prin. Fax 824-5522

American Falls, Power, Pop. 4,393
American Falls JSD 381 1,500/PK-12
827 Fort Hall Ave 83211 208-226-5173
Dr. Ron Bolinger, supt. Fax 226-5754
www.sd381.k12.id.us
American Falls IS 200/4-5
254 Taylor St 83211 208-226-5733
Chris Torgesen, prin. Fax 226-5766
Hillcrest ES 500/PK-3
1045 Bennett Ave 83211 208-226-2391
Tina Fehringer, prin. Fax 226-2677
Thomas MS 300/6-8
355 Bannock Ave 83211 208-226-5203
Randy Jensen, prin. Fax 226-5274

Ammon, Bonneville, Pop. 13,621
Bonneville JSD 93
Supt. — See Idaho Falls
Ammon ES 400/K-6
2900 Central Ave 83406 208-525-4465
John Murdoch, prin. Fax 525-4467
Hillview ES 500/K-6
3075 Teton St 83406 208-525-4460
Dr. Elisa Saffle, prin. Fax 525-4461
Mountain Valley ES 500/K-6
2601 Princess Dr 83406 208-552-0866
Lanie Keller, prin. Fax 552-0514
Rimrock ES 400/K-6
4855 Brennan Bnd, 208-552-4667
Steve Cziep, prin. Fax 552-4694
Sandcreek MS 800/7-8
2955 Owen St 83406 208-525-4416
Yvonne Thurber, prin. Fax 525-4438
Woodland Hills ES 500/K-6
4700 Sweetwater Way 83406 208-552-4850
Oliver Roberts, prin. Fax 552-4772

Arbon, Power, Pop. 613
Arbon ESD 383 50/K-6
4405 Arbon Valley Hwy 83212 208-335-2197
Fax 335-2197
www.arbonvalley.com/school-district/
Arbon ES 50/K-6
4405 Arbon Valley Hwy 83212 208-335-2197
Robin Claunch, lead tchr. Fax 335-2197

Arco, Butte, Pop. 974
Butte County JSD 111 400/PK-12
PO Box 89 83213 208-690-3410
Joel Wilson, supt. Fax 527-8950
www.butteschooldistrict.org
Arco ES 200/PK-5
PO Box 675 83213 208-690-3420
Dr. Joel Wilson, admin. Fax 527-8950
Butte County MS 100/6-8
PO Box 695 83213 208-690-3430
Robert Chambers, prin. Fax 527-8246
Other Schools – See Howe

Arimo, Bannock, Pop. 334
Marsh Valley JSD 21 1,300/PK-12
PO Box 180 83214 208-254-3306
Marvin Hansen, supt. Fax 254-9243
sites.google.com/a/mvsd21.org
Marsh Valley MS 200/7-8
12805 S Old Highway 91 83214 208-254-3260
Jason Brower, prin. Fax 254-3631
Other Schools – See Downey, Inkom, Lava Hot Springs, Mc Cammon

Ashton, Fremont, Pop. 1,114
Fremont County JSD 215
Supt. — See Saint Anthony
Ashton ES 300/PK-5
168 S 1st St 83420 208-652-7601
Evan Ricks, prin. Fax 652-7602

Athol, Kootenai, Pop. 677
Lakeland SD 272
Supt. — See Rathdrum
Athol ES 400/PK-6
6333 E Menser Ave 83801 208-683-2231
Kathy Thomas, prin. Fax 683-7064

Bancroft, Caribou, Pop. 366
North Gem SD 149 200/PK-12
PO Box 70 83217 208-648-7848
David Sotutu, supt. Fax 648-7895
www.sd149.com
North Gem ES 100/PK-6
PO Box 70 83217 208-648-7848
David Sotutu, prin. Fax 648-7895

Bellevue, Blaine, Pop. 2,264
Blaine County SD 61
Supt. — See Hailey
Bellevue ES 300/K-5
305 N 5th St 83313 208-578-5080
Mark Sauvageau, prin. Fax 578-5180

Blackfoot, Bingham, Pop. 11,732
Blackfoot SD 55 4,100/PK-12
270 E Bridge St 83221 208-785-8800
Brian Kress, supt. Fax 785-8809
www.d55.k12.id.us
Blackfoot Heritage 6th Grade 300/6-6
50 S Shilling Ave 83221 208-785-8838
Colin Folsom, prin. Fax 785-8840
Groveland ES 300/K-5
375 W 170 N 83221 208-785-8829
Lori Kay, prin. Fax 785-8859
Hughie ECC 50/PK-PK
440 W Judicial St 83221 208-785-8835
Lynette Carter, dir. Fax 785-8816
Mountain View MS 600/7-8
645 Mitchell Ln 83221 208-785-8820
Wes Jensen, prin. Fax 785-8823
Ridge Crest ES 500/K-5
800 Airport Rd 83221 208-785-8894
Randy Martineau, prin. Fax 785-8897
Stalker ES 400/K-5
991 W Center St 83221 208-785-8841
Brandee Hewatt, prin. Fax 785-8855
Stoddard ES 400/K-5
460 York Dr 83221 208-785-8832
Christine Silzly, prin. Fax 785-8834
Wapello ES 200/K-5
195 E 350 N 83221 208-785-8844
Anthony Peterson, prin. Fax 785-8815
Other Schools – See Pocatello

Snake River SD 52 1,800/PK-12
103 S 900 W 83221 208-684-3001
David Kerns, supt. Fax 684-3003
www.snakeriver.org
Moreland ES 300/PK-1
185 N 750 W 83221 208-684-5115
Jane Reynolds, prin. Fax 684-3094
Riverside ES 300/2-3
16 S 700 W 83221 208-684-5102
Janae Van Orden, prin. Fax 684-5193
Rockford ES 100/4-4
1152 W Highway 39 83221 208-684-4451
Dean Bonney, prin. Fax 684-5190
Snake River JHS 300/7-8
918 W Highway 39 83221 208-684-3018
Bryce Salmon, prin. Fax 684-3047
Snake River MS 200/5-6
1060 W 110 S 83221 208-684-5171
Dean Bonney, prin. Fax 684-5199

Bliss, Gooding, Pop. 316
Bliss JSD 234 100/K-12
PO Box 115 83314 208-352-4445
Kevin Lancaster, supt. Fax 352-1954
www.bliss234.org
Bliss S 100/K-12
PO Box 115 83314 208-352-4445
Kevin Lancaster, prin. Fax 352-1954

Boise, Ada, Pop. 200,322
ISD of Boise City 27,000/PK-12
8169 W Victory Rd 83709 208-854-4000
Dr. Don Coberly, supt. Fax 854-4003
www.boiseschools.org
Adams ES 400/PK-6
1725 E Warm Springs Ave 83712 208-854-4190
Jason Adams, prin. Fax 854-4191
Amity ES 700/K-6
10000 W Amity Rd 83709 208-854-4220
Valerie Yhlorn, prin. Fax 854-4221
Collister ES 300/K-6
4426 W Catalpa Dr 83703 208-854-4650
Dr. Gerald Bell, prin. Fax 854-4651
Garfield ES 400/PK-6
1914 S Broadway Ave 83706 208-854-4950
Darryl Gerber, prin. Fax 854-4951
Hawthorne ES 300/PK-6
2401 W Targee St 83705 208-854-5000
James Bright, prin. Fax 854-5001
Hidden Springs ES 400/K-6
5480 W Hidden Springs Dr 83714 208-854-4920
Kurt Thaemert, prin. Fax 854-4921
Highlands ES 300/K-6
3434 N Bogus Basin Rd 83702 208-854-5050
Kristen Duskey, prin. Fax 854-5051
Hillcrest ES 400/K-6
2045 S Pond St 83705 208-854-5080
Jolene Lincoln, prin. Fax 854-5081
Horizon ES 700/PK-6
730 N Mitchell St 83704 208-854-5170
Steve Novotny, prin. Fax 854-5171
Jefferson ES 300/K-6
200 S Latah St 83705 208-854-5260
Ted Totorica, prin. Fax 854-5261
Jordan ES 600/PK-6
6411 W Fairfield Ave 83709 208-854-5580
Joan Bigelow, prin. Fax 854-5581
Koelsch ES 300/PK-6
2015 N Curtis Rd 83706 208-854-5300
Ken Pahlas, prin. Fax 854-5301
Liberty ES 500/K-6
1740 E Bergeson St 83706 208-854-5410
Jennifer Weske, prin. Fax 854-5411
Longfellow ES 300/K-6
1511 N 9th St 83702 208-854-5450
Bryce England, prin. Fax 854-5451
Lowell ES 400/K-6
1507 N 28th St 83703 208-854-5480
Dr. Adria David, prin. Fax 854-5481
Madison ECC 100/PK-PK
2215 W Madison Ave 83702 208-854-5520
Dedra Swanstrom, lead tchr. Fax 854-5521

Mann ES 500/PK-6
5401 W Castle Dr 83703 208-854-4680
Tammy Burks, prin. Fax 854-4681
Maple Grove ES 600/K-6
2800 S Maple Grove Rd 83709 208-854-5540
Kathy Hutchison, prin. Fax 854-5541
Monroe ES 300/K-6
3615 W Cassia St 83705 208-854-5620
Jeff Farley, prin. Fax 854-5621
Mountain View ES 400/K-6
3500 N Cabarton Ln 83704 208-854-5700
Curtis Anderson, prin. Fax 854-5701
Nelson ES 700/PK-6
7701 W Northview St 83704 208-854-4610
Melanie Koch, prin. Fax 854-4611
Owyhee ES 300/K-6
3434 W Pasadena Dr 83705 208-854-5850
Dr. Stacie Curry, prin. Fax 854-5851
Pierce Park ES 400/K-6
5015 N Pierce Park Ln 83714 208-854-5880
Chris Ryan, prin. Fax 854-5881
Riverside ES 600/PK-6
2100 E Victory Rd 83706 208-854-5980
Erin Kubena, prin. Fax 854-5981
Roosevelt ES 300/K-6
908 E Jefferson St 83712 208-854-6030
Julianne Bronner, prin. Fax 854-6031
Shadow Hills ES 600/K-6
8301 W Sloan St 83714 208-854-6060
Dr. Gale Zickefoose, prin. Fax 854-6061
Taft ES 300/K-6
3722 W Anderson St 83703 208-854-6180
Tim Lowe, prin. Fax 854-6181
Trail Wind ES 700/K-6
3701 E Lake Forest Dr 83716 208-854-6320
Beverly Boyd, prin. Fax 854-6321
Valley View ES 500/K-6
3555 N Milwaukee St 83704 208-854-6370
Heather Scott, prin. Fax 854-6371
Washington ES 300/K-6
1607 N 15th St 83702 208-854-6420
Wendi Forrey, prin. Fax 854-6421
White Pine ES 600/PK-6
401 E Linden St 83706 208-854-6530
Tara Coe, prin. Fax 854-6531
Whitney ES 500/K-6
1609 S Owyhee St 83705 208-854-6580
Amy Pinkerman, prin. Fax 854-6581
Whittier ES 500/K-6
301 N 29th St 83702 208-854-6630
Dr. Fernanda Brendefur, prin. Fax 854-6631

West Ada SD
Supt. — See Meridian
Andrus ES 700/K-5
6100 N Park Meadow Way 83713 208-350-4210
Peggy Ellis, prin. Fax 350-4219
Desert Sage ES 700/K-5
9325 W Mossywood Dr 83709 208-350-4020
Lisa Hahle, prin. Fax 350-4039
Donnell S of the Arts 600/K-8
7075 S Five Mile Rd 83709 208-855-4355
Joni Leipf, prin. Fax 855-4364
Frontier ES 400/PK-5
11851 Musket Dr 83713 208-350-4190
Rhonda McDonough, prin. Fax 350-4199
Gateway School of Language & Culture 400/K-8
10901 W McMillan Rd 83713 208-855-4475
Craig Ayala-Marshall, prin. Fax 855-4484
Joplin ES 400/K-5
12081 W De Meyer St 83713 208-855-4345
Debbie Gourley, prin. Fax 855-4354
Lake Hazel ES 500/K-5
11711 W Lake Hazel Rd 83709 208-350-4075
Jennifer Logan, prin. Fax 350-4084
Lake Hazel MS 1,400/6-8
11625 W La Grange St 83709 208-855-4375
Scot Montoya, prin. Fax 855-4399
Pepper Ridge ES 700/K-5
2252 S Sumpter Way 83709 208-855-4130
Joyce Messenger, prin. Fax 855-4139
Pioneer S of the Arts 700/K-5
13255 W Mcmillan Rd 83713 208-855-4100
David Jakious, prin. Fax 855-4109
Scott MS 1,000/6-8
13600 W Mcmillan Rd 83713 208-350-4060
Linda Ventura, prin. Fax 350-4074
Silver Sage ES 400/PK-5
7700 W Snohomish St 83709 208-855-4485
Amy Senethavilay, prin. Fax 855-4494
Spalding STEM Academy 600/PK-5
12311 W Braddock Dr 83709 208-350-4315
Jamie Dobson, prin. Fax 350-4314
Summerwind STEM Academy 400/K-5
3675 N Jullion St 83704 208-350-4315
Joe Palaia, prin. Fax 350-4323
Ustick ES 500/K-5
12435 W Ustick Rd 83713 208-855-4120
Jason Newell, prin. Fax 855-4129

Boise Valley Adventist S 100/PK-8
925 N Cloverdale Rd 83713 208-376-7141
Calvary Christian S 100/PK-8
111 Auto Dr 83709 208-376-0260
William Deakins, prin. Fax 639-7139
Cole Valley Christian S 400/PK-6
8775 W Ustick Rd 83704 208-947-1212
Foothills S of Arts & Sciences 100/PK-9
618 S 8th St 83702 208-331-9260
Katy Young, admin. Fax 331-3082
Petra Christian Academy 50/K-8
3080 Wildwood St 83713 208-373-4872
Ivan Rudyi, prin. Fax 953-7951
Riverstone International School 300/PK-12
5521 E Warm Springs Ave 83716 208-424-5000
Bob Carignan, head sch Fax 424-0033

Sacred Heart S 200/PK-8
3901 W Cassia St 83705 208-344-9738
Brock Carpenter M.Ed., prin. Fax 343-1939
St. Joseph's S 300/K-8
825 W Fort St 83702 208-342-4909
Anthony Quilici, prin. Fax 342-0997
St. Mark's S 300/PK-8
7503 W Northview St 83704 208-375-6654
Donna Gordon, prin. Fax 375-9471
St. Marys S 200/K-8
2620 W State St 83702 208-342-7476
Tammy Emerich, prin. Fax 345-5154

Bonners Ferry, Boundary, Pop. 2,493
Boundary County SD 101 1,500/PK-12
7188 Oak St 83805 208-267-3146
Gary Pflueger, supt. Fax 267-7217
www.bcsd101.com
Boundary County MS 300/6-8
6577 Main St Ste 100 83805 208-267-5852
David Miles, prin. Fax 267-8099
Mt. Hall ES 200/K-5
1275 Highway 1 83805 208-267-5276
Lisa Iverson, prin. Fax 267-2957
Valley View ES 400/PK-5
6750 Augusta St 83805 208-267-5519
Nathan Williams, prin. Fax 267-3388
Other Schools – See Naples

Cornerstone Christian S 50/1-8
PO Box 1877 83805 208-267-1644

Bovill, Latah, Pop. 251
Whitepine JSD 288
Supt. — See Deary
Bovill ES 100/K-3
PO Box 310 83806 208-826-3314
Doug Henderson, prin. Fax 826-3614

Bruneau, Owyhee
Bruneau-Grand View JSD 365 300/PK-12
39678 State Highway 78 83604 208-834-2260
Ryan Cantrell, supt. Fax 834-2516
www.sd365.us
Bruneau ES 100/PK-5
PO Box 277 83604 208-845-2492
Ryan Cantrell, prin. Fax 845-2495
Other Schools – See Grand View

Buhl, Twin Falls, Pop. 4,067
Buhl JSD 412 1,300/PK-12
920 Main St 83316 208-543-6436
Ronald Anthony, supt. Fax 543-6360
www.buhlschools.org
Buhl MS 300/6-8
525 Sawtooth Ave 83316 208-543-8292
Suzanne Wilkin, prin. Fax 543-5137
Popplewell ES 600/PK-5
200 6th Ave N 83316 208-543-8225
Cyndi Cooper, prin. Fax 543-2133

Clover Trinity Lutheran S 50/PK-4
3552 N 1825 E 83316 208-326-5198
Shirley Hadley, lead tchr. Fax 326-5105

Burley, Cassia, Pop. 10,210
Cassia County JSD 151 5,500/PK-12
3650 Overland Ave 83318 208-878-6600
Dr. Gaylen Smyer Ph.D., supt. Fax 878-4231
www.cassiaschools.org
Burley JHS 500/7-8
700 W 16th St 83318 208-878-6613
Steve Copmann, prin. Fax 878-6624
Dworshak ES 600/K-3
102 E 19th St 83318 208-878-6615
Wesley Nyblade, prin. Fax 878-6342
Mountain View ES 600/K-3
333 W 27th St 83318 208-878-6608
Dustin Heath, prin. Fax 878-6609
White Pine IS 800/4-6
1900 Hiland Ave 83318 208-878-6632
Matt Seely, prin. Fax 878-6635
Other Schools – See Albion, Almo, Declo, Malta, Oakley

Calder, Shoshone
Avery SD 394 50/K-8
1 School House Hill 83808 208-245-2479
Robert Vian, supt. Fax 245-2760
www.sd394.com
Calder S 50/K-8
1 School House Hill 83808 208-245-2948
Robert Vian, admin. Fax 245-2760

Caldwell, Canyon, Pop. 45,339
Caldwell SD 132 6,300/K-12
1502 Fillmore St 83605 208-455-3300
Dr. N. Shalene French, supt. Fax 455-3302
www.caldwellschools.org
Jefferson MS 700/6-8
3311 S 10th Ave 83605 208-455-3309
Meghan Wonderlich, prin. Fax 459-6773
Lewis and Clark ES 500/K-5
1102 Laster St 83607 208-455-3345
Leigh Peebles, prin. Fax 455-3346
Lincoln ES 400/K-5
1200 Grant St 83605 208-455-3321
Tricia Stone, prin. Fax 455-3324
Sacajawea ES 500/K-5
1710 N Illinois Ave 83605 208-455-3333
Paul Webster, prin. Fax 455-4462
Syringa MS 700/6-8
1100 Willow St 83605 208-455-3305
Shay Swan, prin. Fax 455-3353
Van Buren ES 600/K-5
3115 Marble Front Rd 83605 208-455-3326
Melissa Langan, prin. Fax 455-3329
Washington ES 600/K-5
2918 Washington Ave 83605 208-455-3317
Rosemary Rettig, prin. Fax 455-3338

Wilson ES 600/K-5
400 E Linden St 83605 208-455-3313
Tabitha Bruegeman, prin. Fax 454-0050

Middleton SD 134
Supt. — See Middleton
Middleton Purple Sage ES 500/PK-5
25709 El Paso Rd 83607 208-455-1148
Mark Hopkins, prin. Fax 459-2416

Notus SD 135 400/K-12
25257 Notus Rd 83607 208-459-7442
Craig Woods, supt. Fax 453-1027
www.notusschools.org
Notus ES 200/K-6
25257 Notus Rd 83607 208-459-7442
Jen Wright, prin. Fax 455-2439

Vallivue SD 139 9,500/PK-12
5207 S Montana Ave 83607 208-454-0445
Dr. Pat Charlton, supt. Fax 454-0293
www.vallivue.org
Central Canyon ES 700/PK-5
16437 S Florida Ave 83607 208-459-3367
Scott Johnstone, prin. Fax 459-3009
Vallivue MS 800/6-8
16412 S 10th Ave 83607 208-454-1426
Brian Lee, prin. Fax 454-7846
West Canyon ES 700/PK-5
19548 Ustick Rd 83607 208-459-6938
Cindy Dodd, prin. Fax 454-9572
Other Schools – See Nampa

Caldwell Adventist S 100/PK-8
2317 Wisconsin Ave 83605 208-459-4313

Cambridge, Washington, Pop. 325
Cambridge JSD 432 100/PK-12
PO Box 39 83610 208-257-3321
Ed Schumacher, supt. Fax 257-3323
Cambridge ES 100/PK-5
PO Box 39 83610 208-257-3312
Marc Scheibe, prin. Fax 257-3323

Carey, Blaine, Pop. 598
Blaine County SD 61
Supt. — See Hailey
Carey S 200/K-12
20 Panther Ln 83320 208-823-4391
John Peck, prin. Fax 823-4310

Cascade, Valley, Pop. 926
Cascade SD 422 300/PK-12
PO Box 291 83611 208-630-6057
Pal Sartori, supt. Fax 382-3797
www.cascadeschools.org
Cascade ES 100/PK-6
PO Box 291 83611 208-630-6057
Joni Stevenson, prin. Fax 382-3797

Castleford, Twin Falls, Pop. 224
Castleford JSD 417 300/PK-12
500 Main St 83321 208-537-6511
Lyle Bayley, supt. Fax 537-6855
www.castlefordschools.com
Castleford S 300/PK-12
500 Main St 83321 208-537-6511
Lyle Bayley, supt. Fax 537-6855

Cataldo, Kootenai
Kellogg JSD 391
Supt. — See Kellogg
Canyon ES 100/K-5
27491 E Schoolhouse Loop 83810 208-682-2749
Jennifer Ferreira, prin. Fax 682-3047

Challis, Custer, Pop. 1,066
Challis JSD 181 400/K-12
PO Box 304 83226 208-879-4231
Peter McPherson, supt. Fax 879-5473
www.d181.k12.id.us
Challis ES 200/K-6
PO Box 304 83226 208-879-2439
Lani Rembelski, prin. Fax 879-5525
Other Schools – See May, Stanley

Chubbuck, Bannock, Pop. 13,624
Pocatello/Chubbuck SD 25
Supt. — See Pocatello
Chubbuck ES 600/K-5
600 Chastain Dr 83202 208-237-2271
A.J. Watson, prin. Fax 237-2292
Ellis ES 500/K-5
5500 Whitaker Rd 83202 208-237-4742
Denise Lane, prin. Fax 237-4748
Tyhee ES 500/K-5
12743 W Tyhee Rd 83202 208-237-0551
Stuart Johnson, prin. Fax 237-0565

Cocolalla, Bonner
Lake Pend Oreille SD 84
Supt. — See Ponderay
Southside ES 200/K-6
PO Box 159 83813 208-263-3020
Jacquelyn Johnson, prin. Fax 265-4836

Coeur d Alene, Kootenai, Pop. 43,078
Coeur D'Alene SD 271 10,400/PK-12
1400 N Northwood Center Ct 83814 208-664-8241
Stan Olson, supt. Fax 664-1748
www.cdaschools.org
Borah ES 400/K-5
632 E Borah Ave 83814 208-664-5844
Kristina Davenport, prin. Fax 769-0725
Bryan ES 400/K-5
802 E Harrison Ave 83814 208-664-3237
Kristen Gorringe, prin. Fax 769-2075
Canfield MS 800/6-8
1800 E Dalton Ave 83815 208-664-9188
Nick Lilyquist, prin. Fax 769-2951

Fernan STEM Academy 600/PK-5
520 N 21st St 83814 208-664-2659
Kathy Livingston, prin. Fax 769-2923
Lakes Magnet MS 600/6-8
930 N 15th St 83814 208-667-4544
Jeff Bengtson, prin. Fax 769-7400
Ramsey Magnet School of Science 700/1-5
1351 W Kathleen Ave 83815 208-765-2010
Crystal Kubista, prin. Fax 769-0747
Skyway ES 600/1-5
6621 N Courcelles Pkwy 83815 208-664-8998
Janice Beauchamp, prin. Fax 664-4658
Sorensen Magnet S for Arts & Humanities 400/K-6
311 N 9th St 83814 208-664-2822
Brett DePew, prin. Fax 765-9692
Winton ES 400/K-5
920 W Lacrosse Ave 83814 208-664-3440
Eileen Blough, prin. Fax 769-2984
Woodland MS 900/6-8
2101 W St Michelle 83815 208-667-5996
David Serwat, prin. Fax 667-5997
Other Schools – See Dalton Gardens, Hayden Lake

Christ the King Lutheran S 100/PK-K
1700 E Pennsylvania Ave 83814 208-765-6736
Beth Atkinson, admin. Fax 664-9233
Coeur D'Alene Christian S 50/PK-8
6439 N 4th St 83815 208-772-7118
Dan DuPey, prin. Fax 772-7118
Holy Family S 200/PK-8
3005 W Kathleen Ave 83815 208-765-4327
Bridgit Arkoosh, prin. Fax 664-2903
Lake City Junior Academy 200/PK-10
111 E Locust Ave 83814 208-667-0877
LAM Christian Academy 100/PK-5
4800 N Ramsey Rd 83815 208-765-8238
Shelly Matthews, prin. Fax 765-6392

Cottonwood, Idaho, Pop. 891
Cottonwood JSD 242 400/PK-12
PO Box 158 83522 208-962-3971
Rene' Forsmann, supt. Fax 962-7780
www.sd242.org
Prairie ES 200/PK-6
PO Box 570 83522 208-962-3521
Rene' Forsmann, prin. Fax 962-7780

Summit Academy 100/PK-12
PO Box 427 83522 208-962-5650
James Hickel, prin. Fax 962-7129

Council, Adams, Pop. 826
Council SD 13 200/PK-12
PO Box 468 83612 208-253-4217
Tim Jensen, supt. Fax 253-4297
www.csd13.org
Council ES 200/PK-6
PO Box 68 83612 208-253-4223
Vickie Green, prin. Fax 253-4577

Craigmont, Lewis, Pop. 493
Highland JSD 305 200/PK-12
PO Box 130 83523 208-924-5211
Brad Baumberger M.Ed., supt. Fax 924-5614
www.sd305.org
Highland S 200/PK-12
PO Box 130 83523 208-924-5211
Dr. Sarah Hatfield, prin. Fax 924-5614

Culdesac, Nez Perce, Pop. 380
Culdesac JSD 342 100/PK-12
600 Culdesac Ave 83524 208-843-5413
Alan Felgenhauer, supt. Fax 843-2719
culsch.org/
Culdesac S 100/PK-12
600 Culdesac Ave 83524 208-843-5413
Chase Woodford, prin. Fax 843-2719

Dalton Gardens, Kootenai, Pop. 2,306
Coeur D'Alene SD 271
Supt. — See Coeur d Alene
Dalton ES 400/K-5
6336 N Mount Carrol St 83815 208-772-5364
Jim Gray, prin. Fax 762-2360

Dayton, Franklin, Pop. 454
West Side JSD 202 700/PK-12
PO Box 39 83232 208-747-3502
Spencer Barzee, supt. Fax 747-3705
www.wssd.k12.id.us
Beutler MS 100/6-8
626 N Westside Hwy 83232 208-747-3303
Spencer Barzee, prin. Fax 747-3637
Lee ES 300/PK-5
4726 W Highway 36 83232 208-747-3764
Melinda Royer, prin. Fax 747-3637

Deary, Latah, Pop. 490
Whitepine JSD 288 200/K-12
PO Box 249 83823 208-877-1408
Tera Reeves, supt. Fax 877-1570
www.sd288.k12.id.us
Other Schools – See Bovill

Declo, Cassia, Pop. 341
Cassia County JSD 151
Supt. — See Burley
Declo ES 400/K-5
120 E Main St 83323 208-654-2391
Kevin Lloyd, prin. Fax 654-2342
Declo JHS 300/6-8
205 E Main St 83323 208-654-9960
Scott Muir, prin. Fax 654-2070

Dietrich, Lincoln, Pop. 330
Dietrich SD 314 300/PK-12
406 N Park St 83324 208-544-2158
Ben Hardcastle, supt. Fax 544-2832
www.sd314.k12.id.us
Dietrich S 300/PK-12
406 N Park St 83324 208-544-2158
Stefanie Shaw, prin. Fax 544-2832

Donnelly, Valley, Pop. 149
McCall-Donnelly JSD 421
Supt. — See Mc Call
Donnelly ES 100/K-5
PO Box 369 83615 208-325-4433
Jacob Olson, prin. Fax 325-5030

Downey, Bannock, Pop. 617
Marsh Valley JSD 21
Supt. — See Arimo
Downey ES 100/PK-6
88 S 4th St E 83234 208-897-5220
Nancy Dalley, prin. Fax 897-5221

Driggs, Teton, Pop. 1,636
Teton County SD 401 1,700/PK-12
PO Box 775 83422 208-228-5923
Monte Woolstenhulme, supt. Fax 354-2250
tsd401.org
Driggs ES 300/K-5
481 N Main St 83422 208-228-5927
Greg Larson, prin. Fax 354-2336
Rendezvous Upper ES 300/4-5
211 E Howard Ave 83422 208-228-5926
Megan Bybee, prin. Fax 354-2852
Teton MS 400/6-8
935 N 5th E 83422 208-228-5925
Brian Ashton, prin. Fax 354-8685
Other Schools – See Tetonia, Victor

Learning Academy of Teton Valley 100/PK-8
1480 S 500 W 83422 208-354-7898
Danielle Wilson, prin.
Table Rock Christian S 50/K-6
PO Box 621 83422 208-354-9674
Roger Shea, hdmstr.

Dubois, Clark, Pop. 673
Clark County SD 161 200/PK-12
PO Box 237 83423 208-374-5215
Paula Gordon, supt. Fax 374-5234
www.clarkcountyschools161.org
Ross ES 100/PK-5
PO Box 237 83423 208-374-5206
Paula Gordon, supt. Fax 374-5103

Eagle, Ada, Pop. 19,545
West Ada SD
Supt. — See Meridian
Eagle ES of the Arts 400/1-5
475 N Eagle Rd 83616 208-855-4365
Cindy Marshall, prin. Fax 855-4374
Eagle Hills ES 500/K-5
650 E Ranch Dr 83616 208-350-4085
Jason Leforgee, prin. Fax 350-4094
Eagle MS 1,300/6-8
1000 W Floating Feather Rd 83616 208-350-4255
Tony Nelson, prin. Fax 350-4269
Galileo STEM Academy 700/K-8
4735 W Saguaro Dr 83616 208-350-4105
Rob Lamb, prin. Fax 350-4119
Seven Oaks ES 400/PK-5
1441 N Sevenoaks Way 83616 208-350-4095
Lil Folkner, prin. Fax 350-4104

Eagle Adventist Christian S 50/K-8
538 W State St 83616 208-938-0093
Montessori Academy 100/PK-6
1400 Park Ln 83616 208-939-6333

Elk City, Idaho, Pop. 200
Mountain View SD 244
Supt. — See Grangeville
Elk City S 50/PK-8
PO Box 419 83525 208-842-2218
Susan Hill, prin. Fax 842-2225

Emmett, Gem, Pop. 6,420
Emmett ISD 221 2,500/K-12
400 S Pine St 83617 208-365-6301
Wayne Rush, supt. Fax 365-2961
emmettschools.org
Carberry ES 500/K-4
1950 E 12th St 83617 208-365-0839
Donna Schwarting, prin. Fax 365-0871
Emmett MS 600/5-8
301 E 4th St 83617 208-365-2921
Richard Winegar, prin. Fax 365-2427
Shadow Butte ES 500/K-5
3900 W Idaho Blvd 83617 208-365-0877
Todd Adams, prin. Fax 365-0887
Other Schools – See Ola, Sweet

Fairfield, Camas, Pop. 404
Camas County SD 121 200/K-12
610 Soldier Rd 83327 208-764-2625
Jim Cobble, supt. Fax 764-9218
www.camascountyschools.org/
Camas County S 100/K-8
610 Soldier Rd 83327 208-764-2472
Nathan Whittle, prin. Fax 764-2018

Fernwood, Benewah
Saint Maries JSD 41
Supt. — See Saint Maries
UpRiver ES 100/K-6
PO Box 249 83830 208-245-3650
Nicole Goucher, prin. Fax 245-3066

Filer, Twin Falls, Pop. 2,469
Filer SD 413 1,500/PK-12
700B Stevens Ave 83328 208-326-5981
Dr. John Graham, supt. Fax 326-3350
www.filer.k12.id.us
Filer ES 500/PK-3
700 Stevens Ave 83328 208-326-4369
Teri Peters, prin. Fax 326-5960
Filer IS 300/4-6
833 W 6th St 83328 208-326-3069
Matt Mahannah, prin. Fax 326-3071
Filer MS 300/7-8
299 Highway 30 83328 208-326-5906
Shane Hild, prin. Fax 326-3385
Other Schools – See Twin Falls

Firth, Bingham, Pop. 462
Firth SD 59 800/PK-12
319 Lincoln St 83236 208-346-6815
Sid Tubbs, supt. Fax 346-6814
www.firthschools.org
Firth MS 200/5-8
410 Roosevelt St 83236 208-346-6240
David Mecham, prin. Fax 346-4306
Johnson ES 300/PK-4
735 N 600 E 83236 208-346-6848
Sid Tubbs, prin. Fax 346-4320

Fruitland, Payette, Pop. 4,599
Fruitland SD 373 1,700/PK-12
PO Box A 83619 208-452-3595
Teresa Fabricius, supt. Fax 452-6430
www.fruitlandschools.org
Fruitland ES 700/PK-5
PO Box A 83619 208-452-3360
Jared Olsen, prin. Fax 452-3363
Fruitland MS 400/6-8
PO Box A 83619 208-452-3350
Shane Burrup, prin. Fax 452-4063

Garden Valley, Boise, Pop. 390
Garden Valley SD 71 200/PK-12
PO Box 710 83622 208-462-3756
Gregory Alexander, supt. Fax 462-3570
www.gvsd.net
Garden Valley S 200/PK-12
PO Box 710 83622 208-462-3756
Gregory Alexander, supt. Fax 462-3570
Lowman ES 50/K-6
PO Box 710 83622 208-259-3333
Gregory Alexander, supt. Fax 259-3333

Genesee, Latah, Pop. 930
Genesee JSD 282 300/K-12
PO Box 98 83832 208-285-1161
Wendy Moore, supt. Fax 285-1495
www.sd282.org/
Genesee S 300/K-12
PO Box 98 83832 208-285-1161
Kelly Caldwell, prin. Fax 285-1495

Georgetown, Bear Lake, Pop. 462
Bear Lake County SD 33
Supt. — See Paris
Georgetown ES 100/K-5
PO Box 100 83239 208-847-0583
Laurel Jensen, prin. Fax 847-0588

Glenns Ferry, Elmore, Pop. 1,301
Glenns Ferry JSD 192 500/PK-12
800 Old Highway 30 83623 208-366-7436
Cody Fisher, supt. Fax 366-7455
www.glennsferryschools.org/
Glenns Ferry ES 200/PK-5
639 N Bannock St 83623 208-366-7434
Rob Spriggs, prin. Fax 366-2056
Glenns Ferry MS 100/6-8
639 N Bannock St 83623 208-366-7438
Rob Spriggs, prin. Fax 366-2056

Gooding, Gooding, Pop. 3,514
Gooding JSD 231 1,200/PK-12
507 Idaho St 83330 208-934-4321
Spencer Larsen, supt. Fax 934-4403
www.goodingschools.org
Gooding ES 500/PK-5
1045 7th Ave W 83330 208-934-4941
Brandee Sabala, prin. Fax 934-4898
Gooding MS 300/6-8
1047 7th Ave W 83330 208-934-8443
Chad Avery, prin. Fax 934-4898

Grace, Caribou, Pop. 908
Grace JSD 148 400/PK-12
PO Box 347 83241 208-425-3984
Jamie Holyoak, supt. Fax 425-3809
www.sd148.org/
Grace ES 200/PK-6
PO Box 347 83241 208-425-3984
Jamie Holyoak, prin. Fax 425-3809
Other Schools – See Thatcher

Grand View, Owyhee, Pop. 441
Bruneau-Grand View JSD 365
Supt. — See Bruneau
Grand View ES 100/PK-5
PO Box 39 83624 208-834-2775
Ryan Cantrell, prin. Fax 834-2529

Grangeville, Idaho, Pop. 3,096
Mountain View SD 244 1,200/PK-12
714 Jefferson St 83530 208-983-0990
Kent Stokes, supt. Fax 983-1245
www.sd244.org
Grangeville ES 500/PK-8
400 S Idaho Ave 83530 208-983-0400
Susan Anderson, prin. Fax 983-3407
Other Schools – See Elk City, Kooskia

SS. Peter & Paul S 100/PK-8
330 S B St 83530 208-983-2182
Leslie McDaniel, prin. Fax 983-0115

Greenleaf, Canyon, Pop. 835

Greenleaf Friends Academy 200/PK-12
PO Box 368 83626 208-459-6346

Hagerman, Gooding, Pop. 864
Hagerman JSD 233 400/K-12
324 N 2nd Ave 83332 208-837-6344
Fax 837-6380
www.hjsd.org
Hagerman ES 200/K-6
324 N 2nd Ave 83332 208-837-4777
Fax 837-4737

Hailey, Blaine, Pop. 7,880
Blaine County SD 61 3,300/K-12
118 W Bullion St 83333 208-578-5000
Dr. GwenCarol Holmes, supt. Fax 578-5110
www.blaineschools.org/
Hailey ES 500/K-5
520 S 1st Ave 83333 208-788-3091
Thad Biggers, prin. Fax 788-2183
Wood River MS 700/6-8
900 N 2nd Ave 83333 208-578-5030
Fritz Peters, prin. Fax 578-5130
Other Schools – See Bellevue, Carey, Ketchum

Hamer, Jefferson, Pop. 44
West Jefferson SD 253
Supt. — See Terreton
Hamer ES 50/K-4
2450 E 2100 N 83425 208-662-5238
Steve Riding, prin. Fax 662-5473

Hansen, Twin Falls, Pop. 1,129
Hansen SD 415 400/PK-12
550 Main St S 83334 208-423-6387
Kristin Beck, supt. Fax 423-6808
www.hansen.k12.id.us
Hansen ES 200/PK-6
550 Main St S 83334 208-423-5475
Heidi Skinner, prin. Fax 423-6808

Harrison, Kootenai, Pop. 203
Kootenai SD 274 200/K-12
13030 E Ogara Rd 83833 208-689-3631
Lynette Ferguson, supt. Fax 689-3641
www.ksd-id.schoolloop.com
Harrison ES 100/K-5
13030 E Ogara Rd 83833 208-689-3511
Lynette Ferguson, prin. Fax 689-3641

Hayden, Kootenai, Pop. 13,034

North Idaho Christian S 200/1-12
251 W Miles Ave 83835 208-772-7546
Cal Booth, admin. Fax 719-3000

Hayden Lake, Kootenai, Pop. 568
Coeur D'Alene SD 271
Supt. — See Coeur d Alene
Atlas ES 500/1-5
3000 W Honeysuckle Ave 83835 208-762-0626
Heather Somers, prin. Fax 762-2596
Hayden Meadows ES 600/K-5
900 E Hayden Ave 83835 208-772-5006
Lisa Pica, prin. Fax 772-0703
Northwest Expedition Academy 400/K-5
9650 N Government Way 83835 208-763-0800
Bill Rutherford, admin. Fax 769-2923

Hazelton, Jerome, Pop. 738
Valley SD 262 600/PK-12
882 Valley Rd 83335 208-829-5333
Eric Anderson, supt. Fax 829-5548
www.valleyvikings.org
Valley S 600/PK-12
882 Valley Rd 83335 208-829-5353
Risa Moffitt, admin. Fax 829-5548

Heyburn, Minidoka, Pop. 3,058
Minidoka County JSD 331
Supt. — See Rupert
Heyburn ES 600/K-5
1151 7th St 83336 208-679-2400
Sanie Baker, prin. Fax 679-5877

Homedale, Owyhee, Pop. 2,586
Homedale JSD 370 1,200/K-12
116 E Owyhee Ave 83628 208-337-4611
Rob Sauer, supt. Fax 337-4911
www.homedaleschools.org
Homedale ES 500/K-4
420 W Washington Ave 83628 208-337-4033
Terri Vasquez, prin. Fax 337-4703
Homedale MS 400/5-8
3437 Johnstone Rd 83628 208-337-5780
Moss Strong, prin. Fax 337-5782

Hope, Bonner, Pop. 85
Lake Pend Oreille SD 84
Supt. — See Ponderay
Hope ES 100/K-6
255 Hope School Rd 83836 208-255-7232
Sherri Hatley, prin. Fax 264-5681

Horseshoe Bend, Boise, Pop. 696
Horseshoe Bend SD 73 300/PK-12
398 School Dr 83629 208-793-2225
Dennis Chesnut, supt. Fax 793-2449
www.hsbschools.org
Horseshoe Bend ES 100/PK-6
398 School Dr 83629 208-793-2225
Dennis Chesnut, admin. Fax 793-2449

Howe, Butte
Butte County JSD 111
Supt. — See Arco
Howe ES 50/K-5
PO Box 60 83244 208-767-3422
Robert Chambers, prin. Fax 527-8950

Idaho City, Boise, Pop. 473
Basin SD 72 400/PK-12
PO Box 227 83631 208-392-4183
John McFarlane, supt. Fax 392-9954
www.idahocityschools.net
Basin ES 200/PK-6
PO Box 227 83631 208-392-6631
Jamie Pilkerton, prin. Fax 392-4198

Idaho Falls, Bonneville, Pop. 55,872
Bonneville JSD 93 10,900/PK-12
3497 N Ammon Rd 83401 208-525-4400
Dr. Charles Shackett, supt. Fax 529-0104
www.d93schools.org
Bridgewater ES 300/K-6
1499 Indian Hollow Dr 83401 208-552-5577
Terri Beseris, prin. Fax 552-5578
Cloverdale ES 500/K-6
3999 Greenwillow Ln 83401 208-525-4450
Jeanne Johnson, prin. Fax 524-0171
Discovery ES 400/K-6
2935 Golden Rod Dr 83401 208-552-7711
Ken Marlowe, prin. Fax 552-7712
Fairview ES 300/K-6
979 E 97th N 83401 208-525-4425
Nicki Pack, prin. Fax 525-4426
Falls Valley ES 600/PK-6
2455 Virlow St 83401 208-525-4455
Tina Orme, prin. Fax 525-4459
Rocky Mountain MS 800/7-8
3443 N Ammon Rd 83401 208-525-4403
Thomas Kennedy, prin. Fax 525-4469
Summit Hills ES K-6
2853 N Lucina Ave 83401 208-552-8500
Tom Gauchay, prin. Fax 552-8501
Tiebreaker ES 400/PK-6
3100 1st St 83401 208-525-4480
Kent Patterson, prin. Fax 525-4482
Ucon ES 400/K-6
10841 N 41st E 83401 208-525-4430
Daniel Page, prin. Fax 525-4477
Other Schools – See Ammon, Iona

Idaho Falls SD 91 10,500/PK-12
690 John Adams Pkwy 83401 208-525-7500
George Boland, supt. Fax 525-7596
www.d91.k12.id.us
Boyes ES 400/K-6
1875 Brentwood Dr 83402 208-525-7630
Pauline Alessi, prin. Fax 525-7633
Bunker ES 300/K-6
1385 E 16th St 83404 208-525-7606
Andrea Williams, prin. Fax 525-7610
Bush ES 500/K-6
380 W Anderson St 83402 208-525-7602
Joshua Newell, prin. Fax 525-7604
Eagle Rock MS 800/7-8
2020 Pancheri Dr 83402 208-525-7700
Matt Hancock, prin. Fax 525-7703
Edgemont Gardens ES 600/K-6
1240 Azalea Dr 83404 208-525-7618
David Webster, prin. Fax 525-7622
Erickson ES 500/K-6
940 Garfield 83401 208-525-7612
Sheila Walter, prin. Fax 525-7629
Fox Hollow ES 600/PK-6
2365 Genevieve Way 83402 208-524-7890
Tammi Utter, prin. Fax 524-7899
Hawthorne ES 300/K-6
520 S Boulevard 83402 208-525-7636
Randy Stocking, prin. Fax 525-7640
Linden Park ES 500/K-6
1305 9th St 83404 208-525-7642
David England, prin. Fax 525-7643
Longfellow ES 500/K-6
2500 S Higbee Ave 83404 208-525-7648
Kristoffer Smith, prin. Fax 525-7647
Sunnyside ES 500/K-6
165 Cobblestone Ln 83404 208-524-7880
Lance Lindley, prin. Fax 524-7889
Taylorview MS 800/7-8
350 Castlerock Ln 83404 208-524-7850
Kathy Smith, prin. Fax 524-7851
Temple View ES 500/K-6
1500 Scorpius Dr 83402 208-525-7660
Sarah Childers, prin. Fax 525-7659
Westside ES 500/K-6
2680 Newman Dr 83402 208-525-7666
Dr. Terry Miller, prin. Fax 525-7671

Holy Rosary S 100/PK-6
161 9th St 83404 208-522-7781
Carina VanPelt M.Ed., prin. Fax 522-7782
Hope Lutheran S 100/PK-6
2071 12th St 83404 208-529-8080
DiAnn Brown, dir. Fax 529-8880
Snake River Montessori S 100/PK-6
2970 1st St 83401 208-524-4730
Watersprings S 500/PK-12
4250 S 25th E 83404 208-542-6250
Katheryn King, prin. Fax 441-6806

Inkom, Bannock, Pop. 843
Marsh Valley JSD 21
Supt. — See Arimo
Inkom ES 300/PK-6
PO Box 430 83245 208-775-3361
Terry Johnson, prin. Fax 775-4436

Iona, Bonneville, Pop. 1,784
Bonneville JSD 93
Supt. — See Idaho Falls
Iona ES 500/K-6
5338 Owens St 83427 208-525-4440
Jason Curtis, prin. Fax 524-4240

Irwin, Bonneville, Pop. 218
Swan Valley ESD 92 100/K-8
PO Box 220 83428 208-483-2405
Michael Jacobson, supt. Fax 483-2415
sd92.k12.id.us
Swan Valley ES 100/K-8
PO Box 220 83428 208-483-2405
Michael Jacobson, prin. Fax 483-2415

Jerome, Jerome, Pop. 10,745
Jerome JSD 261 3,800/PK-12
125 4th Ave W 83338 208-324-2392
Dale Layne, supt. Fax 324-7609
www.jeromeschools.org
Horizon ES 800/PK-3
934 10th Ave E 83338 208-324-4841
Terri Fisher, prin. Fax 324-2015
Jefferson ES 600/K-3
600 N Fillmore St 83338 208-324-8896
Angie Brulotte, prin. Fax 324-8897
Jerome MS 900/6-8
520 10th Ave W 83338 208-324-8134
Landon Marlor, prin. Fax 324-7458
Summit ES 600/4-5
200 10th Ave W 83338 208-324-3396
Eva Meyerhoeffer, prin. Fax 324-3399

Juliaetta, Latah, Pop. 565
Kendrick JSD 283 300/PK-12
305 4th St 83535 208-289-4211
Dr. Lindsay Park Ph.D., supt. Fax 289-4201
www.dist283.org/
Juliaetta ES 100/PK-6
305 4th St 83535 208-276-3422
Dr. Lindsay Park Ph.D., prin. Fax 276-3424

Kamiah, Lewis, Pop. 1,246
Kamiah JSD 304 500/PK-12
1102 Hill St 83536 208-935-2991
Fred Mercer, supt. Fax 935-4005
www.kamiah.org/
Kamiah ES 200/PK-3
1102 Hill St 83536 208-935-4012
Steve Higgins, prin. Fax 935-4014
Kamiah MS 200/4-8
1102 Hill St 83536 208-935-4040
Peggy Flerchinger, prin. Fax 935-4041

Kellogg, Shoshone, Pop. 2,083
Kellogg JSD 391 1,000/K-12
800 Bunker Ave 83837 208-784-1348
Woody Woodford, supt. Fax 786-3331
www.kelloggschools.org
Kellogg MS 300/6-8
810 Bunker Ave 83837 208-784-1311
Jan Bayer, prin. Fax 784-0134
Other Schools – See Cataldo, Pinehurst

Ketchum, Blaine, Pop. 2,665
Blaine County SD 61
Supt. — See Hailey
Hemingway ES 400/K-6
111 8th St W 83340 208-578-5050
Patricia Short, prin. Fax 578-5150

Kimberly, Twin Falls, Pop. 3,233
Kimberly SD 414 1,700/K-12
141 Center St W 83341 208-423-4170
Luke Schroeder, supt. Fax 423-6155
www.kimberly.edu/
Kimberly ES 800/K-5
141 Center St W 83341 208-423-4170
Megan Garner, prin. Fax 423-6753
Kimberly MS 400/6-8
141 Center St W 83341 208-423-4170
Mathew Schvaneveldt, prin. Fax 423-6155

Kooskia, Idaho, Pop. 590
Mountain View SD 244
Supt. — See Grangeville
Clearwater Valley ES 200/PK-5
PO Box 100 83539 208-926-4311
Susan Hill, prin. Fax 926-7883

Kootenai, Bonner, Pop. 661
Lake Pend Oreille SD 84
Supt. — See Ponderay
Kootenai ES 400/PK-6
301 Sprague St 83840 208-255-4076
Kelli Knowles, prin. Fax 263-4699

Kuna, Ada, Pop. 14,851
Kuna JSD 3 5,200/PK-12
711 E Porter St 83634 208-922-1000
Wendy Johnson, supt. Fax 922-5646
www.kunaschools.org
Crimson Point ES 500/PK-6
1941 N Shayla Ave 83634 208-955-0230
Brandon Crusat, prin. Fax 955-0239
Hubbard ES 400/PK-3
311 E Porter St 83634 208-922-1007
Donene Rognlie, prin. Fax 922-1021
Indian Creek ES 300/K-3
911 W 4th St 83634 208-922-1009
Kimberly Barker, prin. Fax 922-1029
Kuna MS 800/7-8
1360 Boise St 83634 208-922-1002
Paul Souza, prin. Fax 922-1030
Reed ES 600/K-6
1670 N Linder Rd 83634 208-955-0275
Kevin Gifford, prin. Fax 955-0279
Ross ES 200/4-6
610 N School Ave 83634 208-922-1011
Cindy Orr, prin. Fax 922-1018
Teed ES 300/4-6
441 E Porter St 83634 208-922-1005
Deb McGrath, prin. Fax 922-1024
Other Schools – See Meridian

Lapwai, Nez Perce, Pop. 1,098
Lapwai SD 341 500/PK-12
404 S Main St 83540 208-843-2622
Dr. David Aiken, supt. Fax 843-7746
www.lapwai.org
Lapwai ES 300/PK-5
404 S Main St 83540 208-843-2960
Teri Wagner, prin. Fax 843-2978

Lava Hot Springs, Bannock, Pop. 405
Marsh Valley JSD 21
Supt. — See Arimo
Lava ES 100/PK-6
PO Box 660 83246 208-776-5281
Nancy Dalley, prin. Fax 776-5204

Leadore, Lemhi, Pop. 105
South Lemhi SD 292 100/PK-12
PO Box 119 83464 208-768-2441
Michael Jacobson, supt. Fax 768-2797
www.leadoreschool.org
Leadore S 100/PK-12
PO Box 119 83464 208-768-2441
Michael Jacobson, prin. Fax 768-2797
Other Schools – See Tendoy

Lenore, Nez Perce
Orofino JSD 171
Supt. — See Orofino
Cavendish Teakean ES 50/K-6
455 Middle Rd 83541 208-476-5393
Jenine Nord, lead tchr. Fax 476-5082

Lewiston, Nez Perce, Pop. 31,213
Lewiston ISD 1 5,000/PK-12
3317 12th St 83501 208-748-3000
Dr. Robert Donaldson, supt. Fax 748-3059
www.lewistonschools.net
Camelot ES 500/K-6
1903 Grelle Ave 83501 208-748-3500
Karla Carper, prin. Fax 748-3519
Centennial ES 500/K-6
815 Burrell Ave 83501 208-748-3550
Tim Coles, prin. Fax 748-3599
McGhee ES 300/K-6
636 Warner Ave 83501 208-748-3600
Mary Wells, prin. Fax 748-3649
McSorley ES 300/K-6
2020 15th St 83501 208-748-3650
Jason Hoffman, prin. Fax 748-3669
Orchard ES 300/K-6
3429 12th St 83501 208-748-3700
Jennifer Gomez, prin. Fax 748-3729
Webster ES 300/K-6
1409 8th St 83501 208-748-3800
Alex Church, prin. Fax 748-3849
Whitman ES 400/PK-6
1840 9th Ave 83501 208-748-3850
Timothy Sperber, prin. Fax 748-3899

All Saints Catholic S 100/PK-6
641 5th Ave 83501 208-743-4411
Dennis Hammrich, prin. Fax 743-9563
Beacon Christian S 100/K-8
615 Stewart Ave 83501 208-743-8361
Cornerstone Christian S 100/K-8
4073 Fairway Dr 83501 208-798-7149
Cyndy Kym, admin. Fax 746-2158

Mc Call, Valley, Pop. 2,959
McCall-Donnelly JSD 421 1,100/PK-12
120 Idaho St 83638 208-634-2161
Jim Foudy, supt. Fax 634-4075
www.mdsd.org
Morgan ES 400/PK-5
125 S Samson Trl 83638 208-634-2219
Valerie Berg, prin. Fax 634-4695
Payette Lakes MS 200/6-8
111 S Samson Trl 83638 208-634-5994
Susan Buescher, prin. Fax 634-5231
Other Schools – See Donnelly

Mc Cammon, Bannock, Pop. 805
Marsh Valley JSD 21
Supt. — See Arimo
Mountain View ES 300/PK-6
PO Box 69 83250 208-254-3223
Nichole Hales, prin. Fax 254-3224

Mackay, Custer, Pop. 515
Mackay JSD 182 200/PK-12
PO Box 390 83251 208-588-2896
Dr. Susan Buescher, supt. Fax 588-2269
www.mackayschools.org
Mackay ES 100/PK-6
PO Box 390 83251 208-588-2834
Nicole Latsch, prin. Fax 588-2269

Malad City, Oneida, Pop. 2,070
Oneida County SD 351 900/PK-12
25 E 50 S Ste A 83252 208-534-6080
Dr. Rich Moore, supt. Fax 534-6080
www.oneidaschooldistrict.org
Malad ES 400/PK-5
250 W 400 N 83252 208-497-5220
B. Hannah, prin. Fax 497-5220
Malad MS 200/6-8
175 Jenkins Ave 83252 208-497-5877
Sheldon Vaughan, prin. Fax 497-5877
Other Schools – See Stone

Malta, Cassia, Pop. 193
Cassia County JSD 151
Supt. — See Burley
Raft River ES 200/PK-6
PO Box 615 83342 208-645-2561
Katerina Loock, prin. Fax 645-2564

Marsing, Owyhee, Pop. 1,018
Marsing JSD 363 900/K-12
PO Box 340 83639 208-649-5411
Norm Stewart, supt. Fax 649-5517
www.marsingschools.org/
Marsing ES 400/K-5
PO Box 340 83639 208-649-5411
Dr. Glen Croft, prin. Fax 649-5520
Marsing MS 200/6-8
PO Box 340 83639 208-649-5411
Nick Ketterling, prin. Fax 649-5519

May, Lemhi
Challis JSD 181
Supt. — See Challis
Patterson ES 50/K-6
13 Patterson Rd 83253 208-876-4277
Brian Robb, lead tchr. Fax 876-4277

Melba, Canyon, Pop. 503
Melba JSD 136 800/PK-12
PO Box 185 83641 208-495-1141
Andy Grover, supt. Fax 495-1142
www.melbaschools.org
Melba ES 400/PK-6
PO Box 185 83641 208-495-2508
Sherry Adams, prin. Fax 495-2367

Menan, Jefferson, Pop. 728
Jefferson County JSD 251
Supt. — See Rigby
Midway ES 400/K-5
623 N 3500 E 83434 208-754-8604
Gary Comstock, prin. Fax 754-4847

Meridian, Ada, Pop. 73,335
Kuna JSD 3
Supt. — See Kuna
Silver Trail ES 600/K-6
2950 W Mason Creek St 83642 208-472-9731
Ken Lilienkamp, prin. Fax 472-9740

West Ada SD 36,800/PK-12
1303 E Central Dr 83642 208-855-4500
Dr. Mary Ann Ranells, supt. Fax 350-5962
www.westada.org
Chaparral ES 600/K-5
1155 N Deer Creek Ln 83642 208-350-4180
Doni Davis, prin. Fax 350-4189
Chief Joseph S of the Arts 600/K-5
1100 E Chateau Dr, 208-350-4200
Gretchen Hart, prin. Fax 350-4209
Discovery ES 500/K-5
2100 E Leighfield Dr, 208-855-4090
Mike Dudley, prin. Fax 855-4096
Heritage MS 1,100/6-8
4990 N Meridian Rd, 208-350-4130
Susan McInerney, prin. Fax 350-4139
Hillsdale ES PK-5
5225 S Stockenham Way 83642 208-350-4432
Khristie Bair, prin. Fax 350-4442
Hunter ES 800/PK-5
2051 W McMillan Rd, 208-855-4285
Julie Prince, prin. Fax 855-4286
Lewis & Clark MS 1,100/6-8
4141 E Pine Ave 83642 208-350-4270
Kelly Davies, prin. Fax 350-4284
McPherson ES 500/K-5
1050 E Amity Rd 83642 208-855-4300
Shannon Murdoch, prin. Fax 855-4309
Meridian ES 500/PK-5
1035 NW 1st St 83642 208-855-4335
Marcus Myers, prin. Fax 855-4344
Meridian MS 1,000/6-8
1507 W 8th St 83642 208-855-4225
Lisa Austin, prin. Fax 855-4248
Morgan STEM Academy 400/K-5
1825 W Chateau Dr, 208-855-4430
Ryan Wilhite, prin. Fax 855-4439
Paramount ES 800/K-5
550 W Producer Dr, 208-350-4120
Dean Brigham, prin. Fax 350-4129
Peregrine ES 600/PK-5
1860 W Waltman St 83642 208-350-4285
John Labbe, prin. Fax 350-4294
Ponderosa ES 600/K-5
2950 N Naomi Ave, 208-855-4040
Fax 855-4048
Prospect ES 800/K-5
4300 N Red Horse Way, 208-350-4000
Joann Grether, prin. Fax 350-4019
River Valley ES 500/K-5
2900 E River Valley St, 208-350-4295
John Ursillo, prin. Fax 350-4304
Sawtooth MS 1,000/6-8
3730 N Linder Rd, 208-855-4200
Kevin Leishman, prin. Fax 855-4224
Siena ES 800/K-5
2870 E Rome Dr 83642 208-350-4370
Kacey Schneidt, prin. Fax 350-4379
Victory MS 6-8
920 W Kodiak Dr 83642 208-350-4443
Brett Heller, prin. Fax 350-4444
Willow Creek ES K-5
6195 N Long Lake Way, 208-350-4410
Jared Christensen, prin.
Other Schools – See Boise, Eagle, Star

Ambrose S 400/K-12
6100 N Locust Grove Rd, 208-323-3888
Kirk VanderLeest, hdmstr. Fax 672-0522
Covenant Academy 50/K-12
2400 E Fairview Ave 83642 208-377-2385
David Barrett, admin. Fax 362-8061
St. Ignatius Catholic S 400/PK-8
6180 N Meridian Rd, 208-888-4759
Andi Kane, prin.

Middleton, Canyon, Pop. 5,406
Middleton SD 134 3,700/PK-12
5 S 3rd Ave W 83644 208-585-3027
Dr. Josh Middleton, supt. Fax 585-3028
www.msd134.org
Middleton Heights ES 500/K-5
611 Cemetery Rd 83644 208-585-3021
Kimberly Atkinson, prin. Fax 585-3080
Middleton MS 900/6-8
511 W Main St 83644 208-585-3251
Andrew Horning, prin. Fax 585-2098
Middleton Mill Creek ES 700/K-5
500 N Middleton Rd 83644 208-585-3065
Lisa Osler, prin. Fax 585-6697
Other Schools – See Caldwell

Midvale, Washington, Pop. 169
Midvale SD 433 100/K-12
PO Box 130 83645 208-355-2234
James Warren, supt. Fax 355-2347
www.midvalerangers.org
Midvale S 100/K-12
PO Box 130 83645 208-355-2234
KyLee Morris, prin. Fax 355-2347

Montpelier, Bear Lake, Pop. 2,578
Bear Lake County SD 33
Supt. — See Paris
Bear Lake MS 300/6-8
633 Washington St 83254 208-847-2255
Dr. Steve Heeder, prin. Fax 847-3626
Winters ES 300/K-5
535 Clay St 83254 208-847-0477
Laurel Jensen, prin. Fax 847-3959

Moscow, Latah, Pop. 23,195
Moscow SD 281 2,400/PK-12
650 N Cleveland St 83843 208-882-1120
Greg Bailey, supt. Fax 883-4440
www.msd281.org
McDonald ES 400/PK-5
2323 E D St 83843 208-882-0228
Kim Mikolajczyk, prin. Fax 892-1216
Moscow MS 600/6-8
1410 E D St 83843 208-882-3577
Kevin Hill, prin. Fax 892-1182
Russell ES 200/3-5
119 N Adams St 83843 208-882-2715
Craig Allen, prin. Fax 892-1241
West Park ES 200/K-2
510 S Home St 83843 208-882-2714
William Marineau, prin. Fax 892-1259
Whitmore ES 300/K-5
110 S Blaine St 83843 208-882-2621
Kendra McMillan, prin. Fax 892-1202

Logos S 400/PK-12
110 Baker St 83843 208-882-1226
Matt Whitling, prin. Fax 209-8511
Palouse Hills Christian S 50/K-8
3148 Tomer Rd 83843 208-882-0350
St. Mary's S 100/K-8
412 N Monroe St 83843 208-882-2121
Jennifer Beller, prin. Fax 882-0970

Mountain Home, Elmore, Pop. 13,628
Mountain Home SD 193 3,400/PK-12
PO Box 1390 83647 208-587-2580
James Gilbert, supt. Fax 587-9896
www.mtnhomesd.org
East ES 500/PK-4
775 N 10th E 83647 208-587-2575
Ryan Kuntz, prin. Fax 587-2576
Hacker MS 600/5-7
550 E Jackson St 83647 208-587-2500
John Clark, prin. Fax 587-2564
North ES 400/PK-4
290 E 12th N 83647 208-587-2585
Anita Straw, prin. Fax 587-2565
West ES 400/K-4
415 W 2nd N 83647 208-587-2595
Nichole Cruser, prin. Fax 587-2693
Other Schools – See Mountain Home AFB, Pine

Desert View Christian S 50/1-8
PO Box 124 83647 208-580-0512

Mountain Home AFB, Elmore, Pop. 3,053
Mountain Home SD 193
Supt. — See Mountain Home
Stephensen ES 200/K-4
200 Gunfighter Ave 83648 208-832-4651
Phil McCluskey, prin. Fax 832-1120

Mullan, Shoshone, Pop. 674
Mullan SD 392 100/K-12
PO Box 71 83846 208-744-1118
Leslie Wells, supt. Fax 744-1119
www.mullanschools.com
Mullan ES 100/K-6
PO Box 71 83846 208-744-1118
Leslie Wells, prin. Fax 744-1119

Murtaugh, Twin Falls, Pop. 114
Murtaugh JSD 418 200/PK-12
PO Box 117 83344 208-432-5451
Michele Capps, supt. Fax 432-5477
www.murtaugh.k12.id.us/
Murtaugh ES 100/PK-5
PO Box 117 83344 208-432-5233
Michele Capps, prin. Fax 432-5551
Murtaugh MS 100/6-8
PO Box 117 83344 208-432-5451
Adam Johnson, prin. Fax 432-5477

Nampa, Canyon, Pop. 79,667
Nampa SD 131 15,400/PK-12
619 S Canyon St 83686 208-468-4600
Dr. Paula Kellerer, supt. Fax 468-4638
www.nsd131.org
Centennial ES 600/K-5
522 Mason Ln 83686 208-468-4627
Dr. Paul Harman, prin. Fax 468-2814
Central ES 500/K-5
1415 5th St S 83651 208-468-4611
Tami Vandeventer, prin. Fax 468-2813
East Valley MS 1,000/6-8
4085 E Greenhurst Rd 83686 208-468-4760
Matt Crist, admin. Fax 468-4762
Endeavor ES 600/K-5
2824 E Victory Rd 83687 208-468-4629
Dominic de la Paz, prin. Fax 468-2822
Greenhurst ES 400/K-5
1701 Discovery Pl 83686 208-468-4612
Gina White, prin. Fax 468-2810
Iowa ES 600/K-5
626 W Iowa Ave 83686 208-468-4621
Chance Whitmore, prin. Fax 468-2815
Lake Ridge ES 600/K-5
615 Burke Ln 83686 208-468-4626
Steve Labau, prin. Fax 468-2824
Lone Star MS 900/6-8
11055 Lone Star Rd 83651 208-468-4745
Greg Heideman, prin. Fax 468-2828
Nampa ECC 100/PK-PK
1701 Discovery Pl 83686 208-498-0560
Gina White, prin. Fax 468-2810
New Horizon Dual Language S 400/K-5
5226 Southside Blvd 83686 208-468-4623
Valerie Cleverly, prin. Fax 468-2825
Owyhee ES 500/K-5
2300 W Iowa Ave 83686 208-468-4616
Charles Silzly, prin. Fax 468-2820
Park Ridge ES 500/K-5
3313 Parkridge Dr 83687 208-468-4622
Amy Taylor, prin. Fax 468-2817
Reagan ES 500/K-5
3400 Southside Blvd 83686 208-468-4619
Ryan Curry, prin. Fax 468-2821
Roosevelt ES 600/K-5
1901 W Roosevelt Ave 83686 208-468-4620
Shawn Tegethoff, prin. Fax 468-2819
Sherman ES 600/K-5
1521 E Sherman Ave 83686 208-468-4628
Dr. Sherry Marsh, prin. Fax 468-2816
Snake River ES 500/K-5
500 Stampede Dr 83687 208-468-4614
Karla Reynolds, prin. Fax 468-2818
South MS 900/6-8
229 W Greenhurst Rd 83686 208-468-4740
Stuart Vickers, prin. Fax 468-2826
West MS 700/6-8
20 S Midland Blvd 83651 208-468-4750
Stefanie Duby, prin. Fax 468-2809
Willow Creek ES 700/K-5
198 N Elementary Ln 83651 208-468-4617
Scott Knopp, prin. Fax 468-4618

Vallivue SD 139
Supt. — See Caldwell
Birch ES 600/PK-5
6900 Birch Ln 83687 208-461-5960
Yvonne Ihli, prin. Fax 461-5957
Desert Springs ES 700/PK-5
18178 Santa Ana Ave 83687 208-466-1555
Lisa Boyd, prin. Fax 466-1497
East Canyon ES 700/PK-5
18408 Northside Blvd 83687 208-466-6929
Katrina McGee, prin. Fax 466-6232
Lakevue ES 600/K-5
12843 Cirrus Dr 83651 208-467-1478
Leeta Hobbs, prin. Fax 467-4327
Sage Valley MS 900/6-8
18070 Santa Ana Ave 83687 208-468-4919
Sean Smith, prin. Fax 468-4904

Calvary Chapel Christian S 100/PK-12
1210 N Middleton Rd 83651 208-467-7116
Nampa Christian ES 300/PK-5
505 W Orchard Ave 83651 208-466-8451
Dr. Greg Wiles, supt. Fax 475-1741
St. Paul's S 200/PK-8
1515 8th St S 83651 208-467-3601
Scott Coulter, prin. Fax 467-6485
Zion Lutheran S 100/PK-8
1012 12th Ave Rd 83686 208-466-9141
Gayle Wollman, hdmstr. Fax 463-4420

Naples, Boundary
Boundary County SD 101
Supt. — See Bonners Ferry
Naples ES 100/K-5
145 Schoolhouse Rd 83847 208-267-2956
Lisa Iverson, prin. Fax 267-2906

New Meadows, Adams, Pop. 492
Meadows Valley SD 11 200/PK-12
PO Box F 83654 208-347-2411
Mike Howard, supt. Fax 347-2624
www.mvsd11.org
Meadows Valley S 200/PK-12
PO Box F 83654 208-347-2118
Mike Howard, supt. Fax 347-2624

New Plymouth, Payette, Pop. 1,508
New Plymouth SD 372 1,000/PK-12
103 SE Avenue 83655 208-278-5740
Kevin Barker, supt. Fax 278-3069
npschoolsidaho.wordpress.com
New Plymouth ES 500/PK-5
704 S Plymouth Ave 83655 208-278-5333
Carrie Aguas, prin. Fax 278-3257
New Plymouth MS 200/6-8
4400 SW 2nd Ave 83655 208-278-5788
Sean King, prin. Fax 278-3773

Nezperce, Lewis, Pop. 463
Nezperce JSD 302 100/PK-12
PO Box 279 83543 208-937-2551
Dennis Kachelmier, supt. Fax 937-2136
www.nezpercesd.us/
Nezperce S 100/PK-12
PO Box 279 83543 208-937-2551
Dennis Kachelmier, prin. Fax 937-2136

Oakley, Cassia, Pop. 762
Cassia County JSD 151
Supt. — See Burley
Oakley ES 200/K-6
PO Box 72 83346 208 862 3203
Brandell Bedke, prin. Fax 862-3380

Ola, Gem
Emmett ISD 221
Supt. — See Emmett
Ola S 50/K-6
PO Box 29 83657 208-584-3589
Stephen Joyner, prin. Fax 365-2961

Oldtown, Bonner, Pop. 183
West Bonner County SD 83
Supt. — See Priest River
Idaho Hill ES 200/K-6
402 E 3rd St S 83822 208-437-4227
Susie Luckey, prin. Fax 437-2290

House of the Lord Christian Academy 100/PK-12
754 Silver Birch Ln 83822 208-437-2184
Candace Craddick, prin. Fax 437-0441
Pend Oreille Valley SDA S 50/K-8
33820 Highway 41 83822 208-437-2638
Pend Orielle Valley SDA S K-8
33820 Highway 41 83822 208-437-2638

Orofino, Clearwater, Pop. 3,071
Orofino JSD 171 900/PK-12
1051 Michigan Ave 83544 208-476-5593
Dr. Michael Garrett, supt. Fax 476-7293
www.sd171.k12.id.us
Orofino ES 400/PK-6
1000 Michigan Ave 83544 208-476-4212
Denise Pomponio, prin. Fax 476-0145
Other Schools – See Lenore, Peck, Weippe

Osburn, Shoshone, Pop. 1,532
Silver Hills ES 300/PK-6
PO Box 2160 83849 208-556-1556
Todd Howard, prin. Fax 556-1557

Paris, Bear Lake, Pop. 510
Bear Lake County SD 33 1,100/PK-12
PO Box 300 83261 208-945-2891
Dr. Gary Brogan, supt. Fax 945-2893
blsd.net
Paris ES 100/PK-5
39 S Fielding St 83261 208-945-2113
Janet Lindsay, prin. Fax 945-2893
Other Schools – See Georgetown, Montpelier

Parma, Canyon, Pop. 1,955
Parma SD 137 1,100/K-12
805 E McConnell Ave 83660 208-779-4069
Jim Norton, supt. Fax 722-7937
www.parmaschools.org
Johnson ES 400/K-4
607 E McConnell Ave 83660 208-779-4069
Diane Hardin, prin. Fax 722-5168
Parma MS 300/5-8
905 E McConnell Ave 83660 208-779-4069
Stoney Winston, prin. Fax 779-4082

Paul, Minidoka, Pop. 1,146
Minidoka County JSD 331
Supt. — See Rupert
Paul ES 500/K-5
201 N 1st St W 83347 208-438-2211
Ellen Austin, prin. Fax 438-8767
West Minico MS 400/6-8
155 S 600 W 83347 208-438-5018
Tim Perrigot, prin. Fax 438-8513

Payette, Payette, Pop. 7,244
Payette JSD 371 1,600/PK-12
20 N 12th St 83661 208-642-9366
Pauline King, supt. Fax 642-9006
www.payetteschools.org/
McCain MS 400/6-8
400 N Iowa Ave 83661 208-642-4122
Rick Hale, prin. Fax 642-2171
Payette PS 500/PK-3
1320 3rd Ave N 83661 208-642-3379
Kipp McKenzie, prin. Fax 642-2169
Westside ES 200/4-5
609 N 5th St 83661 208-642-3241
Mary Bennett, prin. Fax 642-3307

Treasure Valley Seventh-Day Adventist S 50/1-8
PO Box 396 83661 208-642-2410
Valerie Iwasa, lead tchr.

Peck, Nez Perce, Pop. 190
Orofino JSD 171
Supt. — See Orofino
Peck ES 50/K-6
PO Box 48 83545 208-486-7331
Robyn Bonner, lead tchr. Fax 486-7331

Pine, Elmore
Mountain Home SD 193
Supt. — See Mountain Home
Pine ES 50/K-8
160 S Lester Creek Rd 83647 208-653-2311
James Gilbert, prin. Fax 587-9896

Pinehurst, Shoshone, Pop. 1,602
Kellogg JSD 391
Supt. — See Kellogg
Pinehurst ES 300/K-5
201 3rd St 83850 208-682-2193
Mike Groves, prin. Fax 682-2145

Plummer, Benewah, Pop. 956
Plummer/Worley JSD 44 300/PK-12
PO Box 130 83851 208-686-1621
Judi Sharrett, supt. Fax 686-2108
www.pwsd44.com
Lakeside ES 200/PK-6
PO Box 130 83851 208-686-1651
Mike Crabtree, prin. Fax 686-2118

Pocatello, Bannock, Pop. 53,083
Blackfoot SD 55
Supt. — See Blackfoot
Fort Hall ES 200/K-5
RR 6 Box 430 83202 208-237-2207
Kathy Malm, prin. Fax 237-9402

Pocatello/Chubbuck SD 25 12,500/PK-12
3115 Pole Line Rd 83201 208-232-3563
Fax 235-3280
www.sd25.us
Alameda MS 6-8
845 McKinley Ave 83201 208-235-6800
Brandon Vaughan, prin. Fax 235-6801
Edahow ES 300/K-5
2020 Pocatello Creek Rd 83201 208-233-1844
Nick Muckerman, prin. Fax 239-7119
Franklin MS 800/6-8
2271 E Terry St 83201 208-233-5590
Patrick Vereecken, prin. Fax 233-1024
Gate City ES 500/K-5
2288 Hiskey St 83201 208-237-2503
Deanne Dye, prin. Fax 237-2239
Greenacres ES 400/K-5
1250 E Oak St 83201 208-233-2575
Janelle Armstrong, prin. Fax 234-5936
Hawthorne MS 800/6-8
1025 W Eldredge Rd 83201 208-237-1680
Dr. Heidi Kessler, prin. Fax 237-1682
Indian Hills ES 600/K-5
666 Cheyenne Ave 83204 208-232-4086
Jill Pixton, prin. Fax 232-8986
Irving MS 600/6-8
911 N Grant Ave 83204 208-232-3039
Tonya Wilkes, prin. Fax 232-0379
Jefferson ES 400/K-5
1455 Gwen Dr 83204 208-232-2914
Kirk Thomson, prin. Fax 232-0440
Lewis & Clark ES 600/K-5
800 Grace Dr 83201 208-233-2552
Nichole Garza, prin. Fax 233-9672
Lincoln ECC 100/PK-PK
330 Oakwood Dr 83204 208-232-2994
Shantel Delonas, admin. Fax 232-4906
Syringa ES 500/K-5
388 E Griffith Rd 83201 208-237-4040
Rebecca Bullock, prin. Fax 237-4104
Tendoy ES 300/K-5
957 E Alameda Rd 83201 208-233-2921
Janice Nelson, prin. Fax 233-2952
Washington ES 300/K-5
226 S 10th Ave 83201 208-232-2976
Janice Nelson, prin. Fax 232-6663
Wilcox ES 600/K-5
427 Lark Ln 83201 208-237-6050
Brenda Miner, prin. Fax 237-6073
Other Schools – See Chubbuck

Grace Lutheran S 400/PK-9
1350 Baldy Ave 83201 208-237-4142
Robert Raschke, dir. Fax 237-0931
Holy Spirit Catholic S 200/PK-8
540 N 7th Ave 83201 208-232-5763
Nancy Corgiat M.Ed., prin. Fax 234-1624

Ponderay, Bonner, Pop. 1,102
Lake Pend Oreille SD 84 3,800/PK-12
901 N Triangle Dr 83852 208-263-2184
Shawn Woodward, supt. Fax 263-5053
www.lposd.org/
Other Schools – See Cocolalla, Hope, Kootenai, Sagle, Sandpoint

---

Sandpoint Christian S 50/PK-8
477954 Highway 95 83852 208-265-8624
Elizabeth Page, prin. Fax 263-6504

Post Falls, Kootenai, Pop. 26,948
Post Falls SD 273 5,800/PK-12
PO Box 40 83877 208-773-1658
Jerry Keane, supt. Fax 773-3218
www.pfsd.com
Greensferry ES 300/1-5
PO Box 40 83877 208-773-0999
Kathy Baker, prin. Fax 773-8547
Mullan Trail ES 400/1-5
PO Box 40 83877 208-457-0772
Katrina Kelly, prin. Fax 773-8312
Ponderosa ES 600/1-5
PO Box 40 83877 208-773-1508
Scott Ross, prin. Fax 773-0789
Post Falls MS 700/6-8
PO Box 40 83877 208-773-7554
Brad Harmon, prin. Fax 773-0884
Post K 500/PK-K
PO Box 40 83877 208-777-0479
James Shepard, prin. Fax 773-2553
Prairie View ES 700/1-5
PO Box 40 83877 208-773-8327
Janelle Baker, prin. Fax 777-9665

River City MS 600/6-8
PO Box 40 83877 208-457-0933
Michael Yovetich, prin. Fax 457-1673
Seltice ES 400/1-5
PO Box 40 83877 208-773-1681
Kandi Kuck, prin. Fax 777-2572
West Ridge ES 400/1-5
PO Box 40 83877 208-773-7291
Lisa Hoffeld, prin. Fax 773-7327

Classical Christian Academy 200/PK-12
2289 W Seltice Way 83854 208-777-4400
CornerStone Christian Academy 100/PK-6
810 N Chase Rd 83854 208-773-5200
Genesis Preparatory Academy 100/K-12
PO Box 1237 83877 208-691-0712
Chris Finch, prin. Fax 777-8853

Potlatch, Latah, Pop. 786
Potlatch SD 285 500/K-12
130 6th St 83855 208-875-0327
Jeffrey A. Cirka, supt. Fax 875-1028
www.potlatchschools.org
Potlatch ES 300/K-6
130 6th St 83855 208-875-1331
John Haire, prin. Fax 875-0599

Prairie, Elmore
Prairie ESD 191 50/K-8
1218 W Long Gulch Rd 83647 208-868-3229
Bill Zumstein, chrpsn. Fax 868-3257
prairie191k8.org
Prairie ES 50/K-8
73 Smith Creek Rd 83647 208-868-3229
P. Elaine Faddis, contact Fax 868-3257

Preston, Franklin, Pop. 5,154
Preston JSD 201 2,600/PK-12
105 E 2nd S 83263 208-852-0283
Marc Gee, supt. Fax 852-3976
www.prestonidahoschools.org
Oakwood ES 600/3-5
525 S 4th E 83263 208-852-2233
Kaylynn Hamblin, prin. Fax 852-2234
Pioneer ES 600/PK-2
515 S 4th E 83263 208-852-2050
Lance Harrison, prin. Fax 852-2051
Preston JHS 600/6-8
450 E 800 S 83263 208-852-0751
Curtis Jenson, prin. Fax 852-3510

Priest Lake, Bonner
West Bonner County SD 83
Supt. — See Priest River
Priest Lake ES 50/PK-6
27732 Highway 57 83856 208-443-2555
Paul Anselmo, prin. Fax 443-3845

Priest River, Bonner, Pop. 1,684
West Bonner County SD 83 1,300/PK-12
134 Main St 83856 208-448-4439
Paul Anselmo, supt. Fax 448-4629
www.sd83.org
Priest River ES 400/PK-6
231 Harriet St 83856 208-448-1181
Connie Kimble, prin. Fax 448-1328
Priest River JHS 200/7-8
5709 Highway 2 83856 208-448-1118
Leoni Johnson, prin. Fax 448-1119
Other Schools – See Oldtown, Priest Lake

Rathdrum, Kootenai, Pop. 6,685
Lakeland SD 272 4,200/PK-12
PO Box 39 83858 208-687-0431
Becky Meyer, supt. Fax 687-1884
web.lakeland272.org
Brown ES 400/PK-6
PO Box 10 83858 208-687-0551
John Asher, prin. Fax 687-9355
Garwood ES 300/K-6
PO Box 990 83858 208-687-1265
B.J. DeAustin, prin. Fax 687-4310
Kiefer ES 500/K-6
PO Box 130 83858 208-687-5206
Lynn Paslay, prin. Fax 687-3692
Lakeland JHS 400/7-8
PO Box 98 83858 208-687-0661
Georgeanne Griffith, prin. Fax 687-1510
Twin Lakes ES 300/K-6
PO Box 159 83858 208-687-5870
Patty Morrison, prin. Fax 687-5873
Other Schools – See Athol, Spirit Lake

Rexburg, Madison, Pop. 25,087
Madison SD 321 5,400/PK-12
PO Box 830 83440 208-359-3300
Dr. Geoffrey Thomas, supt. Fax 359-3345
msd321.com
Adams ES 400/K-4
110 N 2nd E 83440 208-359-3335
Kevin Carey M.Ed., prin. Fax 359-3272
Burton ES 600/PK-4
2211 W 1000 S 83440 208-359-3332
Landon Lefevre M.Ed., prin. Fax 359-3345
Hibbard ES 200/K-4
2413 N 3000 W 83440 208-359-3333
William Berry M.Ed., prin. Fax 359-3269
Kennedy ES 400/K-4
60 S 5th W 83440 208-359-3325
Shane Williams M.Ed., prin. Fax 359-3326
Lincoln ES 400/K-4
358 E 2nd S 83440 208-359-3330
Scott Shirley M.Ed., prin. Fax 359-3366
Madison MS 800/5-6
575 W 7th S 83440 208-359-3320
Michael Bone M.Ed., prin. Fax 359-3348
South Fork ES 400/K-4
7163 S 2000 W 83440 208-359-3334
David Wilson, prin. Fax 359-3369

Richfield, Lincoln, Pop. 478
Richfield SD 316 200/PK-12
555 N Tiger Dr 83349 208-487-2241
Mike Smith, supt. Fax 487-2240
sites.google.com/site/richfieldtigers
Richfield S 200/PK-12
555 N Tiger Dr 83349 208-487-2790
Kevin Case, prin. Fax 487-2055

Rigby, Jefferson, Pop. 3,876
Jefferson County JSD 251 4,100/PK-12
3850 E 300 N 83442 208-745-6693
Lisa Sherick, supt. Fax 745-0848
www.sd251.org
Farnsworth ES 700/3-5
305 N 3700 E 83442 208-745-8347
Jeanette Hollis, prin. Fax 745-0144
Harwood ES 300/PK-5
200 W 3rd N 83442 208-745-7613
Paul Lundberg, prin. Fax 745-7995
Jefferson ES 600/K-2
306 N 3700 E 83442 208-745-0758
Dr. Dave Meyer, prin. Fax 745-0762
Rigby MS 300/6-8
290 N 3800 E 83442 208-745-6674
Sherry Simmons, prin. Fax 745-6675
South Fork ES 600/K-5
327 N 4100 E 83442 208-745-7085
Richard Howard, prin. Fax 745-8649
Other Schools – See Menan, Roberts

Riggins, Idaho, Pop. 415
Salmon River JSD 243 100/PK-12
PO Box 872 83549 208-630-6027
Jim Doramus, supt. Fax 630-6026
www.jsd243.org
Riggins ES 100/PK-5
PO Box 872 83549 208-630-6055
Jim Doramus, supt. Fax 630-6056

Ririe, Jefferson, Pop. 653
Ririe JSD 252 500/PK-12
PO Box 508 83443 208-538-7482
Chad Williams, supt. Fax 538-7363
www.ririeschools.org
Ririe ES 300/PK-6
PO Box 548 83443 208-538-5175
Glen Romney, prin. Fax 538-7748

Roberts, Jefferson, Pop. 573
Jefferson County JSD 251
Supt. — See Rigby
Roberts ES 200/K-5
682 N 2858 E 83444 208-228-3111
Teresa Codling, prin. Fax 228-2520

Rockland, Power, Pop. 294
Rockland SD 382 200/K-12
PO Box 119 83271 208-548-2221
Chester Bradshaw, supt. Fax 548-2224
www.rbulldogs.org
Rockland S 200/K-12
PO Box 119 83271 208-548-2221
Chester Bradshaw, prin. Fax 548-2224

Rogerson, Twin Falls
Three Creek JESD 416 50/K-8
49909 Three Creek Rd 83302 208-857-2281
Gus Brackett, chrpsn. Fax 857-2281
Three Creek S 50/K-8
49909 Three Creek Rd 83302 208-857-2281
Dena Pollock, lead tchr. Fax 857-2281

Rupert, Minidoka, Pop. 5,482
Minidoka County JSD 331 4,200/K-12
310 10th St 83350 208-436-4727
Dr. Kenneth Cox, supt. Fax 436-6593
www.minidokaschools.org
East Minico MS 500/6-8
1805 H St 83350 208-436-3178
Bryan McKinney, prin. Fax 436-3235
Rupert ES 600/K-5
202 18th St 83350 208-436-9707
Laurie Copmann, prin. Fax 436-1726
Other Schools – See Acequia, Heyburn, Paul

St. Nicholas S 100/PK-6
PO Box 26 83350 208-436-6320
Wes Remaley M.Ed., prin. Fax 436-0628

Sagle, Bonner
Lake Pend Oreille SD 84
Supt. — See Ponderay
Sagle ES 400/K-6
550 Sagle Rd 83860 208-263-2757
Kathleen Berget, prin. Fax 263-6732

Saint Anthony, Fremont, Pop. 3,512
Fremont County JSD 215 2,200/PK-12
945 W 1st N 83445 208-624-7542
Byron Stutzman, supt. Fax 624-3385
www.sd215.net
Henry's Fork ES 600/PK-5
425 N 3rd W 83445 208-624-7422
DelRay Davenport, prin. Fax 624-7438
Parker-Egin ES 100/K-5
221 N Center St 83445 208-624-7472
Lane Owens, prin. Fax 624-7472
South Fremont JHS 400/6-8
550 N 1st W 83445 208-624-7880
David Marotz, prin. Fax 624-4386
Other Schools – See Ashton, Teton

Saint Maries, Benewah, Pop. 2,361
Saint Maries JSD 41 1,000/PK-12
PO Box 384 83861 208-245-2579
Alica M. Holthaus, supt. Fax 245-3970
www.sd41.org
Heyburn ES 400/PK-5
1405 Main Ave 83861 208-245-2025
Tammi Masters, prin. Fax 245-5418

Saint Maries MS 200/6-8
1315 W Jefferson Ave 83861 208-245-3495
Jeffrey Andersen, prin. Fax 245-0506
Other Schools – See Fernwood

Saint Maries Christian S 50/3-8
201 N 8th St Ste 11 83861 208-245-2274

Salmon, Lemhi, Pop. 3,067
Salmon SD 291 600/PK-12
907 Sharkey St 83467 208-756-4271
Chris Born, supt. Fax 756-6695
www.salmonschools.com
Salmon Pioneer PS 300/PK-5
900 Sharkey St 83467 208-756-3663
John Hamilton, prin. Fax 756-3670

Salmon SDA S 50/1-8
400 Fairmont St 83467 208-756-4439

Sandpoint, Bonner, Pop. 7,221
Lake Pend Oreille SD 84
Supt. — See Ponderay
Farmin Stidwell ES 500/PK-6
1626 Spruce St 83864 208-265-2417
Erik Olson, prin. Fax 265-4610
Northside ES 200/K-6
7881 Colburn Culver Rd 83864 208-263-2734
Perky Smith-Hagadone, prin. Fax 255-2944
Sandpoint MS 500/7-8
310 S Division Ave 83864 208-265-4169
Casey McLaughlin, prin. Fax 263-5525
Washington ES 300/K-6
420 S Boyer Ave 83864 208-263-4759
Dr. Sandy Maras, prin. Fax 263-1453

Sandpoint Jr. Academy 50/1-8
2255 Pine St 83864 208-263-3584
Sandpoint Waldorf S 100/PK-8
PO Box 95 83864 208-265-2683

Shelley, Bingham, Pop. 4,332
Shelley JSD 60 2,200/PK-12
545 Seminary Ave 83274 208-357-3411
Dr. Bryan Jolley, supt. Fax 357-5741
www.shelleyschools.org
Hobbs MS 300/7-8
350 E Pine St 83274 208-357-7667
Dale Clark, prin. Fax 357-3003
Riverview ES 400/PK-PK, 3-
1463 N 800 E 83274 208-357-5625
Ben Lemons, prin. Fax 357-5528
Stuart ES 300/5-6
475 W Center St 83274 208-357-5580
Jared Heath, prin. Fax 357-7631
Sunrise ES 500/K-2
200 E Fir St 83274 208-357-7688
Robyn Elswood, prin. Fax 357-2536

Shoshone, Lincoln, Pop. 1,444
Shoshone JSD 312 400/PK-12
61 E Highway 24 83352 208-886-2381
Dr. Rob Waite, supt. Fax 886-2038
www.shoshonesd.org
Shoshone ES 300/PK-5
61 E Highway 24 83352 208-886-2381
Emily Nelsen, prin. Fax 886-2742

Other Schools – See Osburn

Soda Springs, Caribou, Pop. 3,009
Soda Springs JSD 150 900/K-12
250 E 2nd S 83276 208-547-3371
Dr. Molly Stein, supt. Fax 547-4878
www.sodaschools.org
Thirkill ES 300/K-4
60 E 4th S 83276 208-547-4426
Sue Hansen, prin. Fax 547-2617
Tigert MS 300/5-8
250 E 2nd S Ste B 83276 208-547-4922
Debra Daniels, prin. Fax 547-2619

Spirit Lake, Kootenai, Pop. 1,910
Lakeland SD 272
Supt. — See Rathdrum
Spirit Lake ES 300/K-6
PO Box 189 83869 208-623-2501
Kristie Mitchell, prin. Fax 623-5175
Timberlake JHS 300/7-8
PO Box 1080 83869 208-623-2582
Chris McDougall, prin. Fax 623-2750

Stanley, Custer, Pop. 63
Challis JSD 181
Supt. — See Challis
Stanley S 50/K-8
PO Box 77 83278 208-774-3503
Ashley Baker, lead tchr. Fax 774-3643

Star, Ada, Pop. 5,665
West Ada SD
Supt. — See Meridian
Star ES 500/K-5
700 N Star Rd 83669 208-855-4110
Carla Karnes, prin. Fax 855-4119

Stone, Oneida
Oneida County SD 351
Supt. — See Malad City
Stone ES 50/K-3
10808 S 23000 W 83252 208-698-3585
Rich Moore, prin. Fax 698-3585

Sugar City, Madison, Pop. 1,499
Sugar-Salem JSD 322 1,600/PK-12
PO Box 150 83448 208-356-8802
Alan Dunn, supt. Fax 356-7237
www.sugarsalem.org

Central ES 500/PK-3
PO Box 239 83448 208-356-9351
Robert Potter, prin. Fax 356-0895
Kershaw IS 400/4-6
610 E 3rd N 83448 208-356-0241
Neil Williams, prin. Fax 656-0538
Sugar-Salem JHS 200/7-8
PO Box 180 83448 208-356-4437
Kevin Schultz, prin. Fax 358-9717

Sun Valley, Blaine, Pop. 1,392

Community S 400/PK-12
PO Box 2118 83353 208-622-3955
Ben Pettit, head sch Fax 622-3962

Sweet, Gem
Emmett ISD 221
Supt. — See Emmett
Sweet-Montour S 50/K-5
6600 Sweet Ola Hwy 83670 208-584-3378
Stephen Joyner, prin. Fax 584-3323

Tendoy, Lemhi
South Lemhi SD 292
Supt. — See Leadore
Tendoy ES 50/K-6
PO Box 13 83468 208-768-2441
Michael Jacobson, prin. Fax 768-2797

Terreton, Jefferson
West Jefferson SD 253 500/PK-12
1256 E 1500 N 83450 208-663-4542
Dwight Richins, supt. Fax 663-4543
www.wjsd.org
Terreton S 300/PK-8
1252 E 1500 N 83450 208-663-4393
Jeffrey Haroldsen, prin. Fax 663-4394
Other Schools – See Hamer

Teton, Fremont, Pop. 720
Fremont County JSD 215
Supt. — See Saint Anthony
Teton ES 100/K-5
126 W Main St 83451 208-458-4931
Lane Owens, prin. Fax 624-3385

Tetonia, Teton, Pop. 269
Teton County SD 401
Supt. — See Driggs
Tetonia ES 100/PK-3
PO Box 129 83452 208-228-5930
Megan Christiansen, prin. Fax 456-2288

Thatcher, Franklin
Grace JSD 148
Supt. — See Grace
Thatcher ES 100/1-3
PO Box 14 83283 208-427-6346
Jamie Holyoak, admin. Fax 427-0008

Troy, Latah, Pop. 841
Troy SD 287 300/K-12
PO Box 280 83871 208-835-3791
Brad Malm, supt. Fax 835-3790
www.sd287.k12.id.us
Troy ES 100/K-6
103 Trojan Dr 83871 208-835-4261
Klaire Vogt, prin. Fax 835-4250

Twin Falls, Twin Falls, Pop. 43,303
Filer SD 413
Supt. — See Filer
Hollister ES 100/K-5
2463 Contact Ave 83301 208-655-4215
Kristy Oberg, prin. Fax 655-4214

Twin Falls SD 411 9,900/PK-12
201 Main Ave W 83301 208-733-6900
Dr. Brady Dickinson, supt. Fax 733-6987
www.tfsd.org
Bickel ES 400/K-5
607 2nd Ave E 83301 208-733-4116
Kelli Schroeder, prin. Fax 733-8926
Harrison ES 700/PK-5
600 Harrison St 83301 208-733-4229
Melissa Ardito, prin. Fax 733-4256
Lincoln ES 500/K-5
238 Buhl St N 83301 208-733-1321
Beth Olmstead, prin. Fax 733-4243
Morningside ES 700/K-5
701 Morningside Dr 83301 208-733-6507
Steve Hoy, prin. Fax 733-5407
O'Leary JHS 900/6-8
2350 Elizabeth Blvd 83301 208-733-2155
Ace Marcellus, prin. Fax 733-8666
Oregon Trail ES 700/K-5
660 Park Ave 83301 208-733-8480
Tyler Matlock, prin. Fax 733-8686
Perrine ES 800/K-5
452 Caswell Ave W 83301 208-733-4288
Tammy Rodabaugh, prin. Fax 733-7881
Pillar Falls ES 500/K-5
3105 Stadium Blvd 83301 208-732-7570
Nancy Murphy, prin. Fax 732-7571
Rock Creek ES 500/K-5
850 Federation Rd 83301 208-732-7565
Shari Cowger, prin. Fax 732-7566
Sawtooth ES 700/K-5
1771 Stadium Blvd 83301 208-733-8454
Michelle Combs, prin. Fax 733-5729
South Hills MS 600/6-8
1550 Harison St S 83301 208-732-5160
Ryan Ellsworth, prin. Fax 732-5161
Stuart JHS 900/6-8
644 Caswell Ave W 83301 208-733-4875
Amy McBride, prin. Fax 733-4949

Hilltop SDA S 50/1-8
131 Grandview Dr 83301 208-736-5934
Immanuel Lutheran S 200/PK-5
2055 Filer Ave E 83301 208-733-7820
Michelle Jund, prin. Fax 735-9970
Lighthouse Christian S 300/PK-12
960 Eastland Dr 83301 208-737-1425
Kevin Newbry, supt. Fax 737-4671
St. Edwards Catholic S 200/PK-6
139 6th Ave E 83301 208-734-3872
Angela Hild, prin. Fax 734-1214
Twin Falls Christian Academy 100/K-12
798 Eastland Dr N 83301 208-733-1452
Brent Walker, prin. Fax 734-1417

Victor, Teton, Pop. 1,915
Teton County SD 401
Supt. — See Driggs
Victor ES 200/PK-3
PO Box 169 83455 208-228-5929
Megan Christiansen, prin. Fax 787-2245

Weippe, Clearwater, Pop. 439
Orofino JSD 171
Supt. — See Orofino
Timberline S 100/PK-12
22869 Highway 11 83553 208-435-4411
Jason Hunter, prin. Fax 435-4846

Weiser, Washington, Pop. 5,415
Weiser SD 431 1,600/PK-12
925 Pioneer Rd 83672 208-414-0616
Wil Overgaard, supt. Fax 414-1265
www.weiserschools.org
Park IS 200/4-5
758 E Park St 83672 208-414-2861
Angela Halvorson, prin. Fax 414-0851
Pioneer PS 500/PK-3
624 Pioneer Rd 83672 208-414-3131
Wade Wilson, prin. Fax 414-3198
Weiser MS 400/6-8
320 E Galloway Ave 83672 208-414-2620
Tim Erhard, prin. Fax 414-2094

Wendell, Gooding, Pop. 2,752
Wendell SD 232 1,200/PK-12
PO Box 300 83355 208-536-2418
Greg Lowe, supt. Fax 536-2629
www.wendellschools.org
Wendell ES 500/PK-4
232 N Pocatello St 83355 208-536-6611
Paula Chapman, prin. Fax 536-6602
Wendell MS 400/5-8
920 E Main St 83355 208-536-5531
Brian Jadwin, prin. Fax 536-5957

Wilder, Canyon, Pop. 1,528
Wilder SD 133 400/PK-12
210 A Ave 83676 208-482-6228
Jeff Dillon, supt. Fax 482-6980
www.wilderschools.org
Wilder ES 200/PK-5
210 A Ave 83676 208-482-6220
Jeff Dillon, prin. Fax 482-6980

ILLINOIS

ILLINOIS DEPARTMENT OF EDUCATION
100 N 1st St, Springfield 62777-0002
Telephone 866-262-6663
Fax 217-524-8585
Website http://www.isbe.net

Superintendent of Education Dr. Tony Smith

ILLINOIS BOARD OF EDUCATION
100 N 1st St, Springfield 62777-0002

Chairperson James Meeks

REGIONAL OFFICES OF EDUCATION (ROE)

Adam/Brwn/Cass/Morgn/Pik/Sctt ROE
Deborah Niederhauser, supt. 217-277-2080
507 Vermont St, Quincy 62301 Fax 277-2092
www.wc4.org

Alxndr/Jcksn/Pulsk/Prry/Union ROE
Cheryl Graff, supt., 1001 Walnut St 618-687-7290
Murphysboro 62966 Fax 687-7296
www.roe30.org

Bond/Christn/Effingham/Fayette/Mtgmy ROE
Julie Wollerman, supt. 618-283-5011
1500 W Jefferson St Fax 283-5013
Vandalia 62471
www.roe3.org

Boone/Winnebago ROE
Dr. Lori Fanello, supt. 815-636-3060
300 Heart Blvd, Loves Park 61111 Fax 636-3069
www.bwroe.org

Bureau/Henry/Stark ROE
Angie Zarvell, supt. 309-936-7890
107 S State St, Atkinson 61235 Fax 936-1111
www.bhsroe.org

Calhoun/Greene/Jersey/Macoupin ROE
Michelle Mueller, supt. 217-854-4016
225 E Nicholas St, Carlinville 62626 Fax 854-2032
www.roe40.com

Carroll/Jo Daviess/Stephenson ROE
Aaron Mercier, supt. 815-599-1408
27 S State Ave Ste 101 Fax 297-9032
Freeport 61032
www.roe8.com

Champaign/Ford ROE
Jane Quinlan, supt. 217-893-3219
3358 Big Pine Trail Fax 893-0024
Champaign 61822
www.roe9.k12.il.us/

Clay/Crawford/Jopr/Lwrnce/Rchlnd ROE
Monte Newlin, supt. 618-392-4631
103 W Main St Ste 23, Olney 62450 Fax 392-3993
www.roe12.net

Clintn/Jeffrsn/Marin/Washngtn ROE
Keri Jo Garrett, supt. 618-594-2432
930 Fairfax St Ste B, Carlyle 62231 Fax 594-7192

Clk/Cls/Cumb/Dglas/Edg/Mlt/Shlb ROE
Dr. Bobbi Mattingly, supt. 217-348-0151
730 7th St, Charleston 61920 Fax 348-0171
www.roe11.k12.il.us/

DeKalb ROE
Amanda Christensen, supt. 815-217-0460
2500 N Annie Glidden Rd Fax 217-0467
DeKalb 60115
www.dekalbcounty.org/roe

DeWitt/Livingston/Logan/McLean ROE
Mark Jontry, supt. 309-888-5120
200 W Front St Ste 500 Fax 862-0420
Bloomington 61701
www.roe17.org

Dupage ROE
Darlene Ruscitti, supt. 630-407-5800
421 N County Farm Rd Fax 407-5801
Wheaton 60187
www.dupage.k12.il.us/

Edwds/Gtn/Hdn/Pope/Sln/Wbsh/Wyn/Wt ROE
Lawrence Fillingim, supt. 618-253-5581
512 N Main St, Harrisburg 62946 Fax 252-8472
www.roe20.org

Franklin-Johnson-Massac-Williamson ROE
Lorie LeQuatte, supt. 618-438-9711
901 Public Square, Benton 62812 Fax 435-2861
www.roe21.org

Grundy/Kendall ROE
Christopher Mehochko, supt. 815-941-3247
1320 Union St, Morris 60450 Fax 942-5384
www.roe24.org

Hancck/Fultn/Schuylr/McDonogh ROE
John Meixner, supt. 309-837-4821
130 S Lafayette St Ste 200 Fax 837-2887
Macomb 61455
www.roe26.net

Henderson/Knox/Mercer/Warren ROE
Jodi Scott, supt. 309-734-6822
105 N E St Ste 1, Monmouth 61462 Fax 734-2452
www.roe33.net

Iroquois/Kankakee ROE
Greg Murphy, supt. 815-937-2950
1 Stuart Dr, Kankakee 60901 Fax 937-2921
www.i-kan.org

Kane ROE
Patricia Dal Santo, supt. 630-232-5955
28 N 1st St Ste 201, Geneva 60134 Fax 208-5115
www.kaneroe.org/

Lake ROE
Dr. Roycealee Wood, supt. 847-543-7833
800 Lancer Ln Ste E128 Fax 543-7832
Grayslake 60030
www.lake.k12.il.us

LaSalle/Marshall/Putnam ROE
Christopher Dvorak, supt. 815-434-0780
119 W Madison St, Ottawa 61350 Fax 434-2453
www.roe35.org

Lee/Ogle/Whiteside ROE
Robert Sondgeroth, supt. 815-625-2054
1001 W 23rd St, Sterling 61081 Fax 625-1625
www.roe47.org

Macon/Piatt ROE 39
Matthew Snyder, supt. 217-872-3721
1690 Huston Dr, Decatur 62526 Fax 872-0239
www.maconpiattroe.com/

Madison County ROE
Dr. Robert Daiber, supt. 618-296-4530
157 N Main St, Edwardsville 62025 Fax 692-7018
www.roe41.org

Mason-Tazewell-Woodford ROE
Patrick Durley, supt. 309-477-2290
414 Court St Ste 100, Pekin 61554 Fax 347-3735
www.roe53.net

McHenry ROE
Leslie Schermerhorn, supt. 815-334-4475
2200 N Seminary Ave Fax 338-0475
Woodstock 60098
www.mchenryroe.org/

Menard/Sangamon ROE
Jeff Vose, supt. 217-753-6620
2201 S Dirksen Pkwy Fax 535-3166
Springfield 62703
www.roe51.org

Monroe-Randolph ROE
Kelton Davis, supt. 618-939-5650
107 E Mill St, Waterloo 62298 Fax 939-5332
www.roe45.org

North Cook Intermediate Service Center
Dr. Bruce Brown, dir. 847-824-8300
2340 S River Rd Fax 824-1033
Des Plaines 60018
www.ncisc.org

Peoria ROE
Elizabeth Derry, supt. 309-672-6906
324 Main St Ste 401, Peoria 61602 Fax 672-6053
peoriaroe.org

Rock Island ROE
Tammy Muerhoff, supt. 309-736-1111
3430 Avenue of the Cities Fax 736-1127
Moline 61265
www.riroe.com/

Saint Clair ROE
Susan Sarfaty, supt. 618-825-3900
1000 S Illinois St, Belleville 62220 Fax 825-3999
www.stclair.k12.il.us/

South Cook Intermediate Service Center
Dr. Vanessa Kinder, supt. 708-754-6600
253 W Joe Orr Rd Fax 754-8687
Chicago Heights 60411
www.s-cook.org

Vermilion ROE
Cheryl Reifsteck, supt. 217-431-2668
200 S College St Ste B Fax 431-2671
Danville 61832
www.roe54.k12.il.us/

West Suburb Intermediate Service Center
Kay Poyner Brown, dir. 708-449-4284
4413 Roosevelt Rd Ste 104 Fax 449-4288
Hillside 60162
www.west40.org

Will ROE
Shawn Walsh, supt. 815-740-8360
702 W Maple St, New Lenox 60451 Fax 740-4788
www.willroe.org

PUBLIC, PRIVATE AND CATHOLIC ELEMENTARY SCHOOLS

Abingdon, Knox, Pop. 3,272

Abingdon-Avon CUSD 276 800/PK-12
401 W Latimer St 61410 309-462-2301
Dr. Mike Curry, supt. Fax 462-3870
www.d276.net

Hedding ES 300/PK-5
401 W Latimer St 61410 309-462-2363
Michelle Andrews, prin. Fax 462-2105

Other Schools – See Avon

Addison, DuPage, Pop. 36,491

Addison SD 4 4,200/PK-8
222 N JF Kennedy Dr 60101 630-458-2500
John Langton, supt. Fax 628-8829
www.asd4.org

Addison Early Learning Center PK-PK
650 S Ardmore Ave 60101 630-458-3075
Erin Alexander, prin.

Ardmore ES 200/K-5
644 S Ardmore Ave 60101 630-458-2900
Janet Diaz, prin. Fax 833-3572

Army Trail ES 500/K-5
346 W Army Trail Blvd 60101 630-458-2502
Debra Martello, prin. Fax 628-2516

Fullerton ES 500/K-5
400 S Michigan Ave 60101 630-458-2950
Dr. Carolyn Stange, prin. Fax 833-3949

Indian Trail JHS 1,400/6-8
222 N JF Kennedy Dr Frnt 1 60101 630-458-2600
Craig Bennett, prin. Fax 628-2841

Lake Park ES 400/K-5
330 W Lake Park Dr 60101 630-458-3010
David Smogor, prin. Fax 628-2526

Lincoln ES 500/K-5
720 N Lincoln Ave 60101 630-458-3040
Lina Guio, prin. Fax 628-2524

Stone ES 400/K-5
1404 W Stone Ave 60101 630-628-4020
Cristina Ardizzone, prin. Fax 628-2546

Wesley ES 300/K-5
1111 W Westwood Trl 60101 630-628-4060
Katie Purse, prin. Fax 628-2536

St. Philip the Apostle S 300/PK-8
1233 W Holtz Ave 60101 630-543-4130
Julie Noonan, prin. Fax 458-8750

Akin, Franklin

Akin CCSD 91 100/PK-8
21962 Akin Blacktop, 618-627-2180
Kelly Clark, supt. Fax 627-2119
www.akin.myclassupdates.com

Akin Community Consolidated ES 100/PK-8
21962 Akin Blacktop, 618-627-2180
Kelly Clark, admin. Fax 627-2119

Albers, Clinton, Pop. 1,172

Albers SD 63 200/PK-8
PO Box 104 62215 618-248-5146
Mike Toeben, supt. Fax 248-5659
www.albers.k12.il.us

Albers ES 200/PK-8
PO Box 104 62215 618-248-5146
Mike Toeben, prin. Fax 248-5659

Albion, Edwards, Pop. 1,965
Edwards County CUSD 1 1,000/PK-12
361 W Main St Ste 100 62806 618-445-2814
David Cowger, supt. Fax 445-2272
www.edwardscountyschools.org
Albion S 500/PK-8
361 W Main St 62806 618-445-2327
Preston Nelson, prin. Fax 445-2672
Other Schools – See West Salem

Aledo, Mercer, Pop. 3,626
Mercer County SD 404 1,400/PK-12
1002 SW 6th St 61231 309-582-2238
Scott Petrie, supt. Fax 582-7428
www.mercerschools.org
Apollo ES 400/PK-4
801 SW 9th St 61231 309-582-5350
Bill Fleuette, prin. Fax 582-3457
Mercer County IS 200/5-6
1002 SW 6th St 61231 309-582-2441
Garrett Lefferson, prin. Fax 582-2440
Other Schools – See Joy, New Boston

Alexander, Morgan
Franklin CUSD 1 300/PK-12
PO Box 140 62601 217-478-3011
Andy Stremlau, supt. Fax 478-4921
www.franklinhigh.com
Alexander ES 100/2-5
PO Box 140 62601 217-478-3011
Andrew Stremlau, prin. Fax 478-4921
Other Schools – See Franklin

Alexis, Mercer, Pop. 829
United CUSD 304
Supt. — See Monmouth
United ES - North 200/PK-5
411 W Hunt Ave 61412 309-482-3332
Maggie Wallace, prin. Fax 482-3236

Algonquin, McHenry, Pop. 29,616
CUSD 300 19,100/PK-12
2550 Harnish Dr 60102 847-551-8300
Fred Heid, supt. Fax 551-8413
www.d300.org
Algonquin Lakes ES 600/K-5
1401 Compton Dr 60102 847-854-3900
Christopher Columbaro, prin. Fax 854-3909
Algonquin MS 500/6-8
520 Longwood Dr 60102 847-658-2545
Andrew Reincke, prin. Fax 658-2547
Eastview ES 400/K-5
540 Longwood Dr 60102 847-458-5501
James Zursin, prin. Fax 458-5509
Neubert ES 400/K-5
1100 Huntington Dr 60102 847-658-2540
Peggy Thurow, prin. Fax 658-9809
Westfield Community S 1,400/K-8
2100 Sleepy Hollow Rd 60102 847-532-7600
Ami Engel, prin. Fax 532-7615
Other Schools – See Carpentersville, Gilberts, Hampshire, Lake in the Hills, Sleepy Hollow, West Dundee

Consolidated SD 158 9,200/PK-12
650 Academic Dr 60102 847-659-6158
Dr. John Burkey, supt. Fax 659-6125
www.district158.org/
Conley ES 700/3-5
750 Academic Dr 60102 847-659-3700
Rhonda Maciejewski, prin. Fax 659-3720
Heineman MS 900/6-8
725 Academic Dr 60102 847-659-4300
Jake Litchfield, prin. Fax 659-4320
Mackeben ES 600/K-2
800 Academic Dr 60102 847-659-3400
Anna Hoyou, prin. Fax 659-3420
Other Schools – See Huntley, Lake in the Hills

St. John's Lutheran S 100/PK-8
300 Jefferson St 60102 847-658-9311
Roger Kirsch, prin. Fax 658-5766
St. Margaret Mary S 500/PK-8
119 S Hubbard St 60102 847-658-5313
Alison Mallo, prin. Fax 854-0501

Alhambra, Madison, Pop. 672
Highland CUSD 5
Supt. — See Highland
Alhambra PS 100/PK-3
302 W Main St 62001 618-488-2200
Cynthia Tolbert, prin. Fax 488-2201

Allendale, Wabash, Pop. 474
Allendale CCSD 17 100/PK-8
PO Box 130 62410 618-299-3161
Robert Bowser, supt. Fax 299-2015
www.allendale.wabash.k12.il.us
Allendale ES 100/PK-8
PO Box 130 62410 618-299-3161
Robert Bowser, admin. Fax 299-2015

Alpha, Henry, Pop. 662
Alwood CUSD 225
Supt. — See Woodhull
Alwood ES 200/PK-5
101 E A St 61413 309-629-5011
Reggie Larson, prin. Fax 629-4023

Alsip, Cook, Pop. 19,017
Alsip-Hazelgreen-Oaklawn SD 126 1,500/K-8
11900 S Kostner Ave 60803 708-389-1900
Craig Gwaltney, supt. Fax 396-3793
www.dist126.org
Hazelgreen ES 300/K-6
11751 S Lawler Ave 60803 708-371-5351
Leah Humphrey-Mason, prin. Fax 396-3754
Lane ES 300/K-6
4600 W 123rd St 60803 708-371-0720
Patti Egan, prin. Fax 396-3753
Prairie JHS 300/7-8
11910 S Kostner Ave 60803 708-371-3080
Maureen Paulmeyer, prin. Fax 396-3798
Stony Creek ES 600/K-6
11700 S Kolin Ave 60803 708-371-0220
Nicole Leggett-Gallus, prin. Fax 396-3755

Atwood Heights SD 125 700/PK-8
12150 S Hamlin Ave 60803 708-371-0080
Dr. Thomas Livingston, supt. Fax 371-7847
www.ahsd125.org
Hamlin Upper Grade Center 200/6-8
12150 S Hamlin Ave 60803 708-597-1550
Dr. Lisa West, prin. Fax 396-0515
Other Schools – See Merrionette Park, Oak Lawn

Cook County SD 130
Supt. — See Blue Island
Washington ES 300/K-5
12545 S Homan Ave 60803 708-489-3523
Bridgette McNeal, prin. Fax 385-8467

Altamont, Effingham, Pop. 2,313
Altamont CUSD 10 800/PK-12
7 S Ewing St 62411 618-483-6195
Jeff Fritchtnitch, supt. Fax 483-6303
www.altamontschools.org
Altamont Grade S 500/PK-8
407 S Edwards St 62411 618-483-5171
Doug Hill, prin. Fax 483-6793

Altamont Lutheran Interparish S 100/K-8
7 S Edwards St 62411 618-483-6428
Robinette Flach, prin. Fax 483-6296

Alton, Madison, Pop. 26,887
Alton CUSD 11 5,000/PK-12
PO Box 9028 62002 618-474-2600
Mark Cappel, supt. Fax 463-2126
www.altonschools.org
Alton MS 1,400/6-8
2200 College Ave 62002 618-474-2200
Cindy Inman, prin. Fax 463-2127
East ES 400/3-5
1035 Washington Ave 62002 618-463-2130
Lanea DeConcini, prin. Fax 463-2132
Lovejoy ES 100/K-2
1043 Tremont St 62002 618-463-2057
John Ducey, prin. Fax 463-2138
Smith ES 100/PK-2
2400 Henry St 62002 618-463-2077
Jody Meggos, prin. Fax 462-3810
West ES 400/2-5
1513 State St 62002 618-463-2134
Dr. Brian Saenz, prin. Fax 463-2144
Other Schools – See Godfrey

Mississippi Valley Christian S 100/PK-12
2009 Seminary St 62002 618-462-1071
St. Mary MS 100/6-8
1015 Milton Rd 62002 618-465-9719
Judy Kulp, prin. Fax 465-9726
St. Mary S 400/PK-5
536 E 3rd St 62002 618-465-9719
Judy Kulp, prin. Fax 465-9726
SS. Peter & Paul S 100/PK-8
801 State St 62002 618-465-8711
Harry Cavanaugh, prin. Fax 465-6405

Amboy, Lee, Pop. 2,480
Amboy CUSD 272 700/K-12
11 E Hawley St 61310 815-857-2164
Jeff Thake, supt. Fax 857-4434
www.amboy.net/
Amboy Central ES 300/K-4
30 E Provost St 61310 815-857-3619
Joyce Schamberger, prin. Fax 857-9024
Amboy JHS 200/5-8
140 S Appleton Ave 61310 815-857-3528
Joyce Schamberger, prin. Fax 857-4603

Andalusia, Rock Island, Pop. 1,173
Rockridge CUSD 300
Supt. — See Taylor Ridge
Andalusia ES 200/PK-PK, 3-
112 7th Ave E 61232 309-793-8080
Mike Ruff, prin. Fax 798-9651

Anna, Union, Pop. 4,407
Anna CCSD 37 700/PK-8
301 S Green St 62906 618-833-6812
Charles Goforth, supt. Fax 833-3205
anna37.com/
Anna JHS 300/5-8
301 S Green St 62906 618-833-6415
Mark Laster, prin. Fax 833-6535
Davie ES 200/3-4
301 S Green St 62906 618-833-8022
Mark Laster, prin. Fax 833-6535
Lincoln ES 200/PK-2
108 Warren St 62906 618-833-6851
Mark Laster, prin. Fax 833-3262

Annawan, Henry, Pop. 875
Annawan CUSD 226 400/PK-12
501 W South St 61234 309-935-6781
Kyle Ganson, supt. Fax 935-6065
www.annawan226.org
Annawan ES 300/PK-8
503 W South St 61234 309-935-6623
Wayne Brau, prin. Fax 935-6894

Antioch, Lake, Pop. 14,166
Antioch CCSD 34 3,000/PK-8
964 Spafford St 60002 847-838-8400
Dr. Jay Marino, supt. Fax 838-8404
www.antioch34.com
Antioch ES 400/2-5
817 Main St 60002 847-838-8901
David Shepherd, prin. Fax 838-8904
Antioch Upper Grade S 1,000/6-8
800 Highview Dr 60002 847-838-8310
Joe Koeune, prin. Fax 838-8304
Hillcrest ES 700/PK-1
433 E Depot St 60002 847-838-8000
Lee Gaiser, prin. Fax 838-8004
Petty ES 500/2-5
850 Highview Dr 60002 847-838-8100
Joanna Gerritsen, prin. Fax 838-8104
Other Schools – See Lake Villa

Emmons SD 33 300/K-8
24226 W Beach Grove Rd 60002 847-395-1105
Dr. Eileen Conway, supt. Fax 395-1223
www.emmons33.org
Emmons ES 300/K-8
24226 W Beach Grove Rd 60002 847-395-1105
Dr. Eileen Conway, supt. Fax 395-1223

Grass Lake SD 36 200/PK-8
26177 W Grass Lake Rd 60002 847-395-1550
Dr. Terry O'Brien, supt. Fax 395-8632
www.gls36.org
Grass Lake ES 200/PK-8
26177 W Grass Lake Rd 60002 847-395-1550
Donna Plath, prin. Fax 395-8632

Faith Evangelical Lutheran S 200/PK-8
1275 Main St 60002 847-395-1660
Fax 589-0519

Arcola, Douglas, Pop. 2,899
Arcola CUSD 306 800/PK-12
351 W Washington St 61910 217-268-4963
Thomas Mulligan, supt. Fax 268-3809
www.arcola.k12.il.us
Arcola ES 500/PK-6
351 W Washington St 61910 217-268-4961
Angie Gentry, prin. Fax 268-4719

Pleasant View S 50/K-12
184 N County Road 300E 61910 217-268-3886
Matthew Bontrager, prin.

Arenzville, Cass, Pop. 406

Trinity Lutheran S, PO Box 118 62611 50/PK-6
Lynne Schone, prin. 217-997-5535

Argenta, Macon, Pop. 935
Argenta-Oreana CUSD 1 1,000/PK-12
PO Box 440 62501 217-795-2313
Damian Jones, supt. Fax 795-2174
www.argenta-oreana.org/
Argenta-Oreana MS 200/6-8
PO Box 439 62501 217-795-2163
Patrick Blair, prin. Fax 795-4502
Other Schools – See Oreana

Arlington Heights, Cook, Pop. 74,142
Arlington Heights SD 25 5,300/PK-8
1200 S Dunton Ave 60005 847-758-4900
Dr. Lori Bein, supt. Fax 758-4907
www.sd25.org
Dryden ES 500/K-5
722 S Dryden Pl 60005 847-398-4280
Akemi Sessler, prin. Fax 394-6946
Greenbrier ES 400/PK-5
2330 N Verde Dr 60004 847-398-4272
Donna Bingaman, prin. Fax 394-6291
Ivy Hill ES 500/K-5
2211 N Burke Dr 60004 847-398-4275
Scott Kaese, prin. Fax 394-6556
Olive-Mary Stitt ES 600/K-5
303 E Olive St 60004 847-398-4282
Becky FitzPatrick, prin. Fax 394-6935
Patton ES 500/K-5
1616 N Patton Ave 60004 847-398-4288
Eric Larson, prin. Fax 394-6681
South MS 900/6-8
400 S Highland Ave 60005 847-398-4250
Piper Boston, prin. Fax 394-6260
Thomas MS 900/6-8
1430 N Belmont Ave 60004 847-398-4260
Brian Kaye, prin. Fax 394-6843
Westgate ES 600/K-5
500 S Dwyer Ave 60005 847-398-4292
Brad Carter, prin. Fax 394-6191
Windsor ES 500/K-5
1315 E Miner St 60004 847-398-4297
Shelley Fabrizio, prin. Fax 394-6611

CCSD 59 6,800/PK-8
2123 S Arlington Heights Rd 60005 847-593-4300
Dr. Art Fessler, supt. Fax 593-4409
www.ccsd59.org
Low ES 500/PK-5
1530 S Highland Ave 60005 847-593-4383
Susan Ejma, prin. Fax 593-7291
Other Schools – See Des Plaines, Elk Grove Village, Mount Prospect

Wheeling CCSD 21
Supt. — See Wheeling
Poe ES 400/K-5
2800 N Highland Ave 60004 847-670-3200
Christy Campbell, prin. Fax 670-3216
Riley ES 400/PK-5
1209 E Burr Oak Dr 60004 847-670-3400
Carrie McCulley, prin. Fax 670-3418

Christian Liberty Academy 400/PK-12
502 W Euclid Ave 60004 847-385-2012
Thad Bennett, hdmstr. Fax 259-9972
Our Lady of the Wayside S 600/PK-8
432 S Mitchell Ave 60005 847-255-0050
David Wood, prin. Fax 253-0543
St. James S 500/PK-8
820 N Arlington Heights Rd 60004 224-345-7145
Judith Pappas, prin. Fax 345-7140

St. Peter Lutheran S — 500/PK-8
111 W Olive St 60004 — 847-253-6638
Bruce Rudi, prin. — Fax 259-4185

Armstrong, Vermilion
Armstrong-Ellis Consolidated SD 61 — 100/K-8
PO Box 7 61812 — 217-569-2115
William Mulvaney, supt. — Fax 569-2116
Armstrong-Ellis S — 100/K-8
PO Box 7 61812 — 217-569-2115
Kurt Thornsbrough, prin. — Fax 569-2116

Arthur, Douglas, Pop. 2,280
Arthur CUSD 305 — 1,100/PK-12
301 E Columbia St 61911 — 217-543-2511
Kenneth Schwengel, supt. — Fax 543-2210
www.cusd305.org
Arthur Grade S — 400/PK-8
126 E Lincoln St 61911 — 217-543-2109
Sage Hale, prin. — Fax 543-2308
Other Schools – See Atwood, Lovington

Arthur Christian S — 100/PK-12
1710 State Highway 133 61911 — 217-543-2397
Greg Mast, prin. — Fax 543-3781

Ashkum, Iroquois, Pop. 755
Central CUSD 4 — 1,100/PK-12
PO Box 158 60911 — 815-698-2212
Tonya Evans, supt. — Fax 694-2844
www.clifton-u4.k12.il.us
Ashkum Early Literacy Center — 100/PK-PK
PO Box 158 60911 — 815-698-2212
Andrea Lemenager, prin. — Fax 698-2635
Other Schools – See Chebanse, Clifton

Ashland, Cass, Pop. 1,324
A-C Central CUSD 262 — 400/PK-12
PO Box 260 62612 — 217-476-8112
Timothy Page, supt. — Fax 476-8100
a-ccentral.com
A-C Central MS — 200/5-8
PO Box 260 62612 — 217-476-3313
Steve Groll, prin. — Fax 476-3730
Other Schools – See Chandlerville

Ashley, Washington, Pop. 533
Ashley CCSD 15 — 200/PK-8
450 N Third St 62808 — 618-485-6611
Brian Hodge, supt. — Fax 485-2124
www.ashleyccsd15.org
Ashley Community Consolidated S — 200/PK-8
450 N Third St 62808 — 618-485-6611
Brian Hodge, admin. — Fax 485-2124

Ashmore, Coles, Pop. 778
Charleston CUSD 1
Supt. — See Charleston
Ashmore ES — 100/K-4
PO Box 219 61912 — 217-349-3000
Aaron Lock, prin. — Fax 349-3005

Ashton, Lee, Pop. 967
Ashton-Franklin Center CUSD 275 — 400/PK-12
611 Western Ave 61006 — 815-453-7461
John Zick, supt. — Fax 453-7462
www.afcschools.net
Other Schools – See Franklin Grove

Assumption, Christian, Pop. 1,158
Central A & M CUSD 21 — 800/PK-12
105 N College St 62510 — 217-226-4042
Dr. DeAnn Heck, supt. — Fax 226-4133
www.camraiders.com
Bond ES — 200/PK-5
105 N College St 62510 — 217-226-4022
David Fitzgerald, prin. — Fax 226-4133
Central A & M MS — 200/6-8
404 Colegrove St 62510 — 217-226-4241
Courtney Hiler, prin. — Fax 226-4442
Other Schools – See Moweaqua

Astoria, Fulton, Pop. 1,131
Astoria CUSD 1 — 400/PK-12
402 N Jefferson St 61501 — 309-329-2156
Don Willett, supt. — Fax 329-2214
www.acusd1.org
Astoria ES — 200/PK-5
402 N Jefferson St 61501 — 309-329-2158
Dave Crouse, prin. — Fax 329-2903
Astoria JHS — 100/6-8
402 N Jefferson St 61501 — 309-329-2158
Dave Crouse, prin. — Fax 329-2963

Athens, Menard, Pop. 1,956
Athens CUSD 213 — 1,000/PK-12
501 Warrior Way 62613 — 217-636-8761
Dr. Scott Laird, supt. — Fax 636-8851
www.athens-213.org
Athens JHS — 100/7-8
501 Warrior Way 62613 — 217-636-8380
Matt Rhoades, prin. — Fax 636-8851
Other Schools – See Cantrall

Atlanta, Logan, Pop. 1,677
Olympia CUSD 16
Supt. — See Stanford
Olympia South ES — 300/PK-5
103 NE 5th St 61723 — 217-648-2302
Stacey Rogers, prin. — Fax 648-5248

Atwood, Douglas, Pop. 1,215
Arthur CUSD 305
Supt. — See Arthur
Atwood-Hammond Grade S — 300/PK-8
316 N Illinois St 61913 — 217-578-2229
Kristin Nall, prin. — Fax 578-3314

Auburn, Sangamon, Pop. 4,722
Auburn CUSD 10 — 1,400/PK-12
606 W North St 62615 — 217-438-6164
Darren Root, supt. — Fax 438-6483
www.auburn.k12.il.us
Auburn ES — 400/PK-2
445 N 5th St 62615 — 217-438-6916
Amy Donaldson, prin. — Fax 438-3912
Auburn MS — 300/3-5
601 N 7th St 62615 — 217-438-6919
Matt Grimm, prin. — Fax 438-3700
Other Schools – See Divernon

Augusta, Hancock, Pop. 586
Southeastern CUSD 337 — 500/PK-12
PO Box 215 62311 — 217-392-2172
Todd Fox, supt. — Fax 392-2174
www.southeastern337.com/
Other Schools – See Bowen

Aurora, Kane, Pop. 194,432
Aurora East Unit SD 131 — 14,700/PK-12
417 5th St 60505 — 630-299-5550
Dr. Mark McDonald, supt. — Fax 299-5500
www.d131.org
Allen ES — 800/PK-5
700 S Farnsworth Ave 60505 — 630-299-5200
Robert Pape, prin. — Fax 299-5201
Bardwell ES — 900/PK-5
550 S Lincoln Ave 60505 — 630-299-5300
Twila Garza, prin. — Fax 299-5302
Beaupre ES — 400/K-5
954 E Benton St 60505 — 630-299-5390
Caridad Garcia, prin. — Fax 299-5399
Benavides STEAM Academy — 400/K-1
250 E Indian Trl 60505 — 630-299-7560
Lisa Simoncelli-Bulak, prin.
Brady ES — 500/PK-5
600 Columbia St 60505 — 630-299-5425
Francisco De Los Santos, prin. — Fax 299-5474
Cowherd MS — 1,000/6-8
441 N Farnsworth Ave 60505 — 630-299-5900
Crystal England, prin. — Fax 299-5901
Dieterich ES — 600/PK-5
1141 Jackson St 60505 — 630-299-8280
Paula Ek, prin. — Fax 299-8281
Early Childhood Development Center — 200/PK-PK
278 E Indian Trl 60505 — 630-299-7460
Kathleen Kogut, prin. — Fax 299-7461
Gates ES — 700/PK-5
800 7th Ave 60505 — 630-299-5600
Nitza Carrillo, prin. — Fax 299-5601
Hermes ES — 800/PK-5
1000 Jungles Ave 60505 — 630-299-8200
Scott Dart, prin. — Fax 299-8201
Johnson ES — 400/PK-5
1934 Liberty St, — 630-299-5400
David Ballard, prin. — Fax 299-5401
Krug ES — 300/PK-5
240 Melrose Ave 60505 — 630-299-5280
Noah Little, prin. — Fax 299-5299
Oak Park ES — 700/PK-5
1200 Front St 60505 — 630-299-8250
Annette McMahon, prin. — Fax 299-8251
O'Donnell ES — 500/PK-5
1640 Reckinger Rd 60505 — 630-299-8300
Matt Willigman, prin. — Fax 299-8301
Rodgers Magnet Academy — 400/3-8
157 N Root St 60505 — 630-299-7175
Angela Rowley, prin.
Rollins ES — 500/PK-5
950 Kane St 60505 — 630-299-5480
Glenda Mitrov, prin. — Fax 299-5481
Simmons MS — 1,000/6-8
1130 Sheffer Rd 60505 — 630-299-4150
Mechelle Patterson, prin. — Fax 299-4151
Waldo MS — 900/6-8
56 Jackson St 60505 — 630-299-8400
Jon Simpson, prin. — Fax 299-8401

Aurora West Unit SD 129 — 12,800/PK-12
1877 W Downer Pl 60506 — 630-301-5000
Dr. Jeff Craig, supt. — Fax 844-5710
www.sd129.org/
Freeman ES — 600/K-5
153 S Randall Rd 60506 — 630-301-5002
Crystal Dvorak, prin. — Fax 844-4527
Greenman ES — 700/K-5
729 W Galena Blvd 60506 — 630-301-5004
Cliff Englishharden, prin. — Fax 844-4618
Hall ES — 600/K-5
2001 Heather Dr 60506 — 630-301-5005
Cherie Esposito, prin. — Fax 844-4617
Herget MS — 700/6-8
1550 Deerpath Rd 60506 — 630-301-5006
Cindy Larry, prin. — Fax 301-5222
Hill ES — 600/K-5
724 Pennsylvania Ave 60506 — 630-301-5007
Mike Smith, prin. — Fax 897-4289
Jefferson MS — 800/6-8
1151 Plum St 60506 — 630-301-5009
Shawn Munos, prin. — Fax 844-5711
McCleery ES — 700/K-5
1002 W Illinois Ave 60506 — 630-301-5012
Daniel Ulrich, prin. — Fax 844-9491
Smith ES — 500/K-5
1332 Robinwood Dr 60506 — 630-301-5015
Dr. Pete Clabough, prin. — Fax 896-9442
Todd ECC — 300/PK-PK
100 Oak Ave 60506 — 630-301-5016
Dr. Laurie Klomhaus, prin. — Fax 844-4522
Washington MS — 800/6-8
231 S Constitution Dr 60506 — 630-301-5017
Dr. Brett Burton, prin. — Fax 844-5712
Other Schools – See Montgomery, North Aurora

CUSD 308
Supt. — See Oswego
Bednarcik JHS — 600/6-8
3025 Heggs Rd, — 630-636-2500
John Francis, prin. — Fax 636-2591
Homestead ES — 700/K-5
2830 Hillsboro Blvd, — 630-636-3100
Casey O'Connell, prin. — Fax 636-3168
Wheatlands ES — 700/K-5
2290 Barrington Dr, — 630-636-3500
Jeffrey Gerard, prin. — Fax 636-3591
Wolfs Crossing ES — 600/K-5
3015 Heggs Rd, — 630-636-3700
Allison Sulkson, prin. — Fax 636-3791

Indian Prairie CUSD 204 — 28,600/PK-12
780 Shoreline Dr 60504 — 630-375-3000
Dr. Karen Sullivan, supt. — Fax 375-3009
ipsdweb.ipsd.org
Brooks ES — 800/K-5
2700 Stonebridge Blvd, — 630-375-3200
Terri Russell, prin. — Fax 375-3201
Fischer MS — 1,000/6-8
1305 Long Grove Dr 60504 — 630-375-3100
Jennifer Nonnemacher, prin. — Fax 375-3101
Georgetown ES — 500/K-5
995 Long Grove Dr 60504 — 630-375-3456
Janan Szurek, prin. — Fax 375-3461
Gombert ES — 500/K-5
2707 Ridge Rd 60504 — 630-375-3700
Dr. Jeremy Ricken, prin. — Fax 375-3701
Granger MS — 1,100/6-8
2721 Stonebridge Blvd, — 630-375-1010
Laurie Fiorenza, prin. — Fax 375-1110
McCarty ES — 700/K-5
3000 Village Green Dr 60504 — 630-375-3400
Kevin Schnable, prin. — Fax 375-3401
Prairie Children Preschool — 600/PK-PK
780 Shoreline Dr 60504 — 630-375-3030
Sally Osborne, prin. — Fax 375-3029
Steck ES — 600/K-5
460 Inverness Dr 60504 — 630-375-3500
Elizabeth Pohlmann, prin. — Fax 375-3501
Still MS — 900/6-8
787 Meadowridge Dr 60504 — 630-375-3900
Kimberly Cornish, prin. — Fax 375-3901
Young ES — 700/K-5
800 Asbury Dr, — 630-375-3800
Adrienne Morgan, prin. — Fax 375-3801
Other Schools – See Bolingbrook, Naperville

John C. Dunham STEM Partnership SD — 3-8
405 S Gladstone Ave 60506 — 630-947-1240
Arin Carter, dir.
www.stem.aurora.edu
Dunham STEM Partnership S — 3-8
405 S Gladstone Ave 60506 — 630-947-1240
Arin Carter, dir.

Annunciation of the BVM S — 200/PK-8
1840 Church Rd 60505 — 630-851-4300
Jennifer Wardynski, prin. — Fax 851-4316
Aurora Christian S — 600/PK-12
2255 Sullivan Rd 60506 — 630-892-1551
Dr. Collette House, supt. — Fax 892-1692
Aurora Montessori S — 100/PK-K
3180 N Aurora Rd, — 630-898-4346
Karen Zehnal, head sch — Fax 898-7048
Cosmic Montessori S — 100/PK-5
4100 Westbrook Dr 60504 — 630-585-8881
Covenant Christian S — 100/PK-8
10 N Edgelawn Dr 60506 — 630-801-7955
Phil Lundquist, prin. — Fax 801-7904
Fox Valley Montessori S — 100/PK-6
850 N Commonwealth Ave 60506 — 630-896-7557
Denise Monnier, prin. — Fax 896-8104
Holy Angels S — 500/PK-8
720 Kensington Pl 60506 — 630-897-3613
Tonya Forbes, prin. — Fax 897-8233
Montessori Childrens Garden — 100/PK-3
2300 Montgomery Rd 60504 — 630-820-1010
Teresa Heinen, prin. — Fax 820-1010
Our Lady of Good Counsel S — 300/PK-8
601 Talma St 60505 — 630-851-4400
Karen Behrns, prin. — Fax 851-8220
Resurrection Lutheran S — 100/PK-8
2567 W Sullivan Rd 60506 — 630-907-1313
Bradley Essig, prin. — Fax 907-1008
St. Joseph S — 200/PK-8
706 High St 60505 — 630-844-3781
Nancy Coughlin, prin. — Fax 844-3656
St. Pauls Lutheran S — 100/PK-8
85 S Constitution Dr 60506 — 630-896-3250
Diane Katz, prin.
St. Peter S — 100/K-8
915 Sard Ave 60506 — 630-892-1283
Robert Williams, prin. — Fax 892-4836
St. Rita of Cascia S — 200/PK-8
770 Old Indian Trl 60506 — 630-892-0200
Elizabeth Faxon, prin. — Fax 892-4236
St. Therese of Jesus S — 100/PK-8
255 N Farnsworth Ave 60505 — 630-898-0620
Michael Neis, prin. — Fax 898-3087

Aviston, Clinton, Pop. 1,932
Aviston SD 21 — 400/PK-8
350 S Hull St 62216 — 618-228-7245
Dr. Tami Kampwerth, supt. — Fax 228-7121
www.avistonk-8.org
Aviston ES — 400/PK-8
350 S Hull St 62216 — 618-228-7245
Dr. Tami Kampwerth, supt. — Fax 228-7121

Avon, Fulton, Pop. 778
Abingdon-Avon CUSD 276
Supt. — See Abingdon
Abingdon-Avon MS — 100/6-8
320 E Woods St 61415 — 309-465-3621
Kristi Anderson, prin. — Fax 465-7194
Avon ES — 100/PK-5
400 E Woods St 61415 — 309-465-3851
Kristi Anderson, prin. — Fax 465-9055

Bannockburn, Lake, Pop. 1,556
Bannockburn SD 106 — 200/K-8
2165 Telegraph Rd 60015 — 847-945-5900
Dr. Scott Herrmann, supt. — Fax 945-5909
www.bannockburnschool.org

Bannockburn S 200/K-8
2165 Telegraph Rd 60015 847-945-5900
Debbie Barnes, prin. Fax 945-5909

Barrington, Cook, Pop. 10,188
Barrington CUSD 220 8,800/PK-12
310 James St 60010 847-381-6300
Dr. Brian Harris, supt. Fax 381-6337
www.barrington220.org
Barrington Early Learning Center 200/PK-K
40 E Dundee Rd 60010 224-770-4300
Barbara Romano, prin. Fax 304-4392
Barrington MS Prairie Campus 1,100/6-8
40 E Dundee Rd 60010 847-304-3990
Travis Lobbins, prin. Fax 304-3986
Barrington MS Station Campus 1,000/6-8
215 Eastern Ave 60010 847-756-6400
Kristen Paul, prin. Fax 842-1343
Countryside ES 400/K-5
205 W County Line Rd 60010 847-381-1162
Dr. Micah Korb, prin. Fax 304-3927
Grove Avenue ES 500/K-5
900 S Grove Ave 60010 847-381-1888
Katie Matthews, prin. Fax 304-3922
Hough Street ES 300/K-5
310 S Hough St 60010 847-381-1108
James Aalfs, prin. Fax 304-3919
Lines ES 500/K-5
217 John Snow Ave 60010 847-381-7850
Dr. Kenneth Hyllberg, prin. Fax 304-3918
Roslyn Road ES 400/K-5
224 Roslyn Rd 60010 847-381-4148
Paul Kirk, prin. Fax 304-3923
Other Schools – See Carpentersville, North Barrington, South Barrington

---

Atonement Christian Day S 50/PK-K
909 E Main St 60010 847-382-6360
Cynthia Clanton, dir. Fax 381-2427
St. Anne S 400/PK-8
319 Franklin St 60010 847-381-0311
Dawn Kapka, prin. Fax 381-0384

Barry, Pike, Pop. 1,297
Western CUSD 12 600/PK-12
401 McDonough St 62312 217-335-2323
Jessica Funk, supt. Fax 335-2212
www.westerncusd12.org
Western Barry ES 300/PK-5
401 McDonough St 62312 217-335-2323
Connie Thomas, prin. Fax 335-2211
Other Schools – See Kinderhook

Bartelso, Clinton, Pop. 594
Bartelso ESD 57 100/K-8
PO Box 267 62218 618-765-2164
Tom Siegler, supt. Fax 765-2712
www.bartelsobraves.com
Bartelso S 100/K-8
PO Box 267 62218 618-765-2164
Tom Siegler, supt. Fax 765-2712

Bartlett, Cook, Pop. 40,574
SD U-46
Supt. — See Elgin
Bartlett ES 600/K-6
111 E North Ave 60103 630-213-5545
Lorelei Keltner, prin. Fax 213-5544
Centennial ES 500/PK-6
234 E Stearns Rd 60103 630-213-5632
Sarah Rabe, prin. Fax 213-5630
Eastview MS 900/7-8
321 N Oak Ave 60103 630-213-5550
Donald Donner, prin. Fax 213-5563
Hawk Hollow ES 400/K-6
235 Jacaranda Dr 60103 630-540-7676
Noelle Dupuis, prin. Fax 372-3365
Independence Early Learning S 300/PK-PK
200 E Taylor Ave 60103 630-213-5629
Lisa Bergbreiter, prin. Fax 213-5584
Liberty ES 700/PK-6
1375 W Bartlett Rd 60103 630-540-7680
Juanita Jimenez, prin. Fax 540-7666
Nature Ridge ES 700/K-6
1899 Westridge Blvd 60103 630-372-4647
Charlotte Coleman, prin. Fax 372-4654
Prairieview ES 400/K-6
285 Mayflower Ln 60103 630-213-5603
Paul Flatley, prin. Fax 213-5588
Sycamore Trails ES 600/PK-6
1025 Sycamore Ln 60103 630-213-5641
Lisa Cardenas, prin. Fax 213-5599

Bartonville, Peoria, Pop. 6,361
Bartonville SD 66 300/PK-8
600 S Adams St 61607 309-697-3253
Lan Eberle, supt. Fax 697-3254
www.bgs66.org
Bartonville ES 300/PK-8
6000 S Adams St 61607 309-697-3253
Lan Eberle, admin. Fax 697-3254

Monroe SD 70 300/K-8
5137 W Cisna Rd 61607 309-697-3120
Darrick Reiley, supt. Fax 697-3185
monroe70.org
Monroe ES 300/K-8
5137 W Cisna Rd 61607 309-697-3120
Carrie Kleist, prin. Fax 697-3185

Oak Grove SD 68 300/PK-8
6018 W Lancaster Rd 61607 309-697-3367
Dr. Loren Baele, supt. Fax 633-2381
www.og68.org
Oak Grove S 200/PK-8
6018 W Lancaster Rd 61607 309-697-0621
Dr. Loren Baele, prin. Fax 633-4523

Batavia, Kane, Pop. 25,733
Batavia Unit SD 101 6,100/PK-12
335 W Wilson St 60510 630-937-8800
Dr. Lisa Hichens, supt. Fax 937-8801
www.bps101.net
Gustafson ES 500/PK-5
905 Carlisle Rd 60510 630-937-8000
Dr. Tim McDermott, prin. Fax 937-8001
Hoover - Wood ES 400/K-5
1640 Wagner Rd 60510 630-937-8300
Gina Greenwald, prin. Fax 937-8301
McWayne ES 500/K-5
3501 Hapner Way 60510 630-937-8100
Jeff Modaff, prin. Fax 937-8101
Nelson ES 500/K-5
334 William Wood Ln 60510 630-937-8400
Nicole Prentiss, prin. Fax 937-8401
Rotolo MS 1,500/6-8
1501 S Raddant Rd 60510 630-937-8700
Bryan Zwemke, prin. Fax 937-8701
Storm ES 500/K-5
305 N Van Nortwick Ave 60510 630-937-8200
Anne Paonessa, prin. Fax 937-8201
White ES 400/K-5
800 N Prairie St 60510 630-937-8500
Dr. Kevin Skomer, prin. Fax 937-8501

Holy Cross S PK-8
2300 Main St 60510 630-593-5290
Mike Puttin, prin. Fax 593-5289
Immanuel Lutheran S 300/PK-8
950 Hart Rd 60510 630-406-0157
Donna Laughlin, prin. Fax 879-7614
Montessori Academy 100/PK-8
595 S River St 60510 630-879-2586
George Markham, head sch

Beach Park, Lake, Pop. 13,341
Beach Park CCSD 3 2,300/PK-8
11315 W Wadsworth Rd 60099 847-599-5070
Dr. Robert DiVirgilio, supt. Fax 263-2133
www.bpd3.org
Beach Park MS 800/6-8
40667 N Green Bay Rd 60099 847-596-5860
John Fredrickson, prin. Fax 731-2402
Howe ES 400/K-5
10271 W Beach Rd 60087 847-599-5362
Dr. April Miller, prin. Fax 623-5286
Murphy ES 400/K-5
11315 W Wadsworth Rd 60099 847-599-5052
Gabe Cappozzo, prin. Fax 360-8635
Oak Crest ES 300/PK-5
38550 N Lewis Ave 60099 847-599-5519
Lisa Schaffer, prin. Fax 623-0560
Other Schools – See Wadsworth

Our Lady of Humility S 300/PK-8
10601 W Wadsworth Rd 60099 847-746-3722
Patrick Browne, prin. Fax 731-2870

Beardstown, Cass, Pop. 6,084
Beardstown CUSD 15 1,400/PK-12
500 E 15th St 62618 217-323-3099
Ron Gilbert, supt. Fax 323-5190
www.beardstown.com
Gard ES 400/K-4
400 E 15th St 62618 217-323-1364
Randi Cowell, prin. Fax 323-1364
Grand Avenue S 100/PK-PK
1301 Grand Ave 62618 217-323-1510
Lori Young, prin. Fax 323-5984

Beardstown Christian Academy 100/PK-8
1421 Beard St 62618 217-323-1685
Jeremy Norton, admin. Fax 323-1421

Beckemeyer, Clinton, Pop. 1,034
Breese ESD 12
Supt. — See Breese
Beckemeyer ES 200/2-4
PO Box 307 62219 618-227-8242
Kerrick Rahm, prin. Fax 227-8587

Bedford Park, Cook, Pop. 575
Summit SD 104
Supt. — See Summit
Walker ES 200/K-4
7735 W 66th Pl 60501 708-458-7150
Amanda Deaton, prin. Fax 458-8466

Beecher, Will, Pop. 4,314
Beecher CUSD 200U 1,000/PK-12
PO Box 338 60401 708-946-2266
Joffroy McCartney, supt. Fax 946-3404
www.beecher200u.org/
Beecher ES 400/PK-5
PO Box 308 60401 708-946-2202
Nicole Black, prin. Fax 946-6075
Beecher JHS 200/6-8
101 E Church Rd 60401 708-946-3412
Michael Meyer, prin. Fax 946-2763

Zion Lutheran S 100/PK-8
PO Box 369 60401 708-946-2272
Paul Eggert, prin. Fax 946-2611

Beecher City, Effingham, Pop. 461
Beecher City CUSD 20 300/PK-12
438 E State Highway 33 62414 618-487-5100
Scott Cameron, supt. Fax 487-5242
www.bcity.efingham.k12.il.us
Beecher City ES 100/PK-5
438 E State Highway 33 62414 618-487-5108
Rosa Milleville, prin.

Belleville, Saint Clair, Pop. 43,276
Belle Valley SD 119 600/PK-8
2465 Amann Dr 62220 618-236-5200
R. Dane Gale, supt. Fax 236-4550
www.bv119.net
Belle Valley S 600/PK-8
2465 Amann Dr 62220 618-236-5200
Kathy Goetter Ed.D., prin. Fax 236-4550

Belleville SD 118 3,700/PK-8
105 W A St 62220 618-233-2830
Matt Klosterman, supt. Fax 233-8355
www.belleville118.org
Central JHS 400/7-8
1801 Central School Rd 62220 618-233-5377
Rocky Horrighs, prin. Fax 233-5440
Douglas ES 300/K-6
125 Carlyle Ave 62220 618-233-2417
Geoffrey Schwalenberg, prin. Fax 236-0593
Franklin ES 200/K-6
301 N 2nd St 62220 618-233-2413
Jon Boente, prin. Fax 236-2704
Jefferson ES 400/K-6
1400 N Charles St 62221 618-233-3798
Jamerson McCloskey, prin. Fax 236-2873
Lincoln ES 500/K-6
820 Royal Heights Rd 62226 618-233-2414
Edmund Langen, prin. Fax 236-2597
Raab ES 200/K-6
1120 Union Ave 62220 618-234-4330
Jamie Buss, prin. Fax 236-2768
Roosevelt ES 300/K-6
700 W Cleveland Ave 62220 618-233-1608
Craig Hayes, prin. Fax 233-1757
Union ES 500/K-6
20 S 27th St 62226 618-233-4132
Lori Taylor, prin. Fax 236-2548
Washington S 200/PK-PK
400 S Charles St 62220 618-277-2017
Jamie Buss, prin. Fax 277-2504
Westhaven ES 500/K-6
118 Westhaven School Rd 62220 618-257-9201
Kelly Harter, prin. Fax 257-9310
West JHS 300/7-8
840 Royal Heights Rd 62226 618-234-8200
Gustavo Cotto, prin. Fax 234-8220

Harmony Emge SD 175 900/PK-8
7401 Westchester Dr 62223 618-397-8444
Dr. Pam Leonard, supt. Fax 397-8446
www.harmony175.org/
Ellis ES 400/PK-3
250 Illini Dr 62223 618-538-6114
Terri Kraemer, prin. Fax 538-6118
Emge JHS 200/7-8
7401 Westchester Dr 62223 618-397-6557
Dave Deets, prin. Fax 397-3011
Harmony Intermediate Center 300/4-6
7401 Westchester Dr 62223 618-397-3747
Dave Deets, prin. Fax 397-3011

Mascoutah CUSD 19
Supt. — See Mascoutah
Wingate ES PK-5
150 Wingate Blvd 62221 618-746-4802
Randy Blakely, prin. Fax 235-4421

Signal Hill SD 181 400/PK-8
40 Signal Hill Pl 62223 618-397-0325
Dr. Janice Kunz, supt. Fax 397-2828
www.signalhill181.org
Signal Hill S 400/PK-8
40 Signal Hill Pl 62223 618-397-0325
Brooke Wiemers, prin. Fax 397-2828

Whiteside SD 115 1,400/PK-8
111 Warrior Way 62221 618-239-0000
Peggy Burke, supt. Fax 239-9240
www.wssd115.org
Whiteside ES 800/PK-4
2028 Lebanon Ave 62221 618-239-0000
Nathan Rakers, prin. Fax 233-7931
Whiteside MS 600/5-8
111 Warrior Way 62221 618-239-0000
Monica Laurent, prin. Fax 239-9240

Blessed Sacrament S 200/PK-8
8809 W Main St 62223 618-397-1111
Claire Hatch, prin. Fax 397-8431
French Academy 200/PK-12
219 W Main St 62220 618-233-7542
Phillip Paeltz, hdmstr. Fax 233-0541
Notre Dame Academy - Cathedral Campus 200/PK-8
200 S 2nd St 62220 618-233-6414
Linda Hobbs, prin. Fax 233-3587
Notre Dame Academy - St. Augustine Cmps 100/PK-8
1900 W Belle St 62226 618-234-4958
Linda Hobbs, prin. Fax 234-3360
Our Lady Queen of Peace S 200/PK-8
5915 N Belt W 62223 618-234-1206
Michelle Tidwell, prin. Fax 234-6123
St. Teresa S 300/PK-8
1108 Lebanon Ave 62221 618-235-4066
Skip Birdsong, prin. Fax 235-7930
Zion Lutheran S 300/PK-8
1810 McClintock Ave 62221 618-234-0275
Ananda Baron, prin. Fax 233-2972

Bellwood, Cook, Pop. 18,875
Bellwood SD 88 2,300/PK-8
640 Eastern Ave 60104 708-344-9344
Mark Holder, supt. Fax 344-9416
sd88.org
Lincoln ES 400/K-5
3420 Jackson St 60104 708-544-3373
Rosalind Banks, prin. Fax 544-0062
Marshall ES 400/K-5
2501 Oak St 60104 708-544-6995
Sarah Kilgore, prin. Fax 544-3338
McKinley ES 400/K-5
3317 Butterfield Rd 60104 708-410-3609
Andrew Maisonneuve, prin. Fax 544-0134
Roosevelt MS 500/6-8
2500 Oak St 60104 708-410-3906
Paul Glover, prin. Fax 544-0192
Other Schools – See Melrose Park, Stone Park

Berkeley SD 87
Supt. — See Berkeley
Jefferson PS 400/PK-2
225 46th Ave 60104 708-449-3165
Nancy Tortora, prin. Fax 649-3046

Meca Christian ES 100/PK-8
425 Bohland Ave 60104 708-547-9980
Glennetta Crowder, prin. Fax 547-8715

Belvidere, Boone, Pop. 25,242
Belvidere CUSD 100 8,100/PK-12
1201 5th Ave 61008 815-544-8513
Daniel Woestman, supt. Fax 544-8513
www.district100.com
Belvidere Central MS 1,000/6-8
8787 Beloit Rd 61008 815-544-0190
Nicole Difford, prin. Fax 544-1128
Belvidere South MS 900/6-8
919 E 6th St 61008 815-544-3175
Ben Commore, prin. Fax 544-2780
Lincoln ES 600/K-5
1011 Bonus Ave 61008 815-544-2671
Elizabeth Marchini, prin. Fax 547-4222
Meehan ES 700/K-5
1401 E 6th St 61008 815-547-3546
Michael Yates, prin. Fax 547-3946
Perry ES 300/K-5
633 W Perry St 61008 815-544-9274
Frank Mandera, prin. Fax 544-1459
Washington Academy 900/PK-8
1031 5th Ave 61008 815-544-3124
Sarah Brenner, prin. Fax 544-4182
Whitman ES 800/K-5
8989 Beloit Rd 61008 815-544-3357
Theresa Lozdoski, prin. Fax 547-7258
Other Schools – See Caledonia

Immanuel Lutheran S 300/PK-8
1225 E 2nd St 61008 815-547-5346
Judy Schaefer, prin. Fax 544-5704
St. James S 200/PK-8
320 Logan Ave 61008 815-547-7633
Dr. Kathleen Miller, prin. Fax 544-2294

Bement, Piatt, Pop. 1,710
Bement CUSD 5 400/PK-12
201 S Champaign St 61813 217-678-4200
Sheila Greenwood, supt. Fax 678-4251
www.bement.k12.il.us
Bement ES 200/PK-5
201 S Champaign St 61813 217-678-4200
Sheila Greenwood, prin. Fax 678-4251
Bement MS 100/6-8
201 S Champaign St 61813 217-678-4200
Douglas Kepley, prin. Fax 678-4251

Bensenville, DuPage, Pop. 18,131
Bensenville SD 2 1,800/PK-8
210 S Church Rd 60106 630-766-5940
Dr. James Stelter Ed.D., supt. Fax 766-6099
www.bsd2.org
Blackhawk MS 700/6-8
250 S Church Rd 60106 630-766-2601
Dr. Perry Finch, prin. Fax 766-7612
Johnson ES 300/K-5
252 Ridgewood Ave 60106 630-766-2605
Missy Baglarz, prin. Fax 595-3609
Tioga ES 800/PK-5
212 W Memorial Rd 60106 630-766-2602
Carlos Azcoitia, prin. Fax 766-4114

Holy Family S 200/PK-8
145 E Grand Ave 60106 630-766-0116
Linda Kelly, prin. Fax 766-0181
Zion-Concord Lutheran S 100/PK-8
865 S Church Rd 60106 630-766-0228
Matt Tuomi, prin. Fax 766-3902

Benson, Woodford, Pop. 423
Roanoke-Benson CUSD 60
Supt. — See Roanoke
Roanoke-Benson JHS 200/5-8
PO Box 137 61516 309-394-2233
John Streit, prin. Fax 394-2612

Benton, Franklin, Pop. 7,012
Benton CCSD 47 1,200/PK-8
1000 Forrest St 62812 618-439-3136
Dr. Stephen Smith, supt. Fax 435-4840
www.benton47.org
Benton ES 800/PK-4
1000 E McKenzie St 62812 618-438-7181
Tammy McCollum, prin. Fax 439-6112
Benton MS 400/5-8
1000 Forrest St 62812 618-438-4011
Tammy McCollum, prin. Fax 435-2152

Berkeley, Cook, Pop. 5,108
Berkeley SD 87 2,700/PK-8
1200 N Wolf Rd 60163 708-449-3350
Dr. Terri Bresnahan, supt. Fax 547-3341
www.berkeley87.org
MacArthur MS 500/6-8
1310 N Wolf Rd 60163 708-449-3185
Dr. Kermit Blakley, prin. Fax 649-3780
Sunnyside IS 500/3-5
5412 Saint Charles Rd 60163 708-449-3170
Kevin Grochowski, prin. Fax 649-3770
Other Schools – See Bellwood, Northlake

Berwyn, Cook, Pop. 56,069
Berwyn North SD 98 3,400/PK-8
6633 16th St 60402 708-484-6200
Dr. Carmen Ayala, supt. Fax 795-2482
www.bn98.org
Havlicek ES 700/PK-5
6401 15th St 60402 708-795-2451
Jessica Hartless, prin. Fax 795-0386
Jefferson ES 700/PK-5
7035 16th St 60402 708-795-2454
Stephanie Mitchell, prin. Fax 795-2465
Lincoln MS 1,100/6-8
6432 16th St 60402 708-795-2475
Michelle Smith, prin. Fax 795-2880
Prairie Oak ES 1,000/PK-5
1427 Oak Park Ave 60402 708-795-2442
Charlie DeLeonardis, prin. Fax 795-2443

Berwyn South SD 100 3,900/PK-8
3401 Gunderson Ave 60402 708-795-2300
Mary Havis, supt. Fax 795-2317
www.bsd100.org
Emerson ES 400/PK-5
6850 W 31st St 60402 708-795-2322
Jean Suchy, prin. Fax 795-0821
Freedom MS 600/6-8
3016 Ridgeland Ave 60402 708-795-5800
James Calabrese, prin. Fax 795-5806
Heritage MS 500/6-8
6850 31st St 60402 708-749-6110
Allison Boutet, prin. Fax 749-6124
Hiawatha ES 500/PK-5
6539 26th St 60402 708-795-2327
Jodi Meyer, prin. Fax 795-1270
Irving ES 600/PK-5
3501 Clinton Ave 60402 708-795-2334
William Davini, prin. Fax 795-2336
Komensky ES 500/PK-5
2515 Cuyler Ave 60402 708-795-2342
Mariana Nicasio, prin. Fax 795-1254
Pershing ES 500/PK-5
6537 37th St 60402 708-795-2349
Diona Iacobazzi, prin. Fax 795-1277
Piper ES 300/K-5
2435 Kenilworth Ave 60402 708-795-2364
Samantha Shuman, prin. Fax 795-0140

Lectura Montessori S 100/PK-6
6823 Roosevelt Rd 60402 708-393-6102
St. Leonard S 200/PK-8
3322 Clarence Ave 60402 708-749-3666
Veronica Skelton Cash, prin. Fax 749-7981
St. Odilo S 200/PK-8
6617 23rd St 60402 708-484-0755
William Donegan, prin. Fax 484-3088

Bethalto, Madison, Pop. 9,426
Bethalto CUSD 8 2,500/PK-12
610 Texas Blvd 62010 618-377-7200
Dr. Jill Griffin, supt. Fax 377-2845
www.bethalto.org
Bethalto East PS 500/PK-1
309 Albers Pl 62010 618-377-7250
Todd Hannford, prin. Fax 377-4107
Parkside PS 400/2-3
600 E Central St 62010 618-377-4100
Kim Heinz, prin. Fax 377-4105
Trimpe MS 600/6-8
910 2nd St 62010 618-377-7240
Dr. Kelly McClain, prin. Fax 377-7218
Other Schools – See Moro

Our Lady Queen of Peace S 200/PK-8
618 N Prairie St 62010 618-377-6401
Eve Remiszewski, prin. Fax 377-6146
Zion Lutheran S 300/PK-8
625 Church Dr 62010 618-377-5507
Joseph Snyder, prin. Fax 377-3630

Bethany, Moultrie, Pop. 1,345
Okaw Valley CUSD 302 600/PK-12
PO Box 97 61914 217-665-3232
Kent Stauder, supt. Fax 665-3601
www.okawvalley.org
Okaw Valley ES 200/PK-4
PO Box 98 61914 217-665-3541
Doug McCausland, prin. Fax 665-3511
Other Schools – See Findlay

Biggsville, Henderson, Pop. 300
West Central CUSD 235 900/PK-12
1514 US Route 34 61418 309-627-2371
Paula Markey, supt. Fax 627-2453
www.wc235.k12.il.us
West Central ECC 100/PK-PK
1514 US Route 34 61418 309-627-2371
Paula Markey, prin. Fax 627-2453
West Central ES 400/K-5
1514 US Route 34 61418 309-627-2339
Kathy Lafary, prin. Fax 627-9919
Other Schools – See Stronghurst

Big Rock, Kane, Pop. 710
Hinckley-Big Rock CUSD 429
Supt. — See Hinckley
Hinckley-Big Rock MS 200/6-8
PO Box 247 60511 630-556-4180
Jeff Strouss, prin. Fax 556-4181

Bismarck, Vermilion, Pop. 578
Bismarck-Henning CUSD 1 800/PK-12
PO Box 350 61814 217-759-7261
Scott Watson, supt. Fax 759-7942
www.bismarck.k12.il.us
Bismarck-Henning ES 300/PK-4
PO Box 50 61814 217-759-7251
Laura Girton, prin. Fax 759-7263
Bismarck-Henning JHS 300/5-8
PO Box 350 61814 217-759-7301
Rusty Campbell, prin. Fax 759-7313

Bloomingdale, DuPage, Pop. 21,714
Bloomingdale SD 13 1,200/PK-8
164 Euclid Ave 60108 630-893-9590
Dr. Jon Bartelt, supt. Fax 893-1818
www.sd13.org
Du Jardin ES 400/K-5
166 Euclid Ave 60108 630-894-9200
Mark Dwyer, prin. Fax 893-9545
Erickson ES 500/PK-5
277 Springfield Dr 60108 630-529-2223
Patrick Haugens, prin. Fax 893-9849
Westfield MS 400/6-8
149 Fairfield Way 60108 630-529-6211
Stefan Larsson, prin. Fax 893-9336

CCSD 93 3,800/PK-8
230 Covington Dr 60108 630-893-9393
William Shields Ed.D., supt. Fax 539-3450
www.ccsd93.com
CCSD 93 ECC 200/PK-PK
280 Old Gary Ave 60108 630-307-3750
Rosary Horne, prin. Fax 307-3845
Stratford MS 600/6-8
251 Butterfield Dr 60108 630-671-4300
Patrick Dawson, prin. Fax 671-4399
Other Schools – See Carol Stream, Hanover Park

Marquardt SD 15
Supt. — See Glendale Heights
Winnebago ES 500/PK-5
195 Greenway Dr 60108 630-351-3416
Jon Pokora, prin. Fax 307-6524

St. Isidore S 300/PK-8
431 W Army Trail Rd 60108 630-529-9323
Cyndi Collins, prin. Fax 529-8882

Bloomington, McLean, Pop. 74,597
Bloomington SD 87 5,600/PK-12
300 E Monroe St 61701 309-827-6031
Dr. Barry Reilly, supt. Fax 827-5717
www.district87.org
Bent ES 400/K-5
904 N Roosevelt Ave 61701 309-828-4315
Jeff Geringer, prin. Fax 828-3587
Bloomington JHS 1,200/6-8
901 Colton Ave 61701 309-827-0086
Sherri Thomas, prin. Fax 829-0084
Irving ES 300/K-5
602 W Jackson St 61701 309-827-8091
Christina Brock-Lammers, prin. Fax 829-2295
Oakland ES 500/K-5
1605 E Oakland Ave 61701 309-662-4302
David LaFrance, prin. Fax 663-4385
Raymond S of Early Education 200/PK-PK
1402 W Olive St 61701 309-827-0308
Danel Behrends-Harr, prin.
Sheridan ES 400/K-5
1403 W Walnut St 61701 309-828-2359
Jenifer McGowan, prin. Fax 829-3209
Stevenson ES 500/K-5
2106 Arrowhead Dr 61704 309-663-2351
Katy Hansen, prin. Fax 827-3613
Washington ES 500/K-5
1201 E Washington St 61701 309-829-7034
Jeffrey Lockenvitz, prin. Fax 829-1207

McLean County Unit SD 5
Supt. — See Normal
Benjamin ES 600/K-5
6006 Ireland Grove Rd, 309-557-4410
Marlys Bennington, prin. Fax 557-4511
Brigham Early Learning Center 100/PK-K
201 Brigham School Rd 61704 309-557-4411
Kris Pennington, prin. Fax 557-4512
Cedar Ridge ES 500/K-5
2808 Breezewood Blvd 61704 309-557-4413
Karrah Jensen, prin. Fax 557-4514
Evans JHS 700/6-8
2901 Morrissey Dr 61704 309-557-4406
Christopher McGraw, prin. Fax 557-4507
Fox Creek ES 400/K-5
3910 Timberwolf Trl, 309-557-4416
Julia Schoonover, prin. Fax 557-4517
Northpoint ES 700/K-5
2602 E College Ave 61704 309-557-4420
Matt Harr, prin. Fax 557-4521
Pepper Ridge ES 400/K-5
2602 Danbury Dr, 309-557-4423
Tina Fogal, prin. Fax 557-4524

Cornerstone Christian Academy 400/PK-12
PO Box 1608 61702 309-662-9900
Doug Pavey, head sch Fax 662-9904
Corpus Christi Catholic S 500/PK-8
705 N Roosevelt Ave 61701 309-828-7151
Gwendolyn Roche, prin. Fax 827-8131
St. Mary S 200/PK-8
603 W Jackson St 61701 309-828-5954
Jamie Hartrich, prin. Fax 829-3061
Trinity Lutheran S 400/PK-8
1102 W Hamilton Rd 61704 309-829-7513
Shawn Hoffmann, prin. Fax 834-3237

Blue Island, Cook, Pop. 23,417
Cook County SD 130 3,800/PK-8
12300 Greenwood Ave 60406 708-385-6800
Dr. Tina Halliman, supt. Fax 385-8467
www.district130.org/
Kerr MS 400/6-8
12915 Maple Ave 60406 708-385-5959
Carl Gmazel, prin. Fax 371-6812
Lincoln ES 400/K-3
2140 Broadway St 60406 708-385-5370
Carol Crum, prin. Fax 385-8467
Revere IS 200/4-5
12331 Gregory St 60406 708-385-4450
Constance Grason, prin. Fax 385-8467
Revere PS 500/K-3
2300 123rd Pl 60406 708-489-3533
Carrie Tisch, prin. Fax 385-8467
Veterans Memorial MS 400/6-8
12320 Greenwood Ave 60406 708-489-6630
Michael Steele, prin. Fax 489-3522
Whittier ES 200/4-5
13043 Maple Ave 60406 708-385-6170
Danielle Graber, prin. Fax 371-2354
Other Schools – See Alsip, Crestwood

Council Oak Montessori S — 100/PK-8
PO Box 175 60406 — 773-779-7606
St. Benedict S — 200/PK-8
2324 New St 60406 — 708-385-2016
Melissa Wilson, prin. — Fax 385-4490

Blue Mound, Macon, Pop. 1,145
Meridian CUSD 15
Supt. — See Macon
Meridian ES — 300/PK-5
PO Box 350 62513 — 217-692-2535
Lori Guebert, prin. — Fax 692-2013

Bluffs, Scott, Pop. 708
Scott-Morgan CUSD 2 — 200/PK-12
PO Box 230 62621 — 217-754-3351
Kevin Blankenship, supt. — Fax 754-3908
www.bluffs-school.com/
Bluffs ES — 100/PK-5
PO Box 230 62621 — 217-754-3714
Joseph Kuhlmann, prin. — Fax 754-3908
Bluffs JHS — 50/6-8
PO Box 230 62621 — 217-754-3815
Joseph Kuhlmann, prin. — Fax 754-3908

Bluford, Jefferson, Pop. 685
Bluford Unit SD 318 — 400/K-12
901 6th St 62814 — 618-732-8242
John Ashby, supt. — Fax 732-6114
www.busd318.org
Bluford Grade S — 300/K-8
901 6th St 62814 — 618-732-8242
Kevin Westall, prin. — Fax 732-6114

Farrington CCSD 99 — 100/K-8
20941 E Divide Rd 62814 — 618-755-4414
Sandra Kabat, supt. — Fax 755-4461
Farrington S — 100/K-8
20941 E Divide Rd 62814 — 618-755-4414
Sandra Kabat, supt. — Fax 755-4461

Bolingbrook, Will, Pop. 71,637
Indian Prairie CUSD 204
Supt. — See Aurora
Builta ES — 400/K-5
1835 Apple Valley Rd 60490 — 630-226-4400
Kim Stephens, prin. — Fax 226-4401

Plainfield CCSD 202
Supt. — See Plainfield
Liberty ES — 800/K-5
1401 Essington Rd 60490 — 815-609-3037
Michelle Imbordino, prin. — Fax 609-5963

Valley View CUSD 365U
Supt. — See Romeoville
Addams MS — 700/6-8
905 Lily Cache Ln 60440 — 630-759-7200
Teresa Burrell, prin. — Fax 759-6362
Brooks MS — 1,200/6-8
350 Blair Ln 60440 — 630-759-6340
Dr. Keith Wood, prin. — Fax 759-6360
Humphrey MS — 700/6-8
777 Falconridge Way 60440 — 630-972-9240
Dan Laverty, prin. — Fax 739-8521
Independence ES — 700/K-5
230 S Orchard Dr 60440 — 630-759-7282
Jackie Mitchem, prin. — Fax 759-6366
McGee ES — 600/K-5
179 Commonwealth Dr 60440 — 630-759-4300
Anthony Valenza, prin. — Fax 759-6363
Oak View ES — 600/K-5
150 N Schmidt Rd 60440 — 630-759-9300
Bob Pinciak, prin. — Fax 759-6359
Pioneer ES — 800/K-5
1470 Raven Dr 60490 — 630-771-2420
Carmen Killingsworth, prin. — Fax 771-0199
Salk ES — 600/K-5
500 King Arthur Way 60440 — 630-739-3603
Alyson Ewald, prin. — Fax 739-8518
Tibbott ES — 700/K-5
520 Gary Dr 60440 — 630-739-7155
Ana Wilson, prin. — Fax 739-8522
Ward ES — 500/PK-5
200 Recreation Dr 60440 — 630-972-9200
Ted Warpinski, prin. — Fax 972-9420
Wood View ES — 500/K-5
197 Winston Dr 60440 — 630-739-0185
Jessica McCaslin, prin. — Fax 739-8517

Midwest Christian Montessori Academy — 50/PK-6
151 E Briarcliff Rd 60440 — 630-783-8644
Eileen Contos, dir. — Fax 783-8639
St. Dominic S — 300/PK-8
420 E Briarcliff Rd 60440 — 630-739-1633
Sr. Marie Isaac Staub, prin. — Fax 739-5989

Bonfield, Kankakee, Pop. 378
Herscher CUSD 2
Supt. — See Herscher
Bonfield ES — 300/PK-1
522 E Smith St 60913 — 815-933-6995
Molly Wepprecht, prin. — Fax 936-4125

Bourbonnais, Kankakee, Pop. 18,268
Bourbonnais ESD 53 — 2,200/PK-8
281 W John Casey Rd 60914 — 815-929-5100
Daniel R. Hollowell Ed.D., supt. — Fax 939-0481
www.besd53.org
Bourbonnais Upper Grade Center — 500/7-8
200 W John Casey Rd 60914 — 815-929-5200
Jeffrey Gindy, prin. — Fax 935-7849
Levasseur ES — 300/K-4
601 W Bethel Dr 60914 — 815-929-4500
Jenn Longtin, prin. — Fax 935-7856
Liberty IS — 500/5-6
1600 Career Center Rd 60914 — 815-929-5000
Mary Bicknell, prin. — Fax 929-2467
Shabbona ES — 300/K-4
321 N Convent St 60914 — 815-929-4700
Jon Hodge, prin. — Fax 935-7846
Shepard ES — 500/PK-4
325 N Convent St 60914 — 815-929-4600
Shirley Padera, prin. — Fax 935-7834

Saint George CCSD 258 — 500/K-8
5200 E Center St 60914 — 815-933-1503
Helen Boehrnsen, supt. — Fax 802-3102
www.sg258.com
Saint George ES — 500/K-8
5200 E Center St 60914 — 815-933-1503
Christine Johnston, prin. — Fax 933-1562

Bishop McNamara Catholic S — 300/PK-6
324 E Marsile St 60914 — 815-933-7758
Nicole Gernon, prin. — Fax 933-1884
Kankakee Valley Montessori S — 50/PK-6
718 River Place Dr 60914 — 815-365-2868
Lidia Lehnus, pres.
St. Paul Lutheran S — 200/PK-8
1780 Career Center Rd 60914 — 815-932-0312
James Krupski, prin. — Fax 932-7588

Bowen, Hancock, Pop. 488
Southeastern CUSD 337
Supt. — See Augusta
Southeastern ES — 300/PK-6
PO Box 247 62316 — 217-842-5236
Tecia Lantz, prin. — Fax 842-5248

Braceville, Grundy, Pop. 777
Braceville SD 75 — 200/K-8
209 N Mitchell St 60407 — 815-237-8040
Michael Perrott, supt. — Fax 237-8044
Braceville ES — 200/K-8
209 N Mitchell St 60407 — 815-237-8040
Susan Avery, prin. — Fax 237-8044

Bradford, Stark, Pop. 767
Bradford CUSD 1 — 200/PK-8
345 Silver St 61421 — 309-897-4441
Chad Gripp, supt. — Fax 897-8361
bradfordschool.net
Bradford ES — 100/PK-5
345 Silver St 61421 — 309-897-4441
Chad Gripp, admin. — Fax 897-8361
Bradford JHS — 100/6-8
115 High St 61421 — 309-897-2801
Chad Gripp, admin. — Fax 897-4451

Bradley, Kankakee, Pop. 15,644
Bradley SD 61 — 1,600/PK-8
111 N Crosswell Ave 60915 — 815-933-3371
Dr. Scott Goselin M.Ed., supt. — Fax 939-6601
www.bradleyschools.com/
Bradley Central MS — 500/6-8
260 N Wabash Ave 60915 — 815-939-3564
Mark Kohl, prin. — Fax 939-6603
Bradley East ES — 700/PK-2
610 Liberty St 60915 — 815-933-2233
Michael Hahs, prin. — Fax 933-3810
Bradley West ES — 500/3-5
200 W State St 60915 — 815-933-2216
Trisha Anderson, prin. — Fax 933-2071

Bishop McNamara Catholic S — 300/PK-6
247 N Center Ave 60915 — 815-933-8013
Dana Berg, prin. — Fax 933-2775

Braidwood, Will, Pop. 6,143
Reed-Custer CUSD 255U — 1,600/PK-12
255 S Comet Dr 60408 — 815-458-2307
Mark Mitchell, supt. — Fax 458-4106
www.rc255.net
Reed-Custer ES — 500/PK-5
162 S School St 60408 — 815-458-2145
Heather Faletti, prin. — Fax 458-4106
Reed-Custer MS — 400/6-8
407 S Comet Dr 60408 — 815-458-2868
Shane Trager, prin. — Fax 458-4118

Breese, Clinton, Pop. 4,414
Breese ESD 12 — 600/PK-8
777 Memorial Dr 62230 — 618-526-7128
Jeff Strieker, supt. — Fax 526-2787
d12bobcats.org
Breese S — 500/PK-8
777 Memorial Dr 62230 — 618-526-7128
Kerrick Rahm, prin. — Fax 526-2787
Other Schools – See Beckemeyer

Saint Rose SD 14-15 — 200/PK-8
18004 Saint Rose Rd 62230 — 618-526-7484
Dr. Patricia Cornell, supt. — Fax 526-7168
www.strosedistrict14-15.com/
Saint Rose ES — 200/PK-8
18004 Saint Rose Rd 62230 — 618-526-7484
Dr. Patricia Cornell, prin. — Fax 526-7168

All Saints Academy — 300/PK-8
295 N Clinton St 62230 — 618-526-4323
Dr. Robin Booth, prin. — Fax 526-2547

Bridgeport, Lawrence, Pop. 1,874
Red Hill CUSD 10 — 1,000/PK-12
1250 Judy Ave 62417 — 618-945-2061
Jakie Walker, supt. — Fax 945-7607
redhill.cusd10.org
Bridgeport Grade S — 400/PK-3
1300 N Main St 62417 — 618-945-5721
Tony Gaither, prin. — Fax 945-7111
Other Schools – See Sumner

Bridgeview, Cook, Pop. 16,102
Indian Springs SD 109
Supt. — See Justice
Bridgeview ES — 500/K-6
7800 S Thomas Ave 60455 — 708-496-8713
Candice Del Prete, prin. — Fax 496-1142
Lyle ES — 500/K-6
7801 W 75th St 60455 — 708-496-8722
Nuray Kavustuk, prin. — Fax 728-3120

Ridgeland SD 122
Supt. — See Oak Lawn
Lieb ES — 400/K-5
9101 Pembroke Ln 60455 — 708-599-1050
Gregory Porod, prin. — Fax 599-8189

AQSA S — 200/PK-12
7361 W 92nd St 60455 — 708-598-2700
Tammie Ismail, prin. — Fax 598-2731
Universal S — 600/PK-12
7350 W 93rd St 60455 — 708-599-4100

Brighton, Macoupin, Pop. 2,236
Southwestern CUSD 9 — 1,000/PK-12
PO Box 728 62012 — 618-372-3813
Mark Skertich, supt. — Fax 372-4681
www.piasabirds.net
Brighton North PS — 200/PK-2
PO Box 757 62012 — 618-372-3813
Diane Milner, prin. — Fax 372-4915
Other Schools – See Medora, Piasa, Shipman

Brimfield, Peoria, Pop. 851
Brimfield CUSD 309 — 700/PK-12
PO Box 380 61517 — 309-446-3378
Robert Richardson, supt. — Fax 446-3716
www.brimfield309.com/
Brimfield Grade S — 500/PK-8
PO Box 380 61517 — 309-446-3366
Jeannine Blane, prin. — Fax 446-9500

Bristol, Kendall
Yorkville CUSD 115
Supt. — See Yorkville
Bristol Grade S — 200/K-3
PO Box 177 60512 — 630-553-4383
Kathryn Schafermeyer, prin. — Fax 553-4459

Broadview, Cook, Pop. 7,821
Lindop SD 92 — 400/PK-8
2400 S 18th Ave 60155 — 708-786-6460
Dr. Janiece Jackson, supt. — Fax 345-2923
www.lindop92.net
Lindop ES — 400/PK-8
2400 S 18th Ave 60155 — 708-345-3110
Dr. Sonya Spaulding, prin. — Fax 345-8569

Maywood-Melrose Park-Broadview SD 89
Supt. — See Melrose Park
Roosevelt ES — 200/K-5
1927 S 15th Ave 60155 — 708-450-2047
Kimberly Wright, prin. — Fax 344-1179

Brookfield, Cook, Pop. 18,709
Brookfield Lagrange Park SD 95 — 1,100/K-8
3724 Prairie Ave 60513 — 708-485-0606
Dr. Mark Kuzniewski, supt. — Fax 485-8066
www.district95.org
Gross MS — 400/6-8
3524 Maple Ave 60513 — 708-485-0600
Ryan Evans, prin. — Fax 485-0638
Other Schools – See La Grange Park

La Grange SD 102
Supt. — See La Grange Park
Congress Park ES — 400/K-6
9311 Shields Ave 60513 — 708-482-2430
Claudia Jimenez, prin. — Fax 482-2437

Lyons SD 103
Supt. — See Lyons
Lincoln ES — 500/K-5
4300 Grove Ave 60513 — 708-783-4600
Theresa Silva, prin. — Fax 780-2485

Riverside SD 96
Supt. — See Riverside
Hollywood ES — 100/PK-5
3423 Hollywood Ave 60513 — 708-485-7630
Kim Hefner, prin. — Fax 485-7925

St. Paul Lutheran S — 100/K-8
9035 Grant Ave 60513 — 708-485-0650
Joel Brondos, admin. — Fax 485-7448

Brookport, Massac, Pop. 966
Massac Unit SD 1
Supt. — See Metropolis
Brookport ES — 200/K-6
PO Box 278 62910 — 618-564-2482
Brooke Durham, prin. — Fax 564-3509
Unity S — 200/K-6
6846 Unity School Rd 62910 — 618-564-2582
Brooke Durham, prin. — Fax 564-2014

Brownstown, Fayette, Pop. 753
Brownstown CUSD 201 — 300/PK-12
421 S College Ave 62418 — 618-427-3355
Mike Shackelford, supt. — Fax 427-3704
www.bcusd201.com
Brownstown ES — 200/PK-6
460 W South St 62418 — 618-427-3368
Sherry Harmon, prin. — Fax 427-5247

Brussels, Calhoun, Pop. 140
Brussels CUSD 42 — 100/K-12
PO Box 128 62013 — 618-883-2131
Dr. Mark Martin, supt. — Fax 883-2514
Brussels ES — 100/K-6
PO Box 128 62013 — 618-883-2131
Dr. Mark Martin, prin. — Fax 883-2514

St. Mary S — 100/PK-8
PO Box 39 62013 — 618-883-2124
Brenda Paynic, prin. — Fax 883-2511

Buckley, Iroquois, Pop. 593

St. John's Lutheran S — 100/PK-8
PO Box 148 60918 — 217-394-2422
Timothy Oliver, prin. — Fax 394-2422

Buda, Bureau, Pop. 531
Bureau Valley CUSD 340
Supt. — See Manlius
Bureau Valley South S 300/3-8
PO Box 277 61314 309-895-2037
Kristal LeRette, prin. Fax 895-2200

Buffalo, Sangamon, Pop. 499
Tri-City CUSD 1 600/PK-12
324 W Charles St 62515 217-364-4811
Jill Larson, supt. Fax 364-4896
www.tricityschools.org
Tri-City ES 300/PK-5
324 W Charles St 62515 217-364-4035
Kara Cummins, prin. Fax 364-4812
Tri-City JHS 100/6-8
324 W Charles St 62515 217-364-4530
Christy Kindel, prin. Fax 364-4812

Buffalo Grove, Cook, Pop. 40,915
Aptakisic-Tripp CCSD 102 2,100/PK-8
1231 Weiland Rd 60089 847-353-5660
Dr. Lori Wilcox, supt. Fax 634-5334
www.d102.org
Aptakisic JHS 500/7-8
1231 Weiland Rd 60089 847-353-5500
Eli Rogers, prin. Fax 634-5347
Meridian MS 500/5-6
2195 Brandywyn Ln 60089 847-955-3500
Greg Michels, prin. Fax 634-4229
Pritchett ES 500/PK-4
200 Horatio Blvd 60089 847-353-5700
Dr. Matt Moreland, prin. Fax 215-3259
Tripp ES 600/K-4
850 Highland Grove Dr 60089 847-955-3600
Mary Bhardwaj, prin. Fax 215-3268

Kildeer Countryside CCSD 96 3,100/PK-8
1050 Ivy Hall Ln 60089 847-459-4260
Julie Schmidt, supt. Fax 459-2344
www.kcsd96.org
Ivy Hall ES 400/1-5
1072 Ivy Hall Ln 60089 847-459-0022
Robert Hanrahan, prin. Fax 229-9650
Prairie ES 400/1-5
1530 Brandywyn Ln 60089 847-634-3144
Dr. Christine Pfaff, prin. Fax 821-7571
Twin Groves MS 500/6-8
2600 N Buffalo Grove Rd 60089 847-821-8946
Jessica Barnes, prin. Fax 821-8949
Willow Grove K 300/PK-K
777 Checker Dr 60089 847-541-3660
Jennifer Smith, prin. Fax 821-7572
Other Schools – See Long Grove

Wheeling CCSD 21
Supt. — See Wheeling
Cooper MS 700/6-8
1050 Plum Grove Cir 60089 847-520-2750
Robert Gurney, prin. Fax 419-3071
Kilmer ES 500/PK-5
655 Golfview Ter 60089 847-520-2760
Matthew Lombardo, prin. Fax 520-2601
Longfellow ES 400/K-5
501 S Arlington Heights Rd 60089 847-520-2755
Rick Herrejon, prin. Fax 419-3078

Buffalo Grove Montessori S 100/PK-K
950 Ellen Dr 60089 847-541-8111
Deborah LaPorte, head sch Fax 541-8169
Montessori World of Discovery S 100/PK-5
1395 N Arlington Heights Rd 60089 847-415-2021
St. Mary S 300/PK-8
50 N Buffalo Grove Rd 60089 847-459-6270
Dr. Stephanie Stoneberg, prin. Fax 537-2810
Torah Academy 50/PK-7
720 Armstrong Dr 60089 847-243-8567
Rabbi Shimon Zehnwirth, head sch

Buncombe, Johnson, Pop. 202
Buncombe Consolidated SD 43 100/K-8
PO Box 40 62912 618-658-8830
Vicki Tripp, supt. Fax 658-8830
Buncombe Consolidated S 100/K-8
PO Box 40 62912 618-658-8830
Vicki Tripp, admin. Fax 658-8830

Lick Creek CCSD 16 100/PK-8
7355 Lick Creek Rd 62912 618-833-2545
Dr. Judy Wilson, supt. Fax 833-3201
lickcreekschool.com/
Lick Creek S 100/PK-8
7355 Lick Creek Rd 62912 618-833-2545
Dr. Judy Wilson, supt. Fax 833-3201

Bunker Hill, Macoupin, Pop. 1,760
Bunker Hill CUSD 8 500/PK-12
504 E Warren St 62014 618-585-3116
Dr. Victor Buehler, supt. Fax 585-3212
bhschools.wordpress.com
Wolf Ridge ES 300/PK-7
700 W Orange St 62014 618-585-4831
Stephanie Cann, prin. Fax 585-3123

Burbank, Cook, Pop. 28,566
Burbank SD 111 3,400/PK-8
7600 Central Ave 60459 708-496-0500
Dr. Franzy Fleck, supt. Fax 496-0510
www.bsd111.org
Burbank ES 500/K-6
8235 Linder Ave 60459 708-499-0838
Dr. Sharon Walker-Hood, prin. Fax 499-0502
Byrd ES 300/K-6
8259 Lavergne Ave 60459 708-499-3049
Tom Martin, prin. Fax 499-1002
Fry ES 400/K-6
7805 Mobile Ave 60459 708-599-5554
Mary Rein, prin. Fax 599-1348
Kennedy ES 400/K-6
7644 Central Ave 60459 708-496-0563
Dr. J.R. Entsminger, prin. Fax 496-8365
Liberty JHS 800/7-8
5900 W 81st St 60459 708-952-3255
Mark Antkiewicz, prin. Fax 229-0659
Maddock ES 400/PK-6
8258 Sayre Ave 60459 708-598-0515
Dr. Shwkar Abousweilem, prin. Fax 233-6401
McCord ES 300/K-6
8450 Nashville Ave 60459 708-599-4411
Dr. Nicole Robinson, prin. Fax 233-9104
Tobin ES 300/K-6
8501 Narragansett Ave 60459 708-599-6655
Kristin Welsh, prin. Fax 233-9014

St. Albert the Great S 200/PK-8
5535 State Rd 60459 708-424-7757
Jodi McLawhorn, prin. Fax 636-6477

Burlington, Kane, Pop. 618
Central CUSD 301 3,600/PK-12
PO Box 396 60109 847-464-6005
Dr. Todd Stirn, supt. Fax 464-6021
central301.net
Central MS 300/8-8
PO Box 397 60109 847-464-6000
Carie Walter, prin. Fax 464-0233
Thomas ES 300/PK-5
PO Box 395 60109 847-464-6008
Carrie Ahlstedt, prin. Fax 464-6022
Other Schools – See Elgin, Maple Park

Burnham, Cook, Pop. 4,157
Burnham SD 154-5 200/PK-8
13945 S Green Bay Ave 60633 708-862-8636
Stephen Geraci, supt. Fax 862-8638
www.d1545.org
Burnham ES 200/PK-8
13945 S Green Bay Ave 60633 708-862-8636
Stephen Geraci, prin. Fax 862-8638

Burr Ridge, DuPage, Pop. 10,371
CCSD 180 600/PK-8
15W451 91st St 60527 630-734-6600
Dr. Thomas Schneider, supt. Fax 325-6450
www.ccsd180.org
Burr Ridge MS 300/5-8
15W451 91st St 60527 630-325-5454
Julie Bartell, prin. Fax 325-6450
Other Schools – See Willowbrook

CCSD 181
Supt. — See Clarendon Hills
Elm ES 300/K-5
15W201 60th St 60527 630-861-4000
Jeana Considine, prin. Fax 655-9734

Gower SD 62
Supt. — See Willowbrook
Gower MS 400/5-8
7941 S Madison St 60527 630-323-8275
Tracy Murphy, prin. Fax 323-2055

Pleasantdale SD 107 800/PK-8
7450 Wolf Rd 60527 708-784-2013
Dr. David Palzet, supt. Fax 246-0161
www.d107.org
Pleasantdale MS 300/5-8
7450 Wolf Rd 60527 708-246-3210
Griffin Sonntag, prin. Fax 352-0092
Other Schools – See La Grange

Trinity Lutheran S 100/PK-8
11503 German Church Rd 60527 708-839-1444
Andrew DeWitt, prin. Fax 839-8503

Bushnell, McDonough, Pop. 3,074
Bushnell-Prairie City CUSD 170 800/PK-12
845 Walnut St 61422 309-772-9461
Kathy Dinger, supt. Fax 772-9462
bpcschools.org
Bushnell-Prairie City ES 400/PK-5
345 E Hess St 61422 309-772-9464
Marjorie Rhoades, prin. Fax 772-9466
Bushnell-Prairie City JHS 200/6-8
847 Walnut St 61422 309-772-3123
Dawna Daily, prin. Fax 772-2666

Byron, Ogle, Pop. 3,700
Byron CUSD 226 1,500/PK-12
696 N Colfax St 61010 815-234-5491
Dr. James Hammack, supt. Fax 234-4106
www.byron226.org
Byron MS 400/6-8
850 N Colfax St 61010 815-234-5491
Zack Ettelbrick, prin. Fax 234-4225

Cahokia, Saint Clair, Pop. 14,938
Cahokia CUSD 187 3,600/K-12
1700 Jerome Ln 62206 618-332-3700
Arthur Ryan, supt. Fax 332-3706
www.cusd187.org
8th Grade Academy 200/8-8
1900 Mousette Ln 62206 618-332-5900
Melissa Rebmann, prin. Fax 332-3725
Huffman ES 400/3-5
600 Saint Robert Dr 62206 618-332-3720
Alison Schumacher, prin. Fax 332-3782
Maplewood ES 300/K-2
600 Jerome Ln 62206 618-332-3709
Victoria White, prin. Fax 332-3787
Morris ES 300/K-3
1500 Andrews Dr 62206 618-332-3718
Karen Thompson, prin. Fax 332-3785
Parks S 200/6-6
1900 Mousette Ln 62206 618-332-3796
Gloria Perry, prin. Fax 332-3797
Penniman ES 400/3-5
1820 Jerome Ln 62206 618-332-1915
Wendy Lange, prin. Fax 337-6697
Sauget S of Choice 300/K-8
1700 Jerome Ln 62206 618-332-3820
Trenese Steel, prin. Fax 332-1918
7th Grade Center 200/7-7
1900 Mousette Ln 62206 618-332-3722
John Dozier, prin. Fax 332-3741
Other Schools – See East Saint Louis

Cairo, Alexander, Pop. 2,772
Cairo Unit SD 1 500/PK-12
4201 Sycamore St 62914 618-734-4102
Dr. Andrea Evers, supt. Fax 734-4047
www.cairoschooldistrict1.com
Cairo ES 300/PK-5
3101 Elm St 62914 618-734-1027
Regina Brown, prin. Fax 734-1806

Caledonia, Boone, Pop. 221
Belvidere CUSD 100
Supt. — See Belvidere
Caledonia ES 400/K-5
2311 Randolph St 61011 815-547-1977
Kelly Cotter, prin. Fax 547-3566

Calumet City, Cook, Pop. 36,556
Calumet City SD 155 1,100/K-8
540 Superior Ave 60409 708-862-7665
Dr. Troy Paraday, supt. Fax 868-7555
www.calumetcity155.org/
Wentworth IS 300/3-5
530 Superior Ave 60409 708-868-7926
Julie Hassel, prin. Fax 868-7671
Wentworth JHS 400/6-8
560 Superior Ave 60409 708-862-0750
Ermetra Olawumi, prin. Fax 862-1194
Wilson ES 300/K-2
560 Wentworth Ave 60409 708-862-5166
Deborah Smith, prin. Fax 868-7086

Dolton SD 149 3,000/PK-8
292 Torrence Ave 60409 708-868-8300
Dr. Shelly Davis-Jones, supt. Fax 868-7850
www.schooldistrict149.org/
Braun ES 400/1-6
1655 153rd St 60409 708-868-9470
Jamie Hayes, prin. Fax 868-9466
Creative Communications Academy 200/7-8
1650 Pulaski Rd 60409 708-868-7585
Zarita Beal, prin. Fax 868-7589
School of Fine Arts 200/7-8
1650 Pulaski Rd 60409 708-868-7565
Dellnora Winters, prin. Fax 868-7589
Sibley ES 800/K-6
1550 Sibley Blvd 60409 708-868-1870
Carolyn Franklin, prin. Fax 868-7591
STEM Academy 200/7-8
1650 Pulaski Rd 60409 708-868-7595
James Walton, prin. Fax 868-7589
Other Schools – See Dolton, South Holland

Hoover-Schrum Memorial SD 157 900/PK-8
1255 Superior Ave 60409 708-868-7500
Dr. Donald McKinney, supt. Fax 868-7511
www.hsdist157.org
Hoover ES 600/PK-5
1260 Superior Ave 60409 708-862-4230
Shernita Mays Ph.D., prin. Fax 832-3713
Schrum Memorial MS 300/6-8
485 165th St 60409 708-862-4236
Dr. Shernita Mays, prin. Fax 862-4580

Lincoln ESD 156 1,000/PK-8
410 157th St 60409 708-862-6620
Dr. Darryl Taylor, supt. Fax 862-1227
www.l156.org
Lincoln ES 1,000/PK-8
410 157th St 60409 708-862-6620
Robert Hubbird, prin. Fax 862-1227

Calumet Park, Cook, Pop. 7,781
Calumet Public SD 132 1,200/PK-8
1440 W Vermont Ave 60827 708-388-8920
Dr. Elizabeth Reynolds, supt. Fax 388-2138
www.sd132.org
Burr Oak Academy 400/PK-2
1441 W 124th St 60827 708-824-3090
Dalyn Drown, prin. Fax 388-1211
Burr Oak ES 400/3-5
1440 W 125th St 60827 708-388-8010
Dalyn Drown, prin. Fax 389-5835
Calumet MS 400/6-8
1440 W Vermont Ave 60827 708-388-8820
Andrea Delaney, prin. Fax 388-8557

Cambridge, Henry, Pop. 2,137
Cambridge CUSD 227 500/PK-12
300 S West St 61238 309-937-2144
Thomas Akers, supt. Fax 937-5128
www.district227.org
Cambridge Community ES 300/PK-6
312 S West St 61238 309-937-2028
Shelly Capps, prin. Fax 937-5219

Campbell Hill, Jackson, Pop. 333
Trico CUSD 176 900/PK-12
PO Box 220 62916 618-426-1111
Larry Lovel, supt. Fax 426-3625
www.trico176.org
Trico ES 400/PK-5
PO Box 305 62916 618-426-1111
Jenny Wilson, prin. Fax 426-3988
Trico JHS 200/6-8
PO Box 335 62916 618-426-1111
Ronald Coleman, prin. Fax 426-3712

Camp Point, Adams, Pop. 1,120
Central CUSD 3 800/K-12
2110 Highway 94 N 62320 217-593-7116
Martin Cook, supt. Fax 593-7026
www.cusd3.com
Central ES 200/K-2
2110 Highway 94 N 62320 217-593-7795
Eric Stotts, prin. Fax 593-6514

Central JHS 300/5-8
2110 Highway 94 N 62320 217-593-7741
Erica Smith, prin. Fax 593-7028
Other Schools – See Golden

Canton, Fulton, Pop. 14,563
Canton Union SD 66 2,600/PK-12
20 W Walnut St 61520 309-647-9411
Rolf Sivertsen, supt. Fax 649-5036
www.cantonusd.org
Eastview ES 400/K-4
1490 E Myrtle St 61520 309-647-0136
Bridgette Dennis, prin. Fax 647-3430
Ingersoll MS 800/5-8
1605 E Ash St 61520 309-647-6951
Wayne Krus, prin. Fax 647-6959
Lincoln ES 200/K-4
20 Lincoln Rd 61520 309-647-7594
KiLee McFerren, prin. Fax 647-2043
Westview ES 400/K-4
700 Old West Vine St 61520 309-647-2111
Anne Grzanich, prin. Fax 647-2047

Cantrall, Sangamon, Pop. 137
Athens CUSD 213
Supt. — See Athens
Cantrall ES 300/PK-3
1 Braves Ln 62625 217-487-7312
Eric Szoke, prin. Fax 487-7187
Cantrall IS 200/4-6
155 Claypool St 62625 217-487-9082
Stacey Binegar, prin. Fax 487-9104

Capron, Boone, Pop. 1,363
North Boone CUSD 200
Supt. — See Poplar Grove
Capron ES 100/PK-4
200 N Wooster St 61012 815-569-2314
Allison Louis, prin. Fax 569-2633

Carbondale, Jackson, Pop. 25,058
Carbondale ESD 95 1,500/PK-8
925 S Giant City Rd 62902 618-457-3591
Dr. Elizabeth I. Lewin, supt. Fax 457-2043
www.ces95.org
Carbondale MS 400/6-8
1150 E Grand Ave 62901 618-457-2174
Marilynn Ross, prin. Fax 457-2176
Lewis ES 300/4-5
801 S Lewis Ln 62901 618-457-5393
Kristine Uffelman, prin. Fax 351-9816
Parrish ES 500/PK-1
121 N Parrish Ln 62901 618-457-5781
Jerrah Henson, prin. Fax 457-4661
Thomas ES 300/2-3
1025 N Wall St 62901 618-457-6226
Dr. Carmen Williams-Bonds, prin. Fax 457-5636

Giant City CCSD 130 300/PK-8
1062 Boskydell Rd 62902 618-457-5391
Belinda Hill, supt. Fax 549-5060
www.giants.jacksn.k12.il.us
Giant City ES 300/PK-8
1062 Boskydell Rd 62902 618-457-5391
Belinda Hill, prin. Fax 549-5060

Unity Point CCSD 140 700/PK-8
4033 S Illinois Ave 62903 618-529-4151
Dr. Lori James-Gross, supt. Fax 529-4154
www.up140.jacksn.k12.il.us
Unity Point ES 700/PK-8
4033 S Illinois Ave 62903 618-529-4151
Brenda Jones, prin. Fax 529-4154

Trinity Christian S 100/PK-12
1218 W Freeman St 62901 618-529-3733
Chris Hottensen, prin. Fax 549-8252

Carlinville, Macoupin, Pop. 5,852
Carlinville CUSD 1 1,500/PK-12
829 W Main St 62626 217-854-9823
Dr. Becky Schuchman, supt. Fax 854-2777
www.cusd1.com
Carlinville IS 300/PK-PK, 4-
450 W Buchanan St 62626 217-854-9523
Roy Kulenkamp, prin. Fax 854-3417
Carlinville MS 300/6-8
110 Illinois Ave 62626 217-854-3106
Roy Kulenkamp, prin. Fax 854-4503
Carlinville PS 400/K-3
18456 Shipman Rd 62626 217-854-9849
Elise Schwartz, prin. Fax 854-7867

Carlock, McLean, Pop. 549
McLean County Unit SD 5
Supt. — See Normal
Carlock ES 100/K-5
301 W Washington St 61725 309-557-4412
Laura Delgado, prin. Fax 557-4513

Carlyle, Clinton, Pop. 3,259
Carlyle CUSD 1 1,200/PK-12
1400 13th St 62231 618-594-8283
Joe Novsek, supt. Fax 594-8285
www.carlyle.k12.il.us
Carlyle ES 500/PK-4
951 6th St 62231 618-594-3766
Jay Smith, prin. Fax 594-8110
Carlyle JHS 400/5-8
1631 12th St 62231 618-594-8292
Dustin Bilbruck, prin. Fax 594-8294

Carmi, White, Pop. 5,196
Carmi-White County CUSD 5 1,400/PK-12
211 W Robinson St 62821 618-382-2341
Brad Lee, supt. Fax 384-3207
www.carmischools.org
Carmi-White County JHS 200/7-8
800 W Main St 62821 618-382-4661
Bart King, prin. Fax 382-2453

Jefferson Attendance Center 200/2-3
713 4th St 62821 618-382-7016
Dr. Amy Dixon, prin. Fax 382-7512
Lincoln Attendance Center 300/PK-1
113 10th St 62821 618-384-3421
Amy Atteberry, prin. Fax 382-5138
Prekindergarten Center 100/PK-PK
205 W Main St 62821 618-384-3515
Maryann Stocke, prin. Fax 382-5138
Washington Attendance Center 300/4-6
205 W Main St 62821 618-966-4631
Amy Atteberry, prin. Fax 384-2076

Carol Stream, DuPage, Pop. 38,894
Benjamin SD 25
Supt. — See West Chicago
Evergreen ES 400/PK-4
1041 Evergreen Dr 60188 630-876-7810
Laura Pfanenstiel, prin. Fax 231-4292

CCSD 93
Supt. — See Bloomingdale
Carol Stream ES 300/K-5
422 Sioux Ln 60188 630-588-5400
Geri Serwach, prin. Fax 588-5499
Cloverdale ES 600/K-5
1182 Merbach Dr 60188 630-588-5300
Korrie McCarry, prin. Fax 588-5399
De Shane ES 300/K-5
475 Chippewa Trl 60188 630-588-6300
Peter La Chance, prin. Fax 588-6399
Heritage Lakes ES 400/K-5
925 Woodhill Dr 60188 630-588-6200
Bob Yelaska, prin. Fax 588-6299
Stream MS 600/6-8
283 El Paso Ln 60188 630-588-5200
Julie Tobin, prin. Fax 588-5299
Western Trails ES 400/K-5
860 Idaho St 60188 630-588-6400
Joy Sebastian, prin. Fax 588-6499

SD U-46
Supt. — See Elgin
Spring Trail ES 400/K-6
1384 Spring Valley Dr 60188 630-213-6230
Amy Kendryna, prin. Fax 213-6236

Carpentersville, Kane, Pop. 37,150
Barrington CUSD 220
Supt. — See Barrington
Sunny Hill ES 400/K-5
2500 Helm Rd 60110 847-426-4232
Dr. C. Armendariz-Maxwell, prin. Fax 426-0896

CUSD 300
Supt. — See Algonquin
Carpentersville MS 800/6-8
100 Cleveland Ave 60110 847-426-1380
Dr. Asia Gurney, prin. Fax 426-1404
deLacey Family Educ Center 300/PK-PK
50 Cleveland Ave 60110 847-426-1450
Kelly Burke, dir. Fax 426-1453
Golfview ES 600/K-5
124 Golfview Ln 60110 847-484-2800
Lindsay Sharp, prin. Fax 484-2815
Lakewood ES 400/K-5
1651 Ravine Ln 60110 847-484-2600
Brittany Porsche, prin. Fax 484-2615
Liberty ES 800/K-5
6500 Miller Rd 60110 847-851-8300
Robert Chleboun, prin. Fax 851-8309
Meadowdale ES 400/K-5
14 Ash St 60110 847-484-2900
Dr. Martina Smith, prin. Fax 484-2915
Parkview ES 500/K-5
122 Carpenter Blvd 60110 847-426-1260
Jorge Almodovar, prin. Fax 426-2962
Perry ES 600/K-5
251 Amarillo Dr 60110 847-484-5600
Kristin Sainsbury, prin. Fax 484-5615

Carrier Mills, Saline, Pop. 1,618
Carrier Mills-Stonefort CUSD 2 400/PK-12
7071 US 45 S 62917 618-994-2392
Bryce K. Jerrell, supt. Fax 994-2929
Carrier Mills-Stonefort ES 300/PK-8
PO Box 218 62917 618-994-2413
Geoff Absher, prin. Fax 994-4141

Carrollton, Greene, Pop. 2,475
Carrollton CUSD 1 600/PK-12
950A 3rd St 62016 217-942-5314
Dr. Kerry Cox, supt. Fax 942-9259
www.c-hawks.net
Carrollton Grade S 400/PK-8
721 4th St 62016 217-942-6831
Ronda Smith, prin. Fax 942-6053

St. John the Evangelist S 200/PK-8
426 3rd St 62016 217-942-6814
Julie Lake, prin. Fax 942-6767

Carterville, Williamson, Pop. 5,368
Carterville CUSD 5 2,100/PK-12
306 Virginia Ave 62918 618-985-4826
Keith Liddell, supt. Fax 985-2041
www.cartervillelions.com
Carterville IS 500/4-6
300 School St 62918 618-985-6411
Tom Webb, prin. Fax 985-2402
Carterville JHS 300/7-8
816 S Division St 62918 618-985-2940
Jeff Hartford, prin. Fax 985-2492
Tri-C ES 700/PK-3
1405 W Grand Ave 62918 618-985-8742
Karri Forby, prin. Fax 985-4907

Carthage, Hancock, Pop. 2,577
Carthage ESD 317 400/PK-8
210 S Adams St 62321 217-357-3922
Vicki Hardy, supt. Fax 357-6793
www.cesd317.org
Carthage MS 200/5-8
210 S Adams St 62321 217-357-3914
Jerry Butcher, prin. Fax 357-3755
Carthage PS 300/PK-4
210 S Adams St 62321 217-357-9202
Mike Snowden, prin. Fax 357-0585

Cary, McHenry, Pop. 17,990
Cary CCSD 26 2,500/PK-8
2115 Crystal Lake Rd 60013 224-357-5100
Brian Coleman, supt. Fax 639-3898
www.cary26.org
Briargate ES 400/K-5
100 S Wulff St 60013 224-357-5250
Chad Nass, prin. Fax 516-5516
Cary JHS 1,000/6-8
2109 Crystal Lake Rd 60013 224-357-5150
Kim Qualls, prin. Fax 516-5507
Deer Path ES 500/PK-PK, 1-
2211 Crystal Lake Rd 60013 224-357-5350
Thom Gippert, prin. Fax 516-6355
Three Oaks ES 600/K-5
1514 3 Oaks Rd 60013 224-357-5450
Natalie Wishne, prin. Fax 516-5514

SS. Peter & Paul S 600/PK-8
416 1st St 60013 847-639-3041
Carolyn Strong, prin. Fax 639-5329
Trinity Oaks Christian Academy 200/PK-12
233 Trinity Oaks Way 60013 847-462-5971
Dr. Paul Wrobbel, head sch Fax 462-5972

Casey, Clark, Pop. 2,756
Casey-Westfield CUSD C4 900/PK-12
502 E Delaware Ave 62420 217-932-2184
Dee Scott, supt. Fax 932-5553
www.caseywestfield.org
Monroe ES, 301 E Monroe Ave 62420 500/PK-6
Melissa Meiners, prin. 217-932-2178

Caseyville, Saint Clair, Pop. 4,170
Collinsville CUSD 10
Supt. — See Collinsville
Caseyville ES 300/PK-4
433 S 2nd St 62232 618-346-6205
Chelsea Clark, prin. Fax 343-2743

Metro East Adventist Christian S 1-8
7864 N Illinois St 62232 618-344-1333
Kristina Windham, prin.

Catlin, Vermilion, Pop. 2,025
Salt Fork CUSD 512 700/PK-12
701 1/2 W Vermilion St 61817 217-427-2116
Phil Cox, supt.
www.saltfork.k12.il.us
Salt Fork North ES 300/PK-5
216 N Webster St 61817 217-427-5421
Eric Free, prin. Fax 288-9393
Other Schools – See Sidell

Centralia, Marion, Pop. 12,732
Central City SD 133 300/PK-8
129 Douglas St 62801 618-532-9521
Tim Branon, supt. Fax 533-2219
centralcity.il.schoolwebpages.com
Central City ES 300/PK-8
129 Douglas St 62801 618-532-9521
Tim Branon, prin. Fax 533-2219

Centralia SD 135 1,300/PK-8
400 S Elm St 62801 618-532-1907
Craig Clark, supt. Fax 532-4986
www.ccs135.com
Centralia JHS 500/5-8
900 S Pine St 62801 618-533-7130
Christina Becker, prin. Fax 533-7123
Centralia Pre-Kindergarten Center 50/PK-PK
422 S Elm St 62801 618-532-1907
Craig Clark, prin.
Field Kindergarten Center 200/PK-K
1101 S Locust St 62801 618-533-7133
Brenda Mulvany, prin. Fax 533-7134
Jordan ES 200/1-3
311 Airport Rd 62801 618-533-7145
Craig Bland, prin. Fax 533-7146
Lincoln ES 100/4-4
501 N Elm St 62801 618-533-7135
Van Brentlinger, prin. Fax 533-7136
Schiller ES 200/PK-3
800 W 4th St 62801 618-533-7140
Amanda Marshall, prin. Fax 533-7141

Grand Prairie CCSD 6 100/K-8
21462 N Richview Ln 62801 618-249-6289
Ryan Robinson, supt. Fax 249-8477
Grand Prairie S 100/K-8
21462 N Richview Ln 62801 618-249-6289
Ryan Robinson, prin. Fax 249-8477

North Wamac SD 186 100/K-8
1500 Case St 62801 618-532-1826
Brad Morris, supt. Fax 532-8250
northwamac.com
North Wamac ES 100/K-8
1500 Case St 62801 618-532-1826
Brad Morris, prin. Fax 532-8250

Raccoon Consolidated SD 1 200/PK-8
3601 State Route 161 62801 618-532-7329
Matt Renaud, supt. Fax 532-7336
www.raccoonschool.org
Raccoon ES 200/PK-8
3601 State Route 161 62801 618-532-7329
Matt Renaud, prin. Fax 532-7336

Willow Grove SD 46 200/PK-8
815 W 7th St 62801 618-532-3313
Dave Fults, supt. Fax 532-5638
www.willowgroveschool.com
Willow Grove ES 200/PK-8
815 W 7th St 62801 618-532-3313
Dave Fults, prin. Fax 532-5638

New Horizon Christian S 100/K-8
12 Greenview Church Rd 62801 618-533-6910
Penny Sparks, admin. Fax 533-6911
St. Mary S 100/PK-8
424 E Broadway 62801 618-532-3473
Jason Swann, prin. Fax 532-5180
Trinity Lutheran S 100/PK-8
203 S Pleasant Ave 62801 618-532-5434
Pam Bierbaum, prin. Fax 532-4277

Cerro Gordo, Piatt, Pop. 1,398
Cerro Gordo CUSD 100 400/PK-12
PO Box 79 61818 217-763-5221
Brett Robinson, supt. Fax 763-6562
www.cgbroncos.org
Cerro Gordo ES 200/PK-6
PO Box 79 61818 217-763-2551
Jodi Neaveill, prin. Fax 763-6560

Chadwick, Carroll, Pop. 548
Chadwick-Milledgeville CUSD 399 500/PK-12
15 School St 61014 815-684-5191
Timothy Schurman, supt. Fax 684-5241
www.dist399.net
Chadwick ES 100/4-5
19 School St 61014 815-684-5191
Timothy Schurman, prin. Fax 684-5241
Chadwick JHS 100/6-8
19 School St 61014 815-684-5191
Timothy Schurman, prin. Fax 684-5241
Other Schools – See Milledgeville

Champaign, Champaign, Pop. 78,771
Champaign CUSD 4 9,600/PK-12
703 S New St 61820 217-351-3800
Dr. Susan Zola, supt. Fax 352-3590
www.champaignschools.org
Barkstall ES 500/K-5
2201 Hallbeck Dr 61822 217-373-5580
Peter Foertsch, prin. Fax 373-5587
Bottenfield ES 500/K-5
1801 S Prospect Ave 61820 217-351-3807
Chris Gilbert, prin. Fax 355-2582
Champaign ECC 300/PK-PK
809 N Neil St 61820 217-351-3881
Amy Hayden, prin. Fax 351-3883
Edison MS 700/6-8
306 W Green St 61820 217-351-3771
Angela Schoonover, prin. Fax 355-2564
Franklin MS 600/6-8
817 N Harris Ave 61820 217-351-3819
Sara Sanders, prin. Fax 351-3729
Garden Hills ES 500/K-5
2001 Garden Hills Dr 61821 217-351-3872
Elizabeth Ladd, prin. Fax 355-8180
Howard ES 500/K-5
1117 W Park Ave 61821 217-351-3866
Jeff Dobbs, prin. Fax 359-7036
Jefferson MS 700/6-8
1115 Crescent Dr 61821 217-351-3790
Angelica Franklin, prin. Fax 351-3754
Kenwood ES 400/K-5
1001 Stratford Dr 61821 217-351-3815
Trevor Nadrozny, prin. Fax 355-4944
Robeson ES 400/K-5
2501 Southmoor Dr 61821 217-351-3884
Nicholas Gaines, prin. Fax 351-3751
South Side ES 300/K-5
712 S Pine St 61820 217-351-3890
William Taylor, prin. Fax 373-7318
Stratton Academy of the Arts 500/K-5
902 N Randolph St 61820 217-373-7330
Stephanie Eckels, prin. Fax 373-7337
Washington STEM Academy 400/K-5
606 E Grove St 61820 217-351-3901
Thea Perkins, prin. Fax 373-7350
Westview ES 400/K-5
703 S Russell St 61821 217-351-3905
Nick Swords, prin. Fax 351-3960
Other Schools – See Savoy

Countryside S 100/K-8
4301 W Kirby Ave 61822 217-355-1253
Stephanie Harman, head sch Fax 355-7492
Holy Cross S 300/PK-8
410 W White St 61820 217-356-9521
Christine Ellis, prin. Fax 356-1745
Judah Christian S 500/PK-12
908 N Prospect Ave 61820 217-359-1701
Mike Chitty, admin. Fax 359-0214
Montessori Habitat S 100/PK-8
PO Box 172 61824 217-366-3260
Next Generation S 300/PK-8
2521 Galen Dr 61821 217-356-6995
Chris Bronowski, head sch Fax 356-6345
St. John Lutheran S 200/PK-8
509 S Mattis Ave 61821 217-359-1714
Faith Block, prin. Fax 359-7972
St. Matthew S 400/K-8
1307 Lincolnshire Dr 61821 217-359-4114
Petrece Klein, prin. Fax 359-8319

Chandlerville, Cass, Pop. 551
A-C Central CUSD 262
Supt. — See Ashland
A-C Central ES 200/PK-4
191 S Bluff St 62627 217-458-2224
Deb Rogers, prin. Fax 458-2223

Channahon, Will, Pop. 12,437
Channahon SD 17 1,400/PK-8
24920 S Sage St 60410 815-467-4315
Dr. Nicholas Henkle, supt. Fax 467-4343
csd17.org
Channahon JHS 400/7-8
24917 W Sioux Dr 60410 815-467-4314
Dr. Chad Uphoff, prin. Fax 467-2188
Galloway ES 400/PK-2
24805 W Roberts Rd 60410 815-467-4311
Mary Kelly, prin. Fax 467-3093
Pioneer Path S 300/3-4
24920 S Sage St 60410 815-467-4312
Laura DuBois, prin. Fax 467-8851
Three Rivers S 300/5-6
24150 S Ford Rd 60410 815-467-4313
Susan Kavich, prin. Fax 467-3089

Charleston, Coles, Pop. 21,496
Charleston CUSD 1 2,700/PK-12
410 W Polk Ave 61920 217-639-1000
Todd Vilardo, supt. Fax 639-1005
www.charleston.k12.il.us
Charleston MS 400/7-8
920 Smith Dr 61920 217-639-6000
Tim Keefe, prin. Fax 639-6005
Jefferson ES 600/PK-PK, 4-
801 Jefferson Ave 61920 217-639-7000
Rob Ulm, prin. Fax 639-7005
Sandburg ES 500/1-3
1924 Reynolds Dr 61920 217-639-4000
Kristen Holly, prin. Fax 639-4005
Twain ES 200/PK-K
1021 13th St 61920 217-639-8000
Brandon Miller, prin. Fax 639-8005
Other Schools – See Ashmore

Chatham, Sangamon, Pop. 11,317
Ball Chatham CUSD 5 4,600/PK-12
201 W Mulberry St 62629 217-483-2416
Dr. Douglas A Wood, supt. Fax 483-2940
www.chathamschools.org
Ball ES 700/PK-4
1015 New City Rd 62629 217-483-2414
Tricia Burke, prin. Fax 483-3968
Chatham ES 600/K-4
525 S College St 62629 217-483-2411
Kim Sepich, prin. Fax 483-5270
Glenwood ES 600/K-4
1401 E Plummer Blvd 62629 217-483-6704
Tammi Kuhn, prin. Fax 483-6904
Glenwood IS 700/5-6
465 Chatham Rd 62629 217-483-1183
Elizabeth Gregurich, prin. Fax 483-1254
Glenwood MS 700/7-8
595 Chatham Rd 62629 217-483-2481
Tina Root, prin. Fax 483-4940

St. Joseph Preschool 50/PK-PK
700 E Spruce St 62629 217-483-3772
Diane VanderKooy, dir. Fax 483-4581

Chatsworth, Livingston, Pop. 1,187
Prairie Central CUSD 8
Supt. — See Fairbury
Prairie Central PS East 100/PK-1
PO Box 816 60921 815-635-3555
Shannon McGuckin, prin. Fax 635-3429

Chebanse, Iroquois, Pop. 1,053
Central CUSD 4
Supt. — See Ashkum
Chebanse ES 400/K-4
PO Box 8 60922 815-697-2642
Andrea Lemenager, prin. Fax 697-2448

Chenoa, McLean, Pop. 1,760
Prairie Central CUSD 8
Supt. — See Fairbury
Prairie Central PS West 100/PK-1
700 S Division St 61726 815-945-2971
Dan Groce, prin. Fax 945-2068

Cherry Valley, Winnebago, Pop. 3,095
Rockford SD 205
Supt. — See Rockford
Cherry Valley ES 200/3-5
619 E State St 61016 815-332-4938
Vicki Kested, prin. Fax 332-9661

Chester, Randolph, Pop. 8,526
Chester CUSD 139 1,000/PK-12
1940 Swanwick St 62233 618-826-4509
Brian Pasero, supt. Fax 826-4500
www.chester139.com
Chester ES 600/PK-8
650 Opdyke St 62233 618-826-2354
Tim Lochhead, prin. Fax 826-2805

St. John Lutheran S 200/PK-8
302 W Holmes St 62233 618-826-4345
Wendy Lochhead, prin. Fax 826-4804
St. Mary S 100/PK-8
835 Swanwick St 62233 618-826-3120
Janelle Robinson, prin. Fax 826-3486

Chicago, Cook, Pop. 2,654,865
Central Stickney SD 110 400/PK-8
5001 S Long Ave 60638 708-458-1152
Dr. Christina Leahy, supt. Fax 458-1168
www.sahs.k12.il.us/
Sahs ES 400/PK-8
5001 S Long Ave 60638 708-458-1152
Jennifer Toschi, prin. Fax 458-1168

City of Chicago SD 299 406,100/PK-12
42 W Madison St 60602 773-553-1000
Forrest Claypool, supt. Fax 535-1502
www.cps.edu
Addams ES 900/PK-8
10810 S Avenue H 60617 773-535-6210
Ruth Martini Walsh, prin. Fax 535-6292
Agassiz ES 500/PK-8
2851 N Seminary Ave 60657 773-534-5725
Mira Weber, prin. Fax 534-5784
Albany Park Multicultural MS 300/7-8
4929 N Sawyer Ave 60625 773-534-5108
Hiliana Araceli Leon, prin. Fax 534-5178
Alcott College Prep S 500/PK-8
2625 N Orchard St 60614 773-534-5460
Elias Estrada, prin. Fax 534-5789
Aldridge ES 200/PK-8
630 E 131st St 60827 773-535-5614
Cynthia Treadwell, prin. Fax 535-5613
Ariel Community Academy 600/PK-8
1119 E 46th St 60653 773-535-1996
Dr. Lennette Coleman, prin. Fax 535-1931
Armour ES 300/PK-8
950 W 33rd Pl 60608 773-535-4530
Shelley Cordova, prin. Fax 535-4501
Armstrong International Studies S 1,400/PK-8
2110 W Greenleaf Ave 60645 773-534-2150
Otis Dunson, prin. Fax 534-2192
Ashburn Community ES 500/PK-8
8300 S Saint Louis Ave 60652 773-535-7860
Jewel Diaz, prin. Fax 535-7867
Ashe ES 400/K-8
8505 S Ingleside Ave 60619 773-535-3550
Clyde King, prin. Fax 535-3362
Audubon ES 600/PK-8
3500 N Hoyne Ave 60618 773-534-5470
Meghan Duffy, prin. Fax 534-5785
Avalon Park ES 300/PK-8
8045 S Kenwood Ave 60619 773-535-6615
Takeshi White-James, prin. Fax 535-6660
Avondale-Logandale ES 900/PK-8
3212 W George St 60618 773-534-5350
Evelyn Roman, prin. Fax 534-5349
Azuela ES 900/PK-8
4707 W Marquette Rd 60629 773-535-7395
Carmen Navarro, prin. Fax 535-7397
Barnard ES 300/PK-8
10354 S Charles St 60643 773-535-2625
Patrick MacMahon, prin. Fax 535-2629
Barry ES 800/PK-6
2828 N Kilbourn Ave 60641 773-534-3455
Estuardo Mazin, prin. Fax 534-3489
Barton ES 600/PK-8
7650 S Wolcott Ave 60620 773-535-3260
Augusta Smith, prin. Fax 535-3271
Bass ES 600/PK-8
1140 W 66th St 60621 773-535-3275
Carolyn Jones, prin. Fax 535-3330
Bateman ES 1,000/PK-8
4220 N Richmond St 60618 773-534-5055
Georgia Davos-Vetas, prin. Fax 534-5052
Beasley Academic Magnet S 1,400/PK-8
5255 S State St 60609 773-535-1230
Dr. Kim Brasfield, prin. Fax 535-1248
Beaubien ES 1,200/PK-8
5025 N Laramie Ave 60630 773-534-3500
Michelle Ludford-Naggatz, prin. Fax 534-3517
Beethoven ES 400/PK-8
25 W 47th St 60609 773-535-1480
Marcus Alexander Ed.D., prin. Fax 535-1478
Beidler ES 500/PK-8
3151 W Walnut St 60612 773-534-6811
Ursula Hoskins, prin. Fax 534-6817
Belding ES 600/PK-8
4257 N Tripp Ave 60641 773-534-3590
Heather Smith-Yutzy, prin. Fax 534-3598
Bell ES 1,000/K-8
3730 N Oakley Ave 60618 773-534-5150
Kathleen Miller, prin. Fax 534-5163
Belmont-Cragin ES 600/PK-8
5252 W Palmer St 60639 773-534-2900
Stacey Stewart, prin. Fax 534-2907
Bennett ES 400/PK-8
10115 S Prairie Ave 60628 773-535-5460
Teresa Huggins, prin. Fax 535-5577
Black Magnet S 500/K-8
9101 S Euclid Ave 60617 773-535-6390
Rhonda Butler, prin. Fax 535-6047
Blaine ES 900/PK-8
1420 W Grace St 60613 773-534-5750
Gary Norcross, prin. Fax 534-5748
Bond ES 400/PK-8
7050 S May St 60621 773-535-3480
Valesta Cobbs, prin. Fax 535-3433
Boone ES 800/PK-8
6710 N Washtenaw Ave 60645 773-534-2160
Jaclyn Delaney, prin. Fax 534-2190
Bouchet Math & Science Academy 700/PK-8
7355 S Jeffery Blvd 60649 773-535-0501
Shontae Higginbottom, prin. Fax 535-0559
Bradwell ES of Excellence 800/PK-8
7736 S Burnham Ave 60649 773-535-6600
Tyese Sims, prin. Fax 535-6612
Brenneman ES 500/PK-8
4251 N Clarendon Ave 60613 773-534-5766
Sarah Abedelal, prin. Fax 534-5787
Brentano Math & Science Academy 400/PK-8
2723 N Fairfield Ave 60647 773-534-4100
Seth Lavin, prin. Fax 534-4183
Bridge ES 1,000/PK-8
3800 N New England Ave 60634 773-534-3718
Dr. Christopher Brake, prin. Fax 534-3612
Bright ES 300/PK-8
10740 S Calhoun Ave 60617 773-535-6215
Alicia Lewis, prin. Fax 535-6373
Brighton Park ES 600/PK-8
3825 S Washtenaw Ave 60632 773-535-7237
Sara Haas, prin. Fax 535-7198

Brown Community Academy 300/PK-8
12607 S Union Ave 60628 773-535-5385
Steven Askew, prin. Fax 535-5359

Brown ES 200/PK-8
54 N Hermitage Ave 60612 773-534-7250
Kenya Sadler, prin. Fax 534-7323

Brownell ES 300/PK-6
6741 S Michigan Ave 60637 773-535-3030
Richard Morgan, prin. Fax 535-3413

Brunson Math & Science S 600/PK-8
932 N Central Ave 60651 773-534-6025
Dr. Carol Wilson, prin. Fax 534-6031

Budlong ES 900/PK-8
2701 W Foster Ave 60625 773-534-2591
Noami Nakayama, prin. Fax 534-2544

Burbank ES 900/PK-8
2035 N Mobile Ave 60639 773-534-3000
Dr. Hiram Broyls, prin. Fax 534-3338

Burke ES 400/PK-8
5356 S King Dr 60615 773-535-1325
Jessica Briggs, prin. Fax 535-1913

Burley ES 500/PK-8
1630 W Barry Ave 60657 773-534-5475
Catherine Plocher, prin. Fax 534-5786

Burnham/Anthony Math & Science Academy 600/PK-8
9928 S Crandon Ave 60617 773-535-6530
Dr. Linda Moore, prin. Fax 535-6515

Burnside Scholastic Academy 700/PK-8
650 E 91st Pl 60619 773-535-3300
Kelly Thigpen, prin. Fax 535-3230

Burr ES 400/PK-8
1621 W Wabansia Ave 60622 773-534-4090
William Klee, prin. Fax 534-4718

Burroughs ES 500/PK-8
3542 S Washtenaw Ave 60632 773-535-7226
Richard Morris, prin. Fax 535-7126

Byrne ES 700/K-8
5329 S Oak Park Ave 60638 773-535-2170
Chantel Angeletti, prin. Fax 229-0281

Caldwell ES 300/PK-8
8546 S Cregier Ave 60617 773-535-6300
Danielle Porch, prin. Fax 535-6611

Calmeca Acad Fine Arts & Dual Language 800/PK-8
3456 W 38th St 60632 773-535-7000
Ovidio Villarreal, prin. Fax 535-7010

Cameron ES 800/PK-8
1234 N Monticello Ave 60651 773-534-4290
Stephen Harden, prin. Fax 534-0405

Camras ES 1,000/PK-8
3000 N Mango Ave 60634 773-534-2960
Clariza Dominicci, prin. Fax 534-2963

Canty ES 800/PK-8
3740 N Panama Ave 60634 773-534-1238
Dr. Lucja Mirowska-Kopec, prin. Fax 534-1236

Cardenas ES 700/PK-3
2345 S Millard Ave 60623 773-534-1465
Dr. Jeremy Feiwell, prin. Fax 534-1512

Carnegie ES 700/PK-8
1414 E 61st Pl 60637 773-535-0530
Docilla Pollard, prin. Fax 535-0525

Carroll-Rosenwald ES 500/PK-8
2929 W 83rd St 60652 773-535-9414
Adell Brock, prin. Fax 535-9568

Carson ES 1,200/PK-8
5516 S Maplewood Ave 60629 773-535-9222
Javier Arriola-Lopez, prin. Fax 535-9552

Carter ES 400/PK-8
5740 S Michigan Ave 60637 773-535-0860
Jennifer Laurincik, prin. Fax 535-0698

Carver ES 500/PK-8
901 E 133rd Pl 60827 773-535-5674
Charles Campbell, prin. Fax 535-5455

Casals ES 500/PK-8
3501 W Potomac Ave 60651 773-534-4444
Kristie Langbehn, prin. Fax 534-4559

Cassell ES 400/K-8
11314 S Spaulding Ave 60655 773-535-2640
Eileen Scanlan, prin. Fax 535-2667

Castellanos MS 600/4-8
2524 S Central Park Ave 60623 773-534-1620
Virginia Jimenez, prin. Fax 534-1611

Cather ES 400/PK-8
2908 W Washington Blvd 60612 773-534-6780
Wanda Carey, prin. Fax 534-6727

Chalmers ES 400/PK-8
2745 W Roosevelt Rd 60608 773-534-1720
Romian Crockett, prin. Fax 534-1718

Chappell ES 500/K-8
2135 W Foster Ave 60625 773-534-2390
Joseph Peila, prin. Fax 534-2638

Chase ES 500/PK-8
2021 N Point St 60647 773-534-4185
Raquel Saucedo, prin. Fax 534-4727

Chavez ES 900/PK-8
4747 S Marshfield Ave 60609 773-535-4600
Barton Dassinger, prin. Fax 535-4603

Chicago Academy ES 600/PK-8
3400 N Austin Ave 60634 773-534-3885
John Laughlin, prin. Fax 534-0109

Chopin ES 600/PK-8
2450 W Rice St 60622 773-534-4080
Frederick Williams, prin. Fax 534-4163

Christopher ES 400/K-8
5042 S Artesian Ave 60632 773-535-9375
Katherine Gallagher, prin. Fax 535-9567

Claremont Academy ES 500/PK-8
2300 W 64th St 60636 773-535-8110
Mary Padezanin-Zonca, prin. Fax 535-8108

Clark ES 300/PK-8
1045 S Monitor Ave 60644 773-534-6225
Natasha Buckner, prin. Fax 534-6278

Clay ES 600/PK-8
13231 S Burley Ave 60633 773-535-5600
Jennifer Laurincik, prin. Fax 535-5606

Cleveland ES 700/PK-8
3121 W Byron St 60618 773-534-5130
Debora Ward, prin. Fax 534-5266

Clinton ES 1,100/PK-8
6110 N Fairfield Ave 60659 773-534-2025
Maureen Delgado, prin. Fax 534-2069

Clissold ES 600/K-8
2350 W 110th Pl 60643 773-535-2560
Sean McNichols, prin. Fax 535-2556

Colemon Academy 300/PK-8
1441 W 119th St 60643 773-535-3975
Paulette Williams, prin. Fax 535-3979

Coles Academy 600/PK-8
8441 S Yates Blvd 60617 773-535-6550
Charlie McSpadden, prin. Fax 535-6570

Columbia Explorers Academy 1,100/K-8
4520 S Kedzie Ave 60632 773-535-4050
Eileen Considine, prin. Fax 535-4083

Columbus ES 300/PK-8
1003 N Leavitt St 60622 773-534-4350
Wendy Oleksy, prin. Fax 534-4362

Cook ES 400/PK-8
8150 S Bishop St 60620 773-535-3315
Narineh Gharashor, prin. Fax 535-3383

Coonley ES 700/K-8
4046 N Leavitt St 60618 773-534-5140
Gregory Zurawski, prin. Fax 534-5213

Cooper Dual Language Academy 600/PK-5
1624 W 19th St 60608 773-534-7205
Martha Alba, prin. Fax 534-7245

Corkery ES 600/PK-8
2510 S Kildare Ave 60623 773-534-1650
Carol Devens-Falk, prin. Fax 534-1674

Courtenay Language Arts Center 600/PK-8
4420 N Beacon St 60640 773-534-5790
Macquline King, prin. Fax 534-5799

Crown Community Academy of Fine Arts 300/PK-8
2128 S Saint Louis Ave 60623 773-534-1680
Dr. Lee Jackson, prin. Fax 534-1677

Cuffe Math-Science Tech Academy 500/PK-8
8324 S Racine Ave 60620 773-535-8250
Lakita Reed, prin. Fax 535-3497

Cullen ES 300/K-8
10650 S Eberhart Ave 60628 773-535-5375
Bud Bryant, prin. Fax 535-5366

Curtis ES 600/PK-8
32 E 115th St 60628 773-535-5050
Stephen McClain, prin. Fax 535-5044

Daley Academy 700/PK-8
5024 S Wolcott Ave 60609 773-535-9091
Marla Elitzer, prin. Fax 535-0407

Darwin ES 600/PK-8
3116 W Belden Ave 60647 773-534-4110
Mauricio Segovia, prin. Fax 534-4323

Davis Academy 300/K-8
6740 S Paulina St 60636 773-535-9120
Cheryl Armstrong-Belt, prin. Fax 535-9129

Davis ES 900/PK-8
3014 W 39th Pl 60632 773-535-4540
Rocio Rosales, prin. Fax 535-4510

Dawes ES 1,000/PK-8
3810 W 81st Pl 60652 773-535-2350
Mary Dixon, prin. Fax 535-2367

Decatur Classical ES 300/K-6
7030 N Sacramento Ave 60645 773-534-2200
Susan Kukielka, prin. Fax 534-2191

De Diego Community Academy 900/PK-8
1313 N Claremont Ave 60622 773-534-4451
Jacqueline Menoni, prin. Fax 534-4696

Deneen S of Excellence 600/PK-8
7240 S Wabash Ave 60619 773-535-3035
Karla Kemp, prin. Fax 535-3247

DePriest ES 700/PK-8
139 S Parkside Ave 60644 773-534-6800
Minnie Watson, prin. Fax 534-6799

Dett ES 500/PK-8
2131 W Monroe St 60612 773-534-7160
Lamonica Williams, prin. Fax 534-7291

Dever ES 800/PK-8
3436 N Osceola Ave 60634 773-534-3090
Jason Major, prin. Fax 534-3337

Dewey Academy of Fine Arts 300/PK-8
5415 S Union Ave 60609 773-535-1666
Cleophas Rodgers, prin. Fax 535-1802

Dirksen ES 800/PK-8
8601 W Foster Ave 60656 773-534-1090
Daniel Lucas, prin. Fax 534-1065

Disney II Magnet ES 400/PK-6
3815 N Kedvale Ave 60641 773-534-3750
Kathleen Speth, prin. Fax 534-3757

Disney Magnet ES 1,700/PK-8
4140 N Marine Dr 60613 773-534-5840
Dr. Kathleen Hagstrom, prin. Fax 534-5714

Dixon ES 600/PK-8
8306 S Saint Lawrence Ave 60619 773-535-3834
Terrycita Perry, prin. Fax 535-3811

Doolittle ES 300/PK-8
535 E 35th St 60616 773-535-1040
Kellie Corley, prin. Fax 535-1034

Dore ES 600/PK-8
6108 S Natoma Ave 60638 773-535-2080
Everett Edwards, prin. Fax 535-2084

Drake ES 500/PK-8
2710 S Dearborn St 60616 773-534-9129
Sydney Golliday, prin. Fax 534-9133

Drummond ES 300/PK-8
1845 W Cortland St 60622 773-534-4120
Erica Kittle, prin. Fax 534-4199

Dubois ES 200/PK-8
330 E 133rd St 60827 773-535-5582
Vanessa Williams-Johnson, prin. Fax 535-5587

Dulles S of Excellence 800/PK-8
6311 S Calumet Ave 60637 773-535-0690
Jolene Galpin, prin. Fax 535-0689

Dunne ES 300/PK-8
10845 S Union Ave 60628 773-535-5517
Chandra Byrd-Wright, prin. Fax 535-5018

Durkin Park ES 600/PK-8
8445 S Kolin Ave 60652 773-535-2322
Daniel Redmond, prin. Fax 535-2299

Dvorak S of Excellence 500/PK-8
3615 W 16th St 60623 773-534-1690
LaShawn Whitney, prin. Fax 534-1676

Earhart ES 300/K-8
1710 E 93rd St 60617 773-535-6416
Dr. Brenda DeMar-Williams, prin. Fax 535-6077

Earle ES 500/PK-8
2040 W 62nd St 60636 773-535-9130
Cederrall Petties, prin. Fax 535-9140

Eberhart ES 1,600/PK-8
3400 W 65th Pl 60629 773-535-9190
Nneka Gunn, prin. Fax 535-9494

Ebinger ES 700/PK-8
7350 W Pratt Ave 60631 773-534-1070
Serena Peterson, prin. Fax 534-1088

Edgebrook ES 500/PK-8
6525 N Hiawatha Ave 60646 773-534-1194
Chad Weiden, prin. Fax 534-1170

Edison Park ES 500/PK-8
6220 N Olcott Ave 60631 773-534-0960
Jennifer Farell-Rottman, prin. Fax 534-0969

Edison S Regional Gifted Center 300/K-8
4929 N Sawyer Ave 60625 773-534-0540
Karen Valentine, prin. Fax 534-0539

Edwards ES 1,500/PK-8
4815 S Karlov Ave 60632 773-535-4875
Judith Sauri, prin. Fax 535-4470

Ellington ES 700/PK-8
243 N Parkside Ave 60644 773-534-6361
Shirley Scott, prin. Fax 534-6374

Ericson Scholastic Academy 500/PK-8
3600 W 5th Ave 60624 773-534-6660
Leavelle Abram, prin. Fax 534-6636

Esmond ES 300/PK-8
1865 W Montvale Ave 60643 773-535-2650
Dr. Angela Tucker, prin. Fax 535-2676

Everett ES 200/PK-5
3419 S Bell Ave 60608 773-535-4550
Rodolfo Rojas, prin. Fax 535-4615

Evergreen Academy MS 400/6-8
3537 S Paulina St 60609 773-535-4836
Marian Strok, prin. Fax 535-4853

Evers ES 400/PK-8
9811 S Lowe Ave 60628 773-535-2565
Caroline Ellis, prin. Fax 535-2570

Fairfield Academy 600/PK-8
6201 S Fairfield Ave 60629 773-535-9500
Claudia Lopez, prin. Fax 535-0438

Falconer ES 1,400/PK-6
3020 N Lamon Ave 60641 773-534-3560
James Cosme, prin. Fax 534-3636

Faraday ES 300/PK-8
3250 W Monroe St 60624 773-534-6670
Tawana Wilkes-Williams, prin. Fax 534-6659

Farnsworth ES 600/PK-8
5414 N Linder Ave 60630 773-534-3535
Barbara Oken, prin. Fax 534-3515

Fernwood ES 300/PK-8
10041 S Union Ave 60628 773-535-2700
Robert Towner, prin. Fax 535-2711

Field ES 300/5-8
7019 N Ashland Blvd 60626 773-534-2030
Adrian Dobbins, prin. Fax 534-2189

Finkl ES 500/PK-8
2332 S Western Ave 60608 773-535-5850
Denise Lynch, prin. Fax 535-4409

Fiske ES 500/PK-8
6020 S Langley Ave 60637 773-535-0990
Cynthia Miller, prin. Fax 535-0580

Fort Dearborn ES 400/PK-8
9025 S Throop St 60620 773-535-2680
Sean Clayton, prin. Fax 535-2891

Foster Park ES 400/PK-8
8530 S Wood St 60620 773-535-2725
John Webb, prin. Fax 535-2740

Franklin Fine Arts ES 400/K-8
225 W Evergreen Ave 60610 773-534-8510
Kurt Jones, prin. Fax 534-8022

Frazier International Magnet S 300/K-8
4027 W Grenshaw St 60624 773-534-6880
Charlette Broxton, prin. Fax 534-6616

Fuller ES 300/PK-8
4214 S Saint Lawrence Ave 60653 773-535-1687
Marilyn McCottrell, prin. Fax 535-1689

Fulton ES 500/PK-8
5300 S Hermitage Ave 60609 773-535-9000
Lissette Rua, prin. Fax 535-9464

Funston ES 600/PK-8
2010 N Central Park Ave 60647 773-534-4125
Julie Hallums, prin. Fax 534-4551

Gale Community Academy 400/PK-8
1631 W Jonquil Ter 60626 773-534-2100
Augustine Emuwa, prin. Fax 534-2188

Galileo Scholastic Academy 600/K-8
820 S Carpenter St 60607 773-534-7070
Jodilyn Pinkerton, prin. Fax 534-7109

Gallistel Language Academy 1,300/PK-8
10347 S Ewing Ave 60617 773-535-6540
Kimberly Nelson, prin. Fax 535-6569

Garvey ES 300/PK-8
10309 S Morgan St 60643 773-535-2763
Michelle Miller, prin. Fax 535-2761

Garvy ES 800/K-8
5225 N Oak Park Ave 60656 773-534-1185
Julie McGlade, prin. Fax 534-1124

Gary ES 1,200/PK-PK, 3-
3740 W 31st St 60623 773-534-1455
Alberto Juarez, prin. Fax 534-1435

Gillespie ES 600/PK-8
9301 S State St 60619 773-535-5065
Dr. Michelle Willis, prin. Fax 535-5048

Goethe ES 800/PK-8
2236 N Rockwell St 60647 773-534-4135
Barbara Kargas, prin. Fax 534-4138

Goudy Technology Academy 800/PK-8
5120 N Winthrop Ave 60640 773-534-2480
Pamela Brandt, prin. Fax 534-2588

Graham ES 500/PK-8
4436 S Union Ave 60609 773-535-1308
John Nichols, prin. Fax 535-1424

Gray ES 1,300/PK-8
3730 N Laramie Ave 60641 773-534-3520
Susan Gross, prin. Fax 534-3613

Greeley ES 600/PK-8
832 W Sheridan Rd 60613 773-534-5800
Raquel Gonzalez, prin. Fax 534-5783

Greene ES 600/PK-5
3525 S Honore St 60609 773-535-4560
Patricia Gonzalez, prin. Fax 535-4617

Green ES 300/PK-8
1150 W 96th St 60643 773-535-2575
Tyrone Dowdell, prin. Fax 535-2742

Gregory ES 400/PK-8
3715 W Polk St 60624 773-534-6820
Donella Carter, prin. Fax 534-6484

Gresham ES 300/PK-8
8524 S Green St 60620 773-535-3350
Tosha Jackson, prin. Fax 535-3563

Grimes/Alexander Fleming S 500/PK-8
5450 W 64th Pl 60638 773-535-2364
Judith Carlson, prin. Fax 535-2366

Grissom ES 300/PK-8
12810 S Escanaba Ave 60633 773-535-5380
Dennis Sweeney, prin. Fax 535-5362

Gunsaulus Scholastic Academy 800/PK-8
4420 S Sacramento Ave 60632 773-535-7215
Kiltae Kim, prin. Fax 535-7222

Haines ES 700/PK-8
247 W 23rd Pl 60616 773-534-9200
Catherine Moy, prin. Fax 534-9209

Hale ES 900/PK-8
6140 S Melvina Ave 60638 773-535-2265
Dawn Iles-Gomez, prin. Fax 535-2275

Haley ES 600/PK-8
11411 S Eggleston Ave 60628 773-535-5340
Sherry Pirtle, prin. Fax 535-5351

Hamilton ES 400/PK-8
1650 W Cornelia Ave 60657 773-534-5484
James Gray, prin. Fax 534-5782

Hamline ES 700/PK-8
4747 S Bishop St 60609 773-535-4565
Erik Olson, prin. Fax 535-4546

Hammond ES 500/PK-8
2819 W 21st Pl 60623 773-535-4580
Anamaria Orbe, prin. Fax 535-4579

Hampton Fine & Performing Arts S 600/K-8
3434 W 77th St 60652 773-535-4030
Zaneta Abdul-Ahad, prin. Fax 535-4031

Hanson Park ES 1,500/PK-8
5411 W Fullerton Ave 60639 773-534-3100
David Belanger, prin. Fax 534-3374

Harte ES 400/PK-8
1556 E 56th St 60637 773-535-0870
Shenethe Parks, prin. Fax 535-0666

Harvard S of Excellence 500/PK-8
7525 S Harvard Ave 60620 773-535-3045
Aisha McCarthy, prin. Fax 535-3332

Haugan ES 1,200/PK-6
4540 N Hamlin Ave 60625 773-534-5040
Rosa Valdez, prin. Fax 534-5045

Hawthorne Scholastic Academy 600/K-8
3319 N Clifton Ave 60657 773-534-5550
Nathan Pietrini, prin. Fax 534-5781

Hay Community Academy 500/PK-8
1018 N Laramie Ave 60651 773-534-6000
Latrese Mathis, prin. Fax 534-6035

Hayt ES 1,000/PK-8
1518 W Granville Ave 60660 773-534-2040
Daniel Gomez, prin. Fax 534-2187

Healy ES 1,400/PK-8
3010 S Parnell Ave 60616 773-534-9190
Elizabeth Nessner, prin. Fax 534-9182

Hearst ES 400/PK-8
4640 S Lamon Ave 60638 773-535-2376
Teresa Chrobak-Prince, prin. Fax 535-2341

Hedges ES 800/PK-8
4747 S Winchester Ave 60609 773-535-7360
Raul Magdaleno, prin. Fax 535-4178

Hefferan ES 400/PK-8
4409 W Wilcox St 60624 773-534-6192
Jacqueline Hearns, prin. Fax 534-6190

Henderson ES 400/PK-8
5650 S Wolcott Ave 60636 773-535-9080
Marvis Jackson-Ivy, prin. Fax 535-9115

Hendricks ES 300/PK-8
4316 S Princeton Ave 60609 773-535-1696
Sandee McDonald, prin. Fax 535-1700

Henry ES 700/PK-6
4250 N Saint Louis Ave 60618 773-534-5060
Januario Gutierrez, prin. Fax 534-5042

Hernandez MS for Advancement of Sciences 900/6-8
3510 W 55th St 60632 773-535-8850
Debra Fritz-Fanning, prin. Fax 535-8851

Herzl ES 500/PK-8
3711 W Douglas Blvd 60623 773-534-1480
Tamara Davis, prin. Fax 534-1486

Hibbard ES 1,200/PK-6
3244 W Ainslie St 60625 773-534-5191
Scott Ahlman, prin. Fax 534-5208

Higgins Community Academy 400/PK-8
11710 S Morgan St 60643 773-535-5625
Crystal Dorsey, prin. Fax 535-5623

Hitch ES 600/PK-8
5625 N McVicker Ave 60646 773-534-1189
Adam Stich, prin. Fax 534-1176

Holden ES 500/PK-8
1104 W 31st St 60608 773-535-7200
K. Patsiopoulos, prin. Fax 535-7113

Holmes ES 300/PK-8
955 W Garfield Blvd 60621 773-535-9025
Diedre Coleman, prin. Fax 535-9127

Hope Institute Learning Academy 400/K-5
1628 W Washington Blvd 60612 773-534-7405
Michael Jakubowski, prin. Fax 534-7623

Howe S of Excellence 600/PK-8
720 N Lorel Ave 60644 773-534-6060
Keri Mendez, prin. Fax 534-6080

Hoyne ES 300/K-8
8905 S Crandon Ave 60617 773-535-6425
Michael Hinton, prin. Fax 535-6444

Hughes ES 300/PK-8
4247 W 15th St 60623 773-534-1762
Lucille Howard, prin. Fax 534-1715

Hughes ES 600/PK-8
240 W 104th St 60628 773-535-5075
Kimbreana Taylor-Goode, prin. Fax 535-6520

Hurley ES 800/PK-8
3849 W 69th Pl 60629 773-535-2068
Dolores Cupp, prin. Fax 535-2059

Inter-American Magnet S 700/PK-8
851 W Waveland Ave 60613 773-534-5490
Daniela Bylaitis, prin. Fax 534-5483

Irving ES 500/PK-8
749 S Oakley Blvd 60612 773-534-7295
Valeria Bryant, prin. Fax 534-7289

Jackson ES 300/PK-8
917 W 88th St 60620 773-535-3341
Teresa Nagy, prin. Fax 535-3453

Jackson Language Academy 600/K-8
1340 W Harrison St 60607 773-534-7000
Marilou Rebolledo, prin. Fax 534-9338

Jahn ES 500/PK-8
3149 N Wolcott Ave 60657 773-534-5500
Michael Herring, prin. Fax 534-5533

Jamieson ES 900/PK-8
5650 N Mozart St 60659 773-534-2395
Robert Baughman, prin. Fax 534-2579

Jenner Academy of the Arts 300/PK-8
1119 N Cleveland Ave 60610 773-534-8440
Rhea Bush, prin. Fax 534-8188

Jensen Scholastic Academy 500/PK-8
3030 W Harrison St 60612 773-534-6840
Chinyere Okafor, prin. Fax 534-6722

Johnson ES 400/PK-8
1420 S Albany Ave 60623 773-534-1829
Takia Foster, prin. Fax 534-1355

Joplin ES 500/PK-8
7931 S Honore St 60620 773-535-3425
Alene Mason, prin. Fax 535-3442

Jordan Community S 600/PK-8
7414 N Wolcott Ave 60626 773-534-2220
Gilberto Piedrahita, prin. Fax 534-2231

Jungman ES 300/PK-8
1746 S Miller St 60608 773-534-7375
Suzanne Luzzi, prin. Fax 534-7383

Kanoon Magnet ES 700/PK-8
2233 S Kedzie Ave 60623 773-534-1736
Marin Gonzalez, prin. Fax 534-1740

Keller Gifted Magnet Center 200/1-8
3020 W 108th St 60655 773-535-2636
Delena Little, prin. Fax 535-2635

Kellman Corporate Community S 400/PK-8
3030 W Arthington St 60612 773-534-6602
Sherisse Freeney, prin. Fax 534-6601

Kellogg ES 300/K-8
9241 S Leavitt St 60643 773-535-2590
Cory Overstreet, prin. Fax 535-2596

Kershaw ES 300/PK-8
6450 S Lowe Ave 60621 773-535-3050
Tanya Lynnette Fields, prin. Fax 535-3677

Kilmer ES 800/PK-8
6700 N Greenview Ave 60626 773-534-2115
Jean Papagianis, prin. Fax 534-2186

King Academy of Social Justice 200/PK-8
644 W 71st St 60621 773-535-3875
Jasmine Thurmond, prin. Fax 535-3885

Kinzie ES 700/PK-8
5625 S Mobile Ave 60638 773-535-2425
Dawn Caetta, prin. Fax 535-2086

Kipling ES 400/K-8
9351 S Lowe Ave 60620 773-535-3151
LaWanda Bishop, prin. Fax 535-3187

Kozminski Community S 400/PK-8
936 E 54th St 60615 773-535-0980
Bernadette Glover, prin. Fax 535-0982

Langford Community Academy 400/PK-8
6010 S Throop St 60636 773-535-9180
Lynn McGinnis-Garner, prin. Fax 535-9428

Lara Academy 500/PK-8
4619 S Wolcott Ave 60609 773-535-4389
Paul Schissler, prin. Fax 535-4471

LaSalle II Magnet S 600/PK-8
1148 N Honore St 60622 773-534-0490
Dr. Lauren Albani, prin. Fax 534-0491

LaSalle Language Academy 600/K-8
1734 N Orleans St 60614 773-534-8470
Dr. Beth Bazer, prin. Fax 534-8021

Lavizzo ES 400/PK-8
138 W 109th St 60628 773-535-5300
Tracey Stelly, prin. Fax 535-5313

Lawndale Community Academy 500/PK-8
3500 W Douglas Blvd 60623 773-534-1635
Willard Willette, prin. Fax 534-1644

Lee ES 900/PK-8
6448 S Tripp Ave 60629 773-535-2255
Lisa Epstein, prin. Fax 535-2287

Leland ES 700/PK-8
512 S Lavergne Ave 60644 773-534-6340
Turon Ivy, prin. Fax 534-6040

Lenart Regional Gifted Center 300/PK-8
8101 S La Salle St 60620 773-535-0040
Angela Sims, prin. Fax 535-0048

Lewis ES 500/PK-8
1431 N Leamington Ave 60651 773-534-3060
Aquabah Gonney, prin. Fax 534-3010

Libby ES 500/K-8
5300 S Loomis Blvd 60609 773-535-9050
Rochonda Knox, prin. Fax 535-9383

Lincoln ES 800/K-8
615 W Kemper Pl 60614 773-534-5720
Mark Armendariz, prin. Fax 534-5778

Little Village Academy 900/PK-8
2620 S Lawndale Ave 60623 773-534-1880
Lillian Lazu, prin. Fax 534-1893

Lloyd ES 1,200/PK-5
2103 N Lamon Ave 60639 773-534-3070
Jay Thompson, prin. Fax 534-3388

Locke ES 1,400/PK-8
2828 N Oak Park Ave 60634 773-534-3300
John Fitzpatrick, prin. Fax 534-3168

Lorca ES 900/PK-8
3231 N Springfield Ave 60618 773-534-0950
July Cyrwus, prin. Fax 534-0953

Lovett ES 500/PK-8
6333 W Bloomingdale Ave 60639 773-534-3130
Leviis Haney, prin. Fax 534-3384

Lowell ES 600/PK-8
3320 W Hirsch St 60651 773-534-4300
Gladys Rivera, prin. Fax 534-4306

Lozano ES 300/PK-8
1501 N Greenview Ave, 773-534-4750
Maria Campos, prin. Fax 534-4740

Lyon ES 1,400/K-8
2941 N McVicker Ave 60634 773-534-3120
Clifford Gabor, prin. Fax 534-3375

Madero MS 300/6-8
3202 W 28th St 60623 773-535-4466
Jose Illanes, prin. Fax 535-4469

Madison ES 200/PK-8
7433 S Dorchester Ave 60619 773-535-0551
Allania Moore, prin. Fax 535-0582

Manierre ES 400/PK-8
1420 N Hudson Ave 60610 773-534-8456
Derrick Orr, prin. Fax 534-8020

Mann ES 400/PK-8
8050 S Chappel Ave 60617 773-535-6640
Jeffery Porter, prin. Fax 535-6664

Marquette ES 1,300/PK-8
6550 S Richmond St 60629 773-535-9260
Latarsha Green, prin. Fax 535-9266

Marsh ES 900/PK-8
9822 S Exchange Ave 60617 773-535-6430
Jose Torres, prin. Fax 535-6446

Mason ES 500/PK-8
4217 W 18th St 60623 773-534-1530
Tonya Tolbert, prin. Fax 534-1544

Mayer ES 600/PK-8
2250 N Clifton Ave 60614 773-534-5535
Katie Konieczny, prin. Fax 534-5777

Mays Academy 600/PK-8
6656 S Normal Blvd 60621 773-535-3892
Dr. Patricia McCann, prin. Fax 535-3895

McAuliffe ES 700/PK-8
1841 N Springfield Ave 60647 773-534-4400
Ryan Belville, prin. Fax 534-4744

McClellan ES 300/PK-8
3527 S Wallace St 60609 773-535-1732
Joseph Shoffner, prin. Fax 535-1940

McCormick ES 900/PK-5
2712 S Sawyer Ave 60623 773-535-7252
Flavia Hernandez, prin. Fax 535-7347

McCutcheon ES 500/PK-8
4865 N Sheridan Rd 60640 773-534-2680
Gwyneth Kram, prin. Fax 534-2578

McDade Classical ES 200/K-6
8801 S Indiana Ave 60619 773-535-3669
Daniel Perry, prin. Fax 535-3667

McDowell ES 200/PK-5
1419 E 89th St 60619 773-535-6404
Dr. Jo Easterling-Hood, prin. Fax 535-6434

McKay ES 900/PK-8
6901 S Fairfield Ave 60629 773-535-9340
Dawn Prather-Hawk, prin. Fax 535-9443

McNair S of Excellence 400/PK-8
4820 W Walton St 60651 773-534-8980
Valencia Koker, prin. Fax 534-0668

McPherson ES 800/PK-8
4728 N Wolcott Ave 60640 773-534-2625
Carmen Mendoza, prin. Fax 534-2637

Melody ES 600/PK-8
3937 W Wilcox St 60624 773-534-6850
Tiffany Tillman, prin. Fax 534-6839

Metcalfe Community Academy 500/PK-8
12339 S Normal Ave 60628 773-535-5590
Stephen Fabiyi, prin. Fax 535-5570

Mireles Academy 700/PK-8
9000 S Exchange Ave 60617 773-535-6360
Evelyn Randle-Robbins, prin. Fax 535-6303

Mitchell ES 400/PK-8
2233 W Ohio St 60612 773-534-7655
Nicole Milberg, prin. Fax 534-7633

Mollison ES 500/PK-8
4415 S King Dr 60653 773-535-1804
Hireshemo Clark, prin. Fax 535-1803

Monroe ES 1,000/PK-8
3651 W Schubert Ave 60647 773-534-4155
Ricardo Trujillo, prin. Fax 534-4593

Moos ES 500/PK-8
1711 N California Ave 60647 773-534-4340
Karime Asaf, prin. Fax 534-4535

Morrill Math & Science S 800/PK-8
6011 S Rockwell St 60629 773-535-9288
Rashad Talley, prin. Fax 535-9214

Morton S of Excellence 400/PK-8
431 N Troy St 60612 773-534-6791
Peggie Burnett-Wise, prin. Fax 534-6790

Mt. Greenwood ES 1,000/K-8
10841 S Homan Ave 60655 773-535-2786
Catherine Reidy, prin. Fax 535-2743

Mt. Vernon ES 300/PK-8
10540 S Morgan St 60643 773-535-2825
Raquel Davis, prin. Fax 535-2827

Mozart ES 800/PK-8
2200 N Hamlin Ave 60647 773-534-4160
Sonia Caban, prin. Fax 534-4588

Murphy ES 600/PK-8
3539 W Grace St 60618 773-534-5223
Christine Zelenka, prin. Fax 534-5212

Murray Language Academy 500/K-8
5335 S Kenwood Ave 60615 773-535-0585
Greg Mason, prin. Fax 535-0590

Nash ES 400/PK-8
4837 W Erie St 60644 773-534-6125
Dr. Tresa Dunbar, prin. Fax 534-6105

National Teachers Academy 600/PK-8
55 W Cermak Rd 60616 773-534-9970
Isaac Castelaz, prin. Fax 534-9971

Neil ES 300/PK-8
8555 S Michigan Ave 60619 773-535-3000
Tawane Knox, prin. Fax 535-3010

Nettelhorst ES 800/PK-8
3252 N Broadway St 60657 773-534-5810
Yasmeen Muhammad-Leonard, prin. Fax 534-5776

Newberry Math Science Academy 600/PK-8
700 W Willow St 60614 773-534-8000
Linda Foley, prin. Fax 534-8018

New Field ES 600/PK-4
1707 W Morse Ave 60626 773-534-2760
Carlos Patino, prin. Fax 534-2773

New Sullivan ES 500/PK-8
8331 S Mackinaw Ave 60617 773-535-6585
Kathy McCoy, prin. Fax 535-6561

Nicholson Technology Academy 600/PK-8
6006 S Peoria St 60621 773-535-3285
Derrick Kimbrough, prin. Fax 535-3443

Nightingale ES 1,400/PK-8
5250 S Rockwell St 60632 773-535-9270
Margaret Kouretsos, prin. Fax 535-0430

Ninos Heroes Academic Center 400/PK-8
8344 S Commercial Ave 60617 773-535-6694
Rashone Franklin, prin. Fax 535-6673

Nixon ES 1,100/PK-6
2121 N Keeler Ave 60639 773-534-4375
Sherly Chavarria, prin. Fax 534-4539

Nkrumah Academy 200/K-8
314 W 108th St 60628 773-568-8000
Monique Whittington, prin. Fax 568-8749

Nobel ES 800/PK-8
4127 W Hirsch St 60651 773-534-4365
Manuel Adrianzen, prin. Fax 534-4369

North River ES 400/PK-8
4416 N Troy St 60625 773-534-0590
Jamie Sanchez, prin. Fax 534-0597

Northwest MS 700/6-8
5252 W Palmer St 60639 773-534-3250
Margaret Byrne, prin. Fax 534-3251

Norwood Park ES 400/PK-8
5900 N Nina Ave 60631 773-534-1198
Ryan Coors, prin. Fax 534-1178

Ogden ES 800/PK-5
24 W Walton St 60610 773-534-8110
Dr. Michael Beyer, prin. Fax 534-8017

Oglesby ES 500/PK-8
7646 S Green St 60620 773-535-3060
Kimberly Henderson, prin. Fax 535-3390

O'Keefe ES 600/PK-8
6940 S Merrill Ave 60649 773-535-0600
Melissa Capinegro, prin. Fax 535-0611

Onahan ES 700/PK-8
6634 W Raven St 60631 773-534-1180
Karen Koegler, prin. Fax 534-1163

Oriole Park ES 700/PK-8
5424 N Oketo Ave 60656 773-534-1201
Tim Riff, prin. Fax 534-1066

Orozco ES 600/PK-8
1940 W 18th St 60608 773-534-7215
Efrain Martinez, prin. Fax 534-7329

Ortiz de Dominguez ES 700/PK-2
3000 S Lawndale Ave 60623 773-534-1600
Angelica Herrera-Vest, prin. Fax 534-1415

Otis ES 600/PK-8
525 N Armour St, 773-534-7665
Nancy Mendez, prin. Fax 534-7672

O'Toole ES 400/PK-8
6550 S Seeley Ave 60636 773-535-9040
King Hall, prin. Fax 535-9093

Owen Scholastic Academy 300/K-8
8247 S Christiana Ave 60652 773-535-9330
Dr. Stanley Griggs, prin. Fax 535-9496

Owens Community Academy 500/PK-8
12302 S State St 60628 773-535-5475
Melody Seaton, prin. Fax 535-5483

Palmer ES 900/PK-8
5051 N Kenneth Ave 60630 773-534-3704
Jennifer Dixon, prin. Fax 534-3771

Parker Community Academy 700/PK-8
6800 S Stewart Ave 60621 773-535-3375
Rufina Brown, prin. Fax 535-3336

Park Manor ES 400/PK-8
7037 S Rhodes Ave 60637 773-535-3070
Lachao Merrell, prin. Fax 535-3273

Parkside Community Academy 300/PK-8
6938 S East End Ave 60649 773-535-0940
Cedric Nolen, prin. Fax 535-0966

Pasteur ES 1,200/PK-8
5825 S Kostner Ave 60629 773-535-2270
Gerardo Trujillo, prin. Fax 535-2235

Peck ES 1,600/PK-8
3826 W 58th St 60629 773-535-2450
Okab Hassan, prin. Fax 535-2228

Peirce S of International Studies 1,000/PK-8
1423 W Bryn Mawr Ave 60660 773-534-2440
Lorianne Zaimi, prin. Fax 534-2577

Penn ES 400/PK-8
1616 S Avers Ave 60623 773-534-1665
Dr. Sherryl Moore-Ollie, prin. Fax 534-1673

Perez ES 300/PK-8
1241 W 19th St 60608 773-534-7650
Jessica Johnson, prin. Fax 534-7621

Pershing Magnet S for the Humanities 400/PK-8
3200 S Calumet Ave 60616 773-534-9272
Safurat Giwa, prin. Fax 534-9277

Peterson ES 900/PK-8
5510 N Christiana Ave 60625 773-534-5070
Kate Kane, prin. Fax 534-5077

Piccolo ES 500/PK-8
1040 N Keeler Ave 60651 773-534-4425
Michael Abello, prin. Fax 534-4248

Pickard ES 600/PK-8
2301 W 21st Pl 60608 773-535-7280
Rigo Hernandez, prin. Fax 535-7199

Pilsen Community Academy 400/PK-8
1420 W 17th St 60608 773-534-7675
Leanne Hightower, prin. Fax 534-7797

Pirie Fine Arts & Academic Center 400/PK-6
650 E 85th St 60619 773-535-3435
Senalda Grady, prin. Fax 535-3405

Plamondon ES 200/K-8
2642 W 15th Pl 60608 773-534-1789
Althea Hammond, prin. Fax 534-1858

Poe Classical ES 200/K-6
10538 S Langley Ave 60628 773-535-5525
Eric Dockery, prin. Fax 535-5213

Portage Park ES 1,100/PK-8
5330 W Berteau Ave 60641 773-534-3576
Maureen Ready-Ghuneim, prin. Fax 534-3558

Powell ES 600/K-8
7511 S South Shore Dr 60649 773-535-6650
Sheila Barlow, prin. Fax 535-6602

Prescott ES 300/PK-8
1632 W Wrightwood Ave 60614 773-534-5505
Erin Roche, prin. Fax 534-5542

Prieto Math & Science Academy 1,000/PK-8
2231 N Central Ave 60639 773-534-0210
Mariel Laureano, prin. Fax 534-0211

Pritzker S 700/PK-8
2009 W Schiller St 60622 773-534-4415
Dr. Joenile Albert-Reese, prin. Fax 534-4634

Prussing ES 700/PK-8
4650 N Menard Ave 60630 773-534-3460
George Chipain, prin. Fax 534-3530

Pulaski International S of Chicago 900/PK-8
2230 W McLean Ave 60647 773-534-4391
Diana Racasi, prin. Fax 534-4392

Pullman ES 300/PK-8
11311 S Forrestville Ave 60628 773-535-5395
Dr. Julious Lawson, prin. Fax 535-5393

Randolph S 500/PK-8
7316 S Hoyne Ave 60636 773-535-9015
Elizabeth Meyers, prin. Fax 535-9455

Ravenswood ES 500/PK-8
4332 N Paulina St 60613 773-534-5525
Nathan Manaen, prin. Fax 534-5775

Ray ES 700/PK-8
5631 S Kimbark Ave 60637 773-535-0970
Megan Thole, prin. Fax 535-0842

Reavis ES 300/PK-8
834 E 50th St 60615 773-535-1060
Gail King, prin. Fax 535-1032

Reilly ES 1,100/PK-8
3650 W School St 60618 773-534-5250
Ken Fitzner, prin. Fax 534-5169

Reinberg ES 800/PK-8
3425 N Major Ave 60634 773-534-3465
Edwin Loch, prin. Fax 534-3798

Revere ES 300/PK-8
1010 E 72nd St 60619 773-535-0618
Veronica Thompson, prin. Fax 535-0614

Richardson MS 1,200/5-8
6018 S Karlov Ave 60629 773-535-8640
Martin Anderson, prin.

Robinson ES 100/PK-3
4225 S Lake Park Ave 60653 773-535-1777
Relanda Hobbs, prin. Fax 535-1727

Rogers ES 700/PK-8
7345 N Washtenaw Ave 60645 773-534-2125
Christine Jabbari, prin. Fax 534-2193

Ruggles ES 400/PK-8
7831 S Prairie Ave 60619 773-535-3085
Stephen Parker, prin. Fax 535-3129

Ruiz ES 900/PK-8
2410 S Leavitt St 60608 773-535-4825
Dana Butler, prin. Fax 535-7140

Ryder Math & Science S 400/PK-8
8716 S Wallace St 60620 773-535-3843
Joyce Bristow, prin. Fax 535-3883

Sabin Magnet S 600/K-8
2216 W Hirsch St 60622 773-534-4491
Gwen Kasper-Couty, prin. Fax 534-4511

Salazar Bilingual Center 400/PK-8
160 W Wendell St 60610 773-534-8310
Lourdes Jimenez, prin. Fax 534-8313

Sandoval ES 1,100/PK-5
5534 S Saint Louis Ave 60629 773-535-0457
Wilma David, prin. Fax 535-0467

Saucedo Scholastic Academy 1,300/PK-8
2850 W 24th Blvd 60623 773-534-1770
Virginia Rivera, prin. Fax 534-1356

Sauganash ES 500/K-8
6040 N Kilpatrick Ave 60646 773-534-3470
Christine Munns, prin. Fax 534-3707

Sawyer ES 1,800/K-8
5248 S Sawyer Ave 60632 773-535-0440
Nelly Robles, prin. Fax 535-0445

Sayre Language Academy 600/PK-8
1850 N Newland Ave 60707 773-534-3351
Folasade Adekunle, prin. Fax 534-3394

Scammon ES 900/PK-8
4201 W Henderson St 60641 773-534-3475
Sandra Carlson, prin. Fax 534-3516

Schmid ES 200/PK-8
9755 S Greenwood Ave 60628 773-535-6235
Andrea Black, prin. Fax 535-6092

Schubert ES 1,000/PK-5
2727 N Long Ave 60639 773-534-3080
Therese Cannova, prin. Fax 534-3079

Seward ES 800/PK-8
4600 S Hermitage Ave 60609 773-535-4890
Nora Cadenas, prin. Fax 535-4884

Sheridan Math & Science Academy 500/K-8
533 W 27th St 60616 773-534-9120
John O'Connell, prin. Fax 534-9124

Sherman ES 400/PK-8
1000 W 52nd St 60609 773-535-1757
Mellodie Brown, prin. Fax 535-0343

Sherwood ES 400/PK-8
245 W 57th St 60621 773-535-0829
Alice Buzanis, prin. Fax 535-0872

Shields ES 1,000/PK-4
4250 S Rockwell St 60632 773-535-7285
Michael Pacourek, prin. Fax 535-6829

Shields MS 700/5-8
2611 W 48th St 60632 773-535-7115
Peter Auffant, prin. Fax 535-7296

Shoesmith ES 300/K-6
1330 E 50th St 60615 773-535-1764
Sabrina Gates, prin. Fax 535-1877

Shoop Academy of Math-Science Tech 500/PK-8
11140 S Bishop St 60643 773-535-2715
Salik Mukarram, prin. Fax 535-2714

Skinner North Classical S 400/K-8
640 W Scott St 60610 773-534-8500
Ethan Netterstrom, prin. Fax 534-8502

Skinner West Classical S 900/PK-8
1260 W Adams St 60607 773-534-7790
Deborah Clark, prin. Fax 534-7879

Smith ES 300/PK-8
744 E 103rd St 60628 773-535-5689
Tiffany Brown, prin. Fax 535-5101

Smyser ES 1,000/PK-8
4310 N Melvina Ave 60634 773-534-3711
Jerry Travlos, prin. Fax 534-3555

Smyth ES 500/PK-8
1059 W 13th St 60608 773-534-7180
Ronald Whitmore, prin. Fax 534-7127

Solomon ES 400/PK-8
6206 N Hamlin Ave 60659 773-534-5226
Chris Gamble, prin. Fax 534-5167

Southeast Area ES 400/PK-6
3930 E 105th 60617 773-535-8040
Kenya Underwood, prin. Fax 535-8020

South Loop ES 900/PK-8
1212 S Plymouth Ct 60605 773-534-8690
Tara Shelton, prin. Fax 534-8689

South Shore Fine Arts Academy 500/PK-8
1415 E 70th St 60637 773-535-8340
Vicki Lee, prin. Fax 535-8341

Spencer Technology Academy 800/PK-8
214 N Lavergne Ave 60644 773-534-6150
Kelly Dean, prin. Fax 534-6239

Spry Community S 700/PK-8
2400 S Marshall Blvd 60623 773-534-1700
Elvia Garcia-Graham, prin. Fax 534-1688

Stagg ES 600/PK-8
7424 S Morgan St 60621 773-535-3565
Miyoshi Knox, prin. Fax 535-3564

STEM Magnet Academy 300/K-8
1522 W Fillmore St 60607 773-534-7300
Maria McManus, prin. Fax 534-7302

Stevenson ES 1,300/PK-8
8010 S Kostner Ave 60652 773-535-2280
Paul O'Toole, prin. Fax 535-2339

Stone Scholastic Academy 600/K-8
6239 N Leavitt St 60659 773-534-2045
Barbara Onofrio, prin. Fax 534-2092

Stowe ES 800/PK-8
3444 W Wabansia Ave 60647 773-534-4175
Jimmy Lugo, prin. Fax 534-4167

Suder Montessori Magnet S 400/PK-8
2022 W Washington Blvd 60612 773-534-7685
Alexander Phillips, prin. Fax 534-7933

Sumner Community Academy 400/PK-8
4320 W 5th Ave 60624 773-534-6730
Fatima Cooke, prin. Fax 534-6736

Sutherland ES 700/K-8
10015 S Leavitt St 60643 773-535-2580
Eric Steinmiller, prin. Fax 535-2621

Swift ES 700/PK-8
5900 N Winthrop Ave 60660 773-534-2695
Salvatore Cannella, prin. Fax 534-2575

Talcott ES 500/PK-8
1840 W Ohio St 60622 773-534-7130
Olimpia Bahena, prin. Fax 534-7126

Talman ES 400/PK-8
5450 S Talman Ave 60632 773-535-7850
Jacqueline Medina, prin. Fax 535-7857

Tanner ES 400/PK-8
7350 S Evans Ave 60619 773-535-3870
Nicole White, prin. Fax 535-3874

Tarkington S of Excellence 1,100/PK-8
3330 W 71st St 60629 773-535-4700
Jessica Reisner, prin. Fax 535-4713

Taylor ES 600/PK-8
9912 S Avenue H 60617 773-535-6240
Dr. William Truesdale, prin. Fax 535-6232

Telpochcalli ES 300/PK-8
2832 W 24th Blvd 60623 773-534-1402
Tamara Witzl, prin. Fax 534-1404

Thomas ECC 200/PK-PK
3625 S Hoyne Ave 60609 773-535-4088
Mary Richardson, prin. Fax 535-4085

Thorp ES 400/PK-8
8914 S Buffalo Ave 60617 773-535-6250
Sharrone Travis, prin. Fax 535-6582

Thorp Scholastic Academy 800/K-8
6024 W Warwick Ave 60634 773-534-3640
Efren Toledo, prin. Fax 534-3639

Till Math & Science Academy 400/PK-8
6543 S Champlain Ave 60637 773-535-0570
Terea Peoples, prin. Fax 535-0598

Tilton ES 400/PK-8
223 N Keeler Ave 60624 773-534-6746
Sylvia Hodge, prin. Fax 826-1915

Tonti ES 1,100/PK-5
5815 S Homan Ave 60629 773-535-9280
Gerardo Arriaga, prin. Fax 535-0470

Turner-Drew Language Academy 400/K-8
9300 S Princeton Ave 60620 773-535-5720
Dr. Sabrina Jackson, prin. Fax 535-5203

Twain ES 1,200/PK-8
5134 S Lotus Ave 60638 773-535-2290
Laura Paull, prin. Fax 535-2248
Vanderpoel Magnet ES 300/K-8
9510 S Prospect Ave 60643 773-535-2690
Kia Banks, prin. Fax 535-2677
Volta ES 1,000/PK-8
4950 N Avers Ave 60625 773-534-5080
Roger Johnson, prin. Fax 534-5280
Von Linne ES 600/PK-8
3221 N Sacramento Ave 60618 773-534-5262
Renee Mackin, prin. Fax 534-5287
Wacker ES 200/PK-8
9746 S Morgan St 60643 773-535-2821
Ekaterini Panagakis, prin. Fax 535-2829
Wadsworth ES 500/PK-8
6650 S Ellis Ave 60637 773-535-0730
Rashid Shabazz, prin. Fax 535-0743
Walsh ES 400/PK-8
2015 S Peoria St 60608 773-534-7950
Martin Ryczek, prin. Fax 534-7168
Ward ES 500/PK-8
2701 S Shields Ave 60616 773-534-9050
Karen Anderson, prin. Fax 534-9044
Ward ES 700/PK-8
646 N Lawndale Ave 60624 773-534-6440
Rhea Bush, prin. Fax 534-6718
Warren ES 300/PK-8
9239 S Jeffery Ave 60617 773-535-6625
Margaret Snyder, prin. Fax 535-6698
Washington ES 800/PK-8
3611 E 114th St 60617 773-535-5010
Sergio Ramirez, prin. Fax 535-5124
Washington ES 500/PK-8
9130 S University Ave 60619 773-535-6225
Sherri Walker, prin. Fax 535-6277
Waters ES 600/K-8
4540 N Campbell Ave 60625 773-534-5090
Titia Crespo, prin. Fax 534-5087
Webster ES 300/PK-8
4055 W Arthington St 60624 773-534-6925
Khalid Oluewu, prin. Fax 534-6949
Wells Preparatory Academy 500/PK-8
249 E 37th St 60653 773-535-1204
Jeffery White, prin. Fax 535-1267
Wentworth ES 600/PK-8
1340 W 71st St 60636 773-535-3394
Cynthia Hughes-Hannah, prin. Fax 535-3434
Wescott ES 400/PK-8
409 W 80th St 60620 773-535-3090
Monique Dockery, prin. Fax 535-3099
West Park Academy 600/PK-8
1425 N Tripp Ave 60651 773-534-4940
Martha Irizarry, prin. Fax 534-4945
West Ridge ES 700/PK-8
6700 N Whipple St 60645 773-534-8250
A. Lambrinides-Sofios, prin. Fax 534-8251
Whistler ES 300/PK-8
11533 S Ada St 60643 773-535-5560
Tiffany Phinn, prin. Fax 535-5589
White Career Academy 200/PK-8
1136 W 122nd St 60643 773-535-5672
Maya Sadder, prin. Fax 535-5644
Whitney ES 1,100/PK-8
2815 S Komensky Ave 60623 773-534-1560
Jorge Ruiz, prin. Fax 534-1567
Whittier ES 300/PK-8
1900 W 23rd St 60608 773-535-4590
Antonio Acevedo, prin. Fax 535-4818
Wildwood World Magnet S 400/K-8
6950 N Hiawatha Ave 60646 773-534-1188
Mary Beth Cunat, prin. Fax 534-1144
Woodlawn Community ES 200/PK-6
6657 S Kimbark Ave 60637 773-535-0801
Lawanda Bell, prin. Fax 535-0773
Woodson South ES 400/PK-8
4414 S Evans Ave 60653 773-535-1280
Tamara Littlejohn, prin. Fax 535-1390
Yates ES 700/PK-8
1839 N Richmond St 60647 773-534-4550
Israel Perez, prin. Fax 534-4517
Young ES 1,100/PK-8
1434 N Parkside Ave 60651 773-534-6200
Crystal Bell, prin. Fax 534-6203
Zapata Academy 900/PK-8
2728 S Kostner Ave 60623 773-534-1390
Ruth Garcia, prin. Fax 534-1398

Academy of St. Benedict the African 200/PK-8
6020 S Laflin St 60636 773-776-3316
Patricia Murphy, prin. Fax 776-3715
Akiba-Schechter Jewish Day S 300/PK-8
5235 S Cornell Ave 60615 773-493-8880
Dr. Eliezer Jones, head sch Fax 493-9377
Alphonsus Academy 400/PK-8
1439 W Wellington Ave 60657 773-348-4629
Dr. Casimer Badynee, prin. Fax 348-4829
Ancona S 200/PK-8
4770 S Dorchester Ave 60615 773-924-2356
Ari Frede, head sch Fax 924-8905
Annunciata S 200/PK-8
3750 E 112th St 60617 773-375-5711
Edward Renas, prin. Fax 375-5704
Bennett Day S PK-12
955 W Grand Ave, 312-236-6388
Kate Cicchelli, prin. Fax 268-7383
Bethesda International Academy 100/PK-8
6803 N Campbell Ave 60645 773-743-0800
Patricia Grunde, prin. Fax 743-4415
Brickton Montessori S 100/PK-8
8622 W Catalpa Ave 60656 773-714-0646
Cheryl LaCost, head sch Fax 714-9361
Bridgeport Catholic Academy 300/PK-8
3700 S Lowe Ave 60609 773-376-6223
Caroline Koster, prin. Fax 376-3864
British S of Chicago 800/PK-12
814 W Eastman St, 773-506-2097
Michael Horton, prin.
Cardinal Bernardin ECC 200/PK-3
1651 W Diversey Pkwy 60614 773-975-6330
Barbara Labotka, prin. Fax 975-6339
Catalyst School Circle-Rock 300/PK-8
118 N Central Ave 60644 773-854-1615
Cathy Strokosch, prin. Fax 854-1646
Cheder Lubavitch Hebrew Girls S 100/1-8
2809 W Jarvis Ave 60645 773-465-0863
Leah Perlstein, prin. Fax 973-2119
Chicago City Day S 300/PK-8
541 W Hawthorne Pl 60657 773-327-0900
Galeta Kaar Clayton, head sch Fax 327-6381
Chicago Grammar S 100/PK-8
900 N Franklin St Ste 104 60610 312-944-5600
Chicago Jesuit Academy 100/5-8
5058 W Jackson Blvd 60644 773-638-6103
Thomas Beckley, prin. Fax 638-6107
Chicago Jewish Day S 100/PK-8
5959 N Sheridan Rd 60660 773-271-2700
Judy Finkelstein-Taff, head sch Fax 271-2570
Chicago SDA Academy 100/PK-8
7008 S Michigan Ave 60637 773-873-3005
Marie Smith, prin. Fax 873-6953
Chicago Waldorf S 400/PK-12
1300 W Loyola Ave 60626 773-465-2662
Luke Goodwin, admin. Fax 465-6648
Chicago West Side Christian S 100/PK-8
1240 S Pulaski Rd 60623 773-542-0663
Mary Post, admin. Fax 542-0664
Children of Peace-Holy Trinity S 200/PK-8
1900 W Taylor St Ste 1 60612 312-243-8186
Clair Zaffaroni, prin. Fax 243-8479
Christ the King Lutheran S 50/PK-8
3701 S Lake Park Ave 60653 773-536-1984
Geraldine Brazeal, admin. Fax 536-2387
Christ the King S 300/PK-8
9240 S Hoyne Ave 60643 773-779-3329
Dr. Ann Marie Riordan, prin. Fax 779-3390
Cook S 500/PK-8
226 W Schiller St 60610 312-266-3381
Dr. Michael Roberts, hdmstr. Fax 266-3616
CS Academy College Prep S 100/PK-12
1443 W 63rd St 60636 312-675-8691
Domonique Ziegler, admin. Fax 737-4865
Dachs Bais Yaakov S 500/PK-8
3200 W Peterson Ave 60659 773-583-5329
Ahuva Wainhaus, prin. Fax 583-6530
Daystar S 200/PK-8
1550 S State St 60605 312-791-0001
Destiny Christian ES K-8
8221 S State St 60619 773-488-8788
Dr. Aaron McKenzie, prin. Fax 488-3594
Epiphany S 200/PK-8
4223 W 25th St 60623 773-762-1542
Scott Ernst, prin. Fax 762-2247
GEMS World Academy-Chicago PK-12
350 E South Water St 60601 312-809-8910
Andrew Sherman, head sch
Gloria Dei Lutheran S 50/PK-8
5259 S Major Ave 60638 773-581-5259
Steven Anderson, prin. Fax 767-4670
Grace Christian Academy 100/PK-8
4106 W 28th St 60623 773-762-1234
Carlo Giannotta, prin. Fax 762-4476
Grace English Lutheran S 50/PK-8
2725 N Laramie Ave 60639 773-637-2250
Vicki Helmling, lead tchr. Fax 637-1188
Holy Angels S 100/PK-8
750 E 40th St 60653 773-624-0727
Sean Stalling, prin. Fax 530-9003
Holy Family S 200/PK-8
3415 W Arthington St 60624 773-265-0550
Cheryl Collins, prin. Fax 265-0508
ICC Full Time S 100/PK-8
3333 W Peterson Ave 60659 773-267-6167
Ather Sultana, prin. Fax 267-6168
Immaculate Conception S 300/PK-8
1431 N North Park Ave 60610 773-944-0304
Katie Sullivan, prin. Fax 944-0695
Immaculate Conception S 200/K-8
8739 S Exchange Ave 60617 773-375-4674
Sr. Katia Alcantar, prin. Fax 375-3526
Immaculate Conception S 500/PK-8
7263 W Talcott Ave 60631 773-775-0545
Sue Canzoneri, prin. Fax 775-3822
Intercultural Montessori Language S 100/PK-6
114 S Racine Ave 60607 312-265-1514
Dr. Edina McGivern, dir.
Lake Shore S 200/PK-8
6759 N Greenview Ave 60626 773-561-6707
Farah Essa, dir. Fax 271-4564
Latin S of Chicago 1,100/PK-12
59 W North Blvd 60610 312-582-6000
Randall Dunn, head sch Fax 582-6011
Lycee Francais de Chicago 600/PK-12
1929 W Wilson Ave 60640 773-665-0066
Maternity BVM S 200/PK-8
1537 N Lawndale Ave 60651 773-227-1140
Christina Molina, prin. Fax 227-2939
Midwestern Christian Academy 200/PK-8
3465 N Cicero Ave 60641 773-685-1106
Jeremy Riggs, prin. Fax 685-6541
Montessori Academy of Chicago 200/PK-8
1335 W Randolph St 60607 312-243-0977
Morgan Park Academy 400/PK-12
2153 W 111th St 60643 773-881-6700
Muhammad University of Islam 200/PK-8
7351 S Stony Island Ave 60649 773-643-0700
Jason Karriem, prin.
Near North Montessori S 500/PK-8
1434 W Division St, 773-384-1434
Audrey Perrott, dir. Fax 384-2711
North Park ES 200/PK-8
2017 W Montrose Ave 60618 773-327-3144
Dr. Randy Needlman, prin. Fax 327-0331
North Shore SDA Jr. Academy 100/PK-12
5220 N California Ave 60625 773-769-0733
Harley Peterson, prin. Fax 769-0928
Northside Catholic Academy 300/PK-4
6216 N Glenwood Ave 60660 773-743-6277
Christine Huzenis, prin. Fax 743-6174
Northside Catholic Academy 100/5-8
7318 N Oakley Ave 60645 773-271-2008
Christine Huzenis, prin. Fax 271-3101
Oakdale Christian Academy 300/PK-8
9440 S Vincennes Ave 60620 773-779-9440
Dr. Wytress Richardson, prin. Fax 779-9531
Old St. Mary's S 300/PK-8
1474 S Michigan Ave 60605 312-386-1560
Julie Martin, prin. Fax 386-1578
Our Lady of Grace S 200/PK-8
2446 N Ridgeway Ave 60647 773-342-0170
Sr. Rita Range, prin. Fax 342-5305
Our Lady of Guadalupe S 200/K-8
9050 S Burley Ave 60617 773-768-0999
Carl Ploense, prin. Fax 768-0529
Our Lady of Mt. Carmel Academy 200/PK-8
720 W Belmont Ave 60657 773-525-8779
Shane Staszcuk, prin. Fax 525-7810
Our Lady of Tepayac S 200/PK-8
2235 S Albany Ave 60623 773-522-0024
Patricia Krielaart, prin. Fax 522-4577
Our Lady of the Snows S 200/PK-8
4810 S Leamington Ave 60638 773-735-4810
Joyce Willenborg, prin. Fax 735-6495
Our Saviour Lutheran S 50/PK-K
7151 W Cornelia Ave 60634 773-736-1157
Rev. Chris Browne, admin. Fax 736-1120
Parker S 900/PK-12
330 W Webster Ave 60614 773-353-3000
Daniel Frank Ph.D., prin. Fax 549-4669
Pilgrim Lutheran S 200/PK-8
4300 N Winchester Ave 60613 773-477-4824
Chris Comella, prin. Fax 477-8996
Pope Francis Global Academy North Campus 400/PK-8
6040 W Ardmore Ave 60646 773-763-7080
Terrence O'Rourke, head sch Fax 775-3893
Pope Francis Global Academy South Campus 200/PK-8
6143 W Irving Park Rd 60634 773-736-8806
Terrence O'Rourke, head sch Fax 725-3461
Pope John Paul II Catholic S 200/PK-8
4325 S Richmond St 60632 773-523-6161
Deborah Coffey, prin. Fax 254-9194
Providence - St. Mel S 500/PK-12
119 S Central Park Blvd 60624 773-722-4600
Jeanette Butala, prin. Fax 722-9004
Pui Tak Christian S 200/PK-8
2301 S Wentworth Ave 60616 312-842-8546
Bonnie Ho M.Ed., prin. Fax 842-4304
Queen of All Saints S 600/PK-8
6230 N Lemont Ave 60646 773-736-0567
Kristina Reyes, prin. Fax 736-7142
Queen of Angels S 400/PK-8
4520 N Western Ave 60625 773-769-4211
Julia Kelly, prin. Fax 769-4289
Queen of the Universe S 200/PK-8
7130 S Hamlin Ave 60629 773-582-4266
Mary Porod, prin. Fax 585-7254
Ravenswood Baptist Christian S 100/K-12
4437 N Seeley Ave 60625 773-561-6576
Karl Engle, prin. Fax 561-3080
Rogers Park Montessori S 400/PK-8
1800 W Balmoral Ave 60640 773-271-1700
Fax 271-0771
Sacred Heart S 100/K-8
2926 E 96th St 60617 773-768-3728
Stephen Adams, prin. Fax 768-5034
Sacred Heart Schools 700/K-8
6250 N Sheridan Rd 60660 773-262-4446
Nat Wilburn, head sch Fax 262-6178
St. Agnes of Bohemia S 400/PK-8
2643 S Central Park Ave 60623 773-522-0143
Kaitlin Kysiak, prin. Fax 522-0132
St. Ailbe S 100/PK-8
9037 S Harper Ave 60619 773-734-1386
Alyssa Mostyn, prin. Fax 734-1440
St. Andrew S 400/PK-8
1710 W Addison St 60613 773-248-2500
Allen Ackermann, prin. Fax 248-2709
St. Angela S 500/PK-8
1332 N Massasoit Ave 60651 773-626-2655
Kurt Wittenberg, prin. Fax 626-8156
St. Ann S 200/PK-8
2211 W 18th Pl 60608 312-829-4153
Benny Morten, prin. Fax 829-4155
St. Barbara S 200/PK-8
2867 S Throop St 60608 312-326-6243
Nicole Nolazco, prin. Fax 842-7960
St. Barnabas S 400/PK-8
10121 S Longwood Dr 60643 773-445-7711
Elaine Gaffney, prin. Fax 445-9815
St. Bartholomew S 300/PK-8
4941 W Patterson Ave 60641 773-282-9373
Karen Rebhan-Csuk, prin. Fax 282-4757
St. Bede the Venerable S 500/PK-8
4440 W 83rd St 60652 773-884-2020
Sherry Stewart, prin. Fax 582-3366
St. Benedict Prep S 400/PK-8
3920 N Leavitt St 60618 773-463-6797
Rachel Gemo, admin. Fax 463-0782
St. Bruno S 200/PK-8
4839 S Harding Ave 60632 773-847-0697
Colleen Schrantz, prin. Fax 847-1620
St. Cajetan S 400/PK-8
2447 W 112th St 60655 773-474-7820
Michelle Nitsche, prin. Fax 474-7821
St. Christina S 500/PK-8
3333 W 110th St 60655 773-445-2969
Mary Stokes, prin. Fax 445-0444
St. Clement S 500/PK-8
2524 N Orchard St 60614 773-348-8212
Mari Jo Hanson, prin. Fax 348-4712
St. Constance S 200/PK-8
5841 W Strong St 60630 773-283-2311
Eva Panczyk, prin. Fax 283-3515

St. Daniel the Prophet S 600/PK-8
5337 S Natoma Ave 60638 773-586-1225
Holly Gross, prin. Fax 586-1232
St. Edward S 300/PK-8
4343 W Sunnyside Ave 60630 773-736-9133
Sr. Marie Michelle Hackett, prin. Fax 736-9280
St. Ethelreda S 200/PK-8
8734 S Paulina St 60620 773-238-1757
Denise Spells, prin. Fax 238-6059
St. Eugene S 300/PK-8
7930 W Foster Ave 60656 773-763-2235
Catherine Scotkovsky, prin. Fax 763-2775
St. Ferdinand S 300/PK-8
3131 N Mason Ave 60634 773-622-3022
Denise Akana, prin. Fax 622-2807
St. Francis Borgia S 200/PK-8
3535 N Panama Ave 60634 773-589-1000
Susan Betzolt, prin. Fax 589-0781
St. Gabriel S 200/PK-8
4500 S Wallace St 60609 773-268-6636
Steve Adams, prin. Fax 268-2501
St. Gall S 300/PK-8
5515 S Sawyer Ave 60629 773-737-3454
Caitlin Lee, prin. Fax 737-5592
St. Genevieve S 200/PK-8
4854 W Montana St 60639 773-237-7131
McKenna Corrigan, prin. Fax 237-7265
St. Helen S 400/PK-8
2347 W Augusta Blvd 60622 773-486-1055
Marianne Johnson, prin. Fax 235-3810
St. Hilary S 300/PK-8
5614 N Fairfield Ave 60659 773-561-5885
Kathleen Donovan, prin. Fax 561-6409
St. James Lutheran S 100/PK-8
2101 N Fremont St 60614 773-525-4990
Sheri Meyer M.A., prin. Fax 326-3645
St. Jane De Chantal S 300/PK-8
5201 S McVicker Ave 60638 773-767-1130
Nancy Andrasco, prin. Fax 767-1387
St. Jerome S 200/PK-8
2801 S Princeton Ave 60616 312-842-7668
John Segvich, prin. Fax 842-3506
St. John Berchmans S 300/PK-8
2511 W Logan Blvd 60647 773-486-1334
Margaret Roketenetz, prin. Fax 486-1782
St. John De La Salle Academy 200/PK-8
10212 S Vernon Ave 60628 773-785-2331
Philip Mesina, prin. Fax 785-3630
St. John Fisher S 700/PK-8
10200 S Washtenaw Ave 60655 773-445-4737
Sr. Jean McGrath, prin. Fax 233-3012
St. John's Lutheran S 200/PK-8
4939 W Montrose Ave 60641 773-736-1196
Douglas Markworth, prin. Fax 736-3614
St. Josaphat S 400/PK-8
2245 N Southport Ave 60614 773-549-0909
Marinel Mullins, prin. Fax 549-3127
St. Juliana S 500/PK-8
7400 W Touhy Ave 60631 773-631-2256
Marjorie Marshall, prin. Fax 631-1125
St. Luke Academy 100/PK-8
1500 W Belmont Ave 60657 773-472-3837
Donna Beck, prin. Fax 929-3910
St. Malachy S 300/PK-8
2252 W Washington Blvd 60612 312-733-2252
Bridgid Miller, prin. Fax 733-5703
St. Margaret of Scotland S 200/PK-8
9833 S Throop St 60643 773-238-1088
Kevin Powers, prin. Fax 238-1049
St. Mary of the Angels S 200/PK-8
1810 N Hermitage Ave 60622 773-486-0119
Beth Dolack, prin. Fax 486-0996
St. Mary of the Lake S 300/PK-8
1026 W Buena Ave 60613 773-281-0018
Christine Boyd, prin. Fax 281-0112
St. Mary of the Woods S 400/PK-8
6959 N Hiawatha Ave 60646 773-763-7577
Mary Yamoah, prin. Fax 763-4293
St. Mary Star of the Sea S 200/PK-8
6424 S Kenneth Ave 60629 773-767-6160
Candace Usauskas, prin. Fax 767-7077
St. Matthias S 300/PK-8
4910 N Claremont Ave 60625 773-784-0999
Sheila Klich, prin. Fax 784-3601
St. Monica Academy 400/PK-8
5115 N Mont Clare Ave 60656 773-631-7880
Raymond Coleman, prin. Fax 631-3266
St. Nicholas Cathedral S 100/PK-8
2200 W Rice St 60622 773-384-7243
Anna Cirilli, prin. Fax 384-0028
St. Nicholas of Tolentine S 300/PK-8
3741 W 62nd St 60629 773-735-0772
Dr. Mariagnes Menden, prin. Fax 735-5414
St. Paul Lutheran S 100/PK-8
7621 S Dorchester Ave 60619 773-721-1438
Dr. Robyn Jacks-DuBose, prin. Fax 721-1749
St. Paul Lutheran S 200/PK-8
5650 N Canfield Ave 60631 708-867-5044
Mark Wickboldt, dir. Fax 867-0083
St. Paul Lutheran S 100/PK-8
846 N Menard Ave 60651 773-378-6644
Glen Kuck, prin. Fax 378-7442
St. Philip Lutheran S 200/PK-8
2500 W Bryn Mawr Ave 60659 773-561-9830
Michael Welton, prin. Fax 561-9831
St. Philip Neri S 100/PK-8
2110 E 72nd St 60649 773-288-1138
Linda Sanders, prin. Fax 288-8252
St. Pius V S 200/PK-8
1919 S Ashland Ave 60608 312-226-1590
Nancy Nasko, prin. Fax 226-7265
St. Procopius S 200/PK-8
1625 S Allport St 60608 312-421-5135
Brian O'Rourke, prin. Fax 492-7822
St. Richard S 300/PK-8
5025 S Kenneth Ave 60632 773-582-8083
Michelle Napier, prin. Fax 582-8330

St. Robert Bellarmine S 300/PK-8
6036 W Eastwood Ave 60630 773-725-5133
Carrie Mijal, prin. Fax 725-7611
St. Sabina Academy 300/PK-8
7801 S Throop St 60620 773-483-5000
Helen Dumas, prin. Fax 483-0305
St. Stanislaus Kostka S 200/PK-8
1255 N Noble St, 773-278-4560
Michele Alday, prin. Fax 278-9097
St. Sylvester S 300/PK-8
3027 W Palmer Blvd 60647 773-772-5222
Allyn Doyle, prin. Fax 772-0352
St. Symphorosa S 300/PK-8
6125 S Austin Ave 60638 773-585-6888
Kathy Berry, prin. Fax 585-8411
St. Thecla S 200/PK-8
6323 N Newcastle Ave 60631 773-763-3380
Fr. Gene Dyer, admin. Fax 763-6151
St. Therese S 300/PK-8
247 W 23rd St 60616 312-326-2837
Phyllis Cavallone, prin. Fax 326-6068
St. Thomas of Canterbury S 300/PK-8
5525 N Magnolia Ave 60640 773-271-8655
Christine Boyd, prin. Fax 271-1624
St. Thomas the Apostle S 100/PK-8
5467 S Woodlawn Ave 60615 773-667-1142
Timothy Gallo, prin. Fax 753-7434
St. Viator S 200/PK-8
4140 W Addison St 60641 773-545-2173
Colleen Brewer, prin. Fax 794-1697
St. Walter S 200/PK-8
11741 S Western Ave 60643 773-445-8850
Sharon O'Toole, prin. Fax 445-0277
St. William S 200/PK-8
2559 N Sayre Ave 60707 773-637-5130
Peggy Forgione, prin. Fax 745-4208
Salem Christian S 200/PK-8
2018 N Richmond St 60647 773-227-5580
Hector Quintana, prin. Fax 227-8592
San Miguel MS 100/6-8
1954 W 48th St 60609 773-890-1481
Thaddeus Smith, prin. Fax 254-3382
Santa Lucia S 100/PK-8
3017 S Wells St 60616 312-326-1839
Eileen Sheedy, prin. Fax 326-1945
Tolton Catholic Academy 200/PK-8
7120 S Calumet Ave 60619 773-224-3811
Pamela Sherley, prin. Fax 224-3810
University of Chicago Lab S 1,800/PK-12
1362 E 59th St 60637 773-702-9450
Charlie Abelmann, dir. Fax 702-7455
Urban Prairie Waldorf S 100/1-8
1220 W Lexington St 60607 312-733-5337
Peggy Lofgren, admin.
Visitation S 200/PK-8
900 W Garfield Blvd 60609 773-373-5200
Sr. Jean Matijosaitis, prin. Fax 373-5201
Warde-Old St. Patrick's 400/PK-3
120 S Desplaines St 60661 312-466-0700
Michael Kennedy, head sch Fax 466-0711
Wonder Montessori S 50/PK-1
5644 N Pulaski Rd 60646 773-509-1296
Gwen Ku, dir. Fax 509-1392
Xavier Warde S 400/4-8
751 N State St 60654 312-466-0700
Michael Kennedy, head sch Fax 337-7180
Yeshiva Ohr Boruch 200/PK-8
2620 W Touhy Ave 60645 773-262-0885
Rabbi Moshe Unger, dean Fax 262-2016
Yeshivas Tiferes Tzvi 300/K-8
6317 N California Ave 60659 773-973-6150
Zell Anshe Emet Day S 500/PK-8
3751 N Broadway St 60613 773-281-1858
Noah S. Hartman, head sch Fax 281-4709

Chicago Heights, Cook, Pop. 29,817
Chicago Heights SD 170 3,200/PK-8
30 W 16th St 60411 708-756-4165
Thomas Amadio, supt. Fax 755-3536
www.sd170.com/
Garfield S 400/K-8
140 E 23rd St 60411 708-756-4150
Maricela Ruiz, prin. Fax 756-4643
Greenbriar S 300/K-8
101 W Greenbriar Ave 60411 708-756-4159
Joseph Taylor, prin. Fax 756-4645
Highland Preschool 200/PK-PK
25 W 16th Pl 60411 708-756-0008
Brandi Harvey, prin. Fax 756-1730
Jefferson S 300/K-8
176 E 11th St 60411 708-756-4162
Theresa Brink, prin. Fax 756-0132
Kennedy S 300/K-8
1013 Division St 60411 708-756-4830
Artis McCann, prin. Fax 481-0615
Lincoln-Gavin ES 100/K-4
1520 Center Ave 60411 708-756-4833
Cara Pastere, prin. Fax 758-5879
Roosevelt S 500/K-8
1345 Sunnyside Ave 60411 708-756-4836
Erin Salamon, prin. Fax 756-4646
Washington-McKinley S 600/K-8
25 W 16th Pl 60411 708-756-4843
Gretchen Sutherland, prin. Fax 756-1008
Wilson S 300/K-8
422 W 16th Pl 60411 708-756-4839
Tony Banks, prin. Fax 748-4413
Other Schools – See South Chicago Heights

Flossmoor SD 161 2,300/PK-8
41 E Elmwood Dr 60411 708-647-7000
Dana Smith, supt. Fax 754-2153
www.sd161.org
Serena Hills ES 300/K-5
255 Pleasant Dr 60411 708-647-7300
Dr. Shari Demitrowicz, prin. Fax 756-4465
Other Schools – See Flossmoor

Park Forest SD 163
Supt. — See Park Forest
Obama S of Leadership and STEM 400/4-8
401 Concord Dr 60411 708-668-9100
Ericka Patterson, prin. Fax 283-2358

Cornerstone Christian S 200/PK-8
PO Box 9 60412 708-756-3566
Alison Donald, prin. Fax 756-3678
Deer Creek Christian S 100/PK-8
330 W Highland Dr 60411 708-672-6200
Brian Verwolf, head sch Fax 898-0354
St. Agnes S 300/PK-8
1501 Chicago Rd 60411 708-756-2333
Matthew Lungaro, prin. Fax 709-2693

Chicago Ridge, Cook, Pop. 13,978
Chicago Ridge SD 127-5 1,500/PK-8
6135 108th St 60415 708-636-2000
Dr. Kevin B. Russell, supt. Fax 636-0916
www.crsd1275.org
Finley JHS 400/6-8
10835 Lombard Ave 60415 708-636-2005
Laura Grachan, prin. Fax 636-0045
Ridge Central ES 500/PK-5
10800 Lyman Ave 60415 708-636-2001
Megan Nothnagel, prin. Fax 636-0361
Ridge Lawn ES 600/PK-5
5757 105th St 60415 708-636-2002
Fran Setaro, prin. Fax 636-1062

Chillicothe, Peoria, Pop. 6,048
Illinois Valley Central Unit SD 321 1,700/PK-12
1300 W Sycamore St 61523 309-274-5418
Dr. Chad Allison, supt. Fax 274-5046
www.ivcschools.com/
Chillicothe Elementary Center & JHS 200/4-8
914 W Truitt Ave 61523 309-274-6266
Patrick Auge, prin. Fax 274-2010
South ES 400/PK-3
616 W Hickory St 61523 309-274-4841
Shaun Grant, prin. Fax 274-9715
Other Schools – See Mossville

St. Edwards S 100/PK-8
1221 N 5th St 61523 309-274-2994
Mike Domico, prin. Fax 274-4141

Chrisman, Edgar, Pop. 1,339
Edgar County CUSD 6 300/K-12
23231 IL Highway 1 61924 217-269-2513
James Acklin, supt. Fax 269-3231
www.chrisman.k12.il.us
Chrisman ES 100/K-5
111 N Pennsylvania St 61924 217-269-2022
Kelly Schluter, prin. Fax 269-3222
Chrisman-Scottland JHS 100/6-8
23231 IL Highway 1 61924 217-269-3980
Cole Huber, prin. Fax 269-3231

Christopher, Franklin, Pop. 2,363
Christopher Unit SD 99 600/PK-12
1 Bearcat Dr 62822 618-724-9461
Richard Towers, supt. Fax 724-9400
www.cpher.frnkln.k12.il.us
Christopher ES, 501 S Snider St 62822 400/PK-8
Roy Kirkpatrick, prin. 618-724-7604

Cicero, Cook, Pop. 83,518
Cicero SD 99 13,100/PK-8
5110 W 24th St 60804 708-863-4856
Rodolfo Hernandez, supt. Fax 652-8105
www.cicd99.edu
Burnham ES 1,100/K-6
1630 S 59th Ave 60804 708-652-9577
Jennifer Ferguson, prin. Fax 780-4441
Cicero East S 900/4-6
2324 S 49th Ave 60804 708-652-9440
Jill Miller, prin. Fax 780-4444
Cicero West ES 1,000/PK-3
4937 W 23rd St 60804 708-780-4487
Veronica Morales, prin. Fax 656-2937
Columbus East S 600/3-6
3100 S 54th Ave 60804 708-652-6085
Donata Heppner, prin. Fax 780-4446
Columbus West ES 900/PK-6
5425 W 31st St 60804 708-780-4482
Heriberto Garcia, prin. Fax 780-0735
Drexel ES 600/PK-6
5407 W 36th St 60804 708-652-5532
Luis Illa, prin. Fax 780-4449
Goodwin ES 700/PK-6
2625 S Austin Blvd 60804 708-652-5500
Luis Salto, prin. Fax 780-4452
Liberty ES 800/PK-3
4946 W 13th St 60804 708-780-4475
James Letsos, prin. Fax 780-7062
Lincoln ES 900/PK-6
3545 S 61st Ave 60804 708-652-8889
Gretchen Gorgal, prin. Fax 780-4454
McKinley ES 300/PK-2
5900 W 14th St 60804 708-652-8890
Robert Monech, prin. Fax 780-4458
Roosevelt S 700/3-6
1500 S 50th Ave 60804 708-652-7833
Jill Heyes, prin. Fax 780-4461
Unity JHS 2,700/7-8
2115 S 54th Ave 60804 708-863-8268
Nichole Gross, prin. Fax 656-5652
Warren Park ES 300/PK-6
1225 S 60th Ct 60804 708-780-2299
Raquel Jenke, prin. Fax 780-2298
Wilson ES 900/K-6
2310 S 57th Ave 60804 708-652-2552
Katie Hedrich, prin. Fax 780-4468
Woodbine ES 400/PK-2
3003 S 50th Ct 60804 708-652-8884
Kate Lyman, prin. Fax 780-4470

Our Lady of Charity S — 300/PK-8
3620 S 57th Ct 60804 — 708-652-0262
Lynn LeTourneau, prin. — Fax 652-0601
St. Frances of Rome S — 300/PK-8
1401 S Austin Blvd 60804 — 708-652-2277
Glenn Purpura, prin. — Fax 780-6360

Cisne, Wayne, Pop. 671
North Wayne CUSD 200 — 500/PK-12
PO Box 235 62823 — 618-673-2151
David Reavis, supt. — Fax 673-2152
Cisne MS — 100/5-8
PO Box 69 62823 — 618-673-2156
David Reavis, prin. — Fax 673-2152
Other Schools – See Johnsonville, Mount Erie

Cissna Park, Iroquois, Pop. 841
Cissna Park CUSD 6 — 300/K-12
511 N 2nd St 60924 — 815-457-2171
Dr. Daniel Hylbert, supt. — Fax 457-3033
www.cissnaparkschools.org
Cissna Park ES — 100/K-5
511 N 2nd St 60924 — 815-457-2171
Bethanie Marshall, prin. — Fax 457-3033
Cissna Park JHS — 100/6-8
511 N 2nd St 60924 — 815-457-2171
Mark Portwood, prin. — Fax 457-3033

Clarendon Hills, DuPage, Pop. 8,292
CCSD 181 — 4,000/PK-8
115 55th St 60514 — 630-861-4900
Dr. Don White, supt. — Fax 887-1079
www.d181.org
Clarendon Hills MS — 700/6-8
301 Chicago Ave 60514 — 630-861-4800
Griffin Sonntag, prin. — Fax 887-4267
Prospect ES — 400/K-5
130 N Prospect Ave 60514 — 630-861-4400
Anne Kryger, prin. — Fax 655-9721
Walker ES — 300/K-5
120 Walker Ave 60514 — 630-861-4600
Eric Chisausky, prin. — Fax 887-0387
Other Schools – See Burr Ridge, Hinsdale

Maercker SD 60
Supt. — See Westmont
Holmes ES — 500/PK-2
5800 Holmes Ave 60514 — 630-515-4810
Dominic Sepich, prin. — Fax 515-4815

Notre Dame S — 200/PK-8
66 Norfolk Ave 60514 — 630-323-1642
Mary Ann Feeney, prin. — Fax 654-3255
Seton Montessori S — 300/PK-6
5728 Virginia Ave 60514 — 630-655-1066
Jennifer Nolan, head sch — Fax 654-0182

Clay City, Clay, Pop. 956
Clay City CUSD 10 — 300/PK-12
PO Box 542 62824 — 618-676-1431
Cathy Croy, supt. — Fax 676-1430
www.claycityschools.org
Clay City ES — 200/PK-5
PO Box 542 62824 — 618-676-1431
Ben Borries, prin. — Fax 676-1537
Clay City JHS — 100/6-8
PO Box 542 62824 — 618-676-1431
Ben Borries, prin. — Fax 676-1537

Clifton, Iroquois, Pop. 1,441
Central CUSD 4
Supt. — See Ashkum
Nash MS — 300/5-8
1134 E 3100 North Rd 60927 — 815-694-2323
Brandon Burke, prin. — Fax 694-2830

Clinton, DeWitt, Pop. 7,123
Clinton CUSD 15 — 1,200/PK-12
680 Illini Dr 61727 — 217-935-8321
Curt Nettles, supt. — Fax 935-2300
www.cusd15.org
Clinton ES — 2-5
680 Illini Dr 61727 — 217-935-6772
Sacha Young, prin. — Fax 935-8215
Clinton JHS — 500/6-8
701 Illini Dr 61727 — 217-935-2103
Drew Goebel, prin. — Fax 937-1918
Douglas ES — 200/PK-1
905 E Main St 61727 — 217-935-2987
Beth Wickenhauser, prin. — Fax 935-2525
Lincoln ES — 50/PK-1
407 S Jackson St 61727 — 217-935-6383
Beth Wickenhauser, prin. — Fax 935-3713

Coal City, Grundy, Pop. 5,546
Coal City CUSD 1 — 2,100/PK-12
550 S Carbon Hill Rd 60416 — 815-634-2287
Dr. Kent Bugg, supt. — Fax 634-8775
www.coalcity.k12.il.us
Coal City ECC — 400/PK-1
755 S Carbon Hill Rd 60416 — 815-634-5042
Christopher Spencer, prin. — Fax 634-0669
Coal City ES — 300/2-3
300 N Broadway St 60416 — 815-634-2334
Christopher Spencer, prin. — Fax 634-5036
Coal City IS — 300/4-5
305 E Division St 60416 — 815-634-2182
Tracy Carlson, prin. — Fax 634-4303
Coal City MS — 500/6-8
500 S Carbon Hill Rd 60416 — 815-634-5039
Travis Johnson, prin. — Fax 634-5049

Coal Valley, Rock Island, Pop. 3,687
Moline-Coal Valley CUSD 40
Supt. — See Moline
Bicentennial ES — 300/K-5
1004 1st St 61240 — 309-743-1614
Stephen Etheridge, prin. — Fax 799-7789

Cobden, Union, Pop. 1,130
Cobden Unit SD 17 — 600/PK-12
413 N Appleknocker St 62920 — 618-893-2313
Edwin Shoemate, supt. — Fax 893-4772
www.cobdenappleknockers.com
Cobden ES — 300/PK-5
413 N Appleknocker St 62920 — 618-893-2311
Edwin Shoemate, prin. — Fax 893-4742
Cobden JHS — 200/6-8
413 N Appleknocker St 62920 — 618-893-4031
Crystal Housman, prin. — Fax 893-2138

Coffeen, Montgomery, Pop. 680
Hillsboro CUSD 3
Supt. — See Hillsboro
Coffeen ES — 200/PK-5
PO Box 188 62017 — 217-534-2314
Francine Luckett, prin. — Fax 534-6088

Colchester, McDonough, Pop. 1,398
West Prairie CUSD 103 — 600/PK-12
204 S Hun St 62326 — 309-776-3180
Dr. Carol Kilver, supt. — Fax 776-3194
www.wp103.org
West Prairie MS — 200/5-8
600 S Hun St 62326 — 309-776-3220
Caitlin Watson, prin. — Fax 776-3115
West Prairie South ES — 200/PK-4
310 S Coal St 62326 — 309-776-3790
Jennifer Edholm, prin. — Fax 776-4267
Other Schools – See Good Hope

Colfax, McLean, Pop. 1,054
Ridgeview CUSD 19 — 500/PK-12
300 S Harrison St 61728 — 309-723-5111
Guy Gradert, supt. — Fax 723-6395
www.ridgeview19.org
Ridgeview ES — 300/PK-5
300 S Harrison St 61728 — 309-723-6531
Ben Hutley, prin. — Fax 723-4851

Collinsville, Madison, Pop. 25,082
Collinsville CUSD 10 — 6,900/PK-12
201 W Clay St 62234 — 618-346-6350
Robert Green, supt. — Fax 343-3657
www.kahoks.org
Collinsville MS — 1,000/7-8
9649 Collinsville Rd 62234 — 618-343-2100
Kimberly Jackson, prin. — Fax 343-2102
Dorris IS — 900/5-6
1841 Vandalia St 62234 — 618-346-6311
Kevin Stirnaman, prin. — Fax 343-2787
Jefferson ES — 100/K-4
152 Boskydells Dr 62234 — 618-346-6212
Chelsea Clark, prin. — Fax 343-2747
Kreitner ES — 400/PK-4
9000 College St 62234 — 618-346-6213
Dr. Todd Pettit, prin. — Fax 346-6375
Renfro ES — 600/PK-4
311 Camelot Dr 62234 — 618-346-6265
Laura Bauer, prin. — Fax 346-6379
Summit ES — 100/K-4
408 Willoughby Ln 62234 — 618-346-6222
Dr. Julie Haake, prin. — Fax 343-2755
Twin Echo ES — 200/PK-4
1937 S Morrison Ave 62234 — 618-346-6227
Dr. Julie Haake, prin. — Fax 343-2760
Webster ES — 400/PK-4
108 W Church St 62234 — 618-346-6301
Brad Snow, prin. — Fax 346-6368
Other Schools – See Caseyville, Maryville

Good Shepherd Lutheran S — 400/PK-8
1300 Belt Line Rd 62234 — 618-344-3153
Robert Mayhew, prin. — Fax 344-3156
Holy Cross Lutheran S — 200/PK-8
304 South St 62234 — 618-344-3145
Nancy Lochmann, prin. — Fax 344-1222
SS. Peter & Paul S — 200/PK-8
210 N Morrison Ave 62234 — 618-344-5450
Fax 344-5536

Colona, Henry, Pop. 5,015
Colona SD 190 — 500/PK-8
700 1st St 61241 — 309-792-1232
Carl Johnson, supt. — Fax 792-2249
www.csd190.com
Colona Grade S, 700 1st St 61241 — 500/PK-8
Michael Carlson, prin. — 309-792-1232

Columbia, Monroe, Pop. 9,637
Columbia CUSD 4 — 2,100/PK-12
5 Veterans Pkwy 62236 — 618-281-4772
Dr. Gina Segobiano, supt. — Fax 281-4570
www.columbia4.org
Columbia MS — 700/5-8
100 Eagle Dr 62236 — 618-281-4993
Kevin Moore, prin. — Fax 281-4964
Eagleview ES — 300/PK-1
113 S Rapp Ave 62236 — 618-281-4995
Brad Landgraf, prin. — Fax 281-4775
Parkview ES — 400/2-4
1 Veterans Pkwy 62236 — 618-281-4997
Brad Landgraf, prin. — Fax 281-3605

Immaculate Conception S — 300/PK-8
321 S Metter Ave 62236 — 618-281-5353
Michael Kish, prin. — Fax 281-6044

Concord, Morgan, Pop. 167
Triopia CUSD 27 — 400/PK-12
2204 Concord Arenzville Rd 62631 — 217-457-2283
Steve Eisenhauer, supt. — Fax 457-2297
www.triopiacusd27.org/
Triopia ES — 200/PK-6
2204 Concord Arenzville Rd 62631 — 217-457-2284
Jamie Hobrock, prin. — Fax 457-2277

Congerville, Woodford, Pop. 472
Eureka CUSD 140
Supt. — See Eureka
Congerville ES — 100/K-4
310 E Kauffman St 61729 — 309-448-2347
Randy Berardi, prin. — Fax 448-5122

Cornell, Livingston, Pop. 461
Cornell CCSD 426 — 100/K-8
300 N 7th St 61319 — 815-358-2216
Geoff Schoonover, supt. — Fax 358-2217
www.cornellgradeschool.org
Cornell ES — 100/K-8
300 N 7th St 61319 — 815-358-2216
Geoff Schoonover, prin. — Fax 358-2217

Cortland, DeKalb, Pop. 4,195
DeKalb CUSD 428
Supt. — See DeKalb
Cortland ES — 500/K-5
370 E Lexington Ave 60112 — 815-754-2360
Jennifer Hilliard, prin. — Fax 756-8426

Coulterville, Randolph, Pop. 930
Coulterville Unit SD 1 — 200/PK-12
PO Box 396 62237 — 618-758-2881
Karyn Albers, supt. — Fax 758-2330
Coulterville ES — 100/PK-5
PO Box 396 62237 — 618-758-2881
Brandon Taylor, prin. — Fax 758-2330
Coulterville JHS — 100/6-8
PO Box 396 62237 — 618-758-2881
Brandon Taylor, prin. — Fax 758-2330

Country Club Hills, Cook, Pop. 16,299
Country Club Hills SD 160 — 1,200/PK-8
4411 185th St 60478 — 708-957-6200
Dr. Sandra Thomas, supt. — Fax 957-8686
www.cch160.org
Meadowview ES — 400/4-6
4701 179th St 60478 — 708-957-6220
Dr. Antonia Hill, prin. — Fax 922-2673
Southwood MS — 300/7-8
18635 Lee St 60478 — 708-957-6230
Bridgette Harris, prin. — Fax 799-4033
Sykuta ES — 500/PK-3
4301 180th St 60478 — 708-957-6210
Vernecia Gee-Davis, prin. — Fax 799-2053

Prairie-Hills ESD 144
Supt. — See Markham
Nob Hill ES — 200/PK-5
3701 168th St 60478 — 708-335-9770
Christina Montgomery, prin. — Fax 335-4879

St. John Lutheran S — 100/PK-8
4231 183rd St 60478 — 708-799-7491
Lois Stewart, prin. — Fax 798-4193

Countryside, Cook, Pop. 5,842
La Grange SD 105
Supt. — See La Grange
Ideal ES — 300/K-6
9901 W 58th St 60525 — 708-482-2750
Timothy Sheldon, prin. — Fax 482-2729

Cowden, Shelby, Pop. 628
Cowden-Herrick Community USD 3A — 400/PK-12
PO Box 188 62422 — 217-783-2126
Darrell Gordon, supt. — Fax 783-2126
www.cowden-herrick.k12.il.us
Other Schools – See Herrick

Creal Springs, Williamson, Pop. 526
Marion CUSD 2
Supt. — See Marion
Adams S — 300/PK-8
15470 Lake of Egypt Rd 62922 — 618-996-2181
Kim Burns, prin. — Fax 996-3339

Crescent City, Iroquois, Pop. 613
Crescent Iroquois CUSD 249 — 100/K-8
PO Box 190 60928 — 815-683-2141
Jeffrey Alstadt, supt. — Fax 683-2219
sites.google.com/a/ccgshawks.net/mainpage
Crescent City ES — 100/K-8
PO Box 190 60928 — 815-683-2141
Jeffrey Alstadt, prin. — Fax 683-2219

Crest Hill, Will, Pop. 20,552
Chaney-Monge SD 88 — 300/PK-8
400 Elsie Ave, — 815-722-6673
Andy Siegfried, supt. — Fax 722-7814
www.chaneymonge.us
Chaney-Monge S — 300/PK-8
400 Elsie Ave, — 815-722-6673
Jacelynn Hall, prin. — Fax 722-7814

Richland SD 88A — 1,000/K-8
1919 Caton Farm Rd, — 815-744-7288
Joseph Simpkins, supt. — Fax 744-6196
www.d88a.org
Richland ES — 600/K-4
1919 Caton Farm Rd, — 815-744-6166
Dr. Kelly Whyte, prin. — Fax 725-8491
Richland JHS — 400/5-8
1919 Caton Farm Rd, — 815-744-6166
Dr. Kelly Whyte, prin. — Fax 725-8491

Joliet Montessori S — 100/PK-9
1600 Root St, — 815-741-4180
Heather Bonacorda, head sch — Fax 741-9753

Creston, Ogle, Pop. 654
Creston CCSD 161 — 100/K-8
PO Box 37 60113 — 815-384-3920
Curt Rheingans, supt. — Fax 384-3410
www.crestonschool.org
Creston ES — 100/K-8
PO Box 37 60113 — 815-384-3920
Emily Erickson-Betz, admin. — Fax 384-3410

Crestwood, Cook, Pop. 10,823
Cook County SD 130
Supt. — See Blue Island

Hale IS 200/4-5
5312 135th St 60445 708-385-3399
Churchill Daniels, prin. Fax 293-4088
Hale MS 400/6-8
5220 135th St 60445 708-385-6690
Kiwana Sanders, prin. Fax 385-2417
Hale PS 600/PK-3
5324 135th St 60445 708-385-4690
Alicia Barnes, prin. Fax 293-4087

Crete, Will, Pop. 8,098
Crete-Monee CUSD 201U 4,600/PK-12
1500 S Sangamon St 60417 708-367-8300
Dr. Nathaniel Cunningham, supt. Fax 672-2698
www.cm201u.org
Balmoral ES 500/K-5
1124 W New Monee Rd 60417 708-367-2500
Ghantel Perkins, prin. Fax 672-2613
Crete ES 400/K-5
435 North St 60417 708-367-8430
Erin Lane, prin. Fax 672-2645
Crete-Monee Early Learning Center 200/PK-PK
1500 S Sangamon St 60417 708-367-2770
Kelly Chesta, dir. Fax 672-2762
Other Schools – See Monee, Park Forest, University Park

Illinois Lutheran ES 200/PK-6
448 Cass St 60417 708-672-5969
Scott Sievert, prin. Fax 672-0353
Mother Teresa Catholic Academy 300/PK-8
24201 S Kings Rd 60417 708-672-3093
Anne Murray, prin. Fax 367-0640

Creve Coeur, Tazewell, Pop. 5,361
Creve Coeur SD 76 700/PK-8
400 N Highland St 61610 309-698-3600
Tony Whiston, supt. Fax 698-9827
www.cc76.k12.il.us
Lasalle ES 400/PK-4
300 N Highland St 61610 309-698-3605
Michael McCormick, prin. Fax 698-1499
Parkview JHS 300/5-8
800 Groveland St 61610 309-698-3610
Steven Johnson, prin. Fax 698-3902

Crystal Lake, McHenry, Pop. 40,164
Crystal Lake CCSD 47 7,800/PK-8
300 Commerce Dr 60014 815-459-6070
Kathy Hinz, supt. Fax 459-0263
www.d47.org
Beardsley MS 1,100/6-8
515 E Crystal Lake Ave 60014 815-477-5897
Cathy Alberth, prin. Fax 479-5119
Bernotas MS 1,000/6-8
170 N Oak St 60014 815-459-9210
Steve Scarfe, prin. Fax 479-5116
Canterbury ES 500/K-5
875 Canterbury Dr 60014 815-459-8180
Stacy Graff, prin. Fax 479-5117
Coventry ES 500/K-5
820 Darlington Ln 60014 815-459-4231
Matthew Grubbs, prin. Fax 479-5114
Glacier Ridge ES 600/PK-5
1120 Village Rd 60014 815-477-5518
John Jacobsen, prin. Fax 477-5547
Husmann ES 600/K-5
131 W Paddock St 60014 815-459-7114
Monica Petersen, prin. Fax 479-5110
Indian Prairie ES 600/K-5
651 Village Rd 60014 815-459-2124
Jodie Moss, prin. Fax 479-5118
Lundahl MS 800/6-8
560 Nash Rd 60014 815-459-5971
Angela Compere, prin. Fax 479-5113
North ES 600/K-5
500 W Woodstock St 60014 815-459-0122
Christina Moran, prin. Fax 479-5111
South ES 400/K-5
601 Golf Rd 60014 815-459-1143
Rachael Alt, prin. Fax 479-5112
West ES 600/K-5
100 Briarwood Dr 60014 815-459-2749
Beth Klinsky, prin. Fax 479-5115
Woods Creek ES 600/K-5
1100 Alexandra Blvd 60014 815-356-2720
Amy Marks, prin. Fax 356-2729

Prairie Grove Consolidated SD 46 800/K-8
3223 IL Route 176 60014 815-459-3023
Dr. John Bute, supt. Fax 356-0519
www.dist46.org
Prairie Grove ES 500/K-5
3223 IL Route 176 60014 815-459-3023
Martha Maggiore, prin. Fax 356-0519
Prairie Grove JHS 400/6-8
3225 IL Route 176 60014 815-459-3557
Martha Maggiore, prin. Fax 459-3785

Immanuel Lutheran S 200/PK-8
300 S Pathway Ct 60014 815-459-1444
Edward Bower, prin. Fax 459-1462
Lord and Savior Lutheran S 50/PK-8
9300 Ridgefield Rd 60012 815-455-4175
Joel Moeller, prin. Fax 455-9725
Montessori Pathways S 50/PK-6
133 Illinois St 60014 815-459-6727
Alena Baradzina, prin.
St. Thomas the Apostle S 400/PK-8
265 King St 60014 815-459-0496
Deanne Roy, prin. Fax 459-0591

Cuba, Fulton, Pop. 1,288
CUSD 3 Fulton County 500/PK-12
517 E Madison St 61427 309-785-5021
Angela Simmons, supt. Fax 785-5432
www.cusd3.net
Cuba ES 200/PK-5
652 E Main St 61427 309-785-8054
Angela Simmons, prin. Fax 785-5238
Cuba MS 100/6-8
20325 N State Route 97 61427 309-785-5023
Jeff Braun, prin. Fax 785-5102

Cypress, Johnson, Pop. 231
Cypress SD 64 100/PK-8
4580 Mt Pisgah Road 62923 618-657-2525
Kimberly Shoemaker, supt. Fax 657-2570
www.cypressgradeschool.org
Cypress S 100/PK-8
4580 Mt Pisgah Road 62923 618-657-2525
Kimberly Shoemaker, prin. Fax 657-2570

Dahlgren, Hamilton, Pop. 518
Hamilton County CUSD 10
Supt. — See Mc Leansboro
Dahlgren ES 200/K-6
PO Box 70 62828 618-736-2316
Christina Epperson, prin. Fax 736-2057

Dakota, Stephenson, Pop. 499
Dakota CUSD 201 800/PK-12
400 Campus Dr 61018 815-632-5682
Robert Prusator, supt. Fax 449-2322
www.dakota201.org
Dakota ES 500/PK-6
400 Campus Dr 61018 815-449-2852
Jeff Milburn, prin. Fax 449-2459

Dallas City, Hancock, Pop. 932
Dallas ESD 327 200/PK-8
921 Creamery Hill Rd 62330 217-852-3204
Dr. Ryan Olson, supt. Fax 852-3203
www.dcbulldogs.com
Dallas City S 200/PK-8
921 Creamery Hill Rd 62330 217-852-3201
Alissa Tucker, prin. Fax 852-3203

Dalzell, Bureau, Pop. 707
Dalzell SD 98 100/K-8
307 Chestnut St 61320 815-663-8821
Dr. Bruce Bauer, supt. Fax 664-4515
www.bhsroe.org/site/?page_id=39645
Dalzell ES 100/K-8
307 Chestnut St 61320 815-663-8821
Steve Parker, prin. Fax 664-4515

Damiansville, Clinton, Pop. 479
Damiansville SD 62 100/PK-8
101 E Main St 62215 618-248-5188
Mark Heuring, supt. Fax 248-5910
www.damiansvilleelem.com
Damiansville S 100/PK-8
101 E Main St 62215 618-248-5188
Mark Heuring, prin. Fax 248-5910

Danforth, Iroquois, Pop. 597
Iroquois West CUSD 10
Supt. — See Gilman
Iroquois West ES - Danforth 100/PK-K
PO Box 185 60930 815-269-2230
Ashley Carlson, prin. Fax 269-2521

Danvers, McLean, Pop. 1,140
Olympia CUSD 16
Supt. — See Stanford
Olympia North ES 300/PK-5
205 N State St 61732 309-963-4514
Ben Lee, prin. Fax 963-3969

Danville, Vermilion, Pop. 32,053
Danville CCSD 118 5,100/PK-12
516 N Jackson St 61832 217-444-1000
Dr. Alicia Geddis, supt. Fax 444-1006
www.danville118.org
Denman ES 700/K-4
930 Colfax Dr 61832 217-444-3200
Kimberly Pabst, prin. Fax 444-3204
Edison ES 300/K-4
2101 N Vermilion St 61832 217-444-3350
Mark Goodwin, prin. Fax 444-3354
Garfield ES 300/K-4
1101 N Gilbert St 61832 217-444-1750
Jessica Bradford, prin. Fax 444-1791
Liberty ES 400/K-4
20 E Liberty Ln 61832 217-444-3000
Angelique Simon, prin. Fax 444-3006
Meade Park ES 300/K-4
200 S Kansas Ave 61834 217-444-1925
Chris Rice, prin. Fax 444-1928
Northeast ES 300/K-6
1330 E English St 61832 217-444-3050
Kelly Truex, prin. Fax 444-3080
North Ridge MS 500/7-8
1619 N Jackson St 61832 217-444-3400
Eliza Brooks, prin. Fax 444-3488
South View Upper ES 200/5-6
133 E 9th St 61832 217-444-1800
Mendelle Spesard, prin. Fax 444-1882
Southwest ES 400/PK-4
14794 Catlin Tilton Rd 61834 217-444-3500
Lindsey Prunkard, prin. Fax 444-3507

Oakwood CUSD 76
Supt. — See Oakwood
Oakwood JHS 200/7-8
21600 N 900 East Rd 61834 217-443-2883
John Tosh, prin. Fax 776-2228

Danville Lutheran S 100/PK-8
1930 N Bowman Ave 61832 217-442-5036
Kim Wright, prin. Fax 442-1159
First Baptist Christian S 200/PK-12
1211 N Vermilion St 61832 217-442-2434
Rev. Paul Rebert, admin. Fax 442-8731
Schlarman Academy 500/PK-12
2112 N Vermilion St 61832 217-442-2725
Gail Lewis, prin. Fax 442-0293

Darien, DuPage, Pop. 21,762
Cass SD 63 700/PK-8
8502 Bailey Rd 60561 331-481-4000
Dr. Kerry J. Foderaro, supt. Fax 481-4001
www.cassd63.org
Cass JHS 300/5-8
8502 Bailey Rd 60561 331-481-4020
Christine Marcinkewicz, prin. Fax 481-4021
Concord ES 400/PK-4
1019 Concord Pl 60561 331-481-4010
Dr. Laura Anderson, prin. Fax 481-4011

Center Cass SD 66
Supt. — See Downers Grove
Ide ES 300/K-2
2000 Manning Rd 60561 630-783-5200
Scott Lazar, prin. Fax 971-3367

Darien SD 61 1,600/PK-8
7414 S Cass Ave 60561 630-968-7505
Dr. Robert Carlo, supt. Fax 968-0872
www.darien61.org
Delay ES 600/PK-2
6801 Wilmette Ave 60561 630-852-0200
Lisa M. Kompare, prin. Fax 968-7506
Eisenhower JHS 500/6-8
1410 75th St 60561 630-964-5200
Jacob Buck, prin. Fax 968-8002
Lace ES 500/3-5
7414 S Cass Ave 60561 630-968-2589
Erin Dwyer, prin. Fax 968-5920

Kingswood Academy 200/PK-8
133 Plainfield Rd 60561 630-887-1411
Bernadette McCarthy, prin. Fax 887-1424
Our Lady of Peace S 400/PK-8
709 Plainfield Rd 60561 630-325-9220
Anthony Wilkinson, prin. Fax 325-1995

Decatur, Macon, Pop. 73,849
Decatur SD 61 8,600/PK-12
101 W Cerro Gordo St 62523 217-362-3000
Bobbi Williams, supt. Fax 424-3009
www.dps61.org
Baum ES 400/K-6
801 S Lake Ridge Ave 62521 217-362-3520
Tanya Young, prin. Fax 424-3024
Decatur MS 400/7-8
1 Educational Park 62526 217-362-3250
Deloris Brown, prin. Fax 424-3169
Dennis Lab S 400/PK-8
1499 W Main St 62522 217-362-3510
Matt Andrews, prin. Fax 424-3067
Durfee Technology Magnet S 300/K-6
1077 W Grand Ave 62522 217-362-3500
Dianne Brandt, prin. Fax 424-3135
Enterprise ES 200/PK-6
2115 S Taylor Rd 62521 217-362-3390
Ann Mathieson, prin. Fax 424-3132
Franklin ES 300/K-6
2440 N Summit Ave 62526 217-362-3560
Stephanie Strang, prin. Fax 424-3133
French Academy 300/K-6
520 W Wood St 62522 217-362-3380
Julie Fane, prin. Fax 424-3134
Garfield Montessori S 400/PK-8
300 Meadow Terrace Pl 62521 217-362-3370
Mary Anderson, prin. Fax 424-3148
Harris ES 300/K-6
620 E Garfield Ave 62526 217-362-3360
Sarah Whitlock, prin. Fax 424-3136
Hope Academy 500/PK-8
955 N Illinois St 62521 217-362-3380
Henry Walker, prin. Fax 424-3343
Jefferson MS 500/7-8
4735 E Cantrell St 62521 217-362-3200
Nathan Sheppard, prin. Fax 424-3037
Johns Hill Magnet S 500/K-8
1025 E Johns Ave 62521 217-362-3350
Robert Prange, prin. Fax 424-3192
Muffley ES 400/K-6
88 S Country Club Rd 62521 217-362-3340
Carrie Hogue, prin. Fax 424-3137
Oak Grove ES 300/K-6
2160 W Center St 62526 217-362-3550
Annette Belue, prin. Fax 424-3138
Parsons ES 300/K-6
3591 N MacArthur Rd 62526 217-362-3330
Patricia Paulson, prin. Fax 876-8785
Pershing Early Learning Center 500/PK-PK
2912 N University Ave 62526 217-362-3300
Sarah Knuppel, prin. Fax 876-8322
South Shores ES 300/K-6
2500 S Franklin Street Rd 62521 217-362-3320
Eldon Conn, prin. Fax 424-3176
Stevenson ES 300/K-6
3900 N Neely Ave 62526 217-876-8749
Mary Ann Galligan, prin. Fax 876-8753

Antioch Christian Academy 50/PK-6
3475 N Maple Ave 62526 217-875-0529
Shirley Shaw, prin. Fax 875-5362
Holy Family S 300/PK-8
2400 S Franklin Street Rd 62521 217-423-7049
Debra Alexander, prin. Fax 423-0137
Lutheran School Association 500/K-12
2001 E Mound Rd 62526 217-233-2000
Joel Witt, prin. Fax 233-2000
Our Lady of Lourdes S 200/PK-8
3950 Lourdes Dr 62526 217-877-4408
Christopher Uptmor, prin. Fax 872-3655
St. Patrick S 200/PK-8
412 N Jackson St 62523 217-423-4351
Jan Sweet, prin. Fax 423-7288

Deer Creek, Tazewell, Pop. 696
Deer Creek-Mackinaw CUSD 701
Supt. — See Mackinaw

Deer Creek-Mackinaw IS 300/4-6
506 N Logan St 61733 309-447-6226
Lance Hawkins, prin. Fax 447-5201

Deerfield, Lake, Pop. 18,034
Deerfield SD 109 3,100/PK-8
517 Deerfield Rd 60015 847-945-1844
Dr. Michael Lubelfeld, supt. Fax 945-1853
www.dps109.org
Caruso MS 600/6-8
1801 Montgomery Rd 60015 847-945-8430
Dr. Brian Bullis, prin. Fax 945-1963
Kipling ES 500/K-5
700 Kipling Pl 60015 847-948-5151
Ann Buch, prin. Fax 948-8264
Shepard MS 500/6-8
440 Grove Ave 60015 847-948-0620
Dr. John Filippi, prin. Fax 948-8589
South Park ES 500/PK-5
1421 Hackberry Rd 60015 847-945-5895
Dr. David Sherman, prin. Fax 945-5291
Walden ES 500/K-5
630 Essex Ct 60015 847-945-9660
Dr. Scott Schwartz, prin. Fax 945-0035
Wilmot ES 500/K-5
795 Wilmot Rd 60015 847-945-1075
Eileen Brett, prin. Fax 405-9736

Deerfield Montessori S 50/PK-K
760 North Ave 60015 847-945-7580
Lisa Kambich, hdmstr. Fax 945-8920
Hellenic American Academy 200/PK-8
445 Pine St 60015 847-317-1063
Mary Giannetos, prin. Fax 317-9653

DeKalb, DeKalb, Pop. 43,053
DeKalb CUSD 428 5,900/PK-12
901 S 4th St 60115 815-754-2350
Jamie Craven, supt. Fax 758-6933
dist428.org
Brooks ES 300/K-5
3225 Sangamon Dr 60115 815-754-9936
Brooke Condon, prin. Fax 754-1345
Early Learning & Development Center PK-PK
1515 S 4th St 60115 815-754-2999
Lisa Gorchels, dir. Fax 758-1097
Founders ES 600/K-5
821 S 7th St 60115 815-754-3800
Connie Rohlman, prin. Fax 754-2249
Huntley MS 800/6-8
1515 S 4th St 60115 815-754-2241
Amonaquenette Parker, prin. Fax 758-6062
Jefferson ES 300/K-5
211 McCormick Dr 60115 815-754-2263
Melanie Bickley, prin. Fax 758-1206
Lincoln ES 300/K-5
220 E Sunset Pl 60115 815-754-2212
Jennifer Tallitsch, prin. Fax 758-1279
Littlejohn ES 300/K-5
1121 School St 60115 815-754-2258
Billy Huermo, prin. Fax 758-1065
Rosette MS 500/6-8
650 N 1st St 60115 815-754-2226
Tim Vincent, prin. Fax 758-1097
Tyler ES 200/K-5
1021 Alden Circle 60115 815-754-2389
Andria Mitchell, prin. Fax 758-1244
Other Schools – See Cortland, Malta

St. Mary S 200/PK-8
210 Gurler Rd 60115 815-756-7905
Roseann Feldmann, prin. Fax 758-1459

De Land, Piatt, Pop. 442
Deland-Weldon CUSD 57 200/PK-12
304 E IL Route 10 61839 217-736-2311
Amanda Geary, supt. Fax 736-2654
www.dwschools.org
Other Schools – See Weldon

Delavan, Tazewell, Pop. 1,679
Delavan CUSD 703 500/PK-12
907 S Locust St 61734 309-244-8283
Dr. Andrew Brooks, supt. Fax 244-7696
www.delavanschools.com
Delavan ES 300/PK-6
907 S Locust St 61734 309-244-8283
Staci Harper, prin. Fax 244-7301
Delavan JHS 100/7-8
907 S Locust St 61734 309-244-8285
Dr. Matt Gordon, prin. Fax 244-8694

De Pue, Bureau, Pop. 1,815
DePue Unit SD 103 500/PK-12
PO Box 800 61322 815-447-2121
Chris Dougherty, supt. Fax 447-2067
depueschools.org
DePue ES 300/PK-8
PO Box 800 61322 815-447-2121
Curt Rheingans, supt. Fax 447-2067

De Soto, Jackson, Pop. 1,557
De Soto CCSD 86 300/PK-8
311 Hurst Rd 62924 618-867-2317
Nathaniel Wilson, supt. Fax 867-3233
www.desoto86.org
De Soto ES 300/PK-8
311 Hurst Rd 62924 618-867-2317
Nathaniel Wilson, admin. Fax 867-3233

Des Plaines, Cook, Pop. 57,381
CCSD 59
Supt. — See Arlington Heights
Brentwood ES 400/K-5
260 Dulles Rd 60016 847-593-4401
Dr. Michael Merritt, prin. Fax 593-7184
Devonshire ES 400/K-5
1401 Pennsylvania Ave 60018 847-593-4398
Randy Steinkamp, prin. Fax 593-7183
Friendship JHS 700/6-8
550 Elizabeth Ln 60018 847-593-4350
Jodi Megerle, prin. Fax 593-7182

CCSD 62 4,800/PK-8
777 E Algonquin Rd 60016 847-824-1136
Fax 824-0612
www.d62.org
Algonquin MS 700/6-8
767 E Algonquin Rd 60016 847-824-1205
Dr. Julie Fogarty, prin. Fax 824-1270
Central ES 300/K-5
1526 E Thacker St 60016 847-824-1575
Kelly Krueger, prin. Fax 824-1656
Chippewa MS 700/6-8
123 N 8th Ave 60016 847-824-1503
John Swanson, prin. Fax 824-1514
Cumberland ES 300/K-5
700 E Golf Rd 60016 847-824-1451
Colleen White, prin. Fax 824-0724
Forest ES 600/PK-5
1375 S 5th Ave 60018 847-824-1380
Fax 824-1732
Iroquois Community S 500/K-8
1836 E Touhy Ave 60018 847-824-1308
Dr. Michael Amadei, prin. Fax 824-1310
North ES 600/K-5
1789 Rand Rd 60016 847-824-1399
Denise Fernandez, prin. Fax 824-1768
Orchard Place ES 300/K-5
2727 Maple St 60018 847-824-1255
Jennifer Bautista, prin. Fax 824-1752
Plainfield ES 300/K-5
1850 Plainfield Dr 60018 847-824-1301
Dr. Guillermo Heredia, prin. Fax 824-1547
South ES 200/K-5
1535 Everett Ave 60018 847-824-1566
Amy Cengel, prin. Fax 824-1759
Terrace ES 300/K-5
735 S Westgate Rd 60016 847-824-1501
Dr. Bradley Stein, prin. Fax 824-1764

East Maine SD 63 3,600/PK-8
10150 Dee Rd 60016 847-299-1900
Dr. Scott Clay, supt. Fax 299-9963
www.emsd63.org
Apollo ES 600/PK-6
10100 Dee Rd 60016 847-827-6231
Cassandra Schwartz, prin. Fax 827-1785
Stevenson ES 500/K-6
9000 Capitol Dr 60016 847-298-1622
Howard Sussman, prin. Fax 298-1621
Other Schools – See Glenview, Morton Grove, Niles

Guardian Angel Orthodox Day S 200/PK-6
2350 E Dempster St 60016 847-827-5519
Irene Robaidek, prin. Fax 824-3455
St. Zachary S 200/PK-8
567 W Algonquin Rd 60016 847-437-4022
Caroline Forestor, prin. Fax 758-1064
Science & Arts Academy 300/PK-8
1825 Miner St 60016 847-827-7880
Timothy Costello, head sch Fax 827-7716

Dieterich, Effingham, Pop. 615
Dieterich CUSD 30 400/PK-12
PO Box 187 62424 217-925-5249
Cary Jackson, supt. Fax 925-5447
www.dieterich.k12.il.us
Dieterich ES 200/PK-6
PO Box 187 62424 217-925-5248
Kathy Pattenaude, prin. Fax 925-5447

Divernon, Sangamon, Pop. 1,159
Auburn CUSD 10
Supt. — See Auburn
Auburn JHS 300/6-8
303 E Kenney St 62530 217-628-3414
Mark Dudley, prin. Fax 628-3814

Dix, Jefferson, Pop. 459
Rome CCSD 2 300/PK-8
233 W South St 62830 618-266-7214
Erik Estill, supt. Fax 266-7902
www.rome2.net
Rome Community Consolidated ES 300/PK-8
233 W South St 62830 618-266-7214
Erik Estill, admin. Fax 266-7902

Dixmoor, Cook, Pop. 3,616
West Harvey-Dixmoor SD 147
Supt. — See Harvey
King ES 300/1-4
14600 Seeley Ave 60426 708-385-5400
Taiyuan Banks-Tillmon, prin. Fax 293-1748
Lincoln ES 400/PK-K
14100 Honore Ave 60426 708-597-4160
Taiyuan Banks-Tillmon, prin. Fax 385-2859
Parks MS 400/5-8
14700 Robey Ave 60426 708-371-9575
Patrick Keller, prin. Fax 371-1412

Dixon, Lee, Pop. 15,509
Dixon Unit SD 170 2,600/PK-12
1335 Franklin Grove Rd 61021 815-284-7722
Margo Empen, supt. Fax 284-8576
www.dps170.org
Jefferson ES 400/2-3
800 4th Ave 61021 815-284-7724
Crystal Thorpe, prin. Fax 284-0435
Madison S 400/4-5
618 Division St 61021 815-284-7726
Joey Sagel, prin. Fax 284-1305
Reagan MS 600/6-8
620 Division St 61021 815-284-7725
Andrew Bullock, prin. Fax 284-1711
Washington ES 400/PK-1
703 E Morgan St 61021 815-284-7727
Jeff Gould, prin. Fax 284-0440

Faith Christian S 100/K-12
7571 S Ridge Rd 61021 815-652-4806
Linda Foster, prin. Fax 652-4871
St. Anne S 100/PK-8
1112 N Brinton Ave 61021 815-288-5619
Karen Payan, admin. Fax 288-5820
St. Mary S 200/PK-8
704 S Peoria Ave 61021 815-284-6986
Jean Spohn, prin. Fax 284-6905

Dolton, Cook, Pop. 22,862
Dolton SD 148
Supt. — See Riverdale
Franklin ES 200/K-6
14701 Chicago Rd 60419 708-201-2083
Martez James, prin. Fax 201-2084
Lincoln ES 300/K-6
14151 Lincoln Ave 60419 708-201-2075
Dr. Donald Parker, prin. Fax 849-3758
Lincoln JHS 200/7-8
14151 Lincoln Ave 60419 708-201-2075
Dr. Donald Parker, prin. Fax 849-3758
Roosevelt ES 300/K-6
111 W 146th St 60419 708-201-2070
Steven Chambers, prin. Fax 849-7880
Roosevelt JHS 200/7-8
111 W 146th St 60419 708-201-2071
Steven Chambers, prin. Fax 849-1285

Dolton SD 149
Supt. — See Calumet City
Berger-Vandenberg ES 400/K-6
14833 Avalon Ave 60419 708-841-3606
Gabrielle Herndon, prin. Fax 201-4725
Diekman ES 400/PK-6
15121 Dorchester Ave 60419 708-841-3838
April Davis, prin. Fax 201-4719

Dongola, Union, Pop. 707
Dongola Unit SD 66 200/PK-12
PO Box 190 62926 618-827-3841
Dr. Paige Maginel, supt. Fax 827-4641
dongolaschool.com
Dongola ES 100/PK-5
PO Box 190 62926 618-827-3524
John Goddard, prin. Fax 827-4422
Dongola JHS 50/6-8
PO Box 190 62926 618-827-3524
John Goddard, prin. Fax 827-4422

Donovan, Iroquois, Pop. 304
Donovan CUSD 3 300/PK-12
PO Box 186 60931 815-486-7395
Stephen Westrick, supt. Fax 486-7395
www.donovan.k12.il.us
Donovan ES 100/PK-5
2561 E US Highway 52 60931 815-486-7321
Tina Pitkin, prin. Fax 486-7445
Donovan JHS 50/6-8
PO Box 186 60931 815-486-7395
Tina Pitkin, prin. Fax 486-7030

Dorsey, Madison

St. Peter Lutheran S 50/PK-8
7182 Renken Rd 62021 618-888-2252
Melissa Burns, prin. Fax 888-2353

Downers Grove, DuPage, Pop. 47,147
Center Cass SD 66 1,000/PK-8
699 Plainfield Rd 60516 630-783-5000
Dr. Tim Arnold, supt. Fax 910-0980
www.ccsd66.org/
Lakeview JHS 400/6-8
701 Plainfield Rd 60516 630-985-2700
Paul Windsor, prin. Fax 985-1545
Prairieview ES 400/PK-PK, 3-
699 Plainfield Rd 60516 630-783-5100
Mark Pagel, prin. Fax 910-0803
Other Schools – See Darien

Downers Grove SD 58 5,100/PK-8
1860 63rd St 60516 630-719-5800
Dr. Kari Cremascoli, supt. Fax 719-9857
www.dg58.org
Belle Aire ES 300/K-6
3935 Belle Aire Ln 60515 630-719-5820
Brent Borchelt, prin. Fax 719-9311
El Sierra ES 300/K-6
6835 Fairmount Ave 60516 630-719-5825
Jason Lynde, prin. Fax 719-9281
Fairmount ES 300/K-6
6036 Blodgett Ave 60516 630-719-5830
Lisa Niforatos, prin. Fax 719-1161
Herrick MS 600/7-8
4435 Middaugh Ave 60515 630-719-5810
Matt Neustadt, prin. Fax 719-1628
Highland ES 300/K-6
3935 Highland Ave 60515 630-719-5835
Dr. Bridget Moore, prin. Fax 719-0150
Hillcrest ES 400/K-6
1435 Jefferson Ave 60516 630-719-5840
Michelle Rzepka, prin. Fax 719-0122
Indian Trail ES 400/PK-6
6235 Stonewall Ave 60516 630-719-5845
Robin Bruebach, prin. Fax 719-1275
Kingsley ES 400/K-6
6509 Powell St 60516 630-719-5850
Mark Stange, prin. Fax 719-0982
Lester ES 500/K-6
236 Indianapolis Ave 60515 630-719-5855
Carin Novak, prin. Fax 719-0053
O'Neill MS 500/7-8
635 59th St 60516 630-719-5815
Matthew Durbala, prin. Fax 719-1436
Pierce Downer ES 400/K-6
1436 Grant St 60515 630-719-5860
Christine Clavenna, prin. Fax 719-1176

Puffer ES 400/PK-6
2220 Haddow Ave 60515 630-968-0294
Todd McDaniel, prin. Fax 968-4061
Whittier ES 300/K-6
536 Hill St 60515 630-719-5865
Michael Krugman, prin. Fax 719-1105

Avery Coonley S 400/PK-8
1400 Maple Ave 60515 630-969-0800
Paul Druzinsky, head sch Fax 969-0131
Downers Grove Adventist S 50/PK-8
5524 Lee Ave 60515 630-968-8848
Dr. Patricia Williams, prin.
Downers Grove Christian S 200/PK-8
929 Maple Ave 60515 630-852-0832
Shari Peterson, prin. Fax 852-0880
Good Shepherd Lutheran S 100/PK-8
525 63rd St 60516 630-852-5081
Bryan Scriver, prin. Fax 852-1532
Marquette Manor Baptist Academy 200/PK-12
333 75th St 60516 630-964-5363
Donald Sherwin, admin. Fax 964-5385
St. Joseph S 400/PK-8
4832 Highland Ave 60515 630-969-4306
Rita Stasi, prin. Fax 969-3946
St. Mary of Gostyn S 500/PK-8
440 Prairie Ave 60515 630-968-6155
Chris Tiritilli, prin. Fax 968-6208

Downs, McLean, Pop. 986
Tri-Valley CUSD 3 1,000/PK-12
410 E Washington St 61736 309-378-2351
Dr. David Mouser, supt. Fax 378-2223
tri-valley3.org
Tri-Valley ES 300/PK-3
409 E Washington St 61736 309-378-2031
Sara Burnett, prin. Fax 378-4578
Tri-Valley MS 400/4-8
505 E Washington St 61736 309-378-3414
Brandi Maxedon, prin. Fax 378-3214

Dunlap, Peoria, Pop. 1,372
Dunlap CUSD 323
Supt. — See Peoria
Banner ES 400/K-5
12610 N Allen Rd 61525 309-243-7774
Greg Fairchild, prin. Fax 243-7775
Dunlap Grade S 200/K-5
PO Box 367 61525 309-243-7772
Mandy Ellis, prin. Fax 243-9116
Dunlap MS 600/6-8
13120 N Route 91 61525 309-243-7778
Wes Wolven, prin. Fax 243-1136
Dunlap Valley MS 300/6-8
PO Box 366 61525 309-243-1034
Jason Holmes, prin. Fax 243-9829
Hickory Grove ES 700/PK-5
2514 W Hickory Grove Rd 61525 309-243-8711
Jeremy Etnyre, prin. Fax 243-1075

Dupo, Saint Clair, Pop. 4,069
Dupo CUSD 196 1,200/PK-12
600 Louisa Ave 62239 618-286-3812
Kelly Carpenter Ed.D., supt. Fax 286-5554
www.dupo196.org
Bluffview ES, 905 Bluffview Dr 62239 700/PK-6
Victoria White, prin. 618-286-3311
Dupo JHS, 600 Louisa Ave 62239 200/7-8
William Harris, prin. 618-286-3214

Du Quoin, Perry, Pop. 5,956
Du Quoin CUSD 300 1,400/PK-12
845 E Jackson St 62832 618-542-3856
Dr. Gary Kelly, supt. Fax 542-6614
www.duquoinschools.org
Du Quoin ES 600/K-4
845 E Jackson St 62832 618-542-2646
Diana Rea, prin. Fax 542-6291
Du Quoin MS 400/5-8
845 E Jackson St 62832 618-542-2646
Aaron Hill, prin. Fax 542-4373

Christian Fellowship S 100/PK-12
PO Box 227 62832 618-542-6800
Larry Bullock, admin. Fax 542-6806

Durand, Winnebago, Pop. 1,423
Durand CUSD 322 600/PK-12
200 W South St 61024 815-248-2171
Kurt Alberstett, supt. Fax 248-2599
www.durandbulldogs.com
Durand ES 300/PK-6
200 W South St 61024 815-248-2171
Shanna Rufener, prin. Fax 248-2599
Durand JHS 100/7-8
200 W South St 61024 815-248-2171
Michael Leckowich, prin. Fax 248-2599

Dwight, Livingston, Pop. 4,231
Dwight Common SD 232 600/PK-8
801 S Columbia St 60420 815-584-6216
Dr. Richard Jancek, supt. Fax 584-2950
www.dwight.k12.il.us
Dwight Common ES 600/PK-8
801 S Columbia St 60420 815-584-6220
Ben Bailey, prin. Fax 584-3771

Earlville, LaSalle, Pop. 1,691
Earlville CUSD 9 400/PK-12
PO Box 539 60518 815-246-8361
Rich Faivre, supt. Fax 246-8672
www.earlvillecusd9.org
Earlville S 300/PK-8
PO Box 539 60518 815-246-8361
Jenette Fruit, prin. Fax 246-8672

Serena CUSD 2
Supt. — See Serena
Harding ES 100/K-4
1643 N 40th Rd 60518 815-792-8216
Joe Landers, prin. Fax 792-8003

East Alton, Madison, Pop. 6,171
East Alton SD 13 900/PK-8
210 E Saint Louis Ave 62024 618-433-2051
Virgil Moore, supt. Fax 433-2054
www.easd13.org
East Alton MS 200/6-8
1000 3rd St 62024 618-433-2201
Kelli Decker, prin. Fax 433-2203
Eastwood ES 500/K-5
1030 3rd St 62024 618-433-2199
Matt Stimac, prin. Fax 433-2181
Washington ECC 100/PK-PK
210 E Saint Louis Ave 62024 618-433-2001
Stacey Egan, prin. Fax 433-2096

East Dubuque, Jo Daviess, Pop. 1,681
East Dubuque Unit SD 119 600/PK-12
100 N School Rd 61025 815-747-2111
Tori Lindeman, supt. Fax 747-3516
www.edbqhs.org
East Dubuque ES 400/PK-6
100 N School Rd 61025 815-747-3117
Crissy Johnson, prin. Fax 747-3827

St. Mary S 100/PK-8
701 IL Route 35 N 61025 815-747-3010
Angela Jones, prin. Fax 747-6188

East Dundee, Kane, Pop. 2,833

Immanuel Lutheran S 300/PK-8
5 S Van Buren St 60118 847-428-1010
Sue Domeier, prin. Fax 836-6217

East Moline, Rock Island, Pop. 20,814
East Moline SD 37 2,800/PK-8
3451 Morton Dr 61244 309-792-2887
Kristin Humphries, supt. Fax 792-6010
www.emsd37.org
Glenview MS 1,100/5-8
3100 7th St 61244 309-755-1919
Michael Hawley, prin. Fax 752-2551
Hillcrest ES 300/K-4
451 22nd Ave 61244 309-755-7621
Dalinda Archer, prin. Fax 752-2569
Ridgewood ES 400/K-4
814 30th Ave 61244 309-755-1585
Heidi Lensing, prin. Fax 752-2570
Wells ES 500/PK-4
490 Avenue of the Cities 61244 309-796-1251
Patrick Versluis, prin. Fax 796-1751
Other Schools – See Silvis

Silvis SD 34 600/PK-8
4280 4th Ave 61244 309-792-9325
Dr. Terri VandeWiele Ed.D., supt. Fax 203-1322
silvis34.net
Northeast JHS 200/6-8
4280 4th Ave 61244 309-203-1300
Jim Widdop, prin. Fax 203-1322
Other Schools – See Silvis

East Moline Christian S 400/PK-12
900 46th Ave 61244 309-796-1485
Ronald Patrick, prin. Fax 796-1152
Our Lady of Grace Academy 200/PK-8
603 18th Ave 61244 309-755-9771
Joan Leonard, prin. Fax 755-7407

East Peoria, Tazewell, Pop. 23,021
East Peoria SD 86 1,700/PK-8
601 Taylor St 61611 309-427-5100
Tony Ingold, supt. Fax 698-1364
www.epd86.org
Armstrong-Oakview ES 200/PK-2
1848 Highview Rd 61611 309-427-5300
Ashley Ricca, prin. Fax 694-0829
Bolin ES 200/3-5
428 Arnold Rd 61611 309-427-5350
Daren Lowery, prin. Fax 698-1365
Central JHS 500/6-8
601 Taylor St 61611 309-427-5200
Dustin Schrank, prin. Fax 699-2595
Glendale ES 200/3-5
1000 Bloomington Rd 61611 309-427-5400
Teresa Armstrong, prin. Fax 698-2949
Lincoln ES 200/3-5
801 Springfield Rd 61611 309-427-5450
Chris Kolowski, prin. Fax 698-2969
Shute ES 200/PK-2
300 Briarbrook Dr 61611 309-427-5500
Brad Wood, prin. Fax 698-1362
Wilson ES 200/K-2
300 Oakwood Ave 61611 309-427-5550
Derek Schulze, prin. Fax 698-1369

Riverview CCSD 2 200/PK-8
1421 Spring Bay Rd 61611 309-822-8550
Michelle Lee, supt. Fax 822-8414
www.rgschool.com
Riverview ES 200/PK-8
1421 Spring Bay Rd 61611 309-822-8550
Michelle Lee, prin. Fax 822-8414

Robein SD 85 200/PK-8
200 Campus Ave 61611 309-694-1409
Bradley Bennett, supt. Fax 694-1450
www.robein.org
Robein ES 200/PK-8
200 Campus Ave 61611 309-694-1409
Bradley Bennett, prin. Fax 694-1450

Peoria Christian S - Monroe 300/5-8
109 Barberry Ln 61611 309-681-0500

East Saint Louis, Saint Clair, Pop. 26,776
Cahokia CUSD 187
Supt. — See Cahokia
Lalumier ES 300/K-3
6702 Bond Ave 62207 618-332-3713
Cynthia Schaefer, prin. Fax 332-3811

East St. Louis SD 189 5,800/PK-12
1005 State St 62201 618-646-3000
Arthur Culver, supt. Fax 583-7186
www.estl189.com
Adams ECC 200/PK-PK
501 Katherine Dunham Pl 62201 618-646-3290
Tifani Brown, prin. Fax 646-3298
Avant ES 500/K-4
1915 N 55th St 62204 618-646-3870
Charlotte Edwards, prin. Fax 646-3878
Bush ES 500/K-4
1516 Gross Ave 62205 618-646-3930
Brittany Green, prin. Fax 397-3938
Dunbar ES 500/K-4
1835 Tudor Ave 62207 618-646-3840
Carlynda Coleman, prin. Fax 646-3848
Harper-Wright ES 500/K-4
7710 State St 62203 618-646-3860
Kiaundra Smith, prin. Fax 646-3868
Lincoln MS 600/5-8
12 S 10th St 62201 618-646-3770
Maria Burton, prin. Fax 646-3778
Mason/Clark MS 700/5-8
5510 State St 62203 618-646-3750
Keisa Garrett, prin. Fax 646-3758
Officer ES 400/K-4
558 N 27th St 62205 618-646-3970
Lori Chalmers, prin. Fax 646-3978

Sister Thea Bowman S 100/K-8
8213 Church Ln 62203 618-397-0316
Daniel Nickerson, prin. Fax 397-0337
Unity Lutheran Christian S 100/K-8
1600 N 40th St 62204 618-874-6605
Aaron Dickerson, prin. Fax 874-2707

Edinburg, Christian, Pop. 1,060
Edinburg CUSD 4 300/PK-12
100 E Martin St 62531 217-623-5603
Fred Lamkey, supt. Fax 623-5604
www.ecusd4.com
Edinburg ES 200/PK-6
100 E Martin St 62531 217-623-5603
Michelle Reiss, prin. Fax 623-5604
Edinburg JHS 100/7-8
100 E Martin St 62531 217-623-5603
Michelle Reiss, prin. Fax 623-5604

Edwardsville, Madison, Pop. 23,810
Edwardsville CUSD 7 7,600/PK-12
PO Box 250 62025 618-656-1182
Dr. Lynda Andre, supt. Fax 692-7423
www.ecusd7.org
Columbus ES 400/3-5
315 N Kansas St 62025 618-656-5167
Vince Schlueter, prin. Fax 655-1099
Goshen ES 400/PK-2
101 District Dr 62025 618-655-6250
Mary Miller, prin. Fax 659-9960
LeClaire ES 400/PK-2
801 Franklin Ave 62025 618-656-3825
Dr. Cornelia Smith, prin. Fax 655-1038
Liberty MS 900/6-8
1 District Dr 62025 618-655-6800
Beth Crumbacher, prin. Fax 655-6801
Lincoln MS 800/6-8
145 West St 62025 618-656-0485
Steve Stuart, prin. Fax 659-1268
Nelson ES 300/PK-2
1225 W High St 62025 618-656-8480
Dr. Tanya Patton, prin. Fax 655-1063
Woodland ES 500/3-5
59 S State Route 157 62025 618-692-8790
Tara Fox, prin. Fax 692-7467
Other Schools – See Glen Carbon, Hamel, Moro, Worden

St. Boniface S 300/PK-8
128 N Buchanan St 62025 618-656-6917
Laura Kretzer, prin. Fax 692-8385
St. Mary S 200/PK-8
1802 Madison Ave 62025 618-656-1230
Diane Wepking, prin. Fax 656-1715
Trinity Lutheran S 200/PK-8
600 Water St 62025 618-656-7002
Wesley Jones, prin. Fax 656-5941

Effingham, Effingham, Pop. 12,212
Effingham CUSD 40 2,500/K-12
PO Box 130 62401 217-540-1500
Mark Doan, supt. Fax 540-1510
www.effingham.k12.il.us
Central Grade S 600/2-5
10421 N US Highway 45 62401 217-540-1400
Amy Niebrugge, prin. Fax 540-1454
Early Learning Center 200/K-K
3224 S Banker St 62401 217-540-1460
Jennifer Fox, prin. Fax 540-1484
Effingham JHS 500/6-8
600 S Henrietta St 62401 217-540-1300
Cody Lewis, prin. Fax 540-1362
South Side ES 300/1-2
211 W Douglas Ave 62401 217-540-1530
Cheri Marten, prin. Fax 540-1559

Sacred Heart S 100/PK-8
407 S Henrietta St 62401 217-342-4060
Vicki Wenthe, prin. Fax 342-9251
St. Anthony of Padua S 300/K-8
405 N 2nd St 62401 217-347-0419
Matt Sturgeon, prin. Fax 347-2749

Elburn, Kane, Pop. 5,560
Kaneland CUSD 302
Supt. — See Maple Park

Blackberry Creek ES 400/PK-5
1122 Anderson Rd 60119 630-365-1122
Martne McCoy, prin. Fax 365-3905
Stewart ES 500/PK-5
817 Prairie Valley St 60119 630-365-8170
Laura Garland, prin. Fax 365-0651

Eldorado, Saline, Pop. 4,079
Eldorado CUSD 4 1,200/PK-12
2200A Illinois Ave 62930 618-273-6394
Ryan Hobbs, supt. Fax 273-9311
www.eldorado.k12.il.us/
Eldorado ES 600/PK-5
1100 Alexander St 62930 618-273-9324
Joshua Bradley, prin. Fax 273-9661
Eldorado MS 200/6-8
1907 1st St 62930 618-273-8056
Billy Tippett, prin. Fax 273-2943

Elgin, Kane, Pop. 106,496
Central CUSD 301
Supt. — See Burlington
Country Trails ES 600/K-5
3701 Highland Woods Blvd, 847-717-8000
Jeff King, prin. Fax 717-8006
Prairie Knolls MS 500/6-7
225 Nesler Rd, 847-717-8100
Matthew Haug, prin. Fax 717-8105
Prairie View ES 600/K-5
10N630 Nesler Rd, 847-464-6014
Daniel Schuth, prin. Fax 464-6024

SD U-46 40,200/PK-12
355 E Chicago St 60120 847-888-5000
Tony Sanders, admin. Fax 608-4173
www.u-46.org
Abbott MS 500/7-8
949 Van St 60123 847-888-5160
Kathy Davis, prin. Fax 608-2740
Century Oaks ES 600/K-6
1235 Braeburn Dr 60123 847-888-5181
Dr. Andrea Erickson, prin. Fax 608-2741
Channing ES 600/K-6
63 S Channing St 60120 847-888-5185
Josefina Melendez, prin. Fax 888-7016
Coleman ES 600/K-6
1220 Dundee Ave 60120 847-888-5190
Brian Stark, prin. Fax 608-2743
Creekside ES 600/K-6
655 N Airlite St 60123 847-289-6270
Joanna Sharp, prin. Fax 289-6040
Ellis MS 600/7-8
225 S Liberty St 60120 847-888-5151
Yvette Gonzalez-Collins, prin. Fax 608-2744
Garfield ES 400/PK-6
420 May St 60120 847-888-5192
Dr. Kyle Bunker, prin. Fax 608-2745
Gifford ES 500/K-6
240 S Clifton Ave 60123 847-888-5195
Joseph Corcoran, prin. Fax 608-2763
Highland ES 500/K-6
190 N Melrose Ave 60123 847-888-5280
Steve Johnson, prin. Fax 608-2746
Hillcrest ES 600/K-6
80 N Airlite St 60123 847-888-5282
Teresa Winters, prin. Fax 742-3297
Hilltop ES 700/PK-6
1855 Rohrssen Rd 60120 847-289-6655
Kyle VonSchnase, prin. Fax 888-7199
Huff ES 700/PK-6
801 Hastings St 60120 847-888-5285
Dr. Angelica Ernst, prin. Fax 608-2747
Illinois Park Early Learning S 500/PK-K
1350 Wing St 60123 847-289-6041
Apryl Lowe, prin. Fax 888-5332
Kimball MS 700/7-8
451 N Mclean Blvd 60123 847-888-5290
Alan Tamburrino, prin. Fax 608-2749
Larsen MS 700/7-8
665 Dundee Ave 60120 847-888-5250
Gina Crespo, prin. Fax 888-7172
Lords Park ES 700/PK-6
323 Waverly Dr 60120 847-888-5360
Dr. Hilda Rivera, prin. Fax 608-2750
Lowrie ES 400/PK-6
264 Oak St 60123 847-888-5260
Juan Henderson, prin. Fax 608-2751
McKinley ES 400/K-6
258 Lovell St 60120 847-888-5262
Juan Lira, prin. Fax 608-2752
O'Neal ES 500/PK-6
510 Franklin Blvd 60120 847-888-5266
Marcie Marzullo, prin. Fax 608-2753
Otter Creek ES 700/PK-6
2701 Hopps Rd, 847-888-6995
David Aleman, prin. Fax 888-7607
Washington ES 500/K-6
819 W Chicago St 60123 847-888-5270
Lori Brandes, prin. Fax 608-2754
Other Schools – See Bartlett, Carol Stream, Hanover Park, Hoffman Estates, South Elgin, Streamwood, Wayne

---

Einstein Academy 100/PK-12
747 Davis Rd 60123 847-697-3836
Cathy Ilani, prin. Fax 697-6085
Elgin Academy 500/PK-12
350 Park St 60120 847-695-0300
Seth Hanford, hdmstr. Fax 695-5017
Harvest Christian Academy 600/PK-12
1000 N Randall Rd 60123 847-214-3500
Talbott Behnken, supt. Fax 214-3501
Highland Christian Academy 100/PK-8
2250 W Highland Ave 60123 847-741-5530
St. John's Lutheran S 200/PK-8
109 N Spring St 60120 847-741-7633
Steven Moeller, prin. Fax 741-7687
St. Joseph S 200/PK-8
274 Division St 60120 847-931-2804
Dr. Peter Trumblay, prin. Fax 931-2811

St. Laurence S 200/PK-8
572 Standish St 60123 847-468-6100
Wendy Kelly, prin. Fax 468-6104
St. Mary S 200/K-8
103 S Gifford St 60120 847-695-6609
Barbara Colandrea, prin. Fax 695-6623
St. Thomas More S 300/PK-8
1625 W Highland Ave 60123 847-742-3959
Sonja Keane, prin. Fax 931-1066
Westminster Christian S 500/PK-12
2700 W Highland Ave, 847-695-0310
Steve Hall, head sch Fax 695-0135

Elizabethtown, Hardin, Pop. 296
Hardin County CUSD 1 600/PK-12
PO Box 218 62931 618-287-2411
Richard Morgan, supt. Fax 287-2421
Hardin County ES 300/PK-5
PO Box 218 62931 618-287-2411
Andy Edmondson, prin. Fax 287-6091
Hardin County JHS 100/6-8
PO Box 218 62931 618-287-2411
Andy Edmondson, prin. Fax 287-8381

Elk Grove Village, Cook, Pop. 32,640
CCSD 59
Supt. — See Arlington Heights
Byrd ES 400/K-5
265 Wellington Ave 60007 847-593-4388
Mary Ellen Esser, prin. Fax 593-7188
Clearmont ES 400/K-5
280 Clearmont Dr 60007 847-593-4372
Rachel Solomon, prin. Fax 593-7194
Grove JHS 900/6-8
777 W Elk Grove Blvd 60007 847-593-4367
John Harrington, prin. Fax 472-3001
Rupley ES 500/K-5
305 Oakton St 60007 847-593-4353
Diana O'Donnell, prin. Fax 593-4405
Salt Creek ES 400/K-5
65 JF Kennedy Blvd 60007 847-593-4375
Dr. Nicole Robinson, prin. Fax 593-7390

Schaumburg CCSD 54
Supt. — See Schaumburg
Link ES 600/K-6
900 W Glenn Trl 60007 847-357-5300
Quinn Wulbecker, prin. Fax 357-5301
Mead JHS 700/7-8
1765 Biesterfield Rd 60007 847-357-6000
David Szwed, prin. Fax 357-6001
Stevenson ES 500/PK-6
1414 Armstrong Ln 60007 847-357-5200
Kenneth Haase, prin. Fax 357-5201

Queen of the Rosary S 300/PK-8
690 W Elk Grove Blvd 60007 847-437-3322
Kathleen McGinn, prin. Fax 437-3290

Elkville, Jackson, Pop. 899
Elverado CUSD 196 500/PK-12
PO Box 130 62932 618-568-1321
Kevin Spain, supt. Fax 568-1152
www.elv196.com
Elverado PS 100/PK-2
PO Box 130 62932 618-568-1321
Kevin Spain, prin. Fax 568-1152
Other Schools – See Vergennes

Elmhurst, DuPage, Pop. 43,533
Elmhurst SD 205 8,400/PK-12
162 S York St 60126 630-834-4530
Dr. David Moyer, supt. Fax 617-2345
www.elmhurst205.org/
Bryan MS 700/6-8
111 W Butterfield Rd 60126 630-617-2350
Jacquie Discipio, prin. Fax 617-2232
Churchville MS 500/6-8
155 E Victory Pkwy 60126 630-832-8682
Gina Pogue Reeder, prin. Fax 617-2387
Edison ES 300/K-5
246 S Fair Ave 60126 630-834-4272
James Pluskota, prin. Fax 617-8333
Emerson ES 500/K-5
400 N West Ave 60126 630-834-5562
Michelle Thompson, prin. Fax 993-8883
Field ES 400/K-5
295 N Emroy Ave 60126 630-834-5313
Heidi Thomas, prin. Fax 993-8896
Fischer ES 400/K-5
888 N Wilson St 60126 630-832-8601
Jane Bailey, prin. Fax 993-8890
Hawthorne ES 600/K-5
145 W Arthur St 60126 630-834-4541
Tim Riordan, prin. Fax 993-8886
Jackson ES 400/K-5
925 S Swain Ave 60126 630-834-4544
Christine Trendel, prin. Fax 993-8897
Jefferson ES 400/K-5
360 E Crescent Ave 60126 630-834-6261
Leslie Weber, prin. Fax 993-8888
Lincoln ES 600/K-5
565 S Fairfield Ave 60126 630-834-4548
Jennifer Barnabee, prin. Fax 993-6675
Madison ECC 200/PK-PK
130 W Madison St 60126 630-617-2385
Susan Kondrat, prin. Fax 617-8212
Sandburg MS 700/6-8
345 E Saint Charles Rd 60126 630-834-4534
Linda Fehrenbacher, prin. Fax 617-2380

Salt Creek SD 48
Supt. — See Villa Park
Salt Creek ES 100/PK-1
980 S Riverside Dr 60126 630-832-6122
Gerrie Aulisa, prin. Fax 617-2658

Immaculate Conception S 500/PK-8
132 W Arthur St 60126 630-530-3490
Cathy Linley, prin. Fax 530-9787

Immanuel Lutheran S 200/PK-8
148 E 3rd St 60126 630-832-9302
Paul Trettin, prin. Fax 832-8307
Mary Queen of Heaven PK & K PK-K
426 N West Ave 60126 630-833-9500
Genet Pinkerton, dir. Fax 279-4667
Timothy Christian S 800/PK-8
188 W Butterfield Rd 60126 630-833-4717
Dr. Timothy Hoeksema, prin. Fax 833-9828
Visitation S 500/PK-8
851 S York St 60126 630-834-4931
Dr. Christopher Dransoff, prin. Fax 834-4936

Elmwood, Peoria, Pop. 2,079
Elmwood CUSD 322 700/PK-12
301 W Butternut St 61529 309-742-8464
Dr. Chad Wagner, supt. Fax 742-8812
elmwood322.com
Elmwood ES 400/PK-6
501 N Morgan St 61529 309-742-4261
Anthony Frost, prin. Fax 742-8833
Elmwood JHS 100/7-8
301 W Butternut St 61529 309-742-2851
Tony McCoy, prin. Fax 742-8350

Elmwood Park, Cook, Pop. 24,650
Elmwood Park CUSD 401 2,900/PK-12
8201 W Fullerton Ave 60707 708-452-7292
Dr. Nicolas Wade, supt. Fax 452-9504
www.epcusd401.org/
ECC 200/PK-K
4 W Conti Pkwy 60707 708-583-5860
Joanne Mourikes Rice, prin. Fax 583-5899
Elm MS 400/7-8
7607 W Cortland St 60707 708-452-3550
Dr. Kathleen Porreca, prin. Fax 452-0662
Elmwood ES 600/1-6
2319 N 76th Ave 60707 708-452-3558
Kevin Seibel, prin. Fax 452-5567
Mills ES 700/1-6
2824 N 76th Ave 60707 708-452-3560
Laura Magruder, prin. Fax 452-0349

St. Celestine S 400/PK-8
3017 N 77th Ave 60707 708-453-8234
Jeanine Rocchi, prin. Fax 452-0237

El Paso, Woodford, Pop. 2,782
El Paso-Gridley CUSD 11 1,300/PK-12
97 W 5th St 61738 309-527-4410
Brian Kurz, supt. Fax 527-4040
www.unit11.org
Centennial S 200/3-4
135 W 5th St 61738 309-527-4435
Tim Fairchild, prin. Fax 527-4438
Jefferson Park S 300/PK-2
250 W 3rd St 61738 309-527-4405
Kelly Throneburg, prin. Fax 527-4407
Other Schools – See Gridley

Elwood, Will, Pop. 2,262
Elwood CCSD 203 400/K-8
409 N Chicago Ave 60421 815-423-5588
Cathie Pezanoski, supt. Fax 423-5184
www.elwoodschool.com
Elwood Community Consolidated S 400/K-8
409 N Chicago Ave 60421 815-423-5588
Tonya Peterson, prin. Fax 423-5808

Emden, Logan, Pop. 483
Hartsburg-Emden CUSD 21
Supt. — See Hartsburg
Emden ES, PO Box 267 62635 100/PK-5
Jon Leslie, prin. 217-376-3151

Energy, Williamson, Pop. 1,139

Unity Christian S 200/PK-8
PO Box 310 62933 618-942-3802
William McSparin M.S., prin. Fax 942-7228

Enfield, White, Pop. 596
Norris City-Omaha-Enfield CUSD 3
Supt. — See Norris City
Booth S 200/PK-8
PO Box 39 62835 618-963-2521
Carla Carter, prin. Fax 963-2716

Erie, Whiteside, Pop. 1,588
Erie CUSD 1 700/PK-12
520 5th Ave 61250 309-659-2239
Bradley Cox, supt. Fax 659-2230
www.ecusd.info
Erie ES 300/PK-4
605 6th Ave 61250 309-659-2239
Kali Livengood, prin. Fax 659-2588
Erie MS 200/5-8
500 5th Ave 61250 309-659-2239
Keith Morgan, prin. Fax 659-7254

Eureka, Woodford, Pop. 5,225
Eureka CUSD 140 1,700/PK-12
109 W Cruger Ave 61530 309-467-3737
Robert Bardwell, supt. Fax 467-2377
www.district140.org
Davenport ES 400/PK-4
301 S Main St 61530 309-467-3012
Nancy Ryan, prin. Fax 467-5265
Eureka MS 500/5-8
2005 S Main St 61530 309-467-3771
Kelly Nichols, prin. Fax 467-2052
Other Schools – See Congerville, Goodfield

Evanston, Cook, Pop. 71,880
Evanston/Skokie SD 65 7,600/PK-8
1500 McDaniel Ave 60201 847-859-8000
Dr. Paul Goren, supt. Fax 866-7241
www.district65.net
Chute MS 500/6-8
1400 Oakton St 60202 847-859-8600
James McHolland, prin. Fax 492-7956

Dawes ES 400/K-5
440 Dodge Ave 60202 847-905-3400
Latarsha Green, prin. Fax 492-9841
Dewey ES 500/K-5
1551 Wesley Ave 60201 847-859-8140
Donna Sokolowski, prin. Fax 492-7994
Haven MS 800/6-8
2417 Prairie Ave 60201 847-859-8200
Kathleen Roberson, prin. Fax 492-9983
Hill ECC 400/PK-PK
1500 McDaniel Ave 60201 847-859-8300
Amy Small, admin. Fax 859-8003
King Literary & Fine Arts S 600/K-8
2424 Lake St 60201 847-859-8500
Dr. Jeffrey Brown, prin. Fax 492-1413
Kingsley ES 400/K-5
2300 Green Bay Rd 60201 847-859-8400
Tricia Murray, prin. Fax 492-5868
Lincoln ES 500/K-5
910 Forest Ave 60202 847-905-3500
Michelle Cooney, prin. Fax 492-1870
Lincolnwood ES 400/K-5
2600 Colfax St 60201 847-859-8880
Michelle Bournes-Thomas, prin. Fax 492-7958
Nichols MS 600/6-8
800 Greenleaf St 60202 847-859-8660
Adrian Harries, prin. Fax 492-7880
Oakton ES 400/K-5
436 Ridge Ave 60202 847-859-8800
Wayne Williams, prin. Fax 492-7960
Orrington ES 400/K-5
2636 Orrington Ave 60201 847-859-8780
Jessica Plaza, prin. Fax 492-9003
Walker ES 300/K-5
3601 Church St 60203 847-859-8330
Ginger Lumpkin, prin. Fax 674-7004
Washington ES 500/K-5
914 Ashland Ave 60202 847-905-4900
Kate Ellison, prin. Fax 492-8433
Willard ES 500/K-5
2700 Hurd Ave 60201 847-905-3600
Jerry Michel, prin. Fax 733-2100
Other Schools – See Skokie

Chiaravalle Montessori S 400/PK-8
425 Dempster St 60201 847-864-2190
Robyn McCloud-Springer, head sch Fax 864-2206
Midwest Montessori Demonstration S 50/PK-K
926 Noyes St 60201 847-328-6630
Pope John XXIII S 300/PK-8
1120 Washington St 60202 847-475-5678
Gail Hulse, prin. Fax 475-5683
Roycemore S 300/PK-12
1200 Davis St 60201 847-866-6055
Kevin Smith, hdmstr. Fax 866-6545
St. Athanasius S 300/K-8
2510 Ashland Ave 60201 847-864-2650
Carol McClay, prin. Fax 475-7385
St. Joan of Arc S 200/PK-8
9245 Lawndale Ave 60203 847-679-0660
Craig Scanlon, prin. Fax 679-0689

Evansville, Randolph, Pop. 690
Sparta CUSD 140
Supt. — See Sparta
Evansville Attendance Center 100/K-8
701 Oak St 62242 618-853-4411
Jayson Baker, prin. Fax 853-2243

Evergreen Park, Cook, Pop. 19,576
Evergreen Park ESD 124 1,700/PK-8
2929 W 87th St 60805 708-423-0950
Robert Machak Ed.D., supt. Fax 423-4292
www.d124.org
Central MS 400/7-8
9400 S Sawyer Ave 60805 708-424-0148
Rita Sparks, prin. Fax 229-8406
Northeast ES 300/PK-6
9058 S California Ave 60805 708-422-6501
Jackie Janicke, prin. Fax 229-8410
Northwest ES 300/PK-6
3630 W 92nd St 60805 708-425-9473
Mathew Banach, prin. Fax 229-8407
Southeast ES 300/K-6
9800 S Francisco Ave 60805 708-422-1021
Alice Spingola, prin. Fax 229-8413
Southwest ES 400/K-6
9900 S Central Park Ave 60805 708-424-2444
Patti Bogdan, prin. Fax 229-8416

Most Holy Redeemer S 400/PK-8
9536 S Millard Ave 60805 708-422-8280
Nancy Harmening, prin. Fax 422-4193
Queen of Martyrs S 400/PK-8
3550 W 103rd St 60805 708-422-1540
Kathleen Tomaszewski, prin. Fax 422-1811

Ewing, Franklin, Pop. 307
Ewing Northern CCSD 115 200/PK-8
51 N Main St 62836 618-629-2181
Kristin Ing, admin. Fax 629-2510
www.ewinggradeschool.org/
Ewing Northern S 200/PK-8
51 N Main St 62836 618-629-2181
Kristin Ing, prin. Fax 629-2510

Fairbury, Livingston, Pop. 3,720
Prairie Central CUSD 8 1,600/PK-12
605 N 7th St 61739 815-692-2504
Paula Crane, supt. Fax 692-3195
www.prairiecentral.org
Prairie Central ES 200/2-4
600 S 1st St 61739 815-692-2623
Codi Conway, prin. Fax 692-3726
Other Schools – See Chatsworth, Chenoa, Forrest

Fairfield, Wayne, Pop. 5,118
Fairfield SD 112 700/PK-8
806 N 1st St 62837 618-842-6501
Diana Zurliene, supt. Fax 842-2932
www.fairfieldcolts.com
Center Street S 300/4-8
200 W Center St 62837 618-842-2679
April Smith, prin. Fax 842-4719
North Side ES 400/PK-3
806 N 1st St 62837 618-842-6501
Dr. Scott England, prin. Fax 842-2932

Jasper CCSD 17 100/K-8
2030 County Road 1020 N 62837 618-842-3048
D.M. Mills, supt. Fax 842-3289
www.jasperpolecats.com/
Jasper S 100/K-8
2030 County Road 1020 N 62837 618-842-3048
D.M. Mills, prin. Fax 842-3289

New Hope CCSD 6 200/PK-8
1804 County Road 445 N 62837 618-842-3296
Julie Harrelson, supt. Fax 847-7000
www.newhopepanthers.com/
New Hope S 200/PK-8
1804 County Road 445 N 62837 618-842-3296
Julie Harrelson, prin. Fax 847-7000

Fairview Heights, Saint Clair, Pop. 16,671
Grant CCSD 110 700/PK-8
10110 Old Lincoln Trl 62208 618-398-5577
Matthew Stines, supt. Fax 398-5578
dist110.com
Grant MS 300/5-8
10110 Old Lincoln Trl 62208 618-397-2764
Carla Lasley, prin. Fax 397-7809
Illini ES 400/PK-4
21 Circle Dr 62208 618-398-5552
Travis Klein, prin. Fax 394-9801

Pontiac-William Holliday SD 105 800/PK-8
400 Ashland Ave 62208 618-233-2320
Dr. Julie Brown, supt. Fax 233-0918
www.pwh105.org
Holliday ES 500/K-5
400 Joseph Dr 62208 618-233-7588
Dr. Amy Seelman, prin. Fax 233-1619
Pontiac JHS 200/6-8
400 Ashland Ave 62208 618-233-6004
Joanna Luehmann, prin. Fax 233-0918

Holy Trinity Catholic S East 200/PK-8
504 Fountains Pkwy 62208 618-628-7395
Michael Oslance, prin. Fax 628-1570
True Vine Christian Academy 100/PK-8
5700 Old Collinsville Rd 62208 618-628-8463
Dr. Vincent Rhodes, hdmstr. Fax 628-8493

Farmer City, DeWitt, Pop. 2,018
Blue Ridge CUSD 18 600/PK-12
411 N John St 61842 309-928-9141
Susan Wilson, supt. Fax 928-5478
www.blueridge18.org
Schneider ES 300/PK-3
309 N John St 61842 309-928-2611
Ryan Peyton, prin. Fax 928-2195
Other Schools – See Mansfield

Farmersville, Montgomery, Pop. 724
Panhandle CUSD 2
Supt. — See Raymond
Farmersville ES 50/PK-1
PO Box 170 62533 217-227-3306
Chris Paproth, prin. Fax 227-3246

Farmington, Fulton, Pop. 2,424
Farmington Central CUSD 265 1,400/PK-12
212 N Lightfoot Rd 61531 309-245-1000
Dr. Zac Chatterton, supt. Fax 245-9161
www.dist265.com/
Farmington Central ES 700/PK-5
108 N Lightfoot Rd 61531 309-245-1000
Missy Ryba, prin. Fax 245-9165
Farmington Central JHS 300/6-8
300 N Lightfoot Rd 61531 309-245-1000
Josh Piper, prin. Fax 245-9162

Findlay, Shelby, Pop. 676
Okaw Valley CUSD 302
Supt. — See Bethany
Okaw Valley MS 200/5-8
501 W Division St 62534 217-756-8521
Ross Forlines, prin. Fax 756-8599

Fisher, Champaign, Pop. 1,871
Fisher CUSD 1 600/K-12
801 S 5th St 61843 217-897-6125
Barbara Thompson, supt. Fax 897-6676
www.fisherk12.com
Fisher ES 300/K-6
801 S 5th St 61843 217-897-1133
James Moxley, prin. Fax 897-6676

Flanagan, Livingston, Pop. 1,105
Flanagan-Cornell Unit SD 74 400/PK-12
202 E Falcon Hwy 61740 815-796-2233
Jerry Farris, supt. Fax 796-2856
www.fc74.org
Flanagan ES 200/PK-8
202 E Falcon Hwy 61740 815-796-2261
Jerry Farris, prin. Fax 796-2856

Flora, Clay, Pop. 5,018
Flora CUSD 35 600/PK-12
444 S Locust St 62839 618-662-2412
Joel Hackney, supt. Fax 662-4587
www.floraschools.com
Flora ES PK-5
445 Emory St 62839 618-662-2412
Julie Pearce, prin. Fax 662-8393

Henson JHS 300/6-8
609 N Stanford Rd 62839 618-662-8394
Amy Leonard, prin. Fax 662-8395

Flossmoor, Cook, Pop. 9,246
Flossmoor SD 161
Supt. — See Chicago Heights
Flossmoor Hills ES 300/PK-5
3721 Beech St 60422 708-647-7100
Pat McCraven, prin. Fax 798-8324
Heather Hill ES 300/K-5
1439 Lawrence Cres 60422 708-647-7200
Dr. Keith Davis, prin. Fax 206-2749
Parker JHS 900/6-8
2810 School St 60422 708-647-5400
Fred Hunter, prin. Fax 799-9207
Western Avenue ES 500/PK-5
940 Western Ave 60422 708-647-7400
Dr. Lisa Dallacqua, prin. Fax 206-2350

Flossmoor Montessori S 100/PK-6
740 Western Ave 60422 708-798-4600
Bansari Modi, admin. Fax 798-4021
Infant Jesus of Prague S 400/PK-8
1101 Douglas Ave 60422 708-799-5200
Natalie Formica, prin. Fax 799-5293

Ford Heights, Cook, Pop. 2,726
Ford Heights SD 169 400/PK-8
910 Woodlawn Ave 60411 708-758-1370
Dr. Gregory Jackson, supt. Fax 758-1372
www.fordheights169.org
Cottage Grove Upper Grade Center 200/5-8
800 E 14th St 60411 708-758-1400
Sharon Rivers, prin. Fax 758-0711
Evers PS 200/PK-4
1101 E 10th St 60411 708-758-2520
Monique Johnson, prin. Fax 758-2521

Forest Park, Cook, Pop. 13,818
Forest Park SD 91 900/PK-8
424 Des Plaines Ave 60130 708-366-5700
Dr. Louis Cavallo, supt. Fax 366-5761
www.forestparkschools.org
Field-Stevenson ES 200/3-5
925 Beloit Ave 60130 708-366-5703
Dr. Tiffany Brunson, prin. Fax 366-2091
Forest Park MS 300/6-8
925 Beloit Ave 60130 708-366-5703
Joseph Pisano, prin. Fax 366-2091
Garfield ES 200/PK-2
543 Hannah Ave 60130 708-366-6945
Chyla Weaver, prin. Fax 366-8044
Grant-White ES 100/3-5
147 Circle Ave 60130 708-366-5704
Shannon Roedel, prin. Fax 771-1649
Ross ES 100/K-2
1315 Marengo Ave 60130 708-366-7498
William Milnamow, prin. Fax 771-4232

Forrest, Livingston, Pop. 1,217
Prairie Central CUSD 8
Supt. — See Fairbury
Prairie Central JHS 300/7-8
800 N Wood St 61741 815-657-8660
Keri Jancek, prin. Fax 657-8677
Prairie Central Upper ES 300/5-6
PO Box 496 61741 815-657-8238
James DeMay, prin. Fax 657-8821

Forreston, Ogle, Pop. 1,426
Forrestville Valley CUSD 221 700/PK-12
PO Box 665 61030 815-938-2036
Sheri Smith, supt. Fax 938-9028
www.fvvsd221.org
Forreston ES 200/2-5
PO Box 665 61030 815-938-2301
Jonathan Schneiderman, prin. Fax 938-2471
Other Schools – See German Valley

Forsyth, Macon, Pop. 3,456
Maroa-Forsyth CUSD 2
Supt. — See Maroa
Maroa-Forsyth Grade S 600/PK-5
641 E Shafer St 62535 217-877-2023
Carrie Reynolds, prin. Fax 877-6216

Decatur Christian S 200/PK-12
137 S Grant St 62535 217-877-5636
Randy Grigg, supt. Fax 877-7627

Fox Lake, Lake, Pop. 10,448
Fox Lake Grade SD 114
Supt. — See Spring Grove
Stanton MS 300/5-8
101 Hawthorne Ln 60020 847-973-4200
Jeff Sefcik, prin. Fax 973-4210

Fox River Grove, McHenry, Pop. 4,788
Fox River Grove SD 3 500/PK-8
403 Orchard St 60021 847-516-5100
Dr. Tim Mahaffy, supt. Fax 516-9169
www.dist3.org
Algonquin Road ES 300/PK-4
975 Algonquin Rd 60021 847-516-5101
Dr. Sandy Ozimek, prin. Fax 516-9058
Fox River Grove MS 200/5-8
401 Orchard St 60021 847-516-5105
Eric Runck, prin. Fax 516-5104

Frankfort, Will, Pop. 17,612
Frankfort CCSD 157C 2,500/PK-8
10482 Nebraska St 60423 815-469-5922
Dr. Maura Zinni, supt. Fax 469-8988
www.fsd157c.org
Chelsea ES 800/3-5
22265 S 80th Ave 60423 815-469-2309
Dr. Sharon Nepote, prin. Fax 464-2043
Grand Prairie ES 800/PK-2
10480 Nebraska St 60423 815-469-3366
Eileen Nelson, prin. Fax 469-2899

Hickory Creek MS 900/6-8
22150 116th Ave 60423 815-469-4474
William Seidelmann, prin. Fax 469-7930

Peotone CUSD 207U
Supt. — See Peotone
Peotone IS 50/4-5
9526 W Manhattan Monee Rd 60423 815-469-5744
Joanne Obszanski, prin. Fax 469-6086

Summit Hill SD 161 3,300/PK-8
20100 S Spruce Dr 60423 815-469-9103
Barb Rains, supt. Fax 469-0566
www.summithill.org/
Frankfort Square ES 200/1-4
7710 W Kingston Dr 60423 815-469-3176
Jason Isdonas, prin. Fax 464-2068
Indian Trail ES 500/1-4
20912 S Frankfort Square Rd 60423 815-469-6993
Dana Wright, prin. Fax 806-8352
Rogus ES 800/PK-4
20027 S 88th Ave 60423 815-464-2034
Michael Ruffalo, prin. Fax 464-2250
Summit Hill JHS 800/7-8
7260 W North Ave 60423 815-469-4330
Daniel Pierson, prin. Fax 464-1596
Other Schools – See Mokena, Tinley Park

St. Anthony Preschool 100/PK-PK
7659 W Sauk Trl 60423 815-469-5417
Patricia Smart, dir. Fax 806-9421

Franklin, Morgan, Pop. 598
Franklin CUSD 1
Supt. — See Alexander
Franklin East ES 100/PK-1
412 Wyatt St 62638 217-675-2334
Jason Courier, prin. Fax 675-2396

Franklin Grove, Lee, Pop. 1,012
Ashton-Franklin Center CUSD 275
Supt. — See Ashton
Ashton-Franklin Center ES 200/PK-6
217 S Elm St 61031 815-456-2325
Trina Dillon, prin. Fax 456-2713

Franklin Park, Cook, Pop. 18,209
Franklin Park SD 84 1,200/PK-8
2915 Maple St 60131 847-455-4230
Dr. David H. Katzin, supt. Fax 455-9094
www.d84.org
Hester JHS 400/6-8
2836 Gustav St 60131 847-455-2150
Giffen Trotter, prin. Fax 455-0945
North ES 200/K-5
9500 Gage Ave 60131 847-678-7962
Dr. Cody Huisman, prin. Fax 678-3616
Passow ES 400/K-5
2838 Calwagner St 60131 847-455-6781
Judith Martin, prin. Fax 455-1465
Pietrini ES 300/PK-5
9750 Fullerton Ave 60131 847-455-7960
Lois Fronczke, prin. Fax 455-1809

Mannheim SD 83 2,600/PK-8
10401 Grand Ave 60131 847-455-4413
Kim Petrasek, supt. Fax 451-8290
www.d83.org/
Other Schools – See Melrose Park, Northlake

Freeburg, Saint Clair, Pop. 4,312
Freeburg CCSD 70 800/PK-8
408 S Belleville St 62243 618-539-3188
Tomi Diefenbach, supt. Fax 539-5795
www.frg70.org
Freeburg ES 500/3-8
408 S Belleville St 62243 618-539-3188
Theresa Goscinski, prin. Fax 539-5795
Freeburg Primary Center 300/PK-2
650 S State St 62243 618-539-3188
Theresa Goscinski, prin. Fax 539-6008

St. Joseph S 100/K-8
2 N Alton St 62243 618-539-3930
John Correll, prin. Fax 539-0254

Freeport, Stephenson, Pop. 24,738
Freeport SD 145 4,100/PK-12
501 E South St 61032 815-232-0300
Dr. Michael Schiffman, supt. Fax 235-4177
www.fsd145.org
Blackhawk ES 300/PK-4
1401 S Blackhawk Ave 61032 815-232-0490
Stacey Kleindl, prin. Fax 232-0578
Center ES 300/PK-4
718 E Illinois St 61032 815-232-0480
Danielle Summers, prin. Fax 232-3247
Empire ES 300/PK-4
1325 Empire Ct 61032 815-232-0380
Alice Stech, prin. Fax 232-0577
Freeport MS 700/5-8
701 W Empire St 61032 815-232-0500
Renee Coleman, prin. Fax 232-0536
Jones-Farrar Magnet S 300/K-4
1386 Kiwanis Dr 61032 815-232-0610
Jennifer DeJong, prin. Fax 235-9220
Lincoln-Douglas ES 200/PK-4
1802 W Laurel St 61032 815-232-0370
Matt Bohrer, prin. Fax 232-0379
Sandburg MS 500/5-8
1717 W Eby St 61032 815-232-0340
Ben Asche, prin. Fax 232-1241
Taylor Park ES 300/PK-4
806 E Stephenson St 61032 815-232-0390
Brian Lamm, prin. Fax 232-0399

Aquin Catholic ES 200/PK-6
202 W Pleasant St 61032 815-232-6416
Sr. Jeremy Keesee, prin. Fax 599-8526

Immanuel Lutheran S 200/PK-8
1964 W Pearl City Rd 61032 815-232-3511
Dan Green M.Ed., admin. Fax 233-9158
Open Bible Learning Center 100/PK-6
3800 W Stephenson St 61032 815-235-7216
Dr. Burliss Parker, admin. Fax 235-9232
Tri-County Christian S 100/PK-8
2900 Loras Dr 61032 815-233-1876
Wendy Schardt, admin. Fax 233-4862

Fulton, Whiteside, Pop. 3,442
River Bend CUSD 2 1,000/PK-12
1110 3rd St 61252 815-589-2711
Darryl Hogue Ed.D., supt. Fax 589-4630
www.riverbendschools.org
Early Step Preschool 100/PK-PK
1217 14th St 61252 815-589-2309
Carol Wilkens, prin.
Fulton ES 400/K-5
1301 7th Ave 61252 815-589-2911
Elizabeth Clark, prin. Fax 589-4614
River Bend MS 200/6-8
415 12th St 61252 815-589-2611
Kathleen Schipper, prin. Fax 589-3130

Unity Christian ES 100/K-6
711 10th St 61252 815-589-4196
Christopher Pluister, prin. Fax 589-4430

Gages Lake, Lake, Pop. 9,985
Woodland CCSD 50
Supt. — See Gurnee
Woodland ES East 1,900/1-3
17261 W Gages Lake Rd 60030 847-984-8800
Lisa West, prin. Fax 549-9806
Woodland ES West 2,300/1-3
17371 W Gages Lake Rd 60030 847-984-8900
Ryan Wollberg, prin. Fax 816-0708
Woodland PS 700/PK-K
17366 W Gages Lake Rd 60030 847-984-8700
Stacey Anderson, prin. Fax 816-4511

Galatia, Saline, Pop. 925
Galatia CUSD 1 400/PK-12
200 N Hickory St 62935 618-268-6371
Shain Crank, supt. Fax 268-4196
www.galatiak12.org
Galatia ES 300/PK-6
200 N Hickory St 62935 618-268-6371
Shain Crank, prin. Fax 268-4949
Galatia JHS 100/7-8
200 N McKinley St 62935 618-268-4194
John Cummins, prin. Fax 268-4196

Galena, Jo Daviess, Pop. 3,404
Galena Unit SD 120 800/PK-12
1206 Franklin St 61036 815-777-3086
Greg Herbst, supt. Fax 777-0303
www.gusd120.k12.il.us
Galena MS 200/5-8
1230 Franklin St 61036 815-777-2413
Ben Soat, prin. Fax 777-4259
Galena PS 300/PK-4
219 Kelly Ln 61036 815-777-2200
Jill Muehleip, prin. Fax 777-4842

Tri-State Christian S 200/PK-12
11084 W US Highway 20 61036 815-777-3800
Dr. Tad Nuce, prin. Fax 777-2991

Galesburg, Knox, Pop. 31,321
Galesburg CUSD 205 4,600/PK-12
PO Box 1206 61402 309-343-1151
Dr. John Asplund, supt. Fax 343-1319
www.galesburg205.org
Bright Futures S 200/PK-PK
932 Harrison St 61401 309-973-2031
Jon Bradburn, dir. Fax 342-7260
Churchill JHS 500/6-8
905 Maple Ave 61401 309-973-2002
Tom Hawkins, prin. Fax 342-6384
Gale ES 300/K-5
1131 W Dayton St 61401 309-973-2011
Jennifer Crock-Sibbing, prin. Fax 343-2635
King ES 400/K-5
1018 S Farnham St 61401 309-973-2012
Joan Hoschek, prin. Fax 343-2161
Lombard MS 500/6-8
1220 E Knox St 61401 309-973-2004
Nick Sutton, prin. Fax 342-7135
Nielson ES 400/K-5
547 N Farnham St 61401 309-973-2014
Matthew Leclere, prin. Fax 343-4574
Steele ES 300/K-5
1480 W Main St 61401 309-973-2016
Matt Lingafelter, prin. Fax 343-1259
Willard ES 400/K-5
460 Fifer St 61401 309-973-2015
Tiffany Springer, prin. Fax 343-1712

Costa Catholic S 200/PK-8
2726 Costa Dr 61401 309-344-3151
Joe Buresh, prin. Fax 344-1594
Galesburg Christian S 100/PK-12
1881 E Fremont St 61401 309-343-8008
Robert Nutzhorn, admin. Fax 342-0235

Galva, Henry, Pop. 2,565
Galva CUSD 224 600/PK-12
224 Morgan Rd 61434 309-932-2108
Doug O'Riley, supt. Fax 932-8326
www.galva224.org
Galva ES 300/PK-6
224 Morgan Rd 61434 309-932-2420
Mary Kelly, prin. Fax 932-8716

Gardner, Grundy, Pop. 1,442
Gardner CCSD 72C 200/PK-8
598 N Elm St 60424 815-237-2313
Ron Harris, supt. Fax 237-2114
www.ggs.grundy.k12.il.us

Gardner ES 200/PK-8
598 N Elm St 60424 815-237-2313
Ron Harris, prin. Fax 237-2114

Geff, Wayne
Geff CCSD 14 100/K-8
201 E Lafayette St 62842 618-897-2465
Jill Barger, supt. Fax 897-2565
Geff S 100/K-8
201 E Lafayette St 62842 618-897-2465
Jill Barger, prin. Fax 897-2565

Geneseo, Henry, Pop. 6,533
Geneseo CUSD 228 2,600/PK-12
648 N Chicago St 61254 309-945-0450
Scott Kuffel, supt. Fax 945-0445
www.dist228.org
Geneseo MS 600/6-8
333 E Ogden Ave 61254 309-945-0599
Nathan O'Dell, prin. Fax 945-0580
Millikin ES 400/K-5
920 S Congress St 61254 309-945-0475
Sarah Boone, prin. Fax 945-0480
Northside ES 400/PK-5
415 N Russell Ave 61254 309-945-0625
Alex Kashner, prin. Fax 945-0620
Southwest ES 400/PK-5
715 S Center St 61254 309-945-0652
Brian Hofer, prin. Fax 945-0670

St. Malachy S 100/PK-6
595 E Ogden Ave 61254 309-944-3230
Jack Schlindwein, prin. Fax 944-5319

Geneva, Kane, Pop. 21,261
Geneva CUSD 304 5,800/PK-12
227 N 4th St 60134 630-463-3000
Dr. Kent Mutchler, supt. Fax 463-3009
www.geneva304.org
Fabyan ES 300/K-5
0S350 Grengs Ln 60134 630-444-8600
Lauri Haugen, prin. Fax 444-8609
Geneva 304 Early Learning 100/PK-PK
1415 Viking Dr Ste 100 60134 630-444-8500
Stephanie Martin, coord. Fax 444-8569
Geneva MS North 700/6-8
1357 Viking Dr 60134 630-463-3700
Lawrence Bidlack, prin. Fax 463-3709
Geneva MS South 700/6-8
1415 Viking Dr 60134 630-463-3600
Terry Bleau, prin. Fax 463-3609
Harrison Street ES 400/K-5
201 N Harrison St 60134 630-463-3300
Brenna Westerhoff, prin. Fax 463-3009
Heartland ES 500/K-5
3300 Heartland Dr 60134 630-463-3200
Kimberly Hornberg, prin. Fax 463-3209
Mill Creek ES 400/K-5
0n900 Brundige Dr 60134 630-463-3400
George Petmezas, prin. Fax 463-3409
Western Avenue ES 300/PK-5
1500 Western Ave 60134 630-463-3500
Ron Zeman, prin. Fax 463-3509
Williamsburg ES 500/K-5
1812 Williamsburg Ave 60134 630-463-3100
Dr. Julie Dye, prin. Fax 463-3109

Geneva Christian S PK-6
1745 Kaneville Rd 60134 630-232-8533
Brittany Smith, chrpsn.
Mansio Mens Montessori S 100/PK-K
102 Howard St 60134 630-232-6750
Janet Shanahan, prin. Fax 232-6255
St. Peter S 500/PK-8
1881 Kaneville Rd 60134 630-232-0476
Tricia Weis, prin. Fax 208-5681

Genoa, DeKalb, Pop. 5,138
Genoa-Kingston CUSD 424 1,800/PK-12
980 Park Ave 60135 815-784-6222
Brent O'Daniell, supt. Fax 784-6059
www.gkschools.org
Genoa ES 300/3-5
602 E Hill St 60135 815-784-3742
John Francis, prin. Fax 784-3731
Genoa-Kingston MS 400/6-8
941 W Main St 60135 815-784-5222
Angelo Lekkas, prin. Fax 784-4323
Other Schools – See Kingston

Georgetown, Vermilion, Pop. 3,408
Georgetown-Ridge Farm CUSD 4 1,100/PK-12
502 W Mulberry St 61846 217-662-8488
Dr. Jean Neal, supt. Fax 662-3402
www.grf.k12.il.us
Miller JHS 300/6-8
414 W West St 61846 217-662-6606
Brad Russell, prin. Fax 662-6345
Pine Crest ES 500/PK-5
505 S Kennedy Dr 61846 217-662-6981
Ashley Vaughn, prin. Fax 662-3413

Germantown, Clinton, Pop. 1,266
Germantown SD 60 300/PK-8
PO Box 400 62245 618-523-4253
Robin Becker, supt. Fax 523-7879
www.germantownbulldogs.org
Germantown ES 300/PK-8
PO Box 400 62245 618-523-4253
Robin Becker, prin. Fax 523-7879

Germantown Hills, Woodford, Pop. 3,399
Germantown Hills SD 69 800/K-8
103 Warrior Way, 309-383-2121
Daniel Mair, supt. Fax 383-2123
ghills.metamora.k12.il.us
Germantown Hills ES 200/K-4
103 Warrior Way, 309-383-2121
Dr. Shelli Nafziger, prin. Fax 383-3392

Germantown Hills MS 300/5-8
103 Warrior Way, 309-383-2121
Dimitri Almasi, prin. Fax 383-4739

German Valley, Stephenson, Pop. 461
Forrestville Valley CUSD 221
Supt. — See Forreston
German Valley ES 100/PK-1
PO Box 74 61039 815-362-2279
Jonathan Schneiderman, prin. Fax 362-2235

Gibson City, Ford, Pop. 3,366
Gibson City-Melvin-Sibley CUSD 5 1,000/PK-12
307 N Sangamon Ave 60936 217-784-8296
Jeremy Darnell, supt. Fax 784-8558
www.gcmsk12.org
GCMS ES 500/PK-5
902 N Church St 60936 217-784-4278
Justin Kean, prin. Fax 784-4782
GCMS MS 300/6-8
316 E 19th St 60936 217-784-8731
Kyle Bieldeldt, prin. Fax 784-8726

Gifford, Champaign, Pop. 972
Gifford CCSD 188 200/K-8
PO Box 70 61847 217-568-7733
Rodney Grimsley, supt. Fax 568-7228
www.gifford.k12.il.us
Gifford ES 200/K-8
PO Box 70 61847 217-568-7733
Rodney Grimsley, prin. Fax 568-7228

Gilberts, Kane, Pop. 6,723
CUSD 300
Supt. — See Algonquin
Gilberts ES 700/PK-5
729 Paperback Ln 60136 847-484-5900
Craig Zieleniewski, prin. Fax 484-5915

Gillespie, Macoupin, Pop. 3,280
Gillespie CUSD 7 1,300/PK-12
510 W Elm St 62033 217-839-2464
Joseph Tieman, supt. Fax 839-3353
www.joomla.gcusd7.org
Ben-Gil ES 600/PK-5
340 Kelly St 62033 217-839-4828
Angela Turcol, prin. Fax 839-3598
Gillespie MS, 412 Oregon St 62033 300/6-8
Jill Rosentreter, prin. 217-839-2116

Gilman, Iroquois, Pop. 1,793
Iroquois West CUSD 10 1,000/PK-12
PO Box 67 60938 815-265-4642
Dr. Linda Dvorak, supt. Fax 265-7008
www.iwest.k12.il.us/
Iroquois West ES - Gilman 200/1-3
PO Box 67 60938 815-265-7631
James Harkins, prin. Fax 265-7693
Other Schools – See Danforth, Onarga, Thawville

Girard, Macoupin, Pop. 2,085
North Mac CUSD 34 800/PK-12
525 N 3rd St 62640 217-627-2915
Jay Goble, supt. Fax 627-3519
www.northmacschools.org
North Mac IS 100/3-5
525 N 3rd St 62640 217-627-2419
John Downs, prin. Fax 627-3409
North Mac MS 400/6-8
525 N 3rd St 62640 217-627-2136
Dennis McMillin, prin. Fax 627-3503
Other Schools – See Virden

Glasford, Peoria, Pop. 1,015
Illini Bluffs CUSD 327 900/PK-12
9611 S Hanna City Glasford 61533 309-389-2231
Dr. Roger Alvey, supt. Fax 389-2251
www.illinibluffs.com
Illini Bluffs ES 500/PK-5
9611 S Hanna City Glasford 61533 309-389-5025
Janet Huene, prin. Fax 389-5027
Illini Bluffs MS 200/6-8
9611 S Hanna City Glasford 61533 309-389-3451
Karen Peterson, prin. Fax 389-3454

Glen Carbon, Madison, Pop. 12,692
Edwardsville CUSD 7
Supt. — See Edwardsville
Cassens ES 600/3-5
1014 Glen Crossing Rd 62034 618-655-6150
Martha Richey, prin. Fax 288-9630
Glen Carbon ES 400/PK-2
141 Birger Ave 62034 618-692-7460
Curt Schumacher, prin. Fax 288-1356

Gateway Legacy Christian Academy 100/PK-12
97 Oaklawn Dr 62034 618-288-0452
Melissa Morrison, prin. Fax 288-0453

Glencoe, Cook, Pop. 8,600
Glencoe SD 35 1,200/K-8
620 Greenwood Ave 60022 847-835-7800
Dr. Catherine Wang, supt. Fax 835-7805
www.glencoeschools.org
Central S 600/5-8
620 Greenwood Ave 60022 847-835-7600
Dr. Ryan Mollet, prin. Fax 835-7605
South ES 300/K-2
266 Linden Ave 60022 847-835-6400
Dr. Kelly Zonghetti, prin. Fax 835-6405
West ES 300/3-4
1010 Forestway Dr 60022 847-835-6600
Dr. David Rongey, prin. Fax 835-6605

Glendale Heights, DuPage, Pop. 33,478
Marquardt SD 15 2,700/PK-8
1860 Glen Ellyn Rd 60139 630-469-7615
Dr. Jerry O'Shea Ed.D., supt. Fax 790-1650
www.d15.us/
Black Hawk ES 500/K-5
2101 Gladstone Dr 60139 630-893-5750
Kim Roberts, prin. Fax 307-6525

Hall ES 400/K-5
1447 Wayne Ave 60139 630-469-7720
Karen Marino, prin. Fax 790-5040
Marquardt MS 800/6-8
1912 Glen Ellyn Rd 60139 630-858-3850
Meredith Haugens, prin. Fax 790-5042
Reskin ES 500/K-5
1555 Ardmore Ave 60139 630-469-0612
Davis Rojas, prin. Fax 790-5041
Other Schools – See Bloomingdale

Queen Bee SD 16 2,000/PK-8
1560 Bloomingdale Rd 60139 630-260-6100
Victoria Tabbert, supt. Fax 260-6103
www.queenbee16.org
Americana IS 400/4-5
1629 President St 60139 630-260-6135
Laura Massarella, prin. Fax 510-8570
Glen Hill ES 500/PK-3
1324 Bloomingdale Rd 60139 630-260-6141
Lonna Hancock, prin. Fax 510-8566
Glenside MS 700/6-8
1560 Bloomingdale Rd 60139 630-260-6112
David Benson, prin. Fax 510-8568
Pheasant Ridge ES 400/PK-3
43 E Stevenson Dr 60139 630-260-6147
Angelica Brifcani, prin. Fax 510-8569

St. Matthew S 400/PK-8
1555 Glen Ellyn Rd 60139 630-858-3112
Regina Pestrak, prin. Fax 858-0623

Glen Ellyn, DuPage, Pop. 27,048
CCSD 89 2,000/PK-8
22W600 Butterfield Rd 60137 630-469-8900
Dr. Emily Tammaru, supt. Fax 469-8936
www.ccsd89.org
Arbor View ES 300/PK-5
22W430 Ironwood Dr 60137 630-469-5505
Dr. David Bruno, prin. Fax 790-6073
Glen Crest MS 600/6-8
725 Sheehan Ave 60137 630-469-5220
Kim Price, prin. Fax 469-5250
Park View ES 400/K-5
250 S Park Blvd 60137 630-858-1600
Barbara Peterson, prin. Fax 858-1634
Westfield ES 300/K-5
2S125 Mayfield Ln 60137 630-858-2770
Stacey Hewick, prin. Fax 858-3618
Other Schools – See Wheaton

Glen Ellyn SD 41 3,600/PK-8
793 N Main St 60137 630-790-6400
Dr. Paul Gordon, supt. Fax 790-1867
www.d41.org
Churchill ES 700/PK-5
240 Geneva Rd 60137 630-790-6485
Kari Keith, prin. Fax 790-6498
Forest Glen ES 600/PK-5
561 Elm St 60137 630-790-6490
Scott Klespitz, prin. Fax 790-6468
Franklin ES 600/PK-5
350 Bryant Ave 60137 630-790-6480
Jeffrey Burke, prin. Fax 790-6403
Hadley JHS 1,200/6-8
240 Hawthorne Blvd 60137 630-790-6450
Steve Diveley, prin. Fax 790-6469
Lincoln ES 600/PK-5
380 Greenfield Ave 60137 630-790-6475
Linda Schweikhofer, prin. Fax 790-6404

Montessori Academy of Glen Ellen 100/PK-6
927 N Main St 60137 630-469-4727
Anne Carlson, head sch Fax 469-2761
St. James the Apostle S 200/PK-8
490 S Park Blvd 60137 630-469-8060
Mary Kathryn Warco, prin. Fax 469-1107
St. Petronille S 500/K-8
425 Prospect Ave 60137 630-469-5041
Maureen Aspell, prin. Fax 469-5071

Glenview, Cook, Pop. 44,009
Avoca SD 37
Supt. — See Wilmette
Avoca West ES 400/K-5
235 Beech Dr 60025 847-724-6800
Jessica Hutchison, prin. Fax 724-7323

East Maine SD 63
Supt. — See Des Plaines
Washington ES 400/PK-6
2710 Golf Rd 60025 847-965-4780
Katharine Anderson, prin. Fax 965-4807

Glenview CCSD 34 4,900/PK-8
1401 Greenwood Rd 60026 847-998-5000
Dr. Dane A. Delli, supt. Fax 998-5094
www.glenview34.org
Attea MS 900/6-8
2500 Chestnut Ave 60026 847-486-7700
Mark Richter, prin. Fax 729-6251
Glen Grove ES 500/3-5
3900 Glenview Rd 60025 847-998-5030
Helena Vena, prin. Fax 998-5101
Henking ES 500/PK-2
2941 Linneman St 60025 847-998-5035
Patricia Puetz, prin. Fax 998-9938
Hoffman ES 600/3-5
2000 Harrison St 60025 847-998-5040
Selene Stewart, prin. Fax 998-6840
Lyon ES 500/PK-2
1335 Waukegan Rd 60025 847-998-5045
Kevin Dorken, prin. Fax 998-9701
Pleasant Ridge ES 500/PK-PK, 3-
1730 Sunset Ridge Rd 60025 847-998-5050
Erik Friedman, prin. Fax 998-5532
Springman MS 800/6-8
2701 Central Rd 60025 847-998-5020
Jason Kaiz, prin. Fax 998-4032

Westbrook ES 500/PK-2
1333 Greenwood Rd 60026 847-998-5055
Jeannie Sung, prin. Fax 998-1872

Northbrook/Glenview SD 30
Supt. — See Northbrook
Willowbrook S 300/K-5
2500 Happy Hollow Rd 60026 847-498-1090
Scott Carlson, prin. Fax 272-0893

West Northfield SD 31
Supt. — See Northbrook
Winkelman ES 500/K-5
1919 Landwehr Rd 60026 847-729-5650
Dana Tamez, prin. Fax 729-5654

Our Lady of Perpetual Help S 900/PK-8
1123 Church St 60025 847-724-6990
Amy Mills, prin. Fax 724-7025
St. Catherine Laboure S 300/PK-8
3425 Thornwood Ave 60026 847-724-2240
Jodi Reuter, prin. Fax 724-5805

Glenwood, Cook, Pop. 8,797
Brookwood SD 167 1,200/PK-8
201 E Glenwood Dyer Rd 60425 708-758-5190
Dr. Valorie Moore, supt. Fax 757-2104
www.brookwood167.org
Brookwood JHS 300/7-8
201 E Glenwood Lansing Rd 60425 708-758-5252
Bethany Lindsay, prin. Fax 758-3954
Brookwood MS 300/5-6
200 E Glenwood Lansing Rd 60425 708-758-5350
Onquanette Pierce, prin. Fax 757-4528
Hickory Bend ES 300/K-4
600 E 191st Pl 60425 708-758-4520
Shawn Jackson, prin. Fax 758-0364
Longwood ES 400/PK-4
441 N Longwood Dr 60425 708-757-2100
Reginald Patterson, prin. Fax 757-2104

Glenwood Academy 100/2-8
500 W 187th St 60425 708-754-0175
Mary Hollie, pres. Fax 754-7834

Godfrey, Madison, Pop. 17,742
Alton CUSD 11
Supt. — See Alton
Brown ES 100/K-1
1613 W Delmar Ave 62035 618-463-2175
JoAnn Curvey, prin. Fax 467-0401
Lewis & Clark ES 100/PK-1
6800 Humbert Rd 62035 618-463-2177
Latasha LeFlore-Porter, prin. Fax 467-0604
North ES 400/2-5
5600 Godfrey Rd 62035 618-463-2171
Heather Johnson, prin. Fax 466-5680

Evangelical S 500/PK-8
1212 W Homer M Adams Pkwy 62035 618-466-1599
Maria Baalman, prin. Fax 466-9498
Montessori Children's House 100/PK-6
5800 Godfrey Rd 62035 618-467-3154
Jane Connell, dir. Fax 467-2332
St. Ambrose S 200/PK-8
822 W Homer M Adams Pkwy 62035 618-466-4216
Jean Heil, prin. Fax 466-4575

Golconda, Pope, Pop. 665
Pope County CUSD 1 600/PK-12
125 State Highway 146 W 62938 618-683-2301
Dr. Charles Bleyer, supt. Fax 683-5181
www.popek12.org
Pope County ES 400/PK-8
125 State Highway 146 W 62938 618-683-4011
Ed Blankenship, prin. Fax 683-6022

Golden, Adams, Pop. 633
Central CUSD 3
Supt. — See Camp Point
Central MS 100/3-4
301 Hanna St 62339 217-696-4652
Lorie Obert, prin. Fax 696-4385

Goodfield, Woodford, Pop. 857
Eureka CUSD 140
Supt. — See Eureka
Goodfield ES 100/K-4
308 W Robinson St 61742 309-965-2362
Randy Berardi, prin. Fax 965-2270

Good Hope, McDonough, Pop. 396
West Prairie CUSD 103
Supt. — See Colchester
West Prairie North ES 100/PK-4
100 N Washington St 61438 309-456-3920
Jennifer Edholm, prin. Fax 456-3936

Goreville, Johnson, Pop. 1,046
Goreville CUSD 1 600/PK-12
201 S Ferne Clyffe Rd 62939 618-995-9831
Dr. Steve Webb, supt. Fax 995-9832
www.gorevilleschools.com
Goreville ES 400/PK-8
201 S Ferne Clyffe Rd 62939 618-995-2142
Christi King, prin. Fax 995-1188

Grafton, Jersey, Pop. 656
Jersey CUSD 100
Supt. — See Jerseyville
Grafton ES 300/PK-4
1200 Grafton Hills Dr 62037 618-786-3388
Michelle Brown, prin. Fax 786-2180

Grand Ridge, LaSalle, Pop. 552
Grand Ridge CCSD 95 300/PK-8
400 W Main St 61325 815-249-6225
Ted Sanders, supt. Fax 249-5049
www.grgs95.org
Grand Ridge S 300/PK-8
400 W Main St 61325 815-249-6225
Terry Ahearn, prin. Fax 249-5049

Granite City, Madison, Pop. 29,332
Granite City CUSD 9 4,500/PK-12
1947 Adams St 62040 618-451-5800
Jim Greenwald, supt. Fax 451-6135
www.gcsd9.net
Coolidge JHS 900/7-8
3231 Nameoki Rd 62040 618-451-5826
Patrick Curry, prin. Fax 876-5154
Frohardt ES 200/3-4
2040 Johnson Rd 62040 618-451-5821
Theresa Mitchell, prin. Fax 876-7627
Grigsby IS 1,000/5-6
3801 Cargill Rd 62040 618-931-5544
Donald Stratton, prin. Fax 931-5689
Maryville ES 100/1-2
4651 Maryville Rd 62040 618-931-2044
Mark Lull, prin. Fax 931-6042
Mitchell ES 100/3-4
316 E Chain of Rocks Rd 62040 618-931-0057
Lisa Delaney, prin. Fax 931-0059
Prather ES 100/PK-K
2300 W 25th St 62040 618-451-5823
Dottie Falter, prin. Fax 876-3843
Wilson ES 100/1-2
2400 Wilson Ave 62040 618-451-5817
John Schooley, prin. Fax 451-6889

Holy Family S 200/PK-8
1900 Saint Clair Ave 62040 618-877-5500
Margaret Holland Pennell, prin. Fax 877-5502
Metro East Montessori S 100/PK-9
4405 State Route 162 62040 618-931-2508
Bridget McGuire, head sch Fax 931-5816
St. Elizabeth S 200/PK-8
2300 Pontoon Rd 62040 618-877-3348
Karen Jakich, prin. Fax 877-3352

Grant Park, Kankakee, Pop. 1,318
Grant Park CUSD 6 500/PK-12
PO Box 549 60940 815-465-6013
Dr. John Palan, supt. Fax 465-2505
www.grantparkdragons.org
Grant Park ES 400/PK-8
PO Box 549 60940 815-465-2183
Tracy Planeta, prin. Fax 465-2381

Granville, Putnam, Pop. 1,410
Putnam County CUSD 535 900/PK-12
400 E Silverspoon Ave 61326 815-882-2800
Carl Carlson, supt. Fax 882-2802
www.pcschools535.org
Putnam County PS 200/PK-2
400 E Silverspoon Ave 61326 815-882-2800
Ronda Cross, prin. Fax 882-2801
Other Schools – See Hennepin, Mc Nabb

Graymont, Livingston
Rooks Creek CCSD 425 50/K-8
PO Box 117 61743 815-743-5346
Todd Bean, supt. Fax 743-5394
www.rookscreek.k12.il.us/
Graymont S 50/K-8
PO Box 117 61743 815-743-5346
Todd Bean, prin. Fax 743-5394

Grayslake, Lake, Pop. 20,539
CCSD 46 3,600/K-8
565 Frederick Rd 60030 847-223-3650
Ellen Correll, supt. Fax 223-3695
www.d46.k12.il.us
Frederick MS 700/5-6
595 Frederick Rd 60030 847-543-5300
Eric Detweiler, prin. Fax 548-7768
Grayslake MS 700/7-8
440 N Barron Blvd 60030 847-223-3680
Marcus Smith, prin. Fax 223-3526
Meadowview ES 400/K-4
291 Lexington Ln 60030 847-223-3656
Laura Morgan, prin. Fax 223-3531
Woodview ES 500/K-4
340 N Alleghany Rd 60030 847-223-3668
Cathy Santelle, prin. Fax 223-3525
Other Schools – See Hainesville, Round Lake, Round Lake Beach

Old School Montessori 100/PK-6
144 Commerce Dr 60030 847-223-9606
St. Gilbert S 600/PK-8
231 E Belvidere Rd 60030 847-223-8600
Brian Tekampe, prin. Fax 223-8626
Westlake Christian Academy 200/PK-12
275 S Lake St 60030 847-548-6209
Dr. Michael Healan, prin. Fax 548-6481

Grayville, White, Pop. 1,656
Grayville CUSD 1 300/PK-12
728 W North St 62844 618-375-7114
Sarah Emery, supt. Fax 375-5202
gcusd.com
Wells ES 200/PK-6
704 W North St 62844 618-375-7214
Dr. Melissa Crow, prin. Fax 375-5202

Great Lakes, Lake
North Chicago SD 187
Supt. — See North Chicago
Forrestal ES 200/K-3
2833 E Washington Ave 60088 847-689-6310
Inez Mitchell, prin. Fax 689-3501

Greenfield, Greene, Pop. 1,063
Greenfield CUSD 10 500/PK-12
311 Mulberry St 62044 217-368-2447
Dr. Kevin Bowman, supt. Fax 368-2724
www.greenfieldschools.org/
Greenfield S 300/PK-8
115 Prairie St 62044 217-368-2551
Jeremy Lansaw, prin. Fax 368-2232

Green Oaks, Lake, Pop. 3,768
Oak Grove SD 68 800/K-8
1700 S OPlaine Rd 60048 847-367-4120
Dr. Lonny Lemon Ed.D., supt. Fax 367-4172
www.ogschool.org
Oak Grove ES 800/K-8
1700 S OPlaine Rd 60048 847-367-4120
Andrew Fenton, prin. Fax 367-4172

Green Valley, Tazewell, Pop. 698
Midwest Central CUSD 191
Supt. — See Manito
Midwest Central MS 200/6-8
121 N Church St 61534 309-352-2300
Kyra Fancher, prin. Fax 352-2903

Greenview, Menard, Pop. 765
Greenview CUSD 200 300/PK-12
147 E Palmer St 62642 217-968-2295
Ryan Heavner, supt. Fax 968-2297
www.greenviewschools.org
Greenview ES 100/PK-5
147 E Palmer St 62642 217-968-2295
Tim Turner, prin. Fax 968-2297

Greenville, Bond, Pop. 6,851
Bond County CUSD 2 1,900/PK-12
1008 N Hena St 62246 618-664-0170
Wes Olson, supt. Fax 664-5000
www.bccu2.org
Greenville ES 700/PK-5
800 N Dewey St 62246 618-664-3117
Eric Swingler, prin. Fax 664-5014
Greenville JHS 300/6-8
1200 Junior High Dr 62246 618-664-1226
Gary Brauns, prin. Fax 664-5071
Other Schools – See Pocahontas, Sorento

Gridley, McLean, Pop. 1,415
El Paso-Gridley CUSD 11
Supt. — See El Paso
El Paso-Gridley JHS 300/5-8
403 McLean St 61744 309-747-2156
Robby Tomlinson, prin. Fax 747-2938

Griggsville, Pike, Pop. 1,219
Griggsville-Perry CUSD 4 400/PK-12
PO Box 439 62340 217-833-2352
Dr. Janet Gladu, supt. Fax 833-2354
www.griggsvilleperry.org
Griggsville-Perry ES 200/PK-4
PO Box 439 62340 217-833-2352
Jillian Theis, prin. Fax 833-2354
Other Schools – See Perry

Gurnee, Lake, Pop. 30,557
Gurnee SD 56 2,200/PK-8
3706 Florida Ave 60031 847-336-0800
Dr. John Hutton, supt. Fax 336-1110
www.d56.org
River Trail ES 500/K-8
333 N Oplaine Rd 60031 847-249-6253
Dr. Jennifer Glickley, prin. Fax 249-4662
Spaulding ES 600/PK-2
2000 Belle Plaine Ave 60031 847-662-3701
Dr. Ellen Mauer, prin. Fax 249-6262
Viking MS 600/6-8
4460 Old Grand Ave 60031 847-336-2108
Patrick Jones, prin. Fax 249-0719
Other Schools – See Wadsworth

Woodland CCSD 50 8,600/PK-8
1105 N Hunt Club Rd 60031 847-596-5600
Joy Swoboda, supt. Fax 856-0311
www.dist50.net
Woodland IS 1,400/4-5
1115 N Hunt Club Rd 60031 847-596-5900
Michael Witkowski, prin. Fax 855-9828
Woodland MS 2,300/6-8
7000 Washington St 60031 847-856-3400
Scott Snyder, prin. Fax 856-1306
Other Schools – See Gages Lake

Country Meadows Montessori S 200/PK-8
6151 Washington St 60031 847-244-9352
Mary O'Young, prin. Fax 244-1068
Gurnee Christian S 50/K-8
2190 Fuller Rd 60031 847-623-7773
Roger Alva, prin. Fax 623-7773

Hainesville, Lake, Pop. 3,496
CCSD 46
Supt. — See Grayslake
Prairieview ES 400/K-4
103 E Belvidere Rd 60030 847-543-6200
Vince Murray, prin. Fax 543-4125

Hamel, Madison, Pop. 815
Edwardsville CUSD 7
Supt. — See Edwardsville
Hamel ES 100/K-2
400 W State St 62046 618-633-2242
Matt Sidarous, prin. Fax 633-1702

Hamilton, Hancock, Pop. 2,918
Hamilton CCSD 328 600/PK-12
270 N 10th St 62341 866-332-3880
Joe Yurko, supt. Fax 847-3915
www.hhs328.com
Hamilton ES 300/PK-6
1830 Broadway St 62341 866-332-3880
Eric Bryan, prin. Fax 847-2337
Hamilton JHS 100/7-8
1100 Keokuk St 62341 866-332-3880
Shelli Jennings, prin. Fax 847-3915

Hampshire, Kane, Pop. 5,507
CUSD 300
Supt. — See Algonquin
Hampshire ES 400/K-5
321 Terwilliger Ave 60140 847-683-2171
Nancy Regul, prin. Fax 683-4806
Hampshire MS 900/6-8
560 S State St 60140 847-683-2522
James Szymczak, prin. Fax 683-1030
Wright ES 600/PK-5
1500 Ketchum Rd 60140 847-683-5700
Melanie Gravel, prin. Fax 683-5715

St. Charles Borromeo S 200/PK-8
288 E Jefferson Ave 60140 847-683-3450
Maureen Jackson, prin. Fax 683-3209

Hampton, Rock Island, Pop. 1,846
Hampton SD 29 200/K-8
206 5th St 61256 309-755-0693
Scott McKissick, supt. Fax 755-0694
hampton29.com
Hampton ES 200/K-8
206 5th St 61256 309-755-0693
Scott McKissick, prin. Fax 755-0694

Hanover, Jo Daviess, Pop. 828
River Ridge CUSD 210 500/PK-12
4141 IL Route 84 S 61041 815-858-9005
Bradley Albrecht, supt. Fax 858-9006
www.riverridge210.org
River Ridge ES 300/PK-5
4141 IL Route 84 S 61041 815-858-9005
Beau Buchs, prin. Fax 858-9006
River Ridge MS 100/6-8
4141 IL Route 84 S 61041 815-858-9005
Michael Foltz, prin. Fax 858-9006

Hanover Park, Cook, Pop. 37,237
CCSD 93
Supt. — See Bloomingdale
Johnson ES 400/K-5
1380 Nautilus Ln 60133 630-671-8800
Rosanne Sikich, prin. Fax 671-8899

Keeneyville SD 20 1,500/PK-8
5540 Arlington Dr E 60133 630-894-2250
Dr. Michael Connolly, supt. Fax 894-5187
www.esd20.org
Greenbrook ES 500/PK-5
5208 Arlington Cir 60133 630-894-4544
John Gustafson, prin. Fax 289-1063
Spring Wood MS 500/6-8
5540 Arlington Dr E 60133 630-893-8900
Dr. Roslyn Martin, prin. Fax 894-9658
Other Schools – See Roselle

SD U-46
Supt. — See Elgin
Horizon ES 500/PK-6
1701 Greenbrook Blvd 60133 630-213-5570
Jennifer Schwardt, prin. Fax 213-5564
Laurel Hill ES 500/K-6
1750 Laurel Ave 60133 630-213-5580
Maria Lopez, prin. Fax 213-5569
Ontarioville ES 600/K-6
2100 Elm Ave 60133 630-213-5590
Dr. Elizabeth Ma, prin. Fax 213-5574
Parkwood ES 400/PK-6
2150 Laurel Ave 60133 630-213-5595
Ana Arroyo, prin. Fax 213-5579

Schaumburg CCSD 54
Supt. — See Schaumburg
Einstein ES 500/PK-6
1100 Laurie Ln 60133 630-736-2500
Maribeth Kanoon, prin. Fax 736-2501
Fox ES 400/K-6
1035 Parkview Dr 60133 630-736-3500
Colette Bell, prin. Fax 736-3501
Hanover Highlands ES 400/PK-6
1451 Cypress Ave 60133 630-736-4230
Faith Rivera, prin. Fax 736-4231

Hardin, Calhoun, Pop. 960
Calhoun CUSD 40 400/K-12
PO Box 387 62047 618-576-2722
Dr. Kate Sievers, supt. Fax 576-2641
www.calhoun.k12.il.us
Calhoun ES 300/K-8
52 Poor Farm Hollow Rd 62047 618-576-2341
Kathy Schell, prin. Fax 576-2787

St. Norbert S 100/PK-8
PO Box 525 62047 618-576-2514
Rachael Baalman-Friedel, prin. Fax 576-8074

Harrisburg, Saline, Pop. 8,789
Harrisburg CUSD 3 2,100/PK-12
40 S Main St 62946 618-253-7637
Mike Gauch, supt. Fax 253-2095
www.hbg.saline.k12.il.us
East Side IS 500/3-5
315 E Church St 62946 618-253-7637
Natalie Fry, prin. Fax 253-2087
Harrisburg MS 500/6-8
312 Bulldog Blvd 62946 618-253-7637
John Crabb, prin. Fax 253-2093
West Side PS 600/PK-2
411 W Lincoln St 62946 618-253-7637
Kim Williams, prin. Fax 253-2094

Harristown, Macon, Pop. 1,356
Sangamon Valley CUSD 9
Supt. — See Niantic
Sangamon Valley East ES 200/PK-4
PO Box 79 62537 217-963-2621
Valerie Janvrin, prin. Fax 963-2440

Hartford, Madison, Pop. 1,408
Wood River-Hartford ESD 15
Supt. — See Wood River
Hartford ES 200/PK-5
110 W 2nd St 62048 618-254-9814
Natalie Bouillon, prin. Fax 254-7602

Hartsburg, Montgomery, Pop. 309
Hartsburg-Emden CUSD 21 — 200/PK-12
400 W Front St 62643 — 217-642-5244
Terry Wisniewski, supt. — Fax 642-5333
www.hartem.org
Other Schools – See Emden

Harvard, McHenry, Pop. 9,314
Harvard CUSD 50 — 2,500/PK-12
401 N Division St 60033 — 815-943-4022
Dr. Corey Tafoya, supt. — Fax 943-4282
www.cusd50.org
Crosby ES — 800/K-3
401 Hereley Dr 60033 — 815-943-6125
Debbie Holland, prin. — Fax 943-4230
Harvard JHS — 500/6-8
1301 Garfield St 60033 — 815-943-6466
Maura Bridges, prin. — Fax 943-8521
Jefferson ES — 400/4-5
1200 N Jefferson St 60033 — 815-943-6464
Dr. Judy Floeter, prin. — Fax 943-7495
Washington S — 100/PK-K
305 S Hutchinson St 60033 — 815-943-6367
Steve Torrez, prin. — Fax 943-0293

Harvey, Cook, Pop. 24,990
Harvey SD 152 — 2,300/PK-8
16001 Lincoln Ave 60426 — 708-333-0300
Dr. Margaret Longo, supt. — Fax 333-0349
www.harvey152.org
Angelou ES — 300/K-6
15748 Page Ave 60426 — 708-333-0740
Iretha Brown, prin. — Fax 333-9216
Brooks MS — 500/7-8
14741 Wallace St 60426 — 708-333-6390
Michael Allen, prin. — Fax 333-3177
Bryant ES — 400/K-6
14730 Main St 60426 — 708-331-1390
Marcus Baker, prin. — Fax 225-9510
Holmes ES — 400/K-6
16000 Carse Ave 60426 — 708-333-0440
Doelynn Strong, prin. — Fax 225-9511
Riley Preschool — 200/PK-PK
16001 Lincoln Ave 60426 — 708-210-3960
Dr. Deborah Watson-Hill, prin. — Fax 210-2218
Sandburg ES — 100/K-6
14500 Myrtle Ave 60426 — 708-333-1351
Dr. Deborah Watson-Hill, prin. — Fax 333-9188
Whittier ES — 300/K-6
71 E 152nd St 60426 — 708-331-1130
Roxie Thomas, prin. — Fax 333-9162

South Holland SD 151
Supt. — See South Holland
Taft Primary Center — 400/PK-1
393 E 163rd St 60426 — 708-339-2710
Dr. Regina Hampton, prin. — Fax 210-3254

West Harvey-Dixmoor SD 147 — 1,300/PK-8
191 W 155th Pl 60426 — 708-339-9500
J. Kay Giles, supt. — Fax 596-7020
www.whd147.org
Other Schools – See Dixmoor

Harwood Heights, Cook, Pop. 8,493
Union Ridge SD 86 — 600/PK-8
4600 N Oak Park Ave 60706 — 708-867-5822
Michael Maguire, supt. — Fax 867-5826
www.urs86.org
Union Ridge ES — 600/PK-8
4600 N Oak Park Ave 60706 — 708-867-5822
Michael Maguire, admin. — Fax 867-5826

Havana, Mason, Pop. 3,277
Havana CUSD 126 — 1,100/PK-12
501 S McKinley St 62644 — 309-543-3384
Mathew Plater, supt. — Fax 543-3385
www.havana126.weebly.com
Havana JHS — 300/PK-PK, 5-
801 E Laurel Ave 62644 — 309-543-6677
Chris Snider, prin. — Fax 543-6678
New Central ES — 400/K-4
215 N Pearl St 62644 — 309-543-2241
John Dunker, prin. — Fax 543-6259

Hawthorn Woods, Lake, Pop. 7,541
Lake Zurich CUSD 95
Supt. — See Lake Zurich
Lake Zurich MS North Campus — 700/6-8
95 Hubbard Ln 60047 — 847-719-3600
Todd Jakowitsch, prin. — Fax 719-3620
Loomis ES — 500/K-5
1 Hubbard Ln 60047 — 847-719-3300
Sandy Allen, prin. — Fax 719-3320

St. Matthew Lutheran S — 100/PK-K
24480 N Old McHenry Rd 60047 — 847-438-6103
Doug Duval, admin. — Fax 438-0376

Hazel Crest, Cook, Pop. 13,848
Hazel Crest SD 152-5 — 700/PK-8
1910 W 170th St 60429 — 708-335-0790
Dr. Sheila Harrison-Williams, supt. — Fax 335-3520
www.sd1525.org
White Learning Academy — 600/PK-8
16910 Western 60429 — 708-825-2190
Dr. Cynthia Levy, prin. — Fax 825-0795
Other Schools – See Markham

Prairie-Hills ESD 144
Supt. — See Markham
Chateaux ES — 300/PK-5
3600 Chambord Ln 60429 — 708-335-9776
Glen Greene, prin. — Fax 335-4808
Highlands ES — 300/K-5
3420 Laurel Ln 60429 — 708-335-9773
Tiffany Burnett-Johnson, prin. — Fax 335-1929
Jemison S — 400/K-5
3450 W 177th St 60429 — 708-225-3636
Kevin Johns, prin. — Fax 799-8363

Hebron, McHenry, Pop. 1,203
Alden Hebron SD 19 — 400/PK-12
11915 Price Rd 60034 — 815-648-2442
Dr. Debbie Ehlenburg, supt. — Fax 648-2339
www.alden-hebron.org
Alden-Hebron ES — 200/PK-5
11915 Price Rd 60034 — 815-648-2442
Tiffany Elswick, prin. — Fax 648-2339
Alden-Hebron MS — 100/6-8
9604 Illinois St 60034 — 815-648-2442
Tim Hayunga, prin. — Fax 648-2339

Hennepin, Putnam, Pop. 748
Putnam County CUSD 535
Supt. — See Granville
Putnam County ES — 200/3-5
326 S 5th St 61327 — 815-882-2800
Courtney Balestri, prin. — Fax 925-7435

Henry, Marshall, Pop. 2,442
Henry-Senachwine CUSD 5 — 600/PK-12
1023 College St 61537 — 309-364-3614
Dr. Michael Miller, supt. — Fax 364-2990
www.hscud5.org
Henry-Senachwine Grade S — 400/PK-8
201 Richard St 61537 — 309-364-2531
Dr. Julie Nelson, prin. — Fax 364-2000

Herrick, Shelby, Pop. 436
Cowden-Herrick Community USD 3A
Supt. — See Cowden
Cowden-Herrick ES — 200/K-5
301 N Broadway St 62431 — 618-428-5223
Tina Oldham, prin. — Fax 428-5222

Mid-America Preparatory S — 100/K-12
PO Box 300 62431 — 618-428-5620
Rick Allen, prin. — Fax 428-5604

Herrin, Williamson, Pop. 12,262
Herrin CUSD 4 — 2,500/PK-12
500 N 10th St 62948 — 618-988-8024
Dr. Terry Ryker Ph.D., supt. — Fax 942-6998
www.herrinschools.org
Herrin ES — 700/2-5
5200 Herrin Rd 62948 — 618-942-2744
Bobbi Bigler, prin. — Fax 942-5817
Herrin JHS — 500/6-8
700 S 14th St 62948 — 618-942-7461
Brad Heuring, prin. — Fax 988-8821
North Side Primary Center — 500/PK-1
601 N 17th St 62948 — 618-942-5418
Matt Vienow, prin. — Fax 942-3579

Our Lady of Mt. Carmel S — 300/K-8
300 W Monroe St 62948 — 618-942-4484
Faye Myatt, prin. — Fax 942-2864

Herscher, Kankakee, Pop. 1,577
Herscher CUSD 2 — 1,800/PK-12
PO Box 504 60941 — 815-426-2162
Dr. Richard Decman, supt. — Fax 426-2872
www.hcusd2.org
Herscher IS — 400/PK-PK, 2-
PO Box 504 60941 — 815-426-2242
Brett Miller, prin. — Fax 426-6862
Other Schools – See Bonfield, Kankakee

Heyworth, McLean, Pop. 2,807
Heyworth CUSD 4 — 1,000/PK-12
522 E Main St 61745 — 309-473-3727
Lisa Taylor, supt. — Fax 473-2220
www.husd4.org
Heyworth ES — 500/PK-6
100 S Joselyn St 61745 — 309-473-2822
Brian Bradshaw, prin. — Fax 473-9013

Hickory Hills, Cook, Pop. 13,836
North Palos SD 117
Supt. — See Palos Hills
Conrady JHS — 1,000/6-8
7950 W 97th St 60457 — 708-233-4500
Andy Anderson, prin. — Fax 430-8964
Dorn S — 500/PK-1
7840 W 92nd St 60457 — 708-233-5600
Dr. Eileen McCaffrey, prin. — Fax 430-6649
Glen Oaks ES — 700/2-5
9045 S 88th Ave 60457 — 708-233-6800
Gaylyn Pollard, prin. — Fax 430-6636

St. Patricia S — 200/PK-8
9000 S 86th Ave 60457 — 708-598-8200
Jamie Nowinkski, prin. — Fax 598-8233

Highland, Madison, Pop. 9,807
Highland CUSD 5 — 2,800/PK-12
400 Broadway 62249 — 618-654-2106
Michael Sutton, supt. — Fax 654-5424
www.highlandcusd5.org
Grantfork Upper ES — 50/4-5
400 Broadway 62249 — 618-675-2200
Cynthia Tolbert, prin. — Fax 675-2204
Highland ES — 600/3-5
400 Broadway 62249 — 618-654-2108
Lori Miscik, prin. — Fax 654-1551
Highland MS — 500/6-8
400 Broadway 62249 — 618-651-8800
Dr. Erick Baer, prin. — Fax 654-1551
Highland PS — 600/PK-2
400 Broadway 62249 — 618-654-2107
Julie Korte, prin. — Fax 654-1591
Other Schools – See Alhambra

St. Paul S — 300/PK-8
1416 Main St 62249 — 618-654-7525
Kathy Sherman, prin. — Fax 654-8795

Highland Park, Lake, Pop. 29,398
North Shore SD 112 — 4,400/PK-8
1936 Green Bay Rd 60035 — 224-765-3000
Edward Rafferty, supt. — Fax 765-3083
www.nssd112.org
Braeside ES — 300/K-5
150 Pierce Rd 60035 — 224-765-3400
Joey Hailpern, prin. — Fax 765-3408
Edgewood MS — 600/6-8
929 Edgewood Rd 60035 — 224-765-3200
Matt Eriksen, prin. — Fax 765-3208
Elm Place MS — 400/6-8
2031 Sheridan Rd 60035 — 224-765-3300
Heather Schumacher, prin. — Fax 765-3308
Green Bay ECC — 200/PK-PK
1936 Green Bay Rd 60035 — 224-765-3060
Chelsey Maxwell, prin. — Fax 765-3084
Indian Trail ES — 400/K-5
2075 Saint Johns Ave 60035 — 224-765-3500
Dr. Maria Grable, prin. — Fax 765-3508
Lincoln ES — 200/K-5
711 Lincoln Ave W 60035 — 224-765-3550
Jeanne Banas, prin. — Fax 765-3558
Northwood JHS — 500/6-8
945 North Ave 60035 — 224-765-3600
Joanne Dimitriou, prin. — Fax 765-3608
Ravinia ES — 300/K-5
763 Dean Ave 60035 — 224-765-3700
Courtney Nordstrom, prin. — Fax 765-3708
Red Oak ES — 300/K-5
530 Red Oak Ln 60035 — 224-765-3750
Shawn Tiani, prin. — Fax 765-3758
Sherwood ES — 300/K-5
1900 Stratford Rd 60035 — 224-765-3800
Nicole Bellini, prin. — Fax 765-3808
Thomas ES — 300/K-5
2939 Summit Ave 60035 — 224-765-3900
Maureen Deely, prin. — Fax 765-3908
Other Schools – See Highwood

Highwood, Lake, Pop. 5,342
North Shore SD 112
Supt. — See Highland Park
Oak Terrace ES — 500/K-5
240 Prairie Ave 60040 — 224-765-3100
Amy Cengel, prin. — Fax 765-3108

Hillsboro, Montgomery, Pop. 6,176
Hillsboro CUSD 3 — 1,800/PK-12
1311 Vandalia Rd 62049 — 217-532-2942
David Powell, supt. — Fax 532-3137
www.hillsboroschools.net
Beckemeyer ES — 700/PK-5
1035 Seymour Ave 62049 — 217-532-6994
Zachary Frailey, prin. — Fax 532-5153
Hillsboro JHS — 400/6-8
909 Rountree St 62049 — 217-532-3742
Mark Fenske, prin. — Fax 532-6211
Other Schools – See Coffeen

Hillside, Cook, Pop. 8,034
Hillside SD 93 — 500/K-8
4804 Harrison St 60162 — 708-449-7280
Dr. Kevin Suchinski, supt. — Fax 449-5056
hillside93.sharpschool.com
Hillside S — 500/K-8
4804 Harrison St 60162 — 708-449-6491
Bridget Gainer, prin. — Fax 449-1644

Hillside Montessori S — 100/PK-5
4600 Frontage Rd 60162 — 708-547-8909
Immanuel Christian Academy — 100/PK-8
2329 S Wolf Rd 60162 — 708-562-5580
Matthew Kamien, admin. — Fax 562-6085

Hinckley, DeKalb, Pop. 2,046
Hinckley-Big Rock CUSD 429 — 700/PK-12
700 E Lincoln Ave 60520 — 815-286-7578
Dr. Travis McGuire, supt. — Fax 286-7577
www.hbr429.org
Hinckley-Big Rock ES — 300/PK-5
600 W Lincoln Hwy 60520 — 815-286-3400
Julie Melnyk, prin. — Fax 286-3401
Other Schools – See Big Rock

Hinsdale, DuPage, Pop. 16,548
CCSD 181
Supt. — See Clarendon Hills
Hinsdale MS — 800/6-8
100 S Garfield Ave 60521 — 630-861-4700
Ruben Pena, prin. — Fax 655-9754
Lane ES — 400/K-5
500 N Elm St 60521 — 630-861-4500
Brandon Todd, prin. — Fax 655-9735
Madison ES — 400/K-5
611 S Madison St 60521 — 630-861-4100
Kim Rutan, prin. — Fax 655-9742
Monroe ES — 400/K-5
210 N Madison St 60521 — 630-861-4200
Justin Horne, prin. — Fax 655-9716
Oak ES — 400/PK-5
950 S Oak St 60521 — 630-861-4300
Dr. Martha Henrikson, prin. — Fax 887-0240

Hinsdale Adventist Academy — 300/PK-12
631 E Hickory St 60521 — 630-323-9211
St. Isaac Jogues S — 500/K-8
421 S Clay St 60521 — 630-323-3244
Carol Burlinski, prin. — Fax 655-6676

Hodgkins, Cook, Pop. 1,893
La Grange SD 105
Supt. — See La Grange
Hodgkins ES — 200/PK-6
6516 Kane Ave 60525 — 708-482-2740
John Signatur, prin. — Fax 482-2728

Hoffman, Clinton, Pop. 506

Trinity Lutheran S 100/PK-8
PO Box 200 62250 618-495-2246
Beth Boester, prin. Fax 495-2692

Hoffman Estates, Cook, Pop. 50,808
Palatine CCSD 15
Supt. — See Palatine
Jefferson ES 600/K-6
3805 Winston Dr 60192 847-963-5400
Lawrence Sasso, prin. Fax 963-5406
Whiteley ES 600/K-6
4335 Haman Ave 60192 847-963-7200
Robert Harris, prin. Fax 963-7206

SD U-46
Supt. — See Elgin
Lincoln ES 600/K-6
1650 Maureen Dr 60192 847-289-6639
Abbie Eklund, prin. Fax 888-7195
Timber Trails ES 600/K-6
1675 McDonough Rd 60192 847-289-6640
Dr. Elisa Biancalana, prin. Fax 888-7011

Schaumburg CCSD 54
Supt. — See Schaumburg
Armstrong ES 500/PK-6
1320 Kingsdale Rd, 847-357-6700
Diana Lipman, prin. Fax 357-6701
Churchill ES 400/K-6
1520 Jones Rd 60195 847-357-6300
Steve Kern, prin. Fax 357-6301
Eisenhower JHS 600/7-8
800 Hassell Rd, 847-357-5500
Heather Wilson, prin. Fax 357-5501
Fairview ES 600/K-6
375 Arizona Blvd, 847-357-5700
Judy Gurga, prin. Fax 357-5701
Lakeview ES 600/PK-6
615 Lakeview Ln, 847-357-6600
Dr. Laura Rosenblum, prin. Fax 357-6601
Lincoln Prairie S 400/K-8
500 Hillcrest Blvd, 847-357-5955
Amanda Stochl, prin. Fax 357-5956
MacArthur International Spanish Academy 400/K-6
1800 Chippendale Rd, 847-357-6650
Heidi LaFleur, prin. Fax 357-6651
Muir Literacy Academy 500/K-6
1973 Kensington Ln, 847-357-6444
Carolyn Allar, prin. Fax 357-6445

Montessori Academy of North Hoffman 100/PK-12
1200 Freeman Rd 60192 847-705-1234
Sara Motlagh, head sch Fax 705-0506
St. Hubert S 500/PK-8
255 Flagstaff Ln, 847-885-7702
Kelly Bourrell, prin. Fax 885-0604
Valeo Academy 100/K-12
2500 Beverly Rd 60192 847-645-9300
Dunia Baca, prin. Fax 645-3986

Homer, Champaign, Pop. 1,182
Heritage CUSD 8 500/K-12
512 W 1st St 61849 217-896-2041
Thomas Davis, supt. Fax 896-2338
www.heritage.k12.il.us
Heritage ES 300/K-8
512 W 1st St 61849 217-896-2421
Kristi Sanders, prin. Fax 896-2338

Homer Glen, Will
Homer CCSD 33C 3,400/PK-8
15733 S Bell Rd, 708-226-7600
Dr. Kara Coglianese, supt. Fax 226-7627
www.homerschools.org
Goodings Grove ES 400/1-4
12914 W 143rd St, 708-226-7650
Ann Christie, prin. Fax 301-7288
Hadley MS 800/5-6
15731 S Bell Rd, 708-226-7725
Kristen Schroeder, prin. Fax 226-7733
Homer JHS 800/7-8
15711 S Bell Rd, 708-226-7800
Troy Mitchell, prin. Fax 226-7859
Schilling ES 300/K-4
16025 S Cedar Rd, 708-226-7900
Candis Gasa, prin. Fax 301-1583
Young ES 600/PK-PK, 1-
16240 S Cedar Rd, 708-226-2010
Mike Szopinski, prin. Fax 838-6406
Other Schools – See Lockport

Hometown, Cook, Pop. 4,316
Oak Lawn-Hometown SD 123
Supt. — See Oak Lawn
Hometown ES 400/K-5
8870 S Duffy Ave 60456 708-423-7360
Dr. Kathleen Spreitzer, prin. Fax 499-7679

Homewood, Cook, Pop. 18,862
Homewood SD 153 1,500/PK-8
18205 Aberdeen St 60430 708-799-5661
Dr. Dale Mitchell, supt. Fax 799-1377
www.hsd153.org
Churchill S 400/3-5
1300 190th St 60430 708-798-3424
Nicole Kerr, prin. Fax 798-0417
Hart JHS 500/6-8
18220 Morgan St 60430 708-799-5544
Dr. Scott McAlister, prin. Fax 799-8360
Willow S 600/PK-2
1804 Willow Rd 60430 708-798-3720
Melissa Lawson, prin. Fax 798-0016

Hoopeston, Vermilion, Pop. 5,322
Hoopeston Area CUSD 11 1,300/PK-12
615 E Orange St 60942 217-283-6668
Suzzette Hesser, supt. Fax 283-5431
www.hoopeston.k12.il.us
Greer ES 200/3-5
609 W Main St 60942 217-283-6667
Dan Walder, prin. Fax 283-5431
Hoopeston Area MS 200/6-8
615 E Orange St 60942 217-283-6664
Anne Burton, prin. Fax 283-5431
Maple ES 400/PK-2
500 S 4th St 60942 217-283-6665
Susan Root, prin. Fax 283-5431

Hopkins Park, Kankakee, Pop. 598
Pembroke CCSD 259 300/PK-8
PO Box 546 60944 815-944-5448
John Thomas, supt. Fax 944-6750
www.pembroke.k12.il.us
Smith ES 300/PK-8
4120 S Wheeler Rd 60944 815-944-5219
John Thomas, prin. Fax 944-9214

Hoyleton, Washington, Pop. 528

Trinity Lutheran S 100/PK-8
PO Box 57 62803 618-493-7754
Brett Jones, admin. Fax 493-7754

Hudson, McLean, Pop. 1,821
McLean County Unit SD 5
Supt. — See Normal
Hudson ES 300/K-5
205 S Mclean St 61748 309-557-4419
Scott Myers, prin. Fax 557-4520

Hume, Edgar, Pop. 377
Shiloh CUSD 1 300/PK-12
21751 N 575th St 61932 217-887-2364
Dr. Allen Hall, supt. Fax 887-2448
www.shiloh1.us
Shiloh ES 100/PK-5
21751 N 575th St 61932 217-887-2364
Elizabeth Harbaugh, prin. Fax 887-2209

Huntley, McHenry, Pop. 23,973
Consolidated SD 158
Supt. — See Algonquin
Leggee ES 1,100/K-5
13723 Harmony Rd 60142 847-659-6200
Scott Iddings, prin. Fax 659-6220

Hutsonville, Crawford, Pop. 551
Hutsonville CUSD 1 400/PK-12
500 W Clover St 62433 618-563-4912
Julie Kraemer, supt. Fax 563-9122
hutsonvilletigers.net
Hutsonville ES 300/PK-8
500 W Clover St 62433 618-563-4812
Guy Rumler, prin. Fax 563-9122

Illinois City, Rock Island
Rockridge CUSD 300
Supt. — See Taylor Ridge
Illinois City ES 100/K-2
24017 122nd Ave W 61259 309-793-8090
Sarah Leonard, prin. Fax 791-0710

Illiopolis, Sangamon, Pop. 880
Sangamon Valley CUSD 9
Supt. — See Niantic
Sangamon Valley MS 200/6-8
341 Matilda St 62539 217-486-2241
Cody Trigg, prin. Fax 486-6038
Sangamon Valley West ES 100/PK-5
341 Matilda St 62539 217-486-7521
Brian Britton, prin. Fax 486-5601

Ina, Jefferson, Pop. 2,329
Spring Garden Community Cons SD 178
Supt. — See Mount Vernon
Spring Garden MS 100/4-8
PO Box 129 62846 618-437-5361
Tommi Jo Ryan, prin. Fax 437-5333

Ingleside, See Fox Lake
Big Hollow SD 38 1,800/PK-8
26051 W Nippersink Rd 60041 847-740-1490
Robert Gold, supt. Fax 587-2663
www.bighollow.us
Big Hollow ES 600/2-4
33315 N Fish Lake Rd 60041 847-740-5321
Michelle Dzik, prin. Fax 740-3795
Big Hollow MS 800/5-8
26051 W Nippersink Rd 60041 847-740-5322
Scott Whipple, prin. Fax 740-9021
Big Hollow PS 400/PK-1
33335 N Fish Lake Rd 60041 847-740-5320
Lenayn Janusz, prin.

Gavin SD 37 600/PK-8
25775 W IL Route 134 60041 847-546-2916
Dr. Julie Brua, supt. Fax 546-9584
www.gavin37.org
Gavin Central ES 300/PK-4
36414 N Ridge Rd 60041 847-973-3280
Dr. Jo Ann Amburgey, prin. Fax 973-3285
Gavin South MS 300/5-8
25775 W IL Route 134 60041 847-546-9336
Jason Jurgaitis, prin. Fax 546-9338

St. Bede S 200/PK-8
36399 N Wilson Rd 60041 847-587-5541
Patricia Strang, prin. Fax 587-2713

Inverness, Cook, Pop. 7,291

Holy Family Catholic Academy 400/PK-8
2515 Palatine Rd 60067 847-907-3452
Kate O'Brien, prin. Fax 705-7646

Irvington, Washington, Pop. 654
Irvington CCSD 11 100/K-8
PO Box 130 62848 618-249-6761
David Schulte, supt. Fax 249-6440
www.irvingtongradeschool.com/
Irvington S 100/K-8
PO Box 130 62848 618-249-6761
David Schulte, prin. Fax 249-6440

Island Lake, McHenry, Pop. 7,988
Wauconda CUSD 118
Supt. — See Wauconda
Cotton Creek ES 700/K-5
545 Newport Ct 60042 847-526-4700
Diane Kelly, prin. Fax 526-4725
Matthews MS 500/6-8
PO Box 920 60042 847-526-6210
Robert Taterka, prin. Fax 526-8918

Itasca, DuPage, Pop. 8,539
Itasca SD 10 1,000/PK-8
200 N Maple St 60143 630-773-1232
Craig Benes, supt. Fax 773-1342
www.itasca10.org
Benson PS 300/PK-2
301 E Washington St 60143 630-773-0554
Dr. Dawn Turner, prin. Fax 285-7474
Franzen IS 300/3-5
730 Catalpa Ave 60143 630-773-0100
Jason Taylor, prin. Fax 285-7468
Peacock MS 300/6-8
301 E North St 60143 630-773-0335
Heidi Weeks, prin. Fax 285-7460

St. Luke Lutheran S 200/PK-8
410 S Rush St 60143 630-773-0509
Rev. Alexander Duff, hdmstr. Fax 773-0786

Iuka, Marion, Pop. 488
Iuka CCSD 7 200/PK-8
405 S Main St 62849 618-323-6233
John Consolino, supt. Fax 323-6932
www.iukaschool.com
Iuka S 200/PK-8
405 S Main St 62849 618-323-6233
John Consolino, prin. Fax 323-6932

Jacksonville, Morgan, Pop. 19,003
Jacksonville SD 117 3,400/PK-12
516 Jordan St 62650 217-243-9411
Steve Ptacek, supt. Fax 243-6844
www.jsd117.org
Eisenhower ES 400/K-6
1901 W Lafayette Ave 62650 217-245-5107
Gary Barlow, prin. Fax 243-2433
Jacksonville MS 500/7-8
664 Lincoln Ave 62650 217-243-3383
Beth Brockschmidt, prin. Fax 243-3459
Lincoln ES 300/K-6
320 W Independence Ave 62650 217-245-8720
Barbara Davidsmeyer, prin. Fax 243-3531
North Jacksonville ES 300/K-6
1626 State Highway 78 N 62650 217-245-4084
Lezlie Fuhr, prin. Fax 243-2818
Walnut Court Early Years Program 200/PK-PK
110 Walnut Ct 62650 217-243-2876
Sarah English, dir. Fax 243-2876
Washington ES 300/K-6
524 S Kosciusko St 62650 217-243-6711
Mary Camerer, prin. Fax 243-3055
Other Schools – See Murrayville, South Jacksonville

Our Savior S 300/K-8
455 E State St 62650 217-243-8621
Stephanie VanDeVelde, prin. Fax 245-6185
Salem Lutheran S 100/PK-8
222 E Beecher Ave 62650 217-243-3419
Lisa Aring, prin. Fax 245-0289

Jacob, Jackson

Christ Lutheran S 50/K-8
146 W Jacob Rd 62950 618-763-4664
Karen Hall, prin. Fax 763-4363

Jerseyville, Jersey, Pop. 8,349
Jersey CUSD 100 2,700/PK-12
100 Lincoln Ave 62052 618-498-5561
Brad Tuttle, supt. Fax 498-5265
www.jersey100.org
Illini MS 500/5-7
1101 S Liberty St 62052 618-498-5527
Jason Brunaugh, prin. Fax 498-7079
Jerseyville East ES 400/2-4
201 N Giddings Ave 62052 618-498-3814
Kim Anderson, prin. Fax 498-6805
Jerseyville West ES 400/PK-1
1000 W Carpenter St 62052 618-498-5265
Kristie Hurley, prin. Fax 498-5265
Other Schools – See Grafton

St. Francis/Holy Ghost S 500/PK-8
412 S State St 62052 618-498-4823
Janet Goben, prin. Fax 498-3827

Johnsburg, McHenry, Pop. 6,290
Johnsburg CUSD 12 2,000/PK-12
2222 Church St, 815-385-6916
Dr. Dan Johnson, supt. Fax 385-4715
www.johnsburg12.org
Johnsburg ES 300/3-5
2118 Church St, 815-385-3731
Dr. Bridget Belcastro, prin. Fax 344-7104
Johnsburg JHS 500/6-8
2220 Church St, 815-385-6210
Nancy Hurckes, prin. Fax 344-7106
Other Schools – See Ringwood

St. John the Baptist S 100/PK-8
2304 Church St, 815-385-3959
Julie Stark, prin. Fax 363-3337

Johnsonville, Wayne, Pop. 75
North Wayne CUSD 200
Supt. — See Cisne

Johnsonville ES 100/PK-4
891 County Highway 16 62850 618-673-3044
Julie Bullard, prin. Fax 673-3094

Johnston City, Williamson, Pop. 3,492
Johnston City CUSD 1 900/PK-12
PO Box 147 62951 618-983-8021
Kathy Clark, supt. Fax 983-6034
www.jcindians.org
Jefferson ES 200/PK-2
1108 Grand Ave 62951 618-983-7561
Andria Murrah, prin. Fax 983-6556
Washington MS 300/5-8
100 E 12th St 62951 618-983-7581
Patty Hilliard, prin. Fax 983-6409
Other Schools – See Pittsburg

Joliet, Will, Pop. 145,165
Joliet SD 86 11,900/PK-8
420 N Raynor Ave 60435 815-740-3196
Theresa Rouse Ed.D., supt. Fax 740-6520
www.joliet86.org
Culbertson ES 400/K-5
1521 E Washington St 60433 815-723-0035
Larry Tucker, prin. Fax 740-5454
Cunningham ES 700/K-5
500 Moran St 60435 815-723-0169
Luis Gonzalez, prin. Fax 726-3040
Dirksen JHS 700/6-8
203 S Midland Ave 60436 815-729-1566
Markisha Mitchell, prin. Fax 744-2346
Eisenhower Academy 300/1-5
406 Burke Dr 60433 815-723-0233
Wendy Wolgan, prin. Fax 740-5455
Farragut ES 700/K-5
701 Glenwood Ave 60435 815-723-0394
Brenda Reiter-Gorman, prin. Fax 740-5950
Forest Park Individual Education S 300/PK-5
1220 California Ave 60432 815-723-0414
Jacob Darley, prin. Fax 740-5452
Gompers JHS 900/6-8
1501 Copperfield Ave 60432 815-727-5276
Constance Russell, prin. Fax 726-5341
Hufford JHS 1,100/6-8
1125 N Larkin Ave 60435 815-725-3540
Kyle Sartain, prin. Fax 744-5974
Jefferson ES 500/K-5
2651 Glenwood Ave 60435 815-725-0262
Christopher Latting, prin. Fax 741-7631
Keith ES 400/PK-5
400 4th Ave 60433 815-723-3409
Casonya Henderson, prin. Fax 740-5951
Marshall ES 600/K-5
319 Harwood St 60432 815-727-4919
Lisa Moreno, prin. Fax 727-0274
Marycrest ECC 300/PK-PK
303 Purdue Ct 60436 815-725-1100
Penny Greenwood, prin. Fax 741-7632
Pershing ES 600/K-5
251 N Midland Ave 60435 815-725-0986
Pam George, prin. Fax 741-7633
Sanchez ES 1,000/K-5
1101 Harrison Ave 60432 815-740-2810
Maria Arroyo, prin. Fax 740-2816
Sandburg ES 400/K-5
1100 Lilac Ln 60435 815-725-0281
Saundra Smith, prin. Fax 741-7615
Singleton ES 600/K-5
1451 Copperfield Ave 60432 815-723-0228
Tony Villagomez, prin. Fax 740-5417
Taft ES 500/K-5
1125 Oregon St 60435 815-725-2700
Joy Hopkins, prin. Fax 741-7635
Thigpen ES 600/K-5
207 S Midland Ave 60436 815-741-7629
Kimberly Gordon, prin. Fax 729-6612
Washington JHS & Academy 700/6-8
402 Richards St 60433 815-727-5271
Rolland Jasper, prin. Fax 740-5451
Woodland ES 500/K-5
701 3rd Ave 60433 815-723-2808
Carol Paul, prin. Fax 740-2633

Laraway CCSD 70C 400/PK-8
275 W Laraway Rd 60436 815-727-5115
Dr. Joseph Salmieri, supt. Fax 727-5289
www.laraway70c.org/
Laraway S 300/2-8
275 W Laraway Rd 60436 815-727-5196
Dr. Joseph Salmieri, prin. Fax 727-5289
Oak Valley ES 200/PK-1
1705 Richards St 60433 815-727-2359
Dr. Joseph Salmieri, prin. Fax 727-0927

Minooka CCSD 201
Supt. — See Minooka
Jones ES 500/K-4
800 Barberry Way 60431 815-290-7100
Dr. Rodney Hiser, prin. Fax 290-7120

Plainfield CCSD 202
Supt. — See Plainfield
Aux Sable MS 1,000/6-8
2001 Wildspring Pkwy 60431 815-439-7092
Dr. Christian Rivara, prin. Fax 577-9476
Crystal Lawns ES 400/K-5
2544 Crystal Dr 60435 815-436-9519
Jennifer Jachowicz, prin. Fax 436-8433
Grand Prairie ES 700/K-5
3300 Caton Farm Rd 60431 815-436-7000
Heather Whisler, prin. Fax 436-1233
Jefferson ES 600/K-5
1900 Oxford Way 60431 815-577-2021
Kristen Smith, prin. Fax 254-6862

Troy CCSD 30C
Supt. — See Plainfield
Troy Craughwell ES 500/K-4
3333 Black Rd 60431 815-577-7313
Kathy Barker, prin. Fax 729-7435

Troy Heritage Trail ES 500/PK-4
3389 Longford Dr 60431 815-577-9195
Brooke Allen, prin. Fax 773-2398

Union SD 81 100/K-8
1661 Cherry Hill Rd 60433 815-726-5218
Timothy Baldermann, supt. Fax 726-5056
www.union81.com
Union ES 100/K-8
1661 Cherry Hill Rd 60433 815-726-5218
Tim Baldermann, admin. Fax 726-5056

Cathedral of St. Raymond S 500/PK-8
608 N Raynor Ave 60435 815-722-6626
Marjorie Hill, prin. Fax 727-4668
St. Jude S 200/PK-8
2204 McDonough St 60436 815-729-0288
Lucas Stangler, prin. Fax 729-0344
St. Mary Nativity S 200/PK-8
702 N Broadway St 60435 815-722-8518
Larry White, prin. Fax 726-4071
St. Paul the Apostle S 400/PK-8
130 Woodlawn Ave 60435 815-725-3390
Corie Alimento, prin. Fax 725-3180
St. Peter Lutheran S 50/K-8
310 N Broadway St 60435 815-722-3567
Claudia Pautz, prin. Fax 722-6544

Jonesboro, Union, Pop. 1,793
County of Union SD 43 500/PK-8
309 Cook Ave 62952 618-833-6651
Thomas Stark, supt. Fax 833-8612
www.jonesboro43.com
Jonesboro S 500/PK-8
309 Cook Ave 62952 618-833-5148
Thomas Stark, prin. Fax 833-3410

Joppa, Massac, Pop. 354
Joppa-Maple Grove CUSD 38 300/PK-12
PO Box 10 62953 618-543-9023
William Biggerstaff, supt. Fax 543-9264
joppa38.com
Other Schools – See Metropolis

Joy, Mercer, Pop. 416
Mercer County SD 404
Supt. — See Aledo
Mercer County JHS 200/7-8
203 N Washington St 61260 309-584-4174
Tim Sedam, prin. Fax 584-4257

Junction, Gallatin, Pop. 129
Gallatin CUSD 7 800/PK-12
5175 Highway 13 62954 618-272-3821
Lucinda Schmitt, supt. Fax 272-4101
www.gallatincusd7.com
Gallatin ES 300/PK-4
5175 Highway 13 62954 618-272-7008
Chris Fromm, prin. Fax 272-4101
Gallatin JHS 200/5-8
5175 Highway 13 62954 618-272-7341
Chris Fromm, prin. Fax 272-4101

Justice, Cook, Pop. 12,733
Indian Springs SD 109 3,000/PK-8
7540 S 86th Ave 60458 708-496-8700
Dr. Blair Nuccio, supt. Fax 496-8641
www.isd109.org
Brodnicki ES 700/K-6
8641 W 75th St 60458 708-496-8716
Dr. Kelly Doogan, prin. Fax 496-8173
Player Primary Center 200/PK-1
8600 S Roberts Rd 60458 708-430-8191
Susan Almendarez, prin. Fax 430-8295
Wilkins ES 600/K-6
8001 S 82nd Ave 60458 708-496-8708
Robert Serder, prin. Fax 728-3114
Wilkins JHS 600/7-8
8001 S 82nd Ave 60458 708-496-8708
Joseph Porrey, prin. Fax 728-3114
Other Schools – See Bridgeview

Kankakee, Kankakee, Pop. 26,896
Herscher CUSD 2
Supt. — See Herscher
Limestone MS 600/5-8
963 N 5000W Rd 60901 815-933-2243
Michelle Chavers, prin. Fax 936-4123

Kankakee SD 111 4,800/K-12
240 Warren Ave 60901 815-802-7700
Dr. Genevra A. Walters, supt. Fax 936-8944
www.k111.k12.il.us
Edison PS 200/K-3
1991 E Maple St 60901 815-802-4300
Cheryl O'Leary, prin. Fax 936-4096
Kankakee JHS 700/7-8
2250 E Crestwood St 60901 815-802-5700
Dr. Larry Gray, prin. Fax 935-7272
Kennedy MS 700/3-6
1550 W Calista St 60901 815-802-4000
Cynthia Veronda, prin. Fax 928-7390
King MS 600/3-6
1440 E Court St 60901 815-802-4100
Alicia Young, prin. Fax 933-4548
Lincoln Cultural Center / Montessori 300/K-8
240 Warren Ave 60901 815-802-4800
Chuck Hensley, prin. Fax 933-0710
Steuben ES 300/K-3
520 S Wildwood Ave 60901 815-802-4600
Ana Kasal, prin. Fax 936-4093
Taft PS 500/K-3
1155 W Hawkins St 60901 815-802-4700
Terrence Lee, prin. Fax 933-0684
Twain PS 200/K-3
2250 E Court St 60901 815-802-4500
Ericka Garza, prin. Fax 936-4099

Grace Christian Academy 200/PK-12
2499 Waldron Rd 60901 815-939-4579
Stephen Bull, prin. Fax 939-1334

Kankakee Trinity Academy 200/PK-12
1580 Butterfield Trl 60901 815-935-8080
Brad Prairie, prin. Fax 935-0280

Kansas, Edgar, Pop. 784
Kansas CUSD 3 200/PK-12
PO Box 350 61933 217-948-5174
John Hasten, supt. Fax 948-5577
www.kansas.k12.il.us
Kansas ES 100/PK-6
PO Box 350 61933 217-948-5175
Robert Edwards, prin. Fax 948-5577

Kell, Marion, Pop. 217
Kell CCSD 2 100/PK-8
207 N Johnson St 62853 618-822-6234
Christopher McCann, supt. Fax 822-6733
www.kellgradeschool.com
Kell Grade S 100/PK-8
207 N Johnson St 62853 618-822-6234
Christopher McCann, prin. Fax 822-6733

Kempton, Ford, Pop. 229
Tri-Point CUSD 6-J 400/PK-12
PO Box 128 60946 815-253-6299
Jeff Bryan, supt. Fax 253-6298
www.tripointschools.org
Tri-Point ES 100/PK-3
PO Box 128 60946 815-253-6299
Angela Winger-Bryan, prin. Fax 253-6298
Other Schools – See Piper City

Kenilworth, Cook, Pop. 2,493
Kenilworth SD 38 500/PK-8
542 Abbotsford Rd 60043 847-256-5006
Dr. Crystal LeRoy, supt. Fax 256-4418
www.kenilworth38.org
Sears S 500/PK-8
542 Abbotsford Rd 60043 847-256-5006
Kendra Wallace, prin. Fax 256-4418

Kewanee, Henry, Pop. 12,667
Kewanee CUSD 229 1,700/PK-12
1001 N Main St 61443 309-853-3341
Christopher Sullens Ed.D., supt. Fax 852-5504
www.kcud229.org/
Alexander S 300/K-1
1401 Lake St 61443 309-852-2449
Jason Stabler, prin. Fax 852-0279
Central JHS 400/4-8
215 E Central Blvd 61443 309-853-4290
Jason Anderson, prin. Fax 853-3195
Irving ES 200/2-3
609 W Central Blvd 61443 309-853-3013
Dr. Tammy Brown, prin. Fax 852-0094
Lyle S 100/PK-PK
920 N Burr St 61443 309-853-2741
Deena Brants, coord. Fax 852-0179
Other Schools – See Neponset

Wethersfield CUSD 230 600/PK-12
439 Willard St 61443 309-853-4860
Shane Kazubowski, supt. Fax 856-7976
www.geese230.com
Wethersfield ES 300/PK-6
439 Willard St 61443 309-853-4800
Janean Friedman, prin. Fax 856-8506

Visitation S 100/PK-8
107 S Lexington Ave 61443 309-856-7451
Sheila Cromien, prin. Fax 852-4259

Kickapoo, Peoria

St. Marys of Kickapoo S 100/PK-8
9910 W Knox St 61528 309-691-3015
Rick Pantages, prin. Fax 691-2898

Kincaid, Christian, Pop. 1,483
South Fork SD 14 400/PK-12
PO Box 20 62540 217-237-4333
Ron Graham, supt. Fax 237-2245
www.southforkschools.com/
South Fork ES 200/PK-5
PO Box 20 62540 217-237-4331
Michelle Rogers, prin. Fax 237-2245

Kinderhook, Pike, Pop. 216
Western CUSD 12
Supt. — See Barry
Western JHS 100/6-8
PO Box 189 62345 217-432-8324
Kent Hawley, prin. Fax 432-8003

Kings, Ogle
Kings Consolidated SD 144 100/K-8
100 1st St 61068 815-562-7191
Greg Stott, supt. Fax 562-5405
www.kings144.org
Kings Community Unit S 100/K-8
100 1st St 61068 815-562-7191
Greg Stott, supt. Fax 562-5405

Kingston, DeKalb, Pop. 1,158
Genoa-Kingston CUSD 424
Supt. — See Genoa
Kingston ES 300/PK-2
PO Box 37 60145 815-784-5246
Stefanie Hill, prin. Fax 784-9049

Kinmundy, Marion, Pop. 794
South Central CUSD 401 700/PK-12
PO Box 189 62854 618-547-3414
Kerry Herdes, supt. Fax 547-7790
southcentralschools.org/
South Central ES 300/PK-5
810 E 1st St 62854 618-547-7696
Sara Rose, prin. Fax 547-3144
South Central MS 200/6-8
PO Box 40 62854 618-547-7734
Greg Grinestaff, prin. Fax 547-7441

Kirkland, DeKalb, Pop. 1,732
Hiawatha CUSD 426 600/PK-12
PO Box 428 60146 815-522-6676
Dr. William Mattingly, supt. Fax 522-6619
www.hiawatha426.org/
Hiawatha PreK-8 S 400/PK-8
PO Box 428 60146 815-522-3336
Jared Poynter, prin. Fax 522-3185

Knoxville, Knox, Pop. 2,888
Knoxville CUSD 202 1,100/PK-12
809 E Main St 61448 309-289-2328
Steve Wilder, supt. Fax 289-9614
www.bluebullets.org
Knoxville JHS 400/5-8
701 E Mill St 61448 309-289-4126
Daniel Powell, prin. Fax 289-4128
Woolsey ES 400/PK-4
106 Pleasant Ave 61448 309-289-4134
Tara Bahnks, prin. Fax 289-9300

Lacon, Marshall, Pop. 1,927
Midland CUSD 7
Supt. — See Sparland
Midland ES, 625 6th St 61540 300/PK-4
Krystal Padilla, prin.

Ladd, Bureau, Pop. 1,286
Ladd CCSD 94 200/PK-8
232 E Cleveland St 61329 815-894-2363
Michelle Zeko, supt. Fax 894-2364
www.laddccsd94.com
Ladd Community Consolidated S 200/PK-8
232 E Cleveland St 61329 815-894-2363
David Lawrence, prin. Fax 894-2364

La Grange, Cook, Pop. 15,333
La Grange SD 102
Supt. — See La Grange Park
Cossitt Avenue ES 600/K-6
115 W Cossitt Ave 60525 708-482-2450
Michael Michowski, prin. Fax 482-2734
Ogden Avenue ES 600/K-6
501 W Ogden Ave 60525 708-482-2480
Joe McCauley, prin. Fax 482-2488

La Grange SD 105 1,400/PK-8
701 7th Ave 60525 708-482-2700
Glenn Schlichting Ph.D., supt. Fax 482-2727
www.d105.net
Gurrie MS 300/7-8
1001 S Spring Ave 60525 708-482-2720
Edmond Hood, prin. Fax 482-2724
Seventh Avenue ES 200/PK-6
701 7th Ave 60525 708-482-2730
Erin Hall, prin. Fax 482-2726
Spring Avenue ES 300/K-6
1001 S Spring Ave 60525 708-482-2710
Brian Lawson, prin. Fax 482-2725
Other Schools – See Countryside, Hodgkins

Pleasantdale SD 107
Supt. — See Burr Ridge
Pleasantdale ES 500/PK-4
8100 School St 60525 708-246-4700
Kathleen Tomei, prin. Fax 246-4625

Children's House Montessori S 50/PK-4
1015 E 31st St, 708-325-8246
St. Cletus S 400/PK-8
700 W 55th St 60525 708-352-4820
Tom Chinske, prin. Fax 352-0788
St. Francis Xavier S 600/PK-8
145 N Waiola Ave 60525 708-352-2175
Sharon Garcia, prin. Fax 352-2057
St. John's Lutheran S 200/PK-8
505 S Park Rd 60525 708-354-1690
Teri Lyn Mannes, prin. Fax 354-4910

Lagrange Hlds, Cook
La Grange Highlands SD 106 700/PK-8
1750 W Plainfield Rd 60525 708-246-3085
Dr. Patricia Viniard, supt. Fax 246-0220
www.district106.net
Highlands ES 400/PK-4
5850 Laurel Ave 60525 708-579-6886
Brian Graber, prin. Fax 485-3611
Highlands MS 300/5-8
1850 W Plainfield Rd 60525 708-579-6890
Michael Papierski, prin. Fax 485-3593

La Grange Park, Cook, Pop. 13,395
Brookfield Lagrange Park SD 95
Supt. — See Brookfield
Brook Park ES 700/K-5
1214 Raymond Ave 60526 708-354-3740
Michael Sorensen, prin. Fax 354-3146

La Grange SD 102 3,100/PK-8
333 N Park Rd 60526 708-482-2400
Kyle A. Schumacher Ed.D., supt. Fax 482-2402
www.dist102.k12.il.us
Barnsdale Road S 300/PK-K
920 Barnsdale Rd 60526 708-482-3003
Kathryn Boxell, prin.
Forest Road ES 500/K-6
901 Forest Rd 60526 708-482-2525
Jeff Bergholtz, prin. Fax 352-4573
Park JHS 700/7-8
325 N Park Rd 60526 708-482-2500
Philip Abraham, prin. Fax 352-1170
Other Schools – See Brookfield, La Grange

St. Louise De Marillac S 200/PK-8
1125 Harrison Ave 60526 708-352-2202
AnnMarie Mahay, prin. Fax 352-6654

La Harpe, Hancock, Pop. 1,230
La Harpe Community SD 347 200/PK-8
404 W Main St 61450 217-659-7739
Dr. Ryan Olson, supt. Fax 659-7730
www.laharpeeagles.org
La Harpe ES 100/PK-5
404 W Main St 61450 217-659-3713
Lila McKeown, prin. Fax 659-7730
La Harpe JHS 100/6-8
404 W Main St 61450 217-659-3713
Lila McKeown, prin. Fax 659-7730

Lake Bluff, Lake, Pop. 5,647
Lake Bluff ESD 65 800/PK-8
121 E Sheridan Pl 60044 847-234-9400
Dr. Jean H. Sophie, supt. Fax 234-9403
www.lb65.org
Lake Bluff ES 500/PK-5
350 W Washington Ave 60044 847-234-9405
Margaret St. Claire, prin. Fax 234-4819
Lake Bluff MS 300/6-8
31 E Sheridan Pl 60044 847-234-9407
Nathan Blackmer, prin. Fax 615-9144

Forest Bluff Montessori S 100/PK-8
8 W Scranton Ave 60044 847-295-8338
Paula Lillard Preschlack, dir. Fax 295-2457

Lake Forest, Lake, Pop. 19,130
Lake Forest SD 67 1,900/K-8
300 S Waukegan Rd 60045 847-235-9657
Michael Simeck, supt. Fax 234-5132
www.lakeforestschools.org
Cherokee ES 400/K-4
475 Cherokee Rd 60045 847-234-3805
Jeff McHugh, prin. Fax 615-4467
Deer Path MS - East 500/5-6
95 W Deerpath 60045 847-615-4770
Tom Cardamone, prin. Fax 615-4464
Deer Path MS - West 500/7-8
155 W Deerpath 60045 847-604-7400
Renee DeVore, prin. Fax 234-2389
Everett ES 300/K-4
1111 Everett School Rd 60045 847-234-5713
Angela Sopko Ph.D., prin. Fax 615-4466
Sheridan ES 200/K-4
1360 N Sheridan Rd 60045 847-234-1160
Michelle Shinn Ph.D., prin. Fax 615-4465

Rondout SD 72 200/K-8
28593 N Bradley Rd 60045 847-362-2021
Dr. Jenny Wojcik, supt. Fax 816-2067
www.rondout.org
Rondout ES 200/K-8
28593 N Bradley Rd 60045 847-362-2021
Dr. Jenny Wojcik, prin. Fax 816-2067

East Lake Academy 100/PK-8
13911 W Laurel Dr 60045 847-247-0035
Rosario Echavez, prin. Fax 247-1937
Lake Forest Country Day S 400/PK-8
145 S Green Bay Rd 60045 847-234-2350
Bob Whelan, head sch Fax 234-2352
Montessori S of Lake Forest 100/PK-9
13700 W Laurel Dr 60045 847-918-1000
Ann Jordahl, dir. Fax 918-1304
School of St. Mary MS 300/4-8
185 E Illinois Rd 60045 847-234-0371
Dr. Venette Biancalana, admin. Fax 234-9593
School of St. Mary PS 300/PK-3
900 W Everett Rd 60045 847-283-9800
David Wieters, prin. Fax 283-0742

Lake in the Hills, McHenry, Pop. 28,527
CUSD 300
Supt. — See Algonquin
Lake In The Hills ES 500/K-5
519 Willow St 60156 847-658-2530
Michelle Smith, prin. Fax 658-2563
Lincoln Prairie ES 500/K-5
500 Harvest Gate 60156 847-960-7735
Mark Wetzel, prin. Fax 960-7743

Consolidated SD 158
Supt. — See Algonquin
Chesak ES 900/K-2
10910 Reed Rd 60156 847-659-5700
Dr. Jennifer Zayas, prin. Fax 659-5720
ECC PK-PK
10910 Reed Rd 60156 847-659-5400
Sheryl Pauwels, prin. Fax 659-5316
Marlowe MS 1,400/6-8
9625 Haligus Rd 60156 847-659-4700
Henry Soltesz, prin. Fax 659-4720
Martin ES 1,000/3-5
10920 Reed Rd 60156 847-659-5300
Julie McLaughlin, prin. Fax 659-5320

Lake Villa, Lake, Pop. 8,603
Antioch CCSD 34
Supt. — See Antioch
Oakland ES 500/2-5
818 E Grass Lake Rd 60046 847-838-8600
James Cieciwa, prin. Fax 838-8604

Lake Villa CCSD 41 2,400/PK-8
131 McKinley Ave 60046 847-356-2385
Dr. Lynette Zimmer, supt. Fax 356-2670
www.district41.org
Martin ES 600/PK-6
24750 W Dering Ln 60046 847-245-3400
Dr. Scott Klene, prin. Fax 245-4521
Palombi MS 700/7-8
133 McKinley Ave 60046 847-356-2118
Victor Wight, prin. Fax 356-0833
Thompson ES 500/PK-6
515 Thompson Ln 60046 847-265-2488
Dr. Sandy Keim, prin. Fax 265-2667
Other Schools – See Lindenhurst

Round Lake Area SD 116
Supt. — See Round Lake
K at Pleviak ES 500/K-K
304 E Grand Ave 60046 847-270-9490
Jason Smith, prin. Fax 740-5183

Prince of Peace S 300/PK-8
135 S Milwaukee Ave 60046 847-356-6111
Elizabeth Brown, prin. Fax 356-6121

Lake Zurich, Lake, Pop. 19,359
Lake Zurich CUSD 95 5,800/PK-12
400 S Old Rand Rd 60047 847-438-2831
Dr. Kaine Osburn, supt. Fax 438-6702
www.lz95.org
Adams ES 400/K-5
555 Old Mill Grove Rd 60047 847-438-5986
Claudia Mall, prin. Fax 438-7740
Fox ES 500/K-5
395 W Cuba Rd 60047 847-540-7020
Lisa Gregoire, prin. Fax 540-7032
Lake Zurich MS South Campus 600/6-8
435 W Cuba Rd 60047 847-540-7070
Dave Gardner, prin. Fax 540-9438
Paine ES 400/K-5
50 Miller Rd 60047 847-438-2163
Marie Rothermel, prin. Fax 438-2528
Whitney ES 600/PK-5
100 Church St 60047 847-438-2351
Chris Martelli, prin. Fax 438-2696
Other Schools – See Hawthorn Woods

Quentin Road Christian S 200/PK-12
60 Quentin Rd 60047 847-438-4494
St. Francis De Sales S 500/PK-8
11 S Buesching Rd 60047 847-438-7921
Roy Rash, prin. Fax 438-7114

La Moille, Bureau, Pop. 722
La Moille CUSD 303 300/K-12
801 S Main St 61330 815-638-2018
Dr. Ricardo Espinoza, supt. Fax 638-2186
www.lamoilleschools.org
Allen JHS 100/4-8
801 S Main St 61330 815-638-2233
Chawn Huffaker, prin. Fax 638-2886
Other Schools – See Van Orin

Lanark, Carroll, Pop. 1,444
Eastland CUSD 308 600/PK-12
500 S School Dr 61046 815-493-6301
Dr. Mark Hansen, supt. Fax 493-6303
www.eastland308.com
Other Schools – See Shannon

Lansing, Cook, Pop. 27,924
Lansing ESD 158 2,400/PK-8
18300 Greenbay Ave 60438 708-474-6700
Cecilia Heiberger Ed.D., supt. Fax 474-9976
www.d158.net
Coolidge ES 700/K-5
17845 Henry St 60438 708-474-4320
Pamela Hodgson, prin. Fax 474-8466
Crawl PS 100/PK-1
18300 Greenbay Ave 60438 708-474-4868
Dr. Kim Morley, prin. Fax 474-0149
Memorial JHS 900/6-8
2721 Ridge Rd 60438 708-474-2383
Dr. Keli Ross, prin. Fax 474-8463
Oak Glen ES 500/K-5
2101 182nd St 60438 708-474-1714
Michael Earnshaw, prin. Fax 474-8461
Reavis ES 300/K-5
17121 Roy St 60438 708-474-8523
David Kostopoulos, prin. Fax 474-3071

Sunnybrook SD 171 1,000/PK-8
19266 Burnham Ave 60438 708-895-0750
Dr. Hughes George, supt. Fax 895-8580
www.sd171.org
Hale ES 500/PK-4
19055 Burnham Ave 60438 708-895-3030
Michelle Johnson, prin. Fax 895-2290
Heritage MS 500/5-8
19250 Burnham Ave 60438 708-895-0790
Shalonda Randle, prin. Fax 895-8580

Lansing Christian S 300/PK-8
3660 Randolph St 60438 708-474-1700
Jonathan Postma, prin. Fax 474-1746
Providence Christian Academy 50/K-8
18420 Burnham Ave 60438 219-588-9090
St. Ann S 200/PK-8
3014 Ridge Rd 60438 708-895-1661
Bonnie Hall, prin. Fax 895-6923
St. John's Lutheran S 200/PK-8
18100 Wentworth Ave 60438 708-895-9280
Dave Swanson, prin. Fax 895-9303

La Salle, LaSalle, Pop. 9,462
Dimmick CCSD 175 100/K-8
297 N 33rd Rd 61301 815-223-2933
Ryan Linnig, supt. Fax 223-0169
www.dimmick175.com
Dimmick Community Consolidated S 100/K-8
297 N 33rd Rd 61301 815-223-2933
Ryan Linnig, prin. Fax 223-0169

La Salle ESD 122 1,000/PK-8
1165 Saint Vincents Ave 61301 815-223-0786
Brian DeBernardi, supt. Fax 223-8740
www.lasalleschools.net
Lincoln JHS 300/6-8
1165 Saint Vincents Ave 61301 815-223-0786
Jon Fox, prin. Fax 223-8740
Northwest ES 600/PK-5
1735 Malcolm Ave 61301 815-223-0786
Dr. Karen Steindorf, prin. Fax 224-6961

LaSalle-Peru Christian S 100/PK-12
PO Box 1043 61301 815-223-1037
Wesley Waddle, prin.
Trinity Catholic Academy 200/PK-8
650 4th St 61301 815-223-8523
Jerry Carls, prin. Fax 223-7450

Lawrenceville, Lawrence, Pop. 4,300
Lawrence County CUSD 20 1,200/PK-12
1802 Cedar St 62439 618-943-2326
Doug Daugherty, supt. Fax 943-4092
www.cusd20.com
Parkside ES 600/PK-5
1900 Cedar St 62439 618-943-3922
Julie Hayes, prin. Fax 943-4591
Parkview JHS 300/6-8
1802 Cedar St 62439 618-943-2327
Jeremy Brush, prin. Fax 943-4092

Lebanon, Saint Clair, Pop. 4,302
Lebanon CUSD 9 600/PK-12
200 W Schuetz St 62254 618-537-4611
Patrick Keeney, supt. Fax 537-9588
lcusd9.org/
Lebanon Grade S 300/PK-5
102 W Schuetz St 62254 618-537-4553
Jeff Teasley, prin. Fax 537-2746

Leland, LaSalle, Pop. 971
Leland CUSD 1 300/K-12
370 N Main St 60531 815-495-3821
Jodi Moore, admin. Fax 495-4611
www.leland1.org
Leland ES 200/K-8
370 N Main St 60531 815-495-3231
Jodi Moore, admin. Fax 495-4611

Lemont, DuPage, Pop. 15,866
Lemont-Bromberek Combined SD 113A 1,900/K-8
16100 W 127th St 60439 630-257-2286
Dr. Courtney Orzel, supt. Fax 243-3005
www.sd113a.org
Oakwood ES 600/K-2
1130 Kim Pl 60439 630-257-2286
Kelly Zimmerman, prin. Fax 243-3006
Old Quarry MS 800/6-8
16100 W 127th St 60439 630-257-2286
Johnny Billingsley, prin. Fax 243-3004
River Valley ES 500/3-5
15425 E 127th St 60439 630-257-2286
Debby Lynch, prin. Fax 243-3007

Everest Academy 100/PK-8
11550 Bell Rd 60439 630-243-1995
Lori Broncato, prin. Fax 243-1988
Montessori S of Lemont 100/PK-8
16427 135th St 60439 815-834-0607
Therese Colby, head sch Fax 834-0681
SS. Alphonsus & Patrick S 200/PK-8
20W145 Davey Rd 60439 630-783-2220
Robert Priest, prin. Fax 783-2230
SS. Cyril & Methodius S 500/PK-8
607 Sobieski St 60439 630-257-6488
Shirley Tkachuk, prin. Fax 257-6465

Lena, Stephenson, Pop. 2,887
Lena Winslow CUSD 202 900/PK-12
401 Fremont St 61048 815-369-3100
Dr. Tom Chiles, supt. Fax 369-3102
www.le-win.net
Lena-Winslow ES 400/PK-5
401 Fremont St 61048 815-369-3113
Mary Gerbode, prin. Fax 369-3171
Lena-Winslow JHS 200/6-8
517 Fremont St 61048 815-369-3114
Andrew Lobdell, prin. Fax 369-3162

Le Roy, McLean, Pop. 3,530
Le Roy CUSD 2 800/PK-12
600 E Pine St 61752 309-962-4211
Gary Tipsord, supt. Fax 962-9312
www.leroyk12.org
Le Roy ES 400/PK-6
805 N Barnett St 61752 309-962-4771
Erin Conn, prin. Fax 962-2893
Le Roy JHS 100/7-8
505 E Center St 61752 309-962-2911
Jeff Baughman, prin. Fax 962-8421

Lewistown, Fulton, Pop. 2,366
Lewistown SD 97 500/PK-12
15501 E Avenue L 61542 309-547-5826
Jeanne Davis, supt. Fax 547-5235
www.lewistown97.com
Lewistown ES 300/PK-6
15501 E Avenue L 61542 309-547-2240
Jeanne Davis, prin. Fax 547-5235

Lexington, McLean, Pop. 2,036
Lexington CUSD 7 500/PK-12
100 E Wall St 61753 309-365-4141
Dwight Strickllin, supt. Fax 365-7381
www.lexington.k12.il.us
Lexington ES 200/PK-5
400 N Cherry St 61753 309-365-2741
Paul Deters, prin. Fax 365-8538
Lexington JHS 100/6-8
100 E Wall St 61753 309-365-2711
Paul Deters, prin. Fax 365-5032

Liberty, Adams, Pop. 512
Liberty CUSD 2 700/PK-12
505 N Park St 62347 217-645-3433
Kelle Bunch, supt. Fax 645-3241
www.libertyschool.net
Liberty ES 400/PK-6
505 N Park St 62347 217-645-3481
Jody Obert, prin. Fax 645-3241

Libertyville, Lake, Pop. 20,013
Libertyville SD 70 2,500/PK-8
1381 Lake St 60048 847-362-9695
Dr. Guy Schumacher, supt. Fax 362-3003
www.d70schools.org
Adler Park ES 300/K-5
1740 N Milwaukee Ave 60048 847-362-7275
Kerri Bongle, prin. Fax 362-8158
Butterfield ES 600/PK-5
1441 Lake St 60048 847-362-3120
Dr. Candice Kehoe, prin. Fax 816-5613
Copeland Manor ES 400/K-5
801 7th Ave 60048 847-362-0240
Lori Poelking, prin. Fax 247-8617
Highland MS 1,000/6-8
310 W Rockland Rd 60048 847-362-9020
Jon Hallmark, prin. Fax 362-0870
Rockland ES 300/K-5
160 W Rockland Rd 60048 847-362-3134
Jeff Knapp, prin. Fax 247-8618

Alta Vista Montessori S 100/PK-K
1850 W Winchester Rd 60048 847-918-1621
Sophia Gindler, head sch Fax 918-1921
Children's House of Libertyville PK-6
223 W Golf Rd 60048 847-816-3590
St. John Lutheran S 100/PK-8
501 W Park Ave 60048 847-362-4424
Jon Woldt, prin. Fax 367-9858
St. Joseph S 500/PK-8
221 Park Pl 60048 847-362-0730
Anne Phoenix, prin. Fax 362-8130

Lincoln, Logan, Pop. 14,271
Chester-East Lincoln CCSD 61 300/PK-8
1300 1500th St 62656 217-732-4136
Laura Irwin, supt. Fax 732-3265
www.cel61.com
Chester-East Lincoln ES 300/PK-8
1300 1500th St 62656 217-732-4136
Laura Irwin, prin. Fax 732-3265

Lincoln ESD 27 1,200/PK-8
304 8th St 62656 217-732-2522
Kent Froebe, supt. Fax 732-2198
www.lincoln27.com
Adams S 100/PK-2
1311 Nicholson Rd 62656 217-732-3253
Christa Healy, prin. Fax 732-8098
Central S 200/K-5
100 7th St 62656 217-732-3386
Kelly Bogdanic, prin. Fax 732-9256
Lincoln JHS 400/6-8
208 Broadway St 62656 217-732-3535
Michael Workman, prin. Fax 732-2685
Northwest S 200/K-5
506 11th St 62656 217-732-6819
Christopher Allen, prin. Fax 735-2172
Washington-Monroe S 300/K-5
1002 Pekin St 62656 217-732-4764
Ginger Yeazle, prin. Fax 732-5913

West Lincoln-Broadwell ESD 92 200/PK-8
2695 Woodlawn Rd 62656 217-732-2630
Bailey Climer, supt. Fax 732-3623
www.wlb92.org
West Lincoln-Broadwell S 200/PK-8
2695 Woodlawn Rd 62656 217-732-2630
Bailey Climer, admin. Fax 732-3623

Carroll Catholic S 100/PK-8
111 4th St 62656 217-732-7518
David Welch, prin. Fax 732-7518
Zion Lutheran S 100/PK-8
1600 Woodlawn Rd 62656 217-732-3977
Pamela Fuiten, prin. Fax 732-3398

Lincolnshire, Lake, Pop. 7,186
Lincolnshire-Prairieview SD 103 1,700/PK-8
1370 N Riverwoods Rd 60069 847-295-4030
Dr. Scott Warren, supt. Fax 295-9196
www.d103.org
Half Day ES 400/3-5
239 Olde Half Day Rd 60069 847-634-6463
Jill Mau, prin. Fax 634-1968
Sprague ES 500/PK-2
2425 Riverwoods Rd 60069 847-945-6665
Ann Hofmeier, prin. Fax 945-6718
Wright JHS 800/6-8
1370 N Riverwoods Rd 60069 847-295-1560
Michelle Blackley, prin. Fax 295-7136

Lincolnwood, Cook, Pop. 12,270
Lincolnwood SD 74 1,200/PK-8
6950 N East Prairie Rd 60712 847-675-8234
Dr. Kimberly A. Nasshan, supt. Fax 675-4207
www.sd74.org
Hall ES 400/PK-2
3925 W Lunt Ave 60712 847-675-8235
Ellen Shankar, prin. Fax 675-9378
Lincoln Hall MS 400/6-8
6855 N Crawford Ave 60712 847-675-8240
Dominick Lupo, prin. Fax 675-8124
Rutledge Hall ES 400/3-5
6850 N East Prairie Rd 60712 847-675-8236
Scott Grens, prin. Fax 675-9320

Lindenhurst, Lake, Pop. 14,182
Lake Villa CCSD 41
Supt. — See Lake Villa
Hooper ES 600/PK-6
2400 E Sand Lake Rd 60046 847-356-2151
Dr. Patricia Planic, prin. Fax 356-0934

Millburn CCSD 24
Supt. — See Wadsworth
Millburn MS 600/6-8
640 Freedom Way 60046 847-245-1600
Jake Jorgenson, prin. Fax 265-8198

Lindenwood, Ogle
Eswood CCSD 269 100/K-8
304 Main St 61049 815-393-4477
Joseph Schwartz, supt. Fax 393-4478
www.eswoodschool.org
Eswood S 100/K-8
304 Main St 61049 815-393-4477
Joseph Schwartz, prin. Fax 393-4478

Lisle, DuPage, Pop. 21,980
Lisle CUSD 202 1,500/PK-12
5211 Center Ave 60532 630-493-8000
Keith Filipiak, supt. Fax 971-4054
www.lisle202.org
Lisle JHS 400/6-8
5207 Center Ave 60532 630-493-8200
David Kearney, prin. Fax 493-8209
Schieser ES 400/K-K, 3-5
5205 Kingston Ave 60532 630-493-8100
Melissa Payne, prin. Fax 968-5976
Tate Woods ES 200/PK-PK, 1-
1736 Middleton Ave 60532 630-493-8050
Wesley Gosselink, prin. Fax 971-4069

Naperville CUSD 203
Supt. — See Naperville
Kennedy JHS 1,000/6-8
2929 Green Trails Dr 60532 630-420-3220
Brian Valek, prin. Fax 420-6960

Kindi Academy 100/PK-8
5801 Westview Ln 60532 630-560-4900
St. Joan of Arc S 600/PK-8
4913 Columbia Ave 60532 630-969-1732
Michael Sweeney, prin. Fax 353-4590

Litchfield, Montgomery, Pop. 6,861
Litchfield CUSD 12 1,500/PK-12
1702 N State St 62056 217-324-2157
Debbie Poffinbarger, supt. Fax 324-2158
www.lcusd12.org
Colt ES 200/2-3
615 E Tyler Ave 62056 217-324-3565
Andrea Lee, prin. Fax 324-3703
Litchfield MS 300/6-8
1701 N State St 62056 217-324-4668
Jennifer Thompson, prin. Fax 324-5693
Litchfield Prekindergarten 100/PK-PK
601 S State St 62056 217-324-3514
Adam Favre, prin. Fax 324-2129
Madison Park ES 200/K-1
800 N Chestnut St 62056 217-324-2851
Adam Favre, prin. Fax 324-5562
Russell ES 200/4-5
705 N Jefferson St 62056 217-324-4034
Andrea Lee, prin. Fax 324-3977

Zion Lutheran S 100/PK-8
1301 N State St 62056 217-324-3166
John Schaff, prin. Fax 324-3166

Lockport, Will, Pop. 24,568
Fairmont SD 89 300/PK-8
735 Green Garden Pl 60441 815-726-6318
Dr. Diane Cepela, supt. Fax 726-6157
www.fsd89.org
Fairmont S 300/PK-8
735 Green Garden Pl 60441 815-726-6156
Tamela Daniels, prin. Fax 726-0079

Homer CCSD 33C
Supt. — See Homer Glen
Butler ES 600/1-4
1900 S Farrell Rd 60441 708-226-5155
Melissa Onesto, prin. Fax 836-0667

Lockport SD 91 700/PK-8
808 Adams St 60441 815-838-0737
Donna Gray, supt. Fax 834-4339
www.d91.net/
Kelvin Grove MS 400/4-8
808 Adams St 60441 815-838-0737
John Jennings, prin. Fax 834-4339
Milne Grove ES 300/PK-3
565 E 7th St 60441 815-838-0542
Jaime Koziol, prin. Fax 838-6893

Taft SD 90 300/K-8
1605 S Washington St 60441 815-838-0408
Dr. Pamela Kibbons, supt. Fax 838-7146
www.taft90.org
Taft S 300/K-8
1605 S Washington St 60441 815-838-0408
Dr. Pamela Kibbons, admin. Fax 838-5046

Will County SD 92 1,700/PK-8
708 N State St 60441 815-838-8031
Dr. Peter Sullivan, supt. Fax 838-8034
www.d92.org
Ludwig ES 400/4-5
710 N State St 60441 815-838-8020
Lisa Lyke, prin. Fax 838-3226
Oak Prairie JHS 600/6-8
15161 S Gougar Rd, 815-836-2724
Mark Murray, prin. Fax 834-2178
Reed ES 400/2-3
14939 W 143rd St, 708-301-0692
Catherine Slee, prin. Fax 301-6501
Walsh ES 300/PK-1
514 MacGregor Rd 60441 815-838-7858
Teresa Martin, prin. Fax 838-3346

Crest Hill Christian S 50/PK-9
21514 W Division St 60441 815-730-0664
Lisa Hauck B.A., prin. Fax 730-8389
St. Dennis S 200/PK-8
1201 S Washington St 60441 815-838-4494
Lisa Smith, prin. Fax 838-5435
St. Joseph S 300/PK-8
529 Madison St 60441 815-838-8173
Lynne Scheffler, prin. Fax 838-0504

Lombard, DuPage, Pop. 42,433
DuPage County SD 45
Supt. — See Villa Park
Schafer ES 500/PK-5
700 E Pleasant Ln 60148 630-516-6500
Edith Rivera, prin. Fax 932-6471

Stevenson ES 300/PK-2
18W331 15th St 60148 630-516-7780
Christine Mazaika-Arado, prin. Fax 889-7923
Westmore ES 500/K-5
340 S School St 60148 630-516-7500
John Gibbas, prin. Fax 932-6492
York Center ES 200/3-5
895 E 14th St 60148 630-516-6540
Ellen Bruning, prin. Fax 932-6543

Lombard SD 44 3,100/PK-8
150 W Madison St 60148 630-827-4400
Dr. Patricia Wernet, supt. Fax 620-3798
www.sd44.org
Butterfield ES 400/PK-5
2s500 Gray Ave 60148 630-827-4000
Kristine Walsh, prin. Fax 889-7960
Glenn Westlake MS 1,000/6-8
1514 S Main St 60148 630-827-4500
Philip Wieczorek, prin. Fax 620-3791
Hammerschmidt ES 400/K-5
617 Hammerschmidt Ave 60148 630-827-4200
David Danielski, prin. Fax 620-3733
Madison ES 500/K-5
150 W Madison St 60148 630-827-4100
Yesenia Vazquez, prin. Fax 620-3769
Manor Hill ES 300/K-5
1464 S Main St 60148 630-827-4300
Eric Haren, prin. Fax 889-7964
Park View ES 300/K-5
341 N Elizabeth St 60148 630-827-4040
Roberta Wallerstedt, prin. Fax 620-3749
Pleasant Lane ES 300/K-5
401 N Main St 60148 630-827-4640
Stephanie Loth, prin. Fax 620-3760

College Preparatory S of America 400/PK-12
331 W Madison St 60148 630-889-8000
Dr. Mohammed Taher, prin. Fax 889-8012
Sacred Heart S 200/PK-8
322 W Maple St 60148 630-629-0536
Dr. Joy Packard-Higgins, prin. Fax 629-4752
St. John's Lutheran S 300/PK-8
220 S Lincoln Ave 60148 630-932-3196
Fax 932-4016
St. Pius X S 500/PK-8
601 Westmore Meyers Rd 60148 630-627-2353
Daniel Flaherty, prin. Fax 627-1810
Trinity Lutheran S 100/PK-8
1165 Westmore Meyers Rd 60148 630-627-5601
Chuck Novak, prin. Fax 627-5676

London Mills, Fulton, Pop. 391
Spoon River Valley CUSD 4 400/PK-12
35265 N IL Route 97 61544 309-778-2204
Christopher Janssen, supt. Fax 778-2655
www.spoon-river.k12.il.us
Spoon River Valley ES 200/PK-6
35265 N IL Route 97 61544 309-778-2207
Jody Collier, prin. Fax 778-2655
Spoon River Valley JHS 100/7-8
35265 N IL Route 97 61544 309-778-2201
Jody Collier, prin. Fax 778-2655

Long Grove, Lake, Pop. 7,912
Kildeer Countryside CCSD 96
Supt. — See Buffalo Grove
Country Meadows ES 400/1-5
6360 Gilmer Rd 60047 847-353-8600
Allison Slade, prin. Fax 949-8233
Kildeer Countryside ES 400/1-5
3100 Old McHenry Rd 60047 847-634-3243
Vail Kieser, prin. Fax 229-7570
Woodlawn MS 600/6-8
6362 Gilmer Rd 60047 847-353-8500
Greg Grana, prin. Fax 949-8237

Montessori S of Long Grove 100/PK-6
1115 RFD 60047 847-634-0430
Lyn Pearson, admin. Fax 726-7928

Lostant, LaSalle, Pop. 496
Lostant Community Unit SD 425 100/K-8
PO Box 320 61334 815-368-3392
Dr. Sandra Malahy, supt. Fax 368-3132
www.lostantcomets.org
Lostant ES 100/K-8
PO Box 320 61334 815-368-3392
Dr. Sandra Malahy, admin. Fax 368-3132

Louisville, Clay, Pop. 1,135
North Clay CUSD 25 700/PK-12
PO Box C 62858 618-665-3358
Monty Aldrich, supt. Fax 665-3893
sites.google.com/northclayschools.com/nccusd25
North Clay ES 500/PK-8
PO Box 279 62858 618-665-3393
Jessica Guzman, prin. Fax 665-4803

Lovejoy, Saint Clair, Pop. 732
Brooklyn Unit SD 188 100/PK-12
PO Box 250 62059 618-271-1014
Dr. Ronald Ferrell, supt. Fax 271-7643
www.lovejoy.stclair.k12.il.us
Lovejoy ES 100/PK-5
PO Box 250 62059 618-271-1014
Dr. Ronald Ferrell, prin. Fax 271-9108
Lovejoy MS 50/6-8
PO Box 250 62059 618-271-1014
Dr. Ronald Ferrell, prin. Fax 271-9108

Loves Park, Winnebago, Pop. 23,555
Harlem Unit SD 122
Supt. — See Machesney Park
Harlem MS 1,100/7-8
735 Windsor Rd 61111 815-654-4510
Matthew Cascio, prin. Fax 654-4540
Loves Park ES 300/1-6
344 Grand Ave 61111 815-654-4501
Lisa Clark, prin. Fax 654-4553
Maple ES 300/1-6
1405 Maple Ave 61111 815-654-4502
Tammy Poole, prin. Fax 654-4563
Rock Cut ES 400/1-6
7944 Forest Hills Rd 61111 815-654-4506
Michael Plourde, prin. Fax 654-4574
Windsor ES 400/1-6
935 Windsor Rd 61111 815-654-4507
Anthony Brooks, prin. Fax 654-4585

St. Bridget S 400/PK-8
604 Clifford Ave 61111 815-633-8255
Mary Toldo, prin. Fax 633-5847

Lovington, Moultrie, Pop. 1,122
Arthur CUSD 305
Supt. — See Arthur
Lovington Grade S 200/PK-8
330 S High St 61937 217-873-4318
Brandon Stone, prin. Fax 873-6120

Ludlow, Champaign, Pop. 360
Ludlow CCSD 142 100/K-8
PO Box 130 60949 217-396-5261
Drusilla Lobmaster, supt. Fax 396-8858
Ludlow S 100/K-8
PO Box 130 60949 217-396-5261
Tanya Vipond, prin. Fax 396-8858

Lynwood, Cook, Pop. 8,864
Sandridge SD 172 400/PK-8
2950 Glenwood Dyer Rd 60411 708-895-8339
Tom Smyth, supt. Fax 895-2451
www.sandridgesd172.org/
Sandridge ES 400/PK-8
2950 Glenwood Dyer Rd 60411 708-895-2450
Cynthia Sowles M.A., prin. Fax 895-8654

Lyons, Cook, Pop. 10,580
Lyons SD 103 2,400/K-8
4100 Joliet Ave 60534 708-783-4100
Fax 780-9725
www.sd103.com
Costello ES 300/K-5
4632 Clyde Ave 60534 708-783-4300
Jennifer Bednarczyk, prin. Fax 656-2275
Robinson ES 300/K-5
4431 Gage Ave 60534 708-783-4700
Alberto Molina, prin. Fax 780-0172
Washington MS 800/6-8
8101 Ogden Ave 60534 708-783-4200
Christopher Cybulski, prin. Fax 780-9757
Other Schools – See Brookfield, Stickney

Mc Henry, McHenry, Pop. 26,740
McHenry CCSD 15 4,700/PK-8
1011 N Green St 60050 815-385-7210
R. Alan Hoffman Ed.D., supt. Fax 344-7121
www.d15.org
Duker ES 400/4-5
3711 W Kane Ave 60050 815-344-7125
Alison Kos, prin. Fax 363-5024
Edgebrook ES 500/PK-3
701 N Green St 60050 815-385-3123
Michelle Reinhardt, prin. Fax 363-5025
Hilltop ES 500/K-3
2615 W Lincoln Rd 60051 815-385-4421
Angelena Colon, prin. Fax 363-5027
Landmark ES 300/K-5
3614 Waukegan Rd 60050 815-385-8120
Margaret Carey, prin. Fax 363-5026
McHenry MS 800/6-8
2120 W Lincoln Rd 60051 815-385-2522
Mike Glover, prin. Fax 578-2101
Parkland S 800/6-8
1802 N Ringwood Rd 60050 815-385-8810
Mike Adams, prin. Fax 363-5023
Riverwood ES 800/K-5
300 S Driftwood Trl 60050 815-344-7130
Kathie Robinson, prin. Fax 363-5021
Valley View ES 600/K-5
6515 W IL Route 120 60050 815-385-0640
Amanda Cohn, prin. Fax 363-5022

McHenry Montessori S 100/PK-6
5213 W Elm St 60050 815-344-1015
Lori Lanphier, prin.
Montini MS 200/4-8
1405 N Richmond Rd 60050 815-385-1022
Michael Shukis, prin. Fax 363-7536
Montini Primary Catholic S 200/PK-3
3504 Washington St 60050 815-385-5380
Michael Shukis, prin. Fax 385-5017
Zion Lutheran S 100/PK-3
4206 W Elm St 60050 815-385-4488
Fax 385-0878

Machesney Park, Winnebago, Pop. 23,071
Harlem Unit SD 122 6,900/PK-12
8605 N 2nd St 61115 815-654-4500
Dr. Julie Morris, supt. Fax 654-4600
www.harlem122.org
Machesney IS 400/4-6
8615 N 2nd St 61115 815-654-4509
Abigail Edwards, prin. Fax 637-7421
Marquette ES 300/1-3
8500 Victory Ln 61115 815-654-4503
Brock Morlan, prin. Fax 654-4565
Olson Park ES 400/1-6
1414 Minahan Dr 61115 815-654-4504
Dyonna Johnson, prin. Fax 654-4528
Parker Early Education Center 600/PK-K
808 Harlem Rd 61115 815-654-4559
Amanda Hayes, prin. Fax 654-4613
Ralston ES 400/1-6
710 Ralston Rd 61115 815-654-4505
Taylor Schmit, prin. Fax 654-4572
Other Schools – See Loves Park

Concordia Lutheran S 50/PK-5
7424 N 2nd St 61115 815-633-6450
Joel Koehler, prin. Fax 654-7998

Mackinaw, Tazewell, Pop. 1,936
Deer Creek-Mackinaw CUSD 701 1,100/PK-12
401 E Fifth St 61755 309-359-8965
Dr. Scott Dearman, supt. Fax 359-5291
www.deemack.org/
Deer Creek-Mackinaw Primary / JHS 500/PK-8
102 E Fifth St 61755 309-359-4321
Michele Jacobs, prin. Fax 359-4015
Other Schools – See Deer Creek

Mc Leansboro, Hamilton, Pop. 2,863
Hamilton County CUSD 10 1,200/PK-12
PO Box 369 62859 618-643-2328
Jeff Fetcho, supt. Fax 643-2015
www.unit10.com
East Side ES 500/K-6
501 E Randolph St 62859 618-643-2328
Mark Scott, prin. Fax 643-2070
Hamilton County Preschool 100/PK-PK
204 W Cherry St 62859 618-643-2328
Christina Epperson, prin. Fax 643-5304
Other Schools – See Dahlgren

Mc Nabb, Putnam, Pop. 278
Putnam County CUSD 535
Supt. — See Granville
Putnam County JHS 200/6-8
13183 N 350th Ave 61335 815-882-2800
Michael Olson, prin. Fax 882-2299

Macomb, McDonough, Pop. 18,862
Macomb CUSD 185 2,000/PK-12
323 W Washington St 61455 309-833-4161
Dr. Patrick Twomey, supt. Fax 836-2133
macomb185.org/
Edison ES 400/4-6
521 S Pearl St 61455 309-837-3993
Kellee Sullivan, prin. Fax 837-9992
Lincoln ES 600/K-3
315 N Bonham St 61455 309-833-2095
Kimberly Gillam, prin. Fax 837-7802
MacArthur ECC 100/PK-PK
235 W Grant St 61455 309-833-4273
Kelly Carpenter, prin. Fax 833-5651
Macomb JHS 300/7-8
1525 S Johnson St 61455 309-833-2074
Dana Isackson, prin. Fax 836-1034

St. Paul S 100/PK-6
322 W Washington St 61455 309-833-2470
Laura Cody, prin. Fax 833-2470

Macon, Macon, Pop. 1,126
Meridian CUSD 15 800/PK-12
PO Box 347 62544 217-764-5269
Daniel Brue, supt. Fax 764-5291
www.meridianhawks.net
Meridian MS 200/6-8
PO Box 198 62544 217-764-3367
Andrew Pygott, prin. Fax 764-3902
Other Schools – See Blue Mound

Madison, Madison, Pop. 3,816
Madison CUSD 12 400/PK-12
602 Farrish St 62060 618-877-1712
Dr. Warletta Brookins, supt. Fax 877-2690
www.madisoncusd12.org
Long ES 100/PK-5
1003 Farrish St 62060 618-876-4818
Terrian Fennoy, prin. Fax 877-2696
Madison JHS 100/6-8
600 Farrish St 62060 618-876-6409
Juan Gardner, prin. Fax 877-2693

Mahomet, Champaign, Pop. 7,188
Mahomet-Seymour CUSD 3 3,000/PK-12
PO Box 229 61853 217-586-2161
Dr. Lindsey Hall, supt. Fax 586-7591
www.mscusd.org
Lincoln Trail ES 700/3-5
PO Box 200 61853 217-586-2811
Jeff Starwalt, prin. Fax 586-5072
Mahomet-Seymour JHS 700/6-8
PO Box 560 61853 217-586-4415
Heather Landrus, prin. Fax 586-5869
Middletown Prairie ES 300/PK-K
PO Box 229 61853 217-586-5833
Carol Shallenberger, prin. Fax 586-5834
Sangamon ES 400/1-2
PO Box 198 61853 217-586-4583
Wendy Starwalt, prin. Fax 586-4849

Malden, Bureau, Pop. 361
Malden CCSD 84 100/PK-8
PO Box 216 61337 815-643-2436
Michael Patterson, supt. Fax 643-2132
maldengradeschool.org
Malden S 100/PK-8
PO Box 216 61337 815-643-2436
Michael Patterson, prin. Fax 643-2132

Malta, DeKalb, Pop. 1,142
DeKalb CUSD 428
Supt. — See DeKalb
Malta ES 300/K-5
5068 IL Route 38 60150 815-825-2081
Kristine Baccheschi, prin. Fax 825-2082

Manhattan, Will, Pop. 6,984
Manhattan SD 114 1,300/PK-8
25440 S Gougar Rd 60442 815-478-6093
Russell Ragon, supt. Fax 478-7660
www.manhattan114.org
Manhattan JHS 400/6-8
15606 W Smith Rd 60442 815-478-6090
Ron Pacheco, prin. Fax 478-6094

McDonald ES 400/3-5
200 2nd St 60442 815-478-3310
Ryan McWilliams, prin. Fax 478-4035
Wilson Creek ES 500/PK-2
25440 S Gougar Rd 60442 815-478-4527
Kim Maher, prin. Fax 478-6035

Christs Academy 100/PK-12
22811 S Cedar Rd 60442 815-485-2833
Sharon Meiergerd, prin.
Community Christian S 100/PK-12
22811 S Cedar Rd 60442 815-485-2379
Fax 485-2627
St. Joseph S 200/PK-8
PO Box 70 60442 815-478-3951
Colleen Domke, prin. Fax 478-7412

Manito, Mason, Pop. 1,628
Midwest Central CUSD 191 1,000/PK-12
1010 S Washington St 61546 309-968-6868
Dr. Todd Hellrigel, supt. Fax 968-7916
www.midwestcentral.org
Midwest Central PS 400/PK-5
450 E Southmoor St 61546 309-968-6464
Rodney Norris, prin. Fax 968-7652
Other Schools – See Green Valley

Spring Lake CCSD 606 100/K-6
13650 N Manito Rd 61546 309-545-2241
Dr. Charles Nagel, supt. Fax 545-2695
Spring Lake ES 100/K-6
13650 N Manito Rd 61546 309-545-2241
Dr. Charles Nagel, admin. Fax 545-2695

Manlius, Bureau, Pop. 356
Bureau Valley CUSD 340 1,100/PK-12
PO Box 289 61338 815-445-3101
Eric Lawson, supt. Fax 445-2802
www.bv340.org
Other Schools – See Buda, Walnut, Wyanet

Mansfield, Piatt, Pop. 902
Blue Ridge CUSD 18
Supt. — See Farmer City
Blue Ridge IS & JHS 100/4-8
PO Box 69 61854 217-489-5201
Katie Nichols, prin. Fax 489-9051

Manteno, Kankakee, Pop. 9,119
Manteno CUSD 5 2,200/PK-12
84 N Oak St 60950 815-928-7000
Lisa Harrod, supt. Fax 468-6439
www.manteno5.org/
Manteno ES 800/PK-4
555 W Cook St 60950 815-928-7200
Matthew Glenn, prin. Fax 468-3030
Manteno MS 700/5-8
250 N Poplar St 60950 815-928-7150
David Conrad, prin. Fax 468-8082

Maple Park, Kane, Pop. 1,296
Central CUSD 301
Supt. — See Burlington
Lily Lake ES 200/K-5
5N720 IL Route 47 60151 847-464-6011
Rebecca Jurs, prin. Fax 365-2283

Kaneland CUSD 302 4,600/PK-12
47W326 Keslinger Rd 60151 630-365-5111
Dr. Todd Leden, supt. Fax 365-9428
www.kaneland.org
Other Schools – See Elburn, Montgomery, Sugar Grove

Marengo, McHenry, Pop. 7,571
Marengo-Union Consolidated ESD 165 1,100/PK-8
816 E Grant Hwy 60152 815-568-8323
Lea Damisch, supt. Fax 568-8367
www.marengo165.org
Grant IS 200/4-5
816 E Grant Hwy 60152 815-568-7427
Cheri Heinz, prin. Fax 568-8905
Locust ES 500/PK-3
539 Locust St 60152 815-568-7632
Suellen Lopez, prin. Fax 568-1830
Marengo Community MS 300/6-8
816 E Grant Hwy 60152 815-568-5720
Tracy Beam, prin. Fax 568-7572

Riley CCSD 18 300/K-8
9406 Riley Rd 60152 815-568-8637
Jerry L. Trickett, supt. Fax 568-3709
www.riley18.org
Riley Community Consolidated S 300/K-8
9406 Riley Rd 60152 815-568-8637
Christine Conkling, prin. Fax 568-3709

Zion Lutheran S 300/PK-8
408 Jackson St 60152 815-568-5156
D. Bertrand, prin. Fax 568-6345

Marine, Madison, Pop. 954
Triad CUSD 2
Supt. — See Troy
Marine ES 100/K-5
725 W Division St 62061 618-667-5404
Renee Voegele, prin. Fax 887-4092

Marion, Williamson, Pop. 16,859
Crab Orchard CUSD 3 500/PK-12
19189 Bailey St 62959 618-982-2181
Derek Hutchins, supt. Fax 982-2080
www.cocusd3.org/
Crab Orchard S 400/PK-8
19189 Bailey St 62959 618-982-2181
Sy Stone, prin. Fax 982-2080

Marion CUSD 2 4,000/PK-12
1700 W Cherry St 62959 618-993-2321
Dr. Keith Oates, supt. Fax 997-0943
www.marionunit2.org
Jefferson ES 300/PK-5
700 E Boulevard St 62959 618-997-5766
Kimberly Brave, prin. Fax 993-3287
Lincoln ES 600/PK-5
400 Morningside Dr 62959 618-997-6063
John Fletcher, prin. Fax 997-0459
Longfellow ES 400/PK-5
1400 W Hendrickson St 62959 618-993-3230
Mike Horn, prin. Fax 997-8046
Marion JHS 800/6-8
1609 W Main St 62959 618-997-1317
Rebecca Moss, prin. Fax 997-0477
Washington ES 600/PK-5
420 E Main St 62959 618-993-8534
Thomas Colboth, prin. Fax 997-0460
Other Schools – See Creal Springs

Marion Adventist S 50/K-8
9314 Old Route 13 62959 618-997-1430
Cynthia Ferguson, prin.

Marissa, Saint Clair, Pop. 1,970
Marissa CUSD 40 600/PK-12
1 E Marissa St 62257 618-295-2313
Dr. Kevin Cogdill, supt. Fax 295-2609
www.marissa40.org
Marissa ES 400/PK-6
206 E Fulton St 62257 618-295-2339
Fax 295-3673

Markham, Cook, Pop. 12,287
Hazel Crest SD 152-5
Supt. — See Hazel Crest
Obama Learning Academy 100/PK-8
16448 Park Ave, 708-825-2400
Dr. Vickie Trotter, prin. Fax 825-0804

Prairie-Hills ESD 144 2,600/PK-8
3015 W 163rd St 60428 708-210-2888
Dr. Kimako Patterson, supt. Fax 210-9925
phsd144.net/
Markham Park ES 300/K-5
16239 Lawndale Ave, 708-210-2869
Tiffany Rucker, prin. Fax 210-9201
Prairie-Hills JHS 1,000/6-8
3035 W 163rd St, 708-210-2860
Kenndell Smith, prin. Fax 210-9208
Other Schools – See Country Club Hills, Hazel Crest, Oak Forest

Maroa, Macon, Pop. 1,775
Maroa-Forsyth CUSD 2 1,200/PK-12
PO Box 738 61756 217-794-3488
Dr. John Ahlemeyer, supt. Fax 794-3878
www.mfschools.org
Maroa-Forsyth MS 300/6-8
PO Box 738 61756 217-794-5115
Kristopher Kahler, prin. Fax 794-3351
Other Schools – See Forsyth

Marquette Heights, Tazewell, Pop. 2,798
North Pekin & Marquette Hts SD 102 700/PK-8
51 Yates Rd 61554 309-382-2172
Byron Sondgeroth, supt. Fax 382-2122
www.dist102.org/
Georgetowne MS 200/6-8
51 Yates Rd 61554 309-382-3456
Bob Ketcham, prin. Fax 382-2122
Marquette ES 300/PK-2
100 Joliet Rd 61554 309-382-3612
Jennifer Dietrich, prin. Fax 382-2122
Other Schools – See North Pekin

Marseilles, LaSalle, Pop. 5,061
Marseilles ESD 150 600/PK-8
201 Chicago St 61341 815-795-2162
Brenda Donahue, supt. Fax 795-3415
mes150.org
Marseilles ES 600/PK-8
201 Chicago St 61341 815-795-2428
Jeff Owens, prin. Fax 795-3415

Miller Township CCSD 210 200/K-8
3197 E 28th Rd 61341 815-357-8151
David Hermann, supt. Fax 357-8159
www.miltonpope.net
Pope ES 200/K-8
3197 E 28th Rd 61341 815-357-8151
Mark Giertz, prin. Fax 357-8159

Marshall, Clark, Pop. 3,915
Marshall CUSD 2C 1,300/PK-12
503 Pine St 62441 217-826-5912
Kevin Ross, supt. Fax 826-5170
www.marshall.k12.il.us/
Marshall JHS 200/7-8
806 N 6th St 62441 217-826-2812
Tony Graham, prin. Fax 826-6065
North ES 400/3-6
1001 N 6th St 62441 217-826-2355
Clare Beaven, prin. Fax 826-6127
South ES 300/PK-2
805 S 6th St 62441 217-826-5041
Tony Graham, prin. Fax 826-5822

Martinsville, Clark, Pop. 1,153
Martinsville CUSD 3C 400/PK-12
PO Box K 62442 217-382-4321
Jill Rogers, supt. Fax 382-4183
www.martinsville.k12.il.us/
Martinsville ES 200/PK-6
PO Box 396 62442 217-382-4116
Vickie Norton, prin. Fax 382-5219

Maryville, Madison, Pop. 7,376
Collinsville CUSD 10
Supt. — See Collinsville
Maryville ES 500/PK-4
6900 W Main St 62062 618-346-6262
Carmen Loemker, prin. Fax 343-2750

Maryville Christian S 200/K-11
PO Box 579 62062 618-505-7000
Brian Kamadulski, admin. Fax 500-7005
St. John Neumann S 200/PK-8
142 Wilma Dr 62062 618-345-7230
Michael Palmer, prin. Fax 345-4350

Mascoutah, Saint Clair, Pop. 7,258
Mascoutah CUSD 19 3,700/PK-12
421 W Harnett St 62258 618-566-7414
Dr. Craig Fiegel, supt. Fax 448-0507
msd19.org
Mascoutah ES 1,000/K-5
533 N 6th St 62258 618-566-2152
Kim Enriquez, prin. Fax 566-8543
Mascoutah MS 800/6-8
846 N 6th St 62258 618-566-2305
Bob Stone, prin. Fax 566-2307
Other Schools – See Belleville, Scott AFB

Holy Childhood S 100/K-8
215 N John St 62258 618-566-2922
Claudia Dougherty, prin. Fax 566-2720

Mason City, Mason, Pop. 2,332
Illini Central CUSD 189 800/PK-12
208 N West Ave 62664 217-482-5180
Mike Ward, supt. Fax 482-3121
www.illinicentral.org
Illini Central ECC PK-PK
208 N West Ave 62664 217-482-9846
Tammy Martin, prin.
Illini Central ES 400/PK-5
208 N West Ave 62664 217-482-3269
Tammy Martin, prin. Fax 482-3988
Illini Central MS 200/6-8
208 N West Ave 62664 217-482-3252
Jennifer Durbin, prin. Fax 482-3323

Matherville, Mercer, Pop. 720
Sherrard CUSD 200
Supt. — See Sherrard
Matherville IS 200/5-6
PO Box 639 61263 309-754-8244
Polly Dahlstrom, prin. Fax 754-8245

Matteson, Cook, Pop. 18,630
ESD 159 1,900/PK-8
6202 Vollmer Rd 60443 708-720-1300
Dr. Mable Alfred, supt. Fax 720-3218
www.dist159.com
Powell MS 700/6-8
20600 Matteson Ave 60443 708-283-9600
Kimberly Johnson, prin. Fax 283-0718
Sieden Prairie ES 200/K-5
725 Notre Dame Dr 60443 708-720-2626
LaTonya Rogers-McCaskill, prin. Fax 720-4640
Woodgate ES 300/PK-5
101 Central Ave 60443 708-720-1107
Dr. Nina Gregory-King, prin. Fax 720-3225
Yates ES 400/K-5
6131 Allemong Dr 60443 708-720-1800
Dr. Lisa Woods, prin. Fax 720-0343
Other Schools – See Richton Park

Matteson ESD 162
Supt. — See Richton Park
Huth MS 600/7-8
3718 213th Pl 60443 708-748-0470
Dr. Robert Tomic, prin. Fax 503-1119
Matteson ES 400/K-3
21245 Main St 60443 708-748-0480
Greg Huelsman, prin. Fax 503-0812

Mattoon, Coles, Pop. 18,262
Mattoon CUSD 2 3,500/K-12
1701 Charleston Ave 61938 217-238-8850
Fax 238-8855
www.mattoon.k12.il.us
Mattoon MS 800/6-8
1200 S 9th St 61938 217-238-5800
Jeremie Smith, prin. Fax 238-5805
Riddle ES 800/K-5
4201 Western Ave 61938 217-238-3800
Christy Hild, prin. Fax 238-3805
Williams ES 700/K-5
1709 S 9th St 61938 217-238-2800
Kris Maleske, prin. Fax 238-2805

St. John Lutheran S 200/PK-8
100 Broadway Ave 61938 217-234-4911
Trent Duckett, prin. Fax 234-4925
St. Mary S 100/PK-8
2000 Richmond Ave 61938 217-235-0431
Nicole Durbin, prin. Fax 235-0393

Maywood, Cook, Pop. 23,814
Maywood-Melrose Park-Broadview SD 89
Supt. — See Melrose Park
Emerson ES 300/PK-5
311 Washington Blvd 60153 708-450-2002
Tyrone Smith, prin. Fax 338-3495
Garfield ES 300/PK-5
1514 S 9th Ave 60153 708-450-2009
Marsha Alexander, prin. Fax 344-0593
Irving MS 100/6-8
805 S 17th Ave 60153 708-450-2015
Michelle Hassan, prin. Fax 343-0762
Lincoln ES 500/PK-5
811 Chicago Ave 60153 708-450-2036
Yadira Gomez-Munoz, prin. Fax 344-0986
Washington Dual Language Academy 200/PK-3
1111 Washington Blvd 60153 708-450-2065
Lourdes Perez, prin. Fax 344-1185

Mazon, Grundy, Pop. 1,011
Mazon-Verona-Kinsman ESD 2C 300/PK-8
1013 North St 60444 815-448-2200
Nancy Dillow, supt. Fax 448-3005
www.mvkmavericks.org
Mazon-Verona-Kinsman ES 200/PK-4
1013 North St 60444 815-448-2471
Melanie Elias, prin. Fax 448-2056
Mazon-Verona-Kinsman MS 200/5-8
1013 North St 60444 815-448-2127
Tony DiNello, prin. Fax 448-3005

Medinah, DuPage, Pop. 2,512
Medinah SD 11
Supt. — See Roselle
Medinah IS 200/3-5
7N330 Medinah Rd 60157 630-529-6105
Natalie Czarnecki, prin. Fax 539-3812
Medinah PS 200/K-2
22W300 Sunnyside Rd 60157 630-529-9788
Melissa Langietti, prin. Fax 529-6304

Medora, Jersey, Pop. 414
Southwestern CUSD 9
Supt. — See Brighton
Medora IS 50/5-6
PO Box 178 62063 618-372-3813
Scott Hopkins, prin. Fax 729-4531

Melrose Park, Cook, Pop. 25,229
Bellwood SD 88
Supt. — See Bellwood
Grant ES 400/1-5
1300 N 34th Ave 60160 708-343-0410
Robyn Lee-Diaz, prin. Fax 544-0021

Mannheim SD 83
Supt. — See Franklin Park
Mannheim JHS 900/6-8
2600 Hyde Park Ave 60164 847-455-5020
Timothy Daley, prin. Fax 455-2038
Scott ES 500/K-5
2250 Scott St 60164 847-455-4818
Michael Courington, prin. Fax 455-2039

Maywood-Melrose Park-Broadview SD 89 2,900/PK-8
906 Walton St 60160 708-450-2460
Dr. David Negron, supt. Fax 450-2461
www.maywood89.org
Addams ES 400/PK-5
910 Division St 60160 708-450-2023
Frank Mikl, prin. Fax 344-0982
Melrose Park ES 700/K-5
1715 W Lake St 60160 708-450-2042
Leticia Valadez, prin. Fax 344-1162
Stevenson MS 300/6-8
1630 N 20th Ave 60160 708-450-2053
James Parker, prin. Fax 344-1356
Other Schools – See Broadview, Maywood

Grace Montessori S 50/PK-6
1112 N 9th Ave 60160 708-344-7257
Sacred Heart S 100/PK-8
815 N 16th Ave 60160 708-681-0240
Barbara Ciconte, prin. Fax 681-0454

Mendon, Adams, Pop. 949
CUSD 4 600/PK-12
PO Box 200 62351 217-936-2111
Scott Riddle, supt. Fax 936-2643
www.cusd4.com
Unity ES 100/PK-3
136 W Washington St 62351 217-936-2512
Jerry Ellerman, prin. Fax 936-2124
Unity MS 200/4-8
PO Box 200 62351 217-936-2111
Seth Klusmeyer, prin. Fax 936-2730

Mendota, LaSalle, Pop. 7,312
Mendota CCSD 289 1,200/PK-8
1806 Guiles Ave 61342 815-539-7631
Dr. Kristen School, supt. Fax 538-2927
www.mendota289.org
Blackstone S 300/K-1
1309 Jefferson St 61342 815-539-6888
Stacy Kelly, prin. Fax 539-2370
Lincoln ES 400/2-4
805 4th Ave 61342 815-538-6226
Vicki Johnson, prin. Fax 539-5757
Northbrook S 600/PK-PK, 5-
1804 Guiles Ave 61342 815-539-6237
Paula Daley, prin. Fax 538-3090

Holy Cross S 100/PK-8
1008 Jefferson St 61342 815-539-7003
Anita Kobilsek, prin. Fax 539-9082

Meredosia, Morgan, Pop. 1,040
Meredosia-Chambersburg CUSD 11 200/PK-12
830 Main St 62665 217-584-1744
Thad Walker, supt. Fax 584-1129
www.mcsd11.net
Meredosia-Chambersburg ES 100/PK-5
830 Main St 62665 217-584-1355
Thad Walker, prin. Fax 584-1129
Meredosia-Chambersburg JHS 50/6-8
830 Main St 62665 217-584-1291
Daniel Carie, prin. Fax 584-1129

Merrionette Park, Cook, Pop. 1,874
Atwood Heights SD 125
Supt. — See Alsip
Meadow Lane Intermediate Center 200/3-5
11800 S Meadow Lane Dr 60803 708-388-6958
Damien Aherne, prin. Fax 388-6983

Metamora, Woodford, Pop. 3,585
Metamora CCSD 1 900/PK-8
815 E Chatham St 61548 309-367-2361
Martin Payne, supt. Fax 367-2364
mgs.metamora.k12.il.us
Metamora ES 900/PK-8
815 E Chatham St 61548 309-367-2361
Cathy Costello, prin. Fax 367-2364

St. Mary S 100/PK-8
PO Box 860 61548 309-367-2528
Jim Dansart, prin. Fax 367-2169

Metropolis, Massac, Pop. 6,368
Joppa-Maple Grove CUSD 38
Supt. — See Joppa
Maple Grove ES 200/PK-6
1698 Grand Chain Rd 62960 618-543-7434
Terri Waddell, prin. Fax 543-7486

Massac Unit SD 1 2,200/K-12
PO Box 530 62960 618-524-9376
Jason Hayes, supt. Fax 524-4432
www.massac.org
Franklin ES 200/K-6
1006 Mount Mission Rd 62960 618-524-2243
Rebecca West, prin. Fax 524-2725
Jefferson S 200/K-6
4915 Jefferson School Rd 62960 618-524-4390
Rebecca West, prin. Fax 524-3019
Massac JHS 300/7-8
3028 Old Marion Rd 62960 618-524-2645
Laura Walker, prin. Fax 524-2765
Metropolis ES 500/K-6
1015 Filmore St 62960 618-524-4821
J.R. Conkle, prin. Fax 524-2278
Other Schools – See Brookport

Middletown, Logan, Pop. 320
New Holland-Middletown ESD 88 100/K-8
75 1250th St 62666 217-445-2421
Todd Dugan, supt. Fax 445-2632
www.nhm88.com/
New Holland-Middletown ES 100/K-8
75 1250th St 62666 217-445-2656
Daniel Dugan, prin. Fax 445-2632

Midlothian, Cook, Pop. 14,581
Midlothian SD 143 1,900/PK-8
14959 Pulaski Rd 60445 708-388-6450
Michael Hollingsworth, supt. Fax 388-4793
www.msd143.org
Central Park ES 700/PK-8
3621 151st St 60445 708-385-0045
Colandra Hamilton, prin. Fax 385-7063
Kolmar S 600/K-8
4500 143rd St 60445 708-385-6747
Cathy Thompson, prin. Fax 385-8243
Spaulding ES 100/PK-3
14811 Turner Ave 60445 708-385-4551
Mary Grahovec, prin. Fax 385-7406
Springfield ES 400/PK-6
14620 Springfield Ave 60445 708-388-4121
Adam Thorns, prin. Fax 388-3307

St. Christopher S 200/PK-8
14611 Keeler Ave 60445 708-385-8776
Carol Pretkelis, prin. Fax 385-8102

Milan, Rock Island, Pop. 4,963
Rock Island-Milan SD 41
Supt. — See Rock Island
Jefferson ES 400/K-6
1307 4th St W 61264 309-793-5985
Michael Nitzel, prin. Fax 793-5986

Milford, Iroquois, Pop. 1,300
Milford Area SD 124 700/PK-12
PO Box 304 60953 815-889-5176
Dr. Dale Hastings, supt. Fax 889-5221
www.mpsk12.org
Milford West S 400/K-8
100 S Chicago St 60953 815-889-4174
Michelle Sobkoviak, prin. Fax 889-5503
Other Schools – See Sheldon

St. Paul's Lutheran S 100/PK-8
108 W Woodworth Rd 60953 815-889-4209
Richard Nordmeyer, prin. Fax 889-4364

Millbrook, Kendall, Pop. 329
Newark CCSD 66
Supt. — See Newark
Millbrook JHS 100/5-8
8411 Fox River Dr 60536 630-553-5435
Jan Lenci, prin. Fax 553-1027

Milledgeville, Carroll, Pop. 1,027
Chadwick-Milledgeville CUSD 399
Supt. — See Chadwick
Milledgeville ES 200/PK-3
100 E 8th St 61051 815-225-7141
Brian Maloy, prin. Fax 225-7847

Millstadt, Saint Clair, Pop. 3,983
Millstadt CCSD 160 800/PK-8
211 W Mill St 62260 618-476-1803
Jonathan Green, supt. Fax 476-1893
www.mccsd160.com
Millstadt Consolidated S 500/3-8
211 W Mill St 62260 618-476-1681
Sandi Pegg, prin. Fax 476-3401
Millstadt PS 200/PK-2
105 W Parkview Dr 62260 618-476-7100
Ed Emge, prin. Fax 476-7182

St. James S 200/PK-8
412 W Washington St 62260 618-476-3510
Steve Kidd, admin. Fax 476-1281

Minier, Tazewell, Pop. 1,242
Olympia CUSD 16
Supt. — See Stanford
Olympia West ES 300/PK-5
302 N School St 61759 309-392-2671
Lisa Castleman, prin. Fax 392-2497

Minonk, Woodford, Pop. 2,068
Fieldcrest CUSD 6 1,100/PK-12
1 Dornbush Dr 61760 309-432-2177
Dr. Dan Oakley, supt. Fax 432-3377
www.unit6.org
Fieldcrest PS 200/PK-2
523 Johnson St 61760 309-432-2838
Jason Chaplin, prin. Fax 432-2192
Other Schools – See Toluca, Wenona

Minooka, Grundy, Pop. 10,784
Minooka CCSD 201 4,100/PK-8
PO Box 467 60447 815-467-6121
Dr. Kris Monn, supt. Fax 467-9544
www.min201.org
Aux Sable ES 500/K-4
1004 Misty Creek Dr 60447 815-467-5301
Ciara Manno, prin. Fax 467-2166
Minooka ES 500/1-4
400 W Coady Dr 60447 815-467-2261
Natalie Baxter, prin. Fax 467-1323
Minooka IS 900/5-6
321 W McEvilly Rd 60447 815-467-4692
Jeana Pekol, prin. Fax 467-3121
Minooka JHS 900/7-8
333 W McEvilly Rd 60447 815-467-2136
Sarah Massey, prin. Fax 467-5087
Minooka Primary Center 400/PK-2
305 W Church St 60447 815-467-3167
Teresa Miller, prin. Fax 467-3168
Other Schools – See Joliet, Shorewood

Mokena, Will, Pop. 18,589
Mokena SD 159 1,700/PK-8
11244 Willow Crest Ln 60448 708-342-4900
Dr. Omar Castillo, supt. Fax 479-3143
www.mokena159.org
Mokena ES 600/PK-3
11244 Willow Crest Ln 60448 708-342-4850
Anna Kirchner, prin. Fax 479-3120
Mokena IS 400/4-5
11331 195th St 60448 708-342-4860
David McAtee, prin. Fax 479-3103
Mokena JHS 600/6-8
19815 Kirkstone Way 60448 708-342-4870
Dr. Michael Rolinitis, prin. Fax 479-3122

Summit Hill SD 161
Supt. — See Frankfort
Arbury Hills ES 200/1-4
19651 Beechnut Dr 60448 708-479-2106
Francie Boss, prin. Fax 464-2249

Noonan Elementary Academy 400/PK-8
19131 Henry Dr 60448 708-479-8988
Joseph Dunn, prin. Fax 479-6859
St. Mary S 500/PK-8
11409 195th St 60448 708-326-9330
Beth Cunningham, prin. Fax 326-9331

Moline, Rock Island, Pop. 42,701
Moline-Coal Valley CUSD 40 6,900/PK-12
1619 11th Ave 61265 309-743-1600
Lanty McGuire, supt. Fax 757-3476
www.molineschools.org
Adams ES 300/K-5
3520 53rd St 61265 309-743-1601
Teresa Landon, prin. Fax 757-3580
Butterworth ES 300/K-5
4205 48th St 61265 309-743-1604
Julie Reed, prin. Fax 757-3503
Deere MS 800/6-8
2035 11th St 61265 309-743-1622
Dr. Dusti Adrian, prin. Fax 757-3668
Franklin ES 300/K-5
5312 11th Avenue C 61265 309-743-1607
Michele Pittington, prin. Fax 736-2231
Hamilton ES 100/K-5
700 32nd Ave 61265 309-743-1610
Victoria Diamond-Bohlman, prin. Fax 757-3669
Jefferson ECC 200/PK-PK
3010 26th Ave 61265 309-743-1611
Rachel Fowler, prin. Fax 757-1895
Lincoln-Irving ES 400/K-5
1015 16th Ave 61265 309-743-1612
Blanca Leal, prin. Fax 757-3584
Logan ES 400/K-5
1602 25th St 61265 309-743-1613
Tom Ferguson, prin. Fax 757-3583
Roosevelt ES 300/PK-5
3530 Avenue of the Cities 61265 309-743-1617
Sharon Lantzky, prin. Fax 757-3521
Washington ES 300/K-5
1550 41st St 61265 309-743-1619
Brian Prybil, prin. Fax 757-3665
Willard ES 300/K-5
1616 16th St 61265 309-743-1620
Vicki Diamond-Bohlman, prin. Fax 736-2230
Wilson MS 900/6-8
1301 48th St 61265 309-743-1623
Robert Beem, prin. Fax 757-3586
Other Schools – See Coal Valley

Quad City Christian S - Temple Campus 100/PK-6
2305 7th Ave 61265 309-764-1302
John Mutum, prin. Fax 764-0931
St. Paul Lutheran S 50/PK-8
153 19th Ave 61265 309-762-4494
Robert Pagel, prin. Fax 762-5927
Seton Catholic S 600/PK-8
1320 16th Ave 61265 309-757-5500
Jane Barrett, prin. Fax 762-0545
Villa Montessori S 100/PK-6
2100 48th St 61265 309-764-7047
Renee Detloff, prin. Fax 764-9925

Momence, Kankakee, Pop. 3,244
Momence CUSD 1 — 1,100/PK-12
400 N Pine St 60954 — 815-472-3501
Gary Miller, supt. — Fax 472-3516
www.momence.k12.il.us
Je-Neir ES — 300/K-4
1001 W 2nd St 60954 — 815-472-6646
LaShawn Stewart, prin. — Fax 472-9822
Momence JHS — 300/PK-PK, 5-
801 W 2nd St 60954 — 815-472-4184
Jacqanai Gipson, prin. — Fax 472-3517

Unity Christian S — 50/PK-8
920 W 2nd St 60954 — 815-472-3230
Elizabeth Porte, prin. — Fax 472-3230

Monee, Will, Pop. 5,063
Crete-Monee CUSD 201U
Supt. — See Crete
Monee ES — 500/K-5
25425 S Will Center Rd 60449 — 708-367-2600
JoAnn Jones, prin. — Fax 534-3691

Monmouth, Warren, Pop. 9,279
Monmouth-Roseville CUSD 238 — 1,800/PK-12
105 N E St 61462 — 309-734-4712
Edward Fletcher, supt. — Fax 734-4755
www.mr238.org
Central IS — 300/4-6
401 E 2nd Ave 61462 — 309-734-2213
Becky Ince, prin. — Fax 734-3123
Harding PS — 300/2-3
415 E 9th Ave 61462 — 309-734-4915
Jeff Ewing, prin. — Fax 734-5221
Lincoln PS — 400/PK-1
325 S 11th St 61462 — 309-734-2222
Joe Pilger, prin. — Fax 734-6712
Other Schools – See Roseville

United CUSD 304 — 900/PK-12
1905 100th St 61462 — 309-734-9413
Jeffrey Whitsitt, supt. — Fax 734-0223
united.k12.il.us
United ES - West — 200/PK-5
2140 State Highway 135 61462 — 309-734-8513
Patrick Coate, prin. — Fax 734-8515
United JHS — 200/6-8
2140 State Highway 135 61462 — 309-734-8511
Christopher Schwarz, prin. — Fax 734-6094
Other Schools – See Alexis

Immaculate Conception S — 200/K-8
115 N B St 61462 — 309-734-6037
Randy Frakes, prin. — Fax 734-6082

Monroe Center, Ogle, Pop. 469
Meridian CUSD 223
Supt. — See Stillman Valley
Monroe Center ES — 400/3-5
17500 E Il Route 72 61052 — 815-645-2230
Sarah Hogan, prin. — Fax 393-4530

Montgomery, Kane, Pop. 18,101
Aurora West Unit SD 129
Supt. — See Aurora
Nicholson ES — 400/K-5
649 N Main St 60538 — 630-301-5013
Melena Gaspadarek, prin. — Fax 844-4616

CUSD 308
Supt. — See Oswego
Boulder Hill ES — 500/K-5
163 Boulder Hill Pass 60538 — 630-636-2900
Michael Mitchinson, prin. — Fax 636-2968
Lakewood Creek ES — 800/K-5
2301 Lakewood Crk 60538 — 630-636-3200
Jodi Ancel, prin. — Fax 636-3291
Long Beach ES — 500/K-5
67 Longbeach Rd 60538 — 630-636-3300
Phil Murray, prin. — Fax 636-3391

Kaneland CUSD 302
Supt. — See Maple Park
McDole ES — 600/PK-5
2901 Foxmoor Dr 60538 — 630-897-1961
Patrick Raleigh, prin. — Fax 897-3229

St. Luke's Christian Academy — 200/PK-8
63 Fernwood Rd 60538 — 630-892-0310
Linda King, prin.

Monticello, Piatt, Pop. 5,493
Monticello CUSD 25 — 1,600/PK-12
2 Sage Dr 61856 — 217-762-8511
Dr. Victor Zimmerman, supt. — Fax 762-8534
www.sages.us
Lincoln ES — 300/PK-1
700 N Buchanan St 61856 — 217-762-8511
Mary Vogt, prin. — Fax 762-2733
Monticello MS — 400/6-8
2015 E Washington St 61856 — 217-762-8511
Jeanne Handley, prin. — Fax 762-7765
Washington ES — 300/4-5
3 Sage Dr 61856 — 217-762-8511
Nancy Rosenberry, prin. — Fax 762-8508
Other Schools – See White Heath

Mooseheart, Kane

Mooseheart S — 200/PK-12
255 W James J Davis Dr 60539 — 630-906-3646
Dr. Jeff Szymczak Ph.D., supt. — Fax 906-3617

Moro, Madison
Bethalto CUSD 8
Supt. — See Bethalto
Meadowbrook IS — 400/4-5
111 W Roosevelt Dr 62067 — 618-377-7270
Kimberly Wilks, prin. — Fax 377-7294

Edwardsville CUSD 7
Supt. — See Edwardsville
Midway ES — 200/PK-2
6321 Midway Dr 62067 — 618-692-7446
Matt Sidarous, prin. — Fax 377-2577

Morris, Grundy, Pop. 13,509
Morris SD 54 — 1,100/PK-8
725 School St 60450 — 815-942-0056
Dr. Shannon Dudek, supt. — Fax 416-0581
www.morris54.org
Shabbona MS — 400/5-8
54 White Oak Dr 60450 — 815-942-0056
Christopher Maier, prin. — Fax 318-6900
White Oak ES — 700/PK-4
2001 Dupont Ave 60450 — 815-942-0056
Christopher Maier, prin. — Fax 318-6900

Nettle Creek CCSD 24 C — 100/K-8
8820 Scott School Rd 60450 — 815-942-0511
Al Gegenheimer, supt. — Fax 942-9124
www.nettlecreek.org
Nettle Creek ES — 100/K-8
8820 Scott School Rd 60450 — 815-942-0511
Marissa Darlington, prin. — Fax 942-9124

Saratoga CCSD 60C — 800/PK-8
4040 N Division St 60450 — 815-942-2128
Kathy Perry, supt. — Fax 942-0301
www.sd60c.org
Saratoga ES — 800/PK-8
4040 N Division St 60450 — 815-942-5970
Joe Zweeres, prin. — Fax 942-5953

Immaculate Conception S — 200/PK-8
505 E North St 60450 — 815-942-4111
Kim DesLauriers, prin. — Fax 942-5094

Morrison, Whiteside, Pop. 4,151
Morrison CUSD 6 — 1,100/PK-12
643 Genesee Ave 61270 — 815-772-2064
Scott Vance, supt. — Fax 772-4644
www.morrisonschools.org
Morrison JHS — 200/6-8
300 Academic Dr 61270 — 815-772-7264
Joe Robbins, prin. — Fax 772-2531
Northside ES — 300/PK-2
520 N Genesee St 61270 — 815-772-2153
Jennifer Oetting, prin. — Fax 772-4952
Southside ES — 200/3-5
100 Academic Dr 61270 — 815-772-2183
Jennifer Oetting, prin. — Fax 772-2371

Morrisonville, Christian, Pop. 1,053
Morrisonville CUSD 1 — 300/PK-12
PO Box 13 62546 — 217-526-4431
Dave Meister, supt. — Fax 526-4433
www.mohawks.net
Morrisonville ES — 200/PK-6
PO Box 13 62546 — 217-526-4441
Christy Willman, prin. — Fax 526-4433
Morrisonville JHS — 50/7-8
PO Box 13 62546 — 217-526-4432
Ann Little, prin. — Fax 526-4452

Morton, Tazewell, Pop. 16,106
Morton CUSD 709 — 2,800/PK-12
1050 S 4th Ave Ste 200 61550 — 309-263-2581
Dr. Jeffrey Hill, supt. — Fax 266-6320
www.morton709.org
Brown ES — 300/K-6
2550 N Morton Ave 61550 — 309-266-5309
Faith Waterfield, prin. — Fax 263-7986
Grundy ES — 400/K-6
1100 S 4th Ave 61550 — 309-263-1421
Michael Saunders, prin. — Fax 263-8120
Jefferson ES — 300/K-6
220 E Jefferson St 61550 — 309-263-2650
Kate Wyman, prin. — Fax 284-3031
Lincoln ES — 500/PK-6
100 S Nebraska Ave 61550 — 309-266-6989
Julie Albers, prin. — Fax 263-7877
Morton JHS — 400/7-8
225 E Jackson St 61550 — 309-266-6522
Lee Hoffman, prin. — Fax 284-5031

Bethel Lutheran S — 400/PK-8
325 E Queenwood Rd 61550 — 309-266-6592
John Jacob, prin. — Fax 266-8510
Blessed Sacrament S — 200/K-8
233 E Greenwood St 61550 — 309-263-8442
Mike Birdoes, prin. — Fax 263-8443

Morton Grove, Cook, Pop. 22,739
East Maine SD 63
Supt. — See Des Plaines
Melzer ES — 500/PK-6
9400 Oriole Ave 60053 — 847-965-7474
Jennifer Pacheco, prin. — Fax 965-0539

Golf ESD 67 — 600/PK-8
9401 Waukegan Rd 60053 — 847-966-8200
Dr. Beth Flores, supt. — Fax 966-8290
www.golf67.net
Golf MS — 300/5-8
9401 Waukegan Rd 60053 — 847-965-3740
Karen Chvojka, prin. — Fax 966-9493
Hynes ES — 300/PK-4
9000 Belleforte Ave 60053 — 847-965-4500
Carol Westley, prin. — Fax 965-4565

Morton Grove SD 70 — 900/PK-8
6200 Lake St 60053 — 847-965-6200
Brad Voehringer, supt. — Fax 965-6234
www.mgsd70.org
Park View ES — 900/PK-8
6200 Lake St 60053 — 847 965 6200
Michelle Friedman, prin. — Fax 965-0606

Skokie SD 69
Supt. — See Skokie
Edison ES — 600/3-5
8200 Gross Point Rd 60053 — 847-966-6210
Andrew Carpenter, prin. — Fax 966-6236

Jerusalem Lutheran S — 100/PK-8
6218 Capulina Ave 60053 — 847-965-4750
Duane Vance, prin. — Fax 965-7340
MCC Academy — 400/PK-8
8601 Menard Ave 60053 — 224-534-7638
Habeeb Quadri, prin. — Fax 470-8873

Mossville, Peoria
Illinois Valley Central Unit SD 321
Supt. — See Chillicothe
Mossville Elementary & JHS — 500/PK-8
PO Box 178 61552 — 309-579-2328
Patrick Sell, prin. — Fax 579-2168

Mounds, Pulaski, Pop. 797
Meridian CUSD 101 — 600/PK-12
1401 Mounds Rd 62964 — 618-342-6776
Spencer Byrd, supt. — Fax 342-6856
www.meridian101.com
Meridian ES — 400/PK-5
1401 Mounds Rd 62964 — 618-342-6773
Novella Harris, prin. — Fax 342-6856

Mount Carmel, Wabash, Pop. 7,195
Wabash CUSD 348 — 1,500/PK-12
218 W 13th St 62863 — 618-262-4181
Tim Buss, supt. — Fax 262-7912
www.wabash348.com
Mt. Carmel ES — 300/3-5
1300 N Walnut St 62863 — 618-263-3876
Chris Taylor, prin. — Fax 262-7189
Mt. Carmel Grade S — 300/PK-2
1520 Poplar St 62863 — 618-262-5699
Sheila Odom, prin. — Fax 263-9096
Mount Carmel JHS — 300/6-8
201 N Pear St 62863 — 618-262-8886
Steven Holt, prin. — Fax 262-2302

St. Mary S — 100/PK-8
417 Chestnut St 62863 — 618-263-3183
Cynthia Brogan, prin. — Fax 263-3596

Mount Carroll, Carroll, Pop. 1,702
West Carroll CUSD 314 — 1,100/PK-12
642 S East St 61053 — 815-734-3374
Adam Brumbaugh, supt. — Fax 244-0211
www.wc314.org/
West Carroll MS — 300/5-8
633 S East St 61053 — 815-244-2002
Julie Katzenberger, prin. — Fax 244-1051
Other Schools – See Savanna

Mount Erie, Wayne, Pop. 88
North Wayne CUSD 200
Supt. — See Cisne
Mount Erie ES — 100/K-4
300 School Dr 62446 — 618-854-2611
Donna Williams, prin. — Fax 854-2600

Mount Morris, Ogle, Pop. 2,953
Oregon CUSD 220
Supt. — See Oregon
Rahn JHS — 200/7-8
105 W Brayton Rd 61054 — 815-734-5300
Kip Crandall, prin. — Fax 734-7129

Mount Olive, Macoupin, Pop. 2,093
Mount Olive CUSD 5 — 500/PK-12
804 W Main St 62069 — 217-999-7831
Patrick Murphy, supt. — Fax 999-2150
www.mtoliveschools.org
Mount Olive S — 400/PK-8
804 W Main St 62069 — 217-999-4241
Patrick Murphy, prin. — Fax 999-4302

Mount Prospect, Cook, Pop. 53,352
CCSD 59
Supt. — See Arlington Heights
Early Learning Center — PK-PK
1900 W Lonnquist Blvd 60056 — 847-593-4306
Michele Ramsey, admin. — Fax 593-7199
Forest View ES — 500/PK-5
1901 W Estates Dr 60056 — 847-593-4359
Margaret Weickert, prin. — Fax 593-4360
Frost ES — 500/K-5
1308 S Cypress Dr 60056 — 847-593-4378
Susan Savage, prin. — Fax 593-4365
Holmes JHS — 500/6-8
1900 W Lonnquist Blvd 60056 — 847-593-4390
Rob Bowers, prin. — Fax 593-7386
Jay ES — 400/PK-5
1835 W Pheasant Trl 60056 — 847-593-4385
Mary Beth Niles, prin. — Fax 593-8656

Mount Prospect SD 57 — 2,200/PK-8
701 W Gregory St 60056 — 847-394-7300
Dr. Elaine Aumiller, supt. — Fax 394-7311
www.d57.org
Fairview ES — 400/2-5
300 N Fairview Ave 60056 — 847-394-7320
Daniel Ophus, prin. — Fax 394-7328
Lincoln MS — 700/6-8
700 W Lincoln St 60056 — 847-394-7350
Paul Suminski, prin. — Fax 394-7358
Lions Park ES — 500/2-5
300 E Council Trl 60056 — 847-394-7330
Katherine Kelly, prin. — Fax 394-7338
Westbrook S for Young Learners — 500/PK-1
103 S Busse Rd 60056 — 847-394-7340
Dr. Mary Gorr, prin. — Fax 394-7349

River Trails SD 26 1,300/PK-8
1900 E Kensington Rd 60056 847-297-4120
Dr. Nancy Wagner, supt. Fax 297-4124
www.rtsd26.org
Euclid ES 400/K-5
1211 N Wheeling Rd 60056 847-259-3303
Laura Gammons, prin. Fax 259-3395
Indian Grove ES 400/PK-5
1340 N Burning Bush Ln 60056 847-298-1976
Lynn Fisher, prin. Fax 298-3495
River Trails Early Learning Center PK-PK
1900 E Kensington Rd 60056 224-612-7304
Dr. Miriam Cutler, prin.
River Trails MS 500/6-8
1000 N Wolf Rd 60056 847-298-1750
Keir Rogers, prin. Fax 298-2639

Wheeling CCSD 21
Supt. — See Wheeling
Frost ES 600/PK-5
1805 N Aspen Dr 60056 847-803-4815
Jeff Brusso, prin. Fax 803-4855

St. Emily S 300/PK-8
1400 E Central Rd 60056 847-296-3490
Mary Hemmelman, prin. Fax 296-1155
St. Paul Lutheran S 300/PK-8
18 S School St 60056 847-255-6733
Jennifer Heinze, prin. Fax 255-6834
St. Raymond S 600/PK-8
300 S Elmhurst Ave 60056 847-253-8555
Mary Eileen Ward, prin. Fax 253-8939
Science Academy of Chicago 200/PK-8
501 Midway Dr 60056 847-258-5254
Brianna Bartucci, prin. Fax 378-8242

Mount Pulaski, Logan, Pop. 1,560
Mount Pulaski CUSD 23 500/PK-12
119 N Garden St Ste 2 62548 217-792-7222
Todd Hamm, supt. Fax 792-5551
www.mtpulaski.k12.il.us
Mount Pulaski Grade S 300/PK-8
119 N Garden St Ste 1 62548 217-792-7220
Gene Newton, prin. Fax 792-7221

Zion Lutheran S 100/PK-8
203 S Vine St 62548 217-792-5715
Sara McCormick, coord. Fax 792-5915

Mount Sterling, Brown, Pop. 2,006
Brown County CUSD 1 800/PK-12
503 NW Cross St 62353 217-773-7500
Vicki Phillips, supt. Fax 773-7409
www.bchornets.com/
Brown County ES 400/PK-4
501 NW Cross St 62353 217-773-2624
Shelly Eager, prin. Fax 773-4471
Brown County MS 200/5-8
504 E Main St 62353 217-773-9152
Karen Jirjis, prin. Fax 773-9121

St. Mary S 100/PK-8
408 W Washington St 62353 217-773-2825
Martha Hogge, prin. Fax 773-2399

Mount Vernon, Jefferson, Pop. 14,904
Bethel SD 82 200/K-8
1201 Bethel Rd 62864 618-244-8095
Craig Kujawa, supt. Fax 244-8096
www.bethelschool.net
Bethel S 200/K-8
1201 Bethel Rd 62864 618-244-8095
Craig Kujawa, prin. Fax 244-8096

McClellan CCSD 12 100/K-8
9475 N IL Highway 148 62864 618-244-8072
Brian Brink, supt. Fax 244-8129
McClellan ES 100/K-8
9475 N IL Highway 148 62864 618-244-8072
Brian Brink, prin. Fax 244-8129

Mount Vernon CSD 80 1,700/PK-8
2710 North St 62864 618-244-8080
Aletta Lawrence, supt. Fax 244-8082
www.mtv80.org
Buford Intermediate Education Ctr 300/4-5
623 S 34th St 62864 618-244-8064
Kevin Alvis, prin. Fax 244-8103
Casey MS 400/6-8
1829 Broadway St 62864 618-244-8060
Mary McGreer, prin. Fax 244-8104
Hall Early Education Center 300/PK-PK
301 S 17th St 62864 618-244-8087
Lori Given, prin. Fax 244-8088
Osborne Primary Center 700/K-3
401 N 30th St 62864 618-244-8068
Shannon Marler, prin. Fax 244-8075

Spring Garden Community Cons SD 178 100/K-8
14975 E Bakerville Rd 62864 618-244-8070
Stuart Parks, supt. Fax 244-8071
www.sgd178.org
Spring Garden ES 100/K-3
14975 E Bakerville Rd 62864 618-244-8070
Tommi Jo Ryan, prin. Fax 244-8071
Other Schools – See Ina

Summersville SD 79 300/PK-8
1118 Fairfield Rd 62864 618-244-8079
Mark Zahm, supt. Fax 244-8078
www.summersville79.com/
Summersville S 300/PK-8
1118 Fairfield Rd 62864 618-244-8079
Mark Zahm, prin. Fax 244-8078

St. Mary's S 200/K-8
1416 Main St 62864 618-242-5353
Brett Heinzman, prin. Fax 242-5365

Mount Zion, Macon, Pop. 5,766
Mount Zion CUSD 3 2,400/PK-12
455 Elm St 62549 217-864-2366
Dr. Travis Roundcount, supt. Fax 864-2200
www.mtzion.k12.il.us
McGaughey ES 400/PK-1
1320 W Main St 62549 217-864-2711
Brandi Kelly, prin. Fax 864-4126
Mount Zion Grade S 400/2-3
725 W Main St 62549 217-864-3631
Gary Gruen, prin. Fax 864-6131
Mount Zion IS 600/4-6
310 S Henderson St 62549 217-864-2921
Randall Thacker, prin. Fax 864-5175
Mount Zion JHS 400/7-8
315 S Henderson St 62549 217-864-2369
Julie Marquardt, prin. Fax 864-6829

Moweaqua, Shelby, Pop. 1,822
Central A & M CUSD 21
Supt. — See Assumption
Gregory IS 200/3-5
221 E Pine St 62550 217-768-3860
David Fitzgerald, prin. Fax 768-3797

Mulberry Grove, Bond, Pop. 626
Mulberry Grove CUSD 1 300/PK-12
801 W Wall St 62262 618-326-8812
Brad Turner, supt. Fax 326-8482
www.mgschools.com
Mulberry Grove ES 200/PK-5
801 W Wall St 62262 618-326-8811
Robert Koontz, prin. Fax 326-8482

Mundelein, Lake, Pop. 30,630
Diamond Lake SD 76 1,100/PK-8
500 Acorn Ln 60060 847-566-9221
Dr. Bhavna Sharma-Lewis, supt. Fax 566-5689
www.dist76.org
Diamond Lake ES 300/2-4
25807 N Diamond Lake Rd 60060 847-566-6601
Kurt Preble, prin. Fax 566-9851
Fairhaven ES 300/PK-1
634 Countryside Hwy 60060 847-949-0991
Dr. Juliane Fredericks, prin. Fax 949-6720
West Oak MS 400/5-8
500 Acorn Ln 60060 847-566-9220
Christopher Willeford, prin. Fax 970-3534

Fremont SD 79 2,200/PK-8
28855 N Fremont Center Rd 60060 847-566-0169
Dr. William Robertson, supt. Fax 566-7280
www.fsd79.org
Fremont ES 800/PK-2
28908 N Fremont Center Rd 60060 847-837-0437
Stefan Ladenburger, prin. Fax 837-9540
Fremont IS 700/3-5
28754 N Fremont Center Rd 60060 847-388-3700
Stefan Ladenburger, prin. Fax 388-6900
Fremont MS 700/6-8
28871 N Fremont Center Rd 60060 847-566-9384
Pam Motsenbocker, prin. Fax 566-7805

Mundelein ESD 75 2,000/PK-8
470 N Lake St 60060 847-949-2700
Dr. Andy Henrikson, supt. Fax 949-2727
www.district75.org
Mechanics Grove ES 500/3-5
1200 N Midlothian Rd 60060 847-949-2712
Tanya Fergus, prin. Fax 949-2711
Sandburg MS 600/PK-PK, 6-
855 W Hawley St 60060 847-949-2707
Mark Pilut, prin. Fax 949-2716
Washington ES 500/K-2
122 S Garfield Ave 60060 847-949-2714
Jim Kallieris, prin. Fax 949-2710

Libertyville Montessori S 100/PK-K
450 S Butterfield Rd 60060 847-362-5170
Lynn Hauser, dir. Fax 367-5133
Mundelein Montessori S 100/PK-K
1401 S Lake St 60060 847-566-4345
Carol Hofbauer, prin. Fax 566-4343
St. Mary of the Annunciation S 100/PK-5
22277 W Erhart Rd 60060 847-223-4021
Tammy Kleckner, prin. Fax 223-3489

Murphysboro, Jackson, Pop. 7,754
Murphysboro CUSD 186 1,500/K-12
593 Ava Rd 62966 618-684-3781
Christopher Grode, supt. Fax 684-2465
www.cusd186.org
Carruthers ES 200/3-5
80 Candy Ln 62966 618-687-3231
William Huppert, prin. Fax 687-2811
Logan Attendance Center 300/K-2
320 Watson Rd 62966 618-684-4471
Carla Ehlers, prin. Fax 565-8119
Murphysboro MS 500/6-8
2125 Spruce St 62966 618-684-3041
Jeff Keener, prin. Fax 687-1042

Immanuel Lutheran S 50/PK-8
1915 Pine St 62966 618-684-3012
Jim Zobel, prin. Fax 684-5115
St. Andrew S 100/K-8
723 Mulberry St 62966 618-687-2013
Jenny Martin, prin. Fax 684-4969

Murrayville, Morgan, Pop. 587
Jacksonville SD 117
Supt. — See Jacksonville
Murrayville-Woodson ES 200/K-6
PO Box 170 62668 217-882-3121
Emily English, prin. Fax 882-2141

Naperville, DuPage, Pop. 138,897
Indian Prairie CUSD 204
Supt. — See Aurora
Brookdale ES 600/K-5
1200 Redfield Rd 60563 630-428-6800
Mary Howicz, prin. Fax 428-6801
Clow ES 500/K-5
1301 Springdale Cir 60564 630-428-6060
Kathryn Bennett, prin. Fax 428-6061
Cowlishaw ES 700/K-5
1212 Sanctuary Ln 60540 630-428-6100
Ken Bonomo, prin. Fax 428-6101
Crone MS 1,200/6-8
4020 111th St 60564 630-428-5600
Melissa Couch, prin. Fax 428-5601
Fry ES 600/K-5
3204 Tall Grass Dr 60564 630-428-7400
Laurel Hillman, prin. Fax 428-7401
Graham ES 400/K-5
2315 High Meadow Rd 60564 630-428-6900
Claudette Walton, prin. Fax 428-6901
Gregory MS 900/6-8
2621 Springdale Cir 60564 630-428-6300
Stephen Severson, prin. Fax 428-6301
Hill MS 800/6-8
1836 Brookdale Rd 60563 630-428-6200
Michael Dutdut, prin. Fax 428-6201
Kendall ES 500/K-5
2408 Meadow Lake Dr 60564 630-428-7100
Lena Guerrieri, prin. Fax 428-7101
Longwood ES 400/K-5
30W240 Bruce Ln 60563 630-428-6789
Tracey Ratner, prin. Fax 428-6761
Owen ES 500/K-5
1560 Westglen Dr 60565 630-428-7300
Kim Earlenbaugh, prin. Fax 428-7301
Patterson ES 500/K-5
3731 Lawrence Dr 60564 630-428-6500
Michele Frost, prin. Fax 428-6501
Peterson ES 500/K-5
4008 Chinaberry Ln 60564 630-428-5678
Allison Landstrom, prin. Fax 428-6181
Scullen MS 1,100/6-8
2815 Mistflower Ln 60564 630-428-7000
Leslie Mitchell, prin. Fax 428-7001
Spring Brook ES 700/K-5
2700 Seiler Dr 60565 630-428-6600
David Worst, prin. Fax 428-6601
Watts ES 700/K-5
800 S Whispering Hills Dr 60540 630-428-6700
Brian LeCrone, prin. Fax 428-6701
Welch ES 800/K-5
2620 Leverenz Rd 60564 630-428-7200
Sarah Nowak, prin. Fax 428-7201
White Eagle ES 500/K-5
1585 White Eagle Dr 60564 630-375-3600
Timothy Krahenbuhl, prin. Fax 375-3601

Naperville CUSD 203 17,100/PK-12
203 W Hillside Rd 60540 630-420-6300
Dan Bridges, supt. Fax 420-1066
www.naperville203.org
Beebe ES 600/K-5
110 E 11th Ave 60563 630-420-6332
Christine O'Neil, prin. Fax 420-6962
Ellsworth ES 300/K-5
145 N Sleight St 60540 630-420-6338
Cheryl DeGan, prin. Fax 637-7321
Elmwood ES 600/K-5
1024 Magnolia Ln 60540 630-420-6341
Lisa Polomsky, prin. Fax 637-7348
Highlands ES 600/K-5
525 S Brainard St 60540 630-420-6335
Laura Noon, prin. Fax 420-6957
Jefferson JHS 900/6-8
1525 N Loomis St 60563 630-420-6307
Megan Ptak, prin. Fax 420-6930
Kingsley ES 400/K-5
2403 Kingsley Dr 60565 630-420-3208
Erin Marker, prin. Fax 420-3213
Lincoln JHS 900/6-8
1320 Olympus Dr 60565 630-420-6370
Patrick Gaskin, prin. Fax 637-4582
Madison JHS 700/6-8
1000 River Oak Dr 60565 630-420-4257
Erin Anderson, prin. Fax 420-6402
Maplebrook ES 400/K-5
1630 Warbler Dr 60565 630-420-6381
Ryan DeBora, prin. Fax 420-6638
Meadow Glens ES 400/K-5
1150 Muirhead Ave 60565 630-420-3200
Katy Lynch, prin. Fax 420-6897
Mill Street ES 600/K-5
1300 N Mill St 60563 630-420-6353
Sue Salness, prin. Fax 637-4680
Naper ES 300/K-5
39 S Eagle St 60540 630-420-6345
Julie Beehler, prin. Fax 637-7328
Prairie ES 500/K-5
500 S Charles Ave 60540 630-420-6348
Tracy Dvorchak, prin. Fax 717-0801
Ranch View ES 500/K-5
1651 Ranchview Dr 60565 630-420-6575
Angela Stallion, prin. Fax 420-0915
Reid ECC 400/PK-PK
1011 S Naper Blvd 60540 630-420-6899
Tarah Allen, prin. Fax 637-4033
River Woods ES 500/K-5
2607 River Woods Dr 60565 630-420-6630
Gina Baumgartner, prin. Fax 420-6961
Scott ES 500/K-5
500 Warwick Dr 60565 630-420-6477
Hugh Boger, prin. Fax 420-6471
Steeple Run ES 500/K-5
6S151 Steeple Run Dr 60540 630-420-6385
Josh Louis, prin. Fax 420-6935
Washington JHS 600/5-8
201 N Washington St 60540 630-420-6390
Jon Vogel, prin. Fax 420-6474
Other Schools – See Lisle

All Saints Catholic Academy 500/PK-8
1155 Aurora Ave 60540 630-961-6125
Melissa Santos, prin. Fax 961-3771
Bethany Lutheran S 300/PK-8
1550 Modaff Rd 60565 630-355-6607
Pamela Mueller, prin. Fax 355-2216
Calvary Christian S 300/K-8
9S200 Route 59 60564 630-375-8600
Emery Risdall, prin. Fax 375-8601
Chesterbrook Academy ES 100/K-8
1571 Oswego Rd 60540 630-527-0833
Dawn DeBois-Weber M.A., prin. Fax 527-1204
Covenant Classical S 100/K-11
1852 95th St 60564 630-983-7500
Covenant Classical S 100/K-9
2035 E 75th St 60565 630-963-7500
Camie Perrin, prin.
DuPage Montessori S 200/PK-8
1111 E Warrenville Rd 60563 630-369-6899
Sharon Breen, prin. Fax 369-7306
Naperville Christian Academy 50/PK-12
1451 Raymond Dr Ste 200 60563 630-637-9622
Rebecca Ruff, dir. Fax 355-1828
St. Raphael S 300/K-8
1215 Modaff Rd 60540 630-355-1880
Mavis DeMar, prin. Fax 428-4974
SS. Peter & Paul S 600/K-8
201 E Franklin Ave 60540 630-355-0113
Karen Meskill, prin. Fax 355-9803

Nashville, Washington, Pop. 3,221
Nashville CCSD 49 600/PK-8
750 E Gorman St 62263 618-327-3055
Michael Brink, supt. Fax 327-4503
www.nashville49.org
Nashville ES 600/PK-8
750 E Gorman St 62263 618-327-4304
Chuck Fairbanks, prin. Fax 327-4501

St. Ann S 100/K-8
675 S Mill St 62263 618-327-8741
Pierre Antoine, prin. Fax 327-4904
Trinity-St. John Lutheran S 100/PK-8
680 W Walnut St 62263 618-327-8561
Amy Kurtz, prin. Fax 327-4540

Nauvoo, Hancock, Pop. 1,136
Nauvoo-Colusa CUSD 325 100/PK-8
2461 N State Highway 96 62354 217-453-6639
Dr. Kent Young, supt. Fax 453-6395
www.nauvoo-colusa.com
Nauvoo ES 100/PK-8
2461 N State Highway 96 62354 217-453-2231
Daniel Ayer, prin. Fax 453-6395

SS. Peter & Paul S 100/PK-6
PO Box 160 62354 217-453-2511
Lisa Gray, prin. Fax 453-2015

Neoga, Cumberland, Pop. 1,622
Neoga CUSD 3 500/PK-12
PO Box 280 62447 217-895-2201
Benjamin Johnson, supt. Fax 895-3476
www.neoga.k12.il.us
Neoga ES 200/PK-5
PO Box 310 62447 217-895-2208
Carol Smith, prin. Fax 895-2757

Neponset, Bureau, Pop. 460
Kewanee CUSD 229
Supt. — See Kewanee
Neponset Grade S 100/PK-8
201 W Main St 61345 309-594-2306
Dena Hodge-Bates, prin. Fax 594-2113

Newark, Kendall, Pop. 984
Lisbon CCSD 90 100/K-8
127 S Canal St 60541 815-736-6324
Dr. Michael Rustman, supt. Fax 736-6326
Lisbon ES 100/K-8
127 S Canal St 60541 815-736-6324
Dr. Michael Rustman, prin. Fax 736-6326

Newark CCSD 66 200/K-8
503 Chicago Rd 60541 815-695-5143
Demetra Turman, supt. Fax 695-5776
www.ngsd66.org
Newark ES 100/K-4
503 Chicago Rd 60541 815-695-5143
Demetra Turman, prin. Fax 695-5776
Other Schools – See Millbrook

New Athens, Saint Clair, Pop. 2,032
New Athens CUSD 60 500/PK-12
501 Hanft St 62264 618-475-2174
Brian Karraker, supt. Fax 475-2176
www.na60.org
New Athens ES 200/PK-5
501 Hanft St 62264 618-475-2172
Jim Marlow, prin. Fax 475-2176
New Athens JHS 100/6-8
501 Hanft St 62264 618-475-2172
Jim Marlow, prin. Fax 475-2176

St. Agatha S 100/K-8
207 S Market St 62264 618-475-2170
Sarah Lanham, prin. Fax 475-3177

New Baden, Clinton, Pop. 3,279
Wesclin CUSD 3
Supt. — See Trenton
New Baden ES 200/K-3
700 Marilyn Dr 62265 618-588-3535
James Rahm, prin. Fax 588-4364

New Berlin, Sangamon, Pop. 1,336
New Berlin CUSD 16 900/PK-12
600 N Cedar St 62670 217-488-2040
Adam Ehrman, supt. Fax 488-2043
www.pretzelpride.com
New Berlin ES 500/PK-5
600 N Cedar St 62670 217-488-6054
Casey Wills, prin. Fax 488-6039
New Berlin JHS 200/6-8
PO Box 230 62670 217-488-6011
Megan Doerfler, prin. Fax 488-3207

New Boston, Mercer, Pop. 682
Mercer County SD 404
Supt. — See Aledo
New Boston ES 200/PK-4
301 Jefferson St 61272 309-587-8141
Marcus Bush, prin. Fax 587-3349

New Lenox, Will, Pop. 24,189
New Lenox SD 122 5,400/K-8
102 S Cedar Rd 60451 815-485-2169
Dr. Margaret Manville, supt. Fax 485-2236
www.nlsd122.org
Bentley IS 400/4-6
513 E Illinois Hwy 60451 815-485-4451
Jason Sterritt, prin. Fax 485-7599
Haines ES 400/1-3
155 Haines Ave 60451 815-485-2115
Dr. Michelle Hall, prin. Fax 462-2571
Liberty JHS 700/7-8
151 Lenox St 60451 815-462-7951
Shane Street, prin. Fax 462-0672
Martino JHS 600/7-8
731 E Joliet Hwy 60451 815-485-7593
Dr. Bonnie Groen, prin. Fax 485-9578
Nelson Prairie ES 500/1-3
2366 Nelson Rd 60451 815-462-2874
Tyler Broders, prin. Fax 462-2881
Nelson Ridge IS 500/4-6
2470 Nelson Rd 60451 815-462-2870
Megan Baldermann, prin. Fax 462-2880
Oster-Oakview IS 500/4-6
809 N Cedar Rd 60451 815-485-2125
Theresa Baumann, prin. Fax 462-2572
Spencer Crossing IS 500/4-6
1711 Spencer Rd 60451 815-462-7997
Megan Calleros, prin. Fax 462-0958
Spencer Pointe ES 400/1-3
1721 Spencer Rd 60451 815-462-7988
Dr. Kim Gray, prin. Fax 462-3978
Spencer Trail K 500/K-K
1701 Spencer Rd 60451 815-462-7007
Dr. Lori Motsch, prin. Fax 462-0670
Tyler ES 400/1-3
511 E Illinois Hwy 60451 815-485-2398
Patricia Fisher, prin. Fax 462-2570

Providence Early Education Center 100/PK-K
1800 W Lincoln Hwy 60451 815-485-7129
Laura McErlean, dir. Fax 717 3042
St. Jude S 200/PK-8
241 W 2nd Ave 60451 815-485-2549
Kathleen Winters, prin. Fax 485-0234

Newton, Jasper, Pop. 2,823
Jasper County CUSD 1 1,400/PK-12
609 S Lafayette St 62448 618-783-8459
Andrew D. Johnson, supt. Fax 783-3679
www.cusd1.jasper.k12.il.us
Jasper County JHS 200/7-8
1104 W Jourdan St 62448 618-783-4202
Travis Wyatt, prin. Fax 783-4257
Newton ES 600/1-6
101 Maxwell St 62448 618-783-8464
Kathy Johnson, prin. Fax 783-4106
Other Schools – See Sainte Marie

St. Thomas the Apostle S 100/K-8
306 W Jourdan St 62448 618-783-3517
Jill Bierman, prin. Fax 783-2224

Niantic, Macon, Pop. 703
Sangamon Valley CUSD 9 700/PK-12
PO Box 200 62551 217-668-2338
Robert Meadows, supt. Fax 668-2406
www.sangamonvalley.org
Other Schools – See Harristown, Illiopolis

Niles, Cook, Pop. 29,272
East Maine SD 63
Supt. — See Des Plaines
Gemini JHS 800/7-8
8955 N Greenwood Ave 60714 847-827-1181
Dr. Rene Carranza, prin. Fax 827-3499
Nelson ES 600/K-6
8901 N Ozanam Ave 60714 847-965-0050
Lauren Leitao, prin. Fax 965-7630
Twain ES 400/K-6
9401 N Hamlin Ave 60714 847-296-5341
Lewis Roberts, prin. Fax 296-5345

Niles ESD 71 500/PK-8
6901 W Oakton St 60714 847-966-9280
Dr. John Kosirog, supt. Fax 966-0214
www.culver71.net
Culver S 500/PK-8
6901 W Oakton St 60714 847-966-9280
Peggie Maniscalco, prin. Fax 966-0214

Park Ridge-Niles CCSD 64
Supt. — See Park Ridge
Emerson MS 800/6-8
8101 N Cumberland Ave 60714 847-318-8110
Dr. Jim Morrison, prin. Fax 318-8701
Jefferson S 100/PK-PK
8200 W Greendale Ave 60714 847-318-5360
Lisa Halverson, prin. Fax 318-5442

Childrens Learning World Montessori S 100/PK-6
8101 W Golf Rd 60714 847-470-0370
Rosemary Fish, prin. Fax 470-0934
Logos Christian Academy 200/PK-12
7280 N Caldwell Ave 60714 847-647-9456
Larry Murg, prin. Fax 647-7916

St. John Brebeuf S 300/PK-8
8301 N Harlem Ave 60714 847-966-3266
Elise Matson, prin. Fax 966-5351

Nokomis, Montgomery, Pop. 2,240
Nokomis CUSD 22 700/PK-12
511 Oberle St 62075 217-563-7311
Dr. Scott Doerr, supt. Fax 563-2549
www.nokomis.k12.il.us
North ES 400/PK-5
110 W Hamilton St 62075 217-563-8521
Kevin Reedy, prin. Fax 563-2675

St. Louis S 100/K-8
509 E Union St 62075 217-563-7445
Elaine Wagner, prin. Fax 563-7450

Normal, McLean, Pop. 51,379
ISU Lab SD 1,000/PK-12
ISU Campus Box 5300 61790 309-438-8542
Dr. Ty Wolf, supt. Fax 438-3813
education.illinoisstate.edu/labschools
Metcalf S 400/PK-8
ISU Campus Box 7000 61790 309-438-7621
Dr. Amy Fritson Coffman, prin. Fax 438-2580

McLean County Unit SD 5 13,500/PK-12
1809 Hovey Ave 61761 309-557-4000
Dr. Mark Daniel, supt. Fax 557-4501
www.unit5.org
Chiddix JHS 700/6-8
300 S Walnut St 61761 309-557-4405
Jim Allen, prin. Fax 557-4506
Fairview ES 300/PK-5
416 Fairview St 61761 309-557-4415
Lori Harrison, prin. Fax 557-4516
Glenn ES 300/K-5
306 Glenn Ave 61761 309-557-4418
Maureen Backe, prin. Fax 557-4519
Grove ES 700/K-5
1101 Airport Rd 61761 309-557-4417
Sarah Edwards, prin. Fax 557-4518
Hoose ES 500/K-5
600 Grandview Dr 61761 309-557-4414
Adam Zbrozek, prin. Fax 557-4515
Kingsley JHS 900/6-8
303 Kingsley St 61761 309-557-4407
Shelly Erickson, prin. Fax 557-4508
Oakdale ES 400/PK-5
601 S Adelaide St 61761 309-557-4421
Darrin Cooper, prin. Fax 557-4522
Parkside ES 300/K-5
1900 W College Ave 61761 309-557-4422
Ryan Weichman, prin. Fax 557-4523
Parkside JHS 700/6-8
101 N Parkside Rd 61761 309-557-4408
Dan Lamboley, prin. Fax 557-4509
Prairieland ES 600/K-5
1300 E Raab Rd 61761 309-557-4424
Scott Peters, prin. Fax 557-4525
Sugar Creek ES 500/PK-5
200 N Towanda Ave 61761 309-557-4425
Nicole Combs, prin. Fax 557-4526
Other Schools – See Bloomington, Carlock, Hudson, Towanda

Calvary Christian Academy 300/PK-12
1017 N School St 61761 309-452-7912
Mike Sturgill, head sch Fax 451-0033
Epiphany S 400/PK-8
1002 E College Ave 61761 309-452-3268
Michael Lootens, prin. Fax 454-8087

Norridge, Cook, Pop. 14,463
Norridge SD 80 1,000/K-8
8151 W Lawrence Ave 60706 708-583-2068
Dr. Paul O'Malley, supt. Fax 583-2072
www.norridge80.net
Giles ES 500/5-8
4251 N Oriole Ave 60706 708-453-4847
Stephanie Palmer, prin. Fax 456-0798
Leigh ES 500/K-4
8151 W Lawrence Ave 60706 708-456-8848
Michele Guzik, prin. Fax 583-2053

Pennoyer SD 79 400/PK-8
5200 N Cumberland Ave 60706 708-456-9094
Dr. Kristin Kopta, supt. Fax 456-9098
www.pennoyerschool.org
Pennoyer ES 400/PK-8
5200 N Cumberland Ave 60706 708-456-9094
Gina Sierra, prin. Fax 456-9098

Norris City, White, Pop. 1,272
Norris City-Omaha-Enfield CUSD 3 800/PK-12
PO Box 399 62869 618-378-3222
Matthew Vollman, supt. Fax 378-3286
www.ncoecusd.white.k12.il.us
Norris City-Omaha S 400/K-8
PO Box 399 62869 618-378-3212
Jimmy Foster, prin. Fax 378-3286
Other Schools – See Enfield

North Aurora, Kane, Pop. 16,455
Aurora West Unit SD 129
Supt. — See Aurora
Fearn ES 700/K-5
1600 Hawksley Ln 60542 630-301-5001
Dave Russell, prin. Fax 907-2472
Goodwin ES 400/K-5
18 Poplar Pl 60542 630-301-5003
Robert Halverson, prin. Fax 844-6959
Jewel MS 700/6-8
1501 Waterford Rd 60542 630-301-5010
Dr. Greg Scalia, prin. Fax 907-3161
Schneider ES 500/K-5
304 Banbury Rd 60542 630-301-5014
Olivia Smith, prin. Fax 844-4513

North Aurora SDA ES 50/K-8
950 Mooseheart Rd 60542 630-896-5188
Teresa Smith, prin. Fax 896-5789

North Barrington, Lake, Pop. 2,999
Barrington CUSD 220
Supt. — See Barrington
North Barrington ES 400/K-5
24175 N Grandview Dr 60010 847-381-4340
Austin Johnson, prin. Fax 304-3924

Northbrook, Cook, Pop. 32,798
Northbrook ESD 27 1,200/PK-8
1250 Sanders Rd 60062 847-498-2610
Dr. David Kroeze, supt. Fax 498-5916
www.nb27.org
Hickory Point ES 400/PK-2
500 Laburnum Dr 60062 847-498-3830
Sheila Streets, prin. Fax 480-4837
Shabonee S 400/3-5
1000 Pfingsten Rd 60062 847-498-4970
John Panozzo, prin. Fax 480-4836
Wood Oaks JHS 400/6-8
1250 Sanders Rd 60062 847-272-1900
Robert McElligott, prin. Fax 480-4834

Northbrook SD 28 1,600/PK-8
1475 Maple Ave 60062 847-498-7900
Dr. Larry Hewitt, supt. Fax 498-7970
www.northbrook28.net
Greenbriar ES 400/PK-5
1225 Greenbriar Ln 60062 847-498-7950
Virginia Hiltz, prin. Fax 504-3710
Meadowbrook ES 400/PK-5
1600 Walters Ave 60062 847-498-7940
Pat Thome, prin. Fax 504-3610
Northbrook JHS 600/6-8
1475 Maple Ave 60062 847-498-7920
Scott Meek, prin. Fax 656-1712
Westmoor ES 300/PK-5
2500 Cherry Ln 60062 847-498-7960
Mary Sturgill, prin. Fax 504-3810

Northbrook/Glenview SD 30 1,100/K-8
2374 Shermer Rd 60062 847-498-4190
Dr. Brian Wegley, supt. Fax 498-8981
www.district30.org
Maple S 400/6-8
2370 Shermer Rd 60062 847-400-8900
Dr. Nathan Carter, prin. Fax 272-0979
Wescott S 400/1-5
1820 Western Ave 60062 847-272-4660
Chris Brown, prin. Fax 205-5241
Other Schools – See Glenview

West Northfield SD 31 900/K-8
3131 Techny Rd 60062 847-272-6880
Dr. Alexandra Nicholson, supt. Fax 272-4818
www.district31.net/
Field MS 300/6-8
2055 Landwehr Rd 60062 847-272-6884
Dr. Erin Murphy, prin. Fax 272-1050
Other Schools – See Glenview

Countryside Montessori S 100/PK-8
1985 Pfingsten Rd 60062 847-498-1105
Wendy Calise, head sch Fax 564-1709
St. Norbert S 300/PK-8
1817 Walters Ave 60062 847-272-0051
Geralyn Lawler, prin. Fax 272-5274
Solomon Schechter Day S of Metro Chicago 200/PK-8
3210 Dundee Rd 60062 847-498-2100
Linda Foster, head sch Fax 498-5837

North Chicago, Lake, Pop. 31,474
North Chicago SD 187 2,500/PK-12
2000 Lewis Ave 60064 847-689-8150
John J. Price, supt. Fax 689-7348
d187.org
Alexander ES 200/K-3
1210 Adams St 60064 847-689-7345
Andres Orbe, prin. Fax 578-6018
Green Bay ECC 300/PK-PK
2100 Green Bay Rd 60064 847-775-7100
Nicole Johnson, prin. Fax 775-7233
Katzenmaier Academy 200/4-5
1829 Kennedy Dr 60064 847-689-6330
Michael Grenda, prin. Fax 689-2818
Neal Math Science Academy 600/6-8
1905 Argonne Dr 60064 847-689-6313
Vanessa Campos, prin. Fax 689-6313
Other Schools – See Great Lakes

Northfield, Cook, Pop. 5,375
Sunset Ridge SD 29 500/K-8
525 Sunset Ridge Rd 60093 847-881-9456
Dr. Edward Stange, supt.
www.sunsetridge29.net
Middlefork PS, 405 Wagner Rd 60093 200/K-3
Dr. Mary Frances Greene, prin. 847-881-9500
Sunset Ridge MS 300/4-8
525 Sunset Ridge Rd 60093 847-881-9400
Dr. Ivy Sukenik, prin.

Christian Heritage Academy 500/PK-12
315 Waukegan Rd 60093 847-446-5252
Dr. Hutz Hertzberg, pres. Fax 446-5267

Northlake, Cook, Pop. 12,227
Berkeley SD 87
Supt. — See Berkeley
Northlake MS 400/6-8
202 S Lakewood Ave 60164 708-449-3195
Dr. Sunil Mody, prin. Fax 547-2548
Riley IS 400/3-5
123 S Wolf Rd 60164 708-449-3180
Ives Munoz, prin. Fax 547-2541
Whittier PS 600/PK-2
338 Whitehall Ave 60164 708-449-3175
Dr. Tracy Bodenstab, prin. Fax 547-3313

Mannheim SD 83
Supt. — See Franklin Park
Mannheim ECC PK-K
101 W Diversey Ave 60164 708-455-3611
Shannon Cribaro, dir. Fax 455-0143
Roy ES 600/K-5
533 N Roy Ave 60164 708-562-6400
Joseph Stanislao, prin. Fax 562-9819
Westdale ES 600/K-5
99 W Diversey Ave 60164 847-455-4060
Tara Kjome, prin. Fax 455-2050

St. John Vianney S 200/PK-8
27 N Lavergne Ave 60164 708-562-1466
Paul Kirk M.Ed., prin. Fax 562-0142

North Pekin, Tazewell, Pop. 1,557
North Pekin & Marquette Hts SD 102
Supt. — See Marquette Heights
Rogers ES 200/3-5
109 Rogers Rd 61554 309-382-3401
Jennifer Lindsay, prin. Fax 382-2122

North Riverside, Cook, Pop. 6,608
Komarek SD 94 500/PK-8
8940 W 24th St 60546 708-447-8030
Dr. Brian Ganan, supt. Fax 447-9546
www.komarek94.org
Komarek S 500/PK-8
8940 W 24th St 60546 708-447-8030
Dr. Jason Gold, prin. Fax 447-9546

Oak Brook, DuPage, Pop. 7,720
Butler SD 53 500/PK-8
2801 York Rd 60523 630-573-2887
Dr. Heidi Wennstrom, supt. Fax 573-5374
www.butler53.com
Brook Forest ES 300/PK-5
60 Regent Dr 60523 630-325-6888
Dr. Chad Prosen, prin. Fax 325-8452
Butler JHS 200/6-8
2801 York Rd 60523 630-573-2760
Amy Read, prin. Fax 573-1725

Oakbrook Terrace, DuPage, Pop. 2,106
Salt Creek SD 48
Supt. — See Villa Park
Swartz ES 100/2-4
17W160 16th St 60181 630-834-9256
Gerrie Aulisa, prin. Fax 617-2643

Oakdale, Washington, Pop. 221
Oakdale CCSD 1 100/K-8
280 E Main St 62268 618-329-5292
Charles Peterson, supt. Fax 329-5545
www.oakdalegs.org
Oakdale ES 100/K-8
280 E Main St 62268 618-329-5292
Charles Peterson, admin. Fax 329-5545

Oak Forest, Cook, Pop. 27,551
Arbor Park SD 145 1,500/PK-8
17301 Central Ave 60452 708-687-8040
Dr. Andrea Sala, supt. Fax 687-9498
www.arbor145.org
Arbor Park MS 600/5-8
17303 Central Ave 60452 708-687-5330
Ronald Murabito, prin. Fax 535-4527
Gingerwood ES 300/1-2
16936 Forest Ave 60452 708-560-0092
Camille Hogan, prin. Fax 535-5071
Scarlet Oak ES 300/3-4
5731 Albert Dr 60452 708-687-5822
Scot A. Pierce, prin. Fax 687-4292
Other Schools – See Tinley Park

CCSD 146
Supt. — See Tinley Park
Fierke ES 300/PK-5
6535 Victoria Dr 60452 708-614-4520
Bret Pignatiello, prin. Fax 535-0841

Forest Ridge SD 142 1,600/PK-8
15000 Laramie Ave 60452 708-687-3334
Dr. Paul McDermott, supt. Fax 687-2970
www.d142.org
Foster ES 400/1-5
5931 School St 60452 708-687-4763
Curtis Beringer, prin. Fax 687-2659
Hille MS 500/6-8
5800 151st St 60452 708-687-5550
John Orth, prin. Fax 687-8569
Kerkstra ES 400/1-5
14950 Laramie Ave 60452 708-687-5550
Jeff Kulik, prin. Fax 687-0571
Ridge ECC 200/PK-K
5151 149th St 60452 708-687-2964
Elizabeth Ehrhart, prin. Fax 687-8458

Prairie-Hills ESD 144
Supt. — See Markham
Fieldcrest ES 300/K-5
4100 Wagman St 60452 708-210-2872
Kimberly Cook, prin. Fax 535-0224

St. Damian S 500/PK-8
5300 155th St 60452 708-687-4230
Dr. Marian Stockhausen, prin. Fax 687-8347

Oakland, Coles, Pop. 873
Oakland CUSD 5 300/PK-12
310 Teeter St 61943 217-346-2555
Lance Landeck, supt. Fax 346-2267
www.oak.k12.il.us
Lake Crest S 200/PK-8
310 Teeter St 61943 217-346-2166
Adam Clapp, prin. Fax 346-2267

Oak Lawn, Cook, Pop. 55,942
Atwood Heights SD 125
Supt. — See Alsip
Lawn Manor Primary Center 300/PK-2
4300 W 108th Pl 60453 708-423-3078
Heather Wills, prin. Fax 423-9331

Oak Lawn-Hometown SD 123 3,000/PK-8
4201 W 93rd St 60453 708-423-0150
Dr. Paul Enderle, supt. Fax 423-0160
www.d123.org/
Covington ES 400/K-5
9130 S 52nd Ave 60453 708-423-1530
John Wawczak, prin. Fax 499-7674
Hannum ES 400/K-5
9800 S Tripp Ave 60453 708-423-1690
Anne McGovern, prin. Fax 499-7676
Kolmar Avenue ES 400/PK-5
10425 S Kolmar Ave 60453 708-422-1800
David Creech, prin. Fax 499-7681
Oak Lawn-Hometown MS 1,000/6-8
5345 W 99th St 60453 708-499-6400
Kristin Simpkins, prin. Fax 499-7684
Sward ES 400/K-5
9830 Brandt Ave 60453 708-423-7820
Candice Kramer, prin. Fax 499-7686
Other Schools – See Hometown

Ridgeland SD 122 2,400/PK-8
6500 W 95th St 60453 708-599-5550
Julie Shellberg, supt. Fax 599-5626
www.ridgeland122.com
Columbus Manor ES 400/PK-5
9700 Mayfield Ave 60453 708-424-3481
Meghan Dougherty, prin. Fax 424-9412
Harnew ES 500/PK-5
9101 Meade Ave 60453 708-599-7070
Anthony Gill, prin. Fax 599-9636
Kolb ES 400/K-5
9620 Normandy Ave 60453 708-598-8090
Dan McDermott, prin. Fax 598-6445
Simmons MS 700/6-8
6450 W 95th St 60453 708-599-8540
Tracy Flood, prin. Fax 599-8015
Other Schools – See Bridgeview

St. Catherine of Alexandria S 400/PK-8
10621 Kedvale Ave 60453 708-425-5547
Michelle Edwards, prin. Fax 425-3701
St. Gerald S 400/PK-8
9320 S 55th Ct 60453 708-422-0121
Al Theis, prin. Fax 422-9216
St. Germaine S 300/PK-8
9735 S Kolin Ave 60453 708-425-6063
Kevin Reedy, prin. Fax 425-7463
St. Linus S 400/PK-8
10400 Lawler Ave 60453 708-425-1656
Margaret Hayes, prin. Fax 499-9492
St. Paul Lutheran S 100/PK-8
4660 W 94th St 60453 708-423-1058
Angela Schlie, prin. Fax 423-1588
South Side Baptist S 100/PK-12
5220 W 105th St 60453 708-425-3435
Robert Burckart, prin. Fax 425-9016
Southwest Chicago Christian S Oak Lawn 300/PK-8
10110 Central Ave 60453 708-636-8550
Nathaniel Pettinga, prin. Fax 636-0175

Oak Park, Cook, Pop. 50,159
Oak Park ESD 97 5,800/PK-8
260 Madison St 60302 708-524-3000
Dr. Carol Kelley, supt. Fax 848-8986
www.op97.org
Beye ES 400/K-5
230 N Cuyler Ave 60302 708-524-3070
Jonathan Ellwanger, prin. Fax 524-3069
Brooks MS 900/6-8
325 S Kenilworth Ave 60302 708-524-3050
April Capuder, prin. Fax 524-3036
Hatch ES 300/K-5
1000 N Ridgeland Ave 60302 708-524-3095
Sarah Mendez, prin. Fax 524-3139
Holmes ES 600/PK-5
508 N Kenilworth Ave 60302 708-524-3100
Christine Zelaya, prin. Fax 524-7622
Irving ES 500/K-5
1125 S Cuyler Ave 60304 708-524-3090
John Hodge, prin. Fax 524-3056
Julian MS 900/6-8
416 S Ridgeland Ave 60302 708-524-3040
Dr. Todd Fitzgerald, prin. Fax 524-3035
Lincoln ES 600/K-5
1111 S Grove Ave 60304 708-524-3110
Lisa Carlos, prin. Fax 524-3124
Longfellow ES 600/K-5
715 Highland Ave 60304 708-524-3060
Angela Dolezal, prin. Fax 524-3037
Mann ES 500/K-5
921 N Kenilworth Ave 60302 708-524-3085
Faith Cole, prin. Fax 524-3049
Whittier ES 400/K-5
715 N Harvey Ave 60302 708-524-3080
Keisha Warner, prin. Fax 524-3047

Alcuin Montessori S 200/PK-8
324 N Oak Park Ave 60302 708-366-1882
Gina Gleason, dir. Fax 386-1892
Ascension S 500/PK-8
601 Van Buren St 60304 708-386-7282
Mary Jo Burns, prin. Fax 524-4796
Field School, 931 Lake St 60301 50/PK-1
Jeremy Mann, prin. 708-434-5811
La Casa Montessori S 100/PK-5
514 W Adams 60304 708-613-0514
Gicel Mercado B.A., prin.
St. Giles S 500/PK-8
1034 Linden Ave 60302 708-383-6279
Nancy Zver, prin. Fax 383-9952
SS. Catherine Siena & Lucy S 200/PK-8
27 Washington Blvd 60302 708-386-5286
Sr. Marian Cypser, prin. Fax 386-7328

West Suburban Montessori S PK-6
1039 S East Ave 60304 708-848-2662
Patty Eggerding, head sch

Oakwood, Vermilion, Pop. 1,576
Oakwood CUSD 76 1,000/PK-12
12190 US Route 150 61858 217-446-6081
Gary Lewis, supt. Fax 446-6218
www.oakwood.k12.il.us
Oakwood ES 600/PK-6
PO Box 219 61858 217-354-4221
Nicole Lapenas, prin. Fax 354-2712
Other Schools – See Danville

Oblong, Crawford, Pop. 1,457
Oblong CUSD 4 600/PK-12
PO Box 40 62449 618-592-3933
Jeffery Patchett, supt. Fax 592-3427
www.oblongschools.net
Oblong ES 400/PK-8
600 W Main St 62449 618-592-4225
Dave Parker, prin. Fax 592-4299

Odell, Livingston, Pop. 1,040
Odell CCSD 435 200/PK-8
203 N East St 60460 815-998-2272
Mark Hettmansberger, supt. Fax 998-2619
www.odellschool.org
Odell S 200/PK-8
203 N East St 60460 815-998-2272
Mark Hettmansberger, prin. Fax 998-2619

St. Paul S 100/PK-8
300 S West St 60460 815-998-2194
Richard Morehouse, prin. Fax 998-1514

Odin, Marion, Pop. 1,064
Odin SD 722 300/PK-12
102 S Merritt St 62870 618-775-8266
Jeffrey Humes, supt. Fax 775-8268
www.odinpublicschools.org
Odin S 200/PK-8
102 S Merritt St 62870 618-775-8266
Sam Alli, prin. Fax 775-8268

O Fallon, Saint Clair, Pop. 27,465
Central SD 104 600/PK-8
309 Hartman Ln 62269 618-632-6336
Dawn Elser, supt. Fax 632-0263
www.central104.org
Arthur MS 200/5-8
160 Saint Ellen Mine Rd 62269 618-632-6336
Tron Young, prin. Fax 622-8691
Central ES 400/PK-4
309 Hartman Ln 62269 618-632-6336
Jered Weh, prin. Fax 632-0870

O'Fallon CCSD 90 3,400/PK-8
118 E Washington St 62269 618-632-3666
Carrie Hruby, supt. Fax 632-7864
www.of90.net
Carriel JHS 700/6-8
450 N 7 Hills Rd 62269 618-632-3666
Ellen Hays, prin. Fax 622-2940
Evans ES 300/K-5
802 Dartmouth Dr 62269 618-632-3335
Ryan Keller, prin. Fax 632-1530
Fulton JHS 500/6-8
307 Kyle Rd 62269 618-628-0090
Joi Wills, prin. Fax 624-9390
Hinchcliffe ES 300/K-5
1050 Ogle Rd 62269 618-632-8406
Kristie Belobrajdic, prin. Fax 632-1774
Kampmeyer ES 400/K-5
707 N Smiley St 62269 618-632-6391
Mark Dismukes, prin. Fax 632-7580
Moye ES 700/K-5
1010 Moye School Rd 62269 618-206-2300
Becky Williams, prin. Fax 632-7864
Schaefer ES 400/K-5
505 S Cherry St 62269 618-632-3621
Tracy Duggins, prin. Fax 632-9258

First Baptist Academy 200/K-12
1111 E Highway 50 62269 618-726-6040
Jackye Biehl, admin. Fax 632-8029
St. Clare S 400/K-8
214 W 3rd St 62269 618-632-6327
Clarice McKay, prin. Fax 632-5587

Ogden, Champaign, Pop. 807
Prairieview-Ogden CCSD 197
Supt. — See Royal
Prairieview-Ogden South ES 100/K-6
304 N Market St 61859 217-582-2725
Jeffrey Isenhower, prin. Fax 582-2509

Oglesby, LaSalle, Pop. 3,742
Oglesby ESD 125 600/PK-8
755 Bennett Ave 61348 815-883-9297
Michael Pillion, supt. Fax 883-3568
www.ops125.net
Lincoln ES 500/PK-5
755 Bennett Ave 61348 815-883-8932
Michael Balestri, prin. Fax 883-3568
Washington MS 100/6-8
212 W Walnut St 61348 815-883-3517
Merritt Burns, prin. Fax 883-9282

Holy Family S 100/PK-8
336 Alice Ave 61348 815-883-8916
Jyll Jasiek, prin. Fax 883-8943

Ohio, Bureau, Pop. 504
Ohio CCSD 17 100/K-8
PO Box 478 61349 815-376-4414
Jennifer Hamilton, supt. Fax 376-2102
www.bhsroe.org/site/?page_id=39641
Ohio Community Consolidated ES 100/K-8
PO Box 478 61349 815-376-2934
Jason Wilt, prin. Fax 376-2102

Okawville, Washington, Pop. 1,424
West Washington County CUSD 10 600/PK-12
PO Box 27 62271 618-243-6454
Scott Fuhrhop, supt. Fax 243-6454
www.okawville-k12.org
Okawville ES 300/PK-6
400 S Hanover St 62271 618-243-6157
Leon Spinka, prin. Fax 243-9066

Immanuel Lutheran S 100/PK-8
606 S Hanover St 62271 618-243-6142
Lynn Lukomski, prin. Fax 243-6562

Olney, Richland, Pop. 9,020
Richland County CUSD 1 2,100/PK-12
1100 E Laurel St 62450 618-395-2324
Larry Bussard, supt. Fax 392-4147
www.rccu1.net
Richland County ES 1,000/PK-5
1001 N Holly Rd 62450 618-395-8540
Andrew Thomann, prin. Fax 395-8672
Richland County MS 400/6-8
1099 N Van St 62450 618-395-4372
Cris Edwards, prin. Fax 392-3399

St. Joseph S 200/PK-8
520 E Chestnut St 62450 618-395-3081
Carol Potter, prin. Fax 395-8500

Olympia Fields, Cook, Pop. 4,901
Matteson ESD 162
Supt. — See Richton Park
Arcadia ES 500/K-3
20519 Arcadian Dr 60461 708-747-3535
Stephanie Healy, prin. Fax 503-0961

Homewood Christian Academy 100/PK-8
20820 Western Ave 60461 708-535-1524
Lannaea Alexander, prin. Fax 535-1525

Onarga, Iroquois, Pop. 1,354
Iroquois West CUSD 10
Supt. — See Gilman
Iroquois West MS 200/6-8
303 N Evergreen St 60955 815-268-4355
Duane Ehmen, prin. Fax 268-7608

Oneida, Knox, Pop. 697
ROWVA CUSD 208 700/PK-12
PO Box 69 61467 309-483-3711
Joe Sornberger, supt. Fax 483-6123
www.rowva.k12.il.us
ROWVA ES 400/PK-6
PO Box 69 61467 309-483-6376
Kerry Danner, prin. Fax 483-6378
ROWVA JHS 100/7-8
PO Box 69 61467 309-483-6371
Joe Peters, prin. Fax 483-8223

Opdyke, Jefferson, Pop. 247
Opdyke-Belle-Rive CCSD 5 200/K-8
PO Box 189 62872 618-756-2492
Mark Miller, supt. Fax 756-2792
www.obr5.org
Opdyke-Belle-Rive Grade S 200/K-8
PO Box 189 62872 618-756-2492
Mark Miller, admin. Fax 756-2792

Orangeville, Stephenson, Pop. 784
Orangeville CUSD 203 400/PK-12
201 S Orange St 61060 815-789-4289
Dr. Doug DeSchepper, supt. Fax 789-4709
www.orangevillecusd.com/
Orangeville ES 200/PK-5
310 S East St 61060 815-789-4450
Dr. Douglas DeSchepper, prin. Fax 789-4607
Orangeville JHS 100/6-8
201 S Orange St 61060 815-789-4289
Andrew Janecke, prin. Fax 789-4709

Oreana, Macon, Pop. 867
Argenta-Oreana CUSD 1
Supt. — See Argenta
Argenta-Oreana ES 500/PK-5
400 W South St 62554 217-468-2121
Amanda Ryder, prin. Fax 468-2403

Oregon, Ogle, Pop. 3,686
Oregon CUSD 220 1,400/PK-12
206 S 10th St 61061 815-732-5300
Dr. Thomas Mahoney, supt. Fax 732-2187
www.ocusd.net
Oregon ES 800/PK-6
1150 Jefferson St 61061 815-732-5300
Kolli Virgil, prin. Fax 732-6108
Other Schools – See Mount Morris

Orion, Henry, Pop. 1,846
Orion CUSD 223 1,100/PK-12
PO Box 189 61273 309-526-3388
Joseph Blessman, supt. Fax 526-3711
orionschools.us/
Hanna ES 500/PK-5
PO Box 159 61273 309-526-3386
R.C. Lowe, prin. Fax 526-3864
Orion MS 300/6-8
PO Box 129 61273 309-526-3392
Scott Briney, prin. Fax 526-3872

Orland Hills, Cook, Pop. 7,042

Bernardin S 600/PK-8
9250 W 167th St, 708-403-6525
Mary Iannucilli, prin. Fax 403-8621
Christian Hills S 100/PK-8
9001 159th St, 708-349-7166
Laurence Beadle, prin. Fax 349-9665

Orland Park, Cook, Pop. 56,112
CCSD 146
Supt. — See Tinley Park
Kruse ES 300/PK-5
7617 Hemlock Dr 60462 708-614-4530
Carey Radde, prin. Fax 614-7602

Kirby SD 140
Supt. — See Tinley Park
Fernway Park ES 500/PK-5
16600 S 88th Ave 60462 708-349-3810
Julianne Cosentino, prin. Fax 349-9463

Orland SD 135 5,000/K-8
15100 S 94th Ave 60462 708-364-3306
Dr. D.J. Skogsberg, supt. Fax 873-6479
www.orland135.org
Centennial ES 400/K-3
14101 Creek Crossing Dr 60467 708-364-3444
Beth Hayden, prin. Fax 873-6450
Century JHS 800/6-8
10801 W 159th St 60467 708-364-3500
Dr. Brian Horn, prin. Fax 349-5840
High Point ES 500/3-5
14825 West Ave 60462 708-364-4400
Cheryl Foertsch, prin. Fax 460-5970
Jerling JHS 600/6-8
8851 W 151st St 60462 708-364-3700
Kevin Brown, prin. Fax 873-6457
Liberty ES 400/3-5
8801 W 151st St 60462 708-364-3800
Daniel Prorok, prin. Fax 873-1103
Meadow Ridge ES 600/3-5
10959 W 159th St 60467 708-364-3600
Dana Karczewski, prin. Fax 873-6461
Orland Center ES 300/K-2
9407 W 151st St 60462 708-364-3242
Jennifer Nichols, prin. Fax 873-6453
Orland JHS 500/6-8
14855 West Ave 60462 708-364-4200
Dr. Edward Boswell, prin. Fax 349-5843
Orland Park ES 400/K-2
9960 W 143rd St 60462 708-364-3900
Sue Kuligoski, prin. Fax 460-6139
Prairie ES 500/K-3
14200 S 82nd Ave 60462 708-364-4840
Jeff Nightingale, prin. Fax 873-6451

St. Michael S 500/K-8
14355 Highland Ave 60462 708-349-0068
Paul Smith, prin. Fax 349-2658
Sears Childrens Academy 100/PK-3
16807 108th Ave 60467 708-460-4414
John Sears, prin.

Oswego, Kendall, Pop. 29,822
CUSD 308 17,500/PK-12
4175 State Route 71 60543 630-636-3080
Dr. John W. Sparlin, supt. Fax 636-3688
www.sd308.org
Brokaw Early Learning Center 400/PK-PK
1000 5th St 60543 630-551-9600
Andrew McCree, prin. Fax 551-9619
Churchill ES 600/K-5
520 Secretariat Ln 60543 630-636-3800
Tammie Harmon, prin. Fax 636-3891
Fox Chase ES 600/K-5
260 Fox Chase Dr N 60543 630-636-3000
Sue Tiedt, prin. Fax 636-3078
Hunt Club ES 500/K-5
4001 Hunt Club Dr 60543 630-636-2800
Patrick Haddock, prin. Fax 636-2893
Old Post ES 400/K-5
100 Old Post Rd 60543 630-636-3400
Toia Jones, prin. Fax 636-3491
Plank JHS 900/6-8
510 Secretariat Ln 60543 630-551-9400
James Martin, prin. Fax 551-9691
Prairie Point ES 600/K-5
3650 Grove Rd 60543 630-636-3600
Dr. Jennifer Groves, prin. Fax 636-3612
Southbury ES 600/K-5
820 Preston Ln 60543 630-551-9800
Lindsay Allen, prin. Fax 551-9819
Thompson JHS 1,000/6-8
440 Boulder Hill Pass 60543 630-636-2600
Shannon Lueders, prin. Fax 636-2691
Traughber JHS 1,000/6-8
570 Colchester Dr 60543 630-636-2700
Melinda Renier, prin. Fax 636-2791
Other Schools – See Aurora, Montgomery, Plainfield

Ottawa, LaSalle, Pop. 18,544
Deer Park CCSD 82 100/PK-8
2350 E 1025th Rd 61350 815-434-6930
Randall Vincent, supt. Fax 434-6942
www.deerpark.k12.il.us
Deer Park ES 100/PK-8
2350 E 1025th Rd 61350 815-434-6930
Randall Vincent, prin. Fax 434-6942

Ottawa ESD 141 2,100/PK-8
320 W Main St 61350 815-433-1133
Clovo Threadgill, supt. Fax 433-1888
www.oes141.org
Central IS 400/5-6
711 E McKinley Rd 61350 815-433-3761
Ryan Myers, prin. Fax 433-9572
Jefferson ES 300/K-4
1709 Columbus St 61350 815-434-0726
Nathaniel Pinter, prin. Fax 434-7451
Lincoln ES 500/PK-4
1110 W Madison St 61350 815-434-1250
Ryan Lemberg, prin. Fax 434-2931
McKinley ES 400/PK-4
1320 State St 61350 815-433-1907
Moriah Mott, prin. Fax 433-9124
Shepherd MS 500/7-8
701 E McKinley Rd 61350 815-434-7925
Gary Windy, prin. Fax 433-9447

Rutland CCSD 230 100/K-8
3231 N State Route 71 61350 815-433-2949
Michael Matteson, supt. Fax 433-2322
www.rutlandgradeschool.org
Rutland ES 100/K-8
3231 N State Route 71 61350 815-433-2949
Julie DeFore, prin. Fax 433-2322

Wallace CCSD 195 300/PK-8
1463 N 33rd Rd 61350 815-433-2986
Michael Matteson, supt. Fax 433-2989
wallacegs.org
Wallace ES 300/PK-8
1463 N 33rd Rd 61350 815-433-2986
Toby Coates, prin. Fax 433-2989

Marquette Academy 400/PK-12
1000 Paul St 61350 815-433-0125
Brooke Rick, prin. Fax 433-2632

Palatine, Cook, Pop. 67,495
Palatine CCSD 15 12,500/PK-8
580 N 1st Bank Dr 60067 847-963-3000
Dr. Scott Thompson Ed.D., supt. Fax 963-3200
www.ccsd15.net
Addams ES 700/K-6
1020 E Sayles Dr 60074 847-963-5000
Amy Molinsky, prin. Fax 963-5006
Hunting Ridge ES 600/K-6
1105 W Illinois Ave 60067 847-963-5300
Christine Ortlund, prin. Fax 963-5306
Jordan ES 500/K-6
100 N Harrison Ave 60067 847-963-5500
Jennifer Grosch, prin. Fax 963-5506
Lake Louise ES 800/PK-6
500 N Jonathan Dr 60074 847-963-5600
Jennifer Seoane, prin. Fax 963-5606
Lincoln ES 800/K-6
1021 N Ridgewood Ln 60067 847-963-5700
Mary Beth Knoeppel, prin. Fax 963-5706
Paddock ES 700/PK-6
225 W Washington St 60067 847-963-5800
Rachel Bland, prin. Fax 963-5806
Pleasant Hill ES 500/K-6
434 W Illinois Ave 60067 847-963-5900
David Morris, prin. Fax 963-5906
Sanborn ES 600/PK-6
101 N Oak St 60067 847-963-7000
Erika Johansen, prin. Fax 963-7006
Sundling JHS 700/7-8
1100 N Smith St 60067 847-963-3700
Jason Dietz, prin. Fax 963-3706
Virginia Lake ES 800/K-6
925 N Glenn Dr 60074 847-963-7100
Kristine Seifert, prin. Fax 963-7106
Winston Campus ES 500/PK-6
900 E Palatine Rd 60074 847-963-7500
Andy Tieman, prin. Fax 963-7406
Winston Campus JHS 800/7-8
120 N Babcock Dr 60074 847-963-7400
Dr. Jason Klein Ph.D., prin. Fax 963-7508
Other Schools – See Hoffman Estates, Rolling Meadows

Immanuel Lutheran S 400/PK-8
200 N Plum Grove Rd 60067 847-359-1936
Delaine Schiestel, prin. Fax 359-1583
Quest Academy 300/PK-8
500 N Benton St 60067 847-202-8035
Dr. Khalek Kirkland, head sch Fax 202-8085
St. Theresa S 400/PK-8
445 N Benton St 60067 847-359-1820
Mary Keenley, prin. Fax 705-2084
St. Thomas of Villanova S 200/PK-8
1141 E Anderson Dr 60074 847-358-2110
Mary Brinkman, prin. Fax 776-1435

Palestine, Crawford, Pop. 1,359
Palestine CUSD 3 300/PK-12
100 S Main St 62451 618-586-2713
Chris Long, supt. Fax 586-2905
www.palestine-pioneers.net
Palestine Grade S 200/PK-8
205 S Washington St 62451 618-586-2711
Robbie Kline, prin. Fax 586-5126

Palmyra, Macoupin, Pop. 692
Northwestern CUSD 2 300/PK-12
30953 Route 111 62674 217-436-2210
Patrick Bowman, supt. Fax 436-2701
www.northwestern.k12.il.us
Northwestern ES 200/PK-6
30953 Route 111 62674 217-436-2442
Partick Bowman, prin. Fax 436-2701
Northwestern JHS 100/7-8
30889 Route 111 62674 217-436-2011
Jeff Abell, prin. Fax 436-9112

Palos Heights, Cook, Pop. 12,393
Palos CCSD 118
Supt. — See Palos Park
Palos East ES 800/K-5
7700 W 127th St 60463 708-448-1084
Robert Szklanecki, prin. Fax 923-7077

Palos Heights SD 128 800/PK-8
12809 S McVickers Ave 60463 708-597-9040
Dr. Dawn Green, supt. Fax 597-9089
www.palos128.org
Chippewa ES 200/1-3
12425 S Austin Ave 60463 708-388-7260
Mary Lynn Duffy, prin. Fax 388-2761
Independence JHS 200/6-8
6610 W Highland Dr 60463 708-448-0737
Kevin Kirk, prin. Fax 448-0179
Indian Hill S 100/PK-K
12800 S Austin Ave 60463 708-597-1285
Mary Lynn Duffy, prin. Fax 597-4230
Navajo Heights ES 100/4-5
12401 S Oak Park Ave 60463 708-385-3269
Lynn Adamonis, prin. Fax 385-0429

Landmark Christian Academy 50/K-8
6330 W 127th St 60463 708-623-0332
Ken Darnell, prin. Fax 623-0332
St. Alexander S 300/PK-8
7025 W 126th St 60463 708-448-0408
Cathy Biel, prin. Fax 448-5947

Palos Hills, Cook, Pop. 17,273
North Palos SD 117 3,200/PK-8
7825 W 103rd St 60465 708-598-5500
Dr. Jeannie Stachowiak, supt. Fax 598-5539
www.npd117.net/
Oak Ridge ES 600/2-5
8791 W 103rd St 60465 708-233-5300
Elizabeth Reich, prin. Fax 430-8648
Sorrick S 500/PK-1
7825 W 103rd St 60465 708-599-7760
Sara Olson, prin. Fax 599-7762
Other Schools – See Hickory Hills

Koraes ES 200/PK-8
11025 S Roberts Rd 60465 708-974-3402
Beth Lind, prin. Fax 974-0179

Palos Park, Cook, Pop. 4,788
Palos CCSD 118 1,900/PK-8
8800 W 119th St 60464 708-448-4800
Dr. Anthony Scarsella, supt. Fax 448-4880
www.palos118.org
Palos South MS 600/6-8
13100 S 82nd Ave 60464 708-448-5971
Stuart Wrzesinski, prin. Fax 448-0754
Palos West ES 500/PK-5
12700 S 104th Ave 60464 708-448-6888
Jennifer Peloquin-Biel, prin. Fax 923-7064
Other Schools – See Palos Heights

Pana, Christian, Pop. 5,807
Pana CUSD 8 1,100/PK-12
PO Box 377 62557 217-562-1500
Jason Bauer, supt. Fax 562-1501
www.panaschools.com
Lincoln ES 200/3-5
PO Box 377 62557 217-562-8500
Debra Zueck, prin. Fax 562-9259
Pana JHS 200/6-8
PO Box 377 62557 217-562-6500
Julietta Ellis, prin. Fax 562-6712
Washington ES 300/PK-2
PO Box 377 62557 217-562-7500
Cheri Wysong, prin. Fax 562-9262

Sacred Heart S 100/PK-8
3 E 4th St 62557 217-562-2425
Terry Trader, prin. Fax 562-2942

Paris, Edgar, Pop. 8,761
Paris CUSD 4 500/PK-8
15601 US Highway 150 61944 217-465-5391
Danette Young, supt. Fax 466-1225
www.crestwood.k12.il.us
Crestwood ES 300/PK-5
15601 US Highway 150 61944 217-465-5391
Dan Lynch, prin. Fax 466-1225
Crestwood JHS 200/6-8
15601 US Highway 150 61944 217-465-5391
Dan Lynch, prin. Fax 466-1225

Paris-Union SD 95 1,600/PK-12
300 S Eads Ave 61944 217-465-8448
Jeremy Larson, supt. Fax 463-2243
www.paris95.k12.il.us
Creative Center for Children 100/PK-PK
300 S Eads Ave 61944 217-463-4808
Amy Perry, prin.
Mayo MS 300/6-8
310 E Wood St 61944 217-466-3050
Jeremy Larson, prin. Fax 466-3905
Memorial ES 300/PK-2
509 E Newton St 61944 217-466-6170
Gary Doughan, prin. Fax 466-5586
Wenz ES 300/3-5
437 W Washington St 61944 217-466-3140
Amy Perry, prin. Fax 466-6718

St. Mary Catholic S 100/PK-5
507 Connelly St 61944 217-463-3005
Chery Zuiker, prin. Fax 465-4703

Park Forest, Cook, Pop. 21,337
Crete-Monee CUSD 201U
Supt. — See Crete
Talala ES 300/K-5
430 Talala St 60466 708-367-2560
Michelle Johnson, prin. Fax 672-2620

Matteson ESD 162
Supt. — See Richton Park
Illinois S 500/PK-8
210 Illinois St 60466 708-747-0301
Dr. Carl Cogar, prin. Fax 503-2241
Indiana ES 400/4-6
165 Indiana St 60466 708-747-5300
Dr. Camilla Covington, prin. Fax 503-1012

Park Forest SD 163 1,400/PK-8
242 S Orchard Dr 60466 708-668-9400
Dr. Joyce Carmine, supt. Fax 748-9359
www.sd163.com
Algonquin Primary Center 100/PK-PK
170 Algonquin St 60466 708-668-9202
Regina Nottke, prin. Fax 503-2267
Blackhawk Primary Center 200/K-3
130 Blackhawk Dr 60466 708-668-9500
Bessie Boyd, prin. Fax 481-0917
Mohawk Primary Center 50/K-3
301 Mohawk St 60466 708-668-9300
Karon Nolen, prin. Fax 503-2281
Obama S of Technology and the Arts 500/4-8
215 Wilson St 60466 708-668-9600
Cheryl Muench, prin. Fax 503-2297
21st Century Primary Center 300/K-3
240 S Orchard Dr 60466 708-668-9490
Chrishawn Chinn, prin. Fax 747-0261
Other Schools – See Chicago Heights

South Suburban SDA Christian S 50/PK-8
119 Chestnut St 60466 708-481-8909
Kathryn Kyle, prin. Fax 481-0918

Park Ridge, Cook, Pop. 37,078
Park Ridge-Niles CCSD 64 4,400/PK-8
164 S Prospect Ave 60068 847-318-4300
Dr. Laurie Heinz, supt. Fax 318-4351
www.d64.org
Carpenter ES 400/K-5
300 N Hamlin Ave 60068 847-318-4370
Brett Balduf, prin. Fax 318-4201
Field ES 700/K-5
707 Wisner St 60068 847-318-4385
Jason Bednar, prin. Fax 318-4202
Franklin ES 500/K-5
2401 Manor Ln 60068 847-318-4390
Dr. Claire Kowalczyk, prin. Fax 318-4203
Lincoln MS 700/6-8
200 S Lincoln Ave 60068 847-318-4215
Dr. Anthony Murray, prin. Fax 318-4210
Roosevelt ES 600/K-5
1001 S Fairview Ave 60068 847-318-4235
Dr. Kevin Dwyer, prin. Fax 318-4205
Washington ES 600/K-5
1500 Stewart Ave 60068 847-318-4360
Stephanie Daly, prin. Fax 318-4247
Other Schools – See Niles

Mary Seat of Wisdom S 500/PK-8
1352 S Cumberland Ave 60068 847-825-2500
Julie Due, prin. Fax 825-1943
Montessori Academy of Illinois 50/PK-1
418 W Touhy Ave 60068 847-292-1229
Charlene Alderete, pres. Fax 292-1970
St. Andrews Lutheran S 200/PK-8
260 N Northwest Hwy 60068 847-823-9308
Laura Boggs, admin. Fax 823-1146
St. Paul of the Cross S 700/PK-8
140 S Northwest Hwy 60068 847-825-6366
Nell Agnew, prin. Fax 825-2466

Patoka, Marion, Pop. 584
Patoka CUSD 100 300/PK-12
1220 Kinoka Rd 62875 618-432-5440
David Rademacher, supt. Fax 432-5306
pcusd100.sharpschool.net
Patoka ES 100/PK-6
1220 Kinoka Rd 62875 618-432-5200
Bryan Rainey, prin. Fax 432-5306
Patoka JHS 50/7-8
1220 Kinoka Rd 62875 618-432-5200
Bryan Rainey, prin. Fax 432-5306

Pawnee, Sangamon, Pop. 2,672
Pawnee CUSD 11 600/PK-12
810 4th St 62558 217-625-2471
Gary Alexander, supt. Fax 625-2251
www.pawneeschools.com/
Pawnee S 300/PK-6
810 4th St 62558 217-625-2231
Jenny Mendenhall, prin Fax 625-2251

Paw Paw, Lee, Pop. 862
Paw Paw CUSD 271 200/K-12
PO Box 508 61353 815-627-2841
Stan Adcock, supt. Fax 627-2971
www.2paws.net
Paw Paw ES 100/K-5
PO Box 237 61353 815-627-2841
Stan Adcock, prin. Fax 627-2971

Paxton, Ford, Pop. 4,437
Paxton-Buckley-Loda CUSD 10 1,400/PK-12
PO Box 50 60957 217-379-3314
Clifford McClure, supt. Fax 379-2862
pblunit10.com
Eastlawn ES 300/3-5
PO Box 50 60957 217-379-2000
Barry Wright, prin. Fax 379-2055
Paxton-Buckley-Loda JHS 300/6-8
PO Box 50 60957 217-379-9202
Josh Didier, prin. Fax 379-9169
Peterson ES 300/PK-2
PO Box 50 60957 217-379-2531
Amanda Wetherell, prin. Fax 379-9781

Payson, Adams, Pop. 1,023
Payson CUSD 1 500/PK-12
406 W State St 62360 217-656-3323
Donna Veile, supt. Fax 656-4042
www.cusd1.org
Seymour ES 300/PK-6
404 W State St 62360 217-656-3439
Julie Phelan, prin. Fax 656-4034

Pearl City, Stephenson, Pop. 832
Pearl City CUSD 200 500/PK-12
PO Box 9 61062 815-443-2715
Timothy Thill, supt. Fax 443-2237
www.pcwolves.net/
Pearl City ES 300/PK-6
PO Box 9 61062 815-443-2715
Chris Wallace, prin. Fax 443-2237
Pearl City JHS 100/7-8
PO Box 9 61062 815-443-2715
Dr. Kelly Mandrell, prin. Fax 443-2237

Pecatonica, Winnebago, Pop. 2,172
Pecatonica CUSD 321 900/PK-12
PO Box 419 61063 815-239-1639
William Faller, supt. Fax 239-2125
www.pecschools.com/

Pecatonica Community MS 300/5-8
PO Box 419 61063 815-239-2612
Timothy King, prin. Fax 239-1274
Pecatonica ES 300/PK-4
PO Box 419 61063 815-239-2550
Carrie Brockway, prin. Fax 239-1418

Pekin, Tazewell, Pop. 33,678
Pekin SD 108 3,700/PK-8
501 Washington St 61554 309-477-4700
Dr. Bill Link, supt. Fax 477-4701
www.pekin.net
Altman PS 200/K-3
1730 Highwood Ave 61554 309-477-4715
Lynn Brown, prin. Fax 477-4764
Broadmoor JHS 400/7-8
501 Maywood Ave 61554 309-477-4731
Ty Goss, prin. Fax 477-4739
Dirksen PS 200/K-3
501 Maywood Ave 61554 309-477-4711
Melissa Lard, prin. Fax 477-4760
Edison JHS 400/7-8
1400 Earl St 61554 309-477-4732
Bill Heisel, prin. Fax 477-4738
Jefferson PS 400/K-3
900 S Capitol St 61554 309-477-4712
Jonathan Cox, prin. Fax 477-4761
Pekin Preschool Family Education Center 300/PK-PK
1000 Koch St 61554 309-477-4730
Linda Seth, prin. Fax 477-4737
Smith PS 300/K-3
1314 Matilda St 61554 309-477-4713
Arthur Schroff, prin. Fax 477-4762
Starke PS 300/K-3
1610 Holiday Dr 61554 309-477-4714
Matthew Green, prin. Fax 477-4763
Washington IS 500/4-6
501 Washington St 61554 309-477-4721
Marc Fogal, prin. Fax 477-4729
Willow PS 300/K-3
1110 Veerman St 61554 309-477-4716
Victoria Armbrust, prin. Fax 477-4765
Wilson IS 600/4-6
900 Koch St 61554 309-477-4722
Joshua Norman, prin. Fax 477-4728

Rankin SD 98 200/K-8
13716 5th St 61554 309-346-3182
Dr. Matt Gordon, supt. Fax 346-7928
www.rankin98.org
Rankin ES 200/K-8
13716 5th St 61554 309-346-3182
April McLaughlin, prin. Fax 346-7928

Faith Baptist Christian S 100/PK-12
1501 Howard Ct 61554 309-347-6178
Rev. Shawn Haynie, prin. Fax 347-8716
Good Shepherd Lutheran S 200/PK-8
3201 Court St 61554 309-347-2020
Reva Simpson, prin. Fax 347-9099
St. Joseph S 300/PK-8
300 S 6th St 61554 309-347-7194
Shannon Rogers, prin. Fax 347-7198

Peoria, Peoria, Pop. 111,234
Dunlap CUSD 323 4,200/PK-12
3020 W Willow Knolls Dr 61614 309-691-3955
Dr. Lisa Parker, supt. Fax 691-6764
www.dunlapcusd.net
Ridgeview ES 500/K-5
3903 W Ridgeview Dr 61615 309-692-8260
Todd Jefferson, prin. Fax 692-8357
Wilder-Waite ES 300/K-5
10021 N Pacific St 61615 309-243-7728
Stacy Berg, prin. Fax 243-5272
Other Schools – See Dunlap

Hollis Consolidated SD 328 200/K-8
5613 W Tuscarora Rd 61607 309-697-1325
Lee Ann Meinhold, supt. Fax 697-1334
www.hollis328.net
Hollis Consolidated S 200/K-8
5613 W Tuscarora Rd 61607 309-697-1325
Chad Jones, admin. Fax 697-1334

Limestone Walters CCSD 316 200/K-8
8223 W Smithville Rd 61607 309-697-3035
Timothy Dotson, supt. Fax 697-9466
www.limestonewalters.com
Limestone Walters ES 200/K-8
8223 W Smithville Rd 61607 309-697-3035
Chad Bentley, prin. Fax 697-9466

Norwood ESD 63 400/PK-8
6521 W Farmington Rd 61604 309-676-3523
David Black, supt. Fax 676-6099
www.norwood63.org
Norwood MS 200/5-8
6521 W Farmington Rd 61604 309-676-3683
Joel Kilgus, prin. Fax 676-6099
Norwood PS 200/PK-4
200 S Main St 61604 309-697-6312
Sandra Linhart, prin. Fax 697-6315

Peoria SD 150 13,500/PK-12
3202 N Wisconsin Ave 61603 309-672-6768
Sharon Desmoulin-Kherat, supt. Fax 672-6708
www.psd150.org
Bills MS 200/5-8
6001 N Frostwood Pkwy 61615 309-693-4437
Laura Rodgers, prin. Fax 693-4438
Charter Oak PS 500/K-4
5221 W Timberedge Dr 61615 309-693-4433
Kathy Rodriguez, prin. Fax 693-8701
Franklin PS 500/PK-5
807 W Columbia Ter 61606 309-682-2693
Ann Bond, prin. Fax 682-7283
Glen Oak PS 700/K-6
2100 N Wisconsin Ave 61603 309-672-6518
Magnolia Branscumb, prin. Fax 686-2459
Harrison Community Learning Center 700/K-8
2727 W Krause Ave 61605 309-672-6522
Fabian Daniels, prin. Fax 672-6523
Hines PS 500/K-4
4603 N Knoxville Ave 61614 309-672-6525
Matthew Durr, prin. Fax 672-6526
Hinton ECC 300/PK-1
800 W Romeo B Garrett Ave 61605 309-672-6810
Katie Powers, prin. Fax 676-9831
Jefferson PS 500/PK-6
918 W Florence Ave 61604 309-672-6531
Kary Boerger, prin. Fax 672-6535
Keller PS 400/K-4
6413 N Mount Hawley Rd 61614 309-693-4439
Kendall Turner, prin. Fax 282-0974
Lincoln K-8 S 800/K-8
700 Mary St 61603 309-672-6542
Thomas Blumer, prin. Fax 676-6615
Lindbergh MS 400/5-8
6327 N Sheridan Rd 61614 309-693-4427
Susan Malahy, prin. Fax 693-0499
Northmoor PS 400/PK-4
1819 W Northmoor Rd 61614 309-692-9481
Angela Stockman, prin. Fax 692-9738
Rolling Acres MS 300/5-8
5617 N Merrimac Ave 61614 309-689-1100
Michael Barber, prin. Fax 693-4423
Roosevelt Magnet S 600/PK-8
1704 W Aiken Ave 61605 309-672-6574
Cynthia Clark, prin. Fax 676-7723
Sterling MS 300/5-8
2315 N Sterling Ave 61604 309-672-6557
Dr. Cindy Janovetz, prin. Fax 681-8286
Trewyn S 500/K-8
1419 S Folkers Ave 61605 309-672-6500
Renee Andrews, prin. Fax 673-8537
Von Steuben MS 400/5-8
801 E Forrest Hill Ave 61603 309-672-6561
Thomas Ryan, prin. Fax 685-7631
Washington Gifted MS 300/5-8
3706 N Grand Blvd 61614 309-672-6563
David Poehls, prin. Fax 672-6564
Whittier PS 300/PK-4
1619 W Fredonia Ave 61606 309-672-6569
Julie Deignan, prin. Fax 673-3349
Wilson PS 400/PK-4
1907 W Forrest Hill Ave 61604 309-672-6571
Kelly Schuler, prin. Fax 688-0320
Other Schools – See West Peoria

Pleasant Hill SD 69 200/PK-8
3717 W Malone St 61605 309-637-6829
Dennis MacNamara, supt. Fax 637-8612
www.phill69.com
Pleasant Hill ES 200/PK-8
3717 W Malone St 61605 309-637-6829
Lisa Weaver, prin. Fax 637-8612

Pleasant Valley SD 62 500/PK-8
3314 W Richwoods Blvd 61604 309-679-0634
Dr. Allen Johnson, supt. Fax 674-0165
www.pv62.com
Pleasant Valley ES 300/K-4
4623 W Red Bud Dr 61604 309-673-6750
Tracy Colwell-Forck, prin. Fax 674-0165
Pleasant Valley MS 300/PK-K, 4-8
3314 W Richwoods Blvd 61604 309-679-0634
Kelly Galyean, admin. Fax 679-0652

Aletheia Christian S 50/PK-8
7229 N Knoxville Ave 61614 309-635-9809
Christ Lutheran S 200/PK-8
1311 S Faraday Ave 61605 309-637-1512
Terry Mooney, prin. Fax 637-7829
Concordia Lutheran S 200/K-8
2000 W Glen Ave 61614 309-691-8921
Paul Thompson, prin. Fax 691-2913
Daarul Uloom Islamic S 200/PK-10
4125 W Charter Oak Rd 61615 309-691-9089
Mona Rustom, prin.
Holy Family S 200/K-8
2329 W Reservoir Blvd 61615 309-688-2931
Jill Templin, prin. Fax 681-5687
Montessori S of Peoria 100/PK-6
3601 N North St 61604 309-685-8995
John Meredith Cox, head sch Fax 685-5413
Peoria Academy 300/PK-8
2711 W Willow Knolls Dr 61614 309-692-7570
Peoria Christian S 900/PK-12
3506 N California Ave 61603 309-686-4500
Becky Gardner, admin. Fax 686-2569
St. Jude S 100/PK-6
10811 N Knoxville Ave 61615 309-243-2493
Sr. Maria Christi Nelson, prin. Fax 839-8142
St. Mark S 200/PK-8
711 N Underhill St 61606 309-676-7131
Dr. Noreen Dillon, prin. Fax 677-8060
St. Philomena S 400/PK-8
3216 N Emery Ave 61604 309-685-1208
Jodi Peine, prin. Fax 681-5676
St. Vincent De Paul S 500/PK-8
6001 N University St 61614 309-691-5012
Patsy Santen, prin. Fax 683-1036

Peoria Heights, Peoria, Pop. 5,986
Peoria Heights CUSD 325 800/PK-12
500 E Glen Ave 61616 309-686-8800
Dr. Eric Heath, supt. Fax 686-8801
www.phcusd325.net
Peoria Heights Grade S 500/PK-8
500 E Glen Ave 61616 309-686-8809
Dave Carroll, prin. Fax 686-7272

St. Thomas the Apostle S 400/PK-8
4229 N Monroe Ave 61616 309-685-2533
Maureen Bentley, prin. Fax 681-7262

Peotone, Will, Pop. 4,103
Peotone CUSD 207U 1,400/PK-12
212 W Wilson St 60468 708-258-0991
Steve Stein, supt. Fax 258-0994
www.peotoneschools.org
Connor Shaw Center 100/PK-PK
212 W Wilson St 60468 708-258-0991
Amy Loy, dir. Fax 258-0994
Peotone ES 300/K-3
426 N Conrad St 60468 708-258-6955
Kathy Davis, prin. Fax 258-0455
Peotone JHS 400/6-8
1 Blue Devil Dr 60468 708-258-3246
Scott Wenzel, prin. Fax 258-6669
Other Schools – See Frankfort

Perry, Pike, Pop. 397
Griggsville-Perry CUSD 4
Supt. — See Griggsville
Griggsville-Perry MS 100/5-8
PO Box 98 62362 217-236-9161
Jeff Bourne, prin. Fax 236-7221

Peru, LaSalle, Pop. 10,189
Peru ESD 124 700/PK-8
1800 Church St 61354 815-223-0486
Mark Cross, supt. Fax 223-0490
www.perued.net
Northview ES 300/PK-4
1429 Shooting Park Rd 61354 815-223-2567
Sara McDonald, prin. Fax 223-0618
Parkside MS 400/5-8
1800 Church St 61354 815-223-7723
Lori Madden, prin. Fax 223-0285

Peru Catholic S 200/PK-8
2003 5th St 61354 815-224-1914
Dr. Amy Perona, prin. Fax 223-1354

Petersburg, Menard, Pop. 2,232
PORTA CUSD 202 1,100/PK-12
PO Box 202 62675 217-632-3803
Matthew Brue, supt. Fax 632-3221
www.porta202.org
Petersburg ES 400/PK-2
514 W Monroe St 62675 217-632-7731
Jeffrey Hill, prin. Fax 632-3551
PORTA Central ES 300/3-6
1500 Owen Ave 62675 217-632-7781
Eric Kesler, prin. Fax 632-5103
PORTA JHS 200/7-8
PO Box 202 62675 217-632-3219
Megan Howard, prin. Fax 632-5448

Philo, Champaign, Pop. 1,451
Tolono CUSD 7
Supt. — See Tolono
Unity East ES 300/PK-5
1638 County Road 1000 N 61864 217-684-5218
Jim Carver, prin. Fax 684-5220

St. Thomas S 100/PK-8
311 E Madison St 61864 217-684-2309
Lisa Doughan, prin. Fax 684-2217

Phoenix, Cook, Pop. 1,934
South Holland SD 151
Supt. — See South Holland
Coolidge MS 500/6-8
15500 7th Ave 60426 708-339-5300
Patricia Payne, prin. Fax 339-5327

Piasa, Macoupin
Southwestern CUSD 9
Supt. — See Brighton
Southwestern MS 300/7-8
PO Box 70 62079 618-372-3813
Scott Hopkins, prin. Fax 729-9231

Pinckneyville, Perry, Pop. 5,604
CCSD 204 200/K-8
6067 State Route 154 62274 618-357-2419
Jerry Travelstead, supt. Fax 357-3016
www.ccsd204.org
Community Consolidated ES 200/K-8
6067 State Route 154 62274 618-357-2419
Jerry Travelstead, prin. Fax 357-3016

Pinckneyville SD 50 600/PK-8
301 W Mulberry St 62274 618-357-9096
Tim O'Leary, supt. Fax 357-8731
www.p50.perry.k12.il.us
Pinckneyville ES 300/PK-4
301 W Mulberry St 62274 618-357-5161
Scott Wagner, prin.
Pinckneyville MS 300/5-8
700 E Water St 62274 618-357-2724
Mark Rohlfing, prin.

St. Bruno S 200/PK-8
210 N Gordon St 62274 618-357-8276
Brittany Goldman, prin. Fax 357-6425

Piper City, Ford, Pop. 823
Tri-Point CUSD 6-J
Supt. — See Kempton
Tri-Point MS 200/K-K, 4-8
PO Box 158 60959 815-686-2247
Jay Bennett, prin. Fax 686-2663

Pittsburg, Williamson, Pop. 562
Johnston City CUSD 1
Supt. — See Johnston City
Lincoln ES 50/3-4
20163 Corinth Rd 62974 618-982-2130
Michelle Smiley, prin. Fax 983-2353

Pittsfield, Pike, Pop. 4,559
Pikeland CUSD 10 1,300/PK-12
512 S Madison St 62363 217-285-2147
Paula Hawley, supt. Fax 285-5059
www.pikeland.net

Pikeland Community S 600/3-8
601 Piper Ln 62363 217-285-9462
Lisa Jockisch, prin. Fax 285-9551
Pittsfield South ES 400/PK-2
655 Clarksville Rd 62363 217-285-2431
Angie Ruebush, prin. Fax 285-5479

Plainfield, Will, Pop. 38,856
CUSD 308
Supt. — See Oswego
Grande Park ES 700/K-5
26933 W Grande Park Blvd, 630-551-9700
Sean Smith, prin. Fax 551-9719
Murphy JHS 600/6-8
26923 W Grande Park Blvd, 630-608-5100
Dr. Brent Anderson, prin. Fax 608-5191

Plainfield CCSD 202 28,400/PK-12
15732 S Howard St 60544 815-577-4000
Dr. Ronald Abrell, supt. Fax 436-7824
www.psd202.org
Central ES 900/K-5
23723 Getson Dr 60544 815-436-9278
Linda DiLeo, prin. Fax 436-8415
Creekside ES 700/K-5
13909 S Budler Rd 60544 815-577-4700
Patricia Hudson, prin. Fax 372-0607
Drauden Point MS 900/6-8
1911 Drauden Rd, 815-577-4900
Patrick Flynn, prin. Fax 439-9385
Eagle Pointe ES 800/K-5
24562 Norwood Dr, 815-577-4800
Laura Weed, prin. Fax 609-9403
Eichelberger ES 600/K-5
12450 Essington Rd, 815-577-3606
Trevor Harris, prin. Fax 577-6407
Freedom ES 800/K-5
11600 Heritage Meadows Dr, 815-254-4005
Laurie Boyce, prin. Fax 254-9706
Heritage Grove MS 900/6-8
12425 S Van Dyke Rd, 815-439-4810
Shannon Miller, prin. Fax 436-4661
Indian Trail MS 800/6-8
14723 S Eastern Ave 60544 815-436-6128
John Evans, prin. Fax 436-7536
Jones MS 900/6-8
15320 W Wallin Dr 60544 815-267-3600
Thomas Novinski, prin. Fax 439-7201
Kennedy MS 1,200/6-8
12350 Essington Rd, 815-439-8024
Amandeep Hundal, prin. Fax 254-7375
Lakewood Falls ES 700/K-5
14050 S Budler Rd 60544 815-439-4560
Dr. Tina Olson, prin. Fax 886-0463
Lincoln ES 900/K-5
14740 Meadow Ln 60544 815-577-4500
Casey Hartman, prin. Fax 609-5853
McBeth Learning Center 700/PK-PK
15730 S Howard St 60544 815-439-4288
Kristin Brower, prin. Fax 254-4315
Meadow View ES 700/K-5
2501 Mirage Ave, 815-439-4828
Brian Sorg, prin. Fax 436-3747
Reed ES 700/K-5
2110 Clublands Pkwy, 815-254-2160
Curtis Hudson, prin. Fax 254-9385
Ridge ES 700/K-5
1900 Caton Ridge Dr, 815-577-4630
Dr. Stacey DiBitetto, prin. Fax 609-9387
River View ES 800/K-5
2097 S Bronk Rd, 815-439-4840
Tracey Markowski, prin. Fax 436-4930
Timber Ridge MS 1,100/6-8
2101 S Bronk Rd, 815-439-3410
Dean Kariotakis, prin. Fax 439-3412
Walkers Grove ES 600/K-5
24810 W 135th St 60544 815-439-2885
Jeffrey Schafermeyer, prin. Fax 439-2883
Wesmere ES 600/K-5
2001 Wesmere Pkwy, 815-439-3244
Dr. Deborah Coberley, prin. Fax 439-3413
Other Schools – See Bolingbrook, Joliet

Troy CCSD 30C 4,500/PK-8
5800 Theodore Dr 60586 815-577-6760
Todd Koehl Ph.D., supt. Fax 577-3795
troywebs.troy30c.org
Orenic IS 900/5-6
5820 Theodore Dr, 815-577-6759
Lawrence Piatek, prin. Fax 577-1233
Troy MS 1,000/7-8
5800 Theodore Dr, 815-230-9920
Renee Marski, prin. Fax 577-2867
Other Schools – See Joliet, Shorewood

St. Mary Immaculate S 500/PK-8
15629 S Route 59 60544 815-436-3953
John Garvey, prin. Fax 439-8045

Plano, Kendall, Pop. 10,709
Plano CUSD 88 2,300/PK-12
800 S Hale St 60545 630-552-8978
Dr. Hector Garcia, supt. Fax 552-8548
www.plano88.org/
Centennial ES 400/2-3
800 S West St 60545 630-552-3234
Mike Zeman, prin. Fax 552-0324
Johns ES 500/4-6
430 Mitchell Ct 60545 630-552-9182
Tony Baker, prin. Fax 552-9208
Miller ES 500/PK-1
904 N Lew St 60545 630-552-8504
Laurel Mateyka, prin. Fax 552-3089
Plano MS 300/7-8
804 S Hale St 60545 630-552-3608
Mark Heller, prin. Fax 552-3802

St. Mary S 200/PK-8
817 N Center St 60545 630-552-3345
Joe Scarpino, prin. Fax 552-4385

Pleasant Hill, Pike, Pop. 964
Pleasant Hill CUSD 3 300/PK-12
PO Box 277 62366 217-734-2311
Donald Peebles, supt. Fax 734-2629
www.phwolves.com
Pleasant Hill ES 200/PK-8
PO Box 277 62366 217-734-2311
Ryan Lowe, prin. Fax 734-2629

Pleasant Plains, Sangamon, Pop. 790
Pleasant Plains CUSD 8 1,300/PK-12
PO Box 20 62677 217-626-1041
Matt Runge, supt. Fax 626-1082
www.ppcusd8.org
Farmingdale ES 500/PK-4
2473 N Farmingdale Rd 62677 217-626-1221
Jamie Yates, prin. Fax 626-1839
Pleasant Plains MS 400/5-8
2455 N Farmingdale Rd 62677 217-626-1061
Ben Theilen, prin. Fax 626-2272

Pocahontas, Bond, Pop. 779
Bond County CUSD 2
Supt. — See Greenville
Pocahontas S 200/PK-8
PO Box 189 62275 618-669-2296
Jason Rakers, prin. Fax 669-2627

Polo, Ogle, Pop. 2,326
Polo CUSD 222 600/PK-12
100 S Union Ave 61064 815-946-3815
Christopher Rademacher, supt. Fax 946-2493
polo222.org
Aplington MS 100/6-8
610 E Mason St 61064 815-946-2519
Mark Downey, prin. Fax 946-2537
Centennial ES 300/PK-5
308 S Pleasant Ave 61064 815-946-3811
Melydi Huyett, prin. Fax 946-4233

Pontiac, Livingston, Pop. 11,777
Pontiac CCSD 429 1,300/PK-8
117 W Livingston St 61764 815-842-1533
Brian Dukes, supt. Fax 844-5773
www.pontiac429.org
Central ES 400/PK-1
117 W Livingston St 61764 815-844-3023
Kel Krenz, prin. Fax 844-5773
Lincoln ES 300/2-3
514 S Main St 61764 815-844-3924
Michael Weaver, prin. Fax 844-5773
Pontiac JHS 400/6-8
600 N Morrow St 61764 815-842-4343
Brian Hensley, prin. Fax 844-6230
Washington ES 200/4-5
400 N Morrow St 61764 815-844-3687
Josh DeLong, prin. Fax 844-5773

Pontiac Christian S 100/PK-8
18034 N 2100 East Rd 61764 815-842-1322
Denise Plenert, admin. Fax 844-2033
St. Mary's S 200/K-8
414 N Main St 61764 815-844-6585
Richard Morehouse, prin. Fax 844-6987

Poplar Grove, Boone, Pop. 4,959
North Boone CUSD 200 1,600/PK-12
6248 N Boone School Rd 61065 815-765-3322
Dr. Michael Greenlee, supt. Fax 765-2053
www.nbcusd.org
Manchester ES 100/K-4
3501 Blaine Rd 61065 815-765-2826
Molly Lilja, prin. Fax 765-3334
North Boone MS 300/7-8
17641 Poplar Grove Rd 61065 815-765-9274
Jamison Pearce, prin. Fax 765-9275
North Boone Upper ES 200/5-6
6200 N Boone School Rd 61065 815-765-9006
Jamison Pearce, prin. Fax 765-2496
Poplar Grove ES 300/K-4
208 N State St 61065 815-765-3113
Heather Walsh, prin. Fax 765-1604
Other Schools – See Capron

Port Byron, Rock Island, Pop. 1,628
Riverdale CUSD 100 1,100/PK-12
9624 256th St N 61275 309-523-3184
Ronald Jacobs, supt. Fax 523-3550
riverdaleschools.org
Riverdale ES 600/PK-5
9424 256th St N 61275 309-523-3186
Josh Temple, prin. Fax 523-2870
Riverdale MS 300/6-8
9822 256th St N 61275 309-523-3131
James Jennings, prin. Fax 523-3934

Posen, Cook, Pop. 5,912
Posen-Robbins ESD 143-5 1,700/PK-8
14011 S Harrison Ave 60469 708-388-7200
Dr. Anthony Edison Ed.D., supt. Fax 388-3868
www.prsd1435.org
Gordon ES 500/K-3
14100 S Harrison Ave 60469 708-388-7202
Andrea McKinney M.A., prin. Fax 388-6891
Posen ES 400/4-5
14545 S California Ave 60469 708-388-7204
Emanuel Williams M.A., prin. Fax 388-0075
Other Schools – See Robbins

Potomac, Vermilion, Pop. 742
Potomac CUSD 10 100/PK-8
7915 US Route 136 61865 217-987-6155
Larry Maynard, supt. Fax 987-6663
www.potomac.k12.il.us
Potomac ES 100/PK-8
7915 US Route 136 61865 217-987-6155
Larry Maynard, prin. Fax 987-6663

Prairie du Rocher, Randolph, Pop. 600
Prairie Du Rocher CCSD 134 200/PK-8
714 Middle St 62277 618-284-3530
Dr. Larry Beattie, supt. Fax 284-3444

Prairie Du Rocher S 200/PK-8
714 Middle St 62277 618-284-3530
Dr. Larry Beattie, prin. Fax 284-3444

Princeton, Bureau, Pop. 7,583
Princeton ESD 115 700/PK-8
506 E Dover Rd 61356 815-875-3162
Tim Smith, supt. Fax 875-3101
www.princeton115schools.org
Douglas ES 100/PK-K
220 E Lasalle St 61356 815-872-9741
Bob Bima, prin. Fax 872-0756
Jefferson ES 100/1-2
725 W Putnam St 61356 815-875-4417
J.D. Orwig, prin. Fax 872-0620
Lincoln ES 100/3-4
501 S Euclid Ave 61356 815-875-1164
Bob Bima, prin. Fax 872-0801
Logan JHS 400/5-8
302 W Central Ave 61356 815-875-6415
Amanda Carr, prin. Fax 872-0034

Princeville, Peoria, Pop. 1,723
Princeville CUSD 326 800/PK-12
909 N Town Ave 61559 309-385-2213
Shannon Duling, supt. Fax 385-1823
www.princeville326.org/
Princeville Grade S 600/PK-8
602 N Town Ave 61559 309-385-4994
Shaun Grant, prin. Fax 385-2518

Prophetstown, Whiteside, Pop. 2,069
Prophetstown-Lyndon-Tampico CUSD 3 900/PK-12
79 Grove St 61277 815-537-5101
Chad Colmone, supt. Fax 537-5102
plt3.org
PLT MS 200/6-8
38 Ferry St 61277 815-537-5084
Steven Kastorff, prin. Fax 537-5085
Prophetstown ES 200/PK-3
301 W 3rd St 61277 815-537-2345
Justin Hovey, prin. Fax 537-2417
Other Schools – See Tampico

Prospect Heights, Cook, Pop. 16,131
Prospect Heights SD 23 1,500/PK-8
700 N Schoenbeck Rd 60070 847-870-3850
Don Angelaccio Ed.D., supt. Fax 870-3896
www.d23.org
Eisenhower ES 400/PK-1
700 N Schoenbeck Rd 60070 847-870-3875
Dr. Luke Lambatos, prin. Fax 870-3877
MacArthur MS 500/6-8
700 N Schoenbeck Rd 60070 847-870-3879
Steven Lee, prin. Fax 870-3881
Ross ES 300/2-3
700 N Schoenbeck Rd 60070 847-870-3868
Craig Curtis, prin. Fax 870-3898
Sullivan ES 300/4-5
700 N Schoenbeck Rd 60070 847-870-3865
Traci Meziere, prin. Fax 870-8113

St. Alphonsus Ligouri S 200/PK-8
411 N Wheeling Rd 60070 847-255-5538
Linda Chorazy, prin. Fax 255-0353

Quincy, Adams, Pop. 39,738
Quincy SD 172 5,900/PK-12
1416 Maine St 62301 217-223-8700
Roy Webb, supt. Fax 228-7162
www.qps.org
Adams ES 400/K-3
2001 Jefferson St 62301 217-222-2530
Chrissy Cox, prin. Fax 221-3461
Baldwin IS 1,000/4-5
3000 Maine St 62301 217-223-0003
Melanie Schrand, prin. Fax 228-7148
Berrian ES 200/K-3
1327 S 8th St 62301 217-228-7691
Chrissy Cox, prin. Fax 228-7115
Dewey ES 200/K-3
2040 Cherry St 62301 217-228-7117
Brad Funkenbush, prin. Fax 221-3462
Early Childhood and Family Center 500/PK-PK
401 S 8th St 62301 217-228-7121
Julie Schuckman, prin. Fax 221-3476
Ellington ES 300/K-3
3001 Lindell Ave 62301 217-222-5697
Anne Cashman, prin. Fax 221-3463
Lincoln-Douglas ES 300/K-3
3211 Payson Rd 62305 217-223-8871
Brian Trowbridge, prin. Fax 228-7188
Madison ES 400/K-3
2435 Maine St 62301 217-223-6096
James Sohn, prin. Fax 228-7388
Quincy JHS 900/6-8
100 S 14th St 62301 217-222-3073
Dan Sparrow, prin. Fax 228-7185
Washington ES 300/K-3
1400 N 8th St 62301 217-222-4059
Sara Cramer, prin. Fax 222-8077

Blessed Sacrament Catholic S 200/PK-8
1115 S 7th St 62301 217-228-1477
Christie Dickens, prin. Fax 222-6463
Quincy Christian S 100/PK-12
PO Box 3643 62305 217-223-5698
Susan Hill, admin. Fax 223-5724
St. Dominic S 200/PK-8
4100 Columbus Rd 62305 217-224-0041
Sue Kelley, prin. Fax 224-0042
St. Francis Solanus S 200/K-8
1720 College Ave 62301 217-222-4077
Lori Shepard, prin. Fax 222-5049
St. James Lutheran S 100/PK-8
900 S 17th St 62301 217-222-8267
Nathan Landskroener, prin. Fax 222-3415
St. Peter S 400/PK-8
2500 Maine St 62301 217-223-1120
Cindy Venvertloh, prin. Fax 223-1173

Ramsey, Fayette, Pop. 1,024
Ramsey CUSD 204 500/PK-12
702 W 6th St 62080 618-423-2335
Melissa Ritter, supt. Fax 423-2314
www.ramsey.fayette.k12.il.us
Ramsey ES 300/PK-5
516 W 6th St 62080 618-423-2010
Travis Portz, prin. Fax 423-9024

Ransom, LaSalle, Pop. 384
Allen-Otter Creek CCSD 65 100/K-8
400 S Lane St 60470 815-586-4611
Mary Baima Ed.D., supt. Fax 586-4306
ransomgradeschool.net
Ransom S 100/K-8
400 S Lane St 60470 815-586-4611
Mary Baima Ed.D., prin. Fax 586-4306

Rantoul, Champaign, Pop. 12,421
Rantoul CSD 137 1,600/PK-8
400 E Wabash Ave 61866 217-893-4171
Michelle Ramage, supt. Fax 892-4313
www.rcs137.org
Broadmeadow ES 200/PK-5
500 Sunview Rd 61866 217-892-2194
Michelle Wagner, prin.
Eastlawn ES 300/PK-5
650 N Maplewood Dr 61866 217-892-2131
Dr. Rudy Puente, prin.
Eater JHS, 400 E Wabash Ave 61866 500/6-8
Ryan Green, prin. 217-892-2115
Northview ES 300/PK-5
400 N Sheldon St 61866 217-892-2119
Courtney McClure, prin.
Pleasant Acres ES 300/PK-5
1625 Short St 61866 217-893-4141
Becky Krall, prin.

St. Malachy S 200/PK-8
340 E Belle Ave 61866 217-892-2011
Anastacia Gianessi, prin. Fax 892-5780

Raymond, Montgomery, Pop. 996
Panhandle CUSD 2 400/PK-12
509 N Prairie St 62560 217-229-4215
Aaron Hopper, supt. Fax 229-4216
www.panhandleschools.com
Lincolnwood JHS 100/6-8
507 N Prairie St 62560 217-229-4237
Kendal Elvidge, prin. Fax 229-3005
Raymond ES 100/2-5
505 N Prairie St 62560 217-229-4215
Aaron Hopper, prin. Fax 229-4216
Other Schools – See Farmersville

Red Bud, Randolph, Pop. 3,675
Red Bud CUSD 132 1,000/PK-12
815 Locust St 62278 618-282-3507
Jonathan Tallman, supt. Fax 282-6151
www.redbud132.org
Red Bud ES 600/PK-8
200 W Field Dr 62278 618-282-3858
Ryan McClellan, prin. Fax 282-3965

St. John's Lutheran S 200/PK-8
808 S Main St 62278 618-282-3873
Deitt Schneider, prin. Fax 282-4087
St. John the Baptist S 100/PK-8
519 Hazel St 62278 618-282-3215
Kris Hill, prin. Fax 282-6790
Trinity Lutheran S 100/PK-8
10247 S Prairie Rd 62278 618-282-2881
John Bione, prin. Fax 282-4045

Richmond, McHenry, Pop. 1,854
Nippersink SD 2 1,300/PK-8
4213 US Highway 12 60071 815-678-4242
Dr. Tom Lind, supt. Fax 675-0413
www.nippersinkdistrict2.org
Nippersink MS 500/6-8
10006 N Main St 60071 815-678-7129
Tim Molitor, prin. Fax 678-7210
Richmond Consolidated ES 400/K-5
5815 Broadway St 60071 815-678-4717
Paul Augustyn, prin. Fax 678-2279
Other Schools – See Spring Grove

Richton Park, Cook, Pop. 13,324
ESD 159
Supt. — See Matteson
Armstrong ES 300/K-5
5030 Imperial Dr 60471 708-481-7424
Shahran Spears, prin. Fax 481-7476

Matteson ESD 162 3,000/PK-8
4601 Sauk Trl 60471 708-748-0100
Dr. Blondean Davis, supt. Fax 748-7302
www.sd162.org
Richton Square S 200/PK-K
22700 Richton Square Rd 60471 708-283-2706
Narishea Parham, prin. Fax 283-8594
Sauk ES 400/4-6
4435 S Churchill Dr 60471 708-747-2660
Brenda Calvin, prin. Fax 503-1335
Other Schools – See Matteson, Olympia Fields, Park Forest

Ringwood, McHenry, Pop. 823
Johnsburg CUSD 12
Supt. — See Johnsburg
Ringwood School Primary Center 500/PK-2
4700 School Rd 60072 815-728-0459
Andy Elbert, prin. Fax 728-0690

Riverdale, Cook, Pop. 13,395
Dolton SD 148 2,300/PK-8
114 W 144th St 60827 708-841-2290
Dr. Kevin Nohelty, supt. Fax 841-5048
www.district148.net
ECC 100/PK-PK
560 W 144th St 60827 708-841-2602
Shinora Montgomery, prin. Fax 201-2082
Park ES 200/K-6
14200 S Wentworth Ave 60827 708-849-9440
Dr. Dell McFarlane, prin. Fax 201-2144
Riverdale ES 200/K-4
325 W 142nd St 60827 708-849-7153
Shinora Montgomery, prin. Fax 201-2145
Washington ES 300/K-6
13900 S School St 60827 708-201-2078
Dorothy Jeter, prin. Fax 201-2148
Washington JHS 100/7-8
13900 S School St 60827 708-201-2078
Dorothy Jeter, prin. Fax 201-2148
Other Schools – See Dolton

General George Patton SD 133 300/PK-8
150 W 137th St 60827 708-841-3955
Dr. Carol Kunst, supt. Fax 841-5911
www.district133.org
Patton S 300/K-8
13700 S Stewart Ave 60827 708-841-2420
David Brown, prin. Fax 841-2492
School District 133 Annex 50/PK-PK
150 W 137th St 60827 708-841-3955
Dr. Carol Kunst, supt. Fax 841-5911

River Forest, Cook, Pop. 10,962
River Forest SD 90 1,400/PK-8
7776 Lake St 60305 708-771-8282
Edward Condon Ph.D., supt. Fax 771-8291
www.district90.org
Lincoln ES 400/PK-4
511 Park Ave 60305 708-366-7340
Casey Godfrey, prin. Fax 771-3956
Roosevelt JHS 700/5-8
7560 Oak Ave 60305 708-366-9230
Larry Garstki, prin. Fax 771-3962
Willard ES 300/PK-4
1250 Ashland Ave 60305 708-366-6740
Diane Wood, prin. Fax 366-1416

Grace Lutheran S 200/PK-8
7300 Division St 60305 708-366-6900
William Koehne, prin. Fax 366-0966
Keystone Montessori S 200/PK-8
7415 North Ave 60305 708-366-1080
Victoria Shea, admin. Fax 366-1083
St. Luke S 400/PK-8
519 Ashland Ave 60305 708-366-8587
Timothy Wesley, prin. Fax 366-3831
St. Vincent Ferrer S 200/PK-8
1515 Lathrop Ave 60305 708-771-5905
John Glimco, prin. Fax 771-7114

River Grove, Cook, Pop. 10,116
Rhodes SD 84-5 700/PK-8
8931 Fullerton Ave 60171 708-453-1266
James Prather, supt. Fax 453-0817
www.rhodes.k12.il.us/
Rhodes S 700/PK-8
8931 Fullerton Ave 60171 708-453-6813
Brian McConnell, prin. Fax 452-6324

River Grove SD 85-5 600/K-8
2650 Thatcher Ave 60171 708-453-6172
Dr. Jan Rashid, supt. Fax 453-6186
www.rivergroveschool.org
River Grove ES 600/K-8
2650 Thatcher Ave 60171 708-453-6172
Lisa Skelly, prin. Fax 453-6186

Riverside, Cook, Pop. 8,771
Riverside SD 96 1,600/PK-8
63 Woodside Rd 60546 708-447-5007
Martha Ryan-Toye, supt. Fax 447-3252
www.district96.org
Ames ES 300/K-5
86 Southcote Rd 60546 708-447-0759
Todd Gierman, prin. Fax 447-6904
Blythe Park ES 200/PK-5
735 Leesley Rd 60546 708-447-2168
Casimira Gorman, prin. Fax 447-1703
Central ES 400/K-5
61 Woodside Rd 60546 708-447-1106
Peter Gatz, prin. Fax 447-5030
Hauser JHS 600/6-8
65 Woodside Rd 60546 708-447-3896
April Mahy, prin. Fax 447-5180
Other Schools – See Brookfield

St. Mary S 400/PK-8
97 Herrick Rd 60546 708-442-5747
Barbara Rasinski, prin. Fax 442-0125

Riverton, Sangamon, Pop. 3,413
Riverton CUSD 14 1,400/PK-12
PO Box 1010 62561 217-629-6009
Dr. Lance Thurman, supt. Fax 629-6008
www.rivertonschools.org
Riverton ES 500/PK-4
PO Box 470 62561 217-629-6001
Jaclynn Shoufler, prin. Fax 629-6023
Riverton MS 400/5-8
PO Box 530 62561 217-629-6002
Brad Polanin, prin. Fax 629-6017

Riverwoods, Lake, Pop. 3,639

Riverwoods Montessori S 100/PK-6
3140 Riverwoods Rd 60015 847-945-7582
Lisa Kambich, dir. Fax 948-5136

Roanoke, Woodford, Pop. 2,057
Roanoke-Benson CUSD 60 600/PK-12
PO Box 320 61561 309-923-8921
Rohn Peterson, supt. Fax 923-7508
www.rb60.com/
Sowers ES 200/PK-4
202 W High St 61561 309-923-6241
Rohn Peterson, prin. Fax 923-7638
Other Schools – See Benson

Linn Mennonite Christian S 50/K-12
1594 County Road 1700 N 61561 309-923-5641
Matthew Kennell, pres.

Robbins, Cook, Pop. 5,299
Posen-Robbins ESD 143-5
Supt. — See Posen
Childs ES 200/K-3
14123 S Lydia Ave 60472 708-388-7203
Regina Redd M.A., prin. Fax 489-4368
Kellar JHS 500/6-8
14123 S Lydia Ave 60472 708-388-7201
Dr. Monica Spence, prin. Fax 388-6177
Turner S 200/PK-K
3847 W 135th St 60472 708-388-7205
Angela Craig, prin. Fax 388-0835

Robinson, Crawford, Pop. 7,621
Robinson CUSD 2 1,600/PK-12
PO Box 190 62454 618-544-7511
Josh Quick, supt. Fax 544-9284
www.robinsonschools.com/
Lincoln Grade S 300/3-5
PO Box 190 62454 618-544-3315
Kathy Bemont, prin. Fax 544-3315
Nuttall MS 300/6-8
PO Box 190 62454 618-544-8618
Craig Beals, prin. Fax 544-8618
Washington ES 400/PK-2
PO Box 190 62454 618-544-2233
Jason Stark, prin. Fax 544-2233

New Hebron Christian S 100/PK-8
10755 E 700th Ave 62454 618-544-7619
Susan Wassel, prin. Fax 544-4493

Rochelle, Ogle, Pop. 9,466
Rochelle CCSD 231 1,700/PK-8
444 N 8th St 61068 815-562-6363
Todd Prusator, supt. Fax 562-5500
www.d231.rochelle.net
Central ES 300/PK-5
444 N 8th St 61068 815-562-8251
Justin Adolph, prin. Fax 562-5003
Lincoln ES 400/PK-5
1450 20th St 61068 815-562-4520
Adam Zurko, prin. Fax 561-1005
May ES 200/K-5
1033 N 2nd St 61068 815-562-6331
Becky Cox, prin. Fax 562-2430
Rochelle MS 500/6-8
111 School Ave 61068 815-562-7997
Tony Doyle, prin. Fax 562-8527
Tilton ES 300/K-5
1050 N 9th St 61068 815-562-6665
Jennifer Derricks, prin. Fax 562-2607

St. Paul Lutheran S 200/PK-8
1415 10th Ave 61068 815-562-6323
Fredrick Wren, prin. Fax 561-8074

Rochester, Sangamon, Pop. 3,622
Rochester CUSD 3A 2,300/PK-12
4 Rocket Dr 62563 217-498-6210
Dr. Thomas Bertrand, supt. Fax 498-8045
www.rochester3a.net
Rochester 2-3 ES 300/2-3
456 Education Ave 62563 217-498-6216
Jeff Reed, prin. Fax 498-6217
Rochester EC-1 ES 300/PK-1
707 W Main St 62563 217-498-9778
Jeff Reed, prin. Fax 498-9160
Rochester IS 500/4-6
900 Jack Taylor Dr 62563 217-498-6215
Joe Viola, prin. Fax 498-6218
Rochester JHS 400/7-8
3 Rocket Dr 62563 217-498-9761
Kim Poole, prin. Fax 498-6204

Rockdale, Will, Pop. 1,965
Rockdale SD 84 300/PK-8
715 Meadow Ave 60436 815-725-5321
Dr. Lori Gehrke, supt. Fax 725-3099
www.rockdale.will.k12.il.us
Rockdale ES 300/PK-8
715 Meadow Ave 60436 815-725-5321
Tammy Hafner, prin. Fax 725-3099

Rock Falls, Whiteside, Pop. 9,103
East Coloma-Nelson CESD 20 200/K-8
1602 Dixon Rd 61071 815-625-4400
David Chavira, supt. Fax 625-4624
www.ecoloma.net
East Coloma-Nelson ES 200/K-8
1602 Dixon Rd 61071 815-625-4400
David Chavira, admin. Fax 625-4624

Montmorency CCSD 145 300/PK-8
9415 Hoover Rd 61071 815-625-6616
Alex Moore, supt. Fax 625-8432
sites.google.com/a/mgs145.net/montmorencyschooldistrict145
Montmorency ES 300/PK-8
9415 Hoover Rd 61071 815-625-6616
Shad Hansen, prin. Fax 625-8432

Rock Falls ESD 13 1,100/PK-8
602 4th Ave 61071 815-626-2604
Dan Arickx, supt. Fax 626-2627
www.rfsd13.org
Dillon ES 300/K-2
1901 8th Ave 61071 815-625-3356
Roy Calkins, prin. Fax 625-2943
Merrill ES 300/3-5
600 4th Ave 61071 815-625-4634
Brody Rude, prin. Fax 625-1747

Riverdale PreSchool Center 100/PK-PK
3505 Prophet Rd 61071 815-625-5280
Chelese Palmer, prin. Fax 625-5316
Rock Falls MS 300/6-8
1701 12th Ave 61071 815-626-2626
Kyle Ackman, prin. Fax 626-3198

St. Andrew S 200/PK-8
701 11th Ave 61071 815-625-1456
William Lemmer, prin. Fax 625-1724

Rockford, Winnebago, Pop. 148,827
Rockford SD 205 26,200/PK-12
501 7th St 61104 815-966-3000
Dr. Ehren Jarrett, supt. Fax 966-3193
www.rps205.com
Barbour Language Academy 700/K-8
1506 Clover Ave 61102 815-966-3395
James Robinette, prin. Fax 967-8039
Beyer ES 200/PK-5
333 15th Ave 61104 815-966-3390
Treveda Redmond, prin. Fax 966-3392
Bloom ES 300/K-5
2912 Brendenwood Rd 61107 815-229-2170
Heather Novak, prin. Fax 229-2457
Brookview ES 500/K-5
1750 Madron Rd 61107 815-229-2492
Melanie Wiest, prin. Fax 229-2112
Carlson ES 400/PK-5
4015 Pepper Dr 61114 815-654-4955
Dave Nold, prin. Fax 636-3001
Conklin ES 400/K-5
3003 Halsted Rd 61101 815-654-4860
Sidney Graves, prin. Fax 654-4864
Dennis ECC 400/PK-PK
730 Lincoln Park Blvd 61102 815-490-5410
Jenny Keffer, prin. Fax 966-3751
Eisenhower MS 800/6-8
3525 Spring Creek Rd 61107 815-229-2450
Jeff Carlson, prin. Fax 229-2456
Ellis ES 400/K-5
222 S Central Ave 61102 815-966-3909
Taren Turner, prin. Fax 966-5266
Fairview ECC 700/PK-PK
512 Fairview Ave 61108 815-227-8400
Darcy Dunn, prin. Fax 229-2445
Flinn MS 1,100/6-8
2525 Ohio Pkwy 61108 815-229-2800
Randy Bay, prin. Fax 229-2894
Froberg ES 500/K-5
4555 20th St 61109 815-874-2464
Christina Ulferts, prin. Fax 874-6228
Gregory ES 300/K-5
4820 Carol Ct 61108 815-229-2176
Kristine Leider, prin. Fax 229-2897
Haskell Academy 300/PK-5
515 Maple St 61103 815-966-3355
Loree Leathers, prin. Fax 967-8040
Hillman ES 500/PK-5
3701 Green Dale Dr 61109 815-229-2835
Carolyn Kloss, prin. Fax 229-2807
Johnson ES 500/K-5
3805 Rural St 61107 815-229-2485
Amber Miller, prin. Fax 229-2418
Kennedy MS 700/6-8
520 N Pierpont Ave 61101 815-654-4880
Renneth Richardson, prin. Fax 654-4874
King ES 300/K-5
1306 S Court St 61102 815-966-3740
Greg Midgett, prin. Fax 966-5291
Kishwaukee ES 300/K-5
526 Catlin St 61104 815-966-3380
Aimee Kasper, prin. Fax 966-6372
Lathrop ES 400/K-5
2603 Clover Ave 61102 815-966-3285
Penny El-Azhari, prin. Fax 966-3713
Lemon ES 400/K-5
1993 Mulberry St 61101 815-967-8000
Stephen Francisco, prin. Fax 967-8027
Lincoln MS 700/6-8
1500 Charles St 61104 815-229-2400
Jim Parker, prin. Fax 229-2420
Maria Montessori ES 300/PK-8
2021 Hawthorne Dr 61107 815-654-4906
Candice Collins, prin. Fax 654-4909
Marshall S 600/4-8
4664 N Rockton Ave 61103 815-490-5400
Jessica Powell, prin. Fax 490-5405
McIntosh ES 400/K-5
525 N Pierpont Ave 61101 815-966-3275
Al Gagliano, prin. Fax 966-8922
Nashold ES 400/PK-PK
3303 20th St 61109 815-229-2155
Erin Salberg, prin. Fax 229-2421
Nelson ES 500/K-5
623 15th St 61104 815-229-2190
Rene Mandujano, prin. Fax 489-2790
Riverdahl ES 600/PK-5
3520 Kishwaukee St 61109 815-229-2870
Tommy Gibbons, prin. Fax 229-2891
Rockford Environmental Science Academy 1,000/6-8
1800 Ogilby Rd 61102 815-489-5509
Ben Stover, prin. Fax 966-5360
Rolling Green ES 700/PK-5
3615 W Gate Pkwy 61108 815-229-2881
Holly Lyman, prin. Fax 229-2135
Spring Creek ES 400/K-5
5222 Spring Creek Rd 61114 815-654-4960
Ray Owens, prin. Fax 654-4969
Summerdale ECC 400/PK-PK
3320 Glenwood Ave 61101 815-966-3280
Kristin Martin-Fry, prin. Fax 967-8016
Thompson ES 300/K-5
4949 Marion Ave 61108 815-229-2830
Emma Gipson, prin. Fax 229-2832
Welsh ES 300/PK-5
2100 Huffman Blvd 61103 815-966-3260
Matthew Lerner, prin. Fax 966-3259
West MS 800/6-8
1900 N Rockton Ave 61103 815-966-3200
Maurice Davis, prin. Fax 966-3216
West View ES 400/PK-5
1720 Halsted Rd 61103 815-654-4945
Jake Sayre, prin. Fax 654-4903
Whitehead ES 400/K-5
2325 Ohio Pkwy 61108 815-229-2840
Pam Miner, prin. Fax 229-2419
White Swan ES 300/PK-2
7550 Mill Rd 61108 815-229-2184
Carolyn Timm, prin. Fax 229-2459
Other Schools – See Cherry Valley

Alpine Academy of Rockford 100/PK-6
5001 Forest View Ave 61108 815-227-8894
Robert McVinnie, prin. Fax 227-8899
Alpine Christian S 50/PK-8
325 N Alpine Rd 61107 815-399-0880
Teresa Smith, prin.
Berean Baptist Christian S 200/PK-12
5626 Safford Rd 61101 815-962-4841
Douglas Swanson, admin. Fax 962-4851
Cathedral Baptist S 100/PK-12
5622 35th St 61109 815-874-3883
Thomas Freeman, prin.
Cathedral of St. Peter S 200/PK-8
1231 N Court St 61103 815-963-3620
James Burns, prin. Fax 963-0551
Christian Life Schools 700/PK-12
5950 Spring Creek Rd 61114 815-877-5749
Michael Hoekstra, prin. Fax 877-4358
Holy Family S 500/PK-8
4407 Highcrest Rd 61107 815-398-5331
Corine Gendron, prin. Fax 398-5902
Keith Country Day S 300/PK-12
1 Jacoby Pl 61107 815-399-8823
James Norris, hdmstr. Fax 399-2470
Montessori Private Academy 100/PK-9
8101 Sayer Rd 61108 815-332-8101
Jeffrey Katz, dir. Fax 332-8104
North Love Christian S 200/PK-12
5301 E Riverside Blvd 61114 815-877-6021
Tony Cotelleso, admin. Fax 877-6076
Rockford Christian S 1,200/PK-12
1401 N Bell School Rd 61107 815-391-8000
Randy Taylor, supt. Fax 391-8004
Rockford IQRA S 200/PK-12
5925 Darlene Dr 61109 815-397-6899
Muhammad Kabir, prin. Fax 397-1681
Rockford Lutheran Academy 300/PK-5
1711 Delcy Dr 61107 815-226-4947
Curtis Wudtke, prin. Fax 226-4886
St. Bernadette S 200/PK-8
2300 Bell Ave 61103 815-968-2288
Renee Payne, prin. Fax 987-9453
St. Edward S 200/PK-8
3020 11th St 61109 815-398-2631
Pat Wackenhut, prin. Fax 398-3134
St. James S 200/PK-8
409 N 1st St 61107 815-962-8515
Renee Payne, prin. Fax 962-8526
St. Paul Lutheran S 100/K-8
811 Locust St 61101 815-965-3335
Jason Miller, lead tchr. Fax 965-3335
St. Rita S 300/PK-8
6284 Valley Knoll Dr 61109 815-398-3466
Patrick Flanagan, prin. Fax 398-6104
Spectrum S 200/PK-12
4848 Turner St 61107 815-877-1600
Theodora Middleton, dir. Fax 877-1685

Rock Island, Rock Island, Pop. 37,879
Rock Island-Milan SD 41 6,600/PK-12
2101 6th Ave 61201 309-793-5900
Dr. Michael Oberhaus, supt. Fax 793-5905
rockislandschools.org
Denkmann ES 500/PK-6
4101 22nd Ave 61201 309-793-5922
John Frieden, prin. Fax 793-5988
Edison JHS 400/7-8
4141 9th St 61201 309-793-5920
Christi Thigpen, prin. Fax 793-5919
Field ES 400/K-6
2900 31st Ave 61201 309-793-5935
Dennis Weiss, prin. Fax 793-5936
Hanson ES 400/K-6
4000 9th St 61201 309-793-5930
Dan Coyne-Logan, prin. Fax 793-4195
Longfellow Liberal Arts S 300/K-6
4198 7th Ave 61201 309-793-5975
David Knuckey, prin. Fax 793-5977
Mann Early Learning Center 100/PK-PK
3530 38th Ave 61201 309-793-5928
Nicole Berry, dir. Fax 793-5965
Ridgewood ES 300/K-6
9607 14th St W 61201 309-793-5980
Joey Dilulio, prin. Fax 793-5981
Rock Island Academy 500/PK-6
930 14th St 61201 309-793-5944
Tia Edwards, prin. Fax 793-5909
Rock Island Center for Math & Science 600/PK-6
2101 16th Ave 61201 309-793-5995
Dr. Amy Schelker, prin. Fax 793-5996
Washington JHS 500/7-8
3300 18th Ave 61201 309-793-5915
Kristin Allen, prin. Fax 793-5917
Willard ES 300/K-6
2503 9th St 61201 309-793-5940
Lance Clark, prin. Fax 793-5941
Other Schools – See Milan

Jordan Catholic S 400/PK-8
2901 24th St 61201 309-793-7350
Jacob Smithers, prin. Fax 793-7361

Rockton, Winnebago, Pop. 7,573
Rockton SD 140 1,500/PK-8
1050 E Union St 61072 815-624-7143
Glenn Terry, supt. Fax 624-4640
rockton140.org
Mack MS 500/6-8
11810 Old River Rd 61072 815-624-2611
Autumn Czizek, prin. Fax 624-5900
Rockton ES 500/PK-2
1050 E Union St 61072 815-624-8585
Kindyl Etnyre, prin. Fax 624-1002
Whitman Post ES 500/3-5
1060 E Union St 61072 815-624-4006
Megan Forsythe, prin. Fax 624-2125

Rolling Meadows, Cook, Pop. 23,765
Palatine CCSD 15
Supt. — See Palatine
Central Road ES 600/K-6
3800 Central Rd 60008 847-963-5100
Jenny Garcia-Macko, prin. Fax 963-5106
Kimball Hill ES 600/K-6
2905 Meadow Dr 60008 847-963-5200
Tracey Wrobel, prin. Fax 963-5206
Plum Grove JHS 800/7-8
2600 Plum Grove Rd 60008 847-963-7600
Kerry Wilson Ed.D., prin. Fax 963-7606
Sandburg JHS 600/7-8
2600 Martin Ln 60008 847-963-7800
Douglas Harter, prin. Fax 963-7806
Willow Bend ES 500/K-6
4700 Barker Ave 60008 847-963-7300
Melissa Sabatino, prin. Fax 963-7306

St. Collette S 200/PK-8
3900 Pheasant Dr 60008 847-392-4098
Valerie Zemko, prin. Fax 392-8155

Romeoville, Will, Pop. 38,967
Valley View CUSD 365U 17,500/PK-12
801 W Normantown Rd 60446 815-886-2700
Dr. James Mitchem, supt. Fax 886-7294
www.vvsd.org/
Hermansen ES 600/K-5
101 Wesglen Pkwy 60446 815-886-7581
Loretta Furtute, prin. Fax 886-5593
Hill ES 800/K-5
616 Dalhart Ave 60446 815-886-4343
Jody Ellis, prin. Fax 886-7299
King ES 600/K-5
301 Eaton Ave 60446 815-886-3380
April Vacik, prin. Fax 886-7840
Lukancic MS 600/6-8
725 W Normantown Rd 60446 815-886-2216
Tricia Rollerson, prin. Fax 886-2264
Martinez MS 800/6-8
590 Belmont Dr 60446 815-886-6100
Sarah DeDonato, prin. Fax 886-7264
Skoff ES 800/K-5
775 W Normantown Rd 60446 815-886-8384
Cheryl Lockard, prin. Fax 886-8389
Valley View ECC 200/PK-PK
753 Dalhart Ave 60446 815-886-7827
Jacci Brown, prin. Fax 886-7830
Other Schools – See Bolingbrook

Romeoville Christian Academy 100/PK-12
301 W Normantown Rd 60446 815-886-4850
Mark Widmer, prin.
St. Andrew the Apostle S 200/PK-8
505 Kingston Dr 60446 815-886-5953
Carol Albreski, prin. Fax 293-2016

Roodhouse, Greene, Pop. 1,796
North Greene Unit SD 3
Supt. — See White Hall
North Greene ES 500/PK-6
403 W North St 62082 217-589-4623
Jaclyn Kuchy, prin. Fax 589-4028

Roscoe, Winnebago, Pop. 10,602
Kinnikinnick CCSD 131 1,900/PK-8
5410 Pine Ln 61073 815-623-2837
Keli Freedlund, supt. Fax 623-9285
www.kinn131.org
Kinnikinnick ES 400/4-5
5410 Pine Ln 61073 815-623-2837
Shaun Newmes, prin. Fax 623-1797
Ledgewood ES 400/PK-1
11685 S Gate Rd 61073 815-623-2837
Chad Etnyre, prin. Fax 623-1410
Roscoe MS 700/6-8
6121 Elevator Rd 61073 815-623-2837
Julie Cropp, prin. Fax 623-7604
Stone Creek S 400/2-3
11633 S Gate Rd 61073 815-623-2837
Shane Caiola, prin. Fax 623-3646

Roselle, DuPage, Pop. 22,408
Keeneyville SD 20
Supt. — See Hanover Park
Waterbury ES 500/K-5
355 Rodenburg Rd 60172 630-893-8180
Dr. Deb Guzan, prin. Fax 893-3797

Medinah SD 11 700/K-8
700 E Granville Ave 60172 630-893-3737
Dr. John Butts, supt. Fax 893-4947
www.medinah11.org
Medinah MS 200/6-8
700 E Granville Ave 60172 630-893-3838
George Gouriotis, prin. Fax 893-5198
Other Schools – See Medinah

Roselle SD 12 700/K-8
100 E Walnut St 60172 630-529-2091
Dr. Melissa Kaczkowski, supt. Fax 529-2467
www.sd12.org
Roselle MS 300/6-8
500 S Park St 60172 630-529-1600
Kathleen Schneiter, prin. Fax 529-1882

Spring Hills ES 500/K-5
560 Pinecrest Dr 60172 630-529-1883
Lew Girmscheid, prin. Fax 529-1948

Schaumburg CCSD 54
Supt. — See Schaumburg
Nerge ES 600/PK-6
660 N Woodfield Trl 60172 847-357-5777
Kelly Dvoracek, prin. Fax 357-5778

St. Walter S 700/PK-8
201 W Maple Ave 60172 630-529-1721
Mary Lloyd, prin. Fax 529-9290
Trinity Lutheran S 300/PK-8
405 Rush St 60172 630-894-3263
Dawn Koenig, prin. Fax 894-1430

Rosemont, Cook, Pop. 4,141
Rosemont ESD 78 300/PK-8
6101 Ruby St 60018 847-825-0144
Kevin Anderson, supt. Fax 825-9704
www.rosemont78.org/
Rosemont ES 300/PK-8
6101 Ruby St 60018 847-825-0144
Kevin Anderson, prin. Fax 825-9704

Roseville, Warren, Pop. 986
Monmouth-Roseville CUSD 238
Supt. — See Monmouth
Monmouth-Roseville JHS 200/7-8
200 E Gossett St 61473 309-426-2682
Donald Farr, prin. Fax 426-2303

Rossville, Vermilion, Pop. 1,316
Rossville-Alvin CUSD 7 300/PK-8
350 N Chicago St 60963 217-748-6666
Crystal Johnson, supt. Fax 748-6144
Rossville-Alvin S 300/PK-8
350 N Chicago St 60963 217-748-6666
Crystal Johnson, prin. Fax 748-6121

Round Lake, Lake, Pop. 17,862
CCSD 46
Supt. — See Grayslake
Park S Campus 500/K-8
400 W Townline Rd 60073 847-223-3650
David Dinsmore, prin. Fax 201-1971

Round Lake Area SD 116 7,500/PK-12
884 W Nippersink Rd 60073 847-270-9000
Dr. Constance Collins, supt. Fax 546-3538
www.rlas-116.org
Magee MS 700/6-8
500 N Cedar Lake Rd 60073 847-546-8800
Dr. Lisa Steffen, prin. Fax 740-3836
Preschool at Early Education Center 500/PK-PK
882 W Nippersink Rd 60073 847-270-9920
Janie Metzger, admin. Fax 740-5183
Village ES 400/1-5
880 W Nippersink Rd 60073 847-270-9470
Andrew Wilson, prin. Fax 546-2848
Other Schools – See Lake Villa, Round Lake Beach, Round Lake Heights, Round Lake Park

---

Nature Walk Montessori S PK-8
200 Footpath Ln 60073 224-225-9224
Vicki Promenzio, head sch
St. Joseph S 200/PK-8
118 Lincoln Ave 60073 847-546-1720
Abbie Miller, prin. Fax 546-1720

Round Lake Beach, Lake, Pop. 27,714
CCSD 46
Supt. — See Grayslake
Avon Center ES 400/K-4
1617 N Il Route 83 60073 847-223-3530
Chris Wolk, prin. Fax 223-3532

Round Lake Area SD 116
Supt. — See Round Lake
Ellis ES 800/1-5
720 Central Park Dr 60073 847-270-9900
Beth Kiewicz, prin. Fax 546-2463
Round Lake Beach ES 500/1-5
1421 Ardmore Dr 60073 847-270-9930
Dr. Denise Wilcox, prin. Fax 270-3153

Round Lake Heights, Lake, Pop. 2,629
Round Lake Area SD 116
Supt. — See Round Lake
Indian Hill ES 500/1-5
1920 Lotus Dr 60073 847-270-9970
Raymond Porten, prin. Fax 270-3172
Round Lake MS 1,000/6-8
2000 Lotus Dr 60073 847-270-9400
David Higgs, prin. Fax 270-9419

Round Lake Park, Lake, Pop. 7,416
Round Lake Area SD 116
Supt. — See Round Lake
Murphy ES 700/1-5
220 Greenwood Dr 60073 847-270-9950
Phil Georgia, prin. Fax 546-2394

Roxana, Madison, Pop. 1,531
Roxana CUSD 1 1,500/PK-12
401 Chaffer Ave 62084 618-254-7544
Debra Kreutztrager, supt. Fax 254-7547
www.roxanaschools.org
Central IS 200/3-5
601 Chaffer Ave 62084 618-254-7594
James Miller, prin. Fax 254-7530
Roxana JHS 400/6-8
401 Chaffer Ave 62084 618-254-7560
Dr. Steve Mayerhofer, prin. Fax 254-8107
Other Schools – See South Roxana

Royal, Champaign, Pop. 293
Prairieview-Ogden CCSD 197 200/K-8
PO Box 27 61871 217-583-3300
Victor White Ed.D., supt. Fax 583-3391
www.pvo.k12.il.us/

Prairieview-Ogden North ES 100/K-4
PO Box 27 61871 217-583-3300
Victor White Ed.D., supt. Fax 583-3391
Other Schools – See Ogden, Thomasboro

Rushville, Schuyler, Pop. 3,179
Schuyler-Industry CUSD 5 1,200/PK-12
740 Maple Ave 62681 217-322-4311
Beau Fretueg, supt. Fax 322-4398
www.sid5.com
Schuyler-Industry MS 400/5-8
750 N Congress St 62681 217-322-4311
Jim Shepherd, prin. Fax 322-3938
Washington ES 200/PK-1
100 Buchanan St 62681 217-322-4311
Marcy Wort, prin. Fax 322-3195
Webster ES 200/2-4
310 N Monroe St 62681 217-322-4311
Marcy Wort, prin. Fax 322-2391

Saint Anne, Kankakee, Pop. 1,243
Saint Anne CCSD 256 300/PK-8
PO Box 530 60964 815-427-8190
Charlie Stegall, supt. Fax 427-6019
www.sags256.org
Saint Anne S 300/PK-8
PO Box 530 60964 815-427-8153
Scott Strong, prin. Fax 427-6019

Saint Charles, Kane, Pop. 32,580
Saint Charles CUSD 303 13,300/PK-12
201 S 7th St 60174 331-228-2000
Dr. Jason Pearson, supt. Fax 228-2001
www.d303.org
Anderson ES 400/PK-5
35W071 Villa Maria Rd 60174 331-228-3300
P. Gonzalez-Martinez, prin. Fax 228-3301
Bell-Graham ES 500/K-5
4N505 Fox Mill Blvd 60175 331-228-2100
Patti Palagi, prin. Fax 228-2101
Davis PS 500/PK-2
1125 S 7th St 60174 331-228-2200
Denise Liechty, prin. Fax 228-2201
Ferson Creek ES 600/PK-5
38W160 Bolcum Rd 60175 331-228-2300
Kelly Sculles, prin. Fax 228-2301
Fox Ridge ES 400/PK-5
1905 E Tyler Rd 60174 331-228-2400
Amy Stuckey, prin. Fax 228-2401
Haines MS 1,100/6-8
305 S 9th St 60174 331-228-3100
Pamela Jensen, prin. Fax 228-3101
Lincoln ES 300/K-5
211 S 6th Ave 60174 331-228-2500
Christine Balaskovits, prin. Fax 228-2501
Munhall ES 500/K-5
1400 S 13th Ave 60174 331-228-2600
Jarrod Buxton, prin. Fax 228-2601
Richmond IS 500/3-5
300 S 12th St 60174 331-228-2800
Rosa Ascharya, prin. Fax 228-2801
Thompson MS 900/6-8
705 W Main St 60174 331-228-3100
Timothy Loversky, prin. Fax 228-3401
Wild Rose ES 500/K-5
36W730 Red Haw Ln 60174 331-228-3000
Bob Allison, prin. Fax 228-3001
Wredling MS 1,300/6-8
1200 Dunham Rd 60174 331-228-3400
Steve Morrill, prin. Fax 228-3401
Other Schools – See South Elgin, Wasco, West Chicago

Bridges Montessori Academy 100/PK-K
716 Oak St 60174 630-513-9742
Jan Dangles, dir. Fax 587-6298
St. Patrick S 500/K-8
118 N 5th St 60174 630-584-6367
Lisa Brown, prin. Fax 584-9759

Saint Elmo, Fayette, Pop. 1,414
Saint Elmo CUSD 202 500/PK-12
1200 N Walnut St 62458 618-829-3264
Deborah Philpot, supt. Fax 829-5161
www.stelmo.org
Saint Elmo ES 300/PK-6
519 W 2nd St 62458 618-829-3263
Sean Hannagan, prin. Fax 829-5161
Saint Elmo JHS 100/7-8
300 W 12th St 62458 618-829-3227
Brian Garrard, prin. Fax 829-5161

Sainte Marie, Jasper, Pop. 242
Jasper County CUSD 1
Supt. — See Newton
Sainte Marie ES 100/PK-K
PO Box 157 62459 618-455-3219
Josh Benefiel, prin. Fax 455-3223

Saint Jacob, Madison, Pop. 1,092
Triad CUSD 2
Supt. — See Troy
Saint Jacob ES 200/K-5
PO Box 217 62281 618-644-2541
Jay Simpson, prin. Fax 644-5474
Triad MS 800/6-8
9539 US Highway 40 62281 618-644-5511
Matt Noyes, prin. Fax 644-9435

Saint Joseph, Champaign, Pop. 3,931
Saint Joseph CCSD 169 900/PK-8
PO Box 409 61873 217-469-2291
Todd Pence, supt. Fax 469-8906
www.stjoe.k12.il.us
Saint Joseph ES 500/PK-4
PO Box 409 61873 217-469-2291
Mike Sennert, prin. Fax 469-8906
Saint Joseph MS 400/5-8
PO Box 409 61873 217-469-2334
Chris Graham, prin. Fax 469-2537

Saint Libory, Saint Clair, Pop. 604
Saint Libory Consolidated SD 30 100/K-8
PO Box 323 62282 618-768-4923
Dr. Thomas Rude, supt. Fax 768-4518
www.stlibory30.org
Saint Libory ES 100/K-8
PO Box 323 62282 618-768-4923
Dr. Thomas Rude, admin. Fax 768-4518

Saint Peter, Fayette, Pop. 359

St. Peter Lutheran S 100/PK-8
701 E 3rd St 62880 618-349-8888
Lawrence Urban, prin. Fax 349-8888

Salem, Marion, Pop. 7,393
Salem SD 111 1,100/PK-8
1300 Hawthorn Rd 62881 618-548-7702
Leslie Foppe, supt. Fax 548-7714
www.salem111.com
Franklin Park MS 600/PK-PK, 4-
1325 N Franklin St 62881 618-548-7704
Tyler Lux, prin. Fax 548-7712
Hawthorn ES 400/K-3
1300 Hawthorn Rd 62881 618-548-7702
Marty Adams, prin. Fax 548-7714

Selmaville CCSD 10 200/K-8
3185 Selmaville Rd 62881 618-548-2416
Robin Brooks, supt. Fax 548-6063
www.selmaville.com
Selmaville North ES 200/K-8
3185 Selmaville Rd 62881 618-548-2416
Robin Brooks, prin. Fax 548-6063

St. Theresa of Avila S 100/K-8
190 N Ohio Ave 62881 618-548-3492
Marcia Stinde, prin. Fax 548-9673

Sandoval, Marion, Pop. 1,257
Sandoval CUSD 501 500/PK-12
859 W Missouri Ave 62882 618-247-3233
Dr. Jennifer Garrison, supt. Fax 247-3243
www.sandoval501.org
Sandoval ES 300/PK-6
300 E Perry Ave 62882 618-247-3450
Annie Gray, prin. Fax 247-3161
Sandoval JHS 100/7-8
859 W Missouri Ave 62882 618-247-3361
Annie Gray, prin. Fax 247-3235

Sandwich, DeKalb, Pop. 7,330
Sandwich CUSD 430 2,200/PK-12
720 S Wells St 60548 815-786-2187
Rick Schmitt, supt. Fax 786-6229
www.sandwich430.org
Dummer S 300/4-5
422 S Wells St 60548 815-786-8498
Lynette Ford, prin. Fax 786-1920
Haskin ES 200/PK-3
720 S Wells St 60548 815-786-8812
Dawn Greenacre, prin. Fax 786-8986
Prairie View ES 200/K-3
1201 Castle St 60548 815-786-8811
Sherrie Stricklin, prin. Fax 786-7404
Sandwich MS 500/6-8
600 S Wells St 60548 815-786-2138
B.J. Richardson, prin. Fax 786-6606
Woodbury ES 200/K-3
322 E 3rd St 60548 815-786-6316
Jennifer Kern, prin. Fax 786-2691

Sauk Village, Cook, Pop. 10,221
CCSD 168 1,500/PK-8
21899 Torrence Ave 60411 708-758-1610
Dr. Donna Leak, supt. Fax 758-5929
www.d168.org
Rickover JHS 500/6-8
22151 Torrence Ave 60411 708-758-1900
Chantel Bullock, prin. Fax 758-1601
Strassburg ES 400/3-5
2002 223rd St 60411 708-758-4754
Desiree Tunstall, prin. Fax 758-2202
Wagoner ES 600/PK-2
1831 215th Pl 60411 708-758-3322
Kathleen Hansen, prin. Fax 758-0801

Saunemin, Livingston, Pop. 417
Saunemin CCSD 438 100/PK-8
39 Main St 61769 815-832-4421
Dr. Christopher Maier, supt. Fax 832-4435
www.saunemin.org
Saunemin ES 100/PK-8
39 Main St 61769 815-832-4421
Dr. Christopher Maier, prin. Fax 832-4435

Savanna, Carroll, Pop. 3,017
West Carroll CUSD 314
Supt. — See Mount Carroll
West Carroll PS 400/PK-4
2215 Wacker Rd 61074 815-273-7747
Andrew Jordan, prin. Fax 273-3846

Savoy, Champaign, Pop. 7,113
Champaign CUSD 4
Supt. — See Champaign
Busey ES 500/K-5
304 Prairie Rose Ln 61874 217-351-3811
Jeff Scott, prin. Fax 351-3723

Montessori S of Champaign-Urbana 100/PK-6
1403 Regency Dr E 61874 217-356-1818
George Cook, admin. Fax 356-4818

Scales Mound, Jo Daviess, Pop. 373
Scales Mound CUSD 211 200/PK-12
210 Main St 61075 815-845-2215
William Caron, supt. Fax 845-2238
www.scalesmound.net

Scales Mound ES 100/PK-5
210 Main St 61075 815-845-2215
Dr. Matthew Wiederholt, prin. Fax 845-2238
Scales Mound JHS 50/6-8
210 Main St 61075 815-845-2215
Dr. Matthew Wiederholt, prin. Fax 845-2238

Schaumburg, Cook, Pop. 72,713
Schaumburg CCSD 54 13,900/PK-8
524 E Schaumburg Rd 60194 847-357-5000
Andrew DuRoss, supt. Fax 357-5152
www.sd54.org
Addams JHS 700/7-8
700 S Springinsguth Rd 60193 847-357-5900
Chris Bingen, prin. Fax 357-5901
Aldrin ES 600/PK-6
617 Boxwood Dr 60193 847-357-5400
Mary Botterman, prin. Fax 357-5401
Blackwell ES 500/K-6
345 N Walnut Ln 60194 847-357-5555
Jillian Sagan, prin. Fax 357-5556
Campanelli ES 500/PK-6
310 S Springinsguth Rd 60193 847-357-5333
Amy Christie, prin. Fax 357-5334
Collins ES 600/K-6
407 Summit Dr 60193 847-357-6100
Nell Haack, prin. Fax 357-6101
Dirksen ES 400/K-6
116 W Beech Dr 60193 847-357-5600
Joann Kort, prin. Fax 357-5601
Dooley ES 400/K-6
622 Norwood Ln 60193 847-357-6250
Beth Erbach, prin. Fax 357-6251
Enders-Salk ES 500/K-6
345 N Salem Dr 60194 847-357-6400
Mike Henry, prin. Fax 357-6401
Frost JHS 600/7-8
320 W Wise Rd 60193 847-357-6800
Scott Ross, prin. Fax 357-6801
Hale ES 400/K-6
1300 W Wise Rd 60193 847-357-6200
Brian Kaszewicz, prin. Fax 357-6201
Hoover ES 700/K-6
315 N Springinsguth Rd 60194 847-357-5800
John Schmelzer, prin. Fax 357-5801
Keller JHS 500/7-8
820 Bode Rd 60194 847-357-6500
Tom Barbini, prin. Fax 357-6501
Other Schools – See Elk Grove Village, Hanover Park, Hoffman Estates, Roselle

---

Acarath Montessori Center 100/PK-4
22 Kristin Dr 60195 847-397-0111
Judith Budinger, dir. Fax 397-3403
St. Peter Lutheran S 300/PK-8
208 E Schaumburg Rd 60194 847-885-7636
Steve Kielke, prin. Fax 882-9157
Schaumburg Christian S 1,200/PK-12
200 N Roselle Rd 60194 847-885-3230

Schiller Park, Cook, Pop. 11,679
Schiller Park SD 81 1,400/PK-8
9760 Soreng Ave 60176 847-671-1816
Dr. Kimberly Boryszewski, supt. Fax 671-1872
www.sd81.org
Kennedy ES 700/PK-3
3945 Wehrman Ave 60176 847-671-0250
Melissa Kartsimas, prin. Fax 671-0256
Lincoln MS 400/6-8
9750 Soreng Ave 60176 847-678-2916
Constance Stavrou, prin. Fax 678-4059
Washington ES 300/4-5
4835 Michigan Ave 60176 847-671-1922
Tiffany Leiva, prin. Fax 671-1972

St. Maria Goretti S 200/PK-8
10050 Ivanhoe Ave 60176 847-678-2560
Claudia Mendez, prin. Fax 678-2919

Scott AFB, Saint Clair, Pop. 3,423
Mascoutah CUSD 19
Supt. — See Mascoutah
Scott ES 900/PK-5
4732 Patriots Landing 62225 618-746-4738
Susanne Riechmann, prin. Fax 746-2186

Seneca, LaSalle, Pop. 2,330
Seneca CCSD 170 500/PK-8
174 Oak St 61360 815-357-8744
Eric Misener, supt. Fax 357-1516
www.sgs170.org
Seneca ES North Campus 300/PK-4
174 Oak St 61360 815-357-8744
Lynn McGhee, prin. Fax 357-1516
Seneca MS South Campus 200/5-8
174 Oak St 61360 815-357-8744
Shane Severson, prin. Fax 357-1078

Serena, LaSalle
Serena CUSD 2 700/K-12
PO Box 107 60549 815-496-2850
Marty Felesena, supt. Fax 496-6630
www.unit2.net
Serena MS 200/5-8
PO Box 107 60549 815-496-9250
Aaron Rios, prin. Fax 496-2987
Other Schools – See Earlville, Sheridan

Sesser, Franklin, Pop. 1,900
Sesser-Valier CUSD 196 700/PK-12
4626 State Highway 154 62884 618-625-5105
Dr. Jason D. Henry, supt. Fax 625-6696
sv196.org
Sesser-Valier ES 300/PK-5
4626 State Highway 154 62884 618-625-5105
Judy L. Logsdon, prin. Fax 625-3040
Sesser-Valier JHS 200/6-8
4626 State Highway 154 62884 618-625-5105
Judy L. Logsdon, prin. Fax 625-3040

Shabbona, DeKalb, Pop. 921
Indian Creek CUSD 425 600/PK-12
506 S Shabbona Rd 60550 815-824-2197
Chad Willis, supt. Fax 824-2199
www.indiancreekschools.org
Indian Creek ES 200/PK-4
301 W Cherokee Ave 60550 815-824-2343
David Mantzke, prin. Fax 824-2343
Other Schools – See Waterman

Shannon, Carroll, Pop. 753
Eastland CUSD 308
Supt. — See Lanark
Eastland ES 400/PK-6
601 S Chestnut St 61078 815-864-2300
Angela Mahoney, prin. Fax 864-2281

Shelbyville, Shelby, Pop. 4,676
Shelbyville CUSD 4 1,200/PK-12
720 W Main St 62565 217-774-4626
Denise Bence, supt. Fax 774-2521
www.shelbyville.k12.il.us/
Main Street ES 300/PK-PK, 1-
225 W Main St 62565 217-774-4731
Ryan Scott, prin. Fax 774-3016
Moulton MS 400/4-8
1101 W North 6th St 62565 217-774-2169
Russell Tomblin, prin. Fax 774-3042
Shelbyville K 100/K-K
1001 W North 6th St 62565 217-774-3926
Ryan Scott, prin. Fax 774-5836

Sheldon, Iroquois, Pop. 1,067
Milford Area SD 124
Supt. — See Milford
Milford East ES 50/PK-PK
150 S Randolph St 60966 815-429-3317
MIchelle Sobkoviak, prin. Fax 429-3458

Sheridan, LaSalle, Pop. 2,125
Serena CUSD 2
Supt. — See Serena
Sheridan ES 200/K-4
PO Box 328 60551 815-496-2002
Randy Goodbred, prin. Fax 496-9521

Sheridan SDA S 50/1-8
3904 E 2603rd Rd 60551 815-830-3308
Laura Damon, lead tchr.

Sherman, Sangamon, Pop. 4,106
Williamsville CUSD 15
Supt. — See Williamsville
Sherman ES 600/PK-4
312 South St 62684 217-496-2021
Janis Lindsey, prin. Fax 496-2473

Sherrard, Mercer, Pop. 637
Sherrard CUSD 200 1,600/PK-12
PO Box 369 61281 309-593-4075
Dr. Samuel Light, supt. Fax 593-4078
www.sherrard.us
Sherrard ES 200/K-4
209 1st St 61281 309-593-2917
Konnie Fry, prin. Fax 593-2409
Sherrard JHS 300/7-8
4701 176th Ave 61281 309-593-2135
Richard Basala, prin. Fax 593-2143
Other Schools – See Matherville, Viola

Shiloh, Saint Clair, Pop. 12,229
Shiloh Village SD 85 600/PK-8
125 Diamond Ct 62269 618-632-7434
Dale Sauer, supt. Fax 632-8343
www.shiloh.stclair.k12.il.us
Shiloh MS 300/5-8
1 Wildcat Xing 62269 618-632-7434
Darin Loepker, prin. Fax 622-9350
Shiloh Village S 300/PK-4
125 Diamond Ct 62269 618-632-7434
Tiana Montgomery, prin. Fax 632-8343

Shipman, Macoupin, Pop. 621
Southwestern CUSD 9
Supt. — See Brighton
Shipman ES 50/3-4
PO Box 229 62685 618-372-3813
Diane Milner, prin. Fax 836-7014

Shirland, Winnebago
Shirland CCSD 134 100/K-8
PO Box 99 61079 815-629-2000
Dr. John Ulferts, supt. Fax 629-2100
www.shirland134.org
Shirland ES 100/K-8
PO Box 99 61079 815-629-2000
Dr. John Ulferts, prin. Fax 629-2100

Shorewood, Will, Pop. 15,392
Minooka CCSD 201
Supt. — See Minooka
Walnut Trails ES 500/K-4
301 Wynstone Dr, 815-725-9360
Dr. Kathleen Cheshareck, prin. Fax 725-9366

Troy CCSD 30C
Supt. — See Plainfield
Troy Cronin ES 500/PK-4
210 E Black Rd, 815-577-7314
Jill Howard, prin. Fax 729-7441
Troy Hofer ES 500/K-4
910 Vertin Blvd, 815-577-6758
Kristin Copes, prin. Fax 267-8180
Troy Shorewood ES 500/PK-4
210 School Rd, 815-577-7312
Colleen Connolly, prin. Fax 729-7447

Holy Family S 300/PK-8
600 Brook Forest Ave, 815-725-8149
Anthony Simone, prin. Fax 725-8649

Trinity Christian S 600/PK-8
901 Shorewood Dr, 815-577-9310
Jon Vugteveen, admin. Fax 577-9695

Sidell, Vermilion, Pop. 607
Salt Fork CUSD 512
Supt. — See Catlin
Salt Fork JHS 100/6-8
7087 N 600 East Rd 61876 217-288-9306
Brian Allensworth, prin. Fax 288-9393
Salt Fork South ES 200/PK-5
7087 N 600 East Rd 61876 217-288-9306
Brian Allensworth, prin. Fax 288-9393

Sigel, Shelby, Pop. 373

St. Michael the Archangel S 100/K-8
PO Box 8 62462 217-844-2231
Nicholas Niemerg, prin. Fax 844-2323

Silvis, Rock Island, Pop. 7,322
Carbon Cliff-Barstow SD 36 300/PK-8
2002 Eagle Ridge Dr 61282 309-792-2002
Andy Richmond, supt. Fax 792-2244
www.ccb36.com
Eagle Ridge S 300/PK-8
2002 Eagle Ridge Dr 61282 309-792-2002
Ted Trueblood, prin. Fax 792-2244

East Moline SD 37
Supt. — See East Moline
Bowlesburg ES 400/K-4
2221 10th St 61282 309-792-2947
Jeff Fairweather, prin. Fax 792-9658

Silvis SD 34
Supt. — See East Moline
Barr ES, 1305 5th Ave 61282 400/PK-5
Michael Hughes, prin. 309-792-0639

Skokie, Cook, Pop. 62,756
East Prairie SD 73 500/PK-8
7634 E Prairie Rd 60076 847-673-1141
Theresa Madl, supt. Fax 324-4367
www.eps73.net
East Prairie S 500/PK-8
3907 Dobson St 60076 847-673-1141
Erin Stein, prin. Fax 673-1186

Evanston/Skokie SD 65
Supt. — See Evanston
Rhodes S of Global Studies 400/K-8
3701 Davis St 60076 847-859-8440
Lauren Norwood, prin. Fax 674-3926

Fairview SD 72 700/PK-8
7040 Laramie Ave 60077 847-929-1050
Dr. Cindy Whittaker, supt. Fax 929-1060
www.fairview.k12.il.us
Fairview South ES 700/PK-8
7040 Laramie Ave 60077 847-929-1048
Michael Lopatka, prin. Fax 929-1058

Skokie SD 68 1,800/PK-8
9440 Kenton Ave 60076 847-676-9000
Dr. James Garwood, supt. Fax 676-9232
www.skokie68.org
Devonshire ES 400/K-5
9040 Kostner Ave 60076 847-676-9280
Hal Schmeisser, prin. Fax 676-4031
Highland ES 400/K-5
9700 Crawford Ave 60076 847-676-9380
Dr. Karen Bradley, prin. Fax 676-4048
Old Orchard JHS 600/PK-PK, 6-
9310 Kenton Ave 60076 847-676-9010
Dr. Robyn Huemmer, prin. Fax 676-3827
Stenson ES 400/K-5
9201 Lockwood Ave 60077 847-676-9480
Susan O'Neil, prin. Fax 967-9386

Skokie SD 69 1,700/PK-8
5050 Madison St 60077 847-675-7666
Margaret Clauson, supt. Fax 675-7675
www.skokie69.net
Lincoln JHS 600/6-8
7839 Lincoln Ave 60077 847-676-3545
Lorenzo Cervantes, prin. Fax 676-3595
Madison ES 600/PK-2
5100 Madison St 60077 847-675-3048
Kristen Ulery, prin. Fax 675-1691
Other Schools – See Morton Grove

Skokie SD 73-5 1,000/PK-8
8000 E Prairie Rd 60076 847-324-0509
Kate Donegan, supt. Fax 673-1282
www.sd735.org
McCracken MS 300/6-8
8000 E Prairie Rd 60076 847-673-1220
Allison Stein, prin. Fax 673-1282
Meyer S 200/PK-K
8100 Tripp Ave 60076 847-673-1223
Dr. Alison Gordon, prin. Fax 933-4382
Middleton ES 500/1-5
8300 Saint Louis Ave 60076 847-673-1222
Courtney Goodman, prin. Fax 673-1256

Arie Crown Hebrew S 700/PK-8
4600 Main St 60076 847-982-9191
Rabbi Eli Samber, prin. Fax 982-9525
Cheder Lubavitch Boys Hebrew S 300/PK-8
5201 Howard St 60077 847-675-6777
Rabbi R. Zalman Twersky, prin. Fax 674-6095
Hillel Torah North Suburban Day S 400/PK-8
7120 Laramie Ave 60077 847-674-6533
Rabbi Menachem Linzer, prin. Fax 674-8313
Skokie Montessori S 50/PK-6
8401 North Karlov Avenue 60076 847-679-4614
Joji Arellano-Escanilla, prin. Fax 679-4815
Tzemach Tzedek S 50/PK-8
5130 Touhy Ave 60077 773-413-9770

Sleepy Hollow, Kane, Pop. 3,267
CUSD 300
Supt. — See Algonquin
Sleepy Hollow ES 500/K-5
898 Glen Oak Dr 60118 847-426-1460
Jason Lentz, prin. Fax 426-1290

Smithton, Saint Clair, Pop. 3,673
Smithton CCSD 130 500/PK-8
PO Box 395 62285 618-233-6863
Dr. Susan Homes, supt. Fax 233-8413
www.smithton.stclair.k12.il.us
Smithton ES 500/PK-8
PO Box 395 62285 618-233-6863
Vicki Norton, prin. Fax 233-8413

St. John the Baptist S 100/PK-8
10 S Lincoln St 62285 618-233-0581
Roy Monti, prin. Fax 937-2287

Somonauk, DeKalb, Pop. 1,867
Somonauk CUSD 432 800/PK-12
501 W Market St 60552 815-498-2314
Jay Streicher, supt. Fax 498-9523
www.somonauk.net
Somonauk MS 300/5-8
510 W Lasalle St 60552 815-498-1866
Justin Snider, prin. Fax 498-1647
Wood ES 300/PK-4
320 Maple St 60552 815-498-2338
Christine Pruski, prin. Fax 498-9361

Sorento, Bond, Pop. 494
Bond County CUSD 2
Supt. — See Greenville
Sorento S 200/PK-8
PO Box 68 62086 217-272-4111
Kara Carpenter, prin. Fax 272-4591

South Barrington, Cook, Pop. 4,448
Barrington CUSD 220
Supt. — See Barrington
Rose ES 500/K-5
61 W Penny Rd 60010 847-844-1200
Derek Straight, prin. Fax 844-1443

South Beloit, Winnebago, Pop. 7,705
Prairie Hill CCSD 133 800/PK-8
6605 Prairie Hill Rd 61080 815-389-3957
Wes Heiar, supt. Fax 389-6107
www.prairiehill.org
Prairie Hill ES 400/PK-4
14714 Willowbrook Rd 61080 815-389-3957
Kevin Finnegan, prin. Fax 389-8582
Willowbrook MS 400/5-8
6605 Prairie Hill Rd 61080 815-389-3957
Steve Heidel, prin. Fax 389-6107

South Beloit CUSD 320 1,000/PK-12
850 Hayes Ave 61080 815-389-3478
Scott Fisher, supt. Fax 389-3477
www.sbsobos.org/
Blackhawk ES 100/5-6
840 Blackhawk Blvd 61080 815-389-4001
Michael McCoy, prin. Fax 389-8811
Clark ES 200/PK-1
464 Oak Grove Ave 61080 815-389-2311
Eric Mowbray, prin. Fax 389-9002
Riverview ES 200/2-4
306 Miller St 61080 815-389-1231
Ryan Amendt, prin. Fax 389-9067
South Beloit JHS 200/7-8
840 Blackhawk Blvd 61080 815-389-1421
Michael McCoy, prin. Fax 389-8811

St. Peter S 50/PK-8
320 Elmwood Ave 61080 815-389-3193
Erica Schwartz, prin. Fax 389-2274

South Chicago Heights, Cook, Pop. 4,072
Chicago Heights SD 170
Supt. — See Chicago Heights
Grant S 300/K-8
2712 Miller Ave 60411 708-756-4156
Marco Pellillo, prin. Fax 756-4644

Steger SD 194
Supt. — See Steger
Steger Primary Center 100/PK-1
3341 Miller Ave 60411 708-753-4100
Stephanie Winborn, prin. Fax 753-1921

South Elgin, Kane, Pop. 21,549
SD U-46
Supt. — See Elgin
Clinton ES 500/K-6
770 Mill St 60177 847-888-7045
John Oliver, prin. Fax 608-2742
Fox Meadow ES 800/K-6
1275 Jenna Dr 60177 847-888-7182
Sjoukje Brown, prin. Fax 888-7194
Kenyon Woods MS 1,000/7-8
1515 Raymond St 60177 847-289-6685
Lisa Olsem, prin. Fax 628-6166
Willard ES 400/K-6
370 W Spring St 60177 847-888-5275
Julie Leston, prin. Fax 608-2755

Saint Charles CUSD 303
Supt. — See Saint Charles
Corron ES 500/K-5
455 Thornwood Way 60177 331-228-6900
Amanda Clark, prin. Fax 228-6903

South Holland, Cook, Pop. 21,729
Dolton SD 149
Supt. — See Calumet City
New Beginnings Learning Academy 400/K-6
15703 Clyde Ave 60473 708-768-5200
Karen Slate, prin. Fax 768-5209

South Holland SD 150 700/PK-8
848 E 170th St 60473 708-339-4240
Dr. Jerry Jordan, supt. Fax 339-4244
www.sd150.org
Greenwood ES 400/PK-3
16800 Greenwood Ave 60473 708-339-4433
William Kolloway, prin. Fax 339-3942
McKinley JHS 300/4-8
16949 Cottage Grove Ave 60473 708-339-8500
Jerome Ferrell, prin. Fax 331-5805

South Holland SD 151 1,500/PK-8
525 E 162nd St 60473 708-339-1516
Dr. Teresa D. Hill, supt. Fax 331-7600
www.shsd151.org
Eisenhower ES 300/2-3
16001 Minerva Ave 60473 708-339-5900
Dr. Rhonda Towner, prin. Fax 210-3252
Madison ES 300/4-5
15700 Orchid Dr 60473 708-339-2117
Jerald McNair, prin. Fax 210-3250
Other Schools – See Harvey, Phoenix

Apostolic Kingdom Christian Academy 100/PK-8
16511 S Park Ave 60473 708-331-8206
Fax 331-9842
Calvary Academy 300/K-8
16300 State St 60473 708-333-5471
Karen Pender, admin. Fax 333-5771
Calvin Christian S 200/PK-8
528 E 161st Pl 60473 708-331-5027
Randy Moes, prin. Fax 331-8728
Christ Our Savior S 200/PK-8
900 E 154th St 60473 708-333-8173
Karen Brodzik, prin. Fax 333-3247
Laren Montessori S 50/PK-K
425 E 164th St 60473 708-339-4274

South Jacksonville, Morgan, Pop. 3,290
Jacksonville SD 117
Supt. — See Jacksonville
South Jacksonville ES 400/K-6
1700 S West St, 217-245-5514
Kelly Zoellner, prin. Fax 245-2804

South Pekin, Tazewell, Pop. 1,134
South Pekin SD 137 200/PK-8
PO Box 430 61564 309-348-3695
Seth Mingus, supt. Fax 348-3162
www.spgs.net
South Pekin ES 200/PK-8
PO Box 430 61564 309-348-3695
Seth Mingus, prin. Fax 348-3162

South Roxana, Madison, Pop. 2,033
Roxana CUSD 1
Supt. — See Roxana
South PS 300/PK-2
414 Indiana Ave 62087 618-254-7591
Ryan Tusek, prin. Fax 254-7592

Bethel Christian Academy 100/PK-12
PO Box 87207 62087 618-254-0188
Tera Brasel, prin. Fax 254-2067

South Wilmington, Grundy, Pop. 680
South Wilmington CCSD 74 100/K-8
PO Box 459, 815-237-2281
Cynthia Christensen, supt. Fax 237-2713
South Wilmington Consolidated S 100/K-8
PO Box 459, 815-237-2281
Cynthia Christensen, admin. Fax 237-2713

Sparland, Marshall, Pop. 403
Midland CUSD 7 700/PK-12
901 Hilltop Dr 61565 309-469-2061
Bill Wrenn, supt. Fax 469-2063
midland-7.info
Midland MS 200/5-8
901 Hilltop Dr 61565 309-469-3131
Adam Janssen, prin. Fax 469-5701
Other Schools – See Lacon

Sparta, Randolph, Pop. 4,242
Sparta CUSD 140 900/PK-12
203B Dean Ave 62286 618-443-5331
Dr. Gabrielle Schwemmer, supt. Fax 443-2023
www.sparta.k12.il.us
Sparta Lincoln S 400/PK-8
203A Dean Ave 62286 618-443-5331
Amy Price, prin. Fax 443-2892
Other Schools – See Evansville

Springfield, Sangamon, Pop. 113,193
Springfield SD 186 14,900/PK-12
1900 W Monroe St 62704 217-525-3000
Jennifer Gill, supt. Fax 525-3005
www.sps186.org/
Addams ES 400/K-5
10 Babiak Ln 62702 217-787-3144
Michael Grossen, prin. Fax 535-2754
Black Hawk ES 300/K-5
2500 S College St 62704 217-525-3195
Terrance Jordan, prin. Fax 525-3168
Butler ES 400/K-5
1701 S MacArthur Blvd 62704 217-787-3189
Tracy Gage, prin. Fax 788-6250
Dell ES 200/K-5
850 W Lake Shore Dr, 217-525-3223
Jamar Scott, prin. Fax 525-3216
Dubois ES 500/K-5
120 S Lincoln Ave 62704 217-787-3066
Donna Jefferson, prin. Fax 788-6538
Early Learning Center 700/PK-PK
2501 S 1st St 62704 217-525-3163
Charlena Jackson, prin. Fax 525-7955
Enos ES 300/K-5
524 W Elliott Ave 62702 217-525-3208
Claudia Johnson, prin. Fax 525-3262
Fairview ES 300/K-5
2200 E Ridgely Ave 62702 217-525-3211
Patricia Nikson, prin. Fax 525-3286
Feitshans ES 500/PK-5
1101 S 15th St 62703 217-525-3030
Erica Filipiak, prin. Fax 525-3333
Franklin MS 800/6-8
1200 Outer Park Dr 62704 217-787-3006
Tod Davis, prin. Fax 525-7937
Graham ES 300/PK-5
900 W Edwards St 62704 217-525-3220
Steven Miller, prin. Fax 525-3348
Grant MS 600/6-8
1800 W Monroe St 62704 217-525-3170
Cindy Baugher, prin. Fax 525-3390
Harvard Park ES 500/PK-5
2501 S 11th St 62703 217-525-3214
James Hayes, prin. Fax 525-3280
Iles ES 500/1-8
1700 S 15th St 62703 217-525-3226
Kenyatta Revelle, prin. Fax 525-4408
Jefferson MS 600/6-8
3001 S Allis St 62703 217-585-5810
Karen Stapleton-Crump, prin. Fax 525-3293
Laketown ES 200/K-5
1825 Lee St 62703 217-585-5819
Renee Colwell, prin. Fax 525-3231
Lee S 200/PK-5
1201 Bunn Ave 62703 217-585-5828
Nathan Kochanowski, prin. Fax 535-2755
Lincoln Magnet MS 300/6-8
300 S 11th St 62703 217-525-3236
Nichole Heyen, prin. Fax 525-3294
Lindsay ES 500/K-5
3600 Fielding Dr, 217-546-0200
Jennifer Hanson, prin. Fax 747-5774
Marsh ES 300/PK-5
1100 Avon Dr 62704 217-525-3242
Kathy Wanless, prin. Fax 525-3360
Matheny-Withrow ES 300/K-5
1200 S Pope Ave 62703 217-525-3245
Kathy Hulcher, prin. Fax 525-3137
McClernand ES 300/K-5
801 N 6th St 62702 217-525-3247
Michelle Robertson, prin. Fax 525-7925
Ridgely ES 400/PK-5
2040 N 8th St 62702 217-525-3259
Ken Gilmore, prin. Fax 525-7932
Sandburg ES 300/K-5
2051 Wabash Ave 62704 217-787-3112
Keith Kincaid, prin. Fax 535-2759
Southern View ES 200/K-5
3338 S 5th St 62703 217-525-3267
Alicia Miller, prin. Fax 525-3268
Washington MS 700/6-8
2300 E Jackson St 62703 217-525-3182
Vincent Turner, prin. Fax 525-3319
Wilcox ES 300/K-5
2000 Hastings Rd 62702 217-525-3281
Douglas Goss, prin. Fax 525-3308

Blessed Sacrament S 400/K-8
748 W Laurel St 62704 217-522-7534
Kathy Wear, prin. Fax 522-7542
Calvary Academy 300/PK-12
1730 W Jefferson St 62702 217-546-5987
Cathedral Grade S 100/PK-8
815 S 6th St 62703 217-523-2652
Anthony Cerveny, prin. Fax 523-2750
Christ the King S 400/PK-8
1920 Barberry Dr 62704 217-546-2159
Pamela Fahey, prin. Fax 546-0291
Concordia Lutheran S 100/PK-8
2300 E Wilshire Rd 62703 217-529-3309
Janet Burmeister, prin. Fax 529-3096
Little Flower Catholic S 300/PK-8
900 Adlai Stevenson Dr 62703 217-529-4511
William Moredock, prin. Fax 529-0405
Montessori Children's House 100/PK-6
4147 Sandhill Rd 62702 217-544-7702
Suzanne Harris, dir. Fax 544-5502
Montessori Schoolhouse 100/PK-6
717 Rickard Rd 62704 217-787-5505
Nils Westholm, prin.
Our Savior's Lutheran S 200/PK-8
2645 Old Jacksonville Rd 62704 217-546-4531
Jill Gerberding, prin.
St. Agnes S 400/PK-8
251 N Amos Ave 62702 217-793-1370
Sr. Mary Joan Sorge, prin. Fax 793-1238
St. Aloysius S 200/PK-8
2125 N 21st St 62702 217-544-4553
Tom Weir, prin. Fax 544-1680
St. Patrick S 50/PK-5
1800 South Grand Ave E 62703 217-523-7670
Lori Loveless, prin. Fax 523-0760
Springfield Christian S 400/PK-8
2850 Cider Mill Ln 62702 217-698-1933
Jeremiah Auble, supt. Fax 698-1931
Trinity Lutheran S 200/PK-8
515 S MacArthur Blvd 62704 217-787-2323
Pamela Sausaman, prin. Fax 787-1145

Spring Grove, McHenry, Pop. 5,732
Fox Lake Grade SD 114 800/PK-8
29067 W Grass Lake Rd 60081 847-973-4114
Heather Friziellie, supt. Fax 973-4010
www.foxlake114.org
Lotus ES 500/PK-4
29067 W Grass Lake Rd 60081 847-973-4100
Matt Peters, prin. Fax 973-4110
Other Schools – See Fox Lake

Nippersink SD 2
Supt. — See Richmond
Spring Grove ES 300/PK-5
2018 Main Street Rd 60081 815-678-6750
Chris Pittman, prin. Fax 678-6760

Spring Grove Montessori S 50/PK-6
2014 Main Street Rd 60081 815-675-3338

Spring Valley, Bureau, Pop. 5,488
Spring Valley CCSD 99 600/PK-8
800 N Richards St 61362 815-664-4242
James Hermes, supt. Fax 664-2205
www.sv99.org
Kennedy S 600/PK-8
800 N Richards St 61362 815-664-4601
Kimberly Lisanby-Barber, prin. Fax 664-4213

Stanford, McLean, Pop. 590
Olympia CUSD 16 1,800/PK-12
903 E 800 North Rd 61774 309-379-6011
Dr. Andrew S. Wise, supt. Fax 379-2328
www.olympia.org
Olympia MS 400/6-8
911 E 800 North Rd 61774 309-379-5941
Andrew Walsh, prin. Fax 379-5411
Other Schools – See Atlanta, Danvers, Minier

Staunton, Macoupin, Pop. 5,081
Staunton CUSD 6 1,200/PK-12
801 N Deneen St 62088 618-635-2962
Dan Cox, supt. Fax 635-2994
www.stauntonschools.org
Staunton ES 500/PK-5
801 N Deneen St 62088 618-635-3831
Nancy Werden, prin. Fax 635-4637
Staunton JHS 300/6-8
801 N Deneen St 62088 618-635-3831
Nancy Werden, prin. Fax 635-4637

Zion Lutheran S 100/PK-8
220 W Henry St 62088 618-635-3060
David Manning, prin. Fax 635-3994

Steeleville, Randolph, Pop. 2,076
Steeleville CUSD 138 400/PK-12
609 S Sparta St 62288 618-965-3469
Dr. Stephanie Mulholland, supt. Fax 965-3433
www.steeleville138.org
Steeleville S 300/PK-8
609 S Sparta St 62288 618-965-3469
Dr. Stephanie Mulholland, prin. Fax 965-3433

St. Mark's Lutheran S 100/PK-8
504 N James St 62288 618-965-3838
Larry Luedders, prin. Fax 965-3060

Steger, Will, Pop. 9,382
Steger SD 194 800/PK-8
3753 Park Ave 60475 708-755-0022
Dr. Patricia Hahto, supt. Fax 755-9512
www.sd194.org
Columbia Central MS 500/5-8
94 Richton Rd 60475 708-755-0021
Mike Smith, prin. Fax 755-1877
Steger Intermediate Center 200/2-4
3411 Hopkins 60475 708-753-4200
Janet Inglese, prin. Fax 755-1884
Other Schools – See South Chicago Heights

Sterling, Whiteside, Pop. 15,098
Sterling CUSD 5 3,300/PK-12
410 E Le Fevre Rd 61081 815-626-5050
Tad Everett, supt. Fax 622-4113
www.sterlingpublicschools.org
Challand MS 700/6-8
1700 6th Ave 61081 815-626-3300
Matt Birdsley, prin. Fax 622-4173
Franklin ES 400/PK-2
1510 E 25th St 61081 815-625-5755
Amy Springman, prin. Fax 622-4187
Jefferson ES 400/K-2
806 E Le Fevre Rd 61081 815-625-6402
Heather Wittenauer, prin. Fax 622-4191
Lincoln ES 300/3-5
1501 E 6th St 61081 815-625-1449
Cindy Frank, prin. Fax 622-4196
Washington ES 400/3-5
815 W Le Fevre Rd 61081 815-625-2372
Lindsy Stumpenhorst, prin. Fax 622-4199

Christ Lutheran S 200/PK-8
2000 18th Ave 61081 815-625-3800
Brandi Spreeman, prin. Fax 625-3585
St. Mary S 200/PK-8
6 W 6th St 61081 815-625-2253
Rebecca Schmitt, prin. Fax 625-8942

Steward, Lee, Pop. 255
Steward ESD 220 100/K-8
PO Box 76 60553 815-396-2413
Lowell Taylor, supt. Fax 396-2407
www.stewardschool220.org
Steward ES 100/K-8
PO Box 76 60553 815-396-2413
Lowell Taylor, supt. Fax 396-2407

Stewardson, Shelby, Pop. 732

Trinity Lutheran S 100/PK-8
PO Box 307 62463 217-682-3881
Kent Rincker, prin. Fax 682-3881

Stickney, Cook, Pop. 6,725
Lyons SD 103
Supt. — See Lyons
Edison ES 300/K-5
4100 Scoville Ave 60402 708-783-4400
Dr. Janice Bernard, prin. Fax 780-0035
Home ES 200/K-5
4400 Home Ave 60402 708-783-4500
Kim Ontiveros, prin. Fax 780-0041

Stillman Valley, Ogle, Pop. 1,114
Meridian CUSD 223 1,800/PK-12
207 W Main St 61084 815-645-2230
Dr. Phillip Caposey, supt. Fax 645-4325
www.meridian223.org
Highland ES 400/PK-2
410 S Hickory St 61084 815-645-2230
Mike Coulahan, prin. Fax 645-8200
Meridian JHS 400/6-8
207 W Main St 61084 815-645-2230
Jill Davis, prin. Fax 645-8181
Other Schools – See Monroe Center

Stockton, Jo Daviess, Pop. 1,848
Stockton CUSD 206 600/PK-12
540 N Rush St 61085 815-947-3391
Dr. David Gilliland, supt. Fax 947-2673
www.stocktonschools.com
Stockton ES 300/PK-4
236 N Pearl St 61085 815-947-3321
Colleen Fox, prin. Fax 947-3055
Stockton MS 200/5-8
500 N Rush St 61085 815-947-3702
Brad Fox, prin. Fax 947-2114

Stone Park, Cook, Pop. 4,913
Bellwood SD 88
Supt. — See Bellwood
ECC 200/PK-K
1801 N 36th Ave 60165 708-544-2815
Judith Arman, prin. Fax 544-0062

Stonington, Christian, Pop. 930
Taylorville CUSD 3
Supt. — See Taylorville
Stonington ES 300/PK-4
500 E North 62567 217-325-3216
Anita Brown, prin. Fax 325-3783

Strasburg, Shelby, Pop. 465
Stewardson-Strasburg CUSD 5A 300/PK-12
2806 E 600 North Rd 62465 217-682-3355
Dr. Michele Lindenmeyer, supt. Fax 682-3305
www.stew-stras.org
Stewardson-Strasburg ES 200/PK-8
2806 E 600 North Rd 62465 217-682-3621
Justin Deters, prin. Fax 682-3305

Streamwood, Cook, Pop. 39,124
SD U-46
Supt. — See Elgin
Canton MS 600/7-8
1100 Sunset Cir 60107 630-213-5525
Jeff Smith, prin. Fax 213-5709
Glenbrook ES 500/K-6
315 Garden Cir 60107 630-213-5555
Cheryl DeRoo, prin. Fax 213-5548
Hanover Countryside ES 500/K-6
6 S Bartlett Rd 60107 630-213-5560
Jack Shepherd, prin. Fax 213-6133
Heritage ES 500/K-6
507 Arnold Ave 60107 630-213-5565
Catherine Fletcher, prin. Fax 213-5549
Oakhill ES 500/K-6
502 S Oltendorf Rd 60107 630-213-5585
Laura Alegria, prin. Fax 213-5573
Ridge Circle ES 500/K-6
420 Ridge Cir 60107 630-213-5600
Janelle Raine, prin. Fax 213-9407
Sunnydale ES 400/K-6
716 Sunnydale Blvd 60107 630-213-5610
Maria Valdovinos-Bhatia, prin. Fax 213-5594
Tefft MS 900/7-8
1100 Shirley Ave 60107 630-213-5535
Luis Fernando DeLeon, prin. Fax 213-5646

St. John the Evangelist S 200/PK-8
513 Parkside Cir 60107 630-289-3040
Mary Billmeyer, prin. Fax 289-3026

Streator, LaSalle, Pop. 13,509
Streator ESD 44 1,800/PK-8
1520 N Bloomington St 61364 815-672-2926
Dr. Matthew Wilkinson, supt. Fax 673-2032
www.ses44.net
Centennial ES 400/2-4
614 Oakley Ave 61364 815-672-2747
Anne McDonnell, prin. Fax 672-0594
Kimes ES 300/PK-1
1207 Reading St 61364 815-672-2496
Laura Dawson, prin. Fax 672-1344
Northlawn JHS 800/5-8
202 E 1st St 61364 815-672-4558
Gail Russell, prin. Fax 672-8109

Woodland CUSD 5 500/PK-12
5800 E 3000 North Rd 61364 815-672-5974
Ryan McGuckin, supt. Fax 673-1630
www.woodland5.com
Woodland ES 400/PK-8
5800 E 3000 North Rd 61364 815-672-2909
Jodi Peterson, prin.

St. Michael the Archangel-Streator 100/PK-8
410 S Park St 61364 815-672-3847
Emily Blumenshine, prin. Fax 673-3590

Stronghurst, Henderson, Pop. 875
West Central CUSD 235
Supt. — See Biggsville
West Central MS 200/6-8
PO Box 179 61480 309-924-1681
Julia Burns, prin. Fax 924-1122

Sugar Grove, Kane, Pop. 8,881
Kaneland CUSD 302
Supt. — See Maple Park
Harter MS 1,100/6-8
1601 N Esker Dr 60554 630-466-8400
Brian Faulkner, prin. Fax 466-1999

Shields ES 600/PK-5
85 S Main St 60554 630-466-8500
Shelley Hueber, prin. Fax 466-5320

Sullivan, Moultrie, Pop. 4,417
Sullivan CUSD 300 1,100/PK-12
725 N Main St 61951 217-728-8341
Ted Walk, supt. Fax 728-4139
home.sullivan.k12.il.us
Sullivan ES 500/PK-5
910 N Graham St 61951 217-728-2321
Daniel Allen, prin. Fax 728-4399
Sullivan MS 200/6-8
713 N Main St 61951 217-728-8381
Ted Walk, prin. Fax 728-4139

Summit, Cook
Summit SD 104 1,900/PK-8
6021 S 74th Ave 60501 708-458-0505
Dr. Troy J. Whalen, supt. Fax 458-0532
www.sd104.us
Graves ES 500/PK-4
6021 S 74th Ave 60501 708-458-7260
Hope Durkin, prin. Fax 728-3111
Heritage MS 500/6-8
6021 S 74th Ave 60501 708-458-7590
Robert Bassett, prin. Fax 728-3111
Walsh ES 400/K-4
5640 S 75th Ave 60501 708-458-7165
Christine Smith, prin. Fax 458-7532
Wharton Fifth Grade Center 200/5-5
7555 W 64th St 60501 708-458-0640
Carol Brackins, prin. Fax 458-8467
Other Schools – See Bedford Park

St. Joseph S 200/PK-8
5641 S 73rd Ave 60501 708-458-2927
Lawrence Manetti, prin. Fax 458-9750

Sumner, Lawrence, Pop. 3,166
Red Hill CUSD 10
Supt. — See Bridgeport
Sumner Attendance Center 200/4-6
110 W Locust St 62466 618-936-2412
Todd Tiffany, prin. Fax 936-2742

Swansea, Saint Clair, Pop. 13,123
High Mount SD 116 400/PK-8
1721 Boul Ave 62226 618-233-1054
Mark Halwachs, supt. Fax 233-1136
www.highmountschool.com
High Mount ES 400/PK-8
1721 Boul Ave 62226 618-233-1054
Darin Loepker, prin. Fax 233-1136

Wolf Branch SD 113 900/K-8
410 Huntwood Rd 62226 618-277-2100
Scott Harres, supt. Fax 235-2376
www.wbsd113.org
Wolf Branch ES 400/K-4
125 Huntwood Rd 62226 618-277-2100
Madonna Harris, prin. Fax 277-9786
Wolf Branch MS 400/5-8
410 Huntwood Rd 62226 618-277-2100
Jennifer Poirot, prin. Fax 277-5461

Sycamore, DeKalb, Pop. 17,257
Sycamore CUSD 427 3,700/PK-12
245 W Exchange St Ste 1 60178 815-899-8100
Kathy Countryman, supt. Fax 899-8110
www.syc427.org
North ES 300/K-5
1680 Brickville Rd 60178 815-899-8209
K. Spiewak, prin. Fax 899-8213
North Grove ES 500/K-5
850 Republic Ave 60178 815-899-8124
Ryan Janisch, prin. Fax 899-8114
Southeast ES 300/K-5
718 S Locust St 60178 815-899-8219
Mark Ekstrom, prin. Fax 899-8221
South Prairie ES 300/PK-5
820 Borden Ave 60178 815-899-8299
Kreg Welsey, prin. Fax 899-8292
Sycamore MS 900/6-8
150 Maplewood Dr 60178 815-899-8170
Jim Cleven, prin. Fax 899-8177
West ES 300/K-5
240 S Fair St 60178 815-899-8199
Kristina Crawford, prin. Fax 899-8195

Cornerstone Christian Academy 300/PK-12
355 N Cross St 60178 815-895-8522
Kevin White, admin. Fax 895-8717
St. Mary S 200/PK-8
222 Waterman St 60178 815-895-5215
Jan Benson, prin. Fax 895-5295

Table Grove, Fulton, Pop. 410
V I T CUSD 2 400/PK-12
1502 E US Highway 136 61482 309-758-5138
K. Scot Reynolds, supt. Fax 758-5298
www.vit2.org
V I T ES 200/PK-5
1502 E US Highway 136 61482 309-758-5138
Matt Klaska, prin. Fax 758-5298
V I T JHS 50/6-8
1500 E US Highway 136 61482 309-758-5136
Tracey Korsmeyer, prin. Fax 758-5126

Tamaroa, Perry, Pop. 635
Tamaroa SD 5 100/K-8
PO Box 175 62888 618-496-5513
Phillip R. Hamil, supt. Fax 496-3911
tgs5.com
Tamaroa ES 100/K-8
PO Box 175 62888 618-496-5513
Phillip R. Hamil, supt. Fax 496-3911

Tamms, Alexander, Pop. 620
Egyptian CUSD 5 500/PK-12
20023 Diswood Rd 62988 618-776-5306
Brad Misner, supt. Fax 776-5122
www.egyptianschool.com
Egyptian ES 300/PK-5
20023 Diswood Rd 62988 618-776-5251
Bret Gowin, prin. Fax 776-5122
Egyptian JHS 100/6-8
20023 Diswood Rd 62988 618-776-5251
Bret Gowin, prin. Fax 776-5122

Tampico, Whiteside, Pop. 788
Prophetstown-Lyndon-Tampico CUSD 3
Supt. — See Prophetstown
Tampico ES 200/PK-5
PO Box 637 61283 815-438-2255
Jim Geer, prin. Fax 438-5010

Taylor Ridge, Rock Island
Rockridge CUSD 300 1,100/PK-12
14110 134th Ave W 61284 309-793-8001
Perry Miller, supt. Fax 795-1719
rockridgeschools.org
Rockridge JHS 300/6-8
14110 134th Ave W 61284 309-793-8040
Katy Hasson, prin. Fax 795-9823
Taylor Ridge ES 100/K-2
13227 Turkey Hollow Rd 61284 309-793-8070
Sarah Leonard, prin. Fax 798-5523
Other Schools – See Andalusia, Illinois City

Taylorville, Christian, Pop. 11,116
Taylorville CUSD 3 2,600/PK-12
512 W Spresser St 62568 217-824-4951
Dr. Greggory Fuerstenau, supt. Fax 824-5157
www.taylorvilleschools.com
Central Preschool PK-PK
515 E Bidwell St 62568 217-287-7870
Brandi Bruley, prin. Fax 287-7259
Memorial ES 300/3-4
101 E Adams St 62568 217-287-7929
Nancy Ganci, prin. Fax 287-7696
North ES 400/PK-2
805 N Cherokee St 62568 217-824-3315
Brandi Bruley, prin. Fax 824-5949
Taylorville JHS 800/5-8
120 E Bidwell St 62568 217-824-4924
Kirk Kettelkamp, prin. Fax 824-7180
Other Schools – See Stonington

St. Mary S 100/PK-6
422 S Washington St 62568 217-824-6501
Cathy Robertson, prin. Fax 824-2803
VisionWay Christian S 200/PK-8
1124 N Webster St 62568 217-824-6722
Glenna Tolliver, prin. Fax 824-6622

Teutopolis, Effingham, Pop. 1,530
Teutopolis CUSD 50 1,100/PK-12
PO Box 607 62467 217-857-3535
William Fritcher, supt. Fax 857-6265
www.teutopolisschools.org/
Teutopolis ES 500/PK-6
309 E Main St 62467 217-857-3232
Angie Sheehan, prin. Fax 857-6609
Teutopolis JHS 200/7-8
904 W Water St 62467 217-857-6678
Patrick Drees, prin. Fax 857-6051

Texico, Jefferson
Field CCSD 3 300/PK-8
21075 N Hails Ln 62889 618-755-4611
Gina Ilbery, supt. Fax 755-9701
www.fieldpanthers.com
Field S 300/PK-8
21075 N Hails Ln 62889 618-755-4611
Wayne Stone, prin. Fax 755-9701

Thawville, Iroquois, Pop. 235
Iroquois West CUSD 10
Supt. — See Gilman
Iroquois West Upper ES 200/4-5
PO Box 99 60968 217-387-2291
Christina Duncan, prin. Fax 387-2205

Thomasboro, Champaign, Pop. 1,098
Prairieview-Ogden CCSD 197
Supt. — See Royal
Prairieview-Ogden JHS 100/7-8
2499 County Road 2100 E 61878 217-694-4122
Steve Fiscus, prin. Fax 694-4123

Thomasboro CCSD 130 200/PK-8
201 N Phillips St 61878 217-643-3275
Bonnie McArthur, supt. Fax 643-2022
www.thomasboro.k12.il.us
Thomasboro ES 200/PK-8
201 N Phillips St 61878 217-643-3275
Elizabeth Acton, prin. Fax 643-2022

Thompsonville, Franklin, Pop. 542
Thompsonville CUSD 174 300/K-12
21191 Shawneetown Rd 62890 618-627-2446
Chris Grant, supt. Fax 627-2302
thompsonville.il.schoolwebpages.com/
Thompsonville Grade S 200/K-8
21191 Shawneetown Rd 62890 618-627-2511
Chris Grant, prin. Fax 627-2302

Thompsonville Christian Junior Academy 50/1-10
PO Box 53 62890 618-627-2065
Evelyn Hainey, prin. Fax 627-2065

Thornton, Cook, Pop. 2,283
Thornton SD 154 200/K-8
200 N Wolcott St 60476 708-877-5160
Dr. Thomas Hurlburt, supt. Fax 877-2537
www.wolcottschool.com
Wolcott S 200/K-8
200 N Wolcott St 60476 708-877-2526
Dr. Thomas Hurlburt, prin. Fax 877-2537

Tinley Park, Cook, Pop. 56,069
Arbor Park SD 145
Supt. — See Oak Forest
Kimberly Heights K 200/PK-K
6141 Kimberly Dr 60477 708-532-6434
Eliza Lopez, prin. Fax 532-4495

CCSD 146 2,400/PK-8
6611 171st St 60477 708-614-4500
Dr. Jeff Stawick, supt. Fax 614-8992
www.district146.org
Central MS 700/6-8
18146 Oak Park Ave 60477 708-614-4510
Randy Fortin, prin. Fax 614-7271
Fulton ES, 6601 171st St 60477 600/PK-5
Ron Gonser, prin. 708-614-4525
Memorial ES 400/PK-5
6701 179th St 60477 708-614-4535
Kelly Voliva, prin. Fax 614-7501
Other Schools – See Oak Forest, Orland Park

Kirby SD 140 3,600/PK-8
16931 Grissom Dr 60477 708-532-6462
Julia Mikulich, supt. Fax 532-1512
www.ksd140.org
Bannes ES 400/K-5
16835 Odell Ave 60477 708-532-6466
Terrance Kowalski, prin. Fax 532-8530
Grissom MS 600/6-8
17000 80th Ave 60477 708-429-3030
Deborah Broadwell, prin. Fax 532-8529
Keller ES 400/PK-5
7846 163rd St 60477 708-532-2144
JoAnn Greene, prin. Fax 532-8531
McAuliffe ES 500/PK-5
8944 174th St, 708-429-4565
Annette Szczasny, prin. Fax 532-8533
Millennium ES 600/PK-5
17830 84th Ave, 708-532-3150
Mary Jo Werbiansky, prin. Fax 614-2376
Prairie View MS 600/6-8
8500 175th St, 708-532-8540
Meghan Maurer, prin. Fax 532-8544
Other Schools – See Orland Park

Summit Hill SD 161
Supt. — See Frankfort
Walker IS 700/5-6
19900 80th Ave, 815-464-2285
Laura Goebel, prin. Fax 464-2160

St. George S 300/PK-8
6700 176th St 60477 708-532-2626
Charlotte Pratl, prin. Fax 532-2025
Southwest Chicago Christian S 400/K-8
17171 84th Ave 60477 708-429-7171
Terry Huizenga, prin. Fax 429-7210
Trinity Lutheran S 300/PK-8
6850 159th St 60477 708-532-3529
Gerard Gliege, prin. Fax 532-0799

Toledo, Cumberland, Pop. 1,235
Cumberland CUSD 77 1,000/PK-12
1496 Illinois Route 121 62468 217-923-3132
Todd Butler, supt. Fax 923-3132
www.cumberland.k12.il.us
Cumberland ES 500/PK-4
1496 Illinois Route 121 62468 217-923-3135
Daniel Huffman, prin. Fax 923-5449
Cumberland MS 300/5-8
1496 Illinois Route 121 62468 217-923-3135
Stacy Keyser, prin. Fax 923-5449

Tolono, Champaign, Pop. 3,389
Tolono CUSD 7 1,700/PK-12
PO Box 720 61880 217-485-6510
Andrew Larson, supt. Fax 485-3091
www.unitsevenschools.com
Unity JHS 400/6-8
1121 County Road 800 N 61880 217-485-6735
Laura Fitzgerald, prin. Fax 485-3218
Unity West ES 500/PK-5
1035 County Road 600 N 61880 217-485-3918
Lanee Reichert, prin. Fax 485-3451
Other Schools – See Philo

Toluca, Marshall, Pop. 1,401
Fieldcrest CUSD 6
Supt. — See Minonk
Fieldcrest IS 300/3-5
306 N Maple St 61369 815-452-2318
Molly Allen, prin. Fax 452-2411

Tonica, LaSalle, Pop. 766
Tonica CCSD 79 200/K-8
535 N 1981st Rd 61370 815-442-3420
Charles Schneider, supt. Fax 442-3111
www.tonicagradeschool.org
Tonica ES 200/K-8
535 N 1981st Rd 61370 815-442-3420
Charles Schneider, prin. Fax 442-3111

Toulon, Stark, Pop. 1,289
Stark County CUSD 100
Supt. — See Wyoming
Stark County JHS, PO Box 659 61483 200/6-8
William Lamb, prin. 309-286-3451

Towanda, McLean, Pop. 475
McLean County Unit SD 5
Supt. — See Normal
Towanda ES 200/K-5
PO Box 260 61776 309-557-4426
Scott Vogel, prin. Fax 557-4527

Tremont, Tazewell, Pop. 2,212
Tremont CUSD 702 1,000/PK-12
400 W Pearl St 61568 309-925-3461
Jeff Hinman, supt. Fax 925-5817
www.tremont702.net
Tremont ES 300/PK-4
PO Box 1208 61568 309-925-4841
Becky Hansen, prin. Fax 925-3849
Tremont MS 300/5-8
400 W Pearl St 61568 309-925-3823
Jeremy Garrett, prin. Fax 925-5817

Trenton, Clinton, Pop. 2,693
Wesclin CUSD 3 1,100/PK-12
699 Wesclin Rd 62293 618-224-7583
Jennifer Filyaw, supt. Fax 588-9106
www.wesclin.org
Trenton ES 200/PK-3
308 N Washington St 62293 618-224-9411
Angela Woll, prin. Fax 224-9417
Wesclin MS 200/4-8
10003 State Route 160 62293 618-224-7355
Roger Freeze, prin. Fax 224-7085
Other Schools – See New Baden

Troy, Madison, Pop. 9,707
Triad CUSD 2 3,600/PK-12
203 E Throp St 62294 618-667-5400
Leigh Lewis, supt. Fax 667-8854
www.tcusd2.org
Henning ES 700/PK-5
520 E US Highway 40 62294 618-667-5401
Kay Burrough, prin. Fax 667-5565
Silver Creek ES 600/K-5
209 N Dewey St 62294 618-667-5403
Sandra Padak, prin. Fax 667-5564
Other Schools – See Marine, Saint Jacob

St. Paul Lutheran S 100/PK-8
112 N Border St 62294 618-667-6314
Christopher Lingel, dir. Fax 667-8098

Tunnel Hill, Johnson
New Simpson Hill SD 32 200/PK-8
95 Tunnel Hill Rd, 618-658-8536
Joe Nighswander, supt. Fax 658-5034
newsimpsonhill.com
New Simpson Hill ES 200/PK-8
95 Tunnel Hill Rd, 618-658-8536
Eric Witges, prin. Fax 658-5034

Tuscola, Douglas, Pop. 4,425
Tuscola CUSD 301 1,000/PK-12
409 S Prairie St 61953 217-253-4241
Michael Smith, supt. Fax 253-4522
www.tuscola.k12.il.us/
East Prairie JHS 300/5-8
409 S Prairie St 61953 217-253-2828
Carol Munson, prin. Fax 253-3236
North Ward ES 400/PK-4
1201 N Prairie St 61953 217-253-2712
Jason Wallace, prin. Fax 253-4851

Ullin, Pulaski, Pop. 448
Century CUSD 100 400/K-12
4721 Shawnee College Rd 62992 618-845-3447
Landon Sommer, supt. Fax 845-3476
www.centuryschooldistrict100.com
Century ES 200/K-5
4819 Shawnee College Rd 62992 618-845-3572
Melinda Duke, prin. Fax 845-3586

University Park, Will, Pop. 6,997
Crete-Monee CUSD 201U
Supt. — See Crete
Crete-Monee MS 800/6-8
635 Olmstead Ln, 708-367-2400
Kokona Chrisos, prin. Fax 672-2777
King Magnet ES 300/K-5
1009 Blackhawk Dr, 708-367-4700
Byron Mane, prin. Fax 672-2621

Urbana, Champaign, Pop. 39,989
Urbana SD 116 4,300/PK-12
PO Box 3039 61803 217-384-3636
Dr. Donald Owen Ed.D., supt. Fax 337-4973
www.usd116.org
King ES 300/K-5
1108 Fairview Ave 61801 217-384-3675
Christina Lewandowski, prin. Fax 344-5610
Leal ES 400/K-5
312 W Oregon St 61801 217-384-3618
Spencer Landsman, prin. Fax 384-3622
Paine ES 300/K-5
1801 James Cherry Dr 61802 217-384-3602
Delores Lloyd, prin. Fax 344-1835
Urbana Early Childhood S 300/PK-PK
2202 E Washington St 61802 217-384-3616
Crystal Vowels, prin. Fax 384-3615
Urbana MS 900/6-8
1201 S Vine St 61801 217-384-3685
Scott Woods, prin. Fax 367-3156
Wiley ES 300/K-5
1602 S Anderson St 61801 217-384-3670
Candace Gwin, prin. Fax 384-3559
Williams ES 400/K-5
2102 E Washington St 61802 217-384-3628
Danielle Jackson, prin. Fax 384-3626
Yankee Ridge ES 300/K-5
2102 S Anderson St 61801 217-384-3608
Brian Anderson, prin. Fax 384-3611

Kingswood S 50/K-12
PO Box 834 61803 217-344-5540
Marsh Jones, hdmstr. Fax 344-5535

Utica, LaSalle, Pop. 1,346
Waltham Community CESD 185 200/K-8
946 N 33rd Rd 61373 815-667-4790
Kristine Eager, supt. Fax 667-4462
www.wesd185.org
Waltham North S 200/3-8
946 N 33rd Rd 61373 815-667-4417
Kristine Eager, admin. Fax 667-4462

Waltham South S — K-2
248 W Canal St 61373 — 815-667-4790
Kristine Eager, admin. — Fax 667-9889

Valmeyer, Monroe, Pop. 1,250
Valmeyer CUSD 3 — 500/PK-12
300 S Cedar Bluff Dr 62295 — 618-935-2100
Eric Frankford, supt. — Fax 935-2108
www.valmeyerk12.org
Valmeyer ES — 300/PK-5
300 S Cedar Bluff Dr 62295 — 618-935-2100
Teena Riechmann, prin. — Fax 935-2108
Valmeyer JHS — 100/6-8
300 S Cedar Bluff Dr 62295 — 618-939-2100
Teena Riechmann, prin. — Fax 939-2108

Vandalia, Fayette, Pop. 6,969
Vandalia CUSD 203 — 1,100/PK-12
1109 N 8th St 62471 — 618-283-4525
Rich Well, supt. — Fax 283-4107
www.vandals203.org
Vandalia ES — 200/PK-3
1017 W Fletcher St 62471 — 618-283-5166
Stacy Mesnard, prin. — Fax 283-9479
Vandalia JHS — 500/4-8
1011 W Fletcher St 62471 — 618-283-5151
Brian Kern, prin. — Fax 283-8165

Van Orin, Bureau
La Moille CUSD 303
Supt. — See La Moille
Van Orin ES — 100/K-3
PO Box 7 61374 — 815-638-3141
Chawn Huffaker, prin. — Fax 638-3242

Venice, Madison, Pop. 1,866
Venice CUSD 3 — 100/K-8
300 4th St 62090 — 618-274-7953
Dr. Cullen Cullen, supt. — Fax 274-7953
www.veniceschools.org/
Venice ES — 100/K-8
300 4th St 62090 — 618-274-7953
Dr. Cullen Cullen, prin. — Fax 274-7953

Vergennes, Jackson, Pop. 291
Elverado CUSD 196
Supt. — See Elkville
Elverado IS — 100/3-5
PO Box 35 62994 — 618-684-3527
Belinda Conner, prin. — Fax 687-3363
Elverado JHS — 100/6-8
PO Box 35 62994 — 618-684-3527
Belinda Conner, prin. — Fax 687-3363

Vernon Hills, Lake, Pop. 24,688
Hawthorn CCSD 73 — 4,000/K-8
841 W End Ct 60061 — 847-990-4200
Nicholas Brown, supt. — Fax 367-3290
www.hawthorn73.org
Hawthorn Aspen ES — 400/K-5
500 N Aspen Dr 60061 — 847-990-4300
Bill Fredricksen, prin. — Fax 816-6931
Hawthorn ES North — 400/K-5
301 W Hawthorn Pkwy 60061 — 847-990-4500
Kathryn Waggoner, prin. — Fax 367-3297
Hawthorn ES South — 700/K-5
430 N Aspen Dr 60061 — 847-990-4800
Dr. Jill Martin, prin. — Fax 918-9251
Hawthorn MS North — 600/6-8
201 W Hawthorn Pkwy 60061 — 847-990-4400
Robert Collins, prin. — Fax 367-8124
Hawthorn MS South — 700/6-8
600 N Aspen Dr 60061 — 847-990-4100
Robert Natale, prin. — Fax 816-9259
Hawthorn S of Dual Language — 400/K-5
810 N Aspen Dr 60061 — 847-990-4900
Dr. James Tohme, prin. — Fax 990-4999
Hawthorn Townline ES — 600/K-5
810 N Aspen Dr 60061 — 847-990-4901
Dr. Victoria Kieffer, prin. — Fax 990-4999

Vienna, Johnson, Pop. 1,414
Vienna SD 55 — 500/PK-8
PO Box 427 62995 — 618-658-8638
Greg Frehner, supt. — Fax 658-9036
www.viennagradeschool.com/
Vienna S — 500/PK-8
PO Box 427 62995 — 618-658-8286
Greg Frehner, supt. — Fax 658-9036

Villa Grove, Douglas, Pop. 2,492
Villa Grove CUSD 302 — 600/PK-12
400 N Sycamore St 61956 — 217-832-2261
Norm Tracy, supt. — Fax 832-8615
www.vg302.org
Villa Grove ES — 400/PK-6
400 N Sycamore St 61956 — 217-832-2261
Sara Jones, prin. — Fax 832-8615
Villa Grove JHS — 100/7-8
400 N Sycamore St 61956 — 217-832-2261
Sara Jones, prin. — Fax 832-8615

Villa Park, DuPage, Pop. 21,596
DuPage County SD 45 — 3,400/PK-8
255 W Vermont St 60181 — 630-516-7700
Dr. Anthony Palmisano, supt. — Fax 530-1624
www.d45.org
Ardmore ES — 500/K-5
225 S Harvard Ave 60181 — 630-516-7370
Regina Leeberg, prin. — Fax 530-3660
Jackson MS — 700/6-8
301 W Jackson St 60181 — 630-516-7600
Jill Amrhein, prin. — Fax 530-6271
Jefferson MS — 400/6-8
255 W Vermont St 60181 — 630-516-7800
Raul Gaston, prin. — Fax 993-6348
North ES — 400/K-5
150 W Sunset Ave 60181 — 630-516-7776
Fred Leinweber, prin. — Fax 530-1385
Other Schools – See Lombard

Salt Creek SD 48 — 500/PK-8
1110 S Villa Ave 60181 — 630-279-8400
Dr. John Correll, supt. — Fax 279-6167
www.saltcreek48.org
Albright MS — 200/5-8
1110 S Villa Ave 60181 — 630-279-6160
Scott Jackson, prin. — Fax 279-1614
Other Schools – See Elmhurst, Oakbrook Terrace

Islamic Foundation S — 700/PK-12
300 W Highridge Rd 60181 — 630-941-8800
Khalida Baste, prin. — Fax 941-0114
St. Paul Christian Day Care & K — 50/PK-K
545 S Ardmore Ave 60181 — 630-832-0420
Fax 832-7656
Seton Academy — 50/PK-5
350 N Westmore Ave 60181 — 630-279-4101
Mary Thornton, prin.

Viola, Mercer, Pop. 949
Sherrard CUSD 200
Supt. — See Sherrard
Winola ES — 300/PK-4
1804 17th Ave 61486 — 309-596-2114
Kari Roberts, prin. — Fax 596-2979

Virden, Macoupin, Pop. 3,404
North Mac CUSD 34
Supt. — See Girard
North Mac ES — 200/PK-2
755 W Fortune St 62690 — 217-965-5424
Michele Cimarossa, prin. — Fax 965-4342

Virginia, Cass, Pop. 1,600
Virginia CUSD 64 — 200/PK-12
651 S Morgan St 62691 — 217-452-3085
Gary DePatis, supt. — Fax 452-3088
virginia64.com
Virginia ES — 200/PK-5
651 S Morgan St 62691 — 217-452-3363
Kara Bowman, prin. — Fax 452-3088

Wadsworth, Lake, Pop. 3,763
Beach Park CCSD 3
Supt. — See Beach Park
Newport ES — 300/K-5
15872 W 21st St 60083 — 847-599-5330
Shaton Wolverton, prin. — Fax 599-0893

Gurnee SD 56
Supt. — See Gurnee
Prairie Trail ES — 500/3-5
13600 W Wadsworth Rd 60083 — 847-623-4333
Kevin Simmons, prin. — Fax 623-4456

Millburn CCSD 24 — 1,400/PK-8
18550 W Millburn Rd 60083 — 847-356-8331
Dr. Jason Lind, supt. — Fax 356-9722
www.millburn24.net/
Millburn ES — 900/PK-5
18550 W Millburn Rd 60083 — 847-356-8331
Bennett Walshire, prin. — Fax 356-9722
Other Schools – See Lindenhurst

St. Patrick S — 600/PK-8
15020 W Wadsworth Rd 60083 — 847-623-8446
Mary Vitulli, prin. — Fax 623-3119

Walnut, Bureau, Pop. 1,404
Bureau Valley CUSD 340
Supt. — See Manlius
Bureau Valley North S — 400/PK-8
323 S Main St 61376 — 815-379-2900
Kristie Cady, prin. — Fax 379-9285

Waltonville, Jefferson, Pop. 432
Waltonville CUSD 1 — 400/PK-12
804 W Knob St 62894 — 618-279-7211
Ellie Rush, supt. — Fax 279-3291
www.wcusd1.org
Waltonville ES — 300/PK-8
802 W Knob St 62894 — 618-279-7221
Dana Waggoner, prin. — Fax 279-7771

Warren, Jo Daviess, Pop. 1,421
Warren CUSD 205 — 400/PK-12
311 S Water St 61087 — 815-745-2653
Shawn Teske, supt. — Fax 745-2037
www.205warren.net
Warren ES — 200/PK-5
311 S Water St 61087 — 815-745-2653
Shawn Teske, prin. — Fax 745-2037

Warrensburg, Macon, Pop. 1,195
Warrensburg-Latham CUSD 11 — 1,000/PK-12
430 W North St 62573 — 217-672-3514
Dr. Kristen Kendrick-Weikle, supt. — Fax 672-8468
www.wl.k12.il.us
Warrensburg-Latham ES — 500/PK-5
101 S West St 62573 — 217-672-3612
Laura Anderson, prin. — Fax 672-3321
Warrensburg-Latham MS — 200/6-8
425 W North St 62573 — 217-672-3321
Paul Hoffman, prin. — Fax 672-3770

Warrenville, DuPage, Pop. 12,933
CUSD 200
Supt. — See Wheaton
Bower ES — 500/K-5
4S241 River Rd 60555 — 630-393-9413
Mark Kohlmann, prin. — Fax 393-9403
Hubble MS — 800/6-8
3S600 Herrick Rd 60555 — 630-821-7900
Jon Pilkington, prin. — Fax 821-7901
Johnson ES — 500/K-5
2S700 Continental Dr 60555 — 630-393-1787
Derick Edwards, prin. — Fax 393-7064

Carmel Montessori Academy — 50/PK-12
3S238 State Route 59 60555 — 630-393-2995
Four Winds Waldorf S — 100/PK-8
30W160 Calumet Ave W 60555 — 630-836-9400
Jocelyne Roy, admin.
St. Irene S — 200/PK-8
3S601 Warren Ave 60555 — 630-393-9303
Margaret Detwiler, prin. — Fax 393-7009

Warsaw, Hancock, Pop. 1,585
Warsaw CUSD 316 — 400/PK-12
340 S 11th St 62379 — 217-256-4282
Bob Gound, supt. — Fax 256-4282
warsawschool.com
Warsaw ES, 340 S 11th St 62379 — 200/PK-6
Bill Knowles, prin. — 217-256-4614

Wasco, Kane
Saint Charles CUSD 303
Supt. — See Saint Charles
Wasco ES — 400/K-5
4N782 School St 60183 — 331-228-2900
Barbara Stokke, prin. — Fax 228-2901

Washburn, Marshall, Pop. 1,146
Lowpoint-Washburn CUSD 21 — 400/PK-12
PO Box 580 61570 — 309-248-7522
Parker Dietrich, supt. — Fax 248-7518
www.lwdistrict21.com
Lowpoint-Washburn ES — 200/PK-6
PO Box 580 61570 — 309-248-7221
Duane Schupp, prin. — Fax 248-7906

Washington, Tazewell, Pop. 14,931
Central SD 51 — 1,300/PK-8
1301 Eagle Ave 61571 — 309-444-3943
Dale Heidbreder, supt. — Fax 444-9898
www.central51.net
Central IS — 700/4-8
1301 Eagle Ave 61571 — 309-444-3943
Brian Hoelscher, prin. — Fax 444-3414
Central PS — 600/PK-3
1400 Newcastle Rd 61571 — 309-444-3580
Brett Lawless, prin. — Fax 444-3670

District 50 Schools — 800/PK-8
304 E Almond Dr 61571 — 309-745-8914
Dr. Chad Allaman, supt. — Fax 745-5417
www.d50schools.com
Hensey ES, 304 E Almond Dr 61571 — 400/PK-3
Josh Zaiser, prin. — 309-745-3625
Manor MS, 1014 School St 61571 — 400/4-8
Cathy Trimble, prin. — 309-745-3921

Washington SD 52 — 1,000/PK-8
303 Jackson St 61571 — 309-444-4182
Patreak Minasian, supt. — Fax 444-8538
www.d52schools.com
Lincoln Grade S — 600/PK-4
303 Jackson St 61571 — 309-444-2326
Jon Smith, prin. — Fax 444-8538
Washington MS — 400/5-8
1100 N Main St 61571 — 309-444-3361
Daniel Foehrkolb, prin. — Fax 444-3941

St. Patrick S — 300/PK-8
100 Harvey St 61571 — 309-444-4345
Doreen Shipman, prin. — Fax 444-7100

Waterloo, Monroe, Pop. 9,722
Waterloo CUSD 5 — 2,700/PK-12
302 Bellefontaine Dr 62298 — 618-939-3453
Brian Charron, supt. — Fax 939-4578
www.wcusd5.net
Gardner ES — 400/4-5
1 Ed Gardner Pl 62298 — 618-939-3060
Dawn Ivers, prin. — Fax 939-3065
Rogers ES — 400/2-3
200 Rogers St 62298 — 618-939-3454
Brian Smith, prin. — Fax 939-7980
Waterloo JHS — 600/6-8
200 Bellefontaine Dr 62298 — 618-939-3457
Nick Schwartz, prin. — Fax 939-1383
Zahnow ES — 400/PK-1
301 Hamacher St 62298 — 618-939-3458
Mary Gardner, prin. — Fax 939-1377

SS. Peter & Paul S — 300/PK-8
217 W 3rd St 62298 — 618-939-7217
Lisa Buchheit, prin. — Fax 939-5994

Waterman, DeKalb, Pop. 1,482
Indian Creek CUSD 425
Supt. — See Shabbona
Indian Creek MS — 200/5-8
335 E Garfield St 60556 — 815-264-7712
Steven Simpson, prin. — Fax 264-7826

Watseka, Iroquois, Pop. 5,192
Iroquois County CUSD 9 — 900/PK-12
1411 W Lafayette St 60970 — 815-432-4931
James Bunting, supt. — Fax 432-6889
www.watseka-u9.k12.il.us
Davis ES — 200/PK-1
495 N 4th St 60970 — 815-432-2112
Heather Gerth, prin. — Fax 432-2112
Kendall ES — 100/2-4
535 E Porter Ave 60970 — 815-432-4581
Dawn Garner, prin. — Fax 432-4581
Raymond MS — 200/5-8
101 W Mulberry St 60970 — 815-432-2115
Bradley Welch, prin. — Fax 432-6896

Wauconda, Lake, Pop. 13,421
Wauconda CUSD 118 — 4,500/PK-12
555 N Main St 60084 — 847-526-7690
Dr. Daniel J. Coles, supt. — Fax 526-1019
www.d118.org
Crown ES — 900/PK-5
620 W Bonner Rd 60084 — 847-526-7100
Karrie Diol, prin. — Fax 487-3596
Wauconda ES — 600/PK-5
225 Osage St 60084 — 847-526-6671
Debra Monroe, prin. — Fax 487-3598

Wauconda MS 500/6-8
215 Slocum Lake Rd 60084 847-526-2122
Daniel Stoller, prin. Fax 487-3597
Other Schools – See Island Lake

Da Vinci Waldorf S 100/PK-8
150 W Bonner Rd 60084 847-526-1372
Frassati Academy 6-8
316 W Mill St 60084 847-487-5600
Tammy Kleckner, prin. Fax 487-5611
Transfiguration S 100/PK-5
316 W Mill St 60084 847-526-6311
Tammy Kleckner, prin. Fax 526-4637

Waukegan, Lake, Pop. 87,117
Waukegan CUSD 60 16,700/PK-12
1201 N Sheridan Rd 60085 224-303-1000
Theresa Plascencia, supt.
www.wps60.org
Abbott MS 800/6-8
1319 Washington St 60085 224-303-2360
Carl Hagman, prin. Fax 399-8512
Benny MS 600/6-8
1401 Montesano Ave 60087 224-303-2460
Shanie Keelean, prin. Fax 399-8524
Carman-Buckner ES 700/PK-5
520 Helmholz Ave 60085 224-303-1500
Roberto Silva, prin. Fax 399-8514
Clark ES 300/K-5
601 Blanchard Rd 60087 224-303-1570
Gladys Rodriguez, prin. Fax 399-8522
Clearview ES 700/K-5
1700 Delaware Rd 60087 224-303-1600
Daniel Hill, prin. Fax 399-8526
Cooke Magnet ES 500/K-5
522 Belvidere Rd 60085 224-303-1700
Stephanie Jensen, prin. Fax 399-8528
Glen Flora ES 500/K-5
1110 Chestnut St 60085 224-303-1800
Zenaida Figueroa, prin. Fax 399-8532
Glenwood ES 700/K-5
2500 Northmoor Ave 60085 224-303-2010
Cabrina Williams-Leneau, prin. Fax 399-8504
Greenwood ES 400/PK-5
1919 North Ave 60087 224-303-2080
Joyce Meyer, prin. Fax 399-8534
Hyde Park ES 300/K-5
1525 Hyde Park Ave 60085 224-303-1970
Brian Carr, prin. Fax 399-8500
Jefferson MS 900/6-8
600 S Lewis Ave 60085 224-303-2560
Dr. Chaun Johnson, prin. Fax 399-8516
Juarez MS 800/6-8
201 N Butrick St 60085 224-303-2660
Nelson Campos, prin. Fax 399-8506
Lightfoot Early Learning Center 200/PK-PK
1721 N McAree Rd 60085 224-303-1400
Nicole Session, prin. Fax 399-8601
Little Fort ES 600/PK-5
1775 Blanchard Rd 60087 224-303-3700
Amy Grossman, prin. Fax 399-8510
Lyon Magnet ES 500/K-5
800 S Elmwood Ave 60085 224-303-2300
Amanda Pryce, prin. Fax 399-8530
McCall ES 500/PK-5
3215 N McAree Rd 60087 224-303-1760
Carol May, prin. Fax 399-8502
North ES 600/PK-5
410 Franklin St 60085 224-303-2160
Nicole Lemberger, prin. Fax 399-8518
Oakdale ES 600/PK-5
2230 N McAree Rd 60087 224-303-1860
Catalina Quiones-Nelson, prin. Fax 399-8508
Washington ES 600/K-5
110 S Orchard Ave 60085 224-303-2220
Jason Siegellak, prin. Fax 399-8536
Webster MS 700/6-8
930 New York St 60085 224-303-2760
Yvonne Brown, prin. Fax 399-8540
Whittier ES 700/K-5
901 N Lewis Ave 60085 224-303-1900
Jennifer delaSanchez, prin. Fax 399-8538

Daniels Christian Academy 50/PK-7
3601 N Lewis Ave 60087 847-263-8147
Patti Carlsen, prin. Fax 263-8377
Immanuel Evangelical Lutheran S 50/PK-8
1310 N Frolic Ave 60085 847-249-0011
David Zank, prin. Fax 249-0011
Lake County Baptist S 200/PK-12
1550 W Yorkhouse Rd 60087 847-623-7600
Timothy Kowach, prin. Fax 623-2085
Most Blessed Trinity Academy 300/PK-8
510 Grand Ave 60085 847-623-4110
Sandra Anderson, prin. Fax 599-0477
St. Anastasia S 300/PK-8
629 W Glen Flora Ave 60085 847-623-8320
Dr. Kristine Hillmann, prin. Fax 623-0556

Waverly, Morgan, Pop. 1,296
Waverly CUSD 6 300/PK-12
201 N Miller St 62692 217-435-8121
Dustin Day, supt. Fax 435-3431
www.waverlyscotties.com
Waverly ES 200/PK-6
499 W Elm St 62692 217-435-2331
Dustin Day, prin. Fax 435-2321

Wayne, DuPage, Pop. 2,406
SD U-46
Supt. — See Elgin
Wayne ES 400/K-6
5N443 School St 60184 630-736-7100
Dr. Marybeth DeLaMar, prin. Fax 213-5619

Wayne City, Wayne, Pop. 1,023
Wayne City CUSD 100 500/PK-12
302 Mill St 62895 618-895-3103
Myron Caudle, supt. Fax 895-2331
www.waynecity100.org
Wayne City ES 300/PK-6
302 Mill St 62895 618-895-3103
Jeff Mitchell, prin. Fax 895-2331

Weldon, DeWitt, Pop. 425
Deland-Weldon CUSD 57
Supt. — See De Land
Deland-Weldon ES 100/PK-6
2311 N 300 East Rd 61882 217-736-2401
Amanda Geary, prin. Fax 736-2654
Deland-Weldon MS 50/7-8
2311 N 300 East Rd 61882 217-736-2401
Matt Goldman, prin. Fax 736-2654

Wenona, Marshall, Pop. 1,053
Fieldcrest CUSD 6
Supt. — See Minonk
Fieldcrest MS 300/6-8
102 W Elm St 61377 815-853-4331
Nathan Lorton, prin. Fax 853-4786

Westchester, Cook, Pop. 16,532
Westchester SD 92-5 1,200/K-8
9981 Canterbury St 60154 708-450-2700
Philip Salemi, supt. Fax 450-2718
www.sd925.org
Westchester IS 400/3-5
10900 Canterbury St 60154 708-562-1011
Shawn Barrett, prin. Fax 562-0299
Westchester MS 400/6-8
1620 Norfolk Ave 60154 708-450-2735
Gregory Leban, prin. Fax 450-2752
Westchester PS 400/K-2
2400 Downing Ave 60154 708-562-1509
Stephanie DelFiacco, prin. Fax 562-1547

Divine Infant Jesus S 200/PK-8
1640 Newcastle Ave 60154 708-865-0122
Leonard Gramarossa, prin. Fax 865-9495
Divine Providence S 200/PK-8
2500 Mayfair Ave 60154 708-562-2258
Karen Foleno, prin. Fax 562-9171

West Chicago, DuPage, Pop. 26,802
Benjamin SD 25 700/PK-8
28W250 Saint Charles Rd 60185 630-876-7800
Dr. Philip Ehrhardt, supt. Fax 876-3325
www.bendist25.org
Benjamin MS 300/5-8
28W300 Saint Charles Rd 60185 630-876-7820
Michael Fitzgerald, prin. Fax 231-3886
Other Schools – See Carol Stream

Saint Charles CUSD 303
Supt. — See Saint Charles
Norton Creek ES 400/PK-5
2033 Smith Rd 60185 331-228-2700
Anthony White, prin. Fax 228-2701

West Chicago ESD 33 4,400/PK-8
312 E Forest Ave 60185 630-293-6000
Dr. Charles Johns, supt. Fax 293-6088
www.wego33.org
Currier ES 500/K-5
800 Garys Mill Rd 60185 630-293-6600
Mark Truckenbrod, prin. Fax 562-2579
Early Learning Center 200/PK-PK
300 E Forest Ave 60185 630-293-6000
Sandra Warner, prin. Fax 231-7605
Educare of West Dupage 100/PK-PK
851 Pearl Rd 60185 630-957-5500
Eugenie Matula, prin.
Gary ES 600/K-5
130 E Forest Ave 60185 630-293-6010
Stephanie Drake, prin. Fax 562-2583
Indian Knoll ES 400/K-5
0N645 Indian Knoll Rd 60185 630-293-6020
Jennifer Tapia, prin. Fax 562-2584
Leman MS 1,300/6-8
238 E Hazel St 60185 630-293-6060
Emily Crement, prin. Fax 562-2586
Pioneer ES 400/K-5
615 Kenwood Ave 60185 630-293-6040
Gloria Trejo, prin. Fax 562-2587
Turner ES 400/K-5
750 Ingalton Ave 60185 630-293-6050
John Rodriguez, prin. Fax 562-2589
Wegner ES 500/K-5
1180 Marcella Ln 60185 630-293-6400
Karen Apostoli, prin. Fax 562-2590
Other Schools – See Winfield

West Dundee, Kane
CUSD 300
Supt. — See Algonquin
Dundee Highlands ES 400/PK-5
407 S 5th St 60118 847-426-1480
Karen Cumpata, prin. Fax 426-1935
Dundee MS 1,000/6-8
4200 W Main St 60118 847-426-1485
Jeff Herb, prin. Fax 426-4008

Children's House Montessori S 50/PK-3
417 W Main St 60118 847-426-3570
Donna Butcher, dir. Fax 317-6628
St. Catherine of Siena S 200/PK-8
845 W Main St 60118 847-426-4808
Colleen Cannon, prin. Fax 426-0437

Western Springs, Cook, Pop. 12,882
Western Springs SD 101 1,500/PK-8
4225 Wolf Rd 60558 708-246-3700
Dr. Brian Barnhart, supt. Fax 482-2581
www.d101.org
Field Park ES 300/PK-5
4335 Howard Ave 60558 708-246-7675
Brad Promisel, prin. Fax 482-2581
Forest Hills ES 300/PK-5
5020 Central Ave 60558 708-246-7678
Rachel Corrough, prin. Fax 482-2589
Laidlaw ES 400/K-5
4072 Forest Ave 60558 708-246-7673
Erin DeBartolo, prin. Fax 482-2496
McClure JHS 500/6-8
4225 Wolf Rd 60558 708-246-7590
F. Daniel Chick, prin. Fax 246-4370

St. John of the Cross S 600/PK-8
708 51st St 60558 708-246-4454
Kathleen Gorman, prin. Fax 246-9010

West Frankfort, Franklin, Pop. 8,100
Frankfort CUSD 168 1,900/PK-12
900 N Cherry St 62896 618-937-2421
Matthew Donkin, supt. Fax 932-2025
www.wfschools.org
Central JHS 300/7-8
1600 E 9th St 62896 618-937-2444
Charley Cass, prin. Fax 937-2445
Denning ES 500/PK-2
1401 W 6th St 62896 618-937-2464
Susan Glodich, prin. Fax 937-2465
Frankfort IS 500/3-6
800 N Cherry St 62896 618-937-1412
Natalie Fry, prin. Fax 932-2646

St. John the Baptist S 100/PK-8
702 E Poplar St 62896 618-937-2017
Kevin Spiller, prin. Fax 937-2287

Westmont, DuPage, Pop. 24,243
CUSD 201 1,400/PK-12
133 S Grant St 60559 630-468-8000
Kevin Carey, supt. Fax 969-9022
www.cusd201.org
Manning ES 400/PK-5
200 N Linden Ave 60559 630-468-8050
Lindsay Pietrczal, prin. Fax 969-2492
Miller ES 200/K-5
125 W Traube Ave 60559 630-468-8300
Tim Wyller, prin. Fax 969-5401
South ECC 50/PK-PK
133 S Grant St 60559 630-468-8400
Fax 968-2156
Westmont JHS 400/6-8
944 Oakwood Dr 60559 630-468-8200
John Jonak, prin. Fax 654-2203

Maercker SD 60 1,300/PK-8
1 S Cass Ave Ste 202 60559 630-515-4840
Sean Nugent, supt. Fax 515-4845
www.maercker.org
Maercker ES 400/3-5
5827 S Cass Ave 60559 630-515-4820
Margo Giannoulis, prin. Fax 515-4825
Other Schools – See Clarendon Hills, Willowbrook

Holy Trinity S 200/PK-8
108 S Linden Ave 60559 630-971-0184
Dr. Pamela Simon, prin. Fax 971-1175

West Peoria, Peoria, Pop. 4,328
Peoria SD 150
Supt. — See Peoria
Coolidge MS 400/5-8
2708 W Rohmann Ave 61604 309-672-6506
Mervyn Swanson, prin. Fax 673-7605

West Salem, Edwards, Pop. 893
Edwards County CUSD 1
Supt. — See Albion
West Salem S 200/PK-8
PO Box 367 62476 618-456-8881
Dale Schmittler, prin. Fax 456-3510

Westville, Vermilion, Pop. 3,171
Westville CUSD 2 1,300/PK-12
125 W Ellsworth St 61883 217-267-3141
Dr. Seth Miller, supt. Fax 267-3144
www.gowestville.org
Giacoma ES 700/PK-6
200 S Walnut 61883 217-267-2154
Pam Dalenberg, prin. Fax 267-3484
Westville JHS 200/7-8
412 Moses Ave 61883 217-267-2185
Jared Ellison, prin. Fax 267-3621

Wheaton, DuPage, Pop. 51,936
CCSD 89
Supt. — See Glen Ellyn
Briar Glen ES 300/K-5
1800 Briarcliffe Blvd 60189 630-545-3300
Mitch Dubinsky, prin. Fax 665-2847

CUSD 200 13,100/PK-12
130 W Park Ave 60189 630-682-2002
Dr. Jeff Schuler, supt. Fax 682-2227
www.cusd200.org
Edison MS 700/6-8
1125 S Wheaton Ave 60189 630-682-2050
Rachel Bednar, prin. Fax 682-2337
Emerson ES 300/K-5
119 S Woodlawn St 60187 630-682-2055
Debra Klein, prin. Fax 682-2372
Franklin MS 700/6-8
211 E Franklin St 60187 630-682-2060
David Bendis, prin. Fax 682-2340
Hawthorne ES 300/K-5
334 E Wakeman Ave 60187 630-682-2065
Danielle Moran, prin. Fax 682-2392
Jefferson ECC 200/PK-PK
130 N Hazelton Ave 60187 630-682-2474
Stephanie Farrelly, prin. Fax 462-1914
Lincoln ES 500/K-5
630 Dawes Ave 60189 630-682-2075
Jeff Mitchem, prin. Fax 682-2367
Longfellow ES 400/K-5
311 W Seminary Ave 60187 630-682-2080
Sean Walsh, prin. Fax 682-2342

Lowell ES 400/K-5
312 S President St 60187 630-682-2085
Kathleen Melton, prin. Fax 682-2245
Madison ES 400/K-5
1620 Mayo Ave 60189 630-682-2095
Tim Callahan, prin. Fax 682-2435
Monroe MS 800/6-8
1855 Manchester Rd 60187 630-682-2285
Bryan Buck, prin. Fax 682-2331
Sandburg ES 400/K-5
1345 Jewell Rd 60187 630-682-2105
Aaron Bacon, prin. Fax 682-2350
Washington ES 400/K-5
911 Bridle Ln 60187 630-682-2222
Jennifer Craig, prin. Fax 682-2333
Whittier ES 400/K-5
218 W Park Ave 60189 630-682-2185
Christopher Silagi, prin. Fax 682-2409
Wiesbrook ES 500/K-5
2160 Durfee Rd 60189 630-682-2190
Dr. Brian Turyna, prin. Fax 682-2339
Other Schools – See Warrenville, Winfield

Clapham S, PO Box 209 60187 100/PK-12
Kathy Bailey, admin. 630-547-5125
Dupage Montessori S 50/PK-K
300 E Cole Ave 60187 630-653-1221
Sharon Breen, dir. Fax 653-0578
St. Michael S 600/PK-8
314 W Willow Ave 60187 630-665-1454
Adam Ferguson, prin. Fax 665-1491
Wheaton Montessori S 100/PK-9
1980 N Gary Ave 60187 630-653-5100
Rebecca Lingo, hdmstr. Fax 653-5699

Wheeling, Cook, Pop. 37,130
Wheeling CCSD 21 6,800/PK-8
999 W Dundee Rd 60090 847-537-8270
Dr. Kate Hyland, supt. Fax 520-2848
www.ccsd21.org
Field ES 600/K-5
51 Saint Armand Ln 60090 847-520-2780
Luis Bonilla, prin. Fax 419-3077
Hawthorne ECC 200/PK-PK
200 Glendale St 60090 847-465-7290
Raquel Kim, prin. Fax 465-7296
Holmes MS 800/6-8
221 S Wolf Rd 60090 847-520-2790
Martin Hopkins, prin. Fax 419-3073
London MS 700/6-8
1001 W Dundee Rd 60090 847-520-2745
Luis Correa, prin. Fax 520-2842
Tarkington ES 500/K-5
310 Scott St 60090 847-520-2775
Dr. Joe Arduino, prin. Fax 419-3074
Twain ES 600/PK-5
515 E Merle Ln 60090 847-520-2785
Rita Janus, prin. Fax 419-3080
Whitman ES 600/PK-5
133 Wille Ave 60090 847-520-2795
Gwen Gage, prin. Fax 520-2607
Other Schools – See Arlington Heights, Buffalo Grove, Mount Prospect

---

Bell Montessori S 100/PK-8
9300 Capitol Dr 60090 847-850-5490

White Hall, Greene, Pop. 2,509
North Greene Unit SD 3 900/PK-12
250 E Sherman St 62092 217-374-2842
Mark Scott, supt. Fax 374-2849
www.northgreene.com
Other Schools – See Roodhouse

White Heath, Piatt, Pop. 289
Monticello CUSD 25
Supt. — See Monticello
White Heath ES 200/2-3
300 W High St 61884 217-762-8511
Emily Weidner, prin. Fax 762-8333

Williamsfield, Knox, Pop. 574
Williamsfield CUSD 210 300/PK-12
325 W Kentucky Ave 61489 309-639-2219
Tim Farquer, supt. Fax 639-2618
www.billtown.org
Williamsfield ES 100/PK-5
325 W Kentucky Ave 61489 309-639-2216
Zack Binder, prin.
Williamsfield MS 100/6-8
325 W Kentucky Ave 61489 309-639-2216
Zack Binder, prin.

Williamsville, Sangamon, Pop. 1,465
Williamsville CUSD 15 1,500/PK-12
800 S Walnut St 62693 217-566-2014
Tip Reedy, supt. Fax 566-2183
www.wcusd15.org
Williamsville JHS 300/6-8
500 S Walnut St 62693 217-566-3600
Clay Shoufler, prin. Fax 566-2475
Williamsville MS 100/5-5
504 S Walnut St 62693 217-566-4070
Clay Shoufler, prin. Fax 566-2183
Other Schools – See Sherman

Willowbrook, DuPage, Pop. 8,420
CCSD 180
Supt. — See Burr Ridge
Jeans ES 400/PK-4
16W631 91st St 60527 630-325-8186
Tracy Ritchey, prin. Fax 325-9576

Gower SD 62 900/PK-8
7700 Clarendon Hills Rd 60527 630-986-5383
Dr. Victor Simon, supt. Fax 323-3074
www.gower62.com
Gower West ES 500/PK-4
7650 Clarendon Hills Rd 60527 630-323-6446
Gina Rodewald, prin. Fax 323-6494
Other Schools – See Burr Ridge

Maercker SD 60
Supt. — See Westmont
Westview Hills MS 400/6-8
630 65th St 60527 630-515-4830
Amber Quirk, prin. Fax 515-4835

Willow Springs, Cook, Pop. 5,466
Willow Springs SD 108 400/K-8
8345 Archer Ave 60480 708-839-6828
Frank Patrick, supt. Fax 839-8399
www.willowspringsschool.org
Willow Springs ES 400/K-8
8345 Archer Ave 60480 708-839-6828
Lori Smuda, prin. Fax 839-8399

Wilmette, Cook, Pop. 26,500
Avoca SD 37 700/PK-8
2921 Illinois Rd 60091 847-251-3587
Kevin Jauch, supt. Fax 251-7742
avoca37.org
Murphy MS 300/PK-PK, 6-
2921 Illinois Rd 60091 847-251-3617
Matthew Palcer, prin. Fax 251-4179
Other Schools – See Glenview

Wilmette SD 39 3,700/PK-8
615 Locust Rd 60091 847-256-2450
Ray Lechner, supt. Fax 256-1920
www.wilmette39.org
Central ES 500/K-4
900 Central Ave 60091 847-251-3252
Melanie Horowitz, prin. Fax 251-4086
Harper ES 400/K-4
1101 Dartmouth St 60091 847-251-6754
Sue Kick, prin. Fax 251-4176
Highcrest MS 900/5-6
569 Hunter Rd 60091 847-853-2900
Kelly Jackson, prin. Fax 256-0083
McKenzie ES 500/K-4
649 Prairie Ave 60091 847-251-2295
Rachel Filippi, prin. Fax 251-4067
Romona ES 500/PK-4
600 Romona Rd 60091 847-256-0211
Cindy Anderson, prin. Fax 251-4153
Wilmette JHS 800/7-8
620 Locust Rd 60091 847-256-7280
Kelly Jackson, prin. Fax 256-0204

Baker Demonstration S 300/PK-8
201 Sheridan Rd 60091 847-425-5800
Carly Andrews, hdmstr. Fax 425-5801
St. Francis Xavier S 400/PK-8
808 Linden Ave 60091 847-256-0644
Colleen Barrett, prin. Fax 256-0753
St. Joseph S 300/PK-8
1740 Lake Ave 60091 847-256-7870
Laszlo Katona, prin. Fax 256-9514

Wilmington, Will, Pop. 5,660
Wilmington CUSD 209U 1,500/PK-12
209U Wildcat Ct 60481 815-926-1751
Dr. Matthew Swick, supt. Fax 926-1692
www.wilmington.will.k12.il.us
Bruning ES 300/PK-1
1910 Bruning Dr 60481 815-926-1683
Beth Norman, prin. Fax 476-0130
Stevens IS 400/2-5
221 Ryan St 60481 815-926-1689
Venita Dennis, prin. Fax 476-4406
Wilmington MS 300/6-8
715 S Joliet St 60481 815-476-2189
Adam Spicer, prin. Fax 476-1941

St. Rose S 100/PK-8
626 S Kankakee St 60481 815-476-6220
Linda Bland, prin. Fax 476-5644

Winchester, Scott, Pop. 1,579
Winchester CUSD 1 700/PK-12
149 S Elm St 62694 217-742-3175
David Roberts, supt.
www.winchesterschools.net
Winchester ES, 283 S Elm St 62694 500/PK-8
Andy Stumpf, prin. 217-742-9551

Windsor, Shelby, Pop. 1,177
Windsor CUSD 1 400/PK-12
1424 Minnesota Ave 61957 217-459-2636
Erik Van Hoveln, supt. Fax 459-2661
www.windsor.k12.il.us
Windsor ES 200/PK-6
808 Wisconsin Ave 61957 217-459-2447
Brian Lee, prin. Fax 459-2408

Winfield, DuPage, Pop. 8,924
CUSD 200
Supt. — See Wheaton
Pleasant Hill ES 600/K-5
1N220 Pleasant Hill Rd 60190 630-682-2100
Christy Frederick, prin. Fax 682-2366

West Chicago ESD 33
Supt. — See West Chicago
Winfield Preschool PK-PK
0S150 Winfield Rd 60190 630-909-4954
Sandy Warner, prin.

Winfield SD 34 300/PK-8
0S150 Winfield Rd 60190 630-909-4900
Dr. Matt Rich Ed.D., supt. Fax 260-2382
www.winfield34.org
Winfield Central S 200/3-8
0S150 Park St 60190 630-909-4960
Dawn Reinke, prin. Fax 933-9236
Winfield PS 100/PK-2
0S150 Winfield Rd 60190 630-909-4910
Dawn Reinke, prin. Fax 260-2382

St. John the Baptist S 300/PK-8
0S259 Church St 60190 630-668-2625
Mickey Tovey, prin. Fax 668-7176

Wheaton Christian Grammar S 500/K-8
1N350 Taylor Dr 60190 630-668-1385
Stephen Clum, head sch Fax 668-2475

Winnebago, Winnebago, Pop. 3,067
Winnebago CUSD 323 1,500/PK-12
304 E McNair Rd 61088 815-335-2456
Dr. John Schwuchow, supt. Fax 335-7574
www.winnebagoschools.org
McNair ES 300/3-5
304 E McNair Rd 61088 815-335-1607
Sean Monahan, prin. Fax 335-7574
Simon ES 300/PK-2
309 S Benton St 61088 815-335-2318
Frank Mandera, prin. Fax 335-3127
Winnebago MS 300/6-8
407 N Elida St 61088 815-335-2364
Catherine Finley, prin. Fax 335-1437

Winnetka, Cook, Pop. 12,045
Winnetka SD 36 1,800/K-8
1235 Oak St 60093 847-446-9400
Dr. Trisha Kocanda, supt. Fax 446-9408
www.winnetka36.org
Crow Island ES 400/K-4
1112 Willow Rd 60093 847-446-0353
Dr. Julie Pfeffer, prin. Fax 446-9021
Greeley ES 300/K-4
275 Fairview Ave 60093 847-446-6060
Susan Hugebeck, prin. Fax 501-5737
Hubbard Woods ES 300/K-4
1110 Chatfield Rd 60093 847-446-0920
Beth Carmody, prin. Fax 501-6124
Skokie S 400/5-6
520 Glendale Ave 60093 847-441-1750
Kelly Tess, prin. Fax 441-2193
Washburne MS 400/7-8
515 Hibbard Rd 60093 847-446-5892
Dave Kanne, prin. Fax 446-1380

North Shore Country Day S 500/PK-12
310 Green Bay Rd 60093 847-446-0674
Dr. Thomas Flemma, head sch Fax 446-0675
Sacred Heart S 300/PK-8
1095 Gage St 60093 847-446-0005
Kristen Fink, prin. Fax 446-4961
SS. Faith Hope & Charity S 300/PK-8
180 Ridge Ave 60093 847-446-0031
Kathleen Carden, prin. Fax 446-9064

Winthrop Harbor, Lake, Pop. 6,595
Winthrop Harbor SD 1 600/K-8
500 North Ave 60096 847-731-3085
Patricia Goodwin, supt. Fax 731-3156
www.whsd1.org
North Prairie JHS 300/5-8
500 North Ave 60096 847-731-3089
Carrie Nottingham, prin. Fax 731-3152
Westfield S 300/K-4
2309 9th St 60096 847-872-5438
Summer Poepping, prin. Fax 746-1477

Wolf Lake, Union
Shawnee CUSD 84 200/PK-12
3365 N State Route 3 62998 618-833-5709
Shelly Clover-Hill, supt. Fax 833-4171
www.shawneedistrict84.com/
Shawnee ES 100/PK-5
3365 N State Route 3 62998 618-833-4975
Amy Reynolds, prin. Fax 565-2231

Wonder Lake, McHenry, Pop. 3,980
Harrison SD 36 400/PK-8
6809 McCullom Lake Rd 60097 815-653-2311
Dr. Susan Wings, supt. Fax 653-1712
www.hsd36.org
Harrison ES 400/PK-8
6809 McCullom Lake Rd 60097 815-653-2311
Anne Huff, prin. Fax 653-1712

Wood Dale, DuPage, Pop. 13,602
Wood Dale SD 7 1,200/PK-8
543 N Wood Dale Rd 60191 630-595-9510
Dr. John Corbett, supt. Fax 595-5625
www.wd7.org
Early Childhood Education Center 200/PK-PK
543 N Wood Dale Rd 60191 630-694-1174
Constance Tadel, prin. Fax 238-0387
Oakbrook ES 300/K-2
170 S Wood Dale Rd 60191 630-766-6336
Timothy Shermak, prin. Fax 766-2174
Westview ES 400/3-5
200 N Addison Rd 60191 630-766-8040
Alan Buttimer, prin. Fax 766-2094
Wood Dale JHS 400/6-8
655 N Wood Dale Rd 60191 630-766-6210
Shelly Skarzynski, prin. Fax 766-1839

Holy Ghost S 200/PK-8
260 N Wood Dale Rd 60191 630-766-4508
Dr. Tony Jimenez, prin. Fax 860-7697

Woodhull, Henry, Pop. 803
Alwood CUSD 225 400/PK-12
301 E 5th Ave 61490 309-334-2719
Shannon Bumann, supt. Fax 334-2925
www.alwood.net
Other Schools – See Alpha

Woodlawn, Jefferson, Pop. 691
Woodlawn Unit SD 209 500/PK-12
300 N Central St 62898 618-735-2631
David Larkin, supt. Fax 735-2032
www.woodlawnschools.org
Woodlawn Grade S 400/PK-8
301 S Central St 62898 618-735-2661
Tammy Beckham, prin. Fax 242-2720

Woodridge, DuPage, Pop. 34,058
Woodridge SD 68 3,000/PK-8
7925 Janes Ave 60517 630-985-7925
Patrick Broncato, supt.
www.woodridge68.org
Edgewood ES 400/PK-6
7900 Woodridge Dr 60517 630-985-3603
Tanya Hughes, prin. Fax 380-4147
Goodrich ES 400/K-6
3450 Hobson Rd 60517 630-969-7271
Dr. Paul Scaletta, prin. Fax 380-4148
Jefferson JHS 600/7-8
7200 Janes Ave 60517 630-852-8010
Justin Warnke, prin. Fax 380-4149
Meadowview ES 400/PK-6
2525 Mitchell Dr 60517 630-969-2390
Dr. Kelly Neylon, prin. Fax 380-4150
Murphy ES 400/PK-6
7700 Larchwood Ln 60517 630-985-3797
Jacob Engler, prin. Fax 380-4151
Sipley ES 400/PK-6
2806 83rd St 60517 630-985-7150
Dr. Donald Mrozik, prin. Fax 380-4152
Willow Creek ES 400/PK-6
2901 Jackson Dr 60517 630-852-5055
Kurt Kramer, prin. Fax 380-4153

St. Scholastica S 300/K-8
7720 Janes Ave 60517 630-985-2515
Liz Driscoll, prin. Fax 985-2395

Wood River, Madison, Pop. 10,543
Wood River-Hartford ESD 15 700/PK-8
501 E Lorena Ave 62095 618-254-0607
Dr. Patrick Anderson Ed.D., supt. Fax 254-9048
www.wrh15.org/
Lewis-Clark ES 300/K-5
501 E Lorena Ave 62095 618-254-4354
Kelly Bohnenstiehl, prin. Fax 254-7601
Lewis-Clark JHS 200/6-8
501 E Lorena Ave 62095 618-254-4355
Radena Lemmon, prin. Fax 254-7600
Other Schools – See Hartford

Woodstock, McHenry, Pop. 24,445
Woodstock CUSD 200 6,500/PK-12
227 W Judd St 60098 815-338-8200
Michael Moan Ed.D., supt. Fax 338-2005
www.woodstockschools.org/
Creekside MS 800/6-8
3201 Hercules Rd 60098 815-337-5200
Michael Wheatley, prin. Fax 206-0476
Dean Street ES 300/1-5
600 Dean St 60098 815-338-1133
Vicki Larson Ed.D., prin. Fax 338-3089
Dierzen Early Learning Center 700/PK-K
2045 N Seminary Ave 60098 815-338-8883
Tricia Bogott, prin. Fax 337-5431
Endres ES 500/1-5
2181 N Seminary Ave 60098 815-337-8177
Keri Pala, prin. Fax 338-5765
Greenwood ES 400/1-5
4618 Greenwood Rd 60098 815-648-2606
Thomas Wollpert, prin. Fax 648-4808
Northwood MS 600/6-8
2121 N Seminary Ave 60098 815-338-4900
Jeremy Schaaf, prin. Fax 337-2150
Olson ES 500/1-5
720 W Judd St 60098 815-338-0473
Diana Frisbie, prin. Fax 338-8142
Prairiewood ES 400/1-5
3215 Hercules Rd 60098 815-337-5300
Jared Skorburg, prin. Fax 206-0479
Westwood ES 300/1-5
14124 W South Street Rd 60098 815-337-8173
Ryan Hart, prin. Fax 337-8175

Crystal Lake Montessori S 200/PK-8
3013 S Country Club Rd 60098 815-338-0013
Nancy Bauerband, admin. Fax 338-8588
St. Mary S 300/PK-8
313 N Tryon St 60098 815-338-3598
Vince Sossong, prin. Fax 338-3408

Worden, Madison, Pop. 1,030
Edwardsville CUSD 7
Supt. — See Edwardsville
Worden ES 300/3-5
110 N Main St 62097 618-692-7442
Dr. Beth Renth, prin. Fax 459-2174

St. Paul Lutheran S 50/PK-8
6961 W Frontage Rd 62097 618-633-2202
Kate Thoelke, prin. Fax 633-1709

Worth, Cook, Pop. 10,649
Worth SD 127 1,100/PK-8
11218 S Ridgeland Ave 60482 708-448-2800
Dr. Rita Wojtylewski, supt. Fax 448-6215
www.worthschools.org
Worth ES 400/K-5
11158 S Oak Park Ave 60482 708-448-2801
Tim Hathhorn, prin. Fax 448-6023
Worth JHS 300/6-8
11151 S New England Ave 60482 708-448-2803
Joseph Zampillo, prin. Fax 448-6155
Worthridge S 50/PK-PK
11218 S Ridgeland Ave 60482 708-448-2800
Dr. Rita Wojtylewski, prin. Fax 448-6215
Worthwoods ES 300/PK-5
11000 S Oketo Ave 60482 708-448-2802
Linda Esposito, prin. Fax 448-5623

Wyanet, Bureau, Pop. 984
Bureau Valley CUSD 340
Supt. — See Manlius
Bureau Valley ES Wyanet 200/PK-2
PO Box 341 61379 815-699-2251
Kristal LeRette, prin. Fax 699-7046

Wyoming, Stark, Pop. 1,418
Stark County CUSD 100 800/PK-12
300 W Van Buren St 61491 309-695-6123
Jerry Klooster, supt.
www.stark100.com
Stark County ES 300/PK-5
300 W Van Buren St 61491 309-695-5181
Jenna Bibb, prin. Fax 695-4302
Other Schools – See Toulon

Yorkville, Kendall, Pop. 16,715
Yorkville CUSD 115 5,200/PK-12
PO Box 579 60560 630-553-4382
Dr. Tim Shimp, supt. Fax 553-4398
www.y115.org
Autumn Creek ES 500/K-6
2377 Autumn Creek Blvd 60560 630-553-4048
Mayra Johnson, prin. Fax 553-4060
Bristol Bay ES 600/K-6
427 Bristol Bay Dr 60560 630-553-5121
Katie Spallasso, prin. Fax 882-6267
Circle Center ES 500/K-3
901 Mill St 60560 630-553-4388
Gina Isabelli, prin. Fax 553-4456
Grande Reserve ES 500/K-6
3142 Grande Trl 60560 630-553-5513
Robert Battey, prin. Fax 553-5030
Yorkville Grade S 200/PK-3
201 W Somonauk St 60560 630-553-4390
Melissa Lewis, prin. Fax 553-4450
Yorkville IS 600/4-6
103 E Schoolhouse Rd 60560 630-553-4594
Steve Bjork, prin. Fax 553-4596
Yorkville MS 900/7-8
920 Prairie Crossing Dr 60560 630-553-4544
Lisa Adler, prin. Fax 553-5181
Other Schools – See Bristol

Cross Lutheran S 300/PK-8
8535 State Route 47 60560 630-553-7861
Susan Lopez, prin. Fax 553-2580
Parkview Christian Academy 200/PK-12
201 W Center St 60560 630-553-5158
Deborah Benson, supt. Fax 553-3370
Peaceful Pathways Montessori S 50/PK-9
8250 State Route 71 60560 630-553-4263

Zeigler, Franklin, Pop. 1,781
Zeigler-Royalton CUSD 188 600/PK-12
PO Box 38 62999 618-596-5841
Quent Hamilton, supt. Fax 596-6789
www.zr188.org
Zeigler-Royalton ES 300/PK-6
PO Box 87 62999 618-596-2121
Leigh Bailey, prin. Fax 596-2075
Zeigler-Royalton JHS 100/7-8
PO Box 87 62999 618-596-2121
Leigh Bailey, prin. Fax 596-2075

Zion, Lake, Pop. 23,535
Zion ESD 6 2,800/PK-8
2800 29th St 60099 847-872-5455
Dr. Keely Roberts, supt. Fax 746-1280
www.zion6.com
Beulah Park ES 400/K-6
1910 Gilboa Ave 60099 847-746-1429
Lynn Butera, prin. Fax 746-7803
East ES 200/K-6
2913 Elim Ave 60099 847-872-5425
Charmekia Edelstein, prin. Fax 872-8130
Elmwood ES 400/K-6
3025 Ezra Ave 60099 847-746-1491
Deidre Garnett, prin. Fax 746-0052
Lakeview S 300/PK-PK
2200 Bethesda Blvd 60099 847-872-0255
Cheryl Caesar, prin. Fax 731-1389
Shiloh Park ES 500/K-6
2635 Gabriel Ave 60099 847-746-8136
Robert Schulz, prin. Fax 731-8453
West ES 600/K-6
2412 Jethro Ave 60099 847-746-8222
Nicholas Heckel, prin. Fax 731-8490
Zion Central JHS 600/7-8
1716 27th St 60099 847-746-1431
Tanya Housing, prin. Fax 746-9750

Our Savior's Lutheran S 100/PK-8
1800 23rd St 60099 847-872-5922
John Kujath B.S., prin. Fax 872-5539

INDIANA

INDIANA DEPARTMENT OF EDUCATION
151 W Ohio St Ste X, Indianapolis 46204
Telephone 317-232-6610
Fax 317-232-8004
Website http://www.doe.in.gov

Superintendent of Public Instruction Dr. Jennifer McCormick

INDIANA BOARD OF EDUCATION
200 W Washington St Ste 229, Indianapolis 46204-2731

Chairperson Dr. Jennifer McCormick

EDUCATIONAL SERVICE CENTERS (ESC)

Central Indiana ESC
Dr. Kevin M. Caress, dir. 317-759-5555
6036 Lakeside Blvd Bldg A
Indianapolis 46278
www.ciesc.k12.in.us

East Central ESC
Larry John, dir., 1601 Indiana Ave 765-825-1247
Connersville 47331 Fax 825-2532
www.ecesc.k12.in.us/

Northern Indiana ESC
Ted Chittum, dir. 574-254-0111
56535 Magnetic Dr Fax 254-0148
Mishawaka 46545
www.niesc.k12.in.us/

Northwest Indiana ESC
Edward Schoenfelt, dir. 219-926-5555
48 W 900 N, Chesterton 46304 Fax 926-5553
www.nwiesc.k12.in.us/

Region 8 ESC
Joshua Wenning, dir. 260-423-0030
1027 W Rudisill Blvd Ste D1 Fax 423-0031
Fort Wayne 46807
www.r8esc.k12.in.us/

Southern Indiana ESC
Judy Bueckert, dir. 812-482-6641
1102 Tree Lane Dr, Jasper 47546 Fax 482-6652
www.siec.k12.in.us/

Wabash Valley ESC
Dr. Dennis Cahill, dir. 765-463-1589
3061 Benton St Fax 463-1580
West Lafayette 47906
www.esc5.k12.in.us/

West Central ESC
Valerie Buchanan, dir. 765-653-2727
PO Box 21, Greencastle 46135 Fax 653-7897
www.wciesc.k12.in.us/

William E. Wilson ESC
Dr. Phil Partenheimer, dir. 812-256-8000
PO Box 217, Charlestown 47111 Fax 256-8012
www.wesc.k12.in.us/

PUBLIC, PRIVATE AND CATHOLIC ELEMENTARY SCHOOLS

Acton, Marion
Franklin Township Community SC
Supt. — See Indianapolis
Acton ES 500/K-5
8010 Acton Rd 46259 317-862-6108
Brook Wessel-Burke, prin. Fax 862-7251

Advance, Boone, Pop. 471

Trinity Christian S, PO Box 5 46102 50/PK-8
Vonda Phelps, prin. 765-366-6754

Akron, Kosciusko, Pop. 1,159
Tippecanoe Valley SC 2,000/PK-12
8343 S State Road 19 46910 574-598-2759
Brett Boggs, supt. Fax 598-2773
www.tvsc.k12.in.us
Akron ES 400/K-5
202 E Rural St 46910 574-598-2367
Chrissy Mills, prin. Fax 598-2361
Tippecanoe Valley MS 500/6-8
11303 W 800 S 46910 574-598-2200
Scott Backus, prin. Fax 598-2266
Other Schools – See Mentone

Albany, Delaware, Pop. 2,138
Delaware Community SC
Supt. — See Muncie
Albany ES 300/K-5
700 W State St 47320 765-789-6102
Joe Schmaltz, prin. Fax 789-6349

Albion, Noble, Pop. 2,325
Central Noble Community SC 1,000/K-12
200 E Main St 46701 260-636-2175
Alan Middleton, supt. Fax 636-7918
www.centralnoble.k12.in.us
Albion ES 300/K-5
202 Cougar Ct 46701 260-636-7538
Jeff Harper, prin. Fax 636-7740
Other Schools – See Wolflake

Alexandria, Madison, Pop. 5,088
Alexandria Community SC 1,600/PK-12
202 E Washington St 46001 765-724-4496
Melissa Brisco, supt. Fax 724-5049
www.alex.k12.in.us
Alexandria-Monroe ES 400/PK-2
800 N Central Ave 46001 765-724-7788
Matt Hensley, prin. Fax 724-7788
Alexandria-Monroe IS 500/3-6
308 W 11th St 46001 765-724-4166
Mark Bartmas, prin. Fax 724-5045

St. Mary S 100/K-8
820 W Madison St 46001 765-724-4459
Marca Budzenski, prin. Fax 724-9711

Amo, Hendricks, Pop. 400
Mill Creek Community SC
Supt. — See Clayton
Mill Creek West ES 300/K-5
PO Box 128 46103 317-539-9255
Celina Clements, prin. Fax 303-1909

Anderson, Madison, Pop. 54,768
Anderson Community SC 6,700/PK-12
1600 Hillcrest Ave 46011 765-641-2000
Dr. Tim Smith, supt. Fax 641-2080
www.acsc.net
Anderson ES 600/K-5
2035 Raible Ave 46011 765-641-2092
Matthew Goen, prin. Fax 641-2110
Eastside ES 500/1-5
844 N Scatterfield Rd 46012 765-641-2101
Dr. Valarie Scott, prin. Fax 641-2118
Edgewood ES 300/K-5
3525 Winding Way 46011 765-641-2119
Judi Shafer, prin. Fax 641-2055
Erskine ES 600/K-5
811 W 60th St 46013 765-641-2114
Scott Merkel, prin. Fax 641-2100
Highland MS 1,500/6-8
2108 E 200 N 46012 765-641-2059
David Tijerina, prin. Fax 641-2064
Killbuck Kindergarten K-K
3070 E 300 N 46012 765-378-0560
Sharon Buchanan, prin. Fax 378-0711
Southview Preschool Center 300/PK-PK
4500 Main St 46013 765-641-2360
Shelley Caldwell, prin. Fax 640-5162
Tenth Street ES 500/1-5
3124 E 10th St 46012 765-641-2103
David Suchocki, prin. Fax 641-2167
Valley Grove ES 600/1-5
2160 S 300 E 46017 765-378-3393
Melissa Illuzzi, prin. Fax 378-7683

Frankton-Lapel Community SD 3,000/PK-12
7916 W 300 N 46011 765-734-1261
Bobby Fields, supt. Fax 734-1129
www.flcs.k12.in.us/
Other Schools – See Frankton, Lapel

Anderson Christian S 200/PK-12
5401 S Madison Ave 46013 765-649-0123
Steve Cash, admin. Fax 649-3844
Cross Street Christian S 50/PK-8
2318 W Cross St 46011 765-649-4141
Holy Cross S 100/PK-1
2825 Lincoln St 46016 765-642-8428
Tina Neal, prin. Fax 643-6470
Holy Cross S 200/2-8
1115 Pearl St 46016 765-642-1848
Tina Neal, prin. Fax 642-1828
Indiana Christian Academy 100/PK-12
432 W 300 N 46012 765-643-7884
Kevin Plew, prin. Fax 683-4200
Liberty Christian S 300/PK-6
2025 Hillcrest Dr 46012 765-644-7773
Jay McCurry, supt. Fax 644-7778

Andrews, Huntington, Pop. 1,129
Huntington County Community SC
Supt. — See Huntington
Andrews ES 400/K-5
509 E Jefferson St 46702 260-786-3021
Amy Rudolf, prin. Fax 786-3537

Angola, Steuben, Pop. 8,487
Metropolitan SD of Steuben County 3,000/K-12
400 S Martha St 46703 260-665-2854
Dr. Brent Wilson, supt. Fax 665-9155
www.msdsteuben.k12.in.us
Angola MS 700/6-8
1350 E Maumee St 46703 260-665-9581
Ryan Bounds, prin. Fax 665-9583
Carlin Park ES 300/K-5
800 Williams St 46703 260-665-2014
Marie Floyd, prin. Fax 665-7053
Hendry Park ES 400/K-5
805 S Washington St 46703 260-665-3215
Lisa Bauer, prin. Fax 665-5584
Ryan Park ES 400/K-5
1000 S John McBride Ave 46703 260-668-8873
Amy Heavin, prin. Fax 668-8823
Other Schools – See Pleasant Lake

Arcadia, Hamilton, Pop. 1,652
Hamilton Heights SC 2,300/PK-12
PO Box 469 46030 317-984-3538
Dr. Derek Arrowood, supt. Fax 984-3042
www.hhschuskies.org
Hamilton Heights ES 500/3-5
PO Box 400 46030 317-984-3547
Julie Griffey, prin. Fax 984-3540
Hamilton Heights MS 500/6-8
PO Box 609 46030 317-984-3588
Bret Bailey, prin. Fax 984-3231
Hamilton Heights PS 500/PK-2
PO Box 419 46030 317-984-1530
Julie Griffey, prin. Fax 984-1544

Arcola, Allen
Northwest Allen County SD
Supt. — See Fort Wayne
Arcola ES 200/K-5
11006 Arcola Rd 46704 260-625-3161
Kathleen Perfect, prin. Fax 625-3975

Argos, Marshall, Pop. 1,665
Argos Community SD 600/PK-12
410 N First St 46501 574-892-5139
Ned Speicher, supt. Fax 892-6527
www.argos.k12.in.us/
Argos Community ES 300/PK-6
600 Yearick St 46501 574-892-5136
Becky Vamos, prin. Fax 892-6527

Arlington, Rush, Pop. 429
Rush County SD
Supt. — See Rushville
Arlington ES 200/K-6
2533 N 700 W 46104 765-663-2416
Julie Innis, prin. Fax 663-2723

Ashley, DeKalb, Pop. 968
DeKalb County Central United SC
Supt. — See Waterloo
Country Meadow ES 200/PK-5
2410 County Road 10 46705 260-920-1017
Fax 587-9232

Attica, Fountain, Pop. 3,214
Attica Consolidated SC 800/PK-12
205 E Sycamore St 47918 765-762-7000
Dr. Robert Boyd, supt. Fax 762-7007
www.attica.k12.in.us
Attica ES 500/PK-6
500 E Washington St 47918 765-762-7000
Dusty Goodwin, prin. Fax 762-7019

Auburn, DeKalb, Pop. 12,632
DeKalb County Central United SC
Supt. — See Waterloo
McKenney-Harrison ES 600/PK-5
320 Van Auken St 46706 260-920-1015
Marcus Wagner, prin. Fax 925-4668
Watson ES 600/PK-5
901 Eckhart Ave 46706 260-920-1014
Pam Shoemaker, prin. Fax 925-5612

Lakewood Park Christian S 500/PK-12
5555 County Road 29 46706 260-925-1393
Dr. Ed Yoder, supt. Fax 925-5010

Aurora, Dearborn, Pop. 3,721
South Dearborn Community SC 2,700/PK-12
6109 Squire Pl 47001 812-926-2090
Dr. John Mehrle, supt. Fax 926-4216
www.sdcsc.k12.in.us
Aurora ES 600/PK-6
6098 Squire Pl 47001 812-926-2090
Mary Bailey, prin. Fax 926-0863
Manchester ES 300/K-6
9387 State Road 48 47001 812-926-2090
Janet Platt, prin. Fax 926-2513
South Dearborn MS 500/7-8
5850 Squire Pl 47001 812-926-2090
Jason Cheek, prin. Fax 926-2149
Other Schools – See Dillsboro, Moores Hill

St. John Lutheran S 100/PK-8
222 Mechanic St 47001 812-926-2656
Terri Schmeltzer, admin. Fax 926-7603
St. Mary S 100/K-8
211 4th St 47001 812-926-1558
James Tush, prin. Fax 926-2590

Austin, Scott, Pop. 4,251
Scott County SD 1 1,300/K-12
PO Box 9 47102 812-794-8750
Robert Anderson, supt. Fax 794-8765
www.scsd1.com/
Austin ES 500/K-5
401 S Highway 31 47102 812-794-8743
Beverly Turner, prin. Fax 794-8788
Austin MS 300/6-8
401 S Highway 31 47102 812-794-8740
David Deaton, prin. Fax 794-8739

Avilla, Noble, Pop. 2,387
East Noble SC
Supt. — See Kendallville
Avilla ES 400/PK-6
PO Box 9 46710 260-897-2301
David Pine, prin. Fax 897-3729

Oak Farm Montessori S 200/PK-9
502 Lemper Rd 46710 260-897-4270
Megan O'Sullivan, head sch Fax 897-4212
St. Marys S 100/K-8
PO Box 109 46710 260-897-3481
Jane Sandor, prin. Fax 897-3706

Avon, Hendricks, Pop. 12,177
Avon Community SC 8,800/PK-12
7203 E US Highway 36 46123 317-544-6000
Dr. Margaret Hoernemann, supt. Fax 544-6001
www.avon-schools.org
Avon IS East 700/5-6
174 S State Road 267 46123 317-544-5800
Dr. Jennifer Shayotovich, prin. Fax 544-5801
Avon IS West 700/5-6
176 S State Road 267 46123 317-544-5900
Dustin LeMay, prin. Fax 544-5901
Avon MS North 700/7-8
1251 N Dan Jones Rd 46123 317-544-5500
Susan Green, prin. Fax 544-5501
Avon MS South 800/7-8
7199 E US Highway 36 46123 317-544-5700
Dan Chapin, prin. Fax 544-5701
Cedar ES 700/K-4
685 S State Road 267 46123 317-544-6200
Kevin Gray, prin. Fax 544-6201
Hickory ES 500/K-4
907 S State Road 267 46123 317-544-6300
Scott Collins, prin. Fax 544-6301
Maple ES 300/PK-4
7237 E US Highway 36 46123 317-544-6400
Nikki Harrison, prin. Fax 544-6401
Pine Tree ES 400/K-4
7866 E County Road 100 S 46123 317-544-6500
Karie Mize, prin. Fax 544-6501
River Birch ES 800/K-4
5456 E County Road 75 N 46123 317-544-6800
Kris Kingery, prin. Fax 544-6801
Sycamore ES 400/K-4
7878 E County Road 100 N 46123 317-544-6600
Nicole Harris, prin. Fax 544-6601
White Oak ES 300/K-4
7221 E US Highway 36 46123 317-544-6700
Annette Patchett, prin. Fax 544-6701

Kingsway Christian S 600/PK-8
7979 E County Road 100 N 46123 317-272-2227
Dr. Julie Giardino, admin. Fax 272-3412
Our Shepherd Lutheran S 200/PK-8
9201 E County Road 100 N 46123 317-271-9100
Jeff Huntington, prin. Fax 271-3084

Bainbridge, Putnam, Pop. 737
North Putnam Community SD 1,600/PK-12
PO Box 169 46105 765-522-6218
Daniel Noel Ed.D., supt. Fax 522-3562
www.nputnam.k12.in.us
Bainbridge ES 400/PK-5
412 N Washington St 46105 765-522-6233
Rodney Simpson, prin. Fax 522-2903
Other Schools – See Roachdale

Bargersville, Johnson, Pop. 3,950
Center Grove Community SC
Supt. — See Greenwood
Maple Grove ES 800/K-5
3623 W Whiteland Rd 46106 317-881-0561
Brooke Phillips, prin. Fax 889-2553

Franklin Community SC
Supt. — See Franklin
Union ES 200/K-4
3990 W Division Rd 46106 317-422-5223
Katie Smith, prin. Fax 422-5068

Batesville, Franklin, Pop. 6,459
Batesville Community SC 2,200/PK-12
PO Box 121 47006 812-934-2194
Paul Ketcham, supt. Fax 933-0833
www.batesvilleinschools.com
Batesville IS 500/3-5
707 Columbus Ave 47006 812-934-5701
Devon Phillips, prin. Fax 933-0734
Batesville MS 500/6-8
201 N Mulberry St 47006 812-934-5175
Dave Strouse, prin. Fax 933-0834
Batesville PS 500/PK-2
760 State Road 46 W 47006 812-934-4509
Brad Stoneking, prin. Fax 933-0936

St. Louis S 400/PK-8
17 E Saint Louis Pl 47006 812-934-3310
Chad Moeller, prin. Fax 934-6202

Battle Ground, Tippecanoe, Pop. 1,327
Tippecanoe SC
Supt. — See Lafayette
Battle Ground ES 500/K-5
303 Main St 47920 765-567-2200
John Pearl, prin. Fax 567-4577

Bedford, Lawrence, Pop. 13,252
North Lawrence Community SD 5,100/PK-12
PO Box 729 47421 812-279-3521
Gary Conner, supt. Fax 275-1577
www.nlcs.k12.in.us
Bedford MS 600/6-8
1501 N St 47421 812-279-9781
David Schlegel, prin. Fax 277-3218
Fayetteville ES 200/K-5
223 Old Farm Rd 47421 812-279-2370
Rhonda Hackler, prin. Fax 278-7602
Lincoln ES 300/K-5
2014 F St 47421 812-275-6311
Angela Girgis, prin. Fax 277-7722
Needmore ES 200/K-5
278 Trogdon Ln 47421 812-279-2192
Wendy Butterfield, prin. Fax 277-1624
Parkview IS 200/3-5
2024 16th St 47421 812-275-3301
Amanda May, prin. Fax 277-7721
Parkview PS 300/PK-2
1701 Brian Lane Way 47421 812-275-2333
Dr. Theresa Lemons, prin. Fax 277-7720
Shawswick ES 300/K-5
71 Shawswick School Rd 47421 812-279-3115
Hein Tlustek, prin. Fax 275-0543
Shawswick MS 200/6-8
71 Shawswick School Rd 47421 812-275-6121
James Pentzer, prin. Fax 275-3458
Stalker ES 300/K-5
420 W St 47421 812-275-4821
Brian Perry, prin. Fax 277-7726
Other Schools – See Heltonville, Oolitic, Springville

St. Vincent De Paul S 200/PK-8
923 18th St 47421 812-279-2540
Teresa Underwood, prin. Fax 276-4880

Beech Grove, Marion, Pop. 13,930
Beech Grove CSD 2,900/PK-12
5334 Hornet Ave 46107 317-788-4481
Dr. Paul Kaiser, supt. Fax 782-4065
www.bgcs.k12.in.us
Beech Grove MS 500/7-8
1248 Buffalo St 46107 317-784-6640
Thomas Gearhart, prin. Fax 781-2926
Central ES 500/2-3
1000 Main St 46107 317-784-4565
Craig Buckler, prin. Fax 781-2930
Hornet Park ES 500/PK-1
5249 Hornet Ave 46107 317-780-5050
Erin Probus, prin. Fax 780-5053
South Grove IS 600/4-6
851 S 9th Ave 46107 317-786-7687
Tonya Reid, prin. Fax 781-2933

Holy Name S 300/PK-8
21 N 17th Ave 46107 317-784-9078
Robert Kitchens, prin. Fax 788-3616

Berne, Adams, Pop. 3,972
South Adams SD 1,300/PK-12
1075 Starfire Way 46711 260-589-3133
Scott Litwiller, supt. Fax 589-2065
www.southadams.k12.in.us
South Adams ES 600/PK-5
1012 Starfire Way 46711 260-589-1101
Shellie Miller, prin. Fax 589-2112
South Adams MS 300/6-8
1212 Starfire Way 46711 260-589-1102
Jeff Rich, prin. Fax 589-2112

Bicknell, Knox, Pop. 2,893
North Knox SC 1,300/K-12
11110 N State Road 159 47512 812-735-4434
Dr. Darrel Bobe, supt. Fax 328-6262
www.nknox.k12.in.us
North Knox PS 300/K-2
215 E 4th St 47512 812-735-2547
Scott Sturgeon, prin. Fax 735-2348
Other Schools – See Bruceville

Birdseye, Dubois, Pop. 413
Southeast Dubois County SC
Supt. — See Ferdinand
Pine Ridge ES 200/PK-4
4613 S Pine Ridge Rd 47513 812-817-0900
Ryan Haas, prin. Fax 326-2016

Bloomfield, Greene, Pop. 2,386
Bloomfield SD 900/K-12
PO Box 266 47424 812-384-4507
Jeff Gibboney, supt. Fax 384-0172
www.bsd.k12.in.us
Bloomfield ES 500/K-6
PO Box 266 47424 812-384-4271
Matt Britton, prin. Fax 384-2405

Eastern Greene SD 1,300/PK-12
1471 N State Road 43 47424 812-825-5722
Ted Baechtold, supt. Fax 825-9413
www.egreene.k12.in.us/
Eastern Greene ES 500/PK-4
10503 E State Road 54 47424 812-825-5623
Sharon Abts, prin. Fax 825-3891
Eastern Greene MS 400/5-8
10503 E State Road 54 47424 812-825-5010
Dennis Massengill, prin. Fax 825-7386

Bloomington, Monroe, Pop. 78,128
Monroe County Community SC 10,900/PK-12
315 E North Dr 47401 812-330-7700
Judith DeMuth Ed.D., supt. Fax 330-7813
www.mccsc.edu
Arlington Heights ES 300/PK-6
700 W Parrish Rd 47404 812-330-7747
Micah Heath, prin. Fax 330-7748
Batchelor MS 500/7-8
900 W Gordon Pike 47403 812-330-7763
Eric Gilpin, prin. Fax 330-7766
Binford ES 500/3-6
2300 E 2nd St 47401 812-330-7741
Jennifer Anderson, prin. Fax 330-7834
Childs ES 500/PK-6
2211 S High St 47401 812-330-7756
Chris Finley, prin. Fax 349-4798
Clear Creek ES 400/PK-6
300 W Clear Creek Dr 47403 812-824-2811
Susan Petty, prin. Fax 824-9265
Fairview ES 400/PK-6
627 W 8th St 47404 812-330-7732
Marti Golglazier, prin. Fax 330-7818
Grandview ES 400/PK-6
2300 S Endwright Rd 47403 812-825-3009
Lisa Roberts, prin. Fax 825-3302
Highland Park ES 300/PK-6
900 S Park Square Dr 47403 812-825-7673
Cassidy Rockhill, prin. Fax 825-4907
Jackson Creek MS 600/7-8
3980 S Sare Rd 47401 812-330-2451
David Pillar, prin. Fax 330-2457
Lakeview ES 500/PK-6
9090 S Strain Ridge Rd 47401 812-824-7061
Angela Evans, prin. Fax 824-9280
Marlin ES 200/K-6
1655 E Bethel Ln 47408 812-330-7750
Tim Dowling, prin. Fax 330-7822
Rogers ES 400/K-2
2200 E 2nd St 47401 812-330-7767
Mark Conrad, prin. Fax 330-7820
Summit ES 500/PK-6
1450 W Countryside Ln 47403 812-330-2011
Nick McGinnis, prin. Fax 330-2022
Templeton ES 500/PK-6
1400 S Brenda Ln 47401 812-330-7735
Rebecca Mungle, prin. Fax 330-7779
Tri-North MS 600/7-8
1000 W 15th St 47404 812-330-7745
Dr. Gale Hill, prin. Fax 330-7799
University ES 500/PK-6
1111 N Russell Rd 47408 812-330-7753
Dr. Gretchen Morgan, prin. Fax 330-7770
Other Schools – See Unionville

Richland-Bean Blossom Community SC
Supt. — See Ellettsville
Edgewood IS 500/3-5
7600 W Reeves Rd 47404 812-876-2219
Jennifer Lee, prin. Fax 876-2269
Edgewood PS 600/K-2
7700 W Reeves Rd 47404 812-876-9600
Brenda Whitaker, prin. Fax 876-9611

Adventist Christian ES 50/K-8
2230 N Martha St 47408 812-260-8588
Janelle Ruba, prin.
Bloomington Montessori S 200/PK-6
1835 S Highland Ave 47401 812-336-2800
Roger Meridith, head sch Fax 336-2183
Clear Creek Christian S 100/K-6
530 Church Ln 47403 812-824-2567
Penny Adams, prin. Fax 824-6032
Covenant Christian S 100/PK-12
4000 E Moores Creek Rd 47401 812-287-8833
Rob Akers, head sch Fax 333-2445
Harmony S 200/PK-12
PO Box 1787 47402 812-334-8349
Steve Bonchek, dir. Fax 333-3435
Lighthouse Christian Academy 200/K-12
1201 W That Rd 47403 812-824-2000
Joyce Huck B.A., prin. Fax 824-2017

St. Charles Boromeo S 400/PK-8
2224 E 3rd St 47401 812-336-5853
Madonna Paskash, prin. Fax 349-0300

Bluffton, Wells, Pop. 9,806
Bluffton-Harrison Metropolitan SD 1,500/PK-12
805 E Harrison Rd 46714 260-824-2620
Wayne Barker, supt. Fax 824-6011
www.bhmsd.org
Bluffton-Harrison ES 600/PK-4
1100 E Spring St 46714 260-824-0333
Julie Meitzler, prin. Fax 824-0512
Bluffton-Harrison MS 400/5-8
1500 Stogdill Rd 46714 260-824-3536
Rick Mettler, prin. Fax 824-6014

Northern Wells Community SD
Supt. — See Ossian
Lancaster Central ES 500/PK-5
275 E Jackson St N 46714 260-565-3135
Ginger Butcher, prin. Fax 565-3945

Boone Grove, Porter
Porter Township SC
Supt. — See Valparaiso
Boone Grove ES 200/4-5
325 W 550 S 46302 219-462-1032
Edward Ivanyo, prin. Fax 476-4376
Boone Grove MS 400/6-8
325 W 550 S 46302 219-464-4828
Robert Lichtenberger, prin. Fax 465-0999

Boonville, Warrick, Pop. 6,171
Warrick County SC 9,900/K-12
PO Box 809 47601 812-897-0400
Brad Schneider, supt. Fax 897-6033
www.warrick.k12.in.us/
Boonville MS 700/6-8
555 N Yankeetown Rd 47601 812-897-1420
Abbie Redmon, prin. Fax 897-6584
Loge ES 400/K-5
915 N 4th St 47601 812-897-2230
Lynn Pierce, prin. Fax 897-6052
Oakdale ES 500/K-5
802 S 8th St 47601 812-897-3710
Jamie Pryor, prin. Fax 897-6049
Other Schools – See Chandler, Elberfeld, Lynnville, Newburgh, Tennyson

Borden, Clark, Pop. 799
West Clark Community SC
Supt. — See Sellersburg
Borden ES 400/K-6
PO Box 230 47106 812-967-2548
Lisa Hawkins, prin. Fax 967-5824

Boswell, Benton, Pop. 777
Benton Community SC
Supt. — See Fowler
Boswell ES 100/PK-6
414 W Main St 47921 765-869-5523
Gail Lange, prin. Fax 869-4384

Bourbon, Marshall, Pop. 1,801
Triton SC 1,000/K-12
100 Triton Dr 46504 574-342-2255
Donna Burroughs, supt. Fax 342-8165
www.triton.k12.in.us/
Triton ES 500/K-6
200 Triton Dr 46504 574-342-2355
Jeremy Riffle, prin. Fax 342-0053

Brazil, Clay, Pop. 7,835
Clay Community SD 4,400/PK-12
1013 S Forest Ave 47834 812-443-4461
Jeffery Fritz, supt. Fax 442-0849
www.clay.k12.in.us
East Side ES 300/PK-5
936 E National Ave 47834 812-448-8755
Lisa Froderman, prin. Fax 443-1126
Forest Park ES 300/PK-5
800 S Alabama St 47834 812-443-7621
Dustin Jorgensen, prin. Fax 442-0204
Jackson Township ES 300/K-5
1860 E County Road 600 N 47834 812-986-2177
Bradford Ennen, prin. Fax 443-1406
Meridian Street ES 300/PK-5
410 N Meridian St 47834 812-448-8560
Karen Phillips, prin. Fax 442-0410
North Clay MS 800/6-8
3450 W State Road 340 47834 812-448-1530
Robert Boltinghouse, prin. Fax 442-0608
Staunton ES 300/K-5
6990 N County Road 425 W 47834 812-448-8270
Sheryl Jordan, prin. Fax 446-1038
Van Buren ES 200/K-5
2075 E County Road 1200 N 47834 812-448-1362
Gail Williams, prin. Fax 448-3602
Other Schools – See Clay City

Cornerstone Christian Academy 100/PK-5
PO Box 185 47834 812-446-4416
Linda Somheil, prin. Fax 448-3878

Bremen, Marshall, Pop. 4,550
Bremen Public SD 1,500/K-12
512 W Grant St 46506 574-546-3929
Dr. James White, supt. Fax 546-6303
www.bps.k12.in.us
Bremen Elementary-Middle S 1,000/K-8
700 W South St 46506 574-546-3554
Larry Yelaska, prin. Fax 546-2194

St. Paul's Lutheran S 100/PK-8
605 S Center St 46506 574-546-2790
James Russell, prin. Fax 546-3242

Bristol, Elkhart, Pop. 1,559
Elkhart Community SD
Supt. — See Elkhart
Bristol ES 500/PK-6
705 Indiana St 46507 574-848-7421
Jill Balcom, prin. Fax 848-7422

Middlebury Community SD
Supt. — See Middlebury
York ES 300/K-3
13549 State Road 120 46507 574-825-5312
Yvonne Buller, prin. Fax 825-0146

Brooklyn, Morgan, Pop. 1,588
Metro SD of Martinsville
Supt. — See Martinsville
Brooklyn ES 200/K-4
251 N Church St 46111 317-831-2150
Jennifer Teare, prin. Fax 831-2226

Brookston, White, Pop. 1,541
Frontier SC
Supt. — See Chalmers
Frontier ES 400/K-6
811 S Railroad St 47923 765-563-3901
Carmen Bordner, prin. Fax 563-6938

Brookville, Franklin, Pop. 2,579
Franklin County Community SC 2,800/PK-12
225 E 10th St 47012 765-647-4128
Dr. Debbie Howell, supt. Fax 647-2417
www.fccsc.k12.in.us
Brookville ES 500/PK-5
10160 Oxford Pike 47012 765-647-3503
Myla Brack, prin. Fax 647-2659
Franklin County MS 400/6-8
9092 Wildcat Ln 47012 765-647-6040
Christopher Bundy, prin. Fax 647-4960
Other Schools – See Cedar Grove, Laurel

St. Michael S 200/PK-8
275 High St 47012 765-647-4961
Cindy Johnson, prin. Fax 647-6802

Brownsburg, Hendricks, Pop. 20,984
Brownsburg Community SC 8,000/PK-12
310 S Stadium Dr 46112 317-852-5726
Jim Snapp, supt. Fax 852-1015
www.brownsburg.k12.in.us
Brown ES 500/K-5
340 S Stadium Dr 46112 317-852-1498
Casey Patterson, prin. Fax 858-2171
Brownsburg East MS 1,200/6-8
1250 Airport Rd 46112 317-852-2386
Shane Hacker, prin. Fax 852-1023
Brownsburg ECC 200/PK-PK
111 Eastern Ave 46112 317-852-1046
Jennifer Newingham, coord. Fax 852-1048
Brownsburg West MS 800/6-8
1555 S Odell St 46112 317-852-3143
Laurie Johnson, prin. Fax 858-4100
Cardinal ES 500/PK-5
3590 Hornaday Rd 46112 317-852-1036
Marc Gianfagna, prin. Fax 858-4117
Delaware Trail ES 500/PK-5
3680 Hornaday Rd 46112 317-852-1062
Jennifer Greene, prin. Fax 858-4118
Eagle ES 800/K-5
555 Sycamore St 46112 317-852-1050
Ryan Hoover, prin. Fax 858-4119
Reagan ES 700/K-5
4845 Bulldog Way 46112 317-852-1060
Scott Chambers, prin. Fax 852-1064
White Lick ES 600/K-5
1400 S Odell St 46112 317-852-3126
Susan Wise, prin. Fax 858-4120

Bethesda Christian S 400/PK-12
7950 N County Road 650 E 46112 317-858-2820
Chad Smith, head sch Fax 858-2819
St. Malachy S 400/PK-8
7410 N County Road 1000 E 46112 317-852-2242
Angela Bostrom, prin. Fax 852-3604

Brownstown, Jackson, Pop. 2,921
Brownstown Central Community SC 1,700/PK-12
608 W Commerce St 47220 812-358-4271
Greg Walker, supt. Fax 358-5303
www.btownccs.k12.in.us
Brownstown Central MS 400/6-8
520 W Walnut St 47220 812-358-4947
Doug McClure, prin. Fax 358-3940
Brownstown ES 700/PK-5
612 S Base Rd 47220 812-358-3680
Chrystal Street, prin. Fax 358-9099

Lutheran Central S 100/K-8
415 N Elm St 47220 812-358-2512
Jonathan Sprengel, prin. Fax 358-9905

Bruceville, Knox, Pop. 473
North Knox SC
Supt. — See Bicknell
North Knox IS 400/3-6
7820 N Camp Arthur Rd 47516 812-324-2291
Don Osburn, prin. Fax 324-9002

Bryant, Jay, Pop. 250
Jay SC
Supt. — See Portland
Bloomfield ES 200/K-5
350 E 500 N 47326 260-726-9417
Ben Dues, prin. Fax 726-4680

Bunker Hill, Miami, Pop. 866
Maconaquah SC 2,300/PK-12
7932 S Strawtown Pike 46914 765-689-9131
Dr. Douglas Arnold, supt. Fax 689-0995
www.maconaquah.k12.in.us
Maconaquah ES 700/2-5
7784 S Strawtown Pike 46914 765-689-9131
Kelly McPike, prin. Fax 689-9693
Maconaquah MS 500/6-8
594 E 800 S 46914 765-689-9131
Craig Jernagan, prin. Fax 689-9360
Other Schools – See Peru

Burnettsville, White, Pop. 342
Twin Lakes SC
Supt. — See Monticello
Eastlawn ES 200/PK-5
47 S 1300 E 47926 574-943-3637
Karla Cronk, prin. Fax 943-3618

Butler, DeKalb, Pop. 2,658
DeKalb County Eastern Community SD 1,400/K-12
300 E Washington St 46721 260-868-2125
Dr. Jeffrey Stephens, supt. Fax 868-2562
www.dekalbeastern.com
Butler ES 400/K-6
1025 S Broadway St 46721 260-868-2123
Kim Clark, prin. Fax 868-1709
Other Schools – See Saint Joe

Cambridge City, Wayne, Pop. 1,861
Western Wayne SD
Supt. — See Pershing
Lincoln MS 300/6-8
205 E Parkway Dr 47327 765-478-5840
Renee Lakes, prin. Fax 478-3265
Western Wayne ES 500/PK-5
801 E Delaware St 47327 765-478-3622
Jessica Neill, prin. Fax 478-4332

Camby, Morgan
Mooresville Consolidated SC
Supt. — See Mooresville
North Madison ES 700/K-6
7456 E Hadley Rd 46113 317-831-9214
Stephanie McGaha, prin. Fax 831-9238

Campbellsburg, Washington, Pop. 579
West Washington SC 800/PK-12
8026 W Batt Rd 47108 812-755-4996
Keith Nance, supt. Fax 755-4843
www.westwashingtonschools.org
West Washington ES 400/PK-6
8030 W Batts Rd 47108 812-755-4934
Tom Rosenbaum, prin. Fax 755-4788

Cannelton, Perry, Pop. 1,540
Cannelton CSD 200/PK-12
109 S 3rd St Ste A 47520 812-547-2637
Alva Sibbitt Ed.D., supt. Fax 547-4142
www.cannelton.k12.in.us
Bennett Early Learning Center 50/PK-K
411 Washington St 47520 812-548-4599
Brian Garrett, prin. Fax 548-2291
Myers ES 100/1-5
615 Taylor St 47520 812-547-4126
Brian Garrett, prin. Fax 548-2291

Carlisle, Sullivan, Pop. 689
Southwest SC
Supt. — See Sullivan
Carlisle S 300/K-8
PO Box 649 47838 812-398-3851
Glenda Jones, prin. Fax 398-2221

Carmel, Hamilton, Pop. 77,695
Carmel Clay SD 15,900/PK-12
5201 E Main St 46033 317-844-9961
Dr. Nicholas D. Wahl, supt. Fax 844-9965
www.ccs.k12.in.us
Carmel ES 500/PK-5
101 4th Ave SE 46032 317-844-0168
Megan Klinginsmith, prin. Fax 571-4024
Carmel MS 1,200/6-8
300 S Guilford Rd 46032 317-846-7331
Deanna Pitman, prin. Fax 571-4067
Cherry Tree ES 700/PK-5
13989 Hazel Dell Pkwy 46033 317-846-3086
Chris Atkinson, prin. Fax 571-4053
Clay MS 1,200/6-8
5150 E 126th St 46033 317-844-7251
Todd Crosby, prin. Fax 571-4020
College Wood ES 800/K-5
12415 Shelborne Rd 46032 317-733-6430
Kathy Olsen, prin. Fax 733-6445
Creekside MS 1,500/6-8
3525 W 126th St 46032 317-733-6420
Tim Phares, prin. Fax 733-6422
Forest Dale ES 700/PK-5
10721 W Lakeshore Dr 46033 317-844-4948
Sara Inskeep, prin. Fax 571-4031
Mohawk Trails ES 600/K-5
4242 E 126th St 46033 317-844-1158
Kate Fagan, prin. Fax 571-4034
Prairie Trace ES 600/K-5
14200 River Rd 46033 317-571-7925
Jill Schipp, prin. Fax 571-7926
Smoky Row ES 600/PK-5
900 W 136th St 46032 317-571-4084
Lila Jay, prin. Fax 571-4088
Towne Meadow ES 700/K-5
10850 Towne Rd 46032 317-733-2645
Kim Barrett, prin. Fax 733-2655
West Clay ES 700/K-5
3495 W 126th St 46032 317-733-6500
Jennifer Szuhaj, prin. Fax 733-6501
Woodbrook ES 600/K-5
4311 E 116th St 46033 317-846-4225
Kelly Davis, prin. Fax 571-4037
Other Schools – See Indianapolis

Carmel SDA S 1-8
14535 Carey Rd 46033 317-566-9762
Coram Deo Academy 100/K-12
651 W Main St 46032 317-844-4224
Beth Fetters, dir.
Our Lady of Mt. Carmel S 700/K-8
14596 Oak Ridge Rd 46032 317-846-1118
Sr. Mary Emily Knapp, prin. Fax 582-2375

Cayuga, Vermillion, Pop. 1,146
North Vermillion Community SC 700/K-12
5551 N Falcon Dr 47928 765-492-4033
Daniel Nelson, supt. Fax 492-7001
www.nvc.k12.in.us
North Vermillion ES 400/K-6
5585 N Falcon Dr 47928 765-492-7010
Brian Byrum, prin. Fax 492-7017

Cedar Grove, Franklin, Pop. 154
Franklin County Community SC
Supt. — See Brookville
Mt. Carmel S 500/K-6
6178 Johnson Fork Rd 47016 765-647-4191
Marla Stevens, prin. Fax 647-4009

Cedar Lake, Lake, Pop. 11,431
Crown Point Community SC
Supt. — See Crown Point
MacArthur ES 500/K-5
12900 Fairbanks St 46303 219-662-3600
Marian Buchko, prin. Fax 374-7567

Hanover Community SC 2,100/K-12
PO Box 645 46303 219-374-3500
Thomas Taylor, supt. Fax 374-4411
www.hanover.k12.in.us
Ball ES 500/K-5
13313 Parrish Ave 46303 219-374-3700
Ryan Eckart, prin. Fax 374-4430
Hanover Central MS 500/6-8
10631 W 141st Ave 46303 219-374-3900
Deb Snedden, prin. Fax 374-8926
Lincoln ES 500/K-5
12245 W 109th Ave 46303 219-374-3600
Frank Zaremba, prin. Fax 365-1432

Celestine, Dubois
Northeast Dubois County SC
Supt. — See Dubois
Celestine ES 100/K-4
6748 E Main Cross St 47521 812-678-2777
Brenda Ferguson, prin. Fax 634-1266

Centerville, Wayne, Pop. 2,522
Centerville-Abington Community SD 1,800/PK-12
115 W South St 47330 765-855-3475
Philip Stevenson, supt. Fax 855-2524
www.centerville.k12.in.us
Centerville-Abington ES 500/3-6
200 W South St 47330 765-855-5132
Kelly VanWinkle, prin. Fax 855-5719
Centerville-Abington JHS 300/7-8
509 Willow Grove Rd 47330 765-855-5113
Rick Schauss, prin. Fax 855-5207
Hamilton ES 400/PK-2
1281 S Round Barn Rd 47330 765-966-3911
Lee Stienbarger, prin. Fax 966-4491

Central, Harrison
South Harrison Community SD
Supt. — See Corydon
Heth-Washington ES 200/K-6
2450 Heth Washington Rd SW 47110 812-732-4766
Nissa Ellett, prin. Fax 732-8840

Chalmers, White, Pop. 504
Frontier SC 700/K-12
PO Box 809 47929 219-984-5009
Dan Sichting, supt. Fax 984-5022
www.frontier.k12.in.us
Other Schools – See Brookston

Chandler, Warrick, Pop. 2,857
Warrick County SC
Supt. — See Boonville
Chandler ES 500/K-5
401 S Jaycee St 47610 812-925-6021
Stephanie Henrich, prin. Fax 925-3273

Charlestown, Clark, Pop. 7,449
Greater Clark County SD
Supt. — See Jeffersonville
Charlestown MS 500/6-8
8804 High Jackson Rd 47111 812-256-6363
Karen Wesely, prin. Fax 256-7282
Jennings ES 500/PK-5
603 Market St 47111 812-256-7284
Adrienne Bach, prin. Fax 256-7291
Pleasant Ridge ES 500/K-5
1250 Monroe St 47111 812-256-7286
Sara Porter, prin. Fax 256-7290

Charlottesville, Hancock
Eastern Hancock County Community SC 1,100/K-12
10370 E County Road 250 N 46117 317-467-0064
Dr. Vicki McGuire, supt. Fax 936-5516
www.easternhancock.org
Eastern Hancock ES 500/K-5
10450 E County Road 250 N 46117 317-936-5829
Amanda Pyle, prin. Fax 936-5318
Eastern Hancock MS 300/6-8
10380 E County Road 250 N 46117 317-936-5324
David Pfaff, prin. Fax 936-5050

Chesterton, Porter, Pop. 12,902
Duneland SC 5,900/K-12
601 W Morgan Ave 46304 219-983-3600
Dr. Ginger Bolinger, supt. Fax 983-3614
www.duneland.k12.in.us
Bailly ES 400/K-4
800 S 5th St 46304 219-983-3670
Kevin Zeck, prin. Fax 983-3679
Brummit ES 300/K-4
2500 Indian Boundary Rd 46304 219-983-3660
Antonino Cammarata, prin. Fax 983-3669
Chesterton MS 1,000/7-8
651 W Morgan Ave 46304 219-983-3776
Mike Megyesi, prin. Fax 983-3798
Liberty ES 500/K-4
50-1 W 900 N 46304 219-983-3650
Christy Jarka, prin. Fax 983-3659
Liberty IS 400/5-6
50 W 900 N 46304 219-983-3690
Greg Guernsey, prin. Fax 983-3709
Westchester IS 500/5-6
1050 S 5th St 46304 219-983-3710
Shawn Longacre, prin. Fax 983-3729
Other Schools – See Porter, Valparaiso

St. Patrick S 300/PK-8
640 N Calumet Rd 46304 219-926-1707
Rev. James Meade, prin. Fax 921-1922

Chrisney, Spencer, Pop. 476
North Spencer County SC
Supt. — See Lincoln City
Chrisney ES 200/PK-6
PO Box 97 47611 812-362-8200
Julie Kemp, prin. Fax 362-8201

Churubusco, Whitley, Pop. 1,774
Smith-Green Community SD 1,200/PK-12
222 W Tulley St 46723 260-693-2007
Daniel Hile, supt. Fax 693-6434
www.sgcs.k12.in.us/
Churubusco ES 500/PK-5
3 Eagle Dr 46723 260-693-2188
Dan Hile, prin. Fax 693-2683

Cicero, Hamilton, Pop. 4,762

Cicero Adventist ES 100/1-8
24089 State Road 19 46034 317-984-3252
Fax 984-3252

Clarksville, Clark, Pop. 21,221
Clarksville Community SC 1,400/PK-12
200 Ettel Ln 47129 812-282-7753
Tina Bennett, supt. Fax 282-7754
www.ccsc.k12.in.us/
Clarksville ES 500/PK-4
700 N Randolph Ave 47129 812-282-1447
Mindy Dablow, prin. Fax 280-5019
Clarksville MS 400/5-8
101 Ettel Ln 47129 812-282-8235
Nikki Bullington, prin. Fax 280-5004

Greater Clark County SD
Supt. — See Jeffersonville
Parkwood ES 500/PK-5
748 Spicewood Dr 47129 812-945-2387
Brandon Winebrenner, prin. Fax 945-4072

St. Anthony of Padua S 300/PK-8
320 N Sherwood Ave 47129 812-282-2144
Stephany Tucker, prin. Fax 282-2169

Clay City, Clay, Pop. 856
Clay Community SD
Supt. — See Brazil
Clay City ES 400/K-6
681 Lankford St 47841 812-939-3120
Michael Owens, prin. Fax 939-3170

Claypool, Kosciusko, Pop. 430
Warsaw Community SC
Supt. — See Warsaw
Claypool ES 400/PK-6
2024 W 700 S 46510 574-566-2300
Melissa Rees, prin. Fax 371-5002

Clayton, Hendricks, Pop. 965
Mill Creek Community SC 1,500/PK-12
6631 S County Road 200 W 46118 317-539-9200
Jim Diagostino, supt. Fax 303-1811
www.mccsc.k12.in.us/
Cascade MS 400/6-8
6423 S County Road 200 W 46118 317-539-9285
Eric Sieferman, prin. Fax 303-1907
Mill Creek East ES 400/PK-5
4740 Iowa St 46118 317-539-9225
Wendy Myers, prin. Fax 303-1908
Other Schools – See Amo

Clinton, Vermillion, Pop. 4,826
South Vermillion Community SC 1,800/PK-12
PO Box 387 47842 765-832-2426
David Chapman, supt. Fax 832-7391
www.svcs.k12.in.us
Central ES 400/PK-5
208 S 9th St 47842 765-832-7731
Ryan Jenkins, prin. Fax 832-5327
Pyle ES 200/PK-5
72 E 1100 S 47842 765-832-7718
Broc Leslie, prin. Fax 832-5321
South Vermillion MS 400/6-8
900 Wildcat Dr 47842 765-832-7727
Angela Harris, prin. Fax 832-5316
Van Duyn ES 200/K-5
15095 S Rangeline Rd 47842 765-832-7761
Ronda Foster, prin. Fax 832-5324

Cloverdale, Putnam, Pop. 2,143
Cloverdale Community SD 1,200/PK-12
310 E Logan St 46120 765-795-4664
Greg Linton, supt. Fax 795-5166
www.cloverdale.k12.in.us
Cloverdale ES 400/PK-4
311 E Logan St 46120 765-795-4339
Brad Sandy, prin. Fax 795-5449
Cloverdale MS 400/5-8
312 E Logan St 46120 765-795-2900
Stacey Baugh, prin. Fax 795-2901

Columbia City, Whitley, Pop. 8,635
Whitley County Consolidated SD 4,000/PK-12
107 N Walnut St 46725 260-244-5772
Dr. Patricia O'Connor, supt. Fax 244-4590
www.wccsonline.com
Coesse ES 300/K-5
2250 S 500 E 46725 260-244-3351
Michelle Urban, prin. Fax 244-4086
Indian Springs MS 800/6-8
1692 S State Road 9 46725 260-244-5148
Jan Boylen, prin. Fax 244-4710
Little Turtle ES 500/K-5
1710 S State Road 9 46725 260-244-3343
Kurt Kehmeyer, contact Fax 244-3229
Northern Heights ES 500/K-5
5209 N State Road 109 46725 260-691-2371
Wesley Mullett, prin. Fax 691-3228
Raber ES 400/PK-5
700 E Jackson St 46725 260-244-5857
Julie Turpin, prin. Fax 244-4059

Faith Christian Academy of Whitley Co. 50/PK-8
1550 E State Road 205 46725 260-248-4872
Rev. Larry Schmoekel, admin. Fax 244-4634

Columbus, Bartholomew, Pop. 43,281
Bartholomew Consolidated SC 11,500/PK-12
1200 Central Ave 47201 812-376-4220
Dr. Jim Roberts Ed.D., supt. Fax 376-4486
www.bcsc.k12.in.us
Central MS 800/7-8
725 7th St 47201 812-376-4287
Randall Gratz, prin. Fax 376-4511
Clifty Creek ES 600/PK-6
4625 E 50 N 47203 812-376-4342
Michael Parsons, prin. Fax 376-4305
Columbus Signature Acad - Fodrea Campus 300/PK-6
2775 Illinois Ave 47201 812-376-4321
Lyndsey Linneweber, prin. Fax 376-4501
Columbus Signature Acad - Lincoln 300/K-6
750 5th St 47201 812-376-4447
Brett Findley, prin. Fax 376-4446
Johnson Early Education Ctr 50/PK-PK
1209 Sycamore St 47201 812-376-4569
Shane Yates, dir.
Mt. Healthy ES 400/K-6
12150 S State Road 58 47201 812-342-2463
Amy Wetherald, prin. Fax 342-0584
Northside MS 900/7-8
1400 27th St 47201 812-376-4405
Amy Dixon, prin. Fax 376-4479
Parkside ES 800/PK-6
1400 Parkside Dr 47203 812-376-4314
Chris Smith, prin. Fax 376-4324
Richards ES 600/K-6
3311 Fairlawn Dr 47203 812-376-4311
Darin Sprong, prin. Fax 376-4505
Rockcreek ES 400/PK-6
13000 E 200 S 47203 812-579-5221
Jennifer Dettmer, prin. Fax 579-6488
Schmitt ES 800/PK-6
2675 California St 47201 812-376-4307
Brett Boezeman, prin. Fax 376-4506
Smith ES 500/K-6
4505 Waycross Dr 47203 812-376-4317
Jay Payne, prin. Fax 376-4502
Southside ES 900/PK-6
1320 W 200 S 47201 812-376-4423
Jeff Backmeyer, prin. Fax 376-4507
Other Schools – See Taylorsville

ABC-Stewart Montessori S 200/PK-6
6691 W State Road 46 47201 812-342-3029
Mike Gorday, dir. Fax 342-0296
Columbus Christian S 200/PK-12
3170 Indiana Ave 47201 812-372-3780
Rev. Kendall Wildey, admin. Fax 372-3878
St. Bartholomew S 400/K-8
1306 27th St 47201 812-372-6830
Helen Heckman, prin. Fax 376-0377
St. Peter Lutheran S 400/K-8
719 5th St 47201 812-372-5266
Scott Schumacher, prin. Fax 372-7556
White Creek Lutheran S 100/K-8
16270 S 300 W 47201 812-342-6832
Janice Buss, prin. Fax 342-6832

Commiskey, Jennings
Jennings County SC
Supt. — See North Vernon
Graham Creek ES 300/K-6
7910 S County Road 90 W 47227 812-346-4179
Todd Hearne, prin. Fax 346-8482

Connersville, Fayette, Pop. 13,304
Fayette County SC 3,800/PK-12
1401 Spartan Dr 47331 765-825-2178
Scott Collins, supt. Fax 825-8060
fayettein.schooldesk.net
Connersville MS 600/7-8
1900 N Grand Ave 47331 765-825-1139
Beth Denham, prin. Fax 827-4346
Eastview ES 300/PK-6
401 S Fountain St 47331 765-825-5541
James Small, prin. Fax 827-1584
Everton ES 300/K-6
2440 E Everton Rd 47331 765-825-5840
Bryan Jennings, prin. Fax 825-4275
Fayette Central ES 400/PK-6
2928 N County Road 225 W 47331 765-825-6261
Kathy McCarty, prin. Fax 825-5956
Frazee ES 300/K-6
600 W 3rd St 47331 765-825-6811
Mia McCreary, prin. Fax 827-4805
Grandview ES 400/PK-6
2620 Iowa Ave 47331 765-825-2981
Carla Hubbard, prin. Fax 825-4703
Maplewood ES 300/K-6
1800 N Eastern Ave 47331 765-825-3941
Stephanie McCann, prin. Fax 825-8583

St. Gabriel S 100/PK-6
224 W 9th St 47331 765-825-7951
Sue Barth, prin. Fax 827-4347

Converse, Miami, Pop. 1,252
Oak Hill United SC 1,600/K-12
PO Box 550 46919 765-395-3341
Joel Martin, supt. Fax 395-3343
www.ohusc.k12.in.us
Converse ES 400/K-6
PO Box 489 46919 765-395-3341
Valree Kinch, prin. Fax 395-7830
Oak Hill JHS 300/7-8
7760 W Delphi Pike Ste 27 46919 765-395-3341
Greg Perkins, prin. Fax 391-1397
Other Schools – See Swayzee, Sweetser

Corydon, Harrison, Pop. 3,080
South Harrison Community SD 3,100/K-12
315 S Harrison Dr 47112 812-738-2168
Dr. Mark Eastridge, supt. Fax 738-2158
www.shcsc.k12.in.us/
Corydon Central JHS 400/7-8
377 Country Club Rd 47112 812-738-4184
Jason Toler, prin. Fax 738-5752
Corydon ES 500/K-3
125 Beechmont Dr NE 47112 812-738-4183
Tamela Brewer, prin. Fax 738-7963
Corydon IS 400/4-6
100 High School Rd 47112 812-738-6548
Sandra Joseph, prin. Fax 738-6420
Other Schools – See Central, Elizabeth, New Middletown

St. Joseph S 100/PK-6
512 N Mulberry St 47112 812-738-4549
Julie Crone, prin. Fax 738-2722

Covington, Fountain, Pop. 2,619
Covington Community SC 1,000/PK-12
601 Market St 47932 765-793-4877
Kirk Booe M.S., supt. Fax 793-5209
www.covington.k12.in.us/
Covington ES 500/PK-5
1110 7th St 47932 765-793-2254
Alison Karrfalt, prin. Fax 793-5214
Covington MS 200/6-8
514 Railroad St 47932 765-793-4451
Steve Reynolds, prin. Fax 793-5217

Crawfordsville, Montgomery, Pop. 15,708
Crawfordsville Community SD 1,900/PK-12
1000 Fairview Ave 47933 765-362-2342
Scott Bowling, supt. Fax 364-3237
www.cville.k12.in.us
Crawfordsville MS 6-8
705 Wallace Ave 47933 765-362-2992
Brent Bokhart, prin. Fax 364-3212
Hoover ES 400/4-5
1301 S Elm St 47933 765-362-2691
Marci Galinowski, prin. Fax 362-1149
Hose ES 400/K-1
800 Fairview Ave 47933 765-362-2886
Carol Starlin, prin. Fax 362-3957
Nicholson ES 300/2-3
1010 Lane Ave 47933 765-362-2607
Jennifer Coyle, prin. Fax 361-0767
Willson S 200/PK-PK
500 E Jefferson St 47933 765-362-0005
Marci Galinowski, dir. Fax 364-3220

North Montgomery Community SC 2,000/PK-12
480 W 580 N 47933 765-359-2112
Dr. Colleen Moran, supt. Fax 359-2111
www.nm.k12.in.us/
Northridge MS 500/6-8
482 W 580 N 47933 765-364-1071
Steve Renzino, prin. Fax 362-7985
Pleasant Hill ES 300/PK-5
6895 N 100 W 47933 765-339-4403
Anthony Tharp, prin. Fax 339-4600
Sommer ES 300/K-5
3794 W US Highway 136 47933 765-362-3979
Suzi Gephart, prin. Fax 362-5619
Sugar Creek ES 300/K-5
4702 E 300 N 47933 765-794-4855
Cris McCoy, prin. Fax 794-4578

South Montgomery Community SC 1,600/PK-12
6425 US 231 S 47933 765-866-0203
Dr. Shawn Greiner, supt. Fax 866-0736
www.southmont.k12.in.us
New Market ES 400/PK-6
410 N 3rd St 47933 765-866-0740
Chris Larson, prin. Fax 866-2031
Southmont JHS 300/7-8
6460 S US Highway 231 47933 765-866-2023
Anna Roth, prin. Fax 866-2045
Other Schools – See Ladoga, New Ross

Crothersville, Jackson, Pop. 1,577
Crothersville Community SD 500/K-12
201 S Preston St 47229 812-793-2601
Dr. Terry Goodin, supt. Fax 793-3004
www.crothersville.k12.in.us
Crothersville ES 200/K-5
109 S Preston St 47229 812-793-2622
Drew Markel, prin. Fax 793-3004

Crown Point, Lake, Pop. 27,010
Crown Point Community SC 8,000/PK-12
200 E North St 46307 219-663-3371
Dr. Teresa Eineman, supt. Fax 662-3414
www.cps.k12.in.us
Ball ES 500/K-5
720 W Summit St 46307 219-663-0047
Nicholas Ciochina, prin. Fax 662-4320
Colonel John Wheeler MS 900/6-8
401 W Joliet St 46307 219-663-2173
Mark Gianfermi, prin. Fax 662-4378
Eisenhower ES 600/PK-5
1450 S Main St 46307 219-663-8800
Mary Ann Chapko, prin. Fax 662-4333
Lake Street ES 400/K-5
475 Lake St 46307 219-663-5683
Cindy Wise, prin. Fax 662-4329
Robinson ES 500/K-5
601 Pettibone St 46307 219-663-2525
Barbara Merrill, prin. Fax 662-4365
Ross ES 500/3-5
11319 Randolph St 46307 219-663-3010
Jennifer Stolarz, prin. Fax 662-3529
Taft MS 900/6-8
1000 S Main St 46307 219-663-1507
Michael Hazen, prin. Fax 662-4349
Winfield ES 500/K-2
13128 Montgomery St 46307 219-663-2287
Jillian Alonzo, prin. Fax 663-1138
Other Schools – See Cedar Lake

Avicenna Academy PK-8
9803 Colorado St 46307 219-736-7100
Amanda Arceo, head sch Fax 736-7401
Indiana Horizon Academy 100/PK-2
9803 Colorado St 46307 219-796-9490
Lama Almoazen, prin. Fax 627-6114
Northwest Adventist Christian S 50/K-8
10570 Randolph St 46307 219-663-4472
St. Mary Catholic Community S 500/PK-8
405 E Joliet St 46307 219-663-0676
L. Thomas Ruiz, prin. Fax 663-1347
Trinity Lutheran S 200/PK-8
250 S Indiana Ave 46307 219-663-1578
Christine Miller, prin. Fax 663-1586

Culver, Marshall, Pop. 1,330
Culver Community SC 700/K-12
700 School St 46511 574-842-3364
Karen Shuman, supt. Fax 842-4615
www.culver.k12.in.us
Culver ES 500/K-5
401 School St 46511 574-842-3389
Erin Proskey, prin. Fax 842-3380

Dale, Spencer, Pop. 1,586
North Spencer County SC
Supt. — See Lincoln City
Turnham Education Center 300/PK-6
PO Box 432 47523 812-937-4300
Jennifer Jazyk, prin. Fax 937-4317

Daleville, Delaware, Pop. 1,631
Daleville Community SD 800/K-12
14300 W 2nd St 47334 765-378-3329
Paul Garrison M.S., supt. Fax 378-3649
www.daleville.k12.in.us
Daleville ES 400/K-6
8600 S Bronco Dr 47334 765-378-0251
Kimberly Beard M.A., prin. Fax 378-4085

Danville, Hendricks, Pop. 8,895
Danville Community SC 2,600/PK-12
200 Warrior Way 46122 317-745-2212
Dr. Tracey Shafer, supt. Fax 745-3924
www.danville.k12.in.us
Danville Community MS 800/5-8
1425 W Lincoln St 46122 317-745-5491
Marsha Webster, prin. Fax 745-3949
North ES 500/PK-2
398 Urban St 46122 317-745-2610
Karen Perkins, prin. Fax 745-3921
South ES 400/3-4
1375 W Lincoln St 46122 317-745-2131
Tina Noe, prin. Fax 745-3918

Dayton, Tippecanoe, Pop. 1,406
Tippecanoe SC
Supt. — See Lafayette
Dayton ES 400/K-5
PO Box 187 47941 765-447-5004
Courtney Wildoner, prin. Fax 448-6212

Decatur, Adams, Pop. 9,334
North Adams Community SD 1,800/PK-12
625 Stadium Dr 46733 260-724-7146
Brent Lehman, supt. Fax 724-4777
www.nadams.k12.in.us
Bellmont MS 500/5-8
1200 E North Adams Dr 46733 260-724-3137
Scott Miller, prin. Fax 724-4495
Northwest ES 300/2-4
1109 Dayton St 46733 260-724-3633
Keith Dicke, prin. Fax 724-9247
Southeast ES 300/PK-1
901 Everhart Dr 46733 260-724-3118
Aaron Baker, prin. Fax 724-3956

St. Joseph S 300/PK-8
127 N 4th St 46733 260-724-2765
Jeffrey Kieffer, prin. Fax 724-4953
St. Peter Immanuel S 100/PK-8
3845 E 1100 N 46733 260-623-6115
Greg Becker, prin. Fax 623-3865
Wyneken Memorial Lutheran S 200/PK-8
11565 N US Highway 27 46733 260-639-6177
Andrew Gavrun, prin. Fax 639-3050
Zion Lutheran S 100/PK-8
1022 W Monroe St 46733 260-728-9995
Mitch Hill, prin. Fax 724-9440

Delphi, Carroll, Pop. 2,860
Delphi Community SC 1,500/PK-12
501 Armory Rd 46923 765-564-2100
Greg Briles, supt. Fax 564-6919
www.delphi.k12.in.us/
Delphi Community ES 700/PK-5
300 W Vine St 46923 765-564-3895
Debbie Metzger, prin. Fax 564-2341
Delphi Community MS 300/6-8
401 Armory Rd 46923 765-564-3411
Sarah Tislow, prin. Fax 564-2135

Demotte, Jasper, Pop. 3,774
Kankakee Valley SC
Supt. — See Wheatfield
DeMotte ES 700/K-3
PO Box 340 46310 219-987-2789
Chris Richie, prin. Fax 987-4789

North Newton SC
Supt. — See Morocco
Lincoln ES 400/K-6
10280 N 450 E 46310 219-345-3458
Kelly Shepherd, prin. Fax 345-3488

DeMotte Christian S 200/PK-8
PO Box 430 46310 219-987-3721
Devon Brinks, prin. Fax 987-3724

Denver, Miami, Pop. 480
North Miami Community SD 1,000/K-12
394 E 900 N 46926 765-985-3891
Nicholas Eccles, supt. Fax 985-3904
www.nmcs.k12.in.us/
North Miami ES 500/K-6
632 E 900 N 46926 765-985-2251
Matt Storm, prin. Fax 985-2058

Deputy, Jefferson, Pop. 84
Madison Consolidated SD
Supt. — See Madison
Deputy ES 100/PK-4
PO Box 108 47230 812-274-8007
Janet McCreary, prin. Fax 274-8447

Dillsboro, Dearborn, Pop. 1,312
South Dearborn Community SC
Supt. — See Aurora
Dillsboro ES 300/PK-6
13200 North St 47018 812-926-2090
Samuel Melton, prin. Fax 432-5203

Dubois, Dubois, Pop. 488
Northeast Dubois County SC 1,000/PK-12
5379 E Main St 47527 812-678-2781
William Hochgesang, supt. Fax 678-4418
www.nedubois.k12.in.us
Dubois ES 300/PK-4
5533 E Saint Raphael St 47527 812-678-3011
Brenda Ferguson, prin. Fax 678-2013
Dubois MS 300/5-8
4550 N 4th St 47527 812-678-2181
Ryan Case, prin. Fax 678-2282
Other Schools – See Celestine

Dugger, Sullivan, Pop. 917
Dugger Union Community School Corp K-12
7356 E County Road 50 S 47848 812-648-7109
Darin Simpson, supt. Fax 648-7112
www.duggerunionschools.org
Dugger Union Community S K-12
7356 E County Road 50 S 47848 812-648-7109
Darin Simpson, prin. Fax 648-7112

Dunkirk, Jay, Pop. 2,346
Jay SC
Supt. — See Portland
West Jay MS 300/6-8
140 E Highland Ave 47336 765-768-7648
Mike Crull, prin. Fax 768-6152
Westlawn ES 200/K-5
234 W Pearl St 47336 765-768-6075
Jeff Davis, prin. Fax 768-7984

Dyer, Lake, Pop. 16,198
Lake Central SC
Supt. — See Saint John
Bibich ES 500/PK-4
14600 81st Ave 46311 219-322-1185
Deann Logan, prin. Fax 864-2381
Kahler MS 1,000/5-8
600 Joliet St 46311 219-865-3535
Ken Newton, prin. Fax 865-4428
Protsman ES 700/PK-4
1121 Harrison Ave 46311 219-322-2040
Glenn Brown, prin. Fax 865-4437

Protestant Reformed Christian S 200/K-8
10790 Calumet Ave 46311 219-558-2660
Ryan Van Overloop, admin.

East Chicago, Lake, Pop. 29,444
School City of East Chicago 4,000/PK-12
1401 E 144th St 46312 219-391-4100
Dr. Paige McNulty, supt. Fax 391-4126
www.scec.k12.in.us
Block MS 300/7-8
2700 Cardinal Dr 46312 219-391-4084
Dee Etta Wright, prin. Fax 391-4282
Gosch PreK Early Learning Center 500/PK-PK
4001 Indianapolis Blvd 46312 219-391-4172
Erica Glenn, prin. Fax 391-4272
Harrison ES 500/K-6
4411 Magoun Ave 46312 219-391-4192
Jessica Peters, prin. Fax 391-4280
Lincoln ES 600/K-6
3551 Block Ave 46312 219-391-4096
Nancy Sharp, prin. Fax 391-4274
McKinley ES 600/K-6
4825 Magoun Ave 46312 219-391-4186
David Alvarado, prin. Fax 391-4278
Washington ES 300/K-6
2400 Cardinal Dr 46312 219-391-4077
Andrea Hogan, prin. Fax 391-4269

St. Stanislaus S 300/PK-8
4930 Indianapolis Blvd 46312 219-398-1316
Anne Ruiz, prin. Fax 398-9080

Eaton, Delaware, Pop. 1,779
Delaware Community SC
Supt. — See Muncie
Eaton ES 300/K-5
200 NE Union St 47338 765-396-3301
Greg Kile, prin. Fax 396-3641

Eckerty, Crawford
Crawford County Community SC
Supt. — See Marengo
West Crawford ES 100/PK-5
5600 W Patoka School Rd 47116 812-338-2916
Lisa Smith, prin. Fax 338-2917

Edinburgh, Johnson, Pop. 4,440
Edinburgh Community SC 900/PK-12
202 Keeley St 46124 812-526-2681
Dr. William A. Glentzer, supt. Fax 526-0271
www.ecsc.k12.in.us
East Side ES 500/PK-5
810 E Main Cross St 46124 812-526-9771
Andrew Scholl, prin. Fax 526-3433
Edinburgh Community MS 200/6-8
300 Keeley St 46124 812-526-3418
Kevin Rockey, prin. Fax 526-3439

Elberfeld, Warrick, Pop. 615
Warrick County SC
Supt. — See Boonville
Elberfeld ES 200/K-5
45 S 5th St 47613 812-983-4221
Holly Arnold, prin. Fax 983-4221

Elizabeth, Harrison, Pop. 161
South Harrison Community SD
Supt. — See Corydon
South Central ES 300/K-5
6595 E Highway 11 SE 47117 812-969-2973
Sharon Mathes, prin. Fax 969-2236

Elkhart, Elkhart, Pop. 49,305
Baugo Community SD 1,900/K-12
29125 County Road 22 46517 574-293-8583
James DuBois, supt. Fax 294-2171
www.baugo.org/
Jimtown ES 400/K-2
58901 County Road 3 46517 574-522-0379
Jeff Deak, prin. Fax 522-3899
Jimtown IS 600/3-6
58703 County Road 3 46517 574-294-2158
Marci Brubaker, prin. Fax 522-7649
Jimtown JHS 300/7-8
58903 County Road 3 46517 574-294-6586
Michael Stout, prin. Fax 294-8557

Concord Community SD 5,200/K-12
59040 Minuteman Way 46517 574-875-5161
John Trout, supt. Fax 875-8762
www.concord.k12.in.us
Concord East Side ES 600/K-4
57156 County Road 13 46516 574-875-8517
Shad Hartsough, prin. Fax 875-5985
Concord IS 700/5-6
59197 County Road 13 46517 574-830-0300
Michael Wagner, prin. Fax 830-0302
Concord JHS 900/7-8
59397 County Road 11 46517 574-875-5122
Rob Zook, prin. Fax 875-1089
Concord Ox-Bow ES 500/K-4
23525 County Road 45 46516 574-875-8538
Kent Myers, prin. Fax 875-4108
Concord South Side ES 400/K-4
23702 Arlene Ave 46517 574-875-6565
Lisa Kendall, prin. Fax 875-4208
Concord West Side ES 500/K-4
230 W Mishawaka Rd 46517 574-293-2531
Gerard Donlon, prin. Fax 293-9507

Elkhart Community SD 13,000/PK-12
2720 California Rd 46514 574-262-5500
Dr. Robert Haworth, supt. Fax 262-5733
www.elkhart.k12.in.us
Beardsley ES 500/PK-6
1027 McPherson St 46514 574-262-5575
Valerie Priller, prin. Fax 262-5576
Beck ES 500/PK-6
818 McDonald St 46516 574-295-4830
Tracey Kizyma-Whitmyer, prin. Fax 295-4839
Cleveland ES 700/K-6
53403 County Road 1 46514 574-262-5580
Kelly Carmichael, prin. Fax 262-5582
Daly ES 600/K-6
1735 Strong Ave 46514 574-295-4870
Joshua Nice, prin. Fax 295-4877
Eastwood ES 500/K-6
2605 County Road 15 46514 574-262-5583
Kevin Beveridge, prin. Fax 262-5585
Feeser ES 600/PK-6
26665 County Road 4 46514 574-262-5586
Micah Lambert, prin. Fax 262-5588
Hawthorne ES 500/PK-6
501 W Lusher Ave 46517 574-295-4820
Mary Teeter, prin. Fax 295-4828
Monger ES 400/K-6
1100 E Hively Ave 46517 574-295-4860
April Walker, prin. Fax 295-4865
Moran MS 600/7-8
200 W Lusher Ave 46517 574-295-4805
Cynthia Bonner, prin. Fax 295-4807
North Side MS 600/7-8
300 Lawrence St 46514 574-262-5570
Sara Jackowlak, prin. Fax 262-5573
Osolo ES 500/PK-6
24975 County Road 6 46514 574-262-5590
Gary Gardner, prin. Fax 262-5799
Pinewood ES 700/K-6
3420 E Bristol St 46514 574-262-5595
Melinda Shaw, prin. Fax 262-5745
Riverview ES 400/K-6
2509 Wood St 46516 574-295-4850
Barbara Cripe, prin. Fax 295-4901
Roosevelt STEAM Academy 700/PK-6
201 W Wolf Ave 46516 574-295-4840
Howard Edwards, prin. Fax 295-4845
West Side MS 600/7-8
101 S Nappanee St 46514 574-295-4815
Kristie Stutsman, prin. Fax 295-4812
Woodland ES 600/PK-6
1220 County Road 3 46514 574-262-5578
Jonathan LeVan, prin. Fax 262-5746
Other Schools – See Bristol

Elkhart Adventist Christian S 50/K-8
3601 E Bristol St 46514 574-266-9018
Elkhart Christian Academy 400/PK-12
25943 County Road 22 46517 574-293-1609
Jerry Stayton M.Ed., supt. Fax 293-3238
St. Thomas the Apostle S 400/PK-8
1331 N Main St 46514 574-264-4855
Annette Mitchell, prin. Fax 262-8477
St. Vincent De Paul S 200/PK-8
1114 S Main St 46516 574-293-8451
Tara Lundy, prin. Fax 295-9702
Trinity Lutheran S 300/PK-8
30888 County Road 6 46514 574-674-8800
Sandy Price, prin. Fax 674-6410

Ellettsville, Monroe, Pop. 6,255
Richland-Bean Blossom Community SC 2,800/PK-12
600 Edgewood Dr 47429 812-876-7100
Dr. Mike Wilcox, supt. Fax 876-7020
www.rbbcsc.k12.in.us/
Edgewood ECC 100/PK-PK
8045 W State Road 46 47429 812-876-6325
Melissa Lancaster, dir. Fax 876-5424
Edgewood JHS 600/6-8
851 W Edgewood Dr 47429 812-876-2005
Donna Atkinson, prin. Fax 876-8985
Other Schools – See Bloomington, Stinesville

Elnora, Daviess, Pop. 631
North Daviess Community SD 1,200/K-12
5494 E State Road 58 47529 812-636-8000
Robert Bell, supt. Fax 636-7546
www.ndaviess.k12.in.us
North Daviess ES 700/K-6
5498 E State Road 58 47529 812-636-8000
Renee Judy, prin. Fax 636-7444

Elwood, Madison, Pop. 8,510
Elwood Community SC 1,300/PK-12
1306 N Anderson St 46036 765-552-9861
Dr. Christopher Daughtry, supt. Fax 552-8088
www.elwood.k12.in.us
Elwood ES 400/PK-2
940 N 19th St 46036 765-552-7381
Beverly Groover, prin. Fax 552-2628
Elwood IS 400/3-6
1207 N 19th St 46036 765-552-7378
Teresa Boucher, prin. Fax 552-2017

Eminence, Morgan
Eminence Community SC 400/PK-12
PO Box 135 46125 765-528-2101
Laura Penman, supt. Fax 528-2262
www.eminence.k12.in.us
Eminence ES 200/PK-5
PO Box 105 46125 765-528-2222
Corey Scott, prin. Fax 528-2276

Evansville, Vanderburgh, Pop. 114,065
Evansville-Vanderburgh SC 22,800/PK-12
951 Walnut St 47713 812-435-8453
Dr. David Smith, supt. Fax 435-8421
district.evscschools.com
Caze ES 500/PK-5
2013 S Green River Rd 47715 812-477-5567
Jared Turney, prin. Fax 435-8894
Cedar Hall Community S 600/PK-8
2100 N Fulton Ave 47710 812-435-8223
Joseph Schlosser, prin. Fax 435-8225
Culver Family Learning Center 200/PK-PK
1301 Judson St 47713 812-435-8219
Terry Green, prin. Fax 435-8374
Cynthia Heights ES 500/K-5
7225 Cynthiana Rd 47720 812-435-8740
Chastity Nisbeth, prin. Fax 963-1120
Delaware ES 500/PK-6
700 N Garvin St 47711 812-435-8227
Julie Underwood, prin. Fax 435-8398
Dexter ES 400/K-5
917 S Dexter Ave 47714 812-476-1321
DeKarla Owens, prin. Fax 435-8896
Evans ES 500/PK-6
2727 N Evans Ave 47711 812-435-8330
Antionette Hamilton, prin. Fax 435-8886
Fairlawn ES 400/K-5
2021 S Alvord Blvd 47714 812-476-4997
Beth Mortis, prin. Fax 474-6908
Glenwood Leadership Academy 500/K-8
901 Sweetser Ave 47713 812-435-8242
Tamara Skinner, prin. Fax 435-0978
Harper ES 500/K-5
21 S Alvord Blvd 47714 812-476-1308
Sara O'Daniel, prin. Fax 435-8884
Hebron ES 900/K-5
4400 Bellemeade Ave 47714 812-477-8915
Michael Taylor, prin. Fax 474-6981
Helfrich Park MS 600/6-8
2603 W Maryland St 47712 812-435-8246
Cory Herrin, prin. Fax 435-8249
Highland ES 1,000/K-5
6701 Darmstadt Rd 47710 812-867-6401
Martin Brown, prin. Fax 435-8868
Lincoln S 300/PK-8
635 Lincoln Ave 47713 812-435-8235
Ronnetha Darrett, prin. Fax 435-8872
Lodge Community S 500/K-8
2000 Lodge Ave 47714 812-477-5319
Robert Eberhart, prin. Fax 435-8859
McGary MS 300/6-8
1535 Joyce Ave 47714 812-476-3035
Dale Naylor, prin. Fax 474-6919
North JHS 900/7-8
15325 Highway 41 N 47725 812-435-0975
Aaron Huff, prin. Fax 435-8887
Oak Hill ES 800/K-6
7700 Oak Hill Rd 47725 812-867-6426
Lisa Shanks, prin. Fax 435-8862
Perry Heights MS 400/6-8
5800 Hogue Rd 47712 812-435-8326
Jeanette Lindauer, prin. Fax 435-8363
Plaza Park MS 700/6-8
7301 Lincoln Ave 47715 812-476-4971
Shane Browder, prin. Fax 474-6922
Scott ES 900/PK-6
14940 Old State Rd 47725 812-867-2427
Kimber Scarlett, prin. Fax 435-8865
Stockwell ES 600/K-5
2501 N Stockwell Rd 47715 812-477-5345
Tijuanna Tolliver, prin. Fax 435-8864
Stringtown ES 500/K-5
4720 Stringtown Rd 47711 812-435-8320
Doug Mills, prin. Fax 435-8857
Tekoppel ES 500/K-5
111 N Tekoppel Ave 47712 812-435-8333
Robert White, prin. Fax 435-8880
Thompkins MS 700/6-8
1300 W Mill Rd 47710 812-435-8323
Nichole Alcorn, prin. Fax 435-8588
Vogel ES 700/K-6
1500 Oak Hill Rd 47711 812-477-6109
Brian Baumeyer, prin. Fax 474-6909
Washington MS 400/6-8
1801 Washington Ave 47714 812-477-8983
Michele Branson, prin. Fax 474-6930
Wertz ES 300/PK-5
1702 S Red Bank Rd 47712 812-435-8312
Nathan Steele, prin. Fax 435-8314
West Terrace ES 600/K-5
8000 W Terrace Dr 47712 812-435-8733
Katie White, prin. Fax 435-8869

Annunciation S at Christ the King 200/PK-8
3101 Bayard Park Dr 47714 812-476-1792
Matthew Moore, prin. Fax 475-6804
Annunciation S at Holy Spirit 200/PK-8
1760 Lodge Ave 47714 812-477-9082
David Memmer, prin. Fax 469-6636
Corpus Christi S 300/PK-8
5530 Hogue Rd 47712 812-422-1208
Martha Craig, prin. Fax 422-1243
Evansville Christian S 600/PK-8
4400 Lincoln Ave 47714 812-477-7777
Mike Allen, head sch Fax 469-0261
Evansville Day S 50/PK-12
3400 N Green River Rd 47715 812-476-3039
Jarin Jaffee, head sch Fax 476-4061
Evansville Lutheran S 200/K-8
111 E Virginia St 47711 812-424-7252
Tony Shull, prin. Fax 424-7340
Good Shepherd S 300/PK-8
2301 N Stockwell Rd 47715 812-476-4477
Kristen Girton, prin. Fax 476-4495
Holy Redeemer S 200/PK-8
918 W Mill Rd 47710 812-422-3688
Tim McIntosh, prin. Fax 424-7166
Holy Rosary S 400/PK-8
1303 S Green River Rd 47715 812-477-2271
Joan Fredrich, prin. Fax 471-7230
Montessori Academy of Evansville 100/PK-K
4611 Adams Ave 47714 812-479-1776
Resurrection S 300/PK-8
5301 New Harmony Rd 47720 812-963-6148
Theresa Berendes, prin. Fax 963-1141
St. Benedict Cathedral S 500/PK-8
530 S Harlan Ave 47714 812-425-4596
Sr. Hank Carley, prin. Fax 463-5206
St. Joseph S 200/PK-8
6130 W Saint Joseph Rd 47720 812-963-3335
Melba Wilderman, prin. Fax 963-3335
Westside Catholic S Sacred Heart Campus 100/PK-PK
2735 W Franklin St 47712 812-425-0874
Danielle Carter, prin. Fax 425-0883
Westside Catholic S St. Agnes Campus 100/K-5
1620 Glendale Ave 47712 812-423-9115
Danielle Carter, prin. Fax 423-1953
Westside Catholic S St. Boniface Campus 100/6-8
2031 W Michigan St 47712 812-422-1014
Danielle Carter, prin. Fax 422-1057

Fairland, Shelby, Pop. 314
Northwestern Cons SD of Shelby County 1,400/PK-12
4920 W 600 N 46126 317-835-7461
Chris Hoke, supt. Fax 835-4441
www.nwshelbyschools.org
Triton Central ES 600/PK-4
4976 W 600 N 46126 317-835-3003
James Hough, prin. Fax 835-3005
Triton Central MS 400/5-8
4740 W 600 N 46126 317-835-3006
Bobby Thompson, prin. Fax 835-3008

Fairmount, Grant, Pop. 2,932
Madison-Grant United SC 1,100/PK-12
11580 S E 00 W 46928 765-948-4143
Dr. Scott Deetz Ph.D., supt. Fax 948-4150
www.mgusc.k12.in.us
Park ES 400/K-6
500 S Sycamore St 46928 765-948-5232
Emily Tracy, prin. Fax 948-5240
Other Schools – See Summitville

Farmersburg, Sullivan, Pop. 1,110
Northeast SC
Supt. — See Hymera
Northeast North ES 200/K-5
PO Box 689 47850 812-696-2176
Dawn McKillop, prin. Fax 696-2433

Ferdinand, Dubois, Pop. 2,150
North Spencer County SC
Supt. — See Lincoln City
Hanks ES 300/PK-6
19260 N State Road 162 47532 812-357-5091
Jody Schmitt, prin. Fax 357-5092

Southeast Dubois County SC 1,400/PK-12
432 E 15th St 47532 812-817-0900
Richard Allen, supt. Fax 367-1075
www.sedubois.k12.in.us
Ferdinand ES 300/PK-4
402 E 8th St 47532 812-817-0900
Stacy Kitchin, prin. Fax 367-1194
Other Schools – See Birdseye, Huntingburg

Fillmore, Putnam, Pop. 525
South Putnam Community SD
Supt. — See Greencastle
Fillmore ES 100/PK-5
161 S Main St 46128 765-246-6136
Debbie Steffy, prin. Fax 246-6912

Fishers, Hamilton, Pop. 75,207
Hamilton Southeastern SD 20,100/PK-12
13485 Cumberland Rd 46038 317-594-4100
Dr. Allen Bourff, supt. Fax 594-4109
www.hse.k12.in.us
Brooks ES 700/PK-4
12451 Brooks School Rd, 317-915-4250
Dana Kaminski, prin. Fax 915-4259
Cumberland Road ES 600/K-4
13535 Cumberland Rd 46038 317-594-4170
Lisa Lederach, prin. Fax 594-4179
Fall Creek ES 800/K-4
12131 Olio Rd, 317-594-4180
Amy Jackson, prin. Fax 594-4189
Fall Creek IS 1,200/5-6
12011 Olio Rd, 317-915-4220
Randall Schoeff, prin. Fax 915-4229
Fall Creek JHS 7-8
12001 Olio Rd, 317-594-4390
Kim Lippe, prin. Fax 594-4399
Fishers ES 500/K-4
11442 Lantern Rd 46038 317-594-4160
Brian Sloan, prin. Fax 594-4169
Fishers JHS 1,100/7-8
13257 Cumberland Rd 46038 317-594-4150
Crystal Thorpe, prin. Fax 594-4159
Geist ES 800/K-4
14051 E 104th St, 317-915-4260
Christi L. Thomas, prin. Fax 915-4269
Hamilton Southeastern Intermediate JHS 1,200/5-8
12278 Cyntheanne Rd, 317-594-4120
Tim Mankin, prin. Fax 594-4129
Harrison Parkway ES 500/1-4
14135 Harrison Pkwy 46038 317-915-4210
Andrea Burke, prin. Fax 915-4219
Hoosier Road ES 800/K-4
11300 E 121st St, 317-915-4240
William Hurst, prin. Fax 915-4249
Lantern Road ES 500/K-4
10595 Lantern Rd, 317-594-4140
Danielle Thompson, prin. Fax 594-4149
New Britton ES 600/K-4
8660 E 131st St 46038 317-594-4130
Lori Mankin, prin. Fax 594-4139
Riverside IS 1,000/5-6
11014 Eller Rd 46038 317-594-4320
Danielle Chastain, prin. Fax 594-4329
Riverside JHS 1,000/7-8
10910 Eller Rd 46038 317-915-4280
Rob Huesing, prin. Fax 915-4289
Sand Creek ES 800/PK-4
11420 E 131st St 46038 317-915-4270
Peter English, prin. Fax 915-4279
Sand Creek IS 1,100/5-6
11550 E 131st St 46038 317-915-4230
Brent Farrell, prin. Fax 915-4239
Thorpe Creek ES 900/K-4
14642 E 126th St, 317-594-4310
Sara Curran, prin. Fax 594-4319
Other Schools – See Noblesville

Community Montessori S 100/PK-8
9069 E 141st St 46038 317-774-8551
Carrie Wisser, head sch Fax 774-8991
Fishers Montessori S 50/PK-K
PO Box 615 46038 317-849-9519
St. Louis de Montfort S 500/PK-8
11421 Hague Rd 46038 317-842-1125
Scott Stewart, prin. Fax 842-1126

Flora, Carroll, Pop. 2,010
Carroll Consolidated SC 1,100/PK-12
2 S 3rd St 46929 574-967-4113
Keith Thackery, supt. Fax 967-3831
www.carroll.k12.in.us
Carroll ES 600/PK-6
105 S 225 E 46929 574-967-4881
Amanda Redmon, prin. Fax 967-4882

Floyds Knobs, Floyd
New Albany Floyd County Consolidated SD
Supt. — See New Albany
Floyds Knobs ES 600/K-4
4484 Scottsville Rd 47119 812-542-5505
Mike Losey, prin. Fax 542-4787

St. Mary of the Knobs S 200/PK-7
3033 Martin Rd 47119 812-923-1630
Tracy Jansen, prin. Fax 923-0310

Fort Branch, Gibson, Pop. 2,743
South Gibson SC 2,000/K-12
1029 W 650 S 47648 812-753-4230
Dr. Stacey Humbaugh, supt. Fax 753-4081
www.sgibson.k12.in.us
Fort Branch Community S 500/K-8
7670 S Eastview Ln 47648 812-753-3641
Mark Wahl, prin. Fax 753-4174
Other Schools – See Haubstadt, Owensville

Holy Cross S 200/PK-5
202 S Church St 47648 812-753-3280
John Hollis, prin. Fax 753-3034

Fortville, Hancock, Pop. 3,887
Mt. Vernon Community SC 3,500/PK-12
1806 W State Road 234 46040 317-485-3100
Dr. Shane Robbins, admin. Fax 485-3113
www.mvcsc.k12.in.us
8th Grade Academy 300/8-8
8112 N 200 W 46040 317-485-3131
Ben Williams, prin. Fax 482-0027
Fortville ES 500/PK-5
8414 N 200 W 46040 317-485-3180
Stacy Muffler, prin. Fax 485-3185
Mini-Marauder Preschool PK-PK
1806 W State Road 234 46040 317-485-3100
Laura Durig, prin. Fax 485-3113
Mt. Vernon MS 600/6-7
1862 W State Road 234 46040 317-485-3160
Ben Williams, prin. Fax 485-3171
Other Schools – See Greenfield, Mc Cordsville

Fort Wayne, Allen, Pop. 246,159
East Allen County SD
Supt. — See New Haven
Cedarville ES 700/K-3
12225 Hardisty Rd 46845 260-446-0110
Dr. Brad Bakle, prin. Fax 446-0113
Harding JHS 300/7-8
6501 Wayne Trce 46816 260-446-0240
Danielle Newman, prin. Fax 446-0249
Prince Chapman Academy 600/3-6
4808 E Paulding Rd 46816 260-446-0270
Pat McCann, prin. Fax 446-0275
Southwick ES 500/PK-2
6500 Wayne Trce 46816 260-446-0250
Diamond Robinson, prin. Fax 446-0253

Fort Wayne Community SD 30,300/PK-12
1200 S Clinton St 46802 260-467-1000
Dr. Wendy Robinson, supt. Fax 467-1980
fortwayneschools.org
Abbett ES 400/PK-5
4325 Smith St 46806 260-467-5800
Jennifer Enrietto, prin. Fax 467-5833
Adams ES 300/PK-5
3000 New Haven Ave 46803 260-467-5850
Federa Smith, prin. Fax 467-5881
Arlington ES 500/K-5
8118 Saint Joe Center Rd 46835 260-467-6000
Dave Weber, prin. Fax 467-6043
Blackhawk MS 900/6-8
7200 E State Blvd 46815 260-467-4885
Kara Froning, prin. Fax 467-4943
Bloomingdale ES 300/K-5
1300 Orchard St 46808 260-467-6700
Anne Miller, prin. Fax 467-6748
Brentwood ES 500/PK-5
3710 Stafford Dr 46805 260-467-6775
Sara Wertman, prin. Fax 467-6848
Bunche Montessori ES 200/PK-PK
1111 Greene St 46803 260-467-4790
Tamara Mullins, prin. Fax 467-4816
Croninger ES 600/K-5
6700 Trier Rd 46815 260-467-6050
Carrie Kennedy, prin. Fax 467-6091
Fairfield ES 600/PK-5
2825 Fairfield Ave 46807 260-467-5900
Lindsay Amstutz Martin, prin. Fax 467-5953
Forest Park ES 600/K-5
2004 Alabama Ave 46805 260-467-6850
Steve Jones, prin. Fax 467-6923
Franke Park ES 600/K-5
828 Mildred Ave 46808 260-467-6925
Brian Howard, prin. Fax 467-6998
Glenwood Park ES 600/K-5
4501 Vance Ave 46815 260-467-6200
Stephany Bourne, prin. Fax 467-6237
Haley ES 600/PK-5
2201 Maplecrest Rd 46815 260-467-4510
Brandon White, prin. Fax 467-4558
Harris ES 400/K-5
4501 Thorngate Dr 46835 260-467-6300
Jana Ankenbruck, prin. Fax 467-6338
Harrison Hill ES 600/K-5
355 S Cornell Cir 46807 260-467-7000
Shawn Smiley, prin. Fax 467-7073
Holland ES 600/PK-5
7000 Red Haw Dr 46825 260-467-7075
J.R. Ankenbruck, prin. Fax 467-7148
Indian Village ES 500/PK-5
3835 Wenonah Ln 46809 260-467-5200
Jay Peters, prin. Fax 467-5237
Irwin ES 300/K-5
3501 S Anthony Blvd 46806 260-467-5310
Ingrid Laidroo-Martin, prin. Fax 467-5341
Jefferson MS 700/6-8
5303 Wheelock Rd 46835 260-467-4825
Jeff King, prin. Fax 467-4883
Kekionga MS 500/6-8
2929 Engle Rd 46809 260-467-6600
Robin Peterman, prin. Fax 467-6658
Lakeside MS 500/6-8
2100 Lake Ave 46805 260-467-8625
Alan Jones, prin. Fax 467-8672
Lane MS 500/6-8
4901 Vance Ave 46815 260-467-4400
Mark Bailey, prin. Fax 467-4437
Lincoln ES 700/K-5
1001 E Cook Rd 46825 260-467-5400
Frank Kline, prin. Fax 467-5441
Lindley ES 500/K-5
2201 Ardmore Ave 46802 260-467-5350
Mary Kinniry, prin. Fax 467-5384
Maplewood ES 400/K-5
2200 Maplewood Rd 46819 260-467-7150
Jennifer Evans, prin. Fax 467-7223
Memorial Park MS 700/6-8
2200 Maumee Ave 46803 260-467-5300
Brad Crozier, prin. Fax 467-5298
Miami MS 800/6-8
8100 Amherst Dr 46819 260-467-8560
Adam Swinford, prin. Fax 467-8606

Northcrest ES 400/PK-5
5301 Archwood Ln 46825 260-467-5450
Diane Pelkington, prin. Fax 467-5486
Northwood MS 700/6-8
1201 E Washington Center Rd 46825 260-467-2930
Austin Couch, prin. Fax 467-2987
Portage MS 500/6-8
3521 Taylor St 46802 260-467-4500
Michael Christner, prin. Fax 467-4497
Price ES 500/PK-5
1901 W State Blvd 46808 260-467-4950
Ben Hartman, prin. Fax 467-4994
St. Joseph Central ES 500/K-5
6341 Saint Joe Center Rd 46835 260-467-6100
Bill Critell, prin. Fax 467-6135
Scott Academy 400/PK-5
950 E Fairfax Ave 46806 260-467-8050
Megan Fryman, prin. Fax 467-8077
Shambaugh ES 400/K-5
5320 Rebecca St 46835 260-467-6150
Shannon Rodgers, prin. Fax 467-6187
Shawnee MS 900/6-8
1000 E Cook Rd 46825 260-467-6525
Matt Schiebel, prin. Fax 467-6527
South Wayne ES 400/PK-5
810 Cottage Ave 46807 260-467-8100
Brenda West, prin. Fax 467-8134
Study ES 300/K-5
2414 Brooklyn Ave 46802 260-467-8500
Tim Bobay, prin. Fax 467-8532
Towles IS 600/1-8
420 E Paulding Rd 46816 260-467-4300
Tim Captain, prin. Fax 467-4364
Washington Center ES 500/K-5
1936 W Wallen Rd 46818 260-467-6250
Keith Goldfuss, prin. Fax 467-6252
Washington ES 200/PK-5
1015 W Washington Blvd 46802 260-467-8150
Da Nene Neff, prin. Fax 467-8178
Waynedale ES 500/PK-5
7201 Elzey St 46809 260-467-8820
Justin Arkkelin, prin. Fax 467-8852
Weisser Park ES 600/1-5
902 Colerick St 46806 260-467-8875
Kent Martz, prin. Fax 467-8924
Young ECC 300/PK-K
1026 E Pontiac St 46803 260-467-8950
Melissa Plumb, prin. Fax 467-8972

Metro SD of Southwest Allen County 7,000/K-12
4824 Homestead Rd 46814 260-431-2051
Dr. Philip Downs, supt. Fax 431-2063
www.sacs.k12.in.us
Aboite ES 500/K-5
5004 Homestead Rd 46814 260-431-2101
Richelle Miller, prin. Fax 431-2199
Covington ES 800/K-5
2430 W Hamilton Rd S 46814 260-431-0501
Fred Graf, prin. Fax 431-0599
Deer Ridge ES 400/K-5
1515 S Scott Rd 46814 260-431-0701
Jennifer Sprague, prin. Fax 431-0799
Haverhill ES 400/K-5
4725 Weatherside Run 46804 260-431-2901
Jeanine Kleber, prin. Fax 431-2229
Summit MS 700/6-8
4509 Homestead Rd 46814 260-431-2502
Josh St. John, prin. Fax 431-2599
Whispering Meadow ES 500/K-5
415 Mission Hill Dr 46804 260-431-2601
Nicole Veit, prin. Fax 431-2699
Woodside MS 1,000/6-8
2310 W Hamilton Rd S 46814 260-431-2701
Jerry Schillinger, prin. Fax 431-2799
Other Schools – See Roanoke

Northwest Allen County SD 6,900/PK-12
13119 Coldwater Rd 46845 260-637-3155
Dr. Christopher Himsel, supt. Fax 637-8355
www.nacs.k12.in.us
Carroll MS 900/6-8
4027 Hathaway Rd 46818 260-637-5159
Brandon Basham, prin. Fax 637-5478
Cedar Canyon ES 500/PK-5
15011 Coldwater Rd 46845 260-637-6101
Kim Lochmueller, prin. Fax 637-6120
Eel River ES 500/K-5
12723 Bethel Rd 46818 260-338-5395
Brad Zern, prin. Fax 338-5396
Hickory Center ES 400/PK-5
3606 Baird Rd 46818 260-637-3758
Kate Johanningsmeier, prin. Fax 637-2081
Maple Creek MS 800/6-8
425 Union Chapel Rd 46845 260-338-0802
Bill Toler, prin. Fax 338-0369
Oak View ES 400/K-5
13123 Coldwater Rd 46845 260-637-5117
Pam Kaylor, prin. Fax 637-5055
Perry Hill ES 500/K-5
13121 Coldwater Rd 46845 260-637-3158
Barbara Ihnen, prin. Fax 637-8347
Other Schools – See Arcola, Huntertown

Ascension Lutheran S 100/PK-8
8811 Saint Joe Rd 46835 260-486-2226
Mary Eifert, prin. Fax 486-5793
Blackhawk Christian S 700/PK-12
7400 E State Blvd 46815 260-493-7400
Linda Pearson, admin. Fax 493-5107
Canterbury S 900/PK-12
3210 Smith Rd 46804 260-436-0746
William Ennist, hdmstr. Fax 436-5137
Central Christian S 100/PK-8
5801 Schwartz Rd 46835 260-493-0193
Julie Smith, admin.
Concordia Lutheran S 400/PK-8
4245 Lake Ave 46815 260-426-9922
Michael Rosin, prin. Fax 422-3415

Emmanuel St. Michael Lutheran S 300/K-8
1123 Union St 46802 260-422-6712
Jacob Pennekamp, prin. Fax 422-3553
Emmaus Lutheran S 100/PK-8
8626 Covington Rd 46804 260-459-7722
Keith Martin, prin. Fax 459-7766
Holy Cross Lutheran S 400/PK-8
3425 Crescent Ave 46805 260-483-3173
Cecily Chandler, prin. Fax 484-9115
Lutheran South Unity S 200/K-8
5401 S Calhoun St 46807 260-744-0459
Krista F. Nagy, prin. Fax 745-9265
Most Precious Blood S 200/PK-8
1529 Barthold St 46808 260-424-4832
Stanley Liponoga, prin. Fax 426-5904
Our Lady of Good Hope S K-8
7215 Saint Joe Rd 46835 260-485-5289
Jill Perkins, prin. Fax 485-4463
Queen of Angels S 200/PK-8
1600 W State Blvd 46808 260-483-8214
Rebecca Elswerky, prin. Fax 471-0005
St. Charles Borromeo S 700/K-8
4910 Trier Rd 46815 260-484-3392
Rob Sordelet, prin. Fax 482-2006
St. Elizabeth Ann Seton S PK-8
10650 Aboite Center Rd 46804 260-432-4001
Lois Widner, prin. Fax 432-6899
St. John the Baptist S 300/K-8
4500 Fairfield Ave 46807 260-456-3321
Beatrice Royal, prin. Fax 745-8115
St. Joseph Hessen Cassel S 100/PK-8
11521 Old Decatur Rd 46816 260-639-3580
Rose Worman, prin. Fax 639-3675
St. Joseph S 300/PK-8
2211 Brooklyn Ave 46802 260-432-4000
Cristy Jordan, prin. Fax 432-8642
St. Jude S 500/PK-8
2110 Pemberton Dr 46805 260-484-4611
Michael Obergfell, prin. Fax 969-1607
St. Paul Lutheran S 200/K-8
1125 Barr St 46802 260-424-0049
Fax 969-2052
St. Peter Lutheran S 200/PK-8
7810 Maysville Rd 46815 260-749-5811
Michelle Kidd, prin. Fax 749-9967
St. Therese S 200/K-8
2222 Lower Huntington Rd 46819 260-747-2343
Nick Bobay, prin. Fax 747-4767
St. Vincent De Paul S 700/K-8
1720 E Wallen Rd 46825 260-489-3537
Cheryl Klinker, prin. Fax 489-5318
Suburban Bethlehem Lutheran S 200/PK-8
6318 W California Rd 46818 260-483-9371
Richard Brune, prin. Fax 471-2159

Fountain City, Wayne, Pop. 783
Northeastern Wayne SD 1,000/PK-12
PO Box 406 47341 765-847-2821
Laura Blessing, supt. Fax 847-5355
www.nws.k12.in.us
Northeastern ES 500/PK-5
534 W Wallace Rd 47341 765-847-2595
Samuel Pritchard, prin. Fax 847-5470
Northeastern MS 6-8
7295 N US Highway 27 47341 765-847-1337
Dawn Sonsini, prin. Fax 847-2875

Fowler, Benton, Pop. 2,292
Benton Community SC 1,900/PK-12
PO Box 512 47944 765-884-0850
Gregg Hoover, supt. Fax 884-1614
www.benton.k12.in.us
Other Schools – See Boswell, Otterbein, Oxford

Sacred Heart S 100/PK-6
607 N Washington Ave 47944 765-884-0710
Kristy Gross, prin. Fax 884-0710

Francesville, Pulaski, Pop. 873
West Central SC 900/K-12
PO Box 578 47946 219-567-9161
Don Street, supt. Fax 567-9761
www.wcsc.k12.in.us
West Central ES 400/K-5
1842 S US Highway 421 47946 219-567-9741
Dan Zylstra, prin. Fax 567-9445
West Central MS 200/6-8
1850 S US Highway 421 47946 219-567-2534
Pat Culp, prin. Fax 567-9535

Francisco, Gibson, Pop. 461
East Gibson SC
Supt. — See Oakland City
Francisco ES 100/K-6
302 E Main St 47649 812-782-3207
Dr. Peter Humbaugh, prin. Fax 782-3342

Frankfort, Clinton, Pop. 16,300
Clinton Prairie SC 1,100/K-12
2390 S County Rd 450 W 46041 765-659-1339
Amanda Whitlock, supt. Fax 659-5305
www.clintonprairie.com
Clinton Prairie ES 600/K-6
2500 S County Road 450 W 46041 765-654-4473
Joe Walker, prin. Fax 659-9560

Frankfort Community SC 3,200/PK-12
2400 E Wabash St 46041 765-654-5585
Donald DeWeese, supt. Fax 659-6220
www.frankfortschools.org
Blue Ridge PS 500/PK-2
1910 S Jackson St 46041 765-659-3822
Karie Cloe, prin. Fax 659-2993
Frankfort MS 800/6-8
329 N Maish Rd 46041 765-659-3321
Kelly Berenda, prin. Fax 659-6260
Green Meadows IS 400/3-5
1900 S Jackson St 46041 765-659-3233
Brian Johnson, prin. Fax 659-3889

Suncrest ES 700/PK-5
1608 W Kyger St 46041 765-659-6265
Stephanie West, prin. Fax 659-6244

Franklin, Johnson, Pop. 23,366
Clark-Pleasant Community SC
Supt. — See Whiteland
Clark ES 600/K-5
5764 E 700 N 46131 317-535-8503
Jenni Baker, prin. Fax 535-5521

Franklin Community SC 5,000/PK-12
998 Grizzly Cub Dr 46131 317-738-5800
David Clendening, supt. Fax 738-5812
www.franklinschools.org
Creekside ES 600/K-4
700 E State Road 44 46131 317-346-8800
Dr. Mark Heiden, prin. Fax 738-5767
Custer Baker IS 700/5-6
101 W State Road 44 46131 317-346-8600
David Beck, prin. Fax 346-8611
Franklin Community MS 800/7-8
625 Grizzly Cub Dr 46131 317-346-8400
Rita Holman, prin. Fax 346-8411
Needham ES 400/K-4
1399 Upper Shelbyville Rd 46131 317-738-5780
Dylan Purlee, prin. Fax 738-5787
Northwood ES 500/PK-4
965 Grizzly Cub Dr 46131 317-346-8900
Elizabeth Sargent, prin. Fax 738-5757
Webb ES 300/K-4
1400 Webb Ct 46131 317-738-5790
Cheryl Moran, prin. Fax 738-5797
Other Schools – See Bargersville

St. Rose of Lima S 200/PK-8
114 Lancelot Dr 46131 317-738-3451
Rebecca Floyd, prin. Fax 738-3583

Frankton, Madison, Pop. 1,842
Frankton-Lapel Community SD
Supt. — See Anderson
Frankton ES 900/PK-6
1303 State Road 128 E 46044 765-754-7545
Ronda Podzielinski, prin. Fax 754-8598

Fremont, Steuben, Pop. 2,131
Fremont Community SD 1,000/K-12
PO Box 665 46737 260-495-5005
Dr. William Stitt, supt. Fax 495-9798
fremontschoolsin.com
Fremont ES 300/K-4
PO Box 625 46737 260-495-4385
Barbara Wheeler, prin. Fax 495-2133
Fremont MS 300/5-8
PO Box 770 46737 260-495-6100
Greg Mohler, prin. Fax 495-7301

French Lick, Orange, Pop. 1,754
Springs Valley Community SC 900/K-12
498 S Larry Bird Blvd 47432 812-936-4474
Anthony Whitaker, supt. Fax 936-9392
www.svalley.k12.in.us
Springs Valley ES 400/K-5
356 S Larry Bird Blvd 47432 812-936-4400
Julie Woolsey, prin. Fax 936-9788

Fulton, Fulton, Pop. 332
Caston SC 800/K-12
PO Box 8 46931 574-857-2035
Lucinda Douglass, supt. Fax 857-6035
www.caston.k12.in.us/
Caston ES 400/K-6
PO Box 128 46931 574-857-3025
Katie Miller, prin. Fax 857-6035

Garrett, DeKalb, Pop. 6,210
Garrett-Keyser-Butler Community SD 1,800/K-12
801 E Houston St 46738 260-357-3185
Tonya Weaver, supt. Fax 357-4565
www.gkb.k12.in.us
Garrett MS 400/6-8
801 E Houston St 46738 260-357-5745
Lucas Fielden, prin. Fax 357-3575
Ober ES 700/K-5
801 E Houston St 46738 260-357-3112
Kristi Surfus, prin. Fax 357-3317

St. Joseph S 100/K-6
301 W Houston St 46738 260-357-5137
Kris Call, prin. Fax 357-5138

Gary, Lake, Pop. 78,995
Gary Community SC 6,500/PK-12
1988 Polk St 46407 219-881-5401
Dr. Cheryl Pruitt, supt. Fax 881-4102
www.garycsc.k12.in.us
Bailly Prep Academy 500/K-8
4621 Georgia St 46409 219-980-6326
Dr. Lucille Washington, prin. Fax 981-4463
Banneker Achievement Center 500/K-6
301 N Parke St 46403 219-938-1750
Sarah Givens, prin. Fax 939-3514
Bethune ECC 500/PK-PK
2367 E 21st Ave 46407 219-886-6542
Ava Ligon, prin. Fax 883-2231
Beveridge ES 400/K-6
1234 Cleveland St 46404 219-977-2123
Cheryl Ramsey, prin. Fax 977-2449
Glen Park Academy for Learning 500/K-6
5002 Madison St 46408 219-881-3620
Alicia Skinner-Kelley, prin. Fax 980-0161
Jefferson ES 500/K-6
601 Jackson St 46402 219-886-6570
Michael Buckner, prin. Fax 881-2050
Marquette ES 600/K-6
6401 Hemlock Ave 46403 219-881-3610
Ava Ligon, prin. Fax 939-3966
Williams ES 500/K-8
1320 E 19th Ave 46407 219-881-3600
Jacqueline Bowman, prin. Fax 881-4101

Lake Ridge New Tech SC 1,900/K-12
6111 W Ridge Rd 46408 219-838-1819
Dr. Sharon Johnson-Shirley, supt. Fax 989-[illegible]
www.lakeridge.k12.in.us
Hosford Park New Tech ES 300/K-5
4735 Arthur St 46408 219-980-3390
J. Eric Worthington, prin. Fax 980-3671
Lake Ridge New Tech MS 400/6-8
3601 W 41st Ave 46408 219-980-0730
Greg Mikulich, prin. Fax 980-0731
Longfellow New Tech ES 500/K-5
4500 Calhoun St 46408 219-923-7004
Deborah Carlson, prin. Fax 923-7103

Ambassador Christian Academy 300/PK-8
900 W Ridge Rd 46408 219-887-4473
Dr. Vercena Stewart, admin. Fax 887-1749
Ascension Lutheran Christian S [illegible]
1150 W 49th Ave 46408 219-887-5031
Dr. Sue Zientara, prin.

Gas City, Grant, Pop. 5,872
Mississinewa Community SC 2,500/PK-12
424 E South A St 46933 765-674-8528
Tab McKenzie, supt. Fax 674-8529
www.olemiss.k12.in.us
Baskett MS 600/6-8
125 N Broadway St 46933 765-674-8536
Jamie Eckstein, prin. Fax 677-4452
Northview ES 700/2-5
725 E North H St 46933 765-677-4400
Stephanie Lockwood, prin. Fax 677-4733
Other Schools – See Jonesboro

Gaston, Delaware, Pop. 858
Wes-Del Community SD 900/K-12
10290 N County Road 600 W 47342 765-358-4006
Michael Bush, supt. Fax 358-4065
www.wes-del.k12.in.us
Wes-Del ES 400/K-5
500 E Jackson St 47342 765-358-3079
Tracy Shafer, prin. Fax 358-3573

Georgetown, Floyd, Pop. 2,851
New Albany Floyd County Consolidated SD
Supt. — See New Albany
Georgetown ES 600/K-4
8800 High St 47122 812-951-2901
Rhonda Benz, prin. Fax 941-3420
Highland Hills MS 1,500/5-8
3492 Edwardsville Galena Rd 47122 812-542-8501
Steve Griffin, prin. Fax 542-4792

Goshen, Elkhart, Pop. 31,231
Fairfield Community SD 2,100/K-12
67240 County Road 31 46528 574-831-2188
Steve Thalheimer, supt. Fax 831-5698
www.fairfield.k12.in.us
Benton ES 400/K-6
68350 County Road 31 46526 574-831-2192
Dan Sharp, prin. Fax 831-2200
Other Schools – See Millersburg, New Paris

Goshen Community SD 6,500/PK-12
613 E Purl St 46526 574-533-8631
Dr. Diane Woodworth, supt. Fax 533-2505
www.goshenschools.org/
Chamberlain ES 400/K-5
428 N 5th St 46528 574-534-2691
Kimberly Branham, prin. Fax 534-5918
Chandler ES 500/K-5
419 S 8th St 46526 574-533-5085
Cheryl Williams, prin. Fax 533-1702
Goshen MS 1,500/6-8
1216 S Indiana Ave 46526 574-533-0391
Lori Shreiner, prin. Fax 534-3042
Model ES 600/K-5
412 S Greene Rd 46526 574-533-7677
Tami Hicks, prin. Fax 534-4220
Parkside ES 400/K-5
1202 S 7th St 46526 574-533-7765
Betts McFarren, prin. Fax 533-1648
Prairie View ES 500/PK-5
1730 Regent St 46526 574-534-4710
Donna Wiktorowski, prin. Fax 534-4862
Waterford ES 500/K-5
65560 State Road 15 46526 574-533-6811
Katrina Overton, prin. Fax 533-1408
West Goshen ES 400/K-5
215 Dewey Ave 46526 574-533-7855
Lori Line, prin. Fax 533-1362

Middlebury Community SD
Supt. — See Middlebury
Jefferson ES 400/K-3
18565 County Road 20 46528 574-822-5399
Curt Schwartz, prin. Fax 533-3731

Clinton Christian S 100/PK-12
61763 County Road 35 46528 574-642-3940
Matt Blosser, admin. Fax 642-3674
St. John the Evangelist S 200/PK-5
117 W Monroe St 46526 574-533-9480
Mattie Willerton, prin. Fax 533-1814

Gosport, Owen, Pop. 821
Spencer-Owen Community SD
Supt. — See Spencer
Gosport ES 200/K-6
201 N 9th St 47433 812-879-4694
Carol Watson, prin. Fax 879-4032

Granger, Saint Joseph, Pop. 29,968
Penn-Harris-Madison SC
Supt. — See Mishawaka
Discovery MS 900/6-8
10050 Brummitt Rd 46530 574-674-6010
Sheryll Harper, prin. Fax 679-4214
Frank ES 400/K-5
13111 Adams Rd 46530 574-272-0340
Debra Hildreth, prin. Fax 273-3806

Horizon ES 600/K-5
10060 Brummitt Rd 46530 574-679-9788
Tressa Decker, prin. Fax 674-8395
Northpoint ES 600/K-5
50800 Cherry Rd 46530 574-271-8598
Diane Wirth, prin. Fax 968-6003
Prairie Vista ES 500/K-5
15400 Brick Rd 46530 574-271-0055
Keely Twibell, prin. Fax 273-1846

Granger Christian S 200/PK-12
52025 Gumwood Rd 46530 574-272-5815
Mark Wever, lead tchr. Fax 968-2664
Peace Lutheran S 50/PK-8
16791 Cleveland Rd 46530 574-273-8260
Bradley Pleuss, prin.
St. Pius X S 500/PK-8
52553 Fir Rd 46530 574-272-4935
Elaine Holmes, prin. Fax 855-5400

Greencastle, Putnam, Pop. 10,164
Greencastle Community SC 2,000/PK-12
PO Box 480 46135 765-653-9771
Jeffrey Hubble, supt. Fax 653-1282
www.greencastle.k12.in.us
Deer Meadow PS 300/PK-2
1000 Deer Meadow Dr 46135 765-653-3518
Michael McHugh, prin. Fax 653-1150
Greencastle MS 500/6-8
400 Percy L Julian Dr 46135 765-653-9774
Scott Wetlz, prin. Fax 653-5381
Ridpath PS 200/K-2
711 S Central Ave 46135 765-653-3315
Emily Johnson, prin. Fax 653-9236
Tzouanakis IS 400/3-5
500 Linwood Dr 46135 765-653-4700
Jon Strube, prin. Fax 653-6449

South Putnam Community SD 900/PK-12
3999 S US Highway 231 46135 765-653-3119
Bruce Bernhardt, supt. Fax 653-7476
www.sputnam.k12.in.us
Central ES 400/K-5
1888 E US Highway 40 46135 765-653-6175
Todd Gowen, prin. Fax 653-2532
Other Schools – See Fillmore

Peace Lutheran S 50/PK-5
PO Box 778 46135 765-653-6995
Cynthia Pienta, dir. Fax 653-6995

Greenfield, Hancock, Pop. 20,372
Greenfield-Central Community SD 4,600/PK-12
110 W North St 46140 317-462-4434
Dr. Harold Olin, supt. Fax 467-4227
www.gcsc.k12.in.us
Eden ES 200/K-3
8185 N State Road 9 46140 317-326-3117
Devon Marine, prin. Fax 326-2191
Greenfield Central JHS 800/7-8
1440 N Franklin St 46140 317-477-4616
Dan Jack, prin. Fax 477-4617
Greenfield IS 500/4-6
204 W Park Ave 46140 317-462-6827
James Bever, prin. Fax 467-6730
Harris ES 300/K-3
200 W Park Ave 46140 317-462-6731
Jan Kehrt, prin. Fax 467-6733
Stephens ES 500/PK-3
1331 N Blue Rd 46140 317-462-4491
Matthew Davis, prin. Fax 467-6735
Weston ES 400/K-3
140 Polk Ave 46140 317-462-1492
Shane Bryant, prin. Fax 467-6738
Other Schools – See Maxwell

Mt. Vernon Community SC
Supt. — See Fortville
Mt. Comfort ES 500/K-5
5694 W 300 N 46140 317-894-7667
Casey Dodd, prin. Fax 894-7702

Southern Hancock County Community SC
Supt. — See New Palestine
Brandywine ES 300/PK-6
413 E 400 S 46140 317-462-7396
Dr. Rhonda Peterson, prin. Fax 467-0174

St. Michael S 300/PK-8
519 Jefferson Blvd 46140 317-462-6380
Ruth Hittel, prin. Fax 462-2571

Greensburg, Decatur, Pop. 11,380
Decatur County Community SD 2,100/PK-12
2020 N Montgomery Rd 47240 812-663-4595
Dr. S. Jarrod Burns, supt. Fax 663-4168
www.decaturco.k12.in.us
North Decatur ES 600/K-6
3300 N State Road 3 47240 812-663-9215
Robert Smith, prin. Fax 663-4168
South Decatur ES 500/PK-6
9302 S County Road 420 W 47240 812-591-3115
Marty Layden, prin. Fax 663-4168

Greensburg Community SC 2,300/K-12
1312 W Westridge Pkwy 47240 812-663-4774
Tom Hunter, supt. Fax 663-5713
www.greensburg.k12.in.us
Greensburg Community JHS 600/6-8
505 E Central Ave 47240 812-663-7523
Matt Clifford, prin. Fax 663-9425
Greensburg ES 1,000/K-5
900 Big Blue Ave 47240 812-663-8112
Kara Holdsworth, prin. Fax 662-6516

Good Shepherd Christian Academy 50/PK-6
209 W Washington St 47240 812-663-2410
Janet Hodson, admin. Fax 663-6599

St. Mary S 200/PK-8
1331 Hunter Robbins Way 47240 812-663-2804
Nancy Buening, prin. Fax 663-6088

Greentown, Howard, Pop. 2,402
Eastern Howard SC 1,100/K-12
221 W Main St Ste 1 46936 765-628-3391
Dr. Keith Richie Ed.D., supt. Fax 628-5017
www.eastern.k12.in.us
Eastern ES 600/K-5
308 S Harrison St 46936 765-628-7866
Randy Maurer, prin. Fax 628-2405
Eastern MS 6-8
421 S Harrison St 46936 765-628-5030
Lindsey Brown, prin. Fax 628-5031

Greenville, Floyd, Pop. 588
New Albany Floyd County Consolidated SD
Supt. — See New Albany
Greenville ES 400/K-4
7025 Cross St 47124 812-542-5504
Wendy Ivey, prin. Fax 542-4786

Greenwood, Johnson, Pop. 48,867
Center Grove Community SC 7,700/K-12
4800 W Stones Crossing Rd 46143 317-881-9326
Dr. Richard Arkanoff, supt. Fax 881-0241
www.centergrove.k12.in.us
Center Grove ES 700/K-5
2455 S Morgantown Rd 46143 317-881-1720
Krista Nelson, prin. Fax 885-4535
Center Grove MS Central 1,000/6-8
4900 W Stones Crossing Rd 46143 317-882-9391
Craig Smith, prin. Fax 885-4534
Center Grove MS North 900/6-8
202 N Morgantown Rd 46142 317-885-8800
Scott Johnson, prin. Fax 885-3388
North Grove ES 600/K-5
3280 W Fairview Rd 46142 317-881-5653
Brian Proctor, prin. Fax 885-4547
Pleasant Grove ES 600/K-5
5199 W Fairview Rd 46142 317-887-8525
Trael Kelly, prin. Fax 885-4605
Sugar Grove ES 700/K-5
4135 W Smith Valley Rd 46142 317-887-4707
Dr. Davin Harpe, prin. Fax 885-5249
Other Schools – See Bargersville

Clark-Pleasant Community SC
Supt. — See Whiteland
Clark Pleasant MS 1,000/6-8
1354 E Worthsville Rd 46143 317-535-7121
Tim Rinehold, prin. Fax 535-2064
Grassy Creek ES 500/K-5
2111 Sheek Rd 46143 317-535-3980
Kurt Saugstad, prin. Fax 888-8774

Greenwood Community SC 3,800/PK-12
605 W Smith Valley Rd 46142 317-889-4060
Dr. Kent DeKoninck, supt. Fax 889-4068
gws.k12.in.us
Greenwood MS 900/6-8
1584 Averitt Rd 46143 317-889-4040
Chris Sutton, prin. Fax 889-4044
Greenwood Northeast ES 300/K-5
99 Crestview Dr 46143 317-889-4080
Amy Sander, prin. Fax 889-4087
Isom Central ES 400/K-5
50 E Broadway St 46143 317-889-4070
Sondra Wooton, prin. Fax 889-4115
Southwest ES 500/K-5
619 W Smith Valley Rd 46142 317-889-4090
Beth Guilfoy, prin. Fax 889-4111
Westwood ES 400/PK-5
899 S Honey Creek Rd 46143 317-859-4200
David Ennis, prin. Fax 859-4209

Greenwood Christian Academy 400/PK-12
835 W Worthsville Rd 46143 317-215-5300
Bruce Peters, hdmstr. Fax 535-1070
Greenwood Christian S 300/PK-6
2045 Averitt Rd 46143 317-881-9970
Ellen Sheets, admin. Fax 859-5234
Greenwood Montessori Children's House S 50/PK-3
622 N Madison Ave # 6 46142 317-289-1962
Our Lady of the Greenwood S 400/PK-8
399 S Meridian St 46143 317-881-1300
Kent Clady, prin. Fax 885-5005
SS. Francis & Clare of Assisi S 400/PK-8
5901 Olive Branch Rd 46143 317-859-4673
Betty Popp, prin. Fax 859-4678

Griffith, Lake, Pop. 16,641
Griffith Public SD 2,400/PK-12
PO Box 749 46319 219-924-4250
Dr. Peter Morikis, supt. Fax 922-5933
www.griffith.k12.in.us
Beiriger ES 400/K-6
601 N Lillian St 46319 219-924-4030
Ashley Cotton, prin. Fax 922-6154
Griffith MS 400/7-8
600 N Raymond St 46319 219-924-4280
Dustin Nelson, prin. Fax 922-5927
Ready ES 400/K-6
1345 N Broad St 46319 219-838-4214
Christine Brenner, prin. Fax 838-4237
Wadsworth ES 400/PK-6
600 N Jay St 46319 219-923-4488
Melanie McClure, prin. Fax 838-6770

St. Mary S 200/PK-8
525 N Broad St 46319 219-924-8633
Rebecca Maskovich, prin. Fax 922-2279

Hagerstown, Wayne, Pop. 1,765
Nettle Creek SC 1,100/PK-12
297 E Northmarket St 47346 765-489-4543
Dr. William Doering, supt. Fax 489-4914
nettlecreekschools.com
Hagerstown ES 600/PK-6
299 N Sycamore St 47346 765-489-4555
Tiffani Hokey, prin. Fax 489-6275

Hamilton, DeKalb, Pop. 1,521
Hamilton Community SD 400/K-12
903 S Wayne St 46742 260-488-2513
Dr. Nicole Singer, supt. Fax 488-2348
www.hcs.k12.in.us
Hamilton Community ES 200/K-6
903 S Wayne St 46742 260-488-2101
Greg Piatt, prin. Fax 488-3634

Hamlet, Starke, Pop. 787
Oregon-Davis SC 600/PK-12
5998 N 750 E 46532 574-867-2111
Dr. Donald Harman, supt. Fax 867-8191
www.od.k12.in.us
Oregon-Davis ES 300/PK-6
5860 N 750 E 46532 574-867-2711
William Bennett, prin. Fax 867-2721

Hammond, Lake, Pop. 79,563
Hammond CSD 13,400/PK-12
41 Williams St 46320 219-933-2400
Dr. Walter Watkins, supt. Fax 933-2495
www.hammond.k12.in.us
Columbia ES 300/K-5
1238 Michigan St 46320 219-933-2461
Lynn Lange, prin. Fax 554-4577
Edison ES 600/PK-5
7025 Madison Ave 46324 219-933-2464
Lela Simmons, prin. Fax 554-4578
Eggers MS 700/6-8
5825 Blaine Ave 46320 219-933-2449
Rhoderick Poats, prin. Fax 554-4575
Harding ES 600/PK-5
3211 165th St 46323 219-989-7351
Lori Owens, prin. Fax 554-4580
Hess ES 600/PK-5
3640 Orchard Dr 46323 219-989-7355
Erica Robinson, prin. Fax 554-4581
Irving ES 700/PK-5
4727 Pine Ave 46327 219-933-2467
Re Nae Robinson, prin. Fax 554-4582
Jefferson ES 400/PK-5
6940 Northcote Ave 46324 219-989-7353
Denise Eismin, prin. Fax 554-4583
Kenwood ES 300/K-5
6416 Hohman Ave 46324 219-933-2469
Amy Yoos, prin. Fax 554-4584
Lafayette ES 500/PK-5
856 Sibley St 46320 219-933-2472
Colette Weitknecht, prin. Fax 554-4585
Lincoln ES 600/PK-5
4221 Towle Ave 46327 219-933-2475
Yolanda Bracey, prin. Fax 554-4586
Maywood ES 400/PK-5
1001 165th St 46324 219-933-2477
Dameca Harrison, prin. Fax 554-4587
Morton ES 500/K-5
7006 Marshall Ave 46323 219-989-7336
Timothy Sieman, prin. Fax 554-4588
O'Bannon ES 600/PK-5
1317 173rd St 46324 219-989-7360
Allison Lenzo, prin. Fax 554-4589
Scott MS 800/6-8
3635 173rd St 46323 219-989-7340
Colleen Bergren, prin. Fax 554-4576
Wallace ES 400/PK-5
6235 Jefferson Ave 46324 219-933-2479
Conja Halliburton, prin. Fax 554-4590
Other Schools – See Whiting

Montessori Childrens Schoolhouse 200/PK-6
5935 Hohman Ave 46320 219-932-5666
St. Casimir S 300/PK-8
4329 Cameron Ave 46327 219-932-2686
Renata Gajardo, prin. Fax 932-4458
St. John Bosco S 300/PK-8
1231 171st Pl 46324 219-845-6226
Mark Kielbania, prin. Fax 989-7946

Hanover, Jefferson, Pop. 3,496
Southwestern-Jefferson County Cons SC 1,300/PK-12
239 S Main Cross St 47243 812-866-6250
Trevor Jones, supt. Fax 866-6256
www.swjcs.us
Southwestern ES 700/PK-5
273 S Main Cross St 47243 812-866-6200
Karla Gauger, prin. Fax 866-6205
Southwestern MS 300/6-8
167 S Main Cross St 47243 812-866-6220
Jason Watson, prin. Fax 866-4680

Hartford City, Blackford, Pop. 6,115
Blackford County SD 1,800/PK-12
668 W 200 S 47348 765-348-7550
Chad Yencer, supt. Fax 348-7552
www.bcs.k12.in.us
Blackford JHS 300/7-8
800 W Van Cleve St 47348 765-348-7590
Melissa Blossom, prin. Fax 348-7593
North Side ES 300/4-6
400 E McDonald St 47348 765-348-7595
Kevin Biddle, prin. Fax 348-7552
Southside ES 400/PK-3
1515 S Monroe St 47348 765-348-7584
Craig Campbell, prin. Fax 348-7580
Other Schools – See Montpelier

Haubstadt, Gibson, Pop. 1,567
South Gibson SC
Supt. — See Fort Branch
Haubstadt Community S 400/K-8
158 E 1025 S 47639 812-768-6487
John Obermeier, prin. Fax 768-5020

St. James S 200/PK-8
12394 S 40 W 47639 812-867-2661
Angela Johnson, prin. Fax 867-2696

SS. Peter & Paul S 200/PK-5
210 N Vine St 47639 812-768-6775
Kalyn Herrmann, prin. Fax 768-5039

Hayden, Jennings, Pop. 519
Jennings County SC
Supt. — See North Vernon
Hayden ES 300/K-6
55 S County Road 685 W 47245 812-346-2813
Brent Comer, prin. Fax 346-6295

Hebron, Porter, Pop. 3,695
Metro SD of Boone Township 1,200/K-12
307 S Main St 46341 219-996-4771
Dr. Nathan H. Kleefisch, supt. Fax 996-5777
www.hebronschools.k12.in.us/
Hebron ES 600/K-5
307 S Main St 46341 219-996-4771
James Martin, prin. Fax 996-5777
Hebron MS 300/6-8
307 S Main St 46341 219-996-4771
Jeff Brooks, prin. Fax 996-5777

Porter Township SC
Supt. — See Valparaiso
Porter Lakes ES 400/K-3
208 S 725 W 46341 219-306-8076
Kevin Donnell, prin. Fax 306-8636

Heltonville, Lawrence
North Lawrence Community SD
Supt. — See Bedford
Heltonville ES 100/K-5
580 Diamond Rd 47436 812-834-6632
Christy Wintczak, prin. Fax 834-0704

Henryville, Clark, Pop. 1,892
West Clark Community SC
Supt. — See Sellersburg
Henryville ES 700/PK-6
215 N Ferguson St 47126 812-294-4806
Dr. Glenn Riggs, prin. Fax 294-4940

Highland, Lake, Pop. 23,446
Town of Highland SD 3,200/K-12
9145 Kennedy Ave 46322 219-924-7400
Brian J. Smith, supt. Fax 922-5637
www.highland.k12.in.us
Highland MS 800/6-8
2941 41st St 46322 219-922-5620
Terry Mucha, prin. Fax 922-2270
Johnston ES 300/K-5
8220 5th St 46322 219-923-2428
Ryan Erdelac, prin. Fax 838-9866
Merkley ES 300/K-5
9340 5th St 46322 219-922-5640
Rose Alexander, prin. Fax 922-5638
Southridge ES 400/K-5
9221 Johnston St 46322 219-922-5650
R. Hufford, prin. Fax 922-5639
Warren ES 300/K-5
2901 100th St 46322 219-922-5660
James Boylan, prin. Fax 922-5674

Highland Christian S 500/PK-8
3040 Ridge Rd 46322 219-838-0356
Robert Payne, prin. Fax 838-7817
Our Lady of Grace S 200/PK-8
3025 Highway Ave 46322 219-838-2901
Mark Topp, prin. Fax 972-6389

Hobart, Lake, Pop. 28,672
River Forest Community SC 1,000/K-12
3250 Michigan St 46342 219-962-2909
Dr. Steven Disney, supt. Fax 962-4951
www.rfcsc.k12.in.us
Meister ES 200/K-5
3300 Jay St 46342 219-962-1103
Gina Wagenblast, prin. Fax 962-1459
River Forest MS 100/6-8
3300 Indiana St 46342 219-962-7751
Randall Horka, prin. Fax 962-8338
Other Schools – See Lake Station

School City of Hobart 4,100/PK-12
32 E 7th St 46342 219-942-8885
Dr. Peggy Buffington, supt. Fax 942-0081
www.hobart.k12.in.us
Early Learning Center at George Earle 300/PK-K
400 N Wilson St 46342 219-942-7263
Sara Gutierrez, prin. Fax 942-0249
Hobart MS 1,000/6-8
36 E 8th St 46342 219-942-8541
Nikki Neeley, prin. Fax 947-7194
Liberty ES 400/1-5
130 N Liberty St 46342 219-942-4251
Amy Turley, prin. Fax 942-0346
Martin ES 800/1-5
301 E 10th St 46342 219-947-7869
Kacey Allen, prin. Fax 942-0411
Ridge View ES 300/1-5
3333 W Old Ridge Rd 46342 219-942-5614
Lori Anderson, prin. Fax 942-0600

Montessori Academy in the Oaks 100/PK-6
2109 57th St 46342 219-942-9410
Trinity Lutheran S 100/PK-8
891 S Linda St 46342 219-942-3147
Maria Bunte, prin. Fax 942-6637

Holland, Dubois, Pop. 622
Southwest Dubois County SC
Supt. — See Huntingburg
Holland ES 200/PK-5
408 N Meridian St 47541 812-536-2441
John Seger, prin. Fax 536-2282

Hope, Bartholomew, Pop. 2,080
Flat Rock-Hawcreek SC 900/PK-12
9423 N State Road 9 47246 812-546-4922
Shawn Price, supt. Fax 546-5617
www.flatrock.k12.in.us

Hope IS 500/PK-6
9575 N State Road 9 47246 812-546-5001
Jessica Poe, prin. Fax 546-0603

Howe, Lagrange, Pop. 791
Lakeland SC
Supt. — See Lagrange
Lima-Brighton ES 300/K-5
201 Market St 46746 260-499-2440
Traci Blaize, prin. Fax 562-2840

Huntertown, Allen, Pop. 4,733
Northwest Allen County SD
Supt. — See Fort Wayne
Huntertown ES 500/K-5
15330 Lima Rd 46748 260-637-3181
Joseph Meyer, prin. Fax 637-8348

Huntingburg, Dubois, Pop. 6,020
Southeast Dubois County SC
Supt. — See Ferdinand
Cedar Crest IS 200/5-6
4770 S State Road 162 47542 812-817-0900
Mark Jahn, prin. Fax 481-2963

Southwest Dubois County SC 1,800/PK-12
113 N Jackson St 47542 812-683-3971
Mike Eineman, supt. Fax 683-2752
www.swdubois.k12.in.us
Huntingburg ES 600/K-5
501 W Sunset Dr 47542 812-683-1172
Chad Whitehead, prin. Fax 683-5605
Southridge MS 400/6-8
1112 S Main St 47542 812-683-3372
Kelly Murphy, prin. Fax 683-2817
Other Schools – See Holland

Huntington, Huntington, Pop. 17,196
Huntington County Community SC 5,900/PK-12
2485 Waterworks Rd 46750 260-356-8312
Randy Harris, supt. Fax 358-2222
www.hccsc.k12.in.us
Crestview MS 600/6-8
1151 W 500 N 46750 260-356-6210
Chuck Werth, prin. Fax 358-2232
Flint Springs ES 500/PK-5
1360 E Tipton St 46750 260-356-7612
Aimee Lunsford, prin. Fax 358-2228
Lancaster ES 400/K-5
2932 W 300 S 46750 260-468-2816
Melinda Otwinowski, prin. Fax 468-4273
Lincoln ES 500/K-5
2037 E Taylor St 46750 260-356-2914
Christopher Tillett, prin. Fax 358-2234
Northwest ES 300/K-5
4524 W 800 N 46750 260-344-1455
Mark DuBois, prin. Fax 344-1035
Riverview MS 700/6-8
2465 Waterworks Rd 46750 260-356-0910
James Bragg, prin. Fax 358-2243
Other Schools – See Andrews, Roanoke, Warren

Huntington Catholic S 200/PK-8
960 Warren St 46750 260-356-1926
Derek Boone, prin. Fax 359-8419

Hymera, Sullivan, Pop. 795
Northeast SC 800/PK-12
PO Box 493 47855 812-383-5761
Dr. Mark Baker, supt. Fax 383-4591
www.nesc.k12.in.us/
Northeast East ES 100/PK-5
PO Box 494 47855 812-383-4671
Dr. Kirk Freeman, prin. Fax 383-7213
Other Schools – See Farmersburg, Shelburn

Indianapolis, Marion, Pop. 800,178
Carmel Clay SD
Supt. — See Carmel
Orchard Park ES 700/PK-5
10404 Orchard Park Dr S 46280 317-848-1918
Rhonda Turner, prin. Fax 571-4043

Franklin Township Community SC 9,100/PK-12
6141 S Franklin Rd 46259 317-862-2411
Dr. David Shaffer, supt. Fax 862-7238
www.ftcsc.k12.in.us
Adams ES 500/K-5
7341 E Stop 11 Rd 46259 317-862-2065
Lynlie Schoene, prin. Fax 862-7255
Arlington ES 600/K-5
5814 S Arlington Ave 46237 317-782-4274
Melissa Morris, prin. Fax 784-6698
Bunker Hill ES 600/PK-5
6620 Shelbyville Rd 46237 317-787-3421
Dr. Kent Pettet, prin. Fax 781-9163
Franklin Township MS East 1,200/6-8
10440 Indian Creek Rd S 46259 317-803-8100
Chase Huotari, prin. Fax 803-8199
Franklin Township MS West 900/6-8
7620 E Edgewood Ave 46239 317-862-2446
Matt Vandermark, prin. Fax 862-7271
Kitley ES 1,000/PK-5
8735 Indian Creek Rd S 46259 317-803-5900
Dr. Joseph Brown, prin. Fax 803-5970
South Creek ES 700/K-5
9010 E Southport Rd 46259 317-860-4700
Toni Stevenson, prin. Fax 860-4770
Thompson Crossing ES 600/K-5
7525 E Thompson Rd 46239 317-860-4600
Jeff Murphy, prin. Fax 860-4610
Other Schools – See Acton

Indianapolis SD 25,800/PK-12
120 E Walnut St 46204 317-226-4000
Dr. Lewis Ferebee, supt. Fax 226-4936
www.myips.org
Arlington Woods S 99 500/PK-6
5801 E 30th St 46218 317-226-4299
Tihesha Gutherie, prin. Fax 226-3711

Bellamy Pre-School Center 100/PK-PK
9501 E 36th Pl 46235 317-226-4102
Joyce Buntin, prin.
Blaker ES 200/PK-6
1349 E 54th St 46220 317-226-4255
Arthur Hinton, prin. Fax 226-4811
Brandes ES 300/PK-6
4065 Asbury St 46227 317-226-4265
Lauren Johnson, prin. Fax 226-3392
Brochhausen ES 400/PK-6
5801 E 16th St 46218 317-226-4288
Carmen Sharp, prin. Fax 226-3637
Brookside ES 600/K-6
3150 E 10th St 46201 317-226-4254
Erin Simpson, prin. Fax 226-3368
Buck ES 500/K-6
2701 N Devon Ave 46219 317-226-4294
Dr. Edward Brown, prin. Fax 226-3687
Carver S 300/K-8
2411 Indianapolis Ave 46208 317-226-4287
Mark Nardo, prin.
Center for Inquiry S 2 400/K-8
725 N New Jersey St 46202 317-226-4202
Andrea Hunley, prin. Fax 226-3740
Center for Inquiry S 27 300/PK-8
545 E 19th St 46202 317-226-4227
Brandi Herbert, prin. Fax 226-4808
Center for Inquiry S 70 K-5
510 46th St 46205 317-226-4270
Christine Collier, prin.
Center for Inquiry S 84 400/K-8
440 E 57th St 46220 317-226-4284
Kathleen Miller, prin. Fax 226-3460
Christian Park ES 400/K-6
4700 English Ave 46201 317-226-4282
Andre Gillespie, prin. Fax 226-3435
Cold Spring ES 300/K-6
3650 Cold Spring Rd 46222 317-226-4155
Carrie Bruns, prin. Fax 226-4157
Donnan ES 500/K-8
1202 E Troy Ave 46203 317-217-1979
Michael Dunagan, prin. Fax 217-1984
Edison S of the Arts K-8
777 S White River Pkwy W Dr 46221 317-226-4992
Emerson ES 400/PK-6
321 N Linwood Ave 46201 317-226-4258
Susan Kertes, prin. Fax 226-3375
Fairbanks ES 500/K-6
8620 Montery Rd 46226 317-226-4105
Paula Peterson, prin. Fax 226-2018
Farrington ES 600/PK-6
4326 Patricia St 46222 317-226-4261
Carole Wilson-Frye, prin. Fax 226-4078
Foster ES 600/PK-8
653 N Somerset Ave 46222 317-226-4267
Tanasha Franklin, prin. Fax 226-3393
Frost ES 400/PK-7
5301 Roxbury Rd 46226 317-226-4106
Tina Foster, prin. Fax 226-4551
Gambold Preschool PK-PK
3725 Kiel Ave 46224 317-226-4000
Tammy Bowman, prin.
Garfield ES 600/K-8
307 Lincoln St 46225 317-226-4231
Ann Toombs Heiple, prin. Fax 226-3336
Global Preparatory Academy at Riverside 400/K-8
2033 Sugar Grove Ave 46202 317-226-4244
Mariama Carson, prin. Fax 226-3469
Gregg ES 600/PK-6
2302 E Michigan St 46201 317-226-4215
Ross Pippin, prin. Fax 226-4600
Harshman Magnet MS 400/7-8
1501 E 10th St 46201 317-226-4101
James Larkin, prin. Fax 226-3444
IPS/Butler Lab S PK-6
3330 N Pennsylvania St 46205 317-226-4260
Ronald Smith, prin. Fax 226-4201
Irving ES 500/PK-8
1250 E Market St 46202 317-226-4214
Karen Hastings, prin. Fax 226-4430
Jennings ES 300/K-6
6150 Gateway Dr 46254 317-226-4109
Kevin McMahan, prin. Fax 226-3734
Julian ES 200/K-6
5435 E Washington St 46219 317-226-4257
Debra Ashley, prin. Fax 226-3371
Longfellow Medical/STEM MS 300/7-8
510 Laurel St 46203 317-226-4000
Eric Parquet, prin. Fax 226-3756
Lowell ES 600/PK-6
3426 Roosevelt Ave 46218 317-226-4251
Jennifer Pearson, prin. Fax 226-3312
McClellan ES 500/PK-8
5111 Evanston Ave 46205 317-226-4291
Kathryn Lause, prin. Fax 226-4544
McKinley ES 600/PK-6
1733 Spann Ave 46203 317-226-4239
Stacy Coleman, prin. Fax 226-4400
Miller ES 500/PK-6
2251 Sloan Ave 46203 317-226-4114
Daria Parham, prin. Fax 226-3511
Nicholson ES 500/PK-6
3651 N Kiel Ave 46224 317-226-4296
Mary Siefert, prin. Fax 226-4543
Parker S 300/PK-8
2353 Columbia Ave 46205 317-226-4256
Christine Rembert, prin. Fax 226-3370
Penn ES 800/PK-6
1720 W Wilkins St 46221 317-226-4249
Corye Franklin, prin. Fax 226-3683
Phelan Leadership Academy 100/PK-6
3920 Baker Dr 46235 317-226-4103
Agnes Aleobua, prin. Fax 226-3049
Phillips ES 400/PK-8
1163 N Belmont Ave 46222 317-226-4263
Paul Wirth, prin. Fax 226-3303
Potter ES 300/K-6
1601 E 10th St 46201 317-226-4274
Tim Clevenger, prin. Fax 226-3421

Pyle ES 400/PK-6
3351 W 18th St 46222 317-226-4290
Valerie Allen, prin. Fax 226-4539
Riley ES 500/PK-8
150 W 40th St 46208 317-226-4243
Bakari Posey, prin. Fax 226-3352
Russell ES 400/PK-6
3445 Central Ave 46205 317-226-4248
Sam Crishell, prin. Fax 226-2027
Sidener Gifted Academy 300/2-8
2424 Kessler Boulevard E Dr 46220 317-226-4259
Troy Watkins, prin. Fax 226-3059
Skillen ES 500/PK-6
1410 Wade St 46203 317-226-4234
Angela Ludlum, prin. Fax 226-4876
SUPER S at Douglas 400/PK-8
2020 Dawson St 46203 317-226-4219
Aleicha Ostler, prin. Fax 226-4762
Torrence ES 300/PK-6
5050 E 42nd St 46226 317-226-4283
Heather Haskett, prin. Fax 226-4994
Wallace ES 300/PK-6
3307 Ashway Dr 46224 317-226-4107
Jeremy Baugh, prin. Fax 226-3733
Webster ES 500/K-8
1450 S Reisner St 46221 317-226-4246
Karen Linn, prin. Fax 226-4377
Wilde ES 700/K-6
5002 W 34th St 46224 317-226-4279
Joyce Akridge, prin. Fax 226-2007

Metro SD of Decatur Township 6,100/PK-12
5275 Kentucky Ave 46221 317-856-5265
Nathan Davis Ed.D., admin. Fax 856-2156
www.msddecatur.k12.in.us
Blue Academy 600/1-6
5650 Mann Rd 46221 317-856-5265
Stephanie Hofer, prin. Fax 856-2183
Decatur ES 500/1-6
3425 Foltz St 46221 317-241-0183
Katie Gordon, prin. Fax 241-7580
Decatur MS 900/7-8
5108 S High School Rd 46221 317-856-5274
Kyle Barrentine, prin. Fax 856-2163
Gold Academy 600/1-6
5650 Mann Rd 46221 317-856-5265
Jana Anderson, prin. Fax 856-2197
Liberty ECC 500/PK-K
4640 Santa Fe Dr 46241 317-243-7559
Susan Bryant, prin. Fax 486-4208
Valley Mills ES 600/1-6
5101 S High School Rd 46221 317-856-6363
Michael Gath, prin. Fax 856-2142
Other Schools – See West Newton

Metro SD of Pike Township 11,000/PK-12
6901 Zionsville Rd 46268 317-293-0393
Dr. Flora Reichanadter, supt. Fax 297-7896
www.pike.k12.in.us
Central ES 700/K-5
7001 Zionsville Rd 46268 317-298-2778
Erica Porter, prin. Fax 299-1261
College Park ES 400/K-5
2811 Barnard St 46268 317-347-7400
Stephane Bordelon, prin. Fax 299-1262
Deer Run ES 700/K-5
5401 N High School Rd 46254 317-299-1266
Eric Elmore, prin. Fax 328-7231
Eagle Creek ES 500/K-5
6905 W 46th St 46254 317-291-1311
Kevin Kempton, prin. Fax 328-7234
Eastbrook ES 700/K-5
7625 New Augusta Rd 46268 317-298-2784
Larry Huff, prin. Fax 872-0562
Fishback Creek Public Academy 600/PK-5
8301 W 86th St 46278 317-347-8470
Lisa Steele, prin. Fax 347-8471
Guion Creek ES 800/K-5
4301 W 52nd St 46254 317-298-2780
Pamela Conley, prin. Fax 290-0406
Guion Creek MS 900/6-8
4401 W 52nd St 46254 317-293-4549
Dr. Maggie Bishop, prin. Fax 298-2794
Lincoln MS 800/6-8
5353 W 71st St 46268 317-291-9499
Dan Kuznik, prin. Fax 297-1673
New Augusta Public Academy North 800/6-8
6450 Rodebaugh Rd 46268 317-388-7700
Curtis Wright, prin. Fax 388-7786
New Augusta Public Academy South 500/K-5
6250 Rodebaugh Rd 46268 317-387-4325
Nikki Henson, prin. Fax 388-7838
Snacks Crossing ES 600/PK-5
5455 W 56th St 46254 317-295-7200
Fabrice Decaudin, prin. Fax 298-0686

Metro SD of Warren Township 12,400/PK-12
975 N Post Rd 46219 317-869-4300
Dr. Dena Cushenberry Ed.D., supt. Fax 869-4399
www.warren.k12.in.us
Brookview ES 600/K-4
1550 Cumberland Rd 46229 317-532-3050
Charles Woods, prin. Fax 532-3089
Creston Intermediate Academy 600/5-6
10925 Prospect St 46239 317-869-1319
Jina Simmons, prin. Fax 532-6899
Creston MS 600/7-8
10925 Prospect St 46239 317-532-6800
Chad Reedy, prin. Fax 532-6899
Eastridge ES 400/K-4
10930 E 10th St 46229 317-532-3150
Robin LeClaire, prin. Fax 532-3189
Grassy Creek ES 500/K-4
10330 Prospect St 46239 317-532-3100
Christina Merchant, prin. Fax 532-3139
Hawthorne ES 500/K-4
8301 Rawles Ave 46219 317-532-3950
Greg Butler, prin. Fax 532-3989

Lakeside ES 600/K-4
9601 E 21st St 46229 317-532-2850
Jeff Hoog, prin. Fax 532-2889
Liberty Park ES 500/K-4
8425 E Raymond St 46239 317-532-1850
Jason Brooks, prin. Fax 532-1895
Lowell ES 500/K-4
2150 S Hunter Rd 46239 317-532-3900
Kim Griffin, prin. Fax 532-3939
Pleasant Run ES 500/K-4
1800 N Franklin Rd 46219 317-532-3800
Travis Koomler, prin. Fax 532-3839
Raymond Park Intermediate Academy 600/5-6
8575 E Raymond St 46239 317-532-8966
Carey Storm, prin. Fax 532-8999
Raymond Park MS 600/7-8
8575 E Raymond St 46239 317-532-8900
Dr. John Kleine, prin. Fax 532-8999
Stonybrook Intermediate Academy 600/5-6
11300 Stony Brook Dr 46229 317-532-8803
Mychael Spencer, prin. Fax 532-8899
Stonybrook MS 600/7-8
11300 Stony Brook Dr 46229 317-532-8800
Nathan Day, prin. Fax 532-8899
Sunny Heights ES 500/K-4
11149 Stony Brook Dr 46229 317-532-2900
Bart Lewis, prin. Fax 532-2938
Warren ECC 300/PK-PK
1401 N Mitthoeffer Rd 46229 317-869-4750
Annemarie Fessler, prin. Fax 869-4752

Metropolitan SD of Lawrence Township 14,900/PK-12
6501 Sunnyside Rd 46236 317-423-8200
Dr. Shawn Smith, supt. Fax 543-3534
www.ltschools.org/
Belzer MS 1,100/7-8
7555 E 56th St 46226 317-964-6200
Andrew Harsha, prin. Fax 543-3355
Beverland Early Learning Center PK-K
11650 Fox Rd 46236 317-964-4000
Jered Pennington, prin. Fax 823-5230
Beverland ES 700/1-6
11650 Fox Rd 46236 317-964-4000
Jered Pennington, prin. Fax 823-5230
Brook Park Early Learning Center PK-K
5249 David St 46226 317-423-8215
Erika Radford, prin. Fax 964-5407
Brook Park ES 700/1-6
5259 David St 46226 317-964-4100
Alicia Gatewood, prin. Fax 543-3525
Castle Early Learning Center 1,300/PK-K
8510 E 82nd St 46256 317-423-8216
Stephanie LaPlante, prin. Fax 964-5408
Castle ES 700/1-6
8502 E 82nd St 46256 317-964-4600
Carla Johnson, prin. Fax 570-4301
Crestview ES 400/1-6
7600 E 71st St 46256 317-964-4200
Kimberly Brown, prin. Fax 576-6172
Fall Creek Valley MS 1,100/7-8
9701 E 63rd St 46236 317-964-6600
Kathryn Luessow, prin. Fax 823-5497
Forest Glen ES 700/K-6
6333 Lee Rd 46236 317-964-4900
Jerome Lahlou, prin. Fax 823-5455
Harrison Hill ES 600/1-6
7510 E 53rd St 46226 317-964-4300
Natalie Stewart, prin. Fax 543-3315
Indian Creek ES 700/1-6
10833 E 56th St 46235 317-964-4400
Kevin Kemper, prin. Fax 823-3400
Oaklandon ES 600/1-6
6702 Oaklandon Rd 46236 317-964-4800
Jennifer Sheets, prin. Fax 823-5227
Skiles Test ES 500/1-6
7001 Johnson Rd 46220 317-964-4700
Justin Hunter, prin. Fax 576-6171
Sunnyside ES 700/1-6
6345 Sunnyside Rd 46236 317-964-4500
Tierney Anderson, prin. Fax 823-3418
Winding Ridge Early Learning Center PK-K
11845 E 46th St 46235 317-423-8217
Conni Davis, prin. Fax 964-5409
Winding Ridge ES 600/1-6
11825 E 46th St 46235 317-964-6800
Alicia Harris, prin. Fax 964-6809

Metropolitan SD of Washington Township 11,200/PK-12
8550 Woodfield Crossing 46240 317-845-9400
Dr. Nikki Woodson, supt. Fax 205-3384
www.msdwt.k12.in.us
Allisonville ES 800/1-5
4900 E 79th St 46250 317-845-9441
Michael Pomerenke, prin. Fax 576-5255
Crooked Creek ES 600/K-5
2150 Kessler Boulevard West 46228 317-259-5478
Keana Parquet, prin. Fax 259-5453
Eastwood MS 800/6-8
4401 E 62nd St 46220 317-259-5401
Sean Taylor, prin. Fax 259-5407
Fox Hill ES 800/K-5
802 Fox Hill Dr 46228 317-259-5371
Erica Beard, prin. Fax 259-5383
Greenbriar ES 800/K-5
8201 Ditch Rd 46260 317-259-5445
Jamie Alexander, prin. Fax 259-5494
Hilltop Learning Center 100/PK-PK
1915 E 86th St 46240 317-259-5458
Carletha Yarrell, coord. Fax 259-5229
Nora ES 800/K-5
1000 E 91st St 46240 317-844-5436
Amber Walters, prin. Fax 571-7172
Northview MS 800/6-8
8401 Westfield Blvd 46240 317-259-5421
Matt Kaiser, prin. Fax 259-5431
Spring Mill ES 700/K-5
8250 Spring Mill Rd 46260 317-259-5462
Subha Balagopal, prin. Fax 259-5484

Strange ES 600/K-5
3660 E 62nd St 46220 317-259-5465
Maravene Inman, prin. Fax 259-5469
Westlane MS 900/6-8
1301 W 73rd St 46260 317-259-5412
Bill Pitcock, prin. Fax 259-5409

Metropolitan SD of Wayne Township 16,000/PK-12
1220 S High School Rd 46241 317-988-8600
Jeffrey Butts Ph.D., supt. Fax 243-5744
www.wayne.k12.in.us
Bridgeport ES 700/PK-6
9035 W Morris St 46231 317-988-6200
Dr. Angela Lewis, prin. Fax 988-6299
Chapel Glen ES 700/PK-6
701 Lansdowne Rd 46234 317-988-6500
Marc Coapstick, prin. Fax 988-6589
Chapel Hill 7th & 8th Grade Center 1,200/7-8
7320 W 10th St 46214 317-988-8800
Sheri Patterson, prin. Fax 988-8949
Chapelwood ES 700/K-6
1129 N Girls School Rd 46214 317-988-6400
Heather Pierce, prin. Fax 243-5681
Garden City ES 1,000/PK-6
4901 Rockville Rd 46224 317-988-8300
Dr. Pamela Hardy, prin. Fax 988-8399
Lynhurst 7th & 8th Grade Center 1,200/7-8
2805 S Lynhurst Dr 46241 317-988-8100
Dan Wilson, prin. Fax 243-5532
Maplewood ES 700/PK-6
1643 Dunlap Ave 46241 317-988-6600
Moira Clark, prin. Fax 243-5724
McClelland ES 800/PK-6
6740 W Morris St 46241 317-988-8000
Jennifer Nichols, prin. Fax 484-3123
North Wayne ES 800/PK-6
6950 W 34th St 46214 317-988-6100
Aretha Britton, prin. Fax 988-6199
Rhoades ES 800/PK-6
502 S Auburn St 46241 317-988-6700
Karen Boatright, prin. Fax 243-5718
Robey ES 800/PK-6
8700 W 30th St 46234 317-988-6000
Ben Markley, prin. Fax 988-6089
Stout Field ES 800/PK-6
3820 W Bradbury Ave 46241 317-988-6800
Tim Wickard, prin. Fax 243-5698
Westlake ES 800/PK-6
271 N Sigsbee St 46214 317-988-6900
Dennisha Murff, prin. Fax 484-3122

Perry Township SD 14,600/PK-12
6548 Orinoco Ave 46227 317-789-3700
Patrick Mapes, supt. Fax 789-3709
www.perryschools.org
Bryan ES 700/PK-5
4355 E Stop 11 Rd 46237 317-789-2600
Dana Dehart, prin. Fax 865-2693
Burkhart ES 500/K-5
5701 Brill Rd 46227 317-789-3600
Darlene Hardesty, prin. Fax 780-4285
Glenns Valley ES 700/PK-5
8239 Morgantown Rd 46217 317-789-2800
David Rohl, prin. Fax 865-2685
Gray-Edison ES 600/K-5
5225 Gray Rd 46237 317-789-4300
Douglas Smith, prin. Fax 789-4309
Homecroft ES 600/K-5
1551 Southview Dr 46227 317-789-3500
Jody Matthews, prin. Fax 780-4292
Lincoln ES 800/K-5
5241 Brehob Rd 46217 317-789-3800
Whitney Wilkowski, prin. Fax 780-4345
MacArthur ES 700/K-5
454 E Stop 11 Rd 46227 317-789-2500
Starlena Hardimon, prin. Fax 865-2679
Parks ES 600/K-5
7525 Wellingshire Blvd 46217 317-789-2900
David Henriott, prin. Fax 859-5750
Perry Meridian 6th Grade Academy 600/6-6
202 W Meridian School Rd 46217 317-789-1300
John Ralston, prin. Fax 859-5752
Perry Meridian MS 1,100/7-8
202 W Meridian School Rd 46217 317-789-4100
Jonathan Romine, prin. Fax 865-2710
Southport 6th Grade Academy 500/6-6
5715 S Keystone Ave 46227 317-789-1400
Kimberly Campbell, prin. Fax 780-4401
Southport ES 500/K-5
261 Anniston Dr 46227 317-789-3300
Jeffrey Spencer, prin. Fax 780-4299
Southport MS 1,000/7-8
5715 S Keystone Ave 46227 317-789-4600
Stephanie Quinlan, prin. Fax 780-4302
Young ES 700/K-5
5740 McFarland Rd 46227 317-789-3400
Andrea Korreck, prin. Fax 780-4338
Other Schools – See Southport

Calvary Christian S 200/PK-12
3639 S Keystone Ave 46227 317-789-8710
Charles Barcus, admin. Fax 789-8718
Calvary Lutheran S 200/PK-8
6111 Shelby St 46227 317-783-2305
Stephen Rensner, prin. Fax 789-3039
Capitol City SDA S 50/PK-8
2143 Boulevard Pl 46202 317-602-3524
Jennifer Bolejack, prin. Fax 602-3529
Central Catholic S 200/PK-8
1155 Cameron St 46203 317-783-7759
Ruth Hurrle, prin. Fax 781-5964
Central Christian Academy 200/PK-12
2565 Villa Ave 46203 317-788-1587
David Sexauer, head sch Fax 781-4758
Children's Habitat Montessori S PK-6
801 W 73rd St 46260 317-726-5584
Susan Michal, head sch
Christ the King S 400/K-8
5858 Crittenden Ave 46220 317-257-9366
Ed Seib, prin. Fax 715-4781

Colonial Christian S 200/PK-12
8140 Union Chapel Rd 46240 317-253-0649
Crosspointe Christian Academy 200/PK-12
220 Country Club Rd 46234 317-271-1600
Emmaus Lutheran S 50/PK-6
1224 Laurel St 46203 317-632-1486
Fax 632-2620
Gray Road Christian S 200/PK-6
5500 Gray Rd 46237 317-786-3559
Ann Wall, prin. Fax 789-4046
Hasten Hebrew Academy of Indianapolis 100/PK-8
6602 Hoover Rd 46260 317-251-1261
Miriam Gettinger, prin. Fax 479-3123
Heritage Christian S 1,400/PK-12
6401 E 75th St 46250 317-849-3441
Jeff Freeman, admin. Fax 594-5863
Holy Angels S 100/PK-6
2822 Dr Mrtn Lthr Kng Jr St 46208 317-926-5211
Matthew Goddard, prin. Fax 926-5219
Holy Cross Central S 200/PK-8
125 N Oriental St 46202 317-638-9068
Matthew Gring, prin. Fax 638-0116
Holy Cross Lutheran S 300/PK-8
8115 Oaklandon Rd 46236 317-826-1234
Karen Geiger, prin. Fax 826-0640
Holy Spirit S 400/PK-8
7241 E 10th St 46219 317-352-1243
Rita Parsons, prin. Fax 351-1822
Horizon Christian S 300/PK-12
7702 Indian Lake Rd 46236 317-823-4538
Michael Slack, head sch Fax 823-2396
Horizon Christian S Shepherd Campus 200/K-5
4107 E Washington St 46201 317-823-4538
Sonna Dumas, prin. Fax 823-2396
Immaculate Heart of Mary S 400/K-8
317 E 57th St 46220 317-255-5468
Ronda Swartz, prin. Fax 475-7379
Indianapolis Junior Academy 100/PK-8
2910 E 62nd St 46220 317-251-0560
Norris Ncube, prin. Fax 251-6486
Indianapolis Southside Christian Academy K-8
4801 Shelbyville Rd 46237 317-207-4182
International S of Indiana 600/PK-12
4330 Michigan Rd 46208 317-923-1951
David Garner, hdmstr. Fax 923-1910
Lumen Christi Catholic S 100/PK-12
580 E Stevens St 46203 317-632-3174
Robert Collins, admin. Fax 636-2522
Nativity S 400/PK-8
3310 S Meadow Dr 46239 317-357-1459
Terri Bianchini, prin. Fax 357-9175
Oaks Academy - Fall Creek 200/PK-5
2301 N Park Ave 46205 317-931-3043
Bruce Crawford, head sch Fax 931-3050
Orchard S 600/PK-8
615 W 64th St 46260 317-251-9253
Thomas Rosenbluth, hdmstr. Fax 254-8454
Our Lady of Lourdes S 300/PK-8
30 S Downey Ave 46219 317-357-3316
Chris Kolakovich, prin. Fax 357-0980
Park Tudor S 1,000/PK-12
7200 N College Ave 46240 317-415-2700
Gareth Vaughan, head sch Fax 254-2714
St. Anthony S PK-8
349 N Warman Ave 46222 317-636-3739
Cindy Greer, prin. Fax 636-3740
St. Barnabas S 500/PK-8
8300 Rahke Rd 46217 317-881-7422
Carissa Maddox, prin. Fax 887-8933
St. Christopher S 200/PK-6
5335 W 16th St 46224 317-241-6314
Karen King, prin. Fax 244-6678
St. Joan of Arc S 300/PK-8
500 E 42nd St 46205 317-283-1518
Janet Andriole, prin. Fax 931-3380
St. John Lutheran S 200/PK-8
6630 Southeastern Ave 46203 317-352-9196
Rick Kerr, prin. Fax 352-9740
St. Jude S 500/K-8
5375 McFarland Rd 46227 317-784-6828
Joe Shelburn, prin. Fax 780-7594
St. Lawrence S 200/PK-8
6950 E 46th St 46226 317-543-4923
Sarah Watson, prin. Fax 543-4929
St. Luke S 600/K-8
7650 N Illinois St 46260 317-255-3912
Elizabeth Kissel, prin. Fax 254-3210
St. Mark S 200/PK-8
541 E Edgewood Ave 46227 317-786-4013
Rusty Albertson, prin. Fax 783-9574
St. Matthew S 300/PK-8
4100 E 56th St 46220 317-251-3997
David Smock, prin. Fax 251-3997
St. Michael - St Gabriel Archangels S 200/PK-8
3352 W 30th St 46222 317-926-0516
Liz Ramos, prin. Fax 921-3282
St. Monica S 500/PK-8
6131 Michigan Rd 46228 317-255-7153
Eric Schommer, prin. Fax 222-5911
St. Philip Neri S 200/PK-8
545 Eastern Ave 46201 317-636-0134
Kari Buchinger, prin. Fax 636-3231
St. Pius X S 400/K-8
7200 Sarto Dr 46240 317-466-3361
Alec Mayer, prin. Fax 466-3354
St. Richard's Episcopal S 300/PK-8
33 E 33rd St 46205 317-926-0425
Peter Harding, head sch Fax 921-3367
St. Roch S 300/PK-8
3603 S Meridian St 46217 317-784-9144
Amy Wilson, prin. Fax 784-7051
St. Simon the Apostle S 800/PK-8
8155 Oaklandon Rd 46236 317-826-6000
Cathlene Darragh, prin. Fax 826-6020
St. Therese Little Flower S 200/PK-8
1401 N Bosart Ave 46201 317-353-2282
Kevin Gawrys, prin. Fax 322-7702

St. Thomas Aquinas S 200/K-8
4600 N Illinois St 46208 317-255-6244
Cara Swinefurth, prin. Fax 255-6106
Southport Presbyterian Christian S 200/PK-5
7525 McFarland Blvd 46237 317-534-2929
Shana Hoffman M.Ed., prin. Fax 534-2923
Suburban Christian S 100/PK-12
722 E County Line Rd 46227 317-888-3366
Jeremy Wilhelm, prin. Fax 884-4025
Sycamore S 400/PK-8
1750 W 64th St 46260 317-202-2500
Diane Borgmann, head sch Fax 202-2501
Trinity Christian S 100/K-12
440 Saint Peter St 46201 317-631-3194
Sharon Ragan, prin. Fax 631-7230
Trinity Lutheran S 200/PK-8
8540 E 16th St 46219 317-897-0243
Matt Riley, prin. Fax 897-5277

Ireland, Dubois
Greater Jasper Consolidated SD
Supt. — See Jasper
Ireland ES 600/PK-5
2386 N 500 W 47545 812-482-7751
Ray Mehling, prin. Fax 482-7765

Jamestown, Boone, Pop. 953
Western Boone County Community SD
Supt. — See Thorntown
Wells ES 500/PK-6
5046 S State Road 75 46147 765-485-6311
Tricia Stanley, prin. Fax 676-5012

Jasonville, Greene, Pop. 2,204
Metro SD Shakamak 800/K-12
9233 Shakamak School Rd 47438 812-665-3550
Mike Mogan, supt. Fax 665-5001
www.shakamak.k12.in.us/
Shakamak ES 500/K-6
9233 Shakamak School Rd 47438 812-665-3550
Jeff Gambill, prin. Fax 665-5001

Jasper, Dubois, Pop. 14,939
Greater Jasper Consolidated SD 3,200/PK-12
1520 Saint Charles St 47546 812-482-1801
Dr. Tracy Lorey, supt. Fax 482-3388
www.gjcs.k12.in.us
Fifth Street ES 400/PK-2
401 W 5th St 47546 812-482-1406
Ryan Erny, prin. Fax 482-1413
Jasper MS 800/6-8
3600 N Portersville Rd 47546 812-482-6454
David Hubster, prin. Fax 482-6457
Tenth Street ES 400/3-5
328 W 10th St 47546 812-482-2529
Kent Taylor, prin. Fax 482-2043
Other Schools – See Ireland

Holy Trinity S 300/PK-2
1385 W 6th St 47546 812-482-4461
Tyler Lemen, prin. Fax 482-7762
Holy Trinity S 200/3-8
990 Church Ave 47546 812-482-5050
Tyler Lemen, prin. Fax 481-9909

Jeffersonville, Clark, Pop. 43,626
Greater Clark County SD 10,500/PK-12
2112 Utica Sellersburg Rd 47130 812-283-0701
Dr. Andrew Melin, supt. Fax 288-4804
www.gcs.k12.in.us
Bridgepoint ES 400/PK-5
420 Ewing Ln 47130 812-288-4858
Jacqueline Diaz, prin. Fax 288-2852
Jefferson ES 400/PK-5
2710 Hamburg Pike 47130 812-288-4855
Jennifer Korfhage, prin. Fax 288-4870
Maple ES 300/PK-5
429 Division St 47130 812-288-4860
Denise Ellnor, prin. Fax 288-4899
Northaven ES 400/PK-5
1907 Oakridge Dr 47130 812-288-4865
Laura Morris, prin. Fax 288-4862
Parkview MS 800/6-8
1600 Brigman Ave 47130 812-288-4844
Jeremy Stewart, prin. Fax 288-2849
Riverside ES 500/K-5
17 Laurel Dr 47130 812-288-4868
Beth Kimmel, prin. Fax 288-4894
River Valley MS 900/6-8
2220 Veterans Pkwy 47130 812-288-4848
Michelle Dyer, prin. Fax 288-4851
Spring Hill ES 200/PK-5
201 E 15th St 47130 812-288-4874
Virenda Cunningham-Leste, prin. Fax 288-4876
Utica ES 500/PK-5
210 Maplehurst Dr 47130 812-288-4878
Kathy Gilland, prin. Fax 288-2846
Wilson ES 500/PK-5
2915 Charlestown Pike 47130 812-288-4888
April Holder, prin. Fax 288-4895
Other Schools – See Charlestown, Clarksville, New Washington

Sacred Heart S 200/PK-8
1842 E 8th St 47130 812-283-3123
Frank Barlag, prin. Fax 284-6678

Jonesboro, Grant, Pop. 1,733
Mississinewa Community SC
Supt. — See Gas City
Westview ES 500/PK-1
709 W 6th St 46938 765-677-4437
Bruce Smith, prin. Fax 677-4449

King's Academy 100/K-12
1201 S Water St 46938 765-674-1722
Latrese Moffitt, hdmstr. Fax 674-7322

Kendallville, Noble, Pop. 9,716
East Noble SC 3,800/PK-12
126 W Rush St 46755 260-347-2502
Ann Linson, supt. Fax 347-0111
www.eastnoble.net
East Noble MS 600/7-8
401 E Diamond St 46755 260-347-0100
Andrew Deming, prin. Fax 347-7168
North Side ES 400/K-6
302 Harding St 46755 260-347-1354
Stephanie Leasure, prin. Fax 347-3319
South Side ES 400/PK-6
1350 Sherman St 46755 260-349-2200
Jeff Harper, prin. Fax 349-2210
Wayne Center ES 300/PK-6
1231 E Appleman Rd 46755 260-347-2548
Jaime Carroll, prin. Fax 347-7172
Other Schools – See Avilla, Rome City

St. John Lutheran S 200/PK-8
301 S Oak St 46755 260-347-2444
Tim Walz, prin. Fax 349-2854

Kentland, Newton, Pop. 1,729
South Newton SC 900/PK-12
13232 S 50 E 47951 219-474-5184
Kenneth Rudnick, supt. Fax 474-6966
www.newton.k12.in.us/
South Newton ES 400/PK-5
13188 S 50 E 47951 219-474-5167
Casey Hall, prin. Fax 474-3621
South Newton MS 200/6-8
13100 S 50 E 47951 219-474-5167
Tansey Mulligan, prin. Fax 474-3624

Kingsford Heights, LaPorte, Pop. 1,396
La Porte Community SC
Supt. — See La Porte
Kingsford Heights ES 200/K-5
460 Evanston Rd 46346 219-393-3116
Marcia Alexander, prin. Fax 393-5082

Knightstown, Henry, Pop. 2,153
C.A. Beard Memorial SC 1,000/K-12
8139 W US Highway 40 46148 765-345-5101
Jediah Behny, supt. Fax 345-5103
www.cabeard.k12.in.us
Knightstown ES 200/K-3
8632 S State Road 109 46148 765-345-2151
Danielle Carmichael, prin. Fax 345-7134
Knightstown IS 400/4-8
1 Panther Trl 46148 765-345-5455
K. Gardner, prin. Fax 345-5523

Knox, Starke, Pop. 3,653
Knox Community SC 2,000/PK-12
2 Redskin Trl 46534 574-772-1000
Dr. William Reichhart, supt. Fax 772-1608
www.knox.k12.in.us
Knox Community ES 1,000/PK-5
210 W Culver Rd 46534 574-772-1633
Glenn Barnes, prin. Fax 772-1646
Knox Community MS 500/6-8
901 S Main St 46534 574-772-1654
David Miller, prin. Fax 772-1664

Kokomo, Howard, Pop. 44,079
Kokomo SC 6,800/PK-12
PO Box 2188 46904 765-455-8000
Dr. Jeff Hauswald, supt. Fax 455-8018
www.kokomo.k12.in.us
Bon Air Elementary Technology Academy 500/K-5
2800 N Apperson Way 46901 765-454-7030
Paula Concus, prin. Fax 454-7034
Bon Air MS Technology Academy 300/6-8
2796 N Apperson Way 46901 765-454-7025
Amanda Landrum, prin. Fax 454-7034
Boulevard Elementary STEM S 300/PK-5
1901 W Boulevard 46902 765-455-8070
David Buckalew, prin. Fax 455-8079
Central Middle (KEY) International S 400/6-8
303 E Superior St 46901 765-454-7000
Holly Herrera, prin. Fax 454-7007
Haynes ES 800/PK-5
910 S Cooper St 46901 765-454-7050
Kathi Hoover, prin. Fax 454-7052
Lafayette Park International ES 600/PK-5
919 Korby St 46901 765-454-7060
Tammy Tickfer, prin. Fax 454-7062
Maple Crest Middle STEM S 600/6-8
2727 S Washington St 46902 765-455-8085
Thomas Hughes, prin. Fax 455-8062
Pettit Park 1-1 Elem Technology Academy 400/PK-5
901 W Havens St 46901 765-454-7075
Kelly Wright, prin. Fax 454-7078
Sycamore (KEY) International ES 600/K-5
1600 E Sycamore St 46901 765-454-7090
LaShaya Williams, prin. Fax 454-7093
Wallace ES of Integrated Arts 200/K-5
2326 W Jefferson St 46901 765-454-7095
Charley Hinkle, prin. Fax 454-7206

Northwestern SC 1,700/K-12
3075 N Washington St 46901 765-452-3060
Ryan Snoddy, supt. Fax 452-3065
nwsc.k12.in.us
Howard ES 300/K-6
3526 N 300 E 46901 765-454-2326
Rhonda Lanie, prin. Fax 868-8395
Northwestern ES 600/K-6
4223 W 350 N 46901 765-454-2335
Ron Owings, prin. Fax 454-2334
Northwestern MS 300/7-8
3431 N 400 W 46901 765-454-2323
Brett Davis, prin. Fax 457-2324

Taylor Community SC 1,100/PK-12
3750 E 300 S 46902 765-453-3035
Chris Smith, supt. Fax 455-8531
www.taylor.k12.in.us
Taylor ES 400/PK-5
5500 Wea Dr 46902 765-453-3800
Jeremy Luna, prin. Fax 455-5173
Taylor MS 300/6-8
3794 E 300 S 46902 765-455-5186
Heather Hord, prin. Fax 455-5157

Acacia Academy 100/K-8
830 S Main St 46901 765-457-5545
Redeemer Lutheran S 100/PK-8
705 E Southway Blvd 46902 765-864-6466
Ruth Lavrenz, prin. Fax 864-6468
SS. Joan of Arc & Patrick S 300/PK-8
3155 S 200 W 46902 765-865-9960
Nick Kanable, prin. Fax 865-9962

Kouts, Porter, Pop. 1,870
East Porter County SC 2,500/K-12
PO Box 370 46347 219-766-2214
Dr. Rod Gardin, supt. Fax 766-2885
www.eastporter.k12.in.us
Kouts ES 400/K-5
PO Box 699 46347 219-766-2231
Patti Eich, prin. Fax 766-3763
Other Schools – See Valparaiso

Ladoga, Montgomery, Pop. 977
South Montgomery Community SC
Supt. — See Crawfordsville
Ladoga ES 200/K-6
418 E Taylor St 47954 765-942-2203
Belle Gabbard, prin. Fax 942-2204

Lafayette, Tippecanoe, Pop. 65,793
Lafayette SC 7,500/K-12
2300 Cason St 47904 765-771-6000
Les Huddle, supt. Fax 771-6049
www.lsc.k12.in.us
Earhart ES 500/K-4
3280 S 9th St 47909 765-772-4740
Ryan Habben, prin. Fax 772-4744
Edgelea ES 600/K-4
2910 S 18th St 47909 765-772-4780
Karen Combs, prin. Fax 772-4786
Glen Acres ES 400/K-4
3767 Kimberly Dr 47905 765-771-6150
Megan Hatke, prin. Fax 771-6154
Lafayette Tecumseh JHS 1,000/7-8
2101 S 18th St 47905 765-772-4750
Brandon Hawkins, prin. Fax 772-4763
Miami ES 500/K-4
2401 Beck Ln 47909 765-772-4800
Amanda Henry, prin. Fax 772-4804
Miller ES 400/K-4
700 S 4th St 47905 765-476-2930
Debbie Patterson, prin. Fax 476-2934
Murdock ES 300/K-4
2100 Cason St 47904 765-771-6120
Janell Uerkwitz, prin. Fax 771-6126
Oakland ES 300/K-4
611 S 21st St 47905 765-771-6130
Matt Rhoda, prin. Fax 771-6143
Sunnyside IS 1,000/5-6
530 N 26th St 47904 765-771-6100
Matt Brown, prin. Fax 771-6113
Vinton ES 400/K-4
3101 Elmwood Ave 47904 765-771-6140
Cindy Preston, prin. Fax 771-6144

Tippecanoe SC 12,300/K-12
21 Elston Rd 47909 765-474-2481
Dr. Scott Hanback, supt. Fax 474-0533
www.tsc.k12.in.us
Cole ES 200/K-5
6418 E 900 S 47909 765-523-2141
Michael Pinto, prin. Fax 523-2864
East Tipp MS 500/6-8
7501 E 300 N 47905 765-589-3566
Shaad Buss, prin. Fax 589-3129
Hershey ES 600/K-5
7521 E 300 N 47905 765-589-3907
Linda Fields, prin. Fax 589-8628
Mayflower Mill ES 500/K-5
200 E 500 S 47909 765-538-3875
Shannon Cauble, prin. Fax 538-2014
Mintonye ES 500/K-5
2000 W 800 S 47909 765-538-2780
Robert Skaggs, prin. Fax 538-2988
Southwestern MS 400/6-8
2100 W 800 S 47909 765-538-3025
Karen Shuman, prin. Fax 538-2877
Wainwright MS 300/6-8
7501 E 700 S 47905 765-269-8350
Dr. Neal McCutcheon, prin. Fax 269-8359
Wea Ridge ES 700/K-5
1333 E 430 S 47909 765-471-9321
Michael Gabauer, prin. Fax 471-9329
Wea Ridge MS 700/6-8
4410 S 150 E 47909 765-471-2164
Fred Roop, prin. Fax 474-5347
Woodland ES 500/K-5
3200 E 450 S 47909 765-269-8220
Bruce Hall, prin. Fax 471-0251
Wyandotte ES 400/K-5
5865 E 50 S 47905 765-772-7000
Mary Beth Fitzgerald, prin. Fax 447-5463
Other Schools – See Battle Ground, Dayton, West Lafayette

Faith Christian S 700/PK-12
5526 State Road 26 E 47905 765-447-2727
Scott Grass, supt. Fax 449-3737
Lafayette Christian S 300/PK-8
525 N 26th St 47904 765-447-3052
Jon Rugenstein, prin. Fax 448-1850

St. Boniface S 100/4-6
813 North St 47901 765-742-7913
Sr. Lenore Schwartz, prin. Fax 423-4988
St. James Lutheran S 100/K-8
615 N 8th St 47901 765-742-6464
Jacob Rogers, prin. Fax 742-4642
St. Lawrence S 300/PK-6
1902 Meharry St 47904 765-742-4450
Jody Williams, prin. Fax 742-4450
St. Mary Cathedral S 200/PK-3
1200 South St 47901 765-742-6302
Kim Delaney, prin. Fax 742-7060

Lagrange, Lagrange, Pop. 2,609
Lakeland SC 2,200/K-12
825 E 075 N 46761 260-499-2400
Dr. Eva Merkel, supt. Fax 463-4800
www.lakeland.k12.in.us
Lakeland MS 500/6-8
1055 E 075 N 46761 260-499-2480
Bradley Targgart, prin. Fax 463-2648
Parkside ES 500/K-5
1 Lemaster Cir 46761 260-499-2430
Susan Mueller, prin. Fax 463-3730
Other Schools – See Howe, Wolcottville

Prairie Heights Community SC 1,400/K-12
305 S 1150 E 46761 260-351-3214
Jeff Reed, supt. Fax 351-3614
www.ph.k12.in.us/
Prairie Heights ES 500/K-4
455 S 1150 E 46761 260-351-3214
Alecia Pfefferkorn, prin. Fax 351-2182
Prairie Heights MS 400/5-8
395 S 1150 E 46761 260-351-2334
Andy Arndt, prin. Fax 351-2334

Lake Station, Lake, Pop. 12,350
Lake Station Community SD 1,500/K-12
2500 Pike St 46405 219-962-1159
Dr. Tom Cripliver, supt. Fax 962-4011
www.lakes.k12.in.us
Bailey ES 400/K-6
2100 Union St 46405 219-962-1302
Terry Kolopanis, prin. Fax 962-5222
Hamilton ES 300/1-6
2900 Lake St 46405 219-962-1824
Tara Gordon, prin. Fax 962-4559
Polk ES 200/1-6
2460 Vermillion St 46405 219-962-1360
Eduardo Zamarron, prin. Fax 962-4603

River Forest Community SC
Supt. — See Hobart
Evans ES 300/K-5
2915 E 35th Ave 46405 219-962-1608
Andrew Wielgus, prin. Fax 962-1643

Laketon, Wabash, Pop. 617
Manchester Community SD
Supt. — See North Manchester
Manchester IS 400/4-6
20 W Woodring Rd 46943 260-982-8685
Randy Self, prin. Fax 982-8085

Lake Village, Newton, Pop. 764
North Newton SC
Supt. — See Morocco
Lake Village ES 200/K-6
3281 W 950 N 46349 219-992-3311
Joan Seager, prin. Fax 992-2404

Lakeville, Saint Joseph, Pop. 778
Union-North United SC 1,100/K-12
22601 Tyler Rd 46536 574-784-8141
Mitchell Mawhorter, supt. Fax 784-2181
www.unorth.k12.in.us
Laville ES 600/K-6
12645 Tyler Rd 46536 574-784-2311
Kenneth Shirley, prin. Fax 784-8051

Lamar, Spencer
North Spencer County SC
Supt. — See Lincoln City
Lincoln Trail ES 300/PK-6
13726 N State Road 245 47550 812-544-2929
Ben Lawalin, prin. Fax 544-2930

Lanesville, Harrison, Pop. 557
Lanesville Community SC 700/K-12
2725 Crestview Ave NE 47136 812-952-2555
Steve Morris, supt. Fax 952-3762
www.lanesville.k12.in.us/
Lanesville ES 300/K-6
2725 Crestview Ave NE 47136 812-952-3000
Lisa Hammond, prin. Fax 952-3762

St. John's Lutheran S 100/PK-8
1507 St Johns Church Rd NE 47136 812-952-2737
Mark Ploss, prin. Fax 952-3269

Lapel, Madison, Pop. 2,035
Frankton-Lapel Community SD
Supt. — See Anderson
Lapel ES 700/PK-5
2865 S State Road 13 46051 765-534-3101
Genny Zetterberg, prin. Fax 203-9931
Lapel MS 300/6-8
2883 S State Road 13 46051 765-534-3137
Bill Chase, prin. Fax 203-9937

La Porte, LaPorte, Pop. 21,655
La Porte Community SC 6,400/K-12
1921 A St 46350 219-362-7056
Mark Francesconi, supt. Fax 324-9347
www.lpcsc.k12.in.us
Boston MS 700/6-8
1000 Harrison St 46350 219-326-6930
Deborah Carter, prin. Fax 324-7108
Crichfield ES 500/K-5
336 W Johnson Rd 46350 219-362-2020
Donna Biggs, prin. Fax 324-1399

Hailmann ES 400/K-5
1001 Ohio St 46350 219-362-2080
Denise Sanders, prin. Fax 362-8102
Handley ES 400/K-5
408 W 10th St 46350 219-362-2561
Pamela Upp, prin. Fax 362-1428
Indian Trail ES 300/K-5
3214 S State Road 104 46350 219-369-9016
Kimberly Rehlander, prin. Fax 369-1290
Kesling MS 800/6-8
306 E 18th St 46350 219-362-7507
Bill Wilmsen, prin. Fax 324-5712
Kingsbury ES 400/K-5
802 W 400 S 46350 219-362-1823
Elizabeth Antos, prin. Fax 324-6727
Lincoln ES 300/K-5
402 Harrison St 46350 219-362-3755
Diane Szynal, prin. Fax 324-6297
Riley ES 400/K-5
516 Weller Ave 46350 219-362-3235
Christopher Alber, prin. Fax 362-4903
Other Schools – See Kingsford Heights

Door Prairie Adventist Christian S 100/PK-8
1480 Boyd Blvd 46350 219-362-6959
Jennifer Semillano, lead tchr. Fax 362-6959
St. John's Lutheran S 100/PK-8
111 Kingsbury Ave 46350 219-362-6692
David Wippich, prin. Fax 362-4742

Larwill, Whitley, Pop. 280
Whitko Community SC 1,600/K-12
710 N State Road 5 Ste B 46764 260-327-3677
Steven Clason, supt. Fax 327-3238
www.whitko.org
Whitko MS 400/6-8
710 N State Road 5 46764 260-327-3603
Dr. Eugene Sweeney, prin. Fax 327-3805
Other Schools – See Pierceton, South Whitley

Laurel, Franklin, Pop. 512
Franklin County Community SC
Supt. — See Brookville
Laurel S 500/PK-6
PO Box 322 47024 765-698-3851
Lisa Baudendistel, prin. Fax 698-2611

Lawrenceburg, Dearborn, Pop. 4,938
Lawrenceburg Community SC 2,000/K-12
300 Tiger Blvd 47025 812-537-7200
Karl Galey, supt. Fax 537-0759
www.lburg.k12.in.us
Central ES 500/3-5
500 Short St 47025 812-537-7279
Staci Knigga, prin. Fax 537-7063
Greendale MS 500/6-8
200 Tiger Blvd 47025 812-537-7259
Jayme Herbert, prin. Fax 537-6385
Lawrenceburg PS 500/K-2
400 Tiger Blvd 47025 812-537-7239
Tammy Gregory, prin. Fax 537-5746

Sunman-Dearborn Community SC
Supt. — See Saint Leon
Bright ES 400/K-5
22593 Stateline Rd 47025 812-637-4600
Norb Goessling, prin. Fax 637-4606

St. Lawrence S 200/K-8
524 Walnut St 47025 812-537-3690
Michael Odar, prin. Fax 537-9685

Leavenworth, Crawford, Pop. 233
Crawford County Community SC
Supt. — See Marengo
South Crawford ES 200/PK-5
346 E State Road 62 47137 812-739-2210
Alan Cox, prin. Fax 739-2211

Lebanon, Boone, Pop. 15,595
Lebanon Community SC 3,500/K-12
1810 N Grant St 46052 765-482-0380
Dr. Robert Taylor, supt. Fax 483-3053
www.leb.k12.in.us/
Central ES 400/K-5
515 E Williams St 46052 765-482-2000
Rebecca Outcalt, prin. Fax 483-3059
Harney ES 500/K-5
1500 Garfield St 46052 765-482-5940
Dr. Janet Yonts, prin. Fax 483-3062
Lebanon MS 800/6-8
1800 N Grant St 46052 765-482-3400
Doyle Dunshee, prin. Fax 483-3049
Perry-Worth ES 400/K-5
3900 E 300 S 46052 317-769-3286
Amber Targgart, prin. Fax 769-5236
Stokes ES 500/K-5
1005 Hendricks Dr 46052 765-482-5950
Kelly Sollman, prin. Fax 483-3056

Leesburg, Kosciusko, Pop. 550
Warsaw Community SC
Supt. — See Warsaw
Leesburg ES 500/PK-6
6250 N Old State Road 15 46538 574-453-4121
Nathan Polston, prin. Fax 371-5004

Leo, Allen
East Allen County SD
Supt. — See New Haven
Leo ES 600/4-6
14811 Wayne St 46765 260-446-0170
William Diehl, prin. Fax 446-0173

Leopold, Perry
Perry Central Community SC 1,200/PK-12
18677 Old State Road 37 47551 812-843-5576
Mary Roberson, supt. Fax 843-4746
www.pccs.k12.in.us/
Perry Central ES 700/PK-6
18677 Old State Road 37 47551 812-843-5122
Ray James, prin. Fax 843-5242

Lexington, Scott, Pop. 350
Scott County SD 2
Supt. — See Scottsburg
Lexington ES 200/K-5
7980 E Walnut St 47138 812-752-8924
Nick South, prin. Fax 889-2094

Liberty, Union, Pop. 2,110
Union County/College Corner JSD 1,200/K-12
107 S Layman St 47353 765-458-7471
Christopher Winchell, supt. Fax 458-5647
www.uc.k12.in.us
Liberty ES 400/K-5
501 Eaton St 47353 765-458-5521
Kathy Sourbeer, prin. Fax 458-6223
Union County MS 300/6-8
488 E State Road 44 47353 765-458-7438
Ronald Ross, prin. Fax 458-6041

Ligonier, Noble, Pop. 4,376
West Noble SC 2,500/K-12
5050 N US Highway 33 46767 260-894-3191
Galen Mast, supt. Fax 894-3260
westnoble.k12.in.us/
West Noble ES 600/2-4
5294 N US Highway 33 46767 260-894-3191
Mark Yoder, prin. Fax 894-3199
West Noble MS 800/5-8
5194 N US Highway 33 46767 260-894-3191
Melanie Tijerina, prin. Fax 894-4703
West Noble PS 400/K-1
500 W Union St 46767 260-894-3191
Brian Shepherd, prin. Fax 894-3189

Lincoln City, Spencer
North Spencer County SC 2,000/PK-12
PO Box 316 47552 812-937-2400
Daniel Scherry, supt. Fax 937-7187
www.nspencer.k12.in.us
Heritage Hills MS 300/7-8
PO Box 1777 47552 812-937-4472
Chad Schnieders, prin. Fax 937-4327
Other Schools – See Chrisney, Dale, Ferdinand, Lamar

Linton, Greene, Pop. 5,354
Linton-Stockton SC 1,400/K-12
801 1st St NE 47441 812-847-6020
Nick Karazsia, supt. Fax 847-8659
www.lssc.k12.in.us/
Linton-Stockton ES 700/K-5
900 4th St NE 47441 812-847-6039
Kent Brewer, prin. Fax 847-6030
Linton-Stockton MS 300/6-8
109 I St NE 47441 812-847-6022
Lisa Hollingsworth, prin. Fax 847-6032

Lizton, Hendricks, Pop. 481
North West Hendricks SD 1,900/PK-12
PO Box 70 46149 317-994-4100
Richard King, supt. Fax 994-5963
www.hendricks.k12.in.us/
Tri-West MS 500/6-8
555 W US Highway 136 46149 317-994-4200
Ryan Nickoli, prin. Fax 994-4230
Other Schools – See North Salem, Pittsboro

Logansport, Cass, Pop. 18,151
Logansport Community SC 4,200/PK-12
2829 George St 46947 574-722-2911
Michele Starkey, supt. Fax 753-0143
www.lcsc.k12.in.us
Columbia 6th Grade Academy 500/6-6
1300 N 3rd St 46947 574-753-3797
Greg Grostefon, prin. Fax 753-6159
Columbia ES 500/K-5
20 E Columbia St 46947 574-753-3432
Angela Crook, prin. Fax 753-6072
Fairview ES 400/PK-5
846 S Cicott St 46947 574-722-5288
Christine Hess, prin. Fax 753-6318
Franklin ES 400/K-5
410 W Miami Ave 46947 574-722-3200
Michael Miller, prin. Fax 722-1172
Landis ES 700/K-5
1 Landis Ln 46947 574-722-5466
Rita McLochlin, prin. Fax 753-5513
Logansport JHS 500/7-8
2901 Usher St 46947 574-753-7115
Jeff Canady, prin. Fax 753-5826

Loogootee, Martin, Pop. 2,735
Loogootee Community SC 800/K-12
PO Box 282 47553 812-295-2595
Chip Mehaffey, supt. Fax 295-5595
www.loogootee.k12.in.us/
Loogootee ES 300/K-4
101 Costello Dr 47553 812-295-2833
Dara Chezem, prin. Fax 295-9008
Loogootee MS 100/5-8
201 Brooks Ave 47553 812-295-3254
Lacey Wade, prin. Fax 295-3694

Lowell, Lake, Pop. 9,196
Tri-Creek SC 3,400/K-12
19290 Cline Ave 46356 219-696-6661
Dr. Debra K. Howe, supt. Fax 696-2150
www.tricreek.k12.in.us
Lake Prairie ES 400/K-5
11601 W 181st Ave 46356 219-696-7541
Lisa Stoelb, prin. Fax 690-2616
Lowell MS 900/6-8
19250 Cline St 46356 219-696-7701
Rebecca Pavich, prin. Fax 690-2620
Oak Hill ES 500/K-5
425 S Nichols St 46356 219-696-9285
Stacey Schwuchow, prin. Fax 690-2621
Three Creeks ES 500/K-5
670 S Burr St 46356 219-696-5740
Connie Bales, prin. Fax 696-3051

Lynn, Randolph, Pop. 1,088
Randolph Southern SC 500/K-12
1 Rebel Dr 47355 765-874-1181
Donnie Bowsman, supt. Fax 874-1298
www.rssc.k12.in.us
Randolph Southern ES 200/K-6
3 Rebel Dr 47355 765-874-1141
Daniel Allen, prin. Fax 874-1298

Lynnville, Warrick, Pop. 881
Warrick County SC
Supt. — See Boonville
Lynnville ES 200/K-5
320 E 4th St 47619 812-922-3828
Gene Raber, prin. Fax 922-5646
Tecumseh MS 200/6-8
5300 W State Road 68 47619 812-922-0122
Keith Paige, prin.

Lyons, Greene, Pop. 736
White River Valley SD
Supt. — See Switz City
WRV MS 100/5-8
2926 S State Road 67 47443 812-659-3915
Jimmy Beasley, prin. Fax 659-2599

Mc Cordsville, Hancock, Pop. 4,677
Mt. Vernon Community SC
Supt. — See Fortville
Mc Cordsville ES 500/K-5
7177 N 600 W 46055 317-336-7760
Stephanie Miller, prin. Fax 336-7765

Mackey, Gibson, Pop. 104
East Gibson SC
Supt. — See Oakland City
Barton Township ES 100/K-6
PO Box 48 47654 812-795-2292
Dr. Peter Humbaugh, prin. Fax 795-2254

Madison, Jefferson, Pop. 11,775
Madison Consolidated SD 3,000/PK-12
2421 Wilson Ave 47250 812-274-8001
William Narwold, supt. Fax 274-8507
www.madison.k12.in.us
Madison Consolidated JHS 700/5-8
701 8th St 47250 812-274-8003
Jill Mires, prin. Fax 274-8403
Madison ECC PK-PK
2325 Cherry Dr 47250 812-273-8528
Tara McKay, prin. Fax 273-6622
Middleton ES 300/PK-4
714 W Main St 47250 812-274-8005
Tracy Ahlbrand, prin. Fax 274-8405
Muncie ES 600/PK-4
800 Lanier Dr 47250 812-274-8004
David Horvath, prin. Fax 274-8677
Rykers Ridge ES 200/PK-4
2485 N Rykers Ridge Rd 47250 812-274-8006
Melissa Demaree, prin. Fax 274-8406
Other Schools – See Deputy

Christian Academy of Madison 100/PK-12
477 W Hutchinson Ln 47250 812-273-5000
Anna Gosman, admin. Fax 265-0700
Pope John XXIII S 300/PK-6
221 W State St 47250 812-273-3957
Curt Gardner, prin. Fax 265-4566

Marengo, Crawford, Pop. 809
Crawford County Community SC 1,000/PK-12
5805 E Administration Rd 47140 812-365-2135
Woodrow DeRossett Ph.D., supt. Fax 365-2783
www.cccs.k12.in.us/
Carwford County MS 50/6-8
177 S 2nd St 47140 812-365-2116
Amy Belcher, prin. Fax 365-2814
Other Schools – See Eckerty, Leavenworth, Milltown

Marion, Grant, Pop. 29,023
Eastbrook Community SC 1,600/K-12
560 S 900 E 46953 765-664-0624
Brett Garrett, supt. Fax 664-0626
eastbrook.k12.in.us
Eastbrook JHS 300/7-8
560 S 900 E 46953 765-668-7136
Elizabeth Duckwall, prin. Fax 668-7137
Other Schools – See Upland, Van Buren

Marion Community SD 3,700/PK-12
750 W 26th St 46953 765-662-2546
Brad Lindsay, supt. Fax 651-2043
www.marion.k12.in.us
Allen ES 400/PK-4
1115 E Bradford St 46952 765-664-7355
Anthony Williams, prin. Fax 651-2059
Kendall ES 400/PK-4
2009 W Kem Rd 46952 765-662-7364
David Khalouf, prin. Fax 651-2093
Marian Little Giants Preschool PK-PK
720 N Miller Ave 46952 765-651-2048
Kerri Wortinger, coord. Fax 651-2080
Marshall IS 600/5-6
720 N Miller Ave 46952 765-664-0507
Michael Wingert, prin. Fax 651-2086
McCulloch JHS 500/7-8
3528 S Washington St 46953 765-674-6917
Melissa Pogue, prin. Fax 674-8943
Riverview ES 400/PK-4
513 W Buckingham Dr 46952 765-662-2427
Lendon Schwartz, prin. Fax 651-4665
Slocum ES 400/PK-4
2909 S Torrence St 46953 765-664-0589
Anne Liddick, prin. Fax 651-2061

Lakeview Christian S 300/PK-12
5316 S Western Ave 46953 765-677-4266
St. Paul S 100/PK-6
1009 W Kem Rd 46952 765-662-2883
Cindy Mauman, prin. Fax 664-5953

Marshall, Parke, Pop. 323
North Central Parke Community SC 1,300/K-12
1497 E State Road 47 47859 765-597-2750
Dr. Thomas Rohr, supt. Fax 597-2755
www.ncp.k12.in.us
Turkey Run ES 200/K-6
1551 E State Road 47 47859 765-597-2760
Roberta Hobbs, prin. Fax 597-2813
Other Schools – See Rockville

Martinsville, Morgan, Pop. 11,701
Metro SD of Martinsville 4,300/PK-12
389 E Jackson St 46151 765-342-6641
Dr. Michele Moore, supt. Fax 342-6877
msdmartinsville.org
Bell Intermediate Academy 200/6-6
1459 E Columbus St 46151 765-342-6675
Jeremy Ogden, prin. Fax 349-5236
Centerton ES 200/PK-4
6075 High St 46151 317-831-3410
Reneae Staley, prin. Fax 831-3439
Green Township ES 300/PK-4
6275 Maple Grove Rd 46151 765-342-0505
Paul Spahr, prin. Fax 352-4102
Poston Road ES 400/PK-4
139 E Poston Rd 46151 765-342-8408
Jill Vlcan, prin. Fax 352-4154
Smith ES 300/PK-4
1359 E Columbus St 46151 765-342-8488
Kyle Stout, prin. Fax 349-5255
South ES 400/PK-6
500 E Mahalasville Rd 46151 765-349-1486
Melody Meyer, prin. Fax 349-5247
Wooden MS 400/7-8
109 E Garfield Ave 46151 765-342-6628
Eric Bowlen, prin. Fax 349-5232
Other Schools – See Brooklyn, Paragon

Mooresville Consolidated SC
Supt. — See Mooresville
Waverly ES 400/PK-6
8525 Waverly Rd 46151 317-831-9218
Warren DuBois, prin. Fax 831-9235

Tabernacle Christian S 100/PK-12
2189 Burton Ln 46151 765-342-0501
Kenny Roll, prin. Fax 342-0502

Maxwell, Hancock
Greenfield-Central Community SD
Supt. — See Greenfield
Maxwell IS 500/4-6
102 N Main St 46154 317-326-3121
Jobie Whitaker, prin. Fax 326-4711

Medora, Jackson, Pop. 677
Medora Community SC 200/PK-12
PO Box 369 47260 812-966-2210
Roger Bane, supt. Fax 966-2217
www.medorahornets.org/
Medora ES 100/PK-6
PO Box 248 47260 812-966-2201
Austin Absher, prin. Fax 966-2209

Mentone, Kosciusko, Pop. 988
Tippecanoe Valley SC
Supt. — See Akron
Mentone ES 500/PK-5
PO Box 457 46539 574-598-2590
Randy Dahms, prin. Fax 598-2575

Merrillville, Lake, Pop. 34,497
Merrillville Community SC 6,700/PK-12
6701 Delaware St 46410 219-650-5300
Dr. Jeffery Studebaker, supt. Fax 650-5320
www.mvsc.k12.in.us
Fieler ES 400/K-4
407 W 61st Ave 46410 219-650-5301
Lynne Peters, prin. Fax 650-5411
Iddings ES 600/K-4
7249 Van Buren St 46410 219-650-5302
Teri Crussen, prin. Fax 650-5422
Merrillville IS 1,000/5-6
1400 W 61st Ave 46410 219-650-5306
Kara Bonin, prin. Fax 650-5463
Miller ES 400/K-4
5901 Waite St 46410 219-650-5303
Jennifer Griffin, prin. Fax 650-5431
Pierce MS 1,100/7-8
199 E 70th Ave 46410 219-650-5308
Christine Kibler-Wheeler, prin. Fax 650-5483
Salk ES 700/K-4
3001 W 77th Ave 46410 219-650-5304
Kathleen Sapyta, prin. Fax 650-5442
Wood ES 300/PK-4
6100 E 73rd Ave 46410 219-650-5305
Alison Petralia, prin. Fax 650-5451

Aquinas S at St. Andrew's 200/PK-8
801 W 73rd Ave 46410 219-769-2049
Lisa Gutierrez, prin. Fax 769-8543

Michigan City, LaPorte, Pop. 30,502
Michigan City Area SD 4,900/K-12
408 S Carroll Ave 46360 219-873-2000
Dr. Barbara Eason-Watkins, supt. Fax 873-2072
www.mcas.k12.in.us
Barker MS 300/7-8
319 Barker Rd 46360 219-873-2057
Daniel Caudle, prin. Fax 873-3099
Coolspring ES 300/K-6
9121 W 300 N 46360 219-873-2073
Kimberly Palmer, prin. Fax 873-2219
Edgewood ES 300/K-6
502 Boyd Cir 46360 219-873-2079
Peggy Thomas, prin. Fax 873-2019
Joy ES 400/K-6
1600 E Coolspring Ave 46360 219-873-2090
Lisa Suter, prin. Fax 873-2170

Knapp ES 300/K-6
321 Bolka Ave 46360 219-873-2096
Jennifer Neal, prin. Fax 873-2212
Krueger MS 300/7-8
2001 Springland Ave 46360 219-873-2061
Justin Biggs, prin. Fax 873-2063
Lake Hills ES 400/K-6
201 Ferguson Rd 46360 219-873-2105
Connie Bachmann, prin. Fax 873-2166
Marsh ES 300/K-6
401 E Homer St 46360 219-873-2102
Marsha Tappan, prin. Fax 873-2103
Pine ES 300/K-6
1660 County Line Rd 46360 219-873-2114
Zach Huber, prin. Fax 873-2113
Springfield ES 200/K-6
3054 W 800 N 46360 219-873-2117
Lisa Emshwiller, prin. Fax 877-3064

Notre Dame Catholic S 200/PK-8
1000 Moore Rd 46360 219-872-6216
Dr. Donovan Garletts, prin. Fax 872-6216
Queen of All Saints S 200/PK-8
1715 E Barker Ave 46360 219-872-4420
Marie Arter, prin. Fax 872-1943
St. Paul Lutheran S 200/K-8
818 Franklin St 46360 219-874-7409
Rebecca Cole, prin. Fax 874-6462
St. Stanislaus Kostka S 100/PK-8
1506 Washington St 46360 219-872-2258
Chris Evans, prin. Fax 872-2295

Michigantown, Clinton, Pop. 463
Clinton Central SC 1,000/K-12
PO Box 118 46057 765-249-2515
Ralph Walker, supt. Fax 249-2504
www.clinton.k12.in.us/
Clinton Central ES 600/K-6
PO Box 238 46057 765-249-2244
Dr. Betsy Biederstedt, prin. Fax 249-2349

Middlebury, Elkhart, Pop. 3,377
Middlebury Community SD 4,400/K-12
56853 Northridge Dr 46540 574-825-9425
Jane Allen, supt. Fax 825-9426
www.mcsin-k12.org/
Heritage IS 700/4-5
56647 Northridge Dr 46540 574-822-5396
Kari Dyer, prin. Fax 825-2038
Middlebury ES 300/K-3
432 S Main St 46540 574-825-2158
Marion Hostetler, prin. Fax 825-7959
Northridge MS 1,000/6-8
56691 Northridge Dr 46540 574-825-9531
Robby Goodman, prin. Fax 825-9154
Orchard View ES 400/K-3
56734 Northridge Dr 46540 574-825-5405
Joshua Yoder, prin. Fax 825-5479
Other Schools – See Bristol, Goshen

Middletown, Henry, Pop. 2,295
Shenandoah SC 1,400/PK-12
5100 N Raider Rd 47356 765-354-2266
Ron Green, supt. Fax 354-2274
www.shenandoah.k12.in.us/
Shenandoah ES 600/PK-5
5256 N Raider Rd 47356 765-354-6636
Brent Kinsey, prin. Fax 354-3102
Shenandoah MS 300/6-8
5156 N Raider Rd 47356 765-354-6638
Greg Allen, prin. Fax 354-3120

Milan, Ripley, Pop. 1,874
Milan Community SC 1,200/K-12
412 E Carr St 47031 812-654-2365
Jane Rogers M.S., supt. Fax 654-2441
www.milan.k12.in.us
Milan ES 500/K-4
418 E Carr St 47031 812-654-2922
Cinda Ahlrich, prin. Fax 654-2796
Milan IS 5-6
609 N Warpath Dr 47031 812-654-1616
Patrick Murphy, prin. Fax 654-2368
Milan MS 300/7-8
609 N Warpath Dr 47031 812-654-1616
Patrick Murphy, prin. Fax 654-2368

Milford, Kosciusko, Pop. 1,544
Wawasee Community SC
Supt. — See Syracuse
Milford S 600/K-8
PO Box 548 46542 574-658-9444
Cynthia Kaiser, prin. Fax 658-3429

Millersburg, Elkhart, Pop. 900
Fairfield Community SD
Supt. — See Goshen
Millersburg Elementary MS 400/K-8
PO Box 238 46543 574-642-3074
Teresa Zook, prin. Fax 642-3918

Milltown, Crawford, Pop. 803
Crawford County Community SC
Supt. — See Marengo
East Crawford ES 200/PK-5
518 Speed Rd 47145 812-633-4335
Camie Wiseman, prin. Fax 633-4336

Milroy, Rush, Pop. 599
Rush County SD
Supt. — See Rushville
Milroy ES 200/K-6
300 N Walnut St 46156 765-629-2323
Nancy Schroeder, prin. Fax 629-2250

Mishawaka, Saint Joseph, Pop. 46,961
Penn-Harris-Madison SC 10,300/K-12
55900 Bittersweet Rd 46545 574-259-7941
Dr. Jerry Thacker, supt. Fax 258-9547
www.phmschools.org
Bittersweet ES 400/K-5
55860 Bittersweet Rd 46545 574-259-6341
Robert Thompson, prin. Fax 254-2866
Disney ES 500/K-5
4015 Filbert Rd 46545 574-259-2486
Ryan Towner, prin. Fax 257-8468
Elm Road ES 500/K-5
59400 Elm Rd 46544 574-259-3743
Dr. Lisa Soto-Kile, prin. Fax 258-9384
Grissom MS 600/6-8
13881 Kern Rd 46544 574-633-4061
Nathan Boyd, prin. Fax 633-2134
Meadows Edge ES 300/K-5
16333 Kern Rd 46544 574-255-9347
Kent Mikel, prin. Fax 968-6005
Rogers ES 300/K-5
56219 Currant Rd 46545 574-259-5231
Christina Campbell, prin. Fax 254-9087
Schmucker MS 1,000/6-8
56045 Bittersweet Rd 46545 574-259-5661
Lavon Dean-Null, prin. Fax 259-0807
Other Schools – See Granger, Osceola, Wakarusa

School City of Mishawaka 5,000/K-12
1402 S Main St 46544 574-254-4500
Dr. A. Dean Speicher, supt. Fax 254-4585
www.mishawaka.k12.in.us
Battell ES 300/K-6
715 E Broadway St 46545 574-254-3900
Matthew Wood, prin. Fax 254-3982
Beiger ES 500/K-6
1600 E 3rd St 46544 574-254-4700
Dan Towner, prin. Fax 254-4781
Emmons ES 400/K-6
1306 S Main St 46544 574-254-4600
Brad Addison, prin. Fax 254-4680
Hums ES 300/K-6
3208 Harrison Rd 46544 574-254-3800
Jeffrey Yohe, prin. Fax 254-3882
LaSalle ES 500/K-6
1511 Milburn Blvd 46544 574-254-4800
Michael Babcock, prin. Fax 254-4882
Liberty ES 500/K-6
600 Pregel Dr 46545 574-254-3700
Janine Mabry, prin. Fax 258-3089
Twin Branch Model S 300/K-6
3810 Lincolnway E 46544 574-254-3500
Shelley Brandenburg, prin. Fax 254-3582
Young MS 700/7-8
1801 N Main St 46545 574-254-3600
C. Mike Fisher, prin. Fax 258-3021

Covenant Christian S 100/PK-8
54790 Fir Rd 46545 574-255-5972
Barbara Hesselink, admin. Fax 255-5196
Mishawaka Catholic S 200/PK-8
230 S Spring St 46544 574-255-5554
Jennifer Schwab, prin. Fax 255-6381
Montessori Academy at Edison Lakes 200/PK-8
530 E Day Rd 46545 574-256-5313
Queen of Peace S 200/PK-3
4508 Vistula Rd 46544 574-255-0392
Jill Patrick, prin. Fax 255-1029
South Bend Hebrew S 100/PK-8
206 W 8th St 46544 574-255-3351
Rabbi Reuven Pelberg, prin. Fax 255-7553

Mitchell, Lawrence, Pop. 4,315
Mitchell Community SD 1,700/PK-12
441 N 8th St 47446 812-849-4481
Dr. Steve Phillips, supt. Fax 849-2133
www.mitchell.k12.in.us
Burris ES 400/3-5
1755 Hancock Ave 47446 812-849-2509
Jessica Jones, prin. Fax 849-5638
Hatfield ES 400/PK-2
1081 Teke Burton Dr 47446 812-849-3834
Renee Childress, prin. Fax 849-5722
Mitchell JHS 400/6-8
1010 W Bishop Blvd 47446 812-849-3747
Jennifer Caruso, prin. Fax 849-5841

Modoc, Randolph, Pop. 190
Union SC 400/K-12
8707 W US Highway 36 47358 765-853-5464
Alan Hayne, supt. Fax 853-5070
www.usc.k12.in.us
Union ES 200/K-6
8707 W US Highway 36 47358 765-853-5481
Michael Huber, prin. Fax 853-5070

Monon, White, Pop. 1,750
North White SC 600/K-12
402 E Broadway St 47959 219-253-6618
Dr. Teresa L. Gremaux, supt. Fax 253-6488
www.nwhite.k12.in.us/
North White ES 200/K-5
304 E Broadway St 47959 219-253-6663
Melissa McIntire, prin. Fax 253-8178

Monroe, Adams, Pop. 839
Adams Central Community SD 1,200/PK-12
222 W Washington St 46772 260-692-6193
Dr. Lori M. Stiglitz, supt. Fax 692-6198
www.accs.k12.in.us/
Adams Central ES 600/PK-5
222 W Washington St 46772 260-692-6629
Terri Laurent, prin. Fax 692-6148
Adams Central MS 300/6-8
222 W Washington St 46772 260-692-6151
Chad Smekens, prin. Fax 692-6192

Monroeville, Allen, Pop. 1,229
East Allen County SD
Supt. — See New Haven
Heritage ES 500/K-6
12050 Houk Rd 46773 260-446-0160
Karen Charters, prin. Fax 446-0163

St. John Emmanuel Lutheran S 100/PK-8
12912 Franke Rd 46773 260-639-0123
Alex Gruen, prin. Fax 639-7383
St. Joseph S 100/K-8
401 Monroe St 46773 260-623-3447
Gale Powelson, prin. Fax 623-3447

Monrovia, Morgan, Pop. 1,058
Monroe-Gregg SD 1,500/PK-12
135 S Chestnut St 46157 317-996-3720
Dr. William Roberson, supt. Fax 996-2977
www.m-gsd.org/
Monrovia ES 700/PK-5
395 S Chestnut St 46157 317-996-2246
Melissa York, prin. Fax 996-4199
Monrovia MS 400/6-8
215 S Chestnut St 46157 317-996-2352
Micah Elliott, prin. Fax 996-3429

Montezuma, Parke, Pop. 1,013
Southwest Parke Community SC 1,000/K-12
4851 S Coxville Rd 47862 765-569-2073
Dr. Philip Harrison, supt. Fax 569-0309
www.swparke.k12.in.us
Montezuma ES 200/K-6
PO Box 400 47862 765-245-2303
Jami Britton, prin. Fax 245-2354
Other Schools – See Rosedale

Montgomery, Daviess, Pop. 341
Barr-Reeve Community SD 800/K-12
PO Box 97 47558 812-486-3220
Travis Madison, supt. Fax 486-3509
www.barr.k12.in.us
Barr-Reeve ES 200/2-5
PO Box 129 47558 812-486-3224
Dena Lengacher, prin. Fax 486-2336
Barr-Reeve PS 200/K-1
PO Box 127 47558 812-486-3235
Dena Lengacher, prin. Fax 486-3216

Monticello, White, Pop. 5,324
Twin Lakes SC 2,400/PK-12
565 S Main St 47960 574-583-7211
Michael Galvin, supt. Fax 583-2679
www.tlschools.com
Meadowlawn ES 600/K-5
715 W Ohio St 47960 574-583-7720
Rev. Trent Provo, prin. Fax 583-7791
Oaklawn ES 300/K-5
402 E South St 47960 574-583-5651
Jennifer Lingenfelter, prin. Fax 583-5360
Roosevelt MS 600/6-8
721 W Broadway St 47960 574-583-5552
Rod Coffing, prin. Fax 583-3675
Other Schools – See Burnettsville

Montpelier, Blackford, Pop. 1,783
Blackford County SD
Supt. — See Hartford City
Montpelier S 200/K-6
107 E Monroe St 47359 765-728-2402
Jim Fox, prin. Fax 728-2403

Moores Hill, Dearborn, Pop. 588
South Dearborn Community SC
Supt. — See Aurora
Moores Hill ES 200/PK-6
14733 Main St 47032 812-926-2090
Dr. Leanna Phillippe, prin. Fax 744-5660

Mooresville, Morgan, Pop. 9,219
Mooresville Consolidated SC 4,600/PK-12
11 W Carlisle St 46158 317-831-0950
Dr. David Marcotte, supt. Fax 831-9202
www.mooresvilleschools.org
Armstrong ES 600/K-6
1000 State Road 144 46158 317-831-9210
Paul Spencer, prin. Fax 831-9230
Hadley MS 700/7-8
200 W Carlisle St 46158 317-831-9208
Jacob Allen, prin. Fax 831-9249
Newby Memorial ES 400/K-6
240 N Monroe St 46158 317-831-9212
Krista Nelson, prin. Fax 831-9234
Northwood ES 600/K-6
630 N Indiana St 46158 317-831-9216
Erin Bechtold, prin. Fax 831-9233
Other Schools – See Camby, Martinsville

Mooresville Christian Academy 200/PK-8
4271 E State Road 144 46158 317-831-0799
Rick Brewer, head sch Fax 831-0799

Morgantown, Brown, Pop. 982
Brown County SC
Supt. — See Nashville
Helmsburg ES 200/PK-4
5378 Helmsburg School Rd 46160 812-988-6651
Kelli Bruner, prin. Fax 988-0852

Morocco, Newton, Pop. 1,125
North Newton SC 1,400/K-12
PO Box 8 47963 219-285-2228
Destin Haas, supt. Fax 285-2708
www.nn.k12.in.us/
Morocco ES 200/K-6
PO Box 50 47963 219-285-2258
Sherri Cripe, prin. Fax 285-6429
Other Schools – See Demotte, Lake Village

Morristown, Shelby, Pop. 1,211
Shelby Eastern SD
Supt. — See Shelbyville
Morristown ES 300/PK-5
PO Box 910 46161 765-763-6648
John Corn, prin. Fax 763-6969

Mount Summit, Henry, Pop. 346
Blue River Valley SD 600/PK-12
PO Box 217 47361 765-836-4816
Eric Creviston, supt. Fax 836-4817
www.brv.k12.in.us
Other Schools – See New Castle

Mount Vernon, Posey, Pop. 6,543
Metro SD of Mt. Vernon 2,200/PK-12
1000 W 4th St 47620 812-838-4471
Dr. Tom Kopatich, supt. Fax 833-5179
www.mvschool.org
Farmersville ES 200/PK-5
4065 Highway 69 S 47620 812-838-6593
Dr. Elizabeth Johns, prin. Fax 838-4826
Marrs ES 300/K-5
9201 Highway 62 47620 812-985-2082
Gregory DeWeese, prin. Fax 985-9453
Mount Vernon JHS 500/6-8
701 Tile Factory Rd 47620 812-833-2077
Chad Rodgers, prin. Fax 833-2083
West ES 400/K-5
1105 W 4th St 47620 812-833-2072
Amanda Wilson, prin. Fax 833-2095

St. Matthew S 100/PK-5
401 Mulberry St 47620 812-838-3621
Vickie Wannemuehler, prin. Fax 838-6971
St. Philip S 200/PK-8
3420 Saint Phillips Rd S 47620 812-985-2447
Megan Howington, prin. Fax 985-2457

Muncie, Delaware, Pop. 68,179
Cowan Community SC 800/K-12
9401 S Nottingham St 47302 765-289-4866
Dennis Chambers, supt. Fax 284-0315
www.cowan.k12.in.us
Cowan ES 400/K-6
1000 W County Road 600 S 47302 765-289-7129
Timothy Brown, prin. Fax 741-5958

Delaware Community SC 2,600/K-12
9750 N County Rd 200 E 47303 765-284-5074
Reece Mann, supt. Fax 284-5259
www.delcomschools.org
Delta MS 600/6-8
9800 N County Rd 200 E 47303 765-747-0869
Kelly Brown, prin. Fax 213-2131
Royerton ES 500/K-5
1401 E Royerton Rd 47303 765-282-2044
Doug Marshall, prin. Fax 288-3584
Other Schools – See Albany, Eaton

Muncie Community SD 5,800/K-12
2500 N Elgin St 47303 765-747-5211
Dr. Steven Baule, supt. Fax 747-5341
www.muncie.k12.in.us
East Washington Academy 400/K-5
1000 E Washington St 47305 765-747-5434
Jason Rees, prin. Fax 281-6740
Grissom Memorial ES 500/K-5
3201 S Macedonia Ave 47302 765-747-5401
Melissa DeWitt, prin. Fax 747-5403
Longfellow ES 300/K-5
1900 E Centennial Ave 47303 765-747-5410
Gerry Moore, prin. Fax 751-0661
Muncie Southside MS 1,000/6-8
1601 E 26th St 47302 765-747-5320
Kelli Turner, prin. Fax 747-5325
Northside MS 700/6-8
2400 W Bethel Ave 47304 765-747-5290
Eric Grim, prin. Fax 751-0616
North View ES 300/K-5
807 W Yale Ave 47304 765-747-5422
Jennifer Roberts, prin. Fax 751-0615
South View ES 500/K-5
2100 S Franklin St 47302 765-747-5226
Kara Miller, prin. Fax 751-0671
West View ES 300/K-5
3401 W Gilbert St 47304 765-747-5437
Eric Ambler, prin. Fax 747-5406

University Schools, Supt. — None
Dr. William Sharp, supt.
Burris Laboratory S 600/K-12
2201 W University Ave 47306 765-285-1131
Dawn Miller, prin. Fax 285-8620

Heritage Hall Christian S 200/PK-12
6401 W River Rd 47304 765-289-6371
David Stein, admin. Fax 213-2245
St. Lawrence S 100/PK-5
2801 E 16th St 47302 765-282-9353
Rob Frey, prin. Fax 282-0475
St. Mary S 200/PK-8
2301 W Gilbert St 47303 765-288-5878
Elisha Schlabach, prin. Fax 284-3685

Munster, Lake, Pop. 23,303
Town of Munster SD 4,100/K-12
8616 Columbia Ave 46321 219-836-9111
Dr. Jeffrey Hendrix, supt. Fax 836-3215
www.munster.us
Eads ES 600/K-5
8000 Jackson Ave 46321 219-836-8635
Linda Bevil, prin. Fax 836-3217
Elliott ES 400/K-5
8718 White Oak Ave 46321 219-838-5250
Nicole Guernsey, prin. Fax 838-7867
Hammond ES 600/K-5
1301 Fran Lin Pkwy 46321 219-838-2060
Kelly Boersma, prin. Fax 838-7964
Wright MS 1,000/6-8
8650 Columbia Ave 46321 219-836-6260
Dr. Andrew Sargent, prin. Fax 836-0501

St. Paul's Lutheran S 200/PK-8
8601 Harrison Ave 46321 219-836-6270
Barb Mertens, prin. Fax 836-3724

St. Thomas More S 600/PK-8
8435 Calumet Ave 46321 219-836-9151
Jay Harker, prin. Fax 836-0982

Nappanee, Elkhart, Pop. 6,570
Wa-Nee Community SD 3,000/K-12
1300 N Main St 46550 574-773-3131
Dr. Scot Croner, supt. Fax 773-5593
www.wanee.org
Nappannee ES 400/K-5
755 E Van Buren St 46550 574-773-7421
Randy Cripe, prin. Fax 773-2199
Woodview ES 500/K-5
800 E Woodview Dr 46550 574-773-3117
Alan Thompson, prin. Fax 773-3011
Other Schools – See Wakarusa

Nashville, Brown, Pop. 795
Brown County SC 2,100/PK-12
PO Box 38 47448 812-988-6601
Dr. Laura Hammack, supt. Fax 988-5403
browncountyschools.com
Brown County IS 300/5-6
PO Box 157 47448 812-988-6607
Trent Austin, prin. Fax 988-5417
Brown County JHS 400/7-8
PO Box 578 47448 812-988-6605
Brian Garman, prin. Fax 988-5415
Van Buren ES 300/PK-4
4045 State Road 135 S 47448 812-988-6658
Christy Wrightsman, prin. Fax 988-5418
Other Schools – See Morgantown, Nineveh

New Albany, Floyd, Pop. 35,385
New Albany Floyd County Consolidated SD 11,300/PK-12
PO Box 1087 47151 812-949-4200
Dr. Bruce Hibbard, supt. Fax 949-6900
www.nafcs.k12.in.us
Children's Academy Early Learning Center 100/PK-PK
1111 Pearl St 47150 812-542-5506
Geradine Schultze, dir. Fax 542-4788
Fairmont ES 300/K-4
1725 Abbeydell Ave 47150 812-542-5501
Susie Gahan, prin. Fax 542-4783
Grant Line ES 600/K-4
4811 Grant Line Rd 47150 812-542-5502
Kyle Lanoue, prin. Fax 542-4784
Green Valley ES 300/K-4
2230 Green Valley Rd 47150 812-542-5503
Brian Kehrer, prin. Fax 542-4785
Hazelwood MS 1,000/5-8
1021 Hazelwood Ave 47150 812-542-8502
Jessica Waters, prin. Fax 542-4793
Jones ES 300/K-4
600 E 11th St 47150 812-542-5508
Tammy Swarens, prin. Fax 542-4790
Mt. Tabor ES 700/K-4
800 Mount Tabor Rd 47150 812-542-5507
Scott Hughes, prin. Fax 542-4789
Scribner MS 900/5-8
910 Old Vincennes Rd 47150 812-542-8503
Keith Bush, prin. Fax 542-4794
Slate Run ES 400/K-4
1452 Slate Run Rd 47150 812-542-5509
Amy Niemeier, prin. Fax 542-4791
Other Schools – See Floyds Knobs, Georgetown, Greenville

Christian Academy of Indiana 700/PK-12
1000 Academy Dr 47150 812-944-6200
Darin Long, prin. Fax 944-6903
Holy Family S 400/PK-8
217 W Daisy Ln 47150 812-944-6090
Gerald Ernstberger, prin. Fax 944-7299
Our Lady of Perpetual Help S 300/PK-8
1752 Scheller Ln 47150 812-944-7676
Mary Ann Bennett, prin. Fax 948-2944

Newburgh, Warrick, Pop. 3,276
Warrick County SC
Supt. — See Boonville
Castle ES 900/K-5
3077 Highway 261 47630 812-853-8878
Marty Watson, prin. Fax 853-6061
Castle North MS 800/6-8
2800 State Route 261 47630 812-853-7347
John Bertram, prin. Fax 858-1089
Castle South MS 700/6-8
3711 Casey Rd 47630 812-490-7930
Jim Hood, prin. Fax 490-7925
Newburgh ES 600/K-5
306 State St 47630 812-853-8921
Kurt Krodel, prin. Fax 853-6866
Sharon ES 700/K-5
7300 Sharon Rd 47630 812-853-3349
Ashlee Bruggenschmidt, prin. Fax 853-6955
Yankeetown ES 300/K-5
7422 Yankeetown Rd 47630 812-853-8500
David McConnell, prin. Fax 858-1296

Newburgh Christian S 50/PK-12
4156 State Road 261 47630 812-842-0455
St. John the Baptist S 400/PK-8
725 Frame Rd 47630 812-490-2000
Elizabeth Flatt, prin. Fax 490-2020

New Carlisle, Saint Joseph, Pop. 1,830
New Prairie United SC 2,900/K-12
5327 N Cougar Rd 46552 574-654-7273
Dr. Paul White, supt. Fax 654-7274
www.npusc.k12.in.us
New Prairie MS 700/6-8
5325 N Cougar Rd 46552 574-654-3070
Janet Scott, prin. Fax 654-7009
Olive Township ES 500/K-5
300 W Bon St 46552 574-654-7531
Tara Bush, prin. Fax 654-7964
Other Schools – See Rolling Prairie

New Castle, Henry, Pop. 17,809
Blue River Valley SD
Supt. — See Mount Summit
Blue River Valley ES 300/PK-6
4713 N Hillsboro Rd 47362 765-836-4851
Todd Reagan, prin. Fax 836-3258

New Castle Community SC 3,400/K-12
322 Elliott Ave 47362 765-521-7201
Fax 521-7268
www.nccsc.k12.in.us
Eastwood ES 200/1-6
806 S 22nd St 47362 765-521-7205
Jacob White, prin. Fax 593-6643
New Castle MS 600/7-8
601 Parkview Dr 47362 765-521-7230
Kirk Amman, prin. Fax 521-7269
Parker ES 400/K-6
1819 Roosevelt Ave 47362 765-521-7209
Lora Wilson, prin. Fax 593-6609
Riley ES 300/1-6
1201 Riley Rd 47362 765-521-7211
Nicholas Middleton, prin. Fax 593-6646
Sunnyside ES 200/K-3
2601 S 14th St 47362 765-521-7213
Jean Ann McAllister, prin. Fax 593-6647
Westwood ES 300/1-6
1015 S Greensboro Pike 47362 765-521-7215
James Carson, prin. Fax 593-6648
Wright ES 400/K-6
1950 Washington St 47362 765-521-7217
Tony Personett, prin. Fax 593-6649

New Haven, Allen, Pop. 14,574
East Allen County SD 8,800/PK-12
1240 State Road 930 E 46774 260-446-0100
Marilyn Hissong, supt. Fax 446-0107
www.eacs.k12.in.us
New Haven IS 500/3-5
1065 Woodmere Dr 46774 260-446-0190
Alicia Gatewood, prin. Fax 446-0193
New Haven MS 500/6-8
900 Prospect Ave 46774 260-446-0230
Chad Houser, prin. Fax 446-0236
New Haven PS 500/K-2
1445 Berwick Ln 46774 260-446-0150
Renita Peters, prin. Fax 446-0153
Other Schools – See Fort Wayne, Leo, Monroeville, Woodburn

Central Lutheran S 300/PK-8
900 Green St 46774 260-493-2502
Kevin Creutz, prin. Fax 493-2503
St. John the Baptist S 300/PK-8
204 S Rufus St 46774 260-749-9903
Janice Comito, prin. Fax 749-6047
St. Louis Academy 100/PK-8
15529 Lincoln Hwy E 46774 260-749-5815
Vanessa Diller, prin. Fax 749-5815

New Middletown, Harrison, Pop. 91
South Harrison Community SD
Supt. — See Corydon
New Middletown ES 100/K-6
2460 New Middletown Rd SE 47160 812-968-3225
Wendy Carter, prin. Fax 968-3017

New Palestine, Hancock, Pop. 2,034
Southern Hancock County Community SC 3,300/PK-12
PO Box 508 46163 317-861-4463
Dr. Lisa Lantrip, supt. Fax 861-2142
corp.newpal.k12.in.us/
Doe Creek MS 500/7-8
PO Box 478 46163 317-861-4487
James Voelz, prin. Fax 861-2136
New Palestine ES 600/PK-6
PO Box 538 46163 317-861-5287
Katy Eastes, prin. Fax 861-2146
Sugar Creek ES 700/PK-6
PO Box 558 46163 317-861-6747
Kari Shelton, prin. Fax 861-8656
Other Schools – See Greenfield

Zion Lutheran S 200/PK-8
6513 W 300 S 46163 317-861-4210
Kristie Sombke, prin. Fax 861-8153

New Paris, Elkhart, Pop. 1,488
Fairfield Community SD
Supt. — See Goshen
New Paris ES 400/K-6
18665 County Road 46 46553 574-831-2196
Lisa Litwiller, prin. Fax 831-3160

New Ross, Montgomery, Pop. 338
South Montgomery Community SC
Supt. — See Crawfordsville
Walnut ES 200/PK-6
3548 S 775 E 47968 765-362-0542
Eric Brewer, prin. Fax 362-0545

New Washington, Clark, Pop. 563
Greater Clark County SD
Supt. — See Jeffersonville
New Washington ES 300/PK-6
PO Box 130 47162 812-293-3331
Darcie Goodin, prin. Fax 293-5808

New Whiteland, Johnson, Pop. 5,409
Clark-Pleasant Community SC
Supt. — See Whiteland
Break-O-Day ES 500/K-5
900 Sawmill Rd 46184 317-535-7536
Trina Lake, prin. Fax 535-0817
Sawmill Woods ES 300/PK-PK
700 Sawmill Rd 46184 317-535-2069
J. Wolfe, prin. Fax 535-5530

Nineveh, Brown
Brown County SC
Supt. — See Nashville

Sprunica ES 300/PK-4
3611 Sprunica Rd 46164 812-988-6625
Abbie Oliver Ph.D., prin. Fax 988-0940

Noblesville, Hamilton, Pop. 51,089
Hamilton Southeastern SD
Supt. — See Fishers
Durbin ES 400/K-4
18000 Durbin Rd 46060 765-534-3188
Linda Ededuwa, prin. Fax 534-4238

Noblesville SD 9,800/PK-12
18025 River Rd, 317-773-3171
Dr. Beth Niedermeyer, supt. Fax 773-7845
www.noblesvilleschools.org
Dell ES 700/PK-5
3025 Westfield Rd, 317-773-2914
Karen Carter, prin. Fax 773-2916
Hinkle Creek ES 900/PK-5
595 S Harbour Dr, 317-776-0840
Jack Lawrence, prin. Fax 776-6267
Noble Crossing ES 700/PK-5
5670 Noble Crossing Pkwy E, 317-773-2850
Pat Haney, prin. Fax 773-2854
Noblesville East MS 1,000/6-8
1625 Field Dr 46060 317-773-0782
Ryan Rich, prin. Fax 776-6261
Noblesville West MS 1,300/6-8
19900 Hague Rd, 317-776-7792
Stacey Swan, prin. Fax 776-7797
North ES 500/K-5
440 N 10th St 46060 317-773-0482
Rob Lugo, prin. Fax 776-6274
Promise Road ES 700/K-5
14975 Promise Rd 46060 317-773-7060
Kelly Treinen, prin. Fax 773-7058
Stony Creek ES 600/PK-5
1350 Greenfield Ave 46060 317-773-0582
Heidi Karst, prin. Fax 776-6270
White River ES 700/PK-5
19000 Cumberland Rd 46060 317-770-2080
Rebecca Dicus, prin. Fax 770-2081

Legacy Christian S 200/PK-10
470 Lakeview Dr 46060 317-776-4186
Jodi Monroe, dir. Fax 776-4189
Our Lady of Grace S 400/PK-8
9900 E 191st St 46060 317-770-5660
Michelle Boyd, prin. Fax 770-5663

North Judson, Starke, Pop. 1,752
North Judson-San Pierre SC 900/K-12
801 Campbell Dr 46366 574-896-2155
Dr. Annette Zupin, supt. Fax 896-2156
www.njsp.k12.in.us
North Judson-San Pierre ES 500/K-6
809 W Talmer Ave 46366 574-896-2128
Julie Berndt, prin. Fax 896-2129

St. Peter Lutheran S 100/PK-8
810 W Talmer Ave 46366 574-896-5933
Rhonda Reimers M.Ed., prin. Fax 896-2082

North Liberty, Saint Joseph, Pop. 1,859
John Glenn SC
Supt. — See Walkerton
North Liberty ES 500/K-6
400 School Dr 46554 574-656-8123
Randy Romer, prin. Fax 656-8345

North Manchester, Wabash, Pop. 6,040
Manchester Community SD 1,600/K-12
404 W 9th St 46962 260-982-7518
Mike Pettibone, supt. Fax 982-4583
www.mcs.k12.in.us
Manchester ES 500/K-3
301 S River Rd 46962 260-982-7541
Dr. Joseph Rodgers, prin. Fax 982-8020
Other Schools – See Laketon

North Salem, Hendricks, Pop. 512
North West Hendricks SD
Supt. — See Lizton
North Salem ES 200/K-5
PO Box 69 46165 317-994-3000
Tiffany Cox, prin. Fax 994-3030

North Vernon, Jennings, Pop. 6,629
Jennings County SC 4,600/K-12
34 W Main St 47265 812-346-4483
Teresa Brown, supt. Fax 346-4490
www.jcsc.org
Brush Creek ES 400/K-6
4275 E US Highway 50 47265 812-458-6582
Floyd Bowman, prin. Fax 458-6357
Jennings County MS 700/7-8
820 W Walnut St 47265 812-346-4940
Nick Hill, prin. Fax 346-4497
North Vernon ES 700/K-6
810 W Walnut St 47265 812-346-4903
Nicole Johnson, prin. Fax 346-4863
Sand Creek ES 400/K-6
1450 W County Road 500 N 47265 812-352-9343
Carrie Manowitz, prin. Fax 352-0674
Other Schools – See Commiskey, Hayden, Scipio

St. Mary S 200/PK-8
209 Washington St 47265 812-346-3445
Lisa Vogel, prin. Fax 346-5930

North Webster, Kosciusko, Pop. 1,129
Wawasee Community SC
Supt. — See Syracuse
North Webster ES 500/PK-5
5745 N 750 E 46555 574-834-7644
Lee Snider, prin. Fax 834-1046

Oakland City, Gibson, Pop. 2,406
East Gibson SC 900/PK-12
941 S Franklin St 47660 812-749-4755
Dr. Henry Brewster, supt. Fax 749-3343
www.egsc.k12.in.us
Oakland City ES 300/PK-6
945B S Franklin St 47660 812-749-6133
Matt Malin, prin. Fax 749-4633
Wood Memorial JHS 100/7-8
945A S Franklin St 47660 812-749-4715
Dr. Kevin Smith, prin. Fax 749-4988
Other Schools – See Francisco, Mackey

Oolitic, Lawrence, Pop. 1,177
North Lawrence Community SD
Supt. — See Bedford
Dollens ES 200/K-5
903 Hoosier Ave 47451 812-275-3885
Kelli Terrell, prin. Fax 277-3219
Oolitic MS 300/6-8
903 Hoosier Ave 47451 812-275-7551
Steve Underwood, prin. Fax 277-3219

Orleans, Orange, Pop. 2,135
Orleans Community SD 900/K-12
173 Marley St 47452 812-865-2688
Gary McClintic, supt.
www.orleans.k12.in.us/
Orleans ES 500/K-6
637 E Washington St 47452 812-865-2688
James Ellis, prin. Fax 865-3844

Osceola, Saint Joseph, Pop. 2,415
Penn-Harris-Madison SC
Supt. — See Mishawaka
Moran ES 500/K-5
305 N Beech Rd 46561 574-674-8504
Frank Anglin, prin. Fax 674-4375

Osgood, Ripley, Pop. 1,609
Jac-Cen-Del Community SC 900/PK-12
723 N Buckeye St 47037 812-689-4114
Timothy W. Taylor, supt. Fax 689-7423
www.jaccendel.k12.in.us
Jac-Cen-Del ES 500/PK-6
4544 N US Highway 421 47037 812-689-4144
Travis Rohrig, prin. Fax 689-6512

Ossian, Wells, Pop. 3,255
Northern Wells Community SD 2,400/PK-12
312 N Jefferson St 46777 260-622-4125
Dr. Scott Mills, supt. Fax 622-7893
www.nwcs.k12.in.us
Norwell MS 500/6-8
1100 E US Highway 224 46777 260-543-2218
Tim Wilson, prin. Fax 543-2510
Ossian ES 600/PK-5
213 S Jefferson St 46777 260-622-4179
Susanne Tieman, prin. Fax 622-7161
Other Schools – See Bluffton

Bethlehem Lutheran S 100/K-8
7545 N 650 E 46777 260-597-7366
Mark Schallhorn, prin. Fax 597-7366

Otterbein, Benton, Pop. 1,252
Benton Community SC
Supt. — See Fowler
Otterbein ES 300/K-6
PO Box 368 47970 765-583-4401
Richard Brown, prin. Fax 583-2428

Owensville, Gibson, Pop. 1,273
South Gibson SC
Supt. — See Fort Branch
Owensville Community S 500/K-8
6569 S State Road 65 47665 812-724-3705
Michael Woods, prin. Fax 724-4201

Oxford, Benton, Pop. 1,155
Benton Community SC
Supt. — See Fowler
Prairie Crossing ES 500/K-6
2758 S 400 E 47971 765-884-3000
Tony Coleman, prin. Fax 884-3030

Palmyra, Harrison, Pop. 914
North Harrison Community SC
Supt. — See Ramsey
Morgan ES 500/K-5
12225 State Road 135 NW 47164 812-364-6138
Megan Reynolds, prin. Fax 364-4085

Paoli, Orange, Pop. 3,640
Paoli Community SC 1,600/PK-12
501 Elm St 47454 812-723-4717
Fax 723-5100
www.paoli.k12.in.us
Throop ES 800/PK-6
301 Elm St 47454 812-723-3537
Wes Whitfield, prin. Fax 723-0384

Paragon, Morgan, Pop. 646
Metro SD of Martinsville
Supt. — See Martinsville
Paragon ES 300/PK-4
520 W Union 46166 765-537-2276
Tiffany Johnson, prin. Fax 537-2105

Parker City, Randolph, Pop. 1,400
Monroe Central SC 1,000/K-12
1918 N 1000 W 47368 765-468-6868
Adrian Moulton, supt. Fax 468-6578
www.monroecentral.org
Monroe Central ES 500/K-6
10421 W State Road 32 47368 765-468-7725
Julie Northcutt, prin. Fax 468-8409

Patricksburg, Owen
Spencer-Owen Community SD
Supt. — See Spencer
Patricksburg ES 200/K-6
PO Box 212 47455 812-859-4525
Tabitha Freeman, prin. Fax 859-4535

Pekin, Washington, Pop. 1,385
East Washington SC 1,500/K-12
1050 N Eastern School Rd 47165 812-967-3926
Dennis Stockdale, supt. Fax 967-5797
www.ewsc.k12.in.us
East Washington ES 600/K-4
1020 N Eastern School Rd 47165 812-967-2929
Debbie Esarey, prin. Fax 967-5707
East Washington MS 500/5-8
1100 N Eastern School Rd 47165 812-967-5000
Amber King, prin. Fax 967-5737

Pendleton, Madison, Pop. 4,212
South Madison Community SC 4,500/PK-12
203 S Heritage Way 46064 765-778-2152
Joseph Buck, supt. Fax 778-8207
www.smadison.k12.in.us
East ES 800/K-6
893 E US Highway 36 46064 765-779-4445
Andrew Kruer, prin. Fax 779-4594
Maple Ridge ES 700/K-6
8537 S 650 W 46064 765-778-3818
John Lord, prin. Fax 778-8677
Pendleton ES 900/PK-6
327 S East St 46064 765-778-2117
Eric Schill, prin. Fax 778-1712
Pendleton Heights MS 800/7-8
7450 S 300 W 46064 765-778-2139
Daniel Joyce, prin. Fax 778-0557

Pershing, Wayne, Pop. 406
Western Wayne SD 1,000/PK-12
PO Box 217 47370 765-478-5375
Dr. Robert Mahon, supt. Fax 478-4577
www.wwayne.k12.in.us
Other Schools – See Cambridge City

Peru, Miami, Pop. 11,168
Maconaquah SC
Supt. — See Bunker Hill
Pipe Creek ES 400/PK-1
3036 W 400 S 46970 765-473-3121
Laura Fulton, prin. Fax 473-7074

Peru Community SC 2,200/PK-12
35 W 3rd St 46970 765-473-3081
Sam Watkins Ed.D., supt. Fax 472-5129
www.peru.k12.in.us
Blair Pointe Upper ES 700/3-6
300 Blair Pike 46970 765-473-4741
Linda Watkins, prin. Fax 472-5155
Elmwood Primary Learning Center 500/PK-2
515 N Wayne St 46970 765-473-7335
Kristi Eddy, prin. Fax 472-5158
Peru JHS 400/7-8
30 Daniel St 46970 765-473-3084
Sheri Spiker, prin. Fax 473-4007

Petersburg, Pike, Pop. 2,365
Pike County SC 1,800/PK-12
211 S 12th St 47567 812-354-8731
Suzanne Blake, supt. Fax 354-7138
www.pcsc.k12.in.us
Petersburg ES 500/PK-5
1415 E Alford St 47567 812-354-6876
Rick King, prin. Fax 354-8718
Pike Central MS 500/6-8
1814 E State Road 56 47567 812-354-8478
Mindy Keeker, prin. Fax 354-9559
Other Schools – See Winslow

Pierceton, Kosciusko, Pop. 1,004
Whitko Community SC
Supt. — See Larwill
Pierceton ES 300/K-5
PO Box 94 46562 574-594-2210
Mike McClain, prin. Fax 594-3523

Pine Village, Warren, Pop. 217
Metro SD of Warren County
Supt. — See Williamsport
Pine Village ES 100/K-6
3756 E State Road 26 47975 765-385-2651
Gail Anderson, prin. Fax 385-0124

Pittsboro, Hendricks, Pop. 2,886
North West Hendricks SD
Supt. — See Lizton
Pittsboro ES 300/3-5
206 N Meridian St 46167 317-994-2000
Jeremy Brooks, prin. Fax 892-2010
Pittsboro PS 300/PK-2
540 Osborne Ave 46167 317-994-2100
Jennifer Hollingsworth, prin. Fax 994-4320

Plainfield, Hendricks, Pop. 27,200
Plainfield Community SC 5,100/PK-12
985 Longfellow Ln 46168 317-839-2578
Scott Olinger, supt. Fax 838-3664
www.plainfield.k12.in.us
Brentwood ES 500/K-5
1630 Oliver Ave 46168 317-839-4802
Nicole Walker, prin. Fax 838-3991
Central ES 600/K-5
110 Wabash St 46168 317-839-7707
Julie Thacker, prin. Fax 838-3646
Clarks Creek ES 700/K-5
401 Elm Dr 46168 317-839-0120
Marisa Donovan, prin. Fax 838-7316
Little Quakers Academy PK-PK
401 Elm Dr 46168 317-754-2375
Fax 203-4525
Plainfield Community MS 1,300/6-8
709 Stafford Rd 46168 317-838-3966
Jerry Goldsberry, prin. Fax 838-3965
Van Buren ES 500/K-5
225 Shaw St 46168 317-839-2575
Ray Helmuth, prin. Fax 838-3993

St. Susanna S 300/PK-8
1212 E Main St 46168 317-839-3713
Michele Tillery, prin. Fax 838-7718

Pleasant Lake, Steuben
Metropolitan SD of Steuben County
Supt. — See Angola
Pleasant Lake ES 200/K-5
PO Box 69 46779 260-475-5055
John Curtis, prin. Fax 475-5673

Plymouth, Marshall, Pop. 9,894
Plymouth Community SC 3,700/PK-12
611 Berkley St 46563 574-936-3115
Andrew Hartley, supt. Fax 936-3160
www.plymouth.k12.in.us/
Jefferson ES 300/PK-4
401 Klinger St 46563 574-936-2443
Angela Mills, prin. Fax 936-3532
Lincoln JHS 600/7-8
220 N Liberty St 46563 574-936-3113
Reid Gault, prin. Fax 936-3574
Menominee ES 400/K-4
815 Discovery Ln 46563 574-936-2001
Steven Boyer, prin. Fax 936-2822
Riverside IS 500/5-6
905 Baker St 46563 574-936-3787
Jeni Hirschy, prin. Fax 936-2822
Washington Discovery Academy 400/K-4
1500 Lake Ave 46563 574-936-4072
Lauren Cooper, prin. Fax 936-4073
Webster ES 400/K-4
1101 S Michigan St 46563 574-936-2520
Carrie McGuire, prin. Fax 935-4976

St. Michael S 100/PK-6
612 N Center St 46563 574-936-4329
Amy Weidner, prin. Fax 936-1151

Poneto, Wells, Pop. 166
Southern Wells Community SD 900/K-12
9120 S 300 W 46781 765-728-5537
Steve Darnell, supt. Fax 728-8124
www.swraiders.com
Southern Wells ES 400/K-6
9120 S 300 W 46781 765-728-2121
Cari Whicker, prin. Fax 728-8124

Portage, Porter, Pop. 36,264
Portage Township SD 8,000/K-12
6240 US Highway 6 46368 219-762-6511
Amanda Alaniz, supt. Fax 762-3263
www.portage.k12.in.us
Aylesworth ES 500/K-5
5910 Central Ave 46368 219-763-8010
Jeff King, prin. Fax 764-6363
Central ES 500/K-5
2825 Russell St 46368 219-763-8015
Amanda Alaniz, prin. Fax 764-6542
Crisman ES 500/K-5
6161 Old Porter Rd 46368 219-763-8020
Scott Hufford, prin. Fax 764-6592
Fegely MS 800/6-8
5384 Stone Ave 46368 219-763-8150
Tom Martin, prin. Fax 763-8157
Jones ES 400/K-5
2374 McCool Rd 46368 219-763-8025
Kristen Doty, prin. Fax 764-6642
Kyle ES 500/K-5
2701 Hamstrom Rd 46368 219-763-8030
Michael Sopko, prin. Fax 764-6692
Myers ES 400/K-5
3100 Willowdale Rd 46368 219-763-8035
Jon Evers, prin. Fax 764-6742
Willowcreek MS 1,100/6-8
5962 Central Ave 46368 219-763-8090
Michelle Stewart, prin. Fax 762-3455
Other Schools – See Valparaiso

Nativity of Our Savior S 200/PK-8
2929 Willowcreek Rd 46368 219-763-2400
Sally Skowronski, prin. Fax 764-3225
Portage Christian S 200/PK-12
3040 Arlene St 46368 219-762-8962
Larry Pender, supt. Fax 763-9931

Porter, Porter, Pop. 4,795
Duneland SC
Supt. — See Chesterton
Yost ES 400/K-4
100 W Beam St 46304 219-983-3640
Anne Stillman, prin. Fax 983-3649

Portland, Jay, Pop. 6,162
Jay SC 3,500/PK-12
1976 W Tyson Rd 47371 260-726-9341
Jeremy Gulley, supt. Fax 726-4959
www.jayschools.k12.in.us
East ES 200/K-5
705 E Tallman St 47371 260-726-9418
Andy Schemenaur, prin. Fax 726-9839
East Jay MS 600/6-8
225 E Water St 47371 260-726-9371
Lee Newman, prin. Fax 726-2383
Haynes ES 200/K-5
827 W High St 47371 260-726-8890
Erica Tomano, prin. Fax 726-3587
Shanks ES 300/K-5
414 E Floral Ave 47371 260-726-8868
Craig Campbell, prin. Fax 729-5111
Other Schools – See Bryant, Dunkirk, Redkey

Poseyville, Posey, Pop. 1,039
Metro SD of North Posey County 1,400/PK-12
101 N Church St 47633 812-874-2243
Dr. Todd Camp, supt. Fax 874-8806
www.northposey.k12.in.us/
North ES 400/PK-6
63 W Fletchall St 47633 812-874-2710
Shannon Macmunn, prin. Fax 874-8811
North Posey JHS 200/7-8
5800 High School Rd 47633 812-673-4244
Steve Kavanaugh, prin. Fax 673-6622
Other Schools – See Wadesville

Princeton, Gibson, Pop. 8,390
North Gibson SC 1,900/PK-12
1104 N Embree St 47670 812-385-4851
Dr. Brian Harmon, supt. Fax 386-1531
www.ngsc.k12.in.us
Princeton Community IS 500/3-5
1108 N Embree St 47670 812-386-1221
David McClary, prin. Fax 386-1577
Princeton Community MS 500/6-8
1106 N Embree St 47670 812-385-2020
Noah Velthouse, prin. Fax 386-6746
Princeton Community PS North 300/1-2
813 W Archer Rd 47670 812-386-1222
Mary Williams, prin. Fax 385-2593
Princeton Community PS South PK-K
215 W Water St 47670 812-385-4772
Mary Williams, prin. Fax 385-4682

St. Joseph S 200/PK-5
427 S Stormont St 47670 812-385-2228
Dan Gilbert, prin. Fax 385-2590

Ramsey, Harrison
North Harrison Community SC 2,200/PK-12
1260 Highway 64 NW 47166 812-347-2407
Dr. Lance Richards, supt. Fax 347-2870
www.nhcs.k12.in.us
North Harrison ES 500/PK-5
1115 W Whiskey Run Rd NW 47166 812-347-2419
Lisa Jones, prin. Fax 347-2489
North Harrison MS 500/6-8
1180 Highway 64 NW 47166 812-347-2421
Nathan Freed, prin. Fax 347-2835
Other Schools – See Palmyra

Redkey, Jay, Pop. 1,340
Jay SC
Supt. — See Portland
Redkey ES 200/PK-5
PO Box 6 47373 765-369-2571
Julie Gregg, prin. Fax 369-2089

Remington, Jasper, Pop. 1,161
Tri-County SC
Supt. — See Wolcott
Tri-County PS 200/K-2
300 E Michigan St 47977 219-261-2214
Elaine Hall, prin. Fax 261-2221

Rensselaer, Jasper, Pop. 5,800
Rensselaer Central SC 1,700/PK-12
900 E Washington St 47978 219-866-7822
Curtis D. Craig, supt. Fax 866-8360
www.rensselaerschools.org
Rensselaer Central MS 400/6-8
1106 E Bomber Dr 47978 219-866-4661
Eric Huffman, prin. Fax 866-2103
Rensselaer Central PS 400/PK-2
1144 N Melville St 47978 219-866-5441
Jennifer Norris, prin. Fax 866-8135
Van Rensselaer ES 300/3-5
902 E Washington St 47978 219-866-8212
Chad Wynn, prin. Fax 866-8215

St. Augustine S 100/PK-5
328 N McKinley Ave 47978 219-866-5480
Bruce Schooler, prin. Fax 866-5663

Richland, Spencer, Pop. 423
South Spencer County SC
Supt. — See Rockport
Luce ES 200/K-5
1057 N County Road 700 W 47634 812-359-4401
Lori Hermann, prin. Fax 359-4402

Richmond, Wayne, Pop. 35,381
Richmond Community SC 5,300/PK-12
300 Hub Etchison Pkwy 47374 765-973-3300
Todd Terrill, supt. Fax 973-3417
www.rcs.k12.in.us
Charles ES 500/K-4
2400 Reeveston Rd 47374 765-973-3441
Kirsten Phillips, prin. Fax 973-3701
Crestdale ES 500/PK-4
701 Crestdale Dr 47374 765-973-3415
Elizabeth Markward, prin. Fax 973-3702
Fairview ES 300/PK-4
60 NW L St 47374 765-973-3442
Adam McDaniel, prin. Fax 973-3704
Starr ES 400/PK-4
301 N 19th St 47374 765-973-3426
Karrianne Polk-Meek, prin. Fax 973-3711
Test IS 700/5-8
33 S 22nd St 47374 765-973-3412
Stacy Mopps, prin. Fax 973-3712
Vaile ES 400/PK-4
300 S 14th St 47374 765-973-3433
Rae Ann Turner, prin. Fax 973-3713
Westview ES 300/PK-4
1707 SW A St 47374 765-973-3445
Tammy Rhoades, prin. Fax 973-3714
Worth IS 700/5-8
222 NW 7th St 47374 765-973-3495
Nichole Vandervort, prin. Fax 973-3703

Community Christian S 100/PK-8
PO Box 1393 47375 765-935-3215
Kim Soots, admin. Fax 598-5152
Richmond Friends S 50/PK-8
607 W Main St 47374 765-966-5767
Marcie Roberts, head sch
Richmond SDA S 50/1-8
4358 US Highway 35 N 47374 765-935-1033
Seton Catholic S 200/PK-6
801 W Main St 47374 765-962-4877
Kimberly Becker, prin. Fax 962-5381

Ridgeville, Randolph, Pop. 790
Randolph Central SC
Supt. — See Winchester
Deerfield ES 200/K-5
213 W State Road 28 47380 765-857-2554
Laura Miller, prin. Fax 857-2606

Riley, Vigo, Pop. 218
Vigo County SC
Supt. — See Terre Haute
Riley ES 400/PK-5
PO Box 127 47871 812-462-4449
Claire Marchase, prin. Fax 894-2054

Rising Sun, Ohio, Pop. 2,292
Rising Sun-Ohio County Community SD 800/K-12
110 S Henrietta St 47040 812-438-2655
Branden Roeder, supt. Fax 438-4636
www.risingsun.k12.in.us
Ohio County S 600/K-8
436 S Mulberry St 47040 812-438-2626
Teresa George, prin. Fax 438-2456

Switzerland County SC
Supt. — See Vevay
Switzerland County ES 500/PK-6
12862 State Road 250 47040 812-534-3128
Sally Weales, prin. Fax 534-2042

Roachdale, Putnam, Pop. 922
North Putnam Community SD
Supt. — See Bainbridge
North Putnam MS 400/6-8
8905 N County Road 250 E 46172 765-522-2900
Scott Miller, prin. Fax 522-2863
Roachdale ES 300/K-5
305 S Indiana St 46172 765-522-1732
Beth Waterman, admin. Fax 522-2094

Roanoke, Huntington, Pop. 1,695
Huntington County Community SC
Supt. — See Huntington
Roanoke ES 300/K-5
423 W Vine St 46783 260-672-2806
Seth Parker, prin. Fax 672-3391

Metro SD of Southwest Allen County
Supt. — See Fort Wayne
Lafayette Meadows ES 500/K-5
11420 Ernst Rd 46783 260-431-0601
Jonny Fodolo, prin. Fax 431-0609

Aboite Christian S 50/PK-8
14615 Winters Rd 46783 260-672-8544
Sheldon Schultz, admin. Fax 672-8544

Rochester, Fulton, Pop. 6,144
Rochester Community SC 1,900/PK-12
PO Box 108 46975 574-223-2159
Jana Vance, supt. Fax 223-4909
www.zebras.net
Columbia ES 500/PK-2
PO Box 108 46975 574-223-2501
Jason Snyder, prin. Fax 223-0530
Riddle ES 400/3-5
PO Box 108 46975 574-223-2880
Luke Biernacki, prin. Fax 223-1539
Rochester Community MS 400/6-8
PO Box 108 46975 574-223-2280
Oscar Haughs, prin. Fax 223-1531

Rockport, Spencer, Pop. 2,241
South Spencer County SC 1,300/PK-12
321 S 5th St 47635 812-649-2591
Dr. Richard Rutherford, supt. Fax 649-4249
www.sspencer.k12.in.us
Rockport-Ohio ES 300/PK-5
200 S 6th St 47635 812-649-2201
Kari Ford, prin. Fax 649-2202
South Spencer MS 300/6-8
1298 N Orchard Rd 47635 812-649-2203
Scot French, prin. Fax 649-9630
Other Schools – See Richland

St. Bernard S 200/PK-8
547 Elm St 47635 812-649-2501
Beth Strodel, prin. Fax 649-4176

Rockville, Parke, Pop. 2,594
North Central Parke Community SC
Supt. — See Marshall
Rockville ES 400/K-6
406 Elm St 47872 765-569-5363
Kristin Robinson, prin. Fax 569-5181

Rolling Prairie, LaPorte, Pop. 580
New Prairie United SC
Supt. — See New Carlisle
Prairie View ES 300/K-5
6434 E 700 N 46371 574-654-7258
Rhonda Myers, prin. Fax 778-9237
Rolling Prairie ES 500/K-5
605 E Michigan St 46371 219-778-2018
Rebecca Bartlett, prin. Fax 778-4911

Rome City, Noble, Pop. 1,358
East Noble SC
Supt. — See Kendallville
Rome City ES 300/PK-6
PO Box 218 46784 260-854-3241
Heather Green, prin. Fax 854-9404

Rosedale, Parke, Pop. 714
Southwest Parke Community SC
Supt. — See Montezuma
Rosedale ES 300/K-6
613 E Central St 47874 765-548-2454
Diana Spence, prin. Fax 548-2608

Rossville, Clinton, Pop. 1,638
Rossville Consolidated SD 700/K-12
PO Box 11 46065 765-379-2990
Dr. James Hanna, supt. Fax 379-3014
www.rcsd.k12.in.us
Rossville ES 500/K-5
PO Box 530 46065 765-379-2119
Chad Dennison, prin. Fax 379-9236

Royal Center, Cass, Pop. 854
Pioneer Regional SC 900/K-12
PO Box 577 46978 574-643-2605
Charles Grable, supt. Fax 643-9977
www.pioneer.k12.in.us
Pioneer ES 500/K-6
PO Box 517 46978 574-643-2255
Dr. Beth Dean, prin. Fax 643-4029

Rushville, Rush, Pop. 6,250
Rush County SD 2,500/PK-12
330 W 8th St 46173 765-932-4186
Matthew Vance, supt. Fax 938-1608
rcs.rushville.k12.in.us/
Rush MS 400/7-8
1601 N Sexton St 46173 765-932-2968
Maria Peek, prin. Fax 938-2011
Rushville East ES 300/K-6
390 W 16th St 46173 765-938-1616
Austin Theobald, prin. Fax 938-2417
Rushville West ES 300/PK-6
410 W 16th St 46173 765-938-1509
Patrick Anderson, prin. Fax 938-1703
Other Schools – See Arlington, Milroy

St. Mary S 100/PK-6
226 E 5th St 46173 765-932-3639
Sherri Kirschner, prin. Fax 938-1322

Russiaville, Howard, Pop. 1,087
Western SC 2,600/K-12
2600 S 600 W 46979 765-883-5576
Randy McCracken, supt. Fax 883-7946
www.western.k12.in.us
Western IS 600/3-5
2607 S 600 W 46979 765-883-5554
Pat Quillen, prin. Fax 883-7946
Western MS 700/6-8
2600 S 600 W 46979 765-883-5566
Tracy Horrell, prin. Fax 883-4531
Western PS 600/K-2
2671 S 600 W 46979 765-883-5528
Steve Arthur, prin. Fax 883-7946

Saint Joe, DeKalb, Pop. 458
DeKalb County Eastern Community SD
Supt. — See Butler
Riverdale ES 300/K-6
6127 State Road 1 46785 260-337-5464
Brennen Kitchen, prin. Fax 337-5114

Saint John, Lake, Pop. 14,717
Lake Central SC 9,700/PK-12
8260 Wicker Ave 46373 219-365-8507
Dr. Lawrence Veracco, supt. Fax 365-6406
www.lcsc.us
Clark MS 1,100/5-8
8915 W 93rd Ave 46373 219-365-9203
Scott Graber, prin. Fax 365-9348
Kolling ES 700/PK-4
8801 Wicker Ave 46373 219-365-8577
Cassandra Cruz, prin. Fax 365-6402
Other Schools – See Dyer, Schererville

Crown Point Christian S 500/PK-8
10550 Park Pl 46373 219-365-5694
Michael Wiersma, admin. Fax 365-5729
St. John Evangelist S 400/PK-8
9400 Wicker Ave 46373 219-365-5451
Brianne Oliver, prin. Fax 365-6173

Saint Leon, Franklin, Pop. 670
Sunman-Dearborn Community SC 3,400/K-12
1 Trojan Pl Ste B 47012 812-623-2291
Dr. Andrew Jackson, supt. Fax 623-3341
www.sunmandearborn.k12.in.us
Sunman-Dearborn MS 600/6-8
8356 Schuman Rd, Brookville IN 47012
812-576-3500
Matt Maple, prin. Fax 576-3506
Other Schools – See Lawrenceburg, Sunman, West Harrison

Salem, Washington, Pop. 6,263
Salem Community SD 1,500/K-12
500 N Harrison St 47167 812-883-4437
Dr. D. Lynn Reed, supt. Fax 883-1031
www.salemschools.com/
Salem MS 400/6-8
1001 N Harrison St 47167 812-883-3808
Ray Oppel, prin. Fax 883-8049
Shrum ES 400/K-5
1101 N Shelby St 47167 812-883-3700
Brent Minton, prin. Fax 883-9118

Schererville, Lake, Pop. 28,917
Lake Central SC
Supt. — See Saint John
Grimmer MS 900/5-8
225 W 77th Ave 46375 219-865-6985
John Alessia, prin. Fax 865-4423
Homan ES 600/PK-4
210 E Joliet St 46375 219-322-4451
Kathi Tucker, prin. Fax 865-4442
Peifer ES 500/PK-4
1824 Cline Ave 46375 219-322-5335
Douglas DeLaughter, prin. Fax 865-4426
Watson ES 500/PK-4
333 W 77th Ave 46375 219-322-1365
Michelle Lavin, prin. Fax 865-4431

St. Michael S 300/PK-8
16 W Wilhelm St 46375 219-322-4531
Colleen Kennedy, prin. Fax 322-1710

Scipio, Jennings, Pop. 153
Jennings County SC
Supt. — See North Vernon
Scipio ES 300/K-6
6320 N State Highway 7 47273 812-392-2055
Donna Eaton, prin. Fax 392-2564

Scottsburg, Scott, Pop. 6,707
Scott County SD 2 2,700/PK-12
375 E Mcclain Ave 47170 812-752-8946
Dr. Marc Slaton, supt. Fax 752-8951
www.scsd2.k12.in.us/
Johnson ES 200/PK-5
4235 E State Road 256 47170 812-752-8923
C. Routt, prin. Fax 794-4979
Scottsburg ES 500/K-5
49 N Hyland St 47170 812-752-8922
Deb Yost, prin. Fax 752-9620
Scottsburg MS 600/6-8
425 S 3rd St 47170 812-752-8926
Kristin Nass, prin. Fax 752-8864
Vienna-Finley ES 300/K-5
445 E Ivan Rogers Dr 47170 812-752-8925
Tiffany Barrett, prin. Fax 752-5379
Other Schools – See Lexington

Sellersburg, Clark, Pop. 6,055
West Clark Community SC 4,700/PK-12
601 Renz Ave 47172 812-246-3375
Dr. Chad Schenck, supt. Fax 246-9731
www.wclark.k12.in.us
Silver Creek ES 800/2-5
503 N Indiana Ave 47172 812-246-3312
Christopher Kane, prin. Fax 246-7435
Silver Creek MS 700/6-8
495 N Indiana Ave 47172 812-246-4421
Al Eckert, prin. Fax 246-7430
Silver Creek PS 400/PK-1
8604 Commerce Park Dr 47172 812-248-7250
Sandy Myers, prin. Fax 248-7251
Other Schools – See Borden, Henryville

St. John Paul II S 200/PK-7
105 Saint Paul St 47172 812-246-3266
Karen Haas, prin. Fax 246-7632

Selma, Delaware, Pop. 856
Liberty-Perry Community SC 1,100/K-12
PO Box 337 47383 765-282-5615
Bryan Rausch, supt. Fax 281-3733
www.libertyperry.org
Selma ES 500/K-5
PO Box 336 47383 765-282-2455
Joel Mahaffey, prin. Fax 281-3730
Selma MS 300/6-8
10501 E County Road 167 S 47383 765-288-7242
Dennis Thompson, prin. Fax 281-3727

Seymour, Jackson, Pop. 17,275
Seymour Community SD 4,300/PK-12
1638 S Walnut St 47274 812-522-3340
Robert Hooker, supt. Fax 522-8031
www.scsc.k12.in.us
Brown ES 500/K-5
550 Miller Ln 47274 812-522-5539
Tony Hack, prin. Fax 522-4544
Cortland ES 100/K-5
6687 N County Road 400 E 47274 812-522-7483
Lori Lister, prin. Fax 522-6164
Emerson ES 300/K-5
500 Emerson Dr 47274 812-522-2596
Julie Kelly, prin. Fax 523-3338
Seymour-Jackson ES 700/PK-5
508 B Ave E 47274 812-522-5709
Justin Brown, prin. Fax 522-7095
Seymour MS 1,000/6-8
920 N Obrien St 47274 812-522-5453
J.B. Royer, prin. Fax 523-8134
Seymour-Redding ES 500/PK-5
1700 N Ewing St 47274 812-522-5621
Jake Shaffner, prin. Fax 522-1593

Immanuel Lutheran S 300/1-8
520 S Chestnut St 47274 812-522-1301
Dr. Todd Behmlander, prin. Fax 523-2186
St. Ambrose S 100/PK-8
301 S Chestnut St 47274 812-522-3522
Michelle Neibert-Levine, prin. Fax 522-3545
St. John's Sauers Lutheran S 100/PK-8
1058 S County Road 460 E 47274 812-523-3131
Jonathan Baumgartel, prin. Fax 524-0612
Zion Lutheran S 100/PK-K
1501 Gaiser Dr 47274 812-552-5911
Christina Heiss, prin. Fax 523-7526

Sharpsville, Tipton, Pop. 600
Tri-Central Community School Corporation 900/PK-12
4774 N 200 W 46068 765-963-2585
Dave Driggs, supt. Fax 963-3042
www.tccs.k12.in.us
Tri Central ES 300/PK-5
2115 W 500 N 46068 765-963-5885
Matthew Miller, prin. Fax 963-3072

Shelburn, Sullivan, Pop. 1,220
Northeast SC
Supt. — See Hymera
Northeast MS 200/6-8
620 N Washington St 47879 812-397-5390
J.T. Roberts, prin. Fax 397-2886

Shelbyville, Shelby, Pop. 18,951
Shelby Eastern SD 1,300/PK-12
2451 N 600 E 46176 765-544-2246
Dr. Robert Evans, supt. Fax 544-2247
www.ses.k12.in.us
Other Schools – See Morristown, Waldron

Shelbyville Central SD 4,000/PK-12
803 Saint Joseph St 46176 317-392-2505
Dr. David Adams, supt. Fax 392-5737
www.shelbycs.k12.in.us
Coulston ES 600/PK-5
121 N Knightstown Rd 46176 317-398-3185
James Conner, prin. Fax 392-5721
Hendricks ES 700/PK-5
1111 Saint Joseph St 46176 317-398-7432
Pat Lumbley, prin. Fax 392-5725
Loper ES 700/PK-5
901 Loper Dr 46176 317-398-9725
Brent Baker, prin. Fax 392-5732
Shelbyville MS 900/6-8
1200 W McKay Rd 46176 317-392-2551
Ryan Mikus, prin. Fax 392-5713

Southwestern Cons SD of Shelby County 600/PK-12
3406 W 600 S 46176 317-729-5746
Dr. Paula Maurer, supt. Fax 729-5330
www.swshelby.k12.in.us
Southwestern ES 300/PK-6
3406 W 600 S 46176 317-729-5320
Joshua Edwards, prin. Fax 729-5370

St. Joseph S 100/PK-5
127 E Broadway St 46176 317-398-4202
Bethany Fewell, prin. Fax 398-0270

Sheridan, Hamilton, Pop. 2,630
Sheridan Community SD 1,100/PK-12
24795 Hinesley Rd 46069 317-758-4172
Dr. David Mundy, supt. Fax 758-6248
www.scs.k12.in.us/
Sheridan ES 500/PK-5
24795 Hinesley Rd 46069 317-758-4491
Dean Welbaum, prin. Fax 758-2409
Sheridan MS 200/6-8
3030 W 246th St 46069 317-758-6780
Jane Newblom, prin. Fax 758-2435

Shipshewana, Lagrange, Pop. 654
Westview SC
Supt. — See Topeka
Meadowview ES 400/K-4
7950 W 050 S 46565 260-768-7702
Toni Whitney, prin. Fax 768-7906
Shipshewana-Scott ES 400/K-4
PO Box 217 46565 260-768-4158
Ian Zuercher, prin. Fax 768-4159

Shoals, Martin, Pop. 746
Shoals Community SC 600/PK-12
11741 Ironton Rd 47581 812-247-2060
Dr. Candace Roush, supt. Fax 247-2278
shoals.k12.in.us
Shoals Community ES 300/PK-5
11749 Ironton Rd 47581 812-247-2085
Shannon Wagoner, prin. Fax 247-9913
Shoals Community MS 100/6-8
11741 Ironton Rd 47581 812-247-2060
Austin Malone, prin. Fax 247-2278

South Bend, Saint Joseph, Pop. 97,691
South Bend Community SC 18,900/PK-12
215 S Dr ML King Blvd 46601 574-393-6000
Dr. Kenneth Spells, supt. Fax 283-8143
www.sb.school
Brown Intermediate Center 400/4-8
737 Beale St 46616 574-393-3800
Joseph Somers, prin. Fax 283-5581
Clay Intermediate Center 500/5-8
52900 Lily Rd 46637 574-393-4300
Frances Beard, prin. Fax 243-7151
Coquilliard Traditional S 400/K-4
1245 N Sheridan St 46628 574-393-2000
William Gergely, prin. Fax 283-8613
Darden Primary Center 600/K-4
18645 Janet Dr 46637 574-243-7335
Patricia Karban, prin. Fax 243-7338
Dickinson Intermediate Fine Arts Academy 600/5-8
4404 Elwood Ave 46628 574-393-3900
Thomas Sims, prin. Fax 283-7633
Edison Intermediate Center 500/5-8
2701 Eisenhower Ave 46615 574-393-4400
Michael Budzinski, prin. Fax 283-8903
Greene Intermediate Center 300/5-8
24702 Roosevelt Rd 46614 574-393-4000
Keith Lewis, prin. Fax 283-7903
Hamilton Traditional S 400/K-4
1530 E Jackson Rd 46614 574-393-2100
Kathy Sanders, prin. Fax 231-5675
Harrison Primary Center 600/K-4
3302 W Western Ave 46619 574-393-3000
Fax 283-7303
Hay Primary Center 500/K-4
19685 Johnson Rd 46614 574-393-2200
Brian Harris, prin. Fax 231-5738
Jackson Intermediate Center 600/5-8
5001 Miami St 46614 574-393-4500
Francois Bayingana, prin. Fax 231-5605
Jefferson Traditional S 600/5-8
528 S Eddy St 46617 574-393-4100
Carmen Williams, prin. Fax 283-8703
Kennedy Primary Academy 700/K-4
609 N Olive St 46628 574-393-3100
William Waskom, prin. Fax 283-7441
LaSalle Intermediate Academy 900/5-8
2701 Elwood Ave 46628 574-393-4700
Melinda Ehmer, prin. Fax 283-7513
Lincoln Primary Center 500/K-4
1425 E Calvert St 46613 574-393-2300
Nicole Medich, prin. Fax 283-8963
Madison Primary Center 500/K-4
832 N Lafayette Blvd 46601 574-393-3200
Deb Martin, prin. Fax 283-8328
Marquette Primary Montessori Academy 600/PK-4
1818 Bergan St 46628 574-393-2400
Deb Cyrier, prin. Fax 283-8373

Marshall Intermediate Center 500/5-8
1433 Byron Dr 46614 574-393-4200
Tiana Batiste-Waddell, prin. Fax 231-5804
McKinley Primary Center 500/K-4
228 N Greenlawn Ave 46617 574-393-3300
Jesus Pedraza, prin. Fax 283-8573
Monroe Primary Center 400/K-4
312 Donmoyer Ave 46614 574-393-2500
Jennie Mast, prin. Fax 231-5834
Muessel Primary Center 400/PK-4
1021 Blaine Ave 46616 574-393-3400
Fax 283-7803
Navarre Intermediate Center 700/5-8
4702 Ford St 46619 574-393-4600
Angela Buysse, prin. Fax 283-7351
Nuner Primary Center 300/K-4
2716 Pleasant St 46615 574-393-2600
Elizabeth Willkom, prin. Fax 283-7853
Perley Primary Fine Arts Academy 200/K-4
740 N Eddy St 46617 574-393-3500
Jill VanDriessche, prin. Fax 283-8738
Swanson Primary Center 300/K-4
17677 Parker Dr 46635 574-393-2700
Matt Emery, prin. Fax 243-7253
Tarkington Traditional S 300/K-4
3414 Hepler St 46635 574-393-3600
Tania Grimes, prin. Fax 243-7213
Warren Primary Center 300/K-4
55400 Quince Rd 46619 574-283-7950
Gretchen McEndarfer, prin. Fax 283-7953
Wilson Primary Center 400/K-4
56660 Oak Rd 46619 574-393-3700
Cheryl Batteast, prin. Fax 283-7407

Christ the King S 500/K-8
52473 IN State Route 933 46637 574-272-3922
Stephen Hoffman, prin. Fax 273-6702
Clark S 300/PK-8
3123 Miami St 46614 574-291-4200
Melissa Grubb, head sch Fax 299-4170
Community Baptist Christian S 200/PK-12
5715 Miami St 46614 574-291-3620
Corpus Christi S 300/PK-8
2817 Corpus Christi Dr 46628 574-272-9868
Maggie Mackowiak, prin. Fax 272-9894
Good Shepherd Montessori S 100/PK-8
1101 E Jefferson Blvd 46617 574-288-0098
Holy Cross S 300/PK-8
1020 Wilber St 46628 574-234-3422
Angela Budzinski, prin. Fax 237-6725
Holy Family S 300/PK-8
56407 Mayflower Rd 46619 574-289-7375
Joseph Miller, prin. Fax 289-7386
Our Lady of Hungary S 200/PK-8
735 W Calvert St 46613 574-289-3272
Kevin Goralczyk, prin. Fax 289-3272
Resurrection Lutheran Academy 100/PK-8
6840 Nimtz Pkwy 46628 574-272-2200
Michelle Megyese, prin. Fax 968-0345
St. Adalbert S 200/PK-8
519 S Olive St 46619 574-288-6645
Andrew Currier, prin. Fax 251-2788
St. Anthony De Padua S 300/K-8
2310 E Jefferson Blvd 46615 574-233-7169
Karen Bogol, prin. Fax 233-7290
St. John the Baptist S 100/PK-8
3616 Saint Johns Way 46628 574-232-9849
Derek Boone, prin. Fax 232-9855
St. Joseph S 400/K-8
216 N Hill St 46617 574-234-0451
George Azar, prin. Fax 234-0524
St. Jude S 200/PK-8
19657 Hildebrand St 46614 574-291-3820
Stephen Donndelinger, prin. Fax 299-3051
St. Matthew Cathedral S 300/K-8
1015 E Dayton St 46613 574-289-4535
Sr. Gianna Marie Webber, prin. Fax 289-4539
South Bend Junior Academy 50/K-8
1910 Altgeld St 46614 574-287-3713
Thomas Huntress, prin.

Southport, Marion, Pop. 1,691
Perry Township SD
Supt. — See Indianapolis
Winchester Village ES 600/K-5
1900 E Stop 12 Rd 46227 317-789-2700
Natalie Bohannon, prin. Fax 865-2703

South Whitley, Whitley, Pop. 1,743
Whitko Community SC
Supt. — See Larwill
South Whitley ES 300/K-5
406 W Wayne St 46787 260-723-6342
Bryan Emmert, prin. Fax 723-5165

Speedway, Marion, Pop. 11,556
Town of Speedway SD 1,700/PK-12
5335 W 25th St 46224 317-244-0236
Kenneth Hull, supt. Fax 486-4843
www.speedwayschools.org
Allison ES 300/K-6
5240 W 22nd St 46224 317-244-9836
Jay Bedwell, prin. Fax 486-4847
Fisher ES 200/PK-6
5151 W 14th St 46224 317-241-6543
Mary Snapp, prin. Fax 486-4845
Newby ES 200/K-6
1849 N Whitcomb Ave 46224 317-241-0572
Lance Schnaus, prin. Fax 486-4848
Speedway JHS 200/7-8
5151 W 14th St 46224 317-244-3359
Eric Rosebrough, prin. Fax 486-4845
Wheeler ES 300/K-6
5700 Meadowood Dr 46224 317-291-4274
Brenda Wolfe, prin. Fax 291-4515

Spencer, Owen, Pop. 2,205
Spencer-Owen Community SD 2,700/PK-12
205 E Hillside Ave 47460 812-829-2233
Dr. Chad Briggs, supt. Fax 829-6614
www.socs.k12.in.us
McCormick's Creek ES 400/K-6
1601 Flatwoods Rd 47460 812-828-6000
Matt Cazzell, prin. Fax 828-6010
Owen Valley MS 400/7-8
626 W State Highway 46 47460 812-829-2249
Aaron LaGrange, prin. Fax 829-6635
Spencer ES 700/PK-6
151 E Hillside Ave 47460 812-829-2253
Brittany Greene, prin. Fax 829-6629
Other Schools – See Gosport, Patricksburg

Springville, Lawrence
North Lawrence Community SD
Supt. — See Bedford
Springville ES 200/K-5
PO Box 61 47462 812-279-1388
John Hudson, prin. Fax 278-7703

Stinesville, Monroe, Pop. 195
Richland-Bean Blossom Community SC
Supt. — See Ellettsville
Stinesville ES 200/K-5
7973 W Main St 47464 812-876-2474
Glen Hopkins, prin. Fax 876-2475

Straughn, Henry, Pop. 222
South Henry SC 800/K-12
6972 S State Road 103 47387 765-987-7882
Wesley Hammond, supt. Fax 987-7589
www.shenry.k12.in.us/
Tri ES 400/K-6
6972 S State Road 103 47387 765-987-7090
Nick Kimmel, prin. Fax 987-7487

Sullivan, Sullivan, Pop. 4,203
Southwest SC 1,800/PK-12
PO Box 510 47882 812-268-6311
Chris Stitzle, supt. Fax 268-6312
www.swest.k12.in.us
Sullivan ES 600/PK-5
351 W Frakes St 47882 812-268-3341
Samantha Phegley, prin. Fax 268-5624
Sullivan MS 300/6-8
415 W Frakes St 47882 812-268-4000
Dustin Hitt, prin. Fax 268-5368
Other Schools – See Carlisle

Summitville, Madison, Pop. 954
Madison-Grant United SC
Supt. — See Fairmount
Summitville ES 300/PK-6
405 E Mill St 46070 765-536-2875
Wendy Smedley, prin. Fax 536-2636

Sunman, Ripley, Pop. 1,030
Sunman-Dearborn Community SC
Supt. — See Saint Leon
Sunman ES 400/K-5
925 N Meridian St 47041 812-623-2235
Pamela Chambers, prin. Fax 623-4330

St. Nicholas S 100/K-8
6459 E Saint Nicholas Dr 47041 812-623-2348
Daniel Swygart, prin. Fax 623-0066

Swayzee, Grant, Pop. 973
Oak Hill United SC
Supt. — See Converse
Swayzee ES 300/K-6
PO Box 217 46986 765-395-3341
Rob Martin, prin. Fax 391-1390

Sweetser, Grant, Pop. 1,215
Oak Hill United SC
Supt. — See Converse
Sweetser ES 200/K-6
PO Box 230 46987 765-384-4371
Nijaul Drollinger, prin. Fax 391-1386

Switz City, Greene, Pop. 291
White River Valley SD 500/PK-12
PO Box 1470 47465 812-659-1424
Dr. Robert Hacker, supt. Fax 659-2283
www.wrv.k12.in.us
Other Schools – See Lyons, Worthington

Syracuse, Kosciusko, Pop. 2,781
Wawasee Community SC 3,100/PK-12
1 Warrior Path Bldg 2 46567 574-457-3188
Dr. Thomas Edington, supt. Fax 457-4962
www.wawasee.k12.in.us/
Syracuse ES 500/K-5
502 W Brooklyn St 46567 574-457-4484
Eric Speicher, prin. Fax 457-4486
Wawasee MS 500/6-8
9850 N State Road 13 46567 574-457-8839
Susan Mishler, prin. Fax 457-3575
Other Schools – See Milford, North Webster

Taylorsville, Bartholomew, Pop. 914
Bartholomew Consolidated SC
Supt. — See Columbus
Taylorsville ES 600/PK-6
PO Box 277 47280 812-526-5448
Sydell Gant, prin. Fax 526-2233

Tell City, Perry, Pop. 7,212
Tell City-Troy Township SC 1,500/PK-12
837 17th St 47586 812-547-3300
John Scioldo, supt. Fax 547-9704
www.tellcity.k12.in.us
Tell ES 900/PK-6
1235 31st St 47586 812-547-9727
Laura Noble, prin. Fax 547-9746

Tennyson, Warrick, Pop. 279
Warrick County SC
Supt. — See Boonville
Tennyson ES 100/K-5
323 N Main St 47637 812-567-4715
Tim Long, prin. Fax 567-4715

Terre Haute, Vigo, Pop. 59,043
Vigo County SC 15,500/PK-12
PO Box 3703 47803 812-462-4011
Daniel Tanoos, supt. Fax 462-4115
www.vigoschools.org/
Davis Park ES 400/K-5
310 S 18th St 47807 812-462-4425
Dr. Tammy Roeschlein, prin. Fax 462-4400
Deming ES 300/K-5
1750 8th Ave 47804 812-462-4431
Karen McDonald, prin. Fax 462-4285
De Vaney ES 500/K-5
1011 S Brown Ave 47803 812-462-4497
Michelle Nutter, prin. Fax 462-4317
Dixie Bee ES 600/K-5
1655 E Jessica Dr 47802 812-462-4445
Mika Cassell, prin. Fax 462-4447
Farrington Grove ES 500/K-5
1826 S 6th St 47802 812-462-4423
William Smith, prin. Fax 462-4424
Franklin ES 400/PK-5
1600 Dr Iverson C Bell Ln 47807 812-462-4441
Bettina Galey-Horrall, prin. Fax 462-4438
Fuqua ES 400/PK-5
1111 E Wheeler Ave 47802 812-462-4304
Mary Beth Harris, prin. Fax 462-4306
Honey Creek MS 800/6-8
6601 S Carlisle St 47802 812-462-4372
Nolan Cox, prin. Fax 462-4367
Hoosier Prairie ES 400/K-5
2800 W Harlan Dr 47802 812-462-4236
Jennifer Russell, prin. Fax 462-4233
Lost Creek ES 600/PK-5
6701 Wabash Ave 47803 812-462-4441
Linda Biggs, prin. Fax 877-4815
Meadows ES 300/PK-5
55 S Brown Ave 47803 812-462-4301
Cassandra Cook, prin. Fax 462-4303
Otter Creek MS 900/6-8
4801 N Lafayette St 47805 812-462-4391
Sarah Gore, prin. Fax 462-4388
Ouabache ES 300/PK-5
501 Maple Ave 47804 812-462-4493
Hailey Ringwald, prin. Fax 462-4214
Rio Grande ES 500/PK-5
5555 E Rio Grande Ave 47805 812-462-4307
Susan Lewis, prin. Fax 462-4309
Scott MS 500/6-8
1000 Grant St 47802 812-462-4381
Scotia Brown, prin. Fax 462-4370
Sugar Grove ES 400/PK-5
2800 Wallace Ave 47802 812-462-4416
Teresa Stuckey, prin. Fax 462-4471
Terre Town ES 700/PK-5
2121 Boston Ave 47805 812-462-4385
Cinda Taylor, prin. Fax 462-4413
Wilson MS 900/6-8
301 S 25th St 47803 812-462-4396
Steve Joseph, prin. Fax 232-2217
Other Schools – See Riley, West Terre Haute

St. Patrick S 300/PK-8
449 S 19th St 47803 812-232-2157
Patty Mauer, prin. Fax 478-9384
Terre Haute Adventist S 50/K-8
900 S 29th St 47803 812-232-1339

Thorntown, Boone, Pop. 1,514
Western Boone County Community SD 1,800/PK-12
1201 N State Road 75 46071 765-482-6333
Rob Ramey, supt.
www.weboschools.org
Thorntown ES 400/PK-6
200 W Mill St 46071 765-485-2447
Pam Taylor, prin. Fax 436-2630
Other Schools – See Jamestown

Tipton, Tipton, Pop. 5,058
Tipton Community SC 1,700/PK-12
1051 S Main St 46072 765-675-2147
Kevin Emsweller, supt. Fax 675-3857
www.tcsc.k12.in.us
Tipton ES 800/PK-5
1099 S Main St 46072 765-675-7397
Kathryn Heaston, prin. Fax 675-6211
Tipton MS 400/6-8
817 S Main St 46072 765-675-7521
Shayne Clark, prin. Fax 675-9027

Topeka, Lagrange, Pop. 1,128
Westview SC 2,300/K-12
1545 S 600 W 46571 260-768-4404
Dr. Randall Zimmerly, supt. Fax 768-7368
www.westview.k12.in.us
Topeka ES 400/K-4
PO Box 39 46571 260-593-2897
Becky Siegel, prin. Fax 593-2899
Westview ES 400/5-6
1715 S 600 W 46571 260-768-7717
Juli Leeper, prin. Fax 768-7737
Other Schools – See Shipshewana

Trafalgar, Johnson, Pop. 1,089
Nineveh-Hensley-Jackson United SC 1,800/PK-12
802 S Indian Creek Dr 46181 317-878-2100
Dr. Tim Edsell, supt. Fax 878-2109
www.indiancreekschools.com/
Indian Creek ES 400/PK-2
1002 S Indian Creek Dr 46181 317-878-2150
Keith Grant, prin. Fax 878-5486
Indian Creek IS 400/3-5
1000 S Indian Creek Dr 46181 317-878-2160
Andrea Perry, prin. Fax 878-2165
Indian Creek MS 500/6-8
801 W Indian Creek Dr 46181 317-878-2130
Sean Zachery, prin. Fax 878-2149

Union City, Randolph, Pop. 3,547
Randolph Eastern SC 900/PK-12
731 N Plum St 47390 765-964-4994
Lisa Smith, supt. Fax 964-6590
www.resc.k12.in.us/
North Side ES 500/PK-6
905 N Plum St 47390 765-964-6430
Mark Winkle, prin. Fax 964-3445

Union Mills, LaPorte
South Central Community SC 900/PK-12
9808 S 600 W 46382 219-767-2263
Linda Wiltfong, supt. Fax 767-2260
www.scentral.k12.in.us/
South Central ES 500/PK-6
9808 S 600 W 46382 219-767-2269
Benjamin Anderson, prin. Fax 767-2260

Unionville, Monroe
Monroe County Community SC
Supt. — See Bloomington
Unionville ES 200/PK-6
8144 E State Road 45 47468 812-332-0175
Lily Albright, prin. Fax 339-2717

Upland, Grant, Pop. 3,790
Eastbrook Community SC
Supt. — See Marion
Eastbrook South ES 400/K-6
694 S Second St 46989 765-998-2550
Miriam Dalton, prin. Fax 998-2740

Valparaiso, Porter, Pop. 31,160
Duneland SC
Supt. — See Chesterton
Jackson ES 300/K-4
811 N 400 E 46383 219-983-3680
Dr. Linda Rugg, prin. Fax 983-3689

East Porter County SC
Supt. — See Kouts
Morgan Township ES 300/K-5
299 S State Road 49 46383 219-462-5883
Jessica Niebel, prin. Fax 462-4014
Washington Township ES 400/K-5
383 E State Road 2 46383 219-464-3598
Rik Ihssen, prin. Fax 465-1753

Portage Township SD
Supt. — See Portage
Saylor ES 300/K-5
331 Midway Dr 46385 219-763-8040
John Zack, prin. Fax 764-6792
South Haven ES 400/K-5
395 Midway Dr 46385 219-763-8045
Phil Misecko, prin. Fax 764-6842

Porter Township SC 1,500/K-12
248 S 500 W 46385 219-477-4933
Dr. Stacey Schmidt, supt. Fax 477-4834
www.ptsc.k12.in.us
Other Schools – See Boone Grove, Hebron

Union Township SC 1,500/K-12
599 W 300 N Ste A 46385 219-759-2531
John Hunter, supt. Fax 759-3250
www.union.k12.in.us
Simatovich ES 300/K-5
424 W 500 N 46385 219-759-2508
Leigh Barnes, prin. Fax 759-6634
Union Center ES 300/K-5
272 N 600 W 46385 219-759-2544
Michael Rosta, prin. Fax 759-6360
Union Township MS 400/6-8
599 W 300 N 46385 219-759-2562
Jerry Lasky, prin. Fax 759-4359

Valparaiso Community SD 6,400/K-12
3801 Campbell St 46385 219-531-3000
Dr. E. Ric Frataccia Ed.D., supt. Fax 531-3009
www.valpo.k12.in.us
Central ES 400/K-5
653 Hayes Leonard Rd 46383 219-531-3030
Calli Dado, prin. Fax 531-1251
Cooks Corner ES 300/K-5
358 Bullseye Lake Rd 46383 219-531-3040
Elaina Miller, prin. Fax 531-3041
Flint Lake ES 500/K-5
4106 Calumet Ave 46383 219-531-3160
Dr. Erin Hawkins, prin. Fax 531-3164
Franklin MS 900/6-8
605 Campbell St 46385 219-531-3020
Jeannie Sienkowski, prin. Fax 531-3026
Heavilin ES 400/K-5
2450 Heavilin Rd 46385 219-531-3060
Dr. Bonnie Stephens, prin. Fax 531-3068
Jefferson ES 300/K-5
1700 Roosevelt Rd 46383 219-531-3130
David Muniz, prin. Fax 531-3131
Jefferson MS 700/6-8
1600 Roosevelt Rd 46383 219-531-3140
Elizabeth Krutz, prin. Fax 531-3146
Memorial ES 300/K-5
1052 Park Ave 46385 219-531-3090
Debra Misecko, prin. Fax 531-3094
Northview ES 300/K-5
257 Northview Dr 46383 219-531-3100
Loren Hershberger, prin. Fax 531-3108
Parkview ES 300/K-5
1405 Wood St 46383 219-531-3110
Anne Wodetzki, prin. Fax 531-3112

Immanuel Lutheran S 300/PK-8
1700 Monticello Park Dr 46383 219-462-8207
Joshua Bachman, prin. Fax 531-2238
St. Paul Catholic S 400/PK-8
1755 Harrison Blvd 46385 219-462-3374
Jane Scupham, prin. Fax 477-1763
South Haven Christian S 100/PK-12
786 Juniper Rd 46385 219-759-5313
Michael Owney, prin. Fax 759-1577

Victory Christian Academy 300/PK-12
3805 LaPorte Ave 46383 219-548-8803
Rick Jones, admin. Fax 548-7413

Van Buren, Grant, Pop. 857
Eastbrook Community SC
Supt. — See Marion
Eastbrook North ES 300/K-6
504 S 1st St 46991 765-934-3551
Chris McKim, prin. Fax 934-3552

Veedersburg, Fountain, Pop. 2,156
Southeast Fountain SC 1,200/PK-12
744 E US Highway 136 47987 765-294-2254
Doug Allison, supt. Fax 294-3200
www.sefschools.org/
Southeast Fountain ES 600/PK-6
780 E US Highway 136 47987 765-294-2216
Darren Haas, prin. Fax 294-3206

Versailles, Ripley, Pop. 2,089
South Ripley Community SC 1,200/K-12
PO Box 690 47042 812-689-6282
Robert D. Moorhead, supt. Fax 689-6760
www.sripley.k12.in.us
South Ripley ES 600/K-6
1568 S Benham Rd 47042 812-689-5383
Amy Linkel, prin. Fax 689-6415
South Ripley JHS 200/7-8
1589 S Benham Rd 47042 812-689-0909
Destiny Rutzel, prin. Fax 689-6970

Vevay, Switzerland, Pop. 1,662
Switzerland County SC 1,500/PK-12
1040 W Main St 47043 812-427-2611
Michael Jones, supt. Fax 427-2044
www.switzsc.org
Jefferson-Craig ES 300/PK-6
1002 W Main St 47043 812-427-2170
Tony Spoores, prin. Fax 427-3260
Switzerland County MS 200/7-8
1004 W Main St 47043 812-427-3809
Sean McGarvey, prin. Fax 427-3807
Other Schools – See Rising Sun

Vincennes, Knox, Pop. 18,142
South Knox SC 1,200/K-12
6116 E State Road 61 47591 812-726-4440
Tim Grove, supt. Fax 743-2110
www.sknox.k12.in.us
South Knox ES 700/K-6
6078 E State Road 61 47591 812-743-2591
Alan Drew, prin. Fax 726-4585

Vincennes Community SC 2,700/PK-12
1712 S Quail Run Rd 47591 812-882-4844
Gregory T. Parsley, supt. Fax 885-1427
www.vcsc.k12.in.us
Clark MS 600/6-8
1926 S Richard Bauer Dr 47591 812-882-5172
Ryan Clark, prin. Fax 885-1419
Franklin ES 500/K-5
2600 Wabash Ave 47591 812-882-8176
Melissa Pancake, prin. Fax 885-1440
Riley ES 200/K-5
1008 Upper 11th St 47591 812-882-7953
Susan Marchino, prin. Fax 885-1451
Tecumseh-Harrison ES 300/K-5
2116 N 2nd St 47591 812-882-8458
Jonathan Connor, prin. Fax 885-1422
Vigo ES 400/PK-5
1513 Main St 47591 812-882-5817
Kelley McCarty, prin. Fax 885-1454

Flaget S 200/PK-5
800 Vigo St 47591 812-882-5460
Lori Wissel, prin. Fax 882-5596

Wabash, Wabash, Pop. 10,549
Metro SD of Wabash County 2,100/K-12
204 N 300 W 46992 260-563-8050
Mike Keaffaber, supt. Fax 569-6836
www.msdwc.k12.in.us
Metro North ES 300/K-3
3844 W 200 N 46992 260-563-8050
Janette Moore, prin. Fax 569-6838
Sharp Creek ES 200/4-6
264 W 200 N 46992 260-563-8050
Jay Snyder, prin. Fax 569-6841
Southwood ES 400/K-6
840 E State Road 124 46992 260-563-8050
Phil Boone, prin. Fax 569-6842

Wabash CSD 1,300/PK-12
PO Box 744 46992 260-563-2151
Jason Callahan, supt. Fax 563-2066
www.apaches.k12.in.us
Neighbours ES 500/PK-4
1545 N Wabash St 46992 260-563-2345
Danielle Miller, prin. Fax 563-8883
Wabash MS 300/5-8
150 Colerain St 46992 260-563-4137
Scott Bumgardener, prin. Fax 569-9805

St. Bernard S 100/PK-6
191 N Cass St 46992 260-563-5746
Theresa Carroll, prin. Fax 563-4898

Wadesville, Posey
Metro SD of North Posey County
Supt. — See Poseyville
South Terrace ES 300/PK-6
8427 Haines Rd 47638 812-985-3180
Kelly Carlton, prin. Fax 985-3146

St. Wendel S 100/K-8
4725 St Wendel Cynthiana Rd 47638 812-963-3958
Hallie Scheu, prin. Fax 963-3061

Wakarusa, Elkhart, Pop. 1,739
Penn-Harris-Madison SC
Supt. — See Mishawaka
Madison ES 100/K-5
66030 Dogwood Rd 46573 574-633-4531
Kevin McMillen, prin. Fax 633-4987

Wa-Nee Community SD
Supt. — See Nappanee
Northwood MS 700/6-8
PO Box 367 46573 574-862-2710
Bart Rice, prin. Fax 862-2327
Wakarusa ES 600/K-5
400 N Washington St 46573 574-862-2000
John Payne, prin. Fax 862-2095

Waldron, Shelby, Pop. 796
Shelby Eastern SD
Supt. — See Shelbyville
Waldron ES 300/PK-5
PO Box 38 46182 765-525-6505
Lisa Speidel, prin. Fax 525-4591

Walkerton, Saint Joseph, Pop. 2,125
John Glenn SC 1,900/PK-12
101 John Glenn Dr 46574 574-586-3129
Richard Reese, supt. Fax 586-2660
www.jgsc.k12.in.us
Urey MS 300/7-8
407 Washington St 46574 574-586-3184
Mark Maudlin, prin. Fax 586-3714
Walkerton ES 400/PK-6
805 Washington St 46574 574-586-3186
Tim Davis, prin. Fax 586-3280
Other Schools – See North Liberty

Walton, Cass, Pop. 1,033
Southeastern SC 1,500/PK-12
100 S Main St 46994 574-626-2525
Dr. Tim Garland, supt. Fax 626-2751
www.sescschools.net
Cass ES 400/PK-5
6540 E State Road 218 46994 574-626-2504
Barrett Bates, prin. Fax 626-3483

Wanatah, LaPorte, Pop. 1,033
Tri Township School Corp 400/K-12
PO Box 249 46390 219-754-2461
Tim Somers, supt. Fax 754-2511
www.tritownship.k12.in.us
Wanatah Public S 300/K-8
PO Box 249 46390 219-733-2815
Teri Detering, prin. Fax 733-9974

Warren, Huntington, Pop. 1,231
Huntington County Community SC
Supt. — See Huntington
Salamonie ES 200/K-5
1063 E 900 S 46792 260-468-3093
Dawn Morgan, prin. Fax 375-3435

Warsaw, Kosciusko, Pop. 13,362
Warsaw Community SC 7,100/PK-12
1 Administration Dr 46580 574-371-5098
David Hoffert Ed.D., supt. Fax 371-5046
www.warsaw.k12.in.us
Edgewood MS 600/7-8
900 S Union St 46580 574-371-5096
JoElla Smyth, prin. Fax 371-5010
Eisenhower ES 500/K-6
1900 S County Farm Rd 46580 574-269-7440
Chris Gensinger, prin. Fax 371-5011
Harrison ES 600/K-6
1300 Husky Trl 46582 574-269-7533
Matt Deeds, prin. Fax 371-5007
Lakeview MS 600/7-8
848 E Smith St 46580 574-269-7211
Amy Sivley, prin. Fax 371-5013
Lincoln ES 500/K-6
203 N Lincoln St 46580 574-267-7474
Cathy Snyder, prin. Fax 371-5005
Madison ES 500/K-6
1436 W 300 N 46582 574-267-6231
Tom Kline, prin. Fax 371-5006
Washington STEM Academy 500/K-6
423 Kincaide St 46580 574-371-5097
Tom Ray, prin. Fax 371-5009
Other Schools – See Claypool, Leesburg, Winona Lake

Sacred Heart S 200/PK-6
135 N Harrison St 46580 574-267-5874
Jim Faroh, prin. Fax 267-5136
Warsaw Christian S 100/PK-6
909 S Buffalo St 46580 574-267-5788
Doug Buller, admin. Fax 267-1486

Washington, Daviess, Pop. 11,354
Washington Community SD 2,600/K-12
301 E South St 47501 812-254-5536
Dr. Dan Roach, supt. Fax 254-8346
www.washingtoncommunityschools.org
Dunn ES 400/K-6
801 NW 11th St 47501 812-254-8366
Jeanette Lobeck, prin. Fax 254-9420
Griffith ES 500/K-6
803 E National Hwy 47501 812-254-8360
Tom Lee, prin. Fax 253-8362
North ES 400/K-6
600 NE 6th St 47501 812-254-8363
Jay Wildman, prin. Fax 254-6955
Veale ES 200/K-6
326 E 450 S 47501 812-254-3968
Brenda Butcher, prin. Fax 254-4273
Washington JHS 400/7-8
210 NE 6th St 47501 812-254-2682
Mark Arnold, prin. Fax 254-8381

Washington Catholic ES 100/PK-4
310 NE 2nd St 47501 812-254-3845
Amy Cline, prin. Fax 254-8741

Waterloo, DeKalb, Pop. 2,205
DeKalb County Central United SC 3,700/PK-12
3326 County Road 427 46793 260-920-1011
Steven E. Teders, supt. Fax 837-7767
www.dekalbcentral.net
DeKalb MS 900/6-8
3338 County Road 427 46793 260-920-1013
Matt Vince, prin. Fax 837-7812
Waterloo ES 300/PK-5
300 E Douglas St 46793 260-920-1016
Julia Tipton, prin. Fax 837-7051
Other Schools – See Ashley, Auburn

Westfield, Hamilton, Pop. 29,609
Westfield Washington SD 6,700/PK-12
1143 E 181st St 46074 317-867-8000
Dr. Sherry Grate, supt. Fax 867-0929
www.wws.k12.in.us
Carey Ridge ES 500/PK-4
16231 Carey Rd 46074 317-867-6200
Andy Hilton, prin. Fax 867-2363
Maple Glen ES 600/PK-4
17171 Ditch Rd 46074 317-896-4700
Fax 867-2952
Monon Trail ES 200/K-4
19400 Tomlinson Rd 46074 317-867-8600
Mike Hall, prin. Fax 867-3730
Oak Trace ES 600/PK-4
16504 Oak Ridge Rd 46074 317-867-6400
Robin Lynch, prin. Fax 867-4361
Shamrock Springs ES 400/PK-4
747 W 161st St 46074 317-867-7400
Robb Hedges, prin. Fax 867-1724
Washington Woods ES 400/PK-4
17950 Grassy Branch Rd 46074 317-867-7900
Dr. Scott Williams, prin. Fax 867-1501
Westfield IS 1,100/5-6
326 W Main St 46074 317-867-6500
Annette Patchett, prin. Fax 896-1987
Westfield MS 1,100/7-8
345 W Hoover St 46074 317-867-6600
Ryan Haughey, prin. Fax 867-1407

St. Maria Goretti S 500/PK-8
17104 Spring Mill Rd 46074 317-896-5582
Vince Barnes, prin. Fax 867-0783

West Harrison, Dearborn, Pop. 289
Sunman-Dearborn Community SC
Supt. — See Saint Leon
North Dearborn ES 600/K-5
27650 Sawmill Rd 47060 812-576-1900
Jeffrey Bond, prin. Fax 576-1901

West Lafayette, Tippecanoe, Pop. 29,004
Tippecanoe SC
Supt. — See Lafayette
Battle Ground MS 600/6-8
6100 N 50 W 47906 765-269-8140
Jodi Day, prin. Fax 269-8215
Burnett Creek ES 600/K-5
5700 N 50 W 47906 765-463-2237
Matt Ridenour, prin. Fax 463-2691
Klondike ES 1,000/K-5
3311 Klondike Rd 47906 765-463-5505
Scott Peters, prin. Fax 497-0023
Klondike MS 400/6-8
3307 Klondike Rd 47906 765-463-2544
Christine Cannon, prin. Fax 497-9413

West Lafayette Community SC 2,200/K-12
1130 N Salisbury St 47906 765-746-1602
Dr. Rocky Killion, supt. Fax 746-1644
www.wl.k12.in.us/
Cumberland ES 600/K-3
600 Cumberland Ave 47906 765-464-3212
Kimberly Bowers, prin. Fax 464-3210
Happy Hollow ES 500/4-6
1200 N Salisbury St 47906 765-746-0500
Margaret Psarros, prin. Fax 746-0507

Montessori S of Greater Lafayette 100/PK-3
PO Box 2311 47996 765-464-1133

West Lebanon, Warren, Pop. 721
Metro SD of Warren County
Supt. — See Williamsport
Warren Central ES 300/K-6
1224 S State Road 263 47991 765-893-4525
Mike Holland, prin. Fax 893-8355

West Newton, Marion
Metro SD of Decatur Township
Supt. — See Indianapolis
West Newton ES 600/1-6
7529 Mooresville Rd 46183 317-856-5237
Susan Strube, prin. Fax 856-2148

West Terre Haute, Vigo, Pop. 2,213
Vigo County SC
Supt. — See Terre Haute
Fayette ES 200/K-5
9400 N Beech Pl 47885 812-462-4451
Janel Bonomo, prin. Fax 462-4453
Sugar Creek Consolidated ES 300/K-5
4226 W Old US 40 47885 812-462-4443
Suzanne Marrs, prin. Fax 462-4444
West Vigo ES 300/PK-5
501 W Olive St 47885 812-462-4418
Angileah Bark, prin. Fax 462-4410
West Vigo MS 500/6-8
4750 W Sarah Myers Dr 47885 812-462-4361
Julie Lautenschlager, prin. Fax 462-4358

Westville, LaPorte, Pop. 5,829
Metro SD of New Durham Township 900/PK-12
207 E Valparaiso St 46391 219-785-2239
Dr. Curtiss Strietelmeier, supt. Fax 785-4584
www.westville.k12.in.us/
Westville ES 500/PK-6
207 E Valparaiso St 46391 219-785-2532
Brian Ton, prin. Fax 785-6135

Wheatfield, Jasper, Pop. 846
Kankakee Valley SC 3,500/K-12
PO Box 278 46392 219-987-4711
Dr. Aaron Case, supt. Fax 987-4710
www.kv.k12.in.us
Kankakee Valley IS 500/4-5
12345 N 550 W 46392 219-987-2027
John Shank, prin. Fax 987-3207
Kankakee Valley MS 800/6-8
5258 W State Road 10 46392 219-987-8810
Adam Metzger, prin. Fax 987-2540
Wheatfield ES 400/K-3
PO Box 158 46392 219-956-3221
Cathy Vollmer, prin. Fax 956-4689
Other Schools – See Demotte

Whiteland, Johnson, Pop. 4,117
Clark-Pleasant Community SC 5,700/PK-12
50 Center St 46184 317-535-7579
Dr. Patrick Spray, supt. Fax 535-4931
www.cpcsc.k12.in.us
Pleasant Crossing ES 700/K-5
3030 N 125 W 46184 317-535-3244
Terry Magnuson, prin. Fax 535-0706
Whiteland ES 400/K-5
120 Center St 46184 317-535-4211
Cirsten Lewis, prin. Fax 535-2091
Other Schools – See Franklin, Greenwood, New Whiteland

Whitestown, Boone, Pop. 2,806
Zionsville Community SC
Supt. — See Zionsville
Boone Meadow ES 200/PK-PK, 4-
5555 S Main St 46075 317-873-2226
Tom Hundley, prin. Fax 769-6909
Zionsville West MS 900/5-8
5565 S 700 E 46075 317-873-1240
Kris Devereaux, prin. Fax 769-6909

Traders Point Christian S 600/PK-12
5608 Whitestown Pkwy 46075 317-769-2450
Ron Evans, head sch Fax 769-2466

Whiting, Lake, Pop. 4,948
Hammond CSD
Supt. — See Hammond
Franklin ES 300/K-5
1000 116th St 46394 219-659-1241
Regina Ellis, prin. Fax 554-4579

School City of Whiting 1,200/PK-12
1500 Center St 46394 219-659-0656
Cynthia Scroggins, supt. Fax 473-4008
www.whiting.k12.in.us
Hale ES 500/PK-5
1831 Oliver St 46394 219-659-0738
Julie Pearson, prin. Fax 473-1343
Whiting MS 300/6-8
1800 New York Ave 46394 219-473-1344
Erin Nolan-Higgins, prin. Fax 473-4017

St. John the Baptist S 400/PK-8
1844 Lincoln Ave 46394 219-659-3042
Scott Tabernacki, prin. Fax 473-7553

Williamsport, Warren, Pop. 1,888
Metro SD of Warren County 1,100/K-12
101 N Monroe St 47993 765-762-3364
Ralph Shrader, supt. Fax 762-6623
www.msdwarco.k12.in.us/
Williamsport ES 200/K-6
206 E Monroe St 47993 765-762-2500
Kelly Laffoon, prin. Fax 762-0371
Other Schools – See Pine Village, West Lebanon

Winamac, Pulaski, Pop. 2,467
Eastern Pulaski Community SC 1,300/K-12
711 School Dr 46996 574-946-4010
Dan L. Foster, supt. Fax 946-4510
www.epulaski.k12.in.us/
Eastern Pulaski ES 600/K-5
815 School Dr 46996 574-946-3955
Jill Collins, prin. Fax 946-4510
Winamac Community MS 300/6-8
715 School Dr 46996 574-946-6525
Ryan Dickinson, prin. Fax 946-4219

Winchester, Randolph, Pop. 4,890
Randolph Central SC 1,500/K-12
103 N East St 47394 765-584-1401
Lisa Chalfant, supt. Fax 584-1403
www.rc.k12.in.us
Baker ES 200/K-2
600 S Oak St 47394 765-584-5581
Cynthia Winkle, prin. Fax 584-7900
Driver MS 400/6-8
700 N Union St 47394 765-584-4671
Thomas Osborn, prin. Fax 584-8204
Willard ES 200/3-5
615 W South St 47394 765-584-9171
Jeremy Duncan, prin. Fax 584-5212
Other Schools – See Ridgeville

Winona Lake, Kosciusko, Pop. 4,854
Warsaw Community SC
Supt. — See Warsaw
Jefferson ES 500/PK-6
1 Jefferson Dr 46590 574-267-7361
Kyle Carter, prin. Fax 371-5003

Winslow, Pike, Pop. 859
Pike County SC
Supt. — See Petersburg
Winslow ES 300/PK-5
301 E Porter St 47598 812-789-2209
Ritchie Luker, prin. Fax 789-2795

Wolcott, White, Pop. 982
Tri-County SC 800/K-12
105 N 2nd St 47995 219-279-2418
Dr. Kathy Goad, supt. Fax 279-2242
www.trico.k12.in.us
Tri-County IS 200/3-6
200 W North St 47995 219-279-2138
Brian Hagan, prin. Fax 279-2026
Other Schools – See Remington

Wolcottville, Lagrange, Pop. 994
Lakeland SC
Supt. — See Lagrange
Wolcott Mills ES 200/K-5
108 E Myers St 46795 260-499-2450
Vanessa Wyss, prin. Fax 854-3089

Wolflake, Noble
Central Noble Community SC
Supt. — See Albion
Wolf Lake ES 200/K-5
PO Box 67 46796 260-635-2432
Robby Morgan, prin. Fax 635-2372

Woodburn, Allen, Pop. 1,511
East Allen County SD
Supt. — See New Haven
Woodlan ES 300/K-6
17117 Woodburn Rd 46797 260-446-0280
G. Michael Chen, prin. Fax 446-0283

Woodburn Lutheran S 100/PK-8
PO Box 159 46797 260-632-5493
David Van Spankeren, prin. Fax 632-0005

Worthington, Greene, Pop. 1,456
White River Valley SD
Supt. — See Switz City
WRV ES 200/PK-4
484 W Main St 47471 812-875-3839
Andrea Staggs, prin. Fax 875-2199

Yoder, Allen

St. Aloysius S 100/K-8
14607 Bluffton Rd 46798 260-622-7151
Tina Voors, prin. Fax 622-7961

Yorktown, Delaware, Pop. 9,307
Yorktown Community SC 2,400/K-12
2311 S Broadway St 47396 765-759-2720
Dr. Gregory Hinshaw, supt. Fax 759-7894
www.yorktown.k12.in.us
Pleasant View ES 500/K-2
9101 W River Rd 47396 765-759-2800
Kathy Ray, prin. Fax 759-3258
Yorktown ES 500/3-5
8810 W Smith St 47396 765-759-2770
Heather Lucas, prin. Fax 759-4038
Yorktown MS 600/6-8
8820 W Smith St 47396 765-759-2660
Heath Dudley, prin. Fax 759-3243

Zionsville, Boone, Pop. 13,972
Zionsville Community SC 6,100/PK-12
900 Mulberry St 46077 317-873-2858
Scott Robison, supt. Fax 873-8003
www.zcs.k12.in.us
Eagle ES 400/PK-4
350 N Sixth St 46077 317-873-1234
Christine Squier, prin. Fax 873-5868
Pleasant View ES 800/PK-4
4700 S 975 E 46077 317-873-2376
Chad Smith, prin. Fax 873-1250
Stonegate ES 500/PK-4
7312 W Stonegate Dr 46077 317-873-8050
Connie Largent, prin. Fax 769-4975
Union ES 600/PK-4
11750 E 300 S 46077 317-733-4007
Jennifer Raycroft, prin. Fax 733-4008
Zionsville MS 1,000/5-8
900 N Ford Rd 46077 317-873-2426
Sean Conner, prin. Fax 733-4001
Other Schools – See Whitestown

IOWA

IOWA DEPARTMENT OF EDUCATION
400 E 14th St, Des Moines 50319-0146
Telephone 515-281-5294
Fax 515-242-5988
Website educateiowa.gov/

Director of Education Ryan Wise

IOWA BOARD OF EDUCATION
400 E 14th St, Des Moines 50319-1004

President Charles Edwards

AREA EDUCATION AGENCIES (AEA)

Central Rivers AEA
Julie Davies, dir. 319-273-8200
1521 Technology Pkwy Fax 273-8229
Cedar Falls 50613
www.centralriversaea.org

Grant Wood AEA 10
Joseph Crozier, admin. 319-399-6700
4401 6th St SW Fax 399-6457
Cedar Rapids 52404
www.aea10.k12.ia.us

Great Prairie AEA
Dr. Cindy Yelick, admin. 641-682-8591
2814 N Court St, Ottumwa 52501 Fax 682-9083
www.gpaea.k12.ia.us

Green Hills AEA
Dr. Lane Plugge, admin. 712-366-0503
PO Box 1109, Council Bluffs 51502 Fax 366-7772
www.ghaea.org

Heartland AEA 11
Dr. Jon Sheldahl, admin. 515-270-9030
6500 Corporate Dr Fax 270-5383
Johnston 50131
www.heartlandaea.org

Keystone AEA 1
Patrick Heiderscheit, admin. 563-245-1480
1400 2nd St NW, Elkader 52043 Fax 245-1484
www.aea1.k12.ia.us

Mississippi Bend AEA 9
William Decker, admin. 563-359-1371
729 21st St, Bettendorf 52722 Fax 359-5967
www.mbaea.org

Northwest AEA
Dr. Tim Grieves, admin. 800-352-9040
1520 Morningside Ave Fax 222-6123
Sioux City 51106
www.nwaea.org

Prairie Lakes AEA 8
Jeff Herzberg, admin. 712-335-3588
500 NE 6th St, Pocahontas 50574 Fax 335-5871
www.plaea.org

PUBLIC, PRIVATE AND CATHOLIC ELEMENTARY SCHOOLS

Ackley, Hardin, Pop. 1,584
AGWSR Community SD 600/PK-12
918 4th Ave 50601 641-847-2611
Marty Jimmerson, supt. Fax 847-2612
www.agwsr.org
AGWSR ES 200/K-5
918 4th Ave 50601 641-847-2611
Teresa Keninger, prin. Fax 847-2612
Cougars Den Preschool Center 100/PK-PK
413 State St 50601 641-847-2699
Teresa Keninger, dir. Fax 847-2699
Other Schools – See Wellsburg

Adair, Guthrie, Pop. 778
Adair-Casey Community SD 200/PK-8
3384 Indigo Ave 50002 641-746-2241
Steve Smith, supt. Fax 746-2243
acgcschools.org
AC/GC JHS 50/7-8
3384 Indigo Ave 50002 641-746-2241
Cynthia Jensen, prin. Fax 746-2243
Adair-Casey ES 200/PK-6
3384 Indigo Ave 50002 641-746-2242
Cynthia Jensen, prin. Fax 746-2243

Adel, Dallas, Pop. 3,654
Adel DeSoto Minburn Community SD 1,600/PK-12
215 N 11th St 50003 515-993-4283
Greg Dufoe, supt. Fax 993-1921
www.admschools.org
Adel ES 400/PK-2
1608 Grove St 50003 515-993-4285
Kimberly Anderson, prin. Fax 993-4403
ADM MS 400/6-8
801 Nile Kinnick Dr S 50003 515-993-3490
Kim Timmerman, prin. Fax 993-1956
Other Schools – See De Soto

Afton, Union, Pop. 842
East Union Community SD 500/PK-12
1916 High School Dr 50830 641-347-5215
Lance Ridgely, supt. Fax 347-5514
www.east-union.k12.ia.us
East Union ES 300/PK-5
1916 High School Dr 50830 641-347-5411
Joan Gordon, prin. Fax 347-5514

Akron, Plymouth, Pop. 1,468
Akron Westfield Community SD 600/PK-12
PO Box 950 51001 712-568-2616
Randy Collins, supt. Fax 568-2997
akron-westfield.com
Akron Westfield ES 300/PK-5
PO Box 950 51001 712-568-3322
Cathy Bobier, prin. Fax 568-2997
Akron Westfield MS 100/6-8
PO Box 950 51001 712-568-2020
Derek Briggs, prin. Fax 568-2997

Albert City, Buena Vista, Pop. 695
Albert City-Truesdale Community SD 100/PK-6
PO Box 98 50510 712-843-5416
Rob Olsen, supt. Fax 843-2195
www.albertct.k12.ia.us
Albert City-Truesdale ES 100/PK-6
PO Box 98 50510 712-843-5416
Sarah Voyles, prin. Fax 843-5551

Albia, Monroe, Pop. 3,726
Albia Community SD 1,200/PK-12
701 Washington Ave E 52531 641-932-2161
Kevin Crall, supt. Fax 932-5192
albiacsd.org
Albia JHS 200/7-8
503 B Ave E 52531 641-932-2161
Richard Montgomery, prin. Fax 932-7069
Grant Center ES 300/K-2
520 S Clinton St 52531 641-932-2161
Billy Strickler, prin. Fax 932-5192
Kendall Center Preschool 100/PK-PK
701 Washington Ave E 52531 641-932-2161
Kevin Crall, prin. Fax 932-5192
Lincoln Center ES 300/3-6
222 N 2nd St 52531 641-932-2161
Joellen Breon, prin. Fax 932-5192

Alburnett, Linn, Pop. 663
Alburnett Community SD 500/PK-12
PO Box 400 52202 319-842-2266
Dani Trimble, supt. Fax 842-2398
www.alburnettcsd.org
Alburnett ES 300/PK-5
PO Box 400 52202 319-842-2261
Josh Henriksen, prin. Fax 842-2398

Alden, Hardin, Pop. 774
Alden Community SD 300/PK-6
PO Box 48 50006 515-859-3395
John Robbins, supt. Fax 859-3395
www.ifacadets.net
Alden ES 300/PK-6
PO Box 48 50006 515-859-3394
Kyle Fett, prin. Fax 859-3395

Algona, Kossuth, Pop. 5,513
Algona Community SD 1,400/PK-12
600 S Hale St 50511 515-295-3528
Marty Fonley, supt. Fax 295-5166
www.algona.k12.ia.us
Algona MS 400/5-8
601 S Hale St 50511 515-295-7207
James Rotert, prin. Fax 295-9273
Bryant ES 200/1-2
121 E North St 50511 515-295-7773
Brad Sudol, prin. Fax 295-5824
Godfrey ES 200/PK-K
124 N Main St 50511 515-295-3586
Stacy Mueller, prin. Fax 295-5328
Wallace ES 200/3-4
729 E Kennedy St 50511 515-295-7296
Brad Sudol, prin. Fax 295-6068

Seton S 300/PK-3
808 E Lucas St 50511 515-295-3509
Kristi Hough, prin. Fax 295-5688

Alleman, Polk, Pop. 426
North Polk Community SD 1,500/PK-12
13960 NE 6th Ave 50007 515-984-3400
Dr. Dan Mart Ph.D., supt. Fax 685-2002
www.northpolk.org
North Polk Central ES 400/PK-5
311 NE 141st Ave 50007 515-984-3400
Morgan Miller, prin. Fax 685-2304
North Polk MS 300/6-8
315 NE 141st Ave 50007 515-984-3400
Jon Richards, prin. Fax 685-3520
Other Schools – See Polk City

Allison, Butler, Pop. 1,024
North Butler Community SD 400/PK-12
PO Box 428 50602 319-267-2205
Joel Foster, supt. Fax 267-2926
www.northbutler.k12.ia.us/
North Butler ES 200/PK-6
PO Box 428 50602 319-267-2212
Laura Tracy, prin. Fax 267-2926

Alta, Buena Vista, Pop. 1,871
Alta-Aurelia Community SD 500/PK-12
101 W 5th St 51002 712-200-1010
Lynn Evans, supt. Fax 200-1602
www.alta-aurelia.org
Alta ES 300/PK-4
1009 S Main St 51002 712-200-1400
Kurt Hanna, prin. Fax 200-2459
Other Schools – See Aurelia

Alton, Sioux, Pop. 1,209
MOC-Floyd Valley Community SD
Supt. — See Orange City
MOC-Floyd Valley MS 300/6-8
1104 5th Ave 51003 712-756-4128
Cam Smith, prin. Fax 756-4100

Spalding Catholic S 100/PK-6
PO Box 436 51003 712-756-4532
Maureen Berg, prin. Fax 756-4532

Altoona, Polk, Pop. 14,333
Southeast Polk Community SD
Supt. — See Pleasant Hill
Altoona ES 400/PK-5
301 6th St SW 50009 515-967-3771
Steven Stotts, prin. Fax 967-2079
Centennial ES 500/PK-5
910 7th Ave SE 50009 515-967-2109
Lori Waddell, prin. Fax 967-7076
Clay ES 500/PK-5
3200 1st Ave S 50009 515-967-4198
Lea Morris, prin. Fax 967-2018
Willowbrook ES 500/PK-5
300 17th Ave SW 50009 515-967-7512
Robin Norris, prin. Fax 967-1620

Amana, Iowa, Pop. 442
Clear Creek Amana Community SD
Supt. — See Oxford
Amana ES 200/PK-5
3023 220th Trl 52203 319-622-3255
Ben Macumber, prin. Fax 622-3108

Ames, Story, Pop. 57,846
Ames Community SD 4,400/PK-12
2005 24th St 50010 515-268-6600
Dr. Tim Taylor, supt. Fax 268-6633
www.ames.k12.ia.us
Ames MS 900/6-8
3915 Mortensen Rd 50014 515-268-2400
Dan Fox, prin. Fax 268-2419

Edwards ES 300/K-5
820 Miller Ave 50014 515-239-3760
David Peterson, prin. Fax 239-3814
Fellows ES 500/K-5
1400 Mckinley Dr 50010 515-239-3765
Brandon Schrauth, prin. Fax 239-3837
Meeker ES 400/K-5
300 20th St 50010 515-239-3770
Steve Flynn, prin. Fax 239-3812
Mitchell ES 300/K-5
3521 Jewel Dr 50010 515-239-3775
Justin Jeffs, prin. Fax 239-3823
Northwood Preschool Center 200/PK-PK
3012 Duff Ave 50010 515-268-2470
Kristin Barber, prin. Fax 268-2475
Sawyer ES 400/K-5
4316 Ontario St 50014 515-239-3790
Dr. Sue Lawler, prin. Fax 239-3815

Ames Christian S 100/PK-6
925 S 16th St 50010 515-233-0772
Floyd Athay, admin. Fax 232-0005
St. Cecilia S 200/PK-5
2900 Hoover Ave 50010 515-232-5290
Ervin Rowlands, prin. Fax 233-6423

Anamosa, Jones, Pop. 5,484
Anamosa Community SD 1,300/PK-12
200 S Garnavillo St 52205 319-462-4321
Lisa Beames, supt. Fax 462-4322
www.anamosa.k12.ia.us
Anamosa MS 400/5-8
200 S Garnavillo St 52205 319-462-3553
Linda Vaughn, prin. Fax 462-3309
Strawberry Hill ES 500/PK-4
203 Hamilton St 52205 319-462-3549
Val Daily, prin. Fax 462-5317

St. Patrick S 100/PK-6
216 N Garnavillo St 52205 319-462-2688
Jayne Intlekofer, prin. Fax 462-3239

Andrew, Jackson, Pop. 431
Andrew Community SD 200/PK-8
PO Box 230 52030 563-672-3221
Chris Fee, supt. Fax 672-9750
www.andrew.k12.ia.us
Andrew ES 100/PK-5
PO Box 230 52030 563-672-3221
Tara Notz, prin. Fax 672-9750
Andrew MS 100/6-8
PO Box 230 52030 563-672-3221
Tara Notz, prin. Fax 672-9750

Anita, Cass, Pop. 970
CAM Community SD 400/PK-12
1000 Victory Park Rd 50020 712-762-3231
Dr. Casey Berlau, supt. Fax 762-3713
www.camcougars.org
CAM North ES 100/PK-5
709 McIntyre Dr 50020 712-762-3231
Brian Fogleman, prin. Fax 762-3249
Other Schools – See Massena

Ankeny, Polk, Pop. 45,034
Ankeny Community SD 10,500/PK-12
PO Box 189 50021 515-965-9600
Dr. Bruce Kimpston, supt. Fax 965-4234
www.ankenyschools.org
Ashland Ridge ES 700/K-5
2600 NW Ash Dr, 515-965-9594
Mark Moss, prin. Fax 965-9593
Crocker ES 600/PK-5
2910 SW Applewood St, 515-965-9710
Dr. Tom Muhlenbruck, prin. Fax 965-9714
East ES 400/PK-5
710 SE 3rd St 50021 515-965-9660
Andrew Burg, prin. Fax 965-9663
Northeast ES 700/PK-5
1705 NE Trilein Dr 50021 515-965-9620
Tara Owen, prin. Fax 965-9621
Northwest ES 400/PK-5
1202 W 1st St, 515-965-9680
Travis Busby, prin. Fax 965-9683
Parkview MS 700/6-7
105 NW Pleasant St, 515-965-9640
Jeff Schumacher, prin. Fax 965-9648
Prairie Ridge MS 800/6-7
1010 NW Prairie Ridge Dr, 515-965-9705
James Wichman, prin. Fax 965-9708
Prairie Trail ES 700/PK-5
1850 SW College Ave, 515-965-9605
Dr. Pam Dodge, prin. Fax 289-2825
Rock Creek ES 500/PK-5
3800 NW Abilene Rd, 515-965-9650
Al Neppl, prin.
Southeast ES 700/K-5
1005 SE Trilein Dr 50021 515-965-9650
Ben Muller, prin. Fax 965-9653
Terrace ES 400/PK-5
310 NW School St, 515-965-9670
Matthew Dunsbergen, prin. Fax 965-9672
Westwood ES 700/PK-5
2920 NW 9th St, 515-965-9690
Joel Martin, prin. Fax 965-9693

Ankeny Christian Academy 300/PK-12
1604 W 1st St, 515-965-8114
Dr. Steve Robinson, admin. Fax 965-8210
St. Luke the Evangelist S 50/K-5
1102 NW Weigel Dr, 515-985-7074
Tonya Eaton, prin.

Anthon, Woodbury, Pop. 561
Maple Valley-Anthon Oto Community SD
Supt. — See Mapleton
Anthon ES 100/PK-5
110 W Division St 51004 712-373-5244
Jane Ellis, prin. Fax 373-5326
Maple Valley-Anthon Oto MS 100/6-8
110 W Division St 51004 712-373-5244
Jane Ellis, prin. Fax 373-5326

Aplington, Butler, Pop. 1,123
Aplington-Parkersburg Community SD
Supt. — See Parkersburg
Aplington ES 200/3-5
215 10th St 50604 319-347-6621
Amy May, prin. Fax 347-2395
Aplington-Parkersburg MS 200/6-8
215 10th St 50604 319-347-6621
Brian Buseman, prin. Fax 347-2395

Arlington, Fayette, Pop. 428
Starmont Community SD 600/PK-12
3202 40th St 50606 563-933-4598
Troy Heller, supt. Fax 933-2134
www.starmont.k12.ia.us
Starmont ES 300/PK-5
3202 40th St 50606 563-933-2238
Sandy Klaus, prin. Fax 933-2134
Starmont MS 100/6-8
3202 40th St 50606 563-933-2218
Jason Yessak, prin. Fax 933-2134

Armstrong, Emmet, Pop. 919
North Union SD 600/PK-12
600 4th Ave 50514 515-868-3542
Travis Schueller, supt. Fax 868-3550
www.northunion.k12.ia.us
Other Schools – See Fenton, Swea City

Arnolds Park, Dickinson, Pop. 1,120
Okoboji Community SD
Supt. — See Milford
Okoboji MS 300/5-8
10 W Broadway St 51331 712-332-5641
Ryan Cunningham, prin. Fax 332-7180

Atkins, Benton, Pop. 1,665
Benton Community SD
Supt. — See Van Horne
Atkins ES 200/PK-3
217 4th Ave 52206 319-446-7525
Jason West, prin. Fax 446-7966

Atlantic, Cass, Pop. 7,038
Atlantic Community SD 1,500/PK-12
1100 Linn St 50022 712-243-4252
Steve Barber, supt. Fax 243-8023
www.atlanticiaschools.org
Atlantic MS 300/6-8
1100 Linn St 50022 712-243-1330
Josh Rasmussen, prin. Fax 243-7732
Schuler ES 200/4-5
501 E 11th St 50022 712-243-1370
James Northwick, prin. Fax 243-2120
Washington ES 500/PK-3
500 E 14th St 50022 712-243-5234
Stacey Hornung, prin. Fax 243-5275

Audubon, Audubon, Pop. 2,169
Audubon Community SD 600/PK-12
800 3rd Ave 50025 712-563-2607
Brett Gibbs, supt. Fax 563-3607
www.audubon.k12.ia.us/
Audubon ES 200/PK-4
600 Tracy St 50025 712-563-3751
Sam Graeve, prin. Fax 563-3607

Aurelia, Cherokee, Pop. 1,026
Alta-Aurelia Community SD
Supt. — See Alta
Alta-Aurelia MS 200/5-8
300 Ash St 51005 712-434-5595
Jeannie Henningsen, prin. Fax 434-2053
Aurelia ES 100/PK-4
300 Ash St 51005 712-434-5595
Jeannie Henningsen, prin. Fax 434-2053

Avoca, Pottawattamie, Pop. 1,501
AHSTW Community SD 600/PK-12
768 S Maple St 51521 712-343-6364
Jesse Ulrich, supt. Fax 343-2170
www.ahstwschools.org
AHSTW ES 300/PK-6
768 S Maple St 51521 712-343-6364
Sarah Kock, prin. Fax 343-2170

Barnum, Webster, Pop. 190
Manson Northwest Webster Community SD
Supt. — See Manson
Manson Northwest Webster ES 400/PK-6
303 Pierce St 50518 515-542-3211
Bret Larson, prin. Fax 542-3214

Baxter, Jasper, Pop. 1,091
Baxter Community SD 400/PK-12
PO Box 189 50028 641-227-3102
Todd Martin, supt. Fax 227-3217
www.baxter.k12.ia.us
Baxter ES 200/PK-5
PO Box 189 50028 641-227-3102
Josh Russell, prin. Fax 227-3217

Bedford, Taylor, Pop. 1,430
Bedford Community SD 500/PK-12
PO Box 234 50833 712-523-2656
Joe Drake, supt. Fax 523-3166
www.bedford.k12.ia.us
Bedford ES 200/PK-5
PO Box 234 50833 712-523-2116
Dana Nally, prin. Fax 523-2308

Belle Plaine, Benton, Pop. 2,512
Belle Plaine Community SD 600/PK-12
707 7th St 52208 319-444-3611
Chad Straight, supt. Fax 444-3617
www.belle-plaine.k12.ia.us
Longfellow ES 300/PK-6
707 7th St 52208 319-444-3002
Heather Coover, prin. Fax 444-3064

Bellevue, Jackson, Pop. 2,180
Bellevue Community SD 700/PK-12
1601 State St 52031 563-872-4001
Dr. Tom Meyer, supt. Fax 872-3216
www.bellevue.k12.ia.us
Bellevue ES 300/PK-6
100 S 3rd St 52031 563-872-4001
Jeanette Hartung-Schroed, prin. Fax 872-5049

Marquette HS 100/PK-12
502 Franklin St 52031 563-872-3356
Geoffery Kaiser, prin. Fax 872-3285

Belmond, Wright, Pop. 2,355
Belmond-Klemme Community SD 800/PK-12
411 10th Ave NE 50421 641-444-4300
Dan Frazier, supt. Fax 444-4524
www.bkcsd.org
Jacobson ES 500/PK-6
1004 7th St NE 50421 641-444-4300
Mark Young, prin. Fax 444-4360

Bennett, Cedar, Pop. 403
Bennett Community SD 100/PK-6
PO Box D 52721 563-890-2226
David Larson, supt. Fax 890-2937
www.bennett.k12.ia.us/
Bennett ES 100/PK-6
PO Box D 52721 563-890-2226
David Larson, supt. Fax 890-2937

Bettendorf, Scott, Pop. 32,699
Bettendorf Community SD 4,500/PK-12
PO Box 1150 52722 563-359-3681
Michael Raso, supt. Fax 359-3685
www.bettendorf.k12.ia.us
Armstrong ES 300/PK-5
3311 Central Ave 52722 563-359-8275
David Hlas, prin. Fax 359-5228
Bettendorf MS 1,000/6-8
2030 Middle Rd 52722 563-359-3686
Lisa Reid, prin. Fax 359-3855
Hoover ES 400/K-5
3223 S Hampton Dr 52722 563-332-8636
Karen Allison, prin. Fax 332-5148
Jefferson ES 200/PK-5
610 Holmes St 52722 563-359-8261
Lana LaSalle, prin. Fax 359-6641
Norton ES 400/K-5
4485 Greenbrier Dr 52722 563-332-8936
Brian Walthart, prin. Fax 332-9619
Twain ES 300/PK-5
1620 Lincoln Rd 52722 563-359-8263
Caroline Olson, prin. Fax 355-2735
Wood ES 300/PK-5
1423 Hillside Dr 52722 563-359-8277
John Cain, prin. Fax 359-5254

Pleasant Valley Community SD 4,300/PK-12
525 Belmont Rd 52722 563-332-5550
Jim Spelhaug, supt. Fax 332-4372
www.pleasval.k12.ia.us
Hopewell ES 400/K-6
3900 Hopewell Ave 52722 563-449-5771
Christopher Welch, prin. Fax 332-0255
Pleasant View ES 600/K-6
6333 Crow Creek Rd 52722 563-332-5575
Steven Cotton, prin. Fax 332-0223
Riverdale Heights ES 600/K-6
2125 Devils Glen Rd 52722 563-332-0525
Jennifer Gertson, prin. Fax 332-0224
Other Schools – See Le Claire

Lourdes Catholic S 300/PK-8
1453 Mississippi Blvd 52722 563-359-3466
Jennifer Alongi, prin. Fax 823-1595
Morning Star Academy 200/PK-12
1426 Tanglefoot Ln 52722 563-359-5700
Rob Spykstra, hdmstr. Fax 359-5737
Rivermont Collegiate 200/PK-12
1821 Sunset Dr 52722 563-359-1366
Max Roach, hdmstr. Fax 359-7576

Blairsburg, Hamilton, Pop. 214
Northeast Hamilton Community SD 100/PK-6
606 Illinois St 50034 515-325-6234
Mike Sherwood, supt. Fax 325-6235
www.ne-hamilton.k12.ia.us
Northeast Hamilton ES 100/PK-6
606 Illinois St 50034 515-325-6234
Mike Kruger, prin. Fax 325-6235

Blakesburg, Wapello, Pop. 295
Eddyville-Blakesburg-Fremont Comm SD
Supt. — See Eddyville
Blakesburg ES 100/PK-6
407 Wilson St 52536 641-938-2202
Sheryl Friedman, admin. Fax 938-2613

Bloomfield, Davis, Pop. 2,620
Davis County Community SD 1,300/PK-12
608 S Washington St 52537 641-664-2200
Dan Maeder, supt. Fax 664-2221
www.dcmustangs.com/
Davis County ES 600/PK-4
500 E North St 52537 641-664-2200
Melissa Carson-Roark, prin. Fax 664-1764
Davis County MS 300/5-8
500 E North St 52537 641-664-2200
Bradley McCloskey, prin. Fax 664-1767

Blue Grass, Scott, Pop. 1,438
Davenport Community SD
Supt. — See Davenport
Blue Grass ES 300/K-5
226 W Sycamore St 52726 563-723-6200
Diane Simmons, prin. Fax 445-5964

Bode, Humboldt, Pop. 299
Twin Rivers Community SD 100/PK-5
PO Box 153 50519 515-379-1309
Greg Darling, supt. Fax 379-1645
www.trv.k12.ia.us
Twin Rivers ES 100/PK-5
PO Box 121 50519 515-379-1309
Donald Hasenkamp, prin. Fax 379-1645

Bondurant, Polk, Pop. 3,802
Bondurant-Farrar Community SD 1,100/PK-12
300 Garfield St SW 50035 515-967-7819
Dr. Rich Powers, supt. Fax 967-7847
www.bfschools.org
Anderson ES 300/PK-PK, 3-
400 Garfield St SW 50035 515-967-7494
Mel Hewitt, prin. Fax 957-9099
Bondurant-Farrar MS 400/6-8
300 Garfield St SW 50035 515-967-3711
Mike Kramer, prin. Fax 957-9924
Morris ES K-2
600 Garfield St SW 50035 515-967-6361
Benjiman Anderson, prin. Fax 967-5088

Boone, Boone, Pop. 12,525
Boone Community SD 2,100/PK-12
500 7th St 50036 515-433-0750
Dr. Bradley Manard, supt. Fax 433-0753
boone.k12.ia.us/
Boone MS 600/5-8
1640 1st St 50036 515-433-0020
Scott Kelley, prin. Fax 433-0026
Franklin ES 400/2-4
1903 Crawford St 50036 515-433-0860
Trish Carlson, prin. Fax 433-0950
Lincoln ES 100/K-1
711 W Mamie Eisenhower Ave 50036 515-433-0800
Autumn Seiler, prin. Fax 433-0753
Page ES 200/PK-1
102 S Boone St 50036 515-433-0840
Autumn Seiler, prin. Fax 433-0753

United Community SD 300/PK-6
1284 U Ave 50036 515-432-5319
Tim Salmon, supt. Fax 432-8930
www.united.k12.ia.us
United North ES 100/PK-1
1284 U Ave 50036 515-432-5393
Tim Salmon, prin. Fax 432-8930
United South ES 100/2-6
1284 U Ave 50036 515-432-5319
Tim Salmon, prin. Fax 432-8930

Sacred Heart S 200/PK-8
1111 Marshall St 50036 515-432-4124
Susan Eldridge, prin. Fax 433-9927
Trinity Lutheran S, 712 12th St 50036 100/PK-8
Cindy Pezzetti, prin. 515-432-6912

Boyden, Sioux, Pop. 706
Boyden-Hull Community SD
Supt. — See Hull
Boyden ES 300/K-6
PO Box 129 51234 712-725-2381
Thomas Kerr, prin. Fax 725-2082

Britt, Hancock, Pop. 2,051
West Hancock Community SD 700/PK-12
PO Box 278 50423 641-843-3833
Wayne Kronemann, supt. Fax 843-4717
www.whancock.org/
West Hancock ES 300/PK-4
PO Box 278 50423 641-843-3833
Michele DeHart, prin. Fax 843-4717
Other Schools – See Kanawha

Bronson, Woodbury, Pop. 318
Lawton-Bronson Community SD
Supt. — See Lawton
Bronson ES 400/PK-6
113 W 1st St 51007 712-948-3361
Chad Shook, prin. Fax 948-3211

Brooklyn, Poweshiek, Pop. 1,455
Brooklyn-Guernsey-Malcom Community SD 600/PK-12
1090 Jackson St 52211 641-522-7058
Brad Hohensee, supt. Fax 522-7211
www.brooklyn.k12.ia.us
Brooklyn-Guernsey-Malcom ES 300/PK-6
1090 Jackson St 52211 641-522-9268
Mary Sherwood, prin. Fax 522-7009

Buffalo, Scott, Pop. 1,251
Davenport Community SD
Supt. — See Davenport
Buffalo ES 200/PK-5
329 Dodge St 52728 563-723-6300
Heidi Gilliland, prin. Fax 445-5966

Buffalo Center, Winnebago, Pop. 902
North Iowa Community SD 500/PK-12
111 3rd Ave NW 50424 641-562-2525
Cory Myer, supt. Fax 562-2921
www.northiowa.org
North Iowa ES 200/PK-4
111 3rd Ave NW 50424 641-562-2525
Jill Schutjer, prin. Fax 562-2921
North Iowa MS 100/5-8
111 3rd Ave NW 50424 641-562-2525
Jill Schutjer, prin. Fax 562-2921

Burlington, Des Moines, Pop. 24,989
Burlington Community SD 3,800/PK-12
1429 West Ave 52601 319-753-6791
Patrick Coen, supt. Fax 753-6796
www.bcsds.org
Black Hawk ES 500/PK-5
2804 S 14th St 52601 319-753-5300
Chris Richards, prin. Fax 753-5097
Corse ES 300/PK-5
700 S Starr Ave 52601 319-753-2707
Mark Taylor, prin. Fax 753-9862
Grimes ES 400/PK-5
800 South St 52601 319-753-0420
Joe Rector, prin. Fax 753-6039
Leopold MS 400/6-8
3075 Sunnyside Ave 52601 319-752-8390
Mark Yeoman, prin. Fax 752-8447
North Hill ES 400/PK-5
825 N 9th St 52601 319-753-6363
Tim Cradic, prin. Fax 753-6901
Stone MS 6-8
3000 Mason Rd 52601 319-752-4393
Angela Butler, prin. Fax 752-7437
Sunnyside ES 500/PK-5
2040 Sunnyside Ave 52601 319-753-5244
Tim Bolander, prin. Fax 753-1856

Great River Christian S 100/PK-12
426 Harrison Ave 52601 319-753-2255
Dr. Tim Ahern, admin. Fax 753-2030
Notre Dame ES 300/PK-5
700 S Roosevelt Ave 52601 319-752-3776
Bill Maupin, prin. Fax 752-8690

Burnside, Webster
Southeast Webster-Grand Community SD 300/PK-8
PO Box 49 50521 515-359-2235
Brian Johnson, supt. Fax 359-2236
www.southeastvalley.org
Other Schools – See Dayton

Bussey, Marion, Pop. 420
Twin Cedars Community SD 400/PK-12
2204 Highway G71 50044 641-944-5241
Brian VanderSluis, supt. Fax 944-5824
www.twincedarscsd.org
Twin Cedars ES 200/PK-6
2204 Highway G71 50044 641-944-5245
Brian VanderSluis, prin. Fax 944-5824

Calamus, Clinton, Pop. 426
Calamus-Wheatland Community SD
Supt. — See Wheatland
Calamus-Wheatland ES 300/PK-6
PO Box 158 52729 563-246-2221
Lonnie Luepker, prin. Fax 246-2680

Calmar, Winneshiek, Pop. 970
South Winneshiek Community SD 500/PK-12
PO Box 430 52132 563-562-3269
Kris Einck, supt. Fax 562-3260
www.southwinn.com
Other Schools – See Ossian

C F S Consolidated S 50/PK-3
PO Box 815 52132 563-562-3291
Kathryn Schmitt, prin. Fax 562-3292

Camanche, Clinton, Pop. 4,417
Camanche Community SD 1,100/PK-12
702 13th Ave 52730 563-259-3000
Thomas Parker, supt. Fax 259-3005
www.camanche.k12.ia.us
Camanche ES 400/PK-4
508 11th Pl 52730 563-259-3016
Aimee Dohse, prin. Fax 259-3053
Camanche MS 300/5-8
1400 9th St 52730 563-259-3014
Justin Shaffer, prin. Fax 259-3031

Cambridge, Story, Pop. 820
Ballard Community SD
Supt. — See Huxley
Ballard East ES 400/3-5
505 W 4th St 50046 515-220-4306
Michael Manock, prin. Fax 220-4310

Carlisle, Warren, Pop. 3,818
Carlisle Community SD 2,100/PK-12
430 School St 50047 515-989-3589
Bryce Amos, supt. Fax 989-3075
carlislecsd.org
Carlisle ES 700/PK-3
430 School St 50047 515-989-0339
Barb Niemeyer, prin. Fax 989-3075
Carlisle MS 500/6-8
325 Scotch Ridge Rd 50047 515-989-0833
John Elkin, prin. Fax 989-4521
Other Schools – See Hartford

Carroll, Carroll, Pop. 9,988
Carroll Community SD 1,500/PK-12
1026 N Adams St 51401 712-792-8001
Rob Cordes, supt. Fax 792-8008
www.carroll.k12.ia.us
Adams ES 100/3-4
1026 N Adams St 51401 712-792-8040
Sue Ruch, prin. Fax 792-8008
Carroll MS 400/5-8
3203 N Grant Rd 51401 712-792-8020
Jerry Raymond, prin. Fax 792-8024
Fairview ES 600/PK-2
525 E 18th St 51401 712-792-8030
Sue Ruch, prin. Fax 792-8074

Kuemper Catholic Grade S 300/PK-3
201 S Clark St 51401 712-792-3610
Ted Garringer, prin. Fax 792-8072
Kuemper Catholic Grade S 200/4-5
116 S East St 51401 712-792-8071
Ted Garringer, prin. Fax 792-8072
Kuemper Catholic MS 200/6-8
1519 N West St 51401 712-792-2123
Ted Garringer, prin. Fax 792-3365

Carson, Pottawattamie, Pop. 809
Riverside Community SD 700/PK-12
PO Box 218 51525 712-484-2212
Dr. Timothy Mitchell, supt. Fax 484-3957
www.riversideschools.org
Riverside Community IS 100/4-6
PO Box 218 51525 712-484-2291
Jamie Meek, prin. Fax 484-3957
Other Schools – See Oakland

Carter Lake, Pottawattamie, Pop. 3,735
Council Bluffs Community SD
Supt. — See Council Bluffs
Carter Lake ES 400/PK-5
1000 Willow Dr 51510 712-347-5876
Doreen Knuth, prin. Fax 347-5273

Cascade, Dubuque, Pop. 2,146
Western Dubuque Community SD
Supt. — See Farley
Cascade ES 200/PK-6
110 Harrison St SE 52033 563-852-3335
Dan Wendler, prin. Fax 852-7322

Aquin Catholic S 300/PK-8
PO Box 460 52033 563-852-3331
Vicki Palmer, prin. Fax 852-5269

Cedar Falls, Black Hawk, Pop. 38,680
Cedar Falls Community SD 5,200/PK-12
1002 W 1st St 50613 319-553-3000
Dr. Andy Pattee, supt. Fax 277-0614
www.cfschools.org/
Cedar Heights ES 500/PK-6
2417 Rainbow Dr 50613 319-553-2855
Brian Ortman, prin. Fax 268-2355
Hansen ES 500/PK-6
616 Holmes Dr 50613 319-553-2775
Tara Estep, prin. Fax 268-2347
Lincoln ES 600/PK-6
321 W 8th St 50613 319-553-2950
Ralph Bryant, prin. Fax 266-2827
North Cedar ES 300/PK-6
2419 Fern Ave 50613 319-553-2810
Katherine Johnston, prin. Fax 268-2336
Orchard Hill ES 400/PK-6
3909 Rownd St 50613 319-553-2465
Andrea Christopher, prin. Fax 268-2353
Southdale ES 600/PK-6
627 Orchard Dr 50613 319-553-2900
Kim Cross, prin. Fax 266-3448

St. Patrick S 200/PK-8
615 Washington St 50613 319-277-6781
Bev Mach, prin. Fax 266-5806
Valley Lutheran S 100/K-12
4520 Rownd St 50613 319-266-4565
Brian L'Heureux, head sch Fax 266-4054

Cedar Rapids, Linn, Pop. 122,869
Cedar Rapids Community SD 16,400/PK-12
2500 Edgewood Rd NW 52405 319-558-2000
Dr. Brad Buck, supt.
www.cr.k12.ia.us
Arthur ES, 2630 B Ave NE 52402 400/PK-5
Angi Hoyer, prin. 319-558-2264
Cleveland ES 400/PK-5
2200 1st Ave NW 52405 319-558-2463
Denise Pape, prin.
Coolidge ES, 6225 1st Ave SW 52405 500/PK-5
Greg O'Connell, prin. 319-558-2167
Erskine ES, 600 36th St SE 52403 400/K-5
Annette Zimmerman, prin. 319-558-2364
Franklin MS, 300 20th St NE 52402 600/6-8
Lucas Ptacek, prin. 319-558-2452
Garfield ES 300/PK-5
1201 Maplewood Dr NE 52402 319-558-2169
Joy Long, prin.
Gibson ES, 6101 Gibson Dr NE 52411 500/PK-5
Shannon Kehoe, prin. 319-558-2920
Grant ES, 254 Outlook Dr SW 52404 400/PK-5
Monica Frey, prin. 319-558-2020
Harding MS, 4801 Golf St NE 52402 800/6-8
Linda Reysack, prin. 319-558-2254
Harrison ES, 1310 11th St NW 52405 400/PK-5
Trista Manternach, prin. 319-558-2269
Hoover ES 400/PK-5
4141 Johnson Ave NW 52405 319-558-2369
Clint Stone, prin.
Jackson ES, 1300 38th St NW 52405 400/PK-5
Nicholas Duffy, prin. 319-558-2471
Johnson ES, 355 18th St SE 52403 400/PK-5
Candace Lynch, prin. 319-558-2174
Kenwood ES, 3700 E Ave NE 52402 400/PK-5
David Brandon, prin. 319-558-2273
Madison ES 300/K-5
1341 Woodside Dr NW 52405 319-558-2473
Jim Girdner, prin.
McKinley MS 500/6-8
620 10th St SE 52403 319-558-2348
Jason Martinez, prin. Fax 398-2347
Pierce ES, 4343 Marilyn Dr NE 52402 400/PK-5
Kathleen Ziegler, prin. 319-558-2373
Roosevelt MS, 300 13th St NW 52405 600/6-8
Autumn Pino, prin. 319-558-2153
Taft MS, 5200 E Ave NW 52405 600/6-8
Gary Hatfield, prin. 319-558-2243
Taylor ES, 720 7th Ave SW 52404 300/PK-5
Andrea Scott, prin. 319-558-2477
Truman ES, 441 W Post Rd NW 52405 300/PK-5
Tammi Kuba, prin. 319-558-2375
Van Buren ES 400/PK-5
2525 29th St SW 52404 319-558-2377
Kent Ryan, prin. Fax 654-8647
Wilson MS, 2301 J St SW 52404 400/6-8
Jenifer Phelan, prin. 319-558-2156
Wood ES, 645 26th St SE 52403 300/K-5
Cindy Stock, prin. 319-558-2467
Wright ES 400/PK-5
1524 Hollywood Blvd NE 52402 319-558-2278
Brian Krob, prin.
Other Schools – See Hiawatha

College Community SD 5,200/PK-12
401 76th Ave SW 52404 319-848-5200
John Speer, supt. Fax 848-4019
www.prairiepride.org
Prairie Creek IS 800/5-6
401 76th Ave SW 52404 319-848-5310
Eric Townsley, prin. Fax 848-5323
Prairie Crest ES 500/PK-4
401 76th Ave SW 52404 319-848-5280
Jennifer Nurre, prin. Fax 848-4019
Prairie Heights ES 600/PK-4
401 76th Ave SW 52404 319-848-5230
Matthew Russell, prin. Fax 848-5254
Prairie Hill ES PK-4
401 76th Ave SW 52404 319-848-5330
Scott Schipper, prin. Fax 848-5327
Prairie Ridge ES 600/PK-4
401 76th Ave SW 52404 319-848-5100
Amy Beach, prin. Fax 848-5103
Prairie View ES 500/PK-4
401 76th Ave SW 52404 319-848-5260
Michael Hansen, prin. Fax 848-4019

Linn-Mar Community SD
Supt. — See Marion
Bowman Woods ES 400/K-5
151 Boyson Rd NE 52402 319-447-3240
Tina March, prin. Fax 373-2592

All Saints S 300/PK-5
720 29th St SE 52403 319-363-4110
Megan Boomgarden, prin. Fax 363-9547
Andrews Christian Academy 50/K-8
2773 Edgewood Rd 52411 319-393-1664
Cedar Valley Christian S 200/PK-12
3636 Cottage Grove Ave SE 52403 319-366-7462
Jeffrey Pospisil, prin. Fax 247-0037
Good Shepherd Lutheran S 50/K-8
2900 42nd St NE 52402 319-393-5656
Emily Seeber, prin.
Holy Family - LaSalle MS 100/6-8
3700 1st Ave NW 52405 319-396-7792
Kimberly Graven, prin. Fax 390-6527
Holy Family - St. Jude Center 400/PK-5
3700 1st Ave NW 52405 319-396-7818
Jamie Larson, prin. Fax 362-0952
Holy Family - St. Ludmila S 100/PK-5
215 21st Ave SW 52404 319-362-1943
Jamie Larson, prin. Fax 364-4149
Newton Christian Academy 200/PK-9
1635 Linmar Dr NE 52402 319-362-9512
Dean Ridder, head sch Fax 362-5610
Regis MS 500/6-8
735 Prairie Dr NE 52402 319-363-1968
Beth Globokar, prin. Fax 247-6099
St. Matthew S 300/PK-5
2244 1st Ave NE 52402 319-362-3021
Joseph Wolf, prin. Fax 362-7946
St. Pius X / St. Elizabeth Ann Seton S 400/PK-5
4901 Council St NE 52402 319-393-4507
Brian O'Donnell, prin. Fax 393-9424
Summit S 100/PK-8
1010 Regent St NE 52402 319-294-2036
Trinity Lutheran S 200/PK-8
1361 7th Ave SW 52404 319-362-6952
Mark Mueller M.Ed., prin. Fax 366-1569

Center Point, Linn, Pop. 2,394
Center Point-Urbana Community SD 1,500/PK-12
PO Box 296 52213 319-849-1102
Matt Berninghaus, supt. Fax 849-2312
www.cpuschools.org/
Center Point-Urbana MS 300/6-8
PO Box 296 52213 319-849-1102
Brent Winterhof, prin. Fax 849-1758
Center Point-Urbana PS 400/PK-2
PO Box 296 52213 319-849-1102
Ann Wooldridge, prin. Fax 849-3811
Other Schools – See Urbana

Centerville, Appanoose, Pop. 5,460
Centerville Community SD 1,400/PK-12
PO Box 370 52544 641-856-0601
Tom Rubel, supt. Fax 856-0656
www.centervilleschools.org
Centerville Community Preschool 50/PK-PK
603 N 10th St 52544 641-856-0749
Dianne Fatka, prin.
Central ES 200/K-1
320 Drake Ave 52544 641-856-0709
Dianne Fatka, prin. Fax 856-0881
Howar JHS 200/6-8
850 S Park Ave 52544 641-856-0760
Karen Swanson, prin. Fax 856-0761
Lakeview ES 400/2-5
1800 S 11th St 52544 641-856-0637
Terri Schofield, prin. Fax 856-0641

Central City, Linn, Pop. 1,249
Central City Community SD 400/PK-12
400 Barber St 52214 319-438-6181
Dr. Tim Cronin, supt. Fax 438-6110
www.central-city.k12.ia.us
Central City ES 200/PK-5
400 Barber St 52214 319-438-6181
Amy Smith, prin. Fax 438-6110
Central City MS 100/6-8
400 Barber St 52214 319-438-6181
Jason McLaughlin, prin. Fax 438-6110

Chariton, Lucas, Pop. 4,293
Chariton Community SD 1,300/PK-12
PO Box 738 50049 641-774-5967
Paula Wright, supt. Fax 774-8511
www.chariton.k12.ia.us/
Chariton MS 300/6-8
1300 N 16th St 50049 641-774-5114
Joe Ortega, prin. Fax 774-4109
Columbus ES 300/PK-2
1215 Linden Ave 50049 641-774-4712
Derek Philips, prin. Fax 774-0988
Van Allen ES 300/3-5
1129 Ashland Ave 50049 641-774-5047
Joshua Morgan, prin. Fax 774-5717

Charles City, Floyd, Pop. 7,583
Charles City Community SD 1,200/PK-12
500 N Grand Ave 50616 641-257-6500
Dr. Dan Cox, supt. Fax 257-6509
www.charlescityschools.org
Charles City MS 400/6-8
1200 1st Ave 50616 641-257-6530
Rick Gabel, prin. Fax 228-9842
Lincoln ES 100/3-5
600 5th Ave 50616 641-257-6560
Marcia DeVore, prin. Fax 257-6562
Washington ES 200/PK-2
1406 N Grand Ave 50616 641-257-6570
Kara Shannon, prin. Fax 257-6573

Immaculate Conception S 200/PK-6
1203 Clark St 50616 641-228-1225
Lynette Hackett, prin. Fax 228-7692

Charter Oak, Crawford, Pop. 501
Charter Oak-Ute Community SD 300/PK-8
321 Main St 51439 712-678-3325
Rollie Wiebers, supt. Fax 678-3626
co-u.net
Charter Oak-Ute ES 100/PK-5
321 Main St 51439 712-678-3777
Adam Eggeling, prin. Fax 678-3626
Charter Oak-Ute JHS 100/6-8
321 Main St 51439 712-678-3325
Adam Eggeling, prin. Fax 678-3626

Cherokee, Cherokee, Pop. 5,205
Cherokee Community SD 1,000/PK-12
600 W Bluff St 51012 712-225-6767
Kimberly Lingenfelter, supt. Fax 225-6769
www.ccsd.k12.ia.us/
Cherokee MS 300/5-8
206 Indian St 51012 712-225-6750
Scot Aden, prin. Fax 225-4841
Roosevelt ES 400/PK-4
929 N Roosevelt Ave 51012 712-225-6760
Valery Fuhrman, prin. Fax 225-4202

Churdan, Greene, Pop. 379
Paton-Churdan Community SD 200/PK-12
PO Box 157 50050 515-389-3111
Kreg Lensch, supt. Fax 389-3113
www.paton-churdan.k12.ia.us
Paton-Churdan ES 100/PK-5
PO Box 157 50050 515-389-3111
Annie Smith, prin. Fax 389-3113

Clarinda, Page, Pop. 5,483
Clarinda Community SD 1,200/PK-12
PO Box 59 51632 712-542-5165
Deron Stender, supt. Fax 542-3802
www.clarinda.k12.ia.us
Clarinda MS 300/5-8
PO Box 59 51632 712-542-2132
Josh Porter, prin. Fax 542-5949
Garfield ES 400/PK-4
PO Box 59 51632 712-542-4510
Cynthia Opperman, prin. Fax 542-5949

Clarinda Lutheran S 100/K-8
707 W Scidmore St 51632 712-542-3657
Merrilee Sump, prin. Fax 542-3657

Clarion, Wright, Pop. 2,837
Clarion-Goldfield-Dows Community SD 1,000/PK-12
120 Central Ave E 50525 515-532-3423
Dr. Robert Olson, supt. Fax 209-3751
www.clargold.org
Clarion-Goldfield-Dows ES 500/PK-5
319 3rd Ave NE 50525 515-532-2873
Tricia Rosendahl, prin. Fax 532-2628
Clarion-Goldfield-Dows MS 200/6-8
300 3rd Ave NE 50525 515-532-2412
Steve Haberman, prin. Fax 532-2741

Clarksville, Butler, Pop. 1,422
Clarksville Community SD 300/PK-12
318 N Mather St 50619 319-278-4008
Randy Strabala, supt. Fax 278-4618
www.clarksville.k12.ia.us/
Clarksville ES 200/PK-6
318 N Mather St 50619 319-278-4560
Eric Eckerman, prin. Fax 278-4618

Clear Lake, Cerro Gordo, Pop. 7,667
Clear Lake Community SD 1,500/PK-12
1529 3rd Ave N 50428 641-357-2181
Doug Gee, supt. Fax 357-2182
www.clearlakeschools.org
Clear Creek ES 600/K-5
901 S 14th St 50428 641-357-5288
Sally Duesenberg, prin. Fax 357-5701
Clear Lake MS 300/6-8
1601 3rd Ave N 50428 641-357-6114
Steve Kwikkel, prin. Fax 357-8353
Suncot ES, 408 Marc Hill Dr 50428 200/PK-PK
Sally Duesenberg, admin.

Clear Lake Classical ES 50/K-7
113 Lakeview Meadows Ct 50428 630-854-3006

Clinton, Clinton, Pop. 26,311
Clinton Community SD 2,800/PK-12
1401 12th Ave N 52732 563-243-9600
Gary DeLacy, supt. Fax 243-2415
www.clinton.k12.ia.us
Bluff ES 400/PK-5
1421 S Bluff Blvd 52732 563-242-1606
Kristine Cooley, prin. Fax 243-0480
Clinton MS, 1350 14th St NW 52732 6-8
Dan Boyd, prin. 563-243-0466
Eagle Heights ES 500/K-5
1350 Main Ave 52732 563-243-4288
Rhett Weis, prin. Fax 243-4289
Jefferson ES 400/PK-5
720 4th Ave S 52732 563-243-0479
Theresa Zahs, prin. Fax 243-0462
Whittier ES 300/PK-5
1310 2nd Ave S 52732 563-243-3230
Brian Kenney, prin. Fax 243-0461

Prince of Peace Catholic S 300/PK-12
312 S 4th St 52732 563-242-1663
Nancy Peart, prin. Fax 243-8272

Clive, Polk, Pop. 15,239
Waukee Community SD
Supt. — See Waukee
Shuler ES 700/PK-5
16400 Douglas Pkwy 50325 515-987-8597
Joel Fey, prin. Fax 987-1536

West Des Moines Community SD
Supt. — See West Des Moines
Crestview S of Inquiry 500/PK-6
8355 Franklin Ave 50325 515-633-5700
John Villotti, dir. Fax 633-5799
Indian Hills JHS 700/7-8
9401 Indian Hills Dr 50325 515-633-4700
Shane Christensen, prin. Fax 633-4799

Colesburg, Delaware, Pop. 400
Edgewood-Colesburg Community SD
Supt. — See Edgewood
Edgewood-Colesburg ES 300/PK-6
PO Box 125 52035 563-856-2415
Rob Busch, prin. Fax 856-2113

Colfax, Jasper, Pop. 2,079
Colfax-Mingo Community SD 700/PK-12
204 N League Rd 50054 515-674-3646
Jim Verlengia, supt. Fax 674-3921
www.colfax-mingo.k12.ia.us
Colfax-Mingo ES 400/PK-6
20 W Broadway St 50054 515-674-3465
Brian Summy, prin. Fax 674-4396

College Springs, Page, Pop. 207
South Page Community SD 200/PK-12
PO Box 98 51637 712-582-3212
Tim Hood, supt. Fax 582-3217
www.southpageschools.com
South Page ES 100/PK-5
PO Box 98 51637 712-582-3212
Denise Green, prin. Fax 582-3217

Collins, Story, Pop. 491
Collins-Maxwell Community SD
Supt. — See Maxwell
Collins-Maxwell ES 200/PK-5
416 4th Ave 50055 641-385-2440
Chad Grandon, prin. Fax 385-2447

Colo, Story, Pop. 872
Colo Nesco Comm SD 500/PK-12
PO Box 136 50056 641-377-2282
Steve Gray, supt. Fax 377-2283
www.colo-nesco.k12.ia.us
Other Schools – See Zearing

Columbus Junction, Louisa, Pop. 1,878
Columbus Community SD 800/PK-12
1208 Colton St 52738 319-728-2911
Gary Benda, supt. Fax 728-8750
www.columbuscsd.org
Columbus Community JHS 100/6-8
1004 Colton St 52738 319-728-2233
Tyler Hotz, prin. Fax 728-2205
Roundy ES 500/PK-5
1212 Colton St 52738 319-728-6218
Paul Southwell, prin. Fax 728-2134

Conrad, Grundy, Pop. 1,100
BCLUW Community SD 600/K-12
PO Box 670 50621 641-366-2819
Ben Petty, supt. Fax 366-2175
www.bcluw.k12.ia.us
BCLUW ES 200/K-4
PO Box 670 50621 641-366-2811
Mitchell Parker, prin. Fax 366-2177
Other Schools – See Union

Coon Rapids, Carroll, Pop. 1,296
Coon Rapids-Bayard Community SD 400/PK-12
PO Box 297 50058 712-999-2207
Brett Gibbs, supt. Fax 999-7740
www.crbcrusaders.org
Coon Rapids-Bayard ES 200/PK-4
PO Box 297 50058 712-999-2208
Larry Frakes, prin. Fax 999-7740

Coralville, Johnson, Pop. 18,406
Iowa City Community SD
Supt. — See Iowa City
Borlaug ES 400/PK-6
1000 Kennedy Pkwy, 319-688-1155
Celeste Shoppa, prin. Fax 688-1156
Coralville Central ES 400/PK-6
501 6th St 52241 319-688-1100
Andy Gahan, prin. Fax 688-1101
Kirkwood ES 400/PK-6
1401 9th St 52241 319-688-1120
Anita Gerling, prin. Fax 688-1121
Northwest JHS 700/7-8
1507 8th St 52241 319-688-1060
Laura Cottrell, prin. Fax 688-1069
Wickham ES 500/K-6
601 Oakdale Blvd 52241 319-688-1175
Amber Daubs, prin. Fax 688-1176

Montessori S of Iowa City 100/PK-6
374 Holiday Rd 52241 319-338-9650

Corning, Adams, Pop. 1,626
Southwest Valley SD
Supt. — See Villisca
Corning ES 200/PK-5
1012 10th St 50841 641-322-4020
Linda Kwirant-Brecht, prin. Fax 322-5149

Correctionville, Woodbury, Pop. 815
River Valley Community SD 400/PK-12
PO Box 8 51016 712-372-4420
Ken Slater, supt. Fax 372-4677
www.rvwolverines.org
Other Schools – See Washta

Corydon, Wayne, Pop. 1,578
Wayne Community SD 600/PK-12
102 N Dekalb St 50060 641-872-2184
Dave Daughton, supt. Fax 872-2091
www.wayne.k12.ia.us
Wayne ES 300/PK-6
102 N Dekalb St 50060 641-872-1034
Boyd Sinclair, prin. Fax 872-2543

Council Bluffs, Pottawattamie, Pop. 61,150
Council Bluffs Community SD 8,900/PK-12
300 W Broadway Ste 1600 51503 712-328-6446
Dr. Vickie Murillo, supt. Fax 328-6548
www.cb-schools.org
Bloomer ES 500/PK-5
210 S 7th St 51501 712-328-6519
Casey Moran, prin. Fax 328-6545
College View ES 500/PK-5
1225 College Rd 51503 712-328-6452
Sue Rice, prin. Fax 328-6465
Edison ES 400/PK-5
2218 3rd Ave 51501 712-328-6516
Mike Naughton, prin. Fax 328-6507
Franklin ES 400/PK-5
3130 Avenue C 51501 712-328-6469
Kevin Brown, prin. Fax 328-6468
Hoover ES 500/K-5
1205 N Broadway 51503 712-328-6537
Brittney Hettrick, prin. Fax 328-6539
Kirn MS 900/6-8
100 North Ave 51503 712-328-6454
Kerry Newman, prin. Fax 328-6554
Lewis & Clark ES 200/PK-5
1603 Grand Ave 51503 712-328-6471
Teresa Hamilton, prin. Fax 328-6563
Longfellow ES 500/PK-5
2011 S 10th St 51501 712-328-6522
Garry Milbourn, prin. Fax 328-6524
Roosevelt ES 400/PK-5
517 N 17th St 51501 712-328-6528
Brett Abbotts, prin. Fax 328-6566
Rue ES 400/PK-5
3326 6th Ave 51501 712-328-6540
Amy Glime, prin. Fax 328-6556
Wilson MS 900/6-8
715 N 21st St 51501 712-328-6476
Kim Kazmierczak, prin. Fax 328-6479
Other Schools – See Carter Lake, Crescent

Lewis Central Community SD 3,200/PK-12
4121 Harry Langdon Blvd 51503 712-366-8202
Dr. Mark Schweer, supt. Fax 366-8315
www.lewiscentral.org/
Kreft PS 500/PK-1
3206 Renner Dr 51501 712-366-8367
Barb Grell, prin. Fax 366-8294
Lewis Central MS 700/6-8
3820 Harry Langdon Blvd 51503 712-366-8251
Jim Dermody, prin. Fax 366-8324
Titan Hill IS 900/2-5
4125 Harry Langdon Blvd 51503 712-366-8280
Kent Stopak, prin. Fax 366-8302

Heartland Christian S 100/PK-12
400 Wright Rd 51501 712-322-5817
Larry Gray, dir. Fax 322-4287
St. Albert IS 200/4-5
400 Gleason Ave 51503 712-323-3703
Anne Jensen, prin. Fax 322-0399
St. Albert S 300/PK-3
400 Gleason Ave 51503 712-323-3703
Anne Jensen, prin. Fax 322-0399

Crawfordsville, Washington, Pop. 263
Waco Community SD
Supt. — See Wayland
Waco ES 300/PK-6
200 S Main St 52621 319-658-2931
Vicki Reynolds, prin. Fax 658-3104

Crescent, Pottawattamie, Pop. 616
Council Bluffs Community SD
Supt. — See Council Bluffs
Crescent ES 100/K-5
401 E Welch St 51526 712-545-3566
Janine Crain, prin. Fax 545-4492

Cresco, Howard, Pop. 3,829
Howard-Winneshiek Community SD 900/PK-12
1000 Schroder Dr 52136 563-547-2762
Ted Ihns, supt. Fax 547-5973
www.howard-winn.k12.ia.us
Crestwood ECC 50/PK-PK
1135 Canterbury St 52136 563-547-5424
Sara Grimm, prin.
Crestwood ES 400/K-8
1000 4th Ave E 52136 563-547-2340
Terese Jurgensen, prin. Fax 547-2679

Notre Dame S 200/PK-6
221 2nd Ave E 52136 563-547-4513
Wendy Schatz, prin. Fax 547-3835

Creston, Union, Pop. 7,756
Creston Community SD 1,500/PK-12
801 N Elm St 50801 641-782-7028
Steve McDermott, supt. Fax 782-7020
www.crestonschools.org
Creston ECC 100/PK-K
901 N Elm St 50801 641-782-2724
Callie Anderson, prin. Fax 782-5852
Creston ES 500/1-5
805 Academic Ave 50801 641-782-1155
Scott Driskell, prin. Fax 782-6983
Creston MS 300/6-8
805 Academic Ave 50801 641-782-2129
Brad Baker, prin. Fax 782-6983

Mayflower Heritage Christian S 100/K-8
604 E Townline St 50801 641-782-0026
Karla Powers, admin. Fax 782-9577
St. Malachy S 200/PK-8
403 W Clark St 50801 641-782-7125
Jennifer Simmons, prin. Fax 782-5924

Dakota City, Humboldt, Pop. 834
Humboldt Community SD 1,400/PK-12
PO Box 130 50529 515-332-1330
Greg Darling, supt. Fax 332-4478
www.humboldt.k12.ia.us
Mease ES 200/PK-K
23 3rd St N 50529 515-332-3578
George Bruder, prin. Fax 332-7151
Other Schools – See Humboldt

Dallas, See Melcher
Melcher-Dallas Community SD
Supt. — See Melcher
Melcher-Dallas ES 200/PK-6
1003 Park St 50062 641-947-3151
Mike Horstman, prin. Fax 947-4032

Dallas Center, Dallas, Pop. 1,610
Dallas Center-Grimes Community SD 2,600/PK-12
PO Box 512 50063 515-992-3866
Scott Grimes, supt. Fax 992-3079
dcgschools.com
Dallas Center ES 400/K-5
PO Box 400 50063 515-992-3838
Debra Cales, prin. Fax 992-3467
Dallas Center-Grimes MS 300/6-7
PO Box 608 50063 515-992-4343
Jerry Hlas, prin. Fax 992-4076
Other Schools – See Grimes

Danbury, Woodbury, Pop. 347

Danbury Catholic S 50/K-6
602 Peach St 51019 712-883-2244
Amy Seuntjens, prin. Fax 883-2458

Danville, Des Moines, Pop. 929
Danville Community SD 600/PK-12
419 S Main St 52623 319-392-4223
Dr. Thomas Ward, supt. Fax 392-8390
www.danvillecsd.org
Danville ES 400/PK-6
419 S Main St 52623 319-392-4221
Steve Ita, prin. Fax 392-8702

Davenport, Scott, Pop. 96,534
Davenport Community SD 15,400/PK-12
1606 Brady St 52803 563-445-5000
Dr. Arthur Tate, supt. Fax 445-5950
www.davenportschools.org
Adams ES 600/K-5
3029 N Division St 52804 563-723-6100
Laura Finn, prin. Fax 445-5963
Buchanan ES 400/PK-5
4515 N Fairmount St 52806 563-723-6250
Rachel Ivory, prin. Fax 445-5965
Childrens Village at Hayes 50/PK-PK
622 S Concord St 52802 563-723-6550
Tammy Conrad, admin. Fax 445-5973
Childrens Village at Hoover 100/PK-PK
1002 Spring St 52803 563-336-7850
Tammy Conrad, admin. Fax 445-5967
Childrens Village West 200/PK-PK
1757 W 12th St 52804 563-336-7800
Tammy Conrad, admin. Fax 445-5968
Eisenhower ES 500/K-5
2827 Jersey Ridge Rd 52803 563-723-6350
Dave Martin, prin. Fax 445-5969
Fillmore ES 400/PK-5
7307 Pacific St 52806 563-723-6400
Natalie Milo, prin. Fax 445-5970
Garfield ES 500/K-5
902 E 29th St 52803 563-723-6450
Thomas Green, prin. Fax 445-5971
Harrison ES 600/K-5
1032 W 53rd St 52806 563-723-6500
Lisa Baxter, prin. Fax 445-5972
Hayes ES 400/PK-5
622 S Concord St 52802 563-723-6600
Sara Gott, prin. Fax 445-5973
Jackson ES 400/K-5
1307 Wisconsin Ave 52804 563-723-6650
Teresa Bechen, prin. Fax 445-5974
Jefferson ES 400/K-5
1027 N Marquette St 52804 563-723-6700
Kamie Montoya, prin. Fax 445-5975
Madison ES 400/K-5
116 E Locust St 52803 563-723-6750
Steve Mielenhausen, prin. Fax 445-5976
McKinley ES 400/K-5
1716 Kenwood Ave 52803 563-723-6800
Aaron Vincent, prin. Fax 445-5977
Monroe ES 500/K-5
1926 W 4th St 52802 563-723-6850
Ben Driscoll, prin. Fax 445-5978
Smart IS 500/6-8
1934 W 5th St 52802 563-445-5100
Jim Caparula, prin. Fax 445-5957
Sudlow IS 700/6-8
1414 E Locust St 52803 563-445-5150
Tonya Wilkins, prin. Fax 445-5958
Truman ES 400/PK-5
5506 N Pine St 52806 563-723-6900
Cory Williams, prin. Fax 445-5979
Washington ES 300/K-5
1608 E Locust St 52803 563-723-6150
Diana Allen, prin. Fax 445-5980
Williams IS 700/6-8
3040 N Division St 52804 563-445-5250
Garet Egel, prin. Fax 445-5960
Wilson ES 500/K-5
2002 N Clark St 52804 563-723-6950
Shari Larsen, prin. Fax 445-5981
Wood IS 700/6-8
5701 N Division St 52806 563-445-5300
Sheri Simpson-Schultz, prin. Fax 445-5961
Other Schools – See Blue Grass, Buffalo, Walcott

All Saints S 400/PK-8
1926 N Marquette St 52804 563-324-3205
Jeanne VonFeldt, prin. Fax 324-9331
Kennedy Catholic S 400/PK-8
1627 W 42nd St 52806 563-391-3030
Chad Steimle, prin. Fax 388-5206
St. Paul the Apostle S 500/PK-8
1007 E Rusholme St 52803 563-322-2923
Julie Delaney, prin. Fax 322-2530
Trinity Lutheran S 300/PK-8
1122 W Central Park Ave 52804 563-322-5224
Bill Meyer, prin. Fax 324-9153

Dayton, Webster, Pop. 832
Southeast Webster-Grand Community SD
Supt. — See Burnside
Dayton ES 200/PK-4
PO Box 26 50530 515-547-2314
Daniel Grandfield, prin. Fax 547-2213
Southeast Valley MS 100/5-8
30850 Paragon Ave 50530 515-359-2235
Greg Slininger, prin. Fax 359-2236

Decorah, Winneshiek, Pop. 8,056
Decorah Community SD 1,600/PK-12
510 Winnebago St 52101 563-382-4208
Michael Haluska, supt. Fax 387-0753
www.decorah.k12.ia.us
Cline ES 300/K-2
101 Claiborne Dr 52101 563-382-3125
Rick Varney, prin. Fax 387-4059
Decorah MS 500/5-8
405 Winnebago St 52101 563-382-8427
Justin Albers, prin. Fax 387-4052
Lee ES 300/3-4
210 Vernon St 52101 563-382-3771
Sarah Tobiason, prin. Fax 382-8171
West Side ECC 50/PK-PK
301 Center St 52101 563-382-4451
Rick Varney, prin. Fax 387-0716

North Winneshiek Community SD 200/PK-6
3495 N Winn Rd 52101 563-735-5411
Tim Dugger, supt. Fax 735-5430
www.n-winn.k12.ia.us/
North Winneshiek ES 100/PK-6
3495 N Winn Rd 52101 563-735-5411
Cheryl Miller, prin. Fax 735-5430

St. Benedict S 200/PK-8
402 Rural Ave 52101 563-382-4668
Stephen Haluska, prin. Fax 382-3193

Delhi, Delaware, Pop. 456
Maquoketa Valley Community SD 700/PK-12
PO Box 186 52223 563-922-9422
Doug Tuetken, supt. Fax 922-9502
www.maquoketa-v.k12.ia.us
Delhi ES 200/3-5
PO Box 186 52223 563-922-9411
Brenda Becker, prin. Fax 922-9502
Maquoketa Valley MS 200/6-8
PO Box 186 52223 563-922-9411
Troy Osterhaus, prin. Fax 922-9502
Other Schools – See Earlville, Hopkinton

Delmar, Clinton, Pop. 521
Delwood Community SD 200/PK-6
PO Box 292 52037 563-674-4164
Todd Hawley, supt. Fax 674-4134
sites.google.com/a/delwood.k12.ia.us/delwood-csd/
Delwood ES 200/PK-6
PO Box 292 52037 563-674-4164
Todd Hawley, admin. Fax 674-4134

Denison, Crawford, Pop. 8,238
Denison Community SD 2,100/K-12
819 N 16th St 51442 712-263-2176
Michael Pardun, supt. Fax 263-5233
www.denison.k12.ia.us
Denison Broadway ES 300/4-5
1515 Broadway 51442 712-263-3103
Trevor Urich, prin. Fax 263-3187
Denison ES 600/K-3
38 N 20th St 51442 712-263-3104
Christopher Schulz, prin. Fax 263-8360
Denison MS 500/6-8
1201 N 16th St 51442 712-263-9393
Patricia Ryan, prin. Fax 263-5418

St. Rose of Lima S 100/PK-5
1012 2nd Ave S 51442 712-263-5408
Patty Lansink, prin. Fax 263-9370
Zion Lutheran S 100/PK-8
1004 1st Ave S 51442 712-370-3766
Merrilee Sump, admin. Fax 263-6010

Denver, Bremer, Pop. 1,773
Denver Community SD 800/PK-12
PO Box 384 50622 319-984-6323
Brad Laures, supt. Fax 984-5345
www.denver-cyclones.com
Denver Early ES 50/PK-PK
PO Box 384 50622 319-984-5611
Chris Ward, prin. Fax 984-5345
Denver ES 400/K-5
PO Box 384 50622 319-984-5611
Chris Ward, prin. Fax 984-5630
Denver MS 200/6-8
PO Box 384 50622 319-984-6041
Paul Gebel, prin. Fax 984-5630

Des Moines, Polk, Pop. 197,701
Des Moines Independent Community SD 32,900/PK-12
2323 Grand Ave 50312 515-242-7911
Thomas Ahart, supt. Fax 242-7679
www.dmschools.org
Brody MS 700/6-8
2501 Park Ave 50321 515-242-8443
Thomas Hoffman, prin. Fax 244-0927
Brubaker ES 600/K-5
2900 E 42nd St 50317 515-242-8405
Adams Mark, prin. Fax 265-5690
Callanan MS 600/6-8
3010 Center St 50312 515-242-8101
Dawn Stahly, prin. Fax 242-8103
Capitol View ES 600/PK-5
320 E 16th St 50316 515-242-8402
Marsha Kerper, prin. Fax 262-3471
Carver Community ES 600/K-5
700 E University Ave 50316 515-242-8418
Jill Burnett-Requist, prin. Fax 262-1095
Cattell ES 400/K-5
3101 E 12th St 50316 515-242-8403
Tiona Sandbulte, prin. Fax 266-1605
Edmunds ES 400/PK-5
950 15th St 50314 515-243-1174
Jaynette Rittman, prin. Fax 244-1568
Findley ES 300/PK-5
3025 Oxford St 50313 515-242-8407
Barbara Adams, prin. Fax 244-7410
Franklin Taylor Education Center PK-K
1801 16th St 50314 515-242-8424
Susan Guest, prin.
Garton ES 600/PK-5
2820 E 24th St 50317 515-242-8408
Renita Lord, prin. Fax 263-0046
Goodrell MS 600/6-8
3300 E 29th St 50317 515-242-8444
Peter LeBlanc, prin. Fax 264-9057
Greenwood ES 400/K-5
316 37th St 50312 515-242-8410
Andrea Safina, prin. Fax 277-5673
Hanawalt ES 400/K-5
225 56th St 50312 515-242-8411
Kelly Schofield, prin. Fax 255-1792
Harding MS 700/6-8
203 E Euclid Ave 50313 515-242-8445
Joy Linquist, prin. Fax 244-3566
Hiatt MS 600/6-8
1430 E University Ave 50314 515-242-8450
Debra Chapman, prin. Fax 266-6390
Hillis ES 500/PK-5
2401 56th St 50310 515-242-8412
Renee Gelfond, prin. Fax 279-5003
Howe ES 300/K-5
2900 Indianola Ave 50315 515-242-8413
Jill Burke, prin. Fax 288-4128
Hoyt MS 500/6-8
2700 E 42nd St 50317 515-242-8446
Deborah Markert, prin. Fax 265-5059
Hubbell ES 400/K-5
800 42nd St 50312 515-242-8414
Carrie Belt, prin. Fax 242-8290
Jackson ES 400/K-5
3825 Indianola Ave 50320 515-242-8415
Cynthia Wissler, prin. Fax 244-2880
Jefferson ES 400/K-5
2425 Watrous Ave 50321 515-242-8416
Mary Minard, prin. Fax 287-8601
King ES 400/K-5
1849 Forest Ave 50314 515-242-8417
Kisha Barnes, prin. Fax 288-1382
Lovejoy ES 300/K-5
801 E Kenyon Ave 50315 515-242-8419
Michelle Pospeshil, prin. Fax 285-0279
Madison ES 400/PK-5
806 Hoffman Ave 50316 515-242-8420
Cory Heaberlin, prin. Fax 265-6080
McCombs MS 700/6-8
201 County Line Rd 50320 515-242-8447
Nancy Croy, prin. Fax 287-2644
McKee Education Center 200/PK-K
2115 E 39th St 50317 515-323-8628
Susan Guest, prin.
McKinley ES 300/PK-5
1610 SE 6th St 50315 515-242-8423
Lois Brass, prin. Fax 282-1327
Meredith MS 700/6-8
4827 Madison Ave 50310 515-242-7250
Victor Colemon, prin. Fax 242-8291
Merrill MS 700/6-8
5301 Grand Ave 50312 515-242-8448
Alex Hanna, prin. Fax 274-9691
Mitchell ECC, 111 Porter Ave 50315 400/PK-K
Susan Guest, prin. 515-242-8424
Monroe ES 600/PK-5
3015 Francis Ave 50310 515-242-8425
Laurel Prior Sweet, prin. Fax 279-4331
Moore ES 300/K-5
3716 50th St 50310 515-242-8426
Beth Sloan, prin. Fax 278-5707
Morris ES 600/K-5
1401 Geil Ave 50315 515-242-8421
Sherry Amos, prin. Fax 285-1868
Moulton ES 500/PK-5
1541 8th St 50314 515-242-8427
Eric Van Dorin, prin. Fax 288-1346
Oak Park ES 400/K-5
3928 6th Ave 50313 515-242-8428
Jill Bryson, prin. Fax 244-0302
Park Avenue ES 500/K-5
3141 SW 9th St 50315 515-242-8429
Dianna Anderson, prin. Fax 244-8238
Perkins ES 400/K-5
4301 College Ave 50311 515-242-8430
Dan Koss, prin. Fax 274-1367
Phillips ES 400/PK-5
1701 Lay St 50317 515-242-8431
Kristy Fitzgerald, prin. Fax 265-3406
River Woods ES 600/PK-5
2929 SE 22nd St 50320 515-242-8433
Traci Shipley, prin. Fax 244-2386
Samuelson ES 500/K-5
3929 Bel Aire Rd 50310 515-242-8441
Cindy Roerig, prin. Fax 331-0971
South Union ES 600/K-5
4201 South Union St 50315 515-242-8409
Bill Szakacs, prin. Fax 953-0486
Stowe ES 400/K-5
1411 E 33rd St 50317 515-242-8435
Jennifer Williams, prin. Fax 266-0285
Studebaker ES 500/PK-5
300 E County Line Rd 50320 515-242-8436
Brian Crook, prin. Fax 287-1740
Walnut Street ES 300/PK-5
901 Walnut St 50309 515-242-8438
Amy Laug, prin. Fax 242-8372
Weeks MS 600/6-8
901 E Park Ave 50315 515-242-8449
Audrey Rieken, prin. Fax 288-6755
Willard ES 500/PK-5
2941 Dean Ave 50317 515-242-8439
Julie Kruse, prin. Fax 265-1388
Windsor ES 400/K-5
5912 University Ave 50311 515-242-8440
Robert Nichols, prin. Fax 279-5372
Woodlawn Education Center 300/PK-K
4000 Lower Beaver Rd 50310 515-242-8213
Angela Constable, prin.
Wright ES 300/K-5
5001 SW 14th St 50315 515-242-8442
Michelle Hurlburg, prin. Fax 285-6247
Other Schools – See Pleasant Hill, Windsor Heights

Saydel Community SD 1,400/PK-12
5740 NE 14th St 50313 515-264-0866
Doug Wheeler, supt. Fax 264-0869
www.saydel.k12.ia.us
Cornell ES 500/PK-4
5817 NE 3rd St 50313 515-244-8173
Brian Vaughan, prin. Fax 244-0084
Woodside MS 400/5-8
5810 NE 14th St 50313 515-265-3451
Joshua Heyer, prin. Fax 265-0950

Southeast Polk Community SD
Supt. — See Pleasant Hill
Delaware ES 600/PK-5
4401 E 46th St 50317 515-262-3197
Kevin Walker, prin. Fax 264-8239

Bergman Academy 100/PK-8
100 45th St 50312 515-274-0453
Christ the King S 200/PK-8
701 Wall Ave 50315 515-285-3349
Chuckie Geilenfeld, prin. Fax 285-0381
Des Moines Adventist S 50/K-8
2317 Watrous Ave 50321 515-285-7729
Karma Roberts, prin. Fax 285-7729
Grand View Christian S 400/K-12
2905 NE 46th Ave 50317 319-777-3977
Richard McWilliams, prin. Fax 777 3660
Holy Family S 200/PK-8
1265 E 9th St 50316 515-262-8025
Martin Flaherty, prin. Fax 262-9665
Holy Trinity S 500/PK-8
2922 Beaver Ave 50310 515-255-3162
Anne Franklin, prin. Fax 255-1381
Mt. Olive Lutheran S 100/PK-8
5625 Franklin Ave 50310 515-277-0247
Cory Emily, prin. Fax 274-2723
St. Anthony S 300/PK-8
16 Columbus Ave 50315 515-243-1874
Dr. Joseph Cordaro, prin. Fax 243-4467
St. Augustin S 300/PK-8
4320 Grand Ave 50312 515-279-5947
Dr. Nancy Dowdle, prin. Fax 279-8049
St. Joseph S 300/PK-8
2107 E 33rd St 50317 515-266-3433
Phyllis Konchar, prin. Fax 266-2860
St. Theresa S 300/PK-8
5810 Carpenter Ave 50311 515-277-0178
Ellen Stemler, prin. Fax 255-2415

De Soto, Dallas, Pop. 1,040
Adel DeSoto Minburn Community SD
Supt. — See Adel
DeSoto IS 300/3-5
PO Box 39 50069 515-834-2424
Jodi Banse, prin. Fax 834-2056

De Witt, Clinton, Pop. 5,259
Central DeWitt Community SD 1,500/PK-12
PO Box 110 52742 563-659-0700
Dr. Dan Peterson, supt. Fax 659-0707
www.cd-csd.org
Central DeWitt IS 300/4-6
PO Box 110 52742 563-659-4780
Bill Petsche, prin. Fax 659-4765
Central DeWitt MS 200/7-8
PO Box 110 52742 563-659-0735
George Pickup, prin. Fax 659-0766
Ekstrand ES 400/PK-3
PO Box 110 52742 563-659-0750
Mike Miller, prin. Fax 659-0751

St. Joseph S 200/PK-8
417 6th Ave 52742 563-659-3812
Sharon Roling, prin. Fax 659-1565

Dexter, Dallas, Pop. 611
West Central Valley Community SD
Supt. — See Stuart
Dexter ES 200/K-5
PO Box 157 50070 515-789-4480
David Arnold, prin. Fax 789-4613

Diagonal, Ringgold, Pop. 330
Diagonal Community SD 100/PK-12
403 W 2nd St 50845 641-734-5331
Karleen Stephens, supt. Fax 734-5729
www.diagonal.k12.ia.us
Diagonal ES 100/PK-5
403 W 2nd St 50845 641-734-5331
Karleen Stephens, prin. Fax 734-5729

Dike, Grundy, Pop. 1,205
Dike-New Hartford Community SD 800/PK-12
PO Box D 50624 319-989-2552
Larry Hunt, supt. Fax 989-2735
dnhcsd.org
Dike ES 300/PK-4
PO Box D 50624 319-989-2487
Thomas Textor, prin. Fax 989-2723
Other Schools – See New Hartford

Donahue, Scott, Pop. 343
North Scott Community SD
Supt. — See Eldridge
Glenn ES 300/PK-6
PO Box 168 52746 563-282-9627
Kelly Rohlf, prin. Fax 282-9720

Donnellson, Lee, Pop. 907
Central Lee Community SD 1,100/PK-12
2642 Highway 218 52625 319-835-9510
Andy Crozier, supt. Fax 835-3910
www.centrallee.org
Central Lee ES 500/PK-5
2642 Highway 218 52625 319-835-9510
Heather Fuger, prin. Fax 835-5020
Central Lee MS 200/6 8
2642 Highway 218 52625 319-835-9510
Kim Ensminger, prin. Fax 835-5020

Doon, Lyon, Pop. 576

Doon Christian S 50/K-8
614 Rice Ave 51235 712-726-3404
Sharla Tubergen, prin. Fax 726-3404

Douds, Van Buren, Pop. 151
Van Buren Community SD
Supt. — See Keosauqua
Van Buren ES 300/PK-6
14574 Jefferson St 52551 641-936-4321
Mary Dawn Schuck, prin. Fax 936-4619

Dow City, Crawford, Pop. 510
Boyer Valley Community SD
Supt. — See Dunlap
Boyer Valley ES 200/PK-5
212 S School St 51528 712-674-3248
Mike Weber, prin. Fax 674-3792

Dubuque, Dubuque, Pop. 56,421
Dubuque Community SD 10,700/PK-12
2300 Chaney Rd 52001 563-552-3000
Stan Rheingans, supt. Fax 552-3026
www.dbqschools.org
Audubon ES 300/PK-5
605 Lincoln Ave 52001 563-552-3300
Ed Glaser, prin. Fax 552-3301
Bryant ES 300/PK-5
1280 Rush St 52003 563-552-3400
Chris McCarron, prin. Fax 552-3401
Carver ES 600/PK-5
2007 Radford Rd 52002 563-552-4500
Joe Maloney, prin. Fax 552-4501
Eisenhower ES 500/PK-5
3170 Spring Valley Rd 52001 563-552-3500
Andy Ferguson, prin. Fax 552-3501
Fulton ES 300/PK-5
2540 Central Ave 52001 563-552-3650
Dr. Chris Nugent, prin. Fax 552-3651
Hoover ES 300/PK-5
3259 Saint Anne Dr 52001 563-552-3700
Kathleen Walech-Haas, prin. Fax 552-3701
Irving ES 600/PK-5
2520 Pennsylvania Ave 52001 563-552-3800
Susan Meehan, prin. Fax 552-3801
Jefferson MS 600/6-8
1105 Althauser Ave 52001 563-552-4700
Kelly Molony, prin. Fax 552-4701
Kennedy ES 600/PK-5
2135 Woodland Dr 52002 563-552-3900
Dr. Donna Loewen, prin. Fax 552-3901
Lincoln ES 300/PK-5
555 Nevada St 52001 563-552-4050
T.J. Potts, prin. Fax 552-4051
Marshall ES 300/PK-5
1450 Rhomberg Ave 52001 563-552-4100
Sheila Schmidt, prin. Fax 552-4101
Roosevelt MS 1,100/6-8
2001 Radford Rd 52002 563-552-5000
Jeff Johll, prin. Fax 552-5001
Sageville ES 300/PK-5
12015 Sherrill Rd 52002 563-552-4300
Jean McDonald, prin. Fax 552-4301
Table Mound ES 500/PK-5
100 Tower Dr 52003 563-552-4400
Matthew Hull, prin. Fax 552-4401

Washington MS 700/6-8
51 N Grandview Ave 52001 563-552-4800
Mark Burns, prin. Fax 552-4801

Dubuque Lutheran S 50/K-5
2145 John F Kennedy Rd 52002 563-588-0614
Kevin Kuske, prin. Fax 588-3475
Holy Ghost S 100/PK-5
2981 Central Ave 52001 563-556-1511
Todd Wessels, prin. Fax 556-4768
Mazzuchelli Catholic MS 400/6-8
2005 Kane St 52001 563-582-1198
Phil Bormann, prin. Fax 582-5428
Resurrection S 300/PK-5
4320 Asbury Rd 52002 563-583-9488
Denise Grant, prin. Fax 557-7995
St. Anthony/Our Lady of Guadalupe S 100/PK-5
2175 Rosedale Ave 52001 563-556-4194
Lori Apel, prin. Fax 585-1987
St. Columbkille S 300/PK-5
1198 Rush St 52003 563-582-3532
Barb Roling, prin. Fax 583-4884

Dunkerton, Black Hawk, Pop. 848
Dunkerton Community SD 500/PK-12
509 S Canfield St 50626 319-822-4295
Jim Stanton, supt. Fax 822-9456
www.dunkerton.k12.ia.us
Dunkerton ES 300/PK-6
509 S Canfield St 50626 319-822-4295
Patrick Carlin, prin. Fax 822-9456

Dunlap, Harrison, Pop. 1,032
Boyer Valley Community SD 500/PK-12
1102 Iowa Ave 51529 712-643-5702
Doug Gee, supt. Fax 643-2279
www.boyer-valley.k12.ia.us
Other Schools – See Dow City

Durant, Cedar, Pop. 1,820
Durant Community SD 700/K-12
408 7th St 52747 563-785-4432
Duane Bennett, supt. Fax 785-4611
www.durant.k12.ia.us
Durant ES 200/K-4
408 7th St 52747 563-785-4433
Rebecca Stineman, prin. Fax 785-6558
Durant MS 200/5-8
408 7th St 52747 563-785-4433
Rebecca Stineman, prin. Fax 785-6558

Dyersville, Dubuque, Pop. 4,031
Western Dubuque Community SD
Supt. — See Farley
Dyersville ES 300/PK-4
813 12th Ave SW 52040 563-875-8484
Linda Martin, prin. Fax 875-8265

Archbishop Hennessy Catholic S 100/PK-6
1623 300th Ave 52040 563-875-7572
Steven Cornelius, prin. Fax 875-6140
St. Francis Xavier S 400/PK-6
203 2nd St SW 52040 563-875-7376
Peter Smith, prin. Fax 875-7037

Dysart, Tama, Pop. 1,367
Union Community SD
Supt. — See La Porte City
Dysart-Geneseo ES 200/K-5
PO Box 159 52224 319-476-7110
Mark Albertsen, prin. Fax 476-2260
Union MS 300/6-8
PO Box 159 52224 319-476-5100
Mark Albertsen, prin. Fax 476-2385

Eagle Grove, Wright, Pop. 3,540
Eagle Grove Community SD 800/PK-12
325 N Commercial Ave 50533 515-448-4749
Jess Toliver, supt. Fax 448-3156
www.eagle-grove.k12.ia.us
Blue MS 200/5-8
1015 NW 2nd St 50533 515-448-4767
Scott Jeske, prin. Fax 448-5527
Eagle Grove ES 400/PK-4
425 N Fort Ave 50533 515-448-3126
Joseph Erickson, prin. Fax 603-6571

Earlham, Madison, Pop. 1,435
Earlham Community SD 600/K-12
PO Box 430 50072 515-758-2235
Michael Wright, supt. Fax 758-2215
ecsdcards.com/
Earlham ES 300/K-6
PO Box 430 50072 515-758-2213
Jason Hammen, prin. Fax 758-2215
Earlham MS 100/7-8
PO Box 430 50072 515-758-2214
Jennifer Knight, prin. Fax 758-2215

Earlville, Delaware, Pop. 810
Maquoketa Valley Community SD
Supt. — See Delhi
Earlville ES 100/PK-4
226 Prospect 52041 563-923-3225
Brenda Becker, prin. Fax 923-3305

Early, Sac, Pop. 548
Schaller-Crestland Community SD
Supt. — See Schaller
Ridge View MS 200/6-8
PO Box 377 50535 712-273-5185
Jarod Mozer, prin. Fax 273-5120

Eddyville, Wapello, Pop. 1,011
Eddyville-Blakesburg-Fremont Comm SD 900/PK-12
PO Box 429 52553 641-969-4226
Dean Cook, supt. Fax 969-4547
www.rocketsk12.org
Eddyville-Blakesburg-Fremont JHS 100/7-8
1301 Berdan Ext 52553 641-938-2202
Steve Noble, prin. Fax 938-2613
Eddyville ES 300/PK-6
702 Vance St 52553 641-969-4281
Jil Nelson, prin. Fax 969-5318
Other Schools – See Blakesburg, Fremont

Edgewood, Clayton, Pop. 857
Edgewood-Colesburg Community SD 600/PK-12
PO Box 315 52042 563-928-6411
Rob Busch, supt. Fax 928-6414
www.edge-cole.k12.ia.us
Other Schools – See Colesburg

Eldon, Wapello, Pop. 923
Cardinal Community SD 700/PK-12
4045 Ashland Rd 52554 641-652-7531
Joel Pedersen, supt. Fax 652-3143
www.cardinalcomet.com
Cardinal ES 300/PK-5
5414 Hwy 16 52554 641-652-3591
Heather Buckley, prin. Fax 652-3173

Eldora, Hardin, Pop. 2,695
South Hardin SD 600/PK-12
1010 Edgington Ave 50627 641-939-5631
Jay Mathis, supt. Fax 939-3667
www.southhardin.k12.ia.us
Eldora-New Providence ES 300/PK-5
1100 10th St 50627 641-939-9350
Annie Bradford, prin. Fax 939-5664
Other Schools – See Hubbard, Radcliffe

Eldridge, Scott, Pop. 5,557
North Scott Community SD 3,000/PK-12
251 E Iowa St 52748 563-285-4819
Joe Stutting, supt. Fax 285-6075
www.north-scott.k12.ia.us
Armstrong ES 300/K-6
212 S Parkview Dr 52748 563-285-8223
Tim Green, prin. Fax 285-6169
North Scott JHS 500/7-8
502 S 5th St 52748 563-285-8272
John Hawley, prin. Fax 285-6045
White ES 500/K-6
121 S 5th St 52748 563-285-4544
Bernie Brustkern, prin. Fax 285-6173
Other Schools – See Donahue, Long Grove, Princeton

Elgin, Fayette, Pop. 680
Valley Community SD 300/K-8
23493 Canoe Rd 52141 563-426-5501
Duane Willhite, supt. Fax 426-5502
www.valley.k12.ia.us
North Fayette Valley MS 100/6-8
23493 Canoe Rd 52141 563-426-5551
Micah Gearhart, prin. Fax 426-5502
Valley ES 200/K-5
23493 Canoe Rd 52141 563-426-5891
Micah Gearhart, prin. Fax 426-5502

Elkader, Clayton, Pop. 1,265
Central Community SD 500/PK-12
400 1st St NW 52043 563-245-1751
Nick Trenkamp, supt. Fax 245-1763
www.central.k12.ia.us/
Central ES 200/PK-5
400 1st St NW 52043 563-245-1472
Nick Trenkamp, prin. Fax 245-1763

Elk Horn, Shelby, Pop. 661
Exira-Elk Horn-Kimballton Community SD 400/PK-12
PO Box 388a 51531 712-764-4616
Trevor Miller, supt. Fax 764-4626
www.exira-ehk.k12.ia.us/
Exira-Elk Horn-Kimballton ES 100/PK-3
PO Box 388a 51531 712-764-4616
Rochelle Bruns, prin. Fax 764-4626
Other Schools – See Exira

Elk Run Heights, Black Hawk, Pop. 1,095
Waterloo Community SD
Supt. — See Waterloo
Elk Run ECC 100/PK-PK
316 McCoy Rd 50707 319-433-2660
Charletta Sudduth, prin. Fax 433-2922

Elliott, Montgomery, Pop. 349
Griswold Community SD
Supt. — See Griswold
Elliott ES 100/PK-5
PO Box 140 51532 712-767-2221
Nigel Horton, prin. Fax 767-2211

Emmetsburg, Palo Alto, Pop. 3,872
Emmetsburg Community SD 800/PK-12
205 King St 50536 712-852-3201
Amanda Schmidt, supt. Fax 852-3338
www.e-hawks.org
Emmetsburg MS 200/5-8
205 King St 50536 712-852-2892
Tracie Christensen, prin. Fax 852-3811
West ES 300/PK-4
602 Call St 50536 712-852-4485
Joe Carter, prin. Fax 852-3420

Emmetsburg Catholic S 100/PK-8
1903 Broadway St 50536 712-852-3464
Jean Hyslop, prin. Fax 852-3464

Epworth, Dubuque, Pop. 1,855
Western Dubuque Community SD
Supt. — See Farley
Epworth ES 200/PK-4
PO Box 270 52045 563-876-5514
Dan Butler, prin. Fax 876-3208

Essex, Page, Pop. 789
Essex Community SD 200/PK-12
111 Forbes St 51638 712-379-3117
Paul Croghan, supt. Fax 379-3200
www.ehs-ees.com/
Essex ES 100/PK-5
111 Forbes St 51638 712-379-3114
Rob Brecht, prin. Fax 379-3200

Estherville, Emmet, Pop. 6,305
Estherville Lincoln Central Comm SD 1,200/PK-12
1814 7th Ave S 51334 712-362-2692
Tara Paul, supt. Fax 362-2410
www.estherville.k12.ia.us
DeMoney ES 400/PK-4
109 S 17th St 51334 712-362-2181
Shane Kalous, prin. Fax 362-7842
Estherville Lincoln Central MS 400/5-8
1430 1st Ave S 51334 712-362-2335
David McCaulley, prin. Fax 362-7822

Evansdale, Black Hawk, Pop. 4,640
Waterloo Community SD
Supt. — See Waterloo
Bunger MS 400/6-8
157 S Roosevelt Rd 50707 319-433-2550
Rachel Savage, prin. Fax 433-2564
Poyner ES 500/K-5
1138 Central Ave 50707 319-433-1534
Jennifer Willand, prin. Fax 433-1535

Exira, Audubon, Pop. 839
Exira-Elk Horn-Kimballton Community SD
Supt. — See Elk Horn
Exira-Elk Horn-Kimballton MS 200/PK-K, 4-8
PO Box 335 50076 712-268-5318
Rochelle Bruns, prin. Fax 268-5319

Fairbank, Buchanan, Pop. 1,107
Wapsie Valley Community SD 800/PK-12
2535 Viking Ave 50629 319-638-6711
Jim Stanton, supt. Fax 638-7061
www.wapsievalleyschools.com
Fairbank ES 200/PK-6
311 N 5th St 50629 319-635-2071
Josh Sinram, prin. Fax 635-2501
Rural S 1 50/K-8
1099 Amish Blvd 50629 319-635-2071
Josh Sinram, prin. Fax 635-2501
Rural S 2 50/K-8
CR C57 and Amish Blvd 50629 319-635-2071
Josh Sinram, prin. Fax 635-2501
Rural S 3 50/K-8
1503 130th St 50629 319-635-2071
Josh Sinram, prin. Fax 635-2501
Rural S 4 50/K-8
1153 Denison Ave 50629 319-635-2071
Josh Sinram, prin. Fax 635-2501
Other Schools – See Readlyn

Fairfield, Jefferson, Pop. 9,274
Fairfield Community SD 1,700/PK-12
403 S 20th St 52556 641-472-2655
Dr. Laurie Noll, supt. Fax 472-0269
www.fairfieldsfuture.org/
Fairfield MS 500/5-8
404 W Fillmore Ave 52556 641-472-5019
Laura Atwood, prin. Fax 472-5301
Pence ES 300/2-4
1000 S 6th St 52556 641-472-2957
Chuck Benge, prin. Fax 472-6506
Washington ES 300/PK-1
406 E Madison Ave 52556 641-472-2110
Jeff Eeling, prin. Fax 469-5774

Maharishi S 200/PK-12
804 Dr Robert Keith Wallace 52556 641-472-9400
Richard Beall Ph.D., head sch Fax 472-1211

Farley, Dubuque, Pop. 1,531
Western Dubuque Community SD 3,200/PK-12
PO Box 68 52046 563-744-3885
Rick Colpitts, supt. Fax 744-3093
www.wdbqschools.org
Drexler Middle IS 800/5-8
PO Box 279 52046 563-744-3371
Fax 744-3711
Farley ES 200/PK-4
PO Box 279 52046 563-744-3308
Lori Grimoskas, prin. Fax 744-9190
Other Schools – See Cascade, Dyersville, Epworth, Peosta

Seton Catholic - St. Joseph S 100/6-8
PO Box 249 52046 563-744-3290
Mary Smock, prin. Fax 744-3450

Farmington, Van Buren, Pop. 661
Harmony Community SD 200/PK-6
33727 Route J40 52626 319-592-3600
Kerry Phillips, supt. Fax 592-3690
www.harmonycsd.org
Harmony ES 200/PK-6
33727 Route J40 52626 319-592-3235
Kerry Phillips, prin. Fax 592-3690

Farnhamville, Calhoun, Pop. 367
Prairie Valley Community SD
Supt. — See Gowrie
Prairie Valley ES 300/PK-4
3116 Zearing Ave 50538 515-467-5700
Jim Duncan, prin. Fax 467-5646

Fayette, Fayette, Pop. 1,319
North Fayette Community SD
Supt. — See West Union
Fayette ES 100/5-6
PO Box 10 52142 563-425-3303
Travis Elliott, prin. Fax 425-3304

Fenton, Kossuth, Pop. 279
North Union SD
Supt. — See Armstrong
North Union ES Sentral Campus 200/PK-5
308 310th St 50539 515-889-2261
Karl Dearie, prin. Fax 889-2264

Fontanelle, Adair, Pop. 671
Nodaway Valley Community SD
Supt. — See Greenfield

Nodaway Valley MS 200/5-8
112 S 1st St 50846 641-745-2291
Cameron Wendt, prin. Fax 745-3501

Forest City, Winnebago, Pop. 4,101
Forest City Community SD 1,200/PK-12
PO Box 270 50436 641-585-2323
Darwin Lehmann, supt. Fax 585-5218
www.forestcity.k12.ia.us
Forest City ES 500/PK-5
1405 W I St 50436 641-585-2670
Brad Jones, prin. Fax 585-5903
Forest City MS 300/6-8
216 W School St 50436 641-585-4772
Zach Dillavou, prin. Fax 585-3432

Fort Dodge, Webster, Pop. 24,736
Fort Dodge Community SD 3,200/PK-12
104 S 17th St 50501 515-576-1161
Dr. Douglas Van Zyl, supt. Fax 576-1988
www.fdschools.org
Butler ES 500/K-4
945 S 18th St 50501 515-574-5882
Steph Anderson, prin. Fax 574-5813
Cooper ES 300/K-4
2420 14th Ave N 50501 515-574-5602
Bruce Hartley, prin. Fax 574-5518
Duncombe ES 400/K-4
416 S 10th St 50501 515-576-5623
Patrick Reding, prin. Fax 576-8774
Feelhaver ES 200/K-4
1300 14th Ave N 50501 515-574-5680
Nancy Cross, prin. Fax 574-5513
Fort Dodge MS 500/5-6
800 N 32nd St 50501 515-574-5691
Ryan Flaherty, prin. Fax 576-3160
Riverside Early Learning Center 200/PK-K
733 F St 50501 515-574-5740
Tabitha Acree, prin. Fax 955-8818

Community Christian S 100/PK-8
2406 9 1/2 Ave S 50501 515-573-3011
Maurita Aubrey, admin. Fax 576-7698
St. Edmond S 500/PK-5
2321 6th Ave N 50501 515-576-5182
Linda Mitchell, prin. Fax 573-3601
St. Paul Lutheran S 100/PK-8
1217 4th Ave S 50501 515-955-7208
Julie Mann, prin. Fax 573-7839

Fort Madison, Lee, Pop. 10,836
Fort Madison Community SD 2,000/PK-12
PO Box 1423 52627 319-372-7252
Erin Slater, supt. Fax 372-7255
www.fmcsd.org
Fort Madison MS 700/4-8
502 48th St 52627 319-372-4687
Todd Dirth, prin. Fax 372-0378
Lincoln ES 300/K-3
1326 Avenue E 52627 319-372-2896
Tracy King, prin. Fax 372-8927
Richardson ES 300/PK-3
3301 Avenue L 52627 319-372-2765
Emily Wilson, prin. Fax 376-2284

Fredericksburg, Chickasaw, Pop. 923
Sumner-Fredericksburg Community SD
Supt. — See Sumner
Fredericksburg ES 100/K-5
401 E High St 50630 563-237-5364
Jill Glenn, prin. Fax 237-5888
Sumner-Fredericksburg MS 200/6-8
401 E High St 50630 563-237-5334
Jill Glenn, prin. Fax 237-6329

Fremont, Mahaska, Pop. 740
Eddyville-Blakesburg-Fremont Comm SD
Supt. — See Eddyville
Fremont ES 100/PK-6
525 E Main St 52561 641-933-4211
Lindy Hammes, admin. Fax 933-4123

Galva, Ida, Pop. 433
Galva-Holstein Community SD
Supt. — See Holstein
Galva-Holstein Upper ES 100/3-5
207 Noll St 51020 712-368-4353
Mike Richard, prin. Fax 368-4843

Garnavillo, Clayton, Pop. 742
Clayton Ridge Community SD
Supt. — See Guttenberg
Clayton Ridge MS 200/4-7
PO Box 9 52049 563-964-2321
Shane Wahls, prin. Fax 964-2756

Garner, Hancock, Pop. 3,097
Garner-Hayfield-Ventura Community SD 800/PK-12
PO Box 449 50438 641-923-2718
Tyler Williams, supt. Fax 923-3825
www.ghvschools.org
Garner-Hayfield-Ventura ES 400/PK-4
PO Box 449 50438 641-923-2831
Michael Meyering, prin. Fax 923-2031
Other Schools – See Ventura

Garwin, Tama, Pop. 518
GMG Community SD 500/PK-12
306 Park St 50632 641-499-2239
Ben Petty, supt. Fax 499-2159
www.garwin.k12.ia.us
Other Schools – See Green Mountain

George, Lyon, Pop. 1,076
George-Little Rock Community SD 400/PK-12
PO Box 6 51237 712-475-3311
Steve Barber, supt. Fax 475-3574
george-littlerock.org
George ES 100/PK-3
PO Box 6 51237 712-475-3675
Kevin Range, prin. Fax 475-3594
Other Schools – See Little Rock

Gilbert, Story, Pop. 1,068
Gilbert Community SD 1,400/PK-12
103 Mathews Dr 50105 515-232-3740
Lindsey Beecher, supt. Fax 827-5400
www.gilbert.k12.ia.us
Gilbert ES 400/PK-2
109 Rothmoor Dr 50105 515-232-3744
Staci Edwards, prin. Fax 313-5093
Gilbert IS 300/3-5
103 Mathews Dr 50105 515-232-3748
Amy Griffin, prin. Fax 313-1520
Gilbert MS 300/6-8
201 E Mathews Dr 50105 515-232-0540
Chris Billings, prin. Fax 827-7420

Gilbertville, Black Hawk, Pop. 708

Immaculate Conception S 200/3-8
311 16th Ave 50634 319-296-1089
Sharon Mayer, prin. Fax 296-3847

Gilman, Marshall, Pop. 508
East Marshall Community SD 800/PK-12
PO Box 159 50106 641-498-7481
Anthony Ryan, supt. Fax 498-2035
www.e-marshall.k12.ia.us
East Marshall MS 300/4-8
PO Box 159 50106 641-498-7483
Robert Schelp, prin. Fax 498-2180
Other Schools – See Laurel

Gilmore City, Humboldt, Pop. 500
Gilmore City-Bradgate Community SD 50/PK-6
402 SE E Ave 50541 515-373-6619
Jeff Herzberg, supt. Fax 373-6092
www.gcbagreatstartclosetohome.com/
Gilmore City ES 50/PK-6
402 SE E Ave 50541 515-373-6124
Jeffrey Fenske, prin. Fax 373-6092

Glenwood, Mills, Pop. 5,209
Glenwood Community SD 2,000/PK-12
103 Central St Ste 300 51534 712-527-9034
Devin Embray, supt. Fax 527-4287
www.glenwoodschools.org
Glenwood MS 400/6-8
400 Sivers Rd 51534 712-527-4887
Heidi Stanley, prin. Fax 527-3411
Northeast ES 500/PK-2
901 N Vine St 51534 712-527-4875
Sherry Herron, prin. Fax 527-4054
West ES 400/3-5
707 Sharp St 51534 712-527-4886
Eugenia Wickham, prin. Fax 527-5486

Glidden, Carroll, Pop. 1,142
Glidden-Ralston Community SD 300/PK-12
PO Box 488 51443 712-659-3411
Krog Lensch, supt. Fax 659-2248
www.glidden-ralston.k12.ia.us
Glidden-Ralston ES 200/PK-6
PO Box 488 51443 712-659-3411
Dirk Troutman, prin. Fax 659-2248

Goose Lake, Clinton, Pop. 238
Northeast Community SD 800/PK-12
PO Box 66 52750 563-577-2249
Neil Gray, supt. Fax 577-2450
www.northeast.k12.ia.us
Northeast ES 400/PK-5
PO Box 66 52750 563-577-2249
Dr. Eric Brown, prin. Fax 577-2450

Gowrie, Webster, Pop. 1,027
Prairie Valley Community SD 600/PK-12
PO Box 49 50543 515-352-5575
Brian Johnson, supt. Fax 352-5573
www.prairievalley.k12.ia.us
Other Schools – See Farnhamville

Graettinger, Palo Alto, Pop. 839
Graettinger-Terril Community SD 300/PK-12
PO Box 58 51342 712-859-3286
Andrew Woiwood, supt. Fax 859-3509
www.gtschools.k12.ia.us/
Other Schools – See Terril

Granger, Dallas, Pop. 1,237
Woodward-Granger Community SD 1,200/PK-12
1904 State St 50109 515-999-8022
Brad Anderson, supt. Fax 999-8025
wghawks.school
Woodward-Granger Early Learning Center 300/PK-1
2200 State St 50109 515-999-8058
Matt Brummond, prin.
Woodward-Granger ES 200/2-5
2002 Oak St 50109 515-999-2357
Matt Brummond, prin. Fax 999-9299
Other Schools – See Woodward

Greenfield, Adair, Pop. 1,975
Nodaway Valley Community SD 700/PK-12
410 NW 2nd St 50849 641-743-6127
Casey Berlau, supt. Fax 343-7173
www.nodawayvalley.org/
Nodaway Valley East ES 300/PK-4
324 NW 2nd St 50849 641-743-6136
Connie Lundy, prin. Fax 743-8458
Other Schools – See Fontanelle

Green Mountain, Marshall, Pop. 123
GMG Community SD
Supt. — See Garwin
GMG ES 300/PK-6
1710 Wallace Ave 50632 641-474-2251
Chris Frimml, prin. Fax 474-2253

Grimes, Polk, Pop. 8,166
Dallas Center-Grimes Community SD
Supt. — See Dallas Center
Heritage ES PK-6
500 NE Beaverbrooks Blvd 50111 515-300-9627
Diann Williamson, admin.

North Ridge ES 400/K-5
400 NW 27th St 50111 515-986-5674
April Heitland, prin. Fax 986-5376
South Prairie ES 500/K-5
PO Box 650 50111 515-986-4057
Patty Morris, prin. Fax 986-4532

Grinnell, Poweshiek, Pop. 9,024
Grinnell-Newburg Community SD 1,700/PK-12
1333 Sunset St 50112 641-236-2700
Dr. Janet Stutz, supt. Fax 236-2699
www.grinnell-k12.org
Bailey Park ES 200/K-2
210 8th Ave 50112 641-236-2770
Jennifer Donels, prin. Fax 236-2682
Davis ES 200/3-4
818 Hamilton Ave 50112 641-236-2790
Brian Conway, prin. Fax 236-2785
Fairview ES 300/PK-2
1310 Hobart St 50112 641-236-2780
Sarah Seney, prin. Fax 236-2674
Grinnell Community MS 500/5-8
132 East St S 50112 641-236-2750
Sara Hegg-Dunne, prin. Fax 236-2732

Central Iowa Christian S 100/K-8
201 380th Ave 50112 641-236-3000
Janna Voss, prin.

Griswold, Cass, Pop. 1,029
Griswold Community SD 600/PK-12
PO Box 280 51535 712-778-2152
David Henrichs, supt. Fax 778-4145
www.griswoldschools.org/
Other Schools – See Elliott, Lewis

Grundy Center, Grundy, Pop. 2,679
Grundy Center Community SD 500/PK-12
1301 12th St 50638 319-825-5418
Jerry Schutz, supt. Fax 825-5419
www.spartanpride.net
Grundy Center ES 300/PK-4
903 9th St 50638 319-825-5461
Brian Sammons, prin. Fax 825-6817

Guthrie Center, Guthrie, Pop. 1,559
Guthrie Center Community SD 500/PK-12
906 School St 50115 641-332-2972
Steve Smith, supt. Fax 332-2973
www.acgcschools.org
Guthrie Center ES 300/PK-6
900 N 4th St 50115 641-332-2720
Diane Flanery, prin. Fax 332-2721

Guttenberg, Clayton, Pop. 1,910
Clayton Ridge Community SD 800/PK-12
PO Box 520 52052 563-252-2341
Shane Wahls, supt. Fax 252-2656
www.claytonridge.k12.ia.us
Clayton Ridge ES 200/PK-3
PO Box 520 52052 563-252-1747
Andy Peterson, prin. Fax 252-2656
Other Schools – See Garnavillo

St. Mary S 100/PK-8
PO Box 100 52052 563-252-1577
Joanne Hedemann, prin. Fax 252-4065

Hamburg, Fremont, Pop. 1,176
Nishnabotna SD 300/PK-8
309 S St 51640 712-382-2703
Dr. Mike Wells, supt. Fax 382-1922
www.nishbd.org/
Hamburg MS 6-8
309 S St 51640 712-382-2017
Dr. Mike Wells, prin. Fax 382-1922
Simons ES 200/PK-5
309 S St 51640 712-382-2017
Mike Wells, prin. Fax 382-1922

Hampton, Franklin, Pop. 4,420
Hampton-Dumont Community SD 1,200/PK-12
601 12th Ave NE 50441 641-456-2175
Todd Lettow, supt. Fax 456-5750
www.hdcsd.org
Hampton-Dumont MS 400/4-8
601 12th Ave NE 50441 641-456-4735
Anthony Spradlin, prin. Fax 456-2023
North Side ES 100/PK-K
114 11th Pl NE 50441 641-456-4481
Ellen Pickhinke, prin. Fax 456-4173
South Side ES 300/1-3
507 4th Ave SE 50441 641-456-2261
Ellen Pickhinke, prin. Fax 456-5753

Harlan, Shelby, Pop. 5,057
Harlan Community SD 1,600/PK-12
2102 Durant St 51537 712-755-2152
Justin Wagner, supt. Fax 755-7312
www.harlan.k12.ia.us
Harlan Community MS 400/6-8
2108 Durant St 51537 712-755-3196
Bill Mueller, prin. Fax 755-3699
Harlan IS 400/3-5
1401 19th St 51537 712-755-2725
Jeff Moser, prin. Fax 755-7880
Harlan PS 400/PK-2
2105 Durant St 51537 712-755-5903
Scott Frohlich, prin. Fax 755-3661

Shelby County Catholic S 200/PK-6
2005 College Pl 51537 712-755-5634
Josh DeWeerd, prin. Fax 755-3332

Hartford, Warren, Pop. 765
Carlisle Community SD
Supt. — See Carlisle
Hartford Upper ES 300/4-5
500 N Vine St 50118 515-989-0316
Timothy Norton, prin. Fax 989-3897

Hartley, O'Brien, Pop. 1,644
Hartley-Melvin-Sanborn Community SD 600/PK-12
300 N 8th Ave W 51346 712-928-3406
Bill Thompson, supt. Fax 928-3536
www.hartley-ms.k12.ia.us
Hartley-Melvin-Sanborn ES 300/PK-4
240 1st St SE 51346 712-928-2020
Cathy Jochims, prin. Fax 928-3536
Other Schools – See Sanborn

Hastings, Mills, Pop. 151
East Mills Community SD 400/PK-12
58962 380th St 51540 712-624-8700
Paul Croghan, supt. Fax 624-8279
www.emschools.org
East Mills ES 200/PK-6
58962 380th St 51540 712-624-8696
James Dick, prin. Fax 624-8095

Hawarden, Sioux, Pop. 2,534
West Sioux Community SD 700/PK-12
1300 Falcon Dr 51023 712-551-1461
Ryan Kramer, supt. Fax 551-1367
www.westsiouxschools.org/
Hawarden ES 200/2-5
806 13th St 51023 712-551-1454
Carrie Thonstad, prin. Fax 551-2829
West Sioux MS 200/6-8
1300 Falcon Dr 51023 712-551-1022
Heidi Vasquez, prin. Fax 551-1367
Other Schools – See Ireton

Hiawatha, Linn, Pop. 6,851
Cedar Rapids Community SD
Supt. — See Cedar Rapids
Hiawatha ES, 603 Emmons St 52233 400/PK-5
Stephen Probert, prin. 319-558-2172
Nixon ES, 200 Nixon Dr 52233 400/PK-5
Deeann Crozier, prin. 319-558-2188

Hills, Johnson, Pop. 688
Iowa City Community SD
Supt. — See Iowa City
Hills ES 100/PK-6
PO Box 218 52235 319-688-1105
Lisa TeBockhorst, prin. Fax 688-1106

Hinton, Plymouth, Pop. 925
Hinton Community SD 700/PK-12
PO Box 128 51024 712-947-4329
Pete Stuerman, supt. Fax 947-4427
www.hintonschool.com/
Hinton ES 300/PK-3
PO Box 128 51024 712-947-4327
Kathy Rhodes, prin. Fax 947-4333
Hinton MS 200/4-8
PO Box 128 51024 712-947-4328
Brian DeJong, prin. Fax 947-4947

Holstein, Ida, Pop. 1,384
Galva-Holstein Community SD 500/PK-12
PO Box 320 51025 712-368-4353
Jon Wiebers, supt. Fax 368-4843
www.rvraptors.org/
Galva-Holstein ES 100/PK-2
PO Box 320 51025 712-368-4353
Mike Richard, prin. Fax 368-4843
Other Schools – See Galva

Holy Cross, Dubuque, Pop. 372

LaSalle Catholic S - Holy Cross Center 100/PK-6
PO Box 368 52053 563-870-2405
Susan Hucker, prin. Fax 870-4101

Hopkinton, Delaware, Pop. 624
Maquoketa Valley Community SD
Supt. — See Delhi
Johnston ES 100/PK-4
PO Box 390 52237 563-926-2701
Ann Norton, prin. Fax 926-2093

Hospers, Sioux, Pop. 691
MOC-Floyd Valley Community SD
Supt. — See Orange City
Hospers ES 200/K-5
201 4th Ave S 51238 712-752-8480
Marcia DeGraaf, prin. Fax 752-8498

Hubbard, Hardin, Pop. 843
South Hardin SD
Supt. — See Eldora
South Hardin MS 200/6-8
PO Box 129 50122 641-864-2211
Joseph Taylor, prin. Fax 864-2422

Hudson, Black Hawk, Pop. 2,275
Hudson Community SD 500/K-12
PO Box 240 50643 319-988-3233
Dr. Anthony Voss, supt. Fax 988-3235
hudsonpiratepride.com
Hudson ES 300/K-6
PO Box 240 50643 319-988-3239
Mark Schlatter, prin. Fax 988-3235

Hull, Sioux, Pop. 2,161
Boyden-Hull Community SD 600/K-12
PO Box 678 51239 712-439-2711
Steve Grond, supt. Fax 439-1419
www.boyden-hull.k12.ia.us
Other Schools – See Boyden

Hull Christian S 200/PK-8
PO Box 550 51239 712-439-2273
Randy Ten Pas, prin. Fax 990-0581
Hull Protestant Reformed Christian S 200/K-8
218 2nd St 51239 712-439-2490

Humboldt, Humboldt, Pop. 4,652
Humboldt Community SD
Supt. — See Dakota City
Humboldt MS 400/5-8
1400 Wildcat Rd 50548 515-332-2812
Brenda Geitzenauer, prin. Fax 332-2023
Taft ES 400/1-4
612 2nd Ave N 50548 515-332-3216
George Bruder, prin. Fax 332-7102

St. Mary S 200/PK-6
303 3rd St N 50548 515-332-2134
Cindy Edge, prin. Fax 332-1487

Humeston, Wayne, Pop. 485
Mormon Trail Community SD 200/PK-12
PO Box 156 50123 641-877-2521
Fax 877-3400
www.mormontrailcsd.org
Mormon Trail ES 100/PK-6
PO Box 156 50123 641-877-2521
Becky Stripe, prin. Fax 877-3400

Huxley, Story, Pop. 3,264
Ballard Community SD 1,700/PK-12
PO Box 307 50124 515-597-2811
Herman Maxey, supt. Fax 597-2965
www.ballard.k12.ia.us
Ballard Community MS 400/6-8
PO Box 307 50124 515-597-2815
Thomas Maher, prin. Fax 597-2818
Other Schools – See Cambridge, Slater

Ida Grove, Ida, Pop. 2,129
Odebolt-Arthur/Battle Creek-Ida Grove SD 1,000/PK-12
900 John Montgomery Dr 51445 712-364-3687
Terry Kenealy, supt. Fax 364-3609
www.oabcig.org
Battle Creek-Ida Grove ES 400/PK-5
403 Barnes St 51445 712-364-2360
Alan Henderson, prin. Fax 364-3103
Other Schools – See Odebolt

Independence, Buchanan, Pop. 5,911
Independence Community SD 1,300/PK-12
1207 1st St W 50644 319-334-7400
Jean Peterson, supt. Fax 334-7404
www.independence.k12.ia.us/
East ES 300/K-2
1103 1st St W 50644 319-334-7425
Dr. Danielle Meyer, prin. Fax 334-7427
ECC 50/PK-PK
1011 1st St W 50644 319-334-4780
Dr. Danielle Meyer, prin. Fax 334-4868
West ES 400/3-6
1301 1st St W 50644 319-334-7430
Cherilynn Reed, prin. Fax 334-7433

St. John S 100/PK-8
314 3rd St NE 50644 319-334-7173
Jim Gieryng, prin. Fax 334-9088

Indianola, Warren, Pop. 14,597
Indianola Community SD 3,600/PK-12
1304 E 2nd Ave 50125 515-961-9500
Art Sathoff, supt. Fax 961-9505
www.indianola.k12.ia.us
Emerson ES 400/K-5
1109 E Euclid Ave 50125 515-961-9550
Mark Timmerman, prin. Fax 961-9555
Indianola MS 800/6-8
403 S 15th St 50125 515-961-9530
Annette Jauron, prin. Fax 961-9535
Irving ES 400/K-5
500 W Clinton Ave 50125 515-961-9560
AmyJo Naughton, prin. Fax 961-9566
Whittier ES 400/PK-5
1306 W Salem Ave 50125 515-961-9570
Ed Johnson, prin. Fax 961-9575
Wilder ES 500/K-5
2303 W Euclid Ave 50125 515-961-9540
Craig Sexton, prin. Fax 961-9544

Victory Christian Academy 100/PK-8
805 N 1st St 50125 515-962-1632

Inwood, Lyon, Pop. 809
West Lyon Community SD 900/PK-12
1787 Iowa 182 Ave 51240 712-753-4917
Jim Hargens, supt. Fax 753-4928
www.wlwildcats.org
West Lyon ES 600/PK-6
1787 Iowa 182 Ave 51240 712-753-4917
Tim Snyder, prin. Fax 753-4928
West Lyon JHS 100/7-8
1787 Iowa 182 Ave 51240 712-753-4917
Doug Jiskoot, prin. Fax 753-4928

Inwood Christian S 100/PK-8
PO Box C 51240 712-753-4541
Arlyn Schaap, prin. Fax 753-2434

Iowa City, Johnson, Pop. 66,297
Iowa City Community SD 13,100/PK-12
1725 N Dodge St 52245 319-688-1000
Stephen Murley, supt. Fax 688-1009
www.iowacityschools.org
Alexander ES PK-7
3571 Sycamore St 52240 319-688-1095
Chris Gibson, prin. Fax 688-1096
Hoover ES 300/PK-6
2200 E Court St 52245 319-688-1110
Dennis Harnack, prin. Fax 688-1111
Horn ES 500/K-6
600 Koser Ave 52246 319-688-1115
Kristin Cannon, prin. Fax 688-1116
Lemme ES 400/K-6
3100 E Washington St 52245 319-688-1125
Eliza Proctor, prin. Fax 688-1126
Lincoln ES 200/PK-6
300 Teeters Ct 52246 319-688-1130
Ann Langenfeld, prin. Fax 688-1131
Longfellow ES 300/K-6
1130 Seymour Ave 52240 319-688-1135
Chris Pisarik, prin. Fax 688-1136
Lucas ES 400/K-6
830 Southlawn Dr 52245 319-688-1140
Ken Turnis, prin. Fax 688-1141
Mann ES 300/PK-6
521 N Dodge St 52245 319-688-1145
Julie Robinson, prin. Fax 688-1146
Shimek ES 200/PK-6
1400 Grissell Pl 52245 319-688-1160
Elizabeth Bruening, prin. Fax 688-1161
Southeast JHS 800/7-8
2501 Bradford Dr 52240 319-688-1070
Michelle Cook, prin. Fax 688-1079
Twain ES 400/PK-6
1355 Deforest Ave 52240 319-688-1165
Jeremy Negus, prin. Fax 688-1166
Weber ES 500/K-6
3850 Rohret Rd 52246 319-688-1170
Yaa Appiah-McNulty, prin. Fax 688-1171
Wood ES 600/PK-6
1930 Lakeside Dr 52240 319-688-1180
Joe Divoky, prin. Fax 688-1181
Other Schools – See Coralville, Hills, North Liberty

Faith Academy Iowa 100/K-5
1030 Cross Park Ave 52240 319-351-4860
Doug Fern, head sch
Regina ES 500/PK-6
2120 Rochester Ave 52245 319-337-5739
Celeste Vincent, prin. Fax 337-4109
Willowwind S, 950 Dover St 52245 100/PK-6
Paul Pressler, head sch 319-338-6061

Iowa Falls, Hardin, Pop. 5,192
Iowa Falls Community SD 1,200/PK-12
710 North St 50126 641-648-6400
Dr. John Robbins, supt. Fax 648-6401
www.ifacadets.net
Pineview ES 300/PK-2
1510 Washington Ave 50126 641-648-6410
Ryan Robison, prin. Fax 648-6411
Riverbend MS 200/7-8
1124 Union St 50126 641-648-6430
Jeff Burchfield, prin. Fax 648-6432
Rock Run ES 200/3-5
710 North St 50126 641-648-6420
Mike Swartzendruber, prin. Fax 648-6422

Ireton, Sioux, Pop. 608
West Sioux Community SD
Supt. — See Hawarden
Ireton ES 200/PK-1
PO Box 248 51027 712-278-2374
Carrie Thonstad, prin. Fax 278-2383

Ireton Christian S 100/PK-8
104 5th St 51027 712-278-2245
Marlin Schoonhoven M.S., prin. Fax 278-2245

Irwin, Shelby, Pop. 339
IKM-Manning Community SD
Supt. — See Manning
IKM-Manning ES 100/PK-4
PO Box 217 51446 712-782-3126
Sharon Whitson, prin. Fax 782-3128

Jackson Junction, Winneshiek, Pop. 58
Turkey Valley Community SD 400/PK-12
3219 Highway 24 52171 563-776-6011
Jay Jurrens, supt. Fax 776-4271
www.turkey-v.k12.ia.us
Turkey Valley ES 200/PK-6
3219 Highway 24 52171 563-776-6011
Carol Knoll, prin. Fax 776-4271

Janesville, Bremer, Pop. 923
Janesville Consolidated SD 400/PK-12
PO Box 478 50647 319-987-2581
B.J. Meaney, supt. Fax 987-2824
www.janesville.k12.ia.us
Janesville ES 200/PK-8
PO Box 478 50647 319-987-2581
Krista Pugh, prin. Fax 987-2824

Jefferson, Greene, Pop. 4,314
Greene County Community SD 1,000/PK-12
204 W Madison St 50129 515-386-4168
Tim Christensen, supt. Fax 386-3591
www.gccsd.k12.ia.us
Greene County ES 400/PK-4
401 E Russell St 50129 515-386-3178
Scott Johnson, prin. Fax 386-3483
Greene County MS 200/5-8
203 W Harrison St 50129 515-386-8126
Shawn Zanders, prin. Fax 386-4412

Jesup, Buchanan, Pop. 2,492
Jesup Community SD 1,000/PK-12
PO Box 287 50648 319-827-1700
Nathan Marting, supt. Fax 827-3905
www.jesup.k12.ia.us
Jesup ES 400/PK-4
PO Box 287 50648 319-827-1700
Brian Pottebaum, prin. Fax 827-3905
Jesup MS 200/5-8
PO Box 287 50648 319-827-1700
Lisa Loecher, prin. Fax 827-3905
Perry #1 S 50/K-8
PO Box 287 50648 319-827-1700
Brian Pottebaum, prin. Fax 827-3905
Prairie Grove S 50/K-8
PO Box 287 50648 319-827-1700
Brian Pottebaum, prin. Fax 827-3905
Triumph S 50/K-8
PO Box 287 50648 319-827-1700
Brian Pottebaum, prin. Fax 827-3905

St. Anthanasius S 100/PK-8
PO Box 288 50648 319-827-1314
Jennifer Sornson, prin. Fax 827-1124

Jewell, Hamilton, Pop. 1,204
South Hamilton Community SD 700/PK-12
315 Division St 50130 515-827-5479
Kenneth Howard, supt. Fax 827-5368
www.s-hamilton.k12.ia.us
South Hamilton ES 400/PK-6
404 Blaine St 50130 515-827-5096
Paul D. Hemphill, prin. Fax 827-5868

Johnston, Polk, Pop. 17,014
Johnston Community SD 6,600/PK-12
PO Box 10 50131 515-278-0470
Dr. Corey Lunn, supt. Fax 278-5884
www.johnstoncsd.org
Beaver Creek ES 700/PK-5
PO Box 10 50131 515-278-6228
Eric Toot, prin. Fax 278-1049
Horizon ES 700/PK-5
PO Box 10 50131 515-986-1121
Lindsey Cornwell, prin. Fax 986-1131
Lawson ES 700/PK-5
PO Box 10 50131 515-278-0478
Thomas Bartello, prin. Fax 278-4851
Summit MS 1,000/6-7
PO Box 10 50131 515-986-0318
Chris Billings, prin. Fax 986-0952
Timber Ridge ES 500/K-5
PO Box 10 50131 515-331-4379
Kelley Harrison, prin. Fax 331-9093
Wallace ES 500/PK-5
PO Box 10 50131 515-278-6977
Suzanne Pearson, prin. Fax 278-9894

Kalona, Washington, Pop. 2,347
Mid-Prairie Community SD
Supt. — See Wellman
Mid-Prairie East ES 300/PK-2
702 6th St 52247 319-656-2243
Robin Foster, prin. Fax 656-2238
Mid-Prairie MS 300/5-8
713 F Ave 52247 319-656-2241
Marc Pennington, prin. Fax 656-2207

Kanawha, Hancock, Pop. 646
West Hancock Community SD
Supt. — See Britt
West Hancock MS 200/5-8
PO Box 130 50447 641-762-3261
Ruth Verbrugge, prin. Fax 843-4717

Kanawha Christian S 50/K-8
470 E 5th St 50447 641-762-3322
Janna Voss, prin. Fax 762-8362

Keokuk, Lee, Pop. 10,499
Keokuk Community SD 1,900/PK-12
1721 Franklin St 52632 319-524-1402
Christine Barnes, supt. Fax 524-1114
www.keokukschools.org
Hawthorne ES 600/K-3
2940 Decatur St 52632 319-524-3503
Michael Marsden, prin. Fax 526-5946
Keokuk MS 400/6-8
2002 Orleans Ave 52632 319-524-3737
Layne Billings, prin. Fax 524-1511
Torrence Preschool 100/PK-PK
1721 Fulton St 52632 319-524-1953
Nicole Nemecek, admin.
Washington ES 200/4-5
116 N 8th St 52632 319-524-1953
Nicole Nemecek, prin. Fax 526-3081

Keokuk Catholic ES 100/PK-5
2981 Plank Rd 52632 319-524-5450
Darren MacArthur, prin. Fax 524-7725

Keosauqua, Van Buren, Pop. 1,003
Van Buren Community SD 600/PK-12
503 Henry St 52565 319-293-3334
Dr. Pam Ewell, supt. Fax 293-3301
www.van-buren.k12.ia.us
Other Schools – See Douds

Keota, Keokuk, Pop. 998
Keota Community SD 300/PK-12
PO Box 88 52248 641-636-2189
Jim Henrich, supt. Fax 636-3009
www.keota.k12.ia.us
Keota ES 200/PK-6
PO Box 88 52248 641-636-2323
Josh Smith, prin. Fax 636-3009

Keystone, Benton, Pop. 621
Benton Community SD
Supt. — See Van Horne
Keystone ES 50/PK-3
280 4th St 52249 319-442-3221
Ryan Junge, prin. Fax 442-3702

Kingsley, Plymouth, Pop. 1,392
Kingsley-Pierson Community SD 400/K-12
PO Box 520 51028 712-378-2861
Scott Bailey, supt. Fax 378-3729
www.k-pcsd.org
Kingsley ES 200/K-4
322 Quest Ave 51028 712-378-2861
Robert Wiese, prin. Fax 378-3729
Other Schools – See Pierson

Knoxville, Marion, Pop. 7,242
Knoxville Community SD 1,600/PK-12
309 W Main St 50138 641-842-6551
Cassi Pearson, supt. Fax 842-2109
www.knoxville.k12.ia.us
Knoxville MS 400/6-8
102 N Lincoln St 50138 641-842-3315
Brian McNeill, prin. Fax 842-5754

Northstar ES 400/3-5
407 W Larson St 50138 641-842-6527
John Keitges, prin. Fax 828-8052
West ES 300/PK-2
306 S Park Lane Dr 50138 641-842-2185
Dr. Linda Abbott, prin. Fax 842-6029

Lacona, Warren, Pop. 360
Southeast Warren Community SD
Supt. — See Liberty Center
Southeast Warren IS 100/4-6
519 N Washington Ave 50139 641-534-4701
John Burrell, prin. Fax 534-1300

Lake Mills, Winnebago, Pop. 2,090
Lake Mills Community SD 700/PK-12
102 S 4th Ave E 50450 641-592-0881
Chad Kohagen, supt. Fax 592-0883
www.lake-mills.org
Lake Mills ES 300/PK-5
102 S 4th Ave E 50450 641-592-1882
Karl Wagner, prin. Fax 592-0883
Lake Mills MS 200/6-8
102 S 4th Ave E 50450 641-592-0894
James Scholbrock, prin. Fax 592-0883

Lake Park, Dickinson, Pop. 1,094
Harris-Lake Park Community SD 400/PK-12
PO Box 8 51347 712-832-3809
Andy Irwin, supt. Fax 832-3812
www.harris-lp.k12.ia.us
Harris-Lake Park ES 200/PK-5
PO Box 277 51347 712-832-3437
Judith Brueggeman, prin. Fax 832-3640

Lake View, Sac, Pop. 1,137
East Sac County SD 1,000/PK-12
PO Box 110 51450 712-665-5000
Barb Kruthoff, supt. Fax 665-5021
www.eastsac.k12.ia.us/
Other Schools – See Sac City, Wall Lake

Lamoni, Decatur, Pop. 2,266
Lamoni Community SD 400/PK-12
202 N Walnut St 50140 641-784-3342
Chris Coffelt, supt. Fax 784-6548
lamoni.k12.ia.us
Lamoni ES 200/PK-5
202 N Walnut St 50140 641-784-3422
Alan Dykens, prin. Fax 784-6548
Lamoni MS 100/6-8
202 N Walnut St 50140 641-784-7299
Alan Dykens, prin. Fax 784-6548

Lansing, Allamakee, Pop. 998
Eastern Allamakee Community SD 400/PK-12
569 Center St 52151 563-538-4201
Dale Crozier, supt. Fax 538-4969
www.e-allamakee.k12.ia.us/
Lansing MS 100/6-8
569 Center St 52151 563-538-4201
Mary Hogan, prin. Fax 538-4969
Other Schools – See New Albin

La Porte City, Black Hawk, Pop. 2,264
Union Community SD 1,200/PK-12
200 Adams St 50651 319-342-2674
Travis Fleshner, supt. Fax 342-2393
www.union.k12.ia.us/
La Porte City ES 300/PK-5
515 Fillmore St 50651 319-342-3033
Todd Parker, prin. Fax 342-3816
Other Schools – See Dysart

Latimer, Franklin, Pop. 507
CAL Community SD 200/PK-12
1441 Gull St 50452 641-579-6087
Todd Lettow, supt. Fax 579-6408
www.cal.k12.ia.us
CAL ES 100/PK-5
1441 Gull St 50452 641-579-6085
Steve Lane, prin. Fax 579-6408

St. Paul's Lutheran S 50/K-8
PO Box 609 50452 641-579-6046
Steve Lane, prin. Fax 579-6285

Laurel, Marshall, Pop. 238
East Marshall Community SD
Supt. — See Gilman
East Marshall ES 300/PK-3
PO Box 10 50141 641-476-3342
Cathy DeBondt, prin. Fax 476-3904

Laurens, Pocahontas, Pop. 1,251
Laurens-Marathon Community SD 300/PK-12
300 W Garfield St 50554 712-841-5000
Scott Williamson, supt. Fax 841-5010
www.laurens-marathon.k12.ia.us
Laurens-Marathon ES 200/PK-5
300 W Garfield St 50554 712-841-5000
Troy Oehlertz, prin. Fax 841-5010
Laurens-Marathon MS 100/6-8
300 W Garfield St 50554 712-841-5000
Troy Oehlertz, prin. Fax 841-5010

Lawton, Woodbury, Pop. 902
Lawton-Bronson Community SD 600/PK-12
100 Tara Way 51030 712-944-5183
Randy Collins, supt. Fax 944-5568
www.lb-eagles.org
Other Schools – See Bronson

Le Claire, Scott, Pop. 3,701
Pleasant Valley Community SD
Supt. — See Bettendorf
Bridgeview ES 300/PK-6
316 S 12th St 52753 563-332-0215
Tony Hiatt, prin. Fax 332-0218
Cody ES 300/K-6
2100 Territorial Rd 52753 563-332-0210
Laurie Brasche, prin. Fax 332-0213

Pleasant Valley JHS 700/7-8
3501 Wisconsin St 52753 563-332-0200
Trampus Budde, prin. Fax 332-0205

Le Mars, Plymouth, Pop. 9,729
Le Mars Community SD 2,100/PK-12
940 Lincoln St SW 51031 712-546-4155
Dr. Steve Webner, supt. Fax 546-5934
www.lemars.k12.ia.us
Clark ES 300/PK-5
940 Lincoln St SW 51031 712-546-8121
Patti Kruger, prin. Fax 546-8122
Franklin ES 300/K-5
940 Lincoln St SW 51031 712-546-4185
Patti Kruger, prin. Fax 546-4186
Kluckhohn ES 400/K-5
940 Lincoln St SW 51031 712-546-7064
Scott Parry, prin. Fax 546-7069
Le Mars MS 500/6-8
940 Lincoln St SW 51031 712-546-7022
Steve Shanks, prin. Fax 546-7024

Gehlen S 200/PK-6
709 Plymouth St NE 51031 712-546-4181
Lorie Nussbaum, prin. Fax 546-9384

Lenox, Taylor, Pop. 1,401
Lenox Community SD 500/PK-12
600 S Locust St 50851 641-333-2244
David Henrichs, supt. Fax 333-2247
www.lenoxschools.org
Lenox ES 300/PK-6
600 S Locust St 50851 641-333-2244
Derek Morris, prin. Fax 333-2247

Leon, Decatur, Pop. 1,972
Central Decatur Community SD 800/PK-12
1201 NE Poplar St 50144 641-446-4819
Chris Coffelt, supt. Fax 446-7990
www.centraldecatur.org
Central Decatur North ES 200/3-6
1203 NE Poplar St 50144 641-446-4452
Amy Whittington, prin. Fax 446-8729
Central Decatur South ES 200/PK-2
201 SE 6th St 50144 641-446-6521
Amy Whittington, prin. Fax 446-3856

Letts, Louisa, Pop. 371
Louisa-Muscatine Community SD 700/PK-12
14478 170th St 52754 319-726-3541
Mike Van Sickle, supt. Fax 726-3334
www.lmcsd.org
Louisa-Muscatine ES 500/PK-6
14506 170th St 52754 319-726-3634
Aimee Wedeking, prin. Fax 726-4600

Lewis, Cass, Pop. 426
Griswold Community SD
Supt. — See Griswold
Lewis ES 100/PK-5
PO Box 50 51544 712-769-2221
Nigel Horton, prin. Fax 769-2211

Liberty Center, Warren
Southeast Warren Community SD 500/PK-12
PO Box 19 50145 641-466-3510
Delane Galvin, supt. Fax 466-3525
www.se-warren.k12.ia.us
Other Schools – See Lacona, Milo

Lisbon, Linn, Pop. 2,132
Lisbon Community SD 700/PK-12
PO Box 839 52253 319-455-2075
Patrick Hocking, supt. Fax 455-2733
www.lisbon.k12.ia.us
Lisbon ES 400/PK-6
PO Box 839 52253 319-455-2659
Aaron Becker, prin. Fax 455-2733
Lisbon MS 100/7-8
PO Box 839 52253 319-455-2659
Aaron Becker, prin. Fax 455-2733

Little Rock, Lyon, Pop. 458
George-Little Rock Community SD
Supt. — See George
George-Little Rock MS 100/6-8
PO Box 247 51243 712-479-2771
Molly Schilling, prin. Fax 479-2770
Little Rock ES 100/PK-PK, 4-
PO Box 247 51243 712-479-2771
Molly Schilling, prin. Fax 479-2770

Logan, Harrison, Pop. 1,523
Logan-Magnolia Community SD 700/PK-12
1200 N 2nd Ave 51546 712-644-2250
Tom Ridder, supt. Fax 644-2934
www.lomaschools.org
Logan-Magnolia ES 400/PK-6
1200 N 2nd Ave 51546 712-644-2168
Tom Ridder, prin. Fax 644-2501

Lone Tree, Johnson, Pop. 1,281
Lone Tree Community SD 500/PK-12
PO Box 520 52755 319-629-4212
Kenneth Crawford, supt. Fax 629-4324
www.lone-tree.k12.ia.us
Lone Tree ES 200/PK-5
PO Box 520 52755 319-629-4213
Amber Jacque, prin. Fax 629-4324

Long Grove, Scott, Pop. 807
North Scott Community SD
Supt. — See Eldridge
Shepard ES 400/PK-6
220 W Grove St 52756 563-285-8041
Sherri Marceau, prin. Fax 285-6172

Lowden, Cedar, Pop. 787
North Cedar Community SD
Supt. — See Stanwood
Lowden ES 100/PK-6
PO Box 250 52255 563-941-5383
Jennifer Horman, prin. Fax 941-7533

Lu Verne, Kossuth, Pop. 260
Lu Verne Community SD 100/PK-6
PO Box 69 50560 515-882-3357
Jon Hueser, supt. Fax 882-3417
www.luverne.k12.ia.us
Lu Verne ES 100/PK-6
PO Box 69 50560 515-882-3357
Jon Hueser, prin. Fax 882-3417

Mc Gregor, Clayton, Pop. 856
MFL MarMac Community SD
Supt. — See Monona
MFL MarMac MS 200/4-8
PO Box 504 52157 563-873-3463
Denise Mueller, prin. Fax 873-2371

Madrid, Boone, Pop. 2,521
Madrid Community SD 600/K-12
201 N Main St 50156 515-795-1400
Brian Horn, supt. Fax 795-2121
madrid.k12.ia.us
Madrid ES 300/K-6
213 W 1st St 50156 515-795-3240
Gayle Strickland, prin. Fax 795-2121
Madrid JHS 100/7-8
599 N Kennedy Ave 50156 515-795-3240
Kevin Williams, prin. Fax 795-4408

Mallard, Palo Alto, Pop. 273
West Bend - Mallard Community SD
Supt. — See West Bend
West Bend - Mallard ES 100/K-4
414 Micawber St 50562 712-425-3452
Brian Rodemeyer, prin. Fax 425-3413

Manchester, Delaware, Pop. 5,134
West Delaware County Community SD 1,500/PK-12
701 New St 52057 563-927-3515
Dr. Kristen Rickey, supt. Fax 927-2785
www.w-delaware.k12.ia.us
Lambert ES 500/PK-4
1001 Doctor St 52057 563-927-3515
Rudi Hameister, prin. Fax 927-9235
West Delaware MS 400/5-8
1101 Doctor St 52057 563-927-3515
Doug Koerperich, prin. Fax 927-9115

St. Mary S 200/PK-6
132 W Butler St 52057 563-927-3689
Maureen Albritton, prin. Fax 927-9949

Manly, Worth, Pop. 1,311
Central Springs Community SD 800/PK-12
PO Box 190 50456 641-454-2211
Steve Ward, supt. Fax 454-2212
www.centralsprings.net/
Central Springs ES @ Manly 200/PK-3
PO Box 190 50456 641-454-3283
Bill Carlson, prin. Fax 454-2212
Other Schools – See Nora Springs

Manning, Carroll, Pop. 1,493
IKM-Manning Community SD 600/PK-12
209 10th St 51455 712-655-3781
Trevor Miller, supt. Fax 655-3311
www.ikm-manning.k12.ia.us/
IKM-Manning MS 200/4-8
209 10th St 51455 712-655-3761
Sharon Whitson, prin. Fax 654-9282
Other Schools – See Irwin

Manson, Calhoun, Pop. 1,685
Manson Northwest Webster Community SD 800/PK-12
PO Box 387 50563 712-469-2202
Justin Daggett, supt. Fax 469-2298
www.mnwcougars.com
Other Schools – See Barnum

Mapleton, Monona, Pop. 1,204
Maple Valley-Anthon Oto Community SD 700/PK-12
501 S 7th St 51034 712-881-1315
Steve Oberg, supt. Fax 881-1316
www.mvaoschool.com
Mapleton ES 200/PK-5
501 S 7th St 51034 712-881-1319
Mahlon Carothers, prin. Fax 881-1320
Other Schools – See Anthon

Maquoketa, Jackson, Pop. 5,978
Maquoketa Community SD 1,400/PK-12
612 S Vermont St 52060 563-652-4984
Chris Hoover, supt. Fax 652-6958
www.maquoketaschools.org
Briggs ES 200/3-5
400 W Quarry St 52060 563-652-4996
Patrick Bollman, prin. Fax 652-0231
Cardinal ES 300/PK-2
1003 Pershing Rd 52060 563-652-5157
Sherri Walker, prin. Fax 652-6507
Maquoketa MS 300/6-8
200 E Locust St 52060 563-652-4956
Christine Snell, prin. Fax 652-6885

Sacred Heart S 100/PK-6
806 Eddy St 52060 563-652-3743
Jennifer Litterer, prin. Fax 652-2698

Marcus, Cherokee, Pop. 1,110
Marcus-Meriden-Cleghorn Community SD 300/PK-12
PO Box 667 51035 712-376-4171
Jan Brandhorst, supt. Fax 376-4302
www.mmcruroyals.org
MMCRU ES Marcus 200/PK-4
PO Box 667 51035 712-376-2615
Jason Toenges, prin. Fax 376-2819

Marengo, Iowa, Pop. 2,516
Iowa Valley Community SD 600/PK-12
359 E Hilton St 52301 319-642-7714
Donita Joens, supt. Fax 642-3023
www.iowa-valley.k12.ia.us
Iowa Valley ES 300/PK-6
151 E May St 52301 319-642-3812
Cynthia Miller, prin. Fax 642-3023

Marion, Linn, Pop. 34,170
Linn-Mar Community SD 6,900/PK-12
2999 N 10th St 52302 319-447-3000
Dr. Quintin Shepherd Ph.D., supt. Fax 377-9252
www.linnmar.k12.ia.us/
Echo Hill ES 500/K-5
400 Echo Hill Rd 52302 319-730-3560
Dan Ludwig, prin. Fax 447-0481
Excelsior MS 900/6-8
3555 N 10th St 52302 319-447-3130
John Christian, prin. Fax 373-4930
Indian Creek ES 500/K-5
2900 Indian Creek Rd 52302 319-447-3270
Marilee McConnell, prin. Fax 373-9233
Linn Grove ES 500/PK-5
2301 50th St 52302 319-730-3500
Chad Buchholz, prin. Fax 447-0950
Novak ES 500/PK-5
401 29th Ave 52302 319-447-3300
Carol O'Donnell, prin. Fax 373-9144
Oak Ridge MS 700/6-8
4901 Alburnett Rd 52302 319-447-3410
Travis Axeen, prin. Fax 373-3222
Wilkins ES 400/K-5
2127 27th St 52302 319-447-3380
Amanda Potter, prin. Fax 373-9195
Other Schools – See Cedar Rapids, Robins

Marion ISD 2,000/PK-12
777 S 15th St 52302 319-377-4691
Joseph Chris Dyer, supt. Fax 377-4692
www.marion-isd.org
Longfellow ES, 2900 8th Ave 52302 PK-2
Nicole Harmer, admin. 319-377-0183
Marion IS 300/3-4
2301 3rd Ave 52302 319-373-4766
Mike Murphy, prin. Fax 373-4767
Starry ES 300/K-2
700 S 15th St 52302 319-377-4698
Annette Maier, prin. Fax 377-9492
Vernon MS 600/5-8
1350 4th Ave 52302 319-377-9401
Phillip Cochran, prin. Fax 377-7670

St. Joseph S 200/PK-8
1430 14th St 52302 319-377-6348
Casey Kettmann, prin. Fax 377-9358

Marshalltown, Marshall, Pop. 27,096
Marshalltown Community SD 5,100/PK-12
1002 S 3rd Ave 50158 641-754-1000
Dr. Theron Schutte, supt. Fax 754-1003
www.marshalltown.k12.ia.us
Anson ES 400/PK-4
1016 S 3rd Ave 50158 641-754-1020
Ronnie Manis, prin. Fax 754-1027
Fisher ES 400/PK-4
2001 S 4th St 50158 641-754-1030
Mark Lee, prin. Fax 754-1037
Franklin ES 400/PK-4
1315 W Main St 50158 641-754-1041
Timothy Holmgren, prin. Fax 754-1043
Hoglan ES 400/PK-4
2306 S 3rd Ave 50158 641-754-1060
Amy Williams, prin. Fax 754-1062
Lenihan IS 700/5-6
212 W Ingledue St 50158 641-754-1160
Kyle Young, prin. Fax 754-1190
Miller MS 700/7-8
125 S 11th St 50158 641-754-1110
Patrick Rial, prin. Fax 754-1115
Rogers ES 300/PK-4
406 Summit St 50158 641-754-1070
Michael Jurgensen, prin. Fax 754-1072
Woodbury ES 400/PK-4
8 N 7th Ave 50158 641-754-1080
Anel Garza, prin. Fax 754-1083

Marshalltown Christian S 50/K-8
PO Box 1514 50158 641-753-8824
Bethany Wirin, dir.
St. Francis Catholic S 200/PK-6
310 Columbus Dr 50158 641-753-7977
Matthew Herrick, prin. Fax 753-0337

Martensdale, Warren, Pop. 462
Martensdale-St. Marys Community SD 600/PK-12
PO Box 350 50160 641-764-2466
Tom Wood, supt. Fax 764-2100
www.mstm.us/
Martensdale-St. Marys ES 300/PK-6
PO Box 350 50160 641-764-2621
Beth Happe, prin. Fax 764-2100

Mason City, Cerro Gordo, Pop. 27,653
Mason City Community SD 4,000/PK-12
1515 S Pennsylvania Ave 50401 641-421-4400
Dave Versteeg, supt. Fax 421-4424
www.masoncityschools.org
Adams MS 600/7-8
29 S Illinois Ave 50401 641-421-4420
Jerrold Siglin, prin. Fax 423-5240
Harding ES 400/PK-4
1239 N Rhode Island Ave 50401 641-421-4406
Brooke Brunsvold, prin. Fax 421-2006
Hoover ES 400/PK-4
1123 8th St NW 50401 641-421-4408
Barbara Wells, prin. Fax 421-2012
Jefferson ES 400/PK-4
1421 4th St SE 50401 641-421-4411
Lindsey Millsap, prin. Fax 421-2011
Lincoln IS 600/5-6
1625 S Pennsylvania Ave 50401 641-421-4423
Teresa Schlichting, prin. Fax 423-3387
Roosevelt ES 500/PK-4
313 15th St SE 50401 641-421-4415
Dan Arjes, prin. Fax 423-5731

Newman Catholic S 500/PK-8
2000 S McKinley Ave 50401 641-423-3101
Janet Avery, prin. Fax 422-1181
North Iowa Christian S 50/K-12
680 6th St SE 50401 641-423-6440
Jason Miner, prin.

Massena, Cass, Pop. 355
CAM Community SD
Supt. — See Anita
CAM MS 100/6-8
207 E 6th St 50853 712-779-2212
Larry Hunt, prin. Fax 779-3365
CAM South ES 100/PK-5
207 E 6th St 50853 712-779-2211
Larry Hunt, prin. Fax 779-3365

Maxwell, Story, Pop. 916
Collins-Maxwell Community SD 500/PK-12
400 Metcalf St 50161 515-387-1115
Ottie Maxey, supt. Fax 387-8842
www.collins-maxwell.k12.ia.us
Other Schools – See Collins

Maynard, Fayette, Pop. 516
West Central Community SD 300/PK-12
PO Box 54 50655 563-637-2283
Fred Matlage, supt. Fax 637-2294
www.w-central.k12.ia.us
West Central ES 200/PK-8
PO Box 54 50655 563-637-2283
Josh Bahr, prin. Fax 637-2294

Mechanicsville, Cedar, Pop. 1,134
North Cedar Community SD
Supt. — See Stanwood
Mechanicsville ES 200/PK-6
609 125th St 52306 563-432-6933
Jennifer Horman, prin. Fax 432-6666

Mediapolis, Des Moines, Pop. 1,547
Mediapolis Community SD 800/PK-12
PO Box 358 52637 319-394-3101
Greg Ray, supt. Fax 394-3021
www.meposchools.org/
Mediapolis ES 400/PK-5
PO Box 358 52637 319-394-3101
David Van Ness, prin. Fax 394-9753
Mediapolis MS 200/6-8
PO Box 358 52637 319-394-3101
Roger Thornburg, prin. Fax 394-9198

Melcher, Marion, Pop. 1,280
Melcher-Dallas Community SD 400/PK-12
PO Box 489 50163 641-947-3731
Randy Alger, supt. Fax 947-5002
mdcsd-ia.schoolloop.com
Melcher-Dallas JHS 100/7-8
PO Box 158 50163 641-947-3731
Randy Alger, prin. Fax 947-2203
Other Schools – See Dallas

Miles, Jackson, Pop. 440
Easton Valley SD
Supt. — See Preston
Easton Valley ES 300/PK-6
PO Box 340 52064 563-682-7131
Patty Schmidt, prin. Fax 682-7194

Milford, Dickinson, Pop. 2,878
Okoboji Community SD 1,000/PK-12
PO Box 147 51351 712-338-4757
Todd Abrahamson, supt. Fax 338-4758
www.okobojischools.org
Okoboji ES 500/PK-4
PO Box 147 51351 712-338-2458
Justin Bouse, prin. Fax 338-4758
Other Schools – See Arnolds Park

Milo, Warren, Pop. 768
Southeast Warren Community SD
Supt. — See Liberty Center
Southeast Warren PS 200/PK-3
PO Box 135 50166 641-942-6216
John Burrell, prin. Fax 942-6308

Missouri Valley, Harrison, Pop. 2,810
Missouri Valley Community SD 800/PK-12
109 E Michigan St 51555 712-642-2706
Brent Hoesing, supt. Fax 642-2456
www.movalleyschools.org
Missouri Valley ES 400/PK-5
602 N 9th St 51555 712-642-2279
Robin Holtz, prin. Fax 642-2656
Missouri Valley MS 200/6-8
607 Lincoln Hwy 51555 712-642-2707
Brad Nichols, prin. Fax 642-3738

Mitchellville, Polk, Pop. 2,231
Southeast Polk Community SD
Supt. — See Pleasant Hill
Mitchellville ES 200/PK-5
308 Elm Ave NW 50169 515-967-4274
Joseph Nelson, prin. Fax 967-4934

Mondamin, Harrison, Pop. 398
West Harrison Community SD 300/PK-12
410 Pine St 51557 712-646-2231
Julie Trepa, supt. Fax 646-2891
www.westharrison.school
West Harrison ES 100/PK-3
410 Pine St 51557 712-646-2016
Brandt Snakenberg, prin. Fax 646-2891

Monona, Clayton, Pop. 1,540
MFL MarMac Community SD 700/PK-12
PO Box 1040 52159 563-539-4795
Dr. Dale Crozier, supt. Fax 539-4913
www.mflmarmac.k12.ia.us

MFL MarMac ES 300/PK-3
PO Box 1040 52159 563-539-2032
Kathy Koether, prin. Fax 539-4913
Other Schools – See Mc Gregor

Monroe, Jasper, Pop. 1,82[illegible]
PCM Community SD 1,200/PK-12
PO Box 610 [illegible]70 641-259-2751
Brad Jer[illegible]and, supt. Fax 259-2753
www[illegible]monroe.k12.ia.us
M[illegible]roe ES 300/PK-5
PO Box 610 50170 641-259-2314
Ryan Roozeboom, prin. Fax 259-2944
Other Schools – See Prairie City

Montezuma, Poweshiek, Pop. 1,455
Montezuma Community SD 500/PK-12
PO Box 580 50171 641-623-5185
Dave Hoeger, supt. Fax 623-5733
montezuma-schools.org
Montezuma ES 300/PK-6
PO Box 580 50171 641-623-5129
Darin Jones, prin. Fax 623-5733
Montezuma JHS 100/7-8
PO Box 580 50171 641-623-5121
Brian Moretz, prin. Fax 623-5733

Monticello, Jones, Pop. 3,779
Monticello Community SD 1,100/PK-12
711 S Maple St 52310 319-465-5963
Brian Jaeger, supt. Fax 465-4092
www.monticello.k12.ia.us/
Carpenter ES 300/2-4
615 N Gill St 52310 319-465-3551
Denny Folken, prin. Fax 465-4446
Monticello MS 300/5-8
217 S Maple St 52310 319-465-3575
Brent Meier, prin. Fax 465-6959
Shannon ES 200/PK-1
321 W South St 52310 319-465-5425
Denny Folken, prin. Fax 465-3370

Sacred Heart S 200/PK-6
234 N Sycamore St 52310 319-465-4605
William R. Spencer II, prin. Fax 465-6183

Moravia, Appanoose, Pop. 658
Moravia Community SD 400/PK-12
505 N Trussell Ave 52571 641-724-3241
Brad Breon, supt. Fax 724-0629
www.moravia.k12.ia.us
Moravia ES 200/PK-6
505 N Trussell Ave 52571 641-724-3311
Kay Singley, prin. Fax 724-3591

Morning Sun, Louisa, Pop. 828
Morning Sun Community SD 100/K-6
PO Box 129 52640 319-868-7701
Mike Peterson, supt. Fax 868-7703
www.mscsd.org
Morning Sun ES 100/K-6
PO Box 129 52640 319-868-7701
Mike Peterson, supt. Fax 868-7703

Moulton, Appanoose, Pop. 600
Moulton-Udell Community SD 200/PK-12
305 E 8th St 52572 641-642-3665
Brian VanderSluis, supt. Fax 642-3461
sites.google.com/a/moulton-udell.org/m-u_district/
Moulton ES 100/PK-6
305 E 8th St 52572 641-642-3665
Shane Brown, prin. Fax 642-3461

Mount Ayr, Ringgold, Pop. 1,687
Mount Ayr Community SD 600/PK-12
1001 E Columbus St 50854 641-464-0500
Joe Drake, supt. Fax 464-2325
www.mtayrschools.org
Mount Ayr ES 300/PK-6
607 E Jefferson St 50854 641-464-0537
Chris Elwood, prin. Fax 464-2325

Mount Pleasant, Henry, Pop. 8,462
Mount Pleasant Community SD 2,000/PK-12
400 E Madison St 52641 319-385-7750
John Henriksen, supt. Fax 385-7788
www.mt-pleasant.k12.ia.us
Harlan ES 200/K-5
400 E Madison St 52641 319-385-7762
Michael Gossen, prin. Fax 385-7759
Lincoln ES 300/K-5
400 E Madison St 52641 319-385-7765
Lori LaFrenz, prin. Fax 385-7331
Mount Pleasant MS 500/6-8
400 E Madison St 52641 319-385-7730
Nathan Lange, prin. Fax 385-7735
Van Allen ES 300/PK-5
400 E Madison St 52641 319-385-7771
Donald LeBlanc, prin. Fax 385-1167
Other Schools – See Salem

Mount Pleasant Christian S 100/PK-12
1505 E Washington St 52641 319-385-8613
Tina Hill, admin. Fax 385-8415

Mount Vernon, Linn, Pop. 4,439
Mount Vernon Community SD 1,400/PK-12
525 Palisades Rd SW 52314 319-895-8845
Dr. Greg Batenhorst, supt. Fax 895-8875
www.mountvernon.k12.ia.us
Mount Vernon MS 400/5-8
525 Palisades Rd SW 52314 319-895-6254
Bob Haugse, prin. Fax 895-8134
Washington ES 600/PK-4
615 5th Ave SW 52314 319-895-6251
Kate Stanton, prin. Fax 895-0348

Moville, Woodbury, Pop. 1,596
Woodbury Central Community SD 600/PK-12
408 S 4th St 51039 712-873-3128
Doug Glackin, supt. Fax 873-3162
www.woodbury-central.k12.ia.us
Moville ES 300/PK-5
408 S 4th St 51039 712-873-3128
Dyane Mathers, prin. Fax 873-3162
Woodbury Central MS 100/6-8
408 S 4th St 51039 712-873-3128
Don Bormann, prin. Fax 873-3162

Murray, Clarke, Pop. 756
Murray Community SD 400/PK-12
PO Box 187 50174 641-447-2517
Alan Miller, supt. Fax 447-2313
www.murraycsd.org
Murray ES 200/PK-6
PO Box 187 50174 641-447-2517
Tara Page, prin. Fax 447-2313

Muscatine, Muscatine, Pop. 22,599
Muscatine Community SD 5,000/PK-12
2900 Mulberry Ave 52761 563-263-7223
Dr. Jerry Riibe, supt. Fax 263-7729
www.muscatine.k12.ia.us
Central MS 600/6-8
901 Cedar St 52761 563-263-7784
Terry Hogenson, prin. Fax 263-0145
Colorado ES 300/PK-5
149 Colorado St 52761 563-263-4998
Gretchen Price, prin. Fax 263-0273
Franklin ES 300/PK-5
210 Taylor St 52761 563-263-5040
Jason Wester, prin. Fax 262-3923
Grant ES 300/PK-5
705 Barry Ave 52761 563-263-7005
Jessica Freers, prin. Fax 263-1030
Jefferson ES 400/PK-5
403 E 9th St 52761 563-263-8800
Corry Spies, prin. Fax 264-0757
Madison ES 300/K-5
1820 1st Ave 52761 563-263-6062
Stephanie Zillig, prin. Fax 263-0212
McKinley ES 300/PK-5
621 Kindler Ave 52761 563-263-9049
Joelle McConnaha, prin. Fax 264-1271
Mulberry ES 300/PK-5
3211 Mulberry Ave 52761 563-263-8143
Mary Beilke, prin. Fax 263-8487
West MS 600/6-8
600 Kindler Ave 52761 563-263-0411
Susan O'Donnell, prin. Fax 263-6645

Saints Mary & Mathias Catholic S 200/PK-5
2407 Cedar St 52761 563-263-3264
Benjamin Nietzel, prin. Fax 263-6700

Nashua, Chickasaw, Pop. 1,656
Nashua-Plainfield Community SD 600/PK-12
PO Box 569 50658 641-435-4835
Randy Strabala, supt. Fax 435-4835
www.nashua-plainfield.k12.ia.us
Nashua-Plainfield ES 300/PK-3
PO Box 569 50658 641-435-4114
Michelle Arneson, prin. Fax 435-4886
Other Schools – See Plainfield

Neola, Pottawattamie, Pop. 840
Tri-Center Community SD 700/PK-12
33980 310th St 51559 712-485-2257
Dr. Angie Huseman, supt. Fax 485-2411
www.tctrojans.org
Tri-Center ES 400/PK-5
33980 310th St 51559 712-485-2271
Jami Helgenberger, prin. Fax 485-2027
Tri-Center MS 200/6-8
33980 310th St 51559 712-485-2211
Chad Harder, prin. Fax 485-2402

Nevada, Story, Pop. 6,711
Nevada Community SD 1,600/PK-12
1035 15th St 50201 515-382-2783
Dr. Steven Gray, supt. Fax 382-2836
www.nevadacubs.org
Central ES 700/PK-4
1035 15th St 50201 515-382-2383
Chris DeNeui, prin. Fax 382-5345
Nevada MS 500/5-8
1035 15th St 50201 515-382-2751
Chris Schmidt, prin. Fax 382-2836

Nevada SDA S 50/K-8
224 6th St 50201 515-215-1092

New Albin, Allamakee, Pop. 520
Eastern Allamakee Community SD
Supt. — See Lansing
New Albin ES 200/PK-5
PO Box 28 52160 563-544-4246
Chad Steckel, prin. Fax 544-4247

Newell, Buena Vista, Pop. 875
Newell-Fonda Community SD 300/PK-12
PO Box 297 50568 712-272-3324
Rob Olsen, supt. Fax 272-4276
www.newell-fonda.k12.ia.us
Newell-Fonda S 200/PK-8
PO Box 297 50568 712-272-3324
Dick Jungers, prin. Fax 272-4276

Newhall, Benton, Pop. 874

Central Lutheran S 200/PK-8
PO Box 190 52315 319-223-5271
Nichole Perez, prin. Fax 223-5257

New Hampton, Chickasaw, Pop. 3,557
New Hampton Community SD 1,100/PK-12
710 W Main St 50659 641-394-2134
Jay Jurrens, supt. Fax 394-2921
www.new-hampton.k12.ia.us
New Hampton ES 400/PK-4
206 W Main St 50659 641-394-5858
Brenda Ferrie, prin. Fax 394-2662
New Hampton MS 300/5-8
206 W Main St 50659 641-394-2259
Matt Manson, prin. Fax 394-2662

St. Joseph Community S 200/PK-8
216 N Broadway Ave 50659 641-394-2865
Christina Carlton, prin. Fax 394-5154

New Hartford, Butler, Pop. 512
Dike-New Hartford Community SD
Supt. — See Dike
Dike-New Hartford JHS 200/6-8
PO Box 214 50660 319-983-2206
Brian Petullo, prin. Fax 983-2207
New Hartford ES 100/PK-5
PO Box 214 50660 319-983-2206
Brian Petullo, prin. Fax 983-2207

New London, Henry, Pop. 1,877
New London Community SD 500/PK-12
PO Box 97 52645 319-367-0512
Chad Wahls, supt. Fax 367-0513
www.new-london.k12.ia.us
Clark ES 200/PK-5
PO Box 97 52645 319-367-0507
Todd Palmatier, prin. Fax 367-0506

New Sharon, Mahaska, Pop. 1,287
North Mahaska Community SD 600/PK-12
PO Box 89 50207 641-637-4187
Angela Livezey, supt. Fax 637-4559
nmwarhawks.org
North Mahaska ES 300/PK-6
PO Box 89 50207 641-637-4041
Angela Livezey, prin. Fax 637-2657

Newton, Jasper, Pop. 15,101
Newton Community SD 2,600/PK-12
1302 1st Ave W 50208 641-792-5809
Bob Callaghan, supt. Fax 792-9159
www.newton.k12.ia.us
Aurora Heights ES 100/K-4
310 E 23rd St S 50208 641-792-7324
Jim Gilbert, prin. Fax 792-7701
Berg MS 500/5-8
1900 N 5th Ave E 50208 641-792-7741
Lisa Sharp, prin. Fax 792-7779
Hough ES 500/K-4
700 N 4th Ave E 50208 641-792-3982
Jolene Comer, prin. Fax 792-1504
Jefferson ES 400/PK-4
112 Thomas Jefferson Dr 50208 641-792-2498
Trisca Mick, prin. Fax 792-2716
Wilson IS 100/K-4
801 S 8th Ave W 50208 641-792-7311
Todd Schuster, prin. Fax 792-0186

Newton Christian S 100/K-8
1710 N 11th Ave E 50208 641-792-1924
Mary Patterson, prin. Fax 792-1924

Nora Springs, Floyd, Pop. 1,424
Central Springs Community SD
Supt. — See Manly
Central Springs ES @ Nora Springs 200/PK-3
PO Box 367 50458 641-749-5301
Bill Carlson, prin. Fax 749-5898
Central Springs MS 200/4-8
PO Box 367 50458 641-749-5301
Robert Hoffman, prin. Fax 749-5898

North English, Iowa, Pop. 1,037
English Valleys Community SD 500/PK-12
PO Box 490 52316 319-664-3634
Donita Joens, supt. Fax 664-3636
www.english-valleys.k12.ia.us
English Valleys ES 300/PK-6
PO Box 490 52316 319-664-3638
Amy Andreassen, prin. Fax 664-3636

North Liberty, Johnson, Pop. 13,098
Clear Creek Amana Community SD
Supt. — See Oxford
North Bend ES 500/K-5
PO Box 350 52317 319-626-3950
Brenda Parker, prin. Fax 626-3959

Iowa City Community SD
Supt. — See Iowa City
Garner ES 500/K-6
80 Birch Ct 52317 319-688-1190
Nick Proud, prin. Fax 688-1191
North Central JHS 500/7-8
180 Forevergreen Rd E 52317 319-688-1210
Colby Miller, prin. Fax 688-1219
Penn ES 500/K-6
230 N Dubuque St 52317 319-688-1150
Kristy Heffner, prin. Fax 688-1151
Van Allen ES 500/PK-6
170 Abigail Rd 52317 319-688-1185
Eric Ewald, prin. Fax 688-1186

Heritage Christian S 200/PK-8
2551 Blackberry St 52317 319-626-4777
Michael Annis, admin. Fax 626-4778

Northwood, Worth, Pop. 1,968
Northwood-Kensett Community SD 600/PK-12
PO Box 289 50459 641-324-2021
Michael Crozier, supt. Fax 324-2092
www.nwood-kensett.k12.ia.us
Northwood-Kensett ES 300/PK-6
PO Box 289 50459 641-324-1127
Brian Costello, prin. Fax 324-1353

Norwalk, Warren, Pop. 8,841
Norwalk Community SD 2,200/PK-12
380 Wright Rd 50211 515-981-0676
Duane Magee, supt. Fax 981-0559
www.norwalk.k12.ia.us

Lakewood ES 600/3-5
9210 Happy Hollow Dr 50211 515-981-1850
Jill Anderson, prin. Fax 256-7823
Norwalk MS 400/6-7
200 Cherry St 50211 515-981-0435
Beth Ward, prin. Fax 981-0771
Oviatt ES 600/PK-2
713 School Ave 50211 515-981-1005
Sheila Taylor, prin. Fax 981-1007

Norway, Benton, Pop. 541
Benton Community SD
Supt. — See Van Horne
Norway ES 200/4-6
100 School Dr 52318 319-227-7142
G. Robert Arnold, prin. Fax 227-7969

Oakland, Pottawattamie, Pop. 1,517
Riverside Community SD
Supt. — See Carson
Riverside Community ES 300/PK-3
708 Glass St 51560 712-482-6296
Jamie Meek, prin. Fax 482-6646

Odebolt, Sac, Pop. 1,011
Odebolt-Arthur/Battle Creek-Ida Grove SD
Supt. — See Ida Grove
Odebolt-Arthur/Battle Creek-Ida Grove MS 100/6-8
600 S Maple St 51458 712-668-2827
Doug Mogensen, prin. Fax 668-2631
Odebolt-Arthur ES 200/PK-5
600 S Maple St 51458 712-668-2289
Doug Mogensen, prin. Fax 668-2631

Oelwein, Fayette, Pop. 6,310
Oelwein Community SD 1,300/PK-12
307 8th Ave SE 50662 319-283-3536
Josh Ehn, supt. Fax 283-4497
oelwein.k12.ia.us
Little Husky Learning Center 200/PK-K
317 8th Ave SE Ste D 50662 319-283-2302
Mary Beth Steggall, prin. Fax 283-4497
Oelwein MS 200/6-8
300 12th Ave SE 50662 319-283-3015
Mary Beth Steggall, prin. Fax 283-9813
Parkside ES 100/1-1
301 6th Ave SW 50662 319-283-1245
Shannon Harrelson, prin. Fax 283-4497
Wings Park ES 400/2-5
111 8th Ave NE 50662 319-283-1982
Shannon Harrelson, prin. Fax 283-4497

Sacred Heart S 200/PK-6
601 1st Ave SW 50662 319-283-1366
Sr. Kelley Harbach, prin. Fax 283-5279

Ogden, Boone, Pop. 2,032
Ogden Community SD 700/PK-12
PO Box 250 50212 515-275-2894
Jon Hueser, supt. Fax 275-4537
www.ogdenschools.org
Howe ES 200/PK-4
PO Box 250 50212 515-275-2795
Dave Neubauer, prin. Fax 275-4914
Ogden MS 200/5-8
PO Box 250 50212 515-275-2912
Dave Neubauer, prin. Fax 275-2908

Olin, Jones, Pop. 696
Olin Consolidated SD 100/PK-6
212 Trilby St 52320 319-484-2170
Dave Larson, supt. Fax 484-2258
www.olin.k12.ia.us
Olin ES 100/PK-6
212 Trilby St 52320 319-484-2170
Lindsey Given, prin. Fax 484-2258

Onawa, Monona, Pop. 2,968
West Monona Community SD 500/PK-12
1314 15th St 51040 712-433-2043
Julie Trepa, supt. Fax 433-3803
www.westmonona.org
West Monona ES 200/PK-5
611 4th St 51040 712-433-1393
Mary Black, prin. Fax 433-3379
West Monona MS 100/6-8
1314 15th St 51040 712-433-9098
Joshua Vanderflught, prin. Fax 433-1142

Orange City, Sioux, Pop. 5,966
MOC-Floyd Valley Community SD 1,400/PK-12
PO Box 257 51041 712-737-4873
Russ Adams, supt. Fax 737-8789
www.mocfv.org
Orange City ES 400/PK-5
312 1st St SW 51041 712-737-4606
Mike Landhuis, prin. Fax 737-8006
Other Schools – See Alton, Hospers

Orange City Christian S 300/PK-8
604 3rd St SW 51041 712-737-2274
Jason Alons, prin. Fax 737-8608

Orient, Adair, Pop. 408
Orient-Macksburg Community SD 100/PK-12
PO Box 129 50858 641-337-5061
Norene Bunt, supt. Fax 337-5013
www.o-mschools.org
Orient-Macksburg Community S 100/PK-12
PO Box 129 50858 641-337-5061
Teresa Thompson, prin. Fax 337-5606

Osage, Mitchell, Pop. 3,601
Osage Community SD 1,000/PK-12
820 Sawyer Dr 50461 641-732-5381
Barb Schwamman, supt. Fax 732-5381
www.osage.k12.ia.us
Lincoln ES 400/PK-4
515 Chase St 50461 641-732-5856
Greg Adams, prin. Fax 732-5857
Osage MS 300/5-8
820 Sawyer Dr 50461 641-732-3127
Jay Marley, prin. Fax 732-5450

Osceola, Clarke, Pop. 4,887
Clarke Community SD 1,500/PK-12
802 N Jackson St 50213 641-342-4969
Steve Seid, supt. Fax 342-6101
www.clarke.k12.ia.us
Clarke Community ES 900/PK-6
420 E Jefferson St 50213 641-342-6320
Jill Kiger, prin. Fax 342-4861
Clarke MS 200/7-8
800 N Jackson St 50213 641-342-4221
Jeff Sogard, prin. Fax 342-1528

Oskaloosa, Mahaska, Pop. 11,273
Oskaloosa Community SD 2,400/PK-12
PO Box 710 52577 641-673-8345
Russell Reiter, supt. Fax 673-8370
www.oskaloosa.k12.ia.us
Oskaloosa Community Preschool 100/PK-PK
508 S 7th St 52577 641-676-1632
Mike Dursky, prin. Fax 676-3783
Oskaloosa ES 1,100/PK-5
1801 Orchard Ave 52577 641-673-8092
Mike Dursky, prin. Fax 672-3776
Oskaloosa MS 500/6-8
1704 N 3rd St 52577 641-673-8308
Andy Hotek, prin. Fax 673-3779

Oskaloosa Christian S 200/PK-8
726 N E St 52577 641-672-2174
Joe Venema M.Ed., prin. Fax 672-1451

Ossian, Winneshiek, Pop. 842
South Winneshiek Community SD
Supt. — See Calmar
South Winneshiek ES 200/PK-5
PO Box 298 52161 563-532-9365
Jason Halverson, prin. Fax 532-9855
South Winneshiek MS 100/6-8
PO Box 298 52161 563-532-9365
Jason Halverson, prin. Fax 532-9855

St. Francis DeSales S 100/PK-8
414 E Main St 52161 563-532-9352
Kristin Kriener, prin. Fax 532-9353

Ottumwa, Wapello, Pop. 24,651
Ottumwa Community SD 4,500/PK-12
1112 N Van Buren Ave 52501 641-684-6596
Nicole Kooiker, supt. Fax 684-6522
www.ottumwaschools.com
Douma ES, 307 W Mary St 52501 300/K-1
Amy Taylor, prin. 641-684-4668
Eisenhower ES 200/K-5
2624 Marilyn Rd 52501 641-684-5617
Dana Warnecke, prin. Fax 684-4534
Evans MS 1,000/6-8
812 Chester Ave 52501 641-684-6511
Steve Zimmerman, prin. Fax 684-7386
James ES 200/K-5
1001 N Benton St 52501 641-684-5411
Jay Green, prin. Fax 682-6539
Liberty ES 700/2-5
50 Traxler Dr 52501 641-682-4502
Dawn Sievertsen, prin. Fax 682-9251
Mann ES 300/K-5
1523 N Court St 52501 641-684-4661
Jody Williams, prin. Fax 684-6419
Ottumwa Community Preschool 200/PK-PK
608 E Williams St 52501 641-684-7179
Fax 683-2650
Wilson ES 300/K-5
1102 E 4th St 52501 641-684-5441
Jeff Hendred, prin. Fax 684-4934

Ottumwa Christian S PK-12
438 McKinley Ave 52501 641-683-9119
Arnold VanWardhuizen, prin. Fax 683-1084
Seton Catholic S 100/PK-5
117 E 4th St 52501 641-682-8826
James Wessling, prin. Fax 682-6202

Oxford, Johnson, Pop. 790
Clear Creek Amana Community SD 2,000/PK-12
PO Box 487 52322 319-828-4510
Tim Kuehl, supt. Fax 828-4743
www.ccaschools.org
Clear Creek ES 500/PK-5
PO Box 488 52322 319-828-4505
Matt Leeman, prin. Fax 828-8140
Other Schools – See Amana, North Liberty, Tiffin

Oxford Junction, Jones, Pop. 496
Midland Community SD
Supt. — See Wyoming
Midland ES 300/PK-5
PO Box F 52323 563-488-2292
Angela Ruley, prin. Fax 826-2681

Packwood, Jefferson, Pop. 200
Pekin Community SD 600/PK-12
1062 Birch Ave 52580 319-695-3707
Dave Harper, supt. Fax 695-5130
www.pekincsd.org
Pekin ES 300/PK-5
1062 Birch Ave 52580 641-695-3707
Kim Ledger, prin. Fax 695-5130

Panora, Guthrie, Pop. 1,114
Panorama Community SD 500/PK-12
PO Box 39 50216 641-755-4144
Shawn Holloway, supt. Fax 755-3008
www.panoramaschools.org
Panorama ES 400/PK-5
401 Panther Dr 50216 641-755-2021
Liz Ratcliff, prin. Fax 755-3715

Parkersburg, Butler, Pop. 1,860
Aplington-Parkersburg Community SD 900/PK-12
610 N Johnson St 50665 319-346-1571
Jon Thompson, supt. Fax 346-1012
www.a-pcsd.net
Parkersburg ES 300/PK-2
602 Lincoln St 50665 319-346-2446
Amy May, prin. Fax 346-2255
Other Schools – See Aplington

Paullina, O'Brien, Pop. 1,052
South O'Brien Community SD 600/PK-12
PO Box 638 51046 712-949-2115
Dan Moore, supt. Fax 949-2149
www.soswolverines.org
Other Schools – See Primghar

Zion-St. John Lutheran S 100/PK-8
PO Box 249 51046 712-949-3915
Daniel Hoey, prin. Fax 949-3657

Pella, Marion, Pop. 10,224
Pella Community SD 2,300/PK-12
210 E University St 50219 641-628-1111
Greg Ebeling, supt. Fax 628-1116
www.pellaschools.org
Jefferson IS 500/4-6
801 E 13th St 50219 641-628-8267
Brian Miller, prin. Fax 628-8241
Lincoln ES 300/PK-3
1111 N Main St 50219 641-628-3970
Rich Schulte, prin. Fax 628-8712
Madison ES 600/PK-3
950 E University St 50219 641-628-4638
John Steddom, prin. Fax 628-9183
Pella Community MS 300/7-8
613 E 13th St 50219 641-628-4784
Josh Manning, prin. Fax 628-6804

Pella Christian Grade S 500/PK-8
216 Liberty St 50219 641-628-2414
David TeGrotenhuis, head sch Fax 628-9506
Peoria Christian S 50/K-8
110 Peoria West St 50219 641-625-4131
Craig Rapinchuk, admin. Fax 625-4131

Peosta, Dubuque, Pop. 1,367
Western Dubuque Community SD
Supt. — See Farley
Peosta ES 300/PK-5
8522 Burds Rd 52068 563-588-9010
Melissa O'Brien, prin. Fax 588-9013

Seton Catholic - St. John S 300/PK-5
PO Box 249 52068 563-556-5967
Mary Smock, prin. Fax 556-7579

Perry, Dallas, Pop. 7,599
Perry Community SD 1,800/PK-12
1102 Willis Ave Ste 200 50220 515-465-4656
Clark Wicks, supt. Fax 465-4025
www.perry.k12.ia.us/
Perry ES 800/PK-5
1600 8th St 50220 515-465-5656
Ned Menke, prin. Fax 465-7769
Perry MS 400/6-8
1200 18th St 50220 515-465-3531
Shaun Kruger, prin. Fax 465-8555

St. Patrick S 100/PK-8
1302 5th St 50220 515-465-4186
Eddie Diaz, prin. Fax 465-9808

Pierson, Woodbury, Pop. 361
Kingsley-Pierson Community SD
Supt. — See Kingsley
Pierson ES 50/5-5
321 4th St 51048 712-375-5939
Robert Wiese, prin. Fax 375-5771
Pierson MS 100/6-8
321 4th St 51048 712-375-5939
Robert Wiese, prin. Fax 375-5771

Plainfield, Bremer, Pop. 430
Nashua-Plainfield Community SD
Supt. — See Nashua
Nashua-Plainfield IS 100/4-6
417 Main St 50666 319-276-4451
Michelle Arneson, prin. Fax 276-3541

Pleasant Hill, Polk, Pop. 8,612
Des Moines Independent Community SD
Supt. — See Des Moines
Pleasant Hill ES 300/PK-5
4801 E Oakwood Dr 50327 515-242-8432
Terrie Price, prin. Fax 265-8344

Southeast Polk Community SD 6,900/PK-12
8379 NE University Ave 50327 515-967-4294
Dirk Halupnik, supt. Fax 967-4257
www.southeastpolk.org/
Four Mile ES 500/K-5
670 SE 68th St 50327 515-265-1972
Randy Mohning, prin. Fax 262-1933
Southeast Polk JHS 1,000/7-8
8325 NE University Ave 50327 515-967-5509
Mike Dailey, prin. Fax 967-1676
Spring Creek 6th Grade Center 500/6-6
8031 NE University Ave 50327 515-967-5533
Scott Bauer, prin. Fax 967-5572
Other Schools – See Altoona, Des Moines, Mitchellville, Runnells

Pleasantville, Marion, Pop. 1,681
Pleasantville Community SD 700/PK-12
415 Jones St 50225 515-848-0555
Dr. Tony Aylsworth, supt. Fax 848-0561
www.pvillecsd.org
Pleasantville ES 300/PK-5
415 Jones St 50225 515-848-0566
Tom Roff, prin. Fax 848-0570

Pleasantville MS 200/6-8
415 Jones St 50225 515-848-0528
Gary Friday, prin. Fax 848-0561

Pocahontas, Pocahontas, Pop. 1,776
Pocahontas Area Community SD 500/PK-12
202 1st Ave SW 50574 712-335-4311
Joseph Kramer, supt. Fax 335-4206
www.pocahontas.k12.ia.us/
All Star-T Preschool 50/PK-PK
910 W Elm Ave 50574 712-335-4025
Aaron Davidson, prin.
Pocahontas ES 100/K-6
202 1st Ave SW 50574 712-335-4311
Aaron Davidson, prin. Fax 335-4206

Pocahontas Catholic S 100/K-6
305 SW 3rd St 50574 712-335-3603
Terry Eisenbarth, prin. Fax 335-3603

Polk City, Polk, Pop. 3,381
North Polk Community SD
Supt. — See Alleman
North Polk West ES 400/PK-4
1400 W Broadway St 50226 515-984-3400
Ann Mills, prin. Fax 984-9414

Postville, Allamakee, Pop. 2,192
Postville Community SD 600/PK-12
PO Box 717 52162 563-864-7651
Tim Dugger, supt. Fax 864-7659
www.postvilleschools.com
Darling ES 400/PK-6
PO Box 717 52162 563-864-7651
Ryan Zurbriggen, prin. Fax 864-7659

Bais Chaya Mushka/Oholei Menachem 100/PK-9
PO Box 1025 52162 563-864-3632

Prairie City, Jasper, Pop. 1,659
PCM Community SD
Supt. — See Monroe
PCM MS 300/6-8
PO Box 490 50228 515-994-2686
Blake Kielman, prin. Fax 994-2686
Prairie City ES 300/PK-5
PO Box 490 50228 515-994-2377
Stephanie Verhelst, prin. Fax 994-3280

Preston, Jackson, Pop. 1,004
Easton Valley SD 400/PK-12
321 W School St 52069 563-689-4221
Chris Fee, supt. Fax 689-4222
www.eastonvalleycsd.com
Other Schools – See Miles

Primghar, O'Brien, Pop. 893
South O'Brien Community SD
Supt. — See Paullina
South O'Brien ES 400/PK-6
PO Box P 51245 712-957-3755
Mike Morran, prin. Fax 957-0205

Princeton, Scott, Pop. 869
North Scott Community SD
Supt. — See Eldridge
Grissom ES 200/PK-6
500 Lost Grove Rd 52768 563-289-4404
Michael Kline, prin. Fax 289-9016

Protivin, Howard, Pop. 283

Trinity Catholic S 100/K-6
PO Box 246 52163 563-569-8556
Jim Zajicek, prin. Fax 569-8477

Radcliffe, Hardin, Pop. 544
South Hardin SD
Supt. — See Eldora
Hubbard-Radcliffe ES 200/PK-5
PO Box 410 50230 515-899-2111
Patricia Heinz, prin. Fax 899-2116

Readlyn, Bremer, Pop. 806
Wapsie Valley Community SD
Supt. — See Fairbank
Readlyn ES 100/PK-6
PO Box 280 50668 319-279-3323
Josh Sinram, prin. Fax 279-3187

Community Lutheran S 100/PK-8
2681 Quail Ave 50668 319-279-3968
Nicholas Muench, prin. Fax 279-3168

Redfield, Dallas, Pop. 817
West Central Valley Community SD
Supt. — See Stuart
West Central Valley MS 200/6-8
PO Box B 50233 515-833-2331
Anthony Lohse, prin. Fax 833-2629

Red Oak, Montgomery, Pop. 5,681
Red Oak Community SD 1,200/PK-12
2011 N 8th St 51566 712-623-6600
Tom Messinger, supt. Fax 623-6603
www.redoakschooldistrict.com
Inman PS 300/PK-3
900 Inman Dr 51566 712-623-6635
Gayle Allensworth, prin. Fax 623-6638
Red Oak MS 300/6-8
308 E Corning St 51566 712-623-6620
Nathan Perrien, prin. Fax 623-6626
Washington IS 200/4-5
400 W 2nd St 51566 712-623-6630
Gayle Allensworth, prin. Fax 623-6634

Reinbeck, Grundy, Pop. 1,657
Gladbrook-Reinbeck Community SD 300/PK-12
600 Blackhawk St 50669 319-345-2712
David Hill, supt.
www.gr-rebels.net
Gladbrook-Reinbeck ES 200/PK-6
300 Cedar St 50669 319-345-2822
Bradi Johnson, prin. Fax 345-2242

Remsen, Plymouth, Pop. 1,653
Remsen-Union Community SD 200/PK-8
511 Roosevelt Ave 51050 712-786-1101
Jan Brandhorst, supt. Fax 786-1104
www.mmcruroyals.org
MMCRU MS 100/5-8
511 Roosevelt Ave 51050 712-786-1101
Tobias Young, prin. Fax 786-1104
Remsen-Union ES 200/PK-4
511 Roosevelt Ave 51050 712-786-1101
Tobias Young, prin. Fax 786-1194

St. Catherine & St. Mary S 200/PK-8
321 Fulton St 51050 712-786-1160
Jeff Burkey, prin. Fax 786-1167

Riceville, Howard, Pop. 779
Riceville Community SD 100/PK-12
912 Woodland Ave 50466 641-985-2288
Dr. Steve Nicholson, supt. Fax 985-4171
www.riceville.k12.ia.us
Riceville Community S 100/PK-12
912 Woodland Ave 50466 641-985-2288
Cory Schumann, prin. Fax 985-4171

Riverside, Washington, Pop. 985
Highland Community SD 700/PK-12
1715 Vine Ave 52327 319-648-3822
Dr. Mike Jorgensen, supt. Fax 648-4055
www.highland.k12.ia.us
Highland ES 300/PK-5
220 Schnoebelen St 52327 319-648-2821
Jane O'Leary, prin. Fax 648-5503
Highland MS 200/6-8
1715 Vine Ave 52327 319-648-5018
Angela Hazelett, prin. Fax 648-4055

Robins, Linn, Pop. 3,107
Linn-Mar Community SD
Supt. — See Marion
Westfield ES 500/K-5
901 E Main St 52328 319-447-3350
Ed Rodgers, prin. Fax 832-1581

Rockford, Floyd, Pop. 856
Rudd-Rockford-Marble Rock Community SD 500/PK-12
PO Box 218 50468 641-756-3610
Keith Turner, supt. Fax 756-2369
www.rockford.k12.ia.us
Rudd-Rockford-Marble Rock ES 200/PK-6
PO Box 218 50468 641-756-3508
Makaela Hoffman, prin. Fax 756-2369

Rock Rapids, Lyon, Pop. 2,533
Central Lyon Community SD 700/PK-12
1010 S Greene St 51246 712-472-2664
David Ackerman, supt. Fax 472-2115
www.centrallyon.org
Central Lyon ES 400/PK-5
1010 S Greene St 51246 712-472-2664
Steve Harman, prin. Fax 472-2346
Central Lyon MS 100/6-8
1010 S Greene St 51246 712-472-2664
Jason Engleman, prin. Fax 472-2346

Rock Valley, Sioux, Pop. 3,334
Rock Valley Community SD 800/PK-12
1712 20th Ave 51247 712-476-2701
Chad Janzen, supt. Fax 476-2125
www.rvcsd.org
Rock Valley ES 400/PK-5
1712 20th Ave 51247 712-476-2769
Donald Ortman, prin. Fax 476-2125

Netherlands Reformed Christian S 400/K-12
712 20th Ave SE 51247 712-476-2821
Daniel Breuer, prin. Fax 476-5438
Rock Valley Christian S 200/PK-8
1405 17th St 51247 712-476-2615
Brad Vis, prin. Fax 476-2777

Rockwell, Cerro Gordo, Pop. 1,034
West Fork SD 600/PK-12
PO Box 60 50469 641-822-3234
Darrin Strike, supt. Fax 822-4882
www.westforkschool.org
West Fork ES - Rockwell 100/PK-PK, 2-
PO Box 60 50469 641-822-3233
Tracy Peterson, prin. Fax 822-3273
West Fork MS 200/5-8
PO Box 60 50469 641-822-3234
Tracy Peterson, prin. Fax 822-3273
Other Schools – See Sheffield

Rockwell City, Calhoun, Pop. 1,695
South Central Calhoun Community SD 900/PK-12
1000 Tonawanda St 50579 712-297-7341
Jeff Kruse, supt. Fax 297-7320
www.scc.k12.ia.us
South Central Calhoun ES 300/PK-3
330 Brower St 50579 712-297-8621
Nicole McChesney, prin. Fax 297-7181
South Central Calhoun MS 300/4-8
1000 Tonawanda St 50579 712-297-8111
Marc DeMoss, prin. Fax 297-7320

Roland, Story, Pop. 1,275
Roland-Story Community SD
Supt. — See Story City
Roland-Story MS 300/5-8
206 S Main St 50236 515-388-4348
Brian Town, prin. Fax 388-4435

Royal, Clay, Pop. 436
Clay Central/Everly Community SD 300/PK-12
PO Box 110 51357 712-933-2241
Dennis McClain, supt. Fax 933-2243
www.claycentraleverly.org
Clay Central/Everly ES 200/PK-6
PO Box 110 51357 712-933-2241
Dennis McClain, prin. Fax 933-2243

Runnells, Polk, Pop. 500
Southeast Polk Community SD
Supt. — See Pleasant Hill
Runnells ES 200/K-5
6575 SE 116th St 50237 515-966-2068
Mike Nicodemus, prin. Fax 966-2396

Ruthven, Palo Alto, Pop. 734
Ruthven-Ayrshire Community SD 200/PK-12
PO Box 159 51358 712-837-5211
Andrew Woiwood, supt. Fax 837-5210
www.ruthven.k12.ia.us
Ruthven-Ayrshire ES 100/PK-4
PO Box 159 51358 712-837-5211
Andrew Woiwood, prin. Fax 837-5210

Sac City, Sac, Pop. 2,191
East Sac County SD
Supt. — See Lake View
East Sac County ES 200/PK-4
400 S 16th St 50583 712-662-7200
Mike Fischer, prin. Fax 662-6245
East Sac County MS 300/5-8
300 S 11th St 50583 712-662-3259
Denny Olhausen, prin. Fax 662-4323

Saint Ansgar, Mitchell, Pop. 1,101
St. Ansgar Community SD 700/PK-12
PO Box 398 50472 641-713-4681
Jody Gray, supt. Fax 713-4042
www.st-ansgar.k12.ia.us
Saint Ansgar ES 300/PK-5
PO Box 369 50472 641-713-2331
Scott Cakerice, prin. Fax 713-2037
Saint Ansgar MS 100/6-8
PO Box 398 50472 641-713-4720
Lynn Baldus, prin. Fax 713-4042

Salem, Henry, Pop. 379
Mount Pleasant Community SD
Supt. — See Mount Pleasant
Salem ES 100/PK-5
412 E Jackson St 52649 319-258-7799
Michael Gossen, admin. Fax 258-4050

Sanborn, O'Brien, Pop. 1,402
Hartley-Melvin-Sanborn Community SD
Supt. — See Hartley
Hartley-Melvin-Sanborn MS 200/5-8
PO Box 557 51248 712-930-3281
Mark Dorhout, prin. Fax 930-5414

Sanborn Christian S 100/PK-8
405 W 2nd St 51248 712-729-3288
Anthony Minderhoud, prin.

Schaller, Sac, Pop. 764
Schaller-Crestland Community SD 400/PK-8
PO Box 249 51053 712-275-4267
Jon Wiebers, supt. Fax 275-4269
www.rvraptors.org
Schaller-Crestland ES 200/PK-5
PO Box 249 51053 712-275-4267
Jarod Mozer, prin. Fax 275-4269
Other Schools – See Early

Schleswig, Crawford, Pop. 871
Schleswig Community SD 200/PK-8
PO Box 250 51461 712-676-3313
Fax 676-3539
www.schleswig.k12.ia.us
Schleswig ES 100/PK-4
PO Box 250 51461 712-676-3314
David Galvin, prin. Fax 676-3539
Schleswig MS 100/5-8
PO Box 250 51461 712-676-3313
David Galvin, prin. Fax 676-3539

Sergeant Bluff, Woodbury, Pop. 4,152
Sergeant Bluff-Luton Community SD 1,600/PK-12
201 Port Neal Rd 51054 712-943-4338
Rod Earleywine, supt. Fax 943-1131
www.sblschools.com
Sergeant Bluff-Luton ES 400/3-5
201 Port Neal Rd 51054 712-943-5563
Jenni McCrory, prin. Fax 943-1131
Sergeant Bluff-Luton MS 400/6-8
208 Port Neal Rd 51054 712-943-4235
Bill McKelvey, prin. Fax 943-8780
Sergeant Bluff-Luton PS 400/PK-2
206 D St 51054 712-943-5564
Kelly Adams, prin. Fax 943-1161

Seymour, Wayne, Pop. 696
Seymour Community SD 300/PK-12
100 S Park Ave 52590 641-898-2291
Brad Breon, supt. Fax 898-7500
www.seymourcsd.org
Seymour ES 200/PK-6
100 S Park Ave 52590 641-898-2291
Jamie Houser, prin. Fax 898-7500

Sheffield, Franklin, Pop. 1,165
West Fork SD
Supt. — See Rockwell
West Fork ES 100/PK-1
PO Box 617 50475 641-892-4461
Tracy Peterson, prin. Fax 892-4335

Sheldon, O'Brien, Pop. 5,156
Sheldon Community SD 1,000/PK-12
1700 E 4th St 51201 712-324-2504
Robin W. Spears, supt. Fax 324-5607
sheldonschools.com
East ES 400/PK-4
501 Normal College Ave 51201 712-324-4337
Jason Groendyke, prin. Fax 324-4338

Sheldon MS 300/5-8
310 23rd Ave 51201 712-324-4346
Cindy Barwick, prin. Fax 324-4347

St. Patrick S 100/PK-8
1020 4th Ave 51201 712-324-3181
Joe Mueting, prin. Fax 324-3559
Sheldon Christian S 100/PK-8
1425 E 9th St 51201 712-324-2429
Peter Van Velzen, prin. Fax 324-8444

Shell Rock, Butler, Pop. 1,275
Waverly-Shell Rock Community SD
Supt. — See Waverly
Shell Rock ES 200/PK-4
214 N Cherry St 50670 319-885-4311
Micky Bahlmann, prin. Fax 885-6111

Shellsburg, Benton, Pop. 969
Vinton-Shellsburg Community SD
Supt. — See Vinton
Shellsburg ES 300/PK-5
PO Box C 52332 319-436-4728
Ryan Davis, prin. Fax 436-2294

Shenandoah, Page, Pop. 5,088
Shenandoah Community SD 1,000/PK-12
304 W Nishna Rd 51601 712-246-1581
Dr. Kerri Nelson Ed.D., supt. Fax 246-3722
www.shenandoah.k12.ia.us
Shenandoah ES 400/PK-4
601 Dr Creighton Cir 51601 712-246-2520
Tiffany Spiegel, prin. Fax 246-2496
Shenandoah MS 300/5-8
601 Dr Creighton Cir 51601 712-246-2520
Jason Shaffer, prin. Fax 246-2496

Sibley, Osceola, Pop. 2,785
Sibley-Ocheyedan Community SD 800/PK-12
120 11th Ave NE 51249 712-754-2533
Bill Boer, supt. Fax 754-2534
www.thegenerals.org
Sibley-Ocheyedan ES 400/PK-4
416 9th Ave 51249 712-754-3636
Cory Jenness, prin. Fax 754-3994
Sibley-Ocheyedan MS 200/5-8
120 11th Ave NE 51249 712-754-2542
Fax 754-3651

Sidney, Fremont, Pop. 1,125
Sidney Community SD 400/PK-12
PO Box 609 51652 712-374-2141
Tim Hood, supt. Fax 374-2013
www.sidneyschools.org
Sidney ES 200/PK-6
PO Box 609 51652 712-374-2647
Shannon Wehling, prin. Fax 374-2648

Sigourney, Keokuk, Pop. 2,051
Sigourney Community SD 600/PK-12
909 E Pleasant Valley St 52591 641-622-2025
Dave Harper, supt. Fax 622-2319
www.sigourneyschools.com
Sigourney ES 300/PK-6
509 S Jefferson St 52591 641-622-2350
Deanna Hutchings, prin. Fax 622-3604

Sioux Center, Sioux, Pop. 7,004
Sioux Center Community SD 1,100/PK-12
550 9th St NE 51250 712-722-2985
Pat O'Donnell, supt. Fax 722-2986
www.scwarriors.org
Kinsey ES 500/PK-4
550 9th St NE 51250 712-722-1541
Troy Lentell, prin. Fax 722-0583
Sioux Center MS 300/5-8
550 9th St NE 51250 712-722-3783
Julie Schley, prin. Fax 722-3782

Sioux Center Christian S 400/PK-8
PO Box 165 51250 712-722-0777
Josh Bowar, head sch Fax 722-0782

Sioux City, Woodbury, Pop. 80,564
Sioux City Community SD 11,800/PK-12
627 4th St 51101 712-279-6667
Dr. Paul Gausman, supt. Fax 279-6690
www.siouxcityschools.org
Bryant ES 400/K-5
1114 W 27th St 51103 712-279-6819
Mary Kay Kollars, prin. Fax 279-6748
Clark ECC 100/PK-K
4315 Hamilton Blvd 51104 712-239-7030
Amy Denney, prin. Fax 224-4021
East MS 1,000/6-8
5401 Lorraine Ave 51106 712-274-4030
Dr. Michael Rogers, prin. Fax 274-4668
Hunt ES 300/K-5
615 20th St 51104 712-279-6833
Amy Gilbert, prin. Fax 279-6052
Irving ES 800/K-5
901 Floyd Blvd 51105 712-279-6834
Maria Ruelas, prin. Fax 279-6092
Leeds ES 600/PK-5
3919 Jefferson St 51108 712-239-7034
Angela Bemus, prin. Fax 239-7036
Liberty ES 800/PK-5
1623 Rebecca St 51103 712-279-6845
Stacie Henderson, prin. Fax 279-6808
Loess Hill ES K-5
1717 Casselman St 51103 712-279-6843
John Beeck, prin. Fax 279-6846
Morningside ES K-5
3601 Bushnell Ave 51106 712-274-4048
Dawn Stansbury, prin. Fax 224-7479
Nodland ES 200/K-2
5000 Mayhew Ave 51106 712-274-4044
Blair Taylor, prin. Fax 266-8934
North MS 1,000/6-8
2101 Outer Dr N 51108 712-279-6804
Shawn Chesteen, prin. Fax 277-5941
Perry Creek ES 1-5
3601 Country Club Blvd 51104 712-279-6836
Amy Denney, prin.
Riverside ES 400/PK-5
2303 Riverside Blvd 51109 712-279-6811
Dr. Angela Holcomb, prin. Fax 277-6139
Spalding Park ES 600/PK-5
4101 Stone Ave 51106 712-274-4043
Mimi Moore, prin. Fax 274-4036
Sunnyside ES 200/3-5
2700 S Maple St 51106 712-274-4047
Blair Taylor, prin. Fax 274-4680
Unity ES 500/PK-5
1901 Unity Ave 51105 712-279-6839
Eric Kilburn, prin. Fax 279-6130
West MS 900/6-8
3301 W 19th St 51103 712-279-6813
Katie Towler, prin. Fax 277-6138

Holy Cross S / Blessed Sacrament Ctr 300/3-8
3030 Jackson St 51104 712-277-4739
Michael Sweeney, prin. Fax 258-3698
Holy Cross S - St. Michael Ctr 100/PK-2
4105 Harrison St 51108 712-239-1090
Michael Sweeney, prin. Fax 239-8546
Mater Dei S - Immaculate Conception Ctr 200/PK-5
3719 Ridge Ave 51106 712-276-6216
Mary Fischer, prin. Fax 274-1221
Mater Dei S - Nativity Center 100/6-8
4243 Natalia Way 51106 712-274-0268
Mary Fischer, prin. Fax 274-0377
Sacred Heart S 300/K-8
5010 Military Rd 51103 712-233-1624
Kate Connealy, prin. Fax 233-1469
St. Paul Lutheran S 50/PK-5
612 Jennings St 51101 712-258-6325
Alyce Strong Davis, prin. Fax 252-1141
Siouxland Christian S 200/PK-12
6000 Gordon Dr 51106 712-276-4732
Steven Peters, supt. Fax 276-4752

Sioux Rapids, Buena Vista, Pop. 775
Sioux Central Community SD 600/PK-12
4440 US Highway 71 50585 712-283-2571
Scott Williamson, supt. Fax 283-2989
www.siouxcentral.org
Sioux Central ES 300/PK-6
4440 US Highway 71 50585 712-283-2571
Kari Schmidt, prin. Fax 283-2285
Sioux Central MS 100/7-8
4440 US Highway 71 50585 712-283-2571
Jeff Scharn, prin. Fax 283-2285

Slater, Story, Pop. 1,487
Ballard Community SD
Supt. — See Huxley
Ballard West ES 400/PK-2
105 E Main St 50244 515-228-3890
Jennifer Johnson, prin. Fax 228-3892

Sloan, Woodbury, Pop. 970
Westwood Community SD 500/PK-12
1000 Rebel Way 51055 712-428-3355
Jay Lutt, supt. Fax 428-3246
www.wwrebels.org
Westwood ES 300/PK-6
1000 Rebel Way 51055 712-428-3200
Jay Lutt, prin. Fax 428-3246

Solon, Johnson, Pop. 2,019
Solon Community SD 1,400/PK-12
301 S Iowa St 52333 319-624-3401
Davis Eidahl, supt. Fax 624-2518
www.solon.k12.ia.us
Lakeview ES 600/PK-4
111 N Chabal St 52333 319-624-3401
Jodi Rickels, prin. Fax 624-4176
Solon MS 400/5-8
1775 Racine Ave 52333 319-624-3401
Mike Herdliska, prin. Fax 624-2518

Spencer, Clay, Pop. 11,130
Spencer Community SD 1,400/PK-12
PO Box 200 51301 712-262-8950
Terry Hemann, supt. Fax 262-1116
www.spenceriowaschools.com/
Fairview Park ES 100/2-3
PO Box 200 51301 712-262-4842
Lucas DeWitt, prin. Fax 262-1116
Johnson ES 200/PK-1
PO Box 200 51301 712-262-2710
Tim Wagner, prin. Fax 262-1116
Lincoln ES 100/4-5
PO Box 200 51301 712-262-3752
Cindy Devlaeminck, prin. Fax 262-1116
Spencer MS 400/6-8
PO Box 200 51301 712-262-3345
Pat Hamilton, prin. Fax 264-3444

Iowa Great Lakes Lutheran S 50/K-6
1311 E 18th St 51301 712-262-8237
Stephan Gonzales, prin. Fax 262-8396
Sacred Heart S, PO Box 817 51301 200/PK-6
Ronald Olberding, prin. 712-262-6428

Spillville, Winneshiek, Pop. 366

C F S Consolidated S 100/4-8
PO Box 68 52168 563-562-3617
Kathryn Schmitt, prin. Fax 562-3292

Spirit Lake, Dickinson, Pop. 4,786
Spirit Lake Community SD 1,300/PK-12
2701 Hill Ave 51360 712-336-2820
Dr. David Smith Ed.D., supt. Fax 336-4641
www.spirit-lake.k12.ia.us/
Spirit Lake ES 500/PK-4
2701 Hill Ave 51360 712-336-2822
Kasey Huebner, prin. Fax 336-8966
Spirit Lake MS 400/5-8
2701 Hill Ave 51360 712-336-1370
Terry Bruinsma, prin. Fax 336-4758

Springville, Linn, Pop. 1,066
Springville Community SD 400/PK-12
400 Academy St 52336 319-854-6197
Pat Hocking, supt. Fax 854-6199
www.springville.k12.ia.us
Springville ES 200/PK-5
400 Academy St 52336 319-854-6195
Shannon Robertson, prin. Fax 854-6199

Stanton, Montgomery, Pop. 688
Stanton Community SD 200/K-12
PO Box 400 51573 712-829-2162
Dr. Chris Herrick, supt. Fax 829-2164
www.stantonschools.com
Stanton ES 100/K-5
PO Box 400 51573 712-829-2171
Kevin Blunt, prin. Fax 829-2717

Stanwood, Cedar, Pop. 676
North Cedar Community SD 600/PK-12
PO Box 247 52337 563-942-3358
Mark Dohmen, supt. Fax 942-0014
www.north-cedarstu.org
Other Schools – See Lowden, Mechanicsville

State Center, Marshall, Pop. 1,450
West Marshall Community SD 900/PK-12
PO Box 670 50247 641-483-2660
Jacy Large, supt. Fax 483-2665
www.w-marshall.k12.ia.us
West Marshall ES 500/PK-5
PO Box 370 50247 641-483-2671
Nanette Smith, prin. Fax 483-9951
West Marshall MS 200/6-8
PO Box 340 50247 641-483-2165
Casey Christensen, prin. Fax 483-3095

Storm Lake, Buena Vista, Pop. 10,411
Storm Lake Community SD 2,400/PK-12
PO Box 638 50588 712-732-8060
Dr. Carl Turner Ed.D., supt. Fax 732-8063
www.slcsd.org
East ECC 100/PK-K
PO Box 638 50588 712-732-8076
Kellie Anderson, prin. Fax 732-8108
Storm Lake ES 900/PK-4
PO Box 638 50588 712-732-8074
Julie Kwikkel, prin. Fax 732-8111
Storm Lake MS 600/5-8
PO Box 638 50588 712-732-8080
Jay Slight, prin. Fax 732-8084

St. Marys S 100/PK-5
312 Seneca St 50588 712-732-1856
Diane Jones, prin. Fax 732-4590

Story City, Story, Pop. 3,411
Roland-Story Community SD 1,100/PK-12
1009 Story St 50248 515-733-4301
Matt Patton, supt. Fax 733-2131
rolandstory.school
Roland-Story ES 400/PK-4
900 Hillcrest Ave 50248 515-733-4386
Kate Hartzler, prin. Fax 733-5357
Other Schools – See Roland

Stratford, Hamilton, Pop. 737
Stratford Community SD 100/PK-6
PO Box 190 50249 515-838-2208
Mike Sherwood, supt. Fax 838-1938
www.stratford.k12.ia.us
Stratford ES 100/PK-6
PO Box 190 50249 515-838-2208
Josh Culberson, prin. Fax 838-1938

Stuart, Guthrie, Pop. 1,630
West Central Valley Community SD 900/PK-12
3299 White Pole Rd 50250 515-523-2187
Dr. David Arnold, supt. Fax 523-1166
www.wcv.k12.ia.us
Stuart ES 300/PK-5
320 NE 3rd St 50250 515-523-1018
Cory Wenthe, prin. Fax 523-1174
Other Schools – See Dexter, Redfield

Sully, Jasper, Pop. 821
Lynnville-Sully Community SD 500/K-12
PO Box 210 50251 641-594-4445
Shane Ehresman, supt. Fax 594-2770
www.lshawks.org
Lynnville-Sully ES 200/K-5
PO Box 210 50251 641-594-4445
Teri Bowlin, prin. Fax 594-2770
Lynnville-Sully MS 100/6-8
PO Box 210 50251 641-594-4445
Teri Bowlin, prin. Fax 594-2770

Sully Christian S 50/K-8
12629 S 92nd Ave E 50251 641-594-4180
Angela Veenstra, lead tchr. Fax 594-3799

Sumner, Bremer, Pop. 2,021
Sumner-Fredericksburg Community SD 900/PK-12
802 W 6th St 50674 563-578-3341
Fred Matlage, supt. Fax 578-3424
www.sfcougars.k12.ia.us
Durant ES 300/PK-5
601 W 5th St 50674 563-578-3354
Kurt Volker, prin. Fax 578-3424
Other Schools – See Fredericksburg

Swea City, Kossuth, Pop. 535
North Union SD
Supt. — See Armstrong
North Union MS 100/6-8
PO Box 567 50590 515-272-4361
Julie Runksmeier, prin. Fax 272-4391

Tabor, Fremont, Pop. 1,036
Fremont-Mills Community SD 500/PK-12
PO Box 310 51653 712-629-2325
Dr. Christopher Herrick, supt. Fax 629-5155
www.fmtabor.org
Fremont-Mills ES 300/PK-6
PO Box 310 51653 712-629-6555
Allyson Forney, prin. Fax 629-5155

Tama, Tama, Pop. 2,803
South Tama County Community SD 1,400/PK-12
1702 Harding St 52339 641-484-4811
Jeff Berger, supt. Fax 484-4861
www.s-tama.k12.ia.us
South Tama County ES 600/PK-4
1611 Country Club Dr 52339 641-484-3999
Stacy Stull, prin. Fax 484-3744
Other Schools – See Toledo

Terril, Dickinson, Pop. 361
Graettinger-Terril Community SD
Supt. — See Graettinger
Graettinger-Terril ES 200/PK-5
PO Box 128 51364 712-859-3286
Chris Myers, prin. Fax 859-3509

Thornburg, Keokuk, Pop. 67
Tri-County Community SD 300/PK-12
PO Box 17 50255 641-634-2408
Chad Straight, supt. Fax 634-2145
www.tri-countyschools.com
Tri-County ES 100/PK-6
PO Box 17 50255 641-634-2632
Clay Harrold, prin. Fax 634-2145
Tri-County JHS 50/7-8
PO Box 17 50255 641-634-2636
Clay Harrold, prin. Fax 634-2145

Tiffin, Johnson, Pop. 1,895
Clear Creek Amana Community SD
Supt. — See Oxford
Clear Creek Amana MS 400/6-8
PO Box 530 52340 319-545-4490
Brad Fox, prin. Fax 545-4094
Tiffin ES PK-5
PO Box 620 52340 319-545-2081
Dan Dvorak, prin. Fax 545-2092

Tipton, Cedar, Pop. 3,193
Tipton Community SD 1,000/PK-12
400 E 6th St 52772 563-886-6121
Dr. Marlene Johnson, supt. Fax 886-2341
www.tipton.k12.ia.us
Tipton ES 400/PK-4
400 E 6th St 52772 563-886-6131
Lori Foley, prin. Fax 886-2555
Tipton MS 300/5-8
400 E 6th St 52772 563-886-6025
Troy Smock, prin. Fax 886-2555

Toledo, Tama, Pop. 2,265
South Tama County Community SD
Supt. — See Tama
South Tama County MS 300/5-8
201 S Green St 52342 641-484-4121
Benjamin Adams, prin. Fax 484-2699

Traer, Tama, Pop. 1,686
North Tama County Community SD 500/PK-12
605 Walnut St 50675 319-478-2265
David Hill, supt. Fax 478-2917
www.n-tama.k12.ia.us
North Tama ES 200/PK-6
605 Walnut St 50675 319-478-2265
Craig Josh Youel, prin. Fax 478-2917

Treynor, Pottawattamie, Pop. 919
Treynor Community SD 800/K-12
PO Box 369 51575 712-487-3414
Lou Howell, supt. Fax 487-3332
www.treynorschools.org
Treynor ES 400/K-5
PO Box 369 51575 712-487-3422
Jill Kay, prin. Fax 487-3625
Treynor MS 200/6-8
PO Box 369 51575 712-487-3181
Jenny Berens, prin. Fax 487-3567

Tripoli, Bremer, Pop. 1,304
Tripoli Community SD 400/PK-12
209 8th Ave SW 50676 319-882-4202
Troy Heller, supt. Fax 882-3103
www.tripoli.k12.ia.us
Tripoli ES 200/PK-5
209 8th Ave SW 50676 319-882-4203
Sarah Figanbaum, prin. Fax 882-3649

Troy Mills, Linn
North Linn Community SD 500/PK-12
PO Box 200 52344 319-224-3291
Chris Fenster, supt. Fax 224-3727
www.northlinncsd.org
North Linn ES 200/PK-5
PO Box 200 52344 319-224-3291
Chris Fenster, prin. Fax 224-3264
North Linn MS 200/6-8
PO Box 200 52344 319-224-3291
Scott Beaty, prin. Fax 224-3232

Truro, Madison, Pop. 481
Interstate 35 Community SD 900/PK-12
PO Box 79 50257 641-765-4291
Kevin Fiene, supt. Fax 765-4593
www.i-35.k12.ia.us
Interstate 35 ES 400/K-5
PO Box 200 50257 641-765-4901
Geoff Tessau, prin. Fax 765-4905
Interstate 35 MS 200/6-8
PO Box 200 50257 641-765-4908
Steve Kaster, prin. Fax 765-4905
Little Roadrunner Preschool 50/PK-PK
PO Box 200 50257 641-765-4901
Geoff Tessau, prin. Fax 765-4593

Underwood, Pottawattamie, Pop. 909
Underwood Community SD 700/PK-12
PO Box 130 51576 712-566-2332
Edward Hawks, supt. Fax 566-2070
www.underwoodeagles.org/
Underwood ES 300/PK-5
PO Box 130 51576 712-566-2326
Jeffrey Privia, prin. Fax 566-2963
Underwood MS 200/6-8
PO Box 130 51576 712-566-2332
Beau Jacobsen, prin. Fax 566-2070

Union, Hardin, Pop. 394
BCLUW Community SD
Supt. — See Conrad
BCLUW MS 200/5-8
704 Commercial St 50258 641-486-5371
Dirk Borgman, prin. Fax 486-5372

Urbana, Benton, Pop. 1,434
Center Point-Urbana Community SD
Supt. — See Center Point
Center Point-Urbana IS 300/3-5
202 Main St 52345 319-849-1102
Jon Hasleiet, prin. Fax 443-2764

Urbandale, Polk, Pop. 38,851
Urbandale Community SD 4,100/PK-12
11152 Aurora Ave 50322 515-457-5000
Steve Bass, supt. Fax 457-5018
www.urbandaleschools.com
Jensen ES 200/K-5
6301 Aurora Ave 50322 515-457-5100
Brad Paul, prin. Fax 457-5104
Karen Acres ES 200/K-5
3500 74th St 50322 515-457-5700
Lara Justmann, prin. Fax 457-5704
Olmsted ES 500/PK-5
7110 Prairie Ave 50322 515-457-5800
Elyse Brimeyer, prin. Fax 457-5804
Rolling Green ES 300/PK-5
8100 Airline Ave 50322 515-457-5900
Julia Taylor, prin. Fax 457-5904
Urbandale MS 900/6-8
7701 Aurora Ave 50322 515-457-6600
Loren DeKruyf, prin. Fax 457-6610
Valerius ES 200/K-5
3305 92nd St 50322 515-457-6500
Meredith Mauro, prin. Fax 457-6504
Webster ES 600/PK-5
12955 Aurora Ave 50323 515-331-8600
Erin Shearer, prin. Fax 331-8604

Waukee Community SD
Supt. — See Waukee
Walnut Hills ES 700/PK-5
4240 156th St 50323 515-987-3585
Lyndsay Marron, prin. Fax 987-9784

Des Moines Christian S 1,000/PK-12
13007 Douglas Pkwy Ste 100 50323 515-252-2480
Cade Lambert, supt. Fax 251-6911
St. Pius X S 400/PK-8
3601 66th St 50322 515-276-1061
Mary Jo Kever, prin. Fax 276-0350

Van Horne, Benton, Pop. 678
Benton Community SD 1,200/PK-12
PO Box 70 52346 319-228-8701
Gary Zittergruen, supt. Fax 228-8254
www.benton.k12.ia.us
Benton Community MS 200/7-8
PO Box 70 52346 319-228-8701
Kal Goodchild, prin. Fax 228-8747
Other Schools – See Atkins, Keystone, Norway

Van Meter, Dallas, Pop. 1,006
Van Meter Community SD 800/K-12
PO Box 257 50261 515-996-9960
Deron Durflinger, supt. Fax 996-2488
www.vmbulldogs.com/
Van Meter ES 300/K-5
PO Box 257 50261 515-996-2221
Cody Tibbetts, prin. Fax 996-2488

Ventura, Cerro Gordo, Pop. 712
Garner-Hayfield-Ventura Community SD
Supt. — See Garner
Garner-Hayfield-Ventura IS 5-6
300 S Main Str 50482 641-829-4482
Debra Steenhard, prin. Fax 829-3906
Garner-Hayfield-Ventura JHS 7-8
110 S Main St 50482 641-829-4484
Debra Steenhard, prin. Fax 829-3995

Victor, Iowa, Pop. 887
H-L-V Community SD 400/PK-12
402 5th St 52347 319-647-2161
Brad Hohensee, supt. Fax 647-2164
www.hlv.k12.ia.us
H-L-V ES 200/PK-6
402 5th St 52347 319-647-2161
Cory Lahndorf, prin. Fax 647-2164

Villisca, Montgomery, Pop. 1,244
Southwest Valley SD 800/PK-12
406 E 3rd St 50864 712-826-2552
William Stone, supt. Fax 826-4072
www.southwestvalley.org
Enarson ES 100/PK-5
219 Central Ave 50864 712-826-5982
Lora Top, prin. Fax 826-4133
Southwest Valley MS 200/6-8
406 E 3rd St 50864 712-826-2552
Lora Top, prin. Fax 826-4072
Other Schools – See Corning

Vinton, Benton, Pop. 5,202
Vinton-Shellsburg Community SD 1,600/PK-12
1502 C Ave 52349 319-436-4728
Mary Jo Hainstock, supt. Fax 472-3889
www.vscsd.org
Tilford ES 500/PK-4
308 E 13th St 52349 319-436-4728
Jim Murray, prin. Fax 472-2742
Vinton-Shellsburg MS 300/6-8
212 W 15th St 52349 319-436-4728
Shelly Petersen, prin. Fax 472-4014
Other Schools – See Shellsburg

Walcott, Scott, Pop. 1,613
Davenport Community SD
Supt. — See Davenport
Walcott ES 200/K-5
545 E James St 52773 563-445-5200
Mike Lawler, prin. Fax 445-5959
Walcott IS 400/6-8
545 E James St 52773 563-445-5200
Mike Lawler, prin. Fax 445-5959

Wall Lake, Sac, Pop. 818
East Sac County SD
Supt. — See Lake View
East Sac County ES 200/PK-4
PO Box 40 51466 712-664-2627
Mike Fischer, prin. Fax 664-2607

Wapello, Louisa, Pop. 2,049
Wapello Community SD 700/PK-12
406 Mechanic St 52653 319-523-3641
Mike Peterson, supt. Fax 523-8151
www.wapello.k12.ia.us
Wapello ES 300/PK-6
505 N Cedar St 52653 319-523-5571
Brett Nagle, prin. Fax 523-8125
Wapello JHS 100/7-8
501 Buchanan Ave 52653 319-523-8131
Steve Bohlen, prin. Fax 523-4408

Washington, Washington, Pop. 7,169
Washington Community SD 1,700/PK-12
PO Box 926 52353 319-653-6543
Jeff Dicks, supt. Fax 653-5685
www.washington.k12.ia.us
Lincoln ES 300/3-5
606 S 4th Ave 52353 319-653-3691
Teresa Beenblossom, prin. Fax 653-6800
Stewart ES 400/PK-2
821 N 4th Ave 52353 319-653-3244
Adam Miller, prin. Fax 653-5313
Washington MS 500/6-8
PO Box 490 52353 319-653-5414
Curt Mayer, prin. Fax 653-7350

St. James S 100/PK-6
616 W 2nd St 52353 319-653-3631
Beth McBride, prin. Fax 653-4019

Washta, Cherokee, Pop. 247
River Valley Community SD
Supt. — See Correctionville
River Valley ES 300/PK-5
PO Box 151 51061 712-447-6318
Melissa Holtz, prin. Fax 447-6374

Waterloo, Black Hawk, Pop. 66,424
Waterloo Community SD 10,900/PK-12
1516 Washington St 50702 319-433-1800
Dr. Jane Lindaman, supt. Fax 433-1886
www.waterloo.k12.ia.us
Becker ES 600/PK-5
1239 Sheldon St 50701 319-433-2180
Melissa Steggall, prin. Fax 433-2187
Carver Academy 500/6-8
1505 Logan Ave 50703 319-433-2500
Stephanie Mohorne, prin. Fax 433-2548
Central MS 500/6-8
1350 Katoski Dr 50701 319-433-2100
Ross Bauer, prin. Fax 433-2149
Cunningham S for Excellence 400/PK-5
1224 Mobile St 50703 319-433-2600
Lucy Evans, prin. Fax 433-2603
Henry ES 500/K-5
312 Rachael St 50701 319-433-2860
Jacob Young-Kent, prin. Fax 433-3040
Highland ES 500/PK-5
812 Idaho St 50703 319-433-2630
Matthew Willand, prin. Fax 433-2633
Hoover MS 800/6-8
630 Hillcrest Rd 50701 319-433-2830
Michael Fisher, prin. Fax 433-2843
Irving ES 400/PK-5
1115 W 5th St 50702 319-433-2800
Amy Schmidt, prin. Fax 433-2829
Kingsley ES 500/K-5
201 Sunset Rd 50701 319-433-2210
Amber Dietz, prin. Fax 433-2216
Kittrell ES 600/PK-5
1304 Oregon St 50702 319-433-2910
Audrey Wallican-Green, prin. Fax 433-2916
Lincoln ES 500/PK-5
302 Cedar Bend St 50703 319-433-1990
Brad Schweppe, prin. Fax 433-1997
Lowell ES 400/K-5
1628 Washington St 50702 319-433-1900
Carrie Heinzerling, prin. Fax 433-1905
Orange ES 600/PK-5
5805 Kimball Ave 50701 319-433-2880
Sunni Hart, prin. Fax 433-2888
Other Schools – See Elk Run Heights, Evansdale

Blessed Maria Assunta Pallotta MS 6-8
3225 W 9th St 50702 319-232-6592
Tom Novotney, prin. Fax 232-6963
Blessed Sacrament S 200/PK-5
600 Stephan Ave 50701 319-233-7863
Angie Beck, prin. Fax 233-8237
Sacred Heart S 100/PK-5
620 W 5th St 50702 319-234-6593
Angie Beck, prin. Fax 235-7987
St. Edward S 300/PK-5
139 E Mitchell Ave 50702 319-233-6202
Aaron Becker, prin. Fax 235-2898

Waterloo Christian S 100/PK-12
1307 W Ridgeway Ave 50701 319-235-9309
Ryan Hall, head sch Fax 833-4780

Waterville, Allamakee, Pop. 144
Allamakee Community SD
Supt. — See Waukon
Waterville ES 100/PK-5
115 Main St 52170 563-535-7245
Julie Askelson, prin. Fax 535-7110

Waukee, Dallas, Pop. 13,637
Waukee Community SD 8,200/PK-12
560 SE University Ave 50263 515-987-5161
Dr. Cindi McDonald, supt. Fax 987-2701
www.waukeeschools.org
Eason ES 600/K-5
605 SE Boone Dr 50263 515-987-5200
Clint Prohaska, prin. Fax 987-2707
Ragan ES PK-5
645 NE Dartmoor Dr 50263 515-987-0435
Matthew Tobie, prin. Fax 987-9566
Waukee ES 600/PK-5
850 6th St 50263 515-987-5193
Nicole Johnson, prin. Fax 987-5194
Waukee MS 600/6-7
905 Warrior Ln 50263 515-987-5177
Adam Shockey, prin. Fax 987-2741
Waukee South MS 600/6-7
2350 SE La Grant Pkwy 50263 515-987-3222
Doug Barry, prin. Fax 987-3233
Other Schools – See Clive, Urbandale, West Des Moines

Waukon, Allamakee, Pop. 3,873
Allamakee Community SD 1,100/PK-12
1059 3rd Ave NW 52172 563-568-3409
Dave Herold, supt. Fax 568-2677
www.allamakee.k12.ia.us/
East Campus ES 200/3-5
107 6th St NW 52172 563-568-6304
Joseph Griffith, prin. Fax 568-6410
Waukon MS 200/6-8
1059 3rd Ave NW 52172 563-568-6321
Jennifer Garin, prin. Fax 568-2677
West Campus ES 300/PK-2
953 3rd Ave NW 52172 563-568-6375
Joseph Griffith, prin. Fax 568-2677
Other Schools – See Waterville

St. Patrick S 100/PK-6
200 2nd St SW 52172 563-568-2415
Katie Fahey, prin. Fax 568-2170

Waverly, Bremer, Pop. 9,752
Waverly-Shell Rock Community SD 2,100/PK-12
1415 4th Ave SW 50677 319-352-3630
Dr. Ed Klamfoth, supt. Fax 352-5676
www.wsr.k12.ia.us
Carey ES, 220 9th Ave NW 50677 200/K-4
Micky Bahlmann, prin. 319-352-2855
Southeast ES, PO Box 96 50677 200/K-4
Christi Lines, prin. 319-352-3582
Waverly-Shell Rock MS 700/5-8
501 Heritage Way 50677 319-352-3632
Jeremy Langner, prin. Fax 352-5199
West Cedar ES, PO Box 117 50677 200/K-4
Christi Lines, prin. 319-352-2754
Other Schools – See Shell Rock

St. Paul's Lutheran S 200/PK-6
301 1st St NW 50677 319-352-1484
Dr. Kris Meyer, prin. Fax 352-3999

Wayland, Henry, Pop. 957
Waco Community SD 500/PK-12
PO Box 158 52654 319-256-6200
Jeff Dicks, supt. Fax 256-6211
www.wacocsd.org
Other Schools – See Crawfordsville

Webster City, Hamilton, Pop. 7,961
Webster City Community SD 1,600/PK-12
PO Box 10 50595 515-832-9200
Mike Sherwood, supt. Fax 832-9204
www.webster-city.k12.ia.us
Pleasant View ES 300/PK-1
PO Box 10 50595 515-832-9241
Mindy Mossman, prin. Fax 832-9244
Sunset Heights ES 300/2-4
PO Box 10 50595 515-832-9245
Kelli Reis, prin. Fax 832-9248
Webster City MS 400/5-8
PO Box 10 50595 515-832-9220
Jerry Buseman, prin. Fax 832-9225

St. Thomas Aquinas S 100/PK-6
624 Dubuque St 50595 515-832-1346
Duane Siepker, prin. Fax 832-1212

Wellman, Washington, Pop. 1,387
Mid-Prairie Community SD 1,300/PK-12
PO Box 150 52356 319-646-6093
Mark Schneider, supt. Fax 646-2093
www.mid-prairie.k12.ia.us
Mid-Prairie West ES 300/PK-K, 3-4
PO Box H 52356 319-646-2984
William Poock, prin. Fax 646-2987
Other Schools – See Kalona

Wellsburg, Grundy, Pop. 703
AGWSR Community SD
Supt. — See Ackley
AGWSR Wellsburg Attendance Center 200/K-8
609 S Monroe St 50680 641-869-5121
Jason Gabel, prin. Fax 869-3426

Timothy Christian S 100/K-8
PO Box 70 50680 641-869-3679
Rebecca Johnson, admin. Fax 869-3510

West Bend, Palo Alto, Pop. 779
West Bend - Mallard Community SD 400/K-12
PO Box 247 50597 515-887-7821
Amanda Schmidt, supt. Fax 887-7853
www.west-bend.k12.ia.us
West Bend - Mallard MS 100/5-8
PO Box 247 50597 515-887-7831
Paul Peppmeier, prin. Fax 887-7853
Other Schools – See Mallard

West Branch, Cedar, Pop. 2,295
West Branch Community SD 900/PK-12
148 N Oliphant St 52358 319-643-7213
Kevin Hatfield, supt. Fax 643-7122
www.west-branch.k12.ia.us
Hoover ES 400/PK-4
148 N Oliphant St 52358 319-643-7211
Jess Burger, prin. Fax 643-7228
West Branch MS 300/5-8
225 N Maple St 52358 319-643-5324
Sara Oswald, prin. Fax 643-5447

West Burlington, Des Moines, Pop. 2,909
West Burlington ISD 900/PK-12
607 Ramsey St 52655 319-752-8747
David Schmitt, supt. Fax 754-9382
www.wbschools.us
West Burlington ES 500/PK-5
545 Ramsey St 52655 319-754-5726
Theresa Ritters, prin. Fax 758-6768
West Burlington JHS 200/6-8
408 W Van Weiss Blvd 52655 319-752-7138
Bruce Snodgrass, prin. Fax 754-0075

West Des Moines, Polk, Pop. 55,623
Waukee Community SD
Supt. — See Waukee
Brookview ES 600/K-5
8000 EP True Pkwy 50266 515-987-5166
Stephanie Angelino, prin. Fax 987-5168
Maple Grove ES 500/PK-5
1455 98th St 50266 515-987-3363
Kim Tierney, prin. Fax 987-3903
Woodland Hills ES 500/PK-5
1120 S 95th St 50266 515-987-5196
Scott Shumaker, prin. Fax 987-7560

West Des Moines Community SD 9,000/PK-12
3550 Mills Civic Pkwy 50265 515-633-5000
Dr. Lisa Remy, supt. Fax 633-5099
www.wdmcs.org
Crossroads Park ES 600/K-6
1050 50th St 50266 515-633-5600
Robert G. Davis, prin. Fax 633-5699
Fairmeadows ES 600/K-6
807 23rd St 50265 515-633-6500
Brandon Pierce, prin. Fax 633-6599
Hillside ES 600/K-6
713 8th St 50265 515-633-6200
Dr. Graham Jones, prin. Fax 633-6299
Jordan Creek ES 800/PK-6
4105 Fuller Rd 50265 515-633-5200
Paul Wenger, prin. Fax 633-5299
Stilwell JHS 700/7-8
1601 Vine St 50265 515-633-6000
Eric Boyle, prin. Fax 633-6099
Western Hills ES 600/PK-6
600 39th St 50265 515-633-5900
George Panosh, prin. Fax 633-5999
Westridge ES 600/PK-6
5500 EP True Pkwy 50266 515-633-5400
Nathan Ballagh, prin. Fax 633-5499
Other Schools – See Clive, Windsor Heights

Iowa Christian Academy 300/PK-12
2501 Vine St 50265 515-221-3999
Dr. Brenda Hillman, admin. Fax 225-2387
Sacred Heart S 500/PK-8
1601 Grand Ave 50265 515-223-1284
Jane Kinney, prin. Fax 223-9413
St. Francis of Assisi S 700/K-8
7075 Ashworth Rd 50266 515-457-7167
Misty Hade, prin. Fax 440-1042

West Liberty, Muscatine, Pop. 3,704
West Liberty Community SD 1,200/PK-12
111 W 7th St 52776 319-627-2116
Joseph Potts, supt. Fax 627-2963
www.wl.k12.ia.us
Early Childhood Center 200/PK-K
111 W 7th St 52776 319-627-5089
Missy Johnson, dir. Fax 627-2039
West Liberty ES 400/1-5
806 N Miller St 52776 319-627-4243
Jennifer Laughlin, prin. Fax 627-2099
West Liberty MS 300/6-8
203 E 7th St 52776 319-627-2118
Vicki Vernon, prin. Fax 627-2092

West Point, Lee, Pop. 961

Holy Trinity S 200/K-6
413 Avenue C 52656 319-837-6131
Michael Sheerin, prin. Fax 837-8112

Westside, Crawford, Pop. 299
Ar-We-Va Community SD 200/PK-12
108 Clinton St 51467 712-663-4311
Jeff Kruse, supt. Fax 663-4312
www.ar-we-va.k12.ia.us
Ar-We-Va ES 100/PK-5
108 Clinton St 51467 712-663-4313
Rosemary Cameron, prin. Fax 663-4312

West Union, Fayette, Pop. 2,464
North Fayette Community SD 800/PK-12
PO Box 73 52175 563-422-3851
Duane Willhite, supt. Fax 422-3854
www.nfvschools.com
West Union ES 300/PK-4
400 N Pine St 52175 563-422-3851
Travis Elliott, prin. Fax 422-3085
Other Schools – See Fayette

Wheatland, Clinton, Pop. 762
Calamus-Wheatland Community SD 500/PK-12
PO Box 279 52777 563-374-1292
Lonnie Luepker, supt. Fax 374-1080
www.cal-wheat.k12.ia.us
Other Schools – See Calamus

Whiting, Monona, Pop. 758
Whiting Community SD 200/PK-12
PO Box 295 51063 712-455-2468
Randy Collins, supt. Fax 455-2601
www.whitingcsd.org
Whiting ES 100/PK-6
PO Box 295 51063 712-455-2468
Al Laboranti, prin. Fax 455-2601

Williamsburg, Iowa, Pop. 3,044
Williamsburg Community SD 1,200/PK-12
PO Box 120 52361 319-668-1059
Dr. Chad Garber, supt. Fax 668-9311
www.williamsburg.k12.ia.us
Welsh ES 600/PK-6
PO Box 270 52361 319-668-2301
David Widmer, prin. Fax 668-9552

Lutheran Interparish S 200/PK-8
PO Box 750 52361 319-668-1711
Mark Grewe, prin. Fax 668-9054

Wilton, Muscatine, Pop. 2,767
Wilton Community SD 800/PK-12
1002 Cypress St 52778 563-732-2035
Joe Burnett, supt. Fax 732-4121
www.wiltoncsd.org/
Wilton ES 500/PK-6
1002 Cypress St 52778 563-732-2880
Denise Austin, prin. Fax 732-4181

Windsor Heights, Polk, Pop. 4,791
Des Moines Independent Community SD
Supt. — See Des Moines
Cowles ES 400/PK-8
6401 College Ave, 515-242-7818
Todd Johnson, prin. Fax 242-7358

West Des Moines Community SD
Supt. — See West Des Moines
Clive Learning Academy 500/PK-6
1600 73rd St, 515-633-5800
Janelle Green, dir. Fax 633-5899

Winfield, Henry, Pop. 1,123
Winfield-Mt. Union Community SD 500/PK-12
PO Box E 52659 319-257-7700
Jeff Maeder, supt. Fax 257-7714
wmucsd.org
Winfield ES 200/PK-5
PO Box E 52659 319-257-7702
Gabriel Wylder, prin. Fax 257-7703

Winterset, Madison, Pop. 5,159
Winterset Community SD 1,800/PK-12
PO Box 30 50273 515-462-2718
Dr. Susan Meade, supt. Fax 462-2732
www.winterset.k12.ia.us
Winterset ES 600/PK-3
404 S 2nd Ave 50273 515-462-1551
Jennifer Berns, prin. Fax 462-5025
Winterset JHS 300/7-8
720 Husky Dr 50273 515-462-3336
Doug Hinrichs, prin. Fax 462-2178
Winterset MS 400/4-6
706 W School 50273 515-462-3010
Wendy Sawyer, prin. Fax 462-4149

Winthrop, Buchanan, Pop. 845
East Buchanan Community SD 600/PK-12
414 5th St N 50682 319-935-3767
Daniel Fox, supt. Fax 935-3749
www.eastbuchananschools.com
East Buchanan ES 300/PK-5
414 5th St N 50682 319-935-3660
Daniel Fox, prin. Fax 935-3749
East Buchanan MS 100/6-8
414 5th St N 50682 319-935-3367
Eric Dockstader, prin. Fax 935-3615

Woodbine, Harrison, Pop. 1,455
Woodbine Community SD 500/PK-12
501 Weare St 51579 712-647-2411
Dr. Chris Anderson, supt. Fax 647-2526
sites.google.com/a/woodbine.k12.ia.us/flashy-tiger
Woodbine ES 300/PK-6
501 Weare St 51579 712-647-2440
Chris Anderson, prin. Fax 647-2824

Woodward, Dallas, Pop. 1,006
Woodward-Granger Community SD
Supt. — See Granger
Woodward-Granger MS 200/6-8
306 W 3rd St 50276 515-438-4263
Amy Bidwell, prin. Fax 438-2497

Wyoming, Jones, Pop. 513
Midland Community SD 500/PK-12
PO Box 109 52362 563-488-2292
Doug Tuetken, supt. Fax 488-2253
www.midland.k12.ia.us
Other Schools – See Oxford Junction

Zearing, Story, Pop. 553
Colo-Nesco Comm SD
Supt. — See Colo
Colo-Nesco ES 200/PK-4
407 N Center St 50278 641-487-7411
Ty Adams, prin. Fax 487-7414

KANSAS

KANSAS DEPARTMENT OF EDUCATION
900 SW Jackson St, Topeka 66612
Telephone 785-296-3202
Fax 785-296-7933
Website http://www.ksde.org

Commissioner of Education Randy Watson

KANSAS BOARD OF EDUCATION
120 SE 10th Ave, Topeka 66612-1103

Chairperson Jim Porter

PUBLIC, PRIVATE AND CATHOLIC ELEMENTARY SCHOOLS

Abilene, Dickinson, Pop. 6,690
Abilene USD 435 1,700/PK-12
PO Box 639 67410 785-263-2630
Dr. Denise Guy, supt. Fax 263-7610
www.abileneschools.org/
Abilene MS 400/6-8
500 NW 14th St 67410 785-263-1471
Ron Wilson, prin. Fax 263-4443
Eisenhower ES 4-5
1101 N Vine St 67410 785-263-1643
Ethan Gruen, prin. Fax 263-3223
Kennedy ES 300/PK-1
1501 N Kuney St 67410 785-263-1088
Twyla Sprouse, prin. Fax 263-3078
McKinley ES 200/2-3
112 N Rogers St 67410 785-263-2311
Tom Schwartz, prin. Fax 263-7610

Chapman USD 473
Supt. — See Chapman
Blue Ridge ES 100/K-5
1539 Highway 18 67410 785-598-2226
Kara Spittles, prin. Fax 598-2287
Rural Center ES 50/K-4
902 1400 Ave 67410 785-479-2213
Cynthia Markley, prin. Fax 479-2213

St. Andrew S 100/PK-5
301 S Buckeye Ave 67410 785-263-2453
Christina Bacon, prin. Fax 263-3884

Agra, Phillips, Pop. 263
Thunder Ridge SD 110
Supt. — See Kensington
Thunder Ridge MS 100/PK-PK, 4-
941 Kansas Ave 67621 785-638-2244
Beth Norris, prin. Fax 638-2254

Alma, Wabaunsee, Pop. 821
Wabaunsee USD 329 500/PK-12
PO Box 157 66401 785-765-3394
Brad Starnes, supt. Fax 765-3624
www.usd329.com
Alma ES 100/PK-4
215 E 9th St 66401 785-765-3349
Jan Hutley, prin. Fax 765-3956
Other Schools – See Maple Hill, Paxico

St. John Lutheran S 50/K-8
PO Box 368 66401 785-765-3914
Merv Dehning, prin. Fax 765-7777

Almena, Norton, Pop. 407
Northern Valley USD 212 200/PK-12
PO Box 217 67622 785-669-2445
Ken Tharman, supt. Fax 669-2263
www.nvhuskies.org
Almena ES 100/PK-4
PO Box 217 67622 785-664-2446
Marvin Gebhard, prin. Fax 664-4060
Other Schools – See Long Island

Altamont, Labette, Pop. 1,042
Labette County USD 506 1,600/PK-12
PO Box 189 67330 620-784-5326
Dr. John Wyrick, supt. Fax 784-5879
www.usd506.org
Altamont S 200/PK-8
PO Box 306 67330 620-784-5511
Tiffany Flatt, prin. Fax 784-2675
Other Schools – See Bartlett, Edna, Mound Valley, Parsons

Alta Vista, Wabaunsee, Pop. 442
Morris County USD 417
Supt. — See Council Grove
Prairie Heights ES 100/K-6
801 Center St 66834 785-499-6313
Valerie Gehrer, prin. Fax 499-5342

Altoona, Wilson, Pop. 399
Altoona-Midway USD 387
Supt. — See Buffalo
Altoona-Midway ES 100/PK-4
PO Box 128 66710 620-568-5725
Kim Reazin, prin. Fax 568-5755

Americus, Lyon, Pop. 875
North Lyon County USD 251 400/K-12
PO Box 527 66835 620-443-5116
Aron Dody, supt. Fax 443-5659
www.usd251.org
Americus S 200/K-8
PO Box 497 66835 620-443-5165
Corey Wiltz, prin. Fax 443-5840
Other Schools – See Reading

Andale, Sedgwick, Pop. 920
Renwick USD 267 1,900/PK-12
PO Box 68 67001 316-444-2165
Tracy Bourne, supt. Fax 445-2241
www.usd267.com
Andale ES 400/K-8
500 Rush Ave 67001 316-444-2628
Tad Hatfield, prin. Fax 445-2252
Other Schools – See Colwich, Garden Plain

Andover, Butler, Pop. 11,537
Andover USD 385 9,900/PK-12
1432 N Andover Rd 67002 316-218-4660
Brett White, supt. Fax 733-3604
www.usd385.org
Andover Central MS 600/6-8
903 E Central Ave 67002 316-218-4710
Tim Hayden, prin. Fax 266-8878
Andover MS 600/6-8
1628 N Andover Rd 67002 316-218-4610
Deb Regier, prin. Fax 733-4165
Cottonwood ES 400/K-5
1747 N Andover Rd 67002 316-218-4620
Shari Rooks, prin. Fax 733-3648
Meadowlark ES 400/K-5
1411 N Main St 67002 316-218-4630
Dana Matheny, prin. Fax 733-3651
Prairie Creek ES 300/PK-5
654 S YMCA Dr 67002 316-218-4630
Shelley Jonas, prin. Fax 733-3651
Sunflower ES 400/K-5
616 E Douglas Ave 67002 316-218-4730
Rita Decker, prin. Fax 266-8890
Other Schools – See Wichita

Anthony, Harper, Pop. 2,226
Chaparral Schools USD 361 800/PK-12
PO Box 486 67003 620-842-5183
Josh Swartz, supt. Fax 842-5307
www.usd361.org/
Anthony ES 300/PK-6
215 S Springfield Ave 67003 620-842-3743
Rachel Oliver, prin. Fax 842-5236
Other Schools – See Harper

Argonia, Sumner, Pop. 493
Argonia USD 359 200/PK-12
202 E Allen St 67004 620-435-6311
Dr. Julie McPherron, supt. Fax 435-6623
www.argonia359.org
Argonia ES 100/PK-5
202 E Allen St 67004 620-435-6716
Dr. Julie McPherron, prin. Fax 435-6623

Arkansas City, Cowley, Pop. 11,966
Arkansas City USD 470 2,800/PK-12
PO Box 1028 67005 620-441-2000
Dr. Ron Ballard, supt. Fax 441-2009
www.usd470.com
Adams ES 300/PK-5
1201 N 10th St 67005 620-441-2040
Robert Onolio, prin. Fax 441-2044
Arkansas City MS 600/6-8
400 E Kansas Ave 67005 620-441-2030
William Pfannenstiel, prin. Fax 441-2036
C-4 ES 100/PK-5
11945 292nd Rd 67005 620-441-2045
Amy Hutto, prin. Fax 441-2049
I X L ES 200/PK-5
6758 322nd Rd 67005 620-441-2055
Sheryl Loods, prin. Fax 441-2059
Jefferson ES 300/PK-5
131 E Osage Ave 67005 620-441-2060
Cheryl Carter, prin. Fax 441-2064
Roosevelt ES 200/PK-5
300 N B St 67005 620-441-2070
Pamela Barbour, prin. Fax 441-2074
Willard ES 300/PK-5
201 N 4th St 67005 620-441-2050
Rosann Meier, prin. Fax 441-2054

Ark City Christian Academy 100/PK-12
PO Box 1181 67005 620-442-0022
Lisa Holland, prin. Fax 442-0034
Sacred Heart Catholic S 100/PK-5
312 S B St 67005 620-442-6550
Eva Harmon, prin. Fax 441-0935

Arma, Crawford, Pop. 1,474
Northeast USD 246 500/K-12
PO Box 669 66712 620-347-4116
Greg Gorman, supt. Fax 347-4087
www.usd246.org
Northeast ES 300/K-8
PO Box 669 66712 620-347-8461
Terry Cleland, prin. Fax 347-4140

Ashland, Clark, Pop. 841
Ashland USD 220 200/PK-12
PO Box 187 67831 620-635-2220
Jamie Wetig, supt. Fax 635-2637
www.usd220.net
Ashland ES 100/PK-6
PO Box 187 67831 620-635-2722
Jason Endicott, prin. Fax 635-2851
Ashland JHS 50/7-8
PO Box 187 67831 620-635-2814
Jamie Wetig, prin. Fax 635-2637

Atchison, Atchison, Pop. 10,700
Atchison USD 409 1,700/PK-12
626 Commercial St 66002 913-367-4384
Dr. Susan Myers, supt. Fax 367-2246
www.usd409.net
Atchison ES 900/PK-5
825 N 17th St 66002 913-367-1161
Kent Michel, prin. Fax 367-1602
Atchison MS 400/6-8
301 N 5th St 66002 913-367-5363
Chad Bilderback, prin. Fax 367-1302

St. Benedict Catholic S 200/PK-8
201 Division St 66002 913-367-3503
Diane Liebsch, prin. Fax 367-9324
Trinity Lutheran S 100/PK-8
611 N 8th St 66002 913-367-4763
Lisa Brookover, prin. Fax 367-4823

Attica, Harper, Pop. 621
Attica USD 511 200/PK-12
PO Box 415 67009 620-254-7915
Charles Keller, supt. Fax 254-7872
www.usd511.net
Puls ES 100/PK-5
PO Box 415 67009 620-254-7915
Charles Keller, supt. Fax 254-7872

Atwood, Rawlins, Pop. 1,181
Rawlins County USD 105 300/PK-12
205 N 4th St Ste 1 67730 785-626-3236
Tom Dolenz, supt. Fax 626-3083
www.usd105.org
Rawlins County ES 200/PK-6
205 N 4th St 67730 785-626-3217
Tom Dolenz, prin. Fax 626-1011

Auburn, Shawnee, Pop. 1,187
Auburn Washburn USD 437
Supt. — See Topeka
Auburn ES 400/PK-6
810 Commercial St 66402 785-339-4400
Melinda Patterson, prin. Fax 339-4425

Augusta, Butler, Pop. 9,098
Augusta USD 402 2,300/PK-12
2345 Greyhound Dr 67010 316-775-5484
Dr. John Black, supt. Fax 775-5035
www.usd402.com

Augusta MS 500/6-8
1001 State St 67010 316-775-6383
Matthew Ward, prin. Fax 775-3853
Ewalt ES 400/PK-5
2340 Greyhound Dr 67010 316-775-0056
Kristie Thackery, prin. Fax 775-1556
Garfield ES 300/PK-5
1053 Osage St 67010 316-775-6601
Trever Lockamy, prin. Fax 775-1669
Lincoln ES 300/K-5
1812 Cron St 67010 316-775-5415
Lyle Dosser, prin. Fax 775-5355
Robinson ES 200/K-5
1301 Helen St 67010 316-775-7561
Greg Taylor, prin. Fax 775-0867

St. James Catholic S 100/PK-7
1010 Belmont Ave 67010 316-775-5721
Richard Guy, prin. Fax 775-7160

Axtell, Marshall, Pop. 393
Prairie Hills USD 113
Supt. — See Sabetha
Axtell ES 100/PK-8
504 Pine St 66403 785-736-2237
Jayson Tynon, prin. Fax 736-2295

Baldwin City, Douglas, Pop. 4,416
Baldwin City USD 348 1,400/PK-12
PO Box 67 66006 785-594-2721
Paul Dorathy, supt. Fax 594-3408
www.usd348.com/
Baldwin ES - Intermediate Center 300/3-5
PO Box 67 66006 785-594-2446
Dan Wallsmith, prin. Fax 594-2447
Baldwin ES - Primary Center 400/PK-2
PO Box 67 66006 785-594-2444
Dr. Deb Ehling-Gwin, prin. Fax 594-2445
Baldwin JHS 300/6-8
PO Box 67 66006 785-594-2448
Derek Bland, prin. Fax 594-2449

Barnes, Washington, Pop. 159
Barnes USD 223 500/PK-12
PO Box 188 66933 785-763-4231
Brian Cordel, supt. Fax 763-4461
www.usd223.org
Other Schools – See Hanover, Linn

Bartlett, Labette, Pop. 69
Labette County USD 506
Supt. — See Altamont
Bartlett S 100/K-8
PO Box 4676 67332 620-226-3414
Tim Traxson, prin. Fax 226-3340

Basehor, Leavenworth, Pop. 4,548
Basehor-Linwood USD 458 2,200/K-12
PO Box 282 66007 913-724-1396
David Howard, supt. Fax 724-2709
www.usd458.org
Basehor ES 200/K-2
15602 Leavenworth Rd 66007 913-724-1038
Tiffany Lynch, prin. Fax 724-1492
Basehor IS 200/3-5
PO Box 498 66007 913-724-1279
Teri Boyd, prin. Fax 662-7089
Basehor-Linwood MS 500/6-8
15900 Conley Rd 66007 913-724-2976
Amy Garver, prin. Fax 955-7074
Glenwood Ridge ES 300/K-5
17550 157th Ter 66007 913-724-3536
Jan Hancock, prin. Fax 724-3539
Other Schools – See Linwood

Baxter Springs, Cherokee, Pop. 3,956
Baxter Springs USD 508 1,000/PK-12
1108 Military Ave 66713 620-856-2375
David Pendergraft, supt. Fax 856-3943
www.usd508.org
Central ES 300/3-6
1501 Park Ave 66713 620-856-3311
Robert Womack, prin. Fax 856-3792
Lincoln ES 300/PK-2
801 Lincoln Ave 66713 620-856-3322
Kenneth Boeckman, prin. Fax 856-4173

Bazine, Ness, Pop. 329
Western Plains USD 106
Supt. — See Ransom
Western Plains South ES 100/PK-8
PO Box 218 67516 785-398-2535
Rhonda Heim, prin. Fax 398-2492

Bel Aire, Sedgwick, Pop. 6,561
Wichita USD 259
Supt. — See Wichita
Isely Traditional Magnet S 500/K-5
5256 N Woodlawn Blvd 67220 316-973-8200
Kathy Stybr, prin. Fax 973-8210

Resurrection Catholic S 200/PK-8
4900 N Woodlawn Blvd 67220 316-744-3576
Kori Heiman, prin. Fax 744-1582
Sunrise Christian Academy 500/PK-12
5500 E 45th St N 67220 316-744-9262
Dr. Robert Lindsted, supt. Fax 744-7449

Belle Plaine, Sumner, Pop. 1,652
Belle Plaine USD 357 600/PK-12
PO Box 760 67013 620-488-2288
Dr. James Sutton, supt. Fax 488-3517
www.usd357.org
Belle Plaine ES 300/PK-4
PO Box 338 67013 620-488-2617
Midge Simmons, prin. Fax 488-3976
Belle Plaine MS 200/5-8
PO Box 457 67013 620-488-2222
Morey Balzer, prin. Fax 488-3391

Belleville, Republic, Pop. 1,978
Republic County USD 109 500/K-12
PO Box 469 66935 785-527-5621
Michael Couch, supt. Fax 527-5375
www.usd109.org/
Belleville East ES 200/K-5
PO Box 469 66935 785-527-2330
Katie Struebing, prin. Fax 527-2121

Beloit, Mitchell, Pop. 3,807
Beloit USD 273 800/PK-12
PO Box 547 67420 785-738-3261
Jeff Travis, supt. Fax 738-4103
www.usd273.org
Beloit ES 500/PK-6
PO Box 586 67420 785-738-3581
Brady Dean, prin. Fax 738-3357

St. John Catholic S 100/K-6
712 E Main St 67420 785-738-3941
Marcy Kee, prin. Fax 738-4462

Bennington, Ottawa, Pop. 670
Twin Valley USD 240 500/PK-12
PO Box 38 67422 785-488-3325
Fred Van Ranken, supt. Fax 488-3326
www.usd240.org
Bennington ES 200/PK-6
PO Box 8 67422 785-488-3323
Craig Gantenbein, prin. Fax 488-2939
Other Schools – See Tescott

Bentley, Sedgwick, Pop. 524
Halstead-Bentley USD 440
Supt. — See Halstead
Bentley PS 200/K-3
PO Box 65 67016 316-796-0210
Adam Conard, prin. Fax 796-9958

Benton, Butler, Pop. 874
Circle USD 375
Supt. — See Towanda
Circle Benton ES 200/K-6
PO Box 39 67017 316-778-1151
Dorsey Burgess, prin. Fax 536-2249
Circle MS 300/7-8
14697 SW 20th St 67017 316-778-1470
Brenda Young, prin. Fax 536-2249

Berryton, Shawnee
Shawnee Heights USD 450
Supt. — See Tecumseh
Berryton ES 500/PK-6
2921 SE 69th St 66409 785-861-1300
Stacey Giebler, prin. Fax 861-1315

Bird City, Cheyenne, Pop. 441
Cheylin USD 103 100/K-12
PO Box 28 67731 785-734-2341
Steve Raymer M.Ed., supt. Fax 734-2489
www.cheylin.com/
Cheylin West ES 100/K-6
PO Box 28 67731 785-734-2351
Steve Raymer M.Ed., prin. Fax 734-2489

Blue Rapids, Marshall, Pop. 1,010
Valley Heights USD 498
Supt. — See Waterville
Valley Heights ES 100/3-6
508 Chestnut St 66411 785-363-7693
Robert Green, prin. Fax 363-7713

Bonner Springs, Wyandotte, Pop. 7,122
Bonner Springs USD 204 2,500/PK-12
PO Box 435 66012 913-422-5600
Daniel Brungardt, supt. Fax 422-4193
www.usd204.net
Bonner Springs ES 400/K-5
212 S Neconi Ave 66012 913-441-1777
Kim Mitchell, prin. Fax 441-3447
Clark MS 600/6-8
PO Box 336 66012 913-422-5115
Tammy DeLaRosa, prin. Fax 422-1644
McDanield Learning Center PK-PK
110 S Nettleton St 66012 913-422-7970
Fax 441-5510
Other Schools – See Edwardsville, Kansas City

Brewster, Thomas, Pop. 303
Brewster USD 314 100/PK-12
PO Box 220 67732 785-694-2236
Fax 694-2746
usd314.weebly.com
Brewster ES 50/PK-6
PO Box 220 67732 785-694-2236
Fax 694-2746

Brookville, Saline, Pop. 257
Ell-Saline USD 307 500/K-12
PO Box 157 67425 785-225-6813
Jerry Minneman, supt. Fax 225-6815
www.ellsaline.org
Other Schools – See Salina

Bucklin, Ford, Pop. 775
Bucklin USD 459 200/PK-12
PO Box 8 67834 620-826-3828
Kelly Lampe, supt. Fax 826-3377
www.bucklinschools.com
Bucklin ES 100/PK-4
PO Box 8 67834 620-826-3241
Kelly Lampe, prin. Fax 826-9966

Bucyrus, Miami, Pop. 191

Holy Rosary Wea S 200/PK-8
22705 Metcalf Ave 66013 913-533-2462
Nick Antista, prin. Fax 533-2460

Buffalo, Wilson, Pop. 229
Altoona-Midway USD 387 200/PK-12
20584 US 75 Hwy 66717 620-537-7721
Brent Kaempfe, supt. Fax 302-2080
www.usd387.org
Other Schools – See Altoona

Buhler, Reno, Pop. 1,319
Buhler USD 313 1,700/PK-12
406 W 7th St 67522 620-543-2258
Mike Berblinger, supt. Fax 543-2510
www.usd313.org
Buhler Grade S 300/PK-5
808 N Main St 67522 620-543-2240
Melissa Kennedy, prin. Fax 543-2154
Other Schools – See Hutchinson

Burden, Cowley, Pop. 531
Central USD 462 300/PK-12
PO Box 128 67019 620-438-2218
Rick Shaffer, supt. Fax 438-2217
www.usd462.org
Central ES 200/PK-6
1045 N Oak St 67019 620-438-3195
Jennifer Ray, prin. Fax 438-3198

Burlingame, Osage, Pop. 917
Burlingame USD 454 300/PK-12
100 Bloomquist Dr Ste A 66413 785-654-3328
Allen Konicek, supt. Fax 654-3570
www.usd454.net
Burlingame ES 200/PK-6
100 Bloomquist Dr Ste A 66413 785-654-3713
Tamara Buche, prin. Fax 654-3119

Burlington, Coffey, Pop. 2,635
Burlington USD 244 900/PK-12
200 S 6th St 66839 620-364-8478
Craig Marshall, supt. Fax 364-8548
www.usd244ks.org
Burlington ES 300/PK-4
706 Niagara St 66839 620-364-8882
Darla Long, prin. Fax 364-2999
Burlington MS 300/5-8
720 Cross St 66839 620-364-2156
Matt Thomsen, prin. Fax 364-8560

Burrton, Harvey, Pop. 886
Burrton USD 369 200/PK-12
PO Box 369 67020 620-463-3840
Joan Simoneau, supt. Fax 463-2636
burrton.usd369.org
Burrton ES 100/PK-5
PO Box 369 67020 620-463-3840
Joan Simoneau, prin. Fax 463-2636

Bushton, Rice, Pop. 274
Central Plains USD 112
Supt. — See Holyrood
Central Plains MS 100/5-8
500 S Main St 67427 620-562-3596
Jane Oeser, prin. Fax 562-3248

Caldwell, Sumner, Pop. 1,059
Caldwell USD 360 300/PK-12
22 N Webb St 67022 620-845-2585
Alan Jamison, supt. Fax 845-2610
www.usd360.com
Caldwell ES 100/PK-5
1 N Osage St 67022 620-845-2585
Aaron Roop, prin. Fax 845-2332

Caney, Montgomery, Pop. 2,080
Caney Valley USD 436 800/PK-12
700 E Bullpup Blvd 67333 620-879-9200
Blake Vargas, supt. Fax 879-9209
www.caney.com
Lincoln Memorial ES 500/PK-6
201 E 1st Ave 67333 620-879-9240
Kenneth Eckelberry, prin. Fax 879-9247

Canton, McPherson, Pop. 732
Canton-Galva USD 419 200/K-12
PO Box 317 67428 620-628-4901
John Denk, supt. Fax 628-4380
usd419.org
Other Schools – See Galva

Carbondale, Osage, Pop. 1,411
Santa Fe Trail USD 434
Supt. — See Scranton
Carbondale Attendance Center 300/4-8
315 N 4th St 66414 785-836-7188
Michael Flax, prin. Fax 836-7696

Cassoday, Butler, Pop. 126
Flinthills USD 492
Supt. — See Rosalia
Flinthills PS 100/K-2
200 N Washington 66842 620-735-4428
Larry Gawith, prin. Fax 735-4429

Cawker City, Mitchell, Pop. 462
Waconda USD 272 200/PK-12
PO Box 326 67430 785-781-4328
Troy Damman, supt. Fax 781-4318
www.usd272.org
Lakeside ES 100/PK-5
PO Box 46 67430 785-781-4911
James Giesbrecht, prin. Fax 781-4861
Other Schools – See Tipton

Cedar Vale, Chautauqua, Pop. 554
Cedar Vale USD 285 200/PK-12
PO Box 458 67024 620-758-2265
Lance Rhodd, supt. Fax 758-2647
www.cvs285.net
Cedar Vale ES 100/PK-5
PO Box 458 67024 620-758-2265
Jackie Burdette, prin. Fax 758-2647

Centralia, Nemaha, Pop. 501
Vermillion USD 380
Supt. — See Vermillion
Centralia ES 200/PK-6
507 John Riggins Ave 66415 785-857-3324
Larry Glatczak, prin. Fax 857-3847

Chanute, Neosho, Pop. 8,951
Chanute USD 413 1,900/PK-12
315 Chanute 35 Pkwy 66720 620-432-2500
Richard Proffitt, supt. Fax 431-6810
www.usd413.org
Chanute ES 900/K-5
500 Osa Martin Blvd 66720 620-432-2560
Gary Wheeler, prin. Fax 432-2542
Lincoln Early Learning Center 100/PK-PK
1000 W Main St 66720 620-432-2550
Matt Koester, prin. Fax 432-2552
Royster MS 400/6-8
400 W Main St 66720 620-432-2520
Lori Kiblinger, prin. Fax 431-7841

St. Patrick Catholic S 100/PK-6
409 S Malcolm Ave 66720 620-431-4020
Mary Durand, prin. Fax 431-6587

Chapman, Dickinson, Pop. 1,368
Chapman USD 473 1,000/K-12
PO Box 249 67431 785-922-6521
Jerry Hodson, supt. Fax 922-6446
usd473.net
Chapman ES 200/K-5
PO Box 249 67431 785-922-7171
David Warner, prin. Fax 922-7079
Chapman MS 300/6-8
PO Box 249 67431 785-922-6555
Trent Horn, prin. Fax 922-6601
Other Schools – See Abilene, Enterprise

Chase, Rice, Pop. 461
Chase-Raymond USD 401 200/PK-12
313 E Avenue C 67524 620-938-2913
Glenna Grinstead, supt. Fax 938-2622
www.usd401.com/
Chase ES 100/PK-5
313 E Avenue C 67524 620-938-2996
Gene Short, prin. Fax 938-1107
Raymond JHS 50/6-8
313 E Avenue C 67524 620-938-2923
Brock Hampton, prin. Fax 938-2456

Cheney, Sedgwick, Pop. 2,072
Cheney USD 268 800/PK-12
100 W 6th Ave 67025 316-542-3512
David Grover, supt. Fax 542-0326
www.cheney268.com
Cheney ES 400/PK-5
100 W 6th Ave 67025 316-542-3137
Sherri Conrad, prin. Fax 542-3520
Cheney MS 200/6-8
100 W 6th Ave 67025 316-542-0060
Amy Wallace, prin. Fax 542-0608

St. Paul Lutheran S 50/PK-8
PO Box 278 67025 316-542-3584
Rebecca Hillman, lead tchr. Fax 542-0115

Cherokee, Crawford, Pop. 696
Cherokee USD 247 500/PK-12
506 S Smelter St 66724 620-457-8350
Brad Miner Ed.D., supt. Fax 457-8428
www.usd247.com
Southeast JHS 200/5-8
206 W Magnolia St 66724 620-457-8315
Joseph Martin, prin. Fax 457-8380
Other Schools – See Weir

Cherryvale, Montgomery, Pop. 2,326
Cherryvale USD 447 900/PK-12
618 E 4th St 67335 620-336-8130
Dr. Shelly Kiblinger, supt. Fax 336-8133
www.usd447schools.org
Lincoln Central ES 400/PK-6
401 E Main St 67335 620-336-8140
Steve Pefley, prin. Fax 336-8159
Other Schools – See Thayer

Chetopa, Labette, Pop. 1,068
Chetopa - St. Paul USD 505 400/PK-12
430 Elm St 67336 620-236-7244
Dr. Bobbi Williams, supt. Fax 236-4271
www.usd505.org
Chetopa ES 100/PK-5
430 Elm St 67336 620-236-7244
Lonnie Moser, prin. Fax 236-4271
Other Schools – See Saint Paul

Cimarron, Gray, Pop. 2,164
Cimarron-Ensign USD 102 600/K-12
PO Box 489 67835 620-855-7743
Michael Stegman, supt. Fax 855-7745
www.cimarronschools.net
Cimarron ES 400/K-6
PO Box 489 67835 620-855-3343
Rocky Stewart, prin. Fax 855-3219

Clay Center, Clay, Pop. 4,283
Clay Center USD 379 1,400/K-12
PO Box 97 67432 785-632-3176
Michael Folks, supt. Fax 632-5020
www.usd379.org/
Clay Center Community MS 200/6-8
935 Prospect St 67432 785-632-3232
Keith Hoffman, prin. Fax 632-6013
Garfield ES 200/4-5
815 4th St 67432 785-632-2125
Keith Hoffman, prin. Fax 632-5912
Lincoln ES 400/K-3
1020 Grant Ave 67432 785-632-2156
Matt Weller, prin. Fax 632-2158
Other Schools – See Wakefield

Clearwater, Sedgwick, Pop. 2,443
Clearwater USD 264 1,200/PK-12
PO Box 248 67026 620-584-2091
Paul Becker, supt. Fax 584-6705
www.usd264.org
Clearwater ES West 400/PK-3
PO Box 248 67026 620-584-2081
Mike Welty, prin. Fax 584-3523
Clearwater Intermediate Center 300/4-6
PO Box 248 67026 620-584-5188
Kelly Bielefeld, prin. Fax 584-6113
Clearwater MS 200/7-8
PO Box 248 67026 620-584-2036
Kelly Bielefeld, prin. Fax 584-2199

Clifton, Washington, Pop. 552
Clifton-Clyde USD 224
Supt. — See Clyde
Clifton-Clyde ES 100/K-3
PO Box B 66937 785-455-3319
Eric Sacco, prin. Fax 455-3572
Clifton-Clyde MS 100/PK-PK, 4-
PO Box A 66937 785-455-3323
Eric Sacco, prin. Fax 455-3524

Clyde, Cloud, Pop. 706
Clifton-Clyde USD 224 300/PK-12
616 N High St Ste 2 66938 785-446-2098
Art Baker, supt. Fax 446-3000
www.usd224.com
Other Schools – See Clifton

Coffeyville, Montgomery, Pop. 9,654
Coffeyville USD 445 1,700/PK-12
615 Ellis St 67337 620-252-6400
Craig A. Correll Ed.D., supt. Fax 252-6807
www.cvilleschools.com
Community ES 1,000/K-6
102 S Cline Rd 67337 620-252-6430
Jennifer Bright, prin. Fax 251-3701
Hamm ECC PK-PK
200 Walnut St 67337 620-251-1147
Amanda Cavaness, prin. Fax 251-4933
Roosevelt MS 300/7-8
1000 W 8th St 67337 620-252-6420
Jeffrey Pegues, prin. Fax 252-6844

Holy Name Catholic S 100/PK-6
406 Willow St 67337 620-251-0480
Lisa Payne, prin. Fax 251-1651

Colby, Thomas, Pop. 5,323
Colby USD 315 900/K-12
600 W 3rd St 67701 785-460-5000
Katina Brenn, supt. Fax 460-5050
www.colbyeagles.org
Colby ES 400/K-5
210 N Grant Ave 67701 785-460-5100
Robb Ross, prin. Fax 460-5150
Colby MS 200/6-8
750 W 3rd St 67701 785-460-5200
Robb Ross, prin. Fax 460-5250

Heartland Christian S 100/PK-12
1995 W 4th St 67701 785-460-6419
Dr. Mark Gundlach, admin. Fax 460-8337
Sacred Heart S 100/PK-5
1150 W 6th St 67701 785-460-2813
Alice Ziegler, prin. Fax 460-9688

Coldwater, Comanche, Pop. 813
South Central USD 300 300/K-12
PO Box 721 67029 620-582-2181
Michael Baldwin, supt. Fax 582-2540
www.usd300ks.com
Other Schools – See Protection

Colony, Anderson, Pop. 394
Crest USD 479 200/PK-12
PO Box 305 66015 620-852-3540
Chuck Mahon, supt. Fax 852-3542
www.usd479.org
Crest ES 200/PK-8
PO Box 325 66015 620-852-3529
Travis Hermreck, prin. Fax 852-3539

Columbus, Cherokee, Pop. 3,208
Columbus USD 493 1,100/PK-12
802 S Highschool Ave 66725 620-429-3661
David Carriger, supt. Fax 429-2673
www.usd493.com
Central S 400/4-8
810 S Highschool Ave 66725 620-429-3943
James Bolden, prin. Fax 429-2882
Highland ES 100/2-3
319 N Highschool Ave 66725 620-429-3032
Amber Wheeler, prin. Fax 429-1445
Park ES 200/PK-1
724 Garfield St 66725 620-429-3905
Steve Jameson, prin. Fax 429-1094

Colwich, Sedgwick, Pop. 1,314
Renwick USD 267
Supt. — See Andale
Colwich ES 300/PK-8
PO Box 248 67030 316-796-1331
Tige Stone, prin. Fax 796-0665
St. Marks ES 300/K-8
19001 W 29th St N 67030 316-796-1466
Chris White, prin. Fax 796-0293

Concordia, Cloud, Pop. 5,314
Concordia USD 333 1,100/PK-12
217 W 7th St 66901 785-243-3518
Quentin Breese, supt. Fax 243-8883
www.usd333.com
Concordia ES 500/PK-4
1500 E 9th St 66901 785-243-8853
Derek Holmes, prin. Fax 243-8856
Concordia MS 200/5-6
436 W 10th St 66901 785-243-2114
Krystal Breese, admin. Fax 243-8844

Conway Springs, Sumner, Pop. 1,251
Conway Springs USD 356 600/K-12
110 N Monnett St 67031 620-456-2961
Clay Murphy, supt. Fax 456-3173
www.usd356.org
Conway Springs MS 100/6-8
112 N Cranmer St 67031 620-456-2965
Ryan Rusco, prin. Fax 456-3313
Trueblood ES 200/K-5
111 N Highland St 67031 620-456-2966
Ronald Ronnau, prin. Fax 456-3312

St. Joseph Catholic S 100/K-6
218 N 5th St 67031 620-456-2270
Joel Arnold, prin. Fax 456-2272

Copeland, Gray, Pop. 310
Copeland USD 476 100/PK-8
PO Box 156 67837 620-668-5565
Jay Zehr, supt. Fax 668-5568
www.usd371.org
Copeland ES 50/PK-5
PO Box 156 67837 620-668-5565
Jay Zehr, prin. Fax 668-5568
South Gray JHS 50/6-8
PO Box 156 67837 620-668-5565
Jay Zehr, prin. Fax 668-5568

Cottonwood Falls, Chase, Pop. 897
Chase County USD 284 400/PK-12
PO Box 569 66845 620-273-6303
Jeff Kohlman, supt. Fax 273-6717
www.usd284.org/
Other Schools – See Strong City

Council Grove, Morris, Pop. 2,159
Morris County USD 417 600/PK-12
17 Wood St 66846 620-767-5192
Doug Conwell, supt. Fax 767-5444
www.usd417.net
Council Grove ES 300/PK-6
706 E Main St 66846 620-767-6851
Heather Honas, prin. Fax 767-5260
Other Schools – See Alta Vista

Courtland, Republic, Pop. 285
Pike Valley USD 426
Supt. — See Scandia
Pike Valley ES 100/K-5
PO Box 320 66939 785-374-4221
Mike Gritten, prin. Fax 374-4268
Pike Valley JHS 100/6-8
PO Box 320 66939 785-374-4221
Mike Gritten, prin. Fax 374-4268

Cunningham, Kingman, Pop. 450
Cunningham USD 332 200/PK-12
PO Box 67 67035 620-298-3271
Robert Reed, supt. Fax 298-2562
www.usd332.org
Cunningham ES 100/PK-6
PO Box 98 67035 620-298-2462
Robert Reed, prin. Fax 298-2320

Damar, Rooks, Pop. 131
Palco USD 269 50/PK-12
PO Box 38 67632 785-737-4635
Larry Lysell M.S., supt. Fax 737-4636
www.usd269.net
Damar ES PK-5
PO Box 38 67632 785-839-4265
Larry Lysell M.S., prin. Fax 839-4278

Deerfield, Kearny, Pop. 694
Deerfield USD 216 300/PK-12
803 Beech St 67838 620-426-8516
Dr. Daniel Slack, supt. Fax 426-7890
www.usd216.org
Deerfield ES 100/PK-5
901 Beech 67838 620-426-8301
Shane Burns, prin. Fax 426-8207
Deerfield MS 100/6-8
803 Beech 67838 620-426-7901
Tammie Sabata, prin. Fax 426-6903

Denton, Doniphan, Pop. 142
Doniphan West USD 111 200/PK-12
642 Highway 20 E 66017 785-442-3671
Mike Newman, supt. Fax 442-3289
www.usd111.org
Doniphan West ES 100/PK-6
642 Highway 20 E 66017 785-359-6526
Julie Crum, prin. Fax 359-6522

Derby, Sedgwick, Pop. 21,570
Derby USD 260 6,500/PK-12
120 E Washington St 67037 316-788-8400
Heather Bohaty, supt. Fax 788-8526
www.derbyschools.com
Derby Hills ES 400/PK-5
2230 N Woodlawn Blvd 67037 316-788-8540
James Moffett, prin. Fax 788-8536
Derby MS 1,100/7-8
801 E Madison Ave 67037 316-788-8580
Clinton Shipley, prin. Fax 788-8553
Derby North MS 6-8
3100 N Rock Rd 67037 316-788-8400
Jeff Smith, prin. Fax 788-8527
El Paso ES 400/K-5
900 E Crestway Ave 67037 316-788-8545
Carla Schartz, prin. Fax 788-8495
Park Hill ES 400/K-5
1500 E Woodbrook Ln 67037 316-788-8095
Sandy Rusher, prin. Fax 788-8098
Pleasantview ES 300/K-5
1101 N Georgie Ave 67037 316-788-8555
Yvonne Rothe, prin. Fax 788-8496

Swaney ES 300/PK-5
501 E English St 67037 316-788-8560
Kurt Geilenfeldt, prin. Fax 788-8494
Tanglewood ES 700/PK-5
830 N Ridgecrest Rd 67037 316-788-8565
Shannon Demel, prin. Fax 788-8493
Other Schools – See Wichita

Faith Lutheran S 100/PK-6
208 S Derby Ave 67037 316-788-1715
Cheryl Voss, lead tchr. Fax 789-0043
St. Mary's Parish Catholic S 300/PK-8
2306 E Meadowlark Blvd 67037 316-788-3151
Richard Montgomery, prin. Fax 788-6895

De Soto, Johnson, Pop. 5,615
De Soto USD 232 7,000/PK-12
35200 W 91st St 66018 913-667-6200
Frank Harwood, supt. Fax 667-6201
www.usd232.org
Lexington Trails MS 300/6-8
8800 Penner Ave 66018 913-667-6260
Steve Ludwig, prin. Fax 667-6261
Starside ES 400/K-5
35400 W 91st St 66018 913-667-6270
Kris Meyer, prin. Fax 667-6271
Other Schools – See Lenexa, Shawnee

Dexter, Cowley, Pop. 275
Dexter USD 471 100/PK-12
PO Box 97 67038 620-876-5415
K.B. Criss, supt. Fax 876-5548
www.usd471.org
Dexter ES 100/PK-5
PO Box 97 67038 620-876-5415
K.B. Criss, prin. Fax 876-5548

Dighton, Lane, Pop. 1,017
Dighton USD 482 300/PK-12
PO Box 878 67839 620-397-2835
Dr. Kelly Arnberger, supt. Fax 397-5932
www.usd482.org
Dighton ES 200/PK-6
PO Box 1029 67839 620-397-5319
Dr. Kelly Arnberger, prin. Fax 397-5631

Dodge City, Ford, Pop. 26,977
Dodge City USD 443 6,400/K-12
PO Box 460 67801 620-371-1070
Dr. Fred Dierksen, supt. Fax 227-1687
www.usd443.org
Beeson ES 400/K-5
1700 W Beeson Rd 67801 620-471-2113
Martha Mendoza, prin. Fax 227-1745
Central ES 300/K-5
1100 Central Ave 67801 620-471-2104
Bill Pittman, prin. Fax 227-1721
Comanche MS 700/6-8
1601 1st Ave 67801 620-371-1100
Marc Woofter, prin. Fax 339-4802
Dodge City MS 700/6-8
2000 6th Ave 67801 620-471-2100
Mike King, prin. Fax 227-1731
Linn ES 500/K-5
1900 Linn St 67801 620-471-2114
Amy Olivares, prin. Fax 227-1722
Miller ES 400/K-5
1100 Avenue G 67801 620-471-2102
Tim Skinner, prin. Fax 227-1723
Northwest ES 400/K-5
2100 6th Ave 67801 620-471-2115
Kim Armstrong, prin. Fax 227-1724
Ross ES 500/K-5
3001 6th Ave 67801 620-471-2103
Amy Loder, prin. Fax 227-1781
Soule ES 300/K-5
401 Soule St 67801 620-471-2116
Greg Preston, prin. Fax 227-1719
Sunnyside ES 400/K-5
511 Sunnyside Ave 67801 620-471-2112
John Montford, prin. Fax 227-1727
Wilroads Gardens ES 100/K-5
11558 E Main Rd 67801 620-471-2101
Erica Teran, prin. Fax 227-1728

Sacred Heart Cathedral S 200/PK-8
905 Central Ave 67801 620-227-6532
Lynee Habiger, prin. Fax 227-3221

Douglass, Butler, Pop. 1,675
Douglass USD 396 700/PK-12
921 E 1st St 67039 316-747-3300
Robert Reynolds, supt. Fax 747-3305
www.usd396.net/
Seal ES 300/PK-5
320 S Chestnut St 67039 316-747-3350
Kim McCune, prin. Fax 747-3359
Sisk MS 200/6-8
950 E 1st St 67039 316-747-3340
Scott Dunham, prin. Fax 747-3346

Easton, Leavenworth, Pop. 251
Easton USD 449 700/PK-12
32502 Easton Rd 66020 913-651-9740
Tim Beying, supt. Fax 324-5237
www.easton449.org
Pleasant Ridge ES 300/PK-5
20753 Easton Rd 66020 913-651-5595
Tim Beying, prin. Fax 324-5237
Pleasant Ridge MS 200/6-8
32504 Easton Rd 66020 913-651-5522
Amanda Brimer, prin. Fax 324-5237

Edgerton, Johnson, Pop. 1,614
Gardner Edgerton USD 231
Supt. — See Gardner
Edgerton ES 200/PK-4
400 W Nelson St 66021 913-856-3500
Nancy Woolery, prin. Fax 856-3577

Edna, Labette, Pop. 412
Labette County USD 506
Supt. — See Altamont
Edna S 200/PK-8
PO Box 220 67342 620-922-7210
Tim Traxson, prin. Fax 922-3417

Edwardsville, Wyandotte, Pop. 4,244
Bonner Springs USD 204
Supt. — See Bonner Springs
Edwardsville ES 400/K-5
1700 S 104th St 66111 913-422-4036
Tracy Copeland, prin. Fax 422-7165

Effingham, Atchison, Pop. 540
Atchison County Community USD 377 600/PK-12
PO Box 289 66023 913-833-5050
Dr. Andrew Gaddis, supt. Fax 833-5210
www.usd377.org
Atchison County Community ES 300/PK-6
PO Box 289 66023 913-833-4420
Mandi McMillan, prin. Fax 833-5210

Elbing, Butler, Pop. 228

Berean Academy 300/PK-12
PO Box 70 67041 316-799-2211
Emir A. Ruiz Esparza M.Ed., head sch Fax 799-2601

El Dorado, Butler, Pop. 12,711
Circle USD 375
Supt. — See Towanda
Circle Oil Hill ES 300/K-6
2700 W 6th Ave 67042 316-320-9515
Misty Gawith, prin. Fax 536-2249

El Dorado USD 490 1,700/PK-12
124 W Central Ave 67042 316-322-4800
Sue Givens, supt. Fax 322-4801
www.eldoradoschools.org
El Dorado MS 400/6-8
440 E Wildcat Way 67042 316-322-4820
Karla King, prin. Fax 322-4821
Grandview ES 200/K-5
1300 Lawndale Ave 67042 316-322-4830
Susan Holthaus, prin. Fax 322-4831
Jefferson ES 100/PK-1
1216 W 3rd Ave 67042 316-322-4840
Chad Schuetz, prin. Fax 322-4841
Lincoln ES 100/2-5
522 W 5th Ave 67042 316-322-4850
Chad Schuetz, prin. Fax 322-4851
Skelly ES 200/PK-5
951 Skelly St 67042 316-322-4860
Stan Ruff, prin. Fax 322-4861

Elkhart, Morton, Pop. 2,178
Elkhart USD 218 1,200/PK-12
PO Box 999 67950 620-697-2195
Rex Richardson, supt. Fax 697-2607
www.usd218.org
Elkhart ES 200/PK-4
PO Box 999 67950 620-697-2133
Lynn Thrall, prin. Fax 697-2768
Elkhart MS 100/5-8
PO Box 999 67950 620-697-2197
Diane Finn, prin. Fax 697-4828

Ellinwood, Barton, Pop. 2,100
Ellinwood USD 355 500/K-12
300 N Schiller Ave 67526 620-564-3226
Ben Jacobs, supt. Fax 564-2206
www.usd355.org/
Ellinwood ES 300/K-6
310 E 6th St 67526 620-564-2750
Julie Ann Josserand, prin. Fax 564-2667
Ellinwood MS 100/7-8
210 E 2nd St 67526 620-564-3136
Mark Cook, prin. Fax 564-2816

St. Joseph S 100/K-8
111 W 3rd St 67526 620-564-2721
Marlene Clayton, lead tchr. Fax 564-2714

Ellis, Ellis, Pop. 2,048
Ellis USD 388 400/PK-12
PO Box 256 67637 785-726-4281
Robert Young, supt. Fax 726-4677
www.usd388.k12.ks.us
Washington Grade S 300/PK-6
100 E 13th St 67637 785-726-3136
John Befort, prin. Fax 726-3137

St. Marys S 100/K-6
605 Monroe St 67637 785-726-3185
April Pfeifer, prin. Fax 726-3166

Ellsworth, Ellsworth, Pop. 3,090
Ellsworth USD 327 600/K-12
PO Box 306 67439 785-472-5561
Dale Brungardt, supt. Fax 472-5563
www.usd327.org
Ellsworth ES 200/K-4
110 E 3rd St 67439 785-472-5554
Patrick Schroeder, prin. Fax 472-8118
Other Schools – See Kanopolis

Elwood, Doniphan, Pop. 1,173
Riverside USD 114 700/PK-12
PO Box 49 66024 913-365-5632
Michael Newman, supt. Fax 365-5967
www.usd114.org
Riverside IS 100/3-5
PO Box 368 66024 913-365-6735
Robert Hampton, prin. Fax 365-3503
Riverside MS 200/6-8
PO Box 368 66024 913-365-6735
Robert Hampton, prin. Fax 365-3503
Other Schools – See Wathena

Emporia, Lyon, Pop. 24,437
Emporia USD 253 4,000/PK-12
PO Box 1008 66801 620-341-2200
Kevin Case, supt. Fax 341-2205
www.usd253.org
Emporia MS 900/6-8
2300 Graphic Arts Rd 66801 620-341-2335
Steven Bazan, prin. Fax 341-2341
Logan Avenue ES 200/K-5
521 S East St 66801 620-341-2264
Jessica Griffin, prin. Fax 341-2267
Maynard ECC PK-PK
19 Constitution St 66801 620-341-2260
Keva Scheib, prin. Fax 341-2261
Riverside ES 400/K-5
327 S West St 66801 620-341-2276
Jared Giffin, prin. Fax 341-2279
Timmerman ES 400/K-5
2901 Timmerman Dr 66801 620-341-2270
Kim Kirk, prin. Fax 341-2272
Village ES 500/K-5
2302 W 15th Ave 66801 620-341-2282
Judy Stanley, prin. Fax 341-2285
Walnut ES 300/K-5
801 Grove Ave 66801 620-341-2288
Jami Dakin, prin. Fax 341-2291
White ES 200/K-8
902 Exchange St 66801 620-341-2294
Tell Kirk, prin. Fax 341-2296

Emporia Christian S 100/PK-8
1325 C of E Dr 66801 620-342-5353
Larry Ellis M.S., prin. Fax 342-8686
Sacred Heart S 100/K-6
102 Cottonwood St 66801 620-343-7394
Michelle Barnhart, prin. Fax 342-0450

Enterprise, Dickinson, Pop. 834
Chapman USD 473
Supt. — See Chapman
Enterprise ES 100/K-5
PO Box 247 67441 785-263-8248
Kara Spittles, prin. Fax 263-8281

Enterprise Adventist S 50/K-8
PO Box 367 67441 785-200-6224

Erie, Neosho, Pop. 1,145
Erie-Galesburg USD 101 500/PK-12
PO Box 137 66733 620-244-3264
Steve Woolf, supt. Fax 244-3664
www.usd101.com
Erie ES 300/PK-5
410 W 3rd St 66733 620-244-5161
Ronnie Williams, prin. Fax 244-3560
Other Schools – See Galesburg

Eskridge, Wabaunsee, Pop. 526
Mission Valley USD 330 300/PK-12
PO Box 158 66423 785-449-2297
William Clark, supt. Fax 409-6216
www.mv330.org
Mission Valley ES 200/PK-6
12913 Mission Valley Rd 66423 866-557-6686
Brett Fenton, prin. Fax 409-6219
Mission Valley JHS 100/7-8
12913 Mission Valley Rd 66423 866-557-6686
Rod Hasenbank, prin. Fax 409-6218

Eudora, Douglas, Pop. 5,992
Eudora USD 491 1,600/PK-12
PO Box 500 66025 785-542-4910
Steve Splichal, supt. Fax 542-4909
www.eudoraschools.org/
Eudora ES 800/PK-5
PO Box 602 66025 785-542-4940
Amy DeLaRosa, prin. Fax 542-4950
Eudora MS 400/6-8
PO Box 701 66025 785-542-4960
Denise Kendall, prin. Fax 542-4970

Eureka, Greenwood, Pop. 2,592
Eureka USD 389 700/PK-12
216 N Main St 67045 620-583-5588
Scott Hoyt, supt. Fax 583-8200
www.usd389.net
Marshall ES 400/PK-6
1015 N Jefferson St 67045 620-583-5537
Stacy Coulter, prin. Fax 583-8206

Yates Memorial SDA S 50/1-8
PO Box 307 67045 620-583-7529

Everest, Brown, Pop. 283
South Brown County USD 430
Supt. — See Horton
Everest MS 200/5-8
221 S 7th St 66424 785-548-7536
Jackie Wenger, prin. Fax 548-7538

Fort Leavenworth, Leavenworth, Pop. 1,300
Ft. Leavenworth USD 207 1,900/PK-9
207 Education Way 66027 913-651-7373
Dr. Keith Mispagel, supt. Fax 758-6010
www.usd207.org
Bradley ES 500/PK-6
1 Bradley Cir 66027 913-651-6915
Dr. Michaela Culkin, prin. Fax 758-6090
Eisenhower ES 500/PK-6
1 Eisenhower Cir 66027 913-651-6663
Cindy Wepking, prin. Fax 758-6077
MacArthur ES 500/PK-6
1 McArthur Loop 66027 913-651-6517
Tyler Fowler, prin. Fax 758-6028

Fort Riley, Geary, Pop. 7,475
Geary County USD 475
Supt. — See Junction City

Fort Riley ES 300/K-5
28000 Rifle Range Rd 66442 785-717-4450
Becky Coy, prin. Fax 717-4451
Fort Riley MS 700/6-8
4020 1st Division Rd 66442 785-717-4500
Heather Oentrich, prin. Fax 717-4501
Jefferson ES 200/K-5
4720 Jackson Ave 66442 785-717-4550
Melanie Laster, prin. Fax 717-4551
Morris Hill ES 200/K-5
4400 1st Division Rd 66442 785-717-4650
Kenny Upham, prin. Fax 717-4651
Seitz ES 700/K-5
27500 Rifle Range Rd 66442 785-717-6500
Jodi Testa, prin. Fax 717-6501
Ware ES 700/K-5
6795 Thomas Ave 66442 785-717-4600
Dr. Deb Gustafson, prin. Fax 717-4601

Fort Scott, Bourbon, Pop. 7,870
Ft. Scott USD 234 1,900/PK-12
424 S Main St 66701 620-223-0800
Bob Beckham, supt. Fax 223-2760
www.usd234.org
Fort Scott MS 500/6-8
1105 E 12th St 66701 620-223-3262
Brian Weilert, prin. Fax 223-2760
Fort Scott Preschool Center 50/PK-PK
409 S Judson St 66701 620-223-8965
Rick Scholes, admin. Fax 223-2760
Scott ES 500/K-2
316 W 10th St 66701 620-223-0450
Joy McGhee, prin. Fax 223-2760
Ware ES 400/3-5
900 E 3rd St 66701 620-223-3380
Stephanie Witt, prin. Fax 223-2760

St. Mary's Catholic S 50/PK-5
702 S Eddy St 66701 620-223-6060
Krista Gorman, prin. Fax 223-6060

Fowler, Meade, Pop. 579
Fowler USD 225 200/PK-12
PO Box 170 67844 620-646-5661
Jeff Bollinger, supt. Fax 646-5713
www.usd225.org
Fowler ES 100/PK-6
PO Box 170 67844 620-646-5234
Corrine McDowell, prin. Fax 646-5713

Frankfort, Marshall, Pop. 726
Vermillion USD 380
Supt. — See Vermillion
Frankfort ES 200/PK-6
PO Box 203 66427 785-292-4486
Dean Dalinghaus, prin. Fax 292-4036

Fredonia, Wilson, Pop. 2,433
Fredonia USD 484 500/PK-12
PO Box 539 66736 620-378-4177
Brian Smith, supt. Fax 378-4345
www.fredoniaks.com
Lincoln ES 300/PK-6
713 N 9th St 66736 620-378-4138
Tim Woodcock, prin. Fax 378-3707

Frontenac, Crawford, Pop. 3,381
Frontenac USD 249 900/PK-12
208 S Cayuga St 66763 620-231-7551
Rick Simoncic, supt. Fax 231-1312
www.frontenac249.org
Frontenac JHS 200/6-8
208 S Cayuga St 66763 620-232-6370
Mike Martin, prin. Fax 231-1312
Layden ES 500/PK-5
200 E Lanyon St 66763 620-231-7790
Courtney McCartney, prin. Fax 231-3727

Galena, Cherokee, Pop. 2,973
Galena USD 499 900/PK-12
702 E 7th St 66739 620-783-4499
Dr. Brian Smith, supt. Fax 783-5547
www.usd499.org
Galena MS 200/6-8
702 E 7th St 66739 620-783-4499
Lisa Scarrow, prin. Fax 783-5214
Liberty ES 200/3-5
702 E 7th St 66739 620-783-4499
Susan New, prin. Fax 783-5433
Spring Grove ES 200/PK-2
702 E 7th St 66739 620-783-4499
Mike Strickland, prin. Fax 783-2804

Galesburg, Neosho, Pop. 125
Erie-Galesburg USD 101
Supt. — See Erie
Galesburg MS 100/6-8
PO Box 147 66740 620-763-2470
Jared Han, prin. Fax 763-2224

Galva, McPherson, Pop. 861
Canton-Galva USD 419
Supt. — See Canton
Canton-Galva ES 100/K-6
PO Box 96 67443 620-654-3321
James Struber, prin. Fax 654-3335

Garden City, Finney, Pop. 26,301
Garden City USD 457 7,100/PK-12
1205 Fleming St 67846 620-805-7000
Dr. Steve Karlin Ed.D., supt. Fax 805-7190
www.gckschools.com
Barker ES 100/K-6
5585 N Jennie Barker Rd 67846 620-805-7700
Karen Murrell, prin. Fax 805-7748
Brown ES 400/K-4
1110 E Pine St 67846 620-805-7200
Julie Koerperich, prin. Fax 805-7298
Buffalo Jones ES 300/K-4
708 N Taylor Ave 67846 620-805-7300
Rafaela Solis, prin. Fax 805-7348
Garfield ECC PK-PK
121 W Walnut St 67846 620-805-7500
Josh Guymon, prin. Fax 805-7549
Good MS 800/7-8
1412 N Main St 67846 620-805-8100
Brad Springston, prin. Fax 805-8150
Hubert ES 300/K-6
1205 A St 67846 620-805-8400
Martha Darter, prin. Fax 805-8474
Matthews ES 200/K-4
111 E Johnson St 67846 620-805-7550
Carma Harman, prin. Fax 805-7598
Ornelas ES 400/K-4
3401 E Spruce St 67846 620-805-7900
Tracy Leiker, prin. Fax 805-7998
Plymell ES 100/K-6
20 W Plymell Rd 67846 620-805-7800
Linda Finch, prin. Fax 805-7848
Scheuerman ES 200/K-4
1901 W Wilcox St 67846 620-805-7350
Christy Botts, prin. Fax 805-7398
Sitts Intermediate Center 500/5-6
3101 N Belmont Pl 67846 620-805-8200
Barbara Hauschild, prin. Fax 805-8298
Stones Intermediate Center 400/5-6
401 N Jennie Barker Rd 67846 620-805-8300
Janet Smith, prin. Fax 805-8398
Walker ES 300/K-4
805 W Fair St 67846 620-805-7600
Phil Keidel, prin. Fax 805-7698
Wilson ES 400/K-4
1709 E Labrador Blvd 67846 620-805-7400
Skyla Wehkamp, prin. Fax 805-7498
Wilson ES 200/K-4
1401 Harding Ave 67846 620-805-7750
Melinda Stewart, prin. Fax 805-7798

High Plains Christian S 50/1-8
2710 N Fleming St 67846 620-275-9356
St. Dominic S 200/PK-6
617 J C St 67846 620-276-8981
Trina Delgado, prin. Fax 276-2086
St. Mary S 100/PK-6
503 Saint John St 67846 620-276-2241
Michelle Mead, prin. Fax 276-7067

Garden Plain, Sedgwick, Pop. 838
Renwick USD 267
Supt. — See Andale
Garden Plain ES 300/PK-8
PO Box 375 67050 316-531-2261
Jennifer Campbell, prin. Fax 535-8868

Gardner, Johnson, Pop. 18,628
Gardner Edgerton USD 231 5,300/PK-12
PO Box 97 66030 913-856-2000
Pam Stranathan, supt. Fax 856-2069
www.usd231.com
Gardner ES 300/PK-4
218 E Shawnee St 66030 913-856-3300
Jason Watkins, prin. Fax 856-3385
Grand Star ES 300/PK-4
401 E Grand St 66030 913-856-3750
Amy Bybee, prin. Fax 856-3751
Madison ES 500/PK-4
800 W Madison St 66030 913-856-0400
Matthew Wachel, prin. Fax 856-0490
Moonlight ES 300/PK-4
17960 S Moonlight Rd 66030 913-856-3100
Ryan Horne, prin. Fax 856-3136
Nike ES 300/PK-4
19500 S Gardner Rd 66030 913-856-3000
Bruce Haber, prin. Fax 856-3085
Pioneer Ridge MS 800/5-8
16200 S Kill Creek Rd 66030 913-856-3850
Linda Miesner, prin. Fax 856-2097
Sunflower ES 300/PK-4
775 N Center St 66030 913-856-3700
Dr. Jason Jones, prin. Fax 856-3701
Trail Ridge MS 5-8
495 E Grand St 66030 913-856-3550
John Martin, prin. Fax 856-3552
Wheatridge MS 800/5-8
318 E Washington St 66030 913-856-2900
Carl Garrett, prin. Fax 856-2980
Other Schools – See Edgerton

Garnett, Anderson, Pop. 3,385
Garnett USD 365 900/PK-12
PO Box 328 66032 785-448-6155
Donald Blome, supt. Fax 448-6157
www.usd365.org
Garnett ES 300/K-6
403 W Home Run Dr 66032 785-448-3177
Krista Hedrick, prin. Fax 448-6861
Other Schools – See Greeley, Westphalia

St. Rose Philippine Duchesne S 100/K-8
530 E 4th Ave 66032 785-448-3423
Michelle Gavin, prin. Fax 448-3164

Girard, Crawford, Pop. 2,739
Girard USD 248 1,000/PK-12
415 N Summit St 66743 620-724-4325
Blaise Bauer, supt. Fax 724-8446
www.girard248.org/
Girard MS 200/6-8
415 N Summit St 66743 620-724-4114
Brannon Kidd, prin. Fax 724-4610
Haderlein ES 500/PK-5
415 N Summit St 66743 620-724-4327
Mark LaTurner, prin. Fax 724-6266

Glasco, Cloud, Pop. 493
Southern Cloud USD 334
Supt. — See Miltonvale
Glasco ES 100/K-8
PO Box 158 67445 785-568-2291
Regina Wallace, prin. Fax 568-2239

Goddard, Sedgwick, Pop. 4,232
Goddard USD 265 5,300/K-12
PO Box 249 67052 316-794-4000
Dr. Justin Henry, supt. Fax 794-2222
www.goddardusd.com
Apollo ES 400/K-4
PO Box 159 67052 316-794-4090
Scott May, prin. Fax 794-4091
Challenger IS 300/5-6
PO Box 277 67052 316-794-4040
Jess Herbig, prin. Fax 794-4266
Davidson ES 500/K-4
PO Box 278 67052 316-794-4260
Matt Cavanaugh, prin. Fax 794-4280
Discovery IS 400/5-6
PO Box 248 67052 316-794-4030
Ryan Jilka, prin. Fax 794-4064
Earhart ES 400/K-4
PO Box 319 67052 316-794-4080
Tracy Giddens, prin. Fax 794-4062
Eisenhower MS 500/7-8
PO Box 349 67052 316-794-4150
Jerold Longabaugh, prin. Fax 794-4063
Explorer ES 400/K-4
PO Box 217 67052 316-794-4181
Don Howell, prin. Fax 794-4182
Goddard MS 400/7-8
PO Box 279 67052 316-794-4230
Lisa Hogarth, prin. Fax 794-4254
Oak Street ES 400/K-4
PO Box 188 67052 316-794-4200
Ashley Miller, prin. Fax 794-4220

Holy Spirit Catholic S 100/PK-8
18218 W US Highway 54 67052 316-794-8139
Kelly Bright, prin. Fax 794-2055

Goessel, Marion, Pop. 530
Goessel USD 411 300/K-12
PO Box 68 67053 620-367-4601
John Fast, supt. Fax 367 4603
www.usd411.org
Goessel ES 100/K-5
PO Box 68 67053 620-367-8118
John Fast, prin. Fax 367-8156

Goodland, Sherman, Pop. 4,416
Goodland USD 352 700/K-12
PO Box 509 67735 785-890-2397
Bill Biermann, supt. Fax 890-8504
www.usd352.org
North ES 100/3-6
700 E 4th St 67735 785-890-6558
Emmet Rudolph, prin. Fax 890-8532
West ES 300/K-2
PO Box 509 67735 785-890-6103
Michelle Williams, prin. Fax 890-8526

Grainfield, Gove, Pop. 277
Wheatland USD 292 100/PK-12
PO Box 165 67737 785-673-4213
Gary Kraus, supt. Fax 673-4234
www.usd292.org
Wheatland ES 100/PK-4
PO Box 174 67737 785-673-4365
Gary Kraus, prin. Fax 673-4371

Great Bend, Barton, Pop. 15,763
Great Bend USD 428 3,000/PK-12
201 S Patton Rd 67530 620-793-1500
Khris Thexton, supt. Fax 793-1585
www.usd428.net
Eisenhower ES 300/K-6
1212 Garfield St 67530 620-793-1501
Laurie Harwood, prin. Fax 793-1644
Great Bend MS 400/7-8
1919 Harrison St 67530 620-793-1510
David Reiser, prin. Fax 793-1549
Jefferson ES 300/K-6
2716 24th St 67530 620-793-1502
Kip Wilson, prin. Fax 793-1588
Lincoln ES 300/K-6
5630 Broadway Ave 67530 620-793-1503
Misty Straub, prin. Fax 793-1612
Park ES 300/K-6
1801 Williams St 67530 620-793-1505
Phil Heeke, prin. Fax 793-1545
Riley ES 400/PK-6
1515 10th St 67530 620-793-1506
JoAnn Blevins, prin. Fax 793-1544

Central Kansas Christian Academy 100/K-8
215 McKinley St 67530 620-792-3477
Dottie Dozier, admin. Fax 793-3438
Great Bend SDA S 50/K-8
7 SW 30 Ave 67530 620-793-9247
Holy Family S 200/PK-6
4200 Broadway Ave 67530 620-793-3265
Karen Moeder, prin. Fax 792-1397

Greeley, Anderson, Pop. 297
Garnett USD 365
Supt. — See Garnett
Greeley ES 100/PK 6
101 S Mary 66033 785-867-3460
Debbie Alford, prin. Fax 867-2420

Greensburg, Kiowa, Pop. 767
Kiowa County USD 422 400/PK 12
710 S Main St 67054 620-723-2145
Staci Derstein, supt. Fax 723-2705
www.usd422.org
Kiowa County ES 200/PK-8
730 S Main St 67054 620-723-2332
Brian Deterding, prin. Fax 723-2705

Gridley, Coffey, Pop. 338
Le Roy-Gridley USD 245
Supt. — See Le Roy

Gridley ES — 100/PK-5
PO Box 426 66852 — 620-836-2182
Jay Applegate, prin. — Fax 836-4041
Southern Coffey County JHS — 50/6-8
PO Box 426 66852 — 620-836-2151
Jay Applegate, prin. — Fax 836-4041

Grinnell, Gove, Pop. 259
Grinnell USD 291 — 100/K-8
PO Box 68 67738 — 785-824-3277
Ragena Mize, supt. — Fax 824-3215
usd291.com
Grinnell ES — 50/K-4
PO Box 129 67738 — 785-824-3296
Dr. Ragena Mize, prin. — Fax 824-3215
Grinnell MS — 50/5-8
PO Box 68 67738 — 785-824-3277
Ragena Mize, prin. — Fax 824-3215

Gypsum, Saline, Pop. 398
Southeast of Saline USD 306 — 700/K-12
5056 E Highway K4 67448 — 785-536-4291
Greg Mann, supt. — Fax 536-4247
www.usd306.k12.ks.us
Southeast Saline ES — 400/K-6
5056 E Highway K4 67448 — 785-536-4215
Cassie Gorman, prin. — Fax 536-4292

Halstead, Harvey, Pop. 2,058
Halstead-Bentley USD 440 — 800/K-12
521 W 6th St 67056 — 316-835-2641
Thomas Alstrom, supt. — Fax 835-2305
www.usd440.com
Halstead MS — 300/4-8
221 W 6th St 67056 — 316-835-2694
Ron Barry, prin. — Fax 835-2469
Other Schools – See Bentley

Hamilton, Greenwood, Pop. 262
Hamilton USD 390 — 100/K-12
2596 W Rd N 66853 — 620-678-3244
Greg Markowitz, supt. — Fax 678-3321
www.hamilton390.net
Hamilton ES — 50/K-6
2596 W Rd N 66853 — 620-678-3410
David Kehres, prin. — Fax 678-3321

Hanover, Washington, Pop. 680
Barnes USD 223
Supt. — See Barnes
Hanover S — 200/PK-8
209 E North St 66945 — 785-337-2281
Brian Cordel, prin. — Fax 337-2307

St. Johns S — 100/1-8
100 S Church St 66945 — 785-337-2368
Timothy Rundle, prin. — Fax 337-8950

Harper, Harper, Pop. 1,464
Chaparral Schools USD 361
Supt. — See Anthony
Harper ES — 200/PK-6
1317 Walnut St 67058 — 620-896-7614
Bill Giesen, prin. — Fax 896-7983

Hartford, Lyon, Pop. 364
Southern Lyon County USD 252 — 500/PK-12
PO Box 278 66854 — 620-392-5519
Dr. Michael Argabright, supt. — Fax 392-5841
www.usd252.org/
Other Schools – See Neosho Rapids, Olpe

Haven, Reno, Pop. 1,205
Haven USD 312 — 800/K-12
PO Box 130 67543 — 620-465-3445
Clark Wedel, supt. — Fax 465-3595
www.havenschools.com
Haven ES — 300/K-6
PO Box 489 67543 — 620-465-2501
Alice Glendening, prin. — Fax 465-2775
Haven MS — 100/7-8
PO Box B 67543 — 620-465-2587
Marty Nienstedt, prin. — Fax 465-2588
Other Schools – See Partridge

Haviland, Kiowa, Pop. 699
Haviland USD 474 — 100/PK-8
PO Box 243 67059 — 620-862-5256
Mark Clodfelter, supt. — Fax 862-5260
www.usd474.org/
Haviland ES — 100/PK-8
PO Box 243 67059 — 620-862-5277
Mark Clodfelter, prin. — Fax 862-5260

Hays, Ellis, Pop. 20,202
Hays USD 489 — 2,800/PK-12
323 W 12th St 67601 — 785-623-2400
John Thissen, supt. — Fax 623-2409
www.usd489.com/
Early Childhood Connections - Washington — 100/PK-PK
305 Main St 67601 — 785-623-2430
Donna Hudson-Hamilton, dir. — Fax 623-2432
Hays MS — 600/6-8
201 E 29th St 67601 — 785-623-2450
Craig Pallister, prin. — Fax 623-2456
Lincoln ES — 200/K-5
1906 Ash St 67601 — 785-623-2500
Elaine Rohleder, prin. — Fax 623-2507
McCarthy ES — 400/K-5
1401 Hall St 67601 — 785-623-2510
Vicki Gile, prin. — Fax 623-2518
Roosevelt ES — 400/K-5
2000 MacArthur Rd 67601 — 785-623-2520
Lee Keffer, prin. — Fax 623-2526
Wilson ES — 400/K-5
101 E 28th St 67601 — 785-623-2550
Anita Scheve, prin. — Fax 623-2556

Holy Family S — 400/PK-6
1800 Milner St 67601 — 785-625-3131
Rachel Wentling, prin. — Fax 625-2098
Maranatha Christian S — 50/K-8
1410 Toulon Ave 67601 — 785-625-3975

Haysville, Sedgwick, Pop. 10,516
Haysville USD 261 — 5,200/PK-12
1745 W Grand Ave 67060 — 316-554-2200
Dr. John Burke, supt. — Fax 554-2230
www.usd261.com
Freeman ES — 300/PK-5
1731 W Grand Ave 67060 — 316-554-2265
Dr. Donna Ferguson, prin. — Fax 554-2295
Haysville MS — 600/6-8
900 W Grand Ave 67060 — 316-554-2251
Dr. Mike Maurer, prin. — Fax 554-2258
Haysville West MS — 700/6-8
1956 W Grand Ave 67060 — 316-554-2370
Ildo Martins, prin. — Fax 554-2377
Nelson ES — 400/PK-5
245 N Delos Ave 67060 — 316-554-2273
Mike Mitchener, prin. — Fax 554-2275
Prairie ES — 400/PK-5
7101 S Meridian St 67060 — 316-554-2350
David Engelking, prin. — Fax 554-2357
Rex ES — 500/PK-5
1100 W Grand Ave 67060 — 316-554-2281
Brian Howard, prin. — Fax 554-2043
Other Schools – See Wichita

St. Cecilia Catholic S — 100/PK-8
1912 W Grand Ave 67060 — 316-522-0461
Gerard Hamilton, prin. — Fax 524-6183

Healy, Lane, Pop. 233
Healy USD 468 — 100/PK-12
5006 N Dodge Rd 67850 — 620-398-2248
Larry Lysell, supt. — Fax 398-2435
www.usd468.org
Healy ES — 50/PK-6
5006 N Dodge Rd 67850 — 620-398-2248
Beverly Roemer, prin. — Fax 398-2435

Herington, Dickinson, Pop. 2,456
Herington USD 487 — 500/PK-12
19 N Broadway 67449 — 785-258-2263
Ron Wilson, supt. — Fax 258-2982
www.heringtonschools.org
Herington ES — 200/PK-5
1403 N D St 67449 — 785-258-3234
Donalyn Biehler, prin. — Fax 258-2915
Herington MS — 100/6-8
1317 N D St 67449 — 785-258-2448
Brandi Hendrix, prin. — Fax 258-3976

Hesston, Harvey, Pop. 3,645
Hesston USD 460 — 800/K-12
PO Box 2000 67062 — 620-327-4931
Ben Proctor, supt. — Fax 327-7157
www.hesstonschools.org
Hesston ES — 300/K-4
PO Box 2000 67062 — 620-327-7102
Alisa Krehbiel, prin. — Fax 327-7153
Hesston MS — 300/5-8
PO Box 2000 67062 — 620-327-7111
Greg Heinrichs, prin. — Fax 327-7115

Hiawatha, Brown, Pop. 3,067
Hiawatha USD 415 — 900/PK-12
PO Box 398 66434 — 785-742-2224
Lonnie Moser, supt. — Fax 742-2301
www.hiawathaschools.org
Hiawatha ES — 400/PK-4
600 Miami St 66434 — 785-742-7181
Tom Schmitz, prin. — Fax 742-2545
Hiawatha MS — 200/5-8
307 S Morrill Ave 66434 — 785-742-4172
David Coufal, prin. — Fax 742-1744

Hill City, Graham, Pop. 1,438
Graham County USD 281 — 400/PK-12
PO Box 309 67642 — 785-421-2135
Jim Hickel, supt. — Fax 421-5657
www.usd281.com
Hill City ES — 200/PK-6
216 N 4th Ave 67642 — 785-421-3425
Jim Hickel, prin. — Fax 421-4144

Hillsboro, Marion, Pop. 2,935
Durham-Hillsboro-Lehigh USD 410 — 400/PK-12
416 S Date St 67063 — 620-947-3184
Max Heinrichs, supt. — Fax 947-3475
www.usd410.net
Hillsboro ES — 300/PK-5
812 E A St 67063 — 620-947-3184
Evan Yoder, prin. — Fax 947-3263

Hoisington, Barton, Pop. 2,656
Hoisington USD 431 — 800/PK-12
165 W 3rd St 67544 — 620-653-4134
Bill Lowry, supt. — Fax 653-4073
www.usd431.net
Hoisington MS — 200/5-8
360 W 11th St 67544 — 620-653-4951
Patricia Reinhardt, prin. — Fax 653-4483
Lincoln ES — 100/3-4
516 N Pine St 67544 — 620-653-4549
Alan Charles, prin. — Fax 653-4384
Roosevelt ES — 300/PK-2
315 N Vine St 67544 — 620-653-4470
Alan Charles, prin. — Fax 653-4394

Holcomb, Finney, Pop. 2,058
Holcomb USD 363 — 1,000/PK-12
PO Box 8 67851 — 620-277-2629
Jean Rush, supt. — Fax 277-2010
www.usd363.com/
Holcomb ES — 200/3-5
PO Box 1025 67851 — 620-277-2257
Deana Novack, prin. — Fax 277-0239
Holcomb MS — 200/6-8
PO Box 89 67851 — 620-277-2699
Tyler Helton, prin. — Fax 277-2746
Wiley ES — 300/PK-2
PO Box 37 67851 — 620-277-4431
Deana Novack, prin. — Fax 277-4424

Holton, Jackson, Pop. 3,248
Holton USD 336 — 1,100/PK-12
PO Box 352 66436 — 785-364-3650
Robert Davies, supt. — Fax 364-3975
www.holtonks.net
Holton ES — 500/PK-5
812 W 5th St 66436 — 785-364-3251
Beth Smith, prin. — Fax 364-4844
Holton MS — 200/6-8
900 Iowa Ave 66436 — 785-364-2441
Michael Kimberlin, prin. — Fax 364-5460

North Jackson USD 335 — 400/PK-12
12692 266th Rd 66436 — 785-364-2194
Adrianne Walsh, supt. — Fax 364-4346
www.jhcobras.net
Jackson Heights ES — 200/PK-6
12763 266th Rd 66436 — 785-364-2244
Adrianne Walsh, prin. — Fax 364-4712

Holyrood, Ellsworth, Pop. 439
Central Plains USD 112 — 600/PK-12
PO Box 168 67450 — 785-252-3695
Greg Clark, supt. — Fax 252-3697
www.usd112.org
Central Plains ES — 100/PK-4
600 S Main St 67450 — 785-252-3666
Jane Oeser, prin. — Fax 252-3653
Other Schools – See Bushton, Wilson

Hope, Dickinson, Pop. 357
Rural Vista USD 481
Supt. — See White City
Hope ES — 100/PK-8
PO Box 218 67451 — 785-366-7221
Mike Teeter, prin. — Fax 366-7115

Horton, Brown, Pop. 1,718
South Brown County USD 430 — 600/PK-12
522 Central Ave 66439 — 785-486-2611
Jason Cline, supt. — Fax 486-2496
usd430.org
Horton ES — 200/PK-4
300 E 16th St 66439 — 785-486-2616
Judy Dickman, prin. — Fax 486-2527
Other Schools – See Everest

Howard, Elk, Pop. 671
West Elk USD 282 — 300/PK-12
PO Box 607 67349 — 620-374-2113
Bert Moore, supt. — Fax 374-2414
westelk.us
Howard West Elk S — 300/PK-12
PO Box 278 67349 — 620-374-2147
Martin Burke, prin. — Fax 374-2116

Hoxie, Sheridan, Pop. 1,186
Hoxie USD 412 — 400/PK-12
PO Box 348 67740 — 785-675-3258
James Howard, supt. — Fax 675-2126
www.hoxie.org
Hoxie ES — 300/PK-6
PO Box 348 67740 — 785-675-3254
James Howard, prin. — Fax 675-2126

Hoyt, Jackson, Pop. 649
Royal Valley USD 337
Supt. — See Mayetta
Royal Valley ES — 400/PK-4
PO Box 68 66440 — 785-986-6286
Noah Slay, prin. — Fax 986-6333

Hugoton, Stevens, Pop. 3,876
Hugoton USD 210 — 1,100/PK-12
529 S Main St 67951 — 620-544-4397
Adrian Howie, supt. — Fax 544-7138
www.usd210.org
Hugoton IS — 300/3-6
304 E 6th St 67951 — 620-544-4376
Elise Heger, prin. — Fax 544-4871
Hugoton MS — 200/7-8
115 W 11th St 67951 — 620-544-4341
Tyson Eslinger, prin. — Fax 544-4856
Hugoton PS — 400/PK-2
304 E 6th St 67951 — 620-544-4376
Tiffany Boxum, prin. — Fax 544-4871

Heritage Christian Academy — 50/PK-7
PO Box 744 67951 — 620-544-7005
Misty Martin, prin. — Fax 544-8748

Humboldt, Allen, Pop. 1,917
Humboldt USD 258 — 700/PK-12
801 New York St 66748 — 620-473-3121
Kay Lewis, supt. — Fax 473-2023
www.usd258.net
Humboldt ES — 300/PK-5
1100 Central St 66748 — 620-473-2461
Staci Hudlin, prin. — Fax 473-2642
Humboldt MS — 200/6-8
1105 Bridge St 66748 — 620-473-3348
Stephanie Splechter, prin. — Fax 473-3141

Hutchinson, Reno, Pop. 41,132
Buhler USD 313
Supt. — See Buhler
Plum Creek ES — PK-5
901 E 43rd Ave 67502 — 620-662-5535
John Schulte, prin. — Fax 694-1032
Prairie Hills MS — 400/6-8
3200 Lucille Dr 67502 — 620-662-6027
Todd Fredrickson, prin. — Fax 694-1002
Union Valley ES — 400/PK-5
2501 E 30th Ave 67502 — 620-662-4891
Paul Erickson, prin. — Fax 694-1022

Hutchinson USD 308 4,500/PK-12
1520 N Plum St 67501 620-615-4000
Gary Price, supt. Fax 615-4010
www.usd308.com
Avenue A ES 200/PK-6
111 S Madison St 67501 620-615-4950
Beth Redinger, prin. Fax 615-4952
Faris ES 300/K-6
301 E 10th Ave 67501 620-615-5000
Daniel Ackland, prin. Fax 615-5002
Graber ES 300/PK-6
1600 N Cleveland St 67501 620-615-5050
Kelley McCall, prin. Fax 615-5055
Hutchinson Magnet S at Allen 300/K-6
403 W 10th Ave 67501 620-615-4900
Bryan Cunningham, prin. Fax 615-4902
Hutchinson MS 7 7-7
210 E Avenue A 67501 620-615-4700
Jeff Shearon, prin. Fax 615-4702
Hutchinson MS 8 400/8-8
200 W 14th Ave 67501 620-615-4800
Bruce Hurford, prin. Fax 615-4802
Lincoln ES 300/PK-6
315 E Bigger St 67501 620-615-5100
Darla Fisher, prin. Fax 615-5107
McCandless ES 500/K-6
700 N Baker St 67501 620-615-5150
Sherri Hart, prin. Fax 615-5162
Morgan ES 500/K-6
100 W 27th Ave 67502 620-615-5200
Kayla Wiedeman, prin. Fax 615-5214
Wiley ES 300/K-6
900 W 21st Ave 67502 620-615-5250
Alberto Carrillo, prin. Fax 615-5262

Nickerson USD 309 1,100/PK-12
4501 W 4th Ave 67501 620-663-7141
Dr. Dawn Johnson, supt. Fax 663-7148
www.usd309ks.org
Reno Valley MS 200/7-8
1616 Wilshire Dr 67501 620-662-4573
Vince Naccarato, prin. Fax 662-6708
Other Schools – See Nickerson, South Hutchinson

Central Christian S 200/PK-12
1910 E 30th Ave 67502 620-663-2174
Tim Kuhns, supt. Fax 663-2176
Holy Cross Catholic S 300/PK-6
2633 Independence Rd 67502 620-665-6168
Amy Wagoner, prin. Fax 665-0368

Independence, Montgomery, Pop. 9,137
Independence USD 446 2,000/K-12
517 N 10th St 67301 620-332-1800
Rusty Arnold, supt. Fax 332-1811
www.indyschools.com
Eisenhower ES 500/K-2
501 Spruce St 67301 620-332-1854
Brad Carroll, prin. Fax 332-1859
Independence MS 400/6-8
300 W Locust St 67301 620-332-1836
Mark Hayward, prin. Fax 332-1841
Jefferson S 500/3-5
2101 N 13th St 67301 620-332-1875
Jim Moseley, prin. Fax 332-1878

St. Andrew Catholic S 200/PK-8
215 N Park Blvd 67301 620-331-2870
Becky Brown, prin. Fax 331-6496
Zion Lutheran S 100/PK-8
301 S 11th St 67301 620-332-3331
Eric Pralle, prin. Fax 332-3330

Ingalls, Gray, Pop. 304
Ingalls USD 477 200/PK-12
PO Box 99 67853 620-335-5136
Randy Rockhold, supt. Fax 335-5678
www.ingallsusd477.com/
Ingalls ES 100/PK-5
PO Box 99 67853 620-335-5134
Randy Rockhold, prin. Fax 335-5678

Inman, McPherson, Pop. 1,343
Inman USD 448 400/PK-12
PO Box 129 67546 620-585-6441
Scott Friesen, supt. Fax 585-2797
www.usd448.com
Inman ES 200/PK-6
PO Box 277 67546 620-585-6441
Jo McFadden, prin. Fax 585-2797

Iola, Allen, Pop. 5,562
Iola USD 257 700/PK-12
305 N Washington Ave 66749 620-365-4700
Stacey Fager, supt. Fax 365-4708
www.usd257.org
Iola Lower MS 5-6
600 East St 66749 620-365-4785
Brad Crusinbery, prin. Fax 365-4770
Iola Upper MS 200/7-8
600 East St 66749 620-365-4785
Brad Crusinbery, prin. Fax 365-4770
Jefferson ES 100/1-2
300 S Jefferson Ave 66749 620-365-4840
Lori Maxwell, prin. Fax 365-4845
Lincoln ES 100/3-4
700 N Jefferson Ave 66749 620-365-4820
Andy Gottlob, prin. Fax 365-4829
McKinley ES 50/PK-K
209 S Kentucky St 66749 620-365-4860
Angie Linn, prin. Fax 365-5790

Jetmore, Hodgeman, Pop. 861
Hodgeman County USD 227 300/PK-12
PO Box 398 67854 620-357-8301
Doug Chaney, supt. Fax 357-8437
www.usd227.org/
Hodgeman County ES 200/PK-6
PO Box 398 67854 620-357-8396
Doug Chaney, prin. Fax 357-8437

Johnson, Stanton, Pop. 1,483
Stanton County USD 452 400/PK-12
PO Box C 67855 620-492-6226
Kim Novack, supt. Fax 492-1326
www.usd452.org
Stanton County ES 200/PK-6
PO Box C 67855 620-492-6216
Andrea Jones, prin. Fax 492-1549

Junction City, Geary, Pop. 21,775
Geary County USD 475 8,200/PK-12
PO Box 370 66441 785-717-4000
Dr. Corbin Witt, supt. Fax 717-4003
www.usd475.org/
Early Childhood Center PK-PK
1803 Elmdale Ave 66441 785-717-4730
Stephanie Bogenhagen, prin.
Eisenhower ES 300/K-5
1625 Saint Marys Rd 66441 785-717-4340
Susan Kamphaus, prin. Fax 717-4341
Franklin ES 200/K-5
410 W 2nd St 66441 785-717-4380
Amy Roether, prin. Fax 717-4381
Grandview ES 100/K-5
109 E Grandview Dr 66441 785-717-4470
Lynn Shinault, prin. Fax 717-4471
Junction City MS 1,000/6-8
700 Wildcat Ln 66441 785-717-4400
Mary Wright, prin. Fax 717-4401
Lincoln ES 200/K-5
300 Lincoln School Dr 66441 785-717-4570
Kathi Teeter, prin. Fax 717-4571
Sheridan ES 300/K-5
429 W Ash St 66441 785-717-4670
Dixie Coleman, prin. Fax 717-4671
Spring Valley ES 400/K-5
1601 Hickory Ln 66441 785-717-4790
Sierra Jackson, prin. Fax 717-4791
Washington ES 300/K-5
1500 N Washington St 66441 785-717-4690
Jennifer Black, prin. Fax 717-4691
Westwood ES 300/K-5
1600 N Eisenhower Dr 66441 785-717-4150
Kim Dressman, prin. Fax 717-4151
Other Schools – See Fort Riley, Milford

St. Xaviers Catholic S 200/K-12
200 N Washington St 66441 785-238-2841
Shawn Augustine, prin. Fax 238-5021

Kanopolis, Ellsworth, Pop. 479
Ellsworth USD 327
Supt. — See Ellsworth
Kanopolis MS 100/5-6
PO Box 37 67454 785-472-4477
Patrick Schroeder, prin. Fax 472-4068

Kansas City, Wyandotte, Pop. 142,097
Bonner Springs USD 204
Supt. — See Bonner Springs
Delaware Ridge ES 400/PK-5
1601 N 130th St 66109 913-441-2126
Clark McCracken, prin. Fax 422-4193

Kansas City USD 500 20,500/PK-12
2010 N 59th St 66104 913-551-3200
Dr. Cynthia Lane, supt. Fax 551-3217
www.kckps.org
Argentine MS 600/6-8
2123 Ruby Ave 66106 913-627-6750
Jereme Brueggeman, prin. Fax 627-6783
Arrowhead MS 500/6-8
1715 N 82nd St 66112 913-627-6600
Laurie Boyd, prin. Fax 627-6654
Banneker ES 400/PK-5
2026 N 4th St 66101 913-627-4700
Dr. Tyrone Bates, prin. Fax 627-4776
Bethel ES 200/K-5
7850 Yecker Ave 66109 913-627-3000
Janice McConnell, prin. Fax 627-3046
Caruthers ES 300/PK-5
1100 Waverly Ave 66104 913-627-4750
Molly Struzzo, prin. Fax 627-4786
Central MS 600/6-8
925 Ivandale St 66101 913-627-6150
Dionandre Josenberger, prin. Fax 627-6152
Coronado MS 400/6-8
1735 N 64th Ter 66102 913-627-6300
Jewell Ragsdale, prin. Fax 627-6358
Douglass ES 400/PK-5
1310 N 9th St 66101 913-627-5100
Leala Taylor, prin. Fax 627-5108
Edison ES 400/PK-5
1000 Locust St 66103 913-627-4900
Cynthia Cop, prin. Fax 722-7486
Eisenhower MS 500/6-8
2901 N 72nd St 66109 913-627-6450
Samia Guess, prin. Fax 627-6455
Emerson ES 200/K-5
1429 S 29th St 66106 913-627-5900
Brett Bernard, prin. Fax 627-5937
Fiske ES 500/K-5
625 S Valley St 66105 913-627-4850
Dr. Joe Graham, prin. Fax 627-4876
Grant ES 300/K-5
1510 N 4th St 66101 913-627-4300
Dr. Jennifer Malone, prin. Fax 627-4303
Hazel Grove ES 500/K-5
2401 N 67th St 66104 913-627-7000
Trasi Sorrells, prin. Fax 627-7027
Huyck ES 200/K-5
1530 N 83rd St 66112 913-627-4650
Colleen Dudley, prin. Fax 627-4686
KCK ECC PK-PK
1708 N 55th St 66102 913-627-6590
Heather Turi, prin. Fax 596-1990
Kennedy ES 400/K-5
2600 N 72nd St 66109 913-627-4950
Dr. Bob Wilcox, prin. Fax 627-4986
Lindbergh ES 200/K-5
641 N 57th St 66102 913-627-5150
Dr. Iva Lee Colgan, prin. Fax 627-5176
McKinley ES 200/K-5
1301 Armstrong Ave 66102 913-627-7350
Valerie Castillo, prin. Fax 627-7380
Morse ECC PK-PK
912 S Baltimore St 66105 913-627-6550
Debi Apple, prin. Fax 627-6566
New Chelsea ES 600/K-5
2500 Wood Ave 66104 913-627-5000
Canise Salinas, prin. Fax 627-5013
New Stanley ES 300/K-5
3604 Metropolitan Ave 66106 913-627-3950
Shonielle Roberson, prin. Fax 627-3976
Northwest MS 700/6-8
2400 N 18th St 66104 913-627-4000
Dr. Carnest Mitchell, prin. Fax 627-4052
Parker ES 200/K-5
3334 Haskell Ave 66104 913-627-4200
Angela Diobildo-Sharp, prin. Fax 627-4201
Pearson ES 600/PK-5
310 N 11th St 66102 913-627-3150
Lori Cooper, prin. Fax 627-3176
Prentis ES 200/K-5
2337 S 14th St 66103 913-627-5250
Sharon Potts, prin. Fax 627-5276
Quindaro ES 400/K-5
2800 Farrow Ave 66104 913-627-4400
Stacey Chatmon, prin. Fax 627-4409
Rosedale MS 600/6-8
3600 Springfield St 66103 913-627-6900
Travis Helm, prin. Fax 627-6957
Rushton ES 400/K-5
2605 W 43rd Ave 66103 913-627-3050
Dr. Tamekia McCauley, prin. Fax 627-3088
Silver City ES 300/PK-5
2515 Lawrence Ave 66106 913-627-4550
Dr. Deanne Letourneau, prin. Fax 627-4576
Stony Point North ES 300/K-5
8200 Elizabeth Ave 66112 913-627-4500
Jane Martin, prin. Fax 627-4537
Stony Point South ES 300/K-5
150 S 78th St 66111 913-627-4600
Susan Hendricks, prin. Fax 627-4626
Twain ES 300/K-5
2300 Minnesota Ave 66102 913-627-5200
Sandra Egidy, prin. Fax 627-5246
Ware ES 300/K-5
4820 Oakland Ave 66102 913-627-5950
Monica Randle, prin. Fax 627-5986
Watson Jr ECC PK-PK
6611 Waverly Ave 66104 913-627-0360
Dennis McCall, prin. Fax 596-5480
Welborn ES 500/K-5
5200 Leavenworth Rd 66104 913-627-4450
Collette Chaney, prin. Fax 627-4477
West MS 400/6-8
2600 N 44th St 66104 913-627-6000
Elvira Randle, prin. Fax 627-6053
White Church ES 300/K-5
2226 N 85th St 66109 913-627-4250
Michael Sechler, prin. Fax 627-4276
White ES 300/K-5
2600 N 43rd Ter 66104 913-627-6250
Angela Wright, prin. Fax 627-6282
Whittier ES 600/K-5
295 S 10th St 66102 913-627-6400
Geri Cunningham, prin. Fax 627-6449
Willard ES 500/K-5
3400 Orville Ave 66102 913-627-6100
Sarah Pike, prin. Fax 627-6126

Piper-Kansas City USD 203 1,900/PK-12
3130 N 122nd St 66109 913-721-2088
Tim Conrad, supt. Fax 721-3573
www.piperschools.com
Piper East ES 300/4-5
4410 N 107th St 66109 913-721-5000
Jenny Golden, prin. Fax 721-5336
Piper ES 700/PK-3
3131 N 122nd St 66109 913-721-1243
Bilee Jo Grable, prin. Fax 721-3656
Piper MS 400/6-8
4420 N 107th St 66109 913-721-1144
Stephen Mercer, prin. Fax 721-1526

Turner USD 202 4,000/PK-12
800 S 55th St 66106 913-288-4100
Dr. Jason Dandoy, supt. Fax 288-3401
www.turnerusd202.org/
Junction ES 300/PK-5
2570 S 42nd St 66106 913-288-3600
Christina Compton, prin. Fax 288-3601
Midland Trail ES 600/PK-5
3101 S 51st St 66106 913-288-3500
Aron Attebery, prin. Fax 288-3501
Oak Grove ES 500/PK-5
5340 Oak Grove Rd 66106 913-288-3900
James Polk, prin. Fax 288-3901
Turner ES 600/PK-5
1800 S 55th St 66106 913-288-3400
Tara Hudson, prin. Fax 288-3402
Turner MS 600/7-8
1312 S 55th St 66106 913-288-4000
Bill Weber, prin. Fax 288-4001
Turner Sixth Grade Academy 300/6-6
6425 Riverview Ave 66102 913-288-3800
Matt Spring, prin. Fax 288-3801

Christ the King S 300/PK-8
3027 N 54th St 66104 913-287-8883
Cathy Fithian, prin. Fax 287-7409
Holy Name S 200/PK-8
1007 Southwest Blvd 66103 913-722-1032
Amanda Vega-Mavec, prin. Fax 722-4175
Lindsay SDA S 50/PK-8
3310 Garfield Ave 66104 913-342-4435
Tonya Anderson, admin. Fax 342-6040

Open Door Christian S 50/PK-8
3033 N 103rd Ter 66109 913-334-7777
Teresa Christopher, prin. Fax 334-0678
Our Lady of Unity S 100/K-8
2646 S 34th St 66106 913-262-7022
Nancy Butters, prin. Fax 262-7836
Resurrection S at the Cathedral 300/PK-8
425 N 15th St 66102 913-371-8101
Lynda Higgins, prin. Fax 371-2151
St. Patrick S 300/PK-8
1066 N 94th St 66112 913-299-8131
Felicia Torres, prin. Fax 299-2845

Kensington, Smith, Pop. 463
Thunder Ridge SD 110 200/PK-12
128 S Kansas St 66951 785-476-2218
Jeff Yoxall, supt. Fax 476-2258
usd110.net
Thunder Ridge ES 100/K-3
128 S Kansas St 66951 785-476-3241
Jeff Yoxall, prin. Fax 476-2258
Other Schools – See Agra

Kingman, Kingman, Pop. 3,142
Kingman-Norwich USD 331 1,000/PK-12
115 N Main St 67068 620-532-3134
Dr. Robert Diepenbrock Ed.D., supt. Fax 532-3251
www.knusd331.com
Kingman ES 300/PK-5
607 N Spruce St 67068 620-532-3186
Bill Kelley, prin. Fax 532-5137
Kingman MS 200/6-8
607 N Spruce St 67068 620-532-3186
Amy Wallace, prin. Fax 532-5137
Other Schools – See Norwich

St. Patrick Catholic S 200/PK-8
630 W D Ave 67068 620-532-2791
Bob Lyall, prin. Fax 532-2392

Kinsley, Edwards, Pop. 1,435
Kinsley-Offerle USD 347 400/PK-12
120 W 8th St 67547 620-659-3646
Becky Burcher, supt. Fax 659-2669
www.usd347.org/
Other Schools – See Offerle

Kiowa, Barber, Pop. 1,012
South Barber County USD 255 300/PK-12
512 Main St 67070 833-722-7237
Dr. Andi Williams, supt. Fax 825-4145
www.southbarber.com
South Barber ES 200/PK-6
913 Main St 67070 833-722-7237
Eric Stoddard, prin. Fax 825-4620

Kismet, Seward, Pop. 456
Kismet-Plains USD 483 700/PK-12
17222 Mustang Rd 67859 620-563-7103
Elton Argo, supt. Fax 563-7348
www.usd483.net
Kismet ES 200/K-2
PO Box 336 67859 620-563-7248
Jerrilynn Wood, prin. Fax 563-7035
Southwestern Heights JHS 200/6-8
17222 Mustang Rd 67859 620-563-7100
Kurt Stanfield, prin. Fax 563-7342
Other Schools – See Plains

La Crosse, Rush, Pop. 1,335
La Crosse USD 395 300/K-12
PO Box 778 67548 785-222-2505
Bill Keeley, supt. Fax 222-3240
www.usd395.org
La Crosse ES 200/K-6
PO Box 700 67548 785-222-2622
Bill Keeley, prin. Fax 222-3432
La Crosse MS 50/7-8
PO Box 810 67548 785-222-2528
Kathy Keeley, prin. Fax 222-3480

LaCygne, Linn, Pop. 1,138
Prairie View USD 362 900/PK-12
13799 KS Highway 152, 913-757-2677
Rex Bollinger, supt. Fax 757-4442
www.pv362.org
LaCygne ES 200/PK-5
710 Walnut St, 913-757-4417
Cindy Dziadosz, prin. Fax 757-4581
Prairie View MS 200/6-8
13667 KS Highway 152, 913-757-4497
Ken Bolt, prin. Fax 757-2728
Other Schools – See Parker

Lakin, Kearny, Pop. 2,182
Lakin USD 215 600/PK-12
1003 W Kingman Ave 67860 620-355-6761
Mike Ward, supt. Fax 355-7317
www.usd215.org
Lakin ES 300/PK-4
PO Box 26 67860 620-355-6191
Mindi Brennaman, prin. Fax 355-6491
Lakin MS 200/5-8
1201 W Kingman Ave 67860 620-355-6973
Cody Calkins, prin. Fax 355-8313

Langdon, Reno, Pop. 42
Fairfield USD 310 300/PK-12
16115 S Langdon Rd 67583 620-596-2152
Nathan Reed, supt. Fax 596-2835
www.usd310.org
Fairfield ES 100/PK-5
16115 S Langdon Rd 67583 620-596-2152
Betsy McKinney, prin. Fax 596-2835
Fairfield MS 100/6-8
16115 S Langdon Rd 67583 620-596-2615
Jason Briar, prin. Fax 596-2835

Lansing, Leavenworth, Pop. 10,978
Lansing USD 469 2,500/PK-12
200 E Mary St 66043 913-727-1100
Dr. Darrel Stufflebeam Ed.D., supt. Fax 727-1619
www.usd469.net
Lansing ES 1,100/PK-5
450 W Mary St 66043 913-727-1128
Vickie Kelly, prin. Fax 727-6577
Lansing MS 600/6-8
220 Lion Ln 66043 913-727-1197
Kerry Brungardt, prin. Fax 727-1349

Larned, Pawnee, Pop. 3,979
Ft. Larned USD 495 1,000/PK-12
120 E 6th St 67550 620-285-3185
Jon Flint, supt. Fax 285-2973
www.usd495.net
Hillside ES 100/PK-K
502 W 5th St 67550 620-285-2311
Lea Harding, prin. Fax 285-8429
Larned MS 300/5-8
904 Corse Ave 67550 620-285-8430
Shane Sundahl, prin. Fax 285-8433
Northside ES 100/3-4
1604 State St 67550 620-285-2141
Lea Harding, prin. Fax 285-2584
Phinney ES 200/1-2
523 E 12th St 67550 620-285-3181
Lea Harding, prin. Fax 285-8439
Tri-County ECC PK-PK
723 State St 67550 620-285-2938
Lea Harding, prin. Fax 285-2521

Lawrence, Douglas, Pop. 84,434
Lawrence USD 497 11,700/PK-12
110 McDonald Dr 66044 785-832-5000
Dr. Anna Stubblefield Ed.D., supt. Fax 832-5016
www.usd497.org
Broken Arrow ES 300/K-5
2704 Louisiana St 66046 785-832-5600
Brian McCaffrey, prin. Fax 832-5602
Cordley ES 300/K-5
1837 Vermont St 66044 785-832-5640
Scott Cinnamon, prin. Fax 832-5658
Deerfield ES 500/K-5
101 Lawrence Ave 66049 785-832-5660
Joni Appleman, prin. Fax 832-5663
Hillcrest ES 300/K-5
1045 Hilltop Dr 66044 785-832-5720
Tammy Becker, prin. Fax 832-5722
Hughes ES 500/K-5
1101 George William Way 66049 785-832-5890
Jackie Mickel, prin. Fax 832-5898
Kennedy ES 400/PK-5
1605 Davis Rd 66046 785-832-5760
Chalita Middleton, prin. Fax 832-5762
Lawrence Liberty Memorial Central MS 400/6-8
1400 Massachusetts St 66044 785-832-5400
Jeff Harkin, prin. Fax 832-5403
Lawrence South MS 600/6-8
2734 Louisiana St 66046 785-832-5450
Keith Jones, prin. Fax 832-5453
Lawrence Southwest MS 700/6-8
2511 Inverness Dr 66047 785-832-5550
Kristen Ryan, prin. Fax 832-5554
Lawrence West MS 600/6-8
2700 Harvard Rd 66049 785-832-5500
Brad Kempf, prin. Fax 832-5504
New York ES 200/K-5
936 New York St 66044 785-832-5780
Nancy DeGarmo, prin. Fax 832-5784
Pinckney ES 200/K-5
810 W 6th St 66044 785-832-5800
Kristi Hill, prin. Fax 832-5802
Prairie Park ES 400/K-5
2711 Kensington Rd 66046 785-832-5740
David Williams, prin. Fax 832-5742
Quail Run ES 400/K-5
1130 Inverness Dr 66049 785-832-5820
Philip Thies, prin. Fax 832-5823
Schwegler ES 400/K-5
2201 Ousdahl Rd 66046 785-832-5860
Jared Comfort, prin. Fax 832-5863
Sunflower ES 500/K-5
2521 Inverness Dr 66047 785-832-5870
Howard Diacon, prin. Fax 832-5873
Sunset Hill ES 300/K-5
901 Schwarz Rd 66049 785-832-5880
Jeremy Philipp, prin. Fax 832-5882
Woodlawn ES 200/K-5
508 Elm St 66044 785-832-5920
Jeanne Fridell, prin. Fax 832-5922

Corpus Christi Catholic S 300/PK-8
6001 Bob Billings Pkwy 66049 785-331-3374
Mary Mattern, prin. Fax 865-3933
Prairie Moon Waldorf S 100/PK-7
1853 E 1600 Rd 66044 785-841-8800
Raintree Montessori S 200/PK-6
4601 Clinton Pkwy 66047 785-843-6800
St. John S 300/PK-8
1208 Kentucky St 66044 785-843-9511
Patricia Newton, prin. Fax 843-7143
Veritas Christian S 100/PK-12
256 N Michigan St 66044 785-749-0083
Dr. Michael Chivalette, head sch Fax 749-0580

Leavenworth, Leavenworth, Pop. 33,833
Leavenworth USD 453 3,400/PK-12
PO Box 969 66048 913-684-1400
Mike Roth, supt. Fax 684-1407
www.usd453.org
Anthony ES 400/PK-5
570 Evergreen St 66048 913-684-1500
Ryan Bodensteiner, prin. Fax 684-1503
Brewer ES 300/PK-5
401 N 17th St 66048 913-684-1490
Craig Idacavage, prin. Fax 684-1494
Lawson ES 300/PK-5
820 N 5th St 66048 913-684-1570
Laura Batson, prin. Fax 684-1574
Leavenworth ES 500/PK-5
1925 Vilas St 66048 913-684-1470
Kevin Lunsford, prin. Fax 684-1474
Warren MS 400/6-8
PO Box 7 66048 913-684-1530
Scott Kedrowski, prin. Fax 684-1539

St. Paul Lutheran S 200/PK-8
320 N 7th St 66048 913-682-5553
Fax 682-5647
Xavier S 300/PK-6
541 Muncie Rd 66048 913-682-3135
Evie Porter, prin. Fax 682-5262

Leawood, Johnson, Pop. 31,391
Blue Valley USD 229
Supt. — See Overland Park
Leawood ES 500/K-5
2400 W 123rd St 66209 913-239-6600
Amie Ralston, prin. Fax 239-6648
Leawood MS 500/6-8
2410 W 123rd St 66209 913-239-5300
Chris Legleiter, prin. Fax 239-5348
Mission Trail ES 400/K-5
13200 Mission Rd 66209 913-239-6700
Debbie Bond, prin. Fax 239-6748
Prairie Star ES 500/PK-5
3800 W 143rd St 66224 913-239-7100
Amy Farthing, prin. Fax 239-7148
Prairie Star MS 600/6-8
14201 Mission Rd 66224 913-239-5600
Stacey Sperry, prin. Fax 239-5648

Cure of Ars S 700/PK-8
9403 Mission Rd 66206 913-648-2620
Andrew Legler, prin. Fax 648-3810
Nativity S 500/PK-8
3700 W 119th St 66209 913-338-4330
Dr. Maureen Huppe, prin. Fax 338-2050
St. Michael the Archangel S 700/K-8
14201 Nall Ave, 913-402-3950
Michael Cullinan, prin. Fax 851-8221

Lebo, Coffey, Pop. 937
Lebo-Waverly USD 243
Supt. — See Waverly
Lebo ES 100/PK-5
PO Box 45 66856 620-256-6161
Duane Ford, prin. Fax 256-6342

Lecompton, Douglas, Pop. 617
Perry USD 343
Supt. — See Perry
Lecompton ES 200/2-4
PO Box 108 66050 785-887-6343
Connie Thornton, prin. Fax 887-6755

Lenexa, Johnson, Pop. 47,046
De Soto USD 232
Supt. — See De Soto
Mill Creek MS 700/6-8
8001 Mize Blvd 66227 913-667-3512
Josh Kindler, prin. Fax 422-9229

Olathe USD 233
Supt. — See Olathe
Manchester Park ES 600/K-5
9810 Prairie Creek Rd 66220 913-780-7540
Sean Bohon, prin. Fax 780-7549

Shawnee Mission USD 512
Supt. — See Shawnee Mission
Rising Star ES 600/K-6
8600 Candlelight Ln 66215 913-993-4500
Kristie Darby, prin. Fax 993-4599
Rosehill ES 600/K-6
9801 Rosehill Rd 66215 913-993-4800
Cory Strathman, prin. Fax 993-4899
Shawanoe ES 400/K-6
11230 W 75th St 66214 913-993-5100
Dominic Flora, prin. Fax 993-5199

Christ Preparatory Academy 100/K-12
15700 W 87th Street Pkwy 66219 913-831-1345
Ron Lawlor, admin. Fax 438-1402
Holy Trinity S 700/K-8
13600 W 92nd St 66215 913-888-3250
Scott Merfen, prin. Fax 438-2572

Leon, Butler, Pop. 678
Bluestem USD 205 500/PK-12
625 S Mill Rd 67074 316-742-3261
Joel Lovesee, supt. Fax 742-9265
www.usd205.com
Bluestem ES 300/PK-6
501 S Mill Rd 67074 316-742-3291
Dexter Carpenter, prin. Fax 742-9966

Leoti, Wichita, Pop. 1,520
Leoti USD 467 400/PK-12
PO Box 967 67861 620-375-4677
Keith Higgins, supt. Fax 375-2304
www.leoti.org/
Wichita County ES 300/PK-6
PO Box 807 67861 620-375-2314
Keith Higgins, prin. Fax 375-2589

Le Roy, Coffey, Pop. 552
Le Roy-Gridley USD 245 200/PK-12
PO Box 278 66857 620-964-2212
Russ Mildward, supt. Fax 964-2413
usd245ks.org/
Le Roy ES 50/PK-2
PO Box 188 66857 620-964-2608
Russ Mildward, prin. Fax 964-2413
Other Schools – See Gridley

Lewis, Edwards, Pop. 449
Lewis USD 502 100/PK-6
PO Box 97 67552 620-324-5547
Mike McDermeit, supt. Fax 324-5297
usd502.com
Lewis ES 100/PK-6
PO Box 97 67552 620-324-5547
Mike McDermeit, prin. Fax 324-5297

Liberal, Seward, Pop. 20,195
Liberal USD 480 4,200/PK-12
PO Box 949 67905 620-604-1010
Renae Hickert, supt. Fax 604-1011
www.usd480.net
Bright Start Early Learning Center 300/PK-PK
836 S Jordan Ave 67901 620-604-2000
Cindy Jones, prin. Fax 604-2001
Cottonwood ES 400/K-5
1100 W 11th St 67901 620-604-2700
Traci Mettlen, prin. Fax 604-2701
Eisenhower MS 6-8
2000 N Western Ave 67901 620-604-1400
Randi Jones, prin. Fax 604-1401
MacArthur ES 200/K-5
624 S Holly Dr 67901 620-604-1700
Jennifer Workman, prin. Fax 604-1701
Meadowlark ES 400/K-5
1200 N Calvert 67901 620-604-2100
Shawna Evans, prin. Fax 604-2101
Prairie View ES K-5
615 Warren Ave 67901 620-604-1800
Kendra Haskell, prin. Fax 604-1801
Rogers MS 300/6-8
721 Griffith St 67901 620-604-1300
Jason Diseker, prin. Fax 604-1301
Sunflower ES 600/K-5
310 W Pine St 67901 620-604-2800
Jon Schneider, prin. Fax 604-2801

Lincoln, Lincoln, Pop. 1,283
Lincoln USD 298 400/PK-12
PO Box 289 67455 785-524-4436
Kathy Robertson, supt. Fax 524-3080
www.usd298.com
Lincoln ES 200/PK-6
304 S 4th St 67455 785-524-4487
Stephen Koch, prin. Fax 524-5454

Lindsborg, McPherson, Pop. 3,384
Smoky Valley USD 400 1,100/PK-12
126 S Main St 67456 785-227-2981
Glen Suppes, supt. Fax 227-2982
www.smokyvalley.org/
Smoky Valley MS 300/5-8
401 N Cedar St 67456 785-227-4249
Garrett Scritchfield, prin. Fax 227-3650
Soderstrom ES 300/PK-4
227 N Washington St 67456 785-227-2945
Eric Sjogren, prin. Fax 227-2946

Linn, Washington, Pop. 406
Barnes USD 223
Supt. — See Barnes
Linn S 200/PK-8
300 Parkview St 66953 785-348-5531
Tyler Ayers, prin. Fax 348-5534

Linn Lutheran S 50/PK-PK, 1-
112 Church St 66953 785-348-5792
David Beikmann, prin. Fax 348-5895

Linwood, Leavenworth, Pop. 365
Basehor-Linwood USD 458
Supt. — See Basehor
Linwood ES 100/K-5
215 Park St 66052 913-723-3212
Cindy Hiebert, prin. Fax 723-3449

Little River, Rice, Pop. 556
Little River USD 444 400/PK-12
PO Box 218 67457 620-897-6325
Brent Garrison, supt. Fax 897-6788
usd444.ss5.sharpschool.com
Little River JHS 100/7-8
PO Box 8 67457 620-897-6201
Audrey Johnson, prin. Fax 897-6203
Other Schools – See Windom

Logan, Phillips, Pop. 588
Logan USD 326 200/K-12
PO Box 98 67646 785-689-7595
Michael Gower, supt. Fax 689-7517
www.logan326.net
Logan ES 100/K-6
PO Box 98 67646 785-689-4631
David Kirkendall, prin. Fax 689-7517

Long Island, Phillips, Pop. 134
Northern Valley USD 212
Supt. — See Almena
Long Island MS 100/5-8
PO Box 98 67647 785-854-7681
Marvin Gebhard, prin. Fax 854-7684

Longton, Elk, Pop. 339
Elk Valley USD 283 100/PK-12
PO Box 87 67352 620-642-2811
Jason Crawford, supt. Fax 642-6551
www.usd283.org
Elk Valley ES 100/PK-5
PO Box 87 67352 620-642-3021
Jason Crawford, prin. Fax 642-2092

Lost Springs, Marion, Pop. 64
Centre USD 397 300/PK-12
2382 310th St 66859 785-983-4304
Susan Beeson, supt. Fax 983-4352
www.usd397.com
Centre K-12 S 300/PK-12
2374 310th St 66859 785-983-4321
Susan Beeson, prin. Fax 983-4012

Louisburg, Miami, Pop. 4,257
Louisburg USD 416 1,800/PK-12
PO Box 550 66053 913-837-1700
Dr. Brian Biermann, supt. Fax 837-1701
www.usd416.org
Broadmoor ES 400/3-5
PO Box 367 66053 913-837-1900
Chris McLean, prin. Fax 837-1919
Louisburg MS 400/6-8
PO Box 308 66053 913-837-1800
Michael Isaacsen, prin. Fax 837-1801
Rockville ES 500/PK-2
PO Box 219 66053 913-837-1970
Dr. Pam Best, prin. Fax 837-1978

Lucas, Russell, Pop. 391
Sylvan Grove USD 299
Supt. — See Sylvan Grove
Lucas-Sylvan Unified ES 200/PK-6
PO Box 8 67648 785-525-6244
Jude Stecklein, prin. Fax 525-6245

Lyndon, Osage, Pop. 1,040
Lyndon USD 421 400/K-12
PO Box 488 66451 785-828-4413
Cheryl Cook, supt. Fax 828-3686
www.usd421.org
Lyndon ES 300/K-8
PO Box 488 66451 785-828-4622
Jennifer Hamlet, prin. Fax 828-4110

Lyons, Rice, Pop. 3,662
Lyons USD 405 800/PK-12
800 S Workman St 67554 620-257-5196
Bill Day, supt. Fax 257-5197
www.usd405.com
Lyons Central ES 200/3-5
501 W Lincoln St 67554 620-257-5612
Bob Turner, prin. Fax 257-7032
Lyons MS 200/6-8
501 E American Rd 67554 620-257-3961
Derek Carlson, prin. Fax 257-3518
Lyons Park ES 200/PK-2
121 S Workman St 67554 620-257-5624
John Cannon, prin. Fax 257-7042

Macksville, Stafford, Pop. 542
Macksville USD 351 200/PK-12
PO Box 487 67557 620-348-3415
Greg Rinehart M.Ed., supt. Fax 348-3217
www.usd351.com
Macksville ES 100/PK-6
PO Box 308 67557 620-348-2835
Greg Rinehart M.Ed., prin. Fax 348-3217

Mc Louth, Jefferson, Pop. 860
Mc Louth USD 342 600/PK-12
PO Box 40 66054 913-796-2201
Steve Lilly, supt. Fax 796-6440
www.mclouth.org
Mc Louth ES 300/PK-5
PO Box 40 66054 913-796-6152
Jerome Johnson, prin. Fax 796-6440
Mc Louth MS 100/6-8
PO Box 40 66054 913-796-6122
Janna Davis, prin. Fax 796-6124

Mc Pherson, McPherson, Pop. 12,895
Mc Pherson USD 418 2,400/PK-12
514 N Main St 67460 620-241-9400
Mark Crawford, supt. Fax 241-9410
www.mcpherson.com
Eisenhower ES 300/PK-5
301 Wickersham Dr 67460 620-241-9430
Chris Allen, prin. Fax 241-9431
Lincoln ES 300/PK-5
900 N Ash St 67460 620-241-9540
Cody Rierson, prin. Fax 241-9542
Mc Pherson MS 600/6-8
700 E Elizabeth St 67460 620-241-9450
Brandon Simmelink, prin. Fax 241-9456
Roosevelt ES 300/PK-5
800 S Walnut St 67460 620-241-9550
Todd Beam, prin. Fax 241-9552
Washington ES 300/PK-5
128 N Park St 67460 620-241-9560
Jill Beam, prin. Fax 241-9565

Elyria Christian S 200/PK-12
1644 Comanche Rd 67460 620-241-2994
Allen Siemens, admin. Fax 241-1238
St. Joseph Catholic S 100/PK-6
520 E Northview Ave 67460 620-241-3913
Peggy Bahr, prin. Fax 245-9677

Madison, Greenwood, Pop. 687
Madison-Virgil USD 386 300/PK-12
PO Box 398 66860 620-437-2910
Ryan Bradbury, supt. Fax 437-2916
www.usd386.net
Madison ES 100/PK-6
PO Box 398 66860 620-437-2918
Cindy Hadicke, prin. Fax 437-2919

Maize, Sedgwick, Pop. 3,313
Maize USD 266 6,900/K-12
905 W Academy Ave 67101 316-722-0614
Chad Higgins, supt. Fax 722-8538
www.usd266.com
Maize Central ES 900/K-5
304 W Academy Ave 67101 316-722-0427
David Jennings, prin. Fax 722-8307
Maize ES 400/K-5
305 Jones St 67101 316-722-8230
Kyle White, prin. Fax 722-5456
Maize MS 800/6-8
4600 N Maize Rd 67101 316-729-2461
Brian Thompson, prin. Fax 729-2479
Pray-Woodman ES 600/K-K, 2-5
605 W Academy Ave 67101 316-721-0902
Nils Gabrielson, prin. Fax 721-0486

Vermillion ES 400/K-5
501 S James Ave 67101 316-722-0266
Michael Dome, prin. Fax 722-5020
Other Schools – See Wichita

Manhattan, Riley, Pop. 50,618
Manhattan-Ogden USD 383 6,400/PK-12
2031 Poyntz Ave 66502 785-587-2000
Dr. Marvin Wade, supt. Fax 587-2006
www.usd383.org
Anthony MS 500/7-8
2501 Browning Ave 66502 785-587-2890
Vickie Kline, prin. Fax 587-2899
Arnold ES 500/PK-6
1435 Hudson Ave 66503 785-587-2020
Larry Liotta, prin. Fax 587-2023
Bergman ES 500/K-6
3430 Lombard Dr 66503 785-587-2865
Lori Martin, prin. Fax 587-2869
Bluemont ES 200/K-6
714 Bluemont Ave 66502 785-587-2030
Kathy Stitt, prin. Fax 587-2034
Eisenhower MS 400/7-8
800 Walters Dr 66502 785-587-2880
Tracy Newell, prin. Fax 587-2888
Lee ES 400/K-6
701 Lee St 66502 785-587-2050
Dr. Nancy Kole, prin. Fax 587-2057
Marlatt ES 400/K-6
2715 Hobbs Dr 66502 785-587-2060
Brett Nelson, prin. Fax 587-2064
Northview ES 500/K-6
300 Griffith Dr 66502 785-587-2070
Dr. Cleion Morton, prin. Fax 587-2075
Roosevelt ES 500/PK-6
1401 Houston St 66502 785-587-2090
Andrea Tiede, prin. Fax 587-2139
Wilson ES 300/K-6
312 N Juliette Ave 66502 785-587-2170
Deb Nauerth, prin. Fax 587-2173
Other Schools – See Ogden

Flint Hills Christian S 100/PK-12
3905 Green Valley Rd 66502 785-776-2223
Tim McDonald, admin. Fax 776-3016
Manhattan Catholic S 200/K-8
306 S Juliette Ave 66502 785-565-5050
Scott Hulshoff, prin. Fax 565-5055

Mankato, Jewell, Pop. 856
Rock Hills USD 107 300/PK-12
109 E Main St 66956 785-378-3102
Nadine Smith, supt. Fax 378-3438
www.usd107.org/
Rock Hills ES 200/PK-6
109 E Main St 66956 785-378-3822
Nadine Smith, prin. Fax 378-3467

Maple Hill, Wabaunsee, Pop. 600
Wabaunsee USD 329
Supt. — See Alma
Maple Hill ES 100/K-4
PO Box 68 66507 785-256-4223
Jan Hutley, prin. Fax 256-4129

Marion, Marion, Pop. 1,911
Marion-Florence USD 408 500/K-12
101 N Thorp St 66861 620-382-2117
Lee Leiker, supt. Fax 382-2118
www.usd408.com
Marion ES 200/K-5
1400 E Lawrence St 66861 620-382-3771
Justin Wasmuth, prin. Fax 382-6012
Marion MS 100/6-8
125 S Lincoln St 66861 620-382-6070
Missy Stubenhofer, prin. Fax 382-6073

Marysville, Marshall, Pop. 3,251
Marysville USD 364 800/PK-12
211 S 10th St 66508 785-562-5308
Bill Mullins, supt. Fax 562-5309
www.usd364.org
Marysville ES 400/PK-6
1010 Carolina St 66508 785-562-3641
Jason Wheeler, prin. Fax 562-3411

Good Shepherd Lutheran S 100/PK-8
206 S 17th St 66508 785-562-3181
Terry Harries, prin. Fax 562-3679
St. Gregory S 100/PK-6
207 N 14th St Ste A 66508 785-562-2831
Karen Farrell, prin. Fax 562-4039

Mayetta, Jackson, Pop. 325
Royal Valley USD 337 900/PK-12
PO Box 219 66509 785-966-2246
Aaric Davis, supt. Fax 966-2490
www.rv337.com/
Royal Valley MS 300/5-8
PO Box 189 66509 785-966-2251
John Linn, prin. Fax 966-2833
Other Schools – See Hoyt

Meade, Meade, Pop. 1,700
Meade USD 226 400/PK-12
PO Box 400 67864 620-873-2081
Kenneth Harshberger, supt. Fax 873-2201
www.usd226.org/
Meade ES 300/PK-8
PO Box 400 67864 620-873-2671
Tyler Flavin, prin. Fax 873-2752

Medicine Lodge, Barber, Pop. 1,980
Barber County North USD 254 500/PK-12
PO Box 288 67104 620-886-3370
Mark Buck, supt. Fax 886-3640
www.usd254.org/
Medicine Lodge Grade S 300/PK-6
320 N Walnut St 67104 620-886-5608
Ryan Cunningham, prin. Fax 886-5990

Melvern, Osage, Pop. 380
Marais Des Cygnes Valley USD 456 — 200/K-12
PO Box 158 66510 — 785-549-3521
Ted Hessong, supt. — Fax 549-3659
www.usd456.org
Other Schools – See Quenemo

Meriden, Jefferson, Pop. 803
Jefferson West USD 340 — 900/PK-12
PO Box 267 66512 — 785-484-3444
A. Patton Happer, supt. — Fax 484-3148
www.usd340.org
Jefferson West ES — 300/PK-4
PO Box 265 66512 — 785-484-2455
Wesley Sturgeon, prin. — Fax 484-3340
Jefferson West MS — 300/5-8
PO Box 410 66512 — 785-484-2900
John Hamon, prin. — Fax 484-2904

Milford, Geary, Pop. 487
Geary County USD 475
Supt. — See Junction City
Milford ES — 100/K-5
PO Box 76 66514 — 785-717-4170
Phyllis Boller, prin. — Fax 717-4171

Miltonvale, Cloud, Pop. 532
Southern Cloud USD 334 — 200/K-12
PO Box 334 67466 — 785-427-3334
Roger Perkins, supt. — Fax 427-2422
www.sc334.org
Miltonvale ES — 100/K-6
PO Box 394 67466 — 785-427-3250
Roger Perkins, prin. — Fax 427-3125
Other Schools – See Glasco

Minneapolis, Ottawa, Pop. 2,009
North Ottawa County USD 239 — 600/K-12
PO Box 257 67467 — 785-392-2167
Chris Vignery, supt. — Fax 392-3038
www.usd239.org
Minneapolis ES — 300/K-6
PO Box 48 67467 — 785-392-2111
Pat Anderson, prin. — Fax 392-2198

Minneola, Clark, Pop. 728
Minneola USD 219 — 300/K-12
PO Box 157 67865 — 620-885-4372
Mark Walker, supt. — Fax 885-4509
www.usd219.org/
Minneola S — 200/K-8
PO Box 157 67865 — 620-885-4571
Donna Roetzer, prin. — Fax 885-4509

Mission, Johnson, Pop. 9,093
Shawnee Mission USD 512
Supt. — See Shawnee Mission
Highlands ES — 300/K-6
6200 Roe Ave 66205 — 913-993-3300
Lea Ann Combs, prin. — Fax 993-3399
Rushton ES — 400/K-6
6001 W 52nd St 66202 — 913-993-4900
Amy Simeonov, prin. — Fax 993-4999

Montezuma, Gray, Pop. 959
Montezuma USD 371 — 200/PK-12
PO Box 355 67867 — 620-846-2283
Jay Zehr, supt. — Fax 846-2294
www.usd371.org
Montezuma ES — 100/PK-5
PO Box 355 67867 — 620-846-2283
Tim Skinner, prin. — Fax 846-2294

Moran, Allen, Pop. 543
Marmaton Valley USD 256 — 300/K-12
128 W Oak St 66755 — 620-237-4250
Kenneth McWhirter, supt. — Fax 237-4576
www.usd256.org
Marmaton Valley ES — 100/K-6
128 W Oak St 66755 — 620-237-4381
Ken McWhirter, prin. — Fax 237-4576

Moscow, Stevens, Pop. 304
Moscow USD 209 — 200/K-12
PO Box 158 67952 — 620-598-2205
Stuart Moore, supt. — Fax 598-2233
usd209.weebly.com
Moscow ES — 100/K-5
PO Box 130 67952 — 620-598-2224
Stuart Moore, prin. — Fax 598-2233

Mound City, Linn, Pop. 679
Jayhawk USD 346 — 600/PK-12
PO Box 278 66056 — 913-795-2247
Dr. Royce Powelson, supt. — Fax 795-2185
www.usd346.org/
Jayhawk ES — 300/PK-6
PO Box 305 66056 — 913-795-2519
Mark Proffitt, prin. — Fax 795-2105

Moundridge, McPherson, Pop. 1,722
Moundridge USD 423 — 400/K-12
PO Box K 67107 — 620-345-5500
George Leary, supt. — Fax 345-8617
www.usd423.org
Moundridge ES — 200/K-4
PO Box F 67107 — 620-345-5500
JoAnn Browne, prin. — Fax 345-5408
Moundridge MS — 100/5-8
PO Box 607 67107 — 620-345-5500
JoAnn Browne, prin. — Fax 345-5307

Mound Valley, Labette, Pop. 393
Labette County USD 506
Supt. — See Altamont
Mound Valley S — 200/PK-8
402 Walnut St 67354 — 620-328-3121
Melissa Green, prin. — Fax 328-2078

Mount Hope, Sedgwick, Pop. 799

St. Joseph Catholic S — 100/PK-8
12917 E Maple Grove Rd 67108 — 316-444-2548
Erin Hohl, prin. — Fax 444-2448

Mulvane, Sedgwick, Pop. 5,964
Mulvane USD 263 — 1,800/PK-12
PO Box 130 67110 — 316-777-1102
Brad Rahe, supt. — Fax 777-1103
www.usd263.com
Mulvane Grade S — 400/3-5
411 SE Louis Dr 67110 — 316-777-1981
Raquel Greer, prin. — Fax 777-2799
Mulvane MS — 400/6-8
915 Westview Dr 67110 — 316-777-2022
Traci Becker, prin. — Fax 777-4967
Munson PS — 500/PK-2
1007 Westview Dr 67110 — 316-777-0151
Deana Waltrip, prin. — Fax 777-2798

St. Michael Pre-School — PK-PK
525 E Main St 67110 — 316-777-4221
Joyce Abel, dir. — Fax 777-9456

Natoma, Osborne, Pop. 333
Paradise USD 399 — 100/PK-12
PO Box 100 67651 — 785-885-4843
Larry Geist, supt. — Fax 885-4523
www.usd399.com
Natoma ES — 100/PK-6
PO Box 10 67651 — 785-885-4478
Larry Geist, admin. — Fax 885-4479

Neodesha, Wilson, Pop. 2,454
Neodesha USD 461 — 700/PK-12
PO Box 88 66757 — 620-325-2610
Juanita Erickson, supt. — Fax 325-2368
www.neodesha.k12.ks.us
Heller ES — 200/PK-3
415 N 8th St 66757 — 620-325-3066
Melissa Johnson, prin. — Fax 325-2933
North Lawn ES — 200/4-6
620 W Granby Ave 66757 — 620-325-3011
Hannah Wright, prin. — Fax 325-8106

Neosho Rapids, Lyon, Pop. 260
Southern Lyon County USD 252
Supt. — See Hartford
Neosho Rapids ES — 100/PK-5
240 N Commercial St 66864 — 620-342-7783
Douglas Hes, prin. — Fax 341-9464

Ness City, Ness, Pop. 1,441
Ness City USD 303 — 300/PK-12
414 E Chestnut St 67560 — 785-798-2210
Derek Reinhardt, supt. — Fax 798-3581
www.nesscityschools.org
Ness City ES — 200/PK-6
500 E Chestnut St 67560 — 785-798-2222
Derek Reinhardt, prin. — Fax 798-3581

Sacred Heart S — 100/PK-8
510 S School St 67560 — 785-798-3530
Don Ruda, prin. — Fax 798-3004

Newton, Harvey, Pop. 18,716
Newton USD 373 — 3,500/K-12
308 E 1st St 67114 — 316-284-6200
Dr. Deborah Hamm, supt. — Fax 284-6207
usd373-ks.schoolloop.com
Chisholm MS — 500/7-8
900 E 1st St 67114 — 316-284-6260
Bobbi Jo Grieb, prin. — Fax 284-6267
Northridge ES — 200/K-4
1900 Windsor Dr 67114 — 316-284-6540
Amy Wells, prin. — Fax 284-6545
Santa Fe 5/6 Center — 600/5-6
130 W Broadway St 67114 — 316-284-6270
Jenifer Smith, prin. — Fax 284-6596
Slate Creek ES — 300/K-4
901 E 4th St 67114 — 316-284-6550
Tenae Alfaro, prin. — Fax 284-6556
South Breeze ES — 300/K-4
1020 Old Main St 67114 — 316-284-6560
Jannan Plummer, prin. — Fax 284-6565
Sunset ES — 300/K-4
619 Boyd Ave 67114 — 316-284-6570
Debbie Watson, prin. — Fax 284-6575

St. Mary Catholic S — 200/PK-8
101 E 9th St 67114 — 316-282-1974
Philip Stutey, prin. — Fax 283-3642

Nickerson, Reno, Pop. 1,065
Nickerson USD 309
Supt. — See Hutchinson
Nickerson ES — 300/PK-6
400 N Nickerson St 67561 — 620-422-3215
Amy Jones, prin. — Fax 422-3216

Norton, Norton, Pop. 2,877
Norton USD 211 — 700/PK-12
105 E Waverly St 67654 — 785-877-3386
Phillip Wilson, supt. — Fax 877-2030
www.usd211.org/
Eisenhower ES — 400/PK-6
1100 Eisenhower Dr 67654 — 785-877-5113
Corey Roy, prin. — Fax 877-6516
Norton JHS — 100/7-8
706 Jones Ave 67654 — 785-877-5851
Dustin McEwen, prin. — Fax 877-3771

Nortonville, Jefferson, Pop. 629
Jefferson County North USD 339
Supt. — See Winchester
Jefferson County North ES — 300/PK-8
100 Charger Ln 66060 — 913-886-3870
Matthew Stapp, prin. — Fax 886-6280

Norwich, Kingman, Pop. 478
Kingman-Norwich USD 331
Supt. — See Kingman
Norwich ES — 100/PK-5
PO Box 10 67118 — 620-478-2235
Wayne Morrow, prin. — Fax 478-2879
Norwich MS — 100/6-8
PO Box 10 67118 — 620-478-2235
Wayne Morrow, prin. — Fax 478-2879

Oakley, Logan, Pop. 2,023
Oakley USD 274 — 400/PK-12
621 Center Ave Ste 103 67748 — 785-671-4588
Ken Bockwinkel, supt. — Fax 671-3044
www.oakleyschoolsks.com/
Oakley ES — 200/PK-4
115 W 6th St 67748 — 785-671-3842
Craig Wamsley, prin. — Fax 671-4574
Oakley MS — 100/5-8
611 Center Ave 67748 — 785-671-3820
Craig Wamsley, prin. — Fax 671-3010

St. Joseph ES — 100/PK-6
725 Freeman Ave 67748 — 785-672-4451
Rebecca Scheck, prin. — Fax 671-3919

Oberlin, Decatur, Pop. 1,774
Oberlin USD 294 — 400/PK-12
131 E Commercial St 67749 — 785-475-3805
Dr. Troy Pitsch, supt. — Fax 475-3076
www.usd294.org
Oberlin ES — 200/PK-6
201 W Ash St 67749 — 785-475-2122
Dr. Troy Pitsch, prin. — Fax 475-2579

Offerle, Edwards, Pop. 199
Kinsley-Offerle USD 347
Supt. — See Kinsley
Kinsley-Offerle ES — 200/PK-6
325 S Elm St 67563 — 620-659-2866
Brenna Dooley, prin. — Fax 659-3468

Ogden, Riley, Pop. 1,970
Manhattan-Ogden USD 383
Supt. — See Manhattan
Ogden ES — 200/PK-6
PO Box 851 66517 — 785-587-2080
Jim Armendariz, prin. — Fax 587-2085

Olathe, Johnson, Pop. 122,644
Blue Valley USD 229
Supt. — See Overland Park
Liberty View ES — 600/K-5
14800 S Greenwood St 66062 — 913-239-7700
Stacey Eubanks, prin. — Fax 239-7748

Olathe USD 233 — 27,900/PK-12
PO Box 2000 66063 — 913-780-7000
John Allison, supt. — Fax 780-8011
www.olatheschools.com
Arbor Creek ES — 600/K-5
16150 S Brougham Dr 66062 — 913-780-7300
Dr. Melanie DeMoss, prin. — Fax 780-7309
Black Bob ES — 300/PK-5
14701 S Brougham Dr 66062 — 913-780-7310
Trisha Putthoff, prin. — Fax 780-7319
Briarwood ES — 300/PK-5
14101 S Brougham Dr 66062 — 913-780-7330
Chris Korb, prin. — Fax 780-7339
Brougham ES — 400/PK-5
15500 S Brougham Dr 66062 — 913-780-7350
Stephanie Conklin, prin. — Fax 780-7359
California Trail MS — 800/6-8
13775 W 133rd St 66062 — 913-780-7220
Mike Wiley, prin. — Fax 780-7229
Cedar Creek ES — 600/K-5
11150 S Clare Rd 66061 — 913-780-7360
Tim Reves, prin. — Fax 780-7369
Central ES — 300/K-5
324 S Water St 66061 — 913-780-7370
Dana Hinds, prin. — Fax 780-7379
Chisholm Trail MS — 700/6-8
16700 W 159th St 66062 — 913-780-7240
Mike Wolgast, prin. — Fax 780-7249
Clearwater Creek ES — 500/PK-5
930 S Clearwater Creek Dr 66061 — 913-780-7380
Randy Smith, prin. — Fax 780-7389
Countryside ES — 400/K-5
15800 W 124th Ter 66062 — 913-780-7390
Amy Hercules, prin. — Fax 780-7395
Fairview ES — 300/PK-5
600 N Marion St 66061 — 913-780-7430
Andrew Dimmitt, prin. — Fax 780-7439
Forest View ES — 500/PK-5
12567 S Canyon Dr 66061 — 913-780-7440
Dr. Mark Heck, prin. — Fax 780-7449
Frontier Trail MS — 800/6-8
15300 W 143rd St 66062 — 913-780-7210
Dr. Rod Smith, prin. — Fax 780-7216
Green Springs ES — 300/PK-5
14675 S Alden St 66062 — 913-780-7450
Dr. Todd Wheat, prin. — Fax 780-7457
Havencroft ES — 300/K-5
1700 E Sheridan St 66062 — 913-780-7470
Aaron Miller, prin. — Fax 780-7479
Heatherstone ES — 500/PK-5
13745 W 123rd St 66062 — 913-780-7480
Dr. Ruth Waggoner, prin. — Fax 780-7489
Heritage ES — 300/PK-5
1700 E Pawnee Dr 66062 — 913-780-7490
Scott McFarland, prin. — Fax 780-7499
Indian Creek ES — 400/K-5
15800 Indian Creek Pkwy 66062 — 913-780-7510
Dr. Liz Harrison, prin. — Fax 780-7519
Indian Trail MS — 700/6-8
1440 E 151st St 66062 — 913-780-7230
Dr. Sarah Guerrero, prin. — Fax 780-7234
Madison Place ES — 500/PK-5
16651 Warwick St 66062 — 913-780-7520
Dr. Gary Stevenson, prin. — Fax 780-7529

Mahaffie ES 500/PK-5
1300 N Nelson Rd 66061 913-780-7530
Peggy Head, prin. Fax 780-7539
Meadow Lane ES 400/PK-5
21880 College Blvd 66061 913-780-7550
Brian Lowe, prin. Fax 780-7559
Millbrooke ES PK-5
11751 S Sunnybrook Blvd 66061 913-780-7560
Stephanie Dansco, admin. Fax 780-7563
Mission Trail MS 6-8
1001 N Persimmon Dr 66061 913-780-7260
Rachelle Waters, prin. Fax 780-7269
Northview ES 300/K-5
905 N Walker Ln 66061 913-780-7570
Dr. Jill Smith, prin. Fax 780-7579
Oregon Trail MS 500/6-8
1800 W Dennis Ave 66061 913-780-7250
Anne Hawks, prin. Fax 780-7256
Pioneer Trail MS 700/6-8
15100 W 127th St 66062 913-780-7270
Elaine Carpenter, prin. Fax 780-7278
Prairie Center ES 400/K-5
629 N Persimmon Dr 66061 913-780-7610
Chris Lucas, prin. Fax 780-7619
Prairie Trail MS 800/6-8
21600 W 107th St 66061 913-780-7280
Rick Sola, prin. Fax 780-7289
Ravenwood ES 700/K-5
12211 S Clinton St 66061 913-780-7640
Christi Gottschalk, prin. Fax 780-7649
Regency Place ES 600/K-5
13250 S Greenwood St 66062 913-780-7620
Greg Oborny, prin. Fax 780-7629
Ridgeview ES 300/PK-5
1201 E Elm St 66061 913-780-7630
Kim Thorup, prin. Fax 780-7639
Rolling Ridge ES 500/PK-5
1500 W Elm Ter 66061 913-780-7650
John Ernst, prin. Fax 780-7659
Santa Fe Trail MS 700/6-8
1100 N Ridgeview Rd 66061 913-780-7290
J.J. Libal, prin. Fax 780-7296
Scarborough ES 300/K-5
2000 S Lindenwood Dr 66062 913-780-7670
Jami Veatch, prin. Fax 780-7675
Sunnyside ES 500/K-5
16025 S Lindenwood Dr 66062 913-780-7680
David Kearney, prin. Fax 780-7689
Tomahawk ES 400/K-5
13820 S Brougham Dr 66062 913-780-7690
Christy James, prin. Fax 780-7699
Walnut Grove ES 400/PK-5
11800 S Pflumm Rd 66062 913-780-7710
Natalie DeWeese, prin. Fax 780-7719
Washington ES 400/K-5
1202 N Ridgeview Rd 66061 913-780-7730
T.J. Ulmer, prin. Fax 780-7739
Westview ES 300/PK-5
500 S Troost St 66061 913-780-7750
Jonathon Bell, prin. Fax 780-7759
Woodland ES 400/PK-5
11601 S Woodland St 66061 913-780-7770
Stacy Shipley, prin. Fax 780-7778
Other Schools – See Lenexa, Overland Park

Spring Hill USD 230
Supt. — See Spring Hill
Prairie Creek ES 300/K-5
17077 W 165th St 66062 913-592-7255
Jody Cole, prin. Fax 393-4849

Prince of Peace S 600/K-8
16000 W 143rd St 66062 913-764-0650
Jane Shriver, prin. Fax 393-0819
St. Paul S 100/PK-8
920 S Honeysuckle Dr 66061 913-764-0619
Tonia Helm, prin. Fax 768-6040

Olpe, Lyon, Pop. 541
Southern Lyon County USD 252
Supt. — See Hartford
Olpe ES 200/PK-6
PO Box 203 66865 620-475-3277
Shane Clark, prin. Fax 475-3244

Olsburg, Pottawatomie, Pop. 217
Blue Valley USD 384
Supt. — See Randolph
McCormick ES 100/K-4
PO Box 68 66520 785-468-3551
Brady Burton, prin. Fax 468-3669

Onaga, Pottawatomie, Pop. 694
Onaga-Havensville-Wheaton USD 322 300/PK-12
PO Box 60 66521 785-889-4614
Adam McDaniel, supt. Fax 889-4662
www.usd322.org
Onaga ES 200/PK-8
PO Box 70 66521 785-889-7101
Adam McDaniel, prin. Fax 889-7101

Osage City, Osage, Pop. 2,899
Osage City USD 420 600/K-12
520 Main St 66523 785-528-3176
Troy Hutton, supt. Fax 528-3932
www.usd420.org
Osage City ES 300/K-5
420 S 4th St 66523 785-528-3171
Dena Paul, prin. Fax 528-2986
Osage City MS 200/6-8
420 S 5th St 66523 785-528-3175
Tim Riemann, prin. Fax 528-2980

Osawatomie, Miami, Pop. 4,349
Osawatomie USD 367 1,300/PK-12
1200 Trojan Dr 66064 913-755-4172
Gary French, supt. Fax 755-2031
www.usd367.org/
Osawatomie MS 300/6-8
428 Pacific Ave 66064 913-755-4155
Dan Welch, prin. Fax 755-2197
Swenson Early Childhood Education Center 200/PK-K
1901 Parker Ave 66064 913-755-3220
Andrea Manes, prin. Fax 755-2031
Trojan ES 400/1-5
1901 Parker Ave 66064 913-755-4133
Jeff White, prin. Fax 755-4080

Osborne, Osborne, Pop. 1,422
Osborne County USD 392 300/PK-12
213 W Adams St 67473 785-346-2145
Keith Hall, supt. Fax 346-2448
www.usd392.com
Osborne ES 200/PK-6
234 N 3rd St 67473 785-346-5491
Keith Hall, prin. Fax 346-2668

Oskaloosa, Jefferson, Pop. 1,096
Oskaloosa USD 341 600/PK-12
404 Park St 66066 785-863-2539
Jon Pfau, supt. Fax 863-3080
www.usd341.org
Oskaloosa ES 300/PK-6
404 Park St 66066 785-863-2254
Patrick Foster, prin. Fax 863-9246

Oswego, Labette, Pop. 1,768
Oswego USD 504 400/PK-12
PO Box 129 67356 620-795-2126
Douglas Beisel, supt. Fax 795-4871
www.usd504.org
Oswego Neosho Heights ES 200/PK-6
PO Box 129 67356 620-795-4541
James Gilpin, prin. Fax 795-4591

Otis, Rush, Pop. 278
Otis-Bison USD 403 200/PK-12
PO Box 227 67565 785-387-2201
Roger W. Lowry, supt. Fax 387-2203
www.usd403.org/
Otis-Bison ES 100/PK-6
PO Box 288 67565 785-387-2371
Mark Goodheart, prin. Fax 387-2646

Ottawa, Franklin, Pop. 12,279
Ottawa USD 290 2,400/PK-12
1404 S Ash St 66067 785-229-8010
Dr. Jeanne Stroh, supt. Fax 229-8019
www.usd290.org
Field ES 300/PK-5
720 S Tremont Ave 66067 785-229-8050
Shannan Fanning, prin. Fax 229-8059
Garfield ES 400/K-5
1213 S College St 66067 785-229-8060
Carmen Schaefer, prin. Fax 229-8069
Lincoln ES 500/PK-5
1102 N Milner St 66067 785-229-8080
Austin Entress, prin. Fax 229-8089
Ottawa MS 600/6-8
1230 S Ash St 66067 785-229-8030
Derek Bland, prin. Fax 229-8039

Sacred Heart ES 100/PK-5
426 S Cedar St 66067 785-242-4297
Lisa Blaes, prin. Fax 242-0820

Overbrook, Osage, Pop. 1,048
Santa Fe Trail USD 434
Supt. — See Scranton
Overbrook Attendance Center 200/K-3
PO Box 324 66524 785-665-7135
David Fernkopf, prin. Fax 665-7189

Overland Park, Johnson, Pop. 169,666
Blue Valley USD 229 22,000/PK-12
PO Box 23901 66283 913-239-4000
Dr. Todd White, supt. Fax 239-4150
district.bluevalleyk12.org
Aubry Bend MS 700/6-8
12501 W 175th St 66221 913-624-2300
Diana Tate, prin. Fax 624-2348
Blue River ES 500/PK-5
5101 W 163rd Ter, 913-239-6000
Deborah Kelly, prin. Fax 239-6048
Blue Valley MS 500/6-8
5001 W 163rd Ter, 913-239-5100
Roxana Rogers, prin. Fax 239-5148
Cedar Hills ES 600/PK-5
9100 W 165th St, 913-239-3300
Steve Marsh, prin. Fax 239-3348
Cottonwood Point ES 600/K-5
10521 W 129th St 66213 913-239-6100
Jennifer Spencer, prin. Fax 239-6148
Harmony ES 600/PK-5
14140 Grant St 66221 913-239-6200
Cathy Austin Ed.D., prin. Fax 239-6248
Harmony MS 600/6-8
10101 W 141st St 66221 913-239-5200
Sheila Albers, prin. Fax 239-5248
Heartland ES 400/K-5
12775 Goodman St 66213 913-239-6300
Jennifer Luzenske, prin. Fax 239-6348
Indian Valley ES 400/K-5
11600 Knox St 66210 913-239-6400
Kristin Venable, prin. Fax 239-6448
Lakewood ES 600/K-5
14600 Lamar Ave 66223 913-239-6500
Nancy Layton, prin. Fax 239-6548
Lakewood MS 700/6-8
6601 Edgewater Dr 66223 913-239-5800
Steve Heinauer, prin. Fax 239-5848
Morse ES 400/PK-5
15201 Monrovia St 66221 913-239-6800
Steve Frazell, prin. Fax 239-6848
Oak Hill ES 400/K-5
10200 W 124th St 66213 913-239-6900
Gretchen Anderson Ph.D., prin. Fax 239-6948
Overland Trail ES 600/PK-5
6225 W 133rd St 66209 913-239-7000
Doris Moore, prin. Fax 239-7048
Overland Trail MS 700/6-8
6201 W 133rd St 66209 913-239-5400
Shelly Nielsen, prin. Fax 239-5448
Oxford MS 600/6-8
12500 Switzer Rd 66213 913-239-5500
Linda Crosthwait, prin. Fax 239-5548
Stanley ES 300/K-5
6121 W 158th St 66223 913-239-7200
Desiree Rios, prin. Fax 239-7248
Sunrise Point ES 400/K-5
15800 Roe Blvd 66224 913-239-7500
David Sanders, prin. Fax 239-7548
Sunset Ridge ES 500/K-5
14901 England St 66221 913-239-7400
Sondra Wallace, prin. Fax 239-7448
Timber Creek ES 600/K-5
16451 Flint St 66221 913-239-7800
Pam Bakke Ed.D., prin. Fax 239-7848
Valley Park ES 500/PK-5
12301 Lamar Ave 66209 913-239-7600
Jennifer Griffith, prin. Fax 239-7648
Other Schools – See Leawood, Olathe, Stilwell

Olathe USD 233
Supt. — See Olathe
Bentwood ES 300/K-5
13000 Bond St 66213 913-780-7320
Dr. Catherine McDonald, prin. Fax 897-8839
Pleasant Ridge ES 400/PK-5
12235 Rosehill St 66213 913-780-7590
Krystal Actkinson, prin. Fax 897-8807

Shawnee Mission USD 512
Supt. — See Shawnee Mission
Apache ES 600/PK-6
8910 Goddard St 66214 913-993-1600
Britt Pumphrey, prin. Fax 993-1699
Brookridge ES 600/K-6
9920 Lowell Ave 66212 913-993-2400
Dr. Sue Adams, prin. Fax 993-2499
Diemer ES 300/K-6
9600 Lamar Ave 66207 913-993-3100
Wendy Baumgardner, prin. Fax 993-3199
East Antioch ES 400/PK-6
7342 Lowell Ave 66204 913-993-3200
Felicia Netolicky, prin Fax 993-3299
Oak Park - Carpenter ES 500/K-6
10000 Nieman Rd 66214 913-993-4100
Jennifer Gill, prin. Fax 993-4199
Overland Park ES 400/K-6
8150 Santa Fe Dr 66204 913-993-4200
Karen Faucher, prin. Fax 993-4299
Pawnee ES 400/K-6
9501 W 91st St 66212 913-993-4300
Justin Green, prin. Fax 993-4399
Santa Fe Trail ES 300/PK-6
7100 Lamar Ave 66204 913-993-5000
Kristal Leiker, prin. Fax 993-5099
Tomahawk ES 300/K-6
6301 W 78th St 66204 913-993-5500
Brian Watson, prin. Fax 993-5599
Trailwood ES 400/PK-6
5101 W 95th St 66207 913-993-5600
Gregory Lawrence, prin. Fax 993-5699

Ascension S 600/K-8
9510 W 127th St 66213 913-851-2531
Becky Wright, prin. Fax 851-2518
Bethany Lutheran S 100/K-8
9101 Lamar Ave 66207 913-648-2228
Sharon Fries, admin. Fax 648-2283
Brookridge Day S 100/PK-3
9555 Hadley Dr 66212 913-649-2228
Christ Lutheran S 100/K-8
11720 Nieman Rd 66210 913-754-5888
Steve Vandemark M.Ed., prin. Fax 345-9707
Heritage Christian Academy 400/PK-6
9333 W 159th St 66221 913-681-7622
Rick Lukianuk J.D., pres. Fax 851-8056
Holy Cross S 400/PK-8
8101 W 95th St 66212 913-381-7408
Allison Carney, prin. Fax 381-1312
Holy Spirit S 400/PK-8
11300 W 103rd St 66214 913-492-2582
Michele Watson, prin. Fax 492-9613
John Paul II Catholic S 300/PK-8
6915 W 71st St 66204 913-432-6350
Jenny Yankovich, prin. Fax 432-5081
Mt. Olive Lutheran S 50/PK-8
9514 Perry Ln 66212 913-888-6293
Dan Douglas, prin. Fax 492-2326
Overland Christian S 100/PK-12
7401 Metcalf Ave 66204 913-722-0272
Chad Pollard, admin. Fax 213-5616
Small Beginnings Montessori S 200/PK-3
15801 Metcalf Ave 66223 913-851-2223

Oxford, Sumner, Pop. 1,034
Oxford USD 358 300/PK-12
PO Box 937 67119 620-455-2227
Catherine Wilson Ed.D., supt. Fax 455-3680
www.usd358.com
Oxford ES 200/PK-6
PO Box 1000 67119 620-455-2422
Terri Wiseman, prin. Fax 455-3842

Paola, Miami, Pop. 5,476
Paola USD 368 1,900/K-12
1115 E 303rd St 66071 913-294-8000
Judy Welter, supt. Fax 294-8001
www.usd368.org/
Cottonwood ES 400/K-2
709 Hedge Ln 66071 913-294-8050
Natalie Ball, prin. Fax 294-8051

Paola MS 500/6-8
405 N Hospital Dr 66071 913-294-8030
Mark Bloustine, prin. Fax 294-8031
Sunflower ES 400/3-5
1401 E 303rd St 66071 913-294-8040
Staci Wokutch, prin. Fax 294-8041

Holy Trinity S 100/PK-8
601 E Chippewa St 66071 913-294-3286
Michelle Olson, prin. Fax 294-5286

Park City, Sedgwick, Pop. 7,073
Wichita USD 259
Supt. — See Wichita
Chisholm Trail ES 500/PK-5
6015 N Independence St 67219 316-973-9400
Larry Perlman, prin. Fax 973-9410

Parker, Linn, Pop. 275
Prairie View USD 362
Supt. — See LaCygne
Parker ES 200/PK-5
421 N Center Ave 66072 913-898-3160
Mark Staab, prin. Fax 898-2058

Parsons, Labette, Pop. 10,094
Labette County USD 506
Supt. — See Altamont
Meadow View S 400/PK-8
1377 21000 Rd 67357 620-421-1857
Chris Kastler, prin. Fax 421-0379

Parsons USD 503 1,400/PK-12
PO Box 1056 67357 620-421-5950
Linda Proehl, supt. Fax 421-5954
www.vikingnet.net
Garfield ES 200/2-3
300 S 14th St 67357 620-421-3530
Misty Russell, prin. Fax 423-8838
Guthridge ES 200/4-5
1020 S 31st St 67357 620-421-6800
Kurt Friess, prin. Fax 423-8843
Lincoln ES 300/PK-1
1800 Dirr Ave 67357 620-421-3510
Shelley Gardner, prin. Fax 423-8831
Parsons MS 300/6-8
2719 Main St 67357 620-421-4190
Lori Ray, prin. Fax 423-8822

St. Patrick Catholic S 100/PK-8
1831 Stevens Ave 67357 620-421-0710
Emilio Aita, prin. Fax 421-2429

Partridge, Reno, Pop. 242
Haven USD 312
Supt. — See Haven
Partridge ES 100/K-6
PO Box 98 67566 620-567-2641
Delon Martens, prin. Fax 567-2816

Paxico, Wabaunsee, Pop. 208
Wabaunsee USD 329
Supt. — See Alma
Paxico MS 100/5-6
PO Box 128 66526 785-636-5343
Steve Oliver, prin. Fax 636-5276
Wabaunsee JHS 100/7-8
PO Box 128 66526 785-636-5353
Steve Oliver, prin. Fax 636-5116

Peabody, Marion, Pop. 1,179
Peabody-Burns USD 398 300/PK-12
506 N Elm St 66866 620-983-2198
Ron Traxson, supt. Fax 983-2247
www.usd398.net
Peabody-Burns ES 100/PK-5
506 N Elm St 66866 620-983-2188
Ronald Traxson, prin. Fax 983-2247

Perry, Jefferson, Pop. 910
Perry USD 343 800/PK-12
PO Box 729 66073 785-597-5138
J.B Elliott, supt. Fax 597-2254
www.usd343.net
Perry ES 100/PK-1
PO Box 168 66073 785-597-5156
Connie Thornton, prin. Fax 597-5157
Perry-Lecompton MS 200/5-8
PO Box 31 66073 785-597-5159
Mike Maloun, prin. Fax 597-5014
Other Schools – See Lecompton

Phillipsburg, Phillips, Pop. 2,555
Phillipsburg USD 325 600/PK-12
240 S 7th St 67661 785-543-5281
Mike Gower, supt. Fax 543-2271
www.usd325.com
Phillipsburg ES 200/PK-4
300 Nebraska Ave 67661 785-543-2174
Crystal Laurin, prin. Fax 543-5332
Phillipsburg MS 200/5-8
647 7th St 67661 785-543-5114
Chris Look, prin. Fax 543-2934

Pittsburg, Crawford, Pop. 19,561
Pittsburg USD 250 2,900/K-12
PO Box 75 66762 620-235-3100
Destry Brown, supt. Fax 235-3106
www.usd250.org
Lakeside ES 400/K-5
709 S College St 66762 620-235-3140
Rhonda White, prin. Fax 235-3145
Meadowlark ES 400/K-5
1602 E 20th St 66762 620-235-3130
Becky Bedene, prin. Fax 235-3134
Nettels ES 400/K-5
2012 S Homer St 66762 620-235-3160
Diane Jackson, prin. Fax 235-3163
Pittsburg MS 600/6-8
1310 N Broadway St 66762 620-235-3240
Terry Smith, prin. Fax 235-3248
Westside ES 300/K-5
430 W 5th St 66762 620-235-3170
Ann Lee, prin. Fax 235-3174

St. Mary's ES 300/PK-6
301 E 9th St 66762 620-231-6941
Nancy Hicks, prin. Fax 231-0690

Plains, Meade, Pop. 1,136
Kismet-Plains USD 483
Supt. — See Kismet
Plains ES 200/PK-PK, 3-
PO Box 337 67869 620-563-7285
Ryan Kisner, prin. Fax 563-7873

Plainville, Rooks, Pop. 1,886
Plainville USD 270 300/PK-12
203 SE Cardinal Ave 67663 785-434-4678
Gail Dunbar, supt. Fax 434-7404
www.usd270.net
Plainville ES 200/PK-8
203 SE Cardinal Ave 67663 785-434-4508
Gail Dunbar, prin. Fax 434-2096

Sacred Heart S 100/PK-6
300 N Washington St 67663 785-434-2157
Laura Foss, prin. Fax 434-2480

Pleasanton, Linn, Pop. 1,187
Pleasanton USD 344 400/K-12
PO Box 480 66075 913-352-8534
Travis Laver, supt. Fax 352-6588
www.usd344.org/
Pleasanton ES 200/K-6
PO Box 480 66075 913-352-8531
Dave Thomas, prin. Fax 352-6588

Pomona, Franklin, Pop. 819
West Franklin USD 287 600/PK-12
510 E Franklin St 66076 785-566-3396
Jerry Turner, supt. Fax 566-8325
www.usd287.org
West Franklin ES at Appanoose 200/PK-5
600 Shawnee Rd 66076 785-566-3386
Christine Robertson, prin. Fax 566-3750
West Franklin MS 100/6-8
331 Tyler St 66076 785-566-3541
Rick Smith, prin. Fax 566-3634
Other Schools – See Williamsburg

Potwin, Butler, Pop. 434
Remington-Whitewater USD 206
Supt. — See Whitewater
Remington ES at Potwin 200/PK-4
PO Box 277 67123 620-752-3239
Tammy Sweatland, prin. Fax 752-3611

Prairie Village, Johnson, Pop. 21,158
Shawnee Mission USD 512
Supt. — See Shawnee Mission
Belinder ES 500/K-6
7230 Belinder Ave 66208 913-993-1800
Steve Yeoman, prin. Fax 993-1899
Briarwood ES 600/K-6
5300 W 86th St 66207 913-993-2200
Chris Lash, prin. Fax 993-2299

Kansas City Christian S 400/K-12
4801 W 79th St 66208 913-648-5227
St. Ann S 400/K-8
7241 Mission Rd 66208 913-660-1101
Mike Riley, prin. Fax 660-1132

Pratt, Pratt, Pop. 6,720
Pratt USD 382 1,100/K-12
401 S Hamilton St 67124 620-672-4500
Suzan Patton, supt. Fax 672-4509
www.usd382.com
Liberty MS 300/5-8
300 S Iuka St 67124 620-672-4530
Tony Helfrich, prin. Fax 672-4539
Southwest ES 400/K-4
1100 W 8th St 67124 620-672-4520
Jason May, prin. Fax 672-4529

Skyline USD 438 400/PK-12
20269 W US Highway 54 67124 620-672-5651
Becca Flowers, supt. Fax 672-9377
skylineschools.org
Skyline ES 300/PK-6
20269 W US Highway 54 67124 620-672-5651
Becca Flowers, prin. Fax 672-9377

Pretty Prairie, Reno, Pop. 669
Pretty Prairie USD 311 300/PK-12
PO Box 218 67570 620-459-6241
Randy Hendrickson, supt. Fax 459-6810
www.usd311.com
Pretty Prairie ES 100/PK-4
PO Box 98 67570 620-459-6621
Kevin Hedrick, prin. Fax 459-6616
Pretty Prairie MS 100/5-8
PO Box 307 67570 620-459-6911
Kevin Hedrick, prin. Fax 459-6729

Protection, Comanche, Pop. 508
South Central USD 300
Supt. — See Coldwater
South Central ES 100/K-5
PO Box 38 67127 620-622-4545
Matt Jellison, prin. Fax 622-4844
South Central MS 100/6-8
PO Box 38 67127 620-622-4545
Matt Jellison, prin. Fax 622-4844

Quenemo, Osage, Pop. 378
Marais Des Cygnes Valley USD 456
Supt. — See Melvern
Marais Des Cygnes Valley ES 100/K-5
PO Box 139 66528 785-759-3512
Twila Wollenberg, prin. Fax 759-3515

Quinter, Gove, Pop. 912
Quinter USD 293 300/PK-12
PO Box 540 67752 785-754-2470
Kari Kephart, supt. Fax 754-3365
www.quinterschools.org
Quinter ES 200/PK-6
PO Box 540 67752 785-754-3741
Kari Kephart, supt. Fax 754-3365

Randolph, Riley, Pop. 158
Blue Valley USD 384 200/K-12
PO Box 98 66554 785-293-5256
Brady Burton, supt. Fax 293-5607
www.usd384.org/
Randolph MS 50/5-8
PO Box 38 66554 785-293-5253
Marion Mazouch, prin. Fax 293-5607
Other Schools – See Olsburg

Ransom, Ness, Pop. 292
Western Plains USD 106 100/PK-12
100 School St 67572 785-731-2352
Dr. Jeff Jones, supt. Fax 731-2235
www.usd106.org
Western Plains North ES 50/PK-5
100 School St 67572 785-731-2352
Jeff Jones, prin. Fax 731-2235
Other Schools – See Bazine

Reading, Lyon, Pop. 231
North Lyon County USD 251
Supt. — See Americus
Reading S 100/K-5
424 1st St 66868 620-699-3827
Peggy Fort, prin. Fax 699-3361

Rexford, Thomas, Pop. 229
Golden Plains USD 316
Supt. — See Selden
Golden Plains MS 50/6-8
PO Box 100 67753 785-687-3265
Mary Ellen Welshhon, prin. Fax 687-2285

Richmond, Franklin, Pop. 461
Central Heights USD 288 600/PK-12
3521 Ellis Rd 66080 785-869-3455
Brian Spencer, supt. Fax 869-2675
www.usd288.org
Central Heights ES 200/PK-5
3521 Ellis Rd 66080 785-869-3355
Ann Collins, prin. Fax 869-2675
Central Heights MS 100/6-8
3521 Ellis Rd 66080 785-869-3455
Buddy Welch, prin. Fax 869-2675

Riley, Riley, Pop. 930
Riley County USD 378 800/PK-12
PO Box 326 66531 785-485-4000
Cliff Williams, supt. Fax 485-2860
www.usd378.org
Riley County ES 500/PK-8
PO Box 248 66531 785-485-4010
Teresa Grant, prin. Fax 485-2929

Riverton, Cherokee, Pop. 874
Riverton USD 404 800/PK-12
PO Box 290 66770 620-848-3386
Todd Berry, supt. Fax 848-9853
www.usd404.org/
Riverton ES 400/PK-5
PO Box 260 66770 620-848-4078
Keith Wilson, prin. Fax 848-4025
Riverton MS 200/6-8
PO Box 260 66770 620-848-3355
Zachery Martin, prin. Fax 848-3288

Roeland Park, Johnson, Pop. 6,575

St. Agnes S 300/PK-8
5130 Mission Rd 66205 913-262-1686
Jane Sullivan, prin. Fax 384-1567

Rolla, Morton, Pop. 432
Rolla USD 217 200/PK-12
PO Box 167 67954 620-593-4344
Kim Mauk, supt. Fax 593-4250
www.usd217.org
Rolla ES 100/PK-5
PO Box 167 67954 620-593-4731
Kim Mauk, prin. Fax 593-4025

Rosalia, Butler, Pop. 169
Flinthills USD 492 300/K-12
PO Box 188 67132 620-476-2237
Jeremy Boldra, supt. Fax 476-2253
www.usd492.org
Flinthills IS 100/3-6
PO Box 188 67132 620-476-2218
Larry Gawith, prin. Fax 476-2391
Flinthills MS 50/7-8
806 SE Rosalia Rd 67132 620-476-2218
Larry Gawith, prin. Fax 476-2391
Other Schools – See Cassoday

Rose Hill, Butler, Pop. 3,842
Rose Hill USD 394 1,700/PK-12
104 N Rose Hill Rd 67133 316-776-3300
Randal Chickadonz, supt. Fax 776-3309
www.usd394.com
Rose Hill IS 300/3-5
104 N Rose Hill Rd 67133 316-776-3330
Kevin Collier, prin. Fax 776-3335
Rose Hill MS 400/6-8
104 N Rose Hill Rd 67133 316-776-3320
Kay Walker, prin. Fax 776-3319
Rose Hill PS 400/PK-2
104 N Rose Hill Rd 67133 316-776-3340
Terri Reilly, prin. Fax 776-3379

Rossville, Shawnee, Pop. 1,132
Kaw Valley USD 321
Supt. — See Saint Marys

Rossville ES 300/PK-6
PO Box 248 66533 785-584-6188
Travis VanVleck, prin. Fax 584-6695

Rozel, Pawnee, Pop. 156
Pawnee Heights USD 496 700/K-12
PO Box 98 67574 620-527-4212
Daniel Binder, supt. Fax 527-4215
www.phtigers.net
Pawnee Heights S 700/K-12
PO Box 97 67574 620-527-4211
Daniel Binder, prin. Fax 527-4215

Russell, Russell, Pop. 4,436
Russell County USD 407 800/K-12
802 N Main St 67665 785-483-2173
Angela Lawrence, supt. Fax 483-2175
www.usd407.org
Bickerdyke ES 200/2-5
348 N Maple St 67665 785-483-6066
Jim Moeder, prin. Fax 483-5982
Ruppenthal MS 200/6-8
400 N Elm St 67665 785-483-3174
Gaylon Walter, prin. Fax 483-5386
Simpson ES 100/K-1
1323 N Main St 67665 785-483-6180
Jim Moeder, prin. Fax 483-5459

Sabetha, Nemaha, Pop. 2,538
Prairie Hills USD 113 1,100/PK-12
1619 S US Old Highway 75 66534 785-284-2175
Todd Evans, supt. Fax 284-3739
www.usd113.org
Sabetha ES 400/PK-5
101 Oregon St 66534 785-284-3448
Sara Toedman, prin. Fax 284-2480
Sabetha MS 200/6-8
751 Blue Jay Blvd 66534 785-284-2151
Matthew Garber, prin. Fax 284-0061
Other Schools – See Axtell, Wetmore

Saint Francis, Cheyenne, Pop. 1,327
St. Francis Community USD 297 300/K-12
PO Box 1110 67756 785-332-8182
Robert Schiltz, supt. Fax 332-8181
www.usd297.org/
Saint Francis ES 100/K-5
PO Box 1110 67756 785-332-8143
Darla Raile, prin. Fax 332-8144

Saint George, Pottawatomie, Pop. 611
Rock Creek USD 323
Supt. — See Westmoreland
Saint George ES 400/PK-6
PO Box 31 66535 785-494-2482
Debbie Edwards, prin. Fax 494-2481

Saint John, Stafford, Pop. 1,281
St. John-Hudson USD 350 300/K-12
505 N Broadway St 67576 620-549-3564
Joshua P. Meyer, supt. Fax 549-3964
www.usd350.com
Saint John ES 200/K-6
505 N Broadway St 67576 620-549-3518
Josh Meyer, prin. Fax 549-3964

Saint Marys, Pottawatomie, Pop. 2,562
Kaw Valley USD 321 1,300/PK-12
411 W Lasley St 66536 785-437-2254
Kerry Lacock, supt. Fax 437-3155
www.usd321.com
Saint Marys ES 400/PK-6
312 S Grand Ave 66536 785-437-6159
Jennifer Rueger, prin. Fax 437-3165
Other Schools – See Rossville

Saint Paul, Neosho, Pop. 622
Chetopa - St. Paul USD 505
Supt. — See Chetopa
Saint Paul ES 100/K-6
318 1st St 66771 620-449-2245
Craig Bagshaw, prin. Fax 449-8960

Salina, Saline, Pop. 46,386
Ell-Saline USD 307
Supt. — See Brookville
Ell-Saline ES 300/K-6
1757 N Halstead Rd 67401 785-827-8891
Dana Sprinkle, prin. Fax 825-7355

Salina USD 305 7,000/PK-12
PO Box 797 67402 785-309-4700
Dr. James Hardy, supt. Fax 309-4737
www.usd305.com
Coronado ES 400/K-5
2725 E Ray Ave 67401 785-309-4100
Krista Linenberger, prin. Fax 309-4101
Cottonwood ES 400/K-5
215 S Phillips Ave 67401 785-309-4600
Kyle Griffitts, prin. Fax 309-4601
Heusner ES 400/K-5
1300 Norton St 67401 785-309-4200
Lori Munsell, prin. Fax 309-4201
Kennedy Early Learning Center PK-PK
700 Jupiter Ave 67401 785-309-5000
Lesa Larson, dir. Fax 309-5001
Lakewood MS 800/6-8
1135 E Lakewood Cir 67401 785-309-4000
Bonnie Welty, prin. Fax 309-4001
Meadowlark Ridge ES 400/K-5
2200 Glen Ave 67401 785-309-4300
Deena Hilbig, prin. Fax 309-4301
Oakdale ES 500/K-5
811 E Iron Ave 67401 785-309-4310
Angela Dorzweiler, prin. Fax 309-4311
Salina South MS 800/6-8
2015 Simmons St 67401 785-309-3900
Dustin Dooley, prin. Fax 309-3901
Schilling ES 400/K-5
3121 Canterbury Dr 67401 785-309-4400
Darrell Burgoon, prin. Fax 309-4401
Stewart ES 400/K-5
2123 Roach St 67401 785-309-4450
DeAnna Ryberg, prin. Fax 309-4451
Sunset ES 400/K-5
1510 W Republic Ave 67401 785-309-4520
Lonny Schropp, prin. Fax 309-4521

Cornerstone Classical S 50/PK-8
830 S 9th 67401 785-643-4460
St. Marys S 400/PK-6
304 E Cloud St 67401 785-827-4200
Nick Compagnone, prin. Fax 827-7765
Salina Christian Academy 200/PK-12
1009 Highland Ave 67401 785-452-9929
Charlene Jackson, prin. Fax 825-2506

Satanta, Haskell, Pop. 1,111
Satanta USD 507 300/PK-12
PO Box 279 67870 620-649-2234
Mike Ward, supt. Fax 649-2668
www.usd507.org
Satanta ES 200/PK-5
PO Box 129 67870 620-649-2612
Steven Taton, prin. Fax 649-2627

Scandia, Republic, Pop. 370
Pike Valley USD 426 200/K-12
PO Box 291 66966 785-335-2206
Mary Treaster, supt. Fax 335-2219
www.pikevalley.com
Other Schools – See Courtland

Scott City, Scott, Pop. 3,797
Scott County USD 466 900/PK-12
704 S College St 67871 620-872-7600
Jamie Rumford, supt. Fax 872-7609
www.usd466.com
Scott City ES 400/PK-4
410 E 8th St 67871 620-872-7660
Shawn Roberts, prin. Fax 872-7669
Scott City MS 300/5-8
809 W 9th St 67871 620-872-7640
Jana Irvin, prin. Fax 872-7649

Scranton, Osage, Pop. 706
Santa Fe Trail USD 434 1,000/PK-12
104 S Burlington Ave 66537 785-793-2256
Steve Pegram, supt. Fax 793-2828
www.usd434.org
Scranton Attendance Center 200/PK-PK
104 S Burlingame Ave 66537 785-793-2256
Steve Pegrem, admin. Fax 793-2828
Other Schools – See Carbondale, Overbrook

Sedan, Chautauqua, Pop. 1,096
Chautauqua County Community USD 286 400/PK-12
302 Sherman St 67361 620-725-3187
Nathan Hinrichs, supt. Fax 725-5642
www.usd286.org
Sedan ES 200/PK-6
404 Sherman St 67361 620-725-5611
Kay Hill, prin. Fax 725-5614

Sedgwick, Harvey, Pop. 1,672
Sedgwick USD 439 400/K-12
PO Box K 67135 316-772-5783
Larry Roth, supt. Fax 772-0274
www.usd439.com
Wright ES 300/K-6
PO Box K 67135 316-772-5783
Pat Breckunitch, prin. Fax 772-5294

Selden, Sheridan, Pop. 219
Golden Plains USD 316 200/PK-12
PO Box 199 67757 785-386-4559
Mary Ellen Welshhon, supt. Fax 386-4562
usd316.k12.ks.us/
Golden Plains ES 100/PK-5
PO Box 199 67757 785-386-4560
Mary Ellen Welshhon, prin. Fax 386-4562
Other Schools – See Rexford

Seneca, Nemaha, Pop. 1,982
Nemaha Central USD 115 600/PK-12
318 Main St 66538 785-336-6101
Darrel Kohlman, supt. Fax 336-2268
www.usd115.org
Nemaha Central S 400/PK-8
110 N 11th St 66538 785-336-2173
Dr. Amy Beck, prin. Fax 336-2174

SS. Peter & Paul S 200/PK-8
409 Elk St 66538 785-336-2727
Todd Leonard, prin. Fax 336-3817

Sharon Springs, Wallace, Pop. 741
Wallace County USD 241 200/PK-12
521 N Main St 67758 785-852-4252
Brian McVay, supt. Fax 852-4603
www.usd241.org/
Sharon Springs S 100/PK-8
521 N Main St 67758 785-852-4267
Brian McVay, supt. Fax 852-4603

Shawnee, Johnson, Pop. 60,803
De Soto USD 232
Supt. — See De Soto
Belmont ES 400/PK-5
5805 Belmont Dr 66226 913-667-1810
Pam Hargrove, prin. Fax 667-1811
Clear Creek ES 500/K-5
5815 Monticello Rd 66226 913-422-8700
Andrew Frye Ed.D., prin. Fax 422-3484
Horizon ES 500/K-5
7210 Chouteau St 66227 913-667-3535
Steve Crutchfield, prin. Fax 422-9694
Mize ES 400/K-5
7301 Mize Rd 66227 913-441-0880
Gerri Balthazor, prin. Fax 441-9452
Monticello Trails MS 700/6-8
6100 Monticello Rd 66226 913-422-1100
Melissa Hansen, prin. Fax 422-4990
Prairie Ridge ES 500/K-5
22405 Clear Creek Pkwy 66226 913-667-1800
Kristel Fulcher, prin. Fax 667-3612
Riverview ES 500/K-5
21550 W 47th St 66226 913-441-0808
Beth Mildren, prin. Fax 441-1179

Shawnee Mission USD 512
Supt. — See Shawnee Mission
Benninghoven ES 600/K-6
6720 Caenen Ave 66216 913-993-1900
Mary Riley, prin. Fax 993-1999
Broken Arrow ES 400/K-6
5901 Alden St 66216 913-993-2300
Mike Brewer, prin. Fax 993-2399
Marsh ES 500/K-6
5642 Rosehill Rd 66216 913-993-3400
Kasey Weishaar, prin. Fax 993-3499
Nieman ES 600/K-6
10917 W 67th St 66203 913-993-4000
Stan Anderson, prin. Fax 993-4099

Good Shepherd S 400/PK-8
12800 W 75th St 66216 913-631-0400
Ann McGuff, prin. Fax 631-3539
Grace Christian Academy 50/K-5
7230 Quivira Rd 66216 913-268-6363
Phil Ellsworth, dir. Fax 268-6307
Hope Lutheran S 200/PK-8
6308 Quivira Rd 66216 913-631-6940
Nancy Jankowski, prin. Fax 268-9525
Maranatha Christian Academy 300/PK-3
15000 W 63rd St 66216 913-631-9286
Janet Fogh, head sch Fax 631-2324
Midland Adventist Academy 100/K-12
6915 Maurer Rd 66217 913-268-7400
Sacred Heart of Jesus S 400/K-8
21801 Johnson Dr 66218 913-422-5520
Maureen Engen, prin. Fax 745-0290
St. Joseph S 500/K-8
11505 Johnson Dr 66203 913-631-7730
Dr. Stephanie Hill, prin. Fax 631-3608

Shawnee Mission, See Merriam
Shawnee Mission USD 512 27,000/PK-12
8200 W 71st St 66204 913-993-6200
Dr. Kenny Southwick, supt. Fax 993-6247
www.smsd.org
Bluejacket-Flint ES 500/PK-6
11615 W 49th Ter 66203 913-993-2000
Teddi Pendland, prin. Fax 993-2099
Brookwood ES 400/K-6
3411 W 103rd St 66206 913-993-2500
Kevin Frick, prin. Fax 993-2599
Comanche ES 500/K-6
8200 Grant Ln 66204 913-993-2800
Melissa Green, prin. Fax 993-2899
Corinth ES 500/K-6
8301 Mission Rd 66206 913-993-2900
Chris Lowe, prin. Fax 993-2999
Crestview ES 300/K-6
6101 Craig St 66202 913-993-3000
John Bartel, prin. Fax 993-3099
Hocker Grove MS 800/7-8
10400 Johnson Dr 66203 913-993-0200
Ben Pretz, prin. Fax 993-0399
Indian Hills MS 800/7-8
6400 Mission Rd 66208 913-993-0400
Dr. Scott Sherman, prin. Fax 993-0599
Indian Woods MS 800/7-8
9700 Woodson Dr 66207 913-993-0600
David Conrady, prin. Fax 993-0799
McAuliffe ES 500/K-6
15600 W 83rd St 66219 913-993-3500
Michael Orr, prin. Fax 993-3599
Merriam Park ES 500/K-6
6100 Mastin St 66203 913-993-3600
Chaussee Druen, prin. Fax 993-3699
Mill Creek ES 400/K-6
13951 W 79th St 66215 913-993-3700
Michelle Lord, prin. Fax 993-3799
Prairie ES 400/K-6
6642 Mission Rd 66208 913-993-4400
Kristen Shipp, prin. Fax 993-4499
Roesland ES 400/K-6
4900 Parish Dr 66205 913-993-4700
Jennifer Woolever, prin. Fax 993-4799
Sunflower ES 600/PK-6
8955 Loiret Blvd 66219 913-993-5400
Dr. Ryan Kalie, prin. Fax 993-5499
Trailridge MS 800/7-8
7500 Quivira Rd 66216 913-993-1000
Heath Sigg, prin. Fax 993-1199
Westridge MS 900/7-8
9300 Nieman Rd 66214 913-993-1200
Jeremy McDonnell, prin. Fax 993-1399
Other Schools – See Lenexa, Mission, Overland Park, Prairie Village, Shawnee, Westwood

Silver Lake, Shawnee, Pop. 1,409
Silver Lake USD 372 700/PK-12
PO Box 39 66539 785-582-4026
Tim Hallacy, supt. Fax 582-5259
www.silverlakeschools.org/
Silver Lake ES 400/PK-6
PO Box 39 66539 785-582-4081
Ronda Pegram, prin. Fax 582-5259

Smith Center, Smith, Pop. 1,647
Smith Center USD 237 400/PK-12
216 S Jefferson St 66967 785-282-6665
Joshua Lanning, supt. Fax 282-6518
www.usd237.com
Smith Center ES 200/PK-6
216 S Jefferson St 66967 785-282-6614
Michelle Stamm, prin. Fax 282-5212

Solomon, Dickinson, Pop. 1,069
Solomon USD 393 — 300/PK-12
113 E 7th St 67480 — 785-655-2541
Justin Coup, supt. — Fax 655-2505
www.usd393.net
Solomon ES — 100/PK-6
411 N Pine St 67480 — 785-655-2521
Shalon Worcester, prin. — Fax 655-2505

South Haven, Sumner, Pop. 360
South Haven USD 509 — 200/PK-12
PO Box 229 67140 — 620-892-5216
Dorsey Burgess, supt. — Fax 892-5814
www.usd509.org/
South Haven ES — 100/PK-5
PO Box 229 67140 — 620-892-5215
Dorsey Burgess, prin. — Fax 892-5814

South Hutchinson, Reno, Pop. 2,403
Nickerson USD 309
Supt. — See Hutchinson
South Hutchinson ES — 300/PK-6
405 S Poplar St 67505 — 620-665-8441
Julie Schrum, prin. — Fax 663-7481

Spearville, Ford, Pop. 771
Spearville USD 381 — 400/K-12
PO Box 338 67876 — 620-385-2676
Daryl Stegman, supt. — Fax 385-2614
www.usd381.org/
Spearville ES — 200/K-5
PO Box 337 67876 — 620-385-2556
Christopher Korbe, prin. — Fax 385-2566

Spring Hill, Johnson, Pop. 5,340
Spring Hill USD 230 — 2,800/PK-12
101 E South St 66083 — 913-592-7200
Dr. Wayne Burke, supt. — Fax 592-7270
www.usd230.org
Spring Hill ES — 500/PK-5
300 S Webster St 66083 — 913-592-7277
Tammy Endecott, prin. — Fax 592-5483
Spring Hill MS — 500/6-8
301 E South St 66083 — 913-592-7288
Rodney Sprague, prin. — Fax 592-5424
Wolf Creek ES — 400/K-5
19250 S Ridgeview Rd 66083 — 913-592-7233
Michelle Hackney, admin. — Fax 592-4356
Other Schools – See Olathe

Stafford, Stafford, Pop. 1,029
Stafford USD 349 — 200/PK-12
PO Box 400 67578 — 620-234-5243
Dr. Mary Jo Taylor, supt. — Fax 234-6986
www.stafford349.com
Stafford ES — 100/PK-5
PO Box 400 67578 — 620-234-5255
Kimberly Woolf, prin. — Fax 234-5185

Sterling, Rice, Pop. 2,287
Sterling USD 376 — 500/PK-12
PO Box 188 67579 — 620-278-3621
Dr. Fred Dierksen, supt. — Fax 278-3882
www.usd376.com
Sterling ES — 300/PK-6
218 S 5th St 67579 — 620-278-3112
Brennan Riffel, prin. — Fax 278-2913

Stilwell, Johnson
Blue Valley USD 229
Supt. — See Overland Park
Pleasant Ridge MS — 600/6-8
9000 W 165th St 66085 — 913-239-5700
Phoebe Lewis, prin. — Fax 239-5748
Stilwell ES — 300/K-5
6410 W 199th St 66085 — 913-239-7300
Pam DeVuyst, prin. — Fax 239-7348

Stockton, Rooks, Pop. 1,312
Stockton USD 271 — 300/PK-12
201 N Cypress St 67669 — 785-425-6367
Shelly Swayne, supt. — Fax 425-6923
www.usd271.com
Stockton ES — 200/PK-8
201 N Cypress St 67669 — 785-425-6120
Stacey Green M.S., prin. — Fax 425-7407

Strong City, Chase, Pop. 479
Chase County USD 284
Supt. — See Cottonwood Falls
Chase County ES — 200/PK-6
410 Palmer St 66869 — 620-273-6676
Pam Bevan, prin. — Fax 273-6690

Sublette, Haskell, Pop. 1,442
Sublette USD 374 — 400/PK-12
PO Box 670 67877 — 620-675-2277
Rex Bruce, supt. — Fax 675-2652
www.usd374.org/
Sublette ES — 300/PK-6
PO Box 550 67877 — 620-675-2286
Rachel Lee, prin. — Fax 675-2296

Sylvan Grove, Lincoln, Pop. 277
Sylvan Grove USD 299 — 300/PK-12
504 W 4th St 67481 — 785-526-7175
Jude Stecklein, supt. — Fax 526-7182
www.usd299.org/
Other Schools – See Lucas

Syracuse, Hamilton, Pop. 1,789
Syracuse USD 494 — 500/PK-12
PO Box 1187 67878 — 620-384-7872
Kenneth Bridges, supt. — Fax 384-7692
www.usd494.org
Syracuse ES — 300/PK-6
PO Box 1187 67878 — 620-384-5203
Matthew Holland, prin. — Fax 384-7660

Tecumseh, Shawnee
Shawnee Heights USD 450 — 3,600/PK-12
4401 SE Shawnee Heights Rd 66542 — 785-379-5800
Dr. Martin Stessman, supt. — Fax 379-5810
www.usd450.net
Shawnee Heights MS — 600/7-8
4335 SE Shawnee Heights Rd 66542 — 785-379-5830
Tim Urich, prin. — Fax 379-5848
Tecumseh North ES — 400/PK-6
314 SE Stanton Rd 66542 — 785-379-5910
Sara Glotzbach, prin. — Fax 379-5915
Tecumseh South ES — 500/PK-6
3346 SE Tecumseh Rd 66542 — 785-379-5950
Scott Dial, prin. — Fax 379-5965
Other Schools – See Berryton, Topeka

Tescott, Ottawa, Pop. 315
Twin Valley USD 240
Supt. — See Bennington
Tescott Grade S — 100/PK-6
PO Box 196 67484 — 785-283-4774
Steven Kimmi, prin. — Fax 283-4347

Thayer, Neosho, Pop. 481
Cherryvale USD 447
Supt. — See Cherryvale
Thayer S — 100/K-8
300 W Wilson St 66776 — 620-839-5203
Tim Seibel, prin. — Fax 839-5384

Tipton, Mitchell, Pop. 210
Waconda USD 272
Supt. — See Cawker City
Tipton Community S — 50/K-8
PO Box 154 67485 — 785-373-5355
Chris Moddelmog, prin.

Tonganoxie, Leavenworth, Pop. 4,915
Tonganoxie USD 464 — 1,800/PK-12
330 E 24/40 Highway 66086 — 913-416-1400
Tonya Phillips, supt. — Fax 416-1408
www.tong464.org
Tonganoxie ES — 700/PK-5
1180 S East St 66086 — 913-416-1480
Ty Poell, prin. — Fax 416-1488
Tonganoxie MS — 500/6-8
824 E Washington St 66086 — 913-416-1470
Mark Altman, prin. — Fax 416-1478

Genesis Christian S — 200/PK-8
PO Box 994 66086 — 913-845-9498
Mendy Lietzen, admin. — Fax 845-9498

Topeka, Shawnee, Pop. 122,701
Auburn Washburn USD 437 — 7,300/PK-12
5928 SW 53rd St 66610 — 785-339-4000
Dr. Scott McWilliams, supt. — Fax 339-4025
www.usd437.net
Farley ES — 600/PK-6
6701 SW 33rd St 66614 — 785-408-8300
Dr. Marcy Cassidy, prin. — Fax 408-8325
Indian Hills ES — 500/PK-6
7445 SW 29th St 66614 — 785-339-4500
Heather Calvert, prin. — Fax 339-4525
Pauline Central PS — 500/PK-3
6625 SW Westview Rd 66619 — 785-339-4700
Alan Hageman, prin. — Fax 339-4725
Shideler ES — 500/K-6
4948 SW Wanamaker Rd 66610 — 785-339-4600
Jeff Freeman, prin. — Fax 339-4625
Wanamaker ES — 500/PK-6
6630 SW 10th Ave 66615 — 785-339-4800
Marc Sonderegger, prin. — Fax 339-4825
Washburn Rural MS — 900/7-8
5620 SW 61st St 66619 — 785-339-4300
Mark Koepsel, prin. — Fax 339-4325
Other Schools – See Auburn, Wakarusa

Seaman USD 345 — 3,400/PK-12
901 NW Lyman Rd 66608 — 785-575-8600
Dr. Steve Noble, supt. — Fax 575-8620
www.usd345.com
Elmont ES — 300/K-6
6432 NW Elmont Rd 66618 — 785-286-8450
Joel Wells, prin. — Fax 286-8453
Logan ES, 1124 NW Lyman Rd 66608 — 600/PK-6
Rebecca Kramer, prin. — 785-575-8700
Northern Hills ES — K-6
5620 NW Topeka Blvd 66617 — 785-286-2992
Courtney Hickman, prin.
North Fairview ES — 300/PK-6
1941 NE 39th St 66617 — 785-286-8500
Kelli Finnegan, prin. — Fax 286-8503
Seaman MS — 600/7-8
5530 NW Topeka Blvd 66617 — 785-286-8400
Annie Diederich, prin. — Fax 286-8403
West Indianola ES — 300/K-6
4201 NW Brickyard Rd 66618 — 785-286-8550
Tami Wade, prin. — Fax 286-8560

Shawnee Heights USD 450
Supt. — See Tecumseh
Shawnee Heights ES — 500/PK-6
2410 SE Burton St 66605 — 785-357-5400
Rebecca Hummer, prin. — Fax 357-5415

Topeka USD 501 — 13,500/PK-12
624 SW 24th St 66611 — 785-295-3000
Dr. Tiffany Anderson, supt. — Fax 575-6160
www.topekapublicschools.net
Chase MS — 500/6-8
2250 NE State St 66616 — 785-295-3840
Kelley Norman, prin. — Fax 575-6632
Eisenhower MS — 500/6-8
3305 SE Minnesota Ave 66605 — 785-274-6160
Leosha Giardina, prin. — Fax 274-4603
French MS — 500/6-8
5257 SW 33rd St 66614 — 785-438-4150
Kelli Hoffman, prin. — Fax 271-3609
Highland Park Central ES — 400/K-5
2717 SE Illinois Ave 66605 — 785-235-7000
Pilar Mejia, prin. — Fax 575-6649
Jardine MS — 500/6-8
2600 SW 33rd St 66611 — 785-274-6330
Mike Haire, prin. — Fax 274-4768
Landon MS — 500/6-8
731 SW Fairlawn Rd 66606 — 785-438-4220
David Boggs, prin. — Fax 271-3737
Lowman Hill ES — 300/PK-5
1101 SW Garfield Ave 66604 — 785-235-7060
Christine Saunders, prin. — Fax 575-6884
McCarter ES — 400/K-5
5512 SW 16th St 66604 — 785-438-4660
Katherine Cooney, prin. — Fax 271-3760
McClure ES — 300/K-5
2529 SW Chelsea Dr 66614 — 785-438-4340
Dr. Jennifer Gordon, prin. — Fax 271-3794
McEachron ES — 400/PK-5
4433 SW 29th Ter 66614 — 785-438-4430
Victor Williams, prin. — Fax 271-3774
Meadows ES — 600/PK-5
201 SW Clay St 66606 — 785-235-7150
Nicole Johnson, prin. — Fax 291-1515
Quincy ES — 200/K-5
1500 NE Quincy St 66608 — 785-235-7420
Susan Liotta, prin. — Fax 575-6820
Randolph ES — 400/PK-5
1400 SW Randolph Ave 66604 — 785-438-4480
Karen Williams, prin. — Fax 575-6837
Robinson MS — 400/6-8
1125 SW 14th St 66604 — 785-295-3770
Tammy Hazelton, prin. — Fax 575-6720
Ross ES — 500/K-5
1400 SE 34th St 66605 — 785-274-6280
Melissa Blevins, prin. — Fax 274-4674
Scott Dual Language Magnet ES — 600/PK-5
401 SE Market St 66607 — 785-235-7480
Sarah Lucero, prin. — Fax 291-1615
State Street ES — 500/PK-5
500 NE Sumner St 66616 — 785-235-7280
Sarah Sharp, prin. — Fax 575-6854
Stout ES — 300/K-5
2303 SW College Ave 66611 — 785-438-4710
John Litfin, prin. — Fax 575-6864
Whitson ES — 500/PK-5
1725 SW Arnold Ave 66604 — 785-438-4570
Keelin Pierce, prin. — Fax 271-3782
Williams Science and Fine Arts Magnet ES — 600/K-5
1301 SE Monroe St 66612 — 785-235-7330
Kyrstin Bervert, prin. — Fax 291-1710

Cair Paravel Latin S — 300/PK-12
635 SW Clay St 66606 — 785-232-3878
Melody Congdon, head sch — Fax 232-0047
Christ the King S — 400/K-8
5973 SW 25th St 66614 — 785-272-2220
Relynn Reynoso, prin. — Fax 272-9255
Heritage Christian S — 200/PK-12
2000 NW Clay St 66608 — 785-286-0427
Janeal Lischke, prin. — Fax 286-9898
Holy Family S - East Campus — 200/K-8
1725 NE Seward Ave 66616 — 785-234-8980
Stacey McBride, prin. — Fax 234-6778
Holy Family S - West Campus — 50/PK-PK
210 NE Branner St 66616 — 785-233-9171
Stacey McBride, prin.
Mater Dei S — 200/PK-8
934 SW Clay St 66606 — 785-233-1727
Andrea Hillebert, prin. — Fax 233-1728
Most Pure Heart of Mary S — 500/K-8
1750 SW Stone Ave 66604 — 785-272-4313
Eric White, prin. — Fax 272-1138
St. Matthew S — 200/K-8
1000 SE 28th St 66605 — 785-235-2188
Heather Stessman, prin. — Fax 235-2207
Topeka Collegiate S — 200/PK-8
2200 SW Eveningside Dr 66614 — 785-228-0490
Dr. Lyn Rantz, head sch — Fax 228-0504
Topeka Lutheran S — 100/PK-8
701 SW Roosevelt St 66606 — 785-357-0382
Christopher Francik, prin. — Fax 357-7338
Topeka SDA S — 50/K-8
2431 SW Wanamaker Rd 66614 — 785-272-9474

Towanda, Butler, Pop. 1,426
Circle USD 375 — 1,700/K-12
PO Box 9 67144 — 316-541-2577
James Johnson, supt. — Fax 536-2249
www.usd375.org
Circle Towanda IS — 200/3-6
516 North St 67144 — 316-541-2281
Terri Turner, prin. — Fax 536-2249
Circle Towanda PS — K-2
501 N 6th St 67144 — 316-541-2755
Terri Turner, prin. — Fax 536-2249
Other Schools – See Benton, El Dorado, Wichita

Tribune, Greeley, Pop. 735
Greeley County USD 200 — 200/PK-12
400 W Lawrence St 67879 — 620-376-4211
Stuart Holmes, supt. — Fax 376-2465
greeleycountyschools.ks.schoolinsites.com
Greeley County ES — 100/PK-5
400 W Lawrence St 67879 — 620-376-4274
Stuart Holmes, prin. — Fax 376-2465

Troy, Doniphan, Pop. 1,001
Troy USD 429 — 300/PK-12
PO Box 190 66087 — 785-985-3950
Patrick McKernan M.S., supt. — Fax 985-3688
www.troyusd.org/
Troy ES — 200/PK-6
PO Box 130 66087 — 785-985-3538
Patrick McKernan M.S., prin. — Fax 985-3688

Tyro, Montgomery, Pop. 209

Tyro Community Christian S 100/K-12
PO Box 308 67364 620-289-4450
Terry Byrd, admin. Fax 289-4283

Udall, Cowley, Pop. 727
Udall USD 463 400/PK-12
303 S Seymour St 67146 620-782-3355
Kim Stephens, supt. Fax 782-9690
www.usd463.org/
Udall ES 200/PK-5
308 W 3rd St 67146 620-782-3632
Kim Stephens, prin. Fax 782-3108
Udall MS 100/6-8
301 W 4th St 67146 620-782-3623
Brian Rowley, prin. Fax 782-9689

Ulysses, Grant, Pop. 6,107
Ulysses USD 214 1,800/PK-12
111 S Baughman St 67880 620-356-3655
David Younger, supt. Fax 356-5181
www.ulysses.org
Hickok ES 500/PK-2
810 N Missouri St 67880 620-356-3919
A.C. Barker, prin. Fax 424-1075
Kepley MS 400/6-8
113 N Colorado St 67880 620-356-3025
Juan Perez, prin. Fax 356-3024
Sullivan ES 400/3-5
600 W Nebraska Ave 67880 620-356-1742
Scott Meitler, prin. Fax 424-1074

Uniontown, Bourbon, Pop. 268
Uniontown USD 235 500/PK-12
601 5th St 66779 620-756-4302
Bret Howard, supt. Fax 756-4492
www.uniontown235.org
West Bourbon ES 200/PK-6
602 5th St 66779 620-756-4335
Tyler Jackman, prin. Fax 756-4373

Valley Center, Sedgwick, Pop. 6,673
Valley Center USD 262 2,700/PK-12
143 S Meridian Ave 67147 316-755-7000
Cory Gibson, supt. Fax 755-7001
www.usd262.net
Abilene ES 300/K-4
522 N Abilene Ave 67147 316-755-7020
Mark Hoy, prin. Fax 755-7021
Valley Center IS 400/5-6
737 N Meridian Ave 67147 316-755-7050
Greg Lehr, prin. Fax 755-7051
Valley Center MS 400/7-8
800 N Meridian Ave 67147 316-755-7060
Greg Mittman, prin. Fax 755-7061
West ES 400/PK-4
501 N Sheridan Ave 67147 316-755-7030
Pete Bastian, prin. Fax 755-7031
Wheatland ES 400/K-4
800 N Meadow Rd 67147 316-755-7040
Adelyn Soellner, prin. Fax 755-7041

Valley Falls, Jefferson, Pop. 1,187
Valley Falls USD 338 400/PK-12
700 Oak St 66088 785-945-3214
Loren Feldkamp, supt. Fax 945-6780
www.usd338.com
Valley Falls ES 300/PK-8
700 Oak St 66088 785-945-3221
Susan Grey, prin. Fax 945-6780

Vermillion, Marshall, Pop. 108
Vermillion USD 380 600/PK-12
209 School St 66544 785-382-6216
Mischel Miller, supt. Fax 382-6213
www.usd380.com
Other Schools – See Centralia, Frankfort

Victoria, Ellis, Pop. 1,204
Victoria USD 432 300/K-12
PO Box 139 67671 785-735-9212
David Ottley, supt. Fax 735-9229
www.usd432.org/
Victoria ES 200/K-6
602 10th St 67671 785-735-2870
David Ottley, prin. Fax 735-9204

Wakarusa, Shawnee, Pop. 256
Auburn Washburn USD 437
Supt. — See Topeka
Pauline South IS 300/4-6
7035 SW Morrill Rd 66546 785-339-4750
Chris Holman, prin. Fax 339-4775

Wakeeney, Trego, Pop. 1,842
WaKeeney USD 208 400/PK-12
612 Junction Ave 67672 785-743-2145
Tavis Desormiers, supt. Fax 743-2071
www.tregoeagles.com/
Trego Grade S 300/PK-8
612 Junction Ave 67672 785-743-2472
Tavis Desormiers, prin. Fax 743-5244

Wakefield, Clay, Pop. 948
Clay Center USD 379
Supt. — See Clay Center
Wakefield ES 200/K-8
PO Box 40 67487 785-461-5437
Thomas DeBauche, prin. Fax 461-5892

Wamego, Pottawatomie, Pop. 4,265
Wamego USD 320 1,500/PK-12
1008 8th St 66547 785-456-7643
Tim Winter, supt. Fax 456-8125
www.usd320.com
Central ES 400/PK-2
900 7th St 66547 785-456-7271
Teri Dow, prin. Fax 456-7172
Wamego MS 300/6-8
1701 Kaw Valley Rd 66547 785-456-7682
Vici Jennings, prin. Fax 456-2944
West ES 400/3-5
1911 6th St 66547 785-456-8333
Amy Flinn, prin. Fax 456-7267

Washington, Washington, Pop. 1,122
Washington County USD 108 400/PK-12
101 W College St 66968 785-325-2261
Denise O'Dea, supt. Fax 325-2771
www.usd108.org/
Washington ES 200/PK-6
101 W College St 66968 785-325-2261
Amy Hoover, prin. Fax 325-2801

Waterville, Marshall, Pop. 672
Valley Heights USD 498 400/K-12
PO Box 89 66548 785-363-2398
John Bergkamp, supt. Fax 363-2269
www.valleyheights.org/
Valley Heights ES 100/K-2
PO Box 389 66548 785-363-2530
Robert Green, prin. Fax 363-2758
Other Schools – See Blue Rapids

Wathena, Doniphan, Pop. 1,344
Riverside USD 114
Supt. — See Elwood
Riverside PS 200/PK-2
PO Box 38 66090 785-989-4425
Robert Blair, prin. Fax 989-3341

Waverly, Coffey, Pop. 580
Lebo-Waverly USD 243 500/PK-12
PO Box 457 66871 785-733-2651
Cory Reese, supt. Fax 733-2707
www.usd243ks.org
Waverly ES 100/PK-5
PO Box 589 66871 785-733-2551
Dr. Susan Brenner, prin. Fax 733-2707
Other Schools – See Lebo

Weir, Cherokee, Pop. 675
Cherokee USD 247
Supt. — See Cherokee
Southeast ES 100/PK-4
PO Box 308 66781 620-396-8211
Tammie Hall, prin. Fax 396-8160

Wellington, Sumner, Pop. 7,956
Wellington USD 353 1,600/K-12
PO Box 648 67152 620-326-4300
Mark Whitener, supt. Fax 326-4304
www.usd353.com/
Eisenhower ES 200/K-5
924 N Plum St 67152 620-326-4340
Kelly Adams, prin. Fax 326-6322
Kennedy ES 200/K-5
501 N Woodlawn St 67152 620-326-4350
Stephanie Smith, prin. Fax 326-7813
Lincoln ES 200/K-5
104 S F St 67152 620-326-4360
Erin Sweetwood, prin. Fax 326-3273
Washington ES 100/K-5
1100 N Washington Ave 67152 620-326-4370
Ann Shinliver, prin. Fax 326-6480
Wellington MS 400/6-8
605 N A St 67152 620-326-4320
Jamie Ybarra, prin. Fax 326-4390

Wellsville, Franklin, Pop. 1,818
Wellsville USD 289 800/PK-12
602 Walnut St 66092 785-883-2388
Jerald Henn, supt. Fax 883-4453
www.wellsville-usd289.org
Wellsville ES 400/PK-5
218 Ash St 66092 785-883-2996
Jason Townsend, prin. Fax 883-4850
Wellsville MS 200/6-8
602 Walnut St 66092 785-883-4350
Randy Fox, prin. Fax 883-2260

Weskan, Wallace, Pop. 159
Weskan USD 242 100/PK-12
219 Coyote Blvd 67762 785-943-5222
Dave Hale, supt. Fax 943-5303
www.weskanschools.org/
Weskan ES 50/PK-6
219 Coyote Blvd 67762 785-943-5222
Dave Hale, supt. Fax 943-5303

Westmoreland, Pottawatomie, Pop. 771
Rock Creek USD 323 900/PK-12
PO Box 70 66549 785-457-3732
Kevin Logan, supt. Fax 457-3701
www.rockcreekschools.org
Westmoreland ES 100/PK-6
PO Box 350 66549 785-457-3462
Scott Harshbarger, prin. Fax 457-3701
Other Schools – See Saint George

Westphalia, Coffey, Pop. 154
Garnett USD 365
Supt. — See Garnett
Westphalia S 100/K-8
500 Liberty St 66093 785-489-2511
Debbie Alford, prin. Fax 489-2491

Westwood, Johnson, Pop. 1,478
Shawnee Mission USD 512
Supt. — See Shawnee Mission
Westwood View ES 300/K-6
2511 W 50th St 66205 913-993-5800
Kathy Keith, prin. Fax 993-5899

Wetmore, Nemaha, Pop. 364
Prairie Hills USD 113
Supt. — See Sabetha
Wetmore Attendance Center 100/PK-8
PO Box AB 66550 785-866-2860
Rick Schnacker, prin. Fax 866-5450

White City, Morris, Pop. 611
Rural Vista USD 481 300/PK-12
PO Box 98 66872 785-349-2964
Ralph Blevins, supt. Fax 349-2965
www.usd481.org
White City ES 100/PK-8
PO Box 8 66872 785-349-2211
Joel Kahnt, prin. Fax 349-2965
Other Schools – See Hope

Whitewater, Butler, Pop. 694
Remington-Whitewater USD 206 500/PK-12
PO Box 243 67154 316-799-2115
James Regier, supt. Fax 799-2307
www.usd206.org
Remington MS 200/5-8
PO Box 99 67154 316-799-2131
Bob Friesen, prin. Fax 799-2581
Other Schools – See Potwin

Wichita, Sedgwick, Pop. 369,464
Andover USD 385
Supt. — See Andover
Martin ES 400/K-5
2342 N 159th St E 67228 316-218-4720
Crystal Hummel, prin. Fax 733-3682
Wheatland ES 500/K-5
15200 E 21st St N 67230 316-218-4820
Elton Armbrister, prin. Fax 218-4821

Circle USD 375
Supt. — See Towanda
Circle Greenwich ES 300/K-6
3250 N Greenwich Rd 67226 316-315-4000
Don Coffman, prin. Fax 536-2249

Derby USD 260
Supt. — See Derby
Cooper ES 300/PK-5
4625 S Juniper St 67216 316-554-0934
Liz Garrett, prin. Fax 524-9407
Oaklawn ES 300/PK-5
5000 S Clifton Ave 67216 316-554-0704
Jarrod Craig, prin. Fax 524-9411
Wineteer ES 400/K-5
8801 E Ent Dr 67210 316-684-9373
Melissa Young, prin. Fax 687-2418

Haysville USD 261
Supt. — See Haysville
Clark ES 500/PK-5
1900 W 55th St S 67217 316-554-2333
Carla Wulf, prin. Fax 554-2340
Oatville ES 400/PK-5
4335 S Hoover Rd 67215 316-554-2290
Natalie Rust, prin. Fax 554-2292

Maize USD 266
Supt. — See Maize
Maize South ES 600/K-5
3404 N Maize Rd 67205 316-462-8300
Meg Thimmesch, prin. Fax 462-8301
Maize South MS 900/6-8
3403 N Tyler Rd 67205 316-722-0421
Gillian Macias, prin. Fax 722-4077

Wichita USD 259 47,900/PK-12
201 N Water St 67202 316-973-4000
John Allison, supt. Fax 973-4595
www.usd259.org
Adams ES 400/K-5
1002 N Oliver Ave 67208 316-973-2650
Theresa Manning, prin. Fax 973-2660
Allen ES 500/K-5
1881 Elpyco St 67218 316-973-1750
Molly Nespor, prin. Fax 973-1760
Allison Traditional Magnet MS 500/6-8
221 S Seneca St 67213 316-973-4800
Mitch Linn, prin. Fax 973-4810
Anderson ES 600/K-5
2945 S Victoria Ave 67216 316-973-1900
Lynn Simnitt, prin. Fax 973-1910
Beech ES 500/K-5
1830 S Cypress St 67207 316-973-9800
Laura Drouhard, prin. Fax 973-9810
Benton ES 400/K-5
338 S Woodchuck St 67209 316-973-3300
Christy O'Toole, prin. Fax 973-3305
Black Traditional Magnet ES 400/PK-5
1045 N High St 67203 316-973-3500
Janet Tilton, prin. Fax 973-3510
Bostic Traditional Magnet ES 300/K-5
8103 E Gilbert St 67207 316-973-1800
Jane Walker, prin. Fax 973-1810
Brooks Technology & Arts Magnet MS 600/6-8
3802 E 27th St N 67220 316-973-6450
Renee Erickson, prin. Fax 973-6581
Buckner Performing Arts ES 400/K-5
3530 E 27th St N 67220 316-973-9350
Bettina Banks, prin. Fax 973-9360
Caldwell ES 500/PK-5
1441 S Edgemoor St 67218 316-973-0800
Patty Daman, prin. Fax 973-0810
Cessna ES 400/K-5
2101 W 45th St S 67217 316-973-6900
Matt Snodgrass, prin. Fax 973-6910
Clark ES 300/K-5
650 S Apache Dr 67207 316-973-5850
Lichelle Alford, prin. Fax 973-5860
Cleaveland Traditional Magnet ES 300/K-5
3345 W 33rd St S 67217 316-973-8750
Michelle Wilkes, prin. Fax 973-8760
Cloud ES 700/PK-5
1212 W 25th St N 67204 316-973-9200
Patricia Brown, prin. Fax 973-9210
Coleman MS 500/6-8
1544 N Governeour Rd 67206 316-973-6600
Jeff Freund, prin. Fax 973-6699
College Hill ES 400/K-5
211 N Clifton Ave 67208 316-973-9600
Kathleen Paterson, prin. Fax 973-9610

Colvin ES 800/PK-5
2820 S Roosevelt St 67210 316-973-7600
Michele Ingenthron, prin. Fax 973-7610
Curtis MS 700/6-8
1031 S Edgemoor St 67218 316-973-7350
Stephanie Wasko, prin. Fax 973-7410
Dodge Literacy Magnet ES 500/K-5
4801 W 2nd St N 67212 316-973-3150
Susan Rosell, prin. Fax 973-3160
Earhart Environmental Magnet ES 400/K-5
4401 N Arkansas Ave 67204 316-973-3250
Chris Waterbury, prin. Fax 973-3256
Enders Open Magnet ES 400/K-5
3030 S Osage Ave 67217 316-973-6750
Hannelore Burdette, prin. Fax 973-6760
Enterprise ES 500/PK-5
3605 S Gold St 67217 316-973-6800
Keli Gustafson, prin. Fax 973-6805
Franklin ES 300/K-5
214 S Elizabeth St 67213 316-973-9850
Susanne Smith, prin. Fax 973-9860
Gammon ES 400/K-5
3240 N Rushwood St 67226 316-973-4900
Mendie Vicin, prin. Fax 973-4910
Gardiner ES 600/PK-5
1951 S Laura St 67211 316-973-1700
Heather Swartz, prin. Fax 973-1710
Griffith ES 500/K-5
1802 S Bluff St 67218 316-973-8900
Linda Brown, prin. Fax 973-8910
Hadley MS 700/6-8
1101 N Dougherty Ave 67212 316-973-7800
Amy Johnson, prin. Fax 973-7816
Hamilton MS 600/6-8
1407 S Broadway Ave 67211 316-973-5350
Justin Kasel, prin. Fax 973-5360
Harry Street ES 400/K-5
1605 S Market St 67211 316-973-0700
Julie Bettis, prin. Fax 973-0712
Hyde Intl Studies Communications ES 300/K-5
210 N Oliver Ave 67208 316-973-0650
Anne Clemens, prin. Fax 973-0660
Irving ES 500/PK-5
1642 N Market St 67214 316-973-0050
Heather Vincent, prin. Fax 973-0070
Jackson ES 400/K-5
2717 N Woodlawn Blvd 67220 316-973-1200
Kamiel Evans, prin. Fax 973-1210
Jardine STEM Magnet MS 400/6-8
3550 E Ross Pkwy 67210 316-973-4300
Lura Atherly, prin. Fax 973-4310
Jefferson ES 400/PK-5
4615 E Orme St 67218 316-973-3000
Janice Wilson, prin. Fax 973-3010
Kelly Liberal Arts Academy 400/K-5
3143 S Millwood Ave 67217 316-973-4150
Brian Huffman, prin. Fax 973-4160
Kensler ES 600/PK-5
1030 N Wilbur Ln 67212 316-973-1350
Julie Scott, prin. Fax 973-1360
Lawrence ES 400/K-5
3440 W Maple St 67213 316-973-9900
Carol Dunne, prin. Fax 973-9910
Linwood ES 500/K-5
1654 S Hydraulic St 67211 316-973-8100
Trina Wynn, prin. Fax 973-8110
Little ECC PK-PK
1613 N Piatt Ave 67214 316-973-5300
Shonda Hayes, prin. Fax 973-5310
L'Overture Technology Magnet ES 300/K-5
1539 N Ohio Ave 67214 316-973-5050
Greg Croomes, prin. Fax 973-5060
Mann Dual Language Magnet S 600/K-8
1243 N Market St 67214 316-973-3100
Vanessa Martinez, prin. Fax 973-3128
Marshall MS 500/6-8
1510 N Payne Ave 67203 316-973-9000
Ron Stubbs, prin. Fax 973-9010
Mayberry Cultural & Fine Arts Magnet MS 600/6-8
207 S Sheridan St 67213 316-973-5800
Eric Hofer-Holdeman, prin. Fax 973-5808
McAuliffe S 600/K-8
2055 S 143rd St E 67230 316-973-9985
Shawn Springer, prin. Fax 973-9995
McCollom ES 500/K-5
1201 N Waddington Ave 67212 316-973-0350
Shane Walck, prin. Fax 973-0360
Mclean Science/Tech Magnet ES 300/K-5
2277 N Marigold Ln 67204 316-973-8250
Cindy Graves, prin. Fax 973-8260
Mead MS 600/6-8
2601 E Skinner St 67211 316-973-8500
Toby Martin, prin. Fax 973-8503
Minneha Core Knowledge ES 600/K-5
701 N Webb Rd 67206 316-973-8800
Chris Wendt, prin. Fax 973-8810
Mueller Aerospace Magnet ES 500/PK-5
2500 E 18th St N 67214 316-973-8300
Judy Wright, prin. Fax 973-8310
OK ES 300/K-5
1607 N West St 67203 316-973-0600
Jamie Allison, prin. Fax 973-0610

Ortiz ES 300/K-5
3361 N Arkansas Ave 67204 316-973-9785
Kristina Bowyer, prin. Fax 973-9795
Park ES 300/PK-5
1025 N Main St 67203 316-973-5250
Jeanna Hernandez, prin. Fax 973-5260
Parks Academy 400/K-8
2201 E 25th St N 67219 316-973-7500
Amanda Kingrey, prin. Fax 973-7510
Payne ES 300/K-5
1601 S Edwards St 67213 316-973-7850
Donna Simpson, prin. Fax 973-7860
Peterson ES 500/PK-5
9710 W Central Ave 67212 316-973-0400
Tamara Alexander, prin. Fax 973-0410
Pleasant Valley ES 300/K-5
2000 W 29th St N 67204 316-973-5200
Kari Wiechman, prin. Fax 973-5210
Pleasant Valley MS 600/6-8
2220 W 29th St N 67204 316-973-8000
Victoria Manning, prin. Fax 973-8008
Price - Harris Communications Magnet ES 400/K-5
706 N Armour St 67206 316-973-1650
Dave Saunders, prin. Fax 973-1660
Riverside Leadership Magnet ES 300/PK-5
1001 N Porter Ave 67203 316-973-4050
Brandi Flisram, prin. Fax 973-4060
Robinson MS 800/6-8
328 N Oliver Ave 67208 316-973-8600
Amy Champlin, prin. Fax 973-8625
Seltzer ES 500/K-5
11660 E Lincoln St 67207 316-973-4001
Angie Brown, prin. Fax 973-4010
Spaght Magnet Academy 500/K-5
2316 E 10th St N 67214 316-973-7300
Laquita Lugrand, prin. Fax 973-7310
Stanley ES 400/PK-5
1749 S Martinson St 67213 316-973-1300
Bruce Shelton, prin. Fax 973-1310
Stucky MS 600/6-8
4545 N Broadview Cir 67220 316-973-8400
Jennifer Sinclair, prin. Fax 973-8410
Truesdell MS 1,000/6-8
2464 S Glenn Ave 67217 316-973-3900
Terrell Davis, prin. Fax 973-3904
Washington ES 500/K-5
424 N Pennsylvania Ave 67214 316-973-1150
Stacey Hall, prin. Fax 973-1160
White ES 700/PK-5
5148 S Kansas St 67216 316-973-1250
Paula Rodriguez, prin. Fax 973-1260
Wilbur MS 900/6-8
340 N Tyler Rd 67212 316-973-1100
Mark Jolliffe, prin. Fax 973-1090
Woodland Health & Wellness Magnet ES 300/K-5
1705 N Salina Ave 67203 316-973-0100
Michelle Cuda, prin. Fax 973-0110
Woodman ES 700/PK-5
2500 S Hiram Ave 67217 316-973-0200
Nicki Vossman, prin. Fax 973-0210
Other Schools – See Bel Aire, Park City

All Saints Catholic S 200/PK-8
3313 Grand St 67218 316-682-6021
Joyce Fredericksen, prin. Fax 682-8734
Annoor Islamic S 100/PK-9
6655 E 34th St N 67226 316-685-5768
Blessed Sacrament Catholic S 400/PK-8
125 N Quentin St 67208 316-684-3752
Dan Dester, prin. Fax 687-1082
Central Christian Academy 700/PK-9
2900 N Rock Rd 67226 316-688-1161
Michael Hunter, head sch Fax 691-8853
Christ the King Catholic S 100/PK-8
4501 W Maple St 67209 316-943-0111
Cindy Chrisman, prin. Fax 943-0147
Classical S of Wichita 300/K-12
6355 Willowbrook St 67218 316-773-9279
Compass Star Montessori 50/K-6
3500 N Rock Rd Bldg 2700 67226 316-213-2253
Holy Cross Lutheran S 200/PK-8
600 N Greenwich Rd 67206 316-684-4431
Karen Boettcher, prin. Fax 684-2847
Holy Savior Catholic Academy 200/PK-8
4640 E 15th St N 67208 316-684-2141
Dr. Delia Shropshire, prin. Fax 684-4318
Independent S 500/PK-12
8317 E Douglas Ave 67207 316-686-0152
Dr. Milt Dougherty, head sch Fax 686-3918
Magdalen Catholic S 500/PK-8
2221 N 127th St E 67226 316-634-1572
Kristin Schmitz, prin. Fax 634-6957
St. Anne Catholic S 200/PK-8
1121 W Regal St 67217 316-522-6131
Pam Stead, prin. Fax 469-0096
St. Catherine of Siena Catholic S K-8
3660 N Ridge Rd 67205 316-719-2917
Jeremy Barr, prin. Fax 719-2930
St. Elizabeth Ann Seton Catholic S 700/K-8
645 N 119th St W 67235 316-721-5693
David Charles, prin. Fax 721-1723

St. Francis of Assisi Catholic S 800/PK-8
853 N Socora St 67212 316-722-5171
Mary Carter, prin. Fax 722-0492
St. Joseph Catholic S 100/PK-8
139 S Millwood St 67213 316-261-5860
Ellen Albert, prin. Fax 261-5804
St. Jude Catholic S 200/PK-8
3030 N Amidon Ave 67204 316-838-0800
Danelle Urban, prin. Fax 838-0866
St. Margaret Mary Catholic S 200/PK-8
2635 S Pattie St 67216 316-267-4911
Theresa Lam, prin. Fax 267-1707
St. Patrick Catholic S 200/PK-8
2023 N Arkansas Ave 67203 316-262-4071
Brandon Relph, prin. Fax 262-6217
St. Peter Catholic S 400/PK-8
11010 Southwest Blvd 67215 316-524-6585
Brenda Hickok, prin. Fax 524-1656
St. Thomas Aquinas Catholic S 700/PK-8
1215 N Stratford Ln 67206 316-684-9201
Mary Sweet, prin. Fax 684-7421
Three Angels SDA S 50/K-8
4558 N Hydraulic St 67219 316-832-1010
Wichita Adventist Christian Academy 50/K-10
2725 S Osage Ave 67217 316-267-9472
Wichita Collegiate S 1,000/PK-12
9115 E 13th St N 67206 316-634-0433
Tom Davis, hdmstr. Fax 634-0598
Wichita Friends S 50/PK-1
14700 W US Highway 54 67235 316-729-0303
Pamela Chambers, head sch Fax 558-8034

Williamsburg, Franklin, Pop. 389
West Franklin USD 287
Supt. — See Pomona
West Franklin ES at Williamsburg 100/PK-5
PO Box 7 66095 785-746-5777
Braden Anshutz, prin. Fax 746-5250

Wilson, Ellsworth, Pop. 759
Central Plains USD 112
Supt. — See Holyrood
Wilson ES 100/PK-6
PO Box K 67490 785-658-3555
Kenroy Wilson, prin. Fax 658-2205

Winchester, Jefferson, Pop. 551
Jefferson County North USD 339 500/PK-12
310 5th St 66097 913-774-2000
Denise Jennings, supt. Fax 774-2027
www.usd339.net
Other Schools – See Nortonville

Windom, McPherson, Pop. 127
Little River USD 444
Supt. — See Little River
Windom ES 200/PK-6
PO Box 67 67491 620-489-6241
Jon Paden, prin. Fax 489-6434

Winfield, Cowley, Pop. 11,966
Winfield USD 465 2,000/PK-12
1407 Wheat Rd 67156 620-221-5100
Dr. J.K. Campbell, supt. Fax 221-0508
www.usd465.com
Country View ES 100/K-5
16300 151st Rd 67156 620-221-5155
Desaree Groene, prin. Fax 221-5156
Irving ES 200/K-5
311 Harter St 67156 620-221-5140
Jeff Everett, prin. Fax 221-5142
Lowell ES 200/K-5
1404 Millington St 67156 620-221-5136
Cassandra Davis, prin. Fax 221-5191
Whittier ES 300/K-5
1400 Mound St 67156 620-221-5150
Marcia McIntire, prin. Fax 221-5154
Winfield Early Learning Center 200/PK-PK
400 E 9th Ave 67156 620-221-5170
Desaree Groene, prin. Fax 221-5169
Winfield MS 400/6-8
130 Viking Blvd 67156 620-221-5130
David Hammer, prin. Fax 221-5147

Holy Name Catholic S 100/PK-6
700 Fuller St 67156 620-221-0230
Kim Porter, prin. Fax 221-4047
Trinity Lutheran S 100/PK-6
910 Mound St 67156 620-221-1820
Mark Schotte, prin. Fax 221-3779

Winona, Logan, Pop. 161
Triplains USD 275 100/K-12
PO Box 97 67764 785-846-7869
Lamar Bergsten, supt. Fax 846-7767
triplains.weebly.com
Winona S 100/K-8
PO Box 97 67764 785-846-7496
Lamar Bergsten, admin. Fax 846-7767

Yates Center, Woodson, Pop. 1,379
Woodson USD 366 500/PK-12
PO Box 160 66783 620-625-8804
Greg Brown, supt. Fax 625-8806
www.usd366.net
Yates Center ES 400/PK-8
PO Box 160 66783 620-625-8860
Galen Craghead, prin. Fax 625-8851

KENTUCKY

KENTUCKY DEPARTMENT OF EDUCATION
500 Mero St, Frankfort 40601-1957
Telephone 502-564-4770
Fax 502-564-5680
Website http://www.education.ky.gov

Commissioner of Education Dr. Stephen Pruitt

KENTUCKY BOARD OF EDUCATION
500 Mero St Ste 1, Frankfort 40601-1957

Chairperson William Twyman

PUBLIC, PRIVATE AND CATHOLIC ELEMENTARY SCHOOLS

Adairville, Logan, Pop. 833
Logan County SD
Supt. — See Russellville
Adairville S 300/PK-8
226 School St 42202 270-539-7711
Kristina Rice, prin. Fax 539-3121

Albany, Clinton, Pop. 1,999
Clinton County SD 1,700/PK-12
2353 N Highway 127 42602 606-387-6480
Charlotte Nasief, supt. Fax 387-5437
www.clinton.kyschools.us
Albany ES 500/K-4
819 3rd St 42602 606-387-5828
Tim Armstrong, prin. Fax 387-4930
Clinton County MS 500/5-8
169 Middle School Rd 42602 606-387-6466
Angela Sloan, prin. Fax 387-6469
ECC 200/PK-K
204 King Dr 42602 606-387-4283
Sheldon Harlan, prin. Fax 387-3105

Alexandria, Campbell, Pop. 8,396
Campbell County SD 4,800/PK-12
101 Orchard Ln 41001 859-635-2173
Dr. David Rust, supt. Fax 448-2439
www.campbell.kyschools.us/
Campbell County MS 1,100/6-8
8000 Alexandria Pike 41001 859-635-6077
Jason Smith, prin. Fax 448-4863
Campbell Ridge ES 600/K-5
2500 Grandview Rd 41001 859-448-4780
Anthony Mazzei, prin. Fax 448-4788
Grants Lick ES 300/PK-5
944 Clayridge Rd 41001 859-635-2129
David Enzweiler, prin. Fax 448-4871
Reiley ES 400/K-5
10631 Alexandria Pike 41001 859-635-2118
Susan Rath, prin. Fax 448-4852
Other Schools – See Cold Spring

St. Mary S 300/PK-8
9 S Jefferson St 41001 859-635-9539
Matt Grosser, prin. Fax 448-4824

Allen, Floyd, Pop. 192
Floyd County SD
Supt. — See Prestonsburg
Allen ES 500/K-8
PO Box 930 41601 606-874-2165
Rachel Crider, prin. Fax 874-5565

Alvaton, Warren
Warren County SD
Supt. — See Bowling Green
Alvaton ES 600/PK-6
6350 Old Scottsville Rd 42122 270-843-8067
Sarah Johnson, prin. Fax 842-1668

Anchorage, Jefferson, Pop. 2,325
Anchorage ISD 400/K-8
11400 Ridge Rd 40223 502-245-8927
Kelley Ransdell, supt. Fax 245-2124
www.anchorage-school.org
Anchorage S 400/K-8
11400 Ridge Rd 40223 502-245-2121
Andrew Terry, prin. Fax 245-6249

Argillite, Greenup
Greenup County SD
Supt. — See Greenup
Argillite ES 300/K-5
4157 State Route 1 41121 606-473-7213
Thomas Crump, prin. Fax 473-1057

Ary, Perry
Perry County SD
Supt. — See Hazard
Robinson S 300/PK-8
13150 KY Highway 476 41712 606-378-7761
Jamie Fugate, prin. Fax 378-4350

Ashland, Boyd, Pop. 21,270
Ashland ISD 3,000/PK-12
PO Box 3000 41105 606-327-2706
Sean Howard, supt. Fax 327-2705
www.ashland.kyschools.us
Ashland MS 500/6-8
2800 Kansas St 41102 606-327-2727
David Greene, prin. Fax 327-2765
Ashland Preschool 200/PK-PK
1820 Hickman St 41101 606-327-2715
Teresa Conway, prin. Fax 327-8895
Crabbe ES 300/K-5
520 17th St 41101 606-327-2730
Jamie Campbell, prin. Fax 327-2759
Hager ES 300/K-5
1600 Blackburn Ave 41101 606-327-2731
Phillip Caudill, prin. Fax 327-2788
Oakview ES 400/K-5
3111 Blackburn Ave 41101 606-327-2733
Rebecca Howell, prin. Fax 327-2756
Poage ES 200/PK-5
3215 S 29th St 41102 606-327-2734
Katie Holbrook, prin. Fax 327-2770
Russell ES 300/K-5
1100 Russell St 41101 606-327-2735
Shawn Thornbury, prin. Fax 327-2763

Boyd County SD 3,400/PK-12
1104 Bob McCullough Dr 41102 606-928-4141
R. Brock Walter, supt. Fax 928-4771
www.boyd.kyschools.us
Boyd County MS 700/6-8
1226 Summitt Rd 41102 606-928-9547
Kimberly Fitch, prin. Fax 928-2067
Cannonsburg ES 300/PK-5
12219 Midland Trail Rd 41102 606-928-7131
Jon Stevens, prin. Fax 928-2685
Early Childhood Learning Center - North 100/PK-PK
1100 Bob McCullough Dr 41102 606-928-8001
Carla Malone, dir. Fax 928-4410
Early Childhood Learning Center - South 100/PK-PK
12862 State Route 180 41102 606-929-5500
Carla Malone, dir. Fax 929-5568
Summit ES 500/K-5
830 State Route 716 41102 606-928-6533
Ben Maynard, prin. Fax 928-5234
Other Schools – See Catlettsburg

Fairview ISD 800/PK-12
2201 Main St W 41102 606-324-3877
Michael Taylor, supt. Fax 324-2288
www.fairview.kyschools.us
Fairview ES 400/PK-6
258 Mcknight St 41102 606-325-1528
Christi Dornon, prin. Fax 326-1777

Holy Family S 100/PK-12
932 Winchester Ave 41101 606-324-7040
Ann Kempf, prin. Fax 324-6888
Rose Hill Christian S 200/PK-12
1001 Winslow Rd 41102 606-324-6105
Dr. Jerry Foster, admin. Fax 324-6420

Auburn, Logan, Pop. 1,325
Logan County SD
Supt. — See Russellville
Auburn S 700/PK-8
221 College St 42206 270-542-4181
David Ward, prin. Fax 542-7921

Augusta, Bracken, Pop. 1,171
Augusta ISD 300/PK-12
307 Bracken St 41002 606-756-2545
Lisa McCane, supt. Fax 756-2149
www.augusta.kyschools.us
Augusta S 100/PK-12
207 Bracken St 41002 606-756-2105
Robin Kelsch, prin. Fax 756-3000

St. Augustine S 100/PK-8
203 E 4th St 41002 606-756-3229
Jane Walton, prin. Fax 756-2530

Barbourville, Knox, Pop. 3,119
Barbourville ISD 700/PK-12
PO Box 520 40906 606-546-3120
Kay Dixon, supt. Fax 546-3452
www.barbourvilleind.com
Barbourville Independent S 700/PK-12
PO Box 520 40906 606-546-3129
Paul Middleton, prin. Fax 546-3337

Knox County SD 4,400/PK-12
200 Daniel Boone Dr 40906 606-546-3157
Kelly Sprinkles, supt. Fax 546-2819
www2.knoxkyschools.com
Central ES 500/PK-6
1000 KY 3439 40906 606-546-3496
Eric Hubbard, prin. Fax 546-3761
Hampton ES 300/PK-6
60 KY 3441 40906 606-546-4169
Brian Frederick, prin. Fax 546-9202
Knox County MS 500/7-8
311 N Main St 40906 606-545-5267
Jeremy Ledford, prin. Fax 546-2161
Lay ES 400/PK-6
220 N Allison Ave 40906 606-546-6524
Keith Broughton, prin. Fax 546-3993
Other Schools – See Corbin, Flat Lick, Girdler

Bardstown, Nelson, Pop. 11,437
Bardstown ISD 2,800/PK-12
308 N 5th St 40004 502-331-8800
Brent Holsclaw, supt. Fax 331-8830
www.bardstown.kyschools.us
Bardstown ECC 300/PK-PK
980 Templin Ave 40004 502-331-8804
Michelle Sharp, prin. Fax 331-8830
Bardstown ES 600/3-5
420 N 5th St 40004 502-331-8801
Paul Bowling, prin. Fax 331-8831
Bardstown MS 500/6-8
410 N 5th St 40004 502-331-8803
Dr. Ryan Clark, prin. Fax 331-8833
Bardstown PS 700/K-2
1000 Templin Ave 40004 502-331-8810
Michelle Ryan, prin. Fax 331-8834

Nelson County SD 4,700/PK-12
288 Wildcat Ln 40004 502-349-7000
Tom Brown, supt. Fax 349-7004
nelson.kyschools.us
Foster Heights ES 700/K-5
211 E Muir Ave 40004 502-349-7030
Jeremy Hill, prin. Fax 349-7031
Nelson County Early Learning Center 200/PK-PK
1200 Cardinal Dr 40004 502-350-3914
Holly Walker, prin. Fax 348-5380
Old Kentucky Home MS 400/6-8
301 Wildcat Ln 40004 502-349-7040
Robin Handloser, prin. Fax 349-7042
Other Schools – See Bloomfield, Boston, Coxs Creek, New Haven

---

Bluegrass Christian Academy 100/PK-8
2580 Springfield Rd 40004 502-348-3900
Ed Hardin, prin. Fax 348-6650
St. Joseph S 400/PK-8
320 W Stephen Foster Ave 40004 502-348-5994
Margaret Bowen, prin. Fax 348-4694

Bardwell, Carlisle, Pop. 716
Carlisle County SD 800/PK-12
4557 State Route 1377 42023 270-628-3800
Jay Simmons, supt. Fax 628-5477
www.carlisle.kyschools.us
Carlisle County ES 400/PK-5
4557 State Route 1377 42023 270-628-3800
Jessica Thomas, prin. Fax 628-0126
Carlisle County MS 200/6-8
4557 State Route 1377 42023 270-628-3800
DeeAnne Arant, prin. Fax 628-3974

Barlow, Ballard, Pop. 654
Ballard County SD 1,400/PK-12
3465 Paducah Rd 42024 270-665-8400
Casey Allen, supt. Fax 665-9844
www.ballard.kyschools.us

Ballard County ES 600/K-5
3383 Paducah Rd 42024 270-665-8400
Stephanie Wood, prin. Fax 665-9168
Ballard County MS 300/6-8
3565 Paducah Rd 42024 270-665-8400
Amber Parker, prin. Fax 665-5153
Other Schools – See La Center

Baxter, Harlan
Harlan County SD
Supt. — See Harlan
Rosspoint ES 400/K-8
132 Highway 522 40806 606-573-4600
Bryan Howard, prin. Fax 573-9596

Beattyville, Lee, Pop. 1,296
Lee County SD 500/K-12
PO Box 668 41311 606-464-5000
Dr. Jim Evans Ed.D., supt. Fax 464-5009
www.lee.kyschools.us
Lee County Elementary School 200/K-5
1665 Highway 11 S 41311 606-464-5020
Maureen Patrick, prin. Fax 464-8829

Beaver Dam, Ohio, Pop. 3,367
Ohio County SD
Supt. — See Hartford
Beaver Dam ES 700/PK-6
183 E US Highway 62 42320 270-274-4478
Ginger Tichenor, prin. Fax 274-3886
Southern ES 300/PK-6
3836 S US Highway 231 42320 270-274-3462
Summer Hines, prin. Fax 274-4420

Bedford, Trimble, Pop. 584
Trimble County SD 1,300/K-12
116 Wentworth Ave 40006 502-255-3201
Steve Miracle, supt. Fax 255-5105
www.trimble.kyschools.us
Bedford ES 400/K-6
204 Mount Pleasant Rd 40006 502-255-3217
Shannon Stark, prin. Fax 255-5109
Trimble County MS 200/7-8
1089 Highway 421 N 40006 502-255-7361
Tracy Poe, prin. Fax 255-5102
Other Schools – See Milton

Beechmont, Muhlenberg, Pop. 686
Muhlenberg County SD
Supt. — See Powderly
Muhlenberg South ES 500/PK-5
2005 US Highway 431 S 42323 270-476-2204
Grayson Wells, prin. Fax 476-1411

Belfry, Pike
Pike County SD
Supt. — See Pikeville
Belfry ES 500/K-5
PO Box 500 41514 606-353-7296
Jill Maynard, prin. Fax 353-7092
Belfry MS 500/6-8
PO Box 850 41514 606-353-9688
Jeremy Howard, prin. Fax 353-9327

Bellevue, Campbell, Pop. 5,875
Bellevue ISD 700/PK-12
219 Center St 41073 859-261-2108
Robb Smith, supt. Fax 261-1708
www.bellevue.kyschools.us
Grandview ES 400/PK-5
500 Grandview Ave 41073 859-261-4355
Angela Young, prin. Fax 261-1707

Holy Trinity S PK-5
235 Division St 41073 859-291-6937
James Hubbard, prin. Fax 291-6970

Benton, Marshall, Pop. 4,312
Marshall County SD 4,400/PK-12
86 High School Rd 42025 270-527-8628
Trent Lovett, supt. Fax 527-0804
www.marshall.kyschools.us
Benton ES 600/PK-5
208 W 11th St 42025 270-527-3373
Kevin Jackson, prin. Fax 527-5995
Central ES 500/PK-5
115 Jim Goheen Dr 42025 270-527-0796
Christopher Mott, prin. Fax 527-7713
Jonathan ES 200/PK-5
9207 US Highway 68 E 42025 270-354-6462
Annessa Roberts, prin. Fax 354-5262
Sharpe ES 400/PK-5
8400 US Highway 68 W 42025 270-898-2852
Jackie Reid, prin. Fax 898-2972
South Marshall ES 300/PK-5
155 Sid Darnall Rd 42025 270-527-1581
Scott Pullen, prin. Fax 527-7757
South Marshall MS 200/6-8
2211 US Highway 641 S 42025 270-527-3828
Shannon Solomon, prin. Fax 527-7616
Other Schools – See Calvert City

Christian Fellowship S 100/PK-12
1343 US Highway 68 E 42025 270-527-8377
Bill Rowley, prin. Fax 527-2872

Berea, Madison, Pop. 13,252
Berea ISD 900/PK-12
3 Pirate Pkwy 40403 859-986-8446
Mike Hogg, supt. Fax 986-1839
www.berea.kyschools.us
Berea Community ES 600/PK-5
2 Pirate Pkwy 40403 859-986-4065
Paula Gordon, prin. Fax 986-0727

Madison County SD
Supt. — See Richmond
Farristown MS 500/6-8
751 Farristown Industrial 40403 859-387-8600
Alicia Hunter, prin. Fax 985-0025
Foley MS 400/6-8
275 Glades Rd 40403 859-625-6140
Lora Hardy, prin. Fax 986-3362
Johnson ES 500/PK-5
109 Oakwood Dr 40403 859-387-3400
Glenna Carter, prin. Fax 986-8405
Kingston ES 600/PK-5
2845 Battlefield Memorial 40403 859-625-6091
Darlene Young, prin. Fax 986-4653
Silver Creek ES 500/PK-PK, 1-
75 Old US 25 N 40403 859-987-3200
Angie Barnes, prin. Fax 986-1932

Betsy Layne, Floyd, Pop. 680
Floyd County SD
Supt. — See Prestonsburg
Betsy Layne ES 600/K-8
PO Box 128 41605 606-263-6272
John Kidd, prin. Fax 263-6277

Beverly, Bell

Red Bird Christian S 200/PK-12
70 Queendale Ctr 40913 606-598-3155
Michael R. Hensley, head sch Fax 598-3151

Blackey, Letcher, Pop. 120
Letcher County SD
Supt. — See Whitesburg
Letcher ES 400/K-5
160 LHS Dr, 606-633-2524
Wendy Mullins-Rutherford, prin. Fax 633-8190
Letcher MS 200/6-8
160 Letcher High School Dr 41804 606-633-7812
Ricky Warf, prin. Fax 633-5731

Blaine, Lawrence, Pop. 47
Lawrence County SD
Supt. — See Louisa
Blaine ES 200/PK-8
600 Highway 2562 41124 606-652-3624
Shawn Jennings, prin. Fax 652-3626

Bledsoe, Harlan
Harlan County SD
Supt. — See Harlan
Green Hills ES 200/PK-8
PO Box 9 40810 606-558-3533
Jonathan Perkins, prin. Fax 558-3960

Bloomfield, Nelson, Pop. 831
Nelson County SD
Supt. — See Bardstown
Bloomfield ES 300/K-5
360 Arnold Ln 40008 502-349-7211
Stephanie Smith, prin. Fax 349-7210
Bloomfield MS 400/6-8
96 Arnold Ln 40008 502-349-7201
Rodney Morgeson, prin. Fax 349-7203

Bonnieville, Hart, Pop. 251
Hart County SD
Supt. — See Munfordville
Bonnieville S 300/PK-8
7874 N Dixie Hwy 42713 270-531-1111
Georgia Bryson, prin. Fax 531-3331

Booneville, Owsley, Pop. 81
Breathitt County SD
Supt. — See Jackson
Highland-Turner ES 200/PK-6
10355 Highway 30 W 41314 606-295-7128
Sabrina McElroy, prin. Fax 295-2710

Owsley County SD 900/PK-12
14 Old KY 11 41314 606-593-6363
Dr. Timothy Bobrowski, supt. Fax 593-6368
www.owsley.kyschools.us
Owsley County ES 400/K-6
372 KY 28 41314 606-593-5186
Sylvia Havicus, prin. Fax 593-6758
Owsley County Preschool 100/PK-PK
122 Baker Ln 41314 606-593-5101
Pamela Chandler, dir. Fax 593-5129

Boston, Nelson, Pop. 266
Nelson County SD
Supt. — See Bardstown
Boston ES 300/K-8
130 Wilson Creek Rd 40107 502-833-4644
Dana Cull, prin. Fax 833-4645

Bowling Green, Warren, Pop. 56,664
Bowling Green ISD 4,000/PK-12
1211 Center St 42101 270-746-2200
Gary Fields, supt. Fax 746-2205
www.bgreen.kyschools.us/
Bowling Green JHS 900/6-8
900 Campbell Ln 42104 270-746-2290
Cynthia West, prin. Fax 746-2295
Cherry ES 300/PK-5
1001 Liberty Way 42104 270-746-2230
Kory Twyman, prin. Fax 746-2235
Dishman McGinnis ES 300/PK-5
375 Glen Lily Rd 42101 270-746-2250
Michael Wix, prin. Fax 842-3188
Gray ES 400/K-5
610 Wakefield St 42103 270-746-2280
Dr. Byron Darnall, prin. Fax 746-2285
McNeill ES 400/K-5
1800 Creason St 42101 270-746-2260
Kelli Brooks, prin. Fax 746-2265
Parker-Bennett-Curry ES 500/PK-5
165 Webb Dr 42101 270-746-2270
Delvagus Jackson, prin. Fax 746-2275

Warren County SD 13,900/PK-12
PO Box 51810 42102 270-781-5150
Rob Clayton, supt. Fax 781-2392
www.warrencountyschools.org/
Briarwood ES 700/PK-6
265 Lovers Ln 42103 270-782-5554
Lori Morris, prin. Fax 746-9264
Bristow ES 600/PK-6
6151 Louisville Rd 42101 270-842-1960
Chris Stunson, prin. Fax 782-6543
Cumberland Trace ES 400/PK-6
830 Cumberland Trace Rd 42103 270-781-1356
JoAnna Jones, prin. Fax 781-7036
Drakes Creek MS 600/7-8
704 Cypress Wood Ln 42104 270-843-0165
Daryl Woods, prin. Fax 782-6138
Lost River ES 700/PK-6
450 Modern Way 42101 270-746-0334
Jim Goff, prin. Fax 796-2849
Moss MS 500/7-8
2565 Russellville Rd 42101 270-843-0166
David Nole, prin. Fax 843-8512
Natcher ES 600/PK-6
1434 Cave Mill Rd 42104 270-842-1364
Matt Thornhill, prin. Fax 842-1563
Plano ES 600/PK-6
2650 Plano Rd 42104 270-467-0411
Ben Frasier, prin. Fax 467-0526
Richards ES 600/K-6
2100 Elrod Rd 42104 270-904-1901
Stephanie Martin, prin. Fax 904-6469
Richardsville ES 400/PK-6
1775 Richardsville Rd 42101 270-777-3232
Brian Womack, prin. Fax 777-3463
Rich Pond ES 300/PK-6
530 Richpond Rd 42104 270-781-9627
Dan Costellow, prin. Fax 846-3041
Rockfield ES 700/PK-6
7597 Russellville Rd 42101 270-843-8437
Monte Cassady, prin. Fax 843-8708
South Warren MS 600/7-8
295 Richpond Rd 42104 270-467-7510
Laura Hudson, prin. Fax 467-7516
212 Academy 5-6
303 Lovers Ln 42103 270-781-5150
Fax 781-2392
Warren East MS 500/7-8
7031 Louisville Rd 42101 270-843-0181
David Cloyd, prin. Fax 781-8565
Warren ES 700/PK-6
1846 Loop St 42101 270-781-2385
Josh Porter, prin. Fax 793-0414
Other Schools – See Alvaton, Oakland, Smiths Grove

Anchored Christian S 100/PK-12
1807 Cave Mill Rd 42104 270-781-9077
Bowling Green Christian Academy 100/PK-12
1730 Destiny Ln 42104 270-782-9552
April Scipio, admin. Fax 782-9585
Foundation Christian Academy 200/PK-8
2480 Three Springs Rd 42104 270-780-6100
Holy Trinity Lutheran S 100/PK-6
553 Ashmoor Ave 42101 270-843-1001
Bill Hiskey, dir. Fax 843-7466
St. Joseph S 300/PK-8
416 Church Ave 42101 270-842-1235
Rodney Schwartz, prin. Fax 842-9072

Brandenburg, Meade, Pop. 2,585
Meade County SD 5,100/PK-12
1155 Old Ekron Rd 40108 270-422-7500
Dr. John Millay, supt. Fax 422-5494
www.meade.kyschools.us
Brandenburg PS 700/PK-3
750 Broadway St 40108 270-422-7545
Gloria Bertrand, prin. Fax 422-5235
Pepper MS 800/7-8
1085 Old Ekron Rd 40108 270-422-7530
Chad Butler, prin. Fax 422-5515
Wilson ES 500/4-6
1075 Old Ekron Rd 40108 270-422-7540
Donna Foushee, prin. Fax 422-3941
Other Schools – See Ekron, Payneville

Bremen, Muhlenberg, Pop. 196
Muhlenberg County SD
Supt. — See Powderly
Bremen ES 400/PK-5
PO Box 10 42325 270-525-6686
Grant Sharp, prin. Fax 525-3380

Brodhead, Rockcastle, Pop. 1,198
Rockcastle County SD
Supt. — See Mount Vernon
Brodhead ES 500/PK-5
PO Box 187 40409 606-758-8512
Derrick Bussell, prin. Fax 758-8514

Brooks, Bullitt, Pop. 2,375
Bullitt County SD
Supt. — See Shepherdsville
Brooks ES 500/PK-5
1430 Brooks Hill Rd 40109 502-869-2000
Melissa Boyle, prin. Fax 957-5498

Brooksville, Bracken, Pop. 638
Bracken County SD 1,300/PK-12
348 W Miami St 41004 606-735-2523
Jeff Aulick, supt. Fax 735-3640
www.bracken.k12.ky.us
Bracken County MS 300/6-8
167 Parsley Dr 41004 606-735-3425
Clay King, prin. Fax 735-2057
Taylor ES 600/PK-5
140 Gibson Dr 41004 606-735-2169
Bobbi Jo Brothers, prin. Fax 735-2058

Brownsville, Edmonson, Pop. 829
Edmonson County SD 2,000/PK-12
PO Box 129 42210 270-597-2101
Patrick Waddell, supt. Fax 597-2103
www.edmonson.k12.ky.us
Edmonson County 5/6 Center 300/5-6
191 W Center St 42210 270-597-3900
Alan Talley, prin. Fax 597-3903
Edmonson County MS 300/7-8
210 Wild Cat Way 42210 270-597-2932
Brandon Prunty, prin. Fax 597-2182
Other Schools – See Smiths Grove, Sweeden

Buckhorn, Perry, Pop. 162
Perry County SD
Supt. — See Hazard
Buckhorn S 400/K-12
18392 KY Highway 28 41721 606-398-7176
Tim Wooton, prin. Fax 398-7930

Burgin, Mercer, Pop. 946
Burgin ISD 300/PK-12
PO Box B 40310 859-748-4000
Will Begley, supt. Fax 748-4010
www.burgin.kyschools.us
Burgin S 300/PK-12
PO Box B 40310 859-748-5282
Chris LeMonds, prin. Fax 748-4002

Burkesville, Cumberland, Pop. 1,484
Cumberland County SD 1,000/K-12
810 N Main St 42717 270-864-3377
Dr. Kirk Biggerstaff, supt. Fax 864-5803
www.cland.k12.ky.us
Cumberland County ES 500/K-5
150 Glasgow Rd 42717 270-864-4390
Lisa Perdue, prin. Fax 864-2756
Cumberland County MS 200/6-8
908 N Main St 42717 270-864-5818
Dr. Tim Parson, prin. Fax 864-2590

Burlington, Boone, Pop. 15,646
Boone County SD
Supt. — See Florence
Burlington ES 800/K-5
5946 N Orient St 41005 859-334-4440
Kim Gilbert, prin. Fax 334-4446
Camp Ernst MS 1,000/6-8
6515 Camp Ernst Rd 41005 859-534-4000
Stephanie Hagerty, prin. Fax 534-4001
Kelly ES 200/K-5
6775 McVille Rd 41005 859-334-4450
Kathleen Gutzwiller, prin. Fax 334-4454
Stephens ES 700/PK-5
5687 N Bond Rd 41005 859-334-4460
Adele Gormley, prin. Fax 334-4463

Immaculate Heart of Mary S 700/PK-8
5876 Veterans Way 41005 859-689-4303
Nancy Marcos, prin. Fax 689-5636

Burna, Livingston, Pop. 254
Livingston County SD
Supt. — See Smithland
Livingston County MS 200/6-8
1370 US Highway 60 E 42028 270-988-3263
Lisa Huddleston, prin. Fax 988-2518
North Livingston County ES 200/PK-5
1372 US Highway 60 E 42028 270-988-4000
Sheri Henson, prin. Fax 988-4779

Burnside, Pulaski, Pop. 602
Pulaski County SD
Supt. — See Somerset
Burnside ES 400/PK-5
435 E Lakeshore Dr 42519 606-561-4250
April Mounce, prin. Fax 561-4562

Butler, Pendleton, Pop. 586
Pendleton County SD
Supt. — See Falmouth
Northern ES 500/PK-5
925 Highway 177 E 41006 859-472-7341
Darell Pugh, prin. Fax 472-6548
Sharp MS 600/6-8
35 Wright Rd 41006 859-472-7000
David Sledd, prin. Fax 472-7011

Cadiz, Trigg, Pop. 2,498
Trigg County SD 2,100/PK-12
202 Main St 42211 270-522-6075
Travis Hamby, supt. Fax 522-7782
www.trigg.kyschools.us
Trigg County IS 500/3-5
205 Main St 42211 270-522-2220
Brian Futrell, prin. Fax 522-2234
Trigg County MS 500/6-8
206 Lafayette St 42211 270-522-2210
Amy Breckel, prin Fax 522-2203
Trigg County PS 500/PK-2
205 Main St 42211 270-522-2700
Lindsey Kinslow, prin. Fax 522-6165

Calhoun, McLean, Pop. 758
McLean County SD 1,600/K-12
PO Box 245 42327 270-273-5257
Terry Hayes, supt. Fax 273-5259
www.mclean.kyschools.us
Calhoun ES 300/K-5
755 Main St 42327 270-273-3264
Amy Bell, prin. Fax 273-5060
McLean County MS 400/6-8
1901 State Route 136 E 42327 270-273-5191
Karen Solise, prin. Fax 273-9876
Other Schools – See Livermore, Sacramento

California, Campbell, Pop. 88

SS. Peter & Paul S 200/PK-8
2160 California Cross Rd 41007 859-635-4382
Nicole Herrmann, prin. Fax 635-9184

Calvert City, Marshall, Pop. 2,542
Marshall County SD
Supt. — See Benton
Calvert City ES 300/PK-5
PO Box 215 42029 270-395-4664
Todd Anderson, prin. Fax 395-4027
North Marshall MS 600/6-8
3110 US Highway 95 42029 270-395-7108
Aimee Lepisto, prin. Fax 395-5449

Campbellsburg, Henry, Pop. 798
Henry County SD
Supt. — See New Castle
Campbellsburg ES 400/K-5
270 Cardinal Dr 40011 502-845-8630
Amy Treece, prin. Fax 845-8631

Campbellsville, Taylor, Pop. 8,884
Campbellsville ISD 1,100/PK-12
136 S Columbia Ave 42718 270-465-4162
Kirby Smith, supt. Fax 465-3918
www.cville.kyschools.us
Campbellsville ES 400/PK-3
315 Roberts Rd 42718 270-465-4561
Elisha Rhodes, prin. Fax 789-3827
Campbellsville MS 500/4-8
230 W Main St 42718 270-465-5121
Zach Lewis, prin. Fax 789-3718

Taylor County SD 2,100/PK-12
1209 E Broadway St 42718 270-465-5371
Roger D. Cook, supt. Fax 789-3954
www.taylor.kyschools.us
Taylor County IS 50/3-5
1207 E Broadway 42718 270-465-5691
Donna Wiilliams, prin. Fax 465-5731
Taylor County MS 600/6-8
300 Ingram Ave 42718 270-465-2877
Danita Johnson, prin. Fax 789-1753
Taylor County Primary Center 600/PK-2
106 Ingram Ave 42718 270-465-0449
Melissa Long, prin. Fax 465-6219

Kentucky Christian Academy 100/PK-8
2046 Old Columbia Rd 42718 270-789-2462
Lori Eubank, admin. Fax 789-4451

Campsprings, Campbell

St. Joseph S 50/PK-PK
6829 Four Mile Rd 41059 859-635-5652
Marily Gomez, dir. Fax 635-7336

Campton, Wolfe, Pop. 434
Wolfe County SD 1,300/K-12
PO Box 160 41301 606-668-8002
Kenny Bell, supt. Fax 668-8050
www.wolfe.kyschools.us
Campton ES 400/K-6
PO Box 810 41301 606-668-8102
Sam Dunn, prin. Fax 668-8150
Wolfe County MS 200/7-8
PO Box 460 41301 606-668-8152
Nick Brooks, prin. Fax 668-8100
Other Schools – See Hazel Green, Rogers

Bethany Christian S 50/PK-6
66 Bethany Rd 41301 606-668-6355
Candice Burnette, supt. Fax 668-7315

Caneyville, Grayson, Pop. 601
Grayson County SD
Supt. — See Leitchfield
Caneyville ES 500/PK-5
521 E Maple St 42721 270-879-4211
George Meredith, prin. Fax 879-9022

Carlisle, Nicholas, Pop. 1,984
Nicholas County SD 1,200/PK-12
395 W Main St 40311 859-289-3770
Robert Bell, supt. Fax 289-3777
www.nicholas.kyschools.us
Nicholas County ES 700/PK-6
133 School Dr 40311 859-289-3785
Stacey Allison, prin. Fax 289-6240

Carrollton, Carroll, Pop. 3,864
Carroll County SD 1,900/K-12
813 Hawkins St 41008 502-732-7070
Ronald Livingood Ed.D., supt. Fax 732-7073
www.carroll.kyschools.us
Carroll County MS 400/6-8
408 5th St 41008 502-732-7080
Dana Oak, prin. Fax 732-7107
Cartmell ES 400/3-5
1708 Highland Ave 41008 502-732-7085
Jeannie Rohrer, prin. Fax 732-7100
Winn PS 500/K-2
907 Hawkins St 41008 502-732-7090
Donna Monroe, prin. Fax 732-7091

Christian Academy of Carrollton 100/PK-12
1703 Easterday Rd 41008 502-732-4734
Katie Matson, admin. Fax 732-4732

Catlettsburg, Boyd, Pop. 1,845
Boyd County SD
Supt. — See Ashland
Catlettsburg ES 300/PK-5
3348 Court St 41129 606-739-5515
Jeffrey Frasure, prin. Fax 739-8625

Ponderosa ES 400/K-5
16701 Ponderosa Dr 41129 606-928-2330
Brian Eerenberg, prin. Fax 928-2337

Cave City, Barren, Pop. 2,196
Caverna ISD 800/PK-12
1102 N Dixie Hwy 42127 270-773-2530
Cornelius Faulkner, supt. Fax 773-2524
www.caverna.k12.ky.us
Caverna ES 400/PK-5
1106 N Dixie Hwy 42127 270-773-3671
Tina Southwood, prin. Fax 773-4120
Other Schools – See Horse Cave

Cawood, Harlan, Pop. 729
Harlan County SD
Supt. — See Harlan
Cawood ES 300/K-8
PO Box 308 40815 606-573-2502
Melinda Sergent, prin. Fax 573-4779

Cecilia, Hardin, Pop. 563
Hardin County SD
Supt. — See Elizabethtown
Cecilia Valley ES 300/PK-5
931 E Main St 42724 270-862-3287
Carlena Sheeran, prin. Fax 862-3497
Lakewood ES 600/PK-5
265 Learning Place Ln 42724 270-862-4516
Shelee Clark, prin. Fax 862-3807
West Hardin MS 600/6-8
10471 Leitchfield Rd 42724 270-862-3924
Mike Lawson, prin. Fax 862-3647

Centertown, Ohio, Pop. 422
Ohio County SD
Supt. — See Hartford
Western ES 300/PK-6
4008 State Route 85 E 42328 270-274-7643
Keith Brown, prin. Fax 274-7271

Central City, Muhlenberg, Pop. 5,889
Muhlenberg County SD
Supt. — See Powderly
Central City ES 500/PK-5
1501 N 2nd St 42330 270-754-4474
Janet Higgs, prin. Fax 754-9570

Clarkson, Grayson, Pop. 867
Grayson County SD
Supt. — See Leitchfield
Clarkson ES 700/PK-5
310 Millerstown St 42726 270-242-3061
Shannon Cates, prin. Fax 242-9425

Clay, Webster, Pop. 1,168
Webster County SD
Supt. — See Dixon
Clay ES 300/PK-6
210 College St 42404 270-664-2227
Susan Owens, prin. Fax 639-0329

Clay City, Powell, Pop. 1,064
Powell County SD
Supt. — See Stanton
Clay City ES 500/K-5
PO Box 670 40312 606-663-3315
Suzanne Meadows, prin. Fax 663-3404

Clearfield, Rowan
Rowan County SD
Supt. — See Morehead
Clearfield ES 300/K-5
460 McBrayer Rd 40313 606-784-5792
Misty Litton, prin. Fax 783-0557

Clinton, Hickman, Pop. 1,362
Hickman County SD 800/PK-12
416 N Waterfield Dr 42031 270-653-2341
Casey Henderson, supt. Fax 653-6007
www.hickman.kyschools.us
Hickman County ES 400/PK-6
416 McMorris St 42031 270-653-4067
Richard Todd, prin. Fax 653-4069

Cloverport, Breckinridge, Pop. 1,138
Cloverport ISD 400/PK-12
PO Box 37 40111 270-788-3910
Keith Haynes, supt. Fax 788-6290
www.cloverport.kyschools.us
Fraize MS 100/6-8
301 Poplar St 40111 270-788-3388
Scott Adcock, prin. Fax 788-6640
Natcher ES 200/PK-5
301 Poplar St 40111 270-788-3388
Scott Adcock, prin. Fax 788-6640

Cold Spring, Campbell, Pop. 5,876
Campbell County SD
Supt. — See Alexandria
Cline ES 300/K-5
5586 E Alexandria Pike 41076 859-781-4544
Connie Ryle, prin. Fax 442-3592
Crossroads ES 600/K-5
475 Cross Roads Blvd 41076 859-441-9174
Kim Visse, prin. Fax 442-3581

St. Joseph S 400/K-8
4011 Alexandria Pike 41076 859-441-2025
Susan Greis, prin. Fax 441-2057

Columbia, Adair, Pop. 4,378
Adair County SD 2,600/PK-12
1204 Greensburg St 42728 270-384-2476
Dr. Pamela Stephens, supt. Fax 384-5841
www.adair.kyschools.us
Adair County ES 600/3-5
870 Indian Dr 42728 270-384-0077
Steve Burton, prin. Fax 384-0079
Adair County MS 600/6-8
322 General John Adair Dr 42728 270-384-5308
Alma Rich, prin. Fax 384-2168

Adair County PS — 600/PK-2
158 Col Casey Dr 42728 — 270-384-3367
Patty Jones, prin. — Fax 384-6668

Corbin, Whitley, Pop. 7,232
Corbin ISD — 3,000/PK-12
108 Roy Kidd Ave 40701 — 606-528-1303
David Cox, supt. — Fax 523-1747
www.corbinschools.org
Corbin ES — 400/3-4
710 W 8th St 40701 — 606-528-4367
Chris Webb, prin. — Fax 215-5177
Corbin IS — 400/5-6
404 17th St 40701 — 606-528-1651
Bill Jones, prin. — Fax 524-3141
Corbin MS — 500/7-8
706 S Kentucky Ave 40701 — 606-523-3619
Cindy Davis, prin. — Fax 523-5093
Corbin Preschool — 100/PK-PK
614 Master St 40701 — 606-523-3612
Megan Moses, dir. — Fax 523-3618
Corbin PS — 600/K-2
3551 5th Street Rd 40701 — 606-523-3638
Travis Wilder, prin. — Fax 523-3640

Knox County SD
Supt. — See Barbourville
Lynn Camp ES — 600/PK-6
366 N KY 830 40701 — 606-523-1814
Anthony Pennington, prin. — Fax 523-0872

Laurel County SD
Supt. — See London
Hunter Hills ES — 600/K-5
8325 S US Highway 25 40701 — 606-862-4655
Brian Bond, prin. — Fax 862-4658

Whitley County SD
Supt. — See Williamsburg
Oak Grove ES — 700/PK-6
4505 Cumberland Falls Hwy 40701 — 606-549-7867
Tonya Faulkner, prin. — Fax 528-0968

Corydon, Henderson, Pop. 703
Henderson County SD
Supt. — See Henderson
Chandler ES — 400/PK-5
11215 US Highway 60 W 42406 — 270-533-1760
Brandy Haley, prin. — Fax 533-9128

Covington, Kenton, Pop. 39,321
Covington ISD — 4,100/PK-12
25 E 7th St 41011 — 859-392-1000
Alvin Garrison, supt. — Fax 292-5970
covington.kyschools.us
Biggs ECC — 300/PK-PK
1124 Scott St 41011 — 859-292-5895
Elizabeth Miller, dir. — Fax 292-5956
Carlisle ES — 500/K-5
910 Holman Ave 41011 — 859-292-5812
Tara Bell, prin. — Fax 292-5983
Holmes MS — 800/6-8
2500 Madison Ave 41014 — 859-392-1100
Jeanetta Stacy, prin. — Fax 292-5810
Latonia ES — 400/K-5
3901 Huntington Ave 41015 — 859-292-5825
Joann James, prin. — Fax 292-5918
Ninth District ES — 400/K-5
2800 Indiana Ave 41015 — 859-292-5823
Scott Shepard, prin. — Fax 655-6933
Sixth District ES — 500/K-5
1901 Maryland Ave 41014 — 859-292-5819
Brian Walz, prin. — Fax 655-6979
Swing ES — 400/K-5
501 W 19th St 41014 — 859-292-5821
Scott Alter, prin. — Fax 655-6937

Calvary Christian S — 400/PK-12
5955 Taylor Mill Rd 41015 — 859-356-9201
Dr. Bill Dickens, hdmstr. — Fax 356-8962
Cornerstone Classical Christian Academy — 50/K-6
3800 Church St 41015 — 859-360-3558
Holy Cross S — 200/K-8
3615 Church St 41015 — 859-581-6599
Lisa Timmerding, prin. — Fax 392-3992
Holy Family S — 100/K-8
338 E 16th St 41014 — 859-581-0290
Beth Vieth, prin. — Fax 581-0624
Prince of Peace S — 100/K-8
625 Pike St 41011 — 859-431-5153
Sr. Suzanne Rose, prin. — Fax 291-8632
St. Augustine S — 100/K-8
1840 Jefferson Ave 41014 — 859-261-5564
Katherine Nienaber, prin. — Fax 261-5402

Coxs Creek, Nelson
Nelson County SD
Supt. — See Bardstown
Coxs Creek ES — 500/K-5
5635 Louisville Rd 40013 — 502-349-7050
Haley Victery, prin. — Fax 349-7024

St. Gregory S — 100/PK-8
350 Samuels Loop 40013 — 502-348-9583
Camille Boone, prin. — Fax 348-9597

Crab Orchard, Lincoln, Pop. 825
Lincoln County SD
Supt. — See Stanford
Crab Orchard ES — 300/PK-5
137 Lancaster St 40419 — 606-355-2331
Dreama Tomlison, prin. — Fax 355-2058

Crescent Springs, Kenton, Pop. 3,705

Northern Kentucky Montessori Academy — 100/PK-6
2625 Anderson Rd 41017 — 859-331-3725
St. Joseph S — 300/PK-8
2474 Lorraine Ct 41017 — 859-578-2742
Sally Zeck, prin. — Fax 578-2754

Crestwood, Oldham, Pop. 4,447
Oldham County SD — 11,900/PK-12
6165 W Highway 146 40014 — 502-241-3500
Greg Schultz, supt. — Fax 241-3209
www.oldham.kyschools.us/
Camden Station ES — 400/K-5
6401 W Highway 146 40014 — 502-241-1271
Stu Martin, prin. — Fax 241-1273
Centerfield ES — 400/K-5
4512 Centerfield Dr 40014 — 502-241-1772
Julie Scott, prin. — Fax 241-5502
Crestwood ES — 600/K-5
6500 W Highway 146 40014 — 502-241-8401
Candace McDaniel, prin. — Fax 241-5501
East Oldham MS — 600/6-8
1201 E Highway 22 40014 — 502-222-8480
Mark Robson, prin. — Fax 222-8489
Kenwood Station ES — 600/K-5
6321 Veterans Memorial Pkwy 40014 — 502-241-1452
Eric Davis, prin. — Fax 241-1650
Locust Grove ES — 700/K-5
1231 E Highway 22 40014 — 502-222-3521
Andy Moore, prin. — Fax 222-3530
South Oldham MS — 700/6-8
6403 W Highway 146 40014 — 502-241-0320
Steve Emerson, prin. — Fax 241-1438
Other Schools – See Goshen, La Grange, Prospect

Jubilee Academy — 100/K-12
7505 Kavanaugh Rd 40014 — 502-498-5900
Kristie Eldridge, head sch

Crofton, Christian, Pop. 723
Christian County SD
Supt. — See Hopkinsville
Crofton ES — 300/K-6
12145 S Madisonville Rd 42217 — 270-887-7190
Lori Dexter, prin. — Fax 424-9192

Cub Run, Edmonson
Hart County SD
Supt. — See Munfordville
Cub Run S — 200/PK-8
170 E Gap Hill Rd 42729 — 270-524-2925
Lori Chapman, prin. — Fax 524-0531

Cumberland, Harlan, Pop. 2,210
Harlan County SD
Supt. — See Harlan
Cumberland ES — 600/PK-8
322 Golf Course Rd 40823 — 606-589-2511
Shelia Hall, prin. — Fax 589-2610

Custer, Breckinridge
Breckinridge County SD
Supt. — See Hardinsburg
Custer ES — 200/PK-5
PO Box 9 40115 — 270-756-3040
James Luttrell, prin. — Fax 756-3041

Cynthiana, Harrison, Pop. 6,302
Harrison County SD — 3,000/PK-12
308 Webster Ave 41031 — 859-234-7110
Andy Dotson, supt. — Fax 234-8164
www.harrison.kyschools.us
Eastside ES — 400/PK-5
1226 US Highway 62 E 41031 — 859-234-7121
Melissa Miles, prin. — Fax 234-7189
Harrison County MS — 700/6-8
269 Education Dr 41031 — 859-234-7123
Michael McIntire, prin. — Fax 234-8385
Northside ES — 300/PK-5
2415 US Highway 27 N 41031 — 859-234-7114
Sharon Hill, prin. — Fax 234-7167
Southside ES — 300/PK-5
106 Education Dr 41031 — 859-234-7120
Todd Harp, prin. — Fax 234-7176
Westside ES — 300/PK-5
1585 KY Highway 356 41031 — 859-234-7115
Jon Hoskins, prin. — Fax 234-7199

St. Edward S — 50/PK-6
107 N Walnut St 41031 — 859-234-2731
Debbie Henson, prin. — Fax 234-9823

Danville, Boyle, Pop. 15,790
Boyle County SD — 2,600/PK-12
101 Citation Dr Suite C 40422 — 859-236-6634
Mike LaFavers, supt. — Fax 236-8624
www.boyle.kyschools.us
Boyle County MS — 700/6-8
1651 Perryville Rd 40422 — 859-236-4212
Steve Karsner, prin. — Fax 236-9596
Woodlawn ES — 500/PK-5
1661 Perryville Rd 40422 — 859-236-7688
Bernice Bates, prin. — Fax 236-7360
Other Schools – See Junction City, Perryville

Danville ISD — 1,800/PK-12
152 E Martin L King Blvd 40422 — 859-238-1300
Dr. Keith Look, supt. — Fax 238-1330
www.danvilleschools.net
Bate MS — 400/6-8
460 Stanford Ave 40422 — 859-238-1305
Sheri Satterly, prin. — Fax 238-1343
Hogsett ES — 400/PK-5
300 Waveland Ave 40422 — 859-238-1313
Leo Labrillazo, prin. — Fax 238-1341
Rogers ES — 300/K-5
410 E Main St 40422 — 859-238-1316
Robin Kelly, prin. — Fax 238-1342
Toliver ES — 300/K-5
209 N Maple Ave 40422 — 859-238-1319
Ron Ballard, prin. — Fax 238-1334

Danville Christian Academy — 200/PK-12
2170 Shakertown Rd 40422 — 859-236-2177
James Ward, hdmstr. — Fax 236-6759
Danville Montessori S — 100/PK-6
PO Box 651 40423 — 859-236-9310

Dawson Springs, Hopkins, Pop. 2,724
Dawson Springs ISD — 600/PK-12
118 E Arcadia Ave 42408 — 270-797-3811
Leonard Whalen, supt. — Fax 797-5201
www.dsprings.k12.ky.us
Dawson Springs ES — 300/PK-6
317 Eli St 42408 — 270-797-2991
Jennifer Ward J.D., prin. — Fax 797-5202

Dayton, Campbell, Pop. 5,244
Dayton ISD — 900/PK-12
200 Clay St 41074 — 859-491-6565
Jay Brewer, supt. — Fax 292-3995
www.dayton.kyschools.us
Lincoln ES — 600/PK-6
701 5th Ave 41074 — 859-292-7492
Heather Dragan, prin. — Fax 292-7481

Denniston, Menifee
Menifee County SD
Supt. — See Frenchburg
Botts ES — 200/PK-5
PO Box 39 40316 — 606-768-8052
Jeremy McNabb, prin. — Fax 768-8100

Dixon, Webster, Pop. 785
Webster County SD — 2,300/PK-12
28 State Route 1340 42409 — 270-639-5083
Dr. Rachel Yarbrough, supt. — Fax 639-0117
www.webster.kyschools.us
Dixon ES — 300/K-6
277 State Route 1340 42409 — 270-639-9080
Eric Wheatley, prin. — Fax 639-0129
Webster County MS — 300/7-8
1928 US Highway 41A S 42409 — 270-639-9496
Cyndi Boggs, prin. — Fax 639-9498
Other Schools – See Clay, Providence, Sebree

Dorton, Pike
Pike County SD
Supt. — See Pikeville
Dorton S, PO Box 260 41520 — 300/K-8
Thomas Pinion, prin. — 606-639-6521

Dry Ridge, Grant, Pop. 2,166
Grant County SD
Supt. — See Williamstown
Crittenden Mt. Zion ES — 500/K-5
270 Crittenden Mt Zion Rd 41035 — 859-428-2171
Nancy Livingood, prin. — Fax 428-1890
Dry Ridge ES — 500/K-5
275 School Rd 41035 — 859-824-4484
Bobbie Jo Pelfrey, prin. — Fax 824-4924
Grant County MS — 800/6-8
305 School Rd 41035 — 859-824-7161
Hallie Booth, prin. — Fax 824-7163
Sherman ES — 500/K-5
3987 Dixie Hwy 41035 — 859-428-5500
Jamie Kinmon, prin. — Fax 428-4200

Earlington, Hopkins, Pop. 1,367
Hopkins County SD
Supt. — See Madisonville
Earlington ES — 300/PK-5
1976 Championship Dr 42410 — 270-825-6154
Wendy Mitchell, prin. — Fax 825-6029

East Bernstadt, Laurel, Pop. 710
East Bernstadt ISD — 500/PK-8
PO Box 128 40729 — 606-843-7373
Vicki Jones, supt. — Fax 843-6249
www.e-bernstadt.k12.ky.us
East Bernstadt S — 500/PK-8
PO Box 128 40729 — 606-843-6221
Teresa Smith, prin. — Fax 843-7671

Laurel County SD
Supt. — See London
Hazel Green ES — 300/K-5
2515 Highway 1394 40729 — 606-862-4647
Brad Mullins, prin. — Fax 862-4648

Eastern, Floyd
Floyd County SD
Supt. — See Prestonsburg
Duff-Allen Central ES — 300/K-8
PO Box 129 41622 — 606-358-0110
Wes Halbert, prin. — Fax 358-0112

Eddyville, Lyon, Pop. 2,514
Lyon County SD — 900/K-12
217 Jenkins Rd 42038 — 270-388-9715
Russ Tilford, supt. — Fax 388-4962
www.lyon.kyschools.us
Lyon County ES — 400/K-5
201 W Fairview Ave 42038 — 270-388-9715
Amy Perdue, prin. — Fax 388-9011
Lyon County MS — 200/6-8
111 W Fairview Ave 42038 — 270-388-9715
Robert Richey, prin. — Fax 388-0517

Edgewood, Kenton, Pop. 8,503
Kenton County SD
Supt. — See Fort Wright
Caywood ES — 700/PK-5
3300 Turkeyfoot Rd 41017 — 859-341-7062
Kelly Conner, prin. — Fax 344-3151
Hinsdale ES — 700/K-5
440 Dudley Pike 41017 — 859-341-8226
Angela Castleman, prin. — Fax 341-0759
Turkey Foot MS — 1,100/6-8
3230 Turkeyfoot Rd 41017 — 859-341-0216
Ray Stanley, prin. — Fax 341-7217

St. Pius X S 500/K-8
348 Dudley Pike 41017 859-341-4900
Jill Lonnemann, prin. Fax 341-3440

Edmonton, Metcalfe, Pop. 1,584
Metcalfe County SD 1,300/PK-12
709 W Stockton St 42129 270-432-3171
Dr. Benny Lile, supt. Fax 432-3170
www.metcalfe.kyschools.us
Metcalfe County ES 500/PK-5
703 W Stockton St 42129 270-432-2051
Michael Gill, prin. Fax 432-4678
Metcalfe County MS 400/6-8
208 Randolph St Lot 1 42129 270-432-3359
Allen Trotter, prin. Fax 432-5828

Ekron, Meade, Pop. 124
Meade County SD
Supt. — See Brandenburg
Ekron ES 400/K-6
2500 Haysville Rd 40117 270-422-7570
Joan Cooke, prin. Fax 828-5447
Flaherty ES 300/4-6
2615 Flaherty Rd 40117 270-422-7565
Georgia Taylor, prin. Fax 828-3632
Flaherty PS 500/K-3
2635 Flaherty Rd 40117 270-422-7575
Rikki Hanger, prin. Fax 828-5848

Elizabethtown, Hardin, Pop. 27,593
Elizabethtown ISD 2,500/PK-12
219 Helm St 42701 270-765-6146
Jon Ballard, supt. Fax 765-2158
www.etown.k12.ky.us
Helmwood Heights ES 400/1-5
307 Cardinal Dr 42701 270-769-1328
Jessica Turner, prin. Fax 763-0735
Morningside ES 500/1-5
313 Morningside Dr 42701 270-769-3359
Karla Buckingham, prin. Fax 763-0017
Panther Academy 300/PK-K
634 N Mulberry St 42701 270-765-3007
Kelly Graham, prin. Fax 769-3620
Stone MS 600/6-8
323 Morningside Dr 42701 270-769-6343
Jennifer Burnham, prin. Fax 769-6749

Hardin County SD 14,700/PK-12
65 W A Jenkins Rd 42701 270-769-8800
Teresa Morgan, supt. Fax 769-8888
www.hardin.kyschools.us
Bluegrass MS 600/6-8
170 W A Jenkins Rd 42701 270-765-2658
Michael Elmore, prin. Fax 769-7935
Burkhead ES 700/PK-5
1323 Saint John Rd 42701 270-769-5983
Hal Bender, prin. Fax 737-0989
Heartland ES 600/PK-5
2300 Nelson Dr 42701 270-769-8930
Emily Campbell, prin. Fax 769-8949
Lincoln Trail ES 500/PK-5
3154 Bardstown Rd 42701 270-737-7227
Gena Jeffries, prin. Fax 769-0246
New Highland ES 600/PK-5
110 W A Jenkins Rd 42701 270-737-6612
Daniel Mullins, prin. Fax 769-0183
Other Schools – See Cecilia, Glendale, Radcliff, Rineyville, Sonora, Vine Grove

St. James Regional S 400/PK-8
401 Robinbrooke blvd 42701 270-765-7011
Sr. Marie Hannah Seiler, prin. Fax 765-5745

Elkhorn City, Pike, Pop. 977
Pike County SD
Supt. — See Pikeville
Elkhorn City S 500/K-8
180 Cougar Dr 41522 606-754-4542
James Mercer, prin. Fax 754-7436

Elkton, Todd, Pop. 2,020
Todd County SD 2,100/PK-12
205 Airport Rd 42220 270-265-2436
Wayne Benningfield, supt. Fax 265-5414
www.todd.kyschools.us
North Todd ES 500/PK-5
7300 Greenville Rd 42220 270-277-6800
Yvonne Rundall, prin. Fax 277-9919
Todd County MS 500/6-8
515 W Main St 42220 270-265-2511
Les Broady, prin. Fax 265-9414
Other Schools – See Guthrie

Eminence, Henry, Pop. 2,433
Eminence ISD 700/PK-12
291 W Broadway St 40019 502-845-5427
Buddy Berry, supt. Fax 845-1310
www.eminence.kyschools.us
Eminence ES 300/PK-5
254 W Broadway St 40019 502-845-5427
Michael Doran, prin. Fax 845-1310

Emmalena, Knott
Knott County SD
Supt. — See Hindman
Emmalena ES 200/PK-8
8343 Highway 550 W 41740 606-251-3651
Jeffery Honeycutt, prin. Fax 251-3674

Eolia, Letcher
Letcher County SD
Supt. — See Whitesburg
Boggs ES 100/PK-8
PO Box 87 40826 606-633-4654
Freddie Terry, prin. Fax 633-8102

Erlanger, Kenton, Pop. 17,704
Erlanger-Elsmere ISD 2,200/PK-12
500 Graves Ave 41018 859-727-2009
Dr. Kathlyn Burkhardt, supt. Fax 727-5653
www.erlanger.kyschools.us
Arnett ES 200/PK-5
3552 Kimberly Dr 41018 859-727-1488
Amanda New, prin. Fax 342-2481
EES Early Learning Options PK-PK
450 Bartlett St 41018 859-342-2427
Matthew Engel, admin.
Howell ES 300/K-5
909 Central Row Rd 41018 859-727-1108
Michael Goodenough, prin. Fax 342-2354
Lindeman ES 300/K-5
558 Erlanger Rd 41018 859-727-1188
Angela Gabbard, prin. Fax 342-2451
Miles ES 300/K-5
208 Sunset Ave 41018 859-727-2231
Joshua Jackson, prin. Fax 342-2371
Tichenor MS 500/6-8
305 Bartlett Ave 41018 859-727-2255
Mac Cooley, prin. Fax 342-2425

Mary Queen of Heaven S 200/PK-8
1130 Donaldson Hwy 41018 859-371-8100
Lynn Mowery, prin. Fax 371-3362
St. Henry S 300/PK-8
3825 Dixie Hwy 41018 859-342-2551
Susan Pastor-Richard, prin. Fax 342-2554

Eubank, Pulaski, Pop. 311
Pulaski County SD
Supt. — See Somerset
Eubank ES 300/PK-5
285 W Highway 70 42567 606-379-2712
Lisa Black, prin. Fax 379-5304

Evarts, Harlan, Pop. 947
Harlan County SD
Supt. — See Harlan
Black Mountain ES 400/PK-8
1555 Highway 215 40828 606-837-2214
Bonnie Lefevers, prin. Fax 837-9930
Evarts ES 400/K-8
132 Keister St 40828 606-837-2386
Sherry Anglian, prin. Fax 837-8535

Ewing, Fleming, Pop. 263
Fleming County SD
Supt. — See Flemingsburg
Ewing ES 300/K-6
5651 Elizaville Rd 41039 606-267-2601
Michelle Hunt, prin. Fax 267-6024

Ezel, Morgan, Pop. 235
Morgan County SD
Supt. — See West Liberty
Ezel ES 200/K-5
PO Box 9 41425 606-725-8202
Carol Rose, prin. Fax 725-8250

Fairdale, Jefferson, Pop. 6,563
Jefferson County SD
Supt. — See Louisville
Coral Ridge ES 500/PK-5
10608 National Tpke 40118 502-485-8234
Barbara James, prin. Fax 313-3439
Fairdale ES 600/K-5
10104 Mitchell Hill Rd 40118 502-485-8247
Pam Gooch, prin. Fax 313-3453

Falmouth, Pendleton, Pop. 2,146
Pendleton County SD 2,400/PK-12
2525 US Highway 27 N 41040 859-654-6911
Dr. R. Anthony Strong, supt. Fax 654-6143
www.pendleton.kyschools.us
Southern ES 500/PK-5
320 Fairgrounds Rd 41040 859-654-6981
Mark Hegyi, prin. Fax 654-2906
Other Schools – See Butler

Fancy Farm, Graves, Pop. 457
Graves County SD
Supt. — See Mayfield
Fancy Farm ES 200/PK-6
270 State Route 339 S 42039 270-674-4020
Janet Throgmorton, prin. Fax 623-6393

Fedscreek, Pike
Pike County SD
Supt. — See Pikeville
Feds Creek S 200/K-8
221 Fedscreek Rd 41524 606-835-4757
Daren Stiltner, prin. Fax 835-1382

Fern Creek, Jefferson, Pop. 16,406
Jefferson County SD
Supt. — See Louisville
Fern Creek ES 800/K-5
8815 Ferndale Rd 40291 502-485-8250
Stephen Burch, prin. Fax 313-3457

Flatgap, Johnson
Johnson County SD
Supt. — See Paintsville
Flat Gap ES 300/PK-6
1450 KY Route 689 E 41219 606-265-3110
Chris Pierce, prin. Fax 265-4409

Flat Lick, Knox, Pop. 952
Knox County SD
Supt. — See Barbourville
Dewitt ES 200/PK-6
138 KY 718 40935 606-542-4274
Marcie Walker, prin. Fax 542-4279
Flat Lick ES 200/PK-6
110 KY 3085 40935 606-542-4712
Steve Partin, prin. Fax 542-4737

Flatwoods, Greenup, Pop. 7,339
Russell ISD
Supt. — See Russell
Russell-McDowell IS 400/3-5
1900 Long St 41139 606-836-8186
Pamela Wright, prin. Fax 836-3547

Flemingsburg, Fleming, Pop. 2,619
Fleming County SD 2,300/K-12
211 W Water St 41041 606-845-5851
Brian Creasman, supt. Fax 849-3158
www.fleming.kyschools.us
Flemingsburg ES 600/K-6
245 W Water St 41041 606-845-9871
Kristen Manning, prin. Fax 845-2404
Simons MS 400/7-8
242 W Water St 41041 606-845-9331
Jesse Bacon, prin. Fax 849-2309
Other Schools – See Ewing, Hillsboro, Wallingford

Florence, Boone, Pop. 29,280
Boone County SD 20,000/PK-12
8330 US Highway 42 41042 859-283-1003
Randy Poe Ed.D., supt. Fax 282-2376
www.boone.kyschools.us
Collins ES 700/K-5
9000 Spruce Dr 41042 859-282-2350
T.W. Loring, prin. Fax 282-2356
Erpenbeck ES 700/K-5
9001 Wetherington Blvd 41042 859-384-7200
Pat Berry, prin. Fax 384-5376
Florence ES 700/PK-5
103 Center St 41042 859-282-2610
Lisa Resing, prin. Fax 282-2615
Jones MS 700/6-8
8000 Spruce Dr 41042 859-282-4610
Tony Pastura, prin. Fax 282-2364
Ockerman ES 800/PK-5
8250 US Highway 42 41042 859-282-4620
Kim Best, prin. Fax 282-4625
Ockerman MS 900/6-8
8300 US Highway 42 41042 859-282-3240
Darla Payne, prin. Fax 282-3242
Yealey ES 600/PK-5
10 Yealey Dr 41042 859-282-3333
Renee Turner, prin. Fax 282-3337
Other Schools – See Burlington, Hebron, Union

Heritage Academy 200/PK-12
7216 US Highway 42 41042 859-525-0213
St. Paul S 400/PK-8
7303 Dixie Hwy 41042 859-647-4070
Kemberly Markham, prin. Fax 647-4073

Fordsville, Ohio, Pop. 520
Ohio County SD
Supt. — See Hartford
Fordsville ES 300/PK-6
PO Box 139 42343 270-276-3601
April Porter, prin. Fax 276-9556

Fort Mitchell, Kenton, Pop. 8,095
Beechwood ISD 1,300/PK-12
50 Beechwood Rd 41017 859-331-3250
Dr. Mike Stacy, supt. Fax 331-7528
www.beechwood.kyschools.us
Beechwood ES 700/PK-6
54 Beechwood Rd 41017 859-331-1220
Zach Ashley, prin. Fax 426-3743

Blessed Sacrament S 600/K-8
2407 Dixie Hwy 41017 859-331-3062
Maureen Hannon, prin. Fax 344-7323

Fort Thomas, Campbell, Pop. 16,124
Fort Thomas ISD 2,900/PK-12
28 N Fort Thomas Ave 41075 859-781-3333
Karen Cheser, supt. Fax 442-4016
www.fortthomas.kyschools.us
Highlands MS 700/6-8
2350 Memorial Pkwy 41075 859-441-5222
Michael Howton, prin. Fax 441-4210
Johnson ES 400/PK-5
1180 N Fort Thomas Ave 41075 859-441-2444
Ashley Dikeos, prin. Fax 572-4948
Moyer ES 500/K-5
219 Highland Ave 41075 859-441-1180
Dawn Laber, prin. Fax 441-9440
Woodfill ES 400/K-5
1025 Alexandria Pike 41075 859-441-0506
Keith Faust, prin. Fax 441-2755

St. Catherine of Siena S 200/K-8
23 Rossford Ave 41075 859-572-2680
Doug Lonneman, prin. Fax 572-2699
St. Thomas S 200/PK-8
428 S Fort Thomas Ave 41075 859-572-4641
Deborah Flamm, prin. Fax 572-4644

Fort Wright, Kenton, Pop. 5,642
Kenton County SD 13,800/PK-12
1055 Eaton Dr 41017 859-344-8888
Dr. Henry Webb, supt. Fax 344-1531
www.kenton.kyschools.us/
Fort Wright ES 500/K-5
501 Farrell Dr 41011 859-331-7742
Tina Wartman, prin. Fax 331-7763
Other Schools – See Edgewood, Independence, Morning View, Ryland Heights, Taylor Mill, Villa Hills

St. Agnes S 400/K-8
1322 Sleepy Hollow Rd 41011 859-261-0543
Richard Hoyt, prin. Fax 261-9778

Fourmile, Bell
Bell County SD
Supt. — See Pineville

Lone Jack S Center 200/PK-8
101 Creech Hollow Rd 40939 606-337-9461
Brian Crawford, prin. Fax 337-8136

Frakes, Bell
Bell County SD
Supt. — See Pineville
Frakes School Center 200/PK-8
29 Henderson Settlement 40940 606-337-2921
Terry Wilson, prin. Fax 337-2928

Frankfort, Franklin, Pop. 24,820
Frankfort ISD 800/PK-12
959 Leestown Ln 40601 502-875-8661
Dr. Houston Barber, supt. Fax 875-8663
www.frankfort.k12.ky.us
Frankfort Ind. Early Learning Academy 100/PK-PK
959 Leestown Ln 40601 502-875-8661
Heidi Givens, dir. Fax 875-8663
Second Street S 500/K-8
506 W 2nd St 40601 502-875-8658
Dewey Hensley, prin. Fax 875-8665

Franklin County SD 6,300/PK-12
190 Kings Daughters Dr 40601 502-695-6700
Mark Kopp, supt. Fax 695-6708
www.franklin.kyschools.us
Bondurant MS 600/6-8
300 Bondurant Dr 40601 502-875-8440
Casey Sparrow, prin. Fax 875-8442
Bridgeport ES 500/PK-5
10 Doctors Dr 40601 502-875-8430
Stacy Rutledge, prin. Fax 875-8432
Collins Lane ES 500/PK-5
1 Cougar Ln 40601 502-875-8410
Jennifer Perkins, prin. Fax 875-8412
Early Learning Village - East 400/PK-K
200 Laralan Ave 40601 502-352-2585
Larry Murphy, prin. Fax 352-2586
Elkhorn ES 400/1-5
928 E Main St 40601 502-695-6730
Matt Osborne, prin. Fax 695-6731
Elkhorn MS 800/6-8
1060 E Main St 40601 502-695-6740
Jeff Rhode, prin. Fax 695-6745
Hearn ES 500/1-5
300 Copperleaf Blvd 40601 502-695-6760
Tina Cooper, prin. Fax 695-6762
Peaks Mill ES 400/1-5
100 Peaks Mill Rd 40601 502-875-8450
Dana Blankenship, prin. Fax 875-8452
Westridge ES 500/PK-5
200 Oakridge Dr 40601 502-875-8420
Tracey Cline, prin. Fax 875-8422

Capital Day S 200/PK-8
120 Deepwood Dr 40601 502-227-7121
Tim Corkran, head sch Fax 227-7558
Frankfort Christian Academy 300/PK-12
1349 US Highway 421 S 40601 502-695-0744
Carrie Beth Tigges, admin. Fax 695-8725
Good Shepherd S 100/PK-8
75 Shepherd Way 40601 502-223-5041
Dr. Michele Ulrich Ph.D., prin. Fax 223-2755

Franklin, Simpson, Pop. 8,221
Simpson County SD 2,900/PK-12
430 S College St 42134 270-586-8877
Dr. James Flynn, supt. Fax 586-2011
www.simpson.kyschools.us
Franklin ES 200/PK-K
211 S Main St 42134 270-586-3241
Rachel Fairman, prin. Fax 586-2042
Franklin Simpson MS 700/6-8
322 S College St 42134 270-586-4401
Craig Delk, prin. Fax 586-2048
Lincoln ES 400/4-5
601 John J Johnson Ave 42134 270-586-7133
Joyce Pais, prin. Fax 586-2045
Simpson ES 600/1-3
721 Witt Rd 42134 270-586-4414
Michael Barnum, prin. Fax 598-6059

Frenchburg, Menifee, Pop. 482
Menifee County SD 1,100/PK-12
PO Box 110 40322 606-768-8002
Timothy Spencer, supt. Fax 768-8050
www.menifee.kyschools.us
Menifee County ES 500/K-8
57 Indian Creek Rd 40322 606-768-8351
Tonya Means, prin. Fax 768-8355
Other Schools – See Denniston

Fulton, Fulton, Pop. 2,370
Fulton ISD 400/PK-12
304 W State Line St 42041 270-472-1553
Dr. DeAnna Miller, supt. Fax 472-6921
www.fultonind.kyschools.us
Carr ES 300/PK-5
400 W State Line St 42041 270-472-1637
R.B. Mays, prin. Fax 472-2277

Gamaliel, Monroe, Pop. 374
Monroe County SD
Supt. — See Tompkinsville
Gamaliel ES 300/PK-5
320 W Main St 42140 270-457-2341
Kathy Taylor, prin. Fax 457-2702

Garrison, Lewis, Pop. 863
Lewis County SD
Supt. — See Vanceburg
Garrison ES 400/PK-6
PO Box 547 41141 606-757-2122
Dale McDowell, prin. Fax 757-2161

Georgetown, Scott, Pop. 28,525
Scott County SD 8,900/PK-12
PO Box 578 40324 502-863-3663
Dr. Kevin Hub, supt. Fax 863-5367
www.scott.kyschools.us
Eastern ES 500/PK-5
3407 Newtown Pike 40324 502-863-0275
Corrie Kemper, prin. Fax 863-0537
Garth ES 500/PK-5
501 S Hamilton St 40324 502-863-1170
Damon Stefanic, prin. Fax 867-0794
Georgetown MS 500/6-8
730 S Hamilton St 40324 502-863-3805
Cari Boyd, prin. Fax 867-1372
Lemons Mill ES 300/PK-5
300 School House St 40324 502-867-6700
Lori Mays, prin. Fax 863-4766
Mason ES 700/PK-5
350 Champion Way 40324 502-570-3050
Shane Pickerill, prin. Fax 570-0391
Northern ES 400/PK-5
3600 Cincinnati Rd 40324 502-868-5007
Rachelle Schjoll, prin. Fax 863-6654
Royal Spring MS 800/6-8
332 Champion Way 40324 502-570-2390
John Noll, prin. Fax 863-3621
Scott County MS 800/6-8
1036 Cardinal Dr 40324 502-863-7202
Jennifer Sutton, prin. Fax 863-7452
Scott County Preschool Center 300/PK-PK
1300 Long Lick Pike 40324 502-868-0411
Jennifer Smith, prin. Fax 863-2843
Southern ES 600/PK-5
1200 Fairfax Way 40324 502-863-0772
Bryan Blankenship, prin. Fax 863-3421
Western ES 800/PK-5
1901 Frankfort Rd 40324 502-863-1393
Brent Allen, prin. Fax 867-0840
Other Schools – See Stamping Ground

Providence Christian Academy 300/PK-9
172 Southgate Dr 40324 502-868-9393
Kathleen Mallory, head sch Fax 370-4766
St. John S 200/PK-8
106 Military St 40324 502-863-2607
Dan Mardell, prin. Fax 863-2259

Girdler, Knox
Knox County SD
Supt. — See Barbourville
Girdler ES 400/K-6
PO Box 259 40943 606-546-4859
Jason Jordan, prin. Fax 546-4366

Glasgow, Barren, Pop. 13,692
Barren County SD 4,800/PK-12
202 W Washington St 42141 270-651-3787
Bo Matthews, supt. Fax 651-8836
www.barren.kyschools.us
Barren County MS 700/7-8
555 Trojan Trl 42141 270-651-4909
Lori Downs, prin. Fax 651-5137
Eastern ES 400/PK-6
4601 New Salem Rd 42141 270-678-2722
Erika DeVore, prin. Fax 678-5885
North Jackson ES 500/PK-6
2002 N Jackson Hwy 42141 270-629-2300
Jeannie London, prin. Fax 629-2301
Red Cross ES 700/PK-6
215 Parkview Dr 42141 270-659-2400
Michael Davis, prin. Fax 659-0052
Temple Hill ES 300/PK-6
8788 Tompkinsville Rd 42141 270-427-2611
John Hall, prin. Fax 427-4176
Other Schools – See Hiseville, Lucas, Park City

Glasgow ISD 2,000/PK-12
PO Box 1239 42142 270-651-6757
Keith Hale, supt. Fax 651-9791
www.glasgow.kyschools.us
Glasgow MS 500/6-8
105 Scottie Dr 42141 270-651-2256
Randy Wilkinson, prin. Fax 651-3090
Highland ES 500/PK-5
164 Scottie Dr 42141 270-659-0432
Jennifer Myers, prin. Fax 659-0478
South Green ES 400/PK-5
300 James T Rogers Dr 42141 270-651-3806
BobbiSue Holmes, prin. Fax 651-8957

Glasgow Christian Academy 200/PK-12
600 Old Cavalry Dr 42141 270-651-7729
Tracy Shaw, prin. Fax 651-6811

Glendale, Hardin
Hardin County SD
Supt. — See Elizabethtown
East Hardin MS 700/6-8
129 College St 42740 270-369-7370
Brittany Nickell, prin. Fax 369-6380

Goshen, Oldham, Pop. 900
Oldham County SD
Supt. — See Crestwood
Harmony ES 500/K-5
1901 S Highway 1793 40026 502-228-2228
Suellen Hackmiller, prin. Fax 228-2231
North Oldham MS 800/6-8
1801 S Highway 1793 40026 502-228-9998
Carrie Pitsenberger, prin. Fax 228-0985

Grayson, Carter, Pop. 4,170
Carter County SD 4,700/PK-12
228 S Carol Malone Blvd 41143 606-474-6696
Ronnie Dotson, supt. Fax 474-6125
www.cartercountyschools.org
Carter City ES 100/PK-5
13321 State Rte 2 41143 606-474-6696
Jo Ashworth, prin. Fax 474-2044
East Carter MS 600/6-8
1 Spirit Ln 41143 606-474-6696
Matt Stanfield, prin. Fax 474-4027
Heritage ES 400/PK-5
4863 S State Highway 1 41143 606-474-6696
J.C. Perkins, prin. Fax 474-2025
Prichard ES 700/PK-5
401 E Main St 41143 606-474-6696
Jason McGlone, prin. Fax 474-8557
Other Schools – See Olive Hill, Rush

Greensburg, Green, Pop. 2,133
Green County SD 1,600/K-12
PO Box 369 42743 270-932-6601
Jim Frank, supt. Fax 932-3624
gcsdistrict.blogspot.com
Green County IS 400/3-5
PO Box 136 42743 270-932-6613
Crystal Hedgespeth, prin. Fax 299-2228
Green County MS 400/6-8
PO Box 176 42743 270-932-6615
Philip West, prin. Fax 932-7617
Green County PS 400/K-2
PO Box 150 42743 270-932-6619
Ben Davenport, prin. Fax 932-6172

Greenup, Greenup, Pop. 1,174
Greenup County SD 2,900/K-12
45 Musketeer Dr 41144 606-473-9819
Sherry Horsley, supt. Fax 473-5710
www.greenup.kyschools.us/
Greysbranch ES 400/K-5
1487 Ohio River Rd 41144 606-473-9653
Misty Tackett, prin. Fax 473-6645
Other Schools – See Argillite, South Shore, Wurtland

Greenville, Muhlenberg, Pop. 4,256
Muhlenberg County SD
Supt. — See Powderly
Greenville ES 500/PK-5
201 E Main Cross St 42345 270-338-4830
Stacie Jones, prin. Fax 338-4847
Longest ES 500/PK-5
1020 N Main St 42345 270-338-2842
Brent Hardison, prin. Fax 338-3002
Muhlenberg North MS 600/6-8
1000 N Main St 42345 270-338-3550
Jerry Rager, prin. Fax 338-2911
Muhlenberg South MS 500/6-8
200 Pritchett Dr 42345 270-338-4650
Brian Lile, prin. Fax 338-0151

Christian Academy of ACTSchools 50/K-8
PO Box 405 42345 270-338-1630
Emily Carder, head sch

Grethel, Floyd
Floyd County SD
Supt. — See Prestonsburg
Stumbo ES 300/K-8
6945 KY Route 979 41631 606-263-6200
Donna Robinson, prin. Fax 263-6206

Guthrie, Todd, Pop. 1,397
Todd County SD
Supt. — See Elkton
South Todd ES 600/PK-5
4115 Guthrie Rd 42234 270-265-5785
Doug Cotton, prin. Fax 265-3808

Hagerhill, Johnson
Johnson County SD
Supt. — See Paintsville
Porter ES 400/PK-6
7210 S KY Route 321 41222 606-789-2545
Heather Butcher, prin. Fax 789-6837

Hanson, Hopkins, Pop. 738
Hopkins County SD
Supt. — See Madisonville
Hanson ES 600/K-5
121 Eastlawn Rd 42413 270-825-6158
Aaron Clark, prin. Fax 825-6121

Happy, Perry
Perry County SD
Supt. — See Hazard
Combs S 400/PK-8
9165 S KY Highway 15 41746 606-476-2518
Joshua Baker, prin. Fax 476-8502

Hardin, Marshall, Pop. 610

New Covenant Christian Academy 100/PK-8
PO Box 348 42048 270-437-3170

Hardinsburg, Breckinridge, Pop. 2,302
Breckinridge County SD 2,800/PK-12
86 Airport Rd 40143 270-756-3000
Nick Carter, supt. Fax 756-6888
www.breck.kyschools.us
Hardinsburg ES 500/PK-5
419 E 3rd St 40143 270-756-3020
Will Parker, prin. Fax 756-3021
Other Schools – See Custer, Harned, Irvington, Mc Daniels

St. Romuald S 300/PK-8
408 N Highway 259 40143 270-756-5504
Rob Cox, prin. Fax 756-2099

Hardyville, Hart, Pop. 154
Hart County SD
Supt. — See Munfordville
Memorial S 300/PK-8
1400 N Jackson Hwy 42746 270-528-2271
Allen Poynter, prin. Fax 528-2273

Harlan, Harlan, Pop. 1,720
Harlan County SD 4,200/PK-12
251 Ball Park Rd 40831 606-573-4330
Brent Roark, supt. Fax 573-5767
www.harlan.kyschools.us
Cawood ES 300/PK-8
279 Ball Park Rd 40831 606-573-5029
John Carter, prin. Fax 573-2424
Other Schools – See Baxter, Bledsoe, Cawood, Cumberland, Evarts, Wallins Creek

Harlan ISD 800/PK-12
420 E Central St 40831 606-573-8700
Charles Morton, supt. Fax 573-8711
www.harlan-ind.k12.ky.us
Harlan ES 300/K-4
420 E Central St 40831 606-573-8700
Vickie Anderson, prin. Fax 573-8720
Sunshine Preschool 100/PK-PK
304 Surgener St 40831 606-573-8700
Pat Bryson, prin. Fax 573-8749

Harned, Breckinridge
Breckinridge County SD
Supt. — See Hardinsburg
Breckinridge County MS 600/6-8
PO Box 39 40144 270-756-3060
Jayme Knochel, prin. Fax 756-3061

Harrodsburg, Mercer, Pop. 8,110
Mercer County SD 2,200/PK-12
530 Perryville St 40330 859-733-7000
Dennis Davis, supt. Fax 733-7004
www.mercer.kyschools.us/
King MS 700/6-8
937 Moberly Rd 40330 859-733-7060
Terry Gordon, prin. Fax 733-7064
Mercer County ES 400/PK-2
741 Tapp Rd 40330 859-733-7040
Lee Ann Divine, prin. Fax 733-7044
Mercer County IS 400/3-5
1101 Moberly Rd 40330 859-733-7080
Dana Cobb, prin. Fax 733-7084

Hartford, Ohio, Pop. 2,636
Ohio County SD 4,200/PK-12
PO Box 70 42347 270-298-3249
Scott Lewis, supt. Fax 298-3886
www.ohio.kyschools.us/
Alexander ES 700/PK-6
1250 Oakwood Dr 42347 270-298-3462
Alicia Storm, prin. Fax 298-9354
Ohio County MS 600/7-8
1404 S Main St 42347 270-274-7893
Chip Schrader, prin. Fax 274-7320
Other Schools – See Beaver Dam, Centertown, Fordsville, Horse Branch

Hawesville, Hancock, Pop. 930
Hancock County SD 1,700/PK-12
83 State Route 3543 42348 270-927-6914
Kyle Estes, supt. Fax 927-6916
www.hancock.kyschools.us
South Hancock ES 300/PK-5
8631 State Route 69 42348 270-927-6762
Michael Swihart, prin. Fax 927-9400
Other Schools – See Lewisport

Hazard, Perry, Pop. 4,362
Hazard ISD 900/K-12
705 Main St 41701 606-436-3911
Sandra Johnson, supt. Fax 436-2742
www.hazard.kyschools.us
Eversole ES 300/K-4
601 Broadway St 41701 606-436-4721
James Hughes, prin. Fax 439-3726
Hazard MS 300/5-8
325 School St 41701 606-436-4421
Kevin Combs, prin. Fax 435-0407

Knott County SD
Supt. — See Hindman
Cordia S 200/K-12
6050 Lotts Creek Rd 41701 606-785-4457
Jonathan Mullins, prin. Fax 785-4669

Perry County SD 4,000/PK-12
315 Park Ave 41701 606-439-5814
Jonathan Jett, supt. Fax 439-2512
www.perry.kyschools.us/
East Perry ES 700/PK-8
301 Perry Circle Rd 41701 606-436-3423
Clifford McIntyre, prin. Fax 439-3353
Other Schools – See Ary, Buckhorn, Happy, Leatherwood, Viper

Hazel Green, Wolfe, Pop. 228
Wolfe County SD
Supt. — See Campton
Red River Valley ES 200/K-6
PO Box 219 41332 606-662-8252
Brian Creech, prin. Fax 662-8200

Hebron, Boone, Pop. 5,808
Boone County SD
Supt. — See Florence
Conner MS 1,100/6-8
3300 Cougar Path 41048 859-334-4410
James Brewer, prin. Fax 334-4435
Goodridge ES 800/PK-5
3330 Cougar Path 41048 859-334-4420
Jennifer Patrick, prin. Fax 334-4422
North Pointe ES 500/PK-5
875 N Bend Rd 41048 859-334-7000
Michael Shires, prin. Fax 334-7010
Thornwilde ES 600/PK-5
1760 Elmburn Ln 41048 859-586-3900
Pam Thamann, prin. Fax 586-0295

Henderson, Henderson, Pop. 28,141
Henderson County SD 7,600/PK-12
1805 2nd St 42420 270-831-5000
Marganna Stanley, supt. Fax 831-5009
www.henderson.kyschools.us
Bend Gate ES 500/PK-5
920 Bend Gate Rd 42420 270-831-5040
Deborah Harman, prin. Fax 831-5043
Cairo ES 300/K-5
10694 US Highway 41A 42420 270-533-1286
Brooke Shappell, prin. Fax 533-4827
East Heights ES 600/PK-5
1776 Adams Ln 42420 270-831-5070
Erika Odom, prin. Fax 831-5072
Henderson County North MS 900/6-8
1707 2nd St 42420 270-831-5060
Rebecca Johnson, prin. Fax 831-5064
Henderson County South MS 700/6-8
800 S Alves St 42420 270-831-5050
Ryan Reusch, prin. Fax 831-5058
Jefferson ES 400/K-5
315 Jackson St 42420 270-831-5090
Crissy Sandefur, prin. Fax 831-5091
Johnson Early Learning Center 400/PK-PK
631 N Green St 42420 270-854-0140
Ginger Ashby, admin. Fax 831-5199
Niagara ES 300/K-5
13043 State Route 136 E 42420 270-831-5142
Paige O'Nan, prin. Fax 826-0416
South Heights ES 500/K-5
1199 Madison St 42420 270-831-5081
Robin Carroll, prin. Fax 831-5082
Other Schools – See Corydon, Spottsville

Holy Name S 500/PK-8
628 2nd St 42420 270-827-3425
Scottie Koonce, prin. Fax 827-4027

Herndon, Christian
Christian County SD
Supt. — See Hopkinsville
South Christian ES 600/K-6
12340 Herndon Oak Grove Rd 42236 270-887-7350
Cherise Brummer, prin. Fax 271-9276

Hickman, Fulton, Pop. 2,360
Fulton County SD 600/PK-12
2780 Moscow Ave 42050 270-236-3923
Aaron Collins, supt. Fax 236-2184
www.fulton.kyschools.us
Fulton County Elementary MS 400/PK-8
2750 Moscow Ave 42050 270-236-3923
Julie Jackson, prin. Fax 236-9523

Highland Heights, Campbell, Pop. 6,806

Cornerstone Montessori S 100/PK-6
2048 Alexandria Pike, 859-491-9960

Hi Hat, Floyd
Floyd County SD
Supt. — See Prestonsburg
South Floyd ES K-8
299 Mt Raider Dr 41636 606-263-6175
Denise Isaac, prin. Fax 452-2155

Hillsboro, Fleming
Fleming County SD
Supt. — See Flemingsburg
Hillsboro ES 200/K-6
PO Box 8 41049 606-876-2251
Carol Thompson, prin. Fax 876-2478

Hindman, Knott, Pop. 768
Knott County SD 2,400/PK-12
1156 Hindman Byp 41822 606-785-3153
Kimberly King, supt. Fax 785-0800
www.knott.kyschools.us
Hindman ES 600/PK-8
PO Box 816 41822 606-785-5872
Wes Moore, prin. Fax 785-5860
Other Schools – See Emmalena, Hazard, Littcarr, Mousie, Topmost

Hiseville, Barren, Pop. 239
Barren County SD
Supt. — See Glasgow
Hiseville ES 300/PK-6
PO Box 29 42152 270-453-2611
Shari Alexander, prin. Fax 453-2612

Hitchins, Carter

Carter Christian Academy 50/PK-12
3547 State Highway 773 41146 606-475-1919
Nikki Rice, admin. Fax 475-0551

Hodgenville, Larue, Pop. 3,149
LaRue County SD 2,400/PK-12
208 College St 42748 270-358-4111
Sam Sanders, supt. Fax 358-3053
www.larue.kyschools.us
Hodgenville ES 600/PK-5
33 Eagle Ln 42748 270-358-3506
Eric Hughes, prin. Fax 358-8800
LaRue County MS 600/6-8
911 S Lincoln Blvd 42748 270-358-3196
Jason Detre, prin. Fax 358-3946
Lincoln ES 500/PK-5
2101 Lincoln Farm Rd 42748 270-358-4112
Karen Downs, prin. Fax 358-4142

Hopkinsville, Christian, Pop. 30,860
Christian County SD 6,800/K-12
PO Box 609 42241 270-887-7000
Mary Ann Gemmill, supt. Fax 887-1316
www.christian.kyschools.us
Christian County MS 600/7-8
215 Glass Ave 42240 270-887-7070
Kevin Crider, prin. Fax 887-1189
Freedom ES K-6
831 North Dr 42240 270-887-7150
Brooke Stinson, prin. Fax 887-1287
Hopkinsville MS 500/7-8
434 Koffman Dr 42240 270-887-7130
Wendy Duvall, prin. Fax 887-1234
Indian Hills ES 500/K-6
313 Blane Dr 42240 270-887-7230
Tonya Oakley, prin. Fax 887-1199
King ES 700/K-6
14405 Martin Lther King Way 42240 270-887-7310
Anita Hopson, prin. Fax 890-6014
Millbrooke ES 500/K-6
415 Millbrooke Dr 42240 270-887-7270
Anissa Hendricks, prin. Fax 887-1214
Sinking Fork ES 300/K-6
5005 Princeton Rd 42240 270-887-7330
Kathleen Carter, prin. Fax 887-1217
Other Schools – See Crofton, Herndon, Pembroke

Grace Episcopal Church K 50/PK-K
216 E 6th St 42240 270-885-8757
Rev. Alice Nichols, admin.
Heritage Christian Academy 500/PK-12
8349 Eagle Way 42240 270-885-2417
Linda Garris, hdmstr. Fax 885-0094
SS. Peter & Paul S 200/PK-8
902 E 9th St 42240 270-886-0172
Katie Wyatt, prin. Fax 887-9924
University Heights Academy 400/PK-12
1300 Academy Dr 42240 270-886-0254

Horse Branch, Ohio
Ohio County SD
Supt. — See Hartford
Horse Branch ES 200/PK-6
11980 US Highway 62 E 42349 270-274-4662
Tim Swift, prin. Fax 274-7866

Horse Cave, Hart, Pop. 2,268
Caverna ISD
Supt. — See Cave City
Caverna MS 200/6-8
2278 S Dixie St 42749 270-773-4665
Barry Nesbitt, prin. Fax 773-4668

Hart County SD
Supt. — See Munfordville
LeGrande S 200/PK-8
70 Legrande School Rd 42749 270-786-2746
Jerri Harper, prin. Fax 786-5747

Hoskinston, Leslie
Leslie County SD
Supt. — See Hyden
Stinnett ES 400/PK-8
12975 Highway 421 40844 606-374-3641
Teresa Wilder, prin. Fax 374-6655

Howardstown, Nelson

St. Ann S 50/K-8
7500 Howardstown Rd 40051 502-549-7310
Lois Cecil, prin.

Hustonville, Lincoln, Pop. 401
Lincoln County SD
Supt. — See Stanford
Hustonville ES 400/PK-5
PO Box 6 40437 606-346-3831
Gwen Lawson, prin. Fax 346-2201

Hyden, Leslie, Pop. 362
Leslie County SD 1,900/PK-12
PO Box 949 41749 606-672-2397
Linda Rains, supt. Fax 672-4224
www.leslie.kyschools.us
Mountain View ES 500/PK-8
170 Bear Trl 41749 606-672-2425
Heather Gay, prin. Fax 672-6545
Other Schools – See Hoskinston, Wooton, Yeaddiss

Independence, Kenton, Pop. 24,387
Kenton County SD
Supt. — See Fort Wright
Beech Grove ES 600/PK-5
1029 Bristow Rd 41051 859-371-1636
Michael Jacks, prin. Fax 371-7958
Kenton ES 700/K-5
11246 Madison Pike 41051 859-356-3781
Mary Beth Huss, prin. Fax 356-5397
Summit View Academy 800/PK-8
5006 Madison Pike 41051 859-363-4700
Lesley Smith, prin. Fax 363-4703
Twenhofel MS 800/6-8
11846 Taylor Mill Rd 41051 859-356-5559
Shannon Gross, prin. Fax 356-1137
White's Tower ES 500/PK-5
2977 Harris Pike 41051 859-356-9668
Anthony Procaccino, prin. Fax 356-6799

Community Christian Academy 300/PK-12
11875 Taylor Mill Rd 41051 859-356-7990
Tara Bates, prin. Fax 356-7991
St. Cecilia S 200/PK-8
5313 Madison Pike 41051 859-363-4314
Rob Detzel, prin. Fax 363-4315

Inez, Martin, Pop. 715
Martin County SD 2,300/PK-12
PO Box 366 41224 606-298-3572
Larry James, supt. Fax 298-3732
www.martin.kyschools.us
Eden ES 500/PK-5
179 Eden Ln 41224 606-298-3471
Jeremy Hall, prin. Fax 298-0901
Inez ES 300/K-5
5000 Elementary Dr 41224 606-298-3428
Michael Marcum, prin. Fax 298-0386

Other Schools – See Warfield

Irvine, Estill, Pop. 2,691
Estill County SD — 2,500/PK-12
PO Box 930 40336 — 606-723-2181
Jeff Saylor, supt. — Fax 723-6029
www.estill.kyschools.us/
Estill County MS — 500/6-8
51 Patriot Dr 40336 — 606-723-5136
Tim Burkhart, prin. — Fax 723-2041
Estill Springs ES — 400/K-2
314 Main St 40336 — 606-723-7703
Jessica Mullins, prin. — Fax 723-7683
South Irvine S — 300/PK-PK
1000 S Irvine Rd 40336 — 606-723-4700
Stephen Willis, admin. — Fax 723-6724
West Irvine IS 1 — 600/3-5
155 Riverview Rd 40336 — 606-723-4800
Charlotte Arvin, prin. — Fax 723-5350

Irvington, Breckinridge, Pop. 1,157
Breckinridge County SD
Supt. — See Hardinsburg
Irvington ES — 400/PK-5
1 Wildcat Way 40146 — 270-756-3050
Jon Miller, prin. — Fax 756-3051

Isonville, Elliott
Elliott County SD
Supt. — See Sandy Hook
Isonville ES — 100/K-6
5980 S KY 32 41149 — 606-738-8152
Dolly Fannin, prin. — Fax 738-8150

Jackson, Breathitt, Pop. 2,211
Breathitt County SD — 2,100/PK-12
PO Box 750 41339 — 606-666-2491
Phillip Watts, supt. — Fax 666-2493
www.breathitt.kyschools.us
L.B.J. ES — 700/PK-6
90 L B J Rd 41339 — 606-666-7181
William Noble, prin. — Fax 666-7778
Sebastian MS — 300/7-8
244 L B J Rd 41339 — 606-666-8894
Reggie Hamilton, prin. — Fax 666-5336
Other Schools – See Booneville, Lost Creek

Jackson ISD — 400/PK-12
940 Highland Ave 41339 — 606-666-4979
James Yount, supt. — Fax 666-4350
www.jacksonind.net
Jackson City S — 400/PK-12
940 Highland Ave 41339 — 606-666-5164
Jerry Allen, prin. — Fax 666-2555

Mt. Carmel S — 100/K-12
75 Mill Creek Lawson Rd 41339 — 606-666-5008
David Munson, head sch — Fax 666-4612

Jamestown, Russell, Pop. 1,780
Russell County SD — 3,100/PK-12
404 S Main St 42629 — 270-343-3191
Michael Ford, supt. — Fax 343-3072
www.russell.kyschools.us
Jamestown ES — 500/PK-5
342 S Main St 42629 — 270-343-3966
Diane Blankenship, prin. — Fax 343-3350
Other Schools – See Russell Springs

Jeffersontown, Jefferson, Pop. 25,990
Jefferson County SD
Supt. — See Louisville
Tully ES — 700/PK-5
3300 College Dr 40299 — 502-485-8338
Linda Dauenhauer, prin. — Fax 313-3543

Jenkins, Letcher, Pop. 2,198
Jenkins ISD — 600/PK-12
PO Box 74 41537 — 606-832-2183
Michael Genton, supt. — Fax 832-2181
www.jenkins.kyschools.us
Jenkins ES — 300/PK-5
11497 Highway 805 41537 — 606-832-2711
Stacy Collier, prin. — Fax 832-4191

Junction City, Boyle, Pop. 2,215
Boyle County SD
Supt. — See Danville
Junction City ES — 300/PK-5
250 School St 40440 — 859-936-7524
Pamela Shunk, prin. — Fax 854-0250

Keavy, Laurel
Laurel County SD
Supt. — See London
Keavy ES — 300/K-5
598 W Highway 312 40737 — 606-862-4672
Tonya Ford, prin. — Fax 862-4673

Kimper, Pike
Pike County SD
Supt. — See Pikeville
Kimper S — 200/K-8
8151 State Highway 194 E 41539 — 606-631-1509
David Griffith, prin.

Kona, Letcher
Letcher County SD
Supt. — See Whitesburg
Potter ES — 500/K-5
55 Kona Dr 41858 — 606-855-7544
Amber Stewart, prin. — Fax 855-4929

La Center, Ballard, Pop. 984
Ballard County SD
Supt. — See Barlow
Ballard County Preschool Headstart — 100/PK-PK
PO Box 120 42056 — 270-665-8400
DiAnna Corrigan, prin. — Fax 665-9168

La Grange, Oldham, Pop. 7,910
Oldham County SD
Supt. — See Crestwood
Buckner ES — 500/K-5
4307 Brown Blvd 40031 — 502-222-3712
Elizabeth Dant, prin. — Fax 222-3713
La Grange ES — 600/K-5
500 W Jefferson St 40031 — 502-222-9454
Heather Thomas, prin. — Fax 222-0685
Oldham County MS — 800/6-8
4305 Brown Blvd 40031 — 502-222-1451
Alissa Richards, prin. — Fax 222-5178
Oldham County Preschool — 300/PK-PK
4309 Brown Blvd 40031 — 502-222-3700
Jessica Kasten, prin. — Fax 222-6651

Lancaster, Garrard, Pop. 3,397
Garrard County SD — 2,700/PK-12
322 W Maple Ave 40444 — 859-792-3018
Corey Keith, supt. — Fax 792-4733
www.garrard.kyschools.us
Camp Robinson ES — 500/PK-5
279 N Camp Dick Rd 40444 — 859-792-6136
Scott Bolin, prin. — Fax 792-8908
Garrard MS — 600/6-8
304 W Maple Ave 40444 — 859-792-2108
Andrew Pickerill, prin. — Fax 792-9618
Lancaster ES — 500/PK-5
205 Lexington St 40444 — 859-792-3047
Tracie Bottoms, prin. — Fax 792-4855
Other Schools – See Paint Lick

Lawrenceburg, Anderson, Pop. 10,349
Anderson County SD — 3,900/PK-12
1160 Bypass N 40342 — 502-839-3406
Sheila Mitchell, supt. — Fax 839-2501
www.anderson.kyschools.us
Anderson County MS — 800/6-8
1 Mustang Trl 40342 — 502-839-9261
Jeanna Rose, prin. — Fax 839-2534
Saffell Street ES — 500/1-5
210 Saffell St 40342 — 502-839-3565
Todd Wooldridge, prin. — Fax 839-2539
Sparrow ECC — 300/PK-K
1154 Bypass N 40342 — 502-839-2504
Janice Meredith, prin. — Fax 839-2533
Turner ES — 600/K-5
1411 Fox Creek Rd 40342 — 502-839-2500
Wayne Reese, prin. — Fax 839-2520
Ward ES — 500/1-5
1150 Bypass N 40342 — 502-839-4236
Bobby Murphy, prin. — Fax 839-2506

Christian Academy of Lawrenceburg — 100/PK-12
126 N Main St 40342 — 502-839-9992
Sandra Bowman, prin. — Fax 839-3728

Leatherwood, Perry
Perry County SD
Supt. — See Hazard
Leatherwood S — 200/K-8
7777 KY Highway 699 41731 — 606-675-4431
Kenny Roark, prin. — Fax 675-6888

Lebanon, Marion, Pop. 5,374
Marion County SD — 3,200/PK-12
755 E Main St 40033 — 270-692-3721
Taylora Schlosser, supt. — Fax 692-1899
www.marion.kyschools.us
Calvary ES — 300/K-5
3345 Highway 208 40033 — 270-692-3676
Paul Terrell, prin. — Fax 692-0766
Glasscock ES — 400/PK-5
773 E Main St 40033 — 270-692-3223
Angie Akers, prin. — Fax 692-1895
Lebanon ES — 400/PK-5
420 W Main St 40033 — 270-692-3883
Donna Royse, prin. — Fax 692-6028
Marion County MS — 300/6-7
1155 Highway 327 40033 — 270-692-4578
Buffy Mann, prin. — Fax 692-1176
Other Schools – See Loretto

St. Augustine S — 100/PK-8
236 S Spalding Ave 40033 — 270-692-2063
Paul Terrell, prin. — Fax 692-6597

Lebanon Junction, Bullitt, Pop. 1,783
Bullitt County SD
Supt. — See Shepherdsville
Lebanon Junction ES — 500/PK-5
10920 S Preston Hwy 40150 — 502-869-2200
Daniel Mullins, prin. — Fax 833-3727

Leitchfield, Grayson, Pop. 6,624
Grayson County SD — 4,400/PK-12
PO Box 4009 42755 — 270-259-4011
Doug Robinson, supt. — Fax 259-4756
www.graysoncountyschools.com
Grayson County MS — 1,000/6-8
726 John Hill Taylor Dr 42754 — 270-259-4175
Gary Parker, prin. — Fax 259-5875
Lawler ES — 400/PK-5
100 Charlie Crain Ln 42754 — 270-259-9322
Alicia Brooks, prin. — Fax 259-0690
Wilkey ES — 600/PK-5
130 Wallace Ave 42754 — 270-259-4058
Jonathan Williams, prin. — Fax 259-6332
Other Schools – See Caneyville, Clarkson

St. Paul S, 1812 Saint Paul Rd 42754 — 50/PK-9
Kim Smith, prin. — 270-242-7483

Lewisburg, Logan, Pop. 797
Logan County SD
Supt. — See Russellville
Lewisburg S — 500/PK-8
750 Stacker St 42256 — 270-755-4823
Josh Matthews, prin. — Fax 755-4870

Lewisport, Hancock, Pop. 1,650
Hancock County SD
Supt. — See Hawesville
Hancock County MS — 400/6-8
100 State Route 271 S 42351 — 270-927-6712
Diane Hatchett, prin. — Fax 927-9895
North Hancock ES — 600/PK-5
330 Frank Lutrell Rd 42351 — 270-295-6330
Paul Poole, prin. — Fax 295-6332

Lexington, Fayette, Pop. 288,987
Fayette County SD — 40,600/PK-12
1126 Russell Cave Rd 40505 — 859-381-4100
Emmanuel Caulk, supt. — Fax 381-4303
www.fcps.net
Academy for Leadership at Millcreek ES — 500/PK-5
1212 Reva Ridge Way 40517 — 859-381-3527
Dr. Greg Ross, prin. — Fax 381-3529
Allen ES — 500/PK-5
1901 Appomattox Rd 40504 — 859-381-3456
Greg Williams, prin. — Fax 381-3459
Arlington ES — 400/PK-5
122 Arceme Ave 40505 — 859-381-3030
Kim Lippert, prin. — Fax 381-3027
Ashland ES — 400/K-5
195 N Ashland Ave 40502 — 859-381-3243
Ann Ingram, prin. — Fax 381-3252
Athens-Chilesburg ES — 800/K-5
930 Jouett Creek Dr 40509 — 859-381-4955
Peggy Henderson, prin. — Fax 381-4965
Beaumont MS — 1,100/6-8
2080 Georgian Way 40504 — 859-381-3094
Denis Beall, prin. — Fax 381-3109
Breckinridge ES — 600/PK-5
2101 Saint Mathilda Dr 40502 — 859-381-3273
Michael Price, prin. — Fax 381-3284
Brown ES — 400/PK-5
555 E Fifth St 40508 — 859-381-4990
Jay Jones, prin. — Fax 381-3166
Bryan Station MS — 600/6-8
1865 Wickland Dr 40505 — 859-381-3288
Robin Kirby, prin. — Fax 381-3292
Cardinal Valley ES — 700/PK-5
218 Mandalay Rd 40504 — 859-381-3340
Kevin Disney, prin. — Fax 381-3341
Cassidy ES — 700/K-5
1125 Tates Creek Rd 40502 — 859-381-3018
Rhonda Fister, prin. — Fax 381-3019
Clark MS — 900/6-8
3341 Clays Mill Rd 40503 — 859-381-3036
Jennifer Kendall, prin. — Fax 381-3037
Clays Mill ES — 600/K-5
2319 Clays Mill Rd 40503 — 859-381-3355
Grant Davis, prin. — Fax 381-3359
Coventry Oak ES — K-5
2441 Huntly Pl 40511 — 859-381-3195
Shamiah Ford, prin. — Fax 381-3221
Crawford MS — 400/6-8
1813 Charleston Dr 40505 — 859-381-3370
Mike Jones, prin. — Fax 381-3378
Deep Springs ES — 600/PK-5
1919 Brynell Dr 40505 — 859-381-3069
Adam Kirk, prin. — Fax 381-3364
Dixie Magnet ES — 600/PK-5
1940 Eastland Pkwy 40505 — 859-381-3116
Robin Steiner, prin. — Fax 381-3127
Fayette County Preschool Center — PK-PK
465 Springhill Dr 40504 — 859-381-4080
Garden Springs ES — 500/K-5
2151 Garden Springs Dr 40504 — 859-381-3388
Joey Sheroan, prin. — Fax 381-3400
Glendover ES — 600/K-5
710 Glendover Rd 40502 — 859-381-3403
Dr. Cathy Fine, prin. — Fax 381-3417
Harrison ES — 400/K-5
161 Bruce St 40507 — 859-381-3418
Tammie Franks, prin. — Fax 381-3286
Hayes MS — 1,100/6-8
260 Richardson Pl 40509 — 859-381-4920
Dave Hoskins, prin. — Fax 381-4937
Lansdowne ES — 700/K-5
336 Redding Rd 40517 — 859-381-3500
Jennifer Fish, prin. — Fax 381-3711
Leestown MS — 700/6-8
2010 Leestown Rd 40511 — 859-381-3181
Joe Gibson, prin. — Fax 381-3180
Lexington Traditional Magnet S — 600/6-8
350 N Limestone 40508 — 859-381-3192
Larry Caudill, prin. — Fax 381-3199
Liberty ES — 800/K-5
2585 Liberty Rd 40509 — 859-381-4979
Gerry Brooks, prin. — Fax 381-3468
Marks ES — 600/PK-5
3277 Pepperhill Rd 40502 — 859-381-3470
Rebecca Puckett, prin. — Fax 381-3472
Maxwell Spanish Immersion Magnet ES — 500/K-5
301 Woodland Ave 40508 — 859-381-3516
Robert Crawford, prin. — Fax 381-3517
Meadowthorpe ES — 500/PK-5
1710 N Forbes Rd 40511 — 859-381-3521
Stephanie Urbanek, prin. — Fax 381-3525
Morgan ES — PK-5
1150 Passage Mound Way 40509 — 859-381-3165
Sarah Woodford, prin. — Fax 381-3167
Morton MS — 800/6-8
1225 Tates Creek Rd 40502 — 859-381-3533
Ronda Runyon, prin. — Fax 381-3536
Northern ES — 500/PK-5
340 Rookwood Pkwy 40505 — 859-381-3541
Meredith Ramage, prin. — Fax 381-3966
Parks ES — 700/K-5
1251 Beaumont Centre Ln 40513 — 859-381-3132
Leslie Thomas, prin. — Fax 381-3146
Picadome ES — 500/PK-5
1642 Harrodsburg Rd 40504 — 859-381-3563
Jennifer Hutchison, prin. — Fax 381-3565

Russell Cave ES 300/K-5
3375 Russell Cave Rd 40511 859-381-3571
Amber Catron, prin. Fax 381-3575
Sandersville ES 700/K-5
3025 Sandersville Rd 40511 859-381-4980
Matt Marsh, prin. Fax 381-3712
School for Creative and Performing Arts 300/4-8
400 Lafayette Pkwy 40503 859-381-3332
Beth Randolph, prin. Fax 381-3334
Southern ES 700/PK-5
340 Wilson Downing Rd 40517 859-381-3589
Leigh Ann McLaughlin, prin. Fax 381-3590
Southern MS 600/6-8
400 Wilson Downing Rd 40517 859-381-3582
Kevin Payne, prin. Fax 381-3588
Squires ES 600/K-5
3337 Squire Oak Dr 40515 859-381-3002
Sabrina Adkins, prin. Fax 381-3005
Stonewall ES 600/K-5
3215 Cornwall Dr 40503 859-381-3079
Bill Gatliff, prin. Fax 381-3080
Tates Creek ES 600/PK-5
1113 Centre Pkwy 40517 859-381-3606
Carrie Paul, prin. Fax 381-3772
Tates Creek MS 1,000/6-8
1105 Centre Pkwy 40517 859-381-3052
Eric Thornsbury, prin. Fax 381-3053
Todd ES 500/PK-5
551 Parkside Dr 40505 859-381-3512
Freda Asher, prin. Fax 381-3720
Veterans Park ES 600/K-5
4351 Clearwater Way 40515 859-381-3161
Molly Dabney, prin. Fax 381-3151
Washington ES 400/PK-5
707 Howard St 40508 859-381-3263
Veda Stewart, prin. Fax 381-3267
Wellington ES 700/PK-5
3280 Keithshire Way 40503 859-381-3000
Julie Strange, prin. Fax 381-3222
Winburn MS 600/6-8
1060 Winburn Dr 40511 859-381-3967
Whitney Allison, prin. Fax 381-3971
Yates ES 500/PK-5
695 E New Circle Rd 40505 859-381-3613
Twanjua Jones, prin. Fax 381-3615

Christ the King S 500/PK-8
412 Cochran Rd 40502 859-266-5641
Paula Smith, prin. Fax 266-4547
Community Montessori S 100/PK-8
725 Stone Rd 40503 859-277-4805
Lexington Christian Academy 1,600/PK-12
450 W Reynolds Rd 40503 859-422-5700
Mark Sisk, hdmstr Fax 223-3769
Lexington Junior Academy 50/K-8
968 Lane Allen Rd 40504 859-278-0295
Lexington S 500/PK-8
1050 Lane Allen Rd 40504 859-278-0501
Charles Baldecchi, head sch Fax 278-8604
Mary Queen of Holy Rosary S 400/PK-8
605 Hill N Dale Rd 40503 859-277-3030
Becky Brown, prin. Fax 278-1784
Providence Montessori S 200/PK-8
1209 Texaco Rd 40508 859-255-7330
Sayre S 500/PK-12
194 N Limestone 40507 859-254-1361
Stephen Manella, head sch Fax 231-0508
Seton Catholic S 500/PK-8
1740 Summerhill Dr 40515 859-273-7827
Anna Martin, prin. Fax 273-0115
SS. Peter & Paul Regional S 400/PK-8
423 W Short St 40507 859-254-9257
Jeanne Miller, pres. Fax 254-9050
Summit Christian Academy 100/PK-8
2780 Clays Mill Rd 40503 859-277-0503
Linda Nelson, prin. Fax 472-1405
Trinity Christian Academy 400/PK-12
3900 Rapid Run Dr 40515 859-271-0079
David Kirkendall, head sch Fax 271-2134

Liberty, Casey, Pop. 2,153
Casey County SD 2,300/PK-12
1922 N US 127 42539 606-787-6941
Marion Sowders, supt. Fax 787-5231
www.casey.kyschools.us
Casey County MS 400/7-8
1673 E KY 70 42539 606-787-6769
Jeff Emerson, prin. Fax 787-5337
Jones Park ES 400/PK-6
6295 E KY 70 42539 606-787-1217
William Streeval, prin. Fax 787-0558
Liberty ES 400/K-6
75 College St 42539 606-787-6961
David McFadden, prin. Fax 787-2136
Walnut Hill ES 500/PK-6
2834 S US 127 42539 606-787-0045
Matthew Willoughby, prin. Fax 787-1546

Littcarr, Knott
Knott County SD
Supt. — See Hindman
Carr Creek ES 300/K-8
8596 Highway 160 S 41834 606-642-3833
Dwight Creech, prin. Fax 642-3786

Livermore, McLean, Pop. 1,348
McLean County SD
Supt. — See Calhoun
Livermore ES 300/K-5
PO Box 9 42352 270-278-2522
Carrie Ellis, prin. Fax 278-2363

London, Laurel, Pop. 7,883
Laurel County SD 9,200/PK-12
718 N Main St 40741 606-862-4600
Doug Bennett Ed.D., supt. Fax 862-4601
www.laurel.k12.ky.us
Bush ES 500/PK-5
1832 E Laurel Rd 40741 606-862-4618
Lisa Sibert, prin. Fax 862-4619
Camp Ground ES 300/K-5
6800 Barbourville Rd 40744 606-862-4625
Mark Wells, prin. Fax 862-4626
Cold Hill ES 300/K-5
4012 W Laurel Rd 40741 606-862-4632
Jason Faulkner, prin. Fax 862-4633
Colony ES 400/K-5
3656 Somerset Rd 40741 606-862-4639
Chad Davis, prin. Fax 862-4640
Johnson ES 300/K-5
1781 McWhorter Rd 40741 606-862-4664
Jamie Gilliam, prin. Fax 862-4665
London ES 600/K-5
600 N Main St 40741 606-862-4679
Mary Bowling, prin. Fax 862-4681
North Laurel MS 1,100/6-8
101 Johnson Rd 40741 606-862-4715
Steve Morris, prin. Fax 862-4717
South Laurel MS 1,100/6-8
223 S Laurel Rd 40744 606-862-4745
Jeffrey Reed, prin. Fax 862-4746
Sublimity ES 300/K-5
900 Sublimity School Rd 40744 606-862-4692
Kristina Thomas, prin. Fax 862-4693
Wyan-Pine Grove ES 400/K-5
2330 Keavy Rd 40744 606-862-5400
Jeff Durham, prin. Fax 862-5401
Other Schools – See Corbin, East Bernstadt, Keavy

Cornerstone Christian S 100/PK-8
PO Box 848 40743 606-862-0509
Joe Allen, prin. Fax 862-4902

Loretto, Marion, Pop. 707
Marion County SD
Supt. — See Lebanon
West Marion ES 500/PK-5
8175 Loretto Rd 40037 270-699-4320
Robby Peterson, prin. Fax 699-4323

Lost Creek, Breathitt
Breathitt County SD
Supt. — See Jackson
Roberts-Caney ES 300/PK-6
115 Red Skin Run 41348 606-666-7775
Jason Fugate, prin. Fax 666-8307

Riverside Christian S 50/K-12
114 Riverside School Rd 41348 606-666-2359
Meg Plummer, prin. Fax 666-5211

Louisa, Lawrence, Pop. 2,448
Lawrence County SD 2,500/PK-12
50 Bulldog Ln 41230 606-638-9671
Dr. Robbie Fletcher, supt. Fax 638-0128
www.lawrence.kyschools.us
Fallsburg ES 400/PK-8
6869 N Highway 3 41230 606-686-2351
Sara Bowen, prin. Fax 686-2355
Louisa East ES 500/2-5
235 E Powhaton St 41230 606-638-4574
Anna Prince, prin. Fax 638-9095
Louisa MS 400/6-8
9 Bulldog Ln 41230 606-638-4090
Joe Cecil, prin. Fax 638-4865
Louisa West ES 400/PK-1
201 S Boone St 41230 606-638-4726
Debbie DeLong, prin. Fax 638-4725
Other Schools – See Blaine

Louisville, Jefferson, Pop. 248,762
Bullitt County SD
Supt. — See Shepherdsville
Maryville ES 400/PK-5
4504 Summers Dr 40229 502-869-2400
Ruth Esterle, prin. Fax 955-5753
Overdale ES 600/PK-5
651 Overdale Dr 40229 502-869-2800
Dana Brown, prin. Fax 957-2419

Jefferson County SD 96,700/PK-12
PO Box 34020 40232 502-485-3011
Dr. Martin Pollio, supt. Fax 485-3991
www.jefferson.kyschools.us
Atkinson Academy 400/PK-5
2811 Duncan St 40212 502-485-8203
Stephanie Nutter, prin. Fax 313-3408
Auburndale ES 600/PK-5
5749 New Cut Rd 40214 502-485-8204
KaTonya Parker, prin. Fax 313-3409
Audubon Traditional ES 600/K-5
1051 Hess Ln 40217 502-485-8205
Tiffany Marshall, prin. Fax 313-3410
Barret Traditional MS 600/6-8
2561 Grinstead Dr 40206 502-485-8207
Tom Wortham, prin. Fax 313-3412
Bates ES 600/PK-5
7601 Bardstown Rd 40291 502-485-8208
Alecia Dunn, prin. Fax 313-3413
Blake ES 500/PK-5
3801 Bonaventure Blvd 40219 502-485-8210
Susan Glenn, prin. Fax 313-3415
Bloom ES 500/K-5
1627 Lucia Ave 40204 502-485-8211
Jack Jacobs, prin. Fax 313-3417
Blue Lick ES 500/PK-5
9801 Blue Lick Rd 40229 502-485-8212
Amy Uhlman, prin. Fax 313-3418
Bowen ES 700/K-5
1601 Roosevelt Ave 40242 502-485-8213
Lisa Wathen, prin. Fax 313-3420
Brandeis ES 600/PK-5
2817 W Kentucky St 40211 502-485-8214
Shervita West, prin. Fax 313-3421
Breckinridge-Franklin ES 400/K-5
1351 Payne St 40206 502-485-8215
Cathy Bosemer, prin. Fax 313-3422
Brown S 700/K-12
546 S 1st St 40202 502-485-8216
Angela Parsons, prin. Fax 313-3404
Byck ES 600/PK-5
2328 Cedar St 40212 502-485-8221
Carla Kolodey, prin. Fax 313-3426
Camp Taylor ES 500/PK-5
1446 Belmar Dr 40213 502-485-8222
John Shanton, prin. Fax 313-3427
Cane Run ES 400/PK-5
3951 Cane Run Rd 40211 502-485-8223
Kim Coslow, prin. Fax 313-3428
Carrithers MS 500/6-8
4320 Billtown Rd 40299 502-485-8224
Marcela Williams, prin. Fax 313-3429
Carter Traditional ES 600/K-5
3600 Bohne Ave 40211 502-485-8225
Jamie Wyman, prin. Fax 313-3447
Chancey ES 700/K-5
4301 Murphy Ln 40241 502-485-8387
Ronda Cosby, prin. Fax 313-3432
Chenoweth ES 500/PK-5
3622 Brownsboro Rd 40207 502-485-8227
Laketa Clay, prin. Fax 313-3433
Cochrane ES 500/PK-5
2511 Tregaron Ave 40299 502-485-8231
Jason Hobbs, prin. Fax 313-3436
Cochran ES 400/PK-5
500 W Gaulbert Ave 40208 502-485-8230
Tim Foster, prin. Fax 313-3435
Coleridge-Taylor Montessori ES 600/PK-5
1115 W Chestnut St 40203 502-485-8232
Meg Thomas, prin. Fax 313-3437
Conway MS 900/6-8
6300 Terry Rd 40258 502-485-8233
Gregory Fehr, prin. Fax 313-3438
Crums Lane ES 500/PK-5
3212 Crums Ln 40216 502-485-8236
Anna Byrd, prin. Fax 313-3441
Dixie ES 400/PK-5
10201 Casalanda Dr 40272 502-485-8238
Stephen Howard, prin. Fax 313-3444
Dunn ES 600/K-5
2010 Rudy Ln 40207 502-485-8240
Dr. Tracy Barber, prin. Fax 313-3446
Eisenhower ES 600/PK-5
5300 Jessamine Ln 40258 502-485-8244
Julie Cummings, prin. Fax 313-3450
Engelhard ES 400/PK-5
1004 S 1st St 40203 502-485-8246
Ryan McCoy, prin. Fax 313-3451
Farmer ES 800/PK-5
6405 Gellhaus Ln 40299 502-485-8625
Shannon Conlon, prin. Fax 313-3454
Farnsley MS 1,200/6-8
3400 Lees Ln 40216 502-485-8242
Linda Hudson, prin. Fax 313-3456
Field ES 400/PK-5
120 Sacred Heart Ln 40206 502-485-8252
Deborah Rivera, prin. Fax 485-8576
Foster Traditional Academy 600/K-5
1401 S 41st St 40211 502-485-8253
Letisha Young, prin. Fax 313-3460
Frayser ES 400/PK-5
1230 Larchmont Ave 40215 502-485-8255
Sarah Carmichael-Miller, prin. Fax 313-3461
Frost Sixth Grade Academy 200/6-6
4601 Valley Station Rd 40272 502-485-8256
Faith Stroud, prin. Fax 313-3462
Gilmore Lane ES 300/PK-5
1281 Gilmore Ln 40213 502-485-8257
Samuel Cowan, prin. Fax 313-3464
Goldsmith ES 600/PK-5
3520 Goldsmith Ln 40220 502-485-8258
Jeremy Renner, prin. Fax 313-3465
Greathouse/Shryock Traditional ES 600/K-5
2700 Browns Ln 40220 502-485-8259
Karla Davis, prin. Fax 313-3466
Greenwood ES 600/PK-5
5801 Greenwood Rd 40258 502-485-8260
Dylan Owens, prin. Fax 313-3467
Gutermuth ES 400/PK-5
1500 Sanders Ln 40216 502-485-8261
Laura Mullaney, prin. Fax 313-3468
Hartstern ES 500/PK-5
5200 Morningside Way 40219 502-485-8262
Duan Wright, prin. Fax 313-3469
Hawthorne ES 500/PK-5
2301 Clarendon Ave 40205 502-485-8263
Jessica Rosenthal, prin. Fax 313-3470
Hazelwood ES 500/PK-5
1325 Bluegrass Ave 40215 502-485-8264
Tom Peterson, prin. Fax 313-3471
Highland MS 1,200/6-8
1700 Norris Pl 40205 502-485-8266
Thomas Aberli, prin. Fax 313-3472
Indian Trail ES 400/PK-5
3709 E Indian Trl 40213 502-485-8268
Joseph Wood, prin. Fax 313-3474
Jacob ES 700/PK-5
3701 E Wheatmore Dr 40215 502-485-8271
Michael Terry, prin. Fax 313-3476
Jefferson County Traditional MS 900/6-8
1418 Morton Ave 40204 502-485-8272
Teri Reed, prin. Fax 313-3477
Jefferson MS 900/6-8
1501 Rangeland Rd 40219 502-485-8273
Kimberly Gregory, prin. Fax 313-3541
Jeffersontown ES 800/PK-5
3610 Cedarwood Way 40299 502-485-8274
Brooke Schilling, prin. Fax 313-3479
Johnsontown Road ES 400/PK-5
7201 Johnsontown Rd 40272 502-485-8278
Malinda Dutkowski, prin. Fax 313-3482

Johnson Traditional MS 900/6-8
2509 Wilson Ave 40210 502-485-8277
Beverly Johnson, prin. Fax 313-3481
Kammerer MS 1,100/6-8
7315 Wesboro Rd 40222 502-485-8279
David Armour, prin. Fax 313-3483
Kennedy Montessori ES 600/PK-5
3800 Gibson Ln 40211 502-485-8280
Kimberly Jones, prin. Fax 313-3486
Kenwood ES 600/PK-5
7420 Justan Ave 40214 502-485-8283
Jill Handley, prin. Fax 313-3487
Kerrick ES 400/PK-5
2210 Upper Hunters Trce 40216 502-485-8284
LaWanda Hazard-Irvin, prin. Fax 313-3488
King ES 500/PK-5
4325 Vermont Ave 40211 502-485-8285
Stephanie White, prin. Fax 313-3489
Klondike Lane ES 600/PK-5
3807 Klondike Ln 40218 502-485-8286
Mark Boyer, prin. Fax 313-3490
Knight MS 400/6-8
9803 Blue Lick Rd 40229 502-485-8287
Catherine Gibbs, prin. Fax 313-3491
Lassiter MS 900/6-8
8200 Candleworth Dr 40214 502-485-8288
Jonathan Cesler, prin. Fax 313-3492
Laukhuf ES 500/PK-5
5100 Capewood Dr 40229 502-485-8289
Michele Yates, prin. Fax 313-3495
Lincoln ES 500/PK-5
930 E Main St 40206 502-485-8291
Susan French-Epps, prin. Fax 313-3496
Lowe ES 600/K-5
210 Oxfordshire Ln 40222 502-485-8293
Austin Allain, prin. Fax 313-3497
Luhr ES 500/PK-5
6900 Fegenbush Ln 40228 502-485-8295
Lynley Schroering, prin. Fax 313-3498
Maupin ES 500/PK-5
1312 Catalpa St 40211 502-485-8310
Maria Holmes, prin. Fax 313-3500
McFerran Preparatory Academy 900/PK-5
1900 S 7th St 40208 502-485-8297
Desiree Bush, prin. Fax 313-3501
Meyzeek MS 1,100/6-8
828 S Jackson St 40203 502-485-8299
Chris Burba, prin. Fax 313-3503
Mill Creek ES 500/PK-5
3816 Dixie Hwy 40216 502-485-8301
Michelle Pennix, prin. Fax 313-3505
Minors Lane ES 400/PK-5
8510 Minor Ln 40219 502-485-8303
Erika Walker, prin. Fax 313-3507
Newburg MS 1,000/6-8
4901 Exeter Ave 40218 502-485-8306
Nicole Adell, prin. Fax 313-3509
Noe MS 1,300/6-8
121 W Lee St 40208 502-485-8307
Jennifer Cave, prin. Fax 313-3511
Okolona ES 300/PK-5
7606 Preston Hwy 40219 502-485-8309
Karen Stearman, prin. Fax 313-3513
Olmsted Academy North 600/6-8
4530 Bellevue Ave 40215 502-485-8331
Ryan Rodosky, prin. Fax 313-3514
Olmsted Academy South 700/6-8
5650 Southern Pkwy 40214 502-485-8270
Angela Allen, prin. Fax 313-3515
Orman ECC 200/PK-PK
900 S Floyd St 40203 502-485-7008
Darrell White, prin. Fax 485-6910
Portland ES 300/PK-5
3410 Northwestern Pkwy 40212 502-485-8313
Angela Hosch, prin. Fax 313-3517
Price ES 500/PK-5
5001 Garden Green Way 40218 502-485-8315
Shuvon Ray, prin. Fax 313-3519
Ramsey MS 900/6-8
6409 Gellhaus Ln 40299 502-485-8391
Darryl Farmer, prin. Fax 313-3520
Rangeland ES 500/PK-5
1701 Rangeland Rd 40219 502-485-8317
Mashelle Kiggins, prin. Fax 313-3521
Roosevelt/Perry ES 400/PK-5
1615 W Broadway 40203 502-485-8319
Nichole Marshall, prin. Fax 313-3406
Rutherford ES 600/PK-5
301 Southland Blvd 40214 502-485-8320
Kenya Natsis, prin. Fax 313-3525
St. Matthew's ES 600/K-5
601 Browns Ln 40207 502-485-8321
Scottie Collier, prin. Fax 313-3537
Sanders ES 500/PK-5
8408 Terry Rd 40258 502-485-8322
Pam Cooper, prin. Fax 313-3526
Schaffner Traditional ES 600/PK-5
2701 Crums Ln 40216 502-485-8217
Zachary Eckles, prin. Fax 313-3527
Semple ES 500/PK-5
724 Denmark St 40215 502-485-8324
Danielle Randle, prin. Fax 313-3528
Shacklette ES 400/PK-5
5310 Mercury Dr 40258 502-485-8325
Kevin Garner, prin. Fax 313-3530
Shelby ES 700/K-5
735 Ziegler St 40217 502-485-8327
Kim Goff, prin. Fax 313-3532
Slaughter ES 400/PK-5
3805 Fern Valley Rd 40219 502-485-8328
Kathy Pendleton, prin. Fax 313-3533
Smyrna ES 600/PK-5
6401 Outer Loop 40228 502-485-8329
Dr. Tiffany Stith, prin. Fax 313-3534
Stopher ES 800/PK-5
14417 Aiken Rd 40245 502-485-8281
Dr. Brigitte Owens, prin. Fax 313-3539

Trunnell ES 600/PK-5
7609 Saint Andrews Church 40214 502-485-8337
Stephanie Smith, prin. Fax 313-3542
Unseld ECC 400/PK-PK
5216 Ilex Ave 40213 502-968-7222
Hollie Smith, prin. Fax 485-8989
Watson Lane ES 400/PK-5
7201 Watson Ln 40272 502-485-8341
Sean Russell, prin. Fax 313-3403
Watterson ES 600/PK-5
3900 Breckenridge Ln 40218 502-485-8342
Carol Ferry, prin. Fax 313-3548
Wellington ES 500/PK-5
4800 Kaufman Ln 40216 502-485-8343
Brandi Carney, prin. Fax 313-3549
Western MS 500/6-8
2201 W Main St 40212 502-485-8345
Kymberly Rice, prin. Fax 313-3551
Westport MS 900/6-8
8100 Westport Rd 40222 502-485-8346
Jodie Zeller, prin. Fax 313-3552
Wheatley ES 400/PK-5
1107 S 17th St 40210 502-485-8348
William Bunton, prin. Fax 313-3554
Wheeler ES 700/PK-5
5700 Cynthia Dr 40291 502-485-8349
Penny Espinosa, prin. Fax 313-3555
Wilder ES 600/K-5
1913 Herr Ln 40222 502-485-8350
Bill Perkins, prin. Fax 313-3556
Wilkerson ES 500/PK-5
5601 Johnsontown Rd 40272 502-485-8351
Traci Durbin, prin. Fax 313-3557
Wilt ES 500/PK-5
6700 Price Lane Rd 40229 502-485-8353
Ben Pinnick, prin. Fax 313-3558
Young ES 500/PK-5
3526 W Muhammad Ali Blvd 40212 502-485-8354
Erica Lawrence, prin. Fax 313-3559
Other Schools – See Fairdale, Fern Creek, Jeffersontown, Lyndon, Middletown, Prospect, Valley Station

---

Ascension S 200/PK-8
4600 Lynnbrook Dr 40220 502-451-2535
Terry Mullaney, prin. Fax 451-2535
Beth Haven Christian S 200/PK-12
5515 Johnsontown Rd 40272 502-937-3516
John Baker, head sch Fax 937-3364
Chance S 200/PK-5
4200 Lime Kiln Ln 40222 502-425-6904
Christian Academy of Louisville 300/PK-5
3110 Rock Creek Dr 40207 502-897-3372
Krystal Morrow, prin. Fax 897-3207
Christian Academy of Louisville 1,700/PK-12
700 S English Station Rd 40245 502-244-3225
Tim Greener, supt. Fax 244-1824
Christian Academy of Louisville 200/PK-8
8307 St Andrews Church Rd 40258 502-447-6500
Anna Carson, prin. Fax 447-6508
Covenant Classical Academy 50/K-12
13902 Factory Ln 40245 502-243-0404
R. Lance Harris, hdmstr.
Evangel Christian S 200/K-12
5400 Minor Ln 40219 502-968-7744
Joe Washington, prin. Fax 400-1906
Highlands Latin S 600/K-12
10901 Shelbyville Rd 40243 502-742-4789
Holy Angels Academy 100/K-12
12201 Old Henry Rd 40223 502-254-9440
Joseph Norton, head sch
Holy Family Preschool 200/PK-PK
3934 Poplar Level Rd 40213 502-458-4531
Janice Northcutt, dir. Fax 456-9198
Holy Spirit S 400/PK-8
322 Cannons Ln 40206 502-893-7700
Doris Swenson, prin. Fax 893-8078
Holy Trinity S 700/PK-8
423 Cherrywood Rd 40207 502-897-2785
Jack Richards, prin. Fax 896-0990
Immaculata Classical Academy PK-12
6010 Preston Hwy 40219 502-365-3545
Justin Fout, prin.
John Paul II Academy 300/PK-8
3525 Goldsmith Ln 40220 502-452-1712
Lynn Wilt, prin. Fax 451-2462
Kentucky Country Day S 1,000/PK-12
4100 Springdale Rd 40241 502-423-0440
Brad Lyman, head sch Fax 423-0445
Landmark Christian Academy 200/K-12
6502 Johnsontown Rd 40272 502-933-3300
Louisville Collegiate S 700/PK-12
2427 Glenmary Ave 40204 502-479-0340
Dr. James Calleroz White, head sch Fax 454-8549
Louisville Jewish Day S 50/PK-8
1622 Almara Cir 40205 502-494-3774
Louisville Jr. Academy 50/PK-12
2988 Newburg Rd 40205 502-452-2965
David Matthews, prin. Fax 742-0829
Minnis Junior Academy 50/PK-8
PO Box 1478 40201 502-774-2108
Klossmeryl C. Francois M.Ed., prin. Fax 515-2464
Montessori S of Louisville 200/PK-8
10263 Champion Farms Dr 40241 502-640-8585
Jennifer Cattell, head sch Fax 413-5699
Nativity Academy at St. Boniface 100/6-8
529 E Liberty St 40202 502-855-3300
Thomas Kallay, prin. Fax 562-2192
Notre Dame Academy 400/PK-8
1927 Lewiston Dr 40216 502-447-3155
Elaine Bachman, prin. Fax 447-5515
Our Lady of Lourdes S 500/PK-8
510 Breckenridge Ln 40207 502-895-5122
Jennifer Barz, prin. Fax 893-5051
Our Savior Lutheran S 200/PK-8
8307 Nottingham Pkwy 40222 502-426-0864
Wesley Wrucke, prin. Fax 394-0648

Portland Christian S 200/PK-12
8509 Westport Rd 40242 502-429-3727
Jodell Seay, dir. Fax 326-2682
Sacred Heart Model S 400/PK-8
3107 Lexington Rd 40206 502-896-3931
Dr. Michael Bratcher, prin. Fax 896-3932
Sacred Heart Preschool 200/PK-K
3105 Lexington Rd 40206 502-896-3941
Lisa Houghlin, dir. Fax 896-3966
Sacred Heart S for the Arts 200/K-12
3105 Lexington Rd 40206 502-897-1816
Dr. Anna Jo Paul, dir. Fax 896-3927
St. Agnes S 400/PK-8
1800 Newburg Rd 40205 502-458-2850
Julianna Daly, prin. Fax 459-5215
St. Albert the Great S 700/PK-8
1395 Girard Dr 40222 502-425-1804
Ellen Martin, prin. Fax 394-9896
St. Andrew Academy 200/PK-8
7724 Columbine Dr 40258 502-935-4578
Nicole Rouse, prin. Fax 933-2204
St. Athanasius S 500/PK-8
5915 Outer Loop 40219 502-969-2345
Marjorie Reece, prin. Fax 966-8974
St. Bernard S 500/PK-8
7500 Tangelo Dr 40228 502-239-5178
Fred Klausing, prin. Fax 239-9025
St. Edward S 400/PK-8
9610 Sue Helen Dr 40299 502-267-6633
David Bennett, prin. Fax 267-4474
St. Francis of Assisi S 300/K-8
1938 Alfresco Pl 40205 502-459-3088
Steve Frommeyer, prin. Fax 456-9462
St. Francis S 100/PK-12
233 W Broadway 40202 502-736-1000
Alexandra Thurstone, head sch Fax 736-1049
St. Gabriel the Archangel S 800/PK-8
5503 Bardstown Rd 40291 502-239-5535
Pam Huelsman, prin. Fax 231-1464
St. James S 200/PK-8
1818 Edenside Ave 40204 502-454-0330
Jennifer Zimmerman, prin. Fax 454-0330
St. Lawrence Child Enrichment Center PK-PK
1925 Lewiston Dr 40216 502-449-4021
Suzanne Stewart, dir.
St. Leonard S 200/PK-8
440 Zorn Ave 40206 502-897-5265
Mary Parola, prin. Fax 897-5125
St. Margaret Mary S 800/K-8
7813 Shelbyville Rd 40222 502-426-2635
Wendy Sims, prin. Fax 426-1504
St. Martha S 500/PK-8
2825 Klondike Ln 40218 502-491-3171
Michael Bickett, prin. Fax 495-6107
St. Michael S 600/PK-8
3703 Stone Lakes Dr 40299 502-267-6155
Stacy Tackett, prin. Fax 267-1652
St. Nicholas Academy 400/PK-8
5501 New Cut Rd 40214 502-368-8506
Kathy DeLozier, prin. Fax 380-5453
St. Patrick S 600/PK-8
1000 N Beckley Station Rd 40245 502-244-7083
Dr. Nathan Sturtzel, prin. Fax 719-0369
St. Paul S 200/PK-8
6901 Dixie Hwy 40258 502-935-5511
Jennifer Burba, prin. Fax 935-5596
St. Raphael the Archangel S 400/PK-8
2131 Lancashire Ave 40205 502-456-1541
Jill Tabor, prin. Fax 451-3632
St. Rita S 200/PK-8
8709 Preston Hwy 40219 502-969-7067
Neil Huleswede, prin. Fax 968-0510
St. Stephen Martyr S 300/PK-8
2931 Pindell Ave 40217 502-635-7141
Bridget Britt, prin. Fax 635-1576
Sayers Classical Academy 200/K-12
PO Box 18001 40261 502-231-4655
Valiant Christian Academy 100/PK-12
5627 New Cut Rd 40214 502-368-0080
Kristine Salvo, admin. Fax 361-5179
Valor Traditional Academy 100/K-12
11501 Schlatter Rd 40291 502-239-3345
Walden S 200/K-12
4238 Westport Rd 40207 502-893-0433
Alison Tyler, head sch Fax 895-8668
Waldorf S of Louisville 100/PK-8
8005 New La Grange Rd 40222 502-327-0122
Whitefield Academy 700/PK-12
7711 Fegenbush Ln 40228 502-239-2509
Gary Mounce, head sch Fax 239-3144

Lowes, Graves, Pop. 97
Graves County SD
Supt. — See Mayfield
Lowes ES 300/PK-6
6775 State Route 440, 270-674-4840
Ryan Marchetti, prin. Fax 674-5189

Lucas, Barren
Barren County SD
Supt. — See Glasgow
Tracy ES 300/PK-6
2477 Austin Tracy Rd 42156 270-646-2236
Joey Bunch, prin. Fax 646-2291

Ludlow, Kenton, Pop. 4,360
Ludlow ISD 900/PK-12
525 Elm St 41016 859-261-8210
Mike Borchers, supt. Fax 291-6811
www.ludlow.kyschools.us/
Goetz ES 500/PK-6
512 Oak St 41016 859-261-2100
Jason Steffen, prin. Fax 655-8793

Lyndon, Jefferson, Pop. 10,751
Jefferson County SD
Supt. — See Louisville

Norton ES 700/K-5
8101 Brownsboro Rd 40241 502-485-8308
Tim Hagan, prin. Fax 313-3512
Taylor ES 500/K-5
9620 Westport Rd 40241 502-485-8336
Dwayne Roberts, prin. Fax 313-3561

Mc Daniels, Breckinridge
Breckinridge County SD
Supt. — See Hardinsburg
Johnson ES 200/K-5
PO Box 51 40152 270-756-3070
Michael Broadbent, prin. Fax 756-3071

Mc Kee, Jackson, Pop. 793
Jackson County SD 2,200/PK-12
3331 Hwy 421 S 40447 606-287-7181
Mike Smith, supt. Fax 287-8469
www.jackson.kyschools.us
Jackson County MS 500/6-8
PO Box 1329 40447 606-287-8351
Dr. Brad Kerby, prin. Fax 287-8360
Mc Kee ES 400/PK-5
PO Box 429 40447 606-287-7157
Tim Truett, prin. Fax 287-4775
Other Schools – See Sandgap, Tyner

Mc Kinney, Lincoln
Lincoln County SD
Supt. — See Stanford
Mc Kinney ES 200/PK-5
PO Box 67 40448 606-346-4741
Jeff Craiger, prin. Fax 346-9905

Madisonville, Hopkins, Pop. 19,131
Hopkins County SD 7,000/PK-12
320 S Seminary St 42431 270-825-6000
Deanna D. Ashby, supt. Fax 825-6072
www.hopkins.kyschools.us
Browning Springs MS 400/6-8
357 W Arch St 42431 270-825-6006
Jason Clark, prin. Fax 825-6009
Grapevine ES 300/K-5
1150 Hayes Ave 42431 270-825-6012
Ann Elkins, prin. Fax 825-6026
Madison MS 600/6-8
510 Brown Rd 42431 270-825-6160
Timothy Roy, prin. Fax 825-6016
Pride Avenue ES 400/K-5
861 Pride Ave 42431 270-825-6030
Kristy Saint, prin. Fax 825-6031
Stuart ES 500/K-5
1710 Anton Rd 42431 270-825-6033
Brandon McClain, prin. Fax 825-6120
West Broadway ES 500/PK-5
127 W Broadway St 42431 270-825-6036
Amy Smith, prin. Fax 825-6025
Other Schools – See Earlington, Hanson, Nebo, Nortonville

Christ the King S 100/PK-8
1500 Kingsway Dr 42431 270-821-8271
Beth Herrmann, prin. Fax 825-9394

Manchester, Clay, Pop. 1,245
Clay County SD 3,400/PK-12
128 Richmond Rd 40962 606-598-2168
William Sexton, supt. Fax 598-7829
www.clay.kyschools.us
Burning Springs ES 300/PK-6
9847 N Highway 421 40962 606-598-3138
Kendra Hooker, prin. Fax 598-0079
Clay County MS 500/7-8
239 Richmond Rd 40962 606-598-1810
Steven Burchfield, prin. Fax 598-1230
Goose Rock ES 200/PK-6
364 Highway 1524 40962 606-598-3740
Jerry Combs, prin. Fax 598-3758
Hacker ES 300/PK-6
84 Hooker Rd 40962 606-598-3338
Todd McDaniel, prin. Fax 598-7119
Manchester ES 500/PK-6
1908 N Highway 421 40962 606-598-3444
Dwight Harris, prin. Fax 598-8786
Paces Creek ES 300/PK-6
1983 S Highway 421 40962 606-598-6333
James Gray, prin. Fax 598-0359
Other Schools – See Oneida

Appalachian Christian Academy 50/K-8
168 SDA School Rd 40962 606-598-5427
Carol Peasley, prin. Fax 599-1187

Marion, Crittenden, Pop. 3,006
Crittenden County SD 1,200/K-12
601 W Elm St 42064 270-965-3525
Vince Clark, supt. Fax 965-9064
www.crittenden.kyschools.us/
Crittenden County ES 600/K-5
120 Autumn Ln 42064 270-965-2244
Jenni Gilkey, prin. Fax 965-4113
Crittenden County MS 300/6-8
519 W Gum St 42064 270-965-5221
Tom Radivonyk, prin. Fax 965-5082

Martin, Floyd, Pop. 630
Floyd County SD
Supt. — See Prestonsburg
May Valley ES 400/K-5
481 Stephens Branch Rd 41649 606-285-0883
Kathy Shepherd, prin. Fax 285-0884

Mayfield, Graves, Pop. 9,719
Graves County SD 4,300/PK-12
2290 State Route 121 N 42066 270-328-2656
Kim Dublin, supt. Fax 674-2656
www.graves.kyschools.us
Central ES 400/PK-6
2262 State Route 121 N 42066 270-328-4900
Tiffany Williams, prin. Fax 247-4626
Farmington ES 300/PK-6
7730 State Route 121 S 42066 270-674-4830
Melissa Paul, prin. Fax 345-2163
Graves County MS 800/7-8
625 Jimtown Rd 42066 270-328-4890
Jonathan Miller, prin. Fax 251-3693
Sedalia ES 300/PK-6
5252 State Route 97 42066 270-674-4850
Robert Braden, prin. Fax 328-8266
Other Schools – See Fancy Farm, Lowes, Symsonia, Wingo

Mayfield ISD 1,600/PK-12
914 E College St 42066 270-247-3868
Joe Henderson, supt. Fax 247-3854
www.mayfield.kyschools.us
Mayfield ES 800/PK-4
1004 Backusburg Rd 42066 270-247-8696
Heather Dublin, prin. Fax 247-0017
Mayfield MS 300/5-8
112 W College St 42066 270-247-7521
Kim Reed, prin. Fax 247-8297

Northside Baptist Christian S 100/PK-12
711 N 12th St 42066 270-247-0516
Jenny Page, prin. Fax 247-7125

Maysville, Mason, Pop. 8,803
Mason County SD 2,800/PK-12
PO Box 130 41056 606-564-5563
Rick Ross, supt. Fax 564-5392
www.masoncoschools.com
Mason County IS 600/3-5
720 Clarks Run Rd 41056 606-759-2000
Robbie Kimble, prin. Fax 759-2001
Mason County MS 600/6-8
420 Chenault Dr 41056 606-564-6748
Justin Moore, prin. Fax 564-5958
Straub ES 700/PK-2
387 Chenault Dr 41056 606-564-9047
Robert Moore, prin. Fax 564-3345

St. Patrick S 300/PK-12
318 Limestone St 41056 606-564-5949
Wesley Cooper, prin. Fax 564-8795

Melbourne, Campbell, Pop. 401

St. Philip S 100/K-8
1400 Mary Ingles Hwy 41059 859-441-3423
Kimberly Brewer, prin. Fax 441-2611

Middlesboro, Bell, Pop. 10,068
Bell County SD
Supt. — See Pineville
Yellow Creek School Center 500/PK-8
4840 W Cumberland Ave 40965 606-248-1794
Barbara Warren, prin. Fax 248-6399

Middlesboro ISD 1,300/PK-12
PO Box 959 40965 606-242-8800
Steve Martin, supt. Fax 242-8805
www.mboro.kyschools.us
Middlesboro ES 400/PK-4
3400 Cumberland Ave 40965 606-242-8860
Randy Rose Ed.D., prin. Fax 242-8865
Middlesboro MS 400/5-8
4400 W Cumberland Ave 40965 606-242-8880
William Jones, prin. Fax 242-8885

Middletown, Jefferson, Pop. 7,092
Jefferson County SD
Supt. — See Louisville
Crosby MS 1,400/6-8
303 Gatehouse Ln 40243 502-485-8235
Michael Kelly, prin. Fax 313-3440
Hite ES 500/PK-5
12408 Old Shelbyville Rd 40243 502-485-8267
Sheri Barnett, prin. Fax 313-3473
Middletown ES 600/PK-5
218 N Madison Ave 40243 502-485-8300
Justin Matson, prin. Fax 313-3504

Midway, Woodford, Pop. 1,609
Woodford County SD
Supt. — See Versailles
Northside ES 300/PK-5
500 Northside Dr 40347 859-879-4690
Ryan Asher, prin. Fax 846-4716

Milton, Trimble, Pop. 563
Trimble County SD
Supt. — See Bedford
Milton ES 300/K-6
9245 Highway 421 N 40045 502-268-3322
Amy Shinn, prin. Fax 268-5316

Monticello, Wayne, Pop. 6,123
Wayne County SD 2,900/PK-12
1025 S Main St 42633 606-348-8484
Wayne Roberts, supt. Fax 348-0734
www.wayne.kyschools.us
Bell ES 500/1-2
278 Kenny Davis Blvd 42633 606-348-8150
Derrick Harris, prin. Fax 348-7871
Monticello ES 200/3-5
160 College St 42633 606-340-3900
Stewart York, prin. Fax 348-1974
Walker Early Learning Center 500/PK-K
1080 S Main St 42633 606-348-4251
Angela Ballinger, prin. Fax 348-0168
Wayne County MS 700/6-8
95 Champion Dr 42633 606-348-6691
Melissa Gossage, prin. Fax 348-5495

Morehead, Rowan, Pop. 6,756
Rowan County SD 3,400/PK-12
415 W Sun St 40351 606-784-8928
Marvin Moore, supt. Fax 783-1011
www.rowan.kyschools.us/
Hogge ES 200/K-5
5955 Cranston Rd 40351 606-784-4604
Brandy Breeze, prin. Fax 784-2456
McBrayer ES 500/K-5
550 Viking Dr 40351 606-784-1204
Rhonda Banks, prin. Fax 784-3567
Rodburn ES 500/K-5
91 Christy Crk 40351 606-784-3000
Andrea Murray, prin. Fax 783-7264
Rowan County MS 700/6-8
555 Viking Dr 40351 606-784-8911
Jay Padula, prin. Fax 784-5579
Rowan County Preschool & Early Education 200/PK-PK
455 W Sun St 40351 606-784-7721
Shirley Burge, dir. Fax 783-9994
Other Schools – See Clearfield

Lakeside Christian Academy 200/PK-12
2535 US Highway 60 W 40351 606-784-2751
Jared DeAtley, admin. Fax 784-0056

Morganfield, Union, Pop. 3,234
Union County SD 2,400/PK-12
510 S Mart St 42437 270-389-1694
Patricia Sheffer, supt. Fax 389-9806
www.union.kyschools.us
Morganfield ES 500/PK-5
511 S Mart St 42437 270-389-2611
Ryan Scott, prin. Fax 389-2994
Union County MS 500/6-8
4465 US Highway 60 W 42437 270-389-0224
Jeremy Roach, prin. Fax 389-0245
Other Schools – See Sturgis, Uniontown

John Paul II S 200/PK-8
PO Box 224 42437 270-389-1898
Beth Hendrickson, prin. Fax 389-1834

Morgantown, Butler, Pop. 2,380
Butler County SD 2,200/PK-12
203 N Tyler St 42261 270-526-5624
Scott Howard, supt. Fax 526-5625
www.butlerschools.net
Butler County MS 500/6-8
PO Box 10 42261 270-526-5647
Tim Freeman, prin. Fax 526-3238
Morgantown ES 700/PK-5
PO Box 337 42261 270-526-3361
Chad Flener, prin. Fax 526-2868
North Butler ES 400/PK-5
5539 Brownsville Rd 42261 270-526-8936
Josh Belcher, prin. Fax 526-8941

Morning View, Kenton
Kenton County SD
Supt. — See Fort Wright
Piner ES 300/PK-5
2845 Piner Ridge Rd 41063 859-356-2155
Christi Jefferds, prin. Fax 356-6203

Mount Olivet, Robertson, Pop. 297
Robertson County SD 400/PK-12
1762 Sardis Rd 41064 606-724-5431
Sanford Holbrook, supt. Fax 724-5921
school.robertson.k12.ky.us
Robertson County S 400/PK-12
1760 Sardis Rd 41064 606-724-5421
James Johnson, prin. Fax 724-5225

Mount Sterling, Montgomery, Pop. 6,810
Montgomery County SD 4,900/PK-12
640 Woodford Dr 40353 859-497-8760
Dr. Matthew Thompson, supt. Fax 497-8780
www.montgomery.kyschools.us
Camargo ES 600/PK-4
4307 Camargo Rd 40353 859-497-8776
Dorothy Dennie, prin. Fax 497-9730
Mapleton ES 700/K-4
809 Indian Mound Dr 40353 859-497-8752
Dawn Cockrell, prin. Fax 497-8756
McNabb MS 700/7-8
3570 Indian Mound Dr 40353 859-497-8770
Paula Stafford, prin. Fax 497-9683
Montgomery County Early Learning Center 100/PK-PK
212 N Maysville St 40353 859-497-8724
Leslee Toy, admin. Fax 499-4240
Montgomery County IS 700/5-6
1040 Maysville Rd 40353 859-497-8703
Mark Crain, prin. Fax 497-8585
Mount Sterling ES 600/K-4
6601 Indian Mound Rd 40353 859-497-8730
Brandy Holley, prin. Fax 497-8704

Christian Traditional S 100/PK-5
PO Box 364 40353 859-498-1565
Heather Hartgrove, prin.

Mount Vernon, Rockcastle, Pop. 2,459
Rockcastle County SD 2,900/PK-12
245 Richmond St 40456 606-256-2125
David Pensol, supt. Fax 256-2126
www.rockcastle.kyschools.us
Mount Vernon ES 700/PK-5
PO Box 1530 40456 606-256-2953
J.D. Bussell, prin. Fax 256-3948
Rockcastle County MS 700/6-8
PO Box 1730 40456 606-256-5118
Marcus Reppert, prin. Fax 256-2622
Roundstone ES 300/PK-5
6701 N Wilderness Rd 40456 606-256-2235
Chris Bishop, prin. Fax 256-2259
Other Schools – See Brodhead

Mount Washington, Bullitt, Pop. 9,010
Bullitt County SD
Supt. — See Shepherdsville
Crossroads ES 500/PK-5
156 Erin Cir 40047 502-869-7400
Julie Skeens, prin. Fax 538-0494
Eastside MS 600/6-8
6925 Highway 44 E 40047 502-869-5000
Troy Wood, prin. Fax 538-0659
Mt. Washington ES 500/PK-5
9234 Highway 44 E 40047 502-869-3000
Terri Lewis, prin. Fax 538-2744
Mt. Washington MS 500/6-8
269 Water St 40047 502-869-5200
Shawn Pickett, prin. Fax 538-0703
Old Mill ES 400/PK-5
11540 Highway 44 E 40047 502-869-3200
Les McIntosh, prin. Fax 538-6641
Pleasant Grove ES 600/PK-5
6415 Highway 44 E 40047 502-869-3400
Melissa Whicker, prin. Fax 538-8732

Mousie, Knott
Knott County SD
Supt. — See Hindman
Jones Fork ES 200/PK-8
PO Box 129 41839 606-946-2132
Jared Huff, prin. Fax 946-2629

Munfordville, Hart, Pop. 1,588
Hart County SD 2,300/PK-12
25 Quality St 42765 270-524-2631
Ricky Line, supt. Fax 524-2634
www.hart.kyschools.us
Munfordville S 500/PK-8
505 W Union St 42765 270-524-4651
Anthony Boone, prin. Fax 524-4652
Other Schools – See Bonnieville, Cub Run, Hardyville, Horse Cave

Murray, Calloway, Pop. 17,409
Calloway County SD 3,300/PK-12
PO Box 800 42071 270-762-7300
Tres Settle, supt. Fax 762-7310
www.calloway.kyschools.us
Calloway County MS 700/6-8
2112 College Farm Rd 42071 270-762-7355
Amy Turner, prin. Fax 762-7360
Calloway County Preschool 200/PK-PK
2106 College Farm Rd Ste A 42071 270-762-7410
Leisha Barlow, prin. Fax 762-7412
East Calloway ES 300/K-5
1169 Pottertown Rd 42071 270-762-7325
Monica Price, prin. Fax 762-7330
North Calloway ES 600/K-5
2928 Brinn Rd 42071 270-762-7335
Melinda Hendley, prin. Fax 762-7340
Southwest Calloway ES 500/K-5
3426 Wiswell Rd W 42071 270-762-7345
Jodi Butler, prin. Fax 762-7350

Murray ISD 1,500/PK-12
208 S 13th St 42071 270-753-4363
Coy Samons, supt. Fax 759-4906
www.murray.kyschools.us
Murray ES 500/PK-3
111 S Broach St 42071 270-753-5022
Denise Whitaker, prin. Fax 753-3856
Murray MS 600/4-8
801 Main St 42071 270-753-5125
Bob Horne, prin. Fax 753-9039

Nancy, Pulaski
Pulaski County SD
Supt. — See Somerset
Nancy ES 400/K-5
240 Highway 196 42544 606-636-6338
Michael Gregg, prin. Fax 636-6841

Nazareth, Nelson

St Joseph Montessori Childrens Center 100/PK-K
PO Box 44 40048 502-348-1540
Kathleen Filkins, admin. Fax 331-4050

Nebo, Hopkins, Pop. 235
Hopkins County SD
Supt. — See Madisonville
West Hopkins S 400/K-8
2695 Rabbit Ridge Rd 42441 270-825-6130
Eric Stone, prin. Fax 249-9454

Neon, Letcher, Pop. 749
Letcher County SD
Supt. — See Whitesburg
Fleming Neon MS 200/6-8
PO Box 425 41840 606-855-7864
Ronny Goins, prin. Fax 855-4485

New Castle, Henry, Pop. 887
Henry County SD 2,200/PK-12
326 S Main St 40050 502-845-8600
Terry Price, supt. Fax 845-8601
www.henry.kyschools.us
Henry County ECC 100/PK-PK
182 S Property Rd 40050 502-845-8656
Stephanie Melton, prin. Fax 845-1232
Henry County MS 500/6-8
1124 Eminence Rd 40050 502-845-8660
Lucia Hughes, prin. Fax 845-8661
New Castle ES 300/K-5
182 S Property Rd 40050 502-845-8650
Austin Hunsaker, prin. Fax 845-8651
Other Schools – See Campbellsburg, Pleasureville

New Haven, Nelson, Pop. 839
Nelson County SD
Supt. — See Bardstown
New Haven ES 400/K-8
489 High St 40051 502-349-7232
Kevin Payton, prin. Fax 349-7231

St. Catherine Academy 100/PK-8
413 N 1st St 40051 502-549-3680
Jo Renee O'Bryan, prin. Fax 549-5410

Newport, Campbell, Pop. 14,797
Newport ISD 1,800/PK-12
30 W 8th St 41071 859-292-3001
Kelly Middleton, supt. Fax 292-3073
www.newportwildcats.org
Newport IS 400/3-6
95 W 9th St 41071 859-292-3021
Joshua Snapp, prin. Fax 292-0222
Newport PS 500/PK-2
1102 York St 41071 859-292-3011
Matt Atkins, prin. Fax 292-0771

Holy Trinity JHS 50/6-8
840 Washington Ave 41071 859-292-0487
James Hubbard, prin. Fax 431-8745

Nicholasville, Jessamine, Pop. 27,423
Jessamine County SD 8,100/PK-12
871 Wilmore Rd 40356 859-885-4179
Matt Moore, supt. Fax 887-4811
www.jessamine.k12.ky.us
Brookside ES 500/PK-5
199 Brookside Dr 40356 859-887-2012
JonAnn Horn, prin. Fax 885-9934
East Jessamine MS 900/6-8
901 Union Mill Rd 40356 859-885-5561
Tracy Devney, prin. Fax 887-1797
Jessamine Early Learning Village 900/PK-K
851 Wilmore Rd 40356 859-887-5358
Gina Bernard, prin. Fax 887-0041
Nicholasville ES 500/PK-5
414 W Maple St 40356 859-885-5351
Sara Crum, prin. Fax 885-1011
Red Oak ES 500/PK-5
921 Union Mill Rd 40356 859-885-0616
Andrea McNeal, prin. Fax 885-0921
Rosenwald Dunbar ES 600/PK-5
1500 Wilmore Rd 40356 859-885-6670
Beth Carpenter, prin. Fax 887-2052
Warner ES 500/PK-5
821 Wilmore Rd 40356 859-885-3085
Dr. Kim Brockman, prin. Fax 881-5655
West Jessamine MS 900/6-8
1400 Wilmore Rd 40356 859-885-2244
Matt Albertson, prin. Fax 885-8078
Other Schools – See Wilmore

North Middletown, Bourbon, Pop. 636
Bourbon County SD
Supt. — See Paris
North Middletown ES 200/PK-5
PO Box 67 40357 859-987-2052
Gail Graves, prin. Fax 362-4047

Nortonville, Hopkins, Pop. 1,195
Hopkins County SD
Supt. — See Madisonville
South Hopkins MS 400/6-8
9140 Hopkinsville Rd 42442 270-825-6125
Stuart Fitch, prin. Fax 825-6085
Southside ES 500/PK-5
9220 Hopkinsville Rd 42442 270-825-6143
Millie Seiber, prin. Fax 825-6111

Oakland, Warren, Pop. 224
Warren County SD
Supt. — See Bowling Green
Oakland ES 300/PK-6
2494 Church St 42159 270-563-4719
DeeAnna Crump, prin. Fax 563-2210

Olive Hill, Carter, Pop. 1,580
Carter County SD
Supt. — See Grayson
Olive Hill ES 500/PK-5
PO Box 540 41164 606-474-6696
Cherri Keaton, prin. Fax 286-5982
Tygart Creek ES 400/PK-5
19743 W US Highway 60 41164 606-474-6696
Joshua Mabry, prin. Fax 286-8193
West Carter County MS 500/6-8
150 Warrior Dr 41164 606-474-6696
Ryan Tomolonis, prin. Fax 286-8556

Olmstead, Logan
Logan County SD
Supt. — See Russellville
Olmstead S 400/PK-8
1170 Olmstead Rd 42265 270-726-3811
Bonnie Watson, prin. Fax 726-1591

Oneida, Clay, Pop. 406
Clay County SD
Supt. — See Manchester
Big Creek ES 200/PK-6
523 N Highway 66 40972 606-598-2812
Nadine Couch, prin. Fax 598-2853
Oneida ES 100/PK-6
435 Newfound Rd 40972 606-847-4212
Brandon Hibbard, prin. Fax 847-4340

Owensboro, Daviess, Pop. 55,842
Daviess County SD 11,500/PK-12
PO Box 21510 42304 270-852-7000
Matt Robbins, supt. Fax 852-7010
www.daviess.kyschools.us/
Audubon ES 500/PK-5
300 Worthington Rd 42301 270-852-7150
Caleb York, prin. Fax 852-7160
Burns ES 600/PK-5
4514 Goetz Dr 42301 270-852-7170
Heather Newman, prin. Fax 852-7180
Burns MS 800/6-8
4610 Goetz Dr 42301 270-852-7400
Dane Ferguson, prin. Fax 852-7410
College View MS 800/6-8
5061 New Hartford Rd 42303 270-852-7500
Jennifer Crume, prin. Fax 852-7510
Country Heights ES 400/PK-5
4961 State Route 54 42303 270-852-7250
Stacy Harper, prin. Fax 852-7260
Daviess County MS 900/6-8
1415 E 4th St 42303 270-852-7600
Kelly Skeens, prin. Fax 852-7610
Deer Park ES 500/PK-5
4959 New Hartford Rd 42303 270-852-7270
Robin Nalley, prin. Fax 852-7280
East View ES 500/PK-5
6104 State Route 405 42303 270-852-7350
Sonya Simpson, prin. Fax 852-7360
Highland ES 700/PK-5
2909 Highway 54 42303 270-852-7370
Leslie Peveler, prin. Fax 852-7380
Meadow Lands ES 600/PK-5
3500 Hayden Rd 42303 270-852-7450
Kevin Lowe, prin. Fax 852-7460
Sorgho ES 500/PK-5
5390 KY Route 56 42301 270-852-7470
Laura Cecil, prin. Fax 852-7480
Tamarack ES 500/PK-5
1733 Tamarack Rd 42301 270-852-7550
Carrie Munsey, prin. Fax 852-7560
West Louisville ES 400/PK-5
8400 State Route 56 42301 270-852-7650
Nathan Satterly, prin. Fax 852-7660
Other Schools – See Utica, Whitesville

Owensboro ISD 5,100/PK-12
450 Griffith Ave 42301 270-686-1000
Dr. Nicholas Brake, supt. Fax 684-5756
www.owensboro.kyschools.us
Cravens ES 300/K-4
2741 Cravens Ave 42301 270-686-1010
Cortney Inklebarger, prin. Fax 683-9678
Estes ES 500/PK-4
1675 Leitchfield Rd 42303 270-686-1030
Shari Flagg, prin. Fax 686-1176
Foust ES 400/K-4
601 Foust Ave 42301 270-686-1060
Janie Moseley, prin. Fax 686-1021
Hager Preschool 400/PK-PK
1701 W 7th St 42301 270-686-1125
Sherry Baber, coord. Fax 686-1161
Newton Parrish ES 400/K-4
510 W Byers Ave 42303 270-686-1100
Steve Bratcher, prin. Fax 926-9637
Owensboro MS - North Campus 600/7-8
1300 Booth Ave 42301 270-686-1130
Anita Burnette, prin. Fax 686-1173
Owensboro MS - South Campus 700/5-6
2631 S Griffith Ave 42301 270-686-1130
Patrick Tines, prin. Fax 686-1183
Sutton ES 400/K-4
2060 Lewis Ln 42301 270-686-1140
Danna Johnson, prin. Fax 686-1158

Owensboro Catholic MS 200/7-8
2540 Christie Pl 42301 270-683-0480
David Kessler, prin. Fax 683-0495
Owensboro S 4-6 Campus 300/4-6
525 E 23rd St 42303 270-683-6989
Tracy Conkright, prin. Fax 684-5956
Owensboro S K-3 Campus 400/K-3
4017 Frederica St 42301 270-684-7583
Lori Whitehouse, prin. Fax 684-4938

Owenton, Owen, Pop. 1,301
Owen County SD 2,000/PK-12
1600 Highway 22 E 40359 502-484-3934
Dr. Robert Stafford, supt. Fax 484-9095
www.owen.kyschools.us
Bowling MS 600/5-8
2380 Highway 22 E 40359 502-484-5701
Donette Gaines, prin. Fax 484-3044
Owen County Lower/Upper ES 400/PK-4
1960 Highway 22 E 40359 502-484-3417
Sharen Hubbard, prin. Fax 484-5764

Owingsville, Bath, Pop. 1,507
Bath County SD 2,100/PK-12
405 W Main St 40360 606-674-6314
Harvey Tackett, supt. Fax 674-2647
www.bath.kyschools.us
Bath County MS 500/6-8
335 W Main St 40360 606-674-8165
Todd Neace, prin. Fax 674-2676
Crossroads ES 400/PK-5
4755 E Highway 60 40360 606-674-2101
Lorinda Jamison, prin. Fax 674-2080
Owingsville ES 600/PK-5
50 Chenault Dr 40360 606-674-2722
Mark Leet, prin. Fax 674-6621

Paducah, McCracken, Pop. 24,294
McCracken County SD 6,100/PK-12
5347 Benton Rd 42003 270-538-4000
Brian Harper, supt. Fax 538-4001
www.mccracken.kyschools.us/
Concord ES 600/PK-5
5184 Hinkleville Rd 42001 270-538-4050
Ginger Stewart, prin. Fax 538-4051
Hendron Lone Oak ES 400/PK-3
2501 Marshall Ave 42003 270-538-4110
Jon Reid, prin. Fax 538-4111
Lone Oak ES 500/PK-3
301 Cumberland Ave 42001 270-538-4120
Jill Darnall, prin. Fax 538-4121
Lone Oak IS 500/4-5
300 Cumberland Ave 42001 270-538-4160
Marc Mavigliano, prin.
Lone Oak MS 700/6-8
225 John E Robinson Dr 42001 270-538-4130
Brent Buchanan, prin. Fax 538-4131

Reidland ES 200/PK-3
5741 Benton Rd 42003 270-538-4180
Paul Lamb, prin. Fax 538-4181
Reidland IS 4-5
5349 Benton Rd 42003 270-538-4210
Paula Grubbs, prin. Fax 538-4211
Reidland MS 400/6-8
5351 Benton Rd 42003 270-538-4190
Randy Layne, prin. Fax 538-4191
Other Schools – See West Paducah

Paducah ISD 3,100/PK-12
PO Box 2550 42002 270-444-5600
Donald Shively, supt. Fax 444-5607
www.paducah.kyschools.us/
Clark ES 500/K-5
3401 Buckner Ln 42001 270-444-5730
Steve Ybarzabal, prin. Fax 444-5737
McNabb ES 500/K-5
2100 Park Ave 42001 270-444-5750
Teresa Spann, prin. Fax 444-5772
Morgan ES 400/K-5
2200 S 28th St 42003 270-444-5760
Vicki Conyer, prin. Fax 444-5763
Paducah MS 700/6-8
342 Lone Oak Rd 42001 270-444-5710
Allene Houston-Jones, prin. Fax 444-5709
Paducah Preschool 200/PK-PK
1350 S 6th St 42003 270-444-5780
Kristy Lewis, dir. Fax 444-5781

Community Christian Academy 200/K-12
110 Lebanon Church Rd 42003 270-554-1651
Anna Thomas, prin. Fax 554-8968
St. Mary ES 300/PK-5
377 Highland Blvd 42003 270-442-1681
Lisa Clark, prin. Fax 442-7920
St. Mary MS 100/6-8
1243 Elmdale Rd 42003 270-442-1681
Jennifer Smith, prin. Fax 442-7920

Paint Lick, Garrard
Garrard County SD
Supt. — See Lancaster
Paint Lick ES 400/PK-5
6798 Richmond Rd 40461 859-792-2122
Liz Erwin, prin. Fax 792-4873

Paintsville, Johnson, Pop. 3,422
Johnson County SD 3,700/PK-12
253 N Mayo Trl 41240 606-789-2530
Thom Cochran, supt. Fax 789-2506
www.johnson.kyschools.us/
Central ES 300/PK-6
1715 Euclid Ave 41240 606-789-2541
Robin Halsey, prin. Fax 789-2527
Johnson County MS 600/7-8
251 N Mayo Trl 41240 606-789-4133
Joey Estep, prin. Fax 789-4135
Other Schools – See Flatgap, Hagerhill, Staffordsville, Wittensville

Paintsville ISD 700/PK-12
305 2nd St 41240 606-789-2654
David Gibson, supt. Fax 789-7412
www.paintsville.kyschools.us
Paintsville ES 300/PK-6
325 2nd St 41240 606-789-2651
Katie Webb, prin. Fax 789-2575

Our Lady of the Mountains S 100/PK-1
405 3rd St 41240 606-789-3661
Jayme Runyon, prin. Fax 789-3661

Paris, Bourbon, Pop. 8,356
Bourbon County SD 3,000/PK-12
3343 Lexington Rd 40361 859-987-2180
Amy Baker, supt. Fax 987-2182
www.bourbon.kyschools.us
Bourbon Central ES 600/PK-5
367 Bethlehem Rd 40361 859-987-2195
Keith Madill, prin. Fax 987-2104
Bourbon County MS 600/6-8
3339 Lexington Rd 40361 859-987-2189
Travis Earlywine, prin. Fax 987-5854
Bourbon County Preschool 300/PK-PK
369 Bethlehem Rd 40361 859-987-2183
Melinda Malin, dir. Fax 987-5867
Cane Ridge ES 500/PK-5
8000 Martin Luther King 40361 859-987-2106
Dana Hill, prin. Fax 987-2107
Other Schools – See North Middletown

Paris ISD 700/PK-12
310 W 7th St 40361 859-987-2160
Ken Bicknell, supt. Fax 987-6749
www.paris.kyschools.us
Paris ES 400/PK-5
1481 S Main St 40361 859-987-2166
Thomas Reed, prin. Fax 987-2176
Paris MS 100/6-8
304 W 7th St 40361 859-987-2163
Jami Dailey, prin. Fax 987-2164
Paris Preschool 50/PK-PK
1481 S Main St 40361 859-987-2166
Amanda Evans, dir. Fax 987-6749

St. Mary S 100/PK-5
1121 Main St 40361 859-987-3815
Lucy Marsh, prin. Fax 987-3815

Park City, Barren, Pop. 534
Barren County SD
Supt. — See Glasgow
Park City ES 400/PK-6
PO Box 45 42160 270-749-5665
Anthony Janes, prin. Fax 749-5074

Payneville, Meade
Meade County SD
Supt. — See Brandenburg
Payneville ES 200/K-6
520 Rhodelia Rd 40157 270-422-7550
Marie Barr, prin. Fax 496-4774

Pembroke, Christian, Pop. 850
Christian County SD
Supt. — See Hopkinsville
Pembroke ES 400/K-6
1600 Pembroke Oak Grove Rd 42266 270-887-7290
Dana Gary, prin. Fax 475-9897

Perryville, Boyle, Pop. 746
Boyle County SD
Supt. — See Danville
Perryville ES 200/PK-5
418 W 4th St 40468 859-936-7500
Chris Slone, prin. Fax 332-2324

Pewee Valley, Oldham, Pop. 1,437

Pewee Valley Junior Academy 50/PK-8
103 La Grange Rd 40056 502-241-4354
St. Aloysius S 500/PK-8
122 Mount Mercy Dr 40056 502-241-8516
Maryann Hayslip, prin. Fax 243-2241

Phelps, Pike, Pop. 888
Pike County SD
Supt. — See Pikeville
Phelps ES 400/K-6
PO Box 529 41553 606-456-7716
Angela Lester, prin. Fax 456-8200

Philpot, Daviess

Carrico Memorial S 100/PK-8
9546 State Route 144 42366 270-281-5526
Martha Warren, prin. Fax 281-9556

Pikeville, Pike, Pop. 6,797
Pike County SD 9,000/K-12
316 S Mayo Trl 41501 606-433-9200
Reed Adkins, supt. Fax 432-3321
www.pike.kyschools.us
Johns Creek S 700/K-8
8302 Meta Hwy 41501 606-631-1097
Chad Thompson, prin. Fax 631-9604
Millard S 700/K-8
8015 Millard Hwy 41501 606-437-3380
Mike Potter, prin. Fax 433-9677
Mullins S 800/K-8
101 Tiger Way 41501 606-432-2733
Gary Fields, prin. Fax 432-2393
Valley ES, 163 Douglas Pkwy 41501 900/K-8
James Tackett, prin. 606-639-4392
Other Schools – See Belfry, Dorton, Elkhorn City, Fedscreek, Kimper, Phelps, Sidney

Pikeville ISD 1,200/PK-12
148 2nd St 41501 606-432-8161
Jerry Green, supt. Fax 432-2119
www.pikeville.kyschools.us
Pikeville ES 600/PK-6
105 Bailey Blvd 41501 606-432-4196
Robert Jones, prin. Fax 432-1234

Christ Central S 50/PK-8
PO Box 2154 41502 606-432-9565
G. Janet Burnette, admin. Fax 432-6747
St. Francis of Assisi S 100/PK-6
147 Bryan St 41501 606-437-6117
Fr. Richard Watson, prin. Fax 437-6822

Pine Knot, McCreary, Pop. 1,596
McCreary County SD
Supt. — See Stearns
McCreary County Preschool South 100/PK-PK
119 E Highway 92 42635 606-354-3590
Dr. Aaron Anderson Ed.D., prin. Fax 376-9696
Pine Knot ES Building 1 400/K-3
119 E Highway 92 42635 606-354-2161
Rebecca Blakley, prin. Fax 354-4466
Pine Knot ES Building 2 400/4-6
6519 S Highway 1651 42635 606-354-2511
Rebecca Blakley, prin. Fax 354-9353

Pineville, Bell, Pop. 1,711
Bell County SD 2,800/PK-12
PO Box 340 40977 606-337-7051
Yvonne Gilliam, supt. Fax 337-1412
www.bell.kyschools.us
Bell Central S Center 600/PK-8
9821 US Highway 25 E 40977 606-337-3104
Jennifer Blankenship, prin. Fax 337-0808
Page School Center 400/PK-8
239 Page School Rd 40977 606-337-5207
Will Lefevers, prin. Fax 337-9534
Other Schools – See Fourmile, Frakes, Middlesboro, Stoney Fork

Pineville ISD 500/PK-12
401 W Virginia Ave 40977 606-337-5701
Russell Thompson, supt. Fax 337-9983
www.pineville.kyschools.us
Pineville ES 300/PK-6
401 W Virginia Ave 40977 606-337-5701
Justin Daniels, prin. Fax 337-4395

Pippa Passes, Knott, Pop. 530

Buchanan S 100/K-12
100 Purpose Rd 41844 606-368-6108

Pleasureville, Henry, Pop. 817
Henry County SD
Supt. — See New Castle

Eastern ES 200/K-5
6928 Bethlehem Rd 40057 502-845-8640
Angela Denny, prin. Fax 845-8641

Powderly, Muhlenberg, Pop. 738
Muhlenberg County SD 5,300/PK-12
510 W Main St 42367 270-338-2871
Robby Davis, supt. Fax 338-0529
www.mberg.k12.ky.us/
Other Schools – See Beechmont, Bremen, Central City, Greenville

Prestonsburg, Floyd, Pop. 3,226
Floyd County SD 6,000/K-12
106 N Front Ave 41653 606-886-2354
Steve Trimble, supt. Fax 886-8862
www.floyd.kyschools.us
Adams MS 400/6-8
2520 S Lake Dr 41653 606-886-2671
Thomas Poe, prin. Fax 886-7026
Prestonsburg ES 700/K-5
140 Clark Dr 41653 606-886-3891
Brent Rose, prin. Fax 886-9081
Other Schools – See Allen, Betsy Layne, Eastern, Grethel, Hi Hat, Martin

Princeton, Caldwell, Pop. 6,185
Caldwell County SD 2,100/PK-12
PO Box 229 42445 270-365-8000
Randy McCarty, supt. Fax 365-5742
www.caldwell.kyschools.us/
Caldwell County ES 400/3-5
105 Educational Dr 42445 270-365-8030
Ronnie Martin, prin. Fax 365-3164
Caldwell County MS 500/6-8
440 Beckner Ln 42445 270-365-8020
Steve Smiley, prin. Fax 365-9573
Caldwell County PS 600/PK-2
1000 Marion Rd 42445 270-365-8040
Daniel Bean, prin. Fax 365-7038

Prospect, Oldham, Pop. 4,648
Jefferson County SD
Supt. — See Louisville
Norton Commons ES K-5
10941 Kings Crown Dr 40059 502-485-8367
Allyson Vitato, prin. Fax 313-3562

Oldham County SD
Supt. — See Crestwood
Goshen ES 700/K-5
12518 Ridgemoor Dr 40059 502-228-0101
Lisa Peters, prin. Fax 228-3777

St. Mary Academy 300/PK-8
11311 Saint Mary Ln 40059 502-315-2555
Lisa Kelly, prin. Fax 326-3655

Providence, Webster, Pop. 3,114
Webster County SD
Supt. — See Dixon
Providence ES 400/PK-6
470 S Broadway St 42450 270-667-7041
Greg Bowles, prin. Fax 667-5893

Raceland, Greenup, Pop. 2,412
Raceland-Worthington ISD 1,100/PK-12
600 Rams Blvd 41169 606-836-2144
Larry Coldiron, supt. Fax 833-5807
www.raceland.kyschools.us
Campbell ES 300/PK-3
550 Rams Blvd 41169 606-836-3844
Jill Imes, prin. Fax 494-2417
Other Schools – See Worthington

Radcliff, Hardin, Pop. 20,329
Hardin County SD
Supt. — See Elizabethtown
Meadow View ES 500/1-5
1255 W Vine St 40160 270-352-0500
Althea Hurt, prin. Fax 352-0526
North MS 600/6-8
100 Trojan Way 40160 270-352-3340
Jeff Lowman, prin. Fax 352-3341
North Park ES 600/PK-K
1080 S Logsdon Pkwy 40160 270-351-4464
Beth Brandenburg, prin. Fax 351-7270
Radcliff ES 400/1-5
1145 S Dixie Blvd 40160 270-352-3350
Chris Corder, prin. Fax 352-3351
Woodland ES 500/1-5
6000 S Woodland Dr 40160 270-352-5828
Dawn Tarquinio, prin. Fax 352-5835

North Hardin Christian S 500/PK-12
1298 Rogersville Rd 40160 270-351-7700

Richmond, Madison, Pop. 30,594
Madison County SD 9,900/PK-12
PO Box 768 40476 859-624-4500
Elmer Thomas, supt. Fax 624-4508
www.madison.kyschools.us
Boone ES 400/1-5
710 N 2nd St 40475 859-625-6070
Eddie Sexton, prin. Fax 624-4589
Carson ES 500/1-5
450 Tates Creek Rd 40475 859-625-6103
Ken Clark, prin. Fax 624-4526
Caudill MS 600/6-8
1428 Robert R Martin Bypass 40475 859-625-6172
Che Haselwood, prin. Fax 623-2652
Clark-Moores MS 500/6-8
1143 Berea Rd 40475 859-624-4545
Michael Reister, prin. Fax 624-4534
Kirksville ES 500/PK-PK, 1-
2399 Lancaster Rd 40475 859-624-4582
Starla Browne, prin. Fax 624-4595
Madison Kindergarten Academy 100/PK-K
300 Bond St 40475 859-625-6050
Shelly Boulden, prin. Fax 624-4541

Madison MS 400/6-8
101 Summit St 40475 859-624-4550
Amie Gallion, prin. Fax 624-4543
Marshall ES 500/PK-PK, 1-
1442 Dr Robert R Martin Byp 40475 859-625-6076
Abby White, prin. Fax 624-4021
White Hall ES 600/1-5
2166 Lexington Rd 40475 859-625-6134
Monica Eversole, prin. Fax 624-4512
Other Schools – See Berea, Waco

St. Mark S 100/PK-5
115 Parrish Ave 40475 859-623-2989
Cathy Cornett, prin. Fax 626-5492

Rineyville, Hardin
Hardin County SD
Supt. — See Elizabethtown
Rineyville ES 600/PK-5
275 Rineyville School Rd 40162 270-737-7371
Stephanie Lucas, prin. Fax 737-0916

Rockholds, Whitley, Pop. 388
Whitley County SD
Supt. — See Williamsburg
Whitley County North ES 400/PK-6
6670 Highway 26 40759 606-549-7869
Larry Brown, prin. Fax 523-5383

Rogers, Wolfe
Wolfe County SD
Supt. — See Campton
Rogers ES 200/K-6
1745 KY 715 S 41365 606-668-8302
Amanda Perry, prin. Fax 668-8350

Rush, Boyd
Carter County SD
Supt. — See Grayson
Star ES 100/PK-5
8249 E US Highway 60 41168 606-474-6696
Charles Baker, prin. Fax 475-9595

Russell, Greenup, Pop. 3,354
Russell ISD 2,000/PK-12
409 Belfonte St 41169 606-836-9679
M. Sean Horne, supt. Fax 836-2865
www.russellind.kyschools.us
Russell MS 500/6-8
707 Red Devil Ln 41169 606-836-8135
Shawn Moore, prin. Fax 836-0614
Russell PS 500/PK-2
710 Red Devil Ln 41169 606-836-0007
Phillip Cassity, prin. Fax 834-9300
Other Schools – See Flatwoods

Russell Springs, Russell, Pop. 2,403
Russell County SD
Supt. — See Jamestown
Russell County MS 700/6-8
2258 S Highway 127 42642 270-866-2224
Wayne Ackerman, prin. Fax 866-8679
Russell Springs ES 700/PK-5
1554 N Highway 127 42642 270-866-3587
Keith Emerson, prin. Fax 866-7456
Salem ES 300/PK-5
1409 S Highway 76 42642 270-866-6197
Kimberlee Webb, prin. Fax 866-3687

Russellville, Logan, Pop. 6,795
Logan County SD 3,600/PK-12
PO Box 417 42276 270-726-2436
Paul Mullins, supt. Fax 726-8892
www.logan.kyschools.us
Chandlers S 500/PK-8
6000 Morgantown Rd 42276 270-542-4139
Robbie Davis, prin. Fax 542-4108
Other Schools – See Adairville, Auburn, Lewisburg, Olmstead

Russellville ISD 1,000/PK-12
355 S Summer St 42276 270-726-8405
Bart Flener M.A., supt. Fax 726-4036
www.russellville.kyschools.us/
Stevenson ES 500/PK-5
1000 N Main St 42276 270-726-8425
Robin Cornelius M.A., prin. Fax 726-1109

Ryland Heights, Kenton, Pop. 1,013
Kenton County SD
Supt. — See Fort Wright
Ryland Heights ES 600/PK-5
3845 Stewart Dr 41015 859-356-9270
Sara Callahan, prin. Fax 356-2846

Sacramento, McLean, Pop. 462
McLean County SD
Supt. — See Calhoun
Gatton Phillips ES 100/K-5
PO Box 288 42372 270-736-2343
Jon Farley, prin. Fax 736-5520

Salyersville, Magoffin, Pop. 1,875
Magoffin County SD 2,300/PK-12
PO Box 109 41465 606-349-6117
Scott Helton, supt. Fax 349-3417
www.magoffin.kyschools.us
North Magoffin ES 500/PK-6
1991 Highway 460 W 41465 606-349-2847
Keith Isaac, prin. Fax 349-6466
Salyersville Grade S 500/PK-6
204 Hornet Dr 41465 606-349-3411
Gary Helton, prin. Fax 349-3483
South Magoffin ES 300/PK-6
171 Half Mountain Rd 41465 606-884-7325
Mark Rice, prin. Fax 884-7322
Whitaker MS 300/7-8
201 Hornet Dr 41465 606-349-5190
Garland Yates, prin. Fax 349-5139

Sandgap, Jackson
Jackson County SD
Supt. — See Mc Kee
Sand Gap ES 300/PK-5
PO Box 320 40481 606-965-3171
Barbara Masters, prin. Fax 965-2917

Sandy Hook, Elliott, Pop. 666
Elliott County SD 1,000/K-12
PO Box 767 41171 606-738-8002
Debbie Stephens Ed.D., supt. Fax 738-8000
www.elliott.kyschools.us
Lakeside ES 200/K-6
155 Lakeside School Rd 41171 606-738-8202
Megan West, prin. Fax 738-8249
Sandy Hook ES 300/K-6
PO Box 708 41171 606-738-8402
Jill Copley, prin. Fax 738-8450
Other Schools – See Isonville

Science Hill, Pulaski, Pop. 689
Science Hill ISD 500/PK-8
6007 N Highway 27 42553 606-423-3341
Jimmy Dyehouse, supt. Fax 423-3313
www.sciencehill.kyschools.us
Science Hill S 500/PK-8
6007 N Highway 27 42553 606-423-3341
Jimmy Dyehouse, admin. Fax 423-3313

Scottsville, Allen, Pop. 4,154
Allen County SD 3,300/PK-12
570 Oliver St 42164 270-618-3181
Randall Jackson, supt. Fax 618-3185
www.allen.kyschools.us
Allen County IS 700/4-6
720 Oliver St 42164 270-618-8200
Shawn Holland, prin. Fax 618-8205
Allen County PS 1,100/PK-3
721 New Gallatin Rd 42164 270-618-7200
Tim Wilson, prin. Fax 618-7206
Bazzell MS 500/7-8
201 New Gallatin Rd 42164 270-622-7140
Melissa Towery, prin. Fax 622-4649

Sebree, Webster, Pop. 1,571
Webster County SD
Supt. — See Dixon
Sebree ES 400/PK-6
61 N State St 42455 270-835-7891
Dawn Forker, prin. Fax 639-0374

Shelbyville, Shelby, Pop. 13,656
Shelby County SD 7,000/PK-12
PO Box 159 40066 502-633-2375
Dr. James Neihof, supt. Fax 633-1988
www.shelby.kyschools.us
Clear Creek ES 600/K-5
279 Chapel Hl 40065 502-633-3452
Kim Willhoite, prin. Fax 647-0232
Northside ECC, 821 College St 40065 200/PK-PK
Brenda Musick, prin. 502-633-5123
Painted Stone ES 600/K-5
150 Warriors Way 40065 502-647-4505
Artavia Acklin, prin. Fax 647-4508
Shelby County East MS 500/6-7
600 Rocket Ln 40065 502-633-1478
Jennifer Cox, prin. Fax 633-6981
Shelby County West MS 500/6-7
100 Warriors Way 40065 502-633-4869
Lorri Stivers, prin. Fax 647-4525
Southside ES 300/K-5
728 Ginkgo Dr 40065 502-633-4460
Susanne Burkhardt, prin. Fax 633-4462
Wright ES 500/K-5
500 Rocket Ln 40065 502-633-5222
Seth Green, prin. Fax 647-0243
Other Schools – See Simpsonville, Waddy

Cornerstone Christian Academy 200/PK-12
3850 Frankfort Rd 40065 502-633-4070
David Ladner, hdmstr. Fax 633-4605

Shepherdsville, Bullitt, Pop. 11,048
Bullitt County SD 13,300/PK-12
1040 Highway 44 E 40165 502-869-8000
Keith Davis, supt. Fax 543-3608
www.bullittschools.org
Bernheim MS 500/6-8
700 Audubon Dr 40165 502-869-4000
Katie Stephens, prin. Fax 543-5299
Bullitt Lick MS 500/6-8
555 W Blue Lick Rd 40165 502-869-5400
Kevin Connors, prin. Fax 543-1685
Cedar Grove ES 500/PK-5
1900 Cedar Grove Rd 40165 502-869-3800
Gayle Korfhage, prin. Fax 543-3691
Freedom ES 500/PK-5
4682 N Preston Hwy 40165 502-869-3600
Matthew Treadway, prin. Fax 955-8866
Hebron MS 400/6-8
3300 E Hebron Ln 40165 502-869-4200
Kelland Garland, prin. Fax 957-6014
Roby ES 500/PK-5
1148 Highway 44 E 40165 502-869-7200
Brittany Knipp, prin. Fax 543-2328
Shepherdsville ES 600/PK-5
527 W Blue Lick Rd 40165 502-869-7000
Patrick Durham, prin. Fax 543-7838
Zoneton MS 500/6-8
797 Old Preston Hwy N 40165 502-869-4400
Ann Ford, prin. Fax 955-7027
Other Schools – See Brooks, Lebanon Junction, Louisville, Mount Washington, West Point

---

Little Flock Christian Academy 200/K-12
5500 N Preston Hwy 40165 502-957-7686
Rick Grice, prin. Fax 957-4122

Sidney, Pike
Pike County SD
Supt. — See Pikeville
Bevins ES 300/K-5
17275 E Big Creek Rd 41564 606-353-7078
Amy Swiney, prin. Fax 353-0884

Siler, Whitley
Whitley County SD
Supt. — See Williamsburg
Whitley County East ES 200/PK-6
PO Box 949 40763 606-549-7097
Mike Partin, prin. Fax 549-7098

Silver Grove, Campbell, Pop. 1,083
Silver Grove ISD 200/PK-12
PO Box 444 41085 859-441-3894
Dennis Maines, supt. Fax 441-3033
www.silvergrove.kyschools.us
Silver Grove S 200/PK-12
PO Box 444 41085 859-441-3873
Wesley Murray, prin. Fax 441-4299

Simpsonville, Shelby, Pop. 2,432
Shelby County SD
Supt. — See Shelbyville
Simpsonville ES 600/K-5
6725 Shelbyville Rd 40067 502-722-8855
Jill Tingle, prin. Fax 722-9607

Corpus Christi Classical Academy PK-12
7010 Shelbyville Rd 40067 502-722-8090
Kathy Fehder, prin. Fax 722-8099

Smithland, Livingston, Pop. 299
Livingston County SD 1,300/PK-12
127 E Adair St 42081 270-928-2111
Victor Zimmerman, supt. Fax 928-2112
www.livingston.kyschools.us
South Livingston ES 500/PK-5
850 Cutoff Rd 42081 270-928-3500
Rebecca Dunning, prin. Fax 928-3530
Other Schools – See Burna

Smiths Grove, Warren, Pop. 694
Edmonson County SD
Supt. — See Brownsville
South Edmonson ES 500/PK-4
1058 Chalybeate School Rd 42171 270-597-2379
Jamie Woosley, prin. Fax 597-9031

Warren County SD
Supt. — See Bowling Green
North Warren ES 400/PK-6
420 College St 42171 270-563-2041
Debra Lasala, prin. Fax 563-3971

Somerset, Pulaski, Pop. 11,017
Pulaski County SD 8,700/PK-12
PO Box 1055 42502 606-679-1123
Steve Butcher, supt. Fax 679-1438
www.pulaski.net
Memorial Education Center 700/PK-PK
222 Langdon St 42501 606-678-4100
Amy Smith, prin.
Northern ES 400/K-5
6155 Highway 39 42503 606-423-1040
Julie Shepperd, prin. Fax 423-1042
Northern MS 800/6-8
650 Oak Leaf Ln 42503 606-678-5230
Shelly Hargis, prin. Fax 678-2729
Oak Hill ES 500/K-5
1755 WTLO Rd 42503 606-679-2014
Matt Cook, prin. Fax 677-0044
Pulaski ES 600/K-5
107 W University Dr 42503 606-678-4713
Angela Wilson, prin. Fax 679-9388
Shopville ES 400/K-5
10 Shopville Rd 42503 606-274-4411
Kent Mayfield, prin. Fax 274-5186
Southern ES 700/K-5
198 Enterprise Dr 42501 606-678-5229
Keith Patrick, prin. Fax 678-8517
Southern MS 1,000/6-8
200 Enterprise Dr 42501 606-679-6855
Brett McQueary, prin. Fax 679-2270
Other Schools – See Burnside, Eubank, Nancy

Somerset ISD 1,600/PK-12
305 College St 42501 606-679-4451
Kyle Lively, supt. Fax 678-0864
www.somerset.kyschools.us
Hopkins ES 600/PK-4
210 May St 42501 606-678-8707
Mike Reynolds, prin. Fax 678-3062
Meece MS 500/5-8
210 Barnett St 42501 606-678-5821
Calvin Rollyson, prin. Fax 678-2934

Somerset Christian S 300/PK-12
815 Grand Central Blvd 42503 606-451-1600
John Hale, prin. Fax 677-9850

Sonora, Hardin, Pop. 507
Hardin County SD
Supt. — See Elizabethtown
Creekside ES 600/PK-5
151 Horseshoe Bend Rd 42776 270-369-8460
Meredith Weipert, prin. Fax 369-8573

Southgate, Campbell, Pop. 3,718
Southgate ISD 200/PK-8
6 William F Blatt Ave 41071 859-441-0743
Greg Duty, supt. Fax 441-6735
www.southgate.kyschools.us
Southgate S 200/PK-8
6 William F Blatt Ave 41071 859-441-0743
Eddie Franke, prin. Fax 441-6735

St. Therese S 300/K-8
2516 Alexandria Pike 41071 859-441-0449
Dorothy O'Leary, prin. Fax 441-0449

S Portsmouth, Greenup

Harvest Christian Academy 100/K-12
PO Box 398 41174 606-932-3007
Ashley Pelfrey, admin. Fax 453-1635

South Shore, Greenup, Pop. 1,096
Greenup County SD
Supt. — See Greenup
McKell ES 500/K-5
28978 US 23 Hwy 41175 606-932-3383
Aaron Collier, prin. Fax 473-3438
McKell MS 300/6-8
129 Bulldog Ln 41175 606-932-3221
Nathan Sutton, prin. Fax 932-9844

Spottsville, Henderson, Pop. 322
Henderson County SD
Supt. — See Henderson
Spottsville ES 500/K-5
9190 US Highway 60 E 42458 270-831-5136
Sarah Estabrook, prin. Fax 831-5138

Springfield, Washington, Pop. 2,454
Washington County SD 1,700/PK-12
120 Mackville Hl 40069 859-336-5470
Dr. Robin Cochran Ed.D., supt. Fax 336-5480
www.washington.kyschools.us
Washington County ES 400/PK-5
601 Lincoln Park Rd 40069 859-336-5490
Dr. Jennifer Miller Ed.D., prin. Fax 336-0446
Washington County MS 200/6-8
603 Lincoln Park Rd 40069 859-336-5483
Tyler Howard, prin. Fax 336-5477
Other Schools – See Willisburg

St. Dominic S 200/PK-8
309 W Main St 40069 859-336-7165
Pamela Breunig, prin. Fax 336-7169

Staffordsville, Johnson
Johnson County SD
Supt. — See Paintsville
Highland ES 500/PK-6
649 US Highway 23 S 41256 606-297-3674
Brenton Dials, prin. Fax 297-6080

Stamping Ground, Scott, Pop. 637
Scott County SD
Supt. — See Georgetown
Stamping Ground ES 300/PK-5
3233 Main St 40379 502-570-8800
Maria Bennett, prin. Fax 570-8804

Stanford, Lincoln, Pop. 3,439
Lincoln County SD 4,000/PK-12
PO Box 265 40484 606-365-2124
Michael Rowe, supt. Fax 365-1660
www.lincoln.kyschools.us
Lincoln County MS 600/6-8
285 Education Way 40484 606-365-8400
Billy Harris, prin. Fax 365-8600
Stanford ES 500/PK-5
101 Old Fort Rd 40484 606-365-2191
Brandi Hon, prin. Fax 365-1533
Other Schools – See Crab Orchard, Hustonville, Mc Kinney, Waynesburg

Stanton, Powell, Pop. 2,713
Powell County SD 2,400/PK-12
PO Box 430 40380 606-663-3300
Michael Tate, supt. Fax 663-3303
www.powell.kyschools.us
Bowen ES 200/K-5
5099 Campton Rd 40380 606-663-3313
Julie Foster, prin. Fax 663-3314
Powell County MS 600/6-8
770 W College Ave 40380 606-663-3308
Tiffany Anderson, prin. Fax 663-3683
Stanton ES 400/PK-5
651 Breckenridge St 40380 606-663-3311
James Crase, prin. Fax 663-3305
Other Schools – See Clay City

Stearns, McCreary, Pop. 1,397
McCreary County SD 3,000/PK-12
120 Raider Way 42647 606-376-2591
Michael Cash, supt. Fax 376-5584
www.mccreary.kyschools.us
McCreary County MS 500/7-8
180 Raider Way 42647 606-376-5081
Kenneth Waters, prin. Fax 376-9580
Other Schools – See Pine Knot, Whitley City

Stoney Fork, Bell
Bell County SD
Supt. — See Pineville
Right Fork School Center 200/PK-8
5296 Highway 221 40988 606-337-3271
Bobbi Collotte Carter, prin. Fax 337-5100

Sturgis, Union, Pop. 1,862
Union County SD
Supt. — See Morganfield
Sturgis ES 400/PK-5
1101 N Grant St 42459 270-333-4088
Michelle Hall, prin. Fax 333-4820

Sweeden, Edmonson
Edmonson County SD
Supt. — See Brownsville
Kyrock ES 300/PK-4
5720 KY Highway 259 N 42285 270-286-4013
Shaun Stice, prin. Fax 286-4603

Symsonia, Graves, Pop. 607
Graves County SD
Supt. — See Mayfield
Symsonia ES 300/PK-6
11730 State Route 131 42082 270-674-4860
Alison Gregory, prin. Fax 851-4386

Taylor Mill, Kenton, Pop. 6,506
Kenton County SD
Supt. — See Fort Wright
Taylor Mill ES 600/K-5
5907 Taylor Mill Rd 41015 859-356-2566
Melody Stacy, prin. Fax 356-5750
Woodland MS 700/6-8
5399 Old Taylor Mill Rd 41015 859-356-7300
Jerry Cline, prin. Fax 356-7595

St. Anthony S 100/K-8
485 Grand Ave 41015 859-431-5987
Veronica Schweitzer, prin. Fax 431-5972
Taylor Mill Christian Academy 50/K-8
5235 Taylor Mill Rd 41015 859-905-0077

Taylorsville, Spencer, Pop. 749
Spencer County SD 2,900/PK-12
207 W Main St 40071 502-477-3250
Charles Adams, supt. Fax 477-3259
www.spencer.kyschools.us
Spencer County ES 800/PK-5
1265 Mount Washington Rd 40071 502-477-6950
Gary Kidwell, prin. Fax 477-6955
Spencer County MS 700/6-8
1263 Mount Washington Rd 40071 502-477-3260
Matt Mercer, prin. Fax 477-6796
Taylorsville ES 400/PK-5
420 Highview Dr 40071 502-477-3339
Steven Rucker, prin. Fax 477-3214

Tollesboro, Lewis
Lewis County SD
Supt. — See Vanceburg
Tollesboro ES 300/PK-6
2431 W KY 10 41189 606-798-3231
Woody Underwood, prin. Fax 798-2515

Tompkinsville, Monroe, Pop. 2,360
Monroe County SD 1,900/PK-12
309 Emberton St 42167 270-487-5456
Amy Thompson, supt. Fax 487-5571
www.monroe.kyschools.us
Carter ES 200/PK-5
3888 Edmonton Rd 42167 270-487-5621
Jeff Blythe, prin. Fax 487-9515
Monroe County MS 400/6-8
600 S Main St 42167 270-487-9624
Jon Michael Clemmons, prin. Fax 487-9534
Tompkinsville ES 400/PK-5
420 Elementary School Rd 42167 270-487-6472
Heather Geralds, prin. Fax 487-9203
Other Schools – See Gamaliel

Topmost, Knott
Knott County SD
Supt. — See Hindman
Beaver Creek ES 300/K-8
8000 Highway 7 S 41862 606-447-2833
Jody Keens, prin. Fax 447-2366

Tyner, Jackson
Jackson County SD
Supt. — See Mc Kee
Tyner ES 500/PK-5
PO Box 190 40486 606-364-5105
Tim Johnson, prin. Fax 364-2656

Union, Boone, Pop. 5,294
Boone County SD
Supt. — See Florence
Gray MS 1,000/6-8
10400 US Highway 42 41091 859-384-5333
Todd Novak, prin. Fax 384-5318
Longbranch ES 800/PK-5
2805 Longbranch Rd 41091 859-384-4500
Erika Bowles, prin. Fax 384-2945
Mann ES 800/PK-5
10435 US Highway 42 41091 859-384-5000
Connie Crigger, prin. Fax 384-5007
New Haven ES 800/PK-5
10854 US Highway 42 41091 859-384-5325
Mary Goble, prin. Fax 384-5253

St. Timothy S, PO Box 120 41091 50/PK-8
Deb Thomas, prin. 859-384-1100

Uniontown, Union, Pop. 978
Union County SD
Supt. — See Morganfield
Uniontown ES 200/PK-5
PO Box 517 42461 270-822-4462
Tamala Howard, prin. Fax 822-4286

Utica, Daviess
Daviess County SD
Supt. — See Owensboro
Southern Oaks ES 400/PK-5
7525 US Highway 431 42376 270-852-7570
Jennifer Humphrey, prin. Fax 852-7580

Valley Station, Jefferson, Pop. 22,840
Jefferson County SD
Supt. — See Louisville
Layne ES 500/PK-5
9831 East Ave 40272 502-485-8290
Ron Marshall, prin. Fax 313-3494
Medora ES 400/PK-5
11801 Deering Rd 40272 502-485-8298
Beth White, prin. Fax 313-3402
Stonestreet ES 500/PK-5
10007 Stonestreet Rd 40272 502-485-8333
Donald Boemker, prin. Fax 313-3538

Stuart Academy 700/7-8
4603 Valley Station Rd 40272 502-485-8334
Laura Dalton, prin. Fax 313-3540

Vanceburg, Lewis, Pop. 1,503
Lewis County SD 2,400/PK-12
PO Box 159 41179 606-796-2811
Jamie Weddington, supt. Fax 796-3081
www.lewis.kyschools.us/
Laurel ES 100/PK-6
116 Laurel School Rd 41179 606-796-2214
Chad Kidwell, prin. Fax 796-0805
Lewis County Central ES 500/PK-5
86 Walter St 41179 606-796-2831
Stacy Kidwell, prin. Fax 796-3103
Lewis County MS 500/6-8
PO Box 69 41179 606-796-6228
Bill Allen, prin. Fax 796-6255
Other Schools – See Garrison, Tollesboro

Verona, Boone, Pop. 1,443
Walton-Verona ISD
Supt. — See Walton
Walton-Verona ES 600/PK-4
15066 Porter Rd 41092 859-485-4181
Rob Hartman, prin. Fax 485-1977

Versailles, Woodford, Pop. 8,423
Woodford County SD 4,100/PK-12
330 Pisgah Rd 40383 859-879-4600
D. Scott Hawkins, supt. Fax 873-1614
ilearn.woodfordschools.org/
Huntertown ES 600/PK-5
120 Woodburn Hall Dr 40383 859-879-4680
Elaine Kaiser, prin. Fax 873-6292
Simmons ES 500/PK-5
830 Tyrone Pike 40383 859-879-4670
Tiffany Cook, prin. Fax 873-6914
Southside ES 500/PK-5
1300 Troy Pike 40383 859-879-4660
Jason McAllister, prin. Fax 873-4571
Woodford County MS 900/6-8
100 School House Rd 40383 859-879-4650
Tracy Bruno, prin. Fax 873-4436
Other Schools – See Midway

St. Leo S 200/PK-8
255 Huntertown Rd 40383 859-873-4591
Dr. Helena DiBiasie Ph.D., prin. Fax 873-1495
Versailles Montessori S 100/PK-5
480 Pinckard Pike 40383 859-873-1998
Woodford Christian S 100/K-5
320 Hope Ln 40383 859-873-0288
Cara Meadows, prin. Fax 873-0566

Villa Hills, Kenton, Pop. 7,410
Kenton County SD
Supt. — See Fort Wright
River Ridge ES 1,100/PK-5
2772 Amsterdam Rd 41017 859-341-5260
Jena Smiddy, prin. Fax 341-5962

Villa Madonna Academy 300/K-6
2500 Amsterdam Rd 41017 859-331-6333
Soshana Bosley, prin. Fax 331-8615

Vine Grove, Hardin, Pop. 4,350
Hardin County SD
Supt. — See Elizabethtown
Alton MS 700/6-8
100 Country Club Rd 40175 270-877-2135
Jama Bennett, prin. Fax 877-6297
Vine Grove ES 400/1-5
309 1st St 40175 270-877-5410
Allison Scherer, contact Fax 877-5411

Viper, Perry
Perry County SD
Supt. — See Hazard
Viper S 200/PK-8
20 Eddington Ln 41774 606-436-3837
Kent Campbell, prin. Fax 436-0426

Virgie, Pike, Pop. 279

Valley Christian Academy 50/PK-6
4908 Longfork Rd 41572 606-639-9101
Jessica Hall, admin. Fax 639-8921

Waco, Madison
Madison County SD
Supt. — See Richmond
Waco ES 400/PK-5
359 Waco Loop Rd 40385 859-387-3600
Venessa Worley, prin. Fax 369-3819

Waddy, Shelby
Shelby County SD
Supt. — See Shelbyville
Heritage ES 500/PK-5
8300 Frankfort Rd 40076 502-829-5242
J.J. Black, prin. Fax 829-9605

Wallingford, Fleming
Fleming County SD
Supt. — See Flemingsburg
Ward ES 200/K-6
12811 Morehead Rd 41093 606-876-2061
Terra Greer, prin. Fax 876-4487

Wallins Creek, Harlan, Pop. 156
Harlan County SD
Supt. — See Harlan
Wallins ES 400/PK-8
PO Box 10 40873 606-664-3444
Bristol Belcher, prin. Fax 664-3478

Walton, Boone, Pop. 3,572
Walton-Verona ISD 1,600/PK-12
16 School Rd 41094 859-485-4181
Dr. Robert Storer, supt. Fax 485-1810
wv.kyschools.us
Walton-Verona MS 500/5-8
32 School Rd 41094 859-485-4181
Eric Morwessel, prin. Fax 485-7739
Other Schools – See Verona

St. Joseph Academy 200/PK-8
48 Needmore St 41094 859-485-6444
Sr. Elizabeth Ann Barkett, prin. Fax 485-4262

Warfield, Martin, Pop. 269
Martin County SD
Supt. — See Inez
Martin County Headstart Center 100/PK-PK
33 Warfield Elementary Loop 41267 606-395-7007
Dena James, dir. Fax 395-7006
Martin County MS 500/6-8
130 Middle School Dr 41267 606-395-5900
Brent Haney, prin. Fax 395-5902
Warfield ES 300/K-5
33 Warfield Elementary Loop 41267 606-395-5121
Shane Stafford, prin. Fax 395-5980

Warsaw, Gallatin, Pop. 1,574
Gallatin County SD 1,700/PK-12
75 Boardwalk 41095 859-567-1820
Larry Hammond, supt. Fax 567-4528
www.gallatin.kyschools.us
Gallatin County Lower ES 500/PK-2
25 Boaz Dr 41095 859-567-6340
Joe Wright, prin. Fax 567-6205
Gallatin County MS 400/6-8
88 Pawprint Path 41095 859-567-5860
John Ritchie, prin. Fax 567-6107
Gallatin County Upper ES 400/3-5
50 Pawprint Path 41095 859-567-2060
Shonda Dunn, prin. Fax 567-2715

Waynesburg, Lincoln
Lincoln County SD
Supt. — See Stanford
Highland ES 300/PK-5
75 Tick Ridge Rd 40489 606-365-2768
James Carrier, prin. Fax 365-5809
Waynesburg ES 300/PK-5
345 KY Highway 328 W 40489 606-379-6413
Dr. Amy Rigsby, prin. Fax 365-5810

West Liberty, Morgan, Pop. 3,396
Morgan County SD 2,100/K-12
155 University Dr 41472 606-743-8002
C. Thomas Potter Ed.D., supt. Fax 743-8050
www.morgan.kyschools.us
East Valley ES 200/K-5
7585 Highway 172 41472 606-522-8152
Amanda Lee, prin. Fax 522-8200
Morgan Central ES 300/K-5
3201 Highway 460 W 41472 606-743-8552
Ashley Pelfrey, prin. Fax 743-8599
Morgan County MS 500/6-8
380 Road To Success 41472 606-743-8102
Terry Whitt, prin. Fax 743-8150
Wrigley ES 300/K-5
7490 Highway 7 41472 606-743-8302
Vickie Oldfield, prin. Fax 743-8350
Other Schools – See Ezel

West Paducah, McCracken
McCracken County SD
Supt. — See Paducah
Heath ES 400/PK-5
4365 Metropolis Lake Rd 42086 270-538-4060
Laine Cooper, prin. Fax 538-4061
Heath MS 500/6-8
4330 Metropolis Lake Rd 42086 270-538-4070
Matthew Blackwell, prin. Fax 538-4071

West Point, Hardin, Pop. 790
Bullitt County SD
Supt. — See Shepherdsville
Nichols ES 200/PK-5
10665 Highway 44 W 40177 502-869-2600
Annemarie Landry, prin. Fax 922-3372

West Point ISD 200/PK-8
PO Box 367 40177 502-922-4797
Mickey Brangers, supt. Fax 922-9372
www.westpoint.kyschools.us
West Point Independent S 200/PK-8
PO Box 367 40177 502-922-4797
Lisa Storey, prin. Fax 922-9372

Whitesburg, Letcher, Pop. 2,131
Letcher County SD 3,200/PK-12
224 Parks St 41858 606-633-4455
Tony Sergent, supt. Fax 633-4724
www.letcher.kyschools.us
Cowan ES 400/K-8
PO Box 767 41858 606-633-7195
William Mike, prin. Fax 633-0763
West Whitesburg ES 400/PK-5
330 Parks St 41858 606-633-9538
Stacy Isaac, prin. Fax 633-1085
Whitesburg MS 200/6-8
366 Parks St 41858 606-633-2761
Henry Frazier, prin. Fax 633-4137
Other Schools – See Blackey, Eolia, Kona, Neon

Whitesville, Daviess, Pop. 544
Daviess County SD
Supt. — See Owensboro
Whitesville ES 400/PK-5
9656 State Route 54 42378 270-852-7670
Cindy Appleby, prin. Fax 852-7680

St. Mary of the Woods S 200/PK-8
10521 Franklin St 42378 270-233-5253
Sr. Emily Hernandez, prin. Fax 233-9360

Whitley City, McCreary, Pop. 1,160
McCreary County SD
Supt. — See Stearns
McCreary County Preschool North PK-PK
2819 N Highway 27 42653 606-354-3590
Dr. Aaron Anderson Ed.D., admin. Fax 354-9696
Whitley City ES 600/PK-6
2819 N Highway 27 42653 606-376-2690
Foster Jones, prin. Fax 376-4150

Williamsburg, Whitley, Pop. 5,159
Whitley County SD 4,600/PK-12
300 Main St 40769 606-549-7000
Scott Paul, supt. Fax 549-7006
www.whitley.kyschools.us
Boston ES 300/PK-6
3291 Highway 1804 40769 606-549-7872
Carolyn Lawson, prin. Fax 786-3302
Pleasant View ES 300/PK-6
5554 S Highway 25W 40769 606-549-7085
Bobby Gibbs, prin. Fax 549-7086
Whitley County Central IS 400/3-6
2940 N Highway 25 W 40769 606-549-8011
Susan Brashear, prin. Fax 549-8112
Whitley County Central PS 400/PK-2
520 Boulevard Of Champions 40769 606-549-7060
Brandon Anderson, prin. Fax 549-7065
Whitley County MS 700/7-8
351 Boulevard Of Champions 40769 606-549-7050
Stuart Conlin, prin. Fax 549-7055
Other Schools – See Corbin, Rockholds, Siler

Williamsburg ISD 900/PK-12
1000 Main St 40769 606-549-6044
Dr. Amon Couch, supt. Fax 549-6015
www.wburg.kyschools.us
Williamsburg S 900/PK-12
1000 Main St 40769 606-549-6044
Tim Melton, prin. Fax 549-6015

Williamstown, Grant, Pop. 3,887
Grant County SD 3,800/K-12
820 Arnie Risen Blvd 41097 859-824-3323
Matt Morgan, supt. Fax 824-3508
www.grant.kyschools.us
Mason Corinth ES 400/K-5
225 Heekin Rd 41097 859-824-9510
Leanne Adkins, prin. Fax 824-4225
Other Schools – See Dry Ridge

Williamstown ISD 900/PK-12
300 Helton St 41097 859-824-7144
Misty Middleton, supt. Fax 824-3237
www.williamstown.kyschools.us/
Williamstown ES 400/PK-5
300 Helton St 41097 859-824-3760
Jeremy Dodd, prin. Fax 824-3745
Williamstown JHS 200/6-8
300 Helton St 41097 859-824-4421
Brandy Feagan, prin. Fax 824-3745

Willisburg, Washington, Pop. 281
Washington County SD
Supt. — See Springfield
North Washington ES 500/PK-8
5658 Highway 433 40078 859-375-4038
Amanda Mattingly, prin. Fax 375-0214

Wilmore, Jessamine, Pop. 3,637
Jessamine County SD
Supt. — See Nicholasville
Wilmore ES 600/K-5
150 Campground Ln 40390 859-858-3134
Dawn Floyd, prin. Fax 858-3108

Winchester, Clark, Pop. 18,061
Clark County SD 4,000/PK-12
1600 W Lexington Ave 40391 859-744-4545
Paul Christy, supt. Fax 745-3935
www.clark.kyschools.us
Baker IS 200/5-6
1645 Martin Luther King Jr 40391 859-745-5190
Josh Mounts, prin. Fax 744-1238
Campbell JHS 300/7-8
620 Boone Ave 40391 859-745-5200
Dustin Howard, prin. Fax 745-2027
Clark County Preschool 300/PK-PK
30 Beckner St 40391 859-744-1722
Kara Davies, prin.
Conkwright ES K-5
360 Mt Sterling Rd 40391 859-745-8900
Julie Bonfield, prin. Fax 745-3908
Justice ES 500/K-4
350 Mount Sterling Rd 40391 859-745-8800
Susan Hillman, prin. Fax 745-1635
Shearer ES 400/K-4
244 E Broadway St 40391 859-744-4978
Mark Rose, prin. Fax 745-3933
Strode Station ES 600/K-4
1750 Martin Luther King Jr 40391 859-745-3915
Janet Brown, prin. Fax 745-3094

Calvary Christian S 300/PK-8
15 Redwing Dr 40391 859-744-0817
Ned Hess, prin. Fax 744-9204
St. Agatha Academy 100/PK-8
244 S Main St 40391 859-744-6484
John Pica, prin. Fax 744-0268

Wingo, Graves, Pop. 616
Graves County SD
Supt. — See Mayfield
Wingo ES 300/PK-6
449 Lebanon St 42088 270-674-4870
Scott Bradley, prin. Fax 376-2223

Wittensville, Johnson
Johnson County SD
Supt. — See Paintsville
Castle Memorial ES 400/PK-6
3936 N US Highway 23 41274 606-297-3738
Steve Young, prin. Fax 297-7411

Wooton, Leslie
Leslie County SD
Supt. — See Hyden
Muncy ES 300/PK-8
PO Box 140 41776 606-279-4155
Merlene Lewis, prin. Fax 279-3772

Worthington, Greenup, Pop. 1,591
Raceland-Worthington ISD
Supt. — See Raceland
Worthington ES 200/4-6
800 Center Ave 41183 606-836-8014
Kyle Russell, prin. Fax 836-3449

Wurtland, Greenup, Pop. 983
Greenup County SD
Supt. — See Greenup
Wurtland ES 200/K-5
611 East St 41144 606-836-6987
Steven Branim, prin. Fax 836-5375
Wurtland MS 300/6-8
700 Center St 41144 606-836-1023
Amanda Powell, prin. Fax 836-3939

Yeaddiss, Leslie
Leslie County SD
Supt. — See Hyden
Hayes Lewis ES 200/PK-8
PO Box 70 41777 606-279-4121
Patrick Morgan, prin. Fax 279-3876

LOUISIANA

LOUISIANA DEPARTMENT OF EDUCATION
PO Box 94064, Baton Rouge 70804-9064
Telephone 225-342-3602
Fax 225-342-7316
Website http://www.louisianabelieves.com

Superintendent of Education John White

LOUISIANA BOARD OF EDUCATION
PO Box 94064, Baton Rouge 70804-9064

President Gary Jones

PUBLIC, PRIVATE AND CATHOLIC ELEMENTARY SCHOOLS

Abbeville, Vermilion, Pop. 12,038
Vermilion Parish SD 9,000/PK-12
PO Box 520 70511 337-898-5770
Jerome Puyau, supt. Fax 898-0939
www.vpsb.net
Eaton Park ES 700/PK-2
1502 Sylvester St 70510 337-893-4978
Angela Godwin, prin. Fax 898-1274
Forked Island/E Broussard S 300/PK-8
19635 Columbus Rd 70510 337-642-9100
Patricia Gaspard, prin. Fax 642-9120
Herod ES 500/3-5
120 Odea St 70510 337-893-4258
Lysonia Robertson, prin. Fax 893-4275
LeBlanc ES 600/PK-5
4511 E LA Hwy 338 70510 337-937-8110
Susan Stephen, prin. Fax 937-8761
Meaux ES 400/PK-5
12419 LA Hwy 696 70510 337-893-3901
Dawn Amy, prin. Fax 893-7112
Seventh Ward ES 300/PK-5
12012 Audubon Rd 70510 337-893-5875
Natalie Hebert, prin. Fax 893-8984
Williams MS 600/6-8
1105 Prairie Ave 70510 337-893-3943
Dana Primeaux, prin. Fax 893-5190
Other Schools – See Erath, Gueydan, Kaplan, Maurice, Rayne

Mt. Carmel S 400/PK-8
405 Park Ave 70510 337-898-0859
Jacqueline Trahan, prin. Fax 893-5968

Abita Springs, Saint Tammany, Pop. 2,315
St. Tammany Parish SD
Supt. — See Covington
Abita Springs ES 700/PK-3
22410 Level St 70420 985-892-8184
Rebecca Stogner, prin. Fax 892-2757
Abita Springs MS 400/4-6
72079 Maple St 70420 985-892-2070
Edward Strohmeyer, prin. Fax 893-2304

Albany, Livingston, Pop. 1,080
Livingston Parish SD
Supt. — See Livingston
Albany Lower ES 500/PK-2
PO Box 970 70711 225-567-9281
Kathy Rodosta, prin. Fax 567-2972
Albany MS 600/5-8
PO Box 1210 70711 225-567-5231
Rachel Jenkins, prin. Fax 567-9177
Albany Upper ES 300/3-4
PO Box 1750 70711 225-567-5030
Deborah Tate, prin. Fax 567-5085

Alexandria, Rapides, Pop. 46,974
Rapides Parish SD 22,600/PK-12
PO Box 1230 71309 318-487-0888
Nason Authement, supt. Fax 449-3167
www.rpsb.us
Acadian ES - New Vision Academy 200/K-5
310 Richmond Dr 71302 318-487-1202
Tracy Vorrice, prin. Fax 449-1954
Alexandria Magnet MS 500/6-8
122 Maryland Ave 71301 318-445-5343
Dennis Stewart, prin. Fax 442-8650
Brame MS 900/6-8
4800 Dawn St 71301 318-443-3688
Mollie Fontenot, prin. Fax 442-3966
Brasher ES 500/PK-6
601 Cloverleaf Blvd 71303 318-442-0878
Angie Franklin, prin. Fax 487-8052
Cherokee ES 700/PK-5
5700 Prescott Rd 71301 318-442-1987
Bonnie Lord, prin. Fax 442-4767
Hadnot-Hayes STEM ES 200/PK-5
4020 Aaron St 71302 318-445-0031
Shannon Carmouche, prin. Fax 484-6174
Hall Magnet ES 200/PK-5
3111 Jones Ave 71302 318-443-9093
Emmett Jefferson, prin. Fax 442-7104
Horseshoe Drive ES - New Vision Academy 300/PK-5
2905 Horseshoe Dr 71301 318-443-0579
Catherine Lewis, prin. Fax 448-4788
Huddle ES - New Vision Academy 400/PK-6
505 Texas Ave 71301 318-442-7921
Tonya Normand, prin. Fax 442-5498
Martin Park ES 300/PK-5
4203 Lisa St 71302 318-448-1695
Cynthia Corley, prin. Fax 448-0511
Nachman ES 600/K-5
4102 Wakefield Blvd 71303 318-445-7725
Rebecca Warren, prin. Fax 448-3890
North Bayou Rapides - New Vision Academy 300/PK-6
5500 England Dr 71303 318-445-4260
Alyson Smith, prin. Fax 442-1662
Patrick ES 200/PK-5
1402 Reed Ave 71301 318-443-5443
Laquanta Jones, prin. Fax 561-2008
Peabody Montessori ES 400/PK-6
2416 3rd St 71302 318-442-5012
Rena Linzay, prin. Fax 487-6704
Phoenix Magnet ES 600/K-6
4500 Lincoln Rd 71302 318-445-6296
John Grimes, prin. Fax 442-2213
Poland S 400/PK-8
3348 Highway 457 71302 318-445-9224
Deborah Heltman, prin. Fax 442-7582
Redwine ES - New Vision Academy 200/PK-6
1323 Vance Ave 71301 318-442-3177
Carlessa White, prin. Fax 473-9300
Rosenthal Montessori ES 300/PK-6
1951 Monroe St 71301 318-442-5791
Naomi Jones, prin. Fax 443-1667
Rugg ES 300/PK-5
1319 Bush Ave 71301 318-442-4536
Vickie Smith, prin. Fax 445-8476
Smith Magnet MS 500/6-8
3100 Jones Ave 71302 318-445-6241
Dr. Norvella Williams, prin. Fax 445-9255
Other Schools – See Ball, Deville, Elmer, Forest Hill, Glenmora, Lecompte, Lena, Pineville, Woodworth

---

Alexandria Country Day S 500/PK-8
5603 Bayou Rapides Rd 71303 318-448-1475
Nancy Rials M.Ed., admin. Fax 442-7924
Grace Christian S 400/PK-12
4900 Jackson St 71303 318-449-9031
Kay Blackburn, prin. Fax 443-1034
Montessori Education Center 200/PK-8
4209 N Bolton Ave 71303 318-445-0138
Joelle Flaherty, head sch Fax 445-0165
Our Lady of Prompt Succor S 500/PK-6
420 21st St 71301 318-487-1862
Johanna Tassin, prin. Fax 473-9321
St. Frances Cabrini S 100/PK-8
2215 E Texas Ave 71301 318-448-3333
Nina Vincent, prin. Fax 448-3343

Amite, Tangipahoa, Pop. 4,112
Tangipahoa Parish SD 20,000/PK-12
59656 Puleston Rd 70422 985-748-7153
Mark Kolwe, supt. Fax 748-8587
www.tangischools.org
Amite Elementary Magnet S 600/PK-4
301 Vernon Ave 70422 985-748-6953
Gary Porter, prin. Fax 748-8609
Amite Westside Middle Magnet S 400/5-8
401 W Oak St 70422 985-748-9073
Ashley Walker, prin. Fax 748-9225
Other Schools – See Hammond, Independence, Kentwood, Loranger, Natalbany, Ponchatoula, Roseland, Tickfaw

---

Oak Forest Academy 700/PK-12
600 Walnut St 70422 985-748-4321
Jason Brabham, admin. Fax 748-4320

Anacoco, Vernon, Pop. 864
Vernon Parish SD
Supt. — See Leesville
Anacoco ES 500/PK-6
4726 Port Arthur Ave 71403 337-239-3040
Kevin Dowdle, prin. Fax 239-6245

Angie, Washington, Pop. 242
Washington Parish SD
Supt. — See Franklinton
Ray ES 400/PK-5
30523 Wesley Ray Rd 70426 985-986-3131
Kewanda August, prin. Fax 986-3122

Arabi, Saint Bernard, Pop. 3,513
St. Bernard Parish SD
Supt. — See Chalmette
Arabi ES 700/PK-5
7200 Alexander Ave 70032 504-218-5058
Carla Carollo, prin. Fax 252-4858

Arcadia, Bienville, Pop. 2,890
Bienville Parish SD 2,200/PK-12
PO Box 418 71001 318-263-9416
William Britt, supt. Fax 263-3100
www.bpsb.us/
Crawford ES 300/PK-5
935 Daniel St 71001 318-263-8757
Laverne Wilson, prin. Fax 263-9010
Other Schools – See Bienville, Castor, Gibsland, Ringgold, Saline

Arnaudville, Saint Landry, Pop. 1,048
St. Landry Parish SD
Supt. — See Opelousas
Arnaudville ES 200/5-8
PO Box 770 70512 337-754-5320
Mary Miller, prin. Fax 754-5326

Athens, Claiborne, Pop. 242

Mount Olive Christian S 100/PK-12
15349 Highway 9 71003 318-258-5661
Linda Lee Gantt, prin. Fax 258-5662

Atlanta, Winn, Pop. 159
Winn Parish SD
Supt. — See Winnfield
Atlanta S 200/PK-12
118 School Rd 71404 318-628-4613
Denise Young, prin. Fax 628-4247

Avondale, Jefferson, Pop. 4,884
Jefferson Parish SD
Supt. — See Harvey
Ford MS 700/6-8
435 S Jamie Blvd 70094 504-436-2474
Amy Schayot, prin. Fax 436-0604
Strehle ES 400/PK-5
178 Millie Dr 70094 504-436-1920
Terri Howard, prin. Fax 436-9264

Baker, East Baton Rouge, Pop. 13,732
City of Baker SD 1,700/PK-12
14750 Plank Rd 70714 225-774-5795
Dr. Herman Brister, supt. Fax 774-5797
www.bakerschools.org
Bakerfield ES 300/PK-5
2550 South St 70714 225-775-1493
Candace Jenkins, prin. Fax 775-0022
Baker Heights ES 400/PK-5
3750 Harding St 70714 225-775-1496
LaKesha Reese-Penn, prin. Fax 774-4629
Baker MS 400/6-8
5903 Groom Rd 70714 225-775-9750
Roy Walker, prin. Fax 775-9753
Park Ridge Academic Magnet S 200/K-8
5905 Groom Rd 70714 225-775-5924
Tammy Armand-Golden, prin. Fax 774-0154

East Baton Rouge Parish SD
Supt. — See Baton Rouge
White Hills ES 200/K-5
5300 Bentley Dr 70714 225-775-5891
Dawn Brewster, prin. Fax 775-0557

Baldwin, Saint Mary, Pop. 2,394
St. Mary Parish SD
Supt. — See Centerville
Boudreaux MS 300/6-8
18333 Highway 182 70514 337-924-7990
Magdalene Drexler, prin. Fax 924-7999
Raintree ES 600/PK-5
PO Box 120 70514 337-923-0494
Donald Sanders, prin. Fax 923-6859

Ball, Rapides, Pop. 3,932
Rapides Parish SD
Supt. — See Alexandria
Ball ES 300/PK-6
89 Camp Livingston Rd 71405 318-640-5394
Lisa Lowery, prin. Fax 640-9396
Paradise ES 500/PK-6
5010 Monroe Hwy 71405 318-640-1033
Christy Dugas, prin. Fax 641-1315
Tioga JHS 700/7-8
1150 Tioga Rd 71405 318-640-9412
Rebecca Pippen, prin. Fax 640-0126

Basile, Evangeline, Pop. 1,791
Evangeline Parish SD
Supt. — See Ville Platte
Stewart ES 400/PK-4
1032 Belton St 70515 337-432-6412
Christine Bacon, prin. Fax 432-6791

Baskin, Franklin, Pop. 250
Franklin Parish SD
Supt. — See Winnsboro
Baskin S 400/PK-8
1926 Highway 857 71219 318-248-2381
Ashley Schulte, prin. Fax 248-2187

Bastrop, Morehouse, Pop. 11,255
Morehouse Parish SD 2,700/PK-12
PO Box 872 71221 318-281-5784
Hazel Sellers B.A., supt. Fax 283-3456
www.mpsb.us
Adams ES 200/K-3
804 Kammell St 71220 318-281-5244
Wendy Coleman, prin. Fax 281-7240
Morehouse JHS 300/4-7
1001 W Madison Ave 71220 318-281-0776
Alvin Williams, prin. Fax 283-1846
Morehouse Magnet S 300/PK-8
909 Larche Ln 71220 318-281-3126
Carla Martin, prin. Fax 281-3181
Pine Grove ES 200/PK-3
7261 Pine Grove Loop Rd 71220 318-281-1289
Karmen Murry, prin. Fax 281-5295
Other Schools – See Mer Rouge

Prairie View Academy 300/K-12
9942 Edwin St 71220 318-281-7044
Perry Kelly, prin. Fax 281-4113

Batchelor, Pointe Coupee
Pointe Coupee Parish SD
Supt. — See New Roads
Upper Pointe Coupee S 300/PK-8
4739 LA Highway 419 70715 225-492-2555
Myron Brown, prin. Fax 618-4938

Baton Rouge, East Baton Rouge, Pop. 226,740
Central Community SD 4,400/PK-12
PO Box 78094 70837 225-262-1919
Michael Faulk, supt. Fax 262-1989
www.centralcss.org
Central IS 1,000/3-5
12636 Sullivan Rd 70818 225-261-1390
Rhonda Taylor, prin. Fax 261-1080
Central MS 900/6-8
12656 Sullivan Rd 70818 225-261-2237
Susan Watts, prin. Fax 261-9973
Tanglewood ES 700/1-2
9352 Rustling Oaks Dr 70818 225-261-3454
Julie Stevens, prin. Fax 261-3535
Other Schools – See Greenwell Springs

East Baton Rouge Parish SD 40,600/PK-12
PO Box 2950 70821 225-922-5400
Warren Drake, supt. Fax 922-5499
www.ebrschools.org
Audubon ES 500/PK-5
10730 Goodwood Blvd 70815 225-272-2620
Nakia Perkins, prin. Fax 272-2581
Baton Rouge Foreign Lang Immersion S 300/PK-5
802 Mayflower St 70802 225-343-6630
Cheryl Miller, prin. Fax 344-4962
Baton Rouge Visual & Performing Arts ES 400/PK-5
2040 S Acadian Thruway 70808 225-344-0084
Candice Hartley, prin. Fax 343-6227
Belfair Montessori Magnet S 300/PK-8
4451 Fairfields Ave 70802 225-356-6191
Jamar Jackson, prin. Fax 355-8418
Bernard Terrace ES 400/PK-5
241 Edison St 70806 225-343-5769
Demetric Alexander, prin. Fax 338-0534
Broadmoor ES 600/PK-5
4510 Bawell St 70808 225-925-0343
Lawrence Harris, prin. Fax 926-4689
Broadmoor MS 400/6-8
1225 Sharp Rd 70815 225-272-0540
Daniel Edwards, prin. Fax 272-0195
Brookstown Middle Magnet Academy 6-8
4375 E Brookstown Dr 70805 225-355-6556
James Smith, prin. Fax 355-6503
Brownfields ES 400/PK-5
11615 Ellen Dr 70811 225-775-3527
Sandy Shepard, prin. Fax 774-5437
Buchanan ES 500/PK-5
1222 E Buchanan St 70802 225-343-4585
Charlotte Britten, prin. Fax 343-4673
Capitol ES 500/PK-5
4141 Gus Young Ave 70802 225-343-9364
Mona Collins, prin. Fax 344-5861
Capitol MS 400/6-8
5100 Greenwell Springs Rd 70806 225-231-9292
Viola Jackson, prin. Fax 231-9291
Cedarcrest-Southmoor ES 600/PK-5
10187 Twin Cedars St 70816 225-293-9950
Cherryl Matthews, prin. Fax 293-5028
Claiborne ES 700/PK-5
4707 Denham St 70805 225-357-9712
Rochelle Anderson, prin. Fax 357-7141
Crestworth ES 300/PK-5
11200 Avenue F 70807 225-778-1317
Cleo Perry, prin. Fax 778-1114
Delmont Pre K K Center 400/PK-K
5300 Douglas Ave 70805 225-355-2106
Joan Campbell, dean Fax 359-6515
DuFrocq S 600/PK-5
330 S 19th St 70806 225-334-7653
Mary Robvais, prin. Fax 334-7656
Forest Heights Academy of Excellence 400/PK-5
7447 Sumrall Dr 70812 225-355-5681
Myra Varmall, prin. Fax 357-0646
Glasgow MS 700/6-8
1676 Glasgow Ave 70808 225-925-2942
Erin Howard, prin. Fax 928-3565
Glen Oaks Park ES 600/PK-5
2401 72nd Ave 70807 225-356-4521
Bernard Williams, prin. Fax 356-8821
Greenbrier ES 400/PK-5
12203 Canterbury Dr 70814 225-275-4260
Shayla Hollins, prin. Fax 275-6570
Highland ES 300/PK-5
280 Sunset Blvd 70808 225-766-1272
Justin Robicheaux, prin. Fax 769-0630
Howell Park ES 400/PK-5
6125 Winbourne Ave 70805 225-356-0104
R. Washington-Scott, prin. Fax 357-8134
Jefferson Terrace ES 500/PK-5
9902 Cal Rd 70809 225-293-3210
Zane Whittington, prin. Fax 291-6627
La Belle Aire ES 600/PK-5
12255 Tams Dr 70815 225-275-7480
Cynthia Lipscomb, prin. Fax 272-6322
LaSalle ES 400/PK-5
8000 Lasalle Ave 70806 225-927-6130
Suzanne Navo, prin. Fax 923-1247
Magnolia Woods ES 500/PK-5
760 Maxine Dr 70808 225-769-6845
Kim DiPalma, prin. Fax 769-3340
Mayfair Lab S 200/K-5
9880 Hyacinth Ave 70810 225-761-7849
Christa Bordelon, prin. Fax 766-4507
McKinley Magnet MS 700/6-8
1550 Eddie Robinson Sr Dr 70802 225-388-0089
Sean Joffrion, prin. Fax 387-1434
Melrose ES 600/PK-5
1348 Valcour Dr 70806 225-926-2353
Olga Pack, prin. Fax 927-7808
Merrydale ES 400/PK-5
6700 Rio Dr 70812 225-355-0346
Sherna Lumar, prin. Fax 355-6217
North Banks MS of Excellence 6-8
5959 Cadillac St 70811 225-357-3371
Beverly Tate, prin. Fax 356-2665
Park ES 400/PK-5
2700 Fuqua St 70802 225-344-2145
Stephanie Tate, prin. Fax 343-1244
Park Forest ES 600/PK-5
10717 Elain Dr 70814 225-272-0814
Alicia Franklin, prin. Fax 275-3194
Park Forest MS 900/6-8
3760 Aletha Dr 70814 225-275-6650
Curtis Walker, prin. Fax 275-3058
Parkview ES 700/PK-5
5660 Parkforest Dr 70816 225-753-5615
Carla Parks, prin. Fax 751-6546
Polk ES 200/PK-5
408 E Polk St 70802 225-383-2611
Cheryl Miller, prin. Fax 338-0471
Progress ES 400/PK-5
855 Progress Rd 70807 225-775-4986
LaShawn Stewart, prin. Fax 774-2028
Riveroaks ES 400/PK-5
950 Fontainbleau Dr 70819 225-275-4600
Erica Aguillard, prin. Fax 272-2447
Ryan ES 500/PK-5
10337 Elmgrove Garden Dr 70807 225-775-2407
LaDarrion Jackson, prin. Fax 778-2709
Scotlandville Pre-Engineering Academy 500/6-8
9147 Elmgrove Garden Dr 70807 225-775-0776
Shalika Scott, prin. Fax 775-2104
Sharon Hills ES 400/PK-5
6450 Guynell Dr 70811 225-355-6522
Angela Sanders, prin. Fax 355-4428
Shenandoah ES 500/PK-5
16555 Appomattox Ave 70817 225-753-3560
Amy Butler, prin. Fax 756-0521
Sherwood MS Academic Magnet 800/6-8
1020 Marlbrook Dr 70815 225-272-3090
Jamie Noel, prin. Fax 273-9459
Southeast MS 800/6-8
15000 S Harrells Ferry Rd 70816 225-753-5930
Amber Boyd, prin. Fax 756-8601
Twin Oaks ES 500/PK-5
819 Trammell Dr 70815 225-275-6620
Cesar Rico, prin. Fax 275-2828
University Terrace ES 300/PK-5
575 W Roosevelt St 70802 225-387-2328
Pamela Marshall, prin. Fax 387-3324
Villa Del Ray ES 400/PK-5
9765 Cuyhanga Pkwy 70815 225-924-1606
Joy Abernathy-Dyer, prin. Fax 926-6806
Wedgewood ES 700/PK-5
2330 Aspenwood Dr 70816 225-753-7301
Toni Wilson, prin. Fax 756-8418
Westdale Hts Academic Magnet S 400/PK-5
2000 College Dr 70808 225-926-5421
Catasha Edwards, prin. Fax 926-9885
Westdale MS 1,200/6-8
5650 Claycut Rd 70806 225-924-1308
Jeremy Couvillion, prin. Fax 926-9929
Westminister ES 400/PK-5
8935 Westminister Dr 70809 225-927-2930
Norman St. Amant, prin. Fax 927-4009
Wildwood ES 500/PK-5
444 Halfway Tree Rd 70810 225-766-6002
Natalie Jadid, prin. Fax 769-6803
Winbourne ES 500/1-5
4503 Winbourne Ave 70805 225-355-4446
Brenda Wilkinson, prin. Fax 355-6570
Woodlawn ES 800/PK-5
8160 Antioch Rd 70817 225-756-3861
Janice Lindsey, prin. Fax 756-3684
Woodlawn MS 1,000/6-8
14939 Tiger Bend Rd 70817 225-751-0436
Shelly Colvin, prin. Fax 753-0159
Other Schools – See Baker, Pride

Southern University Lab S 500/PK-12
129 Swan St 70813 225-771-3490
Dr. Ronnie Harrison, dir. Fax 771-2782
www.sulabschool.com
Southern University Lab S 500/PK-12
129 Swan St 70813 225-771-3490
Dr. Ronnie Harrison, dir. Fax 771-2782

Baton Rouge International S 300/PK-12
5015 Auto Plex Dr 70809 225-293-4338
Nathalie Guyon, prin. Fax 293-4307
Baton Rouge Lutheran S 200/PK-8
10925 Florida Blvd 70815 225-272-1288
Harmon Butler, prin. Fax 272-8504
Bethany Christian S 200/PK-5
10877 Rieger Rd 70809 225-412-5335
Stephanie Edmonds, prin. Fax 412-5336
Brighton S 200/K-12
12108 Parkmeadow Ave 70816 225-291-2524
Christ Presbyterian S 50/PK-8
8025 Antioch Rd 70817 225-751-2065
Church Academy Baton Rouge Campus 600/PK-12
2037 Quail Dr 70808 225-769-6760
Chelsea Bertrand M.Ed., hdmstr. Fax 769-8068
Dunham S 800/PK-12
11111 Roy Emerson Dr 70810 225-767-7097
Steven Eagleton, hdmstr. Fax 767-7056
Elan Vital Montessori S 50/PK-6
5228 Perkins Rd 70808 225-767-6620
Katie Guell, dir.
Episcopal S of Baton Rouge 900/PK-12
3200 Woodland Ridge Blvd 70816 225-753-3180
Hugh McIntosh, head sch Fax 756-0507
Family Christian Academy 200/K-12
PO Box 262550 70826 225-768-3026
Warren Smith, admin. Fax 768-3213
Greater Mt. Olive Christian Academy 100/K-3
3155 Victoria Dr 70805 225-355-5155
Beverly Wallace, prin.
Hosanna Christian Academy 200/PK-8
8850 Goodwood Blvd 70806 225-926-4885
Russell Marino, dir. Fax 926-4104
Jones Creek Adventist Academy 50/PK-8
4363 Jones Creek Rd 70817 225-751-8219
MLK Christian Academy 100/K-8
4295 Prescott Ct 70805 225-356-7407
Most Blessed Sacrament S 500/K-8
8033 Baringer Rd 70817 225-751-0273
Cheri Gioe, prin. Fax 753-7259
Our Lady of Mercy Catholic S 800/PK-8
400 Marquette Ave 70806 225-924-1054
Chris Porche, prin. Fax 923-2201
Parkview Baptist S 1,400/PK-12
5750 Parkview Church Rd 70816 225-291-2500
Dr. Don Mayes, supt. Fax 293-4135
Redemptorist St Gerard S 200/PK-8
3655 Saint Gerard Ave 70805 225-355-1437
C.J. Laird, prin. Fax 355-1879
Riverdale Christian Academy 200/PK-8
2791 Oneal Ln 70816 225-753-6722
Daniel McCulloch, prin. Fax 751-4341
Runnels S 800/PK-12
17255 S Harrells Ferry Rd 70816 225-215-5706
Sacred Heart of Jesus S 500/PK-8
2251 Main St 70802 225-383-7481
C.J. Laird, prin. Fax 383-1810
St. Aloysius S 1,200/PK-8
2025 Stuart Ave 70808 225-383-3871
Erin Candilora, prin. Fax 383-4500
St. Francis Xavier S 100/PK-8
1150 S 12th St 70802 225-387-6639
Paula Fabre, prin. Fax 383-1215
St. George S 1,100/K-8
7880 Saint George Dr 70809 225-293-1298
Jack Nelson, prin. Fax 293-4886
St. James Episcopal Day S 300/PK-5
PO Box 3011 70821 225-344-0805
Lauren Ray, head sch Fax 343-4873
St. Jean Vianney S 500/K-8
16266 S Harrells Ferry Rd 70816 225-751-1831
Wendy Ross, prin. Fax 752-8774
St. Jude the Apostle S 600/PK-8
9150 Highland Rd 70810 225-769-2344
Michelle Gardiner, prin. Fax 769-0671
St. Louis King of France S 200/PK-8
2311 N Sherwood Forest Dr 70815 225-273-3932
Paula Johnson, prin. Fax 273-3978
St. Lukes Episcopal Day S 400/PK-8
8833 Goodwood Blvd 70806 225-927-8601
Greg Hutchinson, head sch Fax 928-2542
St. Thomas More S 900/K-8
11400 Sherbrook Dr 70815 225-275-2820
Dr. Judy Armstrong, prin. Fax 275-0376
Trinity Episcopal Day S 200/PK-5
3550 Morning Glory Ave 70808 225-387-0398
Linda Brown, head sch Fax 387-3145
Victory Academy 300/PK-8
3953 N Flannery Rd 70814 225-272-8339
Sue Cashio, prin. Fax 272-0674

Belcher, Caddo, Pop. 263
Caddo Parish SD
Supt. — See Shreveport
Herndon Magnet S 700/PK-8
11845 Gamm Rd 71004 318-221-7676
Tom Thomas, prin. Fax 296-4554

Bell City, Calcasieu
Calcasieu Parish SD
Supt. — See Lake Charles
Bell City S 600/K-12
PO Box 100 70630 337-217-4500
Scott Nunez, prin. Fax 217-4501

Belle Chasse, Plaquemines, Pop. 12,371
Plaquemines Parish SD 4,100/PK-12
1484 Woodland Hwy 70037 504-595-6400
Denis Rousselle, supt. Fax 398-9990
www.ppsb.org
Belle Chasse MS 800/5-8
13476 Highway 23 70037 504-595-6640
Joe Williamson, prin. Fax 656-2399
Belle Chasse PS 1,100/PK-4
539 F Edward Hebert Blvd 70037 504-595-6620
Shelley Ritz, prin. Fax 393-8068
Other Schools – See Boothville, Braithwaite, Port Sulphur

Our Lady of Perpetual Help S 200/PK-7
8970 Highway 23 70037 504-394-0757
Kirsch Wilberg, prin. Fax 394-1627

Belle Rose, Assumption, Pop. 1,892
Assumption Parish SD
Supt. — See Napoleonville
Belle Rose MS 200/5-8
PO Box 229 70341 225-473-8917
Iris Breaux, prin. Fax 473-8429
Belle Rose PS 300/PK-4
7100 Highway 308 S 70341 225-473-7706
Angela Gregoire, prin. Fax 473-8868

Benton, Bossier, Pop. 1,921
Bossier Parish SD 22,000/PK-12
PO Box 2000 71006 318-549-5000
Scott Smith, supt. Fax 549-5004
www.bossierschools.org
Benton ES 800/K-5
562 Highway 162 71006 318-549-5170
Amy Gates, prin. Fax 549-5183
Benton MS 800/6-8
6140 Highway 3 71006 318-549-5310
Dr. Kyle Machen, prin. Fax 549-5323
Kingston ES, 349 Fairburn Ave 71006 K-5
Andrew Coleman, prin. 318-759-2500
Other Schools – See Bossier City, Elm Grove, Haughton, Plain Dealing, Princeton

Berwick, Saint Mary, Pop. 4,860
St. Mary Parish SD
Supt. — See Centerville
Berwick ES 500/PK-5
400 Texas St 70342 985-384-8355
Debbie Tompkins, prin. Fax 384-5427
Berwick JHS 400/6-8
3955 Bourgeois Dr 70342 985-384-5664
Tim Hymel, prin. Fax 384-5663

Bienville, Bienville, Pop. 218
Bienville Parish SD
Supt. — See Arcadia
Bienville S 50/PK-1
325 Main St 71008 318-385-7591
Billy Rogers, prin. Fax 385-7750

Bogalusa, Washington, Pop. 12,052
Bogalusa City SD 1,800/PK-12
1705 Sullivan Dr 70427 985-281-2100
Lisa Tanner, supt. Fax 735-8828
www.bogschools.org
Byrd Avenue PS 300/K-2
1600 Byrd Ave 70427 985-281-2130
Melissa Moses, prin. Fax 735-6258
Central ES 500/3-5
420 Spartans Ave 70427 985-281-2232
Deanna Brown M.Ed., prin. Fax 735-6430
Denhamtown PreKindergarten 100/PK-PK
1101 Avenue M 70427 985-281-2194
Barbara Greely, coord. Fax 735-0093

Annunciation S 200/PK-7
511 Avenue C 70427 985-735-6643
Veda Matthews, prin. Fax 735-6619
Ben's Ford Christian School 500/PK-12
59253 Mount Pleasant Rd 70427 985-735-0387
Maureen Gaddy, prin. Fax 735-0382

Boothville, Plaquemines, Pop. 801
Plaquemines Parish SD
Supt. — See Belle Chasse
Boothville-Venice ES 400/PK-6
1 Oiler Dr, 504-595-6455
Maria Prout, prin Fax 534-1799

Bossier City, Bossier, Pop. 59,796
Bossier Parish SD
Supt. — See Benton
Apollo ES 700/K-5
2400 Viking Dr 71111 318-549-6010
Laura Leflett, prin. Fax 549-6023
Bellaire ES 400/K-3
1310 Bellaire Blvd 71112 318-549-6300
Alyshia Coulson, prin. Fax 549-6313
Bossier ES 400/PK-5
1000 Traffic St 71111 318-549-6350
Treska Mitchell, prin. Fax 549-6363
Central Park ES 400/PK-5
900 Central Park Dr 71112 318-549-6400
Suzette Hadden, prin. Fax 549-6413
Cope MS 800/6-8
4814 Shed Rd 71111 318-549-5380
Judy Grooms, prin. Fax 549-5393
Curtis ES 400/4-5
5600 Barksdale Blvd 71112 318-549-6450
Terri Bird, prin. Fax 549-6463
Elm Grove MS 1,000/6-8
4301 Panther Dr 71112 318-759-2400
Jennifer Armond, prin. Fax 759-2409
Greenacres MS 800/6-8
2220 Airline Dr 71111 318-549-6210
Arthur James, prin. Fax 549-6223
Kerr ES 600/PK-5
1700 Airline Dr 71112 318-549-6560
Janet Doughty, prin. Fax 549-6573
Legacy ES 900/K-5
4830 Swan Lake Rd 71111 318-759-2000
Kimmie Smith, prin. Fax 759-2003
Lewis ES 600/K-5
4701 Modica Lott Rd 71111 318-759-2100
Lisa Burns, prin. Fax 759-2103
Meadowview ES 500/PK-5
4312 Shed Rd 71111 318-549-5640
Janice Williams, prin. Fax 549-5653
Plantation Park ES 700/PK-5
2410 Plantation Dr 71111 318-549-5700
Tonya Hilburn, prin. Fax 549-5713
Rusheon MS 600/6-8
2401 Old Minden Rd 71112 318-549-6610
Lorenza Baker, prin. Fax 549-6623
Stockwell Place ES 800/K-5
5801 Shed Rd 71111 318-549-5820
Brooke Nolte, prin. Fax 549-5833
Sun City ES 600/K-3
4230 Van Deeman St 71112 318-549-7000
Kimberly Tuminello, prin. Fax 549-7011
Waller ES 600/PK-5
1130 Patricia Dr 71112 318-549-6850
Lisa Nix, prin. Fax 549-6863

Providence Classical Academy 500/PK-12
4525 Old Brownlee Rd 71111 318-820-9465
Howard Davis, prin. Fax 742-3379

Bourg, Terrebonne, Pop. 2,533
Terrebonne Parish SD
Supt. — See Houma
Bourg ES 500/PK-4
4413 St Andrew St 70343 985-594-3663
Jennifer Blanchard, prin. Fax 594-9665

Boutte, Saint Charles, Pop. 3,028

Boutte Christian Academy 200/PK-7
13271 Highway 90 70039 985-785-2447
Linda Davis, prin. Fax 785-6641

Braithwaite, Plaquemines
Plaquemines Parish SD
Supt. — See Belle Chasse
Phoenix S 200/PK-12
12700 Highway 39 70040 504-595-6480
Kristie Williams, prin. Fax 333-7073

Lynn Oaks S 100/PK-8
1 Lynn Oaks Dr 70040 504-682-3171
Troy Dean, prin. Fax 682-3173

Branch, Acadia, Pop. 385
Acadia Parish SD
Supt. — See Crowley
Branch S 300/PK-8
PO Box 450 70516 337-334-5708
Marlene Courvelle, prin. Fax 334-7352

Breaux Bridge, Saint Martin, Pop. 8,038
St. Martin Parish SD 7,800/PK-12
625 Corporate Blvd 70517 337-332-2105
Dr. Lottie Beebe, supt.
www.saintmartinschools.org
Breaux Bridge ES 400/3-5
915 Saint Charles St 70517 337-332-1270
Joy Cormier, prin. Fax 332-1274
Breaux Bridge JHS 200/6-8
100 Martin St 70517 337-332-2844
Denise Frederick, prin. Fax 332-4831
Breaux Bridge PS 800/PK-2
1020 E Bridge St 70517 337-332-1821
Jill Bozeman, prin. Fax 332-2547
Teche ES 400/4-6
2439 Main Hwy 70517 337-667-6400
Latonia Cretian, prin. Fax 667-7428
Other Schools – See Cecilia, Morgan City, Parks, Saint Martinville

---

St. Bernard S 500/PK-8
251 E Bridge St 70517 337-332-5350
John Paul Masterson, prin. Fax 332-5894

Bridge City, Jefferson, Pop. 7,624
Jefferson Parish SD
Supt. — See Harvey
Harris ES 400/PK-5
1805 Bridge City Ave 70094 504-436-4626
Leigh Ann Chiasson, prin. Fax 436-6046

Broussard, Lafayette, Pop. 8,078
Lafayette Parish SD
Supt. — See Lafayette
Broussard MS 600/5-8
1325 S Morgan Ave 70518 337-521-7870
John Mouton, prin. Fax 521-7871
Drexel ES 600/PK-4
409 Saint Deporres St 70518 337-521-7650
Denise Soileau, prin. Fax 521-7651

St. Cecilia S 500/PK-8
302 W Main St 70518 337-837-6363
George Fontenot, prin. Fax 837-3688

Brusly, West Baton Rouge, Pop. 2,561
West Baton Rouge Parish SD
Supt. — See Port Allen
Brusly ES 600/PK-2
400 S Labauve Rd 70719 225-749-2126
Taya Loupe, prin. Fax 749-0510
Brusly MS 400/6-8
601 N Kirkland St 70719 225-749-3123
Callie Kershaw, prin. Fax 749-8570
Lukeville Upper ES 500/3-5
6123 LA Highway 1 S 70719 225-749-8386
Judith Brock, prin. Fax 749-9240

Bunkie, Avoyelles, Pop. 4,132
Avoyelles Parish SD
Supt. — See Marksville
Bunkie ES 400/PK-6
311 Pershing Ave 71322 318-346-7292
Liza Jacobs, prin. Fax 346-6164

St. Anthony of Padua S 200/PK-8
116 S Knoll Ave 71322 318-346-2739
Martha Coulon, prin. Fax 346-9191

Bush, Saint Tammany
St. Tammany Parish SD
Supt. — See Covington
Fifth Ward S 500/PK-8
81419 Highway 21 70431 985-886-3273
Christopher Oufnac, prin. Fax 886-2228

Calhoun, Ouachita, Pop. 674
Ouachita Parish SD
Supt. — See Monroe
Calhoun ES 500/PK-2
237 Calhoun School Rd 71225 318-644-1114
Shirley Buford, prin. Fax 644-7146
Calhoun MS 500/6-8
191 Highway 80 E 71225 318-644-5840
Buddy Canal, prin. Fax 644-5418
Central ES 500/3-5
1163 Highway 151 S 71225 318-644-5842
Carmen Banks, prin. Fax 644-5756

Calvin, Winn, Pop. 236
Winn Parish SD
Supt. — See Winnfield
Calvin S 300/PK-12
PO Box 80 71410 318-727-8784
Paula Jones, prin. Fax 727-9224

Cameron, Cameron, Pop. 399
Cameron Parish SD 1,300/PK-12
PO Box 1548 70631 337-775-5784
Charles Adkins, supt. Fax 775-5097
www.camsch.org
Johnson Bayou S 100/PK-12
6304 Gulf Beach Hwy 70631 337-569-2138
Brenda Sanders, prin. Fax 569-2673
Other Schools – See Grand Chenier, Hackberry, Lake Charles

Campti, Natchitoches, Pop. 1,035
Natchitoches Parish SD
Supt. — See Natchitoches
Fairview-Alpha ES 400/PK-6
1439 Highway 71 71411 318-476-4616
Brooke Williams, prin. Fax 476-4558

Cankton, Saint Landry, Pop. 473
St. Landry Parish SD
Supt. — See Opelousas
Cankton ES 500/K-4
602 Main St 70584 337-668-4465
Edward Limoges, prin. Fax 668-4435

Carencro, Lafayette, Pop. 7,438
Lafayette Parish SD
Supt. — See Lafayette
Carencro Heights ES 600/PK-5
601 Teema Rd 70520 337-521-7640
Alysia Messa, prin. Fax 521-7641
Carencro MS 600/6-8
4301 N University Ave 70520 337-521-7880
Jeffrey Janette, prin. Fax 521-7881

Carencro Catholic S 400/PK-8
200 W Saint Peter St 70520 337-896-8973
Andre Angelle, prin. Fax 896-1931

Castor, Bienville, Pop. 258
Bienville Parish SD
Supt. — See Arcadia
Castor S 600/PK-12
PO Box 69 71016 318-544-7271
Dr. James Guin, prin. Fax 544-9077

Cecilia, Saint Martin, Pop. 1,957
St. Martin Parish SD
Supt. — See Breaux Bridge
Cecilia JHS 400/6-8
PO Box 129 70521 337-667-6226
Charee Theriot, prin. Fax 667-7352
Cecilia PS 700/PK-2
PO Box 97 70521 337-667-6700
Suzanne LeBoeuf, prin. Fax 667-7756

Centerville, Saint Mary
St. Mary Parish SD 9,200/PK-12
PO Box 170 70522 337-836-9661
Leonard Armato, supt. Fax 836-5461
www.stmaryk12.net
Centerville S 600/PK-12
PO Box 59 70522 337-836-5103
Kristy Estay, prin. Fax 836-9594
Other Schools – See Baldwin, Berwick, Franklin, Morgan City, Patterson

Central, East Baton Rouge, Pop. 26,615

Central Private S 300/PK-12
12801 Centerra Ct, 225-261-3341
Wayne Cook, prin. Fax 261-3490

Chalmette, Saint Bernard, Pop. 16,314
St. Bernard Parish SD 7,000/PK-12
200 E Saint Bernard Hwy 70043 504-301-2000
Doris Voitier, supt. Fax 301-2010
www.stbernard.k12.la.us

Chalmette ES 700/PK-5
75 E Chalmette Cir 70043 504-304-0370
Elizabeth Winslow, prin. Fax 265-8046
Jackson MS 600/6-8
201 8th St 70043 504-301-1500
Montrelle Sinegar, prin. Fax 301-1510
Lacoste ES 700/PK-5
1625 Missouri St 70043 504-304-5747
Stacie Alfonso, prin. Fax 302-1223
Meraux ES 700/PK-5
4004 Paris Rd 70043 504-556-0900
Natalie Albers, prin. Fax 556-0910
Other Schools – See Arabi, Meraux, Saint Bernard, Violet

Our Lady of Prompt Succor S 400/PK-7
2305 Fenelon St 70043 504-271-2953
Annette Accomando, prin. Fax 271-1490

Chataignier, Evangeline, Pop. 358
Evangeline Parish SD
Supt. — See Ville Platte
Chataignier S 400/PK-8
PO Box 189 70524 337-885-3173
Peggy Edwards, prin. Fax 885-2236

Chauvin, Terrebonne, Pop. 2,885
Terrebonne Parish SD
Supt. — See Houma
Lacache MS 400/5-8
5266 Highway 56 70344 985-594-3945
Mark Thibodeaux, prin. Fax 594-4128
Upper Little Caillou ES 600/PK-4
4824 Highway 56 70344 985-594-4071
Trisha Melancon, prin. Fax 594-7504

Choudrant, Lincoln, Pop. 836
Lincoln Parish SD
Supt. — See Ruston
Choudrant ES 400/K-6
160 Walker Rd 71227 318-768-4106
Charles Hogan, prin. Fax 768-2679

Church Point, Acadia, Pop. 4,487
Acadia Parish SD
Supt. — See Crowley
Church Point ES 700/PK-5
415 E Lougarre St 70525 337-684-5722
Ruby Privat, prin. Fax 684-3587
Church Point MS 300/6-8
340 W Martin Luther King Dr 70525 337-684-6381
Cheri Baggett, prin. Fax 684-0123
Richard S 400/PK-8
1616 Charlene Hwy 70525 337-684-3339
April Briscoe, prin. Fax 684-6892

Our Mother of Peace S 300/PK-8
218 N Rogers St 70525 337-684-5780
Debbie Fontenot, prin. Fax 684-6983

Clarks, Caldwell, Pop. 1,011

Old Bethel Christian Academy 100/PK-12
PO Box 95 71415 318-649-0281
Sandra Richmond, prin. Fax 649-0281

Clinton, East Feliciana, Pop. 1,628
East Feliciana Parish SD 1,800/PK-12
PO Box 397 70722 225-683-8277
Carlos Sam, supt. Fax 683-3320
www.efpsb.k12.la.us
Clinton ES 300/PK-5
PO Box 366 70722 225-683-8293
Ebony Montgomery, prin. Fax 683-6197
East Feliciana MS 300/6-8
PO Box 166 70722 225-683-3321
Casey Smith, prin. Fax 683-5115
Other Schools – See Jackson, Slaughter

Silliman Institute 400/PK-12
PO Box 946 70722 225-683-5383
Ann Kent, admin. Fax 683-6728

Cloutierville, Natchitoches
Natchitoches Parish SD
Supt. — See Natchitoches
Cloutierville S 300/PK-8
155 Schoolhouse Rd 71416 318-379-2577
Carolyn Benefield, prin. Fax 379-1117

Colfax, Grant, Pop. 1,531
Grant Parish SD 3,100/PK-12
PO Box 208 71417 318-627-3274
Sheila Jackson, supt. Fax 627-6235
www.gpsb.org
Colfax ES 300/PK-6
301 3rd St 71417 318-627-3254
Laurie Croom, prin. Fax 627-3245
Other Schools – See Dry Prong, Georgetown, Montgomery, Pollock

Columbia, Caldwell, Pop. 387
Caldwell Parish SD 1,500/PK-12
PO Box 1019 71418 318-649-2689
John Gullatt, supt. Fax 649-0636
www.caldwelledu.org/
Caldwell Parish JHS 400/6-8
114 Trojan Dr 71418 318-649-2340
Kim Adams, prin. Fax 649-2341
Caldwell Parish Pre-K Center PK-PK
182 Spartan Dr 71418 318-649-6139
Ashly Roberts, prin. Fax 649-0508
Columbia ES 200/K-5
PO Box 1679 71418 318-649-2654
Rhonda Whitten, prin. Fax 649-7589
Union Central ES 200/K-6
PO Box 1439 71418 318-649-2569
Rebekah Meredith, prin. Fax 649-2522
Other Schools – See Grayson

Converse, Sabine, Pop. 416
Sabine Parish SD
Supt. — See Many
Converse S 600/PK-12
PO Box 10 71419 318-567-2673
Cynthia Mary, prin. Fax 567-3400

Cottonport, Avoyelles, Pop. 1,987
Avoyelles Parish SD
Supt. — See Marksville
Cottonport ES 500/PK-6
950 Lemoine St 71327 318-876-3404
Wendy Adams, prin. Fax 876-3762

St. Mary's Assumption S 200/PK-8
850 Front St 71327 318-876-3651
Nathan Laborde, prin. Fax 876-2955

Cotton Valley, Webster, Pop. 997
Webster Parish SD
Supt. — See Minden
North Webster Upper ES 100/3-5
PO Box 457 71018 318-832-4716
Beatha Brantley, prin. Fax 832-5273

Coushatta, Red River, Pop. 1,958
Red River Parish SD 1,500/PK-12
PO Box 1369 71019 318-932-4081
Alison N. Hughes, supt. Fax 932-4367
www.rrbulldogs.com/
Red River ES 800/PK-5
1001 Ashland Rd 71019 318-932-9290
S. Deville, prin. Fax 932-9289
Red River JHS 300/6-8
915 E Carrol St 71019 318-932-5265
Mike Peter, prin. Fax 932-9959

Riverdale Academy 300/PK-12
100 Riverdale Rd 71019 318-932-5876
Jamie Lawrence, prin. Fax 932-4355

Covington, Saint Tammany, Pop. 8,662
St. Tammany Parish SD 37,700/PK-12
PO Box 940 70434 985-892-2276
Trey Folse, supt. Fax 898-3267
www.stpsb.org
Covington ES 600/PK-3
325 S Jackson St 70433 985-892-4311
Melissa Eason, prin. Fax 871-1480
Lee Road S 800/PK-8
79131 Highway 40 70435 985-892-3636
Kalinda Fauntleroy, prin. Fax 892-3169
Lyon ES 600/PK-3
1615 N Florida St 70433 985-892-0869
Jeanine Barnes, prin. Fax 892-7971
Pine View MS 700/4-6
1200 W 27th Ave 70433 985-892-6204
Stacie Trepagnier, prin. Fax 893-3736
Pitcher JHS 300/7-8
415 S Jefferson Ave 70433 985-892-3021
Amy Burns, prin. Fax 892-1188
Other Schools – See Abita Springs, Bush, Folsom, Lacombe, Madisonville, Mandeville, Pearl River, Slidell

---

Christ Episcopal S 100/PK-K
120 S New Hampshire St 70433 985-892-9156
Reina Gardner, head sch Fax 871-1626
Christ Episcopal S 400/1-12
80 Christwood Blvd 70433 985-871-9902
John Morvant, hdmstr. Fax 871-9912
Holy Trinity Lutheran S 100/PK-PK
1 N Marigold Dr 70433 985-892-6146
Debby Nelson, dir. Fax 892-3012
Kehoe-France Northshore S 300/PK-7
25 Patricia Dr 70433 985-892-4415
Brad Humphreys, prin. Fax 875-7636
Northlake Christian S 800/PK-12
70104 Wolverine Dr 70433 985-635-0400
Monty Fontenot M.Ed., head sch Fax 893-4363
St. Peter S 800/PK-7
130 E Temperance St 70433 985-892-1831
Michael Kraus, prin. Fax 898-2185

Crowley, Acadia, Pop. 13,095
Acadia Parish SD 10,100/PK-12
PO Box 309 70527 337-783-3664
John Bourque, supt. Fax 783-3761
www.acadia.k12.la.us
Crowley K 300/PK-K
1119 N Parkerson Ave 70526 337-783-4670
Ida Yeager, prin. Fax 783-4696
Crowley MS 600/6-8
401 W Northern Ave 70526 337-783-5305
Chad Lemelle, prin. Fax 783-5338
North Crowley ES 400/1-5
820 W 15th St 70526 337-783-8755
Pamela Dequeant, prin. Fax 783-5135
Ross ES 300/1-5
1809 W Hutchinson Ave 70526 337-783-0927
Paula Cutrer, prin. Fax 783-6349
South Crowley ES 300/1-5
1102 S Parkerson Ave 70526 337-783-1300
April Mixon, prin. Fax 783-8025
Other Schools – See Branch, Church Point, Egan, Estherwood, Evangeline, Iota, Mermentau, Morse, Rayne

---

Northside Christian S 300/K-12
809 E Northern Ave 70526 337-783-3620
Brandon Bergeron, prin. Fax 788-3461
Redemptorist S 200/PK-8
606 S Avenue N 70526 337-783-4466
Cynthia Habetz, prin. Fax 788-0961
St. Michael S 400/PK-8
805 E Northern Ave 70526 337-783-1410
Sandi Dore, prin. Fax 783-8547

Crowville, Franklin
Franklin Parish SD
Supt. — See Winnsboro
Crowville S 500/PK-8
PO Box 128 71230 318-722-3244
Sandra King, prin. Fax 722-3552

Cut Off, Lafourche, Pop. 5,828
Lafourche Parish SD
Supt. — See Thibodaux
Cut Off ES 500/PK-5
177 W 55th St 70345 985-632-3116
Kristine Collins, prin. Fax 632-3219

Delcambre, Vermilion, Pop. 1,846
Iberia Parish SD
Supt. — See New Iberia
Delcambre ES 500/PK-5
706 Martin Luther King Jr 70528 337-685-2376
Jodi Romero, prin. Fax 685-4811

Delhi, Richland, Pop. 2,885
Richland Parish SD
Supt. — See Rayville
Delhi ES 200/PK-4
509 Main St 71232 318-878-2269
Joan Rhodes, prin. Fax 878-0222
Delhi MS 200/5-8
106 Toombs St 71232 318-878-3748
Shirley McDade, prin. Fax 878-3749

Denham Springs, Livingston, Pop. 10,120
Livingston Parish SD
Supt. — See Livingston
Denham Springs ES 500/K-5
306 N Range Ave 70726 225-665-5855
Rhonda Delee, prin. Fax 664-8672
Denham Springs JHS 900/6-8
401 Hatchell Ln 70726 225-665-8898
Bryan Wax, prin. Fax 665-8601
Eastside ES 500/PK-5
9735 Lockhart Rd 70726 225-791-8581
Kelly Lebauve, prin. Fax 791-8582
Freshwater ES 400/K-5
1025 Cockerham Rd 70726 225-665-5371
Julie Dugas, prin. Fax 664-6577
Gray's Creek ES 500/PK-5
11400 LA Highway 1033 70726 225-667-1808
Melissa Dougherty, prin. Fax 667-3597
Juban Parc ES 500/K-5
12555 Brown Rd 70726 225-665-4079
Shanna Steed, prin. Fax 665-4114
Juban Parc JHS 600/6-8
12470 Brown Rd 70726 225-664-1001
Gregory Hayden, prin. Fax 664-5000
Live Oak JHS 7-8
35086 Old Hwy 16 70706 225-667-4195
Daniel Desselle, prin. Fax 667-4196
North Live Oak ES 900/PK-5
36605 Outback Rd 70706 225-667-3135
Michell Stone, prin. Fax 667-1994
Northside ES 400/PK-5
1090 Robbie St 70726 225-664-4223
JoAnn Cook, prin. Fax 664-5660
Seventh Ward ES 300/PK-5
24495 LA Highway 16 70726 225-665-5815
Stacey Milton, prin. Fax 665-7280
South Fork ES 400/K-5
23300 Walker South Rd 70726 225-664-2281
Mary Raborn, prin. Fax 664-2282
Southside ES 500/PK-5
1129 S Range Ave 70726 225-665-5500
Laura Williams, prin. Fax 667-3171
Southside JHS 500/6-8
26535 LA Highway 16 70726 225-664-4221
Wesley Partin, prin. Fax 664-3307
Vincent ES 400/PK-5
7686 Vincent Rd 70726 225-665-8198
Lynette Wheat, prin. Fax 665-9713

Amite Christian Academy 300/PK-7
7100 Amite Church Rd 70706 225-665-2060
Paul Miceli, prin. Fax 665-5730

Dequincy, Calcasieu, Pop. 3,178
Calcasieu Parish SD
Supt. — See Lake Charles
DeQuincy ES 300/3-5
1605 W 4th St 70633 337-217-4650
Ellizabeth Holder, prin. Fax 217-4651
DeQuincy MS 300/6-8
1603 W 4th St 70633 337-217-4770
Denise Doyle, prin. Fax 217-4771
DeQuincy PS 400/PK-2
304 McNeese St 70633 337-217-4650
Amanda Guerrero, prin. Fax 217-4652

Deridder, Beauregard, Pop. 10,238
Beauregard Parish SD 6,000/PK-12
PO Box 938 70634 337-463-5551
Timothy Cooley M.Ed., supt. Fax 463-6735
www.beau.k12.la.us
Carver ES 400/2-3
220 Martin Luther King Dr 70634 337-463-7380
Pamela March, prin. Fax 463-2119
DeRidder JHS 600/6-8
415 N Frusha Dr 70634 337-463-9083
David Wentzel, prin. Fax 463-7696
East Beauregard ES 400/K-5
5368 Highway 113 70634 337-328-8551
Mark Weldon, prin. Fax 328-8803
Hanchey ES 500/PK-1
611 N Frusha Dr 70634 337-463-4479
Teresa Parmley, prin. Fax 463-4482
Pine Wood ES 400/4-5
815 Mel Branch Mem Dr 70634 337-463-8810
Jimmy Maricle, prin. Fax 463-2515
Other Schools – See Longville, Merryville, Singer

Des Allemands, Saint Charles, Pop. 2,462
St. Charles Parish SD
Supt. — See Luling

Allemands ES 300/PK-2
1471 WPA Rd 70030 985-758-7427
Lisa Perrin, prin. Fax 758-2221

Destrehan, Saint Charles, Pop. 11,371
St. Charles Parish SD
Supt. — See Luling
Hurst MS 700/6-8
170 Road Runner Ln 70047 985-764-6367
Jason Madere, prin. Fax 764-2678
New Sarpy ES 400/PK-2
130 Plantation Rd 70047 985-764-1275
Claire Brauninger, prin. Fax 764-6942
Schoeffner ES 400/3-5
140 Plantation Rd 70047 985-725-0123
Vanessa Terry, prin. Fax 725-0131

St. Charles Borromeo S 400/PK-7
13396 River Rd 70047 985-764-9232
Rachel Hafford, prin. Fax 764-3726

Deville, Rapides, Pop. 1,751
Rapides Parish SD
Supt. — See Alexandria
Buckeye ES 500/PK-2
PO Box 529 71328 318-466-3233
Karla Tumminello, prin. Fax 466-3288
Lawrence Upper ES 400/3-5
PO Box 509 71328 318-466-5858
Dwayne Floyd, prin. Fax 466-9204

Dodson, Winn, Pop. 331
Winn Parish SD
Supt. — See Winnfield
Dodson S 300/PK-12
PO Box 97 71422 318-628-2172
Virginia Parker, prin. Fax 628-7515

Donaldsonville, Ascension, Pop. 7,399
Ascension Parish SD 21,400/PK-12
1100 Webster St 70346 225-391-7000
David Alexander, supt. Fax 391-7001
www.apsb.org
Donaldsonville PS 500/PK-2
38210 Highway 3089 70346 225-391-7600
Dr. Tennille Lange, prin. Fax 391-7601
Lowery ES 400/3-5
2389 Highway 1 S Ste B 70346 225-391-7500
Karen Daigle, prin. Fax 473-2539
Lowery MS 400/6-8
2389 Highway 1 S Ste A 70346 225-391-7550
Daryl Comery, prin. Fax 473-2514
Other Schools – See Geismar, Gonzales, Prairieville, Saint Amant, Sorrento

---

Ascension Catholic S 300/PK-6
618 Iberville St 70346 225-473-8540
John Beck, admin. Fax 264-6193

Doyline, Webster, Pop. 803
Webster Parish SD
Supt. — See Minden
Doyline S 500/PK-12
376 College St 71023 318-745-3673
Leroy Hamilton, prin. Fax 745-3695

Dry Prong, Grant, Pop. 434
Grant Parish SD
Supt. — See Colfax
Grant JHS 400/7-8
17773 Highway 167 71423 318-899-5697
Robert Smith, prin. Fax 899-7346
South Grant ES 500/K-6
1000 Highway 1241 71423 318-641-1882
Shana Delrie, prin. Fax 641-1899

Dubach, Lincoln, Pop. 952
Lincoln Parish SD
Supt. — See Ruston
Dubach ES 100/PK-5
7710 Fellowship Rd 71235 318-777-3470
Pamela Pruden, prin. Fax 777-8409

Dubberly, Webster, Pop. 273
Webster Parish SD
Supt. — See Minden
Central ES 600/PK-6
5701 Highway 531 71024 318-377-2591
Guy Sanders, prin. Fax 377-2592

Dulac, Terrebonne, Pop. 1,389
Terrebonne Parish SD
Supt. — See Houma
Grand Caillou MS 300/6-8
2161 Grand Caillou Rd, 985-876-7172
Judy Gaspard, prin. Fax 876-7279

Duson, Lafayette, Pop. 1,682
Lafayette Parish SD
Supt. — See Lafayette
Burke ES 600/PK-5
2845 Ridge Rd 70529 337-521-7630
Loretta Williams-Durand, prin. Fax 521-7631
Duson ES 200/PK-5
PO Box 7 70529 337-521-7660
Connie Fontenot, prin. Fax 521-7661
Judice MS 500/6-8
2645 S Fieldspan Rd 70529 337-521-7890
Sonjie Fontenot, prin. Fax 521-7891
Ridge ES 700/PK-5
2901 S Fieldspan Rd 70529 337-521-7800
Rhonda Dickerson, prin. Fax 521-7801

Edgard, Saint John the Baptist, Pop. 2,428
St. John The Baptist Parish SD
Supt. — See Reserve
West St. John ES 300/PK-7
PO Box 130 70049 985-497-3347
Chantell Walker, prin. Fax 497-5755

Effie, Avoyelles
Avoyelles Parish SD
Supt. — See Marksville
Lafargue ES 700/PK-6
3366 Highway 107 71331 318-253-9591
Sharice Sullivan, prin. Fax 253-4545

Egan, Acadia, Pop. 628
Acadia Parish SD
Supt. — See Crowley
Egan S 200/PK-8
2166 Egan Hwy 70531 337-783-4148
Neal Young, prin. Fax 788-3774

Elizabeth, Allen, Pop. 531
Allen Parish SD
Supt. — See Oberlin
Elizabeth S 400/PK-12
PO Box 580 70638 318-634-5341
Keith Morgan, prin. Fax 634-5218

Elmer, Rapides
Rapides Parish SD
Supt. — See Alexandria
Oak Hill HS 400/K-12
7362 Highway 112 71424 318-793-2014
Mark Roberts, prin. Fax 793-8589

Elm Grove, Bossier
Bossier Parish SD
Supt. — See Benton
Elm Grove ES 500/PK-5
1541 Old Highway 71 71051 318-549-6500
Kimberley Meeder, prin. Fax 549-6513

Elton, Jefferson Davis, Pop. 1,103
Jefferson Davis Parish SD
Supt. — See Jennings
Elton ES 300/PK-5
614 Powell St 70532 337-584-2892
David Harper, prin. Fax 584-2052

Epps, West Carroll, Pop. 844
West Carroll Parish SD
Supt. — See Oak Grove
Epps S 300/PK-12
PO Box 277 71237 318-926-3624
Penny Hale, prin. Fax 926-5655

Erath, Vermilion, Pop. 2,099
Vermilion Parish SD
Supt. — See Abbeville
Dozier ES 500/PK-5
415 W Primeaux St 70533 337-937-6915
Karla Toups, prin. Fax 937-0630
Erath MS 500/6-8
800 S Broadway St 70533 337-937-4441
Wendy Stoute, prin. Fax 937-5125

Estherwood, Acadia, Pop. 878
Acadia Parish SD
Supt. — See Crowley
Estherwood S 200/PK-7
214 Jefferson Ave 70534 337-783-6788
Stan Baggett, prin. Fax 783-9653

Eunice, Saint Landry, Pop. 10,256
St. Landry Parish SD
Supt. — See Opelousas
Central MS 400/5-6
602 S Martin L King Dr 70535 337-457-5895
Ranolviaun Landry, prin. Fax 457-8452
East ES 300/K-4
550 Brother J Rd 70535 337-457-2215
Gina Lagrange, prin. Fax 457-2257
Eunice ES 300/K-4
451 S 9th St 70535 337-457-2380
Mary Dupre, prin. Fax 457-2389
Eunice JHS 400/7-8
751 W Oak Ave 70535 337-457-7386
Dwanetta Scott, prin. Fax 457-1764
Glendale ES 300/PK-4
900 W Dean St 70535 337-457-4121
Laura Lombas, prin. Fax 457-0308
Highland ES 200/PK-4
1341 Duck Ave 70535 337-457-5161
Lorie Ledoux, prin. Fax 457-0207

St. Edmund S 300/PK-6
331 N 3rd St 70535 337-457-5988
Joseph Feucht, prin. Fax 457-5989

Evangeline, Acadia
Acadia Parish SD
Supt. — See Crowley
Evangeline S 300/PK-8
1448 Old Evangeline Hwy 70537 337-824-1308
Chad Latiolais, prin. Fax 824-7193

Evans, Vernon
Vernon Parish SD
Supt. — See Leesville
Evans S 400/PK-12
18829 Highway 111 70639 337-286-5289
Kathy Bass, prin. Fax 286-9298

Farmerville, Union, Pop. 3,818
Union Parish SD 2,100/PK-12
PO Box 308 71241 318-368-9715
Dr. George Cannon, supt. Fax 368-1012
www.unionpsd.org
Union Parish ES 700/PK-5
7195 Highway 33 71241 318-368-9542
Dr. Crystal Washington, prin. Fax 368-6081
Union Parish JHS 300/6-8
606 Bernice St 71241 318-368-9235
David Gray, prin. Fax 368-1989

Union Christian Academy 200/PK-12
110 W Hill St 71241 318-368-8890
Bill Ritz, pres. Fax 368-2920

Fenton, Jefferson Davis, Pop. 364
Jefferson Davis Parish SD
Supt. — See Jennings
Fenton S 100/PK-8
PO Box 250 70640 337-756-2326
Cassidy Juneau, prin. Fax 756-2500

Ferriday, Concordia, Pop. 3,491
Concordia Parish SD
Supt. — See Vidalia
Ferriday JHS 300/6-8
201 Martin Luther King Blvd 71334 318-757-8695
Toyua Watson, prin. Fax 757-8696
Ferriday Lower ES 400/PK-2
110 Bateman Dr 71334 318-757-3293
Julia Walker, prin. Fax 757-8947
Ferriday Upper ES 300/3-5
151 Martin Luther King Blvd 71334 318-757-3105
Betty Marsalis, prin. Fax 757-1924

Florien, Sabine, Pop. 616
Sabine Parish SD
Supt. — See Many
Florien S 600/PK-12
500 High School Rd 71429 318-586-3681
Eddie Jones, prin. Fax 586-3822

Folsom, Saint Tammany, Pop. 708
St. Tammany Parish SD
Supt. — See Covington
Folsom ES 400/PK-5
82144 Highway 25 70437 985-796-3820
Lesa Bodnar, prin. Fax 796-0165
Folsom JHS 200/6-8
83055 Hay Hollow Rd 70437 985-796-3724
Sharon Garrett, prin. Fax 796-3701

Forest, West Carroll, Pop. 348
West Carroll Parish SD
Supt. — See Oak Grove
Forest S 600/PK-12
PO Box 368 71242 318-428-3672
Lisa Smith, prin. Fax 428-8875

Forest Hill, Rapides, Pop. 809
Rapides Parish SD
Supt. — See Alexandria
Forest Hill ES 400/PK-6
PO Box 400 71430 318-748-6844
Amber Eskew, prin. Fax 748-6848

Fort Necessity, Franklin
Franklin Parish SD
Supt. — See Winnsboro
Fort Necessity S 300/PK-8
PO Box 159 71243 318-723-4793
Sherrie Roberts, prin. Fax 723-4343

Fort Polk, Vernon
Vernon Parish SD
Supt. — See Leesville
North Polk ES 500/PK-K
4978 University Pkwy 71459 337-537-5109
Elsee Ashworth, prin. Fax 537-8429

Franklin, Saint Mary, Pop. 7,561
St. Mary Parish SD
Supt. — See Centerville
Foster ES 300/PK-5
101 2nd St 70538 337-828-1905
Dawn Chaisson, prin. Fax 828-9063
Franklin JHS 300/6-8
525 Morris St 70538 337-828-0855
J. Bertrand Ina, prin. Fax 828-5095
LaGrange ES 200/PK-5
2129 Chatsworth Rd 70538 337-828-1991
Kiante Gunner, prin. Fax 828-1999

St. John S 200/PK-5
924 Main St 70538 337-828-2648
Sheri Higdon, prin. Fax 828-2112

Franklinton, Washington, Pop. 3,833
Washington Parish SD 5,300/PK-12
PO Box 587 70438 985-839-3436
Darrell Fairburn, supt. Fax 839-5464
www.wpsb.org
Enon ES 300/PK-5
14058 Highway 16 70438 985-839-3976
Jacqueline Boone, prin. Fax 839-3402
Franklinton ES 500/3-5
345 Jaquar Dr 70438 985-839-3580
Janene Hollen, prin. Fax 839-5149
Franklinton JHS 700/6-8
617 Main St 70438 985-839-3501
Tiffany Hughes-Smith, prin. Fax 839-6912
Franklinton PS 600/PK-2
610 T W Barker Dr 70438 985-839-5674
Aylene Crain, prin. Fax 839-9546
Thomas ES 600/PK-5
30341 Highway 424 70438 985-848-2881
Steven Knight, prin. Fax 848-5497
Other Schools – See Angie, Mount Hermon

Bowling Green S 400/PK-12
700 Varnado St 70438 985-839-5317
Beverly Young, admin. Fax 839-5668

French Settlement, Livingston, Pop. 1,104
Livingston Parish SD
Supt. — See Livingston
French Settlement ES 500/PK-6
15810 LA Highway 16 70733 225-698-6848
Lindy Gill, prin. Fax 698-6849

Galliano, Lafourche, Pop. 7,495
Lafourche Parish SD
Supt. — See Thibodaux
Galliano ES 500/PK-5
PO Box 517 70354 985-632-7211
Dr. Ragan Lorraine, prin. Fax 632-3577

Garyville, Saint John the Baptist, Pop. 2,796
St. John The Baptist Parish SD
Supt. — See Reserve
Garyville/Mt. Airy Math/Science Magnet S 300/K-8
240 Highway 54 70051 985-535-5400
Terran Perry, prin. Fax 535-5017
St. John Child Development Center 100/PK-PK
117 Stebbins St 70051 985-535-3917
Patricia Triche, dir. Fax 535-6406

Geismar, Ascension
Ascension Parish SD
Supt. — See Donaldsonville
Dutchtown MS 800/6-8
13078 Highway 73 70734 225-391-7800
Doug Walker, prin. Fax 621-2351
Dutchtown PS 800/PK-5
13046 Highway 73 70734 225-391-7850
Patricia Espinoza, prin. Fax 621-2383
Spanish Lake PS 800/K-5
13323 Bluff Rd 70734 225-391-7650
Britton Colon, prin. Fax 391-7651

Georgetown, Grant, Pop. 323
Grant Parish SD
Supt. — See Colfax
Georgetown S 200/PK-12
PO Box 99 71432 318-827-5306
Jennifer Winslett, prin. Fax 827-9481

Gibsland, Bienville, Pop. 966
Bienville Parish SD
Supt. — See Arcadia
Gibsland-Coleman S 200/K-12
PO Box 70 71028 318-843-6247
Samuel Andrews, prin. Fax 843-9804

Gibson, Terrebonne
Terrebonne Parish SD
Supt. — See Houma
Gibson ES 200/PK-6
6357 S Bayou Black Dr 70356 985-575-3260
LaCest Campbell, prin. Fax 575-3277

Gilbert, Franklin, Pop. 516
Franklin Parish SD
Supt. — See Winnsboro
Gilbert S 500/PK-8
PO Box 900 71336 318-435-5961
Anna Tarver, prin. Fax 435-3739

Glenmora, Rapides, Pop. 1,328
Rapides Parish SD
Supt. — See Alexandria
Glenmora HS 300/K-12
PO Box 697 71433 318-748-8145
Carrol Babb, prin. Fax 748-8146
Plainview S 300/PK-12
10935 Highway 112 71433 318-634-5944
Sonia Rasmussen, prin. Fax 634-5389

Golden Meadow, Lafourche, Pop. 2,060
Lafourche Parish SD
Supt. — See Thibodaux
Golden Meadow Lower ES 300/PK-2
118 Alcide St 70357 985-475-7385
Kelly Adams, prin. Fax 475-7865
Golden Meadow MS 400/6-8
630 S Bayou Dr 70357 985-475-7314
Hennessy Melancon, prin. Fax 475-6623
Golden Meadow Upper ES 200/3-5
124 N 3rd St 70357 985-475-7669
Buffy Boura, prin. Fax 475-7769

Goldonna, Natchitoches, Pop. 429
Natchitoches Parish SD
Supt. — See Natchitoches
Goldonna S 200/PK-8
PO Box 231 71031 318-727-9449
Mona Bamburg, prin. Fax 727-9449

Gonzales, Ascension, Pop. 9,648
Ascension Parish SD
Supt. — See Donaldsonville
Carver PS 600/PK-5
11310 Legacy Oaks Ln 70737 225-391-6800
Rhonda Gillard, prin. Fax 391-6801
Central MS 700/6-8
14101 Roddy Rd 70737 225-391-6400
Monica Hills, prin. Fax 621-2682
Central PS 800/PK-5
41469 Highway 621 70737 225-391-7700
Christina Knight, prin. Fax 391-7701
Duplessis PS 700/PK-5
38101 Highway 621 70737 225-391-6650
Jennifer Board, prin. Fax 677-5984
Gonzales MS 600/6-8
1502 W Orice Roth Rd 70737 225-391-6450
Lori Charlet, prin. Fax 621-2509
Gonzales PS 500/PK-5
521 N Burnside Ave 70737 225-391-6700
Dr. Roddy Melancon, prin. Fax 621-2663
Pecan Grove PS 500/PK-5
1712 Pecan Grove Ave 70737 225-391-7450
Amy Champagne, prin. Fax 644-6985

Ascension Christian ES 400/PK-6
10473 Airline Hwy 70737 225-644-3110
Mark Pellegrin M.S., supt. Fax 647-2368
St. Theresa S 300/4-8
212 E New River St 70737 225-647-2803
Christine Musso, prin. Fax 647-7814

Gramercy, Saint James, Pop. 3,592
St. James Parish SD
Supt. — See Lutcher
Gramercy ES 600/PK-6
601 E Second St 70052 225-258-4800
Kay Dornier, prin. Fax 869-3107

Grand Cane, DeSoto, Pop. 242

Central S 100/K-12
PO Box 187 71032 318-858-3319
Sherri Troegel, prin. Fax 858-6394

Grand Chenier, Cameron
Cameron Parish SD
Supt. — See Cameron
South Cameron S 300/PK-12
753 Oak Grove Hwy 70643 337-542-4628
Bobbye Delaney, prin. Fax 542-4419

Grand Coteau, Saint Landry, Pop. 940
St. Landry Parish SD
Supt. — See Opelousas
Grand Coteau ES 300/PK-4
PO Box K 70541 337-662-5421
Brandon Bobb, prin. Fax 662-5439

St. Ignatius S 400/PK-8
PO Box J 70541 337-662-3325
Cynthia Prather, prin. Fax 662-3349
School of the Sacred Heart 500/PK-12
PO Box 310 70541 337-662-5275
Dr. Yvonne Adler, head sch Fax 662-3011

Grand Isle, Jefferson, Pop. 1,269
Jefferson Parish SD
Supt. — See Harvey
Grand Isle S 100/PK-12
PO Box 995 70358 985-787-2577
Dr. Christine Templet, prin. Fax 787-3878

Grant, Allen
Allen Parish SD
Supt. — See Oberlin
Fairview S 400/PK-12
PO Box 216 70644 318-634-5354
Melanie Chapman, prin. Fax 634-5357

Grayson, Caldwell, Pop. 529
Caldwell Parish SD
Supt. — See Columbia
Grayson ES 300/K-5
5237 Highway 126 E 71435 318-649-2703
Maria Guerrero, prin. Fax 649-2765

Greensburg, Saint Helena, Pop. 714
St. Helena Parish SD 800/PK-12
PO Box 540 70441 225-222-4349
Dr. Kelli Joseph Ed.D., supt. Fax 222-4937
www.sthpk-12.net
St. Helena Arts and Technology Academy 200/3-6
1798 Highway 1042 70441 225-222-4364
Bernard McPherson, prin. Fax 222-4399
St. Helena Early Learning Center 300/PK-2
1590 Highway 1042 70441 225-222-3715
Donna Jackson, admin. Fax 222-3466

Greenwell Springs, East Baton Rouge
Central Community SD
Supt. — See Baton Rouge
Bellingrath Hills ES 500/PK-K
6612 Audusson Dr 70739 225-261-4093
Laurie Gehling, prin. Fax 261-4047

St. Alphonsus Liquori S 400/PK-8
13940 Greenwell Springs Rd 70739 225-261-5299
Dr. Cynthia Ryals, prin. Fax 261-2795

Gretna, Jefferson, Pop. 17,467
Jefferson Parish SD
Supt. — See Harvey
Cox ES 400/PK-5
2630 Belle Chasse Hwy 70056 504-394-5890
Shelita Jones, prin. Fax 392-3115
Douglass ES PK-5
1400 Huey P Long Ave 70053 504-374-6010
Lauren Rodriguez, prin. Fax 374-6021
Gretna #2 Academy 400/PK-5
701 Amelia St 70053 504-366-3582
Tamara Warner, prin. Fax 364-1268
Gretna MS 700/6-8
910 Gretna Blvd 70053 504-366-0120
D'Amica George, prin. Fax 366-8807
Hart ES 400/PK-5
2001 Hancock St 70053 504-366-4346
Janeen Weston, prin. Fax 366-2054
Johnson/Gretna Park ES 600/PK-5
1130 Gretna Blvd 70053 504-366-1660
Michelle Montagnino, prin. Fax 366-0143
McDonogh 26 ES 400/PK-5
1200 Jefferson St 70053 504-362-9929
Demetria Hamilton, prin. Fax 368-2114
Ruppel Academy for Advanced Studies 300/6-8
815 Huey P Long Ave 70053 504-361-8905
Emily Miller, prin. Fax 361-0792
Solis ES, 2850 Mount Laurel Dr 70056 800/PK-5
Vicki Esquivel, prin. 504-392-7867

Cahill Academy 500/PK-8
3101 Wall Blvd 70056 504-392-0902
Mary Cahill, prin. Fax 392-3813
Muslim Academy 200/1-12
440 Realty Dr 70056 504-433-1960
Nabil Abukhader, prin. Fax 433-7875
St. Anthony S 200/PK-7
900 Franklin Ave 70053 504-367-0689
JoAnna Russo, prin. Fax 361-0054
St. Cletus S 600/PK-7
3610 Claire Ave 70053 504-366-3538
Jill Grabert, prin. Fax 366-0011

Gueydan, Vermilion, Pop. 1,385
Vermilion Parish SD
Supt. — See Abbeville
Owens ES 200/PK-5
203 13th St 70542 337-536-6541
Anita Dupuis, prin. Fax 536-6481

Hackberry, Cameron, Pop. 1,258
Cameron Parish SD
Supt. — See Cameron
Hackberry S 200/PK-12
1390 School St 70645 337-762-3305
Michelle Dunham, prin. Fax 762-3304

Hahnville, Saint Charles, Pop. 3,314
St. Charles Parish SD
Supt. — See Luling
Carver Early Learning Center 100/PK-PK
337 Gum St 70057 985-783-6617
Dr. Tanesha Abdin, dir. Fax 783-6626

Hammond, Tangipahoa, Pop. 19,799
Tangipahoa Parish SD
Supt. — See Amite
Greenville Park Leadership Academy 500/PK-8
111 J W Davis Dr 70403 985-345-2654
Dr. Kay Williams, prin. Fax 542-4215
Hammond Eastside Magnet S 1,000/PK-8
45050 River Rd 70401 985-345-8481
Stephen Labbe, prin. Fax 345-0641
Hammond Westside Montessori S 1,200/PK-8
2500 Westpark Ave 70403 985-345-6857
Jason Oller, prin. Fax 542-0704
Southeastern Louisiana University Lab S 200/K-8
1200 N General Pershing St 70402 985-549-2185
Patricia Williams, prin. Fax 549-2771
Woodland Park Elementary Magnet S 500/PK-K
1000 S Range Rd 70403 985-542-6373
Tangee Daugereaux, prin. Fax 542-9959

Emmanuel SDA S 50/PK-8
702 N Cherry St 70401 985-345-7713
Tiangela Williams, prin.
Holy Ghost S 800/PK-8
507 N Oak St 70401 985-345-0977
Donna Wallette, prin. Fax 542-6545
Trafton Academy 200/PK-8
PO Box 2845 70404 985-542-7212
Susan B. Day, prin. Fax 542-7213

Harahan, Jefferson, Pop. 9,205
Jefferson Parish SD
Supt. — See Harvey
Harahan ES 600/PK-5
6723 Jefferson Hwy 70123 504-737-3918
Stephanie Scott, prin. Fax 737-2028

Faith Lutheran S 100/PK-8
300 Colonial Club Dr 70123 504-737-9554
Gregory Wood, prin. Fax 737-9599
St. Rita S 400/PK-7
194 Ravan Ave 70123 504-737-0744
Miriam Daniel, prin. Fax 738-2184

Harrisonburg, Catahoula, Pop. 340
Catahoula Parish SD 1,500/PK-12
PO Box 690 71340 318-744-5727
Dr. Gwile Freeman, supt. Fax 744-9221
cpsbla.org/
Harrisonburg HS 300/K-12
PO Box 710 71340 318-744-5273
Brenda Higdon, prin. Fax 744-5273
Other Schools – See Jonesville, Sicily Island

Harvey, Jefferson, Pop. 20,018
Jefferson Parish SD 45,100/PK-12
501 Manhattan Blvd 70058 504-349-7600
Isaac Joseph, supt. Fax 349-7960
jpschools.org
Pittman ES 600/PK-5
3800 13th St 70058 504-340-4937
Angelia Grabert, prin. Fax 340-4531
St. Ville ES PK-5
1121 Pailet Ave 70058 504-366-1708
Terrah Harrison, prin. Fax 374-5220
Woodland West ES 700/PK-5
2143 Mars St 70058 504-366-5308
Latonga Toney, prin. Fax 366-6962
Other Schools – See Avondale, Bridge City, Grand Isle, Gretna, Harahan, Jefferson, Kenner, Lafitte, Marrero, Metairie, River Ridge, Terrytown, Waggaman, Westwego

---

St. Rosalie S 700/PK-7
617 2nd Ave 70058 504-341-4342
Caren Creppel, prin. Fax 347-0271

Haughton, Bossier, Pop. 3,398
Bossier Parish SD
Supt. — See Benton
Haughton MS 1,000/6-8
395 S Elm St 71037 318-549-5560
Richard Warren, prin. Fax 549-5573
Platt ES 600/2-3
4680 Highway 80 71037 318-549-5870
Cathy Turner, prin. Fax 549-5883
Rodes ES 700/PK-1
4670 Highway 80 71037 318-549-5940
Lisle Meador, prin. Fax 549-5952

Haynesville, Claiborne, Pop. 2,308
Claiborne Parish SD
Supt. — See Homer
Haynesville ES 200/PK-4
9777 Highway 79 71038 318-624-1084
Jane Brown, prin. Fax 624-0597

Claiborne Academy 300/PK-12
6741 Highway 79 71038 318-927-2747
Scott Johnston, hdmstr. Fax 927-4519

Holden, Livingston
Livingston Parish SD
Supt. — See Livingston
Holden S 600/K-12
30120 LA 441 Hwy 70744 225-567-9367
Kristine Rountree, prin. Fax 567-5248

Homer, Claiborne, Pop. 3,200
Claiborne Parish SD 1,700/PK-12
PO Box 600 71040 318-927-3502
William Kennedy, supt. Fax 927-9184
www.claibornepsb.org
Homer ES 400/PK-4
624 Pelican Dr 71040 318-927-2393
Twyla Hilton, prin. Fax 927-2302
Homer JHS 200/5-8
612 Pelican Dr 71040 318-927-2826
Sue Barfield, prin. Fax 927-4376
Other Schools – See Haynesville, Summerfield

Hornbeck, Vernon, Pop. 464
Vernon Parish SD
Supt. — See Leesville
Hornbeck S 400/PK-12
PO Box 9 71439 318-565-4440
Raymond Jones, prin. Fax 565-4136

Houma, Terrebonne, Pop. 33,132
Lafourche Parish SD
Supt. — See Thibodaux
Bayou Blue ES 700/PK-4
1916 Bayou Blue Rd 70364 985-879-4378
Becky Plaisance, prin. Fax 879-1787
Bayou Blue MS 500/5-8
196 Mazerac St 70364 985-851-1952
Andre Adams, prin. Fax 851-1849

Terrebonne Parish SD 18,400/PK-12
PO Box 5097 70361 985-876-7400
Philip Martin, supt. Fax 872-0054
www.tpsd-la.schoolloop.com
Acadian ES 800/PK-4
1020 Saadi St 70363 985-876-0612
Dr. Monica Breaux, prin. Fax 876-0652
Bayou Black ES 200/PK-6
4449 Bayou Black Dr 70360 985-872-2460
Melynda Rodrigue, prin. Fax 872-3433
Broadmoor ES 600/PK-6
1010 Broadmoor Ave 70364 985-879-1042
Melissa Soileau, prin. Fax 879-2108
Coteau-Bayou Blue ES 800/PK-6
2550 Coteau Rd 70364 985-868-4267
Tess Daigle, prin. Fax 868-4425
Dularge ES 300/PK-6
621 Bayou Dularge Rd 70363 985-876-0176
Cheryl Degruise, prin. Fax 876-0177
East Houma ES 300/PK-3
222 Connely St 70363 985-872-1990
Melanie Wallis, prin. Fax 879-4900
Elysian Fields MS 400/4-6
700 Hibernia Pl 70363 985-876-2041
Markita Grant, prin. Fax 876-9741
Evergreen JHS 800/7-8
5000 W Main St 70360 985-876-2606
Kelly Burlette, prin. Fax 868-4395
Grand Caillou ES 600/PK-5
3933 Grand Caillou Rd 70363 985-879-3001
Amanda Callahan, prin. Fax 879-3009
Honduras ES 300/PK-3
530 Grand Caillou Rd 70363 985-872-5695
Anita Dufrene, prin. Fax 868-4727
Legion Park ES 400/PK-6
710 Williams Ave 70364 985-876-2272
Sharri McGuire M.Ed., prin. Fax 876-2352
Mulberry ES 1,000/PK-6
450 Cougar Dr 70360 985-872-5328
Gwen Ferguson, prin. Fax 872-5445
Oaklawn JHS 500/7-8
2215 Acadian Dr 70363 985-872-2904
Torrey Carter, prin. Fax 917-1917
Oakshire ES 700/PK-6
5459 Vicari St 70364 985-876-1007
Dawn Fleniken, prin. Fax 851-4710
Park ES 700/PK-6
6639 Lisa Park Ave 70364 985-876-1055
Terez LeBlanc, prin. Fax 868-6373
Southdown ES 400/PK-6
1124 Saint Charles St 70360 985-872-9429
Kanika Smith, prin. Fax 879-1841
Village East MS 200/4-6
315 Lafayette Woods Blvd 70363 985-868-4900
Roneka Coleman, prin. Fax 851-5059
Other Schools – See Bourg, Chauvin, Dulac, Gibson, Montegut, Schriever

---

Covenant Christian Academy 200/K-12
144 Rue Des Affaires 70364 985-851-7567
Jason Hutchinson M.Ed., prin. Fax 851-1087
Houma Christian S 400/PK-12
109 Valhi Blvd 70360 985-851-7423
James Champagne, prin. Fax 872-4958
Maria Immacolata S 200/PK-7
324 Estate Dr 70364 985-876-1631
Prissy Davis, prin. Fax 876-1608
Messiah Montessori S 100/PK-12
PO Box 20027 70360 985-857-8808
St. Bernadette S 400/PK-7
309 Funderburk Ave 70364 985-872-3854
Lydia Landry, prin. Fax 872-5780
St. Francis De Sales Cathedral S 700/PK-7
PO Box 8034 70361 985-868-6646
Kelli Cazayoux, prin. Fax 851-5896
St. Gregory Barbarigo S 200/PK-7
441 Sixth St 70364 985-876-2038
Dr. Cindy Martin, prin. Fax 879-2789
St. Matthew's Episcopal S 200/PK-7
266 Gabasse St 70360 985-872-5573

Independence, Saint Helena, Pop. 1,638
Tangipahoa Parish SD
Supt. — See Amite
Independence High Magnet S 300/PK-8
300 W 2nd St 70443 985-878-4376
Donnis Casanave, prin. Fax 878-4848
Independence Leadership Academy 500/PK-8
221 Tiger Ave 70443 985-878-4946
Lisa Raiford, prin. Fax 878-4827

Mater Dolorosa S 200/PK-8
509 Pine St 70443 985-878-4295
Cheryl Santangelo, prin. Fax 878-4888

Iota, Acadia, Pop. 1,481
Acadia Parish SD
Supt. — See Crowley
Iota ES 600/PK-5
470 W Kennedy Ave 70543 337-779-2581
Charles Barbier, prin. Fax 779-3489
Iota MS 300/6-8
426 S 5th St 70543 337-779-2536
Lee Ann Wall, prin. Fax 779-2594

St. Francis S 200/PK-8
490 Saint Joseph Ave 70543 337-779-2527
Michael Darbonne, prin. Fax 779-2309

Iowa, Calcasieu, Pop. 2,909
Calcasieu Parish SD
Supt. — See Lake Charles
Watson ES 1,000/PK-8
201 E First St 70647 337-217-4670
Patricia Schooler, prin. Fax 217-4671

Jackson, East Feliciana, Pop. 3,776
East Feliciana Parish SD
Supt. — See Clinton
Jackson ES 300/PK-5
3505 Highway 10 70748 225-634-5933
Megan Phillips, prin. Fax 634-2224

Jeanerette, Iberia, Pop. 5,487
Iberia Parish SD
Supt. — See New Iberia
Jeanerette ES 200/PK-6
600 Ira St 70544 337-276-6355
Devon Jones, prin. Fax 276-7266
Saint Charles Street ES 400/PK-6
1921 Saint Charles St 70544 337-276-9712
Allison O'Donnell, prin. Fax 276-9713

Jefferson, Jefferson, Pop. 11,058
Jefferson Parish SD
Supt. — See Harvey
Jefferson ES 400/PK-5
4440 Jefferson Hwy 70121 504-733-9461
Kathy McLeod, prin. Fax 733-8177
Riverdale MS 800/6-8
3900 Jefferson Hwy 70121 504-828-2706
Celest Cunningham, prin. Fax 833-5125

Jena, LaSalle, Pop. 3,373
LaSalle Parish SD 2,700/PK-12
PO Box 90 71342 318-992-2161
Janet Tullos, supt. Fax 992-8457
www.lasallepsb.com
Goodpine MS 300/3-5
12642 Highway 84 W 71342 318-992-5665
Janet Tullos, prin. Fax 992-5508
Jena ES 400/PK-2
758 E Sharbono Rd 71342 318-992-5175
Deedra Zeagler, prin. Fax 992-2386
Jena JHS 400/6-8
PO Box 920 71342 318-992-5815
Rhonda Russell, prin. Fax 992-6392
Nebo ES 200/PK-8
300 Highway 777 71342 318-992-4416
Deborah Mayo, prin. Fax 992-0202
Other Schools – See Olla, Trout, Urania

Jennings, Jefferson Davis, Pop. 10,205
Jefferson Davis Parish SD 5,900/PK-12
PO Box 640 70546 337-824-1834
Kirk Credeur, supt. Fax 824-9737
www.jeffersondavis.org
Hathaway S 500/PK-12
4040 Pine Island Hwy 70546 337-824-4452
Tanya Gaudet, prin. Fax 824-2769
Jennings ES 600/3-6
620 Florence St 70546 337-824-4972
Laurie Duhon, prin. Fax 824-4989
Ward ES 600/PK-2
208 Shankland Ave 70546 337-824-1235
Suzanne Doucet, prin. Fax 824-3155
Other Schools – See Elton, Fenton, Lacassine, Lake Arthur, Roanoke, Welsh

---

Bethel Christian S 200/PK-12
15147 Highway 102 70546 337-824-0020
Chris Wales, prin. Fax 824-0579
Our Lady Immaculate Catholic S 200/PK-8
600 Roberts Ave 70546 337-824-1743
Rebecca Chapman, prin. Fax 824-1752

Jonesboro, Jackson, Pop. 4,648
Jackson Parish SD 2,300/PK-12
PO Box 705 71251 318-259-4456
David Claxton, supt. Fax 259-2527
www.jpsb.us
Jonesboro-Hodge MS 300/5-8
440 Old Winnfield Rd 71251 318-259-6611
Dr. Jacqueline Mason, prin. Fax 259-9699
Southside ES 400/PK-4
2105 S Polk Ave 71251 318-259-4489
Dr. Jeananne Smith, prin. Fax 259-9758
Weston S 700/PK-12
213 Highway 505 71251 318-259-7313
Ritchie Tolar, prin. Fax 259-1056
Other Schools – See Quitman

Jonesville, Catahoula, Pop. 2,258
Catahoula Parish SD
Supt. — See Harrisonburg
Central S 100/K-12
244 Larto Bayou Rd 71343 318-339-7574
Johnnie Adams, prin. Fax 339-7925
Jonesville ES 400/PK-4
1219 Cora Dr 71343 318-339-8588
Glenda Barker, prin. Fax 339-9260
Jonesville JHS 200/5-7
802 Johnson St 71343 318-339-9604
Lanel Sharp B.A., prin. Fax 339-8289

Kaplan, Vermilion, Pop. 4,526
Vermilion Parish SD
Supt. — See Abbeville
Kaplan ES 600/PK-4
608 N Eleazar Ave 70548 337-643-7965
Andrea Ford, prin. Fax 643-2821
Rost MS 400/5-8
112 W 6th St 70548 337-643-8545
Sandy Huval, prin. Fax 643-7013

Maltrait Memorial S 100/PK-8
1 Crusader Sq 70548 337-643-7765
Renee Meaux, prin. Fax 643-7765

Keithville, Caddo
Caddo Parish SD
Supt. — See Shreveport
Keithville S 1,000/PK-8
12201 Mansfield Rd 71047 318-925-1005
Billy Williams, prin. Fax 925-2691

Kenner, Jefferson, Pop. 65,713
Jefferson Parish SD
Supt. — See Harvey
Alexander ES 600/PK-5
600 W Esplanade Ave 70065 504-469-7326
Leslie Harrison, prin. Fax 464-1058
Audubon ES 500/PK-5
200 W Loyola Dr 70065 504-466-0525
Dr. Emily Anderson, prin. Fax 464-1901
Chateau Estates ES 600/PK-8
4121 Medoc Dr 70065 504-464-5662
Deirdre Winkler, prin. Fax 464-6819
Clancy-Maggiore ES for the Arts 500/PK-5
2100 Maine Ave 70062 504-469-3664
Danesha Dorsey, prin. Fax 469-0216
Greenlawn Terrace ES 500/PK-5
1500 38th St 70065 504-468-1016
Mary Defusco, prin. Fax 468-5962
Roosevelt MS 600/6-8
3315 Maine Ave 70065 504-443-1361
Dr. Eric Greely, prin. Fax 443-3425
Schneckenburger ES 400/PK-5
26 Earnest Ave 70065 504-443-1236
Christi Rome, prin. Fax 443-6321
Washington Montessori S 300/PK-5
606 Clay St 70062 504-464-9111
Darlene Turnbull, prin. Fax 466-7420
Woods ES 300/PK-5
1037 31st St 70065 504-466-6252
Janine Holmes, prin. Fax 467-9441

Islamic S of Greater New Orleans 100/PK-8
2420 Illinois Ave 70062 504-466-4055
Dr. Siham Elsegelny, prin. Fax 466-4830
Our Lady of Perpetual Help S 200/PK-8
531 Williams Blvd 70062 504-464-0531
Patti Waddell, prin. Fax 464-0725
St. Elizabeth Ann Seton S 500/PK-7
4119 Saint Elizabeth Dr 70065 504-468-3524
Joan Kathmann, prin. Fax 469-6014

Kentwood, Tangipahoa, Pop. 2,191
Tangipahoa Parish SD
Supt. — See Amite
Chesbrough ES 400/PK-5
68495 Highway 1054 70444 985-229-6377
Rosalyn Varnado, prin. Fax 229-7234
Dillon Leadership Academy 400/PK-6
1459 I 55 Service Rd 70444 985-229-8225
Hugh Wallace, prin. Fax 229-5699
Spring Creek ES 400/PK-5
72961 Highway 1061 70444 985-229-8363
Evelyn Showers, prin. Fax 229-1130
Sumner MS 400/6-8
15649 Highway 440 70444 985-310-2152
Brenda Johnson, prin. Fax 229-4257

Kilbourne, West Carroll, Pop. 412
West Carroll Parish SD
Supt. — See Oak Grove
Kilbourne S 300/PK-12
PO Box 339 71253 318-428-3721
Truman Smith, prin. Fax 428-3860

Kinder, Allen, Pop. 2,412
Allen Parish SD
Supt. — See Oberlin
Kinder ES 600/PK-4
412 N 12th St 70648 337-738-2454
Marla Sanders, prin. Fax 738-5526
Kinder MS 400/5-8
414 N 12th St 70648 337-738-3223
Tracey Odom, prin. Fax 738-3425

Krotz Springs, Saint Landry, Pop. 1,194
St. Landry Parish SD
Supt. — See Opelousas
Krotz Springs S 300/K-8
PO Box 456 70750 337-566-3585
Ramiea Robinson, prin. Fax 566-1524

Labadieville, Assumption, Pop. 1,837
Assumption Parish SD
Supt. — See Napoleonville
Labadieville MS 300/5-8
2747 Highway 1 70372 985-526-4227
Corey Crochet, prin. Fax 526-4163
Labadieville PS 400/PK-4
3045 Highway 1 70372 985-526-8220
Brandee Gros, prin. Fax 526-8558

Lacassine, Jefferson Davis, Pop. 475
Jefferson Davis Parish SD
Supt. — See Jennings
Lacassine S 700/PK-12
PO Box 50 70650 337-588-4205
Christina Fontenot, prin. Fax 588-4283

Lacombe, Saint Tammany, Pop. 8,364
St. Tammany Parish SD
Supt. — See Covington
Bayou Lacombe MS 200/4-6
PO Box 787 70445 985-882-5416
Raymond Morris, prin. Fax 882-0056
Chahta-Ima ES 300/PK-3
27488 Pichon Rd 70445 985-882-7541
Gary Marlbrough, prin. Fax 882-7567

Lafayette, Lafayette, Pop. 118,722
Lafayette Parish SD 30,500/PK-12
PO Box 2158 70502 337-521-7000
Dr. Donald Aguillard, supt. Fax 233-0977
www.lpssonline.com
Acadian MS 400/5-8
4201 Moss St 70507 337-521-7840
Rollan Moore, prin. Fax 521-7841
Alleman MS 1,100/5-8
600 Roselawn Blvd 70503 337-521-7850
Jennifer Gardner, prin. Fax 521-7851
Boucher ES 700/PK-5
400 Patterson St 70501 337-521-7610
Irma Trosclair, prin. Fax 521-7611
Breaux MS 700/6-8
1400 S Orange St 70501 337-521-7860
Chad Guillory, prin. Fax 521-7861
Broadmoor ES 700/PK-4
609 Broadmoor Blvd 70503 337-521-7620
David Zielinski, prin. Fax 521-7621
Evangeline ES 700/PK-4
610 E Butcher Switch Rd 70507 337-521-7670
Felice Williams, prin. Fax 521-7671
Faulk ES 500/PK-5
711 E Willow St 70501 337-521-7680
Stephanie Reiners, prin. Fax 521-7681
Lafayette MS 500/6-8
1301 W University Ave 70506 337-521-7900
Tia Trahan, prin. Fax 521-7901
Live Oak ES 700/K-5
3020 N University Ave 70507 337-521-7730
Patricia Thompson, prin. Fax 521-7731
Martin MS 700/5-8
401 Broadmoor Blvd 70503 337-521-7910
Jeanne Hebert, prin. Fax 521-7911
Montgomery ES 600/PK-5
600 Foreman Dr 70506 337-521-7750
Janine Lafleur, prin. Fax 521-7751
Myrtle Place ES 300/K-5
1100 Myrtle Pl 70506 337-521-7760
Catherine Bricelj, prin. Fax 521-7761
Ossun ES 800/K-5
400 Rue Scholastique 70507 337-521-7770
Kelli Clause, prin. Fax 521-7771
Plantation ES 500/K-5
1801 Kaliste Saloom Rd 70508 337-521-7780
Ann Herrmann, prin. Fax 521-7781
Prairie ES 1,000/PK-5
2910 Ambassador Caffery Pky 70506 337-521-7790
Cayce Booher, prin. Fax 521-7791
Truman ECC 500/PK-PK
200 Clara St 70501 337-521-7810
Stephanie Francis, prin. Fax 521-7811
Woodvale ES 600/K-4
100 Leon Dr 70503 337-521-7830
Monique Vidos, prin. Fax 521-7831
Other Schools – See Broussard, Carencro, Duson, Milton, Scott, Youngsville

---

Ascension Episcopal S 700/PK-12
1030 Johnston St 70501 337-233-9748
Paul Quick, hdmstr. Fax 269-9768
Cathedral Carmel S 800/PK-8
848 Saint John St 70501 337-235-5577
Kay Aillet, prin. Fax 261-9493
Christ Church Academy 50/PK-6
800 Jefferson Blvd 70501 985-992-9890
Rev. Joseph Garner, admin.
Episcopal S of Acadiana PK-5
721 E Kaliste Saloom Rd 70508 337-993-2263
Dr. Paul Baker, head sch Fax 993-3706
Family Life Christian Academy 100/PK-7
2223 Dulles Dr 70506 337-988-0032
Sara Aloisio, prin. Fax 988-1637
First Baptist Christian S 200/PK-9
201 W Convent St 70501 337-237-1546
Susan Emerson, prin. Fax 237-9970
Holy Cross Little Shepherds ELC PK-PK
415 Robley Dr 70503 337-984-2636
Sandy Gallo, prin. Fax 988-3790
Holy Family S 200/PK-8
200 Saint John St 70501 337-235-0267
Rogers Griffin, prin. Fax 235-0558
Lafayette Christian Academy 800/PK-12
220 Portland Ave 70507 337-234-9860
Our Lady of Fatima S 900/PK-8
2315 Johnston St 70503 337-235-2464
Angela Isaacs, prin. Fax 235-1320
St. Genevieve ES 400/PK-4
201 Elizabeth Ave 70501 337-234-5257
Rebecca Trouille, prin. Fax 237-6065
St. Genevieve MS 200/5-8
91 Teurlings Dr 70501 337-266-5553
Julie Zaunbrecher, prin. Fax 266-5775
St. Mary Early Learning Center 200/PK-PK
419 Doucet Rd 70503 337-984-3750
Michelle Guidry, prin. Fax 981-8442
St. Pius S 700/PK-8
205 E Bayou Pkwy 70508 337-237-3139
Donna Lemaire, prin. Fax 232-3455
SS. Leo & Seton S 600/PK-8
502 Saint Leo St 70501 337-234-5510
Kimberly Gothreaux, prin. Fax 234-3676
Westminster Christian Academy 700/PK-6
111 Goshen Ln 70508 337-988-6489
Scott Davis, head sch Fax 284-3648

Lafitte, Jefferson, Pop. 956
Jefferson Parish SD
Supt. — See Harvey
Kerner ES 400/PK-5
4924 City Park Dr 70067 504-689-4136
Suzanne Bordlee, prin. Fax 689-7666

Lake Arthur, Jefferson Davis, Pop. 2,693
Jefferson Davis Parish SD
Supt. — See Jennings
Lake Arthur ES 500/PK-6
500 Mill Ave 70549 337-774-3323
Donna Woods, prin. Fax 774-3189

Lake Charles, Calcasieu, Pop. 70,438
Calcasieu Parish SD 32,100/PK-12
PO Box 800 70602 337-217-4000
Karl Bruchhaus, supt. Fax 217-4051
www.cpsb.org
Barbe ES 300/PK-5
400 Penn St 70601 337-217-4600
Sharon Ruffin-Hardy, prin. Fax 217-4601
Brentwood ES 400/PK-5
3825 Brentwood St 70607 337-217-4610
Julee Spann, prin. Fax 217-4611
Clifton ES 300/PK-5
100 N Prater St 70601 337-217-4420
Pamela Bell, prin. Fax 217-4421
College Oaks ES 300/PK-5
3618 Ernest St 70605 337-217-4560
Willona Jackson, prin. Fax 217-4561
Combre-Fondel ES 300/PK-5
2115 Fitzenreiter Rd 70601 337-217-4890
Mildred Smith, prin. Fax 217-4891
Cooley Magnet ES 300/K-5
2711 Common St 70601 337-217-4680
Emily Alcock, prin. Fax 217-4681
Dolby ES 400/PK-5
817 Jefferson Dr 70605 337-217-4730
Laura Phenice, prin. Fax 217-4731
Fairview ES 300/PK-5
3955 Gerstner Memorial Blvd 70607 337-217-4490
Kuricheses Alexander, prin. Fax 217-4491
Gillis ES 800/PK-5
916 Topsy Rd 70611 337-217-4780
Timothy Savoy, prin. Fax 217-4781
Henry Heights ES 400/PK-5
3600 Louisiana Ave 70607 337-217-4620
Michael Juneau, prin. Fax 217-4621
Hunter Head Start PK-PK
2200 Elder St 70601 337-217-4213
Bridget Roberson, prin. Fax 217-4214
Johnson ES 300/PK-5
500 Malcolm St 70601 337-217-4900
Anya Miller, prin. Fax 217-4901
Kaufman ES 400/PK-5
301 Tekel Rd 70607 337-217-4740
Nicole Adaway, prin. Fax 217-4741
Kennedy ES 200/PK-5
2001 Russell St 70615 337-217-4760
Dr. Dinah Robinson, prin. Fax 217-4761
LeBleu Settlement ES 400/K-5
6509 Highway 3059 70615 337-217-4880
Carmen Lopez, prin. Fax 217-4881
Molo Magnet MS 300/6-8
2300 Medora St 70601 337-217-4710
Shonna Anderson, prin. Fax 217-4711
Moss Bluff ES 1,000/PK-5
215 School St 70611 337-217-4640
Shauna Burkhead, prin. Fax 217-4641
Moss Bluff MS 1,000/6-8
297 Park Rd 70611 337-217-4570
Kendall Fontenot, prin. Fax 217-4571
Nelson ES 600/K-5
1001 Country Club Rd 70605 337-217-4790
Adam Caldwell, prin. Fax 217-4791
Oak Park ES 400/PK-5
2001 18th St 70601 337-217-4850
Shaalom St. Mary, prin. Fax 217-4851
Oak Park MS 500/6-8
2200 Oak Park Blvd 70601 337-217-4830
Martin Guillory, prin. Fax 217-4831
Prien Lake ES 600/K-5
3741 Nelson Rd 70605 337-217-4910
Julie Ortego, prin. Fax 217-4911
St. John ES 800/K-5
5566 Elliott Rd 70605 337-217-4870
Sandy Matthews, prin. Fax 217-4871
Watkins ES 200/PK-5
2501 7th Ave 70601 337-217-4590
Phyllis Godfrey, prin. Fax 217-4591
Watson ES 400/PK-5
1300 5th St 70601 337-217-4860
Shaunte Guillory, prin. Fax 217-4861
Welsh MS 1,200/6-8
1500 W Mcneese St 70605 337-217-4410
Bobby Thompson, prin. Fax 217-4412
White MS 600/6-8
1000 E McNeese St 70607 337-217-4810
Owen Clanton, prin. Fax 217-4811
Wilson ES 200/PK-5
1400 Opelousas St 70601 337-217-4750
Debora Garrick, prin. Fax 217-4751
Other Schools – See Bell City, Dequincy, Iowa, Starks, Sulphur, Vinton, Westlake

Cameron Parish SD
Supt. — See Cameron
Grand Lake S 800/PK-12
1039 Highway 384 70607 337-905-2231
Holly Castile, prin. Fax 905-2961

Bishop Noland Episcopal Day S 400/PK-8
803 N Division St 70601 337-433-5246
Rev. Frances Kay, admin. Fax 436-1248
Covenant Grace Academy 50/K-12
2110 E McNeese St 70607 337-474-2424
Marla Pennick, admin. Fax 474-2424
First Baptist Christian Academy 100/K-8
282 Old Highway 171 70611 337-855-9075
Shanna Eggleston, prin. Fax 855-8484
Hamilton Christian S 300/PK-12
1415 8th St 70601 337-439-1178
Dr. Wayne McEntire, prin. Fax 433-1877
Immaculate Conception Cathedral S 400/PK-8
1536 Ryan St 70601 337-433-3497
Christina Jarreau, prin. Fax 433-5056
Our Lady Queen of Heaven S 700/PK-8
3908 Creole St 70605 337-477-7349
JoAnn Wallwork, prin. Fax 477-7384
St. Margaret S 300/PK-8
2510 Enterprise Blvd 70601 337-436-7959
Wendy Wicke, prin. Fax 436-9932
St. Theodore Holy Family Catholic S 100/PK-8
785 Sam Houston Jones Pkwy 70611 337-855-9465
Jennifer Bellon, prin. Fax 855-2809

Lake Providence, East Carroll, Pop. 3,969
East Carroll Parish SD 1,100/PK-12
PO Box 792 71254 318-559-2222
Dr. Voleria Millikin, supt. Fax 559-3864
www.e-carrollschools.org
Griffin Middle Academy 200/6-8
1205 Charles D Jones Blvd 71254 318-559-1395
Christopher Smith, prin. Fax 559-0679
Southside ES 600/PK-5
1307 Charles D Jones Blvd 71254 318-559-0325
Muriel Williams, prin. Fax 559-5853

Briarfield Academy 200/PK-12
301 Riddle Ln 71254 318-559-2360

Laplace, Saint John the Baptist, Pop. 29,464
St. John The Baptist Parish SD
Supt. — See Reserve
Lake Pontchartrain ES 600/PK-8
400 Ory Dr 70068 985-652-2003
Jason Beber, prin. Fax 652-2989
LaPlace ES 1,000/K-8
393 Greenwood Dr 70068 985-652-5552
Dr. Fawn Ukpolo, prin. Fax 652-3979
Ory Communication Arts Magnet S 400/K-8
182 W 5th St 70068 985-651-3700
Christal Sylvain, prin. Fax 651-3712
Watkins ES 500/PK-8
938 Highway 628 70068 985-652-1593
Antoinette Robinet, prin. Fax 652-1578

Ascension of Our Lord S 200/PK-7
1809 Greenwood Dr 70068 985-652-4532
Toni Ruiz, prin. Fax 651-5151
St. Joan of Arc S 600/PK-7
412 Fir St 70068 985-652-6310
Jeff Montz, prin. Fax 652-6390

Larose, Lafourche, Pop. 7,283
Lafourche Parish SD
Supt. — See Thibodaux
Larose-Cut Off MS 500/6-8
13356 W Main St 70373 985-693-3273
Samantha Lagarde, prin. Fax 693-3270
North Larose ES 400/PK-5
175 Richardel Dr 70373 985-693-3445
Celeste Leboeuf, prin. Fax 693-3256
South Larose ES 300/PK-5
154 W 25th St 70373 985-693-7597
Holly Bouzigard, prin. Fax 693-8141

Holy Rosary S 300/PK-8
PO Box 40 70373 985-693-3342
Scott Bouzigard, prin. Fax 693-3348

Lecompte, Rapides, Pop. 1,209
Rapides Parish SD
Supt. — See Alexandria
Raymond ES 200/PK-6
PO Box 429 71346 318-776-5489
Jill Summers, prin. Fax 776-9459

Leesville, Vernon, Pop. 6,343
Vernon Parish SD 8,900/PK-12
201 Belview Rd 71446 337-239-3401
James Williams, supt. Fax 238-5777
www.vpsb.k12.la.us
East Leesville ES 500/PK-1
203 Belview Rd 71446 337-239-4966
Ramona Bennett, prin. Fax 239-7082
Hicks S 300/PK-12
1296 Hicks School Rd 71446 337-239-9645
Rhonda Roberts, prin. Fax 239-6149
Leesville JHS 500/7-8
480 Berry Ave 71446 337-239-3874
Angel Williams, prin. Fax 238-4113
Parkway ES 1-4
3585 University Pkwy 71446 337-239-3363
Dione Bradford, prin. Fax 239-0049
Pickering ES 900/PK-6
116 Lebleu Rd 71446 337-537-3394
Leigh Lansdale, prin. Fax 537-2293
Vernon MS 400/5-6
1410 Nona St 71446 337-238-1505
Henry Lacking, prin. Fax 239-2291
West Leesville ES 400/2-4
1200 Abe Allen Memorial Dr 71446 337-239-2330
Kristie Beasley, prin. Fax 239-0979
Other Schools – See Anacoco, Evans, Fort Polk, Hornbeck, Pitkin, Rosepine, Simpson

---

Faith Training Christian Academy 400/PK-12
603 E Mechanic St 71446 337-329-1569
Wayne Chance, prin. Fax 239-1044

Lena, Rapides
Rapides Parish SD
Supt. — See Alexandria
Northwood HS 700/PK-12
8830 Highway 1 N 71447 318-793-8021
Kelli Welch, prin. Fax 793-8503

Leonville, Saint Landry, Pop. 1,081
St. Landry Parish SD
Supt. — See Opelousas
Leonville S 700/K-8
PO Box 30 70551 337-879-2385
Barbara Roberson, prin. Fax 879-7914

Livingston, Livingston, Pop. 1,758
Livingston Parish SD 25,300/PK-12
PO Box 1130 70754 225-686-7044
Homer Wentzel, supt. Fax 686-3052
www.lpsb.org
Doyle ES 700/PK-6
PO Box 130 70754 225-686-2416
Donna Sibley, prin. Fax 686-1500
Frost ES 300/K-8
19672 LA Highway 42 70754 225-698-3780
Stacey Wise, prin. Fax 698-3126
Other Schools – See Albany, Denham Springs, French Settlement, Holden, Maurepas, Springfield, Walker, Watson

Lockport, Lafourche, Pop. 2,549
Lafourche Parish SD
Supt. — See Thibodaux
Lockport Lower ES 500/PK-2
1421 Crescent Ave 70374 985-532-2846
Myra Ougel, prin. Fax 532-2820
Lockport MS 300/6-8
720 Main St 70374 985-532-2597
Ashleigh Landry, prin. Fax 532-5811
Lockport Upper ES 300/3-5
201 School St 70374 985-532-3223
Ann Hodson, prin. Fax 532-6353

Holy Savior S 200/PK-8
201 Church St 70374 985-532-2536
Tricia Thibodaux, prin. Fax 532-2269

Logansport, DeSoto, Pop. 1,527
DeSoto Parish SD
Supt. — See Mansfield
Logansport S 700/PK-12
PO Box 549 71049 318-697-4338
Mary Register, prin. Fax 697-1120
Stanley S 400/PK-12
14323 Highway 84 71049 318-697-2664
Brian Anderson, prin. Fax 697-5984

Longville, Beauregard, Pop. 621
Beauregard Parish SD
Supt. — See Deridder
South Beauregard ES 400/PK-3
12378 Highway 171 70652 337-725-6302
Chad Schulz, prin. Fax 725-3837
South Beauregard Upper ES 400/4-6
12378 Highway 171 70652 337-725-4354
Wesley Henry, prin. Fax 725-4247

Loranger, Tangipahoa
Tangipahoa Parish SD
Supt. — See Amite
Loranger ES 800/PK-3
54101 Martin St 70446 985-878-4538
Mary Adams, prin. Fax 878-4864
Loranger MS 700/5-8
54123 Allman St 70446 985-878-9455
Catherine Perry, prin. Fax 878-4907

Loreauville, Iberia, Pop. 881
Iberia Parish SD
Supt. — See New Iberia
Loreauville ES 600/PK-6
PO Box 425 70552 337-229-6363
Gannon Dooley, prin. Fax 229-6861

Luling, Saint Charles, Pop. 11,952
St. Charles Parish SD 9,100/PK-12
13855 River Rd 70070 985-785-6289
Felecia Gomez-Walker, supt. Fax 785-1025
www.stcharles.k12.la.us
Lakewood ES 600/3-5
501 E Heather Dr 70070 985-785-1161
Kelli Oertling, prin. Fax 785-2426
Luling ES 600/PK-5
904 Sugarhouse Rd 70070 985-785-6086
Sam Buhler, prin. Fax 785-9933
Mimosa Park ES 400/PK-2
222 Birch St 70070 985-785-8266
Michele deBruler, prin. Fax 785-1299
Smith MS 300/6-8
281 Judge Edward Dufresne 70070 985-331-1018
Harold Blood, prin. Fax 331-9385
Other Schools – See Des Allemands, Destrehan, Hahnville, Norco, Paradis, Saint Rose

Lutcher, Saint James, Pop. 3,521
St. James Parish SD 3,800/PK-12
PO Box 338 70071 225-258-4500
Edward Cancienne Ph.D., supt. Fax 869-8845
www.stjames.k12.la.us
Lutcher ES 100/PK-6
PO Box P 70071 225-869-3661
Becky Louque, prin. Fax 869-9404
Other Schools – See Gramercy, Paulina, Saint James, Vacherie

Madisonville, Saint Tammany, Pop. 704
St. Tammany Parish SD
Supt. — See Covington
Lancaster ES 700/3-5
133 Pine Creek Dr 70447 985-792-0156
Susannah Welch, prin. Fax 792-5716
Madisonville ES 800/PK-2
317 Highway 1077 70447 985-845-3671
Phyllis Stephens, prin. Fax 845-1393
Madisonville JHS 600/6-8
PO Box 850 70447 985-845-3355
Patricia Welch-Nelson, prin. Fax 845-9018

Mamou, Evangeline, Pop. 3,194
Evangeline Parish SD
Supt. — See Ville Platte
Mamou ES 500/PK-4
1205 4th St 70554 337-468-3123
Mitchell Fontenot, prin. Fax 468-2722

Mandeville, Saint Tammany, Pop. 11,401
St. Tammany Parish SD
Supt. — See Covington
Fountainebleau JHS 900/7-8
100 Hurricane Aly 70471 985-875-7501
Kelly Grunditz, prin. Fax 875-7650
Lake Harbor MS 700/4-6
1700 Viola St 70448 985-674-4440
Susan Patin, prin. Fax 674-6762
Magnolia Trace ES 400/2-3
1405 Highway 1088 70448 985-626-8238
Melanie Edwards, prin. Fax 626-0209
Mandeville ES 600/PK-3
519 Massena St 70448 985-626-3950
Chantelle Smith, prin. Fax 674-0886
Mandeville JHS 700/7-8
639 Carondelet St 70448 985-626-4428
Mary Ann Cucchiara, prin. Fax 674-0401
Mandeville MS 800/4-6
2525 Soult St 70448 985-626-8778
Mary Hart, prin. Fax 626-1640
Marigny ES 500/PK-1
1715 Viola St 70448 985-674-3011
Leslie Martin M.Ed., prin. Fax 674-3015
Monteleone JHS 500/7-8
63000 Blue Marlin Dr 70448 985-951-8088
Sheri Jones, prin. Fax 951-8083
Pontchartrain ES 800/PK-3
1500 W Causeway Approach 70471 985-626-3748
Henry Heier, prin. Fax 626-4231
Tchefuncte MS 800/4-6
1530 W Causeway Approach 70471 985-626-7118
Dr. Mitchell Stubbs, prin. Fax 674-0773
Woodlake ES 600/PK-3
1620 Livingston St 70448 985-626-8842
Lelia Parker, prin. Fax 624-9404

Cedarwood S 300/PK-7
607 Heavens Dr 70471 985-845-7111
Mary Queen of Peace Catholic S 500/PK-7
1515 W Causeway Approach 70471 985-674-2466
Sybil Skanci, prin. Fax 674-1441
Our Lady of the Lake S 800/PK-7
316 Lafitte St 70448 985-626-5678
Frank Smith, prin. Fax 626-4337

Mangham, Richland, Pop. 672
Richland Parish SD
Supt. — See Rayville
Mangham ES 400/PK-5
PO Box 388 71259 318-248-2575
Sandra Jones, prin. Fax 248-2273
Mangham JHS 200/6-8
810 McConnel St 71259 318-248-2729
Connie Williams, prin. Fax 248-2931

Mansfield, DeSoto, Pop. 4,973
DeSoto Parish SD 4,900/PK-12
201 Crosby St 71052 318-872-2836
Dr. Cade Brumley, supt. Fax 872-1324
www.desotopsb.com
Mansfield ES 700/PK-4
1915 McArthur Dr 71052 318-872-1772
Malekah Morgan, prin. Fax 872-9610
Mansfield MS 500/5-8
1915 McArthur Dr 71052 318-872-1309
Grayson Collins, prin. Fax 872-1319
Other Schools – See Logansport, Stonewall

Many, Sabine, Pop. 2,778
Sabine Parish SD 4,300/PK-12
PO Box 1079 71449 318-256-9228
Dr. Sara Ebarb, supt. Fax 256-0105
www.sabine.k12.la.us
Many ES 400/PK-4
1501 Natchitoches Hwy 71449 318-256-3450
Tene Leach, prin. Fax 256-0190
Many JHS 400/5-8
1801 Natchitoches Hwy 71449 318-256-3573
Madeline Owens, prin. Fax 256-2846
Other Schools – See Converse, Florien, Negreet, Noble, Pleasant Hill, Zwolle

Maringouin, Iberville, Pop. 1,094
Pointe Coupee Parish SD
Supt. — See New Roads
Valverda ES 800/PK-6
1653 Valverda Rd 70757 225-637-2695
Kim Canezaro, prin. Fax 637-2595

Marksville, Avoyelles, Pop. 5,505
Avoyelles Parish SD 5,900/PK-12
221 Tunica Dr W 71351 318-253-5982
Blaine Dauzat, supt. Fax 253-5178
www.avoyellespsb.com
Marksville ES 700/PK-6
430 W Waddil St 71351 318-253-7464
Dawn Pitre, prin. Fax 253-9818
Other Schools – See Bunkie, Cottonport, Effie, Plaucheville, Simmesport

Marrero, Jefferson, Pop. 32,762
Jefferson Parish SD
Supt. — See Harvey
Collins Montessori 500/PK-5
500 Pine St 70072 504-347-0254
Jenenne Coulon, prin. Fax 347-0597
Ellender ES 500/PK-8
4501 E Ames Blvd 70072 504-341-9469
Cherie Soileau-Varisco, prin. Fax 348-0054
Estelle ES 700/PK-8
2800 Barataria Blvd 70072 504-347-3727
Alisha Gilbert, prin. Fax 340-4014
Janet ES 600/PK-5
2500 Bent Tree Blvd 70072 504-340-0487
Karen Doyle, prin. Fax 341-0548
Lincoln ES for the Arts 500/PK-8
1429 Ames Blvd 70072 504-340-8489
Karen Favorite, prin. Fax 347-1506
Marrero Academy for Advanced Studies 400/PK-5
2820 Mount Kennedy Dr 70072 504-347-4739
Londa Foster, prin. Fax 348-3707
Marrero MS 800/6-8
4100 7th St 70072 504-341-5842
Christina Conforto, prin. Fax 341-0004
Truman MS 800/6-8
5417 Ehret Rd 70072 504-341-0961
Terry Johnson, prin. Fax 347-4497
Wall ES 400/PK-5
2001 Bonnie Ann Dr 70072 504-340-4941
Richelle Christ, prin. Fax 341-5094

Concordia Lutheran S 200/PK-8
6700 Westbank Expy 70072 504-347-4155
Felicia Macon, prin. Fax 348-9345
Conquering Word Christian Academy 200/PK-12
812 Avenue F 70072 504-328-2273
Carolyn Treaudo Ph.D., prin. Fax 328-2204
Immaculate Conception S 700/PK-7
4520 Sixth St 70072 504-347-4409
Sr. Kim DiMarco, prin. Fax 341-2766
Visitation of Our Lady S 800/PK-7
3520 Ames Blvd 70072 504-347-3377
Carolyn Levet, prin. Fax 341-5378

Marthaville, Natchitoches
Natchitoches Parish SD
Supt. — See Natchitoches
Marthaville S 300/PK-8
PO Box 148 71450 318-472-6141
Micah Nicholson, prin. Fax 472-6592

Maurepas, Livingston
Livingston Parish SD
Supt. — See Livingston
Maurepas S 400/K-12
PO Box 39 70449 225-695-6111
Kenny Kraft, prin. Fax 695-3265

Maurice, Vermilion, Pop. 953
Vermilion Parish SD
Supt. — See Abbeville
North Vermilion MS 6-8
11609 LA Highway 699 70555 337-893-1583
Joan Romero, prin. Fax 893-1585
Picard ES 600/PK-5
203 S Albert St 70555 337-893-3887
Paulette Gaspard, prin. Fax 893-3850

Meraux, Saint Bernard, Pop. 5,703
St. Bernard Parish SD
Supt. — See Chalmette
Davies ES 700/PK-5
4101 Mistrot St 70075 504-267-7890
Donna Schultz, prin. Fax 267-7888
Trist MS 600/6-8
1 Pirates Cv 70075 504-872-9402
Denise Pritchard, prin. Fax 872-9426

Mermentau, Acadia, Pop. 647
Acadia Parish SD
Supt. — See Crowley
Mermentau S 200/PK-7
PO Box 250 70556 337-824-1943
Marie Broussard, prin. Fax 824-1958

Mer Rouge, Morehouse, Pop. 626
Morehouse Parish SD
Supt. — See Bastrop
Delta S 300/PK-5
PO Box 162 71261 318-647-3443
Georgia White, prin. Fax 647-5631

Merryville, Beauregard, Pop. 1,088
Beauregard Parish SD
Supt. — See Deridder
Merryville HS 500/K-12
7061 Highway 110 W 70653 337-825-8046
Donnie Love, prin. Fax 825-6443

Metairie, Jefferson, Pop. 136,499
Jefferson Parish SD
Supt. — See Harvey
Adams MS 800/6-8
5525 Henican Pl 70003 504-887-5240
Fax 887-0173
Airline Park Acad for Advanced Studies 400/PK-5
6201 Camphor St 70003 504-888-0969
Tiffani LeBouef, prin. Fax 454-6281
Birney ES 600/PK-5
4829 Hastings St 70006 504-885-1044
Jewel Jackson, prin. Fax 888-3314
Bissonet Plaza ES 700/PK-5
6818 Kawanee Ave 70003 504-887-0470
Audrey Easley, prin. Fax 887-5693
Bridgedale ES 500/PK-5
808 Zinnia Ave 70001 504-888-6807
Benjamin Moscona, prin. Fax 454-8788
Bunche ES 100/K-5
8101 Simon St 70003 504-737-3132
Monya Criddle, prin. Fax 737-7606
Dolhonde ES 400/PK-5
219 Severn Ave 70001 504-837-5370
Lisa Savage, prin. Fax 834-1256
Ellis ES 600/PK-8
801 Brockenbraugh Ct 70005 504-833-7254
Julie Berner, prin. Fax 833-9378
Green Park ES 500/PK-5
1409 N Upland Ave 70003 504-466-0205
Sandy Phillips, prin. Fax 469-3978
Harris MS 800/6-8
911 Elise Ave 70003 504-733-0867
Dawn Matherne, prin. Fax 733-0953

Hearst ES 700/PK-5
5208 Wabash St 70001 504-887-8814
Valentine Williams, prin. Fax 885-9117
Keller ES 500/PK-5
5301 Irving St 70003 504-887-3836
Barbara Hodgson, prin. Fax 455-1866
Matas ES 600/PK-8
1201 Elise Ave 70003 504-733-6200
Scott Deemer, prin. Fax 734-8520
Meisler MS 800/6-8
3700 Cleary Ave 70002 504-888-5832
Semaj Allen-Raymond M.Ed., prin. Fax 888-5855
Metairie Academy for Advanced Studies 400/PK-5
201 Metairie Rd 70005 504-833-5539
Lisa Babin, prin. Fax 838-6241
Riviere ES 500/PK-5
1564 Lake Ave 70005 504-835-8439
John Starr, prin. Fax 835-8943

Atonement Lutheran S 300/PK-8
6500 Riverside Dr 70003 504-887-0225
Douglas Molin, prin. Fax 887-0225
Crescent City Christian S 300/PK-12
4828 Utica St 70006 504-885-4700
Ecole Classique S 300/PK-12
5236 Glendale St 70006 504-887-3507
Sal Federico, hdmstr. Fax 887-8140
Greater New Orleans Christian Academy K-10
5220 Irving St 70006 504-302-7940
Kehoe-France Day S 700/PK-7
720 Elise Ave 70003 504-733-0472
Janet Pananos, prin. Fax 733-0477
Metairie Park Country Day S 800/PK-12
300 Park Rd 70005 504-837-5204
Matt Neely, hdmstr. Fax 837-0015
Our Lady of Divine Providence S 300/PK-7
917 N Atlanta St 70003 504-466-0591
Elvina DiBartolo, prin. Fax 466-0671
Ridgewood Preparatory S 300/PK-12
201 Pasadena Ave 70001 504-835-2545
Milton Montgomery, hdmstr. Fax 837-1864
St. Angela Merici S 400/PK-7
835 Melody Dr 70002 504-835-8491
Paige Bennett, prin. Fax 835-4463
St. Ann S 800/PK-7
4921 Meadowdale St 70006 504-455-8383
Susan Kropog, prin. Fax 455-9572
St. Benilde S 200/PK-7
1801 Division St 70001 504-833-9894
John Downey, prin. Fax 834-4380
St. Catherine of Siena S 900/PK-7
400 Codifer Blvd 70005 504-831-1166
Kimberly Kilroy, prin. Fax 833-8982
St. Christopher S 700/PK-8
3900 Derbigny St 70001 504-837-6871
Ruth Meche, prin. Fax 834-0522
St. Clement of Rome S 500/PK-7
3978 W Esplanade Ave S 70002 504-888-0386
Dr. Patricia Speeg, prin. Fax 885-8273
St. Edward the Confessor S 500/PK-7
4901 W Metairie Ave 70001 504-888-6353
Dr. Thomas Becker, prin. Fax 456-0960
St. Francis Xavier S 400/PK-7
215 Betz Pl 70005 504-833-1471
Barbara Martin, prin. Fax 833-1498
St. Louis King of France S 200/PK-7
1600 Lake Ave 70005 504-833-8224
Pamela Schott, prin. Fax 838-9938
St. Martin's Episcopal S 500/PK-12
225 Green Acres Rd 70003 504-733-0353
Merry Sorrells, head sch Fax 736-8800
St. Mary Magdalen S 400/PK-7
6421 W Metairie Ave 70003 504-733-1433
Valerie Rodriguez, prin. Fax 736-0727
St. Philip Neri S 600/PK-7
6600 Kawanee Ave 70003 504-887-5600
Dr. Carol Stack, prin. Fax 456-6857
Torah Academy 50/PK-8
5210 W Esplanade Ave 70006 504-456-6429
Yosi Chesney, dir. Fax 662-1573
Victory Christian Academy 200/PK-8
5708 Airline Dr 70003 504-733-5087
Michelle Nichols, prin. Fax 734-3381

Milton, Lafayette, Pop. 2,994
Lafayette Parish SD
Supt. — See Lafayette
Milton ES 1,000/K-8
PO Box 239 70558 337-521-7740
Kimberly Etie, prin. Fax 521-7741

Minden, Webster, Pop. 12,925
Webster Parish SD 6,600/PK-12
PO Box 520 71058 318-377-7052
Johnny Rowland, supt. Fax 377-4114
www.websterpsb.org
Harper ES 500/K-1
618 Germantown Rd 71055 318-377-7548
Janene Ashley, prin. Fax 377-7552
Jones ES 400/2-3
620 District Dr 71055 318-377-1815
Valerie Finley, prin. Fax 377-5257
Phillips MS 300/PK-PK, 6-
811 Durwood Dr 71055 318-377-0315
Amanda Thomas, prin. Fax 377-0049
Richardson ES 400/4-5
515 W Todd St 71055 318-377-2213
Oreata Banks, prin. Fax 377-2219
Webster JHS 500/7-8
700 E Union St 71055 318-377-3847
Bewanichi Sheppard, prin. Fax 377-1943
Other Schools – See Cotton Valley, Doyline, Dubberly, Sarepta, Shongaloo, Springhill

---

Glenbrook S 400/K-12
1674 Country Club Cir 71055 318-377-2135
Darden Gladney, hdmstr. Fax 377-0578

Monroe, Ouachita, Pop. 48,278
Monroe City SD 8,200/PK-12
PO Box 4180 71211 318-325-0601
Dr. Brent Vidrine, supt. Fax 812-3604
www.mcschools.net
Berg Jones Lane ES 400/PK-6
3000 Burg Jones Ln 71202 318-325-8982
Lashondra Allen, prin. Fax 325-2302
Carroll Magnet JHS 300/7-8
2913 Renwick St 71201 318-322-1683
Robert Rash, prin. Fax 322-0833
Carver ES 400/PK-6
1700 Orange St 71202 318-322-4245
Valeria Benson, prin. Fax 323-4592
Clark Magnet ES 500/PK-6
1207 Washington St 71201 318-322-8976
Dr. Brian Bush, prin. Fax 338-7983
Cypress Point University ES 500/PK-6
6701 Mosswood Dr 71203 318-345-5666
Mary DeWitt, prin. Fax 345-3224
Faulk ES 300/PK-6
2110 Jackson St 71202 318-322-1300
Cleveland Mouton, prin. Fax 387-7803
Foster ES 400/PK-6
1310 Richwood Road 1 71202 318-325-7979
Jennifer Harris, prin. Fax 329-9275
Hall ES 300/PK-2
1000 Plum St 71202 318-322-8501
Lametria Robinson, prin. Fax 361-0928
Humble ES 500/3-6
3800 Westminister Ave 71201 318-325-7659
Kendrick January, prin. Fax 361-9448
Jefferson Upper ES 300/3-6
1001 Pecan St 71202 318-410-1378
Jacqueline Anderson, prin. Fax 387-2863
King JHS 300/7-8
3716 Nutland Rd 71202 318-387-1825
Jerry Mayhall, prin. Fax 325-4285
Lee JHS 500/7-8
1600 N 19th St 71201 318-323-1143
Dana Mullins, prin. Fax 325-5236
Lexington ES 600/PK-2
1905 Spencer Ave 71201 318-322-9753
Toni McCarty, prin. Fax 361-5170
Ruffin ES 500/PK-6
1801 Parkview Dr 71202 318-322-3447
Sylvia Brass, prin. Fax 322-5951
Shelling ES 400/PK-6
4200 Elm St 71203 318-322-9533
Vickie Williams, prin. Fax 323-2596

Ouachita Parish SD 20,000/PK-12
PO Box 1642 71210 318-432-5000
Dr. Don Coker Ed.D., supt. Fax 432-5221
www.opsb.net
East Ouachita MS 6-8
859 Swartz Fairbanks Rd 71203 318-432-2150
Keshea Jones, prin.
Hayes ES 600/PK-6
3631 Old Sterlington Rd 71203 318-343-4560
Holly Wilkes, prin. Fax 343-4573
Lakeshore ES 600/PK-6
550 Balboa Dr 71203 318-343-1173
Dr. Scott Crain, prin. Fax 345-0870
Ouachita JHS 1,000/6-8
5500 Blanks St 71203 318-345-5100
Charles Wright, prin. Fax 345-3308
Richwood MS 500/6-8
5855 Highway 165 Byp 71202 318-432-2000
Orlando Freemont, prin. Fax 432-2049
Robinson ES 500/PK-5
5101 Reddix Ln 71202 318-322-1784
Dr. Harrington Watson, prin. Fax 325-3639
Shady Grove ES 300/PK-5
2204 Ticheli Rd 71202 318-323-9941
Jerlyn Bobo, prin. Fax 388-4470
Swartz Lower ES 400/K-2
235 Swartz School Rd 71203 318-343-8883
Margaret Haman, prin. Fax 343-2932
Swartz Upper ES 400/3-6
400 Lincoln Hill Dr 71203 318-343-1723
Janita Maxwell, prin. Fax 343-5087
Swayze ES 300/PK-5
2400 Burg Jones Ln 71202 318-325-1357
Dr. Dana Jenkins, prin. Fax 387-9532
Other Schools – See Calhoun, Sterlington, West Monroe

Geneva Academy 100/PK-12
2507 Oliver Rd 71201 318-805-0116
Grace Episcopal S 200/PK-8
1400 N 4th St 71201 318-322-5837
Dr. Beth Ricks Ph.D., hdmstr. Fax 322-6956
Jesus the Good Shepherd S 400/PK-6
900 Good Shepherd Ln 71201 318-325-8569
Lisa Patrick, prin. Fax 325-9730
Ouachita Christian S 800/PK-12
7065 Highway 165 N 71203 318-325-6000
Bobby Stokes, hdmstr. Fax 387-7000
Our Lady of Fatima S 100/PK-6
3202 Franklin St 71201 318-387-1851
Carryn Wiggins Ed.D., prin. Fax 325-7595
QuesTECH Learning 50/2-12
2401 Oliver Rd 71201 318-322-6000
River Oaks S 300/PK-12
600 Finks Hideaway Rd 71203 318-343-4185
Dr. David Nordman, hdmstr. Fax 343-1107

Montegut, Terrebonne, Pop. 1,507
Terrebonne Parish SD
Supt. — See Houma
Montegut ES 300/PK-4
1137 Highway 55 70377 985-594-3657
Andrea Rodrigue, prin. Fax 594-5941
Montegut MS 600/5-8
138 Dolphin St 70377 985-594-5886
Jennifer Pitre, prin. Fax 594-9666
Pointe-Aux-Chenes ES 200/PK-4
1236 Highway 665 70377 985-594-2131
Cindy Chauvin, prin. Fax 594-6849

Monterey, Concordia, Pop. 437
Concordia Parish SD
Supt. — See Vidalia
Monterey S 500/PK-12
PO Box 127 71354 318-386-2214
Dena Hale, prin. Fax 386-7356

Montgomery, Grant, Pop. 714
Grant Parish SD
Supt. — See Colfax
Verda ES 200/PK-6
2580 Highway 122 71454 318-646-3146
Paxton Teddlie, prin. Fax 646-3146

Mooringsport, Caddo, Pop. 772
Caddo Parish SD
Supt. — See Shreveport
Mooringsport ES 300/PK-5
PO Box 310 71060 318-996-6992
Debra Kurkiewicz, prin. Fax 996-7676

Moreauville, Avoyelles, Pop. 900

Sacred Heart S 400/PK-8
PO Box 179 71355 318-985-2772
Sr. Sandra Norsworthy, prin. Fax 985-2164

Morgan City, Saint Mary, Pop. 12,212
Assumption Parish SD
Supt. — See Napoleonville
Bayou L'Ourse PS 200/PK-4
1397 Highway 662 70380 985-631-9268
Lori Pennison, prin. Fax 631-2011

St. Martin Parish SD
Supt. — See Breaux Bridge
Stephensville S 100/PK-8
3243 Highway 70 70380 985-385-1366
Candice Grivet, prin. Fax 385-1369

St. Mary Parish SD
Supt. — See Centerville
Aucoin ES 300/PK-5
739 Julia St 70380 985-631-2464
Shantell Toups, prin. Fax 631-1008
Bayou Vista ES 400/PK-5
1155 Delmar Rd 70380 985-395-3758
Carmen Lagarde, prin. Fax 395-8862
Maitland ES 300/PK-5
1907 Federal Ave 70380 985-384-4986
Tonia Verrette, prin. Fax 384-4989
Morgan City JHS 600/6-8
911 Marguerite St 70380 985-384-5922
Joseph Stadalis, prin. Fax 385-4170
Norman ES 300/PK-5
900 Spruce St 70380 985-384-0877
Shannon Hoffpauir, prin. Fax 384-0889
Wyandotte ES 300/PK-5
2 Glenwood St 70380 985-384-0724
Barbara Leleux, prin. Fax 384-1590

Holy Cross ES 300/PK-6
2100 Cedar St 70380 985-384-1933
Amanda Talbot, prin. Fax 384-3270

Morse, Acadia, Pop. 812
Acadia Parish SD
Supt. — See Crowley
Morse S 200/PK-7
PO Box 247 70559 337-783-5391
Sheila Reed, prin. Fax 783-6562

Mount Hermon, Washington
Washington Parish SD
Supt. — See Franklinton
Mount Hermon S 500/PK-12
36119 Highway 38 70450 985-877-4642
Dawn Seal, prin. Fax 877-4710

Napoleonville, Assumption, Pop. 653
Assumption Parish SD 3,800/PK-12
4901 Highway 308 70390 985-369-7251
Earl Martinez, supt. Fax 369-2530
www.assumptionschools.com
Napoleonville MS 300/5-8
4847 Highway 1 70390 985-369-6587
Shawn Preston, prin. Fax 369-6595
Napoleonville PS 400/PK-4
185 Highway 1008 70390 985-369-6396
Stacy Garrison, prin. Fax 369-9926
Other Schools – See Belle Rose, Labadieville, Morgan City, Pierre Part

Natalbany, Tangipahoa, Pop. 2,949
Tangipahoa Parish SD
Supt. — See Amite
Natalbany MS 500/4-8
47370 Morrison Blvd 70451 985-345-0854
Darlene Hammer, prin. Fax 345-3246

Natchitoches, Natchitoches, Pop. 17,968
Natchitoches Parish SD 6,300/PK-12
PO Box 16 71458 318-352-2358
Dale Skinner, supt. Fax 352-8138
www.nat.k12.la.us
East Natchitoches IS 300/4-6
1001 E 5th St 71457 318-352-4516
Dr. Alvin Brossette, prin. Fax 352-4515
Natchitoches JHS 400/6-8
1621 Welch St 71457 318-238-0066
Edwin Mason, prin. Fax 238-0067
Natchitoches Magnet S 300/1-8
800 Koonce St 71457 318-357-1252
Stephonie French, prin. Fax 354-1122
NSU Elementary Lab S 300/PK-5
1 Caldwell Dr NSU Campus 71497 318-357-6973
Caron Coleman, prin. Fax 357-6979
NSU Middle Lab S 200/6-8
Tec Pod Bldg NSU 71497 318-357-4509
Ben LaGrone, prin. Fax 357-4260

Vaughn ES 500/PK-5
1500 Gold St 71457 318-352-2369
Kristie Irchirl, prin. Fax 352-0565
Weaver ES 600/PK-3
520 Saint Maurice Ln 71457 318-352-3623
Sandy Irchirl, prin. Fax 352-7319
Other Schools – See Campti, Cloutierville, Goldonna, Marthaville, Provencal

St. Mary's S 400/PK-12
1101 E 5th St 71457 318-352-8394
Andrea Harrell, prin. Fax 352-5798

Negreet, Sabine
Sabine Parish SD
Supt. — See Many
Negreet S 500/PK-12
PO Box 14 71460 318-256-2349
Chad Crow, prin. Fax 256-5868

Newellton, Tensas, Pop. 1,181
Tensas Parish SD
Supt. — See Saint Joseph
Newellton ES 200/PK-8
400 Verona St 71357 318-467-5109
Fax 467-5108

New Iberia, Iberia, Pop. 30,160
Iberia Parish SD 13,900/PK-12
1500 Jane St 70563 337-365-2341
Dale Henderson, supt. Fax 365-6996
www.iberia.k12.la.us
Anderson MS 500/7-8
1059 Anderson St 70560 337-365-3932
Dwalyn Jackson, prin. Fax 367-8285
Belle Place MS 500/7-8
4110 Loreauville Rd 70563 337-364-2141
Curtis Coquat, prin. Fax 365-9463
Caneview ES 600/PK-6
5301 Highway 90 E 70560 337-369-6517
Chantel Helms, prin. Fax 359-8971
Center Street ES 500/PK-6
1520 Center St 70560 337-369-9059
Kyla Aucoin, prin. Fax 369-9719
Coteau ES 400/PK-6
2414 Coteau Rd 70560 337-369-3653
Consuela Roberson, prin. Fax 369-6427
Daspit Road ES 500/PK-6
1103 Daspit Rd 70563 337-364-2371
Darla David, prin. Fax 364-8313
Dodson Street ES 300/PK-6
420 Dodson St 70563 337-369-3738
Angela Louviere, prin. Fax 365-1663
Iberia MS 600/7-8
613 Weeks Island Rd 70560 337-364-3927
Dina Bourque, prin. Fax 365-9681
Jefferson Island Road ES 600/PK-6
6007 Jefferson Island Rd 70560 337-365-1120
Tabitha Schwarz, prin Fax 365-6723
Johnston-Hopkins ES 600/PK-6
1200 S Hopkins St 70560 337-369-9687
Mona Atchison, prin. Fax 369-9872
Magnolia ES 600/PK-6
3116 E Admiral Doyle Dr 70560 337-369-6120
Paige Bullock, prin. Fax 365-5589
North Lewis ES 700/PK-6
604 N Lewis St 70563 337-369-6132
Tim Rosamond, prin. Fax 367-9327
North Street ES 300/PK-6
121 N North St 70560 337-369-6636
Bryan Hudson, prin. Fax 369-6394
Park ES 300/PK-6
1609 W Admiral Doyle Dr 70560 337-369-6189
Verdna Rogers, prin. Fax 365-6738
Pesson Addition ES 500/PK-6
619 Broussard St 70560 337-369-9907
Alfreda Jackson, prin. Fax 369-9950
Sugarland ES 400/PK-6
2403 Jefferson Island Rd 70560 337-365-9624
Cheryl Broussard, prin. Fax 364-8074
Other Schools – See Delcambre, Jeanerette, Loreauville

Assembly Christian S 300/PK-12
4219 E Admiral Doyle Dr 70560 337-364-4340
Rev. Armand Prentiss, prin. Fax 364-8310
Epiphany Day S 100/PK-5
120 Jefferson St 70560 337-364-6841
Cheryl Boutte Ph.D., head sch Fax 365-8209
Highland Baptist Christian S 500/PK-12
708 Angers St 70563 337-364-2273
Tim Sensley, admin. Fax 369-6303
St. Edward S 400/PK-3
175 Porter St 70560 337-369-6764
Karon Bonin, prin. Fax 369-0634

New Orleans, Orleans, Pop. 338,397
Orleans Parish SD 11,700/PK-12
3520 General Degaulle Dr 70114 504-304-3520
Dr. Henderson Lewis Ph.D., supt. Fax 309-2865
opsb.us
Bethune ES 400/PK-6
2401 Humanity St 70122 504-324-7076
Mary Haynes-Smith, prin. Fax 483-3291
Franklin Math-Science ES 800/PK-8
1116 Jefferson Ave 70115 504-304-3932
Charlotte Matthew, prin. Fax 304-6257
Jackson ES 100/PK-5
2405 Jackson Ave 70113 504-359-6950
Latasha Skidmore, prin. Fax 379-6076

Academy of the Sacred Heart 800/PK-12
4521 Saint Charles Ave 70115 504-891-1943
Sr. Melanie Guste, head sch Fax 891-9939
Bishop McManus Academy 200/PK-8
13123 I 10 Service Rd 70128 504-246-5121
Dr. Toni-Lynn Tyson, prin. Fax 246-5564
Calvary Baptist S 100/PK-8
2401 General DeGaulle Dr 70114 504-367-6465
Marsha Price, prin. Fax 367-6632
Christian Brothers S 200/PK-7
4600 Canal St 70119 504-488-4426
Richard Neider, prin.
Christian Brothers S 300/5-7
8 Friederichs Ave 70124 504-486-6770
Michael Prat, prin. Fax 486-1053
Ecole Bilingue de la Nouvelle-Orleans 200/PK-8
812 General Pershing St 70115 504-896-4500
Pauline Dides, prin. Fax 896-9610
Good Shepherd Nativity Mission S 100/K-7
353 Baronne St 70112 504-598-9399
Thomas Moran, prin. Fax 598-9346
Holy Cross PS PK-4
5601 Elysian Fields Ave 70122 504-942-3100
Sean Martin, hdmstr. Fax 570-6655
Holy Name of Jesus S 600/PK-7
6325 Cromwell Pl 70118 504-861-1466
Jessica Dwyer, prin. Fax 861-1480
Holy Rosary Academy 100/K-7
2437 Jena St 70115 504-482-7173
Cheryl Orillion, prin. Fax 482-7229
McGehee S 500/PK-12
2343 Prytania St 70130 504-561-1224
Eileen Powers, head sch Fax 525-7910
McMillian's FIRST Steps CDC/Academy 300/PK-8
2601 S Claiborne Ave 70125 504-822-1266
Linda McMillian, prin. Fax 822-1269
Newman S 900/PK-12
1903 Jefferson Ave 70115 504-899-5641
Dale Smith, head sch Fax 896-8597
New Orleans Adventist Academy 50/K-8
4500 Gawain Dr 70127 504-240-2227
Doris Smith, prin. Fax 240-2692
Resurrection of Our Lord S 500/PK-7
4861 Rosalia Dr 70127 504-243-2257
Vickie Helmstetter, prin. Fax 241-5532
St. Alphonsus S 200/PK-7
2001 Constance St 70130 504-523-6594
Sr. Monica Ellerbusch, prin. Fax 523-8769
St. Andrew's Episcopal S 100/PK-8
8012 Oak St 70118 504-861-3743
Melville Brown, head sch Fax 861-3973
St. Andrew the Apostle S 600/PK-7
3131 Eton St 70131 504-394-4171
Patience Clasen, prin. Fax 391-3627
St. Benedict the Moor S 100/PK-4
5010 Piety Dr 70126 504-288-2745
Drue Dumas, prin. Fax 282-9386
St. Dominic S 500/PK-7
6326 Memphis St 70124 504-482-4123
Ashley Seatter, prin. Fax 486-3870
St. George's Episcopal S 400/PK-8
923 Napoleon Ave 70115 504-891-5509
Dr. Robert Eichberger, hdmstr. Fax 895-1225
St. Joan of Arc S 300/PK-7
919 Cambronne St 70118 504-861-2887
Dionne Frost, prin. Fax 866-9588
St. John Lutheran S 100/PK-8
3937 Canal St 70119 504-488-6641
Bethany Gonski, prin. Fax 482-2101
St. Leo the Great S 200/PK-7
1501 Abundance St 70119 504-943-1482
Carmel Mire, prin. Fax 944-5895
St. Marys Academy 500/PK-12
6905 Chef Menteur Hwy 70126 504-245-0200
Sr. Jennie Jones, prin. Fax 245-0422
St. Paul's Episcopal S 200/PK-8
6249 Canal Blvd 70124 504-488-1319
Charleen Schwank, head sch Fax 304-8315
St. Peter Claver S 200/PK-7
1020 N Prieur St 70116 504-822-8191
Lawrence Houston, prin. Fax 822-2692
St. Pius X S 400/PK-7
6600 Spanish Fort Blvd 70124 504-282-2811
Deirdre Macnamara, prin. Fax 282-3043
St. Rita S 200/PK-7
65 Fontainebleau Dr 70125 504-866-1777
Shanda Theriot, prin. Fax 861-8512
St. Stephen S 200/PK-7
1027 Napoleon Ave 70115 504-891-1927
Rosie Kendrick, prin. Fax 891-1928
Stuart Hall S for Boys 300/PK-7
2032 S Carrollton Ave 70118 504-861-1954
Kevin Avin M.Ed., prin. Fax 861-5389
Trinity Episcopal S 400/PK-8
1315 Jackson Ave 70130 504-525-8661
Rev. Gary Taylor, head sch Fax 523-4837
Ursuline Academy S 300/PK-7
2635 State St 70118 504-866-5260
Shanna Gosey, prin. Fax 866-5293
Waldorf S of New Orleans 100/PK-8
517 Soraparu St Apt 101 70130 504-525-2420
Lisa Lynde, admin. Fax 525-3223

New Roads, Pointe Coupee, Pop. 4,804
Pointe Coupee Parish SD 2,900/PK-12
PO Box 579 70760 225-638-8674
Kevin Lemoine, supt. Fax 638-3237
www.pcpsb.net
Rosenwald ES 300/PK-6
1100 New Roads St 70760 225-638-6341
Natalie Aguillard, prin. Fax 638-7148
Other Schools – See Batchelor, Maringouin, Rougon

Catholic ES of Pointe Coupee 400/PK-6
304 Napoleon St 70760 225-638-9313
Melissa Cline, prin. Fax 638-6471
False River Academy 500/PK-12
201 Major Pkwy 70760 225-638-3783
Ashley Allen, prin. Fax 638-8555

Noble, Sabine, Pop. 244
Sabine Parish SD
Supt. — See Many
Ebarb S 300/PK-12
5340 Highway 482 71462 318-645-9402
Darrin Dyess, prin. Fax 645-4689

Norco, Saint Charles, Pop. 3,040
St. Charles Parish SD
Supt. — See Luling
Norco ES 300/PK-5
102 5th St 70079 985-764-7079
Becky Weber, prin. Fax 764-7962

Sacred Heart of Jesus S 100/PK-7
453 Spruce St 70079 985-764-9958
Laura DeLaneuville, prin. Fax 764-0041

Oakdale, Allen, Pop. 7,688
Allen Parish SD
Supt. — See Oberlin
Oakdale ES 600/PK-4
1515 Highway 1153 71463 318-335-0690
Kay Randolph, prin. Fax 335-2823
Oakdale MS 400/5-8
124 S 13th St 71463 318-335-1558
Jarrett Granger, prin. Fax 335-4690

Oak Grove, West Carroll, Pop. 1,714
West Carroll Parish SD 2,200/PK-12
314 E Main St 71263 318-428-2378
Richard Strong, supt. Fax 428-3775
www.wcpsb.com
Oak Grove ES 500/PK-5
206 Tiger Dr 71263 318-428-4810
Joanna Beard, prin. Fax 428-4884
Other Schools – See Epps, Forest, Kilbourne

Oberlin, Allen, Pop. 1,727
Allen Parish SD 4,300/PK-12
PO Box C 70655 337-639-4311
Michael Doucet, supt. Fax 639-2346
www.allen.k12.la.us
Oberlin ES 300/PK-6
110 S 4th St 70655 337-639-2241
Misty Alexander, prin. Fax 639-5561
Other Schools – See Elizabeth, Grant, Kinder, Oakdale, Reeves

Olla, LaSalle, Pop. 1,375
LaSalle Parish SD
Supt. — See Jena
Olla ES 400/PK-5
PO Box 1188 71465 318-495-5163
Debbie Gauthier, prin. Fax 495-5272

Opelousas, Saint Landry, Pop. 16,425
St. Landry Parish SD 14,200/PK-12
PO Box 310 70571 337-948-3657
Patrick Jenkins, supt. Fax 942-0204
www.slp.k12.la.us
Grolee ES 500/K-6
1540 W Grolee St 70570 337-942-3130
Brandon Singleton, prin. Fax 942-2332
Lawtell S 800/K-8
1010 School Rd 70570 337-543-2315
Clentrice Charles, prin. Fax 543-7901
Northeast ES 500/PK-6
1125 Mamie St 70570 337-942-5390
Daphne Guillory, prin. Fax 942-5390
North ES 300/PK-6
308 W Martin Luther King Jr 70570 337-942-2629
Michele Thibodeaux, prin. Fax 948-6284
Opelousas JHS 400/7-8
730 S Market St 70570 337-942-4957
Chastity Wilson, prin. Fax 942-2659
Park Vista ES 900/K-6
PO Box 2059 70571 337-942-7456
Joseph Joubert, prin. Fax 948-7352
Plaisance ES 300/5-8
3264 Highway 167 70570 337-826-3335
Monica Fabre, prin. Fax 826-7062
South Street ES 300/K-6
409 E South St 70570 337-942-8127
Elsie Semien, prin. Fax 942-3386
Southwest ES 400/PK-6
1203 Burr St 70570 337-942-9892
Marcella Fisher, prin. Fax 942-1763
Other Schools – See Arnaudville, Cankton, Eunice, Grand Coteau, Krotz Springs, Leonville, Palmetto, Port Barre, Sunset, Washington

Family Worship Christian Acadmey 100/PK-12
PO Box 1463 70571 337-942-1563
Alysia Richard, prin. Fax 942-1521
Opelousas Catholic S 700/PK-12
428 E Prudhomme St 70570 337-942-5404
Marty Heintz, prin. Fax 942-5922
Westminster Christian Academy 700/PK-12
186 Westminster Dr 70570 337-948-8607
Scott Davis, head sch Fax 948-8983

Paincourtville, Assumption, Pop. 906

St. Elizabeth Interparochial S 200/PK-8
PO Box M 70391 985-369-7402
Paula Simoneaux, prin. Fax 369-1527

Palmetto, Saint Landry, Pop. 157
St. Landry Parish SD
Supt. — See Opelousas
Palmetto ES 300/PK-4
PO Box 200 71358 337-623-4482
Kellie Rabalais, prin. Fax 623-3939

Paradis, Saint Charles, Pop. 1,269
St. Charles Parish SD
Supt. — See Luling
Martin MS 800/6-8
434 South St 70080 985-758-7579
Steven Guitterrez, prin. Fax 758-7570
Vial ES 300/3-5
510 Louisiana St 70080 985-758-2771
Angelle Babin, prin. Fax 758-2773

Parks, Saint Martin, Pop. 645
St. Martin Parish SD
Supt. — See Breaux Bridge

Parks MS 400/5-8
1010 Saint Louis Dr Ste A 70582 337-845-4753
Dr. Wanda Phillips, prin. Fax 845-5532
Parks PS 600/PK-4
1034 Main St 70582 337-845-4663
Julie Laviolette, prin. Fax 845-4198

Patterson, Saint Mary, Pop. 6,020
St. Mary Parish SD
Supt. — See Centerville
Patterson JHS 500/4-8
1101 1st St 70392 985-395-6772
Mark Spradling, prin. Fax 395-6773
Watts ES 600/PK-3
1307 3rd St 70392 985-395-5976
Sheryl Gibbons, prin. Fax 395-2588

Paulina, Saint James, Pop. 1,167
St. James Parish SD
Supt. — See Lutcher
Paulina ES 700/PK-6
2756 LA 44 70763 225-258-4700
Hollie Folse, prin. Fax 869-5290

St. Peter Chanel Interparochial S 200/PK-8
2590 LA 44 70763 225-869-5778
Paula Poche, prin. Fax 869-8131

Pearl River, Saint Tammany, Pop. 2,460
St. Tammany Parish SD
Supt. — See Covington
Creekside JHS 600/6-8
65434 Highway 41 70452 985-863-5882
Lisa Virga, prin. Fax 863-7658
Little Pearl ES 100/PK-K
63829 Highway 11 70452 985-863-5906
Dr. April Whitfield, prin. Fax 863-6217
Riverside ES 500/1-5
38480 Sullivan Dr 70452 985-863-3141
Mary Lou Jordan, prin. Fax 863-9811
Sixth Ward ES 400/PK-5
72360 Highway 41 70452 985-863-7126
Brian Hirstius, prin. Fax 863-2074

Pierre Part, Assumption, Pop. 3,145
Assumption Parish SD
Supt. — See Napoleonville
Pierre Part MS 300/5-8
3321 Highway 70 S 70339 985-252-6359
Wanda Templet, prin. Fax 252-3918
Pierre Part PS 400/PK-4
3321 Highway 70 S 70339 985-252-9415
Nancy Rousseau, prin. Fax 252-4180

Pine Prairie, Evangeline, Pop. 1,598
Evangeline Parish SD
Supt. — See Ville Platte
Pine Prairie S 800/PK-12
PO Box 200 70576 337-599-2300
Charles Johnson, prin. Fax 599-2003

Pineville, Rapides, Pop. 14,277
Rapides Parish SD
Supt. — See Alexandria
Barron ES 900/PK-6
3655 Holloway Rd 71360 318-445-6860
Richard Dewees, prin. Fax 445-6850
Goff ES 300/PK-6
6900 Shreveport Hwy 71360 318-640-3416
Cecelia Montiel, prin. Fax 640-3425
Moore ES 100/PK-K, 6-6
207 Griffith St 71360 318-445-7151
Laurie Johnson, prin. Fax 445-7156
Pineville ES 300/PK-6
835 Main St 71360 318-442-8154
Erin Stokes, prin. Fax 442-8172
Pineville JHS 700/7-8
501 Edgewood Dr 71360 318-640-0512
Michael Yoist, prin. Fax 640-9692
Ruby-Wise ES 400/PK-6
5279 Old Marksville Hwy 71360 318-443-6089
Harry Welch, prin. Fax 443-5709
Tioga ES 600/PK-6
4310 Pardue Rd, 318-640-9494
Crystal Furniss, prin. Fax 641-8752

Alpine Christian S 100/PK-6
7215 Shreveport Hwy 71360 318-640-3804
Lisa Roberts, prin. Fax 640-4645

Pitkin, Vernon, Pop. 566
Vernon Parish SD
Supt. — See Leesville
Pitkin S 500/PK-12
7239 Highway 463 70656 318-358-3121
Kevin Lambright, prin. Fax 358-3580

Plain Dealing, Bossier, Pop. 996
Bossier Parish SD
Supt. — See Benton
Martin ES 200/PK-5
600 S Perrin St 71064 318-759-2800
Stacy Crawford, prin. Fax 759-2804

Plaquemine, Iberville, Pop. 7,074
Iberville Parish SD 5,000/PK-12
PO Box 151 70765 225-687-4341
Arthur Joffrion Ed.D., supt. Fax 687-5408
www.ipsb.net
Crescent S 500/PK-8
62575 Bayou Rd 70764 225-659-2437
Allison Junot, prin. Fax 659-7242
Iberville ES 1,200/PK-6
58650 Iron Farm Rd 70764 225-687-2217
Jeanne Medine, prin. Fax 687-2266
Math Science & Arts West Academy K-12
57955 Saint Louis Rd 70764 225-687-6845
Elvis Cavalier, admin. Fax 687-6826
Other Schools – See Rosedale, Saint Gabriel, White Castle

St. John S 300/PK-8
58645 Saint Clement Ave 70764 225-687-6616
Cherie Schlatre, prin. Fax 687-6280

Plaucheville, Avoyelles, Pop. 243
Avoyelles Parish SD
Supt. — See Marksville
Plaucheville ES 600/PK-6
PO Box 60 71362 318-922-3311
Tonenikea Wilson, prin. Fax 922-3608

St. Joseph S 200/PK-12
PO Box 59 71362 318-922-3401
Billy Albritton, prin. Fax 922-3776

Pleasant Hill, Sabine, Pop. 710
Sabine Parish SD
Supt. — See Many
Pleasant Hill S 300/PK-12
PO Box 8 71065 318-796-3670
Jarrad Rivers, prin. Fax 796-2034

Pollock, Grant, Pop. 458
Grant Parish SD
Supt. — See Colfax
Pollock ES 600/PK-6
4001 Highway 8 71467 318-765-3511
Rebecca Durand, prin. Fax 765-3762

Ponchatoula, Tangipahoa, Pop. 6,436
Tangipahoa Parish SD
Supt. — See Amite
Cooper S 800/PK-8
42530 Highway 445 70454 985-542-6182
Anthony Sciortino, prin. Fax 542-8096
Perrin Early Learning Center 300/PK-K
350 W Ash St 70454 985-386-9734
Patricia Foster, prin. Fax 386-3069
Ponchatoula JHS 800/7-8
315 E Oak St 70454 985-370-5322
Bobby Matthews, prin. Fax 370-5327
Reeves ES 700/3-4
18026 Sisters Rd 70454 985-386-6433
Reginald Elzy, prin. Fax 386-9620
Tucker Memorial ES 700/1-2
310 S 3rd St 70454 985-386-6449
Amber Gardner, prin. Fax 386-9663
Vinyard ES 700/5-6
40105 Dunson Rd 70454 985-386-6364
Melissa Ryan, prin. Fax 386-2553

St. Joseph S 400/PK-8
175 N 8th St 70454 985-386-6421
Danette Ragusa, prin. Fax 386-0560

Port Allen, West Baton Rouge, Pop. 5,131
West Baton Rouge Parish SD 3,900/PK-12
3761 Rosedale Rd 70767 225-343-8309
Wes Watts, supt. Fax 387-2101
www.wbrschools.net
Chamberlin ES 300/PK-4
6024 Section Rd 70767 225-627-6691
Elizabeth Sarradet, prin. Fax 627-9306
Cohn ES 200/3-5
805 N 14th St 70767 225-343-7164
Cassandra Brou, prin. Fax 383-8587
Devall MS 100/5-8
11851 N River Rd 70767 225-627-4268
Laree Taylor, prin. Fax 627-4278
Port Allen ES 400/PK-2
609 Rosedale Rd 70767 225-343-7586
Michael Wright, prin. Fax 343-4607
Port Allen MS 200/6-8
610 Rosedale Rd 70767 225-383-5777
Jessica Major, prin. Fax 346-5030
Other Schools – See Brusly

Holy Family S 400/PK-8
335 N Jefferson Ave 70767 225-344-4100
Michael Comeau, prin. Fax 344-1928

Port Barre, Saint Landry, Pop. 2,017
St. Landry Parish SD
Supt. — See Opelousas
Port Barre ES 500/K-4
PO Box 310 70577 337-585-6172
Tiffany Perry, prin. Fax 585-3646

Port Sulphur, Plaquemines, Pop. 1,706
Plaquemines Parish SD
Supt. — See Belle Chasse
South Plaquemines ES 300/PK-6
218 School Rd 70083 504-595-6415
Stacey Barrett, prin. Fax 564-1335

Prairieville, Ascension, Pop. 26,585
Ascension Parish SD
Supt. — See Donaldsonville
Galvez MS 600/6-8
42018 Highway 933 70769 225-391-6350
Michelle Bourque, prin. Fax 391-6370
Galvez PS 600/PK-5
16093 Henderson Bayou Rd 70769 225-391-6600
Toni Hardy, prin. Fax 621-2447
Lakeside PS 600/PK-5
16500 Highway 431 70769 225-391-7750
Laurent Thomas, prin. Fax 391-7751
Oak Grove PS 900/PK-5
17550 Old Jefferson Hwy 70769 225-391-6750
Eve Frederic, prin. Fax 621-2370
Prairieville MS 900/6-8
16200 Highway 930 70769 225-391-6300
Dina Davis, prin. Fax 673-4883
Prairieville PS 800/PK-5
40228 Parker Rd 70769 225-391-7400
Carol Smith, prin. Fax 391-7401

St. John PS 400/PK-3
37407 Duplessis Rd 70769 225-647-2803
Kim Naquin, prin. Fax 673-6803

Pride, East Baton Rouge
East Baton Rouge Parish SD
Supt. — See Baton Rouge
Northeast ES 300/PK-6
16477 Pride Port Hudson Rd 70770 225-654-5113
Janet Shows, prin. Fax 654-6538

Princeton, Bossier
Bossier Parish SD
Supt. — See Benton
Princeton ES 600/4-5
1895 Winfield Rd 71067 318-549-5750
Andrea Spinney, prin. Fax 549-5763

Provencal, Natchitoches, Pop. 594
Natchitoches Parish SD
Supt. — See Natchitoches
Provencal S 500/PK-8
PO Box 429 71468 318-472-6174
Mary Yount, prin. Fax 472-9642

Quitman, Jackson, Pop. 180
Jackson Parish SD
Supt. — See Jonesboro
Quitman S 700/PK-12
PO Box 38 71268 318-259-2698
William Carter, prin. Fax 259-1139

Raceland, Lafourche, Pop. 10,053
Lafourche Parish SD
Supt. — See Thibodaux
Raceland Lower ES 500/PK-2
144 Bowie Rd 70394 985-537-6837
Rebecca Werner-Johnson, prin. Fax 537-3101
Raceland MS 300/6-8
PO Box C 70394 985-537-5140
Hiram Bailey, prin. Fax 537-5182
Raceland Upper ES 300/3-5
PO Box 370 70394 985-537-5142
Tina Guidry, prin. Fax 537-5354

St. Mary's Nativity S 300/PK-8
3492 Nies St 70394 985-537-7544
Marissa Bagala, prin. Fax 537-4020

Rayne, Acadia, Pop. 7,834
Acadia Parish SD
Supt. — See Crowley
Armstrong MS 400/6-8
700 Martin Luther King Blvd 70578 337-334-3377
Marshall Thibodeaux, prin. Fax 334-2681
Central Rayne K 200/PK-K
507 N Polk St 70578 337-334-3669
Christy Higginbotham, prin. Fax 334-8783
Mire S 600/PK-8
5484 Mire Hwy 70578 337-873-6602
Samuel Babineaux, prin. Fax 873-4620
Petitjean ES 400/1-3
4039 Crowley Rayne Hwy 70578 337-334-9501
Kimberly Cummins, prin. Fax 334-9517
South Rayne ES 300/4-5
101 E Branche St 70578 337-334-3610
Donna Duhon, prin. Fax 334-4993

Vermilion Parish SD
Supt. — See Abbeville
Indian Bayou S 200/PK-5
1603 LA Highway 700 70578 337-334-4070
Phyllis Doguet, prin. Fax 334-4237

Rayne Catholic S 400/PK-8
407 S Polk St 70578 337-334-5657
Gregory Dubois, prin. Fax 334-3301

Rayville, Richland, Pop. 3,658
Richland Parish SD 3,300/PK-12
PO Box 599 71269 318-728-5964
Sheldon Jones, supt. Fax 728-6366
www.richland.k12.la.us
Holly Ridge S 200/K-8
2306 Highway 183 71269 318-728-6495
Mildred Davis, prin. Fax 728-6465
Rayville ES 400/PK-5
1 Learning Pl 71269 318-728-2029
Stephanie Walker, prin. Fax 728-2099
Rayville JHS 200/6-8
225 Highway 3048 71269 318-728-3618
Nettie Ranel, prin. Fax 728-9374
Other Schools – See Delhi, Mangham, Start

Riverfield Academy 300/PK-12
115 Riverfield Dr 71269 318-728-3281
Sherri Slade, admin. Fax 728-3285

Reeves, Allen, Pop. 230
Allen Parish SD
Supt. — See Oberlin
Reeves S 300/PK-12
13770 Highway 113 70658 337-666-2414
Brenda Green, prin. Fax 666-2812

Reserve, Saint John the Baptist, Pop. 9,667
St. John The Baptist Parish SD 6,000/PK-12
PO Box AL 70084 985-536-1106
Kevin George, supt. Fax 536-1109
www.stjohn.k12.la.us
East St. John ES 600/4-8
1880 Highway 44 70084 985-536-8450
Stacy Bradford, prin. Fax 536-2040
Fifth Ward ES 500/K-3
158 Panther Dr 70084 985-536-4221
Drenean Brown, prin. Fax 536-1706
Other Schools – See Edgard, Garyville, Laplace

Riverside Academy 800/PK-12
332 Railroad Ave 70084 985-536-4246
Michael Coburn, prin. Fax 536-2127
St. Peter S 100/PK-7
188 W 7th St 70084 985-536-4296
Marie Comeaux, prin. Fax 536-4305

Ridgecrest, Concordia, Pop. 691
Concordia Parish SD
Supt. — See Vidalia
Academy for Math Science & Technology 200/1-8
200 Robert Webber Dr 71334 318-757-2135
Nancy Anders, prin. Fax 757-4651

Ringgold, Bienville, Pop. 1,471
Bienville Parish SD
Supt. — See Arcadia
Ringgold ES 300/PK-5
4044 Bienville Rd Ste A 71068 318-894-2911
Dorothy Foster, prin. Fax 894-2912

River Ridge, Jefferson, Pop. 13,340
Jefferson Parish SD
Supt. — See Harvey
Hazel Park/Hilda Knoff ES 400/PK-5
8809 Jefferson Hwy 70123 504-737-6163
Meredith Lagasse, prin. Fax 738-9153

Curtis Christian S 800/PK-12
10125 Jefferson Hwy 70123 504-737-4621
J.T. Curtis M.Ed., hdmstr. Fax 737-7326
St. Matthew the Apostle S 500/PK-7
10021 Jefferson Hwy 70123 504-737-4604
Dennis Panepinto, prin. Fax 738-7985

Roanoke, Jefferson Davis, Pop. 537
Jefferson Davis Parish SD
Supt. — See Jennings
Welsh-Roanoke JHS 300/6-8
8150 Highway 90 70581 337-753-2317
Rae Daigle, prin. Fax 753-2245

Rosedale, Iberville, Pop. 789
Iberville Parish SD
Supt. — See Plaquemine
North Iberville ES 300/PK-6
PO Box 200 70772 225-625-2522
Terri Harris, prin. Fax 625-6559

Roseland, Tangipahoa, Pop. 1,114
Tangipahoa Parish SD
Supt. — See Amite
Roseland Montessori S 300/PK-6
12516 Time Ave 70456 985-748-9307
Rhonda Vacarro, prin. Fax 748-9250

Rosepine, Vernon, Pop. 1,651
Vernon Parish SD
Supt. — See Leesville
Rosepine ES 800/PK-6
PO Box 578 70659 337-463-4203
Sandra Blakeway, prin. Fax 463-4246

Rougon, Pointe Coupee
Pointe Coupee Parish SD
Supt. — See New Roads
Rougon ES 600/PK-8
13258 LA Highway 416 70773 225-627-4291
Marcie Cazayoux, prin. Fax 627-5111

Ruston, Lincoln, Pop. 21,600
A.E. Phillips Lab S 400/K-8
PO Box 10168 71272 318-257-3469
Fax 257-3676
aep.latech.edu/
Phillips Lab S 400/K-8
PO Box 10168 71272 318-257-3469
Joanne Hood, prin. Fax 257-3676

Lincoln Parish SD 5,600/PK-12
410 S Farmerville St 71270 318-255-1430
Michael Milstead, supt. Fax 255-3203
www.lincolnschools.org
Cypress Springs ES 500/3-5
1040 Saratoga St 71270 318-255-0791
Mary Wilks-Kilgore, prin. Fax 255-0596
Glen View ES 600/K-2
1601 Bittersweet Ave 71270 318-255-5724
Jana Comstock, prin. Fax 255-5744
Hillcrest ES 400/K-2
301 E Kentucky Ave 71270 318-255-0550
Patrice Hilton, prin. Fax 255-0578
Lewis ES 300/6-6
1000 Mitchell Ave 71270 318-255-5963
John Young, prin. Fax 251-1947
Lincoln Parish ECC 200/PK-PK
801 E Mississippi Ave 71270 318-513-1470
Kathi Pesnell, dir. Fax 513-1478
Ruston ES 400/3-5
200 N Bernard St 71270 318-255-4714
Amanda Brown, prin. Fax 255-4728
Ruston JHS 600/7-8
481 Tarbutton Rd 71270 318-251-1601
Daryl Savage, prin. Fax 254-5235
Other Schools – See Choudrant, Dubach, Simsboro

Bethel Christian S 100/PK-12
2901 Winona Dr 71270 318-255-1112
Nancy Stevenson, admin. Fax 513-1113
Cedar Creek S 600/PK-12
2400 Cedar Creek Dr 71270 318-255-7707
Andrew Yepson, head sch Fax 251-2846
Montessori S of Ruston 100/PK-8
700 Woodward Ave 71270 318-251-1590
Chad Fredrick, dir. Fax 251-1576

Saint Amant, Ascension
Ascension Parish SD
Supt. — See Donaldsonville
Lake ES 1,000/K-8
14185 Highway 431 70774 225-391-6550
Jeremy Muse, prin. Fax 621-2476
Saint Amant MS 500/6-8
44317 Highway 429 70774 225-391-6500
Christy Bourgeois, prin. Fax 621-2593
Saint Amant PS 600/PK-5
44365 Highway 429 70774 225-391-7950
Paiseley Morgan, prin. Fax 391-7951

Saint Bernard, Saint Bernard
St. Bernard Parish SD
Supt. — See Chalmette
Gauthier ES 600/PK-5
1200 E LA 46 70085 504-272-0700
Lisa Young, prin. Fax 272-0710
Saint Bernard MS 300/6-8
2601 Torres Dr 70085 504-267-7878
Angela Seibert, prin. Fax 267-7886

Saint Francisville, West Feliciana, Pop. 1,749
West Feliciana Parish SD 2,200/PK-12
PO Box 1910 70775 225-635-3891
Hollis Milton, supt. Fax 635-0108
www.wfpsb.org
Bains ES 600/2-5
PO Box 1940 70775 225-635-3272
Jodi Lemoine, prin. Fax 635-3303
Bains Lower ES 400/PK-1
PO Box 2130 70775 225-635-4696
Dr. Andrea Mathis, prin. Fax 635-5345
West Feliciana MS 500/6-8
PO Box 690 70775 225-635-3898
Jovanka Chatman, prin. Fax 635-6925

Saint Gabriel, Iberville, Pop. 6,621
Iberville Parish SD
Supt. — See Plaquemine
East Iberville S 600/PK-12
3285 Highway 75 70776 225-642-5410
Calvin Nicholas, prin. Fax 642-9607
Math Science & Arts East Academy 300/K-12
1825 Highway 30 70776 225-238-0150
Charles Johnson, dir.

Saint James, Saint James, Pop. 827
St. James Parish SD
Supt. — See Lutcher
Fifth Ward ES 200/PK-6
8184 Villavaso St 70086 225-473-9537
Chakira Brown, prin. Fax 473-3799

Saint Joseph, Tensas, Pop. 1,163
Tensas Parish SD 700/PK-12
PO Box 318 71366 318-766-3269
Paul E. Nelson Ph.D., supt. Fax 766-3634
tensasedu.org
Tensas ES 200/PK-6
PO Box 318 71366 318-766-3346
Dr. Terri McGruder, prin. Fax 766-3377
Other Schools – See Newellton

Tensas Academy 200/PK-12
PO Box 555 71366 318-766-4384
Shannon Capdepon, head sch Fax 766-3559

Saint Martinville, Saint Martin, Pop. 6,047
St. Martin Parish SD
Supt. — See Breaux Bridge
Catahoula ES 200/PK-5
1016A Catahoula School Hwy 70582 337-394-3641
Tiffany Francis, prin. Fax 394-3632
Early Learning Center 400/PK-1
1004 S M L King Jr Dr 70582 337-394-4763
Jessica Landry, prin. Fax 394-6115
St. Martinville JHS 400/6-8
7190 Main Hwy 70582 337-394-4764
Edward Boyd, prin. Fax 394-9619
St. Martinville PS 600/2-5
716 N Main St 70582 337-394-6254
Sarah Allen, prin. Fax 394-8018

Saint Rose, Saint Charles, Pop. 8,003
St. Charles Parish SD
Supt. — See Luling
Cammon MS 300/6-8
234 Pirate Dr 70087 504-467-4536
Tamika Green, prin. Fax 468-3873
Saint Rose ES 700/PK-5
230 Pirate Dr 70087 504-464-9254
Shonda Honor-Harris, prin. Fax 468-8064

Saline, Bienville, Pop. 271
Bienville Parish SD
Supt. — See Arcadia
Saline S 300/PK-12
PO Box 129 71070 318-576-3215
Scott Canady, prin. Fax 576-9068

Sarepta, Webster, Pop. 889
Webster Parish SD
Supt. — See Minden
North Webster JHS 500/6-8
6041 Highway 2 71071 318-847-4301
Cynthia Hair, prin. Fax 847-4891

Schriever, Terrebonne, Pop. 6,745
Terrebonne Parish SD
Supt. — See Houma
Caldwell MS 400/4-6
445 Highway 311 70395 985-868-2565
Ronald Foret, prin. Fax 448-3963
Schriever ES 600/PK-3
2052 W Main St 70395 985-868-1199
Miranda Babin, prin. Fax 446-1323

Scott, Lafayette, Pop. 8,472
Lafayette Parish SD
Supt. — See Lafayette
James ES 900/PK-5
1500 W Willow St 70583 337-521-7700
Dana Schmersahl, prin. Fax 521-7701
Judice ES 400/K-5
5801 Cameron St 70583 337-521-7710
Mia Lemaire, prin. Fax 521-7711
Scott MS 600/5-8
116 Marie St 70583 337-521-7930
Venus Soileau, prin. Fax 521-7931
Westside ES 400/K-4
912 Delhomme Ave 70583 337-521-7820
Lisa Thomas, prin. Fax 521-7821

SS. Peter & Paul S 200/PK-8
1301 Old Spanish Trl 70583 337-504-3400
Dr. Robert Richard Ph.D., prin. Fax 504-4995

Shongaloo, Webster, Pop. 182
Webster Parish SD
Supt. — See Minden
North Webster Lower ES 200/PK-2
229 Highway Alt 2 71072 318-846-2541
Rick McWilliams, prin. Fax 846-2891

Shreveport, Caddo, Pop. 196,498
Caddo Parish SD 35,700/PK-12
PO Box 32000 71130 318-603-6300
Dr. T. Lamar Goree, supt. Fax 631-5241
www.caddoschools.org
Arthur Circle ES 400/PK-5
261 Arthur Ave 71105 318-861-3537
Ramona Myrick, prin. Fax 869-3395
Atkins ES 300/PK-5
7611 Saint Vincent Ave 71106 318-868-2810
Belinda Stewart, prin. Fax 861-7778
Bickham MS 700/6-8
7240 Old Mooringsport Rd 71107 318-929-4106
Amanda Wall, prin. Fax 929-2416
Blanchard ES 600/PK-5
402 Birch St 71107 318-929-2691
Rhonda Bass, prin. Fax 929-1702
Broadmoor MS Laboratory 600/6-8
441 Atlantic Ave 71105 318-861-2403
Renata Mahoney, prin. Fax 865-4142
Caddo Heights Math/Science ES 500/PK-5
1702 Corbitt St 71108 318-636-9610
Eric Hill, prin. Fax 636-7537
Caddo Middle Career & Technology S 200/6-8
6310 Clift Ave 71106 318-868-2753
Monte Demars, prin. Fax 868-2755
Caddo Parish Magnet MS 1,300/6-8
7635 Cornelious Ln 71106 318-868-6588
Robin Debusk, prin. Fax 865-6125
Cherokee Park ES 400/PK-6
2010 E Algonquin Trl 71107 318-221-6782
Tangela Sylvie, prin. Fax 221-1748
Claiborne Fundamental ES 400/PK-5
2345 Claiborne Ave 71103 318-222-2580
Ellen Hall, prin. Fax 221-1680
Clark ES PK-6
351 Hearne Ave 71103 318-425-8742
Kenya Roberts, prin. Fax 425-1151
Creswell ES 500/PK-5
2901 Creswell Ave 71104 318-222-5935
Tracey Harris, prin. Fax 674-8134
Eden Gardens Fundamental ES 500/PK-5
626 Eden Blvd 71106 318-861-7654
Sydney Allen, prin. Fax 868-7213
Eighty-First Street ECE Center 200/PK-K
8108 Fairfield Ave 71106 318-865-3596
Deborah Alexander, prin. Fax 865-7519
Fairfield Magnet ES 400/PK-5
6215 Fairfield Ave 71106 318-868-9826
Pamela Graham, prin. Fax 861-0662
Fair Park MS 700/6-8
3222 Greenwood Rd 71109 318-635-8181
Dr. Matthew Mitchell, prin. Fax 631-1982
Forest Hill ES 600/PK-5
2005 Francais Dr 71118 318-686-1783
Angela Douglas, prin. Fax 688-4212
Judson Fundamental ES 400/PK-5
3809 Judson St 71109 318-635-1132
Dr. Karon Rankin-Manning, prin. Fax 635-1240
Midway Professional Development Center 200/PK-5
3840 Greenwood Rd 71109 318-636-1861
Marvin Rainey, prin. Fax 636-3427
Mooretown Professional Development Ctr 300/PK-5
3913 Powell St 71109 318-631-7297
Shelia Gladney, prin. Fax 631-0195
North Highlands ES 400/PK-5
885 Poleman Rd 71107 318-221-6346
Lynette Hampton, prin. Fax 227-1426
Northside ES 400/PK-6
1845 Linear St 71107 318-221-3896
Dr. Cindy Frazier, prin. Fax 425-3485
Oak Park ES 200/PK-5
4331 Henry St 71109 318-635-2141
Marjorie Manuel, prin. Fax 636-6336
Pine Grove ES 400/PK-6
1700 Caldwell St 71107 318-424-7191
Travis Smith, prin. Fax 425-2539
Queensborough ES 400/PK-5
2701 Catherine St 71109 318-631-8784
Marco French, prin. Fax 631-7357
Ridgewood MS 700/6-8
2001 Ridgewood Dr 71118 318-686-0383
Scott Aymond, prin. Fax 686-0390
Riverside ES 400/PK-5
625 Dixie Garden Dr 71105 318-865-3576
Cheryl Jones-Hart, prin. Fax 865-3721
Shreve Island ES 700/PK-5
836 Sewanee Pl 71105 318-869-2335
Glen Colvin, prin. Fax 861-2256
Southern Hills ES 800/PK-5
9075 Kingston Rd 71118 318-686-1974
Jesse Scott, prin. Fax 688-4459
South Highlands Magnet ES 500/PK-5
831 Erie St 71106 318-865-5119
Mary Harris, prin. Fax 861-6264
Steere ES 400/PK-5
4009 Youree Dr 71105 318-865-5675
Brandy Holcomb, prin. Fax 861-7823
Stoner Hill ES 200/PK-5
2127 C E Galloway Blvd 71104 318-222-5317
Michelle Franklin, prin. Fax 222-8710
Summerfield ES 700/PK-5
3131 Ardis Taylor Dr 71118 318-686-1930
LeAnn Skinner, prin. Fax 688-6960
Summer Grove ES 800/PK-5
2955 Bert Kouns Industrl Lp 71118 318-686-1754
Pamela Bloomer, prin. Fax 688-6971

Sunset Acres ES 200/PK-5
6514 W Canal Blvd 71108 318-631-7121
William Fields, prin. Fax 636-5185
Timmons ES 300/PK-5
1410 Greenwood Mooringsport 71107 318-929-3950
Mary McWherter, prin. Fax 929-7178
Turner ES 1,100/PK-6
5904 W 70th St 71129 318-688-4380
Dr. Darrell Webb, prin. Fax 671-5230
University ES 900/PK-5
9900 Smitherman Dr 71115 318-797-2240
Kasie Mainiero, prin. Fax 797-0894
Walnut Hill S 1,800/PK-8
9360 Woolworth Rd 71129 318-687-6610
Julia O'Neal, prin. Fax 688-6522
Werner Park ES 100/PK-5
2715 Corbitt St 71108 318-635-9633
Shunda Huff, prin. Fax 621-9846
Westwood ES 400/PK-5
7325 Jewella Ave 71108 318-686-5489
Lynn Gardner, prin. Fax 688-7802
Youree Drive MS 1,000/6-8
6008 Youree Dr 71105 318-868-5324
Jenifer Guerrero, prin. Fax 861-5086
Other Schools – See Belcher, Keithville, Mooringsport, Vivian

---

Ascension Classical S K-3
5075 Dixie Garden Dr 71105 318-423-6104
Calvary Baptist Academy 1,100/K-12
9333 Linwood Ave 71106 318-687-4923
Fax 688-2437
Colquitt Christian Academy 50/K-8
3217 Colquitt Rd 71118 318-688-5081
Evangel Christian Academy 800/PK-12
7425 Broadacres Rd 71129 318-688-7061
Jerry Erickson, hdmstr. Fax 688-7322
First Baptist Church S 400/PK-8
533 Ockley Dr 71106 318-869-2361
Dr. James Gillespie, head sch Fax 869-0125
Montessori S for Shreveport 200/PK-8
2605 C E Galloway Blvd 71104 318-861-6777
Angie Day, prin. Fax 865-5793
St. John Berchmans S 300/PK-8
947 Jordan St 71101 318-221-6005
Jennifer Deason, prin. Fax 425-0648
St. Joseph S 500/PK-8
1210 Anniston Ave 71105 318-865-3585
Dr. Judith McGimsey, prin. Fax 868-1859
St. Marks Cathedral S 300/PK-8
2785 Fairfield Ave 71104 318-221-7454
Dr. Chris Carter, head sch Fax 221-7060
Southfield S 400/PK-8
1100 Southfield Rd 71106 318-868-5375
Gordon Walker, hdmstr. Fax 869-0890
Word Of God Academy 200/PK-12
2820 Summer Grove Dr 71118 318-687-9003
Cathy Jiles, prin. Fax 687-9607

Sicily Island, Catahoula, Pop. 519
Catahoula Parish SD
Supt. — See Harrisonburg
Sicily Island HS 300/PK-12
PO Box 128 71368 318-389-5337
Marguerita Krause, prin. Fax 389-5309

Simmesport, Avoyelles, Pop. 2,139
Avoyelles Parish SD
Supt. — See Marksville
Riverside ES 400/PK-6
529 Norwood St 71369 318-941-2699
Jessica Gauthier, prin. Fax 941-2140

Simpson, Vernon, Pop. 631
Vernon Parish SD
Supt. — See Leesville
Simpson S 300/PK-12
PO Box 8 71474 337-383-7810
Lee Coriell, prin. Fax 383-7655

Simsboro, Lincoln, Pop. 828
Lincoln Parish SD
Supt. — See Ruston
Simsboro S 600/K-12
1 Tiger Dr 71275 318-247-6265
Rusty Farrar, prin. Fax 247-6276

Singer, Beauregard, Pop. 282
Beauregard Parish SD
Supt. — See Deridder
Singer HS 300/K-12
153 Highway 110 E 70660 337-463-5908
Theresa Harlow, prin. Fax 463-0199

Slaughter, East Feliciana, Pop. 983
East Feliciana Parish SD
Supt. — See Clinton
Slaughter ES 500/PK-6
PO Box 60 70777 225-654-4527
Kimberly Glascock, prin. Fax 654-2838

Slidell, Saint Tammany, Pop. 26,521
St. Tammany Parish SD
Supt. — See Covington
Abney ECC 300/PK-K
829 Kostmayer Ave 70458 985-649-1858
Kimberly Blanks, prin. Fax 641-6096
Abney ES 900/1-5
825 Kostmayer Ave 70458 985-643-4044
Stephanie Jackson, prin. Fax 847-9509
Alton ES 200/PK-5
38276 N 5th Ave 70460 985-863-5353
Schanette Hebert, prin. Fax 863-5818
Bayou Woods ES 400/PK-3
35614 Liberty Dr 70460 985-641-1901
Kathryn McDowell, prin. Fax 639-0923
Bonne Ecole ES 800/PK-6
900 Rue Verand 70458 985-643-0674
April Owens Ph.D., prin. Fax 847-1299
Boyet JHS 800/7-8
59295 Rebel Dr 70461 985-643-3775
John Priola, prin. Fax 643-9470
Brock ES 300/PK-5
259 Brakefield St 70458 985-643-5166
Rose Smith, prin. Fax 646-1798
Clearwood JHS 600/4-8
130 Clearwood Dr 70458 985-641-8200
Alan Bennett, prin. Fax 641-7122
Cypress Cove ES 700/PK-1
540 S Military Rd 70461 985-641-3033
Lisa Dial, prin. Fax 641-8366
Florida Avenue ES 600/PK-6
342 Florida Ave 70458 985-643-1605
Kimberley Burgoyne, prin. Fax 641-2917
Honey Island ES 700/2-3
500 S Military Rd 70461 985-641-3557
Mary Jane Smith, prin. Fax 649-0959
Little Oak MS 1,000/4-6
59241 Rebel Dr 70461 985-641-6510
Kimberly Vanderklis, prin. Fax 641-6511
Mayfield ES 800/PK-6
31820 Highway 190 W 70460 985-643-5693
Kerri Soo, prin. Fax 649-3389
Park MS 300/4-6
35708 Liberty Dr 70460 985-643-8593
Patrick Mallory, prin. Fax 649-3910
St. Tammany JHS 600/6-8
701 Cleveland Ave 70458 985-643-1592
Vincent DiCarlo, prin. Fax 643-5873
Slidell JHS 700/7-8
333 Pennsylvania Ave 70458 985-641-5914
Patrick Mackin, prin. Fax 641-6397
Whispering Forest ES 500/PK-3
300 Spiehler Rd 70458 985-641-3400
Maureen Leonard, prin. Fax 641-3424

First Baptist Christian S 200/1-12
4141 Pontchartrain Dr 70458 985-643-3725
Mona Nelson, prin. Fax 445-1690
Our Lady of Lourdes S 500/PK-7
345 Westchester Pl 70458 985-643-3230
Michael Buras, prin. Fax 645-0648
St. Margaret Mary S 600/PK-7
1050 Robert Blvd Ste A 70458 985-643-4612
Cathy Canter, prin. Fax 643-4659

Sorrento, Ascension, Pop. 1,385
Ascension Parish SD
Supt. — See Donaldsonville
Sorrento PS 500/PK-5
42211 N City Park Dr 70778 225-391-6900
Robin Anderson, prin. Fax 391-6901

Springfield, Livingston, Pop. 483
Livingston Parish SD
Supt. — See Livingston
Springfield ES 600/PK-4
PO Box 9 70462 225-294-3398
Catherine Martin, prin. Fax 294-6920
Springfield MS 400/5-8
PO Box 40 70462 225-294-3306
Michael Dykes, prin. Fax 294-3307

Springhill, Webster, Pop. 5,214
Webster Parish SD
Supt. — See Minden
Browning ES 400/PK-2
505 Herrington Dr 71075 318-539-5663
Andre Washington, prin. Fax 539-9867
Brown Upper ES 300/3-5
804 4th St SW 71075 318-539-2818
Jessica Spence, prin. Fax 539-5427

Starks, Calcasieu, Pop. 662
Calcasieu Parish SD
Supt. — See Lake Charles
Starks S 400/PK-12
PO Box 69 70661 337-217-4820
Cary Smith, prin. Fax 217-4821

Start, Richland, Pop. 900
Richland Parish SD
Supt. — See Rayville
Start S 500/PK-8
883 Charleston Dr 71279 318-728-2074
Joyce Davis, prin. Fax 728-9291

Sterlington, Ouachita, Pop. 1,568
Ouachita Parish SD
Supt. — See Monroe
Sterlington ES 600/K-5
9040 Highway 165 N 71280 318-432-2050
Katy Wheeler, prin. Fax 432-2099
Sterlington MS 300/6-8
206 High Ave 71280 318-432-2100
Marty Bumgart, prin. Fax 432-2149

Stonewall, DeSoto, Pop. 1,797
DeSoto Parish SD
Supt. — See Mansfield
North DeSoto Lower ES 500/PK-1
2623 Highway 171 71078 318-925-2383
Bridget Flanders, prin. Fax 925-9373
North DeSoto MS 500/6-8
PO Box 310 71078 318-925-4520
Randall Simmons, prin. Fax 925-4719
North DeSoto Upper ES 500/2-5
2535 Highway 171 71078 318-925-1610
Bruce Burback, prin. Fax 925-2970

Sulphur, Calcasieu, Pop. 20,056
Calcasieu Parish SD
Supt. — See Lake Charles
Cypress Cove ES 500/PK-5
700 Currie Dr 70665 337-217-4970
Edlynn Hamilton, prin. Fax 217-4971
Frasch ES 600/K-5
540 S Huntington St 70663 337-217-4550
Michelle LeBlanc, prin. Fax 217-4551
Henning ES 400/PK-5
774 Henning Dr 70663 337-217-4840
Dea Kay, prin. Fax 217-4841
Key ES 400/K-5
1201 E Burton St 70663 337-217-4660
Laura Ledoux, prin. Fax 217-4661
LeBlanc MS/Drost Special 400/6-8
1100 N Crocker St 70663 337-217-4510
Joseph David, prin. Fax 217-4511
Lewis MS 900/6-8
1752 Cypress St 70663 337-217-4700
Dan Sylvest, prin. Fax 217-4701
Maplewood ES 1,000/PK-8
4401 Maplewood Dr 70663 337-217-4920
Doyce Brinkley, prin. Fax 625-4921
Vincent ES 400/PK-5
1634 Beglis Pkwy 70663 337-217-4690
Joy Fox, prin. Fax 217-4691
Vincent Settlement ES 400/PK-5
1072 Vincent Settlement Rd 70665 337-217-4580
Carla Williams, prin. Fax 217-4581

Our Lady's S 200/PK-8
1111 Cypress St 70663 337-527-7828
Trevor Donnelly, prin. Fax 528-3778

Summerfield, Claiborne
Claiborne Parish SD
Supt. — See Homer
Summerfield S 300/PK-12
PO Box 158 71079 318-927-3621
Shane Lee, prin. Fax 927-9160

Sunset, Saint Landry, Pop. 2,868
St. Landry Parish SD
Supt. — See Opelousas
Sunset ES 400/5-8
236 Church Hill St 70584 337-662-3194
Marquet Rideau, prin. Fax 662-3478

Tallulah, Madison, Pop. 7,266
Madison Parish SD 1,200/PK-12
301 S Chestnut St 71282 318-574-3616
Benita Young, supt. Fax 574-3667
www.madisonpsb.org
Madison MS 300/7-8
1233 Madison High Dr S 71282 318-574-0933
Erika January, prin. Fax 574-9199
Tallulah ES 200/PK-3
1100 Johnson St 71282 318-574-0732
Kimberly Pittman, prin. Fax 574-0489
Wright ES 200/4-6
809 Wyche St 71282 318-574-4430
Glenda Douglas, prin. Fax 574-3029

Tallulah Academy-Delta Christian S 300/PK-12
700 Wood St 71282 318-574-2606
Mary Lynn Watson, head sch Fax 574-3390

Terrytown, Jefferson, Pop. 22,887
Jefferson Parish SD
Supt. — See Harvey
Boudreaux ES 600/PK-5
950 Behrman Hwy 70056 504-393-8732
Kiplyn Pereira, prin. Fax 394-4836
Livaudais MS 700/6-8
925 Lamar Ave 70056 504-393-7544
Davon Hayes, prin. Fax 393-9610
Terrytown ES 900/PK-5
550 E Forest Lawn Dr 70056 504-376-8928
Teresita Diaz, prin. Fax 376-2389

Christ the King S 300/PK-7
2106 Deerfield Rd 70056 504-367-3601
Dawn Swear, prin. Fax 367-3679

Thibodaux, Lafourche, Pop. 14,384
Lafourche Parish SD 13,300/PK-12
PO Box 879 70302 985-446-5631
Dr. JoAnn Matthews, supt. Fax 446-0801
www.lpsd.k12.la.us
Bayou Boeuf ES 300/PK-5
4138 Highway 307 70301 985-633-2352
Kenn Robichaux, prin. Fax 633-2359
Chackbay ES 300/PK-5
101 School Ln 70301 985-633-2348
Robby Lee, prin. Fax 633-4710
East Thibodaux MS 400/6-8
802 E 7th St 70301 985-446-5616
Tanya Richard, prin. Fax 446-5610
Lafargue ES 100/2-3
700 Plantation Rd 70301 985-447-9292
Monica Tauzin, prin. Fax 447-4243
St. Charles ES 300/PK-5
1690 Highway 1 70301 985-446-6862
A. Pitonyak-Delcambre, prin. Fax 446-8591
Sixth Ward MS 300/6-8
1865 Choctaw Rd 70301 985-633-2449
Kenneth Delcambre, prin. Fax 633-7373
South Thibodaux ES 200/4-5
200 Iris St 70301 985-446-8471
Diane Smith, prin. Fax 447-1792
Thibodaux ES 200/PK-1
700 E 7th St 70301 985-446-6116
Robin Bourgeois, prin. Fax 447-8234
West Thibodaux MS 500/6-8
1111 E 12th St 70301 985-446-6889
Gregory Cook, prin. Fax 447-1777
Other Schools – See Cut Off, Galliano, Golden Meadow, Houma, Larose, Lockport, Raceland

---

St. Genevieve S 500/PK-7
807 Barbier Ave 70301 985-447-9291
Chris Knobloch, prin. Fax 447-9883
St. Joseph S 700/PK-7
501 Cardinal Dr 70301 985-446-1346
Gerard Rodrigue, prin. Fax 449-0760

Tickfaw, Tangipahoa, Pop. 685
Tangipahoa Parish SD
Supt. — See Amite
Midway ES 800/PK-3
48405 Highway 51 70466 985-345-2376
Wanda Davis, prin. Fax 345-3107
Nesom S 400/PK-8
14417 Highway 442 W 70466 985-345-2166
Charlotte Tillman, prin. Fax 345-3731

Trout, LaSalle
LaSalle Parish SD
Supt. — See Jena
Fellowship ES 200/PK-8
1650 Highway 773 71371 318-992-5177
Brandy Brunson, prin. Fax 992-0049

Urania, LaSalle, Pop. 1,308
LaSalle Parish SD
Supt. — See Jena
LaSalle JHS 200/6-8
PO Box 520 71480 318-495-3474
Stephanie Clark, prin. Fax 495-3478

Vacherie, Saint James, Pop. 2,354
St. James Parish SD
Supt. — See Lutcher
Sixth Ward ES 300/PK-6
3245 Valcour Aime St 70090 225-265-3942
Kimberly Gales, prin. Fax 265-8609
Vacherie ES 300/PK-6
13440 Highway 644 70090 225-265-3674
Julie Waguespack, prin. Fax 265-7263

Vidalia, Concordia, Pop. 4,268
Concordia Parish SD 3,700/PK-12
PO Box 950 71373 318-336-4226
Loretta Blankenstein, supt. Fax 336-5875
www.cpsbla.us
Vidalia JHS 400/6-8
210 Gillespie St 71373 318-336-6227
Christine Washington, prin. Fax 336 6229
Vidalia Lower ES 500/PK-2
300 Stampley St 71373 318-336-6220
Sandra Cobb, prin. Fax 336-6214
Vidalia Upper ES 300/3-5
1 Concordia Ave 71373 318-336-6224
Jana Lincecum, prin. Fax 336-8922
Other Schools – See Ferriday, Monterey, Ridgecrest

Ville Platte, Evangeline, Pop. 7,370
Evangeline Parish SD 6,100/PK-12
1123 Te Mamou Rd 70586 337-363-6651
Darwan Lazard, supt. Fax 363-8086
www.epsb.com
Bayou Chicot S 800/PK-8
4576 Highway 167 N 70586 337-461-2607
Mary-Christine Fontenot, prin. Fax 461-2601
Stephens Montessori S 300/PK-6
1500 Martin Luther King Dr 70586 337-363-4745
Melanie Bordelon, prin. Fax 363-6242
Vidrine S 300/PK-8
5094 Vidrine Rd 70586 337-363-4280
Anita West, prin. Fax 363-6828
Ville Platte ES 500/PK-4
708 High School Dr 70586 337-363-3068
Sally Moreaux, prin. Fax 363-7317
Other Schools – See Basile, Chataignier, Mamou, Pine Prairie

Christian Heritage Academy 100/PK-12
607 Prosper St 70586 337-363-7690
Sue Pomier, prin. Fax 363-7699
Sacred Heart S 500/K-8
532 E Main St 70586 337-363-3445
Virginia Morein, prin. Fax 363-3551

Vinton, Calcasieu, Pop. 3,128
Calcasieu Parish SD
Supt. — See Lake Charles
Vinton ES 500/PK-5
1610 Hampton St 70668 337-217-4520
Lori Young, prin. Fax 217-4521
Vinton MS 200/6-8
900 Horridge St 70668 337-217-4720
Gena Granger, prin. Fax 217-4721

Violet, Saint Bernard, Pop. 4,893
St. Bernard Parish SD
Supt. — See Chalmette
Smith ES 400/PK-5
6701 E Saint Bernard Hwy 70092 504-302-1000
Dedra Bailey, prin. Fax 302-1005

Vivian, Caddo, Pop. 3,629
Caddo Parish SD
Supt. — See Shreveport
North Caddo ES 600/PK-8
100 W Kentucky Ave 71082 318-375-3271
Judy Langley, prin. Fax 375-2499

Waggaman, Jefferson, Pop. 9,897
Jefferson Parish SD
Supt. — See Harvey
Cherbonnier/Rillieux ES 300/PK-5
700 Dandelion Dr 70094 504-431-9740
Cristin Menyweather, prin. Fax 431-1236
Live Oak Manor ES 300/PK-5
220 Acadia Dr 70094 504-431-7924
Myrtle Weber, prin. Fax 431-1116

Walker, Livingston, Pop. 6,061
Livingston Parish SD
Supt. — See Livingston
Milton ES 700/K-5
31450 Walker Rd N 70785 225-664-9711
Joshua Day, prin. Fax 665-4415
North Corbin ES 600/K-5
PO Box 328 70785 225-686-9169
Glenda Newman, prin. Fax 686-9170
North Corbin JHS 700/6-8
32725 N Corbin Rd 70785 225-686-2038
Carolyn Vosburg, prin. Fax 686-2690
South Walker ES 700/K-5
13745 Milton Ln 70785 225-665-0446
Belinda Avant, prin. Fax 665-0816
Walker ES 600/PK-5
PO Box 188 70785 225-665-5534
Bonnie Cox, prin. Fax 665-9951
Westside JHS 600/6-8
12615 Burgess Ave 70785 225-665-8259
Stephen Link, prin. Fax 665-8283

Washington, Saint Landry, Pop. 948
St. Landry Parish SD
Supt. — See Opelousas
Grand Prairie ES 400/PK-4
669 Highway 363 70589 337-826-3391
Robert Fontenot, prin. Fax 826-5674
Washington ES 200/PK-8
1530 Highway 10 70589 337-826-3393
Brenda Lavergne, prin. Fax 826-5276

Watson, Livingston, Pop. 1,038
Livingston Parish SD
Supt. — See Livingston
Live Oak ES 600/PK-5
PO Box 620 70786 225-665-6702
Michelle Wheeler, prin. Fax 664-7910
Live Oak MS 1,000/5-6
PO Box 470 70786 225-664-3211
Ryan Hodges, prin. Fax 664-1551
South Live Oak ES 600/PK-5
PO Box 500 70786 225-667-9330
Amy Savage, prin. Fax 667-2713

Welsh, Jefferson Davis, Pop. 3,178
Jefferson Davis Parish SD
Supt. — See Jennings
Welsh ES 500/PK-5
222 Bourgeois St 70591 337-734-2351
Arlene Heinen, prin. Fax 734-2704

Westlake, Calcasieu, Pop. 4,510
Calcasieu Parish SD
Supt. — See Lake Charles
Arnett MS 400/6-8
400 Sulphur Ave 70669 337-217-4630
Max Caldarera, prin. Fax 217-4631
Western Heights ES 300/PK-5
1100 Elizabeth St 70669 337-217-4930
Beth Flanagan, prin. Fax 217-4931
Westwood ES 600/K-5
1900 Sampson St 70669 337-217-4940
Gerald Treme, prin. Fax 217-4941

West Monroe, Ouachita, Pop. 12,872
Ouachita Parish SD
Supt. — See Monroe
Boley ES 200/PK-5
2213 Cypress St 71291 318-387-7378
Sandy Bates, prin. Fax 387-7465
Claiborne ES 800/PK-5
1011 Wallace Dean Rd 71291 318-396-8200
Kevin Welch, prin. Fax 396-8604
Crosley ES 200/PK-K
700 Natchitoches St 71291 318-325-3634
Tracey Flaherty, prin. Fax 322-7951
Drew ES 500/PK-5
1132 Ole Highway 15 71291 318-396-7186
Sharyl Boudreau, prin. Fax 397-1923
Good Hope MS 700/6-8
400 Good Hope Rd 71291 318-396-9693
Twainna Calhoun, prin. Fax 397-5110
Highland ES 300/PK-5
1501 Wellerman Rd 71291 318-396-1213
Jan Mercer, prin. Fax 397-1927
Kiroli ES 500/PK-5
700 Kiroli Rd 71291 318-396-1118
Carolyn Norris, prin. Fax 396-0804
Lenwil ES 300/PK-5
112 Arrant Rd 71292 318-323-3604
Lisa Vige, prin. Fax 323-7796
Pinecrest S 300/PK-8
3604 Highway 557 71292 318-325-4331
Don Tumey, prin. Fax 325-4459
Riser ES 400/PK-5
100 Price Dr 71292 318-387-0577
Nicole Zordan, prin. Fax 387-6801
Riser MS 500/6-8
100 Price Dr 71292 318-387-0567
Rodney Lloyd, prin. Fax 387-9072
Riverbend ES 500/1-5
700 Austin Ave 71292 318-361-0155
Dwayne Lathan, prin. Fax 329-9614
Welch ES 500/PK-5
199 Caldwell Rd 71291 318-397-1100
Sharon Sanders, prin. Fax 397-1383
West Ridge MS 700/6-8
6977 Cypress St 71291 318-397-8444
Jennifer Nichols, prin. Fax 397-9376
Woodlawn ES 600/K-5
5946 Jonesboro Rd 71292 318-325-1578
Cathy Jackson, prin. Fax 325-1579
Woodlawn JHS 300/6-8
175 Woodlawn School Rd 71292 318-325-1574
Charles Dykes, prin. Fax 325-9858

Claiborne Christian S 400/PK-12
334 Laird St 71291 318-396-7968
Lee Taylor, head sch Fax 397-0567
Northeast Baptist S 200/PK-12
5225 I 20 Service Rd 71292 318-325-2077

Westwego, Jefferson, Pop. 8,397
Jefferson Parish SD
Supt. — See Harvey
Butler ES 500/PK-5
300 Fourth St 70094 504-341-1351
Denise Rehm, prin. Fax 347-2583
Pitre ES 400/PK-5
1525 Spruce St 70094 504-341-6517
Wesley Taylor, prin. Fax 341-9527
Thibodeaux ES 400/PK-5
537 Avenue D 70094 504-341-1451
Diedra Miller, prin. Fax 341-4087
Worley MS 800/6-8
801 Spartan Ln 70094 504-348-4964
Michelle Biagas, prin. Fax 348-7057

Our Lady of Prompt Succor S 200/PK-7
531 Avenue A 70094 504-341-9505
Sr. Anna Bui, prin. Fax 341-9508

White Castle, Iberville, Pop. 1,872
Iberville Parish SD
Supt. — See Plaquemine
Dorseyville ES 400/PK-6
31505 Highway 1 70788 225-545-3805
Kelli Barbee, prin. Fax 545-2534

Winnfield, Winn, Pop. 4,766
Winn Parish SD 2,400/PK-12
PO Box 430 71483 318-628-6936
Steve Bartlett, supt. Fax 628-1699
www.winnpsb.org
Winnfield K, 1607 Maple St 71483 200/PK-K
Candy Polk, prin. 318-628-4134
Winnfield MS 400/6-8
685 Thomas Mill Rd 71483 318-628-2765
Brent Carpenter, prin. Fax 628-1838
Winnfield PS 500/1-4
401 S Saint John St 71483 318-628-4105
Amy Dantzler, prin. Fax 628-4108
Other Schools – See Atlanta, Calvin, Dodson

Winnsboro, Franklin, Pop. 4,862
Franklin Parish SD 3,000/PK-12
7293 Prairie Rd 71295 318-435-9046
Dr. Lanny Johnson, supt. Fax 435-3392
www.fpsb.us
Winnsboro ES 500/PK-5
1310 Warren St 71295 318-435-5066
Ronnie Lofton, prin. Fax 435-5063
Other Schools – See Baskin, Crowville, Fort Necessity, Gilbert

---

Family Community Christian S 500/PK-12
2023 Highway 15 71295 318-435-4791
Elizabeth Rigdon, prin. Fax 435-4792
Franklin Academy 200/PK-12
2110 Loop Rd 71295 318-435-9520
Phil Jackson, prin. Fax 435-9508

Woodworth, Rapides, Pop. 1,087
Rapides Parish SD
Supt. — See Alexandria
Dormon S PK-8
8906 Highway 165 S 71485 318-473-4066
Monica Helmer, prin. Fax 473-1890

Youngsville, Lafayette, Pop. 8,025
Lafayette Parish SD
Supt. — See Lafayette
Gallet ES 1,100/PK-5
2901 E Milton Ave 70592 337-521-7690
Monique Chargois, prin. Fax 521-7691
Lindon ES 900/PK-4
603 Avenue B 70592 337-521-7720
Cheri Fontenot, prin. Fax 521-7721
Youngsville MS 700/5-8
600 Church St 70592 337-521-7940
Renee Nunez, prin. Fax 521-7941

Youngsville Christian S 100/PK-10
623 Lafayette St 70592 337-856-8693
Daina Jackson, admin. Fax 856-8675

Zachary, East Baton Rouge, Pop. 14,763
Zachary Community SD 4,700/PK-12
3755 Church St 70791 225-658-4969
Scott Devillier, supt. Fax 658-5261
www.zacharyschools.org
Copper Mill ES 400/5-6
1300 Independence Blvd 70791 225-658-1288
Angela Cassard, prin. Fax 658-1298
Northwestern ES 400/K-K
4200 Rollins Rd 70791 225-654-2786
Kelli Day, prin. Fax 654-6613
Northwestern MS 800/7-8
5200 E Central Ave 70791 225-654-9201
Deborah Brian, prin. Fax 658-2025
Rollins Place ES 800/1-2
4488 Rollins Place Rd 70791 225-658-1940
Jennifer Marangos, prin. Fax 658-8207
Zachary Early Learning Center 200/PK-PK
4400 Rollins Place Rd 70791 225-654-6011
Martha Davis, prin. Fax 654-6392
Zachary ES 400/3-4
3775 Hemlock St 70791 225-654-4036
Keisha Thomas, prin. Fax 654-8746

Zwolle, Sabine, Pop. 1,697
Sabine Parish SD
Supt. — See Many
Zwolle ES 500/PK-6
PO Box 768 71486 318-645-6294
Cynthia Lewing, prin. Fax 645-7455

MAINE

MAINE DEPARTMENT OF EDUCATION
23 State House Sta, Augusta 04333
Telephone 207-624-6600
Fax 207-624-6700
Website http://www.maine.gov/doe/

Commissioner of Education Robert Hasson

MAINE BOARD OF EDUCATION
23 State House Sta, Augusta 04333

Chairperson Martha Harris

PUBLIC, PRIVATE AND CATHOLIC ELEMENTARY SCHOOLS

Acton, York
Acton SD 200/PK-8
700 Milton Mills Rd 04001 207-636-2100
Jonathan Ross, supt. Fax 636-3045
www.actonschool.org
Acton ES 200/PK-8
700 Milton Mills Rd 04001 207-636-2100
Jonathan Ross, admin. Fax 636-3045

Addison, Washington
RSU 37 / MSAD 37
Supt. — See Harrington
Merritt S 100/PK-6
518 Indian River Rd 04606 207-483-2229
Lorna Greene, prin. Fax 488-4572

Albion, Kennebec
RSU 49 / MSAD 49
Supt. — See Fairfield
Albion ES 100/K-6
20 School St 04910 207-437-2616
Lori Lee, prin. Fax 437-2001

Alexander, Washington
AOS 77 - SCSS
Supt. — See Eastport
Alexander S 100/PK-8
1430 Airline Rd 04694 207-454-2623
Trevor Flood, prin. Fax 454-7760

Alfred, York
RSU 57 / MSAD 57
Supt. — See Waterboro
Alfred ES 200/K-5
21 Sanford Rd 04002 207-324-3831
Cindy Pellerin, prin. Fax 490-9732

Alton, Penobscot
RSU 34
Supt. — See Old Town
Alton ES 100/PK-4
22 Argyle Rd 04468 207-394-2331
Cheryl Leonard, prin. Fax 394-2352

Andover, Oxford
Andover SD 50/PK-5
PO Box 70 04216 207-392-4381
Alton Hadley, supt. Fax 392-1500
andoverschoolmaine.org
Andover ES 50/PK-5
PO Box 70 04216 207-392-4381
Karen Thurston, prin. Fax 392-1500

Anson, Somerset, Pop. 746
RSU 74 / MSAD 74
Supt. — See North Anson
Schenck ES 100/PK-5
PO Box 317 04911 207-696-3100
Jean Butler, prin. Fax 696-3656

Arundel, York
RSU 21
Supt. — See Kennebunk
Day S 200/K-5
600 Limerick Rd 04046 207-284-4677
Kyle Keenan, prin. Fax 284-5832

Ashland, Aroostook, Pop. 707
RSU 32 / MSAD 32 300/PK-12
PO Box 289 04732 207-435-3661
Gehrig Johnson Ph.D., supt. Fax 435-8421
www.sad32.org
Ashland District S 300/PK-12
PO Box 369 04732 207-435-3481
Joel Hall, prin. Fax 435-6417

Athens, Somerset
AOS 94 - S46HRSD
Supt. — See Dexter
Athens Community S 100/PK-8
8 Fox Hill Rd 04912 207-654-2561
Edward Ellis, lead tchr. Fax 654-2109

Auburn, Androscoggin, Pop. 22,603
Auburn SD 3,600/PK-12
PO Box 800 04212 207-784-6431
Katherine Grondin, supt. Fax 333-6628
www.auburnschl.edu
Auburn MS 500/7-8
38 Falcon Dr 04210 207-333-6654
Celena Ranger, prin. Fax 784-1359
East Auburn Community ES 200/PK-6
15 Andrew Dr 04210 207-782-4142
Dr. Sue Dorris, prin. Fax 782-0173
Fairview ES 500/PK-6
397 Minot Ave 04210 207-784-3559
Celeste Beaudet, prin. Fax 786-0787
Park Avenue ES 400/PK-6
161 Park Ave 04210 207-333-6657
Vickie Gaylord, prin. Fax 786-6782
Sherwood Heights ES 400/PK-6
32 Sherwood Dr 04210 207-783-8526
Kim Taylor, prin. Fax 784-1574
Walton ES 300/PK-6
92 Mary Carroll St 04210 207-784-1528
Mike Davis, prin. Fax 784-1520
Washburn ES 300/K-6
35 Lake Auburn Ave 04210 207-784-5467
Andrew Bard, prin. Fax 784-5468

Augusta, Kennebec, Pop. 18,710
Augusta SD 2,300/PK-12
40 Pierce Dr 04330 207-626-2468
James Anastasio, supt. Fax 626-2444
www.augustaschools.org
Farrington ES 400/K-6
249 Eastern Ave 04330 207-626-2480
Teresa Beaudoin, prin. Fax 626-2479
Gilbert ES 400/PK-6
16 Sunset Ave 04330 207-626-2491
Sue Dionne, prin. Fax 626-2538
Hussey ES 200/K-5
12 Gedney St 04330 207-626-2461
Troy Alexander, prin. Fax 626-2539
Lincoln ES 300/K-6
30 Lincoln St 04330 207-626-2483
Heather Gauthier, prin. Fax 626-2535

Unorganized Territories SD 100/PK-8
23 State House Sta 04333 207-624-6892
Dr. Shelley Lane, dir. Fax 624-6891
www.maine.gov/education/eut
Other Schools – See Connor Twp, Edmunds, Kingman

St. Michael S 200/PK-8
56 Sewall St 04330 207-623-3491
Kevin Cullen, prin. Fax 623-2971

Aurora, Hancock
AOS 47
Supt. — See Orrington
Airline Community S 50/PK-8
26 Great Pond Rd 04408 207-584-3012
Andrew Bryan, lead tchr. Fax 584-5112

Baileyville, Washington
AOS 90 - EMASS 600/PK-12
PO Box 580 04694 207-427-6913
William Braun, supt. Fax 427-3166
sites.google.com/site/aos90aos90
Woodland ES 100/PK-6
23 Fourth Ave 04694 207-427-3882
Amanda Belanger, prin. Fax 427-3632
Other Schools – See Lee, Princeton, Topsfield, Winn

Bangor, Penobscot, Pop. 32,402
Bangor SD 3,800/PK-12
73 Harlow St 04401 207-992-4152
Dr. Betsy Webb, supt. Fax 992-4163
www.bangorschools.net
Cohen MS 400/6-8
304 Garland St 04401 207-941-6230
Michael Missbrenner, prin. Fax 941-6235
Doughty MS 400/6-8
143 5th St 04401 207-941-6220
Edward Hackett, prin. Fax 947-7606
Downeast ES 400/PK-3
100 Moosehead Blvd 04401 207-941-6240
Albert Mooers, prin. Fax 941-6242
Fairmount ES 300/4-5
58 13th St 04401 207-941-6260
Ryan Enman, prin. Fax 941-6269
Fourteenth Street ES 200/PK-3
224 14th St 04401 207-941-6350
Daniel Chadbourne, prin. Fax 941-6289
Fruit Street ES 300/PK-3
175 Fruit St 04401 207-941-6270
Richard Fournier, prin. Fax 941-6273
Lincoln ES 200/PK-3
45 Forest Ave 04401 207-941-6280
John Tennett, prin. Fax 992-9770
Snow ES 200/4-5
435 Broadway 04401 207-941-6290
Brian Bannen, prin. Fax 941-6299
Vine Street ES 200/PK-3
66 Vine St 04401 207-941-6300
Lynn Silk, prin. Fax 992-2448

All Saints S - St. John Campus 100/4-8
PO Box 1749 04402 207-942-0955
Joseph Gallant, prin. Fax 942-2398
All Saints S - St. Mary Campus 100/PK-3
PO Box 1749 04401 207-942-0955
Joseph Gallant, prin. Fax 942-2398
Bangor Christian S 300/PK-12
1476 Broadway 04401 207-947-7356
Dr. Jeffrey Benjamin, hdmstr. Fax 262-9528

Bar Harbor, Hancock, Pop. 2,528
AOS 91 - MDIRSS 1,500/K-12
1081 Eagle Lake Rd 04609 207-288-5049
Dr. Marc Gousse, supt. Fax 288-5071
www.mdirss.org
Conners/Emerson S 400/K-8
11 Eagle Lake Rd 04609 207-288-3631
Barbara Neilly, prin. Fax 288-3597
Other Schools – See Bass Harbor, Frenchboro, Islesford, Northeast Harbor, Southwest Harbor, Swans Island, Trenton

Bass Harbor, Hancock
AOS 91 - MDIRSS
Supt. — See Bar Harbor
Tremont Consolidated S 100/K-8
119 Tremont Rd 04653 207-244-7777
Jandrea True, prin. Fax 244-7023

Bath, Sagadahoc, Pop. 8,327
RSU 1 2,000/PK-12
34 Wing Farm Pkwy 04530 207-443-6601
Dr. Patrick Manuel, supt. Fax 443-8295
www.rsu1.org/
Bath MS 400/6-8
6 Old Brunswick Rd 04530 207-443-8270
Brandon Ward, prin. Fax 443-8273
Dike-Newell ES 300/PK-2
3 Wright Dr 04530 207-443-8285
Jennifer Vose, prin. Fax 443-8288
Fisher-Mitchell ES 200/3-5
597 High St 04530 207-443-8265
Ross Berkowitz, prin. Fax 443-4167
Other Schools – See Phippsburg, Woolwich

Beals, Washington
Moosabec Community SD & Union 103
Supt. — See Jonesport
Beals ES 100/PK-8
PO Box 220 04611 207-497-5449
Christopher Crowley, prin. Fax 497-2334

Belfast, Waldo, Pop. 6,555
RSU 71 1,700/PK-12
PO Box 325 04915 207-338-1960
Dr. Paul Knowles, supt. Fax 338-4597
www.rsu71.org
East Belfast ES 100/PK-5
14 Swan Lake Ave 04915 207-338-4220
Abigail Hartford, prin. Fax 338-6711
Howard MS 400/6-8
173 Lincolnville Ave 04915 207-338-3320
Bruce Bailey, prin. Fax 338-5588
Stevens ES 300/PK-5
31 Elementary Ave 04915 207-338-3510
Glen Widmer, prin. Fax 338-4091
Other Schools – See Morrill, Searsmont, Swanville

Belgrade, Kennebec
RSU 18
Supt. — See Oakland
Belgrade Central S 300/PK-5
158 Depot Rd 04917 207-495-2321
Gwen Bacon, prin. Fax 495-2723

Benton, Kennebec
RSU 49 / MSAD 49
Supt. — See Fairfield
Benton ES 600/K-6
68 School Dr 04901 207-453-4240
Brian Wedge, prin. Fax 453-4242

Berwick, York, Pop. 2,140
RSU 60 / MSAD 60
Supt. — See North Berwick
Hussey PS 400/K-3
20 Blackberry Hill Rd 03901 207-698-4465
Audra Beauvais, prin. Fax 698-5069
Knowlton S 100/4-5
8 Noble Ln 03901 207-698-1188
Elva Lovejoy, prin. Fax 698-4401
Noble MS 500/6-7
46 Cranberry Meadow Rd 03901 207-698-1320
Michael Roberts, prin. Fax 698-4400

Bethel, Oxford
RSU 44 / MSAD 44 800/K-12
1 Parkway Ste 204 04217 207-824-2185
David Murphy Ed.D., supt. Fax 824-2725
www.sad44.org
Crescent Park ES 200/K-5
19 Crescent St 04217 207-824-2839
Elaine Ferland, prin. Fax 824-0265
Telstar MS 200/6-8
284 Walkers Mills Rd 04217 207-824-2136
Mark Kenney, prin. Fax 824-0496
Other Schools – See Bryant Pond

Biddeford, York, Pop. 20,950
Biddeford SD 2,500/PK-12
18 Maplewood Ave 04005 207-282-8280
Jeremy Ray, supt. Fax 284-7956
biddefordschools.me
Biddeford IS 400/4-5
335 Hill St 04005 207-282-5957
Debra Kenney, prin. Fax 282-8289
Biddeford MS 600/6-8
25 Tigor Way 04005 207-282-6400
Scott Descoteaux, prin. Fax 282-6040
Biddeford PS 500/1-3
320 Hill St 04005 207-282-8285
Margaret Pitts, prin. Fax 286-9225
Kennedy Memorial ES 200/PK-K
64 West St 04005 207-282-4134
Lindsey Nadeau, prin. Fax 284-7199

Dayton SD 100/PK-5
18 Maplewood Ave 04005 207-282-8280
Jeremy Ray, supt. Fax 284-7956
sites.google.com/a/daytonschooldept.org
Other Schools – See Dayton

St. James S 200/PK-8
25 Graham St 04005 207-282-4084
Nancy Naimey, prin. Fax 286-3693

Bingham, Somerset, Pop. 749
RSU 83 / MSAD 13 200/PK-12
PO Box 649 04920 207-672-5502
Virginia Rebar, supt. Fax 672-5502
www.sad13.org
Quimby MS 50/5-8
PO Box 649 04920 207-672-5500
Samuel Harper, prin. Fax 672-5502
Other Schools – See Moscow

Blue Hill, Hancock, Pop. 936
Union SD 93 500/PK-8
PO Box 630 04614 207-374-9927
Mark Hurvitt, supt. Fax 374-2951
www.schoolunion93.org
Blue Hill Consolidated S 200/PK-8
60 High St 04614 207-374-2202
Michelle Schildroth, prin. Fax 374-2919
Other Schools – See Brooksville, Castine, Penobscot, Surry

Bay S 100/PK-8
PO Box 950 04614 207-374-2187
Marcia Diamond, dir. Fax 374-5717

Boothbay Harbor, Lincoln, Pop. 1,073
AOS 98 - RCSS 800/PK-12
51 Emery Ln 04538 207-633-2874
Robert Webster, supt. Fax 633-5458
www.aos98schools.org
Boothbay Region ES 400/PK-8
238 Townsend Ave 04538 207-633-5097
Mark Tess, prin. Fax 633-7130
Other Schools – See Edgecomb, Georgetown, Southport

Bowdoin, Sagadahoc
RSU 75 / MSAD 75
Supt. — See Topsham
Bowdoin Central ES 200/K-5
1460 Main St 04287 207-666-5779
Ryan Keith, prin. Fax 666-3139

Bowdoinham, Sagadahoc, Pop. 705
RSU 75 / MSAD 75
Supt. — See Topsham
Bowdoinham Community ES 200/K-5
23 Cemetery Rd 04008 207-666-5546
Christopher Lajoie, prin. Fax 666-3160

Bradley, Penobscot
RSU 34
Supt. — See Old Town

Rand ES 100/PK-4
55 Highland Ave 04411 207-827-2508
Cheryl Leonard, prin. Fax 827-2508

Brewer, Penobscot, Pop. 9,320
Brewer SD 1,700/PK-12
261 Center St 04412 207-989-3160
Cheri Towle, supt. Fax 989-8622
www.breweredu.org
Brewer Community S 1,000/PK-8
92 Pendleton St 04412 207-404-5700
William Leithiser, prin. Fax 404-5730

Bridgton, Cumberland, Pop. 2,035
RSU 61 / MSAD 61 1,800/K-12
900 Portland Rd 04009 207-647-3048
Alan Smith, supt. Fax 647-5682
www.lakeregionschools.org
Stevens Brook ES 300/K-5
14 Frances Bell Dr 04009 207-647-5675
Cheryl Turpin, prin. Fax 647-8172
Other Schools – See Naples, Sebago

Brooklin, Hancock
Union SD 76
Supt. — See Deer Isle
Brooklin S 100/PK-8
PO Box 120 04616 207-359-2133
Jill Blake, prin. Fax 359-2303

Brooks, Waldo
RSU 3 / MSAD 3
Supt. — See Unity
Morse Memorial ES 100/PK-5
27 School St 04921 207-722-3636
Matthew Houghton, prin. Fax 722-3052

Brooksville, Hancock
Union SD 93
Supt. — See Blue Hill
Brooksville ES 100/PK-8
1527 Coastal Rd 04617 207-326-8500
Cammie Lepper, prin. Fax 326-9195

Brownville, Piscataquis
AOS 43
Supt. — See Lagrange
Brownville ES 100/K-5
774 Main Rd 04414 207-965-8184
Carol Smith, prin. Fax 965-8363

Brunswick, Cumberland, Pop. 14,835
Brunswick SD 2,400/K-12
46 Federal St 04011 207-319-1900
Paul Perzanoski, supt. Fax 725-1700
www.brunswick.k12.me.us
Brunswick JHS 500/6-8
65 Columbia Ave 04011 207-319-1930
Walter Wallace, prin. Fax 721-0602
Coffin ES 400/K-1
20 Barrows St 04011 207-319-1950
Steve Ciembroniewicz, prin. Fax 725-1704
Stowe ES 700/2-5
44 McKeen St 04011 207-319-1960
Heather Blanchard, prin. Fax 837-6941

St. Johns S 200/PK-8
37 Pleasant St 04011 207-725-5507
Timothy Forti, prin. Fax 798-4792

Bryant Pond, Oxford
RSU 44 / MSAD 44
Supt. — See Bethel
Woodstock ES 100/K-5
224 Rumford Ave 04219 207-665-2228
Jessica Wilkey, prin. Fax 665-2229

Forestdale Christian S 50/K-8
25 Perkins Valley Rd 04219 207-674-2934

Bucksport, Hancock, Pop. 2,843
RSU 25 1,100/PK-12
62 Mechanic St 04416 207-469-7311
James Boothby, supt. Fax 469-6640
www.rsu25.org/
Bucksport MS 300/5-8
100 Miles Ln 04416 207-469-6647
Todd West, prin. Fax 469-2068
Jewett S 100/PK-K
66 Bridge St 04416 207-469-6644
Susan Lamoreau, prin. Fax 469-6657
Miles Lane ES 300/1-4
52 Miles Ln 04416 207-469-6666
Christina Ellis, prin. Fax 469-6659

Buxton, York
RSU 6 / MSAD 6 3,800/PK-12
94 Main St 04093 207-929-3831
Paul Penna, supt. Fax 646-9748
www.bonnyeagle.org
Bonny Eagle MS 900/6-8
92 Sokokis Trl 04093 207-929-3833
Benjamin Harris, prin. Fax 459-5150
Buxton Center ES 600/K-5
912 Long Plains Rd 04093 207-929-3836
Kimberly O'Donnell, prin. Fax 575-2524
Other Schools – See Hollis Center, Limington, Standish, Steep Falls

Calais, Washington, Pop. 3,074
Calais SD 600/PK-12
32 Blue Devil Hl 04619 207-454-7561
Ronald Jenkins, supt. Fax 454-2296
www.calaisschools.org
Calais ES 300/PK-6
53 Garfield St 04619 207-454-2000
Arlene Carter, prin. Fax 454-2708

Camden, Knox, Pop. 3,526
MSAD 28 800/K-8
7 Lions Ln 04843 207-236-3358
Maria Libby, supt. Fax 236-7810
www.fivetowns.net/sad/
Camden-Rockport MS 400/5-8
34 Knowlton St 04843 207-236-7805
Jaime Stone, prin. Fax 236-7815
Other Schools – See Rockport

Children's House Montessori S 50/PK-4
58 Elm St 04843 207-236-2911

Canaan, Somerset
RSU 54 / MSAD 54
Supt. — See Skowhegan
Canaan ES 200/PK-6
178 Main St 04924 207-474-3901
Steven Swindells, prin. Fax 474-6385

Cape Elizabeth, Cumberland, Pop. 8,854
Cape Elizabeth SD 1,700/K-12
320 Ocean House Rd 04107 207-799-2217
Howard Colter, supt. Fax 799-2914
www.cape.k12.me.us
Cape Elizabeth MS 500/5-8
14 Scott Dyer Rd 04107 207-799-8176
Troy Eastman, prin. Fax 767-0832
Pond Cove ES 600/K-4
12 Scott Dyer Rd 04107 207-799-7339
Jason Manjourides, prin. Fax 799-8171

Caribou, Aroostook, Pop. 8,094
RSU 39 1,600/PK-12
75 Bennett Dr Ste 3 04736 207-496-6311
Timothy Doak, supt. Fax 498-3261
www.rsu39.org
Caribou MS 300/4-8
21 Glenn St 04736 207-493-4240
Leland Caron, prin. Fax 493-4243
Teague Park ES 200/PK-3
59 Glenn St 04736 207-493-4248
Cheryl Hallowell, prin. Fax 493-4262
Other Schools – See Limestone

Carmel, Penobscot
RSU 87 / MSAD 23 700/PK-8
44 Plymouth Rd 04419 207-848-5173
John Backus, supt. Fax 848-5190
www.rsu87.org
Caravel MS 200/6-8
520 Irish Rd 04419 207-848-3615
Mark Turner, prin. Fax 848-0884
Carmel ES 200/PK-5
50 Plymouth Rd 04419 207-848-3383
Candice Devlin, prin. Fax 848-3113
Other Schools – See Levant

Castine, Hancock, Pop. 1,015
Union SD 93
Supt. — See Blue Hill
Adams S 50/PK-8
PO Box 29 04421 207-326-8608
Sheila Irvine, prin. Fax 326-0665

Caswell, Aroostook
Caswell SD 50/K-8
1025 Van Buren Rd 04750 207-325-4611
William Dobbins, supt. Fax 325-3371
www.caswellme.org
Barnes ES 50/PK-8
1025 Van Buren Rd 04750 207-325-4611
Krystina Davenport, prin. Fax 325-3371

Chebeague Island, Cumberland
Chebeague Island SD 50/PK-6
14 School House Rd 04017 207-846-4162
Mike Pulsifer, supt. Fax 829-5465
www.chebeague.org
Chebeague Island ES 50/PK-6
14 School House Rd 04017 207-846-4162
Mike Pulsifer, prin. Fax 829-5465

Chelsea, Kennebec
Sheepscot Valley RSU 12
Supt. — See Somerville
Chelsea ES 300/PK-8
566 Togus Rd 04330 207-582-2214
Patricia Metta, prin. Fax 588-2489

Cherryfield, Washington
Cherryfield SD, PO Box 58 04622 100/PK-8
Katherine Mayo, supt. 207-546-7770
cherryfieldschool.weebly.com
Cherryfield ES 100/PK-8
85 School St 04622 207-546-7949
Katherine Mayo, prin. Fax 546-7949

Cliff Island, See Portland
Portland SD
Supt. — See Portland
Cliff Island ES 50/K-5
PO Box 8 04019 207-766-2885
Renee Bourgione-Serio, lead tchr. Fax 766-2134

Clinton, Kennebec, Pop. 1,404
RSU 49 / MSAD 49
Supt. — See Fairfield
Clinton ES 200/K-6
75 Morrison Ave 04927 207-426-2181
Catherine Gordon, prin. Fax 426-9166

Connor Twp, Aroostook
Unorganized Territories SD
Supt. — See Augusta
Connor Consolidated ES 50/PK-6
1581 Van Buren Rd 04736 207-496-4521
Heather Anderson, prin. Fax 496-0012

Corinna, Penobscot
RSU 19
Supt. — See Newport

Corinna ES 100/PK-4
42 Stetson Rd 04928 207-278-4263
Ellen Surprenant, prin. Fax 278-4265

Corinth, Penobscot
RSU 64 / MSAD 64 600/PK-12
PO Box 279 04427 207-285-3334
Rhonda Sperrey, supt. Fax 285-3307
www.rsu64schools.org
Central ES PK-5
118 Main St 04427 207-285-0325
Dawn Nickerson, prin. Fax 285-7970
Central MS 300/6-8
PO Box 19 04427 207-285-3177
Jonathan Perry, prin. Fax 285-4350

Cornish, York

Ossipee Valley Christian S 50/PK-8
1890 North Rd 04020 207-793-4005
Scott Weirick, hdmstr. Fax 793-2904

Cumberland Center, Cumberland, Pop. 2,477
RSU 51 / MSAD 51 1,900/K-12
PO Box 6A 04021 207-829-4800
Jeff Porter, supt. Fax 829-4802
www.msad51.org
Greely MS 4-5 200/4-5
351 Tuttle Rd 04021 207-829-4815
Carol MacArthur, prin. Fax 829-4819
Greely MS 6-8 500/6-8
351 Tuttle Rd 04021 207-829-4815
Mar-E Trebilcock, prin. Fax 829-4819
Wilson S 600/K-3
353 Tuttle Rd 04021 207-829-4825
Susan Robbins, prin. Fax 829-2254

Cumberland Foreside, Cumberland

Friends S of Portland 100/PK-8
11 US Route 1, 207-781-6321

Cushing, Knox
RSU 13
Supt. — See Rockland
Cushing Community S 100/K-5
54 Cross Rd 04563 207-354-2312
Dawn Jones, prin. Fax 354-0014

Cutler, Washington
AOS 96 - MBASS
Supt. — See Machias
Bay Ridge ES 100/PK-8
PO Box 240 04626 207-259-3347
Darlene Wheeler, prin. Fax 259-3812

Damariscotta, Lincoln, Pop. 1,134
AOS 93 - CLCSS 1,000/PK-8
767 Main St Ste 1-A 04543 207-563-3044
James Hodgkin, supt. Fax 563-8276
www.aos93.org
Great Salt Bay Community S 500/K-8
559 Main St 04543 207-563-3091
Kim Schaff, prin. Fax 563-6974
Other Schools – See Jefferson, Nobleboro, Pemaquid, South Bristol

Danforth, Washington
RSU 84 / MSAD 14 100/PK-12
31A Houlton Rd 04424 207-448-2882
Terry A. Comeau, supt. Fax 448-7235
www.eastgrandschool.org
East Grand S 100/PK-12
31 Houlton Rd 04424 207-448-2260
Margaret White, prin. Fax 448-2417

Dayton, York
Dayton SD
Supt. — See Biddeford
Dayton Consolidated ES 100/PK-5
21 Clarks Mills Rd 04005 207-499-2283
Kimberly Sampietro, prin. Fax 499-7356

Dedham, Hancock
AOS 47
Supt. — See Orrington
Dedham S 200/PK-8
2065 Main Rd, 207-843-6498
Jeffrey Paul, prin. Fax 843-4330

Deer Isle, Hancock
Union SD 76 100/PK-12
251 N Deer Isle Rd 04627 207-348-9100
Chris Elkington, supt. Fax 359-8451
www.su76.org
Deer Isle - Stonington ES 200/K-8
249 N Deer Isle Rd 04627 207-348-6301
Tara McKechnie, prin. Fax 348-6304
Other Schools – See Brooklin, Sedgwick

Denmark, Oxford
RSU 72 / MSAD 72
Supt. — See Fryeburg
Brownfield-Denmark ES 100/K-4
637 W Main St 04022 207-452-2360
Terri Mahanor, lead tchr. Fax 452-2372

Dexter, Penobscot, Pop. 2,129
AOS 94 - S46HRSD 1,200/PK-12
175 Fern Rd Ste 1 04930 207-924-6000
Kevin Jordan, supt. Fax 924-7660
www.aos94.org
Ridge View Community S 700/PK-8
175 Fern Rd 04930 207-924-6000
Jerry Kiesman, prin. Fax 924-7668
Other Schools – See Athens, Harmony

Dixfield, Oxford, Pop. 1,056
RSU 56 PK-12
147 Weld St 04224 207-562-4300
rsu56.org

Dirigo MS 200/6-8
45 Middle School Dr 04224 207-562-7552
Michael Poulin, prin. Fax 562-8329
Other Schools – See Peru

Webb River SDA S K-8
PO Box 605 04224 207-562-9997

Dover Foxcroft, Piscataquis, Pop. 3,077
RSU 68 / MSAD 68 700/PK-8
63 Harrison Ave Ste C 04426 207-564-6535
Stacy Shorey, supt. Fax 564-3487
www.sedomocha.org
Se Do Mo Cha ES 400/PK-4
63 Harrison Ave 04426 207-564-6535
Julie Kimball, prin. Fax 564-6529
Se Do Mo Cha MS 300/5-8
63 Harrison Ave 04426 207-564-6535
Julie Kimball, prin. Fax 564-6531

Dresden, Lincoln
RSU 2
Supt. — See Hallowell
Dresden ES 100/PK-5
86 Cedar Grove Rd 04342 207-737-2559
Christie Jernigan, prin. Fax 737-4392

Durham, Androscoggin
RSU 5
Supt. — See Freeport
Durham Community S 400/PK-8
654 Hallowell Rd 04222 207-353-9333
William Pidden, prin. Fax 353-2731

Dyer Brook, Aroostook
RSU 50 700/PK-12
922 Dyer Brook Rd, 207-757-8223
Todd Leroy, supt. Fax 757-8257
www.rsu50.org
Southern Aroostook Community S 300/PK-12
922 Dyer Brook Rd, 207-757-8206
Jon Porter, prin. Fax 757-7313
Other Schools – See Stacyville

Eastbrook, Hancock
RSU 24
Supt. — See Sullivan
Cave Hill S 100/PK-8
1205 Eastbrook Rd 04634 207-565-3638
Brenda Jordan, prin. Fax 565-2370

East Machias, Washington
AOS 96 - MBASS
Supt. — See Machias
Elm Street S 200/PK-8
PO Box 229 04630 207-255-8692
Tony Maker, prin. Fax 255-5800

East Millinocket, Penobscot, Pop. 1,552
East Millinocket SD 400/PK-12
45 North St 04430 207-746-3500
Eric Steeves M.Ed., supt. Fax 746-3516
eastmillinocketschools.org
Myrick ES 100/PK-4
45 North St 04430 207-746-3511
Curt Ring M.Ed., prin. Fax 746-3516

Millinocket SD 500/PK-12
199 State St 04430 207-723-6400
Frank Boynton, supt. Fax 447-6599
www.millinocketschools.org
Other Schools – See Millinocket

Katahdin Christian Academy 50/PK-6
PO Box 375 04430 207-447-9470

Easton, Aroostook
Easton SD 200/PK-12
PO Box 126 04740 207-488-7700
Roger Shaw, supt. Fax 488-2840
eastonschools.org
Easton ES 100/PK-6
PO Box 126 04740 207-488-7700
Larry Worcester, prin. Fax 488-2840

Eastport, Washington, Pop. 1,291
AOS 77 - SCSS 600/PK-12
PO Box 190 04631 207-853-2567
Kenneth Johnson, supt. Fax 853-6260
Eastport ES 100/PK-8
100 High St 04631 207-853-6252
Paul Theriault, prin. Fax 853-6264
Other Schools – See Alexander, Lubec, Pembroke, Perry

East Waterboro, York
RSU 57 / MSAD 57
Supt. — See Waterboro
Massabesic MS 700/6-8
134 Old Alfred Rd 04030 207-247-6121
Mark Fisher, prin. Fax 247-8621
Waterboro ES 500/K-5
340 Sokokis Trl 04030 207-247-6126
Christine Bertinet, prin. Fax 247-6127

Eddington, Penobscot
RSU 63 / MSAD 63
Supt. — See Holden
Eddington ES 100/PK-1
440 Main Rd 04428 207-843-6010
Don Spencer, prin. Fax 843-4317

Edgecomb, Lincoln
AOS 98 - RCSS
Supt. — See Boothbay Harbor
Edgecomb Eddy ES 100/PK-6
157 Boothbay Rd 04556 207-882-5515
Ira Michaud, prin. Fax 882-5948

Center for Teaching and Learning 100/K-8
119 Cross Point Rd 04556 207-882-9706
Maggie Limm, head sch Fax 882-6413

Edmunds, Washington
Unorganized Territories SD
Supt. — See Augusta
Edmunds Consolidated S 100/PK-8
21 Harrison Rd, 207-726-4478
Trudy Newcomb, prin. Fax 726-0932

Eliot, York
RSU 35 / MSAD 35 2,300/PK-12
180 Depot Rd 03903 207-439-2438
Dr. Mary Nash, supt. Fax 439-2531
www.rsu35.org
Eliot ES 300/PK-3
1298 State Rd 03903 207-439-9004
Maureen Goering, prin. Fax 439-5380
Marshwood MS 500/6-8
626 Harold L Dow Hwy 03903 207-439-1399
Anthony Bourbon, prin. Fax 439-3504
Other Schools – See South Berwick

Seacoast Waldorf S 50/PK-8
403 Harold L Dow Hwy 03903 207-686-3140
Deirdre McEachern, dir.

Ellsworth, Hancock, Pop. 7,675
Ellsworth SD 1,300/PK-12
66 Main St Ste 201 04605 207-664-7100
Daniel Higgins, supt. Fax 669-6032
www.ellsworthschools.org
Ellsworth ES 800/PK-8
20 Forrest Ave 04605 207-667-6241
James Newett, prin. Fax 667-6246

Hancock SD 200/K-8
66 Main St Ste 201 04605 207-664-7199
Katrina Kane, supt. Fax 669-6243
www.hancockgrammar.org
Other Schools – See Hancock

Lamoine Consolidated SD 100/K-8
66 Main St Ste 201 04605 207-664-7199
Katrina Kane, supt. Fax 669-6242
www.lamoineconsolidated.org
Other Schools – See Lamoine

Etna, Penobscot
RSU 19
Supt. — See Newport
Etna-Dixmont S 300/PK-8
2100 Dixmont Rd 04434 207-992-0735
Jane Stork, prin. Fax 234-4190

Fairfield, Kennebec, Pop. 2,598
RSU 49 / MSAD 49 2,200/PK-12
8 School St 04937 207-453-4200
Dr. Dean Baker, supt. Fax 453-0110
www.msad49.org
Fairfield PS 200/PK-K
63 High St 04937 207-453-4220
Lori Lee, prin. Fax 453-4218
Lawrence JHS 400/7-8
7 School St 04937 207-453-4200
Roberta Hersom, prin. Fax 453-4214
Other Schools – See Albion, Benton, Clinton

Kennebec Montessori S 100/PK-6
38 Sheridan Rd 04937 207-453-6055
Rebecca Green, head sch Fax 453-8155

Falmouth, Cumberland, Pop. 1,834
Falmouth SD 2,100/K-12
51 Woodville Rd 04105 207-781-3200
Nate Barnes, supt. Fax 781-5711
www.falmouthschools.org
Falmouth ES 900/K-5
58 Woodville Rd 04105 207-781-3988
Gloria Noyes, prin. Fax 347-3130
Falmouth MS 500/6-8
52 Woodville Rd 04105 207-781-3740
Janet Adams, prin. Fax 321-0108

Farmington, Franklin, Pop. 4,199
RSU 9 - Mt. Blue Regional SD 2,200/PK-12
129 Seamon Rd 04938 207-778-6571
Dr. Thomas Ward, supt. Fax 778-4160
www.mtbluersd.org/
Cascade Brook ES 200/3-5
162 Learning Ln 04938 207-778-4821
Dr. Nichole Goodspeed, prin. Fax 778-5809
Mallet ES 400/PK-3
116 Middle St 04938 207-778-3529
Tracy Williams, prin. Fax 778-5823
Mt. Blue MS 400/6-8
269 Middle St 04938 207-778-3511
James Black, prin. Fax 778-5810
Other Schools – See New Sharon, Wilton

Fayette, Kennebec
Fayette SD 100/PK-5
2023 Main St, 207-685-4770
Joe Mattos, supt. Fax 685-4756
www.maranacook.org/fayette/
Fayette Central ES 100/PK-5
2023 Main St, 207-685-4770
Tara Blue, prin. Fax 685-4756

Fort Fairfield, Aroostook, Pop. 1,799
MSAD 20 500/PK-12
28 High School Dr Ste B 04742 207-473-4455
Timothy Doak, supt. Fax 473-4095
www.msad20.org
Fort Fairfield ES 300/PK-5
76 Brunswick Ave 04742 207-472-3290
Suzanne Parks, prin. Fax 472-3282

Fort Kent, Aroostook, Pop. 2,423
MSAD 27 900/PK-12
84 Pleasant St Ste 1 04743 207-834-3189
Benjamin Sirois, supt. Fax 834-3395
www.sad27.org/

Fort Kent ES 400/PK-6
108 Pleasant St 04743 207-834-3456
Gary Stevens, prin. Fax 834-5169
Valley Rivers MS 100/7-8
84 Pleasant St 04743 207-834-5540
John Kaleta, prin. Fax 834-2723

Freeport, Cumberland, Pop. 1,447
RSU 5 1,900/PK-12
17 West St 04032 207-865-0928
Dr. Becky Foley, supt. Fax 865-2855
rsu5.org
Freeport MS 300/6-8
19 Kendall Ln 04032 207-865-6051
Raymond Grogan, prin. Fax 865-2902
Mast Landing ES 300/3-5
20 Molly Mauk St 04032 207-865-4561
Emily Grimm, prin. Fax 865-2909
Morse Street ES 300/PK-2
21 Morse St 04032 207-865-6361
Julie Nickerson, prin. Fax 865-2903
Other Schools – See Durham, Pownal

Maine Coast Waldorf S 200/PK-8
57 Desert Rd 04032 207-865-3900
Christine Sloan, admin. Fax 865-6822
Pine Tree Academy 200/PK-12
67 Pownal Rd 04032 207-865-4747

Frenchboro, Hancock
AOS 91 - MDIRSS
Supt. — See Bar Harbor
Frenchboro ES 50/K-8
22 High Rd 04635 207-334-2944
Lindsay Eysnogle, prin. Fax 334-2937

Frenchville, Aroostook
RSU 33 / MSAD 33 300/PK-12
PO Box 9 04745 207-543-7334
Lisa Bernier, supt. Fax 543-6242
www.msad33.org
Levesque ES 100/PK-6
PO Box 489 04745 207-543-7302
Lisa Bernier, prin. Fax 543-6185

Friendship, Knox
RSU 40 / MSAD 40
Supt. — See Union
Friendship Village ES 100/K-6
PO Box 100 04547 207-832-5057
Christina Labbe, prin. Fax 832-7389

Fryeburg, Oxford, Pop. 1,595
RSU 72 / MSAD 72 800/K-8
25 Molly Ockett Dr 04037 207-935-2600
Jay Robinson, supt. Fax 935-3787
www.msad72.org
Ockett S 300/K-8
25 Molly Ockett Dr 04037 207-935-2401
Mark Schrader, prin. Fax 935-4470
Other Schools – See Denmark, Lovell

Gardiner, Kennebec, Pop. 5,663
MSAD 11 2,100/PK-12
150 Highland Ave 04345 207-582-5346
Patricia Hopkins, supt. Fax 582-8305
www.msad11.org
Gardiner Regional MS 500/6-8
161 Cobbossee Ave 04345 207-582-1326
Todd Sanders, prin. Fax 582-6823
Richards ES 200/PK-2
279 Brunswick Ave 04345 207-582-3612
Karen Moody, prin. Fax 582-3175
Other Schools – See Pittston, Randolph, South Gardiner, West Gardiner

Georgetown, Sagadahoc
AOS 98 - RCSS
Supt. — See Boothbay Harbor
Georgetown Central S 100/PK-6
PO Box 469 04548 207-371-2160
Matt Carlson, prin. Fax 371-2595

Glenburn, See Bangor
Glenburn SD 400/PK-8
983 Hudson Rd 04401 207-942-4405
Christine Boone, supt. Fax 942-4250
www.glenburnschool.us
Glenburn S 400/PK-8
991 Hudson Rd 04401 207-947-8769
Tom Sullivan, prin. Fax 947-3867

Gorham, Cumberland, Pop. 6,775
Gorham SD 2,700/K-12
75 South St Ste 2 04038 207-222-1000
Heather Perry, supt. Fax 839-8885
www.gorhamschools.org
Gorham MS 600/6-8
106 Weeks Rd 04038 207-222-1220
Robert Riley, prin. Fax 839-4092
Great Falls ES 500/K-5
73 Justice Way 04038 207-222-1050
Rebecca Fortier, prin. Fax 892-6301
Narragansett ES 200/K-5
284 Main St 04038 207-222-1250
Cynthia Remick, prin. Fax 839-5018
Village ES 400/K-5
12 Robie St 04038 207-222-1300
Brian Porter, prin. Fax 839-5029

Gray, Cumberland, Pop. 877
RSU 15 / MSAD 15 2,000/K-12
14 Shaker Rd 04039 207-657-3335
Dr. Craig King, supt. Fax 657-2040
www.msad15.org
Gray-New Gloucester MS 700/5-8
31 Libby Hill Rd 04039 207-657-4994
Sherry Levesque, prin. Fax 657-5219
Russell ES 300/K-2
8 Gray Park 04039 207-657-4929
Cynthia Reichert, prin. Fax 657-2286
Other Schools – See New Gloucester

Greenbush, Penobscot
Greenbush SD 100/PK-8
129 Military Rd 04418 207-826-2000
Gwen Smith, supt. Fax 826-2001
hsdgreenbush.org
Dunn ES 100/PK-8
129 Military Rd 04418 207-826-2000
Gwen Smith, prin. Fax 826-2001

Greene, Androscoggin
RSU 52 / MSAD 52
Supt. — See Turner
Greene Central ES 400/PK-6
41 Main St 04236 207-946-5681
Mark McDonough, prin. Fax 946-3281

Greenville, Piscataquis, Pop. 1,245
Greenville SD 100/PK-12
PO Box 100 04441 207-695-3708
Jim Chasse, supt. Fax 695-3709
www.ghslakers.org
Greenville Consolidated S 100/PK-12
PO Box 100 04441 207-695-2666
Kelly MacFadyen M.Ed., prin. Fax 695-4614

Guilford, Piscataquis, Pop. 885
RSU 80 / MSAD 4 700/PK-12
9 Campus Dr 04443 207-876-3444
Raymond Freve, supt. Fax 876-3446
www.sad4.org
Piscataquis Community ES 400/PK-8
25 Campus Dr 04443 207-876-4301
Anita Wright, prin. Fax 876-4291

Hallowell, Kennebec, Pop. 2,343
RSU 2 1,800/PK-12
7 Reed St 04347 207-622-6351
William Zima, supt. Fax 622-7866
www.kidsrsu.org
Hall-Dale ES 400/PK-5
26 Garden Ln 04347 207-623-8677
James Charette, prin. Fax 623-6246
Other Schools – See Dresden, Monmouth, Richmond

Hampden, Penobscot, Pop. 4,292
RSU 22 2,100/PK-12
24 Main Rd N 04444 207-862-3255
Richard Lyons, supt. Fax 862-2789
www.rsu22.us
McGraw ES 300/PK-2
20 Main Rd N 04444 207-862-3830
Kristin Briggs, prin. Fax 862-5649
Reeds Brook MS 300/6-8
28A Main Rd S 04444 207-862-3540
Don Roux, prin. Fax 862-3551
Weatherbee ES 300/3-5
22 Main Rd N 04444 207-862-3254
Jennifer Cyr, prin. Fax 862-3141
Other Schools – See Newburgh, Winterport

Hancock, Hancock
Hancock SD
Supt. — See Ellsworth
Hancock Grammer S 200/K-8
33 Cemetery Rd 04640 207-422-6231
Michael Benjamin, prin. Fax 422-6568

Harmony, Somerset
AOS 94 - S46HRSD
Supt. — See Dexter
Harmony ES 100/K-8
PO Box 100 04942 207-683-2211
Lori Poirier, prin. Fax 683-5241

Harpswell, Cumberland
RSU 75 / MSAD 75
Supt. — See Topsham
Harpswell Community ES 200/K-5
308 Harpswell Islands Rd 04079 207-729-5177
Kerry Bailey, prin. Fax 725-7567

Harrington, Washington
RSU 37 / MSAD 37 500/PK-12
1020 Sacarap Rd 04643 207-483-2734
Ronald Ramsay, supt. Fax 483-6051
www.msad37.me
Harrington ES 100/PK-6
1227 US Highway 1A 04643 207-483-6681
Susan Meserve, prin. Fax 483-4589
Other Schools – See Addison, Milbridge

Harrison, Cumberland
Oxford Hills SD
Supt. — See South Paris
Harrison ES 100/3-6
309 Naples Rd 04040 207-583-2357
Margaret Emery, prin. Fax 583-9149

Hartland, Somerset, Pop. 799
RSU 19
Supt. — See Newport
Somerset Valley MS 200/3-8
45 Blake St 04943 207-938-4770
Denise Kimball, prin. Fax 938-2114

Hebron, Oxford
Oxford Hills SD
Supt. — See South Paris
Hebron Station S 100/PK-6
884 Station Rd 04238 207-966-3323
Donald Thorne, prin. Fax 966-3142

Hermon, See Bangor
Hermon SD 1,200/PK-12
31 Billings Rd 04401 207-848-4000
Patricia Duran, supt. Fax 848-5226
www.hermon.net
Hermon ES 400/PK-4
235 Billings Rd 04401 207-848-4000
Jenny Perry, prin. Fax 848-2100
Hermon MS 300/5-8
29 Billings Rd 04401 207-848-4000
Micah Grant, prin. Fax 848-2163

North Star Christian S 50/1-8
42 Orion Way 04401 207-848-2331

Hiram, Oxford
RSU 55 / MSAD 55 900/K-12
137 S Hiram Rd 04041 207-625-2490
Carl Landry, supt. Fax 625-7065
www.sad55.org
Sacopee Valley ES 200/K-3
213 S Hiram Rd 04041 207-625-8116
Monique Sullivan, prin. Fax 625-8399
Sacopee Valley MS 300/4-8
137 S Hiram Rd 04041 207-625-2450
Michael Lane, prin. Fax 625-2465

Hodgdon, Aroostook
RSU 70 / MSAD 70 400/PK-12
175 Hodgdon Mills Rd 04730 207-532-3015
Scott Richardson, supt. Fax 532-2679
www.msad70.org
Mill Pond S 300/PK-6
147 Hodgdon Mills Rd 04730 207-532-9228
Loreen Wiley, prin. Fax 532-4090

Holden, Penobscot
RSU 63 / MSAD 63 500/PK-8
202 Kidder Hill Rd 04429 207-843-7851
Susan Smith, supt. Fax 843-7295
www.edline.net/pages/rsu63
Holbrook MS 300/5-8
202 Kidder Hill Rd 04429 207-843-7769
Richard Modery, prin. Fax 843-4328
Holden ES 100/2-4
590 Main Rd 04429 207-843-7828
Don Spencer, prin. Fax 843-4329
Other Schools – See Eddington

Hollis Center, York
RSU 6 / MSAD 6
Supt. — See Buxton
Hollis S 300/K-5
554 River Rd 04042 207-929-3838
Clay Gleason, prin. Fax 544-1916

Hope, Knox
Union SD 69 500/PK-8
444 Camden Rd 04847 207-763-3818
Dianne Halprin, supt. Fax 763-4262
www.fivetowns.net/union/
Hope ES 200/PK-8
34 Highfield Rd 04847 207-785-4081
Danielle Fagonde, prin. Fax 785-2671
Other Schools – See Lincolnville, Union

Houlton, Aroostook, Pop. 4,790
RSU 29 / MSAD 29 1,100/PK-12
PO Box 190 04730 207-532-6555
Ellen Schneider, supt. Fax 532-6481
www.rsu29.org
Houlton ES 400/PK-2
60 South St 04730 207-532-2285
Candace Crane, prin. Fax 521-0360
Houlton Southside ES 300/3-5
65 South St 04730 207-532-6027
Cindy Peterson, prin. Fax 521-0356

Greater Houlton Christian Academy 100/PK-12
27 School St 04730 207-532-0736
R. Thomas Zimmerman, head sch Fax 532-9553

Howland, Penobscot, Pop. 1,083
AOS 43
Supt. — See Lagrange
Hichborn MS 100/6-8
23 Cross St 04448 207-732-3113
Carol Marcinkus, prin. Fax 732-8331

Isle au Haut, Knox
Isle Au Haut SD
Supt. — See Sargentville
Isle Au Haut Rural S 50/K-8
PO Box 56B 04645 207-335-2521
Christian Elkington, prin.

Islesboro, Waldo
Islesboro School Department 100/K-12
PO Box 118 04848 207-734-2251
Patrick Phillips, supt. Fax 734-8159
ics.islesboro.k12.me.us
Islesboro Central S 100/K-12
PO Box 118 04848 207-734-2251
Heather Knight, prin. Fax 734-8159

Islesford, Hancock
AOS 91 - MDIRSS
Supt. — See Bar Harbor
Bryan S 50/K-8
PO Box 8 04646 207-244-3961
Fax 244-3961

Jackman, Somerset
RSU 82 / MSAD 12 200/K-12
606 Main St 04945 207-668-5291
Dr. William Crumley, supt. Fax 668-4482
www.sad12.org
Forest Hills Consolidated S 200/K-12
606 Main St 04945 207-668-5291
Thad A. Lacasse, prin. Fax 668-4482

Jay, Franklin
RSU 73
Supt. — See Livermore Falls
Spruce Mountain ES 300/3-5
12 Tiger Dr 04239 207-897-5719
Christopher Hollingswort, prin. Fax 897-6375

Spruce Mountain MS 400/6-8
23 Community Dr 04239 207-897-4319
Scott Albert, prin. Fax 897-3513

Jefferson, Lincoln
AOS 93 - CLCSS
Supt. — See Damariscotta
Jefferson Village S 200/K-8
48 Washington Rd 04348 207-549-7491
Lynsey Johnston, prin. Fax 549-5011

Jonesboro, Washington
AOS 96 - MBASS
Supt. — See Machias
Jonesboro ES 100/PK-8
57 School Rd 04648 207-434-2602
Greg Marsh, prin. Fax 434-2602

Jonesport, Washington
Moosabec Community SD & Union 103 200/PK-12
127 Snare Creek Ln 04649 207-497-2154
Beth Anne Lorigan, supt. Fax 497-2703
www.union103.org
Jonesport ES 100/PK-8
139 Snare Creek Ln 04649 207-497-2830
Melissa Tenney, prin. Fax 497-5912
Other Schools – See Beals

Kennebunk, York, Pop. 5,151
RSU 21 2,400/K-12
177 Alewive Rd 04043 207-985-1100
Katie Hawes, supt. Fax 985-1104
www.rsu21.net
Kennebunk ES 500/K-3
177 Alewive Rd 04043 207-985-4402
Ryan Quinn, prin. Fax 985-6082
Kennebunk MS 500/6-8
60 Thompson Rd 04043 207-467-8004
Jeff Rodman, prin. Fax 467-9059
Sea Road ES 300/4-5
29 Sea Rd 04043 207-985-1105
Stephen Marquis, prin. Fax 985-4274
Other Schools – See Arundel, Kennebunkport

Kennebunkport, York, Pop. 1,232
RSU 21
Supt. — See Kennebunk
Kennebunkport Consolidated ES 200/K-5
25 School St 04046 207-967-2121
Karen Bubar, prin. Fax 985-5179

Kingfield, Franklin
RSU 58 / MSAD 58
Supt. — See Phillips
Kingfield ES 200/PK-8
102 Salem Rd 04947 207-265-4132
Jaime Ela, prin. Fax 265-2010

Kingman, Penobscot
Unorganized Territories SD
Supt. — See Augusta
Kingman ES 50/PK-5
25 Park St 04451 207-765-2500
Rhonda Irish, prin. Fax 765-2008

Kittery, York, Pop. 4,483
Kittery SD 1,100/K-12
200 Rogers Rd 03904 207-475-1334
Eric Waddell, supt. Fax 439-5407
www.kitteryschools.com
Shapleigh MS 400/4-8
43 Stevenson Rd 03904 207-439-2572
Anne Ellis, prin. Fax 439-9958
Other Schools – See Kittery Point

Kittery Point, York, Pop. 1,008
Kittery SD
Supt. — See Kittery
Mitchell PS 400/K-3
PO Box 176 03905 207-439-1707
Marcelle Durost, prin. Fax 439-9198

Lagrange, Penobscot
AOS 43 1,300/PK-12
22 Howland Rd 04453 207-943-7317
Michael Wright, supt. Fax 943-5314
www.aos43.com
Other Schools – See Brownville, Howland, Milo, West Enfield

Lamoine, Hancock
Lamoine Consolidated SD
Supt. — See Ellsworth
Lamoine Consolidated S 100/K-8
53 Lamoine Beach Rd 04605 207-667-8578
Dawn McPhail, prin. Fax 667-3860

Lebanon, York
RSU 60 / MSAD 60
Supt. — See North Berwick
Lebanon ES 400/K-5
53 Upper Guinea Rd 04027 207-457-1299
Patti Gilley, prin. Fax 457-1829

Lee, Penobscot
AOS 90 - EMASS
Supt. — See Baileyville
Mt. Jefferson JHS 100/5-8
61 Winn Rd 04455 207-738-2866
Pamela Hamilton, prin. Fax 738-3817

Leeds, Androscoggin
RSU 52 / MSAD 52
Supt. — See Turner
Leeds Central ES 200/PK-6
1185 Route 106 04263 207-524-5151
Danielle Harris, prin. Fax 524-2184

Levant, Penobscot
RSU 87 / MSAD 23
Supt. — See Carmel
Smith ES 200/PK-5
169 S Levant Rd 04456 207-884-7444
Lorri Day, prin. Fax 884-6201

Lewiston, Androscoggin, Pop. 35,657
Lewiston SD 5,200/PK-12
36 Oak St 04240 207-795-4100
William T. Webster, supt. Fax 795-4177
www.lewistonpublicschools.org/
Farwell ES 400/K-6
110 Farwell St 04240 207-795-4110
Amanda Winslow, prin. Fax 753-6407
Geiger ES 700/PK-6
601 College St 04240 207-795-4160
Cindy Gish, prin. Fax 753-6409
Lewiston MS 700/7-8
75 Central Ave 04240 207-795-4180
Jana Mates, prin. Fax 753-1789
Longley ES 400/K-6
145 Birch St 04240 207-795-4120
Kristie Clark, prin. Fax 795-4122
Martel ES 300/K-6
880 Lisbon St 04240 207-795-4130
Stephen Whitfield, prin. Fax 753-6408
McMahon ES 600/PK-6
151 N Temple St 04240 207-795-4140
Amber Eliason, prin. Fax 795-4146
Montello ES 700/PK-6
407 East Ave 04240 207-795-4150
James Cliffe, prin. Fax 795-4176

Central Maine Christian Academy 100/PK-12
390 Main St 04240 207-777-0007
Patricia St. Hilaire, prin. Fax 777-0007
St. Dominic Academy - Lewiston 400/PK-6
17 Baird Ave 04240 207-783-9323
Marianne Pelletier, prin. Fax 783-9491

Liberty, Waldo
RSU 3 / MSAD 3
Supt. — See Unity
Walker Memorial ES 100/PK-5
33 W Main St 04949 207-589-4208
Lisa Roux, prin. Fax 589-3421

Limestone, Aroostook, Pop. 1,068
RSU 39
Supt. — See Caribou
Limestone Community S 300/PK-8
93 High St 04750 207-325-4742
Susan White, prin. Fax 325-4969

Limington, York
RSU 6 / MSAD 6
Supt. — See Buxton
Emery Jr Memorial S 200/PK-5
908 Cape Rd 04049 207-637-2056
Douglas Parker, prin. Fax 611-9861

Lincoln, Penobscot, Pop. 2,837
RSU 67 1,000/PK-12
25 Reed Dr 04457 207-794-6500
Dr. Keith Laser, supt. Fax 794-2600
www.rsu67.org
Burr ES 300/PK-3
23 Ella P Burr St 04457 207-794-3014
Christina Doore, prin. Fax 794-2602
Mattanawcook JHS 300/4-8
41 School St 04457 207-794-8935
Christopher Cowing, prin. Fax 794-2601

Greater Lincoln Christian Academy 50/K-8
PO Box 597 04457 207-794-6867
Dolores Dill, prin.

Lincolnville, Waldo
Union SD 69
Supt. — See Hope
Lincolnville Central S 200/K-8
523 Hope Rd 04849 207-763-3366
Paul Russo, prin. Fax 763-3455

Lisbon, See Lisbon Falls
Lisbon SD 1,300/PK-12
19 Gartley St 04250 207-353-6711
Rick Green, supt. Fax 353-3032
www.lisbonschoolsme.org
Lisbon Community S 600/PK-5
33 Mill St 04250 207-353-4132
Robert Kahler, prin. Fax 353-4815
Other Schools – See Lisbon Falls

Lisbon Falls, Androscoggin, Pop. 4,031
Lisbon SD
Supt. — See Lisbon
Sugg MS 300/6-8
4 Sugg Dr 04252 207-353-3055
Darren Akerman, prin. Fax 353-3053

Litchfield, Kennebec, Pop. 275
RSU 4
Supt. — See Wales
Libby-Tozier ES 200/PK-2
466 Academy Rd 04350 207-268-4137
Kelli Rogers, prin. Fax 268-2680
Ricker MS 300/3-5
573 Richmond Rd 04350 207-268-4136
Christine Lajoie-Cameron, prin. Fax 268-4318

Livermore, See Livermore Falls
RSU 73
Supt. — See Livermore Falls
Spruce Mountain ES 500/PK-2
107 Gibbs Mill Rd 04253 207-897-3355
Kevin Harrington, prin. Fax 897-3690

Livermore Falls, Androscoggin, Pop. 1,558
RSU 73 1,600/PK-12
9 Cedar St 04254 207-897-6722
Kenneth Healey, supt. Fax 897-2362
rsu73.com
Other Schools – See Jay, Livermore

Long Island, See Portland
Long Island SD 50/K-5
33 Fern Ave 04050 207-766-4414
Barbara Powers, supt. Fax 766-4414
school.long-island.lib.me.us
Long Island ES 50/K-5
33 Fern Ave 04050 207-766-4414
Paula Johnson, admin. Fax 766-4414

Lovell, Oxford
RSU 72 / MSAD 72
Supt. — See Fryeburg
New Suncook ES 200/K-4
95 Main St 04051 207-925-6711
Rhonda Poliquin, prin. Fax 925-1168

Lubec, Washington, Pop. 345
AOS 77 - SCSS
Supt. — See Eastport
Lubec Consolidated S 100/PK-8
44 South St 04652 207-733-5591
Lovina Wormell, prin. Fax 733-2004

Lyman, York
RSU 57 / MSAD 57
Supt. — See Waterboro
Lyman ES 300/K-5
39 Schoolhouse Rd 04002 207-499-7228
Cindy Pellerin, prin. Fax 499-2981

Machias, Washington, Pop. 1,257
AOS 96 - MBASS 800/PK-12
291 Court St 04654 207-255-6585
Scott Porter, supt. Fax 255-8054
www.aos96.org
Gaffney S 400/PK-8
15 Rose Gaffney Rd 04654 207-255-3411
Joyce Fragale, prin. Fax 255-0346
Other Schools – See Cutler, East Machias, Jonesboro, Machiasport, Wesley, Whiting

Machiasport, Washington
AOS 96 - MBASS
Supt. — See Machias
Ft. O'Brien S 100/PK-8
PO Box 37 04655 207-255-4575
Susan Almendinger, prin. Fax 255-3190

Madawaska, Aroostook, Pop. 2,953
Madawaska SD 500/PK-12
328 Saint Thomas St Ste 201 04756 207-728-3346
Gisele Dionne, supt. Fax 728-7823
www.madawaskaschools.org
Madawaska ES 300/PK-6
353 11th Ave 04756 207-728-3635
Lise Pelletier, prin. Fax 728-3444

Madison, Somerset, Pop. 2,594
RSU 59 / MSAD 59 700/PK-12
205 Main St 04950 207-696-3323
Bonnie Levesque, supt. Fax 696-5631
sites.google.com/a/msad59.org/rsu59/
Madison ES 300/PK-4
43 Learners Ln 04950 207-696-4607
Scott Mitchell, prin. Fax 696-5639
Madison JHS 200/5-8
205 Main St 04950 207-696-3381
Ryan Arnold, prin. Fax 696-5640

Manchester, Kennebec
RSU 38
Supt. — See Readfield
Manchester ES 200/PK-5
17 School St 04351 207-622-2949
Janet Delmar, prin. Fax 622-0616

Mapleton, Aroostook, Pop. 681
RSU 79 / MSAD 1
Supt. — See Presque Isle
Mapleton ES 200/PK-5
1642 Main St 04757 207-764-1589
Daniel Duprey, prin. Fax 764-6429

Mars Hill, Aroostook, Pop. 965
RSU 42 / MSAD 42 400/PK-12
PO Box 1006 04758 207-425-3771
Elaine Boulier, supt. Fax 429-8461
msad42.org
Fort Street ES 200/PK-6
PO Box 509 04758 207-429-8514
Dawn Matthews, prin. Fax 429-8462

Matinicus, Knox, Pop. 117
RSU 65 / MSAD 65
Supt. — See Sedgwick
Matinicus ES, PO Box 194 04851 50/K-8
Lewis Collins, admin. 207-366-3526

Mechanic Falls, Androscoggin, Pop. 2,202
RSU 16
Supt. — See Poland
Elm Street S 300/PK-6
129 Elm St 04256 207-345-3381
Catherine Folan, prin. Fax 346-6224

Medway, Penobscot
Medway SD 5-8
25 Middle School Dr 04460 207-746-3470
Dawn Pray, supt. Fax 746-9435
Medway MS 100/5-8
25 Middle School Dr 04460 207-746-3470
Dawn Pray M.Ed., prin. Fax 746-9435

Mexico, Oxford, Pop. 1,718
RSU 10
Supt. — See Rumford
Meroby ES 300/PK-5
21 Cross St 04257 207-364-3714
Kim Fuller, prin. Fax 369-0156

Mountain Valley MS 300/6-8
58 Highland Ter 04257 207-364-7926
Ryan Casey, prin. Fax 364-5608

Milbridge, Washington
RSU 37 / MSAD 37
Supt. — See Harrington
Milbridge ES 100/PK-6
39 Washington St 04658 207-546-2210
Maria White, prin. Fax 546-7399

Milford, Penobscot, Pop. 2,192
Milford School Department 300/PK-8
13 School St 04461 207-827-2252
J. Underwood, supt. Fax 827-5454
www.lewislibbyschool.org
Libby S 300/PK-8
13 School St 04461 207-827-2252
Trish Clark, prin. Fax 827-5454

Millinocket, Penobscot, Pop. 4,427
Millinocket SD
Supt. — See East Millinocket
Granite Street ES 300/PK-5
191 Granite St 04462 207-723-6425
Francis Boynton, prin. Fax 723-6425

Milo, Piscataquis, Pop. 1,832
AOS 43
Supt. — See Lagrange
Milo ES 300/PK-5
18 Belmont St 04463 207-943-2122
Kristina Dumond, prin. Fax 943-5330

Minot, Androscoggin
RSU 16
Supt. — See Poland
Minot Consolidated S 300/PK-6
23 Shaw Hill Rd 04258 207-346-6471
Kaitlynn Brown, prin. Fax 345-9535

Monhegan, Lincoln
Monhegan Plt SD
Supt. — See Winthrop
Monhegan Island S 50/PK-8
PO Box 8 04852 207-594-5895
Mandy Metrano, lead tchr. Fax 594-5895

Monmouth, Kennebec
RSU 2
Supt. — See Hallowell
Cottrell ES 200/PK-3
169 Academy Rd 04259 207-933-4426
Leticia Goucher, prin. Fax 933-7279
Monmouth MS 300/4-8
117 Academy Rd 04259 207-933-9002
Melissa Burnham-Barter, prin. Fax 933-7252

Monroe, Waldo
RSU 3 / MSAD 3
Supt. — See Unity
Monroe ES 100/PK-5
36 W Main St 04951 207-525-3504
Matthew Houghton, prin. Fax 525-8599

Morrill, Waldo, Pop. 644
RSU 71
Supt. — See Belfast
Weymouth ES 100/PK-1
2 S Main St 04952 207-342-5300
Lori Smail, prin. Fax 342-5301

Moscow, Somerset
RSU 83 / MSAD 13
Supt. — See Bingham
Moscow ES 100/PK-4
125 Canada Rd 04920 207-672-5572
Samuel Harper, prin. Fax 672-3003

Mount Vernon, Kennebec
RSU 38
Supt. — See Readfield
Mount Vernon ES 100/PK-5
1507 North Rd 04352 207-293-2261
Janet Delmar, prin. Fax 293-3205

Naples, Cumberland, Pop. 423
RSU 61 / MSAD 61
Supt. — See Bridgton
Lake Region MS 400/6-8
204 Kansas Rd 04055 207-647-8403
Matthew Lokken, prin. Fax 647-0991
Songo Locks ES 500/K-5
25 Songo School Rd 04055 207-693-6828
Cheryl Cline, prin. Fax 693-4000

Newburgh, Penobscot
RSU 22
Supt. — See Hampden
Newburgh ES 100/PK-PK
2220 Western Ave 04444 207-234-2781
Dawn Moore, admin.

New Gloucester, Cumberland
RSU 15 / MSAD 15
Supt. — See Gray
Dunn ES 300/3-4
667 Morse Rd 04260 207-657-5050
Geoffrey Robbins, prin. Fax 657-7068
Memorial ES 200/K-2
86 Intervale Rd 04260 207-926-4322
Amanda Hennessey, prin. Fax 926-4324

Newport, Penobscot, Pop. 1,726
RSU 19 2,200/PK-12
PO Box 40 04953 207-368-5091
Michael Hammer, supt. Fax 368-2192
www.rsu19.org
Newport ES 300/PK-4
142 Elm St 04953 207-368-4470
Lori Merrow, prin. Fax 368-3274

Sebasticook Valley MS 300/5-8
337 Williams Rd 04953 207-368-4592
Angela Brown, prin. Fax 368-4598
Other Schools – See Corinna, Etna, Hartland, Saint Albans

New Sharon, Franklin
RSU 9 - Mt. Blue Regional SD
Supt. — See Farmington
Cape Cod Hill ES 200/PK-5
516 Cape Cod Hill Rd 04955 207-778-3031
Darlene Paine, prin. Fax 778-6910

Nobleboro, Lincoln
AOS 93 - CLCSS
Supt. — See Damariscotta
Nobleboro Central S 100/K-8
194 Center St 04555 207-563-3437
Ann Hassett, prin. Fax 563-6569

Damariscotta Montessori S 100/PK-8
93 Center St 04555 207-563-2168
Chip DeLorenzo, head sch Fax 563-3871

Norridgewock, Somerset, Pop. 1,411
RSU 54 / MSAD 54
Supt. — See Skowhegan
Mill Stream ES 400/PK-6
26 Mercer Rd 04957 207-634-3121
Terry Atwood, prin. Fax 634-4294

Riverview Memorial S 50/K-10
201 Mercer Rd 04957 207-634-2641

North Anson, Somerset
RSU 74 / MSAD 74 700/PK-12
PO Box 219 04958 207-635-2727
Kenneth Coville, supt. Fax 635-3599
www.sad74.k12.me.us
Carrabec Community S 300/K-8
PO Box 187 04958 207-635-2209
Thomas Desjardins, prin. Fax 635-2048
Other Schools – See Anson, Solon

North Berwick, York, Pop. 1,596
RSU 60 / MSAD 60 2,900/PK-12
PO Box 819 03906 207-676-2234
Steven Connolly, supt. Fax 676-3229
www.msad60.org
North Berwick ES 300/PK-5
25 Varney Rd 03906 207-676-9811
Michael Archambault, prin. Fax 676-3213
Other Schools – See Berwick, Lebanon

Northeast Harbor, Hancock
AOS 91 - MDIRSS
Supt. — See Bar Harbor
Mt. Desert ES 200/K-8
PO Box 308 04662 207-276-3348
Gloria Delsandro, prin. Fax 276-5830

North Haven, Knox
RSU 7 / MSAD 7 100/PK-12
93 Pulpit Harbor Rd 04853 207-867-4707
Robert England, supt. Fax 867-4438
www.nhcshawks.org
North Haven Community S 100/PK-12
93 Pulpit Harbor Rd 04853 207-867-4707
Amy Marx, prin. Fax 867-4438

Northport, Waldo
Northport SD 100/K-8
56 Bayside Rd 04849 207-338-3430
Dr. Judith Lucarelli, supt. Fax 338-5985
www.drinkwaterschool.org
Drinkwater ES 100/K-8
56 Bayside Rd 04849 207-338-3430
Todd Martin, prin. Fax 338-5985

Norway, Oxford, Pop. 2,676
Oxford Hills SD
Supt. — See South Paris
Rowe ES 500/PK-6
219 Main St 04268 207-743-5183
Daniel Hart, prin. Fax 743-5324

Oakland, Kennebec, Pop. 2,571
RSU 18 2,900/PK-12
41 Heath St 04963 207-465-7384
Carl Gartley, supt. Fax 465-9130
www.rsu18.org/
Atwood PS 300/PK-2
19 Heath St 04963 207-465-3411
Jennifer McGee, prin. Fax 465-9133
Messalonskee MS 500/6-8
33 School Bus Dr 04963 207-465-2167
Mark Hatch, prin. Fax 465-9683
Williams ES 200/3-5
55 Pleasant St 04963 207-465-2965
Melanie Smith, prin. Fax 465-4986
Other Schools – See Belgrade, Sidney, South China

Old Orchard Beach, York, Pop. 8,527
RSU 23 700/PK-12
28 Jameson Hill Rd 04064 207-934-5751
John Suttie, supt. Fax 934-1917
www.rsu23.org
Jameson ES 200/PK-2
20 Jameson Hill Rd 04064 207-934-2891
Barbara Fletcher, prin. Fax 934-3710
Loranger MS 300/3-8
148 Saco Ave 04064 207-934-4848
Michael Flaherty, prin. Fax 934-3712

Old Town, Penobscot, Pop. 7,682
RSU 34 1,500/PK-12
156 Oak St Ste 2 04468 207-827-7171
David Walker, supt. Fax 827-3922
www.rsu34.org/

Leonard MS 300/6-8
156 Oak St 04468 207-827-3900
David Crandall, prin. Fax 827-3935
Old Town ES 600/PK-5
576 Stillwater Ave 04468 207-827-1544
Jeanna Tuell, prin. Fax 827-1549
Other Schools – See Alton, Bradley

Stillwater Montessori S 100/PK-5
1024 Stillwater Ave 04468 207-827-2404
Joseph Alex, dir. Fax 827-2404

Orono, Penobscot, Pop. 9,316
RSU 26 800/PK-12
10 Goodridge Dr 04473 207-866-7110
Meredith Higgins, supt. Fax 866-4217
www.rsu26.org
Adams ES 300/PK-5
6 Goodridge Dr 04473 207-866-2151
Darcie Fournier, prin. Fax 866-3664
Orono MS 200/6-8
14 Goodridge Dr 04473 207-866-2350
Heath Kennie, prin. Fax 866-7111

Orrington, Penobscot
AOS 47 600/PK-8
19 School St 04474 207-825-3364
James Stoneton, supt. Fax 825-3393
sites.google.com/a/cdsedu.org/aos47/
Center Drive S 400/PK-8
17 School St 04474 207-825-3697
Judith Marvin, prin. Fax 825-4525
Other Schools – See Aurora, Dedham

Otis, Hancock
Otis SD 100/PK-8
105 Otis Rd 04605 207-537-2203
Terrance Mccannell, supt. Fax 537-3127
sites.google.com/a/beechhillschool.org/bhs
Beech Hill S 100/PK-8
105 Otis Rd 04605 207-537-2203
Nichole Pothier, prin. Fax 537-3127

Otisfield, Oxford
Oxford Hills SD
Supt. — See South Paris
Otisfield Community ES 100/K-6
416 Powhatan Rd 04270 207-627-4208
Tiffany Karnes, prin. Fax 627-4208

Owls Head, Knox
RSU 13
Supt. — See Rockland
Owls Head Central S 100/3-5
54 Ash Point Dr 04854 207-594-5650
Benjamin Tripp, prin. Fax 594-4105

Oxford, Oxford, Pop. 1,240
Oxford Hills SD
Supt. — See South Paris
Oxford ES 400/PK-6
PO Box 839 04270 207-539-4456
Tiffany Karnes, prin. Fax 539-2922

Palermo, Waldo
Sheepscot Valley RSU 12
Supt. — See Somerville
Palermo Consolidated ES 100/K-8
501 Route 3 04354 207-993-2352
Dale Haywood, prin. Fax 993-2354

Peaks Island, See Portland
Portland SD
Supt. — See Portland
Peaks Island ES 100/K-5
4 Church Ave 04108 207-766-2528
Renee Bourgione-Serio, lead tchr. Fax 766-5619

Pemaquid, Lincoln
AOS 93 - CLCSS
Supt. — See Damariscotta
Bristol Consolidated S 200/PK-8
2153 Bristol Rd 04558 207-677-2678
Jennifer Ribeiro, prin. Fax 677-3428

Pembroke, Washington
AOS 77 - SCSS
Supt. — See Eastport
Charlotte ES 50/PK-8
1006 Ayers Jct Rd 04666 207-454-2668
Peggy White, prin. Fax 454-7399
Pembroke ES 100/PK-8
36 US Route 1 04666 207-726-5564
Dr. Deborah Jamieson, prin. Fax 726-5139

Penobscot, Hancock
Union SD 93
Supt. — See Blue Hill
Penobscot S 100/PK-8
PO Box 60 04476 207-326-9421
Jay Corbin, prin. Fax 326-9422

Perry, Washington
AOS 77 - SCSS
Supt. — See Eastport
Perry ES 100/PK-8
1587 US Route 1 04667 207-853-2522
Linda Green, prin. Fax 853-4539

Peru, Oxford, Pop. 1,541
RSU 56
Supt. — See Dixfield
Dirigo ES 400/PK-5
117 Auburn Rd 04290 207-562-4207
Charles Swan, prin. Fax 562-8775

Phillips, Franklin
RSU 58 / MSAD 58 700/PK-12
1401 Rangeley Rd 04966 207-639-2086
Susan Pratt M.Ed., supt. Fax 639-5120
www.msad58.org

Phillips ES 200/PK-8
1401 Rangeley Rd 04966 207-639-2909
Jeffrey Pillsbury, prin. Fax 639-4139
Other Schools – See Kingfield, Strong

Phippsburg, Sagadahoc
RSU 1
Supt. — See Bath
Phippsburg ES 100/PK-5
1047 Main Rd 04562 207-389-1514
Sandra Gorsuch-Plummer, prin. Fax 389-1516

Pittsfield, Somerset, Pop. 3,092
RSU 53 / MSAD 53 700/PK-12
167 School St Ste A 04967 207-487-5107
Jason I. Tardy, supt. Fax 487-6310
www.msad53.org/
Manson Park ES 100/PK-K
179 Lancey St 04967 207-487-2281
Sarah Allen, prin.
Vickery ES 300/1-4
170 School St 04967 207-487-5575
Sarah Allen, prin. Fax 487-6155
Warsaw MS 300/5-8
167 School St 04967 207-487-5145
Sharon Littlefield, prin. Fax 487-4511

Pittston, Kennebec
MSAD 11
Supt. — See Gardiner
Pittston Consolidated ES 200/K-5
1023 Pittston School St, 207-582-6268
Sarah Duffy, prin. Fax 582-6334

Poland, Androscoggin
RSU 16 1,800/PK-12
3 Aggregate Rd 04274 207-998-2727
Tina Meserve, supt. Fax 998-2753
www.rsu16.org
Poland Community ES 500/PK-6
1250 Maine St 04274 207-998-4915
Richard Benoit, prin. Fax 998-4998
Whittier MS 300/7-8
1457 Maine St 04274 207-998-3462
Shawn Vincent, prin. Fax 998-3481
Other Schools – See Mechanic Falls, Minot

Portland, Cumberland, Pop. 64,466
Portland SD 7,000/PK-12
353 Cumberland Ave 04101 207-874-8100
Xavier Botana, supt. Fax 874-8199
www.portlandschools.org
East End Community S 400/PK-5
195 North St 04101 207-874-8228
Marcia Gendron, prin. Fax 874-8234
Hall ES 500/PK-5
23 Orono Rd 04102 207-874-8205
Dawn Kenniston, prin. Fax 874-8243
King MS 500/6-8
92 Deering Ave 04102 207-874-8140
Caitlin LeClair, prin. Fax 874-8290
Lincoln MS 500/6-8
522 Stevens Ave 04103 207-874-8145
Suellyn Santiago, prin. Fax 874-8288
Longfellow ES 400/PK-5
432 Stevens Ave 04103 207-874-8195
Terrence Young, prin. Fax 874-8284
Lyseth ES 500/K-5
175 Auburn St 04103 207-874-8215
Lenore Williams, prin. Fax 874-8218
Moore MS 500/6-8
171 Auburn St 04103 207-874-8150
Ben Donaldson, prin. Fax 874-8272
Ocean Avenue ES 400/K-5
150 Ocean Ave 04103 207-874-8180
Beverly Coursey, prin. Fax 756-8496
Presumpscot ES 300/PK-5
69 Presumpscot St 04103 207-874-8220
Cynthia Loring, prin. Fax 874-8286
Reiche Community ES 400/K-5
166 Brackett St 04102 207-874-8175
Christine Keegan, lead tchr. Fax 874-8177
Riverton ES 500/PK-5
1600 Forest Ave 04103 207-874-8210
Ann Hanna, prin. Fax 874-8271
Other Schools – See Cliff Island, Peaks Island

Breakwater S 100/PK-8
856 Brighton Ave 04102 207-772-8689
David Sullivan, head sch Fax 772-1327
St. Brigid S 400/PK-8
695 Stevens Ave 04103 207-797-7073
William Burke, prin. Fax 797-7078
Waynflete S 600/PK-12
360 Spring St 04102 207-774-5721
Geoff Wagg, head sch Fax 772-4782

Pownal, Cumberland
RSU 5
Supt. — See Freeport
Pownal ES 100/PK-5
587 Elmwood Rd 04069 207-688-4832
Lisa Demick, prin. Fax 688-4872

Presque Isle, Aroostook, Pop. 9,565
RSU 79 / MSAD 1 1,800/PK-12
PO Box 1118 04769 207-764-4101
Brian Carpenter, supt. Fax 764-4103
www.sad1.org/
Pine Street ES 400/PK-2
50 Pine St 04769 207-764-8104
Loretta Clark, prin. Fax 768-3446
Presque Isle MS 400/6-8
569 Skyway St 04769 207-764-4474
Anne Blanchard, prin. Fax 768-3447
Zippel ES 300/3-5
42 Griffin St 04769 207-764-8106
Christopher Hallett, prin. Fax 768-3089
Other Schools – See Mapleton

Cornerstone Christian Academy 50/PK-12
PO Box 743 04769 207-768-6222
Jay Levesque, head sch Fax 768-6224

Princeton, Washington
AOS 90 - EMASS
Supt. — See Baileyville
Princeton ES 100/PK-8
289 Main St 04668 207-796-2253
Charity Williams, prin. Fax 796-8014

Prospect Harbor, Hancock
RSU 24
Supt. — See Sullivan
Peninsula S 200/PK-8
71 Main St 04669 207-963-2003
Sally Leighton, prin. Fax 963-2276

Randolph, Kennebec, Pop. 1,754
MSAD 11
Supt. — See Gardiner
Hamlin ES 100/K-5
2 School St 04346 207-582-4252
Sara Hess, lead tchr. Fax 582-1696

Rangeley, Franklin
RSU 78 200/K-12
43 Mendolia Rd 04970 207-864-3311
Dr. William Richards Ed.D., supt. Fax 864-2451
www.rangeleyschool.org
Rangeley Lakes Regional S 200/K-12
43 Mendolia Rd 04970 207-864-3311
William Richards, prin. Fax 560-9410

Raymond, Cumberland
RSU 14 - Windham Raymond
Supt. — See Windham
Jordan-Small MS 200/5-8
423 Webbs Mills Rd 04071 207-655-4743
Randolph Crockett, prin. Fax 655-6952
Raymond ES 200/K-4
434 Webbs Mills Rd 04071 207-655-8672
Randolph Crockett, prin. Fax 655-8664

Readfield, Kennebec
RSU 38 1,300/PK-12
45 Millard Harrison Dr 04355 207-685-3336
Dr. Donna H. Wolfrom, supt. Fax 685-4703
www.maranacook.org/
Maranacook Community MS 300/6-8
2100 Millard Harrison Dr 04355 207-685-3128
Rick Hogan, prin. Fax 685-9876
Readfield ES 200/PK-5
84 South Rd 04355 207-685-4406
Jeffrey Boston, prin. Fax 685-5521
Other Schools – See Manchester, Mount Vernon, Wayne

Richmond, Sagadahoc, Pop. 1,737
RSU 2
Supt. — See Hallowell
Buker ES 200/PK-5
28 High St 04357 207-737-4748
Thomas McKee, prin. Fax 737-2563

Rockland, Knox, Pop. 7,144
RSU 13 1,200/PK-12
28 Lincoln St 04841 207-596-6620
John McDonald, supt. Fax 596-2004
www.rsu13.org
South S 300/PK-5
30 Broadway 04841 207-596-2020
Justin Bennett, prin. Fax 546-2026
Other Schools – See Cushing, Owls Head, South Thomaston, Thomaston

---

Pen Bay Christian S 100/PK-6
1 Waldo Ave 04841 207-596-6460
Cynthia Wallace, admin.

Rockport, Knox
MSAD 28
Supt. — See Camden
Camden-Rockport ES 400/K-4
11 Childrens Way 04856 207-236-7809
Chris Walker-Spencer, prin. Fax 236-7820

Ashwood Waldorf S 100/PK-8
180 Park St 04856 207-236-8021
Riley S, PO Box 159 04856 100/PK-9
Rebecca Clapp, dir. 207-596-6405

Rumford, Oxford, Pop. 4,160
RSU 10 2,700/PK-12
799 Hancock St 04276 207-562-7254
Deborah Alden, supt. Fax 562-7059
rsu10.org/rsu10
Rumford ES 300/PK-5
121 Lincoln Ave 04276 207-364-8155
Jill Bartash, prin. Fax 369-9446
Other Schools – See Mexico, Sumner

Holy Savior S 50/PK-8
115 Maine Ave 04276 207-364-2528
Fax 364-3713

Sabattus, Androscoggin
RSU 4
Supt. — See Wales
Oak Hill MS 300/6-8
40 Ball Park Rd 04280 207-375-6961
Benjamin Wilson, prin. Fax 375-8871
Sabattus PS 200/PK-2
36 No Name Pond Rd 04280 207-375-4525
Kelli Rogers, prin. Fax 375-8154

Saco, York, Pop. 18,250
Saco SD 1,900/K-8
90 Beach St 04072 207-284-4505
Dominic DePatsy, supt. Fax 284-5951
sacoschools.org
Burns ES 600/3-5
135 Middle Street Ext 04072 207-284-5081
Dr. Timothy Kane, prin. Fax 284-0282
Fairfield ES 300/K-2
75 Beach St 04072 207-282-1322
Maureen McMullin, prin. Fax 284-1751
Saco MS 700/6-8
40 Buxton Rd 04072 207-282-4181
Brian Campbell, prin. Fax 286-1807
Young ES 300/K-2
36 Tasker St 04072 207-284-7053
Dr. Peter Harrison, prin. Fax 282-1510

Lombard Christian S 1-8
46 Cleveland St 04072 207-282-5004

Saint Albans, Somerset
RSU 19
Supt. — See Newport
St. Albans Consolidated ES 100/PK-2
129 Hartland Rd 04971 207-938-4581
Fax 938-5530

Sanford, York, Pop. 9,565
Sanford SD 3,100/K-12
917 Main St Ste 200 04073 207-324-2810
David Theoharides, supt. Fax 324-5742
www.sanford.org
Lafayette ES 100/K-3
69 Brook St 04073 207-324-4160
Sharon Remick, prin. Fax 490-0346
Sanford JHS 600/6-8
708 Main St 04073 207-324-3114
Pam Lydon, prin. Fax 490-5139
Smith ES 400/K-3
248 Twombley Rd 04073 207-324-7586
Chuck Potter M.Ed., prin. Fax 490-5138
Willard S 400/1-5
668 Main St 04073 207-324-8454
Deb Gaudreau, prin. Fax 490-5130
Other Schools – See Springvale

St. Thomas S 100/PK-7
69 North Ave 04073 207-324-5832
Donna Jacques, prin. Fax 324-2549

Sargentville, Hancock
Isle Au Haut SD 50/K-8
9 Caterpillar Hill Rd 04673 207-348-9100
Chris Elkington, supt. Fax 359-8451
www.isleauhaut.org/island-walk/school/
Other Schools – See Isle au Haut

Scarborough, Cumberland, Pop. 4,340
Scarborough SD 3,200/K-12
PO Box 370 04070 207-730-4100
Julie Kukenberger, supt. Fax 730-4104
www.scarboroughschools.org
Blue Point ES 200/K-2
174 Pine Point Rd 04074 207-730-5300
Kelly Mullen-Martin, prin. Fax 730-5331
Eight Corners ES 200/K-2
22 Mussey Rd 04074 207-730-5200
Anne Lovejoy, prin. Fax 730-5229
Pleasant Hill ES 200/K-2
143 Highland Ave 04074 207-730-5250
Barbara Hathorn, prin. Fax 730-5251
Scarborough MS 800/6-8
21 Quentin Dr 04074 207-730-4800
Diane Nadeau, prin. Fax 730-4804
Wentworth IS 700/3-5
20 Quentin Dr 04074 207-730-4600
Kelli Crosby, prin. Fax 730-4607

Searsmont, Waldo
RSU 71
Supt. — See Belfast
Ames ES 100/2-5
165 New England Rd 04973 207-342-5100
Lori Smail, prin. Fax 342-5101

Searsport, Waldo, Pop. 985
RSU 20 500/K-12
6 Mortland Rd 04974 207-548-6643
Chris Downing, supt. Fax 548-2310
www.rsu20.org
Searsport District MS 200/6-8
26 Mortland Rd 04974 207-548-2313
Marianne DeRaps, prin. Fax 548-2354
Searsport ES 200/K-5
30 Mortland Rd 04974 207-548-2317
Larry Clement, prin. Fax 548-2329

Sebago, Cumberland
RSU 61 / MSAD 61
Supt. — See Bridgton
Sebago ES 100/K-5
283 Sebago Rd 04029 207-787-3701
Kirsten Goff, prin. Fax 787-2472

Sedgwick, Hancock
RSU 65 / MSAD 65 50/K-8
547 Graytown Rd 04676 207-326-3234
William Shuttleworth, supt.
Other Schools – See Matinicus

Union SD 76
Supt. — See Deer Isle
Sedgwick ES 100/PK-8
272 Snows Cove Rd 04676 207-359-5002
Dr. John Dow, prin. Fax 359-5071

Shapleigh, York, Pop. 1,911
RSU 57 / MSAD 57
Supt. — See Waterboro
Shapleigh Memorial S 100/PK-5
467 Shapleigh Corner Rd 04076 207-636-1751
Timothy Stinson, prin. Fax 636-2980

Sidney, Kennebec
RSU 18
Supt. — See Oakland
Bean S 300/PK-5
2896 Middle Rd 04330 207-547-3395
Dr. Nancy Reynolds, prin. Fax 547-4438

Skowhegan, Somerset, Pop. 6,196
RSU 54 / MSAD 54 2,700/PK-12
196 W Front St 04976 207-474-9508
Brent Colbry, supt. Fax 474-7422
www.msad54.org/
Bloomfield ES 300/1-4
140 Academy Cir 04976 207-474-6221
Jean Pillsbury, prin. Fax 474-7427
North ES 200/PK-K
33 Jewett St 04976 207-474-2907
Anita Hopkins, admin. Fax 474-8648
Skowhegan Area MS 500/6-8
155 Academy Cir 04976 207-474-3339
Zachary Longyear, prin. Fax 474-9588
Smith ES 200/4-5
40 Heselton St 04976 207-474-9822
Anita Hopkins, prin. Fax 858-4883
Other Schools – See Canaan, Norridgewock

Solon, Somerset
RSU 74 / MSAD 74
Supt. — See North Anson
Solon ES 100/PK-5
PO Box 146 04979 207-643-2491
Jean Butler, prin. Fax 643-2718

Somerville, Lincoln
Sheepscot Valley RSU 12 900/PK-8
665 Patricktown Rd Ste 2 04348 207-549-3261
Howard Tuttle, supt. Fax 549-3082
www.svrsu.org/
Other Schools – See Chelsea, Palermo, Whitefield, Windsor

South Berwick, York
RSU 35 / MSAD 35
Supt. — See Eliot
Central ES 400/PK-3
197 Main St 03908 207-384-2333
Nina D'Aran, prin. Fax 384-2678
Marshwood Great Works S 300/4-5
49 Academy St 03908 207-384-4010
Gerald Burnell, prin. Fax 384-4035

Berwick Academy 600/PK-12
31 Academy St 03908 207-384-2164
Greg Schneider, head sch Fax 384-3332

South Bristol, Lincoln
AOS 93 - CLCSS
Supt. — See Damariscotta
South Bristol S 100/K-8
2024 State Route 129 04568 207-644-8177
Scott White, prin. Fax 644-8171

South China, Kennebec
RSU 18
Supt. — See Oakland
China MS 200/5-8
773 Lakeview Dr 04358 207-445-1500
Lois Bowden, prin. Fax 445-3278
China PS 300/PK-4
763 Lakeview Dr 04358 207-445-1550
Darlene Pietz, prin. Fax 445-3541

South Freeport, Cumberland

L'Ecole Franaise du Maine 100/PK-6
PO Box 737 04078 207-865-3308
Willy LeBihan, hdmstr.

South Gardiner, See Gardiner
MSAD 11
Supt. — See Gardiner
River View Community ES 200/3-5
PO Box 9 04359 207-582-3402
Albert Ghoreyeb, prin. Fax 582-8674

South Paris, Oxford, Pop. 2,214
Oxford Hills SD 3,500/PK-12
232 Main St # 2 04281 207-743-8972
Rick Colpitts, supt. Fax 743-2878
www.msad17.org
Oxford Hills MS 500/7-8
100 Pine St 04281 207-743-5946
Paul Bickford, prin. Fax 743-8048
Paris ES 400/PK-6
4 Hathaway Rd 04281 207-744-0318
Mary Peterson, prin. Fax 743-7803
Other Schools – See Harrison, Hebron, Norway, Otisfield, Oxford, Waterford, West Paris

Southport, Lincoln
AOS 98 - RCSS
Supt. — See Boothbay Harbor
Southport Central ES 50/PK-6
PO Box 279 04576 207-633-3132
Lisa Clarke, prin. Fax 633-9850

South Portland, Cumberland, Pop. 24,549
South Portland SD 3,100/PK-12
130 Wescott Rd 04106 207-871-0555
Ken Kunin, supt. Fax 871-0559
www.spsd.org
Brown ES 300/PK-5
37 Highland Ave 04106 207-799-5196
Margaret Hawkins, prin. Fax 767-7742
Dyer ES 300/K-5
52 Alfred St 04106 207-799-4845
Elizabeth Fowler, prin. Fax 767-7716
Kaler ES 200/PK-5
165 S Kelsey St 04106 207-799-3214
Bonnie Hicks, prin. Fax 767-7728
Mahoney MS 300/6-8
240 Ocean St 04106 207-799-7386
Carrie Stilphen, prin. Fax 767-7731
Memorial MS 400/6-8
120 Wescott Rd 04106 207-773-5629
Megan Welter, prin. Fax 772-4597
Skillin ES 400/PK-5
180 Wescott Rd 04106 207-773-7375
Bethany Connolly, prin. Fax 775-2904
Small ES 300/K-5
87 Thompson St 04106 207-799-7676
Diane Lang, prin. Fax 767-7738

Greater Portland Christian S 100/PK-12
1338 Broadway 04106 207-767-5123
John Bishop, head sch Fax 767-5124
Holy Cross S 200/PK-8
436 Broadway 04106 207-799-6661
Christine L'Abbe, prin. Fax 799-8345

South Thomaston, Knox
RSU 13
Supt. — See Rockland
Butler S 100/K-2
54 Spruce Head Rd 04858 207-594-7666
Benjamin Tripp, prin. Fax 594-4036

Southwest Harbor, Hancock, Pop. 708
AOS 91 - MDIRSS
Supt. — See Bar Harbor
Pemetic ES 200/K-8
PO Box 255 04679 207-244-5502
Rhonda Fortin, prin. Fax 244-0367

Springvale, York, Pop. 3,215
Sanford SD
Supt. — See Sanford
Lamb ES 500/K-6
233 Shaws Ridge Rd 04083 207-324-8481
Steve Bussiere, prin. Fax 490-5144

Stacyville, Penobscot
RSU 50
Supt. — See Dyer Brook
Katahdin ES 200/PK-6
805 Station Rd, 207-365-4285
Marie Robinson, prin. Fax 365-7606

Standish, Cumberland, Pop. 464
RSU 6 / MSAD 6
Supt. — See Buxton
Jack ES 200/4-5
15 Northeast Rd 04084 207-642-4885
Virginia Day, prin. Fax 797-7708
Libby ES 300/PK-3
45 Fort Hill Rd 04084 207 642 2600
Virginia Day, prin. Fax 624-6256

Steep Falls, Cumberland, Pop. 1,126
RSU 6 / MSAD 6
Supt. — See Buxton
Steep Falls ES 100/K-3
781 Boundary Rd 04085 207 675 3321
Douglas Parker, prin. Fax 607-8885

Steuben, Washington
RSU 24
Supt. — See Sullivan
Lewis S 100/PK-8
15 Village Rd 04680 207-546-2430
Dr. Joanne Harriman, prin. Fax 546-2774

Stratton, Franklin
Flagstaff RSU / Eustis School Dept 100/PK-8
65 School St 04982 207-246-2283
Michael Shea, supt. Fax 246-6598
www.strattonschool.org
Stratton S 100/PK-8
65 School St 04982 207-246-2283
Barry London, prin. Fax 246-6598

Strong, Franklin
RSU 58 / MSAD 58
Supt. — See Phillips
Strong ES 200/PK-8
110 N Main St 04983 207-684-3521
Felecia Pease, prin. Fax 684-3340

Sullivan, Hancock
RSU 24 900/PK-12
2165 US Hwy 1 04664 207-422-2017
Michael Eastman, supt. Fax 422-2029
www.rsu24.org
Mountain View S 200/PK-8
512 Bert Gray Rd 04664 207-422-3200
Chris Beals, prin. Fax 422-6881
Other Schools – See Eastbrook, Prospect Harbor, Steuben

Sumner, Oxford
RSU 10
Supt. — See Rumford
Hartford-Sumner ES 300/PK-6
145 Main St 04292 207-388-2681
Ryan Wilkins, prin. Fax 388-2882

Surry, Hancock
Union SD 93
Supt. — See Blue Hill
Surry S 100/PK-8
754 N Bend Rd 04684 207-667-9358
Fred Cole, prin. Fax 667-3296

Swans Island, Hancock
AOS 91 - MDIRSS
Supt. — See Bar Harbor
Swans Island ES 50/K-8
116 Rose Hill Rd 04685 207-526-4300
Crystal DaGraca, prin. Fax 526-4501

Swanville, Waldo
RSU 71
Supt. — See Belfast
Nickerson ES 100/PK-5
18 Town House Rd 04915 207-338-1858
Abigail Hartford, prin. Fax 338-2181

Tenants Harbor, Knox
St. George Municipal School Unit 200/K-8
PO Box 153 04860 207-372-6900
Mike Felton, supt. Fax 372-6312
stgeorgemsu.org
St. George S 200/K-8
PO Box 153 04860 207-372-6900
Christine Miller, coord. Fax 372-6312

Thomaston, Knox, Pop. 1,856
RSU 13
Supt. — See Rockland
Oceanside MS 100/6-8
47 Valley St 04861 207-354-2502
William Gifford, prin. Fax 354-2369
Thomaston Grammar S 100/K-5
65 Watts Ln 04861 207-354-6353
Ainsley Riley, prin. Fax 354-6238

Thorndike, Waldo
RSU 3 / MSAD 3
Supt. — See Unity
Mt. View ES 200/K-5
573 Mount View Rd 04986 207-568-7541
Charles Brown, prin. Fax 568-7590
Mt. View MS 300/6-8
575 Mount View Rd 04986 207-568-7561
Quinton Donahue, prin. Fax 568-7590

Topsfield, Washington
AOS 90 - EMASS
Supt. — See Baileyville
East Range II S 50/K-8
187 School Rd 04490 207-796-2665
Donna Gagnon, prin. Fax 796-2421

Topsham, Sagadahoc, Pop. 5,854
RSU 75 / MSAD 75 2,500/K-12
50 Republic Ave 04086 207-729-9961
Bradley Smith, supt. Fax 725-9354
www.link75.org/
Mt. Ararat MS 600/6-8
66 Republic Ave 04086 207-729-2950
Joshua Ottow, prin. Fax 729-2964
Williams-Cone ES 200/K-5
19 Perkins St 04086 207-725-4391
Randa Rineer, prin. Fax 725-6408
Woodside ES 300/K-5
42 Barrows Dr 04086 207-725-1243
Rick Dedek, prin. Fax 721 9206
Other Schools – See Bowdoin, Bowdoinham, Harpswell

Trenton, Hancock
AOS 91 - MDIRSS
Supt. — See Bar Harbor
Trenton ES 100/K-8
51 School Rd 04605 207-667-8447
Michael Zboray, prin. Fax 667-0146

Troy, Waldo
RSU 3 / MSAD 3
Supt. — See Unity
Troy S 100/K-6
733 Bangor Rd 04987 207-948-2280
Lisa Roux, prin. Fax 948-5211

Turner, Androscoggin
RSU 52 / MSAD 52 2,000/PK-12
486 Turner Ctr Rd 04282 207-225-1000
Kimberly Brandt, supt. Fax 225-5608
www.msad52.org
Tripp MS 300/7-8
65 Matthews Way 04282 207-225-1070
Gail Marine, prin. Fax 225-2102
Turner ES 200/3-6
91 Matthews Way 04282 207-225-1050
Kelly Marston, prin. Fax 225-4559
Turner PS 300/PK-2
59 Cobb Rd 04282 207-225-1030
Theresa Gillis, prin. Fax 225-3989
Other Schools – See Greene, Leeds

Union, Knox
RSU 40 / MSAD 40 1,800/PK-12
PO Box 701 04862 207-785-2277
Steve Nolan, supt. Fax 785-3119
www.msad40.org
Union ES 100/PK-6
1070 Heald Hwy 04862 207-785-4330
Christina Wotton, prin. Fax 785-2277
Other Schools – See Friendship, Waldoboro, Warren, Washington

Union SD 69
Supt. — See Hope
Appleton Village S 100/K-8
737 Union Rd 04862 207-785-4504
Susan Stilwell, prin. Fax 785-3036

Unity, Waldo, Pop. 459
RSU 3 / MSAD 3 1,400/PK-12
84 School St 04988 207-948-6136
Dr. Paul Austin, supt. Fax 948-6173
www.rsu3.org
Other Schools – See Brooks, Liberty, Monroe, Thorndike, Troy

Van Buren, Aroostook, Pop. 1,897
RSU 88 / MSAD 24 300/PK-12
169 Main St Ste 101 04785 207-868-2746
Elaine Boulier, supt. Fax 868-5420
www.msad24.org
Van Buren District ES 200/PK-8
169 Main St 04785 207-868-2733
Karen Dubois, prin. Fax 868-3537

Vassalboro, Kennebec
AOS 92 - KVCS
Supt. — See Waterville
Vassalboro Community S — 400/K-8
1116 Webber Pond Rd 04989 — 207-923-3100
Dianna Gram, prin. — Fax 923-3104

Veazie, See Bangor
Veazie SD — 200/PK-8
1040 School St 04401 — 207-947-6573
Matthew Cyr, supt. — Fax 947-6570
www.veaziecs.org
Veazie Community S — 200/PK-8
1040 School St 04401 — 207-947-6573
Matthew Cyr, prin. — Fax 974-6570

Vinalhaven, Knox
RSU 8 / MSAD 8 — 200/PK-12
22 Arcola Ln 04863 — 207-863-4800
Roy Crawford, supt. — Fax 863-4572
www.vinalhavenschool.org
Vinalhaven S — 200/PK-12
22 Arcola Ln 04863 — 207-863-4800
Ann Kirkpatrick, prin. — Fax 863-4572

Waldoboro, Lincoln, Pop. 1,207
RSU 40 / MSAD 40
Supt. — See Union
Medomak MS — 300/7-8
318 Manktown Rd 04572 — 207-832-5028
Kate Race, prin. — Fax 832-5710
Miller ES — 300/PK-6
145 Kalers Corner St 04572 — 207-832-2103
Julia Levensaler, prin. — Fax 832-2101

Wales, Androscoggin
RSU 4 — 1,500/PK-12
971 Gardiner Rd 04280 — 207-375-4273
James Hodgkin, supt. — Fax 375-2522
www.rsu4.org
Other Schools – See Litchfield, Sabattus

Warren, Knox
RSU 40 / MSAD 40
Supt. — See Union
Warren Community S — 300/PK-6
117 Eastern Rd 04864 — 207-273-2001
Deborah Howard, prin. — Fax 273-3207

Washburn, Aroostook, Pop. 987
RSU 45 / MSAD 45 — 400/PK-12
33 School St 04786 — 207-455-8301
Brian Carpenter, supt. — Fax 455-8217
www.msad45.net
Washburn District ES — 300/PK-8
33 School St 04786 — 207-455-4504
Melanie Cote, prin. — Fax 455-8217

Washington, Knox
RSU 40 / MSAD 40
Supt. — See Union
Prescott Memorial S — 100/K-6
100 Waldoboro Rd 04574 — 207-845-2424
Nancy Stover, prin. — Fax 845-2748

Waterboro, York
RSU 57 / MSAD 57 — 3,200/PK-12
86 West Rd 04087 — 207-247-3221
Larry Malone, supt. — Fax 247-3477
www.rsu57.org
Other Schools – See Alfred, East Waterboro, Lyman, Shapleigh, West Newfield

Waterford, Oxford
Oxford Hills SD
Supt. — See South Paris
Waterford Memorial ES — 100/PK-2
148 Valley Rd 04088 — 207-583-4418
Margaret Emery, prin. — Fax 583-9146

Waterville, Kennebec, Pop. 15,358
AOS 92 - KVCS — 3,600/PK-12
25 Messalonskee Ave 04901 — 207-873-4281
Eric Haley, supt. — Fax 872-5531
www.aos92.org/
Hall ES — 200/4-5
27 Pleasant St 04901 — 207-872-8071
Barbara Jordan, prin. — Fax 872-6129
Mitchell ES — 700/PK-3
58 Drummond Ave 04901 — 207-873-0695
Allan Martin, prin. — Fax 872-6172
Waterville JHS — 400/6-8
100 W River Rd 04901 — 207-873-2144
Carol Gilley, prin. — Fax 873-5752
Other Schools – See Vassalboro, Winslow

Mt. Merici Academy — 200/PK-8
152 Western Ave 04901 — 207-873-3773
Victoria Duguay, prin. — Fax 873-6377
Temple Academy — 200/PK-12
60 W River Rd 04901 — 207-873-5325

Wayne, Kennebec
RSU 38
Supt. — See Readfield
Wayne ES — 100/K-5
48 Pond Rd 04284 — 207-685-3634
Jeffrey Boston, prin. — Fax 685-9172

Wells, York
Wells-Ogunquit Community SD — 1,300/K-12
1460 Post Rd 04090 — 207-646-8331
James Daly, supt. — Fax 646-4236
www.k12wocsd.net
Wells ES — 400/K-4
276 Sanford Rd 04090 — 207-646-5953
April Noble, prin. — Fax 646-2592
Wells JHS — 400/5-8
1470 Post Rd 04090 — 207-646-5142
Robert Griffin, prin. — Fax 646-2899

Wesley, Washington
AOS 96 - MBASS
Supt. — See Machias
Wesley S — 50/K-8
13 Whining Pines Dr 04686 — 207-255-3263
Mitchell Look, prin. — Fax 255-0902

West Bath, Sagadahoc
West Bath SD — K-5
126 New Meadows Rd 04530 — 207-443-9145
Emily Thompson, supt. — Fax 443-6305
www.westbathschool.org
West Bath ES — 100/K-5
126 New Meadows Rd 04530 — 207-443-9145
Emily Thompson, prin. — Fax 443-6305

Westbrook, Cumberland, Pop. 17,059
Westbrook SD — 2,500/PK-12
117 Stroudwater St 04092 — 207-854-0800
Dr. Peter Lancia, supt. — Fax 854-0809
www.westbrookschools.org
Canal ES — 300/PK-4
102 Glenwood Ave 04092 — 207-854-0840
Vickie Hebert, prin. — Fax 854-0855
Congin ES — 400/PK-4
410 Bridge St 04092 — 207-854-0844
John Dickerson, prin. — Fax 854-0846
Saccarappa ES — 300/PK-4
110 Huntress Ave 04092 — 207-854-0847
Brian Mazjanis, prin. — Fax 854-0849
Westbrook MS — 800/5-8
471 Stroudwater St 04092 — 207-854-0830
Laurie Wood, prin. — Fax 854-0858

West Enfield, Penobscot
AOS 43
Supt. — See Lagrange
Enfield Station ES — 300/PK-5
561 Hammett Rd 04493 — 207-732-4141
Angela Priest, prin. — Fax 732-5319

West Gardiner, Kennebec
MSAD 11
Supt. — See Gardiner
Thompson ES — 300/PK-5
309 Spears Corner Rd 04345 — 207-724-3930
Kady Gould, prin. — Fax 724-3934

West Newfield, York
RSU 57 / MSAD 57
Supt. — See Waterboro
Line ES — 300/PK-5
818 Water St 04095 — 207-793-4100
Timothy Stinson, prin. — Fax 793-2425

West Paris, Oxford
Oxford Hills SD
Supt. — See South Paris
Gray ES — 100/PK-4
170 Main St 04289 — 207-674-2332
Elizabeth Clarke, prin. — Fax 674-3084

Whitefield, Lincoln
Sheepscot Valley RSU 12
Supt. — See Somerville
Whitefield S — 200/PK-8
164 Grand Army Rd 04353 — 207-549-5251
Josh McNaughton, prin. — Fax 549-4566

Whiting, Washington
AOS 96 - MBASS
Supt. — See Machias
Whiting Village S — 50/PK-8
PO Box 2 04691 — 207-733-4617
Scott Johnson, prin. — Fax 733-7582

Wilton, Franklin, Pop. 2,160
RSU 9 - Mt. Blue Regional SD
Supt. — See Farmington
Academy Hill ES — 200/2-5
585 Depot St 04294 — 207-645-4488
Keith Acedo, prin. — Fax 645-3844
Cushing ES — 100/PK-1
21 Cushing Dr 04294 — 207-645-2442
Keith Acedo, prin. — Fax 645-5102

Windham, Cumberland, Pop. 13,020
RSU 14 - Windham Raymond — 3,300/K-12
228 Windham Center Rd 04062 — 207-892-1800
Sanford Prince, supt. — Fax 892-1805
www.rsu14.org
Manchester ES — 400/4-5
709 Roosevelt Trl 04062 — 207-892-1830
Danielle Donnini, prin. — Fax 892-1834
Windham MS — 600/6-8
408 Gray Rd 04062 — 207-892-1820
Drew Patin, prin. — Fax 892-1826
Windham PS — 800/K-3
404 Gray Rd 04062 — 207-892-1840
Dr. Kyle Rhoads, prin. — Fax 892-1838
Other Schools – See Raymond

Windham Christian Academy — 100/PK-12
1051 Roosevelt Trl 04062 — 207-892-2244
Roy Mickelson, prin. — Fax 893-1289

Windsor, Kennebec
Sheepscot Valley RSU 12
Supt. — See Somerville
Windsor S — 300/PK-8
366 Ridge Rd 04363 — 207-445-2356
Maggie Allen, prin. — Fax 445-3494

Winn, Penobscot
AOS 90 - EMASS
Supt. — See Baileyville
Lee/Winn ES — 100/PK-4
1009 Route 168 04495 — 207-738-3060
Pamela Hamilton, prin. — Fax 738-3070

Winslow, Kennebec, Pop. 7,626
AOS 92 - KVCS
Supt. — See Waterville
Winslow ES — 500/PK-5
285 Benton Ave 04901 — 207-872-1967
Kyle Price, prin. — Fax 873-6522
Winslow JHS — 300/6-8
6 Danielson St 04901 — 207-872-1973
Jason Briggs, prin. — Fax 872-1977

St. John S — 100/PK-8
15 S Garand St 04901 — 207-872-7115
Valerie Wheeler, prin. — Fax 872-2500

Winterport, Waldo, Pop. 1,327
RSU 22
Supt. — See Hampden
Smith ES — 300/PK-4
319 S Main St 04496 — 207-223-4282
Dawn Moore, prin. — Fax 223-2267
Wagner MS — 100/5-8
19 Williams Way 04496 — 207-223-4309
Dr. Richard Glencross, prin. — Fax 223-4325

Winthrop, Kennebec, Pop. 2,622
Monhegan Plt SD — 50/PK-8
15 Hillside Ave 04364 — 207-844-0666
Melanie Chasse, supt.
www.monheganschool.org
Other Schools – See Monhegan

Winthrop SD — 800/PK-12
17A Highland Ave 04364 — 207-377-2296
Gary Rosenthal, supt. — Fax 377-2708
www.winthropschools.org
Winthrop ES — 400/PK-5
23 Highland Ave 04364 — 207-377-2241
Jeffrey Ladd, prin. — Fax 377-4671
Winthrop MS — 200/6-8
400 Rambler Rd 04364 — 207-377-2249
Karen Criss, prin. — Fax 377-3667

Wiscasset, Lincoln, Pop. 1,086
Wiscasset School Department — 300/PK-12
225 Gardiner Rd 04578 — 207-882-4104
Dr. Heather Wilmot, supt. — Fax 882-4123
www.wiscassetschools.org
Wiscasset ES — 100/PK-6
83 Federal St 04578 — 207-882-7767
Stacy White, prin. — Fax 882-8279

Woodland, Aroostook, Pop. 931
Union SD 122 — 200/PK-8
843 Woodland Center Rd # 3 04736 — 207-498-8436
Karla Michaud, supt. — Fax 498-6349
www.schoolunion122.net
Woodland S — 100/PK-8
844 Woodland Center Rd 04736 — 207-496-2981
Susan Schloeman, prin. — Fax 496-6913

Woolwich, Sagadahoc, Pop. 2,570
RSU 1
Supt. — See Bath
Woolwich Central S — 400/PK-8
137 Nequasset Rd 04579 — 207-443-9739
Jason Libby, prin. — Fax 443-9792

Yarmouth, Cumberland, Pop. 5,801
Yarmouth SD — 1,500/K-12
101 McCartney St 04096 — 207-846-5586
Andrew Dolloff, supt. — Fax 846-2339
www.yarmouthschools.org
Harrison MS — 500/5-8
220 McCartney St 04096 — 207-846-2499
Joan Adler, prin. — Fax 846-2489
Rowe ES — 200/K-1
52 School St 04096 — 207-846-3771
Susan Lobel, prin. — Fax 846-2325
Yarmouth ES — 300/2-4
121 McCartney St 04096 — 207-846-3391
Ryan Gleason, prin. — Fax 846-2330

North Yarmouth Academy — 300/PK-12
148 Main St 04096 — 207-846-9051
Benjamin Jackson, head sch — Fax 846-8829

York, York, Pop. 9,818
York SD — 1,800/K-12
469 US Route 1 03909 — 207-363-3403
Dr. Debra Dunn, supt. — Fax 363-5602
www.yorkschools.org
Coastal Ridge ES — 300/2-4
1 Coastal Ridge Dr 03909 — 207-363-1800
Sean Murphy, prin. — Fax 363-1816
Village ES — 300/K-2
124 York St 03909 — 207-363-4870
Beth Hutchins, prin. — Fax 363-1818
York MS — 600/5-8
30 Organug Rd 03909 — 207-363-4214
Barbara Maling, prin. — Fax 363-1815

Brixham Montessori Friends S — 100/PK-5
18 Brickyard Ct 03909 — 207-351-2700

MARYLAND

MARYLAND DEPARTMENT OF EDUCATION
200 W Baltimore St, Baltimore 21201-2595
Telephone 410-767-0600
Fax 410-333-6033
Website http://www.marylandpublicschools.org

Superintendent of Schools Karen Salmon

MARYLAND BOARD OF EDUCATION
200 W Baltimore St, Baltimore 21201-2549

President Andrew Smarick

PUBLIC, PRIVATE AND CATHOLIC ELEMENTARY SCHOOLS

Aberdeen, Harford, Pop. 14,190
Harford County SD
Supt. — See Bel Air
Aberdeen MS 1,100/6-8
111 Mount Royal Ave 21001 410-273-5510
DeAnn Webb, prin. Fax 273-5542
Bakerfield ES 400/PK-5
36 Baker St 21001 410-273-5518
Tara Dedeaux, prin. Fax 273-5547
Hall's Cross Roads ES 500/PK-5
203 E Bel Air Ave 21001 410-273-5524
Christina Douglass, prin. Fax 273-5555
Lisby ES at Hillsdale 400/PK-5
810 Edmund St 21001 410-273-5530
Christine Langrehr, prin. Fax 273-5561

St. Joan of Arc S 200/K-8
230 S Law St 21001 410-575-7319
Virginia Bahr, prin. Fax 272-1959

Abingdon, Harford
Harford County SD
Supt. — See Bel Air
Abingdon ES 800/PK-5
399 Singer Rd 21009 410-638-3910
Dr. Stacey Gerringer, prin. Fax 638-3914
James ES 400/K-5
1 Laurentum Pkwy 21009 410-638-3900
Rebecca Reese, prin. Fax 638-3906
Paca/Old Post Road ES 800/PK-5
2706 Philadelphia Rd 21009 410-612-2033
Tammy Bosley, prin. Fax 612-1587

New Covenant Christian S 200/PK-12
128 Saint Marys Church Rd 21009 443-512-0771
Jean Armstrong, prin. Fax 569-3846

Accident, Garrett, Pop. 323
Garrett County SD
Supt. — See Oakland
Accident ES 200/PK-5
534 Accident Bittinger Rd 21520 301-746-8863
Jessica Fratz, prin. Fax 746-8570
Northern MS 300/6-8
371 Pride Pkwy 21520 301-746-8165
David Yoder, prin. Fax 746-8865

Accokeek, Prince George's, Pop. 10,314
Prince George's County SD
Supt. — See Upper Marlboro
Accokeek Academy 500/PK-4
14500 Berry Rd 20607 301-203-3200
Judy Adams, prin. Fax 203-3207
Accokeek Academy 800/5-8
14500 Berry Rd 20607 301-203-3200
Judy Adams, prin. Fax 203-3207

Adamstown, Frederick, Pop. 2,325
Frederick County SD
Supt. — See Frederick
Carroll Manor ES 500/PK-5
5624 Adamstown Rd 21710 240-236-3800
Kim Huffer, prin. Fax 236-3801

Adelphi, Prince George's, Pop. 14,821
Prince George's County SD
Supt. — See Upper Marlboro
Adelphi ES 600/PK-6
8820 Riggs Rd 20783 301-431-6250
Chelsea Hill, prin. Fax 445-8468
Buck Lodge MS 800/7-8
2611 Buck Lodge Rd 20783 301-431-6290
Kenneth Nance, prin. Fax 431-6294
Cherokee Lane ES 500/K-6
9000 25th Ave 20783 301-445-8415
Sheena Hardy, prin. Fax 445-8442
Cool Spring ES 700/PK-6
8910 Riggs Rd 20783 301-431-6200
Cameron Millspaugh, prin. Fax 445-8407
Jones ES 1,000/PK-6
2405 Tecumseh St 20783 301-408-7900
Dr. Karen Woodson, prin. Fax 408-7904

Annapolis, Anne Arundel, Pop. 37,674
Anne Arundel County SD 78,600/PK-12
2644 Riva Rd 21401 410-222-5000
Dr. George Arlotto, supt. Fax 222-5602
www.aacps.org
Annapolis ES 300/PK-5
180 Green St 21401 410-222-1600
Bobbie Kesecker, prin. Fax 222-1601
Annapolis MS 700/6-8
1399 Forest Dr 21403 410-267-8658
Sean McElhaney, prin. Fax 267-8924
Bates MS 800/6-8
701 Chase St 21401 410-263-0270
Paul DeRoo, prin. Fax 263-0205
Cape St. Claire ES 700/K-5
931 Blue Ridge Dr, 410-222-1685
Janet Lancaster, prin. Fax 222-1672
Eastport ES 300/PK-5
420 Fifth St 21403 410-222-1605
Susan Gallagher, prin. Fax 222-1609
Georgetown East ES 400/PK-5
111 Dogwood Rd 21403 410-222-1610
Andre Dillard, prin. Fax 222-1612
Germantown ES 700/PK-5
200 Windell Ave 21401 410-222-1615
Karen Soneira, prin. Fax 222-1617
Hillsmere ES 500/PK-5
3052 Arundel on the Bay Rd 21403 410-222-1622
Kimberly Terry, prin. Fax 295-0479
Mills-Parole ES 600/PK-5
1 George & Marion Phelps Ln 21401 410-222-1626
Ginger Henley, prin. Fax 222-1614
Monarch Academy Annapolis 600/K-5
2000 Capital Dr 21401 443-449-2757
Susan Myers, prin.
Rolling Knolls ES 400/PK-5
1985 Valley Rd 21401 410-222-5820
Shira Dowling, prin. Fax 222-5828
Tyler Heights ES 500/PK-5
200 Janwall St 21403 410-222-1630
Julia Walsh, prin. Fax 222-1683
West Annapolis ES 200/K-5
505 Melvin Ave 21401 410-222-1635
Sue Errichiello, prin. Fax 222-1654
Windsor Farm ES 600/K-5
591 Broadneck Rd, 410-222-1690
Jason Otte, prin. Fax 222-8681
Other Schools – See Arnold, Baltimore, Crofton, Crownsville, Davidsonville, Deale, Edgewater, Fort Meade, Gambrills, Glen Burnie, Hanover, Jessup, Laurel, Linthicum Heights, Lothian, Millersville, Odenton, Pasadena, Severn, Severna Park, Shady Side, Tracys Landing

---

Annapolis Area Christian Lower S K-5
710 Ridgely Ave 21401 410-846-3504
Elizabeth Williams, prin. Fax 573-6866
Annapolis Area Christian MS 6-8
716 Bestgate Rd 21401 410-846-3506
Rick Slenk, prin. Fax 573-6866
Chesapeake Montessori S 100/PK-8
30 Old Mill Bottom Rd N, 410-757-4740
Key S 700/PK-12
534 Hillsmere Dr 21403 410-263-9231
Matthew Nespole, hdmstr. Fax 280-5516
Montessori International Childrens House 100/PK-6
1641 N Winchester Rd, 410-757-7789
St. Anne's S of Annapolis 200/PK-8
3112 Arundel on the Bay Rd 21403 410-263-8650
Lisa Nagel, head sch Fax 280-8720
St. Margaret's Day S 100/PK-K
1605 Pleasant Plains Rd, 410-757-2333
Tricia McVeigh, dir. Fax 757-5334
St. Martin's Lutheran S of Annapolis 200/PK-8
1120 Spa Rd 21403 410-269-1955
James Moorhead, head sch Fax 280-2024
St. Mary's S 800/K-8
111 Duke of Gloucester St 21401 410-263-2869
Rebecca Zimmerman, prin. Fax 269-6513

Arnold, Anne Arundel, Pop. 22,629
Anne Arundel County SD
Supt. — See Annapolis
Arnold ES at Severn River MS 400/K-5
241 Peninsula Farm Rd 21012 410-222-1670
Shauna Kauffman, prin. Fax 222-1672
Belvedere ES 500/PK-5
360 Broadwater Rd 21012 410-975-9432
Tara Lambden, prin. Fax 975-9830
Broadneck ES 800/K-5
470 Shore Acres Rd 21012 410-222-1680
John Noon, prin. Fax 222-1676
Magothy River MS 700/6-8
241 Peninsula Farm Rd 21012 410-544-0926
Christopher Mirenzi, prin. Fax 544-1867
Severn River MS 800/6-8
241 Peninsula Farm Rd 21012 410-544-0922
Richard Tubman, prin. Fax 315-8006

Arnold Christian Academy 50/K-8
365 Jones Station Rd 21012 410-544-1882
Kelly Hurd, prin. Fax 544-5765
Severn S 200/PK-5
1185 Baltimore Annapolis 21012 410-647-7700
Douglas Lagarde, hdmstr. Fax 647-6088

Ashton, Montgomery

Mater Amoris Montessori S 100/PK-6
PO Box 97 20861 301-774-7468
Charlotte Shea, dir. Fax 774-5232

Baldwin, Baltimore
Baltimore County SD
Supt. — See Towson
Carroll Manor ES 300/PK-5
4434 Carroll Manor Rd 21013 410-887-5947
William Cirrincione, prin. Fax 887-5948

Baltimore, Baltimore, Pop. 609,299
Anne Arundel County SD
Supt. — See Annapolis
Belle Grove ES 200/PK-5
4502 Belle Grove Rd 21225 410-222-6589
Tamara Kelly, prin. Fax 222-6500
Brooklyn Park ES 400/PK-5
200 14th Ave 21225 410-222-6590
E. Rodney Walker, prin. Fax 222-6581
Brooklyn Park MS 700/6-8
200 Hammonds Ln 21225 410-636-2967
Beth Shakan, prin. Fax 636-1774
Park ES 500/PK-5
201 E 11th Ave 21225 410-222-6593
Sandra Blondell, prin. Fax 222-6596

Baltimore CSD 77,600/PK-12
200 E North Ave 21202 443-984-2000
Sonja Santelises Ed.D., admin. Fax 396-8898
www.bcps.k12.md.us
Abbottston ES 200/PK-5
1300 Gorsuch Ave 21218 410-984-2685
Cathleen Miles, prin.
Arlington ES 500/PK-8
3705 W Rogers Ave 21215 410-396-0567
Emily Hunter, prin. Fax 396-0072
Armistead Gardens ES 600/PK-8
5001 E Eager St 21205 410-396-9090
Cera Doering-Rebello, prin. Fax 488-6270
Arundel ES 400/PK-8
2400 Round Rd 21225 410-396-1379
Rochelle Machado, prin. Fax 396-1836
Barclay ES 500/PK-8
2900 Barclay St 21218 410-396-6387
Armanda Carr, prin. Fax 396-6200
Barrister ES 300/PK-5
1327 Washington Blvd 21230 410-396-5973
David Wunder, prin. Fax 545-3272
Bay-Brook ES 500/PK-8
4301 10th St 21225 410-396-1357
Monique Reese, prin. Fax 396-8430
Beechfield ES 700/PK-8
301 S Beechfield Ave 21229 410-396-0525
Rene Browning, prin. Fax 396-0426
Belmont ES 400/PK-5
1406 N Ellamont St 21216 410-396-0579
Tiffany Etheridge, prin. Fax 545-7841
Brehms Lane ES 800/PK-5
3536 Brehms Ln 21213 410-396-9150
Diya Hafiz, prin. Fax 396-5999
Brent ES 300/PK-8
100 E 26th St 21218 410-396-6509
Pamela Smith, prin. Fax 396-6038

Callaway ES 300/PK-5
3701 Fernhill Ave 21215 410-396-0604
Miguel Del Toro, prin. Fax 545-7847

Calverton ES 700/PK-8
1100 Whitmore Ave 21216 410-396-0581
Martia Cooper, prin. Fax 545-7849

Carter ES 300/PK-8
820 E 43rd St 21212 410-396-6271
Shantay McKinily, prin. Fax 323-7624

Cecil ES 400/PK-5
2000 Cecil Ave 21218 410-396-6385
Aleesha Manning, prin. Fax 396-7193

Cherry Hill ES 400/PK-8
844 Roundview Rd 21225 410-396-1392
Tracey Garrett, prin.

Coldstream Park ES 400/PK-8
1400 Exeter Hall Ave 21218 410-396-6443
Alzata Spencer, prin. Fax 396-6206

Coleman ES 400/PK-5
2400 Windsor Ave 21216 410-396-0764
Carlillian Thompson, prin. Fax 225-3035

Coleridge-Taylor ES 400/PK-5
507 W Preston St 21201 410-396-0783
Bettye Adams, prin. Fax 396-0975

Collington Square ES 600/PK-8
1409 N Collington Ave 21213 410-396-9198
Fax 396-8632

Cross Country ES 800/PK-8
6100 Cross Country Blvd 21215 410-396-0602
Lashella Stanfield, prin. Fax 545-7850

Curtis Bay ES 600/PK-8
4301 W Bay Ave 21225 410-396-1397
Mark Bongiovanni, prin. Fax 396-5263

Dickey Hill ES 400/PK-8
5025 Dickey Hill Rd 21207 410-396-0610
Aaron Clark, prin. Fax 396-0017

Edgecombe Circle ES 400/PK-5
2835 Virginia Ave 21215 410-396-0550
Gloria Pulley, prin. Fax 545-7867

Edgewood ES 300/PK-5
1900 Edgewood St 21216 410-396-0532
Kimberly Sollers, prin. Fax 396-0681

Eutaw-Marshburn ES 300/PK-5
1624 Eutaw Pl 21217 410-396-0779
Tiffany Cole, prin. Fax 396-0397

Fallstaff ES 400/PK-8
3801 Fallstaff Rd 21215 410-396-0682
Faith Hibbert, prin. Fax 545-1737

Farring ES 600/PK-8
300 Pontiac Ave 21225 410-396-1404
Benjamin Crandall, prin. Fax 396-5218

Federal Hill Preparatory Academy 300/PK-5
1040 William St 21230 410-396-1207
Sara Long, prin. Fax 396-3532

Fort Worthington ES 300/K-8
2710 E Hoffman St 21213 410-396-9161
Monique Debi, prin. Fax 396-6341

Franklin Square ES 300/PK-8
1400 W Lexington St 21223 410-396-0795
Terry Patton, prin. Fax 396-0999

Frederick ES 300/PK-5
2501 Frederick Ave 21229 410-396-0830
Harold Henry, prin. Fax 396-8073

Furley ES 400/PK-5
5001 Sinclair Ln 21206 410-396-9094
Greta Cephas, prin. Fax 545-7844

Gardenville ES 400/PK-5
5300 Belair Rd 21206 410-396-6382
Anthony Brooks, prin. Fax 396-8081

Garrett Heights ES 400/PK-8
2800 Ailsa Ave 21214 410-396-6361
Deborah Moffett, prin. Fax 396-0428

Gilmor ES, 1311 N Gilmor St 21217 400/PK-5
Curtis Durham, prin. 410-396-0820

Glenmount ES 500/PK-8
6211 Walther Ave 21206 410-396-6366
Benjamin Mosley, prin. Fax 396-6760

Graceland Park-O'Donnell Heights S 400/PK-8
6300 ODonnell St 21224 410-396-9083
Johanna Mullally, prin. Fax 396-9364

Grove Park ES 300/PK-8
5545 Kennison Ave 21215 410-396-0822
Tracye Carter, prin. Fax 545-7845

Guilford ES 400/PK-8
4520 York Rd 21212 410-396-6358
Brian Pluim, prin. Fax 396-6212

Gwynns Falls ES 400/PK-5
2700 Gwynns Falls Pkwy 21216 410-396-0638
Nikomar Mosley, prin. Fax 545-7853

Hamilton ES 700/PK-8
6101 Old Harford Rd 21214 410-396-6375
Patricia Otway-Drummond, prin. Fax 545-7870

Hamilton ES 300/PK-5
800 Poplar Grove St 21216 410-396-0520
Brandon Pinkney, prin. Fax 396-1803

Hampden ES 300/PK-8
3608 Chestnut Ave 21211 410-396-6004
Katrina Foster, prin. Fax 545-7774

Harford Heights ES 600/PK-5
1919 N Broadway 21213 410-396-9341
Danielle Cromartie, prin. Fax 396-9060

Harlem Park ES 400/PK-8
1401 W Lafayette Ave 21217 410-396-0633
Denisha Logan, prin. Fax 396-0619

Harris ES 500/PK-5
1400 N Caroline St 21213 410-396-1452
Shandra Worthy-Owens, prin. Fax 396-3019

Hazelwood ES 400/PK-8
4517 Hazelwood Ave 21206 410-396-9098
Amanda Rice, prin. Fax 545-7868

Height ES 200/PK-5
2011 Linden Ave 21216 410-396-0837
Tamara Hanson, prin. Fax 396-0184

Henderson ES 400/K-8
2100 Ashland Ave 21205 443-642-2060
Deborah Ptak, prin.

Henson ES 300/PK-5
1600 N Payson St 21217 410-396-0776
Travis Miller, prin. Fax 396-7840

Heritage Early Learning Center PK-PK
2801 Saint Lo Dr 21213 410-396-6644

Highlandtown ES 600/PK-8
3223 E Pratt St 21224 410-396-9381
Nancy Fagan, prin. Fax 396-1178

Highlandtown ES 400/PK-8
231 S Eaton St 21224 443-642-2792
Denise Ashley, prin.

Hilton ES 400/PK-5
3301 Carlisle Ave 21216 410-396-0634
Danielle Henson, prin. Fax 396-0892

Holabird ES 400/PK-8
1500 Imla St 21224 410-396-9086
Stephanie Novak, prin. Fax 396-7588

Jefferson ES 500/PK-8
605 Dryden Dr 21229 410-396-0534
Danielle Davis, prin. Fax 545-7846

Johnson ES 500/PK-8
100 E Heath St 21230 410-396-1575
James Dedinger, prin. Fax 545-7345

Johnston Square ES 400/PK-5
1101 Valley St 21202 410-396-1477
Raymond Braxton, prin. Fax 396-5251

Key ES 500/PK-8
1425 E Fort Ave 21230 410-396-1503
Corey Basmajian, prin. Fax 545-6720

King ES 400/PK-8
3750 Greenspring Ave 21211 410-396-0756
Rachel Brunson, prin. Fax 396-0576

Lakeland ES 800/PK-8
2921 Stranden Rd 21230 410-396-1406
Najib Jammal, prin. Fax 396-0015

Lakewood ES 200/PK-K
2625 E Federal St 21213 410-396-9158
Teresa Cooper, prin. Fax 276-5083

Liberty ES 400/PK-5
3901 Maine Ave 21207 410-396-0571
Joseph Manko, prin. Fax 396-0396

Lockerman-Bundy ES 300/PK-5
301 N Pulaski St 21223 410-396-1364
Kimberly Hill, prin. Fax 545-7877

Lyndhurst ES 300/PK-6
201 N Bend Rd 21229 410-396-0503
Sherelle Lowe, prin. Fax 396-0439

McHenry ES 400/PK-8
31 S Schroeder St 21223 410-396-1621
Christophe Turk, prin. Fax 396-1668

Medfield Heights ES 400/PK-5
4300 Buchanan Ave 21211 410-396-6460
Amber Kilcoyne, prin. Fax 545-7873

Montebello ES, 2040 E 32nd St 21218 700/PK-8
Lorna Hanley, prin. 410-396-6576

Moravia Park ES 800/PK-5
6201 Frankford Ave 21206 410-396-9096
Tadem Daniels, prin. Fax 396-8075

Morrell Park ES 500/PK-8
2601 Tolley St 21230 410-396-3426
Nichelle Johnson, prin. Fax 396-0016

Mosher ES 300/PK-5
2400 W Mosher St 21216 410-396-0506
Octavia Hopkins, prin. Fax 396-7841

Mt. Royal ES 800/K-8
121 McMechen St 21217 410-396-0864
Job Grotsky, prin. Fax 396-0309

Mount Washington ES 600/K-8
1801 Sulgrave Ave 21209 410-396-6354
Ashley Cook, prin. Fax 396-0147

New Song Academy 100/PK-8
1530 Presstman St 21217 410-728-2091
Lisa Brown, dir. Fax 728-0829

Nicholas ES 300/PK-5
201 E 21st St 21218 410-396-4525
Danielle Adams, prin. Fax 396-5975

North Bend ES 500/PK-8
181 North Bend Rd 21229 410-396-0376
Patricia Burrell, prin. Fax 396-0380

Northwood ES 700/PK-5
5201 Loch Raven Blvd 21239 410-396-6377
Erita Adams, prin. Fax 545-7852

Paca ES 500/PK-5
200 N Lakewood Ave 21224 410-396-9148
Olia Hardy, prin. Fax 545-7838

Pimlico ES 500/PK-8
3910 Barrington Rd 21207 410-396-0876
LaJuan Alston, prin. Fax 396-0925

Pinderhughes ES 300/PK-8
701 Gold St 21217 410-396-0800
Federico Adams, prin. Fax 396-0342

Pitts-Ashburton ES 400/PK-8
3935 Hilton Rd 21215 410-396-0636
Erica Fortson, prin. Fax 396-0206

Roach ES 200/PK-5
3434 Old Frederick Rd 21229 410-396-0511
Renata Plummer, prin. Fax 396-0740

Rodman ES 200/PK-5
3510 W Mulberry St 21229 410-396-0508
David Guzman, prin. Fax 396-0702

Rodwell ES 400/PK-5
3501 Hillsdale Rd 21207 410-396-0940
Samuel Rather, prin. Fax 396-0854

Rogers ES 600/PK-8
100 N Chester St 21231 410-396-9300
Marc Martin, prin. Fax 396-9164

Rognell Heights ES 300/PK-8
4300 Sidehill Rd 21229 410-396-0528
Nakeisha Savage, prin. Fax 396-8456

Roland Park ES 1,400/PK-8
5207 Roland Ave 21210 410-396-6420
Nicholas D'Ambrosio, prin. Fax 396-7662

Ruhrah ES 700/PK-8
701 Rappolla St 21224 410-396-9125
Mary Donnelly, prin. Fax 396-8105

Sinclair Lane ES 400/PK-5
3880 Sinclair Ln 21213 410-396-9117
Roxanne Thorn-Lumpkins, prin. Fax 545-7525

Stadium S, 1300 Gorsuch Ave 21218 200/6-8
Shana Hall, dir. 443-984-2682

Steuart Hill Academy 300/PK-5
30 S Gilmor St 21223 410-396-1387
Tanyaneka Lipscomb, prin. Fax 396-6953

Tench Tilghman ES 400/PK-8
600 N Patterson Park Ave 21205 410-396-9247
Jael Yon, prin. Fax 396-9451

Vanguard Collegiate MS 300/6-8
5000 Truesdale Rd 21206 443-642-2069
Esther Wallace, prin.

Violetville ES 500/PK-8
1207 Pine Heights Ave 21229 410-396-1416
Lauren Brown, prin. Fax 396-0838

Walk ES 1,100/PK-8
1235 Sherwood Ave 21239 410-396-6380
James Sargent, prin. Fax 396-6294

Washington ES, 800 Scott St 21230 300/PK-5
Bridget Wrightson, prin. 410-396-1445

Washington MS 300/6-8
1301 McCulloh St 21217 410-396-7734
Misha Scott, prin. Fax 396-0552

Waverly ES 400/PK-8
3400 Ellerslie Ave 21218 410-396-6394
Tanya Green, prin. Fax 396-6161

Westport Academy 300/PK-8
2401 Nevada St 21230 410-396-3396
Melody Locke, prin.

Windsor Hills ES 300/PK-8
4001 Alto Rd 21216 410-396-0595
Joshua Bailey, prin. Fax 545-7843

Winterling ES 400/PK-5
220 N Bentalou St 21223 410-396-1385
Nikia Carter, prin. Fax 545-7878

Woodhome ES 400/PK-8
7300 Moyer Ave 21234 410-396-6398
Shontel Douglas, prin. Fax 396-7792

Woodson ES 400/PK-8
2501 Seabury Rd 21225 410-396-1366
Tracey Pratt, prin. Fax 396-3062

Yorkwood ES 400/PK-5
5931 Yorkwood Rd 21239 410-396-6364
Tonya Combs Redd, prin. Fax 396-6262

Baltimore County SD
Supt. — See Towson

Arbutus ES 400/PK-5
1300 Sulphur Spring Rd 21227 410-887-1400
Brent Grabill, prin. Fax 887-1401

Arbutus MS 800/6-8
5525 Shelbourne Rd 21227 410-887-1402
Michelle Feeney, prin. Fax 536-1164

Baltimore Highlands ES 600/PK-5
4200 Annapolis Rd 21227 410-887-0919
Brian Williams, prin. Fax 789-2502

Battle Grove ES 400/PK-5
7828 Saint Patricia Ln 21222 410-887-7500
Jennifer Gounaris, prin. Fax 887-7501

Bear Creek ES 500/PK-5
1601 Melbourne Rd 21222 410-887-7007
Cheryl Thim, prin. Fax 887-7111

Bedford ES 300/PK-5
7407 Dorman Dr 21208 410-887-1200
Christina Connolly, prin. Fax 887-1201

Berkshire ES 500/PK-5
7431 Poplar Ave 21224 410-887-7008
Cheryl Brooks, prin. Fax 284-5345

Campfield Early Learning Center 200/PK-PK
6834 Alter St 21207 410-887-1227
Mari Morris, prin. Fax 887-1230

Carney ES 600/PK-5
3131 E Joppa Rd 21234 410-887-5228
Barbara McLennan, prin. Fax 887-5229

Chadwick ES 500/PK-5
1918 Winder Rd 21244 410-887-1300
Bonnie Hess, prin. Fax 277-9837

Charlesmont ES 400/PK-5
7800 W Collingham Dr 21222 410-887-7004
Marsha Ayres, prin. Fax 887-7355

Chase ES 400/PK-5
11701 Eastern Ave 21220 410-887-5940
Tara Wilkins, prin. Fax 887-5941

Chesapeake Terrace ES 300/PK-5
2112 Lodge Farm Rd 21219 410-887-7505
Shandra Patrick, prin. Fax 887-7555

Colgate ES 400/PK-5
401 51st St 21224 410-887-7010
Erin Dicello, prin. Fax 887-7012

Cromwell Valley ES Regional Magnet 400/K-5
825 Providence Rd 21286 410-887-4888
Catherine Thomas, prin. Fax 887-4889

Deep Creek ES 400/PK-5
1101 E Homberg Ave 21221 410-887-0110
Laura Kelly, prin. Fax 391-6547

Deep Creek MS 800/6-8
1000 S Marlyn Ave 21221 410-887-0112
Thomas Baker, prin. Fax 391-6534

Dogwood ES 600/K-5
7215 Dogwood Rd 21244 410-887-6808
Johari Toe, prin. Fax 298-2720

Dumbarton MS 1,000/6-8
300 Dumbarton Rd Ste 1 21212 410-887-3176
Susan Harris, prin. Fax 583-7020

Dundalk ES 700/PK-5
2717 Playfield St 21222 410-887-7013
Michael Parker, prin. Fax 887-7015

Dundalk MS 500/6-8
7400 Dunmanway 21222 410-887-7018
Seth Barish, prin. Fax 887-7284

Edgemere ES 500/PK-5
7201 N Point Rd 21219 410-887-7507
Jennifer Lynch, prin. Fax 887-7508

Edmondson Heights ES 500/PK-5
1600 Langford Rd 21207 410-887-0818
Juliet McDivitt, prin. Fax 869-0240

Elmwood ES 600/PK-5
531 Dale Ave 21206 410-887-5232
Jeffrey Hogan, prin. Fax 887-5233

Essex ES 500/PK-5
100 Mace Ave 21221 410-887-0117
Amy Grabner, prin. Fax 887-0118

Featherbed Lane ES 600/PK-5
6700 Richardson Rd 21207 410-887-1302
Renee Johnson, prin. Fax 277-9879

Fort Garrison ES 400/K-5
3310 Woodvalley Dr 21208 410-887-1203
Karen Harris, prin. Fax 887-1204

Fullerton ES 600/PK-5
4400 Fullerton Ave 21236 410-887-5234
Candace Winterson, prin. Fax 661-4813
Glenmar ES 400/PK-5
9700 Community Dr 21220 410-887-0127
Delores Tedeschi, prin. Fax 391-6130
Golden Ring MS 600/6-8
6700 Kenwood Ave 21237 410-887-0130
Lawrence Rudolph, prin. Fax 682-6750
Grange ES 400/PK-5
2000 Church Rd 21222 410-887-7043
Nancy Wenzl, prin. Fax 887-7044
Gunpowder ES 500/PK-5
9540 Holiday Manor Rd 21236 410-887-5121
Wendy Cunningham, prin. Fax 248-3177
Halethorpe ES 500/PK-5
4300 Maple Ave 21227 410-887-1406
Jill Carter, prin. Fax 887-7407
Halstead Academy 500/PK-5
1111 Halstead Rd 21234 410-887-3210
Jenifer Noll, prin. Fax 887-3220
Harford Hills ES 400/PK-5
8902 Old Harford Rd 21234 410-887-5236
Mildred Guild, prin. Fax 887-5237
Hawthorne ES 600/PK-5
125 Kingston Rd 21220 410-887-0138
Dwan Pinamonti, prin. Fax 686-8368
Hebbville ES 400/PK-5
3335 Washington Ave 21244 410-887-0708
Sandra Wilkins, prin. Fax 887-0709
Hillcrest ES 800/PK-5
1500 Frederick Rd 21228 410-887-0820
Douglas Elmendorf, prin. Fax 887-0821
Holabird MS 700/6-8
1701 Delvale Ave 21222 410-887-7049
Julie Dellone, prin. Fax 887-7275
Johnnycake ES 700/PK-5
5910 Craigmont Rd 21228 410-887-0823
Bre-Anne Fortkamp, prin. Fax 887-1048
Lansdowne ES 500/PK-5
2301 Alma Rd 21227 410-887-1408
Stephen Price, prin. Fax 887-1468
Lansdowne MS 700/6-8
2400 Lansdowne Rd 21227 410-887-1411
Frank Dunlap, prin. Fax 887-1412
Loch Raven Technical Academy 800/6-8
8101 La Salle Rd 21286 410-887-3518
Stacey Johnson, prin. Fax 821-6398
Logan ES 600/PK-5
7601 Dunmanway 21222 410-887-7052
Stephen Bender, prin. Fax 282-6357
Mars Estates ES 400/PK-5
1500 E Homberg Ave 21221 410-887-0154
Sharon Whitlock, prin. Fax 887-0156
Martin Boulevard ES 300/PK-5
210 Riverton Rd 21220 410-887-0158
Janet Mahoney, prin. Fax 391-7266
McCormick ES 400/PK-5
5101 Hazelwood Ave 21206 410-887-0500
Ligeri Kourtesis, prin. Fax 887-0504
Middleborough ES 400/PK-5
313 West Rd 21221 410-887-0160
Jamie Basignani, prin. Fax 887-0161
Middle River MS 800/6-8
800 Middle River Rd 21220 410-887-0165
Shannon Parker, prin. Fax 887-0167
Middlesex ES 500/PK-5
142 Bennett Rd 21221 410-887-0170
Lori Hutchison, prin. Fax 887-0469
Milbrook ES 400/PK-5
4300 Crest Heights Rd 21215 410-887-1225
Jeffrey Tessier, prin. Fax 887-6744
Northwest Academy of Health Science 600/6-8
4627 Old Court Rd 21208 410-887-0742
Dr. Katina Webster, prin. Fax 887-0670
Norwood ES 500/PK-5
1700 Delvale Ave 21222 410-887-7055
Patrice Goldys, prin. Fax 887-7057
Oakleigh ES 600/PK-5
1900 White Oak Ave 21234 410-887-5238
Sharon Mason, prin. Fax 665-6379
Oliver Beach ES 300/PK-5
12912 Cunninghill Cove Rd 21220 410-887-5943
Molly Bissell, prin. Fax 887-5944
Orems ES 400/PK-5
711 Highvilla Rd 21221 410-887-0172
Marcia Wolf, prin. Fax 887-0173
Parkville MS 1,000/6-8
8711 Avondale Rd 21234 410-887-5250
Erin O'Toole-Trivas, prin. Fax 887-5315
Perry Hall ES 700/PK-5
9021 Belair Rd 21236 410-887-5105
Donna Bergin, prin. Fax 887-5106
Perry Hall MS 1,600/6-8
4300 Ebenezer Rd 21236 410-887-5100
Lisa Perry, prin. Fax 887-5152
Pikesville MS 1,000/6-8
7701 Seven Mile Ln 21208 410-887-1207
Kalisha Miller, prin. Fax 887-1259
Pine Grove ES 500/PK-5
2701 Summit Ave 21234 410-887-5267
Diane Richmond, prin. Fax 887-5268
Pine Grove MS 900/6-8
9200 Old Harford Rd 21234 410-887-5270
Tina Nelson, prin. Fax 668-5237
Pleasant Plains ES 600/PK-6
8300 Pleasant Plains Rd 21286 410-887-3549
Joyce Albert, prin. Fax 887-8088
Powhatan ES 300/PK-5
3300 Kelox Rd 21207 410-887-1330
Deborea Montgomery, prin. Fax 277-0402
Red House Run ES 500/PK-5
1717 Weyburn Rd 21237 410-887-0506
Drue Whitney, prin. Fax 887-0507
Relay ES 500/PK-5
5885 Selford Rd 21227 410-887-1426
Lisa Dingle, prin. Fax 887-1434
Riderwood ES 500/PK-5
1711 Landrake Rd 21204 410-887-3568
Kathy DeHart, prin. Fax 887-4667

Riverview ES 500/PK-5
3298 Kessler Rd 21227 410-887-1428
Mary Maddox, prin. Fax 887-1465
Rodgers Forge ES 400/K-5
250 Dumbarton Rd 21212 410-887-3582
Melissa Fanshaw, prin. Fax 832-5431
Sandalwood ES 600/PK-5
900 S Marlyn Ave 21221 410-887-0174
Mark Bongiovanni, prin. Fax 391-6349
Sandy Plains ES 600/PK-5
8330 Kavanagh Rd 21222 410-887-7070
Kevin Harrington, prin. Fax 887-7107
Scotts Branch ES 600/K-5
8220 Tawnmoore Rd 21244 410-887-0761
Nashae Bennett, prin. Fax 887-0675
Seneca ES 500/PK-5
545 Carrollwood Rd 21220 410-887-5945
Jason Feiler, prin. Fax 887-5946
Seven Oaks ES 400/PK-5
9220 Seven Courts Dr 21236 410-887-6257
Carol Wingard, prin. Fax 256-0379
Shady Spring ES 600/PK-5
8868 Goldenwood Rd 21237 410-887-0509
Kenneth Dunaway, prin. Fax 886-7619
Southwest Academy 800/6-8
6200 Johnnycake Rd 21207 410-887-0825
Karen Barnes, prin. Fax 887-0829
Sparrows Point MS 500/6-8
7400 N Point Rd 21219 410-887-7524
Shannon Washington, prin. Fax 477-6953
Stemmers Run MS 700/6-8
201 Stemmers Run Rd 21221 410-887-0177
Bryan Thanner, prin. Fax 918-1787
Stoneleigh ES 700/PK-5
900 Pemberton Rd 21212 410-887-3600
Heather Hollenbeck, prin. Fax 887-3601
Stricker MS 800/6-8
7855 Trappe Rd 21222 410-887-7038
Brian Wagner, prin. Fax 285-1864
Sudbrook Magnet MS 1,000/6-8
4300 Bedford Rd 21208 410-887-6720
Gordon Webb, prin. Fax 887-6737
Summit Park ES 500/PK-5
6920 Diana Rd 21209 410-887-1210
Karen Gieron, prin. Fax 887-1256
Sussex ES 400/PK-5
515 S Woodward Dr 21221 410-887-0182
Thomas Bowser, prin. Fax 887-0183
Victory Villa ES 400/PK-5
8200 Old Philadelphia Rd 21237 410-809-0184
Margaret Roberts, prin. Fax 809-0185
Villa Cresta ES 700/PK-5
2600 Rader Ave 21234 410-887-5275
Kevin Connelly, prin. Fax 887-5277
Wellwood International S 500/K-5
2901 Smith Ave 21208 410-887-1212
Jodi O'Neill, prin. Fax 887-1213
Westchester ES 600/K-5
2300 Old Frederick Rd 21228 410-887-1088
Phillip Byers, prin. Fax 887-1089
Winand ES 500/PK-5
8301 Scotts Level Rd 21208 410-887-0763
Debita Basu, prin. Fax 887-0730
Windsor Mill MS 500/6-8
8300 Windsor Mill Rd 21244 410-887-0618
Harvey Chambers, prin. Fax 496-1308
Winfield ES 500/K-5
8300 Carlson Ln 21244 410-887-0766
Aricka Porter, prin. Fax 496-3275
Woodbridge ES 500/PK-5
1410 Pleasant Valley Dr 21228 410-887-0857
Lori Phelps, prin. Fax 887-0912
Woodholme ES 900/K-5
300 Mount Wilson Ln 21208 410-887-6700
Teresa Young, prin. Fax 887-6762
Woodlawn MS 600/6-8
3033 Saint Lukes Ln 21207 410-887-1304
Rochelle Archelus, prin. Fax 298-4352
Woodmoor ES 600/PK-5
3200 Elba Dr 21207 410-887-1318
Franchesca Brown, prin. Fax 887-1320

Al-Rahmah S 300/K-12
6631 Johnnycake Rd 21244 410-719-0921
Archbishop Borders S 100/PK-8
3500 Foster Ave 21224 410-276-6534
Alicia Freeman, prin. Fax 276-6915
Arlington Baptist S 200/PK-12
3030 N Rolling Rd 21244 410-655-9300
Johnnie Whitehead, prin. Fax 496-3901
Baltimore Actors' Theatre Conservatory 50/K-12
300 Dumbarton Rd Ste 2 21212 410-337-8519
Dr. Walter Anderson, hdmstr. Fax 337-8582
Baltimore Junior Academy 100/PK-8
3006 W Cold Spring Ln 21215 410-542-6758
Baltimore-White Marsh Adventist S 50/PK-12
7427 Rossville Blvd 21237 410-663-1819
Bethlehem Christian Day S 100/PK-8
4815 Hamilton Ave 21206 410-488-8963
Beth Tfiloh Dahan Community S 900/PK-12
3300 Old Court Rd 21208 410-486-1905
Bnos Yisroel S of Baltimore 400/PK-12
6300 Park Heights Ave 21215 443-524-3200
Boys Latin S of Maryland 600/K-12
822 W Lake Ave 21210 410-377-5192
Christopher Post, hdmstr. Fax 377-4312
Bryn Mawr S 800/PK-12
109 W Melrose Ave 21210 410-323-8800
Sue Sadler, head sch Fax 323-0301
Calvert S 600/K-8
105 Tuscany Rd 21210 410-243-6054
Andrew Holmgren, hdmstr. Fax 243-0249
Cambridge S 200/K-8
110 Sudbrook Ln 21208 410-486-3686
Cardinal Shehan S 400/PK-8
5407 Loch Raven Blvd 21239 410-433-2775
Fametta Jackson, prin. Fax 323-6131
Emmanuel Lutheran S 100/K-8
929 Ingleside Ave 21228 410-744-0015
Susan Miller, prin. Fax 744-1199

First English Lutheran Preschool & K 100/PK-K
3807 N Charles St 21218 410-235-5887
Jenny Barrett, dir. Fax 235-5117
Friends S of Baltimore 1,000/PK-12
5114 N Charles St 21210 410-649-3200
Matthew Micciche, head sch Fax 649-3213
Gilman S 1,000/K-12
5407 Roland Ave 21210 410-323-3800
Henry Smyth, hdmstr. Fax 864-2812
GreenMount S 100/K-8
501 W 30th St 21211 410-235-6295
Liz Baker, head sch Fax 467-6672
Hampden Christian S 50/PK-8
1234 W 36th St 21211 410-338-2889
Reuben Petersheim, dir.
Holy Angels S 200/PK-8
1201 S Caton Ave 21227 443-602-3200
Kathleen Filippelli, prin. Fax 602-3210
Krieger Schechter Day S 400/K-8
8100 Stevenson Rd 21208 410-486-8640
Mother Seton Academy 100/6-8
2215 Greenmount Ave 21218 410-563-2833
Sr. Margaret Juskelis, pres. Fax 563-7354
Mt. Pleasant Christian S 100/PK-5
6000 Radecke Ave 21206 410-325-4827
Brenda Haynes Ph.D., dir. Fax 325-2655
Mt. Zion Baptist Christian S 100/PK-12
2000 E Belvedere Ave 21239 410-426-2309
Our Lady of Hope / St. Luke S 300/PK-8
8003 North Boundary Rd 21222 410-288-2793
Sr. Irene Pryle, prin. Fax 288-2850
Our Lady of Mt. Carmel S 400/PK-8
1702 Old Eastern Ave 21221 410-686-0859
Christine Olszewski, prin. Fax 686-4916
Our Lady of Victory S 400/PK-8
4416 Wilkens Ave 21229 410-242-3688
Lois Gorman, prin. Fax 242-8867
Park S of Baltimore 900/PK-12
2425 Old Court Rd 21208 410-339-7070
Daniel Paradis, head sch Fax 339-4125
Pilgrim Christian Day S 100/PK-5
7200 Liberty Rd 21207 410-484-9240
Sam Pettijohn, prin. Fax 484-6692
Rabbi Benjamin Steinberg MS 300/6-8
6300 Smith Ave 21209 443-548-7700
Rabbi Naftoli Hexter, prin.
Roland Park Country S 700/PK-12
5204 Roland Ave 21210 410-323-5500
Caroline Blatti, head sch Fax 323-2164
Rosedale Baptist S 300/PK-12
9202 Philadelphia Rd 21237 410-687-6844
St. Casimir S 200/PK-8
1035 S Kenwood Ave 21224 410-342-2681
Noreen Heffner, prin. Fax 342-5715
St. Francis of Assisi S 200/PK-8
3617 Harford Rd 21218 410-467-1683
John D'Adamo, prin. Fax 467-9503
St. Ignatius Loyola Academy 100/6-8
300 E Gittings St 21230 410-539-8268
Teresa Scott, prin. Fax 539-4821
St. Joseph S 500/PK-8
8416 Belair Rd 21236 410-256-8026
Ken Pipkin, prin. Fax 529-7234
St. Michael - St. Clement S 200/PK-8
10 Willow Ave 21206 410-668-8797
Paul Kristoff, prin. Fax 663-9277
St. Pius X S 300/PK-8
6432 York Rd 21212 410-427-7400
Jennifer Ripley, prin. Fax 372-0552
St. Ursula S 600/PK-8
8900 Harford Rd 21234 410-665-3533
Deborah Glinowiecki, prin. Fax 661-1620
School of Cathedral of Mary our Queen 500/K-8
111 Amberly Way 21210 410-464-4100
Michael Wright M.Ed., prin. Fax 464-4137
Sisters Academy of Baltimore 100/5-8
139 1st Ave 21227 410-242-1212
Eileen Copple, prin. Fax 242-5104
SS. James & John S 300/PK-8
1012 Somerset St 21202 410-342-3222
LaUanah Cassell, prin. Fax 732-1323
Waldorf S of Baltimore 200/PK-8
4801 Tamarind Rd 21209 410-367-6808
Yeshivas Chofetz Chaim - Talmudical Acad 800/PK-12
4445 Old Court Rd 21208 410-484-6600

Bel Air, Harford, Pop. 9,934
Harford County SD 37,700/PK-12
102 S Hickory Ave 21014 410-838-7300
Barbara Canavan, supt. Fax 893-2478
www.hcps.org
Bel Air ES 500/PK-5
30 E Lee St 21014 410-638-4160
Dr. Dyann Mack, prin. Fax 638-4320
Bel Air MS 1,300/6-8
99 Idlewild St 21014 410-638-4140
Natalie Holloway, prin. Fax 638-4144
Emmorton ES 600/K-5
2502 S Tollgate Rd 21015 410-638-3920
Rebecca Spencer, prin. Fax 638-3926
Fountain Green ES 500/K-5
517 S Fountain Green Rd 21015 410-638-4220
Alison Donnelly, prin. Fax 638-4347
Hickory ES 700/K-5
2100 Conowingo Rd 21014 410-638-4170
R. Bradley Stinar, prin. Fax 638-4172
Homestead/Wakefield ES 900/PK-5
900 S Main St Bldg B 21014 410-638-4175
Christopher Cook, prin. Fax 638-4319
Prospect Mill ES 500/K-5
101 Prospect Mill Rd 21015 410-638-3817
Karen Jankowiak, prin. Fax 638-3816
Red Pump ES 700/K-5
600 Red Pump Rd 21014 410-638-4252
A. Blaine Hawley, prin. Fax 638-4261
Ring Factory ES 600/K-5
1400 Emmorton Rd 21014 410-638-4186
Meridith Dunlap, prin. Fax 638-4318
Southampton MS 1,300/6-8
1200 Moores Mill Rd 21014 410-638-4150
Charles Hagan, prin. Fax 638-4305

Other Schools – See Aberdeen, Abingdon, Belcamp, Churchville, Darlington, Edgewood, Fallston, Forest Hill, Havre de Grace, Jarrettsville, Joppa, Pylesville, Street, White Hall

---

Bridges Montessori S PK-6
2529 Conowingo Rd 21015 410-836-0833
Harford Day S 300/PK-8
715 Moores Mill Rd 21014 410-838-4848
Gray Smith Ed.D., head sch Fax 836-5918
St. Margaret MS 300/6-8
1716 E Churchville Rd Ste A 21015 410-877-9660
Madeleine Hobik, prin. Fax 420-9322
St. Margaret S 500/PK-5
205 N Hickory Ave 21014 410-879-1113
Madeleine Hobik, prin. Fax 838-5879

Belcamp, Harford, Pop. 900
Harford County SD
Supt. — See Bel Air
Church Creek ES 800/PK-5
4299 Church Creek Rd 21017 410-273-5550
Harley Main, prin. Fax 273-5558

Beltsville, Prince George's, Pop. 16,294
Prince George's County SD
Supt. — See Upper Marlboro
Beltsville Academy 1,000/PK-8
4300 Wicomico Ave 20705 301-572-0630
Leslie Lowe, prin. Fax 572-0671
Calverton ES 800/PK-5
3400 Beltsville Rd 20705 301-572-0640
Dr. Monique Lamar Ed.D., prin. Fax 572-0673
Fuchs ECC 400/PK-PK
11011 Cherry Hill Rd 20705 301-572-0600
Diedra Tramel, prin. Fax 572-0602
King MS 700/6-8
4545 Ammendale Rd 20705 301-572-0650
Rotunda Floyd-Cooper, prin. Fax 572-0668
Vansville ES 800/PK-5
6813 Ammendale Way 20705 301-931-2830
Tom Smith, prin. Fax 931-2840

Beltsville Adventist S 200/K-8
4230 Ammendale Rd 20705 301-937-2933
Wendy Pega, prin. Fax 595-2431
St. Joseph S 200/PK-8
11011 Montgomery Rd 20705 301-937-7154
Dr. Janine Bertolotti, prin. Fax 937-1467

Berlin, Worcester, Pop. 4,357
Worcester County SD
Supt. — See Newark
Berlin IS 700/4-6
309 Franklin Ave 21811 410-632-5320
Tom Sites, prin. Fax 632-5329
Buckingham ES 500/PK-4
100 Buckingham Rd 21811 410-632-5300
Karin Marx, prin. Fax 632-5309
Decatur MS 600/7-8
9815 Seahawk Rd 21811 410-632-3401
Lynne Barton, prin. Fax 641-3274
Showell ES 600/PK-3
11318 Showell School Rd 21811 410-632-5350
Diane Shorts, prin. Fax 632-5359

Most Blessed Sacrament Catholic S 300/PK-8
11242 Racetrack Rd 21811 410-208-1600
Mark Record, prin. Fax 208-4957
Worcester Preparatory S 500/PK-12
PO Box 1006 21811 410-641-3575
Dr. Barry Tull, hdmstr. Fax 641-3586

Berwyn Heights, Prince George's, Pop. 3,012
Prince George's County SD
Supt. — See Upper Marlboro
Berwyn Heights ES 500/PK-6
6200 Pontiac St 20740 240-684-6210
Amanda Alerich, prin. Fax 684-6216

Bethesda, Montgomery, Pop. 59,121
Montgomery County SD
Supt. — See Rockville
Ashburton ES 800/PK-5
6314 Lone Oak Dr 20817 240-740-1300
Gregory Mullenholz, prin. Fax 897-2517
Bannockburn ES 400/K-5
6520 Dalroy Ln 20817 240-740-1270
Kate Bradley, prin. Fax 320-6559
Bethesda ES 500/K-5
7600 Arlington Rd 20814 240-204-5300
Lisa Seymour, prin. Fax 657-4973
Bradley Hills ES 600/K-5
8701 Hartsdale Ave 20817 240-204-5210
Karen Caroscio, prin. Fax 571-6969
Burning Tree ES 500/K-5
7900 Beech Tree Rd 20817 240-740-1750
Dr. Judith Lewis, prin. Fax 320-6538
Carderock Springs ES 400/PK-5
7401 Persimmon Tree Ln 20817 240-740-0540
Jae Lee, prin. Fax 469-1115
North Bethesda MS 900/6-8
8935 Bradmoor Dr 20817 240-740-2100
Alton Sumner, prin. Fax 571-3881
Pyle MS 1,400/6-8
6311 Wilson Ln 20817 301-320-6540
Christopher Nardi, prin. Fax 320-6647
Seven Locks ES 400/K-5
9500 Seven Locks Rd 20817 240-740-0940
Dr. James Virga, prin. Fax 469-1041
Wayside ES 500/K-5
5701 Grosvenor Ln 20814 240-740-0240
Donna Michela, prin. Fax 740-2370
Westbrook ES 400/K-5
5110 Allan Ter 20816 240-740-1040
Karen Cox, prin. Fax 320-6615
Westland MS 1,200/6-8
5511 Massachusetts Ave 20816 301-320-6515
Alison Serino, prin. Fax 320-7054
Wood Acres ES 800/K-5
5800 Cromwell Dr 20816 240-740-1120
Marita Sherburne, prin. Fax 320-6536
Wyngate ES 800/K-5
9300 Wadsworth Dr 20817 240-740-1080
Travis Wiebe, prin. Fax 571-3870

Harbor S 100/PK-2
7701 Bradley Blvd 20817 301-365-1100
Dr. Kendra Sun-Alperin, head sch Fax 365-7491
Holton-Arms S 600/3-12
7303 River Rd 20817 301-365-5300
Susanna Jones, hdmstr. Fax 365-6085
Landon S 700/3-12
6101 Wilson Ln 20817 301-320-3200
Jim Neill, hdmstr. Fax 320-2787
Little Flower S 300/PK-8
5601 Massachusetts Ave 20816 301-320-3273
Sr. Rosemaron Rynn, prin. Fax 320-2867
Lone Oak Montessori S 100/PK-6
PO Box 341210 20827 301-469-4888
Mater Dei S 200/1-8
9600 Seven Locks Rd 20817 301-365-2700
William McMurtrie, hdmstr. Fax 365-2710
Norwood S 500/PK-8
8821 River Rd 20817 301-365-2595
Dr. Matthew Gould, hdmstr. Fax 841-4636
Our Lady of Lourdes S 300/PK-8
7500 Pearl St 20814 301-654-5376
Patricia McGann, prin. Fax 654-2568
Primary Day S 100/PK-2
7300 River Rd 20817 301-365-4355
Scott W.C. Lawrence, head sch Fax 469-8611
Rochambeau The French International S 1,100/PK-12
9600 Forest Rd 20814 301-530-8260
Catherine Levy, head sch Fax 564-5779
St. Bartholomew S 200/PK-8
6900 River Rd 20817 301-229-5586
Frank English, prin. Fax 229-8654
St. Jane De Chantel S 500/K-8
9525 Old Georgetown Rd 20814 301-530-1221
Elizabeth Hamilton, prin. Fax 530-1688
Stone Ridge S of the Sacred Heart 700/PK-12
9101 Rockville Pike 20814 301-657-4322
Catherine Karrels, head sch Fax 657-4393
Washington Episcopal S 300/PK-8
5600 Little Falls Pkwy 20816 301-652-7878
Danny Vogelman, head sch Fax 652-7255
Washington Waldorf S 200/PK-12
4800 Sangamore Rd 20816 301-229-6107
Woods Academy 300/PK-8
6801 Greentree Rd 20817 301-365-3080
Joseph Powers, hdmstr. Fax 469-6439

Bladensburg, Prince George's, Pop. 9,010
Prince George's County SD
Supt. — See Upper Marlboro
Bladensburg ES 800/PK-6
4915 Annapolis Rd 20710 301-985-1450
Judith Haughton-Williams, prin. Fax 985-1457
Port Towns ES 1,000/PK-6
4351 58th Ave 20710 301-985-1480
Michelle Marek, prin. Fax 985-1470
Rogers Heights ES 700/PK-6
4301 58th Ave 20710 301-985-1860
Barbara Bottoms, prin. Fax 985-1868

Boonsboro, Washington, Pop. 3,310
Washington County SD
Supt. — See Hagerstown
Boonsboro ES 600/K-5
5 Campus Ave 21713 301-766-8013
Matthew Wagner, prin. Fax 432-4359
Boonsboro MS 800/6-8
1 JH Wade Dr 21713 301-766-8038
Gary Willow, prin. Fax 432-2644
Greenbrier ES 200/K-5
21222 San Mar Rd 21713 301-766-8170
Jennifer Scarberry-Price, prin. Fax 745-3321

Bowie, Prince George's, Pop. 52,916
Prince George's County SD
Supt. — See Upper Marlboro
Chapel Forge ECC 200/PK-PK
12711 Milan Way 20715 301-805-2740
Elyse Hurley, prin. Fax 805-6672
Heather Hills ES 400/2-5
12605 Heming Ln 20716 301-805-2730
Nema Manuel, prin. Fax 805-2733
High Bridge ES 400/K-5
7011 High Bridge Rd 20720 301-805-2690
William Kelly, prin. Fax 805-2693
Kenilworth ES 300/K-5
12520 Kembridge Dr 20715 301-805-6600
Kristie Clark, prin. Fax 805-6605
Northview ES 700/PK-5
3700 Northview Dr 20716 301-218-1520
Jason Simmons, prin. Fax 218-3071
Ogle MS 900/6-8
4111 Chelmont Ln 20715 301-805-2641
Glenise Marshall, prin. Fax 805-6674
Pointer Ridge ES 500/K-5
1110 Parkington Ln 20716 301-390-0220
Dr. Mary Stephenson, prin. Fax 390-0281
Rockledge ES 400/PK-5
7701 Laurel Bowie Rd 20715 301-805-2720
Roger Prince, prin. Fax 805-2718
Tasker MS 900/6-8
4901 Collington Rd 20715 301-805-2660
Kendra Hill, prin. Fax 805-2663
Tulip Grove ES 400/K-5
3501 Moylan Dr 20715 301-805-2680
Jaime Whitfield-Coffen, prin. Fax 805-6689
Whitehall ES 500/K-5
3901 Woodhaven Ln 20715 301-805-1000
Prentice Christian, prin. Fax 805-1006
Yorktown ES 300/K-5
7301 Race Track Rd 20715 301-805-6610
Dr. Taryn Savoy, prin. Fax 805-6626

Belair Baptist Christian Academy 50/PK-12
2801 Belair Dr 20715 301-262-0578
Dr. Gary Kohl, admin. Fax 262-0579
Bowie Montessori Children's House 200/PK-8
5004 Randonstone Ln 20715 301-262-3566
Cornerstone Christian Academy 100/PK-8
16010 Annapolis Rd 20715 301-262-7683
Stephanie Iszard M.Ed., prin. Fax 262-5200
Grace Christian S 300/K-8
7210 Race Track Rd 20715 301-262-0158
Jack Wilson, prin. Fax 262-4156
St. Pius X Regional S 700/PK-8
14710 Annapolis Rd 20715 301-262-0203
Janet Schrom, prin. Fax 805-8875

Bradshaw, Baltimore

St. Stephen S 300/PK-8
8028 Bradshaw Rd 21087 410-592-7617
Mary Patrick, prin. Fax 592-7330

Brandywine, Prince George's, Pop. 6,567
Prince George's County SD
Supt. — See Upper Marlboro
Baden ES 300/PK-6
13601 Baden Westwood Rd 20613 301-888-1188
Antron Huff, prin. Fax 888-2205
Brandywine ES 400/PK-5
14101 Brandywine Rd 20613 301-372-0100
Teri Lee, prin. Fax 372-0729
Gwynn Park MS 500/6-8
8000 Dyson Rd 20613 301-372-0120
Danielle Moore, prin. Fax 372-0119

Brookeville, Montgomery, Pop. 129
Montgomery County SD
Supt. — See Rockville
Greenwood ES 500/K-5
3336 Gold Mine Rd 20833 240-740-3420
Cheryl Bunyan, prin. Fax 924-3296

Brooklandville, Baltimore

St. Paul's S 800/PK-12
PO Box 8100 21022 410-825-4400
David Faus, hdmstr. Fax 427-0390

Brunswick, Frederick, Pop. 5,703
Frederick County SD
Supt. — See Frederick
Brunswick ES 600/PK-5
400 Central Ave 21716 240-236-2900
Justin McConnaughey, prin. Fax 236-2901
Brunswick MS 600/6-8
301 Cummings Dr 21716 240-236-5400
Jay Schill, prin. Fax 236-5401

Bryantown, Charles, Pop. 646
Charles County SD
Supt. — See La Plata
Martin ES 600/PK-5
6315 Olivers Shop Rd 20617 301-274-3182
Robert Opiekun, prin. Fax 274-3765

St. Mary S 200/PK-8
13735 Notre Dame Pl 20617 301-932-6883
Sharon Caniglia, prin. Fax 274-0626

Burtonsville, Montgomery, Pop. 8,050
Montgomery County SD
Supt. — See Rockville
Banneker MS 800/6-8
14800 Perrywood Dr 20866 301-989-5747
Dr. Otis Lee, prin. Fax 879-1032
Burtonsville ES 600/K-5
15516 Old Columbia Pike 20866 301-989-5654
Kimberly Kimber, prin. Fax 989-5707

Resurrection Church Preschool 100/PK-PK
3315 Greencastle Rd 20866 301-236-9529
Susan Quinn, dir. Fax 236-5204

California, Saint Mary's, Pop. 11,416
St. Mary's County SD
Supt. — See Leonardtown
Evergreen ES 700/PK-5
43765 Evergreen Way 20619 301-863-4060
Jamie Jameson, prin. Fax 863-4074

Callaway, Saint Mary's

King's Christian Academy 300/PK-12
20738 Point Lookout Rd 20620 301-994-3080
Kevin Fry, admin. Fax 994-3087

Cambridge, Dorchester, Pop. 12,038
Dorchester County SD 4,800/PK-12
700 Glasgow St 21613 410-228-4747
Dr. Diana Mitchell, supt. Fax 228-1847
dcps.k12.md.us
Choptank ES 400/PK-5
1103 Maces Ln 21613 410-228-4950
Emma Pinkett, prin. Fax 221-1497
Hoyer ECC PK-PK
1405 Glasgow St 21613 410-221-5268
Chareka Harris, admin. Fax 228-0534
Maces Lane MS 500/6-8
1101 Maces Ln 21613 410-228-2111
Dr. Mike Collins, prin. Fax 221-5278
Maple ES 400/PK-5
5225 Egypt Rd 21613 410-228-8577
Dr. Patricia Prosser, prin. Fax 221-6584
Sandy Hill ES 500/PK-5
1503 Glasgow St 21613 410-228-7978
Vaughn Evans, prin. Fax 228-8738
Other Schools – See Church Creek, Hurlock, Secretary, Vienna

Camp Springs, Prince George's, Pop. 18,674

New Chapel Christian Academy 300/PK-6
5601 Old Branch Ave 20748 301-899-0877
St. Philip the Apostle S 300/PK-8
5414 Henderson Way 20746 301-423-4740
Stephen Lamont, prin. Fax 423-4716

Capitol Heights, Prince George's, Pop. 4,271
Prince George's County SD
Supt. — See Upper Marlboro
Bayne ES 400/K-5
7010 Walker Mill Rd 20743 301-499-7020
Erica Bennett, prin. Fax 808-4499
Bradbury Heights ES 500/PK-6
1401 Glacier Ave 20743 301-817-0570
Lynnette Walker, prin. Fax 817-0573
Brooks ES 200/K-6
1301 Brooke Rd 20743 301-817-0480
Anita Stoddard, prin. Fax 817-0481
Capitol Heights ES 200/K-5
601 Suffolk Ave 20743 301-817-0494
Nina Lattimore, prin. Fax 817-0931
Carmody Hills ES 500/PK-5
401 Jadeleaf Ave 20743 301-808-8180
Yolanda Clark, prin. Fax 808-8188
Gray ES 400/PK-6
4949 Addison Rd 20743 301-636-8400
Cheryl Franklin, prin. Fax 636-8409
Hall Academy 500/PK-8
5200 Marlboro Pike 20743 301-817-2933
Darryl Evans, prin. Fax 817-2946
Seat Pleasant ES 300/K-6
6411 G St 20743 301-925-2330
LaChonta Richardson, prin. Fax 925-2337
Walker Mill MS 700/6-8
800 Karen Blvd 20743 301-808-4055
Erin Cribbs, prin. Fax 808-4039
Wheatley ECC 300/PK-PK
8801 Ritchie Dr 20743 301-808-8100
Julie Orgettas, prin. Fax 808-4490

Cascade, Washington
Washington County SD
Supt. — See Hagerstown
Cascade ES 200/K-5
14519 Pennersville Rd 21719 301-766-8066
Denise Kuhna, prin. Fax 241-4037

Catonsville, Baltimore, Pop. 40,573
Baltimore County SD
Supt. — See Towson
Catonsville ES 500/PK-5
106 Bloomsbury Ave 21228 410-809-0800
Linda Miller, prin. Fax 809-1050
Catonsville MS 800/6-8
2301 Edmondson Ave 21228 410-887-0803
Michael Thorne, prin. Fax 887-1036
Westowne ES 600/PK-5
401 Harlem Ln 21228 410-809-0854
John Palmer, prin. Fax 887-0856

St. Agnes S 300/PK-8
603 Saint Agnes Ln, 410-747-4070
Robert Costante, prin. Fax 747-0138
St. Mark S 400/PK-8
26 Melvin Ave 21228 410-744-6560
Stephanie Rattell, prin. Fax 747-3188
St. Paul Lutheran S 200/PK-5
2001 Old Frederick Rd 21228 410-747-1924
Ron Scherch, prin. Fax 747-7248

Cecilton, Cecil, Pop. 652
Cecil County SD
Supt. — See Elkton
Cecilton ES 300/PK-5
251 W Main St 21913 410-275-1000
Meghan Pugh, prin. Fax 275-1271

Centreville, Queen Anne's, Pop. 4,193
Queen Anne's County SD 7,600/PK-12
202 Chesterfield Ave 21617 410-758-2403
Dr. Andrea M. Kane, supt. Fax 758-8200
qacps.schoolwires.net
Centreville ES 500/PK-2
213 Homewood Ave 21617 410-758-1320
Theresa Farnell, prin. Fax 758-4443
Centreville MS 500/6-8
231 Ruthsburg Rd 21617 410-758-0883
Lawrence Dunn, prin. Fax 758-4447
Kennard ES 500/3-5
420 Little Kidwell Ave 21617 410-758-1166
Michelle Carey, prin. Fax 758-3317
Other Schools – See Church Hill, Grasonville, Stevensville, Sudlersville

Chaptico, Saint Mary's
St. Mary's County SD
Supt. — See Leonardtown
Dynard ES 500/PK-5
23510 Bushwood Rd 20621 301-769-4804
Dr. Joseph Beavers, prin. Fax 769-4808

Charlestown, Cecil, Pop. 1,173
Cecil County SD
Supt. — See Elkton
Charlestown ES 200/PK-5
550 Baltimore St 21914 410-996-6240
George Whisner, prin. Fax 996-6242

Chesapeake Beach, Calvert, Pop. 5,608
Calvert County SD
Supt. — See Prince Frederick
Beach ES 600/PK-5
7900 Old Bayside Rd 20732 410-257-1512
Dr. Michael Shisler, prin. Fax 257-0502

Chesapeake City, Cecil, Pop. 671
Cecil County SD
Supt. — See Elkton
Bohemia Manor MS 500/6-8
2757 Augustine Herman Hwy 21915 410-885-2095
Dr. Ann Little, prin. Fax 885-2485
Chesapeake City ES 300/K-5
214 3rd St 21915 410-885-2085
Alan Loman, prin. Fax 885-2644

Chester, Queen Anne's, Pop. 4,091

St. Christopher's Preschool PK-PK
1861 Harbor Dr 21619 410-643-7186
Sandra Romanek, dir. Fax 643-4055

Chestertown, Kent, Pop. 5,140
Kent County SD
Supt. — See Rock Hall
Garnett ES 200/PK-5
320 Calvert St 21620 410-778-6890
Brenda Rose, prin. Fax 778-5707
Kent County MS 400/6-8
402 E Campus Ave 21620 410-778-1771
Mary Helen Spiri, prin. Fax 778-6541

Chester River Adventist S 50/1-8
305 N Kent St 21620 410-778-2193
Tammy Charles, lead tchr.
Kent S 200/PK-8
6788 Wilkins Ln 21620 410-778-4100
Nancy Mugele, head sch Fax 778-7357

Cheverly, Prince George's, Pop. 5,989
Prince George's County SD
Supt. — See Upper Marlboro
Spellman ES 500/PK-6
3324 64th Ave 20785 301-925-1944
Brandi Smith, prin. Fax 925-1951

St. Ambrose S 200/PK-8
6310 Jason St 20785 301-773-0223
Nelson Abreu, prin. Fax 773-9647

Chevy Chase, Montgomery, Pop. 2,759
Montgomery County SD
Supt. — See Rockville
Chevy Chase IS 500/3-6
4015 Rosemary St 20815 301-657-4994
Jody Smith, prin. Fax 657-4980
North Chevy Chase IS 400/3-6
3700 Jones Bridge Rd 20815 240-204-5280
Renee Wallace-Stevens, prin. Fax 951-6658
Rock Creek Forest ES 600/PK-5
8330 Grubb Rd 20815 240-839-3201
Jennifer Lowndes, prin. Fax 839-3257
Somerset ES 500/K-5
5811 Warwick Pl 20815 240-740-1100
Kelly Morris, prin. Fax 657-4907

Concord Hill S 100/PK-3
6050 Wisconsin Ave 20815 301-654-2626
James Carroll, head sch Fax 654-1374
Oneness Family Montessori S 100/PK-12
6701 Wisconsin Ave 20815 301-652-7751
Andrew Kutt, head sch

Childs, Cecil

Mt. Aviat Academy 200/PK-8
399 Childs Rd 21916 410-398-2206
Sr. John Elizabeth Callaghan, prin. Fax 398-8063

Church Creek, Dorchester, Pop. 122
Dorchester County SD
Supt. — See Cambridge
South Dorchester S 200/PK-8
3485 Golden Hill Rd 21622 410-397-3434
Jennifer Ruark, prin. Fax 397-3595

Church Hill, Queen Anne's, Pop. 722
Queen Anne's County SD
Supt. — See Centreville
Church Hill ES 300/PK-5
631 Main St 21623 410-556-6681
Jacquelyn Wilhelm, prin. Fax 556-6508

Churchville, Harford
Harford County SD
Supt. — See Bel Air
Churchville ES 400/K-5
2935 Level Rd 21028 410-638-3800
Audrey Vohs, prin. Fax 638-3834

Clarksburg, Montgomery, Pop. 13,276
Montgomery County SD
Supt. — See Rockville
Clarksburg ES 300/PK-5
13530 Redgrave Pl 20871 301-353-8060
Carl Bencal, prin. Fax 353-0878
Little Bennett ES 1,000/PK-5
23930 Burdette Forest Rd 20871 301-540-5535
Shawn Miller, prin. Fax 540-5792
Rocky Hill MS 1,100/6-8
22401 Brick Haven Way 20871 301-353-8282
Dr. Cynthia Eldridge, prin. Fax 601-3197
Wells MS 6-8
11701 Little Seneca Pkwy 20871 301-284-4800
Barbara Woodward, prin.
Wims ES K-4
12520 Blue Sky Dr 20871 240-406-1670
Sean McGee, prin. Fax 540-8531

Clarksville, Howard
Howard County SD
Supt. — See Ellicott City
Clarksville ES 500/K-5
12041 Clarksville Pike 21029 410-313-7050
Robin Malcotti, prin Fax 313-7054
Clarksville MS 600/6-8
6535 S Trotter Rd 21029 410-313-7057
Joelle Miller, prin. Fax 531-5105
Pointers Run ES 800/PK-5
6600 S Trotter Rd 21029 410-313-7142
Lenore Schiff, prin. Fax 313-7147

St. Louis S 500/PK-8
12500 State Route 108 21029 410-531-6664
Theresa Weiss, prin. Fax 531-6690

Clear Spring, Washington, Pop. 356
Washington County SD
Supt. — See Hagerstown
Clear Spring ES 400/PK-5
12627 Broadfording Rd 21722 301-766-8074
Sharon Palm, prin. Fax 842-3663
Clear Spring MS 400/6-8
12628 Broadfording Rd 21722 301-766-8094
Christine Korbeil, prin. Fax 842-3826

Clinton, Prince George's, Pop. 35,163
Prince George's County SD
Supt. — See Upper Marlboro
Clinton Grove ES 400/PK-5
9420 Temple Hill Rd 20735 301-599-2414
Jamila Mannie, prin. Fax 599-2412
Decatur MS 700/6-8
8200 Pinewood Dr 20735 301-449-4950
Charity Magruder Ed.D., prin. Fax 449-2105
Evans ES 400/PK-5
6720 Old Alexandria Ferry 20735 301-599-2480
Sonya Gaston, prin. Fax 599-2561
Randall ES 400/PK-5
5410 Kirby Rd 20735 301-449-4980
Suzette Brooks-Butler, prin. Fax 449-2124
Waldon Woods ES 500/K-6
10301 Thrift Rd 20735 301-599-2540
Nicole Crumpler, prin. Fax 599-2544

Grace Brethren Christian S 600/PK-12
6501 Surratts Rd 20735 301-868-1600
George Hornickel, dir. Fax 868-9475
St. John the Evangelist S 200/PK-8
8912 Old Branch Ave 20735 301-868-2010
Ann Gillespie, prin. Fax 856-8941
St. Mary S of Piscataway 200/PK-8
13407 Piscataway Rd 20735 301-292-2522
Scott Farren, prin. Fax 292-2534

Cockeysville, Baltimore, Pop. 20,195
Baltimore County SD
Supt. — See Towson
Cockeysville MS 800/6-8
10401 Greenside Dr 21030 410-887-7626
Deborah Magness, prin. Fax 887-7628
Padonia International ES 500/PK-5
9834 Greenside Dr 21030 410-887-7646
Melissa Didonato, prin. Fax 887-7647
Warren ES 400/K-5
900 Bosley Rd 21030 410-887-7665
Jason Barnett, prin. Fax 887-7666

St. Joseph S 300/K-8
105 Church Ln 21030 410 683 0600
Margaret Dates, prin. Fax 628-6814

College Park, Prince George's, Pop. 29,403
Prince George's County SD
Supt. — See Upper Marlboro
Hollywood ES 400/PK-5
9811 49th Ave 20740 301-513-5900
April Lee, prin. Fax 513-5383
Paint Branch ES 400/PK-6
5101 Pierce Ave 20740 301-513-5300
Emmett Hendershot, prin. Fax 513-5303

Al-Huda S 500/PK-12
5301 Edgewood Rd 20740 301-982-2402
Friends Community S 200/K-8
5901 Westchester Park Dr 20740 301-441-2100
Larry Clements, head sch Fax 441-2105
Holy Redeemer S 300/PK-8
4902 Berwyn Rd 20740 301-474-3993
Maria Bovich, prin. Fax 441-8137

Columbia, Howard, Pop. 95,623
Howard County SD
Supt. — See Ellicott City
Atholton ES 400/K-5
6700 Seneca Dr 21046 410-313-6853
Shawna Holden, prin. Fax 313-7410
Bryant Woods ES 300/K-5
5450 Blue Heron Ln 21044 410-313-6859
Kelley Hough, prin. Fax 313-6864
Clemens Crossing ES 500/K-5
10320 Quarterstaff Rd 21044 410-313-6866
Ed Cosentino, prin. Fax 313-6869
Cradlerock ES 500/PK-5
6700 Cradlerock Way 21045 410-313-7610
Jason McCoy, prin. Fax 313-7634
Guilford ES 500/K-5
7335 Oakland Mills Rd 21046 410-880-5930
Jonathan Davis, prin. Fax 880-5935
Harper's Choice MS 500/6-8
5450 Beaverkill Rd 21044 410-313-6929
Adam Eldridge, prin. Fax 313-5612
Jeffers Hill ES 400/K-5
6001 Tamar Dr 21045 410-313-6872
Patricia Schifflett, prin. Fax 313-6875
Lake Elkhorn MS 500/6-8
6680 Cradlerock Way 21045 410-313-7600
Martin Vandenberge, prin. Fax 313-7633
Longfellow ES 400/K-5
5470 Hesperus Dr 21044 410-313-6879
Laurel Marsh, prin. Fax 313-7106
Oakland Mills MS 400/6-8
9540 Kilimanjaro Rd 21045 410-313-6937
Katherine Orlando, prin. Fax 313-7447
Phelps Luck ES 500/K-5
5370 Old Stone Ct 21045 410-313-6886
Michelle Leader, prin. Fax 313-6889

Running Brook ES 500/PK-5
5215 W Running Brook Rd 21044 410-313-6893
Troy Todd, prin. Fax 313-6898
Steven's Forest ES 400/K-5
6045 Stevens Forest Rd 21045 410-313-6900
Ernesto Diaz, prin. Fax 313-6903
Swansfield ES 600/K-5
5610 Cedar Ln 21044 410-313-6907
Maisha Strong, prin. Fax 313-6910
Talbott Springs ES 400/K-5
9550 Basket Ring Rd 21045 410-313-6915
Nancy Thompson, prin. Fax 313-6921
Thunder Hill ES 500/K-5
9357 Mellenbrook Rd 21045 410-313-6922
Martha Bowen, prin. Fax 313-6926
Waterloo ES 600/PK-5
5940 Waterloo Rd 21045 410-313-5014
Sean Martin, prin. Fax 313-5017
Wilde Lake MS 500/6-8
10481 Cross Fox Ln 21044 410-313-6957
Anne Swartz, prin. Fax 313-6963

Atholton Adventist Academy 200/PK-10
6520 Martin Rd 21044 410-740-2425
Celebration Christian Academy 50/PK-5
6080 Foreland Garth 21045 410-997-2384
Robin Davis, prin. Fax 997-1954
Children's Manor Montessori S 50/PK-K
9008 Red Branch Rd 21045 410-730-3100
Columbia Academy 200/PK-8
10350 Old Columbia Rd 21046 410-312-7413
Gan Israel Hebrew S 50/PK-1
770 Howes Ln 21044 410-740-2424
Love of Learning Montessori S 100/PK-3
9151 Rumsey Rd 21045 410-715-9600

Conowingo, Cecil
Cecil County SD
Supt. — See Elkton
Conowingo ES 500/PK-5
471 Rowlandsville Rd 21918 410-996-6040
Catherine Kelly-Riser, prin. Fax 996-6059

Cordova, Talbot, Pop. 554
Talbot County SD
Supt. — See Easton
Chapel District ES 400/PK-5
11430 Cordova Rd 21625 410-822-2391
Laura Griffith, prin. Fax 822-2039

Crellin, Garrett
Garrett County SD
Supt. — See Oakland
Crellin ES 100/PK-5
115 Kendall Dr 21550 301-334-4704
Dr. Dana McCauley, prin. Fax 334-4704

Cresaptown, Allegany, Pop. 4,546
Allegany County SD
Supt. — See Cumberland
Cresaptown ES 300/PK-5
13202 Sixth Ave 21502 301-729-0212
Scott Llewellyn, prin. Fax 729-1264

Crisfield, Somerset, Pop. 2,671
Somerset County SD
Supt. — See Westover
Woodson ES 600/PK-5
281A Woodson School Rd 21817 410-968-1295
Kirstin Gibson, prin. Fax 968-1420

Crofton, Anne Arundel, Pop. 26,494
Anne Arundel County SD
Supt. — See Annapolis
Crofton ES 600/K-5
1405 Duke of Kent Dr 21114 410-222-5800
Jazmin Lawhorn, prin. Fax 222-5802
Crofton Meadows ES 400/K-5
2020 Tilghman Dr 21114 410-721-9453
Julie Little-McVearry, prin. Fax 721-5821
Crofton Woods ES 600/K-5
1750 Urby Dr 21114 410-222-5805
Lynn Birus, prin. Fax 451-3021
Nantucket ES 800/K-5
2350 Nantucket Dr 21114 410-451-6120
Alexis McKay, prin. Fax 451-6145

Crownsville, Anne Arundel, Pop. 1,733
Anne Arundel County SD
Supt. — See Annapolis
South Shore ES 300/K-5
1376 Fairfield Loop Rd 21032 410-222-3865
Stacy Shafran, prin. Fax 923-6730

Indian Creek Lower S 400/PK-6
680 Evergreen Rd 21032 410-923-3660
Richard Branson Ed.D., head sch Fax 923-0670

Cumberland, Allegany, Pop. 20,280
Allegany County SD 8,600/PK-12
PO Box 1724 21501 301-759-2000
Dr. David Cox Ed.D., supt. Fax 759-2029
www.acpsmd.org
Bel Air ES 200/PK-5
14401 Barton Blvd SW 21502 301-729-2992
Autumn Eirich, prin. Fax 729-5024
Braddock MS 600/6-8
909 Holland St 21502 301-777-7990
Danny Carter, prin. Fax 777-9741
Humbird ES 300/PK-5
120 E Mary St 21502 301-724-8842
Heather Morgan, prin. Fax 759-4506
Northeast ES 300/PK-5
11001 Forest Ave NE 21502 301-724-3285
Dan Clark, prin. Fax 724-7308
South Penn ES 500/PK-5
500 E Second St 21502 301-777-1755
Scott Sisler, prin. Fax 777-1334
Washington MS 700/6-8
200 N Massachusetts Ave 21502 301-777-5360
Kendra Kenney, prin. Fax 777-8452

West Side ES 400/PK-5
425 Paca St 21502 301-724-0340
Dr. Molly Stewart, prin. Fax 724-1651
Other Schools – See Cresaptown, Flintstone, Frostburg, LaVale, Lonaconing, Mount Savage, Westernport

---

Beginnings Montessori S 50/PK-6
16 Howard St 21502 301-722-2220
Bishop Walsh S 400/PK-12
700 Bishop Walsh Rd 21502 301-724-5360
Raymond Kiddy, prin. Fax 722-0555
Calvary Christian Academy 300/PK-12
14517 McMullen Hwy SW 21502 301-729-0791
Daniel Thompson, admin. Fax 729-1648
Lighthouse Christian Academy 100/PK-12
2020 Bedford St 21502 301-777-7375

Damascus, Montgomery, Pop. 14,848
Montgomery County SD
Supt. — See Rockville
Baker MS 500/7-8
25400 Oak Dr 20872 240-207-2440
Dr. Louise Worthington, prin. Fax 253-7020
Clearspring ES 600/PK-5
9930 Moyer Rd 20872 240-740-2580
Holly Gilbertson, prin. Fax 253-2068
Damascus ES 300/K-5
10201 Bethesda Church Rd 20872 301-253-7080
William Collins, prin. Fax 253-8717
Rockwell ES 400/PK-5
24555 Cutsail Dr 20872 301-253-7088
Cheryl Ann Clark, prin. Fax 253-7084

Darlington, Harford, Pop. 406
Harford County SD
Supt. — See Bel Air
Darlington ES 100/K-5
2119 Shuresville Rd 21034 410-638-3700
Alberta Porter, prin. Fax 638-3701

Harford Christian S 400/PK-12
PO Box 88 21034 410-457-5103

Darnestown, Montgomery, Pop. 6,599

Mary of Nazareth S 500/PK-8
14131 Seneca Rd 20874 301-869-0940
Michael Friel, prin. Fax 869-0942

Davidsonville, Anne Arundel
Anne Arundel County SD
Supt. — See Annapolis
Davidsonville ES 700/K-5
962 W Central Ave 21035 410-222-1655
Colleen Harris, prin. Fax 222-1682

Dayton, Howard
Howard County SD
Supt. — See Ellicott City
Dayton Oaks ES 600/PK-5
4691 Ten Oaks Rd 21036 410-313-1571
Carol DeBord, prin. Fax 313-1572

Deale, Anne Arundel, Pop. 4,872
Anne Arundel County SD
Supt. — See Annapolis
Deale ES 300/K-5
759 Masons Beach Rd 20751 410-222-1695
John Barzal, prin. Fax 222-1696

Deal Island, Somerset, Pop. 465
Somerset County SD
Supt. — See Westover
Deal Island ES 100/PK-5
23275 Lola Wheatley Rd 21821 410-784-2449
Ted Gibson, prin. Fax 784-2411

Delmar, Wicomico, Pop. 2,915
Wicomico County SD
Supt. — See Salisbury
Delmar ES 800/PK-5
811 S 2nd St 21875 410-677-5178
Judy Nicholson, prin. Fax 677-5184

Denton, Caroline, Pop. 4,304
Caroline County SD 5,500/PK-12
204 Franklin St 21629 410-479-1460
Dr. Patricia Saelens, supt. Fax 479-0108
www.cl.k12.md.us
Denton ES 600/PK-5
303 Sharp Rd 21629 410-479-1660
Roger Banko, prin. Fax 479-4220
Lockerman MS 800/6-8
410 Lockerman St 21629 410-479-2760
Nicole VonDenBosch, prin. Fax 479-3594
Other Schools – See Federalsburg, Greensboro, Preston, Ridgely

Derwood, Montgomery, Pop. 2,283
Montgomery County SD
Supt. — See Rockville
Sequoyah ES 400/K-5
17301 Bowie Mill Rd 20855 301-840-5335
Dr. Barbara Jasper, prin. Fax 840-5356

Dickerson, Montgomery
Montgomery County SD
Supt. — See Rockville
Monocacy ES 200/K-5
18801 Barnesville Rd 20842 301-972-7990
Kristin Alban, prin. Fax 972-7995

Barnesville S of Arts & Sciences 200/PK-8
21830 Peach Tree Rd 20842 301-972-0341
Susanne Johnson, head sch Fax 972-4076

District Heights, Prince George's, Pop. 5,730
Prince George's County SD
Supt. — See Upper Marlboro
Concord ES 300/PK-6
2004 Concord Ln 20747 301-817-0488
Dana Doggett, prin. Fax 817-0922

District Heights ES 400/PK-5
2200 County Rd 20747 301-817-0484
Marlowe Blount-Rich, prin. Fax 817-0561
Key ES 600/PK-5
2301 Scott Key Dr 20747 301-817-7970
Judie Strawbridge, prin. Fax 817-7979

Easton, Talbot, Pop. 15,604
Talbot County SD 4,600/PK-12
PO Box 1029 21601 410-822-0330
Dr. Kelly Griffith, supt. Fax 820-4260
www.tcps.k12.md.us/
Easton ES - Dobson 500/PK-1
305 Glenwood Ave 21601 410-822-0550
Lisa Kline, prin. Fax 822-9508
Easton ES - Moton 600/2-5
307 Glenwood Ave 21601 410-822-0686
James Redman, prin. Fax 822-1890
Easton MS 800/6-8
201 Peach Blossom Ln 21601 410-822-2910
Norby Lee, prin. Fax 822-7210
Other Schools – See Cordova, Saint Michaels, Tilghman, Trappe

---

Country S 300/K-8
716 Goldsborough St 21601 410-822-1935
Neil Mufson, hdmstr. Fax 822-1971
SS. Peter & Paul S 400/PK-8
900 High St 21601 410-822-2251
Dr. Faye Schilling, prin. Fax 820-0136

Edgewater, Anne Arundel, Pop. 8,834
Anne Arundel County SD
Supt. — See Annapolis
Central ES 700/K-5
130 Stepney Ln 21037 410-222-1075
Kirk Greubel, prin. Fax 222-1078
Central MS 1,000/6-8
221 Central Ave E 21037 410-956-5800
Mildred Beall, prin. Fax 956-1266
Edgewater ES 500/K-5
121 Washington Rd 21037 410-222-1660
Kellie Schell-Ramey, prin. Fax 222-1663
Mayo ES 300/K-5
1260 Mayo Ridge Rd 21037 410-222-1666
Kathleen Fitzgerald, prin. Fax 956-0070

St. Andrew's UM Day S 300/PK-8
4B Wallace Manor Rd 21037 410-266-0952
Mark Wagner, head sch Fax 266-0986

Edgewood, Harford, Pop. 24,585
Harford County SD
Supt. — See Bel Air
Deerfield ES 800/PK-5
2307 Willoughby Beach Rd 21040 410-612-1535
Gregory Lane, prin. Fax 612-1573
Edgewood ES 400/PK-5
2100 Cedar Dr 21040 410-612-1540
Cynthia Womack-Ross, prin. Fax 612-2013
Edgewood MS 1,100/6-8
2311 Willoughby Beach Rd 21040 410-612-1518
Melissa Mickey, prin. Fax 612-1523

Eldersburg, Carroll, Pop. 30,093

St. Stephen's Classical Christian Acad 100/PK-8
2275 Liberty Rd 21784 410-795-1249
John Dykes, hdmstr. Fax 795-8820

Elkridge, Howard, Pop. 15,025
Howard County SD
Supt. — See Ellicott City
Deep Run ES 700/PK-5
6925 Old Waterloo Rd 21075 410-313-5000
Denise Lancaster, prin. Fax 313-5005
Ducketts Lane ES 600/K-5
6501 Ducketts Ln 21075 410-313-5050
Heidi Balter, prin. Fax 313-4580
Elkridge ES 800/K-5
7075 Montgomery Rd 21075 410-313-5006
Michael Caldwell, prin. Fax 313-5074
Elkridge Landing MS 700/6-8
7085 Montgomery Rd 21075 410-313-5040
Gina Cash, prin. Fax 313-5045
Mayfield Woods MS 800/6-8
7950 Red Barn Way 21075 410-313-5022
Melissa Shindel, prin. Fax 313-5029
Rockburn ES 700/PK-5
6145 Montgomery Rd 21075 410-313-5030
Lauren Bauer, prin. Fax 313-5036

St. Augustine S 300/PK-8
5990 Old Washington Rd 21075 410-796-3040
Denise Ball, prin. Fax 579-1165
Tarbiyah Academy K-6
6785 Business Pkwy 21075 844-827-2492
Rasha El-Haggan, head sch Fax 724-2234

Elkton, Cecil, Pop. 14,914
Cecil County SD 15,300/PK-12
201 Booth St 21921 410-996-5400
D'Ette Devine Ed.D., supt. Fax 996-5454
www.ccps.org
Cecil Manor ES 500/PK-5
971 Elk Mills Rd 21921 410-996-5090
Anthony Petinga, prin. Fax 996-5647
Cherry Hill MS 500/6-8
2535 Singerly Rd 21921 410-996-5020
Joseph Harbert, prin. Fax 996-5435
Elk Neck ES 400/K-5
41 Racine School Rd 21921 410-996-5030
Karen Adair, prin. Fax 996-5648
Elkton MS 600/6-8
615 North St 21921 410-996-5010
Megan Frunzi, prin. Fax 996-5639
Gilpin Manor ES 500/PK-5
203 Newark Ave 21921 410-996-5040
Kecia Nesmith, prin. Fax 996-5412

Holly Hall ES 600/PK-5
233 Whitehall Rd 21921 410-996-5050
Regina Roberts, prin. Fax 996-5408
Kenmore ES 300/K-5
2475 Singerly Rd 21921 410-996-5060
Joshua Mangold, prin. Fax 996-5467
Leeds ES 400/PK-5
615 Deaver Rd 21921 410-996-5070
Nikole MacDowell, prin. Fax 996-5290
Thomson Estates ES 500/PK-5
203 E Thomson Dr 21921 410-996-5080
Matthew Stephen, prin. Fax 996-5272
Other Schools – See Cecilton, Charlestown, Chesapeake City, Conowingo, North East, Perryville, Port Deposit, Rising Sun

---

Immaculate Conception S 300/PK-8
452 Bow St 21921 410-398-2636
Jeanne Dinkle, prin. Fax 398-1190
Tri-State Christian Academy 300/PK-12
146 Appleton Rd 21921 410-398-6444
Keith Wilson, head sch Fax 688-4847

Ellicott City, Howard, Pop. 64,049
Howard County SD 52,300/PK-12
10910 Clarksville Pike 21042 410-313-6600
Dr. Renee Foose, supt. Fax 313-6674
www.hcpss.org
Bellows Spring ES 600/K-5
8125 Old Stockbridge Dr 21043 410-313-5057
Carol Hahn, prin. Fax 313-5060
Bonnie Branch MS 700/6-8
4979 Ilchester Rd 21043 410-313-2580
Cherolyn Jones, prin. Fax 313-2586
Burleigh Manor MS 700/6-8
4200 Centennial Ln 21042 410-313-2507
Antoinette Roberson, prin. Fax 313-2513
Centennial Lane ES 700/K-5
3825 Centennial Ln 21042 410-313-2800
Amanda Wadsworth, prin. Fax 313-2804
Dunloggin MS 600/6-8
9129 Northfield Rd 21042 410-313-2831
Jeffrey Fink, prin. Fax 313-2530
Ellicott Mills MS 800/6-8
4445 Montgomery Rd 21043 410-313-2839
Christopher Rattay, prin. Fax 313-2845
Folly Quarter MS 500/6-8
13500 Triadelphia Rd 21042 410-313-1506
Scott Conroy, prin. Fax 313-1509
Hollifield Station ES 700/PK-5
8701 Stonehouse Dr 21043 410-313-2550
Lisa Booth, prin. Fax 313-2557
Ilchester ES 800/PK-5
4981 Ilchester Rd 21043 410-313-2524
Joy Byrd-Butler, prin. Fax 313-2527
Manor Woods ES 700/K-5
11575 Frederick Rd 21042 410-313-7165
James Weisner, prin. Fax 313-7170
Northfield ES 700/K-5
9125 Northfield Rd 21042 410-313-2806
Tiffany Tresler, prin. Fax 313-2810
Patapsco MS 600/6-8
8885 Old Frederick Rd 21043 410-313-2848
Cynthia Dillon, prin. Fax 313-2852
St. John's Lane ES 700/K-5
2960 Saint Johns Ln 21042 410-313-2813
Vicky Sarro, prin. Fax 313-2817
Triadelphia Ridge ES 500/K-5
13400 Triadelphia Rd 21042 410-313-2560
Lisa Smithson, prin. Fax 313-2566
Veterans ES 800/K-5
4355 Montgomery Rd 21043 410-313-1700
Robert Bruce, prin. Fax 313-1709
Waverly ES 800/PK-5
10220 Wetherburn Rd 21042 410-313-2819
Kathy Jacobs, prin. Fax 313-2824
Worthington ES 500/K-5
4570 Roundhill Rd 21043 410-313-2825
Kelli Jenkins, prin. Fax 313-2829
Other Schools – See Clarksville, Columbia, Dayton, Elkridge, Fulton, Glenwood, Hanover, Jessup, Laurel, Marriottsville, West Friendship, Woodbine

---

Children's Manor Montessori S 200/PK-5
4465 Montgomery Rd 21043 410-461-6070
Glenelg Country S 800/PK-12
12793 Folly Quarter Rd 21042 410-531-8600
Gregory Ventre, head sch Fax 531-7363
Our Lady of Perpetual Help S 200/PK-8
4801 Ilchester Rd 21043 410-744-4251
Victor Pellechia, prin. Fax 788-5210
Resurrection / St. Paul S 500/PK-8
3155 Paulskirk Dr 21042 410-461-9111
Karen Murphy, prin. Fax 461-8621
St. John's Parish Day S 300/PK-5
9130 Frederick Rd 21042 410-465-7644
Dr. Chip Prehn, head sch Fax 465-7748
Trinity S 400/PK-8
4985 Ilchester Rd 21043 410-744-1524
Sr. Catherine Phelps, prin. Fax 744-3617

Emmitsburg, Frederick, Pop. 2,774
Frederick County SD
Supt. — See Frederick
Emmitsburg ES 300/PK-5
300 S Seton Ave 21727 240-236-1750
Mary Ann Wiles, prin. Fax 236-1751

Mother Seton S 300/PK-8
100 Creamery Rd 21727 301-447-3161
Sr. Brenda Monahan, prin. Fax 447-3914

Essex, Baltimore, Pop. 38,225

St. Stephens Christian Academy 50/PK-3
1525 Old Eastern Ave 21221 410-772-3447
Rev. William Gray, head sch Fax 780-0393

Ewell, Somerset
Somerset County SD
Supt. — See Westover
Ewell ES 50/PK-7
4005 Smith Island Rd 21824 410-968-0534
Janet Evans, lead tchr. Fax 968-0280

Fallston, Harford, Pop. 8,862
Harford County SD
Supt. — See Bel Air
Fallston MS 900/6-8
2303 Carrs Mill Rd 21047 410-638-4129
Dr. Anthony Bess, prin. Fax 638-4237
Youths Benefit ES 1,000/K-5
1901 Fallston Rd 21047 410-638-4190
Thomas Smith, prin. Fax 638-4193

Federalsburg, Caroline, Pop. 2,672
Caroline County SD
Supt. — See Denton
Federalsburg ES 500/PK-5
302 S University Ave 21632 410-754-5344
Dr. Yolanda Holloway, prin. Fax 754-5504
Richardson MS 400/6-8
25390 Richardson Rd 21632 410-754-5263
Robert Willoughby, prin. Fax 754-5695

Finksburg, Carroll
Carroll County SD
Supt. — See Westminster
Sandymount ES 400/K-5
2222 Old Westminster Pike 21048 410-751-3215
Shakira Murphy, prin. Fax 751-3925

Gerstell Academy 300/PK-12
2500 Old Westminster Pike 21048 410-861-3000
John Polasko, pres. Fax 861-3006

Flintstone, Allegany, Pop. 177
Allegany County SD
Supt. — See Cumberland
Flintstone ES 200/PK-5
22000 National Pike NE 21530 301-478-2434
Sharon Morgan, prin. Fax 777-0612

Forest Hill, Harford
Harford County SD
Supt. — See Bel Air
Forest Hill ES 500/PK-5
2407 Rocks Rd 21050 410-638-4166
Marc Hamilton, prin. Fax 638-4234
Forest Lakes ES 500/K-5
100 Osborne Pkwy 21050 410-638-4262
Victoria Elliott, prin. Fax 638-4265

Forestville, Prince George's, Pop. 12,138
Prince George's County SD
Supt. — See Upper Marlboro
Jackson Academy 600/K-8
3500 Regency Pkwy 20747 301-817-0310
Veonca Richardson, prin. Fax 817-0339
Longfields ES 400/PK-6
3300 Newkirk Ave 20747 301-817-0455
Carmen Bell, prin. Fax 817-0934
Massie Academy 700/PK-8
3301 Regency Pkwy 20747 301-669-1120
Michelle Pegram, prin. Fax 669-6536
North Forestville ES 300/PK-6
2311 Ritchie Rd 20747 301-499-7098
Falecia McMillian, prin. Fax 808-4488

Fort Meade, Anne Arundel, Pop. 8,776
Anne Arundel County SD
Supt. — See Annapolis
MacArthur MS 1,000/6-8
3500 Rockenbach Rd 20755 410-674-0032
Eugene Whiting, prin. Fax 674-8021
Manor View ES 300/K-5
2900 MacArthur Rd 20755 410-222-6504
Barry Gruber, prin. Fax 222-6513
Meade Heights ES 300/PK-5
1925 Reece Rd 20755 410-222-6509
Tiffany Foster, prin. Fax 519-1277
Meade MS 700/6-8
1103 26th St 20755 410-674-2355
Christine DeGuzman, prin. Fax 674-6590
Pershing Hill ES 600/1-5
7600 29th Division Rd 20755 410-222-6519
Christopher Wooleyhand, prin. Fax 222-6527
West Meade Early Education Center 300/PK-K
7722 Ray St 20755 410-222-6545
Carole Janesko, prin. Fax 222-6518

Fort Washington, Prince George's, Pop. 23,030
Prince George's County SD
Supt. — See Upper Marlboro
Apple Grove ES 500/PK-6
7400 Bellefield Ave 20744 301-449-4966
Beth Linn, prin. Fax 449-2106
Avalon ES 400/PK-6
7302 Webster Ln 20744 301-449-4970
Veda McCoy, prin. Fax 449-2114
Dent ES 200/PK-6
2700 Corning Ave 20744 301-702-3850
Yolanda Coleman, prin. Fax 702-7574
Fort Foote ES 300/PK-6
8300 Oxon Hill Rd 20744 301-749-4230
Marilyn Goldsmith, prin. Fax 749-4236
Ft. Washington Forest ES 200/PK-5
1300 Fillmore Rd 20744 301-203-1123
Mark Dennison, prin. Fax 203-1129
Gourdine MS 500/6-8
8700 Allentown Rd 20744 301-449-4940
Leatriz Covington, prin. Fax 449-4948
Indian Queen ES 300/PK-6
9551 Fort Foote Rd 20744 301-749-4250
Aundrea McCall, prin. Fax 749-4252
Oxon Hill MS 600/6-8
9570 Fort Foote Rd 20744 301-749-4270
Wendell Coleman, prin. Fax 749-4286

Potomac Landing ES 400/K-5
12500 Fort Washington Rd 20744 301-203-1114
Kimberly Corprew, prin. Fax 203-3226
Rose Valley ES 400/K-5
9800 Jacqueline Dr 20744 301-449-4990
LaTonya Williams, prin. Fax 449-4766
Tayac ES 400/PK-5
8600 Allentown Rd 20744 301-449-4840
Dr. Saundra Mayo-Carr, prin. Fax 449-4785

National Christian Academy 300/PK-12
6700 Bock Rd 20744 301-567-9507
Andrew Stewart, prin. Fax 567-7332

Frederick, Frederick, Pop. 63,120
Frederick County SD 40,400/PK-12
191 S East St 21701 301-696-6820
Dr. Theresa Alban, supt. Fax 696-6823
www.fcps.org
Ballenger Creek ES 700/PK-5
5250 Kingsbrook Dr 21703 240-236-2500
Kristen Canning, prin. Fax 236-2501
Ballenger Creek MS 700/6-8
5525 Ballenger Creek Pike 21703 240-236-5700
Jeneen Stewart, prin. Fax 236-5701
Centerville ES 900/K-5
3601 Carriage Hill Dr 21704 240-566-0100
Tracy Hilliard, prin. Fax 566-0101
Crestwood MS 600/6-8
7100 Foxcroft Dr 21703 240-566-9000
Neal Case, prin. Fax 566-9001
Hillcrest ES 1,000/PK-5
1285 Hillcrest Dr 21703 240-236-3200
Kimberly Seiss, prin. Fax 236-3201
Johnson MS 500/6-8
1799 Schifferstadt Blvd 21701 240-236-4900
Maggie Gilgallon, prin. Fax 236-4901
Lincoln ES 500/PK-5
200 Madison St 21701 240-236-2650
Kathryn Golightly, prin. Fax 236-2651
Monocacy ES 600/PK-5
7421 Hayward Rd 21702 240-236-1400
Troy Barnes, prin. Fax 236-1401
Monocacy MS 800/6-8
8009 Opossumtown Pike 21702 240-236-4700
Dr. Stephanie Ware, prin. Fax 236-4701
North Frederick ES 600/PK-5
1010 Fairview Ave 21701 240-236-2000
DeVeda Cooley, prin. Fax 236-2001
Orchard Grove ES 600/PK-5
5898 Hannover Dr 21703 240-236-2400
Shirley Olsen, prin. Fax 236-2401
Parkway ES 200/K-5
300 Carroll Pkwy 21701 240-236-2600
Stephanie Brown, prin. Fax 236-2601
Spring Ridge ES 500/PK-5
9051 Ridgefield Dr 21701 240-236-1600
Pattie Barnes, prin. Fax 236-1601
Tuscarora ES 800/K-5
6321 Lambert Ct 21703 240-566-0000
Kimberly Mazaleski, prin. Fax 566-0001
Urbana ES 700/K-5
3554 Urbana Pike 21704 240-236-2200
Tess Blumenthal, prin. Fax 236-2201
Waverley ES 600/PK-5
201 Waverley Dr 21702 240-236-3900
Jan Hollenbeck, prin. Fax 236-3901
West Frederick MS 800/6-8
515 W Patrick St 21701 240-236-4000
Frank Vetter, prin. Fax 236-4050
Whittier ES 700/K-5
2400 Whittier Dr 21702 240-236-3100
Amy Schwiegerath, prin. Fax 236-3101
Yellow Springs ES 500/K-5
8717 Yellow Springs Rd 21702 240-236-1700
Jana Strohmeyer, prin. Fax 236-1701
Other Schools – See Adamstown, Brunswick, Emmitsburg, Ijamsville, Jefferson, Keymar, Libertytown, Middletown, Monrovia, Mount Airy, Myersville, New Market, Sabillasville, Thurmont, Walkersville, Woodsboro

---

Banner S 200/PK-8
1730 N Market St 21701 301-695-9320
Frederick Adventist Academy 100/PK-8
6437 Jefferson Pike 21703 301-663-0363
New Life Christian S 200/PK-12
5909 Jefferson Pike 21703 301-663-8418
Kristi Mitchell, prin. Fax 698-1583
St. John Regional Catholic S 600/PK-8
8414 Opossumtown Pike 21702 301-662-6722
Karen Smith, prin. Fax 695-7024
Trinity S of Frederick 100/K-8
6040 New Design Rd 21703 301-228-2333
Warner James, head sch Fax 228-2687

Freeland, Baltimore
Baltimore County SD
Supt. — See Towson
Prettyboy ES 400/PK-5
19810 Middletown Rd 21053 410-887-1900
Nicole Norris, prin. Fax 887-1901

Friendsville, Garrett, Pop. 491
Garrett County SD
Supt. — See Oakland
Friendsville ES 100/PK-5
841 1st Ave 21531 301-746-5100
Ed Wildesen, prin. Fax 746 5065

Frostburg, Allegany, Pop. 8,847
Allegany County SD
Supt. — See Cumberland
Beall ES 500/PK-5
3 E College Ave 21532 301-689-3636
Robert Stevenson, prin. Fax 689-8006
Frost ES 200/PK-5
260 Shaw St 21532 301-689-5168
Kim Smith, prin. Fax 689-1735

Garrett County SD
Supt. — See Oakland
Route 40 ES 100/PK-5
17764 National Pike 21532 301-689-6132
Candy Maust, prin. Fax 687-0261

Fruitland, Wicomico, Pop. 4,731
Wicomico County SD
Supt. — See Salisbury
Bennett MS 900/6-8
532 S Division St 21826 410-677-5140
Liza Hastings, prin. Fax 677-5133
Fruitland IS 400/3-5
208 W Main St 21826 410-677-5805
Jon Shearer, prin. Fax 677-5890
Fruitland PS 500/PK-2
301 N Division St 21826 410-677-5171
Dave Harris, prin. Fax 677-5176

Fulton, Howard, Pop. 1,957
Howard County SD
Supt. — See Ellicott City
Fulton ES 700/PK-5
11600 Scaggsville Rd 20759 410-880-5957
Sharon Lewandowski, prin. Fax 880-5969
Lime Kiln MS 600/6-8
11650 Scaggsville Rd 20759 410-880-5988
Lucy Lublin, prin. Fax 880-5996

Gaithersburg, Montgomery, Pop. 57,995
Montgomery County SD
Supt. — See Rockville
Brown Station ES 500/PK-5
18100 Washington Grove Ln 20877 240-740-0260
Mary Jo Powell, prin. Fax 740-2360
Carson ES 1,000/PK-5
100 Tschiffely Square Rd 20878 240-740-1840
Deneise Hammond, prin. Fax 740-1846
Darnestown ES 300/PK-5
15030 Turkey Foot Rd 20878 301-284-4260
Mark Craemer, prin. Fax 548-7527
Diamond ES 600/K-5
4 Marquis Dr 20878 240-740-2120
Dan Walder, prin. Fax 840-4506
DuFief ES 300/PK-5
15001 Dufief Dr 20878 301-279-4980
Brent Mascott, prin. Fax 279-4983
Fields Road ES 500/PK-5
1 School Dr 20878 301-840-7131
Erica Williams, prin. Fax 548-7523
Flower Hill ES 500/PK-5
18425 Flower Hill Way 20879 301-840-7161
Lamar Whitmore, prin. Fax 840-7165
Forest Oak MS 800/6-8
651 Saybrooke Oaks Blvd 20877 301-670-8242
Shahid Muhammad, prin. Fax 840-5322
Gaithersburg ES 800/PK-5
35 N Summit Ave 20877 301-840-7136
Meredith McNerney, prin. Fax 548-7524
Gaithersburg MS 500/7-8
2 Teachers Way 20877 301-840-4554
Ann Dolan Rindner, prin. Fax 840-4570
Goshen ES 600/K-5
8701 Warfield Rd 20882 301-840-8165
Yolanda Allen, prin. Fax 840-8167
Jones Lane ES 500/PK-5
15110 Jones Ln 20878 301-840-8160
Carole Sample, prin. Fax 840-8162
Lakelands Park MS 1,000/6-8
1200 Main St 20878 301-670-1400
Deborah Higdon, prin. Fax 670-1418
Laytonsville ES 500/K-5
21401 Laytonsville Rd 20882 240-740-1660
Donna Sagona, prin. Fax 840-7147
Marshall ES 600/PK-5
12260 McDonald Chapel Dr 20878 301-670-8282
Pamela Nazzaro, prin. Fax 670-8256
Resnik ES 600/PK-5
7301 Hadley Farms Dr 20879 301-670-8200
Latricia Thomas, prin. Fax 840-7135
Ridgeview MS 400/7-8
16600 Raven Rock Dr 20878 301-406-1300
Daniel Garcia, prin. Fax 840-4679
Rosemont ES 500/PK-5
16400 Alden Ave 20877 301-840-7123
Keely Cooke, prin. Fax 548-7512
Shady Grove MS 600/6-8
8100 Midcounty Hwy 20877 240-740-1440
Alana Murray, prin. Fax 548-7535
South Lake ES 800/PK-5
18201 Contour Rd 20877 301-337-3450
Celeste King, prin. Fax 840-4549
Stedwick ES 600/PK-5
10631 Stedwick Rd 20886 301-840-7187
Dr. Margaret Pastor, prin. Fax 548-7532
Strawberry Knoll ES 600/PK-5
18820 Strawberry Knoll Rd 20879 301-840-7112
Patrick Scott, prin. Fax 840-7114
Summit Hall ES 600/PK-5
101 W Deer Park Rd 20877 301-284-4150
Lisa Henry, prin. Fax 548-7543
Washington Grove ES 400/PK-5
8712 Oakmont St 20877 240-740-0300
Susan Barranger, prin. Fax 840-4523
Whetstone ES 700/PK-5
19201 Thomas Farm Rd 20886 240-740-1060
Vicky Casey, prin. Fax 840-7185
Woodfield ES 300/K-5
24200 Woodfield Rd 20882 240-207-2550
Stephanie Brant, prin. Fax 391-6298

Avalon S 200/K-12
200 W Diamond Ave 20877 301-963-8022
Kevin Davern, hdmstr. Fax 963-8027
Church of the Redeemer Christian S 300/PK-8
19425 Woodfield Rd 20879 240-238-1500
Carol Bell, prin. Fax 238-1489
Covenant Life S 300/PK-12
7503 Muncaster Mill Rd 20877 301-869-4500
Jamie Leach, hdmstr. Fax 948-4920
Mother of God S 200/PK-8
20501 Goshen Rd 20879 301-990-2088
Hall Miller, pres. Fax 947-0574
St. Martin of Tours S 200/PK-8
115 S Frederick Ave 20877 301-990-2441
Anthony Sahadi, prin. Fax 990-2688

Galena, Kent, Pop. 602
Kent County SD
Supt. — See Rock Hall
Galena ES 200/PK-5
114 S Main St 21635 410-810-2510
Amy Crowding, prin. Fax 648-6881

Gambrills, Anne Arundel, Pop. 2,747
Anne Arundel County SD
Supt. — See Annapolis
Crofton MS 1,100/6-8
2301 Davidsonville Rd 21054 410-793-0280
Nuria Williams, prin. Fax 793-0295
Four Seasons ES 500/PK-5
979 Waugh Chapel Rd 21054 410-222-6501
Sharon Ferralli, prin. Fax 222-6503

School of the Incarnation 800/K-8
2601 Symphony Ln 21054 410-519-2285
Lisa Shipley, prin. Fax 519-2286

Garrett Park, Montgomery, Pop. 967

Holy Cross S 200/PK-8
PO Box 249 20896 301-949-0053
Lisa Kane, prin. Fax 949-5074

Germantown, Montgomery, Pop. 83,263
Montgomery County SD
Supt. — See Rockville
Cedar Grove ES 700/K-5
24001 Ridge Rd 20876 301-253-7000
Lee Derby, prin. Fax 253-0933
Clemente MS 1,100/6-8
18808 Waring Station Rd 20874 301-284-4750
Jeffrey Brown, prin. Fax 601-0370
Clopper Mill ES 500/PK-5
18501 Cinnamon Dr 20874 240-740-2180
Lawrence Chep, prin. Fax 353-8068
Daly ES 600/PK-5
20301 Brandermill Dr 20876 240-740-0600
Nora Dietz, prin. Fax 353-0872
Fox Chapel ES 600/PK-5
19315 Archdale Rd 20876 240-740-0680
Diana Zabetakis, prin. Fax 353-0873
Germantown ES 300/K-5
19110 Liberty Mill Rd 20874 301-353-8050
Amy Bryant, prin. Fax 601-0393
Gibbs ES 700/K-5
12615 Royal Crown Dr 20876 240-740-0740
Kim Bosnic, prin. Fax 353-0890
Great Seneca Creek ES 700/PK-5
13010 Dairymaid Dr 20874 301-353-8500
Scott Curry, prin. Fax 515-3044
King MS 600/6-8
13737 Wisteria Dr 20874 301-353-8080
Christopher Wynne, prin. Fax 601-0399
Kingsview MS 1,000/6-8
18909 Kingsview Rd 20874 301-601-4611
Dyan Harrison, prin. Fax 601-4610
Lake Seneca ES 500/PK-5
13600 Wanegarden Dr 20874 240-740-0280
Teri Johnson, prin. Fax 353-0932
Matsunaga ES 1,000/PK-5
13902 Bromfield Rd 20874 301-601-4350
James Sweeney, prin. Fax 601-4358
McAuliffe ES 700/PK-5
12500 Wisteria Dr 20874 301-353-0910
Wanda Coates, prin. Fax 353-0923
McNair ES 800/PK-5
13881 Hopkins Rd 20874 301-353-0854
Sherry Moses, prin. Fax 353-0964
Neelsville MS 900/6-8
11700 Neelsville Church Rd 20876 301-353-8064
Vicky Lake-Parcan, prin. Fax 353-8094
Ride ES 500/PK-5
21301 Seneca Crossing Dr 20876 301-353-0994
Elise Burgess, prin. Fax 601-0349
Waters Landing ES 700/K-5
13100 Waters Landing Dr 20874 240-740-1020
Srelyne Harris, prin. Fax 601-0392

Butler Montessori 100/PK-8
15951 Germantown Rd 20874 301-977-6600
Fellowship Christian S 100/PK-3
18901 Waring Station Rd 20874 301-540-3110
Rebecca Prater, prin. Fax 540-3115

Glenarden, Prince George's, Pop. 5,916
Prince George's County SD
Supt. — See Upper Marlboro
Glenarden Woods ES 500/2-5
7801 Glenarden Pkwy 20706 301-925-1300
Cecelia Jones-Bowlding, prin. Fax 925-1304
Woods ES 700/PK-6
3000 Church St 20706 301-925-2840
Stephanie Barber, prin. Fax 925-2844

Glen Burnie, Anne Arundel, Pop. 65,521
Anne Arundel County SD
Supt. — See Annapolis
Corkran MS 500/6-8
7600 Quarterfield Rd 21061 410-222-6493
Adam Zetwick, prin. Fax 761-3853
Cromwell ES 300/1-5
525 Wellham Ave 21061 410-222-6920
Kathryn Maxa, prin. Fax 222-6923
Ferndale ECC 100/PK-K
105 Packard Ave 21061 410-222-6927
Lisa Rice, prin. Fax 222-6929
Freetown ES 500/PK-5
7904 Freetown Rd 21060 410-222-6900
Amanda Edmonds, prin. Fax 222-6902
Glen Burnie Park ES 500/PK-5
500 Marlboro Rd 21061 410-222-6400
Colleen McFarland, prin. Fax 222-6418
Glendale ES 400/PK-5
105 Carroll Rd 21060 410-222-6404
Kristy Snyder, prin. Fax 222-6471
Hilltop ES, 415 Melrose Ave 21061 700/PK-5
Kelly Thomas, prin. 410-222-6409
Lee ES 500/K-5
400 A St SW 21061 410-222-6435
Lisa Koennel, prin. Fax 222-6437
Marley ES 700/PK-5
715 Cooper Rd 21060 410-222-6414
Kristie Battista, prin. Fax 222-6413
Marley MS 800/6-8
10 Davis Ct 21060 410-761-0934
Kimberly Winterbottom, prin. Fax 761-0736
North Glen ES 200/PK-5
615 W Furnace Branch Rd 21061 410-222-6416
Richard Rogers, prin. Fax 222-6419
Oakwood ES 300/PK-5
330 Oak Manor Dr 21061 410-222-6420
Edmund Kling, prin. Fax 222-6421
Point Pleasant ES 600/PK-5
1035 Dumbarton Rd 21060 410-222-6425
Christopher Gordon, prin. Fax 222-6459
Rippling Woods ES 600/PK-5
530 Nolfield Dr 21061 410-222-6440
Tammy Scott, prin. Fax 969-1240
Solley ES 700/PK-5
7608 Solley Rd 21060 410-222-6473
Jeffery Haynie, prin. Fax 222-6467
Southgate ES 700/PK-5
290 Shetlands Ln 21061 410-222-6445
Bonnie Myers, prin. Fax 222-6446
Woodside ES 300/PK-5
160 Funke Rd 21061 410-222-6910
Susan Barrie, prin. Fax 222-6917

St. Paul's Lutheran S 400/PK-8
308 Oak Manor Dr 21061 410-766-5790
Julie Bourgeois, prin. Fax 766-9059
Slade Regional Catholic S 800/PK-8
120 Dorsey Rd 21061 410-766-7130
Alexa Cox, prin. Fax 787-0594

Glenn Dale, Prince George's, Pop. 13,111
Prince George's County SD
Supt. — See Upper Marlboro
Glenn Dale ES 500/K-5
6700 Glenn Dale Rd 20769 301-805-2750
Heather Porterfield, prin. Fax 805-2753

Holy Trinity Episcopal Day S 500/PK-8
11902 Daisy Ln 20769 301-464-3215
Michael Mullin, head sch Fax 464-9725
Reid Temple Christian Academy 300/PK-8
11400 Glenn Dale Blvd 20769 301-860-6570
Dr. Donnette Dais, head sch Fax 262-3650

Glenwood, Howard
Howard County SD
Supt. — See Ellicott City
Bushy Park ES 600/PK-5
14601 Carrs Mill Rd 21738 410-313-5500
Molly Ketterer, prin. Fax 313-5505
Glenwood MS 500/6-8
2680 Route 97 21738 410-313-5520
Robert Motley, prin. Fax 313-5534

Glyndon, Baltimore

Sacred Heart S 700/PK-8
PO Box 3672 21071 410-833-0857
Jeanne Cossentino, prin. Fax 833-0914

Grantsville, Garrett, Pop. 758
Garrett County SD
Supt. — See Oakland
Grantsville ES 200/PK-5
120 Grant St 21536 301-895-5173
Nicole Miller, prin. Fax 746-8662

Grasonville, Queen Anne's, Pop. 3,341
Queen Anne's County SD
Supt. — See Centreville
Grasonville ES 500/PK-5
5435 Main St 21638 410-827-8070
Carol Kamp, prin. Fax 827-4695

Great Mills, Saint Mary's
St. Mary's County SD
Supt. — See Leonardtown
Greenview Knolls ES 400/PK-5
45711 Military Ln 20634 301-863-4095
Elizabeth Servello, prin. Fax 863-4099

Little Flower S 300/PK-8
20410 Point Lookout Rd 20634 301-994-0404
Barbara Stirling, prin. Fax 994-2055

Greenbelt, Prince George's, Pop. 22,408
Prince George's County SD
Supt. — See Upper Marlboro
Greenbelt ES 600/PK-5
66 Ridge Rd 20770 301-513-5911
Monica Gaines, prin. Fax 513-5319
Greenbelt MS 1,200/6-8
6301 Breezewood Dr 20770 301-513-5040
Daria Valentine, prin. Fax 513-5097
Kennedy French Immersion S 600/K-8
8950 Edmonston Rd 20770 301-918-8660
Parfait Awono, prin. Fax 760-3904
Springhill Lake ES 800/K-5
6060 Springhill Dr 20770 301-513-5996
Natasha Jenkins, prin. Fax 513-5314

Greensboro, Caroline, Pop. 1,871
Caroline County SD
Supt. — See Denton

Greensboro ES 800/PK-5
625 N Main St 21639 410-482-6251
Dawn Swann, prin. Fax 482-8880

Hagerstown, Washington, Pop. 37,853
Washington County SD 22,000/PK-12
10435 Downsville Pike 21740 301-766-2800
Dr. Boyd Michael, supt. Fax 766-2829
www.wcps.k12.md.us
Bester ES 500/PK-5
385 Mill St 21740 301-766-8001
Kristen English, prin. Fax 766-8010
Doub ES 300/1-5
1221 S Potomac St 21740 301-766-8130
Catherine Poling, prin. Fax 791-4291
Eastern ES 500/3-5
1320 Yale Dr 21742 301-766-8122
Kristi Bachtell, prin. Fax 739-5066
Fountaindale ES 400/K-5
901 Northern Ave 21742 301-766-8156
Teri Williamson, prin. Fax 745-3041
Fountain Rock ES 200/K-5
17145 Lappans Rd 21740 301-766-8146
Nicole Paylor, prin. Fax 223-5759
Hager ES PK-5
12615 Sedgwick Way 21740 301-766-8440
Kathy Stiles, prin.
Hicks MS 800/6-8
1321 S Potomac St 21740 301-766-8110
Michael Telemeco, prin. Fax 766-8116
Lincolnshire ES 600/PK-5
17545 Lincolnshire Rd 21740 301-766-8206
Jamie Hade, prin. Fax 766-8981
Monroe PS 700/PK-2
1311 Yale Dr 21742 301-766-8668
Kathleen Forrest, prin. Fax 766-8679
Northern MS 800/6-8
701 Northern Ave 21742 301-766-8258
Beth Allshouse, prin. Fax 766-8259
Old Forge ES 300/K-5
21615 Old Forge Rd 21742 301-766-8273
Dana Peake, prin. Fax 745-6130
Pangborn ES 700/K-5
195 Pangborn Blvd 21740 301-766-8282
Eric Meredith, prin. Fax 797-5905
Paramount ES 400/K-5
19410 Longmeadow Rd 21742 301-766-8289
Laura Barnes, prin. Fax 766-8749
Potomac Heights ES 200/K-5
301 E Magnolia Ave 21742 301-766-8305
Carl Stark, prin. Fax 739-9353
Rockland Woods ES 600/K-5
18201 Rockland Dr 21740 301-766-8485
Hope Fuss, prin. Fax 766-8498
Salem Avenue ES 700/PK-5
1323 Salem Ave 21740 301-766-8313
Thomas Garner, prin. Fax 791-4382
Western Heights MS 700/6-8
1300 Marshall St 21740 301-766-8403
Matthew Mauriello, prin. Fax 791-4136
Other Schools – See Boonsboro, Cascade, Clear Spring, Hancock, Knoxville, Maugansville, Sharpsburg, Smithsburg, Williamsport

Broadfording Christian Academy 300/PK-12
13535 Broadfording Church 21740 301-797-8886
William Wyand, supt. Fax 797-3155
Grace Academy 400/PK-12
13321 Cearfoss Pike 21740 301-733-2033
Warren Barrett, prin. Fax 733-4706
Heritage Academy 200/PK-12
12215 Walnut Pt W 21740 301-582-2600
Dave Hobbs, prin. Fax 582-2603
Mt. Aetna SDA S 100/PK-8
10207 Crystal Falls Dr 21740 301-824-3875
St. Mary Catholic S 200/PK-8
218 W Washington St 21740 301-733-1184
Patricia McDermott, prin. Fax 745-4997

Hampstead, Carroll, Pop. 6,228
Carroll County SD
Supt. — See Westminster
Hampstead ES 400/PK-5
3737 Shiloh Rd 21074 410-751-3420
Arlene Moore, prin. Fax 751-3438
North Carroll MS 600/6-8
2401 Hanover Pike 21074 410-751-3440
Ralph Billings, prin. Fax 751-3464
Shiloh MS 700/6-8
3675 Willow St 21074 410-386-4570
Scott Lavender, prin. Fax 386-4579
Spring Garden ES 500/K-5
700 Boxwood Dr 21074 410-751-3433
Wendy Leishear, prin. Fax 751-3475

Hancock, Washington, Pop. 1,530
Washington County SD
Supt. — See Hagerstown
Hancock ES 300/PK-5
290 W Main St 21750 301-766-8178
Michelle Gest, prin. Fax 678-5698

Hanover, Anne Arundel
Anne Arundel County SD
Supt. — See Annapolis
Hebron-Harman ES 800/PK-5
7660 Ridge Chapel Rd 21076 410-859-4510
Rebecca Blasingame-White, prin.

Howard County SD
Supt. — See Ellicott City
Viaduct MS 6-8
7000 Banbury Dr 21076 410-313-8711
Shiney Ann John, prin. Fax 313-8091

Havre de Grace, Harford, Pop. 12,505
Harford County SD
Supt. — See Bel Air
Havre De Grace ES 400/PK-5
600 S Juniata St 21078 410-939-6616
Ronald Wooden, prin. Fax 939-6632

Havre De Grace MS 500/6-8
401 Lewis Ln 21078 410-939-6608
James Johnson, prin. Fax 939-6613
Meadowvale ES 600/PK-5
910 Graceview Dr 21078 410-939-6622
Mark Warfield, prin. Fax 939-6635
Roye-Williams ES 500/PK-5
201 Oakington Rd 21078 410-273-5536
Rose Martino, prin. Fax 273-5559

Hebron, Wicomico, Pop. 1,068
Wicomico County SD
Supt. — See Salisbury
Westside IS 400/2-5
8000 Quantico Rd 21830 410-677-5118
Chris Nunzio, prin. Fax 677-5138

Hillcrest Heights, Prince George's, Pop. 16,224

Holy Family S 200/PK-8
2200 Callaway St, 301-894-2323
Michelle Taylor, prin. Fax 894-7100

Hollywood, Saint Mary's
St. Mary's County SD
Supt. — See Leonardtown
Hollywood ES 600/PK-5
44345 Joy Chapel Rd 20636 301-373-4350
Jennifer Gilman, prin. Fax 373-4355

St. John S 200/PK-8
43900 Saint Johns Rd 20636 301-373-2142
Susan McDonough, prin. Fax 373-4500

Huntingtown, Calvert
Calvert County SD
Supt. — See Prince Frederick
Huntingtown ES 500/K-5
4345 Huntingtown Rd 20639 410-550-9360
Brock Fulton, prin. Fax 286-4005
Plum Point ES 400/K-5
1245 Plum Point Rd 20639 410-550-9730
Beth Morton, prin. Fax 286-4021
Plum Point MS 700/6-8
1475 Plum Point Rd 20639 410-550-9170
Kelley Adams, prin. Fax 286-4009

Calverton S 400/PK-12
300 Calverton School Rd 20639 410-535-0216
Christopher Hayes, head sch Fax 535-6934
Good News Preschool PK-PK
885 Cox Rd 20639 410-414-8304
Patricia O'Toole, dir. Fax 535-9057

Hurlock, Dorchester, Pop. 2,049
Dorchester County SD
Supt. — See Cambridge
Hurlock ES 500/PK-5
301 Charles St 21643 410-943-3303
Linda Wilson, prin. Fax 943-8917
North Dorchester MS 400/6-8
5745 Cloverdale Rd 21643 410-943-3322
Leslie Tolley, prin. Fax 943-3214

Hyattsville, Prince George's, Pop. 17,068
Prince George's County SD
Supt. — See Upper Marlboro
Chavez Spanish Immersion 200/K-6
6609 Riggs Rd 20782 301-853-5694
Anna Addis, prin. Fax 853-5696
Chillum ES 200/PK-5
1420 Chillum Rd 20782 301-853-0825
Ryan Daniel, prin. Fax 853-0857
Felegy ES PK-5
6110 Editors Park Dr 20782 301-386-1610
Dr. Trevor Liburd, prin. Fax 760-3883
Hyattsville ES 500/PK-5
5311 43rd Ave 20781 301-209-5800
Teresa Bay, prin. Fax 985-1499
Hyattsville MS 800/6-8
6001 42nd Ave 20781 301-209-5830
Thornton Boone, prin. Fax 209-5849
Langley Park/McCormick ES 800/PK-6
8201 15th Ave 20783 301-445-8423
Kina Flood, prin. Fax 445-8425
Lewisdale ES 700/PK-5
2400 Banning Pl 20783 301-445-8433
Patricia Haith, prin. Fax 431-5654
Orem MS 700/6-8
6100 Editors Park Dr 20782 301-853-0840
Theresa Merrifield, prin. Fax 853-0839
Parks ES 900/K-6
6111 Ager Rd 20782 301-445-8090
Rhonda Summey, prin. Fax 445-8099
Ridgecrest ES 700/PK-6
6120 Riggs Rd 20783 301-853-0820
Denise Dunn, prin. Fax 853-0861
University Park ES 600/PK-6
4315 Underwood St 20782 301-985-1898
Toi Davis, prin. Fax 927-1181
Woodridge ES 300/PK-6
5001 Flintridge Dr 20784 301-918-8585
Viola Harris, prin. Fax 918-4462

Peters Adventist S 100/PK-8
6303 Riggs Rd 20783 301-559-6710
St. Jerome Academy 300/PK-8
5207 42nd Pl 20781 301-277-4568
Daniel Flynn, prin. Fax 683-6080

Hydes, Baltimore

St. John the Evangelist S 200/PK-8
13311 Long Green Pike 21082 410-592-9585
Christine Blake, prin. Fax 817-4548

Ijamsville, Frederick, Pop. 350
Frederick County SD
Supt. — See Frederick

Oakdale ES 600/PK-5
5830 Oakdale School Rd 21754 240-236-3300
Kimberly Clifford, prin. Fax 236-3301
Oakdale MS 600/6-8
5810 Oakdale School Rd 21754 240-236-5500
Mita Badshah, prin. Fax 236-5501
Urbana MS 800/6-8
3511 Pontius Ct 21754 240-566-9200
Peter Daddone, prin. Fax 566-9201
Windsor Knolls MS 800/6-8
11150 Windsor Rd 21754 240-236-5000
Brian Vasquenza, prin. Fax 236-5001

Friends Meeting S 100/K-12
3232 Green Valley Rd 21754 301-798-0288
Trevor Harris, coord. Fax 798-0299

Indian Head, Charles, Pop. 3,706
Charles County SD
Supt. — See La Plata
Henson MS 700/6-8
3535 Livingston Rd 20640 301-375-8550
Christina Caballero, prin. Fax 375-9216
Indian Head ES 500/PK-5
4200 Indian Head Hwy 20640 301-743-5454
Timothy Rosin, prin. Fax 743-5080
Parks ES 800/PK-5
3505 Livingston Rd 20640 301-375-7444
Gregory Miller, prin. Fax 375-9106
Smallwood MS 500/6-8
4990 Indian Head Hwy 20640 301-743-5422
Kathy Kiessling, prin. Fax 753-8421

Jarrettsville, Harford, Pop. 2,870
Harford County SD
Supt. — See Bel Air
Jarrettsville ES 500/K-5
3818 Norrisville Rd 21084 410-692-7800
Kathleen Garafola, prin. Fax 692-7801
North Bend ES 400/PK-5
1445 North Bend Rd 21084 410-692-7815
Robin Payne, prin. Fax 692-7826

Jefferson, Frederick, Pop. 2,084
Frederick County SD
Supt. — See Frederick
Valley ES 400/PK-5
3519 Jefferson Pike 21755 240-236-3000
Tracy Poquette, prin. Fax 236-3001

Jessup, Howard, Pop. 7,088
Anne Arundel County SD
Supt. — See Annapolis
Jessup ES 500/PK-5
2900 Elementary School Ln 20794 410-222-6490
Anita Dempsey, prin. Fax 222-6492

Howard County SD
Supt. — See Ellicott City
Bollman Bridge ES 800/PK-5
8200 Savage Guilford Rd 20794 410-880-5920
Rhonda Inskeep, prin. Fax 880-5923
Patuxent Valley MS 700/6-8
9151 Vollmerhausen Rd 20794 410-880-5840
Rick Robb, prin. Fax 880-5843

Joppa, Harford, Pop. 12,356
Harford County SD
Supt. — See Bel Air
Joppatowne ES 600/PK-5
407 Trimble Rd 21085 410-612-1546
H. Earl Gaskins, prin. Fax 612-1578
Magnolia ES 500/PK-5
901 Trimble Rd 21085 410-612-1553
Patricia Mason, prin. Fax 612-1576
Magnolia MS 700/6-8
299 Fort Hoyle Rd 21085 410-612-1525
Michael Quigg, prin. Fax 612-1598
Riverside ES 500/PK-5
211 Stillmeadow Dr 21085 410-612-1560
Christopher Yancone, prin. Fax 612-1559

Trinity Lutheran Christian S 300/PK-8
1100 Philadelphia Rd 21085 410-679-4000
Rev. John Austin, hdmstr. Fax 679-3472

Kensington, Montgomery, Pop. 2,142
Montgomery County SD
Supt. — See Rockville
Garrett Park ES 700/K-5
4810 Oxford St 20895 240-740-0700
Daniel Tucci, prin. Fax 929-2008
Kensington-Parkwood ES 700/PK-5
4710 Saul Rd 20895 301-571-6949
Candace Ross, prin. Fax 571-6953
Newport Mill MS 600/6-8
11311 Newport Mill Rd 20895 301-929-2244
Panagiota Tsonis, prin. Fax 929-2274
Rock View ES 700/PK-5
3901 Denfeld Ave 20895 240-740-0920
Kristine Alexander, prin. Fax 929-5986
Silver Creek MS 6-7
3701 Saul Rd 20895 240-740-2200
Dr. Traci Townsend, prin. Fax 740-2260

Brookewood S 100/1-12
10401 Armory Ave 20895 301-949-7997
Richard McPherson, hdmstr. Fax 949-0069
Grace Episcopal Day S 50/PK-5
9411 Connecticut Ave 20895 301-949-5860
Jennifer Danish, head sch Fax 949-8398
Holy Redeemer S 400/PK-8
9715 Summit Ave 20895 301-942-3701
Colleen Ryan, prin. Fax 942-4981

Keymar, Frederick
Frederick County SD
Supt. — See Frederick
New Midway ES 3-5
12226 Woodsboro Pike 21757 240-236-1500
Guiseppe DiMonte, prin. Fax 236-1501

Kingsville, Baltimore, Pop. 4,276
Baltimore County SD
Supt. — See Towson
Kingsville ES 400/PK-5
7300 Sunshine Ave 21087 410-887-5949
Carol Ferris, prin. Fax 887-5950

Open Bible Christian Academy 200/PK-12
13 Open Bible Way 21087 410-593-9940
Jill Greenlee, admin. Fax 593-9942
Redeemer Classical Christian S 300/PK-12
6415 Mount Vista Rd 21087 410-592-9625
Terry Cellini, head sch Fax 817-6904
St. Paul's Lutheran S 100/PK-8
12022 Jerusalem Rd 21087 410-592-8100
Wendell Robson, prin. Fax 592-3282

Knoxville, Washington
Washington County SD
Supt. — See Hagerstown
Pleasant Valley ES 200/K-5
1707 Rohrersville Rd 21758 301-766-8297
Adrienne Mayonado, prin. Fax 432-8777

Landover, Prince George's, Pop. 22,690
Prince George's County SD
Supt. — See Upper Marlboro
Columbia Park ES 500/PK-6
1901 Kent Village Dr 20785 301-925-1322
Michelle Tyler-Skinner, prin. Fax 925-1327
Dodge Park ES 500/PK-6
3401 Hubbard Rd 20785 301-883-4220
Josette Moise, prin. Fax 883-4223
Gholson MS 700/6-8
900 Nalley Rd 20785 301-883-8390
Jacqueline Marshall-Hall, prin. Fax 883-8394
Highland Park ES 500/PK-6
6501 Lowland Dr 20785 301-333-0980
Wanda Robinson, prin. Fax 333-0992
Hoyer Montessori S 200/PK-8
929 Hill Rd 20785 301-808-4420
Tracey Spivey-White, prin. Fax 808-8869
Kenmoor ECC 50/PK-PK
3211 82nd Ave 20785 301-925-1970
Alma Ezell-Lawson, prin. Fax 925-2364
Kenmoor MS 700/6-8
2500 Kenmoor Dr 20785 301-925-2300
Maha Fadli, prin. Fax 925-2317
Paca ES 300/K-5
7801 Sheriff Rd 20785 301-925-1330
Dorothy Clowers, prin. Fax 925-1338
Pullen Academy 700/K-8
700 Brightseat Rd 20785 301-808-8160
Pamela Adams, prin. Fax 808-8166
Rice ES 700/PK-5
950 Nalley Rd 20785 301-636-6340
Mickelli Dunn, prin. Fax 636-6344

Highland Park Christian Academy 200/PK-8
6801 Sheriff Rd 20785 301-773-4079
Niesha Wright, prin. Fax 773-2626
SHABACH Christian Academy 200/PK-8
3600 Brightseat Rd 20785 301-583-5330
Washington United Christian Academy 100/PK-8
6421 Old Landover Rd 20785 301-807-9397

Landover Hills, Prince George's, Pop. 1,641
Prince George's County SD
Supt. — See Upper Marlboro
Cooper Lane ES 500/PK-6
3817 Cooper Ln 20784 301-925-1350
Dr. Kishawn Smith, prin. Fax 925-2360
Glenridge ES 800/PK-6
7200 Gallatin St 20784 301-918-8740
Dr. Gloria McCoy, prin. Fax 918-8547

St. Mary S 200/PK-8
7207 Annapolis Rd 20784 301-577-0031
Christian Buchleitner, prin. Fax 577-5485

Lanham Seabrook, Prince George's, Pop. 16,792
Prince George's County SD
Supt. — See Upper Marlboro
Gaywood ES 500/PK-5
6701 97th Ave 20706 301-918-8730
Damien Goings, prin. Fax 918-8560
Goddard Montessori S 500/PK-8
9850 Good Luck Rd 20706 301-918-3515
Deatrice Womack, prin. Fax 918-8670
Johnson MS 1,000/6-8
5401 Barker Pl 20706 301-918-8680
Rodney McBride, prin. Fax 918-8688
Magnolia ES 500/PK-6
8400 Nightingale Dr 20706 301-918-8770
Phyllis Gillens, prin. Fax 918-8772
McHenry ES 800/PK-5
8909 McHenry Ln 20706 301-918-8760
Harold McCray, prin. Fax 918-8638
Reed ES 400/K-5
9501 Greenbelt Rd 20706 301-918-8716
Nicole Warner, prin. Fax 918-8559
Seabrook ES 300/PK-5
6001 Seabrook Rd 20706 301-918-8542
Clareta Spinks, prin. Fax 918-8543

Academy of St. Matthias the Apostle 200/PK-8
9473 Annapolis Rd 20706 301-577-9412
Patricia Schratz, prin. Fax 577-2060
Lanham Christian S 200/PK-12
8400 Good Luck Rd 20706 301-552-9102
Vanessa Anchan, prin. Fax 552-2021

La Plata, Charles, Pop. 8,508
Charles County SD 27,300/PK-12
PO Box 2770 20646 301-932-6610
Kimberly Hill Ed.D., supt. Fax 932-6651
www.ccboe.com
Matula ES 600/PK-5
6025 Radio Station Rd 20646 301-934-5412
Carrie Richardson, prin. Fax 934-5414
Mitchell ES 700/PK-5
400 Willow Ln 20646 301-934-4687
Sabrina Robinson-Taylor, prin. Fax 753-1649
Somers MS 900/6-8
300 Willow Ln 20646 301-934-4663
Carrie Akins, prin. Fax 934-2982
Other Schools – See Bryantown, Indian Head, Marbury, Nanjemoy, Newburg, Pomfret, Waldorf

Archbishop Neale S 400/PK-8
104 Port Tobacco Rd 20646 301-934-9595
Linda Bourne, prin. Fax 934-8610
Grace Lutheran S 200/PK-8
1200 Charles St 20646 301-932-0963
Jeff Burkee, prin. Fax 934-1459

Largo, Prince George's, Pop. 10,502
Prince George's County SD
Supt. — See Upper Marlboro
Perrywood ES 600/K-5
501 Watkins Park Dr 20774 301-218-3040
Carolyn Poole, prin. Fax 218-3050

Divine Peace Lutheran S 50/K-6
1500 Brown Station Rd 20774 301-350-4522
Fax 350-4520

Laurel, Prince George's, Pop. 24,374
Anne Arundel County SD
Supt. — See Annapolis
Brock Bridge ES 800/PK-5
405 Brock Bridge Rd 20724 301-498-6280
Stacy Gray, prin. Fax 776-0128
Maryland City ES 400/PK-5
3359 Crumpton S 20724 301-725-4256
Laura Cooke, prin. Fax 725-0191
Monarch Global Academy Contract S 800/K-8
430 Brock Bridge Rd 20724 301-886-8648
Donna O'Shea, prin.

Howard County SD
Supt. — See Ellicott City
Forest Ridge ES 700/K-5
9550 Gorman Rd 20723 410-880-5950
Genee Varlack, prin. Fax 880-5956
Gorman Crossing ES 600/K-5
9999 Winter Sun Rd 20723 410-880-5900
Deborah Caldwell, prin. Fax 880-5902
Hammond ES 600/K-5
8110 Aladdin Dr 20723 410-880-5890
Kimberlyn Pratesi, prin. Fax 880-5895
Hammond MS 500/6-8
8100 Aladdin Dr 20723 410-880-5830
Kerry Dufresne, prin. Fax 880-5837
Laurel Woods ES 500/K-5
9250 N Laurel Rd 20723 410-880-5960
Susan Brown, prin. Fax 880-5964
Murray Hill MS 700/6-8
9989 Winter Sun Rd 20723 410-880-5897
Rick Wilson, prin. Fax 317-5048

Prince George's County SD
Supt. — See Upper Marlboro
Bond Mill ES 500/K-5
16001 Sherwood Ave 20707 301-497-3600
Justin Fitzgerald, prin. Fax 497-3606
Deerfield Run ES 600/PK-5
13000 Laurel Bowie Rd 20708 301-497-3610
Mary Wall, prin. Fax 497-3615
Eisenhower MS 900/6-8
13725 Briarwood Dr 20708 301-497-3620
John Mangrum, prin. Fax 497-3637
Harrison ES 300/K-6
13200 Larchdale Rd 20708 301-497-3650
Wanda Williams, prin. Fax 497-7217
Laurel ES 600/PK-5
516 Montgomery St 20707 301-497-3660
Melinda Lee, prin. Fax 497-3657
Montpelier ES 600/PK-5
9200 Muirkirk Rd 20708 301-497-3670
Carla Furlow, prin. Fax 497-5431
Oaklands ES 400/PK-5
13710 Laurel Bowie Rd 20708 301-497-3110
Audrey Briscoe, prin. Fax 497-3114
Scotchtown Hills ES 700/PK-6
15950 Dorset Rd 20707 301-497-3994
Tracie Prevost, prin. Fax 498-6421

First Baptist S of Laurel 200/PK-8
15002 First Baptist Ln 20707 301-490-1076
Pallotti Early Learning Center 100/PK-K
800 Main St 20707 301-776-6471
Alisha Jordan, dir. Fax 776-0019
St. Mary of the Mills S 400/PK-8
106 Saint Marys Pl 20707 301-498-1433
Alisha Jordan, prin. Fax 498-1170

LaVale, Allegany, Pop. 3,505
Allegany County SD
Supt. — See Cumberland
Cash Valley ES 300/PK-5
10601 Cash Valley Rd NW 21502 301-724-6632
Jackie Enright, prin. Fax 724-5297
Parkside ES 300/PK-5
50 Parkside Blvd 21502 301-729-0085
Tracey Wharton, prin. Fax 729-0176

Leonardtown, Saint Mary's, Pop. 2,832
St. Mary's County SD 18,300/PK-12
23160 Moakley St 20650 301-475-5511
James Smith, supt. Fax 475-4270
www.smcps.org
Duke ES 500/PK-5
23595 Hayden Farm Ln 20650 240-309-4658
Beth Ramsey, prin. Fax 309-4663
Leonardtown ES 800/PK-5
22885 Duke St 20650 301-475-0250
Contina Quick-McQueen, prin. Fax 475-0254
Leonardtown MS 900/6-8
24015 Point Lookout Rd 20650 301-475-0230
Dr. Deborah Dennie, prin. Fax 475-0237
Other Schools – See California, Chaptico, Great Mills, Hollywood, Lexington Park, Loveville, Mechanicsville, Park Hall, Ridge, Tall Timbers

Father Andrew White S 300/PK-8
PO Box 1756 20650 301-475-9795
Heather Francisco, prin. Fax 475-3537

Lexington Park, Saint Mary's, Pop. 11,085
St. Mary's County SD
Supt. — See Leonardtown
Carver ES 600/PK-5
46155 Carver School Blvd 20653 301-863-4076
Denise Eichel, prin. Fax 862-1217
Esperanza MS 800/6-8
22790 Maple Rd 20653 301-863-4016
Jennifer Consalvo, prin. Fax 863-4020
Green Holly ES 600/PK-5
46060 Millstone Landing Rd 20653 301-863-4064
Wauchilue Adams, prin. Fax 863-4072
Lexington Park ES 500/PK-5
46763 S Shangri La Dr 20653 301-863-4085
Dr. Rebecca Schou, prin. Fax 863-4089
Spring Ridge MS 1,000/6-8
19856 Three Notch Rd 20653 301-863-4031
Dr. Wendy Zimmerman, prin. Fax 863-4035
Town Creek ES 200/K-5
45805 Dent Dr 20653 301-863-4044
Marie Hankinson, prin. Fax 863-4048

Bay Montessori S 100/PK-8
20525 Willows Rd 20653 301-737-2421

Libertytown, Frederick, Pop. 931
Frederick County SD
Supt. — See Frederick
Liberty ES 300/PK-5
11820 Liberty Rd 21762 240-236-1800
Todd Shaffer, prin. Fax 236-1801

Linthicum Heights, Anne Arundel, Pop. 2,980
Anne Arundel County SD
Supt. — See Annapolis
Lindale MS 800/6-8
415 Andover Rd 21090 410-691-4344
Johnny Nash, prin. Fax 691-4359
Linthicum ES 500/K-5
101 School Ln 21090 410-222-6935
Mary Beth Gormley, prin. Fax 222-6936
Overlook ES 300/PK-5
401 Hampton Rd 21090 410-222-6585
Angela Ricciuti, prin. Fax 636-0548

Friendship Adventist S & CDC 50/PK-8
901 Andover Rd 21090 410-859-3598
St. Philip Neri S 400/PK-8
6401 S Orchard Rd 21090 410-859-1212
Catherine Daley, prin. Fax 859-5480

Lonaconing, Allegany, Pop. 1,197
Allegany County SD
Supt. — See Cumberland
George's Creek ES 300/PK-5
15600 Lower Georges Creek 21539 301-463-6202
Tara Fazenbaker, prin. Fax 463-3124
Westmar MS 300/6-8
16915 Lower Georges Creek 21539 301-463-5751
Stephanie Wesolowski, prin. Fax 463-2231

Lothian, Anne Arundel
Anne Arundel County SD
Supt. — See Annapolis
Lothian ES 400/PK-5
5175 Solomons Island Rd 20711 410-222-1697
Melissa Brown, prin. Fax 222-1699
Southern MS 800/6-8
5235 Solomons Island Rd 20711 410-222-1659
Kevin Buckley, prin. Fax 867-0231

Loveville, Saint Mary's
St. Mary's County SD
Supt. — See Leonardtown
Banneker ES 700/PK-5
27180 Point Lookout Rd 20656 301-475-0260
Audrey Ellis, prin. Fax 475-0262

Lusby, Calvert, Pop. 1,786
Calvert County SD
Supt. — See Prince Frederick
Dowell ES 700/PK-5
12680 HG Trueman Rd 20657 410-535-7802
Jessica Reynolds, prin. Fax 535-7803
Mill Creek MS 500/6-8
12200 Southern Connector 20657 410-550-9190
Beckie Bowen, prin. Fax 286-4024
Patuxent-Appeal ES 400/PK-5
35 Appeal Ln 20657 410-535-7800
Karen Vogel, prin. Fax 326-6996
Southern MS 500/6-8
9615 HG Trueman Rd 20657 410-535-7877
Mandy Blackmon, prin. Fax 535-7879

Lutherville, Baltimore, Pop. 6,362
Baltimore County SD
Supt. — See Towson
Hampton ES 600/K-5
1115 Charmuth Rd 21093 410-887-3205
Patricia Kaiser, prin. Fax 887-3209
Lutherville Laboratory ES 600/PK-5
1700 York Rd 21093 410-887-7800
Richard Corner, prin. Fax 887-7804
Ridgely MS 1,100/6-8
121 E Ridgely Rd 21093 410-887-7650
Susan Truesdell, prin. Fax 887-7834

Greenspring Montessori S 200/PK-8
10807 Tony Dr 21093 410-321-8555
Tamara S. Balis, head sch Fax 321-8566

Manchester, Carroll, Pop. 4,742
Carroll County SD
Supt. — See Westminster

Ebb Valley ES 500/PK-5
3100 Swiper Dr 21102 410-386-1550
Justin Watts, prin. Fax 386-1555
Manchester ES 600/K-5
3224 York St 21102 410-751-3410
Catherine Cramer, prin. Fax 751-3439

Marbury, Charles, Pop. 1,244
Charles County SD
Supt. — See La Plata
Gale-Bailey ES 400/PK-5
4740 Pisgah Marbury Rd 20658 301-743-5491
Verniece Rorie, prin. Fax 743-2119

Mardela Springs, Wicomico, Pop. 336
Wicomico County SD
Supt. — See Salisbury
Northwestern ES 300/PK-5
9975 Sharptown Rd 21837 410-677-5808
Kirby Bryson, prin. Fax 677-5850

Marriottsville, Howard
Howard County SD
Supt. — See Ellicott City
Mount View MS 700/6-8
12101 Woodford Dr 21104 410-313-5545
Allen Cosentino, prin. Fax 313-5551

Maugansville, Washington, Pop. 3,011
Washington County SD
Supt. — See Hagerstown
Maugansville ES 600/PK-5
18023 Maugans Ave 21767 301-766-8230
Erin Wolford, prin. Fax 665-1086

Mechanicsville, Saint Mary's, Pop. 1,477
St. Mary's County SD
Supt. — See Leonardtown
Brent MS 1,000/6-8
29675 Point Lookout Rd 20659 301-884-4635
Janet Fowler, prin. Fax 884-8937
Dent ES 600/PK-5
37840 New Market Turner Rd 20659 301-472-4500
Kelly Courtney, prin. Fax 472-4503
Mechanicsville ES 400/K-5
28585 Three Notch Rd 20659 301-472-4800
Sandra Oliver, prin. Fax 472-4809
Oakville ES 300/PK-5
26410 Three Notch Rd 20659 301-373-4365
Kathryn Miluski, prin. Fax 373-4369
White Marsh ES 200/K-5
29090 Thompson Corner Rd 20659 301-472-4600
Julia Steele, prin. Fax 472-4604

Mother Catherine Spalding Academy 100/PK-8
38833 Chaptico Rd 20659 301-884-3165
Anthony Wojt, prin. Fax 472-4460

Middletown, Frederick, Pop. 4,076
Frederick County SD
Supt. — See Frederick
Middletown ES 500/3-5
201 E Green St 21769 240-236-1100
Randy Perrell, prin. Fax 236-1150
Middletown MS 800/6-8
100 Martha Mason St 21769 240-236-4200
Everett Warren, prin. Fax 236-4250
Middletown PS 400/PK-2
403 Franklin St 21769 240-566-0200
Karen Hopson, prin. Fax 566-0201

St. Thomas More Academy PK-8
103 Prospect St 21769 240-490-5479
Veronica Kosch, dir. Fax 490-7626

Millersville, Anne Arundel
Anne Arundel County SD
Supt. — See Annapolis
Millersville ES 400/K-5
1601 Millersville Rd 21108 410-222-3800
Isaphine Johnson, prin. Fax 222-3802
Old Mill MS North 900/6-8
610 Patriot Ln 21108 410-969-5950
Dennis Kelly, prin. Fax 969-2612
Old Mill MS South 700/6-8
620 Patriot Ln 21108 410-969-7000
Christian Thomas, prin. Fax 969-5157
Shipley's Choice ES 400/K-5
310 Governor Stone Pkwy 21108 410-222-3851
Beth Burke, prin. Fax 222-3885

Rockbridge Academy 300/K-12
911 Generals Hwy 21108 410-923-1171
Roy Griffith, hdmstr. Fax 923-6588

Mitchellville, Prince George's, Pop. 10,692
Prince George's County SD
Supt. — See Upper Marlboro
Just MS 600/7-8
1300 Campus Way N 20721 301-808-4040
Dr. Keary Schoen, prin. Fax 808-4050
Kingsford ES 600/PK-5
1401 Enterprise Rd 20721 301-390-0260
Renee Jones, prin. Fax 390-0274
Lake Arbor ES 500/PK-5
10205 Lake Arbor Way 20721 301-808-5940
Tonya Riggins, prin. Fax 808-5960
Woodmore ES 400/K-5
12500 Woodmore Rd 20721 301-390-0239
Jill Walker, prin. Fax 390-0285

Woodstream Christian Academy 400/PK-12
9800 Lottsford Rd 20721 301-955-1160
Bonita Bailey, dean Fax 955-1169

Monkton, Baltimore
Baltimore County SD
Supt. — See Towson
Hereford MS 900/6-8
712 Corbett Rd 21111 410-887-7902
Cathryn Walrod, prin. Fax 887-7904

St. James Academy 300/K-8
3100 Monkton Rd 21111 410-771-4816
Maureen Walsh, head sch Fax 771-4842

Monrovia, Frederick, Pop. 407
Frederick County SD
Supt. — See Frederick
Green Valley ES 400/K-5
11501 Fingerboard Rd 21770 240-236-3400
Leigh Warren, prin. Fax 236-3401
Kemptown ES 400/K-5
3456 Kemptown Church Rd 21770 240-236-3500
Liz Worch, prin. Fax 236-3501

Montgomery Village, Montgomery, Pop. 30,917
Montgomery County SD
Supt. — See Rockville
Montgomery Village MS 600/6-8
19300 Watkins Mill Rd 20886 301-840-4660
Kisha Logan, prin. Fax 840-6388
Watkins Mill ES 600/PK-5
19001 Watkins Mill Rd 20886 301-840-7181
Dr. Rock Palmisano, prin. Fax 840-5319

Living Grace Christian S 100/K-12
20300 Pleasant Ridge Dr 20886 301-840-9830
Dr. Daniel Switzer, prin. Fax 840-8005

Mount Airy, Carroll, Pop. 9,125
Carroll County SD
Supt. — See Westminster
Mount Airy ES 500/3-5
405 N Main St 21771 410-751-3540
Deborah Winson, prin. Fax 549-6917
Mount Airy MS 700/6-8
102 Watersville Rd 21771 410-751-3554
Karl Streaker, prin. Fax 751-3556
Parr's Ridge ES 500/PK-2
202 Watersville Rd 21771 410-751-3559
Craig Hastings, prin. Fax 549-7221

Frederick County SD
Supt. — See Frederick
Twin Ridge ES 500/PK-5
1106 Leafy Hollow Cir 21771 240-236-2300
Susan Gullo, prin. Fax 236-2301

Mount Airy Christian Academy 400/PK-12
16700 Old Frederick Rd 21771 410-489-4321
Vicky Webster, head sch Fax 489-4492

Mount Rainier, Prince George's, Pop. 7,916
Prince George's County SD
Supt. — See Upper Marlboro
Mount Rainier ES 400/PK-6
4011 32nd St 20712 301-985-1810
Jennifer Till, prin. Fax 760-3669
Stone ES 700/PK-5
4500 34th St 20712 301-985-1890
Dr. Ashanti Foster, prin. Fax 927-1153

Mount Savage, Allegany, Pop. 859
Allegany County SD
Supt. — See Cumberland
Mount Savage S 400/PK-8
13201 New School Rd NW 21545 301-264-3220
Martin Crump, prin. Fax 264-4015

Myersville, Frederick, Pop. 1,611
Frederick County SD
Supt. — See Frederick
Myersville ES 400/K-5
429 Main St 21773 240-236-1900
Kathy Swire, prin. Fax 236-1901
Wolfsville ES 200/PK-5
12520 Wolfsville Rd 21773 240-236-2250
Megan Stein, prin. Fax 236-2251

Nanjemoy, Charles
Charles County SD
Supt. — See La Plata
Mt. Hope/Nanjemoy ES 400/PK-5
9275 Ironsides Rd 20662 301-246-4383
William Miller, prin. Fax 246-9453

Newark, Worcester, Pop. 331
Worcester County SD 6,600/PK-12
6270 Worcester Hwy 21841 410-632-5000
Louis Taylor, supt. Fax 632-0364
www.worcesterk12.com
Other Schools – See Berlin, Ocean City, Pocomoke City, Snow Hill

Newburg, Charles
Charles County SD
Supt. — See La Plata
Higdon ES 400/PK-5
12872 Rock Point Rd 20664 301-934-4091
Kathleen Morgan, prin. Fax 934-1718
Piccowaxen MS 400/6-8
12834 Rock Point Rd 20664 301-934-1977
Wendell Martin, prin. Fax 934-1628

New Carrollton, Prince George's, Pop. 11,918
Prince George's County SD
Supt. — See Upper Marlboro
Carroll MS 1,000/6-8
6130 Lamont Dr 20784 301-918-8640
Emmett Hendershot, prin. Fax 918-8646
Carrollton ES 600/PK-5
8300 Quintana St 20784 301-918-8708
Nancy Schickner, prin. Fax 918-8710
Frost ES 300/K-5
6419 85th Ave 20784 301-918-8792
Dr. Renita Alexander, prin. Fax 918-8566
Lamont ES 600/PK-5
7101 Good Luck Rd 20784 301-513-5205
Massa Washington, prin. Fax 513-5271

New Market, Frederick, Pop. 644
Frederick County SD
Supt. — See Frederick
Deer Crossing ES 700/K-5
10601 Finn Dr 21774 240-236-5900
Heather Michael, prin. Fax 236-5901
New Market ES 700/PK-5
93 W Main St 21774 240-236-1300
Jason Bowser, prin. Fax 236-1301
New Market MS 500/6-8
125 W Main St 21774 240-236-4600
Trese Suter, prin. Fax 236-4650

North Bethesda, Montgomery, Pop. 42,508

Green Acres S 300/PK-8
11701 Danville Dr 20852 301-881-4100
Dr. Neal Brown Ed.D., hdmstr. Fax 881-3319

North East, Cecil, Pop. 3,496
Cecil County SD
Supt. — See Elkton
Bay View ES 600/PK-5
910 N East Rd 21901 410-996-6230
Catherine Dingle, prin. Fax 996-6233
North East ES 500/PK-5
301 E Thomas Ave 21901 410-996-6220
Lisa Lowe, prin. Fax 996-6302
North East MS 800/6-8
200 E Cecil Ave 21901 410-996-6210
Denise Sopa, prin. Fax 996-6236

Tome S 500/K-12
581 S Maryland Ave 21901 410-287-2050
Christine Szymanski, head sch Fax 287-8999

North Potomac, Montgomery, Pop. 23,745
Montgomery County SD
Supt. — See Rockville
Stone Mill ES 600/PK-5
14323 Stonebridge View Dr 20878 301-279-4975
Kimberly Williams, prin. Fax 279-4979
Travilah ES 400/K-5
13801 Dufief Mill Rd 20878 301-840-7153
Susan Shenk, prin. Fax 670-8230

Nottingham, Baltimore

St. Peter's Christian Day S 100/PK-5
7910 Belair Rd 21236 410-665-4521
Carole Hengen, prin. Fax 665-4521

Oakland, Garrett, Pop. 1,908
Garrett County SD 3,900/PK-12
40 S 2nd St 21550 301-334-8900
Barbara L. Baker, supt. Fax 334-7621
garrettcountyschools.org
Broad Ford ES 600/PK-5
607 Harvey Winters Dr 21550 301-334-9445
Dawna Ashby, prin. Fax 334-5774
Southern MS 500/6-8
605 Harvey Winters Dr 21550 301-334-8881
Brooks Elliott, prin. Fax 334-2315
Swan Meadow S 50/K-8
6709 Garrett Hwy 21550 301-334-2059
Connie Uphold, prin. Fax 334-6335
Yough Glades ES 300/PK-5
70 Wolf Acres Dr 21550 301-334-3334
Janet Gregory, prin. Fax 334-6992
Other Schools – See Accident, Crellin, Friendsville, Frostburg, Grantsville

---

Mountaintop SDA S K-8
PO Box 533 21550 301-387-0022

Ocean City, Worcester, Pop. 7,021
Worcester County SD
Supt. — See Newark
Ocean City ES 700/PK-4
12828 Center Dr 21842 410-632-5370
Dawn Rogers, prin. Fax 632-5379

Seaside Christian Academy 50/PK-9
12637 Ocean Gtwy Ste A 21842 410-213-7595
Rev. Terry Davis, admin. Fax 213-8001

Odenton, Anne Arundel, Pop. 35,750
Anne Arundel County SD
Supt. — See Annapolis
Arundel MS 900/6-8
1179 Hammond Ln 21113 410-674-6900
George Lindley, prin. Fax 674-6593
Odenton ES 400/PK-5
1290 Odenton Rd 21113 410-222-6514
Tracey Ahern, prin. Fax 222-6516
Piney Orchard ES 700/K-5
2641 Strawberry Lake Way 21113 410-672-7591
Karen Bailey, prin. Fax 672-7173
Seven Oaks ES 700/PK-5
1905 Town Center Dr 21113 410-222-0937
Farah Springer, prin. Fax 305-2590
Waugh Chapel ES 600/PK-5
840 Sunflower Dr 21113 410-222-6542
Cheryl Cox, prin. Fax 222-6963

Olney, Montgomery, Pop. 33,044
Montgomery County SD
Supt. — See Rockville
Belmont ES 300/K-5
19528 Olney Mill Rd 20832 301-924-3140
Evan Pinkowitz, prin. Fax 924-3233
Brooke Grove ES 400/K-5
2700 Spartan Rd 20832 240-722-1800
Jolynn Tarwater, prin. Fax 924-3161
Farquhar MS 600/6-8
17017 Batchellors Forest Rd 20832 240-740-1200
Joel Beidleman, prin. Fax 774-7505
Olney ES 600/PK-5
3401 Queen Mary Dr 20832 301-924-3126
Carla Glawe, prin. Fax 774-8014
Parks MS 900/6-8
19200 Olney Mill Rd 20832 301-924-3180
Jewel Sanders, prin. Fax 924-3288

Olney Adventist Preparatory S 100/K-8
4100 Olney Laytonsville Rd 20832 301-570-2500
St. John's Episcopal S 200/PK-8
3427 Olney Laytonsville Rd 20832 301-774-6804
Thomas Stevens, head sch Fax 774-2375
St. Peter S 400/PK-8
2900 Olney Sandy Spring Rd 20832 301-774-9112
Mary Whelan, prin. Fax 924-3774
Washington Christian Academy 300/K-12
16227 Batchellors Forest Rd 20832 240-390-0429
James Armistead, head sch Fax 559-0115

Owings, Calvert, Pop. 2,102
Calvert County SD
Supt. — See Prince Frederick
Mt. Harmony ES 600/K-5
900 W Mount Harmony Rd 20736 410-550-9620
Charles Treft, prin. Fax 286-4017
Northern MS 700/6-8
2954 Chaneyville Rd 20736 410-257-1622
Jaime Webster, prin. Fax 257-1623
Windy Hill ES 700/PK-5
9550 Boyds Turn Rd 20736 410-550-9790
Kelly Griffith, prin. Fax 286-4023
Windy Hill MS 700/6-8
9560 Boyds Turn Rd 20736 410-257-1560
James Kurtz, prin. Fax 257-4586

Cardinal Hickey Academy 200/PK-8
1601 W Mount Harmony Rd 20736 410-286-0404
Jennifer Griffith, prin. Fax 286-6334

Owings Mills, Baltimore, Pop. 29,714
Baltimore County SD
Supt. — See Towson
Deer Park ES 500/PK-5
9809 Lyons Mill Rd 21117 410-887-0723
Renee Jenkins, prin. Fax 496-4595
Lyons Mill ES K-5
9435 Lyons Mill Rd 21117 410-887-1719
Maralee Clark, prin.
New Town ES 1,000/PK-5
4924 New Town Blvd 21117 410-887-1541
Sharonda Gregory, prin. Fax 887-1544
Owings Mills ES 900/PK-5
10824 Reisterstown Rd 21117 410-887-1710
Chester Scott, prin. Fax 887-1712
Timber Grove ES 600/PK-5
701 Academy Ave 21117 410-887-1714
Paul Scott, prin. Fax 887-1566

Garrison Forest S 600/PK-12
300 Garrison Forest Rd 21117 410-363-1500
Lila Lohr, head sch Fax 363-8441
Hurwitz ES 700/PK-5
11111 Park Heights Ave 21117 410-363-3300
Jemicy Lower S 200/1-8
11 Celadon Rd 21117 410-653-2700
Ben Shifrin, hdmstr. Fax 653-1972
Liberty Christian S 300/PK-8
11303 Liberty Rd 21117 410-655-5527
Monica Gicking, head sch Fax 655-0209
McDonogh S 1,300/PK-12
8600 McDonogh Rd 21117 443-544-7000
Charles Britton, hdmstr. Fax 581-0155
Yeshivas Kochav Yitzchak 600/PK-8
35 Rosewood Ln 21117 410-654-3500

Oxon Hill, Prince George's, Pop. 17,298
Prince George's County SD
Supt. — See Upper Marlboro
Barnaby Manor ES 500/PK-6
2411 Owens Rd 20745 301-702-7560
Viola Lynch, prin. Fax 702-7529
Flintstone ES 400/PK-5
800 Comanche Dr 20745 301-749-4210
Brandi Stinson, prin. Fax 749-4215
Forest Heights ES 300/PK-6
200 Talbert Dr 20745 301-749-4220
Peter Thompson, prin. Fax 749-4224
Glassmanor ES 300/K-5
1011 Marcy Ave 20745 301-749-4240
Diane Jones, prin. Fax 749-4242
Hanson Montessori S 500/PK-8
6360 Oxon Hill Rd 20745 301-749-4052
Zory Kenon, prin. Fax 749-4054
Oxon Hill ES 300/PK-5
7701 Livingston Rd 20745 301-749-4290
Cynthia Best-Goring, prin. Fax 749-4295
Valley View ES 500/PK-5
5500 Danby Ave 20745 301-749-4350
Kimberly Pettway, prin. Fax 749-4354

St. Columba S 200/K-8
7800 Livingston Rd 20745 301-567-6212
Katrina Fernandez, prin. Fax 567-6907

Park Hall, Saint Mary's
St. Mary's County SD
Supt. — See Leonardtown
Park Hall ES 600/PK-5
20343 Hermanville Rd 20667 301-863-4054
Scott Szczerbiak, prin. Fax 863-4050

Parkton, Baltimore
Baltimore County SD
Supt. — See Towson
Seventh District ES 400/K-5
20300 York Rd 21120 410-887-1902
Heather Denmyer, prin. Fax 887-1903

Our Lady of Grace Preschool 200/PK-PK
18310 Middletown Rd 21120 410-329-6956
Sally Lake, prin. Fax 357-5793

Pasadena, Anne Arundel, Pop. 23,755
Anne Arundel County SD
Supt. — See Annapolis
Bodkin ES 600/K-5
8320 Ventnor Rd 21122 410-437-0464
Rachel Amstutz, prin. Fax 437-0845
Chesapeake Bay MS 1,100/6-8
4804 Mountain Rd 21122 410-437-2400
Michael Dunn, prin. Fax 437-9920
Fort Smallwood ES 400/PK-5
1720 Poplar Ridge Rd 21122 410-222-6450
David Sembly, prin. Fax 222-6452
Fox MS 900/6-8
7922 Outing Ave 21122 410-437-5512
Russell Austin, prin. Fax 360-1511
High Point ES 700/PK-5
924 Duvall Hwy 21122 410-222-6454
Timothy Merritt, prin. Fax 222-6456
Jacobsville ES 600/K-5
3801 Mountain Rd 21122 410-222-6460
April Umile, prin. Fax 222-6498
Lake Shore ES 300/K-5
4531 Mountain Rd 21122 410-222-6465
Linda Toth, prin. Fax 222-6468
Pasadena ES 400/K-5
401 E Pasadena Rd 21122 410-222-6573
Jennifer Quirino, prin. Fax 222-6576
Riviera Beach ES 300/PK-5
8515 Jenkins Rd 21122 410-222-6469
Jason Anderson, prin. Fax 360-4557
Sunset ES 500/PK-5
8572 Fort Smallwood Rd 21122 410-222-6478
Antoinette Carr, prin. Fax 222-6482

St. Jane Frances S 300/PK-8
8513 Saint Jane Dr 21122 410-255-4750
Elena Simmons, prin. Fax 360-6720

Perry Hall, Baltimore, Pop. 27,923
Baltimore County SD
Supt. — See Towson
Chapel Hill ES 800/PK-5
5200 E Joppa Rd 21128 410-887-5119
Jonna Hundley, prin. Fax 887-5119
Joppa View ES 700/PK-5
8727 Honeygo Blvd 21128 410-887-5065
Belinda Tetteris, prin. Fax 887-5066

Perry Hall Christian S 300/PK-12
3919 Schroeder Ave 21128 410-256-4886
Steve Taylor, head sch Fax 256-5451

Perryville, Cecil, Pop. 4,257
Cecil County SD
Supt. — See Elkton
Perryville ES 400/PK-5
901 Maywood Ave 21903 410-996-6020
Jennifer Hammer, prin. Fax 996-6024
Perryville MS 600/6-8
850 Aiken Ave 21903 410-996-6010
Shawn Johnson, prin. Fax 996-6048

Good Shepherd S 100/PK-8
800 Aiken Ave 21903 410-642-6265
Jenifer Pileggi, prin. Fax 642-6522

Phoenix, Baltimore, Pop. 500
Baltimore County SD
Supt. — See Towson
Jacksonville ES 600/PK-5
3400 Hillendale Heights Rd 21131 410-887-7880
Deborah Miller, prin. Fax 683-8919

Pittsville, Wicomico, Pop. 1,382
Wicomico County SD
Supt. — See Salisbury
Pittsville S 500/PK-8
34404 Old Ocean City Rd 21850 410-677-5811
Michael Cody, prin. Fax 677-5895

Pocomoke City, Worcester, Pop. 4,103
Worcester County SD
Supt. — See Newark
Pocomoke ES 400/PK-3
2119 Pocomoke Beltway 21851 410-632-5130
Michael Browne, prin. Fax 632-5139
Pocomoke MS 400/4-8
800 8th St 21851 410-632-5150
Matthew Record, prin. Fax 632-5159

Pomfret, Charles, Pop. 498
Charles County SD
Supt. — See La Plata
Craik ES 500/PK-5
7725 Marshall Corner Rd 20675 301-934-4270
Michelle Beckwith, prin. Fax 934-8096

Poolesville, Montgomery, Pop. 4,780
Montgomery County SD
Supt. — See Rockville
Poole MS 400/6-8
17014 Tom Fox Ave 20837 301-972-7979
Jon Green, prin. Fax 972-7982
Poolesville ES 400/PK-5
19565 Fisher Ave 20837 301-972-7960
Douglas Robbins, prin. Fax 972-7963

Port Deposit, Cecil, Pop. 641
Cecil County SD
Supt. — See Elkton
Bainbridge ES 400/PK-5
41 Preston Dr 21904 410-996-6030
Paula Webster, prin. Fax 996-6033

Port Republic, Calvert
Calvert County SD
Supt. — See Prince Frederick
Mutual ES 500/PK-5
1455 Ball Rd 20676 410-535-7700
Donna House, prin. Fax 535-7701

Potomac, Montgomery, Pop. 43,827
Montgomery County SD
Supt. — See Rockville
Bells Mill ES 600/PK-5
8225 Bells Mill Rd 20854 240-740-0480
Jerri Oglesby, prin. Fax 469-1060
Beverly Farms ES 600/K-5
8501 Postoak Rd 20854 240-740-0200
Spencer DeLisle, prin. Fax 469-1058
Cabin John MS 1,000/6-8
10701 Gainsborough Rd 20854 240-406-1600
Dr. John Taylor, prin. Fax 469-1003
Cold Spring ES 300/K-5
9201 Falls Chapel Way 20854 301-279-8480
Sandra Reece, prin. Fax 279-3226
Hoover MS 1,000/6-8
8810 Postoak Rd 20854 301-968-3740
Dr. Yong-Mi Kim, prin. Fax 469-1013
Potomac ES 500/K-5
10311 River Rd 20854 301-469-1042
Catherine Allie, prin. Fax 469-1045

Bullis S 600/K-12
10601 Falls Rd 20854 301-299-8500
Dr. Gerald Boarman, hdmstr. Fax 299-9050
German S Washington D.C. 600/PK-12
8617 Chateau Dr 20854 301-365-4400
Heights S 500/3-12
10400 Seven Locks Rd 20854 301-365-4300
Alvaro de Vicente, hdmstr. Fax 365-4303
McLean S 400/K-12
8224 Lochinver Ln 20854 301-299-8277
Michael Saxenian, head sch Fax 299-1639
Muslim Community S / Alim Academy 100/PK-12
7917 Montrose Rd 20854 301-340-6713
Our Lady of Mercy S 300/K-8
9222 Kentsdale Dr 20854 301-365-4477
Deborah Thomas, prin. Fax 365-3423
St. Andrew's Episcopal S 500/3-12
8804 Postoak Rd 20854 301-983-5200
Robert Kosasky, head sch Fax 983-4710

Preston, Caroline, Pop. 698
Caroline County SD
Supt. — See Denton
Preston ES 400/PK-5
225 Main St 21655 410-673-2552
Dr. Kari Clow, prin. Fax 673-7301

Prince Frederick, Calvert, Pop. 2,434
Calvert County SD 15,700/PK-12
1305 Dares Beach Rd 20678 410-535-1700
Dr. Daniel Curry, supt. Fax 535-7298
www.calvertnet.k12.md.us
Barstow ES 600/PK-5
295 Williams Rd 20678 443-486-4770
Ramona Crowley, prin. Fax 535-4069
Calvert ES 500/PK-5
1450 Dares Beach Rd 20678 410-535-7311
Kim Harris, prin. Fax 535-7473
Calvert MS 600/6-8
655 Chesapeake Blvd 20678 410-550-8970
Zach Seawell, prin. Fax 286-4007
Other Schools – See Chesapeake Beach, Huntingtown, Lusby, Owings, Port Republic, Saint Leonard, Sunderland

---

Christian Beginnings Preschool 50/PK-PK
105 Vianney Ln 20678 410-586-2151
Marie Chrzanowski, dir. Fax 535-4422

Princess Anne, Somerset, Pop. 3,212
Somerset County SD
Supt. — See Westover
Greenwood ES 500/PK-5
11412 Dryden Rd 21853 410-651-0931
Ashley Walters, prin. Fax 651-4091
Princess Anne ES 400/PK-5
11576 Lankford Ave 21853 410-651-0481
Cortney Monar, prin. Fax 651-4286

Pylesville, Harford, Pop. 684
Harford County SD
Supt. — See Bel Air
North Harford ES 400/PK-5
120 Pylesville Rd 21132 410-638-3670
Lisa Sundquist, prin. Fax 638-3675
North Harford MS 1,000/6-8
112 Pylesville Rd 21132 410-638-3658
Karl Wickman, prin. Fax 638-3669

Quantico, Wicomico, Pop. 132
Wicomico County SD
Supt. — See Salisbury
Westside PS 300/PK-1
6046 Quantico Rd 21856 410-677-5117
Maria Wright, prin. Fax 677-5860

Randallstown, Baltimore, Pop. 31,696
Baltimore County SD
Supt. — See Towson
Church Lane ES Technology 500/K-5
3820 Fernside Rd 21133 410-887-0717
Judith Devlin, prin. Fax 496-0473
Deer Park Magnet MS 1,300/6-8
9830 Winands Rd 21133 410-887-0726
Kandice Taylor, prin. Fax 887-0704
Hernwood ES 400/PK-5
9919 Marriottsville Rd 21133 410-887-0732
Stefanie Fogleman, prin. Fax 521-7679
Randallstown ES 400/PK-5
9013 Liberty Rd 21133 410-887-0746
Lois Stokes, prin. Fax 887-0747

Reisterstown, Baltimore, Pop. 25,217
Baltimore County SD
Supt. — See Towson
Cedarmere ES 500/PK-5
17 Nicodemus Rd 21136 410-887-1100
Laura Brown, prin. Fax 887-6920
Chatsworth ES 400/PK-5
222 New Ave 21136 410-887-1103
Andrea Derrien, prin. Fax 887-1109

Franklin ES 500/PK-5
33 Cockeys Mill Rd 21136 410-887-1111
Benjamin Mertes, prin. Fax 887-6947
Franklin MS 1,300/6-8
10 Cockeys Mill Rd 21136 410-887-1114
Charlyn Maul, prin. Fax 517-2548
Glyndon ES 500/PK-5
445 Glyndon Dr 21136 410-887-1130
Tracy Robinson, prin. Fax 833-1828
Reisterstown ES 500/K-5
223 Walgrove Rd 21136 410-887-1133
Lynne Palmer, prin. Fax 887-6925

Ridge, Saint Mary's
St. Mary's County SD
Supt. — See Leonardtown
Ridge ES 300/PK-5
49430 Airedele Rd 20680 301-872-0200
Honora Batelka, prin. Fax 872-0205

St. Michael S 200/PK-8
PO Box 259 20680 301-872-5454
Lila Hofmeister, prin. Fax 872-4047

Ridgely, Caroline, Pop. 1,595
Caroline County SD
Supt. — See Denton
Ridgely ES 500/PK-5
118 N Central Ave 21660 410-634-2105
Lee Sutton, prin. Fax 634-1789

Rising Sun, Cecil, Pop. 2,742
Cecil County SD
Supt. — See Elkton
Calvert ES 500/K-5
79 Brick Meeting House Rd 21911 410-658-5335
Elsie Harrigan, prin. Fax 658-9130
Rising Sun ES 700/PK-5
500 Hopewell Rd 21911 410-658-5925
Cindy Fitzpatrick, prin. Fax 658-7999
Rising Sun MS 700/6-8
289 Pearl St 21911 410-658-5535
Stuart Hutchinson, prin. Fax 658-9173

Riverdale, Prince George's, Pop. 5,120
Prince George's County SD
Supt. — See Upper Marlboro
Beacon Heights ES 500/PK-6
6929 Furman Pkwy, 301-918-8700
Lila Walker, prin. Fax 918-8707
Riverdale ES 700/K-5
5006 Riverdale Rd, 301-985-1850
Natiqua Riley, prin. Fax 927-1166
Templeton ES 800/PK-5
6001 Carters Ln, 301-985-1880
Ebony Harris, prin. Fax 985-1876
Wirt MS 1,000/6-8
6200 Tuckerman St, 301-985-1720
Rhonda Simley, prin. Fax 985-2135

Rock Hall, Kent, Pop. 1,286
Kent County SD 2,100/PK-12
5608 Boundary Ave 21661 410-778-7113
Dr. Karen Couch, supt. Fax 778-2350
www.kent.k12.md.us
Rock Hall ES 200/PK-5
21203 W Sharp St 21661 410-810-2622
Kris Hemstetter, prin. Fax 639-2998
Other Schools – See Chestertown, Galena

Rockville, Montgomery, Pop. 59,311
Montgomery County SD 149,200/PK-12
850 Hungerford Dr 20850 301-279-3066
Dr. Jack Smith, supt. Fax 279-3192
www.montgomeryschoolsmd.org
Barnsley ES 700/K-5
14516 Nadine Dr 20853 240-740-3260
Andrew Winter, prin. Fax 740-3440
Beall ES 800/PK-5
451 Beall Ave 20850 240-740-1220
Elliot Alter, prin. Fax 279-4999
Brookhaven ES 500/PK-5
4610 Renn St 20853 240-740-0500
Xavier Kimber, prin. Fax 460-2460
Candlewood ES 300/K-5
7210 Osprey Dr 20855 301-284-4200
Dr. Linda Sheppard, prin. Fax 840-7171
Cashell ES 300/K-5
17101 Cashell Rd 20853 240-740-0560
Courtney Jones, prin. Fax 924-3132
College Gardens ES 800/K-5
1700 Yale Pl 20850 301-279-8470
Stacey Rogovoy, prin. Fax 279-8473
Fallsmead ES 600/K-5
1800 Greenplace Ter 20850 240-740-3550
Roni Silverstein, prin. Fax 279-3040
Farmland ES 700/PK-5
7000 Old Gate Rd 20852 240-740-0660
Mary Bliss, prin. Fax 230-5424
Flower Valley ES 500/PK-5
4615 Sunflower Dr 20853 240-740-1780
Gay Melnick, prin. Fax 740-1789
Frost MS 1,200/6-8
9201 Scott Dr 20850 301-279-3949
Dr. Joey Jones, prin. Fax 279-3956
Lakewood ES 600/K-5
2534 Lindley Ter 20850 301-279-8465
Debra Berner, prin. Fax 279-8596
Luxmanor ES 400/K-5
6201 Tilden Ln 20852 240-740-0820
Ryan Forkert, prin. Fax 230-5917
Maryvale ES 600/PK-5
1000 1st St 20850 301-279-4990
Margaret Prin, prin. Fax 279-4993
Meadow Hall ES 400/PK-5
951 Twinbrook Pkwy 20851 301-279-4988
Cabell Lloyd, prin. Fax 517-5887
Mill Creek Towne ES 400/PK-5
17700 Park Mill Dr 20855 240-740-1820
Natasha Bolden, prin. Fax 740-1815

Parkland MS 900/6-8
4610 W Frankfort Dr 20853 301-438-5700
Khanny Yang, prin. Fax 460-2699
Redland MS 500/6-8
6505 Muncaster Mill Rd 20855 240-740-0900
Everett Davis, prin. Fax 670-2231
Ritchie Park ES 500/K-5
1514 Dunster Rd 20854 301-279-8475
M. Catherine Long, prin. Fax 517-5047
Rock Creek Valley ES 400/PK-5
5121 Russett Rd 20853 240-740-1240
Kevin Burns, prin. Fax 460-2196
Tilden MS 500/7-8
11211 Old Georgetown Rd 20852 301-230-5930
Irina LaGrange, prin. Fax 230-5991
Twinbrook ES 600/PK-5
5911 Ridgway Ave 20851 301-230-5925
Karen Johnson, prin. Fax 230-5929
West MS 1,100/6-8
651 Great Falls Rd 20850 301-337-3400
Craig Staton, prin. Fax 517-8216
Wheaton Woods ES 500/PK-5
15101 Bauer Dr 20852 301-929-2018
David Chia, prin. Fax 929-6974
Wood MS 900/6-8
14615 Bauer Dr 20853 301-460-2150
Heidi Slatcoff, prin. Fax 460-2104
Other Schools – See Bethesda, Brookeville, Burtonsville, Chevy Chase, Clarksburg, Damascus, Derwood, Dickerson, Gaithersburg, Germantown, Kensington, Montgomery Village, North Potomac, Olney, Poolesville, Potomac, Sandy Spring, Silver Spring, Takoma Park

---

Berman Hebrew Academy 700/PK-12
13300 Arctic Ave 20853 301-962-9400
Christ Episcopal S 200/PK-8
22 W Jefferson St 20850 301-424-6550
Dr. Caroline Chapin, head sch Fax 424-3516
Montrose Christian S 200/PK-12
5100 Randolph Rd 20852 301-770-5335
Dr. Ken Fentress, chncllr. Fax 881-7345
Primary Montessori Day S 100/PK-3
14138 Travilah Rd 20850 301-309-9532
Redwood Montessori Academy 50/PK-5
1605 Veirs Mill Rd 20851 301-762-2524
St. Elizabeth S 600/PK-8
917 Montrose Rd 20852 301-881-1824
Vincent Spadoni, prin. Fax 881-6035
St. Jude Regional S 200/PK-8
4820 Walbridge St 20853 301-946-7888
Glenn Benjamin, prin. Fax 929-8927
St. Mary S 200/PK-8
600 Veirs Mill Rd 20852 301-762-4179
Debra Eisel, prin. Fax 762-9550
St. Patrick S 200/K-8
4101 Norbeck Rd 20853 301-929-9672
Christie Short, prin. Fax 929-1474
St. Raphael S 300/PK-8
1513 Dunster Rd 20854 301-762-2143
Teri Dwyer, prin. Fax 762-4991
Smith Jewish Day S 800/PK-5
1901 E Jefferson St 20852 301-881-1400
Rabbi Mitchel Malkus, head sch Fax 984-7834

Sabillasville, Frederick, Pop. 352
Frederick County SD
Supt. — See Frederick
Sabillasville ES 100/K-5
16210 Sabillasville Rd # B 21780 240-236-6000
Kate Krietz, prin. Fax 236-6001

Saint Leonard, Calvert, Pop. 739
Calvert County SD
Supt. — See Prince Frederick
Saint Leonard ES 500/K-5
5370 Saint Leonard Rd 20685 410-535-7714
Toni Chapman, prin. Fax 535-7726

Saint Michaels, Talbot, Pop. 1,017
Talbot County SD
Supt. — See Easton
Saint Michaels ES 400/PK-6
100 Seymour Ave 21663 410-745-2882
Indra Bullock, prin. Fax 745-2473

Salisbury, Wicomico, Pop. 29,461
Wicomico County SD 14,400/PK-12
PO Box 1538 21802 410-677-4400
Dr. Donna Hanlin, supt. Fax 677-4444
www.wcboe.org
Beaver Run ES 700/PK-2
31481 Old Ocean City Rd 21804 410-677-5101
Curt Twilley, prin. Fax 677-5188
Chipman ES 400/PK-2
711 Lake St 21801 410-677-5814
Antionette Perry, prin. Fax 677-5882
East Salisbury ES 400/3-5
1201 Old Ocean City Rd 21804 410-677-5803
Glendon Jones, prin. Fax 677-5872
Glen Avenue ES 300/3-5
1615 Glen Avenue Ext 21804 410-677-5806
Lil Giddens, prin. Fax 677-5840
North Salisbury ES 400/3-5
1213 Emerson Ave 21801 410-677-5807
Ruby Brown, prin. Fax 677-5835
Pemberton ES 600/PK-5
1300 Pemberton Dr 21801 410-677-5809
Melissa Eiler, prin. Fax 677-5848
Pinehurst ES 500/PK-5
520 S Pinehurst Ave 21801 410-677-5810
Deborah Emge, prin. Fax 677-5858
Prince Street ES 600/PK-5
400 Prince St 21804 410-677-5813
Jason Miller, prin. Fax 677-5865
Salisbury MS 900/6-8
607 Morris St 21801 410-677-5149
Kris Gosnell, prin. Fax 677-5122
Wicomico Early Learning Center PK-PK
1101 Robert St 21804 410-677-5900
Melva Wright, prin. Fax 677-5904

Wicomico MS 700/6-8
635 E Main St 21804 410-677-5145
Kelley Springston, prin. Fax 677-5197
Other Schools – See Delmar, Fruitland, Hebron, Mardela Springs, Pittsville, Quantico, Willards

---

St. Francis de Sales S 200/PK-8
500 Camden Ave 21801 410-749-9907
Debra Traum, prin. Fax 749-9507
Salisbury Christian S 600/PK-12
807 Parker Rd 21804 410-546-0661
John Petrey M.Ed., head sch Fax 546-4674
Salisbury School 300/PK-12
6279 Hobbs Rd 21804 410-742-4464
Edwin Cowell, hdmstr. Fax 742-9875

Sandy Spring, Montgomery, Pop. 3,092
Montgomery County SD
Supt. — See Rockville
Sherwood ES 500/K-5
1401 Olney Sandy Spring Rd 20860 240-740-0960
Dina Brewer, prin. Fax 924-3294

Sandy Spring Friends S 600/PK-12
16923 Norwood Rd 20860 301-774-7455
Thomas Gibian, head sch Fax 924-1115

Savage, Howard, Pop. 6,765

Bethel Christian Academy 300/PK-8
PO Box 406 20763 301-725-4673
Claire Dant, prin. Fax 617-9277

Secretary, Dorchester, Pop. 531
Dorchester County SD
Supt. — See Cambridge
Warwick ES 300/PK-5
155 Main St 21664 410-943-3588
Marybeth Shellabarger, prin. Fax 943-8152

Severn, Anne Arundel, Pop. 42,378
Anne Arundel County SD
Supt. — See Annapolis
Quarterfield ES 400/PK-5
7967 Quarterfield Rd 21144 410-222-6430
John Birus, prin. Fax 222-6432
Ridgeway ES 600/K-5
1440 Evergreen Rd 21144 410-222-6524
Tracy Prater, prin. Fax 222-6526
Severn ES 400/PK-5
838 Reece Rd 21144 410-551-6220
Heather Garris, prin. Fax 551-6223
Van Bokkelen ES 500/PK-5
1140 Reece Rd 21144 410-222-6535
Selecia Hardy, prin. Fax 222-6549

Annapolis Area Christian Lower S K-5
61 Gambrills Rd 21144 410-846-3505
Karl Graustein, prin. Fax 573-6866

Severna Park, Anne Arundel, Pop. 37,032
Anne Arundel County SD
Supt. — See Annapolis
Benfield ES, 365 Lynwood Dr 21146 500/K-5
Deborah Short, prin. 410-222-6555
Jones ES 300/K-5
122 Hoyle Ln 21146 410-222-6565
Patricia Keffer, prin. Fax 384-9584
McKinsey ES 600/K-5
175 Arundel Beach Rd 21146 410-222-6560
Lenora Fox, prin. Fax 255-3060
Oak Hill ES 600/PK-5
34 Truck House Rd 21146 410-222-6568
Deneen Houghton, prin. Fax 222-6570
Severna Park ES 400/K-5
6 Riggs Ave 21146 410-222-6577
Lorie Barnes, prin. Fax 222-6522
Severna Park MS 1,400/6-8
450 Jumpers Hole Rd 21146 410-647-7900
Sharon Hansen, prin. Fax 431-5376

St. John the Evangelist S 500/PK-8
669 Ritchie Hwy 21146 410-647-2283
Casey Buckstaff, prin. Fax 431-5438
St. Martin's in the Field Episcopal S 200/PK-8
375 Benfield Rd Ste A 21146 410-647-7055
Jamey Hein, head sch Fax 647-7411

Shady Side, Anne Arundel, Pop. 5,701
Anne Arundel County SD
Supt. — See Annapolis
Shady Side ES 500/PK-5
4859 Atwell Rd 20764 410-222-1621
Geoffrey Casey, prin. Fax 867-4941

Sharpsburg, Washington, Pop. 679
Washington County SD
Supt. — See Hagerstown
Sharpsburg ES 300/PK-5
17525 Shepherdstown Pike 21782 301-766-8321
Keith Allshouse, prin. Fax 432-8974

Silver Spring, Montgomery, Pop. 69,258
Montgomery County SD
Supt. — See Rockville
Arcola ES 700/K-5
1820 Franwall Ave 20902 301-287-8585
Emmanuel Jean-Philippe, prin. Fax 649-8592
Argyle MS 800/6-8
2400 Bel Pre Rd 20906 301-460-2400
James Allrich, prin. Fax 460-2423
Bel Pre ES 500/PK-2
13801 Rippling Brook Dr 20906 301-287-8870
Dara Brooks, prin. Fax 460-2148
Briggs-Chaney MS 900/6-8
1901 Rainbow Dr 20905 301-288-8300
Dr. Tamitha Campbell, prin. Fax 989-6020
Burnt Mills ES 500/PK-5
11211 Childs St 20901 301-649-8192
Dr. Stacy Ashton, prin. Fax 649-8097

Cannon Road ES 400/K-5
901 Cannon Rd 20904 240-740-0520
Kristine Donohue, prin. Fax 989-5692
Cloverly ES 400/K-5
800 Briggs Chaney Rd 20905 301-989-5770
Melissa Brunson, prin. Fax 879-1035
Cresthaven ES 500/K-5
1234 Cresthaven Dr 20903 240-740-0580
Sherri Gorden, prin. Fax 431-4660
Drew ES 400/PK-5
1200 Swingingdale Dr 20905 301-989-6030
Wanda Means Harris, prin. Fax 879-1033
Eastern MS 900/6-8
300 University Blvd E 20901 301-650-6650
Matt Johnson, prin. Fax 650-6657
East Silver Spring ES 400/PK-3
631 Silver Spring Ave 20910 240-740-0620
Dr. Adrienne Morrow, prin. Fax 650-6424
Fairland ES 600/K-5
14315 Fairdale Rd 20905 240-740-0640
Lakeisha Lashley, prin. Fax 989-5769
Forest Knolls ES 700/K-5
10830 Eastwood Ave 20901 240-740-1640
Evan Bernstein, prin. Fax 649-8196
Galway ES 800/PK-5
12612 Galway Dr 20904 301-595-2930
Dorothea Fuller, prin. Fax 902-1230
Georgian Forest ES 600/PK-5
3100 Regina Dr 20906 240-740-0720
Sundra Mann, prin. Fax 460-2477
Glenallan ES 500/K-5
12520 Heurich Rd 20902 240-740-0760
Peter Moran, prin. Fax 929-2016
Glen Haven ES 500/PK-5
10900 Inwood Ave 20902 301-649-8051
Dr. Jane Ennis, prin. Fax 649-8540
Greencastle ES 800/PK-5
13611 Robey Rd 20904 240-740-1420
Dr. Ayesha McArthur Moore, prin. Fax 902-1222
Harmony Hills ES 700/PK-5
13407 Lydia St 20906 240-740-0780
Dr. Carole Rawlison, prin. Fax 962-5976
Highland ES 500/PK-5
3100 Medway St 20902 240-740-1770
Scott Steffan, prin. Fax 929-2042
Highland View ES 400/PK-5
9010 Providence Ave 20901 240-740-1990
Galit Zolkower, prin. Fax 650-6506
Jackson Road ES 700/PK-5
900 Jackson Rd 20904 240-740-0800
Sally Ann Macias, prin. Fax 879-1054
Kemp Mill ES 500/PK-5
411 Sisson St 20902 301-649-8046
Bernard James, prin. Fax 649-8216
Key MS 900/6-8
910 Schindler Dr 20903 301-422-5600
Norman Coleman, prin. Fax 434-1375
Lee MS 700/6-8
11800 Monticello Ave 20902 301-649-8100
Kimberly Hayden Williams, prin. Fax 649-8110
Leleck ES at Broad Acres 700/PK-5
710 Beacon Rd 20903 240-740-1900
Dr. Harold Barber, prin. Fax 431-7691
Loiederman MS 800/6-8
12701 Goodhill Rd 20906 301-929-2282
Nicole Sosik, prin. Fax 962-5993
Montgomery Knolls ES 500/PK-2
807 Daleview Dr 20901 240-740-0840
Arienne Clark-Harrison, prin. Fax 431-7669
New Hampshire Estates ES 500/PK-3
8720 Carroll Ave 20903 240-740-1580
Robert Geiger, prin. Fax 431-7644
Nix ES 600/PK-5
1100 Corliss St 20903 301-422-5070
Annette Ffolkes, prin. Fax 422-5072
Oakland Terrace ES 500/K-5
2720 Plyers Mill Rd 20902 301-929-2161
Cheryl Pulliam, prin. Fax 929-6910
Oak View ES 400/3-5
400 E Wayne Ave 20901 301-650-6434
Jeffrey Cline, prin. Fax 650-6453
Page ES 400/PK-5
13400 Tamarack Rd 20904 301-989-5672
Stacey Brown, prin. Fax 879-1036
Pine Crest ES 500/PK-5
201 Woodmoor Dr 20901 240-740-1970
Cheryl Booker, prin. Fax 649-8194
Rosemary Hills ES 600/PK-2
2111 Porter Rd 20910 301-920-9990
Deborah Ryan, prin. Fax 650-6404
Shriver ES 800/PK-5
12518 Greenly St 20906 301-929-4426
Zoraida Brown, prin. Fax 929-4428
Silver Spring International MS 1,000/6-8
313 Wayne Ave 20910 240-740-2750
Karen Bryant, prin. Fax 562-5244
Singer ES, 2600 Hayden Dr 20902 600/K-5
Kyle Heatwole, prin. 240-740-0330
Sligo Creek ES 600/K-5
500 Schuyler Rd 20910 240-740-2800
Diantha Swift, prin. Fax 562-2717
Sligo MS 400/6-8
1401 Dennis Ave 20902 301-287-8890
Cary Dimmick, prin. Fax 649-8145
Stonegate ES 500/PK-5
14811 Notley Rd 20905 301-989-5668
Linda Jones, prin. Fax 989-5671
Strathmore ES 400/3-5
3200 Beaverwood Ln 20906 301-460-2135
Tivinia Nelson, prin. Fax 460-2137
Takoma Park MS 1,000/6-8
7611 Piney Branch Rd 20910 301-650-6444
Alicia Deeny, prin. Fax 650-6430
Viers Mill ES 600/PK-5
11711 Joseph Mill Rd 20906 240-740-1000
Matthew Hawkins, prin. Fax 929-6977
Weller Road ES 600/PK-5
3301 Weller Rd 20906 301-287-8601
Marybeth Mantzouranis, prin. Fax 287-8602
Westover ES 300/K-5
401 Hawkesbury Ln 20904 301-989-5676
Dr. Patricia Kelly, prin. Fax 989-5679
White Oak MS 700/6-8
12201 New Hampshire Ave 20904 301-288-8200
Virginia de los Santos, prin. Fax 989-5696
Woodlin ES 600/K-5
2101 Luzerne Ave 20910 240-740-2820
Craig Jackson, prin. Fax 650-6425

Barrie S 300/PK-12
13500 Layhill Rd 20906 301-576-2800
Jon Kidder, head sch Fax 576-2803
Evergreen S 100/PK-3
10700 Georgia Ave 20902 301-942-5979
Forcey Christian S 600/PK-8
2130 E Randolph Rd 20904 301-622-2281
Cheri Vislay, prin. Fax 622-0204
Paint Branch Montessori S 50/PK-6
10309 New Hampshire Ave 20903 301-434-0373
St. Andrew Apostle S 300/PK-8
11602 Kemp Mill Rd 20902 301-649-3555
Susan Sheehan, prin. Fax 649-2352
St. Bernadette S 400/K-8
80 University Blvd E 20901 301-593-5611
Theodore Ewanciw, prin. Fax 593-9042
St. Francis International S 400/PK-8
1500 Saint Camillus Dr 20903 301-434-2344
Tobias Harkleroad, prin. Fax 434-7726
St. John the Baptist S 300/K-8
12319 New Hampshire Ave 20904 301-622-3076
Brian Blomquist, prin. Fax 622-2453
St. John the Evangelist S 300/K-8
10201 Woodland Dr 20902 301-681-7656
Margaret Durney, prin. Fax 681-0745
Torah S of Greater Washington 300/K-6
2010 Linden Ln 20910 301-962-8003

Smithsburg, Washington, Pop. 2,924
Washington County SD
Supt. — See Hagerstown
Smithsburg ES 400/PK-5
67 N Main St 21783 301-766-8329
Krista Burgan, prin. Fax 824-4462
Smithsburg MS 600/6-8
68 N Main St 21783 301-766-8353
Matt Hoffman, prin. Fax 824-5147

Snow Hill, Worcester, Pop. 2,063
Worcester County SD
Supt. — See Newark
Snow Hill ES 400/PK-3
515 Coulbourne Ln 21863 410-632-5210
Dr. Mary Ann Cooper, prin. Fax 632-5219
Snow Hill MS 400/4-8
522 Coulbourne Ln 21863 410-632-5240
Christina Welch, prin. Fax 632-5249

Solomons, Calvert, Pop. 2,331

Our Lady Star of the Sea S 100/PK-8
PO Box 560 20688 410-326-3171
Mary Bartsch, prin. Fax 326-9478

Sparks, Baltimore
Baltimore County SD
Supt. — See Towson
Sparks ES 600/K-5
601 Belfast Rd 21152 410-887-7900
Pamela Oliver-Jones, prin. Fax 472-3190

Spencerville, Montgomery, Pop. 1,516

Spencerville Adventist Academy 300/PK-12
2502 Spencerville Rd 20868 301-421-9101

Springdale, Prince George's, Pop. 2,957
Prince George's County SD
Supt. — See Upper Marlboro
Ardmore ES 500/PK-5
9301 Ardwick Ardmore Rd 20774 301-925-1311
Georgette Gregory, prin. Fax 925-1318

Stevensville, Queen Anne's, Pop. 6,708
Queen Anne's County SD
Supt. — See Centreville
Bayside ES 400/3-5
301 Church St 21666 410-643-6181
Louisa Welch, prin. Fax 643-6685
Kent Island ES 400/PK-2
110 Elementary Way 21666 410-643-2392
David DuLac, prin. Fax 643-9354
Matapeake ES 500/PK-5
651 Romancoke Rd 21666 410-643-3105
Jennifer Schrecongost, prin. Fax 643-3711
Matapeake MS 400/6-8
671 Romancoke Rd 21666 410-643-7330
Fax 643-7445
Stevensville MS 500/6-8
610 Main St 21666 410-643-3194
Tara Downes, prin. Fax 643-3046

Lighthouse Christian Academy 100/K-8
931 Love Point Rd 21666 410-643-3034

Street, Harford
Harford County SD
Supt. — See Bel Air
Dublin ES 300/PK-5
1527 Whiteford Rd 21154 410-638-3703
Patricia Chenworth, prin. Fax 638-3707

Sudlersville, Queen Anne's, Pop. 476
Queen Anne's County SD
Supt. — See Centreville
Sudlersville ES 300/PK-5
300 S Church St 21668 410-438-3164
Thomas Walls, prin. Fax 438-3551
Sudlersville MS 300/6-8
600 Charles St 21668 410-438-3151
Sean Kenna, prin. Fax 438-3489

Suitland, Prince George's, Pop. 25,409
Prince George's County SD
Supt. — See Upper Marlboro
Beanes ES 400/PK-5
5108 Dianna Dr 20746 301-817-0533
Dana Tutt, prin. Fax 817-0982
Drew-Freeman MS 700/6-8
2600 Brooks Dr 20746 301-817-0900
Dallas Lee, prin. Fax 817-0915
Foulois Academy 600/K-8
4601 Beauford Rd 20746 301-817-0300
Matthew McCrea, prin. Fax 817-0941
Princeton ES 400/PK-6
6101 Baxter Dr 20746 301-702-7650
HeNina Bunch, prin. Fax 702-7658
Suitland ES 500/PK-6
4650 Homer Ave 20746 301-817-3770
Pamela Preston, prin. Fax 817-3791

Sunderland, Calvert
Calvert County SD
Supt. — See Prince Frederick
Sunderland ES 700/PK-5
150 Clyde Jones Rd 20689 410-550-9390
Pam Kasulke, prin. Fax 286-4006

Sykesville, Carroll, Pop. 4,375
Carroll County SD
Supt. — See Westminster
Carrolltowne ES 500/PK-5
6542 Ridge Rd 21784 410-751-3530
Rebecca Dupree, prin. Fax 751-3534
Eldersburg ES 500/PK-5
1021 Johnsville Rd 21784 410-751-3520
Cynthia Bell, prin. Fax 751-3553
Freedom District ES 500/K-5
5626 Sykesville Rd 21784 410-751-3525
Allison Smith, prin. Fax 751-3598
Linton Springs ES 600/PK-5
375 Ronsdale Rd 21784 410-751-3280
Debra Benner, prin. Fax 751-3285
Mechanicsville ES 500/K-5
3838 Sykesville Rd 21784 410-751-3510
Glen Messier, prin. Fax 751-3516
Oklahoma Road MS 800/6-8
6300 Oklahoma Rd 21784 410-751-3600
Erin Brilhart, prin. Fax 751-3604
Piney Ridge ES 600/K-5
6315 Freedom Ave 21784 410-751-3535
Patricia Reed, prin. Fax 751-3539
Sykesville MS 800/6-8
7301 Springfield Ave 21784 410-751-3545
Christian Roemer, prin. Fax 751-3573

Takoma Park, Montgomery, Pop. 16,094
Montgomery County SD
Supt. — See Rockville
Piney Branch ES 300/4-6
7510 Maple Ave 20912 301-891-8000
Rachel Dubois, prin. Fax 891-8011
Rolling Terrace ES 900/PK-5
705 Bayfield St 20912 240-740-1950
Kenneth Marcus, prin. Fax 431-7643
Takoma Park ES 700/PK-3
7511 Holly Ave 20912 240-740-0980
Zadia Gadsden, prin. Fax 650-6526

Prince George's County SD
Supt. — See Upper Marlboro
Carole Highlands ES 700/PK-6
1610 Hannon St 20912 301-431-5660
Jevivvien Ray, prin. Fax 431-5670

Sligo Adventist S 200/K-8
8300 Carroll Ave 20912 301-434-1417

Tall Timbers, Saint Mary's, Pop. 454
St. Mary's County SD
Supt. — See Leonardtown
Piney Point ES 500/PK-5
44550 Tall Timbers Rd 20690 301-994-2205
Glenna Edwards, prin. Fax 994-2207

Taneytown, Carroll, Pop. 6,558
Carroll County SD
Supt. — See Westminster
Northwest MS 500/6-8
99 Kings Dr 21787 410-751-3270
David Watkins, prin. Fax 751-3275
Taneytown ES 400/PK-5
100 Kings Dr 21787 410-751-3260
Christy Farver, prin. Fax 751-3532

Temple Hills, Prince George's, Pop. 7,677
Prince George's County SD
Supt. — See Upper Marlboro
Allenwood ES 400/PK-6
6300 Harley Ln 20748 301-702-3930
Shawna Fagbuyi, prin. Fax 702-7598
Angelou French Immersion S 500/K-8
2000 Callaway St 20748 301-702-3950
Martha Kristy, prin. Fax 894-8515
Chase ES 300/PK-5
5700 Fisher Rd 20748 301-702-7660
Nicholas Ohlson, prin. Fax 702-7631
Hillcrest Heights ES 500/PK-5
4305 22nd Pl 20748 301-702-3800
Traci Brown, prin. Fax 702-3807
Marshall MS 700/6-8
4909 Brinkley Rd 20748 301-702-7540
DeMarco Clark, prin. Fax 702-7555
Overlook Spanish Immersion S 100/K-3
3298 Curtis Dr 20748 301-702-3831
Betsy White, prin. Fax 702-3839
Panorama ES 400/PK-5
2002 Callaway St 20748 301-702-3870
Patricia Wells, prin. Fax 702-7600
Stoddert MS 600/6-8
2501 Olson St 20748 301-702-7500
Michael Gilchrist, prin. Fax 702-7515

Thurmont, Frederick, Pop. 6,091
Frederick County SD
Supt. — See Frederick
Lewistown ES 200/K-5
11119 Hessong Bridge Rd 21788 240-236-3750
Dana Austin, prin. Fax 236-3751
Thurmont ES 300/3-5
805 E Main St 21788 240-236-0900
Christina McKeever, prin. Fax 236-0901
Thurmont MS 600/6-8
408 E Main St 21788 240-236-5100
Danny Enck, prin. Fax 236-5101
Thurmont PS 400/PK-2
7989 Rocky Ridge Rd 21788 240-236-2800
Karen Locke, prin. Fax 236-2801

Tilghman, Talbot
Talbot County SD
Supt. — See Easton
Tilghman ES 100/K-6
21374 Foster Ave 21671 410-886-2391
Joyce Crow, prin. Fax 886-2149

Timonium, Baltimore, Pop. 9,759
Baltimore County SD
Supt. — See Towson
Mays Chapel ES PK-5
12250 Roundwood Rd 21093 410-809-4134
Steve Coco, prin. Fax 252-0127
Pinewood ES 600/PK-5
200 Rickswood Rd 21093 410-887-7663
Beatrice Rueter, prin. Fax 252-1962
Pot Spring ES 600/K-5
2410 Spring Lake Dr 21093 410-887-7648
Jane Martin, prin. Fax 887-7649
Timonium ES 500/PK-5
2001 Eastridge Rd 21093 410-887-7661
Donna Scaccio, prin. Fax 887-7662

Towson, Baltimore, Pop. 54,024
Baltimore County SD 106,800/PK-12
6901 N Charles St 21204 410-887-4554
S. Dallas Dance Ph.D., supt. Fax 887-4309
www.bcps.org
West Towson ES 500/PK-5
6914 N Charles St 21204 410-887-3869
Susan Hershfeld, prin. Fax 887-8036
Other Schools – See Baldwin, Baltimore, Catonsville, Cockeysville, Freeland, Kingsville, Lutherville, Monkton, Owings Mills, Parkton, Perry Hall, Phoenix, Randallstown, Reisterstown, Sparks, Timonium, Upperco, White Marsh

---

Immaculate Conception S 500/PK-8
112 Ware Ave 21204 410-427-4800
Madeline Meaney, prin. Fax 427-4895
Immaculate Heart of Mary S 500/PK-8
8501 Loch Raven Blvd 21286 410-668-8466
Anders Alicea, prin. Fax 668-6171

Tracys Landing, Anne Arundel
Anne Arundel County SD
Supt. — See Annapolis
Traceys ES 400/K-5
20 Deale Rd 20779 410-222-1633
John Trumbule, prin. Fax 867-3709

Trappe, Talbot, Pop. 1,057
Talbot County SD
Supt. — See Easton
White Marsh ES 300/PK-5
4322 Lovers Ln 21673 410-476-3144
Sherry Bowen Ed.D., prin. Fax 476-5187

Union Bridge, Carroll, Pop. 956
Carroll County SD
Supt. — See Westminster
Wolfe ES 400/PK-5
119 N Main St 21791 410-751-3307
Tracy Belski, prin. Fax 751-3309

Upperco, Baltimore
Baltimore County SD
Supt. — See Towson
Fifth District ES 300/PK-5
3725 Mount Carmel Rd 21155 410-887-1726
Robert Findley, prin. Fax 374-5625

Upper Marlboro, Prince George's, Pop. 606
Prince George's County SD 121,700/PK-12
14201 School Ln 20772 301-952-6000
Dr. Kevin Maxwell, admin. Fax 627-6576
www.pgcps.org
Arrowhead ES 400/K-5
2300 Sansbury Rd 20774 301-499-7071
Shannon Feinblatt, prin. Fax 499-7074
Kettering ES 400/PK-5
11000 Layton St 20774 301-808-5977
Joel Nelson, prin. Fax 808-5973
Kettering MS 500/6-8
65 Herrington Dr 20774 301-808-4060
Amin Salaam, prin. Fax 499-3128
Madison MS 800/6-8
7300 Woodyard Rd 20772 301-599-2422
Courtney King, prin. Fax 599-2562
Marlton ES 300/K-5
8506 Old Colony Dr S 20772 301-952-7780
Valerie Gifford, prin. Fax 952-7718
Mattaponi ES 300/K-5
11701 Duley Station Rd 20772 301-599-2442
Stephen Green, prin. Fax 599-2449
Melwood ES 400/K-5
7100 Woodyard Rd 20772 301-599-2500
Andrew Dalton, prin. Fax 599-2507
Obama ES 800/PK-5
12700 Brooke Ln 20772 301-574-4020
Megan Ashworth, prin. Fax 574-4025
Patuxent ES 300/PK-5
4410 Bishopmill Dr 20772 301-952-7700
Glenda Washington, prin. Fax 952-7723
Rosaryville ES 400/K-5
9925 Rosaryville Rd 20772 301-599-2490
Rashida Edwards, prin. Fax 599-2494
Williams Spanish Immersion S 200/K-2
9601 Prince Pl 20774 301-499-3373
Shawn Hintz, prin. Fax 808-4487
Other Schools – See Accokeek, Adelphi, Beltsville, Berwyn Heights, Bladensburg, Bowie, Brandywine, Capitol Heights, Cheverly, Clinton, College Park, District Heights, Forestville, Fort Washington, Glenarden, Glenn Dale, Greenbelt, Hyattsville, Landover, Landover Hills, Lanham Seabrook, Largo, Laurel, Mitchellville, Mount Rainier, New Carrollton, Oxon Hill, Riverdale, Springdale, Suitland, Takoma Park, Temple Hills

---

Excellence Christian S 100/PK-8
9010 Frank Tippett Rd 20772 301-868-1873
Erika Lee Ed.D., prin. Fax 868-1877
Riverdale Baptist S 700/PK-12
1133 Largo Rd 20774 301-249-7000
Delano Brown, head sch Fax 249-3425
Rock Creek Christian Academy 500/PK-12
6707 Woodyard Rd 20772 301-599-9600
Dr. Jeffrey L. Mitchell D.D., pres. Fax 599-9603
St. Mary of the Assumption S 300/PK-8
4610 Largo Rd 20772 301-627-4170
Dr. Steven Showalter, prin. Fax 627-6383

Vienna, Dorchester, Pop. 267
Dorchester County SD
Supt. — See Cambridge
Vienna ES 200/PK-5
4905 Ocean Gateway Rt 731 21869 410-376-3151
Susie Price, prin. Fax 376-3623

Waldorf, Charles, Pop. 64,982
Charles County SD
Supt. — See La Plata
Barnhart ES 600/PK-5
4800 Lancaster Cir 20603 301-645-9053
Ben Kohlhorst, prin. Fax 645-8970
Berry ES 900/PK-5
10155 Berry Rd 20603 301-638-2330
Sandra Taylor, prin. Fax 638-3659
Brown ES 400/PK-5
421 University Dr 20602 301-645-1330
Christienne Warren, prin. Fax 374-9489
Daniel of St. Thomas Jenifer ES 600/PK-5
2820 Jenifer School Ln 20603 301-932-9603
Nancy Seifert, prin. Fax 374-9496
Davis MS 900/6-8
2495 Davis Rd 20603 301-638-0858
Kimberly McClarin, prin. Fax 638-3562
Diggs ES 800/PK-5
2615 Davis Rd 20603 301-638-7202
Debra Calvert, prin. Fax 638-7214
Hanson MS 800/6-8
3165 John Hanson Dr 20601 301-645-4520
Susan McCormick, prin. Fax 870-1182
Malcolm ES 400/PK-5
14760 Poplar Hill Rd 20601 301-645-2691
Wilhelmina Pugh, prin. Fax 638-0054
Mattawoman MS 900/6-8
10145 Berry Rd 20603 301-645-7708
Sonia Jones, prin. Fax 638-0043
Middleton ES 500/PK-5
1109 Copley Ave 20602 301-645-3338
Louis D'Ambrosio, prin. Fax 645-0931
Mudd ES 400/PK-5
820 Stone Ave 20602 301-645-3686
Kimberly Hairston, prin. Fax 374-9581
Neal ES 700/PK-5
12105 Saint Georges Dr 20602 301-638-2617
Deborah Brown, prin. Fax 638-4054
Ryon ES 600/PK-5
12140 Vivian Adams Dr 20601 301-645-3090
Thadine Wright, prin. Fax 374-9583
Stoddert MS 700/6-8
2040 Saint Thomas Dr 20602 301-645-1334
Kenneth Schroeck, prin. Fax 870-1183
Turner ES 500/PK-5
1000 Bannister Cir 20602 301-645-4828
Orlena Whatley, prin. Fax 374-9587
Wade ES 700/PK-5
2300 Smallwood Dr W 20603 301-932-4304
Kevin Jackson, prin. Fax 645-8793

Grace Christian Academy of Maryland 400/PK-12
13000 Zekiah Dr 20601 301-645-0406
Dr. Lorne Wenzel, dir. Fax 645-7463
Our Lady's Little Christians Preschool PK-PK
100 Village St 20602 301-645-7112
Neida Tice, dir. Fax 645-3635
St. Peter S 300/PK-8
3310 Saint Peters Dr 20601 301-843-1955
John West, prin. Fax 843-6371

Walkersville, Frederick, Pop. 5,663
Frederick County SD
Supt. — See Frederick
Glade ES 600/PK-5
9525 Glade Rd 21793 240-236-2100
Lorcan OhEithir, prin. Fax 236-2101
Walkersville ES 700/K-5
83 W Frederick St 21793 240-236-1000
John Ewald, prin. Fax 236-1050
Walkersville MS 800/6-8
55 W Frederick St 21793 240-236-4400
Stacey Hiltner, prin. Fax 236-4401

Westernport, Allegany, Pop. 1,876
Allegany County SD
Supt. — See Cumberland
Westernport ES 300/PK-5
172 Church St 21562 301-359-0511
Alexa Fazenbaker, prin. Fax 359-0411

West Friendship, Howard
Howard County SD
Supt. — See Ellicott City
West Friendship ES 300/K-5
12500 State Route 144 21794 410-313-5512
Kaye Breon, prin. Fax 313-5514

Westminster, Carroll, Pop. 18,162
Carroll County SD 24,800/PK-12
125 N Court St 21157 410-751-3000
Stephen Guthrie, supt. Fax 751-3030
www.carrollk12.org/
Cranberry Station ES 500/PK-5
505 N Center St 21157 410-386-4440
Joseph Dorsey, prin. Fax 386-4444
Friendship Valley ES 500/K-5
1100 Gist Rd 21157 410-751-3650
David Bortz, prin. Fax 751-3655
Moton ES 400/PK-5
1413 Washington Rd 21157 410-751-3610
Darryl Robbins, prin. Fax 751-3927
Runnymede ES 500/PK-5
3000 Langdon Dr 21158 410-751-3203
Martin Tierney, prin. Fax 751-3930
Westminster East MS 700/6-8
121 Longwell Ave 21157 410-751-3656
James Carver, prin. Fax 751-3660
Westminster ES 500/K-5
811 Uniontown Rd 21158 410-751-3222
Whitney Warner, prin. Fax 751-3926
Westminster West MS 900/6-8
60 Monroe St 21157 410-751-3661
Amy Gromada, prin. Fax 751-3667
Winchester ES 600/PK-5
70 Monroe St 21157 410-751-3230
Craig Dunkleberger, prin. Fax 751-3929
Winfield ES 600/PK-5
4401 Salem Bottom Rd 21157 410-751-3242
Erin Sikorski, prin. Fax 751-3243
Other Schools – See Finksburg, Hampstead, Manchester, Mount Airy, Sykesville, Taneytown, Union Bridge

---

Carroll Lutheran S 100/K-8
1738 Old Taneytown Rd 21158 410-848-1050
Linda Billig, prin. Fax 848-0614
Montessori S of Westminster 100/PK-9
1055 Montessori Dr 21158 410-848-6283
Jodi Lupco, dir. Fax 848-3217
North Carroll Community S 100/K-8
401 Stone Rd 21158 410-386-0655
Diane Havighurst, admin. Fax 386-0652
St. John S 400/PK-8
45 Monroe St 21157 410-848-7455
JoMarie Tolj, prin. Fax 848-2822

Westover, Somerset
Somerset County SD 3,200/PK-12
7982A Tawes Campus Dr 21871 410-651-1616
Dr. John Gaddis, supt. Fax 651-2931
www.somerset.k12.md.us
Somerset IS 400/6-7
7970 Tawes Campus Dr 21871 410-621-0161
Brandy Brady, prin. Fax 621-0166
Other Schools – See Crisfield, Deal Island, Ewell, Princess Anne

---

Holly Grove Christian S 500/PK-12
7317 Mennonite Church Rd 21871 410-957-0222
Michael Rohrer, prin. Fax 957-4250

White Hall, Harford
Harford County SD
Supt. — See Bel Air
Norrisville ES 200/K-5
5302 Norrisville Rd 21161 410-692-7810
Jennifer Drumgoole, prin. Fax 692-7812

White Marsh, Baltimore, Pop. 9,320
Baltimore County SD
Supt. — See Towson
Vincent Farm ES 700/K-5
6019 Ebenezer Rd 21162 410-887-2983
Charlene Behnke, prin. Fax 335-4054

White Plains, Charles, Pop. 3,560

Southern Maryland Christian Academy 300/PK-12
PO Box 1668 20695 301-870-2550
Matthew Gaines, dir. Fax 934-2855

Willards, Wicomico, Pop. 938
Wicomico County SD
Supt. — See Salisbury
Willards ES 300/PK-2
36161 Richland Rd 21874 410-677-5819
Regina Rando, prin. Fax 677-5830

Williamsport, Washington, Pop. 2,115
Washington County SD
Supt. — See Hagerstown
Hickory ES 200/PK-5
11101 Hickory School Rd 21795 301-766-8198
Ryan Hench, prin. Fax 582-5799
Springfield MS 900/6-8
334 Sunset Ave 21795 301-766-8389
Jennifer Ruppenthal, prin. Fax 766-8401
Williamsport ES 600/K-5
1 S Clifton Dr 21795 301-766-8415
Dr. Jana Palmer, prin. Fax 223-4142

Woodbine, Howard
Howard County SD
Supt. — See Ellicott City
Lisbon ES 400/K-5
15901 Frederick Rd 21797 410-313-5506
Debra Anoff, prin. Fax 313-5508

Woodsboro, Frederick, Pop. 1,126
Frederick County SD
Supt. — See Frederick
Woodsboro ES 200/PK-2
101 Liberty Rd 21798 240-236-3700
Guiseppe DiMonte, prin. Fax 236-3701

MASSACHUSETTS

MASSACHUSETTS DEPARTMENT OF EDUCATION
75 Pleasant St, Malden 02148
Telephone 781-388-3000
Fax 781-388-3770
Website http://www.doe.mass.edu

Commissioner of Education Jeff Wulfson

MASSACHUSETTS BOARD OF EDUCATION
75 Pleasant St, Malden 02148

Chairperson Paul Sagan

PUBLIC, PRIVATE AND CATHOLIC ELEMENTARY SCHOOLS

Abington, Plymouth, Pop. 15,563
Abington SD 2,000/PK-12
171 Adams St 02351 781-982-2150
Peter Schafer, supt. Fax 982-2157
www.abingtonps.org
Abington Early Education 200/PK-PK
201 Gliniewicz Way 02351 781-982-2195
Lora Monachino, prin. Fax 982-0053
Abington MS 300/5-8
201 Gliniewicz Way 02351 781-982-2170
Matthew MacCurtain, prin. Fax 982-2173
Beaver Brook ES 600/K-2
1 Ralph Hamlin Jr Blvd 02351 781-982-2185
Catherine Zinni, prin. Fax 982-2187
Woodsdale ES 300/3-4
128 Chestnut St 02351 781-982-2180
Jonathan Hawes, prin. Fax 982-2184

St. Bridget S 200/PK-8
455 Plymouth St 02351 781-878-8482
Matthew Collins, prin. Fax 871-4471

Acton, Middlesex
Acton-Boxborough Regional SD 5,800/PK-12
16 Charter Rd 01720 978-264-4700
William McAlduff, supt. Fax 264-3340
www.abschools.org
Conant ES 500/K-6
80 Taylor Rd 01720 978-266-2550
Damian Sugrue, prin. Fax 266-2509
Douglas ES 500/K-6
21 Elm St 01720 978-266-2560
Christopher Whitbeck, prin. Fax 266-2500
Gates ES 400/K-6
75 Spruce St 01720 978-266-2570
Lynne Newman, prin. Fax 263-2573
Grey JHS 900/7-8
16 Charter Rd 01720 978-264-4700
Andrew Shen, prin. Fax 264-3343
Huebner Early Childhood Program PK-PK
15 Charter Rd 01720 978-264-4700
Joseph Gibowicz, coord.
McCarthy-Towne ES 500/K-6
11 Charter Rd 01720 978-264-3377
David Krane, prin. Fax 264-4098
Merriam ES 600/PK-6
11 Charter Rd 01720 978-264-3371
Ed Kaufman, prin. Fax 264-3356
Other Schools – See Boxborough

Acushnet, Bristol, Pop. 3,170
Acushnet SD 1,000/PK-8
708 Middle Rd Ste 1 02743 508-998-0260
Michael Shea, supt. Fax 998-0262
www.acushnetschools.us
Acushnet ES 500/PK-4
800 Middle Rd 02743 508-998-0255
Susan Camphina Beck, prin. Fax 998-0259
Ford MS 500/5-8
708 Middle Rd 02743 508-998-0265
Michelle Silvia, prin. Fax 998-7316

St. Francis Xavier S 200/PK-8
223 Main St 02743 508-995-4313
Michelle Russo, prin. Fax 995-0456

Adams, Berkshire, Pop. 5,421
Adams-Cheshire Regional SD
Supt. — See Cheshire
Hoosac Valley ES 500/K-5
14 Commercial St 01220 413-743-0876
Michelle Colvin, prin. Fax 743-8406

St. Stanislaus Kostka S 100/PK-8
108 Summer St 01220 413-743-1091
Linda Reardon, prin.

Agawam, Hampden, Pop. 28,599
Agawam SD
Supt. — See Feeding Hills
Agawam ECC 100/PK-PK
108 Perry Ln 01001 413-821-0598
Robin Fernandes, prin. Fax 821-0596
Clark ES 400/K-4
65 Oxford St 01001 413-821-0576
Shelley Russell, prin. Fax 821-0594
Doering S 600/5-8
68 Main St 01001 413-789-1400
Susan Federico, prin. Fax 789-7337
Phelps ES 400/K-4
689 Main St 01001 413-821-0587
Noelle Colbert, prin. Fax 786-0497
Robinson Park ES 400/K-4
65 Begley St 01001 413-821-0584
Nicholas Bernier, prin. Fax 786-9793

Allston, See Boston
Boston SD
Supt. — See Boston
Gardner Pilot Academy 400/PK-7
30 Athol St 02134 617-635-8365
Erica Herman, prin. Fax 635-7812
Jackson/Mann S 700/PK-8
40 Armington St 02134 617-635-8532
Andy Tuite, prin. Fax 635-6379

Amesbury, Essex, Pop. 12,109
Amesbury SD 2,300/PK-12
5 Highland St 01913 978-388-0507
Gary S. Reese Ed.D., supt. Fax 388-8315
schools.amesburyma.gov
Amesbury ES 400/PK-4
20 S Hampton Rd 01913 978-388-3659
Walter Helliesen, prin. Fax 388-4961
Amesbury MS 700/5-8
220 Main St 01913 978-388-0515
Michael Curry, prin. Fax 388-1626
Cashman ES 500/PK-4
193 Lions Mouth Rd 01913 978-388-4407
Mary Charette, prin. Fax 388-4479

Sparhawk S 200/K-12
4 Noel St 01913 978-388-5354
Louise Stilphen, hdmstr. Fax 499-4303

Amherst, Hampshire, Pop. 17,824
Amherst SD 1,200/PK-6
170 Chestnut St 01002 413-362-1810
Dr. Michael Morris, supt. Fax 549-6108
www.arps.org
Crocker Farm ES 400/PK-6
280 West St 01002 413-362-1600
Derek Shea, prin. Fax 256-0835
Fort River ES 400/K-6
70 S East St 01002 413-253-9731
Diane Chamberlain, prin. Fax 256-5941
Wildwood ES 400/K-6
71 Strong St 01002 413-549-1400
Nick Yaffe, prin. Fax 549-9519

Amherst-Pelham SD 1,500/7-12
170 Chestnut St 01002 413-362-1810
Dr. Michael Morris, supt. Fax 549-6108
www.arps.org
Amherst Regional MS 500/7-8
170 Chestnut St 01002 413-362-1850
Patty Bode, prin. Fax 549-9812

Pelham SD 100/PK-6
170 Chestnut St 01002 413-362-1810
Dr. Michael Morris, supt. Fax 549-6108
www.arps.org
Other Schools – See Pelham

Amherst Montessori S 100/PK-6
27 Pomeroy Ln 01002 413-253-3101
Shelley Poreda, dir. Fax 253-1620
Common S 100/PK-6
PO Box 2248 01004 413-256-8989
Christine Lindeman, head sch Fax 253-1671

Andover, Essex, Pop. 8,592
Andover SD 5,900/PK-12
36 Bartlet St 01810 978-623-8501
Sheldon Berman Ed.D., supt. Fax 623-8505
www.aps1.net
Andover West MS 600/6-8
70 Shawsheen Rd 01810 978-247-5400
Rebecca Franks, prin. Fax 247-5490
Bancroft ES 500/K-5
15 Bancroft Rd 01810 978-247-9500
Michelle Costa, prin. Fax 247-9590
Doherty MS 600/6-8
50 Bartlet St 01810 978-247-9400
Robin Wilson, prin. Fax 247-9490
High Plain ES 600/K-5
333 High Plain Rd 01810 978-247-8600
Pamela Lathrop, prin. Fax 247-8690
Sanborn ES 400/K-5
90 Lovejoy Rd 01810 978-247-9700
Jason DiCarlo, prin. Fax 247-9790
Shawsheen ES 100/PK-PK
18 Magnolia Ave 01810 978-247-8200
Carol Green, dir. Fax 247-8290
South ES 500/K-5
55 Woburn St 01810 978-247-9800
Tracy Crowley, prin. Fax 247-9890
West ES 700/K-5
58 Beacon St 01810 978-247-5300
Liz Roos, prin. Fax 247-5390
Wood Hill MS 400/6-8
11 Cross St 01810 978-247-8800
Patrick Bucco, prin. Fax 247-8890

Andover S of Montessori 200/PK-8
400 S Main St 01810 978-475-2299
Joanna DeStefanis, head sch Fax 475-1290
Pike S 400/PK-9
34 Sunset Rock Rd 01810 978-475-1197
John Waters, head sch Fax 475-3014
St. Augustine S 400/PK-8
26 Central St 01810 978-475-2414
Paula O'Dea, prin. Fax 470-1327

Arlington, Middlesex, Pop. 41,750
Arlington SD 5,000/PK-12
869 Massachusetts Ave 02476 781-316-3501
Kathleen Bodie, supt. Fax 316-3509
www.arlington.k12.ma.us
Bishop ES 400/K-5
25 Columbia Rd 02474 781-316-3792
Mark McAneny, prin. Fax 316-3747
Brackett ES 500/K-5
66 Eastern Ave 02476 781-316-3705
Stephanie Zerchykov, prin. Fax 316-3710
Dallin ES 500/K-5
185 Florence Ave 02476 781-316-3721
Thad Dingman, prin. Fax 316-3727
Hardy ES 400/K-5
52 Lake St 02474 781-316-3781
Kristin DeFrancisco, prin. Fax 316-3717
Menotomy Preschool 100/PK-PK
869 Massachusetts Ave 02476 781-316-3655
Joyce Schlenger, coord.
Ottoson MS 1,100/6-8
63 Acton St 02476 781-316-3745
Eileen Woods, prin. Fax 641-5436
Peirce ES 300/K-5
85 Park Avenue Ext 02474 781-316-3736
Karen Hartley, prin. Fax 316-3748
Stratton ES 400/K-5
180 Mountain Ave 02474 781-316-3754
Michael Hanna, prin. Fax 316-3666
Thompson ES 400/K-5
187 Everett St 02474 781-316-3768
Karen Donato, prin. Fax 316-1419

Ellis S 200/PK-8
34 Winter St 02474 781-641-5987
Deanne Benson, head sch Fax 641-1052
New Covenant S 50/PK-5
9 Westminster Ave 02474 781-643-5511
Joanna Levy, prin. Fax 347-2220
St. Agnes S 300/PK-8
39 Medford St 02474 781-643-9031
Robert Penta, prin. Fax 643-2834

Ashburnham, Worcester
Ashburnham-Westminster Regional SD 2,300/PK-12
11 Oakmont Dr 01430 978-827-1434
Dr. Gary Mazzola, supt. Fax 827-5969
www.awrsd.org
Briggs ES 500/PK-5
96 Williams Rd 01430 978-827-5750
Andrea McGrath, prin. Fax 827-1411
Overlook MS 600/6-8
10 Oakmont Dr 01430 978-827-1425
Philip Saisa, prin. Fax 827-1423

Other Schools – See Westminster

Ashby, Middlesex
North Middlesex SD
Supt. — See Pepperell
Ashby ES 200/K-4
911 Main St 01431 978-386-7266
Anne Cromwell-Gapp, prin. Fax 386-0973

Ashfield, Franklin
Mohawk Trail SD
Supt. — See Shelburne Falls
Sanderson Academy 100/PK-6
808 Cape St 01330 413-628-4404
Emma Liebowitz, prin. Fax 628-4697

Ashland, Middlesex, Pop. 12,066
Ashland SD 2,600/PK-12
87 W Union St 01721 508-881-0150
James Adams, supt. Fax 881-0161
www.ashland.k12.ma.us
Ashland MS 500/6-8
87 W Union St 01721 508-881-0167
David DiGirolamo, prin. Fax 881-0169
Mindess S 600/3-5
90 Concord St 01721 508-881-0166
Michael Caira, prin. Fax 881-0153
Pittaway S 100/PK-PK
75 Central St 01721 508-881-0160
Patricia White, prin. Fax 881-0148
Warren ES 600/K-2
73 Fruit St 01721 508-881-0188
Peter Regan, prin. Fax 881-0191

MetroWest Christian Academy 100/PK-5
PO Box 229 01721 508-881-7404
Stacy Frye, prin. Fax 881-7467
Pincushion Hill Montessori S 100/PK-6
30 Green St 01721 508-881-2123
Christine Kovago, dir. Fax 881-8004

Athol, Worcester, Pop. 8,127
Athol-Royalston SD 1,200/PK-12
1062 Pleasant St 01331 978-249-2400
Darcy Fernandes, supt. Fax 249-2402
www.arrsd.org
Athol Community ES 200/PK-4
1064 Pleasant St 01331 978-249-2406
Mike Leander, prin. Fax 249-2428
Athol-Royalston MS 400/5-8
1062 Pleasant St 01331 978-249-2430
Thomas Telicki, prin. Fax 249-0055
Other Schools – See Royalston

Attleboro, Bristol, Pop. 42,657
Attleboro SD 5,900/PK-12
100 Rathbun Willard Dr 02703 508-222-0012
David Sawyer, supt. Fax 223-1577
www.attleboroschools.com
Brennan MS 600/5-8
320 Rathbun Willard Dr 02703 508-222-6260
Frederick Souza, prin. Fax 223-1555
Coelho MS 600/5-8
99 Brown St 02703 508-761-7551
Andrew Boles, prin. Fax 399-6506
Early Learning Center 200/PK-PK
7 James St 02703 508-223-1563
Veronica Learned, prin. Fax 223-1589
Fine ES 500/K-4
790 Oakhill Ave 02703 508-222-1419
Patricia Martin, prin. Fax 226-0255
Studley ES 400/K-4
299 Rathbun Willard Dr 02703 508-222-2621
Joanne DiPalma, prin. Fax 226-0419
Thacher ES 400/K-4
160 James St 02703 508-226-4162
Veronica Learned, prin. Fax 226-4165
Wamsutta MS 500/5-8
300 Locust St 02703 508-223-1540
Joseph Connor, prin. Fax 226-2087
Willett ES 400/K-4
32 Watson Ave 02703 508-222-0286
Jeffrey Cateon, prin. Fax 223-1536
Other Schools – See South Attleboro

St. John Evangelist S 300/K-8
13 Hodges St 02703 508-222-5062
Sr. Mary Jane Holden, prin. Fax 223-1737

Auburn, Worcester, Pop. 15,005
Auburn SD 2,400/PK-12
5 West St 01501 508-832-7755
Maryellen Brunelle Ed.D., supt. Fax 832-7757
www.auburn.k12.ma.us
Auburn MS 600/6-8
9 West St 01501 508-832-7722
Joseph Gagnon, prin. Fax 832-8655
Bryn Mawr ES 300/K-2
35 Swanson Rd 01501 508-832-7733
Elizabeth Chamberland Ed.D., prin. Fax 832-7734
Pakachoag S 300/PK-2
110 Pakachoag St 01501 508-832-7788
Jennifer Stanick, prin. Fax 832-7787
Swanson Road IS 600/3-5
10 Swanson Rd 01501 508-832-7744
Susan Lopez Ed.D., admin.

Montessori Childrens House of Auburn 50/PK-K
135 Bryn Mawr Ave 01501 508-832-9262

Auburndale, See Newton
Newton SD
Supt. — See Newtonville
Burr ES 400/K-5
171 Pine St 02466 617-559-9360
Mindy Johal, prin. Fax 552-5562
Williams ES 300/K-5
141 Grove St 02466 617-559-6480
Ayesha Farag, prin. Fax 559-2013

Avon, Norfolk, Pop. 4,558
Avon SD 700/PK-12
1 Patrick Clark Dr 02322 508-588-0230
Paul Zinni, supt. Fax 559-1081
www.apps.avon.k12.ma.us
Butler ES 400/PK-6
1 Patrick Clark Dr 02322 508-587-7009
Darrin Reynolds, prin. Fax 583-7193

Ayer, Middlesex, Pop. 2,780
Ayer Shirley SD 1,700/PK-12
115 Washington St 01432 978-772-8600
Dr. Mary Malone Ed.D., supt. Fax 772-1863
www.asrsd.org
Page Hilltop ES 600/PK-5
115 Washington St 01432 978-772-8600
Fred Deppe, prin. Fax 772-8631
Other Schools – See Shirley

Baldwinville, Worcester, Pop. 2,008
Narragansett Regional SD 1,300/PK-12
462 Baldwinville Rd 01436 978-939-5661
Dr. Chris Casavant, supt. Fax 939-5179
www.nrsd.org
Baldwinville ES 200/2-4
16 School St 01436 978-939-5318
Nathaniel North, prin. Fax 939-4438
Narragansett MS 500/5-8
460 Baldwinville Rd 01436 978-393-5928
Dr. Peter Cushing, prin. Fax 939-8422
Templeton Center ES 100/K-1
460 Baldwinville Rd 01436 978-939-8892
Nathaniel North, prin. Fax 939-1211
Other Schools – See Phillipston

Barnstable, Barnstable, Pop. 48,854

Trinity Christian Academy 100/PK-12
979 Mary Dunn Rd 02630 508-790-0114
Ben Haskell, hdmstr. Fax 790-1293

Barre, Worcester, Pop. 998
Quabbin SD 2,400/PK-12
872 South St 01005 978-355-4668
Dr. Maureen Marshall, supt. Fax 355-6756
www.qrsd.org
Quabbin Regional MS 400/7-8
800 South St 01005 978-355-5042
Susanne Musnicki, prin. Fax 355-6104
Ruggles Lane ES 400/PK-6
105 Ruggles Ln 01005 978-355-2934
Julie Vincentsen, prin. Fax 355-2870
Other Schools – See Gilbertville, Hubbardston, New Braintree, Oakham

Becket, Berkshire
Central Berkshire Regional SD
Supt. — See Dalton
Becket Washington ES 100/PK-5
12 Maple St 01223 413 623 8757
Mary Kay McCloskey, prin. Fax 684-6161

Bedford, Middlesex, Pop. 12,996
Bedford SD 2,500/K-12
97 McMahon Rd 01730 781-275-7588
Jonathan Sills, supt. Fax 275-0885
www.bedford.k12.ma.us
Davis ES 500/K-2
410 Davis Rd 01730 781-275-6804
Beth Benoit, prin. Fax 275-7639
Glenn MS 600/6-8
99 McMahon Rd 01730 781-275-3201
Kevin Tracey, prin. Fax 275-7632
Lane ES 500/3-5
66 Sweetwater Ave 01730 781-275-7606
Robert Ackerman, prin. Fax 275-4722

Belchertown, Hampshire, Pop. 2,339
Belchertown SD 2,400/PK-12
PO Box 841 01007 413-323-0423
Karol Coffin, supt. Fax 323-0448
www.belchertownps.org
Chestnut Hill Community S 600/4-6
59 State St 01007 413-323-0437
Jennifer Champagne, prin. Fax 323-0459
Cold Spring S 200/PK-K
57 S Main St 01007 413-323-0428
Andrea Mastalerz, prin. Fax 323-0493
Jabish Brook MS 400/7-8
62 N Washington St 01007 413-323-0433
Thomas Ruscio, prin. Fax 323-0450
Swift River ES 500/1-3
57 State St 01007 413-323-0471
Robert Kuhn, prin. Fax 323-0492

Bellingham, Norfolk, Pop. 4,778
Bellingham SD 1,900/PK-12
4 Mechanic St 02019 508-883-1706
Peter Marano, supt. Fax 966-2402
www.edlinesites.net/pages/Bellingham_Public_Schools
Bellingham ECC 100/PK-PK
338 Hartford Ave 02019 508-966-2512
Pamela Fuhrman, dir. Fax 966-4679
Memorial MS 600/4-7
130 Blackstone St 02019 508-883-2330
Jeffrey Croteau, prin. Fax 883-2037
South ES 400/K-3
70 Harpin St 02019 508-883-8001
Judith Lamarre, prin. Fax 883-5081
Stall Brook ES 200/K-3
342 Hartford Ave 02019 508-966-0451
Brenda Maurao, prin. Fax 966-4679

Belmont, Middlesex, Pop. 24,057
Belmont SD 4,200/PK-12
644 Pleasant St 02478 617-993-5401
John Phelan, supt. Fax 993-5409
www.belmont.k12.ma.us
Burbank ES 400/K-4
266 School St 02478 617-993-5500
Tricia Clifford, prin. Fax 484-2050
Butler ES 400/K-4
90 White St 02478 617-993-5550
Danielle Betancourt, prin. Fax 484-7921
Chenery MS 1,300/5-8
95 Washington St 02478 617-993-5800
Michael McAllister, prin. Fax 993-5809
Wellington ES 600/PK-4
121 Orchard St 02478 617-993-5600
Amy Spangler, prin. Fax 484-1790
Winn Brook ES 400/K-4
97 Waterhouse Rd 02478 617-993-5700
Janet Carey, prin. Fax 484-2657

Belmont Day S 300/PK-8
55 Day School Ln 02478 617-484-3078
Brendan Largay, hdmstr. Fax 489-1942

Berkley, Bristol
Berkley SD 900/PK-8
21 N Main St 02779 508-822-5220
Thomas Lynch, supt. Fax 823-1772
www.berkleypublicschools.org
Berkley Community S 500/PK-4
59 S Main St 02779 508-822-9550
Jennifer Francisco, prin. Fax 822-3773
Berkley MS 400/5-8
21 N Main St 02779 508-884-9434
Kimberly Hebert, prin. Fax 386-1044

Berlin, Worcester
Berlin-Boylston SD
Supt. — See Boylston
Berlin Memorial ES 200/K-5
34 South St 01503 978-838-2417
John Campbell, prin. Fax 838-2395

Bernardston, Franklin
Pioneer Valley SD
Supt. — See Northfield
Bernardston ES 200/PK-6
37 School Rd 01337 413-648-9356
Bob Clancy, prin. Fax 648-5404

Beverly, Essex, Pop. 38,805
Beverly SD 4,300/PK-12
70 Balch St 01915 978-921-6100
Dr. Steven Hiersche Ed.D., supt. Fax 921-8555
www.beverlyschools.org
Ayers/Ryal Side ES 500/K-5
40 Woodland Ave 01915 978-921-6116
Dr. Debra Lay, prin. Fax 921-1995
Beverly Preschool at McKeown PK-PK
70 Balch St 01915 978-921-6100
Stacy Bucyk, prin. Fax 921-8555
Briscoe MS 900/6-8
7 Sohier Rd 01915 978-921-6103
Matthew Poska, prin. Fax 927-7781
Centerville ES 400/K-5
17 Hull St 01915 978-921-6120
Julie Smith, prin. Fax 921-8571
Cove ES 400/K-5
20 Eisenhower Ave 01915 978-921-6121
Lisa Oliver, prin. Fax 921-8551
Hannah ES 300/K-5
41R Brimbal Ave 01915 978-921-6126
Gabrielle Montevecchi, prin. Fax 921-6084
North Beverly ES 400/K-5
48 Putnam St 01915 978-921-6130
Erin Brown, prin. Fax 921-4007

Harborlight Montessori S 300/PK-8
243 Essex St 01915 978-922-1008
Paul Horovitz, head sch Fax 922-0594
Saints Academy 200/K-8
111 New Balch St 01915 978-922-0048
Daniel Bouchard, prin. Fax 927-6694
Shore Country Day S 400/PK-9
545 Cabot St 01915 978-927-1700
Clair Ward, head sch Fax 927-1822
Urquhart S 200/K-8
74 Hart St 01915 978-927-1064
David Liebamann, head sch Fax 927-1064
Waldorf S at Moraine Farm 100/PK-8
701 Cabot St 01915 978-927-8811

Billerica, Middlesex, Pop. 37,609
Billerica SD 5,200/K-12
365 Boston Rd 01821 978-528-7900
Tim Piwowar, supt. Fax 528-7909
www.billerica.k12.ma.us
Ditson ES 600/K-5
39 Cook St 01821 978-528-8510
Victoria Hatem, prin. Fax 436-9537
Kennedy ES 400/K-5
20 Kimbrough Rd 01821 978-528-8570
David Marble, prin. Fax 436-9567
Locke MS 700/6-8
110 Allen Rd 01821 978-528-8650
Anthony Garas, prin. Fax 528-8659
Marshall MS 700/6-8
15 Floyd St 01821 978-528-8670
Michael Rossi, prin. Fax 528-8679
Parker ES 500/K-5
52 River St 01821 978-528-8610
Suzanne Sullivan, prin. Fax 528-8619
Vining ES 200/K-5
121 Lexington Rd 01821 978-528-8630
Christine Gibelli, prin. Fax 436-9587
Other Schools – See North Billerica

Blackstone, Worcester, Pop. 8,023
Blackstone-Millville Regional SD 1,700/PK-12
175 Lincoln St 01504 508-883-4400
Allen Himmelberger, supt. Fax 883-9892
www.bmrsd.net
Hartnett MS 500/6-8
35 Federal St 01504 508-876-0190
Tonya Curl-Hoard, prin. Fax 876-0198
Kennedy ES 300/K-2
200 Lincoln St 01504 508-876-0118
Steven Tringali, prin. Fax 876-0158

Maloney ES 200/3-5
200 Lincoln St 01504 508-876-0119
Carol Brown, prin. Fax 876-0158
Other Schools – See Millville

Bolton, Worcester
Nashoba Regional SD 3,400/PK-12
50 Mechanic St 01740 978-779-0539
Brooke Clenchy, supt. Fax 779-5537
www.nrsd.net
Sawyer S 800/PK-8
100 Mechanic St 01740 978-779-2821
Joel Bates, prin. Fax 779-0121
Other Schools – See Lancaster, Stow

Boston, Suffolk, Pop. 592,375
Boston SD 54,400/PK-12
2300 Washington St 02119 617-635-9000
Tommy Chang, supt. Fax 635-9059
www.bostonpublicschools.org
Blackstone ES 600/PK-5
380 Shawmut Ave 02118 617-635-8471
Jamel Adkins-Sarif, prin. Fax 635-7975
Eliot S 400/K-8
16 Charter St 02113 617-635-8545
Traci Griffith, prin. Fax 635-8550
Hurley S 300/PK-8
70 Worcester St 02118 617-635-8489
Marjorie Soto, prin. Fax 635-6868
Quincy ES 800/PK-5
885 Washington St 02111 617-635-8497
Cynthia Soo Hoo, prin. Fax 635-7778
Other Schools – See Allston, Brighton, Charlestown, Dorchester, East Boston, Hyde Park, Jamaica Plain, Mattapan, Roslindale, Roxbury, South Boston, West Roxbury

---

Advent S 200/PK-6
15 Brimmer St 02108 617-742-0520
Nicole DuFauchard, head sch Fax 723-2207
British International S of Boston 300/PK-12
416 Pond St 02130 617-522-2261
Darren Nicholas, hdmstr. Fax 522-0385
Kingsley Montessori S 200/PK-6
26 Exeter St 02116 617-226-4900
Renee DuChainey-Farkes M.Ed., head sch Fax 247-1417
Learning Project ES 100/K-6
107 Marlborough St 02116 617-266-8427
Michael McCord, head sch Fax 266-3543
Park Street S 300/PK-6
67 Brimmer St 02108 617-523-7577
Tracy Bradley, head sch Fax 523-7576
St. John S 200/PK-8
9 Moon St 02113 617-227-3143
Karen McLaughlin, prin. Fax 227-2188

Bourne, Barnstable, Pop. 1,380
Bourne SD 2,000/PK-12
36 Sandwich Rd 02532 508-759-0660
Steven Lamarche, supt. Fax 759-1107
www.bourneps.org
Bournedale ES 500/PK-4
41 Ernest Valeri Rd 02532 508-743-3800
Elizabeth Carpenito, prin. Fax 743-3801
Bourne MS 700/5-8
77 Waterhouse Rd 02532 508-759-0690
Melissa Stafford, prin. Fax 759-0695
Peebles ES 300/K-4
70 Trowbridge Rd 02532 508-759-0680
Jane Norton, prin. Fax 759-0683

Boxborough, Middlesex, Pop. 3,343
Acton-Boxborough Regional SD
Supt. — See Acton
Blanchard Memorial ES 400/PK-6
493 Massachusetts Ave 01719 978-263-4569
Dana Labb, supt. Fax 263-0477

Boxford, Essex, Pop. 2,307
Boxford SD 700/PK-6
28 Middleton Rd 01921 978-887-0771
Dr. Scott Morrison, supt. Fax 887-8042
www.tritownschoolunion.com
Cole ES, 26 Middleton Rd 01921 300/PK-2
Brian Middleton-Cox, prin. 978-887-2856
Spofford Pond ES 500/3-6
31 Spofford Rd 01921 978-352-8616
Dr. Kathryn Castonguay, prin. Fax 352-7855

Masconomet SD 2,000/7-12
20 Endicott Rd 01921 978-887-2323
Kevin Lyons, supt. Fax 887-3573
www.masconomet.org
Masconomet Regional MS 700/7-8
20 Endicott Rd 01921 978-887-2323
Dorothy Flaherty, prin. Fax 887-1991

Middleton SD 800/PK-6
28 Middleton Rd 01921 978-887-0771
Dr. Scott Morrison, supt. Fax 887-8042
www.tritownschoolunion.com
Other Schools – See Middleton

Topsfield SD 600/PK-6
28 Middleton Rd 01921 978-887-0771
Dr. Scott Morrison, supt. Fax 887-8042
www.tritownschoolunion.com
Other Schools – See Topsfield

Boylston, Worcester
Berlin-Boylston SD 1,000/K-12
215 Main St 01505 508-869-2837
Nadine Ekstrom, supt. Fax 869-0023
www.bbrsd.org
Boylston ES 300/K-5
200 Sewall St 01505 508-869-2200
Alfred Thompson, prin. Fax 869-6914
Other Schools – See Berlin

Bradford, See Haverhill
Haverhill SD
Supt. — See Haverhill

Greenleaf ES 300/K-2
58 Chadwick St 01835 978-374-3487
Toni Donais, admin. Fax 374-3437
Hunking MS 400/6-8
480 S Main St 01835 978-374-5787
Shannon Nolan, prin. Fax 372-5790

Bradford Christian Academy 100/1-12
97 Oxford Ave 01835 978-373-7900
Victoria Kennedy, head sch Fax 373-7977

Braintree, Norfolk, Pop. 33,800
Braintree SD 5,500/K-12
348 Pond St 02184 781-380-0130
Frank Hackett Ed.D., supt. Fax 380-0146
www.braintreeschools.org
East MS 700/6-8
305 River St 02184 781-380-0170
John Sheehan, prin. Fax 848-4522
Flaherty ES 400/K-5
99 Lakeside Dr 02184 781-380-0180
Stacey Soto, prin. Fax 380-0184
Highlands ES 400/K-5
144 Wildwood Ave 02184 781-380-0190
Dr. Nancy Pelletier, prin. Fax 380-0128
Hollis ES 500/K-5
482 Washington St 02184 781-380-0120
Timothy MacDonald, prin. Fax 380-0122
Liberty ES 500/K-5
49 Proctor Rd 02184 781-380-0210
Tara Boening, prin. Fax 380-0213
Monatiquot K Center 50/K-K
25 Brow Ave 02184 781-380-0220
Donna Anderson, prin. Fax 380-0222
Morrison ES 400/K-5
260 Liberty St 02184 781-380-0230
John Riordan, prin. Fax 380-0233
Ross ES 300/K-5
20 Hayward St 02184 781-380-0240
Frank McGourty, prin. Fax 380-0243
South MS 700/6-8
232 Peach St 02184 781-380-0160
Damon Rainie, prin. Fax 380-0164

Meeting House Montessori S 100/PK-5
85 Washington St 02184 781-356-7877
Caren Chevalier-Putnam, dir. Fax 356-6744
St. Francis of Assisi S 300/PK-8
850 Washington St 02184 781-848-0842
Brian Cote, prin. Fax 356-5309
South Shore SDA S 50/1-8
250 Washington St 02184 781-356-7794
Yaisa Walcott, prin. Fax 843-6295

Brewster, Barnstable, Pop. 1,985
Brewster SD
Supt. — See Orleans
Eddy ES 200/3-5
2298 Main St 02631 508-896-4531
Joanna Hughes, prin. Fax 896-4529
Stony Brook ES 300/PK-2
384 Underpass Rd 02631 508-896-4545
Patricia Allen, prin. Fax 896-4081

Bridgewater, Plymouth, Pop. 7,639
Bridgewater-Raynham Regional SD 5,400/PK-12
166 Mount Prospect St 02324 508-279-2140
Derek Swenson, supt. Fax 697-7012
www.bridge-rayn.org
Bridgewater MS 600/7-8
166 Mount Prospect St 02324 508-279-2100
Lynn Bastoni, prin. Fax 279-2104
Mitchell ES 1,000/PK-3
166 Mount Prospect St 02324 508-279-2120
Heidi Letendre, prin. Fax 279-2133
Williams IS 700/4-6
200 South St 02324 508-697-6968
Nancy Kirk, prin. Fax 697-6775
Other Schools – See Raynham

Brighton, See Boston
Boston SD
Supt. — See Boston
Baldwin Early Learning Center 100/K-1
121 Corey Rd 02135 617-635-8409
Tavia Mead, prin. Fax 635-9544
Edison S 800/K-8
60 Glenmont Rd 02135 617-635-8436
Samantha Varano, prin. Fax 635-8446
Lyon S 100/K-8
50 Beechcroft St 02135 617-635-7945
Deborah Rooney, prin. Fax 635-7949
Winship ES 300/PK-5
54 Dighton St 02135 617-635-8399
Monakatellia Ford, prin. Fax 635-8403

St. Columbkille S 200/K-8
25 Arlington St 02135 617-254-3110
William Gartside, head sch Fax 254-3161
Shaloh House Jewish Day S 100/PK-6
29 Chestnut Hill Ave 02135 617-787-2200
Rabbi Dan Rodkin, dir. Fax 787-4693

Brimfield, Hampden
Brimfield SD
Supt. — See Fiskdale
Brimfield ES 300/PK-6
22 Wales Rd 01010 413-245-7337
Brian Ledbetter, prin. Fax 245-4110

Brockton, Plymouth, Pop. 79,948
Brockton SD 17,000/PK-12
43 Crescent St 02301 508-580-7000
Kathleen Smith, supt. Fax 580-7513
www.brocktonpublicschools.com
Angelo ES 800/K-5
472 N Main St 02301 508-894-4501
Marcia Andrade-Serpa, prin. Fax 894-4500
Arnone Community ES 800/K-6
135 Belmont St 02301 508-894-4440
Colleen Proudler, prin. Fax 894-4464

Ashfield MS 500/6-8
225 Coe Rd 02302 508-580-7268
Barbara Lovell, prin. Fax 580-7072
Baker ES 700/K-5
45 Quincy St 02302 508-894-4427
Valerie Brower, prin. Fax 894-4472
Brookfield ES 700/K-5
135 Jon Dr 02302 508-580-7257
Marguerite Masson, prin. Fax 580-7073
Davis ES 1,100/K-8
380 Plain St 02302 508-580-7360
Darlene Campbell, prin. Fax 580-7074
Downey ES 600/K-5
55 Electric Ave 02302 508-580-7221
John Kelly, prin. Fax 580-7075
East MS 400/6-8
464 Centre St 02302 508-580-7351
Kelly Silva, prin. Fax 580-7090
George ES 900/K-5
180 Colonel Bell Dr 02301 508-580-7913
Natalie Pohl, prin. Fax 580-7917
Gilmore ES 300/K-5
150 Clinton St 02302 508-580-7685
Marybeth O'Brien, prin. Fax 580-7080
Hancock ES 700/K-5
125 Pearl St 02301 508-580-7252
Stephen Shaw, prin. Fax 580-7079
Kennedy ES 600/K-5
900 Ash St 02301 508-580-7278
Brian Rogan, prin. Fax 580-7082
North MS 500/6-8
108 Oak St 02301 508-580-7371
Alison Ramsay, prin. Fax 580-7088
Plouffe Academy 600/6-8
250 Crescent St 02302 508-894-4301
Michelle Nessralla, prin. Fax 894-4300
Raymond S 1,100/K-5
125 Oak St 02301 508-580-7364
Carol McGrath, prin. Fax 580-7085
Russell ECC, 45 Oakdale St 02301 300/PK-K
Joanne Camillo, prin. 508-580-4418
South MS 500/6-8
105 Keith Ave 02301 508-580-7311
Diane Lynch, prin. Fax 580-7089
West MS 600/6-8
271 West St 02301 508-580-7381
Carlton Campbell, prin. Fax 580-7307

Brockton Area SDA S 100/K-8
PO Box 7544 02303 508-586-9955
Convelle Morton, prin. Fax 586-9956
Trinity Catholic Academy - Lower Campus 300/PK-3
631 N Main St 02301 508-583-6231
Kristin Blanchette, prin. Fax 583-6336
Trinity Catholic Academy - Upper Campus 200/4-8
37 Erie Ave 02302 508-583-6225
Susan Degnan, prin. Fax 583-6229

Brookfield, Worcester, Pop. 821
Brookfield SD
Supt. — See Fiskdale
Brookfield ES 300/PK-6
37 Central St 01506 508-867-8774
Kathleen Hosterman, prin. Fax 867-0320

Brookline, Norfolk, Pop. 57,031
Brookline SD 6,800/PK-12
333 Washington St 02445 617-730-2401
Andrew Bott, supt. Fax 730-2601
www.brookline.k12.ma.us
Devotion S 500/K-4
30 Webster St 02446 617-879-4400
David O'Hara, prin. Fax 739-7501
Devotion Upper S 5-8
194 Boylston St 02445
Jennifer Buller, prin.
Driscoll S 600/PK-8
64 Westbourne Ter 02446 617-879-4250
Suzie Talukdar, prin. Fax 739-7502
Lawrence S 700/K-8
27 Francis St 02446 617-879-4300
Warren Blair, prin. Fax 879-4390
Lincoln S 600/PK-8
19 Kennard Rd 02445 617-879-4600
Brian Denitzio, prin. Fax 739-7505
Lynch Center 100/PK-PK
599 Brookline Ave 02445 617-739-7516
Fax 264-6429
Pierce S 800/PK-8
50 School St 02446 617-730-2580
Lesley Ryan-Miller, prin. Fax 264-6468
Runkle S 600/PK-8
50 Druce St 02445 617-879-4650
Genteen Jean-Michel, prin. Fax 739-7675
Other Schools – See Chestnut Hill

Dexter Southfield S 400/PK-12
20 Newton St 02445 617-522-5544
Todd Vincent, hdmstr. Fax 522-8166
Maimonides S 500/K-12
34 Philbrick Rd 02445 617-232-4452
Naty Katz, head sch Fax 566-2061
New England Hebrew Academy 300/PK-8
9 Prescott St 02446 617-731-5330
Esther Ciment, admin. Fax 277-0752
Park S 600/PK-8
171 Goddard Ave 02445 617-277-2456
Cynthia A. Harmon, head sch Fax 232-1261
St. Mary of the Assumption S 200/PK-8
67 Harvard St 02445 617-566-7184
Dr. Theresa Kirk, prin. Fax 731-4078
Torah Academy 200/PK-8
11 Williston Rd 02445 617-731-3196
Rabbi Shmuel Ochs, head sch Fax 731-1042

Burlington, Middlesex, Pop. 24,055
Burlington SD 3,500/K-12
123 Cambridge St 01803 781-270-1800
Dr. Eric Conti, supt. Fax 270-1773
www.bpsk12.org

Fox Hill ES 400/K-5
1 Fox Hill Rd 01803 781-270-1791
Ellen Johnson, prin. Fax 229-5909
Memorial ES 400/K-5
125 Winn St 01803 781-270-1721
Deborah Dressler, prin. Fax 229-5751
Pine Glen ES 300/K-5
1 Pine Glen Way 01803 781-270-1712
John Lyons, prin. Fax 229-5793
Simonds MS 900/6-8
114 Winn St 01803 781-270-1781
Richard Connors, prin. Fax 229-4980
Wyman ES 500/K-5
41 Terrace Hall Ave 01803 781-270-1701
Nicole McDonald, prin. Fax 229-5667

Mount Hope Christian S 300/PK-5
3 McGinnis Dr 01803 781-272-1014
Elaine Driscoll, prin. Fax 272-3830

Buzzards Bay, Barnstable, Pop. 3,756

St. Margaret Regional S 200/K-8
143 Main St 02532 508-759-2213
Joyce Saucier, prin. Fax 759-8776

Byfield, Essex
Triton Regional SD 2,800/PK-12
112 Elm St 01922 978-465-2397
Brian Forget, supt. Fax 465-8599
www.tritonschools.org
Triton Regional MS 400/7-8
112 Elm St 01922 978-463-5845
Alan Macrae, prin. Fax 465-6868
Other Schools – See Newbury, Rowley, Salisbury

Cambridge, Middlesex, Pop. 100,799
Cambridge SD 6,300/PK-12
159 Thorndike St 02141 617-349-6400
Dr. Kenneth Salim, supt. Fax 349-6496
www.cpsd.us
Amigos S 300/PK-8
15 Upton St 02139 617-349-6567
Sarah Marrero, prin. Fax 349-6833
Baldwin ES 300/PK-5
85 Oxford St 02138 617-349-6525
Heidi Cook, prin. Fax 349-6893
Cambridgeport ES 300/PK-5
89 Elm St 02139 617-349-6587
Katie Charner-Laird, prin. Fax 349-6511
Cambridge Street Upper S 300/6-8
158 Spring St 02141 617-349-3050
Manuel Fernandez, prin.
Fletcher-Maynard Academy 200/PK-5
225 Windsor St 02139 617-349-6588
Robin Harris, prin. Fax 349-6595
Graham and Parks ES 400/PK-5
44 Linnaean St 02138 617-349-6577
Tony Byers, prin. Fax 349-6590
Haggerty ES 200/PK-5
110 Cushing St 02138 617-349-6555
Dr. Nancy Campbell, prin. Fax 349-6034
Kennedy-Longfellow ES 300/PK-5
158 Spring St 02141 617-349-6841
Christine Gerber, prin. Fax 349-3242
King ES 200/K-5
102 Putnam Ave 02139 617-349-6562
Gerald Yung, prin. Fax 349-6569
King Open ES 300/PK-5
359 Broadway 02139 617-349-6540
Darrell Williams, prin. Fax 349-6548
Morse ES 300/PK-5
40 Granite St 02139 617-349-6575
Patricia Beggy, prin. Fax 349-6576
Peabody ES 300/PK-5
70 Rindge Ave 02140 617-349-6530
Jennifer Ford, prin. Fax 349-6538
Putnam Avenue Upper S 200/6-8
100 Putnam Ave 02139 617-349-7780
Mirko Chardin, prin.
Rindge Avenue Upper S 300/6-8
70 Rindge Ave 02140 617-349-4060
Julie Craven, prin. Fax 349-6037
Tobin Montessori ES 300/PK-5
197 Vassal Ln 02138 617-349-6600
Jaime Frost, prin. Fax 349-6890
Vassal Lane Upper S 300/6-8
197 Vassal Ln 02138 617-349-6550
Daniel Coplon-Newfield, prin. Fax 349-6686

Buckingham Browne & Nichols S 1,000/PK-12
80 Gerrys Landing Rd 02138 617-800-2135
Geordie Mitchell M.Ed., admin.
Cambridge Friends S 200/PK-8
5 Cadbury Rd 02140 617-354-3880
Chris Gorycki, head sch Fax 876-1815
Cambridge Montessori S 200/PK-8
161 Garden St 02138 617-492-3410
Dr. Ingrid Tucker, head sch Fax 576-5154
Fayerweather Street S 200/PK-8
765 Concord Ave 02138 617-876-4746
Edward Kuh, head sch Fax 520-6700
International School of Boston 600/PK-12
45 Matignon Rd 02140 617-499-1451
Richard Ulffers, head sch Fax 499-1454
St. Paul's Choir S 50/4-8
29 Mount Auburn St 02138 617-868-8658
William McIvor, hdmstr. Fax 354-7092
St. Peter S 200/K-8
96 Concord Ave 02138 617-547-0101
Andrew Malionek, prin. Fax 441-8911
Shady Hill S 500/PK-8
178 Coolidge Hl 02138 617-520-5260
Mark Stanek, hdmstr. Fax 520-9387

Canton, Norfolk, Pop. 18,530
Canton SD 3,200/PK-12
960 Washington St 02021 781-821-5060
Jennifer Fischer-Mueller, supt. Fax 575-6500
www.cantonma.org
Galvin MS 800/6-8
55 Pecunit St 02021 781-821-5070
William Conard, prin. Fax 575-6509
Hansen ES 500/K-5
25 Pecunit St 02021 781-821-5085
Peter Boucher, prin. Fax 821-5662
Kennedy ES 500/K-5
100 Dedham St 02021 781-821-5080
Christine McMahon, prin. Fax 575-6543
Luce ES 600/K-5
45 Independence St 02021 781-821-5075
Robie Peter, prin. Fax 575-6528
Rodman ECC 100/PK-PK
960 Washington St 02021 781-821-5060
Donna Kilday, dir. Fax 575-6500

St. John the Evangelist S 200/PK-8
696 Washington St 02021 781-828-2130
Christopher Flieger, prin. Fax 828-7563

Carlisle, Middlesex
Carlisle SD 600/PK-8
83 School St 01741 978-369-6550
James O'Shea, supt. Fax 371-2400
www.carlisle.k12.ma.us
Carlisle ES 600/PK-8
83 School St 01741 978-369-6550
Dennet Sidell, prin. Fax 371-2400

Carver, Plymouth
Carver SD 1,700/PK-12
3 Carver Square Blvd 02330 508-866-6160
Scott Knief, supt. Fax 866-2920
www.carver.org
Carver ES 800/PK-5
85 Main St 02330 508-866-6210
Ruby Maestas, prin. Fax 866-6845

Centerville, Barnstable, Pop. 9,190
Barnstable SD
Supt. — See Hyannis
Centerville ES 300/K-3
658 Bay Ln 02632 508-790-9890
Matthew Scheufele, prin. Fax 790-9895

Veritas Academy 50/PK-8
1200 Old Stage Rd 02632 508-420-8145
Rev. Michael Beckner M.Ed., dir. Fax 420-8145

Charlemont, Franklin
Hawlemont Regional SD
Supt. — See Shelburne Falls
Hawlemont Regional ES 100/PK-6
10 School St 01339 413-339-8316
Samantha Rutz, prin. Fax 339-5760

Mohawk Trail SD
Supt. — See Shelburne Falls
Heath ES 100/PK-6
18 Jacobs Rd 01339 413-337-5307
Jesse Porter-Henry, prin. Fax 337-5507

Charlestown, See Boston
Boston SD
Supt. — See Boston
Edwards MS 500/6-8
28 Walker St 02129 617-635-8516
Laryssa Doherty, prin. Fax 635-8522
Harvard-Kent ES 600/PK-5
50 Bunker Hill St 02129 617-635-8358
Jason Gallagher, prin. Fax 635-8364
Warren-Prescott S 500/PK-8
50 School St 02129 617-635-8346
Michele Davis, prin. Fax 635-9454

Good Shephard S PK-PK
20 Winthrop St 02129 617-242-8800
Jessica Maxwell M.Ed., dir. Fax 242-0016

Charlton, Worcester
Dudley-Charlton Regional SD
Supt. — See Dudley
Charlton ES 400/PK-1
9 Burlingame Rd 01507 508-248-7774
Lori Pacheco, prin. Fax 248-7003
Charlton MS 800/5-8
2 Oxford Rd 01507 508-248-1423
Dean Packard, prin. Fax 248-1418
Heritage ES 500/2-4
34 Oxford Rd 01507 508-248-4884
Kathleen Pastore, prin. Fax 248-1109

Chatham, Barnstable, Pop. 1,395
Monomoy Regional SD 1,300/PK-12
425 Crowell Rd 02633 508-945-5130
Scott Carpenter, supt. Fax 945-5133
www.monomoy.edu/
Chatham ES 300/PK-4
147 Depot Rd 02633 508-945-5135
Dr. Robin Millen, prin. Fax 945-5138
Monomoy Regional MS 100/5-7
425 Crowell Rd 02633 508-945-5148
Mark Wilson, prin. Fax 945-5143
Other Schools – See Harwich

Chelmsford, Middlesex, Pop. 33,858
Chelmsford SD 5,100/PK-12
230 North Rd 01824 978-251-5100
Dr. Jay Lang, supt. Fax 251-5110
www.chelmsford.k12.ma.us
Byam ES 500/K-4
25 Maple Rd 01824 978-251-5144
Jason Fredette, prin. Fax 251-5150
Center ES 400/K-4
84 Billerica Rd 01824 978-251-5155
Dianna Fulreader, prin. Fax 251-5160
Community Education Center 100/PK-PK
170 Dalton Rd 01824 978-251-5151
Amy Matson, prin. Fax 251-5154
McCarthy MS 900/5-8
250 North Rd 01824 978-251-5122
Kurt McPhee, prin. Fax 251-5130
Parker MS 700/5-8
75 Graniteville Rd 01824 978-251-5133
Dr. Jeffrey Parks, prin. Fax 251-5140
South Row ES 400/K-4
250 Boston Rd 01824 978-251-5177
Dr. Molly McMahon, prin. Fax 251-5180
Other Schools – See North Chelmsford

Chelsea, Suffolk, Pop. 34,185
Chelsea SD 6,100/PK-12
500 Broadway 02150 617-466-4477
Mary Bourque, supt. Fax 889-8361
chelseaschools.com
Berkowitz ES 600/1-4
300 Crescent Ave 02150 617-466-5300
Adam Deleidi, prin. Fax 889-8646
Browne S 500/5-8
180 Walnut St 02150 617-466-5235
Julie Shea, prin. Fax 889-8459
Clark Avenue S 600/5-8
8 Clark Ave 02150 617-466-5100
Michael Talbot, prin. Fax 889-7539
Hooks ES 500/1-4
300 Crescent Ave 02150 617-466-5400
Adele Lubarsky, prin. Fax 889-8647
Kelly ES 600/1-4
300 Crescent Ave 02150 617-466-5350
Magdalena Gleason, prin. Fax 889-8644
Silber Early Learning Center 900/PK-1
99 Hawthorne St 02150 617-466-5150
Jacqueline Maloney, prin. Fax 889-8425
Sokolowski ES 600/1-4
300 Crescent Ave 02150 617-466-5450
Nathaniel Meyers, prin. Fax 889-8470
Wright Science & Technology Acad 500/5-8
180 Walnut St 02150 617-466-5240
Michelle Creamer, prin. Fax 889-8463

St. Rose S 200/PK-8
580 Broadway 02150 617-884-2626
Michelle Butler, prin. Fax 889-2345

Cheshire, Berkshire, Pop. 507
Adams-Cheshire Regional SD 1,400/K-12
191 Church St 01225 413-743-2939
Robert Putnam, supt. Fax 743-4135
www.acrsd.net
Other Schools – See Adams

Chester, Hampden, Pop. 622
Gateway SD
Supt. — See Huntington
Chester ES 100/PK-5
325 Middlefield Rd 01011 413-685-1360
Megan Coburn, prin. Fax 354-9618

Chesterfield, Hampshire
Chesterfield-Goshen SD
Supt. — See Westhampton
New Hingham Regional ES 200/PK-6
30 Smith Rd 01012 413-296-0000
Tim Luce, prin. Fax 296-0003

Chestnut Hill, See Newton
Brookline SD
Supt. — See Brookline
Baker S 800/K-8
205 Beverly Rd 02467 617-879-4500
Dr. Mary Brown, prin. Fax 879-4505
Heath S 600/PK-8
100 Eliot St 02467 617-879-4570
Dr. Asa Sevelius, prin. Fax 739-7570

Brimmer and May S 400/PK-12
69 Middlesex Rd 02467 617-566-7462
Judy Guild, head sch Fax 734-5147
Chestnut Hill S 300/PK-6
428 Hammond St 02467 617-566-4394
Dr. Steven Tobolsky Ph.D., head sch Fax 738-6602

Chicopee, Hampden, Pop. 54,468
Chicopee SD 7,400/PK-12
180 Broadway St 01020 413-594-3410
Richard Rege, supt. Fax 594-3552
www.chicopeeps.org
Barry ES 500/K-5
44 Connell St 01020 413-594-3425
Jonathan Endelos, prin. Fax 594-3468
Belcher ES 300/K-2
125 Montgomery St 01020 413-594-3526
Samuel Karlin, prin. Fax 594-3469
Bellamy MS 900/6-8
314 Pendleton Ave 01020 413-594-3527
Matthew Francis, prin. Fax 594-1837
Bowe ES 400/PK-5
115 Hampden St 01013 413-594-3431
David Drugan, prin. Fax 594-1848
Bowie ES 400/K-5
80 DARE Way 01022 413-594-3532
Norman Burgess, prin. Fax 594-3590
Dupont Memorial MS 6-8
650 Front St 01013 413-594-1881
Kristopher Theriault, prin. Fax 594-1897
Fairview ES 700/K-5
26 Memorial Ave 01020 413-594-3501
Irene Lemieux, prin. Fax 594-3509
Lambert-Lavoie ES 300/K-5
99 Kendall St 01020 413-594-3444
William Holt, prin. Fax 594-3513
Litwin ES 400/K-5
135 Litwin Ln 01020 413-594-3545
Elizabeth Masse, prin. Fax 594-3547
Stefanik ES 400/K-5
720 Meadow St 01013 413-594-3464
Amanda Theriault, prin. Fax 594-3462
Streiber ES 300/K-5
40 Streiber Dr 01020 413-594-3446
January Wilson, prin. Fax 594-3480
Szetela Early Childhood S 300/PK-PK
66 Macek Dr 01013 413-594-3597
Janet Reid, prin. Fax 594-3596

St. Joan of Arc S 200/PK-8
587 Grattan St 01020 413-533-1475
Paula Jenkins, prin. Fax 533-1418
St. Stanislaus S 400/PK-8
534 Front St 01013 413-592-5135
Sr. Cecelia Haier, prin. Fax 598-0187

Chilmark, Dukes
Up-Island Regional SD
Supt. — See Vineyard Haven
Chilmark ES 100/PK-5
PO Box 60 02535 508-645-2562
Susan Stevens, prin. Fax 645-2460

Clarksburg, Berkshire, Pop. 1,745
Clarksburg SD 200/K-8
777 W Cross Rd 01247 413-664-8735
Jon Lev, supt. Fax 664-9942
www.clarksburgschool.org/
Clarksburg ES 200/K-8
777 W Cross Rd 01247 413-663-8735
Tara Barnes, prin. Fax 663-8629

Clinton, Worcester, Pop. 7,209
Clinton SD 1,900/PK-12
150 School St 01510 978-365-4200
Dr. Steven Meyer, supt. Fax 365-5037
clinton.k12.ma.us
Clinton ES 700/PK-3
100 Church St 01510 978-365-4230
Robert Rouleau, prin. Fax 368-7209
Clinton MS 700/4-8
100 W Boylston St 01510 978-365-4220
Annmarie Sargent, prin. Fax 368-7256

Cohasset, Norfolk, Pop. 7,075
Cohasset SD 1,600/PK-12
143 Pond St 02025 781-383-6111
Louise Demas, supt. Fax 383-6507
www.cohassetk12.org
Deer Hill ES 400/3-5
208 Sohier St 02025 781-383-6115
Jennifer de Chiara Ph.D., prin. Fax 383-6791
Osgood ES 400/PK-2
210 Sohier St 02025 781-383-6117
Lisa Farrell, prin. Fax 383-0255

Colrain, Franklin
Mohawk Trail SD
Supt. — See Shelburne Falls
Colrain Central ES 100/PK-6
22 Jacksonville Rd 01340 413-624-3451
Amy Looman, prin. Fax 624-3452

Concord, Middlesex, Pop. 4,700
Concord SD 2,200/PK-8
120 Meriam Rd 01742 978-318-1500
Laurie Hunter, supt. Fax 318-1537
www.concordps.org
Alcott ES 500/K-5
93 Laurel St 01742 978-318-9544
Sharon Young, prin. Fax 371-2000
Concord MS 700/6-8
835 Old Marlboro Rd 01742 978-318-1380
Justin Cameron, prin. Fax 318-1392
Concord Preschool PK-PK
120 Meriam Rd 01742 978-371-2490
Jessica Murphy, dir.
Thoreau ES 500/K-5
29 Prairie St 01742 978-318-1300
Angel Charles, prin. Fax 318-1308
Willard ES 500/K-5
185 Powder Mill Rd 01742 978-318-1340
Matt Lucey, prin. Fax 318-1348

Fenn S 300/4-9
516 Monument St 01742 978-369-5800
Gerard J.G. Ward, admin. Fax 371-7520
Nashoba Brooks S 300/PK-8
200 Strawberry Hill Rd 01742 978-369-4591
Danielle Heard, head sch Fax 287-6038

Conway, Franklin
Conway SD
Supt. — See South Deerfield
Conway ES 200/PK-6
24 Fournier Rd 01341 413-369-4239
Kristen Gordon, prin. Fax 369-4017

Cotuit, Barnstable, Pop. 2,364

Waldorf S of Cape Cod 100/PK-8
140 Old Oyster Rd 02635 508-420-1005
Gary Cannon, admin. Fax 420-0473

Cuttyhunk, Dukes
Gosnold SD
Supt. — See East Falmouth
Cuttyhunk ES, PO Box 27 02713 50/5-6
Michelle Carvalho, prin. 508-997-5408

Dalton, Berkshire, Pop. 7,155
Central Berkshire Regional SD 1,700/PK-12
PO Box 299 01227 413-684-0320
Laurie Casna, supt. Fax 684-4088
www.cbrsd.org
Craneville ES 400/PK-5
71 Park Ave 01226 413-684-0209
Deborah White, prin. Fax 684-0584
Nessacus Regional MS 400/6-8
35 Fox Rd 01226 413-684-0780
Peter Falkowski, prin. Fax 684-4214
Other Schools – See Becket, Hinsdale

St. Agnes Academy 100/PK-8
30 Carson Ave 01226 413-684-3143
James Stankiewicz, hdmstr. Fax 684-3124

Danvers, Essex, Pop. 26,232
Danvers SD 3,600/PK-12
64 Cabot Rd 01923 978-777-4539
Lisa Dana, supt. Fax 777-8931
www.danvers.mec.edu
Great Oak ES 400/K-5
76 Pickering St 01923 978-774-2533
Sharon Burrill, prin. Fax 777-1471
Highlands ES 400/K-5
190 Hobart St 01923 978-774-5011
Paula Jones, prin. Fax 777-5821
Holten-Richmond MS 900/6-8
55 Conant St 01923 978-774-8590
Adam Federico, prin. Fax 762-8686
Riverside ES 400/PK-5
95 Liberty St 01923 978-774-5010
Violetta Powers, prin. Fax 774-7850
Smith ES 300/K-5
15 Lobao Dr 01923 978-774-1350
Tracey Mara, prin. Fax 774-1351
Thorpe ES 300/K-5
1 Avon Rd 01923 978-774-6946
Rita Ward, prin. Fax 739-4417

St. Mary of the Annunciation S 400/PK-8
14 Otis St 01923 978-774-0307
Sean Reardon, prin. Fax 750-4852

Dedham, Norfolk, Pop. 24,346
Dedham SD 2,800/PK-12
100 Whiting Ave 02026 781-310-1100
Michael J. Welch, supt. Fax 320-0193
www.dedham.k12.ma.us
Avery ES 300/1-5
336 High St 02026 781-310-5000
Dr. Clare Sullivan, prin. Fax 326-5899
Dedham MS 700/6-8
70 Whiting Ave 02026 781-310-7000
Karen Hillman, prin. Fax 461-0354
Early Childhood Education Center 300/PK-K
322 Sprague St 02026 781-310-8000
Dr. Paul Sullivan, prin. Fax 326-6445
Greenlodge ES 300/1-5
191 Greenlodge St 02026 781-310-4000
Ashley Bodkins, prin. Fax 461-0034
Oakdale ES 300/1-5
147 Cedar St 02026 781-310-6000
Holli Caulfield, prin. Fax 326-8915
Riverdale ES 200/1-5
143 Needham St 02026 781-310-2000
Edward Paris, prin. Fax 251-0732

Dedham Country Day S 300/PK-8
90 Sandy Valley Rd 02026 781-329-0850
Allison Webster, head sch Fax 329-0551
Rashi S 300/K-8
8000 Great Meadow Rd 02026 617-969-4444
Mallory Rome, head sch Fax 355-7252

Deerfield, Franklin, Pop. 620

Bement S 200/K-9
PO Box 8 01342 413-774-7061
Christopher Wilson, head sch Fax 774-7863

Dighton, Bristol
Dighton-Rehoboth Regional SD
Supt. — See North Dighton
Dighton ES 400/PK-4
1250 Somerset Ave 02715 508-669-4245
Dr. Jeanne Bonneau, prin. Fax 669-4248
Dighton MS 400/5-8
1250R Somerset Ave 02715 508-669-4200
Richard Wheeler, prin. Fax 669-4210

Dorchester, See Boston
Boston SD
Supt. — See Boston
Clap Innovation S 100/K-5
35 Harvest St 02125 617-635-8672
Marcia Riddick, prin. Fax 635-6389
Dever ES 600/K-5
325 Mount Vernon St 02125 617-635-8694
Todd Fishburne, prin. Fax 635-8097
Everett ES 300/PK-5
71 Pleasant St 02125 617-635-8779
Karen Cahill, prin. Fax 635-8780
Frederick MS 600/6-8
270 Columbia Rd 02121 617-635-1650
Pauline Lugira, prin. Fax 635-1637
Greenwood S 400/K-8
189 Glenway St 02121 617-635-8710
Karla Gandiaga, prin. Fax 635-8713
Henderson Inclusion S 200/PK-12
18 Croftland Ave 02124 617-635-6365
Patricia Lampron, prin. Fax 635-6367
Holmes ES 300/K-5
40 School St 02124 617-635-8681
Yeshi Gaskin, prin. Fax 635-8685
Kenny ES 300/PK-5
19 Oakton Ave 02122 617-635-8789
Emily Bryan, prin. Fax 635-8791
King S 500/PK-8
77 Lawrence Ave 02121 617-635-8212
Grace Coleman, prin. Fax 635-9356
Lee Academy 200/PK-3
25 Dunbar Ave 02124 617-635-8618
Amelia Gorman, prin. Fax 635-8621
Lee ES 500/K-8
155 Talbot Ave 02124 617-635-8687
Kimberly Curtis-Crowley, prin. Fax 635-8692
Mather ES 600/PK-5
24 Parish St 02122 617-635-8757
Rochelle Valdez, prin. Fax 635-8762
McCormack MS 700/6-8
315 Mount Vernon St 02125 617-635-8657
Elvis Henriquez, prin. Fax 635-9788
Murphy S 900/PK-8
1 Worrell St 02122 617-635-8781
Courtney Sheppeck, prin. Fax 635-8787
Russell ES 400/PK-5
750 Columbia Rd 02125 617-635-8803
Tamara Blake, prin. Fax 635-9768
Shaw ES 300/PK-3
429 Norfolk St 02124 617-635-8777
Akosua Osey-Bobie, prin. Fax 635-8721
Trotter ES 400/PK-8
135 Humboldt Ave 02121 617-635-8225
Sarita Thomas, prin. Fax 635-7915
Winthrop ES 400/PK-5
35 Brookford St 02125 617-635-8379
Leah Blake, prin. Fax 635-9396

Epiphany S 100/5-8
154 Centre St 02124 617-326-0425
Rev. John Finley, head sch Fax 326-0424
Mother Caroline Academy 100/4-8
515 Blue Hill Ave 02121 617-427-1177
Ed Hudner, dir. Fax 427-7788
St. Brendan S 200/PK-6
29 Rita Rd 02124 617-282-3388
Maura Burke, prin. Fax 822-9152
Saint John Paul II Academy 400/PK-8
239 Neponset Ave 02122 617-265-0019
Kate Brandley, prin. Fax 288-3432
Saint John Paul II Academy 200/PK-8
2222 Dorchester Ave 02124 617-265-0019
Lisa Warshafsky, prin. Fax 296-0144
Saint John Paul II Academy PK-8
790 Columbia Rd 02125 617-265-0019
Claire Sheridan, prin. Fax 288-1372

Douglas, Worcester
Douglas SD 1,200/PK-12
21 Davis St 01516 508-476-7901
Kevin Maines, supt. Fax 476-3719
www.douglas.k12.ma.us
Douglas ES, 19 Davis St 01516 300/2-5
Samuel Cederbaum, dir. 508-476-4200
Douglas MS 300/6-8
21 Davis St 01516 508-476-3332
Brian Delaney, prin. Fax 476-1604
Douglas PS 200/PK-1
17 Gleason Ct 01516 508-476-2154
Cindy Socha, prin. Fax 476-4041

Dover, Norfolk, Pop. 2,253
Dover-Sherborn SD 2,100/PK-12
157 Farm St 02030 508-785-0036
Dr. Andrew Keough, supt. Fax 785-2239
www.doversherborn.org
Chickering ES 500/PK-5
29 Cross St 02030 508-785-0480
Laura Dayal, admin. Fax 785-9748
Dover-Sherborn Regional MS 500/6-8
155 Farm St 02030 508-785-0635
Scott Kellett, prin. Fax 785-0796
Other Schools – See Sherborn

Charles River S 200/PK-8
PO Box 339 02030 508-785-0068
Gretchen Larkin, head sch Fax 785-8290

Dracut, Middlesex, Pop. 25,594
Dracut SD 3,500/PK-12
2063 Lakeview Ave 01826 978-957-2660
Steven Stone, supt. Fax 957-2682
www.dracutps.org
Brookside ES 600/K-5
1560 Lakeview Ave 01826 978-957-0716
Dawn Smith, prin. Fax 957-9726
Campbell ES 600/PK-5
1021 Methuen St 01826 978-459-6186
Angela Kimble, prin. Fax 459-9780
Englesby ES 300/K-5
1580 Lakeview Ave 01826 978-957-9745
Laurie Fahey, prin. Fax 957-8449
Greenmont Avenue ES 400/K-5
37 Greenmont Ave 01826 978-453-1797
Nicholas Botelho, prin. Fax 453-8739
Richardson MS 600/6-8
1570 Lakeview Ave 01826 978-957-3330
Maria McGuinness, prin. Fax 957-4075

Dudley, Worcester, Pop. 3,700
Dudley-Charlton Regional SD 4,000/PK-12
68 Dudley Oxford Rd 01571 508-943-6888
Gregg Desto, supt. Fax 943-1077
www.dcrsd.org
Dudley ES 400/2-4
16 School St 01571 508-943-3351
Diane Seibold, prin. Fax 949-3305
Dudley MS 600/5-8
70 Dudley Oxford Rd 01571 508-943-2224
Christopher Starczewski, prin. Fax 949-0720
Mason Road ES 300/PK-1
20 Mason Rd 01571 508-943-4312
Robin Parmley, prin. Fax 949-1005
Other Schools – See Charlton

Dunstable, Middlesex
Groton-Dunstable Regional SD
Supt. — See Groton
Swallow / Union ES 300/K-4
522 Main St 01827 978-649-7281
Peter Myerson, prin. Fax 649-5078

Duxbury, Plymouth, Pop. 1,793
Duxbury SD 3,200/PK-12
93 Chandler St 02332 781-934-7600
John Antonucci, supt. Fax 934-7644
www.duxbury.k12.ma.us
Alden ES 700/3-5
75 Alden St 02332 781-934-7630
Karen Whitaker, prin. Fax 934-7636
Chandler ES 700/PK-2
93 Chandler St 02332 781-934-7680
Erin Wiesehahn, prin. Fax 934-7675
Duxbury MS 800/6-8
71 Alden St 02332 781-934-7640
Blake Dalton, prin. Fax 934-7608

Bay Farm Montessori Academy 200/PK-8
145 Loring St 02332 781-934-7101
Kevin Clark, head sch Fax 934-7102

East Boston, See Boston
Boston SD
Supt. — See Boston
Adams ES 300/PK-5
165 Webster St 02128 617-635-8383
Joanna McKeigue-Cruz, prin. Fax 635-7822
Alighieri Montessori S 100/PK-6
37 Gove St 02128 617-635-8529
Glenda Colon, prin. Fax 635-7691
Bradley ES 300/K-5
110 Beachview Rd 02128 617-635-8422
Claire Rheaume, prin. Fax 635-6927
East Boston Early Education Center 200/PK-1
135 Gove St 02128 617-635-6456
Olga Frechon, prin. Fax 635-8864
Guild ES 300/K-5
195 Leyden St 02128 617-635-8523
Karen McCarthy, prin. Fax 635-8526
Kennedy ES 300/PK-5
343 Saratoga St 02128 617-635-8466
Kristen Goncalves, prin. Fax 635-8469
McKay S 700/K-8
122 Cottage St 02128 617-635-8510
Jordan Weymer, prin. Fax 635-8515
O'Donnell ES 300/PK-5
33 Trenton St 02128 617-635-8454
C. Sura O'Mard, prin. Fax 635-8459
Otis ES 400/PK-5
218 Marion St 02128 617-635-8372
Paula Goncalves, prin. Fax 635-8376
Umana Academy 700/K-8
312 Border St 02128 617-635-8481
Claudia Gutierrez, prin. Fax 635-9595

East Boston Central Catholic S 200/K-8
69 London St 02128 617-567-7456
Maryann Manfredonia, prin. Fax 567-9559

East Bridgewater, Plymouth, Pop. 11,104
East Bridgewater SD 2,300/PK-12
143 Plymouth St 02333 508-378-8200
Elizabeth Legault, supt. Fax 378-8225
www.ebps.net
Central ES 600/PK-2
107 Central St 02333 508-378-8204
Catherine Byrne, prin. Fax 378-8229
Mitchell MS 700/3-6
435 Central St 02333 508-378-8209
Andrew Gentile, prin. Fax 378-8228

East Brookfield, Worcester, Pop. 1,302
Spencer-East Brookfield SD
Supt. — See Spencer
East Brookfield ES 200/PK-6
410 E Main St 01515 508-885-8536
Ronald Tomlin, prin. Fax 885-8571

East Falmouth, Barnstable, Pop. 5,768
Falmouth SD 3,500/PK-12
340 Teaticket Hwy 02536 508-548-0151
Nancy Taylor, supt. Fax 457-9032
www.falmouth.k12.ma.us
East Falmouth ES 400/K-4
33 Davisville Rd 02536 508-548-1052
Dr. Justine Dale, prin. Fax 548-0301
Other Schools – See Falmouth, North Falmouth, Teaticket

Gosnold SD 50/5-6
263 Hill & Plain Rd 02536 508-400-4687
Dr. Margaret Frieswyk, supt.
Other Schools – See Cuttyhunk

East Freetown, Bristol
Freetown-Lakeville SD
Supt. — See Lakeville
Freetown ES 400/PK-3
43 Bullock Rd 02717 508-763-5121
Michael Ward, prin. Fax 763-3986

Eastham, Barnstable
Eastham SD
Supt. — See Orleans
Eastham ES 200/K-5
200 School House Rd 02642 508-255-0808
William Crosby, prin. Fax 240-5403

Easthampton, Hampshire, Pop. 16,004
Easthampton SD 1,600/PK-12
50 Payson Ave Ste 200 01027 413-529-1500
Nancy Follansbee, supt. Fax 529-1567
www.epsd.us
Center ES 200/K-4
9 School St 01027 413-529-1540
Allison Rebello, prin. Fax 529-1547
Maple ES 200/PK-4
7 Chapel St 01027 413-529-1550
Judy Averill, prin. Fax 529-1599
Pepin ES 200/K-4
4 Park St 01027 413-529-1545
Allison Rebello, prin. Fax 529-1594
White Brook MS 500/5-8
200 Park St 01027 413-529-1530
Meredith Balise, prin. Fax 529-1534

East Longmeadow, Hampden, Pop. 13,367
East Longmeadow SD 2,700/PK-12
180 Maple St 01028 413-525-5450
Gordon Smith, supt. Fax 525-5456
www.eastlongmeadowma.gov/170/School-Department
Birchland Park MS 700/6-8
50 Hanward Hl 01028 413-525-5480
Timothy Allen Ed.D., prin. Fax 525-5320
Mapleshade ES 300/3-5
175 Mapleshade Ave 01028 413-525-5485
Michael Fredette, prin. Fax 525-5321
Meadow Brook ES 500/PK-2
607 Parker St 01028 413-525-5470
Lisa Dakin, prin. Fax 525-5405
Mountain View ES 300/3-5
77 Hampden Rd 01028 413-525-5490
Elaine Santaniello, prin. Fax 525-5405

East Sandwich, Barnstable, Pop. 3,915
Sandwich SD
Supt. — See Sandwich
Oak Ridge ES 300/3-6
260 Quaker Meeting House Rd 02537 508-833-0111
Patricia Hill, prin. Fax 888-0911
Sandwich STEM Academy 500/7-8
365 Quaker Meeting House Rd 02537
James Mulcahy, dir. 508-888-5300

East Taunton, See Taunton
Taunton SD
Supt. — See Taunton
East Taunton ES 600/PK-4
58R Stevens St 02718 508-821-1330
Stephanie Hoye, prin. Fax 821-1334
Martin MS 700/5-7
131 Caswell St 02718 508-821-1250
Elizabeth Rodrigues, prin. Fax 821-1273

East Walpole, Norfolk, Pop. 3,800
Walpole SD
Supt. — See Walpole
Bird MS 500/6-8
625 Washington St 02032 508-660-7226
Bridget Gough, prin. Fax 660-7229
Old Post Road ES 500/K-5
99 Old Post Rd 02032 508-660-7219
David Barner, prin. Fax 660-3114

East Weymouth, Norfolk
Weymouth SD
Supt. — See Weymouth
Adams MS 1,000/5-6
89 Middle St 02189 781-335-1100
Matthew Meehan, prin. Fax 340-2544
Chapman MS 1,000/7-8
1051 Commercial St 02189 781-337-4500
Paul Duprey, prin. Fax 340-2594

Edgartown, Dukes
Martha's Vineyard SD
Supt. — See Vineyard Haven
Edgartown ES 400/K-8
35 Robinson Rd 02539 508-627-3316
John Stevens, prin. Fax 627-7983

Erving, Franklin
Erving SD 200/PK-6
18 Pleasant St 01344 413-423-3337
Jennifer Haggerty, supt. Fax 423-3236
www.union28.org
Erving ES 200/PK-6
28 Northfield Rd 01344 413-423-3326
James Trill, prin. Fax 423-3648

Leverett SD 100/PK-6
18 Pleasant St 01344 413-423-3337
Jennifer Haggerty, supt. Fax 423-3236
www.union28.org
Other Schools – See Leverett

New Salem-Wendell SD 100/PK-6
18 Pleasant St 01344 413-423-3337
Jennifer Haggerty, supt. Fax 423-3236
www.union28.org
Other Schools – See New Salem

Shutesbury SD 200/PK-6
18 Pleasant St 01344 413-423-3337
Jennifer Haggerty, supt. Fax 423-3236
www.shutesburyschool.org
Other Schools – See Shutesbury

Essex, Essex, Pop. 1,454
Manchester Essex Regional SD
Supt. — See Manchester
Essex ES 300/K-5
12 Story St 01929 978-768-7324
Jennifer Roberts, prin. Fax 768-2502

Everett, Middlesex, Pop. 38,826
Everett SD 6,900/PK-12
121 Vine St 02149 617-389-7950
Frederick Foresteire, supt. Fax 394-2408
www.everett.k12.ma.us/
Adams ECC 200/PK-PK
78 Tileston St 02149 617-544-6092
Shannon Doherty, prin. Fax 544-6097
English S 900/K-8
105 Woodville St 02149 617-394-5013
Theresa Tringale, prin. Fax 389-5116
Keverian S 900/K-8
20 Nichols St 02149 617-394-5020
Alexander Naumann, prin. Fax 394-5028
Lafayette S 900/K-8
117 Edith St 02149 617-394-2450
John Obremski, prin. Fax 387-5207
Parlin S 900/K-8
587 Broadway 02149 617-394-2480
Michael McLucas, prin. Fax 389-5827
Webster S 500/PK-4
30 Dartmouth St 02149 617-394-5040
David Brady, prin. Fax 394-5043
Whittier S 600/K-8
337 Broadway 02149 617-394-2410
Michael McLucas, prin. Fax 389-5073

St. Anthony of Padua S 300/PK-8
54 Oakes St 02149 617-389-2448
Maria Giggie, prin. Fax 389-3769

Fairhaven, Bristol, Pop. 16,132
Fairhaven SD 2,000/PK-12
128 Washington St 02719 508-979-4000
Dr. Robert Baldwin, supt. Fax 979-4149
www.fairhavenps.org
East Fairhaven ES 400/PK-5
2 New Boston Rd 02719 508-979-4058
Wendy Weidenfeller, prin. Fax 979-4143
Hastings MS 400/6-8
30 School St 02719 508-979-4063
Dr. Nicholas Bettencourt, prin. Fax 979-4068
Wood ES 500/K-5
60 Sconticut Neck Rd 02719 508-979-4073
Amy Hartley-Matteson, prin. Fax 979-4111

St. Joseph S 200/PK-8
100 Spring St 02719 508-996-1983
Faith Piazza, prin. Fax 996-1998

Fall River, Bristol, Pop. 86,097
Fall River SD 10,300/PK-12
417 Rock St 02720 508-675-8420
Matthew Malone Ph.D., supt. Fax 675-8462
www.fallriverschools.org
Borden ES 600/PK-5
1400 President Ave 02720 508-675-8202
Kate Cobb, prin. Fax 675-8259
Doran ES 600/PK-8
101 Fountain St 02721 508-675-8225
Eric Bradley, prin. Fax 235-2608
Fonseca ES 800/K-5
160 N Wall St 02723 508-675-8177
Alicia Lisi, prin. Fax 675-0889
Greene ES 800/PK-5
409 Cambridge St 02721 508-675-8325
Lourdes Santiago, prin. Fax 675-8328
Kuss MS 800/6-8
52 Globe Mills Ave 02724 508-675-8335
Maria Pontes, prin. Fax 675-1984
LeTourneau ES 600/K-5
323 Anthony St 02721 508 676 2170
Brian Raposo Ed.D., prin. Fax 279-1940
Morton MS 700/6-8
1135 N Main St 02720 508-675-8340
Sheryl Patterson, prin. Fax 675-8414
Silvia ES 800/PK-5
1899 Meridian St 02720 508-675-9811
Anne-Marie Scott, prin. Fax 675-8314
Talbot Innovation MS 800/6-8
124 Melrose St 02723 508-675-8350
Renee Lewis, prin. Fax 675-8356
Tansey ES 300/K-5
711 Ray St 02720 508-675-8206
Christopher Audette, prin. Fax 675-4530
Viveiros ES 800/K-5
525 Slade St 02724 508-675-8300
Tricia Whitty, prin. Fax 672-7514
Watson ES 300/K-5
935 Eastern Ave 02723 508-675-8240
Cathy Carvalho, prin. Fax 235-2674

Espirito Santo S 200/PK-8
143 Everett St 02723 508-672-2229
Andrew Raposo, prin. Fax 672-7724
Holy Name S 200/PK-8
850 Pearce St 02720 508-674-9131
Dr. Patricia Wardell, prin. Fax 679-0571
Holy Trinity S 200/PK-8
64 Lamphor St 02721 508-673-6772
Brenda Gagnon, prin. Fax 730-1864
St. Michael S 200/PK-8
209 Essex St 02720 508 678 0266
Pamela Leary, prin. Fax 324-4433
St. Stanislaus S 200/PK-8
PO Box 300 02724 508-674-6771
Jean Willis, prin. Fax 677-1622

Falmouth, Barnstable, Pop. 3,663
Falmouth SD
Supt. — See East Falmouth
Lawrence MS 500/7-8
113 Lakeview Ave 02540 508-548-0606
Thomas Bushy, prin. Fax 457-9778
Morse Pond MS 600/5-6
323 Jones Rd 02540 508-548-7300
Timothy McLaughlin, prin. Fax 457-1810
Mullen Hall ES 500/K-4
130 Katherine Lee Bates Rd 02540 508-548-0220
Nancy Ashworth, prin. Fax 457-5404

Feeding Hills, Hampden, Pop. 5,450
Agawam SD 4,100/PK-12
1305 Springfield St Ste 1 01030 413-821-0548
Steven Lemanski, supt. Fax 789-1835
www.agawamed.org
Agawam JHS 600/7-8
1305 Springfield St Ste 2 01030 413-821-0561
Norman Robbins, prin. Fax 786-4240
Granger ES 300/K-4
31 S Westfield St 01030 413-821-0581
Cheryl Salomao, prin. Fax 821-0595
Other Schools – See Agawam

Fiskdale, Worcester, Pop. 2,545
Brimfield SD 300/PK-6
320 Brookfield Rd 01518 508-347-3077
Erin Nosek, supt. Fax 347-2697
www.tantasqua.org
Other Schools – See Brimfield

Brookfield SD 300/PK-6
320A Brookfield Rd 01518 508-347-3077
Erin Nosek, supt. Fax 347-2697
www.tantasqua.org
Other Schools – See Brookfield

Holland SD 200/PK-6
320 Brookfield Rd 01518 508-347-3077
Erin Nosek, supt. Fax 347-2697
www.tantasqua.org
Other Schools – See Holland

Sturbridge SD 1,000/PK-6
320 Brookfield Rd 01518 508-347-3077
Erin Nosek, supt. Fax 347-2697
www.tantasqua.org
Other Schools – See Sturbridge

Tantasqua SD 1,800/7-12
320 Brookfield Rd 01518 508-347-3077
Erin Nosek, supt. Fax 347-2697
www.tantasqua.org
Tantasqua Regional JHS 600/7-8
320 Brookfield Rd 01518 508-347-7381
Sean Gilrein, prin. Fax 347-3994

Wales SD 200/PK-6
320A Brookfield Rd 01518 508-347-3077
Erin Nosek, supt. Fax 347-2697
www.tantasqua.org
Other Schools – See Wales

Fitchburg, Worcester, Pop. 39,363
Fitchburg SD 5,000/PK-12
376 South St 01420 978-345-3200
Andre Ravenelle, supt. Fax 348-2305
www.fitchburgschools.org
Crocker ES 600/PK-4
200 Bigelow Rd 01420 978-345-3290
Adam Renda, prin. Fax 345-3233
Longsjo MS 500/5-8
98 Academy St 01420 978-343-2146
Craig Chalifoux, prin. Fax 348-2323
McKay Arts Academy 700/PK-8
67 Rindge Rd 01420 978-665-3187
Lourdes Ramirez, prin. Fax 665-3523
Memorial MS 700/5-8
615 Rollstone St 01420 978-345-3295
Francis Thomas, prin. Fax 343-2121
Reingold ES 700/K-4
70 Reingold Ave 01420 978-345-3287
Martha Clark, prin. Fax 343-2132
South Street ES 600/PK-4
376 South St 01420 978-348-2300
Jonathan Thompson, prin. Fax 345-3292

Applewild S 200/PK-8
120 Prospect St 01420 978-342-6053
Christie Stover, head sch Fax 345-5059
St. Bernard S 200/PK-8
254 Summer St 01420 978-342-1948
Deborah Wright, prin. Fax 342-1153

Florence, See Northampton
Northampton SD
Supt. — See Northampton
Finn Ryan Road ES 200/K-5
498 Ryan Rd 01062 413-587-1550
Sarah Madden, prin. Fax 587-1561
Kennedy MS 600/6-8
100 Bridge Rd 01062 413-587-1489
Lesley Wilson, prin. Fax 587-1495

Florida, Berkshire
Florida SD 100/PK-8
56 N County Rd 01247 413-664-6023
Jon Lev, supt. Fax 663-3593
www.abbottmemorial.org
Abbott Memorial S 100/PK-8
56 N County Rd 01247 413-664-6023
Heidi Dugal, prin. Fax 663-3593

Forestdale, Barnstable, Pop. 4,061
Sandwich SD
Supt. — See Sandwich
Forestdale ES 200/PK-2
151 Route 130 02644 508-477-6600
Marc Smith, prin. Fax 477-7665

Foxboro, Norfolk, Pop. 5,706
Foxborough SD 2,700/PK-12
60 South St 02035 508-543-1660
Debra Spinelli, supt. Fax 543-4793
www.foxborough.k12.ma.us
Ahern MS 900/5-8
111 Mechanic St 02035 508-543-1610
Susan Abrams, prin. Fax 543-1613
Burrell ES 400/PK-4
16 Morse St 02035 508-543-1605
Michele McCarthy, prin. Fax 698-2196
Igo ES 400/K-4
70 Carpenter St 02035 508-543-1680
Michael Stanton, prin. Fax 543-1699
Taylor ES 300/K-4
196 South St 02035 508-543-1607
Moira Rodgers, prin. Fax 543-3261

Sage S 200/PK-8
171 Mechanic St 02035 508-543-9619
Marie Leary, head sch Fax 543-1152

Framingham, Middlesex, Pop. 61,638
Framingham SD 8,300/PK-12
73 Mount Wayte Ave Ste 5 01702 508-626-9117
Robert Tremblay, supt. Fax 877-4240
www.framingham.k12.ma.us
Barbieri ES 600/K-5
100 Dudley Rd 01702 508-626-9187
Susan McGilvray-Rivet, prin. Fax 626-9176
BLOCKS Preschool @ Juniper Hill 300/PK-PK
29 Upper Joclyn Ave 01701 508-788-2380
Rosario Alvarez-O'Neil, prin. Fax 872-1354
Brophy ES 500/K-5
575 Pleasant St 01701 508-626-9158
Frank Rothwell, prin. Fax 628-1305
Cameron MS 500/6-8
215 Elm St 01701 508-879-2290
Michelle Melick, prin. Fax 788-3560
Dunning ES 500/K-5
48 Frost St 01701 508-626-9155
Michelle Schecter, prin. Fax 877-4524
Fuller MS 500/6-8
31 Flagg Dr 01702 508-620-4956
Jose Duarte, prin. Fax 628-1308
Hemenway ES 600/K-5
729 Water St 01701 508-626-9149
Liz Simon, prin. Fax 877-2262
King ES, 454 Water St 01701 100/K-3
Kim Taylor, prin. 508-782-7201
McCarthy ES 600/K-5
8 Flagg Dr 01702 508-626-9161
Jean Nolan, prin. Fax 626-9106
Potter Road ES 500/K-5
492 Potter Rd 01701 508-626-9110
Paula DelPrete, prin. Fax 877-1683
Stapleton ES 400/K-5
25 Elm St 01701 508-626-9143
Amy Bright, prin. Fax 877-4908
Walsh MS 700/6-8
301 Brook St 01701 508-626-9180
Patrick Johnson, prin. Fax 877-1825
Wilson ES 600/K-5
169 Leland St 01702 508-626-9164
John Haidemenos, prin. Fax 620-2965

St. Bridget S 300/K-8
832 Worcester Rd 01702 508-875-0181
Cathleen Chaves, prin. Fax 875-9552
Summit Montessori S 100/PK-6
283 Pleasant St 01701 508-872-3630
Martha Torrence M.Ed., head sch Fax 872-3314

Franklin, Norfolk, Pop. 30,893
Franklin SD 5,800/PK-12
355 E Central St 02038 508-541-5243
Sara Ahern Ed.D., supt. Fax 533-0321
franklindistrict.vt-s.net
Franklin ECDC 100/PK-PK
224 Oak St 02038 508-541-8166
Kelty Kelley, prin. Fax 541-8254
Jefferson ES 400/K-5
628 Washington St 02038 508-541-2140
Sarah Klim, prin. Fax 541-2124
Keller ES 500/K-5
500 Lincoln St 02038 508-553-0322
Eric Stark, prin. Fax 541-2109
Kennedy Memorial ES 400/K-5
551 Pond St 02038 508-541-5260
Dr. Linda Ashley, prin. Fax 541-5260
Mann MS 500/6-8
224 Oak St 02038 508-553-0322
Rebecca Motte, prin. Fax 541-7071
Oak Street ES 500/K-5
224 Oak St 02038 508-541-7890
Kate Peretz, prin. Fax 541-8047
Parmenter ES 400/K-5
235 Wachusett St 02038 508-541-5281
Shannon Barca, prin. Fax 553-0894
Remington MS 500/6-8
628 Washington St 02038 508-541-2130
Brian Wildeman, prin. Fax 541-2124
Sullivan MS 500/6-8
500 Lincoln St 02038 508-553-0322
Beth Wittcoff, prin. Fax 542-2109
Thayer ES 300/K-5
137 W Central St 02038 508-541-5263
Kathleen Gerber, prin. Fax 553-0891

Gardner, Worcester, Pop. 19,860
Gardner SD 1,700/PK-12
70 Waterford St 01440 978-632-1000
Mark Pellegrino, supt. Fax 632-1164
www.gardnerk12.org
Elm Street ES 300/2-4
160 Elm St 01440 978-632-1673
David Fredette, prin. Fax 632-4382
Gardner MS 400/5-7
297 Catherine St 01440 978-632-1603
Arthur Murphy, prin. Fax 632-4234
Waterford Street ES 400/PK-1
62 Waterford St 01440 978-632-1605
F. Dan Hill, prin. Fax 632-4037

Holy Family Academy 300/PK-8
99 Nichols St 01440 978-632-8656
Stephen Chartier, prin. Fax 630-1433

Georgetown, Essex
Georgetown SD 1,000/PK-12
51 North St 01833 978-352-5777
Carol Jacobs, supt. Fax 352-5778
www.georgetown-schools.org/
Penn Brook ES 400/K-6
68 Elm St 01833 978-352-5785
Margaret Maher, prin. Fax 352-5787
Perley ES 200/PK-K
51 North St 01833 978-352-5780
Margaret Maher, prin. Fax 352-5782

Gilbertville, Worcester
Quabbin SD
Supt. — See Barre
Hardwick ES 200/K-6
PO Box 576 01031 413-477-6351
Shelly St. George, prin. Fax 477-6409

St. Aloysius Catholic S PK-8
PO Box 522 01031 413-477-1268
Roberta McQuaid, dir. Fax 477-1271

Gill, Franklin, Pop. 1,583
Gill-Montague SD
Supt. — See Turners Falls
Gill ES 100/K-6
48 Boyle Rd, 413-863-3255
Conor Driscoll, prin. Fax 863-3268

Gloucester, Essex, Pop. 28,371
Gloucester SD 3,100/PK-12
2 Blackburn Dr 01930 978-281-9800
Dr. Richard Safier, supt. Fax 281-9899
www.gloucesterschools.com
Beeman Memorial ES 300/K-5
138 Cherry St 01930 978-281-9825
Jodie Gennodie, prin. Fax 282-3011
East Gloucester ES 300/K-5
8 Davis St 01930 978-281-9830
Amy Pasquarello, prin. Fax 281-9864
Gloucester Preschool 100/PK-PK
2 Blackburn Dr 01930 978-281-9848
Ann-Marie Jordan, prin. Fax 281-9861
O'Maley MS 700/6-8
32 Cherry St 01930 978-281-9850
Debra Lucey, prin. Fax 281-9890
Plum Cove ES 200/K-5
15 Hickory St 01930 978-282-3030
Tammy Morgan, prin. Fax 282-3006
Veterans Memorial ES 200/K-5
11 Webster St 01930 978-281-9820
Matthew Fusco, prin. Fax 281-9717
West Parish ES 400/K-5
10 Concord St 01930 978-281-9835
Telena Imel, prin. Fax 281-9886

Faith Christian S 50/PK-8
384 Washington St 01930 978-283-8856
Jean Lodge, prin. Fax 283-8856

Grafton, Worcester
Grafton SD 3,100/PK-12
30 Providence Rd 01519 508-839-5421
James Cummings Ed.D., supt. Fax 839-7618
www.grafton.k12.ma.us
Grafton MS 500/7-8
22 Providence Rd 01519 508-839-5420
Roseanne Kurposka, prin. Fax 839-8528
Millbury Street ES 700/2-6
105 Millbury St 01519 508-839-0757
Joanne Stocklin, prin. Fax 839-7458
North Street ES 500/2-6
60 North St 01519 508-839-5428
Stephen Wiltshire, prin. Fax 839-8539
Other Schools – See North Grafton, South Grafton

Touchstone Community S 100/PK-8
54 Leland St 01519 508-839-0038
Susan Diller, head sch Fax 839-7331

Granby, Hampshire, Pop. 1,346
Granby SD 900/PK-12
387 E State St 01033 413-467-7193
Sheryl Stanton, supt. Fax 467-3909
www.granbyschoolsma.org
East Meadow ES 200/4-6
393 E State St 01033 413-467-7199
William Lataille, prin. Fax 467-9182
West Street ES 300/PK-3
14 West St 01033 413-467-9235
William Lataille, prin. Fax 467-7163

Great Barrington, Berkshire, Pop. 2,177
Berkshire Hills SD
Supt. — See Stockbridge
Monument Valley Regional MS 400/5-8
313 Monument Valley Rd 01230 413-644-2300
Ben Doren, prin. Fax 644-2394
Muddy Brook Regional ES 400/PK-4
318 Monument Valley Rd 01230 413-644-2350
Mary Berle, prin. Fax 644-2395

Great Barrington Rudolf Steiner S 200/PK-8
35 W Plain Rd 01230 413-528-4015
Michael Junkins, admin. Fax 528-6410

Greenfield, Franklin, Pop. 14,016
Greenfield SD 1,600/PK-12
195 Federal St Ste 100 01301 413-772-1300
Jordana Harper, supt. Fax 774-7940
www.gpsk12.org
Academy for Early Learning at N Parish 100/PK-PK
1 Place Ter 01301 413-772-1390
Fax 772-1337
Discovery S at Four Corners 200/K-4
21 Ferrante Ave 01301 413-772-1378
Jacob Toomey, prin. Fax 772-1329
Federal ES 200/K-4
125 Federal St 01301 413-772-1380
Nancy Putnam, prin. Fax 772-1319
Greenfield MS 300/5-7
195 Federal St 01301 413-772-1360
Gary Tashjian, prin. Fax 772-1367
Math & Science Academy 5-7
195 Federal St 01301 413-772-1360
Gary Tashjian, prin. Fax 772-1367
Newton ES 200/K-4
70 Shelburne Rd 01301 413-772-1370
Melodie Goodwin, prin. Fax 772-1332

Groton, Middlesex, Pop. 1,106
Groton-Dunstable Regional SD 2,600/PK-12
PO Box 729 01450 978-448-5505
Dr. Laura Chesson, supt. Fax 448-9402
www.gdrsd.org
Boutwell S 100/PK-PK
PO Box 730 01450 978-448-2297
Russell Hoyt, prin. Fax 448-8459
Groton-Dunstable Regional MS 900/5-8
PO Box 727 01450 978-448-6155
James Lin, prin. Fax 448-1201
Roche ES 500/K-4
PO Box 738 01450 978-448-6665
Liz Garden, prin. Fax 448-3988
Other Schools – See Dunstable

Country Day S of the Holy Union 200/PK-6
14 Main St 01450 978-448-5646
Mary Hamelin, prin. Fax 448-2392

Groveland, Essex, Pop. 5,214
Pentucket SD
Supt. — See West Newbury
Bagnall ES 600/PK-6
253 School St 01834 978-372-8856
Emily Puteri, prin. Fax 521-8956

Hadley, Hampshire
Hadley SD 600/PK-12
125 Russell St 01035 413-586-0822
Anne McKenzie Ed.D., supt. Fax 582-6453
www.hadleyschools.org
Hadley ES 300/PK-6
21 River Dr 01035 413-584-5011
Dr. Joan Wickman, prin. Fax 582-6457

Hartsbrook S 300/PK-12
193 Bay Rd 01035 413-584-3198
Fax 586-9438

Halifax, Plymouth
Halifax SD
Supt. — See Kingston
Halifax ES 600/K-6
464 Plymouth St 02338 781-293-2581
Kayne Beaudry, prin. Fax 293-6589

Hamilton, Essex
Hamilton-Wenham SD
Supt. — See Wenham
Cutler ES 300/K-5
237 Asbury St 01982 978-468-5330
Jennifer Clifford, prin. Fax 468-5314
Miles River MS 400/6-8
787 Bay Rd 01982 978-468-0362
Craig Hovey, prin. Fax 468-8454
Winthrop ES 300/PK-5
325 Bay Rd 01982 978-468-5340
Christopher Heath, prin. Fax 468-5315

Hampden, Hampden
Hampden-Wilbraham SD
Supt. — See Wilbraham
Burgess MS 300/6-8
85 Wilbraham Rd 01036 413-566-8950
John Derosia, prin. Fax 566-2163
Green Meadows ES 200/K-5
38 North Rd 01036 413-566-3263
Sharon Moberg, prin. Fax 566-2089

Hancock, Berkshire
Shaker Mountain School Union # 70
Supt. — See Richmond
Hancock ES 50/PK-6
3080 Hancock Rd 01237 413-738-5676
John Merselis, prin. Fax 738-5338

Hanover, Plymouth, Pop. 11,912
Hanover SD 2,600/PK-12
188 Broadway 02339 781-878-0786
Matthew Ferron Ed.D., supt. Fax 871-3374
www.hanoverschools.org
Cedar ES 400/PK-4
265 Cedar St 02339 781-878-7228
Michael Oates, prin. Fax 878-1968
Center ES 300/K-2
65 Silver St 02339 781-826-2631
Jane Degrenier, prin. Fax 826-0765
Hanover MS 900/5-8
45 Whiting St 02339 781-871-1122
Daniel Birolini, prin. Fax 871-8792
Sylvester ES 200/3-4
495 Hanover St 02339 781-826-3844
Jane Degrenier, prin. Fax 829-5098

Hanscom AFB, See Bedford
Lincoln SD
Supt. — See Lincoln
Hanscom MS 200/4-8
2 Eglin St 01731 781-274-0050
Erich Ledebuhr, prin. Fax 274-7329
Hanscom PS 400/PK-3
2 Eglin St 01731 781-274-7721
Kristen St. George, prin. Fax 274-6414

Hanson, Plymouth, Pop. 2,089
Whitman-Hanson SD
Supt. — See Whitman
Hanson MS 500/6-8
111 Liberty St 02341 781-618-7575
William Tranter, prin. Fax 618-8815
Indian Head ES 400/3-5
726 Indian Head St 02341 781-618-7065
Elizabeth Wilcox, prin. Fax 618-7094
Maquan ES 400/PK-2
38 School St 02341 781-618-7060
Elizabeth Wilcox, prin. Fax 618-7097

Harvard, Worcester
Harvard SD 1,200/PK-12
39 Mass Ave 01451 978-456-4140
Linda Dwight, supt. Fax 456-8592
www.psharvard.org
Hildreth ES 500/PK-5
27 Mass Ave 01451 978-456-4145
Joshua Myler, prin. Fax 456-3287

Harwich, Barnstable
Monomoy Regional SD
Supt. — See Chatham
Harwich ES 600/PK-4
263 South St 02645 508-430-7216
Samuel Hein, prin. Fax 430-7232

Hatfield, Hampshire, Pop. 1,311
Hatfield SD 500/PK-12
34 School St 01038 413-247-5641
John Robert, supt. Fax 247-0201
hatfieldps.net
Hatfield ES 300/PK-6
33 Main St 01038 413-247-5010
Jennifer Chapin, prin. Fax 247-0482

Haverhill, Essex, Pop. 59,811
Haverhill SD 7,600/PK-12
4 Summer St Ste 104 01830 978-374-3400
James Scully, supt. Fax 374-3422
www.haverhill-ps.org/
Bartlett K Center 100/K-K
551 Washington St 01832 978-469-8735
Toni Donais, admin. Fax 469-8736
Bradford ES 600/K-5
118 Montvale St 01835 978-374-2443
Louise Perry, prin. Fax 374-0529
Consentino S 900/1-8
685 Washington St 01832 978-374-5775
John Mele, prin. Fax 374-3442
Crowell K Center 100/K-K
26 Belmont Ave 01830 978-374-3473
Maureen Gray, admin. Fax 374-3489
Golden Hill ES 500/K-4
140 Boardman St 01830 978-374-5794
Bruce Michitson, prin. Fax 374-3454
Moody Preschool 200/PK-PK
59 Margin St 01832 978-374-3459
Maureen Gray, dir. Fax 374-3496
Nettle MS 500/5-8
150 Boardman St 01830 978-374-5792
Tim Corkery, prin. Fax 374-3441
Pentucket Lake ES 500/K-4
252 Concord St 01830 978-374-2421
Dianne Connolly, prin. Fax 374-0392
Tilton ES 400/1-4
70 Grove St 01832 978-374-3475
Bonnie Antkowiak, prin. Fax 374-3440
Walnut Square ES 100/K-2
645 Main St 01830 978-374-3471
Maureen Gray, prin. Fax 374-3486
Whittier MS 500/5-8
256 Concord St 01830 978-374-5782
Brian Gill, prin. Fax 372-5999
Other Schools – See Bradford

Sacred Hearts S 500/PK-8
31 S Chestnut St 01835 978-372-5451
Kathleen Blain, prin. Fax 372-1110
St. Joseph S 300/PK-8
56 Oak Ter 01832 978-521-4256
Carol Simone, prin. Fax 521-2613

Hingham, Plymouth, Pop. 5,570
Hingham SD 4,200/PK-12
220 Central St 02043 781-741-1500
Dorothy Galo, supt. Fax 749-7457
hinghamschools.com
East ES 600/PK-5
2 Collins Rd 02043 781-741-1570
Anthony Keady, prin. Fax 740-1063
Foster ES 500/K-5
55 Downer Ave 02043 781-741-1520
Deborah Stellar, prin. Fax 741-1522
Hingham MS 1,000/6-8
1103 Main St 02043 781-741-1550
Derek Smith, prin. Fax 749-6297
Plymouth River ES 500/K-5
200 High St 02043 781-741-1530
Melissa Smith, prin. Fax 741-1533
South ES 500/K-5
831 Main St 02043 781-741-1540
Mary Eastwood, prin. Fax 749-5673

Derby Academy, 56 Burditt Ave 02043 300/PK-8
Joseph Perry, head sch 781-749-0746
Old Colony Montessori S 100/PK-6
247 Gardner St 02043 781-749-3698
Mikey Walker, admin. Fax 741-8859
St. Paul S 200/PK-8
18 Fearing Rd 02043 781-749-2407
Lisa Fasano, prin. Fax 749-8053

Hinsdale, Berkshire
Central Berkshire Regional SD
Supt. — See Dalton
Kittredge ES 200/PK-5
80 Maple St 01235 413-655-2525
Kathy Buckley, prin. Fax 655-0184

Holbrook, Norfolk, Pop. 10,445
Holbrook SD, 245 S Franklin St 02343 1,200/PK-12
Julie Hamilton, supt. 781-767-1226
www.holbrook.k12.ma.us
Kennedy ES, 245 S Franklin St 02343 400/PK-5
Mallory Stevens, prin. 781-767-4600

St. Joseph S 300/PK-8
143 S Franklin St 02343 781-767-1544
Gretchen Hawley, prin. Fax 767-3975

Holden, Worcester, Pop. 14,628
Wachusett Regional SD
Supt. — See Jefferson
Davis Hill ES 500/K-5
80 Jamieson Rd 01520 508-829-1754
Jay Norton, prin. Fax 829-2057
Dawson ES 500/PK-5
155 Salisbury St 01520 508-829-6828
Shannon Bischoff, prin. Fax 829-6801
Mayo ES 500/K-5
351 Bullard St 01520 508-829-3203
Julie Carter, prin. Fax 829-5216
Mountview MS 700/6-8
270 Shrewsbury St 01520 508-829-5577
Erik Githmark, prin. Fax 829-3711

Holden Christian Academy 100/PK-8
279 Reservoir St 01520 508-829-4418
Susan Hayward, prin. Fax 829-4665

Holland, Hampden, Pop. 1,439
Holland SD
Supt. — See Fiskdale
Holland ES 200/PK-6
28 Sturbridge Rd 01521 413-245-9644
Jennifer Dold Ph.D., prin. Fax 245-4417

Holliston, Middlesex, Pop. 12,926
Holliston SD 2,800/PK-12
370 Hollis St 01746 508-429-0654
Bradford Jackson, supt. Fax 429-0653
www.holliston.k12.ma.us
Adams MS 700/6-8
323 Woodland St 01746 508-429-0657
David Jordan, prin. Fax 429-0690
Miller ES 600/3-5
235 Woodland St 01746 508-429-0667
David Keim, prin. Fax 429-0699
Placentino ES 700/PK-2
235 Woodland St 01746 508-429-0647
Jaime Slaney, prin. Fax 429-0691

Holyoke, Hampden, Pop. 39,370
Holyoke SD 5,600/PK-12
57 Suffolk St 01040 413-534-2000
Dr. Stephen Zrike, supt. Fax 534-3730
www.hps.holyoke.ma.us
Donahue ES 600/PK-8
210 Whiting Farms Rd 01040 413-534-2069
Marc Swygert, prin. Fax 534-2309
Kelly ES 600/PK-8
216 West St 01040 413-534-2078
Isamar Vargas, prin. Fax 534-2303
Lawrence ES 300/PK-3
156 Cabot St 01040 413-534-2075
Catherine Hourihan, prin. Fax 493-1679
McMahon ES 400/PK-8
75 Kane Rd 01040 413-534-2062
Noreen Ewick, prin. Fax 534-2290
Metcalf S 200/PK-3
2019 Northampton St 01040 413-534-2104
Amy Burke, prin. Fax 493-1639
Morgan S 400/PK-8
596 S Bridge St 01040 413-534-2083
Alyson Lingsch, prin. Fax 534-2148
Peck ES 400/4-8
1916 Northampton St 01040 413-534-2040
Kendra Salvador, prin. Fax 532-8563
Sullivan ES 600/PK-8
400 Jarvis Ave 01040 413-534-2060
John Breish, prin. Fax 534-2304
White ES 400/PK-8
1 Jefferson St 01040 413-534-2058
Jacqueline Glasheen, prin. Fax 534-2293

Blessed Sacrament S 300/PK-8
21 Westfield Rd 01040 413-536-2236
Anne O'Connor, prin. Fax 534-0795
First Lutheran S 100/PK-8
1810 Northampton St 01040 413-532-4272
Marianne Bischoff, prin. Fax 534-4239
Mater Dolorosa S 300/PK-8
25 Maple St 01040 413-532-2831
Linda Rex, prin. Fax 532-8588

Hopedale, Worcester, Pop. 3,687
Hopedale SD 1,300/PK-12
25 Adin St 01747 508-634-2220
Karen Crebase, supt. Fax 478-1471
www.hopedaleschools.org
Bright Beginnings Center 100/PK-PK
6 Park St 01747 508-634-2213
Susan Mulready, dir. Fax 634-2232
Memorial ES 600/K-6
6 Prospect St 01747 508-634-2214
Brian Miller, prin. Fax 634-0695

Hopkinton, Middlesex, Pop. 2,531
Hopkinton SD 3,500/PK-12
89 Hayden Rowe St 01748 508-417-9360
Cathy Macleod, supt. Fax 497-9833
www.hopkinton.k12.ma.us
Center ES 400/K-1
11 Ash St 01748 508-497-9875
Lauren DuBeau, prin. Fax 497-9878
Elmwood ES 500/PK-PK, 2-
14 Elm St 01748 508-497-9860
Anne Carver, prin. Fax 497-9862
Hopkins ES 600/4-5
104 Hayden Rowe St 01748 508-497-9824
Vanessa Bilello, prin. Fax 435-0314
Hopkinton MS 800/6-8
88 Hayden Rowe St 01748 508-497-9830
Alan Keller Ed.D., prin. Fax 497-9803
Hopkinton Preschool 100/PK-PK
88 Hayden Rowe St Ste B 01748 508-497-9806
Lauren DuBeau, prin.

Hubbardston, Worcester
Quabbin SD
Supt. — See Barre
Hubbardston Center ES 300/K-6
8 Elm St 01452 978-928-4487
Jill Peterson, prin. Fax 928-3753

Hudson, Middlesex, Pop. 14,374
Hudson SD 2,900/PK-12
155 Apsley St 01749 978-567-6100
Marco Rodrigues, supt. Fax 567-6123
www.hudson.k12.ma.us
Farley ES 500/PK-4
119 Cottage St 01749 978-567-6153
Melissa Provost, prin. Fax 567-6162
Forest Avenue ES 300/K-4
138 Forest Ave 01749 978-567-6190
David Champigny, prin. Fax 567-6202
Mulready ES 300/PK-4
306 Cox St 01749 978-567-6170
Kelly Sardella, prin. Fax 567-6182
Quinn MS 700/5-7
201 Manning St 01749 978-567-6210
Jason Webster, prin. Fax 567-6232

Hull, Plymouth, Pop. 10,097
Hull SD 1,100/PK-12
180 Harborview Rd 02045 781-925-4400
Michael Devine, supt. Fax 925-8042
www.town.hull.ma.us/public_documents/hullma_schools/index

Jacobs ES — 500/PK-5
180 Harborview Rd 02045 — 781-925-4400
Christine Cappadona, prin. — Fax 925-2938
Memorial MS — 200/6-8
81 Central Ave 02045 — 781-925-2040
Anthony Hrivnak, prin. — Fax 925-8002

Huntington, Hampshire, Pop. 920
Gateway SD — 800/PK-12
12 Littleville Rd 01050 — 413-685-1000
Dr. David Hopson, supt. — Fax 667-8739
www.grsd.org
Gateway Regional MS — 100/6-8
12 Littleville Rd 01050 — 413-685-1200
Jason Finnie, prin. — Fax 667-5669
Littleville ES — 300/PK-5
4 Littleville Rd 01050 — 413-685-1300
Megan Coburn, prin. — Fax 667-5734
Other Schools – See Chester

Hyannis, Barnstable, Pop. 14,120
Barnstable SD — 5,100/PK-12
PO Box 955 02601 — 508-862-4953
Meg Mayo-Brown, supt. — Fax 790-6454
www.barnstable.k12.ma.us
Barnstable IS — 800/6-7
895 Falmouth Rd 02601 — 508-790-6460
James Anderson, prin. — Fax 790-6435
Cobb Early Learning Center — PK-PK
549 W Main St 02601 — 508-790-6493
Nicole Caucci M.Ed., prin. — Fax 790-9833
Hyannis West ES — 300/K-3
549 W Main St 02601 — 508-790-6480
Eleanor Amato, prin. — Fax 790-9844
Other Schools – See Centerville, Marstons Mills, West Barnstable

---

St. John Paul II HS & St. Francis Xavier — 200/K-12
120 High School Rd 02601 — 508-862-6336
Christopher Keavy, prin. — Fax 862-6339

Hyde Park, See Boston
Boston SD
Supt. — See Boston
Channing ES — 300/K-5
35 Sunnyside St 02136 — 617-635-8722
Carline Pignato, prin. — Fax 635-8564
Grew ES — 300/PK-5
40 Gordon Ave 02136 — 617-635-8715
Christine Connolly, prin. — Fax 635-8718
Roosevelt S — 500/PK-8
95 Needham Rd 02136 — 617-635-8676
Lynda Sheridan, prin. — Fax 635-8679

Indian Orchard, See Springfield
Springfield SD
Supt. — See Springfield
Indian Orchard ES — 700/PK-5
95 Milton St 01151 — 413-787-7255
Deanna Suomala, prin. — Fax 787-7283

Ipswich, Essex, Pop. 4,128
Ipswich SD — 2,000/PK-12
1 Lord Sq 01938 — 978-356-2935
Dr. Brian Blake, supt. — Fax 356-0445
www.ipsk12.net
Doyon Memorial ES — 500/PK-5
216 Linebrook Rd 01938 — 978-356-5506
Sheila Conley, prin. — Fax 356-8574
Ipswich MS — 500/6-8
130 High St 01938 — 978-356-3535
David Fabrizio, prin. — Fax 412-8169
Winthrop ES — 500/PK-5
65 Central St 01938 — 978-356-2976
Sheila McAdams, prin. — Fax 356-8739

Jamaica Plain, See Boston
Boston SD
Supt. — See Boston
Boston Teachers Union S — 300/K-8
25 Walk Hill St 02130 — 617-635-7717
Elizabeth Drinan, prin. — Fax 635-6982
Curley S — 800/K-8
40 Pershing Rd 02130 — 617-635-8239
Katherine Grassa, prin. — Fax 635-8244
Hennigan ES — 600/K-8
200 Heath St 02130 — 617-635-8264
Maria Cordon, prin. — Fax 635-8271
Kennedy ES — 400/K-5
7 Bolster St 02130 — 617-635-8127
Christine Copeland, prin. — Fax 635-8130
Manning ES — 200/PK-5
130 Louders Ln 02130 — 617-635-8102
Ethan Burnes, prin. — Fax 635-9348
Mission Hill S — 200/K-8
20 Child St 02130 — 617-635-6384
Ayla Gavins, prin. — Fax 635-6419
West Zone Early Learning Center — 100/PK-1
200 Heath St 02130 — 617-635-8275
Jean Larrabee, prin. — Fax 635-9370

Cross Factor Academy — 200/PK-10
322 Centre St 02130 — 617-522-1841
Michael Dixon Ph.D., head sch — Fax 524-9583
Nativity Prep S — 4-8
39 Lamartine St 02130 — 617-728-0031

Jefferson, Worcester
Wachusett Regional SD — 7,400/PK-12
1745 Main St 01522 — 508-829-1670
Dr. Darryll McCall Ed.D., supt. — Fax 829-1680
www.wrsd.net
ECC — 100/PK-PK
1745 Main St 01522 — 508-829-4766
Patricia Ottaviano, prin. — Fax 829-7576
Other Schools – See Holden, Paxton, Princeton, Rutland, Sterling

Kingston, Plymouth, Pop. 5,491
Halifax SD — 600/K-6
250 Pembroke St 02364 — 781-585-4313
Joy Blackwood, supt. — Fax 585-2994
www.slrsd.org
Other Schools – See Halifax

Kingston SD — 1,100/K-6
250 Pembroke St 02364 — 781-585-4313
Joy Blackwood, supt. — Fax 585-2994
www.slrsd.org
Kingston ES — 400/K-2
150 Main St 02364 — 781-585-3821
Paula Bartosiak, prin. — Fax 582-3858
Kingston IS — 700/3-6
65 Second Brook St 02364 — 781-585-0472
Dr. Lisa McMahon, prin. — Fax 585-0053

Plympton SD — 200/K-6
250 Pembroke St 02364 — 781-585-4313
Joy Blackwood, supt. — Fax 585-2994
www.slrsd.org
Other Schools – See Plympton

Silver Lake Regional SD — 1,800/7-12
250 Pembroke St 02364 — 781-585-4313
Joy Blackwood, supt. — Fax 585-2994
www.slrsd.org
Silver Lake Regional MS — 600/7-8
256 Pembroke St 02364 — 781-582-3555
James Dupille, prin. — Fax 582-3599

Sacred Heart ES — 500/PK-6
329 Bishops Hwy 02364 — 781-585-2114
Kim Stoloski, prin. — Fax 585-6993

Lakeville, Plymouth
Freetown-Lakeville SD — 3,000/PK-12
98 Howland Rd 02347 — 508-923-2000
Richard Medeiros, supt. — Fax 923-0934
www.freelake.org/
Assawompset ES — 500/PK-3
232 Main St 02347 — 508-947-1403
Bethany Pineault, prin. — Fax 947-7068
Austin IS — 500/4-5
112 Howland Rd 02347 — 508-923-3506
Elizabeth Sullivan, prin. — Fax 947-0266
Freetown-Lakeville MS — 800/6-8
96 Howland Rd 02347 — 508-923-3518
David Patota, prin. — Fax 946-2050
Other Schools – See East Freetown

Lancaster, Worcester
Nashoba Regional SD
Supt. — See Bolton
Burbank MS — 200/6-8
1 Hollywood Dr 01523 — 978-365-4558
Laura Friend, prin. — Fax 365-6882
Rowlandson ES — 500/PK-5
103 Hollywood Dr 01523 — 978-368-8482
Sean O'Shea, prin. — Fax 368-8730

Lanesboro, Berkshire
Mt. Greylock Regional SD / S Union 71
Supt. — See Williamstown
Lanesborough ES — 200/PK-6
188 Summer St 01237 — 413-443-0027
Martin McEvoy, prin. — Fax 447-9958

Berkshire Hills SDA S — 50/1-8
900 Cheshire Rd 01237 — 413-443-7777
Mark Bugbee, prin. — Fax 443-7777

Lawrence, Essex, Pop. 75,608
Lawrence SD — 12,800/PK-12
237 Essex St 01840 — 978-975-5905
Jeffrey Riley, supt. — Fax 722-8550
www.lawrence.k12.ma.us
Arlington MS — 500/5-8
150 Arlington St 01841 — 978-975-5930
Robin Finn, prin. — Fax 722-8519
Breen ECC — 300/PK-K
114 Osgood St 01843 — 978-975-5932
Margarita Amy, prin. — Fax 722-8520
Bruce S — 500/3-8
135 Butler St 01841 — 978-975-5935
Cheryl Merz, prin. — Fax 722-8521
Frost ES — 600/K-4
33 Hamlet St 01843 — 978-975-5941
Sarah McLaughlin, prin. — Fax 722-8522
Frost MS — 500/5-8
33 Hamlet St 01843 — 978-722-8810
Ellen Baranowski, prin. — Fax 722-8513
Guilmette ES — 600/1-4
80 Bodwell St 01841 — 978-686-8150
Cheryl Corrigan, prin. — Fax 722-8523
Guilmette MS — 500/5-8
80 Bodwell St 01841 — 978-722-8270
Melissa Spash, prin. — Fax 722-8524
Hennessey ECC — 400/PK-2
122 Hancock St 01841 — 978-975-5950
Alyce Merlino, prin. — Fax 722-8529
Lawlor ECC — 200/K-K
41 Lexington St 01841 — 978-975-5956
Christopher Cody, prin. — Fax 722-8530
Leahy ES — 500/K-5
100 Erving Ave 01841 — 978-975-5959
Ethel Cruz, prin. — Fax 722-8532
Oliver Partnership S — 500/1-5
183 E Haverhill St 01841 — 978-722-8170
Nancy Parchuke, admin. — Fax 722-8575
Parthum ES — 600/K-4
255 E Haverhill St 01841 — 978-691-7200
Maria Calobrisi, prin. — Fax 722-8535
Parthum MS — 500/5-8
255 E Haverhill St 01841 — 978-691-7224
Peter Lefebre, prin. — Fax 722-8536
Rollins ECC — 200/PK-K
451 Howard St 01841 — 978-722-8190
James O'Keefe, prin. — Fax 722-8512

South Lawrence East ES — 600/1-5
165 Crawford St 01843 — 978-975-5970
Lori Butterfield, prin. — Fax 722-8537
Tarbox ES — 300/1-5
59 Alder St 01841 — 978-975-5983
Dr. Ada Ramos, prin. — Fax 722-8539
Wetherbee S — 700/K-8
75 Newton St 01843 — 978-557-2900
Colleen Lennon, prin. — Fax 722-8540

Bellesini Academy — 100/5-8
94 Bradford St 01840 — 978-989-0004
Julie DeFillippo, dir. — Fax 989-9404
Esperanza Academy — 100/5-8
198 Garden St 01840 — 978-686-4673
Annmarie Quezada, head sch — Fax 681-1591
Lawrence Catholic Academy — 500/PK-8
101 Parker St 01843 — 978-683-5822
Sr. Lucy Veilleux, prin. — Fax 683-1165

Lee, Berkshire, Pop. 2,028
Lee SD — 700/PK-12
300A Greylock St 01238 — 413-243-0276
Alfred Skrocki, supt. — Fax 243-4995
www.leepublicschools.net
Lee ES — 300/PK-6
310 Greylock St 01238 — 413-243-0336
Kate Retzel, prin. — Fax 243-8216

St. Mary's S — 100/PK-8
115 Orchard St 01238 — 413-243-1079
Jennifer Masten, prin. — Fax 243-1022

Leeds, See Northampton
Northampton SD
Supt. — See Northampton
Leeds ES — 400/PK-5
20 Florence St 01053 — 413-587-1531
Sal Canata, prin. — Fax 587-1539

Leicester, Worcester, Pop. 10,191
Leicester SD — 1,600/PK-12
1078 Main St 01524 — 508-892-7040
Marilyn Tencza, supt. — Fax 892-7043
www.leicester.k12.ma.us/
Leicester Memorial ES — 400/3-5
11 Memorial Dr 01524 — 508-892-7048
Tina Boss, prin. — Fax 892-7052
Leicester MS — 400/6-8
70 Winslow Ave 01524 — 508-892-7055
Joyce Nelson, prin. — Fax 892-7047
Leicester PS — 400/PK-2
170 Paxton St 01524 — 508-892-7050
Emily Soltysik, prin. — Fax 892-7053

Lenox, Berkshire, Pop. 1,652
Lenox SD — 800/PK-12
6 Walker St Ste 3 01240 — 413-637-5550
Timothy Lee, supt. — Fax 637-5559
www.lenoxps.org
Morris ES — 300/PK-5
129 West St 01240 — 413-637-5570
Peter Bachli, prin. — Fax 637-5511

Berkshire County Christian S — 100/PK-12
PO Box 1980 01240 — 413-637-2474
Heidi Dickerson, prin.
Montessori S of the Berkshires — 100/PK-8
PO Box 422 01240 — 413-637-3662
Todd Covert, head sch

Leominster, Worcester, Pop. 39,624
Leominster SD — 6,200/PK-12
24 Church St 01453 — 978-534-7700
Jim Jolicoeur, supt. — Fax 534-7775
www.leominster.mec.edu/
Appleseed ES — 700/K-5
845 Main St 01453 — 978-534-7765
Margaret O'Hearn-Curran, prin. — Fax 534-7776
Bennett K — 100/PK-PK
145 Pleasant St 01453 — 978-534-7704
James Reilly, prin. — Fax 534-7769
Drake ES — 600/K-5
95 Viscoloid Ave 01453 — 978-534-7751
Andres Vera, prin. — Fax 466-8603
Fall Brook ES — 600/K-5
25 DeCicco Dr 01453 — 978-534-7745
Paula Leger, prin. — Fax 466-9825
Lincoln Preschool — 50/PK-PK
100 DeCicco Dr 01453 — 978-534-7761
James Reilly, prin. — Fax 534-7770
Northwest ES — 700/K-5
45 Stearns Ave 01453 — 978-534-7756
Steven Mammone, prin. — Fax 534-7779
Priest Street K — 100/K-K
115 Priest St 01453 — 978-534-7761
James Reilly, prin. — Fax 534-7770
Samoset MS — 600/6-8
100 DeCicco Dr 01453 — 978-534-7725
Colleen LeClair, prin. — Fax 466-7421
Sky View MS — 900/6-8
500 Kennedy Way 01453 — 978-534-7780
Timothy Blake, prin. — Fax 840-8600

St. Anna S — 200/PK-8
213 Lancaster St 01453 — 978-534-4770
Bobbie French, prin. — Fax 466-1167
St. Leo S — 300/PK-8
120 Main St 01453 — 978-537-1007
Nancy Pierce, prin. — Fax 537-7420

Leverett, Franklin
Leverett SD
Supt. — See Erving
Leverett ES — 100/PK-6
85 Montague Rd 01054 — 413-548-9144
Margot Lacey, prin. — Fax 548-8148

Lexington, Middlesex, Pop. 30,568
Lexington SD 6,600/PK-12
146 Maple St 02420 781-861-2580
Dr. Mary Czajkowski, supt. Fax 863-5829
lps.lexingtonma.org
Bowman ES 500/K-5
9 Philip Rd 02421 781-861-2500
Mary Anton-Oldenburg, prin. Fax 861-2315
Bridge ES 500/K-5
55 Middleby Rd 02421 781-861-2510
Margaret Colella, prin. Fax 861-9257
Clarke MS 900/6-8
17 Stedman Rd 02421 781-861-2450
Anna Monaco, prin. Fax 674-2043
Diamond MS 800/6-8
99 Hancock St 02420 781-861-2460
Jennifer Turner, prin. Fax 274-0174
Estabrook ES 500/K-5
117 Grove St 02420 781-861-2520
Jeffrey LaBroad, prin. Fax 862-5610
Fiske ES 500/K-5
55 Adams St 02420 781-541-5001
Thomas Martellone, prin. Fax 541-5008
Harrington ES 400/PK-5
328 Lowell St 02420 781-860-0012
Donna Bonarrigo, prin. Fax 860-5818
Hastings ES 400/K-5
7 Crosby Rd 02421 781-860-5800
Louise Lipsitz, prin. Fax 860-5242
Lexington Children's Place PK-PK
328 Lowell St 02420 781-860-5823
Elizabeth Billings-Fouhy, dir. Fax 860-5827

Armenian Sisters Academy 100/PK-8
20 Pelham Rd 02421 781-861-8303
Sr. Cecile Keghiayan, prin. Fax 862-8479
Lexington Montessori S 200/PK-8
130 Pleasant St 02421 781-862-8571
Aline Gery, head sch Fax 674-0079
Waldorf S of Lexington 200/PK-8
739 Massachusetts Ave 02420 781-863-1062
Robert Schiappacasse, dir. Fax 863-7221

Leyden, Franklin, Pop. 662
Pioneer Valley SD
Supt. — See Northfield
Rhodes ES 50/PK-6
7 Brattleboro Rd 01301 413-772-6245
Bob Clancy, prin. Fax 772-1030

Lincoln, Middlesex, Pop. 2,850
Lincoln SD 1,300/PK-8
6 Ballfield Rd 01773 781-259-9400
Rebecca McFall, supt. Fax 259-9246
www.lincnet.org/
Lincoln S 700/PK-8
6 Ballfield Rd 01773 781-259-9404
Sharon Hobbs, prin. Fax 259-2637
Other Schools – See Hanscom AFB

Birches S, PO Box 237 01773 50/K-4
Elizabeth Grotenhuis Ph.D., head sch 781-728-5438

Littleton, Middlesex, Pop. 2,867
Littleton SD 1,600/PK-12
PO Box 1486 01460 978-540-2500
Kelly Clenchy, supt. Fax 486-9581
www.littletonps.org/
Littleton MS 400/6-8
55 Russell St 01460 978-486-8938
Cheryl Temple, prin. Fax 952-4547
Russell Street ES 400/3-5
57 Russell St 01460 978-540-2520
Dr. Scott Bazydlo, prin. Fax 952-4539
Shaker Lane ES 400/PK-2
35 Shaker Ln 01460 978-486-3959
Michelle Kane, prin. Fax 952-4550

Oak Meadow S 300/PK-8
2 Old Pickard Ln 01460 978-486-9874
William Perrine L.H.D., head sch Fax 486-3269

Longmeadow, Hampden, Pop. 15,594
Longmeadow SD 2,800/PK-12
535 Bliss Rd 01106 413-565-4200
Dr. M. Martin O'Shea, supt. Fax 565-4215
sites.longmeadow.k12.ma.us/www/
Blueberry Hill ES 500/K-5
275 Blueberry Hill Rd 01106 413-565-4280
Amy Bostian, prin. Fax 565-4283
Center ES 300/K-5
837 Longmeadow St 01106 413-565-4290
Donna Hutton, prin. Fax 565-4292
Glenbrook MS 300/6-8
110 Cambridge Cir 01106 413-565-4250
Nikcole Allen, prin. Fax 565-4277
Williams MS 400/6-8
410 Williams St 01106 413-565-4260
Taylor Wrye, prin. Fax 565-4254
Wolf Swamp Road ES 400/PK-5
62 Wolf Swamp Rd 01106 413-565-4270
Dr. Elizabeth Nelson, prin. Fax 565-4273

Lubavitcher Yeshiva Academy 100/PK-8
1148 Converse St 01106 413-567-8665
Rabbi Noach Kosofsky, prin. Fax 567-2233
St. Mary's Academy 300/PK-8
56 Hopkins Pl 01106 413-567-0907
Joan MacDonald, prin. Fax 567-7695

Lowell, Middlesex, Pop. 102,517
Lowell SD 14,000/PK-12
155 Merrimack St 01852 978-674-4320
Salah Khelfaoui Ph.D., supt. Fax 937-7609
www.lowell.k12.ma.us
Bailey International ES 500/PK-4
175 Campbell Dr 01851 978-937-7644
Kimberly Clements, prin. Fax 459-5314
Bartlett Community Partnership S 500/PK-8
79 Wannalancit St 01854 978-937-8968
Peter Holtz, prin. Fax 441-3745
Butler MS 600/5-8
1140 Gorham St 01852 978-937-8973
Teresa Soares-Pena, prin. Fax 937-2819
Daley MS 700/5-8
150 Fleming St 01851 978-937-8981
Liam Skinner, prin. Fax 937-7610
Greenhalge ES 500/PK-4
149 Ennell St 01850 978-937-7670
James Neary, prin. Fax 441-3724
Lincoln ES 500/PK-4
300 Chelmsford St 01851 978-937-2846
Ruben Carmona, prin. Fax 937-2855
MacAuliffe ES 500/PK-4
570 Beacon St 01850 978-937-2838
David Anderson, prin. Fax 937-2845
McAvinnue ES 500/PK-4
131 Mammoth Rd 01854 978-937-2871
Michael Ducharme, prin. Fax 937-2880
Moody ES 300/K-4
158 Rogers St 01852 978-937-7673
Roberta Keefe, prin. Fax 937-7606
Morey ES 500/PK-4
114 Pine St 01851 978-937-7662
Fred McOsker, prin. Fax 937-7663
Murkland ES 500/PK-4
350 Adams St 01854 978-937-2826
Kevin Andriolo, prin. Fax 937-2835
Pawtucketville Memorial ES 500/PK-4
425 W Meadow Rd 01854 978-937-7667
Mathew McLean, prin. Fax 441-3732
Pyne Arts S 500/PK-8
145 Boylston St 01852 978-937-7639
Wendy Crocker-Roberge, prin. Fax 446-0942
Reilly ES 600/K-4
115 Douglas Rd 01852 978-937-7652
Sean Carabatsos, prin. Fax 446-7423
Robinson MS 700/5-8
110 June St 01850 978-937-8971
Kevin McLaughlin, prin. Fax 937-8988
Rogers STEM Academy 100/PK-5
43 Highland St 01852 978-674-2300
Jason McCrevan, prin. Fax 937-7609
Shaughnessy ES 500/PK-4
1158 Gorham St 01852 978-937-7657
Susan Mulligan, prin. Fax 446-7074
Stoklosa MS 700/5-8
560 Broadway St 01854 978-275-6330
James Cardaci, prin. Fax 275-6343
Sullivan MS 700/5-8
150 Draper St 01852 978-937-8993
Edward Foster, prin. Fax 937-3278
Wang MS 700/5-8
365 W Meadow Rd 01854 978-937-7683
Matthew Stahl, prin. Fax 937-7680
Washington ES 300/PK-4
795 Wilder St 01851 978-937-7635
Cheryl Cunningham, prin. Fax 937-7636

Community Christian Academy 200/PK-12
105 Princeton Blvd 01851 978-453-4738
Jennifer Najem, prin. Fax 453-1506
Hellenic American Academy 100/PK-8
41 Broadway St 01854 978-453-5422
David Conway, dir. Fax 970-3554
Immaculate Conception S 300/PK-8
218 E Merrimack St 01852 978-454-5339
Catherine Fiorino, prin. Fax 454-6593
Lowell Catholic ES PK-8
486 Stevens St 01851 978-452-1794
Maryellen DeMarco, head sch Fax 452-5646
St. Louis de France S 200/K-8
77 Boisvert St 01850 978-458-7594
Vina Troianello M.Ed., prin. Fax 454-9289
St. Michael S 400/K-8
21 6th St 01850 978-453-9511
Scott Bolton, prin. Fax 454-4104
St. Patrick S 100/K-8
311 Adams St 01854 978-458-4232
Sr. Joanne Sullivan, prin. Fax 458-4233
Ste. Jeanne d'Arc S 400/K-8
68 Dracut St 01854 978-453-4114
Sr. Prescille Malo, prin. Fax 454-8304

Ludlow, Hampden, Pop. 18,820
Ludlow SD 2,800/PK-12
63 Chestnut St 01056 413-583-8372
Todd Gazda, supt. Fax 583-5666
www.ludlowps.org
Baird MS 600/6-8
1 Rooney Rd 01056 413-583-5685
Stacy Monette, prin. Fax 583-5636
Chapin Street Campus 400/2-3
766 Chapin St 01056 413-583-5031
Nikki Reed, prin. Fax 583-5627
East Street Campus 400/PK-1
508 East St 01056 413-589-9121
Thomas Welch, prin. Fax 593-5629
Veterans Park Campus 400/4-5
486 Chapin St 01056 413-583-5695
Melissa Knowles, prin. Fax 583-5630

St. John the Baptist S 300/PK-8
217 Hubbard St 01056 413-583-8550
Shelly Rose, prin. Fax 589-0544

Lunenburg, Worcester, Pop. 1,728
Lunenburg SD 1,100/PK-12
1025 Massachusetts Ave 01462 978-582-4100
Loxi Jo Calmes, supt. Fax 582-4103
www.lunenburgschools.net/
Lunenburg MS 6-8
1079 Massachusetts Ave 01462 978-582-4710
Tim Santry, prin. Fax 582-4153
Lunenburg PS 400/PK-2
1401 Massachusetts Ave 01462 978-582-4122
Elaine Blaisdell, prin. Fax 582-4173
Turkey Hill ES 200/3-5
129 Northfield Rd 01462 978-582-4110
Heidi Champagne, prin. Fax 582-4109

Lynn, Essex, Pop. 87,864
Lynn SD 14,300/PK-12
100 Bennett St 01905 781-593-1680
Catherine Latham, supt. Fax 477-7487
www.lynnschools.org/
Aborn ES 200/K-5
409 Eastern Ave 01902 781-477-7320
Patricia Muxie, prin. Fax 581-1058
Breed MS 1,200/6-8
90 OCallaghan Way 01905 781-477-7330
Julie Louf, prin. Fax 581-6985
Brickett ES 300/1-5
123 Lewis St 01902 781-477-7333
Eileen Cole, prin. Fax 596-2665
Callahan ES 500/PK-5
200 OCallaghan Way 01905 781-477-7340
Brian Fay, prin. Fax 581-9248
Cobbet ES, 40 Franklin St 01902 600/K-5
Susanne Garrity, prin. 781-477-7341
Connery ES 600/PK-5
50 Elm St 01905 781-477-7344
Mary Dill, prin. Fax 477-7451
Drewicz ES 500/K-5
34 Hood St 01905 781-477-7350
Patricia Hebert, prin. Fax 477-7353
ECC 300/PK-K, 3-5
90 Commercial St 01905 781-477-7190
Lissa Bloom, prin. Fax 477-7221
Ford S 500/1-5
49 Hollingsworth St 01902 781-477-7375
Joanne Larivee, prin. Fax 477-7378
Harrington ES 600/PK-5
21 Dexter St 01902 781-477-7380
Debra Ruggiero, prin. Fax 477-7383
Hood ES 400/K-5
24 Oakwood Ave 01902 781-477-7390
Gayle Dufour, prin. Fax 593-9746
Ingalls ES 700/K-5
1 Collins Street Ter 01902 781-477-7400
Irene Cowdell, prin. Fax 477-7398
Lincoln-Thomson ES 300/K-5
115 Gardiner St 01905 781-477-7460
Mary Foster, prin. Fax 477-7459
Lynn Woods ES 200/K-5
31 Trevett Ave 01904 781-477-7433
Ellen Fritz, prin. Fax 477-7435
Marshall MS 1,000/6-8
100 Brookline St 01902 781-477-7360
Molly Cohen, prin. Fax 477-7355
Pickering MS 600/6-8
70 Conomo Ave 01904 781-477-7440
Kevin Rittershaus, prin. Fax 477-7202
Sewell-Anderson ES 300/K-5
25 Ontario St 01905 781-477-7444
Mary Panagopoulos, prin. Fax 477-7446
Shoemaker ES 300/PK-5
26 Regina Rd 01904 781-477-7450
Christina Colella, prin. Fax 477-7454
Sisson ES 500/K-5
58 Conomo Ave 01904 781-477-7455
Jane Franklin, prin. Fax 268-0550
Tracy ES 400/1-5
35 Walnut St 01905 781-477-7466
Pattye Griffin, prin. Fax 477-7465
Washington STEM ES 400/K-5
58 Blossom St 01902 339-883-1414
Anthony Frye, prin. Fax 883-1415

North Shore Christian S 200/PK-8
26 Urban St 01904 781-599-2040
Robin Lowe, prin. Fax 595-7444
Sacred Heart S 200/K-8
581 Boston St 01905 781-592-7581
Joanne Eagan, prin. Fax 595-9948
St. Pius V S 500/PK-8
28 Bowler St 01904 781-593-8292
Paul Maestranzi, prin. Fax 593-6973

Lynnfield, Essex, Pop. 11,472
Lynnfield SD 2,200/PK-12
525 Salem St 01940 781-334-9200
Jane Tremblay, supt. Fax 334-9209
www.lynnfield.k12.ma.us
Huckleberry Hill ES 400/PK-4
5 Knoll Rd 01940 781-334-5835
Brian Bemiss, prin. Fax 334-7205
Lynnfield MS 800/5-8
505 Main St 01940 781-334-5810
Stephen Ralston, prin. Fax 334-7203
Lynnfield Preschool 100/PK-K
262 Summer St 01940 781-581-5140
Kara Mauro, prin. Fax 581-5231
Summer Street ES 400/PK-4
262 Summer St 01940 781-334-5830
Gregory Hurray, prin. Fax 334-5817

Our Lady of the Assumption S 400/PK-8
40 Grove St 01940 781-599-4422
James Grocki, prin. Fax 599-9280

Malden, Middlesex, Pop. 56,660
Malden SD 6,500/PK-12
77 Salem St 02148 781-397-6100
John Oteri M.Ed., supt. Fax 397-7276
www.maldenps.org
Beebe S 900/K-8
401 Pleasant St 02148 781-388-0621
Dr. Susan Vatalaro, prin. Fax 388-0623
Ferryway S 900/K-8
150 Cross St 02148 781-388-0659
Abdel Sepulveda, prin. Fax 388-0657
Forestdale S 600/K-8
74 Sylvan St 02148 781-397-7326
Donald Concannon, prin. Fax 397-1509
Linden S 900/K-8
29 Wescott St 02148 781-397-7218
Richard Bransfield, prin. Fax 397-1562

Malden ECC 300/PK-PK
257 Mountain Ave 02148 781-397-7025
Peter Dolan, prin. Fax 321-3495
Salemwood S 1,100/K-8
529 Salem St 02148 781-388-0647
Rebecca Gordon, prin. Fax 397-7319

Cheverus S 300/PK-8
30 Irving St 02148 781-324-6584
Thomas Arria, prin. Fax 324-3322

Manchester, Essex, Pop. 5,286
Manchester Essex Regional SD 1,500/PK-12
PO Box 1407 01944 978-526-4919
Pamela Beaudoin, supt. Fax 526-7585
www.mersd.org
Manchester Essex Regional MS 400/6-8
36 Lincoln St 01944 978-526-2022
Joanne Maino, prin. Fax 526-2046
Memorial ES 400/PK-5
43 Lincoln St 01944 978-526-1908
John Willis, prin. Fax 526-2060
Other Schools – See Essex

Brookwood S 400/PK-8
1 Brookwood Rd 01944 978-526-4500
Laura Caron, head sch Fax 526-9303

Mansfield, Bristol, Pop. 7,170
Mansfield SD 4,300/K-12
2 Park Row 02048 508-261-7500
Teresa Murphy, supt. Fax 261-7509
www.mansfieldschools.com
Jordan/Jackson ES 1,000/3-5
255 East St 02048 508-261-7520
John Nieratko, prin. Fax 261-7528
Qualters MS 1,100/6-8
240 East St 02048 508-261-7530
Suzanne Ryan, prin. Fax 261-7535
Robinson ES 800/K-2
245 East St 02048 508-261-7513
Kerri Sankey, prin. Fax 261-7418

Hands-On Montessori S 100/PK-3
12 Creeden St 02048 508-339-4667
St. Mary's Catholic S 200/K-8
330 Pratt St 02048 508-339-4800
Matthew Bourque, prin. Fax 337-2603

Marblehead, Essex, Pop. 19,576
Marblehead SD 3,100/PK-12
9 Widger Rd 01945 781-639-3140
Maryann Perry, supt. Fax 639-3149
www.marbleheadschools.org
Bell ES 300/1-3
40 Baldwin Rd 01945 781-639-3170
Donna Zaeske, prin. Fax 639-3173
Coffin ES 200/2-3
1 Turner Rd 01945 781-639-3180
Sean Satterfield, prin. Fax 639-3182
Gerry ES 200/K-1
50 Elm St 01945 781-639-3185
Sean Satterfield, prin. Fax 639-3182
Glover ES 300/PK-3
9 Maple St 01945 781-639-3190
Brian Ota, prin. Fax 639-3192
Marblehead Veterans MS 500/7-8
217 Pleasant St 01945 781-639-3120
Matthew Fox, prin. Fax 639-3130
Village S 700/4-6
93 Village St 01945 781-639-3159
Amanda Murphy, prin. Fax 639-9423

Epstein Hillel S 100/K-8
6 Community Rd 01945 781-639-2880
Amy Gold, head sch Fax 631-2832
Tower S 300/PK-8
75 W Shore Dr 01945 781-631-5800
Dr. Andrew Taylor, head sch Fax 631-2292

Marion, Plymouth, Pop. 1,426
Marion SD
Supt. — See Mattapoisett
Sippican ES 500/PK-6
16 Spring St 02738 508-748-0100
Evelyn Rivet, prin. Fax 748-1953

Marlborough, Middlesex, Pop. 36,087
Marlborough SD 4,600/PK-12
17 Washington St 01752 508-460-3509
Maureen Greulich, supt. Fax 485-1142
www.mps-edu.org
ECC 200/PK-PK
17 Washington St 01752 508-460-3503
Andrew Bernabei, prin. Fax 460-3561
Jaworek ES 700/K-4
444 Hosmer St 01752 508-460-3506
Ron Sanborn, prin. Fax 460-3709
Kane ES 700/K-4
520 Farm Rd 01752 508-460-3507
Kalliope Pantazopoulos, prin. Fax 460-3588
Richer ES 600/K-4
80 Foley Rd 01752 508-460-3504
Dr. Robert Skaza, prin. Fax 460-3586
Whitcomb MS 1,400/5-8
25 Union St 01752 508-460-3502
Brian Daniels, prin. Fax 460-3597

Immaculate Conception S 200/PK-8
25 Washington Ct 01752 508-460-3401
Martha McCook, prin. Fax 460-6003

Marshfield, Plymouth, Pop. 4,261
Marshfield SD 4,300/PK-12
76 S River St 02050 781-834-5000
Jeffrey Granatino, supt. Fax 834-5070
www.mpsd.org
Eames Way ES 300/K-5
165 Eames Way 02050 781-834-5090
William Campia, prin. Fax 834-5094
Furnace Brook MS 1,100/6-8
500 Furnace St 02050 781-834-5020
Patrick Sullivan, prin. Fax 834-5899
Martinson ES 400/K-5
275 Forest St 02050 781-834-5025
Leslie Scollins, prin. Fax 834-5003
South River ES 500/K-5
59 Hatch St 02050 781-834-5030
Amy Scolaro, prin. Fax 834-5071
Webster ES 400/PK-5
1456 Ocean St 02050 781-834-5045
Sara Prouty, prin. Fax 834-5072
Winslow ES 400/K-5
60 Regis Rd 02050 781-834-5060
Karen Hubbard, prin. Fax 834-5075

Marstons Mills, Barnstable, Pop. 8,017
Barnstable SD
Supt. — See Hyannis
Barnstable United ES 800/4-5
730 W Barnstable Rd 02648 508-420-2272
Mary Sullivan, prin. Fax 420-0185
West Villages ES 500/K-3
760 W Barnstable Rd 02648 508-420-1100
Kirk Gibbons, prin. Fax 420-1486

Mashpee, Barnstable
Mashpee SD 1,700/PK-12
150A Old Barnstable Rd 02649 508-539-1500
Patricia DeBoer, supt. Fax 477-5805
www.mashpee.k12.ma.us
Coombs ES 400/PK-2
152 Old Barnstable Rd 02649 508-539-1520
Paul Labelle, prin. Fax 539-1530
Mashpee MS 300/7-8
500 Old Barnstable Rd 02649 508-539-3601
Mark Balestracci, prin. Fax 539-3603
Quashnet S 600/3-6
150 Old Barnstable Rd 02649 508-539-1550
MaryKate O'Brien, prin. Fax 539-1556

Mattapan, See Boston
Boston SD
Supt. — See Boston
Chittick ES 300/K-5
154 Ruskindale Rd, 617-635-8652
Michelle Burnett-Herndon, prin. Fax 635-6925
Ellison-Parks Early Education S 200/PK-3
108 Babson St 02126 617-635-7680
Benjamin Rockoff, prin. Fax 635-6491
Mattapan ES K-1
100 Hebron St 02126 617-635-8792
Walter Henderson, prin. Fax 635-8799
Mildred Avenue S 400/K-8
5 Mildred Ave 02126 617-635-1642
Andrew Rollins, prin. Fax 635-1641
Taylor ES 500/PK-5
1060 Morton St 02126 617-635-8731
Jennifer Marks, prin. Fax 635-6877
Young Achievers Science and Math S 500/PK-8
20 Outlook Rd 02126 617-635-6804
Sean Guthrie, prin. Fax 635-6811

Berea SDA Academy 100/PK-8
800 Morton St 02126 617-436-8301
Rosalind Aaron Ph.D., prin. Fax 436-8304
Saint John Paul II Academy 200/PK-8
120 Babson St 02126 617-265-0019
Kathleen Aldridge, prin. Fax 296-1659

Mattapoisett, Plymouth, Pop. 2,949
Marion SD 500/PK-6
135 Marion Rd 02739 508-758-2772
Dr. Douglas White, supt. Fax 758-2802
www.oldrochester.org
Other Schools – See Marion

Mattapoisett SD 500/PK-6
135 Marion Rd 02739 508-758-2772
Dr. Douglas White, supt. Fax 758-2802
www.oldrochester.org
Center ES 300/PK-3
17 Barstow St 02739 508-758-2521
Rosemary Bowman, prin. Fax 758-3153
Old Hammondtown ES 200/4-6
20 Shaw St 02739 508-758-6241
Rosemary Bowman, prin. Fax 758-4667

Old Rochester Regional SD 1,200/7-12
135 Marion Rd 02739 508-758-2772
Dr. Douglas White, supt. Fax 758-2802
www.oldrochester.org
Old Rochester Regional JHS 500/7-8
133 Marion Rd 02739 508-758-4928
Kevin Brogioli, prin. Fax 758-6021

Rochester SD 500/PK-6
135 Marion Rd 02739 508-758-2772
Douglas White, supt. Fax 758-2802
www.oldrochester.org
Other Schools – See Rochester

Maynard, Middlesex, Pop. 9,932
Maynard SD 1,400/PK-12
3R Tiger Dr 01754 978-897-2222
Dr. Robert Gerardi Ed.D., supt. Fax 897-4610
www.maynard.k12.ma.us
Fowler S 500/4-8
3 Tiger Dr 01754 978-897-6700
Sharon Seyller, prin. Fax 897-5737
Green Meadow ES 500/PK-3
5 Tiger Dr 01754 978-897-8246
Donna Dankner, prin. Fax 897-8298

Imago S 100/PK-8
1 Percival St 01754 978-897-0549
Daniel Burbeck, prin. Fax 897-3094

Medfield, Norfolk, Pop. 6,407
Medfield SD 2,700/PK-12
459 Main St Fl 3 02052 508-359-2302
Jeffrey Marsden, supt. Fax 359-9829
www.medfield.net
Blake MS 700/6-8
24 Pound St 02052 508-359-2396
Nathaniel Vaughn, prin. Fax 359-0134
Dale Street S 400/4-5
45 Adams St 02052 508-359-5538
Stephen Grenham, prin. Fax 359-1415
Memorial S 400/PK-1
59 Adams St 02052 508-359-5135
Dr. Melissa Bilsborough, prin. Fax 359-1419
Wheelock S 400/2-3
17 Elm St 02052 508-359-6055
Donna Olson, prin. Fax 359-6174

Medford, Middlesex, Pop. 53,960
Medford SD 4,500/PK-12
489 Winthrop St 02155 781-393-2442
Roy Belson, supt. Fax 393-2322
www.medford.k12.ma.us
Andrews MS 500/6-8
3000 Mystic Valley Pkwy 02155 781-393-2228
Paul D'Alleva, prin. Fax 395-8128
Brooks ES 500/K-5
388 High St 02155 781-393-2166
Suzanne Galusi, prin. Fax 393-2174
Columbus ES 500/K-5
37 Hicks Ave 02155 781-393-2177
Katherine Kay, prin. Fax 393-2187
McGlynn ES 500/PK-5
3002 Mystic Valley Pkwy 02155 781-393-2333
Diane Guarino, prin. Fax 393-5462
McGlynn MS 500/6-8
3004 Mystic Valley Pkwy 02155 781-393-2333
Jacob Edwards, prin. Fax 393-5462
Roberts ES 600/PK-5
35 Court St 02155 781-393-2155
Kirk Johnson, prin. Fax 393-2158

St. Joseph S 500/PK-8
132 High St 02155 781-396-3636
Dr. Robert Murphy, prin. Fax 396-5670
St. Raphael S 400/PK-8
516 High St 02155 781-483-3373
Mark Bedrosian M.Ed., prin. Fax 483-3097

Medway, Norfolk, Pop. 9,931
Medway SD 2,100/PK-12
45 Holliston St 02053 508-533-3222
Armand Pires Ph.D., supt. Fax 533-3226
www.medwayschools.org
Burke Memorial ES 200/2-4
16 Cassidy Ln 02053 508-533-3266
Amanda Luizzi, prin. Fax 533-3261
McGovern ES 300/PK-1
9 Lovering St 02053 508-533-3243
Peggy Yanuskiewicz, prin. Fax 533-3263
Medway MS 800/5-8
45 Holliston St 02053 508-533-3230
Cari Lynne Perchase, prin. Fax 533-3257

St. Joseph Academy PK-K
145 Holliston St 02053 508-533-7771
Lynne Sheehan, dir.

Melrose, Middlesex, Pop. 26,480
Melrose SD 3,700/PK-12
360 Lynn Fells Pkwy 02176 781-662-2000
Cyndy Taymore, supt. Fax 979-2149
www.melroseschools.com
ECC 300/PK-PK
16 Franklin St 02176 781-979-2260
Donna Rosso, dir. Fax 979-2261
Hoover ES 300/K-5
37 Glendower Rd 02176 781-979-2180
Carol Weldin, prin. Fax 979-2183
Lincoln ES 300/K-5
80 W Wyoming Ave 02176 781-979-2250
Jenny Corduck, prin. Fax 979-2259
Mann ES 300/K-5
40 Damon Ave 02176 781-979-2190
Dr. Mary Ellen Cobbs, prin. Fax 979-2194
Melrose Veterans Memorial MS 900/6-8
350 Lynn Fells Pkwy 02176 781-979-2100
Brent Conway, prin. Fax 979-2104
Roosevelt ES 400/K-5
253 Vinton St 02176 781-979-2270
Mary Beth Maranto, prin. Fax 979-2275
Winthrop ES 300/K-5
162 1st St 02176 781-979-2280
John Maynard, prin. Fax 979-2281

St. Mary of the Annunciation S 400/PK-8
4 Myrtle St 02176 781-665-5037
Cindy Boyle, prin. Fax 665-7321

Mendon, Worcester
Mendon-Upton Regional SD 2,400/PK-12
150 North Ave 01756 508-634-1585
Joseph Maruszczak M.Ed., supt. Fax 634-1582
www.mursd.org
Clough ES 500/PK-4
10 North Ave 01756 508-634-1580
Janice Gallagher, prin. Fax 478-9111
Miscoe Hill S 800/5-8
148 North Ave 01756 508-634-1590
Jennifer Mannion, prin. Fax 634-1576
Other Schools – See Upton

Bethany Christian Academy 100/PK-12
15 Cape Rd 01756 508-634-8171
Cheri McCutchen, dir. Fax 478-4706

Merrimac, Essex
Pentucket SD
Supt. — See West Newbury

Donaghue ES 300/3-6
24 Union Street Ext 01860 978-346-8921
Robert Harrison, prin. Fax 346-7839
Sweetsir ES 200/PK-2
104 Church St 01860 978-346-8319
Russell Marino, prin. Fax 346-7844

Methuen, Essex, Pop. 46,662
Methuen SD 6,900/PK-12
10 Ditson Pl 01844 978-722-6000
Judith Scannell, supt. Fax 722-6002
www.methuen.k12.ma.us
Comprehensive Grammar S 1,200/PK-8
100 Howe St 01844 978-722-9051
Christopher Reeve, prin. Fax 722-9053
Marsh Grammar S 1,300/PK-8
309 Pelham St 01844 978-722-9076
Mary Jean Fawcett, prin. Fax 722-9078
Tenney Grammar S 1,300/PK-8
75 Pleasant St 01844 978-722-9026
Mary Beth Grassi, prin. Fax 722-9028
Timony Grammar S 1,400/PK-8
45 Pleasant View St 01844 978-722-9001
Timothy Miller, prin. Fax 722-9003

Fellowship Christian Academy 100/PK-12
1 Fellowship Way 01844 978-686-9373
Joann Spain, admin. Fax 685-7466
Islamic Academy 200/PK-8
125 Oakland Ave 01844 978-975-7335
Sr. Jameelah Shareef M.S., prin.
St. Monica S 200/K-8
212 Lawrence St 01844 978-686-1801
Sr. Suzanne Fondini, prin. Fax 686-3582

Middleboro, Plymouth, Pop. 7,135
Middleborough SD 3,200/PK-12
30 Forest St 02346 508-946-2000
Brian Lynch, supt. Fax 946-2004
www.middleboro.k12.ma.us
Burkland ES 700/1-5
41 Mayflower Ave 02346 508-946-2040
Derek Thompson, prin. Fax 946-2029
Goode ES 700/1-5
31 Mayflower Ave 02346 508-946-2045
Lisa Andrade, prin. Fax 946-8851
Memorial ECC 300/PK-K
219 N Main St 02346 508-946-2032
Holly Hargraves, dir. Fax 946 2030
Nichols MS 800/6-8
112 Tiger Dr 02346 508-946-2020
Martin Geoghegan, prin. Fax 946-2019

Fuller S 50/K-9
6 Plympton St 02346 508-947-3217

Middleton, Essex, Pop. 4,921
Middleton SD
Supt. — See Boxford
Fuller Meadow ES 300/K-2
143 S Main St 01949 978-750-4756
Dr. Diane Carreiro, prin. Fax 777-3352
Howe-Manning ES 500/PK-PK, 3-
26 Central St 01949 978-739-2800
James Sforza, prin. Fax 774-1411

Milford, Worcester, Pop. 23,757
Milford SD 3,500/PK-12
31 W Fountain St 01757 508-478-1100
Kevin McIntyre Ed.D., supt. Fax 478-1459
www.milfordpublicschools.com
Brookside ES 600/K-2
110 Congress St 01757 508-478-1177
Lisa Firth, prin. Fax 634-2375
Memorial ES 400/K-2
12 Walnut St 01757 508-478-1689
Lisa Burns, prin. Fax 634-1486
Shining Star ECC 200/PK-PK
31 W Fountain St 01757 508-478-1135
Dr. Corrie Masterson, coord. Fax 473-4195
Stacy MS 600/6-8
66 School St 01757 508-478-1180
Nancy Angelini, prin. Fax 634-2370
Woodland ES 600/3-5
10 N Vine St 01757 508-478-1186
Timothy Kearnan, prin. Fax 473-4280

Millbury, Worcester, Pop. 12,228
Millbury SD 1,800/PK-12
12 Martin St 01527 508-865-9501
Gregory Myers, supt. Fax 865-0888
www.millburyschools.org
Elmwood Street ES 600/PK-3
40 Elmwood St 01527 508-865-5241
Andrew Hall, prin. Fax 865-0888
Shaw S 400/4-6
58 Elmwood St 01527 508-865-3541
Miriam Friedman, prin. Fax 865-3430

Assumption S 200/PK-8
17 Grove St 01527 508-865-5404
Dr. John Hoogasian, prin. Fax 581-8974

Millis, Norfolk, Pop. 4,081
Millis SD 1,400/PK-12
245 Plain St 02054 508-376-7000
Nancy Gustafson, supt. Fax 376-7020
www.millisps.org
Brown ES 600/PK-4
5 Park Rd 02054 508-376-7003
Jason Phelps, prin. Fax 376-7038
Millis MS 500/5-8
245 Plain St 02054 508-376-7014
Maureen Knowlton, prin. Fax 376-7020

Woodside Montessori Academy 100/PK-8
350 Village St 02054 508-376-5320
Kathleen Gasbarro, hdmstr. Fax 590-6644

Mill River, Berkshire
Southern Berkshire Regional SD
Supt. — See Sheffield
New Marlborough Central ES 100/PK-4
PO Box 280 01244 413-229-8867
Mary Turo, prin. Fax 229-7872

Millville, Worcester
Blackstone-Millville Regional SD
Supt. — See Blackstone
Millville ES 300/PK-5
122 Berthelette Way 01529 508-876-0177
Dr. Paul Haughey, prin. Fax 883-0339

Milton, Norfolk, Pop. 26,216
Milton SD 3,900/PK-12
25 Gile Rd 02186 617-696-4808
Mary C. Gormley, supt. Fax 696-5099
www.miltonps.org
Collicot ES 600/PK-5
80 Edge Hill Rd 02186 617-696-4282
Holly Concannon, prin. Fax 698-3577
Cunningham ES 500/K-5
44 Edge Hill Rd 02186 617-696-4285
Jonathan Redden, prin. Fax 698-3473
Glover ES 600/K-5
255 Canton Ave 02186 617-696-4288
Karen McDavitt, prin. Fax 698-2346
Pierce MS 900/6-8
451 Central Ave 02186 617-696-4568
Dr. Karen Spaulding, prin. Fax 698-2238
Tucker ES 400/PK-5
187 Blue Hills Pkwy 02186 617-696-4291
Dr. Elaine McNeil-Girmai, prin. Fax 698-3374

Delphi Academy 100/PK-8
564 Blue Hill Ave 02186 617-333-9610
Corrine Perkins, head sch Fax 333-9613
Milton Academy 1,000/K-12
170 Centre St 02186 617-898-1798
Todd Bland, hdmstr. Fax 898-1700
St. Agatha S 700/PK-8
440 Adams St 02186 617-696-3548
David Marion, prin. Fax 696-6288
St. Mary of the Hills S 400/PK-8
250 Brook Rd 02186 617-698-2464
Julie Marotta, prin. Fax 696-9346
Thacher Montessori S 200/PK-8
1425 Blue Hill Ave 02186 617-361-2522
Don Grace, head sch Fax 364-0911

Monson, Hampden, Pop. 2,101
Monson SD 1,200/PK-12
PO Box 159 01057 413-267-4150
Cheryl Clarke, supt. Fax 267-4163
www.monsonschools.com
Granite Valley MS 400/5-8
21 Thompson St 01057 413-267-4155
Mary Cioplik, prin. Fax 267-4624
Quarry Hill Community S 400/PK-4
43 Margaret St 01057 413-267-4160
Jennifer Beaudry, prin. Fax 267-4154

Montague, Franklin
Gill-Montague SD
Supt. — See Turners Falls
Great Falls MS 200/6-8
224 Turnpike Rd 01351 413-863-7300
Ann Leonard, prin. Fax 863-7354

Nahant, Essex, Pop. 3,385
Nahant SD 200/PK-6
290 Castle Rd 01908 781-581-1600
Anthony Pierantozzi, supt. Fax 581-0440
www.johnsonschool.org
Johnson ES 200/PK-6
290 Castle Rd 01908 781-581-1600
Kevin Andrews, prin. Fax 581-0440

Nantucket, Nantucket, Pop. 7,268
Nantucket SD 1,500/PK-12
10 Surfside Rd 02554 508-228-7285
W. Michael Cozort, supt. Fax 325-5318
www.npsk.org
Nantucket ES 700/PK-2
30 Surfside Rd 02554 508-228-7290
Kimberly Kubisch, prin. Fax 325-5342
Nantucket IS, 30 Surfside Rd 02554 400/3-5
Evemarie McNeil, admin. 508-228-1089
Peirce MS 300/6-8
10 Surfside Rd 02554 508-228-7283
Peter Cohen, prin. Fax 325-7597

Nantucket New S 100/PK-8
15 Nobadoor Farm Rd 02554 508-228-8569
Jonathan Alden, head sch Fax 825-9811

Natick, Middlesex, Pop. 30,700
Natick SD 5,300/PK-12
13 E Central St 01760 508-647-6500
Dr. Peter Sanchioni Ph.D., supt. Fax 647-6506
www.natickps.org/
Bennett-Hemenway ES 600/K-4
22 E Evergreen Rd 01760 508-647-6580
Karen Ghilani, prin. Fax 652-9951
Brown ES 500/K-4
1 Jean Burke Dr 01760 508-647-6660
Kirk Downing, prin. Fax 647-6668
Johnson ES 200/K-4
99 S Main St 01760 508-647-6680
Jordan Hoffman, prin. Fax 647-6688
Kennedy MS 700/5-8
165 Mill St 01760 508-647-6650
Andrew Zitoli, prin. Fax 647-6658
Lilja ES 400/K-4
41 Bacon St 01760 617-852-5205
Anne Carothers, prin. Fax 647-6572
Memorial ES 400/K-4
107 Eliot St 01760 508-647-6590
Susan Balboni, prin. Fax 647-6598

Natick Preschool 100/PK-PK
15 West St 01760 508-647-6583
MaryBeth Kinkead, prin. Fax 647-8522
Wilson MS 900/5-8
22 Rutledge Rd 01760 508-647-6670
Teresa Carney, prin. Fax 647-6678

Riverbend S 200/PK-8
6 Auburn St 01760 508-655-7333
Christine Price, prin. Fax 655-3867

Needham, Norfolk, Pop. 28,386
Needham SD 5,500/PK-12
1330 Highland Ave 02492 781-455-0400
Dr. Daniel Gutekanst, supt. Fax 455-0417
www.needham.k12.ma.us/
Broadmeadow ES 600/K-5
120 Broad Meadow Rd 02492 781-455-0448
Emily Gaberman, prin. Fax 455-0851
High Rock S 400/6-6
77 Ferndale Rd 02492 781-455-0455
Jessica Downey, prin. Fax 455-0411
Mitchell ES 500/K-5
187 Brookline St 02492 781-455-0466
Gregory Bayse, prin. Fax 455-0871
Newman ES 700/PK-5
1155 Central Ave 02492 781-455-0416
Jessica Peterson, prin. Fax 453-2523
Pollard MS 900/7-8
200 Harris Ave 02492 781-455-0480
Tamatha Bibbo, prin. Fax 455-0413
Other Schools – See Needham Heights

Haddad MS 200/6-8
110 May St 02492 781-449-0133
Jane Abel, head sch Fax 449-8096
St. Joseph S 400/K-5
90 Pickering St 02492 781-444-4459
Charlotte Kelly, prin. Fax 444-0822

Needham Heights, Norfolk
Needham SD
Supt. — See Needham
Eliot ES 400/K-5
135 Wellesley Ave 02494 781-455-0452
Karen Bourn, prin. Fax 455-0852
Hillside ES 400/K-5
28 Glen Gary Rd 02494 781-455-0461
Michael Kascak, prin. Fax 455 0857

New Bedford, Bristol, Pop. 86,721
New Bedford SD 12,500/PK-12
455 County St 02740 508-997-4511
Dr. Pia Durkin Ph.D., supt. Fax 997-0298
www.newbedfordschools.org
Ashley ES 400/K-5
122 Rochambeau St 02745 508-997-4511
Christine Pugliese, prin. Fax 995-9707
Brooks ES 300/PK 5
212 Nemasket St 02740 508-997-4511
Maria Reidy, prin. Fax 991-3659
Campbell ES 300/PK-5
145 Essex St 02745 508-997-4511
Lisa Wheelden, prin. Fax 991-7483
Carney ES 700/PK-5
247 Elm St 02740 508-997-4511
Karen Treadup, prin. Fax 990-2879
Congdon ES 300/K-5
50 Hemlock St 02740 508-997-4511
Darcie Aungst, prin. Fax 999-3959
DeValles ES 400/K-5
120 Katherine St 02744 508-997-4511
Darcie Aungst, prin. Fax 999-4034
Gomes ES 700/PK-5
286 S 2nd St 02740 508-997-4511
Ellyn Gallant, prin. Fax 990-1840
Hathaway ES, 256 Court St 02740 300/PK-5
Richard Leeman, prin. 508-997-4511
Hayden/McFadden ES 600/PK-5
361 Cedar Grove St 02746 508-997-4511
Tammy Morgan, prin. Fax 979-4664
Jacobs ES 200/PK-5
33 Emery St 02744 508-997-4511
Kerry Kennedy, prin. Fax 984-5660
Keith MS 800/6-8
225 Hathaway Blvd 02740 508-997-4511
Joshua Almeida, prin. Fax 996-2040
Lincoln ES 800/K-5
441 Ashley Blvd 02745 508-997-4511
Lina DeJesus, prin. Fax 995-7933
Normandin MS 1,000/6-8
81 Felton St 02745 508-997-4511
Dr. Zachary Abrams, prin. Fax 995-6975
Pacheco ES 400/PK-5
261 Mount Pleasant St 02746 508-997-4511
Justine Medina, prin. Fax 994-7241
Parker ES 300/PK-5
705 County St 02740 508-997-4511
Lynn Dessert, prin. Fax 994-4063
Pulaski ES, 1097 Braley Rd 02745 700/PK-5
Melissa Rego, prin. 508-997-4511
Rodman ES 100/K-5
497 Mill St 02740 508-997-4511
Kim Marshall, prin. Fax 997-1567
Roosevelt MS 700/6-8
119 Frederick St 02744 508-997-4511
Daniel Bossolt, prin. Fax 997-1198
Swift ES 200/K-5
2203 Acushnet Ave 02745 508-997-4511
Tonya Vitorino, prin. Fax 998-0887
Taylor ES, 71 Portland St 02744 200/PK-5
Dr. Rafaela DeFigueiredo, prin. 508-997-4511
Winslow ES 300/K-5
561 Allen St 02740 508-997-4511
Margaret Welch, prin. Fax 999-0489

All Saints Catholic S 200/PK-8
115 Illinois St 02745 508-995-3696
Susan Massoud, prin. Fax 998-0840

Holy Family-Holy Name S 300/PK-8
91 Summer St 02740 508-993-3547
Cecilia Felix, prin. Fax 993-8277
Nativity Prep S 100/5-8
66 Spring St 02740 508-994-3800
Jay Goldrick, prin. Fax 994-3434
Nazarene Christian Academy 200/PK-12
764 Hathaway Rd 02740 508-992-7944
Susan Helm, prin. Fax 328-9513
St. James & St. John S 300/PK-8
180 Orchard St 02740 508-996-0534
Cristina Raposo, prin. Fax 996-3087

New Braintree, Worcester
Quabbin SD
Supt. — See Barre
New Braintree Grade S 100/K-1
15 Memorial Dr 01531 508-867-2553
Patricia Worthington, prin. Fax 867-3331

Newbury, Essex
Triton Regional SD
Supt. — See Byfield
Newbury ES 600/PK-6
63 Hanover St 01951 978-465-5353
Beth Yando, prin. Fax 463-3070

Newburyport, Essex, Pop. 17,171
Newburyport SD 2,100/PK-12
70 Low St 01950 978-465-4456
Susan Viccaro, supt. Fax 462-3495
www.newburyport.k12.ma.us/
Bresnahan ES 500/PK-3
333 High St 01950 978-465-4431
Kristina Davis, prin. Fax 465-2112
Molin Upper ES 300/4-5
70 Low St 01950 978-463-8212
Tara Rossi, prin. Fax 463-3280
Nock MS 500/6-8
70 Low St 01950 978-465-4447
Lisa Furlong, prin. Fax 465-4074

Immaculate Conception S 300/PK-8
1 Washington St 01950 978-465-7780
Mary Reardon, prin. Fax 234-7331

New Salem, Franklin
New Salem-Wendell SD
Supt. — See Erving
Swift River ES 100/PK-6
201 Wendell Rd 01355 978-544-6926
Kelley Sullivan, prin. Fax 544-2253

Newton, Middlesex, Pop. 83,100
Newton SD
Supt. — See Newtonville
Bigelow MS 500/6-8
42 Vernon St 02458 617-552-7800
Todd Harrison, prin. Fax 552-7752
Lincoln-Eliot ES 300/K-5
191 Pearl St 02458 617-559-9540
Danielle Morrissey, prin. Fax 552-5558
Newton ECC 200/PK-PK
150 Jackson Rd 02458 617-559-6050
Kathleen Browning, dir. Fax 559-6026
Oak Hill MS 600/6-8
130 Wheeler Rd 02459 617-559-9200
Dr. John Harutunian, prin. Fax 552-5547
Underwood ES 300/K-5
101 Vernon St 02458 617-559-9660
Kathleen Smith, prin. Fax 552-5552

Jackson S 300/K-6
200 Jackson Rd 02458 617-969-1537
Susan Niden, prin. Fax 244-8596
Mt. Alvernia Academy 300/PK-6
20 Manet Rd 02467 617-527-7540
Barbara Plunkett, prin. Fax 527-7995
Walnut Park Montessori S 100/PK-K
47 Walnut Park 02458 617-969-9208
Nancy Fish, head sch Fax 969-6408

Newton Center, See Newton
Newton SD
Supt. — See Newtonville
Bowen ES 500/K-5
280 Cypress St 02459 617-559-9330
Diana Guzzi, prin. Fax 552-7363
Brown MS 700/6-8
125 Meadowbrook Rd 02459 617-559-6900
John Jordan, prin. Fax 552-7729
Mason-Rice ES 500/K-5
149 Pleasant St 02459 617-559-9570
Jacob Bultema, prin. Fax 552-7315
Memorial-Spaulding ES 400/K-5
250 Brookline St 02459 617-559-9600
Thomas Morris, prin. Fax 552-7944
Ward ES 300/K-5
10 Dolphin Rd 02459 617-559-6450
Elaine Harold, prin. Fax 552-5563

Newton Montessori S 200/PK-6
80 Crescent Ave 02459 617-969-4488
Beth Black, head sch Fax 969-4430
Solomon Schechter Day S 500/PK-8
60 Stein Cir 02459 617-964-7765
Rebecca Lurie, head sch Fax 964-8693

Newton Highlands, See Newton
Newton SD
Supt. — See Newtonville
Countryside ES 500/K-5
191 Dedham St 02461 617-559-9450
Beth Herlihy, prin. Fax 552-5583

Newtonville, See Newton
Newton SD 12,600/PK-12
100 Walnut St 02460 617-559-6100
David Fleishman, supt. Fax 559-6101
www.newton.k12.ma.us

Cabot ES 400/K-5
225 Nevada St 02460 617-559-9400
Eric Sprung, prin. Fax 552-5584
Day MS 900/6-8
21 Minot Pl 02460 617-559-9100
Jacqueline Mann, prin. Fax 559-9103
Mann ES 400/K-5
687 Watertown St 02460 617-559-9510
Mark Nardelli, prin. Fax 559-2004
Zervas ES 300/K-5
225 Nevada St 02460 617-559-6750
Dr. Diana Beck, prin. Fax 552-5546
Other Schools – See Auburndale, Newton, Newton Center, Newton Highlands, Waban, West Newton

Norfolk, Norfolk
King Philip Regional SD 2,100/7-12
18 King St 02056 508-520-7991
Dr. Elizabeth Zielinski, supt.
www.kingphilip.org
King Philip MS 800/7-8
18 King St 02056 508-541-7324
Dr. Susan Gilson, prin. Fax 541-3467

Norfolk SD 900/PK-6
70 Boardman St 02056 508-528-1225
Dr. Ingrid Allardi, supt. Fax 528-3739
www.norfolk.k12.ma.us/
Day ES 400/PK-2
232 Main St 02056 508-541-5475
Linda Balfour, prin. Fax 541-5482
Freeman-Kennedy IS 500/3-6
70 Boardman St 02056 508-528-1266
Lisa Altham-Hickey, prin. Fax 541-5495

North Adams, Berkshire, Pop. 13,389
North Adams SD 1,500/PK-12
37 Main St Ste 200 01247 413-776-1458
Barbara Malkas Ed.D., supt. Fax 776-1685
www.napsk12.org
Brayton ES 500/PK-6
20 Brayton Hill Ter 01247 413-662-3260
John Franzoni, prin. Fax 662-3293
Colegrove Park ES 300/PK-6
24 Church St 01247 413-662-3250
Amy Meehan, prin. Fax 672-3247
Greylock ES 200/PK-6
100 Phelps Ave 01247 413-662-3255
Sandra Cote, prin. Fax 662-3033

Northampton, Hampshire, Pop. 27,865
Northampton SD 2,700/PK-12
212 Main St Rm 200 01060 413-587-1315
Dr. John Provost, supt. Fax 587-1318
www.northampton-k12.us/
Bridge Street ES 300/PK-5
2 Parsons St 01060 413-587-1460
Beth Choquette, prin. Fax 587-1474
Jackson Street ES 300/K-5
120 Jackson St 01060 413-587-1510
Gwen Agna, prin. Fax 587-1524
Other Schools – See Florence, Leeds

Lander-Grinspoon Academy 100/K-6
257 Prospect St 01060 413-584-6622
Montessori S of Northhampton 100/PK-8
51 Bates St 01060 413-586-4538
Mark Dansereau, head sch Fax 586-7047
Smith College Campus S 300/K-6
33 Prospect St 01063 413-585-3270
Chris Marblo, prin. Fax 585-3285

North Andover, Essex, Pop. 22,792
North Andover SD 4,800/PK-12
566 Main St 01845 978-794-1503
Dr. Jennifer Price, supt. Fax 794-0231
www.northandoverpublicschools.com
Atkinson ES 500/PK-5
111 Phillips Brooks Rd 01845 978-794-0124
Greg Landry, prin. Fax 794-2454
Franklin ES 500/K-5
2 Cypress Ter 01845 978-794-1990
Joseph Clarke, prin. Fax 682-0240
Kittredge ES 300/K-5
601 Main St 01845 978-794-1688
Richard Cushing, prin. Fax 794-2514
North Andover MS 1,200/6-8
495 Main St 01845 978-794-1870
Joan McQuade, prin. Fax 794-3619
Sargent ES 600/K-5
300 Abbott St 01845 978-725-3673
Karen Murdoch-Lahey, prin. Fax 725-3678
Thomson ES 300/K-5
266 Waverley Rd 01845 978-794-1545
Christopher Raymond, prin. Fax 794-2508

St. Michael S 500/PK-8
80 Maple Ave 01845 978-686-1862
Susan Reidy Gosselin, prin. Fax 688-5144

North Attleboro, Bristol, Pop. 16,178
North Attleborough SD 4,400/PK-12
6 Morse St 02760 508-643-2100
Scott C. Holcomb, supt. Fax 643-2110
www.naschools.net
Amvet Boulevard ES 400/K-5
70 Amvet Blvd 02760 508-643-2155
Michelle McKeon, prin. Fax 643-2184
Community S 300/K-5
45 S Washington St 02760 508-643-2148
James Gaudette, prin. Fax 643-2179
Early Learning Center 100/PK-PK
25 School St 02760 508-643-2145
Dr. Victoria Ekk, prin. Fax 643-2188
Falls ES 300/K-5
2 Jackson St 02763 508-643-2170
Lee Anne Todd, prin. Fax 643-2185
Martin ES 600/K-5
37 Landry Ave 02760 508-643-2140
Dr. Danielle Klingaman, prin. Fax 643-2186

North Attleboro MS 1,200/6-8
564 Landry Ave 02760 508-643-2130
Craig Juelis, prin. Fax 643-2134
Roosevelt Avenue ES 300/K-5
108 Roosevelt Ave 02760 508-643-2151
John Quinn, prin. Fax 643-2187

St. Mary-Sacred Heart S 300/K-8
57 Richards Ave 02760 508-695-3072
Charlotte Lourenco, prin. Fax 695-9074

North Billerica, Middlesex, Pop. 5,400
Billerica SD
Supt. — See Billerica
Dutile ES 300/K-5
10 Biagiotti Way 01862 978-528-8530
Christine Balzotti, prin. Fax 436-9548
Hajjar ES 500/K-5
59 Rogers St 01862 978-528-8550
Elizabeth Devine, prin. Fax 436-9556

Northborough, Worcester, Pop. 6,020
Northborough-Southborough SD
Supt. — See Southborough
Lincoln Street ES 300/K-5
76 Lincoln St 01532 508-351-7030
Jennifer Parson, prin. Fax 351-7033
Melican MS 600/6-8
145 Lincoln St 01532 508-351-7020
Michelle Karb, prin. Fax 351-7006
Peaslee ES 300/K-5
31 Maple St 01532 508-351-7035
Jill Barnhardt, prin. Fax 351-7037
Proctor ES 300/K-5
26 Jefferson Rd 01532 508-351-7040
Alana Cyr, prin. Fax 351-7007
Zeh ES 300/PK-5
33 Howard St 01532 508-351-7048
Susan Whitten, prin. Fax 393-5125

St. Bernadette S 500/PK-8
266 Main St 01532 508-351-9905
Deborah O'Neil, prin. Fax 351-2941

North Brookfield, Worcester, Pop. 2,236
North Brookfield SD 600/PK-12
10 New School Dr 01535 508-867-9821
Dr. Marilyn Tencza, supt. Fax 867-8148
www.nbschools.org
North Brookfield ES 300/PK-6
10 New School Dr 01535 508-867-8326
Eric Glazier, prin. Fax 867-6255

North Chelmsford, Middlesex
Chelmsford SD
Supt. — See Chelmsford
Harrington ES 500/K-4
120 Richardson Rd 01863 978-251-5166
Michael LaCava, prin. Fax 251-5170

Keystone Montessori S 100/PK-6
55 Middlesex St 01863 978-251-2929

North Dartmouth, Bristol, Pop. 8,000
Dartmouth SD
Supt. — See South Dartmouth
Dartmouth MS 1,000/6-8
366 Slocum Rd 02747 508-997-9333
Darren Doane, prin. Fax 999-7720
Potter ES 400/PK-5
185 Cross Rd 02747 508-996-8250
Heidi Brooks, prin. Fax 990-0250
Quinn ES 700/K-5
529 Hawthorn St 02747 508-997-3178
Kyle Grandfield, prin. Fax 997-6257

Friends Academy 300/PK-8
1088 Tucker Rd 02747 508-999-1356
Benjamin Kennedy, head sch Fax 997-0117

North Dighton, Bristol
Dighton-Rehoboth Regional SD 2,900/PK-12
2700 Regional Rd 02764 508-252-5000
Dr. Anthony C. Azar, supt. Fax 252-5024
www.drregional.org
Other Schools – See Dighton, Rehoboth

North Easton, Bristol, Pop. 4,400
Easton SD 3,400/PK-12
PO Box 359 02356 508-230-3200
Dr. Lisha Cabral, supt. Fax 238-3563
www.easton.k12.ma.us
Easton MS 1,000/6-8
98 Columbus Ave 02356 508-230-3222
R. Luke Carroll, prin. Fax 230-3102
Moreau Hall ES 200/PK-2
360 Washington St 02356 508-230-3235
Thomas Higgins, prin. Fax 238-3237
Parkview S 300/PK-2
50 Spooner St 02356 508-230-3230
Christopher Getchell, prin. Fax 230-3249
Richardson - Olmstead S 400/3-5
101 Lothrop St 02356 508-230-3227
Deborah Hammett, prin. Fax 238-3066
Other Schools – See South Easton

North Falmouth, Barnstable, Pop. 3,017
Falmouth SD
Supt. — See East Falmouth
North Falmouth ES 400/K-4
62 Old Main Rd 02556 508-563-2334
Timothy Adams, prin. Fax 564-7525

Northfield, Franklin, Pop. 1,078
Pioneer Valley SD 1,000/PK-12
97 F Sumner Turner Rd 01360 413-498-2911
Ruth Miller, supt. Fax 498-0045
www.pvrsdk12.org
Northfield ES 200/PK-6
104 Main St 01360 413-498-5842
Megan Desmarais, prin. Fax 498-5459
Other Schools – See Bernardston, Leyden, Warwick

North Grafton, Worcester, Pop. 3,100
Grafton SD
Supt. — See Grafton
North Grafton ES 200/PK-1
46 Waterville St 01536 508-839-5483
Julie Yankauskas-Flynn, prin. Fax 839-1073

North Quincy, See Quincy
Quincy SD
Supt. — See Quincy
Atlantic MS 500/6-8
86 Hollis Ave 02171 617-984-8727
Maureen MacNeil, prin. Fax 984-8646
Montclair ES 400/K-5
8 Belmont St 02171 617-984-8708
Renee Malvesti, prin. Fax 984-8719
Parker ES 300/K-5
148 Billings Rd 02171 617-984-8710
Margaret MacNeil, prin. Fax 984-8624
Squantum ES 400/K-5
50 Huckins Ave 02171 617-984-8706
Stephen Sylvia, prin. Fax 984-8857

Quincy Catholic Academy 400/PK-8
370 Hancock St 02171 617-328-3830
Catherine Cameron, prin. Fax 328-6438

North Reading, Middlesex, Pop. 12,002
North Reading SD 2,600/PK-12
189 Park St 01864 978-664-7810
Jon Bernard, supt. Fax 664-0252
www.north-reading.k12.ma.us/
Batchelder ES 500/K-5
175 Park St 01864 978-664-7814
Sean Killeen, prin. Fax 664-7819
Hood ES 300/K-5
298 Haverhill St 01864 978-664-7816
Glen McKay, prin. Fax 664-7805
Little ES 400/PK-5
7 Barberry Rd 01864 978-664-7820
Christine Molle, prin. Fax 664-3081
North Reading MS 700/6-8
189 Park St 01864 978-664-7806
Catherine O'Connell, prin. Fax 276-0679

North Weymouth, Norfolk
Weymouth SD
Supt. — See Weymouth
Johnson ECC 200/PK-PK
70 Pearl St 02191 781-335-0191
Maura Perez, prin. Fax 340-2533
Wessagusset PS 400/K-4
75 Pilgrim Rd 02191 781-335-2210
Elizabeth Drolet, prin. Fax 335-4379

St. Jerome S 200/K-8
598 Bridge St 02191 781-335-1235
Kathleen Pulco, prin. Fax 340-0256

Norton, Bristol, Pop. 1,899
Norton SD 2,600/PK-12
64 W Main St 02766 508-285-0100
Joseph Baeta, supt. Fax 285-0199
www.norton.k12.ma.us
Norton MS 600/6-8
215 W Main St 02766 508-285-0140
Vincent Hayward, prin. Fax 286-9457
Nourse ES 300/PK-3
38 Plain St 02766 508-285-0110
Catherine Luke, prin. Fax 285-0109
Solmonese ES 500/K-3
315 W Main St 02766 508-285-0120
Riitta Bolton, prin. Fax 285-0130
Yelle ES 400/4-5
64 W Main St 02766 508-285-0190
Anthony Difonso, prin. Fax 285-0187

Legacy Christian Academy 100/PK-12
1 New Taunton Ave 02766 508-952-2997
Katrina Joseph, head sch Fax 952-2977

Norwell, Plymouth
Norwell SD 2,300/PK-12
322 Main St 02061 781-659-8800
Matthew Keegan, supt. Fax 659-8805
www.norwellschools.org
Cole ES 500/PK-5
81 High St 02061 781-659-8823
Eliza Burns, prin. Fax 878-6936
Norwell MS 600/6-8
328 Main St 02061 781-659-8814
Derek Sulc, prin. Fax 659-8822
Vinal ES 500/PK-5
102 Old Oaken Bucket Rd 02061 781-659-8820
Patrick Lenz, prin. Fax 659-8812

Chapman Farm S 6-8
76 Accord Park Dr 02061 781-217-3129
Katy Shamitz, prin.

Norwood, Norfolk, Pop. 27,997
Norwood SD 3,500/PK-12
PO Box 67 02062 781-762-6804
David L. Thomson Ed.D., supt. Fax 762-0229
www.norwood.k12.ma.us/
Balch ES 300/1-5
PO Box 67 02062 781-762-0694
Diane Ferreira, prin. Fax 255-5610
Callahan ES 200/1-5
PO Box 67 02062 781-762-0693
Donna Brown, prin. Fax 255-5611
Cleveland ES 400/1-5
PO Box 67 02062 781-762-6522
Nancy Coppola, prin. Fax 255-7317
Coakley MS 700/6-8
PO Box 67 02062 781-762-7880
Margo Fraczek Ed.D., prin. Fax 255-5630
Oldham ES 200/1-5
PO Box 67 02062 781-769-2417
Wesley Manaday Ed.D., prin. Fax 255-7007
Prescott ES 200/1-5
PO Box 67 02062 781-762-6497
Brianne Killion, prin. Fax 255-7028
Willett ECC 400/PK-K
PO Box 67 02062 781-762-6805
Carolyn Boyce, prin. Fax 762-7245

St. Catherine of Siena S 500/PK-8
249 Nahatan St 02062 781-769-5354
Mary Russo, prin. Fax 769-7905

Oak Bluffs, Dukes
Oak Bluffs SD
Supt. — See Vineyard Haven
Oak Bluffs ES 400/PK-8
PO Box 1325 02557 508-693-0951
Dr. Megan Farrell, prin. Fax 693-5189

Oakham, Worcester
Quabbin SD
Supt. — See Barre
Oakham Center ES 200/2-6
1 Deacon Allen Dr 01068 508-882-3392
Patricia Worthington, prin. Fax 882-0101

Orange, Franklin, Pop. 3,955
Orange SD 500/PK-6
507 S Main St 01364 978-544-6763
Tari Thomas, supt. Fax 544-3450
www.orange-elem.org/
Dexter Park ES 200/3-6
3 Dexter St 01364 978-544-6080
Christopher Dodge, prin. Fax 544-1123
Fisher Hill ES 300/PK-2
59 Dexter St 01364 978-544-0018
Maureen Donelan, prin. Fax 544-5703

Orleans, Barnstable, Pop. 1,586
Brewster SD 500/PK-5
78 Eldridge Park Way 02653 508-255-8800
Thomas M. Conrad, supt. Fax 240-2351
www.nausetschools.org
Other Schools – See Brewster

Eastham SD 200/K-5
78 Eldridge Park Way 02653 508-255-8800
Thomas M. Conrad, supt. Fax 240-2351
www.nausetschools.org
Other Schools – See Eastham

Nauset SD 1,600/6-12
78 Eldridge Park Way 02653 508-255-8800
Thomas M. Conrad, supt. Fax 240-2351
www.nausetschools.org
Nauset Regional MS 600/6-8
70 S Orleans Rd 02653 508-255-0016
Dr. Maxine Minkoff, prin. Fax 240-1105

Orleans SD 200/K-5
78 Eldridge Park Way 02653 508-255-8800
Thomas M. Conrad, supt. Fax 240-2351
www.nausetschools.org
Orleans ES 200/K-5
46 Eldridge Park Way 02653 508-255-0380
Elaine Pender, prin. Fax 255-7943

Wellfleet SD 100/PK-5
78 Eldridge Park Way 02653 508-255-8800
Thomas M. Conrad, supt. Fax 240-2351
www.nausetschools.org
Other Schools – See Wellfleet

Osterville, Barnstable, Pop. 2,911

Bayberry Christian S 50/2-8
2736 Falmouth Rd 02655 508-428-9178
Tina Advani, prin. Fax 428-8921
Cape Cod Academy 300/K-12
50 Osterville-W Barnstable 02655 508-428-5400
Thomas Trigg, head sch Fax 428-0701

Otis, Berkshire
Farmington River Regional SD 100/PK-6
PO Box 679 01253 413-269-4466
Thomas Nadolny, supt. Fax 269-7659
www.farmingtonriverelementary.com
Farmington River ES 100/PK-6
PO Box 679 01253 413-269-4466
Thomas Nadolny, admin. Fax 269-7659

Oxford, Worcester, Pop. 6,042
Oxford SD 1,500/PK-12
4 Maple Rd 01540 508-987-6050
Dr. Kristine Nash Ed.D., supt. Fax 987-6054
www.oxps.org
Barton ES 300/2-4
25 Depot Rd 01540 508-987-6066
Martha Wiley, prin. Fax 987-2364
Chaffee ES 300/PK-1
9 Clover St 01540 508-987-6057
Robert Pelczarzski, prin. Fax 987-5828
Oxford MS 500/5-7
497 Main St 01540 508-987-6074
Amy Belhumeur, prin. Fax 987-2588

Oak Hill Christian S 50/PK-8
PO Box 277 01540 508-987-0287
Crystal Brown, admin. Fax 987-6156

Palmer, Hampden, Pop. 4,069
Palmer SD 1,300/PK-12
24 Converse St Ste 1 01069 413-283-2650
Patricia Gardner, supt. Fax 283-2655
www.palmerschools.org
Old Mill Pond ES 600/PK-5
4107 Main St 01069 413-283-4300
Carolyn Wallace, prin. Fax 283-2619

Paxton, Worcester
Wachusett Regional SD
Supt. — See Jefferson
Paxton Center S 600/K-8
19 West St 01612 508-798-8576
Kathleen McCollumn, prin. Fax 754-6569

Peabody, Essex, Pop. 50,101
Peabody SD 6,100/PK-12
27 Lowell St 01960 978-531-1600
Herbert Levine Ph.D., supt. Fax 536-6590
www.peabody.k12.ma.us/
Brown ES 400/K-5
150 Lynn St 01960 978-536-4100
Elaine Metropolis, prin. Fax 536-4180
Burke ES 300/K-5
127 Birch St 01960 978-536-5400
Lacey Becotte, prin. Fax 536-5410
Carroll ES 600/K-5
60 Northend St 01960 978-536-4200
Tracy Smith, prin. Fax 536-4215
Center ES 400/K-5
18 Irving St 01960 978-536-5475
Jacqueline Orphanos, prin. Fax 536-5490
Higgins MS 1,300/6-8
85 Perkins St 01960 978-536-4800
Todd Bucey, prin. Fax 536-4810
McCarthy S, 76 Lake St 01960 300/PK-5
Raymond Smoyer, prin. 978-536-5625
South Memorial ES 500/PK-5
16 Maple Street Ext 01960 978-536-5700
Dr. Mark Higgins, prin. Fax 536-5710
Welch ES 300/PK-5
50 Swampscott Ave 01960 978-536-5775
Michelle Massa, prin. Fax 536-5845
West Memorial ES 300/PK-5
15 Bow St 01960 978-536-5850
Nick Coler, prin. Fax 536-5860

St. John the Baptist S 500/PK-8
19 Chestnut St 01960 978-531-0444
Maureen Kelleher, prin. Fax 531-3569

Pelham, Hampshire
Pelham SD
Supt. — See Amherst
Pelham ES 100/PK-6
45 Amherst Rd 01002 413-362-1100
Lisa Desjarlais, prin. Fax 253-4108

Pembroke, Plymouth
Pembroke SD 3,300/PK-12
72 Pilgrim Rd 02359 781-829-0832
Erin Obey, supt. Fax 826-6957
www.edlinesites.net/pages/PembrokePS
Bryantville ES 600/K-6
29 Gurney Dr 02359 781-293-5411
Catherine Glaude, prin. Fax 294-4662
Hobomock ES 500/K-6
81 Learning Ln 02359 781-294-0911
Danielle Kay, prin. Fax 293-1281
North Pembroke ES 600/PK-6
72 Pilgrim Rd 02359 781-826-5115
Michael Murphy, prin. Fax 826-4851
Pembroke Community MS 600/7-8
559 School St 02359 781-293-8627
Donna McGarrigle, prin. Fax 294-0916

Pepperell, Middlesex, Pop. 2,459
North Middlesex SD 3,400/PK-12
45 Main St 01463 978-597-8713
Joan Landers, supt. Fax 597-6534
nmrsd.org
Nissitissit MS 600/5-8
33 Chase Ave 01463 978-433-0114
Diane Gleason, prin. Fax 433-0118
Squannacook ECC, 10 Hollis St 01463 100/PK-PK
Tara Hanley, prin. 978-433-6150
Varnum Brook ES 600/K-4
10 Hollis St 01463 978-433-6722
Tara Hanley, prin. Fax 433-8140
Other Schools – See Ashby, Townsend

Petersham, Worcester, Pop. 243
Petersham SD 100/K-6
PO Box 148 01366 978-724-3363
Tari Thomas, supt. Fax 724-6687
www.petershamcenterschool.org/
Petersham Center S 100/K-6
PO Box 148 01366 978-724-3363
Joanne Menard, prin. Fax 724-6687

Phillipston, Worcester, Pop. 1,485
Narragansett Regional SD
Supt. — See Baldwinville
Phillipston Memorial ES 200/PK-4
20 The Cmn 01331 978-249-4969
Chante Jillson, prin. Fax 249-5526

Pittsfield, Berkshire, Pop. 43,503
Pittsfield SD 5,900/PK-12
269 1st St 01201 413-499-9512
Dr. Jason McCandless, supt. Fax 448-2643
www.pittsfield.net
Allendale ES 300/K-5
180 Connecticut Ave 01201 413-448-9650
Brenda Kelley, prin. Fax 499-4766
Capeless ES 200/PK-5
86 Brooks Ave 01201 413-448-9665
Candy Jezewski, prin. Fax 496-9449
Conte Community ES 300/PK-5
200 W Union St 01201 413-448-9660
Kerry Light, prin. Fax 448-9663
Crosby ES 400/PK-5
517 West St 01201 413-448-9670
Aaron Dean, prin. Fax 443-9520
Egremont ES 500/K-5
84 Egremont Ave 01201 413-448-9655
Jared Materas, prin. Fax 442-0886
Herberg MS 600/6-8
501 Pomeroy Ave 01201 413-448-9640
Dr. Gina Coleman, prin. Fax 448-9644
Morningside Community ES 500/PK-5
100 Burbank St 01201 413-448-9690
Jennifer Stokes, prin. Fax 443-8907

Reid MS 500/6-8
950 North St 01201 413-448-9620
Linda Whitacre, prin. Fax 443-1587
Stearns ES 200/K-5
75 Lebanon Ave 01201 413-499-9554
Fax 499-9514
Williams ES 300/K-5
50 Bushey Rd 01201 413-448-9680
Lisa Buchinski, prin. Fax 499-5389

Plainville, Norfolk, Pop. 6,871
Plainville SD 800/PK-6
68 Messenger St 02762 508-699-1300
David Raiche, supt. Fax 699-1302
www.plainville.k12.ma.us
Jackson ES 500/PK-3
68 Messenger St 02762 508-699-1304
Kate Campbell, prin. Fax 696-1303
Wood ES 300/4-6
72 Messenger St 02762 508-699-1312
Robin Roberts-Pratt, prin. Fax 699-1317

Plymouth, Plymouth, Pop. 7,138
Plymouth SD 7,700/PK-12
253 S Meadow Rd 02360 508-830-4300
Dr. Gary Maestas, supt. Fax 746-1873
www.plymouth.k12.ma.us
Cold Spring ES 200/K-5
25 Alden St 02360 508-830-4335
Christine Morgan, prin. Fax 830-4328
Federal Furnace ES 400/K-5
860 Federal Furnace Rd 02360 508-830-4360
Trina Camarao, prin. Fax 830-4362
Hedge ES 200/K-5
258 Standish Ave 02360 508-830-4340
Kristin Wilson, prin. Fax 830-4341
Indian Brook ES 700/K-5
1181 State Rd 02360 508-830-4370
Daniel Harold, prin. Fax 830-4373
Manomet ES 300/K-5
70 Manomet Point Rd 02360 508-830-4380
Dr. Patrick Fraine, prin. Fax 830-4387
Morton ES 600/K-5
6 Lincoln St 02360 508-830-4320
Michael Spencer, prin. Fax 830-4324
Plymouth Community IS 1,000/6-8
117 Long Pond Rd 02360 508-830-4450
Brian Palladino, prin. Fax 830-4464
Plymouth ECC 100/PK-PK
117 Long Pond Rd 02360 508-830-4347
Mary Mello, dir. Fax 830-4446
Plymouth South MS 800/5-8
488 Long Pond Rd 02360 508-224-2725
Steven Morgenweck, prin. Fax 224-5660
South ES 600/K-4
178 Bourne Rd 02360 508-830-4390
Adam Blaisdell, prin. Fax 830-4398
West ES 400/K-5
170 Plympton Rd 02360 508-830-4350
Scott Williams, prin. Fax 830-4442

Plympton, Plymouth
Plympton SD
Supt. — See Kingston
Dennett ES 200/K-6
80 Crescent St 02367 781-585-3659
Peter Veneto, prin. Fax 585-3872

Princeton, Worcester
Wachusett Regional SD
Supt. — See Jefferson
Prince S 400/K-8
170 Sterling Rd 01541 978-464-2110
Tammy Boyle, prin. Fax 464-2112

Provincetown, Barnstable, Pop. 3,374
Provincetown SD 100/PK-8
12 Winslow St 02657 508-487-5000
Dr. Beth Singer, supt. Fax 487-5098
www.provincetownschools.com
Provincetown S 100/PK-8
12 Winslow St 02657 508-487-5000
Kim Pike, prin. Fax 487-5098

Quincy, Norfolk, Pop. 89,796
Quincy SD 9,200/PK-12
34 Coddington St 02169 617-984-8700
Dr. Richard DeCristofaro, supt. Fax 984-8965
www.quincypublicschools.com
Atherton Hough ES 300/K-5
1084 Sea St 02169 617-984-8797
Robin Moreira, prin. Fax 984-8653
Beechwood Knoll ES 400/K-5
225 Fenno St 02170 617-984-8781
Diane O'Keeffe, prin. Fax 984-8636
Bernazzani ES 300/K-5
701 Furnace Brook Pkwy 02169 617-984-8713
Peter Dionne, prin. Fax 984-8657
Broad Meadows MS 300/6-8
50 Calvin Rd 02169 617-984-8723
Daniel Gilbert, prin. Fax 984-8834
Central MS 600/6-8
875 Hancock St 02170 617-984-8725
Rick DeCristofaro, prin. Fax 984-8661
Chiesa ECC PK-PK
100 Brooks Ave 02169 617-984-8777
Erin Perkins, admin. Fax 984-8965
Lincoln-Hancock Community ES 500/PK-4
300 Granite St 02169 617-984-8715
Ruth Witmer, prin. Fax 984-8808
Marshall ES 600/K-4
200 Moody St Ext 02169 617-984-8721
Nicholas Ahearn, prin. Fax 984-8609
Merrymount ES 400/K-5
4 Agawam Rd 02169 617-984-8762
Ann Pegg, prin. Fax 984-8909
Point Webster MS 400/5-8
60 Lancaster St 02169 617-984-6600
Christine Barrett, prin. Fax 984-6609
Snug Harbor Community ES 400/PK-5
333 Palmer St 02169 617-984-8763
Michael Marani, prin. Fax 984-8645
Sterling MS 300/5-8
444 Granite St 02169 617-984-8729
John Franceschini, prin. Fax 984-8640
Other Schools – See North Quincy, Wollaston

Adams Montessori S 100/PK-6
310 Adams St 02169 617-773-8200

Randolph, Norfolk, Pop. 30,586
Randolph SD 2,900/PK-12
40 Highland Ave 02368 781-961-6205
Thomas Anderson, supt. Fax 961-6295
www.randolph.k12.ma.us
Donovan ES 400/K-5
123 Reed St 02368 781-961-6248
Beth Gannon, prin. Fax 961-6266
Kennedy ES 400/PK-5
20 Hurley Dr 02368 781-961-6211
John Licorish, prin. Fax 961-6268
Lyons ES 300/K-5
60 Vesey Rd 02368 781-961-6252
Cindy Lopez, prin. Fax 961-6264
Randolph Community MS 700/6-8
225 High St 02368 781-961-6243
Thea Stovell, prin. Fax 961-6286
Young ES 300/K-5
30 Lou Courtney Dr 02368 781-961-6256
Sara Hosmer, prin. Fax 961-6292

Raynham, Bristol, Pop. 2,100
Bridgewater-Raynham Regional SD
Supt. — See Bridgewater
Laliberte ES 500/2-4
777 Pleasant St 02767 508-824-2731
Dennis Bray, prin. Fax 822-0580
Merrill ES 300/K-1
687 Pleasant St 02767 508-824-2490
Deborah Westell, prin. Fax 880-6720
Raynham MS 700/5-8
420 Titicut Rd 02767 508-977-0504
Charlene Charette, prin. Fax 977-0659

Reading, Middlesex, Pop. 24,477
Reading SD 4,400/PK-12
82 Oakland Rd 01867 781-944-5800
Dr. John Doherty, supt. Fax 942-9149
reading.k12.ma.us/
Barrows ES 400/K-5
16 Edgemont Ave 01867 781-942-9166
Heather Leonard, prin. Fax 942-9119
Birch Meadow ES 400/K-5
27 Arthur B Lord Dr 01867 781-944-2335
Julia Hendrix, prin. Fax 942-9164
Coolidge MS 400/6-8
89 Birch Meadow Dr 01867 781-942-9158
Sarah Marchant, prin. Fax 942-9118
Eaton ES 500/K-5
365 Summer Ave 01867 781-942-9161
LisaMarie Ippolito, prin. Fax 942-9053
Killam ES 500/K-5
333 Charles St 01867 781-944-7831
Sarah Leveque, prin. Fax 942-9186
Parker MS 600/6-8
45 Temple St 01867 781-944-1236
Richele Shankland, prin. Fax 942-9008
RISE Preschool 100/PK-PK
62 Oakland Rd 01867 781-942-9179
Kelley Bostwick, prin. Fax 942-5834
Wood End ES 300/PK-5
85 Sunset Rock Ln 01867 781-942-5420
Joanne King, prin. Fax 942-5428

Rehoboth, Bristol
Dighton-Rehoboth Regional SD
Supt. — See North Dighton
Beckwith MS 600/5-8
330R Winthrop St 02769 508-252-5080
Joseph Pirraglia, prin. Fax 252-5082
Palmer River ES 600/PK-4
326 Winthrop St 02769 508-252-5100
Arlene Miguel, prin. Fax 252-5110

Cedar Brook SDA S 100/PK-8
24 Ralsie Rd 02769 508-252-3930
Sherrie Wall, prin. Fax 252-4378

Revere, Suffolk, Pop. 50,075
Revere SD 6,800/PK-12
101 School St 02151 781-286-8226
Dr. Dianne Kelly, supt. Fax 286-8221
www.revereps.mec.edu
Anthony MS 500/6-8
107 Newhall St 02151 781-388-7520
Joanne Willett, prin. Fax 388-7521
Beachmont Veterans Memorial S 400/PK-5
15 Everard Ave 02151 781-286-8316
Percy Napier, prin. Fax 286-8293
Garfield ES 800/PK-5
176 Garfield Ave 02151 781-286-8296
William Coutts, prin. Fax 286-3560
Garfield MS 500/6-8
176 Garfield Ave 02151 781-286-8298
Samantha Meier, prin. Fax 286-3557
Hill ES 500/K-5
51 Park Ave 02151 781-286-8284
Edward Moccia, prin. Fax 333-2108
Lincoln ES 700/PK-5
68 Tuckerman St 02151 781-286-8270
Jodi Gennodie, prin. Fax 286-8315
Revere ES 500/K-5
395 Revere St 02151 781-286-8278
Barbara Kelly, prin. Fax 286-8279
Rumney Marsh Academy 500/6-8
140 American Legion Hwy 02151 781-388-3500
Richard Gallucci, prin. Fax 485-8443
Whelan Memorial ES 700/K-5
107 Newhall St 02151 781-388-7510
Jamie Flynn, prin. Fax 388-7511

Immaculate Conception S 300/PK-8
127 Winthrop Ave 02151 781-284-0519
Stephen Hanley, prin. Fax 284-3805

Richmond, Berkshire
Shaker Mountain School Union # 70 200/PK-8
1831 State Rd 01254 413-698-4001
Peter Dillon, supt. Fax 698-4003
www.rcscares.org
Richmond Consolidated S 200/PK-8
1831 State Rd 01254 413-698-2207
Monica Zanin, prin. Fax 698-3199
Other Schools – See Hancock

Rochester, Plymouth
Rochester SD
Supt. — See Mattapoisett
Rochester Memorial ES 500/PK-6
16 Pine St 02770 508-763-2049
Derek Medeiros, prin. Fax 763-2623

Rockland, Plymouth, Pop. 16,123
Rockland SD 2,200/K-12
34 MacKinlay Way 02370 781-878-3893
Dr. Alan Cron, supt. Fax 982-1483
rocklandschools.org
Esten ES 300/K-4
733 Summer St 02370 781-878-8336
Marilyn Smith, prin. Fax 871-8451
Jefferson ES 300/K-4
93 George St 02370 781-871-8400
Michelle Scheufele, prin. Fax 871-8449
Memorial Park ES 200/K-4
1 Brian Duffy Way 02370 781-878-1367
Janice Sheehan, prin. Fax 871-8450
Rogers MS 700/5-8
100 Taunton Ave 02370 781-878-4341
Elizabeth Bohn, prin. Fax 871-8448

Calvary Chapel Academy 100/PK-12
PO Box 409 02370 781-871-1043
Kevin Hanlon, hdmstr. Fax 792-3902
Holy Family S 400/K-8
6 Delprete Ave 02370 781-878-1154
Joan Cahalane, prin. Fax 982-2485

Rockport, Essex, Pop. 4,922
Rockport SD 1,000/PK-12
24 Jerdens Ln 01966 978-546-1200
Robert Liebow, supt. Fax 546-1205
www.rpk12.org
Rockport ES 400/PK-5
34 Jerdens Ln 01966 978-546-1220
Todd Simendinger, prin. Fax 546-8140
Rockport MS 300/6-8
26 Jerdens Ln 01966 978-546-1250
Amanda LaMantia, prin. Fax 546-1205

Roslindale, See Boston
Boston SD
Supt. — See Boston
Bates ES 300/K-5
426 Beech St 02131 617-635-8064
Rodolfo Morales, prin. Fax 635-8068
Conley ES 200/K-5
450 Poplar St 02131 617-635-8099
Joseph Foley, prin. Fax 635-6417
Haley ES 300/PK-8
570 American Legion Hwy 02131 617-635-8169
Kathleen Sullivan, prin. Fax 635-8173
Irving MS 400/5-8
105 Cummins Hwy 02131 617-635-8072
Carmen Davis, prin. Fax 635-9363
Mozart ES 200/PK-5
236 Beech St 02131 617-635-8082
Michael Baulier, prin. Fax 635-8087
Philbrick ES 200/PK-5
40 Philbrick St 02131 617-635-8069
Danladi Bobbitt, prin. Fax 635-7927
Sumner ES 500/PK-5
15 Basile St 02131 617-635-8131
Catherine MacCuish, prin. Fax 635-8136

Sacred Heart S 400/PK-8
1035 Canterbury St 02131 617-323-2500
Monica Haldiman, prin. Fax 325-7151

Rowe, Franklin
Rowe SD PK-6
86 Pond Rd 01367 413-512-5100
John Lev, supt. Fax 339-8621
roweschool.com
Rowe ES PK-6
86 Pond Rd 01367 413-512-5100
William Knittle, prin. Fax 339-8621

Rowley, Essex, Pop. 1,401
Triton Regional SD
Supt. — See Byfield
Pine Grove ES 500/PK-6
191 Main St 01969 978-948-2520
Christine Kneeland, prin. Fax 948-2980

North Shore Montessori S 50/PK-6
121 Wethersfield St 01969 978-948-2237
Margaret Henry, dir.

Roxbury, See Boston
Boston SD
Supt. — See Boston
Ellis ES 300/K-5
302 Walnut Ave 02119 617-635-8257
Cynthia Jacobs, prin. Fax 635-8262
Hale ES 200/PK-5
51 Cedar St 02119 617-635-8205
Romaine Mills-Teque, prin. Fax 635-8558
Haynes Early Education Center 200/PK-1
263 Blue Hill Ave 02119 617-635-6446
Donette Wilson-Wood, prin. Fax 635-9795

Hernandez S 400/PK-8
61 School St 02119 617-635-8187
Ana Tavares, prin. Fax 635-8190
Higginson/Lewis S 400/PK-8
131 Walnut Ave 02119 617-635-8247
Darlene Ratliff, prin. Fax 635-8252
Higginson S 100/K-2
160 Harrishof St 02119 617-635-8909
Marie Mullen, prin. Fax 635-8911
Mason ES 200/PK-5
150 Norfolk Ave 02119 617-635-8405
Lauretta Lewis-Medley, prin. Fax 635-8406
Mendell ES 200/PK-5
164 School St 02119 617-635-8234
Julia Bott, prin. Fax 635-8238
Orchard Gardens S 800/PK-8
906 Albany St 02119 617-635-1660
Megan Webb, prin. Fax 635-1634
Timilty MS 600/6-8
205 Roxbury St 02119 617-635-8109
T'Sheba Martin, prin. Fax 635-8115
Tobin S 400/PK-8
40 Smith St 02120 617-635-8393
Efrain Toledano, prin. Fax 635-7900

OLO Perpetual Help Mission Grammar S 200/PK-8
94 Saint Alphonsus St 02120 617-442-2660
Aliece Dutson, prin. Fax 442-3775
St. Patrick S 200/PK-8
131 Mount Pleasant Ave 02119 617-427-3881
Mary Lanata, prin. Fax 427-4529

Royalston, Worcester
Athol-Royalston SD
Supt. — See Athol
Royalston Community ES 200/K-6
96 Winchendon Rd 01368 978-249-2900
Janeth Williams, prin. Fax 249-4110

Russell, Hampden, Pop. 781
Westfield SD
Supt. — See Westfield
Russell ES 200/K-5
155 Highland Ave 01071 413-572-6505
Alison Hamilton, prin. Fax 572-1396

Rutland, Worcester, Pop. 2,084
Wachusett Regional SD
Supt. — See Jefferson
Central Tree MS 400/6-8
281 Main St 01543 508-886-0073
David Cornacchioli, prin. Fax 886-0141
Glenwood ES 400/3-5
65 Glenwood Rd 01543 508-886-0399
Karen Cappucci, prin. Fax 886-0392
Naquag ES 400/K-2
285 Main St 01543 508-886-2901
Dixie Estes, prin. Fax 886-2803

Sagamore, Barnstable, Pop. 3,546

Bridgeview Montessori S 100/PK-6
PO Box 270 02561 508-888-3567
Sandra Nickerson, prin. Fax 888-4940

Salem, Essex, Pop. 40,441
Salem SD 4,300/PK-12
29 Highland Ave 01970 978-740-1212
Margarita Ruiz, supt. Fax 740-3083
www.salemk12.org
Bates ES 300/K-5
53 Liberty Hill Ave 01970 978-740-1250
Thomas Milaschewski, prin. Fax 740-1255
Bowditch S 600/K-8
79 Willson St 01970 978-740-1290
Jose Munoz, prin. Fax 740-1180
Carlton ES 200/K-5
10 Skerry St 01970 978-740-1280
Bethann Jellison, prin. Fax 740-1283
Collins MS 600/6-8
29 Highland Ave 01970 978-740-1191
Glenn Burns, prin. Fax 740-1183
Mann Laboratory ES 300/K-5
33 Loring Ave 01970 978-542-6220
Dr. Chad Leith, prin. Fax 542-8332
Salem ECC, 25 Memorial Dr 01970 100/PK-PK
Nancy Jean Charest, prin. 978-740-1181
Saltonstall S 400/K-8
211 Lafayette St 01970 978-740-1297
Michael Lister, prin. Fax 740-1288
Witchcraft Heights ES 500/K-5
1 Frederick St 01970 978-740-1271
Leanne Smith, prin. Fax 825-3451

Phoenix S 50/K-8
89 Margin St 01970 978-741-0870
Betsye Sargent, head sch Fax 741-5696

Salisbury, Essex, Pop. 4,794
Triton Regional SD
Supt. — See Byfield
Salisbury ES 500/PK-6
100 Lafayette Rd 01952 978-463-5852
James Montanari, prin. Fax 463-8149

Sandwich, Barnstable, Pop. 2,933
Sandwich SD 1,900/PK-12
33 Water St 02563 508-888-1054
Dr. Pamela A. Gould, supt. Fax 888-9505
www.sandwichk12.org
Other Schools – See East Sandwich, Forestdale

Sandwich Montessori S 50/PK-K
284 Cotuit Rd 02563 508-888-4222

Saugus, Essex, Pop. 26,187
Saugus SD 2,800/PK-12
23 Main St 01906 781-231-5000
David DeRousi, supt. Fax 233-9424
www.saugus.k12.ma.us

Belmonte MS 700/6-8
25 Dow St 01906 781-231-5052
Kerry Robbins, prin. Fax 233-5665
Lynnhurst ES 300/K-5
10 Elm St 01906 781-231-5079
Michael Mondello, prin. Fax 233-9420
Oaklandvale ES 200/K-5
266 Main St 01906 781-231-5082
Eric Jones, prin. Fax 231-5085
Veterans Memorial ES 600/PK-5
39 Hurd Ave 01906 781-231-8166
Tracey Ragucci, prin. Fax 231-8502
Waybright ES 200/PK-5
25 Talbot St 01906 781-231-5087
Kelly Moss, prin. Fax 231-5090

Savoy, Berkshire
Savoy SD 50/PK-5
26 Chapel Rd 01256 413-743-1992
Jon Lev, supt. Fax 743-1114
savoyelementary.com
Miller ES 50/PK-5
26 Chapel Rd 01256 413-743-1992
Cathy Chapman, prin. Fax 743-1114

Scituate, Plymouth, Pop. 5,135
Scituate SD 3,000/PK-12
606 Chief Justice Cushing 02066 781-545-8759
Ron Griffin, supt. Fax 545-6291
www.scituate.k12.ma.us
Cushing ES 400/K-6
1 Aberdeen Dr 02066 781-545-8770
Donna Moffat, prin. Fax 545-8776
Gates MS 500/7-8
327 First Parish Rd 02066 781-545-8760
Ryan Lynch, prin. Fax 545-8767
Hatherly ES 300/K-6
72 Ann Vinal Rd 02066 781-545-8780
Mari-An Fitzmaurice, prin. Fax 545-8786
Jenkins ES 600/K-6
54 Vinal Ave 02066 781-545-4910
Jennifer Arnold, prin. Fax 545-8509
Wampatuck ES 400/PK-6
266 Tilden Rd 02066 781-545-8790
Linda Whitney, prin. Fax 545-8797

Inly S 300/PK-8
46 Watch Hill Dr 02066 781-545-5544
Donna Milani Luther, head sch Fax 545-6522

Seekonk, Bristol, Pop. 13,046
Seekonk SD 2,000/PK-12
25 Water Ln 02771 508-399-5106
Arlene Bosco, supt. Fax 399-5128
seekonk.sharpschool.com/
Aitken ES 400/PK-5
165 Newman Ave 02771 508-336-5230
Nancy Gagliardi, prin. Fax 336-0324
Hurley MS 500/6-8
650 Newman Ave 02771 508-761-7570
Dr. William Whalen, prin. Fax 336-9630
Martin ES 400/PK-5
445 Cole St 02771 508-336-7558
Bart Lush, prin. Fax 336-0309

Sharon, Norfolk, Pop. 5,546
Sharon SD 3,400/K-12
75 Mountain St 02067 781-784-1570
Timothy Farmer, supt. Fax 784-1573
www.sharon.k12.ma.us
Cottage Street ES 500/K-5
30 Cottage St 02067 781-784-1580
Kevin Madden, prin. Fax 784-0374
East ES 400/K-5
45 Wilshire Dr 02067 781-784-1551
Dr. Judy Freedberg, prin. Fax 784-7403
Heights ES 500/K-5
454 S Main St 02067 781-784-1595
Lisa Lamore, prin. Fax 784-1599
Sharon MS 800/6-8
75 Mountain St 02067 781-784-1560
Kevin O'Rourke, prin. Fax 784-8432

Islamic Academy of New England 100/PK-5
84 Chase Dr 02067 781-784-0400
Nurizzah Khalil, prin. Fax 784-3614
Striar Hebrew Academy 100/PK-5
100 Ames St 02067 781-784-8724
Rabbi Yehudah Potok, head sch Fax 793-0654

Sheffield, Berkshire
Southern Berkshire Regional SD 800/PK-12
PO Box 339 01257 413-229-8778
Beth Regulbuto, supt. Fax 229-2913
sbrsd.org
Undermountain ES 300/PK-6
PO Box 326 01257 413-229-8754
Mary Turo, prin. Fax 229-3211
Other Schools – See Mill River, South Egremont

Shelburne Falls, Franklin, Pop. 1,695
Hawlemont Regional SD 100/PK-6
24 Ashfield Rd 01370 413-625-0192
Michael Buoniconti, supt. Fax 625-0196
www.mohawkschools.org
Other Schools – See Charlemont

Mohawk Trail SD 1,000/PK-12
24 Ashfield Rd 01370 413-625-0192
Michael Buoniconti, supt. Fax 625-0196
www.mohawkschools.org
Buckland-Shelburne ES 200/PK-6
75 Mechanic St 01370 413-625-2521
Joanne Giguere, prin. Fax 625-2034
Other Schools – See Ashfield, Charlemont, Colrain

Sherborn, Middlesex
Dover-Sherborn SD
Supt. — See Dover
Pine Hill ES 400/PK-5
10 Pine Hill Ln 01770 508-655-0630
Dr. Barbara Brown, prin. Fax 655-2763

Shirley, Middlesex, Pop. 1,415
Ayer Shirley SD
Supt. — See Ayer
Ayer-Shirley MS 400/6-8
1 Hospital Rd 01464 978-772-8600
Roberta Aikey, prin. Fax 425-0474
White ES 400/PK-5
34 Lancaster Rd 01464 978-772-8600
Varsha Desai, prin. Fax 425-2639

Shrewsbury, Worcester, Pop. 25,900
Shrewsbury SD 6,000/PK-12
100 Maple Ave 01545 508-841-8400
Joseph Sawyer, supt. Fax 841-8490
schools.shrewsbury-ma.gov
Beal ECC 300/K-1
1 Maple Ave 01545 508-841-8860
Christian Girardi, prin. Fax 841-8862
Coolidge ES 400/K-4
1 Florence St 01545 508-841-8880
Amy Clouter, prin. Fax 841-8883
Floral Street ES 800/1-4
57 Floral St 01545 508-841-8720
Lisa McCubrey, prin. Fax 841-8721
Oak MS 1,000/7-8
45 Oak St 01545 508-841-1200
Ann Jones, prin. Fax 841-1223
Parker Road Preschool 300/PK-PK
15 Parker Rd 01545 508-841-8646
Lisa Robinson, dir. Fax 841-8787
Paton ES 300/1-4
58 Grafton St 01545 508-841-8626
Wendy Bell, prin. Fax 841-8627
Sherwood MS 1,000/5-6
28 Sherwood Ave 01545 508-841-8670
Jane Lizotte, prin. Fax 841-8671
Spring Street ES 400/K-4
123 Spring St 01545 508-841-8700
Bryan Mabie, prin. Fax 841-8701

Al Hamra Academy PK-8
435 South St 01545 508-845-7000
Sadia Khan, prin. Fax 845-7002
Lilliput ECC 200/PK-1
18 Grafton St 01545 508-842-0430
St. Mary S 300/PK-8
16 Summer St 01545 508-842-1601
Jeanmarie MacDonough, prin. Fax 845-1535
Shrewsbury Montessori S 200/PK-6
55 Oak St 01545 508-842-2116
Kari Cafeo, head sch Fax 845-2491

Shutesbury, Franklin
Shutesbury SD
Supt. — See Erving
Shutesbury ES 200/PK-6
23 W Pelham Rd 01072 413-259-1212
Jacqueline Mendonsa, prin. Fax 259-1531

Somerset, Bristol, Pop. 17,980
Somerset SD 1,700/PK-8
580 Whetstone Hill Rd 02726 508-324-3100
Jeffrey Schoonover, supt. Fax 324-3104
www.somersetschools.org
Chace Street ES 400/PK-5
538 Chace St 02726 508-324-3160
Timothy Plante, prin. Fax 324-3163
North ES 500/K-5
580 Whetstone Hill Rd 02726 508-324-3170
Dr. Paula Manchester, prin. Fax 324-3174
Somerset MS 600/6-8
1141 Brayton Ave 02726 508-324-3140
Pauline Camara Ph.D., prin. Fax 324-3145
South ES 200/K-5
700 Read St 02726 508-324-3180
Fax 324-3182

Somerville, Middlesex, Pop. 71,913
Somerville SD 4,900/PK-12
8 Bonair St 02145 617-629-5200
Mary Skipper, supt. Fax 629-5661
www.somerville.k12.ma.us
Argenziano S at Lincoln Park 600/PK-8
290 Washington St 02143 617-629-5460
Alexander Mathews, prin. Fax 629-5463
Brown ES 300/K-5
201 Willow Ave 02144 617-629-5620
Shawn Maguire, prin. Fax 625-4258
Capuano ECC 400/PK-K
150 Glen St 02145 617-629-5480
Cheryl Piccirelli, prin. Fax 629-5481
East Somerville Community S 600/K-8
50 Cross St 02145 617-629-5400
Dr. Holly Hatch, prin. Fax 629-5401
Healey S 500/PK-8
5 Meacham St 02145 617-629-5420
Bridget Dowling, prin. Fax 776-5423
Kennedy S 400/K-8
5 Cherry St 02144 617-629-5440
Mark Hurrie, prin. Fax 776-8224
West Somerville Neighborhood S 400/PK-8
177 Powder House Blvd 02144 617-629-5600
Kathleen Seward, prin. Fax 666-7676
Winter Hill Community Innovation S 400/PK-8
115 Sycamore St 02145 617-629-5680
Chad Mazza, prin. Fax 623-8492

St. Catherine of Genoa S 300/PK-8
192 Summer St 02143 617-666-9116
Marian Burns, prin. Fax 623-9161

Southampton, Hampshire
Southampton SD
Supt. — See Westhampton
Norris ES 600/PK-6
34 Pomeroy Meadow Rd 01073 413-527-0811
Aliza Pluta, prin. Fax 527-4795

South Attleboro, See Attleboro
Attleboro SD
Supt. — See Attleboro

Hill-Roberts ES — 500/K-4
80 Roy Ave 02703 — 508-399-7560
Frank Rich, prin. — Fax 399-7284

Dayspring Christian Academy — 300/PK-12
1052 Newport Ave 02703 — 508-761-5552
Rev. Jason Detty, admin. — Fax 761-3577

Southborough, Worcester
Northborough-Southborough SD — 4,600/PK-12
53 Parkerville Rd 01772 — 508-486-5115
Christine Johnson, supt. — Fax 486-5123
www.nsboro.k12.ma.us
Finn ES — 300/PK-1
60 Richards Rd 01772 — 508-485-3176
Clayton Ryan, prin. — Fax 229-4449
Neary ES — 300/4-5
53 Parkerville Rd 01772 — 508-481-2300
Kathleen Valenti, prin. — Fax 229-4460
Trottier MS — 500/6-8
49 Parkerville Rd 01772 — 508-485-2400
Keith Lavoie, prin. — Fax 481-1506
Woodward Memorial S — 300/2-3
28 Cordaville Rd 01772 — 508-229-1250
Steven Mucci, prin. — Fax 229-0623
Other Schools – See Northborough

Fay S — 500/PK-9
48 Main St 01772 — 508-485-0100
Robert J. Gustavson, head sch — Fax 481-7872

South Boston, See Boston
Boston SD
Supt. — See Boston
Condon ES — 800/PK-8
200 D St 02127 — 617-635-8608
Robby Chisolm, prin. — Fax 635-8611
Perkins ES — 200/K-5
50 Burke St 02127 — 617-635-8601
Craig Martin, prin. — Fax 635-9774
Perry S — 300/PK-8
745 E 7th St 02127 — 617-635-8840
Geoffrey Rose, prin. — Fax 635-6387
Tynan ES — 400/PK-5
650 E 4th St 02127 — 617-635-8641
Leslie Gant, prin. — Fax 635-9758

South Boston Catholic Academy — 300/PK-6
866 E Broadway 02127 — 617-268-2326
Nancy Carr, prin. — Fax 268-7269

Southbridge, Worcester, Pop. 13,631
Southbridge SD — 1,600/PK-12
25 Cole Ave 01550 — 508-764-5415
Dr. Russell Johnston, supt. — Fax 764-3181
www.southbridgepublic.org
Charlton Street ES — 500/1-5
220 Charlton St 01550 — 508-764-5475
Judy Maisonet, prin. — Fax 764-5491
Eastford Road ES — 300/PK-2
120 Eastford Rd 01550 — 508-764-5460
Mary Skrzypczak, prin. — Fax 764-5495
Southbridge MS, 132 Torrey Rd 01550 — 6-8
Rebecca Sweetman, prin. — 508-764-5440
West Street ES — 400/1-5
156 West St 01550 — 508-764-5470
Kathleen Cadarette, prin. — Fax 764-5493

Trinity Catholic Academy — 200/PK-8
11 Pine St 01550 — 508-765-5991
Josie Citta, prin. — Fax 765-0017

South Dartmouth, Bristol, Pop. 9,850
Dartmouth SD — 3,700/PK-12
8 Bush St 02748 — 508-997-3391
Dr. Bonny L. Gifford, supt. — Fax 991-4184
dartmouthps.schoolfusion.us/
Cushman ES, 746 Dartmouth St 02748 — 100/PK-K
Melissa McHenry, admin. — 508-996-3926
Demello ES — 400/1-5
654 Dartmouth St 02748 — 508-996-6750
Catherine Pavao, prin. — Fax 990-2519
Other Schools – See North Dartmouth

South Deerfield, Franklin, Pop. 1,861
Conway SD — 200/PK-6
113 N Main St # C-101 01373 — 413-665-1155
Lynn M. Carey Ed.D., supt. — Fax 665-8506
www.frsu38.org
Other Schools – See Conway

Deerfield SD — 400/PK-6
113 N Main St # C-101 01373 — 413-665-1155
Lynn M. Carey, supt. — Fax 665-8506
www.frsu38.org
Deerfield ES — 400/PK-6
21 Pleasant St 01373 — 413-665-1131
Jeanine Heil, prin. — Fax 665-2747

Sunderland SD — 200/PK-6
113 N Main St # C-101 01373 — 413-665-1155
Lynn M. Carey Ed.D., supt. — Fax 665-8506
www.frsu38.org
Other Schools – See Sunderland

Whately SD — 100/PK-6
113 N Main St # C-101 01373 — 413-665-1155
Lynn M. Carey Ed.D., supt. — Fax 665-8506
www.frsu38.org
Other Schools – See Whately

South Dennis, Barnstable, Pop. 3,547
Dennis-Yarmouth SD
Supt. — See South Yarmouth
Wixon MS — 200/4-5
901 Route 134 02660 — 508-398-7695
Sean Owen, prin. — Fax 398-7608

South Easton, Bristol
Easton SD
Supt. — See North Easton
Center S — 300/PK-2
388 Depot St 02375 — 508-230-3233
Ann Weintrob, prin. — Fax 230-3240

South Egremont, Berkshire
Southern Berkshire Regional SD
Supt. — See Sheffield
South Egremont ES — 50/K-1
Main St 01258 — 413-229-8754
Mary Turo, prin. — Fax 528-1430

South Grafton, Worcester, Pop. 2,700
Grafton SD
Supt. — See Grafton
South Grafton ES — 300/PK-1
90 Main St 01560 — 508-839-5484
Doreen Parker, prin. — Fax 839-5432

South Hadley, Hampshire, Pop. 5,400
South Hadley SD — 1,900/PK-12
116 Main St 01075 — 413-538-5060
Dr. Nicholas D. Young, supt. — Fax 532-6284
www.southhadleyschools.org
Mosier ES — 400/2-4
101 Mosier St 01075 — 413-538-5077
David Gallagher, prin. — Fax 538-6922
Plains ES — 300/PK-1
00 Lyman St 01075 — 413-538-5068
Hank Skala, prin. — Fax 538-5803
Smith MS — 600/5-8
100 Mosier St 01075 — 413-538-5074
Paul Goodhind, prin. — Fax 538-5003

South Lancaster, Worcester, Pop. 1,842

South Lancaster Academy — 300/PK-12
PO Box 1129 01561 — 978-368-8544

South Walpole, Norfolk
Walpole SD
Supt. — See Walpole
Boyden ES — 400/K-5
1852 Washington St 02071 — 508-660-7216
Brendan Dearborn, prin. — Fax 660-7217

South Weymouth, Norfolk
Weymouth SD
Supt. — See Weymouth
Hamilton PS — 400/K-4
400 Union St 02190 — 781-335-2122
Jeremy Burm, prin. — Fax 335-3552
Talbot PS — 300/K-4
277 Ralph Talbot St 02190 — 781-335-7250
Nathan Thorsteinson, prin. — Fax 337-8228

St. Francis Xavier S — 400/PK-8
234 Pleasant St 02190 — 781-335-6868
Robert Murphy, prin. — Fax 331-4192

Southwick, Hampden
Southwick-Tolland-Granville Regional SD — 1,200/PK-12
86 Powder Mill Rd 01077 — 413-569-5391
Jennifer Willard, supt. — Fax 569-1711
www.stgrsd.org
Powder Mill S — 200/3-6
94 Powder Mill Rd 01077 — 413-569-5951
Kimberley Saso, prin. — Fax 569-1710
Woodland ES — 300/PK-2
80 Powder Mill Rd 01077 — 413-569-6598
Dr. Amy Fouracre, prin. — Fax 569-1721

South Yarmouth, Barnstable, Pop. 10,789
Dennis-Yarmouth SD — 2,700/PK-12
296 Station Ave 02664 — 508-398-7600
Carol Woodbury, supt. — Fax 398-7622
www.dy-regional.k12.ma.us/
Station Avenue ES — 400/K-3
276 Station Ave 02664 — 508-760-5600
Peter Crowell, prin. — Fax 760-5601
Other Schools – See South Dennis, West Dennis, West Yarmouth

St. Pius X S — 200/PK-8
321 Wood Rd 02664 — 508-398-6112
Anne Dailey, prin. — Fax 398-6113

Spencer, Worcester, Pop. 5,615
Spencer-East Brookfield SD — 1,400/PK-12
306 Main St 01562 — 508-885-8500
Jodi Bourassa, supt. — Fax 885-8504
www.sebrsd.org
Knox Trail JHS — 400/5-8
73 Ash St 01562 — 508-885-8550
Jodi Bourassa, prin. — Fax 885-8557
Wire Village ES — 300/K-4
60 Paxton Rd 01562 — 508-885-8524
Linda Stanelun, prin. — Fax 885-8546
Other Schools – See East Brookfield

Springfield, Hampden, Pop. 149,577
Springfield SD — 27,600/PK-12
1550 Main St 01103 — 413-787-7100
Daniel Warwick, supt. — Fax 787-6713
www.springfieldpublicschools.com
Balliet ES — 300/PK-5
52 Rosewell St 01109 — 413-787-7446
Jennifer Montano, prin. — Fax 787-7531
Beal ES — 200/K-5
285 Tiffany St 01108 — 413-787-7544
Deborah Beglane, prin. — Fax 787-7363
Boland ES — 800/PK-5
426 Armory St 01104 — 413-750-2511
Lisa Bakowski, prin. — Fax 750-2396
Bowles ES — 300/K-5
24 Bowles Park 01104 — 413-787-7334
Jose Escribano, prin. — Fax 750-2885
Bradley ES — 500/K-5
22 Mulberry St 01105 — 413-787-7475
Kristen Hughes, prin. — Fax 750-2214
Brightwood ES — 400/K-5
471 Plainfield St 01107 — 413-787-7238
John Doty, prin. — Fax 787-7477
Brookings ES — 300/PK-5
433 Walnut St 01105 — 413-787-7200
Terry Powe, prin. — Fax 787-7996
Brunton ES — 500/PK-5
1801 Parker St 01128 — 413-787-7444
Martha Stetkiewicz, prin. — Fax 787-7205
Chestnut Academy — 800/6-8
355 Plainfield St 01107 — 413-750-2333
Daniel Sullivan, prin. — Fax 750-2351
Chestnut Accelerated MS Talented & Gift — 6-8
355 Plainfield St 01107 — 413-750-2333
Colleen O'Connor, prin. — Fax 750-2351
DeBerry ES — 300/K-5
670 Union St 01109 — 413-787-7582
Elizabeth Fazio, prin. — Fax 787-6824
Dorman ES — 300/K-5
20 Lydia St 01109 — 413-787-7554
Rhonda Stowell-Lewis, prin. — Fax 787-7771
Dryden Veterans Memorial ES — 300/PK-5
190 Surrey Rd 01118 — 413-787-7248
Sheila Hoffman, prin. — Fax 750-2314
Early Childhood Education Center — PK-PK
15 Catherine St 01109 — 413-750-2640
Rosemarie Waltsak, prin. — Fax 750-2647
Ells ES — 200/PK-1
319 Cortland St 01109 — 413-787-7345
Janet Perez-Vergne, prin. — Fax 787-7344
Forest Park MS — 700/6-8
46 Oakland St 01108 — 413-787-7420
Thomas Mazza, prin. — Fax 787-7419
Freedman ES — 300/K-5
90 Cherokee Dr 01109 — 413-787-7443
Medina Ali, prin. — Fax 750-2367
Gerena ES — 700/PK-5
200 Birnie Ave 01107 — 413-787-7320
Cynthia Escribano, prin. — Fax 750-2661
Glenwood ES — 300/K-5
50 Morison Ter 01104 — 413-787-7527
Martha Cahillane, prin. — Fax 787-7468
Glickman ES — 300/K-5
120 Ashland Ave 01119 — 413-750-2756
Elizabeth Bienia, prin. — Fax 750-2765
Harris ES — 600/PK-5
58 Hartford Ter 01118 — 413-787-7254
Shannon Collins, prin. — Fax 787-7333
Homer Street ES — 400/K-5
43 Homer St 01109 — 413-787-7526
Catherine Roberts, prin. — Fax 750-2752
Impact Program — 6-8
355 Plainfield St 01107 — 413-750-2333
Nathaniel Higgins, prin. — Fax 750-2351
Johnson ES — 800/PK-5
55 Catharine St 01109 — 413-787-6687
Darcia Milner, prin. — Fax 787-6697
Kennedy MS — 600/6-8
1385 Berkshire Ave 01151 — 413-787-7510
Desmond Caldwell, prin. — Fax 787-7561
Kensington International ES — 300/K-5
31 Kensington Ave 01108 — 413-787-7522
Margaret Thompson, prin. — Fax 787-7374
Kiley MS — 700/6-8
180 Cooley St 01128 — 413-787-7240
Christopher Sutton, prin. — Fax 787-7247
Liberty ES — 300/K-5
962 Carew St 01104 — 413-787-7299
Robin Bailey-Sanchez, prin. — Fax 750-2331
Lincoln ES — 400/K-5
732 Chestnut St 01107 — 413-787-7314
Mark McCann, prin. — Fax 787-7364
Lynch ES — 300/K-5
315 N Branch Pkwy 01119 — 413-787-7250
Linda Wilson, prin. — Fax 750-2165
Pottenger ES — 500/K-5
1435 Carew St 01104 — 413-787-7266
Valerie Williams, prin. — Fax 787-7006
South End MS, 36 Margaret St 01105 — 300/6-8
Cheryl Despirt, prin. — 413-750-2442
STEM Middle Academy — 300/6-8
60 Alton St 01109 — 413-787-6750
Luis Martinez, prin. — Fax 787-6952
Sumner Avenue ES — 500/PK-5
45 Sumner Ave 01108 — 413-787-7430
James McCann, prin. — Fax 787-6229
Talmadge ES — 300/K-5
1395 Allen St 01118 — 413-787-7249
Carla Lussier, prin. — Fax 750-2743
Van Sickle Academy — 6-8
1170 Carew St 01104 — 413-750-2887
Robert Francesca, prin. — Fax 750-2972
Van Sickle Academy - Rise — 1,000/6-8
1170 Carew St 01104 — 413-750-2887
Anna Breen, prin. — Fax 750-2972
Walsh ES — 300/K-5
50 Empress Ct 01129 — 413-787-7448
Vinnie Regan, prin. — Fax 750-2171
Warner ES — 300/PK-5
493 Parker St 01129 — 413-787-7258
Dr. Ann Stennett, prin. — Fax 750-2213
Washington ES — 500/PK-5
141 Washington St 01108 — 413-787-7551
Lynda Bianchi, prin. — Fax 787-7742
White Street ES — 400/K-5
300 White St 01108 — 413-787-7543
Kristen Hughes, prin. — Fax 787-7349
Zanetti S — 400/PK-8
474 Armory St 01104 — 413-787-7400
Tara Clark, prin. — Fax 787-7701
Other Schools – See Indian Orchard

Academy Hill S — 100/PK-8
1190 Liberty St 01104 — 413-788-0300
Melissa Earls, head sch — Fax 781-4806
Grace Academy — 50/K-12
60 Bowles Park 01104 — 413-241-7305
Pioneer Valley Christian Academy — 300/PK-12
965 Plumtree Rd 01119 — 413-782-8031
Timothy Duff, hdmstr. — Fax 782-8033
Pioneer Valley Montessori S — 100/PK-6
1524 Parker St 01129 — 413-782-3108
Margaret Bagge, head sch — Fax 782-3109

St. Michael's Academy 200/PK-8
153 Eddywood St 01118 413-782-5246
Ann Dougal, prin. Fax 782-8137
Springfield SDA Jr Academy 50/K-10
PO Box 90127 01139 413-731-2220

Sterling, Worcester
Wachusett Regional SD
Supt. — See Jefferson
Chocksett MS 400/5-8
40 Boutelle Rd 01564 978-422-6552
Christopher LaBreck, prin. Fax 422-7720
Houghton ES 500/K-4
32 Boutelle Rd 01564 978-422-2333
Anthony Cipro, prin. Fax 422-2301

Stockbridge, Berkshire
Berkshire Hills SD 1,400/PK-12
PO Box 617 01262 413-298-4017
Dr. Peter Dillon, supt. Fax 298-4672
www.bhrsd.org
Other Schools – See Great Barrington

Berkshire Country Day S 200/PK-9
55 Interlaken Rd 01262 413-637-0755
Paul Lindenmaier, head sch Fax 637-8927

Stoneham, Middlesex, Pop. 21,118
Stoneham SD 1,900/PK-12
149 Franklin St 02180 781-279-3802
John Macero, supt. Fax 279-3818
www.stonehamschools.org
Colonial Park ES 200/PK-4
30 Avalon Rd 02180 781-279-3890
Sarah Hardy, prin. Fax 279-3892
Hood ES 200/PK-4
70 Oak St 02180 781-279-3870
Maura Donoghue, prin. Fax 438-8697
South ES 200/K-4
11 Summer St 02180 781-279-3880
Sharon Bird, prin. Fax 279-2104
Stoneham MS 600/5-8
101 Central St 02180 781-279-3840
Christopher Banos, prin. Fax 279-3843

Greater Boston Academy 200/PK-12
108 Pond St 02180 781-438-4253
David Branum, prin. Fax 438-6857
St. Patrick S 300/PK-8
20 Pleasant St 02180 781-438-2593
Anthony Fontana, prin. Fax 438-2543

Stoughton, Norfolk, Pop. 27,500
Stoughton SD 3,600/PK-12
232 Pearl St 02072 781-344-4000
Dr. Marguerite C. Rizzi Ed.D., supt. Fax 344-3789
www.stoughtonschools.org/
Dawe ES 400/K-5
131 Pine St 02072 781-344-7007
Robert Cancellieri, prin. Fax 344-8271
Gibbons ES 400/K-5
235 Morton St 02072 781-344-7008
Lynne Jardin, prin. Fax 344-2653
Hansen ES 300/K-5
1800 Central St 02072 781-344-7006
Faye Polillio, prin. Fax 344-4927
Jones ECC 100/PK-PK
137 Walnut St 02072 781-344-7003
Heather Tucker, prin. Fax 344-2782
O'Donnell MS 900/6-8
211 Cushing St 02072 781-344-7002
Matt Colantonio, prin. Fax 297-5263
South ES 300/K-5
171 Ash St 02072 781-344-7004
Maureen Mulvey, prin. Fax 344-2876
West ES 400/PK-5
1322 Central St 02072 781-344-7005
Lisa Whelan, prin. Fax 344-2973

Shaloh House Preschool 50/PK-K
50 Ethyl Way 02072 781-344-6334

Stow, Middlesex
Nashoba Regional SD
Supt. — See Bolton
Center S 600/PK-5
403 Great Rd 01775 978-897-0290
Ross Mulkerin, prin. Fax 897-5739
Hale MS 300/6-8
55 Hartley Rd 01775 978-897-4788
Kyle Grady, prin. Fax 897-3631

Sturbridge, Worcester, Pop. 2,233
Sturbridge SD
Supt. — See Fiskdale
Burgess ES 1,000/PK-6
45 Burgess School Rd 01566 508-347-7041
Kathleen Pelley, prin. Fax 347-8237

Sudbury, Middlesex
Sudbury SD 2,900/PK-8
40 Fairbank Rd Ste C 01776 978-639-3211
Anne Wilson, supt. Fax 443-9001
www.sudbury.k12.ma.us
Curtis MS 1,000/6-8
22 Pratts Mill Rd 01776 978-443-1071
Jeff Mela, prin. Fax 443-1098
Haynes ES 400/K-5
169 Haynes Rd 01776 978-443-1093
Sharon MacDonald, prin. Fax 443-7513
Loring ES 500/K-5
80 Woodside Rd 01776 978-579-0870
Scott Johnson, prin. Fax 579-0890
Nixon ES 400/K-5
472 Concord Rd 01776 978-443-1080
Jennifer LaMontagne, prin. Fax 440-0202
Noyes ES 600/PK-5
280 Old Sudbury Rd 01776 978-443-1085
Annette Doyle, prin. Fax 443-6310

Sunderland, Franklin
Sunderland SD
Supt. — See South Deerfield
Sunderland ES 200/PK-6
1 Swampfield Dr 01375 413-665-1151
Benjamin Barshefsky, prin. Fax 665-4545

Sutton, Worcester
Sutton SD 1,600/PK-12
383 Boston Rd 01590 508-581-1600
Theodore Friend, supt. Fax 865-6463
www.suttonschools.net/
Simonian Center for Early Learning 300/PK-2
409 Boston Rd 01590 508-581-1610
Jessica Merriam, prin. Fax 917-0061
Sutton ES 400/3-5
407 Boston Rd 01590 508-581-1620
Denise Harrison, prin. Fax 865-3628
Sutton MS 400/6-8
383 Boston Rd 01590 508-581-1630
Gerard Goyette, prin. Fax 581-1731

Swampscott, Essex, Pop. 13,607
Swampscott SD 2,200/K-12
207 Forest Ave 01907 781-596-8800
Pamela R. H. Angelakis M.Ed., supt. Fax 599-2502
www.swampscott.k12.ma.us
Clarke ES 200/K-4
100 Middlesex Ave 01907 781-596-8812
Jennifer Hunt, prin. Fax 581-5556
Hadley ES 300/K-4
24 Redington St 01907 781-596-8847
Ilana Bebchick, prin. Fax 596-5298
Stanley ES 300/K-4
10 Whitman Rd 01907 781-596-8837
Thomas Daniels, prin. Fax 592-9500
Swampscott MS 700/5-8
207 Forest Ave 01907 781-596-8820
Jason Calichman M.Ed., prin. Fax 593-2126

Swansea, Bristol
Swansea SD 2,100/PK-12
1 Gardners Neck Rd 02777 508-675-1195
John J. Robidoux, supt. Fax 672-1040
www.swanseaschools.org
Brown ES 300/3-5
29 Gardners Neck Rd 02777 508-675-7892
Wendy Williams, prin. Fax 646-4411
Case JHS 500/6-8
195 Main St 02777 508-675-0116
Robert Silveira, prin. Fax 646-4413
Gardner ES 300/K-2
10 Church St 02777 508-675-7899
Nicholas Overy, prin. Fax 646-4410
Hoyle ES 300/PK-2
70 Community Ln 02777 508-679-4049
William Courville, prin. Fax 646-4407
Luther ES 200/3-5
100 Pearse Rd 02777 508-675-7499
Sean Scanlon M.Ed., prin. Fax 646-4408

Taunton, Bristol, Pop. 53,462
Taunton SD 7,900/PK-12
215 Harris St 02780 508-821-1100
Dr. Julie Hackett, supt. Fax 821-1177
www.tauntonschools.org
Bennett ES 300/K-4
47 N Walker St 02780 508-821-1245
Michael Kelleher, prin. Fax 821-1353
Chamberlain ES 600/K-4
480 Norton Ave 02780 508-821-3216
Rose Schwartz, prin. Fax 821-3877
Friedman MS 800/5-7
500 Norton Ave 02780 508-821-1493
Kathy Perry, prin. Fax 821-3185
Galligan ES 300/K-4
15 Sheridan St 02780 508-821-1295
Anabela Jones, prin. Fax 821-1355
Hopewell ES 300/K-4
16 Monroe St 02780 508-821-1240
Tara Gagnon, prin. Fax 821-1356
Leddy Preschool 300/PK-PK
36 2nd St 02780 508-821-1275
Janet Belanger, prin. Fax 821-1366
Mulcahey ES 500/K-4
28 Clifford St 02780 508-821-1255
Christel Torres, prin. Fax 821-1360
Parker MS 400/5-7
60 Williams St 02780 508-821-1111
Michael Byron, prin. Fax 821-1361
Pole ES 700/K-4
215 Harris St 02780 508-821-1260
Lisa Riendeau, prin. Fax 821-1363
Other Schools – See East Taunton

Our Lady of Lourdes S 100/PK-5
52 1st St 02780 508-822-3746
Lisa Gilbert, prin. Fax 822-1450
St. Mary PS 300/PK-5
106 Washington St 02780 508-822-9480
Michael O'Brien, prin. Fax 822-7164
Villa Fatima Preschool 100/PK-PK
90 County St 02780 508-880-7447
Sr. Elizabeth Hayes, prin. Fax 823-0825

Teaticket, Barnstable, Pop. 1,642
Falmouth SD
Supt. — See East Falmouth
Teaticket ES 300/PK-4
45 Maravista Avenue Ext 02536 508-548-1550
Dr. Debra Pincince, prin. Fax 540-4383

Tewksbury, Middlesex, Pop. 11,000
Tewksbury SD 3,700/PK-12
139 Pleasant St 01876 978-640-7800
Christopher Malone, supt. Fax 640-7804
www.tewksbury.k12.ma.us
Dewing ES 500/PK-2
1469 Andover St 01876 978-640-7858
Mary Gerrish, prin. Fax 640-7862
Heath-Brook ES 400/K-2
165 Shawsheen St 01876 978-640-7865
Felicia Wettstone, prin. Fax 640-7869
North Street ES 300/3-4
133 North St 01876 978-640-7875
Karen Cronin, prin. Fax 640-7879
Ryan ES 600/5-6
135 Pleasant St 01876 978-640-7880
Judi McInnes, prin. Fax 640-7888
Trahan ES 300/3-4
12 Salem Rd 01876 978-640-7870
Matthew Castonguay, prin. Fax 640-7874
Wynn MS 700/7-8
1 Griffin Way 01876 978-640-7846
John Weir, prin. Fax 640-7850

Topsfield, Essex, Pop. 2,684
Topsfield SD
Supt. — See Boxford
Proctor ES 300/4-6
60 Main St 01983 978-887-1530
Sarah O'Leary, prin. Fax 887-1531
Steward ES 300/PK-3
261 Perkins Row 01983 978-887-1538
Carroll Willa, prin. Fax 887-7462

Townsend, Middlesex, Pop. 1,114
North Middlesex SD
Supt. — See Pepperell
Hawthorne Brook MS 500/5-8
64 Brookline St 01469 978-597-6914
Stephen Coughlan, prin. Fax 597-0354
Spaulding Mem ES 500/K-4
1 Whitcomb St 01469 978-597-0380
Becky Janda, prin. Fax 597-0386

Truro, Barnstable
Truro SD 100/PK-6
PO Box 2029 02666 508-487-1558
Michael Gradone, supt. Fax 487-4289
www.truromass.org
Truro Central ES 100/PK-6
PO Box 2029 02666 508-487-1558
Robert Beaudet, prin. Fax 487-4289

Turners Falls, Franklin, Pop. 4,349
Gill-Montague SD 900/PK-12
35 Crocker Ave 01376 413-863-9324
Michael Sullivan, supt. Fax 863-4560
www.gmrsd.org
Hillcrest ES 100/PK-1
30 Griswold St 01376 413-863-9526
Sarah Burstein, prin. Fax 863-3284
Sheffield ES 200/2-5
43 Crocker Ave 01376 413-863-9326
Melissa Pitrat, prin. Fax 863-3259
Other Schools – See Gill, Montague

Tyngsboro, Middlesex
Tyngsborough SD 1,800/PK-12
50 Norris Rd 01879 978-649-7488
Dr. Michael Flanagan, supt. Fax 649-7199
www.tyngsboroughps.org
Tyngsborough ES 900/PK-5
205 Westford Rd 01879 978-649-1990
Kerry Cavanaugh, prin. Fax 649-2004
Tyngsborough MS 500/6-8
50 Norris Rd 01879 978-649-3115
Christopher Pollet, prin. Fax 649-8673

Academy of Notre Dame ES 400/PK-8
180 Middlesex Rd 01879 978-649-7611
Elizabeth O'Connell, prin. Fax 649-2909

Upton, Worcester, Pop. 2,982
Mendon-Upton Regional SD
Supt. — See Mendon
Memorial ES 500/PK-4
69 Main St 01568 508-529-1082
Debra Swain, prin. Fax 529-1909

Uxbridge, Worcester, Pop. 3,400
Uxbridge SD 1,900/PK-12
9 N Main St 01569 508-278-8648
Kevin Carney, supt. Fax 278-8612
uxbridgeschools.com
McCloskey MS 500/6-8
62 Capron St 01569 508-278-8634
Leanne DeMarco, prin. Fax 278-8627
Taft ES 500/PK-2
16 Granite St 01569 508-278-8643
Marla Sirois, prin. Fax 278-8646
Whitin ES 400/3-5
120 Granite St 01569 508-278-8640
Lori Fafard, prin. Fax 278-8639

Our Lady of the Valley S 200/PK-8
75 Mendon St 01569 508-278-5851
Marilyn Willand, prin. Fax 278-0391

Vineyard Haven, Dukes, Pop. 1,950
Martha's Vineyard SD 1,000/K-12
4 Pine St 02568 508-693-2007
Dr. Matthew D'Andrea, supt. Fax 693-3190
www.mvypc.org
Other Schools – See Edgartown

Oak Bluffs SD 400/PK-8
4 Pine St 02568 508-693-2007
Matthew D'Andrea, supt. Fax 693-3190
www.mvyps.org
Other Schools – See Oak Bluffs

Tisbury SD 300/PK-8
4 Pine St 02568 508-693-2007
Matthew D'Andrea, supt. Fax 693-3190
www.tisbury.mvyps.org
Tisbury ES 300/PK-8
PO Box 878 02568 508-696-6500
John Custer, prin. Fax 696-7437

Up-Island Regional SD 300/PK-8
4 Pine St 02568 508-693-2007
Dr. Matthew T. D'Andrea, supt. Fax 693-3190
www.mvyps.org
Other Schools – See Chilmark, West Tisbury

Waban, See Newton
Newton SD
Supt. — See Newtonville
Angier ES 400/K-5
1697 Beacon St 02468 617-559-9300
Loreta Lamberti, prin. Fax 559-2014

Wakefield, Middlesex, Pop. 24,651
Wakefield SD 3,400/PK-12
60 Farm St 01880 781-246-6400
Dr. Kim Smith, supt. Fax 245-9164
wakefieldpublicschools.org
Dolbeare ES 400/K-4
340 Lowell St 01880 781-246-6480
Terence J. Liberti, prin. Fax 246-6372
Doyle S 100/PK-PK
11 Paul Ave 01880 781-246-6420
Shannon Blacker, prin. Fax 246-6422
Galvin MS 1,100/5-8
525 Main St 01880 781-246-6410
Adam Colantuoni, prin. Fax 224-5009
Greenwood ES 300/K-4
1030 Main St 01880 781-246-6460
Deborah Collura, prin. Fax 224-5082
Walton ES 200/1-4
18 Davidson Rd 01880 781-246-6494
Elaina Byrne, prin. Fax 246-6429
Woodville ES 400/K-4
30 Farm St 01880 781-246-6469
Michelle Zottoli, prin. Fax 224-5006

Odyssey Day S 100/PK-8
2 Audubon Rd 01880 781-245-6050
St. Joseph S 200/PK-8
15 Gould St 01880 781-245-2081
Dr. Joseph Sullivan, prin. Fax 245-0084

Wales, Hampden
Wales SD
Supt. — See Fiskdale
Wales ES 200/PK-6
PO Box 247 01081 413-245-7748
Richard Zinkus, prin. Fax 245-4422

Walpole, Norfolk, Pop. 5,864
Walpole SD 4,000/PK-12
135 School St 02081 508-660-7200
Lincoln Lynch Ed.D., supt. Fax 668-1167
www.walpole.k12.ma.us/
Elm Street ES 400/K-5
415 Elm St 02081 508-660-7374
Rebecca Brogadir, prin. Fax 660-7379
Feeney Preschool 100/PK-PK
415 Elm St 02081 508-660-7374
Jennifer Bernard, dir. Fax 660-7379
Fisher ES 500/K-5
65 Gould St 02081 508-660-7234
Colleen Duggan, prin. Fax 660-7233
Johnson MS 400/6-8
111 Robbins Rd 02081 508-660-7242
William Hahn, prin. Fax 660-7240
Other Schools – See East Walpole, South Walpole

Blessed Sacrament S 400/PK-8
808 East St 02081 508-668-2336
Jim Spillman, prin. Fax 668-7944

Waltham, Middlesex, Pop. 59,317
Waltham SD 5,200/PK-12
617 Lexington St 02452 781-314-5400
Drew Echelson Ed.D., supt. Fax 314-5411
www.walthampublicschools.org
Fitzgerald ES 500/K-5
140 Beal Rd 02453 781-314-5680
Jennifer Santillo, prin. Fax 314-5691
Kennedy MS 500/6-8
655 Lexington St 02452 781-314-5560
John Cawley, prin. Fax 314-5571
MacArthur ES 400/K-5
494 Lincoln St 02451 781-314-5720
Jane Gately, prin. Fax 314-5731
McDevitt MS 500/6-8
75 Church St 02452 781-314-5590
Michael Sabin, prin. Fax 314-5601
Northeast ES 500/PK-5
70 Putney Ln 02452 781-314-5740
Mary Ellen Tenaglia, prin. Fax 314-5751
Plympton ES 400/K-5
20 Farnsworth St 02451 781-314-5760
Stephen Duffy, prin. Fax 314-5771
Stanley ES 500/PK-5
250 South St 02453 781-314-5620
Jennifer Hacker, prin. Fax 314-5631
Waltham Dual Language S K-K
510 Moody St 02453 781-314-5701
Catherine Carney, admin.
Whittemore ES 400/K-5
30 Parmenter Rd 02453 781-314-5780
Emma Herzog, prin. Fax 314-5791

Our Lady's Academy 300/PK-8
920 Trapelo Rd 02452 781-899-0353
Chandra Minor, prin. Fax 891-8734
St. Jude S 100/K-8
175 Main St 02453 781-899-3644
Sr. Katherine Caughey, prin. Fax 899-3644

Ware, Hampshire, Pop. 6,031
Ware SD 1,300/PK-12
PO Box 240 01082 413-967-4271
Dr. Marlene DiLeo, supt. Fax 967-9580
www.wareps.org
Koziol ES 500/PK-3
4 Gould Rd 01082 413-967-6236
Pamela Iwasinski, prin. Fax 967-4203

Ware MS 300/4-6
239 West St 01082 413-967-6903
Lisa Candito, prin. Fax 967-3182

Wareham, Plymouth, Pop. 19,232
Wareham SD 2,100/PK-12
48 Marion Rd Ste 302 02571 508-291-3500
Kimberly Shaver-Hood, supt. Fax 291-3578
www.warehamps.org
Decas ES 300/K-2
760 Main St 02571 508-291-3530
Bethany Chandler, prin. Fax 291-3533
Minot Forest ES 200/PK-PK, 3-
63 Minot Ave 02571 508-291-3555
Joan Seamans, prin. Fax 291-3529
Wareham MS 800/5-8
4 Viking Dr 02571 508-291-3550
Peter Steedman, prin. Fax 291-3580

Warren, Worcester, Pop. 1,379
Quaboag Regional SD 1,100/PK-12
PO Box 1538 01083 413-436-9256
Dr. Brett Kustigian, supt. Fax 436-9738
www.quaboagrsd.org
Other Schools – See West Brookfield, West Warren

Warwick, Franklin, Pop. 200
Pioneer Valley SD
Supt. — See Northfield
Warwick Community ES 100/PK-6
41 Winchester Rd 01378 978-544-6310
Elizabeth Musgrave, prin. Fax 544-6356

Watertown, Middlesex, Pop. 30,947
Watertown SD 2,700/PK-12
30 Common St 02472 617-926-7700
Dede Galdston Ed.D., supt. Fax 923-1234
www.watertown.k12.ma.us
Cunniff ES 300/PK-5
246 Warren St 02472 617-926-7726
Mena Ciarlone, prin. Fax 924-0420
Hosmer ES 700/PK-5
1 Concord Rd 02472 617-926-7740
Robert LaRoche, prin. Fax 926-3259
Lowell ES 400/PK-5
175 Orchard St 02472 617-926-7770
Stacy Phelan, prin. Fax 926-2676
Watertown MS 500/6-8
68 Waverley Ave 02472 617-926-7783
James Carter, prin. Fax 926-5407

Atrium S, 69 Grove St 02472 100/PK-8
Marshall Carter, head sch 617-926-4156
JCDS Bostons Jewish Community Day S 200/K-8
57 Stanley Ave 02472 617-972-1733
Dr. Susie Tanchel, head sch Fax 972-1736
St. Stephens Armenian S 200/PK-5
47 Nichols Ave 02472 617-926-6979
Houry Boyamian M.Ed., prin. Fax 923-8299

Wayland, Middlesex, Pop. 2,500
Wayland SD 2,700/K-12
PO Box 408 01778 508-358-3763
Arthur Unobskey, supt. Fax 358-7708
www.wayland.k12.ma.us
Claypit Hill ES 600/K-5
40 Adams Ln 01778 508-358-7401
Dr. Christie Harvey, prin. Fax 358-3793
Happy Hollow ES 400/K-5
63 Pequot Rd 01778 508-358-8641
James Lee, prin. Fax 358-3761
Loker ES 200/K-5
47 Loker St 01778 508-358-8601
Brian Jones, prin. Fax 650-4007
Wayland MS 700/6-8
201 Main St 01778 508-655-6670
Betsy Gavron, prin. Fax 655-2548

Veritas Christian Academy 100/K-8
6 Loker St 01778 508-653-1188
Cynthia Wellman, prin. Fax 653-1180

Webster, Worcester, Pop. 11,152
Webster SD 1,200/PK-12
PO Box 430 01570 508-943-0104
Ruthann Goguen, supt. Fax 949-2364
www.webster-schools.org
Park Avenue ES 500/PK-4
58 Park Ave 01570 508-943-4554
Ginger Coleman, prin. Fax 949-1668
Webster MS 300/5-8
75 Poland St 01570 508-943-1922
Michael Zajac, prin. Fax 949-2648

All Saints Academy St. Anne Campus 100/5-8
12 Day St 01570 508-943-2735
David Grenier, prin. Fax 943-6215
All Saints Academy St. Louis Campus 200/PK-4
48 Negus St 01570 508-943-0257
David Grenier, prin. Fax 461-9666
St. Joseph S 100/PK-8
47 Whitcomb St 01570 508-943-0378
Michael Hackenson, prin. Fax 949-0581

Wellesley, Norfolk, Pop. 27,391
Wellesley SD 5,000/PK-12
40 Kingsbury St 02481 781-446-6200
David Lussier, supt. Fax 446-6207
www.wellesley.k12.ma.us
Bates ES 400/K-5
116 Elmwood Rd 02481 781-446-6260
Toni Jolley, prin. Fax 263-1520
Fiske ES 400/PK-5
45 Hastings St 02481 781-446-6265
Rachel McGregor, prin. Fax 263-1519
Hardy ES 300/K-5
293 Weston Rd 02482 781-446-6270
Charlene Cook, prin. Fax 263-1523
Hunnewell ES 300/K-5
28 Cameron St 02482 781-446-6275
Ellen Quirk, prin. Fax 263-1525

Schofield ES 400/K-5
27 Cedar St 02481 781-446-6280
Gerardo Martinez, prin. Fax 263-1527
Sprague ES 400/K-5
401 School St 02482 781-263-1965
Susan Snyder, prin. Fax 263-1963
Upham ES 200/K-5
35 Wynnewood Rd 02481 781-446-6285
Jeffrey Dees, prin. Fax 263-1507
Wellesley MS 1,200/6-8
50 Kingsbury St 02481 781-446-6235
Mark Ito, prin. Fax 446-6208

Tenacre Country Day S 200/PK-6
78 Benvenue St 02482 781-235-2282
Christian Elliot, head sch Fax 237-7057

Wellesley Hills, Norfolk

St. John the Evangelist S 100/PK-6
9 Ledyard St 02481 781-235-0300
Michael Dibbert, prin. Fax 235-0283

Wellfleet, Barnstable
Wellfleet SD
Supt. — See Orleans
Wellfleet ES 100/PK-5
100 Lawrence Rd 02667 508-349-3101
Mary Beth Rodman, prin. Fax 349-1377

Wenham, Essex, Pop. 4,212
Hamilton-Wenham SD 1,900/PK-12
5 School St 01984 978-468-5310
Dr. Michael M. Harvey, supt. Fax 468-7889
www.hwschools.net/
Buker ES 200/K-5
1 School St 01984 978-468-5324
Brian O'Donoghue, prin. Fax 468-5329
Other Schools – See Hamilton

Notre Dame Children's Class S 50/PK-2
74 Grapevine Rd 01984 978-468-1340
Sr. Barbara Beauchamp, prin. Fax 468-0166

West Barnstable, Barnstable, Pop. 1,508
Barnstable SD
Supt. — See Hyannis
West Barnstable ES 300/K-3
2463 Main St 02668 508-362-4949
Karen Cloutier, prin. Fax 362-1740

Westborough, Worcester, Pop. 3,951
Westborough SD 3,600/PK-12
45 W Main St 01581 508-836-7700
Amber Bock, supt. Fax 836-7704
westborough.ma.schoolwebpages.com
Armstrong ES 400/K-3
50 West St 01581 508-836-7760
John Mendes, prin. Fax 836-7723
Fales ES 300/K-3
50 Eli Whitney St 01581 508-836-7770
Maryann Stannard, prin. Fax 836-7773
Gibbons MS 600/7-8
20 Fisher St 01581 508-836-7740
John Foley, prin. Fax 836-7744
Hastings ES 400/PK-3
111 E Main St 01581 508-836-7750
Leigh Becker, prin. Fax 836-7755
Mill Pond IS 900/4-6
6 Olde Hickory Path 01581 508-836-7780
Suzanne Kenny, prin. Fax 836-7788

West Boylston, Worcester, Pop. 6,611
West Boylston SD 900/PK-12
125 Crescent St 01583 508-835-2917
Elizabeth Schaper, supt. Fax 835-8992
www.wbschools.com
Edwards ES 400/PK-5
70 Crescent St 01583 508-835-4461
Richard Meagher, prin. Fax 835-4119

West Bridgewater, Plymouth
West Bridgewater SD 1,300/PK-12
2 Spring St 02379 508-894-1230
Dr. Patricia Oakley, supt. Fax 894-1232
wbridgewaterschools.org
Howard ES 300/4-6
70 Howard St 02379 508-894-1250
Peggy Spencer, prin. Fax 894-1253
MacDonald ES 200/1-3
1 Steppingstone Dr 02379 508-894-1240
Keitha Goulet, prin. Fax 894-1242
Spring Street S 100/PK-K
2 Spring St Ste 1 02379 508-894-1233
Peggy Spencer, prin. Fax 894-1232

New England Baptist Academy 100/PK-12
560 N Main St 02379 508-584-5188
Kevin Hicks, prin. Fax 584-7555

West Brookfield, Worcester, Pop. 1,397
Quaboag Regional SD
Supt. — See Warren
West Brookfield ES 300/PK-6
89 N Main St 01585 508-867-4655
Colleen Mucha, prin. Fax 867-9208

Warren SDA S 50/K-8
1570 Southbridge Rd 01585 413-436-9245
Angela Walton, prin. Fax 436-9245

West Dennis, Barnstable, Pop. 2,192
Dennis-Yarmouth SD
Supt. — See South Yarmouth
Baker ES 400/PK-3
810 Main St 02670 508-398-7690
Kevin Depin, prin. Fax 398-7693

Westfield, Hampden, Pop. 40,552
Westfield SD 5,700/PK-12
94 N Elm St Ste 201 01085 413-572-6403
Stefan Czaporowski, supt. Fax 572-6518
www.schoolsofwestfield.org
Fort Meadow ECC 200/PK-PK
35 White St 01085 413-572-6422
Joanne Hentnick, prin. Fax 572-6540
Franklin Avenue ES 200/K-5
22 Franklin Ave 01085 413-572-6424
Fran St. Peter-Sanft, prin. Fax 564-3156
Gibbs ES 200/K-5
50 W Silver St 01085 413-572-6418
Stacy Burgess, prin. Fax 572-6446
Highland ES 400/K-5
34 Western Ave 01085 413-572-6428
Mary Claire Manning, prin. Fax 572-6849
Munger Hill ES 400/K-5
33 Mallard Ln 01085 413-572-6520
Salvatore Frieri, prin. Fax 562-0875
North MS 700/6-8
350 Southampton Rd 01085 413-572-6441
Katie Bourque, prin. Fax 572-1669
Paper Mill ES 500/K-5
148 Paper Mill Rd 01085 413-572-6519
Cynthia Kennedy, prin. Fax 572-0687
Southampton Road ES 400/K-5
330 Southampton Rd 01085 413-572-6435
Kathy O'Donnell, prin. Fax 572-6873
South MS 600/6-8
30 W Silver St 01085 413-568-1900
Fax 572-4892
Other Schools – See Russell

St. Mary's Parish ES 200/PK-8
35 Bartlett St 01085 413-568-2388
Nichole Nietsche, head sch Fax 568-7460

Westford, Middlesex
Westford SD 5,200/PK-12
23 Depot St 01886 978-692-5560
Everett Olsen, supt. Fax 392-4497
westfordk12.us/
Abbot S 400/3-5
25 Depot St 01886 978-692-5580
Kathleen Huntley, prin. Fax 692-9587
Blanchard MS 600/6-8
14 West St 01886 978-692-5582
Timothy Hislop, prin. Fax 692-5598
Crisafulli ES 400/3-5
13 Robinson Rd 01886 978-392-4483
Sharon Kennelly, prin. Fax 392-8581
Day ES 400/3-5
75 E Prescott St 01886 978-692-5591
Chris Louis Sardella, prin. Fax 692-8476
Millennium Preschool 100/PK-PK
23 Depot St 01886 978-692-5565
Courtney Moran, prin Fax 392-4497
Miller ES 300/K-2
1 Mitchell Way 01886 978-392-4476
Donna Pobuk, prin. Fax 692-5502
Nabnasset S 300/K-2
99 Plain Rd 01886 978-692-5583
Susan DuBois, prin. Fax 392-9618
Robinson S 300/K-2
60 Concord Rd 01886 978-692-5586
Kevin LaCoste, prin. Fax 692-5133
Stony Brook MS 700/6-8
9 Farmers Way 01886 978-692-2708
Christopher Chew, prin. Fax 692-5391

Westhampton, Hampshire
Chesterfield-Goshen SD 200/PK-6
19 Stage Rd 01027 413-527-7200
Craig Jurgensen, supt. Fax 529-9497
hr-k12.org
Other Schools – See Chesterfield

Southampton SD 600/PK-6
19 Stage Rd 01027 413-527-7200
Dr. Craig Jurgensen, supt. Fax 529-9497
www.hr-k12.org
Other Schools – See Southampton

Westhampton SD 100/PK-6
19 Stage Rd 01027 413-527-7200
Dr. Craig Jurgensen, supt. Fax 529-9497
www.westhamptonelementaryschool.org
Westhampton ES 100/PK-6
37 Kings Hwy 01027 413-527-0561
Deane Bates, prin. Fax 529-9753

Williamsburg SD 100/PK-6
19 Stage Rd 01027 413-527-7200
Dr. Craig Jurgensen, supt. Fax 529-9497
www.burgy.org/Pages/WilliamsburgMA_Schools/index
Other Schools – See Williamsburg

Worthington SD PK-6
19 Stage Rd 01027 413-527-7200
Dr. Craig Jurgensen, supt. Fax 529-9497
www.hr-k12.org
Other Schools – See Worthington

Westminster, Worcester
Ashburnham-Westminster Regional SD
Supt. — See Ashburnham
Meetinghouse ES 200/K-1
8 South St 01473 978-874-0163
Patricia Marquis, prin. Fax 874-7305
Westminster ES 400/2-5
9 Academy Hill Rd 01473 978-874-2043
Patricia Marquis, prin. Fax 874-7308

Wachusett Hills Christian S 50/1-8
100 Colony Rd 01473 978-874-6432
Edie Conrad, prin.

West Newbury, Essex
Pentucket SD 2,800/PK-12
22 Main St 01985 978-363-2280
Jeffrey Mulqueen, supt. Fax 363-1165
www.prsd.org
Page ES 400/PK-6
694 Main St Ste 7 01985 978-363-2672
Dustin Gray, prin. Fax 363-2234
Pentucket Regional MS 500/7-8
20 Main St 01985 978-363-2957
Kenneth Kelley, prin. Fax 363-2720
Other Schools – See Groveland, Merrimac

West Newton, See Newton
Newton SD
Supt. — See Newtonville
Franklin ES 400/K-5
125 Derby St 02465 617-559-9500
Joel Jocelyn, prin. Fax 552-5521
Peirce ES 300/K-5
170 Temple St 02465 617-559-9630
Mark Chitty, prin. Fax 552-7318

Fessenden S 500/PK-9
250 Waltham St 02465 617-630-2300
David Stettler, hdmstr. Fax 630-2303

Weston, Middlesex, Pop. 10,200
Weston SD 2,300/PK-12
89 Wellesley St 02493 781-786-5200
Dr. Marguerite Connolly, supt. Fax 786-5209
www.westonschools.org
Country ES 300/PK-3
2 Alphabet Ln 02493 781-786-5400
Erin Maguire, prin. Fax 786-5409
Field ES 400/4-5
16 Alphabet Ln 02493 781-786-5500
Joseph Russo, prin. Fax 786-5509
Weston MS 500/6-8
456 Wellesley St 02493 781-786-5600
John Gibbons, prin. Fax 786-5609
Woodland ES 300/PK-3
10 Alphabet Ln 02493 781-786-5300
Jennifer Faber, prin. Fax 786-5309

Meadowbrook S of Weston 300/PK-8
10 Farm Rd 02493 781-894-1193
Arvind Grover, hdmstr. Fax 894-0557

West Peabody, Essex

Covenant Christian Academy 200/PK-12
83 Pine St 01960 978-535-7100
Andrea Bergstrom, head sch Fax 535-7123

Westport, Bristol, Pop. 13,852
Westport Community SD 800/PK-12
17 Main Rd 02790 508-636-1140
Dr. Ann Marie Dargon Ed.D., supt. Fax 636-1146
www.westportschools.org
Macomber PS 200/PK-2
154 Gifford Rd 02790 508-678-8671
Carolyn Pontes, prin. Fax 673-4284
Westport ES 200/3-6
380 Old County Rd 02790 508-636-1075
Thomas Gastall, prin. Fax 636-1077

Montessori S of the Angels 100/PK-8
PO Box 1570 02790 508-636-0200
Alice Marie Levesque, prin. Fax 636-7200

West Roxbury, See Boston
Boston SD
Supt. — See Boston
Beethoven ES 300/K-2
5125 Washington St 02132 617-635-8149
Edward Puliafico, prin. Fax 635-8155
Kilmer S 500/PK-8
35 Baker St 02132 617-635-8060
Emily Berman, prin. Fax 635-8063
Lyndon S 600/PK-8
20 Mount Vernon St 02132 617-635-6824
Kathleen Tunney, prin. Fax 635-6828
Ohrenberger S 600/3-8
175 W Boundary Rd 02132 617-635-8157
Naomi Krakow, prin. Fax 635-8163

Holy Name S 500/PK-6
535 W Roxbury Pkwy 02132 617-325-9338
Jeanne Caulfield, prin. Fax 325-7885
St. Theresa of Avila S 300/PK-8
40 Saint Theresa Ave 02132 617-323-1050
Jean Leahy, prin. Fax 323-8118

West Springfield, Hampden, Pop. 27,989
West Springfield SD 3,700/PK-12
26 Central St Ste 33 01089 413-263-3289
Michael Richard M.Ed., supt. Fax 739-8748
www.wsps.org
Ashley K 200/PK-K
88 Massasoit Ave 01089 413-263-3323
Kathleen Bailer, prin. Fax 827-0404
Coburn ES 400/1-5
115 Southworth St 01089 413-263-3363
Shelly St. George, prin. Fax 781-2604
Fausey ES 400/1-5
784 Amostown Rd 01089 413-263-3314
Myriam Ulloa-Skolnick, prin Fax 781-6973
Memorial ES 200/1-5
201 Norman St 01089 413-263-3333
Donna Calabrese, prin. Fax 747-5535
Mittineague ES 200/1-5
26 2nd St 01089 413-263-3327
Diane Doe, prin. Fax 739-1718
Tatham ES 200/1-5
61 Laurel Rd 01089 413-263-3330
Paul Heath, prin. Fax 739-1587
West Springfield MS 900/6-8
31 Middle School Dr 01089 413-263-3406
Peter Gillen, prin. Fax 781-0965

St. Thomas Apostle S 400/PK-8
75 Pine St 01089 413-739-4131
Sr. Patricia Hottin, prin. Fax 731-8768

West Tisbury, Dukes
Up-Island Regional SD
Supt. — See Vineyard Haven
West Tisbury S 300/PK-8
PO Box 250 02575 508-696-7738
Donna Lowell-Bettencourt, prin. Fax 696-7739

West Warren, Worcester
Quaboag Regional SD
Supt. — See Warren
Warren Community ES 500/PK-6
51 Schoolhouse Dr 01092 413-436-5983
Stephen Duff, prin. Fax 436-9743

Westwood, Norfolk, Pop. 12,557
Westwood SD 3,200/PK-12
220 Nahatan St 02090 781-326-7500
Emily Parks, supt. Fax 326-8154
www.westwood.k12.ma.us
Deerfield ES 300/K-5
72 Deerfield Ave 02090 781-326-7500
Joshua Baumer, prin. Fax 320-0189
Downey ES 300/PK-5
250 Downey St 02090 781-326-7500
Debra Gallagher, prin. Fax 329-7642
Hanlon ES 200/K-5
790 Gay St 02090 781-326-7500
Sarah Cronin, prin. Fax 326-2702
Jones ES 300/K-5
80 Martha Jones Rd 02090 781-326-7500
Donna Tobin, prin. Fax 255-9277
Sheehan ES 400/K-5
549 Pond St 02090 781-326-7500
Kristen Evans, prin. Fax 769-8046
Thurston MS 800/6-8
850 High St 02090 781-326-7500
Zeffro Gianetti, prin. Fax 326-2709
Westwood Integrated Preschool 50/PK-PK
200 Nahatan St 02090 781-326-7500
Aprile Albertelli, dir. Fax 461-9782

West Yarmouth, Barnstable, Pop. 5,701
Dennis-Yarmouth SD
Supt. — See South Yarmouth
Mattacheese MS 500/6-7
400 Higgins Crowell Rd 02673 508-778-7979
Ann Knell, prin. Fax 778-7987
Small ES 300/PK-3
440 Higgins Crowell Rd 02673 508-778-7975
Patrick Riley, prin. Fax 778-4456

Weymouth, Norfolk, Pop. 53,900
Weymouth SD 6,800/PK-12
111 Middle St 02189 781-335-1460
Jennifer Curtis-Whipple, supt. Fax 335-8777
www.weymouthschools.org
Academy Avenue PS 300/K-4
94 Academy Ave 02189 781-335-4717
Patrick Higgins, prin. Fax 340-2514
Murphy PS 300/K-4
417 Front St 02188 781-331-2862
Patrick Costello, prin. Fax 340-2517
Nash PS 200/K-4
1003 Front St 02190 781-340-2506
Rebecca Kelly, prin. Fax 340-2534
Pingree PS 300/K-4
1250 Commercial St 02189 781-337-2974
Kathleen Guilfoy, prin. Fax 340-2518
Seach PS 400/K-4
770 Middle St 02188 781-335-7589
Nancy Schuhwerk, prin. Fax 335-3098
Other Schools – See East Weymouth, North Weymouth, South Weymouth

First Baptist Christian S 100/PK-8
40 West St 02190 781-335-6232
Elaine Allshouse, admin. Fax 335-7901
Sacred Heart S 300/PK-8
75 Commercial St 02188 781-335-6010
Christopher Beza, prin. Fax 331-7936
South Shore Christian Academy 300/PK-12
45 Broad St 02188 781-331-4340
Dr. Mark Jennings, head sch Fax 331-9956

Whately, Franklin
Whately SD
Supt. — See South Deerfield
Whately ES 100/PK-6
PO Box 158 01093 413-665-7826
Peter Crisafulli, prin. Fax 665-0128

Whitinsville, Worcester, Pop. 6,595
Northbridge SD 2,600/PK-12
87 Linwood Ave 01588 508-234-8156
Dr. Catherine Stickney, supt. Fax 234-8469
www.nps.org/
Balmer ES 600/2-4
21 Crescent St 01588 508-234-8161
Karlene Ross, prin. Fax 234-0808
Northbridge ES 500/PK-1
30 Cross St 01588 508-234-6346
Jill Healy, prin. Fax 234-8499
Northbridge MS 800/5-8
171 Linwood Ave 01588 508-234-8718
John Zywien, prin. Fax 234-9718

Whitinsville Christian S 500/PK-12
279 Linwood Ave 01588 508-234-8211
Lance Engbers, hdmstr. Fax 234-0624

Whitman, Plymouth, Pop. 13,240
Whitman-Hanson SD 4,200/PK-12
610 Franklin St 02382 781-618-7000
Ruth Gilbert-Whitner Ed.D., supt. Fax 618-7099
www.whrsd.org

Conley ES 600/K-5
100 Forest St 02382 781-618-7050
Karen Downey, prin. Fax 618-7092
Duval ES 600/K-5
60 Regal St 02382 781-618-7055
Julie McKillop, prin. Fax 618-7096
Whitman MS 600/6-8
100 Corthell Ave 02382 781-618-7035
George Ferro, prin. Fax 618-7091
Other Schools – See Hanson

Wilbraham, Hampden, Pop. 3,882
Hampden-Wilbraham SD 3,300/PK-12
621 Main St 01095 413-596-3884
Albert G. Ganem, supt. Fax 599-1328
www.hwrsd.org
Mile Tree ES 300/PK-1
625 Main St 01095 413-596-6921
Joanne Wilson, prin. Fax 596-9319
Soule Road ES 300/4-5
300 Soule Rd 01095 413-596-9311
Lisa Curtin, prin. Fax 599-1742
Stony Hill ES 300/2-3
675 Stony Hill Rd 01095 413-599-1950
Monique Dangleis, prin. Fax 596-4497
Wilbraham MS 600/6-8
466 Stony Hill Rd 01095 413-596-9061
Peter Dufresne, prin. Fax 596-9382
Other Schools – See Hampden

Williamsburg, Hampshire
Williamsburg SD
Supt. — See Westhampton
Dunphy ES 100/PK-6
1 Petticoat Hill Rd 01096 413-268-8421
Stacey Jenkins, prin. Fax 268-8420

Williamstown, Berkshire, Pop. 4,791
Mt. Greylock Regional SD / S Union 71 1,200/PK-12
1781 Cold Spring Rd 01267 413-458-9582
Kimberley Grady, supt. Fax 458-2856
www.wlschools.org
Williamstown ES 400/PK-6
115 Church St 01267 413-458-5707
Joelle Brookner, prin. Fax 458-3287
Other Schools – See Lanesboro

Pine Cobble S 100/PK-9
163 Gale Rd 01267 413-458-4680
Susannah Wells, head sch Fax 458-8174

Wilmington, Middlesex, Pop. 22,011
Wilmington SD 3,500/PK-12
161 Church St 01887 978-694-6000
Paul Ruggiero, supt. Fax 694-6005
wpsk12.com
Boutwell Early Education Center 200/PK-K
17 Boutwell St 01887 978-694-6070
Kristen Walsh, prin. Fax 694-6009
North IS 300/4-5
320 Salem St 01887 978-694-6040
Christine McMenimen, prin. Fax 694-6043
Shawsheen ES 400/1-3
298 Shawsheen Ave 01887 978-694-6030
Lisa King, prin. Fax 694-6036
West IS 300/4-5
22 Carter Ln 01887 978-694-6050
Dennis Shaw, prin. Fax 694-6052
Wildwood Early Education Center 200/PK-K
182 Wildwood St 01887 978-694-6010
Charlotte King, dir. Fax 694-6008
Wilmington MS 900/6-8
25 Carter Ln 01887 978-694-6080
Kevin Welch, prin. Fax 694-6085
Woburn Street ES 400/1-3
227 Woburn St 01887 978-694-6020
Jeffrey Strasnick, prin. Fax 694-6014

Abundant Life Christian S 200/PK-8
173 Church St 01887 978-657-8710
Kristen Jones, admin. Fax 658-2739

Winchendon, Worcester, Pop. 4,143
Winchendon SD 1,300/PK-12
175 Grove St 01475 978-616-1450
Steven Haddad, supt. Fax 297-5250
www.winchendonk12.org
Memorial S 300/PK-2
32 Elmwood Rd 01475 978-297-1305
Michelle Therrien, prin. Fax 297-3944
Murdock MS 400/6-8
3 Memorial Dr 01475 978-297-1256
Jessica Vezina, prin. Fax 297-0509
Toy Town ES 300/3-5
175 Grove St 01475 978-297-2005
Mary Alice Aker, prin. Fax 297-3011

Winchester, Middlesex, Pop. 20,931
Winchester SD 4,400/PK-12
40 Samoset Rd 01890 781-721-7004
Judith Evans, supt. Fax 721-0016
www.winchester.k12.ma.us
Ambrose ES 500/K-5
27 High St 01890 781-721-7012
Leigh Petrowsky, prin. Fax 721-5605
Lincoln ES 400/K-5
161 Mystic Valley Pkwy 01890 781-721-2296
Kelly Clough, prin. Fax 721-7040
Lynch ES 500/PK-5
10 Brantwood Rd 01890 781-721-7013
John Dupuis, prin. Fax 721-4480
McCall MS 1,100/6-8
458 Main St 01890 781-721-7026
Jorge Goncalves, prin. Fax 721-0886
Muraco ES 400/K-5
33 Bates Rd 01890 781-721-7030
Leslie West, prin. Fax 721-0244
Vinson-Owen ES 400/K-5
75 Johnson Rd 01890 781-721-7019
Grant Smith, prin. Fax 721-2681

St. Mary S 200/PK-5
162 Washington St 01890 781-729-5515
Michael McCabe, prin. Fax 729-1352

Winthrop, Suffolk, Pop. 18,127
Winthrop SD 2,000/PK-12
1 Metcalf Sq 02152 617-846-5500
Lisa Howard, supt. Fax 539-0891
www.winthrop.k12.ma.us
Cummings ES 500/3-5
40 Hermon St 02152 617-846-5543
Ryan Heraty, prin. Fax 846-6559
Gorman-Ft. Banks ES 500/PK-2
101 Kennedy Rd 02152 617-846-5509
Ilene Pearson, prin. Fax 539-0271
Winthrop MS, 60 Payson St 02152 500/6-8
Brian Curley, prin. 617-846-5507

Woburn, Middlesex, Pop. 37,207
Woburn SD 4,800/PK-12
55 Locust St 01801 781-937-8233
Mark Donovan, supt. Fax 937-0668
www.edline.net/pages/WPS
Altavesta ES 200/K-5
990 Main St 01801 781-937-8235
Wendy Sprague, prin. Fax 937-8273
Goodyear ES 300/K-5
41 Central St 01801 781-937-8236
Kenneth Kessaris, prin. Fax 937-8272
Hurld ES 200/K-5
75 Bedford Rd 01801 781-937-8238
Eileen Mills, prin. Fax 937-8270
Joyce MS 600/6-8
55 Locust St 01801 781-937-8233
Thomas Qualey, prin. Fax 937-8279
Kennedy MS 600/6-8
41 Middle St 01801 781-937-8230
Carl Nelson, prin. Fax 937-8223
Linscott-Rumford ES 200/K-5
86 Elm St 01801 781-937-8239
Ernie Wells, prin. Fax 937-8269
Reeves ES 500/PK-5
240 Lexington St 01801 781-937-8240
Bobbie Finocchio, prin. Fax 937-8268
Shamrock ES 300/PK-5
60 Green St 01801 781-937-8241
Wayne Clark, prin. Fax 937-8267
White ES 300/K-5
36 Bow St 01801 781-937-8242
Kara Martyny, prin. Fax 937-8266
Wyman ES 200/K-5
679 Main St 01801 781-937-8243
Kristen Maloney, prin. Fax 937-8265

St. Charles S 200/PK-8
8 Myrtle St 01801 781-935-4635
Cara Blanchette, prin. Fax 935-3121

Wollaston, See Quincy
Quincy SD
Supt. — See Quincy
Wollaston ES 300/PK-5
205 Beale St 02170 617-984-8791
James Hennessy, prin. Fax 984-8629

Worcester, Worcester, Pop. 175,487
Worcester SD 23,800/PK-12
20 Irving St 01609 508-799-3115
Maureen Binienda, supt. Fax 799-3119
worcesterschools.org
Belmont Street Community ES 500/PK-6
170 Belmont St 01605 508-799-3588
Susan Hodgkins, prin. Fax 799-8204
Burncoat MS 600/7-8
135 Burncoat St 01606 508-799-3390
Lisa Houlihan, prin. Fax 799-8207
Burncoat Street Preparatory S 200/K-6
526 Burncoat St 01606 508-799-3537
Deborah Catamero, prin. Fax 799-8205
Canterbury Street Magnet ES 300/PK-6
129 Canterbury St 01603 508-799-3484
Mary Sealey, prin. Fax 799-8208
Chandler Community ES 400/PK-6
114 Chandler St 01609 508-799-3572
Jessica Boss, prin. Fax 799-8209
Chandler Magnet ES 400/PK-6
525 Chandler St 01602 508-799-3452
Ivonne Perez, prin. Fax 799-8210
City View ES 600/PK-6
80 Prospect St 01605 508-799-3670
Yeu Kue, prin. Fax 799-3521
Clark Street Developmental Learning S 300/PK-6
280 Clark St 01606 508-799-3545
Fjodor Dukaj, prin. Fax 799-8212
Columbus Park Preparatory Academy 500/PK-6
75 Lovell St 01603 508-799-3490
Siobhan Dennis, prin. Fax 799-8213
Elm Park Community ES 500/PK-6
23 N Ashland St 01609 508-799-3568
Ellen Kelley, prin. Fax 799-8216
Flagg Street ES 400/K-6
115 Flagg St 01602 508-799-3522
Mary Labuski, prin. Fax 799-8217
Forest Grove MS 1,000/7-8
495 Grove St 01605 508-799-3420
Kareem Tatum, prin. Fax 799-8218
Gates Lane S of International Studies 700/PK-6
1238 Main St 01603 508-799-3488
Ann Swenson, prin. Fax 799-8219
Goddard Science Technical ES 500/PK-6
14 Richards St 01603 508-799-3594
Karrie Allen, prin. Fax 799-8258
Grafton Street ES 400/PK-6
311 Grafton St 01604 508-799-3478
Tina Schimer, prin. Fax 799-8222
Heard Street Discovery Academy 300/K-6
200 Heard St 01603 508-799-3525
Thomas Brindisi, prin. Fax 799-8226
Hiatt Magnet ES 500/PK-6
772 Main St 01610 508-799-3601
Jyoti Datta, prin. Fax 799-8261
Lake View ES 300/K-6
133 Coburn Ave 01604 508-799-3536
Maureen Power, prin. Fax 799-8228
Lincoln Street ES 300/PK-6
549 Lincoln St 01605 508-799-3504
Shannon Conley, prin. Fax 799-8229
May Street ES 300/K-6
265 May St 01602 508-799-3520
Luke Robert, prin. Fax 799-8230
McGrath ES 300/PK-6
493 Grove St 01605 508-799-3584
Paula Gibb-Severin, prin. Fax 799-8235
Midland Street ES 200/K-6
18 Midland St 01602 508-799-3548
Michele Wilson, prin. Fax 799-8231
Nelson Place ES 500/K-6
35 Nelson Pl 01605 508-799-3506
Monica Poitras, prin. Fax 799-8257
Norrback Avenue ES 600/PK-6
44 Malden St 01606 508-799-3500
Christina Troiano, prin. Fax 799-8234
Quinsigamond ES 800/PK-6
14 Blackstone River Rd 01607 508-799-3502
Debbie Mitchell, prin. Fax 799-3517
Rice Square ES 400/K-6
76 Massasoit Rd 01604 508-799-3556
Susan Donahue, prin. Fax 799-8240
Roosevelt ES 700/PK-6
1006 Grafton St 01604 508-799-3482
Kelly Williamson, prin. Fax 799-8241
Sullivan MS 800/7-8
140 Apricot St 01603 508-799-3350
Dr. Josephine Robertson, prin. Fax 799-8244
Tatnuck Magnet ES 400/PK-6
1083 Pleasant St 01602 508-799-3554
Erin Dobson, prin. Fax 799-8245
Thorndyke Road ES 300/PK-6
30 Thorndyke Rd 01606 508-799-3550
Kathleen Lee, prin. Fax 799-8246
Union Hill ES 500/PK-6
1 Chapin St 01604 508-799-3600
Ish Tabales, prin. Fax 799-8247
Vernon Hill ES 500/PK-6
211 Providence St 01607 508-799-3630
Craig Dottin, prin. Fax 799-8248
Wawecus Road ES 200/K-6
20 Wawecus Rd 01605 508-799-3527
Joanna Loftus, prin. Fax 799-8249
West Tatnuck ES 400/PK-6
300 Mower St 01602 508-799-3596
Ellen Moynihan, prin. Fax 799-8250
Worcester Arts Magnet ES 400/PK-6
315 Saint Nicholas Ave 01606 508-799-3575
Mary Ellen Scanlon, prin. Fax 799-8243
Worcester East MS 700/7-8
420 Grafton St 01604 508-799-3430
Dr. Rose Dawkins, prin. Fax 799-8251

Alhuda Academy 100/PK-8
248 E Mountain St 01606 508-854-4700
Sawsan Berjawi, prin. Fax 854-4711
Bancroft S 500/PK-12
110 Shore Dr 01605 508-854-9227
James P. Cassidy, head sch Fax 853-7824
Nativity S of Worcester 5-8
67 Lincoln St 01605 508-799-0100
Sean Dillon, prin. Fax 799-3951
Our Lady Angels S 300/PK-8
1220 Main St 01603 508-752-5609
Doreen Albert, prin. Fax 798-9634
St. Marys ES 100/PK-6
50 Richland St 01610 508-753-0484
Adam Cormier, prin. Fax 795-0560
St. Peter Central S 400/PK-8
865 Main St 01610 508-791-6496
Meg Kursonis, prin. Fax 770-0818
St. Stephen S 200/PK-8
355 Grafton St 01604 508-755-3209
Joanne Mallozzi, prin. Fax 770-1052
Venerini Academy 300/PK-8
23 Edward St 01605 508-753-3210
Carolyn Polselli, prin. Fax 754-6050
Worcester SDA S, 2 Airport Dr 01602 50/1-8
Tina Jones, prin. 508-753-4732

Worthington, Hampshire
Worthington SD
Supt. — See Westhampton
Conwell ES, 147 Huntington Rd 01098 PK-6
Gretchen Morse-Dobosz, prin. 413-238-5856

Wrentham, Norfolk
Wrentham SD 1,100/PK-6
120 Taunton St 02093 508-384-5430
Dr. Allan Cameron Ph.D., supt. Fax 384-5444
www.wrentham.k12.ma.us
Delaney ES 700/PK-3
120 Taunton St 02093 508-384-5430
Colleen Wagstaff M.Ed., prin. Fax 384-5445
Roderick ES 500/4-6
120 Taunton St 02093 508-384-5435
Dr. Vanessa Beauchaine Ed.D., prin. Fax 384-5446

MICHIGAN

MICHIGAN DEPARTMENT OF EDUCATION
608 W Allegan St, Lansing 48933-1524
Telephone 517-373-3324
Fax 517-335-4565
Website http://www.michigan.gov/mde

Superintendent of Public Instruction Brian Whiston

MICHIGAN BOARD OF EDUCATION
608 W Allegan St, Lansing 48933-1524

President Dr. Cassandra Ulbrich

INTERMEDIATE SCHOOL DISTRICTS (ISD)

Allegan Area ESA
William Brown, supt. 269-512-7700
310 Thomas St, Allegan 49010 Fax 512-7701
www.alleganaesa.org/

Alpena-Montmorency-Alcona ESD
Scott Reynolds, supt. 989-354-3101
2118 US Highway 23 S Fax 356-3385
Alpena 49707
www.amaesd.org

Barry ISD
Richard Franklin, supt. 269-945-9545
535 W Woodlawn Ave Fax 945-2575
Hastings 49058
www.barryisd.org

Bay-Arenac ISD
Deborah Kadish, supt. 989-686-4410
4228 2 Mile Rd, Bay City 48706 Fax 667-3286
www.baisd.net

Berrien RESA
Dr. Kevin Ivers, supt. 269-471-7725
PO Box 364, Berrien Springs 49103 Fax 471-2941
www.berrienresa.org

Branch ISD
Joseph Lopez, supt. 517-279-5730
370 Morse St, Coldwater 49036 Fax 279-5766
www.branch-isd.org

Calhoun ISD
Terance Lunger, supt. 269-781-5141
17111 G Dr N, Marshall 49068 Fax 781-7071
www.calhounisd.org

Charlevoix-Emmet ISD
Jeffrey Crouse, supt. 231-547-9947
8568 Mercer Rd, Charlevoix 49720 Fax 547-5621
www.charemisd.org

Cheboygan-Otsego-Presque Isle ISD
Mary Vratanina, supt. 231-238-9394
6065 Learning Ln Fax 238-8551
Indian River 49749
www.copesd.org/

Clare-Gladwin RESD
Sheryl Presler, supt. 989-386-3851
4041 E Mannsiding Rd Fax 386-3238
Clare 48617
www.cgresd.net/

Clinton County RESA
Dr. Wayne Petroelje, supt. 989-224-6831
1013 S US Highway 27 Ste A Fax 224-9574
Saint Johns 48879
www.ccresa.org

C.O.O.R. ISD
Greg Bush, supt. 989-275-9555
PO Box 827, Roscommon 48653 Fax 275-5881
www.coorisd.net

Copper Country ISD
George Stockero, supt. 906-482-4250
809 Hecla St, Hancock 49930 Fax 487-5915
www.copperisd.org

Delta-Schoolcraft ISD
Doug Leisenring, supt. 906-786-9300
2525 3rd Ave S, Escanaba 49829 Fax 786-9318
www.dsisd.net

Dickinson-Iron ISD
Wendy Warmuth, supt. 906-779-2690
1074 Pyle Dr, Kingsford 49802 Fax 779-2669
www.diisd.org

Eastern Upper Peninsula ISD
Dr. Daniel Reattoir, supt. 906-632-3373
315 Armory Pl Fax 632-1125
Sault Sainte Marie 49783
www.eup.k12.mi.us

Eaton RESA
Cindy Anderson, supt. 517-543-5500
1790 Packard Hwy Fax 543-6633
Charlotte 48813
www.eatonresa.org

Genesee ISD
Lisa Hagel, supt. 810-591-4400
2413 W Maple Ave, Flint 48507 Fax 591-7570
www.geneseeisd.org

Gogebic-Ontonagon ISD
Bruce F. Mayle, supt. 906-575-3438
PO Box 218, Bergland 49910 Fax 575-3373
www.goisd.org/

Gratiot-Isabella RESD
Jan Amsterburg, supt. 989-875-5101
PO Box 310, Ithaca 48847 Fax 875-7531
www.giresd.net/

Hillsdale ISD
Ronna Steel, supt. 517-437-0990
310 W Bacon St, Hillsdale 49242 Fax 439-4388
www.hillsdale-isd.org

Huron ISD
Joseph Murphy, supt. 989-269-6406
1299 S Thomas Rd Ste 1 Fax 269-9218
Bad Axe 48413
www.huronisd.org

Ingham ISD
Dr. Scott Koenigsknecht, supt. 517-676-1051
2630 W Howell Rd, Mason 48854 Fax 676-4930
www.inghamisd.org

Ionia County ISD
Jason Mellema, supt. 616-527-4900
2191 Harwood Rd, Ionia 48846 Fax 527-4731
www.ioniaisd.org

Iosco RESA
Dana McGrew, supt. 989-362-3006
27 N Rempert Rd Fax 362-9076
Tawas City 48763
www.ioscoresa.net/

Jackson County ISD
Kevin Oxley, supt. 517-768-5200
6700 Browns Lake Rd Fax 787-2026
Jackson 49201
www.jcisd.org

Kalamazoo RESA
David Campbell, supt. 269-250-9200
1819 E Milham Ave, Portage 49002 Fax 250-9205
www.kresa.org

Kent ISD
Ron Caniff, supt., 2930 Knapp St NE 616-364-1333
Grand Rapids 49525 Fax 364-1488
www.kentisd.org

Lapeer County ISD
Steven Zott, supt. 810-664-5917
1996 W Oregon St, Lapeer 48446 Fax 664-1011
www.lcisd.k12.mi.us

Lenawee ISD
Mark Haag, supt. 517-265-2119
4107 N Adrian Hwy, Adrian 49221 Fax 265-9875
www.lisd.us

Lewis Cass ISD
Brent Holcomb, supt. 269-445-6204
61682 Dailey Rd, Cassopolis 49031 Fax 445-2981
www.lewiscassisd.org

Livingston ESA
R. Michael Hubert, supt. 517-546-5550
1425 W Grand River Ave Fax 546-7047
Howell 48843
www.livingstonesa.org/

Macomb ISD
Michael DeVault, supt. 586-228-3300
44001 Garfield Rd Fax 286-1523
Clinton Township 48038
www.misd.net

Manistee ISD
Jeff Jennette, supt. 231-723-4264
772 E Parkdale Ave Fax 398-3036
Manistee 49660
www.manistee.org

Marquette-Alger RESA
Deborah Veiht, supt. 906-226-5100
321 E Ohio St, Marquette 49855 Fax 226-5134
www.maresa.org

Mecosta-Osceola ISD
Dr. Mark Klumpp, supt. 231-796-3543
15760 190th Ave Fax 796-3300
Big Rapids 49307
www.moisd.org

Menominee ISD
Michele Lemire, supt. 906-863-5665
1201 41st Ave, Menominee 49858 Fax 863-7776
www.mc-isd.org

Midland County ESA
John Searles, supt. 989-631-5890
3917 Jefferson Ave, Midland 48640 Fax 631-4361
www.midlandesa.org

Montcalm Area ISD
Ron Simon, supt. 989-831-5261
PO Box 367, Stanton 48888 Fax 831-8727
www.maisd.com

Muskegon Area ISD
Dr. John Severson, supt. 231-777-2637
630 Harvey St, Muskegon 49442 Fax 767-7299
www.muskegonisd.org

Newaygo County RESA
Lori Clark, supt. 231-924-0381
4747 W 48th St, Fremont 49412 Fax 924-8910
www.ncresa.org

Oakland ISD
Dr. Wanda Cook-Robinson, supt. 248-209-2000
2111 Pontiac Lake Rd Fax 209-2206
Waterford 48328
www.oakland.k12.mi.us

Ottawa Area ISD
Peter Haines, supt. 616-738-8940
13565 Port Sheldon St Fax 738-8946
Holland 49424
www.oaisd.org

Saginaw ISD
Kathy Stewart, supt. 989-399-7473
3933 Barnard Rd, Saginaw 48603 Fax 793-1571
www.sisd.cc

St. Clair County RESA
Dr. Kevin Miller, supt. 810-364-8990
PO Box 1500, Marysville 48040 Fax 364-7474
www.sccresa.org

St. Joseph County ISD
Dr. Teresa Belote, supt. 269-467-5400
62445 Shimmel Rd Fax 467-4309
Centreville 49032
www.sjcisd.org

Sanilac ISD
Duane Lange Ph.D., supt. 810-648-4700
175 E Aitken Rd, Peck 48466 Fax 648-5784
www.sanilac.k12.mi.us

Shiawassee RESD
David Schulte, supt. 989-743-3471
1025 N Shiawassee St Fax 743-6477
Corunna 48817
www.sresd.org

Traverse Bay Area ISD
Michael Hill, supt. 231-922-6200
1101 Red Dr, Traverse City 49684 Fax 922-6270
www.tbaisd.org

Tuscola ISD
Eugene Pierce, supt. 989-673-2144
1385 Cleaver Rd, Caro 48723 Fax 673-5366
www.tuscolaisd.org/

Van Buren ISD
Jeffrey Mills, supt. 269-674-8091
490 S Paw Paw St Fax 674-8030
Lawrence 49064
www.vbisd.org

Washtenaw ISD
Scott Menzel, supt. 734-994-8100
PO Box 1406, Ann Arbor 48106 Fax 994-2203
washtenawisd.org

Wayne RESA
Randy Liepa, supt. 734-334-1300
33500 Van Born Rd, Wayne 48184 Fax 334-1760
www.resa.net

West Shore ESD
Randy Howes, supt. 231-757-3716
2130 W US Highway 10 Fax 757-2406
Ludington 49431
www.wsesd.org

Wexford-Missaukee ISD
Jeff Jennette, supt. 231-876-2260
9907 E 13th St, Cadillac 49601 Fax 876-2261
www.wmisd.org

PUBLIC, PRIVATE AND CATHOLIC ELEMENTARY SCHOOLS

Ada, Kent
Forest Hills SD
Supt. — See Grand Rapids
Ada ES 400/PK-4
731 Ada Dr SE 49301 616-493-8940
Kimberly Van Antwerp, prin. Fax 493-8947
Ada Vista ES 500/K-4
7192 Bradfield Ave SE 49301 616-493-8970
Jesus Santillan, prin. Fax 493-8979
Central MS 600/7-8
5810 Ada Dr SE 49301 616-493-8750
Charlie Vonk, prin. Fax 493-8764
Central Woodlands 5/6 S 500/5-6
400 Alta Dale Ave SE 49301 616-493-8790
Amy Burton-Major, prin. Fax 493-8795
Eastern MS 400/7-8
2200 Pettis Ave NE 49301 616-493-8850
David Washburn, prin. Fax 493-8839
Goodwillie Environmental 5/6 S 100/5-6
8400 2 Mile Rd NE 49301 616-493-8633
David Washburn, prin. Fax 682-1428

Ada Christian S 500/PK-8
6206 Ada Dr SE 49301 616-676-1289
Melissa Brower, prin. Fax 676-9216
St. Patrick S 100/PK-8
4333 Parnell Ave NE 49301 616-691-8833
Scott Czarnopys, prin. Fax 691-6309

Addison, Lenawee, Pop. 592
Addison Community SD 700/K-12
219 N Comstock St 49220 517-547-6901
Steven Guerra, supt. Fax 547-3838
www.addisonschools.org
Addison ES 400/K-5
219 N Comstock St 49220 517-547-6912
Kathee Santiago, prin. Fax 547-6942
Addison MS 100/6-8
219 N Comstock St 49220 517-547-6951
Julie Yeider, prin. Fax 547-6982

Adrian, Lenawee, Pop. 20,608
Adrian SD 3,000/PK-12
785 Riverside Ave Ste 1 49221 517-263-2115
Robert Behnke, supt. Fax 265-5381
www.theadrianmaples.com
Alexander ES 400/PK-5
520 Cherry St 49221 517-263-9533
Mike Perez, prin. Fax 265-3633
Lincoln ES 300/PK-5
158 S Scott St 49221 517-265-8544
Sam Skeels, prin. Fax 265-8923
Michener ES 300/PK-5
104 Dawes Ave 49221 517-263-9002
Ann Lacasse, prin. Fax 265-9296
Prairie ES 200/K-5
2568 Airport Rd 49221 517-265-5082
Shanan Henline, prin. Fax 265-8310
Springbrook MS 500/6-8
615 Springbrook Ave 49221 517-263-0543
Nate Parker, prin. Fax 265-5984

Madison SD 1,500/PK-12
3498 Treat Hwy 49221 517-263-0741
Ryan Rowe, supt. Fax 265-5635
www.madisonk12.us
Madison ES 800/PK-5
3498 Treat Hwy 49221 517-263-0744
Abby Miller, prin. Fax 265-1849
Madison MS 400/6-8
3498 Treat Hwy 49221 517-263-0743
Brad Anschuetz, prin. Fax 265-1848

Tecumseh SD
Supt. — See Tecumseh
Tecumseh South Early Learning Center 300/PK-1
2780 Sutton Rd 49221 517-423-2367
Meghan Way, prin. Fax 423-1302

Lenawee Christian S 600/PK-12
111 Wolf Creek Hwy 49221 517-265-7590
Michael Crafts, head sch Fax 266-8934
St. Stephen Lutheran S 100/PK-8
632 S Madison St 49221 517-263-1775
Neil Neumann, prin. Fax 265-5605

Akron, Tuscola, Pop. 392
Akron-Fairgrove SD
Supt. — See Fairgrove
Akron-Fairgrove ES 100/K-5
4335 Lynn St 48701 989-691-5141
Rebecca Crosby, prin. Fax 691-1022

Alanson, Emmet, Pop. 721
Alanson SD 300/K-12
7400 North St 49706 231-548-2261
Dean Paul, supt. Fax 548-2132
www.alansonvikings.net
Alanson ES 200/K-5
7400 North St 49706 231-548-2261
Dean Paul, admin. Fax 548-2165
Alanson MS 100/6-8
7400 North St 49706 231-548-2261
Dean Paul, admin. Fax 548-2165

Albion, Calhoun, Pop. 8,323
Marshall SD
Supt. — See Marshall
Harrington ES, 100 S Clark 49224 PK-5
Sandra Kingston, prin. 517-629-9421

Algonac, Saint Clair, Pop. 4,051
Algonac Community SD 900/PK-12
5200 Taft Rd 48001 810-794-9364
Dr. Alan Latosz, supt. Fax 794-0040
algonac.k12.mi.us
Algonquin ES 200/2-6
9185 Marsh Rd 48001 810-794-9317
Brooklynn Lestage, prin. Fax 794-8872
Millside ES 100/K-1
1904 Mill St 48001 810-794-8880
Melissa Hanners, prin. Fax 794-8870
Pointe Tremble ECC PK-PK
9541 Phelps Rd 48001 810-794-3022
Douglas Bishop, dir. Fax 794-8867

Allegan, Allegan, Pop. 4,893
Allegan SD 2,600/PK-12
550 5th St 49010 269-673-5431
Kevin Harness, supt. Fax 673-5463
www.alleganps.org/
Dawson ES, 125 Elm St 49010 300/PK-5
Erin Hafer, prin. 269-673-6925
North Ward ES, 440 River St 49010 300/K-5
Becky Corbett, prin. 269-673-6003
Pine Trails ES, 2950 Center St 49010 300/K-5
Jaym Abraham, prin. 269-673-5379
West Ward ES, 630 Vernon St 49010 300/K-5
Harry Dalm, prin. 269-673-7000
White MS, 3300 115th Ave 49010 600/6-8
James Antoine, prin. 269-673-2241

Allendale, Ottawa, Pop. 17,229
Allendale SD 2,500/PK-12
10505 Learning Ln 49401 616-892-5570
Dr. Garth Cooper, supt. Fax 895-6690
www.allendale.k12.mi.us
Allendale MS 500/6-8
7161 Pleasant View Ct 49401 616-892-5595
Rocky Thompson, prin. Fax 895-9111
Evergreen ES 800/PK-3
10690 Learning Ln 49401 616-892-3465
Rinard Pugh, prin. Fax 892-5798
Oakwood IS 400/4-5
10505 Learning Ln 49401 616-892-3475
Doug Bol, prin. Fax 892-5517

Allendale Christian S 200/PK-8
11050 64th Ave 49401 616-895-5108
Brian Koetje, admin. Fax 895-5109

Allen Park, Wayne, Pop. 27,848
Allen Park SD 3,700/K-12
9601 Vine Ave 48101 313-827-2100
Michael H. Darga, supt. Fax 827-2151
www.apps.k12.mi.us
Allen Park MS 900/6-8
8401 Vine Ave 48101 313-827-2200
Mark Lowe, prin. Fax 827-2251
Arno ES 500/K-5
7500 Fox Ave 48101 313-827-1050
Stephen Zielinski, prin. Fax 827-1085
Bennie ES 400/K-5
17401 Champaign Rd 48101 313-827-1300
Sara Metzger, prin. Fax 827-1342
Lindemann ES 600/K-5
9201 Carter Ave 48101 313-827-1150
Theresa Brown, prin. Fax 827-1185

Melvindale-Northern Allen Park SD
Supt. — See Melvindale
Rogers ES 400/K-1
5000 Shenandoah Ave 48101 313-277-5400
Lisa Tafelski, prin. Fax 277-5405

Inter City Baptist S 300/K-12
4700 Allen Rd 48101 313-928-6900
Jim Hubbard Ed.D., admin. Fax 928-7310
Montessori Children's Center 200/PK-5
4141 Laurence Ave 48101 313-382-2777
Jane Adams, prin. Fax 382-4838
St. Francis Cabrini S 500/K-8
15300 Wick Rd 48101 313-928-6610
Kimberly Young, prin. Fax 928-8502

Alma, Gratiot, Pop. 9,259
Alma SD 2,100/PK-12
1500 Pine Ave 48801 989-463-3111
Donalynn Ingersoll, supt. Fax 466-2943
www.almaschools.net
Hillcrest ES 300/2-3
515 E Elizabeth St 48801 989-463-3111
John Helinski, prin. Fax 466-2852
Luce Road ECC 300/PK-1
6265 N Luce Rd 48801 989-463-3111
Cassie Thelen, prin. Fax 466-6087
Pavlik MS 500/6-8
1700 Pine Ave 48801 989-463-3111
Wade Slavik, prin. Fax 466-7612
Pine Avenue ES 400/4-5
1025 Pine Ave 48801 989-463-3111
LaDawn Showers, prin. Fax 466-5038

St. Mary S 100/PK-6
220 W Downie St 48801 989-463-4579
Lisa Seeley, prin. Fax 463-8297

Almont, Lapeer, Pop. 2,651
Almont Community SD 1,500/K-12
4701 Howland Rd 48003 810-798-8561
William Kalmar, supt. Fax 798-2367
www.almontschools.org
Almont MS 500/5-8
4624 Kidder Rd 48003 810-798-3578
Kimberly VonHiltmayer, prin. Fax 673-9349
Orchard PS 500/K-4
4664 Kidder Rd 48003 810-798-7019
Jennifer Szlachta, prin. Fax 798-3530

Alpena, Alpena, Pop. 10,337
Alpena SD 3,900/K-12
2373 Gordon Rd 49707 989-358-5040
Dr. John VanWagoner, supt. Fax 358-5041
www.alpenaschools.com
Besser ES 300/K-5
375 Wilson St 49707 989-358-5100
Eric Cardwell, prin. Fax 358-5105
Hinks ES 200/K-5
7667 US Highway 23 N 49707 989-358-5560
Sharon Miller, prin. Fax 358-5565
Lincoln ES 100/K-5
309 W Lake St 49707 989-358-5900
Hans Stevens, prin. Fax 358-5905
Thunder Bay JHS 1,000/6-8
3500 S Third Ave 49707 989-358-5400
Steve Genschaw, prin. Fax 358-5499
White ES 400/K-5
201 N Ripley Blvd 49707 989-358-5950
Melissa LaCombe, prin. Fax 358-5955
Other Schools – See Herron, Ossineke

All Saints Catholic S 100/PK-8
500 N Second Ave 49707 989-354-4911
Roger Pauley, prin. Fax 354-3752
Immanuel Lutheran S 100/PK-8
355 Wilson St 49707 989-354-4805
Eric Frisco M.Ed., prin. Fax 358-1102

Alto, Kent
Caledonia Community SD
Supt. — See Caledonia
Kettle Lake ES 400/K-5
8451 Garbow Dr SE 49302 616-868-6113
Sean McLaughlin, prin. Fax 868-0021

Lowell Area SD
Supt. — See Lowell
Alto ES 500/K-5
6150 Bancroft Ave SE 49302 616-987-2600
Paul Papes, prin. Fax 987-2611

Ann Arbor, Washtenaw, Pop. 109,999
Ann Arbor SD 16,000/PK-12
PO Box 1188 48106 734-994-2200
Dr. Jeanice Swift, supt. Fax 994-2414
www.a2schools.org
Abbot ES 300/K-5
2670 Sequoia Pkwy 48103 734-994-1901
Pamela Sica, prin. Fax 994-4717
Allen ES 400/K-5
2560 Towner Blvd 48104 734-997-1210
Kerry Beal, prin. Fax 997-1257
Angell ES 300/K-5
1608 S University Ave 48104 734-994-1907
Gary Court, prin. Fax 994-8938
Ann Arbor Preschool 100/PK-PK
2775 Boardwalk St 48104 734-994-2303
Michelle Pogliano, prin. Fax 994-2895
Bach ES 400/K-5
600 W Jefferson St 48103 734-994-1949
Alison Epler, prin. Fax 994-8239
Bryant ES 300/K-2
2150 Santa Rosa Dr 48108 734-997-1212
Kathy Morhous, prin. Fax 997-1231
Burns Park ES 400/K-5
1414 Wells St 48104 734-994-1919
Charles Hatt, prin. Fax 994-1548
Carpenter ES 400/K-5
4250 Central Blvd 48108 734-997-1214
Michael Johnson, prin. Fax 997-1226
Clague MS 700/6-8
2616 Nixon Rd 48105 734-994-1976
Che' Carter, prin. Fax 994-1645
Dicken ES 400/K-5
2135 Runnymede Blvd 48103 734-994-1928
Michael Madison, prin. Fax 997-1884
Eberwhite ES 300/K-5
800 Soule Blvd 48103 734-994-1934
William Harris, prin. Fax 996-3014
Forsythe MS 700/6-8
1655 Newport Rd 48103 734-994-1985
Angela Newing, prin. Fax 994-5749
Haisley ES 400/K-5
825 Duncan St 48103 734-994-1937
Kelly House, prin. Fax 994-1371
King ES 400/K-5
3800 Waldenwood Dr 48105 734-994-1940
Mary Cooper, prin. Fax 997-1258
Lakewood ES 300/K-5
344 Gralake Ave 48103 734-994-1953
Edward Latour, prin. Fax 997-1952
Lawton ES 400/K-5
2250 S 7th St 48103 734-994-1946
Shannon Blick, prin. Fax 994-2597
Logan ES 300/K-5
2685 Traver Blvd 48105 734-994-1807
Will Wright, prin. Fax 994-1473
Mitchell ES 300/K-5
3550 Pittsview Dr 48108 734-997-1216
Kevin Karr, prin. Fax 997-1228
Northside ES 200/K-8
912 Barton Dr 48105 734-994-1958
Megan Fenech, prin. Fax 997-1232
Pattengill ES 300/3-5
2100 Crestland St 48104 734-994-1961
Melita Alston, prin. Fax 994-1276
Pittsfield ES 200/K-5
2543 Pittsfield Blvd 48104 734-997-1218
Carol Shakarian, prin. Fax 997-1229
Scarlett MS 500/6-8
3300 Lorraine St 48108 734-997-1220
Gerald Vazquez, prin. Fax 997-1885
Slauson MS 800/6-8
1019 W Washington St 48103 734-994-2004
Lisa Anglin, prin. Fax 994-1681
Tappan MS 700/6-8
2251 E Stadium Blvd 48104 734-994-2011
Dr. Roberta Heyward, prin. Fax 997-1873
Thurston ES 400/K-5
2300 Prairie St 48105 734-994-1970
Natasha York, prin. Fax 994-1742
Wines ES 400/K-5
1701 Newport Rd 48103 734-994-1973
David DeYoung, prin. Fax 996-3023

Ann Arbor Adventist ES 50/1-8
2796 Packard St 48108 734-971-5570
Doreen King, prin. Fax 929-0820
Ann Arbor Christian S 100/PK-8
5500 Whitmore Lake Rd 48105 734-741-4948
Wayne Sit, head sch Fax 929-6629
Clonlara S 50/K-12
1289 Jewett St 48104 734-769-4511
Daycroft Montessori PS 50/PK-K
100 Oakbrook Dr 48104 734-930-0333
Dr. Seth Kopald, head sch Fax 930-0312
Daycroft Montessori S 100/K-8
1095 N Zeeb Rd 48103 734-662-3335
Dr. Seth Kopald, head sch Fax 662-3360
Doughty Montessori S 50/PK-K
416 S Ashley St 48103 734-663-8050
Emerson S 400/K-8
5425 Scio Church Rd 48103 734-665-5662
John Huber, head sch Fax 665-8126
Go Like the Wind S 200/PK-9
3540 Dixboro Ln 48105 734-747-7422
Colleen Carlson, head sch Fax 747-6560
Hebrew Day S of Ann Arbor 100/K-5
2937 Birch Hollow Dr 48108 734-971-4633
Michigan Islamic Academy 200/PK-12
2301 Plymouth Rd 48105 734-665-8882
Sr. Fayzeh Madani, prin. Fax 665-9058
St. Francis of Assisi S 400/PK-8
2270 E Stadium Blvd 48104 734-821-2200
Julie Fantone-Pritzel, prin. Fax 821-2202
St. Paul Lutheran S 300/PK-8
495 Earhart Rd 48105 734-665-0604
Bob Burgess, prin. Fax 665-7809
St. Thomas the Apostle S 300/PK-8
540 Elizabeth St 48104 734-769-0911
Timothy DiLaura, prin. Fax 769-9078
Spiritus Sanctus Academy 200/PK-8
4101 E Joy Rd 48105 734-996-3855
Sr. John Dominic, prin. Fax 996-4270
Steiner S of Ann Arbor 200/PK-8
2775 Newport Rd 48103 734-995-4141
Dr. Sian Owen-Cruise, admin. Fax 995-4383
Summers-Knoll S 100/PK-8
2203 Platt Rd 48104 734-971-7991
Walter Landberg, head sch Fax 971-9663

Armada, Macomb, Pop. 1,714
Armada Area SD 1,700/PK-12
74500 Burk St 48005 586-784-2112
Michael Musary, supt. Fax 784-4268
www.armadaschools.org
Armada MS 500/6-8
23550 Armada Center Rd 48005 586-784-2500
Todd Schafer, prin. Fax 784-8650
Krause ES 400/PK-5
23900 Armada Center Rd 48005 586-784-2600
Kurt Sutton, prin. Fax 784-9147

Arnold, Marquette
Wells Township SD 50/K-8
PO Box 108 49819 906-238-4200
Luann Lohfink, admin. Fax 238-4200
www.wellstownshipschool.org
Wells Township S 50/K-8
PO Box 108 49819 906-238-4200
Luann Lohfink, admin. Fax 238-4200

Ashley, Gratiot, Pop. 562
Ashley Community SD 300/PK-12
PO Box 6 48806 989-847-4000
Jeffrey Rohrer, supt. Fax 847-3500
www.ashleyschools.net/
Ashley ES 100/PK-4
PO Box 6 48806 989-847-2102
Jeffrey Rohrer, supt. Fax 847-4204
Ashley MS 100/5-8
PO Box 6 48806 989-846-2514
Traci Gavenda, prin. Fax 847-4204

Atlanta, Montmorency, Pop. 815
Atlanta Community SD 300/K-12
PO Box 619 49709 989-785-4877
Carl Seiter, supt. Fax 785-2611
www.atlantaschools.us
Atlanta Community S 300/K-12
PO Box 619 49709 989-785-4877
Carl Seiter, prin. Fax 785-2611

Atlantic Mine, Houghton
Stanton Township SD 100/K-8
50870 Holman School Rd 49905 906-482-2797
James Rautiola, supt. Fax 487-5928
www.stanton.k12.mi.us
Holman S 100/K-8
50870 Holman School Rd 49905 906-482-2797
James Rautiola, prin. Fax 487-5928

Auburn, Bay, Pop. 2,077
Bay City SD
Supt. — See Bay City
Auburn ES 600/K-5
301 E Midland Rd 48611 989-662-4921
Stephen Sevener, prin. Fax 662-2205
Forest ECC 50/PK-PK
2169 W Midland Rd 48611 989-496-3430
Sheri Zimmerman, prin. Fax 496-0221
Western MS 900/6-8
500 W Midland Rd 48611 989-662-4489
Amy Bailey, prin. Fax 662-0185

Auburn Area Catholic S 100/PK-5
114 W Midland Rd 48611 989-662-6431
Jessica Reder, prin. Fax 662-3391
Zion Lutheran S 100/PK-8
1557 Seidlers Rd 48611 989-662-4264
Colett Dominowski, admin. Fax 662-7052

Auburn Hills, Oakland, Pop. 20,778
Avondale SD 3,400/K-12
2940 Waukegan St 48326 248-537-6000
Dr. James V. Schwarz, supt. Fax 537-6005
www.avondaleschools.org
Auburn ES 400/K-5
2900 Waukegan St 48326 248-537-6500
Fax 537-6505
Graham ES 400/K-5
2450 Old Salem Rd 48326 248-537-6800
Tony Harris, prin. Fax 537-6805
Other Schools – See Rochester Hills, Troy

Pontiac SD
Supt. — See Pontiac
Rogers ES 400/K-6
2600 Dexter Rd 48326 248-451-7850
Arlee Ewing, prin. Fax 451-7862

Auburn Hills Christian S 200/PK-12
PO Box 214386 48321 248-373-3399
Scott Wickson, prin. Fax 409-2786
Oakland Christian S 700/PK-12
3075 Shimmons Rd 48326 248-373-2700
Roy Townsend, prin. Fax 373-9255

Au Gres, Arenac, Pop. 875
Au Gres-Sims SD 500/PK-12
PO Box 648 48703 989-876-7150
Jeffrey Collier, supt. Fax 876-6752
www.ags-schools.org
Au Gres-Sims ES 200/PK-5
PO Box 648 48703 989-876-7157
Chad Zeien, prin. Fax 876-4684
Au Gres-Sims MS 200/6-8
PO Box 648 48703 989-876-7157
Chad Zeien, prin. Fax 876-4684

Augusta, Kalamazoo, Pop. 868
Galesburg-Augusta Community SD
Supt. — See Galesburg
Galesburg-Augusta MS 300/5-8
750 W Van Buren St 49012 269-484-2020
Shana Wiese, prin. Fax 731-4138

St. Ann Catholic S 50/PK-PK
12648 E D Ave 49012 269-731-4721
Carrie Jewett, admin. Fax 731-4147

Avoca, Saint Clair
Yale SD
Supt. — See Yale
Avoca ES 300/K-5
PO Box 365 48006 810-324-2660
Therese Damman, prin. Fax 324-2843

Bad Axe, Huron, Pop. 3,092
Bad Axe SD 1,100/K-12
200 N Barrio Rd Ste 100 48413 989-269-9938
Gregory Newland, supt. Fax 269-2739
www.badaxeps.org/
Bad Axe ES 300/K-3
404 Hatchet Dr 48413 989-269-2736
Sharon Brighton, prin. Fax 803-9097
Bad Axe JHS 300/4-7
750 S Van Dyke Rd 48413 989-269-2735
Peter Batzer, prin. Fax 269-9001

Church SD 50/K-8
2927 Crockard Rd 48413 989-269-7772
Joseph Murphy, supt. Fax 269-3022
www.huroncountyruralschools.com/church/
Church S 50/K-8
2927 Crockard Rd 48413 989-269-7772
Joseph Murphy, prin. Fax 269-3022

Colfax Township SD 1F 50/K-8
1509 N Van Dyke Rd 48413 989-269-8853
Joseph Murphy, supt. Fax 269-7245
www.huroncountyruralschools.com
Big Burning S 50/K-8
1509 N Van Dyke Rd 48413 989-269-8853
Joseph Murphy, admin. Fax 269-7245

Sigel Township SD 3 50/K-8
4151 Section Line Rd 48413 989-269-8944
Joseph Murphy, supt. Fax 269-8937
www.huroncountyruralschools.com
Adams ES 50/K-8
4151 Section Line Rd 48413 989-269-8944
Joseph Murphy, lead tchr. Fax 269-8937

Verona Mills SD 1F 50/K-8
3487 School St 48413 989-269-7054
Joe Murphy, supt. Fax 269-9033
www.huroncountyruralschools.com
Verona Mills S 50/K-8
3487 School St 48413 989-269-7054
Amy Schweitzer, lead tchr. Fax 269-9033

Baldwin, Lake, Pop. 1,141
Baldwin Community SD 600/PK-12
525 4th St 49304 231-745-4791
Dr. Stiles Simmons, supt. Fax 745-3240
www.baldwin.k12.mi.us
Baldwin ES 300/PK-5
525 4th St 49304 231-745-3261
Rob Dennis, prin. Fax 745-7481
Baldwin JHS 100/6-8
525 4th St 49304 231-745-4683
Calvin Patillo, prin. Fax 745-2898

Bangor, Van Buren, Pop. 1,809
Bangor SD 1,200/K-12
801 W Arlington St 49013 269-427-6800
Lynn Johnson, supt. Fax 427-8274
www.bangorvikings.org
Bangor MS 400/5-8
803 W Arlington St 49013 269-427-6824
Michael Dandron, prin. Fax 427-6892
South Walnut ES 500/K-4
309 S Walnut St 49013 269-427-6863
Karen Bitzer, prin. Fax 427-6893

Bangor Township SD 8 50/K-8
29842 66th St 49013 269-427-8562
Jeffrey Mills, supt. Fax 674-8030
www.bangorschools.org/
Wood S, 29842 66th St 49013 50/K-8
Jeffrey Mills, prin. 269-427-8562

Trinity Lutheran S 50/K-8
115 E Monroe St 49013 269-427-7102
Kevin Lemke S.T.B., prin.

Baraga, Baraga, Pop. 1,981
Baraga Area SD 400/K-12
210 Lyons St 49908 906-353-6664
Richard Sarau, supt. Fax 353-6664
www.baragaschools.org
La Tendresse ES 100/K-5
210 Lyons St 49908 906-353-6663
Timothy Marczak, prin. Fax 353-7454

Barryton, Mecosta, Pop. 353
Chippewa Hills SD
Supt. — See Remus
Barryton ES 200/PK-4
19701 30th Ave 49305 989-382-5311
Amanda Kimball, prin. Fax 382-5387

Bath, Clinton, Pop. 2,052
Bath Community SD 1,000/K-12
PO Box 310 48808 517-641-6721
Jake Huffman, supt. Fax 641-6958
www.bathschools.net
Bath ES 500/K-5
PO Box 310 48808 517-641-6771
Lisa Roedel, prin. Fax 641-7288
Bath MS 300/6-8
PO Box 310 48808 517-641-6781
Lorenda Jonas, prin. Fax 641-4996

Battle Creek, Calhoun, Pop. 50,321
Battle Creek SD 4,000/K-12
3 Van Buren St W 49017 269-965-9500
Kim Parker-DeVauld, supt. Fax 965-9474
www.battlecreekpublicschools.org
Dudley ES 100/K-2
308 Roosevelt Ave W, 269-965-9720
Deborah Linden, prin. Fax 965-9724
Kellogg ES 100/3-5
306 Champion St, 269-965-9773
Fax 965-9780
LaMora Park ES 100/K-2
65 Woodlawn Ave N, 269-965-9725
Sandra Windon, prin. Fax 965-7007
Northwestern MS 500/6-8
176 Limit St, 269-965-9607
Timothy Reese, prin. Fax 965-9525
Post-Franklin ES 200/K-2
20 Newark Ave 49014 269-965-9693
Nneka Daniels, prin. Fax 965-9696
Verona ES 200/3-5
825 Capital Ave NE 49017 269-965-9710
Jennifer Kay, prin. Fax 965-9712
Other Schools – See Springfield

Harper Creek Community SD 2,600/K-12
7454 B Dr N 49014 269-441-6550
Rob Ridgeway, supt. Fax 962-6034
www.harpercreek.net
Beadle Lake ES 300/K-4
8175 C Dr N 49014 269-441-3250
Nneka Daniels, prin. Fax 962-4748
Harper Creek MS 800/5-8
7290 B Dr N 49014 269-441-4750
Kimberly Thayer, prin. Fax 979-4613
Sonoma ES 300/K-4
4640 B Dr S 49015 269-441-7800
Cyndi Mead, prin. Fax 979-6246
Wattles Park ES 300/K-4
132 Wattles Rd S 49014 269-441-5850
Brent Swan, prin. Fax 963-1174

Lakeview SD 3,900/K-12
15 Arbor St 49015 269-565-2400
Blake Prewitt, supt. Fax 565-2408
www.lakeviewspartans.org
Lakeview MS 1,300/5-8
300 28th St S 49015 269-565-3900
Michael Norstrom, prin. Fax 565-3908
Minges Brook ES 300/K-4
435 Lincoln Hill Dr 49015 269-565-4500
Melissa Remillard, prin. Fax 565-4508
Prairieview ES 300/K-4
1675 Iroquois Ave 49015 269-565-4600
Donald Hoaglin, prin. Fax 565-4608
Riverside ES 400/K-4
650 Riverside Dr 49015 269-565-4700
Melissa Martin, prin. Fax 565-4708
Westlake ES 400/K-4
1184 24th St S 49015 269-565-4900
Tamara Jamierson, prin. Fax 565-4908

Pennfield SD 2,100/K-12
8587 Pennfield Rd 49017 269-961-9781
Tim Everett, supt. Fax 961-9799
www.pennfield.net/
Pennfield Dunlap ES 500/3-5
8587 Pennfield Rd 49017 269-961-9789
Sarah Neubecker, prin. Fax 961-9756
Pennfield MS 600/6-8
8587 Pennfield Rd 49017 269-961-9784
Michele Herzing, prin. Fax 441-5535
Pennfield North ES 200/K-2
8587 Pennfield Rd 49017 269-961-9797
Scott Hall, prin. Fax 961-9765
Pennfield Purdy ES 200/K-2
8587 Pennfield Rd 49017 269-961-9795
Jane Haudek, prin. Fax 961-9764

Battle Creek Academy 100/K-12
480 Parkway Dr, 269-965-1278
James Davis, prin. Fax 965-3250
Calhoun Christian S 200/PK-12
20 Woodrow Ave S 49015 269-965-5560
Jeralyn Belote, prin. Fax 965-8038
St. Joseph ES 300/PK-5
47 23rd St N 49015 269-965-7749
Sara Myers, prin. Fax 965-0790
St. Joseph MS 100/6-8
44 25th St N 49015 269-963-4935
Sara Myers, prin. Fax 963-0354

Bay City, Bay, Pop. 33,947
Bangor Township SD 2,400/PK-12
3359 E Midland Rd 48706 989-684-8121
Matthew Schmidt, supt. Fax 684-6000
www.bangorschools.org
Bangor Central S 300/PK-5
208 State Park Dr 48706 989-684-8891
Melissa Vrable, prin. Fax 686-8211
Bangor Lincoln S 300/K-5
2771 N Euclid Ave 48706 989-686-7639
Kurtis Pake, prin. Fax 686-8213
Bangor North Preschool 50/PK-PK
504 Revilo Rd 48706 989-684-4890
Jamie Doran, dir. Fax 686-8217
Bangor West Central S 300/K-5
3175 Wilder Rd 48706 989-684-3373
Craig Pfenninger, prin. Fax 686-8214
McAuliffe MS 600/6-8
3281 Kiesel Rd 48706 989-686-7640
Kevin Biskup, prin. Fax 686-7633

Bay City SD 8,100/PK-12
910 N Walnut St 48706 989-686-9700
Dr. Stephen Bigelow, supt. Fax 686-1047
www.bcschools.net
Hampton ES 500/K-5
1908 W Youngs Ditch Rd 48708 989-893-1100
Kim Offenbecker, prin. Fax 893-6347
Handy MS 1,000/6-8
601 Blend St 48706 989-684-1723
Ryan Boon, prin. Fax 684-1960
Kolb ES 600/PK-5
305 W Crump St 48706 989-893-9518
Michelle Montgomery, prin. Fax 893-0462
Linsday ES 300/PK-5
607 Lasalle St 48706 989-684-0692
Jill Ball, prin. Fax 684-8760
MacGregor ES 400/PK-5
1012 Fremont St 48708 989-892-1558
Brad Pennell, prin. Fax 892-8651
Mackensen ES 300/K-5
5535 Dennis Dr 48706 989-684-4958
Julie Robinson, prin. Fax 684-8598
McAlear Sawden ES 500/PK-5
2300 Midland Rd 48706 989-684-7702
Mike Connors, prin. Fax 684-6464
Washington ES 400/PK-5
1821 McKinley St 48708 989-894-2744
Dr. Bill Tithof, prin. Fax 894-5870
Other Schools – See Auburn

All Saints Central ES 100/PK-5
715 14th St 48708 989-892-4371
Lisa Rhodus, prin. Fax 892-7567
Bethel Lutheran S 100/PK-8
749 N Pine Rd 48708 989-892-4508
Douglas Dast, prin. Fax 892-4508
Faith Lutheran S 200/PK-8
3033 Wilder Rd 48706 989-684-3448
Susie Smith, prin. Fax 684-3545
Immanuel Lutheran S 200/PK-8
247 N Lincoln St 48708 989-893-8521
Janet LaRocque, prin. Fax 893-4172
St. John Amelith Lutheran S 100/PK-8
1664 Amelith Rd 48706 989-686-0176
Jennifer Enge, prin.
St. John Lutheran S 100/PK-8
210 S Alp St 48706 989-684-6442
Michael Falk, prin. Fax 684-6442
St. Paul Lutheran S 100/PK-8
6094 Westside Saginaw Rd 48706 989-684-4450
Gerald Lustila M.Ed., prin. Fax 684-4450
Trinity Lutheran S 100/PK-8
20 E Salzburg Rd 48706 989-662-4891
Susan Klauer, prin. Fax 662-6173
Trinity Lutheran S 100/PK-8
2515 Broadway St 48708 989-894-2092
Philip Haefner, prin. Fax 894-2870
Zion Lutheran S 100/PK-8
1707 S Kiesel St 48706 989-893-5793
Janet LaRocque, prin. Fax 893-4633

Bear Lake, Manistee, Pop. 281
Bear Lake SD 300/K-12
7748 Cody St 49614 231-864-3133
Marlen Cordes, supt. Fax 864-3434
www.bearlake.k12.mi.us
Bear Lake ES 100/K-5
7748 Cody St 49614 231-864-3133
Sarah Harless, prin. Fax 864-3434

Beaver Island, Charlevoix
Beaver Island Community SD 100/K-12
37895 Kings Hwy 49782 231-448-2744
Wil Cwikiel, supt. Fax 448-2919
www.beaverisland.k12.mi.us
Beaver Island Community S 100/K-12
37895 Kings Hwy 49782 231-448-2744
Wil Cwikiel, prin. Fax 448-2919

Beaverton, Gladwin, Pop. 1,061
Beaverton Rural SD 700/K-12
PO Box 529 48612 989-246-3000
Susan Wooden, supt. Fax 435-7631
www.brs.cgresd.net
Beaverton ES 300/K-6
PO Box 529 48612 989-246-3020
Michael Bassage, prin. Fax 246-3420

Belding, Ionia, Pop. 5,669
Belding Area SD 2,000/PK-12
850 Hall St 48809 616-794-4700
Brent Noskey, supt. Fax 794-4730
www.bas-k12.org/
Belding MS 500/6-8
410 Ionia St 48809 616-794-4400
Fax 794-4420
Ellis ES 400/PK-2
100 W Ellis Ave 48809 616-794-4100
Tiffany Jackson, prin. Fax 794-4142
Woodview ES 400/3-5
450 Orchard St 48809 616-794-4750
Bruce Cook, prin. Fax 794-4790

Faith Community Christian S 50/PK-5
9614 Fisk Rd 48809 616-794-3451
Amy Derfler M.Ed., admin.

Bellaire, Antrim, Pop. 1,076
Bellaire SD 400/K-12
204 W Forrest Home Ave 49615 231-533-8141
James Emery, supt. Fax 533-6797
www.bellairepublicschools.com/
Rodger ES 200/K-5
204 W Forrest Home Ave 49615 231-533-8916
Kristi Poel, prin. Fax 533-9214

Belleville, Wayne, Pop. 3,881
Van Buren SD 5,000/PK-12
555 W Columbia Ave 48111 734-697-1016
Peter Kudlak, supt. Fax 697-6385
www.vanburenschools.net
Edgemont ES 500/K-4
125 S Edgemont St 48111 734-697-8002
Fred Abel, prin. Fax 697-6588
Haggerty S 50/PK-PK
13770 Haggerty Rd 48111 734-699-2180
Karen Johnston, admin. Fax 699-2164
McBride MS 700/7-8
47097 McBride Ave 48111 734-697-9171
John Leroy, prin. Fax 697-6573
Owen IS 700/5-6
45201 Owen St 48111 734-697-8711
Melissa Lloyd, prin. Fax 697-6576
Savage ES 400/K-4
42975 Savage Rd 48111 734-699-5050
Lisa Preuss, prin. Fax 697-6520
Tyler ES 400/K-4
42200 Tyler Rd 48111 734-699-5818
Aleisa Pitt, prin. Fax 697-6521
Other Schools – See Ypsilanti

Bellevue, Eaton, Pop. 1,257
Bellevue Community SD 600/K-12
904 W Capital Ave 49021 269-763-9432
John C. Prescott, supt. Fax 763-2300
www.bellevue-schools.com
Bellevue ES 300/K-6
904 W Capital Ave 49021 269-763-9435
John C. Prescott, prin. Fax 763-9008

Belmont, Kent
Rockford SD
Supt. — See Rockford
Belmont ES 300/K-5
6097 Belmont Ave NE 49306 616-863-6362
Jeremy Karel, prin. Fax 863-6356

Assumption BVM S 200/PK-8
6393 Belmont Ave NE 49306 616-361-5483
Domenic Franconi, prin. Fax 361-2553

Benton Harbor, Berrien, Pop. 9,796
Benton Harbor Area SD 1,200/PK-12
PO Box 1107 49023 269-605-1000
Shelly Walker Ed.D., supt. Fax 605-1043
www.bhas.org
Arts & Communications Academy 200/6-8
120 E Napier Ave 49022 269-605-1400
Fred Roseburgh, prin. Fax 605-1403
Discovery Enrichment Center 100/PK-PK
465 S Mccord St 49022 269-605-1600
Dr. David VanDyke, prin. Fax 605-1603
International Academy at Hull 100/K-2
1716 Territorial Rd 49022 269-605-1500
Rita Seay, prin. Fax 605-1503
STEAM Academy at MLK Jr. 200/3-5
750 E Britain Ave 49022 269-605-2400
David Vandyke, prin. Fax 605-2403

Dowagiac UNSD
Supt. — See Dowagiac
Sister Lakes ES 200/K-5
68079 M 152 49022 269-782-4468
Mike Campbell, prin. Fax 944-1811

Brookview Montessori S 100/PK-9
501 Zollar Dr 49022 269-925-3544
Dr. Larry Schanker, dir. Fax 925-3525
River of Life S K-5
275 Pipestone St 49022 269-267-0831
Jessica Concannon, prin.

Benzonia, Benzie, Pop. 484
Benzie County Central SD 1,600/K-12
9300 Homestead Rd 49616 231-882-9653
Matthew Olson, supt. Fax 882-9121
www.benzieschools.net/
Benzie Central MS 300/6-8
9300 Homestead Rd 49616 231-882-4498
David Clasen, prin. Fax 882-7627
Crystal Lake ES 200/K-5
7048 Severence St 49616 231-882-4641
LeeAnn Stephan, prin. Fax 882-7829
Other Schools – See Interlochen, Thompsonville

Berkley, Oakland, Pop. 14,700
Berkley SD
Supt. — See Oak Park
Anderson MS 600/6-8
3205 Catalpa Dr 48072 248-837-8200
Mike Ross, prin. Fax 546-0696
Angell ES 400/K-5
3849 Beverly Blvd 48072 248-837-8500
Vince Gigliotti, prin. Fax 546-0848
Pattengill ES 300/K-5
3540 Morrison Ave 48072 248-837-8700
Meghan Ashkanani, prin. Fax 435-0184
Rogers ES 400/K-5
2265 Hamilton Ave 48072 248-837-8800
Beth Meacham, prin. Fax 546-0634

Berrien Springs, Berrien, Pop. 1,747
Berrien Springs SD 2,300/K-12
PO Box 130 49103 269-471-2891
David Eichberg, supt. Fax 471-2590
www.homeoftheshamrocks.org
Berrien Springs MS 400/6-8
PO Box 130 49103 269-471-2796
Steven Spenner, prin. Fax 471-2590
Mars ES 400/K-2
PO Box 130 49103 269-471-1836
Darla Campbell, prin. Fax 471-8855
Sylvester ES 400/3-5
PO Box 130 49103 269-471-7198
Chelsea Pollyea, prin. Fax 471-8856

Murdoch ES 300/K-8
8885 Garland Ave 49104 269-471-3225
Dr. Evelyn P. Savory Ph.D., prin. Fax 471-6115
Trinity Lutheran S 100/PK-8
9123 George Ave 49103 269-473-1811
Mike Shembarger, prin. Fax 471-7013
Village Adventist ES 200/K-8
409 W Mars St 49103 269-473-5121
Wendy Baldwin, prin. Fax 473-2830

Bessemer, Gogebic, Pop. 1,874
Bessemer City SD 400/PK-12
301 E Sellar St 49911 906-667-0802
David Radovich, supt. Fax 667-0318
www.bessemer.k12.mi.us
Washington ES 200/PK-6
301 E Sellar St 49911 906-663-4515
David Radovich, admin. Fax 667-0318

Bluff View Christian S 50/K-8
507 E Cinnebar St 49911 906-663-6959
Merrie Hellman, prin.

Beverly Hills, Oakland, Pop. 10,098
Birmingham SD 8,100/PK-12
31301 Evergreen Rd 48025 248-203-3000
Dr. Daniel Nerad Ed.D., supt. Fax 203-3009
www.birmingham.k12.mi.us
Berkshire MS 800/6-8
21707 W 14 Mile Rd 48025 248-203-4702
Jason Clinckscale, prin. Fax 203-4802
Beverly ES 400/PK-5
18305 Beverly Rd 48025 248-203-3164
Dr. Jamii Hitchcock, prin. Fax 203-3165
Greenfield ES 300/K-5
31200 Fairfax Ave 48025 248-203-3217
Noelle Davis, prin. Fax 203-3218
Other Schools – See Bingham Farms, Birmingham, Bloomfield Hls, Troy

---

Detroit Country Day MS 400/6-8
22400 Hillview Ln 48025 248-430-1677
Glen Shilling, hdmstr.
Our Lady Queen of Martyrs S 300/PK-8
32460 Pierce St 48025 248-642-2616
Jacqueline Mojeske, prin. Fax 642-3671

Big Bay, Marquette, Pop. 314
Powell Township SD 50/PK-8
PO Box 160 49808 906-345-9355
Daniel Barry, supt. Fax 345-9936
sites.google.com/site/powelltownshipschooldistrict
Powell Township S 50/PK-8
PO Box 160 49808 906-345-9355
Seth Hoopingarner, prin. Fax 345-9936

Big Rapids, Mecosta, Pop. 10,347
Big Rapids SD 1,800/K-12
21034 15 Mile Rd 49307 231-796-2627
Tim Haist, supt. Fax 592-0639
www.brps.org
Big Rapids MS 600/5-8
500 N Warren Ave 49307 231-796-9965
Mitch Cumings, prin. Fax 592-3494
Brookside ES 300/K-4
210 Escott St 49307 231-796-8323
Kara Schafer, prin. Fax 592-3496
Riverview ES 200/2-4
509 Willow Ave 49307 231-796-2550
Renee Kent, prin. Fax 592-8501

St. Mary S 100/PK-8
927 Marion Ave 49307 231-796-6731
J.B. Watters, prin. Fax 796-9293
St. Peter's Lutheran S 100/PK-8
408 W Bellevue St 49307 231-796-8782
Brad Massey, prin. Fax 796-1186

Bingham Farms, Oakland, Pop. 1,083
Birmingham SD
Supt. — See Beverly Hills
Bingham Farms ES 300/K-5
23400 W 13 Mile Rd 48025 248-203-3350
Russell Facione, prin. Fax 203-3394

Birch Run, Saginaw, Pop. 1,524
Birch Run Area SD 1,800/K-12
12450 Church St Ste 2 48415 989-624-9307
David Bush, supt. Fax 624-8503
www.birchrunschools.org
Greene MS 500/5-8
8225 Main St 48415 989-624-5821
Scott Preston, prin. Fax 624-8507
North ES 600/K-4
12440 Church St 48415 989-624-9011
Joe Birkmeier, prin. Fax 624-8504

Birmingham, Oakland, Pop. 19,789
Birmingham SD
Supt. — See Beverly Hills
Derby MS 800/6-8
1300 Derby Rd 48009 248-203-5003
Celeste Nowacki, prin. Fax 203-4948
Midvale ECC, 2121 Midvale St 48009 PK-PK
Laura Tinsley, prin. 248-203-5800
Pierce ES 600/K-5
1829 Pierce St 48009 248-203-4337
James Lalik, prin. Fax 203-4393
Quarton ES 500/K-5
771 Chesterfield Ave 48009 248-203-3425
Jill Ghiardi-Coignet, prin. Fax 203-3430

Holy Name S 400/PK-8
680 Harmon St 48009 248-644-2722
DeAnn Brzezinski, prin. Fax 644-1191
Our Shepherd Lutheran S 300/PK-8
1658 E Lincoln St 48009 248-645-0551
Janet McLoughlin, prin. Fax 645-2427

Blanchard, Isabella
Montabella Community SD
Supt. — See Edmore
Montabella ES 400/PK-6
1456 N County Line Rd 49310 989-427-5414
Michael Moore, prin. Fax 427-5602

Blissfield, Lenawee, Pop. 3,300
Blissfield Community SD 1,200/K-12
630 S Lane St 49228 517-486-2205
Jerry Johnson, supt. Fax 486-5701
www.blissfieldschools.us/
Blissfield ES 600/K-5
640 S Lane St 49228 517-486-2811
Michael Valasek, prin. Fax 486-3348
Blissfield MS 300/6-8
1305 Beamer Rd 49228 517-486-4420
Cris Rupp, prin. Fax 486-4758

Bloomfield Hls, Oakland, Pop. 3,811
Birmingham SD
Supt. — See Beverly Hills
Birmingham Covington S 600/3-8
1525 Covington Rd, 248-203-4425
Mark Morawski, prin. Fax 203-4433
Harlan ES 400/K-5
3595 N Adams Rd, 248-203-3265
Alex Agius, prin. Fax 203-3269
West Maple ES 500/K-5
6275 Inkster Rd, 248-851-2667
Laura Mahler, prin. Fax 203-5109

Bloomfield Hills SD 6,600/PK-12
7273 Wing Lake Rd, 248-341-5400
Dr. Robert Glass, supt. Fax 341-5449
www.bloomfield.org
Bloomfield Hills MS 700/5-8
4200 Quarton Rd, 248-341-6000
Randy English, prin. Fax 341-6099
Bloomin' Kids Preschool at Conant PK-PK
4100 Quarton Rd, 248-341-7075
Lisa Gryglak, admin.
Bloomin' Tots at Fox Hills PK-PK
1661 Hunters Ridge Dr, 248-341-7950
Lisa Gryglak, admin.
Conant ES 400/K-4
4100 Quarton Rd, 248-341-7000
Nicholas Russo, prin. Fax 341-7099
East Hills MS 500/4-8
2800 Kensington Rd, 248-341-6200
Jason Rubel, prin. Fax 341-6299
Eastover ES 500/K-3
1101 Westview Rd, 248-341-7100
Carey Crocker, prin. Fax 341-7199
Way ES 400/K-4
765 W Long Lake Rd, 248-341-7800
Adam Scher, prin. Fax 341-7899
Other Schools – See West Bloomfield

Academy of the Sacred Heart 400/PK-12
1250 Kensington Rd, 248-646-8900
Sr. Bridget Bearss, hdmstr. Fax 646-4143
Bloomfield Christian School 200/K-12
3570 Telegraph Rd, 248-499-7800
Trenton Leach, head sch Fax 457-1520
Cranbrook S 1,700/PK-12
PO Box 801, 248-645-3000
Arlyce Seibert, dir. Fax 645-3524
Detroit Country Day Junior S 200/3-5
3600 Bradway Blvd, 248-430-1074
Glen Shilling, hdmstr.
Detroit Country Day Lower S 300/PK-2
3003 W Maple Rd, 248-430-2740
Glen Shilling, hdmstr.
Roeper S 300/PK-5
41190 Woodward Ave, 248-203-7300
Kari Papadopoulos, head sch Fax 203-7310
St. Hugo of the Hills S 700/K-8
380 E Hickory Grove Rd, 248-642-6131
Sr. Joseph Vincler, prin. Fax 642-4457
St. Regis S 500/K-8
3691 Lincoln Rd, 248-646-2686
Katie Brydges, prin. Fax 644-0944

Bloomingdale, Van Buren, Pop. 446
Bloomingdale SD 1,200/K-12
PO Box 217 49026 269-521-3900
Deb Paquette, supt. Fax 521-3907
www.bdalecards.org
Bloomingdale ES 300/K-5
PO Box 217 49026 269-521-3935
Jennifer Bloomfield, prin. Fax 521-3949
Bloomingdale MS 300/6-8
PO Box 217 49026 269-521-3910
Rick Reo, prin. Fax 521-3958
Other Schools – See Pullman

Boon, Wexford, Pop. 165
Cadillac Area SD
Supt. — See Cadillac
Forest View ES 200/K-4
7840 S 25 Rd 49618 231-876-5100
Carrie Paulen, prin. Fax 876-5121

Boyne City, Charlevoix, Pop. 3,622
Boyne City SD 1,300/K-12
321 S Park St 49712 231-439-8190
Patrick Little M.A., supt. Fax 439-8195
www.boyne.k12.mi.us
Boyne City ES 500/K-4
930 Brockway St 49712 231-439-8300
Lisa King, prin. Fax 439-8251
Boyne City MS 400/5-8
1025 Boyne Ave 49712 231-439-8200
Mike Wilson M.A., prin. Fax 439-8233

Boyne Falls, Charlevoix, Pop. 286
Boyne Falls SD 200/PK-12
PO Box 356 49713 231-549-2211
Cynthia Pineda, supt. Fax 549-2922
www.boynefalls.org
Boyne Falls S 200/PK-12
PO Box 356 49713 231-549-2211
Cynthia Pineda, admin. Fax 549-2922

Breckenridge, Gratiot, Pop. 1,316
Breckenridge Community SD 800/PK-12
PO Box 217 48615 989-842-3182
Kimberly Thompson, supt. Fax 842-3625
breckhuskies.org
Breckenridge ES 300/PK-5
PO Box 217 48615 989-842-3182
Dr. Jennifer Thrush, prin. Fax 842-5655
Breckenridge MS 200/6-8
PO Box 217 48615 989-842-3182
Sheila Pilmore, prin. Fax 842-5761

Brethren, Manistee, Pop. 407
Kaleva Norman Dickson SD 500/K-12
4400 Highbridge Rd 49619 231-477-5353
Marlen Cordes, supt. Fax 477-5351
www.knd.k12.mi.us
Brethren MS 100/7-8
4400 Highbridge Rd 49619 231-477-5354
Jakob Veith, prin. Fax 477-5351
Kaleva Norman Dickson ES 300/K-6
4400 Highbridge Rd 49619 231-477-5353
Jakob Veith, prin. Fax 477-5351

Bridgeport, Saginaw, Pop. 6,811
Bridgeport-Spaulding Community SD 1,200/PK-12
PO Box 657 48722 989-777-1770
Carol W. Selby, supt. Fax 777-4720
www.bscs.k12.mi.us
Other Schools – See Saginaw

Bridgman, Berrien, Pop. 2,260
Bridgman SD 1,000/PK-12
9964 Gast Rd 49106 269-465-5432
Shane Peters, supt. Fax 466-0221
www.bridgmanschools.com
Bridgman ES 400/PK-4
3891 Lake St 49106 269-466-0241
Lori Graves, prin. Fax 466-0248
Reed MS 300/5-8
10254 California Rd 49106 269-465-5410
John Truesdell, prin. Fax 466-0393

Brighton, Livingston, Pop. 7,364
Brighton Area SD 6,000/K-12
125 S Church St 48116 810-299-4000
Greg Gray, supt. Fax 299-4092
www.brightonk12.com/
Hawkins ES 500/K-4
8900 Lee Rd 48116 810-299-3900
Barbara Kiehler, prin. Fax 299-3910
Hilton ES 500/K-4
9600 Hilton Rd 48114 810-299-3950
Jeff Eisele, prin. Fax 299-3960
Hornung ES 500/K-4
4680 Bauer Rd 48116 810-299-4450
Jack Yates, prin. Fax 299-4460
Maltby MS 900/5-6
4740 Bauer Rd 48116 810-299-3600
Scott Brenner, prin. Fax 299-3610
Scranton MS 1,000/7-8
8415 Maltby Rd 48116 810-299-3700
Mark Wilson, prin. Fax 299-3710
Spencer Road ES 400/K-4
10639 Spencer Rd 48114 810-299-4350
Bill Renner, prin. Fax 299-4360

Hartland Consolidated SD
Supt. — See Howell
Hartland Farms IS 900/5-6
581 Taylor Rd 48114 810-626-2500
Mikki Cheney, prin. Fax 626-2501
Lakes ES 500/K-4
687 Taylor Rd 48114 810-626-2700
Anthony Howerton, prin. Fax 626-2701

Cornerstone Christian S 200/PK-8
9455 Hilton Rd 48114 810-494-4040
Dr. Arthur Hunt, head sch Fax 494-4041

Holy Spirit Catholic S 100/PK-8
9565 Musch Rd 48116 810-231-9199
Christine Blandino, prin. Fax 231-6129
Maple Tree Montessori Academy 50/PK-7
2944 S Old US Highway 23 48114 810-225-8321
Patricia Cherry, head sch Fax 225-7258
St. Patrick S 400/K-8
1001 Orndorf Dr 48116 810-229-7946
Jeanine Kenny, prin. Fax 229-6206
Shepherd of the Lakes Lutheran S 100/PK-8
2101 S Hacker Rd 48114 810-227-6473
Juli VanDeven, prin. Fax 227-3566

Brimley, Chippewa
Brimley Area SD 500/K-12
7134 S M 221 49715 906-248-3219
Brian Reattoir, supt. Fax 248-3220
brimley.eup.k12.mi.us
Brimley ES 300/K-6
7134 S M 221 49715 906-248-3217
Peter Routhier, prin. Fax 248-5594

Britton, Lenawee, Pop. 584
Britton Deerfield SD 600/PK-12
201 College Ave 49229 517-451-4581
Stacy Johnson, supt. Fax 451-8595
www.bdschools.us
Britton S 500/PK-12
201 College Ave 49229 517-451-4581
Stacy Johnson, admin. Fax 451-8595
Other Schools – See Deerfield

Bronson, Branch, Pop. 2,313
Bronson Community SD 1,300/K-12
501 E Chicago St 49028 517-369-3260
Richard Hilderley, supt. Fax 369-2802
www.bronsonschools.org
Anderson ES 300/K-2
335 E Corey St 49028 517-369-3234
Harmonee McCrea, prin. Fax 369-2190
Ryan ES 300/3-5
461 Rudd St 49028 517-369-3254
Mark Heifner, prin. Fax 369-2260

St. Marys Assumption S 100/PK-8
204 Albers Rd 49028 517-369-4625
David Kubel, prin. Fax 369-1652

Brooklyn, Jackson, Pop. 1,196
Columbia SD 1,000/PK-12
11775 Hewitt Rd 49230 517-592-6641
Dr. Pamela Campbell, supt. Fax 592-8090
www.myeagles.org
Columbia ES 300/PK-2
320 School St 49230 517-592-6632
Debra Powell, prin. Fax 592-3337
Columbia Upper ES 200/3-6
321 School St 49230 517-592-2181
Christi O'Neil, prin. Fax 592-3447

Brown City, Sanilac, Pop. 1,303
Brown City Community SD 900/PK-12
PO Box 160 48416 810-346-4700
Neil Kohler, supt. Fax 346-3762
www.browncityschools.org
Brown City ES 400/PK-6
PO Box 160 48416 810-346-4700
Sean Hagey, prin. Fax 346-2601

Brownstown, See Flat Rock
Woodhaven-Brownstown SD
Supt. — See Woodhaven
Brownstown MS 800/6-7
20135 Inkster Rd 48174 734-783-3400
Andrew Clark, prin. Fax 783-3407
Gudith ES 400/K-5
22700 Sibley Rd, 734-783-5386
Thomas Martin, prin. Fax 783-5389
Wegienka ES 400/K-5
23925 Arsenal Rd 48134 734-783-3367
Michelle Briegel, prin. Fax 783-3372

Brownstown Twp, Wayne
Gibraltar SD
Supt. — See Woodhaven
Hunter ES 300/PK-5
21320 Roche Rd 48183 734-379-6390
John Kernan, prin. Fax 379-6391

Buchanan, Berrien, Pop. 4,325
Buchanan Community SD 1,400/PK-12
401 W Chicago St 49107 269-695-8401
Timothy J. Donahue, supt. Fax 695-8450
www.buchananschools.com
Buchanan MS 400/5-7
610 W 4th St 49107 269-695-8406
Mark Kurland, prin. Fax 695-8459
Moccasin ES 100/2-4
410 Moccasin St 49107 269-695-8408
Stacey Denison, prin. Fax 695-8427
Ottawa ES 300/PK-1
109 Ottawa St 49107 269-695-8409
Karin Falkenstein, prin. Fax 695-8426

Buckley, Wexford, Pop. 683
Buckley Community SD 400/K-12
305 S 1st St 49620 231-269-3325
Laurie Walles, supt. Fax 269-3833
www.buckleyschools.com
Buckley Community S 400/K-12
305 S 1st St 49620 231-269-3325
Laurie Walles, admin. Fax 269-3833

Burr Oak, Saint Joseph, Pop. 822
Burr Oak Community SD 200/K-12
PO Box 337 49030 269-489-2213
Terry Conklin, supt. Fax 489-5198
burroakcs.org/
Burr Oak ES 100/K-4
PO Box 337 49030 269-489-5181
Kris Owens, prin. Fax 489-5198

Burton, Genesee, Pop. 29,312
Atherton Community SD 900/K-12
3354 S Genesee Rd 48519 810-591-9182
John Ploof, supt. Fax 591-1926
www.athertonschools.org
Atherton ES 400/K-6
3444 S Genesee Rd 48519 810-591-0604
Susanne Carpenter, prin. Fax 591-9456

Bendle SD 1,100/PK-12
3420 Columbine Ave 48529 810-591-2501
John Krolewski, supt. Fax 591-2210
www.bendleschools.org
Bendle MS 300/6-8
2294 E Bristol Rd 48529 810-591-3385
Pete Gleason, prin. Fax 591-2540
South Bendle ES 300/PK-2
4341 Larkin Dr 48529 810-591-0620
Trisha Cherveny, prin. Fax 591-2520
West Bendle ES 300/3-5
4020 Cerdan Dr 48529 810-591-0880
Brock Place, prin. Fax 591-9011

Bentley Community SD 900/K-12
1170 N Belsay Rd 48509 810-591-9100
Christopher Arrington, supt. Fax 591-9102
www.bentleyschools.org
Barhitte ES 400/K-5
6080 Roberta St 48509 810-591-9661
Debra McCollum, prin. Fax 591-9198
Bentley MS 200/6-8
1180 N Belsay Rd 48509 810-591-9043
Brian Eddy, prin. Fax 591-9166

Carman-Ainsworth Community SD
Supt. — See Flint
Dillon ES 300/K-3
1197 E Schumacher St 48529 810-591-3590
Kaire Verbeke, prin. Fax 591-3835

Kearsley Community SD
Supt. — See Flint
Weston ES 400/K-1
2499 Cashin St 48509 810-591-8483
Doug Hibbs, prin. Fax 591-8485

Faithway Christian S 100/PK-12
1225 S Center Rd 48509 810-743-0055
Fax 743-0033
Genesee Christian S 400/PK-12
1223 S Belsay Rd 48509 810-743-3108
Robert Buchalski, prin. Fax 743-3230
Good Shepherd Lutheran S 50/PK-8
5496 Lippincott Blvd 48519 810-742-1131
Daniel Busch, prin. Fax 742-9907
St. Thomas More Academy 100/K-12
6456 E Bristol Rd 48519 810-742-2411
Dan Le Blanc, prin. Fax 742-4803

Byron, Shiawassee, Pop. 573
Byron Area SD 1,000/PK-12
312 W Maple St 48418 810-266-4881
Tricia Murphy-Alderman, supt. Fax 266-5723
www.byron.k12.mi.us
Byron ES 400/PK-6
401 E Maple St 48418 810-266-4671
Jacob Haynes, prin. Fax 266-5011
Byron MS 200/7-8
312 W Maple St 48418 810-266-4422
Grant Hegenauer, prin. Fax 266-4151

Byron Center, Kent, Pop. 5,750
Byron Center SD 3,700/PK-12
8542 Byron Center Ave SW 49315 616-878-6100
Daniel Takens, supt. Fax 878-3283
www.bcpsk12.net
Brown ES 500/K-4
8064 Byron Center Ave SW 49315 616-878-6200
Jack Gitler, prin. Fax 878-6220
Byron Center ECC PK-PK
8542 Byron Center Ave SW 49315 616-878-6100
Erin Tacoma, dir.
Byron Center West MS 500/7-8
8654 Homerich Ave SW 49315 616-878-6500
Jeff Wierzbicki, prin. Fax 878-6520
Countryside ES 500/K-4
8200 Eastern Ave SE 49315 616-878-6900
Jolynne Dobson, prin. Fax 878-6920
Marshall ES 500/K-4
1756 64th St SW 49315 616-878-6300
John Krajewski, prin. Fax 878-6320
Nickels IS 500/5-6
8638 Byron Center Ave SW 49315 616-878-6400
Thomas Trout, prin. Fax 878-6420

Byron Center Christian S 500/PK-8
8840 Byron Center Ave SW 49315 616-878-3347
John Kramer, prin. Fax 878-0019
St. Mary's Visitation S 100/PK-6
2455 146th Ave SW 49315 616-681-9601
Chris Hurley, prin. Fax 681-9919
Zion Christian S 300/PK-12
7555 Byron Center Ave SW 49315 616-878-9472
Todd Hoekstra, admin. Fax 878-9473

Cadillac, Wexford, Pop. 10,183
Cadillac Area SD 3,100/K-12
421 S Mitchell St 49601 231-876-5000
Jennifer Brown, supt. Fax 876-5021
www.cadillac.k12.mi.us
Cadillac JHS 500/7-8
500 Chestnut St 49601 231-876-5700
Michael Outman, prin. Fax 876-5721
Franklin ES 400/K-4
505 Lester St 49601 231-876-5200
Jaime Heuker, prin. Fax 876-5221
Kenwood ES 300/K-4
1700 Chestnut St 49601 231-876-5300
Kelly Buckmaster, prin. Fax 876-5321
Lincoln ES 300/K-4
125 Ayer St 49601 231-876-5400
Kerri Roby, prin. Fax 876-5421
Mackinaw Trail MS 400/5-6
8401 Mackinaw Trl 49601 231-876-5600
Matthew Brown, prin. Fax 876-5621
Other Schools – See Boon

Cadillac Heritage Christian S 100/PK-12
1706 Wright St 49601 231-775-4272
William Goodwill, admin.
Northview Adventist S 50/1-8
202 N Carmel St 49601 231-775-3622
Brenda Mejeur, prin. Fax 775-6233
St. Ann S 200/PK-6
800 W 13th St 49601 231-775-1301
Robert Kellogg, prin. Fax 775-0161

Caledonia, Kent, Pop. 1,496
Caledonia Community SD 4,400/PK-12
9753 Duncan Lake Ave SE 49316 616-891-8185
Randy Rodriguez, supt. Fax 891-9253
www.calschools.org
Caledonia ES 400/K-5
9770 Duncan Lake Ave SE 49316 616-891-8181
Josh Traughber, prin. Fax 891-7019
Duncan Lake ECC 50/PK-PK
9751 Duncan Lake Ave SE 49316 616-891-6220
Mindy Duba, prin. Fax 891-6229
Duncan Lake MS 500/6-8
9757 Duncan Lake Ave SE 49316 616-891-1380
Ryan Graham, prin. Fax 891-0833
Dutton ES 300/K-5
3820 68th St SE 49316 616-698-8982
Shawn Veitch, prin. Fax 698-2117
Emmons Lake ES 400/K-5
8950 Kraft Ave SE 49316 616-528-8100
Tony Silveri, prin. Fax 528-8104
Kraft Meadows MS 500/6-8
9230 Kraft Ave SE 49316 616-891-8649
Steve Uyl, prin. Fax 891-7013
Paris Ridge ES 400/K-5
4690 Paris Ridge Ave SE 49316 616-891-7033
Kris Vydareny, prin. Fax 891-8539
Other Schools – See Alto

Kentwood SD
Supt. — See Kentwood
Explorer ES 500/K-5
2307 68th St SE 49316 616-554-0302
Carrie Tellerico, prin. Fax 554-0970

Dutton Christian S 500/PK-8
6729 Hanna Lake Ave SE 49316 616-698-8660
Daniel Netz, admin. Fax 698-2281

Calumet, Houghton, Pop. 716
Calumet-Laurium-Keweenaw SD 1,400/K-12
57070 Mine St 49913 906-337-0311
Darryl Pierce, supt. Fax 337-1406
clkschools.org
CLK ES 700/K-5
57070 Mine St 49913 906-337-0311
Holly Rivest, admin. Fax 337-5408
Washington MS 300/6-8
57070 Mine St 49913 906-337-0311
Michael Steber, prin. Fax 337-5406

Camden, Hillsdale, Pop. 510
Camden-Frontier SD 500/K-12
4971 W Montgomery Rd 49232 517-368-5991
Scott Riley, supt. Fax 368-5959
www.cfss.org/
Camden Frontier ES 400/K-8
4971 W Montgomery Rd 49232 517-368-5258
Scott Riley, prin. Fax 368-5959

Canton, Wayne, Pop. 81,500
Plymouth-Canton Community SD
Supt. — See Plymouth
Bentley ES 400/K-5
1100 S Sheldon Rd 48188 734-397-6361
Laura Carino, prin. Fax 397-6347
Discovery MS 1,000/6-8
45083 Hanford Rd 48187 734-416-2880
Terry Sawchuk, prin. Fax 416-2895
Dodson ES 500/K-5
205 N Beck Rd 48187 734-981-8003
April Quasarano, prin. Fax 981-9202
Eriksson ES 500/K-5
1275 N Haggerty Rd 48187 734-981-5560
Kevin Learned, prin. Fax 981-2740
Field ES 300/K-5
1000 S Haggerty Rd 48188 734-397-6330
Denise Lilly, prin. Fax 397-6334
Gallimore ES 200/PK-PK, 3-
8375 N Sheldon Rd 48187 734-416-3150
Aimee Bell, prin. Fax 416-7670
Hoben ES 500/K-5
44680 Saltz Rd 48187 734-981-8670
Lisa Johnston, prin. Fax 981-7405
Hulsing ES 500/K-5
8055 Fleet St 48187 734-416-6150
Jennifer Chambers, prin. Fax 455-9530
Liberty MS 6-8
46250 Cherry Hill Rd 48187 734-416-7600
James Hunter, prin. Fax 927-0576
Miller ES 400/K-5
43721 Hanford Rd 48187 734-416-4800
Blair Klco, prin. Fax 416-4801
Tonda ES 500/K-5
46501 Warren Rd 48187 734-416-6100
Deirdre Brady, prin. Fax 416-2018
Workman ES 700/K-5
250 N Denton Rd 48187 734-582-6700
Dr. James Burt, prin. Fax 844-6526

Wayne-Westland Community SD
Supt. — See Westland
Walker-Winter ES 400/K-4
39932 Michigan Ave 48188 734-419-2780
Julie Mytych, prin. Fax 595-2578

All Saints S 500/PK-8
48735 Warren Rd 48187 734-459-2490
Kristen Strausbaugh, prin. Fax 459-0981
Crescent Academy International 500/PK-8
40440 Palmer Rd 48188 734-729-1000
Plymouth Christian Academy 600/PK-12
43065 Joy Rd 48187 734-459-3505
Caryn Huntsman, supt. Fax 459-9997
Schoolhouse Montessori - Canton 100/PK-6
1669 S Haggerty Rd 48188 734-405-2345

Capac, Saint Clair, Pop. 1,866
Capac Community SD 900/PK-12
403 N Glassford St 48014 810-395-3710
Dr. Jeff Terpenning, supt. Fax 395-4858
www.capacschools.us
Capac ES 500/PK-6
351 W Kempf Ct 48014 810-395-3636
Sean Lively, prin. Fax 395-8086

Carleton, Monroe, Pop. 2,303
Airport Community SD 2,100/PK-12
11270 Grafton Rd 48117 734-654-2414
John Krimmel, supt. Fax 654-4014
www.airportschools.com
Eyler ES 300/K-4
1335 Carleton Rockwood Rd 48117 734-654-2121
Steven Krause, prin. Fax 654-9535
Sterling ES 300/PK-4
160 Fessner Rd 48117 734-654-6846
Ryan Duvall, prin. Fax 654-9480
Wagar 5/6 MS 5-6
11200 Grafton Rd 48117 734-654-6205
Craig Freestone, prin. Fax 654-0057
Wagar 7/8 MS 400/7-8
11200 Grafton Rd 48117 734-654-6205
Dan Bondy, prin. Fax 654-0057
Other Schools – See South Rockwood

St. Patrick S 100/K-8
2970 W Labo Rd 48117 734-654-2522
Charles Lenze, prin. Fax 654-8532

Carney, Menominee, Pop. 190
Carney-Nadeau SD 200/PK-12
PO Box 68 49812 906-639-2171
Adam Cocco, supt. Fax 639-2176
www.cnps.us
Carney-Nadeau S 200/PK-12
PO Box 68 49812 906-639-2171
Adam Cocco, admin. Fax 639-2176

Caro, Tuscola, Pop. 4,185
Caro Community SD 1,800/K-12
301 N Hooper St 48723 989-673-3160
Michael Joslyn, supt. Fax 673-6248
www.carok12.org
Caro MS 400/6-8
299 N Hooper St 48723 989-673-3167
JoAnn Nordstrom, prin. Fax 673-1225
McComb ES 400/K-2
303 N Hooper St 48723 989-673-3169
David Wheeler, prin. Fax 673-3883
Schall ES 400/3-5
325 E Frank St 48723 989-673-3168
Michelle Warren, prin. Fax 672-4684

Carson City, Montcalm, Pop. 1,086
Carson City-Crystal Area SD 900/K-12
PO Box 780 48811 989-584-3138
Kevin Murphy, supt. Fax 584-3539
www.carsoncity.k12.mi.us
Carson City-Crystal Upper Elementary MS 400/4-8
PO Box 780 48811 989-584-3903
Duane Lyons, prin. Fax 584-3259
Carson City ES 300/K-3
PO Box 780 48811 989-584-3130
Alexis Shaver, prin. Fax 584-6112

Carsonville, Sanilac, Pop. 513
Carsonville-Port Sanilac SD 500/K-12
100 N Goetze Rd 48419 810-657-9393
James Stewart, supt. Fax 657-9060
www.cpsk12.us
Carsonville-Port Sanilac ES 200/K-5
4115 E Chandler St 48419 810-657-9318
Jennifer Richmond, prin. Fax 657-8966

Casco, Saint Clair
Anchor Bay SD 6,000/PK-12
5201 County Line Rd Ste 100 48064 586-725-2861
Leonard Woodside, supt. Fax 727-9059
www.anchorbay.misd.net
Other Schools – See Chesterfield, Ira, New Baltimore

Caseville, Huron, Pop. 766
Caseville SD 100/K-12
6609 Vine St 48725 989-856-2940
Dr. Kenneth Ewald, supt. Fax 856-3095
www.cpseagles.org
Caseville S 100/K-12
6609 Vine St 48725 989-856-7192
Dr. Kenneth Ewald, prin. Fax 856-8641

Cass City, Tuscola, Pop. 2,395
Cass City SD 1,000/PK-12
4868 Seeger St 48726 989-872-2200
Jeffrey Hartel, supt. Fax 872-5015
www.casscity.k12.mi.us
Campbell ES 600/PK-6
4805 Ale St 48726 989-872-2158
Aaron Fernald, prin. Fax 872-3910

Cassopolis, Cass, Pop. 1,687
Cassopolis SD 900/K-12
725 Center St 49031 269-445-0503
Dr. Angela Piazza, supt. Fax 445-0505
www.cassopolis.k12.mi.us
Adams ES 500/K-6
114 Depot St 49031 269-445-0516
DeeAnn Melville-Voss, prin. Fax 445-0521

Calvin Center SDA S 50/K-8
19088 Brownsville Rd 49031 269-476-2218
Norman Usher, prin. Fax 476-2614

Cedar Lake, Montcalm

Cedar Lake SDA S 50/1-8
PO Box 218 48812 989-427-5614
Alio Santos, prin. Fax 427-0012

Cedar Springs, Kent, Pop. 3,426
Cedar Springs SD 3,300/PK-12
204 E Muskegon St 49319 616-696-1204
Dr. Laura VanDuyn Ed.D., supt. Fax 696-3755
www.csredhawks.org
Beach ES 500/2-3
204 E Muskegon St 49319 616-696-0350
Tricia Shenefield, prin. Fax 696-3182
Cedar Springs MS 500/7-8
204 E Muskegon St 49319 616-696-9100
Sue Spahr, prin. Fax 696-3109
Cedar Trails ES 600/PK-1
204 E Muskegon St 49319 616-696-9884
Beth Whaley, prin. Fax 696-3104
Cedar View ES 500/4-5
204 E Muskegon St 49319 616-696-9102
Carol Franz, prin. Fax 696-3177
Red Hawk ES 200/6-6
204 E Muskegon St 49319 616-696-7330
Miranda Latimer, prin. Fax 696-3123

Cedarville, Mackinac
Les Cheneaux Community SD 300/K-12
PO Box 366 49719 906-484-2256
Randy Schaedig, supt. Fax 484-2072
lescheneaux.eup.k12.mi.us/site/default.aspx?PageID=1
Cedarville S 300/K-12
PO Box 366 49719 906-484-2256
Randy Schaedig, supt. Fax 484-2072

Center Line, Macomb, Pop. 8,060
Center Line SD 2,700/PK-12
26400 Arsenal 48015 586-510-2000
Eve Kaltz, supt. Fax 510-2019
www.clps.org
Wolfe MS 600/6-8
8640 McKinley 48015 586-510-2300
Cassandra Conaton, prin. Fax 510-2319
Other Schools – See Warren

Macomb Christian S 200/PK-12
8155 Ritter 48015 586-751-8980
Dr. Erica Holloman, prin. Fax 751-8980

Central Lake, Antrim, Pop. 931
Central Lake SD 400/PK-12
PO Box 128 49622 231-544-3141
Lenore Weaver, supt. Fax 544-2903
www.clps.k12.mi.us
Central Lake ES 200/PK-5
PO Box 128 49622 231-544-3141
Lenore Weaver, prin. Fax 544-6061

Centreville, Saint Joseph, Pop. 1,388
Centreville SD 800/K-12
PO Box 158 49032 269-467-5220
Stephanie Lemmer, supt. Fax 467-5214
www.cpschools.org
Centreville ES 400/K-6
PO Box 158 49032 269-467-5200
Becky Stauffer, prin. Fax 467-5209
Centreville JHS 100/7-8
PO Box 158 49032 269-467-5210
Matthew Hawkins, prin. Fax 467-5214

Charlevoix, Charlevoix, Pop. 2,468
Charlevoix SD 1,000/PK-12
104 E Saint Marys Dr 49720 231-547-3200
Michael Ritter, supt. Fax 547-0556
www.rayder.net
Charlevoix ES 500/PK-6
13513 Division Ave 49720 231-547-3215
John Haan, prin. Fax 547-3150

St. Mary S 100/PK-8
1005 Bridge St 49720 231-547-9441
Kathleen Dvoracek, prin. Fax 547-6658

Charlotte, Eaton, Pop. 8,946
Charlotte SD 2,600/PK-12
378 State St 48813 517-541-5100
Mark Rosekrans, supt. Fax 541-5105
www.charlottenet.org
Charlotte MS 400/7-8
1068 Carlisle Hwy 48813 517-541-5700
Matthew Maitland, prin. Fax 541-5705
Charlotte Upper ES 600/4-6
1068 Carlisle Hwy 48813 517-541-5770
Mark McGarry, prin. Fax 541-5775
Parkview ES 400/PK-3
301 E Kalamo Hwy 48813 517-543-5780
Kim Caudell, prin. Fax 541-5785
Washington ES 300/PK-3
525 High St 48813 517-541-5170
Scott Martin, prin. Fax 541-5175

Charlotte Adventist Christian S 50/K-8
1510 S Cochran Rd 48813 517-543-0445
Kalicia Clements, prin.

St. Mary S 100/K-7
905 Saint Marys Blvd 48813 517-543-3460
Amanda Wildern, prin. Fax 543-9798

Chassell, Houghton
Chassell Township SD 300/K-12
PO Box 140 49916 906-483-2132
Howard Parmentier, supt. Fax 487-9045
www.chassellschools.org
Chassell Township S 300/K-12
PO Box 140 49916 906-483-2132
Howard Parmentier, supt. Fax 487-9045

Cheboygan, Cheboygan, Pop. 4,714
Cheboygan Area SD 1,200/K-12
PO Box 100 49721 231-627-4436
Troy Reehl, supt. Fax 627-9105
www.chebschools.org
Cheboygan IS 400/3-7
PO Box 100 49721 231-627-7103
Brandie Williams, prin. Fax 627-4151
East ES 100/K-2
PO Box 100 49721 231-627-5211
Michael Duvall, prin. Fax 627-4148

Bishop Baraga S 100/PK-7
623 W Lincoln Ave 49721 231-627-5608
Kitty LaBlance, prin. Fax 627-6048

Chelsea, Washtenaw, Pop. 4,865
Chelsea SD 2,400/PK-12
500 Washington St 48118 734-433-2200
Dr. Julie D. Helber Ed.D., supt. Fax 433-2218
www.chelsea.k12.mi.us
Beach MS 600/6-8
445 Mayer Dr 48118 734-433-2202
Nick Angel, prin. Fax 433-2212
Chelsea ECC PK-PK
500 Washington St 48118 734-433-2208
Lisa Nickel, dir.
North Creek ES 500/PK-2
699 McKinley St 48118 734-433-2203
Luman Strong, prin. Fax 433-2213
South Meadows ES 500/3-5
335 Pierce St 48118 734-433-2205
Stacie Battaglia, prin. Fax 433-2215

Chesaning, Saginaw, Pop. 2,377
Chesaning UNSD 1,500/K-12
PO Box 95 48616 989-845-7020
Mike McGough, supt. Fax 845-3722
www.chesaningschools.net
Big Rock ES 500/K-4
920 E Broad St 48616 989-845-2430
Jill Nieman, prin. Fax 845-5872
Chesaning MS 500/5-8
431 N 4th St 48616 989-845-7040
Melinda Soule, prin. Fax 845-5335

Zion Evangelical Lutheran S 50/PK-8
796 Hampton St 48616 989-845-2377
Hannah Mose, sec. ed.

Chesterfield, Macomb
Anchor Bay SD
Supt. — See Casco
Great Oaks ES 400/K-5
32900 24 Mile Rd 48047 586-725-2038
Ronald Medley, prin. Fax 725-4014

L'Anse Creuse SD
Supt. — See Clinton Township
Burdi ECC PK-PK
29851 24 Mile Rd 48051 586-493-5220
Patrice Wadie, dir. Fax 493-5225
Carkenord ES 400/K-5
27100 24 Mile Rd 48051 586-493-5230
Christopher May, prin. Fax 493-5235
Green ES 500/K-5
47260 Sugarbush Rd 48047 586-493-5280
Karen Nelson, prin. Fax 493-5285
Higgins ES 500/PK-5
29901 24 Mile Rd 48051 586-493-5210
Susan Trebilcock, prin. Fax 493-5215
L'Anse Creuse MS East 800/6-8
30300 Hickey Rd 48051 586-493-5200
Nina Davis, prin. Fax 493-5205

China, Saint Clair
East China SD
Supt. — See East China
Pine River ES 400/K-5
3575 King Rd 48054 810-676-1050
Rachel Card, prin. Fax 676-1060

Clare, Clare, Pop. 3,061
Clare SD 1,500/K-12
201 E State St 48617 989-386-9945
James Walter, supt. Fax 386-6055
www.clare.k12.mi.us
Clare MS 500/5-8
201 E State St 48617 989-386-9979
Steve Newkirk, prin. Fax 386-4008
Clare PS 600/K-4
201 E State St 48617 989-386-3438
Fax 386-1215

Clarkston, Oakland, Pop. 980
Clarkston Community SD 7,800/PK-12
6389 Clarkston Rd 48346 248-623-5400
Dr. Rod Rock, supt. Fax 623-5450
www.clarkston.k12.mi.us
Bailey Lake ES 600/K-5
8051 Pine Knob Rd 48348 248-623-5300
Glenn Gualtieri, prin. Fax 623-5305
Clarkston ECC 100/PK-K
6397 Clarkston Rd 48346 248-623-4350
Lisa Marion, prin. Fax 623-4355
Clarkston ES 400/K-5
6589 Waldon Rd 48346 248-623-5100
Brian Adams, prin. Fax 623-5144

Independence ES 500/K-5
6850 Hubbard Rd 48348 248-623-5500
Nathan Fuller, prin. Fax 623-5554
North Sashabaw ES 300/K-5
5290 Maybee Rd 48346 248-623-4100
Jennifer Johnson, prin. Fax 623-4105
Pine Knob ES 500/K-5
6020 Sashabaw Rd 48346 248-623-3900
Jodi Yeloushan, prin. Fax 623-3905
Sashabaw MS 1,200/6-7
5565 Pine Knob Rd 48346 248-623-4200
Elizabeth Walker, prin. Fax 623-4205
Springfield Plains ES 500/PK-5
8650 Holcomb Rd 48348 248-623-3800
Matthew Gifford, prin. Fax 623-3805
Other Schools – See Davisburg

Cedar Crest Academy 100/PK-8
8970 Dixie Hwy 48348 248-625-7270
Tracy Moen, dir. Fax 625-7212
Everest Collegiate HS & Academy 500/PK-12
5935 Clarkston Rd 48348 248-620-3390
Gregory Reichert, pres. Fax 620-3942

Clawson, Oakland, Pop. 11,609
Clawson SD 1,700/K-12
626 Phillips Ave 48017 248-655-4400
Monique Beels, supt. Fax 655-4422
www.clawsonschools.org
Clawson MS 400/6-8
150 John M Ave 48017 248-655-4250
Adam Schihl, prin. Fax 655-4251
Kenwood ES 300/K-5
240 Nahma Ave 48017 248-655-3838
Amy Carpenter, prin. Fax 655-3802
Schalm ES 500/K-5
940 N Selfridge Blvd 48017 248-655-4949
Bianca Hill, prin. Fax 655-4947

Guardian Angels S 300/PK-8
521 E 14 Mile Rd 48017 248-588-5545
Stephen Turk, prin. Fax 589-7356

Climax, Kalamazoo, Pop. 761
Climax-Scotts Community SD 500/PK-12
372 S Main St 49034 269-746-2400
Douglas Newington, supt. Fax 746-4374
www.csschools.net
Other Schools – See Scotts

Clinton, Lenawee, Pop. 2,302
Clinton Community SD 1,100/PK-12
341 E Michigan Ave 49236 517-456-6501
James Cracraft, supt. Fax 456-4324
ccsweb.clinton.k12.mi.us
Clinton ES 500/K-5
200 E Franklin St 49236 517-456-6504
Todd Baulch, prin. Fax 456-8201
Clinton MS 200/6-8
100 E Franklin St 49236 517-456-6507
Eric Claus, prin. Fax 456-4997
Pray Preschool PK-PK
330 E Michigan Ave 49236 517-456-2010
Mimi Scott, dir. Fax 701-1000

Clinton Township, Macomb, Pop. 95,648
Chippewa Valley SD 15,300/K-12
19120 Cass Ave 48038 586-723-2000
Ron Roberts, supt. Fax 723-2001
www.chippewavalleyschools.org
Algonquin MS 600/6-8
19150 Briarwood Ln 48036 586-723-3500
Walter Kozlowski, prin. Fax 723-3501
Cherokee ES 600/K-5
42900 Rivergate Dr 48038 586-723-4800
Lynn Mair, prin. Fax 723-4801
Erie ES 500/K-5
42276 Romeo Plank Rd 48038 586-723-5400
Dr. Gerard Evanski, prin. Fax 723-5401
Huron ES 500/K-5
15800 Terra Bella St 48038 586-723-5800
Kelly Shock, prin. Fax 723-5801
Miami ES 500/K-5
41290 Kentvale Dr 48038 586-723-6000
Craig Bulgrin, prin. Fax 723-6001
Ottawa ES 400/K-5
18601 Millar Rd 48036 586-723-6600
Duane Lockhart, prin. Fax 723-6601
Wyandot MS 1,000/6-8
39490 Garfield Rd 48038 586-723-4200
Darleen Gauci, prin. Fax 723-4201
Other Schools – See Macomb, Mount Clemens

Clintondale Community SD 2,500/PK-12
35100 Little Mack Ave 48035 586-791-6300
Gregory Green, supt. Fax 791-6786
seatwaitingforyou.com
Clintondale MS 400/6-8
35300 Little Mack Ave 48035 586-791-6300
Ira Hamden, prin. Fax 790-7642
McGlinnen ES 300/K-6
21415 Sunnyview St 48035 586-791-3400
Cathy LaMont, prin. Fax 790-7639
Parker ES 400/PK-6
22055 Quinn Rd 48035 586-791-6900
Shannon King, prin. Fax 790-7641
Rainbow ES 200/K-6
33749 Wurfel St 48035 586-791-3500
Cara Cottrell-Booms, prin. Fax 790-7640

Fraser SD
Supt. — See Fraser
Disney ES 400/K-6
36155 Kelly Rd 48035 586-439-6400
Aaron Sutherland, prin. Fax 439-6401
Salk ES 600/K-6
17601 15 Mile Rd 48035 586-439-6800
Dr. Donna Anderson Ed.D., prin. Fax 439-6801

L'Anse Creuse SD 10,700/PK-12
24076 Frederick Pankow Blvd 48036 586-783-6300
Erik Edoff, supt. Fax 783-6310
www.lc-ps.org
Tenniswood ES 400/K-5
23450 Glenwood St 48035 586-493-5640
Kimberly Vigneron, prin. Fax 493-5645
Other Schools – See Chesterfield, Harrison Township, Macomb

Faith Christian S 100/PK-12
23130 Remick Dr 48036 586-783-9630
Jim Hawkins, prin. Fax 783-9628
St. Luke Lutheran S 100/PK-8
21400 S Nunneley Rd 48035 586-791-1151
Keith Vieregge, prin. Fax 791-1880
St. Thecla S 500/PK-8
20762 S Nunneley Rd 48035 586-791-2170
Geoffrey Fisher, prin. Fax 791-2356
Trinity Lutheran S 400/PK-8
38900 Harper Ave 48036 586-468-8511
Julian Petzold, prin. Fax 468-1226

Clio, Genesee, Pop. 2,597
Clio Area SD 3,300/K-12
430 N Mill St 48420 810-591-0500
Fletcher Spears, supt. Fax 591-0140
www.clioschools.org
Carter MS 1,000/5-8
300 Rogers Ldg 48420 810-591-0503
Neil Bedell, prin. Fax 591-8148
Edgerton ES 400/K-4
11218 N Linden Rd 48420 810-591-7650
Michelle Pyrett, prin. Fax 591-8162
Garner ES 400/K-4
10271 N Clio Rd 48420 810-591-1871
John Lanyi, prin. Fax 591-8163
Lacure ES 400/K-4
12167 N Lewis Rd 48420 810-591-1950
Katrina Mitchell, prin. Fax 591-8168

Coldwater, Branch, Pop. 10,680
Coldwater Community SD 3,000/PK-12
401 Sauk River Dr 49036 517-279-5910
Terry Ann Boguth, supt. Fax 279-7651
www.coldwaterschools.org
Jefferson ES 400/2-3
15 Vans Ave 49036 517-279-5970
Peter Rogovich, prin. Fax 279-2332
Lakeland ES 400/4-5
519 Otis Rd 49036 517-238-2105
Gary Dancer, prin. Fax 238-4022
Larsen ES 500/K-1
25 Parkhurst Ave 49036 517-279-5960
Shawn Caldwell, prin. Fax 279-2516
Legg MS 600/6-8
175 Green St 49036 517-279-5940
Julie Slusher, prin. Fax 279-5945
Lincoln Learning Center 300/PK-PK
70 Tibbits St 49036 517-279-5975
Krista Searls, prin. Fax 279-5977

St. Charles S 100/PK-8
79 Harrison St 49036 517-279-0404
Brenda Mescher, prin. Fax 278-0505

Coleman, Midland, Pop. 1,211
Coleman Community SD 700/K-12
4823 N Coleman Schools Dr 48618 989-465-6060
Jennifer McCormack, supt. Fax 465-9853
www.colemanschools.net
Coleman ES 400/K-6
1010 E Washington St 48618 989-465-6179
Cindy Araway, prin. Fax 465-9852

Coloma, Berrien, Pop. 1,456
Coloma Community SD 900/PK-12
PO Box 550 49038 269-468-2424
Pete Bush, supt. Fax 468-2440
www.ccs.coloma.org
Coloma ES 200/PK-3
PO Box 550 49038 269-468-2420
John Klein, prin. Fax 468-2434
Coloma IS 100/4-5
PO Box 550 49038 269-468-2415
Dr. Darla England, prin. Fax 468-2429
Coloma JHS 100/6-8
PO Box 550 49038 269-468-2405
Wendy Tremblay, prin. Fax 468-2428

Colon, Saint Joseph, Pop. 1,152
Colon Community SD 600/PK-12
400 Dallas St 49040 269-386-2239
Fax 432-2981
www.colonschools.org
Colon ES 300/PK-5
328 E State St 49040 269-432-2121
Martha Hymer, prin. Fax 432-9341
Other Schools – See Leonidas

Columbiaville, Lapeer, Pop. 775
LakeVille Community SD
Supt. — See Otisville
Columbiaville ES 300/3-5
4775 Pine St 48421 810-538-3460
Michael Banyas, prin. Fax 793-6516

Commerce Township, Oakland, Pop. 26,955
Huron Valley SD
Supt. — See Highland
Country Oaks ES 600/PK-5
5070 S Duck Lake Rd 48382 248-684-8075
Gary Hamilton, prin. Fax 684-8275
Oak Valley MS 700/6-8
4200 White Oak Trl 48382 248-684-8101
Brett Myers, prin. Fax 684-8105

Walled Lake Consolidated SD
Supt. — See Walled Lake
Commerce ES 600/K-5
520 Farr St 48382 248-956-3900
Christina Carlin, prin. Fax 956-3905
Smart MS 1,000/6-8
8500 Commerce Rd 48382 248-956-3500
David Tucker, prin. Fax 956-3505

Comstock Park, Kent, Pop. 9,824
Comstock Park SD 2,400/PK-12
101 School St NE 49321 616-254-5001
Ethan Ebenstein, supt. Fax 784-5404
www.cppschools.com
Greenridge ES 300/PK-PK
3825 Oakridge Ave NW 49321 616-254-5700
Jodi Miller, prin. Fax 785-9829
Mill Creek MS 500/6-8
100 Betty St NE 49321 616-254-5100
August Harju, prin. Fax 785-2464
Pine Island ES 500/3-5
6101 Pine Island Dr NE 49321 616-254-5500
Stacy Reehl, prin. Fax 785-4176
Stoney Creek ES 500/K-2
200 Lantern Dr NW 49321 616-254-5600
Jason Rykse, prin. Fax 785-9853

Kenowa Hills SD
Supt. — See Grand Rapids
Alpine ES 400/K-5
4730 Baumhoff Ave NW 49321 616-784-0884
Jason Snyder M.Ed., prin. Fax 784-1228

Holy Trinity S 100/PK-8
1304 Alpine Church Rd NW 49321 616-784-0696
Kathy Rand, prin. Fax 988-9415

Concord, Jackson, Pop. 1,046
Concord Community SD 700/K-12
PO Box 338 49237 517-524-8850
Dan Funston, supt. Fax 524-8613
www.concordschools.net
Concord ES 300/K-5
PO Box 338 49237 517-524-6650
Rebecca Hutchinson, prin. Fax 524-7680
Concord MS 200/6-8
PO Box 338 49237 517-524-8854
Rebecca Hutchinson, prin. Fax 524-7324

Conklin, Ottawa

Divine Providence Academy - St. Joseph 100/PK-8
18768 8th Ave 49403 616-899-5300
Kendra DeYoung, prin. Fax 899-5491
Trinity Lutheran S 50/PK-5
1401 Harding St 49403 616-899-2152
Terri Kober, admin. Fax 899-1112

Constantine, Saint Joseph, Pop. 2,015
Constantine SD 1,400/K-12
1 Falcon Dr 49042 269-435-8900
Steve Wilson, supt. Fax 435-8980
www.constps.org
Constantine MS 300/6-8
260 W 6th St 49042 269-435-8940
Ray Bohm, prin. Fax 435-8982
Eastside ES 400/K-2
935 White Pigeon Rd 49042 269-435-8960
Christina Bainbridge, prin. Fax 435-8984
Riverside ES 300/3-5
600 W 6th St 49042 269-435-8950
Darrin Vandenberg, prin. Fax 435-8983

Cooks, Delta
Big Bay de Noc SD 200/PK-12
8928 00.25 Rd 49817 906-644-2773
Diana Thill, supt. Fax 644-2615
www.bigbayschool.com
Big Bay de Noc S 200/PK-12
8928 00.25 Rd 49817 906-644-2773
Diana Thill, prin. Fax 644-2615

Coopersville, Ottawa, Pop. 4,215
Coopersville Area SD 2,500/PK-12
198 East St 49404 616-997-3200
Ron Veldman, supt. Fax 997-3214
www.coopersvillebroncos.org/
Coopersville East ES 400/1-2
198 East St 49404 616-997-3300
Corey DeRidder, prin. Fax 997-3314
Coopersville MS 600/6-8
198 East St 49404 616-997-3400
Ryan Pfahler, prin. Fax 997-3414
Coopersville South ES 600/3-5
198 East St 49404 616-997-3100
Bernie Stanko, prin. Fax 997-3114
Coopersville West ECC 200/PK-K
198 East St 49404 616-997-3600
Corey DeRidder, prin. Fax 997-3614

Lamont Christian S 100/PK-8
5260 Leonard St 49404 616-677-1757
Joe Oosterheert, prin. Fax 677-2935

Copper Harbor, Keweenaw, Pop. 105
Grant Township SD 2 50/PK-8
PO Box 74 49918 906-289-4447
George Stockero, supt. Fax 289-4447
www.copperharborschool.org/
Copper Harbor S 50/PK-8
PO Box 74 49918 906-289-4447
Diane Trudgeon, lead tchr. Fax 289-4447

Corunna, Shiawassee, Pop. 3,446
Corunna SD 1,200/PK-12
124 N Shiawassee St 48817 989-743-6338
Dave Moore, supt. Fax 743-4474
www.corunna.k12.mi.us
Corunna MS 300/4-7
400 N Comstock St 48817 989-743-5641
Robb Dettman, prin. Fax 743-8761

Meyer ES 200/1-3
100 Hastings St 48817 989-743-4404
Stacy Regan, prin. Fax 743-8854
Peacock Children's Services PK-PK
485 E McArthur St 48817 989-743-8848
April Woodruff, admin. Fax 743-4963
Other Schools – See Vernon

Covert, Van Buren
Covert SD 300/PK-12
35323 M 140 Hwy 49043 269-764-3701
Dr. Bobbi Morehead, supt. Fax 764-8598
www.covertps.org
Covert ES 200/PK-5
35323 M 140 Hwy 49043 269-764-3720
Claire Kliss, prin. Fax 764-3764
Covert MS 100/6-8
35323 M 140 Hwy 49043 269-764-3730
Yolanda Brunt, prin. Fax 764-3754

Croswell, Sanilac, Pop. 2,419
Croswell-Lexington SD 2,300/PK-12
5407 Peck Rd 48422 810-679-1000
Daniel Gilbertson, supt. Fax 679-1005
www.croslex.org
Croswell-Lexington MS 700/5-8
5485 Peck Rd 48422 810-679-1400
Bethany Davis, prin. Fax 679-1405
Frostick ES 500/K-4
57 S Howard Ave 48422 810-679-1100
Colette Moody, prin. Fax 679-1105
Geiger ECC 50/PK-PK
57 S Howard Ave 48422 810-679-1300
Colette Moody, prin. Fax 679-1105
Other Schools – See Lexington

Crystal Falls, Iron, Pop. 1,443
Forest Park SD 500/PK-12
801 Forest Pkwy 49920 906-214-4695
Becky Waters, supt. Fax 875-4660
www.fptrojans.org
Forest Park ES 200/PK-5
801 Forest Pkwy 49920 906-214-4695
Becky Waters, prin. Fax 875-4660

Custer, Mason, Pop. 279
Mason County Eastern SD 500/K-12
18 S Main St 49405 231-757-3733
Paul Shoup, supt. Fax 757-9671
mceschools.com
Mason County Eastern ES 200/K-6
18 S Main St 49405 231-757-3733
Paul Shoup, admin. Fax 757-9671

Dansville, Ingham, Pop. 554
Dansville SD 800/K-12
PO Box 187 48819 517-623-6120
Amy Hodgson, supt. Fax 623-6719
www.dansville.org
Dansville ES 300/K-5
PO Box 187 48819 517-623-6120
Andrew Cox, prin. Fax 623-6665
Dansville MS 200/6-8
PO Box 187 48819 517-623-6120
Tania Dupuis, prin. Fax 623-1087

Davisburg, Oakland
Clarkston Community SD
Supt. — See Clarkston
Andersonville ES 400/K-5
10350 Andersonville Rd 48350 248-623-5200
Kimberly Fletcher, prin. Fax 623-5205

Holly Area SD
Supt. — See Holly
Davisburg ES 300/PK-5
12003 Davisburg Rd 48350 248-328-3500
Denise Kott, prin. Fax 328-3504

Davison, Genesee, Pop. 5,081
Davison Community SD 5,500/K-12
PO Box 319 48423 810-591-0801
Eric Lieske, supt. Fax 591-7813
www.davisonschools.org/
Central ES 600/1-4
600 S State Rd 48423 810-591-0818
Lance Harper, prin. Fax 591-0830
Davison MS 800/7-8
600 S Dayton St 48423 810-591-0848
Shelly Fenner-Krasny, prin. Fax 591-2754
Gates ES 600/1-4
2359 S Irish Rd 48423 810-591-5001
Theresa Wendt, prin. Fax 591-5016
Hahn IS 800/5-6
500 S Dayton St 48423 810-591-0530
Verle Gilbert, prin. Fax 591-1120
Hill ES 300/K-4
404 Aloha St 48423 810-591-0839
Jennifer Torok, prin. Fax 591-9490
Siple ES 400/K-4
9286 E Coldwater Rd 48423 810-591-5104
Christy Flowers, prin. Fax 591-5102
Thomson K 300/K-K
617 E Clark St 48423 810-591-0911
Natalie Miller, prin. Fax 591-0905

Faith Baptist S 300/PK-12
7306 E Atherton Rd 48423 810-653-9661

Dearborn, Wayne, Pop. 94,259
Dearborn SD 17,900/PK-12
18700 Audette St 48124 313-827-3020
Dr. Glenn Maleyko, supt. Fax 827-3137
www.dearbornschools.org
Becker ES 300/PK-5
10821 Henson St 48126 313-827-6950
Rima Hassan, prin. Fax 827-6955
Bryant MS 800/6-8
460 N Vernon St 48128 313-827-2900
Andrew Denison, prin. Fax 827-2905

Cotter ECC 50/PK-PK
13020 Osborne St 48126 313-827-6150
Fax 827-6155
DuVall ES 300/K-5
22561 Beech St 48124 313-827-2750
Robert Attee, prin. Fax 827-2755
Ford ES 800/K-5
16140 Driscoll St 48126 313-827-4700
Adnan Moughni, prin. Fax 827-4705
Ford ES 700/K-5
14749 Alber St 48126 313-827-6400
David Higgins, prin. Fax 827-6405
Geer Park ES 300/K-5
14767 Prospect St 48126 313-827-2300
Lamis Srour, prin. Fax 827-2305
Haigh ES 500/K-5
601 N Silvery Ln 48128 313-827-6200
Zachary Short, prin. Fax 827-6205
Howard ES 400/K-5
1611 N York St 48128 313-827-6350
Dan Blessing, prin. Fax 827-6355
Lindbergh ES 300/K-5
500 N Waverly St 48128 313-827-6300
Zainah Tiba, prin. Fax 827-6305
Long ES 200/K-5
3100 Westwood St 48124 313-827-6100
Veronica Jakubus, prin. Fax 827-6105
Lowrey S 700/K-8
6601 Jonathon St 48126 313-827-1800
Rima Younes, prin. Fax 827-1805
Maples ES 600/K-5
6801 Mead St 48126 313-827-6450
Donna Jakubik, prin. Fax 827-6455
McCollough / Unis S 600/K-8
7801 Maple St 48126 313-827-1700
Heyam Alcodray, prin. Fax 827-1705
McDonald ES 300/K-5
10151 Diversey St 48126 313-827-6700
Amy Modica, prin. Fax 827-6705
Miller ES 500/PK-5
4824 Lois St 48126 313-827-6850
Mahmoud Abu-Rus, prin. Fax 827-6855
Nowlin ES 200/PK-5
23600 Penn St 48124 313-827-6900
Josh Tynan, prin. Fax 827-6905
Oakman ES 300/K-5
7545 Chase Rd 48126 313-827-6500
Mahmoud AbuRus, prin. Fax 827-6505
Salina ES 400/PK-3
2700 Ferney St 48120 313-827-6550
Susan Stanley, prin. Fax 827-6555
Salina IS 500/4-8
2623 Salina St 48120 313-827-6600
Jamel Lawera, prin. Fax 827-6605
Smith MS 600/6-8
23851 Yale St 48124 313-827-2800
Zeina Jebril, prin. Fax 827-2805
Snow ES 400/K-5
2000 Culver Ave 48124 313-827-6250
Amal Alcodray, prin. Fax 827-6255
Stout MS 800/6-8
18500 Oakwood Blvd 48124 313-827-4600
Gregory Oke, prin. Fax 827-4605
Whitmore-Bolles ES 300/PK-5
21501 Whitmore St 48124 313-827-6800
Kristin Waddell, prin. Fax 827-6805
Woodworth MS 900/6-8
4951 Ternes St 48126 313-827-7100
Maysam Alie-Bazzi, prin. Fax 827-7105
Other Schools – See Dearborn Heights

Divine Child S 600/K-8
25001 Herbert Weier Dr 48128 313-562-1090
Sr. Cecilia Bondy, prin. Fax 562-9306
Emmanuel Lutheran S 50/PK-8
22425 Morley Ave 48124 313-561-6265
Paul Baerwolf, prin. Fax 565-4330
Guardian Lutheran S 200/PK-8
24544 Cherry Hill St 48124 313-274-3665
Matthew Dummann, prin. Fax 274-2076
Muslim American Youth Academy 300/PK-8
19500 Ford Rd 48128 313-436-3300
Sacred Heart S 200/K-8
22513 Garrison St 48124 313-561-9192
Gary Yee, prin. Fax 561-1598

Dearborn Heights, Wayne, Pop. 56,336
Crestwood SD 3,400/PK-12
1501 N Beech Daly Rd 48127 313-278-0906
Dr. Laurine VanValkenburg, supt. Fax 278-4774
www.csdm.k12.mi.us/
Highview ES 300/PK-4
25225 Richardson St 48127 313-278-8390
Alice Reinke, prin. Fax 792-0204
Hillcrest ES 300/K-4
7500 N Vernon St 48127 313-278-0425
Fax 792-0202
Kinloch ES 500/K-4
1505 Kinloch St 48127 313-278-4482
Susan Zahul, prin. Fax 792-0203
Riverside MS 1,100/5-8
25900 W Warren St 48127 313-274-0140
Dennis Faletti, prin. Fax 792-0201

Dearborn Heights SD 7 2,600/PK-12
20629 Annapolis St 48125 313-203-1000
Jennifer Mast, supt. Fax 278-1413
www.district7.net
Bedford ES 400/K-1
4650 Croissant St 48125 313-203-4100
Bradley Allen, prin. Fax 278-1980
Best JHS 700/6-8
22201 Powers Ave 48125 313-203-3200
Aaron Mollett, prin. Fax 278-2470
Madison ECC PK-PK
4650 Madison 48125 313-203-4200
Linda Zibbell, prin. Fax 292-3608
Pardee ES 300/4-5
4650 Pardee Ave 48125 313-203-5600
William Murphy, prin. Fax 292-3606

Polk ES 400/2-3
4651 Polk St 48125 313-203-0500
Mark Brenton, prin. Fax 563-7189

Dearborn SD
Supt. — See Dearborn
River Oaks ES 300/K-5
20755 Ann Arbor Trl 48127 313-827-6750
Joe Martin, prin. Fax 827-6755

Westwood Community SD 2,300/K-12
3335 S Beech Daly St 48125 313-565-1900
Sue Carnell, supt. Fax 565-3162
westwoodschools.net
Thorne ES 900/K-6
25251 Annapolis St 48125 313-292-1600
Vickie Patterson, prin. Fax 292-4282
Other Schools – See Inkster

Dearborn Heights Montessori Center 300/PK-8
466 N John Daly Rd 48127 313-359-3000
Kay Neff, hdmstr. Fax 359-3003
St. Anselm S 100/PK-8
17700 W Outer Dr 48127 313-563-3430
Angela Kraetke, prin. Fax 563-2435
St. Linus S 300/PK-8
6466 N Evangeline St 48127 313-274-5320
Christine Sagert, prin. Fax 562-2821
St. Sebastian S 200/PK-8
20700 Colgate St 48125 313-563-6640
Sr. Geraldine Kaczynski, prin. Fax 563-6641

Decatur, Van Buren, Pop. 1,763
Decatur SD 900/K-12
110 Cedar St 49045 269-423-6800
Dr. Patrick Creagan, supt. Fax 423-6849
www.raiderpride.org/
Davis ES 400/K-5
409 N Phelps St 49045 269-423-6950
Kimberly Cugnetti, prin. Fax 423-6999
Decatur MS 200/6-8
405 N Phelps St 49045 269-423-6900
Matthew McLouth, prin. Fax 423-6949

Deckerville, Sanilac, Pop. 821
Deckerville Community SD 600/K-12
2633 Black River St 48427 810-376-3615
Michael Hugan, supt. Fax 376-3115
deckerville.k12.mi.us
Deckerville ES 300/K-6
2633 Black River St 48427 810-376-9785
Yvonne O'Connor, prin. Fax 376-3115

Deerfield, Lenawee, Pop. 875
Britton Deerfield SD
Supt. — See Britton
Deerfield S 200/4-8
PO Box 217 49238 517-447-3015
Stacy Johnson, admin. Fax 447-3216

Deerton, Alger
Autrain-Onota SD 50/PK-8
PO Box 105 49822 906-343-6632
Bryan Tyner, supt. Fax 343-6633
www.autrainonota.com
Autrain-Onota S 50/PK-8
PO Box 105 49822 906-343-6632
Bryan Tyner, prin. Fax 343-6633

Delton, Barry, Pop. 851
Delton Kellogg SD 1,300/K-12
327 N Grove St 49046 269-623-1501
Kyle Corlett, supt. Fax 623-1508
www.dkschools.org
Delton Kellogg ES 500/K-4
327 N Grove St 49046 269-623-1531
Steve Scoville, prin. Fax 623-1538
Delton Kellogg MS 400/5-8
6325 Delton Rd 49046 269-623-1542
April Margaritis, prin. Fax 623-1548

De Tour Village, Chippewa, Pop. 312
De Tour Area SD 100/K-12
PO Box 429 49725 906-297-2421
Angela Reed, supt. Fax 297-3403
detour.eup.k12.mi.us
Other Schools – See Drummond Island

Detroit, Wayne, Pop. 700,219
Detroit SD 52,800/PK-12
7321 2nd Ave Fl 14 48202 313-873-7450
Dr. Nikolai Vitti, supt. Fax 873-7433
detroitk12.org
Academy of the Americas 700/PK-8
5680 Konkel St 48210 313-596-7640
Nicholas Brown, prin. Fax 596-7652
Bagley ES 300/PK-6
8100 Curtis St 48221 313-494-7175
Christa Reeves, prin. Fax 494-7173
Bennett ES 400/PK-5
2111 Mullane St 48209 313-849-3585
Dina Bonomo, prin. Fax 849-1169
Bethune S PK-8
8145 Puritan St 48238 313-494-3830
Alisanda Woods, prin. Fax 494-3829
Blackwell Institute 400/PK-8
9330 Shoemaker St 48213 313-866-4391
Cleo Moody, prin. Fax 866-4386
Bow S 500/PK-8
19801 Prevost St 48235 313-852-0500
DaRhonda Evans, prin. Fax 852-0508
Brewer ES 500/PK-8
18025 Brock St 48205 313-866-2070
Willie Wood, prin. Fax 866-2098
Brown Academy 700/PK-6
11530 E Outer Dr 48224 313-886-2611
Tina Brown, prin. Fax 417-2880
Bunche S 500/PK-8
2715 Macomb St 48207 313-494-8350
Cindy Lang, prin. Fax 866-7943

Burns S 400/PK-8
14350 Terry St 48227 313-852-0534
Cynthia Clayton, prin. Fax 852-0539
Burton International Academy 500/PK-8
2001 Martin Luther King Jr 48208 313-596-3800
Dr. John Wilson, prin. Fax 596-3807
Carleton ES 300/PK-5
11724 Casino St 48224 313-866-8322
Myrina Scott, prin. Fax 866-8333
Carstens S 500/PK-8
13000 Essex Ave 48215 313-866-5500
Donna Thornton, prin. Fax 866-5580
Carver STEM Academy 300/PK-8
18701 Paul St 48228 313-240-6622
Sabrina Evans, prin. Fax 240-8741
Chrysler ES 200/K-5
1445 E Lafayette St 48207 313-494-8440
Wendy Shirley, prin. Fax 494-8367
Clark Preparatory Academy 700/PK-8
15755 Bremen St 48224 313-417-9340
Monica Hester, prin. Fax 417-9345
Clemente Academy 700/PK-5
1551 Beard St 48209 313-849-3489
Maria Hernandez-Martinez, prin. Fax 849-6304
Clippert Academy 500/5-8
1981 McKinstry St 48209 313-849-5009
Kim Gonzalez, prin. Fax 849-5740
Cooke ES 300/PK-6
18800 Puritan St 48223 313-494-7458
Damon Sewell, prin. Fax 494-7759
Davison ES 700/PK-8
2800 E Davison St 48212 313-252-3118
Randall Coleman, prin. Fax 866-0919
Detroit Intl Acad for Young Women 500/K-12
9026 Woodward Ave 48202 313-873-3050
Pamela Askew, prin. Fax 873-3088
Dixon Educational Learning Academy 700/PK-8
8401 Trinity St 48228 313-945-1330
Ivan Branson, prin. Fax 945-1557
Dossin ES 400/PK-8
16650 Glendale St 48227 313-866-9390
Kurtis Brown, prin. Fax 866-9386
DPS Foundation for Early Learners PK-PK
1300 W Canfield St 48201 313-228-0910
Regina Olden, admin. Fax 873-8562
Durfee S 600/PK-8
2425 Tuxedo St 48206 313-252-3070
Latoyea Webb-Harris, prin. Fax 866-0914
Earhart ES 700/PK-8
1000 Scotten St 48209 313-849-3945
Melissa Villarreal, prin. Fax 849-4746
Edison ES 300/PK-5
17045 Grand River Ave 48227 313-852-1066
Marcus Davenport, prin. Fax 852-1060
Ellington Conservatory of Music/Art 700/PK-8
9860 Park Dr 48213 313-866-2860
Rita Davis, prin. Fax 866-2866
Emerson S 700/PK-8
18240 Huntington Rd 48219 313-831-9689
Brenda Carethers, prin. Fax 831-9699
Fisher Magnet Lower Academy 500/PK-4
15510 E State Fair St 48205 313-642-4854
Yvonne Stokes, prin. Fax 642-4855
Fisher Magnet Upper Academy 600/5-8
15491 Maddelein St 48205 313-866-7233
Sean Fisher, prin. Fax 866-7329
Fleming ECC 600/PK-PK
18501 Waltham St 48205 313-347-8923
Wilma Taylor-Costen, prin. Fax 330-7582
Foreign Language Immersion S 700/K-8
6501 W Outer Dr 48235 313-651-2400
Todd Losie, prin. Fax 651-2401
Gardner ES 300/PK-5
6528 Mansfield St 48228 313-581-4615
Shannon Cummings, prin. Fax 581-3713
Garvey Academy 400/PK-8
2301 Van Dyke St 48214 313-866-7400
Shelia Davis, prin. Fax 866-7382
Gompers ES 800/PK-8
14450 Burt Rd 48223 313-494-7495
Bobbie Posey, prin. Fax 494-7636
Greenfield Union S 300/PK-8
420 W 7 Mile Rd 48203 313-866-2999
Curtis Dunlap, prin. Fax 866-2633
Harms ES 500/PK-5
2400 Central St 48209 313-849-3492
Mauro Cruz, prin. Fax 849-4690
Henderson Academy 800/PK-8
16101 W Chicago St 48228 313-852-0512
Deborah Manciel, prin. Fax 852-0523
Holmes S 500/K-8
8950 Crane St 48213 313-866-5644
Tammy Mitchell, prin. Fax 866-2299
Hutchinson ES 500/PK-8
2600 Garland St 48214 313-866-4169
Sharon Williams, prin. Fax 866-4193
King Academic and Performing Arts Acad 900/PK-8
15850 Strathmoor St 48227 313-866-9600
Felicia Cook, prin. Fax 866-9626
Law Academy PK-8
19411 Cliff St 48234 313-866-3400
Shana Murphy, prin. Fax 866-6200
Ludington Magnet MS 500/5-8
19501 Berg Rd 48219 313-494-7577
Allan Cosma, prin. Fax 494-7707
Mackenzie ES 1,000/K-8
10147 W Chicago 48204 313-416-6400
Jason Drain, prin. Fax 873-0755
Mann ES 400/PK-5
19625 Elmira St 48228 313-866-9580
Gwendolyn Frencher, prin. Fax 866-9587
Marquette S 800/PK-8
6145 Canyon St 48236 313-417-9360
Deborah Sinclair, prin. Fax 881-3398
Marshall ES 500/PK-8
15531 Linwood St 48238 313-494-8820
Sharon Lee, prin. Fax 494-7294

Mason ES 600/K-8
19955 Fenelon St 48234 313-866-3700
Philip Vanhooks, prin. Fax 866-3609
Maybury ES 300/PK-5
4410 Porter St 48209 313-849-2014
Kathleen Keenon, prin. Fax 849-2016
Munger ES 800/K-8
5525 Martin St 48210 313-457-6200
Deborah Hurst, prin. Fax 457-6130
Neinas Dual Language Learning Academy 300/K-7
6021 Mcmillan St 48209 313-849-3701
Natalia Russell, prin. Fax 849-4733
Nichols S 300/K-8
3000 Burns St 48214 313-852-0800
Regina Haywood, prin. Fax 852-0811
Noble S 500/PK-8
8646 Fullerton St 48238 313-873-0377
Tonya Norwood, prin. Fax 873-0398
Nolan S PK-8
1150 E Lantz St 48203 313-866-7730
Anissa Kimber, prin. Fax 866-7725
Palmer Park Prep Academy 500/PK-8
3901 Margareta St 48221 313-494-7300
Shirita Hightower, prin. Fax 494-7306
Pasteur ES 400/PK-6
19811 Stoepel St 48221 313-494-7314
Sharon Lawson, prin. Fax 494-7313
Priest ES 700/PK-8
7840 Wagner St 48210 313-849-3705
Lisa Billops, prin. Fax 849-4824
Pulaski S 500/PK-8
19725 Strasburg St 48205 313-866-7022
Desheil Echols, prin. Fax 866-7011
Robeson/Malcolm X Academy 400/PK-8
2585 Grove St 48221 313-494-8100
Dr. Jeffrey Robinson, prin. Fax 494-7089
Sampson Academy 400/PK-8
4700 Tireman St 48204 313-596-4750
Karla Craig, prin. Fax 596-4748
Schulze Academy for Arts & Technology 700/PK-6
10700 Santa Maria St 48221 313-340-4400
Angela Kemp, prin. Fax 340-4401
Scott Academy for Theatre Arts 500/PK-8
18440 Hoover St 48205 313-866-6700
Eric Redwine, prin. Fax 866-2693
Spain S 600/PK-8
3700 Beaubien St 48201 313-494-2081
Frederick Cannon, prin. Fax 494-1508
Thirkell ES 500/PK-6
7724 14th St 48206 313-596-0990
Denise Connelly, prin. Fax 596-0982
Twain S 200/PK-8
12800 Visger St 48217 313-386-5530
Mumtaz Haque, prin. Fax 386-1276
Vernor S 200/PK-6
13726 Pembroke Ave 48235 313-494-7342
Dr. Tonyia Jeanmarie, prin. Fax 494-7341
Wayne ES 300/PK-5
10633 Courville St 48224 313-866-0400
Senta Ray-Conley, prin. Fax 866-2022
Wright Academy 500/PK-4
19299 Berg Rd 48219 313-538-3024
Laura Jawor, prin. Fax 538-3049
Young ES 400/PK-5
15771 Hubbell St 48227 313-852-0725
Melissa Scott, prin. Fax 852-0732
Other Schools – See Redford

Christ the King S 200/PK-8
16800 Trinity St 48219 313-532-1213
Amanda Lund, prin. Fax 532-1050
Cornerstone S 500/PK-12
6861 E Nevada St 48234 313-892-1860
Ernestine Sanders, pres. Fax 892-1861
Detroit Waldorf S 100/PK-8
2555 Burns St 48214 313-822-0300
Gesu S 200/PK-8
17139 Oak Dr 48221 313-863-4677
Christa Laurin, prin. Fax 862-4395
Holy Redeemer S 100/K-8
1711 Junction St 48209 313-841-5230
Mary Beth Kiley, prin. Fax 841-3640
Most Holy Trinity S 200/PK-8
1229 Labrosse St 48226 313-961-8855
Chris Camilleri, prin. Fax 961-5797

De Witt, Clinton, Pop. 4,434
De Witt SD 3,000/PK-12
PO Box 800, 517-668-3000
Dr. John Deiter, supt. Fax 668-3018
www.dewittschools.net/
De Witt JHS 500/7-8
PO Box 800, 517-668-3200
Keith Cravotta, prin. Fax 668-3255
Fuerstenau ECC 200/K-K
PO Box 800, 517-668-3460
Ruth Foster, prin. Fax 668-3484
Herbison Woods ES 400/5-6
PO Box 800, 517-668-3300
Vicky Milner, prin. Fax 668-3355
Schavey Road ES 400/PK-PK, 1-
PO Box 800, 517-668-3500
Emily Palmatier, prin. Fax 668-3555
Scott ES 500/3-4
PO Box 800, 517-668-3400
Linda Reha, prin. Fax 668-3455

Dexter, Washtenaw, Pop. 3,976
Dexter Community SD 3,500/PK-12
7714 Ann Arbor St 48130 734-424-4100
Christopher Timmis, supt. Fax 424-4112
www.dexterschools.org
Bates ES 400/K-2
2704 Baker Rd 48130 734-424-4130
Ryan Bruder, prin. Fax 424-4139
Cornerstone ES 400/PK-2
7480 Dan Hoey Rd 48130 734-424-4120
Craig McCalla, prin. Fax 424-4129
Creekside IS 500/5-6
2615 Baker Rd 48130 734-424-4160
Tammy Reich, prin. Fax 424-4159
Jenkins ECC PK-PK
2801 Baker Rd 48130 734-424-4180
David Teddy, dir. Fax 426-9515
Mill Creek MS 500/7-8
7305 Dexter Ann Arbor Rd 48130 734-424-4150
Jami Bronson, prin. Fax 424-4159
Wylie ES 500/3-4
3060 Kensington St 48130 734-424-4140
Katherine See, prin. Fax 424-4149

Dimondale, Eaton, Pop. 1,201
Holt SD
Supt. — See Holt
Dimondale ES 300/K-4
PO Box 159 48821 517-694-6411
Fax 694-6472

Dollar Bay, Houghton, Pop. 1,072
Dollar Bay-Tamarack City SD 300/K-12
PO Box 371 49922 906-482-5800
Susan Miko, supt. Fax 455-4237
www.dollarbay.k12.mi.us
Davis ES 200/K-6
PO Box 371 49922 906-482-5812
C. Norland, prin. Fax 455-4237

Dorr, Allegan
Hopkins SD
Supt. — See Hopkins
Sycamore ES 300/K-5
2163 142nd Ave 49323 616-681-9189
Amy Mielke, prin. Fax 557-7919

Wayland UNSD
Supt. — See Wayland
Dorr ES 500/PK-4
4159 18th St 49323 616-681-9637
Kevin Zaschak, prin. Fax 503-8877

St. Stanislaus S 100/PK-8
1861 136th Ave 49323 269-793-7204
Shannon Saxton-Murphy, prin. Fax 793-3264

Douglas, Allegan, Pop. 1,221
Saugatuck SD 700/PK-12
PO Box 818 49406 269-857-1444
Rolfe Timmerman, supt. Fax 857-1448
www.saugatuckps.com
Douglas ES 400/PK-5
PO Box 818 49406 269-857-2139
Michaelle Gust, prin. Fax 857-4487

Dowagiac, Cass, Pop. 5,518
Dowagiac UNSD 2,300/K-12
243 S Front St 49047 269-782-4400
Paul Hartsig, supt. Fax 782-4418
www.dowagiacschools.org
Dowagiac MS 500/6-8
243 S Front St 49047 269-782-4440
Sean Wightman Ph.D., prin. Fax 782-4449
Gage ES 300/K-5
243 S Front St 49047 269-782-4460
Bryan Henry, prin. Fax 782-2382
Hamilton ES 300/K-5
243 S Front St 49047 269-782-4450
Heather Nash, prin. Fax 782-9205
Kincheloe ES 300/K-5
243 S Front St 49047 269-782-4464
Cathy Stone, prin. Fax 782-8985
Other Schools – See Benton Harbor

Drummond Island, Chippewa, Pop. 500
De Tour Area SD
Supt. — See De Tour Village
Drummond Island ES 100/K-8
PO Box 39 49726 906-493-5225
Angela Reed, prin. Fax 493-6030

Dryden, Lapeer, Pop. 947
Dryden Community SD 600/K-12
3866 Rochester Rd 48428 810-448-4090
Mary Finnigan, supt. Fax 796-3698
www.dryden.k12.mi.us
Dryden ES 300/K-6
3835 N Mill Rd 48428 810-796-2201
Brian Tresnak, prin. Fax 796-9621

Dundee, Monroe, Pop. 3,916
Dundee Community SD 1,400/PK-12
420 Ypsilanti St 48131 734-529-2350
Edward Manuszak, supt. Fax 529-5606
www.dundeecommunityschools.org
Dundee ES 500/PK-5
420 Ypsilanti St 48131 734-529-2350
August Ost, prin. Fax 529-3741
Dundee MS 400/6-8
420 Ypsilanti St 48131 734-529-2350
Aaron Carner, prin. Fax 529-7380

Durand, Shiawassee, Pop. 3,411
Durand Area SD 1,500/PK-12
310 N Saginaw St 48429 989-288-2681
Craig McCrumb, supt. Fax 288-3553
www.durand.k12.mi.us
Durand MS 400/5-7
9550 E Lansing Rd 48429 989-288-3435
Paula Dobson, prin. Fax 288-5563
Kerr ES 300/2-4
9591 E Monroe Rd 48429 989-288-2805
Amy Holek, prin. Fax 288-3461
Neal ES 200/PK-1
930 W Main St 48429 989-288-2016
Hattie Rainer, prin. Fax 288-3603

Eagle, Clinton, Pop. 123
Grand Ledge SD
Supt. — See Grand Ledge
Wacousta ES 400/1-6
9135 W Herbison Rd 48822 517-925-5940
Christopher Groves, prin. Fax 925-5970

East China, Saint Clair, Pop. 3,216
East China SD 4,400/K-12
1585 Meisner Rd 48054 810-676-1000
Suzanne Cybulla, supt. Fax 676-1037
www.eastchinaschools.org
Other Schools – See China, Fair Haven, Marine City, Saint Clair

East Jordan, Charlevoix, Pop. 2,312
East Jordan SD 700/K-12
PO Box 399 49727 231-536-3131
Matt Stevenson, supt. Fax 536-3310
www.ejps.org
East Jordan ES 400/K-6
PO Box 399 49727 231-536-7564
Carla Winteringham, prin. Fax 536-3379

East Lansing, Ingham, Pop. 47,217
East Lansing SD 2,900/K-12
501 Burcham Dr 48823 517-333-7420
Dori Leyko, supt. Fax 333-7470
www.elps.us
Donley ES 300/K-5
2961 E Lake Lansing Rd 48823 517-333-7370
Tracey Barton, prin. Fax 333-5090
Glencairn ES 100/K-5
939 N Harrison Rd 48823 517-333-7930
Lorraine Ware, prin. Fax 333-5091
MacDonald MS 500/6-8
1601 Burcham Dr 48823 517-333-7600
Amy Martin, prin. Fax 333-5098
Marble ES 300/K-5
729 N Hagadorn Rd 48823 517-333-7860
Sarah Scott, prin. Fax 333-5092
Pinecrest ES 300/K-5
1811 Pinecrest Dr 48823 517-333-7870
Amy Webster, prin. Fax 333-5093
Whitehills ES 100/K-5
621 Pebblebrook Ln 48823 517-333-7900
Fax 333-5096

Greater Lansing Islamic S 200/PK-8
920 S Harrison Rd 48823 517-332-3700
Dr. Jamila Jones, prin. Fax 332-7666
St. Thomas Aquinas S 400/PK-8
915 Alton Rd 48823 517-332-0813
Meghan Loughlin-Krusky, prin. Fax 332-9490

East Leroy, Calhoun
Athens Area SD 600/K-12
4320 K Dr S 49051 269-729-5427
Joseph Huepenbecker, supt. Fax 729-9610
www.athensk12.org
East Leroy ES 300/K-5
4320 K Dr S 49051 269-729-5419
Marvin Taylor, prin. Fax 729-9648

Eastpointe, Macomb, Pop. 31,538
Eastpointe Community SD 3,700/PK-12
24685 Kelly Rd 48021 586-533-3000
Dr. Ryan McLeod, supt. Fax 533-3025
www.eastpointeschools.org
Bellview ES 400/3-5
15800 Bell Ave 48021 586-533-3100
Anthony Sedick, prin. Fax 533-3109
Crescentwood ES 300/K-2
14500 Crescentwood Ave 48021 586-533-3200
Susan Miller, prin. Fax 533-3209
Eastpointe Early Learning Center PK-PK
27350 David Ave 48021 586-533-3000
Keisha Smith, dir.
Eastpointe MS 900/6-8
24701 Kelly Rd 48021 586-533-3600
Stephanie Fleming, head sch Fax 533-3609
Forest Park ES 400/K-2
18361 Forest Ave 48021 586-533-3300
Kimberley Busuttil, prin. Fax 533-3309
Pleasantview ES 400/3-5
16501 Toepfer Dr 48021 586-533-3400
Laurie Hillebrand, prin. Fax 533-3409

South Lake SD
Supt. — See Saint Clair Shores
Koepsell ES 200/K-5
21760 Raven Ave 48021 586-435-1500
Diane Boehm, prin. Fax 445-4322

St. Peter Lutheran S 200/PK-8
23000 Gratiot Ave 48021 586-777-6300
Michele Gapski, prin. Fax 777-0347

East Tawas, Iosco, Pop. 2,763

Holy Family S 100/PK-7
411 Wilkinson St 48730 989-362-5651
Tim St. Aubin, prin. Fax 362-6916

Eaton Rapids, Eaton, Pop. 5,118
Eaton Rapids SD 2,500/K-12
912 Greyhound Dr 48827 517-663-8155
Dr. William DeFrance, supt. Fax 663-2236
www.erpsk12.org
Eaton Rapids MS 600/6-8
815 Greyhound Dr 48827 517-663-8151
Therese Lake, prin. Fax 663-0625
Greyhound Central K 100/K-K
912 Greyhound Dr 48827 517-663-1064
Shawn Towsley, prin. Fax 663-0626
Greyhound IS 500/3-5
805 Greyhound Dr 48827 517-663-9192
Jason Brant, prin. Fax 663-9181
Lockwood ES 300/1-2
810 Greyhound Dr 48827 517-663-8194
Jason Zeller, prin. Fax 663-6836

Eau Claire, Berrien, Pop. 604
Eau Claire SD 900/K-12
6190 W Main St 49111 269-461-6947
David Gray, supt. Fax 461-0089
www.eauclaireps.com

Eau Claire MS 200/6-8
7450 Hochberger Rd 49111 269-461-0083
Scott Pfeiffer, prin. Fax 461-0082
Lybrook ES 400/K-5
6238 W Main St 49111 269-461-6191
Timothy Keathley, prin. Fax 461-6662

Eau Claire SDA S 50/1-8
6562 Naomi Rd 49111 269-944-4132
Sarah Taylor, prin. Fax 944-4132

Eben Junction, Alger
Superior Central SD 400/K-12
PO Box 148 49825 906-439-5531
William Valima, supt. Fax 439-5734
superiorcentralschools.org
Superior Central S 400/K-12
PO Box 148 49825 906-439-5532
William Valima, prin. Fax 439-5243

Ecorse, Wayne, Pop. 9,214
Ecorse SD 900/PK-12
27225 W Outer Dr 48229 313-294-4750
Dr. Josha Talison, supt. Fax 949-0018
ecorse.education
Bunche ES 200/PK-3
503 Hyacinthe St 48229 313-294-4710
Kelley Beck, prin. Fax 949-0018
Grandport MS 200/4-7
4536 6th St 48229 313-294-4720
Patrick Burrage, prin. Fax 949-0020

Edenville, Midland

Edenville SDA S, PO Box 189 48620 50/K-8
R. Jameson, head sch 989-689-3505

Edmore, Montcalm, Pop. 1,174
Montabella Community SD 800/PK-12
PO Box 349 48829 989-427-5148
Shelly Millis, supt. Fax 427-3828
www.montabella.com
Other Schools – See Blanchard

Edwardsburg, Cass, Pop. 1,228
Edwardsburg SD 2,700/K-12
69410 Section St 49112 269-663-3055
Sherman Ostrander, supt. Fax 663-6485
www.edwardsburgpublicschools.org/
Eagle Lake ES 400/2-3
69410 Section St 49112 269-663-1040
Debra Becraft, prin. Fax 699-7653
Edwardsburg IS 400/4-5
69410 Section St 49112 269-663-1063
Daniel Nommay, prin. Fax 663-6156
Edwardsburg MS 700/6-8
69410 Section St 49112 269-663-1031
Fax 663-8638
Edwardsburg PS 400/K-1
69410 Section St 49112 269-663-1037
Carrie McGuire, prin. Fax 663-8361

Elk Rapids, Antrim, Pop. 1,628
Elk Rapids SD 1,300/K-12
707 E 3rd St 49629 231-264-8692
Dr. Stephen Prissel, supt. Fax 264-6538
erschools.com
Cherryland MS 300/6-8
707 E 3rd St 49629 231-264-8991
Terry Starr, prin. Fax 264-9370
Lakeland ES 400/K-5
616 Buckley St 49629 231-264-8289
Bryan McKenna, prin. Fax 264-6132
Other Schools – See Williamsburg

Ellsworth, Antrim, Pop. 341
Ellsworth Community SD 200/PK-12
9467 Park St 49729 231-588-2544
Aaron Gaffney, supt. Fax 588-6183
www.ellsworth.k12.mi.us/
Ellsworth Community S 200/PK-12
9467 Park St 49729 231-588-2544
Aaron Gaffney, admin. Fax 588-6183

Ebenezer Christian S 100/PK-8
PO Box 158 49729 231-588-2111
Ann Hazelwood, admin. Fax 588-2111

Elmira, Antrim
Alba SD 200/PK-12
5935 Elm St 49730 231-584-2000
Richard Satterlee, supt. Fax 584-2001
www.albaschool.org/
Alba S 200/PK-12
5935 Elm St 49730 231-584-2000
Richard Satterlee, supt. Fax 584-2001

Elsie, Clinton, Pop. 962
Ovid-Elsie Area SD 1,300/PK-12
8989 E Colony Rd 48831 989-834-2271
Dr. Ryan Cunningham, supt. Fax 862-5887
www.ovidelsie.org
Knight ES 200/3-5
215 N Tyler Dr 48831 989-862-5170
Cory Gavenda, prin. Fax 862-5995
Ovid-Elsie MS 200/6-8
8989 E Colony Rd 48831 989-834-2271
Randy Barton, prin. Fax 862-4463
Other Schools – See Ovid

Emmett, Saint Clair, Pop. 263
Yale SD
Supt. — See Yale
Farrell-Emmett ES 200/K-5
3300 Kinney Rd 48022 810-384-1300
Robert Watson, prin. Fax 384-8010

Engadine, Mackinac
Engadine Consolidated SD 300/K-12
W13920 Melville St 49827 906-477-6313
Angie McArthur, supt. Fax 477-6643
engadine.eupschools.org
Engadine Consolidated S 300/K-12
W13920 Melville St 49827 906-477-6351
Kendra Feldhusen, prin. Fax 477-6643

Erie, Monroe
Mason Consolidated SD 1,100/PK-12
2400 Mason Eagle Dr 48133 734-848-5475
Andrew Shaw, supt. Fax 848-2516
www.eriemason.k12.mi.us
Central ES 500/PK-5
2400 Mason Eagle Dr 48133 734-848-5595
Debra McCain, prin. Fax 848-2933
Mason MS 200/6-8
2400 Mason Eagle Dr 48133 734-848-4211
Ben Russow, prin. Fax 848-0035

St. Joseph S 100/PK-8
2238 Manhattan St 48133 734-848-6985
Julie Miazgowicz, prin. Fax 848-8215

Escanaba, Delta, Pop. 12,293
Escanaba Area SD 2,400/PK-12
1500 Ludington St 49829 906-786-5411
Dr. Coby W. Fletcher, supt. Fax 786-4469
www.eskymos.com
Escanaba JHS 400/7-8
500 S Lincoln Rd 49829 906-786-6521
Jude VanDamme, prin. Fax 786-2166
Escanaba Upper ES 600/4-6
1500 Ludington St 49829 906-786-7462
Steve Martin, prin. Fax 786-5958
Lemmer ES 400/PK-3
700 S 20th St 49829 906-786-5333
Dr. Matthew Johnson-Reeves, prin. Fax 789-8169
Soo Hill ES 200/K-3
5219 18th Rd 49829 906-786-7035
Paulette Wickham, prin. Fax 789-8163
Webster ES 200/PK-3
1209 N 19th St 49829 906-786-6118
Craig LeClaire, prin. Fax 789-8165

Escanaba SDA S 50/K-8
210 S Lincoln Rd 49829 906-786-3039
Melissa Boryca, prin.
Holy Name Catholic S 300/PK-8
409 S 22nd St 49829 906-786-7550
Joe Carlson, prin. Fax 786-7582

Essexville, Bay, Pop. 3,434
Essexville-Hampton SD 1,700/K-12
303 Pine St 48732 989-894-9700
Matthew T. Cortez, supt. Fax 894-9705
www.e-hps.net
Bush ES 200/K-1
800 Nebobish Ave 48732 989-894-9760
Shannon Flippin, prin. Fax 894-9739
Cramer JHS 600/5-8
313 Pine St 48732 989-894-9740
Jeff Dinauer, prin. Fax 894-9720
Verellen ES 400/2-4
612 W Borton Rd 48732 989-894-9770
Barry Kenniston, prin. Fax 894-9759

Eureka, Clinton
Saint Johns SD
Supt. — See Saint Johns
Eureka ES 100/K-5
7500 N Welling Rd 48833 989-227-4900
Anne-Marie Potter, prin. Fax 227-4999

Evart, Osceola, Pop. 1,857
Evart SD 900/PK-12
PO Box 917 49631 231-734-5594
Shirley Howard, supt. Fax 734-2931
www.evart.k12.mi.us/
Evart ES 300/PK-4
515 N Cedar St 49631 231-734-5595
Sarah Bailey, prin. Fax 734-3218
Evart MS 300/5-8
321 N Hemlock St 49631 231-734-4222
Jason O'Dell, prin. Fax 734-3367

Ewen, Ontonagon
Ewen-Trout Creek SD 300/K-12
14312 Airport Rd 49925 906-813-0620
Alan Tulppo, supt. Fax 813-0621
www.etc.k12.mi.us/
Ewen-Trout Creek ES 100/K-6
14312 Airport Rd 49925 906-813-0620
Alan Tulppo, supt. Fax 813-0621

Fairgrove, Tuscola, Pop. 559
Akron-Fairgrove SD 300/K-12
PO Box 319 48733 989-693-6163
Diane Foster, supt. Fax 693-6560
www.akronfairgrove.org
Other Schools – See Akron

Fair Haven, Saint Clair, Pop. 1,505
East China SD
Supt. — See East China
Palms ES 300/K-5
6101 Palms Rd 48023 810-676-1350
Philip Russell, prin. Fax 676-1360

Fairview, Oscoda
Fairview Area SD 100/K-12
1879 E Miller Rd 48621 989-848-7000
John Sattler, supt. Fax 848-7070
www.fairview.k12.mi.us
Fairview Area S 100/K-12
1879 E Miller Rd 48621 989-848-7009
John Sattler, supt. Fax 848-7070

Farmington, Oakland, Pop. 10,133
Farmington SD 9,000/PK-12
32500 Shiawassee Rd 48336 248-489-3349
Dr. George Heitsch, supt. Fax 489-3348
www.farmington.k12.mi.us
Longacre ES 300/K-5
34850 Arundel Dr 48335 248-489-3733
Rhonda Henry, prin. Fax 489-3730
Other Schools – See Farmington Hills

Farmington Hills, Oakland, Pop. 77,980
Farmington SD
Supt. — See Farmington
Alameda ECC 50/PK-PK
32400 Alameda St 48336 248-489-3808
Kirsten Cicchella, prin. Fax 489-3810
Beechview ES 300/K-5
26850 Westmeath Ct 48334 248-489-3655
Shawndra Hernton, prin. Fax 489-3659
East MS 900/6-8
25000 Middlebelt Rd 48336 248-489-3601
Ken Sanders, prin. Fax 489-3606
Farmington Community ECC PK-PK
30415 Shiawassee Rd 48336 248-489-3373
Kirsten Cicchella, coord. Fax 489-3378
Farmington STEAM Academy 300/K-7
32800 W 12 Mile Rd 48334 248-785-2070
Dyanne Sanders, prin. Fax 737-9135
Forest ES 400/K-5
34545 Old Timber Rd 48331 248-785-2068
Steven Vercellino, prin. Fax 788-2002
Gill ES 500/K-5
21195 Gill Rd 48335 248-489-3690
Christina Suliman, prin. Fax 489-3480
Hillside ES 500/K-5
36801 W 11 Mile Rd 48335 248-489-3773
Rob Kauffman, prin. Fax 489-3781
Kenbrook ES 400/K-5
32130 Bonnet Hill Rd 48334 248-489-3711
Julie Kaminski, prin. Fax 489-3649
Lanigan ES 500/K-5
23800 Tuck Rd 48336 248-489-3722
Gregory Smith, prin. Fax 489-3742
Power Upper ES 400/6-8
34740 Rhonswood St 48335 248-489-3622
Allyson Robinson, prin. Fax 489-3628
Warner Upper ES 400/6-8
30303 W 14 Mile Rd 48334 248-785-2030
Allen Archer, prin. Fax 855-0210
Wood Creek ES 300/K-5
28400 Harwich Dr 48334 248-785-2077
Christopher O'Brien, prin. Fax 851-1526

Concordia Lutheran S - North Campus 100/K-4
20805 Middlebelt Rd 48336 248-474-2488
Judy Schwaegerle, prin. Fax 474-1945
Hillel Day School Metropolitan Detroit 600/PK-8
32200 Middlebelt Rd 48334 248-851-3220
Steve Freedman, head sch Fax 851-5095
Maria Montessori Center 200/PK-6
32450 W 13 Mile Rd 48334 248-851-9695
Shatomi Kerbawy, head sch
Our Lady of Sorrows S 800/PK-8
24040 Raphael Rd 48336 248-476-0977
Meghan Evoy, prin. Fax 615-5567
Red Hill Montessori Academy 100/PK-6
29001 W 13 Mile Rd 48334 248-851-4166
Leila Charlesworth, dir. Fax 851-4237
St. Fabian S 400/K-8
32200 W 12 Mile Rd 48334 248-553-2750
Sharon Szuba, prin. Fax 848-3035

Farwell, Clare, Pop. 865
Farwell Area SD 1,300/PK-12
399 E Michigan St 48622 989-588-9917
Tom House, supt. Fax 588-6440
www.farwellschools.net/
Farwell ES 500/PK-3
268 E Ohio St 48622 989-588-9916
Catheryn Gross, prin. Fax 588-0158
Farwell MS 400/4-7
500 E Ohio St 48622 989-588-9915
Nancy Cairnduff, prin. Fax 588-3337

Felch, Dickinson
North Dickinson County SD 300/K-12
W6588 State Highway M69 49831 906-542-9281
Angel Inglese, supt. Fax 542-6950
www.go-nordics.com
North Dickinson County S 300/K-12
W6588 State Highway M69 49831 906-542-9281
Angel Inglese, admin. Fax 542-6950

Fennville, Allegan, Pop. 1,373
Fennville SD 1,400/PK-12
5 Memorial Dr 49408 269-561-7331
Dirk Weeldreyer, supt. Fax 561-5792
www.fennville.org
Fennville ES 600/PK-5
8 Memorial Dr 49408 269-561-7231
Albert Lombard, prin. Fax 561-2356
Fennville MS 300/6-8
1 Memorial Dr 49408 269-561-7341
Kim Zdybel, prin. Fax 561-2143

Fenton, Genesee, Pop. 11,554
Fenton Area SD 3,400/PK-12
3100 Owen Rd 48430 810-591-4700
Adam J. Hartley, supt. Fax 591-4705
www.fentonschools.org
North Road ES 500/K-5
525 North Rd 48430 810-591-1500
Melissa Lane, prin. Fax 591-1505
Schmidt MS 800/6-8
3255 Donaldson Dr 48430 810-591-7700
Heidi Ciesielski, prin. Fax 591-7705
State Road ES 500/K-5
1161 State Rd 48430 810-591-2400
Barry Tiemann, prin. Fax 591-2405
Tomek-Eastern ES 500/K-5
600 4th St 48430 810 591 6800
Brett Young, prin. Fax 591-6805
World of Wonder Early Learning Program PK-PK
404 W Ellen St 48430 810-591-8349
Linda Mora, dir. Fax 591-8305

Lake Fenton Community SD 2,000/K-12
11425 Torrey Rd 48430 810-591-4141
Julie A. Williams, supt. Fax 591-9866
www.lakefentonschools.org
Lake Fenton MS 500/6-8
11425 Torrey Rd 48430 810-591-2209
Dr. Daniel Ferguson, prin. Fax 591-8475
Torrey Hill IS 400/3-5
12410 Torrey Rd 48430 810-591-3617
Kathleen Conover, prin. Fax 591-3550
West Shore ES 400/K-2
3076 Lahring Rd 48430 810-591-6542
Sonya Shaughnessy, prin. Fax 591-5399

St. John the Evangelist S 400/PK-8
514 Lincoln St 48430 810-629-6551
Rosanne Jodway, prin. Fax 629-2213

Ferndale, Oakland, Pop. 19,252
Ferndale SD 2,800/PK-12
2920 Burdette St 48220 248-586-8651
Dr. Dania Bazzi, supt. Fax 586-8655
www.ferndaleschools.org
Ferndale ECC 50/PK-PK
2920 Burdette St 48220 248-586-8820
Heidi Schmidt, dir. Fax 586-8672
Ferndale Lower ES 300/K-2
2610 Pinecrest Dr 48220 248-548-1950
Diana Keefe, prin. Fax 586-8804
Ferndale MS 300/6-8
725 Pinecrest Dr 48220 248-541-1783
Jason Gillespie, prin. Fax 586-8834
Other Schools – See Oak Park

Hazel Park SD
Supt. — See Hazel Park
Webb ES 300/K-5
2100 Woodward Hts 48220 248-658-5900
Corri Nastasi, prin. Fax 544-5316

Fife Lake, Grand Traverse, Pop. 434
Forest Area Community SD 400/PK-12
7741 Shippy Rd SW 49633 231-369-4191
Joshua Rothwell M.S., supt. Fax 369-4153
www.forestarea.org
Fife Lake ES 100/PK-3
7741 Shippy Rd SW 49633 231-879-3362
Joshua Rothwell M.S., prin. Fax 879-4825
Forest Area MS 100/4-8
7741 Shippy Rd SW 49633 231-369-2884
Lisa Magee, prin. Fax 369-3646

Flat Rock, Wayne, Pop. 9,628
Flat Rock Community SD 1,800/K-12
28639 Division St 48134 734-535-6500
Andrew Brodie, supt. Fax 535-6501
www.flatrockschools.org
Barnes ES 400/3-5
24925 Meadows Ave 48134 734-535-6800
Kirstie Mullins, prin. Fax 535-6801
Bobcean ES 500/K-2
28300 Evergreen St 48134 734-535-6900
Tammy Steffen, prin. Fax 535-6901
Simpson MS 500/6-8
24900 Meadows Ave 48134 734-535-6700
Drew Wilde, prin. Fax 535-6701

Flint, Genesee, Pop. 98,869
Beecher Community SD 1,400/PK-12
1020 W Coldwater Rd 48505 810-591-9200
Ira Rutherford, supt. Fax 591-2522
www.beecherschools.org
Other Schools – See Mount Morris

Carman-Ainsworth Community SD 4,400/K-12
G3475 W Court St 48532 810-591-3700
Dr. Eddie Kindle, supt. Fax 591-3323
www.carman.k12.mi.us
Carman-Ainsworth MS 1,100/6-8
1409 W Maple Ave 48507 810-591-3500
Mary Haslinger, prin. Fax 591-3594
Dye ES 600/K-5
1174 S Graham Rd 48532 810-591-3229
Detra Fields, prin. Fax 591-3310
Randels ES 700/K-5
6022 Brobeck St 48532 810-591-3250
Rick Kalinin, prin. Fax 591-3225
Other Schools – See Burton, Swartz Creek

Flint Community SD 5,000/PK-12
923 E Kearsley St 48503 810-760-1000
Bilal K. Tawwab, supt. Fax 760-7601
www.flintschools.org
Brownell STEM Academy 300/PK-2
6302 Oxley Dr 48504 810-760-1643
Shalonda Byas, prin. Fax 760-1538
Doyle/Ryder ES 400/PK-6
1040 N Saginaw St 48503 810-760-5266
Kevelin Jones, prin. Fax 760-5118
Durant-Tuuri-Mott Community S 500/K-7
1518 University Ave 48504 810-760-1594
Shelly Umphrey, prin. Fax 760-7729
Eisenhower ES 300/PK-6
1235 Pershing St 48503 810-760-1607
Anthony Sitko, prin. Fax 760-7457
Freeman ES 300/PK-6
4001 Ogema Ave 48507 810-760-1797
Anita Steward, prin. Fax 760-6882
Holmes STEM Academy 400/PK-PK, 3-
6602 Oxley Dr 48504 810-760-1968
Eddie Thomas, prin. Fax 760-1624
Neithercut ES 300/K-6
2010 Crestbrook Ln 48507 810-760-1359
Joyce Pratt, prin. Fax 760-5133
Pierce ES 300/PK-6
1101 W Vernon Dr 48503 810-760-1386
Dr. Shamarion Grace, prin. Fax 760-7147
Potter Community S 500/PK-8
2500 N Averill Ave 48506 810-760-1813
Gretchen Shafer, prin. Fax 760-5156

Kearsley Community SD 3,400/PK-12
4396 Underhill Dr 48506 810-591-8000
Patti Yorks, supt. Fax 591-8421
www.kearsleyschools.org
Armstrong MS 800/6-8
6161 Hopkins Rd 48506 810-591-9929
Casey Killingbeck, prin. Fax 591-9944
Buffey ECC 100/PK-PK
4235 Crosby Rd 48506 810-591-3585
Janis Akers, dir. Fax 591-3595
Dowdall ES 400/2-3
3333 Shillelagh Dr 48506 810-591-2274
Kelly Fisher, prin. Fax 591-2276
Fiedler ES 500/4-5
6317 Nightingale Dr 48506 810-591-9925
Kelli Verran, prin. Fax 591-9927
Other Schools – See Burton

Westwood Heights SD 1,300/PK-12
3400 N Jennings Rd 48504 810-591-0870
Peter Toal, supt. Fax 591-4341
www.hamadyhawks.net
Hamady MS 200/7-8
3223 W Carpenter Rd 48504 810-591-0890
Peter Toal, prin. Fax 591-5140
McMonagle ES 400/PK-6
3484 N Jennings Rd 48504 810-591-5145
Dianne Coplin, prin. Fax 591-5149

Fairhaven SDA S 50/K-8
1379 Louis Ave 48505 810-785-4024
First Flint SDA S 50/1-8
G4285 Beecher Rd 48532 810-732-0230
Gayle Stevens, prin. Fax 732-0065
Holy Rosary S 100/K-8
5191 Richfield Rd 48506 810-736-4220
Mark Callahan, prin. Fax 736-1064
St. John Vianney S 200/PK-8
2319 Bagley St 48504 810-235-5687
Linda Warner, prin. Fax 235-2811
St. Paul Lutheran S 200/PK-8
402 S Ballenger Hwy 48532 810-239-6733
Mary Buck, prin. Fax 239-5466
St. Pius X S 200/PK-8
G3139 Hogarth Ave 48532 810-235-8572
R.J. Kaplan, prin. Fax 235-2675

Flushing, Genesee, Pop. 8,256
Flushing Community SD 4,100/PK-12
522 N McKinley Rd 48433 810-591-1180
Timothy Stein, supt. Fax 591-0656
www.flushingschools.org/
Central ES 500/1-6
525 Coutant St 48433 810-591-1901
Robert Steinhaus, prin. Fax 591-0067
Elms ES 500/1-6
6125 N Elms Rd 48433 810-591-7350
John Hagens, prin. Fax 591-0690
Flushing ECC 300/PK-K
409 Chamberlain St 48433 810-591-2326
Theresa Miles, prin. Fax 591-2330
Flushing MS 700/7-8
8100 Carpenter Rd 48433 810-591-2800
Andrew Schmidt, prin. Fax 591-0148
Seymour ES 500/1-6
3088 N Seymour Rd 48433 810-591-5150
Joseph Reinfelder, prin. Fax 591-0595
Springview ES 400/1-6
1233 Springview Dr 48433 810-591-8550
Melissa Killingbeck, prin. Fax 591-8555

St. Robert Bellarmine S 300/PK-8
214 E Henry St 48433 810-659-2503
Matthew Ralbusky, prin. Fax 659-4002

Fort Gratiot, Saint Clair, Pop. 8,968
Port Huron Area SD
Supt. — See Port Huron
Edison ES 500/PK-5
3559 Pollina Ave 48059 810-984-6507
Chris Collins, prin. Fax 958-0624
Fort Gratiot MS 600/6-8
3985 Keewahdin Rd 48059 810-984-6544
Alycia Shagena, prin. Fax 275-1271
Keewahdin ES 600/PK-5
4801 Lakeshore Rd 48059 810-984-6517
Charles Lesser, prin. Fax 213-9831

Fowler, Clinton, Pop. 1,204
Fowler SD 500/PK-12
PO Box 407 48835 989-593-2296
Neil Hufnagel, supt. Fax 593-2358
www.fowlerschools.net
Waldron ES 300/PK-8
PO Box 408 48835 989-593-2160
Paul Minns, prin. Fax 593-2358

Most Holy Trinity S 100/1-8
545 N Maple St 48835 989-593-2616
Anne Hufnagel, prin. Fax 593-2801

Fowlerville, Livingston, Pop. 2,844
Fowlerville Community SD 2,900/PK-12
7677 W Sharpe Rd Ste A 48836 517-223-6000
Wayne Roedel, supt. Fax 223-6022
www.fowlervilleschools.org
Fowlerville JHS 700/6-8
7677 W Sharpe Rd Ste A 48836 517-223-6003
Myriah Lillie, prin. Fax 223-6199
Kreeger ES 700/3-5
7677 W Sharpe Rd Ste A 48836 517-223-6006
Jason Miller, prin. Fax 223-6388
Little Glad ECC PK-PK
7677 W Sharpe Rd Ste A 48836 517-223-6480
Katie Sloan, dir. Fax 223-6484
Smith ES 700/K-2
7677 W Sharpe Rd Ste A 48836 517-223-6005
Kathy Gibson, prin. Fax 223-6444

Frankenmuth, Saginaw, Pop. 4,915
Frankenmuth SD 1,200/PK-12
525 E Genesee St 48734 989-652-9958
Adele Martin, supt. Fax 652-9780
www.fmuthschools.com
List ES 400/PK-4
805 E Genesee St 48734 989-652-6187
Jill Waliczek, prin. Fax 652-7255
Rittmueller MS 300/5-8
965 E Genesee St 48734 989-652-6119
Kristin Hecht, prin. Fax 652-2921

St. Lorenz Lutheran S 500/PK-8
140 Churchgrove Rd 48734 989-652-6141
Michael Bender, prin. Fax 652-9071

Frankfort, Benzie, Pop. 1,275
Frankfort-Elberta Area SD 500/K-12
534 11th St 49635 231-352-4641
Jeffrey Tousley, supt. Fax 352-5066
www.frankfort.k12.mi.us
Frankfort ES 300/K-6
613 Leelanau Ave 49635 231-352-7601
Jeffrey Tousley, prin. Fax 352-0390

Franklin, Oakland, Pop. 3,092

Huda S 300/PK-8
32220 Franklin Rd 48025 248-626-0900
Erum Mohiuddin, prin. Fax 626-7146

Fraser, Macomb, Pop. 14,229
Fraser SD 5,300/PK-12
33466 Garfield Rd 48026 586-439-7000
Dr. David Richards Ph.D., supt. Fax 439-7001
www.fraser.k12.mi.us/
Edison ES 500/K-6
17470 Sewel 48026 586-439-6500
Dr. Kristi Weiss, prin. Fax 439-6501
Eisenhower ES 500/K-6
31275 Eveningside 48026 586-439-6600
Denis Metty, prin. Fax 439-6601
Emerson ES 400/K-6
32151 Danna 48026 586-439-6700
Sam Argiri, prin. Fax 439-6701
Richards MS 900/7-8
33500 Garfield Rd 48026 586-439-7400
Huston Julian, prin. Fax 439-7401
Other Schools – See Clinton Township, Roseville

St. John Lutheran S 200/PK-8
16339 E 14 Mile Rd 48026 586-294-8740
David Waltz, prin. Fax 294-9565

Freeland, Saginaw, Pop. 6,900
Freeland Community SD 1,800/K-12
710 Powley Dr 48623 989-695-5527
Matthew Cairy, supt. Fax 695-5789
www.freelandschools.net
Freeland ES 600/2-6
710 Powley Dr 48623 989-695-5371
Stacey Criner, prin. Fax 695-5789
Freeland Learning Center 400/K-1
307 S 3rd St 48623 989-695-5721
Marcus Hillborg, prin. Fax 695-2508
Freeland MS 300/7-8
8250 Webster Rd 48623 989-692-4032
Renee Wulff, prin. Fax 692-4034

Fremont, Newaygo, Pop. 4,037
Fremont SD 2,100/K-12
450 E Pine St 49412 231-924-2350
Ken Haggart, supt. Fax 924-5264
www.fremont.net
Daisy Brook ES 300/3-5
502 N Division Ave 49412 231-924-4380
Bob Cassiday, prin. Fax 924-9117
Fremont MS 500/6-8
500 Woodrow St 49412 231-924-0230
Kenneth Haggart, prin. Fax 924-9149
Pathfinder ES 500/K-2
109 W 44th St 49412 231-924-7230
Andrea Wood, prin. Fax 924-7231

Newaygo County RESA 200/
4747 W 48th St 49412 231-924-0381
Lori Clark, supt. Fax 924-8910
www.ncresa.org
Other Schools – See Newaygo

Fremont Christian S 100/PK-8
208 Hillcrest Ave 49412 231-924-2740
John Barkel, prin. Fax 924-1240

Fruitport, Muskegon, Pop. 1,081
Fruitport Community SD 2,800/PK-12
3255 E Pontaluna Rd 49415 231-865-4100
Bob Szymoniak, supt. Fax 865-3393
www.fruitportschools.net
ECC PK-PK
3113 Pontaluna Rd 49415 231-865-4102
Pam Bergey, dir. Fax 865-4103
Edgewood ES 500/K-5
3255 Pontaluna Rd 49415 231-865-3171
Amy Upham, prin. Fax 865-4085
Fruitport MS 700/6-8
3113 Pontaluna Rd 49415 231-865-3128
Tim Tiefenbach, prin. Fax 865-4086
Other Schools – See Muskegon

Calvary Christian S 200/PK-12
5873 Kendra Rd 49415 231-865-2141
Thomas Kapanka, admin. Fax 865-8730

Gaines, Genesee, Pop. 375
Swartz Creek Community SD
Supt. — See Swartz Creek
Gaines ES 200/K-5
300 Lansing St 48436 810-591-1076
Jamie Johnston, prin. Fax 591-1099

Galesburg, Kalamazoo, Pop. 1,969
Galesburg-Augusta Community SD 1,100/PK-12
1076 N 37th St 49053 269-484-2000
Wendy Maynard-Somers, supt. Fax 484-2001
www.g-aschools.org
Galesburg-Augusta ES 400/PK-4
315 W Battle Creek St 49053 269-484-2040
Shaun Sportel, prin. Fax 484-2041
Other Schools – See Augusta

Garden City, Wayne, Pop. 27,153
Garden City SD 4,300/PK-12
1333 Radcliff St 48135 734-762-8300
Derek Fisher, supt. Fax 762-8530
www.gardencityschools.com
Douglas ES 500/3-4
6400 Hartel St 48135 734-762-8450
James Bohnwagner, prin. Fax 762-8535
Farmington IS 600/5-6
33411 Marquette St 48135 734-762-8460
Lesley Rodriguez, prin. Fax 762-8536
Garden City MS 600/7-8
1851 Radcliff St 48135 734-762-8400
Kip O'Leary, prin. Fax 762-8532
Lathers ECC & K Center 200/PK-K
28351 Marquette St 48135 734-762-8490
Susan Ford, prin. Fax 762-8539
Memorial ES 500/1-2
30001 Marquette St 48135 734-762-8480
Jennifer Sheldon, prin. Fax 762-8538

Gaylord, Otsego, Pop. 3,564
Gaylord Community SD 3,000/PK-12
615 S Elm Ave 49735 989-705-3080
Brian Pearson, supt. Fax 732-6029
www.gaylordschools.com
Gaylord IS 700/4-6
240 E 4th St 49735 989-731-0856
Rich Marshall, prin. Fax 732-6475
Gaylord MS 500/7-8
600 E 5th St 49735 989-731-0848
Gerald Belanger, prin. Fax 732-2632
GCS Preschool PK-PK
615 S Elm St 49735 989-705-3020
Sherri Ryan, prin. Fax 732-6029
North Ohio ES 400/K-3
912 N Ohio Ave 49735 989-731-2648
Dan Vaara, prin. Fax 731-3387
South Maple ES 500/K-3
650 E 5th St 49735 989-731-0648
Therese Hansen, prin. Fax 731-0095

Otsego Christian S 100/PK-3
PO Box 1365 49734 989-732-8333
Fax 705-7713
St. Mary Cathedral S 300/PK-12
321 N Otsego Ave 49735 989-732-5801
Nicole Hatch, prin. Fax 732-2085

Genesee, Genesee
Genesee SD 800/PK-12
7347 N Genesee Rd 48437 810-591-1650
Melody Strang, supt. Fax 591-1646
www.geneseeschools.org
Haas ES 400/PK-6
7347 N Genesee Rd 48437 810-591-1650
Bethany Zito, prin. Fax 591-1656

Gibraltar, Wayne, Pop. 4,593
Gibraltar SD
Supt. — See Woodhaven
Parsons ES 400/K-5
14473 Middle Gibraltar Rd 48173 734-379-7050
Kelley Villa, prin. Fax 379-7051
Shumate MS 900/6-8
30448 W Jefferson Ave 48173 734-379-7600
Eric Cassie, prin. Fax 379-2370

Gladstone, Delta, Pop. 4,885
Gladstone Area SD 1,500/K-12
400 S 10th St 49837 906-428-2417
Dr. Jay Kulbertis, supt. Fax 789-8457
www.gladstoneschools.com
Cameron ES 300/K-2
803 29th St 49837 906-428-2314
Lori Neurohr, prin. Fax 789-8502
Gladstone MS 400/6-8
300 S 10th St 49837 906-428-2295
Dave Ballard, prin. Fax 789-8404
Jones ES 300/3-5
400 S 10th St 49837 906-428-3660
Kristina Hansen, prin. Fax 789-8464

Gladwin, Gladwin, Pop. 2,897
Gladwin Community SD 1,800/K-12
401 N Bowery Ave 48624 989-426-9255
Rick Seebeck, supt. Fax 426-5981
www.gladwinschools.net
Gladwin ES 400/K-2
600 W 1st St 48624 989-426-7771
Josh Pahl, prin. Fax 426-6036
Gladwin IS 400/3-5
780 W 1st St 48624 989-426-4531
Joe Cote, prin. Fax 426-6037
Gladwin JHS 500/6-8
401 N Bowery Ave 48624 989-426-3808
Kaycie Soderling, prin. Fax 426-6038

Skeels Christian S 100/PK-12
3956 N M 18 48624 989-426-2054
John Shoaf, dir. Fax 426-4411

Glenn, Allegan
Glenn SD 50/K-6
PO Box 69 49416 269-227-3411
Scott Morgan, supt. Fax 227-5375
www.glennpublicschool.org
Glenn ES 50/K-6
PO Box 69 49416 269-227-3411
Scott Morgan, supt. Fax 227-5375

Gobles, Van Buren, Pop. 803
Gobles SD 800/K-12
PO Box 412 49055 269-628-5618
Jeff Rehlander, supt. Fax 628-5306
www.gobles.org/
Gobles ES 400/K-5
PO Box 412 49055 269-628-2131
Terry Breen, prin. Fax 628-5306
Gobles MS 200/6-8
PO Box 412 49055 269-628-2113
Chris Miller, dean Fax 628-5306

Gobles Jr. Academy 50/K-10
32110 6th Ave 49055 269-628-2704
Thomas Coffee, prin. Fax 628-7314

Goodrich, Genesee, Pop. 1,851
Goodrich Area SD 2,000/PK-12
8029 Gale Rd 48438 810-591-2250
Ryan Relken, supt. Fax 591-2550
www.goodrich.k12.mi.us
Goodrich MS 500/6-8
7480 Gale Rd 48438 810-591-4210
Kapeka vonKeltz, prin. Fax 636-7879
Oaktree ES 400/2-5
7500 Gale Rd 48438 810-591-5200
Jasan Bryan, prin. Fax 591-5210
Reid ES 200/PK-1
7501 Seneca St 48438 810-591-3455
Beth Millerschin, prin. Fax 636-2622

Grand Blanc, Genesee, Pop. 8,062
Grand Blanc Community SD 7,700/PK-12
11920 S Saginaw St 48439 810-591-6000
Dr. Clarence Garner, supt. Fax 591-6018
www.grandblancschools.org
Anderson ES 400/K-2
5290 Leroy St 48439 810-591-5829
Barbara Watkins, prin. Fax 591-5833
Brendel ES 500/K-5
223 Bush St 48439 810-591-6137
Dr. Doris Goetz, prin. Fax 591-6149
Cook ES 400/K-2
4434 E Cook Rd 48439 810-591-7910
Tia Dale, prin. Fax 591-7916
Grand Blanc MS East 1,100/6-8
6100 Perry Rd 48439 810-591-4696
Jodi Kruse, prin. Fax 591-0242
Grand Blanc MS West 1,000/6-8
1515 E Reid Rd 48439 810-591-7309
Jeff Neall, prin. Fax 591-0182
Indian Hill ES 500/K-5
11240 Woodbridge Dr 48439 810-591-4100
Jeremy Mitchell, prin. Fax 591-4101
Mason ES 400/3-5
4455 E Cook Rd 48439 810-591-7840
Sonya James, prin. Fax 591-7811
McGrath ES 400/3-5
5288 Todd St 48439 810-591-5827
Barbara Watkins, prin. Fax 591-5824
Myers ES 500/K-5
6085 Sun Valley Dr 48439 810-591-3000
Betsy Kato, prin. Fax 591-3002
Perry Innovation Center 100/2-6
11920 S Saginaw St 48439 810-591-6078
Amber Hall, prin. Fax 591-6095
Perry Pre K 100/PK-PK
11920 S Saginaw St 48439 810-591-6078
Lynn Spaly, dir. Fax 591-6095
Reid ES 500/K-5
2103 E Reid Rd 48439 810-591-7121
Jamie Wagner, prin. Fax 591-7179

Holy Family S 500/PK-8
215 Orchard St 48439 810-694-9072
Theresa Purcell, prin. Fax 694-9405

Grand Haven, Ottawa, Pop. 10,239
Grand Haven Area SD 6,000/PK-12
1415 S Beechtree St 49417 616-850-5000
Andrew Ingall, supt. Fax 850-5010
www.ghaps.org
Ferry ES 300/PK-4
1050 Pennoyer Ave 49417 616-850-5300
Shelly Hammond, prin. Fax 850-5310
Griffin ES 300/PK-4
1700 S Griffin St 49417 616-850-5500
Debra Mann, prin. Fax 850-5510
Lakeshore MS 1,000/7-8
900 Cutler St 49417 616-850-6500
Amanda Sorrelle, prin. Fax 850-6510
Peach Plains ES 400/PK-4
15849 Comstock St 49417 616-850-5800
Kate Drake, prin. Fax 850-5810
Robinson ES 300/PK-4
11801 120th Ave 49417 616-850-5900
Jeffrey Marcus, prin. Fax 850-5910
Rosy Mound ES 300/PK-4
14016 Lakeshore Dr 49417 616-850-6700
Kevin Blanding, prin. Fax 850-6710
White ES 300/PK-4
1400 Wisconsin Ave 49417 616-850-5700
Valerie Livingston, prin. Fax 850-5710
White Pines IS 900/5-6
1400 S Griffin St 49417 616-850-6300
Mike Shelton, prin. Fax 850-6310
Other Schools – See Spring Lake

Grand Haven Christian S 300/PK-8
1102 Grant Ave 49417 616-842-5420
James Onderlinde, prin. Fax 842-6850
St. John Lutheran S 100/PK-8
525 Taylor Ave 49417 616-842-0260
Laura Harvey, admin. Fax 842-0934

Grand Ledge, Eaton, Pop. 7,630
Grand Ledge SD 5,000/PK-12
220 Lamson St 48837 517-925-5400
Dr. Brian Metcalf, supt. Fax 925-5409
www.glcomets.net/
Beagle ES 600/1-6
600 W South St 48837 517-925-5480
Dawn Kennaugh, prin. Fax 925-5523
Hayes MS 800/7-8
12620 Nixon Rd 48837 517-925-5680
Julie Taylor, prin. Fax 925-5730
Holbrook ECC PK-PK
615 Jones St 48837 517-925-5640
Breanna Cleeves, prin. Fax 925-5453
Neff Kindergarten Center 400/K-K
950 Jenne St 48837 517-925-5740
David Averill, prin. Fax 925-5772
Willow Ridge ES 500/1-6
12840 Nixon Rd 48837 517-925-5775
Jim Gee, prin. Fax 925-5811
Other Schools – See Eagle, Lansing

Oneida Township SD 3 50/K-5
8981 Oneida Rd 48837 517-627-7005
Heidi Burtchett, lead tchr.
strangeschool.weebly.com
Strange ES 50/K-5
8981 Oneida Rd 48837 517-749-9832
Diane McNeil, prin. Fax 543-6633

St. Michael S 200/PK-8
325 Edwards St 48837 517-627-2167
Laurie Cathcart, prin. Fax 627-1289

Grand Marais, Alger
Burt Township SD 50/K-12
PO Box 338 49839 906-494-2543
Heidi Homeister, supt. Fax 494-2522
grandmaraisschools.org/
Burt Township S 50/K-12
PO Box 338 49839 906-494-2521
Heidi Homeister, supt. Fax 494-2522

Grand Rapids, Kent, Pop. 182,274
East Grand Rapids SD 3,000/K-12
2915 Hall St SE 49506 616-235-3535
Dr. Sara Shubel, supt. Fax 235-6730
www.egrps.org
Breton Downs ES 400/K-5
2500 Boston St SE 49506 616-235-7552
Caroline Breault-Cannon, prin. Fax 235-6733
East Grand Rapids MS 700/6-8
2425 Lake Dr SE 49506 616-235-7551
Anthony Morey, prin. Fax 235-7587
Lakeside ES 400/K-5
2325 Hall St SE 49506 616-235-7553
Stephanie Thelen, prin. Fax 235-3915
Wealthy ES 400/K-5
1961 Lake Dr SE 49506 616-235-7550
Carlye Allen, prin. Fax 235-3918

Forest Hills SD 10,100/PK-12
6590 Cascade Rd SE 49546 616-493-8800
Daniel Behm, supt. Fax 493-8552
www.fhps.net
Collins ES 400/PK-4
4368 Heather Ln SE 49546 616-493-8900
Mitchell Balingit, prin. Fax 493-8909
Knapp Forest ES 700/PK-6
4243 Knapp Valley Dr NE 49525 616-493-8980
Scott Haid, prin. Fax 493-8989
Meadow Brook ES 500/K-4
1450 Forest Hill Ave SE 49546 616-493-8740
Timothy Shaw, prin. Fax 493-8749
Northern Hills MS 600/7-8
3775 Leonard St NE 49525 616-493-8650
David Simpson, prin. Fax 493-8686
Northern Trails 5/6 S 600/5-6
3777 Leonard St NE 49525 616-493-8990
Dr. Susan Gutierrez, prin. Fax 493-8995
Orchard View ES 600/PK-6
2770 Leffingwell Ave NE 49525 616-493-8930
Tim Fournier, prin. Fax 493-8939
Pine Ridge ES 500/PK-4
3250 Redford Dr SE 49546 616-493-8910
Tamasha James, prin. Fax 493-8919
Thornapple ES 400/K-4
6932 Bridgewater Dr SE 49546 616-493-8920
Greg Shubel, prin. Fax 493-8929
Other Schools – See Ada

Grand Rapids SD 14,800/PK-12
PO Box 117 49501 616-819-2000
Teresa Weatherall Neal M.Ed., supt. Fax 819-3480
www.grps.org/
Aberdeen ES 300/K-8
928 Aberdeen St NE 49505 616-819-2868
Jaime Masco, prin. Fax 819-1111
Alger MS 400/6-8
921 Alger St SE 49507 616-819-6200
Roderick Wade, prin. Fax 819-6201
Blandford S 100/6-6
3143 Milo St NW, 616-819-2555
Greg Ramey, prin. Fax 819-5243
Brookside ES 300/PK-5
2505 Madison Ave SE 49507 616-819-2242
Denishea Neal, prin. Fax 819-6059
Buchanan ES 600/PK-5
1775 Buchanan Ave SW 49507 616-819-2252
Evelyn Ortiz, prin. Fax 819-2249
Burton ES 500/PK-5
2133 Buchanan Ave SW 49507 616-819-2262
Allison Woodside, prin. Fax 819-2284
Burton MS 500/6-8
2133 Buchanan Ave SW 49507 616-819-2269
Lametria Johnson-Eaddy, prin. Fax 819-2282
Campus ES 300/PK-5
710 Benjamin Ave SE 49506 616-819-3525
Bernard Colton, prin. Fax 819-3526
Center of Economicology 100/6-6
1720 Plainfield Ave NE 49505 616-819-2380
Ryan Huppert, prin. Fax 819-2496
Chavez ES 500/PK-5
1205 Grandville Ave SW 49503 616-819-2560
Aimee Garcia, prin. Fax 819-2556

Coit Creative Arts Academy 300/K-5
617 Coit Ave NE 49503 616-819-2390
Jason McGhee, prin. Fax 819-4209
Congress ES 200/PK-5
940 Baldwin St SE 49506 616-819-2201
Erek Kooyman, prin. Fax 819-2203
Dickinson Academy 300/PK-8
448 Dickinson St SE 49507 616-819-2505
Nikki Schellenberg, prin. Fax 819-2502
East Leonard ES 200/K-5
410 Barnett St NE 49503 616-819-2525
Adam Rusticus, prin. Fax 819-2528
Ford Academic Center 200/PK-8
851 Madison Ave SE 49507 616-819-2640
Jerry McComb, prin. Fax 819-2660
Frost Environmental Science Academy 500/PK-12
1460 Laughlin Dr NW 49504 616-819-2550
Greg Ramey, prin. Fax 819-2184
Grand Rapids Montessori at Fountain 300/PK-8
159 College Ave NE 49503 616-819-2405
Kerri Reed, prin. Fax 819-2406
Grand Rapids Montessori at North Park 300/PK-8
3375 Cheney Ave NE 49525 616-819-2848
Robin Sorge, prin. Fax 819-2849
Harrison Park S 900/PK-8
1440 Davis Ave NW 49504 616-819-2565
Troy Wilbon, prin. Fax 819-2567
Ken-O-Sha Park ES 100/PK-5
1353 Van Auken St SE 49508 616-819-2696
Stephanie Villalta, prin. Fax 819-3461
Kent Hills ES 400/PK-5
1445 Emerald Ave NE 49505 616-819-2727
Benjamin Rodgers, prin. Fax 819-2726
King Leadership Academy 400/PK-8
645 Logan St SE 49503 616-819-2600
Tricia Mathes, prin. Fax 819-2596
Mulick Park ES 200/PK-5
1761 Rosewood Ave SE 49506 616-819-2810
Lisa Minnella, prin. Fax 819-2817
Palmer ES 200/PK-5
309 Palmer St NE 49505 616-819-2929
Leanne Lange, prin. Fax 819-2928
Ridgemoor Park Montessori PK-6
2555 Inverness Rd 49546 616-819-5321
Forrest Clift, prin.
Riverside MS 300/6-8
265 Eleanor St NE 49505 616-819-2969
William Martin, prin. Fax 819-2981
Shawmut Hills ES 300/K-8
2550 Burritt St NW 49504 616-819-3055
Timothy Mabin, prin. Fax 819-3056
Sherwood Park Global Studies S 500/K-8
3859 Chamberlain Ave SE 49508 616-819-3095
Sherrie Ross, prin. Fax 819-3099
Sibley ES 400/PK-5
943 Sibley St NW 49504 616-819-3100
Roselyn CharlesMaher, prin. Fax 819-3108
Southwest Community Campus 700/PK-8
801 Oakland Ave SW 49503 616-819-2947
Carols de la Barrera, prin. Fax 819-3630
Stocking ES 300/PK-5
863 7th St NW 49504 616-819-3130
JoAnn Riemersma, prin. Fax 819-2414
Westwood MS 400/6-8
1525 Mount Mercy Dr NW 49504 616-819-3322
Dennis Branson, prin. Fax 819-3301
Zoo ES 100/6-6
1300 Fulton St W 49504 616-819-3344
Greg Ramey, prin. Fax 819-3345

Grandville SD
Supt. — See Grandville
Cummings ES 500/PK-6
4261 Schoolcraft St SW, 616-254-6040
David Martini, prin. Fax 254-6043

Kelloggsville SD 2,100/PK-12
242 52nd St SE 49548 616-538-7460
Samuel Wright, supt. Fax 532-1597
www.kvilleps.org
East Kelloggsville S 400/K-3
4656 Jefferson Ave SE 49548 616-532-1580
Jeff Owen, prin. Fax 532-7487
Kelloggsville Early Childhood Learning 200/PK-PK
977 44th St SW 49509 616-532-1585
Kim Stevens, admin. Fax 532-7437
Kelloggsville MS 500/6-8
4650 Division Ave S 49548 616-532-1575
James Alston, prin. Fax 532-1579
Southeast Kelloggsville S 300/4-5
240 52nd St SE 49548 616-532-1590
Kelly Farkas, prin. Fax 532-7750
West Kelloggsville S 300/K-3
4555 Magnolia Ave SW 49548 616-532-1595
Eric Schilthuis, prin. Fax 532-7475

Kenowa Hills SD 3,300/PK-12
2325 4 Mile Rd NW 49544 616-784-2511
Gerald Hopkins M.Ed., supt. Fax 784-8323
www.khps.org
Kenowa Hills Central ES 700/K-5
4252 3 Mile Rd NW, 616-453-6351
Cherie Horner M.Ed., prin. Fax 453-9686
Kenowa Hills ECC 50/PK-PK
3971 Richmond Ct NW, 616-647-0910
Daniel Brant M.Ed., dir. Fax 647-0911
Kenowa Hills MS 700/6-8
3950 Hendershot Ave NW 49544 616-785-3225
Abby Wiseman M.Ed., prin. Fax 784-2404
Zinser ES 300/K-5
1234 Kinney Ave NW, 616-453-2461
Ross Willick M.Ed., prin. Fax 453-0277
Other Schools – See Comstock Park

Northview SD 3,400/PK-12
4365 Hunsberger Ave NE 49525 616-363-6861
Dr. M Korpak, supt. Fax 363-9609
www.nvps.net
Crossroads MS 500/7-8
4400 Ambrose Ave NE 49525 616-361-3430
Daniel Duba, prin. Fax 363-7868
East Oakview ES 400/K-4
3940 Suburban Shores Dr NE 49525 616-361-3460
David Parmerlee, prin. Fax 361-3458
Highlands MS 400/5-6
4645 Chandy Dr NE 49525 616-361-3440
Jamey Vermaat, prin. Fax 365-6171
North Oakview ES 400/K-4
4300 Costa Ave NE 49525 616-361-3450
Teya Cotter, prin. Fax 365-6161
West Oakview ES 300/PK-4
3880 Stuyvesant Ave NE 49525 616-361-3470
Dan Heitzman, prin. Fax 361-3492

All Saints Academy - ES Campus 200/PK-3
2233 Diamond Ave NE 49505 616-364-9453
Michael Debri, prin. Fax 361-6991
All Saints Academy - MS Campus 100/4-8
1110 4 Mile Rd NE 49525 616-363-7725
Abby Giroux, prin. Fax 363-3086
Grand Rapids Adventist Academy 100/K-12
1151 Oakleigh Rd NW 49504 616-791-9797
Burney Culpepper, prin. Fax 791-7242
Grand Rapids Christian ES PK-5
1630 Griggs St SE 49506 616-574-5900
Ann Bakker, prin. Fax 574-5910
Grand Rapids Christian ES 600/PK-4
1050 Iroquois Dr SE 49506 616-574-6500
Mark Krommendyk, prin. Fax 574-6510
Grand Rapids Christian MS 400/5-8
2036 Chesaning Dr SE 49506 616-574-6300
Eric Burgess, prin. Fax 574-6310
Grand Rapids Hebrew Academy 50/PK-1
2615 Michigan St NE 49506 616-957-0770
Holy Spirit S 300/PK-8
2222 Lake Michigan Dr NW 49504 616-453-2772
Patrick Kalahar, prin. Fax 453-0018
Hope Protestant Reformed Christian S 200/K-9
1545 Wilson Ave SW, 616-453-9717
Ron Koole, prin. Fax 453-9907
Immaculate Heart of Mary S 300/PK-8
1951 Plymouth Ave SE 49506 616-241-4633
Michael Thomasma, prin. Fax 241-4418
Immanuel-St. James Lutheran S 100/PK-8
2066 Oakwood Ave NE 49505 616-363-0505
Jason Alexander, prin. Fax 363-3319
Legacy Christian ES 300/PK-4
520 68th St SE 49548 616-455-0310
Vince Bonnema M.A., admin. Fax 455-6162
Legacy Christian West Campus 200/5-8
67 68th St SW 49548 616-455-3860
Vince Bonnema M.A., admin. Fax 455-1960
Living Stones Academy 100/PK-6
1415 Lyon St NE 49503 616-803-9654
Rev. Aaron Winkle, head sch
NorthPointe Christian ES 300/PK-6
540 Russwood St NE 49505 616-363-4869
Todd Tolsma, head sch Fax 363-5977
Our Savior Lutheran S 100/PK-8
1916 Ridgewood Ave SE 49506 616-949-0710
Rev. Jeremy Swem, prin. Fax 975-7840
Plymouth Christian ES 200/PK-6
1000 Ball Ave NE 49505 616-458-4367
Nathan Bleeker, admin. Fax 458-8532
Potter's House S 400/PK-8
810 Van Raalte Dr SW 49509 616-241-5202
Mark Ponstine, prin. Fax 241-9331
Sacred Heart Academy 100/PK-11
1200 Dayton St SW 49504 616-459-0948
Sean Maltbie, hdmstr. Fax 459-0899
St. Anthony of Padua S 400/PK-8
2510 Richmond St NW 49504 616-453-8229
Julie Whelan, prin. Fax 453-8053
St. Paul the Apostle S 200/PK-8
2750 Burton St SE 49546 616-949-1690
Lori Salva, prin. Fax 949-0836
St. Stephen S 300/PK-8
740 Gladstone Dr SE 49506 616-243-8998
Cindy Thomas, prin. Fax 243-0451
St. Thomas the Apostle S 400/PK-8
1429 Wilcox Park Dr SE 49506 616-458-4228
Suzi Furtwangler, prin. Fax 458-4583
San Juan Diego Academy 100/PK-8
1650 Godfrey Ave SW 49509 616-243-1126
Rick Muniz, prin. Fax 243-0862
Stepping Stones Montessori S 100/PK-6
1110 College Ave NE 49503 616-451-8627
West Side Christian S 400/PK-8
955 Westend Ave NW 49504 616-453-3925
An Kurosu, prin. Fax 453-4150

Grandville, Kent, Pop. 15,098
Grandville SD 5,600/PK-12
3839 Prairie St SW 49418 616-254-6570
Roger Bearup, supt. Fax 254-6580
www.grandville.k12.mi.us
Central ES 200/PK-6
4052 Prairie St SW 49418 616-254-6010
Angie Thornburgh, prin. Fax 254-6013
Century Park Learning Center 500/PK-6
5710 Kenowa Ave SW 49418 616-254-6820
Tonia Shoup, prin. Fax 254-6823
East ES 300/K-6
3413 30th St SW 49418 616-254-6080
Ana Aleman, prin. Fax 254-6083
Grand View ES 600/K-6
3701 52nd St SW 49418 616-254-6120
Emily McAlpine, prin. Fax 254-6123
Grandville MS 900/7-8
3535 Wilson Ave SW 49418 616-254-6610
Ken See, prin. Fax 254-6613

South ES 400/PK-6
3650 Navaho St SW 49418 616-254-6211
Ryan Roberts, prin. Fax 254-6213
West ES 400/K-6
3777 Aaron Ave SW 49418 616-254-6250
Brian Mulder, prin. Fax 254-6253
Other Schools – See Grand Rapids

Grandville Calvin Christian ES 300/PK-6
3934 Wilson Ave SW 49418 616-538-9710
Derek Braman, prin. Fax 538-3553
Grandville Calvin Christian MS 6-8
3740 Ivanrest Ave SW 49418 616-531-7400
Thelma Ensink, prin. Fax 531-7402

Grant, Newaygo, Pop. 889
Grant SD 2,000/PK-12
148 S Elder St 49327 231-834-5621
Jonathan Whan, supt. Fax 834-7146
www.grantps.net
Grant ES 400/2-4
160 E State Rd 49327 231-834-5678
Carol Dawson, prin. Fax 834-9002
Grant MS 600/5-8
96 E 120th St 49327 231-834-5910
Lance Jones, prin. Fax 834-9029
Grant PS 300/PK-1
103 S Elder St 49327 231-834-7382
Carol Dawson, prin. Fax 834-5707

Grant Christian S 100/PK-8
12931 S Poplar Ave 49327 231-834-8445
Dave VanderGoot, prin. Fax 834-9185

Grass Lake, Jackson, Pop. 1,146
Grass Lake Community SD 1,200/PK-12
899 S Union St 49240 517-867-5540
Dr. Ryle Kiser, supt. Fax 522-8195
www.grasslakeschools.com
Grass Lake MS 300/6-8
1000 Grass Lake Rd 49240 517-867-5550
Jeanene Byerly, prin. Fax 522-4775
Long ES 600/PK-5
829 S Union St 49240 517-867-5590
Michelle Clark, prin. Fax 522-8789

Grayling, Crawford, Pop. 1,867
Crawford AuSable SD 1,700/PK-12
1135 N Old 27 49738 989-344-3500
Joseph Powers, supt. Fax 348-6822
www.casdk12.net/
Grayling ES 700/PK-5
306 Plum St 49738 989-344-3655
Gina Brunskill, prin. Fax 348-3544
Grayling MS 400/6-8
500 Spruce St 49738 989-344-3550
Jeffrey Branch, prin. Fax 348-7045

Grayling SDA S 50/1-8
2468 Camp AuSable Rd 49738 989-348-2501
Ben Zork, prin.

Greenville, Montcalm, Pop. 8,316
Greenville SD 3,700/K-12
1414 Chase St 48838 616-754-3686
Linda Van Houten, supt. Fax 754-5374
www.greenville.k12.mi.us
Baldwin Heights ES 500/K-5
821 W Oak St 48838 616-754-3643
Michael Walsh, prin. Fax 754-0272
Cedar Crest ES 300/K-5
622 S Cedar St 48838 616-754-3641
Keisha Peters, prin. Fax 754-0338
Greenville MS 800/6-8
1321 Chase St 48838 616-754-9361
Leigh Acker, prin. Fax 754-2901
Lincoln Heights ES 500/K-5
12420 Lincoln Lake Rd NE 48838 616-754-9167
Katy Beebe, prin. Fax 754-0469
Walnut Hills ES 400/K-5
712 N Walnut St 48838 616-754-3688
Susan Ayres, prin. Fax 754-0484

St. Charles S 200/K-8
502 S Franklin St 48838 616-754-3416
Margaret Karpus, prin. Fax 754-9262

Grosse Ile, Wayne, Pop. 9,781
Grosse Ile Township SD 1,900/K-12
23276 E River Rd 48138 734-362-2555
Joanne Lelekatch, supt. Fax 362-2594
www.gischools.org/
Grosse Ile MS 500/6-8
23270 E River Rd 48138 734-362-2500
Clifton Whitehouse, prin. Fax 362-2596
Meridian ES 400/3-5
26700 Meridian Rd 48138 734-362-2700
Joseph Reimann, prin. Fax 362-2796
Parke Lane ES 400/K-2
21610 Parke Ln 48138 734-362-2600
Audrie Kalisz, prin. Fax 362-2696

Grosse Pointe, Wayne, Pop. 5,336
Grosse Pointe SD 8,300/K-12
389 Saint Clair St 48230 313-432-3000
Dr. Gary Niehaus, supt. Fax 432-3002
www.gpschools.org
Barnes ECC 50/K-K
20090 Morningside Dr 48236 313-432-3800
Sue Lucchese, prin. Fax 432-3802
Brownell MS 700/6-8
260 Chalfonte Ave 48236 313-432-3900
Roger Hunwick, prin. Fax 432-3902
Defer ES 300/K-5
15425 Kercheval Ave 48230 313-432-4000
Lisa Rheaume, prin. Fax 432-4002
Ferry ES 400/K-5
748 Roslyn Rd 48236 313-432-4100
Gloria Hinz, prin. Fax 432-4102

Kerby ES 400/K-5
285 Kerby Rd 48236 313-432-4200
Sara Delgado, prin. Fax 432-4202
Maire ES 300/K-5
740 Cadieux Rd 48230 313-432-4300
Sonja Franchett, prin. Fax 432-4302
Mason ES 300/K-5
1640 Vernier Rd 48236 313-432-4400
Roy Bishop, prin. Fax 432-4402
Monteith ES 500/K-5
1275 Cook Rd 48236 313-432-4500
Shellyann Keelean, prin. Fax 432-4502
Parcells MS 800/6-8
20600 Mack Ave 48236 313-432-4600
Daniel Hartley, prin. Fax 432-4602
Pierce MS 600/6-8
15430 Kercheval Ave 48230 313-432-4700
Chris Clark, prin. Fax 432-4702
Richard ES 400/K-5
176 McKinley Ave 48236 313-432-4900
M. MacDonald-Barrett, prin. Fax 432-4902
Trombly ES 300/K-5
820 Beaconsfield Ave 48230 313-432-5000
Walter Fitzpatrick, prin. Fax 432-5002
Other Schools – See Harper Woods

Grosse Pointe Academy 300/PK-8
171 Lake Shore Rd 48236 313-886-1221
Tommy Adams, head sch Fax 886-8050
Our Lady Star of the Sea S 300/PK-8
467 Fairford Rd 48236 313-884-1070
Julie Aemisegger, prin. Fax 884-0406
St. Clare of Montefalco S 200/PK-8
16231 Charlevoix St 48230 313-647-5100
Ann Tonissen, prin. Fax 647-5105
St. Paul on the Lake S 500/PK-8
170 Grosse Pointe Blvd 48236 313-885-3430
Tina Forsythe, prin. Fax 885-9357
University Liggett S 700/PK-12
1045 Cook Rd 48236 313-884-4444
Joseph P. Healey Ph.D., head sch Fax 884-1775

Gwinn, Marquette, Pop. 1,874
Gwinn Area Community SD 1,400/K-12
50 W State Highway M35 49841 906-346-9283
Thomas Jayne, supt. Fax 346-3616
www.gwinn.k12.mi.us
Gilbert ES 200/K-5
250 W Iron St 49841 906-346-2775
Marci Paulsen, prin. Fax 346-2776
Gwinn MS 200/6-8
50 W State Highway M35 49841 906-346-5914
Sandra Petrovich, prin. Fax 346-0300
Sawyer ES 500/K-5
411 Scorpion Rd 49841 906-346-5567
Marci Paulsen, prin. Fax 346-7126

Hale, Iosco
Hale Area SD 300/K-12
311 N Washington St 48739 989-728-3551
Loren Vannest, supt. Fax 728-9551
www.haleschools.net
Hale S 300/K-8
311 N Washington St 48739 989-728-3551
Loren Vannest, admin. Fax 728-9551

Hamilton, Allegan
Hamilton Community SD 2,500/PK-12
4815 136th Ave 49419 269-751-5148
David Tebo, supt. Fax 751-7116
www.hamiltonschools.us
Bentheim ES 300/K-4
4057 38th St 49419 269-751-5335
Dan Scoville, prin. Fax 751-7537
Hamilton ES 300/PK-4
3472 Lincoln Rd 49419 269-751-5413
Dean Kramer, prin. Fax 751-7554
Hamilton MS 600/5-8
4845 136th Ave 49419 269-751-4436
Rick Frens, prin. Fax 751-8560
Other Schools – See Holland

Hamtramck, Wayne, Pop. 21,353
Hamtramck SD 2,700/PK-12
PO Box 12012 48212 313-872-9270
Thomas Niczay, supt. Fax 872-8679
www.hamtramck.k12.mi.us
Dickinson East ES 700/K-6
3385 Norwalk St 48212 313-873-9437
George Hill, prin. Fax 871-0511
Dickinson West ES 400/K-6
2333 Burger St 48212 313-365-5861
Corey Pitts, prin. Fax 365-4760
Hamtramck ECC 100/PK-K
11680 McDougall St 48212 313-891-3200
Colleen Stevens, prin. Fax 366-0786
Holbrook ES 200/K-6
2361 Alice St 48212 313-872-3203
Myron Miller, prin. Fax 871-2366
Kosciuszko MS 300/7-8
2333 Burger St 48212 313-365-4625
Nuo Ivezaj, prin. Fax 365-4760

Hancock, Houghton, Pop. 4,572
Hancock SD 600/K-12
501 Campus Dr 49930 906-487-5925
Kipp Beaudoin, supt. Fax 455-2255
www.hancockpublicschools.org
Barkell ES 400/K-5
1201 N Elevation St 49930 906-487-9030
Dan Vaara, prin. Fax 455-4142

Hanover, Jackson, Pop. 437
Hanover-Horton SD
Supt. — See Horton
Hanover-Horton ES 500/K-5
131 Fairview St 49241 517-563-0103
Cindy Forgione, prin. Fax 563-0160

Harbor Beach, Huron, Pop. 1,671
Harbor Beach Community SD 500/PK-12
402 S 5th St 48441 989-479-3261
Dr. Shawn Bishop, supt. Fax 479-9521
www.hbpirates.org
Harbor Beach ES 100/PK-5
402 S 5th St 48441 989-479-3261
Tumara Johnston, prin. Fax 479-9521
Harbor Beach MS 100/6-8
402 S 5th St 48441 989-479-3261
Tumara Johnston, prin. Fax 479-9521

Sigel Township SD 4 50/K-8
5754 Section Line Rd 48441 989-479-9266
Joseph Murphy, supt.
Eccles S, 5754 Section Line Rd 48441 50/K-8
Anne Kennedy, lead tchr. 989-479-9266

Our Lady of Lake Huron S 100/PK-8
222 Court St 48441 989-479-3427
David Mausolf, prin. Fax 479-3335
Zion Lutheran S 100/PK-8
299 Garden St 48441 989-479-3615
Cynthia Brown, prin. Fax 479-6551

Harbor Springs, Emmet, Pop. 1,169
Harbor Springs SD 800/PK-12
800 State Rd 49740 231-526-4545
Mark Tompkins, supt. Fax 526-4544
www.harborps.org
Blackbird ES 100/PK-2
421 E Lake St 49740 231-526-4600
Nathan Fairbanks, prin. Fax 526-4630
Harbor Springs MS 200/6-8
800 State Rd 49740 231-526-4700
Brad Plackemeier, prin. Fax 526-4760
Shay ES 200/3-5
175 E Lake St 49740 231-526-4500
Nathan Fairbanks, prin. Fax 526-4534

Harbor Light Christian S 100/PK-12
8333 Clayton Rd 49740 231-347-7859
Ryan Coxon, admin. Fax 347-7703

Harper Woods, Wayne, Pop. 13,876
Grosse Pointe SD
Supt. — See Grosse Pointe
Poupard ES 300/K-5
20655 Lennon St 48225 313-432-4800
Hussain Ali, prin. Fax 432-4802

Harper Woods SD 1,500/PK-12
20225 Beaconsfield St 48225 313-245-3000
Steven McGhee, supt. Fax 839-1249
www.hwschools.org
Beacon ES 400/PK-3
19475 Beaconsfield St 48225 313-245-5343
Janet Gottsleben, prin. Fax 371-4170
Harper Woods MS 200/7-8
20225 Beaconsfield St 48225 313-245-3000
Heath Filber, prin. Fax 839-4360
Tyrone ES 200/4-6
19525 Tyrone St 48225 313-245-3000
Cheryl Puzdrakiewicz, prin. Fax 884-1057

Harris, Menominee
Bark River-Harris SD 700/K-12
PO Box 350 49845 906-466-9981
Jason Lockwood, supt. Fax 466-0107
www.brhschools.org/
Bark River-Harris ES 400/K-6
PO Box 350 49845 906-466-5334
Kelly Harvey, prin. Fax 466-2925

Harrison, Clare, Pop. 2,058
Harrison Community SD 1,500/K-12
PO Box 529 48625 989-539-7871
Richard T. Foote, supt. Fax 539-7491
www.harrisonschools.com/
Harrison MS 300/6-8
PO Box 529 48625 989-539-7194
Kelly Pieprzyk, prin. Fax 539-0460
Hillside ES 300/3-5
PO Box 529 48625 989-539-6902
Andrea Andera, prin. Fax 539-4322
Larson ES 300/K-2
PO Box 529 48625 989-539-3259
Julie Rosekrans, prin. Fax 539-4316

Harrison Township, Macomb, Pop. 24,685
L'Anse Creuse SD
Supt. — See Clinton Township
Graham ES 400/PK-5
25555 Crocker Blvd 48045 586-783-6460
Amy Horgan, prin. Fax 783-6466
L'Anse Creuse MS Central 700/6-8
38000 Reimold St 48045 586-783-6430
Andrea Glynn, prin. Fax 783-6437
L'Anse Creuse MS South 500/6-8
34641 Jefferson Ave 48045 586-493-5620
Paul Lasala, prin. Fax 493-5625
Lobbestael ES 400/PK-5
38495 Prentiss St 48045 586-783-6450
Beverly Polega, prin. Fax 783-6456
South River ES 500/K-5
27733 S River Rd 48045 586-783-6480
Cathy Ciolino, prin. Fax 783-6486
Yacks ES 400/K-5
34700 Union Lake Rd 48045 586-493-5630
Kelly Darlington, prin. Fax 493-5635

Hart, Oceana, Pop. 2,108
Hart SD 1,300/PK-12
301 Johnson St W 49420 231-873-6214
Mark Platt, supt. Fax 873-6244
www.hartschools.net
Diman-Wolf ECC PK-PK
306 Johnson St W 49420 231-873-6330
Amy Stone, dir. Fax 873-5162

Hart MS 400/5-8
308 Johnson St W 49420 231-873-6320
Kevin Ackley, prin. Fax 873-0245
Spitler ES 500/K-4
302 Johnson St W 49420 231-873-6340
Amy Taranko, prin. Fax 873-7042

Oceana Christian S 100/PK-8
3258 N 72nd Ave 49420 231-873-2514
Jean Riley, admin. Fax 873-5096

Hartford, Van Buren, Pop. 2,604
Hartford SD 1,300/PK-12
115 School St 49057 269-621-7000
Andrew Hubbard, supt. Fax 621-3887
www.hpsmi.org/
Hartford MS 300/6-8
141 School St 49057 269-621-7200
Ken Mohney, prin. Fax 621-7260
Redwood ES 700/PK-5
395 Woodside Dr 49057 269-621-7300
Andrew Hubbard, admin. Fax 621-7360

Hartland, Livingston
Hartland Consolidated SD
Supt. — See Howell
Creekside ES 500/K-4
PO Box 408 48353 810-626-2600
Lawrence Pumford, prin. Fax 626-2601
Hartland MS 900/7-8
3250 Hartland Rd 48353 810-626-2400
Steve Livingway, prin. Fax 626-2401
Round ES 300/K-4
11550 Hibner Rd 48353 810-626-2800
Dotty Selix, prin. Fax 626-2801
Village ES 400/K-4
10632 Hibner Rd 48353 810-626-2850
Mary Day, prin. Fax 626-2851

Our Savior Evangelical Lutheran S 100/PK-8
13667 Highland Rd 48353 248-887-3836
Andrea Johnson, prin. Fax 887-3596

Haslett, Ingham, Pop. 18,726
Haslett SD 2,700/K-12
5593 Franklin St 48840 517-339-8242
Steven L. Cook, supt. Fax 339-1360
www.haslett.k12.mi.us/
Haslett MS 600/6-8
1535 Franklin St 48840 517-339-8233
Susan Gillings, prin. Fax 339-4837
Murphy ES 400/2-5
1875 Lake Lansing Rd 48840 517-339-8253
Diane Lindbert, prin. Fax 339-4830
Ralya ES 400/2-5
5645 School St 48840 517-339-8202
Judy Tegreeny, prin. Fax 339-7359
Wilkshire ECC 400/K-1
5750 Academic Way 48840 517-339-8208
Gail Hicks, prin. Fax 339-4832

Hastings, Barry, Pop. 7,265
Hastings Area SD 2,800/PK-12
232 W Grand St 49058 269-948-4400
Dr. Carrie Duits, supt. Fax 948-4425
www.hassk12.org
Central ES 400/PK-5
509 S Broadway St 49058 269-948-4423
Sarah Geukes, prin. Fax 948-4449
Hastings MS 600/6-8
232 W Grand St 49058 269-948-4404
Beth Stevens, prin. Fax 945-6101
Northeastern ES 300/K-5
519 E Grant St 49058 269-948-4421
Eric Heide, prin. Fax 948-4502
Southeastern ES 300/K-5
1300 S East St 49058 269-948-4419
Dana Stein, prin. Fax 948-4504
Star ES 300/K-5
1900 Star School Rd 49058 269-948-4442
Amy Smelker, prin. Fax 948-4448

Barry County Christian S 100/K-12
2999 McKeown Rd 49058 269-948-2151
Brandon Strong, admin. Fax 948-2795
Hastings SDA S, 888 Terry Ln 49058 50/1-8
Renee Truax, prin. 269-945-3896
St. Rose of Lima S 100/PK-6
707 S Jefferson St 49058 269-945-3164
Lori Pearson, prin. Fax 945-0509

Hazel Park, Oakland, Pop. 15,715
Hazel Park SD 2,500/PK-12
1620 E Elza Ave 48030 248-658-5200
Dr. Amy Kruppe, supt. Fax 544-5443
www.hazelparkschools.org
Hazel Park JHS 600/6-8
22770 Highland Ave 48030 248-658-2300
Tammy Scholz, prin. Fax 586-5875
Hoover ES 300/PK-5
23720 Hoover Ave 48030 248-658-5300
Debbie Dimas, prin. Fax 586-5831
United Oaks ES 300/PK-5
1015 E Harry Ave 48030 248-658-2400
Karla Graessley, prin. Fax 658-2405
Webster ECC PK-PK
431 W Jarvis Ave 48030 248-658-5550
Deborah Jones, coord. Fax 544-5421
Other Schools – See Ferndale

Hemlock, Saginaw, Pop. 1,446
Hemlock SD 1,100/PK-12
PO Box 260 48626 989-642-5282
Donald Killingbeck, supt. Fax 642-2773
www.hemlockps.com
Hemlock ES 100/PK-PK
PO Box 260 48626 989-642-5221
Lori Gensch, prin. Fax 642-4146

Hemlock MS 300/5-8
PO Box 260 48626 989-642-5253
Terry Keyser, prin. Fax 642-8239
Ling ES 200/K-4
PO Box 260 48626 989-642-5235
Lori Gensch, prin. Fax 642-8008

St. John Lutheran S 50/PK-8
2290 Pretzer Rd 48626 989-642-5178
Justin Danell, prin. Fax 642-5178
St. Peter Lutheran S 100/PK-8
2440 N Raucholz Rd 48626 989-642-5659
Eric Hagenow, prin. Fax 642-9053

Hermansville, Menominee
North Central Area SD
Supt. — See Powers
North Central ES 200/PK-6
PO Box 159 49847 906-498-7737
Anthony Adams, prin. Fax 498-2235

Herron, Alpena
Alpena SD
Supt. — See Alpena
Wilson ES 200/K-5
4999 S Herron Rd 49744 989-358-5700
Lisa Hilberg, prin. Fax 358-5705

Hesperia, Oceana, Pop. 932
Hesperia Community SD 1,000/K-12
PO Box 338 49421 231-854-6185
Vaughn White, supt. Fax 854-1586
www.hesp.net
Hesperia MS 300/5-8
PO Box 338 49421 231-854-6475
David LaPrairie, prin. Fax 854-6096
St. Clair ES 400/K-4
PO Box 338 49421 231-854-6615
Bryan Mey, prin. Fax 854-6075

Hickory Corners, Kalamazoo, Pop. 316
Gull Lake Community SD
Supt. — See Richland
Kellogg ES 200/PK-2
9594 N 40th St 49060 269-548-3800
Mary Jayne Vavra, prin. Fax 548-3801

Highland, Oakland
Huron Valley SD 9,200/PK-12
2390 S Milford Rd 48357 248-684-8000
Nancy Coratti, supt. Fax 684-8235
www.hvs.org
Heritage ES 600/PK-5
219 Watkins Blvd 48357 248-684-8190
Jenna Stevens, prin. Fax 684-8193
Highland ES 300/PK-5
300 W Livingston Rd 48357 248-684-8070
Patti Woodruff, prin. Fax 684-8269
Spring Mills ES 500/PK-5
3150 Harvey Lake Rd 48356 248-684-8130
Randy Muffley, prin. Fax 684-8189
Other Schools – See Commerce Township, Milford, White Lake

Hillman, Montmorency, Pop. 696
Hillman Community SD 500/K-12
26042 M 32 S 49746 989-742-2908
Cark Seiter, supt. Fax 742-3376
www.hillmanschools.com
Hillman ES 300/K-6
245 E 3rd St 49746 989-742-4537
Dr. Pamela Rader, prin. Fax 742-4509

Hillsdale, Hillsdale, Pop. 8,143
Hillsdale Community SD 1,400/PK-12
30 S Norwood Ave 49242 517-437-4401
Shawn Vondra, supt. Fax 439-4194
www.hillsdaleschools.org
Bailey ECC 300/PK-PK
59 S Manning St 49242 517-437-7369
Shawn Vondra, prin. Fax 437-4319
Davis MS 400/5-8
30 N West St 49242 517-439-4326
Barbara Wheeler, prin. Fax 437-1195
Gier ES 300/K-4
175 Spring St 49242 517-437-7347
Laurie VanOrman, prin. Fax 437-5641

Hillsdale Academy 200/K-12
1 Academy Ln 49242 517-439-8644
Dr. Kenneth Calvert, hdmstr. Fax 607-2794

Holland, Ottawa, Pop. 32,396
Hamilton Community SD
Supt. — See Hamilton
Blue Star ES 300/K-4
3846 58th St 49423 269-751-5630
Teisha Struik-Kothe, prin. Fax 751-2901
Hawkeye Preschool PK-PK
4317 46th St 49423 269-751-5372
Fax 751-5089
Little Hawks Preschool 100/PK-PK
5678 143rd Ave 49423 616-393-0949
Rachel Hucul, admin.
Sandyview ES 100/K-4
4317 46th St 49423 269-751-5372
Jeff Roon, prin. Fax 751-5089

Holland SD 3,800/PK-12
320 W 24th St 49423 616-494-2000
Dr. Brian Davis Ph.D., supt. Fax 392-8225
www.hollandpublicschools.org
East S 700/K-7
373 E 24th St 49423 616-494-2425
Nick Cassidy, prin. Fax 355-0674
Holland ECC 50/PK-PK
925 Central Ave 49423 616-494-2650
Jennifer VanDyke, coord. Fax 393-7653
Holland Heights S 400/K-7
856 E 12th St 49423 616-494-2750
Kevin Derr, prin. Fax 393-7566
Holland Language Academy at Van Raalte K-7
461 Van Raalte Ave 49423 616-494-2600
Iliana Vasquez-Ochoa, prin.
Jefferson S 500/K-7
282 W 30th St 49423 616-494-2500
Maria Yoder, prin. Fax 393-7569
West S 700/K-7
500 W 24th St 49423 616-494-2350
Kathleen Ramirez, prin. Fax 393-7544

West Ottawa SD 6,900/K-12
1138 136th Ave 49424 616-786-2050
Thomas K. Martin, supt.
www.westottawa.net
Great Lakes ES 500/K-5
3200 152nd Ave 49424 616-786-1200
Dave Stefanich, prin.
Harbor Lights MS 900/6-8
1024 136th Ave 49424 616-786-1000
Dennis White, prin.
Lakeshore ES 400/K-5
3765 N 168th Ave 49424 616-786-1400
Lakewood ES 300/K-5
2134 W Lakewood Blvd 49424 616-786-1300
Elizabeth VanderWege, prin.
Macatawa Bay MS 700/6-8
3700 140th Ave 49424 616-786-2000
Anne Armstrong, prin.
North Holland ES 300/K-5
11946 New Holland St 49424 616-786-1500
Kevin Westrate, prin.
Pine Creek ES 400/K-5
1184 136th Ave 49424 616-786-1600
Waukazoo ES 500/K-5
1294 W Lakewood Blvd 49424 616-786-1800
Ami Taylor, prin.
Woodside ES 500/K-5
2591 N Division Ave 49424 616-786-1900
Greg Rutten, prin.
Other Schools – See West Olive

Calvary S of Holland 200/PK-6
518 Plasman Ave 49423 616-396-4494
Cheryl Ward, prin. Fax 396-0326
Corpus Christi S 200/PK-8
12100 Quincy St 49424 616-994-9864
Joanne Jones, prin. Fax 994-9870
Holland Adventist S 50/K-8
11385 Ottogan St 49423 616-396-5941
Sari Butler, prin. Fax 396-5941
Holland Christian MS 200/7-8
850 Ottawa Ave 49423 616-820-3205
Dirk Hollebeek, prin. Fax 820-3210
Pine Ridge Christian S 200/3-6
623 W 40th St 49423 616-820-3505
Timothy Howell, prin. Fax 820-3510
Rose Park Christian S 300/PK-6
556 Butternut Dr 49424 616-820-4055
Rodney Brandsen, prin. Fax 820-4060
South Olive Christian S 100/PK-8
6230 120th Ave 49424 616-875-8224
Paula DeRoos, prin. Fax 875-2287
South Side Christian S 200/PK-2
913 Pine Ave 49423 616-820-3535
Miska Rynsburger, prin. Fax 820-3540

Holly, Oakland, Pop. 5,990
Holly Area SD 3,100/PK-12
920 Baird St 48442 248-328-3100
David M. Nuss, supt. Fax 328-3145
www.hask12.org
Holly ES 300/PK-5
801 E Maple St 48442 248-328-3600
Ryan DeSana, prin. Fax 328-3604
Holly MS 500/6-8
14470 N Holly Rd 48442 248-328-3400
Eric Curl, prin. Fax 328-3404
Patterson ES 400/PK-5
3231 Grange Hall Rd 48442 248-328-3700
Margaret Kraemer, prin. Fax 328-3704
Pioneer ES 300/PK-5
7110 Milford Rd 48442 248-328-3800
Michael Beattie, prin. Fax 328-3804
Other Schools – See Davisburg

Adelphian Junior Academy 50/K-10
PO Box 208 48442 248-634-9481
Nancy Danelson, prin. Fax 634-9222

Holt, Ingham, Pop. 23,336
Holt SD 5,700/PK-12
5780 Holt Rd 48842 517-694-0401
Dr. David G. Hornak, supt. Fax 694-1335
www.hpsk12.net
Elliott ES 400/K-4
4200 Bond Ave 48842 517-699-2106
Erin North, prin. Fax 699-3409
Holt JHS 1,000/7-8
1784 Aurelius Rd 48842 517-694-7117
Marshall Perkins, prin. Fax 694-3535
Hope S 400/5-6
2020 Park Ln 48842 517-699-2194
Jennifer Goodman, prin. Fax 699-3442
Horizon ES 400/K-4
5776 Holt Rd 48842 517-694-4224
Scott Huard, prin. Fax 699-3427
Midway Early Learning Center 300/PK-PK
4552 Spahr St 48842 517-694-3411
Heather Crandall, dir. Fax 699-3417
Sycamore ES 300/K-4
4429 Sycamore St 48842 517-699-2185
Steve Garrison, prin. Fax 699-3449
Washington Woods S 400/5-6
2055 S Washington Rd 48842 517-699-0250
Walt Sutterlin, prin. Fax 699-3438
Wilcox ES 400/K-4
1650 Laurelwood Dr 48842 517-699-0249
Traci Heuhs, prin. Fax 699-3422
Other Schools – See Dimondale

Holt Lutheran S 200/PK-8
2418 Aurelius Rd 48842 517-694-3182
Chelsea Speers, prin. Fax 694-6371

Holton, Muskegon
Holton SD 800/PK-12
6500 4th St 49425 231-821-1700
Adam Bayne, supt. Fax 821-1724
www.holtonschools.com
Holton ES 400/PK-5
6245 Syers Rd 49425 231-821-1825
Erin Byrnes, prin. Fax 821-1849
Holton MS 100/6-8
6477 Syers Rd 49425 231-821-1775
Don Hammond, prin. Fax 821-1824

Homer, Calhoun, Pop. 1,660
Homer Community SD 1,100/K-12
403 S Hillsdale St 49245 517-568-4463
Scott Salow, supt. Fax 568-4468
www.homerschools.net
Fletcher ES 400/K-4
403 S Hillsdale St 49245 517-568-4452
Heather Cahill, prin. Fax 568-5651
Homer MS 400/5-8
403 S Hillsdale St 49245 517-568-4456
Duane Sitkiewicz, prin. Fax 568-7125

Hopkins, Allegan, Pop. 603
Hopkins SD 1,600/K-12
400 S Clark St 49328 269-793-7261
Gary Wood, supt. Fax 557-7919
www.hpsvikings.org
Hopkins ES 400/K-5
400 S Clark St 49328 269-793-7286
Scott VanBonn, prin. Fax 557-7919
Hopkins MS 400/6-8
215 S Clark St 49328 269-793-7407
Scott Stockwell, prin. Fax 557-7919
Other Schools – See Dorr

Horton, Jackson
Hanover-Horton SD 1,200/K-12
10000 Moscow Rd 49246 517-563-0100
John Denney, supt. Fax 563-0150
www.hanoverhorton.org/
Hanover-Horton MS 300/6-8
10000 Moscow Rd 49246 517-563-0102
Denise Bergstrom, prin. Fax 563-9140
Other Schools – See Hanover

Houghton, Houghton, Pop. 7,574
Houghton-Portage Township SD 1,400/K-12
1603 Gundlach Rd 49931 906-482-0451
Doreen Klingbeil, supt. Fax 487-9764
www.hpts.us
Houghton ES 600/K-5
203 W Jacker Ave 49931 906-482-0456
Anders Hill, prin. Fax 487-5941
Houghton MS 300/6-8
1603 Gundlach Rd 49931 906-482-4871
Julie Filpus, prin. Fax 483-2566

Houghton Lake, Roscommon, Pop. 3,390
Houghton Lake Community SD 1,400/PK-12
6001 W Houghton Lake Dr 48629 989-366-2000
Susan Tyer, supt. Fax 422-6606
www.hlcsk12.net
Collins ES 400/PK-3
4451 W Houghton Lake Dr 48629 989-366-2023
Amy Peterson, prin. Fax 366-2077
Houghton Lake MS 400/4-7
4441 W Houghton Lake Dr 48629 989-366-2016
Leif Williams, prin. Fax 366-2078

Howard City, Montcalm, Pop. 1,777
Tri County Area SD
Supt. — See Sand Lake
Edgerton Building 300/PK-PK
412 E Edgerton St 49329 231-937-4391
Melissa Clegg, admin. Fax 937-7077
MacNaughton ES 400/K-2
415 Cedar 49329 231-937-4380
Dan Clegg, prin. Fax 937-4442
Tri County MS 500/6-8
21350 Kendaville Rd 49329 231-937-4318
Steve Johnson, prin. Fax 937-6319

Howell, Livingston, Pop. 9,332
Hartland Consolidated SD 5,500/K-12
9525 E Highland Rd 48843 810-626-2100
Chuck Hughes, supt. Fax 626-2101
www.hartlandschools.us
Other Schools – See Brighton, Hartland

Howell SD 7,600/K-12
411 N Highlander Way 48843 517-548-6200
Erin J. MacGregor, supt. Fax 548-6229
www.howellschools.com
Challenger ES 400/K-5
1066 W Grand River Ave 48843 517-548-6375
David Cherry, prin. Fax 545-1436
Highlander Way MS 1,000/6-8
511 N Highlander Way 48843 517-548-6252
Melanie Post, prin. Fax 545-1455
Hutchings ES 500/K-5
3503 Bigelow Rd, 517-548-1127
Timothy Moore, prin. Fax 548-1763
Northwest ES 400/K-5
1233 Bower St 48843 517-548-6297
Craig Munro, prin. Fax 545-1433
Parker MS 900/6-8
400 Wright Rd 48843 517-552-4600
Patricia Poelke, prin. Fax 552-0106
Southwest ES 500/K-5
915 Gay St 48843 517-548-6288
Jenn Goodwin, prin. Fax 545-1432
Three Fires ES 400/K-5
4125 Crooked Lake Rd 48843 517-548-6387
Robert Starkey, prin. Fax 548-7524

Voyager ES 500/K-5
1450 Byron Rd 48843 517-552-7500
Mindy McGinn, prin. Fax 552-7519

St. Joseph S 300/PK-8
425 E Washington St 48843 517-546-0090
Susan Doyle, prin. Fax 546-8939

Hudson, Lenawee, Pop. 2,276
Hudson Area SD 900/K-12
781 N Maple Grove Ave 49247 517-448-8912
Dr. Michael Osborne Ph.D., supt. Fax 448-8570
www.hudson.k12.mi.us
Hudson MS 200/6-8
771 N Maple Grove Ave 49247 517-445-8912
Michael Beard, prin. Fax 448-8975
Lincoln ES 400/K-5
746 N Maple Grove Ave 49247 517-448-8912
Cindy Godfrey, prin. Fax 448-5801

Sacred Heart S 100/PK-6
208 S Market St 49247 517-448-6405
Anne Atkin, prin. Fax 448-2401

Hudsonville, Ottawa, Pop. 7,024
Hudsonville SD 6,200/PK-12
3886 Van Buren St 49426 616-669-1740
Dr. Nicholas Ceglarek, supt. Fax 669-4878
www.hudsonvillepublicschools.org
Alward ES 500/PK-5
3811 Port Sheldon St 49426 616-669-6700
Fax 662-1470
Baldwin Street MS 800/6-8
3835 Baldwin St 49426 616-669-7750
Joel Olson, prin. Fax 669-7755
Bauer ES 400/PK-5
8136 48th Ave 49426 616-669-6824
Julie VanBergen, prin. Fax 669-4897
Forest Grove ES 300/PK-5
1645 32nd Ave 49426 616-896-9429
John Gillette, prin. Fax 896-1370
Georgetown ES 600/K-5
3909 Baldwin St 49426 616-797-9797
Theresa Reagan, prin. Fax 797-9929
Hudsonville ECC PK-PK
5535 School Ave 49426 616-797-0842
Rebecca VanSomeren, prin.
Jamestown Lower ES 300/PK-2
2522 Greenly St 49426 616-662-1478
Marie DeGroot, prin. Fax 896-1160
Jamestown Upper ES 300/3-5
3291 Lincoln Ct 49426 616-896-9375
Andy Secor, admin. Fax 896-1160
Park ES 400/K-5
5525 Park Ave 49426 616-669-1970
Brian Field, prin. Fax 669-4899
Riley Street MS 600/6-8
2745 Riley St 49426 616-896-1920
Bill Ross, prin. Fax 896-1925
South ES, 4900 40th Ave 49426 400/K-5
Mark Heagle, prin. 616-669-9362

Heritage Christian S 500/K-8
6340 Autumn Dr 49426 616-669-1773
Hudsonville Christian ES 600/PK-5
3435 Oak St 49426 616-669-6689
Dan Pott, supt. Fax 669-7491
Hudsonville Christian MS 300/6-8
3925 Van Buren St 49426 616-669-7487
Mary Broene, prin. Fax 669-2031

Huntington Woods, Oakland, Pop. 6,162
Berkley SD
Supt. — See Oak Park
Burton ES 500/K-5
26315 Scotia Rd, 248-837-8600
Beth Krehbiel, prin. Fax 546-0279

Ida, Monroe
Ida SD 1,400/K-12
3145 Prairie St 48140 734-269-3110
Richard Carsten, supt. Fax 269-2294
www.idaschools.org
Ida ES 500/K-4
7900 Ida St 48140 734-269-3605
Bert Wagner, prin. Fax 269-1334
Ida MS 500/5-8
3143 Prairie St 48140 734-269-2220
Dave Eack, prin. Fax 269-2576

Imlay City, Lapeer, Pop. 3,545
Imlay City Community SD 2,100/PK-12
634 W Borland Rd 48444 810-724-2765
Dr. Stu Cameron, supt. Fax 724-4307
www.icschools.us
Borland ES 500/3-5
500 W Borland Rd 48444 810-724-9813
Megan Cottone, prin. Fax 724-9894
Imlay City MS 500/6-8
495 W 1st St 48444 810-724-9811
Patrick Brown, prin. Fax 724-9896
Weston ES 400/PK-2
275 Weston St 48444 810-724-9812
Devon Caudill, prin. Fax 724-9895

Imlay City Christian S 50/PK-8
7197 E Imlay City Rd 48444 810-724-5695
Karen Hibbler, prin. Fax 724-5355

Indian River, Cheboygan, Pop. 1,930
Inland Lakes SD 700/K-12
4363 S Straits Hwy 49749 231-238-6868
Brad Jacobs, supt. Fax 238-4181
www.inlandlakes.org
Inland Lakes ES 300/K-5
4363 S Straits Hwy 49749 231-238-6868
Cynthia Brown, prin. Fax 238-4981

Inkster, Wayne, Pop. 24,504
Wayne-Westland Community SD
Supt. — See Westland
Hicks ES 500/K-4
100 Helen St 48141 734-419-2660
Amy Gee, prin. Fax 563-8450

Westwood Community SD
Supt. — See Dearborn Heights
Daly ES 200/K-6
25824 Michigan Ave 48141 313-565-0016
Leslie Simmons, prin. Fax 565-2359
Tomlinson MS 300/7-8
25912 Annapolis St 48141 313-565-3393
Kristen Kajoian, prin. Fax 565-0920

Peterson-Warren Academy 100/PK-12
PO Box 888 48141 313-565-5808
Angelita Crawford, lead tchr. Fax 565-7784

Interlochen, Grand Traverse, Pop. 574
Benzie County Central SD
Supt. — See Benzonia
Lake Ann ES 200/K-5
19375 Bronson Lake Rd 49643 231-275-7730
Larry Haughn, prin. Fax 275-7735

Ionia, Ionia, Pop. 11,276
Berlin Township SD 3 50/K-8
6679 S State Rd 48846 616-527-4900
Jason Mellema, supt. Fax 527-4731
www.coonschool.org
Coon S 50/K-8
6679 S State Rd 48846 616-527-4900
Jason Mellema, admin. Fax 527-4731

Easton Twp SD 6 50/K-5
1779 Haynor Rd 48846 616-527-0089
Jason Mellema, supt. Fax 527-4494
www.haynorschool.org/
Haynor ES 50/K-5
1779 Haynor Rd 48846 616-527-0089
Jason Mellema, admin. Fax 527-4494

Ionia SD 3,000/PK-12
250 E Tuttle Rd 48846 616-527-9280
Dr. Ronald Wilson, supt. Fax 527-8846
www.ioniaschools.org
Boyce ES 300/K-5
3550 N State Rd 48846 616-527-0571
Scott Yenchar, prin. Fax 527-8003
Emerson ES 200/PK-5
645 Hackett St 48846 616-527-8018
Jonathan Duley, prin. Fax 527-1741
Ionia MS 700/6-8
438 Union St 48846 616-527-0040
Wayne Piercefield, prin. Fax 527-3380
Jefferson ES 300/PK-5
420 N Jefferson St 48846 616-527-2740
Matt Vogel, prin. Fax 527-8002
Rather ES 300/PK-5
380 E Tuttle Rd 48846 616-527-1720
Darin Magley, prin. Fax 527-8004
Other Schools – See Muir

Ionia Township SD 2 50/K-5
2120 N State Rd 48846 616-527-4900
Jason Mellema, supt. Fax 527-4731
www.northlevalleyschool.org
North LeValley ES 50/K-5
2120 N State Rd 48846 616-527-4900
Jason Mellema, admin. Fax 527-4731

Ionia SDA S, 721 Elmwood Dr 48846 50/K-8
Tamie Hasty, prin. 616-527-1971
SS. Peter & Paul S 100/PK-8
317 Baldie St 48846 616-527-3561
Julie Baty, prin. Fax 527-3562

Ira, Saint Clair
Anchor Bay SD
Supt. — See Casco
Maconce ES 300/K-5
6300 Church Rd 48023 586-725-0284
Sherri Milton-Hoffman, prin. Fax 725-2037

Immaculate Conception S 200/PK-8
7043 Church Rd 48023 586-725-0078
Lawrence Ricard, prin. Fax 725-8240

Iron Mountain, Dickinson, Pop. 7,523
Iron Mountain SD 900/K-12
217 Izzo Mariucci Way 49801 906-779-2600
Raphael Rittenhouse, supt. Fax 779-2676
www.imschools.org
Central MS 200/7-8
300 W B St 49801 906-779-2610
Mark Herman, prin. Fax 779-2638
East ES 100/5-6
300 W B St 49801 906-779-2620
Donny Bianco, prin. Fax 779-2634
North ES 200/K-4
900 5th St 49801 906-779-2626
Donny Bianco, prin. Fax 779-2636

Baraga Catholic S 200/PK-8
406 W B St 49801 906-774-2277
Kevin Weed, prin. Fax 774-8704
Pine Mountain Christian S 50/K-8
N3770 Pine Mountain Rd 49801 906-779-7640
Liz Channell, prin.

Iron River, Iron, Pop. 2,984
West Iron County SD 700/PK-12
601 Garfield Ave 49935 906-265-9218
Christopher Thomson, supt. Fax 265-9736
www.westiron.org
Stambaugh ES 400/PK-5
700 Washington Ave 49935 906-265-6141
Michelle Thomson, prin. Fax 265-9810

Ironwood, Gogebic, Pop. 5,289
Ironwood Area SD 400/K-12
650 E Ayer St 49938 906-932-0200
Timothy Kolesar, supt. Fax 932-9915
www.ironwood.k12.mi.us/
Wright K-12 S 400/K-12
650 E Ayer St 49938 906-932-0932
Denise Woodward, prin. Fax 932-9915

All Saints Catholic Academy 50/PK-6
106 S Marquette St 49938 906-932-3200
Emily Lightfoot, prin. Fax 932-1019

Ishpeming, Marquette, Pop. 6,339
Ishpeming SD 1 800/PK-12
319 E Division St 49849 906-485-5501
Carrie Meyer, supt. Fax 485-1422
www.ishpemingschools.com
Birchview ES 300/PK-4
663 Poplar St 49849 906-485-6341
Bernie Anderson, prin. Fax 485-5925
Ishpeming MS 300/5-8
319 E Division St 49849 906-485-1066
Seth Hoopingarner, prin. Fax 485-4750

NICE Community SD 1,200/K-12
300 S Westwood Dr 49849 906-485-1021
Bryan DeAugustine, supt. Fax 485-4095
www.nice.k12.mi.us/
Aspen Ridge S 800/K-8
350 Aspen Ridge School Rd 49849 906-485-3175
Chris Marana, prin. Fax 485-3182

Ithaca, Gratiot, Pop. 2,877
Ithaca SD 1,300/PK-12
710 N Union St 48847 989-875-3700
Charmian Fletcher, supt. Fax 875-4538
www.ithacaschools.net
North ES 400/3-6
201 E Arcada St 48847 989-875-3047
Renee Sopel, prin. Fax 875-4701
South ES 300/PK-2
400 Webster St 48847 989-875-4741
David Kanine, prin. Fax 875-8701

Ithaca SDA S 50/K-8
937 N Pine River St 48847 989-875-4961
Kari Williams, prin. Fax 875-4961

Jackson, Jackson, Pop. 31,900
East Jackson Community SD 800/K-12
1404 N Sutton Rd 49202 517-764-2090
Steve Doerr, supt. Fax 764-6033
www.eastjacksonschools.org
East Jackson ES 300/K-6
4340 Walz Rd 49201 517-764-1810
Heather Jacobs, prin. Fax 764-6085
East Jackson MS 200/7-8
1566 N Sutton Rd 49202 517-764-6010
Brent Cole, prin. Fax 764-6081

Jackson SD 4,800/K-12
522 Wildwood Ave 49201 517-841-2200
Jeff Beal, supt. Fax 789-8056
www.jpsk12.org/
Bennett ES 200/K-2
820 Bennett St 49202 517-841-2730
Jacquelyn Brock, prin. Fax 768-5901
Cascades ES 100/K-2
1200 S Wisner St 49203 517-841-3900
Martha Kuhn, prin. Fax 768-5902
Dibble ES 300/K-5
3450 Kibby Rd 49203 517-841-3970
Martin DuBois, prin. Fax 768-5903
Frost ES 200/3-5
1226 S Wisner St 49203 517-841-2601
Joe Zessin, prin. Fax 768-6045
Hunt ES 400/K-5
1143 N Brown St 49202 517-841-2610
Mary Jo Raczkowski-Shann, prin. Fax 768-5900
MS at Parkside 1,100/6-8
2400 4th St 49203 517-841-2300
Jeremy Patterson, prin. Fax 768-5968
JPS Montessori Center K-3
205 Seymour Ave 49202 517-841-3870
Julie Baker, prin.
McCulloch Academy 100/K-2
216 E Biddle St 49203 517-841-3940
Julie Baker, prin. Fax 768-5906
Northeast ES 200/3-6
1024 Fleming Ave 49202 517-841-2500
Erik Weatherwax, prin. Fax 768-5911
Sharp Park IB World S 300/K-5
766 Park Rd 49203 517-841-2860
Jasper Lusby, prin. Fax 784-1325

Northwest Community SD 2,800/PK-12
6900 Rives Junction Rd 49201 517-817-4700
Geoff Bontrager, supt. Fax 569-2395
www.nwschools.org/
Northwest Early ES 600/K-2
3735 Lansing Ave 49202 517-817-4705
Mark Short, prin. Fax 768-4505
Northwest ES 600/3-5
3757 Lansing Ave 49202 517-817-4704
Eric Kelly, prin. Fax 789-8467
Northwest Kidder MS 600/6-8
6700 Rives Junction Rd 49201 517-817-4703
Dan Brooks, prin. Fax 569-2931
Northwest Preschool PK-PK
6900 Rives Junction Rd 49201 517-817-4706
Amy Marrison, dir.

Vandercook Lake SD 1,300/K-12
1000 E Golf Ave 49203 517-782-9044
Scott Leach, supt. Fax 788-3690
www.vandyschools.org
Townsend ES 600/K-5
1005 Floyd Ave 49203 517-784-6133
Micki Berg, prin. Fax 788-3695

Jackson Christian ES 100/PK-5
801 Halstead Blvd 49203 517-784-6161
Todd Barney, prin. Fax 784-6322
Queen of Miraculous Medals S 300/K-6
811 S Wisner St 49203 517-782-2664
Elizabeth Hartley, prin. Fax 782-3570
St. John the Evangelist S 200/PK-6
405 E North St 49202 517-784-1714
Kristi Blair, prin. Fax 788-5382
St. Mary Star of the Sea S 200/PK-6
116 E Wesley St 49201 517-784-8811
Matt Berkemeier, prin. Fax 788-3425
Trinity Lutheran S 100/PK-8
4900 McCain Rd 49201 517-750-2105
Lisa Singleton, prin. Fax 750-9945

Jenison, Ottawa, Pop. 16,336
Jenison SD 4,600/PK-12
8375 20th Ave 49428 616-457-8890
Thomas TenBrink, supt. Fax 457-8898
www.jpsonline.org/
Bauerwood ES 600/K-6
1443 Bauer Rd 49428 616-457-1408
Crystal Morse, prin. Fax 457-8491
Bursley ES 400/K-6
1195 Port Sheldon St 49428 616-457-2200
Brent Huck, prin. Fax 457-8489
ECC 100/PK-PK
800 Connie St 49428 616-457-1406
Lee Westervelt, dir. Fax 457-8492
Jenison JHS 700/7-8
8295 20th Ave 49428 616-457-1402
Brett Cataldo, prin. Fax 457-8090
Pinewood ES 400/K-6
2405 Chippewa St 49428 616-457-1407
Rachael Postel-Brown, prin. Fax 457-8490
Rosewood ES 500/K-6
2370 Tyler St 49428 616-669-0011
Lloyd Gingerich, prin. Fax 669-5980
Sandy Hill ES 500/K-6
1990 Baldwin St 49428 616-457-1404
Sara Melton, prin. Fax 457-8493

Jenison Christian S 400/PK-8
7726 Graceland Dr 49428 616-457-3301
Tim Paauw, prin. Fax 457-1430

Johannesburg, Otsego
Johannesburg-Lewiston Area SD 700/K-12
PO Box 69 49751 989-732-1773
Kathleen Makowski, supt. Fax 732-6556
www.jlas.org
Johannesburg ES 300/K-8
PO Box 69 49751 989-731-2040
Nancy Odren, prin. Fax 732-6556
Other Schools – See Lewiston

Jonesville, Hillsdale, Pop. 2,240
Jonesville Community SD 1,500/PK-12
115 East St 49250 517-849-9075
Chellie Broesamle, supt. Fax 849-2434
www.jonesvilleschools.org
Jonesville MS 300/6-8
401 E Chicago St 49250 517-849-3210
Bryan Playford, prin. Fax 849-3213
Williams ES 700/PK-5
440 Adrian Rd 49250 517-849-9175
Joshua McDowell, prin. Fax 849-7306

Kalamazoo, Kalamazoo, Pop. 71,183
Comstock SD 2,100/PK-12
3010 Gull Rd 49048 269-250-8900
Todd Mora, supt. Fax 250-8901
www.comstockps.org
Comstock Northeast MS 500/5-8
1423 N 28th St 49048 269-250-8600
Jemel Hence, prin. Fax 250-8601
Comstock STEM Academy 300/K-8
175 Hunt St 49048 269-250-8560
Christopher Chopp, dir. Fax 250-8561
Green Meadow ES 300/PK-4
6171 E MN Ave 49048 269-250-8960
Susan Caswell, prin. Fax 250-8961
North ES 300/PK-4
3100 N 26th St 49048 269-250-8550
Mark Wilke, prin. Fax 250-8549

Kalamazoo SD 12,300/K-12
1220 Howard St 49008 269-337-0100
Michael Rice, supt. Fax 337-0149
www.kalamazoopublicschools.com
Arcadia ES 400/K-5
932 Boswell Ln 49006 269-337-0530
Gregory Socha, prin. Fax 372-9871
Edison Environmental Science Academy 300/K-5
924 Russell St 49001 269-337-0550
Julie McDonald, prin. Fax 337-1621
El Sol ES 300/K-5
604 W Vine St 49008 269-337-0230
Natalie Wilson, prin. Fax 337-1648
Greenwood ES 100/K-3
3501 Moreland St 49001 269-337-0560
Sylvia Washington, prin. Fax 337-1622
Hillside MS 600/6-8
1941 Alamo Ave 49006 269-337-0570
Atiba McKissack, prin. Fax 337-1618
Indian Prairie ES 200/K-3
3546 Grand Prairie Rd 49006 269-337-0590
Kelly Bertch, prin. Fax 337-1623
King-Westwood ES 500/K-5
1100 Nichols Rd 49006 269-337-0610
Sandie Lundquist, prin. Fax 337-1624
Lincoln International Studies ES 300/K-5
912 N Burdick St 49007 269-337-0640
Linda Howard, prin. Fax 337-1626
Linden Grove MS 800/6-8
4241 Arboretum Pkwy 49006 269-337-1740
Craig McCane, prin. Fax 337-1614
Maple Magnet MS 700/6-8
922 W Maple St 49008 269-337-0730
Dr. Jeffery Boggan, prin. Fax 337-1633
Milwood ES 400/K-5
3400 Lovers Ln 49001 269-337-0660
Craig LeSuer, prin. Fax 337-1627
Milwood Magnet MS 700/6-8
2916 Konkle St 49001 269-337-0670
Mark Tobolski, prin. Fax 337-1628
Northeastern ES 300/K-5
2433 Gertrude St 49048 269-337-0690
William Hawkins, prin. Fax 337-1629
Northglade Montessori Magnet ES 200/K-5
1914 Cobb Ave 49007 269-337-0700
Dale Mogaji, prin. Fax 337-1630
Parkwood-Upjohn ES 500/K-5
2321 S Park St 49001 269-337-0720
Robin Greymountain, prin. Fax 337-1632
Prairie Ridge ES 500/K-5
2294 S 9th St 49009 269-337-0540
Joletta Drake, prin. Fax 372-9839
Spring Valley ES 400/K-5
3530 Mount Olivet Rd 49004 269-337-0750
Lisa Dewey, prin. Fax 337-1634
Washington Writers' Academy 300/K-5
1919 Portage St 49001 269-337-0770
Lanisha Spiller, prin. Fax 337-1635
Winchell ES 500/K-5
2316 Winchell Ave 49008 269-337-0780
Michael Hughes, prin. Fax 337-1636
Woods Lake Magnet ES 500/K-5
3215 Oakland Dr 49008 269-337-0790
Micole Dyson, prin. Fax 337-1637
Woodward ES for Technology & Research 400/K-5
606 Stuart Ave 49007 269-337-0810
Frank Rocco, prin. Fax 337-1638

Otsego SD
Supt. — See Otsego
Alamo ES 200/PK-5
8184 N 6th St 49009 269-692-6150
Nicole Knight-Lucas, prin. Fax 692-6144

Parchment SD
Supt. — See Parchment
North ES 300/K-5
5535 Keyes Dr 49004 269-488-1400
Marcy Patterson, prin. Fax 488-1410
Northwood ES 200/PK-5
600 Edison St 49004 269-488-1300
Dr. Sarah Neumann, prin. Fax 488-1310

Plainwell Community SD
Supt. — See Plainwell
Cooper ES 200/K-5
7559 N 14th St 49009 269-349-2674
Jeff McNutt, prin. Fax 345-5111

Gagie S 200/K-8
615 Fairview Ave 49008 269-342-8008
Dr. Sandra Gagie, dir. Fax 342-1064
Heritage Christian Academy 300/PK-12
6312 Quail Run Dr 49009 269-372-1400
Randal Hadley, admin. Fax 372-6018
Kalamazoo Christian ES 700/PK-8
3800 S 12th St 49009 269-544-2332
Marc Verkaik, prin. Fax 544-2391
Kalamazoo Junior Academy 100/K-10
1601 Nichols Rd 49006 269-342-8943
Kenneth Armstrong, prin. Fax 492-1459
Kazoo S 100/PK-8
1401 Cherry St 49008 269-345-3239
Dr. Sally Read, head sch Fax 345-3235
Montessori S 100/PK-6
750 Howard St 49008 269-349-3248
Providence Christian S 100/K-9
100 Pratt Rd 49001 269-385-4889
Tom Kwekel, prin. Fax 385-4889
St. Augustine Cathedral S 300/PK-8
600 W Michigan Ave 49007 269-349-1945
Dr. Andra Zommers, prin. Fax 349-1085
St. Monica S 400/PK-8
530 W Kilgore Rd 49008 269-345-2444
Rebecca Reits, prin. Fax 345-8534
Tree of Life S 50/K-5
2001 Cameron St 49001 269-718-7428
Adam Sterenberg, prin.

Kalkaska, Kalkaska, Pop. 1,989
Excelsior Township SD 1 50/K-8
5521 M 72 NE 49646 231-922-6200
Fax 922-6270
www.crawfordschool.com
Crawford S 50/K-8
5521 M 72 NE 49646 231-258-2934
Fax 258-4103

Kalkaska SD 1,600/PK-12
315 S Coral St 49646 231-258-9109
Karen Sherwood, supt. Fax 258-4474
www.kpschools.com/
Birch Street ES 400/PK-3
315 S Coral St 49646 231-258-8629
Arica Zenner, prin. Fax 258-3579
Cherry Street IS 200/4-5
315 S Coral St 49646 231-258-9146
Ryan Moore, prin. Fax 258-5149
Kalkaska MS 300/6-8
315 S Coral St 49646 231-258-4040
Staci Short, prin. Fax 258-3576
Other Schools – See Rapid City

Kawkawlin, Bay

St. Bartholomew Lutheran S 100/PK-8
1033 E Beaver Rd 48631 989-684-6751
Mark Boileau, prin. Fax 684-0071

Keego Harbor, Oakland, Pop. 2,899
West Bloomfield SD
Supt. — See West Bloomfield
Roosevelt ES 400/K-5
2065 Cass Lake Rd 48320 248-865-6620
Dennis Rapal, prin. Fax 865-6621

Kent City, Kent, Pop. 1,047
Kent City Community SD 1,300/PK-12
200 N Clover St 49330 616-678-7714
Mike Weiler, supt. Fax 678-4320
www.kentcityschools.org
Kent City ES 700/PK-5
29 College St 49330 616-678-4181
Pam Thomas, prin. Fax 678-7785
Kent City MS 300/6-8
285 N Main St 49330 616-678-4214
Bill Crane, prin. Fax 678-5099

Algoma Christian S 200/PK-12
PO Box 220 49330 616-678-7480
Dr. Brian Hazeltine Ed.D., supt. Fax 678-7484

Kentwood, Kent, Pop. 47,105
Kentwood SD 8,600/PK-12
5820 Eastern Ave SE 49508 616-455-4400
Michael Zoerhoff, supt. Fax 455-4476
www.kentwoodps.org
Bowen ES 300/K-5
4483 Kalamazoo Ave SE 49508 616-455-5220
Blair Feldkamp, prin. Fax 455-6991
Brookwood ES 300/K-5
5465 Kalamazoo Ave SE 49508 616-455-0030
Lorenzo Bradshaw, prin. Fax 455-5778
Challenger ES 300/K-5
2475 52nd St SE 49508 616-698-2524
Teressa Gatza, prin. Fax 698-9089
Crestwood MS 700/6-8
2674 44th St SE 49512 616-455-1200
Donald Dahlquist, prin. Fax 455-2338
Discovery ES 500/K-5
2461 60th St SE 49508 616-871-1080
Deb McNally, prin. Fax 871-1081
Endeavor ES 500/PK-5
5757 East Paris Ave SE 49512 616-554-5241
Mark Bea, prin. Fax 554-5244
Glenwood ES 300/K-5
912 Silverleaf St SE 49508 616-455-2510
Jenny Graham, prin. Fax 455-0320
Hamilton ECC PK-PK
3303 Breton Rd SE 49512 616-493-5693
Lori Eaton, dir. Fax 493-5696
Meadowlawn ES 300/PK-5
4939 Burgis Ave SE 49508 616-534-4608
Tim Hargis, prin. Fax 534-2512
Pinewood MS 700/6-8
2100 60th St SE 49508 616-455-1224
Gary Harmon, prin. Fax 455-2054
Southwood ES 300/K-5
630 66th St SE 49548 616-455-7230
Jeff Overkleeft, prin. Fax 455-7220
Townline ES 300/K-5
100 60th St SE 49548 616-538-4120
Michelle Downs, prin. Fax 538-8770
Valleywood MS 500/6-8
1110 50th St SE 49508 616-538-7670
Mindy Westra, prin. Fax 538-9301
Other Schools – See Caledonia

Trinitas Classical S 100/K-8
1934 52nd St SE 49508 616-855-6518
Peter Marth, hdmstr. Fax 855-6962

Kimball, Saint Clair, Pop. 7,247
Port Huron Area SD
Supt. — See Port Huron
Indian Woods ES 300/PK-5
4975 W Water St 48074 810-984-6515
Cheryl Rogers, prin. Fax 275-1268
Kimball ES 400/PK-5
5801 Griswold Rd 48074 810-984-6519
Kathleen Kish, prin. Fax 272-4461

New Life Christian Academy 200/PK-12
5517 Griswold Rd 48074 810-367-3770
Lee Ann Shimmel, admin. Fax 367-2249

Kinde, Huron, Pop. 445
North Huron SD 400/K-12
21 Main St 48445 989-874-4100
Martin Prout, supt. Fax 874-4109
www.nhuron.org
North Huron S 400/K-12
21 Main St 48445 989-874-4101
Tanya Kramer, prin. Fax 874-4129

Kingsford, Dickinson, Pop. 5,077
Breitung Township SD 1,700/PK-12
2000 W Pyle Dr 49802 906-779-2650
Craig Allen, supt. Fax 779-7703
www.kingsford.org
Kingsford MS 400/5-8
445 Hamilton Ave 49802 906-779-2680
David Holmes, prin. Fax 774-1354
Woodland ES 800/PK-4
2000 W Pyle Dr 49802 906-779-2685
Darren Petschar, prin. Fax 779-7701

Kingsley, Grand Traverse, Pop. 1,450
Kingsley Area SD 1,400/K-12
402 Fenton St 49649 231-263-5261
Keith Smith, supt. Fax 263-5282
www.kingsley.k12.mi.us
Kingsley Area ES 500/K-4
402 Fenton St 49649 231-263-5261
Kristin Goethals, prin. Fax 263-3813
Kingsley Area MS 400/5-8
402 Fenton St 49649 231-263-5261
Karl Hartman, prin. Fax 263-4623

St. Mary of Hannah S 100/PK-6
2912 W M 113 49649 231-263-5288
Richard Gebhard, prin. Fax 263-5288

Kingston, Tuscola, Pop. 436
Kingston Community SD 600/PK-12
5790 State St 48741 989-683-2294
Matt Drake, supt. Fax 683-2081
www.kingstonk12.org
Kingston ES 300/PK-6
3644 Ross St 48741 989-683-2284
Justin Diegel, prin. Fax 683-3318

Laingsburg, Shiawassee, Pop. 1,260
Laingsburg Community SD 1,100/PK-12
205 S Woodhull Rd 48848 517-651-2705
Matthew Shastal, supt. Fax 651-9075
www.laingsburg.k12.mi.us/
Early Childhood Education Center 50/PK-PK
320 E Grand River Rd 48848 517-651-3100
Nikki Lange, prin. Fax 651-3101
Laingsburg ES 500/K-5
117 Prospect St 48848 517-651-5067
Karen Lockwood, prin. Fax 651-2615
Laingsburg MS 300/6-8
112 High St 48848 517-651-5034
Brandon Woodworth, prin. Fax 651-6213

Lake City, Missaukee, Pop. 830
Lake City Area SD 900/K-12
PO Box 900 49651 231-839-4333
Kim Blaszak, supt. Fax 839-5219
www.lakecityschools.net
Lake City ES 200/K-5
PO Box 900 49651 231-839-2665
Kay Gill, prin. Fax 839-6029
Lake City MS 300/6-8
PO Box 900 49651 231-839-7163
Tim Hejnal, prin. Fax 839-6042

Lake Leelanau, Leelanau, Pop. 250

St. Mary S 200/PK-12
PO Box 340 49653 231-256-9636
Megan Glynn, prin. Fax 256-7239

Lake Linden, Houghton, Pop. 992
Lake Linden-Hubbell SD 500/K-12
601 Calumet St 49945 906-296-6211
Craig Sundblad, supt. Fax 296-0943
www.lakelinden.k12.mi.us
Lake Linden Hubbell ES 300/K-6
601 Calumet St 49945 906-296-6211
Brad Codere, coord. Fax 296-0305

Lake Odessa, Ionia, Pop. 1,980
Lakewood SD
Supt. — See Woodland
Lakewood ES 300/1-4
812 Washington Blvd 48849 616-374-8842
Keith Carpenter, prin. Fax 374-1499

St. Edward Preschool PK-PK
531 Jordan Lake St 48849 616-374-8809
Fredia Prysock, coord. Fax 374-1559

Lake Orion, Oakland, Pop. 2,917
Lake Orion Community SD 7,300/K-12
315 N Lapeer St 48362 248-693-5400
Marion Ginopolis, supt. Fax 693-5464
www.lakeorion.k12.mi.us
Carpenter ES 400/K-5
2290 Flintridge St 48359 248-391-3500
Adam Weldon, prin. Fax 391-5461
Orion Oaks ES 600/K-5
1255 Joslyn Rd 48360 248-393-0010
Andrew Towlerton, prin. Fax 393-0018
Paint Creek ES 500/K-5
2800 Indianwood Rd 48362 248-814-1724
Lauren Smith, prin. Fax 814-0209
Scripps MS 600/6-8
385 E Scripps Rd 48360 248-693-5440
Dan Haas, prin. Fax 693-5301
Sims ES 300/K-5
465 E Jackson St 48362 248-693-5460
Kenneth Nuss, prin. Fax 693-5322
Stadium Drive ES 500/K-5
244 Stadium Dr 48360 248-693-5475
Rob Murray, prin. Fax 693-5318
Waldon MS 600/6-8
2509 Waldon Rd 48360 248-391-1100
Randy Groya, prin. Fax 391-5452
Webber ES 500/K-5
3191 W Clarkston Rd 48362 248-391-0400
Jennifer Goethals, prin. Fax 391-5460
Other Schools – See Oakland

Divine Grace Lutheran S 100/PK-8
3000 S Lapeer Rd 48359 248-391-2811
Jesse Nofftz, prin. Fax 391-7649
Good Shepherd Lutheran S 100/PK-8
1950 S Baldwin Rd 48360 248-391-7244
Eric Heins, prin. Fax 391-1680
Lake Orion Baptist S 100/K-12
255 E Scripps Rd 48360 248-693-6203
Tony Bryson, prin. Fax 693-6177
St. Joseph S 400/K-8
703 N Lapeer Rd 48362 248-693-6215
Joseph Zmikly, prin. Fax 693-0958

Lakeport, Saint Clair

St. Edward on the Lake S 100/PK-5
6995 Lakeshore Rd 48059 810-385-4461
Nancy Appel, prin. Fax 385-6070

Lakeview, Montcalm, Pop. 988
Lakeview Community SD 1,300/PK-12
123 5th St 48850 989-352-7221
Kyle Hamlin, supt. Fax 352-8245
www.lakeviewschools.net
Lakeview ES 300/PK-3
9497 Paden Rd 48850 989-352-8021
Kelly Nielsen, prin. Fax 352-7021
Lakeview MS 400/4-7
516 Washington St 48850 989-352-8016
Tim Erspamer, prin. Fax 352-6710

Lambertville, Monroe, Pop. 9,863
Bedford SD
Supt. — See Temperance
Douglas Road ES 600/K-5
6875 Douglas Rd 48144 734-850-6700
Carol Perz, prin. Fax 850-6799
Monroe Road ES 700/K-5
7979 Monroe Rd 48144 734-850-6800
Alex Chapman, prin. Fax 850-6899

LAnse, Baraga, Pop. 1,920
L'Anse Area SD 600/K-12
201 N 4th St 49946 906-524-6000
Susan Tollefson, supt. Fax 524-6001
www.lanseschools.org/
Sullivan ES 300/K-5
201 N 4th St 49946 906-524-6000
Melissa Scroggs, prin. Fax 524-0277

Sacred Heart Catholic S 50/PK-8
433 Baraga Ave 49946 906-524-5157
Christy Miron, prin. Fax 524-5154

Lansing, Ingham, Pop. 108,750
Grand Ledge SD
Supt. — See Grand Ledge
Delta Center ES 600/1-6
305 S Canal Rd 48917 517-925-5540
Lori Bucholz, prin. Fax 925-5579
Delta Mills ECC 100/PK-PK
6816 Delta River Dr 48910 517-925-5600
Breanna Cleeves, dir. Fax 925-5453

Lansing SD 11,700/PK-12
519 W Kalamazoo St 48933 517-755-1000
Yvonne Caamal Canul, supt. Fax 755-2009
www.lansingschools.net
Attwood ES 300/4-6
915 Attwood Dr 48911 517-755-1210
Carla Laws, prin. Fax 755-1219
Averill ES 300/PK-3
3201 Averill Dr 48911 517-755-1220
Kyron Harvell, prin. Fax 755-1229
Cavanaugh ES 200/PK-3
300 W Cavanaugh Rd 48910 517-755-1250
Angela Jackson, prin. Fax 755-1259
Cumberland ES 200/PK-3
2801 Cumberland Rd 48906 517-755-1280
Martha Rusesky, prin. Fax 755-1289
Fairview ES 300/PK-3
815 N Fairview Ave 48912 517-755-1310
Janice Marchal, prin. Fax 755-1319
Forest View ES 200/PK-3
3119 Stoneleigh Dr 48910 517-755-1330
Emily Brown, prin. Fax 755-1339
Gardner Academy 900/4-8
333 Dahlia Dr 48911 517-755-1120
Priscilla Ellis, prin. Fax 755-1129
Gier Park ES 300/PK-3
401 E Gier St 48906 517-755-1360
Rebecca Stephens, prin. Fax 755-1369
Kendon ES 200/PK-3
827 Kendon Dr 48910 517-755-1450
LaDonna Mask, prin. Fax 755-1459
Lewton ES 300/K-6
2000 Lewton Pl 48911 517-755-1460
Dr. Tom Buffett, prin. Fax 755-1469
Lyons ES 300/PK-3
2901 Lyons Ave 48910 517-755-1480
Terry Baker, prin. Fax 755-1489
Mt. Hope ES 200/4-6
1215 E Mount Hope Ave 48910 517-755-1550
Elizabeth Jones, prin. Fax 755-1559
North ES 600/PK-5
333 E Miller Rd 48911 517-755-1710
Ariel Rodriguez-Pena, prin. Fax 755-1719
Pattengill Academy 600/4-6
626 Marshall St 48912 517-755-1130
Tony Forsthoefel, prin. Fax 755-1139
Pleasant View Academy 600/K-8
4501 Pleasant Grove Rd 48910 517-755-1600
Semekia Fowler, prin. Fax 755-1609
Post Oak ES 300/PK-6
2320 Post Oak Ln 48912 517-755-1610
Traci Ojerio, prin. Fax 755-1619
Reo ES 200/PK-3
1221 Reo Rd 48910 517-755-1620
Sarah Odneal, prin. Fax 755-1629
Rich STEM 600/K-8
2600 Hampden Dr 48911 517-755-1100
Sandra Noecker, prin. Fax 755-1169
Riddle ES 100/PK-3
221 Huron St 48915 517-755-1720
Nicole Beard, prin. Fax 755-1729
Sheridan Road ES 300/4-6
16900 Cedar St 48906 517-755-1630
Jessica Benavides, prin. Fax 755-1639
Wexford Montessori Academy 400/K-8
5217 Wexford Rd 48911 517-755-1740
Dr. Nancy Lubeski, prin. Fax 755-1749
Willow ES 200/PK-3
1012 W Willow St 48915 517-755-1680
Steven Lonzo, prin. Fax 755-1689

Waverly Community SD 2,600/PK-12
515 Snow Rd 48917 517-321-7265
Kelly Blake, supt. Fax 321-8577
www.waverlycommunityschools.net
Colt Early Childhood Education Center 200/PK-K
4344 W Michigan Ave 48917 517-323-3777
Shawn Talifarro, prin. Fax 323-9813
Elmwood ES 300/1-4
1533 Elmwood Rd 48917 517-321-3383
Tim Lyman, prin. Fax 321-9318
Waverly East IS 400/5-6
3131 W Michigan Ave 48917 517-484-8830
Vickie Tisdale, prin. Fax 485-4008
Waverly MS 400/7-8
620 Snow Rd 48917 517-321-7240
Michael Moreno, prin. Fax 321-5789
Winans ES 300/1-4
5401 W Michigan Ave 48917 517-321-2371
Helene McNeilly, prin. Fax 323-1840

Emanuel First Lutheran S 100/PK-8
1001 N Capitol Ave 48906 517-485-4547
Daniel Hosbach, prin. Fax 484-7484
Greater Lansing Adventist S 100/PK-10
5330 W St Joe Hwy 48917 517-321-5565
Judy Shull, prin. Fax 321-5580
Immaculate Heart of Mary S 300/PK-8
3830 Rosemont St 48910 517-882-6631
Angela Johnston, prin. Fax 882-5536
Lansing Christian S 600/PK-12
3405 Belle Chase Way 48911 517-882-5779
Wendy Hofman, head sch Fax 882-5849
Montessori Children's House of Lansing 100/PK-6
2100 W Saint Joseph St 48915 517-482-9191
Maureen Newton, prin. Fax 482-0011
New Covenant Christian S 100/PK-12
PO Box 80737 48908 517-323-8903
Fred McGlone, prin. Fax 323-0421
Our Savior Lutheran S 200/PK-8
7910 E St Joe Hwy 48917 517-882-3550
Matthew Couser, prin. Fax 622-1576
Resurrection S 200/PK-8
1527 E Michigan Ave 48912 517-487-0439
Jacob Allstott, prin. Fax 487-3198
St. Gerard S 500/PK-8
4433 W Willow Hwy 48917 517-321-6126
Michelle Piecuch, prin. Fax 323-8046

Lapeer, Lapeer, Pop. 8,708
Lapeer Community SD 3,700/PK-12
250 2nd St 48446 810-667-2400
Matthew Wandrie, supt. Fax 667-2411
www.lapeerschools.org
Kids & Company Preschool 50/PK-PK
3145 W Genesee Rd 48446 810-667-2454
Stefanie Heddy, coord. Fax 245-1090
Lynch ES 400/PK-5
2035 Roods Lake Rd 48446 810-667-2448
Ryan West, prin. Fax 667-2473
Mayfield ES 500/PK-5
302 Plum Creek Rd 48446 810-667-2442
Michael Goetz, prin. Fax 667-2468
Rolland-Warner MS 400/6-7
3145 W Genesee Rd 48446 810-538-2334
Jeff Stanton, prin. Fax 538-3250
Schickler ES 400/PK-5
2020 W Oregon St 48446 810-667-2440
Scott Warren, prin. Fax 667-2469
Turrill ES 500/PK-5
785 S Elm St 48446 810-667-2438
Robert Downey, prin. Fax 667-2470
Other Schools – See Metamora

Bishop Kelley Catholic S 200/PK-8
926 W Nepessing St 48446 810-664-5011
Penny Clemens, prin. Fax 664-5606
St. Paul Lutheran S 100/PK-8
90 Millville Rd 48446 810-664-0046
Raymond Sturm, prin. Fax 245-4082

Lathrup Village, Oakland, Pop. 3,943
Southfield SD
Supt. — See Southfield
MacArthur K-8 University Academy 500/K-8
19301 W 12 Mile Rd 48076 248-746-8590
Vicki Bayne-Perry, prin. Fax 746-8944

Lawrence, Van Buren, Pop. 973
Lawrence SD 600/PK-12
650 W Saint Joseph St 49064 269-674-8233
Gretchen Gendron, supt. Fax 674-8200
www.lawrencetigers.com
Lawrence ES 300/PK-6
714 W Saint Joseph St 49064 269-674-8231
Jennifer Curtis, prin. Fax 674-3545

Lawton, Van Buren, Pop. 1,870
Lawton Community SD 1,000/PK-12
101 Primary Way 49065 269-624-7901
Christopher Rice M.Ed., supt. Fax 624-6489
www.lawtoncs.org
Lawton ES 400/PK-5
101 Primary Way 49065 269-624-7500
Stephanie Brown, prin. Fax 624-5604
Lawton MS 200/6-8
101 Primary Way 49065 269-624-7610
Tim Cerven, prin. Fax 624-5206

Leland, Leelanau, Pop. 377
Leland SD 400/K-12
PO Box 498 49654 231-256-9857
Jason Stowe, supt. Fax 256-9844
www.lelandpublicschools.com
Leland S 400/K-12
PO Box 498 49654 231-256-9857
Charles Gann, prin. Fax 256-9844

Leonard, Oakland, Pop. 402
Oxford Community SD
Supt. — See Oxford
Leonard ES 200/K-5
335 E Elmwood 48367 248-969-5300
Paul McDevitt, prin. Fax 969-5310

Romeo Community SD
Supt. — See Romeo
Hamilton-Parsons ES 400/K-5
69875 Dequindre Rd 48367 586-752-0280
Andrea Hasse, prin. Fax 752-0421

Leonidas, Saint Joseph
Colon Community SD
Supt. — See Colon

Leonidas S 100/K-8
30945 Church St 49066 269-496-7385
Martha Hymer, prin. Fax 432-9341

LeRoy, Osceola, Pop. 252
Pine River Area SD 900/K-12
17445 Pine River Rd 49655 231-829-3141
Matt Lukshaitis, supt. Fax 829-4410
www.pineriver.org/
Pine River Area ES 300/K-3
408 W Gilbert St 49655 231-768-4481
Heidi Hayes, prin. Fax 768-4048
Pine River Area Upper ES 200/4-5
17445 Pine River Rd 49655 231-829-4064
Heidi Hayes, prin. Fax 829-3041

Leslie, Ingham, Pop. 1,824
Leslie SD 1,300/K-12
4141 Hull Rd 49251 517-589-8200
Jeff Manthei, supt. Fax 589-5340
www.lesliek12.net/
Leslie MS 400/5-8
400 Kimball St 49251 517-589-8218
Todd Gonser, prin. Fax 589-5714
Woodworth ES 400/K-4
212 Pennsylvania St 49251 517-589-5151
Jim Dell, prin. Fax 589-5548

Lewiston, Montmorency, Pop. 1,370
Johannesburg-Lewiston Area SD
Supt. — See Johannesburg
Lewiston ES 200/K-5
PO Box 417 49756 989-786-2253
Cynthia Kievit, prin. Fax 786-5315

Lexington, Sanilac, Pop. 1,169
Croswell-Lexington SD
Supt. — See Croswell
Meyer ES 300/K-4
7201 Lake St 48450 810-679-1200
Donna Barrier, prin. Fax 679-1205

Lincoln, Alcona, Pop. 335
Alcona Community SD 700/PK-12
PO Box 249 48742 989-736-6212
Daniel O'Connor, supt. Fax 736-6261
www.alconaschools.net
Alcona ES 400/PK-5
PO Box 249 48742 989-736-8146
Timothy Lee, prin. Fax 736-7031

Lincoln Park, Wayne, Pop. 37,338
Lincoln Park SD 4,800/PK-12
1650 Champaign Rd 48146 313-389-0200
Terry Dangerfield, supt. Fax 389-1322
www.lincolnparkpublicschools.com
Carr ES 300/K-5
3901 Ferris Ave 48146 313-389-0230
Whitney Waskiewicz, prin. Fax 388-9869
Crowley Center 200/PK-PK
2000 Pagel Ave 48146 313-389-0213
Nicole Sexton, dir. Fax 383-2203
Foote ES 300/K-5
3250 Abbott Ave 48146 313-389-0216
Steve Massengill, prin. Fax 389-0997
Hoover ES 200/K-5
3750 Howard St 48146 313-389-0207
Katherine Stepulla, prin. Fax 388-0278
Keppen ES 300/K-5
661 Mill St 48146 313-389-0232
Lisa Clark, prin. Fax 389-3522
LaFayette ES 600/K-5
1360 Lafayette Blvd 48146 313-389-0224
Aaron Currier, prin. Fax 389-0749
Lincoln Park MS 1,100/6-8
2800 Lafayette Blvd 48146 313-389-0757
Daniel Mercer, prin. Fax 389-0761
Paun ES 300/K-5
2821 Bailey Ave 48146 313-389-0218
Leslie Perlaki, prin. Fax 388-2955
Raupp ES 300/K-5
1351 Ethel Ave 48146 313-389-0226
Tara Randall, prin. Fax 388-6429

John Paul II Catholic S 200/PK-8
1590 Riverbank St 48146 313-386-0633
Mariann Lupinacci, prin. Fax 928-1326

Linden, Genesee, Pop. 3,937
Linden Community SD 2,700/PK-12
7205 Silver Lake Rd 48451 810-591-0980
Russ Ciesielski, supt. Fax 591-5587
www.lindenschools.org
Argentine Preschool 300/PK-PK
8483 Silver Lake Rd 48451 810-591-0320
Denice Westervelt, dir. Fax 591-9658
Central ES 100/4-5
7199 Silver Lake Rd 48451 810-591-8410
Michael Gagne, prin. Fax 591-7316
Hyatt ES 300/K-3
325 Stan Eaton Dr 48451 810-591-8180
Cheryl Thomas, prin. Fax 591-4377
Linden ES 300/K-3
400 S Bridge St 48451 810-591-9130
Vicki Makaravage, prin. Fax 591-9143
Linden MS 700/6-8
15425 Lobdell Rd 48451 810-591-0710
Robert Pouch, prin. Fax 591-0155

Linwood, Bay
Pinconning Area SD
Supt. — See Pinconning
Linwood ES 100/K-5
517 W Center St 48634 989-697-5711
Mark Fuhrman, prin. Fax 697-5707

Litchfield, Hillsdale, Pop. 1,359
Litchfield Community SD 300/PK-12
210 Williams St 49252 517-542-2388
Dr. Corey Helgesen Ed.D., supt. Fax 542-2580
www.lcsmi.org
Litchfield ES 100/PK-5
210 Williams St 49252 517-542-2356
Dr. Corey Helgesen Ed.D., prin. Fax 542-2703

Livonia, Wayne, Pop. 95,640
Clarenceville SD 1,900/PK-12
20210 Middlebelt Rd 48152 248-919-0400
Paul Shepich, supt. Fax 919-0430
www.clarencevilleschools.org
Botsford ES 400/PK-5
19515 Lathers St 48152 248-919-0402
Christine Teff, prin. Fax 919-0442
Clarenceville MS 400/6-8
20210 Middlebelt Rd 48152 248-919-0406
Stacey Lown, prin. Fax 919-0436
Grandview ES 400/PK-5
19814 Louise St 48152 248-919-0404
Michelle Barsh, prin. Fax 919-0434

Livonia SD 14,400/PK-12
15125 Farmington Rd 48154 734-744-2500
Andrea Oquist, supt.
www.livoniapublicschools.org
Buchanan ES 400/K-4
16400 Hubbard St 48154 734-744-2690
Jonathan Wennstrom, prin. Fax 744-2692
Cleveland ES 400/K-4
28030 Cathedral St 48150 734-744-2700
Bridget Regan, prin. Fax 744-2702
Coolidge ES 500/K-4
30500 Curtis Rd 48152 248-744-2705
Lawrence Grezak, prin. Fax 744-2707
Emerson MS 700/7-8
29100 W Chicago St 48150 734-744-2665
Ann Owen, prin. Fax 744-2667
Frost MS 800/7-8
14041 Stark Rd 48154 734-744-2670
Anthony Abbate, prin. Fax 744-2672
Grant ES 400/K-4
9300 Hubbard St 48150 734-744-2720
Jennifer Keatts, prin. Fax 744-2722
Holmes MS 800/7-8
16200 Newburgh Rd 48154 734-744-2675
Eric Stromberg, prin. Fax 744-2677
Hoover ES 500/K-4
15900 Levan Rd 48154 734-744-2730
Julie Linn, prin. Fax 744-2732
Jackson ECC 50/PK-PK
32025 Lyndon St 48154 734-744-2813
Carol Carignan, admin. Fax 744-2814
Kennedy ES 300/K-4
14201 Hubbard St 48154 734-744-2745
Dr. Danielle Daniels, prin. Fax 744-2747
Niji-Iro Japanese Immersion ES K-4
36611 Curtis Rd 48152 734-744-2500
Lawrence DeLuca, prin. Fax 744-2574
Randolph ES 300/K-4
14470 Norman St 48154 734-744-2770
Mike Daraskavich, prin. Fax 744-2772
Riley ES 800/5-6
15555 Henry Ruff St 48154 734-744-2680
Kristyn Cousino, prin. Fax 744-2682
Roosevelt ES 400/K-4
30200 Lyndon St 48154 734-744-2775
Bill Green, prin. Fax 744-2777
Rosedale ES 200/K-4
36651 Ann Arbor Trl 48150 734-744-2800
Paula Kohler, prin. Fax 744-2802
Webster ES 200/K-4
32401 Pembroke St 48152 734-744-2795
Lora Boka, prin. Fax 744-2797
Other Schools – See Westland

Brookfield Academy Livonia Campus 50/PK-5
38945 Ann Arbor Rd 48150 734-464-2789
Karen Funyak, prin. Fax 464-3302
Peace Lutheran S 100/PK-8
9415 Merriman Rd 48150 734-422-6930
Geoffrey Kieta, prin. Fax 422-0790
St. Edith S 200/K-8
15089 Newburgh Rd 48154 734-464-1250
Georgene Wojciechowski, prin. Fax 464-6765
St. Michael S 800/K-8
11311 Hubbard St 48150 734-421-7360
Nancy Kuszczak, prin. Fax 466-9713
St. Paul's Lutheran S 100/PK-8
17810 Farmington Rd 48152 734-421-9022
Josh Walker, prin. Fax 421-9022

Lowell, Kent, Pop. 3,710
Lowell Area SD 3,700/K-12
300 High St 49331 616-987-2500
Gregory Pratt, supt. Fax 987-2511
www.lowellschools.com/
Bushnell ES 300/K-1
700 Elizabeth St 49331 616-987-2650
Erin Walters, prin. Fax 987-2661
Cherry Creek ES 500/2-5
12675 Foreman St 49331 616-987-2700
Shelli Otten, prin. Fax 987-2711
Lowell MS 800/6-8
750 Foreman St 49331 616-987-2800
Dan VanderMeulen, prin. Fax 987-2811
Murray Lake ES 500/K-5
3275 Alden Nash Ave NE 49331 616-987-2750
Brent Noskey, prin. Fax 987-2761
Other Schools – See Alto

Ludington, Mason, Pop. 7,926
Ludington Area SD 2,200/PK-12
809 E Tinkham Ave 49431 231-845-7303
Jason J. Kennedy, supt. Fax 843-4930
www.lasd.net
DeJonge MS 500/6-8
706 E Tinkham Ave 49431 231-845-3810
Kristi Zimmerman, prin. Fax 845-3814
Foster ES 500/3-5
505 E Foster St 49431 231-845-3820
Brian Dotson, prin. Fax 845-0146
Franklin ES 300/K-2
721 Anderson St 49431 231-845-3830
Janice Jackoviak, prin. Fax 843-8567
Lakeview ES 200/K-2
502 W Haight St 49431 231-845-3840
Amber Kowatch, prin. Fax 845-0788
Pere Marquette ECC 100/PK-PK
1115 S Madison St 49431 231-845-3850
Julie Marshall, dir. Fax 843-9680

Covenant Christian S 100/PK-8
2980 W US Highway 10 49431 231-845-9183
Thressa Ambrose, admin. Fax 845-9058
Ludington Area Catholic S 100/PK-8
700 E Bryant Rd 49431 231-843-3188
Collin Thompson, prin. Fax 843-2052

Mc Bain, Missaukee, Pop. 651
McBain Rural Agricultural SD 700/PK-12
107 E Maple St 49657 231-825-2165
Steven Brimmer, supt. Fax 825-2119
www.mcbain.org
Mc Bain ES 400/PK-6
107 E Maple St 49657 231-825-2021
Kim VanderVlucht, prin. Fax 825-2436

Northern Michigan Christian S 300/PK-12
128 S Martin St 49657 231-825-2492
Dirk Walhout, supt. Fax 825-2371

Mackinac Island, Mackinac, Pop. 466
Mackinac Island SD 100/PK-12
PO Box 340 49757 906-847-3377
Robert Lohff, supt. Fax 847-3773
mackinac.eup.k12.mi.us
Mackinac Island S 100/PK-12
PO Box 340 49757 906-847-3377
Robert Lohff, admin. Fax 847-3773

Mackinaw City, Emmet, Pop. 794
Mackinaw City SD 200/PK-12
609 W Central Ave 49701 231-436-8211
Jeffrey Curth, supt. Fax 436-5434
www.mackcity.k12.mi.us
Mackinaw City S 200/PK-12
609 W Central Ave 49701 231-436-8211
Jeffrey Curth, supt. Fax 436-5434

Macomb, Macomb, Pop. 22,714
Chippewa Valley SD
Supt. — See Clinton Township
Cheyenne ES 700/K-5
47600 Heydenreich Rd 48044 586-723-5000
Mark Johnson, prin. Fax 723-5001
Fox ES 500/K-5
17500 Millstone Dr 48044 586-723-5600
Frank Bellomo, prin. Fax 723-5601
Iroquois MS 1,100/6-8
48301 Romeo Plank Rd 48044 586-723-3700
Chris Gardner, prin. Fax 723-3701
Mohawk ES 500/K-5
48101 Romeo Plank Rd 48044 586-723-6200
Andrea McVicar, prin. Fax 723-6201
Ojibwa ES 700/K-5
46950 Heydenreich Rd 48044 586-723-6400
Marina Licari, prin. Fax 723-6401
Seneca MS 1,400/6-8
47200 Heydenreich Rd 48044 586-723-3900
Todd Distelrath, prin. Fax 723-3901
Sequoyah ES 800/K-5
18500 24 Mile Rd 48042 586-723-7000
Ted Zotos, prin. Fax 723-2001
Shawnee ES 900/K-5
21555 Vesper Dr 48044 586-723-6800
Sarah Simon, prin. Fax 723-6801

L'Anse Creuse SD
Supt. — See Clinton Township
Atwood ES 700/K-5
45690 North Ave 48042 586-493-5250
Angela Szczepanski, prin. Fax 493-5255
L'Anse Creuse MS North 800/6-8
46201 Fairchild Rd 48042 586-493-5260
Brian Fahning, prin. Fax 493-5265

Utica Community SD
Supt. — See Sterling Heights
Beck Centennial ES 700/K-6
54600 Hayes Rd 48042 586-797-3900
Christine Wilson, prin. Fax 797-3901
Ebeling ES 600/PK-6
15970 Haverhill Dr 48044 586-797-4700
Denise Bailey, prin. Fax 797-4701

Immanuel Lutheran S 500/PK-8
47120 Romeo Plank Rd 48044 586-286-7076
Joel Neumeyer, prin. Fax 286-4243
St. Peter Lutheran S 500/PK-8
17051 24 Mile Rd 48042 586-781-9296
Tim Leinberger, prin. Fax 781-9726

Madison Heights, Oakland, Pop. 28,913
Lamphere SD 2,800/PK-12
31201 Dorchester Ave 48071 248-589-1990
Dale Steen, supt. Fax 589-2618
www.lamphereschools.org
Edmonson ES 300/K-5
621 E Katherine Ave 48071 248-547-5342
Sharon Stephens, prin. Fax 547-6444
Hiller ES 300/K-5
400 E La Salle Ave 48071 248-589-0406
Jennifer Cumiskey, prin. Fax 589-2055
Lamphere Learning Ladder PK-PK
31201 Dorchester Ave 48071 248-589-1990
Jan Figurski, prin. Fax 589-2618
Lessenger ES 300/K-5
30150 Campbell Rd 48071 248-589-0556
Jane Jurvis, prin. Fax 589-8853

Page MS 600/6-8
29615 Tawas St 48071 248-589-3428
Rodney Thomas, prin. Fax 545-1870
Simonds ES 300/K-5
30000 Rose St 48071 248-547-5292
Tina Johnson-Davis, prin. Fax 547-8635

Madison SD 1,300/K-12
26524 John R Rd 48071 248-399-7800
Randy Speck, supt. Fax 399-2229
www.madisondistrict.org
Madison ES 200/K-5
27107 Hales St 48071 248-542-3414
Randy Speck, prin. Fax 543-5466
Wilkinson MS 300/6-8
26524 John R Rd 48071 248-399-0455
Angel Abdulahad, prin. Fax 399-1965

Mancelona, Antrim, Pop. 1,339
Mancelona SD 1,000/PK-12
PO Box 739 49659 231-587-9764
Jeffery DiRosa, supt. Fax 587-9500
www.mancelonaschools.org/
Mancelona ES 400/PK-4
PO Box 739 49659 231-587-8661
Tina Frollo, prin. Fax 587-8699
Mancelona MS 300/5-8
PO Box 739 49659 231-587-9869
Dr. Larry Rager, prin. Fax 587-0615

Manchester, Washtenaw, Pop. 2,074
Manchester Community SD 1,100/K-12
410 City Rd 48158 734-428-9711
Brad Hamilton, supt. Fax 428-9188
www.manchesterschools.us
Klager ES 400/K-6
405 Ann Arbor St 48158 734-428-8321
Jennifer Mayes, prin. Fax 428-7962

Manistee, Manistee, Pop. 6,070
Manistee Area SD 1,300/PK-12
550 Maple St 49660 231-723-3521
Ronald Stoneman, supt. Fax 723-1507
maps.manistee.org
Jefferson ES 300/K-2
515 Bryant Ave 49660 231-723-9285
Julia Raddatz, prin. Fax 723-2021
Kennedy ES 400/3-5
550 Maple St 49660 231-723-3271
Kevin Schmutzler, prin. Fax 723-5879
Madison ECC 100/PK-PK
1309 Madison Rd 49660 231-723-5212
Julia Raddatz, prin. Fax 723-1607

Manistee Catholic Central S 200/PK-12
1200 US Highway 31 S 49660 231-723-2529
Jason Allen, prin. Fax 723-0669
Trinity Lutheran S 100/PK-8
420 Oak St 49660 231-723-8700
Chuck Dillon, prin. Fax 723-9755

Manistique, Schoolcraft, Pop. 2,986
Manistique Area SD 800/PK-12
100 N Cedar St 49854 906-341-4300
Maryann Boddy, supt. Fax 341-2374
www.manistiqueschools.org
Emerald ES 300/PK-5
628 Oak St 49854 906-341-4332
Maryann Boddy, prin. Fax 341-1004

St. Francis de Sales Catholic S 200/PK-8
210 Lake St 49854 906-341-5512
Don Erickson, prin. Fax 341-5512

Manton, Wexford, Pop. 1,266
Manton Consolidated SD 900/K-12
105 5th St 49663 231-824-6411
Leonard Morrow, supt. Fax 824-4101
www.mantonschools.org
Manton ES 300/K-4
105 5th St 49663 231-824-6413
John Katona, prin. Fax 824-3126
Manton MS 300/5-8
105 5th St 49663 231-824-6401
Ryan Hiller, prin. Fax 824-4121

Maple City, Leelanau, Pop. 204
Glen Lake Community SD 800/PK-12
3375 W Burdickville Rd 49664 231-334-3061
Sander Scott, supt. Fax 334-6255
www.glenlakeschools.org
Glen Lake ES 400/PK-6
3375 W Burdickville Rd 49664 231-334-3061
Kimberly Wright, prin. Fax 334-6255

Marcellus, Cass, Pop. 1,184
Marcellus Community SD 700/K-12
PO Box 48 49067 269-646-7655
Nanette Pauley, supt. Fax 646-2700
www.marcelluscs.org/
Marcellus ES 300/K-6
PO Box 48 49067 269-646-9209
Melinda Bohan, prin. Fax 646-5014

Howardsville Christian S 200/PK-12
53441 Bent Rd 49067 269-646-9367
Dave Nelson, admin. Fax 646-7006

Marine City, Saint Clair, Pop. 4,184
East China SD
Supt. — See East China
Belle River ES 400/K-5
1601 Chartier Rd 48039 810-676-1150
Robyn Smith-Herr, prin. Fax 676-1160
Marine City MS 400/6-8
6373 King Rd 48039 810-676-1201
Christopher Ming, prin. Fax 676-1225

Holy Cross S 100/PK-8
618 S Water St 48039 810-765-3591
Dr. Carl Wagner, prin. Fax 765-9074

Marion, Osceola, Pop. 863
Marion SD 500/K-12
PO Box O 49665 231-743-2486
Mort Meier, supt. Fax 743-2890
www.marion.k12.mi.us
Marion ES 300/K-5
PO Box O 49665 231-743-6251
Mort Meier, prin. Fax 743-2955

Marlette, Sanilac, Pop. 1,847
Marlette Community SD 900/PK-12
6230 Euclid St 48453 989-635-7429
Sarah Barratt, supt. Fax 635-7103
www.marletteschools.org
Marlette ES 500/PK-6
6230 Euclid St 48453 989-635-7427
Jason Vislosky, prin. Fax 635-4941

Our Savior Lutheran S 100/PK-8
6770 Marlette St 48453 989-635-0115
Joel Rachow, admin. Fax 635-0112

Marquette, Marquette, Pop. 20,996
Marquette Area SD 3,200/PK-12
1201 W Fair Ave 49855 906-225-4200
William Saunders, supt. Fax 225-5340
www.mapsnet.org
Bothwell MS 700/6-8
1200 Tierney St 49855 906-225-4262
Dan Gannon, prin. Fax 225-4229
Cherry Creek ES 400/K-5
1111 Ortman Rd 49855 906-225-4399
Travis Smith, prin. Fax 225-4326
Graveraet ES 300/K-5
611 N Front St 49855 906-225-4310
Dr. Sarah Kemppainen, prin. Fax 225-4312
Sandy Knoll ES 400/PK-5
401 N 6th St 49855 906-225-4281
Kevin Hooper, prin. Fax 225-4335
Superior Hills ES 400/PK-5
1201 S McClellan Ave 49855 906-225-4295
Robert Anthony, prin. Fax 225-4339

Father Marquette Catholic S 200/PK-4
500 S 4th St 49855 906-225-1129
Mary Jo Scamperle, prin. Fax 225-1987
Father Marquette MS 100/5-8
414 W College Ave 49855 906-226-7912
Mary Jo Scamperle, prin. Fax 225-9962

Marshall, Calhoun, Pop. 6,978
Mar Lee SD 300/K-8
21236 H Dr N 49068 269-781-5412
Chad Holt, supt. Fax 781-9471
www.mar-lee.org/
Mar Lee S 300/K-8
21236 H Dr N 49068 269-781-5412
Chad Holt, prin. Fax 781-9471

Marshall SD 2,400/PK-12
100 E Green St 49068 269-781-1250
Dr. Randy Davis, supt. Fax 789-1813
www.marshall.k12.mi.us
Gordon ES 300/K-5
400 N Gordon St 49068 269-781-1270
Mike Leathead, prin. Fax 789-3700
Hughes ES 300/PK-5
103 W Hughes St 49068 269-781-1275
Matthew Lefebvre, prin. Fax 789-3704
Marshall MS 500/6-8
100 E Green St 49068 269-781-1251
David Turner, prin. Fax 781-6621
Walters ES 300/K-5
705 N Marshall Ave 49068 269-781-1280
Paul Holbrook, prin. Fax 789-3703
Other Schools – See Albion

Martin, Allegan, Pop. 398
Martin SD 500/PK-12
PO Box 241 49070 269-672-7194
Dr. David Harnish, supt. Fax 672-7116
www.martinpublicschools.org
Brandon ES 300/PK-6
PO Box 241 49070 269-672-7253
Rebecca Bullen, prin. Fax 672-5138

East Martin Christian S 100/K-8
516 118th Ave 49070 269-672-5722
Lisa Leep, admin. Fax 672-5736

Marysville, Saint Clair, Pop. 9,889
Marysville SD 2,700/K-12
495 E Huron Blvd 48040 810-364-7731
Dr. Shawn Wightman, supt. Fax 364-3150
www.marysvilleschools.us/
Gardens ES 500/K-5
1070 6th St 48040 810-364-7141
Rebecca Biedermann, prin. Fax 364-2987
Marysville MS 600/6-8
400 Collard Dr 48040 810-364-6336
Jay Schultz, prin. Fax 364-4456
Morton ES 300/K-5
920 Lynwood St 48040 810-364-2990
Kathleen Quain, prin. Fax 364-5983
Washington ES 400/K-5
905 16th St 48040 810-364-7101
Karen Bracey, prin. Fax 364-4456

Mason, Ingham, Pop. 8,111
Mason SD 3,100/K-12
400 S Cedar St 48854 517-676-2484
Ronald Drzewicki, supt. Fax 676-6058
www.masonk12.net
Alaiedon ES 400/K-5
1723 Okemos Rd 48854 517-676-6499
Fax 676-0283
Mason MS 700/6-8
235 Temple St 48854 517-676-6514
Ted Berryhill, prin. Fax 676-0287

North Aurelius ES 500/K-5
115 N Aurelius Rd 48854 517-676-6506
Michael Prelesnik, prin. Fax 676-0293
Steele ES 500/K-5
531 Steele St 48854 517-676-6510
Kevin Dufresne, prin. Fax 676-0295

Mattawan, Van Buren, Pop. 1,954
Mattawan Consolidated SD 3,800/K-12
56720 Murray St 49071 269-668-3361
Dr. Robin Buchler, supt. Fax 668-2372
www.mattawanschools.org
Mattawan Early ES 800/K-2
56720 Murray St 49071 269-668-3361
Rebecca Moore, prin. Fax 668-3364
Mattawan Later ES 900/3-5
56720 Murray St 49071 269-668-3361
Carrie Wendell, prin. Fax 668-3363
Mattawan MS 900/6-8
56720 Murray St 49071 269-668-3361
Chip Schuman, prin. Fax 668-3188

Mayville, Tuscola, Pop. 933
Mayville Community SD 700/PK-12
6250 Fulton St 48744 989-843-6115
Barry Markwart, supt. Fax 843-6988
www.mayville.k12.mi.us
Mayville ES 300/PK-5
106 Orchard St 48744 989-843-6115
Kimberly Morden, prin. Fax 843-7218
Mayville MS 100/6-8
6210 Fulton St 48744 989-843-6115
Barry Markwart, prin. Fax 843-7209

Mecosta, Mecosta, Pop. 427
Chippewa Hills SD
Supt. — See Remus
Mecosta ES 300/PK-4
555 W Main St 49332 231-972-7477
Kyle Talicska, prin. Fax 972-4005

Melvindale, Wayne, Pop. 10,396
Melvindale-Northern Allen Park SD 2,900/K-12
18530 Prospect St 48122 313-389-3300
Dr. Kimberly Soranno, supt. Fax 389-3312
www.melnap.k12.mi.us
Allendale ES 900/2-5
3201 Oakwood Blvd 48122 313-389-4664
Shannon Luppino, prin. Fax 389-8713
Strong MS 700/6-8
3303 Oakwood Blvd 48122 313-389-3330
Donald Fish, prin. Fax 389-2077
Other Schools – See Allen Park

Memphis, Saint Clair, Pop. 1,172
Memphis Community SD 900/PK-12
PO Box 201 48041 810-392-2151
Brad Gudme, supt. Fax 392-3614
www.memphisk12.org/
Memphis ES 400/PK-5
PO Box 201 48041 810-392-2125
Susan Hankins, prin. Fax 392-2324

Mendon, Saint Joseph, Pop. 857
Mendon Community SD 600/K-12
148 Kirby Rd 49072 269-496-9940
Roger Rathburn, supt. Fax 496-8234
www.mendonschools.org
Mendon ES 300/K-5
306 Lane St 49072 269-496-2175
Kate Wall, prin. Fax 496-7021

Menominee, Menominee, Pop. 8,500
Menominee Area SD 1,500/PK-12
1230 13th St 49858 906-863-9951
John Mans, supt. Fax 863-1171
www.menominee.k12.mi.us
Blesch IS 400/3-6
1200 11th Ave 49858 906-863-4466
Scott Martin, prin. Fax 863-1171
Central ES 300/PK-2
1800 18th Ave 49858 906-863-3605
DeeAnne Pohlmann, prin. Fax 863-3554
Menominee JHS 200/7-8
2101 18th St 49858 906-863-9929
Alison Granquist, admin. Fax 863-8883

St. John Paul II Catholic Academy 100/PK-8
2701 17th St 49858 906-863-3190
Michael Muhs, prin. Fax 863-3990

Merrill, Saginaw, Pop. 771
Merrill Community SD 700/PK-12
431 W Alice St 48637 989-643-7261
Sarah Kettelhohn, supt. Fax 643-5570
merrillschools.org
Merrill ES 300/PK-5
431 W Alice St 48637 989-643-7283
Gwen Glazier, prin. Fax 643-5249
Merrill MS 100/6-8
431 W Alice St 48637 989-643-7231
Tara Mager, prin. Fax 643-7942

Mesick, Wexford, Pop. 390
Mesick Consolidated SD 600/K-12
PO Box 275 49668 231-885-1200
Scott Akom, supt. Fax 885-1234
www.mesick.org
Jewett ES 300/K-5
PO Box 275 49668 231-885-1207
Fax 885-2544

Metamora, Lapeer, Pop. 561
Lapeer Community SD
Supt. — See Lapeer
Murphy ES 400/PK-5
1100 Pratt Rd 48455 810-678-2201
Katie Jordan, prin. Fax 678-3393

Michigan Center, Jackson, Pop. 4,596
Michigan Center SD 1,400/K-12
400 S State St 49254 517-764-5778
Brady Cook, supt. Fax 764-9607
www.mccardinals.org/
Arnold ES 300/K-2
400 S State St 49254 517-764-5700
Kelly McCloughan, prin. Fax 764-6623
Keicher ES 400/3-6
400 S State St 49254 517-764-5200
Johanna Pscodna, prin. Fax 764-6624

Middleton, Gratiot
Fulton SD 1,000/PK-12
8060 Ely Hwy 48856 989-236-7300
Paul Hungerford, supt. Fax 236-7660
fultonpirates.net
Fulton ES 300/PK-6
8060 Ely Hwy 48856 989-236-7234
Paul Avery, prin. Fax 236-5607
Fulton MS 100/7-8
8060 Ely Hwy 48856 989-236-7232
Paul Hungerford, prin. Fax 236-7628

Middleville, Barry, Pop. 3,261
Thornapple-Kellogg SD 3,000/PK-12
10051 Green Lake Rd 49333 269-795-5521
Tom Enslen, supt. Fax 795-5401
www.tkschools.org/
Lee ES 500/2-3
840 W Main St 49333 269-795-9747
Angie Jefferson, prin. Fax 795-5587
McFall ES 500/PK-1
509 W Main St 49333 269-795-3637
Jon Washburn, prin. Fax 795-5554
Page ES 500/4-5
3675 Bender Rd 49333 269-795-7944
Michael Gelmi, prin. Fax 795-5501
Thornapple-Kellogg MS 700/6-8
10375 Green Lake Rd 49333 269-795-3349
Brian Balding, prin. Fax 795-5455

Midland, Midland, Pop. 41,135
Bullock Creek SD 1,900/K-12
1420 S Badour Rd 48640 989-631-9022
Shawn Hale, supt. Fax 631-2882
www.bcreek.k12.mi.us
Bullock Creek ES 200/K-2
1037 S Poseyville Rd 48640 989-832-8691
Vicki Mikusko, prin. Fax 832-4014
Bullock Creek MS 400/6-8
644 S Badour Rd 48640 989-631-9260
Curt Moses, prin. Fax 832-4018
Floyd ES 300/K-5
725 S 8 Mile Rd 48640 989-832-2081
Rodney Dishaw, prin. Fax 698-3249
Pine River ES 300/K-K, 3-5
1894 E Pine River Rd 48640 989-631-5121
Debra Bradford, prin. Fax 832-4017

Midland SD 7,600/K-12
600 E Carpenter St 48640 989-923-5001
Michael Sharrow, supt. Fax 923-5003
www.midlandps.org
Adams ES 400/K-5
1005 Adams Dr 48642 989-923-6037
Linda Lipsitt, prin. Fax 923-6035
Central Park ES, 1400 Rodd St 48640 800/K-5
Bridget Hockemeyer, prin. 989-923-6836
Chestnut Hill ES 400/K-5
3900 Chestnut Hill Dr 48642 989-923-6634
Tracy Renfro, prin. Fax 923-6630
Jefferson MS 900/6-8
800 W Chapel Ln 48640 989-923-5873
Ted Davis, prin. Fax 923-5800
Northeast MS 1,000/6-8
1305 E Sugnet Rd 48642 989-923-5772
Dirk DeBoer, prin. Fax 923-5780
Plymouth ES 500/K-5
1105 E Sugnet Rd 48642 989-923-7616
Margaret Doan, prin. Fax 923-7665
Siebert ES 600/K-5
5700 Siebert St 48640 989-923-7835
Paul Schroll, prin. Fax 923-7875
Woodcrest ES 600/K-5
5500 Drake St 48640 989-923-7940
Jeff Pennex, prin. Fax 923-7919

Blessed Sacrament S 200/PK-5
3109 Swede Ave 48642 989-835-6777
Carl Sztuczko, prin. Fax 835-2451
Calvary Baptist Academy 500/PK-12
6100 Perrine Rd 48640 989-832-3341
David Warren, prin. Fax 832-7443
Good Shepherd Lutheran S 50/PK-8
907 Mattes Dr 48642 989-835-4181
Rev. Jacob Behnken, prin. Fax 835-4181
Midland Christian S 100/PK-12
4417 W Wackerly St 48640 989-835-9881
Betsy Haigh, head sch Fax 835-5201
Midland Montessori S 100/PK-2
5709 Eastman Ave 48640 989-835-3921
St. Brigid S 200/K-8
130 W Larkin St 48640 989-835-9481
Maureen Becker, prin. Fax 835-9141
St. John's Lutheran S 100/PK-8
505 E Carpenter St 48640 989-835-7041
Brenda Hoskey, prin. Fax 835-2443

Milan, Monroe, Pop. 5,683
Milan Area SD 2,200/K-12
100 Big Red Dr 48160 734-439-5050
Bryan Girbach, supt. Fax 439-5083
www.milanareaschools.org/
Milan MS 500/6-8
920 North St 48160 734-439-5200
Shanna Spickard, prin. Fax 439-5288
Paddock ES 400/K-2
707 Marvin St 48160 734-439-5100
Sean DeSarbo, prin. Fax 439-5160

Symons ES 400/3-5
432 S Platt Rd 48160 734-439-5300
Kimberly Gillow, prin. Fax 439-5303

Milford, Oakland, Pop. 6,058
Huron Valley SD
Supt. — See Highland
Johnson ES 400/K-5
515 General Motors Rd 48381 248-684-8020
Joshua Gignac, prin. Fax 684-8023
Kurtz ES 500/K-5
1350 Kurtz Dr 48381 248-684-8025
Steve Chisik, prin. Fax 684-8024
Muir MS 800/6-8
425 George St 48381 248-684-8060
Daniel Hurst, prin. Fax 684-8068

Christ Lutheran Preschool & K 50/PK-K
620 General Motors Rd 48381 248-684-6773
Ruth Carlton, dir. Fax 685-7703
West Highland Christian Academy 100/K-12
1116 S Hickory Ridge Rd 48380 248-887-6698
Charley Allen, head sch Fax 629-4267

Millington, Tuscola, Pop. 1,059
Millington Community SD 800/K-12
8537 Gleason St 48746 989-660-2451
Bruce Martin, supt. Fax 660-2445
www.mcsdistrict.com
Kirk ES 400/K-5
8664 Dean Dr 48746 989-660-2432
Karen Moore, prin. Fax 660-2443

St. Paul Lutheran S 200/PK-8
4941 Center St 48746 989-871-4581
Paul Schoenknecht, prin. Fax 871-5573

Mio, Oscoda, Pop. 1,791
Mio-AuSable SD 600/K-12
1110 W 8th St 48647 989-826-2400
James Gendernalik, supt. Fax 826-2415
www.miok12.net
Mio-AuSable ES 300/K-5
1110 W 8th St 48647 989-826-2430
Teresa Cole, admin. Fax 826-2417
Mio-AuSable MS 200/6-8
1110 W 8th St 48647 989-826-2481
James Gendernalik, prin. Fax 826-2416

Moline, Allegan

Moline Christian S 300/PK-8
PO Box 130 49335 616-877-4688
Kevin Sall, prin. Fax 877-4689

Monroe, Monroe, Pop. 20,187
Jefferson SD 1,600/K-12
2400 N Dixie Hwy 48162 734-289-5550
Craig Haugen, supt. Fax 289-5574
www.jeffersonschools.org
Jefferson MS 300/5-8
5102 N Stoney Creek Rd 48162 734-289-5565
Sara Griffin, prin. Fax 289-5596
Sodt ES 100/K-1
2888 Nadeau Rd 48162 734-289-5575
Mike Petty, prin. Fax 289-5600
Other Schools – See Newport

Monroe SD 5,900/PK-12
PO Box 733 48161 734-265-3000
Dr. Julie Everly, supt. Fax 265-3001
www.monroe.k12.mi.us
Arborwood Campus 700/PK-6
1135 Riverview Ave 48162 734-265-4500
Steve Pollzzie, prin. Fax 265-4501
Custer ES 1,100/PK-6
5003 W Albain Rd 48161 734-265-4300
Lisa McLaughlin, prin. Fax 265-4301
Manor ES 500/PK-6
1731 W Lorain St 48162 734-265-4700
Ronda Meier, prin. Fax 265-4701
Monroe MS 900/7-8
503 Washington St 48161 734-265-4000
Jeffrey McVeigh, prin. Fax 265-4001
Raisinville ES 400/PK-6
2300 N Raisinville Rd 48162 734-265-4800
Scott Hoppert, prin. Fax 265-4801
Riverside Learning Center 200/PK-PK
77 N Roessler St 48162 734-265-4900
Barbara Difiore, contact Fax 265-4901
Waterloo ES 300/K-6
1933 S Custer Rd 48161 734-265-5100
Meghan Gibson, prin. Fax 265-5101

Holy Ghost Lutheran S 100/PK-8
3563 Heiss Rd 48162 734-242-0509
Lois Krohe, prin. Fax 242-2701
Meadow Montessori S 200/PK-12
1670 S Raisinville Rd 48161 734-241-9496
Catharine Calder, head sch Fax 241-0829
St. John the Baptist S 100/2-4
521 S Monroe St 48161 734-241-1670
Kyle Kubik, dir. Fax 241-8782
St. Mary MS 200/5-8
151 N Monroe St 48162 734-241-3377
Sheena Zawistowicz, prin. Fax 241-0497
St. Michael the Archangel S 100/PK-1
510 W Front St 48161 734-241-3923
Kyle Kubik, prin. Fax 241-7314
Trinity Lutheran S 100/PK-8
315 Scott St 48161 734-241-1160
Cindy Lucas, prin. Fax 241-6293
Zion Lutheran S 50/PK-8
186 Cole Rd 48162 734-242-1378
Bryan Schneck, prin. Fax 242-7049

Montague, Muskegon, Pop. 2,329
Montague Area SD 1,500/PK-12
4882 Stanton Blvd 49437 231-893-1515
Jeffrey Johnson, supt. Fax 894-6586
www.mapsk12.org
Chisholm MS 400/6-8
4700 Stanton Blvd 49437 231-894-5617
James Perreault, prin. Fax 894-5728
Montague Area Childhood Center 100/PK-K
9151 Dicey St 49437 231-981-4670
Jeff Henderson, prin.
Oehrli ES, 4859 Knudsen St 49437 600/1-5
Jeff Henderson, prin. 231-894-9018

Montrose, Genesee, Pop. 1,644
Montrose Community SD 1,400/PK-12
PO Box 3129 48457 810-591-8800
Dr. Edward Graham Ph.D., supt. Fax 591-7268
www.montroseschools.org
Carter ES 400/PK-4
PO Box 3129 48457 810-591-8842
Cassandra Jackson, prin. Fax 591-7283
Kuehn-Haven MS 400/5-8
PO Box 3129 48457 810-591-8832
Rhonda Barber, prin. Fax 591-7282

Morenci, Lenawee, Pop. 2,192
Morenci Area SD 500/PK-12
788 Coomer St 49256 517-458-7501
Michael McAran, supt. Fax 458-7821
morencibulldogs.org
Morenci ES 300/PK-4
517 E Locust St 49256 517-458-7504
Gail Frey, admin. Fax 458-6364

Morley, Mecosta, Pop. 490
Morley Stanwood Community SD 1,200/K-12
4700 Northland Dr 49336 231-856-4392
Roger Cole, supt. Fax 856-4180
www.morleystanwood.org
Morley Stanwood ES 500/K-5
4808 Northland Dr 49336 231-856-7684
John Nawrot, prin. Fax 856-0139
Morley-Stanwood MS 300/6-8
4700 Northland Dr 49336 231-856-4550
James Nelson, prin. Fax 856-0136

Morrice, Shiawassee, Pop. 914
Morrice Area SD 500/PK-12
111 E Mason 48857 517-625-3142
Scott Williams, supt. Fax 625-3866
www.morrice.k12.mi.us
Morrice ES 300/PK-6
111 E Mason 48857 517-625-3141
Kelly Roe, prin. Fax 625-3866

Mount Clemens, Macomb, Pop. 15,743
Chippewa Valley SD
Supt. — See Clinton Township
Clinton Valley ES 400/K-5
1260 Mulberry St 48043 586-723-5200
Greg Finlayson, prin. Fax 723-5201

Mount Clemens Community SD 1,200/PK-12
167 Cass Ave 48043 586-469-6100
Teresa Davis, supt. Fax 469-5569
www.mtcps.org
King Academy 200/PK-PK
400 Clinton River Dr 48043 586-461-3100
Stacy Tomlingson, admin. Fax 469-7006
Mount Clemens MS 200/6-8
161 Cass Ave 48043 586-461-3300
Joe Gibson, prin. Fax 469-7066
Seminole Academy 400/K-5
1500 Mulberry St 48043 586-461-3900
Elizabeth Manning, prin. Fax 469-7027

St. Mary S 500/PK-8
2 Union St 48043 586-468-4570
Maureen Miscavish, prin. Fax 464-0718

Mount Morris, Genesee, Pop. 2,972
Beecher Community SD
Supt. — See Flint
Dailey Early Head Start Center 200/PK-PK
6236 Neff Rd 48458 810-591-9806
Nerita Adams-Spillers, admin. Fax 244-0130
Dailey ES 300/K-7
6236 Neff Rd 48458 810-591-9357
Lance Sumpter, prin. Fax 591-5632

Mount Morris Consolidated SD 1,800/K-12
12356 Walter St 48458 810-591-8760
Renae Galsterer, supt. Fax 591-7469
www.mtmorrisschools.org
Montague ES 300/2-5
344 W Mount Morris St 48458 810-591-3750
Melissa Bellinger, prin. Fax 591-8079
Moore ES 300/2-5
1201 Wisner St 48458 810-591-6090
John Strickert, prin. Fax 591-8077
Mount Morris MS 400/6-8
12356 Walter St 48458 810-591-7100
Allen Peter, prin. Fax 591-7105
Pinehurst Early ES 300/K-1
1013 Pinehurst Blvd 48458 810-591-2760
Kathy Lintz, prin. Fax 591-8070

St. Mary S 100/PK-8
11208 N Saginaw St 48458 810-686-4790
Rex Hart, prin. Fax 686-4749

Mount Pleasant, Isabella, Pop. 25,361
Beal City Public Schools 700/PK-12
3180 W Beal City Rd 48858 989-644-3901
William Chilman, supt. Fax 644-5847
www.bealcityschools.net
Beal City ES 300/PK-6
3180 W Beal City Rd 48858 989-644-2740
Jason Johnston, prin. Fax 644-5847

Mount Pleasant SD 3,300/K-12
720 N Kinney Ave 48858 989-775-2300
Jennifer Verleger, supt. Fax 775-2309
www.mtpleasant.edzone.net
Fancher ES 300/4-6
801 S Kinney Ave 48858 989-775-2230
Katie Rinke, prin. Fax 775-2234
Ganiard ES 300/K-3
101 S Adams St 48858 989-775-2240
Marcy Stout, prin. Fax 775-2244
McGuire ES 300/4-6
4883 Crosslanes St 48858 989-775-2260
Susan Renaud, prin. Fax 775-2264
Pullen ES 400/K-3
251 S Brown St 48858 989-775-2270
Diane Falsetta, prin. Fax 775-2274
Vowles ES 400/K-4
1560 Watson Rd 48858 989-775-2280
Kim Bishop, prin. Fax 775-2284
West IS 500/7-8
440 S Bradley St 48858 989-775-2220
Dana Calkins, prin. Fax 775-2229

Mount Pleasant SDA S 50/1-8
1730 E Pickard Rd 48858 989-773-3231
Tamara Draves, prin.
Sacred Heart Academy 300/PK-6
200 S Franklin St 48858 989-773-9530
Mary Kay Yonker, prin. Fax 772-9056
Saginaw Chippewa Academy 100/PK-6
7498 E Broadway Rd 48858 989-775-4453
Kara Hotchkiss, prin.
St. Joseph the Worker S 100/K-6
2091 N Winn Rd 48858 989-644-3970
Mary Hauck, prin. Fax 644-2026

Muir, Ionia, Pop. 595
Ionia SD
Supt. — See Ionia
Twin Rivers ES 200/K-5
435 Lou Lemke Ln 48860 616-522-0005
Dayna Ellis, prin. Fax 321-9825

Munising, Alger, Pop. 2,289
Munising SD 700/K-12
810 State Highway M28 W 49862 906-387-2251
Pete Kelto, supt. Fax 387-5416
www.munisingschools.com
Mather ES 300/K-5
411 Elm Ave 49862 906-387-2102
Dee Jay Paquette, prin. Fax 387-4774

Muskegon, Muskegon, Pop. 37,002
Fruitport Community SD
Supt. — See Fruitport
Beach ES 300/K-5
2741 Heights Ravenna Rd 49444 231-773-8996
Courtney Stahl, prin. Fax 777-3455
Shettler ES 400/K-5
2187 Shettler Rd 49444 231-737-7595
Janelle Duffey, prin. Fax 733-1328

Mona Shores SD
Supt. — See Norton Shores
Campbell ES 400/K-5
1355 Greenwich Rd 49441 231-755-2550
Andy Hogston, prin. Fax 759-1260

Muskegon SD 4,300/PK-12
349 W Webster Ave 49440 231-720-2000
Justin Jennings, supt. Fax 720-2050
www.muskegonpublicschools.org
Glenside ECC PK-PK
1213 W Hackley Ave 49441 231-720-2560
Diane Aamodt, prin.
Lakeside ES 500/PK-6
2312 Denmark St 49441 231-720-2300
Gay Monroe, prin. Fax 720-2325
Marquette ES 600/PK-6
480 Bennett St 49442 231-720-2600
Keri Cooper, prin. Fax 720-2658
Moon ES 400/PK-6
1826 Hoyt St 49442 231-720-2700
Okeelah McBride, prin. Fax 720-2735
Muskegon MS 600/7-8
1150 Amity Ave 49442 231-720-3000
Paul Kurdziel, prin. Fax 720-3025
Nelson ES 400/PK-6
550 W Grand Ave 49441 231-720-2200
Brian Gamm, prin. Fax 720-2215
Oakview ES 500/PK-6
1420 Madison St 49442 231-720-2450
L. Williams-Loudermill, prin. Fax 720-2490

Oakridge SD 1,800/PK-12
275 S Wolf Lake Rd 49442 231-788-7100
Tom Livezey, supt. Fax 788-7114
www.oakridgeschools.org
Oakridge Lower ES 600/PK-3
120 N Park St 49442 231-788-7600
Joey Bennink, prin. Fax 788-7614
Oakridge MS 300/7-8
251 S Wolf Lake Rd 49442 231-788-7400
Jason McVoy, prin. Fax 788-7414
Oakridge Upper ES 400/4-6
481 S Wolf Lake Rd 49442 231-788-7500
Troy Moran, prin. Fax 788-7514

Orchard View SD 2,300/PK-12
35 S Sheridan Dr 49442 231-760-1300
Jim Nielsen, supt. Fax 760-1323
www.orchardview.org
Cardinal ES 700/2-5
2310 Marquette Ave 49442 231-760-1700
Brenda Hodge, prin. Fax 760-1655
Orchard View Early ES 400/PK-1
2820 MacArthur Rd 49442 231-760-1850
Tom Hamilton, prin. Fax 760-1840
Orchard View MS 600/6-8
35 S Sheridan Dr 49442 231-760-1500
Hal Holman, prin. Fax 760-1506

Reeths-Puffer SD 3,700/PK-12
991 W Giles Rd 49445 231-744-4736
Steve Edwards, supt. Fax 744-9497
www.reeths-puffer.org
Central ES 400/PK-4
1807 W Giles Rd 49445 231-744-1693
Cody Hamilton, prin. Fax 744-0507
McMillan ECC 200/PK-PK
2885 Hyde Park Rd 49445 231-766-3443
Robyn Fisher, dir. Fax 744-2906
Reeths-Puffer ES 500/K-4
874 E Giles Rd 49445 231-744-4777
Paul Klimsza, prin. Fax 744-2815
Reeths-Puffer IS 600/5-6
1500 N Getty St 49445 231-744-9280
Nate Smith, prin. Fax 744-7922
Other Schools – See North Muskegon, Twin Lake

Michigan Dunes Montessori S 50/PK-3
5248 Henry St 49441 231-798-7293
Muskegon Catholic Central S 200/PK-6
1145 W Laketon Ave 49441 231-755-2201
Stephanie Weber, prin. Fax 755-2744
Muskegon Christian S 300/PK-6
1220 Eastgate St 49442 231-773-3221
Dan DeKam, admin. Fax 773-1647
West Shore Lutheran S 100/PK-8
3225 Roosevelt Rd 49441 231-755-1048
Bradley Feenstra, prin. Fax 755-6942

Napoleon, Jackson, Pop. 1,230
Napoleon Community SD 1,400/K-12
PO Box 308 49261 517-536-8667
James Graham, supt. Fax 536-8006
www.napoleonschools.org
Eby ES 600/K-5
PO Box 308 49261 517-536-8667
Michel McGonegal, prin. Fax 536-8029
Napoleon MS 300/6-8
PO Box 308 49261 517-536-8667
Chris Adams, prin. Fax 536-8005

Nashville, Barry, Pop. 1,609
Maple Valley SD
Supt. — See Vermontville
Fuller Street ES 200/PK-2
251 Fuller St 49073 517-852-9468
Cindy Trebian, prin. Fax 852-1640

Negaunee, Marquette, Pop. 4,500
Negaunee SD 1,500/PK-12
101 S Pioneer Ave 49866 906-475-4157
Dan Skewis, supt. Fax 475-5107
www.negaunee.k12.mi.us
Lakeview ES 600/PK-4
200 Croix St 49866 906-475-7803
Julie Peterson, prin. Fax 475-5764
Negaunee MS 400/5-8
102 W Case St 49866 906-475-7866
Michael McCollum, prin. Fax 475-6408

Marquette Adventist S K-8
270 US Highway 41 E 49866 906-475-4488

Newaygo, Newaygo, Pop. 1,944
Newaygo County RESA
Supt. — See Fremont
Neway Center 100/PK-PK
585 Fremont St 49337 231-652-3700

Newaygo SD 1,600/K-12
PO Box 820 49337 231-652-6984
Dr. Peggy Mathis, supt. Fax 652-6505
www.newaygo.net
Matson Upper ES 400/3-4
PO Box 820 49337 231-652-2100
Adam DeShano, prin. Fax 652-9705
Newaygo MS 500/5-8
PO Box 820 49337 231-652-1285
Steve Bush, prin. Fax 652-9704
Wilsie ES 300/K-2
PO Box 820 49337 231-652-6371
Candy Wells, prin. Fax 652-9706

New Baltimore, Macomb, Pop. 11,927
Anchor Bay SD
Supt. — See Casco
Anchor Bay MS North 1,000/6-8
52805 Ashley Dr 48047 586-725-7373
James Thiede, prin. Fax 725-6760
Anchor Bay MS South 500/6-8
48650 Sugarbush Rd 48047 586-949-4510
Phil Latona, prin. Fax 949-4739
Ashley ES 500/K-5
52347 Ashley St 48047 586-725-2801
Melissa VanHulle, prin. Fax 725-4426
ECC PK-PK
52680 Washington St 48047 586-716-7862
Barbara Healey, admin. Fax 716-7864
Lighthouse ES 500/K-5
51880 Washington St 48047 586-725-6404
Sandra Youngert, prin. Fax 725-4016
Naldrett ES 200/K-5
47800 Sugarbush Rd 48047 586-949-1212
Heidi Stephenson, prin. Fax 598-7666
Schmidt ES 300/K-5
33700 Hooker Rd 48047 586-725-7541
Anne Berglund, prin. Fax 725-7590
Sugarbush ES 300/K-5
48400 Sugarbush Rd 48047 586-598-7660
Yolanda White, prin. Fax 598-7671

Newberry, Luce, Pop. 1,471
Tahquamenon Area SD 700/K-12
700 Newberry Ave 49868 906-293-3226
Fax 293-3709
www.taschools.org
Newberry ES 400/K-6
700 Newberry Ave 49868 906-293-3226
Stacy Price, prin. Fax 293-3709

New Boston, Wayne
Huron SD 2,500/K-12
32044 Huron River Dr 48164 734-782-2441
Richard Naughton, supt. Fax 783-0338
www.huronschools.org
Brown ES 500/K-5
25485 Middlebelt Rd 48164 734-782-2716
Cory Pengelly, prin. Fax 783-0326
Miller ES 500/K-5
18955 Hannan Rd 48164 734-753-4421
Jean Robinson, prin. Fax 753-4270
Renton JHS 600/6-8
31578 Huron River Dr 48164 734-782-2483
Kurt Mrocko, prin. Fax 783-0327

St. John Lutheran S 200/PK-8
28320 Waltz Rd 48164 734-654-6366
Adrienne Thompson, prin. Fax 654-3675
St. Stephen S 200/K-8
18800 Huron River Dr 48164 734-753-4175
Christine Vaughan, prin. Fax 753-4579

New Buffalo, Berrien, Pop. 1,853
New Buffalo Area SD 600/K-12
PO Box 280 49117 269-469-6010
Dr. Jeffrey Leslie, supt. Fax 469-3315
www.nbas.org/
New Buffalo ES 200/K-5
12291 Lubke Rd 49117 269-469-6060
Adam Bowen, prin. Fax 469-6065
New Buffalo MS 100/6-8
PO Box 280 49117 269-469-6003
Wayne Butler, prin. Fax 469-6017

St. Mary of the Lake S 100/PK-PK
704 W Merchant St 49117 269-469-1515
Jamie Bartelheim, dir. Fax 469-3772

New Era, Oceana, Pop. 447
Shelby SD
Supt. — See Shelby
New Era ES 200/4-5
2752 Hillcrest Dr 49446 231-861-2662
Beth Pranger, prin. Fax 861-2473

New Era Christian S 100/PK-8
1901 Oak Ave 49446 231-861-5450
Phillip Moroc, prin. Fax 861-5450

New Haven, Macomb, Pop. 4,447
New Haven Community SD 1,200/PK-12
PO Box 482000 48048 586-749-5123
Todd Robinson, supt. Fax 749-6307
newhaven.misd.net/
New Haven ES 600/PK-5
PO Box 482000 48048 586-749-8360
Robert McCabe, prin. Fax 749-8365
Other Schools – See Ray

New Hudson, Oakland
South Lyon Community SD
Supt. — See South Lyon
Dolsen ES 400/K-5
56775 Rice St 48165 248-573-8400
Megan Goodemoot, prin. Fax 486-4322

New Lothrop, Shiawassee, Pop. 573
New Lothrop Area SD 900/PK-12
PO Box 339 48460 810-638-5091
Dr. Anthony Berthiaume Ph.D., supt. Fax 638-7277
www.newlothrop.k12.mi.us
New Lothrop ES 500/PK-6
PO Box 279 48460 810-638-5026
Michelle Barrett, prin. Fax 638-7289

Newport, Monroe
Jefferson SD
Supt. — See Monroe
North ES 200/2-4
8281 N Dixie Hwy 48166 734-586-6784
Millie Grow, prin. Fax 586-8854

St. Charles S 200/PK-8
8125 Swan Creek Rd 48166 734-586-2531
Catherine Grinn, prin. Fax 586-3900

Niles, Berrien, Pop. 11,170
Brandywine Community SD 1,200/PK-12
1830 S 3rd St 49120 269-684-7150
Karen Weimer, supt. Fax 684-8998
www.brandywinebobcats.org
Brandywine ES, 2428 S 13th St 49120 400/3-6
James Boger, prin. 269-684-8574
Merritt ES 300/PK-2
1620 LaSalle Ave 49120 269-684-6511
Matthew Severin, prin. Fax 684-8940

Niles Community SD 3,600/PK-12
111 Spruce St 49120 269-683-0732
Dr. Dan Applegate Ed.D., supt. Fax 684-6337
nilesschools.schoolwires.net
Ballard ES 700/K-5
1601 W Chicago Rd 49120 269-683-5900
David Eichenberg, prin. Fax 684-9527
Eastside Connections S 300/K-8
315 N 14th St 49120 269-683-2585
Joe Racht, prin. Fax 684-1534
Howard-Ellis ES 500/K-5
2788 Mannix St 49120 269-683-4633
Michelle Asmus, prin. Fax 684-9534
Northside Child Development Center 100/PK-K
2020 N 5th St 49120 269-683-1982
Dr. Zech Hoyt Ed.D., prin. Fax 684-9542
Ring Lardner MS 500/6-8
801 N 17th St 49120 269-683-6610
Adam Burtsfield, prin. Fax 684-9524

Niles Adventist S 100/PK-8
110 N Fairview Ave 49120 269-683-5444
William Crawford, prin. Fax 683-9885

St. Mary S 100/PK-6
217 S Lincoln Ave 49120 269-683-9191
Sharon Gregorski, prin. Fax 683-8118

North Adams, Hillsdale, Pop. 473
North Adams-Jerome SD 300/K-12
4555 Knowles Rd 49262 517-287-4263
Wes Johnson, supt. Fax 287-4722
www.najps.org
North Adams-Jerome ES 100/K-5
4555 Knowles Rd 49262 517-287-4278
Wes Johnson, prin. Fax 287-4275

North Branch, Lapeer, Pop. 1,023
North Branch Area SD 2,400/K-12
PO Box 3620 48461 810-688-3570
James D. Fish, supt. Fax 688-7010
www.nbbroncos.net
Fox ES 400/5-6
PO Box 3620 48461 810-688-3284
Cindy Howe, prin. Fax 688-2930
North Branch ES 800/K-4
PO Box 3620 48461 810-688-3041
Greg Matheson, prin. Fax 688-8320
North Branch MS 400/7-8
PO Box 3620 48461 810-688-4431
Cindy Howe, prin. Fax 688-4344

North Muskegon, Muskegon, Pop. 3,727
North Muskegon SD 1,000/K-12
1600 Mills Ave 49445 231-719-4100
Dr. Curt Babcock, supt. Fax 744-0739
www.nmps.net
North Muskegon ES 500/K-5
1600 Mills Ave 49445 231-719-4200
Steve Sanocki, prin. Fax 719-4207
North Muskegon MS 200/6-8
1507 Mills Ave 49445 231-719-4110
Ken Byard, prin. Fax 719-4156

Reeths-Puffer SD
Supt. — See Muskegon
Reeths-Puffer MS 600/7-8
1911 W Giles Rd 49445 231-744-4721
Jennifer Anderson, prin. Fax 744-6049

Northport, Leelanau, Pop. 512
Northport SD 200/K-12
PO Box 188 49670 231-386-5153
Neil Wetherbee, supt. Fax 386-9838
www.northportps.org
Northport S 200/K-12
PO Box 188 49670 231-386-5153
Neil Wetherbee, supt. Fax 386-9838

Northville, Oakland, Pop. 5,889
Northville SD 7,300/K-12
501 W Main St 48167 248-349-3400
Mary Gallagher, supt. Fax 347-6928
www.northvilleschools.org
Amerman ES 500/K-5
847 N Center St 48167 248-344-8405
Marco Marando, prin. Fax 380-4019
Hillside MS 1,000/6-8
775 N Center St 48167 248-344-8493
William Jones, prin. Fax 334-8480
Meads Mill MS 800/6-8
16700 Franklin Rd, 248-344-8435
Brad O'Neill, prin. Fax 334-1830
Moraine ES 400/K-5
46811 8 Mile Rd 48167 248-344-8473
Denise Bryan, prin. Fax 344-8408
Ridge Wood ES 600/K-5
49775 6 Mile Rd, 248-349-7602
Heather Bauer, prin. Fax 349-4147
Silver Springs ES 500/K-5
19801 Silver Spring Dr 48167 248-344-8410
Katie Booth, prin. Fax 344-8404
Winchester ES 500/K-5
16141 Winchester Dr, 248-344-8415
Kelly Lindsay, prin. Fax 344-8402
Other Schools – See Novi

Northville Christian S 400/PK-8
41355 6 Mile Rd, 248-348-9031
Ken Storey, prin. Fax 348-5423
Our Lady of Victory S 400/K-8
132 Orchard Dr 48167 248-349-3610
Dan Timmis, prin. Fax 380-7247
St. Paul Lutheran S 100/PK-8
201 Elm St 48167 248-349-3146
Jared Weiss, prin. Fax 349-7493

Norton Shores, Muskegon, Pop. 23,577
Mona Shores SD 3,800/K-12
121 Randall Rd 49441 231-780-4751
Greg Helmer, supt. Fax 780-2099
www.monashores.net
Churchill ES 300/K-5
961 Porter Rd 49441 231-798-1276
Lowell Whitaker, prin. Fax 798-2012
Lincoln Park ES 400/K-5
2951 Leon St 49441 231-755-1257
Karen Abraham, prin. Fax 759-2427
Mona Shores MS 900/6-8
1700 Woodside Rd 49441 231-759-8506
Doug Ammeraal, prin. Fax 755-0514
Ross Park ES 400/K-5
121 Randall Rd 49441 231-798-1773
Eve Mills, prin. Fax 798-8741
Other Schools – See Muskegon

Norway, Dickinson, Pop. 2,807
Norway-Vulcan Area SD 700/PK-12
300 Section St 49870 906-563-9552
Louis Steigerwald, supt. Fax 563-5169
www.nvknights.org
Norway ES, 300 Section St 49870 300/PK-4
Rico Meneghini, prin. 906-563-9543
Vulcan MS, 300 Section St 49870 200/5-8
Rico Meneghini, prin. 906-563-9563

Holy Spirit S 100/PK-8
201 Saginaw St 49870 906-563-8817
Melissa Menghini, prin. Fax 563-8854

Novi, Oakland, Pop. 54,165
Northville SD
Supt. — See Northville
Thornton Creek ES 500/K-5
46180 W 9 Mile Rd 48374 248-344-8475
Jennifer Bennett, prin. Fax 344-8423

Novi Community SD 6,300/PK-12
25345 Taft Rd 48374 248-449-1200
Dr. Steven Matthews, supt. Fax 449-1219
www.novi.k12.mi.us
Deerfield ES 400/K-4
26500 Wixom Rd 48374 248-449-1700
Julie Bedford, prin. Fax 449-1709
Novi ECC PK-PK
25745 Taft Rd 48374 248-675-3431
Ann Hansen, coord. Fax 675-3435
Novi Meadows ES 500/5-5
25549 Taft Rd 48374 248-449-1250
Lisa Fenchel, prin. Fax 449-1259
Novi Meadows ES 500/6-6
25299 Taft Rd 48374 248-449-1270
John Brickey, prin. Fax 449-1279
Novi MS 1,100/7-8
49000 W 11 Mile Rd 48374 248-449-1600
Stephanie Schriner, prin. Fax 449-1619
Novi Woods ES 500/K-4
25195 Taft Rd 48374 248-449-1230
David Ascher, prin. Fax 449-1239
Orchard Hills ES 400/K-4
41900 Quince Dr 48375 248-449-1400
Pam Quitiquit, prin. Fax 449-1419
Parkview ES 500/K-4
45825 W 11 Mile Rd 48374 248-449-1220
Jenifer Michos, prin. Fax 449-1229
Village Oaks ES 500/K-4
23333 Willowbrook 48375 248-449-1300
Alexander Ofili, prin. Fax 449-1319

Walled Lake Consolidated SD
Supt. — See Walled Lake
Hickory Woods ES 600/PK-5
30655 Novi Rd 48377 248-956-2600
Patricia Chinn, prin. Fax 956-2605
Meadowbrook ES 600/K-5
29200 Meadowbrook Rd 48377 248-956-2700
Christopher Peal Ph.D., prin. Fax 956-2705

Franklin Road Christian S 300/K-12
40800 W 13 Mile Rd 48377 248-668-7100
Daniel Robinson, admin. Fax 668-7101

Oakland, Oakland
Lake Orion Community SD
Supt. — See Lake Orion
Oakview MS 600/6-8
917 Lake George Rd 48363 248-693-0321
Sarah Manzo, prin. Fax 693-5419

Rochester Community SD
Supt. — See Rochester
Delta Kelly ES 600/K-5
3880 Adams Rd 48363 248-726-3500
Amanda McKay, prin. Fax 726-3505

Eagle Creek Academy 100/PK-8
3739 Kern Rd 48363 248-475-9999
Catherine Hammond, prin. Fax 475-1616

Oakley, Saginaw, Pop. 289

Christ Lutheran S 50/K-8
16070 W Brady Rd 48649 989-845-2611
Alan Schaffer, prin.

Oak Park, Oakland, Pop. 28,448
Berkley SD 4,300/K-12
14700 Lincoln St 48237 248-837-8000
Dennis McDavid, supt. Fax 544-5835
www.berkleyschools.org
Norup International S 800/K-8
14450 Manhattan St 48237 248-837-8300
Paul Yowchuang, prin. Fax 547-5558
Other Schools – See Berkley, Huntington Woods

Ferndale SD
Supt. — See Ferndale
Ferndale Upper ES 200/3-5
24220 Rosewood St 48237 248-547-0880
Katie Jeffrey, prin. Fax 586-8780

Oak Park SD 4,500/PK-12
13900 Granzon St 48237 248-336-7700
Dr. Daveda Colbert, supt. Fax 336-7738
www.oakparkschools.org
Einstein ES 600/PK-5
14001 Northend Ave 48237 248-336-7640
Dr. Joann Wright, prin. Fax 336-7648
Key ES 600/PK-5
23400 Jerome St 48237 248-336-7610
William Washington, prin. Fax 336-7618
Oak Park Preparatory Academy 500/7-8
22180 Parklawn St 48237 248-336-7780
Nickolus South, prin. Fax 336-7738
Pepper ES 400/PK-5
24301 Church St 48237 248-336-7700
Emanuel Haley, prin. Fax 336-7738

Beth Jacob School for Girls 300/K-12
14390 W 10 Mile Rd 48237 248-544-9070
Rabbi Zev Poss, prin. Fax 544-4662

Okemos, Ingham, Pop. 20,807
Okemos SD 4,000/K-12
4406 Okemos Rd 48864 517-706-5000
Alena Zachery-Ross, supt. Fax 349-6235
www.okemosschools.net
Bennett Woods ES 400/K-4
2650 Bennett Rd 48864 517-706-5100
Noelle Palasty, prin. Fax 351-1912
Chippewa MS 600/7-8
4000 Okemos Rd 48864 517-706-4800
Jody Noble, prin. Fax 347-9824
Cornell ES 400/K-4
4371 Cornell Rd 48864 517-706-5300
Tara Fry, prin. Fax 349-2080
Hiawatha ES 400/K-4
1900 Jolly Rd 48864 517-706-4500
Gary Kinzer, prin. Fax 347-6770
Kinawa IS 600/5-6
1900 Kinawa Dr 48864 517-706-4700
Steve Stierley, prin. Fax 347-4189
Okemos Montessori S at Central 300/K-4
4406 Okemos Rd 48864 517-706-5400
Sue Hallman, prin. Fax 349-9833

St. Martha S 100/PK-8
1100 W Grand River Ave 48864 517-349-3322
Monica Dowell, prin. Fax 349-3322

Olivet, Eaton, Pop. 1,574
Olivet Community SD 1,500/K-12
255 First St 49076 269-749-9129
Rocky Aldrich, supt. Fax 749-9701
www.olivetschools.org
Olivet MS 600/4-8
255 First St 49076 269-749-9953
Stephen Williams, prin. Fax 749-9701
Persons ES 400/K-3
4425 W Butterfield Hwy 49076 269-749-4611
Brock Peters, prin. Fax 749-4621

Onaway, Presque Isle, Pop. 861
Onaway Area SD 700/K-12
4549 M 33 49765 989-733-4950
Rod Fullerton, supt. Fax 733-8612
www.onawayschools.com/
Onaway ES 300/K-5
4549 M 33 49765 989-733-4900
Mindy Horn, prin. Fax 733-4949
Onaway MS 200/6-8
4549 M 33 49765 989-733-4850
Marty Mix, prin. Fax 733-4899

Onaway SDA S 50/K-8
PO Box 156 49765 989-733-8600
Brenda Sutherland, prin. Fax 733-9916

Onekama, Manistee, Pop. 404
Onekama Consolidated SD 400/K-12
5016 Main St 49675 231-889-4251
Kevin Hughes, supt. Fax 889-3720
ocs.manistee.org
Onekama ES 200/K-5
5016 Main St 49675 231-889-5521
Gina Hagen, prin. Fax 889-9567

Onsted, Lenawee, Pop. 906
Onsted Community SD 1,500/K-12
10109 Slee Rd 49265 517-467-2173
Steve Head, supt. Fax 467-5600
www.onsted.k12.mi.us
Onsted ES 600/K-5
10109 Slee Rd 49265 517-467-7046
Marsha Davis, prin. Fax 467-5604
Onsted MS 400/6-8
10109 Slee Rd 49265 517-467-2168
Alaina Ellison, prin. Fax 467-5603

Ontonagon, Ontonagon, Pop. 1,473
Ontonagon Area SD 400/K-12
701 Parker Ave 49953 906-813-0614
James Bobula, supt. Fax 813-0615
www.oasd.k12.mi.us
Ontonagon Area S 400/K-12
701 Parker Ave 49953 906-813-0614
James Bobula, admin. Fax 813-0615

Orchard Lake, Oakland

Our Lady of Refuge S 300/PK-8
3750 Commerce Rd 48324 248-682-3422
Robert Pyles, prin. Fax 683-2265

Ortonville, Oakland, Pop. 1,423
Brandon SD 2,900/PK-12
1025 S Ortonville Rd 48462 248-627-1800
Dr. Matthew Outlaw, supt. Fax 627-4533
www.brandonschooldistrict.org
Brandon MS 500/6-8
609 S Ortonville Rd 48462 248-627-1830
Mike Tucker, prin. Fax 627-7201
Harvey-Swanson ES 400/PK-5
209 Varsity Dr 48462 248-627-1850
Andrew Phillips, prin. Fax 627-1858
Oakwood ES 300/K-5
2839 Oakwood Rd 48462 248-627-1880
Coy Stewart, prin. Fax 627-1888

Oscoda, Iosco, Pop. 877
Oscoda Area SD 900/K-12
PO Box 694 48750 989-739-2033
Scott Moore, supt. Fax 739-2325
www.oscodaschools.org
Richardson ES 300/K-6
PO Box 694 48750 989-739-9173
Tamara Pichla, prin. Fax 739-2510

Ossineke, Alpena, Pop. 932
Alpena SD
Supt. — See Alpena

Sanborn ES 200/K-5
12170 US Highway 23 S 49766 989-358-5800
Pauline Burnham, prin. Fax 358-5805

Otisville, Genesee, Pop. 856
LakeVille Community SD 1,400/PK-12
11107 Washburn Rd 48463 810-591-3980
Michael Lytle, supt. Fax 591-6538
www.lakevilleschools.org/
Lakeville MS 300/6-8
11107 Washburn Rd 48463 810-591-3945
Kelli-Ann Fazer, prin. Fax 591-6632
Otisville ES 100/PK-K
11107 Washburn Rd 48463 810-591-3985
Stephanie Stiles, prin. Fax 631-6050
Other Schools – See Columbiaville, Otter Lake

Otsego, Allegan, Pop. 3,879
Otsego SD 2,300/PK-12
400 Sherwood St 49078 269-692-6066
Jeffrey Haase, supt. Fax 692-6074
www.otsegops.org
Dix Street ES 300/PK-5
503 Dix St 49078 269-692-6099
Dr. Mark Rollandini, prin. Fax 692-6130
Otsego MS 600/6-8
540 Washington St 49078 269-692-6199
Melissa Koenig, prin. Fax 692-6228
Washington Street ES 400/PK-5
538 Washington St 49078 269-692-6069
Heather Badders, prin. Fax 692-6123
Other Schools – See Kalamazoo

Otsego Christian Academy 50/PK-11
247 E Allegan St 49078 269-694-6738
Lydia Hutchens, admin.
St. Margaret Catholic S 100/PK-8
736 S Farmer St 49078 269-694-2951
Jan Hall, prin. Fax 694-4520

Ottawa Lake, Monroe
Whiteford Agricultural SD 700/K-12
6655 Consear Rd 49267 734-856-1443
Valerie Orr, supt. Fax 854-6463
www.whiteford.k12.mi.us
Whiteford ES 300/K-5
6655 Consear Rd 49267 734-856-1443
Michaele Shepherd, prin. Fax 856-4724
Whiteford MS 200/6-8
6655 Consear Rd 49267 734-856-1443
Kelli Tuller, prin. Fax 856-2564

Otter Lake, Lapeer, Pop. 379
LakeVille Community SD
Supt. — See Otisville
Otter Lake ES 200/1-2
6313 Hart Lake Rd 48464 810-538-3640
Stephanie Stiles, prin. Fax 793-1854

Ovid, Clinton, Pop. 1,574
Ovid-Elsie Area SD
Supt. — See Elsie
Leonard ES 300/PK-2
732 Mabbit Rd 48866 989-834-5029
Kris Kirby, prin. Fax 834-5242

Owendale, Huron, Pop. 236
Owendale-Gagetown Area SD 200/K-12
7166 E Main St 48754 989-678-4261
Terri Falkenberg, supt. Fax 678-4284
www.owengage.org/
Owendale-Gagetown ES 100/K-5
7166 E Main St 48754 989-678-4141
Terri Falkenberg, prin. Fax 678-0920

Owosso, Shiawassee, Pop. 14,957
Owosso SD 3,300/PK-12
PO Box 340 48867 989-723-8131
Dr. Andrea Tuttle Ed.D., supt. Fax 723-7777
www.owosso.k12.mi.us
Bentley Bright Beginnings ECC 100/PK-PK
1375 W North St 48867 989-725-5770
Amanda Rowell, dir. Fax 729-5694
Bryant ES 500/K-5
925 Hampton St 48867 989-723-4355
Stephen Brooks, prin. Fax 729-5666
Central ES 400/K-5
600 W Oliver St 48867 989-723-2790
Bridgit Spielman, prin. Fax 723-3046
Emerson ES 500/K-5
515 E Oliver St 48867 989-725-7361
Terry Sedlar, prin. Fax 729-5451
Owosso MS 700/6-8
219 N Water St 48867 989-723-3460
Rich Collins, prin. Fax 729-5760

St. Paul S 100/PK-8
718 W Main St 48867 989-725-7766
Laura Heatwole, prin. Fax 725-9824
Salem Lutheran S 100/PK-8
520 W Stewart St 48867 989-725-2234
Anthony Perry, prin. Fax 725-2429

Oxford, Oakland, Pop. 3,399
Oxford Community SD 5,300/PK-12
10 N Washington St 48371 248-969-5000
Tim Throne, supt. Fax 969-5016
www.oxfordschools.org
Axford ES 400/PK-2
74 Mechanic St 48371 248-969-5050
Chad Boyd, prin. Fax 969-5099
Clear Lake ES 500/PK-5
2085 W Drahner Rd 48371 248-969-5200
Brad Bigelow, prin. Fax 969-5216
Lakeville ES 400/PK-5
1400 E Lakeville Rd 48371 248-969-1850
Kristy Gibson-Marshall, prin. Fax 969-1855
Oxford Early Learning Center 100/PK-PK
105 Pontiac St 48371 248-969-5035
Washea Jackson, dir. Fax 969-1881

Oxford ES 500/3-5
109 Pontiac St 48371 248-969-5075
Jeff Brown, prin. Fax 969-5085
Oxford MS 1,100/6-8
1420 E Lakeville Rd 48371 248-969-1800
Dacia Beazley, prin. Fax 969-1840
Other Schools – See Leonard

Painesdale, Houghton
Adams Township SD 400/K-12
PO Box 37 49955 906-482-0599
Tim Keteri, supt. Fax 487-5999
www.adams.k12.mi.us
Other Schools – See South Range

Paradise, Chippewa
Whitefish Township Community SD 50/K-12
7221 N M 123 49768 906-492-3353
Tom McKee, supt. Fax 492-3254
whitefish.eupschools.org
Whitefish Township S 50/K-12
7221 N M 123 49768 906-492-3353
Thomas McKee, prin. Fax 492-3254

Parchment, Kalamazoo, Pop. 1,738
Parchment SD 1,700/PK-12
520 N Orient St 49004 269-488-1050
Matthew Miller, supt. Fax 488-1060
www.parchmentschools.org
Parchment Central ES 300/K-5
516 N Orient St 49004 269-488-1000
Julia Kaemming, prin. Fax 488-1010
Parchment MS 400/6-8
307 N Riverview Dr 49004 269-488-1200
Jason Misner, prin. Fax 488-1210
Other Schools – See Kalamazoo

Paris, Newaygo
Big Jackson SD 50/K-6
4020 13 Mile Rd 49338 231-796-8947
Dr. Lori Clark, supt. Fax 796-2921
bigjackson.ncats.net/
Big Jackson ES 50/K-6
4020 13 Mile Rd 49338 231-796-8947
Rebecca Jackson, admin. Fax 796-2921

Parma, Jackson, Pop. 755
Western SD 2,900/PK-12
1400 S Dearing Rd 49269 517-841-8100
Michael Smajda, supt. Fax 841-8801
www.wsdpanthers.org
Parma ES 400/K-5
385 Elizabeth St 49269 517-841-8600
Susan Haney, prin. Fax 841-8806
Western MS 600/6-8
1400 S Dearing Rd 49269 517-841-8300
Ryan Tripp, prin. Fax 841-8803
Other Schools – See Spring Arbor

Paw Paw, Van Buren, Pop. 3,443
Paw Paw SD 2,200/K-12
119 Johnson Rd 49079 269-415-5200
Sonia Lark, supt. Fax 415-5201
www.ppps.org
Paw Paw Early ES 500/K-2
512 W North St 49079 269-415-5300
Melissa Remillard, prin. Fax 415-5301
Paw Paw Later ES 500/3-5
612 W North St 49079 269-415-5400
Jeremy Davison, prin. Fax 415-5401
Paw Paw MS 500/6-8
313 W Michigan Ave 49079 269-415-5500
Jerry McDaniel, prin. Fax 415-5501

St. Mary S 100/PK-5
508 E Paw Paw St 49079 269-657-3750
Michelle Radomsky, prin. Fax 657-4260
Trinity Lutheran S 100/PK-8
725 Pine St 49079 269-657-5921
Beverly Schafer, dean Fax 657-3359

Peck, Sanilac, Pop. 624
Peck Community SD 400/K-12
222 E Lapeer St 48466 810-378-5171
Frank Johnson, supt. Fax 378-5116
www.peck.k12.mi.us
Peck ES 200/K-6
222 E Lapeer St 48466 810-378-5200
Bill Kerr, prin. Fax 378-5116

Pellston, Emmet, Pop. 782
Pellston SD 600/PK-12
172 N Park St 49769 231-539-8682
Monique Dean, supt. Fax 539-8838
www.pellstonschools.org/
Pellston ES 200/PK-5
172 N Park St 49769 231-539-8421
Monique Dean, prin. Fax 539-8118

Pentwater, Oceana, Pop. 845
Pentwater SD 300/K-12
600 Park St 49449 231-869-4100
Scott Karaptian, supt. Fax 869-4535
www.pentwater.k12.mi.us
Pentwater S 300/K-12
600 Park St 49449 231-869-4100
Scott Karaptian, prin. Fax 869-4535

Perry, Shiawassee, Pop. 2,154
Perry SD 1,300/K-12
2665 W Britton Rd 48872 517-625-3108
Mike Foster, supt. Fax 625-6256
www.perry.k12.mi.us
Perry ES 400/K-4
401 N Watkins 48872 517-625-3101
Jackie Staib, prin. Fax 625-5003
Perry MS 400/5-8
2775 W Britton Rd 48872 517-625-6196
Matt Schmidtfranz, prin. Fax 625-0120

Petersburg, Monroe, Pop. 1,129
Summerfield SD 700/K-12
17555 Ida West Rd 49270 734-279-1035
John Hewitt, supt. Fax 279-1448
www.summerfield.k12.mi.us
Summerfield ES 400/K-6
232 E Elm St 49270 734-279-1013
Jodi Bucher, prin. Fax 279-1017

Petoskey, Emmet, Pop. 5,571
Petoskey SD 2,900/K-12
1130 Howard St 49770 231-348-2100
Dr. John Scholten Ed.D., supt. Fax 348-2342
www.petoskeyschools.org
Central ES 300/K-5
410 State St 49770 231-348-2110
Cal Prins, prin. Fax 348-2402
Lincoln ES 300/K-5
616 Connable Ave 49770 231-348-2120
Mike Frampus, prin. Fax 348-2471
Montessori ES 50/K-5
1560 E Mitchell Rd 49770 231-348-2190
Kim Maves, admin. Fax 347-4304
Ottawa ES 400/K-5
871 Kalamazoo Ave 49770 231-348-2130
Carol Thola, prin. Fax 348-2302
Petoskey MS 700/6-8
801 Northmen Dr 49770 231-348-2150
Jon Wilcox, prin. Fax 348-2234
Sheridan ES 300/K-5
1415 Howard St 49770 231-348-2140
Mark Oberman, prin. Fax 348-2444

Petoskey Montessori S 100/PK-5
1560 E Mitchell Rd 49770 231-348-2190
St. Francis Xavier S 300/PK-8
414 Michigan St 49770 231-347-3651
James Kanine, prin. Fax 347-3610

Pewamo, Ionia, Pop. 454
Pewamo-Westphalia SD
Supt. — See Westphalia
Pewamo ES 200/PK-5
430 W Jefferson St 48873 989-593-3488
Julie Farmer, prin. Fax 593-4118

St. Joseph S 100/1-8
PO Box 38 48873 989-593-3400
Patricia O'Mara, prin. Fax 593-3400

Pickford, Chippewa
Pickford SD 400/K-12
333 S Pleasant St 49774 906-647-6285
Angela Nettleton, supt. Fax 647-3706
pickford.eup.k12.mi.us/
Pickford S 300/K-12
333 S Pleasant St 49774 906-647-4028
Angela Nettleton, prin. Fax 647-3706

Pigeon, Huron, Pop. 1,203
Elkton-Pigeon-Bay Port Laker SD 900/PK-12
6136 Pigeon Rd 48755 989-453-4600
W. Brian Keim, supt. Fax 453-4609
www.lakerschools.org
Laker ES 400/PK-5
6436 Pigeon Rd 48755 989-453-4600
Kathy Dickens, prin. Fax 453-4629
Laker MS 200/6-8
6136 Pigeon Rd 48755 989-453-4600
Jonathon Good, prin. Fax 453-4609

Cross Lutheran S 100/PK-8
200 Ruppert St 48755 989-453-3330
Rev. Tim Loehrke, prin. Fax 453-3331
St. John Evangelical Lutheran S 50/PK-8
7379 Berne Rd 48755 989-453-2861
Rev. Steven Neuman, prin. Fax 453-2884

Pinckney, Livingston, Pop. 2,402
Pinckney Community SD 3,500/K-12
2130 E M 36 48169 810-225-3900
Richard Todd M.A., supt. Fax 225-3905
www.pinckneyschools.org
Country ES 300/K-3
2939 E M 36 48169 810-225-6600
Lester Sharon, prin. Fax 225-6605
Farley Hill ES 300/K-3
8110 Farley Rd 48169 810-225-6400
Yvonne Taylor, prin. Fax 225-6405
Navigator S 800/4-6
2150 E M 36 48169 810-225-5300
Ruth Badalucco, prin. Fax 225-5305
Pathfinder S 600/7-8
2100 E M 36 48169 810-225-5200
Eric Ray, prin. Fax 225-5205

St. Mary S 200/PK-8
10601 Dexter Pinckney Rd 48169 734-878-5616
Veronica Kinsey, prin. Fax 878-2383

Pinconning, Bay, Pop. 1,286
Pinconning Area SD 1,300/PK-12
605 W 5th St 48650 989-308-0500
Michael Vieau, supt. Fax 879-4705
www.pasd.org/
Pinconning Area MS 300/6-8
605 W 5th St 48650 989-308-0503
Brady Palmer, prin. Fax 879-7258
Pinconning Central ES 400/PK-5
605 W 5th St 48650 989-308-0502
John Sanford, prin. Fax 879-2740
Other Schools – See Linwood

St. Michael S 100/PK-8
310 E 2nd St 48650 989-879-3063
Ashley Kanuszewski, prin. Fax 879-3626

Pittsford, Hillsdale
Pittsford Area SD 700/K-12
9304 Hamilton Rd 49271 517-523-3481
Deanna Edens, supt. Fax 523-3467
pittsfordk12.org
Pittsford ES 300/K-6
9304 Hamilton Rd 49271 517-523-3481
Deanna Edens, admin. Fax 523-3467

Pittsford ES 50/1-8
5085 S Waldron Rd 49271 517-523-4143
Andrea Szynkowski, prin.

Plainwell, Allegan, Pop. 3,755
Plainwell Community SD 2,700/PK-12
600 School Dr 49080 269-685-5823
Matthew Montange, supt. Fax 685-1108
www.plainwellschools.org
Gilkey ES 400/PK-5
707 S Woodhams St 49080 269-685-2424
Melissa Preston, prin. Fax 685-9742
Plainwell MS 600/6-8
720 Brigham St 49080 269-685-5813
Tasia Stamos, prin. Fax 685-2099
Starr ES 500/K-5
601 School Dr 49080 269-685-5835
Laurie Lanphear, prin. Fax 685-2027
Other Schools – See Kalamazoo

Plymouth, Wayne, Pop. 8,997
Plymouth-Canton Community SD 16,000/PK-12
454 S Harvey St 48170 734-416-2700
Monica Merritt, supt. Fax 416-4932
www.pccsk12.com
Allen Early Learning Academy PK-PK
11100 N Haggerty Rd 48170 734-416-3050
Peggy Kaczmarek, prin. Fax 416-4816
Bird ES 600/K-5
220 S Sheldon Rd 48170 734-416-3100
Catherine Williams, prin. Fax 455-9521
East MS 800/6-8
1042 S Mill St 48170 734-416-4950
Scott Burek, prin. Fax 416-4949
Farrand ES 400/K-5
41400 Greenbriar Ln 48170 734-582-6900
Carolyn Washington, prin. Fax 420-7022
Isbister ES 400/K-5
9300 N Canton Center Rd 48170 734-416-6050
Lee Harrison, prin. Fax 416-7681
Pioneer MS 800/6-8
46081 Ann Arbor Rd W 48170 734-416-2770
Kevin Rhein, prin. Fax 416-7569
Smith ES 500/K-5
1298 McKinley St 48170 734-416-4850
Dana Jones, prin. Fax 455-9522
West MS 800/6-8
44401 W Ann Arbor Trl 48170 734-416-7550
Clinton Smiley, prin. Fax 416-7648
Other Schools – See Canton

Metropolitan SDA Jr Academy 50/K-10
15585 N Haggerty Rd 48170 734-420-4044
Craig Morgan, prin. Fax 420-3710
Our Lady of Good Counsel S 600/K-8
1151 William St 48170 734-453-3053
Liz Ross, prin. Fax 357-5331
Spiritus Sanctus Academy 200/K-8
10450 Joy Rd 48170 734-414-8430
Sr. Maria Faustina, prin. Fax 414-8495

Pointe Aux Pins, Mackinac
Bois Blanc Pines SD 50/K-8
PO Box 876 49775 906-632-3373
Dr. Daniel Reattoir, supt. Fax 632-1125
boisblanc.eup.k12.mi.us
Pines S 50/K-8
PO Box 876 49775 231-634-7225
Wendy Spray, lead tchr. Fax 634-7225

Pontiac, Oakland, Pop. 57,635
Pontiac SD 4,400/K-12
47200 Woodward Ave 48342 248-451-6800
Kelley Williams, supt. Fax 451-6890
www.pontiac.k12.mi.us
Alcott ES 500/K-6
460 W Kennett Rd 48340 248-451-7910
Dr. Vanessa Carter, prin. Fax 451-7924
Herrington ES 400/K-6
541 Bay St 48342 248-451-7790
Dr. Petrina Hill, prin. Fax 451-7805
Owen ES 400/K-6
1700 Baldwin Ave 48340 248-451-7870
Natashia Smith, prin. Fax 451-8206
Pontiac MS 1,000/7-8
1275 N Perry St 48340 248-451-8010
Shana Jackson, prin. Fax 451-8034
Whitman ES 700/K-6
125 W Montcalm St 48342 248-451-7930
Nelson Henry, prin. Fax 451-7963
Other Schools – See Auburn Hills

Notre Dame Marist Acad - Lower Division 100/PK-5
1425 Giddings Rd 48340 248-373-2573
Diana Atkins, prin. Fax 373-2819
Notre Dame Marist Acad - Middle Division 200/6-8
1300 Giddings Rd 48340 248-373-5371
Brandon Jezdimir, prin. Fax 373-4707

Portage, Kalamazoo, Pop. 44,979
Portage SD 8,700/K-12
8107 Mustang Dr 49002 269-323-5000
Mark T. Bielang, supt. Fax 323-5001
www.portageps.org
Amberly ES 600/K-5
6637 Amberly St 49024 269-323-5900
Andy Fuehr, prin. Fax 323-5990
Angling Road ES 400/K-5
5340 Angling Rd 49024 269-323-6000
Heather Yankovich, prin. Fax 323-6090
Central ES 400/K-5
8422 S Westnedge Ave 49002 269-323-6100
William Dygert, prin. Fax 323-6190
Haverhill ES 400/K-5
6633 Haverhill Ave 49024 269-323-6200
Jeremy Zonts, prin. Fax 323-6290
Lake Center ES 600/K-5
10011 Portage Rd 49002 269-323-6300
Kelly Jensenius, prin. Fax 323-6390
Moorsbridge ES 500/K-5
7361 Moorsbridge Rd 49024 269-323-6400
Lori Kirshman, prin. Fax 323-6490
North MS 600/6-8
5808 Oregon Ave 49024 269-323-5700
Travis Thomsen, prin. Fax 323-5790
Portage Central MS 700/6-8
8305 S Westnedge Ave 49002 269-323-5600
Jeff Hamilton, prin. Fax 323-5690
12th Street ES 600/K-5
6501 S 12th St 49024 269-323-6500
Fax 323-6590
West MS 700/6-8
7145 Moorsbridge Rd 49024 269-323-5800
Denny Roehm, prin. Fax 323-5890
Woodland ES 400/K-5
1401 Woodland Dr 49024 269-323-6600
Allison Taylor, prin. Fax 323-6690

Kalamazoo Country Day S 200/PK-8
4221 E Milham Ave 49002 269-329-0116
Brian Kissman, head sch Fax 329-1850
St. Catherine Catholic Preschool 50/PK-PK
1150 W Centre St 49024 269-327-5165
Nichole McClish, dir. Fax 327-7266
St. Michael Lutheran S 200/PK-8
7211 Oakland Dr 49024 269-327-0512
Greg Johnson, prin. Fax 327-3189

Port Huron, Saint Clair, Pop. 29,088
Port Huron Area SD 9,200/PK-12
PO Box 5013 48061 810-984-3101
James Cain, supt. Fax 984-6606
www.phasd.us
Central MS 900/6-8
200 32nd St 48060 810-984-6533
Bethany Davis, prin. Fax 272-4780
Cleveland ES 300/PK-5
2801 Vanness St 48060 810-984-6500
Michelle Kristick, prin. Fax 272-4787
Crull ES 400/PK-5
2615 Hancock St 48060 810-984-6504
Charles Raski, prin. Fax 989-2733
Garfield ES 500/PK-5
1221 Garfield St 48060 810-984-6509
Julie Alley, prin. Fax 272-4782
Holland Woods MS 600/6-8
1617 Holland Ave 48060 810-984-6548
Abraham Leaver, prin. Fax 989-2713
Michigamme ES 400/K-5
2855 Michigan Rd 48060 810-984-6523
Heidi Bartle, prin. Fax 272-4469
Roosevelt ES 400/PK-5
1112 20th St 48060 810-984-6525
Christopher Johnson, prin. Fax 275-1272
Wilson ES 500/PK-5
834 Chestnut St 48060 810-984-6530
Joseph Kramer, prin. Fax 272-4467
Other Schools – See Fort Gratiot, Kimball

St. Mary/McCormick Academy 200/PK-8
1429 Ballentine St 48060 810-982-7906
Michael Gibson M.Ed., prin. Fax 987-8255

Portland, Ionia, Pop. 3,841
Portland SD 2,000/K-12
1100 Ionia Rd 48875 517-647-4161
William Heath, supt. Fax 647-2975
portland.schooldesk.net
Oakwood ES 500/K-2
500 Oak St 48875 517-647-2991
Elizabeth Findlay, prin. Fax 647-4479
Portland MS 400/6-8
745 Storz St 48875 517-647-2985
Kevin Robydek, prin. Fax 647-2820
Westwood ES 500/3-5
883 Cross St 48875 517-647-2989
Chris Kenroy, prin. Fax 647-1790

St. Patrick S 400/PK-12
122 N West St 48875 517-647-7551
Randy Hodge, prin. Fax 647-4545

Posen, Presque Isle, Pop. 228
Posen Consolidated SD 9 200/K-12
PO Box 187 49776 989-766-2573
Michelle Wesner, supt. Fax 766-2519
www.posen.k12.mi.us
Posen Consolidated ES 100/K-6
PO Box 187 49776 989-766-2573
Michelle Wesner, prin. Fax 766-2519

Potterville, Eaton, Pop. 2,560
Potterville SD 900/K-12
420 N High St 48876 517-645-2662
Dr. Thomas Pillar, supt. Fax 645-0392
www.pps.k12.mi.us
Potterville ES 400/K-4
426 N High St 48876 517-645-2525
Cheri Christensen, prin. Fax 645-0256
Potterville MS 300/5-8
424 N High St 48876 517-645-4777
Nathan Leale, prin. Fax 645-0091

Powers, Menominee, Pop. 422
North Central Area SD 400/PK-12
PO Box 601 49874 906-497-5226
Bruce Tapio, supt. Fax 497-5066
www.ncajets.org
Other Schools – See Hermansville

Prudenville, Roscommon, Pop. 1,664

Our Lady of the Lake Regional Catholic S 100/PK-8
PO Box 800 48651 989-366-5592
Elizabeth Kindermann, prin. Fax 366-1348

Pullman, Allegan
Bloomingdale SD
Supt. — See Bloomingdale
Pullman ES 200/K-5
5582 South Ave 49450 269-236-5235
Melissa Corona, prin. Fax 236-5307

Quincy, Branch, Pop. 1,637
Quincy Community SD 1,200/PK-12
1 Educational Pkwy 49082 517-639-7141
Martin Chard, supt. Fax 639-4273
www.quincyschools.org
Jennings ES 500/PK-4
44 E Liberty St 49082 517-639-9885
Ron Olmsted, prin. Fax 639-3461
Quincy MS 400/5-8
32 Fulton St 49082 517-639-4201
Joshua Haggerty, prin. Fax 639-3701

Rapid City, Kalkaska, Pop. 1,304
Kalkaska SD
Supt. — See Kalkaska
Rapid City ES 100/K-5
5258 River St NW 49676 231-331-6121
Laura Kwekel, prin. Fax 331-4910

Rapid River, Delta
Rapid River SD 400/K-12
10070 US Highway 2 49878 906-474-6411
Dr. Jay Kulbertis, supt. Fax 474-9903
www.rapidriver.k12.mi.us
Rapid River ES 200/K-5
10070 US Highway 2 49878 906-474-6411
William Warning, prin. Fax 474-9903

Ravenna, Muskegon, Pop. 1,203
Ravenna SD 1,100/PK-12
12322 Stafford St 49451 231-853-2231
John Van Loon, supt. Fax 853-2193
www.ravennaschools.org
Beechnau ES 400/PK-4
12322 Stafford St 49451 231-853-2258
Randy Creed, prin. Fax 853-6889
Ravenna MS 300/5-8
2700 S Ravenna Rd 49451 231-853-2268
Mindy Lynch, prin. Fax 853-2629

Divine Providence Academy St. Catherine 50/K-6
3376 Thomas St 49451 231-853-6743
Kendra DeYoung, prin. Fax 853-8673

Ray, Macomb
New Haven Community SD
Supt. — See New Haven
Endeavour S 300/PK-8
22505 26 Mile Rd 48096 586-749-8067
Kristin Guinn, prin. Fax 749-8069

Reading, Hillsdale, Pop. 1,073
Reading Community SD 800/PK-12
PO Box 330 49274 517-283-2166
Chuck North, supt. Fax 283-3519
www.readingrangers.org
Reynolds ES 400/PK-6
221 Strong St 49274 517-283-2188
Dennis Irelan, prin. Fax 283-3973

Redford, Wayne, Pop. 51,100
Detroit SD
Supt. — See Detroit
Ann Arbor Trail Magnet S 400/PK-8
7635 Chatham 48239 313-274-8560
Michele Massey, prin. Fax 274-8074

Redford Union SD 2,700/K-12
17715 Brady 48240 313-242-6000
Dr. Sarena Shivers, supt. Fax 242-6025
www.redfordu.k12.mi.us
Beech ES 700/2-5
19990 Beech Daly Rd 48240 313-342-6100
Susan Shelton, prin. Fax 242-6105
Hilbert MS 600/6-8
26440 Puritan 48239 313-242-4000
Andrew Christopherson, prin. Fax 242-4005
MacGowan ES 300/K-1
18255 Kinloch 48240 313-242-3800
Kathy Robbins, prin. Fax 242-3805

South Redford SD 3,100/PK-12
26141 Schoolcraft 48239 313-535-4000
Brian Galdes, supt. Fax 535-1059
www.southredford.org
Addams ES 300/PK-5
14025 Berwyn 48239 313-532-8064
Michelle Hubbard, prin. Fax 532-2585
Fisher ES 500/PK-5
10000 Crosley 48239 313-532-2455
Amy Davidson, prin. Fax 532-5602
Jefferson ES 300/PK-5
26555 Westfield 48239 313-937-2330
Susan Maurus, prin. Fax 937-0654
Pierce MS 700/6-8
25605 Orangelawn 48239 313-937-8880
Christine Hofer, prin. Fax 937-9486
Shear ECC PK-PK
26141 Schoolcraft 48239 313-535-4000
Lisa Horvatich, dir. Fax 535-4772
Vandenberg ES 300/PK-5
24901 Cathedral 48239 313-532-0300
Lisa Hughes, prin. Fax 532-0327

Concordia Lutheran S - South Campus 50/5-8
9600 Leverne 48239 313-937-2233
Judy Schwaegerle, prin. Fax 937-2233

St. Robert Bellarmine S 200/PK-8
27201 W Chicago 48239 313-937-1655
Linda Kramer, prin. Fax 937-9795
St. Valentine S 200/PK-8
25875 Hope 48239 313-533-7149
Rachel Damuth, prin. Fax 533-3060

Reed City, Osceola, Pop. 2,371
Reed City Area SD 1,500/K-12
225 W Church Ave 49677 231-832-2201
Myra Munroe, supt. Fax 832-2202
www.reedcity.k12.mi.us
Norman ES 700/K-5
338 W Lincoln Ave 49677 231-832-5548
DeAnna Goodman, prin. Fax 832-6194
Reed City MS 400/6-8
233 W Church Ave 49677 231-832-6174
Dean McGuire, prin. Fax 832-6180

Trinity Lutheran S 100/PK-8
19778 US Highway 10 49677 231-832-5186
Fax 832-0107

Reese, Tuscola, Pop. 1,450
Reese SD 800/PK-12
PO Box 389 48757 989-868-9864
Keith Wetters, supt. Fax 868-9570
www.reese.k12.mi.us/
Reese ES 300/PK-5
PO Box 389 48757 989-868-4561
Kristine Krieger, prin. Fax 868-4446
Reese MS 200/6-8
PO Box 389 48757 989-868-4191
Dave Hurst, prin. Fax 868-4091

St. Elizabeth S 100/PK-8
12835 E Washington Rd 48757 989-868-4108
M. Gabriela Costoya, prin. Fax 868-0060
Trinity Lutheran S 100/PK-8
9858 North St 48757 989-868-4501
Levi Bringold, prin. Fax 868-4769

Remus, Mecosta
Chippewa Hills SD 1,900/PK-12
3226 Arthur Rd 49340 989-967-2000
Dr. Michael Bob Grover, supt. Fax 967-2009
www.chsd.us
Chippewa Hills IS 300/5-8
3102 Arthur Rd 49340 989-967-2200
Chi Ethridge, prin. Fax 967-2209
Other Schools – See Barryton, Mecosta, Weidman

St. Michael S 100/PK-6
8944 50th Ave 49340 989-967-3681
Jerry Ward, prin. Fax 967-3061

Republic, Marquette, Pop. 565
Republic-Michigamme SD 100/PK-12
227 Maple St 49879 906-376-2277
Kevin Luokkala, supt. Fax 376-8299
r-mschool.org
Republic-Michigamme S 100/PK-12
227 Maple St 49879 906-376-2277
Kevin Luokkala, supt. Fax 376-8299

Richland, Kalamazoo, Pop. 729
Gull Lake Community SD 2,900/PK-12
10100 E D Ave 49083 269-488-3500
Christopher Rundle, supt. Fax 488-3501
www.gulllakecs.org
Gull Lake MS 700/6-8
9550 M 89 49083 269-548-3600
Carmen Maring, prin. Fax 548-3601
Richland ES 400/K-2
9476 M 89 49083 269-548-3900
Daniel Buckmaster, prin. Fax 548-3901
Ryan IS 600/3-5
9562 M 89 49083 269-548-3700
Rob Woodrow, prin. Fax 548-3701
Other Schools – See Hickory Corners

Richmond, Macomb, Pop. 5,652
Richmond Community SD 1,500/PK-12
35276 Division Rd 48062 586-727-3565
Brian J. Walmsley, supt. Fax 727-2098
www.richmond.k12.mi.us
Lee ES 500/PK-4
68399 S Forest Ave 48062 586-727-2509
David Kochan, prin. Fax 727-9223
Richmond MS 500/5-8
35250 Division Rd 48062 586-727-7552
Keith Bartels, prin. Fax 727-2545

St. Augustine S 100/PK-8
67901 Howard St 48062 586-727-9365
Tina Silvestri, prin. Fax 727-6502
St. Peter Lutheran S 100/PK-8
37601 31 Mile Rd 48062 586-727-9080
Heather Haller, prin. Fax 727-3370

Richville, Tuscola

St. Michael Lutheran S 200/PK-8
PO Box 185 48758 989-868-4809
Daniel Stoelting, prin. Fax 868-4288

River Rouge, Wayne, Pop. 7,623
River Rouge SD 1,600/K-12
1460 Coolidge Hwy 48218 313-297-9600
Dr. Derrick R. Coleman, supt. Fax 297-6525
www.riverrougeschools.org
River Rouge STEM Academy @ Dunn S 200/K-8
163 Burke St 48218 313-297-0500
LaToiya Tolliver-Revell, admin. Fax 297-0541
Sabbath 6-8 Preparatory Academy 300/6-8
340 Frazier St 48218 313-297-9654
Fax 297-5695
Visger K-5 Preparatory Academy 500/K-5
11121 W Jefferson Ave 48218 313-297-9648
Nichole German, prin. Fax 297-5694

Riverside, Berrien
Hagar Township SD 6 100/K-8
PO Box 40 49084 269-849-1343
Sally Woods, supt. Fax 849-0735
www.riversidehagar.org/
Riverside S 100/K-8
PO Box 40 49084 269-849-1343
Sally Woods, prin. Fax 849-0735

Riverview, Wayne, Pop. 12,365
Riverview Community SD 2,800/PK-12
13425 Colvin St Ste 1, 734-285-9660
Dr. Russell Pickell, supt. Fax 285-9822
www.riverviewschools.com
Forest ES 500/PK-5
19400 Hampton St, 734-479-2550
Jason Gribble, prin. Fax 479-2912
Huntington ES 300/K-5
17752 Kennebec St, 734-283-4820
Tim Barlage, prin. Fax 285-6650
Memorial ES 400/K-5
13425 Colvin St Ste 2, 734-285-4080
Angelyn Maxon, prin. Fax 285-6664
Seitz MS 700/6-8
17800 Kennebec St, 734-285-2043
Nicole Munoz, prin. Fax 285-6649

Rochester, Oakland, Pop. 12,556
Rochester Community SD 14,700/K-12
501 W University Dr 48307 248-726-3000
Dr. Robert Shaner, supt. Fax 726-3105
www.rochester.k12.mi.us
Baldwin ES 500/K-5
4325 Bannister Rd 48306 248-726-3200
Cathy Kochanski, prin. Fax 726-3205
Brewster ES 400/K-5
1535 Brewster Rd 48306 248-726-3300
Kelly Dessy, prin. Fax 726-3305
Hugger ES 600/K-5
5050 Sheldon Rd 48306 248-726-3800
Marnie Barker, prin. Fax 726-3805
McGregor ES 400/K-5
1101 1st St 48307 248-726-4000
David Pontzious, prin. Fax 726-4005
Other Schools – See Oakland, Rochester Hills

Holy Family Regional S - North Campus 500/K-3
1240 Inglewood Ave 48307 248-656-1234
Jon Myers, prin. Fax 656-3494
St. John Lutheran S 200/PK-8
1011 W University Dr 48307 248-402-8050
Todd Pehlke, prin. Fax 402-8001

Rochester Hills, Oakland, Pop. 69,733
Avondale SD
Supt. — See Auburn Hills
Avondale MS 700/6-8
1445 W Auburn Rd 48309 248-537-6300
Fax 537-6305
Deerfield ES 400/K-5
3600 Crooks Rd 48309 248-537-6700
David Goetz, prin. Fax 537-6705

Rochester Community SD
Supt. — See Rochester
Brooklands ES 500/K-5
480 E Auburn Rd 48307 248-726-3400
Teresa Simonetti, prin. Fax 726-3405
Hamlin ES 400/K-5
270 W Hamlin Rd 48307 248-726-3600
Gary van Staveren, prin. Fax 726-3605
Hampton ES 500/K-5
530 Hampton Cir 48307 248-726-3700
Ryan Starr, prin. Fax 726-3705
Hart MS 1,100/6-8
6500 Sheldon Rd 48306 248-726-4500
Allison Roberts, prin. Fax 726-4505
Long Meadow ES 600/K-5
450 Allston Dr 48309 248-726-3900
Jeffrey Frankowiak, prin. Fax 726-3905
Meadow Brook ES 400/K-5
2350 Munster Rd 48309 248-726-4100
Seth Berg, prin. Fax 726-4105
Musson ES 400/K-5
3500 Dutton Rd 48306 248-726-4200
Victoria Righter, prin. Fax 726-4205
North Hill ES 600/K-5
1385 Mahaffy Ave 48307 248-726-4300
Dave Murphy, prin. Fax 726-4305
Reuther MS 700/6-8
1430 E Auburn Rd 48307 248-726-4700
Wendy Darga, prin. Fax 726-4705
University Hills ES 400/K-5
600 Croydon Rd 48309 248-726-4400
Amy Grande, prin. Fax 726-4405
Van Hoosen MS 800/6-8
1339 N Adams Rd 48306 248-726-4900
Dan Mooney, prin. Fax 726-4905
West MS 900/6-8
500 Old Perch Rd 48309 248-726-5000
Mike Dillon, prin. Fax 726-5005

Brookfield Academy 200/PK-5
1263 S Adams Rd 48309 248-375-1700
Dawn McComb, prin. Fax 375-1020
Holy Family Regional S - South Campus 600/4-8
2633 John R Rd 48307 248-299-3798
Jon Myers, prin. Fax 299-3843
Rochester Hills Christian S 300/PK-12
3300 S Livernois Rd 48307 248-852-0585
Karen Patton, prin. Fax 852-4757

Rock, Delta
Mid Peninsula SD 200/K-12
5055 Saint Nicholas 31st Rd 49880 906-359-4387
Eric VanDamme, supt. Fax 359-4167
mpswolverines.com
Mid Peninsula S 200/K-12
5055 Saint Nicholas 31st Rd 49880 906-359-4390
Eric VanDamme, prin. Fax 359-4167

Rockford, Kent, Pop. 5,617
Rockford SD 7,800/PK-12
350 N Main St 49341 616-863-6320
Michael Shibler Ph.D., supt. Fax 866-1911
www.rockfordschools.org
Cannonsburg ES 200/K-5
4894 Sturgis Ave NE 49341 616-863-6344
Mike Westgate, prin. Fax 863-6357
Crestwood ES 400/K-5
6350 Courtland Dr NE 49341 616-863-6346
Nicole Reeves, prin. Fax 863-6359
East Rockford MS 800/6-8
8615 9 Mile Rd NE 49341 616-863-6140
Mike Ramm, prin. Fax 863-6565
Lakes ES 500/K-5
6849 Young Ave NE 49341 616-863-6340
Sharon Wells, prin. Fax 863-6358
Meadow Ridge ES 400/PK-5
8100 Courtland Dr NE 49341 616-863-6342
Blake Bowman, prin. Fax 866-7593
North Rockford MS 900/6-8
397 E Division St 49341 616-863-6300
Lissa Weidenfeller, prin. Fax 866-5998
Parkside ES 300/K-5
156 Lewis St 49341 616-863-6360
Larry Watters, prin. Fax 866-2327
Rockford Spanish Immersion 300/K-5
3900 Kroes St NE 49341 616-863-6374
Doug Hoogerland, prin. Fax 866-7132
Roguewood ES 400/K-5
3900 Kroes St NE 49341 616-863-6374
Doug Hoogerland, prin. Fax 866-7132
Valley View ES 600/K-5
405 Summit Ave NE 49341 616-863-6366
Robert Siegel, prin. Fax 866-5995
Other Schools – See Belmont

Our Lady of Consolation S 300/PK-8
4865 11 Mile Rd NE 49341 616-866-2427
Kevin Varner, prin. Fax 866-5475
Rockford Christian S 300/PK-8
6060 Belding Rd NE 49341 616-574-6400
Becky Breuker, prin. Fax 874-9932

Rockwood, Wayne, Pop. 3,246
Gibraltar SD
Supt. — See Woodhaven
Chapman ES 500/K-5
31500 Olmstead Rd 48173 734-379-6380
Leslie Guizzetti, prin. Fax 379-6381

St. Mary S 200/PK-8
32447 Church St 48173 734-379-9285
Sara Furtah, prin. Fax 379-9088

Rogers City, Presque Isle, Pop. 2,809
Rogers City Area SD 600/K-12
1033 W Huron Ave Ste B 49779 989-734-9100
David O'Bryant, supt. Fax 734-7428
www.rcashurons.org
Rogers City ES 200/K-5
532 W Erie St 49779 989-734-9150
Tamara Kuntz, prin. Fax 734-9165

St. Ignatius S 100/1-8
545 S 3rd St 49779 989-734-3443
Amy Rabeau, prin. Fax 734-7671
St. John Lutheran S 50/K-8
145 N 5th St 49779 989-734-3580
Tonya Langlois, prin. Fax 734-2120

Romeo, Macomb, Pop. 3,511
Romeo Community SD 5,200/PK-12
316 N Main St 48065 586-752-0200
Eric Whitney, supt. Fax 752-0228
www.romeo.k12.mi.us
Croswell Center PK-PK
175 Croswell St 48065 586-752-0422
Cheryl Majors, prin. Fax 752-0429
Moore ES 400/K-5
209 Dickenson St 48065 586-752-0260
Roger Bennett, prin. Fax 752-0468
Romeo MS 600/6-8
297 Prospect St 48065 586-752-0240
Brad Martz, prin. Fax 752-0256
Other Schools – See Leonard, Washington

Romulus, Wayne, Pop. 23,107
Romulus Community SD 3,000/PK-12
36540 Grant St 48174 734-532-1602
Marjie McAnally, supt. Fax 532-1611
www.romulus.net
Barth ES 300/PK-5
38207 Barth St 48174 734-532-1253
David Thompson, prin. Fax 532-1251
Halecreek ES 300/K-5
16200 Harrison 48174 734-532-1353
Kristen Fuss, prin. Fax 532-1351
Romulus ES 400/K-5
32200 Beverly Rd 48174 734-532-1453
Gretchen Notaro, prin. Fax 532-1451
Romulus MS 700/6-8
37300 Wick Rd 48174 734-532-1703
Jason Salhaney, prin. Fax 532-1701
Wick ES 400/K-5
36900 Wick Rd 48174 734-532-1503
ShaVonna Johnson, prin. Fax 532-1501

Roscommon, Roscommon, Pop. 1,048
Roscommon Area SD 900/PK-12
PO Box 825 48653 989-275-6600
Catherine Erickson, supt. Fax 275-8227
www.rapsk12.net
Roscommon ES 300/PK-3
PO Box 825 48653 989-275-6610
Kathryn Fuelling, prin. Fax 275-6617
Roscommon MS 200/4-7
PO Box 825 48653 989-275-6640
Kathryn Fuelling, prin. Fax 275-6609

Rose City, Ogemaw, Pop. 648
West Branch-Rose City Area SD
Supt. — See West Branch
Rose City S 200/PK-6
515 Harrington St 48654 989-343-2250
Susan Shepardson, prin. Fax 343-2299

Roseville, Macomb, Pop. 46,120
Fraser SD
Supt. — See Fraser
Dooley ECC 50/PK-PK
16170 Canberra St 48066 586-439-7600
Carrie Wozniak, admin. Fax 439-7601
Twain ES 400/K-6
30601 Calahan Rd 48066 586-439-6900
Laura Woods, prin. Fax 439-6901

Roseville Community SD 4,700/K-12
18975 Church St 48066 586-445-5505
John Kment, supt. Fax 771-1772
www.rcs.misd.net
Dort ES 300/K-5
16225 Dort St 48066 586-445-5750
Donovan Stec, prin. Fax 445-5753
Eastland MS 300/6-8
18700 Frank St 48066 586-445-5702
Major Mickens, prin. Fax 445-5721
Fountain ES 300/K-5
16850 Wellington Ave 48066 586-445-5765
Wayne Johnson, prin. Fax 445-5769
Huron Park ES 400/K-5
18530 Marquette St 48066 586-445-5780
Daniel Schultz, prin. Fax 445-5784
Kaiser ES 200/K-5
16700 Wildwood St 48066 586-445-5785
Kelly Torpey, prin. Fax 445-5789
Kment ES 400/K-5
20033 Washington St 48066 586-445-5756
Paul Schummer, prin. Fax 445-5764
Patton ES 200/K-5
18851 Mckinnon St 48066 586-445-5795
Jeanne Williams, prin. Fax 293-2881
Roseville MS 600/6-8
16250 Martin Rd 48066 586-445-5605
Jason Bettin, prin. Fax 445-5620
Steenland ES 500/K-5
16335 Chestnut St 48066 586-445-5745
Chuck Felker, prin. Fax 445-5809

Royal Oak, Oakland, Pop. 56,180
Royal Oak SD 4,900/PK-12
800 Devillen Ave 48073 248-435-8400
Mary Beth Fitzpatrick, supt. Fax 397-5701
www.royaloakschools.org
Addams ES 500/PK-5
2222 W Webster Rd 48073 248-288-3100
Joseph Youanes, prin. Fax 288-3144
Keller ES 400/K-5
1505 N Campbell Rd 48067 248-542-6500
Marcie Dryden, prin. Fax 541-1260
Northwood ES 500/K-5
926 W 12 Mile Rd 48073 248-541-0229
Angela Ashburn, prin. Fax 541-4709
Oakland ES 300/K-5
2415 Brockton Ave 48067 248-542-4406
Sam Lynch, prin. Fax 542-9289
Oak Ridge ES 400/K-5
506 E 13 Mile Rd 48073 248-588-8353
Dr. Jason Parrott, prin. Fax 588-0750
Royal Oak MS 1,000/6-8
709 N Washington Ave 48067 248-541-7100
Todd Noonan, prin. Fax 541-0408
Upton ES 300/K-5
4400 Mandalay Ave 48073 248-549-4968
John Grzywack, prin. Fax 549-0013

St. Mary S 300/PK-8
628 S Lafayette Ave 48067 248-545-2140
Gabriela Bala, prin. Fax 545-2303
St. Paul Lutheran S 100/PK-8
508 S Williams St 48067 248-546-6555
Harmon Butler, prin. Fax 546-8096
Shrine Catholic ES 500/PK-6
1621 Linwood Ave 48067 248-541-4622
Kathleen Fotiu, prin. Fax 541-6969

Rudyard, Chippewa
Rudyard Area SD 700/PK-12
11185 W 2nd St 49780 906-478-3771
Mark Pavloski, supt. Fax 478-3912
www.rudyard.k12.mi.us
Rudyard ES 400/PK-6
11185 W 2nd St 49780 906-478-3771
Wendy Peterson, prin. Fax 478-4600

Rudyard Christian S 50/1-5
10702 W 17 Mile Rd 49780 906-478-3910
Heather Leep, lead tchr.

Saginaw, Saginaw, Pop. 50,106
Bridgeport-Spaulding Community SD
Supt. — See Bridgeport
Atkins S 400/1-8
3675 Southfield Dr 48601 989-777-1600
Jon Chapman, prin. Fax 777-4652
White ES 200/PK-K
3650 Southfield Dr 48601 989-777-2811
Jon Chapman, prin. Fax 746-0318

Carrollton SD 2,000/PK-12
3211 Carla Dr 48604 989-754-1475
Tim Wilson, supt. Fax 754-1470
www.carrolltonpublicschools.org
Carrollton ES 700/K-5
3211 Carla Dr 48604 989-754-2425
Sarah Coates, prin. Fax 754-2427
Carrollton MS 400/6-8
3211 Carla Dr 48604 989-753-9704
Marc McKenzie, prin. Fax 754-1470
Griffith ECC 200/PK-PK
3211 Carla Dr 48604 989-754-0381
Katrina Priuer, dir. Fax 754-2427

Saginaw SD 6,000/PK-12
550 Millard St 48607 989-399-6500
Nathaniel McClain Ph.D., supt. Fax 399-6635
www.spsd.net
Eddy Academy 300/PK-5
1000 Cathay St 48601 989-399-4300
Eric S. Gordon, prin. Fax 399-4305
Handley S - P.C.A.T. 400/K-5
224 N Elm St 48602 989-399-4250
Mary Couillard, prin. Fax 399-4255
Herig ES 400/PK-5
1905 Houghton Ave 48602 989-399-4350
Jeanine Kowalski, prin. Fax 399-4355
Kempton ES 400/K-5
3040 Davenport Ave 48602 989-399-4600
Diane Dalton, prin. Fax 399-4605
Loomis Math Science Technology Academy 400/PK-5
2001 Limerick St 48601 989-399-4750
Cynthia Townsend, prin. Fax 399-4755
Merrill Park ES 300/PK-5
1800 Grout St 48602 989-399-4800
Lisa Tran, prin. Fax 399-4805
Miller ES 300/PK-5
2020 Brockway St 48602 989-399-4850
Robert Ueberroth, prin. Fax 399-4855
Rouse ES 300/PK-5
435 Randolph St 48601 989-399-5000
Debra Williams, prin. Fax 399-5005
Stone ES 200/PK-5
1006 State St 48602 989-399-5100
Sherry Couture, prin. Fax 399-5105
Thompson MS 500/6-8
3021 Court St 48602 989-399-5600
Rachel Reid, prin. Fax 399-5615
Zilwaukee S 300/PK-8
500 W Johnson St 48604 989-399-5200
Tina Munoz, prin. Fax 399-5205

Saginaw Township Community SD 4,900/K-12
PO Box 6278 48608 989-797-1800
Douglas Trombley, supt. Fax 797-1801
stcs.org
Arrowwood ES 400/3-5
5410 Seidel Rd, 989-797-1835
Richard Sebring, prin. Fax 799-5140
Hemmeter ES 400/K-5
1890 Hemmeter Rd, 989-797-1832
James Bailey, prin. Fax 797-1854
Sherwood ES 500/K-2
3870 Shattuck Rd 48603 989-799-2382
Mark Abenth, prin. Fax 797-1856
Weiss ES 300/3-5
4645 Weiss St 48603 989-793-5226
Kathryn Stanley, prin. Fax 797-1857
Westdale ES 300/K-2
705 S Center Rd, 989-797-1827
Karen Volk, prin. Fax 797-1858
White Pine MS 1,100/6-8
505 N Center Rd, 989-797-1814
Pri Victoria Wandmacher, prin. Fax 797-1859

Swan Valley SD 1,700/PK-12
8380 OHern Rd 48609 989-921-3701
Mat McRae, supt. Fax 921-3705
www.swanvalley.k12.mi.us
Havens ES 300/3-5
457 Van Wormer Rd 48609 989-921-4201
Shelly DuRussel, prin. Fax 921-4205
Shields ES 400/PK-2
6900 Stroebel Rd 48609 989-921-4701
Leland Jennings, prin. Fax 921-4705
Swan Valley MS 400/6-8
453 Van Wormer Rd 48609 989-921-2601
Shelly DuCharme, prin. Fax 921-2605

Bethlehem Lutheran S 100/PK-8
2777 Hermansau Rd 48604 989-755-1144
Dr. Nicole Frederick, prin. Fax 755-3969
Community Baptist Christian S 100/PK-12
8331 Gratiot Rd 48609 989-781-2340
Douglas Jackson, prin. Fax 781-1344
Good Shepherd ECC 100/PK-K
5335 Brockway Rd, 989-793-8252
Wendy Butler, prin. Fax 793-9525
Grace Christian S 100/PK-8
4619 Mackinaw Rd 48603 989-793-2129
Sharon Gamber, prin. Fax 793-2125
Holy Cross Lutheran S 100/PK-8
610 Court St 48602 989-793-9795
Roger Wolter, prin. Fax 793-7441
Immanuel Lutheran S 100/PK-8
8220 E Holland Rd 48601 989-754-4285
Kyle Smith, admin. Fax 754-0454
Nouvel Catholic Central ES 400/PK-8
2136 Berberovich Dr 48603 989-792-2361
Sr. Ann de Guise, prin. Fax 792-0411
Peace Lutheran S 400/PK-8
3161 Lawndale Rd 48603 989-792-2581
Joel Keup, prin. Fax 792-8266
St. John's Lutheran S 50/K-8
4705 Brockway Rd, 989-799-0935
Ken Peterson, prin. Fax 799-0935
St. Paul Lutheran S 100/PK-8
2745 W Genesee Ave 48602 989-799-3271
Kevin Needham, prin. Fax 799-1713
Tri-City SDA S 50/K-8
3955 Kochville Rd 48604 989-790-2508
Esther Nanasi, prin. Fax 790-3721

Saint Charles, Saginaw, Pop. 2,035
Saint Charles Community SD 1,000/PK-12
891 W Walnut St 48655 989-865-9961
Michael Decker, supt. Fax 865-6185
www.stccs.org
Saint Charles ES 400/PK-5
801 W Walnut St 48655 989-865-9210
Mark Benson, prin. Fax 865-2449
Thurston MS 200/6-8
893 W Walnut St 48655 989-865-9927
Shawna Groulx, prin. Fax 865-2429

Saint Clair, Saint Clair, Pop. 5,422
East China SD
Supt. — See East China
Eddy ES 400/K-5
301 N 9th St 48079 810-676-1550
Rick Carlson, prin. Fax 676-1560
Gearing ES 300/K-5
200 N Carney Dr 48079 810-676-1650
Lynda Crandall, prin. Fax 676-1660
Saint Clair MS 600/6-8
4335 Yankee Rd 48079 810-676-1800
Michael Domagalski, prin. Fax 676-1825

St. Mary S 100/PK-8
800 Orchard St 48079 810-329-4150
John Fitzmaurice, prin. Fax 329-5705

Saint Clair Shores, Macomb, Pop. 58,728
Lake Shore SD 3,600/K-12
28850 Harper Ave 48081 586-285-8480
Dr. Joseph DiPonio, supt. Fax 285-8463
www.lakeshoreschools.org
Kennedy MS 800/6-8
23101 Masonic Blvd 48082 586-285-8800
Patrick Donohue, prin. Fax 285-8804
Masonic Heights ES 500/K-5
22100 Masonic Blvd 48082 586-285-8500
George Lewis, prin. Fax 285-8504
Rodgers ES 500/K-5
21601 Lanse St 48081 586-285-8600
Cynthia Sam, prin. Fax 285-8604
Violet ES 500/K-5
22020 Violet St 48082 586-285-8700
Joan Grassi, prin. Fax 285-8704

Lakeview SD 3,900/PK-12
27575 Harper Ave 48081 586-445-4000
Karl Paulson, supt. Fax 445-4029
www.lakeview.misd.net
Ardmore ES 400/K-5
27001 Greater Mack Ave 48081 586-445-4160
Christopher Hahn, prin. Fax 445-4524
ECC, 27575 Harper Ave 48081 PK-PK
Kathryn Neumann, admin. 586-445-4159
Greenwood ES 300/K-5
27900 Joan St 48081 586-445-4178
Sara Dobbelaer, prin. Fax 445-4181
Harmon ES 400/K-5
24800 Harmon St 48080 586-445-4184
Greg Seader, prin. Fax 445-4526
Jefferson MS 900/6-8
27900 Rockwood St 48081 586-445-4130
David Lavender, prin. Fax 445-4041
Princeton ES 500/K-5
20300 Statler St 48081 586-445-4190
Justin Cabe, prin. Fax 445-4399

South Lake SD 1,900/K-12
23101 Stadium Dr 48080 586-435-1600
Ted Von Hiltmayer, supt. Fax 445-4202
www.solake.org
Avalon ES 300/K-5
20000 Avalon St 48080 586-435-1000
Fax 445-4358
Elmwood ES 400/K-5
22700 California St 48080 586-435-1100
Michael Fringer, prin. Fax 445-4338
South Lake MS 400/6-8
21621 California St 48080 586-435-1300
Michael Bruce, prin. Fax 778-3151
Other Schools – See Eastpointe

St. Germaine S 300/PK-8
28250 Rockwood St 48081 586-771-0890
Julie DeGrez, prin. Fax 779-3667
St. Isaac Jogues S 300/PK-8
21100 Madison St 48081 586-771-3525
Sr. Catherine Marie, prin. Fax 778-8183
St. Joan of Arc S 500/PK-8
22415 Overlake St 48080 586-775-8370
Katherine Kalich, prin. Fax 447-3574

Saint Ignace, Mackinac, Pop. 2,280
Moran Township SD 100/K-8
W1828 Gros Cap Rd 49781 906-643-7970
Amy Lester, supt. Fax 643-7240
morantownshipschools.org
Gros Cap S 100/K-8
W1828 Gros Cap Rd 49781 906-643-7970
Amy Lester, admin. Fax 643-7240

Saint Ignace Area SD 600/K-12
W429 Portage St 49781 906-643-8145
Don Gustafson, supt. Fax 643-7873
stignace.eup.k12.mi.us/
Saint Ignace S 400/K-8
W429 Portage St 49781 906-643-7822
Kari Visnaw, prin. Fax 643-0247

Saint Johns, Clinton, Pop. 7,721
Saint Johns SD 3,100/K-12
501 W Sickles St 48879 989-227-4050
Dedrick Martin, supt. Fax 227-4099
www.sjredwings.org
Gateway North ES 300/K-2
915 N Lansing St 48879 989-227-4600
Michael Winkel, prin. Fax 227-4699
Oakview South ES 300/3-5
1400 S Clinton Ave 48879 989-227-4500
James Alspaugh, prin. Fax 227-4599
Riley ES 300/K-5
5935 W Pratt Rd 48879 989-227-5100
Joseph Corr, prin. Fax 227-5199

Saint Johns MS 700/6-8
900 W Townsend Rd 48879 989-227-4300
Adel DiOrio, prin. Fax 227-4399
Other Schools – See Eureka

St. Joseph S 300/K-6
201 E Cass St 48879 989-224-2421
Christopher Wells, prin. Fax 224-1900
St. Peter Lutheran S 100/PK-6
8990 Church Rd 48879 989-224-3178
Karen Schnuell-Ruth, prin. Fax 224-8962

Saint Joseph, Berrien, Pop. 8,211
Saint Joseph SD 2,900/K-12
3275 Lincoln Ave 49085 269-926-3100
Ann Cardon, supt. Fax 429-5042
www.sjschools.org/
Brown ES 300/K-5
2027 Brown School Rd 49085 269-926-3500
Kristen Bawks, prin. Fax 926-3503
Clarke ES 400/K-5
515 E Glenlord Rd 49085 269-926-3600
Michelle Allen, prin. Fax 926-3603
Lincoln ES 400/K-5
1102 Orchard Ave 49085 269-926-3700
Craig Hubble, prin. Fax 926-3703
Upton MS 700/6-8
800 Maiden Ln 49085 269-926-3400
Chad Mandarino, prin. Fax 408-0970

Grace Lutheran S 100/PK-8
404 E Glenlord Rd 49085 269-429-4951
Nate Sievert, prin. Fax 429-4797
Lake Michigan Catholic ES 300/PK-5
3165 Washington Ave 49085 269-429-0227
Larry Hoskins, prin. Fax 429-1461
Lake Michigan Catholic MS 100/6-8
915 Pleasant St 49085 269-983-2511
Gerald Heath, prin. Fax 983-0883
Trinity Lutheran S 200/PK-8
613 Court St 49085 269-983-3056
Terry Bird, prin. Fax 983-0037

Saint Louis, Gratiot, Pop. 7,441
Saint Louis SD 1,100/PK-12
113 E Saginaw St 48880 989-681-2545
Kristi Teall, supt. Fax 681-5894
www.stlouisschools.net
Knause ECC 200/PK-2
121 I and K St 48880 989-681-3535
Stephanie Binder, prin. Fax 681-3387
Nikkari ES 300/3-5
301 W State St 48880 989-681-5131
Eugene Binder, prin. Fax 681-4228
Nurnberger MS 200/6-8
312 Union St 48880 989-681-5155
Shane Brooks, prin. Fax 681-4658

Salem, Washtenaw
South Lyon Community SD
Supt. — See South Lyon
Salem ES 300/K-5
7806 Salem Rd 48175 248-573-8450
Ryan Knapp, prin. Fax 349-5744

Saline, Washtenaw, Pop. 8,661
Saline Area SD 5,200/PK-12
7265 N Ann Arbor St 48176 734-401-4000
Scot Graden, supt. Fax 401-4098
www.salineschools.com
Harvest ES 500/PK-3
1155 Campus Pkwy 48176 734-401-4500
Betty Rosen-Leacher, prin.
Heritage IS 800/4-5
290 Woodland Dr 48176 734-401-4100
Laura Washington, prin. Fax 401-4197
Pleasant Ridge ES 400/PK-3
229 Pleasant Ridge Dr 48176 734-401-4800
Kevin Musson, prin. Fax 401-4870
Saline MS 1,200/6-8
7190 N Maple Rd 48176 734-401-4600
Brad Bezeau, prin. Fax 401-4745
Woodland Meadows ES 400/PK-3
350 Woodland Dr 48176 734-401-4900
Michelle Szczechowicz, prin. Fax 401-4990

Washtenaw Christian Academy 300/PK-12
7200 Moon Rd 48176 734-429-7733

Sand Creek, Lenawee
Sand Creek Community SD 900/PK-12
6518 Sand Creek Hwy 49279 517-436-3108
Steven Laundra, supt. Fax 436-3143
www.sc-aggies.us
McGregor ES 400/PK-5
6850 Sand Creek Hwy 49279 517-436-3121
Vicky Strang, prin. Fax 436-3109

Sand Lake, Montcalm, Pop. 495
Tri County Area SD 2,400/PK-12
PO Box 79 49343 616-636-5454
Allen Cumings M.A., supt. Fax 636-5677
www.tricountyschools.com
Sand Lake ES 500/3-5
15 7th St 49343 616-636-5669
Fran Clemence, prin. Fax 636-4894
Other Schools – See Howard City

Sandusky, Sanilac, Pop. 2,651
Sandusky Community SD 900/PK-12
191 E Pinetree Ln 48471 810-648-3400
Paul Flynn, supt. Fax 648-5113
www.sandusky.k12.mi.us
Sandusky ES 400/PK-6
395 S Sandusky Rd 48471 810-648-2488
Adam Lulis, prin. Fax 648-5221

Sanford, Midland, Pop. 854
Meridian SD 1,100/PK-12
3361 N Meridian Rd 48657 989-687-3200
Craig Carmoney, supt. Fax 687-3222
www.merps.org
Meridian ES 500/K-4
3353 N Meridian Rd 48657 989-687-3500
Joshua Hook, prin. Fax 687-3490
Meridian JHS 400/5-8
3475 N Meridian Rd 48657 989-687-3360
Kent Boxey, prin. Fax 687-3364
Sanford ECC 100/PK-PK
2534 N West River Rd 48657 989-687-3455
Julie Sheets, dir. Fax 687-2658

Saranac, Ionia, Pop. 1,311
Saranac Community SD 1,000/PK-12
225 Pleasant St 48881 616-642-1400
Jason Smith, supt. Fax 642-1405
www.saranac.k12.mi.us
Saranac ES 600/PK-6
250 Pleasant St 48881 616-642-1200
Mike Catrell, prin. Fax 642-1205

Sault Sainte Marie, Chippewa, Pop. 13,362
Sault Sainte Marie Area SD 2,400/PK-12
876 Marquette Ave 49783 906-635-3839
Timothy D. Hall Ed.D., supt. Fax 635-6642
sault.eup.k12.mi.us
Lincoln ES 300/PK-5
810 E 5th Ave 49783 906-635-6626
Sheri McFarlane, prin. Fax 635-6666
Sault Sainte Marie MS 500/6-8
684 Marquette Ave 49783 906-635-6604
Jessica Rondeau, prin. Fax 635-3841
Soo Township ES 300/K-5
5788 S M 129 49783 906-635-6630
Diane Chevillot, prin. Fax 635-6668
Washington ES 300/PK-5
1200 Ryan Ave 49783 906-635-6629
Edward Chevillot, prin. Fax 635-6669

St. Mary Catholic S 100/K-8
360 Maple St 49783 906-635-6141
Hedy Yanni, prin. Fax 635-6934

Sawyer, Berrien
River Valley SD
Supt. — See Three Oaks
Chikaming ES 100/K-2
13742 Three Oaks Rd 49125 269-426-4204
Heidi Clark, prin. Fax 426-8491

Schoolcraft, Kalamazoo, Pop. 1,506
Schoolcraft Community SD 1,100/PK-12
551 E Lyons St 49087 269-488-7390
Dr. Wayne Stitt, supt. Fax 488-7391
www.schoolcraftschools.org
Schoolcraft ES 400/K-4
551 E Lyons St 49087 269-488-7250
Matt Webster, prin. Fax 488-7269
Schoolcraft MS 300/5-8
551 E Lyons St 49087 269-488-7300
Dave Powers, prin. Fax 488-7303
Schoolcraft Preschool 100/PK-PK
551 E Lyons St 49087 269-488-7387
Amie Goldschmeding, prin.

Scotts, Kalamazoo
Climax-Scotts Community SD
Supt. — See Climax
Climax-Scotts ES 200/PK-5
11250 QR Ave E 49088 269-497-2100
Teri Peters, prin. Fax 497-2127

Vicksburg Community SD
Supt. — See Vicksburg
Tobey ES 300/PK-5
8551 Long Lake Dr E 49088 269-321-1600
Mike Barwegen, prin. Fax 321-1655

Scottville, Mason, Pop. 1,185
Mason County Central SD 1,400/PK-12
300 W Broadway Ave 49454 231-757-3713
Jeff Mount, supt. Fax 757-5716
mccschools.org
Mason County Central MS 300/6-8
310 W Beryl St 49454 231-757-3724
John Russell, prin. Fax 757-4820
Mason County Central Upper ES 300/3-5
505 W Maple Ave 49454 231-757-5720
Kevin Kimes, prin. Fax 757-1059
Scottville ES 300/K-2
201 W Maple Ave 49454 231-757-4701
Chris Etchison, prin. Fax 757-4810
Victory ECC 50/PK-PK
4171 N Stiles Rd 49454 231-843-2410
Angela Taylor, dir. Fax 845-1717

Sebewaing, Huron, Pop. 1,753
Unionville-Sebewaing SD 700/PK-12
2203 Wildner Rd 48759 989-883-2360
George Rierson, supt. Fax 883-9021
www.think-usa.org
Unionville-Sebewaing MS 200/6-8
2203 Wildner Rd 48759 989-883-3140
Josh Hahn, prin.
Other Schools – See Unionville

Christ the King Lutheran S 100/2-8
612 E Bay St 48759 989-883-3730
David Kaiser, prin. Fax 883-9171
New Salem Lutheran S 50/K-8
214 E Grove St 48759 989-883-3880
William Mayhew, prin. Fax 883-3880

Shelby, Oceana, Pop. 2,029
Shelby SD 1,500/PK-12
525 N State St 49455 231-861-5211
Dan Bauer, supt. Fax 861-5416
www.shelbypublicschools.net
ECC 100/PK-PK
155 E 6th St 49455 231-861-6629
Teresa Mead, coord. Fax 861-0601
Read ES 400/K-3
155 E 6th St 49455 231-861-5541
Dannielle McGuire, prin. Fax 861-6764
Shelby MS 300/6-8
525 N State St 49455 231-861-4521
Mark Olmstead, prin. Fax 861-0415
Other Schools – See New Era

Shelby Township, Macomb, Pop. 69,500
Utica Community SD
Supt. — See Sterling Heights
Beacon Tree ES 700/K-6
55885 Schoenherr Rd 48315 586-797-7300
Jason Ellis, prin. Fax 797-7301
Crissman ES 600/K-6
53550 Wolf Dr 48316 586-797-4300
Sofia Papastamatis, prin. Fax 797-4301
Duncan ES 800/K-6
14500 26 Mile Rd 48315 586-797-4600
Sharon Coil, prin. Fax 797-4601
Monfort ES 700/K-6
6700 Montgomery Dr 48316 586-797-5700
Brian LaPorte, prin. Fax 797-5701
Morgan ES 600/K-6
53800 Mound Rd 48316 586-797-5800
Sue Lasky, prin. Fax 797-5801
Roberts ES 600/K-6
2400 Belle View Dr 48316 586-797-6100
Patrick Zott, prin. Fax 797-6101
Switzer ES 600/K-6
53200 Shelby Rd 48316 586-797-6400
Jacob Palmer, prin. Fax 797-6401
West Utica ES 600/K-6
5415 W Utica Rd 48317 586-797-6600
Brad Suggs, prin. Fax 797-6601

Peace Lutheran S 300/PK-8
6580 24 Mile Rd 48316 586-731-4120
Carol Stathakis, prin. Fax 731-8935

Shepherd, Isabella, Pop. 1,488
Shepherd SD 1,800/K-12
PO Box 219 48883 989-828-5520
Claire Bunker, supt. Fax 828-5679
www.shepherdschools.net
Shepherd ES 700/K-5
168 E Maple St 48883 989-828-6601
Lou Ann Schmidt, prin. Fax 828-6947
Shepherd MS 400/6-8
150 E Hall St 48883 989-828-6601
Benjamin Brock, prin. Fax 828-6578
Other Schools – See Winn

Sheridan, Montcalm, Pop. 639
Central Montcalm SD
Supt. — See Stanton
Central Montcalm ES 200/PK-1
289 Saint Clair St 48884 989-831-2500
Wilberta Wittkopp, prin. Fax 831-2510

Beth Haven Baptist Academy 100/PK-12
1158 W Carson City Rd 48884 989-291-0555
Phil Hilleman, prin. Fax 527-3122

Skanee, Baraga
Arvon Township SD 50/K-6
21798 Skanee Rd 49962 906-524-7336
Fax 524-7394
www.arvontownshipschool.org
Arvon Township S 50/K-6
21798 Skanee Rd 49962 906-524-7336
Lori Johnson, prin. Fax 524-7394

Sodus, Berrien
Sodus Township SD 5 100/K-8
4439 River Rd 49126 269-925-6757
Laura Lausch, supt. Fax 925-3144
www.riverschoolk8.org
River S 100/K-8
4439 River Rd 49126 269-925-6757
Laura Lausch, prin. Fax 925-3144

Southfield, Oakland, Pop. 70,027
Southfield SD 5,900/PK-12
24661 Lahser Rd 48033 248-746-8500
Derrick Lopez, supt. Fax 746-8540
www.southfieldk12.org
Adler ES 300/K-5
19100 Filmore St 48075 248-746-8870
Alma Deane, prin. Fax 746-8946
Birney K-8 S 700/K-8
27225 Evergreen Rd 48076 248-746-8800
Edward Hill, prin. Fax 746-8561
Bussey Preschool 50/PK-PK
24501 Fredrick St, 248-746-7350
Janice Hill, dir. Fax 746-7354
Levey MS 300/6-8
25300 W 9 Mile Rd, 248-746-8740
Sonia Jackson, prin. Fax 746-8718
McIntyre ES 300/K-5
19600 Saratoga Blvd 48076 248-746-7365
Kimberly Beckwith, prin. Fax 746-7663
Stevenson ES 300/K-5
27777 Lahser Rd 48034 248-746-8840
Sandra LaPerriere, prin. Fax 746-8945
Thompson K-8 S 600/K-8
16300 Lincoln Dr 48076 248-746-7400
Paula Lightsey, prin. Fax 746-7493
Vandenberg ES 400/K-5
16100 Edwards Ave 48076 248-746-7377
Michael Griffin, prin. Fax 746-7617
Other Schools – See Lathrup Village

Farber Hebrew Day S - Yeshivat Akiv 300/PK-12
21100 W 12 Mile Rd 48076 248-386-1625
Rabbi Noam Stein, prin. Fax 386-1632

Southfield Christian S 500/PK-12
28650 Lahser Rd 48034 248-357-3660
Sue Hoffenbacher, supt. Fax 357-5271
Yeshiva Beth Yehuda 200/K-8
15751 Lincoln Dr 48076 248-557-9380
Rabbi Zev Pam, prin. Fax 557-5343
Yeshivas Darchei Torah Boys S 1-8
21550 W 12 Mile Rd 48076 248-357-3560
Yeshivas Darchei Torah Girls S 300/K-12
21550 W 12 Mile Rd 48076 248-948-1080
Sharon Kahn, prin. Fax 948-1825

Southgate, Wayne, Pop. 29,584
Southgate Community SD 4,700/K-12
14600 Dix Toledo Rd 48195 734-246-4600
Leslie Chretian, supt. Fax 283-6791
www.sgate.k12.mi.us
Allen ES 400/K-5
16500 McCann St 48195 734-246-4644
Renne' Chilson, prin. Fax 246-7277
Davidson MS 1,000/6-8
15800 Trenton Rd 48195 734-246-4628
Dennis Kemp, prin. Fax 246-7280
Fordline ES 300/K-5
14775 Fordline St 48195 734-246-4640
Andrea Ball, prin. Fax 246-7259
Grogan ES 500/K-5
13300 Burns St 48195 734-246-4642
Robert Wolsek, prin. Fax 246-7269
Shelters ES 400/K-5
12600 Fordline St 48195 734-246-4631
Sinder Gundick, prin. Fax 246-4653

Christ the King Lutheran S 300/PK-8
15600 Trenton Rd 48195 734-285-9697
Daniel Burk, prin. Fax 285-5275
St. Pius X S 300/PK-8
14141 Pearl St 48195 734-284-6500
Michelle Seward, prin. Fax 285-6525

South Haven, Van Buren, Pop. 4,285
South Haven SD 2,200/PK-12
554 Green St 49090 269-637-0520
Robert Herrera, supt. Fax 637-3025
www.shps.org
Baseline MS 500/6-8
7357 Baseline Rd 49090 269-637-0530
Dr. LaTonya Gill, prin. Fax 639-9689
Lincoln ES 300/PK-3
500 Elkenburg St 49090 269-637-0540
Bennett Tyler, prin. Fax 639-8267
Maple Grove ES 400/K-3
72399 12th Ave 49090 269-637-0549
Kimberly Cross, prin. Fax 637-0550
North Shore ES 300/4-5
7320 N Shore Dr 49090 269-637-0560
Carey Frost, prin. Fax 639-8162

St. Basil S 100/PK-6
94 Superior St 49090 269-637-3529
Jeanne Arbanas, prin. Fax 639-1242
St. Paul Lutheran S 100/PK-8
718 Arbor Ct 49090 269-637-4459
Joseph Greefkes, prin. Fax 639-7109

South Lyon, Oakland, Pop. 11,160
South Lyon Community SD 7,400/PK-12
345 S Warren St 48178 248-573-8127
Melissa Baker, supt. Fax 437-8686
www.slcs.us
Bartlett ES 400/K-5
350 School St 48178 248-573-8300
Emily Testani, prin. Fax 486-4090
Brummer ES 500/K-5
9919 N Rushton Rd 48178 248-573-8520
Stacy Cooper, prin. Fax 486-4355
Centennial MS 900/6-8
62500 W 9 Mile Rd 48178 248-573-8600
Brian Toth, prin. Fax 486-4302
ECC PK-PK
310 N Warren St 48178 248-573-8330
Cathy Craig, dir. Fax 486-4041
Hardy ES 600/K-5
24650 Collingwood Rd 48178 248-573-8650
Cory Heitsch, prin. Fax 486-4070
Kent Lake ES 600/K-5
30181 Kent Lake Rd 48178 248-573-8350
Ray Metcalf, prin. Fax 486-0412
Millennium MS 900/6-8
61526 W 9 Mile Rd 48178 248-573-8200
Kelly Gallagher, prin. Fax 437-4066
Pearson ES 500/K-5
57900 Eleven Mile Rd 48178 248-573-8750
Kimberly Dancer, prin.
Sayre ES 600/K-5
23000 Valerie St 48178 248-573-8500
Jennifer Herbstreit, prin. Fax 437-3826
Other Schools – See New Hudson, Salem

South Range, Houghton, Pop. 742
Adams Township SD
Supt. — See Painesdale
South Range ES 200/K-6
PO Box 69 49963 906-482-0599
Kim Harris, prin. Fax 487-5948

South Rockwood, Monroe, Pop. 1,657
Airport Community SD
Supt. — See Carleton
Ritter ES 300/K-4
5650 Carleton Rockwood Rd 48179 734-379-5335
Dawn Spears, prin. Fax 379-0701

Sparta, Kent, Pop. 4,088
Sparta Area SD 2,600/PK-12
465 S Union St 49345 616-887-8253
Gordie Nickels, supt. Fax 887-9958
www.spartaschools.org
Appleview ES 500/3-5
240 E Spartan Dr 49345 616-887-1743
Mike Birely, prin. Fax 887-7509
Ridgeview ES 600/PK-2
560 W Spartan Dr 49345 616-887-8218
Marialyce Zeerip, prin. Fax 887-1928
Sparta MS 600/6-8
480 S State St 49345 616-887-8211
Brad Wood, prin. Fax 887-1080
White ECC 50/PK-PK
1655 12 Mile Rd NW 49345 616-887-0068
Fax 887-2231

Spring Arbor, Jackson, Pop. 2,850
Western SD
Supt. — See Parma
Bean ES 400/K-5
3201 Noble Rd 49283 517-841-8400
Michael Ykimoff, prin. Fax 841-8804
Warner ES 400/K-5
118 Star Rd 49283 517-841-8500
Ben Gilpin, prin. Fax 841-8805

Springfield, Calhoun, Pop. 5,036
Battle Creek SD
Supt. — See Battle Creek
Springfield MS 500/6-8
1023 Avenue A, 269-965-9640
William Martin, prin. Fax 962-2486
Valley View ES 500/K-5
960 Avenue A, 269-965-9760
Stephanie Bruce, prin. Fax 965-9764

Spring Lake, Ottawa, Pop. 2,288
Grand Haven Area SD
Supt. — See Grand Haven
Lake Hills ES 300/PK-4
18181 Dogwood Dr 49456 616-850-5600
Jason Lawson, prin. Fax 850-5610

Spring Lake SD 2,400/PK-12
345 Hammond St 49456 616-846-5500
Dennis Furton, supt. Fax 846-9830
www.springlakeschools.org
Holmes ES 500/K-4
426 River St 49456 616-846-5504
Sandra Smits, prin. Fax 847-7934
Jeffers ES 400/PK-4
16031 144th St 49456 616-846-5503
Shelley Peets, prin. Fax 414-6204
Spring Lake IS 400/5-6
345 Hammond St 49456 616-846-6845
Ben Lewakowski, prin. Fax 847-7580
Spring Lake MS 400/7-8
345 Hammond St 49456 616-846-5502
Aaron West, prin. Fax 847-7913

St. Mary's S 200/PK-8
430 E Savidge St 49456 616-842-1282
Steve VanHammen, prin. Fax 842-8048

Springport, Jackson, Pop. 785
Springport SD 1,000/PK-12
300 W Main St 49284 517-857-3495
Randall Cook, supt. Fax 857-4179
springportschools.net
Springport ES 500/PK-5
300 W Main St 49284 517-857-3465
Janis Sanford, prin. Fax 857-3499
Springport MS 200/6-8
300 W Main St 49284 517-857-3475
Tanya Newland, prin. Fax 857-3251

Standish, Arenac, Pop. 1,487
Standish-Sterling Community SD 1,600/PK-12
3789 Wyatt Rd 48658 989-846-3670
Darren Kroczaleski, supt. Fax 846-7890
www.standish-sterling.org
Standish-Sterling Central ES 1-6
3789 Wyatt Rd 48658 989-846-4526
Gary Roper, prin. Fax 846-4529
Other Schools – See Sterling

Stanton, Montcalm, Pop. 1,397
Central Montcalm SD 1,700/PK-12
PO Box 9 48888 989-831-2000
Amy Meinhardt, supt. Fax 831-2010
www.central-montcalm.org
Central Montcalm MS 400/6-8
PO Box 9 48888 989-831-2200
Charity Groom, prin. Fax 831-2210
Central Montcalm Upper ES 500/2-5
PO Box 9 48888 989-831-2300
Jane Trimper, prin. Fax 831-2310
Other Schools – See Sheridan

Stephenson, Menominee, Pop. 850
Stephenson Area SD 400/K-12
PO Box 509 49887 906-753-2221
Ron Kraft, supt. Fax 753-4676
www.stephenson.k12.mi.us
Stephenson ES 200/K-5
PO Box 307 49887 906-753-2221
Becky Marciniak, prin. Fax 753-2864

Sterling, Arenac, Pop. 520
Standish-Sterling Community SD
Supt. — See Standish
Sterling ES 300/PK-K
338 W State St 48659 989-654-2367
Clinton Potts, prin. Fax 654-2138

Sterling Heights, Macomb, Pop. 126,870
Utica Community SD 27,900/PK-12
11303 Greendale Dr 48312 586-797-1100
Christine Johns Ed.D., supt. Fax 797-1101
www.uticak12.org
Bemis JHS 1,000/7-8
12500 19 Mile Rd 48313 586-797-2500
Thomas Yaw, prin. Fax 797-2501
Browning ES 400/K-6
12400 19 Mile Rd 48313 586-797-4000
Nina Carver-Hardewich, prin. Fax 797-4001
Burr ES 500/K-6
41460 Ryan Rd 48314 586-797-4100
Jeanne Poleski, prin. Fax 797-4101
Collins ES 400/K-6
12900 Grand Haven Dr 48312 586-797-4200
Jennifer Kleiner, prin. Fax 797-4201
DeKeyser ES 500/K-6
39600 Atkinson Dr 48313 586-797-4400
MaryBeth Merlo, prin. Fax 797-4401
Dresden ES 500/PK-6
11400 Delvin Dr 48314 586-797-4500
Jami Wood, prin. Fax 797-4501
Graebner ES 600/PK-6
41875 Saal Rd 48313 586-797-5000
Gregory Church, prin. Fax 797-5001
Harvey ES 500/K-6
41700 Montroy Dr 48313 586-797-5100
Laurie Pritchard, prin. Fax 797-5101
Havel ES 600/K-6
41855 Schoenherr Rd 48313 586-797-5200
Kristina Barel, prin. Fax 797-5201
Messmore ES 300/K-6
8742 Dill Dr 48312 586-797-5600
Renee Fiema, prin. Fax 797-5601
Oakbrook ES 600/PK-6
12060 Greenway Dr 48312 586-797-5900
Linda Schneider-Rediske, prin. Fax 797-5901
Plumbrook ES 500/K-6
39660 Spalding Dr 48313 586-797-6000
Melissa Labadie, prin. Fax 797-6001
Schuchard ES 700/K-6
2900 Holly Dr 48310 586-797-6200
Stephen Slancik, prin. Fax 797-6201
Schwarzkoff ES 500/K-6
8401 Constitution Blvd 48313 586-797-6300
Amber Fante, prin. Fax 797-6301
Other Schools – See Macomb, Shelby Township, Utica

Warren Consolidated SD
Supt. — See Warren
Angus ES 400/K-5
3180 Hein Dr 48310 586-825-2780
Carlie McClenathan, prin. Fax 698-4321
Black ES 300/K-5
14100 Heritage Rd 48312 586-825-2840
Khris Nedam, prin. Fax 698-4326
Carleton MS 600/6-8
8900 15 Mile Rd 48312 586-825-2590
Eric Kausch, prin. Fax 698-4286
Grissom MS 700/6-8
35701 Ryan Rd 48310 586-825-2560
Joseph Konal, prin. Fax 698-4313
Harwood ES 400/K-5
4900 Southlawn Dr 48310 586-825-2650
Coreen Tremmel, prin. Fax 698-4346
Hatherly Educational Center PK-PK
35201 Davison St 48310 586-825-2880
Deborah Teolis, admin. Fax 698-4351
Holden ES 300/K-6
37565 Calka Dr 48310 586-825-2670
Cheryl Priemer, prin. Fax 698-4356
Jefferson ES 400/K-5
37555 Carol Dr 48310 586-825-2680
Keith Karpinski, prin. Fax 698-4361
Willow Woods ES 400/K-5
11001 Daniel Dr 48312 586-825-2850
Vera Ivezaj, prin. Fax 698-4390

Parkway Christian S 500/PK-12
14500 Metropolitan Pkwy 48312 586-446-9900
Lila Place, head sch Fax 446-9904

Stevensville, Berrien, Pop. 1,138
Lakeshore SD 2,800/PK-12
5771 Cleveland Ave 49127 269-428-1400
Philip Freeman, admin. Fax 428-1574
www.lakeshoreschools.k12.mi.us
Hollywood ES 400/PK-5
143 E John Beers Rd 49127 269-428-1414
Natalie Macerata, prin. Fax 428-1578
Lakeshore MS 700/6-8
1459 W John Beers Rd 49127 269-428-1408
Jason Messenger, prin. Fax 428-1571
Roosevelt ES 400/K-5
2000 El Dorado Dr 49127 269-428-1416
Kristen Pennington, prin. Fax 428-1576
Stewart ES 400/K-5
2750 Orchard Ln 49127 269-428-1418
Lori Kuntz, prin. Fax 428-1580

Christ Lutheran S 100/PK-8
4333 Cleveland Ave 49127 269-429-7111
Neil Webb, prin. Fax 429-3788
St. Paul Lutheran S 100/PK-8
2673 W John Beers Rd 49127 269-429-1546
Paul Ihde, prin. Fax 429-0172

Stockbridge, Ingham, Pop. 1,207
Stockbridge Community SD 1,000/PK-12
305 W Elizabeth St 49285 517-851-7188
Karl Heidrich, supt. Fax 851-8334
panthernet.net
Heritage S 200/3-6
222 Western St 49285 517-851-8600
Shelley Ruh, prin. Fax 851-4676
Smith ES 300/PK-2
100 Price Ave 49285 517-851-7735
Bradley Edwards, prin. Fax 851-4721

Sturgis, Saint Joseph, Pop. 10,748
Nottawa Community SD 100/K-8
26438 M 86 49091 269-467-7153
Ruth Rowe, supt. Fax 467-6069
www.nottawaschool.org
Nottawa Community S 100/K-8
26438 M 86 49091 269-467-7153
Jerome Wolff, prin. Fax 467-6069

Sturgis SD 3,300/K-12
107 W West St 49091 269-659-1500
Dr. Thomas Langdon, supt. Fax 659-1584
www.sturgisps.org/
Congress ES 200/K-2
421 E Congress St 49091 269-659-1565
Nicholas Herblet, prin. Fax 659-1567
Eastwood ES 800/3-5
909 S Franks Ave 49091 269-659-1560
Michael Miller, prin. Fax 659-1555
Sturgis MS 700/6-8
1400 E Lafayette St 49091 269-659-1550
Lauri Pressly, prin. Fax 659-1553
Wall ES 400/K-2
702 E Lafayette St 49091 269-659-1570
Harmonee McCrea, prin. Fax 659-1589
Wenzel ES 200/K-2
403 E Park St 49091 269-659-1575
Nick Herblet, prin. Fax 659-8161

Lake Area Christian S 50/K-12
63590 Borgert Rd 49091 269-651-5135
Sharon Wickey, admin. Fax 651-8648
Trinity Lutheran S 100/PK-8
406 S Lakeview Ave 49091 269-651-4245
Paul Kosman, prin. Fax 659-2909

Suttons Bay, Leelanau, Pop. 604
Suttons Bay SD 600/PK-12
PO Box 367 49682 231-271-8601
Michael Carmean, supt. Fax 271-8691
www.suttonsbayschools.com
Suttons Bay ES 200/PK-5
PO Box 367 49682 231-271-8601
Fax 271-8656

Swartz Creek, Genesee, Pop. 5,666
Carman-Ainsworth Community SD
Supt. — See Flint
Rankin ES 300/K-5
G-3459 Mundy Ave 48473 810-591-4605
Laura Garrison, prin. Fax 591-8440

Swartz Creek Community SD 4,000/PK-12
8354 Cappy Ln 48473 810-591-2300
Benjamin Mainka, supt. Fax 591-2784
www.swartzcreek.org
Crapo Child Development Center PK-PK
8197 Miller Rd 48473 810-591-4373
David Simancek, dir. Fax 591-4343
Dieck ES 300/K-5
2239 Van Vleet Rd 48473 810-591-5271
Bruce Fuller, prin. Fax 591-5273
Elms Road ES 500/K-5
3259 S Elms Rd 48473 810-591-1250
Dave Simonsen, prin. Fax 591-1274
Morrish ES 500/K-5
5055 Maple Ave 48473 810-591-3702
Michele Corbat, prin. Fax 591-0580
Swartz Creek MS 900/6-8
8230 Crapo St 48473 810-591-1705
Kevin Klaeren, prin. Fax 591-1712
Syring ES 300/K-5
5300 Oakview Dr 48473 810-591-1301
Michelle Telliga, prin. Fax 591-1303
Other Schools – See Gaines

Genesee Academy 200/PK-12
9447 Corunna Rd 48473 810-250-7557
Br. Imad Tibi, prin. Fax 250-7556

Tawas City, Iosco, Pop. 1,814
Tawas Area SD 1,100/K-12
245 W M 55 48763 989-984-2250
Jeffrey Hutchison, supt. Fax 984-2253
www.tawas.net
Bolen ES 400/K-4
211 S Plank Rd 48763 989-984-2200
John Klinger, prin. Fax 984-2203
Tawas Area MS 300/5-8
255 W M 55 48763 989-984-2300
Peter Newman, prin. Fax 984-2303

Emanuel Lutheran S 50/PK-8
216 North St W 48763 989-362-3622
Dennis Fricke, prin.

Taylor, Wayne, Pop. 61,678
Taylor SD 7,400/PK-12
23033 Northline Rd 48180 734-374-1200
Ben Williams, supt. Fax 287-6083
www.taylorschools.net
Eureka Heights ES 300/K-5
25125 Eureka Rd 48180 734-946-6597
Stacie Hall, prin. Fax 946-6591
Holland ES 300/K-5
10201 Holland Rd 48180 313-295-5795
Kathy McNiven-King, prin. Fax 295-8375
Hoover MS 500/6-8
27101 Beverly Rd 48180 313-295-5775
Matthew Hall, prin. Fax 295-8354
Johnson ECC PK-PK
20701 Wohlfeil St 48180 313-295-8362
Lee MacKenzie, admin. Fax 295-8376
Kinyon ES 400/K-5
10455 Monroe Blvd 48180 313-295-5802
Susan Sweet, prin. Fax 295-8377
McDowell ES 300/K-5
22929 Brest 48180 734-374-1240
Lynne Borg, prin. Fax 374-1290
Moody ES 400/K-5
8280 Hipp St 48180 313-295-5807
Michelle Hernandez, prin. Fax 295-8358
Myers ES 400/K-5
16201 Lauren St 48180 734-946-6602
Tamara Jones-Jackson, prin. Fax 955-6847
Randall ES 700/K-5
8699 Robert St 48180 313-295-5812
Cynthia Meszaros, prin. Fax 295-8336

Taylor Parks ES 500/K-5
20614 Pinecrest St 48180 734-374-1246
Diane Downie, prin. Fax 388-0655
West MS 600/6-8
10575 William St 48180 313-295-5783
Patricia Kaechele, prin. Fax 291-2203

Oakwood Jr. Academy 50/K-8
26300 Goddard Rd 48180 313-291-6790
Connie Hickman, prin. Fax 291-5483

Tecumseh, Lenawee, Pop. 8,429
Tecumseh SD 2,800/PK-12
212 N Ottawa St 49286 517-424-7318
Dr. Kelly Coffin Ed.D., supt. Fax 423-3847
tps.k12.mi.us
Compass Learning Ctr 900/2-6
307 N Maumee St 49286 517-423-1105
Angel Mensing, prin. Fax 423-1300
Tecumseh East STEAM Center 200/8-8
600 Herrick Park Dr 49286 517-423-2324
Alan Schmidt, prin. Fax 423-1401
Tecumseh North Early Learning Center 300/PK-1
500 S Adrian St 49286 517-423-9744
Carl Lewandowski, prin. Fax 423-1400
Tecumseh West STEAM Center 200/7-7
401 N Van Buren St 49286 517-423-3331
Deidra Thelen, prin. Fax 423-1301
Other Schools – See Adrian

Tekonsha, Calhoun, Pop. 699
Tekonsha Community SD 100/K-12
245 S Elm St 49092 517-767-4121
Jeff Kawaski, supt. Fax 767-3465
www.tekonshaschools.org
Tekonsha JSHS 100/K-12
245 S Elm St 49092 517-767-4121
Jeffrey Kawaski, admin. Fax 767-3465

Temperance, Monroe, Pop. 8,433
Bedford SD 4,600/K-12
1623 W Sterns Rd 48182 734-850-6000
Dr. Mark French, supt. Fax 850-6099
www.mulenation.us
Bedford JHS 1,100/6-8
8405 Jackman Rd 48182 734-850-6200
Roderick Hurley, prin. Fax 850-6299
Jackman Road ES 700/K-5
8008 Jackman Rd 48182 734-850-6600
Sherry Farnan, prin. Fax 850-6699
Other Schools – See Lambertville

State Line Christian S 300/K-12
6320 Lewis Ave 48182 734-847-6771
Steve Hobbins, admin. Fax 847-4968

Thompsonville, Manistee, Pop. 433
Benzie County Central SD
Supt. — See Benzonia
Betsie Valley ES 200/K-5
17936 Cadillac Hwy 49683 231-378-4164
Amiee Erfourth, prin. Fax 378-2538

Three Oaks, Berrien, Pop. 1,589
River Valley SD 500/PK-12
15480 Three Oaks Rd 49128 269-756-9541
William Kearney, supt. Fax 756-6631
www.rivervalleyschools.org/
Three Oaks ES 100/PK-PK, 3-
100 Oak St 49128 269-756-9050
Heidi Clark, prin. Fax 756-1420
Other Schools – See Sawyer

Three Rivers, Saint Joseph, Pop. 7,541
Three Rivers Community SD 2,800/K-12
851 6th Avenue Rd 49093 269-279-1100
Jean Logan, supt. Fax 279-5584
www.trschools.org
Andrews ES 300/K-5
200 S Douglas Ave 49093 269-279-1140
Ben McIntyre, prin. Fax 278-8106
Hoppin ES 300/K-5
415 N Main St 49093 269-279-1142
David Soderquist, prin. Fax 278-6096
Norton ES 300/K-5
59692 Arthur L Jones Rd 49093 269-244-1144
Jennifer Graber, prin. Fax 244-0500
Park ES 400/K-5
53806 Wilbur Rd 49093 269-279-1143
Kevin Faraci, prin. Fax 278-7122
Three Rivers MS 600/6-8
1101 Jefferson St 49093 269-279-1130
Andy Mains, prin. Fax 279-1139

Immaculate Conception S 50/PK-5
601 S Douglas Ave 49093 269-273-2085
Sharon Alexander, prin. Fax 273-1925

Toivola, Houghton
Elm River Township SD 50/K-8
3999 Winona Rd 49965 906-288-3751
George Stockero, supt. Fax 288-3074
www.elmriver.k12.mi.us
Elm River ES 50/K-8
3999 Winona Rd 49965 906-288-3751
Bruce Matson, prin. Fax 288-3074

Traverse City, Grand Traverse, Pop. 14,412
Traverse City Area SD 9,400/PK-12
412 Webster St 49686 231-933-1700
Paul Soma, supt. Fax 933-1721
www.tcaps.net
Blair ES 300/PK-5
1625 Sawyer Rd 49685 231-933-5700
Kirsten Jones-Morgan, prin. Fax 933-5703
Central ES 600/PK-5
301 W Seventh St 49684 231-933-5600
Toby Tisdale, prin. Fax 933-5617
Cherry Knoll ES 400/PK-5
1800 3 Mile Rd N 49696 231-933-8940
Dr. Victoria Derks, prin. Fax 933-8943

Courtade ES 300/PK-5
1111 Rasho Rd 49696 231-933-5800
Katie Bonne, prin. Fax 933-5803
Long Lake ES 300/PK-5
7600 N Long Lake Rd 49685 231-933-7800
Kate Burwinkel, prin. Fax 933-7822
Montessori S at Glenn Loomis 300/PK-6
1009 S Oak St 49684 231-933-5608
Lisa VanLoo, dir. Fax 933-3655
Oak Park ES PK-PK
301 S Garfield Ave 49686 231-933-1759
Jame McCall, admin. Fax 933-1760
Old Mission Peninsula ES 200/PK-5
2699 Island View Rd 49686 231-933-7420
Beth Still, prin. Fax 933-7442
Silver Lake ES 300/PK-5
5858 Culver Rd 49685 231-933-5760
Angela Camp, prin. Fax 933-5789
Traverse City East MS 900/6-8
1776 3 Mile Rd N 49696 231-933-7300
Colleen Smith, prin. Fax 933-6998
Traverse City West MS 1,200/6-8
3950 Silver Lake Rd 49684 231-933-8200
Terry Smith, prin. Fax 933-8205
Traverse Heights ES 200/PK-5
933 Rose St 49686 231-933-6500
Ryan Schrock, prin. Fax 933-6503
Westwoods ES 400/PK-5
1500 Fisher Rd 49685 231-933-7970
Dan Tiesworth, prin. Fax 933-8520
Willow Hill ES 500/PK-5
1250 Hill St 49684 231-933-8540
Angela Sides-McKay, prin. Fax 933-8572
Other Schools – See Williamsburg

Children's House 200/PK-8
5363 N Long Lake Rd 49685 231-929-9325
Michele Shane, head sch Fax 929-9384
Holy Angels S 300/PK-2
130 E Tenth St 49684 231-946-5961
Jessica Lesinski, admin. Fax 946-1878
Immaculate Conception S 200/3-5
314 Vine St 49684 231-947-1252
Maureen DeYoung, prin. Fax 947-2508
Pathfinder S 100/PK-8
11930 S West Bay Shore Dr 49684 231-995-3800
Robert Hansen, head sch Fax 995-3850
St. Elizabeth Ann Seton MS 200/6-8
1601 3 Mile Rd N 49696 231-932-4810
Carl Scholten, prin. Fax 932-4814
Traverse City Christian S 200/PK-12
753 Emerson Rd 49696 231-929-1747
Bart Den Boer, admin. Fax 929-1831
Traverse City SDA S 50/K-8
2055B 4 Mile Rd N 49686 231-947-4640
JanElla Schnepp, prin.
Trinity Lutheran S 100/PK-8
1003 S Maple St 49684 231-946-2721
Rev. Bruce Lucas, prin. Fax 946-4796

Trenton, Wayne, Pop. 18,620
Trenton SD 2,700/K-12
2603 Charlton Rd 48183 734-676-8600
Rodney Wakeham, supt. Fax 676-4851
www.trentonschools.com
Anderson ES 500/K-5
2600 Harrison Ave 48183 734-676-2177
Douglas Mentzer, prin. Fax 692-6354
Arthurs MS 700/6-8
4000 Marian Dr 48183 734-676-8700
Stephanie O'Connor, prin. Fax 676-7364
Hedke ES 500/K-5
3201 Marian Dr 48183 734-692-4563
Vincent Porreca, prin. Fax 692-6355

St. Joseph S 200/K-8
2675 3rd St 48183 734-676-2565
Christen McMillan, prin. Fax 676-9744

Troy, Oakland, Pop. 79,352
Avondale SD
Supt. — See Auburn Hills
Woodland ES 400/K-5
6465 Livernois Rd 48098 248-537-6900
Arryn Schneider, prin. Fax 537-6905

Birmingham SD
Supt. — See Beverly Hills
Pembroke ES 300/K-5
955 Eton Dr 48084 248-203-3888
Susan Crocker, prin. Fax 203-3920

Troy SD 12,000/K-12
4400 Livernois Rd 48098 248-823-4000
Dr. Richard Machesky Ed.D., supt. Fax 823-4013
www.troy.k12.mi.us
Baker MS 700/6-8
1359 Torpey Dr 48083 248-823-4600
Dr. Audra Melton, prin. Fax 823-4613
Barnard ES 500/K-5
3601 Forge Dr 48083 248-823-4300
Melanie Morey, prin. Fax 823-4313
Bemis ES 600/K-5
3571 Northfield Pkwy 48084 248-823-4100
Jeremey Whan, prin. Fax 823-4113
Boulan Park MS 700/6-8
3570 Northfield Pkwy 48084 248-823-4900
Jo Kwasny, prin. Fax 823-4913
Costello ES 300/K-5
1333 Hamman Dr 48085 248-823-3700
Dr. Tammy DiPonio, prin. Fax 823-3713
Hamilton ES 500/K-5
5625 Northfield Pkwy 48098 248-823-4400
Sarah Glasser, prin. Fax 823-4413
Hill ES 300/K-5
4600 Forsyth Dr 48085 248-823-3500
Janice Brzezinski, prin. Fax 823-3513
Larson MS 700/6-8
2222 E Long Lake Rd 48085 248-823-4800
Joseph Duda, prin. Fax 823-4813

Leonard ES 400/K-5
4401 Tallman Dr 48085 248-823-3300
Erin Detmer, prin. Fax 823-3313
Martell ES 500/K-5
5666 Livernois Rd 48098 248-823-3800
John Pagel, prin. Fax 823-3813
Morse ES 500/K-5
475 Cherry Dr 48083 248-823-3200
Stephanie Zendler, prin. Fax 823-3213
Schroeder ES 500/K-5
3541 Jack Dr 48084 248-823-3600
Brian Canfield, prin. Fax 823-3613
Smith MS 600/6-8
5835 Donaldson Dr 48085 248-823-4700
Timothy Fulcher, prin. Fax 823-4713
Troy Union ES 500/K-5
1340 E Square Lake Rd 48085 248-823-3100
Mike Cottone, prin. Fax 823-3113
Wass ES 400/K-5
2340 Willard Dr 48085 248-823-3900
Matt Jansen, prin. Fax 823-3913
Wattles ES 500/K-5
3555 Ellenboro Dr 48083 248-823-3400
Dr. Joyce Brasington, prin. Fax 823-3413

Warren Consolidated SD
Supt. — See Warren
Susick ES 400/K-5
2200 Castleton Dr 48083 586-825-2665
Mary Caruso, prin. Fax 698-4376

Bethany Christian S 300/K-12
2601 John R Rd 48083 248-689-4821
Brookfield Academy 300/PK-5
3950 Livernois Rd 48083 248-689-9565
Lisa Luther, prin. Fax 689-3335
Troy Adventist Academy 50/K-8
2777 Crooks Rd 48084 248-649-3122
Carli Sullivan, prin. Fax 643-0805

Twin Lake, Muskegon, Pop. 1,699
Reeths-Puffer SD
Supt. — See Muskegon
Twin Lake ES 300/PK-4
3175 5th St 49457 231-719-3190
Dawn Schmitt, prin. Fax 828-5028

Ubly, Sanilac, Pop. 853
Ubly Community SD 600/K-12
2020 Union St 48475 989-658-8202
Joseph Candela, supt. Fax 658-2361
www.ublyschools.org
Ubly S 300/K-6
2020 Union St 48475 989-658-8261
Joel Brandel, prin. Fax 658-8564

Union City, Branch, Pop. 1,560
Union City Community SD 1,100/PK-12
430 Saint Joseph St 49094 517-741-8091
Patrick Kreger, supt. Fax 741-5205
www.unioncityschools.org/
Union City ES 400/PK-4
430 Saint Joseph St 49094 517-741-8191
Lori Vaccaro, prin. Fax 741-8415
Union City MS 300/5-8
430 Saint Joseph St 49094 517-741-5381
Brandon Bruce, prin. Fax 741-8513

Unionville, Tuscola, Pop. 505
Unionville-Sebewaing SD
Supt. — See Sebewaing
Unionville-Sebewaing Area ES 300/PK-5
7835 N Unionville Rd 48767 989-883-9147
David Farley, prin. Fax 883-9193

Utica, Macomb, Pop. 4,675
Utica Community SD
Supt. — See Sterling Heights
Flickinger ES 500/K-6
45400 Vanker Ave 48317 586-797-4900
Nancy Brunetz, prin. Fax 797-4901
Wiley ES 600/PK-6
47240 Shelby Rd 48317 586-797-6700
Christopher Cassin, prin. Fax 797-6701

St. Lawrence S 800/PK-8
44429 Utica Rd 48317 586-731-0135
Lisa DiMercurio, prin. Fax 731-5393
Trinity Lutheran S 500/PK-8
45160 Van Dyke Ave 48317 586-731-4490
Bruce Volkert, prin. Fax 731-1071

Vanderbilt, Otsego, Pop. 548
Vanderbilt Area SD 100/PK-12
947 Donovan St 49795 989-983-2561
Richard Heitmeyer, supt. Fax 983-3051
www.vanderbilt.k12.mi.us
Vanderbilt Area S 100/PK-12
947 Donovan St 49795 989-983-2561
Richard Heitmeyer, supt. Fax 983-3051

Vassar, Tuscola, Pop. 2,631
Vassar SD 1,300/PK-12
220 Athletic St 48768 989-823-8535
Dorothy Blackwell, supt. Fax 823-7823
www.vassar.k12.mi.us
Central ES 400/K-5
220 Athletic St 48768 989-823-8566
Lisa Riccobono, prin. Fax 823-7516
Townsend North Preschool 100/PK-PK
220 Athletic St 48768 989-823-7722
Lisa Riccobono, prin. Fax 823-7513

St. Luke's Lutheran S 50/K-8
1056 Wels Ln 48768 989-823-8400
John Lange, prin.

Vermontville, Eaton, Pop. 745
Maple Valley SD 1,100/PK-12
11014 Nashville Hwy 49096 517-852-9699
Michelle Falcon, supt. Fax 852-5076
mvs.k12.mi.us
Maplewood ES 300/3-6
170 Seminary St 49096 517-726-0600
Cindy Trebian, prin. Fax 726-0052
Other Schools – See Nashville

Vernon, Shiawassee, Pop. 776
Corunna SD
Supt. — See Corunna
Reed ES 50/K-K
201 E Washington Ave 48476 989-743-1579
Shannon Toma, prin. Fax 288-0945

Vestaburg, Montcalm
Vestaburg Community SD 600/PK-12
7188 Avenue B 48891 989-268-5353
Brandon Hubbard, supt. Fax 268-5246
www.vcs-k12.net
Vestaburg ES 300/PK-6
7188 Avenue B 48891 989-268-5284
Darby Weaver, prin. Fax 268-5898

Vicksburg, Kalamazoo, Pop. 2,854
Vicksburg Community SD 2,600/PK-12
PO Box 158 49097 269-321-1000
Charles Glaes, supt. Fax 321-1055
www.vicksburgcommunityschools.org/
Indian Lake ES 400/PK-5
11901 S 30th St 49097 269-321-1400
Ruth Hook, prin. Fax 321-1455
Sunset Lake ES 500/PK-5
201 N Boulevard St 49097 269-321-1500
Amie McCaw, prin. Fax 321-1555
Vicksburg MS 600/6-8
348 E Prairie St 49097 269-321-1300
Matt VanDussen, prin. Fax 321-1355
Other Schools – See Scotts

Wakefield, Gogebic, Pop. 1,831
Wakefield-Marenisco SD 300/K-12
715 Putnam St 49968 906-224-9421
Catherine Shamion, supt. Fax 224-1771
www.wmschools.org
Wakefield-Marenisco S 300/K-12
715 Putnam St 49968 906-224-7211
Catherine Shamion, supt. Fax 224-1771

Waldron, Hillsdale, Pop. 534
Waldron Area SD 100/K-12
13380 Waldron Rd 49288 517-286-6251
Mike Potts, supt. Fax 286-6254
www.wassd.org
Waldron Area S 100/K-12
13380 Waldron Rd 49288 517-286-6251
Ken Poling, admin. Fax 286-6254

Walkerville, Oceana, Pop. 238
Walkerville SD 100/PK-12
145 Lathrop St 49459 231-873-4850
Gary Jensen, supt. Fax 873-5615
walkk12.org
Walkerville S 100/PK-12
145 Lathrop St 49459 231-873-4850
Gary Jensen, prin. Fax 873-5615

Walled Lake, Oakland, Pop. 6,836
Walled Lake Consolidated SD 14,600/PK-12
850 Ladd Rd Bldg D 48390 248-956-2000
Kenneth Gutman M.A., supt. Fax 956-2123
www.wlcsd.org
Geisler MS 700/6-8
46720 W Pontiac Trl 48390 248-956-2900
Sheryl Kennedy Ph.D., prin. Fax 956-2905
Glengary ES 400/K-5
3070 Woodbury St 48390 248-956-3100
RosaLeigh Johnson, prin. Fax 956-3105
Guest ES 400/K-5
1655 Decker Rd 48390 248-956-3300
Michelle Fiebke-Lang, prin. Fax 956-3305
Oakley Park ES 400/K-5
2015 E Oakley Park Rd 48390 248-956-4100
Kristin Froning, prin. Fax 956-4105
Walled Lake ES 400/K-5
1055 W West Maple Rd 48390 248-956-4300
Cynthia Nickel, prin. Fax 956-4305
Other Schools – See Commerce Township, Novi, West Bloomfield, White Lake, Wixom

---

Lakes Area Montessori Center 100/PK-5
8605 Richardson Rd 48390 248-360-0500
Suha Zablock, admin. Fax 360-1542
St. Matthew Lutheran S 300/PK-8
2040 S Commerce Rd 48390 248-624-7677
Susan Palka, prin. Fax 624-0685
St. William S 200/K-8
135 Oflaherty St 48390 248-669-4440
Linda Jackson, prin. Fax 669-2245

Warren, Macomb, Pop. 130,738
Center Line SD
Supt. — See Center Line
Crothers ES 300/K-5
27401 Campbell Rd 48093 586-510-2400
Janis Byrn, prin. Fax 510-2409
ECC 50/PK-PK
24580 Cunningham Ave 48091 586-510-2800
Terri Karam, admin. Fax 510-2809
Peck ES 300/K-5
11300 Engleman Rd 48089 586-510-2600
Julian Roper, prin. Fax 510-2609
Roose ES 500/K-5
25310 Masch Ave 48091 586-510-2700
Shannon McBrady, prin. Fax 510-2709

Fitzgerald SD 2,200/PK-12
23200 Ryan Rd 48091 586-757-1750
Barbara VanSweden, supt. Fax 758-0991
www.fitz.k12.mi.us
Chatterton MS 600/6-8
24333 Ryan Rd 48091 586-757-6650
Amanda Clor, prin. Fax 620-6011
Mound Park ES 300/K-5
5356 Toepfer Rd 48091 586-757-7590
Keith Tonn, prin. Fax 620-6085
Schofield ECC PK-PK
21555 Warner Ave 48091 586-757-5150
Theresa Swalec, admin. Fax 620-5946
Westview ES 400/K-5
24077 Warner Ave 48091 586-757-5520
Denye Griessel, prin. Fax 620-6397

Van Dyke SD 2,700/PK-12
23500 Mac Arthur Blvd 48089 586-757-6600
Piper Bognar, supt. Fax 759-9408
www.vdps.net
Carlson ES 500/K-5
12355 Mruk Ave 48089 586-758-8345
Tricia Huey-Rocheleau, prin. Fax 758-7397
Kennedy ECC PK-PK
11333 Kaltz Ave 48089 586-759-9406
Melissa Pluszczynski, prin. Fax 758-7394
Lincoln ES 500/K-5
22100 Federal Ave 48089 586-758-8342
Nicole Susewitz, prin. Fax 758-7381
Lincoln MS 600/6-8
22500 Federal Ave 48089 586-758-8320
Victor Breithaupt, prin. Fax 758-8322
McKinley ES 400/K-5
13173 Toepfer Rd 48089 586-758-8365
Heather Brodi, prin. Fax 427-3658

Warren Consolidated SD 13,700/PK-12
31300 Anita Dr 48093 586-825-2400
Dr. Robert Livernois, supt. Fax 698-4095
www.wcskids.net
Beer MS 700/6-8
3200 Martin Rd 48092 586-574-3175
Marla Otterbacher, prin. Fax 698-4277
Carter MS 800/6-8
12000 Masonic Blvd 48093 586-825-2620
Amy Hendry, prin. Fax 698-4295
Cromie ES 600/K-5
29797 Gilbert Dr 48093 586-574-3160
Mary Ann Figurski, prin. Fax 698-4331
Green Acres ES 500/K-5
4655 Holmes Dr 48092 586-825-2890
Stacey Leavell, prin. Fax 698-4341
Lean ES 600/K-5
2825 Girard Dr 48092 586-574-3230
Kerry Keener, prin. Fax 698-4366
Siersma ES 500/K-6
3100 Donna Ave 48091 586-574-3174
Eric Williamson, prin. Fax 698-4371
Wilde ES 400/K-5
32343 Bunert Rd 48088 586-294-8490
Matt Guinn, prin. Fax 698-4380
Wilkerson ES 500/K-5
12100 Masonic Blvd 48093 586-825-2550
Anthony Viviano, prin. Fax 698-4385
Other Schools – See Sterling Heights, Troy

Warren Woods SD 3,200/PK-12
12900 Frazho Rd 48089 586-439-4400
Stacey Denewith-Fici, supt. Fax 353-0544
www.warrenwoods.misd.net
Briarwood ES 300/K-5
14100 Leisure Dr 48088 586-439-4404
Christine Walter, prin. Fax 445-6335
Pinewood ES 400/K-5
14411 Bade Dr 48088 586-439-4405
Leo Kondziolka, prin. Fax 778-3520
Warren Woods ECC PK-PK
12900 Frazho Rd 48089 586-439-4885
Stacy Santamaria, coord.
Warren Woods MS 800/6-8
13400 E 12 Mile Rd 48088 586-439-4403
Donny Sikora, prin. Fax 574-9830
Westwood ES 500/K-5
11999 Martin Rd 48093 586-439-4406
Melissa Johnson, prin. Fax 573-4813

Crown of Life Lutheran S 50/PK-8
25065 Eureka Dr 48091 586-427-6579
Christopher Holman, prin. Fax 427-6579
Immaculate Conception Ukranian S 200/PK-8
29500 Westbrook Ave 48092 586-574-2480
Romana Tobianski, prin. Fax 574-3497
Peace Lutheran S 100/PK-8
11701 E 12 Mile Rd 48093 586-751-8011
Michele Gapski, prin. Fax 751-8558
St. Anne S 500/PK-8
5920 Arden Ave 48092 586-264-2911
Matthew Marion, prin. Fax 264-4533
Warren Woods Christian S 200/PK-8
14000 E 13 Mile Rd 48088 586-772-8787
Beth Denhart, admin. Fax 772-9078

Washington, Macomb
Romeo Community SD
Supt. — See Romeo
Hevel ES 500/K-5
12700 29 Mile Rd 48094 586-752-5951
Paul Essian, prin. Fax 752-6008
Indian Hills ES 500/K-5
8401 29 Mile Rd 48095 586-752-0290
Lisa Wujcyk, prin. Fax 752-0467
Powell MS 700/6-8
62100 Jewell Rd 48094 586-752-0270
Jeffrey LaPerriere, prin. Fax 752-0276
Washington ES 400/K-5
58230 Van Dyke Rd 48094 586-781-5563
William Bock, prin. Fax 752-0470

Cross of Glory Lutheran S 50/PK-8
61095 Campground Rd 48094 586-781-9870
Douglas Fillner, prin. Fax 781-9870

Waterford, Oakland, Pop. 74,500

Waterford SD 9,200/PK-12
501 N Cass Lake Rd 48328 248-682-7800
Dr. Keith Wunderlich, supt. Fax 706-4888
www.wsdmi.org

Beaumont ES 400/K-5
6532 Elizabeth Lake Rd 48327 248-682-6822
Jennifer Knipper, prin. Fax 738-4723

Cooley ES 400/K-5
2000 Highfield Rd 48329 248-673-0300
Mike Batten, prin. Fax 674-6322

Donelson Hills ES 400/K-5
2690 Wewoka Rd 48328 248-682-9530
Anne Kruse, prin. Fax 738-4703

Grayson ES 400/K-5
3800 W Walton Blvd 48329 248-673-8900
Lynn Bigelman, prin. Fax 674-6319

Haviland ES 300/K-5
5305 Cass Elizabeth Rd 48327 248-682-2620
Michelle Sullivan, prin. Fax 738-4798

Knudsen ES 300/PK-5
5449 Crescent Rd 48327 248-682-7300
Laura Smith, prin. Fax 738-4711

Mason MS 1,300/6-8
3835 W Walton Blvd 48329 248-674-2281
Roger Opsommer, prin. Fax 673-3718

Pierce MS 1,000/6-8
5145 Hatchery Rd 48329 248-674-0331
Yvonne Dixon, prin. Fax 674-4222

Riverside ES 300/K-5
5280 Farm Rd 48327 248-674-0805
Suzanne Grambush, prin. Fax 674-7686

Schoolcraft ES 400/K-5
6400 Maceday Dr 48329 248-623-6211
Cheryl Pocius, prin. Fax 623-2635

Stepanski ECC 50/PK-PK
6010 Hatchery Rd 48329 248-666-9593
Cathy Force, prin. Fax 666-8669

Other Schools – See White Lake

Oakdale Academy 200/PK-12
3200 Beacham Dr 48329 248-481-9039
Paul Rumbuc, head sch

Our Lady of the Lakes S 200/PK-5
5495 Dixie Hwy 48329 248-623-0340
Lauri Hoffman, prin. Fax 623-6650

Waterford SDA S 50/1-8
5725 Pontiac Lake Rd 48327 248-682-6262
Frances Robinson, prin. Fax 682-7164

Watersmeet, Gogebic, Pop. 416

Watersmeet Township SD 200/K-12
PO Box 217 49969 906-358-4504
Dr. Gerald Pease, supt. Fax 358-4713
www.watersmeet.k12.mi.us/

Watersmeet Township S 200/K-12
PO Box 217 49969 906-358-4504
George Peterson, supt. Fax 358-4713

Watervliet, Berrien, Pop. 1,689

Watervliet SD 1,300/PK-12
450 E Red Arrow Hwy 49098 269-463-0300
Kevin Schooley, supt. Fax 463-6809
www.watervlietps.org

North ES 300/3-5
287 W Baldwin Ave 49098 269-463-0820
Joe Allen, prin. Fax 463-7616

South ES 300/PK-2
433 Lucinda Ln 49098 269-463-0860
Carole Fetke, prin. Fax 463-7614

Watervliet MS 300/6-8
450 E Red Arrow Hwy 49098 269-463-0780
Dave Armstrong, prin. Fax 463-6809

Grace Christian S 200/PK-12
325 N M 140 49098 269-463-5545
Robin McBride, prin. Fax 463-5739

Wayland, Allegan, Pop. 3,998

Wayland UNSD 2,800/PK-12
850 E Superior St 49348 269-792-2181
Norman Taylor, supt. Fax 792-1615
waylandunion.org

Baker ES 300/PK-1
507 W Sycamore St 49348 269-792-9208
Celeste Diehm, prin. Fax 792-2092

Pine Street ES 400/5-6
201 Pine St 49348 269-792-1127
Jennifer Moushegian, prin. Fax 503-8877

Steeby ES 300/2-4
435 E Superior St 49348 269-792-2281
Mike Haverdink, prin. Fax 792-2780

Wayland Union MS 500/7-8
701 Wildcat Dr 49348 269-792-2306
Carolyn Whyte, prin. Fax 397-1126

Other Schools – See Dorr

St. Therese S 100/PK-6
430 S Main St 49348 269-792-2016
Hank Leverett, prin. Fax 792-6778

Wayne, Wayne, Pop. 17,081

Wayne-Westland Community SD
Supt. — See Westland

Franklin MS 1,000/7-8
33555 Annapolis St 48184 734-419-2400
Stacy Williamson, prin. Fax 595-2401

Hoover ES 300/K-4
5400 4th St 48184 734-419-2670
John Besek, prin. Fax 595-2498

Roosevelt/McGrath ES 400/K-4
36075 Currier St 48184 734-419-2720
Jennifer Keatts, prin. Fax 595-2126

Taft-Galloway ES 300/K-4
4035 Gloria St 48184 734-419-2760
Dr. Kenneth Schofield, prin. Fax 595-2574

St. Mary S 200/PK-8
34516 W Michigan Ave 48184 734-721-1240
Kathy Sparks, prin. Fax 721-1245

St. Michael Lutheran S 100/PK-8
3003 Hannan Rd 48184 734-728-3315
Diane Hegenauer, admin. Fax 728-9569

Webberville, Ingham, Pop. 1,262

Webberville Community SD 500/PK-12
309 E Grand River Rd 48892 517-521-3422
Brian Friddle, supt. Fax 521-4139
www.webbervilleschools.org

Webberville ES 300/PK-5
202 N Main St 48892 517-521-3071
Jeannette Kiernan, prin. Fax 521-1028

Weidman, Isabella, Pop. 947

Chippewa Hills SD
Supt. — See Remus

Weidman ES 300/PK-4
3311 N School Rd 48893 989-644-3430
Starr Lederer, prin. Fax 644-5113

West Bloomfield, Oakland, Pop. 67,200

Bloomfield Hills SD
Supt. — See Bloomfield Hls

Bloomin' Kids Preschool at Lone Pine PK-PK
3100 Lone Pine Rd 48323 248-341-7375
Lisa Gryglak, admin.

Lone Pine ES 300/K-3
3100 Lone Pine Rd 48323 248-341-7300
Dr. Mary Hillberry, prin. Fax 341-7399

West Hills MS 600/4-8
2601 Lone Pine Rd 48323 248-341-6100
Rob Durecka, prin. Fax 341-6199

Walled Lake Consolidated SD
Supt. — See Walled Lake

Keith ES 700/K-5
2800 Keith Rd 48324 248-956-3700
Marci Augenstein Ph.D., prin. Fax 956-3705

Pleasant Lake ES 600/K-5
4900 Halsted Rd 48323 248-956-2800
Nayal Maktari, prin. Fax 681-9950

Walnut Creek MS 900/6-8
7601 Walnut Lake Rd 48323 248-956-2400
Dr. Patrick Cavanaugh Ph.D., prin. Fax 956-2405

West Bloomfield SD 5,600/K-12
5810 Commerce Rd 48324 248-865-6420
Dr. Gerald Hill, supt. Fax 865-6481
www.wbsd.org

Abbott MS 700/6-8
3380 Orchard Lake Rd 48324 248-865-3670
Amy Hughes, prin. Fax 865-3671

Doherty ES 500/K-2
3575 Walnut Lake Rd 48323 248-865-6020
Scott Long, prin. Fax 865-6021

Gretchko ES 300/K-2
5300 Greer Rd 48324 248-865-6570
Sally Drummond, prin. Fax 865-6571

Orchard Lake MS 800/6-8
6000 Orchard Lake Rd 48322 248-865-4480
Morrison Borders, prin. Fax 865-4481

Scotch ES 500/3-5
5959 Commerce Rd 48324 248-865-3280
James Scrivo, prin. Fax 865-3281

Sheiko ES 600/3-5
4500 Walnut Lake Rd 48323 248-865-6370
Sonja James, prin. Fax 865-6371

Other Schools – See Keego Harbor

Brookfield Academy 100/PK-5
2965 Walnut Lake Rd 48323 248-626-6665
Lisa Winkel, prin. Fax 626-3690

West Branch, Ogemaw, Pop. 2,115

West Branch-Rose City Area SD 2,000/PK-12
PO Box 308 48661 989-343-2000
Philip Mikulski, supt. Fax 343-2006
www.wbrc.k12.mi.us/

Surline ES 600/PK-4
PO Box 308 48661 989-343-2190
Jill Smith, prin. Fax 343-2200

Surline MS 500/5-8
PO Box 308 48661 989-343-2140
Wendy Tuttle, prin. Fax 343-2239

Other Schools – See Rose City

St. Joseph S 200/PK-8
935 W Houghton Ave 48661 989-345-0220
Dave Walby, prin. Fax 345-3030

Westland, Wayne, Pop. 82,217

Livonia SD
Supt. — See Livonia

Cooper ES 700/5-6
28550 Ann Arbor Trl 48185 734-744-2710
Shalonda Owens, prin. Fax 744-2712

Hayes ES 400/K-4
30600 Louise St 48185 734-744-2725
Sheila O'Kane, prin. Fax 744-2727

Johnson ES 500/5-6
8400 N Hix Rd 48185 734-744-2740
DeAnn Urso, prin. Fax 744-2742

Wayne-Westland Community SD 12,400/PK-12
36745 Marquette St 48185 734-419-2000
Dr. Shelley Holt, supt. Fax 595-2123
www.wwcsd.net

Adams Upper ES 800/5-6
33475 Palmer Rd 48186 734-419-2380
Kate Brohl, prin. Fax 595-2374

Edison ES 500/K-4
34505 Hunter Ave 48185 734-419-2600
Christine Swanson, prin. Fax 595-2368

Elliott ES 400/K-4
30800 Bennington St 48186 734-419-2610
Andrea Griffin, prin. Fax 595-2430

Graham ES 400/K-4
1255 S John Hix St 48186 734-419-2620
Jennifer Curry, prin. Fax 595-2483

Hamilton ES 400/K-4
1031 S Schuman St 48186 734-419-2650
Kristin Brickey, prin. Fax 595-2488

Marshall Upper ES 800/5-6
35100 Bayview St 48186 734-419-2275
Kelly Kaminski, prin. Fax 595-2588

Schweitzer ES 400/K-4
2601 Treadwell St 48186 734-419-2750
Jennifer Chambers, prin. Fax 595-2564

Stevenson MS 800/7-8
38501 Palmer Rd 48186 734-419-2350
Fax 595-2692

Stottlemyer ECC 500/PK-PK
34801 Marquette St 48185 734-419-2645
Nancy Ely, dir. Fax 595-2573

Wildwood ES 500/K-4
500 N Wildwood St 48185 734-419-2790
Fax 595-2579

Other Schools – See Canton, Inkster, Wayne

St. John Lutheran S 100/PK-8
2602 S Wayne Rd 48186 734-576-1539
Lori Bartholomew, prin.

St. Matthew Lutheran S 200/PK-8
5885 N Venoy Rd 48185 734-425-0261
Andrea Unger, prin. Fax 425-7932

West Olive, Ottawa

West Ottawa SD
Supt. — See Holland

Sheldon Woods ES 100/K-5
15050 Blair St 49460 616-786-1700
Kevin Westrate, prin.

Westphalia, Clinton, Pop. 918

Pewamo-Westphalia SD 600/PK-12
5101 S Clintonia Rd 48894 989-587-5100
Jeff Wright, supt. Fax 587-5120
www.pwschools.org

Other Schools – See Pewamo

St. Mary S 200/K-6
209 N Westphalia St 48894 989-587-3702
Darren Thelen, prin. Fax 587-3706

White Cloud, Newaygo, Pop. 1,346

White Cloud SD 800/K-12
PO Box 1000 49349 231-689-6591
Barry Seabrook, supt. Fax 689-3210
www.whitecloud.net

White Cloud ES 500/K-5
PO Box 1002 49349 231-689-2300
Lorie Watson, prin. Fax 689-2323

Whitehall, Muskegon, Pop. 2,657

Whitehall SD 2,000/PK-12
541 E Slocum St 49461 231-893-1005
Dr. Jerry McDowell, supt. Fax 894-6450
www.whitehallschools.net

Ealy ES 500/3-5
425 E Sophia St 49461 231-893-1040
Ron Bailey, prin. Fax 894-9060

Shoreline ES 500/PK-2
205 E Market St 49461 231-893-1050
David Hundt, prin. Fax 893-4705

Whitehall MS 500/6-8
401 S Elizabeth St 49461 231-893-1030
C.J. VanWieren, prin. Fax 894-6844

White Lake, Oakland, Pop. 22,608

Huron Valley SD
Supt. — See Highland

Lakewood ES 400/PK-5
1500 Bogie Lake Rd 48383 248-684-8030
Jill Brower, prin. Fax 684-8069

Oxbow ES 400/PK-5
100 Oxbow Lake Rd 48386 248-684-8085
Christopher McAuliffe, prin. Fax 676-8436

White Lake MS 800/6-8
1450 Bogie Lake Rd 48383 248-684-8004
Patrick Borg, prin. Fax 676-8437

Walled Lake Consolidated SD
Supt. — See Walled Lake

Dublin ES 600/K-5
425 Farnsworth Rd 48386 248-956-3800
Jeffrey Drewno, prin. Fax 956-3805

Waterford SD
Supt. — See Waterford

Houghton ES 400/K-5
8080 Elizabeth Lake Rd 48386 248-698-9230
Valerie Grimes, prin. Fax 698-9146

St. Patrick S 500/PK-8
9040 Hutchins St 48386 248-698-3240
Jeremy Clark, prin. Fax 698-4339

White Pigeon, Saint Joseph, Pop. 1,492

White Pigeon Community SD 800/K-12
410 Prairie Ave 49099 269-483-7676
Carrie Erlandson, supt. Fax 483-2256
www.wpcschools.org

Central ES 300/K-5
305 E Hotchin Ave 49099 269-483-7107
Shelly McBride, prin. Fax 483-9882

Whitmore Lake, Washtenaw, Pop. 6,301

Whitmore Lake SD 800/PK-12
8845 Main St 48189 734-449-4464
Tom DeKeyser, supt. Fax 449-5336
www.wlps.net/

Whitmore Lake ES 400/K-6
1077 Barker Rd 48189 734-449-2051
Sue Wanamaker, prin. Fax 449-9376

Whitmore Lake Preschool — PK-PK
8845 Main St 48189 — 734-449-4464
Sue Wanamaker, dir.

Livingston Christian S — 100/PK-12
8877 Main St 48189 — 734-878-9818
Ted Nast, admin.
Livingston Christian S — 200/PK-12
8877 Main St 48189 — 734-878-9818
Theodore Nast, admin.

Whittemore, Iosco, Pop. 377
Whittemore-Prescott Area SD — 900/PK-12
PO Box 250 48770 — 989-756-2500
Joseph Perrera, supt. — Fax 756-2278
www.wpas.net
Whittemore-Prescott ECC — 100/PK-PK
PO Box 250 48770 — 989-756-2400
Fax 756-2278
Whittemore-Prescott ES — 500/K-6
8878 Prescott Rd 48770 — 989-756-2400
Lori Ruthruff, prin. — Fax 756-3097

Williamsburg, Grand Traverse
Elk Rapids SD
Supt. — See Elk Rapids
Mill Creek ES — 200/K-5
9039 Old M 72 49690 — 231-267-9955
Jessica Ziecina, prin. — Fax 267-5215

Traverse City Area SD
Supt. — See Traverse City
Eastern ES — 300/PK-5
3723 Shore Dr 49690 — 231-933-1660
Biz Ruskowski, prin. — Fax 933-1682

Williamston, Ingham, Pop. 3,766
Williamston Community SD — 1,800/PK-12
418 Highland St 48895 — 517-655-4361
Dr. Adam Spina, supt. — Fax 655-7500
www.gowcs.net
Williamston Discovery ES — 300/PK-2
350 Highland St 48895 — 517-655-2855
Patrick VanRemmen, prin. — Fax 655-7504
Williamston Explorer ES — 400/3-5
416 Highland St 48895 — 517-655-2174
Kelly Campbell, prin. — Fax 655-7503
Williamston MS — 400/6-8
3845 Vanneter Rd 48895 — 517-655-4668
Robert Watson, prin. — Fax 655-7502

Memorial Lutheran S — 50/PK-5
2070 E Sherwood Rd 48895 — 517-655-1402
Rev. David Voss, prin. — Fax 655-1402
St. Mary S — 100/PK-5
220 N Cedar St 48895 — 517-655-4038
Richard Lomas, prin. — Fax 655-3855

Wilson, Menominee, Pop. 1,391

Wilson SDA Academy — 50/K-10
N13925 County Road 551 49896 — 906-639-2566
Emily Gibbs, prin. — Fax 639-2566

Winn, Isabella
Shepherd SD
Supt. — See Shepherd
Winn ES — 200/K-5
PO Box 338 48896 — 989-866-2250
Kim Stegman, prin. — Fax 866-2740

Wixom, Oakland, Pop. 13,242
Walled Lake Consolidated SD
Supt. — See Walled Lake
Banks MS — 800/6-8
1760 Charms Rd 48393 — 248-956-2200
Brad Paddock, prin. — Fax 956-2205
Loon Lake ES — 500/K-5
2151 Loon Lake Rd 48393 — 248-956-4000
Anita Qonja, prin. — Fax 956-4005
Wixom ES — 500/K-5
301 N Wixom Rd 48393 — 248-956-3400
Alec Bender, prin. — Fax 956-3405

Wixom Christian S — 100/PK-12
620 N Wixom Rd 48393 — 248-624-4362
Brad Stille, admin. — Fax 624-1068

Wolverine, Cheboygan, Pop. 234
Wolverine Community SD — 300/K-12
PO Box 219 49799 — 231-525-8201
Stephen Seelye, supt. — Fax 525-8591
wolverineschools.org
Wolverine Community ES — 200/K-6
PO Box 219 49799 — 231-525-8201
Stephen Seelye, prin. — Fax 525-8591

Woodhaven, Wayne, Pop. 12,674
Gibraltar SD — 3,700/PK-12
19370 Vreeland Rd 48183 — 734-379-6350
Amy Conway, supt. — Fax 379-6359
www.gibdist.net
Weiss ES — 300/K-5
26631 Reaume St 48183 — 734-379-7060
David Anderson, prin. — Fax 379-7061
Other Schools – See Brownstown Twp, Gibraltar, Rockwood

Woodhaven-Brownstown SD — 4,900/K-12
24821 Hall Rd 48183 — 734-783-3300
Mark Greathead, supt. — Fax 783-3316
www.woodhaven.k12.mi.us
Bates ES — 400/K-5
22811 Gudith Rd 48183 — 734-692-2217
Cherie Godfrey, prin. — Fax 692-2235
Erving ES — 400/K-5
24175 Hall Rd 48183 — 734-692-2212
Caterina Berry, prin. — Fax 692-2211
Yake ES — 300/K-5
16400 Carter Rd 48183 — 734-692-2230
Timothy Podlewski, prin. — Fax 692-2234
Other Schools – See Brownstown

Woodland, Barry, Pop. 422
Lakewood SD — 1,400/PK-12
223 W Broadway St 48897 — 616-374-8043
Randy Fleenor, supt. — Fax 374-8858
www.lakewoodps.org
Lakewood ECC — PK-K
223 W Broadway St 48897 — 269-367-4935
Jodi Duits, prin. — Fax 367-4771
Lakewood MS — 400/5-8
8699 Brown Rd 48897 — 616-374-2400
Kellie Rowland, prin. — Fax 374-2424
Other Schools – See Lake Odessa

Wyandotte, Wayne, Pop. 25,476
Wyandotte SD — 4,500/PK-12
PO Box 130 48192 — 734-759-5000
Dr. Catherine Cost, supt. — Fax 759-6009
www.wyandotte.org
Garfield ES — 400/PK-5
340 Superior Blvd 48192 — 734-759-5500
Krizia Totty, prin. — Fax 759-5509
Jefferson ES — 500/PK-5
1515 15th St 48192 — 734-759-5600
Crystal Eskin, prin. — Fax 759-5609
Monroe ES — 400/PK-5
1501 Grove St 48192 — 734-759-5800
Vicki Wilson, prin. — Fax 759-5809
Washington ES — 400/PK-5
1440 Superior Blvd 48192 — 734-759-6100
Kristin McMaster, prin. — Fax 759-6109
Wilson MS — 1,000/6-8
1275 15th St 48192 — 734-759-5300
Carol Makuch, prin. — Fax 759-5309

Wyoming, Kent, Pop. 70,258
Godfrey-Lee SD — 1,900/PK-12
1324 Burton St SW 49509 — 616-241-4722
Kevin Polston, supt. — Fax 241-4707
www.godfrey-lee.org
Godfrey ES — 400/3-5
1920 Godfrey Ave SW 49509 — 616-243-0533
Andy Steketee, prin. — Fax 475-6618
Lee ECC — 400/PK-2
961 Joosten St SW 49509 — 616-452-8703
Peter Geerling, prin. — Fax 475-6628
Lee MS — 400/6-8
1335 Lee St SW 49509 — 616-452-3296
Kathryn Curry, prin. — Fax 241-4677

Godwin Heights SD — 2,300/K-12
15 36th St SW 49548 — 616-252-2090
William Fetterhoff, supt. — Fax 252-2232
www.godwinschools.org
Godwin Heights MS — 600/5-8
111 36th St SE 49548 — 616-252-2070
Aaron Berlin, prin. — Fax 252-2075
North Godwin ES — 400/K-4
161 34th St SW 49548 — 616-252-2010
Mary Lang, prin. — Fax 252-2011
West Godwin ES — 400/K-4
3546 Clyde Park Ave SW 49509 — 616-252-2030
Steve Minard, prin. — Fax 252-2031

Wyoming SD — 4,300/PK-12
3575 Gladiola Ave SW, — 616-530-7550
Dr. Thomas Reeder, supt. — Fax 530-7557
wyomingps.org
Gladiola ES — 400/K-4
3500 Gladiola Ave SW, — 616-530-7596
David Lyon, prin. — Fax 249-7623
Huntington Woods ECC — PK-PK
4334 Byron Center Ave SW, — 616-530-7537
Dr. Lillian Cummings, dir. — Fax 249-7606
Oriole Park ES — 300/K-4
1420 40th St SW 49509 — 616-530-7558
Dr. Jennifer Slanger, prin. — Fax 249-7624
Parkview ES — 500/K-4
2075 Lee St SW, — 616-530-7572
Katie Jobson, prin. — Fax 249-7625
West ES — 400/K-4
1840 38th St SW, — 616-530-7533
Joshua Baumbach, prin. — Fax 249-7606
Wyoming IS — 600/5-6
1331 33rd St SW 49509 — 616-530-7540
Kirk Bloomquist, prin. — Fax 249-7659

Adams Protestant Reformed Christian S — 400/K-8
5539 Byron Center Ave SW, — 616-531-0748
Rick Mingerink, prin. — Fax 531-5172
AnchorPoint Christian S — 100/PK-6
601 36th St SW 49509 — 616-608-4006
Lael Mulder, prin. — Fax 455-2211
Holy Trinity Evangelical Lutheran S — 100/PK-8
4201 Burlingame Ave SW 49509 — 616-538-1122
Larry Sellnow, prin. — Fax 538-1122
St. John Vianney S — 300/K-8
4101 Clyde Park Ave SW 49509 — 616-532-7001
Gregg Bruno, prin. — Fax 532-1884
Tri-Unity Christian ES — 200/PK-6
5353 Wilson Ave SW 49418 — 616-532-8827

Yale, Saint Clair, Pop. 1,919
Yale SD — 2,000/K-12
198 School Dr 48097 — 810-387-3231
Kenneth Nicholl, supt. — Fax 387-4418
www.ypsd.us/
Yale ES — 300/K-5
200 School Dr 48097 — 810-387-3231
Bill Kryscynski, prin. — Fax 387-9413
Yale JHS — 500/6-8
198 School Dr 48097 — 810-387-3231
Adam Nelson, prin. — Fax 387-9207
Other Schools – See Avoca, Emmett

Emanuel-Redeemer Lutheran S — 50/K-8
11089 Yale Rd 48097 — 810-387-2906
Rev. Greg Sitzman, prin. — Fax 387-2906

Ypsilanti, Washtenaw, Pop. 18,646
Lincoln Consolidated SD — 4,100/PK-12
8970 Whittaker Rd 48197 — 734-484-7000
Sean McNatt, supt. — Fax 484-1212
www.lincolnk12.org
Bishop ES — 600/K-5
8970 Whittaker Rd 48197 — 734-484-7061
Fax 484-7065
Brick ES — 500/1-5
8970 Whittaker Rd 48197 — 734-484-7031
David Northrop, prin. — Fax 484-7049
Childs ES — 600/K-5
7300 Bemis Rd 48197 — 734-484-7035
Jeffery Petzak, prin. — Fax 484-7048
Lincoln ECC — 50/PK-PK
8850 Whittaker Rd 48197 — 734-484-7070
Kerry Shelton, dir. — Fax 484-7047
Lincoln MS — 1,000/6-8
8744 Whittaker Rd 48197 — 734-484-7033
Timothy Green, prin. — Fax 484-7088
Model ES — 100/K-K
8850 Whittaker Rd 48197 — 734-484-7045
Kerry Shelton, prin. — Fax 484-7047

Van Buren SD
Supt. — See Belleville
Rawsonville ES — 500/K-4
3110 S Grove St 48198 — 734-482-9845
Fax 482-3306

Ypsilanti Community SD — 4,200/PK-12
1885 Packard Rd 48197 — 734-221-1210
Dr. Benjamin Edmondson, supt. — Fax 714-1214
www.ycschools.us
Beatty Early Learning Center — PK-K
1661 Leforge Rd 48198 — 734-994-8178
Ginelle Skinner, dir. — Fax 994-8181
Erickson ES — 300/1-5
1427 Levona St 48198 — 734-221-1600
Kelly Mickel, prin. — Fax 221-1603
Estabrook ES — 400/2-8
1555 W Cross St 48197 — 734-221-1900
Raymond Alvarado, prin. — Fax 221-1903
Ford Early Learning Center — 300/PK-1
2440 E Clark Rd 48198 — 734-221-1801
Jeanina Harris, prin. — Fax 221-1803
Holmes ES — 400/2-5
1255 Holmes Rd 48198 — 734-221-2100
Aaron Rose, prin. — Fax 221-2103
Perry Early Learning Center — 300/PK-1
550 Perry St 48197 — 734-221-1700
Connie Thompson, prin. — Fax 221-1703
Washtenaw International Middle Academy — 100/6-8
510 Emerick St 48198 — 734-994-8145
Jessica Garcia, prin. — Fax 484-9719
Ypsilanti Community MS — 700/6-8
235 Spencer Ln 48198 — 734-221-2200
Seth Petty, prin. — Fax 221-2203
Ypsilanti International ES — PK-5
503 Oak St 48198 — 734-221-2400
Cassandra Sheriff, prin. — Fax 221-2403

Calvary Christian Academy — 200/K-12
1007 Ecorse Rd 48198 — 734-482-1990
Cathy White, prin. — Fax 484-5118
Huron Valley Catholic S — 200/PK-8
1300 N Prospect Rd 48198 — 734-483-0366
Timothy Kotyuk, prin. — Fax 483-0372

Zeeland, Ottawa, Pop. 5,407
Zeeland SD — 5,900/PK-12
PO Box 110 49464 — 616-748-3000
Cal De Kuiper, supt. — Fax 748-3035
www.zps.org/
Adams ES — 300/PK-5
7447 Adams St 49464 — 616-748-3475
Nancy Burk, prin. — Fax 688-7500
Cityside MS — 700/6-8
320 E Main Ave 49464 — 616-748-3200
Sarah Huizenga, prin. — Fax 748-3210
Creekside MS — 600/6-8
179 W Roosevelt Ave 49464 — 616-748-3300
C. Greshaw, prin. — Fax 748-3325
Lincoln ES — 400/K-5
60 E Lincoln Ave 49464 — 616-748-3350
Tom De Graaf, prin. — Fax 772-7374
New Groningen ES — 400/K-5
10542 Chicago Dr 49464 — 616-748-3375
Laurie Poll, prin. — Fax 772-7389
Quincy ES — 500/PK-5
10155 Quincy St 49464 — 616-748-4700
Allyson Apsey, prin. — Fax 748-4705
Roosevelt ES — 300/PK-5
175 W Roosevelt Ave 49464 — 616-748-3050
Judy Tuttle, prin. — Fax 748-3054
Woodbridge ES — 500/PK-5
9110 Woodbridge St 49464 — 616-748-3400
Mike Dalman, prin. — Fax 748-1436
Zeeland ECC — 200/PK-PK
140 W McKinley Ave 49464 — 616-748-3275
Ellen Kontowicz, dir. — Fax 748-1428
Zeeland Quest S — 100/K-8
175 W Roosevelt Ave 49464 — 616-748-3050
Leslie Rindfliesch, dir. — Fax 748-3054

Borculo Christian S — 100/PK-8
6830 96th Ave 49464 — 616-875-8152
Deb Miller, admin. — Fax 875-2236
Zeeland Christian S — 900/PK-8
334 W Central Ave 49464 — 616-772-2609
John Buteyn, head sch — Fax 772-2706

MINNESOTA

MN DEPARTMENT OF EDUCATION
1500 Highway 36 W, Roseville 55113-4035
Telephone 651-582-8200
Website education.state.mn.us

Commissioner of Education   Dr. Brenda Cassellius

PUBLIC, PRIVATE AND CATHOLIC ELEMENTARY SCHOOLS

Ada, Norman, Pop. 1,681
Ada-Borup SD 2854   500/PK-12
604 W Thorpe Ave 56510   218-784-5300
Shawn Yates, supt.   Fax 784-3475
www.ada.k12.mn.us
Ada ES   300/PK-6
209 6th St W 56510   218-784-5312
Craig Bahr, prin.   Fax 784-3475

Adams, Mower, Pop. 779
Southland SD 500   500/PK-12
203 NW 2nd St 55909   507-582-3283
Jeff Sampson, supt.   Fax 582-7813
www.isd500.k12.mn.us
ECC, 312 W Main St 55909   PK-PK
Caitlin Bartels, coord.   507-582-3405
Southland MS   100/6-8
203 NW 2nd St 55909   507-582-3568
Scott Hall, prin.   Fax 582-7813
Other Schools – See Rose Creek

Sacred Heart S   100/K-8
PO Box 249 55909   507-582-3120
Darlene Boe, prin.   Fax 582-1033

Adrian, Nobles, Pop. 1,201
Adrian SD 511   600/PK-12
PO Box 40 56110   507-483-2266
Roger Graff, supt.   Fax 483-2342
www.isd511.net
Adrian ES   300/PK-5
PO Box 40 56110   507-483-2225
Russell Lofthus, prin.   Fax 483-2461
Adrian MS   100/6-8
PO Box 40 56110   507-483-2232
Cate Koehne, prin.   Fax 483-2375

Aitkin, Aitkin, Pop. 2,132
Aitkin SD 1   1,200/PK-12
306 2nd St NW 56431   218-927-2115
Brad Kelvington, supt.   Fax 927-4234
home.isd1.org
Aitkin Community Education   PK-12
225 2nd Ave SW 56431   218-927-2115
Krista Olson, dir.
Rippleside ES   600/K-6
225 2nd Ave SW 56431   218-927-4838
Jesse Peterson, prin.   Fax 927-4234

Albany, Stearns, Pop. 2,533
Albany SD 745   1,400/PK-12
PO Box 40 56307   320-845-2171
Greg Johnson, supt.   Fax 845-4017
www.district745.org
Albany Area Early Childhood Education   PK-K
PO Box 40 56307   320-845-2171
Cassandra Nentl, dir.   Fax 845-4017
Albany ES   400/PK-5
PO Box 40 56307   320-845-5200
Ann Schultz, prin.   Fax 845-2165
Other Schools – See Avon

Holy Family S   200/PK-6
PO Box 674 56307   320-845-2011
Bonnie Massmann, prin.   Fax 845-7380

Albert Lea, Freeborn, Pop. 17,797
Albert Lea SD 241   3,200/PK-12
211 W Richway Dr 56007   507-379-4800
Dr. Mike Funk, supt.
www.alschools.org
Halverson ES   400/PK-5
707 E 10th St 56007   507-379-4900
Johanna Thomas, prin.   Fax 379-4958
Hawthorne ES   400/PK-5
1000 E Hawthorne St 56007   507-379-4960
Judith Vitito, prin.   Fax 379-5018
Lakeview ES   400/K-5
902 Abbott St 56007   507-379-5020
Nick Sofio, prin.   Fax 379-5078
Sibley ES   400/K-5
1501 W Front St 56007   507-379-5080
Diane Schultz, prin.   Fax 379-5138
Southwest MS   500/6-7
1601 W Front St 56007   507-379-5240
Steve Kovach, prin.   Fax 379-5338

St. Theodore S, 323 E Clark St 56007   100/PK-5
Sue Amundson, admin.   507-373-9657

Albertville, Wright, Pop. 6,921
Saint Michael-Albertville SD 885   4,800/PK-12
11343 50th St NE 55301   763-497-3180
Dr. Ann-Marie Foucault, supt.   Fax 497-6588
www.stma.k12.mn.us
Albertville PS   400/K-K
5386 Main Ave NE 55301   763-497-2688
Dr. John McDonald, prin.   Fax 497-6593
Saint Michael-Albertville MS West   900/5-8
11343 50th St NE 55301   763-497-4524
Andrew Merfeld, prin.   Fax 497-6566
Other Schools – See Saint Michael

Alden, Freeborn, Pop. 654
Alden-Conger SD 242   500/PK-12
PO Box 99 56009   507-874-3240
Brian Shanks, supt.   Fax 874-2747
www.alden-conger.org
Alden-Conger ES   300/PK-6
PO Box 99 56009   507-874-3240
Brian Shanks, supt.   Fax 874-2747
ECC, PO Box 99 56009   PK-PK
Brian Shanks, dir.   507-874-3240

Alexandria, Douglas, Pop. 10,938
Alexandria SD 206   3,900/PK-12
PO Box 308 56308   320-762-2141
Julie Critz, supt.   Fax 762-2765
www.alexandria.k12.mn.us
Discovery MS   600/6-8
510 McKay Ave N 56308   320-762-7900
Matt Aker, prin.   Fax 762-8347
Early Education Center   100/PK-PK
1410 McKay Ave S Ste 102 56308   320-762-3305
April Larson, coord.
Lincoln ES   500/K-5
1120 Lark St 56308   320-762-3320
Brendan Bogart, prin.   Fax 762-3321
Voyager ES   400/K-5
PO Box 339 56308   320-762-3325
Dana Christenson, prin.   Fax 762-3326
Woodland ES   500/K-5
1410 McKay Ave S Ste 101 56308   320-762-3300
Darla Harstad, prin.   Fax 762-3301
Other Schools – See Carlos, Garfield, Miltona

St. Marys S   200/K-6
421 Hawthorne St 56308   320-763-5861
Troy Sladek, prin.   Fax 763-7992
Zion Lutheran S   100/PK-8
300 Lake St 56308   320-763-4842
Muriel Stark, prin.   Fax 763-3676

Altura, Winona, Pop. 489
Lewiston-Altura SD 857
Supt. — See Lewiston
Lewiston-Altura IS   100/5-6
325 1st Ave SE 55910   507-523-2191
David Riebel, prin.   Fax 796-5127

Andover, Anoka, Pop. 30,071
Anoka-Hennepin SD 11
Supt. — See Anoka
Andover ES   1,300/K-5
14950 Hanson Blvd NW 55304   763-506-1700
Mark VanVoorhis, prin.   Fax 506-1703
Crooked Lake ES   500/K-5
2939 Bunker Lake Blvd NW 55304   763-506-2100
Sam Anderson, prin.   Fax 506-2103
Oak View MS   1,400/6-8
15400 Hanson Blvd NW 55304   763-506-5600
Gary Lundeen, prin.   Fax 506-5603
Rum River ES   1,000/K-5
16950 Verdin St NW 55304   763-506-8200
Deborah Shepard, prin.   Fax 506-8203

Legacy Christian Academy   500/PK-12
3037 Bunker Lake Blvd NW 55304   763-427-4595
Toni Johnson, coord.   Fax 427-3398

Angle Inlet, Lake of the Woods, Pop. 60
Warroad SD 690
Supt. — See Warroad
Angle Inlet ES   50/K-6
17606 Inlet Rd NW 56711   218-223-4161
Brita Comstock, prin.

Annandale, Wright, Pop. 3,201
Annandale SD 876   1,700/PK-12
PO Box 190 55302   320-274-5602
Tim Prom, supt.   Fax 274-5978
www.isd876.org
Annandale ES   800/PK-5
PO Box 190 55302   320-274-8218
Jon Klippenes, prin.   Fax 274-8470
Annandale MS   400/6-8
PO Box 190 55302   320-274-8226
Jeff Erickson, prin.   Fax 274-5978

Anoka, Anoka, Pop. 16,703
Anoka-Hennepin SD 11   37,300/PK-12
2727 N Ferry St 55303   763-506-1000
David Law, supt.   Fax 506-1003
www.ahschools.us
Anoka MS for the Arts-Washington Campus   600/6-6
2171 6th Ave 55303   763-506-4600
Jerri McGonigal, prin.   Fax 506-4603
Anoka MS of the Arts - Fred Moore Campus   1,300/7-8
1523 5th Ave 55303   763-506-5000
Jerri McGonigal, prin.   Fax 506-6003
Franklin ES   400/K-5
215 W Main St 55303   763-506-2600
Brian Erlandson, prin.   Fax 506-2603
Lincoln ES   400/K-5
540 South St 55303   763-506-3100
Michelle Zimmerman, prin.   Fax 506-3103
Wilson ES   500/K-5
1025 Sunny Ln 55303   763-506-4700
Christopher Forrest, prin.   Fax 506-4703
Other Schools – See Andover, Blaine, Brooklyn Center, Brooklyn Park, Champlin, Coon Rapids, Dayton, Ham Lake, Ramsey

Anoka Adventist Christian S   50/K-8
1035 Lincoln St 55303   763-421-6710
Jamie Madden, prin.   Fax 390-0657
Minnesota Renaissance S   100/PK-8
1333 5th Ave 55303   763-323-0741
St. Stephen S   500/PK-8
506 Jackson St 55303   763-421-3236
Diane Morri, prin.   Fax 712-7433

Appleton, Swift, Pop. 1,397
Lac qui Parle Valley SD 2853
Supt. — See Madison
Appleton-Milan ES   200/PK-4
349 S Edquist St 56208   320-289-1114
Maureen Heinecke, prin.   Fax 289-1334

Apple Valley, Dakota, Pop. 47,792
Rosemount-Apple Valley-Eagan ISD 196
Supt. — See Rosemount
Cedar Park Elementary STEM S   700/K-5
7500 Whitney Dr 55124   952-431-8360
John Garcia, prin.   Fax 431-8365
Diamond Path ES of International Studies   800/K-5
14455 Diamond Path 55124   952-423-7695
Lynn Hernandez, prin.   Fax 423-7694
Falcon Ridge MS   1,100/6-8
12900 Johnny Cake Ridge Rd 55124   952-431-8760
Noel Mehus, prin.   Fax 431-8770
Greenleaf ES   900/K-5
13333 Galaxie Ave 55124   952-431-8270
Michelle deKam Palmieri, prin.   Fax 431-8274
Highland ES   700/K-5
14001 Pilot Knob Rd 55124   952-423-7595
Chad Ryburn, prin.   Fax 423-7665
Scott Highlands MS   900/6-8
14011 Pilot Knob Rd 55124   952-423-7581
Daniel Wilharber, prin.   Fax 423-7601
Southview ES   700/K-5
1025 Whitney Dr 55124   952-431-8370
Christine Heilman, prin.   Fax 431-8377
Valley MS - S of STEM   900/6-8
900 Garden View Dr 55124   952-431-8300
Dave McKeag, prin.   Fax 431-8313
Westview ES   400/K-5
225 Garden View Dr 55124   952-431-8380
Tami Staloch-Schultz, prin.   Fax 431-8338

Arden Hills, Ramsey, Pop. 9,377
Mounds View SD 621
Supt. — See Shoreview
Valentine Hills ES   600/1-5
1770 County Road E2 W 55112   651-621-7800
Lindsey Boumgarden, prin.   Fax 621-7805

Argyle, Marshall, Pop. 634
Stephen-Argyle Central SD 2856
Supt. — See Stephen
Argyle ES   200/PK-6
PO Box 279 56713   218-437-6616
Dr. Chris Mills, prin.   Fax 437-6617

Arlington, Sibley, Pop. 2,206
Sibley East SD 2310   1,200/PK-12
PO Box 1000 55307   507-964-2292
James Amsden, supt.   Fax 964-8224
www.sibleyeast.org
Other Schools – See Gaylord

St. Paul's S   100/PK-8
510 W Adams St 55307   507-964-2397
Eric Kaesermann, prin.   Fax 964-2397

Ashby, Grant, Pop. 435
Ashby SD 261 300/PK-12
PO Box 30 56309 218-747-2257
Alan Niemann, supt. Fax 747-2289
www.ashby.k12.mn.us
Ashby ES 100/PK-6
PO Box 30 56309 218-747-2257
Nate Meissner, prin. Fax 747-2289

Atwater, Kandiyohi, Pop. 1,130
ACGC SD 2396
Supt. — See Grove City
ACGC ES 300/PK-4
302 2nd St S 56209 320-974-8841
Kodi Goracke, prin. Fax 974-8410

Audubon, Becker, Pop. 506
Lake Park Audubon ISD 2889
Supt. — See Lake Park
Lake Park Audubon ES 400/K-6
PO Box 338 56511 218-325-0574
Sam Skaaland, prin. Fax 252-5233

Aurora, Saint Louis, Pop. 1,668
Mesabi East SD 2711 1,000/PK-12
601 N 1st St W 55705 218-229-3321
Gregg Allen, supt. Fax 229-3736
www.mesabieast.k12.mn.us/
Mesabi East ES 500/PK-6
601 N 1st St W 55705 218-229-3321
Sam Wilkes, prin. Fax 229-3736

Austin, Mower, Pop. 24,273
Austin SD 492 4,700/PK-12
401 3rd Ave NW 55912 507-460-1900
David Krenz, supt. Fax 460-1939
www.austin.k12.mn.us
Austin Community Learning Center 100/PK-PK
912 1st Ave NE 55912 507-460-1700
Amy Baskin, prin. Fax 460-1711
Banfield ES 500/1-5
301 17th St SW 55912 507-460-1200
Jeff Roland, prin. Fax 460-1205
Ellis MS 700/6-8
1700 4th Ave SE 55912 507-460-1500
Jason Senne, prin. Fax 460-1510
Holton IS 700/5-6
1800 4th Ave SE 55912 507-460-1525
Angi McAndrews, prin. Fax 355-1608
Neveln ES 300/1-5
1918 E Oakland Ave 55912 507-460-1600
Dewitt Schara, prin. Fax 460-1606
Southgate ES 400/1-5
1601 19th Ave SW 55912 507-460-1300
Katie Baskin, prin. Fax 460-1308
Sumner ES 200/1-5
805 8th Ave NW 55912 507-460-1100
Sheila Berger, prin. Fax 460-1105
Woodson Kindergarten Center 400/K-K
1601 4th St SE 55912 507-460-1400
Jessica Cabeen, prin. Fax 460-1407

Pacelli ES 200/PK-5
511 4th Ave NW 55912 507-433-8859
Jean McDermott, prin. Fax 433-6630

Avon, Stearns, Pop. 1,391
Albany SD 745
Supt. — See Albany
Avon ES 400/PK-5
410 Avon Ave N 56310 320-356-7346
Sue Jenkins, prin. Fax 356-2241

Babbitt, Saint Louis, Pop. 1,456
Saint Louis County Schools ISD 2142
Supt. — See Virginia
Northeast Range S 100/PK-12
30 South Dr 55706 218-827-3101
Kelly Engman, prin. Fax 827-3103

Badger, Roseau, Pop. 364
Badger SD 676 300/PK-12
PO Box 68 56714 218-528-3201
Tom Jerome, supt. Fax 528-3366
www.badger.k12.mn.us/
Badger ES 100/PK-6
PO Box 68 56714 218-528-3201
Thomas Jerome, prin. Fax 528-3366

Bagley, Clearwater, Pop. 1,356
Bagley SD 162 1,000/PK-12
202 Bagley Ave NW 56621 218-694-6184
Steve Cairns, supt. Fax 694-3221
www.bagley.k12.mn.us/
Bagley ES 600/PK-6
202 Bagley Ave NW 56621 218-694-6528
Lee Furuseth, prin. Fax 694-3450

Barnesville, Clay, Pop. 2,545
Barnesville SD 146 900/PK-12
PO Box 189 56514 218-354-2217
Scott Loeslie, supt. Fax 354-7260
www.barnesville.k12.mn.us/
Atkinson ES 500/PK-6
PO Box 189 56514 218-354-2300
Todd Henrickson, prin. Fax 354-7797

Barnum, Carlton, Pop. 583
Barnum SD 91 800/PK-12
3675 County Road 140 55707 218-389-6978
David Bottem, supt. Fax 389-3259
isd91.org
Barnum ES 400/PK-6
3813 E North St 55707 218-389-6976
Tom Cawcutt, prin. Fax 389-3259

Barrett, Grant, Pop. 415
West Central Area SD 2342 600/PK-12
301 County Road 2 56311 320-528-7400
Barry Schmidt, supt. Fax 528-2279
www.westcentralareaschools.net
Other Schools – See Elbow Lake, Kensington

Battle Lake, Otter Tail, Pop. 865
Battle Lake SD 542 400/K-12
402 W Summit St 56515 218-864-5215
Jeff Drake, supt. Fax 864-0919
www.battlelake.k12.mn.us/
Battle Lake ES 200/K-8
402 W Summit St 56515 218-864-5217
Jeff Drake, prin. Fax 864-0919

Baudette, Lake of the Woods, Pop. 1,074
Lake of the Woods SD 390 500/PK-12
PO Box 310 56623 218-634-2735
Jeff Nelson, supt. Fax 634-2467
lakeofthewoodsschool.org
Lake of the Woods ES 300/PK-6
PO Box 310 56623 218-634-2056
Jeff Nelson, prin. Fax 634-2467

Baxter, Crow Wing, Pop. 7,503
Brainerd SD 181
Supt. — See Brainerd
Baxter ES 500/PK-4
5546 Fairview Rd 56425 218-454-6400
Steve Lundberg, prin. Fax 454-6401
Forestview MS 1,900/5-8
12149 Knollwood Dr 56425 218-454-6000
Jonathan Anderson, prin. Fax 454-6687

Lake Region Christian S 200/PK-12
7398 Fairview Rd 56425 218-828-1226
Steve Ogren, admin. Fax 828-1643

Bayport, Washington, Pop. 3,433
Stillwater Area SD 834
Supt. — See Stillwater
Andersen ES 300/PK-5
309 4th St N 55003 651-351-6600
Stacey Benz, prin. Fax 351-6695

Beaver Creek, Rock, Pop. 296
Hills-Beaver Creek SD 671
Supt. — See Hills
Hills-Beaver Creek ES 200/PK-5
PO Box 49 56116 507-673-2541
Jason Phelps, prin. Fax 673-2550

Becker, Sherburne, Pop. 4,467
Becker SD 726 2,800/PK-12
12000 Hancock St SE 55308 763-261-4502
Dr. Stephen Malone, supt. Fax 261-4559
www.becker.k12.mn.us
Becker IS 600/3-5
12000 Hancock St SE 55308 763-261-4504
Dr. Christine Glomski, prin. Fax 261-5799
Becker MS 700/6-8
12000 Hancock St SE 55308 763-261-6300
Nancy Helmer, prin. Fax 261-6306
Becker PS 600/PK-2
12000 Hancock St SE 55308 763-261-6330
Dale Christensen, prin. Fax 261-6340

Belgrade, Stearns, Pop. 733
Belgrade-Brooten-Elrosa SD 2364 700/PK-12
PO Box 339 56312 320-254-8211
Matt Bullard, supt. Fax 254-3784
www.bbejaguars.org
Other Schools – See Brooten

Belle Plaine, Scott, Pop. 6,520
Belle Plaine SD 716 1,600/PK-12
130 S Willow St 56011 952-873-2400
Dr. Ryan Laager, supt. Fax 873-6909
www.belleplaine.k12.mn.us/
Belle Plaine Chatfield ES 400/PK-2
330 S Market St 56011 952-873-2401
Kim DeWitte, prin. Fax 873-2598
Belle Plaine JHS 300/7-8
220 S Market St 56011 952-873-2403
Dave Kreft, prin. Fax 378-2420
Belle Plaine Oak Crest ES 500/3-6
1101 W Commerce Dr 56011 952-873-2402
Liann Hanson Ph.D., prin. Fax 378-2430

Our Lady of the Prairie S 50/PK-6
200 E Church St 56011 952-873-6564
Wendi Alessio, prin. Fax 873-6717
Trinity Lutheran S 100/PK-8
500 W Church St 56011 952-873-6320
Daniel Whitney, prin. Fax 873-6545

Bemidji, Beltrami, Pop. 12,863
Bemidji SD 31 5,000/PK-12
502 Minnesota Ave NW 56601 218-333-3100
James Hess Ed.D., supt. Fax 333-3129
www.bemidji.k12.mn.us
Bemidji MS 1,100/6-8
502 Minnesota Ave NW 56601 218-333-3215
Drew Hildenbrand, prin. Fax 333-3333
Bunyan ES 200/PK-K
502 Minnesota Ave NW 56601 218-333-3119
Kathy Van Wert, prin. Fax 333-3456
Central ES 200/K-5
502 Minnesota Ave NW 56601 218-333-3220
Patricia Welte, prin. Fax 333-3205
Lincoln ES 600/K-5
502 Minnesota Ave NW 56601 218-333-3250
Jason Luksik, prin. Fax 333-3480
May ES 400/1-5
502 Minnesota Ave NW 56601 218-333-3240
Ami Aalgaard, prin. Fax 333-3244
Northern ES 500/1-5
502 Minnesota Ave NW 56601 218-333-3260
Wendy Templin, prin. Fax 333-3263
Smith ES 400/K-5
502 Minnesota Ave NW 56601 218-333-3290
Patricia Welte, prin. Fax 333-3296
Other Schools – See Solway

Heartland Christian Academy 50/PK-8
9914 Heartland Cir NW 56601 218-751-1751
Carolyn Johannsen, prin. Fax 333-0260
St. Mark Lutheran S 50/K-8
2220 Anne St NW 56601 218-444-3939
Nathan Bitter, prin.
St. Philips S 300/PK-8
620 Beltrami Ave NW 56601 218-444-4938
Carol Rettinger, prin. Fax 444-1379

Benson, Swift, Pop. 3,222
Benson SD 777 700/PK-12
1400 Montana Ave 56215 320-843-2710
Fax 843-2262
www.benson.k12.mn.us
Benson ES 5-6
1400 Montana Ave 56215 320-843-2710
Mike Knutson, prin. Fax 843-2262
Northside ES 300/PK-4
1800 Nevada Ave 56215 320-842-2717
Brad Johnson, prin. Fax 843-5300

Bertha, Todd, Pop. 494
Bertha-Hewitt SD 786 400/K-12
PO Box 8 56437 218-924-2500
Eric Koep, supt. Fax 924-3252
www.isd786.org
Bertha ES 200/K-6
PO Box 8 56437 218-924-2500
Darren Glynn, prin. Fax 924-3252

Bigfork, Itasca, Pop. 444
Grand Rapids SD 318
Supt. — See Grand Rapids
Bigfork S 100/K-6
PO Box 228 56628 218-743-3444
Scott Patrow, prin. Fax 743-3443

Big Lake, Sherburne, Pop. 9,820
Big Lake SD 727 3,300/PK-12
501 Minnesota Ave 55309 763-262-2536
Steve Westerberg, supt. Fax 262-2539
www.biglakeschools.org
Big Lake MS 700/6-8
601 Minnesota Ave 55309 763-262-2567
Mark Ernst, prin. Fax 262-2563
Independence ES 900/3-5
701 Minnesota Ave 55309 763-262-2537
Darren Kern, prin. Fax 262-2533
Liberty ES 700/PK-2
17901 205th Ave NW 55309 763-262-8100
Caryl Gordy, prin. Fax 262-8185

Birchdale, Koochiching
South Koochiching-Rainy River ISD 363
Supt. — See Northome
Indus ES 100/PK-6
8560 Highway 11 56629 218-634-2425
Laurie Bitter, prin. Fax 634-1334

Bird Island, Renville, Pop. 1,033
BOLD SD 2534
Supt. — See Olivia
BOLD-Bird Island ES 400/K-6
110 S 9th St 55310 320-365-3551
Ann Dettmann, prin. Fax 365-4001

St. Mary S 100/K-8
PO Box 500 55310 320-365-3693
Tracy Bertrand, prin. Fax 365-3142

Blackduck, Beltrami, Pop. 754
Blackduck SD 32 600/PK-12
PO Box 550 56630 218-835-5200
Mark Lundin, supt. Fax 835-4491
blackduck.k12.mn.us
Blackduck ES 300/PK-6
PO Box 550 56630 218-835-5300
Mark Lundin, prin. Fax 835-5351

Blaine, Anoka, Pop. 55,728
Anoka-Hennepin SD 11
Supt. — See Anoka
Jefferson ES 700/K-5
11331 Jefferson St NE 55434 763-506-2900
Mark Hansen, prin. Fax 506-2903
Johnsville ES 700/K-5
991 125th Ave NE 55434 763-506-3000
Scott Johnson, prin. Fax 506-3003
Madison ES 500/K-5
650 Territorial Rd NE 55434 763-506-3300
Dorothy Olsen, prin. Fax 506-3303
Roosevelt MS 1,100/6-8
650 125th Ave NE 55434 763-506-5800
Greg Blodgett, prin. Fax 506-5803
University Avenue ES 600/K-5
9901 University Ave NE 55434 763-506-4500
Anissa Cravens, prin. Fax 506-4503

Spring Lake Park SD 16
Supt. — See Spring Lake Park
Westwood IS 700/4-5
701 91st Ave NE 55434 763-600-5400
Tom Larson, prin. Fax 600-5413
Westwood MS 1,200/6-8
711 91st Ave NE 55434 763-600-5300
Tom Larson, prin. Fax 600-5313

Calvin Christian S 200/K-8
8966 Pierce St NE 55434 763-785-0135
Northside Christian S 100/PK-12
804 131st Ave NE 55434 763-755-3993
Beth Dvorak, prin. Fax 755-4405
Way of the Shepherd Montessori S 100/PK-6
13200 Central Ave NE 55434 763-862-9110
Tricia Menzhuber, prin. Fax 755-7361

Blooming Prairie, Steele, Pop. 1,975
Blooming Prairie SD 756 700/PK-12
202 4th Ave NW 55917 507-583-4426
Barry Olson, supt. Fax 583-7952
www.blossoms.k12.mn.us
Blooming Prairie ES 400/PK-6
123 2nd St NW 55917 507-583-6615
Christopher Staloch, prin. Fax 583-4415

Bloomington, Hennepin, Pop. 80,538
Bloomington SD 271 — 10,200/PK-12
1350 W 106th St 55431 — 952-681-6400
Les Fujitake, supt. — Fax 681-6401
www.bloomington.k12.mn.us/
Hillcrest Community ES — 400/K-5
9301 Thomas Rd S 55431 — 952-681-5300
Calvin Keasling, prin. — Fax 681-5301
Indian Mounds ES — 400/K-5
9801 11th Ave S 55420 — 952-681-6000
Joan Maland, prin. — Fax 681-6001
Normandale Hills ES — 500/K-5
9501 Toledo Ave S 55437 — 952-806-7000
Andrew Vollmuth, prin. — Fax 806-7001
Oak Grove ES — 400/K-5
1301 W 104th St 55431 — 952-681-6800
Brian Cline, prin. — Fax 681-6801
Oak Grove MS — 800/6-8
1300 W 106th St 55431 — 952-681-6600
Brian Ingemann, prin. — Fax 681-6601
Olson ES — 500/K-5
4501 W 102nd St 55437 — 952-806-8800
Paul Meyer, prin. — Fax 806-8801
Olson MS — 900/6-8
4551 W 102nd St 55437 — 952-806-8600
Jeremy Kuhns, prin. — Fax 806-8601
Pond Family Center — PK-PK
9600 3rd Ave S 55420 — 952-681-6200
Jeanna Miller, admin.
Poplar Bridge ES — 500/K-5
8401 Palmer Ave S 55437 — 952-681-5400
Roberto Cantu, prin. — Fax 681-5401
Ridgeview ES — 400/K-5
9400 Nesbitt Ave S 55437 — 952-806-7100
Steve Abrahamson, prin. — Fax 806-7101
Valley View ES — 500/K-5
351 E 88th St 55420 — 952-681-5700
Cori Thompson, prin. — Fax 681-5701
Valley View MS — 700/6-8
8900 Portland Ave S 55420 — 952-681-5800
Megan Willrett, prin. — Fax 681-5801
Washburn ES — 400/K-5
8401 Xerxes Ave S 55431 — 952-681-5500
Andrew Wilkins, prin. — Fax 681-5501
Westwood ES — 400/K-5
3701 W 108th St 55431 — 952-806-7200
Hugh Roberts, prin. — Fax 806-7201

Bethany Academy — 200/K-12
4300 W 98th St 55437 — 952-831-8686
Nancy Johnson, head sch — Fax 831-9568
Bloomington Lutheran S — 200/PK-8
10600 Bloomington Ferry Rd 55438 — 952-941-9047
Mike Butzow, prin. — Fax 941-1242
Nativity of Mary S — 300/PK-8
9901 E Bloomington Fwy 55420 — 952-881-8160
Mindy Reeder, prin. — Fax 881-3032
Ramalynn Academy — PK-8
8800 Queen Ave S 55431 — 952-921-6500
TLC Early Learning Center — 100/PK-K
11000 France Ave S 55431 — 952-884-7955
Barbara Wigstadt, dir.

Blue Earth, Faribault, Pop. 3,328
Blue Earth Area ISD 2860 — 1,000/K-12
315 E 6th St 56013 — 507-526-3188
Evan Gough, supt. — Fax 526-2432
www.blueearth.k12.mn.us
Blue Earth Area ES — 500/K-5
315 E 6th St 56013 — 507-526-3090
Melissa McGuire, prin. — Fax 526-2432
Blue Earth Area MS — 200/6-7
315 E 6th St 56013 — 507-526-3115
Melissa McGuire, prin. — Fax 526-2432

Braham, Isanti, Pop. 1,757
Braham SD 314 — 800/K-12
531 Elmhurst Ave S 55006 — 320-396-3313
Ken Gagner, supt. — Fax 396-3068
www.braham.k12.mn.us
Braham Area ES — 500/K-6
528 8th St SW 55006 — 320-396-3316
Jeffrey Eklund, prin. — Fax 396-3317

Brainerd, Crow Wing, Pop. 13,204
Brainerd SD 181 — 6,400/PK-12
804 Oak St 56401 — 218-454-6900
Laine Larson, supt. — Fax 454-5549
www.isd181.org
Garfield ES — 400/K-4
1120 10th Ave NE 56401 — 218-454-6450
Jodi Kennedy, prin. — Fax 454-6451
Harrison ES — 300/K-4
1515 Oak St 56401 — 218-454-6500
Cathy Nault, prin. — Fax 454-6501
Lowell ES — 400/K-4
704 3rd Ave NE 56401 — 218-454-6550
Todd Sauer, prin. — Fax 454-6551
Riverside ES — 600/K-4
220 NW 3rd St 56401 — 218-454-6800
Jon Clark, prin. — Fax 454-6801
Other Schools – See Baxter, Nisswa

Oak Street Christian S — 50/K-8
2910 Oak St 56401 — 218-828-9660
Jayme Anderson, prin.
St. Francis of the Lakes Catholic S — 200/PK-8
817 Juniper St 56401 — 218-829-2344
Deb Euteneuer, prin. — Fax 829-4157

Brandon, Douglas, Pop. 489
Brandon-Evansville ISD 2908 — 400/PK-12
PO Box 185 56315 — 320-834-4084
Dean Yocum, supt. — Fax 524-2228
www.b-e.k12.mn.us
Brandon ES — 200/PK-3
PO Box 185 56315 — 320-524-2263
Dean Yocum, prin. — Fax 524-2228
Other Schools – See Evansville

Breckenridge, Wilkin, Pop. 3,345
Breckenridge SD 846 — 600/PK-12
810 Beede Ave 56520 — 218-643-6822
Diane Cordes, supt. — Fax 641-4035
www.breckenridge.k12.mn.us
Breckenridge ES — 300/PK-8
810 Beede Ave 56520 — 218-643-6681
Corinna Erickson, prin. — Fax 643-5021

St. Marys S — 100/PK-8
210 4th St N 56520 — 218-643-5443
Linda Johnson, prin. — Fax 643-5443

Breezy Point, Crow Wing, Pop. 2,331
Pequot Lakes SD 186
Supt. — See Pequot Lakes
Eagle View ES — 600/PK-4
6539 County Road 11 56472 — 218-562-6100
Melissa Hesch, prin. — Fax 562-6106

Brewster, Nobles, Pop. 468
Round Lake-Brewster SD — 200/PK-8
PO Box 309 56119 — 507-842-5951
Raymond Hassing, supt. — Fax 842-5365
www.rlb.mntm.org
Round Lake-Brewster ES — 200/PK-6
PO Box 309 56119 — 507-842-5951
Raymond Hassing, prin. — Fax 842-5365
Round Lake-Brewster MS — 50/7-8
PO Box 309 56119 — 507-842-5951
Raymond Hassing, prin. — Fax 842-5365

Brooklyn Center, Hennepin, Pop. 28,921
Anoka-Hennepin SD 11
Supt. — See Anoka
Evergreen Park ES — 500/PK-5
7020 Dupont Ave N 55430 — 763-506-2500
Sheryl Ray, prin. — Fax 506-2503

Brooklyn Center SD 286 — 2,200/PK-12
6300 Shingle Creek Pky #286 55430 — 763-450-3386
Mark Bonine, supt. — Fax 560-2647
www.brooklyncenterschools.org
Brown ES — 1,100/PK-5
1500 59th Ave N 55430 — 763-561-4480
Callie Lalugba, prin. — Fax 560-1674

Osseo Area ISD 279
Supt. — See Maple Grove
Garden City ES — 400/K-5
3501 65th Ave N 55429 — 763-561-9768
David Branch, prin. — Fax 549-2360
Willow Lane ECC — 300/PK-PK
7020 Perry Ave N 55429 — 763-585-7300
Candace Larson, coord. — Fax 585-7303

Robbinsdale SD 281
Supt. — See New Hope
Northport ES — 600/K-5
5421 Brooklyn Blvd 55429 — 763-504-7800
Frederico Rowe, prin. — Fax 504-7809

St. Alphonsus S — 200/K-8
7031 Halifax Ave N 55429 — 763-561-5101
Kari Staples, prin. — Fax 503-3368

Brooklyn Park, Hennepin, Pop. 73,081
Anoka-Hennepin SD 11
Supt. — See Anoka
Monroe ES — 600/K-5
901 Brookdale Dr 55444 — 763-506-3600
Amy Oliver, prin. — Fax 506-3603

Osseo Area ISD 279
Supt. — See Maple Grove
Birch Grove S for the Arts — 500/K-5
4690 Brookdale Dr N 55443 — 763-561-1374
Jeff Zastrow, prin. — Fax 549-2300
Brooklyn MS — 600/6-8
7377 Noble Ave N 55443 — 763-569-7700
Kim Monette, prin. — Fax 569-7707
Crest View ES — 300/PK-5
8200 Zane Ave N 55443 — 763-561-5165
Shawn Stibbins, prin. — Fax 549-2323
Edinbrook ES — 700/K-5
8925 Zane Ave N 55443 — 763-493-4737
Aaron Krueger, prin. — Fax 391-8400
Fair Oaks ES — 400/PK-5
5600 65th Ave N 55429 — 763-533-2246
Phil Sadler, prin. — Fax 549-2350
North View Intl Baccalaureate World MS — 500/6-8
5869 69th Ave N 55429 — 763-585-7200
Diana Bledsoe, prin. — Fax 585-7210
Palmer Lake ES — 600/K-5
7300 W Palmer Lake Dr 55429 — 763-561-1930
Say Billy Chan, prin. — Fax 549-2400
Park Brook ES — 300/K-5
7400 Hampshire Ave N 55428 — 763-561-6870
Scott Taylor, prin. — Fax 549-2410
Woodland ES — 800/PK-5
4501 Oak Grove Pkwy N 55443 — 763-315-6400
Toni Beckler, prin. — Fax 315-6401
Zanewood Community S — 400/PK-5
7000 Zane Ave N 55429 — 763-561-9077
Michael Savage, prin. — Fax 549-2440

Bethany Christian Academy — 100/K-9
2603 Brookdale Dr 55444 — 763-717-8928
Ilya Marchenko, prin.
Maranatha Christian Academy — 700/PK-12
9201 75th Ave N 55428 — 763-488-7900
Brian Sullivan, admin. — Fax 315-7294
St. Vincent De Paul S — 400/K-8
9050 93rd Ave N 55445 — 763-425-3970
Lisa Simon, prin. — Fax 425-2674

Brooten, Stearns, Pop. 739
Belgrade-Brooten-Elrosa SD 2364
Supt. — See Belgrade
Belgrade-Brooten-Elrosa ES — 400/PK-6
PO Box 39 56316 — 320-346-2278
Rick Gossen, prin. — Fax 346-2589

Browerville, Todd, Pop. 779
Browerville SD 787 — 400/PK-12
PO Box 185 56438 — 320-594-2272
Scott Vedbraaten, supt. — Fax 594-8105
www.browerville.k12.mn.us/
Browerville ES — 200/PK-6
PO Box 185 56438 — 320-594-2272
Patrick Sutlief, prin. — Fax 594-8105

Christ the King S — 100/PK-6
PO Box 186 56438 — 320-594-6114
Sarah Becker, dean — Fax 594-6114

Browns Valley, Traverse, Pop. 577
Browns Valley SD 801 — 100/PK-8
PO Box N 56219 — 320-695-2103
Brenda Reed, supt. — Fax 695-2868
www.brownsvalley.k12.mn.us/
Browns Valley ES — 100/PK-4
PO Box N 56219 — 320-695-2103
Brenda Reed, supt. — Fax 695-2868
Browns Valley MS — 50/5-8
PO Box N 56219 — 320-695-2103
Brenda Reed, supt. — Fax 695-2868

Buffalo, Wright, Pop. 15,192
Buffalo-Hanover-Montrose SD — 5,800/K-12
214 1st Ave NE 55313 — 763-682-8700
Scott Thielman, supt. — Fax 682-8785
www.bhmschools.org
Buffalo Community MS — 1,300/6-8
1300 Highway 25 N 55313 — 763-682-8200
Matt Lubben, prin. — Fax 682-8209
Discovery ES — 300/K-5
301 2nd Ave NE 55313 — 763-682-8400
Mat Nelson, prin. — Fax 682-8444
Northwinds ES — 600/K-5
1111 7th Ave NW 55313 — 763-682-8800
Shawn Gombos, prin. — Fax 682-8805
Parkside ES — 500/K-5
207 3rd St NE 55313 — 763-682-8500
Michelle Robinson, prin. — Fax 682-8577
Tatanka STEM ES — 500/K-5
703 8th St NE 55313 — 763-682-8600
Don Metzler, prin. — Fax 682-8671
Other Schools – See Hanover, Montrose

St. Francis Xavier S — 300/PK-8
219 19th St NW 55313 — 763-684-0075
Alisa Louwagie, prin. — Fax 684-4771

Buffalo Lake, Renville, Pop. 721
Buffalo Lake-Hector-Stewart SD 2159 — 600/PK-12
211 3rd St NE 55314 — 320-833-5311
David Hansen, supt. — Fax 833-5311
www.blhsd.org
Buffalo Lake-Hector-Stewart ES — 300/PK-5
PO Box 278 55314 — 320-833-5311
David Hansen, prin. — Fax 833-5312

Burnsville, Dakota, Pop. 58,440
Burnsville-Eagan-Savage ISD 191 — 7,600/K-12
200 W Burnsville Pkwy 55337 — 952-707-2000
Cindy Amoroso, supt. — Fax 707-2002
www.isd191.org
Byrne ES — 500/K-5
11608 River Hills Dr 55337 — 952-707-3500
Lyle Bornsta, prin. — Fax 707-3502
Gideon Pond ES — 400/K-5
613 E 130th St 55337 — 952-707-3000
Chris Bellmont, prin. — Fax 707-3002
Metcalf MS — 400/6-8
2250 Diffley Rd 55337 — 952-707-2400
Kelly Ronn, prin. — Fax 707-2402
Neill ES — 400/K-5
13409 Upton Ave S 55337 — 952-707-3100
Dr. Elizabeth Vaught, prin. — Fax 707-3102
Nicollet MS — 200/6-8
400 E 134th St 55337 — 952-707-2600
Renee Brandner, prin. — Fax 707-2602
Sioux Trail ES — 400/K-5
2801 River Hills Dr 55337 — 952-707-3300
Shannon McParland, prin. — Fax 707-3302
Sky Oaks ES — 500/K-5
100 E 134th St 55337 — 952-707-3700
John Bonneville, prin. — Fax 707-3702
Vista View ES — 400/K-5
13109 County Road 5 55337 — 952-707-3400
Brad Robb, prin. — Fax 707-3402
Other Schools – See Eagan, Savage

Rosemount-Apple Valley-Eagan ISD 196
Supt. — See Rosemount
Echo Park ES — 700/PK-5
14100 County Road 11 55337 — 952-431-8390
Pamela Haldeman, prin. — Fax 431-8333

Good Shepherd Lutheran S — 100/PK-8
151 County Road 42 E 55306 — 952-953-0690
David Retzlaff Ph.B., admin. — Fax 891-3469
Southview Christian S — 100/PK-10
15304 County Road 5 55306 — 952-898-2727
Rayleen Hansen M.A., prin. — Fax 898-0457

Butterfield, Watonwan, Pop. 581
Butterfield SD 836 — 200/PK-12
PO Box 189 56120 — 507-956-2771
Ray Arsenault, supt. — Fax 956-3431
butterfield.k12.mn.us
Butterfield ES — 100/PK-6
PO Box 189 56120 — 507-956-2771
Greg Ewing, prin. — Fax 956-3431

Byron, Olmsted, Pop. 4,841
Byron SD 531 1,700/PK-12
630 1st Ave NW 55920 507-775-2383
Joey Page Ed.D., supt. Fax 775-2385
www.bears.byron.k12.mn.us
Byron IS 300/3-5
501 10th Ave NE 55920 507-775-6620
Abe Rodemeyer, prin. Fax 775-7225
Byron MS 400/6-8
601 4th St NW 55920 507-775-2189
Richard Swanson, prin. Fax 775-2825
Byron PS 500/PK-2
820 7th St NE 55920 507-624-0311
Amanda Durnen, prin. Fax 624-0312

Caledonia, Houston, Pop. 2,844
Caledonia SD 299 700/PK-12
511 W Main St 55921 507-725-3389
Benjamin Barton, supt. Fax 725-3558
www.cps.k12.mn.us/
Caledonia Area MS 100/6-8
825 N Warrior Ave 55921 507-725-3316
Mary Morem, prin. Fax 725-3319
Caledonia ES 300/PK-5
511 W Main St 55921 507-725-5205
Gina Meinertz, prin. Fax 725-3558

St. John's Evangelical Lutheran S 100/PK-8
720 N Marshall St 55921 507-725-3412
Nate Livingston, prin.
St. Mary S 200/PK-8
308 E South St 55921 507-725-3355
Roger Betzold, prin. Fax 725-8355

Cambridge, Isanti, Pop. 7,948
Cambridge-Isanti SD 911 5,200/PK-12
625A Main St N 55008 763-689-6188
Dr. Raymond Queener, supt. Fax 689-6200
www.c-ischools.org
Cambridge IS 600/3-5
428 2nd Ave NW 55008 763-691-6600
Scott Peterson, prin. Fax 691-6699
Cambridge MS 600/6-8
31374 Xylite St NE 55008 763-552-6300
Charlie Burroughs, prin. Fax 552-6399
Cambridge PS 700/PK-2
310 Elm St N 55008 763-691-6500
Rhonda Malecha, prin. Fax 691-6599
Other Schools – See Isanti

Cambridge Christian S 200/PK-12
2211 Old Main St S 55008 763-689-3806
Scott Thune, supt. Fax 689-3807

Campbell, Wilkin, Pop. 158
Campbell-Tintah SD 852 100/PK-12
PO Box 8 56522 218-630-5311
Kyle Edgerton, supt. Fax 630-5881
www.campbell.k12.mn.us
Campbell-Tintah S 100/PK-12
PO Box 8 56522 218-630-5311
Kyle Edgerton, admin. Fax 630-5881

Canby, Yellow Medicine, Pop. 1,782
Canby SD 891 500/PK-12
307 1st St W 56220 507-223-2001
Ryan Nielsen, supt. Fax 223-2011
www.canbymn.org/
Canby ES 300/PK-6
307 1st St W 56220 507-223-2003
Ryan Arndt, prin. Fax 223-2013

St. Peter S 50/PK-6
410 Ring Ave N 56220 507-223-7729
Lori Rangaard, prin. Fax 223-7178

Cannon Falls, Goodhue, Pop. 4,027
Cannon Falls SD 252 1,200/PK-12
820 Minnesota St E 55009 507-263-6800
Beth Giese, supt. Fax 263-2555
www.cannonfallsschools.com
Cannon Falls ES 500/PK-5
1020 Minnesota St E 55009 507-263-6800
Derek Bell, prin. Fax 263-4888

St. Paul S 100/PK-8
30289 59th Avenue Way 55009 507-263-4589
David Noack, prin. Fax 263-4589

Carlos, Douglas, Pop. 501
Alexandria SD 206
Supt. — See Alexandria
Carlos ES 100/K-5
PO Box 129 56319 320-852-7181
Lisa Pikop, prin. Fax 852-7538

Carlton, Carlton, Pop. 843
Carlton ISD 93 500/PK-12
PO Box 310 55718 218-384-4225
Gwen Carman, supt. Fax 384-3543
www.carlton.k12.mn.us
South Terrace ES 200/PK-5
PO Box 310 55718 218-384-4728
Ben Midge, prin. Fax 384-4039

Carver, Carver, Pop. 3,648
Eastern Carver County SD 112
Supt. — See Chaska
Carver ES, 1717 Ironwood Dr 55315 K-5
June Johnson, prin. 952-556-1900
East Union ES 200/K-5
15655 County Road 43 55315 952-556-6800
Jay Woller, prin. Fax 556-6809

Cass Lake, Cass, Pop. 725
Cass Lake-Bena SD 115 1,100/PK-12
208 Central Ave NW 56633 218-335-2204
Rochelle Johnson, supt. Fax 335-2614
www.clbs.k12.mn.us
Cass Lake-Bena ES 500/PK-4
15 4th St NW 56633 218-335-2201
Josh Grover, prin. Fax 335-8538
Cass Lake-Bena MS 300/5-8
15314 State Highway 371 NW 56633 218-335-7851
Sue Chase, prin. Fax 335-1194

Cedar, Anoka
Saint Francis SD 15
Supt. — See Saint Francis
Cedar Creek Community ES 800/K-5
21108 Polk St NE 55011 763-213-8780
Darin Hahn, prin. Fax 434-7679
East Bethel Community ES 600/K-5
21210 Polk St NE 55011 763-213-8900
Angie Scardigli, prin. Fax 434-7627

Centerville, Anoka, Pop. 3,726
Centennial SD 12
Supt. — See Circle Pines
Centerville ES 600/K-5
1721 Westview Ave 55038 763-792-5800
Wayne Whitwam, prin. Fax 792-5850

Champlin, Hennepin, Pop. 22,615
Anoka-Hennepin SD 11
Supt. — See Anoka
Champlin Brooklyn Park Academy 900/K-5
6100 109th Ave N 55316 763-506-6000
Brian Mann, prin. Fax 506-6003
Jackson MS 1,900/6-8
6000 109th Ave N 55316 763-506-5200
Tom Hagerty, prin. Fax 506-5203
Oxbow Creek ES 1,200/K-5
6505 109th Ave N 55316 763-506-3800
Rolf Carlsen, prin. Fax 506-3803

Chanhassen, Carver, Pop. 22,622
Eastern Carver County SD 112
Supt. — See Chaska
Bluff Creek ES 500/K-5
2300 Coulter Blvd 55317 952-556-6600
Joan MacDonald, prin. Fax 556-6609
Chanhassen ES 500/PK-5
7600 Laredo Dr 55317 952-556-6700
Greg Lange, prin. Fax 556-6709

Chapel Hill Academy 300/PK-8
306 W 78th St 55317 952-949-9014
Kassie Grosz, head sch Fax 949-3871
St. Hubert S 700/PK-8
8201 Main St 55317 952-934-6003
Tom Donlon, prin. Fax 906-1229

Chaska, Carver, Pop. 23,347
Eastern Carver County SD 112 9,200/PK-12
11 Peavey Rd 55318 952-556-6100
Dr. Clint Christopher, supt. Fax 556-6109
www.district112.org
Chaska MS East 700/6-8
1600 Park Ridge Dr 55318 952-556-7600
Beth Holm, prin. Fax 556-7609
Chaska MS West 800/6-8
140 Engler Blvd 55318 952-556-7400
Sheryl Hough, prin. Fax 556-7409
Clover Ridge ES 700/K-5
114000 Hundertmark Rd 55318 952-556-6900
Nathan Slinde, prin. Fax 556-6909
Jonathan ES 600/K-5
110300 Pioneer Trl W 55318 952-556-6500
Nancy Wittman-Beltz, prin. Fax 556-6509
Kinder Academy 300/K-K
1800 N Chestnut St 55318 952-556-6300
Lori Warnberg, prin. Fax 556-6309
Pioneer Ridge MS 600/6-8
1085 Pioneer Trl 55318 952-556-7800
Dana Miller, prin. Fax 556-7809
Other Schools – See Carver, Chanhassen, Victoria

Guardian Angels S 200/PK-8
217 W 2nd St 55318 952-227-4010
Sue Lovegreen, prin. Fax 227-4050
St. John's Lutheran S 200/PK-8
300 E 4th St 55318 952-448-2526
Gordon Thomas, admin. Fax 448-9500

Chatfield, Fillmore, Pop. 2,758
Chatfield SD 227 900/PK-12
205 Union St NE 55923 507-867-4210
Edward Harris, supt. Fax 518-0704
www.chatfield.k12.mn.us
Chatfield ES 500/PK-6
11555 Hillside Dr SE 55923 507-867-4521
Craig Ihrke, prin. Fax 518-0702

Chisago City, Chisago, Pop. 4,910
Chisago Lakes SD 2144
Supt. — See Lindstrom
Chisago Lakes PS 500/PK-2
11009 284th St 55013 651-213-2200
Brenda Schell, prin. Fax 213-2250
Lakeside ES 600/3-5
10345 Wyoming Ave 55013 651-213-2300
Sara Johnson, prin. Fax 213-2350

Chisago Lakes Baptist S 100/PK-12
9387 Wyoming Trl 55013 651-257-4587
Michael Elliott, admin. Fax 257-3888

Chisholm, Saint Louis, Pop. 4,873
Chisholm SD 695 700/PK-12
300 3rd Ave SW 55719 218-254-5726
Dr. Janey Blanchard, supt. Fax 254-3741
www.chisholm.k12.mn.us
Chisholm ES 200/4-6
300 3rd Ave SW 55719 218-254-5726
Jeff Hancock, prin. Fax 254-3741
Vaughan-Steffensrud ES 200/PK-3
1000 1st Ave NE 55719 218-254-5726
Jeffrey Hancock, prin. Fax 254-0068

Chokio, Stevens, Pop. 399
Chokio-Alberta SD 771 100/PK-12
PO Box 68 56221 320-324-7131
Dr. David Baukol, supt. Fax 324-2731
www.chokioalberta.k12.mn.us
Chokio-Alberta S 100/PK-12
PO Box 68 56221 320-324-7131
Tate Jerome, prin. Fax 324-2731

Circle Pines, Anoka, Pop. 4,828
Centennial SD 12 6,300/PK-12
4707 North Rd 55014 763-792-6000
Brian Dietz, supt. Fax 792-6050
www.isd12.org
Centennial ES 400/K-5
4657 North Rd 55014 763-792-5300
Kathleen Kaiser, prin. Fax 792-5350
Golden Lake ES 400/K-5
1 School Rd 55014 763-792-5900
Chris Gerst, prin. Fax 792-5950
Other Schools – See Centerville, Lino Lakes

Clara City, Chippewa, Pop. 1,350
MACCRAY SD 700/PK-12
PO Box 690 56222 320-847-2154
Brian Koslofsky, supt. Fax 847-3239
www.maccray.k12.mn.us
Other Schools – See Maynard, Raymond

Clearbrook, Clearwater, Pop. 513
Clearbrook-Gonvick SD 2311 400/PK-12
16770 Clearwater Lake Rd 56634 218-776-3112
Wayne Olson, supt. Fax 776-3117
www.clearbrook-gonvick.k12.mn.us
Clearbrook-Gonvick ES 300/PK-6
16770 Clearwater Lake Rd 56634 218-776-3112
Jeff Burgess, prin. Fax 776-3117

Clear Lake, Sherburne, Pop. 540
Saint Cloud Area SD 742
Supt. — See Saint Cloud
Clearview ES 600/PK-6
7310 State Highway 24 55319 320-743-2241
Sheri Rutar, prin. Fax 743-4407

Cleveland, LeSueur, Pop. 714
Cleveland SD 391 300/PK-12
PO Box 310 56017 507-931-5953
Brian Phillips, supt. Fax 931-9088
cleveland.k12.mn.us/
Cleveland S 300/PK-12
PO Box 310 56017 507-931-5953
Scott Lusk, prin. Fax 931-9088

Climax, Polk, Pop. 262
Climax-Shelly SD 592 100/PK-12
PO Box 67 56523 218-857-2385
Norman Baumgarn, supt. Fax 857-3544
www.climax.k12.mn.us
Climax-Shelly S 100/PK-12
PO Box 67 56523 218-857-2385
Nancy Newcomb, prin. Fax 857-3544

Clinton, Big Stone, Pop. 449
Clinton-Graceville-Beardsley SD 2888 300/PK-12
PO Box 361 56225 320-325-5282
Phil Grant, supt. Fax 325-5509
www.graceville.k12.mn.us
Clinton-Graceville-Beardsley ES 200/PK-6
PO Box 361 56225 320-325-5224
Larry Mischke, prin. Fax 325-5509
Lismore Colony S 50/K-12
PO Box 361 56225 320-325-5583
Larry Mischke, prin. Fax 325-5509

Cloquet, Carlton, Pop. 11,711
Cloquet SD 94 2,400/K-12
302 14th St 55720 218-879-6721
Ken Scarbrough, supt. Fax 879-6724
www.isd94.org
Churchill ES 500/K-4
515 Granite St 55720 218-879-3308
David Wangen, prin. Fax 879-1514
Cloquet MS 500/5-8
509 Carlton Ave 55720 218-879-3328
Tom Brenner, prin. Fax 879-4175
Washington ES 600/K-4
801 12th St 55720 218-879-3369
Robbi Mondati, prin. Fax 879-3360

Queen of Peace S 100/PK-6
102 4th St 55720 218-879-8516
Bill Van Loh, prin. Fax 879-8930

Cohasset, Itasca, Pop. 2,634
Grand Rapids SD 318
Supt. — See Grand Rapids
Cohasset ES 200/K-4
450 Columbus Ave 55721 218-327-5860
Jill Wheelock, prin. Fax 327-5861

Cokato, Wright, Pop. 2,654
Dassel-Cokato SD 466 2,300/PK-12
4852 Reardon Ave SW 55321 320-286-4100
Jeff Powers, supt. Fax 286-4101
www.dc.k12.mn.us
Cokato ES 500/PK-4
200 5th St SW 55321 320-286-4100
Brian Franklin, prin. Fax 286-4131
Dassel-Cokato MS 700/5-8
4852 Reardon Ave SW 55321 320-286-4100
Alisa Johnson, prin. Fax 286-4176
Other Schools – See Dassel

Cold Spring, Stearns, Pop. 3,975
Rocori SD 750 2,000/PK-12
534 5th Ave N 56320 320-685-4185
Scott Staska, supt. Fax 685-4906
www.rocori.k12.mn.us
Cold Spring ES 500/K-5
601 Red River Ave N 56320 320-685-7534
Eric Skanson, prin. Fax 685-4962

Rocori District Education Facility PK-PK
527 Main St 56320 320-685-8631
Stephanie Hillman, dir.
Rocori MS 500/6-8
534 5th Ave N 56320 320-685-3296
Mark Jenson, prin. Fax 685-4968
Other Schools – See Richmond, Rockville

St. Boniface S 300/PK-6
501 Main St 56320 320-685-3541
Sr. Sharon Waldoch, prin. Fax 685-8194

Coleraine, Itasca, Pop. 1,927
Greenway SD 316
Supt. — See Marble
Vandyke ES 400/K-4
PO Box 570 55722 218-245-2510
Sue Hoeft, prin. Fax 245-1824

Cologne, Carver, Pop. 1,500

Zion Lutheran S 100/PK-8
14735 County Road 153 55322 952-466-3379
Chris Dehning, prin. Fax 466-2703

Columbia Heights, Anoka, Pop. 18,748
Columbia Heights SD 13 3,100/PK-12
1440 49th Ave NE 55421 763-528-4500
Kathy Kelly, supt. Fax 571-9203
www.colheights.k12.mn.us
Columbia Academy 700/6-8
900 49th Ave NE 55421 763-586-4701
Duane Berkas, prin. Fax 528-4707
Early Childhood S 100/PK-PK
1460 49th Ave NE 55421 763-528-4423
Karen Kremer, admin.
Highland ES 500/PK-5
1500 49th Ave NE 55421 763-528-4400
Michele DeWitt, prin. Fax 528-4407
Valley View ES 600/PK-5
800 49th Ave NE 55421 763-528-4200
Willie Fort, prin. Fax 528-4207
Other Schools – See Fridley

Immaculate Conception S 100/PK-8
4030 Jackson St NE 55421 763-788-9065
Jane Bona, prin. Fax 788-9066

Comfrey, Brown, Pop. 378
Comfrey SD 81 200/K-12
305 Ochre St W 56019 507-877-3491
Kirsten Hutchison, supt. Fax 877-3492
www.comfreyps.new.rschooltoday.com
Comfrey ES 100/K-6
305 Ochre St W 56019 507-877-3491
Kirsten Hutchison, admin. Fax 877-3492

Cook, Saint Louis, Pop. 560
Saint Louis County Schools ISD 2142
Supt. — See Virginia
North Woods S 300/PK-12
10248 E Olson Rd 55723 218-666-5221
John Vukmanich, prin. Fax 666-5223

Coon Rapids, Anoka, Pop. 59,722
Anoka-Hennepin SD 11
Supt. — See Anoka
Adams ES 600/PK-5
8989 Sycamore St NW 55433 763-506-1600
Dr. Ann Herlofsky, prin. Fax 506-1603
Bye ES 500/K-5
11931 Crooked Lake Blvd NW 55433 763-506-3700
Janel Wahlin, prin. Fax 506-3703
Coon Rapids MS 1,200/6-8
11600 Raven St NW 55433 763-506-4800
Tom Shaw, prin. Fax 506-4803
Eisenhower ES 700/K-5
151 Northdale Blvd NW 55448 763-506-2300
Amy Reed, prin. Fax 506-2303
Hamilton ES 500/K-5
1374 111th Ave NW 55433 763-506-2700
Melissa Monson, prin. Fax 506-2703
Hoover ES 600/K-5
2369 109th Ave NW 55433 763-506-2800
George Vasil, prin. Fax 506-2803
Mississippi ES 500/K-5
10620 Direct River Dr NW 55433 763-506-3500
Ann Sangster, prin. Fax 506-3503
Northdale MS 1,100/6-8
11301 Dogwood St NW 55448 763-506-5400
Jeff Leach, prin. Fax 506-5403
Sand Creek ES 800/K-5
12156 Olive St NW 55448 763-506-4300
Paul Anderson, prin. Fax 506-4303

Cross of Christ Lutheran S 100/PK-8
9931 Foley Blvd NW 55433 763-786-0637
Rev. Ben Pederson, prin. Fax 792-0484
Epiphany S 500/K-8
11001 Hanson Blvd NW 55433 763-754-1750
Michael McGinty, prin. Fax 862-4350

Corcoran, Hennepin, Pop. 5,327

St. John Lutheran S 200/PK-8
9141 County Road 101 55340 763-420-2426
Scott Kloetzke, admin. Fax 420-7198

Cottage Grove, Washington, Pop. 33,853
South Washington County SD 833 17,600/PK-12
7362 E Point Douglas Rd S 55016 651-425-6300
Keith Jacobus Ph.D., supt. Fax 425-6318
www.sowashco.org
Armstrong ES 400/PK-5
8855 Inwood Ave S 55016 651-425-4100
Andrew Caflisch, prin. Fax 425-4115
Cottage Grove ES 600/PK-5
7447 65th St S 55016 651-425-5800
Theresa Blume-Thole, prin. Fax 425-5815
Cottage Grove MS 1,200/6-8
9775 Indian Blvd S 55016 651-425-6800
Elise Block, prin. Fax 425-6828
Crestview/Nuevas Fronteras ES 300/PK-5
7830 80th St S 55016 651-425-3800
Jodi Husting, prin. Fax 425-3815
Grey Cloud ES 700/PK-5
9525 Indian Blvd S 55016 651-425-4200
Laura Loshek, prin. Fax 425-4215
Hillside ES 500/PK-5
8177 Hillside Trl S 55016 651-425-4000
Erin Shadick, prin. Fax 425-4015
Pine Hill ES 400/PK-5
9015 Hadley Ave S 55016 651-425-3900
Jolaine Mast, prin. Fax 425-3915
Other Schools – See Newport, Saint Paul Park, Woodbury

Cottonwood, Lyon, Pop. 1,201
Lakeview SD 2167 600/PK-12
PO Box 107 56229 507-423-5164
Dr. Chris Fenske, supt. Fax 423-5568
www.lakeview2167.com
Lakeview ES 300/PK-6
PO Box 107 56229 507-423-5164
Melissa Wilber, prin. Fax 423-5568

Courtland, Nicollet, Pop. 610

Immanuel Lutheran S 100/PK-8
50605 478th St 56021 507-359-2534
Dan Erdman, prin. Fax 359-3288

Cromwell, Carlton, Pop. 231
Cromwell-Wright SD 95 300/PK-12
PO Box 7 55726 218-644-3737
Nathan Libbon, supt. Fax 644-3992
www.cromwellwright.k12.mn.us
Cromwell-Wright ES 200/PK-6
PO Box 7 55726 218-644-3716
Nathan Libbon, admin. Fax 644-3992

Crookston, Polk, Pop. 7,779
Crookston SD 593 1,300/PK-12
402 W Fisher Ave Ste 593 56716 218-281-5313
Chris Bates, supt. Fax 281-3505
www.crookston.k12.mn.us
Highland ES 500/2-6
801 Central Ave N 56716 218-281-5600
Chris Trostad, prin. Fax 281-6166
Washington ES 200/PK-1
724 University Ave 56716 218-281-2762
Denice Oliver, prin. Fax 281-2784

Cathedral S 100/K-6
702 Summit Ave 56716 218-281-1735
Patricia Jones, prin. Fax 281-1747
Our Savior Lutheran S 50/PK-7
PO Box 477 56716 218-281-5191
Sandra Trittin, prin.

Crosby, Crow Wing, Pop. 2,354
Crosby-Ironton SD 182 1,100/PK-12
711 Poplar St 56441 218-545-8801
Dr. Jamie Skjeveland, supt. Fax 545-8836
www.ci.k12.mn.us
Cuyuna Range ES 600/PK-6
711 Poplar St 56441 218-545-8803
Kurt Becker, prin. Fax 545-8858

Crystal, Hennepin, Pop. 21,394
Robbinsdale SD 281
Supt. — See New Hope
Forest ES 600/K-5
6800 47th Ave N 55428 763-504-7900
Melissa Jackson, prin. Fax 504-7909
Neill ES 500/K-5
6600 Medicine Lake Rd 55427 763-504-7400
Kelly Corbett, prin. Fax 504-7409

St. Raphael S 200/PK-8
7301 Bass Lake Rd 55428 763-504-9450
Ann Coone, prin. Fax 504-9460

Culver, Saint Louis
Saint Louis County Schools ISD 2142
Supt. — See Virginia
South Ridge S 300/PK-12
8162 Swan Lake Rd 55779 218-345-6789
Andrew Bernard, prin. Fax 345-6790

Dakota, Winona, Pop. 321

St. John's Lutheran S 100/PK-8
42685 County Road 12 55925 507-643-6440
Mark Kutz, prin. Fax 643-6007

Dassel, Meeker, Pop. 1,449
Dassel-Cokato SD 466
Supt. — See Cokato
Dassel ES 400/PK-4
PO Box 368 55325 320-286-4100
Debbie Morris, prin. Fax 286-4151

Dawson, Lac qui Parle, Pop. 1,527
Dawson-Boyd SD 378 500/PK-12
848 Chestnut St 56232 320-769-2955
Shane Tappe, supt. Fax 769-4502
dawsonboydschools.org/
Stevens ES 300/PK-6
848 Chestnut St 56232 320-769-4590
Amy Hiedeman, prin. Fax 769-4502

Dayton, Hennepin, Pop. 4,606
Anoka-Hennepin SD 11
Supt. — See Anoka
Dayton ES 500/K-5
12000 S Diamond Lake Rd 55327 763-506-2200
Jessica Whippler, prin. Fax 506-2203

Deephaven, Hennepin, Pop. 3,617

St. Therese S 200/PK-8
18325 Minnetonka Blvd 55391 952-473-4355
Lauren Caton, prin. Fax 261-0630

Deer River, Itasca, Pop. 888
Deer River SD 317 900/PK-12
PO Box 307 56636 218-246-2420
Matt Grose, supt. Fax 246-8948
www.isd317.org
King ES 500/PK-5
PO Box 307 56636 218-246-8860
Jennifer Stefan, prin. Fax 246-8897

Delano, Wright, Pop. 5,379
Delano SD 879 2,400/PK-12
700 Elm Ave E 55328 763-972-3365
Matthew Schoen, supt. Fax 972-6706
www.delano.k12.mn.us
Delano ES 900/PK-4
678 Tiger Dr 55328 763-972-3365
Darren Schuler, prin. Fax 972-6199
Delano MS 700/5-8
700 Elm Ave E 55328 763-972-3365
Barry Voight, prin. Fax 972-6876

Mount Olive Lutheran S 100/PK-8
435 Bridge Ave E 55328 763-972-2442
Nolan Valus, prin. Fax 972-8139
St. Maximilian Kolbe S 100/PK-6
PO Box 470 55328 763-972-2528
Mary Ziebell, prin. Fax 972-6177

Detroit Lakes, Becker, Pop. 8,324
Detroit Lakes SD 22 2,600/PK-12
PO Box 766 56502 218-847-9271
Doug Froke, supt. Fax 847-9273
www.dlschools.net/
Detroit Lakes MS 600/6-8
510 11th Ave 56501 218-847-9228
Michael Suckert, prin. Fax 847-0057
Lincoln Community Ed. ECC Alt
204 Willow St E 56501 218-847-4418
Doug Froke, prin. Fax 847-9794
Roosevelt ES 600/PK-5
510 11th Ave 56501 218-847-1106
Trish Mariotti, prin. Fax 847-1305
Rossman ES 600/PK-5
1221 Rossman Ave 56501 218-847-9268
Jason Kuehn, prin. Fax 847-1481

Adventist Christian S 50/K-8
404 Richwood Rd 56501 218-846-9764
Sandy Daniels, prin.
Holy Rosary S 100/PK-8
1043 Lake Ave 56501 218-847-5306
Mike Connell, prin. Fax 847-6367

Dilworth, Clay, Pop. 3,965
Dilworth-Glyndon-Felton SD 2164 1,500/PK-12
PO Box 188 56529 218-477-6800
Bryan Thygeson, supt. Fax 477-6807
www.dgf.k12.mn.us
Dilworth ES 500/PK-4
PO Box 188 56529 218-477-6801
Peggy Hanson, prin. Fax 477-6807
Dilworth-Glyndon-Felton MS 300/6-8
PO Box 188 56529 218-477-6803
Heidi Critchley, prin. Fax 477-6807
Other Schools – See Glyndon

Dodge Center, Dodge, Pop. 2,647
Triton SD 2125 1,200/PK-12
813 W Highway St 55927 507-418-7530
Brett Joyce, supt. Fax 374-6524
www.triton.k12.mn.us
Triton ES 600/PK-5
813 W Highway St 55927 507-418-7500
Nick Jurrens, prin. Fax 374-2208
Triton MS 300/6-8
813 W Highway St 55927 507-418-7510
Luke Lutterman, prin. Fax 633-8673

Grace Lutheran S 50/PK-2
404 Central Ave N 55927 507-633-2253
Patricia Marquardt B.S., dir. Fax 633-2783
Maranatha Adventist S 50/1-8
414 3rd Ave SW 55927 507-374-6353
Vickie Martin, prin. Fax 374-6353

Duluth, Saint Louis, Pop. 83,742
Duluth ISD 709 8,200/PK-12
215 N 1st Ave E 55802 218-336-8700
William Gronseth, supt. Fax 336-8773
www.isd709.org
Congdon Park ES 500/K-5
3116 E Superior St 55812 218-336-8825
Kathi Kusch Marshall, prin. Fax 336-8829
Homecroft ES 400/K-5
4784 Howard Gnesen Rd 55803 218-336-8865
Amy Worden, prin. Fax 336-8869
Lakewood ES 200/K-5
5207 N Tischer Rd 55804 218-336-8870
Darren Sheldon, prin. Fax 336-8874
Lester Park ES 500/K-5
5300 Glenwood St 55804 218-336-8875
Sue Lehna, prin. Fax 336-8879
Lincoln Park MS 500/6-8
3215 W 3rd St 55806 218-336-8880
Brenda Vatthauer, prin. Fax 336-8894
Lowell ES 400/K-5
2000 Rice Lake Rd 55811 218-336-8895
Jen Larva, prin. Fax 336-8899
MacArthur ES 500/K-5
720 N Central Ave 55807 218-336-8900
Clayton Norman, prin. Fax 336-8904
Myers-Wilkins ES 400/PK-5
1027 N 8th Ave E 55805 218-336-8860
Elisa Maldonado, prin. Fax 336-8864

Ordean East MS 900/6-8
2900 E 4th St 55812 218-336-8940
Gina Kleive, prin. Fax 336-8949
Piedmont ES 500/K-5
2827 Chambersburg Ave 55811 218-336-8950
Beth Shermoen, prin. Fax 336-8954
Stowe ES 400/K-5
715 101st Ave W 55808 218-336-8965
Nathan Glockle, prin. Fax 336-8969

Proctor SD 704
Supt. — See Proctor
Bay View ES 600/PK-5
8708 Vinland St 55810 218-628-4949
Diane Morin, prin. Fax 628-4951
Pike Lake ES 300/K-5
5682 Martin Rd 55811 218-729-8214
Mark Hughes, prin. Fax 729-8215

Holy Rosary S 300/K-8
2802 E 4th St 55812 218-724-8565
Jesse Murray, prin. Fax 724-6201
Lakeview Christian Academy 200/PK-12
155 W Central Entrance 55811 218-723-8844
Todd Benson, admin. Fax 722-7850
Many Rivers Montessori S PK-8
916 E 3rd St 55805 218-464-5570
Mark Niedermier, head sch Fax 464-5569
Montessori S of Duluth PK-6
PO Box 3314 55803 218-728-4600
Daphne Amundson, prin.
St. James Catholic S 100/PK-8
715 N 57th Ave W 55807 218-624-1511
Julieanne Blazevic, prin. Fax 624-3435
St. John the Evangelist S 100/PK-6
1 W Chisholm St 55803 218-724-9392
Peggy Frederickson, prin. Fax 724-9368
St. Michael's Lakeside S 100/PK-5
4628 Pitt St 55804 218-525-1931
Peggy Frederickson, prin. Fax 525-0296
Stone Ridge Christian S 50/1-8
115 E Orange St 55811 218-722-7535
Rudy Carlson, prin.

Eagan, Dakota, Pop. 62,501
Burnsville-Eagan-Savage ISD 191
Supt. — See Burnsville
Rahn ES 400/K-5
4424 Sandstone Dr 55122 952-707-3600
Barbara Borer, prin. Fax 707-3602

Rosemount-Apple Valley-Eagan ISD 196
Supt. — See Rosemount
Black Hawk MS 800/6-8
1540 Deerwood Dr 55122 651-683-8521
Richard Wendorff, prin. Fax 683-8527
Dakota Hills MS 1,200/6-8
4183 Braddock Trl 55123 651-683-6800
Trevor Johnson, prin. Fax 683-6858
Deerwood ES 600/K-5
1480 Deerwood Dr 55122 651-683-6801
Jeremy Sorenson, prin. Fax 683-6808
Glacier Hills ES of Arts and Science 700/K-5
3825 Glacier Hls 55123 651-683-8570
Scott Thomas, prin. Fax 683-8577
Northview ES 400/K-5
965 Diffley Rd 55123 651-683-6820
Kerri Town, prin. Fax 683-6819
Oak Ridge ES 600/K-5
4350 Johnny Cake Ridge Rd 55122 651-683-6970
Cindy Magnuson, prin. Fax 683-6873
Pinewood ES 600/K-5
4300 Dodd Rd 55123 651-683-6980
Cris Town, prin. Fax 683-6870
Red Pine ES 900/K-5
530 Red Pine Ln 55123 651-423-7870
Drew Goeldner, prin. Fax 423-7875
Thomas Lake ES 400/K-5
4350 Thomas Lake Rd 55122 651-683-6890
Mary Jelenik, prin. Fax 683-6884
Woodland ES 500/K-5
945 Wescott Rd 55123 651-683-6990
Lisa Carlson, prin. Fax 683-6883

West St. Paul-Mendota Hts-Eagan SD 197
Supt. — See Mendota Heights
Pilot Knob STEM Magnet S 300/PK-4
1436 Lone Oak Rd 55121 651-403-7900
Adriana Henderson, prin. Fax 403-7910

Faithful Shepherd S 500/K-8
3355 Columbia Dr 55121 651-406-4747
Sheila Hendricks, prin. Fax 406-4743
Trinity Lone Oak Lutheran S 200/PK-8
2950 Highway 55 55121 651-454-1139
Cletus Pfeiffer, prin. Fax 454-0109

Eagle Lake, Blue Earth, Pop. 2,397
Mankato SD 77
Supt. — See Mankato
Eagle Lake ES 400/K-5
500 LeSueur Ave 56024 507-257-3530
Kory Kath, prin. Fax 257-3867

East Grand Forks, Polk, Pop. 8,422
East Grand Forks SD 595 1,800/PK-12
PO Box 151 56721 218-773-3494
Mike Kolness, supt. Fax 773-7408
www.egf.k12.mn.us/
Central MS 400/6-8
PO Box 151 56721 218-773-1141
Lon Ellingson, prin. Fax 773-9112
New Heights ES 500/PK-2
PO Box 151 56721 218-773-0908
Julie Pederson, prin. Fax 773-3150
South Point ES 400/3-5
PO Box 151 56721 218-773-1149
Jim Torkelson, prin. Fax 773-4392

Riverside Christian S 100/PK-8
610 2nd Ave NE 56721 218-773-1770
Brian Marcus, head sch Fax 773-4322
Sacred Heart S 100/K-12
200 3rd St NW 56721 218-773-0230
Jodi Vanderheiden, prin. Fax 773-7042

Eden Prairie, Hennepin, Pop. 59,499
Eden Prairie SD 272 9,100/PK-12
8100 School Rd 55344 952-975-7000
Joshua Swanson Ph.D., supt. Fax 975-7020
www.edenpr.org
Cedar Ridge ES 800/K-6
8905 Braxton Dr 55347 952-975-7800
Joe Epping, prin. Fax 975-7820
Central MS 1,400/7-8
8025 School Rd 55344 952-975-7300
Nathan Swenson, prin. Fax 975-7320
Eagle Heights Spanish Immersion S 800/K-6
13400 Staring Lake Pkwy 55347 952-975-7700
Hernan Moncada, prin. Fax 975-7721
Early Childhood Preschool 100/PK-PK
8040 Mitchell Rd 55344 952-975-6980
Judy Beaton, dir. Fax 975-6921
Eden Lake ES 800/K-6
12000 Anderson Lakes Pkwy 55344 952-975-8400
Tim Beekmann, prin. Fax 975-8420
Forest Hills ES 700/K-6
13708 Holly Rd 55346 952-975-8600
Connie Hytjan, prin. Fax 975-8620
Oak Point ES 800/K-6
13400 Staring Lake Pkwy 55347 952-975-7600
Joel Knorr, prin. Fax 975-7620
Prairie View ES 700/K-6
17255 Peterborg Rd 55346 952-975-8800
Felicia Thames, prin. Fax 975-8820

Agape Christi Academy 50/PK-8
9957 Valley View Rd 55344 952-856-0103
International School of Minnesota 400/PK-12
6385 Beach Rd 55344 952-918-1800
Kenneth Riggs, prin. Fax 918-1801

Eden Valley, Meeker, Pop. 1,031
Eden Valley-Watkins SD 463 1,000/PK-12
298 Brooks St N 55329 320-453-2900
Mark Messman, supt. Fax 453-5600
www.evw.k12.mn.us
Eden Valley ES 500/K-6
901 Stearns Ave E 55329 320-453-2900
Rob Pederson, prin. Fax 453-6457
Other Schools – See Watkins

Edgerton, Pipestone, Pop. 1,174
Edgerton SD 581 300/PK-12
PO Box 28 56128 507-442-7881
Keith Buckridge, supt. Fax 442-8541
www.edgertonpublic.com
Edgerton ES 200/PK-5
PO Box 28 56128 507-442-7881
Keith Buckridge, prin. Fax 442-8541

Edgerton Christian S 200/K-8
PO Box 210 56128 507-442-6181
John Top, prin. Fax 442-3019

Edina, Hennepin, Pop. 47,052
Edina SD 273 8,500/K-12
5701 Normandale Rd 55424 952-848-3900
John Schultz Ed.D., supt. Fax 848-3901
www.edinaschools.org
Concord ES 700/K-5
5900 Concord Ave 55424 952-848-4300
Susan Prather, prin. Fax 848-4301
Cornelia ES 500/K-5
7000 Cornelia Dr 55435 952-848-4600
Lisa Masica, prin. Fax 848-4601
Countryside ES 600/K-5
5701 Benton Ave 55436 952-848-4700
Karen Bergman, prin. Fax 848-4701
Creek Valley ES 600/K-5
6401 Gleason Rd 55439 952-848-3200
Kari Dahlquist, prin. Fax 848-3201
Highlands ES 600/K-5
5505 Doncaster Way 55436 952-848-4500
Kathryn Mahoney, prin. Fax 848-4501
Normandale ES 700/K-5
5701 Normandale Rd 55424 952-848-4100
Chris Holden, prin. Fax 848-4101

Calvin Christian S 400/K-8
4015 Inglewood Ave S 55416 952-927-5304
Steven Groen, supt. Fax 927-4628
Our Lady of Grace S 700/K-8
5051 Eden Ave 55436 952-929-5463
Maureen Trenary, prin. Fax 929-8170

Elbow Lake, Grant, Pop. 1,157
West Central Area SD 2342
Supt. — See Barrett
West Central Area North ES 200/PK-4
411 1st St SE 56531 218-685-4477
Jon Moore, dean Fax 685-4149

Elgin, Wabasha, Pop. 1,079
Plainview-Elgin-Millville ISD 2899
Supt. — See Plainview
Plainview-Elgin-Millville IS 300/4-6
210 2nd St SW 55932 507-876-2213
Clark Olstad, prin. Fax 876-2296
Plainview-Elgin-Millville JHS 200/7-8
70 1st St SE 55932 507-876-2521
Clark Olstad, prin. Fax 876-2110

Elko, Scott, Pop. 533
New Prague Area SD 721
Supt. — See New Prague
Eagle View ES 500/PK-5
25600 Nevada Ave 55020 952-758-6000
Will Remmert, prin. Fax 758-6099

Elk River, Sherburne, Pop. 22,557
Elk River Area SD 728 11,900/K-12
815 Highway 10 55330 763-241-3400
Daniel Bittman, supt. Fax 241-3407
www.isd728.org
Lincoln ES 500/K-5
600 School St NW 55330 763-241-3480
Justin Sperling, prin. Fax 241-3481
Meadowvale ES 600/K-5
12701 Elk Lake Rd NW 55330 763-241-3470
Karen Maschler, prin. Fax 241-3471
Otsego ES 800/K-5
8125 NE River Rd 55330 763-241-3494
Kelly Corbett, prin. Fax 241-3496
Parker ES 500/K-5
500 School St NW 55330 763-241-3500
Scott Lempka, prin. Fax 241-3501
Salk MS 800/6-8
11970 Highland Rd NW 55330 763-241-3455
Julie Athman, prin. Fax 241-3456
Twin Lakes ES 800/K-5
10051 191st Ave NW 55330 763-274-7242
Dan Collins, prin. Fax 274-7243
VandenBerge MS 500/6-8
948 Proctor Ave NW 55330 763-241-3450
Marcia Welch, prin. Fax 241-3552
Other Schools – See Otsego, Rogers, Zimmerman

St. Andrew S 200/PK-5
428 Irving Ave NW 55330 763-441-2216
Sue Scipioni, prin. Fax 441-1146
St. John Lutheran S 100/PK-7
9231 Viking Blvd NW 55330 763-441-6616
Brett Hardecopf, prin. Fax 441-9858

Ellendale, Steele, Pop. 690
NRHEG SD 2168
Supt. — See New Richland
NRHEG ES 500/PK-5
600 School St S 56026 507-684-3181
Doug Anderson, prin. Fax 684-2108

Ellsworth, Nobles, Pop. 460
Ellsworth SD 514 100/PK-12
PO Box 8 56129 507-967-2242
John Willey, supt. Fax 967-2588
www.ellsworth.mntm.org
Ellsworth S 100/PK-12
PO Box 8 56129 507-967-2242
John Willey, prin. Fax 967-2588

Ely, Saint Louis, Pop. 3,405
ISD 696 400/PK-12
600 E Harvey St 55731 218-365-6166
Kevin Abrahamson, supt. Fax 365-6138
www.ely.k12.mn.us
Washington ES 300/PK-5
600 E Harvey St 55731 218-365-6166
Anne Oelke, prin. Fax 365-6138

Erskine, Polk, Pop. 492
Win-E-Mac SD 2609 400/PK-12
23130 345th St SE 56535 218-687-2236
Randy Bruer, supt. Fax 563-2902
www.win-e-mac.k12.mn.us
Win-E-Mac ES 200/PK-6
23130 345th St SE 56535 218-687-2236
Kevin McKeever, prin. Fax 563-2902

Esko, Carlton, Pop. 1,843
Esko SD 99 1,200/PK-12
PO Box 10 55733 218-879-2969
Aaron Fischer, supt. Fax 879-7490
www.esko.k12.mn.us/
Winterquist ES 600/PK-6
PO Box 10 55733 218-879-3361
Brian Harker, prin. Fax 879-7490

Evansville, Douglas, Pop. 609
Brandon-Evansville ISD 2908
Supt. — See Brandon
Brandon-Evansville MS 50/6-8
PO Box 40 56326 218-948-2241
Dean Yocum, prin. Fax 948-2441
Evansville ES 100/4-5
PO Box 40 56326 218-948-2241
Dean Yocum, prin. Fax 948-2441

Eveleth, Saint Louis, Pop. 3,636
Eveleth-Gilbert SD 2154 1,100/PK-12
801 Jones St 55734 218-744-7700
Jeff Carey, supt. Fax 744-4381
www.egschools.org
Franklin ES 400/PK-4
801 Jones St 55734 218-744-7709
Jeff Carey, prin. Fax 744-4381
Other Schools – See Gilbert

Excelsior, Hennepin, Pop. 2,144
Minnetonka SD 276
Supt. — See Minnetonka
Excelsior ES 800/K-5
441 Oak St 55331 952-401-5650
Stacy Decorsey, prin. Fax 401-5657
Minnetonka West MS 1,100/6-8
6421 Hazeltine Blvd 55331 952-401-5300
Dr. Paula Hoff, prin. Fax 401-5350
Minnewashta ES 900/K-5
26350 Smithtown Rd 55331 952-401-5500
Cynthia Andress, prin. Fax 401-5506

Our Savior S 100/PK-K
23290 Highway 7 55331 952-474-5181
Fred Limmel, prin. Fax 470-1985
St. John the Baptist S 100/PK-8
638 Mill St 55331 952-474-5812
Nicholas Fonte, prin. Fax 401-8778

Eyota, Olmsted, Pop. 1,965
Dover-Eyota SD 533 1,100/PK-12
615 South Ave SW 55934 507-545-2125
Michael Carolan, supt. Fax 545-2349
www.desch.org
Dover-Eyota ES 500/PK-5
27 Knowledge Rd SW 55934 507-545-2632
Dr. Jeanne Svobodny, prin. Fax 545-2841
Dover-Eyota MS 300/6-8
615 South Ave SW 55934 507-545-2631
Todd Rowekamp, prin. Fax 545-2218

Fairfax, Renville, Pop. 1,227
GFW SD 2365
Supt. — See Gibbon
GFW MS 200/5-8
300 2nd Ave SE 55332 507-426-7251
Ralph Fairchild, prin. Fax 426-7425

Prairie Lutheran MS 50/5-8
PO Box 130 55332 507-426-7755
Macord Johnson, prin. Fax 426-8372

Fairmont, Martin, Pop. 10,613
Fairmont Area SD 2752 1,700/PK-12
714 Victoria St Ste 103 56031 507-238-4234
Joseph Brown, supt. Fax 235-4050
fairmont.k12.mn.us
Fairmont ES 900/PK-6
714 Victoria St Ste 101 56031 507-238-4487
Jim Davison, prin.

St. James Evangelical Lutheran S 100/PK-8
108 S James St 56031 507-436-5289
Jon Jenks, prin. Fax 436-5547
St. John Vianney S 100/PK-6
911 S Prairie Ave 56031 507-235-5304
Sarah Striemer, prin. Fax 235-9099
St. Paul Lutheran S 200/PK-8
201 Oxford St 56031 507-238-9492
Brian Kube, prin. Fax 238-9492

Falcon Heights, Ramsey, Pop. 5,195
Roseville Area SD 623
Supt. — See Roseville
Falcon Heights ES 500/K-6
1393 Garden Ave 55113 651-646-0021
Beth Behnke, prin. Fax 646-7183

Faribault, Rice, Pop. 23,011
Faribault SD 656 3,700/PK-12
710 17th St SW 55021 507-333-6000
Todd Sesker, supt. Fax 333-6050
www.faribault.k12.mn.us/
Faribault MS 900/6-8
704 17th St SW 55021 507-333-6300
Michael Meihak, prin. Fax 333-6400
Jefferson ES 600/K-5
922 Home Pl 55021 507-333-6500
Yesica Louis, prin. Fax 333-6544
Lincoln ES 500/K-5
510 Lincoln Ave NW 55021 507-333-6600
Brad Palmer, prin. Fax 333-6642
McKinley Pre K PK-PK
930 4th Ave NW 55021 507-333-6460
Christine Gorman, coord. Fax 333-6830
Roosevelt ES 500/K-5
925 Parshall St 55021 507-333-6700
Terry Ronayne, prin. Fax 333-6734

Divine Mercy Catholic S 200/PK-6
15 3rd Ave SW 55021 507-334-7706
Gina Ashley, prin. Fax 332-2669
Faribault Lutheran S 100/K-8
526 4th St NW 55021 507-334-7982
Seth Winter, admin. Fax 334-4208

Farmington, Dakota, Pop. 20,570
Farmington SD 192 6,900/K-12
20655 Flagstaff Ave 55024 651-463-5000
Jay Haugen, supt. Fax 463-5010
www.farmington.k12.mn.us
Akin Road ES 700/K-5
5231 195th St W 55024 651-460-1700
Lisa Reichelt, prin. Fax 460-1710
Boeckman MS 700/6-8
800 Denmark Ave 55024 651-460-1400
Dan Miller, prin. Fax 460-1410
Dodge MS 800/6-8
4200 208th St W 55024 651-460-1500
Chris Bussmann, prin. Fax 460-1510
Farmington ES 700/K-5
500 Maple St 55024 651-463-9000
Kim Bolleson, prin. Fax 463-9010
Gateway Academy 3-8
4100 208th St W 55024 651-463-5004
Barb Duffrin, prin. Fax 463-5021
Meadowview ES 600/K-5
6100 195th St W 55024 651-460-3100
Becky Bican, prin. Fax 460-3110
North Trail ES 700/K-5
5580 170th St W 55024 651-460-1800
Dr. Steven Geis, prin. Fax 460-1810
Riverview ES 800/K-5
4100 208th St W 55024 651-460-1600
Dr. Kim Grengs, prin. Fax 460-1610

Christian Life Academy 200/PK-12
6300 212th St W 55024 651-463-4545
Rev. Darin Kindle, admin. Fax 463-8353

Fergus Falls, Otter Tail, Pop. 12,946
Fergus Falls SD 544 3,100/PK-12
601 Randolph Ave 56537 218-998-0544
Gerald Ness, supt. Fax 755-5000
www.isd544.org
Adams ES 300/1-2
301 W Bancroft Ave 56537 218-998-0544
Scott Colbeck, prin. Fax 755-5000
Cleveland ES 500/3-4
919 Northern Ave 56537 218-998-0544
Tindy Rund, prin. Fax 755-5000
Early Childhood Family Education PK-PK
601 Randolph Ave 56537 218-998-0544
Karen Hanan, dir. Fax 755-5000
Kennedy MS 500/5-8
601 Randolph Ave 56537 218-998-0544
Dean Monke, prin. Fax 755-5000
McKinley S 200/K-1
724 W Laurel Ave 56537 218-998-0544
Scott Colbeck, prin. Fax 755-5000

Morning Son Christian S 200/PK-6
1319 N Cleveland Ave 56537 218-736-2477
Tessa Martinson, prin. Fax 739-9374
Our Lady of Victory S 100/PK-6
426 W Cavour Ave 56537 218-736-6661
Tonya Zierden, prin. Fax 736-4407

Fertile, Polk, Pop. 831
Fertile-Beltrami SD 599 400/PK-12
210 S Mill St 56540 218-945-6933
Brian Clarke, supt. Fax 945-6934
fertilebeltrami.k12.mn.us
Fertile-Beltrami ES 200/PK-6
210 S Mill St 56540 218-945-6953
Nathaniel Messick, prin. Fax 945-6934

Finlayson, Pine, Pop. 312
East Central SD 2580 700/PK-12
61085 State Highway 23 55735 320-245-2289
Andy Almos, supt. Fax 245-5453
www.eastcentral.k12.mn.us
East Central ES 400/PK-5
61085 State Highway 23 55735 320-245-2931
Kris Chryst, prin. Fax 245-2448

Hinckley-Finlayson SD 2165
Supt. — See Hinckley
Finlayson ES 100/PK-6
PO Box 180 55735 320-233-7611
Jeffrey Wilson, prin. Fax 233-6135

Fisher, Polk, Pop. 434
Fisher SD 600 300/PK-12
313 Park Ave 56723 218-891-4105
Evan Hanson, supt. Fax 891-4251
www.fisher.k12.mn.us
Fisher ES 100/PK-6
313 Park Ave 56723 218-891-4105
Evan Hanson, admin. Fax 891-4251

Floodwood, Saint Louis, Pop. 508
Floodwood SD 698 300/PK-12
PO Box 287 55736 218-476-2285
Dr. Rae Villebrun, supt. Fax 476-2813
www.isd698.org
Floodwood ES 100/PK-6
PO Box 287 55736 218-476-2285
Dr. Rae Villebrun, prin. Fax 476-2813

Foley, Benton, Pop. 2,576
Foley SD 51 1,800/PK-12
840 Norman Ave N 56329 320-968-7175
Paul Neubauer, supt. Fax 968-8608
foley.k12.mn.us
Foley ES 600/PK-3
743 Penn St 56329 320-968-7286
Maria Erlandson, prin. Fax 968-8467
Foley IS 700/4-8
840 Norman Ave N 56329 320-968-6251
Eric Bjurman, prin. Fax 968-8608

St. John S 100/PK-6
PO Box 368 56329 320-968-7972
Christine Friederichs, prin. Fax 968-9956

Forest Lake, Washington, Pop. 18,070
Forest Lake SD 831 6,700/PK-12
6100 210th St N 55025 651-982-8100
Dr. Steve Massey, supt. Fax 982-8114
www.flaschools.org
Central Montessori ES 100/K-6
200 4th St SW 55025 651-982-3171
Kelly Tschudy-Lafean, prin. Fax 982-3172
Columbus ES 400/K-6
17345 Notre Dame St NE 55025 651-982-8900
Neal Fox, prin. Fax 982-8957
Forest Lake ES 400/4-6
408 4th St SW 55025 651-982-3200
Kenny Newby, prin. Fax 982-3299
Forest View ES 500/K-3
620 4th St SW 55025 651-982-8200
Scott Urness, prin. Fax 982-8260
Other Schools – See Lino Lakes, Scandia, Wyoming

St. Peter S 300/PK-6
1250 S Shore Dr 55025 651-982-2215
James Morehead, prin. Fax 982-2230

Foreston, Mille Lacs, Pop. 528

Faith Christian S 100/PK-12
11818 160th Ave 56330 320-294-5501
Nathan Johnson, admin. Fax 294-5197

Fosston, Polk, Pop. 1,489
Fosston SD 601 700/PK-12
301 1st St E 56542 218-435-6335
Kevin Ricke, supt. Fax 435-1663
www.fosston.k12.mn.us
Magelssen ES 400/PK-6
700 1st St E 56542 218-435-6036
Dan Boushee, prin. Fax 435-6414

Franklin, Renville, Pop. 491
Cedar Mountain SD 2754
Supt. — See Morgan
Cedar Mountain ES 200/K-5
PO Box 38 55333 507-557-2251
Patti Machart, prin. Fax 557-2116

Frazee, Becker, Pop. 1,295
Frazee-Vergas SD 23 900/PK-12
305 N Lake St 56544 218-334-3181
Terry S. Karger, supt. Fax 334-3182
www.frazee.k12.mn.us/
Frazee-Vergas ES 500/PK-6
305 N Lake St 56544 218-334-3181
Travis Nagel, prin. Fax 334-2115

Freeport, Stearns, Pop. 632

Sacred Heart S 100/PK-6
PO Box 39 56331 320-836-2591
Kristie Harren, prin. Fax 836-2142

Fridley, Anoka, Pop. 26,152
Columbia Heights SD 13
Supt. — See Columbia Heights
North Park ES 500/PK-5
5575 Fillmore St NE 55432 763-528-4300
Jeff Cacek, prin. Fax 528-4307

Fridley SD 14 2,900/K-12
6000 Moore Lake Dr W 55432 763-502-5000
Dr. Peggy Flathmann, supt. Fax 502-5040
www.fridley.k12.mn.us
Fridley MS 800/5-8
6100 Moore Lake Dr W 55432 763-502-5400
Amy Cochran, prin. Fax 502-5440
Hayes ES 600/K-4
615 Mississippi St NE 55432 763-502-5200
John Piotraschke, prin. Fax 502-5240
Stevenson ES 600/K-4
6080 E River Rd 55432 763-502-5300
Daryl Vossler, prin. Fax 502-5340

Spring Lake Park SD 16
Supt. — See Spring Lake Park
Woodcrest Spanish Immersion ES 400/K-5
880 Osborne Rd NE 55432 763-600-5800
Elizabeth Linares, prin. Fax 600-5813

Al-Amal S PK-12
1401 Gardena Ave NE 55432 763-571-8886

Fulda, Murray, Pop. 1,307
Fulda SD 505 300/PK-12
410 N College Ave 56131 507-425-2514
Ann Wendorff, supt. Fax 425-2001
www.fps.mntm.org
Fulda ES 100/PK-6
303 N Lafayette Ave 56131 507-425-2581
Mike Pagel, prin. Fax 425-2001

St. Paul's Lutheran S 50/PK-8
PO Box 394 56131 507-425-2169
Sherri Boehnke, admin.

Garfield, Douglas, Pop. 344
Alexandria SD 206
Supt. — See Alexandria
Garfield ES 100/K-5
PO Box 158 56332 320-762-3350
Lisa Pikop, prin. Fax 834-2260

Gary, Norman, Pop. 212
Norman County East SD 2215
Supt. — See Twin Valley
Norman County East ES 200/PK-6
PO Box 100 56545 218-356-8222
Rob Nudell, prin. Fax 356-8794

Gaylord, Sibley, Pop. 2,288
Sibley East SD 2310
Supt. — See Arlington
Sibley East ES 400/PK-5
PO Box 356 55334 507-237-3318
Marilu Martens, prin. Fax 237-3300

Immanuel Lutheran S 100/PK-8
PO Box 448 55334 507-237-2804
Fax 237-2899

Gibbon, Sibley, Pop. 764
GFW SD 2365 800/PK-12
323 E 11th St 55335 507-834-9813
Tami Martin, supt. Fax 834-6264
www.gfw.k12.mn.us
GFW ES 300/PK-4
323 E 11th St 55335 507-834-6501
Jennifer Thompson, prin. Fax 834-6264
Other Schools – See Fairfax

Prairie Lutheran ES 100/PK-4
1322 1st Ave 55335 507-834-6136
Macord Johnson, prin. Fax 426-8372
St. Peter Lutheran S 50/K-8
63872 240th St 55335 507-834-6676
Ruth Knaack, prin. Fax 834-6676

Gilbert, Saint Louis, Pop. 1,775
Eveleth-Gilbert SD 2154
Supt. — See Eveleth
Eveleth-Gilbert JHS 200/7-8
Summit St 55741 218-744-7770
Todd Griepentrog, prin. Fax 744-4381
Shean ES 200/5-6
Summit St 55741 218-744-7770
Todd Griepentrog, prin. Fax 744-4381

Glencoe, McLeod, Pop. 5,593
Glencoe-Silver Lake SD 2859 1,600/PK-12
1621 16th St E 55336 320-864-2499
Chris Sonju, supt. Fax 864-6320
www.gsl.k12.mn.us

Glencoe-Silver Lake JHS 300/PK-PK, 7-
1621 16th St E 55336 320-864-2456
Dan Svoboda, prin. Fax 864-2475
Lincoln ES 300/K-2
1621 16th St E 55336 320-864-2666
Bill Butler, prin. Fax 864-2682
Other Schools – See Silver Lake

First Evangelical Lutheran S 100/PK-8
925 13th St E 55336 320-864-3317
Dean Scheele, prin. Fax 864-3317

Glenville, Freeborn, Pop. 641
Glenville-Emmons SD 2886 200/K-12
PO Box 38 56036 507-448-2889
Jerry Reshetar, supt. Fax 448-2836
www.geschools.com
Glenville-Emmons ES 100/K-6
240 2nd Ave SW 56036 507-448-3334
Jeff Tietje, prin. Fax 448-2045

Glenwood, Pope, Pop. 2,537
Minnewaska SD 2149 900/PK-12
25122 State Highway 28 56334 320-239-4820
Chip Rankin, supt. Fax 239-1360
www.minnewaska.k12.mn.us
Minnewaska Area ES 300/PK-3
409 4th St SE 56334 320-634-4567
Sarah Suchy, prin. Fax 239-1380
Minnewaska Area IS 200/4-6
25122 State Highway 28 56334 320-239-4800
Sarah Suchy, prin. Fax 239-1362

Glyndon, Clay, Pop. 1,373
Dilworth-Glyndon-Felton SD 2164
Supt. — See Dilworth
Glyndon-Felton ES 400/PK-5
513 Parke Ave S 56547 218-477-6802
Margaux Hylla, prin. Fax 477-6808

Golden Valley, Hennepin, Pop. 19,843
Hopkins SD 270
Supt. — See Hopkins
Meadowbrook ES 600/K-6
5430 Glenwood Ave 55422 952-988-5100
Greta Evans-Becker, prin. Fax 988-5115

Robbinsdale SD 281
Supt. — See New Hope
Noble ES 400/K-5
2601 Noble Ave N 55422 763-504-4000
Jane Byrne, prin. Fax 504-4009
Sandburg MS 1,100/6-8
2400 Sandburg Ln 55427 763-504-8200
Amy O'Hern, prin. Fax 504-8231
School of Engineering and Arts 400/K-5
1751 Kelly Dr 55427 763-504-7200
Heather Hanson, prin. Fax 504-7209

Breck S 1,100/PK-12
123 Ottawa Ave N 55422 763-381-8100
Natalia Hernandez Ed.D., head sch Fax 381-8288
Good Shepherd S 300/K-6
145 Jersey Ave S 55426 763-545-4285
Bob Tift, prin. Fax 545-1896
King of Grace Lutheran S 200/PK-8
6000 Duluth St 55422 763-546-3131
Allen Labitzky, prin. Fax 540-0028

Goodhue, Goodhue, Pop. 1,166
Goodhue SD 253 700/PK-12
510 3rd Ave 55027 651-923-4447
Michael Redmond, supt. Fax 923-4036
www.goodhue.k12.mn.us
Goodhue ES 400/PK-6
510 3rd Ave 55027 651-923-4447
Mark Opsahl, prin. Fax 923-4036

St. John Lutheran S 100/PK-8
36620 County 4 Blvd 55027 651-923-4773
Theodore Glodowski, prin. Fax 923-5015

Goodridge, Pennington, Pop. 132
Goodridge SD 561 200/K-12
PO Box 195 56725 218-378-4133
Galen Clow, supt. Fax 378-4142
www.goodridge.k12.mn.us/
Goodridge ES 100/K-6
PO Box 195 56725 218-378-4133
Becky Carlson, prin. Fax 378-4142

Good Thunder, Blue Earth, Pop. 581
Maple River SD 2135
Supt. — See Mapleton
Maple River West ES 300/PK-5
PO Box 306 56037 507-278-3039
Jon Lewis, prin. Fax 278-4266

Granada, Martin, Pop. 302
Granada - Huntley - East Chain SD 2536 200/PK-12
PO Box 17 56039 507-447-2211
Mandy Fletcher, supt. Fax 447-2214
www.ghec.k12.mn.us
Granada - Huntley - East Chain ES 100/PK-6
PO Box 17 56039 507-447-2211
Mandy Fletcher, supt. Fax 447-2214

Grand Marais, Cook, Pop. 1,315
Cook County SD 166 300/PK-12
101 W 5th St 55604 218-387-2271
Dr. William Crandall, supt. Fax 387-1093
www.cookcountyschools.org
Sawtooth Mountain ES 200/PK-5
101 W 5th St 55604 218-387-2271
Adam Nelson, prin. Fax 387-9667

Grand Meadow, Mower, Pop. 1,132
Grand Meadow SD 495 400/PK-12
PO Box 68 55936 507-754-5318
Paul W. Besel, supt. Fax 754-5608
www.gm.k12.mn.us
Grand Meadow ES 200/PK-4
PO Box 68 55936 507-754-5318
Paul Besel, prin. Fax 754-5608
Grand Meadow MS 100/5-8
PO Box 68 55936 507-754-5318
Jacob Schwarz, prin. Fax 754-5608

Grand Rapids, Itasca, Pop. 10,671
Grand Rapids SD 318 4,000/PK-12
820 NW 1st Ave 55744 218-327-5700
Joni Olson, supt. Fax 327-5702
www.isd318.org
Early Childhood Family Education PK-PK
820 NW 1st Ave 55744 218-327-5850
Jan Reindl, dir. Fax 327-5851
Elkington MS 900/5-8
1000 NE 8th Ave 55744 218-327-5800
Dan Adams, prin. Fax 327-5801
Forest Lake ES 400/K-4
715 NW 7th Ave 55744 218-327-5870
Scott Briske, prin. Fax 327-5871
Murphy ES 400/K-4
822 NE 5th Ave 55744 218-327-5880
Sean Martinson, prin. Fax 327-5881
Southwest ES 400/K-4
601 SW 7th St 55744 218-327-5890
Ken Decoster, prin. Fax 327-5891
Other Schools – See Bigfork, Cohasset

Blackberry SDA S K-8
25321 Dove Ln 55744 218-326-2263
Rachelle Nelson, prin.
St. Joseph's Catholic S 200/PK-6
315 SW 21st St 55744 218-326-6232
Teresa Matetich, prin. Fax 326-6034

Granite Falls, Yellow Medicine, Pop. 2,841
Yellow Medicine East SD 2190 600/K-12
450 9th Ave 56241 320-564-4081
Dr. Rick Clark, supt. Fax 564-4781
isd2190.org/
Raney ES 400/K-5
555 7th Ave 56241 320-564-4427
Lisa Hansen, prin. Fax 564-4082

Greenbush, Roseau, Pop. 717
Greenbush-Middle River SD 2683 400/PK-12
PO Box 70 56726 218-782-2231
Tom Jerome, supt. Fax 782-3141
www.middleriver.k12.mn.us/
Greenbush ES 100/PK-3
PO Box 70 56726 218-782-2232
Eldon Sparby, prin. Fax 782-2165
Other Schools – See Middle River

Greenfield, Hennepin, Pop. 2,751

Salem Lutheran S 100/PK-8
9615 Pioneer Trl 55357 763-498-7283
Jonathan Beilke, prin. Fax 498-7835

Greenwald, Stearns, Pop. 222

St. John-St. Andrew S 100/K-6
PO Box 120 56335 320-987-3491
Mary Miller, prin. Fax 987-3306

Grove City, Meeker, Pop. 630
ACGC SD 2396 700/PK-12
27250 Minnesota Highway 4 56243 320-857-2271
Nels Onstad, supt. Fax 857-2989
www.acgcfalcons.org
Other Schools – See Atwater

Grygla, Marshall, Pop. 220
Grygla SD 447 200/PK-12
PO Box 18 56727 218-294-6155
Galen Clow, supt. Fax 294-6766
www.grygla.k12.mn.us/
Grygla ES 100/PK-6
PO Box 18 56727 218-294-6155
Jamie Lunsetter, prin. Fax 294-6766

Hallock, Kittson, Pop. 976
Kittson Central SD 2171 100/PK-12
PO Box 670 56728 218-843-3682
Bob Jaszczak, supt. Fax 843-2856
www.kittson.k12.mn.us
Kittson Central S 100/PK-12
PO Box 670 56728 218-843-3682
Bob Jaszczak, prin. Fax 843-2856

Halstad, Norman, Pop. 582
Norman County West SD 2527 300/PK-12
225 2nd Ave E 56548 218-456-2151
Shawn Yates, supt. Fax 456-2193
www.ncw.k12.mn.us
Other Schools – See Hendrum

Hamburg, Carver, Pop. 512

Emanuel Lutheran S 100/PK-8
18155 County Road 50 55339 952-467-2780
Todd Bentz, prin. Fax 467-2907

Ham Lake, Anoka, Pop. 15,124
Anoka-Hennepin SD 11
Supt. — See Anoka
McKinley ES 800/K-5
1740 Constance Blvd NE 55304 763-506-3400
Mike Koenig, prin. Fax 506-3403

Hancock, Stevens, Pop. 763
Hancock SD 768 300/K-12
PO Box 367 56244 320-392-5622
Loren Hacker, supt. Fax 392-5156
hancock.k12.mn.us
Hancock ES 200/K-6
PO Box 367 56244 320-392-5622
Tim Pahl, prin. Fax 392-5156

Hanover, Wright, Pop. 2,916
Buffalo-Hanover-Montrose SD
Supt. — See Buffalo
Hanover ES 400/K-5
274 Labeaux Ave 55341 763-682-0823
Brad Koltes, prin. Fax 682-0868

Hastings, Dakota, Pop. 21,783
Hastings SD 200 4,500/K-12
1000 11th St W 55033 651-480-7000
Tim Collins, supt. Fax 480-7001
www.hastings.k12.mn.us
Hastings MS 1,400/5-8
1000 11th St W 55033 651-480-7060
Mark Zuzek, prin. Fax 480-7066
Kennedy ES 500/K-4
1175 Tyler St 55033 651-480-7220
Kyle Latch, prin. Fax 480-7223
McAuliffe ES 500/K-4
1601 12th St W 55033 651-480-7390
Matt Esterby, prin. Fax 480-7393
Pinecrest ES 600/K-4
975 12th St W 55033 651-480-7280
Paul Bakker, prin. Fax 480-7284

Pine Harbor Christian Academy 100/K-8
PO Box 54 55033 651-493-7526
Scott Urban, prin. Fax 493-2576
St. Elizabeth Ann Seton S 400/PK-8
600 Tyler St 55033 651-437-3098
Tim Sullivan, prin. Fax 438-3377

Hawley, Clay, Pop. 2,037
Hawley SD 150 1,000/K-12
PO Box 608 56549 218-483-4647
Phil Jensen, supt. Fax 483-3510
www.hawley.k12.mn.us/
Hawley ES 500/K-6
PO Box 608 56549 218-483-3316
Chris Ellingson, prin. Fax 483-4638
Spring Prairie S 50/K-12
PO Box 608 56549 218-483-3316
Chris Ellingson, prin. Fax 483-4638

Hayfield, Dodge, Pop. 1,321
Hayfield SD 203 600/K-12
9 6th Ave SE 55940 507-477-3235
Gregg Slaathaug, supt. Fax 477-3230
hayfield.k12.mn.us
Hayfield ES 300/K-6
9 6th Ave SE 55940 507-477-3235
Grant Klennert, prin. Fax 477-3204

Henderson, Sibley, Pop. 878
Le Sueur-Henderson SD 2397
Supt. — See Le Sueur
Hilltop ES 200/4-5
PO Box 457 56044 507-665-5900
Amanda Feterl, prin. Fax 248-3838

Hendricks, Lincoln, Pop. 712
Hendricks SD 402 100/PK-12
PO Box 137 56136 507-275-3116
Bruce Houck, supt. Fax 275-3150
hendrickspublicschools.org
Hendricks S 100/PK-12
PO Box 137 56136 507-275-3115
Paul Chick, prin. Fax 275-3150

Hendrum, Norman, Pop. 307
Norman County West SD 2527
Supt. — See Halstad
Norman County West ES 200/PK-6
PO Box 39 56550 218-861-5800
Mary Niklaus, prin. Fax 861-6223

Henning, Otter Tail, Pop. 795
Henning SD 545 400/PK-12
500 School Ave 56551 218-583-2927
Jeremy Olson, supt. Fax 583-2312
www.henning.k12.mn.us
Henning ES 200/PK-6
500 School Ave 56551 218-583-2927
Thomas Williams, prin. Fax 583-2312

Herman, Grant, Pop. 435
Herman-Norcross SD 264 100/K-12
PO Box 288 56248 320-677-2291
Rick Bleichner, supt. Fax 677-2412
herman.mn.schoolwebpages.com
Herman ES 100/K-6
PO Box 288 56248 320-677-2291
Rick Bleichner, admin. Fax 677-2412

Hermantown, Saint Louis, Pop. 9,290
Hermantown SD 700 1,900/PK-12
4307 Ugstad Rd 55811 218-729-9313
Kerry Juntunen, supt. Fax 729-9315
www.isd700.org
Hermantown ECC 50/PK-PK
5028 Miller Trunk Hwy 55811 218-729-9563
Kristal Berg, dir.
Hermantown ES 600/K-4
5365 W Arrowhead Rd 55811 218-729-6891
Deb Reynolds, prin. Fax 729-9870
Hermantown MS 600/5-8
4289 Ugstad Rd 55811 218-729-6690
Jenny Wiese, prin. Fax 729-9890

Heron Lake, Jackson, Pop. 696
Heron Lake-Okabena SD 330
Supt. — See Okabena
Heron Lake-Okabena ES 200/PK-6
PO Box 378 56137 507-793-2307
Paul Bang, prin. Fax 793-2557

Hibbing, Saint Louis, Pop. 16,076
Hibbing SD 701 2,400/K-12
800 E 21st St 55746 218-208-0848
Brad Johnson, supt. Fax 208-0866
www.hibbing.k12.mn.us

Greenhaven ES 300/K-2
323 E 37th St 55746 218-208-0844
Bj Berg, prin. Fax 208-0859
Lincoln ES 700/3-6
1114 E 23rd St 55746 218-208-0842
Robert Bestul, prin. Fax 208-0857
Washington ES 300/K-2
2100 12th Ave E 55746 218-208-0843
Bj Berg, prin. Fax 208-0858

Assumption S 200/PK-6
2310 7th Ave E 55746 218-263-3054
Gabe Johnson, prin. Fax 263-5058
Victory Christian Academy 100/PK-12
206 E 39th St 55746 218-262-6550
Fax 416-1424

Hill City, Aitkin, Pop. 617
Hill City SD 2 200/PK-12
500 Ione Ave 55748 218-697-2394
Pat Rendle, supt. Fax 697-2594
isd002.org
Hill City ES 100/PK-6
500 Ione Ave 55748 218-697-2394
Pat Rendle, prin. Fax 697-2594

Hills, Rock, Pop. 678
Hills-Beaver Creek SD 671 300/PK-12
PO Box 547 56138 507-962-3240
Todd Holthaus, supt. Fax 962-3238
www.hbcpatriots.com
Other Schools – See Beaver Creek

Hills Christian S 50/K-8
PO Box 27 56138 507-962-3297
Barry Miedema, admin. Fax 962-3297

Hinckley, Pine, Pop. 1,722
Hinckley-Finlayson SD 2165 1,000/PK-12
PO Box 308 55037 320-384-6277
Rob Prater, supt. Fax 384-6135
www.hf.k12.mn.us
Hinckley ES 500/PK-6
PO Box 308 55037 320-384-6443
Jeffrey Wilson, prin. Fax 384-6135
Other Schools – See Finlayson

Hokah, Houston, Pop. 568

St. Peter S, PO Box 357 55941 100/PK-8
Rachel Fishel, prin. 507-894-4375

Holdingford, Stearns, Pop. 699
Holdingford SD 738 1,000/PK-12
PO Box 250 56340 320-746-4307
Chris Swenson, supt. Fax 746-2274
www.isd738.org
Holdingford ES 500/PK-6
PO Box 250 56340 320-746-4462
Jim Stang, prin. Fax 746-8174

Hollandale, Freeborn, Pop. 303

Hollandale Christian S 100/K-8
203 Central Ave S 56045 507-889-3321
Enno Haan, prin. Fax 889-3321

Hopkins, Hennepin, Pop. 17,010
Hopkins SD 270 6,800/K-12
1001 Highway 7 55305 952-988-4000
Dr. Rhoda Mhiripiri-Reed, supt. Fax 988-4020
www.hopkinsschools.org
Eisenhower ES 500/K-6
1001 Highway 7 55305 952-988-4300
Paul Domer, prin. Fax 988-4314
Smith ES 500/K-6
801 Minnetonka Mills Rd 55343 952-988-4200
Jody de St. Hubert, prin. Fax 988-4195
XingXing Academy 300/K-5
1001 Highway 7 55305 952-988-4300
Paul Domer, prin. Fax 988-4314
Other Schools – See Golden Valley, Minnetonka

Blake S 1,400/PK-12
110 Blake Rd S 55343 952-988-3400
Dr. Anne Stavney, head sch Fax 988-3455

Houston, Winona, Pop. 978
Houston SD 294 2,300/PK-12
306 W Elm St 55943 507-896-5323
Krin Abraham, supt. Fax 896-3452
www.houston.k12.mn.us
Houston ES 200/PK-6
310 S Sherman St 55943 507-896-5323
Richard Bartz, prin. Fax 896-3222

Howard Lake, Wright, Pop. 1,947
Howard Lake-Waverly-Winsted SD 2687 1,100/PK-12
PO Box 708 55349 320-543-4646
Brad Sellner, supt. Fax 543-4630
www.hlww.k12.mn.us
Howard Lake-Waverly-Winsted MS 300/5-8
PO Box 708 55349 320-543-4660
Jim Schimelpfenig, prin. Fax 543-4632
Other Schools – See Waverly, Winsted

St. James Lutheran S 200/PK-8
PO Box 680 55349 320-543-2630
Jason Roslansky, admin. Fax 543-3063

Hugo, Washington, Pop. 13,110
White Bear Lake Area SD 624
Supt. — See White Bear Lake
Hugo ES 300/K-1
14895 Francesca Ave N 55038 651-653-2798
Jason Healy, prin. Fax 653-2800
Oneka ES 600/2-5
4888 Heritage Pkwy N 55038 651-288-1800
Teresa Dahlem, prin. Fax 288-1899

Hutchinson, McLeod, Pop. 14,005
Hutchinson SD 423 2,900/PK-12
30 Glen St NW 55350 320-587-2860
Daron VanderHeiden, supt. Fax 587-4590
www.isd423.org
Hutchinson MS 700/6-8
1365 S Grade Rd SW 55350 320-587-2854
Todd Grina, prin. Fax 587-2857
Hutchinson Park ES 900/2-5
100 Glen St SW 55350 320-587-2837
Dan Olberg, prin. Fax 587-4821
Hutchinson West ES 500/PK-1
875 School Rd SW 55350 320-587-4470
Anne Broderius, prin. Fax 587-0735

Immanuel Lutheran S 50/PK-8
20917 Walden Ave 55350 320-587-4858
Brian Gephart, prin.
Northwoods S 50/PK-8
95 Academy Ln NW 55350 320-234-5994
Jamie Madden, prin.
Our Savior's Lutheran S 50/PK-5
800 Bluff St NE 55350 320-587-3319
Andrew Boll, prin. Fax 234-7861
St. Anastasia S 100/PK-6
400 Lake St SW 55350 320-587-2490
Julie Shelby, prin. Fax 234-6756

International Falls, Koochiching, Pop. 6,261
International Falls SD 361 1,000/PK-12
1515 11th St 56649 218-283-2571
Kevin Grover, supt. Fax 283-8104
www.isd361.k12.mn.us
Falls ES 500/PK-5
1414 15th Ave 56649 218-283-3487
Melissa Tate, prin. Fax 283-3133

St. Thomas Aquinas S 100/PK-8
810 5th St 56649 218-283-3430
Dawn Flesland, prin. Fax 283-3553

Inver Grove Heights, Dakota, Pop. 33,073
Inver Grove Heights Community ISD 199 3,700/PK-12
2990 80th St E 55076 651-306-7800
David Bernhardson, supt. Fax 306-7295
www.invergrove.k12.mn.us
Hilltop ES 700/PK-5
3201 68th St E 55076 651-306-7400
Sue Vallafskey, prin. Fax 306-7444
Inver Grove Heights MS 900/6-8
8167 Cahill Ave 55076 651-306-7200
Jodi Wendel, prin. Fax 306-7152
Pine Bend ES 600/K-5
9875 Inver Grove Trl 55076 651-306-7701
Quonnol Cooper, prin. Fax 306-7739
Salem Hills ES 300/PK-5
5899 Babcock Trl 55077 651-306-7300
Tina Willette, prin. Fax 306-7321

Iron, Saint Louis, Pop. 85
Saint Louis County Schools ISD 2142
Supt. — See Virginia
Cherry S 200/PK-12
3943 Tamminen Rd 55751 218-258-8991
Michael Johnson, prin. Fax 258-8993

Isanti, Isanti, Pop. 5,155
Cambridge-Isanti SD 911
Supt. — See Cambridge
Isanti IS 500/3-5
101 9th Ave NE 55040 763-552-8800
Mark Ziebarth, prin. Fax 552-8899
Isanti MS 400/6-8
201 Centennial Dr 55040 763-691-8600
Randy Pauly, prin. Fax 691-8662
Isanti PS 500/PK-2
301 Heritage Blvd NW 55040 763-691-8778
Shane Dordal, prin. Fax 691-8700
Minnesota Center S 100/6-8
201 Centennial Dr 55040 763-691-8676
Randy Pauly, prin. Fax 691-8677
School for all Seasons 200/K-5
101 9th Ave NE 55040 763-552-8810
Mark Ziebarth, prin. Fax 552-8899

Isle, Mille Lacs, Pop. 739
Isle SD 473 500/K-12
PO Box 25 56342 320-676-3146
Dean Kapsner, supt. Fax 676-3966
www.isle.k12.mn.us
Nyquist ES 300/K-6
PO Box 25 56342 320-676-3494
Dean Kapsner, prin. Fax 676-3966

Ivanhoe, Lincoln, Pop. 559
Ivanhoe SD 403 100/PK-6
PO Box 9 56142 507-694-1540
Daniel Deitte, supt. Fax 694-1125
www.lincolnhi.org
Lincoln ES 100/PK-6
PO Box 9 56142 507-694-1540
Courtney Frie, prin. Fax 694-1125

Jackson, Jackson, Pop. 3,254
Jackson County Central SD 2895 1,200/PK-12
PO Box 119 56143 507-847-3608
Todd Meyer, supt. Fax 847-3078
www.jccschools.com/
Riverside ES 400/PK-5
820 Park St 56143 507-847-5963
Joel Timmerman, prin. Fax 847-4398
Other Schools – See Lakefield

Janesville, Waseca, Pop. 2,234
Janesville-Waldorf-Pemberton SD 2835 600/PK-12
PO Box 389 56048 507-234-5181
Bill Adams, supt. Fax 234-5796
www.jwp.k12.mn.us
Janesville-Waldorf-Pemberton ES 300/PK-6
PO Box 389 56048 507-234-5181
Jeremy Erler, prin. Fax 234-5796

Trinity Lutheran S 100/PK-8
501 N Main St 56048 507-231-6646
Wade Stockman, prin. Fax 234-6751

Jeffers, Cottonwood, Pop. 359
Red Rock Central SD 2884
Supt. — See Lamberton
Red Rock Central ES 100/PK-4
107 E Clark St 56145 507-628-5521
Deb Altermatt, admin. Fax 628-5546

Jordan, Scott, Pop. 5,361
Jordan SD 717 1,800/PK-12
500 Sunset Dr 55352 952-492-6200
Matthew Helgerson, supt. Fax 492-4445
www.jordan.k12.mn.us
Jordan ES 700/PK-4
815 Sunset Dr 55352 952-492-2336
Melissa Barnett, prin. Fax 492-4446
Jordan MS 500/5-8
500 Sunset Dr 55352 952-492-2332
Ben Bakeberg, prin. Fax 492-4450

St. John the Baptist S 100/PK-6
215 Broadway St N 55352 952-492-2030
Dr. Bonita Jungels, prin. Fax 492-3211

Karlstad, Kittson, Pop. 759
Tri-County SD 2358 200/PK-12
PO Box 178 56732 218-436-2261
Ryan Baron, supt. Fax 436-2263
www.tricounty.k12.mn.us
Karlstad ES 100/PK-6
PO Box 178 56732 218-436-2261
Ryan Baron, prin. Fax 436-2263

Kasson, Dodge, Pop. 5,864
Kasson-Mantorville SD 204 2,100/PK-12
101 16th St NE 55944 507-634-1100
Mark D. Matuska, supt. Fax 634-6661
www.komets.k12.mn.us
Kasson-Mantorville ES 800/PK-4
604 16th St NE 55944 507-634-1234
Ariana Wright, prin. Fax 634-1240
Kasson-Mantorville MS 700/5-8
1400 5th Ave NE 55944 507-634-4030
Erin Kyllo, prin. Fax 634-6485

Keewatin, Itasca, Pop. 1,046
Nashwauk-Keewatin SD 319
Supt. — See Nashwauk
Keewatin ES 300/PK-6
300 W 3rd Ave 55753 218-885-1280
Anne Olson-Reiners, prin. Fax 885-2909

Kelliher, Beltrami, Pop. 261
Kelliher SD 36 100/PK-12
PO Box 259 56650 218-647-8286
Tim Lutz, supt. Fax 647-8660
www.kelliher.k12.mn.us
Kelliher S 100/PK-12
PO Box 259 56650 218-647-8286
Mary Lundin, admin. Fax 647-3110

Kensington, Douglas, Pop. 292
West Central Area SD 2342
Supt. — See Barrett
West Central Area South ES 200/PK-4
31 Central Ave N 56343 320-965-2724
Jon Moore, dean Fax 965-2264

Kenyon, Goodhue, Pop. 1,804
Kenyon-Wanamingo SD 2172
Supt. — See Wanamingo
Kenyon-Wanamingo MS 100/7-8
400 6th St 55946 507-789-6186
Matt Ryan, prin. Fax 789-6188

Kerkhoven, Swift, Pop. 759
Kerkhoven-Murdock-Sunburg SD 775 600/PK-12
PO Box 168 56252 320-264-1411
Martin Heidelberger, supt. Fax 264-1410
www.kms.k12.mn.us
Other Schools – See Murdock

Kimball, Stearns, Pop. 750
Kimball SD 739 600/PK-12
PO Box 368 55353 320-398-5585
Jim Wagner, supt. Fax 398-5595
www.kimball.k12.mn.us/
Kimball ES 300/PK-5
PO Box 368 55353 320-398-5425
Keri Johnson, prin. Fax 398-5433

Holy Cross of Pearl Lake S 100/PK-6
10672 County Road 8 55353 320-398-7885
Missy Johnson, lead tchr. Fax 398-7873

La Crescent, Houston, Pop. 4,750
La Crescent-Hokah SD 300 1,200/PK-12
703 S 11th St 55947 507-895-4484
Kevin Cardille, supt. Fax 895-8560
www.isd300.k12.mn.us
La Crescent-Hokah ES 400/PK-4
504 S Oak St 55947 507-895-4428
Jeffrey Copp, prin. Fax 895-4470
La Crescent MS 300/5-8
1301 Lancer Blvd 55947 507-895-4474
Steve Smith, prin. Fax 895-8597

Crucifixion S 100/PK-6
420 S 2nd St 55947 507-895-4402
Doug Harpenau, prin. Fax 895-4403

Lake Benton, Lincoln, Pop. 676
Lake Benton SD 404 100/PK-6
PO Box 158 56149 507-368-4235
Ann Wendorff, supt. Fax 368-4477
www.lakebentonschool.org/

Lake Benton ES 100/PK-6
PO Box 158 56149 507-368-4235
Ann Wendorff, supt. Fax 368-4477

Pipestone Area SD 2689
Supt. — See Pipestone
Heartland S 50/K-8
2171 100th Ave 56149 507-368-9585
Toni Baartman, prin. Fax 368-9518

Lake City, Wabasha, Pop. 4,995
Lake City SD 813 1,300/PK-12
300 S Garden St 55041 651-345-2198
Erick Enger, supt. Fax 345-3709
www.lake-city.k12.mn.us
Bluff View ES 700/PK-6
1156 W Lakewood Ave 55041 651-345-4551
James Borgschatz, prin. Fax 345-2781

St. John's Lutheran S 100/PK-8
516 W Chestnut St 55041 651-345-4092
David Zabel, prin. Fax 345-4002

Lake Crystal, Blue Earth, Pop. 2,527
Lake Crystal Wellcome Memorial SD 2071 800/PK-12
PO Box 160 56055 507-726-2323
Tom Farrell, supt. Fax 726-2334
www.isd2071.k12.mn.us
Lake Crystal Wellcome Memorial ES 400/PK-5
PO Box 810 56055 507-726-2320
Dan Beert, prin. Fax 726-2003

Lake Elmo, Washington, Pop. 7,919
Stillwater Area SD 834
Supt. — See Stillwater
Lake Elmo ES 700/PK-5
11030 Stillwater Blvd N 55042 651-351-6700
Stephen Gorde, prin. Fax 351-6797
Oak-Land MS 800/6-8
820 Manning Ave N 55042 651-351-8500
Andy Fields, prin. Fax 351-8505

Lakefield, Jackson, Pop. 1,687
Jackson County Central SD 2895
Supt. — See Jackson
Jackson County Central MS 300/6-8
PO Box 338 56150 507-662-6625
Chris Naumann, prin. Fax 662-5083
Pleasantview ES 200/PK-5
PO Box 754 56150 507-662-6218
Tammy Timko, admin. Fax 662-6690

Immanuel Lutheran S 100/PK-8
PO Box 750 56150 507-662-5860
Scott Johnson, prin. Fax 662-5820

Lakeland, Washington, Pop. 1,779
Stillwater Area SD 834
Supt. — See Stillwater
Afton-Lakeland ES 500/K-5
475 Saint Croix Trl S 55043 651-351-6500
Malinda Lansfeldt, prin. Fax 351-6595

Lake Park, Becker, Pop. 774
Lake Park Audubon ISD 2889 700/K-12
PO Box 479 56554 218-325-0574
Dale Hogie, supt. Fax 201-0886
www.lakeparkaudubon.com
Other Schools – See Audubon

Lakeville, Dakota, Pop. 54,640
Lakeville Area SD 194 10,800/K-12
8670 210th St W 55044 952-232-2000
Michael Baumann, supt. Fax 469-6054
isd194.org
Century MS 1,000/6-8
18610 Ipava Ave 55044 952-232-2300
Christopher Endicott, prin. Fax 469-6103
Cherry View ES 500/K-5
8600 175th St W 55044 952-232-3200
Paul Helberg, prin. Fax 469-7245
Eastview ES 600/K-5
18060 Ipava Ave 55044 952-232-2900
Taber Akin, prin. Fax 469-7644
Huddleston ES 500/K-5
9569 175th St W 55044 952-232-3100
Jill Kelly, prin. Fax 469-7280
Impact Academy at Orchard Lake ES 500/K-5
16531 Klamath Trl 55044 952-232-2100
Marilynn Smith, prin. Fax 469-7331
Kennedy ES 600/K-5
21240 Holyoke Ave 55044 952-232-2800
Beth Anderson, prin. Fax 469-7248
Kenwood Trail MS 700/6-8
19455 Kenwood Trl 55044 952-232-3800
Kate Eisenthal, prin. Fax 469-3508
Lake Marion ES 500/K-5
19875 Dodd Blvd 55044 952-232-2700
Bret Domstrand, prin. Fax 469-7180
Lakeview ES 600/K-5
20500 Jacquard Ave 55044 952-232-2600
Pete Otterson, prin. Fax 469-7270
McGuire MS 900/6-8
21220 Holyoke Ave 55044 952-232-2200
Joshua Alexander, prin. Fax 469-7224
Oak Hills ES 600/K-5
8640 165th St W 55044 952-232-2500
Wade Labatte, prin. Fax 469-6304

All Saints S 400/K-8
19795 Holyoke Ave 55044 952-469-3332
Carol Margarit, prin. Fax 469-4484
Christian Heritage Academy 100/PK-8
7320 175th St W 55044 952-953-4155
Gail Wolfe, prin. Fax 997-1543
Glory Academy 50/PK-12
25170 Dodd Blvd 55044 952-985-3659
Rev. Cheryl Engelman, prin.

Lamberton, Redwood, Pop. 817
Red Rock Central SD 2884 400/PK-12
PO Box 278 56152 507-752-7361
Bruce Olson, supt. Fax 752-6133
www.rrcnet.org/default.shtml
Other Schools – See Jeffers

Lancaster, Kittson, Pop. 340
Lancaster SD 356 200/PK-12
401 Central Ave S 56735 218-762-5400
Shannon Hunstad, supt. Fax 762-5512
www.lancaster.k12.mn.us/
Lancaster ES 100/PK-6
401 Central Ave S 56735 218-762-5400
Shannon Hunstad, admin. Fax 762-5512

Lanesboro, Fillmore, Pop. 743
Lanesboro SD 229 400/PK-12
100 Kirkwood St E 55949 507-467-2229
Matt Schultz, supt. Fax 467-3026
www.lanesboro.k12.mn.us
Lanesboro ES 200/PK-6
100 Kirkwood St E 55949 507-467-2229
James Semmen, prin. Fax 467-3026

Laporte, Hubbard, Pop. 104
Laporte SD 306 300/PK-12
315 Main St W 56461 218-224-2288
Kim Goodwin, supt. Fax 224-2905
www.laporte.k12.mn.us
Laporte ES 200/PK-6
315 Main St W 56461 218-224-2288
Kim Goodwin, admin. Fax 224-2905

Le Center, LeSueur, Pop. 2,491
Tri-City United ISD 2905
Supt. — See Montgomery
Tri-City United LeCenter K-8 S 400/PK-8
150 W Tyrone St 56057 507-357-6802
Brian Grensteiner, prin. Fax 357-4825

Le Roy, Mower, Pop. 926
Le Roy-Ostrander SD 499 300/PK-12
406 W Main St 55951 507-324-5743
Jeff Sampson, supt. Fax 324-5149
www.leroy.k12.mn.us
Le Roy-Ostrander ES 200/PK-6
406 W Main St 55951 507-324-5786
Aaron Hungerholt, prin. Fax 324-5004

Lester Prairie, McLeod, Pop. 1,714
Lester Prairie SD 424 400/PK-12
131 Hickory St N 55354 320-395-2521
Jeremy Schmidt, supt. Fax 395-4204
www.lp.k12.mn.us
Lester Prairie ES 200/PK-5
131 Hickory St N 55354 320-395-2521
Nathaniel Boyer, prin. Fax 395-4204

Le Sueur, LeSueur, Pop. 4,019
Le Sueur-Henderson SD 2397 800/PK-12
115 1/2 N 5th St Ste 200 56058 507-665-4600
Brian Gersich, supt. Fax 665-6858
www.isd2397.org
Park ES 300/PK-3
115 N 5th St 56058 507-665-4700
Christine McDonald, prin. Fax 665-8819
Other Schools – See Henderson

St. Anne S 100/PK-5
511 N 4th St 56058 507-665-2489
Diane Lee, prin. Fax 665-3811

Lewiston, Winona, Pop. 1,612
Lewiston-Altura SD 857 700/PK-12
100 County Road 25 55952 507-523-2191
Jennifer Backer-Johnson, supt. Fax 523-3460
www.lewalt.k12.mn.us
Lewiston-Altura ES 300/PK-4
115 S Fremont St 55952 507-523-2191
David Riebel, prin. Fax 523-2609
Other Schools – See Altura

Immanuel Lutheran S 100/PK-8
22591 County Road 25 55952 507-523-3143
E Anderson, prin. Fax 523-1049
St. John Lutheran S, PO Box 9 55952 100/PK-8
Jeffery Essig, prin. 507-523-2508

Lindstrom, Chisago, Pop. 4,380
Chisago Lakes SD 2144 3,400/PK-12
13750 Lake Blvd 55045 651-213-2000
Dean Jennissen, supt. Fax 213-2050
www.isd2144.org
Chisago Lakes MS 800/6-8
13750 Lake Blvd 55045 651-213-2400
Jodi Otte, prin. Fax 213-2051
Other Schools – See Chisago City, Taylors Falls

Lino Lakes, Anoka, Pop. 19,895
Centennial SD 12
Supt. — See Circle Pines
Blue Heron ES 900/K-5
405 Elm St 55014 763-792-6200
Jason Hartmann, prin. Fax 792-6250
Centennial MS 1,500/6-8
399 Elm St 55014 763-792-5400
Robert Stevens, prin. Fax 792-5450
Early Childhood Center PK-PK
575 Birch St 55014 763-792-6120
Sarah Holmboe, coord. Fax 792-6130
Rice Lake ES 500/K-5
575 Birch St 55014 763-792-5700
Bryan Carlson, prin. Fax 792-5750

Forest Lake SD 831
Supt. — See Forest Lake
Lino Lakes ES STEM 500/PK-6
725 Main St 55014 651-982-8850
Scott Geary, prin. Fax 982-8891

Litchfield, Meeker, Pop. 6,688
Litchfield SD 465 1,400/K-12
307 E 6th St Ste 100 55355 320-693-2444
Daniel Frazier, supt. Fax 593-6528
www.litchfield.k12.mn.us
Lake Ripley ES 500/K-4
100 W Pleasure Dr 55355 320-693-2436
Gregg Zender, prin. Fax 593-0227
Litchfield MS 400/5-8
340 E 10th St 55355 320-693-2441
Beckie Simenson, prin. Fax 593-3485

St. Philip S 100/K-5
225 E 3rd St 55355 320-693-6283
Michelle Kramer, prin. Fax 404-1952

Little Canada, Ramsey, Pop. 9,560
Roseville Area SD 623
Supt. — See Roseville
Roseville Area MS 900/7-8
15 County Road B2 E 55117 651-482-5280
Dr. Tyrone Brookins, prin. Fax 482-5299

St. John S of Little Canada 200/PK-8
2621 McMenemy St 55117 651-484-3038
Mary Kay Rowan, prin. Fax 481-1355

Little Falls, Morrison, Pop. 8,197
Little Falls SD 482 2,400/PK-12
1001 5th Ave SE 56345 320-632-2002
Stephen Jones, supt. Fax 632-2012
www.lfalls.k12.mn.us
Lincoln ES 400/PK-5
300 6th St SW 56345 320-616-6200
Larry Edgerton, prin. Fax 616-2144
Lindbergh ES 600/PK-5
101 9th St SE 56345 320-616-3200
Jill Griffith-McRaith, prin. Fax 616-3210
Little Falls Community MS 500/6-8
1000 1st Ave NE 56345 320-616-4200
Wade Mathers, prin. Fax 616-4210
Other Schools – See Randall

Mary of Lourdes MS 100/5-8
205 3rd St NW 56345 320-632-6742
Maria Heymans-Becker, prin. Fax 632-3556
Mary of Lourdes S 200/PK-4
307 4th St SE 56345 320-632-5408
Maria Heymans-Becker, prin. Fax 632-3556

Littlefork, Koochiching, Pop. 646
Littlefork-Big Falls SD 362 200/PK-12
700 Main St 56653 218-278-6614
Jamie Wendt, supt. Fax 278-6615
www.isd362.k12.mn.us
Littlefork-Big Falls S 200/PK-12
700 Main St 56653 218-278-6614
Jamie Wendt, admin. Fax 278-6615

Long Lake, Hennepin, Pop. 1,729
Orono SD 278 2,800/K-12
685 N Old Crystal Bay Rd 55356 952-449-8300
Dr. Karen Orcutt, supt. Fax 449-8399
www.orono.k12.mn.us
Orono IS 600/3-5
685 N Old Crystal Bay Rd 55356 952-449-8470
Dr. Mary Jodl Ernhart, prin. Fax 449-8479
Orono MS 700/6-8
800 N Old Crystal Bay Rd 55356 952-449-8450
Dr. Patricia Wroten, prin. Fax 449-8453
Orono Schumann ES 500/K-2
765 N Old Crystal Bay Rd 55356 952-449-8480
Dr. Adam Lamparske, prin. Fax 449-8499

Long Prairie, Todd, Pop. 3,383
Long Prairie-Grey Eagle SD 2753 900/PK-12
205 2nd St S 56347 320-732-2194
Jon Kringen, supt. Fax 732-3791
www.lpge.k12.mn.us/
Long Prairie-Grey Eagle ES 500/PK-6
205 2nd St S 56347 320-732-2194
Tammy Cebulla, prin. Fax 732-0961

St. Mary of Mount Carmel S 100/PK-6
425 Central Ave 56347 320-357-0813
Linda Kay Dinkel, prin. Fax 732-8023

Lonsdale, Rice, Pop. 3,622
Tri-City United ISD 2905
Supt. — See Montgomery
Tri-City United Lonsdale ES 200/PK-4
1000 Idaho St SW 55046 507-744-3900
Mollie Meyer, prin. Fax 744-3902

Luverne, Rock, Pop. 4,679
Luverne SD 2184 1,200/PK-12
709 N Kniss Ave 56156 507-283-8088
Craig Oftedahl, supt. Fax 283-9681
www.isd2184.net/
Luverne ES 600/PK-5
709 N Kniss Ave 56156 507-283-4497
Stacy Gillette, prin. Fax 283-9681
Luverne MS 300/6-8
709 N Kniss Ave 56156 507-283-4491
Ryan Johnson, prin. Fax 283-9681

Lyle, Mower, Pop. 544
Lyle SD 497 200/PK-12
700 E 2nd St 55953 507-325-2201
Bryan Boysen, supt. Fax 325-4611
www.lyle.k12.mn.us
Lyle ES 100/PK-6
700 E 2nd St 55953 507-325-2201
Bryan Boysen, prin. Fax 325-4611

Lynd, Lyon, Pop. 443
Lynd SD 415 100/PK-8
PO Box 68 56157 507-865-4404
Bruce Houck, supt. Fax 865-4621
www.lyndschool.org

Lynd S 100/PK-8
PO Box 68 56157 507-865-4404
Jason Swenson, prin. Fax 865-4621

Mabel, Fillmore, Pop. 777
Mabel-Canton SD 238 300/PK-12
316 W Fillmore 55954 507-493-5423
Jennifer Backer, supt. Fax 493-5425
www.mabelcanton.k12.mn.us/
Mabel-Canton ES 100/PK-6
316 W Fillmore 55954 507-493-5422
Michelle Weidemann, admin. Fax 493-5425

Mc Gregor, Aitkin, Pop. 390
McGregor ISD 4 400/PK-12
PO Box 160 55760 218-768-2111
Paul Grams, supt. Fax 768-3901
www.mcgregor.k12.mn.us
McGregor ES 200/PK-6
PO Box 160 55760 218-768-2111
Paul Grams, prin. Fax 768-3901

Madelia, Watonwan, Pop. 2,301
Madelia SD 837 500/PK-12
320 Buck Ave SE 56062 507-642-3232
Brian Grenell, supt. Fax 642-3622
www.madelia.k12.mn.us
Madelia ES 300/PK-6
121 E Main St 56062 507-642-3234
Carol Wrightson, prin. Fax 642-8893

St. Marys S 100/PK-6
223 1st St NE 56062 507-642-3324
Jennifer Slater, prin. Fax 642-3899

Madison, Lac qui Parle, Pop. 1,527
Lac qui Parle Valley SD 2853 800/PK-12
2860 291st Ave 56256 320-752-4800
Gregory A. Schmidt, supt. Fax 752-4401
www.lqpv.org
Lac qui Parle Valley MS 100/5-6
2860 291st Ave 56256 320-752-4800
Scott Sawatzky, prin. Fax 752-4409
Madison-Marietta-Nassau ES 100/PK-4
316 W 4th St 56256 320-598-7528
Kipp Stender, prin. Fax 598-3001
Other Schools – See Appleton

Mahnomen, Mahnomen, Pop. 1,108
Mahnomen SD 432 600/PK-12
PO Box 319 56557 218-935-2211
Jeff Bisek, supt. Fax 935-5921
www.mahnomen.k12.mn.us/
Mahnomen ES 300/PK-6
PO Box 319 56557 218-935-2581
Jacob Melby, prin. Fax 935-5951

St. Michaels S 100/PK-6
501 1st St SW 56557 218-935-5222
Sarah Chalich, prin. Fax 935-5222

Mahtomedi, Washington, Pop. 7,538
Mahtomedi SD 832 3,300/PK-12
1520 Mahtomedi Ave 55115 651-407-2000
Dr. Mark Larson, supt. Fax 407-2025
www.mahtomedi.k12.mn.us
Anderson ES 700/3-5
666 Warner Ave S 55115 651-407-2300
Kirsten Bouwens, prin. Fax 407-2325
Mahtomedi MS 800/6-8
8100 75th St N 55115 651-407-2200
Dr. Mike Neubeck, prin. Fax 407-2225
Other Schools – See Stillwater

St. Jude of the Lake S 100/PK-5
600 Mahtomedi Ave 55115 651-426-2562
Cressy Epperly, prin. Fax 653-3662

Mankato, Blue Earth, Pop. 38,565
Mankato SD 77 7,000/K-12
PO Box 8741 56002 507-387-1868
Dr. Sheri Allen Ed.D., supt. Fax 387-4257
www.isd77.org
Bridges Community ES 100/K-5
PO Box 8741 56002 507-387-2800
Robin Courrier, lead tchr. Fax 387-3143
Franklin ES 400/K-5
PO Box 8741 56002 507-345-4287
Travis Olson, prin. Fax 345-4801
Jefferson ES 200/K-5
PO Box 8741 56002 507-388-5480
Scot Johnson, prin. Fax 388-8440
Kennedy ES 400/K-5
PO Box 8741 56002 507-387-2122
Jason Grovom, prin. Fax 387-1005
Parks ES 400/K-5
PO Box 8741 56002 507-387-7672
Michelle Kruize, prin. Fax 387-7673
Prairie Winds MS 500/6-8
PO Box 8741 56002 507-345-6625
Stephen Rustad, prin. Fax 387-2890
Roosevelt ES 400/K-5
PO Box 8741 56002 507-345-4285
Ann Haggerty, prin. Fax 345-1374
Washington ES 400/K-5
PO Box 8741 56002 507-345-3059
Shane Baier, prin. Fax 345-7198
Other Schools – See Eagle Lake, North Mankato

Loyola Catholic S 200/PK-12
145 Good Counsel Dr 56001 507-388-2997
Adam Bemmels, prin. Fax 388-3081
Mt. Olive Lutheran S 100/K-8
1123 Marsh St 56001 507-345-7927
Larry Rude, prin. Fax 345-7463
Risen Savior Lutheran S 100/K-8
502 W 7th St 56001 507-388-6624
Jason Rupnow, prin.

Maple Grove, Hennepin, Pop. 60,235
Osseo Area ISD 279 17,400/PK-12
11200 93rd Ave N 55369 763-391-7000
Kate Maguire, supt. Fax 391-7070
www.district279.org
Arbor View ECC 100/PK-PK
9401 Fernbrook Ln N 55369 763-391-8777
Sally Nault-Maurer, coord. Fax 391-8762
Basswood ES 900/PK-5
15425 Bass Lake Rd 55311 763-494-3858
Patrick Smith, prin. Fax 315-7660
Cedar Island ES 500/PK-5
6777 Hemlock Ln N 55369 763-425-5855
Dan Wald, prin. Fax 315-7680
Elm Creek ES 500/K-5
9830 Revere Ln N 55369 763-425-0577
Elizabeth Ness, prin. Fax 315-7690
Fernbrook ES 800/PK-5
9661 Fernbrook Ln N 55369 763-420-8888
Todd Tischer, prin. Fax 391-8420
Maple Grove MS 1,100/6-8
7000 Hemlock Ln N 55369 763-315-7600
Lisa Hartman, prin. Fax 315-7601
Oak View ES 400/K-5
6710 E Fish Lake Rd 55369 763-425-1881
Ann Mock, prin. Fax 391-8686
Rice Lake ES 600/PK-5
13755 89th Ave N 55369 763-420-4220
Margo Kleven, prin. Fax 315-7370
Rush Creek ES 800/PK-5
8801 County Road 101 N 55311 763-494-4549
Tim Brown, prin. Fax 315-7360
Weaver Lake Science Math & Technology S 600/PK-5
15900 Weaver Lake Rd 55311 763-420-3337
Dennis Palm, prin. Fax 391-8880
Other Schools – See Brooklyn Center, Brooklyn Park, Osseo

Ave Maria Academy 200/PK-8
7000 Jewel Ln N 55311 763-494-5387
Brad Norton, prin. Fax 494-5389
Heritage Christian Academy 500/PK-12
15655 Bass Lake Rd 55311 763-463-2200
Gwen Berge, pres. Fax 463-2299

Maple Lake, Wright, Pop. 2,037
Maple Lake SD 881 900/PK-12
200 Highway 55 E 55358 320-963-3171
Mark Redemske, supt. Fax 963-3170
www.maplelake.k12.mn.us
Maple Lake ES 400/PK-6
200 Highway 55 E 55358 320-963-3024
Andrew Sawatzke, prin. Fax 963-6584

St. Timothy S 100/K-8
241 Star St E 55358 320-963-3417
Dawn McCabe, prin. Fax 963-8804

Mapleton, Blue Earth, Pop. 1,738
Maple River SD 2135 1,000/PK-12
PO Box 515 56065 507-524-3918
Dan Anderson, supt. Fax 524-4882
www.isd2135.k12.mn.us/
Other Schools – See Good Thunder, Minnesota Lake

Maplewood, Ramsey, Pop. 37,068
North St. Paul-Maplewood-Oakdale SD 622
Supt. — See North Saint Paul
Carver ES 500/PK-5
2680 Upper Afton Rd E 55119 651-702-8200
Gena Abrahamson, prin. Fax 702-8291
Gladstone Community S PK-PK
1945 Manton St 55109 651-748-7280
Tracy Tessier, dir.
Glenn MS 800/6-8
1560 County Road B E 55109 651-748-6300
Jill Miklausich, prin. Fax 748-6391
Maplewood MS 700/6-8
2410 Holloway Ave E 55109 651-748-6500
Kevin Wolff, prin. Fax 748-6591
Weaver ES 500/K-5
2135 Birmingham St 55109 651-748-7000
Pangjua Xiong, prin. Fax 748-7091

Roseville Area SD 623
Supt. — See Roseville
Edgerton ES 500/K-6
1929 Edgerton St 55117 651-772-2565
Melissa Sonnek, prin. Fax 772-1510
Harambee ES 400/K-6
30 County Road B E 55117 651-379-2500
Kathy Griebel, prin. Fax 379-2590

Gethsemane Lutheran S 200/PK-8
2410 Stillwater Rd E 55119 651-739-7540
Scott Revoir, prin. Fax 578-0610
Presentation of Mary S 200/PK-8
1695 Kennard St 55109 651-777-5877
Nikki Giel, prin. Fax 777-8283
St. Jerome S 200/PK-8
384 Roselawn Ave E 55117 651-771-8494
Laureen Sherman, prin. Fax 771-3466

Marble, Itasca, Pop. 685
Greenway SD 316 700/PK-12
201 Kate St 55764 218-247-7306
David Pace, supt. Fax 245-6612
www.isd316.org
Marble ECC 50/PK-PK
PO Box 10 55764 218-247-7306
Sue Hoeft, prin. Fax 245-6612
Other Schools – See Coleraine

Marshall, Lyon, Pop. 13,459
Marshall SD 413 2,300/PK-12
401 S Saratoga St 56258 507-537-6924
Scott Monson, supt. Fax 537-6931
www.marshall.k12.mn.us

Marshall MS 600/5-8
401 S Saratoga St 56258 507-537-6938
Mary Kay Thomas, prin. Fax 537-6942
Park Side ES 600/PK-2
1300 E Lyon St 56258 507-537-6948
Darci Love, prin. Fax 537-6953
West Side ES 300/3-4
500 S 4th St 56258 507-537-6962
Jeremy Williams, prin. Fax 537-6966

Holy Redeemer S 300/K-8
501 S Whitney St 56258 507-532-6642
Carol J. DeSmet, prin. Fax 532-2636
Samuel Lutheran S 100/PK-8
500 Village Dr 56258 507-532-2162
John Festerling, prin. Fax 532-2162
True Light Christian S 100/PK-8
PO Box 751 56258 507-532-2762
Laura Hibma, admin. Fax 337-0019

Mayer, Carver, Pop. 1,725

Zion Lutheran S 100/PK-8
209 Bluejay Ave 55360 952-657-2339
Joshua Baumann, admin. Fax 657-2337

Maynard, Chippewa, Pop. 366
MACCRAY SD
Supt. — See Clara City
MACCRAY West ES 200/PK-6
PO Box 276 56260 320-367-2396
Doug Runia, prin. Fax 367-2399

Mazeppa, Wabasha, Pop. 837
Zumbrota-Mazeppa SD 2805 900/PK-12
343 3rd Ave NE 55956 507-732-1400
Gary Anger, supt. Fax 732-1401
www.zmschools.us/
Zumbrota-Mazeppa ES 200/3-6
343 3rd Ave NE 55956 507-732-1420
Quinn Rasmussen, prin. Fax 732-1421
Other Schools – See Zumbrota

Medford, Steele, Pop. 1,228
Medford ISD 763 900/PK-12
750 2nd Ave SE 55049 507-214-6300
Mark Ristau, supt. Fax 451-6474
www.medford.k12.mn.us
Medford ES 500/PK-6
750 2nd Ave SE 55049 507-451-5250
Mark Ristau, prin. Fax 451-6474

Melrose, Stearns, Pop. 3,582
Melrose SD 740 1,400/PK-12
546 5th Ave NE 56352 320-256-5160
Greg Winter, supt. Fax 256-4311
www.isd740.org
Melrose ES 500/PK-5
566 5th Ave NE 56352 320-256-5160
Jim Conrad, prin. Fax 256-3616
Melrose MS 400/6-8
546 5th Ave NE 56352 320-256-5160
Robert Anerson, prin. Fax 256-4311

St. Marys S 100/PK-6
320 5th Ave SE 56352 320-256-4257
Autumn Nelson, prin. Fax 256-4208

Menahga, Wadena, Pop. 1,296
Menahga SD 821 700/PK-12
PO Box 160 56464 218-564-4141
Kevin Wellen, supt. Fax 564-5401
www.menahga.k12.mn.us
Menahga ES 500/PK-4
PO Box 160 56464 218-564-4141
Jeannie Mayer, prin. Fax 564-4502
Menahga MS 5-8
PO Box 160 56464 218-564-4141
Ann Wothe, prin. Fax 564-4502

Mendota Heights, Dakota, Pop. 10,905
West St. Paul-Mendota Hts-Eagan SD 197 4,800/PK-12
1897 Delaware Ave 55118 651-403-7000
Peter Olson-Skog, supt. Fax 403-7010
www.isd197.org
Friendly Hills MS 700/5-8
701 Mendota Heights Rd 55120 651-403-7600
Chris Hiti, prin. Fax 403-7610
Mendota ES 400/PK-4
1979 Summit Ln 55118 651-403-8000
Steve Goldade, prin. Fax 403-8010
Somerset ES 400/PK-4
1355 Dodd Rd 55118 651-403-8200
Libby Huettl, prin. Fax 403-8210
Other Schools – See Eagan, West Saint Paul

Visitation S 600/PK-12
2455 Visitation Dr 55120 651-683-1700
Rene Gavic, head sch Fax 454-7144

Middle River, Marshall, Pop. 301
Greenbush-Middle River SD 2683
Supt. — See Greenbush
Middle River ES 100/PK-4
PO Box 130 56737 218-222-3310
Sharon Schultz, prin. Fax 222-3314

Milaca, Mille Lacs, Pop. 2,899
Milaca SD 912 1,900/PK-12
500 Highway 23 W 56353 320-982-7210
Tim Truebenbach, supt. Fax 982-7179
www.milaca.k12.mn.us/
Milaca ES 1,100/PK-6
500 Highway 23 W 56353 320-982-7301
Steve Voshell, prin. Fax 982-7178

Milroy, Redwood, Pop. 251
Milroy SD 635 100/K-8
PO Box 10 56263 507-336-2563
Wade McKittrick, supt. Fax 336-2568
www.milroy.k12.mn.us

Milroy ES 50/5-6
PO Box 10 56263 507-336-2563
Heidi Sachariason, prin. Fax 336-2568
Milroy JHS 50/7-8
PO Box 10 56263 507-336-2563
Heidi Sachariason, prin. Fax 336-2568

Miltona, Douglas, Pop. 423
Alexandria SD 206
Supt. — See Alexandria
Miltona ES 100/K-5
PO Box 113 56354 877-736-1419
Lisa Pikop, prin. Fax 943-5140

Minneapolis, Hennepin, Pop. 368,444
Minneapolis SD 1 33,300/PK-12
1250 W Broadway Ave 55411 612-668-0000
Ed Graff, supt. Fax 668-0145
www.mpls.k12.mn.us
Andersen United Community S 1,100/PK-8
1098 Andersen Ln 55407 612-668-4200
Denise Wells, prin. Fax 668-4260
Anishinabe Academy 400/PK-5
3100 E 28th St 55406 612-668-0880
Laura Sullivan, prin. Fax 668-0890
Anthony MS 800/6-8
5757 Irving Ave S 55419 612-668-3240
Mai Chang Vue, prin. Fax 668-3250
Anwatin MS 600/6-8
256 Upton Ave S 55405 612-668-2450
Ellen Shulman, prin. Fax 668-2460
Armatage Montessori ES 600/PK-5
2501 W 56th St 55410 612-668-3180
Joan Franks, prin. Fax 668-3190
Bancroft ES 500/PK-5
1315 E 38th St 55407 612-668-3550
Erin Glynn, prin. Fax 668-3560
Barton Open S 700/K-8
4237 Colfax Ave S 55409 612-668-3580
Cynthia Mueller, prin. Fax 668-3590
Bethune Community ES 400/PK-5
919 Emerson Ave N 55411 612-668-2550
Cheryl Martin, prin. Fax 668-2560
Bryn Mawr Community ES 500/PK-5
252 Upton Ave S 55405 612-668-2500
Kristi Ward, prin. Fax 668-2510
Burroughs Community ES 800/K-5
1601 W 50th St 55419 612-668-3280
Ana Bartl, prin. Fax 668-3290
Cityview STEM 50/PK-5
3350 N 4th St 55412 612-668-2270
Renee Montague, prin. Fax 668-2280
Dowling Urban Environmental ES 500/K-5
3900 W River Pkwy 55406 612-668-4410
Lloyd Winfield, prin. Fax 668-4420
Emerson Spanish Immersion ES 500/PK-5
1421 Spruce Pl 55403 612-668-3610
Aaron Arredondo, prin. Fax 668-3620
FAIR S Downtown 500/1-12
10 S 10th St 55403 612-668-1060
Mary Pat Cumming, prin. Fax 668-1099
Field Community MS 500/5-8
4645 4th Ave S 55419 612-668-3640
VaNita Miller, prin. Fax 668-3661
Folwell Performing Arts S PK-8
3611 20th Ave S 55407 612-668-4550
Ronald Salazar, prin. Fax 668-4560
Franklin MS 6-8
1501 Aldrich Ave N 55411 612-668-2600
Karon Cunningham, prin. Fax 668-2649
Green Central Park S 400/PK-5
3416 4th Ave S 55408 612-668-3730
Matthew Arnold, prin. Fax 668-3740
Hale Community ES 600/K-4
1220 E 54th St 55417 612-668-3760
Ryan Fitzgerald, prin. Fax 668-3770
Hall International ES 500/PK-5
1601 Aldrich Ave N 55411 612-668-2650
Pao Vue, prin. Fax 668-2660
Hiawatha Community ES Hiawatha Campus 200/PK-2
4201 42nd Ave S 55406 612-668-4610
Debbie Regnier, prin. Fax 668-4620
Hiawatha Community ES Howe Campus 3-5
3733 43rd Ave S 55406 612-668-4640
Kevin Oldenburg, prin. Fax 668-4650
Hmong International Academy 500/PK-8
1501 30th Ave N 55411 612-668-2250
Debora Golden-Brooks, prin. Fax 668-2260
Jefferson Community S 700/PK-8
1200 W 26th St 55405 612-668-2720
Holly Kleppe, prin. Fax 668-2730
Johnson Community S 600/PK-5
807 27th Ave N 55411 612-668-2930
Amy Luehmann, prin. Fax 668-2940
Kenny Community ES 400/K-5
5720 Emerson Ave S 55419 612-668-3340
Bill Gibbs, admin. Fax 668-3350
Kenwood Community Performing Arts ES 500/K-5
2013 Penn Ave S 55405 612-668-2760
Aura Wharton-Beck, prin. Fax 668-2770
Lake Harriet Community Lower ES 500/K-3
4030 Chowen Ave S 55410 612-668-3210
Merry Tilleson, prin. Fax 668-3220
Lake Harriet Community Upper ES 600/4-8
4912 Vincent Ave S 55410 612-668-3310
Walter Schleisman, prin. Fax 668-3320
Lake Nokomis S - Keewaydin Campus 400/3-8
5209 30th Ave S 55417 612-668-4670
LaShawn Ray, prin. Fax 668-4680
Lake Nokomis S - Wenonah Campus 300/K-2
5625 23rd Ave S 55417 612-668-5040
Kelly Wright, prin. Fax 668-5050
Laney Community S 700/PK-5
3333 Penn Ave N 55412 612-668-2200
Mauri Melander, prin. Fax 668-2210
Lind ES 500/PK-5
5025 Bryant Ave N 55430 612-668-2020
Delon Smith, prin. Fax 668-2030
Loring Community ES 400/PK-5
2600 44th Ave N 55412 612-668-2060
Ryan Gibbs, prin. Fax 668-2070
Lyndale ES 600/PK-5
312 W 34th St 55408 612-668-4000
Andree James, prin. Fax 668-4010
Marcy Open S 700/K-8
415 4th Ave SE 55414 612-668-1020
Donna Andrews, prin. Fax 668-1030
Moede ECC PK-PK
2406 Girard Ave N 55411 612-668-2127
Elizabeth Fields, dir. Fax 668-2146
Northeast MS 600/6-8
2955 Hayes St NE 55418 612-668-1500
Vernon Rowe, prin. Fax 668-1510
Northrop Community ES 500/K-5
4315 31st Ave S 55406 612-668-4520
Amy Jahnke, prin. Fax 668-4530
Olson MS 300/6-8
1607 51st Ave N 55430 612-668-1640
Steve Emerson, prin. Fax 668-1650
Page MS 300/6-8
1 W 49th St 55419 612-668-4040
Erin Rathke, prin. Fax 668-4050
Pillsbury Community ES 600/PK-5
2250 Garfield St NE 55418 612-668-1530
Jonathan Luknic, prin. Fax 668-1540
Pratt Community ES 200/PK-5
66 Malcolm Ave SE 55414 612-668-1122
Nancy Vague, admin. Fax 668-1110
Sanford MS 800/6-8
3524 42nd Ave S 55406 612-668-4900
Emily Palmer, prin. Fax 668-4910
Seward Montessori S 800/K-8
2309 28th Ave S 55406 612-668-4950
Tammy Goetz, prin. Fax 668-4960
Sheridan Arts Magnet ES 500/PK-5
1201 University Ave NE 55413 612-668-1130
Yajaira Guzman Carrero, prin. Fax 668-1140
Sullivan Community Center 700/PK-8
3100 E 28th St 55406 612-668-5000
Jennifer Hedberg, prin. Fax 668-5010
Waite Park Community ES 400/PK-5
1800 34th Ave NE 55418 612-668-1600
Rochelle McGinness, prin. Fax 668-1610
Webster ES PK-2
425 5th St NE 55413 612-668-1210
Ginger Kranz, prin. Fax 668-1220
Whittier International ES 700/PK-5
315 W 26th St 55404 612-668-4170
Norma Gibbs, prin. Fax 668-4180
Windom Open/Spanish Dual Immersion S 500/PK-5
5821 Wentworth Ave 55419 612-668-3370
James Clark, prin. Fax 668-3380

Spring Lake Park SD 16
Supt. — See Spring Lake Park
Northpoint ES 800/K-3
2350 124th Ct NE 55449 763-600-5700
Judi Kahoun, prin. Fax 600-5713

Annunciation S 400/PK-8
525 W 54th St 55419 612-823-4394
Jennifer Cassidy, prin. Fax 824-0998
Ascension S 200/K-8
1726 Dupont Ave N 55411 612-521-3609
Benito Matias, prin. Fax 522-3862
Carondelet Catholic S 400/K-8
3210 W 51st St 55410 612-927-8673
Sue Kerr, prin. Fax 927-7426
City of Lakes Waldorf S 200/PK-8
2344 Nicollet Ave 55404 612-767-1550
Marti Stewart, admin. Fax 767-1551
Hope Academy 300/K-12
2300 Chicago Ave 55404 612-721-6294
Russell Gregg, head sch Fax 722-9048
Lake Country S 300/PK-8
3755 Pleasant Ave 55409 612-827-3707
Paulette Zoe, prin. Fax 827-1332
Minnehaha Academy 500/PK-8
4200 W River Pkwy 55406 612-721-3359
Karen Balmer, prin. Fax 728-7777
Our Lady of Peace S 200/PK-8
5435 11th Ave S 55417 612-823-8253
Paul Berry, prin. Fax 824-7328
Pilgrim Lutheran S 100/PK-8
3901 1st Ave S 55409 612-825-5375
Michelle Cambrice M.Ed., prin.
Risen Christ S 300/K-8
1120 E 37th St 55407 612-822-5329
Liz Ramsey, prin. Fax 729-2336
St. Charles Borromeo S 300/PK-8
2727 Stinson Blvd 55418 612-781-2643
Danny Kieffer, prin. Fax 787-1110
St. Helena S 200/K-8
3200 E 44th St 55406 612-729-9301
Jane Hileman, prin. Fax 729-6016
St. John Paul II Prep S 100/K-8
1630 4th St NE 55413 612-789-8851
Edgar Alfonzo, prin. Fax 789-8773
Trinity First Lutheran S 100/PK-8
1115 E 19th St 55404 612-871-2353
Sarah Wippich, prin. Fax 871-6550
Woodcrest Baptist Academy 100/PK-12
6875 University Ave NE 55432 763-571-6410
Loren Isaacs, admin. Fax 571-3978

Minneota, Lyon, Pop. 1,386
Minneota SD 414 500/K-12
PO Box 98 56264 507-872-6532
Dan Deitte, supt. Fax 872-5172
www.minneotaschools.org/
Minneota ES 200/K-6
PO Box 98 56264 507-872-6122
Jeremy Frie, prin. Fax 872-5172

St. Edward S 100/K-8
210 W 4th St 56264 507-872-6391
Jaci Garvey, prin. Fax 872-5263

Minnesota Lake, Faribault, Pop. 687
Maple River SD 2135
Supt. — See Mapleton
Maple River East ES 200/PK-5
PO Box 218 56068 507-462-3348
Jon Lewis, prin. Fax 462-3219

Minnetonka, Hennepin, Pop. 48,748
Hopkins SD 270
Supt. — See Hopkins
Gatewood ES 500/K-6
14900 Gatewood Dr 55345 952-988-5250
Mark French, prin. Fax 988-5276
Glen Lake ES 500/K-6
4801 Woodridge Rd 55345 952-988-5200
Jeff Radel, prin. Fax 988-5199
Tanglen ES 500/K-6
10901 Hillside Ln W 55305 952-988-4900
Jim Hebeisen, prin. Fax 988-4871

Minnetonka SD 276 9,700/K-12
5621 County Road 101 55345 952-401-5000
Dr. Dennis Peterson, supt. Fax 401-5083
www.minnetonkaschools.org
Clear Springs ES 800/K-5
5701 County Road 101 55345 952-401-6950
Curt Carpenter, prin. Fax 401-6955
Groveland ES 800/K-5
17310 Minnetonka Blvd 55345 952-401-5600
David Parker, prin. Fax 401-5606
Minnetonka East MS 1,200/6-8
17000 Lake Street Ext 55345 952-401-5200
Pete Dymit, prin. Fax 401-5268
Scenic Heights ES 800/K-5
5650 Scenic Heights Dr 55345 952-401-5400
Joe Wacker, prin. Fax 401-5412
Other Schools – See Excelsior, Wayzata

Minnetonka Christian Academy 50/K-8
3520 Williston Rd 55345 952-935-4497
Andrew Carlson, prin. Fax 935-4498
Notre Dame Academy 300/PK-8
13505 Excelsior Blvd 55345 952-358-3500
Ginger Vance, prin. Fax 935-2031

Minnetrista, Hennepin, Pop. 6,316
Westonka SD 277 2,200/PK-12
5901 Sunnyfield Rd E 55364 952-491-8000
Kevin Borg, supt. Fax 491-8012
www.westonka.k12.mn.us
Other Schools – See Mound

Montevideo, Chippewa, Pop. 5,317
Montevideo SD 129 1,300/PK-12
2001 William Ave 56265 320-269-8833
Dr. Luther Heller, supt. Fax 269-8834
www.montevideoschools.org
Montevideo MS 400/4-7
2001 William Ave 56265 320-269-6431
Shawn Huntley, prin. Fax 321-8970
Ramsey ES 300/1-3
501 Hamilton Ave 56265 320-269-6584
Bill Sprung, prin. Fax 269-6585
Sanford Education Center 100/PK-K
412 S 13th St 56265 320-269-6538
Bob Grey, prin. Fax 269-5684

Montgomery, LeSueur, Pop. 2,910
Tri-City United ISD 2905 1,200/PK-12
101 2nd St NE Ste 3 56069 507-364-8100
Teri Preisler, supt. Fax 364-8103
www.tcu2905.us
Tri-City United Montgomery K-8 S 300/PK-8
101 2nd St NE Ste 1 56069 507-364-8119
Deb Dwyer, prin. Fax 364-8411
Other Schools – See Le Center, Lonsdale

Most Holy Redeemer S 100/PK-8
205 Vine Ave W 56069 507-364-7383
George VonDracek, prin. Fax 364-5964

Monticello, Wright, Pop. 12,521
Monticello SD 882 4,200/PK-12
302 Washington St 55362 763-272-2000
Dr. Michael Favor, supt. Fax 272-2009
www.monticello.k12.mn.us
Eastview Education Center 200/PK-K
9375 Fenning Ave NE 55362 763-272-2900
Eric Olson, prin. Fax 272-2909
Little Mountain ES 800/PK-5
9350 Fallon Ave NE 55362 763-272-2600
Gabe Hackett, prin. Fax 272-2609
Monticello MS 900/6-8
800 E Broadway St 55362 763-272-2100
Jeff Scherber, prin. Fax 272-2109
Pinewood ES 1,000/PK-5
1010 W Broadway St 55362 763-272-2400
Linda Borgerding, prin. Fax 272-2409

Montrose, Wright, Pop. 2,802
Buffalo-Hanover-Montrose SD
Supt. — See Buffalo
Montrose ES of Innovation 300/K-5
100 2nd St S 55363 763-682-8345
Tony Steffes, prin. Fax 682-8391

Moorhead, Clay, Pop. 37,202
Moorhead Area SD 152 5,600/K-12
2410 14th St S 56560 218-284-3300
Lynne Kovash Ed.D., supt. Fax 284-3333
www.moorheadschools.org/
Asp ES 900/K-4
910 11th St N 56560 218-284-6300
Chris Triggs, prin. Fax 284-6333
Dodds ES, 4400 24th Ave 56560 K-4
Robin Grooters, prin. 218-284-1300
Hopkins ES 800/K-4
2020 11th St S 56560 218-284-4300
Lynnelle Dirksen, prin. Fax 284-4333

Horizon MS East Campus 1,300/7-8
3601 12th Ave S 56560 218-284-7300
Jeremy Larson Ed.D., prin. Fax 284-7333
Horizon MS West Campus 5-6
3601 12th Ave S 56560 218-284-8300
Carla Smith, admin. Fax 284-8300
Reinertsen ES 800/1-4
1201 40th Ave S 56560 218-284-5300
Josh St. Louis, prin. Fax 284-5333

Park Christian S 300/K-12
300 17th St N 56560 218-236-0500
Chris Nellermoe, pres. Fax 236-7301
St. Joseph S 200/PK-8
1005 2nd Ave S 56560 218-233-0553
Andrew Hilliker, prin. Fax 291-9479

Moose Lake, Carlton, Pop. 2,729
Moose Lake SD 97 600/PK-12
4812 County Road 10 55767 218-485-4435
Bob Indihar, supt. Fax 485-8110
www.mooselake.k12.mn.us
Moose Lake ES 300/PK-6
4812 County Road 10 55767 218-485-4834
Kraig Konietzko, prin. Fax 485-4351

Mora, Kanabec, Pop. 3,511
Mora SD 332 1,700/PK-12
400 Maple Ave E 55051 320-679-6200
Craig Schultz, supt. Fax 679-6209
www.moraschools.org
Mora ES 500/PK-6
200 9th St N 55051 320-679-6240
Randy Qual, prin. Fax 679-6258

Morgan, Redwood, Pop. 873
Cedar Mountain SD 2754 500/K-12
PO Box 188 56266 507-249-5990
Robert Tews, supt. Fax 249-3149
www.cms.mntm.org/
Other Schools – See Franklin

St. Michael S 50/PK-6
PO Box 459 56266 507-249-3192
Jennifer Fischer, prin. Fax 249-2557

Morris, Stevens, Pop. 5,158
Morris SD 769 1,200/PK-12
201 S Columbia Ave 56267 320-589-4840
Richard Lahn, supt. Fax 585-2208
www.morris.k12.mn.us
Morris Area JHS 200/6-8
201 S Columbia Ave 56267 320-589-4400
Bill Kehoe, prin. Fax 589-3203
Morris ES 500/PK-5
151 S Columbia Ave 56267 320-589-1250
Shane Monson, prin. Fax 589-3920

St. Marys S 100/K-6
411 Colorado Ave 56267 320-589-1704
Joseph Ferriero, prin. Fax 589-1703

Morristown, Rice, Pop. 973
Waterville-Elysian-Morristown SD 2143
Supt. — See Waterville
Waterville-Elysian-Morristown ES 100/5-6
PO Box 278 55052 507-685-4222
Anna Braam, prin. Fax 685-2420
Waterville-Elysian-Morristown JHS 100/7-8
PO Box 278 55052 507-685-4222
Anna Braam, prin. Fax 685-2420

Trinity Lutheran S 50/K-6
10500 215th St W 55052 507-685-2200
Lori Gieseke, lead tchr.

Motley, Morrison, Pop. 649
Staples-Motley ISD 2170
Supt. — See Staples
Motley-Staples MS 200/4-7
132 1st Ave N 56466 218-352-6315
John Regan, prin. Fax 352-6508

Mound, Hennepin, Pop. 8,930
Westonka SD 277
Supt. — See Minnetrista
Grandview MS 500/5-7
1881 Commerce Blvd 55364 952-491-8300
Christy Zachow, prin. Fax 491-8303
Hilltop PS 400/PK-4
5700 Game Farm Rd E 55364 952-491-8500
Michael Moch, prin. Fax 491-8503
Shirley Hills PS 500/K-4
2450 Wilshire Blvd 55364 952-491-8400
Scott Eidsness, prin. Fax 491-8403
Westonka ECC PK-PK
5241 Shoreline Dr 55364 952-491-8048
Sarah Grimm, admin. Fax 472-0196

Our Lady of the Lake S 200/PK-8
2411 Commerce Blvd 55364 952-472-1284
Becky Kennedy, prin. Fax 472-9152

Mounds View, Ramsey, Pop. 11,818
Mounds View SD 621
Supt. — See Shoreview
Edgewood MS 600/6-8
5100 Edgewood Dr 55112 651-621-6600
Penny Howard, prin. Fax 621-6605
Pinewood ES 500/1-5
5500 Quincy St 55112 651-621-7500
Andrew Skinner, prin. Fax 621-7505

Mountain Iron, Saint Louis, Pop. 2,818
Mountain Iron-Buhl SD 712 500/PK-12
5720 Marble Ave 55768 218-735-8271
John Klarich, supt. Fax 735-8244
www.mib.k12.mn.us
Merritt ES 300/PK-6
5529 Emerald Ave 55768 218-735-8271
John Klarich, prin. Fax 741-1930

Mountain Lake, Cottonwood, Pop. 2,081
Mountain Lake SD 173 500/PK-12
PO Box 400 56159 507-427-2325
William Strom, supt. Fax 427-3047
www.mountainlake.k12.mn.us
Mountain Lake ES 300/PK-6
PO Box 400 56159 507-427-3151
Jon Schwaegerl, prin. Fax 427-3047

Mountain Lake Christian S 100/PK-12
PO Box 478 56159 507-427-2010
Dr. Michael James, admin. Fax 427-3123

Murdock, Swift, Pop. 275
Kerkhoven-Murdock-Sunburg SD 775
Supt. — See Kerkhoven
Murdock ES 400/PK-6
PO Box 46 56271 320-875-2441
Jeff Keil, prin. Fax 875-2226

Nashwauk, Itasca, Pop. 964
Nashwauk-Keewatin SD 319 600/PK-12
400 2nd St 55769 218-885-1280
Matt Grose, supt. Fax 885-2910
www.isd319.org
Other Schools – See Keewatin

Nett Lake, Saint Louis, Pop. 280
Nett Lake SD 707 100/K-6
13090 Westley Rd, Orr MN 55771 218-757-3102
Steve Thomas, supt. Fax 757-3330
www.nettlakeschool.org
Nett Lake ES 100/K-6
13090 Westley Rd, Orr MN 55771 218-757-3102
James Varichak, prin. Fax 757-3330

Nevis, Hubbard, Pop. 379
Nevis SD 308 300/PK-12
PO Box 138 56467 218-652-3500
Gregg Parks, supt. Fax 652-3505
www.nevis308.org
Nevis S 300/PK-12
PO Box 138 56467 218-652-3500
Brian Michaelson, prin. Fax 652-3505

New Brighton, Ramsey, Pop. 20,903
Mounds View SD 621
Supt. — See Shoreview
Bel Air ES 600/1-5
1800 5th St NW 55112 651-621-6300
Dawn Wiegand, prin. Fax 621-6305
Highview MS 700/6-8
2300 7th St NW 55112 651-621-6700
Dr. Sheila Eller, prin. Fax 621-6705
Kindergarten at Pike Lake Education Ctr K-K
2101 14th St NW 55112 651-621-8060
Ryan Lang, prin. Fax 621-8065
Sunnyside ES 600/1-5
2070 County Road H 55112 651-621-7600
Nathan Flansburg, prin. Fax 621-7605

St. John the Baptist S 400/PK-8
845 2nd Ave NW 55112 651-633-1522
Ann Laird, prin. Fax 633-7404

Newfolden, Marshall, Pop. 366
Marshall County Central SD 441 400/K-12
PO Box 189 56738 218-874-8530
Jeffrey Lund, supt. Fax 874-8581
www.newfolden.k12.mn.us/
Newfolden ES 100/3-6
PO Box 189 56738 218-874-8805
Jeffrey Lund, prin. Fax 874-8581
Other Schools – See Viking

New Hope, Hennepin, Pop. 19,669
Robbinsdale SD 281 11,800/K-12
4148 Winnetka Ave N 55427 763-504-8000
Dr. Carlton Jenkins, supt. Fax 504-8979
www.rdale.org
Meadow Lake ES 600/K-5
8525 62nd Ave N 55428 763-504-7700
Jane Byrne, prin. Fax 504-7709
Robbinsdale Spanish Immersion ES 800/K-5
8808 Medicine Lake Rd 55427 763-504-4400
Elaine Mehdizadeh, prin. Fax 504-4409
Sonnesyn ES 600/K-5
3421 Boone Ave N 55427 763-504-7600
Leia Ward, prin. Fax 504-7609
Other Schools – See Brooklyn Center, Crystal, Golden Valley, Plymouth, Robbinsdale

---

Holy Trinity Lutheran S 100/PK-8
4240 Gettysburg Ave N 55428 763-533-0600
Ryan Rush, prin.

New London, Kandiyohi, Pop. 1,247
New London-Spicer SD 345 1,400/K-12
101 4th Ave SW 56273 320-354-9001
Paul Carlson, supt. Fax 354-2252
www.nls.k12.mn.us
New London-Spicer MS 400/5-8
101 4th Ave SW 56273 320-354-2252
Trish Perry, prin. Fax 354-4244
Prairie Woods ES 500/K-4
101 4th Ave SW 56273 320-354-2252
Randall Juhl, prin. Fax 354-2093

Newport, Washington, Pop. 3,361
South Washington County SD 833
Supt. — See Cottage Grove
Newport ES 300/PK-5
851 6th Ave 55055 651-425-4300
Rich Romano, prin. Fax 425-4315

New Prague, Scott, Pop. 7,228
New Prague Area SD 721 3,900/PK-12
410 Central Ave N 56071 952-758-1700
Tim Dittberner, supt. Fax 758-1799
www.npaschools.org
Falcon Ridge ES 600/K-5
1200 Columbus Ave N 56071 952-758-1600
David Giesen, prin. Fax 758-1699
New Prague MS 900/6-8
721 Central Ave N 56071 952-758-1400
Brad Gregor, prin. Fax 758-1499
Raven Stream ES 600/K-5
300 11th Ave NW 56071 952-758-1500
Patrick Pribyl, prin. Fax 758-1599
Other Schools – See Elko

St. Wenceslaus S 300/PK-8
227 Main St E 56071 952-758-3133
Kim Doyle, prin. Fax 758-2958

New Richland, Waseca, Pop. 1,198
NRHEG SD 2168 1,000/PK-12
306 Ash Ave S 56072 507-465-3205
Dale Carlson, supt. Fax 465-8633
nrheg.k12.mn.us/pages/NRHEG
Other Schools – See Ellendale

New Ulm, Brown, Pop. 13,436
New Ulm SD 1,800/PK-12
414 S Payne St 56073 507-233-6180
Jeff Bertrang, supt. Fax 233-6181
www.newulm.k12.mn.us
Jefferson ES 400/1-4
318 S Payne St 56073 507-233-3500
Adam Kluver, prin. Fax 233-3501
New Ulm MS 300/5-8
414 S Payne St 56073 507-233-6100
Michelle Miller, prin. Fax 233-6101
Washington Learning Center 500/PK-K
910 14th St N 56073 507-233-8300
Dawn Brown, prin. Fax 233-8301

St. Anthony S 200/PK-6
514 N Washington St 56073 507-354-2928
Shelly Bauer, prin. Fax 354-7029
St. Paul's Lutheran S 300/PK-8
126 S Payne St 56073 507-354-2329
Greg Thiesfeldt, prin. Fax 354-6893

New York Mills, Otter Tail, Pop. 1,166
New York Mills SD 553 700/PK-12
PO Box 218 56567 218-385-4201
Blaine Novak, supt. Fax 385-2551
www.nymills.k12.mn.us
New York Mills ES 400/PK-6
PO Box 218 56567 218-385-4208
Judith Brockway, prin. Fax 385-2551

Nicollet, Nicollet, Pop. 1,085
Nicollet SD 507 100/PK-12
PO Box 108 56074 507-232-3411
Jack Eustice, supt. Fax 232-3536
www.isd507.k12.mn.us
Nicollet S 100/PK-12
PO Box 108 56074 507-232-3411
Todd Toulouse, prin. Fax 232-3536

Trinity Lutheran S, 425 6th St 56074 50/PK-8
Joseph Gumm, prin. 507-232-3839

Nisswa, Crow Wing, Pop. 1,960
Brainerd SD 181
Supt. — See Brainerd
Nisswa ES 300/PK-4
5533 Lakers Ln 56468 218-961-6860
Molly Raske, prin. Fax 961-6861

North Branch, Chisago, Pop. 9,994
North Branch Area ISD 138 3,100/PK-12
PO Box 370 55056 651-674-1000
Dr. Deb Henton Ed.D., supt. Fax 674-1010
www.isd318.org
Early Childhood Center 50/PK-PK
PO Box 370 55056 651-674-1220
Erica Bjerketvedt, dir. Fax 674-1210
North Branch Area MS 1,000/5-8
PO Box 370 55056 651-674-1300
Todd Tetzlaff, prin. Fax 674-1310
Sunrise River ES 1,100/K-4
PO Box 370 55056 651-674-1100
Dr. Laura Zimmerman Ed.D., prin. Fax 674-1110

Veritas Academy 50/K-12
34888 Kable Ave 55056 651-462-3894
Dr. Susie Brooks Ed.D., pres. Fax 462-4709

Northfield, Rice, Pop. 19,624
Northfield SD 659 3,900/K-12
1400 Division St S 55057 507-663-0600
Matt Hillmann Ph.D., supt. Fax 663-0611
northfieldschools.org
Bridgewater ES 600/K-5
401 Jefferson Pkwy 55057 507-664-3300
Nancy Antoine, prin. Fax 664-3308
Greenvale Park ES 500/K-5
700 Lincoln Pkwy 55057 507-645-3500
Sam Richardson, prin. Fax 645-3505
Northfield MS 900/6-8
2200 Division St S 55057 507-663-0650
Greg Gelineau, prin. Fax 663-0660
Sibley ES 600/K-5
1400 Maple St 55057 507-645-3470
Scott Sannes, prin. Fax 645-3469

St. Dominic S 200/PK-8
216 Spring St N 55057 507-645-8136
Vicki Marvin, prin. Fax 650-0680

North Mankato, Nicollet, Pop. 13,239
Mankato SD 77
Supt. — See Mankato
Dakota Meadows MS 600/6-8
1900 Howard Dr W 56003 507-387-5077
Carmen Strahan, prin. Fax 387-1119
Hoover ES 500/K-5
1524 Hoover Dr 56003 507-388-5202
Dan Kamphoff, prin. Fax 388-8432
Monroe ES 500/K-5
441 Monroe Ave 56003 507-387-7889
Stephen Johanson, prin. Fax 387-4027

Good Shepherd Lutheran S PK-8
2101 Lorray Dr 56003 507-388-4336
Ben Holten, prin. Fax 388-2160

North Oaks, Ramsey, Pop. 4,424
Mounds View SD 621
Supt. — See Shoreview
Chippewa MS 1,000/6-8
5000 Hodgson Rd, 651-621-6400
Rob Reetz, prin. Fax 621-6405

Northome, Koochiching, Pop. 196
South Koochiching-Rainy River ISD 363 400/PK-12
PO Box 465 56661 218-897-5275
Steven Thomas, supt. Fax 897-5280
www.isd363.org
Northome ES 100/K-6
PO Box 465 56661 218-897-5275
Anthony Kerr, prin. Fax 897-5280
Other Schools – See Birchdale

North Saint Paul, Ramsey, Pop. 11,176
North St. Paul-Maplewood-Oakdale SD 622
10,500/PK-12
2520 12th Ave E 55109 651-748-7622
Christine Osorio, supt. Fax 748-7413
www.isd622.org/
Cowern ES 500/K-5
2131 Margaret St N 55109 651-748-6800
Jennifer Wilson, prin. Fax 748-6891
Richardson ES 500/PK-5
2615 1st St N 55109 651-748-6900
Jenna Peters, prin. Fax 748-6991
Webster ES 400/PK-5
2170 7th Ave E 55109 651-748-7100
Mona Perkins, prin. Fax 748-7191
Other Schools – See Maplewood, Oakdale

Christ Lutheran S 200/PK-8
2475 17th Ave E 55109 651-777-1450
Mark Dobberstein, prin. Fax 748-0723
St. Peter S 300/PK-8
2620 Margaret St N 55109 651-777-3091
Alison Dahlman, prin. Fax 777-7750

Norwood Young America, Carver, Pop. 3,521
Central ISD 108 1,000/PK-12
PO Box 247 55368 952-467-7000
Brian Corlett, supt. Fax 467-7003
raiders.central.k12.mn.us
Central ES 400/PK-5
PO Box 367 55368 952-467-7300
Michael Daugs, prin. Fax 467-7303
Central MS 200/6-8
PO Box 247 55368 952-467-7200
Ron Erpenbach, prin. Fax 467-7203

Oakdale, Washington, Pop. 26,751
North St. Paul-Maplewood-Oakdale SD 622
Supt. — See North Saint Paul
Castle ES 400/PK-5
6675 50th St N 55128 651-748-6700
Bridget Bruner, prin. Fax 748-6791
Eagle Point ES 400/K-5
7850 15th St N 55128 651-702-8300
Shawn Bromeland, prin. Fax 702-8391
Oakdale ES 500/PK-5
821 Glenbrook Ave N 55128 651-702-8500
Tracy Buhl, prin. Fax 702-8591
Skyview Community ES 600/K-5
1100 Heron Ave N 55128 651-702-8100
Travis Barringer, prin. Fax 702-8191
Skyview Community MS 800/6-8
1100 Heron Ave N 55128 651-702-8000
Lynn Pham, prin. Fax 702-8091

Transfiguration S 300/PK-8
6135 15th St N 55128 651-501-2220
Andy Jacobson, prin. Fax 501-2258

Ogema, Becker, Pop. 157
Waubun-Ogema-White Earth SD 435
Supt. — See Waubun
Ogema ES 200/PK-4
PO Box 68 56569 218-473-6174
Laurie Johnson, prin. Fax 983-4200

Ogilvie, Kanabec, Pop. 366
Ogilvie SD 333 500/PK-12
333 School Dr 56358 320-272-5000
Kathy Belsheim, supt. Fax 272-5072
www.ogilvie.k12.mn.us
Ogilvie ES 300/PK-5
333 School Dr 56358 320-272-5050
Alicia Nelson, prin. Fax 272-5072

Okabena, Jackson, Pop. 186
Heron Lake-Okabena SD 330 300/PK-12
PO Box 97 56161 507-853-4507
Paul Bang, supt. Fax 853-4642
www.isd330.org
Other Schools – See Heron Lake

Oklee, Red Lake, Pop. 424
Red Lake County Central ISD 2906 400/PK-12
PO Box 100 56742 218-465-4222
Jim Guetter, supt. Fax 465-4225
www.rlcc2906.org

Other Schools – See Plummer

Olivia, Renville, Pop. 2,461
BOLD SD 2534 700/PK-12
701 9th St S 56277 320-523-1031
John Dotson, supt. Fax 523-2399
www.bold.k12.mn.us
Other Schools – See Bird Island

Onamia, Mille Lacs, Pop. 845
Onamia SD 480 600/K-12
35465 125th Ave 56359 320-532-4174
Jason Vold, supt. Fax 532-4658
www.onamia.k12.mn.us
Onamia ES 300/K-6
35465 125th Ave 56359 320-532-6707
Jason Vold, prin. Fax 532-4658

Ortonville, Big Stone, Pop. 1,887
Ortonville SD 2903 300/PK-12
200 Trojan Dr 56278 320-839-6181
Jeffrey Taylor, supt. Fax 839-3708
www.ortonville.k12.mn.us
Knoll ES 300/PK-6
200 Trojan Dr 56278 320-839-6181
Kristyanna Brandriet, prin. Fax 839-3708

Osakis, Douglas, Pop. 1,728
Osakis SD 213 700/PK-12
PO Box X 56360 320-859-2191
Randal Bergquist, supt. Fax 859-2835
www.osakis.k12.mn.us
Osakis ES 300/PK-4
PO Box X 56360 320-859-2191
Shad Schmidt, prin. Fax 859-2835

St. Agnes S 100/PK-6
PO Box O 56360 320-859-2130
Pat Popisil, prin. Fax 859-5850

Osseo, Hennepin, Pop. 2,385
Osseo Area ISD 279
Supt. — See Maple Grove
Osseo MS 700/6-8
10223 93rd Ave N 55369 763-391-8800
Brian Chance, prin. Fax 391-8801

Otsego, Wright, Pop. 13,320
Elk River Area SD 728
Supt. — See Elk River
Prairie View ES K-8
12200 80th St NE 55330 763-274-6270
Kari Sampson, prin.

Owatonna, Steele, Pop. 25,301
Owatonna SD 761 4,700/K-12
515 W Bridge St 55060 507-444-8600
Jeff Elstad, supt. Fax 444-8688
www.owatonna.k12.mn.us
Lincoln ES 500/K-5
747 Havana Rd 55060 507-444-8100
Fax 444-8199
McKinley ES 500/K-5
1050 22nd St NE 55060 507-444-8200
Justin Kiel, prin. Fax 444-8299
Owatonna MS 700/6-8
500 15th St NE 55060 507-444-8700
Julie Sullivan, prin. Fax 444-8799
Washington ES 500/K-5
423 14th St NE 55060 507-444-8300
Beth Svenby, prin. Fax 444-8399
Wilson ES 600/K-5
325 Meadow Ln 55060 507-444-8400
Melodee Hoffner, prin. Fax 444-8499

St. Marys S, 730 S Cedar Ave 55060 400/PK-8
Jen Swanson, prin. 507-446-2300

Parkers Prairie, Otter Tail, Pop. 1,009
Parkers Prairie ISD 547 500/PK-12
PO Box 46 56361 218-338-6011
Thomas Ames, supt. Fax 338-4077
www.isd547.com
Parkers Prairie ES 300/PK-6
PO Box 46 56361 218-338-4079
Steve Radtke, prin. Fax 338-4078

Park Rapids, Hubbard, Pop. 3,639
Park Rapids SD 309 1,500/PK-12
301 Huntsinger Ave 56470 218-237-6500
Lance Bagstad, supt. Fax 237-6519
www.parkrapids.k12.mn.us
Century ES 700/K-4
501 Helten Ave 56470 218-237-6200
Joleen DeLaHunt, prin. Fax 237-6248
Century MS 400/5-8
501 Helten Ave 56470 218-237-6300
Shawn Andress, prin. Fax 237-6349
White Preschool PK-PK
301 Huntsinger Ave 56470 218-237-6600
Jill Dickinson, prin. Fax 237-6613

Paynesville, Stearns, Pop. 2,410
Paynesville SD 741 700/PK-12
217 W Mill St 56362 320-243-3410
Robert Huot, supt. Fax 243-7525
www.paynesvilleschools.com
Paynesville ES 500/PK-5
205 W Mill St 56362 320-243-3725
David Oehrlein, prin. Fax 243-7525

Pease, Mille Lacs, Pop. 239

Community Christian S 100/PK-8
208 E Main St, 320-369-4239
Tracy Rosenberg, prin. Fax 369-4346

Pelican Rapids, Otter Tail, Pop. 2,413
Pelican Rapids SD 548 900/PK-12
PO Box 642 56572 218-863-5910
Randi Anderson, supt. Fax 863-5915
www.pelicanrapids.k12.mn.us

Viking ES 500/PK-6
PO Box 642 56572 218-863-2911
Edwin Richardson, prin. Fax 863-5358

Pequot Lakes, Crow Wing, Pop. 2,149
Pequot Lakes SD 186 1,600/PK-12
30805 Olson St 56472 218-568-4996
Chris Lindholm, supt. Fax 568-5259
www.isd186.org
Pequot Lakes MS 500/5-8
30805 Olson St 56472 218-568-9357
Michael O'Neil, prin. Fax 568-9202
Other Schools – See Breezy Point

Perham, Otter Tail, Pop. 2,944
Perham-Dent SD 549 1,400/PK-12
200 5th St SE 56573 218-346-4501
Mitch Anderson, supt. Fax 346-4506
www.perham.k12.mn.us
Heart of Lake ES 500/PK-4
810 2nd Ave SW 56573 218-346-5437
Jen Hendrickson, prin. Fax 346-4634
Prairie Wind MS 400/5-8
480 Coney St W 56573 218-346-1700
Scott Bjerke, prin. Fax 346-1704

St. Henry S 100/K-6
253 2nd St SW 56573 218-346-6190
Jason Smith, prin. Fax 346-6190
St. Paul Lutheran S 100/PK-6
500 6th Ave SW 56573 218-346-2300
Jolene Wagner, prin. Fax 346-2306

Pierz, Morrison, Pop. 1,383
Pierz SD 484 1,100/PK-12
112 Kamnic St 56364 320-468-6458
George Weber, supt. Fax 468-6408
www.pierz.k12.mn.us
Pioneer ES 500/PK-6
66 Kamnic St 56364 320-468-6458
Tom Otte, prin. Fax 468-2841

Holy Trinity S 200/PK-6
PO Box 427 56364 320-468-6446
Debra Meyer-Myrum, prin. Fax 468-6446

Pillager, Cass, Pop. 463
Pillager SD 116 500/PK-12
323 E 2nd St 56473 218-746-2100
Michael Malmberg, supt. Fax 746-4236
www.isd116.org
Pillager ES 400/PK-4
323 E 2nd St 56473 218-746-2110
Josh Smith, prin. Fax 746-2134
Pillager MS 100/5-8
323 E 2nd St 56473 218-746-2112
Scott Doss, prin. Fax 746-2153

Pine City, Pine, Pop. 3,072
Pine City SD 578 1,700/K-12
1400 Main St S 55063 320-629-4010
Annette Freiheit, supt. Fax 629-4070
www.pinecity.k12.mn.us
Pine City ES 900/K-6
700 6th Ave SW 55063 320-629-4200
Stephanie Lorsung, prin. Fax 629-4205

Pine Island, Goodhue, Pop. 3,224
Pine Island SD 255 700/PK-12
PO Box 398 55963 507-356-4849
Dr. Tammy Berg, supt. Fax 356-8827
www.pineisland.k12.mn.us
Pine Island S 400/PK-4
PO Box 398 55963 507-356-8581
Dr. Cindy Hansen, prin. Fax 356-6406

Pine River, Cass, Pop. 928
Pine River-Backus SD 2174 900/PK-12
PO Box 610 56474 218-587-4720
David Endicott, supt. Fax 587-4120
www.prbschools.org
Pine River-Backus ES 500/PK-6
PO Box 610 56474 218-587-4447
Richard Aulie, prin. Fax 587-8390

Pipestone, Pipestone, Pop. 4,229
Pipestone Area SD 2689 1,200/PK-12
1401 7th St SW 56164 507-825-5861
Kevin Enerson, supt. Fax 825-6729
www.pas.k12.mn.us
Brown ES 200/PK-1
701 7th St SE 56164 507-825-6756
Toni Baartman, prin. Fax 825-6749
Hill ES 300/2-4
900 6th Ave SW 56164 507-825-6763
Toni Baartman, prin. Fax 825-6757
Pipestone MS 300/5-8
1401 7th St SW 56164 507-825-5861
Cory Strasser, prin. Fax 825-6729
Other Schools – See Lake Benton

Plainview, Wabasha, Pop. 3,322
Plainview-Elgin-Millville ISD 2899 1,500/PK-12
500 W Broadway 55964 507-534-3651
William Ihrke, supt. Fax 534-3907
www.pem.k12.mn.us/
Plainview-Elgin-Millville ES 500/PK-3
600 W Broadway 55964 507-534-4232
Jake Donze, prin. Fax 534-0132
Other Schools – See Elgin

Immanuel Lutheran S 100/PK-8
30 S Wabasha 55964 507-534-2108
Alvin Lutringer, prin. Fax 534-2579

Plummer, Red Lake, Pop. 286
Red Lake County Central ISD 2906
Supt. — See Oklee
Red Lake County Central ES 200/PK-6
PO Box 7 56748 218-465-4222
Andy Fougner, prin. Fax 465-4225

Plymouth, Hennepin, Pop. 69,055
Robbinsdale SD 281
Supt. — See New Hope
Plymouth MS 1,300/6-8
10011 36th Ave N 55441 763-504-7100
Cheri Kulland, prin. Fax 504-7131
Zachary Lane ES 600/K-5
4350 Zachary Ln N 55442 763-504-7300
Randy Moberg, prin. Fax 504-7309

Wayzata SD 284 11,200/PK-12
210 County Road 101 N 55447 763-745-5000
Dr. Chace B. Anderson, supt. Fax 745-5091
www.wayzata.k12.mn.us
Birchview ES 600/K-5
425 Ranchview Ln N 55447 763-745-5300
Sam Fredrickson, prin. Fax 745-5391
Gleason Lake ES 700/PK-5
310 County Road 101 N 55447 763-745-5400
Mary McKasy, prin. Fax 745-5491
Greenwood ES 800/K-5
18005 Medina Rd, 763-745-5500
Brad Gustafson, prin. Fax 745-5591
Kimberly Lane ES 700/K-5
17405 Old Rockford Rd, 763-745-5600
Kari Wehrmann, prin. Fax 745-5691
Meadow Ridge ES 800/K-5
17905 County Road 47, 763-745-7100
Karen Keffeler, prin. Fax 745-7191
Oakwood ES 500/K-5
17340 County Road 6 55447 763-745-5700
Sarabeth Deneui, prin. Fax 745-5791
Plymouth Creek ES 700/K-5
16005 41st Ave N, 763-745-5800
Karla Thompson, prin. Fax 745-5891
Sunset Hill ES 600/K-5
13005 Sunset Trl 55441 763-745-5900
Ross Williams, prin. Fax 745-5991
Wayzata Central MS 1,100/6-8
305 Vicksburg Ln N 55447 763-745-6000
Clark Doten, prin. Fax 745-6091
Wayzata East MS 800/6-8
12000 Ridgemount Ave W 55441 763-745-6200
Paul Paetzel, prin. Fax 745-6291
Other Schools – See Wayzata

Providence Academy 900/PK-12
15100 Schmidt Lake Rd, 763-258-2500
Dr. Todd Flanders, hdmstr. Fax 258-2501

Ponemah, Beltrami, Pop. 722
Red Lake SD 38
Supt. — See Redlake
Ponemah ES 200/PK-8
25039 Abinojii Dr 56666 218-554-7337
Aaron Jabs, prin. Fax 554-7442

Ponsford, Becker
Pine Point SD 25 100/K-8
PO Box 8 56575 218-573-4100
Chris Schulz, supt. Fax 573-4128
www.pinepoint.k12.mn.us
Pine Point S 100/K-8
PO Box 8 56575 218-573-4100
Chris Schulz, prin. Fax 573-4128

Preston, Fillmore, Pop. 1,314
Fillmore Central SD 2198 600/PK-12
PO Box 50 55965 507-765-3845
Richard Keith, supt. Fax 765-3636
www.fillmorecentral.k12.mn.us/
Fillmore Central ES 300/PK-6
PO Box 50 55965 507-765-3809
Heath Olstad, prin. Fax 765-2367

Princeton, Mille Lacs, Pop. 4,614
Princeton SD 477 3,300/PK-12
706 1st St 55371 763-389-2422
Dr. Julia Espe, supt. Fax 389-9142
www.princeton.k12.mn.us
Princeton IS 700/3-5
1202 7th Ave N 55371 763-389-6801
John Beach, prin. Fax 389-6850
Princeton MS 800/6-8
1100 4th Ave N 55371 763-389-6704
Dan Voce, prin. Fax 389-6737
Princeton PS 800/PK-2
1206 7th Ave N 55371 763-389-6901
Gregory Finck, prin. Fax 389-6920

Prinsburg, Kandiyohi, Pop. 492

Central Minnesota Christian S 300/PK-12
PO Box 98 56281 320-978-8700
Peter Van Der Puy, supt. Fax 978-8797

Prior Lake, Scott, Pop. 22,273
Prior Lake - Savage Area SD 719 7,400/K-12
4540 Tower St SE 55372 952-226-0000
Teri Staloch, supt. Fax 226-0059
www.priorlake-savage.k12.mn.us
Edgewood S 200/K-3
5304 Westwood Dr SE 55372 952-226-0900
Richie Kucinski, coord. Fax 226-0949
Five Hawks ES 500/K-5
16620 Five Hawks Ave SE 55372 952-226-0100
Tim Bell, prin. Fax 226-0149
Grainwood ES 300/K-5
5061 Minnesota St SE 55372 952-226-0300
Patrick Glynn, prin. Fax 226-0349
Hidden Oaks MS 900/6-8
15855 Fish Point Rd SE 55372 952-226-0700
Sasha Kuznetsov, prin. Fax 226-0749
Jeffers Pond ES 500/K-5
14800 Jeffers Pass NW 55372 952-226-0600
Dr. Karoline Warner, prin. Fax 226-0649
SAGE Academy 3-5
5370 Westwood Dr SE 55372 952-226-0400
Karen Zwolenski, coord. Fax 226-0449
Twin Oaks MS 800/6-8
15860 Fish Point Rd SE 55372 952-226-0500
Dr. Dan Edwards, prin. Fax 226-0549
Westwood ES 500/K-5
5370 Westwood Dr SE 55372 952-226-0400
Karen Zwolenski, prin. Fax 226-0449
Other Schools – See Savage

St. Michael S 500/PK-8
16280 Duluth Ave SE 55372 952-447-2124
Laurie Maxwell, prin. Fax 447-2132
St. Paul's Lutheran S 100/K-8
5634 Luther Rd SE 55372 952-447-2117
Sue Brown, admin. Fax 447-2119

Proctor, Saint Louis, Pop. 3,021
Proctor SD 704 1,800/PK-12
131 9th Ave 55810 218-628-4934
John Engelking, supt. Fax 628-4937
www.proctor.k12.mn.us
Community Ed. ECC PK-PK
131 9th Ave 55810 218-628-4958
Jedlicka MS 400/6-8
131 9th Ave 55810 218-628-4926
Tim Rohweder, prin. Fax 628-4932
Other Schools – See Duluth

Ramsey, Anoka, Pop. 23,299
Anoka-Hennepin SD 11
Supt. — See Anoka
Ramsey ES 1,300/K-5
15000 Nowthen Blvd NW 55303 763-506-4000
Jeff Clusiau, prin. Fax 506-4003

Randall, Morrison, Pop. 644
Little Falls SD 482
Supt. — See Little Falls
Knight ES 100/K-5
PO Box 185 56475 320-616-5200
Larry Edgerton, prin. Fax 749-2147

Randolph, Dakota, Pop. 430
Randolph SD 195 600/PK-12
PO Box 38 55065 507-263-2151
Michael Kelley, supt. Fax 645-5950
www.randolph.k12.mn.us
Randolph ES 300/PK-6
PO Box 38 55065 507-263-2151
Matt Rutledge, prin. Fax 645-5950

Raymond, Kandiyohi, Pop. 759
MACCRAY SD
Supt. — See Clara City
MACCRAY East ES 200/PK-6
PO Box 215 56282 320-967-4281
Doug Runia, prin. Fax 967-4283

Redlake, Beltrami, Pop. 1,719
Red Lake SD 38 1,300/PK-12
PO Box 499 56671 218-679-3353
Melinda Crowley, supt. Fax 679-2321
www.redlake.k12.mn.us
Red Lake ES 500/PK-5
PO Box 499 56671 218-679-3329
Reed Carlson, prin. Fax 679-3644
Red Lake MS 200/6-8
PO Box 499 56671 218-679-3733
Mark Bensen, prin. Fax 679-2717
Other Schools – See Ponemah

St. Marys Mission S 100/PK-6
PO Box 189 56671 218-679-3388
Greg Ferrin, prin. Fax 679-2231

Red Lake Falls, Red Lake, Pop. 1,407
Red Lake Falls SD 630 400/PK-12
PO Box 399 56750 218-253-2139
Jim Guetter, supt. Fax 253-2135
www.redlakefalls.k12.mn.us
Hughes ES 200/PK-6
PO Box 7 56750 218-253-2161
Chris Bjerklie, prin. Fax 253-4479

Red Wing, Goodhue, Pop. 16,138
Red Wing SD 256 2,700/K-12
2451 Eagle Ridge Dr 55066 651-385-4500
Karsten Anderson, supt. Fax 385-4510
www.rwps.org
Burnside ES 600/2-4
5001 Learning Ln 55066 651-385-4700
Jennifer Bordonaro, prin. Fax 385-4710
Sunnyside ES 500/K-2
1669 Southwood Ave 55066 651-385-4570
Michael Pagel, prin. Fax 385-4576
Twin Bluff MS 600/5-7
2120 Twin Bluff Rd 55066 651-385-4530
Chris Palmatier, prin. Fax 385-4540

St. John Lutheran S 100/PK-8
421 East Ave 55066 651-388-2611
Chris Avila, prin. Fax 388-8325

Redwood Falls, Redwood, Pop. 5,083
Redwood Area SD 2897 1,100/PK-12
100 George Ramseth Dr 56283 507-644-3531
Rick Ellingworth, supt. Fax 644-3057
www.redwoodareaschools.com
Gray ES 400/PK-4
201 McPhail Dr 56283 507-644-2627
Paul van der Hagen, prin. Fax 644-8138
Redwood Valley MS 300/5-8
100 George Ramseth Dr 56283 507-644-3521
Amanda Pederson, prin. Fax 644-3057

St. John Lutheran S 100/PK-8
34719 County Highway 24 56283 507-617-3002
David Gartner, prin. Fax 617-3003

Remer, Cass, Pop. 366
Northland Community SD 118 300/PK-12
316 Main St E 56672 218-566-2351
John McDonald, supt. Fax 566-2053
www.isd118.k12.mn.us
Remer ES 200/PK-6
316 Main St E Rm 500 56672 218-566-2351
Clayton Lindner, prin. Fax 566-2053

Renville, Renville, Pop. 1,277
Renville County West SD 2890 200/K-12
PO Box 338 56284 320-329-8362
Michelle Mortensen, supt. Fax 329-3271
www.rcw.k12.mn.us
Renville County West S 200/K-12
PO Box 338 56284 320-329-8368
Fax 329-8191

Rice, Benton, Pop. 1,253
Sauk Rapids-Rice SD 47
Supt. — See Sauk Rapids
Rice ES 300/PK-5
PO Box 25 56367 320-393-2177
Sue Paasch, prin. Fax 393-2140

Richfield, Hennepin, Pop. 34,223
Richfield SD 280 4,100/PK-12
7001 Harriet Ave 55423 612-798-6000
Steven Unowsky, supt. Fax 798-6057
www.richfieldschools.org
Centennial ES 500/PK-5
7315 Bloomington Ave 55423 612-798-6800
Lee Ann Wise, prin. Fax 798-6827
Richfield Dual Language ES 300/PK-3
7001 Elliot Ave S 55423 612-798-6700
Marta Shahsavand, prin. Fax 798-6727
Richfield MS 900/6-8
7461 Oliver Ave S 55423 612-798-6400
Brian Zambreno, prin. Fax 798-6427
Richfield STEM S 800/PK-5
7020 12th Ave S 55423 612-798-6600
Amy Winter, prin. Fax 798-6664
Sheridan Hills ES 500/PK-5
6400 Sheridan Ave S 55423 612-798-6900
Nancy Stachel, prin. Fax 798-6927

Blessed Trinity S - Nicollet Campus 100/4-8
6720 Nicollet Ave 55423 612-869-5200
Patrick O'Keefe, prin. Fax 767-2191
Blessed Trinity S - Penn Campus 200/PK-3
7540 Penn Ave S 55423 612-866-6906
Patrick O'Keefe, prin. Fax 234-4707

Richmond, Stearns, Pop. 1,413
Rocori SD 750
Supt. — See Cold Spring
Richmond ES 100/K-5
PO Box 489 56368 320-597-2016
Mary Holmberg, prin. Fax 597-2955

SS. Peter & Paul S 100/K-6
PO Box 189 56368 320-597-2565
Jacqueline Walz, prin. Fax 597-4385

Robbinsdale, Hennepin, Pop. 13,450
Robbinsdale SD 281
Supt. — See New Hope
Lakeview ES 400/K-5
4110 Lake Drive Ave N 55422 763-504-4100
Bridget Hall, prin. Fax 504-4109
Robbinsdale MS 1,300/6-8
3730 Toledo Ave N 55422 763-504-4800
George Nolan, prin. Fax 504-4831

Sacred Heart S 300/PK-8
4050 Hubbard Ave N 55422 763-537-1329
Karen Bursey, prin. Fax 537-1486

Rochester, Olmsted, Pop. 104,165
Rochester ISD 535 15,500/PK-12
615 7th St SW 55902 507-328-3000
Michael Munoz, supt. Fax 328-4212
www.rochester.k12.mn.us
Adams MS 1,100/6-8
1525 31st St NW 55901 507-328-5700
Kim McDonald, prin. Fax 280-4726
Bamber Valley ES 900/PK-5
2001 Bamber Valley Rd SW 55902 507-328-3030
Brenda Wichmann, prin. Fax 328-3035
Bishop ES 400/K-5
406 36th Ave NW 55901 507-328-3100
Jared Groehler, prin. Fax 287-7847
Churchill ES, 2240 7th Ave NE 55906 200/K-2
Ryan Eversman, prin. 507-328-3150
Elton Hills ES 500/K-5
1421 Elton Hills Dr NW 55901 507-328-3200
Brant Goetz, prin. Fax 287-7833
Folwell ES, 603 15th Ave SW 55902 300/K-5
Wendy Moritz, prin. 507-328-3220
Franklin ES 200/K-5
1801 9th Ave SE 55904 507-328-3300
George Nemanich, prin. Fax 328-3295
Friedell MS 500/6-8
1200 S Broadway 55904 507-328-5650
Levi Lundak, prin. Fax 328-5635
Gage ES 600/K-5
1300 40th St NW 55901 507-328-3400
Nichole Bergerson, prin. Fax 328-3395
Gibbs ES 800/K-5
5525 56th St NW 55901 507-328-4100
Michelle Schrantz, prin. Fax 328-4105
Hoover ES 200/3-5
369 Elton Hills Dr NW 55901 507-328-3450
Ryan Eversman, prin. Fax 328-3451
Jefferson ES 500/K-5
1201 10th Ave NE 55906 507-328-3500
Chris Lingen, prin. Fax 328-3495
Kellogg MS, 503 17th St NE 55906 800/6-8
Eric Johnson, prin. 507-328-5800

Lincoln S 400/K-8
1122 8th Ave SE 55904 507-328-3550
James Sonju, prin. Fax 328-3545
Longfellow ES 300/K-5
1615 Marion Rd SE 55904 507-328-3600
Kris Davidson, prin. Fax 287-7842
Pinewood ES 300/K-5
1900 Pinewood Rd SE 55904 507-328-3630
Paul Ehling, prin.
Riverside Central ES 700/K-5
506 5th Ave SE 55904 507-328-3700
Matt Ruzek, prin. Fax 328-3701
Sunset Terrace ES 700/PK-5
1707 19th Ave NW 55901 507-328-3770
Heather Hogen, prin. Fax 328-3765
Washington ES 300/K-5
1200 11th Ave NW 55901 507-328-3800
Chad Schroeder, prin.
Willow Creek MS 1,000/6-8
2425 11th Ave SE 55904 507-328-5900
Nancy Denzer, prin. Fax 328-5905

Holy Spirit S 400/PK-8
5455 50th Ave NW 55901 507-288-8818
Lynette Lenoch M.Ed., prin. Fax 288-5155
Resurrection Lutheran S 100/PK-8
4520 19th Ave NW 55901 507-282-8280
Fax 285-9724
Rochester Central Lutheran S 300/PK-8
2619 9th Ave NW 55901 507-289-3267
Suzanne Lagerwaard, prin. Fax 287-6588
Rochester Montessori S 200/PK-8
5099 7th St NW 55901 507-288-8725
Michael Wridt, head sch Fax 288-4186
St. Francis of Assisi S 500/PK-8
318 11th Ave SE 55904 507-288-4816
Barb Plenge, prin. Fax 288-4815
St. John the Evangelist S 300/5-8
424 W Center St 55902 507-282-5248
Erin Widman, prin. Fax 282-1343
St. Pius X S 300/PK-4
1205 12th Ave NW 55901 507-282-5161
Erin Widman, prin. Fax 282-5107
Schaeffer Academy 400/K-12
2700 Schaeffer Ln NE 55906 507-286-1050
Keith E. Phillips, hdmstr. Fax 282-3823

Rockford, Wright, Pop. 4,215
Rockford Area ISD 883 1,500/PK-12
6051 Ash St 55373 763-477-9165
Paul Durand, supt. Fax 477-5833
www.rockford.k12.mn.us
Rockford Elementary Arts Magnet S 700/PK-4
7650 County Road 50 55373 763-477-5837
Brenda Nyhus, prin. Fax 477-5025
Rockford MS Center for Environmental Std 400/5-8
6051 Ash St 55373 763-477-5831
Dr. Bobbi Anderson-Hume, prin. Fax 477-5832

Rockville, Stearns, Pop. 2,436
Rocori SD 750
Supt. — See Cold Spring
Clark ES 100/K-5
PO Box 37 56369 320-251-8651
Sam Court, prin. Fax 251-8430

Rogers, Hennepin, Pop. 8,439
Elk River Area SD 728
Supt. — See Elk River
Hassan ES 800/K-5
14055 Orchid Ave 55374 763-274-7230
Heidi Adamson-Baer, prin. Fax 274-7231
Rogers ES 700/K-5
12521 Main St 55374 763-241-3462
Phil Schreifels, prin. Fax 428-8475
Rogers MS 1,000/6-8
20855 141st Ave N 55374 763-241-3550
Mark Huss, prin. Fax 241-3518

Mary Queen of Peace S 100/PK-5
21201 Church Ave 55374 763-428-2355
Michael Gerard, prin. Fax 428-2062

Rollingstone, Winona, Pop. 663
Winona Area SD 861
Supt. — See Winona
Rollingstone Community ES 100/PK-4
61 Main St 55969 507-689-2171
Dawn Lueck, prin. Fax 689-2934

Roseau, Roseau, Pop. 2,615
Roseau SD 682 1,200/PK-12
509 3rd St NE 56751 218-463-1471
Dr. Larry Guggisberg, supt. Fax 463-3243
www.roseau.k12.mn.us
Roseau ES 700/PK-6
509 3rd St NE 56751 218-463-2746
Wayne LePard, prin. Fax 463-1016

Rose Creek, Mower, Pop. 387
Southland SD 500
Supt. — See Adams
Southland ES 200/K-5
201 1st St NE 55970 507-437-3214
Brian Schoen, prin. Fax 433-2368

Rosemount, Dakota, Pop. 21,334
Rosemount-Apple Valley-Eagan ISD 196 26,600/PK-12
3455 153rd St W 55068 651-423-7700
Jane Berenz, supt. Fax 423-7633
www.district196.org
East Lake ES, 4715 162nd St, PK-5
Miles Haugen, prin. 952-423-7896
Parkview ES 700/K-5
6795 Gerdine Path W 55068 952-431-8350
Nicole Frovik, prin. Fax 431-8346
Rosemount ES 700/K-5
3155 143rd St W 55068 651-423-7690
Tom Idstrom, prin. Fax 423-7668
Rosemount MS 1,200/6-8
3135 143rd St W 55068 651-423-7570
Eric Hansen, prin. Fax 423-7664
Shannon Park ES 800/K-5
13501 Shannon Pkwy 55068 651-423-7670
Erik Davis, prin. Fax 423-7667
Other Schools – See Apple Valley, Burnsville, Eagan

First Baptist S 200/PK-12
14400 Diamond Path W 55068 651-423-2272
Scott Cain, prin. Fax 423-8844
St. Joseph S 200/K-8
13900 Biscayne Ave W 55068 651-423-1658
Kelly Roche, prin. Fax 423-4402

Roseville, Ramsey, Pop. 32,857
Roseville Area SD 623 7,400/K-12
1251 County Road B2 W 55113 651-635-1600
Dr. Aldo Sicoli, supt. Fax 635-1659
www.isd623.org
Brimhall ES 700/K-6
1744 County Road B W 55113 651-638-1958
Penny Bidne, prin. Fax 638-9007
Central Park ES 500/K-6
535 County Road B2 W 55113 651-481-9951
Becky Berkas, prin. Fax 481-7128
Parkview Center S 800/K-8
701 County Road B W 55113 651-487-4360
Kristen Smith Olson, prin. Fax 487-4379
Other Schools – See Falcon Heights, Little Canada, Maplewood, Saint Paul, Shoreview

---

King of Kings Lutheran S 100/PK-8
2330 Dale St N 55113 651-484-9206
Dan Maser, prin. Fax 484-4346
North Heights Christian Academy 200/K-8
2701 Rice St 55113 651-797-7900
Jeff Taylor, prin. Fax 797-7977
St. Rose of Lima S 300/PK-8
2072 Hamline Ave N 55113 651-646-3832
Sean Slaikeu, prin. Fax 647-6437

Rothsay, Wilkin, Pop. 493
Rothsay SD 850 100/PK-12
2040 County Road 52 56579 218-867-2117
Allen Stoeckman, supt. Fax 867-2376
www.rothsay.k12.mn.us
Rothsay S 100/PK-12
2040 County Road 52 56579 218-867-2116
Wade Johnson, prin. Fax 867-2376

Royalton, Morrison, Pop. 1,237
Royalton SD 485 700/PK-12
120 S Hawthorn St 56373 320-584-4000
John Phelps, supt. Fax 584-4249
www.royalton.k12.mn.us
Royalton ECC PK-K
120 S Hawthorn St 56373
Royalton ES 500/1-6
119 N Driftwood St 56373 320-584-4100
Dr. Philipp Gurbada, prin. Fax 584-4163

Rush City, Chisago, Pop. 3,060
Rush City SD 139 900/PK-12
PO Box 566 55069 320-358-4855
Teresa Dupre, supt. Fax 358-1351
www.rushcity.k12.mn.us
Jacobson ES 500/PK-6
PO Box 566 55069 320-358-4724
Jason Mielke, prin. Fax 358-1361

Rushford, Fillmore, Pop. 1,721
Rushford-Peterson SD 239 700/PK-12
PO Box 627 55971 507-864-7785
Charles Ehler, supt. Fax 864-2085
www.r-pschools.com
Rushford-Peterson ES 300/PK-5
PO Box 627 55971 507-864-7787
Angela Shepard, prin. Fax 864-2085

Russell, Lyon, Pop. 338
R T R ISD 2902
Supt. — See Tyler
R T R MS 100/6-8
PO Box 310 56169 507-823-4371
Darren Baartman, admin. Fax 823-4657

Ruthton, Pipestone, Pop. 239
R T R ISD 2902
Supt. — See Tyler
R T R ES 300/PK-5
PO Box B 56170 507-658-3301
Patricia Lindeman, prin. Fax 658-3589

Saint Anthony, Hennepin, Pop. 8,057
Saint Anthony-New Brighton SD 282 1,700/PK-12
3303 33rd Ave NE 55418 612-706-1000
William Robert Laney, supt. Fax 706-1020
www.stanthony.k12.mn.us
Saint Anthony MS 400/6-8
3303 33rd Ave NE 55418 612-706-1032
Renee Corneille, prin. Fax 706-1040
Wilshire Park ES 700/PK-5
3600 Highcrest Rd NE 55418 612-706-1202
Kari Page, prin. Fax 706-1240

Saint Augusta, Stearns

St. Mary Help of Christians S 100/K-6
24560 County Road 7, 320-251-3937
Kelly Kirks, prin. Fax 251-3937

Saint Charles, Winona, Pop. 3,695
Saint Charles SD 858 1,000/PK-12
600 E 6th St 55972 507-932-4420
Jeff Apse, supt. Fax 932-4700
www.scschools.net
Saint Charles ES 500/PK-6
925 Church Ave 55972 507-932-4910
Shane McBroom, prin. Fax 932-4912

Saint Clair, Blue Earth, Pop. 859
Saint Clair SD 75 700/PK-12
PO Box 99 56080 507-245-3501
Tom Bruels, supt. Fax 245-3517
www.stclair.new.rschooltoday.com
Saint Clair ES 400/PK-6
PO Box 99 56080 507-245-3533
Nadine Holland, admin. Fax 245-3378

Saint Cloud, Stearns, Pop. 64,343
Saint Cloud Area SD 742 9,800/PK-12
1000 44th Ave N 56303 320-253-9333
Willie Jett, supt. Fax 529-4343
www.isd742.org
Lincoln ES 400/K-5
336 5th Ave SE 56304 320-251-6343
BriAnne Hern, prin. Fax 251-9488
Madison ES 800/PK-5
2805 9th St N 56303 320-252-4665
Kate Flynn, prin. Fax 252-6971
North JHS 800/6-8
1212 29th Ave N 56303 320-251-2159
Ellen Stewart, prin. Fax 251-7350
Oak Hill Community ES 800/PK-5
2600 County Road 136 56301 320-251-7936
Mike Rivard, prin. Fax 251-5233
South JHS 1,000/6-8
1120 15th Ave S 56301 320-251-1322
Jason Harris, prin. Fax 251-2911
Talahi Community ES 500/K-5
1321 University Dr SE 56304 320-251-7551
Nicole Hansen, prin. Fax 251-5042
Westwood ES 500/K-5
5800 Ridgewood Rd 56303 320-253-1350
Derek Branton, prin. Fax 253-7794
Other Schools – See Clear Lake, Saint Joseph, Waite Park

All Saints Academy St. Cloud Campus 200/PK-6
1215 11th Ave N 56303 320-251-5295
Paula Leider, admin. Fax 251-5295
Calvary Classical Academy 50/K-9
1200 Roosevelt Rd 56301 320-251-4825
Carol Kuhn, hdmstr. Fax 251-5646
Prince of Peace Lutheran S 300/PK-8
4770 County Road 120 56303 320-251-1477
Rev. David Strohschein, admin. Fax 251-8996
Saint Cloud Christian S 200/K-12
430 3rd Ave NE 56304 320-252-8182
Karen Goyette, admin. Fax 656-9678
St. Elizabeth Ann Seton S 200/K-6
1615 11th Ave S 56301 320-251-1988
Kelly Vangsness, prin. Fax 229-2149
St. Katharine Drexel S 300/PK-6
428 2nd St SE 56304 320-251-2376
Erin Hatlestad, prin. Fax 529-3222
St. Wendelin S 100/PK-6
22776 State Highway 15 56301 320-251-9175
Lynn Rasmussen, prin. Fax 654-9030

Saint Francis, Anoka, Pop. 7,077
Saint Francis SD 15 4,800/K-12
4115 Ambassador Blvd NW 55070 763-753-7040
Troy Ferguson, supt. Fax 753-4693
www.isd15.org
Saint Francis ES 700/K-5
22919 Saint Francis Blvd NW 55070 763-213-8670
Ryan Johnson, prin. Fax 753-5180
Saint Francis MS 1,100/6-8
23026 Ambassador Blvd NW 55070 763-213-8500
Bobbi Hume, prin. Fax 753-3821
Other Schools – See Cedar

Crown Christian S 50/PK-8
7515 269th Ave NW 55070 763-856-2099
Rachel Schutte, prin. Fax 856-5997
St. Francis Christian S 100/K-12
22940 Saint Francis Blvd NW 55070 763-753-1230
Jeremy Zajicek, admin.
Trinity Lutheran S 100/PK-8
3812 229th Ave NW 55070 763-753-1234
Rev. Keaton Christiansen, prin. Fax 753-1774

Saint James, Watonwan, Pop. 4,579
Saint James SD 840 1,000/PK-12
PO Box 509 56081 507-375-5974
Becky Cselovszki, supt. Fax 375-7143
www.stjames.k12.mn.us
Armstrong S 100/PK-PK
600 Armstrong Blvd S 56081 507-375-3321
Doug Storbeck, admin. Fax 375-3323
Saint James Northside ES 300/K-5
1273 10th Ave N 56081 507-375-3325
Doug Storbeck, prin. Fax 375-3327

St. Paul's Lutheran S 50/PK-8
315 9th St S 56081 507-375-3809
Jared Christensen, prin. Fax 375-3809

Saint Joseph, Stearns, Pop. 6,430
Saint Cloud Area SD 742
Supt. — See Saint Cloud
Colt's Academy ECC 200/PK-PK
3015 3rd St N 56374 320-253-5828
Julie Midas, dir. Fax 253-5828
Kennedy Community S 700/PK-8
1300 Jade Rd 56374 320-363-7791
Laurie Putnam, prin. Fax 529-4336

All Saints Academy St. Joseph Campus 200/PK-6
32 W Minnesota St 56374 320-363-7769
Karl Terhaar, prin. Fax 363-7760

Saint Louis Park, Hennepin, Pop. 43,914
Saint Louis Park SD 283 4,500/K-12
6425 W 33rd St 55426 952-928-6000
Astein Osie, supt. Fax 928-6020
www.slpschools.org

Aquila ES 600/K-5
8500 W 31st St 55426 952-928-6500
Clarence Pollock, prin. Fax 928-6466
Hobart ES 600/K-5
6500 W 26th St 55426 952-928-6600
Shelley Nielsen, prin. Fax 928-6643
Lindgren ES 500/K-5
4801 W 41st St 55416 952-928-6700
Frank Johnson, prin. Fax 928-6716
Park Spanish Immersion ES 500/K-5
6300 Walker St 55416 952-928-6759
Corey Maslowski, prin. Fax 928-6753
Saint Louis Park MS 1,000/6-8
2025 Texas Ave S 55426 952-928-6300
Les Bork, prin. Fax 928-6383

Groves Academy 200/1-12
3200 Highway 100 S 55416 952-920-6377
Kim Peeples, head sch Fax 920-2068
Heilicher Minneapolis Jewish Day S 400/K-8
4330 Cedar Lake Rd S 55416 952-381-3500
Yoni Binus, head sch Fax 381-3501
Holy Family Academy 200/PK-8
5925 W Lake St 55416 952-925-9193
Jim Grogan, prin. Fax 925-5298
Torah Academy 200/PK-8
2800 Joppa Ave S 55416 952-920-6630
Jordan Ford, prin. Fax 922-7844
Westwood ECC 100/PK-K
9001 Cedar Lake Rd S 55426 952-545-5624
Kellee Nelson, dir.

Saint Michael, Wright, Pop. 16,153
Saint Michael-Albertville SD 885
Supt. — See Albertville
Big Woods ES 600/1-4
13470 Frankfort Pkwy NE 55376 763-497-8025
Lee Brown, prin. Fax 497-6563
Fieldstone ES 700/1-4
5255 Jansen Ave NE 55376 763-497-0904
Jeanette Aanerud, prin. Fax 497-6557
Saint Michael-Albertville MS East 5-8
4862 Naber Ave NE 55376 763-497-2655
Jennifer Kelly, prin. Fax 497-6591
Saint Michael ES 600/PK-4
101 Central Ave W 55376 763-497-4882
Corey Lahr, prin. Fax 497-6592

St. Michael S 400/PK-8
14 Main St N 55376 763-497-3887
Jennifer Haller, prin. Fax 497-9159

Saint Paul, Ramsey, Pop. 275,178
Roseville Area SD 623
Supt. — See Roseville
Little Canada ES 500/K-6
400 Eli Rd 55117 651-490-1353
Garin Bogenholm, prin. Fax 490-1436

Saint Paul SD 625 35,900/PK-12
360 Colborne St 55102 651-767-8100
Dr. Joe Gothard, supt. Fax 293-8586
www.spps.org
Adams Spanish Immersion Magnet ES 700/K-5
615 Chatsworth St S 55102 651-298-1595
Heidi Bernal, prin. Fax 298-1598
American Indian Magnet S 700/PK-8
1075 3rd St E 55106 651-778-3100
Todd Goggleye, prin. Fax 778-3101
Battle Creek Environmental Magnet S 400/PK-5
60 Ruth St S 55119 651-293-8850
Craig Anderson, prin. Fax 293-5396
Battle Creek MS 900/6-8
2121 N Park Dr 55119 651-293-8960
Lanisha Paddock, prin. Fax 293-8866
Capitol Hill Magnet S 1,300/1-8
560 Concordia Ave 55103 651-325-2500
Patrick Bryan, prin. Fax 325-2501
Chelsea Heights ES 400/PK-5
1557 Huron St 55108 651-293-8790
Jill Gebeke, prin. Fax 293-8793
Cherokee Heights West Side S 300/PK-5
694 Charlton St 55107 651-293-8610
Melisa Rivera, prin. Fax 293-8617
Como Park ES 500/PK-5
780 Wheelock Pkwy W 55117 651-293-8820
Christine Vang, prin. Fax 293-8828
Crossroads Montessori S 300/PK-5
543 Front Ave 55117 651-767-8540
Celeste Carty, prin. Fax 312-9003
Daytons Bluff ES 400/PK-5
262 Bates Ave 55106 651-293-8915
Lena Christiansen, prin. Fax 771-3428
Eastern Heights ES 400/PK-5
2001 Margaret St 55119 651-293-8870
Howard Wilson, prin. Fax 293-8982
Expo ES 700/PK-5
540 Warwick St 55116 651-290-8384
Darren Yerama, prin. Fax 293-8639
Farnsworth Aerospace Magnet ES 600/PK-4
1290 Arcade St 55106 651-293-8675
Laura Saatzer, prin. Fax 293-8679
Farnsworth Aerospace Magnet MS 700/5-8
1000 Walsh St 55106 651-293-8880
Hamilton Bell, prin. Fax 293-8888
Four Seasons A+ ES 400/PK-5
318 Moore St 55104 651-290-7595
Heidi George, prin. Fax 293-6575
Frost Lake Magnet ES 500/PK-5
1505 Hoyt Ave E 55106 651-293-8930
Stacey Kadrmas, prin. Fax 293-8932
Galtier Magnet ES 200/PK-5
1317 Charles Ave 55104 651-293-8710
Sharon Hendrix, prin. Fax 293-8973
Groveland Park ES 500/K-5
2045 Saint Clair Ave 55105 651-293-8760
Rebecca Pederson, prin. Fax 293-8653
Hamline ES 300/PK-5
1599 Englewood Ave 55104 651-293-8715
Bobbie Johnson, prin. Fax 293-8718
Hazel Park Prep Academy 600/PK-8
1140 White Bear Ave N 55106 651-293-8970
Delores Henderson, prin. Fax 293-8976
Heights Community S 600/PK-5
1863 Clear Ave 55119 651-293-8815
Chreese Jones, prin. Fax 293-8977
Highland Park ES 400/K-5
1700 Saunders Ave 55116 651-293-8770
Nancy Flynn, prin. Fax 293-8983
Highland Park MS 900/6-8
975 Snelling Ave S 55116 651-293-8950
Charlene Hoff, prin. Fax 293-8953
Highwood Hills ES 300/PK-5
2188 Londin Ln E 55119 651-744-3290
Fatima Lawson, prin.
Hill Montessori Magnet S 400/PK-5
998 Selby Ave 55104 651-293-8720
Maura Brink, prin. Fax 298-1586
Jackson Preparatory Magnet ES 400/PK-5
437 Edmund Ave 55103 651-293-8650
Bee Lee, prin. Fax 228-7742
Johnson Achievement Plus ES 400/PK-5
740 York Ave 55106 651-793-7300
Lisa Gruenewald, prin. Fax 793-7310
L'Etoile Du Nord French Immersion ES 400/2-5
1760 Ames Pl 55106 651-221-1480
Lourdes Flores-Hanson, prin. Fax 744-6971
L'Etoile Du Nord French Immersion PS 200/K-1
1305 Prosperity Ave 55106 651-221-1480
Lourdes Flores-Hanson, prin. Fax 221-1487
Linwood Monroe Arts Plus ES 300/K-3
1023 Osceola Ave 55105 651-293-6606
Bryan Bass, prin. Fax 293-6605
Linwood Monroe Arts Plus MS 600/4-8
810 Palace Ave 55102 651-293-8690
Bryan Bass, prin. Fax 293-8699
Mann ES 400/K-5
2001 Eleanor Ave 55116 651-293-8965
Jim Litwin, prin. Fax 293-8985
Maxfield Magnet ES 300/PK-5
380 Victoria St N 55104 651-293-8680
Ryan Vernosh, prin. Fax 293-5306
Mays International Magnet S 500/PK-5
560 Concordia Ave 55103 651-325-2400
Kirk Morris, prin. Fax 325-2401
Ming Mandarin Immersion Academy 100/K-5
1599 Englewood Ave 55104 651-293-8715
Bobbie Johnson, prin.
Mississippi Creative Arts Magnet ES 500/PK-5
1575 L Orient St 55117 651-293-8840
Be Vang, prin. Fax 293-8843
Murray MS 800/6-8
2200 Buford Ave 55108 651-293-8740
Stacy Theien-Collins, prin. Fax 293-8742
Nokomis Montessori Magnet S North 300/PK-5
985 Ruth St N 55119 651-744-7440
Melissa McCollor, prin. Fax 293-5464
Nokomis Montessori Magnet S South 200/PK-5
525 White Bear Ave N 55106 651-744-5500
Melissa McCollor, prin. Fax 744-5501
Obama Service Learning ES 500/PK-6
707 Holly Ave 55104 651-293-8625
Adrian Pendelton, prin. Fax 293-8669
Parkway Montessori MS 400/6-8
1363 Bush Ave 55106 651-744-1000
Jocelyn Sims, prin. Fax 744-1001
Phalen Lake Hmong Studies Magnet ES 700/PK-5
1089 Cypress St 55106 651-293-8935
Catherine Rich, prin. Fax 293-8978
Ramsey MS 700/6-8
1700 Summit Ave 55105 651-293-8860
Dr. Teresa Vibar, prin. Fax 298-1587
Randolph Heights ES 500/PK-5
348 Hamline Ave S 55105 651-293-8780
Jayne Ropella, prin. Fax 293-8986
Riverview West Side S of Excellence 300/PK-5
160 Isabel St E 55107 651-293-8665
Nancy Paez, prin. Fax 293-5303
Saint Anthony Park ES 500/K-5
2180 Knapp St 55108 651-293-8735
Karen Duke, prin. Fax 293-8737
St. Paul Music Academy 500/PK-5
27 Geranium Ave E 55117 651-293-8795
Barbara Evangelist, prin. Fax 293-8798
Vento ES 500/PK-5
409 Case Ave, 651-293-8685
Scott Masini, prin. Fax 293-8688
Wellstone ES 600/PK-5
1041 Marion St 55117 651-290-8354
Angelica Van Iperen, prin. Fax 290-8357

Capital City Adventist Christian S 50/PK-8
1220 McKnight Rd S 55119 651-739-7484
Elizabeth Rodriguez, prin. Fax 739-6383
Central Lutheran S 200/PK-8
775 Lexington Pkwy N 55104 651-645-8649
Elizabeth Wegner, admin. Fax 645-8640
Christ's Household of Faith S 200/PK-12
355 Marshall Ave 55102 651-265-3400
Vernon Harms, prin. Fax 227-9813
Friends S of Minnesota 200/K-8
1365 Englewood Ave 55104 651-917-0636
Jeanette Lutter-Gardella, prin. Fax 917-0708
Highland Catholic S 400/PK-8
2017 Bohland Ave 55116 651-690-2477
Jane Schmidt, prin. Fax 699-1869
Holy Spirit S 300/PK-8
515 Albert St S 55116 651-698-3353
Dr. Mary Adrian, prin. Fax 698-1605
JOY Academy PK-8
655 Forest St 55106 651-771-6982
Robert Orr, prin. Fax 771-6982
Lubavitch Cheder Day S / Chabad Acad 100/PK-8
1758 Ford Pkwy 55116 651-698-0556
Rabbi Shlomo Bendet, dir. Fax 690-3387
Maternity of Mary-St. Andrew S 200/PK-8
592 Arlington Ave W 55117 651-489-1459
Maggie Quast, prin. Fax 489-3560
Minnesota Waldorf S 200/PK-8
70 County Road B E 55117 651-487-6700
Frances Kane, admin. Fax 487-6800
Mounds Park Academy 600/PK-12
2051 Larpenteur Ave E 55109 651-777-2555
Dr. Bill Hudson, head sch Fax 777-8633
Nativity of Our Lord S 800/PK-8
1900 Stanford Ave 55105 651-699-1311
Kate Wollan, prin. Fax 696-5420
St. Agnes S 500/K-12
530 Lafond Ave 55103 651-925-8700
Dr. Kevin Ferdinandt, head sch Fax 925-8708
St. Mark S 300/PK-8
1983 Dayton Ave 55104 651-644-3380
Zach Zeckser, prin. Fax 644-1923
St. Pascal Baylon S 200/PK-8
1757 Conway St 55106 651-776-0092
Laurie Jennrich, prin. Fax 774-9152
St. Paul Academy & Summit ES 300/K-5
1150 Goodrich Ave 55105 651-696-1560
Bryn Roberts, head sch Fax 296-9470
St. Peter Claver S 100/K-8
1060 Central Ave W 55104 651-621-2273
Terese Shimshock, prin. Fax 647-5394
St. Thomas More S 300/PK-8
1065 Summit Ave 55105 651-224-4836
Pat Lofton, prin. Fax 224-0097
Sunny Hollow Montessori S 100/PK-6
636 Mississippi River Blvd 55116 651-690-2307
Renee Campion, head sch Fax 690-0684

Saint Paul Park, Washington, Pop. 5,176
South Washington County SD 833
Supt. — See Cottage Grove
Oltman MS 700/6-8
1020 3rd St 55071 651-425-3500
Joni Hagebock, prin. Fax 425-3555
Pullman ES 400/PK-5
1260 Selby Ave 55071 651-425-3600
Ed Ross, prin. Fax 425-3615

Hope Christian Academy 100/PK-12
920 Holley Ave Ste 2 55071 651-459-6438
Randy Krussow, prin. Fax 769-2108

Saint Peter, Nicollet, Pop. 11,009
Saint Peter SD 508 1,600/PK-12
100 Lincoln Dr 56082 507-934-5703
Dr. Paul Peterson, supt. Fax 934-2805
www.stpeterschools.org
North ES 600/2-4
815 N 9th St 56082 507-934-3260
Darin Doherty, prin. Fax 934-1865
South ES 500/PK-1
1405 S 7th St 56082 507-934-2754
Doreen Oelke, prin. Fax 934-4830

Ireland S 100/K-6
1801 W Broadway Ave 56082 507-931-2810
Colleen Wenner, prin. Fax 931-9179
St. Peter Lutheran S 50/PK-8
427 W Mulberry St 56082 507-931-1866
James Bakken, prin.

Sandstone, Pine, Pop. 2,776

Harvest Christian S 100/PK-12
PO Box 646 55072 320-245-5330
Jack Allen, admin. Fax 245-5330

Sartell, Stearns, Pop. 15,661
Sartell-St. Stephen SD 748 3,700/K-12
212 3rd Ave N 56377 320-656-3715
Jeff Schwiebert, supt. Fax 656-3765
www.sartell.k12.mn.us
Oak Ridge ES 700/K-4
1111 27th St N 56377 320-258-3693
Kristopher Lynk, prin. Fax 258-3694
Pine Meadow ES 700/K-4
1029 5th St N 56377 320-253-8303
Sara Nelson, prin. Fax 656-3766
Sartell MS 1,200/5-8
627 3rd Ave N 56377 320-253-2200
Kurt Stumpf, prin. Fax 253-1403

St. Francis Xavier S 100/PK-6
PO Box 150 56377 320-252-9940
Kathy Kockler, prin. Fax 259-7090

Sauk Centre, Stearns, Pop. 4,294
Sauk Centre SD 743 1,000/PK-12
903 State Rd 56378 320-352-2284
Patrick Westby, supt. Fax 352-3404
www.isd743.org
Sauk Centre ES 500/PK-6
901 State Rd 56378 320-352-6521
Amy Millard, prin. Fax 352-3404

Holy Family S 200/K-6
231 Sinclair Lewis Ave 56378 320-352-6535
Lynn Peterson, prin. Fax 352-6537

Sauk Rapids, Benton, Pop. 12,559
Sauk Rapids-Rice SD 47 4,100/PK-12
1833 Osauka Rd 56379 320-253-4703
Bruce Watkins, supt. Fax 255-1914
www.isd47.org
Mississippi Heights ES 900/PK-5
1003 4th St S 56379 320-252-0122
Tanya Peterson, prin. Fax 258-1399
Pleasantview ES 700/PK-5
1009 6th Ave N 56379 320-253-0506
Aby Froiland, prin. Fax 253-1444
Sauk Rapids-Rice MS 1,000/6-8
901 1st St S 56379 320-654-9073
Dr. Nate Rudolph, prin. Fax 259-8909
Other Schools – See Rice

Petra Lutheran S 50/K-8
1049 1st Ave N 56379 320-251-0158
Terrence Graf, prin.

Savage, Scott, Pop. 26,220
Burnsville-Eagan-Savage ISD 191
Supt. — See Burnsville
Bishop ES 600/K-5
14400 OConnell Rd 55378 952-707-3900
Ken Essay, prin. Fax 707-3902
Eagle Ridge MS 500/6-8
13955 Glendale Rd 55378 952-707-2800
Erika Nesvig, prin. Fax 707-2802
Hidden Valley ES 500/K-5
13875 Glendale Rd 55378 952-707-3800
Kristine Black, prin. Fax 707-3802
Savage ES 400/K-5
4819 W 126th St 55378 952-707-3200
Jeff Nepsund, prin. Fax 707-3202

Prior Lake - Savage Area SD 719
Supt. — See Prior Lake
Glendale ES 600/K-5
6601 Connelly Pkwy 55378 952-226-0200
Jennifer Molitor, prin. Fax 226-0249
Redtail Ridge ES 600/K-5
15200 Hampshire Ave S 55378 952-226-8003
Barb Yetzer, prin. Fax 226-8049

St. John the Baptist S 600/PK-8
12508 Lynn Ave 55378 952-890-6604
Phil Singewald, prin. Fax 890-9481

Scandia, Washington, Pop. 3,907
Forest Lake SD 831
Supt. — See Forest Lake
Scandia ES 400/PK-6
14351 Scandia Trl N 55073 651-982-3300
Julianne Greiman, prin. Fax 982-3349

Sebeka, Wadena, Pop. 700
Sebeka SD 820 500/PK-12
PO Box 249 56477 218-837-5101
Dave Fjeldheim, supt. Fax 837-5967
www.sebeka.k12.mn.us
Sebeka ES 300/PK-6
PO Box 249 56477 218-837-5101
Dave Fjeldheim, prin. Fax 837-5967

Shakopee, Scott, Pop. 36,163
Shakopee SD 720 7,600/K-12
505 Holmes St S 55379 952-496-5000
Gary Anger, supt. Fax 496-5056
www.shakopee.k12.mn.us
Eagle Creek ES 800/K-5
6855 Woodward Ave 55379 952-496-5922
Josie Koivisto, prin. Fax 496-5935
Jackson ES 800/K-5
14601 Lusitano St 55379 952-496-5802
Doug Schleif, prin. Fax 496-5865
Pearson 6th Grade Center 600/6-6
917 Dakota St S 55379 952-496-5862
Kevin Bjerken, prin. Fax 496-5865
Red Oak ES 700/K-5
7700 Old Carriage Ct 55379 952-496-5952
Mitch Perrine, prin. Fax 496-5955
Sun Path ES 700/K-5
2250 17th Ave E 55379 952-496-5892
Patrick Leonard, prin. Fax 496-5895
Sweeney ES 700/K-5
1001 Adams St S 55379 952-496-5832
Melissa Zahn, prin. Fax 496-5835

Living Hope Lutheran S 100/PK-4
8600 Horizon Dr 55379 952-445-1785
Michael Butzow, prin. Fax 445-1822
Shakopee Area Catholic S 900/PK-8
2700 17th Ave E 55379 952-445-3387
Julie Moran, prin. Fax 445-7256

Sherburn, Martin, Pop. 1,125
Martin County West SD 2448 500/K-12
105 E 5th St 56171 507-764-2330
Allison Schmidt, supt. Fax 764-2335
www.martin.k12.mn.us
Sherburn ES 100/K-4
105 E 5th St 56171 507-764-4461
Allison Schmidt, prin. Fax 764-3652
Other Schools – See Trimont

Shoreview, Ramsey, Pop. 24,520
Mounds View SD 621 9,900/K-12
4570 Victoria St N 55126 651-621-6000
Chris Lennox, supt. Fax 621-6046
www.moundsviewschools.org
Island Lake ES 700/1-5
3555 Victoria St N 55126 651-621-7000
Todd Durand, prin. Fax 621-7005
Kindergarten at Snail Lake Edcuation Ctr K-K
350 Highway 96 W 55126 651-621-8000
Kristi Abbott, prin.
Turtle Lake ES 1,000/1-5
1141 Lepak Ct 55126 651-621-7700
Darin Johnson, prin. Fax 621-7705
Other Schools – See Arden Hills, Mounds View, New Brighton, North Oaks

Roseville Area SD 623
Supt. — See Roseville
Williams ES 500/K-6
955 County Road D W 55126 651-482-8624
Brian Koland, prin. Fax 482-0801

Oak Hill Montessori S 200/PK-8
4665 Hodgson Rd 55126 651-484-8242
St. Odilia S 600/PK-8
3495 Victoria St N 55126 651-484-3364
Brian Ragatz, prin. Fax 789-0067

Silver Bay, Lake, Pop. 1,866
Lake Superior SD 381
Supt. — See Two Harbors
Kelley ES 200/PK-6
137 Banks Blvd 55614 218-226-4437
Joe Nicklay, prin. Fax 226-4860

Silver Lake, McLeod, Pop. 834
Glencoe-Silver Lake SD 2859
Supt. — See Glencoe
Lakeside ES 500/3-6
229 Lake Ave 55381 320-864-2500
Diane Schultz, prin. Fax 327-3122

Slayton, Murray, Pop. 2,140
Murray County Central SD 2169 700/PK-12
2420 28th St 56172 507-836-6183
Joe W. Meyer, supt. Fax 836-6375
www.mcc.mntm.org
Murray County Central West ES 400/PK-6
2640 Forest Ave 56172 507-836-6450
Todd Burlingame, prin. Fax 836-6610

Sleepy Eye, Brown, Pop. 3,585
Sleepy Eye SD 84 600/PK-12
400 4th Ave SW 56085 507-794-7903
John Cselovszki, supt. Fax 794-5404
www.sleepyeyeschools.com
Sleepy Eye ES 300/PK-6
400 4th Ave SW 56085 507-794-7905
John Cselovszki, prin. Fax 794-5457

St. John's Lutheran S 50/PK-8
216 3rd Ave SE 56085 507-794-6200
Daniel Rick, prin. Fax 794-6202
St. Mary ES 200/PK-6
104 Saint Marys St NW 56085 507-794-6141
Mary Gangelhoff, prin. Fax 794-4841

Solway, Beltrami, Pop. 93
Bemidji SD 31
Supt. — See Bemidji
Solway ES 100/1-5
159 Lomen Ave NE 56678 218-467-3232
Tami Wesely, prin. Fax 467-3490

South Saint Paul, Dakota, Pop. 19,660
South St. Paul SD 6 3,100/PK-12
104 5th Ave S 55075 651-457-9400
Dr. Dave Webb, supt. Fax 457-9485
www.sspps.org
Kaposia Education Center ES 800/PK-5
1225 1st Ave S 55075 651-451-9260
Terry Bretoi, prin. Fax 457-9453
Lincoln Center ES 900/PK-5
357 9th Ave N 55075 651-457-9426
Mike Fugazzi, prin. Fax 457-9423

Holy Trinity S 100/PK-8
745 6th Ave S 55075 651-455-8557
Dr. Daniel Gleason, prin. Fax 455-9696

Springfield, Brown, Pop. 2,141
Springfield SD 85 600/PK-12
12 Burns Ave 56087 507-723-4283
Keith Kottke, supt. Fax 723-6407
www.springfield.mntm.org/
Springfield ES 300/PK-6
12 Burns Ave 56087 507-723-4286
Jeff Kuehn, prin. Fax 723-4289

St. Raphael S 50/PK-6
20 W Van Dusen St 56087 507-723-4135
Jennifer Fischer, prin. Fax 723-5409

Spring Grove, Houston, Pop. 1,322
Spring Grove SD 297 400/K-12
PO Box 626 55974 507-498-3221
Rachel Udstuen, supt. Fax 498-3470
www.springgrove.k12.mn.us
Spring Grove ES 200/K-6
PO Box 626 55974 507-498-3223
Nancy Gulbranson, prin. Fax 498-3470

Spring Lake Park, Anoka, Pop. 6,217
Spring Lake Park SD 16 5,300/K-12
1415 81st Ave NE 55432 763-600-5000
Dr. Jeff Ronneberg, supt. Fax 600-5582
www.springlakeparkschools.org
Lighthouse S 50/1-12
7925 Able St NE 55432 763-600-5200
Mike Callahan, admin. Fax 600-5213
Park Terrace ES 700/K-3
8301 Terrace Rd NE 55432 763-600-5600
Kim Fehringer, prin. Fax 600-5613
Other Schools – See Blaine, Fridley, Minneapolis

Spring Valley, Fillmore, Pop. 2,458
Kingsland SD 2137 600/PK-12
705 N Section Ave 55975 507-346-7276
James Hecimovich, supt. Fax 346-7278
www.kingsland.k12.mn.us
Kingsland ES 200/PK-6
705 N Section Ave 55975 507-346-7276
Jim Hecimovich, prin. Fax 346-7278

Staples, Todd, Pop. 2,930
Staples-Motley ISD 2170 800/PK-12
202 Pleasant Ave NE 56479 218-894-5400
Ron Bratlie, supt. Fax 894-1828
www.isd2170.k12.mn.us
Staples-Motley ES 300/PK-3
1025 4th St NE 56479 218-894-2433
Kathy Johnson, prin. Fax 894-1545
Other Schools – See Motley

Sacred Heart S 100/PK-6
324 4th St NE 56479 218-894-2077
Jim Opelia, prin. Fax 894-2994

Stephen, Marshall, Pop. 657
Stephen-Argyle Central SD 2856 300/PK-12
PO Box 68 56757 218-478-3315
Dr. Chris Mills, supt. Fax 478-3537
www.sac.k12.mn.us/
Other Schools – See Argyle

Stewartville, Olmsted, Pop. 5,872
Stewartville SD 534 2,000/PK-12
301 2nd St SW 55976 507-533-1438
Belinda Selfors, supt. Fax 533-4012
www.ssd.k12.mn.us
Bear Cave IS 500/3-5
1021 10th St NW 55976 507-533-1400
Sheila McNeill, prin. Fax 533-7776
Bonner ES 500/K-2
526 5th Ave SE 55976 507-533-1500
Zane McInroy, prin. Fax 533-4836
Central Education Center PK-PK
301 2nd St SW 55976 507-533-1438
Hailey Liffrig, dir. Fax 533-4012
Stewartville MS 400/6-8
440 6th Ave SW 55976 507-533-1666
Steven Gibbs, prin. Fax 533-1490

Stillwater, Washington, Pop. 17,911
Mahtomedi SD 832
Supt. — See Mahtomedi
Mahtomedi Preschool 50/PK-PK
8698 75th St N 55082 651-407-2441
Diane Tich, coord. Fax 407-2125
Wildwood ES 600/K-2
8698 75th St N 55082 651-407-2100
Mark Hamre, prin. Fax 407-2125

Stillwater Area SD 834 8,100/PK-12
1875 Greeley St S 55082 651-351-8301
Denise Pontrelli, supt. Fax 351-8380
www.stillwaterschools.org
Lily Lake ES 500/PK-5
2003 Willard St W 55082 651-351-6800
Nate Cox, prin. Fax 351-6895
Rutherford ES 600/PK-5
115 Rutherford Rd 55082 651-351-6400
Heather Nelson, prin. Fax 351-6495
Stillwater MS 1,100/6-8
523 Marsh St W 55082 651-351-6905
Roderic VanScoy, prin. Fax 351-6999
Stonebridge ES 500/PK-5
900 Owens St N 55082 651-351-8700
Derek Berg, prin. Fax 351-8790
Other Schools – See Bayport, Lake Elmo, Lakeland, Woodbury

St. Croix Catholic S 400/PK-8
621 3rd St S 55082 651-439-5581
Sr. Mary Juliana Cox, prin. Fax 439-8360
Saint Croix Montessori S 100/PK-6
177 Neal Ave N 55082 651-436-2603
Sheri Rylicki, head sch Fax 436-1170
Salem Lutheran S 200/PK-8
14940 62nd St N 55082 651-439-7831
Roger Zolldan, prin. Fax 439-0035

Swanville, Morrison, Pop. 348
Swanville SD 486 300/PK-12
PO Box 98 56382 320-547-5100
Gene Harthan, supt. Fax 547-2576
www.swanville.k12.mn.us/
Swanville ES 200/PK-6
PO Box 98 56382 320-547-5100
Gene Harthan, prin. Fax 547-2576

Taylors Falls, Chisago, Pop. 960
Chisago Lakes SD 2144
Supt. — See Lindstrom
Taylors Falls ES 400/K-5
648 West St 55084 651-213-2100
Jason Riebe, prin. Fax 213-2150

Thief River Falls, Pennington, Pop. 8,403
Thief River Falls SD 564 2,000/PK-12
230 LaBree Ave S 56701 218-681-8711
Bradley Bergstrom, supt. Fax 681-2905
www.trf.k12.mn.us
Challenger ES 900/PK-5
601 County Road 61 56701 218-681-2345
Patrick Marolt, prin. Fax 681-3252
Franklin MS 400/6-8
300 Spruce Ave S 56701 218-681-8813
Bob Wayne, prin. Fax 681-4771

St. Bernards S 100/PK-5
117 Knight Ave N 56701 218-681-1539
Randy Schantz, prin. Fax 681-2261
St. John Lutheran S 50/PK-12
15671 158th St NE 56701 218-681-7753
John Folland, prin.

Tower, Saint Louis, Pop. 489
Saint Louis County Schools ISD 2142
Supt. — See Virginia
Tower-Soudan S 100/PK-6
PO Box 469 55790 218-753-4040
Kelly Engman, prin. Fax 753-6461

Tracy, Lyon, Pop. 2,129
Tracy SD 2904 800/PK-12
934 Pine St 56175 507-629-5500
Chad Anderson, supt. Fax 629-5507
www.tracy.k12.mn.us
Tracy ES 400/PK-6
700 S 4th St 56175 507-629-5518
Michael Munson, prin. Fax 629-5525

St. Mary S 50/PK-6
225 6th St 56175 507-629-3270
Fax 629-3518

Trimont, Martin, Pop. 740
Martin County West SD 2448
Supt. — See Sherburn
Trimont ES 100/K-K, 5-6
PO Box 408 56176 507-639-2071
Chad Brusky, prin. Fax 639-2091

Truman, Martin, Pop. 1,111
Truman SD 458 200/PK-12
PO Box 276 56088 507-776-2111
Dr. Virginia Dahlstrom, supt. Fax 776-3379
www.truman.k12.mn.us
Truman ES 100/PK-6
PO Box 276 56088 507-776-2111
Mark Nass, prin. Fax 776-3379

St. Paul Lutheran S 100/PK-8
114 E 4th St N 56088 507-776-6541
Marty Miller, prin. Fax 776-3060

Twin Valley, Norman, Pop. 807
Norman County East SD 2215 300/PK-12
PO Box 420 56584 218-584-5151
Rob Nudell, supt. Fax 584-5170
www.nce.k12.mn.us
Other Schools – See Gary

Two Harbors, Lake, Pop. 3,693
Lake Superior SD 381 1,400/PK-12
1640 Highway 2 55616 218-834-8201
Dr. Bill Crandall, supt. Fax 834-8239
www.isd381.org
Minnehaha ES 400/PK-5
421 7th St 55616 218-834-8221
Brett Archer, prin. Fax 834-8247
Other Schools – See Silver Bay

Tyler, Lincoln, Pop. 1,129
R T R ISD 2902 600/PK-12
PO Box 659 56178 507-247-5913
Lee Warne, supt. Fax 247-3876
www.rtrschools.org
Other Schools – See Russell, Ruthton

Ulen, Clay, Pop. 535
Ulen-Hitterdal SD 914 300/K-12
PO Box 389 56585 218-596-8853
Todd Cameron, supt. Fax 596-8610
www.ulenhitterdal.k12.mn.us
Ulen-Hitterdal ES 200/K-6
PO Box 389 56585 218-596-8853
Kent Henrickson, prin. Fax 596-8610

Underwood, Otter Tail, Pop. 340
Underwood SD 550 600/PK-12
100 Southern Ave E 56586 218-826-6101
Dr. Jeremiah Olson, supt. Fax 826-6310
www.underwood.k12.mn.us
Underwood ES 300/PK-6
100 Southern Ave E 56586 218-826-6101
Dr. Jeremiah Olson, prin. Fax 826-6310

Upsala, Morrison, Pop. 425
Upsala SD 487 400/PK-12
PO Box 190 56384 320-573-2174
Vern Capelle, supt. Fax 573-2173
www.upsala.k12.mn.us
Upsala ES 200/PK-6
PO Box 190 56384 320-573-2175
Vern Capelle, prin. Fax 573-2173

Vadnais Heights, Ramsey, Pop. 12,047
White Bear Lake Area SD 624
Supt. — See White Bear Lake
Vadnais Heights ES 400/K-5
3645 Centerville Rd 55127 651-653-2858
Sara Svir, prin. Fax 653-2860

Vermillion, Dakota, Pop. 411

St. John the Baptist S 100/PK-6
PO Box 50 55085 651-437-2644
Sr. Mike Strommen, prin. Fax 437-9006

Verndale, Wadena, Pop. 586
Verndale SD 818 500/PK-12
411 SW Brown St 56481 218-445-5184
Paul Brownlow, supt. Fax 445-5185
www.verndale.k12.mn.us
Verndale ES 300/PK-6
411 SW Brown St 56481 218-445-5184
Paul Brownlow, prin. Fax 445-5185

Victoria, Carver, Pop. 7,244
Eastern Carver County SD 112
Supt. — See Chaska
Victoria ES 700/K-5
9300 Red Fox Dr 55386 952-556-3000
Jill Velure, prin. Fax 556-3009

Viking, Marshall, Pop. 100
Marshall County Central SD 441
Supt. — See Newfolden
Viking ES 100/K-2
PO Box 10 56760 218-523-4425
Jeffrey Lund, prin. Fax 523-4428

Virginia, Saint Louis, Pop. 8,491
Saint Louis County Schools ISD 2142 1,000/PK-12
1701 N 9th Ave 55792 218-749-8130
Steven Sallee, supt. Fax 749-8133
isd2142.net
Other Schools – See Babbitt, Cook, Culver, Iron, Tower

Virginia SD 706 1,600/PK-12
411 S 5th Ave 55792 218-742-3901
Dr. Noel Schmidt, supt. Fax 742-3960
www.vmps.org
Parkview Learning Center 500/PK-2
411 S 5th Ave 55792 218-742-3802
Michael Krebsbach, prin. Fax 741-8522
Roosevelt ES 400/3-6
411 S 5th Ave 55792 218-742-3943
William Spelts, prin. Fax 741-8522

Marquette S 100/PK-6
311 3rd St S 55792 218-741-6811
Jean Virant, prin. Fax 741-2158

Wabasha, Wabasha, Pop. 2,493
Wabasha-Kellogg SD 811 600/PK-12
2113 Hiawatha Dr E 55981 651-565-3559
Jim Freihammer, supt. Fax 565-2769
www.wabasha-kellogg.k12.mn.us/
Wabasha-Kellogg ES 300/PK-6
2113 Hiawatha Dr E 55981 651-565-3559
Rob Stewart, prin. Fax 565-2769

St. Felix S 100/PK-6
130 3rd St E 55981 651-565-4446
Eric Sonnek, prin. Fax 565-0244

Wabasso, Redwood, Pop. 691
Wabasso SD 640 400/PK-12
PO Box 69 56293 507-342-5114
Wade McKittrick, supt. Fax 342-5203
isd640.org
Wabasso ES 200/PK-6
PO Box 69 56293 507-342-5114
Wade McKittrick, admin. Fax 342-5203

St. Anne S 100/PK-6
PO Box 239 56293 507-342-5389
Mary Franta, prin. Fax 342-5156

Waconia, Carver, Pop. 10,592
Waconia SD 110 3,300/PK-12
512 Industrial Blvd 55387 952-442-0600
Patrick Devine, supt. Fax 442-0609
www.waconia.k12.mn.us
Bayview ES 700/K-5
24 S Walnut St 55387 952-442-0630
Ann Swanson, prin. Fax 442-0609
Laketown ES, 960 Airport Rd 55387 500/K-5
Nancy Wittman, prin. 952-442-0690
Southview ES 700/PK-5
225 W 4th St 55387 952-442-0620
Khuzana DeVaan, prin. Fax 442-0629
Waconia MS 900/6-8
1400 Community Dr 55387 952-442-0650
Shane Clausen, prin. Fax 442-0659

St. Joseph S 200/PK-8
41 E 1st St 55387 952-442-4500
Bruce Richards, prin. Fax 442-3719
Trinity Lutheran S 400/PK-8
601 E 2nd St 55387 952-442-4165
Kristine Marlatt, admin. Fax 442-4644

Wadena, Wadena, Pop. 4,023
Wadena-Deer Creek SD 2155 800/PK-12
600 Colfax Ave SW 56482 218-632-2155
Lee Westrum, supt. Fax 632-2199
www.wdc2155.k12.mn.us
Wadena-Deer Creek ES 400/PK-4
215 Colfax Ave SW 56482 218-632-2400
Louis Rutten, prin. Fax 632-2499

Waite Park, Stearns, Pop. 6,543
Saint Cloud Area SD 742
Supt. — See Saint Cloud
Discovery ES 500/PK-5
700 7th St S 56387 320-251-7770
Tammy Wilson, prin. Fax 251-1827

Walker, Cass, Pop. 910
Walker-Hackensack-Akeley SD 113 700/PK-12
PO Box 4000 56484 218-547-1311
Eric Pingrey, supt. Fax 547-4298
www.wha.k12.mn.us
Walker-Hackensack-Akeley ES 400/PK-6
PO Box 4000 56484 218-547-4261
Jill McGowan, prin. Fax 547-4367

Immanuel Lutheran S 100/PK-8
4656 State 200 NW 56484 218-547-4139
Janna Kietzman, prin. Fax 547-4139

Walnut Grove, Redwood, Pop. 870
Westbrook-Walnut Grove SD 2898
Supt. — See Westbrook
Walnut Grove ES 200/PK-6
PO Box 278 56180 507-859-2141
Paul Olson, prin. Fax 859-2329

Wanamingo, Goodhue, Pop. 1,081
Kenyon-Wanamingo SD 2172 700/PK-12
225 3rd Ave 55983 507-789-7001
Dr. Jeff Pesta, supt. Fax 789-7032
www.kw.k12.mn.us
Kenyon-Wanamingo ES 300/PK-6
225 3rd Ave 55983 507-824-2211
Katy Schuerman, prin. Fax 789-7033
Other Schools – See Kenyon

Warren, Marshall, Pop. 1,554
Warren-Alvarado-Oslo SD 2176 400/PK-12
224 E Bridge Ave 56762 218-745-5393
Lon Jorgensen, supt. Fax 745-5886
www.wao.k12.mn.us
Warren ES 300/PK-6
224 E Bridge Ave 56762 218-745-4441
Kirk Thorstenson, prin. Fax 745-7659

Warroad, Roseau, Pop. 1,740
Warroad SD 690 1,000/PK-12
510 Cedar Ave NW 56763 218-386-1872
Peter Haapala, supt. Fax 386-1909
www.warroad.k12.mn.us
Warroad ES 600/PK-6
510 Cedar Ave NW 56763 218-386-1877
Brita Comstock, prin. Fax 386-2179
Other Schools – See Angle Inlet

Waseca, Waseca, Pop. 9,257
Waseca SD 829 1,500/PK-12
501 Elm Ave E 56093 507-835-2500
Thomas Lee, supt. Fax 835-1161
www.waseca.k12.mn.us
Hartley ES 500/PK-3
605 7th St NE 56093 507-835-2248
Ben O'Brien, prin. Fax 835-3187
Waseca IS 400/4-6
400 19th Ave NW 56093 507-835-3000
John Huttemier, prin. Fax 835-1161

Sacred Heart S 100/K-4
308 Elm Ave W 56093 507-835-2780
LeAnn Dahle, prin. Fax 833-1498

Watertown, Carver, Pop. 4,128
Watertown-Mayer SD 111 1,600/PK-12
1001 Highway 25 Shls NW 55388 952-955-0480
Ron Wilke, supt. Fax 955-0481
www.wm.k12.mn.us
Watertown-Mayer ES 600/1-5
500 Paul Ave 55388 952-955-0300
Marnie Pauly, prin. Fax 955-0301
Watertown-Mayer MS 400/6-8
1001 Highway 25 Shls NW 55388 952-955-0400
Nick Guertin, prin. Fax 955-0481
Watertown-Mayer PS 200/PK-K
313 Angel Ave NW 55388 952-955-0200
Allison Arndt, dean Fax 955-0201

Christ Community Lutheran S 100/PK-8
512 County Road 10 SE 55388 952-955-1419
Jeff Boehlke, prin. Fax 955-1424

Waterville, LeSueur, Pop. 1,853
Waterville-Elysian-Morristown SD 2143 900/PK-12
500 Paquin St E 56096 507-362-4432
Joel Whitehurst, supt. Fax 362-4561
www.wem.k12.mn.us/
Waterville-Elysian-Morristown ES 400/PK-4
500 Paquin St E 56096 507-362-4439
Bobbie Jo Bastian, prin. Fax 362-4762
Other Schools – See Morristown

Watkins, Meeker, Pop. 962
Eden Valley-Watkins SD 463
Supt. — See Eden Valley
Watkins ES 100/PK-K
161 School Ave S 55389 320-453-2900
Rob Pederson, prin. Fax 453-6457

Waubun, Mahnomen, Pop. 324
Waubun Ogema White Earth SD 435 600/PK-12
PO Box 98 56589 218-473-6171
Lisa Weber, supt. Fax 473-6191
www.waubun.k12.mn.us
Waubun ES 100/5-6
PO Box 98 56589 218-473-6173
Eric Martinez, prin. Fax 473-6190
Other Schools – See Ogema

Waverly, Wright, Pop. 1,345
Howard Lake-Waverly-Winsted SD 2687
Supt. — See Howard Lake
Humphrey ES 200/PK-4
PO Box 248 55390 320-543-4680
Jennifer Olson, prin. Fax 658-4497

Wayzata, Hennepin, Pop. 3,646
Minnetonka SD 276
Supt. — See Minnetonka
Deephaven ES 700/K-5
4452 Vinehill Rd 55391 952-401-6900
Bryan McGinley, prin. Fax 401-6906

Wayzata SD 284
Supt. — See Plymouth
Wayzata West MS 700/6-8
149 Barry Ave N 55391 952-745-6400
Susan Sommerfeld, prin. Fax 745-6491

Blake S - Highcroft Campus 300/PK-5
301 Peavey Ln 55391 952-988-3550
Dr. Anne Stavney, head sch Fax 988-3555
Holy Name of Jesus S 400/PK-6
155 County Road 24 55391 763-473-3675
Martha Laurent, prin. Fax 745-3499
Redeemer Christian Academy 100/PK-8
115 Wayzata Blvd W 55391 952-473-5356
Linda Wiebold, admin. Fax 473-3186
St. Bartholomew S 200/PK-6
630 Wayzata Blvd E 55391 952-473-6189
Patrick Fox, prin. Fax 745-4598

Webster, Rice

Holy Cross S 200/PK-8
6100 37th St W 55088 952-652-6100
Constance Krocak Ed.D., prin. Fax 652-6102

Wells, Faribault, Pop. 2,325
United South Central SD 2134 600/PK-12
PO Box 312 56097 507-553-3134
Keith Fleming, supt. Fax 553-5929
www.usc.k12.mn.us
United South Central ES 300/PK-6
PO Box 312 56097 507-553-5810
Tracey Magnuson, prin. Fax 553-5929

St. Casimir S, 330 2nd Ave SW 56097 100/K-8
Joanne Tibodeau, prin. 507-553-5822

Westbrook, Cottonwood, Pop. 737
Westbrook-Walnut Grove SD 2898 400/PK-12
PO Box 129 56183 507-274-5450
Loy Woelber, supt. Fax 274-6113
www.wwgschools.org
Other Schools – See Walnut Grove

West Saint Paul, Dakota, Pop. 19,105
West St. Paul-Mendota Hts-Eagan SD 197
Supt. — See Mendota Heights
Garlough Environmental Magnet S 400/PK-4
1740 Charlton St 55118 651-403-8100
Susan Powell, prin. Fax 403-8110
Heritage E-STEM Magnet S 800/5-8
121 Butler Ave W 55118 651-403-7400
Karen Allen, prin. Fax 403-7410
Moreland Arts & Health Sciences Magnet S 400/PK-4
217 Moreland Ave W 55118 651-403-7800
Mark Quinn, prin. Fax 403-7810

Community of Saints Regional S 100/K-8
335 Hurley St E 55118 651-457-2510
Bridget Kramer, prin. Fax 457-5049
Crown of Life Lutheran S 200/PK-8
115 Crusader Ave W 55118 651-451-3832
Daniel L. Plath, prin. Fax 451-7579
St. Joseph S 600/PK-8
1138 Seminole Ave 55118 651-457-8550
Greg Wesely, prin. Fax 457-0780
Seton Montessori S PK-K
149 Thompson Ave E 55118 651-343-0155

Wheaton, Traverse, Pop. 1,408
Wheaton Area SD 803 400/PK-12
1700 3rd Ave S 56296 320-563-8283
Daniel Posthumus, supt. Fax 563-4218
www.wheaton.k12.mn.us
Pearson ES 200/PK-5
710 4th Ave N 56296 320-563-8191
Daniel Posthumus, prin. Fax 563-4636

White Bear Township, See White Bear Lake
White Bear Lake Area SD 624
Supt. — See White Bear Lake
Otter Lake ES 600/K-5
1401 County Road H2, White Bear Lake MN 55110
651-653-2831
Cynthia Mueller, prin. Fax 653-2833

White Bear Lake, Ramsey, Pop. 23,270
White Bear Lake Area SD 624 8,100/PK-12
4855 Bloom Ave 55110 651-407-7500
Dr. Wayne Kazmierczak, supt. Fax 407-7566
www.isd624.org
Birch Lake ES 300/K-5
1616 Birch Lake Ave 55110 651-653-2776
Jonathan Luknic, prin. Fax 653-2778
Central MS 1,000/6-8
4857 Bloom Ave 55110 651-653-2888
Timothy Schochenmaier, prin. Fax 653-2885
Lakeaires ES 400/K-5
3963 Van Dyke St 55110 651-653-2809
Cary Krusemark, prin. Fax 653-2811
Lincoln ES 400/K-5
1961 6th St 55110 651-653-2820
Dan Schmidt, prin. Fax 653-2822
Matoska International IB World S 500/K-5
2530 Spruce Pl 55110 651-653-2847
John Leininger, prin. Fax 653-2849
Normandy Park Education Ctr Erly Childhd 100/PK-PK
2482 County Road F E 55110 651-653-3100
Danielle Barkley, admin. Fax 653-3155
Sunrise Park MS 800/6-8
2399 Cedar Ave 55110 651-653-2700
Christina Pierre, prin. Fax 653-2716
Willow Lane ES 400/K-5
3375 Willow Ave 55110 651-773-6170
Chris Streiff, prin. Fax 773-6176
Other Schools – See Hugo, Vadnais Heights, White Bear Township

---

Frassati Catholic Academy 300/PK-8
4690 Bald Eagle Ave 55110 651-429-7771
Patrick Gallivan, prin. Fax 429-9539
Liberty Classical Academy 200/PK-12
3878 Highland Ave 55110 651-772-2777
Rebekah Hagstrom M.A., hdmstr. Fax 776-0393
Magnuson Christian S 100/K-8
4000 Linden St 55110 651-429-5349
Sue Spangenberg, dir. Fax 429-3942
White Bear Montessori S 100/PK-6
1201 County Road E E 55110 651-429-3710
Marnie McPherson, admin. Fax 429-2927

Willmar, Kandiyohi, Pop. 19,385
Willmar SD 347 4,000/K-12
611 5th St SW 56201 320-231-8500
Dr. Jeffrey Holm, supt. Fax 231-1061
www.willmar.k12.mn.us
Kennedy ES 900/K-5
824 7th St NW 56201 320-214-6688
Kristin Dresler, prin. Fax 235-9536
Lakeland ES K-5
1001 Lakeland Dr SE 56201
Gretchen Baumgarn, prin.
Roosevelt ES 1,000/K-5
1800 19th Ave SW 56201 320-231-8470
Lori Lockhart, prin. Fax 231-1170
Willmar MS 900/6-8
201 Willmar Ave SE 56201 320-214-6000
Mark Miley, prin. Fax 235-1254

Community Christian S 200/PK-12
1300 19th Ave SW 56201 320-235-0592
Steve Masseth, head sch Fax 235-0620

Willow River, Pine, Pop. 405
Willow River SD 577 400/PK-12
PO Box 66 55795 218-372-3131
William Peel, supt. Fax 372-3132
www.isd577.org
Willow River ES 200/PK-4
PO Box 66 55795 218-372-3131
William Peel, prin. Fax 372-3132

Windom, Cottonwood, Pop. 4,585
Windom SD 177 1,000/K-12
PO Box 177 56101 507-831-6901
Wayne Wormstadt, supt. Fax 831-6919
www.windom.k12.mn.us
Windom MS 400/4-8
PO Box 177 56101 507-831-6910
Jake Tietje, prin. Fax 831-6909
Winfair ES 400/K-3
PO Box 177 56101 507-831-6925
Jamie Frank, prin. Fax 831-6932

Winnebago, Faribault, Pop. 1,425

Genesis Classical Academy 50/K-6
PO Box 735 56098 507-893-3600
Renee Doyle, prin. Fax 674-3735

Winona, Winona, Pop. 27,243
Winona Area SD 861 3,100/PK-12
903 Gilmore Ave 55987 507-494-0861
Richard Dahman, supt. Fax 494-0863
www.winona.k12.mn.us
Goodview ES 200/PK-4
5100 W 9th St 55987 507-494-2400
Andrea Eisner, prin. Fax 494-2401
Jefferson ES 300/K-4
1268 W 5th St 55987 507-494-2000
Dr. Arthur Williams, prin. Fax 494-2010
Madison ES 200/K-4
515 W Wabasha St 55987 507-494-2200
Andrea Eisner, prin. Fax 494-2201
Washington-Kosciusko ES 300/K-4
365 Mankato Ave 55987 507-494-2100
Dawn Lueck, prin. Fax 494-2101
Winona MS 900/5-8
1570 Homer Rd 55987 507-494-1000
Mark Winter, prin. Fax 494-1002
Other Schools – See Rollingstone

St. Martins Lutheran S 100/PK-8
253 Liberty St 55987 507-452-6928
Sharon Forst, prin. Fax 452-8992
St. Mary PS 50/PK-K
1315 W Broadway St 55987 507-452-2890
Christine Nichols, dir. Fax 452-2898
St. Matthew Lutheran S 100/PK-8
756 W Wabasha St 55987 507-454-3083
Scott Schomberg M.Ed., prin. Fax 452-1676
St. Stanislaus S 200/1-6
602 E 5th St 55987 507-452-3766
Pat Bowlin, prin. Fax 454-1473

Winsted, McLeod, Pop. 2,341
Howard Lake-Waverly-Winsted SD 2687
Supt. — See Howard Lake
Winsted ES 200/PK-4
PO Box 160 55395 320-543-4690
Jennifer Olson, prin. Fax 485-4183

Holy Trinity ES 100/PK-6
PO Box 38 55395 320-485-2182
Dr. Bonita Jungels, prin. Fax 485-4283

Woodbury, Washington, Pop. 60,529
South Washington County SD 833
Supt. — See Cottage Grove
Bailey ES 700/K-5
4125 Woodlane Dr 55129 651-425-4800
Candace Hofstad, prin. Fax 425-4815
Lake MS 1,200/6-8
3133 Pioneer Dr 55125 651-425-6400
Molly Roeske, prin. Fax 425-6428
Liberty Ridge ES 1,000/PK-5
11395 Eagle View Blvd 55129 651-425-5900
Mike Moore, prin. Fax 425-5915
Middleton ES 800/PK-5
9105 Lake Rd 55125 651-425-4900
Sara Palodichuk, prin. Fax 425-4915
Red Rock ES 600/PK-5
3311 Commonwealth Ave 55125 651-425-5600
Jennifer Holt, prin. Fax 425-5615
Royal Oaks ES 500/PK-5
7335 Steepleview Rd 55125 651-425-4700
Dr. Susan Risius, prin. Fax 425-4715
Valley Crossing ES 700/PK-6
9900 Park Xing 55125 651-425-7500
Lela Olson, prin. Fax 425-7515
Woodbury ES 500/PK-5
1251 School Dr 55125 651-425-4600
Connha Classon, prin. Fax 425-4615
Woodbury MS 900/6-8
1425 School Dr 55125 651-425-4500
Kari Lopez, prin. Fax 425-4567

Stillwater Area SD 834
Supt. — See Stillwater
Brookview ES 500/PK-5
11099 Brookview Rd 55129 651-275-2500
Mark Drommerhausen, prin.

New Life Academy 700/PK-12
6758 Bailey Rd 55129 651-459-4121
Clark Gilbert, head sch Fax 459-6194
St. Ambrose of Woodbury S 600/K-8
4125 Woodbury Dr 55129 651-768-3000
Betsy Osterhaus-Hand, prin. Fax 768-3080

Worthington, Nobles, Pop. 12,573
Worthington SD 518 2,800/PK-12
1117 Marine Ave 56187 507-372-2172
John Landgaard, supt. Fax 372-2174
www.isd518.net
Prairie ES 1,200/PK-4
1700 1st Ave SW 56187 507-727-1250
Heidi Meyer, prin. Fax 727-1255
Worthington MS 800/5-8
1401 Crailsheim Dr 56187 507-376-4174
Jeff Luke, prin. Fax 372-1424

St. Marys S 100/K-6
1206 8th Ave 56187 507-376-5236
Jackie Probst, prin. Fax 376-6159
Worthington Christian S 100/PK-8
1770 Eleanor St 56187 507-376-4861
Martha Lubben, lead tchr. Fax 376-4185

Wrenshall, Carlton, Pop. 390
Wrenshall SD 100 300/PK-12
207 Pioneer Dr 55797 218-384-4274
Dr. Kimberly Belcastro, supt. Fax 384-4293
www.wrenshall.k12.mn.us
Wrenshall ES 100/PK-6
207 Pioneer Dr 55797 218-384-4274
Dr. Kimberly Belcastro, prin. Fax 384-4293

Wykoff, Fillmore, Pop. 442

St. Johns Lutheran S 50/PK-8
PO Box 189 55990 507-352-4671
Kevin Meyer, prin. Fax 352-7671

Wyoming, Chisago, Pop. 7,693
Forest Lake SD 831
Supt. — See Forest Lake
Linwood ES 400/PK-6
21900 Typo Creek Dr NE 55092 651-982-1900
Joe Mueller, prin. Fax 982-1955
Wyoming ES 600/PK-6
25701 Forest Blvd 55092 651-982-8000
Curtis Slater, prin. Fax 982-8067

Young America, Carver, Pop. 1,659

St. John's Lutheran S 100/PK-8
27 1st St NW 55397 952-467-3461
David Polzin, prin.

Zimmerman, Sherburne, Pop. 5,145
Elk River Area SD 728
Supt. — See Elk River
Westwood ES 600/3-5
13651 4th Ave S 55398 763-274-3180
Timothy Stowe, prin. Fax 274-3181
Zimmerman ES 600/K-2
25959 4th St W 55398 763-241-3475
Gretchen Fisher, prin. Fax 241-3476

Zumbrota, Goodhue, Pop. 3,200
Zumbrota-Mazeppa SD 2805
Supt. — See Mazeppa
Zumbrota-Mazeppa MS 200/7-8
705 Mill St 55992 507-732-7395
Dave Anderson, prin. Fax 732-4511
Zumbrota-Mazeppa PS 300/PK-2
799 Mill St 55992 507-732-7848
Quinn Rasmussen, prin. Fax 732-4522

Christ Lutheran S 50/K-8
223 E 5th St 55992 507-732-5367
Daniel Kell, prin. Fax 732-7641

MISSISSIPPI

MISSISSIPPI DEPARTMENT OF EDUCATION

PO Box 771, Jackson 39205
Telephone 601-359-1750
Fax 601-359-3242
Website http://www.mde.k12.ms.us

Superintendent of Education   Dr. Carey Wright

MISSISSIPPI BOARD OF EDUCATION

PO Box 771, Jackson 39205

Chairperson   Rosemary Aultman

PUBLIC, PRIVATE AND CATHOLIC ELEMENTARY SCHOOLS

Aberdeen, Monroe, Pop. 5,561
Aberdeen SD 1,200/PK-12
PO Box 607 39730 662-369-4682
Jeff Clay, admin. Fax 369-0728
www.asdms.us
Aberdeen ES 400/PK-3
PO Box 607 39730 662-369-4782
Kristen Fondren, prin. Fax 319-9216
Belle-Shivers MS 200/4-8
PO Box 607 39730 662-369-6241
Martha Jackson, prin. Fax 319-8931

Ackerman, Choctaw, Pop. 1,499
Choctaw County SD 1,400/PK-12
PO Box 398 39735 662-285-4022
Stewart Beard, supt. Fax 285-4049
www.choctaw.k12.ms.us/
Ackerman ES 500/PK-6
8475 MS Highway 15 39735 662-285-4052
Samantha Kelly, prin. Fax 285-4099
Other Schools – See French Camp, Weir

Amory, Monroe, Pop. 7,262
Amory SD 1,700/K-12
PO Box 330 38821 662-256-5991
Ken Byars, supt. Fax 256-6302
www.amoryschools.com/
Amory MS 400/6-8
700 2nd Ave N 38821 662-256-5658
Kenneth Goralczyk, prin. Fax 256-6304
East Amory ES 400/3-5
305 Easthaven Dr 38821 662-256-7191
Kristy Keeton, prin. Fax 256-1647
West Amory ES 400/K-2
704 111th St 38821 662-256-2601
Letricia French, prin. Fax 256-1643

Monroe County SD 2,200/K-12
PO Box 209 38821 662-257-2176
Scott Cantrell, supt. Fax 257-2181
www.mcsd.us
Hatley S 1,000/K-12
60286 Hatley Rd 38821 662-256-4563
Chris Kidd, prin. Fax 256-5626
Other Schools – See Hamilton, Smithville

Anguilla, Sharkey, Pop. 721
South Delta SD
Supt. — See Rolling Fork
South Delta MS 200/6-8
PO Box 487 38721 662-873-6535
Deloris Williams, prin. Fax 873-6073

Arcola, Washington, Pop. 359

Deer Creek S 200/PK-12
PO Box 376 38722 662-827-5165

Ashland, Benton, Pop. 566
Benton County SD 1,200/K-12
PO Box 247 38603 662-224-6252
Steve Bostick, supt. Fax 224-3607
www.benton.k12.ms.us
Ashland ES 300/K-5
768 Lamar Rd 38603 662-224-6622
Sharon Albert, prin. Fax 224-3613
Ashland MS 100/6-8
PO Box 368 38603 662-224-6485
Dr. Rosie Ladd, prin. Fax 224-3609
Other Schools – See Hickory Flat

Avon, Washington
Western Line SD 2,000/PK-12
PO Box 50 38723 662-335-7186
Larry Green, supt. Fax 378-2285
www.westernline.org
Riverside ES 600/PK-6
PO Box 130 38723 662-335-4528
Glenda Triplett-Jackson, prin. Fax 332-5921
Other Schools – See Greenville

Baldwyn, Lee, Pop. 3,256
Baldwyn SD 800/K-12
107 W Main St 38824 662-365-1000
Jason McKay, supt. Fax 365-1003
www.baldwynschools.com
Baldwyn ES 300/K-4
515 Bender Cir 38824 662-365-1010
Rickey Weaver, prin. Fax 365-1034
Baldwyn MS 200/5-8
452 N Fourth St 38824 662-365-1015
Danny Ramsey, prin. Fax 365-1029

Bassfield, Jefferson Davis, Pop. 253
Jefferson Davis County SD
Supt. — See Prentiss
Carver ES 400/K-8
PO Box 460 39421 601-943-5251
Dr. Crystal Haynes, prin. Fax 943-5151

Batesville, Panola, Pop. 7,385
South Panola SD 4,400/PK-12
209 Boothe St 38606 662-563-9361
Tim Wilder, supt. Fax 563-6077
www.spsd.k12.ms.us
Batesville ES 700/PK-1
110 College St 38606 662-563-4596
LaSherry Irby, prin. Fax 563-0028
Batesville IS 600/2-3
200 College St 38606 662-563-7834
LaShunda Hamilton, prin. Fax 563-3462
Batesville JHS 900/6-8
507 Tiger Dr 38606 662-563-4503
Charles Stevenson, prin. Fax 563-8991
Batesville MS 500/4-5
509 Tiger Dr 38606 662-563-1924
Chad Lindamood, prin. Fax 563-3808
Other Schools – See Pope

North Delta S 400/PK-12
330 Green Wave Ln 38606 662-563-4536

Bay Saint Louis, Hancock, Pop. 9,056
Bay St. Louis-Waveland SD 1,900/K-12
200 N 2nd St 39520 228-467-6621
Dr. Vikki Landry, supt. Fax 467-1230
www.bwsd.org/
Bay-Waveland MS 500/6-8
600 Pine St 39520 228-463-0315
Dr. Cherie Labat, prin. Fax 463-2681
North Bay ES 400/3-5
602 Pine St 39520 228-467-4052
Jeremy Weir, prin. Fax 466-4516
Other Schools – See Waveland

Hancock County SD
Supt. — See Kiln
South Hancock ES 600/K-5
6590 Lakeshore Rd 39520 228-467-4655
Rose Jenkins, prin. Fax 467-0618

Holy Trinity S 300/PK-6
301 S Second St 39520 228-467-5158
Janet Buras, prin. Fax 467-9742

Bay Springs, Jasper, Pop. 1,763
West Jasper Consolidated SD 1,400/K-12
PO Box 610 39422 601-764-2280
Warren Woodrow, supt. Fax 764-4490
wjsd-mississippi.schoolloop.com/
Bay Springs ES 300/K-4
PO Box 927 39422 601-764-2016
Hollie Parker, prin. Fax 764-6757
Bay Springs MS 200/5-8
PO Box 587 39422 601-764-3378
Tracy Adcock, prin. Fax 764-2329
Other Schools – See Stringer

Sylva-Bay Academy 300/PK-12
PO Box J 39422 601-764-2157

Beaumont, Perry, Pop. 943
Perry County SD
Supt. — See New Augusta
South Perry ES 200/K-5
1300 Beaumont Brooklyn Rd 39423 601-784-3393
Dr. Anthony O'Neal, prin. Fax 964-8204

Belden, Lee

Tupelo Christian Preparatory S 500/PK-12
5440 Endville Rd 38826 662-844-8604
Ronnie Hill, hdmstr. Fax 823-6972

Belmont, Tishomingo, Pop. 2,002
Tishomingo County Special Municipal SD
Supt. — See Iuka
Belmont S 1,000/K-12
9 School Dr 38827 662-454-7924
Van Roberts, prin. Fax 454-7611

Belzoni, Humphreys, Pop. 2,229
Humphreys County SD 1,700/K-12
PO Box 678 39038 662-247-6000
Elliot Wheeler, supt. Fax 247-1578
www.humphreyscountyschools.com
Greene ES 500/K-2
PO Box 678 39038 662-247-6080
Kandice Jernigan, prin. Fax 247-9328
Humphreys JHS 400/6-8
PO Box 678 39038 662-247-6050
LaMarlon Wilson, prin. Fax 247-2212
McNair Upper ES 400/3-5
PO Box 678 39038 662-247-6060
Nicole Dobbins, prin. Fax 247-4318

Humphreys Academy 100/K-12
PO Box 179 39038 662-247-1572

Benoit, Bolivar, Pop. 477
West Bolivar Cons SD
Supt. — See Rosedale
Brooks S 300/PK-12
PO Box 8 38725 662-742-3257
Barbara Flore, prin. Fax 742-3493

Benton, Yazoo

Benton Academy 200/PK-12
PO Box 308 39039 662-673-9722

Bentonia, Yazoo, Pop. 436
Yazoo County SD
Supt. — See Yazoo City
Bentonia/Gibbs ES 600/K-5
PO Box 247 39040 662-755-2270
Melanie Roberts, prin. Fax 755-9966

Biloxi, Harrison, Pop. 42,823
Biloxi Public SD 5,500/PK-12
PO Box 168 39533 228-374-1810
Arthur McMillan, supt. Fax 435-6289
www.biloxischools.net
Biloxi JHS 1,200/7-8
1921 Tribe Dr 39532 228-435-1421
Scott Powell, prin. Fax 435-1426
Biloxi Upper ES 5-6
1424 Father Ryan Ave 39530 228-432-3700
Kelleigh Reynolds, prin. Fax 432-3715
Davis ES 800/K-4
340 Saint Mary Blvd 39531 228-436-5110
Lona Moffett, prin. Fax 374-6837
Gorenflo ES 300/2-4
771 Elder St 39530 228-436-5145
Dr. Vera Robertson, prin. Fax 374-6224
Nichols ES, 590 Division St 39530 300/PK-1
Melissa Nance, prin. 228-374-7250
North Bay ES 800/K-4
1825 Popps Ferry Rd 39532 228-435-6166
Dr. Laurie Pitre, prin. Fax 436-5185
Popps Ferry ES 600/K-4
364 Nelson Rd 39531 228-436-5135
Dr. Todd Boucher, prin. Fax 388-2313

Harrison County SD
Supt. — See Gulfport
North Woolmarket S 1,000/K-8
16237 Old Woolmarket Rd 39532 228-396-3674
Christy Buchanan, prin. Fax 396-3444
Woolmarket ES 600/K-6
12513 John Lee Rd 39532 228-392-5640
Dr. Dawn Hearn, prin. Fax 392-9868

Jackson County SD
Supt. — See Vancleave
St. Martin ES North 700/K-3
11000 Yellowjacket St 39532 228-392-1387
Dr. Lisa Suarez, prin. Fax 392-6805

Cedar Lake Christian Academy 200/PK-12
11555 Cedar Lake Rd 39532 228-392-9389
Nativity BVM S 200/PK-6
1046 Beach Blvd 39530 228-432-2269
Sr. Mary Jo Mike, prin. Fax 432-9421
Our Lady of Fatima ES 200/PK-6
320 Jim Money Rd 39531 228-388-3602
Cindy Hahn, prin. Fax 385-1140

Blue Mountain, Tippah, Pop. 901
South Tippah SD
Supt. — See Ripley
Blue Mountain S 300/K-12
408 W Mill St 38610 662-685-4706
Karen Letson, prin. Fax 685-4706

Blue Springs, Union, Pop. 228
Union County SD
Supt. — See New Albany
East Union S 900/PK-12
1548 Highway 9 S 38828 662-534-6920
Ray Kennedy, prin. Fax 534-6542

Bogue Chitto, Lincoln, Pop. 518
Lincoln County SD
Supt. — See Brookhaven
Bogue Chitto S 700/K-12
385 Monticello St 39629 601-734-2723
Scott Merrell, prin. Fax 734-6020

Bolton, Hinds, Pop. 565
Hinds County SD
Supt. — See Raymond
Bolton/Edwards S 500/PK-8
9700 I 20 W 39041 601-866-2522
Lashurn Williams, prin. Fax 866-2524

Booneville, Prentiss, Pop. 8,634
Booneville SD 1,300/K-12
201 N 1st St 38829 662-728-2171
Dr. Todd English, supt. Fax 728-4940
boonevilleschools.org
Anderson ES 500/K-4
111 Anderson St 38829 662-728-5465
Laquita McDonald, prin. Fax 728-2959
Booneville MS 400/5-8
300 W George E Allen Dr # B 38829 662-728-5843
Brad Mixon, prin. Fax 728-2427

Prentiss County SD 2,400/K-12
PO Box 179 38829 662-728-4911
Randle Downs, supt. Fax 728-2000
prentisscountyschools.com
Hills Chapel S 500/K-8
8 County Road 2371 38829 662-728-5181
Nicky Marshall, prin. Fax 728-1773
Jumpertown S 300/K-12
717 Highway 4 W 38829 662-728-6378
Anthony Michael, prin. Fax 728-9420
Thrasher S 400/K-12
167 County Road 1040 38829 662-728-5233
Jeff Boren, prin. Fax 728-8107
Other Schools – See Marietta, Wheeler

Boyle, Bolivar, Pop. 642
Cleveland SD
Supt. — See Cleveland
Bell Academy 300/PK-6
1016 Taylor Rd 38730 662-843-4572
Sonya Swafford, prin. Fax 843-1719

Brandon, Rankin, Pop. 21,524
Rankin County SD 18,200/K-12
PO Box 1359 39043 601-825-5590
Dr. Susan Townsend, supt. Fax 825-2618
www.rcsd.ms
Brandon ES 800/4-5
125 Overby St 39042 601-825-4706
Lisa Hudson, prin. Fax 824-9574
Brandon MS 1,200/6-8
408 S College St 39042 601-825-5998
Trey Rein, prin. Fax 825-8402
Highland Bluff ES 700/K-5
5970 Highway 25 39047 601-992-5168
Dr. Amanda Stocks, prin. Fax 992-5553
Northshore ES 600/K-5
110 N Shore Pkwy 39047 601-992-5279
Lee Pambianchi, prin. Fax 992-5359
Oakdale ES 500/K-5
171 Oakdale Rd 39047 601-992-5442
Dr. Lynette McNeil, prin. Fax 992-5429
Pisgah ES 400/K-6
125 Pisgah High Rd 39047 601-829-2937
Heather Dyess, prin. Fax 829-1099
Rouse ES 900/K-1
151 Boyce Thompson Dr 39042 601-825-5437
Kelli Adcock, prin. Fax 824-1081
Stonebridge ES 800/2-3
115 Stonebridge Blvd 39042 601-824-3287
Angela Nichols, prin. Fax 824-9861
Other Schools – See Florence, Flowood, Pelahatchie, Puckett, Richland

Brookhaven, Lincoln, Pop. 12,389
Brookhaven SD 2,900/K-12
PO Box 540 39602 601-833-6661
Ray Carlock, supt. Fax 833-4154
www.brookhavenschools.org
Alexander JHS 400/7-8
713 Beauregard St 39601 601-833-7549
Patrick Hardy, prin. Fax 835-5467
Brookhaven ES 500/3-4
300 S Church St 39601 601-833-3139
Shelley Riley, prin. Fax 833-8170
Lipsey MS 400/5-6
412 Drury Ln 39601 601-833-6148
Rita Robinson, prin. Fax 835-3968
Martin ES 800/K-2
420 Vivian Merritt St 39601 601-833-7359
Rob McCreary, prin. Fax 835-3964

Lincoln County SD 3,100/K-12
PO Box 826 39602 601-835-0011
Mickey Myers, supt. Fax 833-3030
lcsd.k12.ms.us/
Enterprise S 800/K-12
1601 Highway 583 SE 39601 601-833-7284
Terry Brister, prin. Fax 835-1261
Star S 800/K-12
1880 Highway 550 NW 39601 601-833-3473
Robin Case, prin. Fax 833-1254
West Lincoln S 800/K-12
948 Jackson Liberty Dr SW 39601 601-833-4600
John Shows, prin. Fax 833-9909
Other Schools – See Bogue Chitto

Brookhaven Academy 500/PK-12
943 Brookway Blvd Ext 39601 601-833-4041

Brooklyn, Forrest
Forrest County SD
Supt. — See Hattiesburg
South Forrest Attendance Center 700/K-8
8 Burborne St 39425 601-545-7714
Kim Dolan, prin. Fax 544-3002

Brooksville, Noxubee, Pop. 1,213
Noxubee County SD
Supt. — See Macon
Jones ES 300/K-6
PO Box 1005 39739 662-738-5557
Jennifer Slaughter-Willi, prin. Fax 738-5286

Bruce, Calhoun, Pop. 1,918
Calhoun County SD
Supt. — See Pittsboro
Bruce ES 400/PK-3
PO Box 579 38915 662-983-3373
Jeff Patton, prin. Fax 983-3375
Bruce Upper ES 200/4-6
PO Box 1159 38915 662-983-3366
Julia Aron, prin. Fax 983-3376

Buckatunna, Wayne, Pop. 512
Wayne County SD
Supt. — See Waynesboro
Buckatunna S 400/K-8
11 Buckatunna Mount Zion Rd 39322 601-648-2501
Lynn Revette, prin. Fax 648-2519

Burnsville, Tishomingo, Pop. 924
Tishomingo County Special Municipal SD
Supt. — See Iuka
Burnsville ES 400/K-8
23 Washington St 38833 662-427-9226
Lorie McCalmon, prin. Fax 427-9521

Byhalia, Marshall, Pop. 1,278
Marshall County SD
Supt. — See Holly Springs
Byhalia ES 700/K-5
172 Highway 309 N 38611 662-838-6980
Milony Jenkins, prin. Fax 838-3941
Byhalia MS 400/6-8
172 Highway 309 N 38611 662-838-2591
Landon Pollard, prin. Fax 838-5141

Byram, Hinds, Pop. 11,388
Hinds County SD
Supt. — See Raymond
Gary Road ES 900/K-2
7241 Gary Rd 39272 601-373-1319
David Burris, prin. Fax 346-4165
Gary Road IS 900/3-5
7255 Gary Rd 39272 601-372-8150
Ashley Green, prin. Fax 372-5028

Caledonia, Lowndes, Pop. 1,021
Lowndes County SD
Supt. — See Columbus
Caledonia ES 1,000/PK-5
9509 Wolfe Rd 39740 662-356-2050
Roger Hill, prin. Fax 356-2065
Caledonia MS 500/6-8
105 Confederate Dr 39740 662-356-2042
Karen Pittman, prin. Fax 356-2045

Calhoun City, Calhoun, Pop. 1,755
Calhoun County SD
Supt. — See Pittsboro
Calhoun City ES 400/PK-4
PO Box H 38916 662-628-5111
Lisa Langford, prin. Fax 628-6270
Calhoun City MS 200/5-8
PO Box 1546 38916 662-628-1890
Stacia Parker, prin. Fax 628-1896

Camden, Madison
Madison County SD
Supt. — See Ridgeland
Camden ES 200/PK-5
4784 Highway 43 39045 662-468-2833
Fannie Green, prin. Fax 468-3695

Canton, Madison, Pop. 13,125
Canton SD 3,300/K-12
403 Lincoln St 39046 601-859-4110
Cassandra Williams, supt. Fax 859-4023
www.cantonschools.net
Canton ES 300/3-5
740 E Academy St 39046 601-859-2400
Shalondia Washington, prin. Fax 859-6955
Canton S of Arts & Sciences 500/K-5
357 Old Yazoo City Rd 39046 601-855-7819
Chasedy Bergold, prin. Fax 855-7823
Goodloe ES 400/K-5
551 Finney Rd 39046 601-407-1809
C. Monique Lastique, prin. Fax 407-1371
McNeal ES 600/K-2
364 Martin Luther King Dr 39046 601-859-3654
Shannon Whitehead, prin. Fax 859-6956
Nichols MS 400/6-8
529 Mace St 39046 601-859-3741
Tina Manning, prin. Fax 859-6561
Porter MS 300/6-8
551 Finney Rd 39046 601-407-1819
Michael Ellis, prin. Fax 407-1401

Madison County SD
Supt. — See Ridgeland
Branson ES 200/PK-5
3903 Highway 16 E 39046 601-859-2743
Jessica Smith, prin. Fax 859-0173
Madison Crossing ES 700/K-5
300 Yandell Rd 39046 601-898-7710
Terri Thornton, prin. Fax 898-7716
Simmons MS 200/6-8
820 Sulphur Springs Rd 39046 601-855-2406
Kelvin Griffin, prin. Fax 859-7615

Canton Academy 300/PK-12
PO Box 116 39046 601-859-5231

Carriere, Pearl River
Pearl River County SD 3,000/K-12
7441 Highway 11 39426 601-798-7744
Alan Lumpkin, supt. Fax 798-3527
www.prc.k12.ms.us/
Pearl River Central Lower ES 700/K-2
116 Alphabet Ave 39426 601-799-4519
Dr. Sharon Guepet, prin. Fax 799-0350
Pearl River Central MS 700/6-8
7391 Highway 11 39426 601-798-5654
Dr. Lori Burkett, prin. Fax 798-2822
Pearl River Central Upper ES 700/3-5
1592 Henleyfield McNeill Rd 39426 601-798-2864
Darlene Hall, prin. Fax 799-0356

Carrollton, Carroll, Pop. 190
Carroll County SD 800/PK-12
PO Box 256 38917 662-237-9276
Billy Joe Ferguson, supt. Fax 237-9703
www.ccsd.ms
Other Schools – See North Carrollton

Carroll Academy 300/PK-12
PO Box 226 38917 662-237-6858

Carthage, Leake, Pop. 5,025
Leake County SD 2,900/K-12
111 W Main St 39051 601-267-4579
Billy Wilbanks, supt. Fax 267-5283
www.leakesd.org
Leake Central ES 1,100/K-5
603 Highway 16 W 39051 601-267-9148
Keith Moss, prin. Fax 267-5904
Leake Central JHS 500/6-8
801 Martin Luther King Dr 39051 601-267-8909
Peggy Marble, prin. Fax 267-5902
Other Schools – See Walnut Grove

Cedarbluff, Clay
West Point SD
Supt. — See West Point
West Clay County ES 100/K-6
450 Joe Stevens Rd 39741 662-494-2350
Brad Cox, prin. Fax 494-4824

Centreville, Wilkinson, Pop. 1,683
Wilkinson County SD
Supt. — See Woodville
Finch ES 300/PK-5
PO Box 130 39631 601-645-5081
Sharon Robinson, prin. Fax 645-6358
Winans MS 300/6-8
PO Box 610 39631 601-645-0008
Jason Hamilton, prin. Fax 645-0170

Centreville Academy 400/K-12
PO Box 70 39631 601-645-5912
Jason Horne, hdmstr. Fax 645-5940

Charleston, Tallahatchie, Pop. 2,183
East Tallahatchie Consolidated SD 1,200/PK-12
411 E Chestnut St 38921 662-647-5524
Dr. Ben Kennedy, supt. Fax 647-3720
www.etsd.k12.ms.us
Charleston ES 500/PK-4
411 E Chestnut St 38921 662-647-2679
Scarlett Willis, prin. Fax 647-2381
Charleston MS 300/5-8
411 E Chestnut St 38921 662-647-2115
Greg McCord, prin. Fax 647-2380

Strider Academy 100/K-12
3698 MS Highway 32 Central 38921 662-647-5833
Kelvin Newton, hdmstr.

Clarksdale, Coahoma, Pop. 17,884
Clarksdale Municipal SD 3,000/PK-12
PO Box 1088 38614 662-627-8500
Dennis Dupree, supt. Fax 627-8542
www.cmsd.k12.ms.us/
Heidelberg ES 300/K-4
PO Box 1088 38614 662-627-8577
Cornishee Bruce, prin. Fax 627-8548
Higgins MS 500/7-8
PO Box 1088 38614 662-627-8550
Debra Ware, prin. Fax 627-8543
Kirkpatrick ES 200/K-4
PO Box 1088 38614 662-627-8588
SuzAnne Walton, prin. Fax 627-8526
Oakhurst IS 500/5-6
PO Box 1088 38614 662-627-8560
Londeria Hayes, prin. Fax 627-8512

Oliver ES 200/K-4
PO Box 1088 38614 662-627-8605
Elizabeth George, prin. Fax 627-8547
Washington ES 300/PK-4
PO Box 1088 38614 662-627-8567
Brenda Miller, prin. Fax 627-7355

Coahoma County SD 1,500/PK-12
PO Box 820 38614 662-624-5448
Xandra Brooks-Keys, supt. Fax 624-5512
www.coahoma.k12.ms.us
Sherard ES 300/PK-6
3105 Bobo Sherard Rd 38614 662-624-4629
Kevin Carter, prin. Fax 627-7865
Other Schools – See Friars Point, Jonestown, Lyon

Presbyterian Day S 100/PK-6
944 Catalpa St 38614 662-627-7761
St. Elizabeth S 100/PK-6
150 Florence Ave 38614 662-624-4239
Jeannie Roberts, prin. Fax 624-2072

Cleveland, Bolivar, Pop. 12,236
Cleveland SD 3,500/PK-12
305 Merritt Dr 38732 662-843-3529
Jacquelyn Thigpen Ed.D., supt. Fax 579-3090
www.cleveland.k12.ms.us
Cleveland Central MS 7-8
601 Lucy Seaberry Dr 38732 662-843-2338
L'Kenna Whitehead, prin. Fax 843-1900
Nailor ES 400/K-2
600 Cross St 38732 662-843-4528
Jessica Tyson, prin. Fax 843-2293
Parks ES 400/K-6
1301 Terrace Rd 38732 662-843-3166
Cody Shumaker, prin. Fax 843-3155
Pearman ES 300/K-5
420 Robinson Dr 38732 662-843-4484
Authur Johnson, prin. Fax 843-4484
Smith ES 200/3-5
715 S Martin Luther King Dr 38732 662-846-6152
Angela Towers, prin. Fax 545-4895
Other Schools – See Boyle

Bayou Academy 400/PK-12
PO Box 417 38732 662-843-3708
Presbyterian Day S 200/PK-6
1100 W Highway 8 38732 662 843 8698

Clinton, Hinds, Pop. 24,956
Clinton SD 4,900/K-12
PO Box 300 39060 601-924-7533
Dr. Tim Martin Ed.D., supt. Fax 924-6345
www.clintonpublicschools.com
Clinton JHS 800/7-8
711 Lakeview Dr 39056 601-924-0619
Dr. John Wallace, prin. Fax 924-7703
Clinton Park ES 800/K-1
501 Arrow Dr 39056 601-924-5205
Kelli Pope, prin. Fax 925-6237
Eastside ES 700/4-5
453 Arrow Dr 39056 601-924-7261
Cindy Hamil, prin. Fax 925-9005
Lovett MS 400/6-6
2002 W Northside Dr 39056 601-924-5664
Michael Pope, prin. Fax 924-3778
Northside ES 800/2-3
451 Arrow Dr 39056 601-924-7531
Mandy Ambrose, prin. Fax 925-4028

Clinton Christian Academy 200/PK-12
PO Box 330 39060 601-910-5990
Mount Salus Christian S 100/PK-12
PO Box 240 39060 601-924-5863
Br. Bill Maner, head sch Fax 924-3377

Coffeeville, Yalobusha, Pop. 891
Coffeeville SD 600/PK-12
96 Mississippi St 38922 662-675-8941
Dr. Vivian Robinson, supt. Fax 675-5004
www.coffeevilleschools.org
Coffeeville ES 400/PK-7
96 Mississippi St 38922 662-675-2721
Emily Patty, prin. Fax 675-5007

Coldwater, Tate, Pop. 1,663
Tate County SD 2,900/K-12
574 Parkway St 38618 662-562-5861
Dr. Daryl Scoggin, supt. Fax 622-7402
www.tcsdms.org
Coldwater Attendence Center 500/K-12
340 Darnell St 38618 662-622-5561
Timeka Thomas, prin. Fax 622-7253
East Tate ES 700/K-6
6832 E Tate Rd 38618 662-562-4688
Stephanie Franklin, prin. Fax 560-0881
Other Schools – See Sarah

Collins, Covington, Pop. 2,566
Covington County SD 2,900/K-12
PO Box 1269 39428 601-765-4457
Dr. Arnetta Crosby, supt. Fax 765-9402
www.cov.k12.ms.us
Carver MS 300/5-8
PO Box 757 39428 601-765-4908
Lisa Campbell, prin. Fax 765-4100
Collins ES 400/K-4
PO Box 160 39428 601-765-4383
Missy Rogers, prin. Fax 765-2189
Hopewell ES 300/K-6
824 Hopewell Rd 39428 601-765-8568
Turpin Smith, prin. Fax 765-9486
Other Schools – See Mount Olive, Seminary

Collinsville, Lauderdale, Pop. 1,932
Lauderdale County SD
Supt. — See Meridian
West Lauderdale MS 700/5-8
9916 W Lauderdale Rd 39325 601-737-8689
Glenn Boothe, prin. Fax 737-5145

Columbia, Marion, Pop. 6,495
Columbia SD 1,800/K-12
613 Bryan Ave 39429 601-736-2366
Jason Harris Ed.D., supt. Fax 736-2653
www.columbiaschools.org
Columbia ES 300/3-5
401 Mary St 39429 601-736-2362
Robert White, prin. Fax 736-5891
Columbia PS 600/K-2
913 West Ave 39429 601-736-2216
Heather Singley, prin. Fax 731-3764
Jefferson MS 400/6-8
611 Owens St 39429 601-736-2786
Raymond Powell, prin. Fax 731-3762

Marion County SD 2,100/PK-12
1010 Highway 13 N Ste 2 39429 601-736-7193
Wendy Bracey, supt. Fax 736-6274
www.marionk12.org
East Marion ES 400/PK-6
527 E Marion School Rd 39429 601-736-7290
Dr. Portia Hull, prin. Fax 736-7157
Other Schools – See Foxworth

Columbia Academy 600/K-12
1548 Highway 98 E 39429 601-736-6418
Woodlawn Prep S 50/PK-8
1452 Highway 98 E 39429 601-736-4122
Dr. Darin Tubb, prin.

Columbus, Lowndes, Pop. 23,393
Columbus Municipal SD 4,500/PK-12
PO Box 1308 39703 662-241-7400
Dr. Philip Hickman, supt. Fax 241-7453
www.columbuscityschools.org
Columbus MS 900/6-8
175 Highway 373 39705 662-241-7300
Billie Smith, prin. Fax 241-7305
Cook ES 700/PK-5
2217 7th Ave N 39701 662-241-7180
Dr. Tim Wilcox, prin. Fax 241-7182
Fairview Aerospace & Science S 300/PK-5
225 Airline Rd 39702 662-241-7140
Evan Caine, prin. Fax 241-7141
Franklin Medical Sciences & Wellness S 400/PK-5
501 3rd Ave N 39701 662-241-7150
TaWan Williams, prin. Fax 241-7152
Sale International Studies S 400/PK-5
520 Warpath Rd 39702 662-241-7260
Kimberly Blunt, prin. Fax 241-7262
Stokes-Beard Technology/Communication S 500/PK-5
311 Martin Luther King Dr 39701 662-241-7270
Kimberly Gardner, prin. Fax 241-7231

Lowndes County SD 4,900/PK-12
1053 Highway 45 S 39701 662-244-5000
Lynn Wright, supt. Fax 244-5043
www.lowndes.k12.ms.us/
New Hope ES 1,100/PK-5
199 Enlow Dr 39702 662-244-4760
Dr. Christy Adams, prin. Fax 244-4775
New Hope MS 600/6-8
462 Center Rd 39702 662-244-4740
Sam Allison, prin. Fax 244-4758
West Lowndes ES 300/PK-6
1000 Gilmer Wilburn Rd 39701 662-244-5050
Robert Sanders, prin. Fax 328-2912
Other Schools – See Caledonia

Annunciation Catholic S 100/PK-8
223 N Browder St 39702 662-328-4479
Joni House, prin. Fax 328-0430
Heritage Academy 500/K-12
625 Magnolia Ln 39705 662-327-5272

Como, Panola, Pop. 1,273
North Panola SD
Supt. — See Sardis
Como ES 300/PK-5
202 Lewers St 38619 662-526-0396
Victor Henson, prin. Fax 526-5259
North Panola JHS 300/6-8
526 Compress Rd 38619 662-526-5938
Dr. Mario Keys, prin. Fax 526-5990

Corinth, Alcorn, Pop. 14,398
Alcorn SD 3,000/PK-12
PO Box 1420 38835 662-286-5591
Larry Mitchell, supt. Fax 286-7766
www.alcorn.k12.ms.us
Biggersville ES 100/PK-6
571A Highway 45 38834 662-286-6593
Elizabeth White, admin. Fax 286-5735
Kossuth ES 500/PK-4
14 County Road 604 38834 662-286-2761
Charla Essary, admin. Fax 286-6875
Kossuth MS 500/5-8
17 County Road 604 38834 662-286-7093
Samuel Roberts, admin. Fax 286-6837
Other Schools – See Glen

Corinth SD 2,600/PK-12
1204 N Harper Rd 38834 662-287-2425
Edward Lee Childress Ed.D., supt. Fax 286-1885
www.corinth.k12.ms.us
Corinth ES 1,200/PK-4
1910 Droke Rd 38834 662-286-5245
Brian Knippers, prin. Fax 287-0298
Corinth MS 800/5-8
1000 E 5th St 38834 662-286-1261
Nathan Hall, prin. Fax 287-0296

Corinth Adventist S 50/1-8
42B County Road 278 38834 662-286-3600

Crenshaw, Panola, Pop. 880
North Panola SD
Supt. — See Sardis
Crenshaw ES 100/K-5
108 WC Franklin St 38621 662-382-5803
Rachel McKinney-Williams, prin. Fax 382-7122

Crystal Springs, Copiah, Pop. 5,021
Copiah County SD
Supt. — See Hazlehurst
Crystal Springs ES 600/K-3
213 Newton St 39059 601-892-4795
Tracy Boone, prin. Fax 892-4789
Crystal Springs MS 600/4-8
2092 S Pat Harrison Dr 39059 601-892-2722
Donald Regan, prin. Fax 892-9949

Decatur, Newton, Pop. 1,826
Newton County SD 1,800/K-12
15305 Highway 15 39327 601-635-2317
J.O. Amis, supt. Fax 635-4025
www.newton.k12.ms.us
Newton County ES 900/K-5
15881 Highway 15 39327 601-635-2956
Jason Roberson, prin. Fax 635-4074

Newton County Academy 200/PK-12
PO Box 25 39327 601-635-2756

De Kalb, Kemper, Pop. 1,156
Kemper County SD 1,100/PK-12
PO Box 219 39328 601-743-2657
Jackie Pollock, supt. Fax 743-9297
kemper.k12.ms.us
West Kemper ES 500/PK-6
PO Box 250 39328 601-743-2432
Jammy Davis, prin. Fax 743-4232
Other Schools – See Scooba

Kemper Academy 200/PK-12
149 Walnut Ave 39328 601-743-2232

D'Iberville, Harrison, Pop. 9,203
Harrison County SD
Supt. — See Gulfport
D'Iberville ES 800/K-3
4540 Brodie Rd 39540 228-392-2803
Alison Morgan, prin. Fax 392-0557
D'Iberville MS 900/4-8
3320 Warrior Dr 39540 228-392-1746
Matthew Elias, prin. Fax 392-9948

Sacred Heart ES 100/PK-6
10482 Lemoyne Blvd 39540 228-392-4180
Richard Lopez, prin. Fax 392-4859

Drew, Sunflower, Pop. 1,923
Sunflower County Consolidated SD
Supt. — See Indianola
Drew Hunter MS 100/6-8
10 Swoope Rd 38737 662-745-8940
Tony Young, prin. Fax 745-8529
James ES 300/K-5
400 South Blvd 38737 662-745-8892
Barbara Akon, prin. Fax 745-6630

North Sunflower Academy 100/K-12
148 Academy Rd 38737 662-756-4573

Duncan, Bolivar, Pop. 423
North Bolivar Consolidated SD
Supt. — See Mound Bayou
Brooks ES 200/PK-4
PO Box 168 38740 662-395-2254
Doris Hall, prin. Fax 395-2247

Dundee, Tunica
Tunica County SD
Supt. — See Tunica
Dundee ES 200/PK-5
12910 Old Highway 61 S 38626 662-363-1810
Natasha Bates, prin. Fax 363-1695

Durant, Holmes, Pop. 2,658
Durant SD 500/K-12
5 W Madison St 39063 662-653-3175
Glenn Carlisle, supt. Fax 653-6151
durant.k12.ms.us
Durant S 500/K-12
PO Box 669 39063 662-653-3429
Karen Williams, prin. Fax 653-3472

Holmes County SD
Supt. — See Lexington
Williams-Sullivan ES 300/PK-8
14494 Highway 51 39063 662-653-6218
Shem Whigham, prin. Fax 653-1056

Ecru, Pontotoc, Pop. 882
Pontotoc County SD
Supt. — See Pontotoc
North Pontotoc ES 800/PK-4
8324 Highway 15 N 38841 662-489-5613
Terri Smith, prin. Fax 489-9126
North Pontotoc MS 200/7-8
8324 Highway 15 N 38841 662-489-5613
Paul Ross, prin. Fax 489-7068
North Pontotoc Upper ES 300/5-6
1620 Old Highway 15 38841 662-489-2295
Libby Young, prin. Fax 509-8908

Ellisville, Jones, Pop. 4,419
Jones County SD 8,300/K-12
5204 Highway 11 N 39437 601-649-5201
Thomas Parker, supt. Fax 649-1613
www.jones.k12.ms.us/
South Jones ES 1,000/K-6
27 Warrior Rd 39437 601-477-3577
Wade Clark, prin. Fax 477-2700
Other Schools – See Laurel, Moselle

Enterprise, Clarke, Pop. 526
Enterprise SD — 1,000/PK-12
503 S River Rd 39330 — 601-659-7965
Josh Perkins, supt. — Fax 659-3254
www.esd.k12.ms.us/
Enterprise ES — 400/PK-4
103 Short St 39330 — 601-659-7613
Steven Gunn, prin. — Fax 659-7371
Enterprise MS — 300/5-8
105 Short St 39330 — 601-659-7722
Marlon Brannan, prin. — Fax 659-7722

Eupora, Webster, Pop. 2,169
Webster County SD — 1,700/PK-12
95 Clark Ave 39744 — 662-258-5921
Brian Jones, supt. — Fax 258-3134
www.webstercountyschools.org
Eupora ES — 500/PK-6
1 Naron Ave 39744 — 662-258-6735
Chip Powell, prin. — Fax 258-3129
Other Schools – See Mathiston

Falkner, Tippah, Pop. 510
North Tippah SD
Supt. — See Tiplersville
Falkner ES — 300/K-6
20771 Highway 15 38629 — 662-837-3947
Debby Harrison, prin. — Fax 837-0082

Fayette, Jefferson, Pop. 1,609
Jefferson County SD — 1,300/PK-12
PO Box 157 39069 — 601-786-3721
Dr. Bertha L. Watts, supt. — Fax 786-8441
www.jcpsd.net
Jefferson County ES — 500/PK-4
430 Highway 33 39069 — 601-786-6003
LaRondrial Barnes, prin. — Fax 786-2274
Jefferson County JHS — 200/7-8
468 Highway 33 39069 — 601-786-3900
David Day, prin. — Fax 786-2273
Jefferson County Upper ES — 200/5-6
442 Highway 33 39069 — 601-786-8510
Curtis Smith, prin. — Fax 786-3527

Flora, Madison, Pop. 1,878
Madison County SD
Supt. — See Ridgeland
East Flora ES — 300/K-5
PO Box J 39071 — 601-879-8724
Dr. Capucine Robinson, prin. — Fax 879-3158

Tri-County Academy — 300/PK-12
PO Box K 39071 — 601-879-8517
Mark Johnson, hdmstr. — Fax 879-3373

Florence, Rankin, Pop. 4,112
Rankin County SD
Supt. — See Brandon
Florence ES — 600/3-5
285 Highway 469 N 39073 — 601-845-8164
Vallerie Lacey, prin. — Fax 845-1582
Florence MS — 600/6-8
PO Box 159 39073 — 601-845-2862
Jessica Hodges, prin. — Fax 845-2114
McLaurin ES — 600/K-6
2693 Star Rd 39073 — 601-845-2127
Charles Lee, prin. — Fax 845-3251
Steen's Creek ES — 600/K-2
300 Highway 469 N 39073 — 601-845-5724
Catie Gunn, prin. — Fax 845-3549

Flowood, Rankin, Pop. 7,724
Rankin County SD
Supt. — See Brandon
Flowood ES — 600/K-5
102 Winners Cir 39232 — 601-992-6277
Denese Sutton, prin. — Fax 992-2468
Northwest Rankin ES — 500/K-5
500 Vine Dr 39232 — 601-992-0924
Kara Killough, prin. — Fax 992-7112
Northwest Rankin MS — 900/6-8
1 Paw Print Pl 39232 — 601-992-1329
Shea Taylor, prin. — Fax 992-1347

Good Shepherd Lutheran S — 50/PK-5
6035 Highway 25 39232 — 601-992-4752
Carolyn Sawyer, dir.
Hartfield Academy — 400/PK-12
1240 Luckney Rd 39232 — 601-992-5333
David Horner, hdmstr. — Fax 783-9930

Forest, Scott, Pop. 5,620
Forest Municipal SD — 1,500/K-12
325 Cleveland St 39074 — 601-469-3250
Dr. Joseph White, supt. — Fax 469-3101
www.forest.k12.ms.us/
Forest ES — 800/K-4
513 Cleveland St 39074 — 601-469-3073
Stacy Crosby, prin. — Fax 469-8252
Hawkins MS — 400/5-8
803 E Oak St 39074 — 601-469-1474
Marcus Holbert, prin. — Fax 469-8251

Scott County SD — 3,900/K-12
110 Commerce Loop 39074 — 601-469-3861
Tony McGee, supt. — Fax 469-3874
www.scott.k12.ms.us
Scott Central S — 1,000/K-12
2415 Old Jackson Rd 39074 — 601-469-4883
Patrick Henderson, prin. — Fax 469-3746
Other Schools – See Lake, Morton, Sebastopol

Foxworth, Marion, Pop. 592
Marion County SD
Supt. — See Columbia
West Marion ES — 300/4-6
2 W Marion St 39483 — 601-731-2076
Sherrie Williams, prin. — Fax 731-7938
West Marion PS — 400/K-3
PO Box 6 39483 — 601-736-3713
Heather Singley, prin. — Fax 731-2091

French Camp, Choctaw, Pop. 172
Choctaw County SD
Supt. — See Ackerman
French Camp ES — 200/PK-6
300 Church St 39745 — 662-547-7102
Shane Burton, prin. — Fax 547-7119

Friars Point, Coahoma, Pop. 1,198
Coahoma County SD
Supt. — See Clarksdale
Friars Point ES — 200/PK-6
PO Box 600 38631 — 662-383-2477
LaTasha Turner, prin. — Fax 383-0066

Fulton, Itawamba, Pop. 3,914
Itawamba County SD — 3,400/PK-12
605 S Cummings St 38843 — 662-862-2159
Michael Nanney, supt. — Fax 862-4713
www.itawambacountyschools.com
Dorsey Attendance Center — 400/K-8
1 Dorsey School Rd 38843 — 662-862-3663
Fax 862-7210
Itawamba Attendance Center — 900/PK-8
488 Little Indian Rd 38843 — 662-862-4641
Dr. Terry Harbin, prin. — Fax 862-4396
Other Schools – See Golden, Mantachie, Tremont

Gallman, Copiah

Copiah Educational Foundation — 700/PK-12
PO Box 125 39077 — 601-892-3770

Gautier, Jackson, Pop. 18,202
Pascagoula-Gautier SD
Supt. — See Pascagoula
College Park ES — 300/K-4
2617 Ladnier Rd 39553 — 228-522-8829
Suzanne Ros, prin. — Fax 522-8830
Gautier ES — 400/K-4
505 Magnolia Tree Dr 39553 — 228-522-8824
Jessica Coleman, prin. — Fax 522-8825
Gautier MS — 400/7-8
1920 Graveline Rd 39553 — 228-522-8806
Christy Reimsnyder, prin. — Fax 522-8813
Martin Bluff ES — 600/K-4
1306 Roys Rd 39553 — 228-522-8850
Dr. Vickie Hoover, prin. — Fax 522-8852
Singing River Academy — 500/5-6
4601 Gautier Vancleave Rd 39553 — 228-522-8835
Pam Rone, prin. — Fax 522-8839

Glen, Alcorn, Pop. 409
Alcorn SD
Supt. — See Corinth
Alcorn Central ES — 400/PK-4
20 County Road 254 38846 — 662-286-6899
John Anderson, admin. — Fax 287-6487
Alcorn Central MS — 400/5-8
8A County Road 254 38846 — 662-286-3674
Jeff Boren, admin. — Fax 286-6712

Golden, Itawamba, Pop. 190
Itawamba County SD
Supt. — See Fulton
Fairview Attendance Center — 200/K-8
66 Fairview School Rd 38847 — 662-585-3127
Benjie Ewing, prin. — Fax 585-3139

Goodman, Holmes, Pop. 1,376
Holmes County SD
Supt. — See Lexington
Goodman-Pickens ES — 300/K-5
3877 Highway 51 39079 — 662-468-2116
Bridgett Wheaton, prin. — Fax 468-2786

Greenville, Washington, Pop. 34,233
Greenville SD — 6,000/PK-12
PO Box 1619 38702 — 662-334-7000
Dr. Janice Page-Johnson, supt. — Fax 334-7021
www.gvillepublicschooldistrict.com
Akin ES — 500/K-5
361 Bowman Blvd 38701 — 662-334-7161
James Stevens, prin. — Fax 334-2847
Armstrong ES — 300/K-5
528 Redbud St 38701 — 662-334-7121
Yolanda Johnson, prin. — Fax 334-7120
Boyd ES — 500/K-5
1021 S Colorado St 38703 — 662-334-7166
Brigetta Sims, prin. — Fax 334-2872
Coleman MS — 600/6-8
400 Dr Martin L King Blvd 38701 — 662-334-7036
Dianne Zanders, prin. — Fax 334-7040
McBride Pre-K Academy — 100/PK-PK
438 N Poplar St 38701 — 662-334-7136
Fax 334-2874
Solomon Magnet S — 600/6-8
556 Bowman Blvd 38701 — 662-334-7052
Michael Dean, dir. — Fax 334-7053
Stern ES — 200/K-5
522 McAllister St 38701 — 662-334-7130
Samuel Evans, prin. — Fax 378-1821
Trigg ES — 500/K-5
3004 Lincoln Dr 38703 — 662-334-7177
Betty Johnson, prin. — Fax 334-7176
Webb ES — 300/K-5
600 S Harvey St 38701 — 662-334-7146
Debra Reeves, prin. — Fax 334-2879
Weddington ES — 500/K-5
668 Sampson Rd 38701 — 662-334-7101
Tamela Gines, prin. — Fax 334-2879

Western Line SD
Supt. — See Avon
O'Bannon ES — 500/PK-6
PO Box 5816 38704 — 662-332-4830
James Johnson, prin. — Fax 334-1956

Greenville Christian S — 200/PK-12
2064 GCS Rd 38701 — 662-332-0946
Our Lady of Lourdes S — 200/PK-6
1501 V F W Rd 38701 — 662-334-3287
Michelle Gardiner, prin. — Fax 332-9877
Washington S — 700/PK-12
1605 E Reed Rd 38703 — 662-334-4096

Greenwood, LeFlore, Pop. 15,124
Greenwood SD — 2,600/PK-12
PO Box 1497 38935 — 662-453-4231
Dr. Jennifer Wilson, supt. — Fax 455-7409
www.greenwood.k12.ms.us/
Bankston ES — 300/K-6
1312 Grand Blvd 38930 — 662-455-7421
Kirby Love, prin. — Fax 455-7473
Davis ES — 500/K-6
400 Cotton St 38930 — 662-455-7430
Likisha Coleman, prin. — Fax 455-7497
Greenwood MS — 400/7-8
1200 Garrard Ave 38930 — 662-455-3661
Dr. Michael Johnson, prin. — Fax 455-5559
Threadgill ES — 600/PK-6
1001 Broad St 38930 — 662-455-7440
Lachada Robie, prin. — Fax 455-7413
Threadgill PS — K-2
1300 Carrollton Ave 38930 — 662-644-0685
Dawn West, prin. — Fax 453-1092

Leflore County SD — 2,700/PK-12
1901 Highway 82 W 38930 — 662-453-8566
Ilean Richards, supt. — Fax 459-7265
www.lefcsd.org
Brown ES — 300/K-3
3827 County Road 363 38930 — 662-453-8622
EdShundra Gary, prin. — Fax 453-8623
East ES — 500/PK-5
208 Meadowbrook Rd 38930 — 662-453-9182
Aiyotoro Roy, prin. — Fax 451-7734
Elzy JHS — 400/6-8
604 Elzy Ave 38930 — 662-453-9677
Barren Cleark, prin. — Fax 455-0139
Other Schools – See Itta Bena

Pillow Academy — 800/PK-12
69601 Highway 82 W 38930 — 662-453-1266
St. Francis of Assisi S — 100/PK-6
2607 Highway 82 E 38930 — 662-453-9511
Sr. Jackie Lewis, prin. — Fax 453-9060

Grenada, Grenada, Pop. 12,980
Grenada SD — 4,100/PK-12
PO Box 1940 38902 — 662-226-1606
Dr. David Daigneault, supt. — Fax 226-7994
www.gsd.k12.ms.us/
Grenada ES — 1,500/PK-3
250 Pender Dr 38901 — 662-226-2584
Raleigh Wood, prin. — Fax 227-4497
Grenada MS — 900/6-8
28 Jones Rd 38901 — 662-226-5135
Marshall Whittemore, prin. — Fax 227-6106
Grenada Upper ES — 600/4-5
500 Pender Dr 38901 — 662-226-2818
Carole Tharpe, prin. — Fax 227-6107

Kirk Academy — 300/PK-12
PO Box 1008 38902 — 662-226-2791
Dr. Randy Poss, hdmstr. — Fax 226-9066

Gulfport, Harrison, Pop. 66,180
Gulfport SD — 6,300/K-12
2001 Pass Rd 39501 — 228-865-4600
Glen East, supt. — Fax 865-1918
www.gulfportschools.org/
Anniston Avenue ES — 700/K-5
2314 Jones St 39507 — 228-896-6309
John Barnett, prin. — Fax 896-3124
Bayou View ES — 700/K-5
4898 Washington Ave 39507 — 228-865-4625
Tess Lawrence, prin. — Fax 865-1928
Bayou View MS — 800/6-8
212 43rd St 39507 — 228-865-4633
Jonathan Dill, prin. — Fax 867-1967
Central ES — 400/K-5
1043 Pass Rd 39501 — 228-865-4642
Sandra Wilks, prin. — Fax 865-0281
Gaston Point ES — 300/K-5
1526 Mills Ave 39501 — 228-865-4656
Shawn Butler, prin. — Fax 865-4701
Gulfport Central MS — 600/6-8
1310 42nd Ave 39501 — 228-870-1035
Dr. Shannon Doughty, prin. — Fax 870-1041
Pass Road ES — 500/K-5
37 Pass Rd 39507 — 228-865-4659
Simone Fairley, prin. — Fax 863-1549
28th Street ES — 400/K-5
3034 46th Ave 39501 — 228-867-2140
Angela August, prin. — Fax 867-2148
West ES — 400/K-5
4051 15th St 39501 — 228-870-1025
Joshua Lindsey, prin. — Fax 870-1032

Harrison County SD — 14,100/K-12
11072 Highway 49 39503 — 228-539-6500
Roy Gill, supt. — Fax 539-6507
www.harrison.k12.ms.us/
Bel Aire ES — 800/K-6
10531 Klein Rd 39503 — 228-832-7436
Heather Blenden, prin. — Fax 832-5388
Crossroads ES — 600/K-6
10453 Klein Rd 39503 — 228-832-6711
Natasha Williams, prin. — Fax 832-0940
Harrison Central ES — 700/K-3
15451 Dedeaux Rd 39503 — 228-832-2701
Kelly Wawrek, prin. — Fax 831-5357
Lizana ES — 500/K-6
15341 Lizana School Rd 39503 — 228-832-1592
Patsy Brewer, prin. — Fax 831-5354
Lyman ES — 600/K-6
14222 Old Highway 49 39503 — 228-832-2257
Melanie Upton, prin. — Fax 831-5345

North Gulfport MS 500/7-8
4715 Illinois Ave 39501 228-864-5326
Kelly Fuller, prin. Fax 863-9649

Orange Grove ES 400/4-6
11391 Old Highway 49 39503 228-832-2322
Denea Smith, prin. Fax 831-5347

River Oaks ES K-6
14111 Three Rivers Rd 39503 228-831-1660
Dr. Shelly Simmons, prin. Fax 831-9181

Three Rivers ES 900/K-6
13500 Three Rivers Rd 39503 228-831-5359
Tracy Sellers, prin. Fax 831-5361

Other Schools – See Biloxi, D'Iberville, Pass Christian, Saucier

---

Christian Collegiate Academy 300/PK-12
12200 Dedeaux Rd 39503 228-832-4585

St. James ES 300/PK-6
603 West Ave 39507 228-896-6631
Jennifer Broadus, prin. Fax 896-6638

Guntown, Lee, Pop. 2,042

Lee County SD
Supt. — See Tupelo

Guntown MS 800/6-8
1539 Main St 38849 662-348-8800
Casey Dye, prin. Fax 348-8810

Hamilton, Monroe, Pop. 450

Monroe County SD
Supt. — See Amory

Hamilton S 700/K-12
40201 Hamilton Rd 39746 662-343-8307
Tim Dickerson, prin. Fax 343-5813

Hattiesburg, Forrest, Pop. 45,409

Forrest County SD 2,400/K-12
400 Forrest St 39401 601-545-6055
Brian Freeman, supt. Fax 545-6054
www.forrest.k12.ms.us/

Dixie Attendance Center 600/K-8
790 Elks Lake Rd 39401 601-582-4890
Mandy Bailey, prin. Fax 582-5277

North Forrest ES 300/K-6
702 Eatonville Rd 39401 601-584-6466
Quan O'Neal, prin. Fax 544-1779

Rawls Springs Attendance Center 200/K-6
10 Archie Smith Rd 39402 601-268-2217
Dena Ford, prin. Fax 264-7256

Travillion S 300/K-8
316 Travillion Rd 39401 601-584-9303
Kristina Pollard, prin. Fax 582-5785

Other Schools – See Brooklyn

Hattiesburg SD 3,700/PK-12
PO Box 1569 39403 601-582-5078
Dr. Robert Williams, supt. Fax 582-6666
www.hattiesburgpsd.com

Burger MS 600/7-8
174 WSF Tatum Drive Ext 39401 601-582-0536
Tonsa Vaughn, prin. Fax 582-0572

Burney STEAM Academy 50/6-6
901 Ida Ave 39401 601-582-5291
Tangela Rayborn, prin. Fax 544-4366

Christian ES 500/PK-5
2207 W 7th St 39401 601-583-0662
Dr. Vanessa Lofton, prin. Fax 582-6083

Hawkins ES 300/PK-5
526 Forrest St 39401 601-583-4311
Hope Mikell, prin. Fax 583-8840

Rowan ES 400/PK-5
500 Martin Luther King Ave 39401 601-583-0960
Donna Scott, prin. Fax 582-0227

Thames ES 500/PK-5
2900 Jamestown Rd 39402 601-582-6655
Teresa Merwin-Vince, prin. Fax 582-6084

Woodley ES 300/PK-5
2006 Oferral St 39401 601-583-8112
Felica Morris, prin. Fax 582-6081

Lamar County SD
Supt. — See Purvis

Longleaf ES 700/PK-5
5279 W 4th St 39402 601-264-3858
Angela McCarty, prin. Fax 261-6892

Oak Grove Lower ES 700/2-3
1762 Old Highway 24 39402 601-268-3862
Matthew Thomas, prin. Fax 268-8852

Oak Grove MS 1,300/6-8
2543 Old Highway 24 39402 601-264-4634
Patrick Gray, prin. Fax 264-2822

Oak Grove Primary ES 800/PK-1
70 Leaf Ln 39402 601-264-9764
Dahlia Landers, prin. Fax 261-3393

Oak Grove Upper ES 600/4-5
1760 Old Highway 24 39402 601-264-6724
Heather Roland, prin. Fax 264-6771

Presbyterian Christian S 1,000/PK-12
221 Bonhomie Rd 39401 601-582-4956

Sacred Heart S 700/PK-12
608 Southern Ave 39401 601-583-8683
Brian McCrory, head sch Fax 583-8684

Word of Faith Christian Academy 50/PK-4
2105 Country Club Rd 39401 601-545-7735
Dr. Beverly Magee Commodore, prin. Fax 545-7734

Hazlehurst, Copiah, Pop. 3,977

Copiah County SD 2,800/K-12
254 W Gallatin St 39083 601-894-1341
Rickey Clopton, supt. Fax 894-2634
www.copiah.ms/

Other Schools – See Crystal Springs, Wesson

Hazlehurst CSD 1,500/PK-12
119 Robert McDaniel Dr 39083 601-894-1152
Lisa Davis, supt. Fax 894-3170
www.hazlehurst.k12.ms.us

Hazlehurst ES 700/PK-5
112 School Dr 39083 601-894-3463
Kimberly Langston, prin. Fax 894-2629

Hazlehurst MS 300/6-8
112 School Dr 39083 601-894-3463
Kristi Harris, prin. Fax 894-5939

Heidelberg, Jasper, Pop. 716

East Jasper Consolidated SD 900/K-12
PO Box E 39439 601-787-3281
Dr. Nadene Arrington, supt. Fax 787-3410
www.eastjasper.k12.ms.us

Berry ES 500/K-6
PO Box O 39439 601-787-2607
Stacie Collins, prin. Fax 787-2662

Heidelberg JHS 100/7-8
PO Box M 39439 601-787-3665
Delois Bullock, prin. Fax 787-3045

Hernando, DeSoto, Pop. 13,952

DeSoto County SD 32,200/PK-12
5 E South St 38632 662-429-5271
Corey Uselton, supt. Fax 429-4198
www.desotocountyschools.org

Hernando ES 600/PK-1
455 Riley St 38632 662-429-4160
Renee Triplett, prin. Fax 449-1108

Hernando Hills ES 600/2-3
570 McIngvale Rd 38632 662-429-9117
Stephanie Gilder, prin. Fax 429-3607

Hernando MS 900/6-8
700 Dilworth Ln 38632 662-429-4154
Jerry Floate, prin. Fax 429-4189

Oak Grove Central ES 600/4-5
893 W Oak Grove Rd 38632 662-429-4180
Stacey Pirtle, prin. Fax 429-4181

Other Schools – See Horn Lake, Lake Cormorant, Olive Branch, Southaven, Walls

Hickory Flat, Benton, Pop. 592

Benton County SD
Supt. — See Ashland

Hickory Flat S 600/K-12
26 Rebel Dr 38633 662-333-7731
Roger Browning, prin. Fax 333-4127

Hollandale, Washington, Pop. 2,691

Hollandale SD 600/K-12
PO Box 128 38748 662-827-2276
Dr. Mario Willis, supt. Fax 827-5261
www.hollandalesd.org

Sanders ES 300/K-6
PO Box 366 38748 662-827-2024
Jorgell Jones, prin. Fax 827-2056

Holly Springs, Marshall, Pop. 7,662

Holly Springs SD 1,400/PK-12
840 Highway 178 E 38635 662-252-2183
Dr. Irene Walton Turnage, supt. Fax 252-7718
www.hssd.k12.ms.us

Holly Springs IS 300/4-6
655 S Maury St 38635 662-252-2329
Susie Brown, prin. Fax 252-5185

Holly Springs JHS 200/7-8
325 E Falconer Ave 38635 662-252-7737
Letashia White, prin. Fax 252-7751

Holly Springs PS 500/PK-3
405 S Maury St 38635 662-252-1768
Dr. Demeka Norwood, prin. Fax 252-7732

Marshall County SD 3,300/K-12
122 S Spring St 38635 662-252-4271
Dr. Lela S. Hale, supt. Fax 252-5129
www.marshallcountysd.org/

Byers ES 400/K-5
4178 Highway 72 38635 662-851-7826
Bobby Sims, prin. Fax 851-4915

Byers MS 200/6-8
4178 Highway 72 38635 662-851-7826
James Kimbrough, prin. Fax 851-4915

Galena ES 200/K-6
4202 Highway 4 W 38635 662-564-2229
Shoanee Garrison, prin. Fax 564-2231

Other Schools – See Byhalia, Potts Camp

Holy Family S 200/PK-8
395 West St 38635 662-252-1612
Clara Isom, prin. Fax 252-3694

Marshall Academy 300/PK-12
100 Academy Dr 38635 662-252-3449

Horn Lake, DeSoto, Pop. 25,611

DeSoto County SD
Supt. — See Hernando

Horn Lake ES 600/PK-2
6341 Ridgewood Rd 38637 662-393-4608
Cynthia Dunning, prin. Fax 393-0216

Horn Lake IS 1,100/3-5
6585 Horn Lake Rd 38637 662-280-7075
Rosie King, prin. Fax 280-7067

Horn Lake MS 1,000/6-8
6125 Hurt Rd 38637 662-393-7443
Nick Toungett, prin. Fax 342-5039

Shadow Oaks ES 500/PK-2
3780 Shadow Oaks Pkwy 38637 662-393-4585
Michaela Smith, prin. Fax 342-1035

Houlka, Chickasaw, Pop. 621

Chickasaw County SD 500/PK-12
PO Box 480 38850 662-568-3333
Dr. Betsy Collums, supt. Fax 568-2993
chickasaw.k12.ms.us/

Houlka S 500/PK-12
PO Box 480 38850 662-568-2772
Anthony Golding, prin. Fax 568-7931

Houston, Chickasaw, Pop. 3,580

Houston SD 1,800/K-12
PO Box 351 38851 662-456-3332
Tony Cook, supt. Fax 456-5259
www.houstonmsschools.com

Houston Lower ES 500/K-2
123 S Starkville Rd 38851 662-456-3323
Robert Winters, prin. Fax 456-5876

Houston MS 400/6-8
PO Box 192 38851 662-456-5174
John Ellison, prin. Fax 456-2254

Houston Upper ES 400/3-5
452 Pittsboro St 38851 662-456-2797
Trevor Hampton, prin. Fax 456-5840

Indianola, Sunflower, Pop. 10,634

Sunflower County Consolidated SD 4,100/K-12
PO Box 70 38751 662-887-4919
Miskia Davis, supt. Fax 887-5501
www.sunflower.k12.ms.us

Carver Upper ES 600/3-6
404 Jefferson St 38751 662-884-1250
Thelma Green, prin. Fax 887-7086

Lockard ES 600/K-2
302 College Ave 38751 662-884-1260
Daphne Heflin, prin. Fax 887-7710

Other Schools – See Drew, Inverness, Moorhead, Ruleville, Sunflower

---

Indianola Academy 500/PK-12
PO Box 967 38751 662-887-2025

Restoration Ministries Christian Academy 100/PK-12
PO Box 1001 38751 662-887-2040
Jeanette Bolden, prin. Fax 887-2040

Inverness, Sunflower, Pop. 1,017

Sunflower County Consolidated SD
Supt. — See Indianola

Inverness S 100/K-8
PO Box 228 38753 662-265-5752
Brenda Singleton, prin. Fax 265-0027

Itta Bena, LeFlore, Pop. 2,046

Leflore County SD
Supt. — See Greenwood

LeFlore County ES 500/K-6
PO Box 564 38941 662-254-6225
Shajuanda Davis, prin. Fax 254-7942

Iuka, Tishomingo, Pop. 2,992

Tishomingo County Special Municipal SD 3,200/K-12
1620 Paul Edmondson Dr 38852 662-423-3206
Christie Holly, supt. Fax 424-9820
www.tcsk12.com

Iuka ES 500/K-4
1500 Whitehouse Rd 38852 662-423-9290
Joshua McClung, prin. Fax 423-7315

Iuka MS 300/5-8
507 W Quitman St 38852 662-423-3316
Jeremy Reece, prin. Fax 423-2426

Other Schools – See Belmont, Burnsville, Tishomingo

Jackson, Hinds, Pop. 172,074

Jackson SD 28,700/PK-12
PO Box 2338 39225 601-960-8700
Dr. Freddrick Murray, supt. Fax 960-8713
www.jackson.k12.ms.us

Bailey APAC MS 600/6-8
1900 N State St 39202 601-960-5343
Christi Hollingshead, prin. Fax 592-2496

Baker Magnet ES 400/K-5
300 E Santa Clair St 39212 601-371-4327
Dr. Shauna Nicholson-Johnson, prin. Fax 371-4371

Barr ES 100/PK-5
1593 W Capitol St 39203 601-960-5336
Linda Murray, prin. Fax 960-5428

Bates ES 400/K-5
3180 McDowell Road Ext 39204 601-346-1412
Stephen Johnson, prin. Fax 371-1654

Blackburn MS 500/6-8
1311 W Pearl St 39203 601-960-5329
Dr. Valerie Bradley, prin. Fax 360-2601

Boyd ES 600/K-5
4531 Broadmeadow Dr 39206 601-987-3504
LeKeisha Sutton, prin. Fax 987-3682

Brinkley MS 400/6-8
3535 Albermarle Rd 39213 601-987-3573
Larry Armstrong, prin. Fax 987-3746

Brown ES 200/PK-5
146 E Ash St 39202 601-960-5326
Zackery Hodge, prin. Fax 960-4043

Cardozo MS 600/6-8
3180 McDowell Road Ext 39204 601-346-5635
Eliza Lee, prin. Fax 373-0286

Casey ES 400/K-5
2101 Lake Cir 39211 601-987-3510
Rhoda Yoder, prin. Fax 987-4944

Chastain MS 700/6-8
4650 Manhattan Rd 39206 601-987-3550
Harrison Michael, prin. Fax 987-4930

Clausell ES 400/K-5
3330 Harley St 39209 601-960-5319
LaToya Burge Blackshear, prin. Fax 360-2693

Davis IB ES 300/K-5
750 N Congress St 39202 601-960-5333
Dr. Kathleen Grigsby, prin. Fax 592-2494

Dawson ES 400/K-5
4215 Sunset Dr 39213 601-987-3513
Vicki Conley, prin. Fax 987-3683

French ES 300/K-5
311 Joel Ave 39209 601-960-5316
Roshanda Clark, prin. Fax 592-2495

Galloway ES 300/PK-5
186 Idlewild St 39203 601-960-5313
Marvin Davis, prin. Fax 360-2657

George ES 200/K-5
1020 Hunter St 39204 601-960-5339
Carla Thomas, prin. Fax 360-2694

Green ES 400/K-5
610 Forest Ave 39206 601-987-3519
Yavonka McGee, prin. Fax 987-4938

Hardy MS 600/6-8
545 Ellis Ave 39209 601-960-5362
Vertis Holmes, prin. Fax 360-2686

Hopkins ES 400/K-5
170 John Hopkins Rd 39209 601-923-2540
Dr. Carri Pillers, prin. Fax 923-0556

Isable ES 400/PK-5
1716 Isable St 39204 601-960-5310
Catrina Crawford, prin. Fax 360-2695
Johnson ES 500/PK-5
1339 Oak Park Dr 39213 601-987-3501
Faith Strong, prin. Fax 987-4971
Key ES 400/K-5
699 W Mcdowell Rd 39204 601-371-4333
Dionne Woody, prin. Fax 371-4374
Kirksey MS, 5677 Highland Dr 39206 300/6-8
Quita Ware, prin. 601-987-8360
Lake ES 300/PK-5
472 Mount Vernon Ave 39209 601-960-5308
Althea Johnson, prin. Fax 960-5449
Lee ES 300/K-5
330 Judy St 39212 601-371-4336
Dr. Cynthia Veals, prin. Fax 371-1102
Lester ES 300/K-5
2350 Oakhurst Dr 39204 601-371-4339
Delacy Bridges, prin. Fax 371-4737
Marshall ES 400/K-5
2909 Oak Forest Dr 39212 601-371-4342
Helen Person-Young, prin. Fax 371-4729
McLeod ES 500/K-5
1616 Sandlewood Pl 39211 601-987-3597
Claudine Blakey, prin. Fax 956-3948
McWillie ES 400/PK-5
4851 McWillie Cir 39206 601-987-3709
Dr. Sara Harper, prin. Fax 987-4960
North Jackson ES 500/K-5
650 James M Davis Dr 39206 601-987-3528
Kimberly Smith, prin. Fax 987-4976
Northwest Jackson MS 300/6-8
7020 Highway 49 N 39213 601-987-3609
Denese Sutton, prin. Fax 987-4975
Oak Forest ES 500/K-5
1831 Smallwood St 39212 601-371-4330
Lutithia Luckett, prin. Fax 371-4702
Pecan Park ES 400/K-5
415 Claiborne Ave 39209 601-960-5444
Wanda Quon, prin. Fax 592-2490
Peeples MS 500/6-8
2940 Belvedere Dr 39212 601-346-5660
Dr. Kerry Gray, prin. Fax 371-4722
Powell MS 500/6-8
3655 Livingston Rd 39213 601-987-3580
Justin Green, prin. Fax 987-3583
Power APAC 200/4-5
1120 Riverside Dr 39202 601-960-5387
Sandra Reed, prin. Fax 968-5157
Raines ES 400/K-5
156 N Flag Chapel Rd 39209 601-923-2544
Dina Owens, prin. Fax 923-0555
Siwell Road MS 600/6-8
1983 N Siwell Rd 39209 601-923-2550
Donald Boyd, prin. Fax 923-2570
Smith ES 400/K-5
3900 Parkway Ave 39213 601-987-3525
Benjamin Torrey, prin. Fax 987-3546
Spann ES 500/K-5
1615 Brecon Dr 39211 601-987-3532
Nicole Menotti, prin. Fax 987-3719
Sykes ES 400/K-5
3555 Simpson St 39212 601-371-4303
Dr. Wanda Clark, prin. Fax 371-4701
Timberlawn ES 500/K-5
1980 N Siwell Rd 39209 601-923-2556
Jamellah Johnson, prin. Fax 923-0553
Van Winkle ES 500/K-5
1655 Whiting Rd 39209 601-923-2547
Kescher Rankin, prin. Fax 923-2566
Walton ES 400/PK-5
3200 Bailey Ave 39213 601-987-3591
Gwen Gardner, prin. Fax 987-4943
Watkins ES 400/K-5
3915 Watkins Dr 39206 601-987-3594
Dr. Josie Blake, prin. Fax 987-3690
Whitten MS 500/6-8
210 Daniel Lake Blvd 39212 601-371-4309
Paula Epps, prin. Fax 371-4728
Wilkins ES 600/K-5
1970 Castle Hill Dr 39204 601-371-4306
Dr. Jonathan Sutton, prin. Fax 371-4730
Woodville Heights ES 400/K-5
2930 McDowell Road Ext 39204 601-371-4300
Dr. Lynn Horton, prin. Fax 371-4372

Bowman S 100/PK-6
1217 Hattiesburg St 39209 601-352-5441
Shae Robinson, prin. Fax 352-5136
Education Center S 200/K-12
PO Box 55509 39296 601-982-2812
Emmanuel Christian S 200/PK-6
1109 Cooper Rd 39212 601-371-2728
Loretta Horton-Wallace, prin. Fax 372-0560
First Presbyterian Day S 700/K-6
1390 N State St Ste A 39202 601-355-1731
Hillcrest Christian S 500/K-12
4060 S Siwell Rd 39212 601-372-0149
Jackson Academy 1,200/PK-12
PO Box 14978 39236 601-362-9676
Cliff Kling, pres. Fax 364-5722
Mother Goose Christian Academy 200/PK-1
6543 Watkins Dr 39213 601-981-4678
Dr. Earnestine Mason, dir. Fax 981-4688
New Hope Christian S 200/PK-6
5202 Watkins Dr 39206 601-362-4776
Kelli Hart, prin. Fax 362-0938
New Jerusalem Christian S 100/PK-6
5708 Old Canton Rd 39211 601-206-1749
Dr. Joanna Thompson, prin. Fax 206-5706
Redeemer's S PK-3
640 E Northside Dr 39206 601-203-2106
Rogers SDA S 50/K-8
5125 Robinson Rd Ste B 39204 769-257-7041
St. Andrew's Episcopal S 500/PK-4
4120 Old Canton Rd 39216 601-987-9300
Tom Sheppard, head sch Fax 987-9324
St. Richard S 400/PK-6
100 Holly Dr 39206 601-366-1157
Cathy Wilson, prin. Fax 366-4344

Jonestown, Coahoma, Pop. 1,295
Coahoma County SD
Supt. — See Clarksdale
Jonestown ES 200/PK-6
PO Box 26 38639 662-358-4496
Charlette Artis Harris, prin. Fax 358-4491

Kilmichael, Montgomery, Pop. 698
Montgomery County SD
Supt. — See Winona
Montgomery County ES 200/K-6
PO Box 248 39747 662-262-4564
Patricia Cox, prin. Fax 262-4912

Kiln, Hancock, Pop. 2,194
Hancock County SD 4,900/K-12
17304 Highway 603 39556 228-255-0376
Alan Dedeaux, supt. Fax 255-0378
www.hancock.k12.ms.us
East Hancock ES 700/K-5
4221 Kiln Delisle Rd 39556 228-255-6637
Dr. Stacey Lee, prin. Fax 255-8372
Hancock MS 1,100/6-8
7070 Stennis Airport Rd 39556 228-467-1889
Dr. Jessica Taylor, prin. Fax 467-2812
Hancock North Central ES 500/K-5
6122 Cuevas Town Rd 39556 228-255-7641
Chrissy Cuevas, prin. Fax 255-1580
Other Schools – See Bay Saint Louis, Picayune

Kosciusko, Attala, Pop. 7,358
Attala County SD 1,100/PK-12
100 Courthouse Ste 3 39090 662-289-2801
Bryan Weaver, supt. Fax 289-2804
www.attala.k12.ms.us/
Other Schools – See Mc Cool, Sallis

Kosciusko SSD 2,300/K-12
229 W Washington St 39090 662-289-4771
Billy Ellzey, supt. Fax 289-1177
www.ksd.k12.ms.us/
Kosciusko JHS 500/6-8
229 W Washington St 39090 662-289-3737
Jackie McElwain, prin. Fax 289-1177
Kosciusko Lower ES 400/K-1
229 W Washington St 39090 662-289-3364
Michelle Nowell, prin. Fax 289-3364
Kosciusko Middle ES 400/2-3
229 W Washington St 39090 662-289-4653
Chris Terry, prin. Fax 289-4653
Kosciusko Upper ES 400/4-5
229 W Washington St 39090 662-289-2264
Henry Coats, prin. Fax 289-2264

Presbyterian Day S 100/PK-6
603 Smythe St 39090 662-289-3322

Lake, Newton, Pop. 321
Scott County SD
Supt. — See Forest
Lake ES 300/K-4
200 School St 39092 601-775-3011
Lisa Seale, admin. Fax 775-8225
Lake MS 200/5-8
1770 E Scott Rd 39092 601-775-3614
Nancy Butler, prin. Fax 775-8830

Lake Cormorant, DeSoto
DeSoto County SD
Supt. — See Hernando
Lake Cormorant ES 700/PK-5
3285 Wilson Mill Rd 38641 662-781-1135
Carol Smith, prin. Fax 781-9234
Lake Cormorant MS 800/6-8
3203 Wilson Mill Rd 38641 662-781-0778
Lisa Steiner, prin. Fax 781-0688

Lambert, Quitman, Pop. 1,636
Quitman County SD
Supt. — See Marks
Quitman County ES 400/PK-4
PO Box 175 38643 662-326-7186
Dr. Fredrick Robinson, prin. Fax 326-2494

Laurel, Jones, Pop. 18,408
Jones County SD
Supt. — See Ellisville
East Jones ES 800/K-6
108 Northeast Dr 39443 601-425-9799
Sylvia Busby, prin. Fax 425-9118
Glade ES 400/K-6
990 Highway 15 S 39443 601-428-4265
Lisa Ishee, prin. Fax 425-5690
North Jones ES, 650 Trace Rd 39443 800/K-6
Anderle Foster, prin. 601-426-6632
West Jones ES 1,000/K-6
5652 Highway 84 W 39443 601-763-4850
Steve Gieger, prin. Fax 763-4853

Laurel SD 3,100/PK-12
PO Box 288 39441 601-649-6391
Dr. Chuck Benigno, supt. Fax 649-6398
www.laurelschools.org
Davis Magnet ES 400/PK-5
1305 Dr Martin Luther King 39440 601-428-7782
Tammy Griffith, prin. Fax 425-3692
Laurel MS 700/6-8
1600 Grandview Dr 39440 601-428-5312
Leah McCullum, prin. Fax 426-6775
Maddox ES 300/PK-5
600 S 16th Ave 39440 601-426-6437
Angelia Lott, prin. Fax 609-2954
Mason ES 500/K-5
2726 Old Bay Springs Rd 39440 601-428-0393
Rhonda Holloman, prin. Fax 649-2751
Oak Park ES 500/PK-5
1205 Queensburg Ave 39440 601-428-5046
Tito Lanier, prin. Fax 649-6342

Laurel Christian S 500/PK-12
PO Box 8425 39441 601-649-4190
St. Johns S 200/PK-6
520 N 5th Ave 39440 601-428-4350

Leakesville, Greene, Pop. 893
Greene County SD 2,100/PK-12
PO Box 1329 39451 601-394-2364
Charles Breland, supt. Fax 394-5542
www.greene.k12.ms.us
Leakesville ES 500/PK-4
175 Annex Rd 39451 601-394-2493
Shalonda Hollingsworth, prin. Fax 394-5548
Leakesville JHS 400/5-8
620 Main St 39451 601-394-2495
Monica Edwards, prin. Fax 394-5690
Other Schools – See Mc Lain, Richton

Learned, Hinds, Pop. 92

Rebul Academy 100/PK-12
5257 Learned Rd 39154 601-885-6802

Leland, Washington, Pop. 4,449
Leland SD 900/PK-12
408 4th St 38756 662-686-5000
Rev. Jessie King, supt. Fax 686-5029
lelandschooldistrict.schoolinsites.com
Leland ES 400/PK-4
403 E 3rd St 38756 662-686-5013
Maurice Johnson, prin. Fax 686-5043
Leland MS 300/5-8
200 Milam St 38756 662-686-5017
Susie Williams, prin. Fax 686-5042

Lexington, Holmes, Pop. 1,722
Holmes County SD 1,900/PK-12
PO Box 630 39095 662-834-2175
Dr. Angel Meeks, supt. Fax 834-9060
www.holmes.k12.ms.us
Dean ES 700/K-5
96 Rockport Rd 39095 662-834-1333
Valerie Bankhead, prin. Fax 834-4581
Marshall ES 400/K-5
12572 Highway 12 39095 662-235-5226
Karina Peterson, prin. Fax 235-4895
Other Schools – See Durant, Goodman

Central Holmes Christian S 300/PK-12
130 Robert E Lee Dr 39095 662-834-3011

Liberty, Amite, Pop. 726
Amite County SD 1,000/K-12
PO Box 378 39645 601-657-4361
Scotty Whittington, supt. Fax 657-4291
www.amite.k12.ms.us
Amite County ES 600/K-6
PO Box 308 39645 601-657-8311
LeTina Guice, prin. Fax 657-4365

Amite School Center 200/K-12
PO Box 354 39645 601-657-8896

Long Beach, Harrison, Pop. 14,545
Long Beach SD 3,100/K-12
19148 Commission Rd 39560 228-864-1146
Dr. Jay Smith, supt. Fax 863-3196
www.lbsdk12.com
Harper McCaughan ES 700/4-6
19200 Pineville Rd 39560 228-863-0478
Kathryn Standish, prin. Fax 867-1786
Long Beach MS 600/7-8
204 N Cleveland Ave 39560 228-864-3370
Dr. Tim Holland, prin. Fax 867-1789
Quarles ES 500/K-3
111 Quarles St 39560 228-864-3946
Dr. Jan Hansen, prin. Fax 868-6448
Reeves ES 500/K-3
214 Saint Augustine Dr 39560 228-864-9764
Rhonda Powell, prin. Fax 867-1787

Coast Episcopal S 200/PK-6
5065 Espy Ave 39560 228-452-9442
Daren Houck, head sch Fax 452-9446
St. Vincent DePaul S 400/PK-6
4321 Espy Ave 39560 228-222-6000
Carol Church, prin. Fax 222-6003

Louisville, Winston, Pop. 6,587
Louisville Municipal SD 2,800/PK-12
PO Box 909 39339 662-773-3411
Ken McMullan, supt. Fax 773-4013
louisville.k12.ms.us/
Eiland MS 400/6-8
508 Camille Ave 39339 662-773-9001
Jawana Young, prin. Fax 773-4016
Fair ES 600/PK-2
301 N Columbus Ave 39339 662-773-5946
LeAnn Boswell, prin. Fax 773-4012
Louisville ES 400/3-5
300 N Columbus Ave 39339 662-773-3258
Linda Estes, prin. Fax 773-4015
Waiya S 500/K-12
13937 Highway 397 39339 662-773-6770
Belinda Swart, prin. Fax 773-6764
Other Schools – See Noxapater

Grace Christian S 100/PK-12
173 McLeod Rd 39339 662-773-8524
Gale Gregory, hdmstr. Fax 773-4308
Winston Academy 500/PK-12
PO Box 545 39339 662-773-3569

Lucedale, George, Pop. 2,907
George County SD 4,100/PK-12
5152 Main St 39452 601-947-6993
Pam Touchard, supt. Fax 947-8805
www.gcsd.us

Agricola ES 500/K-6
6165 Highway 613 39452 601-947-8447
Dr. Lori Massey, prin. Fax 947-8218
Benndale ES 200/K-6
5204 Highway 26 W 39452 601-766-6341
Jason Woodruff, prin. Fax 945-2938
Central ES 500/K-6
14159 Highway 26 W 39452 601-947-2429
Zach Bost, prin. Fax 947-1421
George County MS 700/7-8
330 Church St 39452 601-947-3106
Kiley Hughes, prin. Fax 947-6004
Hatcher ES 300/PK-3
689 Church St 39452 601-947-3110
Phyllis McDonald, prin. Fax 947-9548
Rocky Creek ES 400/K-6
2183 Rocky Creek Rd 39452 601-947-3886
Stanley Thompson, prin. Fax 766-9962
Taylor IS 300/4-6
159 Mable St 39452 601-947-6065
Debra Joiner, prin. Fax 947-6127

Lumberton, Lamar, Pop. 2,065
Lamar County SD
Supt. — See Purvis
Baxterville S 300/PK-8
1201 Bilbo Rd 39455 601-796-4483
Jarrod Bohannon, prin. Fax 796-5933

Lumberton SD 600/K-12
107 E 10th Ave 39455 601-796-2441
Dr. Linda Smith, supt. Fax 796-2051
www.lumberton.k12.ms.us
Lumberton ES 400/K-8
7922 U S Highway 11 39455 601-796-3721
Carol Jones, prin. Fax 796-7903

Bass Christian S 50/1-8
74 Maranatha Cir 39455 601-794-8867

Lyon, Coahoma, Pop. 350
Coahoma County SD
Supt. — See Clarksdale
Lyon ES 300/PK-6
2020 Roberson Rd 38645 662-624-8544
Crystal Hall-Gooden, prin. Fax 621-8996

Mc Comb, Pike, Pop. 12,696
McComb SD 2,900/PK-12
PO Box 868 39649 601-684-4661
Cederick Ellis Ph.D., supt. Fax 249-4732
www.mccomb.k12.ms.us
Denman JHS 400/7-8
1211 Louisiana Ave 39648 601-684-2387
James Brown, prin. Fax 249-3564
Higgins MS 600/4-6
1000 Elmwood St 39648 601-684-2038
Kelli Little, prin. Fax 249-4734
Kennedy ECC 300/PK-K
207 S Myrtle St 39648 601-684-2889
Felicia Thomas, prin. Fax 249-4739
Otken ES 700/1-3
401 Montana Ave 39648 601-684-3749
Cynthia Lamkin, prin. Fax 684-8304
Other Schools – See Summit

Parklane Academy 900/K-12
1115 Parklane Dr 39648 601-684-8113

Mc Cool, Attala, Pop. 134
Attala County SD
Supt. — See Kosciusko
Greenlee ES 400/PK-6
26050 Highway 12 39108 662-674-5263
Culley Newman, prin. Fax 674-5936

Mc Lain, Greene, Pop. 439
Greene County SD
Supt. — See Leakesville
McLain Attendance Center 200/PK-8
PO Box 39 39456 601-753-2257
Jennifer Pulliam, prin. Fax 753-2266

Macon, Noxubee, Pop. 2,760
Noxubee County SD 1,800/PK-12
PO Box 540 39341 662-726-4527
Roger Liddell Ed.D., supt. Fax 726-2809
www.noxcnty.k12.ms.us
Liddell ES 200/K-4
PO Box 229 39341 662-726-2287
Holli Jenkins, prin. Fax 726-2463
Liddell MS 300/5-8
PO Box 229 39341 662-726-4880
Andrew McFarland, prin. Fax 726-5044
Nash ES 500/PK-4
PO Box 391 39341 662-726-5203
Richard Baliko, prin. Fax 726-3431
Other Schools – See Brooksville

Central Academy 100/PK-12
PO Box 231 39341 662-726-4817

Madden, Leake

Leake Academy 600/PK-12
PO Box 128 39109 601-267-4461

Madison, Madison, Pop. 23,961
Madison County SD
Supt. — See Ridgeland
Germantown MS 700/6-8
202 Calhoun Pkwy 39110 601-859-0376
Chris Perritt, prin. Fax 859-1302
Madison Avenue Lower ES 500/K-2
1199 Madison Ave 39110 601-856-2951
Dr. Brenda Jones, prin. Fax 853-2726
Madison Avenue Upper ES 500/3-5
1209 Madison Ave 39110 601-856-6609
Kim Hurst, prin. Fax 856-7679
Madison MS 1,300/6-8
1365 Mannsdale Rd 39110 601-605-4171
Leatha Phillips, prin. Fax 853-2254
Madison Station ES 900/K-5
459 Reunion Pkwy 39110 601-856-6246
Martha Hanna, prin. Fax 856-5321
Mannsdale ES 700/K-2
443 Mannsdale Rd 39110 601-879-0309
Dr. Emily Mulhollen, prin. Fax 879-0313
Mannsdale Upper ES 400/3-5
371 Mannsdale Rd 39110 601-879-0309
Debra Houghton M.Ed., prin. Fax 879-0313

Madison Ridgeland Academy 900/PK-12
7601 Old Canton Rd 39110 601-856-4455
Termie Land, head sch Fax 853-3835
St. Anthony S 300/PK-6
1585 Old Mannsdale Rd 39110 601-607-7054
Jim Bell, prin. Fax 853-9687

Magee, Simpson, Pop. 4,347
Simpson County SD
Supt. — See Mendenhall
Magee ES 900/K-4
1035 Goodwater Rd NW 39111 601-849-3601
Dr. Paul Lawrence, prin. Fax 849-6207
Magee MS 600/5-8
413 Choctaw St E Ste 100 39111 601-849-3334
Terrell Luckey, prin. Fax 849-6130

Magnolia, Pike, Pop. 2,410
South Pike SD 1,800/PK-12
250 W Bay St 39652 601-783-0430
Dr. Johnnie Vick, supt. Fax 783-6733
www.southpike.org
Gordon Lower ES 500/PK-3
1175 N Clark Ave 39652 601-783-0434
Roxie Baker, prin. Fax 783-2055
Gordon Upper ES 300/4-6
1147 N Clark Ave 39652 601-783-0432
James Coney, prin. Fax 783-2231
South Pike JHS 300/7-8
222 W Myrtle St 39652 601-783-0425
Warren Eyster, prin. Fax 783-2272
Other Schools – See Osyka

Mantachie, Itawamba, Pop. 1,139
Itawamba County SD
Supt. — See Fulton
Mantachie ES 600/PK-6
PO Box 38 38855 662-282-7536
Jamie Dill, prin. Fax 282-7167

Marietta, Prentiss, Pop. 252
Prentiss County SD
Supt. — See Booneville
Marietta S 300/K-8
42 County Road 4070 38856 662-728-4770
Jason Potts, prin. Fax 728-0965

Marks, Quitman, Pop. 1,725
Quitman County SD 1,200/PK-12
PO Box E 38646 662-326-5451
Evelyn W. Jossell, supt. Fax 326-3694
qcschools.com
Quitman County MS 400/5-8
PO Box 290 38646 662-326-6871
Phelton C. Moss, prin. Fax 326-3535
Other Schools – See Lambert

Delta Academy 200/PK-12
PO Box 70 38646 662-326-8164

Mathiston, Webster, Pop. 692
Webster County SD
Supt. — See Eupora
East Webster ES 400/K-6
230 South St 39752 662-263-8373
Kim Stallings, prin. Fax 263-8386

Meadville, Franklin, Pop. 448
Franklin County SD 1,200/PK-12
PO Box 605 39653 601-384-2340
Chris Kent, supt. Fax 384-2393
www.franklincountyschoolsms.com
Franklin County Lower ES 400/PK-3
481 Highway 98 E 39653 601-384-5605
Marsha Webb, prin. Fax 384-3078
Franklin County MS 200/7-8
236 Edison St S 39653 601-384-2441
Lisa Storey, prin. Fax 384-2085
Franklin County Upper ES 200/4-6
409 Highway 98 E 39653 601-384-2940
Susan McGehee, prin. Fax 384-5885

Mendenhall, Simpson, Pop. 2,477
Simpson County SD 4,100/K-12
111 Education Ln 39114 601-847-8000
Greg Paes, supt. Fax 847-8001
www.simpson.k12.ms.us
Mendenhall ES 600/K-4
814 East St 39114 601-847-2621
Rhonda Berry, prin. Fax 847-7192
Mendenhall JHS 500/5-8
730 Dixie Ave 39114 601-847-2296
Kirby Craft, prin. Fax 847-7175
Other Schools – See Magee, Pinola

Simpson County Academy 500/PK-12
124 Academy Cir 39114 601-847-1395

Meridian, Lauderdale, Pop. 40,816
Lauderdale County SD 6,700/PK-12
PO Box 5498 39302 601-693-1683
Randy Hodges, supt. Fax 485-1748
www.lauderdale.k12.ms.us
Clarkdale ES 500/K-4
7000 Highway 145 39301 601-693-4463
Angie McHenry, prin. Fax 483-6329
Clarkdale MS 300/5-8
7000 Highway 145 39301 601-693-4463
Joe Walton, prin. Fax 483-6329
Northeast Lauderdale ES 900/PK-4
6750 Newell Rd 39305 601-485-4882
Lisa Shelly, prin. Fax 482-5198
Northeast MS 700/5-8
7763 Highway 39 39305 601-483-3532
Deborah Brown, prin. Fax 485-0846
Southeast ES 500/K-4
2362 Long Creek Rd 39301 601-486-2500
Ryan Powell, prin. Fax 486-2515
Southeast MS 400/5-8
2535 Old Highway 19 SE 39301 601-485-5751
Marcus Irby, prin. Fax 485-2302
West Lauderdale ES 800/K-4
10350 Highway 495 39305 601-737-2279
Rosemary Harris, prin. Fax 737-8962
Other Schools – See Collinsville

Meridian SD 6,000/PK-12
1019 25th Ave 39301 601-483-6271
Dr. Amy Carter, supt. Fax 484-4917
www.mpsd.k12.ms.us
Carver MS 400/6-8
900 44th Ave 39307 601-484-4482
Felicia Ruffin, prin. Fax 484-3011
Crestwood ES 400/PK-5
730 Crestwood Dr 39301 601-484-4971
Rosalind Operton, prin. Fax 484-5194
Harris ES 700/PK-5
3951 12th St 39307 601-484-4464
Shannon Miller, prin. Fax 484-4994
Magnolia MS 400/6-8
1350 24th St 39301 601-484-4060
Angela McQuarley, prin. Fax 484-5179
Northwest MS 500/6-8
4400 32nd St 39307 601-484-4094
Justus Booth, prin. Fax 484-5180
Oakland Heights ES 500/PK-5
601 59th Ave 39307 601-484-4983
Barbara Young, prin. Fax 484-4986
Parkview ES 600/PK-5
1225 26th St 39305 601-484-4990
Eric Boone, prin. Fax 484-5192
Poplar Springs ES 500/PK-5
4101 27th Ave 39305 601-484-4450
LaVonda Germany, prin Fax 484-5189
West Hills ES 500/PK-5
4100 32nd St 39307 601-484-4472
Candi Robertson, prin. Fax 484-5188

Community Christian S 50/K-8
6256 Highway 39 N 39305 601-485-0715
Lamar S 500/PK-12
544 Lindley Rd 39305 601-482-1345
Russell Christian Academy 400/PK-12
1844D Highway 11 And 80 39301 601-484-5888
St. Patrick S 200/PK-6
2700 Davis St 39301 601-482-6044
Jennifer David, prin. Fax 485-2762

Mize, Smith, Pop. 339
Smith County SD
Supt. — See Raleigh
Mize S 800/K-12
PO Box 187 39116 601-733-2242
John King, prin. Fax 733-9649

Monticello, Lawrence, Pop. 1,561
Lawrence County SD 2,200/K-12
346 Thomas E Jolly Dr W 39654 601-587-2506
Tammy Fairburn, supt. Fax 587-2221
www.lawrence.k12.ms.us
Monticello ES 500/K-4
957 McPherson Dr 39654 601-587-7609
Flavol Rester, prin. Fax 587-4167
Paige MS 400/5-8
1570 W Broad St 39654 601-587-2128
Cassie Bridges, prin. Fax 587-7178
Topeka-Tilton S 400/K-8
853 Highway 27 39654 601-587-4895
Jeff Quin, prin. Fax 587-2367
Other Schools – See Newhebron

Mooreville, Lee, Pop. 646
Lee County SD
Supt. — See Tupelo
Mooreville ES 800/K-5
PO Box 30 38857 662-844-7105
Joanna Peugh, prin. Fax 844-0777
Mooreville MS 400/6-8
PO Box 180 38857 662-680-4894
Roman Doty, prin. Fax 680-4896

Moorhead, Sunflower, Pop. 2,399
Sunflower County Consolidated SD
Supt. — See Indianola
Rosser ES 200/K-5
PO Box 628 38761 662-246-5395
Geneva Benson, prin. Fax 246-8018

Morton, Scott, Pop. 3,416
Scott County SD
Supt. — See Forest
Jack Upper MS 500/5-8
PO Box 500 39117 601-732-6977
Miles Porter, prin. Fax 732-2242
Morton ES 700/K-4
265 E Second Ave 39117 601-732-8529
Debra Herring, prin. Fax 732-1781

Moselle, Jones
Jones County SD
Supt. — See Ellisville
Moselle ES 600/K-6
PO Box 249 39459 601-582-7586
Belinda Beech, prin. Fax 582-7587

Moss Point, Jackson, Pop. 13,562
Jackson County SD
Supt. — See Vancleave

East Central Lower ES 600/K-2
5621 Highway 614 39562 228-588-7060
Becky White, prin. Fax 588-7071
East Central MS 600/6-8
5404 Hurley Wade Rd 39562 228-588-7009
Monique Farrington, prin. Fax 588-7043
East Central Upper ES 600/3-5
5400 Hurley Wade Rd 39562 228-588-7019
Jamie Wade, prin. Fax 588-7046

Moss Point SD 2,200/PK-12
4924 Church St 39563 228-475-4558
Shannon Vincent Ph.D., supt. Fax 474-3302
www.mosspointschools.org/
Magnolia MS 600/6-8
4924 Church St 39563 228-475-1429
Susan Stachowski, prin. Fax 475-2684
Moss Point Escatawpa Upper ES 500/3-5
4924 Church St 39563 228-474-3300
Janice Thomas, prin. Fax 474-3396
Moss Point Kreole PS 600/PK-2
4924 Church St 39563 228-475-3719
Brooks Delk, prin. Fax 474-3312

Mound Bayou, Bolivar, Pop. 1,532
North Bolivar Consolidated SD 1,200/PK-12
201 Green St 38762 662-741-2555
Maurice Smith, supt. Fax 741-2726
www.nbcsd.k12.ms.us
Montgomery ES 300/K-6
201 Green St 38762 662-741-2433
Montresia Cain, prin. Fax 741-2578
Other Schools – See Duncan, Shelby

Mount Olive, Covington, Pop. 971
Covington County SD
Supt. — See Collins
Mt. Olive S 400/K-12
PO Box 309 39119 601-797-3939
O'Tonya Walker, prin. Fax 797-3980

Myrtle, Union, Pop. 482
Union County SD
Supt. — See New Albany
Myrtle S 700/PK-12
1008 Hawk Ave 38650 662-988-2416
Tommy Ozbirn, prin. Fax 988-2001
West Union S 600/PK-12
1610 State Road 30 W 38650 662-534-6745
Russell Taylor, prin. Fax 534-6716

Natchez, Adams, Pop. 15,630
Natchez-Adams SD 4,000/PK-12
10 Homochitto St 39120 601-445-2800
Dr. Fred Butcher, supt. Fax 445-2818
www.natchez.k12.ms.us
Frazier ES 600/K-5
1445 George F West Sr Blvd 39120 601-445-2885
Orisha Mims, prin. Fax 445-2497
Lewis Magnet S 100/6-6
1221 N Dr ML King Jr St 39120 601-445-2927
LaTanya Davis, admin. Fax 445-2966
McLaurin ES 700/PK-5
170 Sgt Prentiss Dr 39120 601-445-2953
Margie Clark, prin. Fax 445-3003
Morgantown MS 200/6-8
101 Cottage Home Dr 39120 601-445-2917
Shemekia Rankin, admin. Fax 445-2912
West ES 500/K-5
161 Lewis Dr 39120 601-445-2891
Jessica Rankin, prin. Fax 445-3010

Adams County Christian S 400/PK-12
300 Chinquapin Ln 39120 601-442-1422
Cathedral S 700/PK-12
701 N Dr ML King Jr St 39120 601-442-2531
Patrick Sanguinetti, prin. Fax 442-0960
Trinity Episcopal Day S 300/PK-12
1 Mallan G Morgan Dr 39120 601-442-5424
Christina Daugherty, hdmstr. Fax 442-3216

Nettleton, Itawamba, Pop. 1,982
Nettleton SD 1,200/K-12
PO Box 409 38858 662-963-2151
Brian Jernigan, supt. Fax 963-7407
www.nettletonschools.com
Nettleton JHS 200/6-8
PO Box 409 38858 662-963-7400
Betsy Grubbs, prin. Fax 963-1525
Nettleton PS 400/K-3
PO Box 409 38858 662-963-2360
Neashatia Buchanan, prin. Fax 963-7413
Nettleton Upper ES 200/4-5
PO Box 409 38858 662-963-7406
Angela Hendrix, prin. Fax 963-7407

New Albany, Union, Pop. 7,897
New Albany SD 2,100/PK-12
301 State Highway 15 N 38652 662-534-1800
Lance Evans, supt. Fax 534-3608
www.newalbanyschools.us
New Albany ES 1,100/PK-5
874 Sam T Barkley Dr 38652 662-534-1840
Jamey Wright, prin. Fax 534-1843
New Albany MS 500/6-8
400 Apple St 38652 662-534-1820
Damon Ladner Ph.D., prin. Fax 534-1819

Union County SD 2,800/PK-12
PO Box 939 38652 662-534-1960
Ken Basil, supt. Fax 534-1961
www.union.k12.ms.us
Ingomar S 700/PK-12
1384 County Road 101 38652 662-534-2680
Roben Denton, prin. Fax 534-3624
Other Schools – See Blue Springs, Myrtle

New Augusta, Perry, Pop. 638
Perry County SD 1,200/PK-12
PO Box 137 39462 601-964-3211
Dr. Scott Dearman, supt. Fax 964-8204
www.pcsdms.com
Perry Central MS 300/6-8
100 8th Ave S 39462 601-964-3226
Kevin Britt, prin. Fax 964-8200
Other Schools – See Beaumont, Petal

Newhebron, Lawrence, Pop. 443
Lawrence County SD
Supt. — See Monticello
New Hebron S 400/K-8
120 Golden Bear Ln 39140 601-694-2151
Christy Alexander, prin. Fax 694-2799

Newton, Newton, Pop. 3,349
Newton Municipal SD 900/K-12
205 School St 39345 601-683-2451
Dr. Nola Bryant, supt. Fax 683-7131
www.nmsd.us
Newton ES 400/K-5
301 W Tatum St 39345 601-683-3979
Kay Killens, prin. Fax 683-7138
Pilate MS 200/6-8
521 E Church St 39345 601-683-3926
Dr. Sharon Hoye, prin. Fax 683-7139

Nicholson, Pearl River, Pop. 3,006
Picayune SD
Supt. — See Picayune
Nicholson ES 400/K-6
1887 Highway 11 S 39463 601-798-6309
Patrick Rutherford, prin. Fax 798-1558

North Carrollton, Carroll, Pop. 470
Carroll County SD
Supt. — See Carrollton
Marshall ES 500/PK-5
PO Box 130 38947 662-237-6840
Fletcher Harges, prin. Fax 237-0080

Noxapater, Winston, Pop. 468
Louisville Municipal SD
Supt. — See Louisville
Noxapater S 400/K-12
220 W Alice St 39346 662-724-4241
Chet Wilkes, prin. Fax 724-4240

Ocean Springs, Jackson, Pop. 17,087
Jackson County SD
Supt. — See Vancleave
St. Martin ES East 700/K-3
7508 Rose Farm Rd 39564 228-875-3204
Nannette Whitehead, prin. Fax 875-3155
St. Martin MS 1,000/6-8
10800 Yellow Jacket Rd 39564 228-818-4833
Stephanie Gruich, prin. Fax 818-0198
St. Martin Upper ES 700/4-5
11000 Yellow Jacket Rd 39564 228-818-2849
Valerie Martino, prin. Fax 818-0425

Ocean Springs SD 5,700/K-12
PO Box 7002 39566 228-875-7706
Dr. Bonita Coleman, supt. Fax 875-7708
www.ossdms.org
Magnolia Park ES 600/K-3
PO Box 7002 39566 228-875-4263
Alison Block, prin. Fax 872-0017
Oak Park ES 500/K-3
PO Box 7002 39566 228-875-5847
Dr. Jennifer Pope, prin. Fax 875-3496
Ocean Springs MS 900/7-8
PO Box 7002 39566 228-872-6210
Adelle Register, prin. Fax 872-9850
Ocean Springs Upper ES 1,300/4-6
PO Box 7002 39566 228-875-4367
Susan Dollar, prin. Fax 872-5048
Pecan Park ES 600/K-3
PO Box 7002 39566 228-875-2851
Christopher LeBatard, prin. Fax 875-0547

St. Alphonsus ES 200/PK-6
504 Jackson Ave 39564 228-875-5329
Dr. Pamala Rogers, prin. Fax 875-3584
Treehouse Montessori Christian S 50/1-6
921 Ocean Ave 39564 228-355-1431

Okolona, Chickasaw, Pop. 2,664
Okolona SSD 700/K-12
411 W Main St 38860 662-447-2353
Dexter Green, supt. Fax 447-9955
okolona.k12.ms.us
Okolona ES 300/K-5
411 W Main St 38860 662-447-5406
Sandra Murray, prin. Fax 447-2700

Olive Branch, DeSoto, Pop. 33,067
DeSoto County SD
Supt. — See Hernando
Center Hill ES 700/PK-5
13662 Center Hill Rd 38654 662-890-7705
Leslie Heyman, prin. Fax 890-7679
Center Hill MS 800/6-8
8756 Forest Hill Irene Ln 38654 662-892-6800
Larry Hood, prin. Fax 892-6810
Chickasaw ES 500/2-3
6391 Chickasaw Dr 38654 662-895-6664
Selina Hall, prin. Fax 893-3434
Lewisburg ES 600/3-5
1717 Craft Rd 38654 662-895-8750
Amanda Samples, prin. Fax 895-8754
Lewisburg MS 700/6-8
1711 Craft Rd 38654 662-892-5050
Brad Meadows, prin. Fax 892-5060
Lewisburg PS 600/PK-2
1707 Craft Rd 38654 662-893-6001
Jeannie Treadway, prin. Fax 893-6006
Olive Branch ES 500/PK-1
9549 Pigeon Roost Rd 38654 662-895-2256
Leighanne Wamble, prin. Fax 893-3299
Olive Branch IS 600/4-5
8631 Pigeon Roost Rd 38654 662-893-1221
Tonja Hellums, prin. Fax 893-1225
Olive Branch MS 800/6-8
6530 Blocker St 38654 662-895-4610
Beth Turner, prin. Fax 895-7358
Overpark ES 700/PK-5
8530 Forest Hill Irene Ln 38654 662-890-8745
Lisa Love, prin. Fax 890-3839
Pleasant Hill ES 800/PK-5
7686 Pleasant Hill Rd 38654 662-890-9654
Jamie Loper, prin. Fax 890-9659

DeSoto County Academy 400/PK-12
100 Academy Dr 38654 662-895-6385
Mildred Waters, prin.

Osyka, Pike, Pop. 439
South Pike SD
Supt. — See Magnolia
Osyka ES 300/K-6
444 Amite St 39657 601-783-0427
Angela Lowery, prin. Fax 542-5350

Oxford, Lafayette, Pop. 18,701
Lafayette County SD 2,700/PK-12
100 Commodore Dr 38655 662-234-3271
Dr. Adam Pugh, supt. Fax 236-3019
www.gocommodores.org
Lafayette ES 700/PK-2
150 Commodore Dr 38655 662-234-5627
Paula Gibbs, prin. Fax 238-7991
Lafayette MS 600/6-8
102 Commodore Dr 38655 662-234-1664
Chad Chism, prin. Fax 232-8736
Lafayette Upper ES 600/3-5
120 Commodore Dr 38655 662-236-3761
Thomas Tillman, prin. Fax 234-0291

Oxford SD 2,700/PK-12
224 Bramlett Blvd 38655 662-234-3541
Brian Harvey, supt. Fax 232-2862
www.oxfordsd.org
Bramlett ES 400/PK-K
225 Bramlett Blvd 38655 662-234-2685
Keri Jo Finnie, prin. Fax 236-2775
Davidson ES 300/3-4
209 Common Wealth Blvd 38655 662-236-4870
Marni Herrington, prin. Fax 236-4874
Oxford ES 300/1-2
1637 Highway 30 E 38655 662-234-3497
Tamara Hillmer, prin. Fax 236-7942
Oxford IS 5-6
501 Martin Luther King Jr 38655 662-236-5508
Steven Hurdle, prin. Fax 236-7944
Oxford MS 600/7-8
222 Bramlett Blvd 38655 662-234-2288
Audra Rester, prin. Fax 236-7337

Oxford University S 100/PK-8
200 OUS Dr 38655 662-234-2200
Regents S of Oxford 200/PK-12
14 County Road 130 38655 662-232-1945
Jason Wood, dir. Fax 232-8818

Pascagoula, Jackson, Pop. 22,125
Pascagoula-Gautier SD 6,900/K-12
PO Box 250 39568 228-938-6491
Wayne Rodolfich, supt. Fax 938-6528
www.pgsd.ms
Arlington ES 400/K-4
3511 Arlington St 39581 228-938-6552
Elizabeth Dock, prin. Fax 938-6551
Beach ES 100/K-4
633 Market St 39567 228-938-6428
Shirley Hunter, prin. Fax 696-6619
Central ES 200/K-4
1100 Dupont Ave 39567 228-938-6559
Angela Burch, prin. Fax 696-6614
Cherokee ES 300/K-4
4102 Scovel Ave 39581 228-938-6547
Tina Bankston, prin. Fax 938-6201
Colmer MS 600/7-8
3112 Eden St 39581 228-938-6473
Dr. Myrick Nicks, prin. Fax 938-6593
Eastlawn ES 300/K-4
2611 Ingalls Ave 39567 228-938-6431
Beth Goff, prin. Fax 938-6433
Jackson ES 300/K-4
3203 Lanier Ave 39581 228-938-6554
Dr. Caterria Payton, prin. Fax 938-6218
Lake ES 100/K-4
4504 Willow St 39567 228-938-6422
Susan Keenum, prin. Fax 696-6618
Lott Academy 600/5-6
2234 Pascagoula St 39567 228-938-6465
Stewart Smirthwaite, prin. Fax 938-6463
Other Schools – See Gautier

Gateway Christian Academy 100/PK-6
PO Box 2295 39569 228-762-4144
Brad Stewart, prin.
Resurrection ES 300/PK-6
3704 Quinn Dr 39581 228-762-7207
Elizabeth Benefield, prin. Fax 762-0611

Pass Christian, Harrison, Pop. 4,509
Harrison County SD
Supt. — See Gulfport
Pineville ES 100/K-6
5192 Menge Ave 39571 228-452-4364
Vivian Bosworth, prin. Fax 452-4605

Pass Christian SD 1,900/K-12
6457 Kiln Delisle Rd 39571 228-255-6200
Carla Evers Ph.D., supt. Fax 255-9302
www.pc.k12.ms.us
DeLisle ES 400/K-5
6303 W Wittman Rd 39571 228-255-6219
Mandy Lacy, prin. Fax 255-6222
Pass Christian ES 500/K-5
270 W Second St 39571 228-452-5200
Dr. Kenitra Ezi, prin. Fax 452-9614

Pass Christian MS 500/6-8
280 W Second St 39571 228-452-5220
Joe Nelson, prin. Fax 452-9616

Pearl, Rankin, Pop. 24,692
Pearl SD 4,000/K-12
3375 Highway 80 E 39208 601-932-7921
Dr. Raymond Morgigno, supt. Fax 932-7929
www.pearl.k12.ms.us/
Northside ES 600/2-3
3600 Harle St 39208 601-932-7971
Nikki Graham, prin. Fax 932-7984
Pearl JHS 900/6-8
200 Mary Ann Dr 39208 601-932-7952
Dr. Jessica Broome, prin. Fax 932-7998
Pearl Lower ES 800/K-1
160 Mary Ann Dr 39208 601-932-7976
Canda Jackson, prin. Fax 932-7978
Pearl Upper ES 600/4-5
400 Treasure Cove 39208 601-932-7981
Gavin Gill, prin. Fax 932-7983

College Drive SDA S 50/1-8
120 College St 39208 601-933-0990
Park Place Christian Academy 400/PK-12
201 Park Place Dr 39208 601-939-6229
Ted Poore, head sch Fax 939-3276

Pelahatchie, Rankin, Pop. 1,321
Rankin County SD
Supt. — See Brandon
Pelahatchie ES 500/K-6
PO Box 599 39145 601-854-8060
Lisa Attkisson, prin. Fax 854-8762

East Rankin Academy 800/PK-12
PO Box 509 39145 601-854-5691
Dan Boyce, hdmstr. Fax 854-5893

Perkinston, Stone
Stone County SD
Supt. — See Wiggins
Perkinston ES 600/K-5
40 2nd St 39573 601-928-3380
Rebecca Puckett, prin. Fax 528-6008

Petal, Forrest, Pop. 10,310
Perry County SD
Supt. — See New Augusta
Runnelstown ES 300/PK-5
9214 Highway 42 39465 601-544-2811
Mike Lott, prin. Fax 543-0933

Petal SD 4,000/K-12
115 E Central Ave 39465 601-545-3002
Dr. Matthew L. Dillon, supt. Fax 584-4700
www.petalschools.com
Petal ES 600/3-4
1179 Highway 42 39465 601-582-7454
Kelli Brown, prin. Fax 584-9400
Petal MS 700/7-8
203 Highway 42 39465 601-584-6301
Michael Hogan, prin. Fax 584-4716
Petal PS 1,000/K-2
60 Herrington Rd 39465 601-554-7244
Tessa Trimm, prin. Fax 554-7246
Petal Upper ES 600/5-6
400 Hillcrest Loop 39465 601-584-7660
Emily Branch, prin. Fax 545-1720

Pheba, Clay

Hebron Christian S 100/PK-12
5100 Henryville Rd 39755 662-494-7513

Philadelphia, Neshoba, Pop. 7,347
Neshoba County SD 3,200/K-12
401 E Beacon St Ste 102 39350 601-656-3752
Dr. Lundy Brantley, supt. Fax 656-3789
www.neshobacentral.com
Neshoba Central ES 1,600/K-5
1002 Saint Francis Dr 39350 601-656-2182
Tiffany Plott, prin. Fax 656-9922
Neshoba Central MS 800/6-8
1000 Saint Francis Dr 39350 601-656-4636
Dr. Kenyon Barron, prin. Fax 389-2989

Philadelphia SD 1,100/K-12
248 Byrd Ave N 39350 601-656-2955
Lisa Hull, supt. Fax 656-3141
www.phillytornadoes.com
Philadelphia ES 700/K-6
406 Stribling St 39350 601-656-1623
Jason Gentry, prin. Fax 656-1302

Picayune, Pearl River, Pop. 10,684
Hancock County SD
Supt. — See Kiln
West Hancock ES 400/K-5
23350 Highway 43 39466 228-586-6054
Katie Warren, prin. Fax 586-6055

Picayune SD 3,400/PK-12
706 Goodyear Blvd 39466 601-798-3230
Dean Shaw, supt. Fax 798-1742
picayune.schooldesk.net
Picayune JHS 600/7-8
702 Goodyear Blvd 39466 601-798-5449
Gen Breeland, prin. Fax 799-4715
Roseland Park ES 500/K-6
1610 Gilcrease Ave 39466 601-798-6824
Kimberly Massengale, prin. Fax 798-1894
South Side ES 300/3-6
1500 Rosa St 39466 601-798-1105
Debra Smith, prin. Fax 798-6032
South Side Lower ES 200/PK-2
400 S Beech St 39466 601-799-0683
Fax 798-6371
West Side ES 400/K-6
111 Kirkwood St 39466 601-798-3625
Mary Williams, prin. Fax 798-1879

Other Schools – See Nicholson

St. Charles Borromeo S PK-7
1006 Goodyear Blvd 39466 601-799-0860
Angela Ingram, prin. Fax 798-7574

Pinola, Simpson
Simpson County SD
Supt. — See Mendenhall
Simpson Central S 500/K-8
755 Simpson Highway 28 W 39149 601-847-2630
Dr. Antoinette Woodall, prin. Fax 847-0954

Pittsboro, Calhoun, Pop. 200
Calhoun County SD 2,500/PK-12
119 W Main St 38951 662-412-3152
Mike Moore, supt. Fax 412-3157
www.calhoun.k12.ms.us
Other Schools – See Bruce, Calhoun City, Vardaman

Calhoun Academy 200/PK-12
10 County Road 406 38951 662-412-2084

Plantersville, Lee, Pop. 1,140
Lee County SD
Supt. — See Tupelo
Plantersville MS 300/5-8
PO Box 129 38862 662-842-4690
Lindsay Brett, prin. Fax 791-0491

Pontotoc, Pontotoc, Pop. 5,537
Pontotoc CSD 2,300/K-12
140 Education Dr 38863 662-489-3336
Dr. Michelle Bivens, supt. Fax 489-7932
www.pontotoc.k12.ms.us
Cox ES 300/3-4
304 Clark St 38863 662-489-2454
Christy Suggs, prin. Fax 489-6239
Pontotoc ES 600/K-2
145 Fred Dowdy Ave 38863 662-489-4973
Avence Pittman, prin. Fax 489-8916
Pontotoc JHS 300/7-8
132 N Main St 38863 662-489-8360
Phil Webb, prin. Fax 489-8947
Pontotoc MS 400/5-6
135 Education Dr 38863 662-489-6056
Gwyn Russell, prin. Fax 489-6197

Pontotoc County SD 3,200/PK-12
354 Center Ridge Dr 38863 662-489-3932
Brock Puckett, supt. Fax 489-2940
www.pcsd.ms
South Pontotoc ES 800/K-5
1523 S Pontotoc Rd 38863 662-489-5941
Lisa Williamson, prin. Fax 489-1757
South Pontotoc MS 400/6-8
1523 S Pontotoc Rd 38863 662-489-5925
Ben Moore, prin. Fax 489-6252
Other Schools – See Ecru

Pope, Panola, Pop. 214
South Panola SD
Supt. — See Batesville
Pope S 500/K-8
PO Box 59 38658 662-563-3732
Jay Cossey, prin. Fax 563-0895

Poplarville, Pearl River, Pop. 2,824
Poplarville SSD 1,900/PK-12
302 Julia St 39470 601-795-8477
Carl Merritt, supt. Fax 795-0712
www.poplarvilleschools.org/
Poplarville Lower ES 400/PK-2
804 Julia St Ste A 39470 601-795-4736
Candace Henderson, prin. Fax 795-6568
Poplarville MS 500/6-8
6 Spirit Dr 39470 601-795-1350
Heidi Dillon, prin. Fax 795-1351
Poplarville Upper ES 400/3-5
1 Todd Cir 39470 601-795-8303
William Payne, prin. Fax 795-3104

Port Gibson, Claiborne, Pop. 1,561
Claiborne County SD 1,600/PK-12
404 Market St 39150 601-437-4232
Dr. Cardell Williams Ph.D., supt. Fax 437-3036
www.claiborne.k12.ms.us/
Port Gibson MS 400/6-8
PO Box 567 39150 601-437-4251
Marvin Harvey, prin. Fax 437-3099
Watson ES 800/PK-5
880 Anthony St 39150 601-437-5070
Antwan Reeves, prin. Fax 437-3044

Potts Camp, Marshall, Pop. 520
Marshall County SD
Supt. — See Holly Springs
Potts Camp MS 200/4-8
7050 Church Ave 38659 662-333-6354
Tana Miller, prin.
Reid PS 300/K-4
160 W Pontotoc Ave 38659 662-333-7774
Leigh Anne Sanderson, prin. Fax 333-7775

Prentiss, Jefferson Davis, Pop. 1,069
Jefferson Davis County SD 1,600/K-12
PO Box 1197 39474 601-792-4267
Will Russell, supt. Fax 792-2251
www.jdcsd.com
Johnson ES 500/K-8
PO Box 1168 39474 601-792-8278
Devonshae Harrien, prin. Fax 792-8149
Other Schools – See Bassfield

Prentiss Christian S 300/K-12
PO Box 1287 39474 601-792-8549
Danny Quick, hdmstr. Fax 792-2560

Puckett, Rankin, Pop. 315
Rankin County SD
Supt. — See Brandon
Puckett ES K-6
PO Box 40 39151 601-825-6140
Nicki Stanley, prin. Fax 825-0015

Purvis, Lamar, Pop. 2,145
Lamar County SD 9,400/PK-12
PO Box 609 39475 601-794-1030
Tess Smith, supt. Fax 794-1012
www.lamarcountyschools.org
Purvis Lower ES 400/PK-2
5976 US Highway 11 39475 601-794-3302
Jackie Cuevas, prin. Fax 794-3317
Purvis MS 400/6-8
PO Box 549 39475 601-794-1068
Frank Bunnell, prin. Fax 794-1037
Purvis Upper ES 400/3-5
310 Mitchell Ave 39475 601-794-2959
Jennifer Moore, prin. Fax 794-1038
Other Schools – See Hattiesburg, Lumberton, Sumrall

Lamar Christian S 300/PK-12
PO Box 880 39475 601-794-0016
Allen Stevens, hdmstr. Fax 794-3726
United Christian Academy 50/4-9
48 Azalea Trl 39475 601-520-1113
Callison Richardson, head sch

Quitman, Clarke, Pop. 2,307
Quitman SD 2,000/PK-12
104 E Franklin St 39355 601-776-2186
Dr. Lynn Weathersby Ph.D., supt. Fax 776-1051
www.quitmanschools.org
Quitman JHS 500/6-8
501 W Lynda St 39355 601-776-6243
Fax 776-1288
Quitman Lower ES 600/PK-2
101 E McArthur St 39355 601-776-6156
Amanda Allen, prin. Fax 776-1035
Quitman Upper ES 400/3-5
300 E Franklin St 39355 601-776-6123
Leah Ivey, prin. Fax 776-1043

Raleigh, Smith, Pop. 1,457
Smith County SD 2,800/K-12
PO Box 308 39153 601-782-4296
Jimmy Hancock, supt. Fax 782-9895
www.smithcountyschools.net
Raleigh ES 700/K-6
201 Whiteoak Ave 39153 601-782-9507
Shelley Bradshaw, prin. Fax 782-9501
Other Schools – See Mize, Taylorsville

Raymond, Hinds, Pop. 1,915
Hinds County SD 6,200/PK-12
13192 Highway 18 39154 601-857-5222
Dr. Delesicia Martin, supt. Fax 857-8548
www.hinds.k12.ms.us/
Carver MS 200/6-8
PO Box 47 39154 601-857-5006
Deborah Newman, prin. Fax 857-4935
Raymond ES 400/K-5
417 Palestine St 39154 601-857-0213
Bobby Taylor, prin. Fax 857-4156
Other Schools – See Bolton, Byram, Terry, Utica

Central Hinds Academy 400/K-12
2894 Raymond Bolton Rd 39154 601-857-5568

Redwood, Warren
Vicksburg Warren SD
Supt. — See Vicksburg
Redwood ES 400/K-6
100 Redwood Rd 39156 601-636-4885
Buddy Wooten, prin. Fax 636-7815

Richland, Rankin, Pop. 6,844
Rankin County SD
Supt. — See Brandon
Richland ES 500/K-2
200 Spell Dr 39218 601-939-4375
Andrea Payne, prin. Fax 939-1991
Richland Upper ES 600/3-6
175 Wilson Dr 39218 601-939-2288
Toby Price, prin. Fax 939-1946

Richton, Perry, Pop. 1,058
Greene County SD
Supt. — See Leakesville
Sand Hill S 400/PK-8
39455 Highway 63 N 39476 601-989-2021
Angela Jones, prin. Fax 394-2022

Richton SD 700/K-12
PO Box 568 39476 601-788-6581
James Clay Anglin, supt. Fax 788-9391
www.richtonschools.com
Richton ES 400/K-6
PO Box 568 39476 601-788-6975
Felicia McCardle, prin. Fax 788-6802

Ridgeland, Madison, Pop. 23,769
Madison County SD 12,600/PK-12
476 Highland Colony Pkwy 39157 601-879-3000
Dr. Ronnie McGehee, supt. Fax 879-3039
www.madison-schools.com/
Highland ES 600/3-5
330 Brame Rd 39157 601-853-8103
Paula Tharp, prin. Fax 853-8109
Olde Towne MS 700/6-8
210 Sunnybrook Rd 39157 601-898-8730
Crystal Chase, prin. Fax 853-8108
Smith ES 700/K-2
306 S Pear Orchard Rd 39157 601-856-6621
Dr. Melissa Philley, prin. Fax 853-2043
Other Schools – See Camden, Canton, Flora, Madison

Christ Covenant S 400/PK-8
752 S Pear Orchard Rd 39157 601-978-2272
Cathy Haynie, head sch Fax 957-2766

Ripley, Tippah, Pop. 5,308
South Tippah SD 2,800/K-12
402 Greenlee Dr 38663 662-837-7156
Frank Campbell, supt. Fax 837-1362
www.stippah.k12.ms.us/
Pine Grove S 600/K-12
3510A County Road 600 38663 662-837-7789
Brad Pounders, prin. Fax 837-8179
Ripley ES 800/K-4
702 Terry St 38663 662-837-7203
Ruby Bennett, prin. Fax 837-1480
Ripley MS 600/5-8
718 S Clayton St 38663 662-837-7959
Patick Mathis, prin. Fax 837-0251
Other Schools – See Blue Mountain

Robinsonville, Tunica
Tunica County SD
Supt. — See Tunica
Robinsonville ES 600/PK-5
7743 Old Highway 61 N 38664 662-357-1077
Donna Smith, prin. Fax 357-1087

Rolling Fork, Sharkey, Pop. 2,129
South Delta SD 900/PK-12
PO Box 219 39159 662-873-4302
Sammie Ivy, supt. Fax 873-6114
www.southdelta.k12.ms.us/
South Delta ES 400/PK-5
138 Weathers Ave 39159 662-873-4849
Valerie Smith, prin. Fax 873-6104
Other Schools – See Anguilla

Sharkey Issaquena Academy 200/K-12
272 Academy Dr 39159 662-873-4241

Rosedale, Bolivar, Pop. 1,864
West Bolivar Cons SD 1,500/PK-12
PO Box 189 38769 662-759-3525
Dr. Beverly Culley, supt. Fax 759-6795
www.wbcsdk12.org
West Bolivar ES 300/K-4
PO Box 429 38769 662-759-3823
Nathan Towers, prin. Fax 759-6795
West Bolivar MS 200/5-8
PO Box 159 38769 662-759-3700
Kym Longstreet, prin. Fax 759-3743
Other Schools – See Benoit, Shaw

Ruleville, Sunflower, Pop. 2,980
Sunflower County Consolidated SD
Supt. — See Indianola
Ruleville Central ES 300/K-5
360 LF Packer Dr 38771 662-756-2548
Latasha Carroll Monroe, prin. Fax 756-2622
Ruleville MS 200/6-8
250 Oscar St 38771 662-756-4698
Tommy Molden, prin. Fax 756-4902

Sallis, Attala, Pop. 134
Attala County SD
Supt. — See Kosciusko
Long Creek ES 300/PK-6
9534 Highway 429 39160 662-289-1630
Dietrich Harmon, prin. Fax 289-4020

Saltillo, Lee, Pop. 4,701
Lee County SD
Supt. — See Tupelo
Saltillo ES 800/3-5
PO Box 1059 38866 662-869-2211
Belinda McKinion, prin. Fax 869-1620
Saltillo PS 800/K-2
PO Box 1525 38866 662-869-3724
Kay Davis, prin. Fax 869-3726

Sarah, Tate
Tate County SD
Supt. — See Coldwater
Strayhorn ES 600/K-6
3402 Highway 4 W 38665 662-562-8637
Stephen Robert Beebe, prin. Fax 562-8631

Sardis, Panola, Pop. 1,686
North Panola SD 1,500/PK-12
470 Highway 51 N 38666 662-487-2305
Cedric Richardson, supt. Fax 487-2050
www.northpanolaschools.org
Green Hill ES 400/K-5
599 W Pearl St 38666 662-487-1074
LaTonya Robinson, prin. Fax 487-2057
Other Schools – See Como, Crenshaw

Saucier, Harrison, Pop. 1,304
Harrison County SD
Supt. — See Gulfport
Saucier ES 400/K-6
24052 1st St 39574 228-832-2440
Cynthia Grimes, prin. Fax 831-5343
West Wortham S 1,200/K-8
20199 W Wortham Rd 39574 228-831-1276
Don Cuevas, prin. Fax 539-5962

Scooba, Kemper, Pop. 727
Kemper County SD
Supt. — See De Kalb
East Kemper ES 200/PK-6
PO Box 97 39358 662-476-8423
Tyresia Brown, prin. Fax 476-8001

Sebastopol, Scott, Pop. 272
Scott County SD
Supt. — See Forest
Sebastopol Attendance Center 600/K-12
PO Box 86 39359 601-625-8654
Kaleb Smith, prin. Fax 625-9426

Seminary, Covington, Pop. 314
Covington County SD
Supt. — See Collins
Seminary ES 500/K-4
PO Box 34 39479 601-722-3355
Angie Palmer, prin. Fax 722-3972
Seminary MS 400/5-8
PO Box 34 39479 601-722-4510
Caprice Smalley, prin. Fax 722-0232

Senatobia, Tate, Pop. 8,076
Senatobia Municipal SD 1,800/K-12
104 McKie St 38668 662-562-4897
Jay Foster, supt. Fax 562-4996
www.senatobiaschools.com
Senatobia ES 600/K-6
301 Marvin St 38668 662-562-9613
Toni Bell, prin. Fax 562-0372

Magnolia Heights S 600/PK-12
1 Chiefs Dr 38668 662-562-4491

Shannon, Lee, Pop. 1,726
Lee County SD
Supt. — See Tupelo
Shannon ES 300/3-5
PO Box 7 38868 662-767-9514
Allen Stanford, prin. Fax 767-8687
Shannon MS 300/6-8
PO Box 349 38868 662-767-3986
Barry Woods, prin. Fax 767-9981
Shannon PS 300/K-2
PO Box 469 38868 662-767-0135
Shelly Brooks, prin. Fax 767-0137

Shaw, Bolivar, Pop. 1,947
West Bolivar Cons SD
Supt. — See Rosedale
McEvans S 300/K-8
PO Box 510 38773 662-754-2611
Nakita Goins, prin. Fax 754-6630

Shelby, Bolivar, Pop. 2,225
North Bolivar Consolidated SD
Supt. — See Mound Bayou
Shelby MS 200/5-8
PO Box 28 38774 662-398-4020
Sonya DeBose, prin. Fax 398-4039

Smithville, Monroe, Pop. 930
Monroe County SD
Supt. — See Amory
Smithville S 600/K-12
60017 Highway 23 38870 662-651-4276
Chad O'Brian, prin. Fax 651-4163

Southaven, DeSoto, Pop. 48,244
DeSoto County SD
Supt. — See Hernando
DeSoto Central ES 700/3-5
2411 Central Pkwy 38672 662-349-6234
Lisa Nye, prin. Fax 349-9387
DeSoto Central MS 1,200/6-8
2611 Central Pkwy 38672 662-349-6660
Byron Williams, prin. Fax 349-1045
DeSoto Central PS 600/PK-2
3210 Getwell Rd 38672 662-912-1300
Colleen Long, prin. Fax 912-1336
Greenbrook ES 600/PK-2
730 Rasco Rd E 38671 662-342-2330
Melynda Crockett, prin. Fax 342-9227
Southaven ES 700/PK-5
8274 Claiborne Dr 38671 662-342-2289
Christy Johnston, prin. Fax 280-9873
Southaven IS 1,200/3-5
175 Rasco Rd E 38671 662-253-0123
Kenneth McKinney, prin. Fax 253-0128
Southaven MS 1,600/6-8
899 Rasco Rd W 38671 662-280-0422
Paul Chrestman, prin. Fax 280-3613
Sullivan ES 600/PK-2
7985 Southaven Cir W 38671 662-393-2919
Bettye Magee, prin. Fax 393-2920

Northpoint Christian S 1,100/PK-12
7400 Getwell Rd 38672 662-349-3096
David Manley, pres. Fax 349-4962
Sacred Heart S 400/PK-8
5150 Tchulahoma Rd 38671 662-349-0900
Bridget Martin, prin. Fax 349-0690

Starkville, Oktibbeha, Pop. 23,580
Starkville-Oktibbeha Consolidated SD 3,900/K-12
401 Greensboro St 39759 662-324-4050
Dr. Eddie Peasant, supt. Fax 324-4068
www.starkvillesd.com
Armstrong MS 1,000/6-8
303 McKee St 39759 662-324-4070
Julie Kennedy, prin. Fax 324-4075
Henderson-Ward-Stewart ES 300/2-4
200 Martin Luther King Jr W 39759 662-324-4160
Diane Baker, prin. Fax 324-6957
Sudduth ES 1,100/K-1
101 Greenfield Dr 39759 662-324-4150
Elizabeth Mosley, prin. Fax 324-6137
Other Schools – See Sturgis

Starkville Academy 700/PK-12
505 Academy Rd 39759 662-323-7814
Jeremy Nicholas, head sch Fax 323-5480
Starkville Christian S 200/PK-12
303 Lynn Ln 39759 662-323-7453
Rev. Randall Witbeck, prin. Fax 323-7571

Steens, Lowndes

Columbus Christian Academy 300/PK-12
6405 Military Rd 39766 662-328-7888
Jay Watts, admin. Fax 328-7750

Stringer, Jasper
West Jasper Consolidated SD
Supt. — See Bay Springs
Stringer S 600/K-12
PO Box 1068 39481 601-428-5508
Jay Arrington, prin. Fax 426-6760

Sturgis, Oktibbeha, Pop. 252
Starkville-Oktibbeha Consolidated SD
Supt. — See Starkville
West ES 200/K-5
127 Sturgis Maben Rd 39769 662-465-7956
Gabrielle Mills, prin. Fax 465-6470

Summit, Pike, Pop. 1,702
McComb SD
Supt. — See Mc Comb
Summit ES 200/K-4
1201 Baldwin St 39666 601-276-3077
Lakya Taylor-Washington, prin. Fax 276-2254

North Pike SD 2,400/K-12
1036 Jaguar Trl 39666 601-276-2216
Dennis Penton, supt. Fax 276-3666
npsd.k12.ms.us/
North Pike ES 900/K-4
1052 Jaguar Trl 39666 601-276-2646
Lori Harrell, prin. Fax 276-2688
North Pike MS 800/5-8
2034 Highway 44 NE 39666 601-684-3283
Allen Barron, prin. Fax 684-3269

Faith Adventist Christian S 1-8
1005 Gordon Covington Rd 39666 601-600-2118

Sumner, Tallahatchie, Pop. 316
West Tallahatchie SD
Supt. — See Webb
Bearden ES 500/K-6
PO Box 189 38957 662-375-8304
Devora Berdin, prin. Fax 375-7234

Sumrall, Lamar, Pop. 1,412
Lamar County SD
Supt. — See Purvis
Sumrall ES 900/K-5
198 Todd Rd 39482 601-758-4289
Danny Sumrall, prin. Fax 758-4203
Sumrall MS 400/6-8
1217 Highway 42 39482 601-758-4416
Terry Smith, prin. Fax 758-4148

Benedict Day S 100/K-8
27 Veritas Ln 39482 601-450-4413

Sunflower, Sunflower, Pop. 1,157
Sunflower County Consolidated SD
Supt. — See Indianola
East Sunflower ES 200/K-5
212 E Claiborne St 38778 662-569-3137
Sawanda Washington, prin. Fax 569-3309

Taylorsville, Smith, Pop. 1,344
Smith County SD
Supt. — See Raleigh
Taylorsville ES 400/K-5
PO Box 8 39168 601-785-2283
Jerel Wade, prin. Fax 785-2282

Terry, Hinds, Pop. 1,052
Hinds County SD
Supt. — See Raymond
Byram MS 1,000/6-8
2009 Byram Bulldog Blvd 39170 601-372-4597
Benjamin Lundy, prin. Fax 346-2383

Tiplersville, Tippah
North Tippah SD 1,300/K-12
PO Box 65 38674 662-223-4384
Bill Brand, supt. Fax 223-5379
www.ntippah.k12.ms.us
Other Schools – See Falkner, Walnut

Tishomingo, Tishomingo, Pop. 335
Tishomingo County Special Municipal SD
Supt. — See Iuka
Tishomingo ES 300/K-8
PO Box 90 38873 662-438-6800
Shannon Edmondson, prin. Fax 438-6321

Tremont, Itawamba, Pop. 462
Itawamba County SD
Supt. — See Fulton
Tremont Attendance Center 300/K-12
320 School Loop Dr 38876 662-652-3391
Dawn Rogers, prin. Fax 652-3994

Tunica, Tunica, Pop. 1,021
Tunica County SD 2,400/PK-12
PO Box 758 38676 662-363-2811
Dr. Margie Pulley, supt. Fax 363-3061
www.tunicak12.org
Tunica ES 500/PK-5
PO Box 1289 38676 662-363-1442
Eva O'Neil, prin. Fax 363-4221
Tunica MS 500/6-8
PO Box 967 38676 662-363-4224
Glen Newson, prin. Fax 357-1058
Other Schools – See Dundee, Robinsonville

Tunica Academy 200/PK-12
PO Box 966 38676 662-363-1051

Tupelo, Lee, Pop. 34,140
Lee County SD 7,100/K-12
PO Box 832 38802 662-841-9144
Jimmy Weeks, supt. Fax 680-6012
www.leecountyschools.us/
Other Schools – See Guntown, Mooreville, Plantersville, Saltillo, Shannon, Verona

Tupelo SD 7,200/PK-12
PO Box 557 38802 662-841-8850
Dr. Gearl Loden, supt. Fax 841-8887
www.tupeloschools.com/
Carver ES 300/K-1
910 N Green St 38804 662-841-8870
Christy Carroll, prin. Fax 841-8877

Joyner ES 400/K-2
1201 Joyner Ave 38804 662-841-8900
Kimberly Foster, prin. Fax 841-8903
King ECC 200/PK-PK
1402 N Green St 38804 662-840-5237
Haley Stewart, prin. Fax 842-2609
Lawhon ES 500/2-5
140 Lake St 38804 662-841-8910
Mark Enis, prin. Fax 840-1856
Lawndale ES 400/3-5
1563 Mitchell Rd 38801 662-841-8890
Melissa Thomas, prin. Fax 840-1837
Milam ES 600/6-6
720 W Jefferson St 38804 662-841-8920
Paul Moton, prin. Fax 841-8929
Parkway ES 400/K-2
628 Rutherford Rd 38801 662-844-6303
Carmen Gary, prin. Fax 841-2957
Pierce Street ES 400/3-5
1008 Pierce St 38801 662-841-8940
Amy Barnett, prin. Fax 841-8959
Rankin ES 300/3-5
1908 Forrest St 38801 662-841-8950
Mitzi Moore, prin. Fax 840-1826
Thomas Street ES 500/K-2
520 S Thomas St 38801 662-841-8960
Cynthia Pike, prin. Fax 841-8965
Tupelo MS 1,100/7-8
1009 Varsity Dr 38801 662-840-8780
Dr. Brock English, prin. Fax 840-1831

Tylertown, Walthall, Pop. 1,598
Walthall County SD 1,900/K-12
814 Morse Ave 39667 601-876-3401
Wade Carney, supt. Fax 876-6982
www.wcsd.k12.ms.us
Dexter ES 200/K-6
927 Highway 48 E 39667 601-876-3985
Allen Dyess, prin. Fax 876-5410
Salem Attendance Center 500/K-12
881 Highway 27 N 39667 601-876-2580
Charles Boyd, prin. Fax 876-4155
Tylertown ES 200/3-6
705 Broad St 39667 601-876-3350
Felecia Prince, prin. Fax 876-3146
Tylertown PS 400/K-2
813 Ball Ave 39667 601-876-2149
Robin Duncan, prin. Fax 876-0066

Union, Newton, Pop. 1,954
Union SD 1,000/PK-12
PO Box 445 39365 601-774-9579
Wayne McDill, supt. Fax 774-0600
www.unioncity.k12.ms.us/
Union ES 400/PK-4
101 Forest St 39365 601-774-8257
Deanna Rush, prin. Fax 774-8187
Union MS 300/5-8
115 James St 39365 601-774-5303
Tyler Hansford, prin. Fax 774-9607

Utica, Hinds, Pop. 817
Hinds County SD
Supt. — See Raymond
Utica S 400/PK-8
PO Box 329 39175 601-885-8765
Willis Smith, prin. Fax 885-2083

Vancleave, Jackson, Pop. 5,787
Jackson County SD 9,300/K-12
PO Box 5069 39565 228-826-1757
Dr. Barry Amacker, supt. Fax 826-3393
www.jcsd.ms
Vancleave Lower ES 500/K-2
12602 Highway 57 39565 228-826-5982
Tanya Posey, prin. Fax 826-2689
Vancleave MS 600/6-8
4725 Bull Dog Ln 39565 228-826-5902
Rhett Ladner, prin. Fax 826-1421
Vancleave Upper ES 600/3-5
13901 Highway 57 39565 228-826-4581
Karen Glass, prin. Fax 826-2015
Other Schools – See Biloxi, Moss Point, Ocean Springs

Vardaman, Calhoun, Pop. 1,309
Calhoun County SD
Supt. — See Pittsboro
Vardaman ES 400/PK-6
114 WB Gregg Dr 38878 662-682-7799
Pamela Lee, prin. Fax 682-7734

Vaughan, Yazoo
Yazoo County SD
Supt. — See Yazoo City
Linwood ES 200/K-5
3439 Vaughan Rd 39179 662-673-9191
Shundria Shaffer Ph.D., prin. Fax 673-9163

Verona, Lee, Pop. 2,965
Lee County SD
Supt. — See Tupelo
Verona ES 400/K-4
PO Box 579 38879 662-566-7266
Amelia Anglin, prin. Fax 566-4247

Vicksburg, Warren, Pop. 23,676
Vicksburg Warren SD 8,200/PK-12
1500 Mission 66 39180 601-638-5122
Chad Shealy, supt. Fax 631-2819
www.vwsd.org
Academy of Innovation 7-8
1315 Grove St 39183 601-636-2539
Jason McKellar, prin. Fax 631-2856
Beechwood ES 400/PK-6
999 Highway 27 39180 601-638-3874
David Adams, prin. Fax 631-2869
Bovina ES 300/K-6
5 Willow Creek Dr 39183 601-619-4454
Miki Ginn, prin. Fax 619-4455
Bowmar Avenue ES 400/K-6
912 Bowmar Ave 39180 601-636-2486
Jason Bennett, prin. Fax 631-2853
Dana Road ES 700/PK-3
1247 Dana Rd 39180 601-619-2340
LaShonda Smith, prin. Fax 619-2343
Sherman Avenue ES 700/PK-3
2145 Sherman Ave 39183 601-638-2409
Dr. Tameka Davis, prin. Fax 638-5169
South Park ES 400/K-6
6530 Nailor Rd 39180 601-636-1271
Latoya Minor, prin. Fax 636-2501
Vicksburg IS 500/3-6
1245 Dana Rd 39180 601-638-4199
Sharon Williams, prin. Fax 638-4416
Vicksburg JHS 600/7-8
1533 Baldwin Ferry Rd 39180 601-636-1966
Katrina Hills, prin. Fax 631-2830
Warren Central IS 500/3-6
2147 Sherman Ave 39183 601-638-5656
Tonya Magee, prin. Fax 638-6358
Warren Central JHS 700/7-8
1630 Baldwin Ferry Rd 39180 601-638-3981
Dr. Cedric Magee, prin. Fax 631-2839
Warrenton ES 400/K-6
809 Belva Dr 39180 601-636-7549
Derrick Reed, prin. Fax 638-6191
Other Schools – See Redwood

Porters Chapel Academy 200/K-12
3460 Porters Chapel Rd 39180 601-638-3733
Vicksburg Catholic S St. Francis Xavier 400/PK-6
1200 Hayes St 39183 601-636-4824
Mary Arledge, prin. Fax 636-3665

Victoria, Marshall

Friendship Christian Academy PK-12
184 Friendship Rd 38679 662-838-4000

Walls, DeSoto, Pop. 1,138
DeSoto County SD
Supt. — See Hernando
Walls ES 700/PK-5
6131 Delta View Rd 38680 662-781-1280
Elisa Goss, prin. Fax 781-3918

Walnut, Tippah, Pop. 762
North Tippah SD
Supt. — See Tiplersville
Chalybeate ES 300/K-8
2471 Highway 354 38683 662-223-4311
Andy Carter, prin. Fax 223-5362
Walnut S 500/K-12
280 Commerce Ave 38683 662-223-6471
Joe McCoy, prin. Fax 223-5275

Walnut Grove, Leake, Pop. 1,907
Leake County SD
Supt. — See Carthage
Leake County ES 400/K-6
1280 School St 39189 601-253-2324
Dr. Jimmy Henderson, prin. Fax 253-2325

Water Valley, Yalobusha, Pop. 3,370
Water Valley SD 1,200/K-12
PO Box 788 38965 662-473-1203
Dr. Michael McInnis, supt. Fax 473-1225
www.wvsd.k12.ms.us
Davidson ES 700/K-6
PO Box 808 38965 662-473-1110
Ezzard Beane, prin. Fax 473-2277

Waveland, Hancock, Pop. 6,261
Bay St. Louis-Waveland SD
Supt. — See Bay Saint Louis
Waveland ES 500/K-2
1101 Saint Joseph St 39576 228-467-6630
Steven Engle, prin. Fax 467-7349

Waynesboro, Wayne, Pop. 4,998
Wayne County SD 3,300/K-12
810 Chickasawhay St 39367 601-735-4871
Bobby Jones, supt. Fax 735-4872
www.wayne.k12.ms.us
Beat Four S 400/K-8
5090 Highway 84 39367 601-735-2124
Tommy Branch, prin. Fax 735-6311
Clara S 400/K-8
40 Clara School Rd 39367 601-735-2065
Donna Hopkins, prin. Fax 735-3633
Wayne Central ES 600/K-4
1022 Azalea Dr 39367 601-735-2205
Eric Smith, prin. Fax 735-6314
Waynesboro MS 500/5-8
155 Wayne St 39367 601-735-3159
Shronda Turner, prin. Fax 735-6316
Other Schools – See Buckatunna

Wayne Academy 300/K-12
PO Box 308 39367 601-735-2921
Charles Hoots, hdmstr. Fax 735-2117

Webb, Tallahatchie, Pop. 557
West Tallahatchie SD 800/K-12
PO Box 129 38966 662-375-9291
Christopher Furdge, supt. Fax 375-9294
www.wtsd.k12.ms.us
Other Schools – See Sumner

Weir, Choctaw, Pop. 459
Choctaw County SD
Supt. — See Ackerman
Weir ES 200/PK-6
351 Marion Kelley Dr 39772 662-547-7079
Robbie Denson, prin. Fax 547-7074

Wesson, Copiah, Pop. 1,907
Copiah County SD
Supt. — See Hazlehurst
Wesson S 1,100/K-12
1048 Grove St 39191 601-643-2221
Marilyn Phillips, prin. Fax 643-2458

West Point, Clay, Pop. 11,257
West Point SD 3,300/K-12
PO Box 656 39773 662-494-4242
Burnell McDonald, supt. Fax 494-8605
www.westpoint.k12.ms.us
Central S 400/5-6
264 E Westbrook St 39773 662-495-2418
Wynesther Cousins, prin. Fax 494-0060
Church Hill ES 500/1-2
2050 W Church Hill Rd 39773 662-494-5900
Cindy Donahoo, prin. Fax 495-2434
East Side K 300/K-K
813 E Broad St 39773 662-494-4691
Jacqueline Gray, prin. Fax 495-6203
Fifth Street JHS 500/7-8
418 5th St 39773 662-494-2191
Richard Bryant, prin. Fax 494-2432
South Side ES 400/3-4
237 Louis Odneal Rd 39773 662-495-6216
Casey Glusenkamp, prin. Fax 495-6219
Other Schools – See Cedarbluff

Oak Hill Academy 400/PK-12
1682 N Eshman Ave 39773 662-494-5043

Wheeler, Prentiss
Prentiss County SD
Supt. — See Booneville
Wheeler S 500/K-12
318 County Road 5011 38880 662-365-2629
Todd Swinney, prin. Fax 365-2535

Wiggins, Stone, Pop. 4,345
Stone County SD 2,600/K-12
214 Critz St N 39577 601-928-7247
Inita Owen, supt. Fax 928-5122
www.stone.k12.ms.us
Stone ES 700/K-5
1652 Central Ave E 39577 601-928-5473
Krista Sablich, prin. Fax 928-5122
Stone MS 700/6-8
532 Central Ave E 39577 601-928-4876
Leslie Cudd, prin. Fax 928-6440
Other Schools – See Perkinston

Gateway Christian Academy 100/PK-12
908 Frontage Dr W 39577 601-528-5454

Winona, Montgomery, Pop. 5,020
Montgomery County SD 300/K-12
PO Box 687 38967 662-283-4533
James Johnson-Waldington, supt. Fax 283-4584
www.mcsdms.net
Other Schools – See Kilmichael

Winona SD 1,100/PK-12
218 Fairground St 38967 662-283-3731
Dr. Teresa Jackson, supt. Fax 283-1003
www.winonaschools.net
Winona ES 700/PK-6
513 S Applegate St 38967 662-283-4129
Tabitha McCrory, prin. Fax 283-1066

Winona Christian S 300/PK-12
1014 S Applegate St 38967 662-283-1169

Woodville, Wilkinson, Pop. 1,088
Wilkinson County SD 1,300/PK-12
PO Box 785 39669 601-888-3582
Kimberly Jackson, supt. Fax 888-3133
wilkinsoncounty.schoolinsites.com/
Wilkinson County ES 300/PK-5
PO Box 1197 39669 601-888-4331
Dr. Regina Harris-McCoy, prin. Fax 888-6335
Other Schools – See Centreville

Wilkinson County Christian Academy 300/K-12
2420 US Highway 61 S 39669 601-888-4313

Yazoo City, Yazoo, Pop. 11,345
Yazoo City Municipal SD 2,200/PK-12
1133 Calhoun Ave 39194 662-746-2125
Dr. Darron Edwards, supt. Fax 746-9210
www.yazoocity.k12.ms.us/
McCoy ES 600/2-4
1835 School Dr 39194 662-746-5800
Dr. Richard Chano, prin. Fax 746-8608
Webster Street ES 500/PK-1
622 E Fourth St 39194 662-746-4093
Jacqueline Ellis, prin. Fax 716-0258
Woolfolk MS 500/5-8
209 E Fifth St 39194 662-746-2904
Torrey Hampton Ed.D., prin. Fax 746-8609

Yazoo County SD 1,700/K-12
94 Panther Dr 39194 662-746-4672
Rebecca Fisher, supt. Fax 746-9270
www.yazoo.k12.ms.us
Yazoo County MS 400/6-8
116 Panther Dr 39194 662-746-1596
Virginia Ables, prin. Fax 746-1616
Other Schools – See Bentonia, Vaughan

Covenant Christian S 100/K-6
PO Box 1108 39194 662-746-8855
Sharon Gilder, prin. Fax 746-8887
Manchester Academy 400/PK-12
2132 Gordon Ave 39194 662-746-5913

MISSOURI

MISSOURI DEPARTMENT OF EDUCATION
PO Box 480, Jefferson City 65102-0480
Telephone 573-751-4212
Fax 573-751-1179
Website http://www.dese.mo.gov

Commissioner of Education Dr. Roger Dorson

MISSOURI BOARD OF EDUCATION
PO Box 480, Jefferson City 65102-0480

President Charles Shields

PUBLIC, PRIVATE AND CATHOLIC ELEMENTARY SCHOOLS

Adrian, Bates, Pop. 1,663
Adrian R-III SD 700/PK-12
PO Box 98 64720 816-297-2710
Don Lile, supt. Fax 297-2980
www.adrian.k12.mo.us
Adrian ES 300/PK-5
PO Box 98 64720 816-297-2158
Connie Reynolds, prin. Fax 297-2980

Advance, Stoddard, Pop. 1,340
Advance R-IV SD 400/PK-12
201 E School St 63730 573-722-3581
Shannon Garner, supt. Fax 722-9886
www.advance.k12.mo.us
Advance ES 200/PK-6
201 E School St 63730 573-722-3564
James Hamlin, prin. Fax 722-5366

Albany, Gentry, Pop. 1,720
Albany R-III SD 500/PK-12
101 W Jefferson St 64402 660-726-3911
Erin Oligschlaeger, supt. Fax 726-5841
www.albany.k12.mo.us
Albany MS 100/6-8
101 W Jefferson St 64402 660-726-3912
Sarah Barmann-Smith, prin. Fax 726-5841
George ES 300/PK-5
202 S East St 64402 660-726-5621
Beth Findley, prin. Fax 726-4107

Alexandria, Clark, Pop. 155
Clark County R-I SD
Supt. — See Kahoka
Running Fox ES 100/K-5
27192 US Highway 61 63430 660-754-6766
Katrina Nixon, prin. Fax 754-6725

Alma, Lafayette, Pop. 395
Santa Fe R-X SD 400/K-12
PO Box 197 64001 660-674-2238
Derek Lark, supt. Fax 674-2239
santafechiefs.k12.mo.us
Other Schools – See Waverly

Trinity Lutheran S 100/PK-8
PO Box 257 64001 660-674-2444
Pam Fetter, prin. Fax 674-2747

Altenburg, Perry, Pop. 350
Altenburg SD 48 100/K-8
PO Box 127 63732 573-824-5857
Debbie Haertling, supt. Fax 824-5122
altenburgps.eduk12.net
Altenburg S 100/K-8
PO Box 127 63732 573-824-5857
Debbie Haertling, prin. Fax 824-5122

Alton, Oregon, Pop. 847
Alton R-IV SD 700/K-12
RR 2 Box 2180 65606 417-778-7216
Dr. Eric Allen, supt. Fax 778-6394
www.alton.k12.mo.us/
Alton ES 400/K-6
RR 2 Box 2181 65606 417-778-7217
Shane Benson, prin. Fax 778-7865

Amazonia, Andrew, Pop. 310
Savannah R-III SD
Supt. — See Savannah
Amazonia ES 100/K-5
845 6th St 64421 816-475-2161
Aimee Addington, prin. Fax 475-2504

Amoret, Bates, Pop. 185
Miami R-I SD 200/K-12
7638 NW State Route J 64722 660-267-3480
Dr. Daniel Johnson, supt. Fax 267-3630
www.miamir1.net
Miami ES 100/K-6
7638 NW State Route J 64722 660-267-3495
Dr. Angela Wiley, prin. Fax 267-3630

Anderson, McDonald, Pop. 1,900
McDonald County R-I SD 3,800/PK-12
100 Mustang Dr 64831 417-845-3321
Dr. Mark Stanton, supt. Fax 845-6972
mcdonaldr1.net
Anderson ES 600/PK-6
512 Chapman St 64831 417-845-3488
Julie Hollaway, prin. Fax 845-7042
Anderson MS 200/7-8
135 Mustang Dr 64831 417-845-1805
Ken Anders, prin. Fax 845-7406
Other Schools – See Jane, Noel, Pineville, Rocky Comfort, South West City

Annapolis, Iron, Pop. 343
South Iron R-I SD 300/PK-12
210 School St 63620 573-598-4241
Donald Wakefield, supt. Fax 598-4210
www.sipanthers.k12.mo.us
South Iron ES 200/PK-6
210 School St 63620 573-598-4240
Cristie Ayers, prin. Fax 598-4210

Appleton City, Saint Clair, Pop. 1,108
Appleton City R-II SD 300/PK-12
408 W 4th St 64724 660-476-2161
Ryan Middleton Ed.D., supt. Fax 476-5564
www.appletoncity.k12.mo.us
Appleton City ES 100/PK-5
408 W 4th St 64724 660-476-2108
Mona Reid, prin. Fax 476-5564

Hudson R-IX SD 100/PK-8
15012 NE State Route 52 64724 660-476-5467
Karen Warmbrodt, admin. Fax 476-5527
Hudson ES 100/PK-8
15012 NE State Route 52 64724 660-476-5467
Karen Warmbrodt, prin. Fax 476-5527

Archie, Cass, Pop. 1,157
Archie R-V SD 500/PK-12
302 W State Route A 64725 816-293-5312
Jeffrey Kramer, supt. Fax 293-5712
www.archie.k12.mo.us
Cass County ES 200/PK-5
302 W State Route A 64725 816-293-5312
Tamara Silvey, prin. Fax 293-5712

Arnold, Jefferson, Pop. 20,546
Fox C-6 SD 11,700/PK-12
745 Jeffco Blvd 63010 636-296-8000
Dr. Jim Wipke, supt. Fax 282-5170
www.fox.k12.mo.us
Earl Early Childhood Learning Ctr 200/PK-PK
849 Jeffco Blvd 63010 636-282-5184
Dr. Robert Townsley, prin. Fax 282-6982
Fox ES 600/K-5
739 Jeffco Blvd 63010 636-296-3396
Lisa Sell, prin. Fax 282-1468
Fox MS 500/6-8
743 Jeffco Blvd 63010 636-296-5077
Aaron Wilken, prin. Fax 282-5171
Lone Dell ES 600/PK-5
2500 Tomahawk Dr 63010 636-282-1470
Luann Domek, prin. Fax 282-1474
Meramec Heights ES 600/PK-5
1340 W Outer 21 Rd 63010 636-296-4385
Dustin Bain, prin. Fax 282-1472
Ridgewood MS 500/6-8
1401 Ridgewood School Rd 63010 636-282-1459
Jamie Cavato, prin. Fax 282-5193
Rockport Heights ES 600/K-5
3871 Jeffco Blvd 63010 636-464-2010
Janine Hueter, prin. Fax 464-0390
Sherwood ES 500/PK-5
1769 Missouri State Rd 63010 636-282-6965
Colleen Cole, prin. Fax 282-1475
Simpson ES 400/K-5
3585 Vogel Rd 63010 636-282-1480
Bryan Clark, prin. Fax 282-5174
Other Schools – See Barnhart, Fenton, Imperial

Holy Child S 200/PK-8
2316 Church Rd 63010 636-296-0055
Dwight Elmore, prin. Fax 296-5639
St. John's Lutheran S 200/PK-8
3511 Jeffco Blvd 63010 636-464-7303
David Florine, prin. Fax 464-8424
Victory Christian Academy 100/K-8
1930 Meyer Drury Dr 63010 636-223-7330
Doug Rose, head sch Fax 223-7332

Ash Grove, Greene, Pop. 1,452
Ash Grove R-IV SD 700/PK-12
100 N Maple Ln 65604 417-751-2534
Dr. Aaron Gerla, supt. Fax 751-2283
www.ashgrove.k12.mo.us
Ash Grove ES 200/PK-3
100 N Maple Ln 65604 417-751-2533
Sheila Cox-Hines, prin. Fax 751-2283
Other Schools – See Bois D Arc

Ashland, Boone, Pop. 3,660
Southern Boone County R-I SD 1,600/PK-12
PO Box 168 65010 573-657-2147
Christopher Felmlee, supt. Fax 657-5513
ashland.k12.mo.us
Southern Boone County ES 400/3-5
PO Box 168 65010 573-657-2145
Amy James, prin. Fax 657-5510
Southern Boone County MS 400/6-8
PO Box 168 65010 573-657-2146
Kevin Kiley, prin. Fax 657-5519
Southern Boone County PS 400/PK-2
PO Box 168 65010 573-657-2148
Brandy Clark, prin. Fax 657-4236

Atlanta, Macon, Pop. 377
Atlanta C-3 SD 200/K-12
600 S Atterberry St 63530 660-239-4212
William Perkins, supt. Fax 239-4205
www.atlanta.k12.mo.us/
Atlanta ES 100/K-6
600 S Atterberry St 63530 660-239-4211
William Perkins, prin. Fax 239-4205

Augusta, Saint Charles, Pop. 251
Washington SD
Supt. — See Washington
Augusta ES 100/K-6
5541 Locust St 63332 636-231-2400
Mary Robertson, prin. Fax 231-2405

Aurora, Lawrence, Pop. 7,398
Aurora R-VIII SD 2,100/PK-12
201 S Madison Ave 65605 417-678-3373
Billy Redus, supt. Fax 678-4043
www.aurorar8.org
Aurora JHS 400/7-8
500 W Olive St 65605 417-678-3630
Kimberly Yeary, prin. Fax 678-2487
Pate ECC 600/PK-2
400 Terrace Dr 65605 417-678-1552
Dr. Mykie Nash, prin. Fax 678-3491
Robinson ES 300/3-4
1034 S Lincoln Ave 65605 417-678-7436
David Mais, prin. Fax 678-6554
Robinson IS 300/5-6
1044 S Lincoln Ave 65605 417-678-5651
Adam Bax, prin. Fax 678-8900

Auxvasse, Callaway, Pop. 978
North Callaway County R-I SD
Supt. — See Kingdom City
Auxvasse S 400/PK-8
PO Box 8 65231 573-386-2217
Nicole Kemp, prin. Fax 386-2039

Ava, Douglas, Pop. 2,954
Ava R-I SD 1,400/PK-12
PO Box 338 65608 417-683-4717
Dr. Jason Dial, supt. Fax 683-6329
www.avaschools.k12.mo.us/
Ava ES 500/PK-4
PO Box 338 65608 417-683-5450
Clint Hall, prin. Fax 683-9010
Ava MS 400/5-8
PO Box 338 65608 417-683-3835
Marcella Swatosh, prin. Fax 683-9101

Plainview R-VIII SD 100/K-8
RR 3 Box 145 65608 417-683-2046
Brenda Reed, supt. Fax 683-3222
www.plainviewschool.org/
Plainview ES 100/K-8
RR 3 Box 145 65608 417-683-2046
Brenda Reed, prin. Fax 683-3222

Avilla, Jasper, Pop. 117
Avilla R-XIII SD 200/K-8
PO Box 7 64833 417-246-5330
Russ Cruzan Ed.D., supt. Fax 246-5432
www.avillapanthers.org
Avilla S 200/K-8
PO Box 7 64833 417-246-5330
Gayla Degraffenreid Ed.D., admin. Fax 246-5432

Bakersfield, Ozark, Pop. 240
Bakersfield R-IV SD 400/PK-12
PO Box 38 65609 417-284-7333
Dr. Amy Britt, supt. Fax 284-7335
www.bakersfield.k12.mo.us
Bakersfield ES 200/PK-5
PO Box 38 65609 417-284-7333
Brian Hollis, prin. Fax 284-7335

Ballwin, Saint Louis, Pop. 29,903
Parkway C-2 SD
Supt. — See Chesterfield
Claymont ES 500/K-5
405 Country Club Dr 63011 314-415-6150
Aaron Wills, prin. Fax 415-6162
ECC PK-PK
14605 Clayton Rd 63011 314-415-6950
Dr. Elena Amirault, dir. Fax 415-6956
Hanna Woods ES 400/K-5
720 Hanna Rd 63021 314-415-6300
Kristy Roberts, prin. Fax 415-6312
Henry ES 400/K-5
700 Henry Ave 63011 314-415-6350
Dr. Lynn Pott, prin. Fax 415-6362
Oak Brook ES 500/PK-5
510 Big Bend Rd 63021 314-415-6550
Dr. Chris Shirley, prin. Fax 415-6562
Sorrento Springs ES 400/K-5
390 Tumulty Dr 63021 314-415-6800
Kathy Stewart, prin. Fax 415-6812

Rockwood R-VI SD
Supt. — See Eureka
Ballwin ES 500/K-5
400 Jefferson Ave 63021 636-207-2533
Dr. Rodney Lewis, prin. Fax 207-2536
Ridge Meadows ES 400/K-5
777 Ridge Rd 63021 636-207-2661
Dr. Amy Digman, prin. Fax 207-2666
Selvidge MS 700/6-8
235 New Ballwin Rd 63021 636-207-2622
Dr. Michael Anselmo, prin. Fax 207-2632
Westridge ES 400/K-5
908 Crestland Dr 63011 636-207-2572
Dr. Dan Gieseler, prin. Fax 207-2577
Woerther ES 500/K-5
314 New Ballwin Rd 63021 636-207-2674
Jane Levy, prin. Fax 207-2681

Al-Salam Day S 300/PK-12
519 Weidman Rd 63011 636-394-8986
Holy Infant S 700/PK-8
248 New Ballwin Rd 63021 636-227-0802
Rebecca McQuaide, prin. Fax 227-9184
Twin Oaks Christian S 300/PK-8
1230A Big Bend Rd 63021 636-861-1901
Debbie Stair, head sch Fax 861-2084

Barnard, Nodaway, Pop. 221
South Nodaway County R-IV SD 200/PK-12
209 Morehouse St 64423 660-652-3221
Johnnie Silkett, supt. Fax 652-3411
www.southnodaway.k12.mo.us
Other Schools – See Guilford

Barnhart, Jefferson, Pop. 5,631
Fox C-6 SD
Supt. — See Arnold
Antonia MS 400/6-8
6798 Saint Lukes Church Rd 63012 636-282-6970
Joe Willis, prin. Fax 282-6971

Windsor C-1 SD
Supt. — See Imperial
Freer ES 200/K-2
1800 Hanover Ln 63012 636-464-2951
Charles Bouzek, prin. Fax 464-4471

Battlefield, Greene, Pop. 5,468
Springfield R-XII SD
Supt. — See Springfield
Wilson's Creek IS 500/5-6
4035 W Weaver Rd 65619 417-523-7800
Karyn Christy, prin. Fax 523-7895

Beaufort, Franklin
Union R-XI SD
Supt. — See Union
Beaufort ES 400/K-6
3200 Highway 50 63013 573-484-3221
Kendra Fennessey, prin. Fax 484-4145

Bell City, Stoddard, Pop. 438
Bell City R-II SD 200/K-12
25254 Walnut St 63735 573-733-4444
Matthew Asher, supt. Fax 733-4114
www.bellcity.k12.mo.us/
Bell City ES 100/K-6
25254 Walnut St 63735 573-733-4444
Patrick Niemczyk, prin. Fax 733-4114

Belle, Maries, Pop. 1,518
Maries County R-II SD 800/K-12
PO Box 819 65013 573-859-3800
Dr. Patrick Call, supt. Fax 859-3883
www.mariesr2.org
Belle ES 300/K-4
PO Box 819 65013 573-859-3326
Melinda Vandevort, prin. Fax 859-3446
Other Schools – See Bland

Belleview, Iron
Belleview R-III SD 100/PK-8
27431 Highway 32 63623 573-697-5702
Judd Marquis, supt. Fax 697-5701
www.belleviewbraves.org
Belleview S 100/PK-8
27431 Highway 32 63623 573-697-5702
Judd Marquis, prin. Fax 697-5701

Belton, Cass, Pop. 22,497
Belton SD 124 4,700/PK-12
110 W Walnut St 64012 816-489-7000
Dr. Andrew Underwood, supt. Fax 489-7005
www.beltonschools.org
Cambridge ES 300/K-4
109 W Cambridge Rd 64012 816-348-1008
Michelle Biondo, prin. Fax 348-1093
Gladden ES 400/K-4
405 Westover Rd 64012 816-489-7530
Amanda Spight, prin. Fax 489-7535
Grace ECC and Education Center 300/PK-PK
614 Mill St 64012 816-348-1514
Jill Brown, prin. Fax 348-1565
Hillcrest STEAM Academy 300/K-6
106 S Hillcrest Rd 64012 816-348-1130
Roxanne Pearson, prin. Fax 348-1135
Kentucky Trail ES 600/K-4
8301 E 163rd St 64012 816-348-1100
Dr. Alisa Seidelman, prin. Fax 348-1105
Mill Creek Upper ES 800/5-6
308 S Cleveland Ave 64012 816-348-1576
Kimberly Mauck, prin. Fax 348-1595
Scott ES 300/K-4
310 S Scott Ave 64012 816-489-7040
Kelly Crumley, prin. Fax 489-7045

Heartland Christian S 100/PK-12
810 S Cedar St 64012 816-331-1000
Claire Baker, prin. Fax 322-2782

Benton, Scott, Pop. 855
Kelso C-7 SD 100/PK-8
1016 State Highway A 63736 573-545-3357
Kimberly Burger, supt. Fax 545-4356
kelsoc-7.k12.mo.us/
Kelso S 100/PK-8
1016 State Highway A 63736 573-545-3357
Kimberly Burger, prin. Fax 545-4356

Scott County R-IV SD 1,000/PK-12
4035 State Highway 77 63736 573-545-3541
Fara Jones, supt. Fax 545-3929
sites.google.com/a/kellyhawks.org/kellyhawks
Scott County ES 500/PK-5
4035 State Highway 77 63736 573-545-3541
Tracy Siebert, prin. Fax 545-3452
Scott County MS 200/6-8
4035 State Highway 77 63736 573-545-3541
Kari Bickings, prin. Fax 545-4386

St. Denis S 100/K-8
PO Box 189 63736 573-545-3017
Karen Powers, prin. Fax 545-9185

Berkeley, Saint Louis, Pop. 8,830
Ferguson-Florissant R-II SD
Supt. — See Florissant
Airport ES 300/K-6
8249 Airport Rd 63134 314-524-3872
Staci Price, prin. Fax 524-3879
Berkeley MS 300/7-8
8300 Frost Ave 63134 314-524-3883
Dr. Mark Weller, prin. Fax 524-3885
Holman ES 200/K-6
8811 Harold Dr 63134 314-428-9695
Aisha Grace, prin. Fax 428-9792

Bernie, Stoddard, Pop. 1,930
Bernie R-XIII SD 500/PK-12
516 W Main Ave 63822 573-293-5333
Dustin Hicks, supt. Fax 293-5731
www.bernie.k12.mo.us
Bernie ES 300/PK-6
121 S Spiker St 63822 573-293-5335
Tommie Ellenburg, prin. Fax 293-6124

Bethany, Harrison, Pop. 3,262
South Harrison County R-II SD 700/PK-12
PO Box 445 64424 660-425-8044
Dennis Eastin, supt. Fax 425-7050
www.shr2.k12.mo.us
South Harrison County ECC 50/PK-PK
PO Box 445 64424 660-425-7539
Kathy Daniel, dir. Fax 425-7842
South Harrison County R-II ES 400/K-5
PO Box 445 64424 660-425-8061
Kathryn Knapp, prin. Fax 425-2130
South Harrison County R-II MS 6-8
PO Box 445 64424 660-425-7467
Shane Jones, prin. Fax 425-7469

Bevier, Macon, Pop. 711
Bevier C-4 SD 200/K-12
400 Bloomington St 63532 660-773-6611
Joan Patrick, supt. Fax 773-6955
bevierc-4.com
Bevier S 100/K-8
400 Bloomington St 63532 660-773-6611
Jason Martie, prin. Fax 773-5565

Billings, Christian, Pop. 1,023
Billings R-IV SD 400/PK-12
118 W Mount Vernon Rd 65610 417-744-2623
Cynthia Brandt, supt. Fax 744-4545
www.billings.k12.mo.us
Billings ES 200/PK-6
118 W Mount Vernon Rd 65610 417-744-2552
Ben Abramovitz, prin. Fax 744-4545

Bismarck, Saint Francois, Pop. 1,531
Bismarck R-V SD 500/PK-12
PO Box 257 63624 573-734-6111
Fax 734-2957
www.bismarckr5.org
Bismarck ES 300/PK-5
PO Box 257 63624 573-734-6111
Carmen Barton, prin. Fax 734-2957

Black Jack, Saint Louis, Pop. 6,797

Salem Lutheran S 100/PK-8
5190 Parker Rd 63033 314-741-8220
Daniel Schwerin, prin. Fax 741-7242

Blackwater, Cooper, Pop. 160
Blackwater R-II SD 100/PK-8
PO Box 117 65322 660-846-2461
Tanya Brown, supt. Fax 846-2431
www.blackwater.k12.mo.us
Blackwater S 100/PK-8
PO Box 117 65322 660-846-2461
Tanya Brown, prin. Fax 846-2431

Bland, Gasconade, Pop. 534
Maries County R-II SD
Supt. — See Belle
Maries County MS 300/5-8
PO Box 10 65014 573-646-3912
Kristin Williams, prin. Fax 646-3148

Bloomfield, Stoddard, Pop. 1,925
Bloomfield R-XIV SD 700/PK-12
505 Court St 63825 573-568-4564
Toni Hill, supt. Fax 568-4565
www.bps14.org
Bloomfield ES 300/PK-4
505 Court St 63825 573-568-4562
Sabrina Skaggs, prin. Fax 568-4563
Bloomfield MS 200/5-8
505 Court St 63825 573-568-4283
Louis Bell, prin. Fax 568-4286

Bloomsdale, Sainte Genevieve, Pop. 518
St. Genevieve County R-II SD
Supt. — See Sainte Genevieve
Bloomsdale ES 300/PK-5
6279 Highway 61 63627 573-883-4500
Lorie Zuspann, prin. Fax 883-5957

St. Agnes S 200/PK-8
PO Box 154 63627 573-483-2506
Erin O'Driscoll, prin. Fax 483-9303

Blue Eye, Stone, Pop. 163
Blue Eye R-V SD 700/PK-12
PO Box 105 65611 417-779-5332
Dr. Doug Arnold, supt. Fax 779-2151
www.blueeye.k12.mo.us
Blue Eye ES 200/PK-4
PO Box 105 65611 417-779-4318
Michael Fransen, prin. Fax 779-3268
Blue Eye MS 200/5-8
PO Box 105 65611 417-779-4299
Teresa Porter, prin. Fax 779-4526

Blue Springs, Jackson, Pop. 51,123
Blue Springs R-IV SD 14,400/K-12
1801 NW Vesper St 64015 816-874-3200
Dr. James Finley, supt. Fax 224-1764
www.bssd.net
Brittany Hill MS 900/6-8
2701 NW 1st St 64014 816-874-3470
Dallas Truex, prin. Fax 224-1704
Bryant ES 400/K-5
1101 SE Sunnyside School Rd 64014 816-874-3730
Jennie Alderman, prin. Fax 224-1343
Cordill-Mason ES 700/K-5
4001 SW Christiansen Dr 64014 816-874-3610
Todd Nurnberg, prin. Fax 224-1372
Franklin ES 600/K-5
111 NE Roanoke Dr 64014 816-874-3690
Dr. Doug Nielsen, prin. Fax 224-1396
Kinder MS 800/6-8
3930 S R D Mize Rd 64015 816-874-3560
Steve Goddard, prin. Fax 224-1309
Lewis ES 500/K-5
717 NW Park Rd 64015 816-874-3650
Lori Reynolds, prin. Fax 224-1347
Moreland Ridge MS 1,000/6-8
900 SW Bishop Dr 64015 816-874-3540
Kevin Grover, prin. Fax 224-1805
Nowlin ES 400/K-5
5020 NW Valley View Rd 64015 816-874-3670
Seth Shippy, prin. Fax 224-1359
Smith ES 500/K-5
1609 SW Clark Rd 64015 816-874-3640
Ramona Dunn, prin. Fax 224-1378
Sunny Pointe ES 500/K-5
3920 S R D Mize Rd 64015 816-874-3700
Nick Goos, prin. Fax 224-7804
Ultican ES 500/K-5
1812 NW Vesper St 64015 816-874-3710
Dr. Abbie Swisher, prin. Fax 224-1490
Walker ES 500/K-5
201 SE Sunnyside School Rd 64014 816-874-3660
Dr. Kelly Flax, prin. Fax 224-1461
Young ES 300/K-5
505 SE Shamrock Ln 64014 816-874-3630
Ryan Crum, prin. Fax 224-1492

Other Schools – See Independence, Lees Summit

Plaza Heights Christian Academy 200/PK-12
1500 SW Clark Rd 64015 816-228-0670
Chuck Lawson, admin. Fax 229-4092
St. John LaLande S 300/PK-8
801 NW R D Mize Rd 64015 816-228-5895
Ann Wright, prin. Fax 228-8979
Timothy Lutheran S 100/PK-8
301 E Wyatt Rd 64014 816-228-5300
Ken Holland, admin. Fax 874-4025

Bois D Arc, Greene
Ash Grove R-IV SD
Supt. — See Ash Grove
Bois D'Arc ES 200/4-6
10315 W State Highway T 65612 417-742-2203
Karie Julian, prin. Fax 742-4460

Bolivar, Polk, Pop. 10,153
Bolivar R-I SD 2,800/PK-12
524 W Madison St 65613 417-326-5291
Dr. Tony Berry, supt. Fax 326-3562
www.bolivarschools.org
Bolivar IS 600/3-5
1300 N Hartford Ave 65613 417-777-5160
Dr. Julie Routh, prin. Fax 777-5434
Bolivar MS 600/6-8
604 W Jackson St 65613 417-326-3811
Dr. Tim Garber, prin. Fax 326-8277
Bolivar PS 700/PK-2
706 N Leonard Pl 65613 417-326-5247
Dr. Tracy Daniels, prin. Fax 326-2394

Polk County Christian S 100/PK-8
PO Box 303 65613 417-777-2330
Karon Burton, admin. Fax 777-5723

Bonne Terre, Saint Francois, Pop. 6,797
North St. Francois County R-I SD 3,200/PK-12
300 Berry Rd 63628 573-431-3300
Dr. Yancy Poorman Ed.D., supt. Fax 358-2377
www.ncsd.k12.mo.us/
North County PS 800/PK-2
405 Hillcrest Dr 63628 573-431-3300
Dr. Chad Lynn, prin. Fax 358-7475
Preschool Center 100/PK-PK
405 Hillcrest Dr 63628 573-431-3300
Dr. Chad Lynn, prin. Fax 358-7475
Other Schools – See Desloge

Bonnots Mill, Osage

St. Mary S 50/1-8
1641 Highway C 65016 573-897-2567
Tatis Taylor, prin. Fax 897-4143

Boonville, Cooper, Pop. 8,135
Boonville R-I SD 1,500/K-12
736 Main St 65233 660-882-7474
Dr. Mark Ficken, supt. Fax 882-5721
www.boonville.k12.mo.us/
Barton ES 300/3-5
814 Locust St 65233 660-882-6527
Brett Frerking, prin. Fax 882-2473
Cole PS 400/K-2
1700 W Ashley Rd 65233 660-882-2744
Leslie Reardon, prin. Fax 882-2898
Elliott MS 300/6-8
700 Main St 65233 660-882-6649
Frederick Smith, prin. Fax 882-8646

SS. Peter & Paul S 200/PK-8
502 7th St 65233 660-882-2589
Alan Lammers, prin. Fax 882-2476

Bosworth, Carroll, Pop. 302
Bosworth R-V SD 100/PK-12
102 E Eldridge St 64623 660-534-7311
Lachrissa Smith, supt. Fax 534-7409
www.bosworthr-v.k12.mo.us/
Bosworth ES 50/PK-6
102 E Eldridge St 64623 660-534-7311
Natalie Ikenberry, prin. Fax 534-7409

Bourbon, Crawford, Pop. 1,624
Crawford County R-I SD 1,000/PK-12
1444 S Old Highway 66 65441 573-732-4426
Patricia L. Thompson, supt. Fax 732-4545
www.warhawks.k12.mo.us
Bourbon ES 400/PK-4
357 Jost St 65441 573-732-5365
Kristi Hale, prin. Fax 732-3196
Bourbon MS 300/5-8
363 Jost St 65441 573-732-4424
Brian Witt, prin. Fax 732-4425

Bowling Green, Pike, Pop. 5,265
Bowling Green R-I SD 1,300/K-12
700 W Adams St 63334 573-324-5441
Dr. Matt Frederickson, supt. Fax 324-2439
www.bgschools.k12.mo.us
Bowling Green ES 500/K-5
700 W Adams St 63334 573-324-2042
Stephanie Bailey, prin. Fax 324-2331
Bowling Green MS 300/6-8
700 W Adams St 63334 573-324-2181
David Koogler, prin. Fax 324-3292
Other Schools – See Frankford

St. Clement S 100/PK-8
21493 Highway 161 63334 573-324-2166
Dr. Larry Twellman, prin. Fax 324-6159

Bradleyville, Taney, Pop. 84
Bradleyville R-I SD 200/PK-12
PO Box 20 65614 417-796-2288
Scott Ewing, supt. Fax 796-2289
Bradleyville ES 100/PK-6
PO Box 20 65614 417-796-2288
Gina Norwine M.Ed., prin. Fax 796-2289

Branson, Taney, Pop. 10,302
Branson R-IV SD 4,600/PK-12
1756 Bee Creek Rd 65616 417-334-6541
Dr. Brad Swofford, supt. Fax 332-2510
www.branson.k12.mo.us
Branson JHS 700/7-8
263 Buccaneer Dr 65616 417-334-3087
Bryan Bronn, prin. Fax 336-3913
Buchanan ES 700/K-3
1000 Buchanan Rd 65616 417-243-2530
Dr. April Hawkins, prin. Fax 334-6613
Buchanan IS 500/4-6
766 Buchanan Rd 65616 417-332-3201
Matt Dean, prin. Fax 332-3224
Cedar Ridge ES 500/1-3
396 Cedar Ridge Dr 65616 417-334-5135
Dr. Michelle Collins, prin. Fax 336-6079
Cedar Ridge IS 500/4-6
308 Cedar Ridge Dr 65616 417-334-5137
Dr. Landon Gray, prin. Fax 336-3652
Cedar Ridge PS 300/PK-K
402 Cedar Ridge Dr 65616 417-336-1887
Dr. Shelly Worley, prin. Fax 336-1889

Brashear, Adair, Pop. 264
Adair County R-II SD 200/K-12
205 W Dewey St 63533 660-323-5272
Shelly Shipman, supt. Fax 323-5250
brashear.k12.mo.us
Adair County R-II ES 100/K-6
205 W Dewey St 63533 660-323-5272
Shelly Shipman, prin. Fax 323-5250

Braymer, Caldwell, Pop. 864
Braymer C-4 SD 300/PK-12
400 Bobcat Ave 64624 660-645-2284
Wade Schroeder, supt. Fax 645-2780
www.braymerbobcats.org
Braymer ES 200/PK-6
400 Bobcat Ave 64624 660-645-2284
Lyndsey Hall, prin. Fax 645-2780

Breckenridge, Caldwell, Pop. 364
Breckenridge R-I SD 100/PK-12
400 W Colfax St 64625 660-644-5715
Brent Skinner, supt. Fax 644-5710
Breckenridge ES 50/PK-6
400 W Colfax St 64625 660-644-5715
Brent Skinner, prin. Fax 644-5710

Brentwood, Saint Louis, Pop. 7,905
Brentwood SD 800/PK-12
1201 Hanley Industrial Ct 63144 314-962-4507
Dr. Brian Lane, supt. Fax 962-7302
www.brentwoodmoschools.org
Brentwood ECC PK-PK
1201 Hanley Industrial Ct 63144 314-262-8521
Nancy Stoverink, prin. Fax 962-7302
Brentwood MS 200/6-8
9127 White Ave 63144 314-962-8238
Dr. Andrew Loiterstein, prin. Fax 968-8724
McGrath ES 200/K-5
2350 Saint Clair Ave 63144 314-962-6824
Dr. Cynthia Neu, prin. Fax 962-6541
Twain ES 200/K-5
8636 Litzsinger Rd 63144 314-962-0613
Trina Petty-Rice, prin. Fax 963-7724

St. Mary Magdalen S 200/PK-8
8750 Magdalen Ave 63144 314-961-0149
Kathy Wiseman, prin. Fax 961-7208

Bridgeton, Saint Louis, Pop. 11,322
Pattonville R-3 SD
Supt. — See Saint Ann
Bridgeway ES 400/K-5
11635 Oakbury Ct 63044 314-213-8012
William Casner, prin. Fax 213-8612

Bronaugh, Vernon, Pop. 241
Bronaugh R-VII SD 200/PK-12
527 E 6th St 64728 417-922-3211
Dr. David Copeland, supt. Fax 922-3308
www.bronaughschools.net
Bronaugh ES 100/PK-6
527 E 6th St 64728 417-922-3211
Jordan Dickey, prin. Fax 922-3308

Brookfield, Linn, Pop. 4,463
Brookfield R-III SD 1,100/PK-12
124A N Pershing Dr 64628 660-258-7443
Dr. Kyle Collins, supt. Fax 258-4711
www.brookfield.k12.mo.us
Brookfield ES 400/PK-4
128 N Pershing Dr 64628 660-258-2241
Tinna Croy, prin. Fax 258-2243
Brookfield MS 300/5-8
126 N Pershing Dr 64628 660-258-7335
Melinda Wilbeck, prin. Fax 258-3064

Broseley, Butler
Twin Rivers R-X SD 1,000/K-12
PO Box 146 63932 573-328-4321
Jeremy Siebert, supt. Fax 328-1070
www.tr10.us
Other Schools – See Fisk, Qulin

Brunswick, Chariton, Pop. 841
Brunswick R-II SD 300/PK-12
1008 County Rd 65236 660-548-3550
Robert Kottman, supt. Fax 548-3029
www.brunswick.k12.mo.us
Brunswick ES 200/PK-6
1008 County Rd 65236 660-548-3777
Susan Duncan, prin. Fax 548-3029

Bucklin, Linn, Pop. 465
Bucklin R-II SD 100/PK-12
26832 Highway 129 64631 660-695-3555
Stephen Coulson, supt. Fax 695-3345
www.bucklin.k12.mo.us/
Bucklin R-II S 100/PK-12
26832 Highway 129 64631 660-695-3225
Nicole Head, prin. Fax 695-3345

Buckner, Jackson, Pop. 3,009
Fort Osage R-I SD
Supt. — See Independence
Buckner ES 400/K-4
013 S Sibley St 64016 816-650-7300
Karen Hile, prin. Fax 650-7305

Buffalo, Dallas, Pop. 3,038
Dallas County R-I SD 1,600/K-12
1323 S Ash St 65622 417-345-2222
Dr. Tim Ryan, supt. Fax 345-8446
www.bisonpride.us
Buffalo MS 500/5-8
926 Truman 65622 417-345-2335
Buck Shockley, prin. Fax 345-5968
Mallory ES 600/K-4
315 S Hickory St 65622 417-345-2350
Cheryl Knox, prin. Fax 345-2350

Bunceton, Cooper, Pop. 348
Cooper County R-IV SD 100/K-12
500 E Main St 65237 660-427-5347
Dr. Mark Spaid, supt. Fax 427-5348
www.bunceton.k12.mo.us
Bunceton ES 100/K-6
500 E Main St 65237 660-427-5415
Jessica Huth, prin. Fax 427-5348

Zion Lutheran S 50/1-8
17321 Lone Elm Rd 65237 660-838-6307
Marcia Toellner, lead tchr.

Bunker, Reynolds, Pop. 405
Bunker R-III SD 200/K-12
PO Box 365 63629 573-689-2507
Melissa Nash, supt. Fax 689-1268
www.bunkerr3.k12.mo.us/
Bunker ES 100/K-6
PO Box 365 63629 573-689-2211
Rachel Gore, prin. Fax 689-1269

Burlington Junction, Nodaway, Pop. 533
West Nodaway R-I SD 300/PK-12
PO Box 260 64428 660-725-4613
Shannon Nolte, supt. Fax 725-4300
www.wnrockets.com/
West Nodaway R-1 ES 100/PK-5
PO Box 260 64428 660-725-4126
Holly Brady, prin. Fax 725-4300

Butler, Bates, Pop. 4,155
Ballard R-II SD 100/K-12
10247 NE State Route 18 64730 816-297-2656
John Siebeneck, supt. Fax 297-4002
www.ballardr2.net
Ballard ES 100/K-6
10247 NE State Route 18 64730 816-297-2656
Eric Hon, prin. Fax 297-4002

Butler R-V SD 1,000/PK-12
420 S Fulton St 64730 660-679-0653
Darin Carter, supt. Fax 200-3010
www.butlerr5.org/
Butler ES 600/PK-6
4 N High St 64730 660-679-6591
Melody Siebeneck, prin. Fax 679-6593

Cabool, Texas, Pop. 2,104
Cabool R-IV SD 700/PK-12
1025 Rogers Ave 65689 417-962-3153
Robin Ritchie, supt. Fax 962-5043
www.cabool.k12.mo.us
Cabool ES 300/PK-4
1025 Rogers Ave 65689 417-962-3153
Aaron Miller, prin. Fax 962-5043
Cabool MS 300/5-8
1025 Rogers Ave 65689 417-962-3153
Cheryl Manning, prin. Fax 962-5043

Cadet, Washington
Kingston SD K-14 700/K-12
10047 Diamond Rd 63630 573-438-4982
Alex McCaul, supt. Fax 438-8813
www.kingston.k12.mo.us
Kingston ES 200/3-5
10047 Diamond Rd 63630 573-438-4982
Jennifer Boyster, prin. Fax 438-8814
Kingston MS 200/6-8
10047 Diamond Rd 63630 573-438-4982
Lampkin Markie, prin. Fax 438-1212
Kingston PS 200/K-2
10047 Diamond Rd 63630 573-438-4982
Marlene King, prin. Fax 438-4664

St. Joachim S 100/PK-8
10121 Crest Rd 63630 573-438-3973
Carmen Litton, prin. Fax 438-3161

Cainsville, Harrison, Pop. 285
Cainsville R-I SD 100/PK-12
PO Box 108 64632 660-893-5213
Richard Smith, supt. Fax 893-5713
cainsville.k12.mo.us
Cainsville ES 100/PK-6
PO Box 108 64632 660-893-5214
Bill Pottorff, prin. Fax 893-5713

Cairo, Randolph, Pop. 287
Northeast Randolph County R-IV SD 400/PK-12
301 W Martin St 65239 660-263-2788
Darren Rapert, supt. Fax 263-5735
www.ner4bearcats.com

Northeast ES 200/PK-5
301 W Martin St 65239 660-263-2828
Kelsey Kearns, prin. Fax 263-5735

Caledonia, Washington, Pop. 130

Valley R-VI SD 300/K-12
1 Viking Dr 63631 573-779-3446
Brad Crocker, supt. Fax 779-3505
www.valleyschooldistrict.org

Valley ES 100/K-6
2 Viking Dr 63631 573-779-3332
Caleb Tiefenauer, prin. Fax 779-3562

Calhoun, Henry, Pop. 463

Calhoun R-VIII SD 100/PK-12
409 S College St 65323 660-694-3422
John Thompson, supt. Fax 694-3501
calhoun.k12.mo.us

Calhoun ECC, 206 W 7th St 65323 PK-PK
Pam Little, dir. 660-694-3344

Calhoun ES 100/K-6
409 S College St 65323 660-694-3422
Christopher Calhoun, prin. Fax 694-3921

California, Moniteau, Pop. 4,221

High Point R-III SD 100/K-8
60909 Highway C 65018 660-489-2213
Marilyn Maier, supt. Fax 489-2412
www.highpointr3.com

High Point ES 100/K-8
60909 Highway C 65018 660-489-2213
Marilyn Maier, supt. Fax 489-2412

Moniteau County R-I SD 1,300/PK-12
211 S Owen St Ste B 65018 573-796-2145
Dwight Sanders, supt. Fax 796-6123
www.californiak12.org/

California ES 600/PK-5
101 S Owen St 65018 573-796-2161
Gary Baker, prin. Fax 796-8650

California MS 300/6-8
211 S Owen St 65018 573-796-2146
Matt Abernathy, prin. Fax 796-8257

Callao, Macon, Pop. 286

Callao C-8 SD 100/K-8
PO Box A 63534 660-768-5541
Pamela Halstead, admin. Fax 768-5699
www.callaoc8.com/

Callao S 100/K-8
PO Box A 63534 660-768-5541
Pamela Halstead, admin. Fax 768-5699

Camden Point, Platte, Pop. 473

North Platte County R-I SD
Supt. — See Dearborn

North Platte ES 200/PK-2
300 Scout St 64018 816-280-3422
Cathy Hubble, prin. Fax 445-3764

Camdenton, Camden, Pop. 3,647

Camdenton R-III SD 4,300/PK-12
PO Box 1409 65020 573-346-9213
Dr. Tim Hadfield, supt. Fax 346-9211
camdentonschools.schoolwires.net/

Camdenton MS 600/7-8
PO Box 1409 65020 573-346-9257
Matt Stacey, prin. Fax 346-9288

Dogwood ES 800/PK-2
PO Box 1409 65020 573-346-9239
Lucinda Varner, prin. Fax 346-9291

Hawthorn ES 500/3-4
PO Box 1409 65020 573-317-3450
Todd Shockley, prin. Fax 317-3452

Oak Ridge IS 600/5-6
PO Box 1409 65020 573-346-9280
Tracy Evans, prin. Fax 346-9286

Other Schools – See Osage Beach, Sunrise Beach

Cameron, Clinton, Pop. 9,834

Cameron R-I SD 1,400/PK-12
423 N Chestnut St 64429 816-632-2170
Dr. Matt Robinson, supt. Fax 632-2612
www.cameron.k12.mo.us

Cameron IS 3-5
915 S Park 64429 816-882-1046
Laurie Mefford, prin. Fax 882-1047

Cameron Veterans MS 400/6-8
1015 S Park 64429 816-882-1042
Tiffani Collins, prin. Fax 882-1043

Parkview ES 500/PK-2
602 S Harris St 64429 816-882-1051
Angela Ormsby, prin. Fax 882-1052

Campbell, Dunklin, Pop. 1,968

Campbell R-II SD 700/PK-12
801 S State Highway 53 63933 573-246-2133
Jay Thornton, supt. Fax 246-3212
www.campbell.k12.mo.us

Campbell ES 400/PK-6
801 S State Highway 53 63933 573-246-3109
Ben Foster, prin. Fax 246-2245

St. Teresa S 100/PK-8
40648 State Highway JJ 63933 573-328-4197
Peggy Ogden, prin. Fax 328-4197

Canton, Lewis, Pop. 2,342

Canton R-V SD 500/PK-12
200 S 4th St 63435 573-288-5216
W.A. Anderson, supt. Fax 288-5442
www.canton.k12.mo.us

Canton ES 300/PK-6
200 S 4th St 63435 573-288-5216
Mark Lyon, prin. Fax 288-5442

Cape Girardeau, Cape Girardeau, Pop. 37,082

Cape Girardeau SD 63 4,300/PK-12
301 N Clark St 63701 573-335-1867
Neil Glass, supt. Fax 335-1820
www.capetigers.com

Blanchard ES 300/PK-4
1829 N Sprigg St 63701 573-335-3030
Dr. Barbara Kohlfeld, prin. Fax 334-1319

Central JHS 600/7-8
1910 Whitener St 63701 573-334-2923
Carla Fee, prin. Fax 332-8746

Central MS 600/5-6
1900 Thilenius St 63701 573-334-6281
Rex Crosnoe, prin. Fax 334-1557

Clippard ES 400/PK-4
2880 Hopper Rd 63701 573-334-5720
Dr. Sydney Herbst, prin. Fax 334-1067

Franklin ES 400/PK-4
1550 Themis St 63701 573-335-5456
Leigh Ragsdale, prin. Fax 334-1140

Jefferson ES 400/PK-4
520 S Minnesota St 63703 573-334-2030
Dr. RaeAnne Alpers, prin. Fax 334-1159

Schrader ES 400/K-4
1360 Randol Ave 63701 573-335-5310
Dr. Ruth Ann Orr, prin. Fax 334-3871

Jackson R-II SD
Supt. — See Jackson

Gordonville ES 100/K-2
653 State Highway Z 63701 573-243-9580
Shauna Criddle, prin. Fax 243-9580

Nell Holcomb R-IV SD 300/K-8
6547 State Highway 177 63701 573-334-3644
Darryl Pannier, supt. Fax 334-9552
www.nellholcomb.k12.mo.us/

Holcomb ES 300/K-8
6547 State Highway 177 63701 573-334-3644
Mike Wortmann, prin. Fax 334-9552

Cape Christian Community S 100/PK-8
1855 Perryville Rd 63701 573-335-8333
Carroll Williams, prin. Fax 335-3161

Eagle Ridge Christian S 200/PK-12
4210 State Highway K 63701 573-339-1335
Janice Margrabe, admin. Fax 339-1390

St. Marys Cathedral S 200/K-8
210 S Sprigg St 63703 573-335-3840
Carol Strattman, prin. Fax 335-4142

St. Vincent de Paul S 400/PK-8
1919 Ritter Dr 63701 573-334-9594
Kay Glastetter, prin. Fax 334-0425

Trinity Lutheran S 200/PK-8
55 N Pacific St 63701 573-334-1068
Melissa Adams, prin. Fax 334-5081

Cardwell, Dunklin, Pop. 704

Southland C-9 SD 400/PK-12
500 S Main St 63829 573-654-3574
Thomas Gotsch, supt. Fax 654-3575
www.southland.k12.mo.us

Southland ES 200/PK-6
500 S Main St 63829 573-654-3564
Kevin Reddick, prin. Fax 654-3565

Carl Junction, Jasper, Pop. 7,264

Carl Junction R-I SD 3,400/PK-12
206 S Roney St 64834 417-649-7026
Dr. Phillip Cook, supt. Fax 649-6594
www.cjr1.org

Carl Junction IS 800/4-6
206 S Roney St 64834 417-649-5760
Gretchen DeMasters, prin. Fax 649-7248

Carl Junction JHS 500/7-8
206 S Roney St 64834 417-649-7246
Scott Sawyer, prin. Fax 649-0022

Carl Junction PS 2-3 500/2-3
206 S Roney St 64834 417-649-7034
Lauri Mead, prin. Fax 649-6566

Carl Junction PS K-1 600/PK-1
206 S Roney St 64834 417-649-7045
Kari Arehart, prin. Fax 649-7981

Carrollton, Carroll, Pop. 3,737

Carrollton R-VII SD 900/PK-12
103 E 9th St 64633 660-542-2769
Dr. Jon Oetinger, supt. Fax 542-3416
www.trojans.k12.mo.us/

Adams PS 200/PK-1
306 N Jefferson St 64633 660-542-2926
Heidi Smith, prin. Fax 542-3692

Carrollton ES 200/2-4
207 E 9th St 64633 660-542-2535
Heidi Smith, prin. Fax 542-3692

Carrollton MS 300/5-8
300 E 9th St 64633 660-542-3472
Brent Dobbins, prin. Fax 542-3169

Carterville, Jasper, Pop. 1,855

Webb City R-VII SD
Supt. — See Webb City

Carterville ES 200/K-4
210 E Hall St 64835 417-673-6080
Jarrett Cook, prin. Fax 673-6082

Carthage, Jasper, Pop. 14,047

Carthage R-IX SD 4,600/PK-12
710 Lyon St 64836 417-359-7000
Dr. Mark Baker, supt. Fax 359-7004
www.carthagetigers.org

Carthage Intermediate Center 700/5-6
2851 S Chapel Rd 64836 417-359-7246
Scott Ragsdale, prin. Fax 359-7408

Carthage JHS 700/7-8
714 S Main St 64836 417-359-7050
Jenny Bogle, prin. Fax 359-7057

Columbian ES 500/K-4
1015 W Macon St 64836 417-359-7060
Bryan Shallenburger, prin. Fax 359-8979

Early Childhood & Pat Center PK-PK
625 E Fairview 64836 417-359-7004
Kim Ensminger, dir.

Fairview ES 500/PK-4
1201 E Fairview Ave 64836 417-359-7070
Ronna Patterson, prin. Fax 359-7074

Pleasant Valley ES 200/K-4
652 County Road 180 64836 417-359-7085
Melony Houlihan, prin. Fax 359-7084

Steadley ES 700/PK-4
1814 W Fir Rd 64836 417-359-7065
Dr. Tom Barlow, prin. Fax 359-7069

Twain ES 300/K-4
1435 S Main St 64836 417-359-7080
Laurel Rosenthal, prin. Fax 359-7079

St. Ann Catholic S 100/PK-6
1156 Grand Ave 64836 417-358-2674
Bonnie Schaeffer, prin. Fax 358-8976

Caruthersville, Pemiscot, Pop. 6,073

Caruthersville SD 18 1,200/PK-12
1711 Ward Ave 63830 573-333-6100
J.J. Bullington, supt. Fax 333-6108
www.cps18.org

Caruthersville ES 600/PK-5
900 Washington Ave 63830 573-333-6133
Bradley Gerling, prin. Fax 333-6137

Caruthersville MS 300/6-8
1705 Ward Ave 63830 573-333-6120
Stephanie McGraw, prin. Fax 333-1835

Pemiscot County R-III SD 100/K-8
1727 County Highway 536 63830 573-333-1856
Joey Watkins, supt. Fax 333-1857
r3.k12.mo.us

Pemiscot County R-III S 100/K-8
1727 County Highway 536 63830 573-333-1856
Joey Watkins, prin. Fax 333-1857

Cassville, Barry, Pop. 3,224

Cassville R-IV SD 1,900/PK-12
1501 Main St 65625 417-847-2221
Dr. Richard Asbill, supt. Fax 847-4009
cassville.k12.mo.us/

Cassville IS 400/3-5
1501 Main St 65625 417-847-4010
Eric White, prin. Fax 847-2226

Cassville MS 400/6-8
1501 Main St 65625 417-847-3136
Jimmie Barton, prin. Fax 847-3156

Thomas ES 500/PK-2
1501 Main St 65625 417-847-2445
Catherine Weaver, prin. Fax 847-2462

Catawissa, Franklin

Meramec Valley R-III SD
Supt. — See Pacific

Nike ES 100/K-5
2264 Highway AP 63015 636-271-1444
David Quanz, prin. Fax 271-1447

Center, Ralls, Pop. 502

Ralls County R-II SD 800/PK-12
21622 Highway 19 63436 573-267-3397
Dr. Tara Lewis, supt. Fax 267-3538
www.rallsr2.k12.mo.us

Ralls County ES 400/PK-5
21700 Highway 19 63436 660-267-3567
Dr. Natalie Gibson, prin.

Twain JHS 200/6-8
21622 Highway 19 63436 573-267-3397
Delores Woodhurst, prin. Fax 267-3538

Centerview, Johnson, Pop. 266

Johnson County R-VII SD 500/PK-12
92 NW State Route 58 64019 660-656-3316
Brett Gray, supt. Fax 656-3633
www.crestridge.org

Crest Ridge ES 300/PK-6
94 NW State Route 58 64019 660-656-3315
Kim Evans, prin. Fax 656-3411

Centerville, Reynolds, Pop. 187

Centerville R-I SD 100/K-8
PO Box 99 63633 573-648-2285
Joseph Minks, supt. Fax 648-2282
www.ces.k12.mo.us/

Centerville S 100/K-8
PO Box 99 63633 573-648-2285
Joseph Minks, supt. Fax 648-2282

Centralia, Boone, Pop. 3,976

Centralia R-VI SD 1,400/PK-12
1399 E Highway 22 Ste B 65240 573-682-3561
Darin Ford, supt. Fax 682-2181
www.centralia.k12.mo.us

Boren MS 300/6-8
110 N Jefferson St 65240 573-682-2617
Nathan Gordon, prin. Fax 682-1500

Centralia IS 300/3-5
550 W Lakeview St 65240 573-682-3451
Jason Lea, prin. Fax 682-2663

Chance ES 300/PK-2
510 S Rollins St 65240 573-682-2014
Tiffani Shuman, prin. Fax 682-1369

Sunnydale Adventist S 50/K-8
6979 Audrain Road 9139 65240 573-682-2811

Chadwick, Christian

Chadwick R-I SD 200/PK-12
PO Box 274 65629 417-634-3588
Dana Comstock, supt. Fax 634-2668
www.chadwick.k12.mo.us/

Chadwick ES 100/PK-6
PO Box 274 65629 417-634-3588
David Aldrich, prin. Fax 634-4040

Chaffee, Scott, Pop. 2,925
Chaffee R-II SD 600/PK-12
517 W Yoakum Ave 63740 573-887-3532
Ken Latham, supt. Fax 887-3926
chaffee.k12.mo.us
Chaffee ES 300/PK-6
408 Elliott Ave 63740 573-887-3244
Sid Atkins, prin. Fax 887-6493

St. Ambrose S 100/K-8
419 S 3rd St 63740 573-887-6711
Laura Enderle, prin. Fax 887-6711

Chamois, Osage, Pop. 395
Osage County R-I SD 200/PK-12
614 S Poplar St 65024 573-763-5666
Lyle Best, supt. Fax 763-5686
www.chamois.k12.mo.us
Osage County ES 100/PK-6
614 S Poplar St 65024 573-763-5446
Dee Luker, prin. Fax 763-5011

Charleston, Mississippi, Pop. 5,882
Charleston R-I SD 1,000/PK-12
PO Box 39 63834 573-683-3776
Dr. Tammy Lupardus, supt. Fax 683-2909
charleston.k12.mo.us
Charleston MS 200/6-8
PO Box 39 63834 573-683-3346
Dr. Kimberley Blissett, prin. Fax 683-2930
Hearnes ES 500/PK-5
PO Box 39 63834 573-683-3728
Angela Zorbas, prin. Fax 683-2915

St. Henry S 100/PK-8
306 Court St 63834 573-683-6218
Mike Eftink, prin. Fax 683-4124

Chesterfield, Saint Louis, Pop. 46,860
Parkway C-2 SD 17,200/PK-12
455 N Woods Mill Rd 63017 314-415-8100
Dr. Keith Marty, supt. Fax 415-8009
www.parkwayschools.net
Green Trails ES 400/K-5
170 Portico Dr 63017 314-415-6250
Dr. Rene Sommers, prin. Fax 415-6262
Highcroft Ridge ES 300/K-5
15380 Highcroft Dr 63017 314-415-6400
Cartelia Lucas, prin. Fax 415-6419
Parkway Central MS 900/6-8
471 N Woods Mill Rd 63017 314-415-7800
Dr. Michael Baugus, prin. Fax 415-7834
Parkway West MS 900/6-8
2312 Baxter Rd 63017 314-415-7400
Anne Miller, prin. Fax 415-7409
River Bend ES 400/K-5
224 River Valley Dr 63017 314-415-6650
Jaime Otto, prin. Fax 415-6669
Shenandoah Valley ES 400/K-5
15399 Appalachian Trl 63017 314-415-6750
Greg Cicotte, prin. Fax 415-6762
Other Schools – See Ballwin, Creve Coeur, Manchester, Maryland Heights

Rockwood R-VI SD
Supt. — See Eureka
Chesterfield ES 400/K-5
17700 Wild Horse Creek Rd 63005 636-537-4342
Dr. Meg Brooks, prin. Fax 537-4347
Kehrs Mill ES 600/K-5
2650 Kehrs Mill Rd 63017 636-537-4359
Dr. Sarah Padberg, prin. Fax 537-4363
Rockwood Center ECC 300/PK-PK
2730 Valley Rd 63005 636-207-2600
Dr. Jane Brown, dir. Fax 207-2607
Wild Horse ES 500/K-5
16695 Wild Horse Creek Rd 63005 636-891-6075
Patrick Fisher, prin. Fax 537-4388

Ascension S 400/PK-8
238 Santa Maria Dr 63005 636-532-1151
Julie Smith, prin. Fax 532-6502
Chesterfield Day S 200/PK-6
1100 White Rd 63017 314-469-6622
Rachana Creeth, head sch Fax 469-7889
Chesterfield Montessori S 100/PK-9
14000 Ladue Rd 63017 314-469-7150
Lisa Trout, head sch Fax 469-7851
Incarnate Word S 400/K-8
13416 Olive Blvd 63017 314-576-5366
Michael Welling, prin. Fax 576-2046

Chilhowee, Johnson, Pop. 315
Chilhowee R-IV SD 100/PK-12
101 SW State Route 2 64733 660-678-2511
Troy Marnholtz, supt. Fax 678-5711
www.chilhowee.k12.mo.us
Chilhowee ES 100/PK-6
101 SW State Route 2 64733 660-678-4511
John Murphy, prin. Fax 678-5711

Shawnee R-III SD 100/K-8
1193 N Highway 13 64733 660-885-3620
Dr. Nancy Akert, supt. Fax 885-3620
sites.google.com/a/shawnee.k12.mo.us/www/
Shawnee ES 100/K-8
1193 N Highway 13 64733 660-885-3620
Dr. Nancy Akert, prin. Fax 885-3620

Chillicothe, Livingston, Pop. 9,375
Chillicothe R-II SD 1,900/K-12
1020 Old Highway 36 W 64601 660-646-4566
Dr. Roger Barnes, supt. Fax 646-6508
www.chillicotheschools.org/
Central ES 300/4-5
321 Elm St 64601 660-646-2359
Melanie Rucker, prin. Fax 646-3832
Chillicothe MS 400/6-8
1529 Calhoun St 64601 660-646-1916
Steve Haley, prin. Fax 646-5065
Dewey ES 300/K-1
905 Dickinson St 64601 660-646-4255
Abby Smith, prin. Fax 646-0801
Field ES 300/2-3
1100 Oak St 64601 660-646-2909
Philip Pohren, prin. Fax 646-6286

Bishop Hogan Memorial S 100/PK-8
1114 Trenton St 64601 660-646-0705
Pam Brobst, prin. Fax 646-0705

Chula, Livingston, Pop. 207
Livingston County R-III SD 100/PK-8
PO Box 40 64635 660-639-3135
Megan Hardie, admin. Fax 639-2171
www.chulaschool.org
Livingston County ES 100/PK-8
PO Box 40 64635 660-639-3135
Megan Hardie, admin. Fax 639-2171

Clarence, Shelby, Pop. 804
Shelby County R-IV SD
Supt. — See Shelbina
Clarence ES 100/PK-5
206 N Shelby St 63437 660-699-3302
Kelly Williams, prin. Fax 699-2168

Clarksburg, Moniteau, Pop. 331
Clarksburg C-2 SD 100/K-8
401 S Highway H 65025 573-787-3511
Nathan Bestgen, supt. Fax 787-3667
www.clarksburg.k12.mo.us
Clarksburg S 100/K-8
401 S Highway H 65025 573-787-3511
Nathan Bestgen, prin. Fax 787-3667

Clarksville, Pike, Pop. 436
Pike County R-III SD 500/PK-12
28176 Highway WW 63336 573-242-3546
Mark Harvey, supt. Fax 485-2393
www.cloptonhawks.com
Clopton ES 200/PK-6
28176 Highway WW 63336 573-485-2488
Linda Henderson, prin. Fax 485-2393

Clarkton, Dunklin, Pop. 1,265
Clarkton C-4 SD 300/PK-12
PO Box 637 63837 573-448-3712
Delane Beckwith, supt. Fax 448-5182
www.clarktonschools.org/
Clarkton ES 200/PK-6
PO Box 637 63837 573-448-3712
Paul Lynch, prin. Fax 448-5182

Clayton, Saint Louis, Pop. 15,572
Clayton SD 2,700/PK-12
2 Mark Twain Cir 63105 314-854-6000
Dr. Sean Doherty, supt. Fax 854-6093
www.claytonschools.net
Captain ES 400/K-5
6345 Northwood Ave 63105 314-854-6100
Jennifer Martin, prin. Fax 854-6190
Family Center 100/PK-PK
301 Gay Ave 63105 314-854-6900
Debra Reilly, dir. Fax 854-6940
Glenridge ES 400/K-5
7447 Wellington Way 63105 314-854-6200
Beth Scott, prin. Fax 854-6290
Meramec ES 400/K-5
400 S Meramec Ave 63105 314-854-6300
Lisa Jackson-Terry, prin. Fax 854-6390
Wydown MS 600/6-8
6500 Wydown Blvd 63105 314-854-6400
Dr. Jamie Jordan, prin. Fax 854-6491

St. Michael S of Clayton 100/PK-8
6345 Wydown Blvd 63105 314-721-4422
Elizabeth Mosher, head sch Fax 721-4448
Wilson S 200/PK-6
400 De Mun Ave 63105 314-725-4999
Thad Falkner, head sch Fax 725-5242

Cleveland, Cass, Pop. 645
Midway R-I SD 400/K-12
5801 E State Route 2 64734 816-250-2994
Gordon Myers, supt. Fax 899-2823
www.midwayk12.net
Midway ES 200/K-6
5801 E State Route 2 64734 816-250-2994
Susan Tinich, prin. Fax 899-2823

Clever, Christian, Pop. 2,109
Clever R-V SD 500/PK-12
103 S Public Ave 65631 417-743-4800
Steve Carvajal, supt. Fax 743-4802
www.cleverbluejays.org
Clever ES 200/PK-8
103 S Public Ave 65631 417-743-4815
Benjy Fenske, prin. Fax 743-4822

Clifton Hill, Randolph, Pop. 111
Westran R-I SD
Supt. — See Huntsville
Westran MS 200/6-8
622 Harlan St 65244 660-261-4511
Mike Aulbur, prin. Fax 261-4292

Climax Springs, Camden, Pop. 124
Climax Springs R-IV SD 200/PK-12
571 Climax Ave 65324 573-347-3905
Nathan Barb, supt. Fax 347-9931
www.csprings.k12.mo.us
Climax Springs ES 100/PK-6
571 Climax Ave 65324 573-347-3005
Caleb Petet, prin. Fax 347-9933

Clinton, Henry, Pop. 8,864
Clinton SD 124 1,800/PK-12
701 S 8th St 64735 660-885-2237
Dr. Adam Willard, supt. Fax 885-7033
www.clintoncardinals.org
Clinton IS 400/3-5
701 S 8th St 64735 660-885-3179
Jarrod Boyles, prin. Fax 885-2437
Clinton MS 400/6-8
701 S 8th St 64735 660-885-3353
Jennifer Paschall, prin. Fax 885-4826
Henry ES 500/PK-2
701 S 8th St 64735 660-885-5585
Sherri Swope, prin. Fax 885-2784

Davis R-XII SD 50/K-8
227 SW Highway T 64735 660-885-2629
Deborah Day, supt. Fax 885-2648
Davis ES 50/K-8
227 SW Highway T 64735 660-885-2629
Deborah Day, admin. Fax 885-2648

Leesville R-IX SD 100/K-8
823 SE Highway 7 64735 660-477-3406
Brian Wishard, supt. Fax 477-9362
www.leesville.k12.mo.us/
Leesville ES 100/K-8
823 SE Highway 7 64735 660-477-3406
Brian Wishard, admin. Fax 477-9362

Clinton Christian Academy 100/PK-9
271 W Division Rd 64735 660-890-2111
Clark Ballard, admin. Fax 885-2191
Golden Valley Adventist S 1-8
2000 Community Dr 64735 660-492-5559
Holy Rosary S 100/PK-8
400 E Wilson St 64735 660-885-4412
Andrea Harris, prin. Fax 885-5791

Cole Camp, Benton, Pop. 1,108
Cole Camp R-I SD 700/PK-12
500 S Keeney St 65325 660-668-4427
Dr. Tim Roling, supt. Fax 668-4703
colecamp.schoolwires.net
Cole Camp ES 200/K-4
500 S Keeney St 65325 660-668-3011
Kevin Shearer, prin. Fax 668-4703
Cole Camp MS 200/5-8
500 S Keeney St 65325 660-668-3502
Tyler Clark, prin. Fax 668-4703
Cole Camp Preschool PK-PK
500 S Keeney St 65325 660-668-3011
Fax 668-4703

Lutheran School Association 100/K-8
204 E Butterfield Trl 65325 660-668-4614
Larry Andersen, prin. Fax 668-0167

Columbia, Boone, Pop. 105,254
Columbia SD 93 17,600/PK-12
1818 W Worley St 65203 573-214-3400
Dr. Peter Stiepleman, supt. Fax 214-3401
www.cpsk12.org
Battle ES K-5
2600 Battle Ave 65202 573-214-3790
Petre Jeri, prin. Fax 214-3791
Benton ES 300/PK-5
1410 Hinkson Ave 65201 573-214-3610
Laura Lewis, prin. Fax 214-3611
Blue Ridge ES 500/PK-5
3700 Woodland Dr 65202 573-214-3580
Kristen Palmer, prin. Fax 214-3581
Cedar Ridge ES 200/K-5
1100 S Roseta Ave 65201 573-214-3510
Angie Chandler, prin. Fax 214-3511
Center for Gifted Education 50/1-5
1010 Rangeline St 65201 573-214-3750
Terry Gaines, dir. Fax 214-3751
Derby Ridge ES 600/PK-5
4000 Derby Ridge Dr 65202 573-214-3270
Bonita Benson, prin. Fax 214-3271
Fairview ES 600/K-5
909 S Fairview Rd 65203 573-214-3590
Diana Demoss, prin. Fax 214-3591
Gentry MS 800/6-8
4200 Bethel St 65203 573-214-3240
Dr. Fairouz Bishara, prin. Fax 214-3241
Grant ES 300/K-5
10 E Broadway 65203 573-214-3520
Jennifer Wingert, prin. Fax 214-3521
Jefferson MS 500/6-8
713 Rogers St 65201 573-214-3210
Dr. Greg Caine, prin. Fax 214-3211
Keeley ES 700/K-5
201 Park De Ville Dr 65203 573-214-3570
Adrienne Patton, prin. Fax 214-3571
Lange MS 700/6-8
2201 Smiley Ln 65202 573-214-3250
Dr. Bernard Solomon, prin. Fax 214-3251
Lee ES 300/K-5
1208 Locust St 65201 573-214-3530
Ed Elsea, prin. Fax 214-3531
Lewis ES 600/PK-5
5801 Arbor Pointe Pkwy 65202 573-214-3200
Michelle Holz, prin. Fax 214-3209
Midway Heights ES 300/K-5
8130 Highway 40 W 65202 573-214-3540
Angie Gerzen, prin. Fax 214-3541
Mill Creek ES 900/K-5
2200 W Nifong Blvd 65203 573-214-3280
Tabetha Rawlings, prin. Fax 214-3281
New Haven ES 300/K-5
3301 New Haven Rd 65201 573-214-3640
Carole Garth, prin. Fax 214-3641
Oakland MS 500/6-8
3405 Oakland Pl 65202 573-214-3220
Helen Porter, prin. Fax 214-3221

Parkade ES 500/PK-5
111 Parkade Blvd 65202 573-214-3630
Amy Watkins, prin. Fax 214-3631
Ralph ES K-5
5801 S Highway KK 65203 573-214-3840
Dr. Tim Majerus, prin. Fax 214-3841
Ridgeway ES 200/K-5
107 E Sexton Rd 65203 573-214-3550
Shari Lawson, prin. Fax 214-3551
Rock Bridge ES 600/PK-5
5151 S Highway 163 65203 573-214-3290
Dr. Ryan Link, prin. Fax 214-3291
Russell Boulevard ES 600/PK-5
1800 W Rollins Rd 65203 573-214-3650
Candace Fowler, prin. Fax 214-3651
Shepard Boulevard ES 600/K-5
2616 Shepard Blvd 65201 573-214-3660
John Elliston, prin. Fax 214-3661
Smithton MS 700/6-8
3600 W Worley St 65203 573-214-3260
Chris Drury, prin. Fax 214-3261
Two Mile Prairie ES 300/K-5
5450 N Route Z 65202 573-214-3560
Patti Raynor, prin. Fax 214-3561
West Boulevard ES 400/PK-5
319 West Blvd N 65203 573-214-3670
Susan Deakins, prin. Fax 214-3671
West MS 600/6-8
401 Clinkscales Rd 65203 573-214-3230
Dr. Melita Walker, prin. Fax 214-3231

Christian Fellowship S 300/PK-12
4600 Christian Fellowship 65203 573-445-8565
Dr. Rick Mueller, admin. Fax 445-8564
College Park Christian Academy 100/PK-9
1114 College Park Dr 65203 573-445-6315
Heidi Jorgenson, prin. Fax 445-6113
Columbia Independent S 400/PK-12
1801 N Stadium Blvd 65202 573-777-9250
Adam Dube, head sch Fax 777-9251
Good Shepherd Lutheran S 100/K-8
2201 W Rollins Rd 65203 573-445-5878
Tammy Mangold, admin. Fax 445-4078
Our Lady of Lourdes Interparish S 600/K-8
817 Bernadette Dr 65203 573-445-6516
Elaine Hassemer, prin. Fax 445-9887

Conception Junction, Nodaway, Pop. 198
Jefferson C-123 SD 100/PK-12
37614 US Highway 136 64434 660-944-2316
Tim Jermain, supt. Fax 944-2315
www.jeffersonc123.org/
Jefferson ES 100/PK-6
37614 US Highway 136 64434 660-944-2417
Tim Jermain, supt. Fax 944-2315

Concordia, Lafayette, Pop. 2,425
Concordia R-II SD 500/PK-12
PO Box 079 64020 660-463-7235
Brent Cooper, supt. Fax 463-1326
www.concordia.k12.mo.us
Concordia ES 300/PK-6
PO Box 879 64020 660-463-2261
Caleb Petet, prin. Fax 463-2413

St. Paul's Lutheran S 200/PK-8
407 S Main St 64020 660-463-7654
Charlie Snider, prin. Fax 463-0037

Conway, Laclede, Pop. 768
Laclede County R-I SD 700/K-12
726 W Jefferson Ave 65632 417-589-2951
Mark Hedger, supt. Fax 589-3202
www.lacledecountyr1.com
Ezard ES 400/K-6
209 S Shiloh Ave 65632 417-589-2171
Melissa Snell, prin. Fax 589-8251

Cooter, Pemiscot, Pop. 468
Cooter R-IV SD 300/K-12
PO Box 218 63839 573-695-3312
Clay Snider, supt. Fax 695-3073
cooter.k12.mo.us
Cooter ES 100/K-6
PO Box 218 63839 573-695-4584
Debbie Morgan, prin. Fax 695-2542

Cosby, Andrew, Pop. 124
Avenue City R-IX SD 200/K-8
18069 Highway 169 64436 816-662-2305
Don Lawrence, supt. Fax 662-3201
www.avenuecityschool.org
Avenue City S 200/K-8
18069 Highway 169 64436 816-662-2305
Rebecca Grimes, prin. Fax 662-3201

Country Club, Andrew, Pop. 2,414
Savannah R-III SD
Supt. — See Savannah
Glenn ES 300/K-5
12401 County Road 438, 816-279-4533
Kelly Warren, prin. Fax 279-0540

Cowgill, Caldwell, Pop. 187
Cowgill R-VI SD 50/PK-8
341 E 6th St 64637 660-255-4415
Betty Vassmer, supt. Fax 255-4224
www.cowgillr6.com/
Cowgill S 50/PK-8
341 E 6th St 64637 660-255-4415
Betty Vassmer, prin. Fax 255-4224

Craig, Holt, Pop. 248
Craig R-III SD 50/K-12
402 N Ward St 64437 660-683-5351
Michael Leach, supt. Fax 683 5769
www.craigr3school.com
Craig R-III S 50/K-12
402 N Ward St 64437 660-683-5431
Jennifer Dyer, prin. Fax 683-5769

Crane, Stone, Pop. 1,443
Crane R-III SD 700/PK-12
PO Box 405 65633 417-723-5300
Dr. Chris Johnson, supt. Fax 723-5551
www.crane.k12.mo.us
Crane ES 400/PK-6
PO Box 405 65633 417-723-5300
Kelli Rogers, prin. Fax 723-5551

Creighton, Cass, Pop. 347
Sherwood Cass R-VIII SD 900/PK-12
PO Box 98 64739 660-499-2834
Dr. Steve Ritter, supt. Fax 499-2624
www.sherwoodk12.net
Sherwood ES 400/PK-5
PO Box 98 64739 660-499-2202
D'Ann Imler, prin. Fax 499-2865
Sherwood MS 200/6-8
PO Box 98 64739 660-499-2239
Brenda Koch, prin. Fax 499-2585

Creve Coeur, Saint Louis, Pop. 17,490
Ladue SD
Supt. — See Saint Louis
Spoede ES 400/K-4
425 N Spoede Rd 63141 314-432-4438
Dr. Kimberly Stallons, prin. Fax 432-6098

Parkway C-2 SD
Supt. — See Chesterfield
Bellerive ES 400/K-5
620 Rue De Fleur Dr 63141 314-415-6050
Dr. Jami Debosch, prin. Fax 415-6062
Craig ES 400/K-5
1492 Craig Rd, Saint Louis MO 63146 314-415-6200
Dr. David Duckworth, prin. Fax 415-6212
Mason Ridge ES 400/K-5
715 S Mason Rd 63141 314-415-6450
Dr. Jennifer Dieken-Buchek, prin. Fax 415-6462
Parkway Northeast MS 900/6-8
181 Coeur De Ville Dr 63141 314-415-7100
Dr. Jenn Sebold, prin. Fax 415-7113
Ross ES 400/K-5
1150 Ross Ave, Saint Louis MO 63146
314-415-6700
Dr. Lisa Luna, prin. Fax 415-6712

Pattonville R-3 SD
Supt. — See Saint Ann
Willow Brook ES 500/K-5
11022 Schuetz Rd, Saint Louis MO 63146
314-213-8018
Marla Wasserman, prin. Fax 213-8618

Andrews Academy 200/PK-6
888 N Mason Rd 63141 314-878-1883
Sam Sciortino Ph.D., hdmstr. Fax 878-0759
St. Monica S 200/PK-8
12132 Olive Blvd 63141 314-434-2173
Genevieve Callier, prin. Fax 434-7689

Crocker, Pulaski, Pop. 1,094
Crocker R-II SD 600/PK-12
PO Box 488 65452 573-736-5000
Gary Doerhoff, supt. Fax 736-5924
www.crockerschools.org
Dye ES 300/PK-6
PO Box 488 65452 573-736-5000
Teresa Helton, prin. Fax 736-2688

Crystal City, Jefferson, Pop. 4,757
Crystal City SD 47 500/K-12
1100 Mississippi Ave 63019 636-937-4411
Philip Harrison, supt. Fax 937-2512
www.crystal.k12.mo.us/
Crystal City ES 300/K-8
600 Mississippi Ave 63019 636-937-4017
Tim Thompson, prin. Fax 937-2229

Cuba, Crawford, Pop. 3,311
Crawford County R-II SD 1,500/K-12
1 Wildcat Pride Dr 65453 573-885-2534
Jon Earnhart, supt. Fax 885-3900
www.cuba.k12.mo.us/
Cuba ES 600/K-4
1 Wildcat Pride Dr 65453 573-885-2534
Dr. Kim Peterson, prin. Fax 885-3900
Cuba MS 500/5-8
1 Wildcat Pride Dr 65453 573-885-2534
Marie Shoemaker, prin. Fax 885-6278

Holy Cross S 100/PK-5
407 School Ave 65453 573-885-4727
Michael Brooks, prin. Fax 885-3501

Curryville, Pike, Pop. 217

Pike County Christian S 50/K-12
PO Box 96 63339 573-324-2700
Frank Welch, admin. Fax 324-2700

Dadeville, Dade, Pop. 228
Dadeville R-II SD 100/K-12
PO Box 188 65635 417-995-2201
Matt Bushey, supt. Fax 995-2110
bearcats.dadeville.k12.mo.us
Dadeville ES 100/K-5
PO Box 188 65635 417-995-2201
Cassy Farmer, prin. Fax 995-2110

Dardenne Pr, Saint Charles, Pop. 11,319
Wentzville R-IV SD
Supt. — See Wentzville
Prairie View ES 600/K-6
1550 Feise Rd, 636-625-2494
David Bates, prin. Fax 625-2491

Immaculate Conception S 800/K-8
2089 Hanley Rd, 636-561-4450
Daniel Mullenschlader, prin. Fax 625-9020

Dearborn, Platte, Pop. 488
North Platte County R-I SD 500/PK-12
212 W 6th St 64439 816-450-3511
Karl Matt, supt. Fax 992-8727
www.nppanthers.org
North Platte JHS, 212 W 6th St 64439 100/6-8
Michelle Johnson, prin. 816-450-3350
Other Schools – See Camden Point, Edgerton

Deepwater, Henry, Pop. 430
Lakeland R-III SD 400/PK-12
12530 Lakeland School Dr 64740 417-644-2223
Mitch Towne, supt. Fax 644-2316
www.lakeland.k12.mo.us
Lakeland ES 200/PK-6
12530 Lakeland School Dr 64740 417-644-2223
Patricia Munsterman, prin. Fax 644-7301

Deering, Pemiscot, Pop. 130
Delta C-7 SD 200/K-12
PO Box 297 63840 573-757-6648
Kenny Copley, supt. Fax 757-9691
www.deltac7.k12.mo.us
Delta C-7 ES 100/K-6
PO Box 297 63840 573-757-6615
Nathan Baker, prin. Fax 757-6201

De Kalb, Buchanan, Pop. 219
Buchanan County R-IV SD 300/PK-12
702 Main St 64440 816-685-3160
Travis Dittemore, supt. Fax 685-3203
www.bcr4.org
Other Schools – See Rushville

Delta, Cape Girardeau, Pop. 421
Delta R-V SD 300/PK-12
PO Box 787 63744 573-794-2500
Dr. Mellisa Heath, supt. Fax 794-2504
www.deltar5schools.com
Delta ES 100/PK-6
PO Box 787 63744 573-794-2440
Kenyon Wright, prin. Fax 794-9024

Desloge, Saint Francois, Pop. 4,987
North St. Francois County R-I SD
Supt. — See Bonne Terre
North County IS 500/5-6
801 Elm St 63601 573-431-3300
Melanie Allen, prin. Fax 518-0569
North County MS 500/7-8
406 E Chestnut St 63601 573 431-3300
Brenda Hampton, prin. Fax 431-5203
Parkside ES 400/3-4
100 N Parkside St 63601 573-431-3300
Brandon Gregory, prin. Fax 431-0250

De Soto, Jefferson, Pop. 6,303
Desoto SD 73 3,100/PK-12
610 Vineland School Rd 63020 636-586-1000
Dr. Josh Isaacson, supt. Fax 586-1009
www.desoto.k12.mo.us
Athena ES 700/K-6
3775 Athena School Rd 63020 636-586-1020
Ron Farrow, prin. Fax 586-1029
De Soto JHS 500/7-8
731 Amvets Dr 63020 636-586-1030
Alex Mahn, prin. Fax 586-1039
Early Childhood Center 200/PK-PK
1812 Rock Rd 63020 636-586-1040
Nancy Schmitz, dir. Fax 586-3320
Vineland ES 900/K-6
650 Vineland School Rd 63020 636-586-1010
Mary Ribble, prin. Fax 586-1019

Sunrise R-IX SD 300/PK-8
4485 Sunrise School Rd 63020 636-586-6660
Dr. Armand Spurgin, supt. Fax 586-3192
www.sunrise-r9.org
Sunrise ES 300/PK-8
4485 Sunrise School Rd 63020 636-586-6660
Dr. Armand Spurgin, supt. Fax 586-3192

St. Rose of Lima S 100/PK-8
523 S 4th St 63020 636-337-7855
Michael Talleur, prin. Fax 337-2394

Des Peres, Saint Louis, Pop. 8,270

St. Paul Lutheran S 200/K-8
1300 N Ballas Rd 63131 314-822-2771
Janet Profilet M.A., prin. Fax 822-6574

Dexter, Stoddard, Pop. 7,773
Dexter R-XI SD 2,100/PK-12
1031 Brown Pilot Ln 63841 573-614-1000
Charles Counts, supt. Fax 614-1002
dexter.k12.mo.us/
Central ES 500/3-5
1213 Central Dr 63841 573-614-1020
Angela Duncan, prin. Fax 614-1021
Hill MS 500/6-8
1107 Brown Pilot Ln 63841 573-614-1010
Scott Kruse, prin. Fax 614-1012
Southwest ES 600/PK-2
915 W Grant St 63841 573-614-1015
Jacinda DeWitt, prin. Fax 614-1017

Diamond, Newton, Pop. 880
Diamond R-IV SD 800/K-12
PO Box 68 64840 417-325-5186
Steve Hubbard, supt. Fax 325 5338
www.diamondwildcats.org/
Diamond ES 300/K-4
PO Box 68 64840 417-325-5189
Brian Duffie, prin. Fax 325-5187

Diamond MS 300/5-8
PO Box 68 64840 417-325-5336
Chris Gold, prin. Fax 325-5333

Dittmer, Jefferson
Northwest R-I SD
Supt. — See High Ridge
Maple Grove ES 400/K-5
7887 Dittmer Ridge Rd 63023 636-274-5327
Kimm O'Connor, prin. Fax 274-0413

Dixon, Pulaski, Pop. 1,508
Dixon R-I SD 1,100/PK-12
106 W 4th St 65459 573-759-7163
Duane Doyle, supt. Fax 759-2506
www.dixonr1.com
Dixon ES 500/PK-5
106 W 4th St 65459 573-759-7163
Lisa Parker, prin. Fax 759-2952
Dixon MS 200/6-8
106 W 4th St 65459 573-759-7163
Mark Parker, prin. Fax 759-6627

Doniphan, Ripley, Pop. 1,976
Doniphan R-I SD 1,500/PK-12
309 Pine St 63935 573-996-3667
Dr. Jennifer Snyder, supt. Fax 996-5865
www.doniphanr1.k12.mo.us
Doniphan ES 600/PK-2
603 E Summit St 63935 573-996-3667
Wesley Johnson, prin. Fax 996-5675
Doniphan IS, 904 Elm St 63935 300/3-5
Krissey Whitlock, prin. 573-996-3667
Doniphan MS 400/6-8
651 E Summit St 63935 573-996-3667
Dr. Fish James, prin. Fax 996-4525

Ripley County R-IV SD 200/PK-8
HC 7 Box 51 63935 573-996-7118
Matt Stahl, supt. Fax 996-7484
www.lonestarschool.org
Ripley County S 200/PK-8
HC 7 Box 51 63935 573-996-7118
Matt Stahl, prin. Fax 996-7484

Dora, Ozark
Dora R-III SD 300/PK-12
613 County Road 379 65637 417-261-2346
Steve Richards, supt. Fax 261-2673
www.dora.org
Dora ES 200/PK-8
613 County Road 379 65637 417-261-2337
Brett Mitchell, prin. Fax 261-2673

Drexel, Bates, Pop. 952
Drexel R-IV SD 300/K-12
PO Box 860 64742 816-657-4715
Terry Mayfield, supt. Fax 657-4798
www.drexel.k12.mo.us
Drexel ES 200/K-6
PO Box 860 64742 816-619-2468
Laurie Jacklovich, prin. Fax 657-4798

Duenweg, Jasper, Pop. 1,057
Joplin SD
Supt. — See Joplin
Joplin ECC 100/PK-PK
202 Malloy Cir 64841 417-625-5290
Melinda St. Clair, prin. Fax 625-5297

Eagleville, Harrison, Pop. 315
North Harrison R-III SD 300/PK-12
12023 Fir St 64442 660-867-5222
Rick Johnson, supt. Fax 867-5263
www.nhr3.net
North Harrison ES 200/PK-6
12023 Fir St 64442 660-867-5214
Rick Johnson, prin. Fax 867-3397

East Lynne, Cass, Pop. 297
East Lynne SD 40 100/PK-8
PO Box 108 64743 816-626-3511
John Brinkley, supt. Fax 869-3505
www.eastlynne40school.org/
East Lynne S 100/PK-8
PO Box 108 64743 816-626-3511
John Brinkley, admin. Fax 869-3505

Easton, Buchanan, Pop. 228
East Buchanan County C-1 SD
Supt. — See Gower
East Buchanan MS 200/6-8
301 N County Park Rd 64443 816-473-2451
David Elms, prin. Fax 473-2604

East Prairie, Mississippi, Pop. 3,146
East Prairie R-II SD 1,200/PK-12
PO Box 10 63845 573-649-3562
Lesli Jones, supt. Fax 649-5455
eastprairie.org
Doyle ES 400/PK-2
402 N Washington St 63845 573-649-2272
Aimee Scruggs, prin. Fax 649-5455
East Prairie JHS 200/7-8
210 E Washington St 63845 573-649-9368
Amanda Dean, prin. Fax 649-9370
Martin ES 300/3-6
510 Wilkinson St 63845 573-649-3521
Cole Byassee, prin. Fax 649-5455

Edgar Springs, Phelps, Pop. 199
Phelps County R-III SD 200/K-8
17790 State Route M 65462 573-435-6293
John Fluhrer, supt. Fax 435-9489
www.pcr3.k12.mo.us
Phelps County S 200/K-8
17790 State Route M 65462 573-435-6293
John Fluhrer, prin. Fax 435-9489

Edgerton, Platte, Pop. 541
North Platte County R-I SD
Supt. — See Dearborn
North Platte IS 100/3-5
900 Lewis St 64444 816-790-3622
Jim Brockhoff, prin. Fax 227-3719

Edina, Knox, Pop. 1,171
Knox County R-I SD 500/PK-12
55701 State Hwy 6 63537 660-397-2228
Andy Turgeon, supt. Fax 397-3998
www.knox.k12.mo.us/
Knox County ES 200/PK-5
55701 State Hwy 6 63537 660-397-2285
Alex Van Delft, prin. Fax 397-3316

Edwards, Benton
Warsaw R-IX SD
Supt. — See Warsaw
South ES 300/PK-5
23395 Highway 7 65326 660-438-5965
Cheri Cross, prin. Fax 438-5976

Eldon, Miller, Pop. 4,478
Eldon R-I SD 2,000/PK-12
112 S Pine St 65026 573-392-8000
Matt Davis, supt. Fax 392-8080
eldonmustangs.org
Eldon MS 300/7-8
1400 N Grand Ave 65026 573-392-8020
Shaun Fischer, prin. Fax 392-9151
Eldon Upper ES 400/4-6
409 E 15th St 65026 573-392-6364
Cody Kliethermes, prin. Fax 392-9152
South ES 700/PK-3
1210 S Maple St 65026 573-392-8030
Michele Herbert, prin. Fax 392-9152

El Dorado Springs, Cedar, Pop. 3,534
El Dorado Springs R-II SD 1,200/PK-12
901 S Grand Ave 64744 417-876-3112
Mark Koca, supt. Fax 876-2128
www.eldo.k12.mo.us/
El Dorado Springs ES 600/PK-5
901 S Grand Ave 64744 417-876-3112
Tracy Lanser, prin. Fax 876-0613
El Dorado Springs MS 300/6-8
901 S Grand Ave 64744 417-876-3112
Brad Steward, prin. Fax 876-2128

El Dorado Christian S 100/PK-12
1600 S Ohio St 64744 417-876-2201
Amy Castor, prin. Fax 876-4913

Ellington, Reynolds, Pop. 979
Southern Reynolds County R-II SD 500/PK-12
1 School St 63638 573-663-3591
Dr. Mike Redlich, supt. Fax 663-2412
www.ellington.k12.mo.us
Southern Reynolds County ES 200/PK-5
1 School St 63638 573-663-2293
Carolyn Bouma, prin. Fax 663-2144

Ellisville, Saint Louis, Pop. 9,012
Rockwood R-VI SD
Supt. — See Eureka
Crestview MS 1,200/6-8
16025 Clayton Rd 63011 636-207-2520
Dr. Gary Jansen, prin. Fax 207-2529
Ellisville ES 600/K-5
1425 Froesel Dr 63011 636-207-2548
Dr. Allison Loy, prin. Fax 207-2553
Green Pines ES 400/K-5
16543 Green Pines Dr 63011 636-458-7255
Dr. Paul Godwin, prin. Fax 458-7262

St. Clare of Assisi S 400/PK-8
15668 Clayton Rd 63011 636-227-8654
Kim Vangel, prin. Fax 394-0359
St. John Lutheran S 500/PK-8
15800 Manchester Rd 63011 636-779-2325
Scott Osbourn, prin. Fax 394-9853

Ellsinore, Carter, Pop. 444
East Carter County R-II SD 700/PK-12
24 S Herren Ave 63937 573-322-5625
Dr. Richard Sullivan, supt. Fax 322-8586
www.ecarter.k12.mo.us
East Carter County R-II ES 300/PK-5
24 S Herren Ave 63937 573-322-5325
Kacie Kendrick, prin. Fax 322-5325
East Carter County R-II MS 200/6-8
24 S Herren Ave 63937 573-322-5420
Theresa Kearbey, prin. Fax 322-5420

Elsberry, Lincoln, Pop. 1,898
Elsberry R-II SD 800/PK-12
PO Box 106 63343 573-898-5554
Dr. Tim Reller, supt. Fax 898-3140
www.elsberryschools.com
Cannon ES 300/PK-4
PO Box 106 63343 573-898-5554
Tracy Kingsley, prin. Fax 898-2977
Cannon MS 300/5-8
PO Box 106 63343 573-898-5554
Jason Miller, prin. Fax 898-5825

Eminence, Shannon, Pop. 585
Eminence R-I SD 300/PK-12
PO Box 730 65466 573-226-3252
Charles James, supt. Fax 226-3250
www.redwingsk12.org
Eminence ES 100/PK-6
PO Box 730 65466 573-226-3281
Rob Harlow, prin. Fax 226-3802

Essex, Stoddard, Pop. 469
Richland R-I SD 200/K-12
24456 State Highway 114 63846 573-283-5332
Frank Killian, supt. Fax 283-5798
www.richland.k12.mo.us/
Richland ES 100/K-6
24456 State Highway 114 63846 573-283-5310
Cara Merritt, prin. Fax 283-5108

Eugene, Cole, Pop. 159
Cole County R-V SD 600/PK-12
14803 Highway 17 65032 573-498-4000
Dawna Burrow, supt. Fax 498-4090
www.coler-v.k12.mo.us
Eugene ES 300/PK-6
14803 Highway 17 65032 573-498-4002
Teresa Messersmith, prin. Fax 498-4090

Our Lady of Snows S 100/PK-8
276 Highway H 65032 573-498-3574
Joshua Vandike, prin. Fax 498-3776

Eureka, Saint Louis, Pop. 10,033
Rockwood R-VI SD 21,900/PK-12
111 E North St 63025 636-733-2000
Dr. Eric Knost, supt. Fax 938-2251
www.rsdmo.org
Blevins ES 400/K-5
25 E North St 63025 636-938-2150
Dr. Sharon Jackson, prin. Fax 938-2170
Eureka ES 300/K-5
442 W 4th St 63025 636-938-2452
Lynn White, prin. Fax 938-2457
Geggie ES 600/K-5
430 Bald Hill Rd 63025 636-938-2458
Dr. Mary Kleekamp, prin. Fax 938-2460
Other Schools – See Ballwin, Chesterfield, Ellisville, Fenton, Glencoe, Grover

---

Most Sacred Heart S 200/PK-8
350 E 4th St 63025 636-938-4602
Monica Wilson, prin. Fax 938-5802
St. Mark's Lutheran S 200/PK-8
500 Meramec Blvd 63025 636-938-4432
Ron Pawlitz, prin. Fax 938-6464

Everton, Dade, Pop. 310
Everton R-III SD 100/K-12
211 E School St 65646 417-535-2221
Dr. Karl Janson, supt. Fax 535-4105
www.evertontigers.org
Everton ES 100/K-5
211 E School St 65646 417-535-2221
Heather Harden, prin. Fax 535-4105

Excelsior Springs, Clay, Pop. 10,839
Excelsior Springs SD 40 2,800/PK-12
300 W Broadway St 64024 816-630-9200
Dr. Dan Hoehn, supt. Fax 630-9203
www.essd40.com
Elkhorn ES 200/K-5
PO Box 248 64024 816-630-9270
Christi Rice, prin. Fax 630-9274
Excelsior Springs MS 600/6-8
PO Box 248 64024 816-630-9230
Mark Bullimore, prin. Fax 630-9236
Lewis ES 600/PK-5
PO Box 248 64024 816-630-9290
Jill Evert, prin. Fax 630-9295
Westview ES 500/K-5
PO Box 248 64024 816-630-9260
Anneliese Gould, prin. Fax 630-9265

Exeter, Barry, Pop. 762
Exeter R-VI SD 300/K-12
101 Locust St 65647 417-835-2922
Dr. Ernest Raney, supt. Fax 835-3201
www.exeter.k12.mo.us/
Exeter ES 200/K-8
101 Locust St 65647 417-835-8922
Tim Jordan, prin. Fax 835-3201

Fairfax, Atchison, Pop. 634
Fairfax R-III SD 100/PK-12
500 E Main St 64446 660-686-2421
Dr. Jeremy Burright, supt. Fax 686-2848
www.fairfaxk12mo.us
Fairfax ES 100/PK-6
500 E Main St 64446 660-686-2851
Dustin Barnes, prin. Fax 686-2848

Fair Grove, Greene, Pop. 1,384
Fair Grove R-X SD 1,100/PK-12
132 N Main St 65648 417-759-2233
Mike Bell, supt. Fax 759-7150
www.fairgroveschools.net
Fair Grove ES 400/PK-4
132 N Main St 65648 417-759-2555
Dr. Charity Hollan, prin. Fax 759-7634
Fair Grove MS 300/5-8
132 N Main St 65648 417-759-2556
Marc Green, prin. Fax 759-9053

Fair Play, Polk, Pop. 467
Fair Play R-II SD 400/PK-12
301 N Walnut St 65649 417-654-2231
Renee Sagaser, supt. Fax 654-5028
www.fairplay.k12.mo.us/
Fair Play ES 200/PK-6
301 N Walnut St 65649 417-654-2233
Betty Spitler, prin. Fax 654-2233

Falcon, Laclede
Gasconade C-4 SD 100/PK-8
32959 Highway 32 65470 417-532-4821
Dr. Jim Bogle, supt. Fax 532-0615
gasconadec4.org
Gasconade ES 100/PK-8
32959 Highway 32 65470 417-532-4821
Dr. Jim Bogle, prin. Fax 532-0615

Farmington, Saint Francois, Pop. 16,061
Farmington R-VII SD 4,000/PK-12
PO Box 570 63640 573-701-1300
Matthew R. Ruble, supt. Fax 701-1309
www.fsdknights.com
Farmington MS 600/7-8
506 S Fleming St 63640 573-701-1330
Dr. Dustin Jenkerson, prin. Fax 701-1339
Jefferson ES 400/1-4
9 Summit Dr 63640 573-701-1360
Stephen Phillips, prin. Fax 701-1369
Lincoln IS 600/5-6
708 S Fleming St 63640 573-701-1340
Stacie Smith, prin. Fax 701-1349
Roosevelt ES 400/1-4
1040 Forster St 63640 573-701-1345
Daniel Thompson, prin. Fax 701-1348
Truman Learning Center 300/PK-K
209 W College St 63640 573-701-1370
Kimberly Johnson, prin. Fax 701-1379
Washington-Franklin ES 400/1-4
409 N Washington St 63640 573-701-1350
Lori Lamb, prin. Fax 701-1359

St. Joseph S 100/PK-8
501 Sainte Genevieve Ave 63640 573-756-6312
Shirley Bieser, prin. Fax 756-0738
St. Paul Lutheran S 300/PK-8
608 E Columbia St 63640 573-756-5147
Dustin Murray, prin. Fax 756-8669

Faucett, Buchanan
Mid-Buchanan County R-V SD 700/PK-12
3221 SE State Route H 64448 816-238-1646
Dr. Cody Hirschi, supt. Fax 238-4150
www.midbuchanan.k12.mo.us
Mid-Buchanan ES 300/PK-6
3221 SE State Route H 64448 816-238-1646
Reesa Smiddy, prin. Fax 238-2029

Fayette, Howard, Pop. 2,632
Fayette R-III SD 500/PK-12
705 Lucky St 65248 660-248-2153
Dr. Tamara Kimball, supt. Fax 248-3702
www.fayette.k12.mo.us/
Clark MS 100/6-8
704 Lucky St 65248 660-248-3800
Brent Doolin, admin. Fax 248-2610
Daly ES 300/PK-5
702 Lucky St 65248 660-248-3800
Cheri Huster, prin. Fax 248-2610

Fenton, Saint Louis, Pop. 3,976
Fox C-6 SD
Supt. — See Arnold
Guffey ES 600/K-5
400 13th St 63026 636-343-7662
Jackie Waller, prin. Fax 343-7664

Rockwood R-VI SD
Supt. — See Eureka
Bowles ES 300/K-5
501 Bowles Ave 63026 636-305-2736
Dr. Danielle Vogelsang, prin. Fax 305-2740
Kellison ES 400/K-5
1626 Hawkins Rd 63026 636-861-7760
Dr. Kimberly Dickens, prin. Fax 861-7761
Rockwood South MS 1,000/6-8
1628 Hawkins Rd 63026 636-861-7723
Dr. Laurie Birkenmeier, prin. Fax 861-7730
Stanton ES 500/K-5
1430 Flora Del Dr 63026 636-861-7766
Dr. Christine Starnes, prin. Fax 861-7767
Uthoff Valley ES 500/K-5
1600 Uthoff Dr 63026 636-305-2717
Dr. Danna Thorne, prin. Fax 305-2721

Our Savior Lutheran S 100/PK-8
1500 San Simeon Way 63026 636-343-7511
Michelle Eggold, prin. Fax 343-4921
St. Paul S 400/PK-8
465 New Smizer Mill Rd 63026 636-343-4333
Francine Nieburg, prin. Fax 343-1769

Ferguson, Saint Louis, Pop. 20,785
Ferguson-Florissant R-II SD
Supt. — See Florissant
Central ES 300/K-6
201 Wesley Ave 63135 314-521-4981
Sheldon Mcafee, prin. Fax 521-4983
Griffith ES 400/K-6
200 Day Dr 63135 314-521-5971
Sean Joyce, prin. Fax 521-2820
Hamilton ES 300/K-6
401 Powell Ave 63135 314-521-6755
Dr. Jill Loyet, prin. Fax 521-6757
Johnson-Wabash ES 400/K-6
685 January Ave 63135 314-524-0280
Carla Leggett, prin. Fax 524-1149
Walnut Grove ES 500/K-6
1248 N Florissant Rd 63135 314-524-8922
Jennifer Andrade, prin. Fax 524-3052

Blessed Teresa of Calcutta S 200/PK-8
150 N Elizabeth Ave 63135 314-522-3888
Adrienne Govero, prin. Fax 595-9274

Festus, Jefferson, Pop. 11,379
Festus R-VI SD 3,000/K-12
1515 Midmeadow Ln 63028 636-937-4920
Dr. Link Luttrell, supt. Fax 937-8525
www.festus.k12.mo.us
Festus ES 900/K-3
1500 Midmeadow Ln 63028 636-937-4063
Darin Siefert, prin. Fax 937-7870
Festus IS 700/4-6
1501 Midmeadow Ln 63028 636-937-4750
Merlin Kearns, prin. Fax 937-6106
Festus MS 400/7-8
1717 W Main St 63028 636-937-5417
Tina Thebeau, prin. Fax 937-4171

Jefferson County R-VII SD 1,000/PK-12
1250 Dooling Hollow Rd 63028 636-937-7940
Clint D. Johnston, supt. Fax 937-9189
www.jr7.k12.mo.us/
Danby-Rush Tower MS 200/6-8
1250 Dooling Hollow Rd 63028 636-937-9188
Cynthia Holdinghausen, prin. Fax 937-9189
Plattin PS 200/PK-2
2400 R-7 School Rd 63028 636-937-7170
Tina Basler, prin. Fax 937-7985
Telegraph IS 300/3-5
1265 Dooling Hollow Rd 63028 636-937-6530
Tina Basler, prin. Fax 937-6835

Our Lady S 300/K-8
1599 Saint Marys Ln 63028 636-931-2963
Tracy Kempfer, prin. Fax 933-2230

Fisk, Butler, Pop. 340
Twin Rivers R-X SD
Supt. — See Broseley
Fisk ES 400/K-8
PO Box 547 63940 573-967-3607
Leann Mann, prin. Fax 967-3679

Florissant, Saint Louis, Pop. 50,980
Ferguson-Florissant R-II SD 12,200/PK-12
1005 Waterford Dr 63033 314-506-9000
Dr. Joseph Davis, supt. Fax 506-9010
www.fergflor.org
Combs ES 300/K-6
300 Saint Jean St 63031 314-831-0411
Tanyaneeka Oglesby, prin. Fax 831-0414
Commons Lane ES 500/K-6
2700 Derhake Rd 63033 314-831-0440
Heather Carroll, prin. Fax 831-0474
Cross Keys MS 900/7-8
14205 Cougar Dr 63033 314-506-9700
Christopher Clark, prin. Fax 506-9701
Duchesne ES 400/K-6
100 S New Florissant Rd 63031 314-831-1911
Dr. Sheila Ward, prin. Fax 831-1914
Early Education Center 400/PK-PK
1005 Waterford Dr 63033 314-506-9066
Shantana Herd, dir. Fax 506-9080
Halls Ferry ES 300/K-6
13585 New Halls Ferry Rd 63033 314-831-1022
Leo Ganahl, prin. Fax 831-1024
Parker Road ES 400/K-6
2800 Parker Rd 63033 314-831-2644
Jane Crawford, prin. Fax 831-2648
Robinwood ES 400/K-6
955 Derhake Rd 63033 314-831-4633
Dr. Malinda Ice, prin. Fax 831-4656
Wedgwood ES 500/K-6
14275 New Halls Ferry Rd 63033 314-831-4551
Exley Warren, prin. Fax 831-4607
Other Schools – See Berkeley, Ferguson, Saint Louis

Hazelwood SD 18,400/PK-12
15955 New Halls Ferry Rd 63031 314-953-5000
Dr. Nettie Collins-Hart, supt. Fax 953-5085
www.hazelwoodschools.org
Barrington ES 400/K-5
15600 Old Halls Ferry Rd 63034 314-953-4050
Dr. Ty McNichols, prin. Fax 953-4063
Brown ES 500/K-5
3325 Chicory Creek Ln 63031 314-953-4100
Marvin Talley, prin. Fax 953-4113
Cold Water ES 400/K-5
1105 Wiethaupt Rd 63031 314-953-4150
D. Luke Dix, prin. Fax 953-4163
Hazelwood Central ECC 200/PK-PK
15955 New Halls Ferry Rd 63031 314-953-4950
Curtis Gunn, coord. Fax 953-4963
Hazelwood Central MS 700/6-8
13450 Old Jamestown Rd 63033 314-953-7400
Steve Richards, prin. Fax 953-7413
Hazelwood East ECC 100/PK-PK
12555 Partridge Run Dr 63033 314-953-7600
Amanda Reading, coord. Fax 953-7631
Hazelwood North MS 800/6-8
4420 Vaile Ave 63034 314-953-7500
Brooks Tony, prin. Fax 953-7513
Hazelwood Northwest MS 800/6-8
1605 Shackelford Rd 63031 314-953-5500
Nicole Huffman, prin. Fax 953-5513
Jamestown ES 400/K-5
13750 Old Jamestown Rd 63033 314-953-4300
Angela Haywood-Gaskin, prin. Fax 953-4313
Jana ES 400/K-5
405 Jana Dr 63031 314-953-4350
Sheilah Fitzgerald, prin. Fax 953-4363
Jury ES 400/K-5
11950 Old Halls Ferry Rd 63033 314-953-4400
Michelle Prather, prin. Fax 953-4463
Lawson ES 400/K-5
1830 Charbonier Rd 63031 314-953-4550
Melissa Adkins, prin. Fax 953-4563
Lusher ES 400/K-5
2015 Mullanphy Ln 63031 314-953-4600
Dr. Julie Melton, prin Fax 953-4613
McCurdy ES 400/K-5
975 Lindsay Ln 63031 314-953-4650
Jason Cox, prin. Fax 953-4663
Townsend ES 300/PK-5
6645 Parker Rd 63033 314-953-4800
Patricia Wilson, prin. Fax 953-4813
Walker ES 300/K-5
1250 Humes Ln 63031 314-953-4900
Dr. John Koeneker, prin. Fax 953-4913
Other Schools – See Hazelwood, Saint Louis

Atonement Lutheran S 300/PK-8
1285 N New Florissant Rd 63031 314-837-1252
Mark Briggs, prin. Fax 837-6754
North County Christian S 300/PK-12
845 Dunn Rd 63031 314-972-6227
Dr. Greg Clark, supt. Fax 972-6220
Sacred Heart K 100/PK-K
751 N Jefferson St 63031 314-837-6939
Mary Gladbach, prin. Fax 837-6954
Sacred Heart S 300/1-8
501 Saint Louis St 63031 314-831-3372
Lois Vollmer, prin. Fax 831-2844
St. Ferdinand S 200/PK-8
1735 Charbonier Rd 63031 314-921-2201
Annamarie Davis, prin. Fax 921-2253
St. Norbert S 500/PK-8
16475 New Halls Ferry Rd 63031 314-839-0948
Pam Gilbert, prin. Fax 839-3053
St. Rose Philippine Duchesne S 300/PK-8
3500 Saint Catherine St 63033 314-921-3023
Ken Morr, prin. Fax 921-6724

Fordland, Webster, Pop. 792
Fordland R-III SD 600/PK-12
1230 School St 65652 417-738-2296
Chris Ford, supt. Fax 767-4483
www.fordland.k12.mo.us
Fordland ES 300/PK-5
252 N Center St 65652 417-738-2223
Jennifer Sitzes, prin. Fax 767-4267
Fordland MS 100/6-8
1230 School St 65652 417-738-2119
Doug Fields, prin. Fax 767-4483

Foristell, Saint Charles, Pop. 494
Wentzville R-IV SD
Supt. — See Wentzville
Wabash ES K-6
100 Golden Gate Pkwy 63348 636-887-3884
Matt Schulte, prin. Fax 887-3087

Wright City R-II SD
Supt. — See Wright City
Wright City East ES 300/K-1
3675 W Meyer Rd 63348 636-463-2710
Dawn Hickman, prin. Fax 463-2711

Forsyth, Taney, Pop. 2,219
Forsyth R-III SD 1,200/PK-12
PO Box 187 65653 417-546-6384
Dr. Jeff Mingus, supt. Fax 546-2204
www.forsythpanthers.org
Forsyth ES 400/PK-4
PO Box 187 65653 417-546-6381
Dr. Kendra Stuart, prin. Fax 546-2696
Forsyth MS 400/5-8
PO Box 187 65653 417-546-6382
Dr. Sandra Goss, prin Fax 546 6043

Fort Leonard Wood, Pulaski, Pop. 14,411
Waynesville R-VI SD
Supt. — See Waynesville
Partridge ES 400/K-5
7078 Young St 65473 573-842-2600
Melissa Vernon, prin. Fax 842-2601
Thayer ES 200/K-5
4273 Thayer St 65473 573-842-2200
Robyn Justice, prin. Fax 842-2201
Williams ECC PK-PK
12225 Pulaski Ave 65473 573-842-2650
Molinda Mitchell, prin. Fax 842-2658
Wood ES 400/K-5
4590 Buckeye Ave 65473 573-842-2625
Melanie Mitchell, prin. Fax 842-2626

Frankford, Pike, Pop. 317
Bowling Green R-I SD
Supt. — See Bowling Green
Frankford ES 100/K-5
500 School St 63441 573-784-2550
Stephanie Bailey, prin. Fax 324-2550

Fredericktown, Madison, Pop. 3,947
Fredericktown R-I SD 1,900/PK-12
704 E Highway 72 63645 573-783-2570
Brett Reutzel, supt. Fax 783-7045
www.fpsk12.org/
Fredericktown ES 500/PK-2
419 Newberry St 63645 573-783-3477
Joe Clauser, prin. Fax 783-8038
Fredericktown IS 400/3-5
905 E Highway 72 63645 573-783-6455
Mary Moyers, prin. Fax 783-8033
Fredericktown MS 400/6-8
805A E Highway 72 63645 573-783-6555
Kenneth Lunsford, prin. Fax 783-8079

Freeburg, Osage, Pop. 435

Holy Family S 100/K-8
PO Box 156 65035 573-744-5200
Debbie Reinkemeyer, prin. Fax 744-9201

Freistatt, Lawrence, Pop. 162

Trinity Lutheran S 100/PK-8
218 N Main St 65654 417-235-5931
Amanda Moennig, prin. Fax 235-5931

Frohna, Perry, Pop. 254

United In Christ Lutheran S 100/PK-8
10158 Highway C 63748 573-824-5218
Cheryl Honoree, prin. Fax 824-5250

Fulton, Callaway, Pop. 12,513
Fulton SD 58 2,200/K-12
2 Hornet Dr 65251 573-590-8000
Dr. Jacque Cowherd, supt. Fax 590-8090
www.fulton58.org
Bartley ES 300/K-5
603 S Business 54 65251 573-590-8300
Connie Epperson, prin. Fax 590-8390
Bush ES 400/K-5
908 Wood St 65251 573-590-8400
Alexandria Engle, prin. Fax 590-8490
Fulton MS 500/6-8
403 E 10th St 65251 573-590-8200
Beth Houf, prin. Fax 590-8290
McIntire ES 400/K-5
706 Hickman Ave 65251 573-590-8500
Amy Crane, prin. Fax 590-8590

Kingdom Christian Academy 200/PK-12
650 E 8th St 65251 573-642-2117
Kevin Browne, admin. Fax 642-2022
St. Peter S 100/PK-8
700 State Road Z 65251 573-642-2839
Teresa Arms, prin. Fax 642-2839

Gainesville, Ozark, Pop. 761
Gainesville R-V SD 700/PK-12
422 Bulldog Dr 65655 417-679-4210
Dr. Jeffrey Hyatt, supt. Fax 679-4270
gainesville.mo.schoolwebpages.com
Gainesville ES 400/PK-6
218 Bulldog Dr 65655 417-679-4416
Jason Morris, prin. Fax 679-2077

Galena, Stone, Pop. 437
Galena R-II SD 500/PK-12
PO Box 286 65656 417-357-6027
Dr. Daniel Humble, supt. Fax 357-0058
www.galena.k12.mo.us/
Galena-Abesville ES 300/PK-6
PO Box 286 65656 417-357-6378
Staci Baker, prin. Fax 357-8807

Gallatin, Daviess, Pop. 1,762
Gallatin R-V SD 500/PK-12
602 S Olive St 64640 660-663-2171
Dr. Bryan Copple, supt. Fax 663-2559
gallatin.k12.mo.us
Gallatin MS 5-8
600 S Olive St 64640 660-663-2172
Tiffany Otto, prin. Fax 663-2559
Searcy ES 300/PK-4
502 S Olive St 64640 660-663-2173
Toni Cox, prin. Fax 663-2559

Galt, Grundy, Pop. 246
Grundy County R-V SD 200/K-12
PO Box 6 64641 660-673-6511
Robert Deaver, supt. Fax 673-6523
Other Schools – See Humphreys

Garden City, Cass, Pop. 1,626

Training Center Christian S 50/PK-12
PO Box 200 64747 816-773-8367
Judy Williams, supt. Fax 862-6052

Gatewood, Ripley
Ripley County R-III SD 100/PK-8
HC 6 Box 200 63942 573-255-3213
Allen Woods, supt. Fax 255-3648
ripleyr3.k12.mo.us
Ripley County R-III S 100/PK-8
HC 6 Box 200 63942 573-255-3213
Allen Woods, admin. Fax 255-3648

Gerald, Franklin, Pop. 1,334
Gasconade County R-II SD
Supt. — See Owensville
Gerald ES 300/PK-5
PO Box 25 63037 573-764-3321
Jennifer Hall, prin. Fax 764-2183

Gideon, New Madrid, Pop. 1,088
Gideon SD 37 300/PK-12
PO Box 227 63848 573-448-3911
James Breece, supt. Fax 448-5197
gideon.k12.mo.us/
Gideon ES 200/PK-6
PO Box 227 63848 573-448-3447
Monica Ward, prin. Fax 448-5153

Gilliam, Saline, Pop. 196
Gilliam C-4 SD 50/K-8
PO Box 8 65330 660-784-2225
Rayetta Self, supt. Fax 784-2238
Gilliam ES 50/K-8
PO Box 8 65330 660-784-2225
Rayetta Self, prin. Fax 784-2238

Gilman City, Daviess, Pop. 381
Gilman City R-IV SD 100/PK-12
141 Lindsey Ave 64642 660-876-5221
Roger Alley, supt. Fax 876-5553
www.gilman.k12.mo.us
Gilman City ES 100/PK-6
141 Lindsey Ave 64642 660-876-5221
Justin Collins, prin. Fax 876-5553

Gladstone, Clay, Pop. 24,544
North Kansas City SD 74
Supt. — See Kansas City
Antioch MS 900/6-8
2100 NE 65th St 64118 816-321-5260
Dr. Stephanie Schnoebelen, prin. Fax 321-5261
Chapel Hill ES 500/K-5
3220 NE 67th Ter 64119 816-321-5040
Enjoli Avila, prin. Fax 321-5041
Linden West ES 500/K-5
7333 N Wyandotte St 64118 816-321-5130
Dr. Shelly Sanders, prin. Fax 321-5131
Meadowbrook ES 600/K-5
6301 N Michigan Ave 64118 816-321-5150
Kathy D'Anza, prin. Fax 321-5151
Oakwood Manor ES 300/K-5
5900 N Flora Ave 64118 816-321-5180
Tanya Donnelly, prin. Fax 321-5181

Oakhill Day S 300/PK-8
7019 N Cherry St 64118 816-436-6228
Suzanne McCanles, head sch Fax 436-0184
St. Andrew the Apostle S 300/PK-8
6415 NE Antioch Rd 64119 816-454-7377
Rebecca Sachen, prin. Fax 453-6393

Glasgow, Howard, Pop. 1,085
Glasgow SD 300/PK-12
860 Randolph St 65254 660-338-2012
Michael Reynolds, supt. Fax 338-2610
www.glasgow.k12.mo.us
Glasgow ES 200/PK-6
860 Randolph St 65254 660-338-2012
Kyra Yung, prin. Fax 338-2610

St. Mary S 100/K-8
501 3rd St 65254 660-338-2258
Kent Monnig, prin. Fax 338-9930

Glencoe, Saint Louis
Rockwood R-VI SD
Supt. — See Eureka
Babler ES 500/K-5
1955 Shepard Rd 63038 636-733-1175
Tim Buss, prin. Fax 458-7347
LaSalle Springs MS 900/6-8
3300 Highway 109 63038 636-938-2425
Deborah Brandt, prin. Fax 938-2434
Rockwood Valley MS 800/6-8
1220 Babler Park Dr 63038 636-458-7324
Dr. Karen Hedrick, prin. Fax 458-7325
Wildwood MS 800/6-8
17401 Manchester Rd 63038 636-458-7360
Dr. Allison Klouse, prin. Fax 458-7372

Glendale, Saint Louis, Pop. 5,865
Kirkwood R-VII SD
Supt. — See Kirkwood
North Glendale ES 600/K-5
765 N Sappington Rd 63122 314-213-6130
Dr. Todd Benben, prin. Fax 213-6173

Golden City, Barton, Pop. 757
Golden City R-III SD 200/PK-12
1208 Walnut St 64748 417-537-4900
Steven Brigham, supt. Fax 537-8717
www.goldencityschools.com/
Golden City ES 100/PK-6
1208 Walnut St 64748 417-537-4272
Jason Kramer, prin. Fax 537-8717

Goodman, McDonald, Pop. 1,167
Neosho R-V SD
Supt. — See Neosho
Goodman ES 300/K-4
117 N School St 64843 417-364-7216
Samantha Hamilton, prin. Fax 451-8685

Gower, Buchanan, Pop. 1,511
East Buchanan County C-1 SD 700/K-12
100 Smith St 64454 816-424-6466
Paul Mensching, supt. Fax 424-3511
www.ebs.k12.mo.us/
East Buchanan ES 300/K-5
100 Smith St 64454 816-424-3111
Josh Barker, prin. Fax 424-3511
Other Schools – See Easton

Graham, Nodaway, Pop. 171
Nodaway-Holt R-VII SD 200/PK-12
318 S Taylor St 64455 660-939-2137
Dr. Jeff Blackford, supt. Fax 939-2200
www.nodholt.k12.mo.us
Other Schools – See Maitland

Grain Valley, Jackson, Pop. 12,604
Grain Valley R-V SD 4,000/PK-12
PO Box 304 64029 816-847-5006
Dr. Marc Snow Ph.D., supt. Fax 229-4831
www.gvr5.net
Grain Valley ECC 100/PK-PK
PO Box 304 64029 816-994-9401
Shannon Jenkins, dir. Fax 994-4902
Grain Valley North MS 300/6-8
PO Box 304 64029 816-994-4800
Theresa Nelson, prin. Fax 994-4899
Grain Valley South MS 600/6-8
PO Box 304 64029 816-229-3499
Jim Myers, prin. Fax 847-5017
Matthews ES 500/K-5
PO Box 304 64029 816-229-4870
James Pinney, prin. Fax 847-5003
Prairie Branch ES 500/K-5
PO Box 304 64029 816-847-5070
Heather Gross, prin. Fax 847-5071
Sni-A-Bar ES 500/K-5
PO Box 304 64029 816-847-5020
Dr. Carrie Reich, prin. Fax 847-5023
Stony Point ES 500/K-5
PO Box 304 64029 816-847-7800
Scott Schmidt, prin. Fax 847-7802

Granby, Newton, Pop. 2,075
East Newton County R-VI SD 1,500/PK-12
22808 E Highway 86 64844 417-472-6231
Ron Mitchell, supt. Fax 472-3500
www.eastnewton.org
Granby S 600/PK-8
PO Box 440 64844 417-472-6279
Bill Kirby, prin. Fax 472-7115
Other Schools – See Stella

Grandview, Jackson, Pop. 23,651
Grandview C-4 SD 4,100/PK-12
13015 10th St 64030 816-316-5000
Dr. Kenny Rodrequez, supt. Fax 316-5050
www.grandviewc4.net
Belvidere ES 300/K-5
15200 White Ave 64030 816-316-5300
Jennifer Harris, prin. Fax 316-5305
Butcher-Greene ES 400/K-5
5302 E 140th St 64030 816-316-5400
Ethel Judon, prin. Fax 316-5445
Conn-West ES 400/K-5
1100 High Grove Rd 64030 816-316-5225
Marcy Simon, prin. Fax 316-5230
Grandview MS 600/6-8
12650 Manchester Ave 64030 816-316-5600
Jacqueline Spencer, prin. Fax 316-5699
High Grove ECC 100/PK-PK
2500 High Grove Rd 64030 816-316-5500
Keri Collison, coord. Fax 316-5505
Meadowmere ES 400/K-5
7010 E 136th St 64030 816-316-5525
Stephen Fielder, prin. Fax 316-5599
Other Schools – See Kansas City

Grandview Christian S 100/K-12
12340 Grandview Rd 64030 816-767-8630

Grant City, Worth, Pop. 858
Worth County R-III SD 300/PK-12
510 East Ave 64456 660-564-3389
Dr. Matthew Martz, supt. Fax 564-2193
wc.k12.mo.us
Worth County ES 200/PK-6
510 East Ave 64456 660-564-3320
Chuck Borey, prin. Fax 564-2193

Gravois Mills, Morgan, Pop. 140
Morgan County R-II SD
Supt. — See Versailles
Morgan County South ES 65038 100/PK-2
Kim Murdock, prin. 573-372-6261
Fax 372-6261

Green City, Sullivan, Pop. 647
Green City R-I SD 300/PK-12
301 N East St 63545 660-874-4128
Tennille Banner, supt. Fax 874-4515
www.greencity.k12.mo.us/
Green City ES 100/PK-6
301 N East St 63545 660-874-4126
Stefani Franklin, prin. Fax 874-5950

Greenfield, Dade, Pop. 1,342
Greenfield R-IV SD 400/PK-12
410 College St 65661 417-637-5321
Jeffery Davis, supt. Fax 637-5805
www.greenfieldwildcats.net
Greenfield ES 300/PK-6
409 N Montgomery St 65661 417-637-5921
Christopher Kell, prin. Fax 637-2844

Green Ridge, Pettis, Pop. 466
Green Ridge R-VIII SD 400/K-12
PO Box 70 65332 660-527-3315
Dr. Jamie Burkhart, supt. Fax 527-3299
greenridge.k12.mo.us
Green Ridge ES 200/K-6
PO Box 70 65332 660-527-3315
Rachel Hammers, prin. Fax 527-3299

Greenville, Wayne, Pop. 503
Greenville R-II SD 800/PK-12
PO Box 320 63944 573-224-3844
Dr. Todd Porter, supt. Fax 224-3412
bears.k12.mo.us
Greenville ES 400/PK-6
PO Box 320 63944 573-224-3617
Scottie Blackburn, prin. Fax 224-3819
Greenville JHS 100/7-8
PO Box 320 63944 573-224-3833
Rick Clubb, prin. Fax 224-3580
Other Schools – See Williamsville

Greenwood, Jackson, Pop. 5,146
Lee's Summit R-VII SD
Supt. — See Lees Summit
Greenwood ES 500/K-6
805 W Main St 64034 816-986-1320
Carrie Jackson, prin. Fax 986-1335

Grover, Saint Louis
Rockwood R-VI SD
Supt. — See Eureka
Fairway ES 500/K-5
480 Old Fairway Dr 63040 636-458-7300
Dr. Lorinda Krey, prin. Fax 458-7350
Pond ES 400/K-5
17200 Manchester Rd 63040 636-458-7264
Dr. Carlos Diaz-Granados, prin. Fax 458-7271

Grovespring, Wright
Hartville R-II SD
Supt. — See Hartville
Grovespring ES 100/K-5
PO Box 100 65662 417-462-3288
Adam Cook, prin. Fax 462-3144

Guilford, Nodaway, Pop. 85
South Nodaway County R-IV SD
Supt. — See Barnard
South Nodaway ES 100/PK-6
34471 State Highway M 64457 660-652-3718
Darbi Bauman, prin. Fax 652-3711

Hale, Carroll, Pop. 409
Hale R-I SD 200/PK-12
PO Box 248 64643 660-565-2417
Clinton Heussner, supt. Fax 565-2418
haleschooldistrict.com

Hale ES 100/PK-6
PO Box 248 64643 660-565-2417
Hollie Burnside, prin. Fax 565-2418

Half Way, Polk, Pop. 165
Halfway R-III SD 300/K-12
2150 Highway 32 65663 417-445-2351
Tim Boatwright, supt. Fax 445-2026
www.halfwayschools.org
Halfway ES 100/K-6
2150 Highway 32 65663 417-445-2215
Karla Spear, prin. Fax 445-6714

Hallsville, Boone, Pop. 1,463
Hallsville R-IV SD 1,400/PK-12
421 Hwy 124 E 65255 573-696-5512
John Downs, supt. Fax 696-3606
www.hallsville.org/
Hallsville IS 400/2-5
411 Hwy 124 E 65255 573-696-5512
Bethany Morris, prin. Fax 696-8990
Hallsville MS 300/6-8
421 Hwy 124 E 65255 573-696-5512
Ty Sides, prin. Fax 696-7238
Hallsville PS 300/PK-1
6401 E Highway 124 65255 573-696-5512
Karen Jimerson, prin. Fax 696-0729

Hamilton, Caldwell, Pop. 1,790
Hamilton R-II SD 700/PK-12
PO Box 130 64644 816-583-2134
Troy Ford, supt. Fax 583-2139
www.hamilton.k12.mo.us/
Hamilton ES 300/PK-5
PO Box 130 64644 816-583-4811
Billie McGraw, prin. Fax 583-7919
Hamilton MS 200/6-8
PO Box 130 64644 816-583-2173
Dave Richman, prin. Fax 583-2686

New York R-IV SD 50/K-8
6061 NE State Route U 64644 816-583-2563
Debra Ellis, supt. Fax 583-4065
nyr4bulldogs.com
New York ES 50/K-8
6061 NE State Route U 64644 816-583-2563
Debra Ellis, prin. Fax 583-4065

Hannibal, Marion, Pop. 17,465
Hannibal SD 60 3,600/PK-12
4650 McMasters Ave 63401 573-221-1258
Susan Johnson, supt. Fax 221-2994
www.hannibal.k12.mo.us
Early Childhood Center PK-PK
544 N Veterans 63401 573-221-3054
Kindra Szarka, admin.
Field ES 200/K-5
1405 Pearl St 63401 573-221-1050
Dr. Meghan Karr, prin. Fax 221-0545
Hannibal MS 800/6-8
4700 Mcmasters Ave 63401 573-221-5840
Matt Nimmo, prin. Fax 221-7779
Oakwood ES 300/K-5
3716 Market St 63401 573-221-2747
Denise Hudson, prin. Fax 221-3753
Stowell ES 300/K-5
500 Union St 63401 573-221-0980
Kyle Gibbs, prin. Fax 221-2994
Twain ES 400/K-5
2800 Bird St 63401 573-221-0768
Karen Wheelan, prin. Fax 221-3726
Veterans ES 500/K-5
790 N Veterans Rd 63401 573-221-0649
Brooke Kelly, prin. Fax 221-1349

Holy Family S 200/PK-8
1113 Broadway 63401 573-221-0456
Sr. Betty Uchytil, prin. Fax 221-6357
St. John's Lutheran S 100/PK-8
1317 Lyon St 63401 573-221-0215
Ann Lear, prin. Fax 221-8384

Hardin, Ray, Pop. 565
Hardin-Central C-2 SD 300/PK-12
PO Box 548 64035 660-398-4394
Trey Cavanah, supt. Fax 398-4396
www.hardin-central.org
Hardin-Central ES 100/PK-6
PO Box 548 64035 660-398-4394
Austin Purvis, prin. Fax 398-4396

Harrisburg, Boone, Pop. 260
Harrisburg R-VIII SD 500/K-12
1000 S Harris St 65256 573-875-5604
Steve Combs, supt. Fax 875-8877
www.harrisburg.k12.mo.us
Harrisburg ES 200/K-5
221 S Harris St 65256 573-875-0290
Rosemary Worthley, prin. Fax 875-8572
Harrisburg MS 100/6-8
233 S Harris St 65256 573-817-5857
Jeff Wardrip, prin. Fax 875-8936

Harrisonville, Cass, Pop. 9,864
Harrisonville R-IX SD 2,700/PK-12
503 S Lexington St 64701 816-380-2727
Frank Dahman, supt. Fax 380-3134
www.harrisonvilleschools.org
Harrisonville ECC 300/PK-K
500 Polar Ln 64701 816-380-4421
Rebecca Campbell, prin. Fax 884-2148
Harrisonville ES 500/1-3
101 Meghan Dr 64701 816-380-4131
Jauna Weber, prin. Fax 884-2938
Harrisonville MS 600/6-8
601 S Highland Dr 64701 816-380-7654
Chris Grantham, prin. Fax 884-5733
McEowen ES 400/4-5
1901 S Halsey Ave 64701 816-380-4545
Julie Dahlstrom, prin. Fax 884-3046

Harrisonville Christian S East Campus 100/PK-4
1606 Chapel Dr 64701 816-884-3318
Chad Culpepper, prin. Fax 884-3040
Harrisonville Christian S West Campus 100/5-8
1202 S Commercial St 64701 816-884-6499
Chad Culpepper, prin. Fax 887-2093

Hartville, Wright, Pop. 610
Hartville R-II SD 700/PK-12
PO Box 460 65667 417-741-7676
Mark Piper, supt. Fax 741-7746
www.hartville.k12.mo.us
Hartville ES 300/PK-6
PO Box 460 65667 417-741-7141
Rodney Cravens, prin. Fax 741-7746
Other Schools – See Grovespring

Harviell, Butler, Pop. 103
Neelyville R-IV SD
Supt. — See Neelyville
Hillview ES 200/PK-2
11001 Highway 160 63945 573-989-3370
Aaron Burton, prin. Fax 989-3975

Hawk Point, Lincoln, Pop. 647
Lincoln County R-III SD
Supt. — See Troy
Hawk Point ES 100/K-5
327 Maple St 63349 636-338-4366
Jennifer Eigenseher, prin. Fax 338-4566

Hayti, Pemiscot, Pop. 2,893
Hayti R-II SD 800/PK-12
PO Box 469 63851 573-359-6500
Jackie Johnson, supt. Fax 359-6502
www.haytir2.org
Mathis ES 300/PK-4
PO Box 469 63851 573-359-6500
Katherine Suddarth, prin. Fax 359-6509
Wallace MS 200/5-8
PO Box 469 63851 573-359-6500
Twanna Jones, prin. Fax 359-6254

Hazelwood, Saint Louis, Pop. 25,088
Hazelwood SD
Supt. — See Florissant
Armstrong ES 400/K-5
6255 Howdershell Rd 63042 314-953-4000
Roger LeBlanc, prin. Fax 953-4013
Garrett ES 400/K-5
1400 Ville Rosa Ln 63042 314-953-4200
Erik Melton, prin. Fax 953-4213
Hazelwood West ECC 100/PK-PK
5323 Ville Maria Ln 63042 314-953-7650
Teri Edwards, dir. Fax 953-7651
Hazelwood West MS 800/6-8
12834 Missouri Bottom Rd 63042 314-953-5800
Lanetra Thomas, prin. Fax 953-5813
McNair ES 400/K-5
585 Coachway Ln 63042 314-953-4700
Dr. Jen Roper, prin. Fax 953-4713
Russell ES 400/PK-5
7350 Howdershell Rd 63042 314-953-4750
Dr. Paul Alvord, prin. Fax 953-4763

ASA Christian Academy 100/PK-6
8390 Latty Ave 63042 314-524-4272
Dr. Janet Strickland, head sch Fax 524-4271

Helena, Andrew
Savannah R-III SD
Supt. — See Savannah
Helena ES 100/K-5
21080 Osage St 64459 816-369-2865
Roxanne Rooney, prin. Fax 369-2404

Herculaneum, Jefferson, Pop. 3,429
Dunklin R-V SD 1,700/K-12
497 Joachim Ave 63048 636-479-5200
Stan Stratton, supt. Fax 479-6208
www.dunklin.k12.mo.us
Senn-Thomas MS 300/6-8
200 Senn Tomas Dr 63048 636-479-5200
Alice Menne, prin. Fax 479-7219
Other Schools – See Pevely

Hermann, Gasconade, Pop. 2,399
Gasconade County R-I SD 1,000/K-12
170 Blue Pride Dr 65041 573-486-2116
Dr. Tracey Hankins, supt. Fax 486-3032
www.hermann.k12.mo.us
Hermann ES 300/K-3
328 W 7th St 65041 573-486-3197
Kendra Brune, prin. Fax 486-3244
Hermann MS 300/4-8
164 Blue Pride Dr 65041 573-486-3121
Nicole Buschmann, prin. Fax 486-5106

St. George S 200/PK-8
133 W 4th St 65041 573-486-5914
Julie Clingman, prin. Fax 486-1914

Hermitage, Hickory, Pop. 457
Hermitage R-IV SD 300/PK-12
PO Box 327 65668 417-745-6418
William Vest, supt. Fax 745-6475
www.hermitage.k12.mo.us/
Hermitage ES 100/PK-5
PO Box 327 65668 417-745-6277
Krissy Friedman, prin. Fax 745-6475
Hermitage MS 100/6-8
PO Box 327 65668 417-745-6417
Krissy Friedman, prin. Fax 745-6475

Higbee, Randolph, Pop. 552
Higbee R-VIII SD 200/K-12
PO Box 128 65257 660-456-7277
Danielle Tuepker, supt. Fax 456-7278
www.higbeeschool.com/
Higbee R-VIII ES 100/K-6
PO Box 128 65257 660-456-7206
Jennifer Juergensmeyer, prin. Fax 456-7207

Higginsville, Lafayette, Pop. 4,706
Lafayette County C-1 SD 1,000/PK-12
805 W 31st St 64037 660-584-3631
David Figg, supt. Fax 584-2622
www.huskers.k12.mo.us
Grandview ES 500/PK-5
705 W 31st St 64037 660-584-7127
Dr. Jennifer Hayes, prin. Fax 584-6094
Lafayette County MS 200/6-8
807b W 31st St 64037 660-584-7161
Jove Stickel, prin. Fax 584-6080

Immanuel Lutheran S 100/PK-8
1500 Lipper Ave 64037 660-584-2854
Rev. Timothy Miille, prin. Fax 584-5914

Highlandville, Christian, Pop. 898
Spokane R-VII SD 800/PK-12
167 Kentling Ave 65669 417-443-2200
Terry Jamieson, supt. Fax 443-2205
www.spokane.k12.mo.us
Highlandville ES 400/PK-5
PO Box 220 65669 417-443-3361
Jennifer Wheeler, prin. Fax 443-2013
Other Schools – See Spokane

High Ridge, Jefferson, Pop. 4,270
Northwest R-I SD 6,600/PK-12
2843 Community Ln 63049 636-677-3473
Dr. Desi Kirchhofer, supt. Fax 677-5480
www.northwestschools.net
Brennan Woods ES 600/K-5
4630 Brennan Rd 63049 636-677-3400
Susan Wingenbach, prin. Fax 677-5440
High Ridge ES 400/K-5
2901 High Ridge Blvd 63049 636-677-3996
Jennifer Baugh, prin. Fax 677-4366
Murphy ES 500/K-5
2101 Valley Dr 63049 636-326-0577
Katie Brettschneider, prin. Fax 343-5786
Woodridge MS 600/6-8
2109 Gravois Rd 63049 636-677-3577
Shannon Umfleet, prin. Fax 677-5581
Other Schools – See Dittmer, House Springs

Hillsboro, Jefferson, Pop. 2,784
Grandview R-II SD 800/K-12
11470 State Road C 63050 636-944-3941
Matt Zoph, supt. Fax 944-5239
www.grandviewr2.com
Grandview ES 300/K-5
11470 State Road C 63050 636-944-3291
Kimberly Bequette, prin. Fax 944-3870
Grandview MS 200/6-8
11470 State Road C 63050 636-944-3931
Allen Davis, prin. Fax 944-5239

Hillsboro R-III SD 3,500/K-12
5 Ridgewood Dr 63050 636-789-0060
Aaron Cornman Ph.D., supt. Fax 789-3216
www.hsdr3.org
Hillsboro ES 500/3-4
13 Hawk Dr 63050 636-789-0040
Kimberly Tooley, prin. Fax 789-3214
Hillsboro IS 500/5-6
10478 Business 21 63050 636-789-0030
Scott Readnour, prin. Fax 789-3213
Hillsboro JHS 500/7-8
12 Hawk Dr 63050 636-789-0020
Heath Allison, prin. Fax 789-3212
Hillsboro PS 800/K-2
101 Leon Hall Pkwy 63050 636-789-0050
Callista Kostine Ed.D., prin. Fax 789-3215

Good Shepherd S 100/PK-8
701 3rd St 63050 636-789-3311
Mariann Jones, prin. Fax 789-9986

Holcomb, Dunklin, Pop. 633
Holcomb R-III SD 600/PK-12
PO Box 190 63852 573-792-3113
Dr. Ashley McMillian, supt. Fax 792-3118
www.holcombschools.com
Holcomb ES 400/PK-6
PO Box 190 63852 573-792-3550
Jason Skelton, prin. Fax 792-3490

Holden, Johnson, Pop. 2,201
Holden R-III SD 1,300/PK-12
1612 S Main St 64040 816-732-5568
Dr. Mike Hough, supt. Fax 732-4336
www.holdenschools.org
Holden ES 600/PK-5
1903 S Market St 64040 816-732-6071
Sarah Burks, prin. Fax 732-2008
Holden MS 300/6-8
301 Eagle Dr 64040 816-732-4125
Ardy Dehdasht, prin. Fax 732-2009

Holliday, Monroe, Pop. 137
Holliday C-2 SD 100/K-8
PO Box 7038 65258 660-266-3412
Daniel Liebhart, supt. Fax 266-3029
hollidayc2school.weebly.com
Holliday ES 100/K-8
PO Box 7038 65258 660-266-3412
Daniel Liebhart, admin. Fax 266-3029

Hollister, Taney, Pop. 4,346
Hollister R-V SD 1,500/PK-12
1914 State Highway BB 65672 417-243-4005
Dr. Brian Wilson, supt. Fax 334-2663
www.hollister.k12.mo.us/
Hollister ECC 300/PK-1
1792 State Highway BB 65672 417-243-4015
Mark Waugh, prin. Fax 334-6293

Hollister ES 400/2-5
1794 State Highway BB 65672 417-243-4025
Henson Nina, prin. Fax 334-5152
Hollister MS 300/6-8
1798 State Highway BB 65672 417-243-4035
Shawn Page, prin. Fax 334-6482

Trinity Christian Academy 100/PK-12
119 Myrtle Ave 65672 417-334-7084
Holly Gregory, prin. Fax 334-1794

Holt, Clay, Pop. 437

Northern Hills Christian Academy 100/PK-8
17211 NE 180th St 64048 816-320-3204
Mike Dye, admin. Fax 320-3226

Holts Summit, Callaway, Pop. 3,172
Jefferson City SD
Supt. — See Jefferson City
Callaway Hills ES 300/K-5
2715 State Road AA 65043 573-896-5051
Todd Shalz, prin. Fax 896-4054
North ES 400/K-5
285 S Summit Dr 65043 573-896-8304
Barbara Martin, prin. Fax 896-4018

Hopkins, Nodaway, Pop. 530
North Nodaway County R-VI SD 300/PK-12
705 E Barnard St 64461 660-778-3411
James Simmelink, supt. Fax 778-3210
www.nnr6.org/
Other Schools – See Pickering

Hornersville, Dunklin, Pop. 654
Senath-Hornersville C-8 SD
Supt. — See Senath
Senath-Hornersville MS 200/5-8
601 School St 63855 573-737-2455
Dustin Benson, prin. Fax 737-2456

House Springs, Jefferson
Northwest R-I SD
Supt. — See High Ridge
Cedar Springs ES 500/K-5
6922 Rivermont Trl 63051 636-671-3330
Cynthia Spurgeon, prin. Fax 671-7244
House Springs ES 600/K-5
4380 Gravois Rd 63051 636-671-3360
Dr. Leigh Ann Parker, prin. Fax 671-7269
Northwest ECC 200/PK-PK
6180 Highway MM 63051 636-671-3382
Cindy Wills, dir. Fax 671-1625
Valley MS 800/6-8
4300 Gravois Rd 63051 636-671-3470
Dayle Burgdorf, prin. Fax 671-0948

Our Lady Queen of Peace S 300/PK-8
4675 Notre Dame Dr 63051 636-671-0247
John Boyd, prin. Fax 671-0418

Houston, Texas, Pop. 2,038
Houston R-I SD 1,000/PK-12
423 W Pine St 65483 417-967-3024
Dr. Allen Moss, supt. Fax 967-4887
www.houston.k12.mo.us
Houston ES 400/PK-5
423 W Pine St 65483 417-967-3024
Jody Jarrett, prin. Fax 967-4885
Houston MS 200/6-8
423 W Pine St 65483 417-967-3024
Amber Stephens, prin. Fax 967-5481

Houstonia, Pettis, Pop. 219
Pettis County R-V SD
Supt. — See Hughesville
Northwest ES 200/K-6
407 W Tuck St 65333 660-568-3315
Joel Sherman, prin. Fax 568-3394

Hughesville, Pettis, Pop. 182
Pettis County R-V SD 300/K-12
16215 Highway H 65334 660-827-0772
Amy Fagg, supt. Fax 827-7162
www.northwest.k12.mo.us
Other Schools – See Houstonia

Humansville, Polk, Pop. 1,030
Humansville R-IV SD 300/PK-12
300 N Oak St 65674 417-754-2535
Tammy Erwin, supt. Fax 754-8565
www.humansville.k12.mo.us
Humansville ES 200/PK-5
300 N Oak St 65674 417-754-2221
Mary Dodson, prin. Fax 754-8565
Humansville MS 6-8
300 N Oak St 65674 417-754-2119
Colleena Frazier, admin. Fax 754-8565

Hume, Bates, Pop. 331
Hume R-VIII SD 200/PK-12
9163 SW 2nd St 64752 660-643-7411
Scott Morrison, supt. Fax 643-7506
www.humer8.k12.mo.us
Hume ES 100/PK-6
9163 SW 2nd St 64752 660-643-7411
Scott Morrison, prin. Fax 643-7506

Humphreys, Sullivan, Pop. 117
Grundy County R-V SD
Supt. — See Galt
Grundy County ES 100/K-6
PO Box 88 64646 660-673-6314
Dr. Anne Billington, prin. Fax 673-6346

Huntsville, Randolph, Pop. 1,540
Westran R-I SD 700/PK-12
228 Huntsville Ave 65259 660-277-4429
Dr. Kelly Shelby, supt. Fax 277-4420
westran.k12.mo.us/
Westran ES 300/PK-5
210 W Depot St 65259 660-277-3666
Mark Harvey, prin. Fax 277-4420
Other Schools – See Clifton Hill

Hurley, Stone, Pop. 177
Hurley R-I SD 200/K-12
PO Box 248 65675 417-369-3271
Dr. Allison Murphy-Pope, supt. Fax 369-2212
www.hurley.k12.mo.us/
Hurley ES 100/K-5
PO Box 248 65675 417-369-3271
Michaela Wilson, prin. Fax 369-2212

Iberia, Miller, Pop. 730
Iberia R-V SD 700/PK-12
201 Pemberton Dr 65486 573-793-6818
Lyndel Whittle, supt. Fax 793-6821
www.iberia.k12.mo.us/
Iberia ES 400/PK-6
201 Pemberton Dr 65486 573-793-6267
Shannon Shelton, prin. Fax 793-6304

Imperial, Jefferson, Pop. 4,673
Fox C-6 SD
Supt. — See Arnold
Antonia ES 600/K-5
3901 Old State Road M 63052 636-942-2181
Mark Rudanovich, prin. Fax 942-3042
Hamrick ES 300/PK-5
4525 E Four Ridge Rd 63052 636-282-6930
Elizabeth Anderson, prin. Fax 282-6934
Hodge ES 400/K-5
2499 Prairie Hollow Rd 63052 636-282-6920
Theresa Jansen, prin. Fax 282-6984
Seckman ES 700/PK-5
2824 Seckman Rd 63052 636-296-2030
Dan Baker, prin. Fax 282-5176
Seckman MS 500/7-8
2840 Seckman Rd 63052 636-296-5707
Dr. Tammy Cardona, prin. Fax 296-5707

Windsor C-1 SD 2,900/K-12
6208 US Highway 61 67 63052 636-464-4400
Dr. Joel Holland Ed.D., supt. Fax 464-4454
windsor.k12.mo.us
Windsor ES 400/K-2
6208 US Highway 61 67 63052 636-464-4408
Denise Funston, prin. Fax 464-4470
Windsor IS 600/3-5
6208 US Highway 61 67 63052 636-464-4451
Dr. Matt Carlton, prin. Fax 464-4472
Windsor MS 700/6-8
6208 US Highway 61 67 63052 636-464-4417
Karl Shininger, prin. Fax 464-4473
Other Schools – See Barnhart

St. Joseph S 300/PK-8
6024 Old Antonia Rd 63052 636-464-9027
Sr. Carol Sansone, prin. Fax 464-8792

Independence, Jackson, Pop. 113,065
Blue Springs R-IV SD
Supt. — See Blue Springs
Yates ES 400/K-5
3600 S Davidson Ave 64055 816-874-3740
Kerri Edwards, prin. Fax 478-6137

Fort Osage R-I SD 5,000/PK-12
2101 N Twyman Rd 64058 816-650-7000
Jason Snodgrass, supt. Fax 650-3888
www.fortosage.net
Blue Hills ES 400/K-4
2101 N Twyman Rd 64058 816-650-7440
Monica Shane, prin. Fax 650-7445
Cler-Mont ES 400/K-4
2101 N Twyman Rd 64058 816-650-7350
Julie Stout, prin. Fax 650-7355
ECC 100/PK-PK
2101 N Twyman Rd 64058 816-650-7480
Karen Harrach, prin. Fax 650-7485
Elm Grove ES 300/K-4
2101 N Twyman Rd 64058 816-650-7400
Pam Fore, prin. Fax 650-7405
Fire Prairie Upper ES 800/5-6
2101 N Twyman Rd 64058 816-650-7158
Suzanne Boyer-Baker, prin. Fax 650-7166
Indian Trails ES 400/K-4
2101 N Twyman Rd 64058 816-650-7645
Emily Cross, prin. Fax 650-7694
Osage Trail MS 800/7-8
2101 N Twyman Rd 64058 816-650-7151
Robbie Shepherd, prin. Fax 650-7152
Other Schools – See Buckner

Independence SD 30 13,600/PK-12
201 N Forest Ave 64050 816-521-5300
Dr. Dale Herl, supt. Fax 521-5680
www.isdschools.org
Benton ES 400/PK-5
429 S Leslie St 64050 816-521-5390
Leslie Hochspring, prin. Fax 521-5634
Bingham MS 400/7-8
1716 S Speck Rd 64057 816-521-5490
Brett Playter, prin. Fax 521-5631
Blackburn ES 500/PK-5
17302 E R D Mize Rd 64057 816-521-5395
Christine Lamb, prin. Fax 521-5635
Bridger MS 300/6-6
18200 E State Route 78 64057 816-521-5375
Dr. Jeff Williams, prin. Fax 521-5632
Bryant ES 300/PK-5
827 W College St 64050 816-521-5400
Dr. Jonathan Pye, prin. Fax 521-5636
Fairmount ES 400/PK-5
120 N Cedar Ave 64053 816-521-5405
Jeff Anger, prin. Fax 521-5637
Glendale ES 500/PK-5
2611 S Lees Summit Rd 64055 816-521-5510
Todd Siebert, prin. Fax 521-5638
Hanthorn S 300/PK-PK
1511 S Kings Hwy 64055 816-521-5485
Amy Cox, prin. Fax 521-5654
Korte ES 600/PK-5
2437 S Hardy Ave 64052 816-521-5430
Ron Alburtus, prin. Fax 521-5641
Little Blue ES 200/PK-5
2020 Quail Dr 64057 816-521-5480
Joe Armin, prin. Fax 521-5692
Luff ES 400/PK-5
3700 S Delaware Ave 64055 816-521-5415
Melissa Carver, prin. Fax 521-5639
Mill Creek ES 300/PK-5
2601 N Liberty St 64050 816-521-5420
Lindsey Miller, prin. Fax 521-5640
Nowlin MS 800/6-8
2800 S Hardy Ave 64052 816-521-5380
Cristin Nowak, prin. Fax 521-5633
Ott ES 400/PK-5
1525 N Noland Rd 64050 816-521-5435
Dr. Ronnee Laughlin, prin. Fax 521-5642
Pioneer Ridge MS 500/7-8
1656 S Speck Rd 64057 816-521-5385
Michael Estes, prin. Fax 521-5630
Procter ES 300/PK-5
1403 W Linden Ave 64052 816-521-5440
Amy Hawley, prin. Fax 521-5643
Randall ES 300/PK-5
509 N Jennings Rd 64056 816-521-5445
Bobby McCutcheon, prin. Fax 521-5644
Santa Fe Trail ES 400/PK-5
1301 Windsor St 64055 816-521-5450
Gilberto Rito, prin. Fax 521-5645
Southern ES 600/PK-5
4300 S Phelps Rd 64055 816-521-5475
Gwenn Tauveli, prin. Fax 521-5646
Spring Branch ES 300/PK-5
20404 E Truman Rd 64056 816-521-5455
Aaron Kirchhoff, prin. Fax 521-5647
Sunshine Center 200/PK-PK
18400 E Salisbury Rd 64056 816-521-5526
Patti White, prin. Fax 521-5686
Sycamore Hills ES 500/PK-5
15208 E 39th St S 64055 816-521-5465
Amber Miller, prin. Fax 521-5649
Three Trails ES 400/PK-5
11801 E 32nd St S 64052 816-521-5470
Kevin Lathrom, prin. Fax 521-5650
Other Schools – See Sugar Creek

Messiah Lutheran S 100/PK-8
613 S Main St 64050 816-254-9409
Eric Eckhoff, prin. Fax 254-9407
Nativity of Mary S 400/PK-8
10021 E 36th Ter S 64052 816-353-0284
Mary Parrish, prin. Fax 356-0286

Ironton, Iron, Pop. 1,442
Arcadia Valley R-II SD 1,000/PK-12
750 Park Dr 63650 573-546-9700
Jim Carver Ed.D., supt. Fax 546-7314
www.avr2.org
Arcadia Valley ES 400/PK-4
700 Park Dr 63650 573-546-9700
Laura Marquis, prin. Fax 546-7388
Arcadia Valley MS 300/5-8
550 Park Dr 63650 573-546-9700
Kent Huddleston, prin. Fax 546-7304

Jackson, Cape Girardeau, Pop. 13,577
Jackson R-II SD 4,700/PK-12
614 E Adams St 63755 573-243-9501
Dr. John Link, supt. Fax 243-9503
www.jacksonr2schools.com
East ES PK-5
455 N Lacey St 63755 573-243-5271
Dr. Jessica Maxwell, prin. Fax 243-5343
Jackson MS 700/6-7
1651 W Independence St 63755 573-243-9543
Janelle Pope, prin. Fax 243-9545
North ES 300/K-5
10730 State Hwy W 63755 573-243-9590
Dr. Lance McClard, prin. Fax 243-9591
Orchard Drive ES 500/K-2
1402 Orchard Dr 63755 573-243-9555
Shanna Wilson, prin. Fax 243-9559
South ES 600/K-5
1701 S Hope St 63755 573-243-9575
Krista Birk, prin. Fax 243-9574
West Lane ES 500/3-5
338 N West Ln 63755 573-243-9565
Samantha Trankler, prin. Fax 243-9572
Other Schools – See Cape Girardeau, Millersville

Immaculate Conception S 200/K-8
300 S Hope St 63755 573-243-5013
Michele Campbell, prin. Fax 243-7216
St. Paul Lutheran S 400/PK-8
216 S Russell St 63755 573-243-5360
Timothy Mirly, prin. Fax 243-4527

Jameson, Daviess, Pop. 124
North Daviess R-III SD 100/PK-12
413 E 2nd St 64647 660-828-4123
Daniel Street, supt. Fax 828-4122
www.northdaviess.org
North Daviess ES 100/PK-6
413 E 2nd St 64647 660-828-4123
Kelly Hightree, prin. Fax 828-4122

Jamesport, Daviess, Pop. 506
Tri-County R-VII SD 100/K-12
904 W Auberry Grv 64648 660-684-6118
David Probasco, supt. Fax 684-6218
www.trico.k12.mo.us/
Tri-County ES 100/K-6
904 W Auberry Grv 64648 660-684-6117
Tinna Croy, prin. Fax 684-6218

Jamestown, Moniteau, Pop. 378
Jamestown C-1 SD — 200/K-12
222 School St 65046 — 660-849-2141
Gretchen Guitard, supt. — Fax 849-2600
www.jamestown.k12.mo.us
Jamestown C-I ES — 100/K-6
222 School St 65046 — 660-849-2141
Steven McDannold, prin. — Fax 849-2600

Jane, McDonald
McDonald County R-I SD
Supt. — See Anderson
White Rock ES — 400/PK-8
1113 E State Highway 90 64856 — 417-226-4446
Tonya Cox, prin. — Fax 226-4447

Jasper, Jasper, Pop. 913
Jasper County R-V SD — 500/K-12
201 W Mercer St 64755 — 417-394-2511
Christina Hess, supt. — Fax 394-9977
www.jasper.k12.mo.us
Jasper County ES — 200/K-6
201 W Mercer St 64755 — 417-394-2301
David Davis, prin. — Fax 394-2001

Jefferson City, Cole, Pop. 42,185
Jefferson City SD — 9,100/PK-12
315 E Dunklin St 65101 — 573-659-3000
Larry Linthacum, supt. — Fax 659-3807
www.jcschools.us
Belair ES — 400/K-5
701 Belair Dr 65109 — 573-659-3155
Elizabeth Milhollin, prin. — Fax 632-3492
Cedar Hill ES — 400/K-5
1510 Vieth Dr 65109 — 573-659-3160
Stacy Fick, prin. — Fax 632-3493
East ES — 400/K-5
1229 E McCarty St 65101 — 573-659-3165
Ryan Day, prin. — Fax 632-3489
Gordon ES — 300/K-5
1101 Jackson St 65101 — 573-659-3170
Christopher Schmitz, prin. — Fax 659-3514
Jefferson MS — 1,000/6-8
1201 Fairgrounds Rd 65109 — 573-659-3250
Shawn Kelsch, prin. — Fax 659-3259
Lawson ES — 600/PK-5
1105 Fairgrounds Rd 65109 — 573-659-3175
Patricia Tavenner, prin. — Fax 632-3487
Lewis and Clark MS — 900/6-8
325 Lewis and Clark Dr 65101 — 573-659-3200
Sherri Thomas, prin. — Fax 659-3209
Moreau Heights ES — 400/K-5
1410 Hough Park St 65101 — 573-659-3180
Suzanna Haugen, prin. — Fax 632-3495
Pioneer ES — 600/K-5
301 Pioneer Trail Dr 65109 — 573-632-3400
Scott Salmons, prin. — Fax 632-3420
South ES — 300/K-5
707 Linden Dr 65109 — 573-659-3185
Angela Otlker, prin. — Fax 632-3497
Southwest ECC — 200/PK-PK
812 Saint Marys Blvd 65109 — 573-659-3190
Nicole Langston, prin. — Fax 632-3498
West ES — 400/K-5
100 Dix Rd 65109 — 573-659-3195
Brandi Fatherley, prin. — Fax 632-3496
Other Schools – See Holts Summit

Immaculate Conception S — 400/PK-8
1208 E McCarty St 65101 — 573-636-7680
Heather Schrimpf, prin. — Fax 635-1833
Immanuel Lutheran S — 100/PK-8
8231 Tanner Bridge Rd 65101 — 573-496-3766
Steve Schumacher, prin.
River Oak Christian Academy — 100/PK-5
3212 Emerald Ln Ste 100 65109 — 573-634-3983
Lisa Smith, admin. — Fax 634-7095
St. Francis Xavier S — 200/K-8
7307 Route M 65101 — 573-395-4612
Michael Buskirk, prin. — Fax 395-4017
St. Joseph Cathedral S — 500/PK-8
2303 W Main St 65109 — 573-635-5024
Spencer Allen, prin. — Fax 635-5238
St. Martin S — 200/PK-8
7206 Saint Martins Blvd 65109 — 573-893-3519
Eddie Mulholland, prin. — Fax 893-7404
St. Peter Interparish S — 500/PK-8
314 W High St 65101 — 573-636-8922
Gayle Trachsel, prin. — Fax 636-8410
Trinity Lutheran S — 300/K-8
812 Stadium Blvd 65109 — 573-636-7807
Steve Gonzales, prin. — Fax 269-8341

Jennings, Saint Louis, Pop. 14,545
Jennings SD — 2,500/PK-12
2559 Dorwood Dr 63136 — 314-653-8000
Dr. Art McCoy, supt. — Fax 653-8030
www.jenningsk12.org
Fairview IS — 200/4-6
7053 Emma Ave 63136 — 314-653-8070
Melisha Carson, prin. — Fax 653-8075
Fairview PS — 300/PK-3
7047 Emma Ave 63136 — 314-653-8070
Melisha Carson, prin. — Fax 653-8075
Hanrahan ES — 200/4-6
8430 Lucas and Hunt Rd 63136 — 314-653-8190
Curt Wrisberg, prin. — Fax 653-8197
Jennings JHS — 400/7-8
8831 Cozens Ave 63136 — 314-653-8150
Dr. Charmyn Andrews, prin. — Fax 653-8168
Northview ES — 500/PK-6
8920 Cozens Ave 63136 — 314-653-8050
Dr. Patricia Guyton, prin. — Fax 653-8055
Woodland ES — 300/PK-3
8420 Sunbury Ave 63136 — 314-653-8170
Curt Wrisberg, prin. — Fax 653-8173

Jonesburg, Montgomery, Pop. 743
Montgomery County R-II SD
Supt. — See Montgomery City
Jonesburg ES — 200/PK-5
106 Smith Rd 63351 — 573-564-2278
Jennifer Krattli, prin. — Fax 782-8704

Joplin, Jasper, Pop. 48,394
Joplin SD — 7,700/PK-12
PO Box 128 64802 — 417-625-5200
Dr. Melinda Moss, supt. — Fax 625-5210
www.joplinschools.org
Columbia ES — 200/K-5
PO Box 128 64802 — 417-625-5325
Shally Lundien, prin. — Fax 625-5329
East MS — 500/6-8
PO Box 128 64802 — 417-625-5280
Jason Cravens, prin. — Fax 625-5284
Eastmorland ES — 300/K-5
PO Box 128 64802 — 417-625-5340
Heather Surbrugg, prin. — Fax 625-5344
Floyd ES — 600/K-5
PO Box 128 64802 — 417-625-5320
Christopher Bozarth, prin. — Fax 625-5324
Irving ES — 500/K-5
PO Box 128 64802 — 417-625-5350
Sarah Mwangi, prin. — Fax 625-5354
Jefferson ES — 300/K-5
PO Box 128 64802 — 417-625-5355
Jason Weaver, prin. — Fax 625-5216
McKinley ES — 200/K-5
PO Box 128 64802 — 417-625-5365
Brian Olivera, prin. — Fax 625-5369
Norman ES — 300/K-5
PO Box 128 64802 — 417-625-5360
Julie Munn, prin. — Fax 625-5364
North MS — 600/6-8
PO Box 128 64802 — 417-625-5270
Matthew Harding, prin. — Fax 625-5273
Royal Heights ES — 300/K-5
PO Box 128 64802 — 417-625-5370
Jill White, prin. — Fax 625-5374
Soaring Heights ES — 300/K-5
PO Box 128 64802 — 417-625-5330
Teresa Adams, prin. — Fax 625-5334
South MS — 700/6-8
PO Box 128 64802 — 417-625-5250
Chris Mitchell, prin. — Fax 625-5256
Stapleton ES — 500/K-5
PO Box 128 64802 — 417-625-5375
Karen Secrist, prin. — Fax 625-5379
West Central ES — 200/PK-5
PO Box 128 64802 — 417-625-5380
Bret Ingle, prin. — Fax 625-5384
Other Schools – See Duenweg

College Heights Christian S — 500/PK-12
4311 Newman Rd 64801 — 417-782-4114
Randy Goldsmith, supt. — Fax 659-9092
Jefferson Independent Day S — 300/PK-12
3401 Newman Rd 64801 — 417-781-5124
Luther S — 100/PK-8
2616 Connecticut Ave 64804 — 417-624-1403
Jeremy Schamber, prin. — Fax 624-2774
St. Mary S — 200/PK-5
3025 S Central City Rd 64804 — 417-623-7051
Ann Hamlet, prin. — Fax 533-7887
St. Peter MS — 100/6-8
931 Byers Ave 64801 — 417-624-5605
Gene Koester, prin. — Fax 624-6254

Kahoka, Clark, Pop. 2,063
Clark County R-I SD — 1,000/PK-12
427 W Chestnut St 63445 — 660-727-2377
Ritchie Kracht, supt. — Fax 727-2035
www.clarkcounty.k12.mo.us/
Black Hawk ES — 400/K-5
751 W Chestnut St 63445 — 660-727-3318
Julie Brotherton, prin. — Fax 727-8017
Clark County ECC — PK-PK
566 E Commercial St 63445 — 660-727-3327
Susan Rossmiller, prin. — Fax 727-2035
Clark County MS — 200/6-8
384 N Jefferson St 63445 — 660-727-3319
Jason Church, prin. — Fax 727-3363
Other Schools – See Alexandria

Shiloh Christian S — 50/K-12
RR 1 Box 68A 63445 — 573-853-4430
Ken Penfield, admin. — Fax 853-4432

Kansas City, Jackson, Pop. 447,224
Center SD 58 — 2,600/PK-12
8701 Holmes Rd 64131 — 816-349-3300
Dr. Sharon Nibbelink, supt. — Fax 349-3431
www.center.k12.mo.us
Boone ES — 300/K-5
8817 Wornall Rd 64114 — 816-349-3613
Anson Baker, prin. — Fax 349-3637
Center ECC — 200/PK-PK
8817 Wornall Rd 64114 — 816-349-3700
Tamara Sandage, prin. — Fax 349-3733
Center ES — 300/K-5
8401 Euclid Ave 64132 — 816-349-3444
Brian Borgmeyer, prin. — Fax 349-3441
Center MS — 500/6-8
326 E 103rd St 64114 — 816-612-4000
Linda Williams, prin. — Fax 612-4053
Indian Creek ES — 300/K-5
9801 Grand Ave 64114 — 816-612-4250
Dr. Angela Price, prin. — Fax 612-4287
Red Bridge ES — 200/K-5
10781 Oak St 64114 — 816-612-4200
Rachelle Hamrick, prin. — Fax 612-4205

Grandview C-4 SD
Supt. — See Grandview
Martin City K-8 S — 800/K-8
201 E 133rd St 64145 — 816-316-5700
Johnny Dodge, prin. — Fax 316-5751

Hickman Mills C-I SD — 4,800/PK-12
9000 Old Santa Fe Rd 64138 — 816-316-7000
Yolanda Cargile Ed.D., supt. — Fax 316-7020
www.hickmanmills.org
Compass ES — 300/1-6
5401 E 103rd St 64137 — 816-316-7750
Dr. Michael Camp, prin. — Fax 316-7745
Dobbs ES — 400/1-6
9400 Eastern Ave 64138 — 816-316-7800
Adrain Howard, prin. — Fax 316-7805
Ervin Early Childhood Learning Center — PK-K
10530 Greenwood Rd 64134 — 816-316-7600
Anna Blancarte, prin.
Ingels ES — 400/1-6
11600 Food Ln 64134 — 816-316-7850
Dr. Sabrina Tillman-Winfrey, prin. — Fax 316-7887
Johnson ES — 300/1-6
10900 Marsh Ave 64134 — 816-316-7900
Connie Moore, prin. — Fax 316-7928
Markley ECC — PK-PK
9201 E Bannister Rd 64134 — 816-316-8500
Dr. Shari Osborn, prin. — Fax 316-8506
Santa Fe ES — 400/1-6
8908 Old Santa Fe Rd 64138 — 816-316-7950
Dr. Craig Merkerson, prin. — Fax 316-7988
Smith-Hale MS — 500/7-8
8925 Longview Rd 64134 — 816-316-7700
Shaunda Fowler, prin. — Fax 316-7704
Symington ES — 400/1-6
8650 Ruskin Way 64134 — 816-316-8050
Dr. Elizabeth Woods, prin. — Fax 316-8051
Truman ES — 400/1-6
9601 James A Reed Rd 64134 — 816-316-8100
Susan Herrera, prin. — Fax 316-8310
Warford ES — 300/1-6
11400 Cleveland Ave 64137 — 816-316-8150
Urban Ray, prin. — Fax 316-8170

Kansas City SD 33 — 12,600/PK-12
2901 Troost Ave 64109 — 816-418-7000
Dr. Mark Bedell, supt. — Fax 418-7766
www.kcpublicschools.org
African-Centered Prep ES — 300/PK-8
6410 Swope Pkwy 64132 — 816-418-1175
Claire Thornton-Poke, prin. — Fax 418-1080
Banneker ES — 300/K-6
7050 Askew Ave 64132 — 816-418-1850
Harrison Neal, prin. — Fax 418-1865
Border Star Montessori ES — 400/PK-6
6321 Wornall Rd 64113 — 816-418-5150
Adriene White, prin. — Fax 418-5165
Carver Dual Language ES — 300/K-6
4600 Elmwood Ave 64130 — 816-418-4925
Michael Coulter, prin. — Fax 418-4930
Central MS — 7-8
3611 E Linwood Blvd 64128 — 816-418-7000
Dr. Bryan Shaw, prin.
Faxon ES — 300/PK-6
1320 E 32nd Ter 64109 — 816-418-6525
Kathleen Snipes, prin. — Fax 418-6530
Foreign Language Academy — 700/K-8
3450 Warwick Blvd 64111 — 816-418-6000
Joell Ramsdell, prin. — Fax 418-6010
Garcia ES — 300/PK-6
1000 W 17th St 64108 — 816-418-8725
Rejeanne Alomenu, prin. — Fax 418-8730
Garfield ES — 500/K-6
436 Prospect Ave 64124 — 816-418-3600
Doug White, prin. — Fax 418-3610
Gladstone ES — 500/K-6
335 N Elmwood Ave 64123 — 816-418-3950
Dana Carter, prin. — Fax 418-3960
Hale Cook ES — 200/PK-5
7302 Pennsylvania Ave 64114 — 816-418-1750
Julie Lynch, prin. — Fax 418-1777
Hartman ES — 300/PK-6
8111 Oak St 64114 — 816-418-1750
Dr. Jessie Kirksey, prin. — Fax 418-1777
Holliday Montessori ES — 400/PK-6
7227 Jackson Ave 64132 — 816-418-1950
Kalinda Bass-Barlow, prin. — Fax 418-1960
James ES — 400/K-6
5810 Scarritt Ave 64123 — 816-418-3700
Mary Bachkora, prin. — Fax 418-3710
King ES — 500/K-6
4848 Woodland Ave 64110 — 816-418-2475
Jarius Jones, prin. — Fax 418-2480
Longfellow ES — 200/PK-6
2830 Holmes St 64109 — 816-418-5325
Jimmie Bullard, prin. — Fax 418-5330
Melcher ES — 400/PK-6
3958 Chelsea Ave 64130 — 816-418-6725
Patricia Hayes, prin. — Fax 418-6730
Northeast MS — 7-8
4904 Independence Ave 64124 — 816-418-7000
Cleora Taylor, prin.
Pitcher ES — 300/PK-6
9915 E 38th Ter 64133 — 816-418-4550
Karol Howard, prin. — Fax 418-4560
Rogers ES — 800/K-6
6400 E 23rd St 64129 — 816-418-4770
Dr. Adriane Blankinship, prin. — Fax 418-4803
Trailwoods ES — 300/PK-6
6201 E 17th St 64126 — 816-418-3250
Leah Starr, prin. — Fax 418-3275
Troost ES — 300/PK-6
1215 E 59th St 64110 — 816-418-1700
Jenise Hampton, prin. — Fax 418-1725
Wheatley ES — 400/PK-6
2415 Agnes Ave 64127 — 816-418-4825
Micah Enders, prin. — Fax 418-4830

Whittier ES 500/K-6
1012 Bales Ave 64127 816-418-3850
Luis Hinojosa, prin. Fax 418-3860
Woodland Early Learning Community S PK-PK
711 Woodland Ave 64106 816-418-5900
Mona Cozart, dir. Fax 418-5905

Lee's Summit R-VII SD
Supt. — See Lees Summit
Summit Pointe ES 600/K-6
13100 E 147 St 64149 816-986-2410
Dr. Heather Kenney, prin. Fax 986-4235

Liberty SD 53
Supt. — See Liberty
Early Childhood Education Center 300/PK-PK
9600 NE 79th St 64158 816-736-5324
Sarah Birk, prin. Fax 736-6781
Kellybrook ES 700/K-5
10701 N Eastern Ave 64157 816-736-5700
Andrea Wilson, prin. Fax 736-5705
Liberty Oaks ES 600/K-5
8150 N Farley Ave 64158 816-736-5600
Debra Slaughter, prin. Fax 736-5605
Shoal Creek ES 900/K-5
9000 NE Flintlock Rd 64157 816-736-7150
Mary Boman, prin. Fax 736-7155

North Kansas City SD 74 19,600/PK-12
2000 NE 46th St 64116 816-321-5000
Dr. Dan Clemens, supt. Fax 321-5005
www.nkcschools.org
Bell Prairie ES 500/K-5
3000 NE 108th St 64156 816-321-5020
Dr. Jessica Martin, prin. Fax 321-5021
Briarcliff ES 300/K-5
4100 N Briarcliff Rd 64116 816-321-5030
Kate Place, prin. Fax 321-5031
Chouteau ES 400/PK-5
3701 N Jackson Ave 64117 816-321-5050
Anjanette Walker, prin. Fax 321-5051
Clardy ES 500/2-5
8100 N Troost Ave 64118 816-321-5060
Raquel Coy, prin. Fax 321-5061
Crestview ES 500/K-5
4327 N Holmes St 64116 816-321-5070
Deyrle Wallace, prin. Fax 321-5071
Davidson ES 400/K-5
5100 N Highland Ave 64118 816-321-5080
Anne Tate, prin. Fax 321-5081
Eastgate MS 700/6-8
4700 NE Parvin Rd 64117 816-321-5270
Dr. Chris McCann, prin. Fax 321-5271
Fox Hill ES 500/K-5
545 NE 106th St 64155 816-321-5090
Branson Bradley, prin. Fax 321-5091
Gashland ES 300/K-1
500 NE 83rd St 64118 816-321-5100
Cindy Lakin, prin. Fax 321-5101
Gracemor ES 900/PK-5
5125 N Sycamore Dr 64119 816-321-5110
Dr. Jose Verduzco, prin. Fax 321-5111
Lakewood ES 200/K-5
4624 N Norton Ave 64117 816-321-5120
Brandon Greason, prin. Fax 321-5121
Maple Park MS 800/6-8
5300 N Bennington Ave 64119 816-321-5280
Brian Van Batavia, prin. Fax 321-5281
Maplewood ES 300/PK-5
6400 NE 52nd St 64119 816-321-5140
Curt Fowler, prin. Fax 321-5141
Nashua ES 400/K-5
221 NE 114th St 64155 816-321-5160
Heather Stukey, prin. Fax 321-5161
New Mark MS 1,100/6-8
515 NE 106th St 64155 816-321-5290
Terri Sherry, prin. Fax 321-5291
Northgate MS 800/6-8
2117 NE 48th St 64118 816-321-5300
P.J. McGinnis, prin. Fax 321-5301
Northview ES 800/K-5
9201 N Indiana Ave 64156 816-321-5170
Dr. Starr Rich, prin. Fax 321-5171
Ravenwood ES 400/K-5
5020 NE 58th St 64119 816-321-5190
Amy Casey, prin. Fax 321-5191
Topping ES 300/K-5
4433 N Topping Ave 64117 816-321-5200
Dr. Dana Miller, prin. Fax 321-5201
West Englewood ES 400/PK-5
1506 NW Englewood Rd 64118 816-321-5210
Tammy Eldridge, prin. Fax 321-5211
Winnwood ES 400/PK-5
4531 NE 44th Ter 64117 816-321-5220
Leah Copeland, prin. Fax 321-5221
Other Schools – See Gladstone, Pleasant Valley

Park Hill SD 10,700/PK-12
7703 NW Barry Rd 64153 816-359-4000
Dr. Jeanette Cowherd, supt. Fax 359-4049
www.parkhill.k12.mo.us
Chinn ES 400/K-5
7100 N Chatham Ave 64151 816-359-4330
Lee Heinerikson, prin. Fax 359-4339
Congress MS 900/7-8
8150 N Congress Ave 64152 816-359-4230
Dr. Timothy Todd, prin. Fax 359-4219
English Landing ES 500/K-5
6500 NW Klamm Dr 64151 816-359-4370
Dr. Kerry Roe, prin. Fax 359-4379
Gerner Family Early Education Center 100/PK-PK
8100 N Congress Ave 64152 816-359-4600
Rachel Ward, coord.
Hawthorn ES 500/K-5
8200 N Chariton Ave 64152 816-359-4390
Brooke Renton, prin. Fax 359-4399
Lakeview MS 800/7-8
6720 NW 64th St 64151 816-359-4220
Kirsten Clemons, prin. Fax 359-4229
Line Creek ES 500/K-5
5801 NW Waukomis Dr 64151 816-359-4320
Betsy Greim, prin. Fax 359-4329
Plaza MS 800/6-6
6501 NW 72nd St 64151 816-359-4210
Dr. Lezlee Ivy, prin. Fax 359-4219
Prairie Point ES 500/K-5
8101 NW Belvidere Pkwy 64152 816-359-4380
Jay Niceswanger, prin. Fax 359-4389
Renner ES 400/K-5
7401 NW Barry Rd 64153 816-359-4350
Dr. Melissa Hensley, prin. Fax 359-4359
Southeast ES 400/K-5
5704 NW Northwood Rd 64151 816-359-4360
Diane Simpson, prin. Fax 359-4369
Tiffany Ridge ES 500/K-5
5301 NW Old Tiffany Springs 64154 816-359-4400
Shawn Fitzmorris, prin. Fax 359-4409
Union Chapel ES 500/K-5
7100 NW Hampton Rd 64152 816-359-4310
Dr. Steven Archer, prin. Fax 359-4319
Other Schools – See Parkville

Platte County R-III SD
Supt. — See Platte City
Barry S 400/5-8
2001 NW 87th Ter 64154 816-436-9623
Merri Beth Means, prin. Fax 468-6046
Pathfinder ES 400/K-4
1951 NW 87th Ter 64154 816-436-6670
Dr. Devin Doll, prin. Fax 436-2130

Raytown C-2 SD
Supt. — See Raytown
Eastwood Hills ES 400/K-5
5290 Sycamore Ave 64129 816-268-7210
Amanda Coleman, prin. Fax 268-7215
Fleetridge ES 400/K-5
13001 E 55th St 64133 816-268-7220
Debbie Kingrey, prin. Fax 268-7225
Little Blue ES 400/K-5
13900 E 61st St 64133 816-268-7740
Dr. Julie Schmidli, prin. Fax 268-7745
Norfleet ES 400/K-5
6140 Norfleet Rd 64133 816-268-7240
Lori Kang, prin. Fax 268-7245
Raytown MS 800/6-8
4900 Pittman Rd 64133 816-268-7360
Dr. Georgetta May, prin. Fax 268-7365
Robinson ES 400/K-5
6707 Woodson Rd 64133 816-268-7260
Elizabeth Arbisi, prin. Fax 268-7265
Westridge ES 400/K-5
8500 E 77th St 64138 816-268-7290
Matthew Jones, prin. Fax 268-7295

Barstow S 700/PK-12
11511 State Line Rd 64114 816-942-3255
Shane Foster, head sch Fax 942-3227
Blue Ridge Christian S 200/PK-12
15701 Calvary Rd 64147 816-358-0950
Kathleen Reynolds, supt.
Calvary Lutheran S 200/PK-8
12411 Wornall Rd 64145 816-595-4020
Michelle Fischer, prin. Fax 361-5979
Faith Academy 100/PK-8
4300 N Corrington Ave 64117 816-455-2847
Dr. Donna Houpe, admin. Fax 455-8041
Faith Christian Academy 300/K-12
3500 NE Prather Rd 64116 816-455-3513
Forerunner Christian Academy 100/PK-12
10415 Chestnut Dr 64137 816-694-1331
Suzanne Clough, head sch
Glad Tidings Christian Academy 50/PK-3
PO Box 300932 64130 816-333-1054
Errolyn Fraser, admin. Fax 333-0396
Holy Cross S 200/PK-8
121 N Quincy Ave 64123 816-231-8874
Barb Deane, prin. Fax 231-7258
Islamic S of Greater Kansas City 300/PK-12
8505 E 99th St 64134 816-763-0322
Luther Academy 100/K-8
7112 N Overland Dr 64151 816-734-1060
Ann Arndt, prin. Fax 734-0485
Northland Christian S 200/PK-12
4214 NW Cookingham Rd 64164 816-548-2222
Richard Rice, supt.
Notre Dame de Sion S of Kansas City 300/PK-8
3823 Locust St 64109 816-753-3810
Dr. Paola Clark, prin. Fax 753-0806
Our Lady of Hope S K-8
4232 Mercier St 64111 816-931-1693
Mary Delac, prin.
Outreach Christian Education 100/PK-8
2900 NE Cates St 64117 816-455-5575
Kathy Taylor, admin. Fax 455-5168
Pembroke Hill S - Wornall Campus 400/PK-5
400 W 51st St 64112 816-936-1200
Dr. Steven J. Bellis, head sch Fax 936-1208
Providence S of Arts PK-2
6422 Woodland Ave 64131 816-287-0411
Marcus Oatis, admin. Fax 569-0209
St. Charles Borromeo S 400/PK-8
804 NE Shady Lane Dr 64118 816-436-1009
Ann Lachowitzer, prin. Fax 436-6293
St. Elizabeth S 500/PK-8
14 W 75th St 64114 816-523-7100
Pat Kollasch, prin. Fax 523-2566
St. Gabriel S 200/PK-8
4737 N Cleveland Ave 64117 816-453-4443
Amy Hogan, prin. Fax 453-6254
St. John Francis Regis S 300/PK-8
8941 James A Reed Rd 64138 816-763-5837
Cally Dahlstrom, prin. Fax 966-1350
St. Patrick S 100/PK-8
1401 NE 42nd Ter 64116 816-453-0971
Julie Hess, prin. Fax 453-5451
St. Pauls Episcopal Day S 400/PK-8
4041 Main St 64111 816-931-8614
Andrew Myler, head sch Fax 931-6860
St. Peter S 500/PK-8
6400 Charlotte St 64131 816-523-4899
Mary Omecene, prin. Fax 523-1248
St. Therese ECC 200/PK-PK
7277 N State Route 9 64152 816-746-1500
Kelly Carroll, dir. Fax 741-4474
St. Therese S 600/K-8
7277 N State Route 9 64152 816-741-5400
Carol Lenz, prin. Fax 741-0533
St. Thomas More S 600/PK-8
11800 Holmes Rd 64131 816-942-5581
Brian Borgmeyer, prin. Fax 941-2450
Visitation S 600/K-8
5134 Baltimore Ave 64112 816-531-6200
Dr. Vincent Cascone, prin. Fax 531-8045
Whitefield Academy 200/PK-12
8929 Holmes 64131 816-444-3567
Dr. Quentin Johnston Ph.D., hdmstr. Fax 822-8405

Kearney, Clay, Pop. 8,257
Kearney R-I SD 3,600/K-12
1002 S Jefferson St 64060 816-628-4116
Dr. William Nicely, supt. Fax 628-4074
www.ksdr1.net
Dogwood ES 500/K-5
1400 Cedar Wood Pkwy 64060 816-903-1400
Janelle Nelson, prin. Fax 628-0016
Hawthorne ES 300/K-5
1815 S Jefferson St 64060 816-628-4114
Annette Shelton, prin. Fax 628-6476
Kearney ES 300/K-5
902 S Jefferson St 64060 816-628-4113
Brian Sloan, prin. Fax 628-4132
Kearney MS 600/6-7
200 E 5th St 64060 816-628-4115
Bart Woods, prin. Fax 628-4424
Southview ES 500/K-5
7 S Campus St 64060 816-628-4652
Rebecca Parks, prin. Fax 628-6173

Kelso, Scott, Pop. 582

St. Augustine S 100/K-8
PO Box 97 63758 573-264-4644
Gerald Landewee, prin. Fax 264-1475

Kennett, Dunklin, Pop. 10,740
Kennett SD 39 2,200/PK-12
510 College Ave 63857 573-717-1100
Chris Wilson, supt. Fax 717-1016
www.kennett.k12.mo.us
ECC 100/PK-PK
205 Wiggs St 63857 573-717-1145
Dr. Kim Short, dir. Fax 717-1102
Kennett MS 500/6-8
510 College Ave 63857 573-717-1105
Ward Billings, prin. Fax 717-1106
Masterson ES 500/K-2
1600 Ely St 63857 573-717-1115
Laurie McAtee, prin. Fax 717-1115
South ES 500/3-5
920 Kennett St 63857 573-717-1130
Kimberly Morgan, prin. Fax 717-1130

Keytesville, Chariton, Pop. 471
Keytesville R-III SD 100/PK-12
27247 Highway 5 65261 660-288-3787
Josh Shoemaker, supt. Fax 288-3110
keytesville.k12.mo.us
Keytesville R-III ES 100/PK-6
27247 Highway 5 65261 660-288-3767
Chad Hall, prin. Fax 288-3110

King City, Gentry, Pop. 1,004
King City R-I SD 300/PK-12
PO Box 189 64463 660-535-4319
Danny Johnson, supt. Fax 535-4765
www.kingcityschools.org
King City ES 200/PK-6
PO Box 189 64463 660-535-4712
Ryan Anderson, prin. Fax 535-4356

Kingdom City, Callaway, Pop. 127
North Callaway County R-I SD 1,100/PK-12
2690 Thunderbird Dr 65262 573-386-2214
Dr. Bryan Thomsen, supt. Fax 386-2169
nc.k12.mo.us
Hatton-McCredie ES 300/K-8
4171 County Road 240 65262 573-642-4333
Christine Biggers, prin. Fax 642-5624
Other Schools – See Auxvasse, Williamsburg

Kingston, Caldwell, Pop. 345
Kingston SD 42 50/PK-8
139 E Lincoln St 64650 816-586-3111
Andrea Hieronymus, admin. Fax 586-3903
www.kingston42.com
Kingston 42 S 50/PK-8
139 E Lincoln St 64650 816-586-3111
Andrea Hieronymus, prin. Fax 586-3903

Kingsville, Johnson, Pop. 264
Kingsville R-I SD 100/K-12
PO Box 7 64061 816-597-3422
Lorna Warren, supt. Fax 597-3702
kingsville.k12.mo.us
Kingsville S 100/K-12
PO Box 7 64061 816-597-3422
Lorna Warren, admin. Fax 597-3702

Kirbyville, Taney, Pop. 203
Kirbyville R-VI SD 300/K-8
6225 E State Highway 76 65679 417-337-8913
Carless Osbourn, supt. Fax 348-0794
www.kirbyville.k12.mo.us

Kirbyville ES 100/K-3
4278 E State Highway 76 65679 417-334-2757
Addie Gaines, prin. Fax 336-2084
Kirbyville MS 200/4-8
6225 E State Highway 76 65679 417-348-0444
Amy Burton, prin. Fax 348-0525

Kirksville, Adair, Pop. 17,170
Kirksville R-III SD 2,600/PK-12
1901 E Hamilton St 63501 660-665-7774
Dr. Damon Kizzire, supt. Fax 626-1448
www.kirksville.k12.mo.us
Kirksville PS 800/PK-2
1815 E Hamilton St 63501 660-665-5691
Ernest Motley, prin. Fax 626-1421
Matthew MS 500/6-8
1515 Cottage Grove Ave 63501 660-665-3793
Dr. Michael Mitchell, prin. Fax 626-1418
Miller ES 500/3-5
2010 E Normal Ave 63501 660-665-2834
Jennifer Botello, prin. Fax 626-1464

Faith Lutheran S 100/PK-8
1820 S Baltimore St 63501 660-665-8166
Janie Fouch, dir. Fax 627-0101
Mary Immaculate S 100/PK-8
712 E Washington St 63501 660-665-1006
Ann Gray, prin. Fax 665-3621

Kirkwood, Saint Louis, Pop. 27,112
Kirkwood R-VII SD 5,900/PK-12
11289 Manchester Rd 63122 314-213-6101
Dr. Michele Condon, supt. Fax 984-0002
www.kirkwoodschools.org
Keysor ES 500/K-5
725 N Geyer Rd 63122 314-213-6120
Dr. Troy Hogg, prin. Fax 213-6172
Kirkwood ECC 300/PK-PK
100 N Sappington Rd 63122 314-213-6136
Melissa Sandbothe, prin. Fax 213-6138
Nipher MS 600/6-8
700 S Kirkwood Rd 63122 314-213-6180
Laura Havener, prin. Fax 213-6178
North Kirkwood MS 600/6-8
11287 Manchester Rd 63122 314-213-6170
Tim Cochran, prin. Fax 213-6177
Robinson ES 500/K-5
803 Couch Ave 63122 314-213-6140
Jennifer Sisul, prin. Fax 213-6174
Tillman ES 500/K-5
230 Quan Ave 63122 314-213-6150
Dr. Maria Stobbe, prin. Fax 213-6175
Westchester ES 500/K-5
1416 Woodgate Dr 63122 314-213-6160
Robert Ricker, prin. Fax 213-6176
Other Schools – See Glendale

Christ Community Lutheran S 600/PK-8
110 W Woodbine Ave 63122 314-822-7774
Jonathan Butterfield, dir. Fax 822-5472
St. Gerard Majella S 400/K-8
2005 Dougherty Ferry Rd 63122 314-822-8844
Chrisell Guthrie, prin. Fax 822-8588
St. Peter S 500/PK-8
215 N Clay Ave 63122 314-821-0460
Dr. John Freitag, prin. Fax 821-0833
Villa Di Maria Montessori S 50/PK-6
1280 Simmons Ave 63122 314-822-2601

Knob Noster, Johnson, Pop. 2,592
Knob Noster R-VIII SD 1,500/PK-12
401 E Wimer St 65336 660-563-3186
Dr. Jerrod Wheeler, supt. Fax 563-3026
www.knobnoster.k12.mo.us
Knob Noster ES 400/PK-4
405 E Wimer St 65336 660-563-3019
Mellon Kristi, prin. Fax 563-3781
Knob Noster MS 400/5-8
211 E Wimer St 65336 660-563-2260
Julie Andrade, prin. Fax 563-3274
Other Schools – See Whiteman AFB

Koshkonong, Oregon, Pop. 200
Oregon-Howell R-III SD 200/K-12
100 School St 65692 417-867-5601
Seth Bryant, supt. Fax 867-1205
www.koshkonongschool.org/
Koshkonong ES 100/K-8
100 School St 65692 417-867-5601
David Miller, prin. Fax 867-3757

Labadie, Franklin
Washington SD
Supt. — See Washington
Labadie ES 100/K-6
2749 Highway T 63055 636-231-2600
Jennifer Pecka, prin. Fax 231-2605

Laddonia, Audrain, Pop. 512
Community R-VI SD 300/PK-12
35063 Highway BB 63352 855-708-7567
Cheryl Mack, supt. Fax 492-6268
www.cr6.net/
Community ES 100/PK-5
35063 Highway BB 63352 855-708-7567
Tammy Angel, prin. Fax 492-6268

Lake Ozark, Camden, Pop. 1,563
School of the Osage R-II SD 1,900/PK-12
PO Box 1960 65049 573-365-4091
Dr. Brent Depee', supt. Fax 365-5748
www.osageschools.org
Heritage ES 500/PK-2
PO Box 1960 65049 573-365-5341
Holly Birdsley, prin. Fax 365-5394
Other Schools – See Osage Beach

Kings Academy 100/PK-5
1700 Bagnell Blvd 65049 573-693-9245
Rayleen Wilson, admin. Fax 365-5356

Lake Saint Louis, Saint Charles, Pop. 14,381
Wentzville R-IV SD
Supt. — See Wentzville
Duello ES 800/K-6
1814 Duello Rd 63367 636-327-6050
Laura Parn, prin. Fax 327-4211
Green Tree ES 700/K-6
1000 Ronald Reagan Dr 63367 636-625-5600
Angela Politte, prin. Fax 625-5610

Lamar, Barton, Pop. 4,398
Lamar R-I SD 1,300/PK-12
202 W 7th St 64759 417-682-3527
Dr. Zach Harris, supt. Fax 682-6013
www.lamar.k12.mo.us
East PS 300/PK-2
202 W 7th St 64759 417-681-0613
Lemert Zachary, prin. Fax 681-0652
Lamar MS 300/6-8
202 W 7th St 64759 417-682-3548
Alan Ray, prin. Fax 682-4409
West ES 300/3-5
202 W 7th St 64759 417-682-3567
Mary Clark, prin. Fax 682-9675

La Monte, Pettis, Pop. 1,113
La Monte R-IV SD 400/PK-12
301 S Washington St 65337 660-347-5439
Dr. Randal E. Bagby, supt. Fax 347-5467
lamonte.k12.mo.us/
La Monte ES 200/PK-6
201 S Washington St 65337 660-347-5621
Jennifer Corson, prin. Fax 347-5467

La Plata, Macon, Pop. 1,336
La Plata R-II SD 300/PK-12
201 W Moore St 63549 660-332-7001
Dr. Craig Noah, supt. Fax 332-7929
laplata.k12.mo.us
La Plata ES 200/PK-6
201 W Moore St 63549 660-332-7003
Lisa Coy, prin. Fax 332-4881

Laquey, Pulaski
Laquey R-V SD 700/PK-12
PO Box 130 65534 573-765-3716
Dr. Randy Caffey, supt. Fax 765-4052
www.laquey.k12.mo.us/
Laquey R-V ES 300/PK-5
PO Box 130 65534 573-765-3245
Michael Mayle, prin. Fax 765-5604
Laquey R-V MS 200/6-8
PO Box 130 65534 573-765-3129
Nicole Hanson, prin. Fax 765-4086

Laredo, Grundy, Pop. 197
Laredo R-VII SD 100/K-8
PO Box C 64652 660-286-2225
Misty Foster, supt. Fax 286-2226
Laredo S 100/K-8
PO Box C 64652 660-286-2225
Misty Foster, admin. Fax 286-2226

Latham, Moniteau
Moniteau County R-V SD 100/K-8
PO Box 367 65050 660-458-6271
Jennifer Fletcher, supt. Fax 458-6604
www.lathambraves.com
Latham ES 100/K-8
PO Box 367 65050 660-458-6271
Jennifer Fletcher, prin. Fax 458-6604

Lathrop, Clinton, Pop. 2,052
Lathrop R-II SD 900/K-12
700 East St 64465 816-528-7500
Chris Fine, supt. Fax 528-7514
www.lathropschools.com
Lathrop ES 400/K-5
700 Center St 64465 816-528-7700
Chauncey Rardon, prin. Fax 528-7759
Lathrop MS 200/6-8
612 Center St 64465 816-528-7600
Andy McNeely, prin. Fax 528-7646

Lawson, Ray, Pop. 2,441
Lawson R-XIV SD 1,200/PK-12
PO Box 157 64062 816-580-7277
Roger Schmitz, supt. Fax 296-7723
lawsoncardinals.org
Lawson MS 400/5-8
PO Box 157 64062 816-580-7279
Tammy Dunn, prin. Fax 296-3164
Southwest ES 400/PK-4
PO Box 157 64062 816-580-7272
Holly Simmons, prin. Fax 296-3202

Leadwood, Saint Francois, Pop. 1,274
West St. Francois County R-IV SD 1,000/PK-12
1124 Main St 63653 573-562-7535
Stacy Stevens, supt. Fax 562-7510
westco.k12.mo.us/
Other Schools – See Park Hills

Lebanon, Laclede, Pop. 14,144
Laclede County C-5 SD 500/PK-8
16050 Highway KK 65536 417-532-4837
Tina Nolan, supt. Fax 588-2100
www.jebc5.k12.mo.us/
Barber S 500/PK-8
16050 Highway KK 65536 417-532-4837
Tina Nolan, prin. Fax 588-2100

Lebanon R-III SD 4,700/PK-12
1310 E Route 66 65536 417-657-6001
David Schmitz, supt. Fax 532-9492
www.lebanon.k12.mo.us
Boswell ES 700/4-5
695 Millcreek Rd 65536 417-657-6004
Rachelle Jennings, prin. Fax 532-4359
Esther ES 900/PK-1
1200 Clark Ave 65536 417-657-6002
Shalyn Howe, prin. Fax 532-8063
Lebanon MS 600/6-8
2700 Buzz Pride Dr 65536 417-657-6005
Tom Merriott, prin. Fax 533-3805
Maplecrest ES 800/2-3
901 Maple Ln 65536 417-657-6003
Bryan Campbell, prin. Fax 533-3802

Lees Summit, Jackson, Pop. 89,308
Blue Springs R-IV SD
Supt. — See Blue Springs
Chapel Lakes ES 500/K-5
3701 NE Independence Ave 64064 816-874-3600
Lizabeth White, prin. Fax 525-9502
Delta Woods MS 700/6-8
4401 NE Lakewood Way 64064 816-874-3580
Steven Cook, prin. Fax 795-5839
Spears ES 600/K-5
201 NE Anderson Dr 64064 816-874-3720
Renee Murry, prin. Fax 478-9799

Lee's Summit R-VII SD 17,900/PK-12
301 NE Tudor Rd 64086 816-986-1000
Dr. Dennis Carpenter, supt. Fax 986-1170
www.lsr7.org
Campbell MS 900/7-8
1201 NE Colbern Rd 64086 816-986-3175
Dr. Sherri Lewis, prin. Fax 986-3245
Cedar Creek ES 500/K-6
2600 SW 3rd St 64081 816-986-1260
Jenifer Opie, prin. Fax 986-1285
Great Beginnings Early Education Center 200/PK-PK
905 NE Bluestem Dr 64086 816-986-2460
Kerry Boehm, dir. Fax 986-2475
Hawthorn Hill ES 600/K-6
2801 SW Pryor Rd 64082 816-986-3380
Carol Germano, prin. Fax 986-3405
Hazel Grove ES 500/K-6
2001 NW Blue Pkwy 64064 816-986-3310
Merrell Kristen, prin. Fax 986-3335
Highland Park ES 500/K-6
400 SE Millstone Ave 64063 816-986-2250
Jodi Mallotte, prin. Fax 986-2275
Lee's Summit ES 300/K-6
110 SE Green St 64063 816-986-3340
Tracy Sample, prin. Fax 986-3355
Longview Farms ES 600/K-6
1001 SW Longview Park Dr 64081 816-986-4180
Dr. Kimberly Hassler, prin. Fax 986-4205
Mason ES 400/K-6
27600 E Colbern Rd 64086 816-986-2330
Beth Ratty, prin. Fax 986-2355
Meadow Lane ES 500/K-6
1421 NE Independence Ave 64086 816-986-3250
Sheryl Cochran, prin. Fax 986-3275
Pleasant Lea ES 600/K-6
700 SW Persels Rd 64081 816-986-1230
Aaron Barnett, prin. Fax 986-1255
Pleasant Lea MS 900/7-8
630 SW Persels Rd 64081 816-986-1175
Janette Miller, prin. Fax 986-1225
Prairie View ES 900/K-6
501 SE Todd George Pkwy 64063 816-986-2280
Amy Fennewald, prin. Fax 986-2325
Richardson ES 600/K-6
800 NE Blackwell Rd 64086 816-986-2220
Lisa Detig, prin. Fax 986-2245
Summit Lakes MS 1,000/7-8
3500 SW Windemere Dr 64082 816-986-1375
Dr. David Mitchell, prin. Fax 986-1435
Sunset Valley ES 500/K-6
1850 SE Ranson Rd 64082 816-986-4240
Greg Johnson, prin. Fax 986-4265
Trailridge ES 500/K-6
3651 SW Windemere Dr 64082 816-986-1290
Jeff Scalfaro, prin. Fax 986-1305
Underwood ES 500/K-6
1125 NE Colbern Rd 64086 816-986-3280
Anna McGraw, prin. Fax 986-3295
Westview ES 400/K-6
200 NW Ward Rd 64063 816-986-1350
Dave Boulden, prin. Fax 986-1365
Woodland ES 400/K-6
12709 Smart Rd 64086 816-986-2360
Stacy James, prin. Fax 986-2385
Other Schools – See Greenwood, Kansas City

Lee's Summit Academy 100/K-12
601 NW Libby Ln 64063 816-399-2026
Bobby King, head sch
Our Lady of the Presentation S 500/PK-8
150 NW Murray Rd 64081 816-251-1150
Jodi Briggs, prin. Fax 251-1155
Summit Christian Academy 700/PK-12
1500 SW Jefferson St 64081 816-525-1480
Linda Harrelson, head sch Fax 525-5402
Summit View Adventist S 50/PK-8
12503 State Route 7 64086 816-697-3443
Matt Daarud B.S., prin.

Leeton, Johnson, Pop. 557
Leeton R-X SD 400/PK-12
500 N Main St 64761 660-653-2301
Susan Crooks, supt. Fax 653-4315
www.leeton.k12.mo.us/
Leeton ES 200/PK-5
500 N Main St 64761 660-653-4731
Heather Shaffer, prin. Fax 653-4315

Leeton MS — 100/6-8
500 N Main St 64761 — 660-653-4314
Bryan Himes, prin. — Fax 653-4315

Leopold, Bollinger
Leopold R-III SD — 200/K-12
PO Box 39 63760 — 573-238-2211
Keenan Kinder, supt. — Fax 238-9868
www.leopold.k12.mo.us
Leopold ES — 100/K-6
PO Box 39 63760 — 573-238-2211
Matt Britt, prin. — Fax 238-9868

Lesterville, Reynolds
Lesterville R-IV SD — 300/PK-12
PO Box 120 63654 — 573-637-2201
James Watts, supt. — Fax 637-2279
www.lesterville.k12.mo.us/
Lesterville ES — 100/PK-6
PO Box 120 63654 — 573-637-2201
Jeremy Myers, prin. — Fax 637-2279

Lewistown, Lewis, Pop. 532
Lewis County C-1 SD — 1,000/PK-12
21504 State Highway 6 63452 — 573-209-3217
John French, supt. — Fax 209-3318
www.lewis.k12.mo.us
Highland ES — 500/PK-6
25189 Heritage Ave 63452 — 573-209-3586
Larry Post, prin. — Fax 209-3370

Lexington, Lafayette, Pop. 4,541
Lexington R-V SD — 900/PK-12
2323 High School Dr Ste A 64067 — 660-259-4369
Dr. Jeff Levy, supt. — Fax 259-4992
www.lexington.k12.mo.us
Bell ES — 400/K-4
400 S 20th St 64067 — 660-259-4341
Kacie Pennington, prin. — Fax 259-2040
ECC — PK-PK
811 S Business Hwy 13 Ste B 64067 — 660-259-2192
Kacie Pennington, dir. — Fax 259-2439
Lexington MS — 300/5-8
1111 S 24th St 64067 — 660-259-4611
Vicky Alves, prin. — Fax 259-2538

Liberal, Barton, Pop. 739
Liberal R-II SD — 500/PK-12
PO Box 38 64762 — 417-843-5115
William Harvey, supt. — Fax 843-6698
www.liberal.k12.mo.us/
Liberal ES — 200/PK-5
PO Box 38 64762 — 417-843-5865
Leticia Fry, prin. — Fax 843-5231
Liberal MS — 100/6-8
PO Box 38 64762 — 417-843-6033
Rachel Miller, prin. — Fax 843-2403

Liberty, Clay, Pop. 28,451
Liberty SD 53 — 11,800/PK-12
8 Victory Ln 64068 — 816-736-5300
Dr. Jeremy Tucker, supt. — Fax 736-5306
www.lps53.org
Discovery MS — 600/6-8
800 Midjay Dr 64068 — 816-736-7300
Dr. Gregory Mees, prin. — Fax 736-7306
Doniphan ES — 400/K-5
1900 Clay Dr 64068 — 816-736-5400
Beth Cunningham, prin. — Fax 736-5403
EPIC ES, 650 Conistor Ln 64068 — K-5
Dr. Michelle Schmitz, prin. — 816-736-5730
Franklin ES — 300/K-5
201 W Mill St 64068 — 816-736-5440
Andy Wright, prin. — Fax 736-5443
Heritage MS — 700/6-8
600 W Kansas St 64068 — 816-736-5380
Scott Carr, prin. — Fax 736-5384
Lewis & Clark ES — 600/K-5
1407 Nashua Rd 64068 — 816-736-5430
Mitch Hiser, prin. — Fax 736-5433
Liberty MS — 700/6-8
1500 S Withers Rd 64068 — 816-736-5410
Katherine Lawson, prin. — Fax 736-5415
Manor Hill ES — 400/K-5
1400 S Skyline Dr 64068 — 816-736-5460
Valerie Utecht, prin. — Fax 736-5464
Ridgeview ES — 500/K-5
701 Thornton St 64068 — 816-736-5450
Tyler Shannon, prin. — Fax 736-5454
Schumacher ES — 700/K-5
425 Claywoods Pkwy 64068 — 816-736-5490
Chris Gabriel, prin. — Fax 736-5494
South Valley MS — 600/6-8
1000 Midjay Dr 64068 — 816-736-7180
Jill Mullen, prin. — Fax 736-7185
Warren Hills ES — 700/K-5
1251 Camille St 64068 — 816-736-5630
Michelle Swierski, prin. — Fax 736-5635
Other Schools – See Kansas City

St. James S — 400/PK-8
309 S Stewart Rd 64068 — 816-781-4428
Jennifer Scanlon-Smith, prin. — Fax 781-0747

Licking, Texas, Pop. 3,111
Licking R-VIII SD — 900/PK-12
125 College Ave 65542 — 573-674-2911
Dr. John Hood, supt. — Fax 674-4064
www.licking.k12.mo.us/
Licking ES — 500/PK-6
125 College Ave 65542 — 573-674-3211
Bradley Cooper, prin. — Fax 674-4064

Lilbourn, New Madrid, Pop. 1,170
New Madrid County R-I SD
Supt. — See New Madrid
Lilbourn ES — 300/PK-5
PO Box 605 63862 — 573-688-2593
Laurie Brittain, prin. — Fax 688-2595

Lincoln, Benton, Pop. 1,178
Lincoln R-II SD — 500/K-12
PO Box 39 65338 — 660-547-3514
Kevin Smith, supt. — Fax 547-3729
www.lincoln.k12.mo.us/
Lincoln ES — 300/K-6
PO Box 39 65338 — 660-547-2222
Rebecca Eifert, prin. — Fax 547-3401

Linn, Osage, Pop. 1,447
Osage County R-II SD — 600/PK-12
141 Wildcat Dr 65051 — 573-897-4200
Dr. Lenice Basham, supt. — Fax 897-3768
www.linn.k12.mo.us
Osage County ES — 300/PK-5
141 Wildcat Dr 65051 — 573-897-4226
Lorie Winslow, prin. — Fax 897-3768

St. George S — 200/PK-8
PO Box 19 65051 — 573-897-3645
Lisa Grellner, prin. — Fax 897-2148

Lockwood, Dade, Pop. 928
Lockwood R-I SD — 300/PK-12
400 W 4th St 65682 — 417-232-4513
Clay Lasater, supt. — Fax 232-4187
www.lockwoodschools.org
Lockwood ES — 200/PK-8
408 Locust St 65682 — 417-232-4528
Joey Graves, prin. — Fax 232-4875

Immanuel Lutheran S — 100/PK-8
PO Box H 65682 — 417-232-4530
Marsha Caldwell, prin. — Fax 232-4476

Lonedell, Franklin
Lonedell R-14 SD — 300/PK-8
7466 Highway FF 63060 — 636-629-4974
Jenny Ulrich, supt. — Fax 629-5561
www.lonedell.org/
Lonedell R 14 S — 300/PK-8
7466 Highway FF 63060 — 636-629-0401
Wayne Dierker, prin. — Fax 629-5561

Lone Jack, Jackson, Pop. 1,030
Lone Jack C-6 SD — 600/PK-12
313 S Bynum Rd 64070 — 816-697-3539
Matthew Tarwater, supt. — Fax 566-3128
www.lonejackc6.net
Lone Jack ES — 300/PK-6
600 N Bynum Rd 64070 — 816-697-2811
Katheryn Butler, prin. — Fax 566-2473

Loose Creek, Osage

Immaculate Conception S — 100/K-8
PO Box 68 65054 — 573-897-3516
Rita Stiefermann, prin. — Fax 897-4271

Louisiana, Pike, Pop. 3,291
BONCL R-X SD — 50/PK-8
23526 Pike 9247 63353 — 573-754-5412
C. Huckstep-Spangler, supt. — Fax 754-7981
www.bonclbluejays.com
BONCL R-X S — 50/PK-8
23526 Pike 9247 63353 — 573-754-5412
C. Huckstep-Spangler, prin. — Fax 754-7981

Louisiana R-II SD — 700/PK-12
3321 Georgia St 63353 — 573-754-4261
Dr. Todd Smith, supt. — Fax 754-4319
louisianarii.org
Louisiana ES — 400/PK-5
500 Haley Ave 63353 — 573-754-6904
Stacy Hamlett, prin. — Fax 754-3122
Louisiana MS — 200/6-8
3321 Georgia St 63353 — 573-754-5340
Nicholas Heggemann, prin. — Fax 754-5377

Ludlow, Livingston, Pop. 131
Southwest Livingston County R-I SD — 200/PK-12
4944 Highway DD 64656 — 660-738-4433
Cinthia Barnes, supt. — Fax 738-4441
www.southwestr1.org/
Southwest Livingston County ES — 100/PK-6
4944 Highway DD 64656 — 660-738-4433
Scott Calhoun, prin. — Fax 738-4115

Macks Creek, Camden, Pop. 238
Macks Creek R-V SD — 400/PK-12
245 State Rd N 65786 — 573-363-5909
Dr. Joshua Phillips, supt. — Fax 363-5981
www.mcreek.k12.mo.us
Macks Creek ES — 200/PK-6
245 State Rd N 65786 — 573-363-5977
Dr. Jori Phillips, prin. — Fax 363-5981

Macon, Macon, Pop. 5,339
Macon County R-I SD — 1,400/PK-12
702 N Missouri St 63552 — 660-385-5719
Scott Jarvis, supt. — Fax 385-7179
www.macon.k12.mo.us
Macon County ES — 700/PK-5
702 N Missouri St 63552 — 660-385-2118
Susan Hazen, prin. — Fax 385-7689
Macon County MS — 300/6-8
702 N Missouri St 63552 — 660-385-2189
Bruce Weimer, prin. — Fax 385-7230

Immaculate Conception S — 100/K-8
401 N Rubey St 63552 — 660-385-2711
Janice Dubbert, prin. — Fax 385-2839

Madison, Monroe, Pop. 551
Madison C-3 SD — 200/PK-12
309 S Thomas St 65263 — 660-291-5115
Shane Stocks, supt. — Fax 291-5006
www.madison.k12.mo.us
Madison ES — 100/PK-6
309 S Thomas St 65263 — 660-291-4515
James Lafferty, prin. — Fax 291-5006

Middle Grove C-1 SD — 50/K-8
11476 Route M 65263 — 660-291-8583
Warren Salmons, supt. — Fax 291-8584
www.middlegrove.k12.mo.us/
Middle Grove ES — 50/K-8
11476 Route M 65263 — 660-291-8583
Warren Salmons, prin. — Fax 291-8584

Maitland, Holt, Pop. 343
Nodaway-Holt R-VII SD
Supt. — See Graham
Nodaway-Holt ES — 100/PK-6
409 Hickory St 64466 — 660-935-2514
Rita Carroll, prin. — Fax 935-2242

Malden, Dunklin, Pop. 4,199
Malden R-I SD — 900/PK-12
505 Burkhart St 63863 — 573-276-5794
Kenneth Cook, supt. — Fax 276-5796
www.malden.k12.mo.us/
Malden ES — 500/PK-6
505 Burkhart St 63863 — 573-276-5791
Kent Luke, prin. — Fax 276-5792

Malta Bend, Saline, Pop. 249
Malta Bend R-V SD — 100/K-12
PO Box 10 65339 — 660-595-2371
John Angelhow, supt. — Fax 595-2430
mbtigers.weebly.com
Malta Bend ES — 50/K-6
PO Box 10 65339 — 660-595-2371
Aaron Feagan, prin. — Fax 595-2430

Manchester, Saint Louis, Pop. 17,723
Parkway C-2 SD
Supt. — See Chesterfield
Barretts ES — 400/PK-5
1780 Carman Rd 63021 — 314-415-6000
Dr. Kelli Moreton, prin. — Fax 415-6012
Carman Trails ES — 400/PK-5
555 S Weidman Rd 63021 — 314-415-6100
Allison Love, prin. — Fax 415-6119
Parkway South MS — 600/6-8
760 Woods Mill Rd 63011 — 314-415-7200
Amy Branson, prin. — Fax 415-7213
Parkway Southwest MS — 700/6-8
701 Wren Ave 63021 — 314-415-7300
Aaron McPherson, prin. — Fax 415-7334
Pierremont ES — 400/K-5
1215 Dauphine Ln 63011 — 314-415-6600
Joseph Hawkinson, prin. — Fax 415-6612
Wren Hollow ES — 400/PK-5
655 Wren Ave 63021 — 314-415-6850
Katie Terbrock, prin. — Fax 415-6869

Christ Prince of Peace S — 300/PK-8
417 Weidman Rd 63011 — 636-394-6840
Joanne Hoormann, prin. — Fax 594-0082
St. Joseph S — 400/PK-8
555 Saint Joseph Ln 63021 — 636-391-1253
Darrel Sturgill, prin. — Fax 391-1462

Mansfield, Wright, Pop. 1,287
Mansfield R-IV SD — 700/PK-12
316 W Ohio St 65704 — 417-924-8458
Dr. Nathan Moore, supt. — Fax 924-3427
www.mansfieldschool.net
Mansfield JHS — 200/6-8
305 W Ohio St 65704 — 417-924-8625
Dr. Gary Greene, prin. — Fax 924-8789
Wilder ES — 300/PK-5
415 W Ohio St 65704 — 417-924-3289
Gina Adams, prin. — Fax 924-3280

Maplewood, Saint Louis, Pop. 7,766
Maplewood Richmond Heights SD — 1,300/PK-12
7539 Manchester Rd 63143 — 314-644-4400
Karen I. Hall, supt. — Fax 781-3160
www.mrhschools.net
Maplewood Richmond Heights ECC — 400/PK-2
2801 Oakland Ave 63143 — 314-644-4405
Dr. Cynthia Hebenstreit, prin. — Fax 781-1896
Maplewood Richmond Heights MS — 100/7-8
7539 Manchester Rd 63143 — 314-644-4406
Dittrich Michael, prin. — Fax 781-4629
Other Schools – See Richmond Heights

Marble Hill, Bollinger, Pop. 1,464
Woodland R-IV SD — 900/K-12
RR 5 Box 3210 63764 — 573-238-3343
Michael Kiehne, supt. — Fax 238-2153
www.woodland.k12.mo.us/
Woodland ES — 400/K-4
RR 5 Box 3210 63764 — 573-238-2822
Misty Dildine, prin. — Fax 238-3319
Woodland MS — 300/5-8
RR 5 Box 3210 63764 — 573-238-2656
Brian Hukel, prin. — Fax 238-0133

Marceline, Linn, Pop. 2,210
Marceline R-V SD — 600/PK-12
400 E Santa Fe Ave 64658 — 660-376-3371
Dr. Gabe Edgar Ed.D., supt. — Fax 376-6001
www.marcelineschools.org
Disney ES — 300/K-5
420 E California Ave 64658 — 660-376-2166
Sarah Dunham, prin. — Fax 376-6026
Marceline MS — 100/6-8
314 E Santa Fe Ave 64658 — 660-376-2411
Matt Finch, prin. — Fax 376-6016
Marceline R-V Early Learning Center — 50/PK-PK
223 E Santa Fe Ave 64658 — 660-376-2422
Dawn Lichtenberg, dir. — Fax 376-6001

Father McCartan Memorial S 100/PK-8
327 S Kansas Ave 64658 660-376-3580
Casey Dillon, prin. Fax 376-2836

Marionville, Lawrence, Pop. 2,171
Marionville R-IX SD 700/PK-12
PO Box 409 65705 417-258-7755
Dr. Larry Brown, supt. Fax 258-2564
www.marionville.us
Marionville ES 300/PK-5
PO Box 409 65705 417-258-2550
Greg Hopkins, prin. Fax 258-2564
Marionville MS 200/6-8
PO Box 409 65705 417-258-2531
Shane Moseman, prin. Fax 258-2564

Marquand, Madison, Pop. 203
Marquand-Zion R-VI SD 200/K-12
205 E Morley 63655 573-783-3388
Scott Blake, supt. Fax 783-3067
mz.k12.mo.us
Marquand ES 100/K-6
205 E Morley 63655 573-783-3388
Scott Blake, prin. Fax 783-3067

Marshall, Saline, Pop. 12,591
Hardeman R-X SD 100/K-8
21051 Highway D 65340 660-837-3400
Paul Vaillancourt, admin. Fax 837-3411
www.hardemanschool.com
Hardeman ES 100/K-8
21051 Highway D 65340 660-837-3400
Paul Vaillancourt, admin. Fax 837-3411

Marshall SD 2,400/PK-12
860 W Vest St 65340 660-886-7414
Dr. Carol Maher, supt. Fax 886-5641
www.marshallschools.com
Benton ES 200/K-1
467 S Ellsworth Ave 65340 660-886-3993
Paige Clouse, prin. Fax 886-7188
Bueker MS 700/5-8
565 S Odell Ave 65340 660-886-6833
Lance Tobin, prin. Fax 886-7529
Early Childhood Learning Center PK-PK
945 N Miami Ave 65340 660-886-9066
Renee Vaught, prin. Fax 831-1989
Eastwood ES 200/K-K, 3-4
313 E Eastwood St 65340 660-886-7100
Amy Heuman, prin. Fax 886-3812
Northwest ES 200/K-K, 4-4
411 N Benton Ave 65340 660-886-2993
Janine Machholz, prin. Fax 886-3875
Southeast ES 200/K-K, 2-2
215 E Mitchell St 65340 660-886-2655
Rendy Maupin, prin. Fax 886-6824

St. Peter S 200/PK-8
368 S Ellsworth Ave 65340 660-886-6390
Mary McCoy, prin. Fax 886-6606

Marshfield, Webster, Pop. 6,529
Marshfield R-I SD 3,100/PK-12
170 State Highway DD 65706 417-859-2120
David Steward, supt. Fax 859-2193
www.mjays.us
Hubble PS 600/PK-1
600 N Locust St 65706 417-859-2120
Laura O'Quinn, prin. Fax 859-7332
Marshfield JHS 700/6-8
660 N Locust St 65706 417-859-2120
Doug Summers, prin. Fax 859-4970
Shook ES 500/4-5
180 State Highway DD 65706 417-859-2120
Heather Sample, prin. Fax 859-5186
Webster ES 400/2-3
650 N Locust St 65706 417-859-2120
Michelle Mitchell, prin. Fax 859-7333

Marthasville, Warren, Pop. 1,124
Washington SD
Supt. — See Washington
Marthasville ES 300/K-6
800 E Main St 63357 636-231-2650
Joselyn Schluss, prin. Fax 231-2605

St. Ignatius S 100/PK-8
19129 Mill Rd 63357 636-932-4444
Dr. Arlesa Leopold, prin. Fax 932-4479
St. Vincent de Paul S 100/PK-8
13495 S State Highway 94 63357 636-433-2466
Mark Spann, prin. Fax 433-2924

Martinsburg, Audrain, Pop. 303

St. Joseph S 100/K-8
401 E Kellett St 65264 573-492-6283
Randy Struck, prin. Fax 492-6346

Maryland Heights, Saint Louis, Pop. 26,834
Parkway C-2 SD
Supt. — See Chesterfield
McKelvey ES 500/K-5
1751 McKelvey Rd 63043 314-415-6500
Dr. Kim Cohen, prin. Fax 415-6512

Pattonville R-3 SD
Supt. — See Saint Ann
Parkwood ES 400/K-5
3199 Parkwood Ln 63043 314-213-8015
Melissa Yount-Ott, prin. Fax 213-8615
Pattonville Heights MS 500/6-8
195 Fee Fee Rd 63043 314-213-8033
Scot Mosher, prin. Fax 213-8633
Remington Traditional S 400/K-8
102 Fee Fee Rd 63043 314-213-8016
Don Furjes, prin. Fax 213-8616

Rose Acres ES 400/K-5
2905 Rose Acres Ln 63043 314-213-8017
Steve Vargo, prin. Fax 213-8617

Holy Spirit S 200/PK-8
3120 Parkwood Ln 63043 314-739-1934
Jill Gould, prin. Fax 739-7703

Maryville, Nodaway, Pop. 11,837
Maryville R-II SD 1,500/PK-12
1429 S Munn Ave 64468 660-562-3255
Becky Albrecht, supt. Fax 562-4113
www.maryville.k12.mo.us
Field ES 600/PK-4
418 E 2nd St 64468 660-562-3233
Brian Lynn, prin. Fax 562-2735
Maryville MS 400/5-8
525 W South Hills Dr 64468 660-562-3244
Kevin Pitts, prin. Fax 562-4138

St. Gregory Barbarigo S 100/PK-8
315 S Davis St 64468 660-582-2462
Susan Martin, prin. Fax 582-2496

Matthews, New Madrid, Pop. 626
New Madrid County R-I SD
Supt. — See New Madrid
Matthews ES 200/PK-5
PO Box 118 63867 573-471-0077
Angela Hanlin, prin. Fax 471-3410

Maysville, DeKalb, Pop. 1,100
Maysville R-I SD 600/K-12
PO Box 68 64469 816-449-2308
Robert Smith, supt. Fax 449-5678
www.maysville.k12.mo.us
Maysville ES 300/K-6
PO Box 68 64469 816-449-2284
Stacy Blythe, prin. Fax 449-5678

Meadville, Linn, Pop. 461
Meadville R-IV SD 200/K-12
PO Box 217 64659 660-938-4111
Ron Holcer, supt. Fax 938-4100
meadvillemoeagles.org/
Meadville ES 100/K-6
PO Box 217 64659 660-938-4112
Misty Burnett, prin. Fax 938-4100

Memphis, Scotland, Pop. 1,807
Scotland County R-I SD 600/PK-12
438 W Lovers Ln 63555 660-465-8531
Ryan Bergeson, supt. Fax 465-8636
scotland.k12.mo.us/
Scotland County ES 300/PK-6
438 W Lovers Ln 63555 660-465-8532
Erin Tallman, prin. Fax 465-8636

Mendon, Chariton, Pop. 171
Northwestern R-I SD 200/PK-12
PO Box 43 64660 660-272-3201
Eric Hoyt, supt. Fax 272-3419
www.northwestern.k12.mo.us
Northwestern ES 100/PK-6
PO Box 43 64660 660-272-3201
Eric Hoyt, admin. Fax 272-3419

Mercer, Mercer, Pop. 315
North Mercer County R-III SD 200/PK-12
PO Box 648 64661 660-382-4214
Dan Owens, supt. Fax 382-4239
www.northmercer.k12.mo.us
North Mercer ES 100/PK-6
PO Box 648 64661 660-382-4214
Wes Guilkey, prin. Fax 382-4239

Mexico, Audrain, Pop. 11,278
Mexico SD 59 2,400/PK-12
2101 Lakeview Rd 65265 573-581-3773
Dr. Zachary Templeton, supt. Fax 581-1794
www.mexicoschools.net
Field ES 400/K-5
704 W Boulevard St 65265 573-581-5268
Amber Crane, prin. Fax 581-0690
Hawthorne ES 400/K-5
1250 W Curtis St 65265 573-581-3064
Melissa Chastain, prin. Fax 581-3065
McMillan ES 200/K-5
1101 E Anderson St 65265 573-581-5029
Rebecca Moppin, prin. Fax 581-3175
Mexico ECC 100/PK-PK
1101 E Anderson St 65265 573-581-3500
Emily Schmidt, dir. Fax 581-1794
Mexico MS 500/6-8
1200 W Boulevard St 65265 573-581-4664
Deb Haag, prin. Fax 581-8440

St. Brendan S 200/PK-8
620 S Clark St 65265 573-581-2443
Kathryn Coulson, prin. Fax 581-2571

Miami, Saline, Pop. 175
Miami R-I SD 50/PK-8
34520 N Highway 41 65344 660-852-3269
Lori Price, supt. Fax 852-3259
www.miami-mustangs.com
Miami R-1 S 50/PK-8
34520 N Highway 41 65344 660-852-3269
Lori Price, supt. Fax 852-3259

Milan, Sullivan, Pop. 1,949
Milan C-2 SD 700/PK-12
373 S Market St 63556 660-265-4414
Dr. Ben Yocom, supt. Fax 265-4315
www.milan.k12.mo.us/
Milan ES 300/PK-6
373 S Market St 63556 660-265-4416
Ashley Pauley, prin. Fax 265-4315

Miller, Lawrence, Pop. 697
Miller R-II SD 500/PK-12
110 W 6th St 65707 417-452-3515
Dr. Dustin Storm, supt. Fax 452-2709
www.millerschools.org
Central ES 300/PK-6
108 S Highway 39 65707 417-452-3512
John Knight, prin. Fax 452-3264

Round Grove Christian Academy 100/PK-12
877 Highway UU 65707 417-452-2324
Tammy McCanless, admin. Fax 452-2573

Millersville, Cape Girardeau
Jackson R-II SD
Supt. — See Jackson
Millersville ES 100/K-3
377 State Highway B 63766 573-243-9585
Dr. Lance McClard, prin. Fax 243-9585

Missouri City, Clay, Pop. 255
Missouri City SD 56 50/K-8
PO Box 259 64072 816-750-4391
Jay Jackson, supt. Fax 750-4394
www.mocity.k12.mo.us/
Missouri City ES 50/K-8
PO Box 259 64072 816-750-4391
Jay Jackson, prin. Fax 750-4394

Moberly, Randolph, Pop. 13,647
Moberly SD 2,300/K-12
926 Kwix Rd 65270 660-269-2600
Dr. Matthew S. Miller, supt. Fax 269-2611
moberly.k12.mo.us
Gratz Brown ES 500/3-5
1320 Gratz Brown St 65270 660-269-2694
Angela Doss, prin. Fax 269-8093
Moberly MS 500/6-8
920 Kwix Rd 65270 660-269-2680
Wes Land, prin. Fax 269-8519
North Park ES 300/K-2
909 Porter St 65270 660-269-2630
Cindy Beltz, prin. Fax 269-8094
South Park ES 300/K-2
701 S 4th St 65270 660-269-2640
Anna Nordmeyer, prin. Fax 269-2695

Maranatha SDA S 50/K-8
1400 E McKinsey St 65270 660-263-8600
St. Pius X S 200/PK-8
210 S Williams St 65270 660-263-5500
Melissa Renfro, prin. Fax 263-5744

Mokane, Callaway, Pop. 182
South Callaway County R-II SD 800/PK-12
10135 State Road C 65059 573-676-5225
Kevin Hillman, supt. Fax 676-5134
www.sc.k12.mo.us/
South Callaway ECC 200/PK-2
10135 State Road C 65059 573-676-5215
Leigh Dunlap B.A., prin. Fax 676-5063
South Callaway ES 200/3-5
10135 State Road C 65059 573-676-5218
Corey Pontius, prin. Fax 676-5953
South Callaway MS 200/6-8
10135 State Road C 65059 573-676-5216
Gary Bonsall, prin. Fax 676-5347

Monett, Barry, Pop. 8,746
Monett R-I SD 2,300/PK-12
900 E Scott St 65708 417-235-7422
Dr. Brad Hanson, supt. Fax 235-1415
www.monettschools.org
Monett Central Park ES 300/3-4
1010 7th St 65708 417-354-2168
Jennifer Wallace, prin. Fax 354-2198
Monett ES 600/PK-2
601 Learning Ln 65708 417-235-3411
Sarah Garner, prin. Fax 235-3086
Monett IS 400/5-6
711 9th St 65708 417-235-6151
Cherie Austin, prin. Fax 236-0248
Monett MS 400/7-8
710 9th St 65708 417-235-6228
Dr. Jonathan Apostol, prin. Fax 235-3278

St. Lawrence S 100/PK-6
407 7th St 65708 417-235-3721
Vicki Irsik, prin. Fax 235-3721

Monroe City, Monroe, Pop. 2,481
Monroe City R-I SD 700/PK-12
401 US Highway 24 36 E 63456 573-735-4631
Tracy Bottoms, supt. Fax 735-2413
monroe.k12.mo.us
Monroe City ES 300/PK-4
420 N Washington St 63456 573-735-4632
Kim Shinn, prin. Fax 735-2413
Monroe City MS 200/5-8
430 N Washington St 63456 573-735-4742
Troy Patterson, prin. Fax 735-2413

Holy Rosary S 200/K-8
620 S Main St 63456 573-735-2422
Sr. Suzanne Walker, prin. Fax 735-3091

Montgomery City, Montgomery, Pop. 2,792
Montgomery County R-II SD 1,300/PK-12
418 N Highway 19 63361 573-564-2278
Michael Gray, supt. Fax 782-8700
www.mc-wildcats.org
Montgomery City ES 400/PK-5
817 N Harper St 63361 573-564-2278
Jeania Burton, prin. Fax 782-8703
Montgomery County MS 300/6-8
418 N Highway 19 63361 573-564-2278
Chris Parker, prin. Fax 782-8702
Other Schools – See Jonesburg

Immaculate Conception S 100/PK-8
407 W 3rd St 63361 573-564-2679
Randy Struck, prin. Fax 564-2305

Montrose, Henry, Pop. 383
Montrose R-XIV SD 100/K-12
307 E 2nd St 64770 660-693-4812
Denise Fast, supt. Fax 693-4594
www.montrose.k12.mo.us
Montrose R-XIV S 100/K-8
307 E 2nd St 64770 660-693-4812
Denise Fast, supt. Fax 693-4594

St. Mary S 50/PK-8
608 Kansas Ave 64770 660-693-4502
Fax 693-4713

Morrisville, Polk, Pop. 377
Marion C. Early R-V SD 600/PK-12
5309 S Main Ave 65710 417-376-2255
Dr. Josh Angel, supt. Fax 376-3243
www.mceonline.net
Early ES 300/PK-5
5309 S Main Ave 65710 417-376-2215
Dr. Brandon Randall, prin. Fax 376-4350
Early JHS 100/6-8
5309 S Main Ave 65710 417-376-2216
Dr. Joel Carey, prin. Fax 376-7622

Moscow Mills, Lincoln, Pop. 2,430
Lincoln County R-III SD
Supt. — See Troy
Cappel ES 400/K-5
121 Hampel Rd 63362 636-356-4246
Dr. Megan Crawmer, prin. Fax 356-0016
Troy South MS 800/6-8
200 S Campus Rd 63362 636-462-5125
Amy Salvo Ed.D., prin. Fax 462-5126

Mound City, Holt, Pop. 1,154
Mound City R-II SD 200/PK-12
708 Nebraska St 64470 660-442-3737
Kenneth Eaton, supt. Fax 442-5941
mndcty.k12.mo.us
Mound City ES 100/PK-8
708 Nebraska St 64470 660-442-5420
Carolyn Hall, prin. Fax 442-5282

Mountain Grove, Wright, Pop. 4,721
Manes R-V SD 50/PK-8
8939 Highway 95 65711 417-668-5313
Mary Holder, supt. Fax 668-5537
www.manes.k12.mo.us/
Manes S 50/PK-8
8939 Highway 95 65711 417-668-5313
Mary Holder, prin. Fax 668-5537

Mountain Grove R-III SD 1,400/K-12
PO Box 806 65711 417-926-3177
Jim Dickey, supt. Fax 926-4564
www.mg.k12.mo.us
Mountain Grove ES 600/K-4
PO Box 806 65711 417-926-3177
Melissa Glenn, prin. Fax 926-7474
Mountain Grove MS 400/5-8
PO Box 806 65711 417-926-3177
Lori Golden, prin. Fax 926-1673

Mountain View, Howell, Pop. 2,694
Mountain View-Birch Tree R-III SD 1,200/PK-12
1054 Old Highway 60 65548 417-934-5408
Dr. Don Christensen, supt. Fax 934-5404
mvbt.k12.mo.us
Birch Tree ES 200/PK-5
1054 Old Highway 60 65548 573-292-3106
Robert Bennett, prin. Fax 292-4421
Liberty MS 300/6-8
1054 Old Highway 60 65548 417-934-2020
Ryan Chowning, prin. Fax 934-1329
Mountain View ES 500/PK-5
1054 Old Highway 60 65548 417-934-2550
Loren Smith, prin. Fax 934-5417

Mount Vernon, Lawrence, Pop. 4,491
Mt. Vernon R-V SD 1,400/K-12
731 S Landrum St 65712 417-466-7573
Scott Cook, supt. Fax 466-7058
www.mtvernon.k12.mo.us
Mount Vernon ES 300/K-2
301 E Blaze Rd 65712 417-466-7512
Christina West, prin. Fax 466-7527
Mount Vernon IS 300/3-5
260 W Highway 174 65712 417-466-2312
Dulcie Price, prin. Fax 466-2336
Mount Vernon MS 300/6-8
731 S Landrum St 65712 417-466-3137
Kevin Kultgen, prin. Fax 466-7058

Myrtle, Oregon
Couch R-I SD 200/PK-12
21922 Missouri 142 65778 417-938-4211
Dr. Sherry McMasters, supt. Fax 938-4267
www.couch.k12.mo.us
Couch ES 100/PK-6
21922 Missouri 142 65778 417-938-4215
Kelly Roberts, prin. Fax 938-4267

Naylor, Ripley, Pop. 602
Naylor R-II SD 400/K-12
101 Batten St 63953 573-399-2505
Terry Arnold, supt. Fax 399-2874
www.nayloreagles.com
Naylor ES 200/K-6
RR 2 Box 512 63953 573-399-2507
Stacey Roach, prin. Fax 399-2307

Neelyville, Butler, Pop. 467
Neelyville R-IV SD 600/PK-12
PO Box 8 63954 573-989-3813
Bradley Hagood, supt. Fax 989-3434
www.neelyville.k12.mo.us
Neelyville ES 200/3-6
PO Box 8 63954 573-989-3814
Aaron Burton, prin. Fax 989-3336
Other Schools – See Harviell

Neosho, Newton, Pop. 11,282
Neosho R-V SD 4,300/PK-12
418 Fairground Rd 64850 417-451-8600
Dan Decker, supt. Fax 451-8604
www.neoshosd.org
Benton ES 500/K-4
1120 Carl Sweeney Rd 64850 417-451-8610
Jody Martin, prin. Fax 451-8607
Carver ES 600/K-4
12350 Norway Rd 64850 417-451-8690
Satotha Burr, prin. Fax 451-8696
Central ES 200/K-4
301 Big Spring Dr 64850 417-451-8620
Christine Cawley, prin. Fax 451-8624
Field K 100/PK-K
302 Smith Ave 64850 417-451-8630
Michael Daugherty, prin. Fax 451-8633
Neosho JHS 300/7-8
14646 Kodiak Rd 64850 417-451-8660
Dr. Jenifer Cryer, prin. Fax 451-8687
Neosho MS 700/5-6
1420 Hale McGinty Dr 64850 417-451-8650
Charity Williams, prin. Fax 451-8649
South ES 200/K-4
1111 Wornall St 64850 417-451-8640
Lee Woodward, prin. Fax 451-8644
Other Schools – See Goodman

Westview C-6 SD 100/K-8
7441 Westview Rd 64850 417-776-2425
Misty Hailey, admin. Fax 776-1994
www.wc6.org
Westview ES 100/K-8
7441 Westview Rd 64850 417-776-2425
Misty Hailey, prin. Fax 776-1994

Neosho Christian S 100/PK-12
903 W South St 64850 417-451-1941
Lowell McInturff, supt. Fax 451-4059
Ozark Christian Academy 50/K-12
PO Box 786 64850 417-451-1100
Amanda Russell, head sch Fax 451-2059

Nevada, Vernon, Pop. 8,266
Nevada R-V SD 2,600/PK-12
811 W Hickory St 64772 417-448-2000
Dr. Tyson Beshore, supt. Fax 448-2006
www.nevada.k12.mo.us
Benton ES 200/2-2
500 E Vernon St 64772 417-448-2070
Brendon Smith, prin. Fax 448-2071
Bryan ES 400/PK-1
400 W Lee St 64772 417-448-2060
Deborah Spaur, prin. Fax 448-2067
Nevada MS 600/6-8
900 N Olive St 64772 417-448-2040
Geoff Stewart, prin. Fax 448-2048
Truman ES 600/3-5
901 W Ashland St 64772 417-448-2080
Misti Raney, prin. Fax 448-1920

St. Mary S 50/PK-4
330 N Main St 64772 417-667-7517
Fax 667-7517

New Bloomfield, Callaway, Pop. 652
New Bloomfield R-III SD 600/PK-12
307 Redwood Dr 65063 573-491-3700
Sarah Wisdom, supt. Fax 491-3696
www.nb.k12.mo.us
New Bloomfield ES 300/PK-6
307 Redwood Dr 65063 573-491-3700
Julia Gerloff, prin. Fax 491-3439

Newburg, Phelps, Pop. 466
Newburg R-II SD 500/PK-12
PO Box C 65550 573-762-9653
Dr. Lynne Reed, supt. Fax 762-3040
www.newburg.k12.mo.us
Newburg ES 300/PK-6
PO Box C 65550 573-762-2721
Russ Mudd, prin. Fax 762-2498

New Cambria, Macon, Pop. 195
Macon County R-IV SD 100/K-12
PO Box 70 63558 660-226-5615
John Dunham, supt. Fax 226-5618
www.mcr4.k12.mo.us/
Macon County ES 50/K-6
PO Box 70 63558 660-226-5615
Zach Bruner, prin. Fax 226-5618

New Franklin, Howard, Pop. 1,064
New Franklin R-I SD 500/PK-12
412 W Broadway 65274 660-848-2141
Dr. David Haggard, supt. Fax 848-2226
www.nfranklin.k12.mo.us/
New Franklin ES 200/PK-5
412 W Broadway 65274 660-848-2112
Dawn Shipp, prin. Fax 848-3061

New Haven, Franklin, Pop. 2,057
Franklin County R-II SD 100/K-8
3128 Highway Y 63068 573-237-2414
Carol Laboube, supt. Fax 237-4838
www.franklincountyr2.k12.mo.us/
Franklin County ES 100/K-8
3128 Highway Y 63068 573-237-2414
Carol Laboube, prin. Fax 237-4838

New Haven SD 500/K-12
100 Park Dr 63068 573-237-3231
Josh Hoener, supt. Fax 237-5959
www.newhavenschools.org
New Haven ES 300/K-6
100 Park Dr 63068 573-237-2141
Kasi Meyer, prin. Fax 237-4471
New Haven MS 100/7-8
100 Park Dr 63068 573-237-2900
Chip Stutzman, prin. Fax 237-5959

Washington SD
Supt. — See Washington
Campbellton ES 200/K-6
3693 Highway 185 63068 636-231-2450
Jennifer Meyer, prin. Fax 231-2455

New Madrid, New Madrid, Pop. 3,072
New Madrid County R-I SD 1,500/PK-12
310 US Highway 61 63869 573-688-2161
Dr. Sam Duncan, supt. Fax 688-2169
www.nmceaglenation.com
Central MS 300/6-8
308 US Highway 61 63869 573-688-2176
Thomas Drummond, prin. Fax 688-2245
New Madrid ES 300/PK-5
PO Box 130 63869 573-748-5568
Bradley Kolwyck, prin. Fax 748-5572
Other Schools – See Lilbourn, Matthews

Immaculate Conception S 100/PK-8
560 Powell Ave 63869 573-748-5123
Lynette Fowler, prin. Fax 748-5150

Newtown, Sullivan, Pop. 178
Newtown-Harris R-III SD 100/PK-12
306 N Main St 64667 660-794-2245
Kimberly Johnson, supt. Fax 794-2730
www.nhtigers.k12.mo.us/
Newtown-Harris ES 100/PK-6
306 N Main St 64667 660-794-2245
Misty Foster, prin. Fax 794-2730

Niangua, Webster, Pop. 404
Niangua R-V SD 300/PK-12
301 Rumsey St 65713 417-473-6101
Thomas Bransfield, supt. Fax 473-1056
www.nianguaschools.com
Niangua ES 200/PK-6
301 Rumsey St 65713 417-473-6101
Lori Allen, prin. Fax 473-1056

Nixa, Christian, Pop. 18,653
Nixa SD 5,900/PK-12
301 S Main St 65714 417-875-5400
Dr. Stephen Kleinsmith, supt. Fax 449-3190
www.nixapublicschools.net
Century ES 400/K-3
732 E North St 65714 417-724-3800
Cara Blevins, prin. Fax 725-7475
Early Childhood Center 200/PK-PK
301 S Main St 65714 417-724-4050
Lara Wilbur, prin. Fax 724-4068
Espy ES 400/K-4
220 S Gregg Rd 65714 417-875-5650
Karrie Long, prin. Fax 725-7448
High Pointe ES 400/K-4
900 Cheyenne Rd 65714 417-225-1600
Marilyn Hanna, prin. Fax 225-1608
Inman IS 400/5-6
1300 N Nicholas Rd 65714 417-449-3210
Liz Gredell, prin. Fax 449-3268
Mathews ES 500/K-4
605 S Gregg Rd 65714 417-449-3110
Brigette Golmen, prin. Fax 725-7474
Nixa JHS 900/7-8
205 North St 65714 417-875-5430
Jared Webster, prin. Fax 875-5426
Summit IS 500/4-6
890 Cheyenne Rd 65714 417-724-4000
Alysia Ackerman, prin. Fax 724-4008
Thomas S of Discovery 500/K-6
312 N Market St 65714 417-875-5600
Dr. Jennifer Chastain, prin. Fax 875-5608

Noel, McDonald, Pop. 1,745
McDonald County R-I SD
Supt. — See Anderson
Noel ES 400/3-8
318 Sulphur St 64854 417-475-3302
Samantha Buckridge, prin. Fax 475-6516
Noel PS 200/PK-2
14762 W State Highway 90 64854 417-475-3900
Deborah Pearson, prin. Fax 475-3955

Norborne, Carroll, Pop. 697
Norborne R-VIII SD 200/PK-12
PO Box 192 64668 660-593-3319
Troy Lentz, supt. Fax 593-3657
www.norborneschools.com
Norborne ES 100/PK-5
PO Box 192 64668 660-593-3616
Kyla Waters, prin. Fax 593-3657

Normandy, Saint Louis, Pop. 4,907
Normandy Schools Collaborative
Supt. — See Saint Louis
Lucas Crossing Elementary Complex 500/1-6
7837 Natural Bridge Rd 63121 314-493-0200
Tiffany McDonnell, prin. Fax 493-0297
Normandy MS 400/7-8
7855 Natural Bridge Rd 63121 314-493-0500
Andrew Miller, prin. Fax 493-0560

St. Ann S 200/PK-8
7532 Natural Bridge Rd 63121 314-381-0113
Jacob Reft, prin. Fax 381-1367

Norwood, Wright, Pop. 654
Norwood R-I SD 500/PK-12
675 N Hawk St 65717 417-746-4101
Shannon Crain, supt. Fax 746-9950
www.norwood.k12.mo.us/
Norwood ES 300/PK-6
675 N Hawk St 65717 417-746-4101
Christy Chadwell, prin. Fax 746-9950

Skyline R-II SD 100/PK-8
RR 72 Box 486 65717 417-683-4874
Jeanne Curtis, supt. Fax 683-5865
www.skylineschool.org
Skyline R-II S 100/PK-8
RR 72 Box 486 65717 417-683-4874
Jeanne Curtis, supt. Fax 683-5865

Novinger, Adair, Pop. 454
Adair County R-I SD 300/K-12
600 Rombauer Ave 63559 660-488-6411
Rick Roberts, supt. Fax 488-5400
www.novinger.k12.mo.us
Adair County ES 100/K-6
600 Rombauer Ave 63559 660-488-6412
Robin Daniels, prin. Fax 488-5400

Oak Grove, Jackson, Pop. 7,672
Oak Grove R-VI SD 2,000/PK-12
601 SE 12th St 64075 816-690-4156
Freddie Doherty, supt. Fax 690-3031
www.oakgrove.k12.mo.us
Oak Grove ES 500/3-5
501 SE 12th St 64075 816-690-4153
Peggy Tiffany, prin. Fax 690-8561
Oak Grove MS 500/6-8
401 SE 12th St 64075 816-690-4154
Tracy Kemp, prin. Fax 690-3976
Oak Grove PS 400/PK-2
500 SE 17th St 64075 816-690-8770
Laura Oyler, prin. Fax 690-6984

Oak Ridge, Cape Girardeau, Pop. 236
Oak Ridge R-VI SD 400/K-12
PO Box 10 63769 573-266-3218
Dr. Adrian Eftink, supt. Fax 266-0133
www.oakridger6schools.com
Oak Ridge R-VI ES 200/K-6
PO Box 10 63769 573-266-3232
Dr. Shawn Nix, prin. Fax 266-0133

Odessa, Lafayette, Pop. 5,180
Odessa R-VII SD 2,100/K-12
701 S 3rd St 64076 816-633-5316
Robert Brinkley, supt. Fax 633-8582
www.odessar7.net
McQuerry ES 500/K-2
607 S 3rd St 64076 816-633-5334
Daniel Armstrong, prin. Fax 633-5327
Odessa MS 500/6-8
607 S 5th St 64076 816-633-1500
Kendra Malizzi, prin. Fax 633-7101
Odessa Upper ES 400/3-5
1100 W Cox School Rd 64076 816-633-5396
Debbie Schweikert, prin. Fax 633-4299

O Fallon, Saint Charles, Pop. 77,920
Francis Howell R-III SD
Supt. — See Saint Charles
Weldon ES 700/K-5
7370 Weldon Spring Rd, 636-851-5500
Bryan Howse, prin. Fax 851-4136

Ft. Zumwalt R-II SD 18,500/PK-12
555 E Terra Ln 63366 636-240-2072
Dr. Bernard DuBray, supt. Fax 272-1059
www.fz.k12.mo.us
Dardenne ES 500/K-5
2621 Highway K, 636-978-4001
Dr. Daniel Boatman, prin. Fax 978-4012
Emge ES 500/K-5
250 Fallon Pkwy, 636-281-0261
Sheila Fraley, prin. Fax 281-0331
Forest Park ES 500/3-5
501 Sunflower Ln 63366 636-272-2704
Dr. Kim McKinley, prin. Fax 281-0007
Ft. Zumwalt North MS 1,000/6-8
210 Virgil St 63366 636-281-2356
Dr. Damon Burkhart, prin. Fax 281-0005
Ft. Zumwalt West MS 1,400/6-8
150 Waterford Crossing Dr, 636-272-6690
Dan Mcquerrey, prin. Fax 272-6361
Mount Hope ES 600/K-5
1099 Mount Hope Ln 63366 636-272-2717
Tania Farran, prin. Fax 281-0003
Mudd ES 400/K-2
610 Prince Ruppert Dr 63366 636-272-2709
Dr. Stephanie Mountain, prin. Fax 281-0008
Ostmann ES 500/K-5
200 Meriwether Lewis Dr, 636-281-3382
Cary Jennings, prin. Fax 281-3372
Pheasant Point ES 500/K-5
3450 Pheasant Meadow Dr, 636-379-0173
Dr. Greg Cicotte, prin. Fax 980-3650
Rock Creek ES 600/K-5
8970 Mexico Rd 63366 636-978-1611
Keith Jennings, prin. Fax 980-1653
Twin Chimneys ES 500/K-5
7396 Twin Chimneys Blvd, 636-240-0093
Jessica Trost, prin. Fax 240-0095
Westhoff ES 600/K-5
900 Homefield Blvd 63366 636-272-6710
Alicia Hooton, prin. Fax 272-6351
Other Schools – See Saint Peters, Wentzville

Wentzville R-IV SD
Supt. — See Wentzville
Crossroads ES 800/K-6
7500 Highway N, 636-625-4537
Damian Fay, prin. Fax 625-4447

Discovery Ridge ES 700/K-6
2523 Sommers Rd 63367 636-561-2354
Laura Bates, prin. Fax 561-2355
Frontier MS 900/7-8
9233 Highway DD, 636-625-1026
Jeri LaBrot, prin. Fax 625-1094
Lakeview ES 700/K-6
2501 Mexico Rd 63366 636-332-2923
Douglas Holler, prin. Fax 332-2924

Assumption S - O'Fallon 500/PK-8
203 W 3rd St 63366 636-240-4474
Laurie Zaleuke, prin. Fax 240-5795
First Baptist Christian Academy 300/PK-6
8750 Veterans Memorial Pkwy 63366 636-272-3220
Brandon Tucker, head sch Fax 240-3067

Old Monroe, Lincoln, Pop. 262

Immaculate Conception S 200/K-8
120 Maryknoll Rd 63369 636-661-5156
Janice Palmer, prin. Fax 665-5307

Olivette, Saint Louis, Pop. 7,540

Immanuel Lutheran Day S 200/PK-8
9733 Olive Blvd 63132 314-993-5004

Oran, Scott, Pop. 1,284
Oran R-III SD 400/K-12
PO Box 250 63771 573-262-2330
Adam Friga, supt. Fax 262-2330
www.oran.k12.mo.us
Oran ES 200/K-6
PO Box 250 63771 573-262-3435
Travis Spane, prin. Fax 262-3874

Guardian Angel S 100/PK-8
PO Box 188 63771 573-262-3583
Katrina Kluesner, prin. Fax 262-3583

Oregon, Holt, Pop. 851
South Holt County R-I SD 300/PK-12
201 S Barbour St 64473 660-446-2282
Bob Ottman, supt. Fax 446-2312
www.southholtr1.com
South Holt County ES 200/PK-6
201 S Barbour St 64473 660-446-2356
Ted Quinlin, prin. Fax 446-2312

Orrick, Ray, Pop. 827
Orrick R-XI SD 400/PK-12
100 Kirkham St 64077 816-770-0094
Aerin O'Dell, supt. Fax 496-3829
www.orrick.k12.mo.us
Orrick ES 200/PK-6
100 Kirkham St 64077 816-770-3922
Angela Bright, prin. Fax 496-3829

Osage Beach, Miller, Pop. 4,299
Camdenton R-III SD
Supt. — See Camdenton
Osage Beach ES 200/PK-4
1241 Nichols Rd 65065 573-348-2461
Bob Currier, prin. Fax 348-2820

School of the Osage R-II SD
Supt. — See Lake Ozark
Osage MS 400/6-8
635 Highway 42 65065 573-552-8326
Tony Slack, prin. Fax 552-8322
Osage Upper ES 400/3-5
626 Highway 42 65065 573-348-0004
Chris Wolf, prin. Fax 348-3058

Osborn, DeKalb, Pop. 422
Osborn R-0 SD 100/K-12
275 Clinton Ave 64474 816-675-2217
Richard Goin, supt. Fax 675-2222
www.osbornwildcats.org
Osborn ES 100/K-6
275 Clinton Ave 64474 816-675-2217
Derek Brady, prin. Fax 675-2222

Osceola, Saint Clair, Pop. 924
Osceola SD 500/PK-12
76 SE Highway WW 64776 417-646-8143
Danny Dewitt, supt. Fax 646-8075
www.osceola.k12.mo.us
Osceola ES 300/PK-6
76 SE Highway WW 64776 417-646-8333
Chris McClimans, prin. Fax 646-8075

Roscoe C-I SD 100/K-8
1515 SW 300 Rd 64776 417-646-2376
Lexie Scott, supt. Fax 646-2856
Roscoe S 100/K-8
1515 SW 300 Rd 64776 417-646-2376
Lexie Scott, supt. Fax 646-2856

Otterville, Cooper, Pop. 446
Otterville R-VI SD 200/K-12
101 W Georgetown St 65348 660-366-4391
Kim Oelrichs, supt. Fax 366-4293
www.ottervillervi.k12.mo.us
Otterville ES 100/K-6
101 W Georgetown St 65348 660-366-4621
Kim Oelrichs, admin. Fax 366-4293

Overland, Saint Louis, Pop. 15,614
Normandy Schools Collaborative
Supt. — See Saint Louis
Washington ES 100/1-6
1730 N Hanley Rd 63114 314-493-0810
Pamela Hollins, prin. Fax 493-0820

Ritenour SD
Supt. — See Saint Louis
Iveland ES 500/K-5
1836 Dyer Ave 63114 314-493-6330
Dr. Connelly Amanda, prin. Fax 429-6721
Ritenour MS 700/6-8
2500 Marshall Ave 63114 314-493-6250
Brian Rich, prin. Fax 429-6726

Owensville, Gasconade, Pop. 2,647
Gasconade County R-II SD 1,900/PK-12
PO Box 536 65066 573-437-2177
Dr. Chuck Garner, supt. Fax 437-5808
www.owensville.k12.mo.us
Owensville ES 600/PK-5
PO Box 536 65066 573-437-2171
Kent Sherrow, prin. Fax 437-5405
Owensville MS 400/6-8
PO Box 536 65066 573-437-2172
Teresa Schulte, prin. Fax 437-6704
Other Schools – See Gerald

Ozark, Christian, Pop. 17,472
Ozark R-VI SD 4,500/K-12
PO Box 166 65721 417-582-5900
Dr. Kevin Patterson, supt. Fax 582-5960
www.ozark.k12.mo.us
Ozark East ES 500/K-5
PO Box 166 65721 417-582-5906
Kent Sappington, prin. Fax 582-5785
Ozark North ES 600/K-5
PO Box 166 65721 417-582-5904
Karen Hood, prin. Fax 582-4786
Ozark South ES 500/K-5
PO Box 166 65721 417-582-5905
Dr. Kim Fitzpatrick, prin. Fax 582-4886
Ozark Upper ES 500/6-7
PO Box 166 65721 417-582-5903
Les Ford, prin. Fax 582-4802
Ozark West ES 500/K-5
PO Box 166 65721 417-582-5907
Sharon Underwood, prin. Fax 582-5761

Pacific, Franklin, Pop. 6,911
Meramec Valley R-III SD 3,400/PK-12
126 N Payne St 63069 636-271-1400
Dr. Edward Hillhouse, supt. Fax 271-1406
www.mvr3.k12.mo.us/
Meramec Valley ECC 100/PK-PK
2001 W Osage St 63069 636-271-1464
Tina Pittman, prin. Fax 271-1456
Meramec Valley MS 500/6-7
195 N Indian Pride Dr 63069 636-271-1425
Russ Rowbottom, prin. Fax 271-1465
Riverbend S 300/8-8
2085 Highway N 63069 636-271-1481
Mathieu Agee, prin. Fax 271-1485
Truman ES 300/K-5
101 Indian Warpath Dr 63069 636-271-1434
Marian Meinhardt, prin. Fax 271-1490
Zitzman ES 500/K-5
255 S Indian Pride Dr 63069 636-271-1440
Ketina Armstrong, prin. Fax 271-1443
Other Schools – See Catawissa, Robertsville, Villa Ridge

St. Bridget of Kildare S 100/PK-8
223 W Union St 63069 636-257-4533
Elizabeth Hanneken, prin. Fax 257-2504

Palmyra, Marion, Pop. 3,541
Palmyra R-I SD 1,100/K-12
PO Box 151 63461 573-769-2066
Kirt Malone, supt. Fax 769-4218
www.palmyra.k12.mo.us
Palmyra ES 400/K-4
PO Box 151 63461 573-769-3736
Lora Hillman, prin. Fax 769-4113
Palmyra MS 400/5-8
PO Box 151 63461 573-769-2174
Michael Kirt Malone, prin. Fax 769-4227

Paris, Monroe, Pop. 1,208
Paris R-II SD 400/PK-12
740 Cleveland St 65275 660-327-4112
Aaron Vitt, supt. Fax 327-4290
www.pariscoyotes.com
Paris ES 200/PK-6
725 Cleveland St 65275 660-327-5116
Wendy Reid, prin. Fax 327-5074
Paris JHS 100/7-8
25678 Business Highway 24 65275 660-327-4563
Chris Willingham, prin. Fax 327-4782

Park Hills, Saint Francois, Pop. 8,642
Central R-III SD 2,100/PK-12
200 High St 63601 573-431-2616
Dr. Desmond Mayberry, supt. Fax 431-2107
www.centralr3.org
Central ES 600/PK-2
900 Saint Francois Ave 63601 573-431-2616
Timothy McCoy, prin. Fax 431-8965
Central MS 500/6-8
801 Columbia St 63601 573-431-2616
Mike Harlow, prin. Fax 431-5393
West ES 500/3-5
403 W Fite St 63601 573-431-2616
Keith Groom, prin. Fax 431-2562

West St. Francois County R-IV SD
Supt. — See Leadwood
West County ES 500/PK-5
625 Chariton Ave 63601 573-562-7558
Todd Watson, prin. Fax 562-7512
West County MS 200/6-8
728 Highway M 63601 573-562-7544
Kevin Coffman, prin. Fax 562-2714

Parkville, Platte, Pop. 5,415
Park Hill SD
Supt. — See Kansas City

Graden ES — 500/K-5
8804 NW Highway 45 64152 — 816-359-4340
Dr. LuAnn Halverstadt, prin. — Fax 359-4349

Pasadena Hills, Saint Louis, Pop. 912
Normandy Schools Collaborative
Supt. — See Saint Louis
Jefferson ES — 200/1-6
4315 Cardwell Dr 63121 — 314-493-0100
Robin Vaulx-Williams, prin. — Fax 493-0110

Patton, Bollinger
Meadow Heights R-II SD — 500/PK-12
RR 5 Box 2365 63662 — 573-866-0060
Dr. John D. Wiggans, supt. — Fax 866-3240
www.meadowheights.k12.mo.us
Meadow Heights ES — 300/PK-6
RR 5 Box 2365 63662 — 573-866-2611
Donna Bristow, prin. — Fax 866-3719

Pattonsburg, Daviess, Pop. 346
Pattonsburg R-II SD — 200/PK-12
PO Box 200 64670 — 660-367-2111
Scott Ireland, supt. — Fax 367-4205
www.pattonsburg.k12.mo.us
Pattonsburg ES — 100/PK-5
PO Box 200 64670 — 660-367-4416
Alan McCrary, prin. — Fax 367-4205

Peculiar, Cass, Pop. 4,532
Raymore-Peculiar R-II SD — 6,600/PK-12
PO Box 789 64078 — 816-892-1300
Dr. Kari Monsees, supt. — Fax 892-1380
www.raypec.k12.mo.us
Peculiar ES — 300/K-5
PO Box 789 64078 — 816-892-1650
Rob Weida, prin. — Fax 892-1655
Raymore-Pecuiar South MS — 6-8
PO Box 789 64078 — 816-892-1500
Randy Randolph, prin. — Fax 892-1501
Shull Early Learning S — 200/PK-PK
PO Box 789 64078 — 816-892-1210
Mary Shatford, dir. — Fax 892-1211
Other Schools – See Raymore

Perryville, Perry, Pop. 8,127
Perry County SD 32 — 2,300/K-12
326 College St 63775 — 573-547-7500
Andrew Comstock, supt. — Fax 547-8572
www.perryville.k12.mo.us
Perry County MS — 700/5-8
326 College St 63775 — 573-547-7500
Milton Wick, prin. — Fax 547-1962
Perryville ES — 900/K-4
326 College St 63775 — 573-547-7500
Emily Koenig, prin. — Fax 547-6445

Immanuel Lutheran S — 200/PK-8
225 W South St 63775 — 573-547-6161
William Unzicker, admin. — Fax 547-8205
St. Vincent de Paul S — 400/PK-6
1007 W Saint Joseph St 63775 — 573-547-4300
Dr. Benjamin Johnson, prin. — Fax 547-1757

Pevely, Jefferson, Pop. 5,377
Dunklin R-V SD
Supt. — See Herculaneum
Pevely ES — 800/K-5
30 Main St 63070 — 636-479-5200
Angela Helms, prin. — Fax 479-7804

Philadelphia, Marion
Marion County R-II SD — 200/PK-12
2905 Highway D 63463 — 573-439-5913
Anthony Degrave, supt. — Fax 439-5914
www.marion.k12.mo.us/
Marion County ES — 100/PK-6
2905 Highway D 63463 — 573-439-5913
Anthony Degrave, admin. — Fax 439-5914

Pickering, Nodaway, Pop. 160
North Nodaway County R-VI SD
Supt. — See Hopkins
North Nodaway ES — 100/PK-5
201 E 6th St 64476 — 660-927-3322
Ashley Yount, prin. — Fax 927-3482

Piedmont, Wayne, Pop. 1,960
Clearwater R-I SD — 1,000/PK-12
RR 4 Box 1004 63957 — 573-223-7426
Deborah Hand, supt. — Fax 223-2932
cwtigers.net
Clearwater ES — 400/PK-4
RR 4 Box 1004 63957 — 573-223-7426
Michael Keller, prin. — Fax 223-7820
Clearwater MS — 300/5-8
RR 4 Box 1004 63957 — 573-223-7426
Lisa Towe, prin. — Fax 223-3117

Pierce City, Lawrence, Pop. 1,276
Pierce City R-VI SD — 700/PK-12
300 N Myrtle St 65723 — 417-476-2555
Dr. Russell Moreland, supt. — Fax 476-5213
www.pcschools.net
Central ES — 300/PK-4
PO Box E 65723 — 417-476-2255
Kristi Marion, prin. — Fax 476-5446
Pierce City MS — 100/5-8
300 N Myrtle St 65723 — 417-476-2842
Charity Rakoski, prin. — Fax 476-5405

St. Mary S — 100/K-8
202 Front St 65723 — 417-476-2824
Judy Harper, prin. — Fax 476-5103

Pilot Grove, Cooper, Pop. 759
Pilot Grove C-4 SD — 300/PK-12
107 School St 65276 — 660-834-6915
Ashley Groepper, supt. — Fax 834-6925
www.pilotgrove.k12.mo.us
Pilot Grove ES — 100/PK-6
107 School St 65276 — 660-834-4115
Lindsay Leonard, prin. — Fax 834-4401
Pilot Grove MS — 50/7-8
107 School St 65276 — 660-834-4415
Randall Glenn, prin. — Fax 834-4401

St. Joseph S — 100/PK-8
405 Harris St 65276 — 660-834-5600
Gary Littrell, prin. — Fax 834-5601

Pineville, McDonald, Pop. 780
McDonald County R-I SD
Supt. — See Anderson
Pineville ES — 200/3-8
202 E 8th St 64856 — 417-223-4346
Tamra Kester, prin. — Fax 223-4195
Pineville PS — 100/PK-2
340 Pleasant Ridge Rd 64856 — 417-223-3303
Thomas Henry, prin. — Fax 223-3305

Plato, Texas, Pop. 109
Plato R-V SD — 600/PK-12
PO Box A 65552 — 417-458-3333
Dr. Kim Hawk, supt. — Fax 458-4706
www.plato.k12.mo.us
Plato ES — 300/PK-5
PO Box A 65552 — 417-458-4700
Veronica Vergara, prin. — Fax 458-4706

Platte City, Platte, Pop. 4,565
Platte County R-III SD — 3,000/PK-12
998 Platte Falls Rd 64079 — 816-858-5420
Dr. Mike Reik, supt. — Fax 858-5593
www.plattecountyschooldistrict.com/
Compass ES — PK-5
401 Kentucky Ave 64079 — 816-858-0712
Chad Searcey, prin. — Fax 858-4982
Platte City MS — 600/6-8
900 Pirate Dr 64079 — 816-858-2036
Dr. Chris Miller, prin. — Fax 858-3748
Siegrist ES — 600/PK-3
1701 Branch St 64079 — 816-858-5977
Jennifer McClure, prin. — Fax 858-3942
Other Schools – See Kansas City

Our Savior Christian Academy — 100/PK-8
14155 N Highway 64079 — 816-866-1597
Holly Anderson, prin.

Plattsburg, Clinton, Pop. 2,263
Clinton County R-III SD — 700/PK-12
800 W Frost St 64477 — 816-539-2183
Dr. Sandy Steggall, supt. — Fax 539-2412
ccr3.k12.mo.us
Clinton County R-III MS — 200/6-8
800 W Frost St 64477 — 816-539-3920
Angie Courtney, prin. — Fax 539-2412
Ellis ES — 300/PK-5
603 W Frost St 64477 — 816-539-2187
Rachel Turner, prin. — Fax 539-3305

Pleasant Hill, Cass, Pop. 7,996
Pleasant Hill R-III SD — 2,100/PK-12
318 Cedar St 64080 — 816-540-3161
Dr. Wesley Townsend, supt. — Fax 540-5135
www.pleasanthillschools.com
Pleasant Hill ES — 300/3-4
327 N Mckissock St 64080 — 816-540-2220
Heidi Mackey, prin. — Fax 987-2040
Pleasant Hill IS — 300/5-6
1204 E 163rd St 64080 — 816-540-3156
Chandra Arbuckle, prin. — Fax 987-6316
Pleasant Hill MS — 300/7-8
1301 E Myrtle St 64080 — 816-540-2149
Greg Reeves, prin. — Fax 987-2017
Pleasant Hill PS — 500/PK-2
304 Eklund St 64080 — 816-540-2119
Sherry Helus, prin. — Fax 987-2752

Pleasant Hope, Polk, Pop. 604
Pleasant Hope R-VI SD — 1,000/PK-12
PO Box 387 65725 — 417-267-2850
Kelly Lowe, supt. — Fax 267-4373
www.phr6.org
Pleasant Hope ES — 300/PK-4
PO Box 387 65725 — 417-267-2277
Michael Methvin, prin. — Fax 267-4304
Pleasant Hope MS — 300/5-8
PO Box 387 65725 — 417-267-7701
Brent Dunning, prin. — Fax 267-9221

Pleasant Valley, Clay, Pop. 2,871
North Kansas City SD 74
Supt. — See Kansas City
Pleasant Valley ECC — 200/PK-PK
6800 Sobbie Rd 64068 — 816-321-5250
Sarah Monfore, prin. — Fax 321-5251

Point Lookout, Taney

School of the Ozarks — 300/K-12
PO Box 17 65726 — 417-690-2325
Brad Dolloff, dean — Fax 690-2327

Polo, Caldwell, Pop. 552
Mirabile C-1 SD — 100/PK-8
2954 SW State Route D 64671 — 816-586-4129
Troy Stemberger, supt. — Fax 586-2029
Mirabile ES — 100/PK-8
2954 SW State Route D 64671 — 816-586-4129
Troy Stemberger, prin. — Fax 586-2029

Polo R-VII SD — 400/K-12
300 W School St 64671 — 660-354-2326
Dr. Beverly Deis, supt. — Fax 354-2910
polo.k12.mo.us/
Polo ES — 100/K-4
300 W School St 64671 — 660-354-2200
Monica Palmer, prin. — Fax 354-3162
Polo MS — 100/5-8
300 W School St 64671 — 660-354-2200
Monica Palmer, prin. — Fax 354-3162

Poplar Bluff, Butler, Pop. 16,562
Poplar Bluff R-I SD — 4,800/PK-12
1110 N Westwood Blvd 63901 — 573-785-7751
Scott Dill, supt. — Fax 785-0336
www.poplarbluffschools.net
Field ES — 300/1-3
711 Nickey St 63901 — 573-785-4047
Jennifer Taylor, prin. — Fax 785-1867
Lake Road ES — 200/1-3
986 Highway AA 63901 — 573-785-4392
Erica Weadon, prin. — Fax 778-0303
Oak Grove ES — 400/1-3
3297 Oak Grove Rd 63901 — 573-785-6589
Jenifer Richardson, prin. — Fax 785-6589
O'Neal ES — 400/1-3
2300 Baugh Ln 63901 — 573-785-3037
Amy Dill, prin. — Fax 785-3037
Poplar Bluff ECC — 200/PK-PK
1235 N Main St 63901 — 573-785-6803
Carol Brotman, dir. — Fax 785-2827
Poplar Bluff JHS — 800/7-8
550 N Westwood Blvd 63901 — 573-785-5602
Bob Case, prin. — Fax 785-5004
Poplar Bluff Kindergarten — 400/K-K
1200 Camp Rd 63901 — 573-785-4905
Carol Brotman, prin. — Fax 785-4423
Poplar Bluff MS — 800/4-6
1300 Victory Ln 63901 — 573-785-5566
Brad Owings, prin. — Fax 785-6748

Sacred Heart S — 100/PK-8
111 N 8th St 63901 — 573-785-5836
Monique Gribbins, prin. — Fax 785-3908
Westwood Baptist Academy — PK-12
419 County Road 5231 63901 — 573-785-2922
Br. Josh Hawley, prin.

Portageville, New Madrid, Pop. 3,162
North Pemiscot County R-I SD
Supt. — See Wardell
Ross ES — 100/K-5
128 State Highway A 63873 — 573-359-0543
Emmons Kim, prin. — Fax 359-0930

Portageville SD — 800/PK-12
904 King Ave 63873 — 573-379-3855
Michael Allred, supt. — Fax 379-5817
www.portageville.k12.mo.us
Portageville ES — 400/PK-5
904 King Ave 63873 — 573-379-5706
K. Taylor, prin. — Fax 379-5817
Portageville MS — 200/6-8
902 King Ave 63873 — 573-379-3853
Barry Branscum, prin. — Fax 379-5817

St. Eustachius S — 100/PK-8
214 W 4th St 63873 — 573-379-3525
Patricia Rone, prin. — Fax 379-3525

Potosi, Washington, Pop. 2,627
Potosi R-III SD — 2,400/PK-12
400 N Mine St 63664 — 573-438-5485
Dr. Shawn McCue, supt. — Fax 438-5487
www.potosir3.org
Evans MS — 400/7-8
303 S Lead St 63664 — 573-438-2101
Brice Wilson, prin. — Fax 438-4635
Potosi ES — 800/PK-3
205 State Highway P 63664 — 573-438-2223
Jennifer Woods, prin. — Fax 438-4370
Trojan IS — 500/4-6
367 Intermediate Dr 63664 — 573-436-8108
Nicole Portell, prin. — Fax 436-8508

Prairie Home, Cooper, Pop. 279
Prairie Home R-V SD — 200/K-12
301 Highway 87 65068 — 660-841-5296
David Heeb, supt. — Fax 841-5513
www.prairiehome.k12.mo.us
Prairie Home ES — 100/K-6
301 Highway 87 65068 — 660-841-5296
Michele Rex, prin. — Fax 841-5513

Princeton, Mercer, Pop. 1,164
Princeton R-V SD — 400/PK-12
1008 E Coleman St 64673 — 660-748-3490
Jerry Girdner, supt. — Fax 748-3212
www.tigertown.k12.mo.us
Princeton ES — 200/PK-6
225 S College Ave 64673 — 660-748-3335
Dana Price, prin. — Fax 748-3334

Purdin, Linn, Pop. 189
Linn County R-I SD — 100/PK-12
PO Box 130 64674 — 660-244-5045
Ryan Livingston, supt. — Fax 244-5025
www.linnr1.k12.mo.us
Linn County R-1 S — 100/PK-12
PO Box 130 64674 — 660-244-5035
Candi Gray, prin. — Fax 244-5025

Purdy, Barry, Pop. 1,081
Purdy R-II SD — 700/K-12
PO Box 248 65734 — 417-442-3216
Dr. Steven Chancellor, supt. — Fax 442-3963
www.purdyk12.com
Purdy ES — 300/K-4
PO Box 248 65734 — 417-442-3217
Julie Dalton, prin. — Fax 442-7988
Purdy MS — 200/5-8
PO Box 248 65734 — 417-442-7066
Derek Banwart, prin. — Fax 442-7067

Puxico, Stoddard, Pop. 867
Puxico R-VIII SD 800/PK-12
481 N Bedford St 63960 573-222-3762
Dr. Kyle Dare, supt. Fax 222-3137
www.puxico.k12.mo.us
Puxico ES 300/PK-5
481 N Bedford St 63960 573-222-3542
Nathan Wills, prin. Fax 222-2441
Puxico JHS 200/6-8
481 N Bedford St 63960 573-222-3058
Jason Hill, prin. Fax 222-6373

Queen City, Schuyler, Pop. 595
Schuyler County R-I SD 600/PK-12
21701 N Highway 63 63561 660-766-2204
Robert Amen, supt. Fax 766-2400
www.schuyler.k12.mo.us
Schuyler County R-I ES 300/PK-6
21701 N Highway 63 63561 660-766-2296
Katherine Wayman, prin. Fax 766-2400

Qulin, Butler, Pop. 449
Twin Rivers R-X SD
Supt. — See Broseley
Qulin ES 300/K-8
406 Connecticut St 63961 573-328-4444
Seth McBroom, prin. Fax 328-4246

Ravenwood, Nodaway, Pop. 439
Northeast Nodaway County R-V SD 200/PK-12
PO Box 206 64479 660-937-3112
Ken Grove, supt. Fax 937-3110
www.nenr5.com
Northeast Nodaway ES 100/PK-6
PO Box 206 64479 660-937-3125
Jason McDowell, prin. Fax 937-3110

Raymondville, Texas, Pop. 354
Raymondville R-VII SD 200/PK-8
PO Box 10 65555 417-457-6237
Dana Buschmann, admin. Fax 457-6318
rvillc.k12.mo.us
Raymondville ES 200/PK-8
PO Box 10 65555 417-457-6237
Dana Buschmann, prin. Fax 457-6318

Raymore, Cass, Pop. 18,776
Raymore-Peculiar R-II SD
Supt. — See Peculiar
Bridle Ridge ES 500/K-5
900 E 195th St 64083 816-892-1700
Missy Mattingly, prin. Fax 892-1701
Creekmoor ES 500/K-5
1501 Creekmoor Dr 64083 816-892-1675
Jerrod Fellhauer, prin. Fax 892-1676
Eagle Glen ES 400/K-5
100 S Foxridge Dr 64083 816-892-1750
Robin Jones, prin. Fax 892-1751
Raymore ES 600/K-5
500 S Madison St 64083 816-892-1925
Jennika Miller, prin. Fax 892-1926
Raymore-Peculiar East MS 1,000/6-8
17509 E State Route 58 64083 816-388-4000
Katie Campbell, prin. Fax 388-4001
Stonegate ES 400/K-5
900 S Foxridge Dr 64083 816-892-1900
Douglas Becker, prin. Fax 892-1901
Timber Creek ES 400/K-5
310 E Calico Dr 64083 816-892-1950
Lovie Driskill, prin. Fax 892-1951

Raytown, Jackson, Pop. 28,561
Raytown C-2 SD 8,900/PK-12
6608 Raytown Rd 64133 816-268-7000
Dr. Allan Markley, supt. Fax 268-7019
www.raytownschools.org/
Blue Ridge ES 400/K-5
6410 Blue Ridge Blvd 64133 816-268-7200
Danielle Miles, prin. Fax 268-7205
Laurel Hills ES 400/K-5
5401 Lane Ave 64133 816-268-7230
Suzanne Brennamen, prin. Fax 268-7235
New Trails Early Learning Center 200/PK-PK
6325 Hunter St 64133 816-268-7430
Donna Denney, prin. Fax 268-7435
Raytown Central MS 600/6-8
10601 E 59th St 64133 816-268-7050
Dr. Jaime Sadich, prin. Fax 268-7055
Raytown South MS 600/6-8
8401 E 83rd St 64138 816-268-7380
Carl Calcara, prin. Fax 268-7385
Southwood ES 400/K-5
8015 Raytown Rd 64138 816-268-7280
Dr. Cathy Miller, prin. Fax 268-7285
Spring Valley ES 400/K-5
8838 E 83rd St 64138 816-268-7270
Dr. Judith Jordan Campbell, prin. Fax 268-7275
Three Trails Preschool PK-PK
8812 E Gregory Blvd 64133 816-268-7145
Tara Baker, admin. Fax 268-7149
Other Schools – See Kansas City

Reeds Spring, Stone, Pop. 896
Reeds Spring R-IV SD 1,900/PK-12
20281 State Highway 413 65737 417-272-8173
Dr. Michael Mason, supt. Fax 272-8656
www.rs-wolves.com
Reeds Spring ES 400/2-4
300 Wolves Ln 65737 417-272-1735
Laura Weber, prin. Fax 272-1754
Reeds Spring MS 300/7-8
345 Morrill Ln 65737 417-272-8245
Travis Kite, prin. Fax 272-8490
Reeds Spring PS 300/K-1
257 Elementary Rd 65737 417-272-3241
Karen Murray, prin. Fax 272-3239
Reeds Springs IS 300/5-6
175 Elementary Rd 65737 417 272 8250
Andrea Chavez, prin. Fax 272-1743
RSEEC-HD/RSEEC-FD PK-PK
257 Elementary Rd 65737 417-272-3241
Karen Murray, prin. Fax 272-3239

Renick, Randolph, Pop. 172
Renick R-V SD 100/PK-8
PO Box 37 65278 660-263-4886
Lisa Borden, supt. Fax 263-4249
www.renick.k12.mo.us
Renick R-V S 100/PK-8
PO Box 37 65278 660-263-4886
Lisa Borden, admin. Fax 263-4249

Republic, Greene, Pop. 14,495
Republic R-III SD 4,800/PK-12
518 N Hampton Ave 65738 417-732-3605
Chance Wistrom, supt. Fax 732-3609
www.republicschools.org
ECC 100/PK-PK
636 N Main Ave 65738 417-732-3670
Misty Kinsey, dir. Fax 732-3679
Lyon ES 500/K-5
201 E State Highway 174 65738 417-732-3630
Casey Mitchell, prin. Fax 732-3639
McCulloch ES 500/K-5
234 E Anderson St 65738 417-732-3620
Amber Shuck, prin. Fax 732-3629
Price ES 400/K-5
518 N Hampton Ave 65738 417-732-3690
Allan Brown, prin. Fax 732-3699
Republic MS 1,100/6-8
1 Tiger Dr 65738 417-732-3640
Allison Dishman, prin. Fax 732-3649
Schofield ES 400/K-5
235 E Anderson St 65738 417-732-3610
Christy Coursey, prin. Fax 732-3619
Sweeny ES 400/K-5
720 N Main Ave 65738 417-732-3670
Dr. Beth Engelhart Ed.D., prin. Fax 732-3679

Rich Fountain, Osage

Sacred Heart S 100/K-8
4309 Highway U 65035 573-744-5898
Linda Neuner, prin. Fax 744-5761

Rich Hill, Bates, Pop. 1,356
Rich Hill R-IV SD 400/K-12
703 N 3rd St 64779 417-395-2418
Heath Oates, supt. Fax 395-2407
www.richhill.k12.mo.us/
Rich Hill ES 200/K-6
320 E Poplar St 64779 417-395-2227
Jani Drake, prin. Fax 395-2963

Richland, Pulaski, Pop. 1,803
Richland R-IV SD 600/PK-12
714 E Jefferson Ave 65556 573-765-3241
Doug Smith, supt. Fax 765-5552
www.richlandbears.us
Richland ES 300/PK-6
714 E Jefferson Ave 65556 573-765-3812
Dr. Tina Turner, prin. Fax 765-5783
Richland JHS 100/7-8
714 E Jefferson Ave 65556 573-765-3711
Dr. Pamela Dawson, prin. Fax 765-5552

Swedeborg R-III SD 100/PK-8
17507 Highway T 65556 573-736-2735
Doug Jacobson, supt. Fax 736-5926
www.swedeborgpanthers.com
Swedeborg ES 100/PK-8
17507 Highway T 65556 573-736-2735
Doug Jacobson, prin. Fax 736-5926

Richmond, Ray, Pop. 5,691
Richmond R-XVI SD 1,600/PK-12
1017 E Main St 64085 816-776-6912
Dr. Mike Aytes, supt. Fax 776 5554
richmond.k12.mo.us
Dear ES 300/PK-1
701 E Main St 64085 816-776-5401
Piper Peterson, prin. Fax 776-2110
Richmond MS 400/6-8
715 S Wellington St 64085 816-776-5841
Jana Fleckenstine, prin. Fax 776-2788
Sunrise ES 500/2-5
401 Matt Waller Dr 64085 816-776-3059
Sara Terrill, prin. Fax 776-2608

Richmond Heights, Saint Louis, Pop. 8,447
Maplewood Richmond Heights SD
Supt. — See Maplewood
Maplewood Richmond Heights ES 500/3-6
1800 Princeton Pl 63117 314-644-4403
Dr. Jason Adams, prin. Fax 644-0315

Immacolata S 300/K-8
8910 Clayton Rd 63117 314-991-5700
Jennifer Stutsman, prin. Fax 991-9354
Little Flower S 200/PK-8
1275 Boland Pl 63117 314-781-4995
Andrew Long, prin. Fax 781-9179

Richwoods, Washington
Richwoods R-VII SD 200/PK-8
10788 State Highway A 63071 573-678-2257
Bethany Deal, supt. Fax 678 5207
www.richwoodsr7.org
Richwoods ES 200/PK-8
10788 State Highway A 63071 573-678-2257
Bethany Deal, supt. Fax 678-5207

Ridgeway, Harrison, Pop. 462
Ridgeway R-V SD 100/PK-12
305 Main St 64481 660-872-6813
Brenda Dougan, supt. Fax 872-6230
www.ridgewayowls.net/
Ridgeway ES 100/PK-6
305 Main St 64481 660-872-6813
Aaron Lewis, prin. Fax 872-6230

Risco, New Madrid, Pop. 338
Risco R-II SD 200/K-12
PO Box 17 63874 573-396-5568
Amy Baker, supt. Fax 396-5503
www.risco.k12.mo.us/
Risco ES 100/K-6
PO Box 17 63874 573-396-5501
Brandon Blankenship, prin. Fax 396-5503

Robertsville, Franklin
Meramec Valley R-III SD
Supt. — See Pacific
Robertsville ES 200/K-5
4000 Highway N 63072 636-271-1448
Keith Orris, prin. Fax 271-1450

Rock Port, Atchison, Pop. 1,303
Rock Port R-II SD 300/K-12
600 S Nebraska St 64482 660-744-6298
Craig Walker, supt. Fax 744-5539
rockport.k12.mo.us
Rock Port ES 200/K-6
600 S Nebraska St 64482 660-744-6294
Steve Waigand, prin. Fax 744-5539

Rockville, Bates, Pop. 161

Zion Lutheran S 50/K-8
10135 SE County Road 9526 64780 660-598-6213
Cynthia Hammons, prin.

Rocky Comfort, McDonald
McDonald County R-I SD
Supt. — See Anderson
Rocky Comfort ES 200/K-8
14814 E State Highway 76 64861 417-628-3781
Steven Sorrell, prin. Fax 628-3784

Rogersville, Greene, Pop. 3,000
Logan-Rogersville R-VIII SD 2,400/PK-12
100 E Front St 65742 417-753-2891
Dr. Shawn B. Randles, supt. Fax 753-3063
logrog.net/
Logan-Rogersville ES 400/2-3
7297 E Farm Road 164 65742 417-882-2626
Dr. Jennifer Katzin, prin. Fax 881-3444
Logan-Rogersville MS 400/7-8
8225 E Farm Road 174 65742 417-753-2896
Dr. Toby Kite, prin. Fax 753-3182
Logan-Rogersville PS 400/PK-1
512 Sentry Dr 65742 417-881-2947
Toni Bass, prin. Fax 753-5027
Logan-Rogersville Upper ES 500/4-6
306 S Mill St 65742 417-753-2996
Teri Jernigan, prin Fax 753-7033

Rolla, Phelps, Pop. 19,067
Rolla SD 31 4,100/PK-12
500A Forum Dr 65401 573-458-0100
Dr. Aaron Zalis, supt. Fax 458-0105
rolla.k12.mo.us
Rolla JHS 600/7-8
1360 Soest Rd 65401 573-458-0130
Monica Fulton, prin. Fax 458-0135
Rolla MS 900/4-6
1111 Soest Rd 65401 573-458-0120
Monica Davis, prin. Fax 458-0124
Truman ES 600/PK-3
1001 E 18th St 65401 573 458 0180
Maragelly Harris, prin. Fax 458-0185
Twain ES 600/PK-3
1100 Mark Twain Dr 65401 573-458-0170
Matt Fridley, prin. Fax 458-0175
Wyman ES 500/PK-3
402 Lanning Ln 65401 573-458-0190
Dr. Corey Ray, prin. Fax 458-0195

Rolla-Immanuel Lutheran S 100/PK-1
807 W 11th St 65401 573-364-3915
Dawn Koenig, admin. Fax 364-3945
St. Patrick S 200/PK-8
19 Saint Patrick Ln 65401 573-364-1162
Michael Brooks, prin. Fax 364-0679

Rosebud, Gasconade, Pop. 404

Immanuel Lutheran S 50/PK-8
300 1st St N 63091 573-764-3495
Fax 764-3495

Rosendale, Andrew, Pop. 143
North Andrew County R-VI SD 400/K-12
9120 Highway 48 64483 816 567 2965
Jim Shultz, supt. Fax 567-2096
northandrew.org
North Andrew ES 200/K-5
9120 Highway 48 64483 816-567-2527
Mark McDaniel, prin. Fax 567-2096
North Andrew MS 100/6-8
9120 Highway 48 64483 816-567-2525
Jason Tolen, prin. Fax 567-2096

Rueter, Taney
Mark Twain R-VIII SD 100/PK-8
37707 US Highway 160 65744 417-785-4323
Joe Donley, supt. Fax 785-9810
www.marktwain.k12.mo.us
Twain ES 100/PK-8
37707 US Highway 160 65744 417-785-4323
Joe Donley, admin. Fax 785-9810

Rushville, Buchanan, Pop. 301
Buchanan County R-IV SD
Supt. — See De Kalb

Rushville ES 200/PK-6
8681 SW State Route 116 64484 816-688-7777
Jennifer Dittemore, prin. Fax 688-7775

Russellville, Cole, Pop. 799
Cole County R-I SD 600/PK-12
13600 Route C 65074 573-782-3534
Perry Gorrell, supt. Fax 782-3545
www.cole.k12.mo.us
Cole County R-I MS 100/6-8
13600 Route C 65074 573-782-4915
Tina Kauffman, prin. Fax 782-3775
Cole County R-I S 300/PK-5
13600 Route C 65074 573-782-4814
Tina Kauffman, prin. Fax 782-3435

Saint Albans, Franklin

Fulton S at St. Albans 100/PK-12
PO Box 78 63073 636-458-6688
Kara Douglass, hdmstr. Fax 458-6660

Saint Ann, Saint Louis, Pop. 12,679
Pattonville R-3 SD 5,700/PK-12
11097 Saint Charles Rock Rd 63074 314-213-8500
Dr. Michael Fulton, supt. Fax 213-8601
psdr3.org
Drummond ES 700/K-5
3721 Saint Bridget Ln 63074 314-213-8419
Jason Van Beers, prin. Fax 213-8619
Holman MS 600/6-8
11055 Saint Charles Rock Rd 63074 314-213-8032
Sarah Moran, prin. Fax 213-8632
Pattonville ECC 100/PK-PK
11097 Saint Charles Rock Rd 63074 314-213-8100
Mary Kreckeler, admin. Fax 213-8630
Other Schools – See Bridgeton, Creve Coeur, Maryland Heights

Ritenour SD
Supt. — See Saint Louis
Buder ES 500/K-5
10350 Baltimore Ave 63074 314-493-6300
Jennifer Singleton, prin. Fax 429-6734
Hoech MS 700/6-8
3312 Ashby Rd 63074 314-493-6200
Dr. Terrance Peterson, prin. Fax 426-3837

Holy Trinity S 200/PK-8
10901 Saint Henry Ln 63074 314-426-8966
Margaret Ahle, prin. Fax 428-7084

Saint Charles, Saint Charles, Pop. 64,512
Francis Howell R-III SD 20,100/PK-12
4545 Central School Rd 63304 636-851-4000
Dr. Mary Hendricks-Harris, supt. Fax 851-4093
www.fhsdschools.org
Barnwell MS 900/6-8
1035 Jungs Station Rd 63303 636-851-4100
David Eckhoff, prin. Fax 851-4095
Becky-David ES 900/K-5
1155 Jungs Station Rd 63303 636-851-4200
Sherri Brown, prin. Fax 851-4097
Castlio ES 900/K-5
1020 Dingledine Rd 63304 636-851-4300
Bridgett Niedringhaus, prin. Fax 851-4099
Central ES 800/K-5
4525 Central School Rd 63304 636-851-5700
Stacey King, prin. Fax 851-4104
Early Childhood Family Education Center 800/PK-PK
2555 Hackmann Rd 63303 636-851-6200
Jane McKinney, prin. Fax 851-6202
Early Childhood Family Education Center 800/PK-PK
4535 Central School Rd 63304 636-851-6400
Marcia Birk, prin. Fax 851-4106
Harvest Ridge ES 800/K-5
1220 Harvest Ridge Dr 63303 636-851-5100
Natalie Deweese, prin. Fax 851-4128
Henderson ES 600/K-5
2501 Hackmann Rd 63303 636-851-5200
Jennette Barker, prin. Fax 851-4131
Hollenbeck MS 600/6-8
4555 Central School Rd 63304 636-851-5400
Woody Borgschulte, prin. Fax 851-4132
Saeger MS 800/6-8
5201 Highway N 63304 636-851-5600
Krisandar Worley, prin. Fax 851-4138
Other Schools – See O Fallon, Saint Peters, Weldon Spring, Wentzville

Orchard Farm R-V SD 1,600/PK-12
3489 Boshertown Rd 63301 636-925-5400
Dr. Thomas Muzzey, supt. Fax 916-3803
www.ofsd.k12.mo.us
Discovery ES 300/K-5
500 Discovery Path Ln 63301 636-757-6800
Betheny Brown, prin. Fax 757-6899
Early Learning Center PK-PK
3489 Boschertown Rd 63301 636-925-5400
Kari Schriber, prin. Fax 916-3788
Orchard Farm ES 500/K-5
2135 Highway V 63301 636-250-5200
Dr. Jerry Oetting, prin. Fax 250-5204
Orchard Farm MS 400/6-8
2195 Highway V 63301 636-250-5300
Keith Klostermann, prin. Fax 250-5306

St. Charles R-VI SD 5,100/PK-12
400 N 6th St 63301 636-443-4000
Dr. Jeff Marion, supt. Fax 443-4001
www.stcharlessd.org
Blackhurst ES 300/PK-4
2000 Elm St 63301 636-443-4500
Steve Wilson, prin. Fax 443-4501
Coverdell ES 300/PK-4
2475 W Randolph St 63301 636-443-4600
Annette Hill, prin. Fax 443-4601
Hardin MS 800/7-8
1950 Elm St 63301 636-443-4300
Dr. Ed Gettemeier, prin. Fax 443-4301
Harris ES 500/PK-4
2800 Old Muegge Rd 63303 636-443-4700
Tyson Plumlee, prin. Fax 443-4701
Jefferson IS 700/5-6
2660 Zumbehl Rd 63301 636-443-4400
Jeremy Shields, prin. Fax 443-4401
Lincoln ES 200/PK-4
625 S 6th St 63301 636-443-4650
Julie Williams, prin. Fax 443-4651
Monroe ES 500/PK-4
2670 Zumbehl Rd 63301 636-443-4800
Kathleen Kostos, prin. Fax 443-4801
Null ES 300/PK-4
435 Yale Blvd 63301 636-443-4900
Dr. Kate Kimsey, prin. Fax 443-4901

Academy of the Sacred Heart 500/PK-8
619 N 2nd St 63301 636-946-6127
Marcia Renken, prin. Fax 949-6659
Immanuel Lutheran S 500/PK-8
115 S 6th St 63301 636-946-0051
Diana Meers M.A., prin. Fax 946-0166
St. Charles Borromeo S 400/K-8
431 Decatur St 63301 636-946-2713
Jackie Voelkl, prin. Fax 946-3096
St. Cletus S 200/K-8
2721 Zumbehl Rd 63301 636-946-7756
Rosann Doherty, prin. Fax 946-6526
St. Joseph S 900/K-8
1351 Motherhead Rd 63304 636-441-0055
Sr. Mary Maksim, prin. Fax 441-9932
Seton Regional Catholic S 200/K-8
1 Seton Ct 63303 636-946-6716
Joanna Collins, prin. Fax 946-2670
SS. Joachim & Ann S 400/PK-8
4110 McClay Rd 63304 636-441-4835
Deborah Pecher, prin. Fax 441-9534
Trinity Lutheran S 50/K-8
4689 N Highway 94 63301 636-250-3654
Esther Loeffler, prin. Fax 250-3355
Zion Lutheran S 300/PK-8
3866 S Old Highway 94 63304 636-441-7424
Marc Debrick, prin.

Saint Clair, Franklin, Pop. 4,665
St. Clair R-XIII SD 2,300/K-12
905 Bardot St 63077 636-629-3500
Kyle Kruse, supt. Fax 629-4466
www.stcmo.org
Murray ES 500/3-5
1044 High School Dr 63077 636-629-3500
Dr. Beth Hill, prin. Fax 629-5739
Saint Clair ES 500/K-2
895 Bardot St 63077 636-629-3500
Sande Racherbaumer, prin. Fax 629-8413
Saint Clair JHS 500/6-8
925 High School Dr 63077 636-629-3500
Eric Lause, prin. Fax 629-1363

St. Clare S 100/PK-8
125 E Springfield Rd 63077 636-629-0413
Kathy Hunt, prin. Fax 629-1440

Sainte Genevieve, Sainte Genevieve, Pop. 4,356
St. Genevieve County R-II SD 1,900/PK-12
375 N 5th St 63670 573-883-4500
Jeffrey Lindsey, supt. Fax 883-5957
www.sgdragons.org
Sainte Genevieve ES 500/PK-5
725 Washington St 63670 573-883-4500
Geri Diesel, prin. Fax 883-5957
Sainte Genevieve MS 400/6-8
211 N 5th St 63670 573-883-4500
Paul Taylor, prin. Fax 883-5957
Other Schools – See Bloomsdale

St. Joseph S 50/PK-5
11822 Zell Rd 63670 573-883-5097
Kathy Bartlow, prin. Fax 883-5970
Valle Catholic S 300/K-8
40A N 4th St 63670 573-883-2403
Jill Metzger, prin. Fax 883-7413

Saint Elizabeth, Miller, Pop. 334
St. Elizabeth R-IV SD 100/PK-12
PO Box 68 65075 573-493-2246
Toni Taylor, supt. Fax 493-2380
www.ste.k12.mo.us
Saint Elizabeth S 100/PK-12
PO Box 68 65075 573-493-2246
Crintina Irwin, prin. Fax 493-2380

Saint James, Phelps, Pop. 4,150
St. James R-I SD 1,800/PK-12
122 E Scioto St 65559 573-265-2300
Dr. Merlyn Johnson, supt. Fax 265-6126
www.stjschools.org/
James ES 900/PK-5
314 S Jefferson St 65559 573-265-2300
Dan Copeland, prin. Fax 265-1504
St. James MS 400/6-8
1 Tiger Dr 65559 573-265-2300
Kaaren Lepper, prin. Fax 265-6302

Saint Joseph, Buchanan, Pop. 74,914
St. Joseph SD 11,300/PK-12
925 Felix St 64501 816-671-4000
Dr. Robert Newhart, supt. Fax 671-4470
www.sjsd.k12.mo.us
Bode MS 500/7-8
720 N Noyes Blvd 64506 816-671-4050
Roberta Dias, prin. Fax 671-4473
Carden Park ES K-6
1510 Duncan St 64503 816-671-4160
Lacey Adams, prin. Fax 671-4163
Coleman ES 500/K-6
3312 Beck Rd 64506 816-671-4100
Gladhart Heather, prin. Fax 671-4101
Edison ES 500/PK-6
515 N 22nd St 64501 816-671-4110
Terri Deayon, prin. Fax 671-4477
Ellison ES 400/K-6
45 SE 85th Rd 64507 816-667-5316
Kara Anderson, prin. Fax 667-5530
Field ES 400/K-6
2602 Gene Field Rd 64506 816-671-4130
Joni Owens, prin. Fax 671-4478
Hosea ES 500/K-6
6401 Gordon Ave 64504 816-671-4180
Dr. Kevin Carroll, prin. Fax 671-4182
Humboldt ES 500/PK-6
1520 N 2nd St 64505 816-671-4190
Leah Richardson, prin. Fax 671-4191
Hyde ES 400/K-6
509 Thompson Ave 64504 816-671-4210
Jaimee Lawrence, prin. Fax 671-4211
Lake Contrary ES 300/PK-6
1800 Alabama St 64504 816-671-4240
Julie Crum, prin. Fax 671-4481
Lindbergh ES 600/PK-6
2812 Saint Joseph Ave 64505 816-671-4250
Dr. Julie Gaddie, prin. Fax 671-4251
Oak Grove ES PK-6
4901 Cook Rd 64505 816-671-4290
Natalie Arnold, prin. Fax 671-4291
Parkway ES 500/K-6
2900 Duncan St 64507 816-671-4310
Heather Beaulieu, prin. Fax 671-4311
Pershing ES 400/K-6
2610 Blackwell Rd 64505 816-671-4320
Tara Wells, prin. Fax 671-4485
Pickett ES 300/PK-6
3923 Pickett Rd 64503 816-671-4330
John Davison, prin. Fax 671-4486
Robidoux MS 400/7-8
4212 Saint Joseph Ave 64505 816-671-4350
Mark Weis, prin. Fax 671-4487
Skaith ES 400/K-6
4701 Schoolside Ln 64503 816-671-4370
Dr. Jennifer Patterson, prin. Fax 671-4488
Spring Garden MS 400/7-8
5802 S 22nd St 64503 816-671-4380
Dr. Lara Gilpin, prin. Fax 671-4489
Truman MS 500/7-8
3227 Olive St Ste 45 64507 816-671-4400
Landi Quinlin, prin. Fax 671-4491
Twain ES 400/PK-6
705 S 31st St 64507 816-671-4270
Dr. Suzanne Tiemann, prin. Fax 671-4483

Cathedral S 200/PK-8
518 N 11th St 64501 816-232-8486
Mary Burgess, prin. Fax 232-8793
Hosanna Christian S 50/K-12
17290 US Highway 71 64505 816-324-2000
St. Francis Xavier S 300/PK-8
2614 Seneca St 64507 816-232-4911
Darin Pollard, prin. Fax 364-0263
St. James S 200/PK-8
120 Michigan Ave 64504 816-238-0281
Richard Soetaert, prin. Fax 238-1758
St. Joseph Christian S 300/PK-12
5401 Gene Field Rd 64506 816-279-1555
Dr. Jason Tindol, supt. Fax 279-4574
St. Paul Lutheran S 300/PK-8
4715 Frederick Ave 64506 816-279-1118
Sue Templeton, prin. Fax 279-1114

Saint Louis, Saint Louis, Pop. 312,138
Affton SD 101 2,400/PK-12
8701 MacKenzie Rd 63123 314-638-8770
Dr. Steve Brotherton, supt. Fax 631-2548
www.afftonschools.net
Affton ECC, 9832 Reavis Rd 63123 PK-PK
Karin Fleming, dir. 314-633-5988
Gotsch IS 500/3-5
8348 S Laclede Station Rd 63123 314-842-1238
Dr. Christine Powers, prin. Fax 633-5991
Mesnier PS 500/K-2
6930 Weber Rd 63123 314-849-5566
Christina Been, prin. Fax 633-5992
Rogers MS 500/6-8
7550 MacKenzie Rd 63123 314-351-9679
Jason Buck, prin. Fax 351-6381

Bayless SD 1,600/PK-12
4530 Weber Rd 63123 314-256-8600
Ronald J. Tucker, supt. Fax 544-6315
baylessk12.org
Bayless ES 800/PK-5
4531 Weber Rd 63123 314-256-8640
Aaron Kohler, prin. Fax 544-6315
Bayless JHS 400/6-8
4530 Weber Rd 63123 314-256-8690
Doug Harness, prin. Fax 544-6315

Ferguson-Florissant R-II SD
Supt. — See Florissant
Bermuda ES 300/K-6
5835 Bermuda Dr 63121 314-524-4821
Matthew Hinzpeter, prin. Fax 524-4827
Cool Valley ES 200/K-6
1351 S Florissant Rd 63121 314-521-5622
Suzette Simms, prin. Fax 521-5624
Ferguson MS 600/7-8
701 January Ave 63135 314-506-9600
Dr. Katherine Chambers, prin. Fax 506-9601
Vogt ES 300/K-6
200 Church St 63135 314-521-6347
Dr. Leslie Thomas-Washington, prin. Fax 521-5938

Hancock Place SD 1,500/K-12
9417 S Broadway 63125 314-544-1300
Dr. Kevin Carl, supt. Fax 631-3752
hancock.k12.mo.us
Hancock Place ES 800/K-5
9101 S Broadway 63125 314-544-1300
Dr. Jill Wright Ed.D., prin. Fax 544-4931
Hancock Place MS 300/6-8
243 W Ripa Ave 63125 314-544-6423
Thomas Dittrich, prin. Fax 544-6470

Hazelwood SD
Supt. — See Florissant
Arrowpoint ES 600/PK-5
2017 Arrowpoint Dr 63138 314-953-5300
Dr. Lisa Strauther, prin. Fax 953-5313
Grannemann ES 400/PK-5
2324 Redman Rd 63136 314-953-4250
Dr. Evelyn Woods, prin. Fax 953-4263
Hazelwood East MS 500/8-8
11300 Dunn Rd 63138 314-953-5700
Dr. Irma Moore, prin. Fax 953-5713
Hazelwood Southeast MS 700/6-8
918 Prigge Rd 63138 314-953-7700
Chauncey Granger, prin. Fax 953-7713
Keeven ES 400/PK-5
11230 Old Halls Ferry Rd 63136 314-953-4450
Ingrid Carter, prin. Fax 953-4463
Larimore ES 500/PK-5
1025 Trampe Ave 63138 314-953-4500
Cameron Coleman, prin. Fax 953-4513
Twillman ES 400/K-5
11831 Bellefontaine Rd 63138 314-953-4850
Germaine Stewart, prin. Fax 953-4863

Ladue SD 4,100/PK-12
9703 Conway Rd 63124 314-994-7080
Dr. Donna Jahnke, supt. Fax 994-0441
www.laduesschools.net
Conway ES 300/K-4
9900 Conway Rd 63124 314-993-2878
Dr. M. Lane Narvaez, prin. Fax 994-3988
Ladue ECC PK-PK
10890 Ladue Rd 63141 314-993-5724
Kerri Wetzel, dir. Fax 432-0980
Ladue Fifth Grade Center 300/5-5
9701 Ladue Rd 63124 314-993-5540
Julie Helm, prin. Fax 983-5539
Ladue MS 1,000/6-8
9701 Conway Rd 63124 314-993-3900
Dr. Tiffany Taylor Johnson, prin. Fax 997-8736
Old Bonhomme ES 400/K-4
9661 Old Bonhomme Rd 63132 314-993-0656
Cheryl Kirchgessner, prin. Fax 994-3987
Reed ES 400/K-4
9060 Ladue Rd 63124 314-991-1456
Dr. Chris Schreiner, prin. Fax 994-3981
Other Schools – See Creve Coeur

Lindbergh SD 6,000/PK-12
4900 S Lindbergh Blvd 63126 314-729-2480
Dr. Jim Simpson, supt. Fax 729-2482
www.lindberghschools.ws/
Concord ES 600/K-5
10305 Concord School Rd 63128 314-729-2436
Megan Stryjewski, prin. Fax 729-2454
Crestwood ES 500/K-5
1020 S Sappington Rd 63126 314-729-2430
Jodi Meese, prin. Fax 729-2432
Dressel ES 600/K-5
10911 Tesson Ferry Rd 63123 314-729-2485
Dr. Craig Hamby, prin. Fax 729-2486
Kennerly ES 500/K-5
10025 Kennerly Rd 63128 314-729-2440
Dr. Todd Morgan, prin. Fax 729-2442
Lindbergh Early Childhood Education PK-PK
4814 S Lindbergh Blvd 63126 314-729-2434
Dr. Charlene Ziegler, dir. Fax 729-2484
Long ES 500/K-5
9021 Sappington Rd 63126 314-729-2450
Dr. Jana Parker, prin. Fax 729-2452
Sappington ES 600/K-5
11011 Gravois Rd 63126 314-729-2460
Craig Hamby, prin. Fax 729-2462
Sperreng MS 700/6-8
12111 Tesson Ferry Rd 63128 314-729-2420
Mark Eggers, prin. Fax 729-2422
Truman MS 700/6-8
12225 Eddie and Park Rd 63127 314-729-2470
Michael Straatman, prin. Fax 729-2472

Mehlville R-IX SD 11,100/PK-12
3120 Lemay Ferry Rd 63125 314-467-5000
Dr. Chris Gaines, supt. Fax 467-5099
www.mehlvilleschooldistrict.com
Beasley ES 400/K-5
3131 Koch Rd 63125 314-467-5400
Andrea Deane, prin. Fax 467-5499
Bernard MS 700/6-8
1054 Forder Rd 63129 314-467-6600
Lori Sullivan, prin. Fax 467-6699
Bierbaum ES 600/K-5
2050 Union Rd 63125 314-467-5500
Nathan Burch, prin. Fax 467-5599
Blades ES 500/K-5
5140 Patterson Rd 63129 314-467-7300
Dr. Jeremy Booker, prin. Fax 467-7399
Buerkle MS 600/6-8
623 Buckley Rd 63125 314-467-6800
Jim Kern, prin. Fax 467-6899
Cary ECC 300/PK-PK
3155 Koch Rd 63125 314-467-5300
Ann Westbrook, prin. Fax 467-5399
Forder ES 400/K-5
623 W Ripa Ave 63125 314-467-5600
Whitney Maus, prin. Fax 467-5699
Hagemann ES 300/K-5
6401 Hagemann Rd 63128 314-467-5700
Dr. Scott Andrews, prin. Fax 467-5799
MOSAIC ES, 3701 Will Ave 63125 300/K-4
Scott Clark, prin. 314-467-7900
Oakville ES 400/K-5
2911 Yaeger Rd 63129 314-467-5800
Dr. Chad Dickemper, prin. Fax 467-5899
Oakville MS 600/6-8
5950 Telegraph Rd 63129 314-467-7400
Mike Salsman, prin. Fax 467-7499
Point ES 500/K-5
6790 Telegraph Rd 63129 314-467-5900
Dr. Shannon Pike, prin. Fax 467-5999
Rogers ES 400/K-5
7700 Fine Rd 63129 314-467-6300
Dr. Patrick Keenoy, prin. Fax 467-6399
Trautwein ES 500/K-5
5011 Ambs Rd 63128 314-467-6400
Shannon Henderson, prin. Fax 467-6499
Washington MS 600/6-8
5165 Ambs Rd 63128 314-467-7600
Justin Reynolds, prin. Fax 467-7699
Wohlwend ES 500/K-5
5966 Telegraph Rd 63129 314-467-6500
Dr. Dave Meschke, prin. Fax 467-6599

Normandy Schools Collaborative 2,500/PK-12
3855 Lucas and Hunt Rd 63121 314-493-0400
Dr. Charles Pearson, supt. Fax 493-0475
www.normandysc.org
Normandy ECC 100/PK-PK
3417 Saint Thomas More Pl 63121 314-493-0880
Dr. Jerri Johnson, prin. Fax 493-0890
Normandy Kindergarten Center 300/K-K
3101 Nordic Dr 63121 314-493-0140
Dannah Steele, prin. Fax 493-0150
Obama ES 300/1-6
3883 Jennings Station Rd 63121 314-493-0850
Netra Taylor-Nichols, prin. Fax 493-0870
Other Schools – See Normandy, Overland, Pasadena Hills

Ritenour SD 6,400/PK-12
2420 Woodson Rd 63114 314-493-6010
Dr. Christopher Kilbride, supt. Fax 426-7144
www.ritenour.k12.mo.us
Kratz ES 600/K-5
4301 Edmundson Rd 63134 314-493-6360
Dorlita Adams, prin. Fax 429-6735
Marion ES 500/K-5
2634 Sims Ave 63114 314-493-6400
Dr. Denean Steward, prin. Fax 429-6720
Marvin ES 500/K-5
3510 Woodson Rd 63114 314-493-6430
Michael Smith, prin. Fax 429-6737
School for Early Childhood PK-PK
3580 Woodson Rd 63114 314-493-6240
Dr. Gyniqua Davis, prin. Fax 429-3688
Wyland ES 500/K-5
2200 Brown Rd 63114 314-493-6460
Lisa Greenstein, prin. Fax 429-6728
Other Schools – See Overland, Saint Ann

Riverview Gardens SD 5,000/PK-12
1370 Northumberland Dr 63137 314-869-2505
Dr. Scott Spurgeon, supt. Fax 388-6002
www.rgsd.k12.mo.us
Central MS 600/6-8
9800 Patricia Barkalow Dr 63137 314-867-2603
Lakena Curtis, prin. Fax 388-6028
Danforth ES 300/K-5
1111 Saint Cyr Rd 63137 314-868-9524
Sheri Schjolberg, prin. Fax 388-6030
Early Childhood Education Center 100/PK-PK
1111 Saint Cyr Rd 63137 314-868-9524
Crystal Hunter, dir. Fax 388-6030
Gibson ES 400/K-5
9926 Fonda Dr 63137 314-869-4845
Dr. Crystal Henderson, prin. Fax 388-6032
Glasgow ES 300/K-5
10560 Renfrew Dr 63137 314-868-4680
Amanda Bell-Greenough, prin. Fax 388-6034
Highland ES 400/K-5
174 Shepley Dr 63137 314-868-4561
Dr. Shauntel Jones, prin. Fax 388-6036
Koch ES 300/K-5
1910 Exuma Dr 63136 314-868-3029
Howard Fields, prin. Fax 388-6038
Lemasters ES 300/K-5
1825 Crown Point Dr 63136 314-868-8192
Kevin Starks, prin. Fax 388-6040
Lewis & Clark ES 200/K-5
10242 Prince Dr 63136 314-868-5205
Jerri Johnson, prin. Fax 388-6042
Meadows ES 200/K-5
9801 Edgefield Dr 63136 314-868-2454
Dr. Stacey Nichols, prin. Fax 388-6044
Moline ES 400/K-5
9865 Winkler Dr 63136 314-868-9829
Carrie Collins, prin. Fax 388-6048
Westview MS 600/6-8
1950 Nemnich Rd 63136 314-867-0410
Valeska Hill, prin. Fax 388-6055

St. Louis City SD 26,300/PK-12
801 N 11th St 63101 314-231-3720
Dr. Kelvin Adams, supt. Fax 345-2661
www.slps.org/
Adams ES 300/PK-6
1311 Tower Grove Ave 63110 314-535-3910
Felecia Miller, prin. Fax 244-1701
Ames Visual/Perf Arts ES 400/PK-5
2900 Hadley St 63107 314-241-7165
Javeeta Parks-Prince, prin. Fax 231-1607
Ashland ES 400/PK-6
3921 N Newstead Ave 63115 314-385-4767
Paula Boddie, prin. Fax 244-1707
Bryan Hill ES 200/PK-5
2128 E Gano Ave 63107 314-534-0370
Sarah Briscoe, prin. Fax 244-1720
Buder ES 400/PK-5
5319 Lansdowne Ave 63109 314-352-4343
Anna Russell, prin. Fax 244-1722
Busch MS of Character & Athletics 300/6-8
5910 Clifton Ave 63109 314-352-1043
Robert Lescher, prin. Fax 244-1729
Carr Lane Visual & Performing Art MS 600/6-8
1004 N Jefferson Ave 63106 314-231-0413
Barrett Taylor, prin. Fax 244-1733
Chapman New American Academy K-8
1616 S Grand Blvd 63104 314-776-3285
Dr. Nicole Conaway, prin. Fax 244-1711
Clay ES 200/PK-5
3820 N 14th St 63107 314-231-9608
Lanor Payne, prin. Fax 244-1740
Columbia ES 300/PK-6
3120 Saint Louis Ave 63106 314-533-2750
Dr. Deshonda Payton, prin. Fax 533-4062
Compton-Drew ILC MS 500/6-8
5130 Oakland Ave 63110 314-652-9282
Nicole Holland, prin. Fax 244-1756
Dewey S International Studies 400/PK-5
6746 Clayton Ave 63139 314-645-4845
Andrew Donovan, prin. Fax 244-1760
Dunbar ES 300/PK-6
1415 N Garrison Ave 63106 314-533-2526
Anthony Virdure, prin. Fax 244-1762
Fanning MS Community Education Center 400/6-8
3417 Grace Ave 63116 314-772-1038
Lisa Brown, prin. Fax 244-1766
Farragut ES 200/PK-6
4025 Sullivan Ave 63107 314-531-1198
Patricia Cox, prin. Fax 244-1767
Ford ES 300/PK-6
1383 Clara Ave 63112 314-383-0836
Michelle McDaniel, prin. Fax 244-1769
Froebel ES 400/PK-5
3709 Nebraska Ave 63118 314-771-3533
Mamie Womack, prin. Fax 771-3590
Gateway ES 600/PK-5
4 Gateway Dr 63106 314-241-8255
Dr. Rose Howard, prin. Fax 244-1788
Gateway MST Prep S 600/6-8
1200 N Jefferson Ave 63106 314-241-2295
Nakia King, prin. Fax 241-7698
Hamilton eMints Academy 400/PK-5
5819 Westminster Pl 63112 314-367-0552
Starlett Frenchie, prin. Fax 244-1793
Henry Downtown Academy 300/PK-6
1220 N 10th St 63106 314-231-7284
Colby Heckendorn, prin. Fax 244-1796
Herzog Pilot Academy 400/K-6
5831 Pamplin Ave 63147 314-385-2212
Sandra Bell, prin. Fax 244-1798
Hickey ES 300/PK-5
3111 Cora Ave 63115 314-383-2550
Phyllis Miller, prin. Fax 383-5164
Hodgen ES 300/PK-6
1616 California Ave 63104 314-771-2539
Brandon Murray, prin. Fax 244-1801
Humboldt Academy 300/3-5
2516 S 9th St 63104 314-772-5566
Jacqueline Russell, prin. Fax 772-3180
Jefferson ES 300/PK-6
1301 Hogan St 63106 314-231-2459
Kristen Taylor, prin. Fax 231-2905
Kennard Classical Jr Academy 400/PK-5
5031 Potomac St 63139 314-353-8875
Dr. Wanda LeFlore, prin. Fax 244-1806
Laclede ES 300/PK-6
5821 Kennerly Ave 63112 314-385-0546
Damaris White, prin. Fax 244-1809
Lexington ES 400/PK-5
5030 Lexington Ave 63115 314-385-2522
Myra Pendleton, prin. Fax 385-4158
Long MS Community Education Center 200/6-8
5028 Morganford Rd 63116 314-481-3440
Steven Mathes, prin. Fax 481-7329
Lyon Academy @ Blow 400/K-8
516 Loughborough Ave 63111 314-353-1349
Ingrid Iskali, prin. Fax 353-9048
Mallinckrodt ES 300/PK-5
6020 Pernod Ave 63139 314-352-9212
Deandre Thomas, prin. Fax 244-1825
Mann eMints Academy 300/PK-6
4047 Juniata St 63116 314-772-4545
Angela Glass, prin. Fax 244-1827
Mason S of Academic & Cultural Literacy 500/PK-6
6031 Southwest Ave 63139 314-645-1201
Deborah Leto, prin. Fax 244-1831
McKinley Classical Junior Academy 200/6-8
2156 Russell Blvd 63104 314-773-0027
Steven Warmack, prin. Fax 244-1834
Meramec ES 300/PK-5
2745 Meramec St 63118 314-353-7145
Jonathan Strong, prin. Fax 353-6783
Monroe eMints Academy 400/PK-6
3641 Missouri Ave 63118 314-776-7315
Sonya Wayne, prin. Fax 776-7339
Mullanphy Investigation Learning Center 500/PK-5
4221 Shaw Blvd 63110 314-772-0994
Kelli Casper, prin. Fax 244-1845
Nance ES 400/PK-6
8959 Riverview Blvd 63147 314-867-0634
Jana Haywood, prin. Fax 244-1874
Oak Hill eMints Academy 400/PK-5
4300 Morganford Rd 63116 314-481-0420
Tina Hamilton, prin. Fax 481-2371
Pamoja Prep Academy 400/PK-8
3935 Enright Ave 63108 314-533-0894
Sean Nichols, prin. Fax 244-1753
Peabody Academy 400/PK-8
1224 S 14th St 63104 314-241-1533
Monica Miller-Seawood, prin. Fax 244-2805
Shaw Visual/Performing Arts ES 400/PK-5
5329 Columbia Ave 63139 314-776-5091
Dr. Lori Craig, prin. Fax 776-5124

Shenandoah ES 200/PK-6
3412 Shenandoah Ave 63104 314-772-7544
Brenda Smith, prin. Fax 244-1866
Sigel ES 300/PK-6
2050 Allen Ave 63104 314-771-0010
Hollie Russell-West, prin. Fax 771-4527
Stix ECC 500/PK-2
647 Tower Grove Ave 63110 314-533-0874
Diane Dymond, prin. Fax 244-1909
Walbridge ES 300/PK-6
5000 Davison Ave 63120 314-383-1829
Mildred Moore, prin. Fax 244-1925
Washington Montessori ES 400/PK-5
1130 N Euclid Ave 63113 314-361-0432
Lisa Small, prin. Fax 244-1927
Wilkinson ECC 300/PK-2
1921 Prather Ave 63139 314-645-1202
Yvette Levy, prin. Fax 645-2618
Woerner ES 400/PK-5
6131 Leona St 63116 314-481-8585
Margaret Meyer, prin. Fax 351-2272
Woodward ES 400/PK-5
725 Bellerive Blvd 63111 314-353-1346
Carla Cunigan, prin. Fax 353-5768

Webster Groves SD
Supt. — See Webster Groves
Bristol ES 500/K-5
20 Gray Ave 63119 314-963-6433
William Senti, prin. Fax 963-6438
Computer ES 100/K-5
701 N Rock Hill Rd 63119 314-963-6460
Howard Fields, prin. Fax 963-6471
Hixson MS 700/7-8
630 S Elm Ave 63119 314-963-6450
Unsun Lee, prin. Fax 918-4624
Steger 6th Grade Center 300/6-6
701 N Rock Hill Rd 63119 314-963-6460
Howard Fields, prin. Fax 963-6471

Abiding Saviour Lutheran S 300/PK-8
4353 Butler Hill Rd 63128 314-892-4408
Zachary Klug, prin. Fax 892-4469
Assumption S - Mattese 300/PK-8
4709 Mattis Rd 63128 314-487-6520
Jennifer Sykora, prin. Fax 487-3598
Central Christian S 300/PK-6
700 S Hanley Rd 63105 314-727-4535
Christian Academy of Greater St. Louis 100/PK-12
11050 N Warson Rd 63114 314-429-7070
Christ Light of the Nations S 200/PK-8
1650 Redman Rd 63138 314-741-0400
Sr. Mary Lawrence, prin. Fax 653-2531
Community S 400/PK-6
900 Lay Rd 63124 314-991-0005
Robert Cooke, head sch Fax 991-1512
Covenant Christian S 200/PK-6
2145 N Ballas Rd 63131 314-787-1036
Rev. John Roberts, head sch Fax 432-3989
Forsyth S 400/PK-6
6235 Wydown Blvd 63105 314-726-4542
Dr. Timothy Burns, head sch Fax 726-0112
Grace Chapel Lutheran S 200/PK-8
10015 Lance Dr 63137 314-867-6564
Eric Brofford, prin. Fax 868-2485
Grace Christian Academy 200/PK-8
2543 Hood Ave 63114 314-455-4114
Rev. Mark Cline, admin. Fax 576-7729
Green Park Lutheran S 300/K-8
4248 Green Park Rd 63125 314-544-4248
Stephen Eggold, prin. Fax 544-0237
HCA St. Michael the Archangel S 100/PK-5
7630 Sutherland Ave 63119 314-647-7159
Kristina Mantych, prin. Fax 644-1433
Hillcrest SDA S 50/K-8
9777 Grandview Dr 63132 314-993-1807
Holy Cross Academy - St. Dominic Savio 300/PK-5
7748 MacKenzie Rd 63123 314-832-4161
Clare Abkemeier, prin. Fax 352-6331
Holy Cross Acad Our Lady of Providence 100/PK-5
8874 Pardee Rd 63123 314-842-2073
Laura Clark, prin. Fax 270-8233
Kirk Day S 300/PK-6
12928 Ladue Rd 63141 314-434-4349
Taylor Clement, head sch Fax 434-0047
Loyola Academy 100/6-8
3851 Washington Blvd 63108 314-531-9091
Ashley Chapman, prin. Fax 531-3603
Marian MS 100/5-8
4130 Wyoming St 63116 314-771-7674
Sr. Sarah Heger, prin. Fax 771-7679
Mary Institute/St. Louis Country Day S 1,200/PK-12
101 N Warson Rd 63124 314-995-7367
Lisa Lyle, head sch
Mirowitz Jewish Community S 100/K-8
348 S Mason Rd 63141 314-576-6177
Cheryl Maayan, head sch Fax 576-3624
Most Holy Trinity Academy 200/K-8
1435 Mallinckrodt St 63107 314-231-9014
Jessica Kilmade, prin. Fax 621-3712
New City S 400/PK-6
5209 Waterman Blvd 63108 314-361-6411
Alexis Wright, head sch Fax 361-1499
Our Lady of Guadalupe S 200/PK-8
1115 S Florissant Rd 63121 314-524-1948
Margaret O'Brien, prin. Fax 522-8461
Our Lady of the Pillar S 200/PK-8
403 S Lindbergh Blvd 63131 314-993-3353
Heather Fanning, prin. Fax 993-2172
Our Redeemer Lutheran S 200/PK-8
9135 Shelley Ave 63114 314-427-3444
Dan Reinitz, prin. Fax 427-8273
Principia S 500/PK-12
13201 Clayton Rd 63131 314-434-2100
Travis Brantingham, prin. Fax 275-3583

Providence Classical Christian Academy 100/K-12
5293 S Lindbergh Blvd 63126 314-842-6846
Jonathan Mattull, hdmstr. Fax 842-8935
Queen of all Saints S 400/PK-8
6611 Christopher Dr 63129 314-846-0506
Shannon Sanchez, prin. Fax 846-4939
Rabbi Epstein Hebrew Academy 200/PK-8
1138 N Warson Rd 63132 314-994-7856
River Roads Lutheran S 100/PK-8
8623 Church Rd 63147 314-388-0300
Yvonne Boyd, prin. Fax 388-3253
Rohan Woods S 100/PK-6
1515 Bennett Ave 63122 314-821-6270
Sam Templin-Page, head sch Fax 821-6878
Rossman S 200/PK-6
12660 Conway Rd 63141 314-434-5877
Patricia Shipley, head sch Fax 434-1668
Sacred Heart Villa PK-K
2108 Macklind Ave 63110 314-771-2224
Kris Doder, prin. Fax 771-1262
St. Ambrose S 300/PK-8
5110 Wilson Ave 63110 314-772-1437
Sr. Barbara Zipoli, prin. Fax 771-4560
St. Catherine Laboure S 500/K-8
9750 Sappington Rd 63128 314-843-2819
Laurie Jost, prin. Fax 843-7687
St. Cecilia S & Academy 200/PK-8
906 Eichelberger St 63111 314-353-2455
Mary Loux, prin. Fax 353-2114
St. Clement of Rome S 300/PK-8
1508 Bopp Rd 63131 314-822-1903
Susan Cunningham, prin. Fax 822-8371
St. Frances Cabrini Academy 200/K-8
3022 Oregon Ave 63118 314-776-0883
Dr. Peter Schroeder, prin. Fax 776-4912
St. Francis of Assisi S 400/PK-8
4550 Telegraph Rd 63129 314-487-5736
Elizabeth Bartolotta, prin. Fax 416-7118
St. Gabriel the Archangel S 500/K-8
4711 Tamm Ave 63109 314-353-1229
Kelly Slattery, prin. Fax 353-6737
St. James the Greater S 200/PK-8
1360 Tamm Ave 63139 314-647-5244
Michael Biggs, prin. Fax 647-8237
St. Justin the Martyr S 200/PK-8
11914 Eddie and Park Rd 63126 314-843-6447
Amy Schroff, prin. Fax 843-9257
St. Louis Catholic Academy 200/PK-8
4720 Carter Ave 63115 314-389-0401
Sandra Morton, prin. Fax 389-7042
St. Louis Unified S 50/K-8
PO Box 3808 63136 314-869-7800
St. Margaret Mary Alacoque S 500/PK-8
4900 Ringer Rd 63129 314-487-1666
Marianne Freiling, prin. Fax 487-4475
St. Margaret of Scotland S 400/PK-8
3964 Castleman Ave 63110 314-776-7837
Juliann Hesed, prin. Fax 776-7955
St. Mark S 200/PK-8
4220 Ripa Ave 63125 314-743-8640
Jill Burkett, prin. Fax 743-8690
St. Michael S of Clayton 100/PK-8
6345 Wydown Blvd 63105 314-721-4422
Elizabeth Mosher, head sch Fax 721-4448
St. Raphael the Archangel S 200/PK-8
6000 Jamieson Ave 63109 314-352-9474
Julie Hayes, prin. Fax 351-7477
St. Roch S 200/PK-8
6040 Waterman Blvd 63112 314-721-2595
Dr. Mark Gilligan, prin. Fax 721-1656
St. Simon the Apostle S 300/PK-8
11019 Mueller Rd 63123 314-842-3848
Karin Hiatt, prin. Fax 849-6355
St. Stephen Protomartyr S 200/PK-8
3929 Wilmington Ave 63116 314-752-4700
Michel Wendell, prin. Fax 752-5165
Salem Lutheran S 200/PK-8
5025 Lakewood Ave 63123 314-353-9242
Robert Kellar, prin. Fax 353-9328
South City Catholic Academy K-8
5821 Pernod Ave 63139 314-752-4171
Laura Hirshman, prin. Fax 351-8562
South City Community S 50/PK-8
4926 Reber Pl 63139 314-667-4311
Brandy Greiner, dir. Fax 667-4311
Ste. Genevieve Du Bois S 200/PK-8
1575 N Woodlawn Ave 63122 314-821-4245
Anthony Van Gessel, prin. Fax 821-1241
Torah Prep Boys S 100/2-8
609 North And South Rd 63130 314-727-3335
Torah Prep Girls S 100/PK-8
8659 Olive Blvd 63132 314-569-2929
Tower Grove Christian S 200/PK-12
4257 Magnolia Ave 63110 314-776-6473
Michael Gregory, head sch Fax 776-4867
Villa Duchesne/Oak Hill S 300/PK-6
801 S Spoede Rd 63131 314-432-2021
Katie Komos, prin. Fax 810-3594
Visitation Academy 600/PK-12
3020 N Ballas Rd 63131 314-625-9100
David Colon, head sch Fax 432-7210
Word of Life Lutheran S 200/PK-8
6535 Eichelberger St 63109 314-832-1244
Alicia Klug, prin. Fax 832-0195

Saint Paul, Saint Charles, Pop. 1,822

St. Paul S 200/PK-8
1235 Church Rd 63366 636-978-1900
Kelly Kaimann, prin. Fax 978-1944

Saint Peters, Saint Charles, Pop. 51,692
Francis Howell R-III SD
Supt. — See Saint Charles
Fairmount ES 900/K-5
1725 Thoele Rd 63376 636-851-4500
Sue Sharp, prin. Fax 851-4107

Warren ES 800/K-5
141 Weiss Rd 63376 636-851-6100
Michele Christopher, prin. Fax 851-6209

Ft. Zumwalt R-II SD
Supt. — See O Fallon
DuBray MS 900/6-8
100 DuBray Dr 63376 636-279-7979
Michael Anderson, prin. Fax 278-4749
Ft. Zumwalt ECC PK-PK
7898 Veterans Memorial Pkwy 63376 636-474-8676
Lynette Cornett, dir. Fax 474-8677
Ft. Zumwalt South MS 1,000/6-8
300 Knaust Rd 63376 636-281-0776
Dr. Monte Massey, prin. Fax 281-0006
Hawthorn ES 600/K-5
166 Boone Hills Dr 63376 636-474-3999
Marc Schultz, prin. Fax 447-9216
Lewis & Clark ES 400/3-5
460 Mcmenamy Rd 63376 636-397-3111
Stephanie Sanker, prin. Fax 397-1454
Mid Rivers ES 500/K-5
7479 Mexico Rd 63376 636-278-2168
Justin Musgrove, prin. Fax 278-2451
Progress South ES 900/K-5
201 Knaust Rd 63376 636-272-2721
Dr. Deb Yerkes, prin. Fax 281-0002
Saint Peters ES 400/K-2
400 Mcmenamy Rd 63376 636-397-3211
Dr. Erin Gruntman, prin. Fax 279-3416

All Saints S 300/PK-8
5 Mcmenamy Rd 63376 636-397-1440
Deborah Hake, prin. Fax 970-3735
Child of God Lutheran S 100/PK-8
650 Salt Lick Rd 63376 636-970-7080
Dr. Melissa Sandfort Ph.D., prin. Fax 970-7083
Living Word Christian ES 200/PK-5
1614 Willott Rd 63376 636-978-1680
Keith Currivean, supt. Fax 329-3033

Saint Robert, Pulaski, Pop. 4,056
Waynesville R-VI SD
Supt. — See Waynesville
Freedom ES 900/K-5
286 Eastlawn Ave 65584 573-842-2100
Carey Drehle, prin. Fax 842-2101

Maranatha Baptist Academy 200/PK-12
200 Acorn Dr 65584 573-336-5972

Saint Thomas, Cole, Pop. 262

St. Thomas the Apostle S 100/PK-8
PO Box 211 65076 573-477-3322
Leroy Heckemeyer, prin. Fax 477-3700

Salem, Dent, Pop. 4,859
Dent-Phelps R-III SD 300/PK-8
27870 Highway C 65560 573-729-4680
Victoria Brooker, supt. Fax 729-8644
www.dentphelps.k12.mo.us/
Dent-Phelps S 300/PK-8
27870 Highway C 65560 573-729-4680
Victoria Brooker, supt. Fax 729-8644

Green Forest R-II SD 200/K-8
6111 Highway F 65560 573-729-3902
Kevin Prugh, supt. Fax 729-4842
www.gfr2.k12.mo.us
Green Forest S 200/K-8
6111 Highway F 65560 573-729-3902
Wanda Tatom, prin. Fax 729-4842

North Wood R-IV SD 200/PK-8
3734 N Highway 19 65560 573-729-4607
Dr. Paul Dodson, admin. Fax 729-8714
www.northwood.k12.mo.us
North Wood R-IV S 200/PK-8
3734 N Highway 19 65560 573-729-4607
Dr. Paul J. Dodson, admin. Fax 729-8714

Oak Hill R-I SD 100/PK-8
6200 S Highway 19 65560 573-729-5618
Douglas Dunn, supt. Fax 729-6982
district.oakhillr1.k12.mo.us
Oak Hill S 100/PK-8
6200 S Highway 19 65560 573-729-5618
Douglas Dunn, prin. Fax 729-6982

Salem R-80 SD 1,200/PK-12
1409 W Rolla Rd 65560 573-729-6642
John McColloch, supt. Fax 729-8493
www.salem.k12.mo.us/
Lynch ES 200/PK-1
101 N Main St 65560 573-729-6642
Kriste Crocker, prin. Fax 729-2433
Salem MS 200/6-8
1400 Tiger Pride Dr 65560 573-729-6642
Kerry Roberts, prin. Fax 729-2720
Salem Upper ES 200/2-5
1601 Doss Rd 65560 573-729-6642
Melanie Wisdom, prin. Fax 729-0284

Salisbury, Chariton, Pop. 1,601
Salisbury R-IV SD 400/K-12
1000 S Maple Ave 65281 660-388-6699
Troy Clawson, supt. Fax 388-6753
www.salisbury.k12.mo.us/
Salisbury ES 200/K-6
305 E 6th St 65281 660-388-6611
Robin Gebhardt, prin. Fax 388-6752

St. Joseph S 100/K-8
105 N Willie Ave 65281 660-388-5518
Cathy Fuemmeler, prin. Fax 388-5518

Sarcoxie, Jasper, Pop. 1,304
Sarcoxie R-II SD 700/K-12
101 S 17th St 64862 417-548-3134
Dr. Kevin Goddard, supt. Fax 548-6165
www.sarcoxie.k12.mo.us/
Wildwood ES 300/K-5
214 S 11th St 64862 417-548-3421
Dusty Feather, prin. Fax 548-6445

Savannah, Andrew, Pop. 5,020
Savannah R-III SD 2,300/K-12
408 W Market St 64485 816-324-3144
Dr. Eric Kurre, supt. Fax 324-5594
www.savannahr3.com
Cline ES 600/K-5
808 W Price Ave 64485 816-324-3915
Troy Dunn, prin. Fax 324-6767
Savannah MS 600/6-8
10500 State Route T 64485 816-324-3126
Clint Howren, prin. Fax 324-6397
Other Schools – See Amazonia, Country Club, Helena

Schell City, Vernon, Pop. 247
Northeast Vernon County R-I SD
Supt. — See Walker
Northeast Vernon County R-I ES 100/PK-6
150 N Hickory St 64783 417-432-3196
Kendall Ogburn, prin. Fax 432-3197

Scott City, Scott, Pop. 4,518
Scott City R-I SD 800/PK-12
3000 Main St 63780 573-264-2381
Brian Lee, supt. Fax 264-2206
scschools.k12.mo.us/
Scott City ES 400/PK-4
3000 Main St 63780 573-264-2131
April Garner, prin. Fax 264-4058
Scott City MS 200/5-8
3000 Main St 63780 573-264-2139
Michael Umfleet, prin. Fax 264-2599

St. Joseph Catholic S 50/PK-8
606 Sycamore St 63780 573-264-2600
Betty Spalding, prin. Fax 264-1325

Sedalia, Pettis, Pop. 20,824
Pettis County R-XII SD 200/PK-8
22675 Depot Rd 65301 660-826-5385
Travis Moore, supt. Fax 826-5452
www.pettisr12.k12.mo.us
Pettis County R-XII S 200/PK-8
22675 Depot Rd 65301 660-826-5385
Patrice Cook, prin. Fax 826-5452

Sedalia SD 200 4,200/PK-12
2806 Matthew Dr 65301 660-829-6450
Bradley Pollitt, supt. Fax 827-8938
www.sedalia200.org
Hunt ES 500/K-4
600 S Warren Ave 65301 660-826-1058
Brendan Eisenmenger, prin. Fax 829-0698
Mann ES 300/K-4
1100 W 16th St 65301 660-826-6441
Todd Fraley, prin. Fax 829-0767
Parkview ES 500/K-4
1901 S New York Ave 65301 660-826-4947
Stephanie Jackson, prin. Fax 829-0873
Pettis County ECC 100/PK-PK
2255 S Ingram Ave 65301 660-827-8955
Grace Kendrick, prin. Fax 827-8957
Sedalia MS 300/5-5
2205 S Ingram Ave 65301 660-829-6500
Sara Pannier, prin. Fax 827-6112
Skyline ES 500/K-4
2505 W 32nd St 65301 660-826-8087
Kelly McFatrich, prin. Fax 829-0916
Smith-Cotton JHS 700/6-8
312 E Broadway Blvd 65301 660-829-6300
Jason Curry, prin. Fax 829-6409
Washington ES 300/K-4
610 S Engineer Ave 65301 660-826-2216
Lisa Volk, prin. Fax 829-0982

Sacred Heart S 100/PK-12
416 W 3rd St 65301 660-827-3800
Dr. Gary Manning, prin. Fax 827-3806
St. Paul's Lutheran S 100/PK-8
701 S Massachusetts Ave 65301 660-826-1925
Rhonda Tull, prin. Fax 826-1925
Sedalia Adventist Academy 50/K-8
29531 Highway 50 65301 660-826-8951

Senath, Dunklin, Pop. 1,752
Senath-Hornersville C-8 SD 900/PK-12
PO Box 370 63876 573-738-2669
Chad Morgan, supt. Fax 738-9845
www.shs.k12.mo.us/
Senath-Hornersville ES 400/PK-4
PO Box 370 63876 573-738-2515
Lori Hoffmann, prin. Fax 738-9845
Other Schools – See Hornersville

Seneca, Newton, Pop. 2,214
Seneca R-VII SD 1,500/PK-12
914 Frisco St 64865 417-776-3426
Jim Cummins, supt. Fax 776-2177
www.senecar7.com
Seneca ECC PK-PK
914 Frisco St 64865 417-776-1201
Dedra Cornett, dir. Fax 776-1202
Seneca ES 500/K-3
914 Frisco St 64865 417-776-2785
Shanna Eidson, prin. Fax 776-1508
Seneca IS 300/4-6
914 Frisco St 64865 417-776-7961
Will King, prin. Fax 776-7963
Seneca JHS 200/7-8
914 Frisco St 64865 417-776-3911
John Whitehead, prin. Fax 776-2673

Seymour, Webster, Pop. 1,885
Seymour R-II SD 800/PK-12
416 E Clinton Ave 65746 417-935-2287
Bruce Denney, supt. Fax 935-4060
www.seymourschool.net
Seymour ES 400/PK-5
425 E Center Ave 65746 417-935-2234
Vicky Denney, prin. Fax 935-2083
Seymour MS 200/6-8
501 E Clinton Ave 65746 417-935-4626
Brian Bell, prin. Fax 935-2848

Victory Academy 100/PK-12
PO Box 309 65746 417-935-2315
Teresa Bruffett, admin. Fax 935-2316

Shelbina, Shelby, Pop. 1,695
Shelby County R-IV SD 600/PK-12
4154 Highway 36 63468 573-588-4961
Tim Maddex, supt. Fax 588-2490
www.cardinals.k12.mo.us
Shelbina ES 200/PK-5
111 W College Ave 63468 573-588-2181
Catherine Stueve, prin. Fax 588-4982
Other Schools – See Clarence

Shelbyville, Shelby, Pop. 547
North Shelby SD 300/PK-12
3071 Highway 15 63469 573-633-2410
Kim Gaines, supt. Fax 633-2138
www.nshelby.k12.mo.us
North Shelby ES 200/PK-6
3071 Highway 15 63469 573-633-2401
Monica Hinshaw, prin. Fax 633-2138

Sheldon, Vernon, Pop. 525
Sheldon R-VIII SD 200/PK-12
100 E Gene Lathrop Dr 64784 417-884-5113
Jason Irwin, supt. Fax 884-5331
www.sheldon.k12.mo.us
Sheldon ES 100/PK 6
100 E Gene Lathrop Dr 64784 417-884-5113
Carolyn Compton, admin. Fax 884-5331

Shell Knob, Barry, Pop. 1,370
Shell Knob ESD 78 100/PK-8
24400 State Highway 39 65747 417-858-6743
Dr. Shelly Fransen Ed.D., supt. Fax 858-3921
www.sks.k12.mo.us/
Shell Knob S 100/PK-8
24400 State Highway 39 65747 417-858-6743
Dr. Shelly Fransen Ed.D., supt. Fax 858-3921

Sikeston, Scott, Pop. 16,008
Scott County Central SD 400/PK-12
20794 US Highway 61 63801 573-471-2686
Dr. Howard Benyon, supt. Fax 471-2029
scottcentral.k12.mo.us
Scott County Central ES 200/PK-6
20794 US Highway 61 63801 573-471-3511
Stacey Russell M.Ed., prin. Fax 471-3515

Sikeston R-6 SD 3,400/K-12
1002 Virginia St 63801 573-472-2581
Thomas Williams, supt. Fax 472-2584
www.sikestonr6.org
Hunter ES 400/1-4
1002 Virginia St 63801 573-472-2200
Kimberly Pinkard, prin. Fax 472-3847
Matthews ES 300/1-4
1002 Virginia St 63801 573-471-0615
Crystal Hartzog, prin. Fax 471-0614
Sikeston 5th and 6th Grade Center 500/5-6
1002 Virginia St 63801 573-471-0792
Sheila Branch, prin. Fax 471-0793
Sikeston 7th and 8th Grade Center 500/7-8
1002 Virginia St 63801 573-471-1720
Frank Staple, prin. Fax 472-8884
Sikeston K 300/K-K
1002 Virginia St 63801 573-471-0653
Jennifer Hobeck, prin. Fax 471-0654
Southeast ES 300/1-4
1002 Virginia St 63801 573-472-0707
Alecia Jordan, prin. Fax 471-1714

Christian Academy 100/PK-12
103 E Kathleen St 63801 573-481-0216
Kevin Self, admin. Fax 481-9485
St. Francis Xavier S 200/PK-8
106 N Stoddard St 63801 573-471-0841
Debbie Pollock, prin. Fax 475-9847

Silex, Lincoln, Pop. 187
Silex R-I SD 300/K-12
PO Box 46 63377 573-384-5227
David Deets, supt. Fax 384-5996
www.silex.k12.mo.us
Silex ES 200/K-6
PO Box 46 63377 573-384-5044
Suzie Plackemeier, prin. Fax 384-5996

St. Alphonsus S 50/PK-8
25 Saint Alphonsus Rd 63377 573-384-5305
Lisa Huber, prin. Fax 384-6190

Slater, Saline, Pop. 1,827
Orearville R-IV SD 100/PK-8
32524 E Highway P 65349 660-529-2481
Dr. Meghan Tichenor, supt. Fax 529-2454
orearvilletigers.k12.mo.us
Orearville S 100/PK-8
32524 E Highway P 65349 660-529-2481
Dr. Meghan Tichenor, prin. Fax 529-2454

Slater SD 400/PK-12
515 Elm St 65349 660-529-2278
Debbie Gonzalez, supt. Fax 529-2279
www.slaterschools.net
Alexander ES 200/PK-8
515 Elm St 65349 660-529-2278
Rebecca Drummond, prin. Fax 529-2279

Smithton, Pettis, Pop. 561
Smithton R-VI SD 400/PK-12
505 S Myrtle Ave 65350 660-343-5316
David Bray, supt. Fax 343-5389
smithton.k12.mo.us
Smithton ES 200/PK-4
505 S Myrtle Ave 65350 660-343-5317
Dawn McNeeley M.S., prin. Fax 343-5389
Smithton MS 5-8
505 S Myrtle Ave 65350 660-343-5316
Brandon Wallace, prin. Fax 343-5389

Smithville, Clay, Pop. 8,290
Smithville R-II SD 2,500/PK-12
655 S Commercial Ave 64089 816-532-0406
Dr. Todd Schuetz, supt. Fax 532-4192
www.smithvilleschooldistrict.net
Horizon ES 600/3-5
695 S Commercial Ave 64089 816-532-4566
Denise Harwood, prin. Fax 532-4409
Maple ES 600/PK-2
600 Maple Ave 64089 816-532-0589
Rena Hawkins, prin. Fax 532-3158
Smithville MS 600/6-8
675 S Commercial Ave 64089 816-532-1122
Tod Winterboer, prin. Fax 532-3210

South West City, McDonald, Pop. 939
McDonald County R-I SD
Supt. — See Anderson
Southwest City ES 400/PK-8
PO Box 189 64863 417-762-3251
Sarah Messley, prin. Fax 762-3165

Sparta, Christian, Pop. 1,734
Sparta R-III SD 800/PK-12
PO Box 160 65753 417-634-4284
Dr. Rocky Valentine, supt. Fax 634-3156
www.sparta.k12.mo.us/
Sparta ES 400/K-4
PO Box 160 65753 417-634-3223
William Chambers, prin. Fax 634-5256
Sparta MS 200/5-8
PO Box 160 65753 417-634-5518
David Baker, prin. Fax 634-3426
Sparta Preschool PK-PK
PO Box 160 65753 417-634-3223
William Chambers, prin. Fax 634-3156

Spickard, Grundy, Pop. 252
Spickard R-II SD 50/PK-8
105 N 4th St 64679 660-485-6121
Burnie Schneiderheinz, supt. Fax 485-6179
www.spickard.k12.mo.us/
Spickard ES 50/PK 8
105 N 4th St 64679 660-485-6121
Danny Johnson, prin. Fax 485-6179

Spokane, Christian, Pop. 175
Spokane R-VII SD
Supt. — See Highlandville
Spokane MS 200/6-8
PO Box 220 65754 417-443-3506
Pamila Rowe, prin. Fax 443-2069

Springfield, Greene, Pop. 154,799
Springfield R-XII SD 25,500/PK-12
1359 E Saint Louis St 65802 417-523-0000
Dr. John Jungmann, supt. Fax 523-0391
www.springfieldpublicschoolsmo.org/
Bingham ES 400/K-5
2126 E Cherry St 65802 417-523-3400
Adam Meador, prin. Fax 523-3495
Bissett ES 300/K-5
3014 W Calhoun St 65802 417-523-2800
Marcie Stallcup, prin. Fax 523-2895
Bowerman ES 300/K-5
2148 N Douglas Ave 65803 417-523-1400
Angela Valchev, prin. Fax 523-1495
Boyd ES 200/K-5
1409 N Washington Ave 65802 417-523-1500
Andrea Fraser, prin. Fax 895-2768
Campbell ES 200/K-5
506 S Grant Ave 65806 417-523-3200
John Mott, prin. Fax 523-3295
Carver MS 800/6-8
3325 W Battlefield St 65807 417-523-6800
Dr. Dana Powers, prin. Fax 523-6895
Cherokee MS 800/6-8
420 E Farm Road 182 65810 417-523-7200
William Powers, prin. Fax 523-7295
Cowden ES 300/PK-5
2927 S Kimbrough Ave 65807 417-523-3500
Cherie Norman, prin. Fax 888-2504
Delaware ES 200/K-5
1505 S Delaware Ave 65804 417-523-3700
Stephanie Young, prin. Fax 523-3795
Disney ES 500/K-5
4100 S Fremont Ave 65804 417-523-3600
Dr. Lynne Miller, prin. Fax 523-3695
Field ES 400/K-5
2120 E Barataria St 65804 417-523-4800
Janell Bagwell, prin. Fax 888-2543
Fremont ES 200/K-5
2814 N Fremont Ave 65803 417-523-1700
James Grandon, prin. Fax 523-1795
Gray ES 500/K-4
2101 W Farm Road 182 65810 417-523-4000
Angela Carder, prin. Fax 888-2694
Harrison ES 400/K-4
3055 W Kildee Ln 65810 417-523-5800
Christine Parker, prin. Fax 523-5895

Hickory Hills ES 400/K-5
4650 E State Highway YY 65802 417-523-7100
Sarah Odom, prin. Fax 523-7195
Hickory Hills MS 500/6-8
4650 E State Highway YY 65802 417-523-7100
Sarah Odom, prin. Fax 523-7195
Holland ES 200/K-5
2403 S Holland Ave 65807 417-523-4100
Gary Tew, prin. Fax 523-4195
Jarrett MS 500/6-8
840 S Jefferson Ave 65806 417-523-6600
Rob Kroll, prin. Fax 523-6695
Jeffries ES 600/K-5
4051 S Scenic Ave 65807 417-523-3900
Liz Cooper, prin. Fax 888-2600
Mann ES 400/K-5
3745 S Broadway Ave 65807 417-523-4400
Teri Peterson, prin. Fax 523-4495
McBride ES 400/K-4
5005 S Farm Road 135 65810 417-523-4500
Lael Streight, prin. Fax 523-4595
McGregor ES 300/K-5
1221 W Madison St 65806 417-523-5700
Sara Shevchuk, prin. Fax 523-5795
Pershing ES 200/K-5
2120 S Ventura Ave 65804 417-523-2400
Ryan Savage, prin. Fax 523-2495
Pershing MS 700/6-8
2120 S Ventura Ave 65804 417-523-2400
Ryan Savage, prin. Fax 523-2495
Pipkin MS 600/6-8
1215 N Boonville Ave 65802 417-523-6000
Rebecca Ash, prin. Fax 523-6195
Pittman ES 300/K-5
2934 E Bennett St 65804 417-523-4700
Laura Batson, prin. Fax 888-2568
Pleasant View ES 200/K-5
2210 E State Highway AA 65803 417-523-2100
Joshua Groves, prin. Fax 523-2395
Pleasant View MS 400/6-8
2210 E State Highway AA 65803 417-523-2100
Joshua Groves, prin. Fax 523-2395
Portland ES 300/K-5
906 W Portland St 65807 417-523-4600
Josh Holt, prin. Fax 895-2094
Reed MS 600/6-8
2000 N Lyon Ave 65803 417-523-6300
Dr. Debbie Grega, prin. Fax 523-6395
Robberson ES 300/K-5
1100 E Kearney St 65803 417-523-1800
Kevin Huffman, prin. Fax 523-1895
Rountree ES 300/K-5
1333 E Grand St 65804 417-523-4900
Amy Patton, prin. Fax 523-4995
Sequiota ES 400/K-5
3414 S Mentor Ave 65804 417-523-5400
Crystal Magers, prin. Fax 523-5495
Shady Dell ECC 500/PK-PK
2757 E Division St 65803 417-523-1300
Melissa Riley, prin. Fax 523-1395
Sherwood ES 300/K-5
2524 S Golden Ave 65807 417-523-3800
Nicole Holt, prin. Fax 523-3895
Sunshine ES 200/K-5
421 E Sunshine St 65807 417-523-5200
David Martin, prin. Fax 523-5295
Truman ES 400/PK-5
3850 N Farm Road 159 65803 417-523-5100
Joellyn Travis, prin. Fax 523-5242
Twain ES 500/K-5
2352 S Weaver Ave 65807 417-523-4300
Stacye Manlove, prin. Fax 888-2584
Watkins ES 300/PK-5
732 W Talmage St 65803 417-523-5000
Janine Forrester, prin. Fax 523-5095
Weaver ES 400/K-5
1461 N Douglas Ave 65802 417-523-1200
Cindy Webster, prin. Fax 895-2128
Weller ES 400/PK-5
1630 N Weller Ave 65803 417-523-1900
Dr. Rebecca Donaldson, prin. Fax 895-2134
Westport ES 400/PK-5
415 S Golden Ave 65802 417-523-3100
Kim Sublett, prin. Fax 523-3195
Westport MS 400/6-8
415 S Golden Ave 65802 417-523-3100
Dr. Justin Herrell, prin. Fax 523-3195
Wilder ES 300/K-5
2526 S Hillsboro Ave 65804 417-523-5300
Jason Steingraber, prin. Fax 888-2616
Williams ES 300/PK-5
2205 W Kearney St 65803 417-523-2000
Jennifer Webb, prin. Fax 523-2095
York ES 200/PK-5
2100 W Nichols St 65802 417-523-3000
Lora Hopper, prin. Fax 895-2149
Other Schools – See Battlefield

Willard R-II SD
Supt. — See Willard
Willard Central ES 400/K-4
2625 N Farm Road 101 65802 417-831-4440
Dr. Shane Medlin, prin. Fax 831-2486
Willard Orchard Hills ES 400/K-4
4595 W Farm Road 140 65802 417-869-0600
Dr. Garrett Prevo, prin. Fax 869-0606
Willard South ES 400/PK-4
4151 W Division St 65802 417-862-6308
Kara Crighton-Smith, prin. Fax 862-4266

Discovery Garden Montessori S 50/PK-5
1515 S National Ave 65804 417-631-4590
Cynthia Barraza, head sch
Grace Classical Academy 200/PK-12
2438 E Cherry St 65802 417-877-7910
Jedidiah Moss, hdmstr. Fax 866-8409
Greenwood Laboratory S 400/K-12
901 S National Ave, 417-836-5124
Dr. Janice Duncan, dir. Fax 836-8449
Immaculate Conception S 500/PK-8
3555 S Fremont Ave 65804 417-881-7000
Theresa Coleman, prin. Fax 881-7087
New Covenant Academy 300/PK-12
3304 S Cox Ave 65807 417-887-9848
Matthew Searson M.A., admin. Fax 887-2419
St. Agnes S 200/PK-8
531 S Jefferson Ave 65806 417-866-5038
Lindsay Paulsell, prin. Fax 866-2906
St. Elizabeth Ann Seton S 200/PK-8
2200 W Republic Rd 65807 417-887-6056
Cheryl Hall, prin. Fax 866-2189
St. Joseph Catholic Academy 100/PK-8
515 W Scott St 65802 417-866-0667
Bonnie Johnson, prin. Fax 866-2862
Springfield Lutheran S 200/PK-8
2852 S Dayton Ave 65807 417-883-5717
Paul Baker, prin. Fax 881-5470
Springfield SDA Junior Academy 50/K-10
704 S Belview Ave 65802 417-862-0833
Summit Prep S of Southwest Missouri 100/PK-12
2155 W Chesterfield Blvd 65807 417-869-8077
Robert Gronniger, head sch Fax 869-8087

Stanberry, Gentry, Pop. 1,181
Stanberry R-II SD 300/PK-12
610 N Park St 64489 660-783-2136
Brian Garner, supt. Fax 783-2177
www.sr2.k12.mo.us
Stanberry R-II ES 200/PK-6
610 N Park St 64489 660-783-2141
Robert Heddinger, prin. Fax 783-2177

Steele, Pemiscot, Pop. 2,134
South Pemiscot County R-V SD 700/PK-12
611 Beasley Rd 63877 573-695-4426
Chris Moore, supt. Fax 695-4427
www.southpemiscot.com
South Pemiscot ES 400/PK-6
611 Beasley Rd 63877 573-695-4781
Jason Williams, prin. Fax 695-7464

Steelville, Crawford, Pop. 1,631
Steelville R-III SD 900/PK-12
PO Box 339 65565 573-775-2175
Mike Whittaker, supt. Fax 775-2179
steelville.k12.mo.us
Steelville ES 400/PK-4
PO Box 339 65565 573-775-2099
Stephanie Billingsley, prin. Fax 775-4940
Steelville MS 300/5-8
PO Box 339 65565 573-775-2176
Curtis Finley, prin. Fax 775-2591

Stella, Newton, Pop. 158
East Newton County R-VI SD
Supt. — See Granby
Triway S 400/PK-8
131 Lentz St 64867 417-628-3227
Jamie Medlin, prin. Fax 628-3226

Stewartsville, DeKalb, Pop. 741
Stewartsville C-2 SD 200/K-12
902 Buchanan St 64490 816-669-3792
Jay Albright, supt. Fax 669-8125
www.stewartsville.k12.mo.us
Stewartsville ES 100/K-6
902 Buchanan St 64490 816-669-3258
Michael Stephenson, prin. Fax 669-8125

Stockton, Cedar, Pop. 1,789
Stockton R-I SD 1,000/K-12
PO Box 190 65785 417-276-5143
Shannon Snow, supt. Fax 276-3765
www.stockton.k12.mo.us/
Stockton ES 300/K-4
PO Box 190 65785 417-276-5141
Doug Crawford, prin. Fax 276-5946
Stockton MS 300/5-8
PO Box 190 65785 417-276-5141
Robert Bolte, prin. Fax 276-6389

Stoutland, Laclede, Pop. 192
Stoutland R-II SD 500/PK-12
7584 State Road T 65567 417-286-3711
Doug Dahman, supt. Fax 286-3153
www.stoutlandschools.com
Stoutland ES 300/PK-6
7584 State Road T 65567 417-286-3711
Samie Hill, prin. Fax 286-4341

Stover, Morgan, Pop. 1,079
Morgan County R-I SD 600/PK-12
701 N Oak St 65078 573-377-2217
Dr. Matt Unger, supt. Fax 377-2211
mcr1.us/
Morgan County R-I ES 400/PK-6
701 N Oak St 65078 573-377-2219
Molly Roe, prin. Fax 377-2211

St. Paul Lutheran S 50/PK-8
407 W 3rd St 65078 573-377-2690
Fax 377-2185

Strafford, Greene, Pop. 2,311
Strafford R-VI SD 1,100/K-12
201 W McCabe St 65757 417-736-7000
John Collins, supt. Fax 736-7016
straffordschools.net
Strafford ES 400/K-5
310 W McCabe St 65757 417-736-7000
Michelle Gardner, prin. Fax 736-7018
Strafford MS 300/6-8
213 W McCabe St 65757 417-736-7000
Marcia Chadwell, prin. Fax 736-7019

Strasburg, Cass, Pop. 141
Strasburg C-3 SD 100/K-8
608 W State Route E 64090 816-680-3333
Larry Arnone, supt. Fax 865-3349
www.strasburg.k12.mo.us
Strasburg S 100/K-8
608 W State Route E 64090 816-680-3333
Larry Arnone, admin. Fax 865-3349

Sturgeon, Boone, Pop. 864
Sturgeon R-V SD 500/PK-12
210 W Patton St 65284 573-687-3515
Shawn Schultz, supt. Fax 687-2116
www.sturgeon.k12.mo.us/
Sturgeon ES 200/PK-4
210 W Patton St 65284 573-687-3519
Brandee Brown, prin. Fax 687-1226
Sturgeon MS 100/5-8
210 W Patton St 65284 573-687-2155
Brandee Brown, prin. Fax 687-1226

Success, Texas
Success R-VI SD 100/PK-8
10341 Highway 17 65570 417-967-2597
David Russell, supt. Fax 967-5774
www.success.k12.mo.us
Success ES 100/PK-8
10341 Highway 17 65570 417-967-2597
David Russell, prin. Fax 967-5774

Sugar Creek, Jackson, Pop. 3,262
Independence SD 30
Supt. — See Independence
Mallinson ES 300/2-5
709 N Forest Ave, 816-521-5530
Dr. Sarah Brown, prin. Fax 521-5693
Sugar Creek ES 200/PK-1
11424 Gill St 64054 816-521-5460
Shellie Dumas, prin. Fax 521-5648

Sullivan, Franklin, Pop. 7,019
Spring Bluff R-XV SD 200/K-8
9374 Highway 185 63080 573-457-8302
Jeannie Jenkins, supt. Fax 457-2070
www.springbluffpirates.com
Spring Bluff S 200/K-8
9374 Highway 185 63080 573-457-8302
Jeannie Jenkins, supt. Fax 457-2070

Strain-Japan R-XVI SD 100/K-8
4640 Highway H 63080 573-627-3243
Anita Studdard, supt. Fax 971-4401
strainjapan.com/
Strain-Japan S 100/K-8
4640 Highway H 63080 573-627-3243
Anita Studdard, supt. Fax 971-4401

Sullivan SD 2,300/PK-12
138 Taylor St 63080 573-468-5171
Dr. Thomas Allen, supt. Fax 468-7720
www.sullivaneagles.org
Sullivan ES 600/2-5
104 W Washington St 63080 573-468-5171
Heather Mueller, prin. Fax 860-2436
Sullivan MS 500/6-8
1156 Elmont Rd 63080 573-468-5191
Patrick Burke, prin. Fax 860-2326
Sullivan PS 400/PK-1
1132 Elmont Rd 63080 573-468-5446
Cynthia Carey, prin. Fax 468-6387

St. Anthony S 100/PK-8
119 W Springfield Rd 63080 573-468-4423
Mary Wooley, prin. Fax 468-3428

Summersville, Texas, Pop. 492
Summersville R-II SD 400/PK-12
PO Box 198 65571 417-932-4045
Rick Stark, supt. Fax 932-5360
www.sville.k12.mo.us
Summersville ES 200/PK-6
PO Box 198 65571 417-932-4613
Lisa Howell, prin. Fax 932-6703

Sunrise Beach, Morgan, Pop. 422
Camdenton R-III SD
Supt. — See Camdenton
Hurricane Deck ES 200/PK-4
59 American Legion Dr 65079 573-374-5369
Christy Glodt, prin. Fax 374-4416

Sweet Springs, Saline, Pop. 1,457
Sweet Springs R-VII SD 500/PK-12
600 E Marshall St 65351 660-335-4860
Donna Wright, supt. Fax 335-4378
sweetsprings.k12.mo.us/
Sweet Springs ES 300/PK-6
600 E Marshall St 65351 660-335-6348
Melanie Schlup, prin. Fax 335-4388

Taneyville, Taney, Pop. 391
Taneyville R-II SD 200/PK-8
302 Myrtle St 65759 417-546-5803
Dr. Tara Roberts, supt. Fax 546-3705
www.taneyvilletigers.com
Taneyville S 200/PK-8
302 Myrtle St 65759 417-546-5803
Garnet Bills, prin. Fax 546-6401

Tarkio, Atchison, Pop. 1,576
Tarkio R-I SD 300/K-12
312 S 11th St 64491 660-736-4161
Karma Coleman, supt. Fax 736-4546
tarkio.k12.mo.us
Tarkio ES 200/K-6
1201 Pine St 64491 660-736-4177
Deborah Taylor, prin. Fax 736-9952

Thayer, Oregon, Pop. 2,197
Thayer R-II SD 700/PK-12
401 E Walnut St 65791 417-264-4600
Tonya Woods, supt. Fax 264-4608
thayer.k12.mo.us/
Thayer ES 400/PK-6
365 E Walnut St 65791 417-264-4600
Jason Andrews, prin. Fax 264-3956

Theodosia, Ozark, Pop. 239
Lutie R-VI SD 100/PK-12
5802 US Highway 160 65761 417-273-4274
Scot Young, supt. Fax 273-4171
lutieschool.org
Lutie ES 100/PK-6
5802 US Highway 160 65761 417-273-4274
Sherry Anstine, prin. Fax 273-4171

Thornfield, Ozark
Thornfield R-I SD 100/K-8
37 County Road 855 65762 417-265-3212
Michael Wallace, supt. Fax 265-3729
Thornfield S 100/K-8
37 County Road 855 65762 417-265-3212
Michael Wallace, prin. Fax 265-3729

Tina, Carroll, Pop. 154
Tina-Avalon R-II SD 200/PK-12
11896 Highway 65 64682 660-622-4211
Jana Holcer, supt. Fax 622-4210
tinaavalon.k12.mo.us/
Tina-Avalon ES 100/PK-6
11896 Highway 65 64682 660-622-4212
William Dow, prin. Fax 622-4210

Tipton, Moniteau, Pop. 3,237
Tipton R-VI SD 600/K-12
305 US Highway 50 E 65081 660-433-5520
Dr. Terry Robinson, supt. Fax 433-5241
tipton.k12.mo.us
Tipton ES 300/K-6
305 US Highway 50 E 65081 660-433-2213
Kelly Kohler, prin. Fax 433-2899

St. Andrew S 100/K-8
118 E Cooper St 65081 660-433-2232
Paul Hinman, prin. Fax 433-5432

Trenton, Grundy, Pop. 5,941
Pleasant View R-VI SD 100/PK-8
128 SE 20th St 64683 660-359-3438
Rebecca Steinhoff, admin. Fax 359-6925
pleasantviewr6.org
Pleasant View ES 100/PK-8
128 SE 20th St 64683 660-359-3438
Rebecca Steinhoff, admin. Fax 359-6925

Trenton R-IX SD 1,200/K-12
1607 Normal St 64683 660-359-3994
Daniel Wiebers, supt. Fax 359-3995
www.trentonr9.k12.mo.us/
Rissler ES 400/K-4
804 W 4th Ter 64683 660-359-2228
Jennifer Boon, prin. Fax 359-3778
Trenton MS 400/5-8
1417 Oklahoma Ave 64683 660-359-4328
Daniel Gott, prin. Fax 359-6554

Troy, Lincoln, Pop. 10,315
Lincoln County R-III SD 6,900/PK-12
951 W College St 63379 636-462-6098
Dr. Mark Penny Ed.D., supt. Fax 462-6099
www.troy.k12.mo.us
Boone ES 400/K-5
1464 Boone St 63379 636-528-1560
Al Slusser, prin. Fax 528-1561
Brown ES 300/K-5
711 W College St 63379 636-462-5078
Mandy Champion, prin. Fax 462-5079
Cuivre Park ES 600/K-5
100 Wieman Ln 63379 636-462-5218
Toni White, prin. Fax 462-5219
Early Childhood Education Center PK-PK
1601 S Main St 63379 636-462-3020
Dr. Kelly Groeber, prin. Fax 462-3021
Lincoln ES 400/K-5
1484 Boone St 63379 636-528-1990
Holly Hite, prin. Fax 528-1991
Main Street ES 500/K-5
51 Main St 63379 636-528-4809
Megan Sanford, prin. Fax 528-2649
Troy MS 1,500/6-8
713 W College St 63379 636-462-4937
Dr. Briscoe Kelly, prin. Fax 462-4938
Other Schools – See Hawk Point, Moscow Mills

First Baptist Christian Academy 100/K-8
1000 Elm Tree Rd 63379 636-528-5967
Karen Ryan, admin. Fax 528-8766
Sacred Heart S 300/PK-8
110 Thompson Dr 63379 636-528-6684
Ann Hoffman, prin. Fax 528-3923

Tuscumbia, Miller, Pop. 203
Miller County R-III SD 200/K-12
PO Box 1 65082 573-369-2375
Jason Price, supt. Fax 369-2833
www.tuscumbialions.k12.mo.us
Miller County ES 200/K-8
PO Box 1 65082 573-369-2375
Randy Gum, prin. Fax 369-2833

Union, Franklin, Pop. 10,024
Union R-XI SD 3,100/K-12
PO Box 440 63084 636-583-8626
Dr. Steve Weinhold, supt. Fax 583-2403
union.k12.mo.us
Central ES 700/K-3
PO Box 440 63084 636-583-3152
Leslie Lause, prin. Fax 583-8173
Clark-Vitt ES 600/4-6
PO Box 440 63084 636-583-6997
Aaron Burd, prin. Fax 583-8517
Union MS 400/7-8
PO Box 440 63084 636-583-5855
Ted Koenigsfeld, prin. Fax 583-6156
Other Schools – See Beaufort

Washington SD
Supt. — See Washington
Clearview ES 300/K-6
1581 Clearview Rd 63084 636-231-2500
Matt Busekrus, prin. Fax 231-2505

Immaculate Conception S 400/PK-8
6 W State St 63084 636-583-2641
Rebecca Tucker, prin. Fax 583-3073

Union Star, DeKalb, Pop. 430
Union Star R-II SD 100/K-12
6132 NW State Route Z 64494 816-593-2294
Rick Calloway, supt. Fax 593-4427
www.usr2.com
Union Star ES 100/K-5
6132 NW State Route Z 64494 816-593-2294
Chris Turpin, prin. Fax 593-4427

Unionville, Putnam, Pop. 1,843
Putnam County R-I SD 700/PK-12
803 S 20th St 63565 660-947-3361
Dr. Heath Halley Ed.D., supt. Fax 947-2912
www.putnamcountyr1.net
Putnam County R-1 ES 300/PK-5
801 S 20th St 63565 660-947-2494
Donna Altiser, prin. Fax 947-2912
Putnam County R-1 MS 200/6-8
802 S 18th St 63565 660-947-3237
Andrew Garber, prin. Fax 947-2912

University City, Saint Louis, Pop. 34,413
School District of University City 3,100/PK-12
8136 Groby Rd 63130 314-290-4000
Sharonica Hardin-Bartley Ph.D., supt.
www.ucityschools.org
Brittany Woods MS 700/6-8
8125 Groby Rd 63130 314-290-4280
Elliott Shostak, prin. Fax 997-1786
Flynn Park ES 400/K-5
7220 Waterman Ave 63130 314-290-4421
Nicalee Stephens, prin. Fax 727-8244
Goldstein Early Education Center 100/PK-PK
737 Kingsland Ave 63130 314-721-2965
Crystal Cauley, admin. Fax 721-2045
Jackson Park ES 400/K-5
7400 Balson Ave 63130 314-290-4450
Rebecca O'Connell, prin. Fax 727-4478
Jordan ES 400/K-5
1500 82nd Blvd, 314-290-4360
Shenelle DuBose, prin. Fax 692-9970
Pershing ES 400/K-5
6761 Bartmer Ave 63130 314-290-4150
Herbert Buie, prin. Fax 725-3562

Agape Academy 300/PK-8
7400 Olive Blvd 63130 314-725-5262
Christ the King S 200/PK-8
7324 Balson Ave 63130 314-725-5855
Susan Hooker, prin. Fax 725-5981
Freedom S 100/PK-5
1483 82nd Blvd, 314-432-7396
Our Lady of Lourdes S 300/K-8
7157 Northmoor Dr, 314-726-3352
Dr. Jeanne Gearon, prin. Fax 727-0503

Urbana, Hickory, Pop. 412
Hickory County R-I SD 500/K-12
20663 US Highway 65 65767 417-993-4241
Dr. Mark Beem, supt. Fax 993-4269
skylineschools.info
Skyline ES 300/K-6
20663 US Highway 65 65767 417-993-4225
Jason Pursley, prin. Fax 993-0216

Valley Park, Saint Louis, Pop. 6,786
Valley Park SD 1,000/PK-12
1 Main St 63088 636-923-3500
Dr. David Knes, supt. Fax 861-1002
www.vp.k12.mo.us
Valley Park ES 500/PK-5
1 Main St 63088 636-923-3500
Dr. Janice Monroe, prin. Fax 225-4518
Valley Park MS 200/6-8
1 Main St 63088 636-923-3624
Kelly Muzzey, prin. Fax 225-1529

Sacred Heart S 300/PK-8
12 Ann Ave 63088 636-225-3824
Angie Lind, prin. Fax 225-8941

Van Buren, Carter, Pop. 813
Van Buren R-I SD 500/PK-12
PO Box 550 63965 573-323-4281
Fax 323-4297
www.vanburen.k12.mo.us
Van Buren ES 300/PK-6
PO Box 550 63965 573-323-4266
Amy Jackson, prin. Fax 323-4537

Vandalia, Audrain, Pop. 3,832
Van-Far R-I SD 600/PK-12
2200 W US Highway 54 63382 573-594-6111
Stephen Hunter, supt. Fax 594-2878
www.vf.k12.mo.us
Van-Far ES 400/PK-6
2122 Audrain Road 557 63382 573-594-2731
Brian Hummel, prin. Fax 594-2133

Verona, Lawrence, Pop. 608
Verona R-VII SD 400/K-12
PO Box 7 65769 417-498-2274
Tony L. Simmons, supt. Fax 498-6590
www.verona.k12.mo.us
Verona ES 200/K-6
PO Box 7 65769 417-498-6418
M. Whitehead, prin. Fax 498-6046

Versailles, Morgan, Pop. 2,421
Morgan County R-II SD 1,500/PK-12
913 W Newton St 65084 573-378-4231
Dr. Joyce Ryerson, supt. Fax 378-5714
www.versaillestigers.org
Morgan County ES 600/PK-5
913 W Newton St 65084 573-378-4272
Kim Murdock, prin. Fax 378-5164
Morgan County MS 300/6-8
913 W Newton St 65084 573-378-5432
Travis Troyer, prin. Fax 378-6610
Other Schools – See Gravois Mills

Viburnum, Iron, Pop. 688
Iron County C-4 SD 400/K-12
35 Highway 49 65566 573-244-5422
Dr. Tim Hager, supt. Fax 244-5424
www.ironc4.k12.mo.us
Viburnum ES 200/K-6
PO Box 368 65566 573-244-5670
Michelle Merseal, prin. Fax 244-5767

Vienna, Maries, Pop. 605
Maries County R-I SD 500/PK-12
PO Box 218 65582 573-422-3304
Joseph Dunlap, supt. Fax 422-3185
www.mariesr1.k12.mo.us
Vienna ES 300/PK-6
PO Box 218 65582 573-422-3365
Sherree Burkholder, prin. Fax 422-3185

Visitation Interparish S 50/K-8
PO Box 269 65582 573-422-3375
Teresa Finnern, prin. Fax 422-3375

Villa Ridge, Franklin, Pop. 2,605
Meramec Valley R-III SD
Supt. — See Pacific
Coleman ES 400/K-5
4536 Coleman Rd 63089 636-742-2133
Lisa Weirich, prin. Fax 742-2281

Crosspoint Christian S 100/PK-12
PO Box 100 63089 636-742-5380
Don Coons, admin. Fax 742-5917
St. John the Baptist S 100/PK-8
5579 Gildehaus Rd 63089 636-583-2392
Gary Menke, prin. Fax 583-6114

Walker, Vernon, Pop. 266
Northeast Vernon County R-I SD 200/PK-12
216 E Leslie Ave 64790 417-465-2221
Charles Naas, supt. Fax 465-2388
www.nevcknights.org
Other Schools – See Schell City

Walnut Grove, Greene, Pop. 659
Walnut Grove R-V SD 300/PK-12
PO Box 187 65770 417-788-2543
Gwenda Barton, supt. Fax 788-1254
www.wgtigers.com
Walnut Grove ES 100/PK-5
PO Box 187 65770 417-788-2543
Christina Bowers, prin. Fax 788-1254

Wardell, Pemiscot, Pop. 423
North Pemiscot County R-I SD 300/K-12
PO Box 38 63879 573-628-3471
Terry Hamilton, supt. Fax 628-3472
www.northpem.k12.mo.us
Other Schools – See Portageville

Wardsville, Cole, Pop. 1,489
Blair Oaks R-II SD 1,200/K-12
6124 Falcon Ln 65101 573-636-2020
Dr. James Jones, supt. Fax 636-2202
www.blairoaks.k12.mo.us
Blair Oaks ES 400/K-4
6124 Falcon Ln 65101 573-634-2808
Kimberley Rodriguez, prin. Fax 634-3240
Blair Oaks MS 300/5-8
6124 Falcon Ln 65101 573-634-2053
Don Jeffries, prin. Fax 636-3509

St. Stanislaus S 200/PK-8
6410 Route W 65101 573-636-7802
Nancy Heberlie, prin. Fax 635-4782

Warrensburg, Johnson, Pop. 18,253
Warrensburg R-VI SD 3,300/PK-12
PO Box 638 64093 660-747-7823
Dr. Scott Patrick, supt. Fax 747-9615
www.warrensburgr6.org
Maple Grove ES 400/PK-2
950 Hamilton St 64093 660-422-5770
John Finnane, prin. Fax 429-0047
Ridge View ES 400/PK-2
215 S Ridgeview Dr 64093 660-747-6013
Melissa Marnholtz, prin. Fax 747-3697
Sterling ES 400/3-5
522 E Gay St 64093 660-747-7478
Christine Johnson, prin. Fax 747-9400
Warren ES 400/3-5
105 S Maguire St 64093 660-747-7160
Lorna Cassell, prin. Fax 747-8062
Warrensburg MS 700/6-8
640 E Gay St 64093 660-747-5612
Jim Elliott, prin. Fax 747-8779

Warrenton, Warren, Pop. 7,746
Warren County R-III SD 3,200/PK-12
385 W Veterans Memorial Pky 63383 636-456-6901
Dr. Jill Schowe, supt. Fax 456-7687
www.warrencor3.org
Black Hawk MS 700/6-8
300 Kuhl Ave 63383 636-456-6903
Lisa Pirrung, prin. Fax 456-1445
Boone ES 500/PK-5
813 Vosholl 63383 636-456-6905
Stacey Goldsmith, prin. Fax 456-6900
Boone ES 500/PK-5
836 South St, 636-456-6904
Steve Weeks, prin. Fax 456-0481
Warrior Ridge ES 500/PK-5
800 Warrior Ave 63383 636-456-6906
Bobbie Russell, prin. Fax 456-6996

Holy Rosary S 100/K-8
716 E Booneslick Rd 63383 636-456-3698
Loraine Racine, prin. Fax 456-6181

Warsaw, Benton, Pop. 2,107
Warsaw R-IX SD 1,300/PK-12
PO Box 248 65355 660-438-7120
Dr. Shawn Poyser, supt. Fax 438-5028
www.warsaw.k12.mo.us
Boise MS 300/6-8
PO Box 1750 65355 660-438-9079
Dr. Eric Findley, prin. Fax 438-2209
Mercer ES 100/PK-K
PO Box 307 65355 660-438-7222
Beth Love, prin. Fax 438-5976
North ES 200/1-5
PO Box 307 65355 660-438-6260
Jill Shelby, prin. Fax 438-3817
Other Schools – See Edwards

Cornerstone Academy of the Ozarks 50/PK-7
PO Box 1093 65355 660-438-6161
Dr. Rebecka Spencer, prin.

Washburn, Barry, Pop. 418
Southwest R-V SD 800/PK-12
529 E Pineville Rd 65772 417-826-5410
Tosha Tilford, supt. Fax 826-5603
www.swr5.net
Southwest ES 300/PK-4
529 E Pineville Rd 65772 417-826-5411
Jeff Payne, prin. Fax 826-5603
Southwest MS 200/5-8
529 E Pineville Rd 65772 417-826-5050
Christy Hermansen, prin. Fax 826-5603

Washington, Franklin, Pop. 13,819
Washington SD 4,000/PK-12
220 Locust St 63090 636-231-2000
Dr. Lori VanLeer, supt. Fax 239-3315
www.washington.k12.mo.us
Early Learning Center PK-PK
831 W Pride Dr 63090 636-231-2850
Dr. Dawn Hellebusch, dir. Fax 231-2855
South Point ES 500/K-6
2300 Southbend Dr 63090 636-231-2700
Aimee Harty, prin. Fax 231-2750
Washington MS 600/7-8
401 E 14th St 63090 636-231-2300
Ron Millheiser, prin. Fax 231-2305
Washington West ES 500/K-6
840 W Pride Dr 63090 636-390-9150
Kim Hunt, prin. Fax 390-9152
Other Schools – See Augusta, Labadie, Marthasville, New Haven, Union

---

Immanuel Lutheran S 200/PK-8
214 W 5th St 63090 636-239-1636
Nick Hopfensperger, admin. Fax 239-0589
Our Lady of Lourdes S 200/PK-8
950 Madison Ave 63090 636-239-5292
Tammi Rohman, prin. Fax 390-9050
St. Francis Borgia S 300/PK-8
225 Cedar St 63090 636-239-2590
Linda Pahl, prin. Fax 239-3501
St. Gertrude S 300/PK-8
6520 Highway YY 63090 636-239-2347
Stephen Young Ed.D., prin. Fax 239-3550

Waverly, Lafayette, Pop. 845
Santa Fe R-X SD
Supt. — See Alma
Santa Fe ES 200/K-6
703 W Walnut St 64096 660-493-2811
Stacey Smith, prin. Fax 493-2421

Waynesville, Pulaski, Pop. 4,531
Waynesville R-VI SD 6,200/PK-12
200 Fleetwood Dr 65583 573-842-2097
Dr. Brian Henry, supt. Fax 433-2967
www.waynesville.k12.mo.us
Waynesville East ES 1,200/PK-5
1501 State Route F 65583 573-842-2150
Heather Hays, prin. Fax 842-2159
Waynesville MS 900/7-8
1001 Historic 66 W 65583 573-842-2550
Michele Sumter, prin. Fax 842-2559
Waynesville Sixth Grade Center 500/6-6
810 Roosevelt St 65583 573-842-2300
Jamie Goforth, prin. Fax 433-2600
Other Schools – See Fort Leonard Wood, Saint Robert

Weaubleau, Hickory, Pop. 411
Weaubleau R-III SD 300/PK-12
509 N Center St 65774 417-428-3668
Dr. Eric Wilken, supt. Fax 428-3004
www.weaubleau.k12.mo.us
Weaubleau ES 200/PK-6
509 N Center St 65774 417-428-3668
Traci Foster, prin. Fax 428-3360

Webb City, Jasper, Pop. 10,693
Webb City R-VII SD 4,100/PK-12
411 N Madison St 64870 417-673-6000
Anthony Rossetti, supt. Fax 673-6007
www.wcr7.org
Field ES 200/3-4
510 S Oronogo St 64870 417-673-6040
Mark Drake, prin. Fax 673-6041
Franklin ECC 50/PK-PK
404 Tracy St 64870 417-673-6070
Trey Moeller, prin. Fax 673-6007
James K 200/K-K
211 W Aylor St 64870 417-673-6075
Amanda Green, prin. Fax 673-6077
Truman ES 300/2-4
810 N Highway D 64870 417-673-6085
Jodi Bennett, prin. Fax 673-6087
Truman Primary Center 200/K-1
800 N Highway D 64870 417-673-6055
Stacy Hollingsworth, prin. Fax 673-6057
Twain ES 200/3-4
1427 W Aylor St 64870 417-673-6050
Jan Shelley, prin. Fax 673-6051
Webb City JHS 600/7-8
807 W 1st St 64870 417-673-6030
Angie Broadus, prin. Fax 673-6037
Webb City MS 700/5-6
603 W Aylor St 64870 417-673-6045
Alicia Zornes, prin. Fax 673-6048
Webster ES 400/1-2
700 N Main St 64870 417-673-6060
Sarah Lee, prin. Fax 673-6061
Other Schools – See Carterville

Webster Groves, Saint Louis, Pop. 22,645
Webster Groves SD 4,600/PK-12
400 E Lockwood Ave 63119 314-961-1233
Dr. John Simpson, supt. Fax 963-6411
www.webster.k12.mo.us
Ambrose Family Center 200/PK-PK
222 W Cedar Ave 63119 314-963-6440
Marty Baker, dir. Fax 968-9259
Avery ES 500/K-5
909 N Bompart Ave 63119 314-963-6425
Dr. Anthony Arnold, prin. Fax 963-6490
Clark ES 300/K-5
9130 Big Bend Blvd 63119 314-963-6444
Joe Hays, prin. Fax 963-6446
Edgar Road ES 400/K-5
1131 Edgar Rd 63119 314-963-6472
Dr. Julie Wuch, prin. Fax 963-6477
Hudson ES 200/K-5
9825 Hudson Ave 63119 314-963-6466
Lisa Hilpert, prin. Fax 963-6478
Other Schools – See Saint Louis

College S 300/PK-8
7825 Big Bend Blvd 63119 314-962-9355
Ed Maggart, hdmstr. Fax 962-5078
Holy Cross Academy Annunciation S 50/6-8
16 W Glendale Rd 63119 314-961-7712
Janet Dolan, prin. Fax 961-2157
Holy Redeemer S 200/PK-8
341 E Lockwood Ave 63119 314-962-8989
Pam Galluzzo, prin. Fax 962-3560
Mary Queen of Peace S 500/K-8
680 W Lockwood Ave 63119 314-961-2891
Michael Nieman, prin. Fax 961-7469
Waldorf S of St. Louis 100/PK-8
915 N Elm Ave 63119 314-962-2129

Weldon Spring, Saint Charles, Pop. 5,401
Francis Howell R-III SD
Supt. — See Saint Charles
Bryan MS 900/6-8
605 Independence Rd 63304 636-851-5800
Suzanne Chester, prin. Fax 851-6208
Early Childhood Family Education Center 900/PK-PK
4810 Meadows Pkwy 63304 636-851-6000
Mary Calkins, prin. Fax 851-6198
Howell MS 800/6-8
825 OFallon Rd 63304 636-851-4800
Ted Huff, prin. Fax 851-4121
Independence ES 800/K-5
4800 Meadows Pkwy 63304 636-851-5900
Emily Pavia, prin. Fax 851-6149

Messiah Lutheran S 300/PK-8
5911 S Highway 94 63304 636-329-1096
Joanie Smith, prin. Fax 329-1098

Wellington, Lafayette, Pop. 797
Wellington-Napoleon R-IX SD 400/K-12
800 Highway 131 64097 816-934-2531
MIndy Hampton, supt. Fax 934-8649
www.wntigers.net
Wellington-Napoleon ES 200/K-5
800 Highway 131 64097 816-240-2631
Justin Mefferd, prin. Fax 934-8649

Wellsville, Montgomery, Pop. 1,206
Wellsville Middletown R-I SD 400/PK-12
900 Burlington St 63384 573-684-2428
Pete Nasir, supt. Fax 684-2018
wmr1.k12.mo.us/
Wellsville-Middleton ES 200/PK-6
900 Burlington St 63384 573-684-2047
Tiffany Gosseen, prin. Fax 684-2018

Wentzville, Saint Charles, Pop. 28,539
Francis Howell R-III SD
Supt. — See Saint Charles
Boone ES 400/K-5
201 W Highway D 63385 636-851-4400
Kevin Armour, prin. Fax 851-4105

Ft. Zumwalt R-II SD
Supt. — See O Fallon
Flint Hill ES K-5
587 Mexico Rd 63385 636-542-7095
Deborah Mueller, prin. Fax 327-6290

Wentzville R-IV SD 14,500/K-12
280 Interstate Dr 63385 636-327-3800
Dr. Curtis Cain, supt. Fax 327-8611
www.wentzville.k12.mo.us
Boone Trail ES 900/K-6
555 E Highway N 63385 636-327-3830
Michelle Cleve, prin. Fax 327-3956
Heritage IS 600/3-6
601 Carr St 63385 636-327-3839
Dr. Todd Kraft, prin. Fax 327-3957
Heritage PS 600/K-2
612 Blumhoff Ave 63385 636-327-3846
Geri Buss, prin. Fax 327-3958
Peine Ridge ES 700/K-6
1107 Peine Rd 63385 636-327-5110
Ryan Andrews, prin. Fax 327-5121
Stone Creek ES K-6
1820 Highway Z 63385 636-887-3898
Dr. Melvin Bishop, prin. Fax 887-3893
Wentzville MS 1,200/7-8
405 Campus Dr 63385 636-327-3815
Dr. Kelly Mantz, prin. Fax 327-3954
Wentzville South MS 1,200/7-8
561 E Highway N 63385 636-327-3928
Scott Swift, prin. Fax 327-3955
Other Schools – See Dardenne Pr, Foristell, Lake Saint Louis, O Fallon

---

Immanuel Lutheran S 400/PK-8
632 E Highway N 63385 636-639-9887
Allison Dolak, prin. Fax 639-9944
St. Joseph S 100/PK-8
1410 Josephville Rd 63385 636-332-5672
Jill Nance, prin. Fax 332-5693
St. Patrick S 500/PK-8
701 S Church St 63385 636-332-9913
Denise Brickler, prin. Fax 887-2065
St. Theodore S 200/K-8
5059 Highway P 63385 636-639-1385
Kelly Cassinger, prin. Fax 327-5115

Weston, Platte, Pop. 1,614
West Platte County R-II SD 600/PK-12
1103 Washington St 64098 816-640-2236
Dr. John Rinehart, supt. Fax 386-2104
www.wpsd.net
Central ES 300/PK-6
1025 Washington St 64098 816-640-2811
Rebecca Henshaw, prin. Fax 386-5888

Westphalia, Osage, Pop. 382
Osage County R-III SD 800/K-12
PO Box 37 65085 573-455-2375
Chuck Woody, supt. Fax 455-9884
www.fatimacomets.org
Fatima ES 300/K-6
PO Box 37 65085 573-455-2395
Karen Keller, prin. Fax 455-9884

St. Joseph S 200/K-8
PO Box 205 65085 573-455-2339
Tammy Ogden, prin. Fax 455-2984

West Plains, Howell, Pop. 11,780
Fairview R-XI SD 500/PK-8
4036 State Route K 65775 417-256-1063
Aaron Sydow, supt. Fax 256-8831
www.fairview.k12.mo.us
Fairview S 500/PK-8
4036 State Route K 65775 417-256-1063
Aaron Sydow, supt. Fax 256-8831

Glenwood R-VIII SD 300/PK-8
10286 State Route 17 65775 417-256-4849
Wayne Stewart, supt. Fax 257-2567
glenwoodmustangs.com
Glenwood ES 300/PK-8
10286 State Route 17 65775 417-256-4849
Wayne Stewart, supt. Fax 257-2567

Howell Valley R-I SD 200/K-8
6461 State Route ZZ 65775 417-256-2268
Marvin Hatley, supt. Fax 257-2953
www.hvpanthers.org
Howell Valley S 200/K-8
6461 State Route ZZ 65775 417-256-2268
Ava Patterson, prin. Fax 256-9696

Junction Hill C-12 SD 200/PK-8
8004 County Road 3010 65775 417-256-4265
John Dern, supt. Fax 256-3588
www.junctionhill.k12.mo.us
Junction Hill S 200/PK-8
8004 County Road 3010 65775 417-256-4265
Denis Knight, prin. Fax 256-3588

Richards R-V SD 500/PK-8
3461 County Road 1710 65775 417-256-5239
Dr. Melonie Bunn, supt. Fax 256-3314
richardsschool.k12.mo.us
Richards ES 500/PK-8
3461 County Road 1710 65775 417-256-5239
Douglas Lansdown, prin. Fax 256-3314

West Plains R-VII SD 2,600/PK-12
305 Valley View Dr 65775 417-256-6150
Dr. John Mulford, supt. Fax 256-8616
wpr7.schoolwires.net
South Fork ES 200/PK-6
3209 US Highway 160 65775 417-256-2836
Dr. Seth Huddleston, prin. Fax 255-1432
West Plains ES 700/PK-4
1136 Allen St 65775 417-256-6150
Donnie Miller, prin. Fax 256-2358

West Plains MS 500/5-8
730 E Olden St 65775 417-256-6150
Dr. Wesley Davis, prin. Fax 256-8907

Ozarks Christian Academy 100/PK-12
PO Box 1620 65775 417-255-1622

Wheatland, Hickory, Pop. 358
Wheatland R-II SD 300/PK-12
PO Box 68 65779 417-282-6433
Tim Judd, supt. Fax 282-5733
sites.google.com/a/wheatland.k12.mo.us/district/
Wheatland R-II ES 200/PK-6
PO Box 68 65779 417-282-5833
Brian Pearson, prin. Fax 282-5733

Wheaton, Barry, Pop. 680
Wheaton R-III SD 400/PK-12
PO Box 249 64874 417-652-3914
Dr. Lance Massey, supt. Fax 652-7355
www.wheatonbulldogs.org/
Wheaton ES 200/PK-6
PO Box 249 64874 417-652-7240
Naomi Austin, prin. Fax 652-7355

Whiteman AFB, Johnson, Pop. 2,433
Knob Noster R-VIII SD
Supt. — See Knob Noster
Whiteman AFB ES 400/PK-4
120 Houx Dr 65305 660-563-3028
Jessica Steward, prin. Fax 563-3443

Wildwood, Saint Louis, Pop. 35,007

Living Water Academy 100/PK-8
17770 Mueller Rd 63038 636-821-2308
Thomas Keller, head sch Fax 821-1709
St. Alban Roe S 500/PK-8
2005 Shepard Rd 63038 636-458-6084
Tara Smith, prin. Fax 405-3026

Willard, Greene, Pop. 5,200
Willard R-II SD 4,400/PK-12
500 Kime St 65781 417-742-2584
Dr. Matthew Teeter, supt. Fax 742-2586
www.willardschools.net
Willard East ES 300/PK-4
518 Kime St 65781 417-742-4639
Melinda Miller, prin. Fax 685-0005
Willard IS 700/5-6
407 Farmer Rd 65781 417-742-4242
Tom Davis, prin. Fax 742-0217
Willard MS 700/7-8
205 S Miller Rd 65781 417-742-2588
Amy Sims, prin. Fax 742-3505
Willard North ES 300/PK-4
409 Farmer Rd 65781 417-742-2597
Amanda Hambey, prin. Fax 742-0139
Other Schools – See Springfield

Williamsburg, Callaway
North Callaway County R-I SD
Supt. — See Kingdom City
Williamsburg ES 200/K-8
10500 Old US Highway 40 63388 573-254-3415
Tammy Thompson, prin. Fax 254-3859

Williamsville, Wayne, Pop. 338
Greenville R-II SD
Supt. — See Greenville
Williamsville ES 100/PK-6
HC 1 Box 6M 63967 573-998-2313
Diane Meyer, prin. Fax 998-2339

Willow Springs, Howell, Pop. 2,140
Willow Springs R-IV SD 1,400/PK-12
215 W 4th St 65793 417-469-3260
William Hall, supt. Fax 469-2507
www.willowspringsschool.com
Willow Springs ES 500/PK-4
215 W 4th St 65793 417-469-2474
Bobby Cottengim, prin. Fax 469-4320
Willow Springs MS 400/5-8
215 W 4th St 65793 417-469-3211
Philip Pietroburgo, prin. Fax 469-1229

Windsor, Henry, Pop. 2,866
Henry County R-I SD 700/PK-12
210 North St 65360 660-647-3533
Dr. Kristee Lorenz, supt. Fax 647-2711
henrycountyr1.k12.mo.us
Windsor ES 400/PK-6
501 S Main St 65360 660-647-5621
Stephany Wasson, prin. Fax 647-5344

Winfield, Lincoln, Pop. 1,383
Winfield R-IV SD 1,500/K-12
100 8th St 63389 636-668-8188
Daniel Williams, supt. Fax 668-8641
www.winfield.k12.mo.us
Winfield IS 400/3-5
100 8th St 63389 636-668-8300
Jeffrey Schultz, prin. Fax 668-6056
Winfield MS 300/6-8
100 8th St 63389 636-668-8001
Tom McCracken, prin. Fax 668-6044
Winfield PS 300/K-2
100 8th St 63389 636-668-8195
Ericka Dixon, prin. Fax 668-6259

Winona, Shannon, Pop. 1,311
Winona R-III SD 500/PK-12
PO Box 248 65588 573-325-8101
Jennifer Mahan-Asplin, supt. Fax 325-8447
www.winonar3.org
Winona ES 300/PK-8
PO Box 248 65588 573-325-8101
Jana Williams, prin. Fax 325-4345

Winston, Daviess, Pop. 258
Winston R-VI SD 200/PK-12
PO Box 38 64689 660-749-5331
Dr. Brian Robinson, supt. Fax 749-5432
www.winston.k12.mo.us
Winston ES 100/PK-6
PO Box 38 64689 660-749-5459
Pamela Madison, prin. Fax 749-5432

Wright City, Warren, Pop. 3,037
Wright City R-II SD 1,600/PK-12
90 Bell Rd 63390 636-745-7200
Dr. David Buck, supt. Fax 745-3613
www.wrightcity.k12.mo.us/
Wright City MS 300/6-8
100 Bell Rd 63390 636-745-7300
Douglas Smith, prin. Fax 745-7304
Wright City West ES 500/2-5
100 Wildcat Dr 63390 636-745-7400
Patrick Wallace, prin. Fax 745-7411
Wright Start Preschool 100/PK-PK
80 Bell Rd 63390 636-791-2150
David Herod, admin.
Other Schools – See Foristell

Liberty Christian Academy 100/PK-12
PO Box 514 63390 636-745-0388
Beverly Wilgus, admin. Fax 745-0390

Zalma, Bollinger, Pop. 122
Zalma R-V SD 200/K-12
HC 2 Box 184 63787 573-722-5504
Gerard Vandeven, supt. Fax 722-9870
zalma.k12.mo.us
Zalma ES 100/K-6
1 School St 63787 573-722-3136
Jeri Bader, prin. Fax 722-9870

MONTANA

MONTANA OFFICE OF PUBLIC INSTRUCTION
PO Box 202501, Helena 59620-2501
Telephone 406-444-3095
Fax 406-444-2893
Website opi.mt.gov

State Superintendent of Public Instruction Elsie Arntzen

MONTANA BOARD OF EDUCATION
PO Box 200601, Helena 59620

Chairperson Sharon Carroll

COUNTY SUPERINTENDENTS OF SCHOOLS

Beaverhead County Office of Education
Linda Marsh, supt. 406-683-3737
2 S Pacific St Ste 7, Dillon 59725 Fax 683-3769

Big Horn County Office of Education
Vicki Gale, supt. 406-665-9820
PO Box 908, Hardin 59034 Fax 665-9823

Blaine County Office of Education
Kelly Mills, supt. 406-357-3270
PO Box 819, Chinook 59523 Fax 357-2199

Broadwater County Office of Education
Douglas Ellis, supt. 406-266-9215
515 Broadway St, Townsend 59644 Fax 266-3674

Carbon County Office of Education
Jane Swanson-Webb, supt. 406-446-1301
PO Box 116, Red Lodge 59068 Fax 446-9155

Carter County Office of Education
Tracey Walker, supt. 406-775-8714
PO Box 352, Ekalaka 59324 Fax 775-8703

Cascade County Office of Education
Patricia Boyle, supt. 406-454-6776
121 4th St N Ste 1A Fax 454-6778
Great Falls 59401
www.cascadecountymt.gov

Chouteau County Office of Education
Mary Lou Tweet, supt. 406-622-3242
PO Box 459, Fort Benton 59442 Fax 622-3028

Custer County Office of Education
Doug Ellingson, supt. 406-874-3421
1010 Main St, Miles City 59301 Fax 874-3452

Daniels County Office of Education
Joan Bjarko, supt. 406-487-2651
PO Box 67, Scobey 59263 Fax 487-5432

Dawson County Office of Education 406-377-3963
, 207 W Bell St, Glendive 59330 Fax 377-2022

Deer Lodge County Office of Education
Michael O'Rourke, supt. 406-563-9178
800 Main St, Anaconda 59711 Fax 563-5476

Fallon County Office of Education
Don Dilworth, supt. 406-778-8158
PO Box 846, Baker 59313 Fax 778-2048

Fergus County Office of Education
Rhonda Long, supt. 406-535-3136
712 W Main St, Lewistown 59457 Fax 535-2819

Flathead County Office of Education
Jack Eggensperger, supt. 406-758-5720
935 1st Ave W, Kalispell 59901 Fax 758-5850

Gallatin County Office of Education
Laura Axtman, supt. 406-582-3090
311 W Main St Rm 107 Fax 582-3093
Bozeman 59715

Garfield County Office of Education
Jessica McWilliams, supt. 406-557-6115
PO Box 28, Jordan 59337 Fax 557-6115

Glacier County Office of Education
Darryl Omsberg, supt. 406-873-2295
1210 E Main St, Cut Bank 59427 Fax 873-9103
www.glaciercountygov.com

Golden Valley County Office of Education
Craig Mattheis, supt. 406-568-2342
107 Kemp St, Ryegate 59074 Fax 568-2428

Granite County Office of Education
Vicki Harding, supt. 406-859-9831
PO Box 9, Philipsburg 59858 Fax 859-3817

Hill County Office of Education
Diane McLean, supt. 406-265-5481
315 4th St, Havre 59501 Fax 265-5487

Jefferson County Office of Education
Garry Pace, supt. 406-225-4114
PO Box H, Boulder 59632 Fax 225-4149

Judith Basin County Office of Education
Julie Anderson Peevey, supt. 406-566-2277
PO Box 307, Stanford 59479 Fax 566-2211

Lake County Office of Education
Carolyn Hall, supt. 406-883-7262
106 4th Ave E, Polson 59860 Fax 883-7283
www.lakemt.gov/

Lewis & Clark County Office of Education
Katrina Chaney, supt. 406-447-8344
316 N Park Ave Ste 221 Fax 447-8398
Helena 59623
www.lccountymt.gov/education

Liberty County Office of Education
Kathy Armstrong, supt. 406-759-5216
PO Box 684, Chester 59522 Fax 759-5996

Lincoln County Office of Education
Nancy Trotter-Higgins, supt. 406-283-2401
512 California Ave, Libby 59923 Fax 293-7760

Madison County Office of Education
Pam Birkeland, supt. 406-843-4280
PO Box 247, Virginia City 59755 Fax 843-5388

McCone County Office of Education
Nita Crockett, supt. 406-485-3590
PO Box 180, Circle 59215 Fax 485-2689

Meagher County Office of Education
Helen Hanson, supt., PO Box 429 406-547-3388
White Sulphur Springs 59645

Mineral County Office of Education
Mary Yarnall, supt. 406-822-3529
PO Box 100, Superior 59872 Fax 822-3579

Missoula County Office of Education
Erin Lipkind, supt. 406-258-3349
438 W Spruce St, Missoula 59802 Fax 258-3973

Musselshell County Office of Education
Kathryn Pfister, supt. 406-323-1470
506 Main St, Roundup 59072 Fax 323-3303

Park County Office of Education
Jo Newhall, supt. 406-222-4148
414 E Callender St Fax 222-4199
Livingston 59047

Petroleum County Office of Education
Pamela Bevis, supt. 406-429-5551
PO Box 226, Winnett 59087 Fax 429-6328

Phillips County Office of Education
Vivian Taylor, supt. 406-654-2010
PO Box 138, Malta 59538 Fax 654-3333

Pondera County Office of Education
Lynn Utterback, supt. 406-271-4055
20 4th Ave SW Ste 307 Fax 271-4070
Conrad 59425

Powder River County Office of Education
Molly Lloyd, supt. 406-436-2488
PO Box 718, Broadus 59317 Fax 436-2151

Powell County Office of Education
Jules Waber, supt. 406-846-9719
409 Missouri Ave Fax 846-3891
Deer Lodge 59722

Prairie County Office of Education
Jamie Smith, supt. 406-635-5577
PO Box 566, Terry 59349 Fax 635-5576

Ravalli County Office of Education
Regina Plettenberg, supt. 406-375-6551
215 S 4th St Ste B, Hamilton 59840 Fax 375-6554

Richland County Office of Education
Gail Anne Staffanson, supt. 406-433-1608
201 W Main St, Sidney 59270 Fax 433-3731

Roosevelt County Office of Education
Jeri Toavs, supt. 406-653-6266
400 2nd Ave S, Wolf Point 59201 Fax 653-6203

Rosebud County Office of Education
Joby Parker, supt. 406-346-2537
PO Box 407, Forsyth 59327 Fax 346-7319

Sanders County Office of Education
Carol Turk, supt. 406-826-4288
PO Box 519, Plains 59859 Fax 826-4299

Sheridan County Office of Education
June Johnson, supt. 406-765-3403
100 W Laurel Ave Fax 765-2609
Plentywood 59254
www.co.sheridan.mt.us

Silver Bow County Office of Education
Cathy Maloney, supt. 406-497-6215
155 W Granite St, Butte 59701 Fax 497-6328

Stillwater County Office of Education
Judy Martin, supt. 406-322-8057
PO Box 1139, Columbus 59019 Fax 322-1118

Sweet Grass County Office of Education
Susan Metcalf, supt. 406-932-5147
PO Box 1310, Big Timber 59011 Fax 932-5112

Teton County Office of Education
Cathy Sessions, supt. 406-466-2907
PO Box 610, Choteau 59422 Fax 466-2138
tetoncomt.org/supofschools

Toole County Office of Education
Boyd Jackson, supt. 406-424-8322
226 1st St S, Shelby 59474 Fax 424-8321
toolecountymt.gov

Treasure County Office of Education
Tamara Kimball, supt. 406-342-5545
PO Box 429, Hysham 59038 Fax 342-5445

Valley County Office of Education
Lynne Nyquist, supt. 406-228-6226
501 Court Sq Ste 2 Fax 228-9027
Glasgow 59230

Wheatland County Office of Education
Susan Beley, supt. 406-632-4816
PO Box 637, Harlowton 59036 Fax 632-4873

Wibaux County Office of Education
Patricia Zinda, supt. 406-796-2481
PO Box 199, Wibaux 59353 Fax 796-2625

Yellowstone County Office of Education
Sherry Long, supt. 406-256-6933
217 N 27th St, Billings 59101 Fax 256-6930
www.co.yellowstone.mt.gov/

PUBLIC, PRIVATE AND CATHOLIC ELEMENTARY SCHOOLS

Absarokee, Stillwater, Pop. 1,134

Absarokee SD 300/PK-12
327 S Woodard Ave 59001 406-328-4583
Dustin Sturm, supt. Fax 328-4077
www.absarokee.k12.mt.us/

Absarokee ES 100/PK-6
327 S Woodard Ave 59001 406-328-4581
Meredith Feddes, prin. Fax 328-4575

Absarokee MS 50/7-8
327 S Woodard Ave 59001 406-328-4583
Dustin Sturm, prin. Fax 328-4077

Alberton, Mineral, Pop. 415

Alberton SD 100/PK-12
PO Box 330 59820 406-722-4413
Clay Acker, supt. Fax 722-3040
alberton.k12.mt.us/

Alberton ES 100/PK-6
PO Box 330 59820 406-722-4413
Kyle Fisher, prin. Fax 722-3040

Alberton MS 50/7-8
PO Box 330 59820 406-722-4413
Kyle Fisher, prin. Fax 722-3040

Alder, Madison, Pop. 103

Alder-Upper Ruby ESD 50/PK-8
PO Box 127 59710 406-843-4280
Pam Birkeland, supt. Fax 843-5388

Alder S 50/PK-8
PO Box 127 59710 406-842-5285
Teresa Murdoch, lead tchr. Fax 842-7149

Alzada, Carter, Pop. 29

Alzada ESD 56, PO Box 8 59311 50/PK-8
Tracey Walker, supt. 406-775-8721

Alzada ES, PO Box 8 59311 50/PK-8
Serena Parnell, lead tchr. 406-828-4445

Anaconda, Deer Lodge, Pop. 9,095
Anaconda SD 1,100/PK-12
1410 W Park Ave 59711 406-563-6361
Dr. Gerry Nolan, supt. Fax 563-7763
www.anacondaschools.org/
Lincoln ES 200/PK-2
1601 Tammany St 59711 406-563-6361
Norah Barney, prin. Fax 563-5729
Moodry IS, 506 Chestnut 59711 200/3-6
Anthony Laughlin, prin. 406-563-5639
Moodry JHS 200/7-8
219 E 3rd St 59711 406-563-6242
Tammy Hurley, prin. Fax 563-5093

Arlee, Lake, Pop. 605
Arlee SD 400/K-12
72220 Fyant St 59821 406-726-3216
Dave Whitesell, supt. Fax 360-8531
www.arleeschools.org
Arlee ES 300/K-6
72220 Fyant St 59821 406-726-3216
Don Holst, prin. Fax 315-4651
Arlee JHS 100/7-8
72220 Fyant St 59821 406-726-3216
James Taylor, prin. Fax 726-3940

Ashland, Rosebud, Pop. 799
Ashland ESD 100/PK-8
PO Box 17 59003 406-784-2568
Augustine Lopez, supt. Fax 784-6138
www.ashlandpublicschool.com
Ashland ES 100/PK-6
PO Box 17 59003 406-784-2568
Kathryn Piller, prin. Fax 784-6138
Ashland MS 50/7-8
PO Box 17 59003 406-784-2568
Kathryn Piller, prin. Fax 784-6138

St. Labre Catholic ES 300/PK-4
PO Box 216 59003 406-784-4580
Crystal Redgrave Ph.D., prin. Fax 784-4565
St. Labre Catholic MS 200/5-8
PO Box 216 59003 406-784-4567
Holly Bailey, prin. Fax 784-4565

Augusta, Lewis and Clark, Pop. 305
Augusta SD 100/PK-12
PO Box 307 59410 406-562-3384
Matt Genger, supt. Fax 562-3898
www.augustaschool.org/
Augusta ES 50/PK-6
PO Box 307 59410 406-562-3384
Matt Genger, prin. Fax 562-3898
Augusta MS 50/7-8
PO Box 307 59410 406-562-3384
Matt Genger, prin. Fax 562-3898

Avon, Powell, Pop. 110
Avon SD 29 50/K-8
PO Box 246 59713 406-492-6191
Fax 492-6191
Avon S 50/K-8
PO Box 246 59713 406-492-6191
Jennifer Wade, lead tchr. Fax 492-6191

Babb, Glacier, Pop. 168
Browning SD
Supt. — See Browning
Babb ES 50/K-6
PO Box 70 59411 406-732-5539
Billie Jo Juneau, prin. Fax 732-9255

Bainville, Roosevelt, Pop. 202
Bainville SD 200/PK-12
PO Box 177 59212 406-769-2321
Renee Rasmussen, supt. Fax 769-3291
www.bainvilleschool.k12.mt.us
Bainville ES 100/PK-6
PO Box 177 59212 406-769-2321
Rhiannon Beery, prin. Fax 769-3291
Bainville MS 50/7-8
PO Box 177 59212 406-769-2321
Rhiannon Beery, prin. Fax 769-3291

Baker, Fallon, Pop. 1,723
Baker SD 400/PK-12
PO Box 659 59313 406-778-3574
Jon Wrzesinski, supt. Fax 778-2785
www.baker.k12.mt.us
Baker MS 100/7-8
PO Box 659 59313 406-778-3329
David Breitbach, prin. Fax 778-2785
Lincoln ES 100/PK-3
PO Box 659 59313 406-778-2022
Bo Lingle, prin. Fax 778-2445
Longfellow MS 100/4-6
PO Box 659 59313 406-778-2426
Bo Lingle, prin. Fax 778-2445

Basin, Jefferson, Pop. 204
Basin ESD 50/PK-6
PO Box 128 59631 406-225-3211
www.basinschool.net/
Basin ES, PO Box 128 59631 50/PK-6
Branna Schmidt, lead tchr. 406-225-3211

Belfry, Carbon, Pop. 215
Belfry SD 50/PK-12
PO Box 210 59008 406-664-3319
Jason Olson, supt. Fax 664-3274
belfrybats.org
Belfry ES 50/PK-6
PO Box 210 59008 406-664-3319
Jason Olson, prin. Fax 664-3274
Belfry MS 50/7-8
PO Box 210 59008 406-664-3319
Jason Olson, prin. Fax 664-3274

Belgrade, Gallatin, Pop. 7,233
Belgrade SD 2,700/PK-12
PO Box 166 59714 406-924-2006
Leland Stocker, supt. Fax 388-0122
www.bsd44.org
Belgrade MS 900/5-8
410 Triple Crown St 59714 406-924-2258
Julie Mickolio, prin. Fax 388-8894
Heck/Quaw ES 400/PK-4
308 N Broadway 59714 406-924-2121
Lori Degenhart, prin. Fax 388-4577
Ridge View ES 500/K-4
117 Green Belt Dr 59714 406-388-4534
Matt Johnston, prin. Fax 388-4569
Saddle Peak ES K-4
PO Box 166 59714 406-924-2006
Barbara Frank, prin. Fax 924-2759

Pass Creek ESD 50/K-8
3747 Pass Creek Rd 59714 406-388-7879
Laura Axtman, supt. Fax 388-7978
Pass Creek S 50/K-8
3747 Pass Creek Rd 59714 406-388-6353
Sid Rider, lead tchr.

Springhill ESD 50/K-8
6020 Springhill Community 59714 406-586-6485
Laura Axtman, supt. Fax 586-6485
Springhill S 50/K-8
6020 Springhill Community 59714 406-586-6485
Terra Spotts, lead tchr. Fax 586-6485

Belt, Cascade, Pop. 585
Belt SD 300/PK-12
PO Box 197 59412 406-277-3351
Kathleen Prody, supt. Fax 277-4466
www.beltschool.com
Belt ES 100/PK-5
PO Box 197 59412 406-277-3351
Kyle Paulson, prin. Fax 277-4466
Belt MS 50/6-8
PO Box 197 59412 406-277-3351
Kyle Paulson, prin. Fax 277-4466
Pleasant Valley S 50/K-8
PO Box 197 59412 406-277-3351
Kyle Paulson, prin. Fax 277-4466

Biddle, Powder River, Pop. 41
Biddle ESD 50/PK-8
PO Box 399 59314 406-427-5290
Biddle S, PO Box 399 59314 50/PK-8
Sherrie Bassett, lead tchr. 406-427-5290

Bigfork, Flathead, Pop. 4,196
Bigfork SD 800/K-12
PO Box 188 59911 406-837-7400
Matt Jensen, supt. Fax 837-7407
www.bigforkschools.org
Bigfork ES 400/K-6
PO Box 188 59911 406-837-7412
Brenda Clarke, prin. Fax 837-7438
Bigfork MS 100/7-8
PO Box 188 59911 406-837-7412
Brenda Clarke, prin. Fax 837-7438

Swan River ESD 100/K-8
1205 Swan Hwy 59911 406-837-4528
Marc Bunker, prin. Fax 837-4055
www.swanriverschool.org
Swan River ES 100/K-6
1205 Swan Hwy 59911 406-837-4528
Marc Bunker, prin. Fax 837-4055
Swan River MS 50/7-8
1205 Swan Hwy 59911 406-837-4528
Marc Bunker, prin. Fax 837-4055

Big Sandy, Chouteau, Pop. 583
Big Sandy SD 200/PK-12
PO Box 570 59520 406-378-2502
Brad Moore, supt. Fax 378-2275
www.bigsandy.k12.mt.us
Big Sandy JHS 50/7-8
PO Box 570 59520 406-378-2502
Brad Moore, prin. Fax 378-2275
Miley ES 100/PK-6
PO Box 570 59520 406-378-2406
Brad Moore, prin. Fax 378-2255

Big Sky, Gallatin, Pop. 2,277

Big Sky Discovery Academy 50/PK-12
PO Box 161548 59716 406-993-2008
Nettie Breuner, dir.

Big Timber, Sweet Grass, Pop. 1,599
Big Timber ESD 300/PK-8
PO Box 887 59011 406-932-5939
Mark Ketcham, supt. Fax 932-4069
www.bigtimber-gs.k12.mt.us
Big Timber ES 200/PK-6
PO Box 887 59011 406-932-5939
Mark Ketcham, prin. Fax 932-4069
Big Timber MS 100/7-8
PO Box 887 59011 406-932-5939
Mark Ketcham, prin. Fax 932-4069

Mc Leod ESD 50/PK-8
346 Otter Creek Rd 59011 406-932-5147
Susan Metcalf, supt. Fax 932-3017
Other Schools – See Mc Leod

Billings, Yellowstone, Pop. 101,668
Billings SD 16,400/PK-12
415 N 30th St 59101 406-281-5065
Terry Bouck, supt. Fax 281-6179
www.billingsschools.org/
Alkali Creek ES 400/PK-6
681 Alkali Creek Rd 59105 406-281-6200
Greg Senitte, prin. Fax 254-0162
Arrowhead ES 500/1-5
2510 38th St W 59102 406-281-6201
Pam Meier, prin. Fax 656-0169
Beartooth ES 500/PK-6
1345 Elaine St 59105 406-281-6202
Travis Niemeyer, prin. Fax 254-1123
Bench ES 400/PK-6
505 Milton Rd 59105 406-281-6203
Sandie Mammenga, prin. Fax 254-1130
Big Sky ES 500/PK-6
3231 Granger Ave E 59102 406-281-6204
Kim Beatty, prin. Fax 656-0247
Bitterroot ES 400/PK-6
1801 Bench Blvd 59105 406-281-6205
Dr. Shanna Henry, prin. Fax 254-1155
Boulder ES 500/PK-6
2202 32nd St W 59102 406-281-6206
Jeri Heard, prin. Fax 656-0287
Broadwater ES 400/PK-5
415 Broadwater Ave 59101 406-281-6207
Justin Huck, prin. Fax 254-0057
Burlington ES 300/1-6
2135 Lewis Ave 59102 406-281-6208
Lori Booke, prin. Fax 656-0357
Castle Rock MS 800/7-8
1441 Governors Blvd 59105 406-281-5800
O'Shean Moran, prin. Fax 254-1116
Central Heights ES 400/PK-6
120 Lexington Dr 59102 406-281-6209
Kyra Gaskill, prin. Fax 656-0878
Eagle Cliffs ES 500/PK-6
1201 Kootenai Ave 59105 406-281-6210
Lorrie Wolverton, prin. Fax 254-1312
Highland ES 300/PK-6
729 Parkhill Dr 59102 406-281-6211
Julie Donald, prin. Fax 254-1412
James MS 700/6-8
1200 30th St W 59102 406-281-6100
Kim Verschoot, prin. Fax 281-6178
Lewis & Clark MS 700/6-8
1315 Lewis Ave 59102 406-281-5900
Jody Sulser, prin. Fax 281-6177
McKinley ES 300/PK-5
820 N 31st St 59101 406-281-6212
Nikki Trahan, prin. Fax 254-1225
Meadowlark ES 700/PK-6
221 29th St W 59102 406-281-6213
Stacy Lemelin, prin. Fax 656-0359
Medicine Crow MS 6-8
900 Barrett Rd 59105 406-281-8600
Nikki Hofmann, prin.
Miles Avenue ES 300/PK-6
1601 Miles Ave 59102 406-281-6214
John English, prin. Fax 656-0625
Newman ES 300/PK-6
605 S Billings Blvd 59101 406-281-6215
Bert Reyes, prin. Fax 254-1075
Orchard ES 400/PK-5
120 Jackson St 59101 406-281-6216
Jeremy Carlson, prin. Fax 254-1723
Poly Drive ES 400/PK-6
2410 Poly Dr 59102 406-281-6217
Kevin Croff, prin. Fax 656-0649
Ponderosa ES 400/PK-6
4188 King Ave E 59101 406-281-6218
Clay Herron, prin. Fax 254-1825
Riverside MS 600/6-8
3700 Madison Ave 59101 406-281-6000
Kevin Kirkman, prin. Fax 255-3534
Rose Park ES 300/PK-6
1812 19th St W 59102 406-281-6219
Tami Concepcion, prin. Fax 254-1404
Sandstone ES 500/PK-6
1440 Nutter Blvd 59105 406-281-6220
Mark Venner, prin. Fax 254-1965
Steele MS 59101 6-8
Washington ES 300/PK-5
1044 Cook Ave 59102 406-281-6221
DeeDee Larsen, prin. Fax 254-1287

Blue Creek ESD 200/PK-6
3652 Blue Creek Rd 59101 406-259-0653
Cathi Rude, supt. Fax 259-9378
www.bluecreekschool.org
Blue Creek ES 200/PK-6
3652 Blue Creek Rd 59101 406-259-0653
Cathi Rude, prin. Fax 259-9378

Canyon Creek ESD 200/PK-8
3139 Duck Creek Rd 59101 406-656-4471
Brent Lipp, supt. Fax 655-1031
www.canyoncreekschool.org
Canyon Creek ES 200/PK-6
3139 Duck Creek Rd 59101 406-656-4471
Brent Lipp, admin. Fax 655-1031
Canyon Creek MS 50/7-8
3139 Duck Creek Rd 59101 406-656-4471
Brent Lipp, admin. Fax 655-1031

Elder Grove ESD 400/K-8
1532 S 64th St W 59106 406-656-2893
Justin Klebe, supt. Fax 651-4346
www.eldergrove.k12.mt.us/
Elder Grove ES 300/K-5
1532 S 64th St W 59106 406-656-2893
Justin Klebe, supt. Fax 651-4346
Elder Grove MS 100/6-8
1532 S 64th St W 59106 406-656-2893
Nathan Schmitz, prin. Fax 651-4346

Elysian ESD 200/PK-8
6416 Elysian Rd 59101 406-656-4101
Bob Whalen, supt. Fax 656-9941
elysianschool.org
Elysian ES 200/PK-6
6416 Elysian Rd 59101 406-656-4101
Luke Shelton, prin. Fax 656-9941

Elysian MS 50/7-8
6416 Elysian Rd 59101 406-656-4101
Luke Shelton, prin. Fax 656-9941

Independent ESD 300/PK-6
2907 Roundup Rd 59105 406-259-8109
Bill Laurent, supt. Fax 259-8541
www.independent.k12.mt.us
Independent ES 300/PK-6
2907 Roundup Rd 59105 406-259-8109
Sheila Chouinard, prin. Fax 259-8541

Lockwood ESD 1,200/PK-8
1932 US Highway 87 E 59101 406-252-6022
Tobin Novasio, supt. Fax 259-2502
www.lockwoodschool.org/
Lockwood IS 400/3-5
1932 US Highway 87 E 59101 406-248-2339
Michael Bowman, prin. Fax 245-8300
Lockwood MS 400/6-8
1932 US Highway 87 E 59101 406-259-0154
Gordon Klasna, prin. Fax 259-3832
Lockwood PS 400/PK-2
1932 US Highway 87 E 59101 406-252-2776
Michael Bowman, prin. Fax 256-0373

Morin ESD 50/K-6
8824 Pryor Rd 59101 406-259-6093
Fax 259-6093
www.morin.k12.mt.us
Morin ES 50/K-6
8824 Pryor Rd 59101 406-259-6093
Tia Schacht, lead tchr. Fax 259-6093

Pioneer ESD, 1937 Dover Rd 59105 100/K-6
Melissa Schnitzmeier, admin. 406-373-5357
www.pioneerschool.us
Pioneer ES, 1937 Dover Rd 59105 100/K-6
Melissa Schnitzmeier, admin. 406-373-5357

Yellowstone Academy ESD 50/PK-8
1750 Ray of Hope Ln 59106 406-656-2198
Michael Sullivan, supt. Fax 656-2802
Yellowstone Academy S 50/PK-8
1750 Ray of Hope Ln 59106 406-656-2198
Mike Sullivan, prin. Fax 656-2328

Billings Christian S 100/PK-12
4519 Grand Ave 59106 406-656-9484
Diann Floth, head sch Fax 655-4880
Central Acres SDA S 50/K-8
3204 Broadwater Ave 59102 406-652-1799
Grace Montessori Academy 200/PK-8
4809 Grand Ave 59106 406-652-1739
Mount Olive Lutheran S 100/PK-8
2336 Saint Johns Ave 59102 406-652-7431
Cheryl Forke, hdmstr. Fax 656-1211
St. Francis IS 200/3-5
1734 Yellowstone Ave 59102 406-656-2300
Timothy Lowe, prin. Fax 656-2301
St. Francis PS 200/PK-2
511 Custer Ave 59101 406-259-6421
Deb Hayes, prin. Fax 245-0176
St. Francis Upper S 200/6-8
205 N 32nd St 59101 406-259-5037
Jim Stanton, prin. Fax 259-7981
Trinity Lutheran S 200/K-8
2802 Belvedere Dr 59102 406-656-1021
Richard Thomas, prin. Fax 656-1936

Birney, Rosebud, Pop. 136
Birney ESD 50/PK-8
PO Box 521 59012 406-984-6247
Fax 984-6270
Birney S 50/PK-8
PO Box 521 59012 406-984-6247
Fax 984-6270

Bloomfield, Dawson
Bloomfield ESD
Supt. — See Glendive
Bloomfield S 50/PK-8
2285 Fas 470 59315 406-583-7575

Bonner, Missoula, Pop. 1,669
Bonner ESD 400/PK-8
PO Box 1004 59823 406-258-6151
James Howard, supt. Fax 258-6153
www.bonner.k12.mt.us
Bonner ES 300/PK-6
PO Box 1004 59823 406-258-6151
Chelley Andres, prin. Fax 258-6153
Bonner MS 100/7-8
PO Box 1004 59823 406-258-6151
James Howard, prin. Fax 258-6153

Potomac ESD 100/PK-8
29750 Potomac Rd 59823 406-244-5581
Fax 244-5840
www.potomacschoolmontana.us/
Potomac ES 100/PK-6
29750 Potomac Rd 59823 406-244-5581
Angie Williams, prin. Fax 244-5840
Potomac MS 50/7-8
29750 Potomac Rd 59823 406-244-5581
Angie Williams, prin. Fax 244-5840

Boulder, Jefferson, Pop. 1,141
Boulder ESD 200/PK-8
PO Box 1346 59632 406-225-3316
Maria Pace, supt. Fax 225-9218
bgs.k12.mt.us
Boulder ES 100/PK-6
PO Box 1346 59632 406-225-3316
Maria Pace, prin. Fax 225-9218
Boulder MS 100/7-8
PO Box 1346 59632 406-225-3316
Maria Pace, prin. Fax 225-9218

Box Elder, Hill, Pop. 80
Box Elder SD 400/PK-12
PO Box 205 59521 406-352-4195
Jeremy MacDonald, supt. Fax 352-3830
Box Elder ES 200/PK-6
PO Box 205 59521 406-352-3222
Mark Irvin, prin. Fax 352-3225
Box Elder MS 100/7-8
PO Box 205 59521 406-352-4195
Melanie Jenkins, prin. Fax 352-3830

Rocky Boy SD 600/PK-12
81 Mission Taylor Rd 59521 406-395-4291
Voyd St. Pierre, supt. Fax 395-4829
www.rockyboy.k12.mt.us
Rocky Boy ES 300/PK-6
81 Mission Taylor Rd 59521 406-395-4474
Josephine Corcoran, prin. Fax 395-4829
Rocky Boy MS 100/7-8
81 Mission Taylor Rd 59521 406-395-4270
Lewis Reese, prin. Fax 395-4829

Bozeman, Gallatin, Pop. 36,568
Anderson ESD 200/PK-8
10040 Cottonwood Rd 59718 406-587-1305
Scott McDowell, supt. Fax 587-2501
www.andersonmt.org/
Anderson ES 200/PK-6
10040 Cottonwood Rd 59718 406-587-1305
Scott McDowell, prin. Fax 587-2501
Anderson MS 50/7-8
10040 Cottonwood Rd 59718 406-587-1305
Scott McDowell, prin. Fax 587-2501

Bozeman SD 5,600/PK-12
404 W Main St 59715 406-522-6000
Robert Watson, supt. Fax 522-6065
www.bsd7.org
Chief Joseph MS 700/6-8
4255 Kimberwicke St 59718 406-522-6300
Brian Ayers, prin. Fax 522-6306
Dickinson ES 500/K-5
2435 Annie St 59718 406-522-6650
Sarah Hayes, prin. Fax 522-6640
Hawthorne ES 300/K-5
114 N Rouse Ave 59715 406-522-6700
Casey Bertram, prin. Fax 522-6730
Hyalite ES 100/K-5
3600 W Babcock St 59718 406-582-6800
Mike Van Vuren, prin. Fax 582-6850
Irving ES 300/PK-5
611 S 8th Ave 59715 406-522-6600
Adrian Advincula, prin. Fax 522-6690
Longfellow ES 300/PK-5
516 S Tracy Ave 59715 406-522-6150
Patrick McClellan, prin. Fax 522-6180
Meadowlark ES PK-5
4415 Durston Rd 59718 406-582-6860
Sharon Navas, prin. Fax 582-6890
Morning Star ES 500/PK-5
830 W Arnold St 59715 406-522-6500
Robin Arnold, prin. Fax 522-6550
Sacajawea MS 600/6-8
3525 S 3rd Rd 59715 406-522-6470
Gordon Grissom, prin. Fax 522-6474
Whittier ES 200/PK-5
511 N 5th Ave 59715 406-522-6750
Darren Schlepp, prin. Fax 522-6780

Cottonwood ESD 50/K-5
13233 Cottonwood Rd 59718 406-763-4903
Fax 763-4903
www.cottonwoodelementary.com
Cottonwood ES 50/K-5
13233 Cottonwood Rd 59718 406-763-4903
Katalin Anderson, lead tchr. Fax 763-4903

LaMotte ESD 100/K-8
841 Bear Canyon Rd 59715 406-586-2838
Fax 585-8626
www.lamotteschool.com
LaMotte ES 100/K-6
841 Bear Canyon Rd 59715 406-586-2838
LeeAnn Burke, prin. Fax 585-8626
LaMotte MS 50/7-8
841 Bear Canyon Rd 59715 406-586-2838
LeeAnn Burke, prin. Fax 585-8626

Malmborg ESD 50/PK-8
375 Jackson Creek Rd 59715 406-586-2759
Fax 586-5735
Malmborg S 50/PK-8
375 Jackson Creek Rd 59715 406-586-2759
Meghan Larson, lead tchr. Fax 586-5735

Monforton ESD 300/PK-8
6001 Monforton School Rd 59718 406-586-1557
Darren Strauch, supt. Fax 587-5049
www.monfortonschool.org/
Monforton IS 100/3-6
6001 Monforton School Rd 59718 406-586-1557
Darren Strauch, supt. Fax 587-5049
Monforton MS 100/7-8
6001 Monforton School Rd 59718 406-586-1557
Darren Strauch, supt. Fax 587-5049
Monforton PS 100/PK-2
6001 Monforton School Rd 59718 406-586-1557
Darren Strauch, supt. Fax 587-5049

Bozeman Summit S 50/PK-6
3001 W Villard St 59718 406-585-3778
Dani Stern, dir. Fax 522-9477
Headwaters Academy 50/6-8
418 W Garfield St 59715 406-585-9997
Joseph Stefani, head sch Fax 585-9992
Heritage Christian S 200/K-12
4310 Durston Rd 59718 406-587-9311
Gerry Goede M.S., admin. Fax 587-1838

Mount Ellis SDA S 50/PK-8
3835 Bozeman Trail Rd 59715 406-587-5430
Petra Academy 100/PK-12
4720 Classical Way 59718 406-582-8165

Brady, Pondera, Pop. 137
Knees ESD
Supt. — See Carter
Knees S, 23831 Brady Rd E 59416 50/K-8
Deborah Manley, lead tchr. 406-734-5312

Bridger, Carbon, Pop. 700
Bridger SD 200/PK-12
429 W Park Ave 59014 406-662-3588
Bill Phillips, supt. Fax 662-3520
www.bridgerscouts.org
Bridger ES 100/PK-6
106 N 4th St 59014 406-662-3588
Bill Phillips, prin. Fax 662-3520
Bridger MS 50/7-8
106 N 4th St 59014 406-662-3588
Jim Goltz, prin. Fax 662-3520

Broadus, Powder River, Pop. 457
Broadus SD 200/PK-12
PO Box 500 59317 406-436-2658
Jim Hansen, supt. Fax 436-2660
www.broadus.net/
Broadus ES 100/PK-6
PO Box 500 59317 406-436-2637
Rosalie Lunby, prin. Fax 436-2660

Broadview, Yellowstone, Pop. 191
Broadview SD 200/PK-12
PO Box 147 59015 406-667-2337
Gary Fisher, supt. Fax 667-2195
www.broadviewschools.org
Broadview ES 100/PK-6
PO Box 147 59015 406-667-2337
Gary Fisher, supt. Fax 667-2195
Broadview MS 50/7-8
PO Box 147 59015 406-667-2337
Gary Fisher, supt. Fax 667-2195

Brockton, Roosevelt, Pop. 255
Brockton SD 100/PK-12
PO Box 198 59213 406-786-3311
Mike Radakovich, supt. Fax 786-3377
www.brockton.k12.mt.us
Gilligan ES 100/PK-6
PO Box 198 59213 406-786-3318
Joel Steinmetz, prin. Fax 786-3377
Gilligan MS 50/7-8
PO Box 198 59213 406-786-3311
Francis LaBounty, prin. Fax 786-3377

Browning, Glacier, Pop. 998
Browning SD 2,000/PK-12
PO Box 610 59417 406-338-2715
John P. Rouse, supt. Fax 338-3200
www.bps.k12.mt.us
Bergan ES 200/PK-1
PO Box 629 59417 406-338-2756
Chuck Pilling, prin. Fax 338-5607
Big Sky S 50/PK-8
Del Bonita Rd 59417 406-336-3790
Billie Jo Juneau, prin. Fax 336-3790
Browning ES 300/2-3
PO Box 689 59417 406-338-2740
Jennifer Wagner, prin. Fax 338-3490
Browning MS 300/7-8
PO Box 610 59417 406-338-2725
Julie Hayes, prin. Fax 338-5320
Chattin ES 200/1-1
PO Box 629 59417 406-338-2758
Chuck Pilling, prin. Fax 338-5625
Napi ES 500/4-6
PO Box 649 59417 406-338-2735
Sicily Bird, prin. Fax 338-3350
Other Schools – See Babb, Cut Bank

De LaSalle Blackfeet S 100/4-8
PO Box 1489 59417 406-338-5290
Br. Dale Mooney, pres. Fax 338-7900

Brusett, Garfield
Pine Grove ESD 50/PK-8
3646 Brusett Rd 59318 406-557-6115
Jessica McWilliams, supt.
Pine Grove S 50/PK-8
9 Seven Blackfoot Rd 59318 406-557-2782

Butte, Silver Bow, Pop. 32,958
Butte SD 4,300/PK-12
111 N Montana St 59701 406-533-2500
Judy Jonart, supt. Fax 533-2526
www.butte.k12.mt.us
East MS 600/7-8
2600 Grand Ave 59701 406-533-2600
Larry Driscoll, prin. Fax 533-2670
Emerson ES 400/PK-6
1924 Phillips Ave 59701 406-533-2800
Brenda Miner, prin. Fax 533-2818
Hillcrest ES 400/K-6
3000 Continental Dr 59701 406-533-2850
Susan Johnson, prin. Fax 533-2858
Kennedy ES 300/PK-6
1101 N Emmett Ave 59701 406-533-2450
Ron Ricketts, prin. Fax 533-2457
Leary ES 300/PK-6
1301 Four Mile View Rd 59701 406-533-2550
Brett Huntsman, prin. Fax 533-2560
West ES 500/PK-6
800 S Emmett Ave 59701 406-533-2700
Pat Kissell, prin. Fax 533-2717
Whittier ES 400/PK-6
2500 Sherman Ave 59701 406-533-2890
J.P. Gallagher, prin. Fax 533-2920

Butte Central ES — 300/PK-8
100 Delaware Ave 59701 — 406-782-4500
Kerrie Hellyer, prin. — Fax 723-4845

Highland View Christian S — 1-8
PO Box 3043 59702 — 406-221-7044

Silver Bow Montessori S — 50/PK-6
1800 Sunset Rd 59701 — 406-494-1033

Bynum, Teton, Pop. 31

Bynum ESD — 50/PK-8
PO Box 766 59419 — 406-469-2373
Fax 469-2253
tetoncomt.org/superintendent-of-schools/superintendent

Bynum S — 50/PK-8
PO Box 766 59419 — 406-469-2373
Susan Luinstra, lead tchr. — Fax 469-2253

Canyon Creek, Lewis and Clark

Trinity ESD — 50/PK-8
PO Box 523 59633 — 406-368-2230
Fax 368-2250
te-k12-mt.schoolloop.com/

Trinity S — 50/PK-8
PO Box 523 59633 — 406-368-2230
Fax 368-2250

Cardwell, Jefferson, Pop. 49

Cardwell ESD — 50/PK-8
80 MT Highway 359 59721 — 406-287-3321
Garry Pace, supt. — Fax 287-9181

Cardwell S — 50/PK-8
80 MT Highway 359 59721 — 406-287-3321
Nancy Veca, lead tchr. — Fax 287-9181

Carter, Chouteau, Pop. 58

Carter ESD — 50/PK-8
PO Box 158 59420 — 406-734-5387

Carter S, PO Box 158 59420 — 50/PK-8
Marjorie Scott, lead tchr. — 406-734-5387

Knees ESD — 50/K-8
1018 Charlson Dr 59420 — 406-734-5312
Other Schools – See Brady

Cascade, Cascade, Pop. 673

Cascade SD — 300/K-12
PO Box 529 59421 — 406-468-9383
Justin Barnes, supt. — Fax 468-2212
www.cascade.k12.mt.us

Cascade ES — 100/K-6
PO Box 529 59421 — 406-468-9383
Siobhan Hathhorn, prin. — Fax 468-2212

Cascade JHS — 50/7-8
PO Box 529 59421 — 406-468-2267
Kevin Sukut, prin. — Fax 468-2212

Charlo, Lake, Pop. 328

Charlo SD — 300/K-12
PO Box 10 59824 — 406-644-2206
Steve Love, supt. — Fax 644-2400
www.charlo.k12.mt.us

Charlo ES — 200/K-6
PO Box 10 59824 — 406-644-2206
Bonnie Perry, prin. — Fax 644-2400

Charlo MS — 50/7-8
PO Box 10 59824 — 406-644-2206
Bonnie Perry, prin. — Fax 644-2400

Chester, Liberty, Pop. 830

Chester-Joplin-Inverness SD — 200/PK-12
PO Box 550 59522 — 406-759-5945
Francis LaBounty, supt. — Fax 759-5867
www.cji.k12.mt.us

Chester-Joplin-Inverness ES — 100/PK-6
PO Box 550 59522 — 406-759-5477
Rita Chvilicek, prin. — Fax 759-5867

Chester-Joplin-Inverness MS — 50/7-8
PO Box 550 59522 — 406-759-5108
Rita Chvilicek, prin. — Fax 759-5867

Sage Creek S — 50/PK-8
PO Box 550 59522 — 406-759-5477
Rita Chvilicek, prin. — Fax 759-5867

Chinook, Blaine, Pop. 1,183

Bear Paw ESD — 50/PK-8
22820 Cleveland Rd 59523 — 406-357-3689

Bear Paw S — 50/PK-8
22820 Cleveland Rd 59523 — 406-395-4436
Kelly Mills, lead tchr.

Chinook SD — 400/PK-12
PO Box 1059 59523 — 406-357-2236
Darin Hannum, supt. — Fax 357-2238
www.chinookschools.org

Chinook MS — 50/7-8
PO Box 1059 59523 — 406-357-2237
Matt Molyneaux, prin. — Fax 357-2238

Meadowlark ES — 200/PK-6
PO Box 1059 59523 — 406-357-2033
Jonathan Martin, prin. — Fax 357-3146
Other Schools – See Havre

Cleveland-Lone Tree ESD — 50/PK-8
22820 Cleveland Rd 59523 — 406-357-3689

Cleveland S — 50/PK-8
22820 Cleveland Rd 59523 — 406-357-2018
Shirley Kienenberger, lead tchr.

Choteau, Teton, Pop. 1,646

Choteau SD — 400/PK-12
204 7th Ave NW 59422 — 406-466-5303
Chuck Gameon, supt. — Fax 466-5305
www.choteauschools.net

Choteau ES — 200/PK-6
102 7th Ave NW 59422 — 406-466-5364
Chuck Gameon, prin. — Fax 466-5362

Choteau MS — 50/7-8
204 7th Ave NW 59422 — 406-466-5303
Dave Jamison, prin. — Fax 466-5305

Circle, McCone, Pop. 606

Circle SD — 200/PK-12
PO Box 99 59215 — 406-485-3600
Willie Thibault, supt. — Fax 485-2332
www.circleschools.org

Bo Peep PS — 100/PK-3
PO Box 99 59215 — 406-485-2140
Craig Widhalm, prin. — Fax 485-2332

Redwater IS — 50/4-6
PO Box 99 59215 — 406-485-2140
Craig Widhalm, prin. — Fax 485-2332

Redwater MS — 50/7-8
PO Box 99 59215 — 406-485-2140
Craig Widhalm, prin. — Fax 485-2332

Vida ESD, PO Box 180 59215 — 50/PK-8
Jackie Becker, supt. — 406-485-3600
Other Schools – See Vida, Wolf Point

Clancy, Jefferson, Pop. 1,638

Clancy ESD — 200/PK-8
PO Box 209 59634 — 406-933-5575
Dave Selvig, supt. — Fax 933-5715
www.clancyschool.org

Clancy ES — 200/PK-6
PO Box 209 59634 — 406-933-5575
Dave Selvig, prin. — Fax 933-5715

Clancy MS — 50/7-8
PO Box 209 59634 — 406-933-5575
Dave Selvig, prin. — Fax 933-5715

Montana City ESD — 400/K-8
11 McClellan Creek Rd 59634 — 406-442-6779
Tony Kloker, supt. — Fax 443-8875
montanacity.schoolwires.com

Montana City ES — 300/K-5
11 McClellan Creek Rd 59634 — 406-442-6779
Daryl Mikesell, prin. — Fax 443-8875

Montana City MS — 200/6-8
11 McClellan Creek Rd 59634 — 406-442-6779
Daryl Mikesell, prin. — Fax 443-8875

Clinton, Missoula, Pop. 1,018

Clinton ESD — 200/PK-8
PO Box 250 59825 — 406-825-3113
Tom Stack, supt. — Fax 825-3114
www.clintoncougars.com

Clinton ES — 200/PK-6
PO Box 250 59825 — 406-825-3113
Tom Stack, prin. — Fax 825-3114

Clinton MS — 50/7-8
PO Box 250 59825 — 406-825-3113
Tom Stack, prin. — Fax 825-3114

Clyde Park, Park, Pop. 288

Shields Valley SD — 200/PK-12
PO Box 40 59018 — 406-578-2535
Randy Russell, supt. — Fax 578-2176
www.shieldsvalleyschools.org/

Shields Valley ES — 100/PK-6
308 S Hannaford 59018 — 406-578-2535
Alan Peterson, prin. — Fax 578-2176

Shields Valley MS — 50/7-8
405 1st St E 59018 — 406-686-4621
Greg Sager, prin. — Fax 686-4937

Cohagen, Garfield

Cohagen ESD, PO Box 113 59322 — 50/PK-8
Jessica McWilliams, supt. — 406-557-6115

Cohagen S, PO Box 113 59322 — 50/PK-8
Joan Caroll, lead tchr. — 406-557-2771

Colstrip, Rosebud, Pop. 2,118

Colstrip SD — 600/PK-12
PO Box 159 59323 — 406-748-4699
Bob Lewandowski, supt. — Fax 748-2268
colstrippublicschools.org

Brattin MS — 100/6-8
PO Box 159 59323 — 406-748-4699
Pax Haslem, prin. — Fax 748-3143

Pine Butte ES — 300/PK-5
PO Box 159 59323 — 406-748-4699
Aaron Skogen, prin. — Fax 748-2551

Columbia Falls, Flathead, Pop. 4,562

Columbia Falls SD — 2,100/K-12
PO Box 1259 59912 — 406-892-6550
Steve Bradshaw, supt. — Fax 892-6552
www.cfmtschools.net

Columbia Falls JHS — 500/6-8
PO Box 1259 59912 — 406-892-6530
Dave Wick, prin. — Fax 892-6528

Glacier Gateway ES — 500/K-5
PO Box 1259 59912 — 406-892-6540
Penni Anello, prin. — Fax 892-6544

Ruder ES — 500/K-5
PO Box 1259 59912 — 406-892-6570
Brenda Krueger, prin. — Fax 892-6563

Deer Park ESD — 100/PK-8
2105 Middle Rd 59912 — 406-892-5388
Fax 892-3504
sites.google.com/a/deerparkedu.org/panthers/

Deer Park ES — 100/PK-6
2105 Middle Rd 59912 — 406-892-5388
Dan Block, prin. — Fax 892-3504

Deer Park MS — 50/7-8
2105 Middle Rd 59912 — 406-892-5388
Dan Block, prin. — Fax 892-3504

Columbus, Stillwater, Pop. 1,857

Columbus SD — 700/PK-12
433 N 3rd St 59019 — 406-322-5373
Jeff Bermes, supt. — Fax 322-5028
www.columbus.k12.mt.us

Columbus ES — 300/PK-5
218 E 1st Ave N 59019 — 406-322-5372
Marlene Deis, prin. — Fax 322-5371

Columbus MS — 200/6-8
415 N 3rd St 59019 — 406-322-5375
Ron Osborne, prin. — Fax 322-5376

Condon, Missoula, Pop. 336

Seeley Lake ESD 34
Supt. — See Seeley Lake

Swan Valley S — 50/K-8
6423 MT Highway 83 59826 — 406-754-2320
Chris Stout, prin. — Fax 754-2627

Conrad, Pondera, Pop. 2,522

Conrad SD — 500/PK-12
220 N Wisconsin St 59425 — 406-278-5521
Sharyl Allen, supt. — Fax 278-3630
www.conradschools.org

Meadowlark ES — 100/PK-2
17 3rd Ave SW 59425 — 406-278-5620
Marie Judisch, prin. — Fax 278-5621

Prairie View ES — 100/3-5
220 N Wisconsin St 59425 — 406-278-5251
Fax 271-5252

Utterback MS — 50/4-8
24 2nd Ave SW 59425 — 406-278-3227
Danele Dyer, prin. — Fax 278-3228

Dutton/Brady SD
Supt. — See Dutton

Midway Colony S — 50/PK-8
605 Healy Spring Rd 59425 — 406-476-3201
Leslee Weber, prin. — Fax 476-3342

Miami ESD — 50/PK-8
400 New Miami Colony Rd 59425 — 406-472-3325

Miami S — 50/PK-8
400 New Miami Colony Rd 59425 — 406-472-3325
Janice Hayworth, lead tchr.

Cooke City, Park, Pop. 73

Cooke City ESD — 50/PK-8
PO Box 1070 59020 — 406-838-2285
Fax 838-2285

Cooke City S — 50/PK-8
PO Box 1070 59020 — 406-838-2285
Soquel Snider, lead tchr. — Fax 838-2285

Corvallis, Ravalli, Pop. 945

Corvallis SD — 1,300/PK-12
PO Box 700 59828 — 406-961-4211
Tim Johnson, supt. — Fax 961-5144
www.corvallis.k12.mt.us

Brown PS — 400/PK-4
PO Box 700 59828 — 406-961-3261
Janice Stranahan, prin. — Fax 961-5147

Corvallis JHS — 200/7-8
PO Box 700 59828 — 406-961-3007
Rich Durgin, prin. — Fax 961-5144

Thomas IS — 200/5-6
PO Box 700 59828 — 406-961-3007
Rich Durgin, prin. — Fax 961-8876

Crow Agency, Big Horn, Pop. 1,597

Hardin SD 17-H & 1
Supt. — See Hardin

Crow Agency ES — 300/PK-5
PO Box 219 59022 — 406-638-2252
Jason Cummins, prin. — Fax 638-7267

Culbertson, Roosevelt, Pop. 690

Culbertson SD — 300/PK-12
PO Box 459 59218 — 406-787-6246
Larry Crowder, supt. — Fax 787-6244
www.culbertsonschool.com

Culbertson ES — 200/PK-6
PO Box 459 59218 — 406-787-6241
Mike Olson, prin. — Fax 787-6244

Culbertson MS — 50/7-8
PO Box 459 59218 — 406-787-6241
Mike Olson, prin. — Fax 787-6244

Custer, Yellowstone, Pop. 158

Custer SD — 100/K-12
PO Box 69 59024 — 406-856-4117
Dr. David Perkins, supt. — Fax 856-4206
www.custerschools.org

Custer ES — 50/K-6
PO Box 69 59024 — 406-856-4117
Dr. David Perkins, supt. — Fax 856-4206

Custer MS — 50/7-8
PO Box 69 59024 — 406-856-4117
Dr. David Perkins, supt. — Fax 856-4206

Cut Bank, Glacier, Pop. 2,736

Browning SD
Supt. — See Browning

Glendale S — 50/PK-8
DelBonita Rd 59427 — 406-336-2635
Billie Jo Juneau, prin. — Fax 336-2635

Cut Bank SD — 700/PK-12
101 3rd Ave SE 59427 — 406-873-2229
Wade Johnson, supt. — Fax 873-4691
www.cutbankschools.net

Cut Bank MS — 200/6-8
101 3rd Ave SE 59427 — 406-873-4421
Gail Hofstad, prin. — Fax 873-4691

Davis ES — 200/PK-3
15 2nd Ave SE 59427 — 406-873-5513
Venus Dodson, prin. — Fax 873-4691

Glacier ES — 50/1-8
451 Tipville Rd 59427 — 406-336-2623
Gail Hofstad, prin. — Fax 873-4691

Hidden Lake ES — 50/PK-8
100 Welch Rd 59427 — 406-336-3696
Gail Hofstad, prin. — Fax 873-4691

Horizon ES — 50/PK-8
100 Horizon Rd 59427 — 406-336-2961
Gail Hofstad, prin. — Fax 873-4691

Jeffries ES — 100/4-5
105 2nd St NW 59427 — 406-873-2411
Venus Dodson, prin. — Fax 873-4691

Zenith ES — 50/PK-8
Zenith Colony Rd, — 406-336-5430
Gail Hofstad, prin. — Fax 873-4691

Mountain View ESD 50/PK-8
PO Box 1169 59427 406-336-2433
Fax 336-2434
Mountain View S 50/PK-8
PO Box 1169 59427 406-336-2433
Fax 336-2434

Darby, Ravalli, Pop. 697
Darby SD 300/PK-12
209 School Dr 59829 406-821-1314
Loyd Rennaker, supt. Fax 821-4977
www.darby.k12.mt.us/
Darby ES 200/PK-6
209 School Dr 59829 406-821-3643
Chris Toynbee, prin. Fax 821-4977
Darby MS 100/7-8
209 School Dr 59829 406-821-3252
J.P. McCrossin, prin. Fax 821-4977

Dayton, Lake, Pop. 84
Upper West Shore ESD 50/PK-6
PO Box 195 59914 406-849-5484
Fax 849-5485
Dayton ES 50/PK-6
PO Box 195 59914 406-849-5484
Jamie Bartel, lead tchr. Fax 849-5485

Decker, Big Horn
Spring Creek ESD 50/PK-8
PO Box 118 59025 406-665-9304
Dennis Gerke, supt. Fax 665-9823
Spring Creek S 50/PK-8
PO Box 118 59025 406-757-2515
Alexis Nikirk, lead tchr. Fax 757-2247

Deer Lodge, Powell, Pop. 3,077
Deer Lodge ESD 400/PK-8
444 Montana Ave 59722 406-846-1553
Rodney Simpson, supt. Fax 846-1599
www.deerlodgeschools.org
Duvall MS 100/7-8
444 Montana Ave 59722 406-846-1684
Rick Chrisman, prin. Fax 846-1599
Speer ES 300/PK-6
444 Montana Ave 59722 406-846-2268
Ann Morani, prin. Fax 846-1599

Denton, Fergus, Pop. 253
Denton SD 100/K-12
PO Box 1048 59430 406-567-2270
Fax 567-2559
www.denton.k12.mt.us
Denton ES 50/K-6
PO Box 1048 59430 406-567-2270
Fax 567-2559
Denton JHS 50/7-8
PO Box 1048 59430 406-567-2270
Fax 567-2559

Dillon, Beaverhead, Pop. 4,039
Dillon ESD 700/PK-8
22 Cottom Dr 59725 406-683-4311
Glen Johnson, supt. Fax 683-4312
www.dillonelem.k12.mt.us/
Dillon MS 200/6-8
14 Cottom Dr 59725 406-683-2368
Randy Shipman, prin. Fax 683-2369
Parkview ES 500/PK-5
22 Cottom Dr 59725 406-683-2373
Greg Fitzgerald, prin. Fax 683-2374

Grant ESD, 526 Chinatown Rd 59725 50/PK-8
Linda Marsh, supt. 406-681-3143
Grant S, 526 Chinatown Rd 59725 50/PK-8
Penny Huxtable, lead tchr. 406-681-3143

Polaris ESD 50/PK-8
19200 MT Highway 278 59725 406-834-3435
Fax 834-3435

Other Schools – See Polaris

Divide, Silver Bow
Divide ESD 50/PK-8
PO Box 9 59727 406-267-3347
Divide S, PO Box 9 59727 50/PK-8
Judith Boyle, lead tchr. 406-267-3347

Dixon, Sanders, Pop. 184
Dixon ESD 50/PK-8
PO Box 10 59831 406-246-3566
Crista Anderson, admin. Fax 246-3379
www.dixonschool.org
Dixon ES 50/PK-6
PO Box 10 59831 406-246-3566
Crista Anderson, prin. Fax 246-3379
Dixon MS 50/7-8
PO Box 10 59831 406-246-3566
Crista Anderson, prin. Fax 246-3379

Dodson, Phillips, Pop. 121
Dodson SD 100/PK-12
PO Box 278 59524 406-383-4361
Gary Weitz, supt. Fax 383-4489
www.dodson.k12.mt.us
Dodson ES 50/PK-6
PO Box 278 59524 406-383-4361
Gary Weitz, supt. Fax 383-4489
Dodson MS 50/7-8
PO Box 278 59524 406-383-4362
Gary Weitz, supt. Fax 383-4489

Drummond, Granite, Pop. 304
Drummond SD 200/K-12
PO Box 349 59832 406-288-3281
Bryan Kott, supt. Fax 288-3299
drummondschool.blackfoot.net/dhs/
Drummond ES 100/K-6
PO Box 349 59832 406-288-3281
Rick Parke, prin. Fax 288-3299
Drummond MS 50/7-8
PO Box 349 59832 406-288-3281
Bryan Kott, prin. Fax 288-3299

Dupuyer, Pondera, Pop. 82
Dupuyer ESD 50/PK-8
PO Box 149 59432 406-472-3297
Fax 472-3256
Dupuyer S 50/PK-8
PO Box 149 59432 406-472-3297
Heidi Owens, lead tchr. Fax 472-3256

Dutton, Teton, Pop. 311
Dutton/Brady SD 200/PK-12
101 2nd St NE 59433 406-476-3424
D.K. Brooks, supt. Fax 476-3342
duttonbradyps.schoolwires.net
Dutton/Brady ES 100/PK-8
101 2nd St NE 59433 406-476-3201
Leslee Weber, prin. Fax 476-3342
Dutton/Brady MS 50/7-8
101 2nd St NE 59433 406-476-3424
D.K. Brooks, admin. Fax 476-3342
Other Schools – See Conrad, Valier

East Glacier Park, Glacier
East Glacier Park SD 50/PK-8
PO Box 150 59434 406-226-5543
Karlona Sheppherd, supt. Fax 226-4269
www.eastglacierschool.com/
East Glacier Park S 50/PK-8
PO Box 150 59434 406-226-5543
Karlona Sheppard, prin. Fax 226-4269

East Helena, Lewis and Clark, Pop. 1,919
East Helena ESD 1,200/PK-8
PO Box 1280 59635 406-227-7700
Ron Whitmoyer, supt. Fax 227-5534
www.ehps.k12.mt.us
Eastgate ES 300/PK-1
PO Box 1280 59635 406-227-7770
Jill MIller, prin. Fax 227-8479
East Valley MS 400/6-8
PO Box 1280 59635 406-227-7740
Dan Rispens, prin. Fax 227-9730
Radley ES 500/2-5
PO Box 1280 59635 406-227-7710
Joseph McMahon, prin. Fax 227-7713

Helena Christian S 200/PK-12
3384 Canyon Ferry Rd 59635 406-442-3821
Ted Clark, admin. Fax 442-0341

Ekalaka, Carter, Pop. 327
Ekalaka SD 100/PK-12
PO Box 458 59324 406-775-8765
Daniel Schrock, supt. Fax 775-8766
www.ekalaka.net
Ekalaka ES 100/PK-6
PO Box 458 59324 406-775-8765
Daniel Schrock, prin. Fax 775-8766
Ekalaka MS 50/7-8
PO Box 458 59324 406-775-8767
Daniel Schrock, prin. Fax 775-8766

Elliston, Powell, Pop. 213
Elliston ESD 27 50/PK-8
PO Box 160 59728 406-492-7676
Elliston S, PO Box 160 59728 50/PK-8
Robin Clark, lead tchr. 406-492-7676

Ennis, Madison, Pop. 828
Ennis SD 300/PK-12
PO Box 517 59729 406-682-4258
Casey Clasna, supt. Fax 682-7751
www.ennisschools.org
Ennis ES 200/PK-6
PO Box 517 59729 406-682-4237
Brian Hilton, prin. Fax 682-7752
Ennis MS 100/7-8
PO Box 517 59729 406-682-4237
Brian Hilton, prin. Fax 682-7752

Eureka, Lincoln, Pop. 1,015
Eureka SD 700/PK-12
PO Box 2000 59917 406-297-5650
Jim Mepham, supt. Fax 297-2644
www.lchigh.net
Eureka ES 200/PK-4
PO Box 2000 59917 406-297-5500
Cari Lucey, prin. Fax 297-2400
Eureka MS 200/5-8
PO Box 2000 59917 406-297-5600
Trevor Utter, prin. Fax 297-5653

Fairfield, Teton, Pop. 690
Fairfield SD 300/K-12
PO Box 399 59436 406-467-2103
Les Meyer, supt. Fax 467-2554
www.fairfield.k12.mt.us/
Fairfield ES 100/K-6
PO Box 399 59436 406-467-2425
Courtney Bake, prin. Fax 467-2554
Fairfield MS 50/7-8
PO Box 399 59436 406-467-2425
Dustin Gordon, prin. Fax 467-2554

Golden Ridge ESD 45 50/PK-8
1374 US Highway 408 59436 406-467-2010
Fax 467-2190
tetoncomt.org/superintendent-of-schools/golden-ridge-
Golden Ridge S 50/PK-8
1374 US Highway 408 59436 406-467-2010
Sara Wood, lead tchr. Fax 467-2190

Greenfield ESD 100/PK-8
590 Mt Highway 431 59436 406-467-2433
Fax 467-3138
greenfieldschool.wixsite.com/greenfield
Greenfield ES 100/PK-6
590 Mt Highway 431 59436 406-467-2433
Paul Wilson, prin. Fax 467-3138
Greenfield MS 50/7-8
590 Mt Highway 431 59436 406-467-2433
Paul Wilson, prin. Fax 467-3138

Fairview, Richland, Pop. 832
Fairview SD 300/PK-12
PO Box 467 59221 406-742-5265
Luke Kloker, supt. Fax 742-3336
fschool.org
Fairview ES 200/PK-6
PO Box 467 59221 406-742-5265
Mark Thompson, prin. Fax 742-8265
Fairview MS 50/7-8
PO Box 467 59221 406-742-5265
Mark Thompson, prin. Fax 742-8265

Fishtail, Stillwater
Fishtail ESD 50/PK-8
PO Box 75 59028 406-328-4277
Fax 328-4277
Fishtail S 50/PK-8
PO Box 75 59028 406-328-4277
Fax 328-4277

Florence, Ravalli, Pop. 755
Florence-Carlton SD 800/PK-12
5602 Old US Highway 93 59833 406-273-6751
Bud Scully, supt.
www.florence.k12.mt.us
Florence-Carlton ES 400/PK-6
5602 Old US Highway 93 59833 406-273-6741
Christine Hulla, prin. Fax 273-0594
Florence-Carlton MS 100/7-8
5602 Old US Highway 93 59833 406-273-0587
Audrey Backus, prin. Fax 273-0545

Floweree, Chouteau
Benton Lake ESD 50/PK-8
17557 Bootlegger Trl 59440 406-452-9023
Benton Lake S 50/PK-8
17557 Bootlegger Trl 59440 406-452-9023
Dawn Dawson, lead tchr.

Forsyth, Rosebud, Pop. 1,757
Forsyth SD 400/PK-12
PO Box 319 59327 406-346-2796
Dinny Bennett, supt. Fax 346-7455
www.forsyth.k12.mt.us
Forsyth ES 200/PK-6
PO Box 319 59327 406-346-2796
Dixie Seleg, prin. Fax 346-7797
Forsyth JHS 100/7-8
PO Box 319 59327 406-346-2796
Shelly Weight, prin. Fax 346-9219

Fort Benton, Chouteau, Pop. 1,439
Ft. Benton SD 300/PK-12
PO Box 399 59442 406-622-5691
Jory Thompson, supt. Fax 622-3305
fortbentonschools.weebly.com
Fort Benton ES 200/PK-6
PO Box 399 59442 406-622-3761
Jory Thompson, prin. Fax 622-5408
Fort Benton JHS 50/7-8
PO Box 399 59442 406-622-3213
Rusty Bowers, prin. Fax 622-5691

Fortine, Lincoln, Pop. 317
Fortine ESD 100/PK-8
PO Box 96 59918 406-882-4531
Fax 882-4057
www.fortineschool.net
Fortine S 100/PK-8
PO Box 96 59918 406-882-4531
Laura Pluid, prin. Fax 882-4057

Fort Shaw, Cascade, Pop. 268
Sun River Valley SD
Supt. — See Simms
Fort Shaw ES 100/PK-5
1 School Loop 59443 406-264-5110
Rick Danelson, prin. Fax 264-5146

Fort Smith, Big Horn, Pop. 155
Hardin SD 17-H & 1
Supt. — See Hardin
Fort Smith ES 50/K-5
PO Box 7827 59035 406-666-2350
Annette Moody, lead tchr. Fax 666-2305

Frazer, Valley, Pop. 360
Frazer SD 100/PK-12
PO Box 488 59225 406-695-2241
Carroll Decoteau, supt. Fax 695-2243
www.frazer.k12.mt.us
Frazer ES 100/PK-6
PO Box 488 59225 406-695-2241
Carroll DeCoteau, admin. Fax 695-2243
Frazer MS 50/7-8
PO Box 488 59225 406-695-2241
Carroll DeCoteau, admin. Fax 695-2243

Lustre ESD 50/PK-8
282 Lustre Rd 59225 406-392-5725
Fax 392-5780
Lustre S 50/PK-8
282 Lustre Rd 59225 406-392-5725
Wes Young, prin. Fax 392-5780

Frenchtown, Missoula, Pop. 1,780
Frenchtown SD 1,200/PK-12
PO Box 117 59834 406-626-2600
Randy Cline, supt. Fax 626-2605
www.ftsd.org
Frenchtown ES 400/PK-4
PO Box 117 59834 406-626-2620
Aaron Griffin, prin. Fax 626-2625
Frenchtown IS 200/5-6
PO Box 117 59834 406-626-2622
Riley Devins, prin. Fax 626-2623

Frenchtown MS 200/7-8
PO Box 117 59834 406-626-2650
Mark McMurray, prin. Fax 626-2654

Froid, Roosevelt, Pop. 181
Froid SD 100/K-12
PO Box 218 59226 406-766-2343
Ken Taylor, supt. Fax 766-2206
Froid ES 50/K-6
PO Box 218 59226 406-766-2342
Ken Taylor, admin. Fax 766-2206
Froid MS 50/7-8
PO Box 218 59226 406-766-2342
Ken Taylor, admin. Fax 766-2206

Fromberg, Carbon, Pop. 437
Fromberg SD 100/PK-12
319 School St 59029 406-668-7611
Teri Harris, supt. Fax 668-7669
frombergpublicschools.com
Fromberg ES 100/PK-6
319 School St 59029 406-668-7755
Teri Harris, admin. Fax 668-7669
Fromberg MS 50/7-8
319 School St 59029 406-668-7315
Teri Harris, admin. Fax 668-7669

Galata, Toole
Galata ESD 50/PK-8
PO Box 76 59444 406-424-8322
Boyd Jackson, supt. Fax 424-8321
Galata S 50/PK-8
PO Box 76 59444 406-432-2123
Fax 432-2123

Liberty ESD 50/PK-8
PO Box 78 59444 406-759-5216
Kathy Armstrong, supt. Fax 759-5996
Liberty ES 50/PK-8
PO Box 78 59444 406-432-5265
Mike Hofer, admin. Fax 432-2582
Riverview ES 50/PK-8
PO Box 78 59444 406-759-5477

Gallatin Gateway, Gallatin, Pop. 845
Big Sky SD 200/PK-12
45465 Gallatin Rd 59730 406-995-4281
Dr. Dustin Shipman, supt. Fax 995-2161
www.bssd72.org
Ophir ES 100/PK-4
45465 Gallatin Rd 59730 406-995-4281
Dr. Dustin Shipman, prin. Fax 995-2161
Ophir MS 100/5-8
45465 Gallatin Rd 59730 406-995-4281
Alexander Ide, prin. Fax 995-2161

Gallatin Gateway ESD 200/PK-8
PO Box 265 59730 406-763-4415
Travis Anderson, supt. Fax 763-4886
www.gallatingatewayschool.com
Gallatin Gateway ES 100/PK-6
PO Box 265 59730 406-763-4415
Travis Anderson, prin. Fax 763-4886
Gallatin Gateway MS 50/7-8
PO Box 265 59730 406-763-4415
Travis Anderson, prin. Fax 763-4886

Gardiner, Park, Pop. 871
Gardiner SD 200/PK-12
510 Stone St 59030 406-848-7261
J.T. Stroder, supt. Fax 848-0606
gardiner.org
Gardiner ES 100/PK-6
510 Stone St 59030 406-848-7563
Mike Baer, prin. Fax 848-0606
Gardiner MS 50/7-8
510 Stone St 59030 406-848-7563
Mike Baer, prin. Fax 848-9489

Garrison, Powell, Pop. 93
Garrison ESD 50/K-6
33 School House Rd 59731 406-846-1043
Fax 846-1043
Garrison ES 50/K-6
33 School House Rd 59731 406-846-1043
Debra Crow, lead tchr. Fax 846-1043

Geraldine, Chouteau, Pop. 255
Geraldine SD 100/PK-12
PO Box 347 59446 406-737-4371
Eric Gustafson, admin. Fax 737-4478
www.geraldine.k12.mt.us
Geraldine ES 50/PK-6
PO Box 347 59446 406-737-4371
Eric Gustafson, prin. Fax 737-4478
Geraldine MS 50/7-8
PO Box 347 59446 406-737-4371
Eric Gustafson, prin. Fax 737-4478

Geyser, Judith Basin, Pop. 87
Geyser SD 58 100/PK-12
PO Box 70 59447 406-735-4368
Dale Bernard, supt. Fax 735-4452
www.geyser.k12.mt.us
Geyser ES 50/PK-6
PO Box 70 59447 406-735-4368
Dale Bernard, admin. Fax 735-4452
Geyser MS 50/7-8
PO Box 70 59447 406-735-4368
Dale Bernard, admin. Fax 735-4452

Gildford, Hill, Pop. 178
Gildford Colony ESD 50/PK-8
PO Box 138 59525 406-376-3249
Gildford Colony S, PO Box 138 59525 50/PK-8
Nancy McKinley, lead tchr. 406-376-3249

North Star SD
Supt. — See Rudyard
North Star ES 100/PK-6
205 3rd St E 59525 406-355-4481
Bart Hawkins, prin. Fax 355-4532

Glasgow, Valley, Pop. 3,170
Glasgow SD 600/PK-12
PO Box 28 59230 406-228-2406
Robert Connors, supt. Fax 228-2407
www.glasgow.k12.mt.us/
Glasgow MS 100/6-8
PO Box 28 59230 406-228-2485
Michael Zoanni, prin. Fax 228-4061
Irle ES 300/PK-5
PO Box 28 59230 406-228-2419
Rachel Erickson, prin. Fax 228-8762

Glen, Beaverhead
Reichle ESD 50/K-8
PO Box 320097 59732 406-683-3737
Linda Marsh, supt. Fax 683-3769
Reichle S 50/K-8
PO Box 320097 59732 406-835-2281
Sue Webster, lead tchr. Fax 835-2095

Glendive, Dawson, Pop. 4,857
Bloomfield ESD 50/PK-8
207 W Bell St 59330 406-377-3963
Jayne Mitchell, supt. Fax 377-2022
Other Schools – See Bloomfield

Deer Creek ESD, 12 Road 564 59330 50/PK-8
Jayne Mitchell, supt. 406-687-3724
Deer Creek S 50/PK-8
12 Road 564 59330 406-687-3724

Glendive SD 1,200/PK-12
PO Box 701 59330 406-377-5293
Stephen Schreibeis, supt. Fax 377-6212
www.glendiveschools.com
Jefferson ES 300/PK-2
PO Box 701 59330 406-377-4155
Jordan Viegut, prin. Fax 377-8944
Lincoln ES 200/3-5
PO Box 701 59330 406-377-2308
John Bole, prin. Fax 377-2309
Washington MS 300/6-8
PO Box 701 59330 406-377-2356
Mark Goyette, prin. Fax 377-2357

Valley View Adventist S 50/K-8
PO Box 389 59330 406-687-3472

Gold Creek, Powell
Gold Creek ESD 50/K-8
825 Gold Creek Rd 59733 406-846-9719
Jules Waber, supt.
Gold Creek S 50/K-8
825 Gold Creek Rd 59733 406-288-3560
Sheri Nelson, lead tchr.

Grass Range, Fergus, Pop. 109
Ayers ESD 50/PK-8
PO Box 100 59032 406-428-2368
Fax 428-2368
Ayers S 50/PK-8
PO Box 100 59032 406-428-2340
Susan Seastrand, lead tchr. Fax 428-2368

Grass Range SD 27 100/PK-12
PO Box 58 59032 406-428-2122
Joe Gaylord, supt. Fax 428-2235
grps.k12.mt.us
Grass Range ES 50/PK-6
PO Box 58 59032 406-428-2341
Joe Gaylord, supt. Fax 428-2235
Grass Range MS 50/7-8
PO Box 58 59032 406-428-2122
Joe Gaylord, supt. Fax 428-2235

Great Falls, Cascade, Pop. 56,542
Great Falls SD 10,400/PK-12
PO Box 2429 59403 406-268-6001
Tammy Lacey, supt. Fax 268-6002
www.gfps.k12.mt.us
Chief Joseph ES 300/K-6
5305 3rd Ave S 59405 406-268-6675
Bobby Ingalls, prin. Fax 268-6955
East MS 700/7-8
4040 Central Ave 59405 406-268-6500
Brad Barringer, prin. Fax 268-6524
Lewis & Clark ES 400/PK-6
3800 1st Ave S 59405 406-268-6705
Jackie Carlson, prin. Fax 268-7003
Lincoln ES 400/PK-6
624 27th St S 59405 406-268-6800
Jon Konen, prin. Fax 268-6819
Longfellow ES 300/PK-6
1100 6th Ave S 59405 406-268-6845
Ryan Hart, prin. Fax 268-7450
Loy ES 400/PK-6
501 57th St N 59405 406-268-6085
Kim Ray, prin. Fax 268-6887
Meadow Lark ES 500/PK-6
2204 Fox Farm Rd 59404 406-268-7300
Teresa Sprague, prin. Fax 268-7304
Morningside ES 300/PK-6
4119 7th Ave N 59405 406-268-6960
Kim DeFrics, prin. Fax 268-7480
Mountain View ES 300/PK-6
3420 15th Ave S 59405 406-268-7305
Carole McKittrick, prin. Fax 268-7336
North MS 700/7-8
2601 8th St NE 59404 406-268-6525
Tara Rosipal, prin. Fax 268-6575
Riverview ES 400/PK-6
100 Smelter Ave NW 59404 406-268-7015
Luke Diekhans, prin. Fax 268-7007
Roosevelt ES 300/PK-6
2501 2nd Ave N 59401 406-268-7045
Rhonda Zobrak, prin. Fax 268-7077
Sacajawea ES 400/PK-6
630 Sacajawea Dr 59404 406-268-7080
Rae Smith, prin. Fax 268-7114
Sunnyside ES 500/K-6
1800 19th St S 59405 406-268-7115
Lance Boyd, prin. Fax 268-7421
Valley View ES 400/PK-6
900 Avenue A NW 59404 406-268-7145
Rachel Cutler, prin. Fax 268-7148
West ES 500/PK-6
1205 1st Ave NW 59404 406-268-7180
Michelle Meredith, prin. Fax 268-7227
Whittier ES 300/PK-6
305 8th St N 59401 406-268-7230
Corri Smith, prin. Fax 268-7243

Five Falls Christian S 50/K-8
2930 Flood Rd 59404 406-452-6883
Foothills Community Christian S 200/PK-12
2210 5th Ave N 59401 406-452-5276
David Culpepper, head sch Fax 452-8606
Holy Spirit Catholic S 200/PK-8
2820 Central Ave 59401 406-761-5775
Jim Wichman, prin. Fax 761-5887
Our Lady of Lourdes S 200/PK-8
1305 5th Ave S 59405 406-452-0551
Sherri Schmitz, prin. Fax 761-7180

Greenough, Missoula
Sunset ESD 50/PK-8
5024 Sunset Hill Rd 59823 406-244-5542
Sunset S, 5024 Sunset Hill Rd 59823 50/PK-8
Toni Hatten, lead tchr. 406-244-5542

Greycliff, Sweet Grass, Pop. 109
Greycliff ESD, PO Box 65 59033 50/PK-8
Susan Metcalf, supt. 406-932-6641
Greycliff S, PO Box 65 59033 50/PK-8
Robin Thomas, lead tchr. 406-932-6641

Hall, Granite
Hall ESD 50/PK-8
109 W Main St 59837 406-859-3218
Margaret Tallon, supt. Fax 859-3262
Hall S 50/PK-8
109 W Main St 59837 406-288-3440
Teresa Kielley, lead tchr. Fax 288-3440

Hamilton, Ravalli, Pop. 4,256
Hamilton SD 1,500/PK-12
217 Daly Ave 59840 406-363-2280
Tom Korst, supt. Fax 363-1843
www.hsd3.org
Daly ES 400/2-5
208 Daly Ave 59840 406-363-2122
Nate Lant, prin. Fax 363-6494
Hamilton MS 400/6-8
209 S 5th St 59840 406-363-2121
Marlin Lowie, prin. Fax 363-7032
Washington ES 200/PK-1
225 N 5th St 59840 406-363-2144
Scott Holland, lead tchr. Fax 363-7420

Blodgett View Christian S 50/1-8
119 Westbridge Rd 59840 406-373-0575
Hamilton Christian Academy 50/PK-8
778 Grantsdale Rd 59840 406-363-4534
Stephanie Beck, prin. Fax 961-9602

Hammond, Carter
Hawks Home ESD 50/PK-8
11 Talcott Ln 59332 406-775-8721
Tracey Walker, supt.
Hammond S 50/PK-8
10851 Highway 212 59332 406-427-5438
Barb Lapke, lead tchr.
Hawks Home S 50/PK-8
1461 Hammond Rd 59332 406-775-6506
Lynnette Wolff, lead tchr.

Hardin, Big Horn, Pop. 3,345
Hardin SD 17-H & 1 1,900/PK-12
401 Park Rd 59034 406-665-9300
Dennis Gerke, supt. Fax 665-9338
www.hardin.k12.mt.us
Hardin IS 300/3-5
631 5th St W 59034 406-665-6390
Larry Johnson, prin. Fax 665-6468
Hardin MS 400/6-8
611 5th St W 59034 406-665-6350
Scott Brokaw, prin. Fax 665-1409
Hardin PS 400/PK-2
314 3rd St W 59034 406-665-9340
Roxanne Not Afraid, prin. Fax 665-9346
Other Schools – See Crow Agency, Fort Smith

Harlem, Blaine, Pop. 770
Harlem SD 600/PK-12
PO Box 339 59526 406-353-2289
Shawn Smith, supt. Fax 353-2674
www.harlem-hs.k12.mt.us
Harlem ES 300/PK-6
PO Box 309 59526 406-353-2258
Shiloh Seymour, prin. Fax 353-2892
Harlem MS 100/7-8
PO Box 339 59526 406-353-2287
Doug Komrosky, prin. Fax 353-2339

North Harlem Colony ESD 50/K-8
755 Hillcrest Rd 59526 406-357-2800
Kelly Mills, supt.
North Harlem S 50/K-8
755 Hillcrest Rd 59526 406-353-2800
Kelly Mills, admin.

Harlowton, Wheatland, Pop. 971
Harlowton SD 300/PK-12
PO Box 288 59036 406-632-4822
Andrew Begger, supt. Fax 632-4416
www.harlowton.k12.mt.us
Hillcrest MS 50/7-8
PO Box 288 59036 406-632-4361
Gregg Wasson, prin. Fax 632-4416

Hillcrest S 200/PK-8
PO Box 288 59036 406-632-4361
Aubrey Miller, prin. Fax 632-4744

Harrison, Madison, Pop. 137
Harrison SD 100/K-12
PO Box 7 59735 406-685-3428
Fred Hofman, supt. Fax 685-3420
sites.google.com/a/harrison.k12.mt.us/hhswildcats/
Harrison ES 50/K-6
PO Box 7 59735 406-685-3428
Fred Hofman, admin. Fax 685-3430
Harrison MS 50/7-8
PO Box 7 59735 406-685-3428
Fred Hofman, admin. Fax 685-3430

Havre, Hill, Pop. 8,979
Chinook SD
Supt. — See Chinook
Hartland S 50/PK-8
2105 Woodpile Rd 59501 406-357-2033
Jonathan Martin, prin. Fax 357-3146

Cottonwood ESD 50/PK-8
PO Box 1024 59501 406-265-5481
Diane McLean, supt. Fax 394-2273
Cottonwood S 50/PK-8
PO Box 1024 59501 406-394-2273
Monica Mattson, lead tchr. Fax 394-2273

Davey ESD, PO Box 1829 59501 50/K-8
Diane McClain, supt. 406-265-6970
Davey ES, PO Box 1829 59501 50/K-8
Denellda Barnekoff, lead tchr. 406-395-4461

Havre SD 2,000/K-12
PO Box 7791 59501 406-265-4356
Andy Carlson, supt. Fax 265-8460
www.havre.k12.mt.us/
Havre MS 500/6-8
1441 11th St W 59501 406-265-9613
Dustin Kraske, prin. Fax 265-4414
Highland Park ES 300/K-1
1207 Washington Ave 59501 406-265-5554
Tracy Pare, prin. Fax 265-5571
Lincoln-McKinley ES 300/2-3
801 4th St 59501 406-265-9619
Holly Bitz, prin. Fax 265-9610
Sunnyside ES 300/4-5
601 14th St 59501 406-265-9671
Carmen Lunak, prin. Fax 395-6835

St. Jude Thaddeus S 100/PK-8
430 7th Ave 59501 406-265-4613
Julanne Gauger, lead tchr. Fax 265-1315

Hays, Blaine, Pop. 831
Hays-Lodge Pole SD 200/PK-12
PO Box 110 59527 406-673-3120
Dr. Margaret Campbell, supt. Fax 673-3415
Hays-Lodge Pole MS 50/7-8
PO Box 110 59527 406-673-3120
Amy Snow, prin. Fax 673-3274
Lodge Pole ES 100/PK-6
PO Box 110 59527 406-673-3120
Amy Snow, prin. Fax 673-3274

St. Paul's Mission Grade S 100/K-6
PO Box 40 59527 406-673-3123

Heart Butte, Pondera, Pop. 576
Heart Butte SD 200/PK-12
PO Box 259 59448 406-338-3344
V. Lee Folley, supt. Fax 338-5832
www.heartbutteschool.com
Heart Butte ES 100/PK-6
PO Box 259 59448 406-338-3344
Steven Schwartz, prin. Fax 338-5832
Heart Butte MS 50/7-8
PO Box 259 59448 406-338-2200
Steven Schwartz, prin. Fax 338-5832

Helena, Lewis and Clark, Pop. 27,530
Helena SD 8,000/PK-12
55 S Rodney St 59601 406-324-2001
George Copps, supt. Fax 324-2035
helenaschools.org
Anderson MS 1,000/6-8
1200 Knight St 59601 406-324-2800
Bruce Campbell, prin. Fax 324-2801
Broadwater ES 300/K-5
900 Hollins Ave 59601 406-324-1130
Sue Sweeney, prin. Fax 324-1131
Bryant ES 200/PK-5
1529 Boulder Ave 59601 406-324-1200
JJ Lamb, prin. Fax 324-1201
Central ES 200/PK-5
1325 Poplar St 59601 406-324-1230
Vanessa Nasset, prin. Fax 324-1231
Darcy ES 300/PK-5
990 Lincoln Rd W 59602 406-324-1410
Brian Cummings, prin. Fax 324-1411
Four Georgians ES 500/PK-5
555 W Custer Ave 59602 406-324-1300
Nick Radley, prin. Fax 324-1301
Hawthorne ES 300/K-5
430 Madison Ave 59601 406-324-1370
Dr. Deb Jacobsen, prin. Fax 324-1371
Helena MS 700/6-8
1025 N Rodney St 59601 406-324-1000
Josh McKay, prin. Fax 324-1001
Jefferson ES 300/PK-5
1023 E Broadway St 59601 406-324-2060
Lona Carter-Scanlon, prin. Fax 324-2061
Kessler ES 300/PK-5
2420 Choteau St 59601 406-324-1700
Craig Crawford, prin. Fax 324-1701
Rossiter ES 500/PK-5
1497 Sierra Rd E 59602 406-324-1500
Kareen Bangert, prin. Fax 324-1501
Smith ES 300/PK-5
2320 5th Ave 59601 406-324-1530
Jill Nyman, prin. Fax 324-1531
Warren ES 300/PK-5
2690 York Rd 59602 406-324-1600
Tim McMahon, prin. Fax 324-1601

Capital View Christian S 50/K-8
3108 McHugh Ln 59602 406-465-6451
First Lutheran S 100/PK-5
2231 E Broadway St 59601 406-442-6913
Stacy Smith, dir. Fax 442-5285
St. Andrew's S 200/K-12
PO Box 231 59624 406-449-3201
Donna Smillie, prin. Fax 449-0129

Helmville, Powell
Helmville ESD 50/PK-8
PO Box 91 59843 406-793-5656
Helmville S, PO Box 91 59843 50/PK-8
Susan Graveley, lead tchr. 406-793-5656

Highwood, Chouteau, Pop. 174
Highwood SD 100/PK-12
160 West St S 59450 406-733-2081
Jane Suberg, supt. Fax 733-2671
www.highwood.k12.mt.us
Highwood ES 50/PK-5
160 West St S 59450 406-733-2081
Jane Suberg, admin. Fax 733-2671
Highwood MS 50/6-8
160 West St S 59450 406-733-2081
Jane Suberg, admin. Fax 733-2671

Hinsdale, Valley, Pop. 212
Hinsdale SD 100/PK-12
PO Box 398 59241 406-364-2314
Ed Sugg, supt. Fax 364-2205
www.hinsdale.k12.mt.us
Hinsdale ES 50/PK-6
PO Box 398 59241 406-364-2314
Edward Sugg, admin. Fax 364-2205
Hinsdale MS 50/7-8
PO Box 398 59241 406-364-2314
Edward Sugg, admin. Fax 364-2205

Hobson, Judith Basin, Pop. 215
Hobson SD 100/PK-12
PO Box 410 59452 406-423-5483
Hugo Anderson, supt. Fax 423-5260
www.hobson.k12.mt.us
Hobson ES 100/PK-6
PO Box 410 59452 406-423-5483
Hugo Anderson, prin. Fax 423-5260
Hobson MS 50/7-8
PO Box 410 59452 406-423-5483
Hugo Anderson, prin. Fax 423-5260

Hot Springs, Sanders, Pop. 493
Hot Springs SD 200/PK-12
PO Box 1005 59845 406-741-3285
Dr. Mike Perry, supt. Fax 741-3287
hssdmt.org/
Hot Springs ES 100/PK-6
PO Box 1005 59845 406-741-2014
Kelly Moore, prin. Fax 741-2015
Hot Springs MS 50/7-8
301 Broadway St 59845 406-741-2962
Kelly Moore, prin. Fax 741-3287

Hysham, Treasure, Pop. 299
Hysham SD 100/PK-12
PO Box 272 59038 406-342-5237
Larry Fink, supt. Fax 342-5257
www.hysham.k12.mt.us
Hysham ES 50/PK-6
PO Box 272 59038 406-342-5237
Larry Fink, admin. Fax 342-5257
Hysham MS 50/7-8
PO Box 272 59038 406-342-5237
Larry Fink, admin. Fax 342-5257

Jackson, Beaverhead
Jackson ESD 50/PK-8
PO Box 835 59736 406-834-3138
Fax 834-3138
Jackson S 50/PK-8
PO Box 835 59736 406-834-3138
Leah Tucker, lead tchr. Fax 834-3138

Joliet, Carbon, Pop. 592
Joliet SD 400/K-12
PO Box 590 59041 406-962-3541
Allison B. Evertz M.Ed., supt. Fax 962-3958
www.jolietschools.org/
Joliet ES 200/K-6
PO Box 590 59041 406-962-3541
Allison B. Evertz M.Ed., prin. Fax 962-3958
Joliet MS 100/7-8
PO Box 590 59041 406-962-3541
Marilyn Vukonich, prin. Fax 962-3958

Jordan, Garfield, Pop. 342
Jordan SD 200/PK-12
PO Box 409 59337 406-557-2259
Nathan Olson, supt. Fax 557-2778
jordanpublicschools.org
Jordan ES 100/PK-6
PO Box 409 59337 406-557-2259
Nathan Olson, prin. Fax 557-2778
Jordan MS 50/7-8
PO Box 409 59337 406-557-2259
Nathan Olson, prin. Fax 557-2778
Kester ESD 50/PK-8
2031 Haxby Rd 59337 406-557-6274
Fax 557-2890
Kester S 50/PK-8
2031 Haxby Rd 59337 406-557-6274
Sarah Bailey, lead tchr. Fax 557-2890

Judith Gap, Wheatland, Pop. 125
Judith Gap SD 50/PK-12
PO Box 67 59453 406-473-2211
Annette Hart, supt. Fax 473-2250
www.judithgap.k12.mt.us/
Judith Gap ES 50/PK-6
PO Box 67 59453 406-473-2211
Annette Hart, supt. Fax 473-2250
Judith Gap MS 50/7-8
PO Box 67 59453 406-473-2211
Annette Hart, supt. Fax 473-2250

Kalispell, Flathead, Pop. 19,453
Cayuse Prairie ESD 200/PK-8
897 Lake Blaine Rd 59901 406-756-4560
Amy Piazzola, supt. Fax 756-4570
cayuseprairie.com
Cayuse Prairie ES 200/PK-6
897 Lake Blaine Rd 59901 406-756-4560
Amy Piazzola, prin. Fax 756-4570
Cayuse Prairie MS 50/7-8
897 Lake Blaine Rd 59901 406-756-4560
Amy Piazzola, prin. Fax 756-4570

Creston ESD 100/PK-6
4495 Mt Highway 35 59901 406-755-2814
Fax 755-2814
crestonschool.com
Creston ES 100/PK-6
4495 Mt Highway 35 59901 406-755-2859
Tami Ward, prin. Fax 755-2814

Evergreen SD 600/PK-8
18 W Evergreen Dr 59901 406-751-1111
Dr. Laurie Barron, supt. Fax 752-2307
www.evergreensd50.com
East Evergreen ES 400/PK-4
18 W Evergreen Dr 59901 406-751-1121
Linda DeVoe, prin. Fax 751-1120
Evergreen JHS 200/5-8
18 W Evergreen Dr 59901 406-751-1131
Kim Anderson, prin. Fax 751-1134

Fair-Mont-Egan ESD 200/PK-8
797 Fairmont Rd 59901 406-755-7072
Christine Anthony, admin. Fax 755-7077
www.fmemontana.net
Fair-Mont-Egan ES 100/PK-6
797 Fairmont Rd 59901 406-755-7072
Christine Anthony, prin. Fax 755-7077
Fair-Mont-Egan MS 50/7-8
797 Fairmont Rd 59901 406-755-7072
Christine Anthony, prin. Fax 755-7077

Helena Flats SD 15 200/K-8
1000 Helena Flats Rd 59901 406-257-2301
Dan Anderson, supt. Fax 257-2304
helenaflats.org
Helena Flats ES 200/K-6
1000 Helena Flats Rd 59901 406-257-2301
Dan Anderson, prin. Fax 257-2304
Helena Flats MS 50/7-8
1000 Helena Flats Rd 59901 406-257-2301
Dan Anderson, prin. Fax 257-2304

Kalispell SD 6,000/PK-12
233 1st Ave E 59901 406-751-3400
Mark Flatau, supt. Fax 751-3416
www.sd5.k12.mt.us
Edgerton ES 600/PK-5
1400 Whitefish Stage 59901 406-751-4040
Merisa Murray, prin. Fax 751-4045
Elrod ES 300/K-5
412 3rd Ave W 59901 406-751-3700
Glenda Armstrong, prin. Fax 751-3705
Hedges ES 400/PK-5
827 4th Ave E 59901 406-751-4090
Brent Benkelman, prin. Fax 751-4095
Kalispell MS 1,100/6-8
205 Northwest Ln 59901 406-751-3800
Tryg Johnson, prin. Fax 751-3805
Peterson ES 400/K-5
1119 2nd St W 59901 406-751-3737
Tracy Ketchum, prin. Fax 751-3740
Russell ES 300/PK-5
227 W Nevada St 59901 406-751-3900
Bill Sullivan, prin. Fax 751-3905

Smith Valley ESD 200/K-8
2901 US Highway 2 W 59901 406-756-4535
Laili Komenda, supt. Fax 756-4534
www.smithvalleyschool.org
Smith Valley ES 200/K-6
2901 US Highway 2 W 59901 406-756-4535
Laili Komenda, admin. Fax 756-4534
Smith Valley MS 50/7-8
2901 US Highway 2 W 59901 406-756-4535
Laili Komenda, admin. Fax 756-4534

West Valley ESD 500/PK-8
2290 Farm To Market Rd 59901 406-755-7239
Cal Ketchum, supt. Fax 755-7300
www.westvalleyschool.com
West Valley ES 400/PK-5
2290 Farm To Market Rd 59901 406-755-7239
Brent Benkelman, prin. Fax 755-7300
West Valley MS 200/6-8
2290 Farm To Market Rd 59901 406-755-7239
Tina Blair, prin. Fax 755-7300

St. Matthews ES 200/PK-8
602 S Main St 59901 406-752-6303
Lauren Smith, prin. Fax 756-8248

Stillwater Christian S 300/PK-12
255 FFA Dr 59901 406-752-4400
Daniel Makowski, head sch Fax 755-4061
Trinity Lutheran S 200/PK-8
495 5th Avenue West N 59901 406-257-6716
Christina Roberts, prin. Fax 257-6717
Valley Adventist Christian S 50/1-8
1275 Helena Flats Rd 59901 406-752-0830

Kila, Flathead, Pop. 375
Kila ESD 200/PK-8
PO Box 40 59920 406-257-2428
Fax 755-6663
www.kilaschool.com/
Kila ES 100/PK-6
PO Box 40 59920 406-257-2428
Jason Christy, prin. Fax 755-6663
Kila MS 50/7-8
PO Box 40 59920 406-257-2428
Jason Christy, prin. Fax 755-6663

Kinsey, Custer
Kinsey ESD, 7 Mastin Rd 59338 100/K-8
Doug Ellingson, supt. 406-874-3420
Kinsey S 100/K-8
7 Mastin Rd 59338 406-232-2440
Shyla Barnosky, lead tchr. Fax 232-2440

Lakeside, Flathead, Pop. 2,629
Somers ESD
Supt. — See Somers
Lakeside ES 400/PK-5
255 Adams St 59922 406-844-2208
John Thies, prin. Fax 844-4609

Lambert, Richland
Lambert SD 100/PK-12
PO Box 260 59243 406-774-3333
Sean Beddow, supt. Fax 774-3335
lps.schoolwires.net
Lambert ES 100/PK-6
PO Box 260 59243 406-774-3333
Kara Triplett, admin. Fax 774-3335
Lambert MS 50/7-8
PO Box 260 59243 406-774-3333
Kara Triplett, admin. Fax 774-3335

Lame Deer, Rosebud, Pop. 2,025
Lame Deer SD 500/PK-12
PO Box 96 59043 406-477-6305
Gerald Chouinard, supt. Fax 477-6535
www.lamedeer.k12.mt.us/
Lame Deer ES 300/PK-6
PO Box 96 59043 406-477-6305
Gerald Chouinard, prin. Fax 477-8234
Lame Deer MS 100/7-8
PO Box 96 59043 406-477-8900
Steve Ewing, prin. Fax 477-8906

Laurel, Yellowstone, Pop. 6,588
Laurel SD 2,000/K-12
410 Colorado Ave 59044 406-628-8623
Linda Filpula, supt. Fax 628-8625
www.laurel.k12.mt.us
Graff ES 300/3-4
417 E 6th St 59044 406-628-6916
Allison Nys, prin. Fax 628-3497
Laurel MS 600/5-8
725 Washington Ave 59044 406-628-6919
Patrick Cates, prin. Fax 628-3350
West ES 500/K-2
502 8th Ave 59044 406-628-6914
Kelly Anderson, prin. Fax 628-3447

Lavina, Golden Valley, Pop. 177
Lavina SD 100/PK-12
PO Box 290 59046 406-636-2761
Duane Walker, supt. Fax 636-4911
www.lavinapublicschools.com
Lavina ES 50/PK-6
PO Box 290 59046 406-636-2761
Duane Walker, admin. Fax 636-4911
Lavina MS 50/7-8
PO Box 290 59046 406-636-2761
Duane Walker, admin. Fax 636-4911

Lewistown, Fergus, Pop. 5,800
Deerfield ESD 50/PK-8
1211 Oro Country Rd 59457 406-538-3852
Deerfield S 50/PK-8
1211 Oro Country Rd 59457 406-538-3852
Traci Manseau, lead tchr.

King Colony ESD 50/PK-8
982 Jenni Rd 59457 406-538-9702
King Colony S 50/PK-8
2370 King Colony Rd 59457 406-538-9702
Vicki Eades, lead tchr.

Lewistown SD 800/K-12
215 7th Ave S 59457 406-535-8777
Thom Peck, supt. Fax 535-7292
www.lewistown.k12.mt.us
Garfield ES 50/K-1
215 7th Ave S 59457 406-535-2366
Matt Lewis, prin. Fax 535-2367
Highland Park ES 100/2-4
215 7th Ave S 59457 406-535-2555
Matt Ventresca, prin. Fax 535-4617
Lewis & Clark ES 200/5-6
215 7th Ave S 59457 406-535-2811
Danny Wirtzberger, prin. Fax 535-2812
Lewistown JHS 200/7-8
215 7th Ave S 59457 406-535-5419
Tim Majerus, prin. Fax 535-2300

Spring Creek Colony ESD 50/PK-8
PO Box 1185 59457 406-538-8022
Fax 538-2819
Spring Creek Colony S 50/PK-8
PO Box 1185 59457 406-538-8022
Fax 538-2819

Libby, Lincoln, Pop. 2,579
Libby SD 1,000/PK-12
724 Louisiana Ave 59923 406-293-8811
Craig Barringer, supt. Fax 293-8812
www.libbyschools.org
Libby ES 600/PK-6
101 Ski Rd 59923 406-293-2763
Ron Goodman, prin. Fax 293-2862

Kootenai Valley Christian S 100/PK-12
1024 Montana Ave 59923 406-293-2303
Ruthanne Dolezal, admin. Fax 293-2303
Libby Adventist Christian S 50/1-8
206 Airfield Rd 59923 406-293-8613

Lima, Beaverhead, Pop. 213
Lima SD 100/PK-12
PO Box 186 59739 406-276-3571
Brian Rayburn, supt. Fax 276-3495
www.limaschoolmt.org
Lima JHS 50/7-8
PO Box 186 59739 406-276-3571
Brian Rayburn, prin. Fax 276-3495
Lima S 50/PK-6
PO Box 186 59739 406-276-3571
Brian Rayburn, prin. Fax 276-3495

Lincoln, Lewis and Clark, Pop. 993
Lincoln SD 100/PK-12
PO Box 39 59639 406-362-4201
Carla Anderson, supt. Fax 362-4030
www.lincolnlynx.com
Lincoln ES 50/PK-6
PO Box 39 59639 406-362-4201
Carla Anderson, prin. Fax 362-4030
Lincoln MS 50/7-8
PO Box 39 59639 406-362-4201
Carla Anderson, prin. Fax 362-4030

Lindsay, Dawson
Lindsay ESD, PO Box 185 59339 50/PK-8
Steve Engebretson, supt. 406-584-7486
Lindsay S, PO Box 185 59339 50/PK-8
Steve Engebretson, prin. 406-584-7486

Livingston, Park, Pop. 6,921
Arrowhead ESD 75 50/PK-8
1489 E River Rd 59047 406-222-4148
Jo Newhall, supt. Fax 222-4199
www.arrowheadk8.org
Arrowhead ES 50/PK-6
1489 E River Rd 59047 406-333-4359
Leah Shannon, lead tchr. Fax 333-4975
Arrowhead MS 50/7-8
1489 E River Rd 59047 406-333-4359
Leah Shannon, lead tchr. Fax 333-4975

Livingston SD 1,400/K-12
132 S B St 59047 406-222-0861
Don Viegut Ph.D., supt. Fax 222-7323
www.livingston.k12.mt.us
East Side ES 300/3-5
401 View Vista Dr 59047 406-222-1773
Bob Stevenson, prin. Fax 222-5243
Sleeping Giant MS 400/6-8
301 View Vista Dr 59047 406-222-3292
Lisa Rosburg, prin. Fax 222-3512
Winans ES 300/K-2
1015 W Clark St 59047 406-222-0192
Susie Hedalen, prin. Fax 222-7239

Pine Creek ESD 50/PK-8
2575 E River Rd 59047 406-581-8446
Kimberly DeBruycker, supt. Fax 222-0059
pinecreekschool.com
Pine Creek ES 50/PK-6
2575 E River Rd 59047 406-222-0059
Monte Silk, lead tchr. Fax 222-0059
Pine Creek MS 50/7-8
2575 E River Rd 59047 406-222-0059
Monte Silk, lead tchr. Fax 222-0059

St. Marys Catholic S 100/PK-8
511 S F St 59047 406-222-3303
Catherine Kirchner, prin. Fax 222-4662
Summit Christian Academy 50/K-12
PO Box 403 59047 406-823-9155

Lodge Grass, Big Horn, Pop. 414
Lodge Grass SD 300/PK-12
PO Box 810 59050 406-639-2304
Victoria Falls Down M.Ed., supt. Fax 639-2388
www.lodgegrass.k12.mt.us
Lodge Grass ES 200/PK-6
PO Box 810 59050 406-639-2333
Melanie Ferguson, prin. Fax 639-2375
Lodge Grass MS 50/7-8
PO Box 810 59050 406-639-2702
Curtis Brien M.Ed., prin. Fax 639-2066

Lolo, Missoula, Pop. 3,815
Lolo ESD 600/PK-8
11395 US Highway 93 S 59847 406-273-0451
Dr. Michael Magone, supt. Fax 273-2628
www.lolo.k12.mt.us
Lolo ES 300/PK-4
11395 US Highway 93 S 59847 406-273-6686
Shawna Kientz, prin. Fax 273-2628
Lolo MS 200/5-8
11395 US Highway 93 S 59847 406-273-6141
Dale Olinger M.Ed., prin. Fax 273-2628

Woodman ESD 50/K-8
18470 Highway 12 W 59847 406-273-6770
Fax 273-6659
Woodman ES 50/K-6
18470 Highway 12 W 59847 406-273-6770
Kelly Hoover, lead tchr. Fax 273-6659
Woodman MS 50/7-8
18470 Highway 12 W 59847 406-273-6770
Kelly Hoover, lead tchr. Fax 273-6659

Loring, Phillips
Malta SD
Supt. — See Malta
Loring Colony S 50/PK-8
6888 Cut Across Rd 59537 406-674-5525
Theodore Schye, prin. Fax 654-2326

Lustre, Valley

Lustre ES 7-8
6 Lustre Grade Ln 59225 406-392-5725
Wes Young, admin. Fax 392-5780

Luther, Carbon
Luther ESD 50/K-8
4 Luther Roscoe Rd 59068 406-446-2480
Fax 446-1172
Luther S 50/K-8
4 Luther Roscoe Rd 59068 406-446-2480
Janis Eckert, lead tchr. Fax 446-1172

Mc Leod, Sweet Grass
Mc Leod ESD
Supt. — See Big Timber
Mc Leod S 50/PK-8
1 Main St 59052 406-932-6164
Diana Baker, lead tchr. Fax 932-6164

Malta, Phillips, Pop. 1,893
Malta SD 500/PK-12
PO Box 670 59538 406-654-1871
Kris Kuehn, supt. Fax 654-2205
www.malta.k12.mt.us/
Malta ES 200/PK-5
706 S 3rd Ave E 59538 406-654-2320
Theodore Schye, prin. Fax 654-2326
Malta JHS 100/6-8
PO Box 670 59538 406-654-2225
Shawn Bleth, prin. Fax 654-2226
Other Schools – See Loring

Manhattan, Gallatin, Pop. 1,493
Amsterdam SD 75 200/K-6
6360 Camp Creek Rd 59741 406-282-7216
Laura Axtman, supt. Fax 282-7724
www.amsterdamschool.org
Amsterdam ES 200/K-6
6360 Camp Creek Rd 59741 406-282-7216
Katherine Dawe, prin. Fax 282-7724

Manhattan SD 600/PK-12
PO Box 425 59741 406-284-6460
Scott Chauvet, supt. Fax 284-6853
manhattan.schoolwires.com
Manhattan ES 300/PK-6
PO Box 425 59741 406-284-3250
Scott Schumacher, prin. Fax 284-4122
Manhattan MS 100/7-8
PO Box 425 59741 406-284-3250
Scott Schumacher, prin. Fax 284-4122

Manhattan Christian S 300/PK-12
8000 Churchill Rd 59741 406-282-7261
Patrick DeJong, supt. Fax 282-7701

Marion, Flathead, Pop. 853
Marion ESD 100/K-8
205 Gopher Ln 59925 406-854-2333
Cherie Stobie, prin. Fax 854-2690
www.marionschoolmt.com
Marion ES 100/K-6
205 Gopher Ln 59925 406-854-2333
Cherie Stobie, prin. Fax 854-2690
Marion MS 50/7-8
205 Gopher Ln 59925 406-854-2333
Cherie Stobie, prin. Fax 854-2690

Pleasant Valley ESD 50/PK-8
7975 Pleasant Valley Rd 59925 406-758-5720
Jack Eggensperger, supt. Fax 858-2250
www.pleasantvalleyschoolmontana.org
Pleasant Valley S 50/PK-8
7975 Pleasant Valley Rd 59925 406-858-2343
Richelle Sheets, lead tchr. Fax 858-2250

Medicine Lake, Sheridan, Pop. 215
Medicine Lake SD 100/PK-12
PO Box 265 59247 406-789-2211
Tiffani Anderson, supt. Fax 789-2213
www.medicinelake.k12.mt.us/
Medicine Lake ES 100/PK-6
PO Box 265 59247 406-789-2211
Tiffani Anderson, supt. Fax 789-2213
Medicine Lake MS 50/7-8
PO Box 265 59247 406-789-2211
Tiffani Anderson, supt. Fax 789-2213

Melrose, Silver Bow
Melrose ESD 50/PK-8
PO Box 128 59743 406-835-2811
Melrose S, PO Box 128 59743 50/PK-8
Lara Chamberlin, lead tchr. 406-835-2811

Melstone, Musselshell, Pop. 96
Melstone SD 100/PK-12
PO Box 97 59054 406-358-2352
Kelly Haaland, supt. Fax 358-2346
melstone.schoolwires.com/
Melstone ES 50/PK-6
PO Box 97 59054 406-358-2352
Kelly Haaland, prin. Fax 358-2346

Melstone MS 50/7-8
PO Box 97 59054 406-358-2352
Kelly Haaland, prin. Fax 358-2346

Melville, Sweet Grass
Melville ESD, PO Box 275 59055 50/PK-8
Susan Metcalf, supt. 406-537-4457
Melville S, PO Box 275 59055 50/PK-8
Ettje Plaggemeyer, lead tchr. 406-537-4457

Miles City, Custer, Pop. 8,282
Kircher ESD 50/PK-7
331 Kircher Creek Rd 59301 406-874-3421
Doug Ellingson, supt.
Kircher ES 50/PK-7
331 Kircher Creek Rd 59301 406-234-2761
Benson Hill, lead tchr.

Miles City SD 1,500/PK-12
1604 Main St 59301 406-234-3840
Keith Campbell, supt. Fax 234-3147
www.milescity.k12.mt.us
Garfield ES 300/PK-6
1015 Milwaukee St 59301 406-234-4310
Laurie Huffman, prin. Fax 234-4311
Highland Park ES 200/PK-3
716 Cale Ave 59301 406-234-3890
Carolyn Hopkins, prin. Fax 234-3892
Jefferson ES 200/PK-3
106 N Strevell Ave 59301 406-234-2888
Carolyn Hopkins, prin. Fax 234-2889
Lincoln ES 200/4-6
210 S Lake Ave 59301 406-234-1697
John Gorton, prin. Fax 234-2081
Washington MS 200/7-8
210 N 9th St 59301 406-234-2084
Derrick Tvedt, prin. Fax 234-7403

SH ESD 50/PK-8
6281 Moon Creek Rd 59301 406-421-5560
SH S, 6281 Moon Creek Rd 59301 50/PK-8
Corinne Osendorph, lead tchr. 406-421-5560

SY ESD 83, 735 Road 664 59301 50/PK-8
Doug Ellingson, supt. 406-874-3421
SY S, 1 Road 664 59301 50/PK-8
Bonnie Crabtree, lead tchr. 406-421-5526

Trail Creek ESD 50/PK-8
1734 Road 506 59301 406-421-5503
Riverview S, 1734 Road 506 59301 50/PK-8
Shannon Marshall, lead tchr. 406-421-5503

Sacred Heart S 100/PK-8
519 N Center Ave 59301 406-234-3850
Bart Freese, prin. Fax 234-5687
Trinity Lutheran Classical S 100/PK-6
221 S Center Ave 59301 406-234-4983
Rev. Howard Schreibeis, hdmstr. Fax 234-8033

Missoula, Missoula, Pop. 65,061
DeSmet ESD 100/K-8
6355 Padre Ln 59808 406-549-4994
Matthew Driessen, admin. Fax 549-6731
www.desmetpadres.org
DeSmet ES 100/K-6
6355 Padre Ln 59808 406-549-4994
Matthew Driessen, prin. Fax 549-6731
DeSmet MS 50/7-8
6355 Padre Ln 59808 406-549-4994
Matthew Driessen, prin. Fax 549-6731

Hellgate ESD 1,800/PK-8
2385 Flynn Ln 59808 406-728-5626
Dr. Doug Reisig, supt. Fax 728-5636
www.hellgate.k12.mt.us
Hellgate ES 900/PK-5
2385 Flynn Ln 59808 406-721-2160
Julia Mclaverty, prin. Fax 728-5636
Hellgate MS 400/6-8
2385 Flynn Ln 59808 406-721-2452
Jamie Courville, prin. Fax 728-0967

Missoula SD 1 8,600/K-12
215 S 6th St W 59801 406-728-2400
Mark Thane, supt. Fax 542-4009
www.mcpsmt.org
Chief Charlo ES 400/K-5
5600 Longview Dr 59803 406-542-4005
Giammona Vincent, prin. Fax 721-2977
Cold Springs ES 500/K-5
2625 Briggs St 59803 406-542-4010
Susan Daniel, prin. Fax 542-4012
Franklin ES 300/K-5
1901 S 11th St W 59801 406-542-4020
Amy Shattuck, prin. Fax 728-7373
Hawthorne ES 400/K-5
2835 S 3rd St W 59804 406-542-4025
Becky Sorenson, prin. Fax 542-4027
Lewis & Clark ES 500/K-5
2901 Park St 59801 406-542-4035
Susan Anderson, prin. Fax 542-4037
Lowell ES 300/K-5
1215 Phillips St 59801 406-542-4040
Brooke Casper, prin. Fax 542-4042
Meadow Hill MS 500/6-8
4210 S Reserve St 59803 406-542-4045
Christina Stevens, prin. Fax 721-4418
Paxson ES 400/K-5
101 Evans Ave 59801 406-542-4055
Peter Halloran, prin. Fax 542-4058
Porter MS 500/6-8
2510 W Central Ave 59804 406-542-4060
Lisa Hendrix, prin. Fax 542-4098
Rattlesnake ES 500/K-5
1220 Pineview Dr 59802 406-542-4050
Pam Wright, prin. Fax 542-4059
Russell ES 400/K-5
3216 S Russell St 59801 406-542-4080
Cindy Christensen, prin. Fax 721-7063
Washington MS 600/6-8
645 W Central Ave 59801 406-542-4085
Kacie Laslovich, prin. Fax 721-7346

Target Range ESD 500/PK-8
4095 South Ave W 59804 406-549-9239
Dr. Corey Austin, supt. Fax 728-8841
www.target.k12.mt.us
Target Range ES 400/PK-5
4095 South Ave W 59804 406-549-9239
Barbara Droessler, prin. Fax 728-8841
Target Range MS 200/6-8
4095 South Ave W 59804 406-549-9239
Barbara Droessler, prin. Fax 728-8841

First Lutheran Classical S PK-8
2808 South Ave W 59804 406-549-3311
Tyler Taylor, lead tchr. Fax 829-3528
Garden City Montessori S 100/PK-5
PO Box 5183 59806 406-240-0290
Missoula International S 200/PK-8
1100 Harrison St 59802 406-542-9924
Julie Lennox, head sch Fax 542-5185
Mountain View ES 50/K-8
1010 Clements Rd 59804 406-543-6223
Sandie Webster, prin.
St. Joseph S 300/K-8
503 Edith St 59801 406-549-1290
Rick Hyland, prin. Fax 543-4034
Valley Christian S 200/PK-12
2526 Sunset Ln 59804 406-549-0482
Dave Entwistle, head sch Fax 549-5047

Molt, Stillwater
Molt ESD 50/K-8
214 Lake Ave 59057 406-322-8057
Judy Martin, supt. Fax 322-1118
Molt S 50/K-8
PO Box 70 59057 406-669-3224
Debra Flynn, lead tchr. Fax 669-3224

Moore, Fergus, Pop. 188
Moore SD 100/PK-12
509 Highland Ave 59464 406-374-2231
Denise Chrest, supt. Fax 374-2490
www.moore.k12.mt.us
Moore ES 100/PK-6
509 Highland Ave 59464 406-374-2231
Denise Chrest, admin. Fax 374-2490
Moore MS 50/7-8
509 Highland Ave 59464 406-374-2231
Denise Chrest, admin. Fax 374-2490

Mosby, Garfield
Ross ESD, 1491 Old Stage Rd 59058 50/PK-8
Jessica McWilliams, supt. 406-557-6115
Ross S, 1491 Old Stage Rd 59058 50/PK-8
Caitlin Fortescue, lead tchr. 406-429-6501

Nashua, Valley, Pop. 284
Nashua SD 100/PK-12
PO Box 170 59248 406-746-3411
William Clter, supt. Fax 746-3458
www.nashua.k12.mt.us
Nashua ES 100/PK-6
PO Box 170 59248 406-746-3411
William Colter, supt. Fax 746-3458
Nashua MS 50/7-8
PO Box 170 59248 406-746-3411
William Colter, supt. Fax 746-3458

Noxon, Sanders, Pop. 210
Noxon SD 200/PK-12
300 Noxon Ave 59853 406-847-2922
Thad Kaiser, supt. Fax 847-8684
noxonschools.com
Noxon ES 100/PK-6
300 Noxon Ave 59853 406-847-2442
Thad Kaiser, prin. Fax 847-2232
Noxon MS 50/7-8
300 Noxon Ave 59853 406-847-2442
Rik Rewerts, prin. Fax 847-2232

Nye, Stillwater
Nye ESD 50/PK-6
PO Box 472 59061 406-328-6138
Nye ES, PO Box 472 59061 50/PK-6
Kathy Currie, lead tchr. 406-328-6138

Opheim, Valley, Pop. 83
Opheim SD 50/PK-12
PO Box 108 59250 406-762-3214
Tony Warren, supt. Fax 762-3348
sites.google.com/site/opheimschool/Home
Opheim ES 50/PK-6
PO Box 108 59250 406-762-3214
Tony Warren, prin. Fax 762-3348
Opheim MS 50/7-8
PO Box 108 59250 406-762-3214
Tony Warren, prin. Fax 762-3348

Ovando, Powell, Pop. 80
Ovando ESD, PO Box 176 59854 50/PK-8
Jules Waber, supt. 406-793-5722
www.ovandoschool.org/
Ovando S, PO Box 176 59854 50/PK-8
Leigh Ann Valiton, lead tchr. 406-793-5722

Pablo, Lake, Pop. 2,090
Ronan SD
Supt. — See Ronan
Pablo ES 300/PK-4
608 4th Ave E 59855 406-676-3390
Ryan Fisher, prin. Fax 675-2833

Park City, Stillwater, Pop. 973
Park City SD 300/PK-12
PO Box 278 59063 406-633-2406
Dan Grabowska, supt. Fax 633-2913
parkcityschools.org
Park City ES 200/PK-6
PO Box 278 59063 406-633-2350
Janet Southworth, prin. Fax 633-2913
Park City MS 50/7-8
PO Box 278 59063 406-633-2350
Jared Delaney, prin. Fax 633-2913

Pendroy, Teton
Pendroy ESD 50/PK-8
PO Box 65 59467 406-469-2387
Fax 469-2386
Pendroy S 50/PK-8
PO Box 65 59467 406-469-2387
Kimberly Hueske, lead tchr. Fax 469-2386

Philipsburg, Granite, Pop. 808
Philipsburg SD 200/PK-12
PO Box 400 59858 406-859-3232
Mike Cutler, supt. Fax 859-3674
pburg.k12.mt.us
Philipsburg ES 100/PK-6
PO Box 400 59858 406-859-3233
Dustin Keltner, prin. Fax 859-3673
Philipsburg MS 50/7-8
PO Box 400 59858 406-859-3232
Mike Cutler, prin. Fax 859-3674

Plains, Sanders, Pop. 1,024
Plains SD 400/PK-12
PO Box 549 59859 406-826-8600
Thomas Chisholm, supt. Fax 826-4439
www.plainsschools.net/
Plains ES 200/PK-6
PO Box 549 59859 406-826-3642
Jim Holland, prin. Fax 826-4439
Plains MS 50/7-8
PO Box 549 59859 406-826-8600
Kevin Meredith, prin. Fax 826-4439

Plentywood, Sheridan, Pop. 1,706
Plentywood SD 400/PK-12
100 E Laurel Ave 59254 406-765-1803
Matt Torix, supt. Fax 765-1175
www.plentywood.k12.mt.us/
Plentywood ES 200/PK-6
100 E Laurel Ave 59254 406-765-1803
Rob Pedersen, prin. Fax 765-1195
Plentywood MS 100/7-8
100 E Laurel Ave 59254 406-765-1803
Rob Pedersen, prin. Fax 765-1195

Plevna, Fallon, Pop. 160
Plevna SD 100/PK-12
PO Box 158 59344 406-772-5666
Jule Walker, supt. Fax 772-5548
www.plevna.k12.mt.us
Plevna ES 100/PK-6
PO Box 158 59344 406-772-5666
Jule Walker, admin. Fax 772-5548
Plevna MS 50/7-8
PO Box 158 59344 406-772-5666
Jule Walker, admin. Fax 772-5548

Polaris, Beaverhead
Polaris ESD
Supt. — See Dillon
Polaris S 50/PK-8
4210 Pioneer Mtns Scenic Rd 59746 406-834-3403
Kristi Knaub, lead tchr. Fax 834-3435

Polson, Lake, Pop. 4,155
Polson SD 1,700/PK-12
111 4th Ave E 59860 406-883-6355
Rex Weltz, supt. Fax 883-6345
www.polson.k12.mt.us
Cherry Valley ES 300/PK-1
107 8th Ave W 59860 406-883-6333
Rhonda Crowl, prin. Fax 883-6332
Linderman ES 400/2-4
312 4th Ave E 59860 406-883-6229
Tim Finkbeiner, prin. Fax 883-6365
Polson MS 300/5-6
1602 2nd St W 59860 406-883-6335
Jesse Yarbrough, prin. Fax 883-6334
Polson MS 300/7-8
1602 2nd St W 59860 406-883-6335
Tom Digiallonardo, prin. Fax 883-6334

Valley View ESD 50/PK-6
42448 Valley View Rd 59860 406-883-7262
Carolyn O. Hall, supt. Fax 883-7262
www.valleyviewschool.net/contact.html
Valley View ES 50/PK-6
42448 Valley View Rd 59860 406-883-2208
Carol Madden, lead tchr. Fax 883-2996

Mission Valley Christian Academy 100/K-12
38907 Mt Highway 35 59860 406-883-6858
Chris Bumgarner, dir. Fax 883-6858

Poplar, Roosevelt, Pop. 787
Poplar SD 700/PK-12
PO Box 458 59255 406-768-6602
James Baldwin, supt. Fax 768-6800
www.poplar.k12.mt.us
Poplar ES 400/PK-4
PO Box 458 59255 406-768-6630
Tom Granbois, prin. Fax 768-6801
Poplar JHS 100/5-8
PO Box 458 59255 406-768-6730
David Allen, prin. Fax 768-6802

Power, Teton, Pop. 174
Power SD 100/PK-12
PO Box 155 59468 406-463-2251
Loren Dunk, supt. Fax 463-2360
www.power.k12.mt.us/
Power ES 100/PK-6
PO Box 155 59468 406-463-2251
Loren Dunk, prin. Fax 463-2360

Power MS 50/7-8
PO Box 155 59468 406-463-2251
Loren Dunk, prin. Fax 463-2360

Vaughn ESD
Supt. — See Vaughn
Hillcrest Colony ES 50/K-8
1124 Wilson Rd 59468 406-463-2236
Jan Cahill, admin.

Pryor, Big Horn, Pop. 610
Pryor SD 100/PK-12
PO Box 229 59066 406-259-7329
Linda Pease, supt. Fax 245-8938
Pryor ES 50/PK-6
PO Box 229 59066 406-259-8011
Linda Pease, admin. Fax 252-9197
Pryor MS 50/7-8
PO Box 229 59066 406-259-7329
Linda Pease, admin. Fax 245-8938

St. Charles Mission S 100/PK-8
PO Box 29 59066 406-259-9976
Bambi Van Dyke, prin. Fax 259-7092

Ramsay, Silver Bow
Ramsay ESD 100/K-8
PO Box 105 59748 406-782-5470
Maury Cook, admin. Fax 723-8905
www.ramsay.k12.mt.us/
Ramsay ES 100/K-6
PO Box 105 59748 406-782-5470
Maury Cook, prin. Fax 723-8905
Ramsay MS 50/7-8
PO Box 105 59748 406-782-5470
Maury Cook, prin. Fax 723-8905

Rapelje, Stillwater
Rapelje SD 50/K-12
PO Box 89 59067 406-663-2215
Jerry Thompson, supt. Fax 663-2299
www.rapelje.k12.mt.us/
Rapelje ES 50/K-6
PO Box 89 59067 406-663-2215
Jerry Thompson, admin. Fax 663-2299
Rapelje MS 50/7-8
PO Box 89 59067 406-663-2215
Jerry Thompson, admin. Fax 663-2299

Red Lodge, Carbon, Pop. 2,091
Red Lodge SD 500/PK-12
PO Box 1090 59068 406-446-2110
John Fitzgerald, supt. Fax 446-2037
redlodge.schoolwires.com/
Mountain View ES 200/PK-5
PO Box 1090 59068 406-446-1804
Doug Mann, prin. Fax 446-0115
Roosevelt JHS 100/6-8
PO Box 1090 59068 406-446-2110
Jason Reimer, prin. Fax 446-3975

Reed Point, Stillwater, Pop. 186
Reed Point SD 100/K-12
PO Box 338 59069 406-326-2245
Michael Ehinger, supt. Fax 326-2339
www.reedpoint.k12.mt.us/
Reed Point ES 50/K-6
PO Box 338 59069 406-326-2228
Michael Ehinger, supt. Fax 326-2339
Reed Point MS 50/7-8
PO Box 338 59069 406-326-2245
Michael Ehinger, supt. Fax 326-2339

Richey, Dawson, Pop. 177
Richey SD 100/PK-12
PO Box 60 59259 406-773-5523
Maureen Simonson, supt. Fax 773-5554
www.richey.k12.mt.us/
Richey ES 50/PK-6
PO Box 60 59259 406-773-5523
Maureen Simonson, prin. Fax 773-5554
Richey MS 50/7-8
PO Box 60 59259 406-773-5680
Maureen Simonson, prin. Fax 773-5554

Roberts, Carbon, Pop. 354
Roberts SD 100/K-12
PO Box 78 59070 406-445-2421
Alexander Ator, supt. Fax 445-2506
www.roberts.k12.mt.us
Roberts ES 100/K-6
PO Box 78 59070 406-445-2421
Alex Ator, prin. Fax 445-2506
Roberts MS 50/7-8
PO Box 78 59070 406-445-2421
Alex Ator, prin. Fax 445-2506

Ronan, Lake, Pop. 1,691
Ronan SD 1,500/PK-12
421 Andrew St NW 59864 406-676-3390
Mark J. Johnston, supt. Fax 676-3392
www.ronank12.edu/
Harvey ES 400/PK-4
421 Andrew St NW 59864 406-676-3390
Ted Madden, prin. Fax 676-3319
Ronan MS 400/5-8
421 Andrew St NW 59864 406-676-3390
Sandra Beal, prin. Fax 676-2852
Other Schools – See Pablo

Glacier View Christian S 50/1-8
36332 Mud Creek Ln 59864 406-676-5142

Rosebud, Rosebud, Pop. 111
Rosebud SD 100/PK-12
PO Box 38 59347 406-347-5353
Michael Silverman, supt. Fax 347-5544
www.rhs12.com
Rosebud ES 50/PK-6
PO Box 38 59347 406-347-5353
Michael Silverman, prin. Fax 347-5544
Rosebud MS 50/7-8
PO Box 38 59347 406-347-5353
Michael Silverman, prin. Fax 347-5544

Roundup, Musselshell, Pop. 1,766
Roundup SD 600/PK-12
700 3rd St W 59072 406-323-1507
Chad Sealey, supt. Fax 323-1927
www.roundup.k12.mt.us
Roundup ES 400/PK-6
401 11th Ave E 59072 406-323-1512
Rick Griffith, prin. Fax 323-1759
Roundup JHS 100/7-8
525 6th Ave W 59072 406-323-2402
Dana Quenzer, prin. Fax 323-1583

Roy, Fergus, Pop. 108
Roy SD 50/K-12
PO Box 9 59471 406-464-2511
Steve Picard, supt. Fax 464-2561
www.roy.k12.mt.us
Roy ES 50/K-6
PO Box 9 59471 406-464-2511
Steve Picard, prin. Fax 464-2561
Roy MS 50/7-8
PO Box 9 59471 406-464-2511
Steve Picard, prin. Fax 464-2561

Rudyard, Hill, Pop. 252
North Star SD 200/PK-12
PO Box 129 59540 406-355-4481
Bart Hawkins, supt. Fax 355-4532
www.northstar.k12.mt.us
North Star MS 50/7-8
PO Box 129 59540 406-355-4481
Bart Hawkins, prin. Fax 355-4532
Other Schools – See Gildford

Ryegate, Golden Valley, Pop. 241
Ryegate SD 50/K-12
PO Box 129 59074 406-568-2211
Park A. Hook, supt. Fax 568-2528
www.ryegateschool.com/
Ryegate ES 50/K-6
PO Box 129 59074 406-568-2211
Park A. Hook, supt. Fax 568-2528
Ryegate MS 50/7-8
PO Box 129 59074 406-568-2211
Park A. Hook, supt. Fax 568-2528

Saco, Phillips, Pop. 189
Saco SD 100/PK-12
PO Box 298 59261 406-527-3531
Wade Sundby, supt. Fax 527-3479
www.sacoschools.k12.mt.us
Saco ES 50/PK-6
PO Box 298 59261 406-527-3531
Gordon Hahn, lead tchr. Fax 527-3479
Saco MS 50/7-8
PO Box 298 59261 406-527-3531
Gordon Hahn, lead tchr. Fax 527-3479

Saint Ignatius, Lake, Pop. 774
St. Ignatius SD 500/PK-12
PO Box 1540 59865 406-745-3811
Jason Sargent, supt. Fax 745-4421
www.stignatiusschools.org
St. Ignatius ES 200/PK-5
PO Box 1540 59865 406-745-3811
T. Arlint, prin. Fax 745-4070
St. Ignatius MS 100/6-8
PO Box 1540 59865 406-745-3811
Shawn Hendrickson, prin. Fax 745-4060

Saint Regis, Mineral, Pop. 301
Saint Regis SD 200/PK-12
PO Box 280 59866 406-649-2311
Joe Steele, supt. Fax 649-2271
sites.google.com/a/stregis.k12.mt.us/stregisschool/
Saint Regis ES 100/PK-6
PO Box 280 59866 406-649-2311
Shaun Ball, prin. Fax 649-2788
Saint Regis MS 50/7-8
PO Box 280 59866 406-649-2311
Shaun Ball, prin. Fax 649-2788

Saint Xavier, Big Horn, Pop. 82

Pretty Eagle Catholic Academy 100/K-8
PO Box 257 59075 406-666-2215
Carla Williamson, prin. Fax 666-2245

Sand Coulee, Cascade, Pop. 209
Centerville SD 300/PK-12
PO Box 100 59472 406-736-5123
John McGee, supt. Fax 736-5210
www.centerville.k12.mt.us/
Big Stone S 50/PK-8
PO Box 100 59472 406-736-5167
Michael Taylor, prin. Fax 736-5210
Centerville ES 100/PK-6
PO Box 100 59472 406-736-5167
Michael Taylor, prin. Fax 736-5210
Centerville MS 50/7-8
PO Box 100 59472 406-736-5167
Michael Taylor, prin. Fax 736-5210

Sand Springs, Garfield
Sand Springs ESD 50/PK-8
160 Twin Buttes Rd 59077 406-557-2774
Sand Springs S 50/PK-8
3194 Highway 200 W 59077 406-557-2774
Nicole Carrels, lead tchr.

Savage, Richland
Savage SD 100/PK-12
PO Box 110 59262 406-776-2317
Lynne Peterson, supt. Fax 776-2260
www.savagepublicschool.com
Savage ES 100/PK-6
PO Box 110 59262 406-776-2317
Angie Nelson, prin. Fax 776-2260
Savage MS 50/7-8
PO Box 110 59262 406-776-2317
Lynne Peterson, admin. Fax 776-2260

Scobey, Daniels, Pop. 996
Scobey SD 300/PK-12
PO Box 10 59263 406-487-2202
Dan Schmidt, supt. Fax 487-2204
www.scobeyschools.com
Scobey ES 100/PK-6
PO Box 10 59263 406-487-2202
Dan Schmidt, prin. Fax 487-2204
Scobey MS 50/7-8
PO Box 10 59263 406-487-2202
Logan Brower, prin. Fax 487-2204

Seeley Lake, Missoula, Pop. 1,625
Seeley Lake ESD 34 200/PK-8
PO Box 840 59868 406-677-2265
Chris Stout, supt. Fax 677-2264
www.sleonline.org
Seeley Lake ES 100/PK-6
PO Box 840 59868 406-677-2265
Chris Stout, prin. Fax 677-2264
Seeley Lake MS 50/7-8
PO Box 840 59868 406-677-2265
Chris Stout, prin. Fax 677-2264
Other Schools – See Condon

Shelby, Toole, Pop. 3,316
Shelby SD 400/PK-12
1010 Oilfield Ave 59474 406-434-2622
Elliott Crump, supt. Fax 434-2959
www.shelbypublicschools.org/
Rose S 50/PK-8
253 Union School Rd 59474 406-424-8910
Elliott Crump, supt. Fax 424-8933
Shelby ES 200/PK-6
901 Valley St 59474 406-424-8910
Erica Allen, prin. Fax 424-8933
Shelby MS 100/7-8
1001 Valley St 59474 406-424-8910
Phil French, prin. Fax 434-7273

Shepherd, Yellowstone, Pop. 501
Shepherd SD 800/PK-12
PO Box 8 59079 406-373-5461
Scott Carter, supt. Fax 373-5284
www.shepherd.k12.mt.us
Shepherd ES 400/PK-5
PO Box 8 59079 406-373-5516
Autumn Kring, prin. Fax 373-5076
Shepherd MS 100/6-8
PO Box 8 59079 406-373-5873
Richard Hash, prin. Fax 373-5648

Sheridan, Madison, Pop. 623
Sheridan SD 200/K-12
PO Box 586 59749 406-842-5302
Micheal Wetherbee, supt. Fax 842-5391
sheridan.k12.mt.us
Sheridan ES 100/K-6
PO Box 586 59749 406-842-5302
Rodney Stout, prin. Fax 842-5391
Sheridan MS 50/7-8
PO Box 586 59749 406-842-5302
Micheal Wetherbee, prin. Fax 842-5391

Sidney, Richland, Pop. 5,107
Brorson ESD 50/K-6
PO Box 145 59270 406-433-1608
Gail Staffanson B.S., supt. Fax 433-3731
Brorson ES 50/K-6
PO Box 145 59270 406-798-3361
Gail Staffanson B.S., supt. Fax 798-3414

Rau ESD 100/K-6
12138 County Road 350 59270 406-482-1088
Paul Richter, admin. Fax 482-1016
www.rauschool.net
Rau ES 100/K-6
12138 County Road 350 59270 406-482-1088
Paul Richter, lead tchr. Fax 482-1016

Sidney SD 1,000/PK-12
200 3rd Ave SE 59270 406-433-4080
Dr. Daniel Farr Ed.D., supt. Fax 433-4358
www.sidney.k12.mt.us/
Central ES 300/K-K, 4-5
200 3rd Ave SE 59270 406-433-4080
Brent Sukut, prin. Fax 433-4358
Sidney MS 300/6-8
200 3rd Ave SE 59270 406-433-4050
Kelly Johnson, prin. Fax 433-4052
West Side ES PK-PK, 1-
200 3rd Ave SE 59270 406-433-2530
Jonathan Skinner, prin. Fax 433-9186

Simms, Cascade, Pop. 343
Sun River Valley SD 200/PK-12
PO Box 380 59477 406-264-5110
Dave Marzolf, supt. Fax 264-5189
www.srvs.k12.mt.us
Other Schools – See Fort Shaw, Sun River

Somers, Flathead, Pop. 1,095
Somers ESD 600/PK-8
315 School Addition Rd 59932 406-857-3301
Joseph Price, supt. Fax 857-3144
www.somersdist29.org
Somers MS 200/6-8
315 School Addition Rd 59932 406-857-3661
Rose McIntyre, prin. Fax 857-3144

Other Schools – See Lakeside

Stanford, Judith Basin, Pop. 400
Stanford SD — 100/PK-12
PO Box 506 59479 — 406-566-2265
Tim Dolphay M.Ed., supt. — Fax 566-2772
www.stanford.k12.mt.us/
Stanford ES — 100/PK-6
PO Box 506 59479 — 406-566-2265
Tim Dolphay M.Ed., admin. — Fax 566-2772
Stanford MS — 50/7-8
PO Box 506 59479 — 406-566-2265
Tim Dolphay M.Ed., admin. — Fax 566-2772
Surprise Creek S — 50/K-8
928 Surprise Creek Rd 59479 — 406-566-2269
Tim Dolphay, admin.

Stevensville, Ravalli, Pop. 1,781
Lone Rock ESD — 300/PK-8
1112 Three Mile Creek Rd 59870 — 406-777-3314
Scott Stiegler, supt. — Fax 777-2770
www.lonerockschool.org
Lone Rock ES — 200/PK-6
1112 Three Mile Creek Rd 59870 — 406-777-3314
Scott Stiegler, prin. — Fax 777-2770
Lone Rock MS — 100/7-8
1112 Three Mile Creek Rd 59870 — 406-777-3314
Scott Stiegler, prin. — Fax 777-2770

Stevensville SD — 800/K-12
300 Park St 59870 — 406-777-5481
Dr. Bob Moore, supt. — Fax 258-1246
www.stevensvilleschool.net/
Stevensville ES — 300/K-3
300 Park St 59870 — 406-777-5613
Jessica Shourd, prin. — Fax 258-1245
Stevensville MS — 100/4-8
300 Park St 59870 — 406-777-5533
Tracey Rogstad, prin. — Fax 258-1242

Sunburst, Toole, Pop. 361
Sunburst SD 2 — 200/K-12
PO Box 710 59482 — 406-937-2811
M. Christina Barbachano, supt. — Fax 937-2828
www.sunburst.k12.mt.us
Hillside Colony S — 50/K-8
PO Box 710 59482 — 406-937-2816
Dan Nau, prin. — Fax 937-4444
Rimrock Colony S — 50/K-8
PO Box 710 59482 — 406-937-2816
Dan Nau, prin. — Fax 937-4444
Sunburst ES — 100/K-6
PO Box 710 59482 — 406-937-2816
Dan Nau, prin. — Fax 937-4444
Sunburst MS — 50/7-8
PO Box 710 59482 — 406-937-2816
M. Christina Barbachano, prin. — Fax 937-4444

Sun River, Cascade, Pop. 116
Sun River Valley SD
Supt. — See Simms
Cascade Colony S — 50/PK-8
508 Birdtail Creek Rd 59483 — 406-264-5104
Rick Danelson, prin. — Fax 264-5265

Superior, Mineral, Pop. 795
Superior SD — 300/PK-12
PO Box 400 59872 — 406-822-3600
Scott Kinney, supt. — Fax 822-3601
ssd3.us
Superior ES — 200/PK-6
PO Box 400 59872 — 406-822-3600
Logan Labbe, prin. — Fax 822-3601
Superior MS — 50/7-8
PO Box 400 59872 — 406-822-4851
Chris Clairmont, prin. — Fax 822-4396

Swan Lake, Flathead, Pop. 111
Swan Lake-Salmon Prairie ESD — 50/PK-8
23187 MT Highway 83 59911 — 406-883-7262
Carolyn O. Hall, supt. — Fax 883-7262
Salmon Prairie S — 50/PK-8
40224 Salmon Prairie Rd 59911 — 406-754-2245
Thomas Hubbard, lead tchr. — Fax 754-2245

Terry, Prairie, Pop. 589
Terry SD — 100/PK-12
PO Box 187 59349 — 406-635-5533
Angela Williams, supt. — Fax 635-5705
www.terry.k12.mt.us
Terry ES — 100/PK-6
PO Box 187 59349 — 406-635-5533
Angela Williams, prin. — Fax 635-5705
Terry MS — 50/7-8
PO Box 187 59349 — 406-635-5595
Angela Williams, prin. — Fax 635-5705

Thompson Falls, Sanders, Pop. 1,286
Thompson Falls SD — 500/PK-12
206 Haley Ave 59873 — 406-827-3323
Jason Slater, supt. — Fax 827-3020
www.thompsonfalls.net
Thompson Falls ES — 200/PK-6
206 Haley Ave 59873 — 406-827-3592
Len Dorscher, prin. — Fax 827-0192
Thompson Falls MS — 100/7-8
206 Haley Ave 59873 — 406-827-3593
Len Dorscher, prin. — Fax 827-0306

Three Forks, Gallatin, Pop. 1,859
Three Forks SD — 500/PK-12
212 E Neal St 59752 — 406-285-3224
Dr. Robert DoBell, supt. — Fax 285-3503
www.tfschools.com
Three Forks ES — 300/PK-6
212 E Neal St 59752 — 406-285-6830
Steven Fanning, prin. — Fax 285-3216
Three Forks MS — 100/7-8
210 E Neal St 59752 — 406-285-3224
Justin Helvik, prin. — Fax 285-3503

Townsend, Broadwater, Pop. 1,847
Townsend SD — 600/PK-12
201 N Spruce St 59644 — 406-441-3454
Erik Wilkerson, supt. — Fax 441-3457
www.townsend.k12.mt.us
Hazelton ES — 300/PK-6
201 N Spruce St 59644 — 406-441-3431
Brad Racht, prin. — Fax 441-3475
Townsend MS — 100/7-8
201 N Spruce St 59644 — 406-441-3431
Brad Racht, prin. — Fax 441-3475

Trego, Lincoln, Pop. 534
Trego ESD — 50/K-8
PO Box 10 59934 — 406-882-4713
Fax 882-4365
Trego S — 50/K-8
PO Box 10 59934 — 406-882-4713
Lori Guckenberg, contact — Fax 882-4365

Trout Creek, Sanders, Pop. 235
Trout Creek SD — 50/PK-8
4 School Ln 59874 — 406-827-3629
Debbie Phillips, admin. — Fax 827-4185
www.troutcreekeagles.org
Trout Creek ES — 50/PK-6
4 School Ln 59874 — 406-827-3629
Debbie Phillips, prin. — Fax 827-4185
Trout Creek MS — 50/7-8
4 School Ln 59874 — 406-827-3629
Debbie Phillips, prin. — Fax 827-4185

Trout Creek Adventist S — 1-8
3020 MT Highway 200 59874 — 406-827-3099

Troy, Lincoln, Pop. 913
McCormick ESD — 50/PK-8
1564 Old US Highway 2 N 59935 — 406-295-4982
Fax 295-6035
McCormick S — 50/PK-8
1564 Old US Highway 2 N 59935 — 406-295-4982
Darcy Koemans, lead tchr. — Fax 295-6035

Troy SD — 400/PK-12
PO Box 867 59935 — 406-295-4606
Dr. Jacob Francom, supt. — Fax 295-4802
troymtk-12.us/
Morrison ES — 200/PK-6
PO Box 867 59935 — 406-295-4321
Diane Rewerts, prin. — Fax 295-8672
Troy MS — 100/7-8
PO Box 867 59935 — 406-295-4520
Dr. Jacob Francom, prin. — Fax 295-5371

Yaak ESD — 50/K-8
29893 Yaak River Rd 59935 — 406-295-9311
Nancy Higgins, supt. — Fax 295-9597
Yaak S — 50/K-8
29893 Yaak River Rd 59935 — 406-295-9311
Diane Downey, lead tchr. — Fax 295-9311

Turner, Blaine, Pop. 56
Turner SD — 100/K-12
PO Box 40 59542 — 406-379-2315
Russ McKenna, supt. — Fax 379-2398
turner.k12.mt.us
Turner ES — 50/K-6
PO Box 40 59542 — 406-379-2219
Russ McKenna, supt. — Fax 379-2398
Turner MS — 50/7-8
PO Box 40 59542 — 406-379-2219
Russ McKenna, supt. — Fax 379-2398

Twin Bridges, Madison, Pop. 367
Twin Bridges SD — 200/PK-12
PO Box 419 59754 — 406-684-5657
Chad Johnson, supt. — Fax 684-5458
www.twinbridges.k12.mt.us
Twin Bridges ES — 100/PK-6
PO Box 419 59754 — 406-684-5613
Tammy Demien, prin. — Fax 684-5458
Twin Bridges MS — 50/7-8
PO Box 419 59754 — 406-684-5613
Tammy Demien, prin. — Fax 684-5458

Ulm, Cascade, Pop. 714
Ulm ESD — 100/PK-8
PO Box 189 59485 — 406-866-3313
Lyndsey Green, supt. — Fax 866-3209
www.ulmschools.com
Fair Haven Colony S — 50/K-8
PO Box 189 59485 — 406-866-3313
Lyndsey Green, prin. — Fax 866-3209
Ulm ES — 100/PK-6
PO Box 189 59485 — 406-866-3313
Lyndsey Green, prin. — Fax 866-3209
Ulm MS — 50/7-8
PO Box 189 59485 — 406-866-3313
Lyndsey Green, prin. — Fax 866-3209

Valier, Pondera, Pop. 489
Dutton/Brady SD
Supt. — See Dutton
Pondera Colony S — 50/PK-8
300 Pondera Colony Rd 59486 — 406-476-3424
Leslee Weber, prin. — Fax 476-3342

Valier SD — 200/PK-12
PO Box 528 59486 — 406-279-3613
Julie Gaffney, supt. — Fax 279-3212
sites.google.com/a/valier.k12.mt.us/homepage/
Kingsbury Colony S — 50/1-8
PO Box 588 59486 — 406-279-3314
Julie Gaffney, prin. — Fax 279-3510
Valier ES — 100/PK-6
PO Box 508 59486 — 406-279-3314
Julie Gaffney, prin. — Fax 279-3314
Valier MS — 50/7-8
PO Box 508 59486 — 406-279-3314
Julie Gaffney, prin. — Fax 279-3510

Vaughn, Cascade, Pop. 628
Vaughn ESD — 100/PK-8
PO Box 279 59487 — 406-965-2231
Jan Cahill, supt. — Fax 965-3703
www.vaughnschool.com
Vaughn ES — 100/PK-6
PO Box 279 59487 — 406-965-2231
Jan Cahill, admin. — Fax 965-3703
Vaughn MS — 50/7-8
PO Box 279 59487 — 406-965-2231
Jan Cahill, admin. — Fax 965-3703
Other Schools – See Power

Victor, Ravalli, Pop. 724
Victor SD — 400/PK-12
425 4th Ave 59875 — 406-642-3221
Lance Pearson, supt. — Fax 642-3446
www.victor.k12.mt.us/
Victor ES — 200/PK-5
425 4th Ave 59875 — 406-642-3551
Danny Johnston, prin. — Fax 642-3446
Victor MS — 100/6-8
425 4th Ave 59875 — 406-642-3221
Danny Johnston, prin. — Fax 642-3446

Vida, McCone
Vida ESD
Supt. — See Circle
Vida S — 50/PK-8
200 Shell St 59274 — 406-525-3374
Sherry Haynie, lead tchr. — Fax 525-3234

Volborg, Custer
South Stacey ESD — 50/PK-8
124 Stacey Rd 59351 — 406-784-2256
South Stacey S — 50/PK-8
124 Stacey Rd 59351 — 406-784-2256
Victoria Neal, lead tchr. — Fax 784-2850

Westby, Sheridan, Pop. 166
Westby SD — 100/PK-12
PO Box 109 59275 — 406-385-2225
Tony Holecek, supt. — Fax 385-2430
www.westbyschool.k12.mt.us/
Westby ES — 50/PK-6
PO Box 109 59275 — 406-385-2225
Tony Holecek, prin. — Fax 385-2430
Westby MS — 50/7-8
PO Box 109 59275 — 406-385-2225
Tony Holecek, prin. — Fax 385-2430

West Glacier, Flathead, Pop. 226
West Glacier ESD — 50/K-6
PO Box 309 59936 — 406-888-5312
Fax 888-5141
www.westglacierelementary.org
West Glacier ES — 50/K-6
PO Box 309 59936 — 406-888-5312
Krista Booher, prin. — Fax 888-5141

West Yellowstone, Gallatin, Pop. 1,235
West Yellowstone SD — 300/K-12
PO Box 460 59758 — 406-646-7617
Kevin Flanagan, supt. — Fax 646-7232
www.westyellowstone.k12.mt.us
West Yellowstone ES — 200/K-6
PO Box 460 59758 — 406-646-7617
Kevin Flanagan, admin. — Fax 646-7232
West Yellowstone MS — 50/7-8
PO Box 460 59758 — 406-646-7617
Brian Smith, prin. — Fax 646-7232

Whitefish, Flathead, Pop. 6,250
Olney-Bissell ESD — 100/PK-8
5955 Farm To Market Rd 59937 — 406-862-2828
Fax 862-2838
www.olneybissellschool.com
Bissell ES — 100/PK-6
5955 Farm To Market Rd 59937 — 406-862-2828
Trevor Dahlman, prin. — Fax 862-2838
Bissell MS — 50/7-8
5955 Farm to Market Rd 59937 — 406-862-2828
Trevor Dahlman, prin. — Fax 862-2838

Whitefish SD — 1,600/PK-12
600 2nd St E 59937 — 406-862-8640
Heather Davis Schmidt, supt. — Fax 862-1507
www.wsd44.org
Muldown ES — 600/PK-4
600 2nd St E 59937 — 406-862-8620
Linda Whitright, prin. — Fax 862-8630
Whitefish MS — 500/5-8
600 2nd St E 59937 — 406-862-8650
Josh Branstetter, prin. — Fax 862-8664

Whitefish Christian Academy — 100/PK-11
820 Ashar Ave 59937 — 406-862-5875

Whitehall, Jefferson, Pop. 1,005
Whitehall SD — 400/PK-12
PO Box 1109 59759 — 406-287-3455
John Sullivan, supt. — Fax 287-3843
whitehall.schoolwires.com/
Whitehall ES — 200/PK-6
PO Box 1109 59759 — 406-287-3882
Britt McLean, prin. — Fax 287-5508
Whitehall JHS — 100/7-8
PO Box 1109 59759 — 406-287-3882
Britt McLean, prin. — Fax 287-5508

White Sulphur Springs, Meagher, Pop. 922
White Sulphur Springs SD — 200/PK-12
PO Box C 59645 — 406-547-3751
Larry Markuson, supt. — Fax 547-3922
www.whitesulphur.k12.mt.us/
White Sulphur Springs ES — 100/PK-6
PO Box C 59645 — 406-547-3751
Jacqueline Boyd, prin. — Fax 547-3922
White Sulphur Springs MS — 50/7-8
PO Box C 59645 — 406-547-3351
Jacqueline Boyd, prin. — Fax 547-2407

Whitewater, Phillips, Pop. 62
Whitewater SD 100/PK-12
PO Box 46 59544 406-674-5418
Darin Cummings, supt. Fax 674-5460
www.whitewater.k12.mt.us
Whitewater ES 50/PK-6
PO Box 46 59544 406-674-5417
Darin Cummings, prin. Fax 674-5460
Whitewater MS 50/7-8
PO Box 46 59544 406-674-5417
Darin Cummings, prin. Fax 674-5460

Wibaux, Wibaux, Pop. 582
Wibaux SD 200/PK-12
121 F St N 59353 406-796-2474
Terry Quintus, supt. Fax 796-2259
wibauxschools.net
Wibaux ES 100/PK-6
415 Nolan Ave W 59353 406-796-2518
Janet Huisman, prin. Fax 796-2635
Wibaux JHS 50/7-8
121 F St N 59353 406-796-2474
Janet Huisman, prin. Fax 796-2259

Willow Creek, Gallatin, Pop. 206
Willow Creek SD 100/PK-12
PO Box 189 59760 406-285-6991
Bonnie Lower, supt. Fax 285-6923
www.willowcreek.k12.mt.us
Willow Creek ES 50/PK-6
PO Box 189 59760 406-285-6991
Bonnie Lower, prin. Fax 285-6923
Willow Creek MS 50/7-8
PO Box 189 59760 406-285-6991
Bonnie Lower, prin. Fax 285-6923

Winifred, Fergus, Pop. 207
Winifred SD 50/PK-12
PO Box 109 59489 406-462-5420
Chad Fordyce, supt. Fax 462-5477
www.winifred.k12.mt.us
Winifred S 50/PK-12
PO Box 109 59489 406-462-5420
Kelli Carlson, prin. Fax 462-5477

Winnett, Petroleum, Pop. 182
Winnett SD 100/PK-12
PO Box 167 59087 406-429-2251
Walt Stevens, supt. Fax 429-7631
www.midrivers.com/~whsrams/
Winnett ES 50/PK-6
PO Box 167 59087 406-429-2251
Walt Stevens, admin. Fax 429-7631
Winnett MS 50/7-8
PO Box 167 59087 406-429-2251
Walt Stevens, admin. Fax 429-7631

Wisdom, Beaverhead, Pop. 98
Wisdom ESD 50/PK-8
PO Box 176 59761 406-689-3227
Fax 689-3217
Wisdom S 50/PK-8
PO Box 176 59761 406-689-3227
Dani Peterson, lead tchr. Fax 689-3217

Wise River, Beaverhead
Wise River ESD 50/PK-8
School House Rd 59762 406-832-3279
Fax 832-3214
Wise River S 50/PK-8
School House Rd 59762 406-832-3279
Betty Jean DeFord, lead tchr. Fax 832-3214

Wolf Creek, Lewis and Clark
Auchard Creek ESD 50/PK-8
9605 US Highway 287 59648 406-447-8344
Katrina Chaney, supt. Fax 447-8398
Auchard Creek S 50/PK-8
9605 US Highway 287 59648 406-562-3528
Katrina Chaney, prin. Fax 562-3722

Wolf Creek ESD 50/PK-6
PO Box 200 59648 406-235-4241
Fax 235-4241
www.wolfcreekschool.com
Wolf Creek ES 50/PK-6
PO Box 200 59648 406-235-4241
Korrin Kenck-Vanderloos, lead tchr. Fax 235-4241

Wolf Point, Roosevelt, Pop. 2,478
Frontier ESD 100/PK-8
6996 Roy St 59201 406-653-7083
Christine Eggar, supt. Fax 653-2508
Frontier ES 100/PK-6
6996 Roy St 59201 406-653-2501
Christine Eggar, admin. Fax 653-2508
Frontier MS 50/7-8
6996 Roy St 59201 406-653-2501
Christine Eggar, admin. Fax 653-2508
Vida ESD
Supt. — See Circle
Prairie Elk Colony S 50/PK-8
1438 Highway 528 59201 406-525-3438
Fax 525-3030

Wolf Point SD 900/PK-12
213 6th Ave S 59201 406-653-2361
Robert Osborne, supt. Fax 653-3405
wolfpointschools.org
Northside IS 200/4-6
710 4th Ave N 59201 406-653-1653
Kathy Adkins, prin. Fax 653-2368
Southside ES 300/PK-3
415 4th Ave S 59201 406-653-1480
Mary Beil, prin. Fax 653-1483
Wolf Point JHS 100/7-8
213 6th Ave S 59201 406-653-1200
Kim Hanks, prin. Fax 653-3104

Worden, Yellowstone, Pop. 573
Huntley Project SD 800/PK-12
1477 Ash St 59088 406-967-2540
Wes Coy, supt. Fax 967-3059
www.huntley.k12.mt.us/
Huntley Project ES 400/PK-6
1477 Ash St 59088 406-967-2540
Clint Croy, prin. Fax 967-2547
Huntley Project MS 100/7-8
2436 N 15th Rd 59088 406-967-2540
Frank Hollowell, prin. Fax 967-3054

Wyola, Big Horn, Pop. 212
Wyola ESD 100/PK-8
PO Box 66 59089 406-343-2722
Linda Brien, supt. Fax 343-5901
www.wyola.k12.mt.us
Wyola ES 100/PK-6
PO Box 66 59089 406-343-2722
Linda Brien, prin. Fax 343-5901
Wyola MS 50/7-8
PO Box 66 59089 406-343-2722
Linda Brien, prin. Fax 343-5901

Zurich, Blaine
Zurich ESD 50/K-8
PO Box 847 59547 406-357-4164
Fax 357-4299
Zurich ES 50/K-8
PO Box 847 59547 406-357-4164
Colleen Overcast, lead tchr. Fax 357-4299

NEBRASKA

NEBRASKA DEPARTMENT OF EDUCATION

PO Box 94987, Lincoln 68509-4987
Telephone 402-471-2295
Fax 402-471-0117
Website http://www.education.ne.gov/

Commissioner of Education Dr. Matthew Blomstedt

NEBRASKA BOARD OF EDUCATION

PO Box 94987, Lincoln 68509-4987

President Patricia Timm

EDUCATIONAL SERVICE UNITS (ESU)

ESU 1
Robert Uhing, admin. 402-287-2061
211 10th St, Wakefield 68784 Fax 287-2065
www.esu1.org/

ESU 2
Dr. Ted DeTurk Ed.D., admin. 402-721-7710
PO Box 649, Fremont 68026 Fax 721-7712
www.esu2.org/

ESU 3
Dr. Dan Schnoes, admin. 402-597-4800
6949 S 110th St, La Vista 68128 Fax 597-4808
www.esu3.org

ESU 4
Jon Fisher, admin. 402-274-4354
919 16th St, Auburn 68305 Fax 274-4356
www.esu4.org

ESU 5
Dr. Brenda McNiff, admin. 402-223-5277
900 W Court St, Beatrice 68310 Fax 223-5279
www.esu5.org

ESU 6
Dr. Dan Shoemake, admin. 800-327-0091
210 5th St, Milford 68405 Fax 761-3279
www.esu6.org

ESU 7
Larianne Polk, admin. 402-564-5753
2657 44th Ave, Columbus 68601 Fax 563-1121
ww2.esu7.org

ESU 8
Bill Mowinkel, admin. 402-887-5041
PO Box 89, Neligh 68756 Fax 887-4604
www.esu8.org

ESU 9
Dr. Kraig Lofquist, admin. 402-463-5611
1117 E South St, Hastings 68901 Fax 463-9555
esu9.org

ESU 10
Wayne Bell, admin. 308-237-5927
PO Box 850, Kearney 68848 Fax 237-5920
www.esu10.org/

ESU 11
Paul Tedesco, admin. 308-995-6585
PO Box 858, Holdrege 68949 Fax 995-6587
www.esu11.org

ESU 13
Dr. Jeff West, admin. 308-635-3696
4215 Avenue I, Scottsbluff 69361 Fax 635-0680
www.esu13.org

ESU 15 308-334-5160
, PO Box 398, Trenton 69044 Fax 334-5581
www.esu15.org

ESU 16
Margene Beatty, admin. 308-284-8481
PO Box 915, Ogallala 69153 Fax 284-8483
www.blogesu16.org

ESU 17
Geraldine Erickson, admin. 402-387-1420
207 N Main St, Ainsworth 69210 Fax 387-1028
www.esu17.org

ESU 18
Steve Joel Ed.D., supt. 402-436-1000
PO Box 82889, Lincoln 68501 Fax 436-1620
www.lps.org

ESU 19
Dr. Julia Allen, admin. 531-299-9463
3215 Cuming St, Omaha 68131
esu19.org

PUBLIC, PRIVATE AND CATHOLIC ELEMENTARY SCHOOLS

Adams, Gage, Pop. 572
Freeman SD 400/PK-12
PO Box 259 68301 402-988-2525
Randy Page, supt. Fax 988-3475
www.freemanpublicschools.org/
Freeman ES 200/PK-6
PO Box 259 68301 402-988-2525
Erin Sieh, prin. Fax 988-3475

Ainsworth, Brown, Pop. 1,710
Ainsworth SD 500/PK-12
PO Box 65 69210 402-387-2333
Darrell Peterson, supt. Fax 387-0525
www.ainsworthschools.org
Ainsworth ES 200/K-4
PO Box 65 69210 402-387-2083
Mike Wentz, prin. Fax 387-0525
Ainsworth Little Paws Preschool 50/PK-PK
PO Box 233 69210
Ainsworth MS 100/5-8
PO Box 65 69210 402-387-2082
Mike Wentz, prin. Fax 387-0525

Albion, Boone, Pop. 1,646
Boone Central SD 500/K-12
PO Box 391 68620 402-395-2134
Nicole Hardwick, supt. Fax 395-2137
www.boonecentral.org
Boone Central ES - Albion 200/K-5
PO Box 391 68620 402-395-2134
Jimmy Feeey, prin. Fax 395-2137
Other Schools – See Petersburg

St. Michael's S 100/PK-8
520 W Church St 68620 402-395-2926
Lisa Schumacher, prin. Fax 395-2926

Allen, Dixon, Pop. 375
Allen Consolidated SD 200/K-12
PO Box 190 68710 402-635-2484
Michael Pattee, supt. Fax 635-2331
www.allenschools.org/
Allen ES 100/K-6
PO Box 190 68710 402-635-2484
Michael Pattee, prin. Fax 635-2331

Alliance, Box Butte, Pop. 8,339
Alliance SD 1,400/PK-12
1604 Sweetwater Ave 69301 308-762-5475
Dr. Troy Unzicker, supt. Fax 762-8249
apschools.schoolfusion.us
Alliance Early Childhood Education 100/PK-PK
1604 Sweetwater Ave 69301 308-762-4425
Laurie Keilwitz, dir. Fax 762-8249
Alliance MS 300/6-8
1604 Sweetwater Ave 69301 308-762-3079
Troy Mach, prin. Fax 762-7302
Emerson ES 300/K-2
1604 Sweetwater Ave 69301 308-762-4093
Susan Cummings, prin. Fax 762-4195
Grandview ES 200/3-5
1604 Sweetwater Ave 69301 308-762-4519
Steve Folchert, prin. Fax 762-4521

Immanuel Lutheran S PK-6
PO Box 715 69301 308-629-1601
Jill Mueller, prin.
St. Agnes Academy 100/PK-8
1104 Cheyenne Ave 69301 308-762-2315
Rodney Wilhelm, prin. Fax 762-7474

Alma, Harlan, Pop. 1,129
Alma SD 300/K-12
PO Box 170 68920 308-928-2131
Jon Davis, supt. Fax 928-2763
almacardinals.org
Alma ES 200/K-6
PO Box 170 68920 308-928-2131
Galen Kronhofman, prin. Fax 928-2763

Amherst, Buffalo, Pop. 248
Amherst SD 300/K-12
PO Box 8 68812 308-826-3131
Tom Moore, supt. Fax 826-4865
amherst.k12.ne.us/
Amherst ES 200/K-6
PO Box 8 68812 308-826-3131
Tom Moore, prin. Fax 826-4865

Ansley, Custer, Pop. 440
Ansley SD 200/PK-12
PO Box 370 68814 308-935-1121
Dave Mroczek Ed.D., supt. Fax 935-9103
ansleynebraska.org
Ansley ES 100/PK-6
PO Box 370 68814 308-935-1121
Lance Bristol, prin. Fax 935-9103

Arapahoe, Furnas, Pop. 1,013
Arapahoe SD 300/PK-12
PO Box 360 68922 308-962-5458
Dr. George Griffith, supt. Fax 962-7481
arapahoewarriors.org
Arapahoe ES 200/PK-6
PO Box 360 68922 308-962-5459
Bob Braithwait, prin. Fax 962-7481

Arcadia, Valley, Pop. 309
Arcadia SD 100/PK-12
PO Box 248 68815 308-789-6522
Jess Underwood Ed.D., supt. Fax 789-6214
www.arcadiapublicschools.org/
Arcadia ES 100/PK-6
PO Box 248 68815 308-789-6522
Jess Underwood Ed.D., admin. Fax 789-6214

Arlington, Washington, Pop. 1,239
Arlington SD 600/K-12
PO Box 580 68002 402-478-4173
Lynn Johnson, supt. Fax 478-4176
www.apseagles.org
Arlington ES 300/K-6
PO Box 580 68002 402-478-4121
Jacqueline Morgan, prin. Fax 478-4176

St. Paul Lutheran S 100/K-8
8951 County Road 9 68002 402-478-4278
Dennis Rosenthal, prin. Fax 478-5378

Arnold, Custer, Pop. 592
Arnold SD 100/K-12
PO Box 399 69120 308-848-2226
Dawn Lewis, supt. Fax 848-2201
blog.arnold.k12.ne.us
Arnold ES 100/K-6
PO Box 399 69120 308-848-2226
Joel Morgan, prin. Fax 848-2201

Arthur, Arthur, Pop. 117
Arthur County SD 100/K-12
PO Box 145 69121 308-764-2253
Barry Schaeffer, supt. Fax 764-2206
www.arthurcountywolves.org
Arthur Lower ES 100/K-6
PO Box 145 69121 308-764-2231
Barry Schaeffer, supt. Fax 764-2206

Ashland, Saunders, Pop. 2,429
Ashland-Greenwood SD 900/PK-12
1842 Furnas St 68003 402-944-2128
Jason Libal, supt. Fax 944-3310
www.agps.org/
Ashland-Greenwood ES 400/PK-5
1200 Boyd St 68003 402-944-7083
Teresa Bray, prin. Fax 944-3515
Ashland-Greenwood MS 200/6-8
1842 Furnas St 68003 402-944-2114
Brad Jacobsen, prin. Fax 944-2116

Atkinson, Holt, Pop. 1,242
West Holt SD 400/K-12
PO Box 457 68713 402-925-2848
Paul Pistulka, supt. Fax 925-2177
www.westholtps.org
Union S 50/K-8
47572 887th Rd 68713 402-925-2435
Douglas Gross, prin. Fax 925-2177
West Holt ES 200/K-6
PO Box 457 68713 402-925-2848
Douglas Gross, prin. Fax 925-2177

St. Joseph S 100/PK-8
PO Box 69 68713 402-925-2104
Erin Jelinek, admin. Fax 925-2104

Auburn, Nemaha, Pop. 3,425
Auburn SD 800/PK-12
1713 J St 68305 402-274-4830
Kevin Reiman, supt. Fax 274-5227
www.auburnpublicschools.org
Auburn MS 200/6-8
1829 Central Ave 68305 402-274-4027
Marty Hughes, prin. Fax 274-4147
Calvert ES 400/PK-5
1713 J St 68305 402-274-4129
Jacquelyn Kelsay, prin. Fax 274-4121

Aurora, Hamilton, Pop. 4,447
Aurora SD 1,200/PK-12
300 L St 68818 402-694-6923
Damon McDonald, supt. Fax 694-5097
aurorahuskies.us
Aurora ES 500/K-5
300 L St 68818 402-694-3167
Mark Standage, prin. Fax 694-5348
Aurora MS 300/6-8
300 L St 68818 402-694-6915
Kenneth Thiele, prin. Fax 694-3815
Aurora Preschool 50/PK-PK
409 J St 68818 402-694-3167

Axtell, Kearney, Pop. 718
Axtell Community SD 200/K-12
PO Box 97 68924 308-743-2415
Rob Gregory, supt. Fax 743-2417
www.axtellwildcats.org
Axtell ES 100/K-5
PO Box 97 68924 308-743-2415
Bill Gilbreath, prin. Fax 743-2417
Axtell MS 100/6-8
PO Box 97 68924 308-743-2415
Bill Gilbreath, prin. Fax 743-2417

Bancroft, Cuming, Pop. 482
Bancroft-Rosalie SD 200/K-12
PO Box 129 68004 402-648-3336
Jon Cerny, supt. Fax 648-3338
www.bancroft-rosalie.org
Bancroft ES 100/K-6
PO Box 129 68004 402-648-3336
Jon Cerny, prin. Fax 648-3338

Bartlett, Wheeler, Pop. 117
Wheeler Central SD 100/PK-12
PO Box 68 68622 308-654-3273
Rodney Olson, supt. Fax 654-3237
www.wbroncs.org
Wheeler Central ES #45 100/PK-6
PO Box 68 68622 308-654-3273
Rodney Olson, prin. Fax 654-3237

Bartley, Red Willow, Pop. 282
Southwest SD 179 300/PK-12
PO Box 187 69020 308-692-3223
Robert Porter, supt. Fax 692-3221
www.swpschools.org/
Other Schools – See Indianola

Bassett, Rock, Pop. 618
Rock County SD 200/K-12
PO Box 448 68714 402-684-3411
Thomas Becker, supt. Fax 684-3671
www.rockcountyschools.org
Bassett Grade S 100/K-6
PO Box 407 68714 402-684-3855
Steve Camp, prin. Fax 684-3808
Pony Lake S 50/K-8
45597 866th Rd 68714 402-244-5450
Steve Camp, prin. Fax 244-5450
Rose Community S 50/K-8
85256 US Highway 183 68714 402-684-3469
Steve Camp, prin. Fax 684-3469

Battle Creek, Madison, Pop. 1,202
Battle Creek SD 400/K-12
PO Box 100 68715 402-675-6905
Jay Bellar, supt. Fax 675-1038
www.battlecreekschools.net
Battle Creek ES 200/K-6
PO Box 100 68715 402-675-8085
Kyle Finke, prin. Fax 675-1038

St. John Lutheran S 100/PK-8
PO Box 67 68715 402-675-3605
Nicholas Onnen, prin. Fax 675-1400

Bayard, Morrill, Pop. 1,198
Bayard SD 400/PK-12
PO Box 607 69334 308-586-1325
Travis Miller, supt. Fax 586-1638
www.bayardpublicschools.org/
Bayard ES 200/PK-6
PO Box 607 69334 308-586-1211
Matthew McLaughlin, prin. Fax 586-1638

Beatrice, Gage, Pop. 12,303
Beatrice SD 2,200/PK-12
320 N 5th St 68310 402-223-1500
Pat Nauroth, supt. Fax 223-1509
www.beatricepublicschools.org
Beatrice Community Preschool PK-PK
201 Cedar St 68310 402-223-1585
Beatrice MS 500/6-8
215 N 5th St 68310 402-223-1545
John Jarosh, prin. Fax 223-1547
Lincoln ES 300/K-5
500 N 19th St 68310 402-223-1575
Kevin Janssen, prin. Fax 223-1576
Paddock Lane ES 300/PK-5
1300 N 14th St 68310 402-223-1566
Elizabeth Replogle, prin. Fax 223-1595
Stoddard ES 300/K-5
400 S 7th St 68310 402-223-1580
Elizabeth Replogle, prin. Fax 223-1597

St. Joseph S 50/K-6
420 N 6th St 68310 402-223-5033
Andrew Haake, prin. Fax 228-0100
St. Paul Lutheran S 100/PK-5
930 Prairie Ln 68310 402-223-3414
Amy Duever, prin. Fax 223-3418

Bellevue, Sarpy, Pop. 48,571
Bellevue SD 9,900/PK-12
2600 Arboretum Dr 68005 402-293-4000
Dr. Jeff Rippe, supt. Fax 293-5002
www.bellevuepublicschools.org
Avery ES 300/PK-6
2107 Avery Rd E 68005 402-293-4460
John Campbell, prin. Fax 293-5700
Barber ES 200/PK-6
1402 Main St 68005 402-293-4560
Amber Dembowski, prin. Fax 293-5704
Belleaire ES 300/PK-6
1200 W Mission Ave 68005 402-293-4510
Nikole Schubauer, prin. Fax 293-5706
Bellevue ES 500/PK-6
12001 Timberridge Dr, 402-827-1840
Brad Wellmann, prin. Fax 827-1860
Betz ES 300/PK-6
605 W 27th Ave 68005 402-293-4585
Katherine Boeve, prin. Fax 293-5702
Birchcrest ES 400/PK-6
1212 Fairfax Rd 68005 402-293-4635
Ron Oltman, prin. Fax 293-5708
Central ES 200/PK-6
510 W 22nd Ave 68005 402-293-4685
Amber Dembowski, prin. Fax 293-5710
Fairview ES 500/PK-6
14110 Tregaron Dr 68123 402-827-5950
Amber Johnson, prin. Fax 827-5948
Fontenelle MS 500/7-8
701 Kayleen Dr 68005 402-293-4360
Doug Schaefer, prin. Fax 293-4450
Ft. Crook ES 300/PK-6
12501 S 25th St 68123 402-293-4710
Meredith Petit, prin. Fax 293-5712
Lawrence ES 500/K-6
13204 S 29th St 68123 402-293-4880
Chad Zavala, prin. Fax 293-5716
LeMay ES 400/PK-6
2726 Kennedy Blvd 68123 402-293-4760
Andrew Miller, prin. Fax 293-5714
Lewis & Clark MS 500/7-8
13502 S 38th St 68123 402-898-8760
Dr. Mike Smith, prin. Fax 898-9018
Mission MS 400/7-8
2202 Washington St 68005 402-293-4260
Dr. Jenny Powell, prin. Fax 293-4350
Sarpy ES 400/PK-6
2908 Vandenberg Ave 68123 402-293-4795
Jeremy Weber, prin. Fax 293-5719
Twin Ridge ES 300/K-6
1400 Sunbury Dr 68005 402-293-4845
Dana Martin, prin. Fax 293-5721
Two Springs ES 400/PK-6
3001 Spring Blvd 68123 402-293-5070
Kelli Berke, prin. Fax 293-5723
Wake Robin ES 300/K-6
700 Lincoln Rd 68005 402-293-4955
Sheri Fillipi, prin. Fax 293-5725

Papillion La Vista Community SD
Supt. — See Papillion
Anderson Grove ES 300/K-6
11820 S 37th St 68123 402-898-0479
Andrew Bell, prin. Fax 898-0481
Golden Hills ES 200/PK-6
2912 Coffey Ave 68123 402-898-0459
Mikaela Vobejda, prin. Fax 898-0461

Cornerstone Christian S 100/K-8
1001 Fort Crook Rd N 68123 402-292-1030
Teri Lynn Schrag, supt. Fax 884-1725
St. Mary S 200/PK-8
903 W Mission Ave 68005 402-291-1694
Patricia Wallinger, prin. Fax 291-9667
St. Matthew the Evangelist S 100/PK-8
12210 S 36th St Ste B 68123 402-291-2030
Lisa DuVall, prin. Fax 292-7421

Bellwood, Butler, Pop. 435
David City SD
Supt. — See David City
Bellwood ES 100/PK-6
PO Box 100 68624 402-538-4805
Danielle Beerbohm, prin. Fax 538-2041

Benkelman, Dundy, Pop. 937
Dundy County-Straton SD 300/PK-12
PO Box 586 69021 308-423-2738
James Kent, supt. Fax 423-2711
www.dcstigers.org
Benkelman S 200/PK-6
PO Box 586 69021 308-423-2216
Michael Rotherham, prin. Fax 423-2320
Other Schools – See Stratton

Bennet, Lancaster, Pop. 712
Palmyra OR 1 SD
Supt. — See Palmyra
Bennet ES 200/K-6
50 Dogwood St 68317 402-782-3535
Linde Walter, prin. Fax 782-3545

Bennington, Douglas, Pop. 1,439
Bennington SD 1,700/K-12
PO Box 309 68007 402-238-3044
Dr. Terry Haack, supt. Fax 238-2185
www.benningtonschools.org
Bennington ES 400/K-5
PO Box 309 68007 402-238-2690
Chad Boyes, prin. Fax 238-2185
Bennington JHS, PO Box 309 68007 6-8
Shawn Hoppes, prin. 402-238-3082
Heritage ES 300/K-5
PO Box 309 68007 402-238-2095
Therese Nelson, prin. Fax 238-3351
Pine Creek ES 400/K-5
PO Box 309 68007 402-238-2372
Shannon Thoendel, prin. Fax 238-2416

Bertrand, Phelps, Pop. 742
Bertrand SD 300/K-12
PO Box 278 68927 308-472-3427
Dr. Dennis Shipp, supt. Fax 472-3429
bertrandvikings.org
Bertrand ES 100/K-6
PO Box 278 68927 308-472-3427
Shaun Kidder, prin. Fax 472-3429

Big Springs, Deuel, Pop. 393
South Platte SD 200/K-12
PO Box 457 69122 308-889-3674
David Spencer, supt. Fax 889-3523
www.southplatteschools.com
South Platte ES 100/K-6
PO Box 457 69122 308-889-3674
David Spencer, admin. Fax 889-3523

Bladen, Webster, Pop. 227
Silver Lake SD
Supt. — See Roseland
Silver Lake ES Bladen 100/K-6
PO Box 127 68928 402-756-1311
Duane Arntt, prin. Fax 756-1313

Blair, Washington, Pop. 7,886
Blair Community SD 2,100/PK-12
PO Box 288 68008 402-426-2610
Rex Pfeil, supt. Fax 426-3110
www.blairschools.org/
Blair Arbor Park ES 300/3-5
PO Box 288 68008 402-426-2735
Mike Janssen, prin. Fax 533-8110
Blair Deerfield ES 200/PK-2
PO Box 288 68008 402-426-5123
Amy Rogers, prin. Fax 427-2499
Blair North ES 100/K-2
PO Box 288 68008 402-426-3835
Amy Rogers, prin. Fax 533-8355
Blair South ES 100/K-2
PO Box 288 68008 402-426-2229
Amy Rogers, prin. Fax 533-8355
Otte Blair MS 600/6-8
PO Box 288 68008 402-426-3678
Chris Stogdill, prin. Fax 426-1788

Bloomfield, Knox, Pop. 1,011
Bloomfield SD 200/PK-12
PO Box 308 68718 402-373-4800
Shane Alexander, supt. Fax 373-2712
www.bloomfieldschools.net
Bloomfield ES 100/PK-6
PO Box 308 68718 402-373-4985
Tabitha Gilsdorf, prin. Fax 307-8053

Blue Hill, Webster, Pop. 925
Blue Hill SD 300/K-12
PO Box 217 68930 402-756-2085
Joel Ruybalid, supt. Fax 756-2086
www.bluehillschools.org
Blue Hill ES 100/K-6
PO Box 217 68930 402-756-2085
Lori Toepfer, prin. Fax 756-2086

Blue Springs, Gage, Pop. 326
Southern SD 1
Supt. — See Wymore
Southern ES 200/K-6
PO Box 158 68318 402-645-3359
Jerry Rempe, prin. Fax 645-3740

Boys Town, Douglas, Pop. 727

Wegner S 50/K-8
14124 Norton Dr 68010 402-498-1820
Andrew Simon, prin. Fax 498-1825

Brady, Lincoln, Pop. 425
Brady SD 200/K-12
PO Box 68 69123 308-584-3317
James McGown, supt. Fax 584-3725
www.bradyschools.org
Brady ES 100/K-6
PO Box 68 69123 308-584-3317
Matt Gordon, prin. Fax 584-3725

Brainard, Butler, Pop. 330
East Butler SD 300/K-12
PO Box 36 68626 402-545-2081
Sam Stecher, supt. Fax 545-2023
www.ebutlertigers.org

Brainard ES 100/K-6
PO Box 36 68626 402-545-2081
Shawn Biltoft, prin. Fax 545-2023
Other Schools – See Dwight

Bridgeport, Morrill, Pop. 1,536
Bridgeport SD 63 500/K-12
PO Box 430 69336 308-262-1470
Chuck Lambert, supt. Fax 262-1284
www.bridgeportschools.org
Bridgeport ES 200/K-6
PO Box 430 69336 308-262-1574
Troy Malone, prin. Fax 262-1284

Broken Bow, Custer, Pop. 3,500
Broken Bow SD 700/PK-12
323 N 7th Ave 68822 308-872-6821
Tom Bailey, supt. Fax 872-2751
www.bbps.org
Broken Bow MS 100/6-8
323 N 7th Ave 68822 308-872-6441
Rusty Kluender, prin. Fax 872-2528
New Discoveries Preschool 50/PK-PK
727 S 6th Ave 68822 308-872-5606
Fax 872-5741
North Park ES 300/PK-5
1135 N H St 68822 308-872-2982
Kimberly Jonas, prin. Fax 872-6349

Bruning, Thayer, Pop. 279
Bruning-Davenport USD
Supt. — See Davenport
Bruning-Davenport ES 50/PK-1
PO Box 70 68322 402-353-4685
Damen Kugel, prin. Fax 353-4445

Burwell, Garfield, Pop. 1,207
Burwell SD 400/PK-12
PO Box 670 68823 308-346-4150
Daniel Bird, supt. Fax 346-5430
www.burwellpublicschools.org
Burwell ES 200/PK-6
PO Box 790 68823 308-346-4431
Darrin Max, prin. Fax 346-5324

Butte, Boyd, Pop. 325
Boyd County SD
Supt. — See Spencer
Boyd County ES - Butte 100/K-4
PO Box 139 68722 402-775-2201
Cindy Johnson, prin. Fax 775-2204

Cairo, Hall, Pop. 780
Centura SD 500/PK-12
PO Box 430 68824 308-485-4258
Julie Otero, supt. Fax 485-4780
centuraps.org
Centura ES 300/PK-6
PO Box 430 68824 308-485-4258
Cory Bohling, prin. Fax 485-4780

Callaway, Custer, Pop. 533
Callaway SD 200/K-12
PO Box 280 68825 308-836-2272
Dawn Lewis, supt. Fax 836-2771
callawaypublicschools.org
Callaway ES 100/K-6
PO Box 280 68825 308-836-2272
Heath Birkel, prin. Fax 836-2771

Cambridge, Furnas, Pop. 1,055
Cambridge SD 300/K-12
PO Box 100 69022 308-697-3322
Gregory Shepard, supt. Fax 697-4880
cambridge.k12.ne.us
Cambridge ES 200/K-6
PO Box 100 69022 308-697-3322
Jarod Albers, prin. Fax 697-4880
Cambridge MS 7-8
PO Box 100 69022 308-697-3322
Jarod Albers, prin. Fax 697-4180

Cedar Bluffs, Saunders, Pop. 604
Cedar Bluffs SD 200/PK-12
PO Box 66 68015 402-628-2060
Harlan Ptomey, supt. Fax 628-2108
www.cedarbluffsschools.org/
Cedar Bluffs ES 100/K-5
PO Box 66 68015 402-628-2060
Ben Hansen, prin. Fax 628-2108
Cedar Bluffs MS 50/6-8
PO Box 66 68015 402-628-2080
Ben Hansen, prin. Fax 628-2108
Cedar Bluffs PreSchool 50/PK-PK
PO Box 66 68015 402-628-2080
Ben Hansen, prin. Fax 628-2108

Central City, Merrick, Pop. 2,899
Central City SD 700/PK-12
PO Box 57 68826 308-946-3055
Jeff Jensen, supt. Fax 946-3149
www.centralcityschoolsne.org
Central City ES 300/PK-4
PO Box 57 68826 308-946-3057
Neely Moser, prin. Fax 946-3149
Central City MS 200/5-8
PO Box 57 68826 308-946-3056
Holee Hanke, prin. Fax 946-2124

Nebraska Christian S 200/PK-12
1847 Inskip Ave 68826 308-946-3836
Joshua Cumpston, admin. Fax 946-3837

Ceresco, Saunders, Pop. 883
Raymond Central SD
Supt. — See Raymond
Ceresco ES 100/K-5
PO Box 10 68017 402-665-3651
Ann Egr, prin. Fax 665-2307

Chadron, Dawes, Pop. 5,665
Chadron SD 900/K-12
602 E 10th St 69337 308-432-0700
Dr. Caroline Winchester, supt. Fax 432-0702
www.chadronschools.org/
Chadron IS 100/3-4
450 Norfolk Ave 69337 308-432-0717
Bill Cogdill, prin. Fax 432-0715
Chadron MS 300/5-8
551 E 6th St 69337 308-432-0708
Nichlas Dressel, prin. Fax 432-0720
Chadron PS 200/K-2
732 Ann St 69337 308-432-0710
Libby Uhing, prin. Fax 432-6985

Prairie View SDA S 50/1-8
5802 Highway 20 69337 308-432-4228
Carlene Lang, prin. Fax 432-6517

Chambers, Holt, Pop. 268
Chambers SD 100/K-12
PO Box 218 68725 402-482-5233
Tedsen Hillman, supt. Fax 482-5234
chambers.esu8.org
Chambers ES 100/K-6
PO Box 218 68725 402-482-5233
Frank Jesse, prin. Fax 482-5234

Chapman, Merrick, Pop. 285
Northwest SD
Supt. — See Grand Island
Chapman S 100/K-8
1003 Cady St 68827 308-986-2215
Jeff Ellsworth, prin. Fax 986-2726

Chappell, Deuel, Pop. 921
Creek Valley SD 300/K-12
PO Box 608 69129 308-874-2911
Ron Howard, supt. Fax 874-2602
www.cvsstorm.com
Creek Valley ES 100/K-6
PO Box 608 69129 308-874-2911
Tessa Fraass, prin. Fax 874-2602

Clarks, Merrick, Pop. 363
High Plains Community SD
Supt. — See Polk
High Plains ES at Clarks 100/K-3
PO Box 205 68628 308-548-2216
Karyee LeSuer, prin. Fax 548-2120
High Plains MS 100/6-8
PO Box 205 68628 308-548-2216
Karyee LeSuer, prin. Fax 548-2120

Clarkson, Colfax, Pop. 655
Clarkson SD 100/PK-12
PO Box 140 68629 402-892-3454
Rich Lemburg, supt. Fax 892-3455
www.clarksonpublicschools.org
Clarkson S 100/PK-12
PO Box 140 68629 402-892-3454
Rich Lemburg, admin. Fax 892-3455

St. John Neumann S 50/PK-6
PO Box 457 68629 402-892-3474
Ann Prokopec, admin. Fax 892-3474

Clearwater, Antelope, Pop. 413
Nebraska USD 1
Supt. — See Orchard
Clearwater S 100/PK-12
PO Box 38 68726 402-485-2505
Mike Sanne, prin. Fax 485-2634

Cody, Cherry, Pop. 150
Cody-Kilgore SD 100/PK-12
PO Box 216 69211 402-823-4190
Adam Lambert, supt. Fax 823-4275
www.cody-kilgore.com
Other Schools – See Kilgore

Valentine SD
Supt. — See Valentine
Cutcomb Lake S 50/K-8
35591 Medicine Lake Rd 69211 402-823-4208
Jeff Sayer, prin. Fax 376-8096

Coleridge, Cedar, Pop. 470
Laurel-Concord-Coleridge SD
Supt. — See Laurel
Laurel-Concord-Coleridge MS 100/5-8
PO Box 37 68727 402-283-4844
Jay Vance, prin. Fax 283-4508

Columbus, Platte, Pop. 21,922
Columbus SD 3,600/PK-12
PO Box 947 68602 402-563-7000
Dr. Troy Loeffelholz, supt. Fax 563-7005
www.columbuspublicschools.org
Centennial ES 400/PK-4
500 Centennial St 68601 402-563-8180
Jackie Herink, prin. Fax 563-8185
Columbus MS 800/5-8
2200 26th St 68601 402-563-7060
Amy Haynes, prin. Fax 563-7068
Emerson ES 300/PK-4
2410 20th St 68601 402-563-7030
Sara Colford, prin. Fax 563-7035
Lost Creek ES 400/PK-4
3772 33rd Ave 68601 402-563-7045
Jeff Bartels, prin. Fax 563-7047
North Park ES 400/K-4
2200 31st St 68601 402-563-7070
Robert Hausmann, prin. Fax 563-7072
West Park ES 300/PK-4
4100 Adamy St 68601 402-563-7075
Paula Lawrence, prin. Fax 563-7077

Lakeview Community SD 600/K-12
3744 83rd St 68601 402-563-2345
Dr. Aaron Plas, supt. Fax 564-5209
www.lakeviewcs.esu7.org
Shell Creek S 200/K-6
16786 280th St 68601 402-564-8008
Josh Graves, prin. Fax 563-4552
Other Schools – See Platte Center

Christ Lutheran S 50/K-8
32312 122nd Ave 68601 402-564-3531
Kathy Petersen, lead tchr. Fax 564-5680
Columbus Christian S 100/PK-8
PO Box 924 68602 402-562-6470
Earl Kirkpatrick, admin.
Immanuel Lutheran S 200/PK-8
2865 26th Ave 68601 402-564-8423
Jody Timm, prin. Fax 564-1162
St. Anthony S 100/PK-6
1719 6th St 68601 402-564-4767
Amy Sokol, prin. Fax 564-5530
St. Bonaventure S 300/PK-6
1604 15th St 68601 402-564-7153
Cheryl Zoucha, prin. Fax 564-2587
St. Isidore S 200/PK-6
3821 20th St 68601 402-564-2604
Amy Evans, prin. Fax 564-8955
St. John Lutheran S 50/PK-8
39346 205th Ave 68601 402-285-0335
Annette Sonntag, prin. Fax 285-0335

Cook, Johnson, Pop. 316
Johnson County Central SD
Supt. — See Tecumseh
Johnson County Central ES - Cook 100/PK-5
PO Box 255 68329 402-864-4181
Jon Rother, prin. Fax 864-2074
Johnson County Central MS 100/6-8
PO Box 255 68329 402-864-4181
Rich Bacon, prin. Fax 864-2074

Cozad, Dawson, Pop. 3,959
Cozad Community SD 900/PK-12
1910 Meridian Ave 69130 308-784-2745
Dr. Joel Applegate, supt. Fax 217-4504
www.cozadschools.net
Cozad Early Education Center 50/PK-PK
420 W 14th St 69130 308-784-3381
Jill Beckenhauer, prin. Fax 217-4563
Cozad ES 300/K-5
420 E 14th St 69130 308-784-3462
Dale Henderson, prin. Fax 217-4507
Cozad MS 200/6-8
1810 Meridian Ave 69130 308-784-2746
Brian Regelin, prin. Fax 217-4506

Crawford, Dawes, Pop. 968
Crawford SD 200/PK-12
908 5th St 69339 308-665-1537
Kirk Hughes, supt. Fax 665-1909
www.cpsrams.org
Crawford ES 100/PK-6
908 5th St 69339 308-665-1928
Barb Edwards, prin. Fax 665-1909

Creighton, Knox, Pop. 1,135
Creighton SD 200/PK-12
PO Box 10 68729 402-358-5000
Robby Thompson, supt. Fax 358-5030
www.creightonpublicschools.org
Creighton ES 100/PK-6
PO Box 10 68729 402-358-5001
Robby Thompson, admin. Fax 358-5030

St. Ludger S 50/PK-6
410 Bryant Ave 68729 402-358-3501
Miranda Hornback, admin. Fax 358-3559

Crete, Saline, Pop. 6,858
Crete SD 1,800/PK-12
920 Linden Ave 68333 402-826-5855
Dr. Mike Waters, supt. Fax 826-5120
www.creteschools.com
Crete ES 800/PK-2
309 E 11th St 68333 402-826-5822
Heather Wendelin, prin. Fax 826-2135
Crete IS 3-5
1700 Glenwood Ave 68333 402-826-5833
Lisa Fye, prin. Fax 826-7789
Crete MS 500/5-8
920 Linden Ave 68333 402-826-5844
Brent Cole, prin. Fax 381-0223

St. James S 100/PK-6
525 E 14th St 68333 402-826-2044
Sr. Mary Alma, prin. Fax 826-2318

Crofton, Knox, Pop. 722
Crofton Community SD 300/K-12
PO Box 429 68730 402-388-2440
Corey Dahl, supt. Fax 388-4265
www.croftonschools.org
Crofton ES 100/K-6
PO Box 429 68730 402-388-4357
Mark Wragge, prin. Fax 388-2457

St. Rose of Lima S 100/PK-8
1302 W 5th St 68730 402-388-4393
Jennifer Fiscus, admin. Fax 388-4393

Crookston, Cherry, Pop. 64
Todd County SD 66-1
Supt. — See Mission, SD
Lakeview ES 100/K-8
26886 299th St 69212 605-429-3339
Bobbi Cox, prin. Fax 429-3309

Culbertson, Hitchcock, Pop. 590
Hitchcock County SD
Supt. — See Trenton
Hitchcock County ES 200/PK-6
PO Box 128 69024 308-278-2131
John Kershaw, prin. Fax 278-3173

Curtis, Frontier, Pop. 926
Medicine Valley SD 200/K-12
PO Box 9 69025 308-367-4106
Alan Garey, supt. Fax 367-4108
www.mvraiders.org/
Medicine Valley ES 100/K-6
PO Box 65 69025 308-367-4210
Steven Gleisberg, prin. Fax 367-4108

Dakota City, Dakota, Pop. 1,900
South Sioux City SD
Supt. — See South Sioux City
Dakota City ES 200/K-5
PO Box 455 68731 402-987-3363
Laura Sulzbach, prin. Fax 987-3363

Dalton, Cheyenne, Pop. 312
Leyton SD 200/K-12
PO Box 297 69131 308-377-2303
Lorrie Miller, supt. Fax 377-2304
www.leytonwarriors.org
Other Schools – See Gurley

Davenport, Thayer, Pop. 289
Bruning-Davenport USD 200/PK-12
PO Box 190 68335 402-364-2225
Dr. Trudy Clark, supt. Fax 364-2477
www.bruningdavenport.org/
Bruning-Davenport ES 50/2-4
PO Box 190 68335 402-364-2225
Damen Kugel, prin. Fax 364-2477
Bruning-Davenport MS 50/5-8
PO Box 190 68335 402-364-2225
Damen Kugel, prin. Fax 364-2477
Other Schools – See Bruning

David City, Butler, Pop. 2,884
David City SD 700/PK-12
750 D St 68632 402-367-4590
Chad Denker, supt. Fax 367-3479
www.davidcitypublicschools.org/
David City ES 300/PK-6
826 E St 68632 402 367 3779
Ernie Valentine, prin. Fax 367-3783
Other Schools – See Bellwood

St. Marys S 300/PK-5
1026 5th St 68632 402-367-3669
Carm Fiala, prin. Fax 367-3703

Daykin, Jefferson, Pop. 166
Meridian SD 200/K-12
PO Box 190 68338 402-446-7265
Randall Kort, supt. Fax 446-7246
www.meridianmustangs.org
Meridian ES 100/K-6
PO Box 190 68338 402-446-7265
Harold Scott, prin. Fax 446-7246

Deshler, Thayer, Pop. 745
Deshler SD 200/K-12
PO Box 547 68340 402-365-7272
Dr. Al Meier, supt. Fax 365-7560
www.deshlerpublicschools.org
Deshler ES 100/K-6
PO Box 547 68340 402-365-7272
Dr. Al Meier, prin. Fax 365-7560

Deshler Lutheran S 100/K-8
PO Box 340 68340 402-365-7858
Todd Voss, admin. Fax 365-7858

De Witt, Saline, Pop. 509
Tri County SD 400/K-12
72520 Highway 103 68341 402-683-2037
Randy Schlueter, supt. Fax 683-2116
www.tricountyschools.org
Tri County ES 200/K-6
72520 Highway 103 68341 402-683-4035
Jesse Gronemeyer, prin. Fax 683-2116

Diller, Jefferson, Pop. 256
Diller-Odell SD
Supt. — See Odell
Diller-Odell ES 100/K-6
PO Box 8 68342 402-793-5570
Matthew Mezger, prin. Fax 793-5173

Dix, Kimball, Pop. 253
Potter-Dix SD
Supt. — See Potter
Potter-Dix ES 100/K-6
PO Box 149 69133 308-682-5226
Michael Williams, prin. Fax 682-5227

Dodge, Dodge, Pop. 607
Howells-Dodge Consolidated SD
Supt. — See Howells
Dodge ES 50/2-6
209 N Ash St 68633 402-693-2207
Mark Ernst, prin. Fax 693-2209

St. Wenceslaus S 50/PK-6
212 N Linden St 68633 402-693-2819
Danielle Klosen, admin. Fax 693-2819

Doniphan, Hall, Pop. 824
Doniphan-Trumbull SD 500/K-12
PO Box 300 68832 402-845-2282
Kirk Russell, supt. Fax 845-6688
www.dtcardinals.org
Doniphan-Trumbull ES 300/K-6
PO Box 300 68832 402-845-2730
Rod Engel, prin. Fax 845-6688

Dorchester, Saline, Pop. 580
Dorchester SD 200/K-12
PO Box 7 68343 402-946-2781
Daryl Schrunk, supt. Fax 946-6271
www.dorchesterschool.org
Dorchester ES 100/K-6
PO Box 7 68343 402-946-2781
Adrian Allen, prin. Fax 946-6271

Dunning, Blaine, Pop. 103
Sandhills SD 100/K-12
PO Box 29 68833 308-538-2224
Dale Hafer, supt. Fax 538-2228
blog.sandhills.k12.ne.us/
Other Schools – See Halsey

Dwight, Butler, Pop. 204
East Butler SD
Supt. — See Brainard
Dwight ES 50/K-6
PO Box 160 68635 402-566-2445
Shawn Biltoft, prin. Fax 545-2023

Eagle, Cass, Pop. 1,014
Waverly SD 145
Supt. — See Waverly
Eagle ES 300/K-5
600 S 1st St 68347 402-781-2210
Megan Flohr, prin. Fax 786-2799

Elba, Howard, Pop. 212
Elba SD 100/PK-12
PO Box 100 68835 308-863-2228
Matthew Palmer, supt. Fax 863-2329
www.elba.k12.ne.us
Elba ES 50/PK-6
PO Box 100 68835 308-863-2228
Matthew Palmer, admin. Fax 863-2329

Elgin, Antelope, Pop. 656
Elgin SD 200/PK-12
PO Box 399 68636 402-843-2455
Daniel Polk, supt. Fax 843-2475
www.elgineagles.org
Elgin ES 100/PK-6
PO Box 399 68636 402-843-2455
Greg Wemhoff, prin. Fax 843-2475

St. Boniface S 100/PK-6
PO Box 179 68636 402-843-5325
Betty Getzfred, prin. Fax 843-2297

Elkhorn, Douglas, Pop. 8,192
Elkhorn SD 6,900/PK-12
20650 Glenn St 68022 402-289-2579
Bary Habrock, supt. Fax 289-2585
www.elkhornweb.org
Arbor View ES K-5
5115 N 208th St 68022 402-289-1007
Troy Sidders, prin. Fax 289-3035
Elkhorn Early Education Center 100/PK-PK
20650 Glenn St 68022 402-289-3790
Fax 289-2585
Elkhorn MS 700/6-8
3200 N 207th Plz 68022 402-289-2428
Deb Garrison, prin. Fax 289-1639
Elkhorn Valley View MS 500/6-8
1313 S 208th St 68022 402-289-0362
Chad Soupir, prin.
Fire Ridge ES 600/K-5
19660 Farnam St 68022 402-289-0735
Deborah Knutson, prin. Fax 289-0741
Hillrise ES 300/K-5
20110 Hopper St 68022 402-289-2602
Debra Madden, prin. Fax 289-1610
Skyline ES 300/K-5
400 S 210th St 68022 402-289-3433
Andrew Luebbe, prin. Fax 289-1652
West Dodge Station ES 400/PK-5
18480 California St 68022 402-289-2773
Pamela Wahl, prin.
Westridge ES 400/K-5
3100 N 206th St 68022 402-289-2559
Ryan Broshar, prin. Fax 289-5725
Other Schools – See Omaha

St. Patrick S 700/PK-8
PO Box 10 68022 402-289-5407
Kami Landenberger, prin. Fax 763-9530

Elm Creek, Buffalo, Pop. 896
Elm Creek SD 300/PK-12
PO Box 490 68836 308-856-4300
Jason Sullivan, supt. Fax 856-4907
elmcreekschools.org
Elm Creek ES 200/PK-6
PO Box 490 68836 308-856-4300
Derrick Pulliam, supt. Fax 856-4907

Elmwood, Cass, Pop. 629
Elmwood-Murdock SD
Supt. — See Murdock
Elmwood-Murdock ES 200/PK-6
400 W F St 68349 402-994-2125
Bruce Friedrich, prin. Fax 994-2078

Elwood, Gosper, Pop. 693
Elwood SD 200/PK-12
PO Box 107 68937 308-785-2491
Daren Hatch, supt. Fax 785-2322
elwood.k12.ne.us
Elwood ES 100/PK-6
PO Box 107 68937 308-785-2491
Kyle Hemmerling, prin. Fax 785-2322

Emerson, Dakota, Pop. 834
Emerson-Hubbard SD 300/PK-12
PO Box 9 68733 402-695-2621
Lindsey Burback, supt. Fax 695-2622
www.emersonhubbardschools.org
Emerson-Hubbard ES 200/PK-6
PO Box 9 68733 402-695-2654
Lindsey Burback, prin. Fax 695-2622

Eustis, Frontier, Pop. 399
Eustis-Farnam SD 200/K-12
PO Box 9 69028 308-486-3991
Steve Sampy, supt. Fax 486-5350
www.efknights.org
Eustis-Farnam ES 100/K-6
PO Box 9 69028 308-486-3991
Nick Hodge, prin. Fax 486-5659

Ewing, Holt, Pop. 385
Ewing SD 100/K-12
PO Box 98 68735 402-626-7235
Ted Hillman, supt. Fax 626-7236
ewing.ne.schoolwebpages.com
Ewing ES 100/K-6
PO Box 98 68735 402-626-7235
Greg Appleby, prin. Fax 626-7236

Exeter, Fillmore, Pop. 589
Exeter-Milligan SD 200/PK-12
PO Box 139 68351 402-266-5911
Paul Sheffield, supt. Fax 266-4811
www.emwolves.org/
Exeter-Miligan ES 50/PK-2
PO Box 139 68351 402-266-5911
Laura Kroll, prin. Fax 266-4811
Other Schools – See Milligan

Fairbury, Jefferson, Pop. 3,893
Fairbury SD 900/PK-12
703 K St 68352 402-729-6104
Stephen Grizzle, supt. Fax 729-6392
www.fairburyjeffs.org
Central ES 300/PK-2
808 F St 68352 402-729-2418
Patty Smith, prin. Fax 729-2467
Jefferson IS 300/3-6
924 K St 68352 402-729-5041
Jeremy Christiansen, prin. Fax 729-5446

Fairfield, Clay, Pop. 385
South Central Nebraska Unified SD 500/PK-12
30671 Highway 14 68938 402-726-2151
Dr. Randall Gilson, supt. Fax 726-2208
www.southcentralunified.org
Sandy Creek ES 200/PK-6
30671 Highway 14 68938 402-726-2412
Jason Searle, prin. Fax 726-2208
Other Schools – See Lawrence

Fairmont, Fillmore, Pop. 560
Fillmore Central SD
Supt. — See Geneva
Fillmore Central MS 200/5-8
PO Box 157 68354 402-268-3411
Steven Adkisson, prin. Fax 268-3491

Falls City, Richardson, Pop. 4,224
Falls City SD 800/PK-12
PO Box 129 68355 402-245-2825
Dr. Tim Heckenlively, supt. Fax 245-2022
www.fctigers.org/
Falls City MS 200/6-8
PO Box 129 68355 402-245-3455
Rick Johnson, prin. Fax 245-2022
Falls City North ES 200/PK-2
2500 Chase St 68355 402-245-2712
Shelly Leyden, prin. Fax 245-4005
Falls City South ES 200/3-5
1000 Fulton St 68355 402-245-4067
John Holys, prin. Fax 245-3476

Sacred Heart S 200/K-12
1820 Fulton St 68355 402-245-4151
Doug Goltz, prin. Fax 245-5217

Firth, Lancaster, Pop. 580
Norris SD 160 2,200/PK-12
25211 S 68th St 68358 402-791-0000
Dr. John Skretta, supt. Fax 791-0025
www.norris160.org
Norris ES 500/PK-4
25211 S 68th St 68358 402-791-0030
Jennifer Piening, prin. Fax 791-0038
Norris IS 500/3-5
25211 S 68th St 68358 402-791-0040
Kristina Morrison, prin. Fax 791-0037
Norris MS 500/5-8
25211 S 68th St 68358 402-791-0020
Mary Jo Leininger, prin. Fax 791-0029

Fordyce, Cedar, Pop. 137

West Catholic S 50/PK-6
303 Omaha St 68736 402-357-3507
Mary Jean Klug, prin. Fax 357-3551

Fort Calhoun, Washington, Pop. 895
Fort Calhoun SD 600/PK-12
5876 County Rd P43 68023 402-468-5591
Dr. Donald Johnson, supt. Fax 468-5593
www.fortcalhounschools.org
Fort Calhoun ES 300/PK-6
5876 County Rd P43 68023 402-468-5714
Drew Wagner, prin. Fax 468-5593

Franklin, Franklin, Pop. 993
Franklin SD 300/PK-12
1001 M St 68939 308-425-6283
Dr. Candace Conradt, supt. Fax 425-6553
fpsflyers.org

Franklin ES 100/PK-6
1001 M St 68939 308-425-6283
Shelley Kahrs, prin. Fax 425-6553

Fremont, Dodge, Pop. 26,088
Fremont SD 4,700/PK-12
130 E 9th St 68025 402-727-3000
Mark Shepard, supt. Fax 727-3002
fremonttigers.org
Bell Field ES 300/K-4
1240 E 11th St 68025 402-727-3178
Chris Raasch, prin. Fax 727-3040
Clarmar ES 200/K-4
1865 E 19th St 68025 402-727-3175
Jason Chicoine, prin. Fax 727-3041
Davenport ECC 100/PK-PK
940 Michael St 68025 402-727-3173
Theresa Muhle, admin. Fax 727-3042
Fremont MS 700/7-8
540 Johnson Rd 68025 402-727-3100
LaVonna Emmanuel, prin. Fax 727-3963
Grant ES 200/K-4
226 N Grant St 68025 402-727-3171
Brent Cudly, prin. Fax 727-3043
Howard ES 300/K-4
240 N Howard St 68025 402-727-3169
Mindy Chandler, prin. Fax 727-3044
Johnson Crossing Academic Center 700/5-6
200 Johnson Rd 68025 402-721-2004
Brent Harrill, admin. Fax 721-2037
Linden ES 300/K-4
1250 N L St 68025 402-727-3150
Diane Beninato, prin. Fax 727-3046
Milliken Park ES 300/K-4
2950 Dale St 68025 402-727-3160
Susan Farkas, prin. Fax 727-3047
Washington ES 200/K-4
515 S Broad St 68025 402-727-3164
Diane Stevens, prin. Fax 727-3049

Archbishop Bergan ES PK-6
1515 Johnson Rd 68025 402-721-9766
Dan Koenig, prin. Fax 721-1180
Trinity Lutheran S 200/K-8
1546 N Luther Rd 68025 402-721-5959
Greg Rathke, prin. Fax 721-5537

Friend, Saline, Pop. 1,022
Friend SD 300/PK-12
PO Box 67 68359 402-947-2781
David Kraus, supt. Fax 947-2026
www.friendbulldogs.org
Friend ES 100/PK-6
PO Box 67 68359 402-947-2781
Alyson Dickinson, prin. Fax 947-2026

Fullerton, Nance, Pop. 1,303
Fullerton SD 300/K-12
PO Box 520 68638 308-536-2431
Jeffrey Anderson, supt. Fax 536-2432
www.fullertonpublicschools.org
Fullerton ES 200/K-8
PO Box 520 68638 308-536-2431
Tammy Carlson, prin. Fax 536-2432

Geneva, Fillmore, Pop. 2,199
Fillmore Central SD 500/K-12
1410 L St 68361 402-759-4955
Mark Norvell, supt. Fax 759-4038
www.fillmorecentral.org
Fillmore Central ES 200/K-4
225 N 17th St 68361 402-759-3184
Aaron Veleba, prin. Fax 759-3110
Other Schools – See Fairmont

Grace Lutheran S 50/K-8
434 N 16th St 68361 402-759-4517

Genoa, Nance, Pop. 992
Twin River SD 400/K-12
PO Box 640 68640 402-993-2274
Dr. John M. Weidner, supt. Fax 993-7718
www.twinriverschools.org
Twin River ES at Genoa 200/K-6
PO Box 640 68640 402-993-2510
Tod Heier, prin. Fax 993-7718
Other Schools – See Silver Creek

Gering, Scotts Bluff, Pop. 8,397
Gering SD 2,000/PK-12
1519 10th St 69341 308-436-3125
Bob Hastings, supt. Fax 436-4301
www.geringschools.net
Geil ES 300/K-6
1600 D St 69341 308-436-2545
Angela Morris, prin. Fax 436-4398
Gering JHS 300/7-8
800 Q St 69341 308-436-3123
Dora Olivares, prin. Fax 436-6010
Gering Preschool/Early Child Development 100/PK-PK
1725 13th St 69341 308-436-2350
Pam Barker, prin. Fax 436-3383
Lincoln ES 400/K-6
1725 13th St 69341 308-436-2350
Pam Barker, prin. Fax 436-3383
Northfield ES 300/PK-6
1900 Flaten Ave 69341 308-436-5555
John Wiedeman, prin. Fax 436-4352

Gibbon, Buffalo, Pop. 1,809
Gibbon SD 600/PK-12
PO Box 790 68840 308-468-6555
Dr. Vern Fisher, supt. Fax 468-5164
www.gibbonpublic.org
Gibbon ES 300/PK-6
PO Box 790 68840 308-468-6546
Rob Alderson, prin. Fax 468-5164

Giltner, Hamilton, Pop. 348
Giltner SD 200/K-12
PO Box 160 68841 402-849-2238
Dr. Stuart Lenz, supt. Fax 849-2440
www.giltner.k12.ne.us
Giltner ES 100/K-6
PO Box 160 68841 402-849-2238
Dr. Stuart Lenz, prin. Fax 849-2440

Gordon, Sheridan, Pop. 1,571
Gordon-Rushville SD 700/PK-12
PO Box 530 69343 308-282-1322
Lori Liggett, supt. Fax 282-2207
www.grmustangs.org
Gordon ES 200/PK-5
PO Box 530 69343 308-282-0216
Casey Slama, prin. Fax 282-1512
Other Schools – See Rushville

Gothenburg, Dawson, Pop. 3,547
Gothenburg SD 900/K-12
1322 Avenue I 69138 308-537-3651
Michael Teahon, supt. Fax 537-3965
www.gothenburgswedes.org
Gothenburg ES 500/K-6
1311 Avenue G 69138 308-537-3651
Allison Jonas, prin. Fax 537-3965

Grand Island, Hall, Pop. 47,867
Grand Island SD 9,500/PK-12
PO Box 4904 68802 308-385-5900
Dr. Tawana Grover, supt. Fax 385-5949
www.gips.org
Barr MS 800/6-8
602 W Stolley Park Rd 68801 308-385-5875
Brian Kort, prin. Fax 385-5880
Dodge ES 500/K-5
641 S Oak St 68801 308-385-5889
Carrie Kolar, prin. Fax 385-5141
Early Learning Center 400/PK-PK
4360 W Capital Ave 68803 308-385-5655
Tara Peterson, admin. Fax 385-5690
Engleman ES 500/K-5
1812 Mansfield Rd 68803 308-385-5902
Jennifer Lohrberg, prin. Fax 385-5726
Gates ES 300/K-5
2700 W Louise St 68803 308-385-5892
Julie Martin, prin. Fax 385-5729
Howard ES 400/K-5
502 W 9th St 68801 308-385-5916
Julie Schnitzler, prin. Fax 385-5959
Jefferson ES 300/K-5
315 Wyandotte St 68801 308-385-5922
Sheree Stockwell, prin. Fax 385-5711
Knickrehm ES 300/K-5
2013 N Oak St 68801 308-385-5927
Kelly Klanecky, prin. Fax 385-5984
Lincoln ES 300/PK-5
805 Beal St 68801 308-385-5924
Maureen Oman, prin. Fax 385-5710
Newell ES 500/K-5
2700 W 13th St 68803 308-385-5905
Andrew Rinaldi, prin. Fax 385-5907
Seedling Mile ES 100/K-5
3208 E Seedling Mile Rd 68801 308-385-5910
Charity LaBrie, prin. Fax 385-5803
Shoemaker ES 400/K-5
4160 W Old Potash Hwy 68803 308-385-5936
Lee Wolfe, prin. Fax 385-5986
Starr ES 300/K-5
1800 S Adams St 68801 308-385-5882
Michael Persampieri, prin. Fax 385-5954
Walnut MS 900/6-8
1600 N Custer Ave 68803 308-385-5990
Rod Foley, prin. Fax 385-5992
Wasmer ES 400/K-5
318 S Clark St 68801 308-385-5920
Tina Godfrey, prin. Fax 385-5749
West Lawn ES 200/K-5
3022 College St 68803 308-385-5930
Darrell Holley, prin. Fax 385-5603
Westridge MS 400/6-8
4111 W 13th St 68803 308-385-5886
Brad Wolfe, prin. Fax 385-5003

Northwest SD 1,500/PK-12
2710 N North Rd 68803 308-385-6398
Matthew Fisher, supt. Fax 385-6393
www.ginorthwest.org
Cedar Hollow S 300/K-8
4900 S Engleman Rd 68803 308-385-6306
Scott Mazour, prin. Fax 385-6308
1 R S 200/K-8
3301 W One-R Rd 68803 308-385-6352
Steve Retzlaff, prin. Fax 385-6358
Lockwood Preschool 50/PK-PK
750 Lockwood Rd 68801 308-384-2042
Jeff Ellsworth, prin.
Other Schools – See Chapman, Saint Libory

Trinity Lutheran S 200/PK-8
208 W 13th St 68801 308-382-5274
Sandra Armstrong, prin. Fax 389-2418

Grant, Perkins, Pop. 1,163
Perkins County SD 400/K-12
PO Box 829 69140 308-352-4735
Phillip Picquet, supt. Fax 352-4769
www.perkinscountyschools.org
Perkins County ES 200/K-5
PO Box 809 69140 308-352-4313
Nicole Long, prin. Fax 352-4955

Perkins County Christian S 50/K-9
PO Box 322 69140 308-352-8309
Jarret Malmkar, pres. Fax 352-4505

Greeley, Greeley, Pop. 461
Central Valley SD 100/PK-12
PO Box 160 68842 308-428-3145
Amy Malander, supt. Fax 428-5395
www.centralvps.org
Other Schools – See Scotia

Gretna, Sarpy, Pop. 4,403
Gretna SD 3,700/PK-12
11717 S 216th St 68028 402-332-3265
Dr. Kevin Riley, supt. Fax 408-2534
www.gretnadragons.org
Gretna ES 500/PK-5
11717 S 216th St 68028 402-332-3341
Travis Lightle, prin. Fax 408-2538
Gretna MS 800/6-8
11717 S 216th St 68028 402-332-3048
Harvey Birky, prin. Fax 408-2536
Thomas ES 500/PK-5
11717 S 216th St 68028 402-332-5578
Bret Basye, prin. Fax 408-2539
Other Schools – See Omaha

Millard SD
Supt. — See Omaha
Reeder ES 600/K-5
19202 Chandler St 68028 402-715-6420
Paige Roberts, prin. Fax 715-6440

Gurley, Cheyenne, Pop. 213
Leyton SD
Supt. — See Dalton
Leyton S 100/K-8
PO Box 178 69141 308-884-2248
Lance Howitt, prin. Fax 884-2300

Hadar, Pierce, Pop. 292

Immanuel Lutheran ES 50/PK-8
PO Box 190 68738 402-371-0685
Rev. Austin Ziche, prin.

Halsey, Thomas, Pop. 72
Sandhills SD
Supt. — See Dunning
Halsey ES 50/K-6
PO Box 99 69142 308-533-2203
Dale Hafer, prin. Fax 533-2204

Hampton, Hamilton, Pop. 420
Hampton SD 200/PK-12
458 5th St 68843 402-725-3117
Holly Herzberg, supt. Fax 725-3334
hamptonhawks.us
Hampton ES 100/PK-6
458 5th St 68843 402-725-3233
Angie Arndt, prin. Fax 725-3334

Hampton Lutheran S 100/PK-6
732 N 3rd St 68843 402-725-3347
Jean Carnoali, prin. Fax 725-3341

Harrisburg, Banner, Pop. 96
Banner County SD 100/PK-12
PO Box 5 69345 308-436-5263
Lana Sides, supt. Fax 436-5252
www.bannercountyschool.org
Banner County ES 100/PK-6
PO Box 5 69345 308-436-5263
Charles Jones, prin. Fax 436-5252

Harrison, Sioux, Pop. 247
Sioux County SD 100/K-12
PO Box 38 69346 308-668-2415
Dr. Brett Gies, supt. Fax 668-2260
www.siouxcountyschools.org
Harrison S 50/K-8
PO Box 38 69346 308-668-2336
Barry Swisher, prin. Fax 668-2335
Other Schools – See Marsland, Morrill

Hartington, Cedar, Pop. 1,550
Hartington - Newcastle SD 300/PK-12
PO Box 75 68739 402-254-3947
Adrian Johnson, supt. Fax 254-3945
hartington.esu1.org
Hartington - Newcastle ES 100/PK-6
PO Box 75 68739 402-254-3947
Sarah Edwards, prin. Fax 254-3945
Other Schools – See Newcastle

East Catholic S 100/PK-6
108 W 889 Rd 68739 402-357-2146
Mary Klug, lead tchr. Fax 357-3758
Holy Trinity S 100/PK-6
PO Box 278 68739 402-254-6496
Terry Kathol, prin. Fax 254-3976

Harvard, Clay, Pop. 1,002
Harvard SD 300/K-12
PO Box 100 68944 402-772-2171
Michael Derr, supt. Fax 772-2204
www.harvardcardinals.org
Harvard ES 100/K-5
PO Box 100 68944 402-772-2171
Michael Derr, prin. Fax 772-2204

Hastings, Adams, Pop. 24,622
Adams Central SD 800/K-12
PO Box 1088 68902 402-463-3285
Shawn Scott, supt. Fax 463-6344
adamscentral.us
Adams County ES 100/K-6
1970 E 12th St 68901 402-463-6107
Lonnie Abbott, prin. Fax 463-6107
Wallace ES 100/K-6
2975 S Baltimore Ave 68901 402-463-5090
Allyson Bohlen, prin. Fax 463-6006
Other Schools – See Juniata

Hastings SD 3,300/PK-12
1924 W A St 68901 402-461-7500
Craig Kautz, supt. Fax 461-7509
www.hastingspublicschools.org
Alcott ES 300/K-5
731 N Baltimore Ave 68901 402-461-7580
Lawrence Tunks, prin. Fax 461-7639
Hastings MS 800/6-8
201 N Marian Rd 68901 402-461-7520
David Essink, prin. Fax 461-7650
Hawthorne ES 300/PK-5
2200 W 9th St 68901 402-461-7540
Amy Kelly, prin. Fax 461-7546
Lincoln ES 300/PK-5
720 S Franklin Ave 68901 402-461-7589
Cara Kimball, prin. Fax 461-7592
Longfellow ES 400/K-5
828 N Hastings Ave 68901 402-461-7584
Irina Belikova-Erickson, prin. Fax 461-7585
Watson ES 200/PK-5
1720 Crane Ave 68901 402-461-7593
Jason Cafferty, prin. Fax 461-7636

St. Michael S 200/K-5
721 Creighton Ave 68901 402-462-6310
Carrie Rasmussen, prin. Fax 462-6035
Zion Lutheran S 100/PK-8
465 S Marian Rd 68901 402-462-5012
David Berens, prin. Fax 462-5375

Hayes Center, Hayes, Pop. 214
Hayes Center SD 100/K-12
PO Box 8 69032 308-286-5600
Tony Primavera, supt. Fax 286-5629
www.hccardinals.org
Hayes Center ES 100/K-6
PO Box 8 69032 308-286-5601
Megan Soundy, prin. Fax 286-5630

Hay Springs, Sheridan, Pop. 560
Hay Springs SD 200/PK-12
PO Box 280 69347 308-638-4434
Russell Lechtenberg, supt. Fax 915-5126
hshawks.com
Hay Springs Early Childhood Development 50/PK-PK
PO Box 280 69347 308-638-4434
Russell Lechtenberg, admin. Fax 915-5126
Hay Springs ES 100/K-5
PO Box 280 69347 308-638-4434
Russell Lechtenberg, prin. Fax 915-5126
Hay Springs MS 50/6-8
PO Box 280 69347 308-638-4434
Russell Lechtenberg, prin. Fax 915-5126

Hebron, Thayer, Pop. 1,566
Thayer Central Community SD 300/PK-12
PO Box 9 68370 402-768-6117
Drew Harris, supt. Fax 768-6110
www.thayercentral.org/
Thayer Central ES 100/PK-6
PO Box 9 68370 402-768-7287
Kurk Wiedel, prin. Fax 768-2572

Hemingford, Box Butte, Pop. 793
Hemingford SD 400/PK-12
PO Box 217 69348 308-487-3328
Casper Ningen, supt. Fax 487-5215
www.hemingfordschools.org
Hemingford ES 200/PK-6
PO Box 217 69348 308-487-3330
Eric Arneson, prin. Fax 487-5215

Henderson, York, Pop. 988
Heartland Community SD 300/K-12
1501 Front St 68371 402-723-4434
Brad Best, supt. Fax 723-4431
www.heartlandschools.org/
Heartland Community ES 200/K-6
1501 Front St 68371 402-723-4434
Sadie Coffey, prin. Fax 723-4431

Herman, Washington, Pop. 268
Tekamah-Herman SD
Supt. — See Tekamah
Herman ES 100/PK-6
20051 County Road 25 68029 402-456-7404
Ben Kreifels, prin. Fax 374-2155

Hershey, Lincoln, Pop. 650
Hershey SD 600/PK-12
PO Box 369 69143 308-368-5572
Jane Davis, supt. Fax 368-5570
www.hpspanthers.org
Hershey ES 300/PK-6
PO Box 369 69143 308-368-5572
Jason Calahan, prin. Fax 368-5570

Hildreth, Franklin, Pop. 376
Wilcox-Hildreth SD
Supt. — See Wilcox
Wilcox-Hildreth MS 50/6-8
613 Nelson St 68947 308-938-2415
Carl Dietz, prin. Fax 938-5335

Holdrege, Phelps, Pop. 5,459
Holdrege SD, PO Box 2002 68949 1,100/K-12
Todd Hilyard, supt. 308-995-8663
www.holdregedusters.org
Holdrege ES, PO Box 2002 68949 400/K-4
Amber Porter, prin. 308-995-4339
Holdrege MS, PO Box 2002 68949 400/5-8
Angie Girard, prin. 308-995-5421

All Saints S 50/PK-4
1206 Logan St 68949 308-995-4590
Rev. Thomas Lux, prin. Fax 995-2217

Homer, Dakota, Pop. 542
Homer Community SD 400/PK-12
PO Box 340 68030 402-698-2377
Gregg Cruickshank, supt. Fax 698-2379
www.homerknights.org
Homer ES 200/PK-6
PO Box 340 68030 402-698-2377
Lora Crowe, prin. Fax 698-2379

Hooper, Dodge, Pop. 820
Logan View SD 300/K-12
2163 County Road G 68031 402-654-3317
Jeremy Klein, supt. Fax 654-3699
www.loganview.org/
Logan View ES 100/K-6
2163 County Road G 68031 402-654-3317
Kevin Kraus, prin. Fax 654-3699

Hoskins, Wayne, Pop. 284

Trinity Lutheran S 50/PK-8
PO Box 100 68740 402-565-4517
Ryan Obry, prin. Fax 565-4517

Howells, Colfax, Pop. 557
Howells-Dodge Consolidated SD 200/PK-12
PO Box 159 68641 402-986-1621
Jeffrey Walburn Ed.D., supt. Fax 986-1261
www.howellsdodgeschools.org
Howells ES 50/PK-1
PO Box 159 68641 402-986-1621
Mark Ernst, prin. Fax 986-1261
Other Schools – See Dodge

Howells Community Catholic S 100/1-6
114 N 6th St 68641 402-986-1689
Carol Vogel, admin. Fax 986-1653

Humboldt, Richardson, Pop. 874
Humboldt Table Rock Steinauer SD 70 300/PK-12
810 Central Ave 68376 402-862-2235
Sherri Edmundson, supt. Fax 862-3135
www.htrstitans.com
Humboldt Table Rock Steinauer S 100/PK-12
810 Central Ave 68376 402-862-2151
Lisa Othmer, prin. Fax 862-2152

Humphrey, Platte, Pop. 758
Humphrey SD 67 200/PK-12
PO Box 278 68642 402-923-1230
Greg Sjuts, supt. Fax 923-1235
www.humphrey.esu7.org
Humphrey ES 100/PK-6
PO Box 278 68642 402-923-1230
Brice King, prin. Fax 923-1235
Other Schools – See Lindsay

St. Francis S 200/PK-12
PO Box 277 68642 402-923-0818
Jennifer Dunn, prin. Fax 923-1590

Hyannis, Grant, Pop. 178
Hyannis Area SD 200/K-12
PO Box 286 69350 308-458-2202
Fax 458-2227
www.disteleven.org
Hyannis ES 100/K-6
PO Box 109 69350 308-458-2202
Bruce Parish, prin. Fax 458-2321

Imperial, Chase, Pop. 2,057
Chase County SD 600/K-12
PO Box 577 69033 308-882-4304
Joseph Lefdal, supt. Fax 882-5629
chasecountyschools.org
Chase County ES 200/K-4
PO Box 577 69033 308-882-4228
Becky Odens, prin. Fax 882-5629
Chase County MS 200/5-8
PO Box 577 69033 308-882-4304
Chad Scheel, prin. Fax 882-5629

Indianola, Red Willow, Pop. 579
Southwest SD 179
Supt. — See Bartley
Southwest ES 200/PK-6
719 E St 69034 308-364-2613
Kathy Latta, prin. Fax 364-2508

Jackson, Dakota, Pop. 214
Ponca SD
Supt. — See Ponca
Jackson ES 100/K-6
PO Box 67 68743 402-632-4276
Bob Hayes, prin. Fax 632-5014

Johnson, Nemaha, Pop. 325
Johnson-Brock SD 300/K-12
PO Box 186 68378 402-868-5235
Jeff Koehler, supt. Fax 868-4785
www.johnsonbrockeagles.org
Johnson ES 200/K-6
PO Box 186 68378 402-868-5235
Lucus Dalinghaus, prin. Fax 868-4785

Juniata, Adams, Pop. 740
Adams Central SD
Supt. — See Hastings
Juniata ES 100/K-6
PO Box 157 68955 402-751-2245
Jennifer Pohlson, prin. Fax 751-2711

Christ Lutheran S 50/K-8
13175 W 70th St 68955 402-744-4991
Doug Eisele, prin. Fax 744-4971

Kearney, Buffalo, Pop. 30,426
Kearney SD 5,300/PK-12
310 W 24th St 68845 308-698-8000
Kent Edwards, supt. Fax 698-8001
www.kearneypublicschools.org
Bright Futures Preschool 100/PK-PK
1511 5th Ave 68845 308-698-8046
Tom Jochum, prin. Fax 698-8054
Bryant ES 200/K-5
1611 C Ave 68847 308-698-8190
Mark Johnson, prin. Fax 698-8192
Buffalo Hills ES 200/K-5
6110 11th Ave 68845 308-698-8290
Tom Jochum, prin. Fax 698-8292
Central ES 300/K-5
300 W 24th St 68845 308-698-8040
Teresa Schnoor, prin. Fax 698-8053
Emerson ES 200/K-5
2705 E Ave 68847 308-698-8270
Megan Schmidt, prin. Fax 698-8273
Glenwood ES 100/K-5
8105 9th Ave 68845 308-698-8240
Tom Jochum, prin. Fax 698-8244
Horizon MS 500/6-8
915 W 35th St 68845 308-698-8120
Kipp Petersen, prin. Fax 698-8143
Kenwood ES 400/K-5
915 16th Ave 68845 308-698-8200
Jill Clevenger, prin. Fax 698-8202
Meadowlark ES 400/K-5
1010 E 53rd St 68847 308-698-8210
Mark Stute, prin. Fax 698-8215
Northeast ES 400/K-5
910 E 34th St 68847 308-698-8230
Cathy Gundersen, prin. Fax 698-8235
Park ES 300/K-5
3000 7th Ave 68845 308-698-8280
Katie Mathews, prin. Fax 698-8283
Sunrise MS 500/6-8
4611 N Ave 68847 308-698-8150
Jeff Ganz, prin. Fax 698-8152
Windy Hills ES 300/K-5
4211 20th Ave 68845 308-698-8220
Nathan Lightle, prin. Fax 698-8224

Faith Christian S of Kearney 100/PK-8
PO Box 3048 68848 308-236-8744
Titus Staples, prin.
Zion Lutheran S 100/PK-8
2421 C Ave 68847 308-234-3410
Anthony Splittgerber, prin. Fax 236-8100

Kenesaw, Adams, Pop. 876
Kenesaw SD 200/K-12
PO Box 129 68956 402-752-3215
Richard Masters, supt. Fax 752-3579
www.kenesawschools.org
Kenesaw ES 100/K-6
PO Box 129 68956 402-752-3215
Richard Masters, admin. Fax 752-3579

Kilgore, Cherry, Pop. 70
Cody-Kilgore SD
Supt. — See Cody
Cody-Kilgore ES 50/PK-5
PO Box 58 69216 402-966-2291
Adam Lambert, prin. Fax 966-2167

Kimball, Kimball, Pop. 2,447
Kimball SD 500/PK-12
901 S Nadine St 69145 308-235-2188
Marshall Lewis, supt. Fax 235-3269
www.kpslonghorns.org
Lynch ES 300/PK-6
1000 E 6th St 69145 308-235-4696
Michael Mitchell, prin. Fax 235-2227

Laurel, Cedar, Pop. 959
Laurel-Concord-Coleridge SD 300/K-12
PO Box 8 68745 402-256-3133
Randall Klooz, supt. Fax 256-9465
www.lccschool.org
Laurel-Concord-Coleridge ES 100/K-4
PO Box 8 68745 402-256-3730
Paige Parsons, prin. Fax 256-9465
Other Schools – See Coleridge

La Vista, Sarpy, Pop. 15,366
Papillion La Vista Community SD
Supt. — See Papillion
Hall ES 400/PK-6
7600 S 72nd St 68128 402-898-0455
Jamie Boyer, prin. Fax 898-0457
La Vista MS 800/7-8
7900 Edgewood Blvd 68128 402-898-0436
Jennifer Carson, prin. Fax 898-0442
La Vista West ES 300/PK-6
7821 Terry Dr 68128 402-898-0463
DerNecia Harris, prin. Fax 898-0465
Parkview Heights ES 400/K-6
7609 S 89th St 68128 402-898-0433
Rachel Stephenson, prin. Fax 898-0435
Portal ES 600/K-6
9920 Brentwood Dr 68128 402-898-0425
Becky Meyers, prin. Fax 898-0426

Lawrence, Nuckolls, Pop. 302
South Central Nebraska Unified SD
Supt. — See Fairfield
Lawrence/Nelson ES 100/PK-6
PO Box 128 68957 402-756-7013
Dana Epley, prin. Fax 756-7120

Leigh, Colfax, Pop. 404
Leigh Community SD 200/K-12
PO Box 98 68643 402-487-3301
Stephanie Petersen, supt. Fax 487-3341
www.leighcommunityschools.org

Leigh ES 100/K-6
PO Box 98 68643 402-487-3301
Stephanie Petersen, admin. Fax 487-2607

Lewiston, Pawnee, Pop. 68
Lewiston SD 200/K-12
306 Tiger Ave 68380 402-865-4675
Adrian Bowen, supt. Fax 865-4875
www.lewistonconsolidated.org
Lewiston ES 100/K-6
306 Tiger Ave 68380 402-865-4675
Adrian Bowen, prin. Fax 865-4875

Lexington, Dawson, Pop. 10,140
Lexington SD 2,900/PK-12
PO Box 890 68850 308-324-4681
John Hakonson Ed.D., supt. Fax 324-2528
www.lexschools.org
Bryan ES 300/K-5
1003 N Harrison St 68850 308-324-3762
Drew Welch, prin. Fax 324-7471
Early Learning Academy 200/PK-PK
1503 Plum Creek Pkwy 68850 308-324-1841
Tracy Naylor, prin. Fax 324-2528
Lexington MS 600/6-8
1100 N Washington St 68850 308-324-2349
Scott West, prin. Fax 324-6612
Morton ES 300/K-5
PO Box 820 68850 308-324-3764
Nikki Edeal, prin. Fax 324-2138
Pershing ES 300/K-5
PO Box 840 68850 308-324-3765
Suzanne Melliger, prin. Fax 324-2665
Sandoz ES 300/K-5
1711 N Erie St 68850 308-324-5540
Kimberly Ide, prin. Fax 324-2350

Lincoln, Lancaster, Pop. 251,784
Lincoln SD 37,300/PK-12
PO Box 82889 68501 402-436-1000
Stephen Joel Ed.D., supt. Fax 436-1084
www.lps.org/
Adams ES 800/PK-5
7401 Jacobs Creek Dr 68512 402-436-1121
Amy Clark, prin. Fax 458-3221
Arnold ES 700/PK-5
5000 Mike Scholl St 68524 402-436-1120
Jodi Frager, prin. Fax 458-3220
Beattie ES 400/PK-5
1901 Calvert St 68502 402-436-1123
Sean Bailey, prin. Fax 458-3223
Belmont ES 700/PK-5
3425 N 14th St 68521 402-436-1124
Kim Rosenthal, prin. Fax 458-3224
Brownell ES 400/PK-5
6000 Aylesworth Ave 68505 402-436-1127
Kelly Apel, prin. Fax 458-3227
Calvert ES 400/PK-5
3709 S 46th St 68506 402-436-1130
Jeff Brehm, prin. Fax 458-3230
Campbell ES 700/K-5
2200 Dodge St 68521 402-436-1129
Julie Lawler, prin. Fax 458-3229
Cavett ES 700/PK-5
7701 S 36th St 68516 402-436-1131
Jeff Vercellino, prin. Fax 458-3231
Clinton ES 500/PK-5
1520 N 29th St 68503 402-436-1132
Angela Luedtke, prin. Fax 458-3232
Culler MS 700/6-8
5201 Vine St 68504 402-436-1210
Michaela Hahn, prin. Fax 458-3210
Dawes MS 400/6-8
5130 Colfax Ave 68504 402-436-1211
Angela Plugge, prin. Fax 458-3211
Eastridge ES 300/K-5
6245 L St 68510 402-436-1135
Traci Boothe, prin. Fax 458-3235
Elliott ES 400/K-5
225 S 25th St 68510 402-436-1136
Kathleen Dering, prin. Fax 458-3236
Everett ES 500/PK-5
1123 C St 68502 402-436-1159
Michael Long, prin. Fax 458-3259
Fredstrom ES 500/K-5
5700 NW 10th St 68521 402-436-1140
Vicki Schulenberg, prin. Fax 458-3240
Goodrich MS 700/6-8
4600 Lewis Ave 68521 402-436-1213
Kelly Schrad, prin. Fax 458-3213
Hartley ES 300/K-5
730 N 33rd St 68503 402-436-1139
Jeff Rust, prin. Fax 458-3239
Hill ES 500/K-5
5230 Tipperary Trl 68512 402-436-1142
Amy Carnie, prin. Fax 458-3242
Holmes ES 400/PK-5
5230 Sumner St 68506 402-436-1143
Haeven Pedersen, prin. Fax 458-3243
Humann ES 600/PK-5
6720 Rockwood Ln 68516 402-436-1145
Gena Licata, prin. Fax 458-3245
Huntington ES 500/PK-5
2900 N 46th St 68504 402-436-1144
Rik Devney, prin. Fax 458-3244
Irving MS 800/6-8
2745 S 22nd St 68502 402-436-1214
Jason Shanahan, prin. Fax 458-3214
Kahoa ES 600/K-5
7700 Leighton Ave 68507 402-436-1147
Terri Nelson, prin. Fax 458-3247
Kloefkorn ES 400/K-5
6601 Glass Ridge Dr 68526 402-436-1148
Polly Bowhay, prin. Fax 458-3248
Kooser ES 700/PK-5
7301 N 13th St 68521 402-436-1146
Ann Jablonski, prin. Fax 458-3246
Lakeview ES 400/PK-5
300 Capitol Beach Blvd 68528 402-436-1149
Scott Nelson, prin. Fax 458-3249
Lefler MS 600/6-8
1100 S 48th St 68510 402-436-1215
Jessie Fries, prin. Fax 458-3215
Lux MS 1,000/6-8
7800 High St 68506 402-436-1220
Duane Dohmen, prin. Fax 458-3292
Maxey ES 600/K-5
5200 S 75th St 68516 402-436-1153
Suzanne Reimers, prin. Fax 458-3253
McPhee ES 300/PK-5
820 Goodhue Blvd 68508 402-436-1150
Betsy Gomez, prin. Fax 458-3250
Meadow Lane ES 500/PK-5
7200 Vine St 68505 402-436-1151
Daniele Schulzkump, prin. Fax 458-3251
Mickle MS 600/6-8
2500 N 67th St 68507 402-436-1216
Gene Thompson, prin. Fax 458-3216
Moore MS 6-8
8700 Yankee Woods Dr 68501 402-436-1225
Dr. Gary Czapla, prin. Fax 458-3225
Morley ES 600/K-5
6800 Monterey Dr 68506 402-436-1154
Molly Bates, prin. Fax 458-3254
Norwood Park ES 200/PK-5
4710 N 72nd St 68507 402-436-1155
Pam Hale, prin. Fax 458-3255
Park MS 800/6-8
855 S 8th St 68508 402-436-1212
Ryan Zabawa, prin. Fax 458-3212
Pershing ES 400/PK-5
6402 Judson St 68507 402-436-1160
Jamie Cook, prin. Fax 436-1471
Pound MS 800/6-8
4740 S 45th St 68516 402-436-1217
Dr. Christopher Deibler, prin. Fax 458-3217
Prescott ES 500/PK-5
1930 S 20th St 68502 402-436-1161
J.J. Wilkins, prin. Fax 458-3261
Pyrtle ES 400/K-5
721 Cottonwood Dr 68510 402-436-1162
Chris Schefdore, prin. Fax 458-3262
Randolph ES 400/K-5
1024 S 37th St 68510 402-436-1163
Kristen Finley, prin. Fax 458-3263
Riley ES 400/PK-5
5021 Orchard St 68504 402-436-1164
Jeff Bjorkman, prin. Fax 458-3264
Roper ES 900/PK-5
2323 S Coddington Ave 68522 402-436-1170
Tim Muggy, prin. Fax 458-3270
Rousseau ES 600/PK-5
3701 S 33rd St 68506 402-436-1165
Dr. Wendy Badje, prin. Fax 458-3265
Saratoga ES 300/PK-5
2215 S 13th St 68502 402-436-1166
Annette Bushaw, prin. Fax 458-3266
Schoo MS 800/6-8
700 Penrose Dr 68521 402-436-1222
Bill Schulenberg, prin. Fax 458-3222
Scott MS 1,000/6-8
2200 Pine Lake Rd 68512 402-436-1218
Dave Knudsen, prin. Fax 458-3218
Sheridan ES 500/K-5
3100 Plymouth Ave 68502 402-436-1167
Dr. DeAnn Currin, prin. Fax 458-3267
West Lincoln ES 400/PK-5
630 W Dawes Ave 68521 402-436-1168
Scott Schwartz, prin. Fax 458-3268
Wysong ES PK-5
7901 Blanchard Blvd 68516 402-436-1185
Randy Oltman, prin. Fax 458-3271
Zeman ES 400/K-5
4900 S 52nd St 68516 402-436-1169
Kristi Schirmer, prin. Fax 458-3108

Blessed Sacrament S 300/PK-8
1725 Lake St 68502 402-476-6202
Danielle Miller, prin. Fax 476-0232
Cathedral of Risen Christ S 300/PK-8
3245 S 37th St 68506 402-489-9621
Jeremy Ekeler, prin. Fax 488-9622
Christ S 100/PK-5
4325 Sumner St 68506 402-483-7774
Mark L'Heureux M.Ed., prin. Fax 483-7776
College View Academy 200/PK-12
5240 Calvert St 68506 402-483-1181
Brian Carlson, prin. Fax 483-5574
Faith Lutheran S 100/PK-5
8701 Adams St 68507 402-466-7402
Krista Barnhouse, prin. Fax 466-3857
Good Shepherd Lutheran S 100/PK-8
3825 Wildbriar Ln 68516 402-423-7677
Lincoln Christian S 600/PK-12
5801 S 84th St 68516 402-488-8888
Dr. Zachary Kassebaum, supt. Fax 486-4527
Messiah Lutheran S 300/PK-5
1800 S 84th St 68506 402-489-3024
Matthew Stueber, prin. Fax 489-3093
North American Martyrs S 500/PK-8
1101 Isaac Dr 68521 402-476-7373
Sr. Janelle Buettner, prin. Fax 476-3040
Parkview Christian S 200/PK-12
4400 N 1st St 68521 402-474-5820
Dr. Michelle Lundgren, supt. Fax 474-5830
Sacred Heart S 200/K-8
540 N 31st St 68503 402-476-1783
Laura Knaus, prin. Fax 476-3040
St. John the Apostle S 300/PK-8
7601 Vine St 68505 402-486-1860
Dennis Martin, prin. Fax 486-4762
St. Joseph S 500/PK-8
1940 S 77th St 68506 402-489-0341
Sr. Mary Mills, prin. Fax 489-3260
St. Mark Lutheran S 50/K-8
3930 S 19th St 68502 402-423-1497
Jeremiah Drews, prin. Fax 817-4481
St. Mary S 100/PK-8
1434 K St 68508 402-476-3987
Dr. Nina Beck, prin. Fax 476-0838
St. Michael S, 9101 S 78th St 68516 K-8
Denise Ray, prin. 402-488-1313
St. Patrick S 100/PK-8
4142 N 61st St 68507 402-466-3710
Leah Bethune, prin. Fax 466-3572
St. Peter S 500/K-8
4500 Duxhall Dr 68516 402-421-6299
Sr. Mary Michael, prin. Fax 421-6507
St. Teresa S 300/K-8
616 S 36th St 68510 402-477-3358
Sr. Anne Braunsroth, prin. Fax 477-3361
Stone SDA S 50/K-8
3800 S 48th St 68506 402-486-2895
Dr. Denise White, prin. Fax 486-2895
Trinity Lutheran S 200/PK-5
1200 N 56th St 68504 402-466-1800
David Geidel, prin. Fax 466-1820

Lindsay, Platte, Pop. 253
Humphrey SD 67
Supt. — See Humphrey
Lindsay Attendance Center 50/K-K
PO Box 62 68644 402-428-2409
Brice King, prin. Fax 923-1235

Holy Family S 100/PK-12
PO Box 158 68644 402-428-3455
Andy Bishop, prin. Fax 428-3231

Litchfield, Sherman, Pop. 262
Litchfield SD 100/PK-12
PO Box 167 68852 308-446-2244
Wade Finley, supt. Fax 446-2244
www.litchfieldpublicschools.org
Litchfield ES 100/PK-6
PO Box 167 68852 308-446-2244
Matthew Drew, prin. Fax 446-2244

Loomis, Phelps, Pop. 377
Loomis SD 200/K-12
PO Box 250 68958 308-876-2111
Sam Dunn, supt. Fax 876-2372
loomiswolves.org
Loomis ES 100/K-6
PO Box 250 68958 308-876-2111
Robert Ridenour, prin. Fax 876-2372

Louisville, Cass, Pop. 1,086
Louisville SD 500/K-12
PO Box 489 68037 402-234-3585
Andrew Farber, supt. Fax 234-2141
www.lpslions.org
Louisville ES 200/K-5
PO Box 489 68037 402-234-4215
Cory Holl, prin. Fax 234-2141
Louisville MS 100/6-8
PO Box 489 68037 402-234-3585
Brett Schwartz, prin. Fax 234-2141

Loup City, Sherman, Pop. 1,023
Loup City SD 300/K-12
PO Box 628 68853 308-745-0120
Blake Dahlberg, supt. Fax 745-0130
blog.loupcity.k12.ne.us
Loup City ES 200/K-6
PO Box 628 68853 308-745-1814
Roger Reikofski, prin. Fax 745-0130

Lynch, Boyd, Pop. 241
Boyd County SD
Supt. — See Spencer
Boyd County ES - Lynch 50/K-6
PO Box 98 68746 402-569-2081
Cindy Johnson, admin. Fax 569-2091
Boyd County S - Lynch 50/K-12
PO Box 98 68746 402-569-2081
Mark Koch, admin. Fax 569-2091

Lyons, Burt, Pop. 845
Lyons-Decatur Northeast SD 200/PK-12
PO Box 526 68038 402-687-2363
Fred Hansen, supt. Fax 687-2472
www.lyonsdecaturschools.org/
Northeast ES 100/PK-6
PO Box 526 68038 402-687-2363
Christopher Lecher, prin. Fax 687-2472

Mc Cook, Red Willow, Pop. 7,616
Mc Cook SD 1,500/PK-12
700 W 7th St 69001 308-344-4400
Grant Norgaard, supt. Fax 217-1530
www.mccookbison.org/
Central ES 200/4-5
604 W 1st St 69001 308-344-4400
Kate Repass, prin. Fax 217-1517
Mc Cook ES 400/PK-3
1500 W 3rd St 69001 308-344-4400
Greg Borland, prin. Fax 217-1498
Mc Cook JHS 300/6-8
800 W 7th St 69001 308-344-4400
Chad Lyons, prin. Fax 217-1483

St. Patrick S 100/PK-8
PO Box 1040 69001 308-345-4546
Rebecca Redl, prin. Fax 345-4546

Mc Cool Junction, York, Pop. 409
Mc Cool Junction SD 300/K-12
PO Box 278 68401 402-724-2231
Curtis Cogswell, supt. Fax 724-2232
www.mcjmustangs.org
Mc Cool Junction ES 100/K-6
PO Box 278 68401 402-724-2231
Curtis Cogswell, prin. Fax 724-2232

Macy, Thurston, Pop. 1,021
UMO N HO N Nation SD 400/PK-12
PO Box 280 68039 402-837-5622
Stacie Hardy, supt. Fax 837-5245
www.unpsk-12.org
UMO N HO N Nation ES 300/PK-5
PO Box 280 68039 402-837-5622
Vincent Hamman, prin. Fax 837-5245
UMO N HO N Nation MS 100/6-8
PO Box 280 68039 402-837-5622
Fax 837-5245

Madison, Madison, Pop. 2,422
Madison SD 600/PK-12
PO Box 450 68748 402-454-3336
Alan Ehlers, supt. Fax 454-2238
www.mpsdragons.org
Madison ES 200/K-5
PO Box 450 68748 402-454-2656
Andrew Offner, prin. Fax 454-3978
Madison MS 100/6-8
PO Box 450 68748 402-454-3336
Karla Kush, prin. Fax 454-2238
Madison Preschool 50/PK-PK
405 E 8th ST 68748 402-454-2656

St. Leonard S 100/PK-6
PO Box 368 68748 402-454-3525
Lisa Jackson, admin. Fax 454-6533
Trinity Lutheran S 100/PK-8
PO Box 969 68748 402-454-2651
Bill Masters, prin. Fax 454-3476

Malcolm, Lancaster, Pop. 378
Malcolm SD 500/K-12
10004 NW 112th St 68402 402-796-2151
Ryan Terwilliger, supt. Fax 796-2178
www.malcolmschools.org
Westfall ES 300/K-6
10000 NW 112th St 68402 402-796-2151
Amber Dolliver, prin. Fax 796-2186

Marsland, Dawes, Pop. 10
Sioux County SD
Supt. — See Harrison
Pink S 50/K-8
1022 River Rd 69354 308-665-1964
Barry Swisher, prin. Fax 665-1964

Maxwell, Lincoln, Pop. 309
Maxwell SD 200/K-12
PO Box 188 69151 308-582-4585
Todd Rhodes, supt. Fax 582-4584
www.maxwellschools.org
Maxwell ES 100/K-6
PO Box 188 69151 308-582-4585
Missy Friend, prin. Fax 582-4584

Maywood, Frontier, Pop. 257
Maywood SD 200/K-12
PO Box 46 69038 308-362-4223
Cynthia Huff, supt. Fax 362-4454
www.maywoodtigers.org
Maywood ES 100/K-6
PO Box 46 69038 308-362-4223
Cynthia Huff, prin. Fax 362-4454

Mead, Saunders, Pop. 567
Mead SD 200/K-12
PO Box 158 68041 402-624-2745
Dr. Dale Rawson, supt. Fax 624-2001
www.meadpublicschools.org/
Mead ES 100/K-6
PO Box 158 68041 402-624-6465
P.J. Quinn, prin. Fax 624-2001

Merna, Custer, Pop. 361
Anselmo-Merna SD 100/K-12
PO Box 68 68856 308-643-2224
Pat Osmond, supt. Fax 643-2243
www.a-mps.org
Anselmo-Merna S 100/K-12
PO Box 68 68856 308-643-2224
Carlie Wells, prin. Fax 643-2243

Milford, Seward, Pop. 2,066
Milford SD 700/PK-12
PO Box C 68405 402-761-3321
Kevin Wingard, supt. Fax 761-3322
www.milfordpublicschools.org/
Milford ES 400/PK-6
PO Box C 68405 402-761-2408
Cory Hartman, prin. Fax 761-3322

Milligan, Fillmore, Pop. 282
Exeter-Milligan SD
Supt. — See Exeter
Exeter-Milligan ES 50/3-6
PO Box 40 68406 402-629-4265
Laura Kroll, prin. Fax 629-4293

Minatare, Scotts Bluff, Pop. 808
Minatare SD 200/PK-12
PO Box 425 69356 308-783-1232
Tim Cody, supt. Fax 783-1050
www.edline.net/pages/Minatare_Public_Schools
Minatare ES 100/K-6
PO Box 425 69356 308-783-1255
Rocky Robbins, prin. Fax 783-2982
Minatare Preschool 50/PK-PK
PO Box 425 69356 308-783-1829

Scottsbluff SD
Supt. — See Scottsbluff
Lake Minatare ES 100/K-5
280548 County Road K 69356 308-783-1134
Mary Burkhalter, prin. Fax 783-1574

Minden, Kearney, Pop. 2,907
Minden SD 800/PK-12
PO Box 301 68959 308-832-2440
Melissa Wheelock, supt. Fax 832-2567
minden.k12.ne.us
Jones MS 300/4-8
PO Box 301 68959 308-832-2338
John Osgood, prin. Fax 832-3236
Minden East ES 300/K-3
PO Box 301 68959 308-832-2460
Sandra Pohl, prin. Fax 832-2567
Minden Preschool 50/PK-PK
PO Box 301 68959 308-832-1666

Mitchell, Scotts Bluff, Pop. 1,691
Mitchell SD 700/PK-12
1819 19th Ave 69357 308-623-1707
Katherine Urbanek, supt. Fax 623-1330
www.mpstigers.com
Mitchell ES 400/PK-6
1439 13th Ave 69357 308-623-2828
Kirk Kuxhausen, prin. Fax 623-1690

Morrill, Scotts Bluff, Pop. 916
Morrill SD 400/PK-12
PO Box 486 69358 308-247-3414
Joseph Sherwood, supt. Fax 247-2196
www.mpslions.org
Morrill ES 200/K-6
PO Box 486 69358 308-247-2176
Keri Homan, prin. Fax 247-2491
Tri Community Preschool 50/PK-PK
PO Box 486 69358 308-247-3413
Keri Homan, dir. Fax 247-2196

Sioux County SD
Supt. — See Harrison
Chalk Butte S 50/K-8
321 SI Rd 69358 308-247-2811
Barry Swisher, prin. Fax 247-2811

Mullen, Hooker, Pop. 506
Mullen SD 200/K-12
PO Box 127 69152 308-546-2223
Mark Sievering, supt. Fax 546-2209
www.mullenpublicschools.org
Mullen ES 100/K-6
PO Box 89 69152 308-546-2292
Justin Moore, prin. Fax 546-2423

Murdock, Cass, Pop. 236
Elmwood-Murdock SD 400/PK-12
300 Wyoming St 68407 402-867-2341
Dan Novak, supt. Fax 867-2009
www.elm.esu3.org
Other Schools – See Elmwood

Murray, Cass, Pop. 456
Conestoga SD 600/PK-12
PO Box 184 68409 402-235-2992
Beth Johnsen, supt. Fax 227-2992
www.conestogacougars.org/
Conestoga ES 400/PK-6
PO Box 68 68409 402-235-2341
Eric Dennis, prin. Fax 235-2345

Nebraska City, Otoe, Pop. 7,192
Nebraska City SD 1,400/PK-12
1700 14th Ave 68410 402-873-6033
Dr. Jeffrey Edwards, supt. Fax 873-6030
www.nebcityps.org
Hayward ES 300/3-5
1700 14th Ave 68410 402-873-6641
Scot Davis, prin. Fax 874-9274
Nebraska City MS 300/6-8
1700 14th Ave 68410 402-873-5591
Craig Taylor, prin. Fax 873-5641
Northside ES 400/PK-2
1700 14th Ave 68410 402-874-9193
Brent Gaswick, prin. Fax 874-9200

Lourdes Central S 200/PK-12
412 2nd Ave 68410 402-873-6154
Curt Feilmeier, prin. Fax 873-3154

Neligh, Antelope, Pop. 1,591
Neligh-Oakdale SD 400/PK-12
PO Box 149 68756 402-887-4166
Scott Gregory, supt. Fax 887-5322
www.nelighoakdaleschools.com
Neligh-Oakdale Eastward ES 200/3-6
PO Box 149 68756 402-887-5290
Mary Schrader, prin. Fax 887-5322
Neligh-Oakdale Westward ES 100/PK-2
PO Box 149 68756 402-887-4754
Mary Schrader, prin. Fax 887-5322

Newcastle, Dixon, Pop. 325
Hartington - Newcastle SD
Supt. — See Hartington
Hartington-Newcastle ES at Newcastle 50/PK-6
PO Box 187 68757 402-355-2231
Sarah Edwards, prin. Fax 355-2635

Newman Grove, Madison, Pop. 715
Newman Grove SD 100/K-12
PO Box 370 68758 402-447-2721
Mikal Shalikow, supt. Fax 447-2445
www.newman.esu8.org
Newman Grove ES 100/K-6
PO Box 370 68758 402-447-6051
Darrell Barnes, prin. Fax 447-2445

Niobrara, Knox, Pop. 360
Niobrara SD 200/K-12
PO Box 310 68760 402-857-3323
Margaret Sandoz, supt. Fax 857-3877
www.niobraraschools.org
Niobrara ES 100/K-4
PO Box 310 68760 402-857-3323
Margaret Sandoz, prin. Fax 857-3877

Santee SD 100/PK-12
206 Frazier Ave E 68760 402-857-2741
Kari Garwood-Daniels, supt. Fax 857-2743
www.santeeschools.org
Santee ES 100/PK-6
206 Frazier Ave E 68760 402-857-2741
Cindy Nagel, prin. Fax 857-2743

Norfolk, Madison, Pop. 23,882
Norfolk SD 4,200/PK-12
PO Box 139 68702 402-644-2500
Jami Jo Thompson, supt. Fax 644-2506
www.norfolkpublicschools.org/
Bel Air ES 300/K-4
PO Box 139 68702 402-644-2539
Trisha Andreasen, prin. Fax 644-2542
Grant ES 200/K-4
PO Box 139 68702 402-644-2544
Fax 644-2545
Jefferson ES 300/K-4
PO Box 139 68702 402-644-2546
Angela Hausmann, prin. Fax 644-2548
Lincoln ES 200/PK-4
PO Box 139 68702 402-644-2550
Michael Andreasen, prin. Fax 644-2552
Norfolk JHS 600/7-8
PO Box 139 68702 402-644-2516
Michael Hart, prin. Fax 644-2519
Norfolk MS 600/5-6
PO Box 139 68702 402-644-2569
Jennifer Robinson, prin. Fax 644-2576
Washington ES 200/K-4
PO Box 139 68702 402-644-2557
Michael Andreasen, prin. Fax 644-2560
Westside ES 200/K-4
PO Box 139 68702 402-644-2561
Angela Baumann, prin. Fax 644-2562
Woodland Park ES 200/K-4
PO Box 139 68702 402-644-2565
Fax 644-2568

Christ Lutheran S 300/PK-8
511 S 5th St 68701 402-371-5536
Steven Stortz, prin. Fax 371-1288
Keystone Christian Academy 50/PK-9
715 W Madison Ave 68701 402-371-3531
Sharon Lotz, admin. Fax 371-4824
Norfolk Catholic S 400/PK-6
2300 W Madison Ave 68701 402-371-4584
William Lafleur, prin. Fax 379-8129
St. Paul Lutheran S 100/PK-8
1010 Georgia Ave 68701 402-371-1233
Mike Paulsen, prin. Fax 379-3646

North Bend, Dodge, Pop. 1,172
North Bend Central SD 600/K-12
PO Box 160 68649 402-652-3268
Dan Endorf, supt. Fax 652-8348
www.nbtigers.org
North Bend ES 300/K-5
PO Box 220 68649 402-652-8122
Tessie Beaver, prin. Fax 652-3474

North Platte, Lincoln, Pop. 24,455
North Platte SD 3,700/PK-12
PO Box 1557 69103 308-535-7100
Dr. Ron Hanson, supt. Fax 535-5300
www.nppsd.org
Adams MS 400/7-8
1200 McDonald Rd 69101 308-535-7112
Dan Helberg, prin. Fax 535-5309
Buffalo ES 200/PK-5
1600 N Buffalo Bill Ave 69101 308-535-7130
Kim Flanders, prin. Fax 535-5363
Cody ES 300/PK-5
2000 W 2nd St 69101 308-535-7132
Jeff Nemecek, prin. Fax 535-5364
Eisenhower ES 200/K-5
3900 W A St 69101 308-535-7134
Mary Derby, prin. Fax 535-5365
Jefferson ES 400/PK-5
700 E 3rd St 69101 308-535-7136
John Byrn, prin. Fax 535-5366
Lake Maloney ES 100/K-5
848 E Correction Line Rd 69101 308-532-9392
Robin Vahle, prin. Fax 534-4371
Lincoln ES 300/PK-5
200 W 9th St 69101 308-535-7138
Matt Irish, prin. Fax 535-5367
Madison MS 100/6-6
1400 N Madison Ave 69101 308-535-7126
Danny McMurtry, prin. Fax 535-5303
McDonald ES 200/K-5
601 McDonald Rd 69101 308-535-7140
Trent Benjamin, prin. Fax 535-5368
Osgood ES 100/K-5
495 W State Farm Rd 69101 308-535-7144
Robin Vahle, prin. Fax 535-5369
Washington ES 200/K-5
600 W 3rd St 69101 308-535-7142
Greg Fruhwirth, prin. Fax 535-5370

Mc Daid ES 200/K-6
PO Box 970 69103 308-532-1874
Pam Wood, prin. Fax 532-8015
Our Redeemer Lutheran S 100/PK-8
1400 E E St 69101 308-532-6421
Wende Carson, prin. Fax 532-0295

Oakland, Burt, Pop. 1,227
Oakland Craig SD 500/PK-12
309 N Davis Ave 68045 402-685-5661
Jeffery Smith, supt. Fax 685-5697
www.ocknights.org
Oakland Craig ES 300/PK-6
400 N Brewster Ave 68045 402-685-5631
Jessica Bland, prin. Fax 685-6734

Oakland Craig JHS 100/7-8
309 N Davis Ave 68045 402-685-5661
Rusty Droescher, prin. Fax 685-5697

Odell, Gage, Pop. 299
Diller-Odell SD 200/K-12
PO Box 188 68415 402-766-4171
Michael Meyerle, supt. Fax 766-4211
www.dillerodell.org
Other Schools – See Diller

Ogallala, Keith, Pop. 4,669
Ogallala SD 500/PK-12
801 E O St 69153 308-284-4060
Michael L. Apple, supt. Fax 284-3981
www.opsd.org/
Prairie View S 200/PK-8
801 E O St 69153 308-284-6087
Steve Bristol, prin. Fax 284-3839

St. Luke S 50/PK-5
406 E 3rd St 69153 308-284-4841
Sr. Loretta Krajewski, prin. Fax 284-9839
St. Paul's Lutheran S 50/PK-5
312 W 3rd St 69153 308-284-2944
Dr. Larry Wooster, lead tchr. Fax 284-2944

Omaha, Douglas, Pop. 399,005
Elkhorn SD
Supt. — See Elkhorn
Elkhorn Grandview MS 6-8
17801 Grand Ave 68116 402-289-9399
Mike Tomjack, prin. Fax 289-9499
Elkhorn Ridge MS 400/6-8
17880 Marcy St 68118 402-334-9302
Kevin Riggert, prin. Fax 334-9378
Manchester ES 400/K-5
2750 N HWS Cleveland Blvd 68116 402-289-2590
Amy Christ, prin. Fax 289-2585
Sagewood ES, 4910 N 177th St 68116 300/K-6
Jan Peterson, prin. 402-289-9078
Spring Ridge ES 600/K-5
17830 Shadow Ridge Dr 68130 402-637-0204
Laurinda Peterson, prin. Fax 637-0207
West Bay ES 300/PK-5
3220 S 188th Ave 68130 402-289-9045
Jen Coltvet, prin. Fax 289-1588

Gretna SD
Supt. — See Gretna
Aspen Creek ES K-5
10325 S 188 St 68136 402-332-5617
Wendi Kistler, prin.
Aspen Creek MS 6-8
18414 Summit Dr 68136 402-332-3866
Stacey Deterding, prin.
Palisades ES 600/PK-5
16820 Chutney Dr 68136 402-895-2194
Salli Wells, prin. Fax 408-3090
Whitetail Creek ES 500/PK-5
19110 Greenleaf St 68136 402-895-3388
Ellen Ridolfi, prin. Fax 408-3091

Millard SD 23,100/PK-12
5606 S 147th St 68137 402-715-8200
Dr. James Sutfin, supt. Fax 715-8409
www.mpsomaha.org
Abbott ES 400/PK-5
1313 N 156th Ave 68118 402-715-2900
Erik Chaussee, prin. Fax 715-2911
Ackerman ES 500/K-5
5110 S 156th St 68135 402-715-8420
James Hanlon, prin. Fax 715-6193
Aldrich ES 500/K-5
506 N 162nd Ave 68118 402-715-2020
Heidi Penke, prin. Fax 715-2035
Andersen MS 900/6-8
15404 Adams St 68137 402-715-8440
Jeff Alfrey, prin. Fax 715-8410
Beadle MS 1,200/6-8
18201 Jefferson St 68135 402-715-6100
John Southworth, prin. Fax 715-6140
Black Elk ES 400/K-5
6708 S 161st Ave 68135 402-715-6200
Jason Farwell, prin. Fax 715-6220
Bryan ES 400/K-5
5010 S 144th St 68137 402-715-8325
Brad Sullivan, prin. Fax 715-6194
Cather ES 400/K-5
3030 S 139th St 68144 402-715-1315
Bethany Case, prin. Fax 715-1432
Cody ES 300/PK-5
3320 S 127th St 68144 402-715-1320
Ryan Saunders, prin. Fax 715-1250
Cottonwood ES 300/K-5
615 Piedmont Dr 68154 402-715-1390
Gina Rudloff, prin. Fax 715-1428
Disney ES 300/K-5
5717 S 112th St 68137 402-715-2350
Cindy Scharff, prin. Fax 715-2358
Hitchcock ES 200/K-5
5809 S 104th St 68127 402-715-2255
Mandy Hartz, prin. Fax 715-1901
Holling Heights ES 400/K-5
6565 S 136th St 68137 402-715-8330
Nancy Nelson, prin. Fax 715-6195
Kiewit MS 900/6-8
15650 Howard St 68118 402-715-1470
Marshall Smith, prin. Fax 715-1490
Millard Central MS 800/6-8
12801 L St 68137 402-715-8225
Dr. Beth Fink, prin. Fax 715-8574
Millard ES 400/K-5
14111 Blondo St 68164 402-715-2955
Roberta Deremer, prin. Fax 715-2970
Millard North MS 800/6-8
2828 S 139th St 68144 402-715-1280
Scott Ingwerson, prin. Fax 715-1275

Montclair ES 500/K-5
2405 S 138th St 68144 402-715-1295
Alicia Kotlarz, prin. Fax 715-1446
Morton ES 300/K-5
1805 S 160th St 68130 402-715-1290
Julie Bergstrom, prin. Fax 715-1311
Neihardt ES 600/PK-5
15130 Drexel St 68137 402-715-8360
Carrie Novotny-Buss, prin. Fax 715-6191
Norris ES 400/K-5
12424 Weir St 68137 402-715-8340
Colleen Ballard, prin. Fax 715-6119
Oaks ES 300/K-5
15228 Shirley St 68144 402-715-1386
Erin Gonzales, prin. Fax 715-1624
Reagan ES 700/K-5
4440 S 198th Ave 68135 402-715-7100
Tara Fabian, prin. Fax 715-7120
Rockwell ES 300/K-5
6370 S 140th Ave 68137 402-715-8246
Joycilyn Rozelle, prin. Fax 715-6197
Rohwer ES 400/K-5
17701 F St 68135 402-715-6225
Nicole Burton, prin. Fax 715-6240
Russell MS 900/6-8
5304 S 172nd St 68135 402-715-8500
Teresa Perkins, prin. Fax 715-8368
Sandoz ES 300/K-5
5959 Oak Hills Dr 68137 402-715-8345
Dawn Marten, prin. Fax 715-8367
Upchurch ES, 8686 S 156th St 68136 700/K-5
Susan Anglemeyer, prin. 402-715-7150
Wheeler ES 500/K-5
6707 S 178th St 68135 402-715-6250
Tracy Logan, prin. Fax 715-6270
Willowdale ES 400/K-5
16901 P St 68135 402-715-8280
Amanda Hunt, prin. Fax 715-8580
Other Schools – See Gretna

Omaha SD 48,800/PK-12
3215 Cuming St 68131 402-557-2222
Mark Evans, supt. Fax 557-2019
district.ops.org
Adams ES 300/K-6
3420 N 78th St 68134 402-572-9072
Mark Kelin, prin. Fax 572-9075
Ashland Park-Robbins ES 800/PK-6
5050 S 51st St 68117 402-734-6001
Jan Martin, prin. Fax 734-6210
Bancroft ES 800/PK-6
2724 Riverview Blvd 68108 402-344-7505
David Milan, prin. Fax 344-7695
Beals ES 400/PK-6
1720 S 48th St 68106 402-554-8570
Nicole Lanum, prin. Fax 554-8546
Belle Ryan ES 300/PK-6
5616 L St 68117 531-299-1080
Charla Johnson, prin. Fax 299-1098
Belvedere ES 500/PK-6
3775 Curtis Ave 68111 402-457-6630
Christina Windsor, prin. Fax 457-6609
Benson West ES 600/K-6
6652 Maple St 68104 402-554-8633
Dr. Monica Green, prin. Fax 554-8616
Beveridge Magnet MS 700/7-8
1616 S 120th St 68144 531-299-4000
Dr. David Lavender, prin. Fax 299-2298
Boyd ES 500/PK-6
8314 Boyd St 68134 402-572-8928
Briana McLeod-Larsen, prin. Fax 572-9001
Bryan MS 800/7-8
8210 S 42nd St 68147 402-557-4100
Darren Rasmussen, prin. Fax 557-4129
Buffet Magnet MS 700/5-8
14101 Larimore Ave 68164 531-299-2320
Dr. Rony Ortega, prin. Fax 299-2338
Castelar ES 600/PK-6
2316 S 18th St 68108 402-344-7794
Adriana Vargas, prin. Fax 344-7884
Catlin Magnet Arts Center 300/PK-6
12736 Marinda St 68144 402-697-0414
William Schmidt, prin. Fax 697-0016
Central Park ES 400/PK-6
4904 N 42nd St 68111 402-457-5277
Scott Sturgeon, prin. Fax 457-5122
Chandler View ES 700/PK-6
7800 S 25th St 68147 402-734-5705
Gregory Eversoll, prin. Fax 734-5609
Columbian ES 300/K-6
330 S 127th St 68154 402-697-1433
Nanette Beller, prin. Fax 697-1273
Conestoga ES 400/PK-6
2115 Burdette St 68110 402-344-7147
Vanita Jarmon, prin. Fax 344-7195
Crestridge Magnet ES 400/K-6
818 Crestridge Rd 68154 531-299-1280
Marjorie Reed-Schmid, prin. Fax 299-1298
Davis MS 400/6-8
8050 N 129th Ave 68142 402-561-6130
Dan Bartels, prin. Fax 299-2358
Dodge ES 400/PK-6
3520 Maplewood Blvd 68134 402-572-9005
Cody Hays, prin. Fax 572-9049
Druid Hill ES 400/PK-6
4020 N 30th St 68111 402-451-8225
Cherice Williams, prin. Fax 453-9744
Dundee ES 600/K-6
310 N 51st St 68132 402-554-8424
Kaye Kennedy, prin. Fax 554-0303
Edison ES 400/PK-6
2303 N 97th St 68134 402-392-7310
Melany Fullenkamp, prin. Fax 299-1378
Field Club ES 600/K-6
3512 Walnut St 68105 402-344-7226
Barbara Wild, prin. Fax 344-7395

Florence ES 300/K-6
4301 N 30th St 68112 402-457-5818
Dan Hoeck, prin. Fax 299-1418
Fontenelle ES 600/PK-6
3905 N 52nd St 68104 402-457-5905
Eric Nelson, prin. Fax 457-6525
Franklin ES 300/PK-6
3506 Franklin St 68111 531-299-1440
Decua Jean-Baptiste, prin. Fax 299-1458
Fullerton Magnet ES 500/K-4
4711 N 138th St 68164 402-498-2787
Craig McGee, prin. Fax 498-0967
Gateway ES 800/PK-6
5610 S 42nd St 68107 402-561-6030
Terry Burton, prin. Fax 502-3449
Gilder ES 400/K-6
3705 Chandler Rd W 68147 402-734-7334
Cassie Schmidt, prin. Fax 734-9973
Gomez-Heritage ES 800/PK-4
5101 S 17th St 68107 402-898-2801
John Campin, prin. Fax 898-1854
Hale MS 300/7-8
6143 Whitmore St 68152 402-557-4200
Darin Williams, prin. Fax 557-4229
Harrison ES 300/K-6
5304 Hamilton St 68132 402-554-8535
Dr. Andrea Haynes, prin. Fax 553-2940
Hartman ES 500/PK-6
5530 N 66th St 68104 402-572-1966
Shelly Burghardt, prin. Fax 572-1653
Highland ES 500/PK-6
2625 Jefferson St 68107 402-734-5711
Gwen Foxall, prin. Fax 734-5821
Indian Hill ES 600/PK-6
3121 U St 68107 531-299-1600
Robert Holzapfel, prin. Fax 299-1608
Jackson ES 300/PK-6
620 S 31st St 68105 402-344-7484
Tynisha Northcutt, prin. Fax 344-7414
Jefferson ES 500/K-6
4065 Vinton St 68105 402-554-6590
Jennifer Schlapia, prin. Fax 553-2956
Joslyn ES 400/PK-6
11220 Blondo St 68164 531-299-1660
Elizabeth Kosch, prin. Fax 299-1678
Kellom ES 500/PK-6
1311 N 24th St 68102 402-344-0441
Carri Hutcherson, prin. Fax 344-0213
Kennedy ES 200/K-6
2906 N 30th St 68111 402-457-5520
Tony Gunter, prin. Fax 457-5031
King ES 300/PK-6
3706 Maple St 68111 402-457-5723
Stephanie Black, prin. Fax 457-4932
King Science/Tech Magnet MS 300/5-8
3720 Florence Blvd 68110 531-299-2380
Maria Buckner, prin. Fax 299-2398
Lewis & Clark MS 700/7-8
6901 Burt St 68132 531-299-2400
Dr. Lisa Sterba, prin. Fax 299-2418
Liberty ES 700/PK-6
2021 Saint Marys Ave 68102 402-898-1697
Ilka Oberst, prin. Fax 898-1698
Lothrop Magnet ES 300/PK-4
3300 N 22nd St 68110 531-299-1780
Gary Westbrook, prin. Fax 299-1798
Marrs Magnet MS 700/5-8
5619 S 19th St 68107 531-299-2420
Bryan Dunne, prin. Fax 299-2439
Masters ES 300/K-6
5505 N 99th St 68134 402-572-1027
Dr. LeDonna Griffin, prin. Fax 572-0952
McMillan Magnet MS 500/7-8
3802 Redick Ave 68112 531-299-2440
Dr. Jeaneen Talbott, prin. Fax 299-2458
Miller Park ES 400/PK-6
5625 N 28th Ave 68111 402-457-5620
Dr. Carrie Rath, prin. Fax 457-5702
Minne Lusa ES 400/PK-6
2728 Ida St 68112 402-457-5611
Kim Jones, prin. Fax 451-4971
Monroe MS 500/7-8
5105 Bedford Ave 68104 531-299-2460
Boris Moore, prin. Fax 299-2479
Morton Magnet MS 600/5-8
4606 Terrace Dr 68134 402-557-4700
Sherri Wehr, prin. Fax 557-4709
Mount View ES 400/PK-6
5322 N 52nd St 68104 402-457-5117
Matthew Williams, prin. Fax 457-5109
Norris MS 800/7-8
2235 S 46th St 68106 531-299-2500
Dr. David Alati, prin. Fax 299-2518
Oak Valley ES 300/PK-6
3109 Pedersen Dr 68144 402-697-0690
Glenn Mitchell, prin. Fax 697-0769
Pawnee ES 400/K-6
7310 S 48th St 68157 402-734-5011
Elizabeth Holland, prin. Fax 734-1365
Picotte ES 500/K-6
14506 Ohio St 68116 402-496-8401
Angela Burns, prin. Fax 496-2108
Pinewood ES 300/PK-6
6717 N 63rd St 68152 402-561-6000
Kristi Reinsch, prin. Fax 561-6009
Ponca ES 200/K-6
11300 N Post Rd 68112 531-299-1960
Jennifer LeClair, prin. Fax 299-1978
Prairie Wind ES 700/K-6
10908 Ellison Ave 68164 402-491-0859
Paula Knutzen-Peatrowsky, prin. Fax 491-0273
Rose Hill ES 300/K-6
5605 Corby St 68104 402-554-6797
Tylee Hanson, prin. Fax 554-8406
Saddlebrook ES 500/PK-5
14850 Laurel Ave 68116 402-933-3915
Jodie Lenser, prin. Fax 502-9108

Sherman ES 200/PK-6
5618 N 14th Ave 68110 402-457-6711
Dana Barker, prin. Fax 457-7965

Skinner Magnet Center 400/PK-5
4304 N 33rd St 68111 531-299-2080
Tarina Cox-Jones, prin. Fax 299-2090

Spring Lake Magnet Center 800/PK-4
4215 S 20th St 68107 402-734-1833
Susan Aguilera-Robles, prin. Fax 734-1715

Springville ES 400/K-6
7400 N 60th St 68152 402-572-0130
Susan Cloyed, prin. Fax 572-9106

Standing Bear ES 600/PK-4
15860 Taylor St 68116 402-827-4362
Lynnette Keyes, prin. Fax 827-7101

Sunny Slope ES 500/PK-6
10828 Old Maple Rd 68164 531-299-2160
Mindi Grim, prin. Fax 299-2178

Wakonda ES 400/PK-6
4845 Curtis Ave 68104 402-457-6737
Ebony Harvey, prin. Fax 299-2198

Walnut Hill ES 500/PK-6
4355 Charles St 68131 402-554-8644
Rocky Parkert, prin. Fax 554-8638

Washington ES 300/PK-6
5519 Mayberry St 68106 402-554-8690
Jean Gilreath, prin. Fax 554-1407

Western Hills Magnet ES 400/K-6
6523 Western Ave 68132 531-299-2240
Heather Hardison, prin. Fax 299-2258

Wilson Focus S 200/3-6
5141 F St 68117 402-733-1785
Bret Anderson, dir. Fax 733-1846

Ralston SD
Supt. — See Ralston

Blumfield ES 400/PK-6
10310 Mockingbird Dr 68127 402-331-0891
Peyton Lewis, prin. Fax 331-1191

Meadows ES 300/PK-6
9225 Berry St 68127 402-339-6655
Lisa Schroeder, prin. Fax 331-1044

Mockingbird ES 400/PK-6
5100 S 93rd St 68127 402-331-6954
Brian Ferguson, prin. Fax 331-6403

Western ES 100/PK-6
6224 H St 68117 402-731-7477
Dr. Josh Wilken, prin. Fax 731-0952

Springfield Platteview Community SD
Supt. — See Springfield

Westmont ES 300/PK-6
13210 Glenn St 68138 402-895-9602
Melissa Hasty, prin. Fax 894-4876

Westside Community SD 6,200/PK-12
909 S 76th St 68114 402-390-2100
Dr. Blane McCann Ph.D., supt. Fax 390-2120
www.westside66.org

Hillside ES 400/K-6
7500 Western Ave 68114 402-390-6450
Cynthia Bailey, prin. Fax 390-2165

Loveland ES 300/K-6
8201 Pacific St 68114 402-390-6455
Stephanie Hornung, prin. Fax 390-2162

Oakdale ES 300/PK-6
9801 W Center Rd 68124 402-390-6460
Glen Jagels, prin. Fax 390-2164

Paddock Road ES 300/PK-6
3535 Paddock Rd 68124 402-390-6465
Scott Becker, prin. Fax 390-2161

Prairie Lane ES 300/PK-6
11444 Hascall St 68144 402-390-6470
Beth Welke, prin. Fax 390-6469

Rockbrook ES 300/PK-6
2514 S 108th St 68144 402-390-6475
Garret Higginbotham, prin. Fax 390-2157

Sunset Hills ES 200/PK-6
9503 Walnut St 68124 402-390-6480
Michelle Patterson, prin. Fax 390-2160

Swanson ES 400/K-6
8601 Harney St 68114 402-390-6485
Jennifer Harr, prin. Fax 390-2159

Underwood Hills ECC PK-PK
9030 Western Ave 68114 402-390-8207
Julie Oelke, dir. Fax 390-2253

Westbrook ES 500/PK-6
1312 Robertson Dr 68114 402-390-6490
Tyler Hottovy, prin. Fax 390-2163

Westgate ES 300/PK-6
7802 Hascall St 68124 402-390-6495
Amanda Moon, prin. Fax 390-2156

Westside MS 900/7-8
8601 Arbor St 68124 402-390-6464
Russ Olsen, prin. Fax 390-6454

All Saints S 100/PK-8
1335 S 10th St 68108 402-346-5757
Marlan Burki, prin. Fax 346-8794

Brownell Talbot S 500/PK-12
400 N Happy Hollow Blvd 68132 402-556-3772
Dr. Kristi Gibbs, head sch Fax 553-2994

Christ the King S 300/PK-8
831 S 88th St 68114 402-391-0977
Christopher Segrell, prin. Fax 391-2418

Concordia Academy 200/K-5
1821 N 90th St 68114 402-592-8005
Nathan Domsch, prin. Fax 399-1682

Gethsemane Lutheran S 100/K-8
4040 N 108th St 68164 402-493-2550
Corey Pederson, prin.

Good Shepherd Lutheran S 100/PK-8
5071 Center St 68106 402-553-6760
Joel Lauber, prin.

Holy Cross S 300/PK-8
1502 S 48th St 68106 402-551-3773
Tawnya Mann, prin. Fax 556-1896

Holy Name S 200/PK-8
2901 Fontenelle Blvd 68104 402-451-5403
Patty Ahlgren, prin. Fax 453-7950

Jesuit Academy 100/4-8
2311 N 22nd St 68110 402-346-4464
Troy Wharton, prin. Fax 341-1817

Lifegate Christian S 400/K-8
15555 W Dodge Rd 68154 402-333-5153
Dan Diercks, supt. Fax 758-6980

Mary Our Queen S 500/PK-8
3405 S 119th St 68144 402-333-8663
Maureen Hoy, prin. Fax 334-3948

Montessori Childrens Academy 100/PK-3
14340 Harrison St 68138 402-502-9118

Montessori Children's Room 200/PK-6
7302 Burt St 68114 402-551-1440
Mary Anderson, head sch Fax 397-5417

Montessori ES of Omaha 50/PK-6
2111 S 67th St Ste 300 68106 402-393-1311
Julie Roy, dir. Fax 513-8196

Omaha Christian Academy 300/PK-12
10244 Wiesman Dr 68134 402-399-9565
Fred Ivey, admin. Fax 399-0248

Omaha Memorial Adventist S 50/1-8
840 N 72nd St 68114 402-397-4642
Fax 393-0125

Our Lady of Lourdes S 300/PK-8
2124 S 32nd Ave 68105 402-341-5604
Megan Fiedler, prin. Fax 341-9957

Sacred Heart S 100/K-8
2205 Binney St 68110 402-455-5858
Mike Jensen, prin. Fax 451-7480

St. Bernadette S 200/PK-8
7600 S 42nd St 68147 402-731-3033
Lynn Schultz, prin. Fax 731-8735

St. Bernard S 200/PK-8
3604 N 65th St 68104 402-553-4993
Dr. Joe Greco, prin. Fax 551-4939

St. Cecilia S 300/PK-8
3869 Webster St 68131 402-556-6655
Julia Pick, prin. Fax 502-3048

St. James-Seton S 600/PK-8
4720 N 90th St 68134 402-572-0339
W. Kelly, prin. Fax 572-0347

St. Joan of Arc S 100/PK-8
7430 Hascall St 68124 402-393-2314
Kayleen Wallace, prin. Fax 393-4405

St. Margaret Mary S 600/K-8
123 N 61st St 68132 402-551-6663
Peggy Grennan, prin. Fax 551-5631

St. Paul Lutheran S 50/PK-8
5020 Grand Ave 68104 402-451-2865
Linda Tripp M.S., prin. Fax 451-6816

St. Philip Neri S 200/PK-8
8202 N 31st St 68112 402-455-8666
Mary Simerly, prin. Fax 453-3620

St. Pius X-St. Leo S 800/PK-8
6905 Blondo St 68104 402-551-6667
Cory Sepich, prin. Fax 551-8123

St. Robert Bellarmine S 600/PK-8
11900 Pacific St 68154 402-334-1929
Sandra Suiter, prin. Fax 333-7188

St. Stephen the Martyr S 900/PK-8
16701 S St 68135 402-896-0754
Dr. Roseanne Williby, prin. Fax 861-4640

St. Thomas More S 300/PK-8
3515 S 48th Ave 68106 402-551-9504
Gary Davis, prin. Fax 551-9507

St. Vincent de Paul S 800/PK-8
14330 Eagle Run Dr 68164 402-492-2111
Dr. Barbara Marchese, prin. Fax 496-9933

St. Wenceslaus S 800/PK-8
15353 Pacific St 68154 402-330-4356
William Huben, prin. Fax 330-1476

SS. Peter & Paul S 100/PK-8
3619 X St 68107 402-731-4713
Andrew Bauer, prin. Fax 731-2633

Trinity Classical Academy 100/PK-5
PO Box 540853 68154 402-979-6822

O Neill, Holt, Pop. 3,676

O'Neill SD 700/PK-12
PO Box 230 68763 402-336-3775
Amy Shane, supt. Fax 336-4890
www.oneillpublicschools.org

O'Neill ES 400/PK-6
PO Box 230 68763 402-336-1400
Jim York, prin. Fax 336-2651

St. Mary S 300/PK-12
300 N 4th St 68763 402-336-4455
Cody Havranek, prin. Fax 336-1281

Orchard, Antelope, Pop. 377

Nebraska USD 1 200/PK-12
PO Box 248 68764 402-893-2068
Dale Martin, supt. Fax 893-2065
neunified1.esu8.org/

Orchard S 50/PK-12
PO Box 269 68764 402-893-3215
Cathy Cooper, prin. Fax 893-2065

Other Schools – See Clearwater, Verdigre

Ord, Valley, Pop. 2,094

Ord SD 500/K-12
320 N 19th St 68862 308-728-5013
Jason Alexander, supt. Fax 728-5108
www.ordps.org

Ord ES 200/K-6
820 S 16th St 68862 308-728-3331
Doug Smith, prin. Fax 728-3749

St. Marys S, 527 N 20th St 68862 100/K-6
Patricia Valasek, lead tchr. 308-728-5389

Osceola, Polk, Pop. 874

Osceola SD 200/K-12
PO Box 198 68651 402-747-3121
Steve Rinehart, supt. Fax 747-3041
www.osceolaschools.org

Osceola ES 100/K-5
PO Box 198 68651 402-747-2091
Brett Webster, prin. Fax 747-3041

Osceola MS 100/6-8
PO Box 198 68651 402-747-3121
Dale Maynard, prin. Fax 747-3041

Polk County Christian S 50/K-8
12986 N Rd 68651 402-747-6561
Kay Kronberg, lead tchr. Fax 747-6561

Oshkosh, Garden, Pop. 869

Garden County SD 200/PK-12
PO Box 230 69154 308-772-3242
Dr. Paula Sissel, supt. Fax 772-3039
www.gardencountyschools.org/

Garden County ES 100/PK-6
PO Box 230 69154 308-772-3336
Dr. Paula Sissel, prin. Fax 772-4059

Osmond, Pierce, Pop. 774

Osmond SD 200/K-12
PO Box 458 68765 402-748-3777
David Hamm, supt. Fax 748-3210
www.osmondtigers.org

Osmond ES 100/K-6
PO Box 458 68765 402-748-3777
Kurt Polt, prin. Fax 748-3210

St. Marys S 50/PK-8
PO Box 427 68765 402-748-3433
Tiffany Guenther, admin. Fax 748-3433

Overton, Dawson, Pop. 592

Overton SD 300/PK-12
PO Box 310 68863 308-987-2424
Mark Aten, supt. Fax 987-2349
www.overtoneagles.org

Overton ES 200/PK-6
PO Box 310 68863 308-987-2424
Brian Fleischman, prin. Fax 987-2349

Oxford, Furnas, Pop. 773

Southern Valley SD 400/K-12
43739 Highway 89 68967 308-868-2222
Darren Tobey, supt. Fax 868-2223
sites.google.com/a/sveagles.org/southern-valley

Southern Valley ES 200/K-6
43737 Highway 89 68967 308-868-2222
Mark Grove, prin. Fax 868-2223

Palisade, Hitchcock, Pop. 351

Wauneta-Palisade SD
Supt. — See Wauneta

Palisade ES 100/K-6
PO Box 329 69040 308-285-3232
Joseph Frecks, prin. Fax 285-3219

Palmer, Merrick, Pop. 470

Palmer SD 300/PK-12
PO Box 248 68864 308-894-3065
Dr. Joel Bohlken, supt. Fax 894-8245
www.palmertigers.org

Palmer ES 200/PK-6
PO Box 248 68864 308-894-3065
Sherise Loeffelbein, prin. Fax 894-8245

Palmyra, Otoe, Pop. 536

Palmyra OR 1 SD 400/K-12
PO Box 130 68418 402-780-5327
Robert Hanger, supt. Fax 780-5328
www.districtor1.org/
Other Schools – See Bennet

Papillion, Sarpy, Pop. 18,478

Papillion La Vista Community SD 10,900/PK-12
420 S Washington St 68046 402-537-6200
Dr. Andrew Rikli, supt. Fax 537-6216
www.paplv.org

Bell ES 500/K-6
7909 Reed St 68046 402-898-0408
Randy Guthmiller, prin. Fax 898-0416

Carriage Hill ES 400/K-6
400 Cedardale Rd 68046 402-898-0449
Kelcy Tapp, prin. Fax 898-0453

Hickory Hill ES 400/K-6
1307 Rogers Dr 68046 402-898-0469
Monica Thompson, prin. Fax 898-0472

Liberty MS, 10820 Wittmuss Dr 68046 7-8
Dr. Troy Juracek, prin. 402-537-6200

Papillion-La Vista ECC 100/PK-PK
1211 N Monroe St 68046 402-514-3243
Jacci Lucas, prin.

Papillion MS 800/7-8
423 S Washington St 68046 402-898-0424
Tim Johnson, prin. Fax 898-0430

Patriot ES 600/K-6
1701 Hardwood Dr 68046 402-898-0405
Matt Hilderbrand, prin. Fax 898-0406

Prairie Queen ES K-6
10520 S 123rd Ave 68046 402-514-3650
Pamela Lowndes, prin. Fax 331-0964

Rumsey Station ES 400/PK-6
110 Eagle Ridge Dr 68133 402-898-0475
Dan Kauk, prin. Fax 898-0418

Tara Heights ES 400/K-6
700 Tara Rd 68046 402-898-0445
Dave Fritson, prin. Fax 898-0447

Trumble Park ES 400/K-6
500 Valley Rd 68046 402-898-0466
Amy Wemhoff, prin. Fax 898-0474

Walnut Creek ES 500/PK-6
720 Fenwick St 68046 402-898-9630
Angelique Gunderson, prin. Fax 898-9634

Other Schools – See Bellevue, La Vista

St. Columbkille S 500/K-8
224 E 5th St 68046 402-339-8706
Brandi Redburn, prin. Fax 592-4147

Pawnee City, Pawnee, Pop. 861
Pawnee City SD 300/K-12
PO Box 393 68420 402-852-2988
Brian Rottinghaus, supt. Fax 852-2993
www.pawneecityschool.com
Pawnee City ES 100/K-6
PO Box 393 68420 402-852-2411
Brian Rottinghaus, prin. Fax 852-2993

Paxton, Keith, Pop. 521
Paxton Consolidated SD 200/K-12
PO Box 368 69155 308-239-4283
Delbert Dack, supt. Fax 239-4359
www.paxtonschools.org
Paxton ES 100/K-6
PO Box 368 69155 308-239-4283
Melissa States, prin. Fax 239-4359

Pender, Thurston, Pop. 991
Pender SD 400/PK-12
609 Whitney St 68047 402-385-3244
Jason Dolliver, supt. Fax 385-3342
www.penderschools.org/
Pender ES 200/PK-6
609 Whitney St 68047 402-385-3244
Kelly Ballinger, prin. Fax 385-3342

Petersburg, Boone, Pop. 329
Boone Central SD
Supt. — See Albion
Boone Central MS 100/6-8
PO Box 240 68652 402-386-5302
Tanner Schutt, prin. Fax 386-5464

Pierce, Pierce, Pop. 1,757
Pierce SD 600/K-12
201 N Sunset St 68767 402-329-4677
Kendall Steffensen, supt. Fax 329-4678
www.piercepublic.org/
Pierce ES 300/K-6
211 N 7th St 68767 402-329-4302
Adam Patrick, prin. Fax 329-4186

Zion Lutheran S 100/PK-8
520 E Main St 68767 402-329-4658
Stacy Johnson, prin. Fax 329-6406

Plainview, Pierce, Pop. 1,240
Plainview SD 300/K-12
PO Box 638 68769 402-582-4993
Darren Arlt, supt. Fax 582-4665
www.plainviewschools.org/
Plainview ES 100/K-6
PO Box 638 68769 402-582-3808
Patty Novicki, prin. Fax 582-4665

Zion Lutheran S 50/PK-6
PO Box 159 68769 402-582-3312
Dawn Williams, lead tchr. Fax 582-3912

Platte Center, Platte, Pop. 327
Lakeview Community SD
Supt. — See Columbus
Platte Center ES 100/K-6
PO Box 109 68653 402-246-3465
Quentin Witt, prin. Fax 246-3044

Plattsmouth, Cass, Pop. 6,376
Plattsmouth SD 1,800/PK-12
1912 Old Highway 34 68048 402-296-3361
Dr. Richard E. Hasty, supt. Fax 296-3361
www.pcsd.org
Plattsmouth ECC 200/PK-PK
1912 Old Highway 34 68048 402-296-5250
Pam Dobrovolny, dir. Fax 296-5202
Plattsmouth ES 600/K-4
1912 Old Highway 34 68048 402-296-4173
Todd Halvorsen, prin. Fax 296-2462
Plattsmouth MS 500/5-8
1912 Old Highway 34 68048 402-296-3174
Mark Smith, prin. Fax 296-2910

St. John the Baptist S 100/PK-8
500 S 18th St 68048 402-296-6230
Linda Monahan, prin. Fax 296-6961

Pleasanton, Buffalo, Pop. 340
Pleasanton SD 300/PK-12
PO Box 190 68866 308-388-2041
Jeff Vetter, supt. Fax 388-2041
pleasantonbulldogs.org
Pleasanton ES 200/PK-6
PO Box 190 68866 308-388-2041
Jeff Vetter, admin. Fax 388-2041

Plymouth, Jefferson, Pop. 409

St. Paul's Lutheran S 100/PK-8
PO Box 247 68424 402-656-4465
Andrew Danner, prin.

Polk, Polk, Pop. 321
High Plains Community SD 200/K-12
PO Box 29 68654 402-765-2271
Brian Tonniges, supt. Fax 765-2272
www.hpcstorm.org
High Plains ES at Polk 50/4-5
PO Box 29 68654 402-765-2271
Cameron Hudson, prin. Fax 765-2272
Other Schools – See Clarks

Immanuel Lutheran ES 50/K-8
2406 E 26th Rd 68654 402-765-7253
Fax 765-7253

Ponca, Dixon, Pop. 947
Ponca SD 400/K-12
PO Box 568 68770 402-755-5700
Jody Phillips, supt. Fax 755-5773
www.poncaschool.org
Ponca ES 100/K-6
PO Box 568 68770 402-755-5700
Bob Hayes, prin. Fax 755-5773
Other Schools – See Jackson

Potter, Cheyenne, Pop. 337
Potter-Dix SD 200/K-12
PO Box 189 69156 308-879-4434
Michael Williams, supt. Fax 879-4566
www.pdcoyotes.org
Other Schools – See Dix

Ralston, Douglas, Pop. 5,872
Ralston SD 3,100/PK-12
8545 Park Dr 68127 402-331-4700
Dr. Mark Adler, supt. Fax 331-4843
www.ralstonschools.org/
Ralston MS 500/7-8
8202 Lakeview St 68127 402-331-4701
Andy Parizek, prin. Fax 331-5376
Seymour ES 200/PK-6
4900 S 79th St 68127 402-331-0540
Jody Blessen, prin. Fax 331-1099
Wildewood ES 300/PK-6
8071 Ralston Ave 68127 402-331-6475
Heather Nebesniak, prin. Fax 331-9099
Other Schools – See Omaha

St. Gerald S 400/K-8
7857 Lakeview St 68127 402-331-4223
Christy Keenan, prin. Fax 331-4523

Randolph, Cedar, Pop. 943
Randolph SD 45 200/PK-12
PO Box 755 68771 402-337-0252
Jeffrey Hoesing, supt. Fax 337-0235
www.randolphpublic.org/
Randolph ES 100/PK-6
PO Box 755 68771 402-337-0385
Mary Miller, prin. Fax 337-0410

Ravenna, Buffalo, Pop. 1,347
Ravenna SD 500/PK-12
PO Box 8400 68869 308-452-3249
Dr. Ken Schroeder, supt. Fax 452-3172
www.ravennabluejays.org
Ravenna ES 200/PK-6
PO Box 8400 68869 308-452-3202
Paul Anderson, prin. Fax 452-3172

Raymond, Lancaster, Pop. 163
Raymond Central SD 500/K-12
1800 W Agnew Rd 68428 402-785-2615
Dr. Derrick Joel, supt. Fax 785-2097
www.rcentral.org
Other Schools – See Ceresco, Valparaiso

Red Cloud, Webster, Pop. 1,006
Red Cloud Community SD 200/K-12
334 N Cherry St 68970 402-746-3413
Brian Hof, supt. Fax 746-3690
www.redcloud.k12.ne.us/
Lincoln ES 100/K-6
334 N Cherry St 68970 402-746-3413
Amy Dallman, prin. Fax 746-3690

Richland, Colfax, Pop. 72
Schuyler Community SD
Supt. — See Schuyler
Richland S 50/K-8
595 Road 3 68601 402-564-6900
Heather Bebout, prin. Fax 564-6900

Roseland, Adams, Pop. 235
Silver Lake SD 200/K-12
PO Box 8 68973 402-756-6611
Mel Crowe, supt. Fax 756-6613
www.silverlakemustangs.org
Other Schools – See Bladen

Rushville, Sheridan, Pop. 866
Gordon-Rushville SD
Supt. — See Gordon
Gordon-Rushville MS 200/6-8
PO Box 590 69360 308-327-2491
Matt Stetson, prin. Fax 327-2504
Rushville ES 100/PK-5
PO Box 590 69360 308-327-2491
Scott Plummer, prin. Fax 327-2504

Saint Edward, Boone, Pop. 704
Saint Edward SD 100/K-12
PO Box C 68660 402-678-2282
Justin Frederick, supt. Fax 678-2284
stedwardpublicschool.ne.schoolinsites.com
Saint Edward ES 100/K-6
PO Box C 68660 402-678-2282
Allison Pritchard, prin. Fax 678-2284

Saint Libory, Howard, Pop. 263
Northwest SD
Supt. — See Grand Island
Saint Libory S 100/K-8
435 Saint Paul Rd 68872 308-687-6475
Michael Herzberg, prin. Fax 687-6358

Saint Paul, Howard, Pop. 2,270
Saint Paul SD 600/K-12
PO Box 325 68873 308-754-4433
John Poppert, supt. Fax 754-5374
www.stpaulpublicschools.org
Saint Paul ES 400/K-6
PO Box 325 68873 308-754-4433
Sara Paider, prin. Fax 754-5374

Sargent, Custer, Pop. 524
Sargent SD 200/K-12
PO Box 366 68874 308-527-4119
Wayne Ruppert, supt. Fax 527-3332
sargentpublicschools.org
Sargent ES 100/K-6
PO Box 366 68874 308-527-4119
Cory Grint, prin. Fax 527-3332

Schuyler, Colfax, Pop. 6,165
Schuyler Community SD 1,800/PK-12
401 Adam St 68661 402-352-2421
Dr. Daniel Hoesing, supt. Fax 352-5552
schuylercommunityschools.org
Fishers 24 S 100/K-8
1098 Road J 68661 402-352-3700
Heather Bebout, prin. Fax 352-3414
Schuyler ES 800/K-5
2404 Denver St 68661 402-352-9940
Bill Comley, prin. Fax 352-9943
Schuyler MS 300/6-8
200 W 10th St 68661 402-352-5514
Michelle Burton, prin. Fax 352-2644
Schuyler Preschool 100/PK-PK
100 E 15th St 68661 402-352-2628
Bill Comley, prin. Fax 352-5976
Other Schools – See Richland

Scotia, Greeley, Pop. 317
Central Valley SD
Supt. — See Greeley
Central Valley ES 100/PK-6
PO Box 307 68875 308-245-3201
Connie Shafer, prin. Fax 245-9133

Scottsbluff, Scotts Bluff, Pop. 14,885
Scottsbluff SD 3,100/PK-12
1722 1st Ave 69361 308-635-6200
Rick Myles, supt. Fax 635-6217
www.sbps.net
Bluffs MS 700/6-8
27 E 23rd St 69361 308-635-6270
Bert Wright, prin. Fax 635-6271
Early Childhood Learning Center 100/PK-PK
2512 2nd Ave 69361 308-635-6293
Lincoln Heights ES 300/K-5
2214 Avenue C 69361 308-635-6252
Jodi Benson, prin. Fax 635-6251
Longfellow ES 400/K-5
2003 5th Ave 69361 308-635-6262
Laurie Bahl, prin. Fax 635-6237
Roosevelt ES 300/K-5
1306 9th Ave 69361 308-635-6259
Jana Mason, prin. Fax 635-6258
Westmoor ES 400/K-5
1722 Avenue K 69361 308-635-6255
Charlotte Browning, prin. Fax 635-6233
Other Schools – See Minatare

Community Christian S 200/PK-6
511 W 14th St 69361 308-632-2230
Deirdre Amundsen, prin. Fax 632-2230
St. Agnes ES, 205 E 23rd St 69361 100/PK-5
Julie Brown, admin. 308-632-6918
Valley View SDA S 50/K-8
401 W 31st St 69361 308-632-8804
Fax 632-8804

Scribner, Dodge, Pop. 841
Scribner-Snyder SD 200/K-12
PO Box L 68057 402-664-2567
Ginger Meyer, supt. Fax 664-2708
www.sstrojans.org
Scribner ES 100/K-6
PO Box L 68057 402-664-2568
Brad Stithem, prin. Fax 664-2708

Seward, Seward, Pop. 6,883
Seward SD 1,400/PK-12
410 South St 68434 402-643-2941
Josh Fields, supt. Fax 643-2941
www.sewardpublicschools.org
Seward ES 500/PK-4
200 E Pinewood Ave 68434 402-643-2968
Jessica Dominy, prin. Fax 643-2969
Seward MS 400/5-8
2401 Karol Kay Blvd 68434 402-643-2986
Kirk Gottschalk, prin. Fax 643-6686

St. John Lutheran S 100/K-8
877 N Columbia Ave 68434 402-643-4535
Amber Fiala, prin. Fax 643-4536
St. Vincent DePaul S 100/PK-4
152 Pinewood Ave 68434 402-643-9525
Allen Brozovsky, prin. Fax 643-2594

Shelby, Polk, Pop. 707
Shelby-Rising City SD 400/PK-12
PO Box 218 68662 402-527-5946
Chester Kay, supt. Fax 527-5133
www.shelby.esu7.org
Shelby-Rising City ES 200/PK-5
PO Box 218 68662 402-527-5946
Denise Glock, prin. Fax 527-5133
Shelby-Rising City MS 100/6-8
PO Box 218 68662 402-527-5946
William Curry, prin. Fax 527-5133

Shelton, Buffalo, Pop. 1,053
Shelton SD 300/K-12
PO Box 610 68876 308-647-6742
Brian Gegg, supt. Fax 647-5233
www.shelton.k12.ne.us

Shelton ES 100/K-6
PO Box 610 68876 308-647-6558
Jeff Kenton, prin. Fax 647-5233

Shickley, Fillmore, Pop. 338
Shickley SD 50/PK-12
PO Box 407 68436 402-627-3375
Bryce Jorgenson, supt. Fax 627-2003
www.shickleypublicschool.com
Shickley S 50/PK-12
PO Box 407 68436 402-627-3375
Derek Ippensen, prin. Fax 627-2003

Sidney, Cheyenne, Pop. 6,700
Sidney SD 1,100/PK-12
1101 21st Ave 69162 308-254-5855
Jay Ehler, supt. Fax 254-5756
www.sidneyraiders.org
Central ES 100/PK-K
1101 21st Ave 69162 308-254-3642
Belinda Westfall, prin. Fax 254-1066
North Ward ES 100/3-4
1101 21st Ave 69162 308-254-2114
Belinda Westfall, prin. Fax 254-5756
Sidney MS 200/7-8
1101 21st Ave 69162 308-254-5853
Brandon Ross, prin. Fax 254-1130
South Ward ES 100/1-2
1101 21st Ave 69162 308-254-3589
Rick Meyer, prin. Fax 254-5756
West ES 200/5-6
1101 21st Ave 69162 308-254-0960
Gene Russel, prin. Fax 254-5298

Silver Creek, Merrick, Pop. 362
Twin River SD
Supt. — See Genoa
Twin River ES at Silver Creek 100/K-6
PO Box 247 68663 308-773-2233
Tod Heier, prin. Fax 773-2234

South Sioux City, Dakota, Pop. 13,178
South Sioux City SD 3,700/K-12
PO Box 158 68776 402-494-2425
Todd Strom, supt. Fax 494-3916
www.ssccardinals.org
Cardinal ES 400/K-5
820 E 29th St 68776 402-494-1662
Daniel Swatek, prin. Fax 494-1968
Covington ES 400/K-5
2116 A St 68776 402-494-4238
Laura Dandurand, prin. Fax 494-6300
Harney ES 400/K-5
1001 Arbor Dr 68776 402-494-1446
Kristin Wilshire, prin. Fax 494-6303
Lewis & Clark ES 200/K-5
801 2nd Ave 68776 402-494-1917
Benjamin Schultz, prin. Fax 494-6301
South Sioux City MS 800/6-8
3625 G St 68776 402-494-3061
Tom McGuire, prin. Fax 494-8427
Swett ES 100/K-5
2300 C St 68776 402-494-3501
Jessica Major, prin. Fax 494-6302
Other Schools – See Dakota City

St. Michael S 200/PK-8
1315 1st Ave 68776 402-494-1526
Sandy Williams, prin. Fax 494-4283

Spalding, Greeley, Pop. 485
Riverside SD 100/PK-12
124 S Ash St 68665 308-358-0640
Dr. Joan Carraher, supt. Fax 358-0211
www.riversideps.org
Spalding ES 100/PK-5
PO Box 220 68665 308-497-2431
Sarah Nordhues, prin. Fax 497-2141

Spalding Academy 100/K-12
PO Box 310 68665 308-497-2103
Amy McKay, prin. Fax 497-2105

Spencer, Boyd, Pop. 452
Boyd County SD 200/K-12
PO Box 109 68777 402-589-1333
Michael Brown, supt. Fax 589-2041
boydcounty.org
Other Schools – See Butte, Lynch

Springfield, Sarpy, Pop. 1,494
Springfield Platteview Community SD 1,100/PK-12
14801 S 108th St 68059 402-592-1300
Brett Richards, supt. Fax 597-8551
www.springfieldplatteview.org
Platteview Central JHS 200/7-8
14801 S 108th St 68059 402-339-5052
Darin Johnson, prin. Fax 339-3166
Springfield ES 300/PK-6
765 Main St 68059 402-253-2245
Kaela Heneger, prin. Fax 253-2003
Other Schools – See Omaha

Springview, Keya Paha, Pop. 242
Keya Paha County SD 100/K-12
PO Box 219 68778 402-497-3501
Dennis Peters, supt. Fax 497-4321
keyapahacountyschools.org
Pleasant View S, PO Box 219 68778 50/K-6
Luke Wroblewski, prin. 402-497-3501
Spring View ES 50/K-6
PO Box 219 68778 402-497-2621
Luke Wroblewski, prin. Fax 497-4321

Stanton, Stanton, Pop. 1,582
Stanton Community SD 500/K-12
PO Box 749 68779 402-439-2233
Dr. Michael J. Sieh Ed.D., supt. Fax 439-2270
www.scs-ne.org/
Stanton ES 200/K-6
PO Box 749 68779 402-439-2639
Mary McKeon, prin. Fax 439-2270

Staplehurst, Seward, Pop. 240

Our Redeemer Lutheran S 50/K-8
425 South St 68439 402-535-2251
Harlan Anson, prin. Fax 535-2421

Stapleton, Logan, Pop. 305
Stapleton SD 200/PK-12
PO Box 128 69163 308-636-2252
Howard Gaffney, supt. Fax 636-2618
www.stapletonschools.org
Stapleton ES 100/PK-6
PO Box 128 69163 308-636-2252
Kristine Walker, prin. Fax 636-2618

Sterling, Johnson, Pop. 476
Sterling SD 200/K-12
PO Box 39 68443 402-866-4761
Dottie Heusman, supt. Fax 866-4771
www.sterlingjets.org
Sterling ES 100/K-5
PO Box 39 68443 402-866-4761
Scott Harrington, prin. Fax 866-4771
Sterling MS 50/6-8
PO Box 39 68443 402-866-4761
Scott Harrington, prin. Fax 866-4771

Stratton, Hitchcock, Pop. 332
Dundy County-Straton SD
Supt. — See Benkelman
Stratton S 50/K-6
PO Box 324 69043 308-276-2281
Michael Rotherham, prin. Fax 276-2129

Stromsburg, Polk, Pop. 1,155
Cross County Community SD 300/PK-12
PO Box 525 68666 402-764-5521
Brent Hollinger, supt. Fax 764-8294
crosscountyschools.org
Cross County ES 200/PK-5
PO Box 525 68666 402-764-5521
Tammy Schaefer, prin. Fax 764-8294

Stuart, Holt, Pop. 586
Stuart SD 200/PK-12
PO Box 99 68780 402-924-3302
Robert Hanzlik, supt. Fax 924-3676
www.stuartbroncos.org
Stuart ES 100/PK-6
PO Box 99 68780 402-924-3302
Robert Hanzlik, prin. Fax 924-3676

Sumner, Dawson, Pop. 234
Sumner-Eddyville-Miller SD 200/PK-12
PO Box 126 68878 308-752-2925
Kevin Finkey, supt. Fax 752-2600
www.semmustangs.org
SEM ES 100/PK-6
PO Box 126 68878 308-752-2925
Kevin Finkey, supt. Fax 752-2600

Superior, Nuckolls, Pop. 1,929
Superior SD 500/PK-12
PO Box 288 68978 402-879-3258
Charles Isom, supt. Fax 879-3022
Superior ES 300/PK-6
PO Box 288 68978 402-879-3025
Douglas Hoins, prin. Fax 879-4054

Sutherland, Lincoln, Pop. 1,283
Sutherland SD 300/PK-12
PO Box 217 69165 308-386-4656
Dan Keyser, supt. Fax 386-2426
www.spssailors.org/
Sutherland ES 200/PK-6
PO Box 217 69165 308-386-4656
Josie Floyd, prin. Fax 386-2426

Sutton, Clay, Pop. 1,500
Sutton SD 400/PK-12
PO Box 590 68979 402-773-5569
Dana Wiseman, supt. Fax 773-5578
www.suttonpublicschool.org
Sutton ES 200/PK-6
PO Box 590 68979 402-773-4423
Shawn Carlson, prin. Fax 773-5578

Sutton Christian S 50/K-8
1004 E Ash St 68979 402-773-4845
David Kauk, admin.

Syracuse, Otoe, Pop. 1,933
Syracuse-Dunbar-Avoca SD 700/PK-12
PO Box P 68446 402-269-2381
Bradley Buller, supt. Fax 269-3028
www.sdarockets.org
Syracuse ES 200/PK-3
PO Box P 68446 402-269-2382
Chris Moore, prin. Fax 269-2224
Syracuse MS 300/4-8
PO Box P 68446 402-269-2388
Tim Farley, prin. Fax 269-2402

Taylor, Loup, Pop. 190
Loup County SD 100/PK-12
PO Box 170 68879 308-942-6115
Wayne Ruppert, supt. Fax 942-6248
www.loupcountyschools.org
Loup County ES 50/PK-6
PO Box 170 68879 308-942-6115
Ken Sheets, prin. Fax 942-6248

Tecumseh, Johnson, Pop. 1,665
Johnson County Central SD 600/PK-12
PO Box 338 68450 402-335-3320
Jack Moles, supt. Fax 335-3346
www.jccentral.org
Johnson County Central ES - Tecumseh 200/PK-4
PO Box 338 68450 402-335-3320
Jon Rother, prin. Fax 335-3346
Other Schools – See Cook

St. Andrew S 50/PK-6
PO Box 386 68450 402-335-2234
Kathi Mercure, lead tchr. Fax 335-2246

Tekamah, Burt, Pop. 1,725
Tekamah-Herman SD 600/PK-12
112 N 13th St 68061 402-374-2157
Dan Gross, supt. Fax 374-2155
www.tekamah.esu2.org
Tekamah ES 200/K-6
112 N 13th St 68061 402-374-2154
Ben Kreifels, prin. Fax 374-2155
Other Schools – See Herman

Thedford, Thomas, Pop. 188
Thedford SD 100/PK-12
PO Box 248 69166 308-645-2230
Gary Cooper, supt. Fax 645-2618
www.thedfordschools.org
Thedford ES 100/PK-6
PO Box 248 69166 308-645-2214
Gary Cooper, prin. Fax 645-2618

Tilden, Madison, Pop. 942
Elkhorn Valley SD 300/PK-12
PO Box 430 68781 402-368-5301
Keith Leckron, supt. Fax 368-5338
www.elkhornvalleyschools.org
Elkhorn Valley ES 200/PK-6
PO Box 430 68781 402-368-5301
Darin Hahne, prin. Fax 368-5338

Tobias, Saline, Pop. 106

Zion Lutheran S 50/PK-8
2245 County Road 400 68453 402-243-2354
Judy Bartels, prin. Fax 243-2354

Trenton, Hitchcock, Pop. 557
Hitchcock County SD 300/PK-12
PO Box 368 69044 308-334-5575
Robert Sattler, supt. Fax 334-5381
www.hcfalcons.org
Other Schools – See Culbertson

Tryon, McPherson, Pop. 153
McPherson County SD 100/K-12
PO Box 38 69167 308-587-2262
Dana Jeppson, supt. Fax 587-2571
www.mcstryon.org
Tryon ES 100/K-7
PO Box 68 69167 308-587-2262
Debra Brownfield, prin. Fax 587-2571

Utica, Seward, Pop. 859
Centennial SD 500/PK-12
PO Box 187 68456 402-534-2291
Tim DeWaard, supt. Fax 534-2291
www.centennialbroncos.org
Centennial ES 300/PK-6
PO Box 187 68456 402-534-2321
Marni Parrack, prin. Fax 534-2291

St. Paul Lutheran S 100/PK-8
1100 D St 68456 402-534-2121
Robert Brauer, prin. Fax 534-2100

Valentine, Cherry, Pop. 2,652
Todd County SD 66-1
Supt. — See Mission, SD
Klein ES 50/K-8
28959 286th Ave 69201 605-378-3854
Jan Epke, lead tchr. Fax 378-1111
Littleburg ES 50/K-8
28406 301st St 69201 605-378-3881
Erin Grant, prin. Fax 378-1109

Valentine SD 600/K-12
431 N Green St 69201 402-376-1780
Jamie Isom, supt. Fax 376-2736
www.valentinecommunityschools.org/
Goose Creek S 50/1-8
39517 Goose Creek School Dr 69201 308-748-2294
Jeff Sayer, prin. Fax 376-8096
Kennedy S 50/K-8
37919 Kennedy Rd 69201 402-376-1666
Jeff Sayer, prin. Fax 376-8096
Valentine ES 200/K-5
615 E 5th St 69201 402-376-3237
Rebecca Berry, prin. Fax 376-1032
Valentine MS 100/6-8
239 N Wood St 69201 402-376-3367
Jeff Sayer, prin. Fax 376-3386
Other Schools – See Cody, Wood Lake

Zion Lutheran S 50/PK-8
224 N Government St 69201 402-376-2745
Brad Jensen, prin. Fax 376-2720

Valley, Douglas, Pop. 1,851
Douglas County West Community SD 700/K-12
PO Box 378 68064 402-359-2583
Melissa Poloncic, supt. Fax 359-4371
www.dcwest.org/
Douglas County West ES 300/K-4
PO Box 378 68064 402-359-2151
Duane Krusemark, prin. Fax 359-5421
Other Schools – See Waterloo

Valparaiso, Saunders, Pop. 562
Raymond Central SD
Supt. — See Raymond
Valparaiso ES 100/K-6
PO Box 68 68065 402-784-3301
Shelly Dostal, prin. Fax 784-3304

Verdigre, Knox, Pop. 565
Nebraska USD 1
Supt. — See Orchard
Verdigre S 100/PK-12
201 S 3rd St 68783 402-668-2275
Chuck Kucera, prin. Fax 668-2276

Waco, York, Pop. 233

Trinity Lutheran S 50/K-8
401 Norval St 68460 402-728-5364
Philip Stern, prin. Fax 728-5433

Wahoo, Saunders, Pop. 4,441
Wahoo SD 1,000/PK-12
2201 N Locust St 68066 402-443-3051
Brandon Lavaley, supt. Fax 443-4731
www.wahooschools.org
Wahoo ES 500/K-5
2056 N Hackberry St 68066 402-443-4250
Jane Wiebold, prin. Fax 443-4916
Wahoo MS 200/6-8
2201 N Locust St 68066 402-443-3101
Marc Kaminski, prin. Fax 443-4731
Wahoo Preschool 50/PK-PK
2056 N Hackberry St 68066 402-443-4250
Fax 443-4916

St. Wenceslaus S 300/PK-6
108 N Linden St 68066 402-443-3336
Mike Weiss, prin. Fax 443-5551

Wakefield, Dixon, Pop. 1,440
Wakefield SD 400/PK-12
PO Box 330 68784 402-287-2012
Mark Bejot, supt. Fax 287-2014
www.wakefieldschools.org/
Wakefield ES 300/PK-6
PO Box 330 68784 402-287-9892
Jerad Wulf, prin. Fax 287-2014

Wallace, Lincoln, Pop. 360
Wallace SD 65 R 200/K-12
151 N Wallace Rd 69169 308-387-4323
Thomas Sandberg, supt. Fax 387-4322
whs.esu16.org
Wallace ES 100/K-6
151 N Wallace Rd 69169 308-387-4323
Thomas Sandberg, prin. Fax 387-4322

Walthill, Thurston, Pop. 761
Walthill SD 300/K-12
PO Box 3C 68067 402-846-5432
Ed Stansberry, supt. Fax 846-5029
walthweb.esu1.org
Walthill ES 200/K-6
PO Box 3C 68067 402-846-5432
Marty Slaughter, prin. Fax 846-5029

Waterloo, Douglas, Pop. 837
Douglas County West Community SD
Supt. — See Valley
Douglas County West MS 200/5-8
800 N Front St 68069 402-779-2646
Jeremy Travis, prin. Fax 779-2534

Wauneta, Chase, Pop. 575
Wauneta-Palisade SD 200/K-12
PO Box 368 69045 308-394-5700
Randy Geier, supt. Fax 394-5962
www.waunetapalisadeschools.org
Wauneta Palisade MS 50/7-8
PO Box 368 69045 308-394-5650
Joseph Frecks, prin. Fax 394-5962
Other Schools – See Palisade

Wausa, Knox, Pop. 629
Wausa SD 200/PK-12
PO Box 159 68786 402-586-2255
Bradley Hoesing, supt. Fax 586-2406
wausaweb.esu1.org
Wausa ES 100/PK-6
PO Box 159 68786 402-586-2255
Tish Hennings, prin. Fax 586-2406

Waverly, Lancaster, Pop. 3,253
Waverly SD 145 1,900/K-12
PO Box 426 68462 402-786-2321
Cory Worrell, supt. Fax 786-2799
www.district145.org
Hamlow ES 300/K-2
PO Box 426 68462 402-786-2341
Michelle Rezek, prin. Fax 786-2799
Waverly IS 300/3-5
PO Box 426 68462 402-786-5340
Craig Patzel, prin. Fax 786-2799
Waverly MS 400/6-8
PO Box 426 68462 402-786-2348
Ross Ricenbaw, prin. Fax 786-2782
Other Schools – See Eagle

Villa Marie S 50/PK-8
7205 N 112th St 68462 402-786-3625
Sr. Jeanette Rerucha, prin. Fax 488-6525

Wayne, Wayne, Pop. 5,585
Wayne SD 700/PK-12
611 W 7th St 68787 402-375-3150
Mark Lenihan, supt. Fax 375-5251
www.wayneschools.org
Wayne Early Learning Center PK-PK
803 Providence Rd 68787 402-833-1450
Misty Beair, prin.
Wayne ES 500/K-6
312 Douglas St 68787 402-375-3854
Russ Plager, prin. Fax 375-1702

St. Mary S 50/PK-6
420 E 7th St 68787 402-375-2337
Stacy Uttecht, prin. Fax 375-5782

Weeping Water, Cass, Pop. 1,042
Weeping Water SD 300/PK-12
PO Box 206 68463 402-267-2445
Dr. Ken Heinz Ed.D., supt. Fax 267-5217
www.weepingwaterps.org/
Weeping Water ES 200/PK-5
PO Box 206 68463 402-267-2435
Dawn DeTurk, prin. Fax 267-5217
Weeping Water MS 6-8
PO Box 206 68463 402-267-2445
Gary Wockenfuss, prin. Fax 267-5217

Weston, Saunders, Pop. 321

St. John Nepomucene S 100/K-6
PO Box 10 68070 402-642-5234
Linda Maly, lead tchr. Fax 642-5590

West Point, Cuming, Pop. 3,356
West Point SD 600/PK-12
1200 E Washington St 68788 402-372-5860
Bill McAllister, supt. Fax 372-5458
www.wpcadets.org
West Point ES 300/PK-4
1200 E Washington St 68788 402-372-5507
Doug Moran, prin. Fax 372-5318

Guardian Angels/Central Catholic S 200/PK-6
419 E Decatur St 68788 402-372-5328
Kate Hagemann, prin. Fax 372-3563
St. Paul Lutheran S 100/PK-8
325 N Colfax St 68788 402-372-2355
Kari Penrose, prin. Fax 372-2742

Wilber, Saline, Pop. 1,843
Wilber-Clatonia SD 600/PK-12
PO Box 487 68465 402-821-2266
Ray Collins, supt. Fax 821-3013
www.wilber-clatonia.org
Wilber ES 300/PK-6
PO Box 487 68465 402-821-2141
Christine Radcliff, prin. Fax 821-3013

Wilcox, Kearney, Pop. 354
Wilcox-Hildreth SD 200/K-12
PO Box 190 68982 308-478-5265
Carl Dietz, supt. Fax 478-5260
whfalcons.org
Wilcox-Hildreth ES 100/K-5
PO Box 206 68982 308-478-5265
Justin Patterson, prin. Fax 478-5260
Other Schools – See Hildreth

Winnebago, Thurston, Pop. 756
Winnebago SD 500/K-12
PO Box KK 68071 402-878-2224
Dan Fehringer, supt. Fax 878-2472
sites.google.com/a/winnebagok12.org/winnebagok12/
Winnebago ES 300/K-6
PO Box KK 68071 402-878-2224
Breann Haney, prin. Fax 878-2472

St. Augustine Mission S 100/K-8
PO Box GG 68071 402-878-2291
Donald Blackbird, prin. Fax 878-2760

Winside, Wayne, Pop. 419
Winside SD 200/PK-12
203 Crawford Ave 68790 402-286-4466
Michael Shoff Ed.D., supt. Fax 286-4466
www.winsidewildcats.org
Winside ES 100/PK-6
203 Crawford Ave 68790 402-286-4466
Sarah Remm, prin. Fax 286-4582

Wisner, Cuming, Pop. 1,154
Wisner-Pilger SD 400/K-12
PO Box 580 68791 402-529-3249
Chad Boyer, supt. Fax 529-3477
www.wisnerpilger.org
Wisner-Pilger ES 200/K-6
PO Box 580 68791 402-529-6465
Mark Porter, prin. Fax 529-6460

Wood Lake, Cherry, Pop. 63
Valentine SD
Supt. — See Valentine
Wood Lake S 50/K-8
PO Box 697 69221 402-967-3395
Jeff Sayer, prin. Fax 376-8096

Wood River, Hall, Pop. 1,319
Wood River Rural SD 500/K-12
PO Box 518 68883 308-583-2249
Dr. James Haley Ed.D., supt. Fax 583-2395
www.woodriver.k12.ne.us/
Wood River ES 200/K-5
PO Box 488 68883 308-583-2525
Betty Smith, prin. Fax 583-2668
Wood River Rural MS 100/6-8
PO Box 518 68883 308-583-2249
Terry Zessin, prin. Fax 583-2395

Wymore, Gage, Pop. 1,431
Southern SD 1 400/K-12
PO Box 237 68466 402-645-3326
Chris Prososki, supt. Fax 645-8049
www.southernschools.org
Other Schools – See Blue Springs

Wynot, Cedar, Pop. 165
Wynot SD 200/K-12
PO Box 157 68792 402-357-2121
Jeff Messersmith, supt. Fax 357-2524
www.wynotpublicschools.org
Wynot ES 100/K-4
PO Box 157 68792 402-357-2121
Jeff Messersmith, prin. Fax 357-2524
Wynot MS 50/5-8
PO Box 157 68792 402-357-2121
Jeff Messersmith, prin. Fax 357-2524

York, York, Pop. 7,673
York SD 1,200/PK-12
1715 N Delaware Ave 68467 402-362-6655
Dr. Mike Lucas, supt. Fax 362-6943
www.yorkpublic.org/
Preschool Learning Academy of York PK-PK
1501 Washington Ave 68467 402-362-6655
Kris Friesen, prin.
York ES 500/PK-5
1501 Washington Ave 68467 402-362-1414
Kris Friesen, prin. Fax 362-5488
York MS 300/6-8
1730 N Delaware Ave 68467 402-362-6655
Kenny Loosvelt, prin. Fax 362-6831

Emmanuel-Faith Lutheran S 100/PK-8
806 N Beaver Ave 68467 402-362-6575
Justin Bangert, admin.
St. Joseph S 100/K-8
428 N East Ave 68467 402-362-3021
Rochelle Geiger, prin. Fax 362-4067

Yutan, Saunders, Pop. 1,169
Yutan SD 400/K-12
1200 2nd St 68073 402-625-2243
Stanford Hendricks, supt. Fax 625-2812
www.yutanpublicschools.com
Yutan ES 200/K-6
902 2nd St 68073 402-625-2141
Trevor Hoegh, prin. Fax 625-2462

NEVADA

NEVADA DEPARTMENT OF EDUCATION

700 E Fifth St, Carson City 89701-5096
Telephone 775-687-9200
Fax 775-687-9101
Website http://www.doe.nv.gov/

Superintendent of Instruction Steve Canavero

NEVADA BOARD OF EDUCATION

700 E Fifth St, Carson City 89701-5096

President Elaine Wynn

PUBLIC, PRIVATE AND CATHOLIC ELEMENTARY SCHOOLS

Alamo, Lincoln, Pop. 1,045
Lincoln County SD
Supt. — See Panaca
Pahranagat Valley ES 100/PK-5
PO Box 170 89001 775-725-3351
Brian Higbee, prin. Fax 725-3355

Amargosa Valley, Nye, Pop. 350
Nye County SD
Supt. — See Tonopah
Amargosa Valley S 100/PK-8
777 E Amargosa Farm Rd 89020 775-372-5324
Rob Williams, prin. Fax 372-5314

Austin, Lander, Pop. 191
Lander County SD
Supt. — See Battle Mountain
Austin S 50/K-12
PO Box 160 89310 775-964-2467
Michelle Caramella, lead tchr. Fax 964-1206

Baker, White Pine, Pop. 68
White Pine County SD
Supt. — See Ely
Baker ES 50/3-6
PO Box 120 89311 775-234-7333
Robert Bischoff, prin. Fax 234-7157

Battle Mountain, Lander, Pop. 3,594
Lander County SD 800/PK-12
PO Box 1300 89820 775-635-2886
Dan Lantis, supt. Fax 635-5347
www.lander.k12.nv.us
Battle Mountain ES 400/PK-5
PO Box 1390 89820 775-635-2889
Lorrie Sparks, prin. Fax 635-8795
Lemaire JHS 100/6-8
PO Box 1360 89820 775-635-8114
Dr. Toby Melver, prin. Fax 635-8803
Other Schools – See Austin

Beatty, Nye, Pop. 983
Nye County SD
Supt. — See Tonopah
Beatty S 100/PK-8
PO Box 369 89003 775-553-2902
Rob Williams, prin. Fax 553-2646

Blue Diamond, Clark, Pop. 274
Clark County SD
Supt. — See Las Vegas
Blue Diamond ES 50/K-5
6 Diamond St 89004 702-875-4226
Shawn Paquette, prin. Fax 875-4053

Boulder City, Clark, Pop. 14,662
Clark County SD
Supt. — See Las Vegas
Garrett MS 500/6-8
1200 Avenue G 89005 702-799-8290
Jamey Hood, prin. Fax 799-8252
King ES 400/3-5
888 Adams Blvd 89005 702-799-8260
Anthony Gelsone, prin. Fax 799-8269
Mitchell ES 400/K-2
900 Avenue B 89005 702-799-8280
Benjamin Day, prin. Fax 799-8272

Grace Christian Academy 50/K-5
512 California Ave 89005 702-293-3536
Devon Tilman, admin. Fax 294-8050

Bunkerville, Clark, Pop. 1,271
Clark County SD
Supt. — See Las Vegas
Bowler ES 600/K-5
451 Vincen Leavitt Ave 89007 702-346-1900
Christopher Jenkins, prin. Fax 346-1914

Caliente, Lincoln, Pop. 1,102
Lincoln County SD
Supt. — See Panaca
Caliente ES 100/PK-6
PO Box 767 89008 775-726-3772
Cherry Florence, prin. Fax 726-3880

Carlin, Elko, Pop. 2,339
Elko County SD
Supt. — See Elko
Carlin S 100/K-12
PO Box 730 89822 775-754-6317
Thomas Cunningham, prin. Fax 754-2175

Carson City, Carson City, Pop. 54,098
Carson City SD 7,500/K-12
PO Box 603 89702 775-283-2000
Richard Stokes, supt. Fax 283-2090
www.carsoncityschools.com
Bordewich/Bray ES 600/K-5
110 Thompson St 89703 775-283-2400
Karen Simms, prin. Fax 283-2490
Carson MS 1,100/6-8
1140 W King St 89703 775-283-2800
Dan Sadler, prin. Fax 283-2890
Eagle Valley MS 600/6-8
4151 E Fifth St 89701 775-283-2600
Lee Conley, prin. Fax 283-2690
Empire ES 600/K-5
1260 Monte Rosa Dr 89701 775-283-1100
Susan Squires, prin. Fax 283-1190
Fremont ES 500/K-5
1511 Firebox Rd 89701 775-283-1200
Casey Gilles, prin. Fax 283-1290
Fritsch ES 600/K-5
504 Bath St 89703 775-283-1400
Dan Brown, prin. Fax 283-1490
Seeliger ES 600/K-5
2800 S Saliman Rd 89701 775-283-2200
Paula Zona, prin. Fax 283-2290
Twain ES 600/K-5
2111 Carriage Crest Dr 89706 775-283-1000
Ruthlee Caloiaro, prin. Fax 283-1090

Douglas County SD
Supt. — See Minden
Jacks Valley ES 400/K-5
701 Jacks Valley Rd 89705 775-267-3267
Pam Gilmartin, prin. Fax 267-3211

Bethlehem Lutheran S 200/PK-8
1837 Mountain St 89703 775-882-5252
Lonnie Karges, prin. Fax 882-3664
St. Teresa of Avila S 200/PK-8
567 S Richmond Ave 89703 775-882-2079
Peggy Burger, prin. Fax 882-6135

Crescent Valley, Eureka, Pop. 386
Eureka County SD
Supt. — See Eureka
Crescent Valley ES 50/PK-6
444 Fourth St 89821 775-468-0213
Bruce Williams, prin. Fax 468-2005

Dayton, Lyon, Pop. 8,727
Lyon County SD
Supt. — See Yerington
Dayton ES 500/PK-6
285 Dayton Valley Rd 89403 775-246-6262
Leslie Peters, prin. Fax 246-6264
Dayton IS 400/7-8
315 Dayton Valley Rd 89403 775-246-6250
Kevin Kranjcec, prin. Fax 246-6253
Riverview ES 400/PK-6
1200 Ferretto Pkwy 89403 775-246-6170
Barbara Harris, prin. Fax 246-6299
Sutro ES 400/PK-6
190 Dayton Village Pkwy 89403 775-246-6270
Cory Sandberg, prin. Fax 246-6276

Denio, Humboldt, Pop. 46
Humboldt County SD
Supt. — See Winnemucca
Denio S 50/K-8
PO Box 76 89404 775-941-0376
Laura Molini, prin. Fax 941-0376

Duckwater, White Pine
Nye County SD
Supt. — See Tonopah
Duckwater S 50/K-8
2 Duckwater Rd 89314 775-863-0277
Lynette Huston, lead tchr. Fax 863-0149

Dyer, Esmeralda, Pop. 249
Esmeralda County SD
Supt. — See Goldfield
Dyer ES 50/PK-8
PO Box 129 89010 775-572-3250
John Scates, lead tchr. Fax 572-3310

Elko, Elko, Pop. 17,970
Elko County SD 8,800/K-12
PO Box 1012 89803 775-738-5196
Jeff Zander, supt. Fax 738-5857
www.ecsdnv.net
Adobe MS 600/7-8
3375 Jennings Way 89801 775-738-3375
Colby Corbitt, prin. Fax 738-3860
Elko Grammar S 2 400/K-4
1055 7th St 89801 775-738-7161
Sean Stanton, prin. Fax 778-9144
Flag View IS 600/5-6
777 Country Club Dr 89801 775-738-7236
Bobby Steensen, prin. Fax 753-3876
Mountain View ES 500/K-4
3300 Argent Ave 89801 775-738-1844
Jeanne Jackson, prin. Fax 738-2561
Northside ES 400/K-4
1645 Sewell Dr 89801 775-738-7255
Krista Chamberlin, prin. Fax 738-7251
Southside ES 600/K-4
501 S 9th St 89801 775-738-3731
Mikel Lopategui, prin. Fax 738-9507
Other Schools – See Carlin, Jackpot, Owyhee, Ruby Valley, Spring Creek, Tuscarora, Wells, West Wendover

Ely, White Pine, Pop. 4,185
White Pine County SD 1,300/K-12
1135 Avenue C 89301 775-289-4851
Adam Young, supt. Fax 289-3999
www.whitepine.k12.nv.us
Norman ES 400/K-5
1001 11th St E 89301 775-289-4847
Cammie Briggs, prin. Fax 289-4850
White Pine MS 300/6-8
844 Aultman St 89301 775-289-4841
Susan Jensen, prin. Fax 289-1565
Other Schools – See Baker, Lund, Mc Gill

Eureka, Eureka, Pop. 600
Eureka County SD 200/PK-12
PO Box 249 89316 775-237-5373
Dan Wold, supt. Fax 237-5014
www.eureka.k12.nv.us
Eureka ES 100/PK-6
PO Box 249 89316 775-237-5700
Bruce Williams, prin. Fax 237-7026
Other Schools – See Crescent Valley

Fallon, Churchill, Pop. 8,201
Churchill County SD 2,500/PK-12
690 S Maine St 89406 775-423-0462
Dr. Sandra Sheldon, supt. Fax 423-9581
www.churchill.k12.nv.us
Best ES 200/2-3
750 E Williams Ave 89406 775-423-3159
Keith Boone, prin. Fax 423-0407
Churchill County MS 800/6-8
650 S Maine St 89406 775-423-7701
Scott Meihack, prin. Fax 423-8010
Lahontan ES 100/K-1
1099 Merton Dr 89406 775-423-1999
Gregg Malkovich, prin. Fax 423-8774
Northside Early Learning Center 100/PK-PK
340 Venturacci Ln 89406 775-423-3463
John Johnson, prin. Fax 423-1240
Numa ES 200/4-5
601 Discovery Dr 89406 775-428-1996
Shawn Purrell, prin. Fax 428-1699

Fallon SDA ES 50/K-8
380 E Front St 89406 775-423-4185

Logos Christian Academy 100/K-8
PO Box 952 89407 775-428-1825
Jack Beach, prin. Fax 428-6490

Fernley, Lyon, Pop. 18,657
Lyon County SD
Supt. — See Yerington
Cottonwood ES 600/PK-4
925 Farm District Rd 89408 775-575-3414
James Huckaby, prin. Fax 575-3417
East Valley ES 400/PK-4
4180 Farm District Rd 89408 775-575-3332
BillieJo Hogan, prin. Fax 575-3342
Fernley ES 400/PK-4
450 Hardie Ln 89408 775-575-3420
Chanen Cross, prin. Fax 575-3428
Fernley IS 500/5-6
320 US Highway 95A S 89408 775-575-3390
Rob Jacobson, prin. Fax 575-3394
Silverland MS 500/7-8
1100 Jasmine Ln 89408 775-575-1575
Ryan Cross, prin. Fax 575-1566

Gabbs, Nye, Pop. 259
Nye County SD
Supt. — See Tonopah
Gabbs S 50/PK-12
PO Box 147 89409 775-285-2692
David Dispensa, prin. Fax 285-2381

Gardnerville, Douglas, Pop. 5,526
Douglas County SD
Supt. — See Minden
Carson Valley MS 500/6-8
1477 US Highway 395 N 89410 775-782-2265
Bob Been, prin. Fax 782-7341
Gardnerville ES 400/K-5
1290 Toler Ave 89410 775-782-5117
Shannon Brown, prin. Fax 782-2115
Meneley ES 500/K-5
1446 Muir Dr, 775-265-3154
Becky Rugger, prin. Fax 265-7193
Pau-Wa-Lu MS 400/6-8
701 Long Valley Rd, 775-265-6100
David Whittemore, prin. Fax 265-1653
Scarselli ES 500/K-5
699 Long Valley Rd, 775-265-2222
Susan McNeall, prin. Fax 265-1218

Faith Christian Academy 100/K-8
1004 Dresslerville Rd, 775-265-0688
Jill Crandall, admin. Fax 265-0688

Gerlach, Washoe, Pop. 206
Washoe County SD
Supt. — See Reno
Gerlach S 50/K-12
555 E Sunset Blvd 89412 775-557-2326
Gia Maraccini, prin. Fax 557-2587

Goldfield, Esmeralda, Pop. 263
Esmeralda County SD 100/PK-8
PO Box 560 89013 775-485-6382
Rodriguez Broadnax, supt. Fax 572-3310
www.esmeraldacountyschools.com
Goldfield ES 50/K-8
PO Box 560 89013 775-485-6382
Denys Khalevskyy, lead tchr. Fax 485-3511
Other Schools – See Dyer, Silverpeak

Goodsprings, Clark, Pop. 218
Clark County SD
Supt. — See Las Vegas
Goodsprings ES 50/K-6
385 San Pedro St 89019 702-874-1378
Dawna O'Dea-Alexander, prin. Fax 874-1802

Hawthorne, Mineral, Pop. 3,168
Mineral County SD 500/PK-12
PO Box 1540 89415 775-945-2403
Walter Hackford, supt. Fax 945-3709
www.mineral.k12.nv.us
Hawthorne ES 200/PK-6
PO Box 1060 89415 775-945-1000
Stephanie Keuhey, prin. Fax 945-1009
Hawthorne JHS 100/7-8
PO Box 938 89415 775-945-3332
Jeff Wales, prin. Fax 945-3371
Other Schools – See Schurz

Henderson, Clark, Pop. 247,241
Clark County SD
Supt. — See Las Vegas
Bartlett ES 700/K-5
1961 Wigwam Pkwy 89074 702-799-5750
Brodie Christian, prin. Fax 799-5739
Brown JHS 900/6-8
307 Cannes St 89015 702-799-8900
Wendy Phelps, prin. Fax 799-3511
Burkholder MS 800/6-8
355 W Van Wagenen St 89015 702-799-8080
Christopher Hermes, prin. Fax 799-8088
Cox ES 600/K-5
280 Clark Dr 89074 702-799-5730
Tara Imboden, prin. Fax 799-5759
Dooley ES 500/K-5
1940 Chickasaw Dr, 702-799-8060
Mary Scialabba, prin. Fax 799-8076
Galloway ES 600/K-5
701 Skyline Rd, 702-799-8920
Maureen Langenbach, prin. Fax 799-8927
Gibson ES 500/K-5
271 Leisure Cir 89074 702-799-8730
Kristian Ryerson, prin. Fax 799-0791
Greenspun JHS 1,400/6-8
140 N Valle Verde Dr 89074 702-799-0920
Jacqueline Carducci, prin. Fax 799-0925
Hinman ES 600/K-5
450 E Merlayne Dr 89011 702-799-8990
Shannon Williamson, prin. Fax 799-0599
Kesterson ES 600/K-5
231 Bailey Island Dr 89074 702-799-6300
Jacqueline Walker, prin. Fax 799-6306
Lamping ES 700/K-5
2551 Summit Grove Dr 89052 702-799-1330
Robert Solomon, prin. Fax 799-1347
Mack ES 600/K-5
3170 Laurel Ave 89014 702-799-7760
Nancy Heavey, prin. Fax 799-8795
Mannion MS 1,600/6-8
155 E Paradise Hills Dr, 702-799-3020
Todd Petersen, prin. Fax 799-3501
McCaw ES 500/K-5
330 Tin St 89015 702-799-8930
Jennifer Furman-Born, prin. Fax 799-8910
McDoniel ES 500/K-5
1831 Fox Ridge Dr 89014 702-799-7788
Darla Richards, prin. Fax 799-0948
Miller MS 1,700/6-8
2400 Cozy Hill Cir 89052 702-799-2260
Nicole Lehman-Donadio, prin. Fax 799-1309
Morrow ES 700/K-5
1070 Featherwood Ave 89015 702-799-3550
Michelle Adams, prin. Fax 799-3556
Newton ES 600/K-5
571 Greenway Rd 89015 702-799-0500
Majorie DiCamillo, prin. Fax 799-0511
Roberts ES 800/K-5
227 Charter Oak St 89074 702-799-1320
Deborah Harbin, prin. Fax 799-1326
Sewell ES 800/K-5
700 E Lake Mead Pkwy 89015 702-799-8940
Virginia Ratliff, prin. Fax 799-8965
Smalley ES 800/K-5
304 E Paradise Hills Dr, 702-799-8090
Heather Ford-Skramstad, prin. Fax 799-8094
Taylor ES 900/K-5
2655 Siena Heights Dr 89052 702-799-6892
Nicole Coloma, prin. Fax 799-2276
Taylor ES 500/K-5
144 Westminster Way 89015 702-799-8950
Kimberly Basham, prin. Fax 799-8984
Thorpe ES 400/K-2
1650 Patrick Ln 89014 702-799-0740
Chelsea Gibson, prin. Fax 799-0775
Treem ES 400/3-5
1698 Patrick Ln 89014 702-799-8760
Yvette Tippetts, prin. Fax 799-0916
Twitchell ES 1,000/K-5
2060 Desert Shadow Trl 89012 702-799-6860
Michelle Woolridge, prin. Fax 799-6864
Vanderburg ES 900/K-5
2040 Desert Shadow Trl 89012 702-799-0540
Catherine Maggiore, prin. Fax 799-0546
Walker International ES 600/K-5
850 Scholar St, 702-799-0570
Shaun Cochran-Hall, prin. Fax 799-0537
Wallin ES 1,000/K-5
2333 Canyon Retreat Dr, 702-799-5776
Anna Hurst, prin. Fax 799-5752
Webb MS 1,800/6-8
2200 Reunion Ave 89052 702-799-1305
Paula Naegle, prin. Fax 799-1310
White MS 1,400/6-8
1661 Galleria Dr 89014 702-799-0777
Andrea Katona, prin. Fax 799-7690
Wolff ES 900/PK-5
1001 Seven Hills Dr 89052 702-799-2230
Linnea Westwood, prin. Fax 799-2257

American Heritage Academy 100/PK-12
2100 Olympic Ave 89014 702-949-5614
Laurel Beckstead, hdmstr. Fax 949-0273
Calvary Chapel Green Vlly Christian Acad 100/K-12
2615 W Horizon Ridge Pkwy 89052 702-456-2422
Bill Adams, prin. Fax 456-2515
DJ's Community Christian Academy 50/K-8
95 S Arroyo Grande Blvd 89012 702-263-9646
Debra Jo Abendroth B.A., prin. Fax 269-0670
Foothills Montessori S 300/PK-8
1401 Amador Ln 89012 702-407-0790
Karen Kolb, dir. Fax 407-0775
Green Valley Christian S 600/PK-12
711 Valle Verde Ct 89014 702-454-4056
Stephanie Smith, prin. Fax 454-6275
Henderson International S 400/PK-12
1165 Sandy Ridge Ave 89052 702-818-2100
Seth Ahlborn, hdmstr. Fax 616-2065
Lake Mead Christian Academy 600/PK-12
540 E Lake Mead Pkwy 89015 702-565-5831
Gayle Blakeley, admin. Fax 566-6206
Yeshiva Day S of Las Vegas 50/PK-8
55 N Valle Verde Dr 89074 702-838-8003

Imlay, Pershing, Pop. 171
Pershing County SD
Supt. — See Lovelock
Imlay ES 50/K-5
PO Box 86 89418 775-538-7360
Shea Murphy, prin. Fax 538-7360

Incline Village, Washoe, Pop. 8,627
Washoe County SD
Supt. — See Reno
Incline ES 400/K-5
915 Northwood Blvd 89451 775-832-4250
Daniel Zimmerman, prin. Fax 832-4255
Incline MS 200/6-8
931 Southwood Blvd 89451 775-832-4220
Sharon Kennedy, prin. Fax 832-4210

Lake Tahoe S 100/PK-8
995 Tahoe Blvd 89451 775-831-5828
Ruth Glass, head sch Fax 831-5825

Indian Springs, Clark, Pop. 947
Clark County SD
Supt. — See Las Vegas
Indian Springs S 100/K-12
PO Box 1088 89018 702-799-0932
Brian Wiseman, prin. Fax 879-3142

Jackpot, Elko, Pop. 1,175
Elko County SD
Supt. — See Elko
Jackpot S 100/K-12
PO Box 463 89825 775-755-2374
Brian Messmer, prin. Fax 755-2291

Las Vegas, Clark, Pop. 562,567
Clark County SD 310,300/PK-12
5100 W Sahara Ave 89146 702-799-5000
Pat Skorkowsky, supt. Fax 799-5125
www.ccsd.net
Adams ES 500/K-5
580 N Fogg St 89110 702-799-8800
Mark Connors, prin. Fax 799-2115
Adcock ES 600/K-5
6350 Hyde Ave 89107 702-799-4185
Wendy DeMille, prin. Fax 799-4172
Alamo ES 900/K-5
7455 El Camino Rd 89139 702-799-2590
Todd Lindberg, prin. Fax 799-2622
Allen ES 500/K-5
8680 W Hammer Ln 89149 702-799-4580
Juanita Frasier, prin. Fax 799-4586
Bailey ES 800/K-5
4525 Jimmy Durante Blvd 89122 702-799-7510
Brenton Lago, prin. Fax 799-7515
Bailey MS 1,200/6-8
2500 N Hollywood Blvd 89156 702-799-4811
Nathalie Burgess, prin. Fax 799-4807
Bass ES 900/PK-5
10377 Rancho Destino Rd, 702-799-2220
Kevin Gilmore, prin. Fax 799-1372
Batterman ES 900/K-5
10135 W Quail Ave 89148 702-799-1920
Christopher Sparrow, prin. Fax 799-1912
Beatty ES 600/K-5
8685 Hidden Palms Pkwy 89123 702-799-5700
Jennifer Lepore, prin. Fax 799-5711
Becker MS 1,300/6-8
9151 Pinewood Hills Dr 89134 702-799-4460
Amy Smith, prin. Fax 799-4470
Beckley ES 900/K-5
3223 Glenhurst Dr 89121 702-799-7700
Shannon Brown, prin. Fax 799-0792
Bell ES 800/K-5
2900 Wilmington Way 89102 702-799-5910
Jaymes Aimetti, prin. Fax 799-5916
Bendorf ES 800/K-5
3550 Kevin St 89147 702-799-4440
Joanna Gerali-Schwartz, prin. Fax 799-4319
Berkley ES K-5
9850 Copper Edge Rd 89148 702-799-2525
Diane Lewis, prin.
Bilbray ES 700/K-5
9370 Brent Ln 89143 702-799-4646
Aalya Page, prin. Fax 799-4538
Blackhurst ES K-5
11141 S Pioneer Way, 702-799-1252
Jennifer Boccia, prin.
Bonner ES 900/K-5
765 Crestdale Ln 89144 702-799-6050
Michelle Case, prin. Fax 799-6056
Booker ES 500/K-5
2277 N Martin L King Blvd 89106 702-799-4720
Marcus Mason, prin. Fax 799-4727
Bozarth ES 1,000/K-5
7431 Egan Crest Dr, 702-799-6608
Fax 799-6618
Bracken ES 500/K-5
1200 N 27th St 89101 702-799-7095
Kathleen Decker, prin. Fax 799-7102
Brinley MS 900/6-8
2480 Maverick St 89108 702-799-4550
Brett Booth, prin. Fax 799-4549
Brookman ES 700/K-5
6225 E Washington Ave 89110 702-799-7250
Darren Hall, prin. Fax 799-7241
Bryan ES 600/K-5
8050 Cielo Vista Ave 89128 702-799-1460
Kori Deal, prin. Fax 799-1469
Bryan ES 600/K-5
8255 W Katie Ave 89147 702-799-1270
Leslie Brinks, prin. Fax 799-1276
Bunker ES 700/K-5
6350 Peak Dr 89108 702-799-3420
Pauline Mills, prin. Fax 799-3476
Cadwallader MS 1,500/6-8
7775 Elkhorn Rd 89131 702-799-6692
Mindi Martinez, prin. Fax 799-4536
Cambeiro ES 600/K-5
2851 Harris Ave 89101 702-799-1700
Pamela Simone, prin. Fax 799-1706
Canarelli MS 1,900/6-8
7808 S Torrey Pines Dr 89139 702-799-1340
Monica Lang, prin. Fax 799-5715
Cannon JHS 900/6-8
5850 Euclid St 89120 702-799-5600
Warren McKay, prin. Fax 799-5644
Carl ES 700/K-5
5625 Corbett St 89130 702-799-6650
Brenda Swann, prin. Fax 799-6659
Carson ES 400/K-5
1735 D St 89106 702-799-7113
Ayoka Snipes, prin. Fax 799-0401
Cartwright ES 700/K-5
1050 E Gary Ave 89123 702-799-1350
Amy Siembida, prin. Fax 799-1356
Cashman MS 1,600/6-8
4622 W Desert Inn Rd 89102 702-799-5880
Misti Taton, prin. Fax 799-5947
Christensen ES 600/K-5
9001 Mariner Cove Dr 89117 702-799-4390
Angela Jacobs, prin. Fax 799-1413

Conners ES 800/K-5
3810 Shadow Peak St 89129 702-799-1402
Steve Piccininni, prin. Fax 799-1414
Cortez ES 900/K-5
4245 E Tonopah Ave 89115 702-799-2180
Belinda Jones, prin. Fax 799-3219
Cortney JHS 1,300/6-8
5301 E Hacienda Ave 89122 702-799-2400
David Rose, prin. Fax 799-2407
Cox ES 800/K-5
3855 Timberlake Dr 89115 702-799-4990
Laure Forsberg, prin. Fax 799-4997
Crestwood ES 700/K-5
1300 Pauline Way 89104 702-799-7890
Jacqueline Richardson, prin. Fax 799-7884
Culley ES 800/K-5
1200 N Mallard St 89108 702-799-4800
Ellen Stayman, prin. Fax 799-0611
Cunningham ES 700/K-5
4145 Jimmy Durante Blvd 89122 702-799-8780
Joyce Brooks, prin. Fax 799-0881
Dailey ES 700/K-5
2001 E Reno Ave 89119 702-799-5690
M. Olivia Egemba, prin. Fax 799-5698
Darnell ES 700/K-5
9480 W Tropical Pkwy 89149 702-799-6630
Patricia Cobb, prin. Fax 799-6651
Dearing ES 800/K-5
3046 Ferndale St 89121 702-799-7710
Christine Beaird, prin. Fax 799-8798
Decker ES 700/K-5
3850 Redwood St 89103 702-799-5920
Alice Roybal-Benson, prin. Fax 799-5924
Derfelt ES 700/K-5
1900 S Lisa Ln 89117 702-799-4370
Rick DiTondo, prin. Fax 799-4341
Deskin ES 600/K-5
4550 N Pioneer Way 89129 702-799-4600
Ron Schroder, prin. Fax 799-4609
Detwiler ES 700/K-5
1960 Ferrell St 89106 702-799-1830
Deborah Palermo, prin. Fax 799-3106
Diaz ES 700/K-5
4450 E Owens Ave 89110 702-799-2120
Rebecca Tschinkel, prin. Fax 799-2143
Diskin ES 600/K-5
4220 Ravenwood Dr 89147 702-799-5930
Fax 799-5925
Dondero ES 700/K-5
4450 Ridgeville St 89103 702-799-5940
Melonie Poster, prin. Fax 799-1210
Earl ES 900/K-5
1463 Marion Dr 89110 702-799-7310
Gina Harvey, prin. Fax 799-8817
Earl ES 700/K-5
6650 W Reno Ave 89118 702-799-8181
Belinda Schauer, prin. Fax 799-8188
Edwards ES 700/K-5
4551 Diamond Head Dr 89110 702-799-7320
Emily Petosa, prin. Fax 799-8890
Eisenberg ES 600/K-5
7770 W Delhi Ave 89129 702-799-4680
Janie McKee, prin. Fax 799-4677
Escobedo MS 1,200/6-8
9501 Echelon Point Dr 89149 702-799-4560
Stefanie Machin, prin. Fax 799-4568
Faiss MS 1,400/6-8
9525 W Maule Ave 89148 702-799-6850
Roger West, prin. Fax 799-6852
Ferron ES 500/K-5
4200 Mountain Vista St 89121 702-799-7720
Joseph Uy, prin. Fax 799-0798
Fertitta MS 1,500/6-8
9905 W Mesa Vista Ave 89148 702-799-1900
Cailin Ellis, prin. Fax 799-5688
Fine ES 900/K-5
6635 W Cougar Ave 89139 702-799-6882
Stephanie Taylor, prin. Fax 799-6889
Fong ES 800/K-5
2200 James Bilbray Dr 89108 702-799-4890
Jamie Agresti, prin. Fax 799-0694
Forbuss ES 1,100/K-5
8601 S Grand Canyon Dr, 702-799-6840
Shawn Paquette, prin. Fax 799-6844
Fremont Professional Development MS 900/6-8
1100 E Saint Louis Ave 89104 702-799-5558
Ann Schiller, prin. Fax 799-5566
French ES 400/K-5
3235 E Hacienda Ave 89120 702-799-7730
Tammy Villarreal-Crabb, prin. Fax 799-0757
Frias ES 800/K-5
5800 Broken Top Ave 89141 702-799-2298
Fax 799-6859
Fyfe ES 500/K-5
4101 W Bonanza Rd 89107 702-799-4191
Roann Triana, prin. Fax 799-0379
Garehime ES 600/K-5
3850 N Campbell Rd 89129 702-799-6000
Ryan Lewis, prin. Fax 799-6012
Garside JHS 1,200/6-8
300 S Torrey Pines Dr 89107 702-799-4245
Scarlett Perryman, prin. Fax 799-4296
Gehring ES 600/K-5
1155 E Richmar Ave 89123 702-799-6899
Amy Yacobovsky, prin. Fax 799-6891
Gibson MS 1,200/6-8
3900 W Washington Ave 89107 702-799-4700
Jennifer Jaeger, prin. Fax 799-4705
Givens ES 1,100/K-5
655 Park Vista Dr 89138 702-799-1430
Daniel Hungerford, prin. Fax 799-1485
Goldfarb ES 700/K-5
1651 Orchard Valley Dr 89142 702-799-1550
Jacqueline Gillespie, prin. Fax 799-1556
Goolsby ES 800/K-5
11175 W Desert Inn Rd 89135 702-799-2520
Kimberly Cunningham, prin. Fax 799-1233

Gragson ES 800/K-5
555 N Honolulu St 89110 702-799-7330
Lucia Valenzuela, prin. Fax 799-7339
Gray ES 500/K-5
2825 S Torrey Pines Dr 89146 702-799-5950
Elizabeth Chandler, prin. Fax 799-5058
Griffith ES 600/K-5
324 Essex Dr 89107 702-799-4200
Lori Andrews, prin. Fax 799-0319
Guinn MS 800/6-8
4150 S Torrey Pines Dr 89103 702-799-5900
Georgia Taton, prin. Fax 799-5905
Hancock ES 500/K-5
1661 Lindell Rd 89146 702-799-4205
Fax 799-4183
Harmon ES 800/K-5
5351 Hillsboro Ln 89120 702-799-7740
Shannon Schumm, prin. Fax 799-7748
Harney MS 1,800/6-8
1580 S Hollywood Blvd 89142 702-799-3240
Susan Echols, prin. Fax 799-3286
Harris ES 700/K-5
3620 S Sandhill Rd 89121 702-799-7750
Shawn Nielsen, prin. Fax 799-0785
Hayes ES 800/K-5
9620 W Twain Ave 89147 702-799-6030
Mikie Young, prin. Fax 799-4466
Heard Academy, 4497 Kell Ln 89110 K-5
Rebecca Lyon, prin. 702-799-4920
Heckethorn ES 700/K-5
5150 Whispering Sands Dr 89131 702-799-6690
Mike Houle, prin. Fax 799-6674
Herr ES 700/K-5
6475 Eagle Creek Ln 89156 702-799-8860
Kristofer Huffman, prin. Fax 799-8884
Hewetson ES 1,000/K-5
701 N 20th St 89101 702-799-7896
Ariel Villalobos, prin. Fax 799-8526
Hickey ES 800/K-5
2450 N Hollywood Blvd 89156 702-799-1899
Ronalyn Napier, prin. Fax 799-1612
Hill ES 700/K-5
560 E Eldorado Ln 89123 702-799-5720
Jennifer Reynolds, prin. Fax 799-5719
Hoggard ES 500/K-5
950 N Tonopah Dr 89106 702-799-4740
Stacey Scott-Cherry, prin. Fax 799-4884
Hollingsworth ES 700/K-5
1776 E Ogden Ave 89101 702-799-1660
Kathleen Decker, prin. Fax 799-1666
Hummel ES 800/K-5
9800 Placid St, 702-799-6810
Erica Etienne, prin. Fax 799-6803
Hyde Park MS 1,700/6-8
900 Hinson St 89107 702-799-4260
Anna Belknap, prin. Fax 799-0348
Iverson ES 800/K-5
1575 S Hollywood Blvd 89142 702-799-7260
Laura Dickensheets, prin. Fax 799-7329
Jacobson ES 600/K-5
8400 Boseck Dr 89145 702-799-4320
Amber Brookins, prin. Fax 799-4359
Jeffers ES 800/K-5
2320 Clifford St 89115 702-799-2100
Heather Lenz, prin. Fax 799-2110
Johnson JHS 1,200/6-8
7701 Ducharme Ave 89145 702-799-4480
George Anas, prin. Fax 799-4497
Jydstrup ES 600/K-5
5150 Duneville St 89118 702-799-8140
Christina Miani, prin. Fax 799-8198
Kahre ES 500/K-5
7887 W Gowan Rd 89129 702-799-4660
Sherian McGlothen, prin. Fax 799-4666
Katz ES 700/K-5
1800 Rock Springs Dr 89128 702-799-4330
Kelly Reed, prin. Fax 799-4306
Keller ES 700/K-5
5445 Cedar Ave 89110 702-799-2140
Audrey Carroll, prin. Fax 799-2145
Keller MS 1,300/6-8
301 N Fogg St 89110 702-799-3220
Debbie Brockett, prin. Fax 799-3226
Kelly ES 300/K-5
1900 J St 89106 702-799-4750
Alaina Criner, prin. Fax 799-0699
Kim ES 600/K-5
7600 Peace Way 89147 702-799-5990
Cathleen Furtado, prin. Fax 799-5979
King ES 500/K-5
2260 Betty Ln 89156 702-799-7390
Wanda Hentrow, prin. Fax 799-7299
Knudson MS 1,300/6-8
2400 Atlantic St 89104 702-799-7470
Lezlie Koepp, prin. Fax 799-0157
Lake ES 1,000/K-5
2904 Meteoro St, 702-799-5530
Larry McHargue, prin. Fax 799-0260
Lawrence JHS 1,500/6-8
4410 S Juliano Rd 89147 702-799-2540
Revelyn Smothers, prin. Fax 799-2563
Leavitt MS 1,500/6-8
4701 Quadrel St 89129 702-799-4699
Keith Wipperman, prin. Fax 799-4528
Lied MS 1,200/6-8
5350 W Tropical Pkwy 89130 702-799-4620
Derek Fialkiewicz, prin. Fax 799-4626
Long ES 800/K-5
2000 S Walnut Rd 89104 702-799-7456
Kathleen Decker, prin. Fax 799-7460
Lowman ES 700/K-5
4225 N Lamont St 89115 702-799-4930
Louis Markouzis, prin. Fax 799-4927
Lummis ES 500/K-5
9000 Hillpointe Rd 89134 702-799-4380
Lisa McKenrick, prin. Fax 799-4310

Lunt ES 600/K-5
2701 Harris Ave 89101 702-799-8360
Lisa Drakulich, prin. Fax 799-8372
Lynch ES 800/K-5
4850 Kell Ln 89115 702-799-8820
Stephanie Morgan, prin. Fax 799-8895
Mack MS 1,400/6-8
4250 Karen Ave 89121 702-799-2005
Roxanne Kelley, prin. Fax 799-2412
Manch ES 700/K-5
4351 N Lamont St 89115 702-799-4900
Anthony Nunez, prin. Fax 799-4904
Martin MS 1,500/6-8
200 N 28th St 89101 702-799-7922
Amanda Lobkowicz, prin. Fax 799-7959
Mathis ES, 4351 Lamont St 89115 K-5
Joseph Rekrut, prin. 702-799-4900
May ES 600/K-5
6350 W Washburn Rd 89130 702-799-4690
Bridget Leatherman, prin. Fax 799-4544
McMillan ES 600/K-5
7000 Walt Lott Dr 89128 702-799-4350
Antoinette Irby, prin. Fax 799-4307
McWilliams ES 700/K-5
1315 Hiawatha Rd 89108 702-799-4770
Andrea Womack, prin. Fax 799-3170
Mendoza ES 800/K-5
2000 S Sloan Ln 89142 702-799-8680
Fax 799-7464
Miller ES 700/1-5
4851 E Lake Mead Blvd 89115 702-799-8830
Lene Muth, prin. Fax 799-3259
Molasky JHS 1,300/6-8
7801 W Gilmore Ave 89129 702-799-3400
Spencer Beals, prin. Fax 799-3407
Monaco MS 1,300/6-8
1870 N Lamont St 89115 702-799-3670
Lisa Medina, prin. Fax 799-3202
Moore ES 700/PK-5
491 N Lamb Blvd 89110 702-799-3270
Cheryl Butera, prin. Fax 799-3269
Mountain View ES 500/K-5
5436 Kell Ln 89156 702-799-7350
Kimberly Ann Fiszer, prin. Fax 799-7398
Neal ES 600/K-5
6651 W Azure Dr 89130 702-799-2200
Denise Murray, prin. Fax 799-4576
Ober ES 800/PK-5
3035 Desert Marigold Ln 89135 702-799-6077
Melissa Baker, prin. Fax 799-6704
O'Callaghan MS 1,400/6-8
1450 Radwick Dr 89110 702-799-7340
Scott Fligor, prin. Fax 799-8870
O'Roarke ES 800/K-5
8455 OHare Rd 89143 702-799-6600
Kody Barto, prin. Fax 799-6612
Orr MS 900/6-8
1562 E Katie Ave 89119 702-799-5573
Anthony Nunez, prin. Fax 799-0297
Paradise Professional Development ES 600/K-5
900 Cottage Grove Ave 89119 702-799-5660
Annemarie Stover, prin. Fax 895-2038
Park ES 900/K-5
931 Franklin Ave 89104 702-799-7904
Miriam Benitez, prin. Fax 799-7949
Parson ES 400/K-5
4100 Thom Blvd 89130 702-799-4530
Chris Prosen, prin. Fax 799-4540
Petersen ES 800/K-5
3650 Cambridge St, 702-799-1120
Krista Yarberry, prin. Fax 799-3397
Piggott ES 500/K-5
9601 Red Hills Rd 89117 702-799-4450
David Hudzick, prin. Fax 799-1410
Pittman ES 600/K-5
6333 Fargo Ave 89107 702-799-4213
Kathy Konowalow, prin. Fax 799-0315
Red Rock ES 700/K-5
408 Upland Blvd 89107 702-799-4223
Stephanie Wong, prin. Fax 799-4164
Reed ES 600/K-5
2501 Winwood St 89108 702-799-4777
Cynthia Marlowe, prin. Fax 799-0680
Reedom ES 1,100/K-5
10025 Rumrill St, 702-799-5702
Kalandra Sheppard, prin. Fax 799-5722
Rhodes ES 600/K-5
7350 Tealwood St 89131 702-799-3450
Rebecca Lucero, prin. Fax 799-3456
Ries ES 1,000/K-5
9805 Lindell Rd 89141 702-799-1240
Adrian Quinonez, prin. Fax 799-1275
Robison MS 1,100/6-8
825 Marion Dr 89110 702-799-7300
Immer Ravalo, prin. Fax 799-7302
Rogers ES 700/K-5
5535 S Riley St 89148 702-799-6870
Melissa Gutierrez, prin. Fax 799-2222
Rogich MS 1,800/6-8
235 N Pavilion Center Dr 89144 702-799-6040
Susan Harrison, prin. Fax 799-6094
Ronnow ES 800/K-5
1100 Lena St 89101 702-799-7159
Chris Popek, prin. Fax 799-7164
Ronzone ES 900/K-5
5701 Stacey Ave 89108 702-799-4780
Lori McGaughey, prin. Fax 799-4788
Roundy ES 800/K-5
2755 Mohawk St 89146 702-799-5890
John Haynal, prin. Fax 799-5899
Rowe ES 600/K-5
4338 S Bruce St 89119 702-799-5540
Dustin Mancl, prin. Fax 799-0299
Rundle ES 800/K-5
425 N Christy Ln 89110 702-799-7380
Lenette Reece, prin. Fax 799-7327

Saville MS 1,500/6-8
8101 N Torrey Pines Dr 89131 702-799-3460
Sean Davis, prin. Fax 799-4511
Sawyer MS 1,300/6-8
5450 Redwood St 89118 702-799-5980
Gregory Mingo, prin. Fax 799-5969
Scherkenbach ES 600/K-5
9371 Iron Mountain Rd 89143 702-799-3401
David Sanders, prin. Fax 799-3433
Schofield MS 1,300/6-8
8625 Spencer St 89123 702-799-2290
Terri Knepp, prin. Fax 799-5717
Schorr ES 900/K-5
11420 Placid St, 702-799-1380
Jacqueline Brown, prin. Fax 799-1377
Silvestri JHS 1,600/6-8
1055 E Silverado Ranch Blvd, 702-799-2240
Merry Sillitoe, prin. Fax 799-2247
Smith ES 800/PK-5
5150 E Desert Inn Rd 89122 702-799-3700
Carey Roybal-Benson, prin. Fax 799-3711
Smith ES 500/K-5
7101 Pinedale Ave 89145 702-799-4300
Robert Hinchliffe, prin. Fax 799-4436
Snyder ES, 8951 W Ford Ave 89148 K-5
Shawn Paquette, prin. 702-799-6840
Snyder ES 900/K-5
4317 E Colorado Ave 89104 702-799-3750
Jennifer Haynal, prin. Fax 799-3723
Stanford ES 600/K-5
5350 Harris Ave 89110 702-799-7272
Ryan Merritt, prin. Fax 799-7303
Staton ES 900/PK-5
1700 Sageberry Dr 89144 702-799-6720
Lindsay Tomlinson, prin. Fax 799-6070
Steele ES 900/K-5
6995 W Eldorado Ln 89113 702-799-2201
Martha Slack, prin. Fax 799-2204
Stuckey ES 900/K-5
4905 Chartan Ave 89141 702-799-2274
Joelle Mills, prin. Fax 799-2295
Sunrise Acres ES 800/K-5
211 N 28th St 89101 702-799-7912
Margarita Gamboa, prin. Fax 799-8556
Tanaka ES 1,000/K-5
9135 W Maule Ave 89148 702-799-2504
Tony Davis, prin. Fax 799-1289
Tarkanian MS 1,600/6-8
5800 W Pyle Ave 89141 702-799-6801
Reece Oswalt, prin. Fax 799-6805
Tarr ES 600/K-5
9400 W Gilmore Ave 89129 702-799-6710
Alyson Jones, prin. Fax 799-4317
Tate ES 700/K-5
2450 Lincoln Rd 89115 702-799-7360
Sarah Popek, prin. Fax 799-7287
Thiriot ES 600/K-5
5700 W Harmon Ave 89103 702-799-2550
Sonya Holdsworth, prin. Fax 799-2545
Thomas ES 700/K-5
1560 Cherokee Ln, 702-799-5550
Dennis Kubala, prin. Fax 799-1160
Thompson ES 700/K-5
7351 N Campbell Rd 89149 702-799-3430
Shawn Halland, prin. Fax 799-3432
Tobler ES 500/K-5
6510 Buckskin Ave 89108 702-799-4500
Gary Prince, prin. Fax 799-4520
Tomiyasu ES 500/K-5
5445 Annie Oakley Dr 89120 702-799-7770
Renee Muraco, prin. Fax 799-0726
Twin Lakes ES 600/K-5
1205 Silver Lake Dr 89108 702-799-4790
Hilary Jones, prin. Fax 799-4899
Ullom ES 700/K-5
4869 Sun Valley Dr 89121 702-799-7780
Marcell Farnsworth, prin. Fax 799-0719
Vassilliadis ES K-5
215 Antelope Ridge Dr 89138 702-799-1420
Paul Catania, prin. Fax 799-1421
Vegas Verdes ES 500/K-5
4000 El Parque Ave 89102 702-799-5960
John Haynal, prin. Fax 799-5975
Von Tobel MS 1,100/6-8
2436 N Pecos Rd 89115 702-799-7280
Leonardo Amador, prin. Fax 799-7286
Ward ES 700/K-5
1555 E Hacienda Ave 89119 702-799-5650
Lea Chua, prin. Fax 799-5658
Ward ES 800/K-5
5555 Horse Dr 89131 702-799-4501
Theresa Douglas, prin. Fax 799-4503
Warren ES 700/K-5
6451 Brandywine Way 89107 702-799-4233
Jonathan Herring, prin. Fax 799-0317
Wasden ES 600/K-5
2831 Palomino Ln 89107 702-799-4239
Scott DuChateau, prin. Fax 799-4252
Wengert ES 600/K-5
2001 Winterwood Blvd 89142 702-799-8600
Kimberly Swoboda, prin. Fax 799-0116
West Prep S 1,300/K-12
1950 Pink Rose St 89106 702-799-3120
Danny Eichelberger, prin. Fax 799-1858
Whitney ES 600/K-5
5005 Keenan Ave 89122 702-799-7790
Sherrie Gahn, prin. Fax 799-0933
Wiener ES 700/K-5
450 E Eldorado Ln 89123 702-799-5760
Michael Blume, prin. Fax 799-5770
Williams ES 300/K-5
1030 J St 89106 702-799-4760
Cynthia Ireland, prin. Fax 799-4765
Woodbury MS 900/6-8
3875 E Harmon Ave 89121 702-799-7660
Lakeisha Young, prin. Fax 799-0805
Woolley ES 700/K-5
3955 Timberlake Dr 89115 702-799-4970
Darryl Wyatt, prin. Fax 799-2199
Wright ES 1,200/K-5
8425 Bob Fisk Ave, 702-799-5701
Maribel McAdory, prin. Fax 799-5708
Wynn ES 900/K-5
5655 Edna Ave 89146 702-799-8160
John Haynal, prin. Fax 799-8146
Other Schools – See Blue Diamond, Boulder City, Bunkerville, Goodsprings, Henderson, Indian Springs, Laughlin, Logandale, Mesquite, Moapa, Mt Charleston, North Las Vegas, Overton, Sandy Valley, Searchlight

---

Abundant Life Christian Academy 50/K-8
1720 J St 89106 702-647-2777
Adelson Educational Campus 500/PK-12
9700 Hillpointe Rd 89134 702-255-4500
Rabbi Joyce Raynor Ph.D., head sch Fax 255-7232
Calvary Chapel Christian S 600/PK-12
7175 W Oquendo Rd 89113 702-248-8879
John Trevino M.Ed., supt. Fax 220-8694
Calvary Christian Learning Academy 200/PK-8
2900 N Torrey Pines Dr 89108 702-655-1385
Tonya Hennington, prin. Fax 655-2932
Challenger S 300/K-8
1725 E Serene Ave 89123 702-990-7300
Challenger S 400/K-8
9900 Isaac Newton Ln 89129 702-878-6418
CornerStone Christian Academy 400/PK-8
5825 Eldora Ave Ste B 89146 702-939-5050
Linda Rosek, dir. Fax 507-0699
Dawson S 600/PK-8
10845 W Desert Inn Rd 89135 702-949-3600
Carola Wittmann Ph.D., head sch Fax 838-1818
Desert Torah Academy 200/PK-12
1312 Vista Dr 89102 702-259-1000
Faith Lutheran Academy 300/K-5
2700 S Town Center Dr 89135 702-921-2777
Diana Bartholomew, prin. Fax 921-2730
Far West Academy 100/K-12
4660 N Rancho Dr 89130 702-430-2722
Br. David Lamb, head sch
First Good Shepard Lutheran S 200/PK-5
301 S Maryland Pkwy 89101 702-382-8610
Terri Humphrey, prin. Fax 384-4168
Good Samaritan Christian Academy 100/PK-5
8425 W Windmill Ln 89113 702-407-6749
Miriam Dake, dir. Fax 407-0195
International Christian Academy 400/PK-8
8100 Westcliff Dr 89145 702-869-1109
Lisa Adams, prin. Fax 242-3206
Lamb of God Lutheran S 300/PK-5
6232 N Jones Blvd 89130 702-645-1626
Sanna Klipfel, prin. Fax 645-6031
Las Vegas Day S 900/PK-8
3275 Red Rock St 89146 702-362-1180
Las Vegas Junior Academy 100/K-10
6059 W Oakey Blvd 89146 702-871-7208
Liberty Baptist Academy 200/K-12
6501 W Lake Mead Blvd 89108 702-647-4522
John Shorer, admin. Fax 647-8083
Meadows S 900/PK-12
8601 Scholar Ln 89128 702-254-1610
Jeremy Gregersen, head sch Fax 254-2452
Merryhill S at Spanish Trail 100/K-5
5055 S Durango Dr 89113 702-889-2803
Kim Roden, prin. Fax 889-2810
Merryhill S at Summerlin 100/K-5
2160 Snow Trl 89134 702-242-8838
Montessori Visions Academy 100/PK-K
3551 E Sunset Rd 89120 702-451-9801
Lori Bossy M.Ed., head sch Fax 451-0049
Montessori Visions Academy PK-12
1905 E Warm Springs 89119 702-451-9801
Lori Bossy M.Ed., head sch Fax 451-0049
Mountain Heights Montessori 100/PK-3
3412 S Decatur Blvd 89102 702-475-8348
Mountain View Christian S 300/PK-12
3900 E Bonanza Rd 89110 702-452-1300
Dr. Crystal McClanahan, supt. Fax 452-9006
Mountain View Lutheran S 200/PK-5
9550 W Cheyenne Ave 89129 702-233-9323
Kris Schneider, prin. Fax 360-2009
Omar Haikal Islamic Academy 200/PK-8
485 E Eldorado Ln 89123 702-614-9002
Lori Wood, prin. Fax 614-8002
Our Lady of Las Vegas S 700/PK-8
3046 Alta Dr 89107 702-802-2323
Phyllis Joyce, prin. Fax 802-2324
Redeemer Lutheran S 50/PK-2
1730 N Pecos Rd 89115 702-642-5176
Michelle Hurley, prin. Fax 642-3548
St. Anne S 300/PK-8
1813 S Maryland Pkwy 89104 702-735-2586
Mary Beth Zentner, prin. Fax 735-8357
St. Elizabeth Ann Seton S 500/K-8
1807 Pueblo Vista Dr 89128 702-804-8328
Helen Silva, prin. Fax 228-8906
St. Francis de Sales S 300/K-8
1111 N Michael Way 89108 702-647-2828
Marisa Delgado, prin. Fax 647-0284
St. Viator S 700/PK-8
4246 S Eastern Ave 89119 702-732-4477
Tracy Brunelle, prin. Fax 732-4418
Solomon Schechter Day S 100/K-6
10700 Havenwood Ln 89135 702-804-1333
Southern Highlands Preparatory S 200/K-8
11500 Southern Highlands Pk 89141 702-617-6030
Spring Valley Christian Academy 50/K-12
7570 Peace Way 89147 702-873-3216
Word of Life Christian Academy 300/PK-12
3520 N Buffalo Dr 89129 702-645-1180
Rev. Kelly Marchello, prin. Fax 396-0293

Laughlin, Clark, Pop. 7,092
Clark County SD
Supt. — See Las Vegas
Bennett ES 300/K-5
2750 Needles Hwy 89029 702-298-3378
Dawn Estes, prin. Fax 299-0405

Logandale, Clark
Clark County SD
Supt. — See Las Vegas
Bowler ES 600/K-5
1415 W Whipple Rd 89021 702-398-3233
Shawna Jessen, prin. Fax 398-3278

Lovelock, Pershing, Pop. 1,824
Pershing County SD 700/K-12
PO Box 389 89419 775-273-7819
Russell Fecht, supt. Fax 273-2668
www.pershing.k12.nv.us
Lovelock ES 300/K-5
PO Box 621 89419 775-273-2176
Ted Wells, prin. Fax 273-1250
Pershing County MS 200/6-8
PO Box 1020 89419 775-273-1200
Shea Murphy, prin. Fax 273-3191
Other Schools – See Imlay

Lund, White Pine, Pop. 277
White Pine County SD
Supt. — See Ely
Lund ES 100/K-6
PO Box 129 89317 775-238-5200
Robert Bischoff, prin. Fax 238-0208

Mc Dermitt, Humboldt, Pop. 172
Humboldt County SD
Supt. — See Winnemucca
Mc Dermitt ES 100/K-6
PO Box 98 89421 775-532-8761
Doc Welter, prin. Fax 532-8017

Mc Gill, White Pine, Pop. 1,125
White Pine County SD
Supt. — See Ely
Mc Gill ES 100/K-5
PO Box 1296 89318 775-235-7722
Robert Bischoff, prin. Fax 235-7036

Mesquite, Clark, Pop. 15,069
Clark County SD
Supt. — See Las Vegas
Hughes MS 600/6-8
550 Hafen Ln 89027 702-346-3250
Maurice Perkins, prin. Fax 346-3095
Virgin Valley ES 700/K-5
200 Woodbury Ln 89027 702-346-5761
Cathy Davis, prin. Fax 346-5049

Minden, Douglas, Pop. 2,948
Douglas County SD 5,100/K-12
1638 Mono Ave 89423 775-782-5134
Teri White, supt. Fax 782-8562
www.dcsd.k12.nv.us
Minden ES 300/K-5
1170 Baler St 89423 775-782-5510
Ken Stoll, prin. Fax 782-5551
Pinon Hills ES 400/K-5
1479 Stephanie Way 89423 775-267-3622
Jason Reid, prin. Fax 267-3846
Other Schools – See Carson City, Gardnerville, Zephyr Cove

Grace Christian Academy 100/K-8
2320 Heybourne Rd 89423 775-782-7811
Rachela Fazio, prin. Fax 782-0866

Moapa, Clark
Clark County SD
Supt. — See Las Vegas
Perkins ES 200/K-5
PO Box 189 89025 702-864-2444
Holly Lee, prin. Fax 864-2566

Mt Charleston, Clark
Clark County SD
Supt. — See Las Vegas
Lundy ES 50/K-5
4405 Yellow Pine Ave, 702-872-5438
Brian Wiseman, prin. Fax 872-0510

North Las Vegas, Clark, Pop. 207,375
Clark County SD
Supt. — See Las Vegas
Antonello ES 600/K-5
1101 W Tropical Pkwy 89031 702-799-8380
Domenic Russo, prin. Fax 799-8355
Bridger MS 1,400/6-8
2505 N Bruce St 89030 702-799-7185
Laura Willis, prin. Fax 799-7074
Bruner ES 700/K-5
4289 Allen Ln 89032 702-799-0620
Catherine Conger, prin. Fax 799-0610
Cahlan ES 800/K-5
2801 Fort Sumter Dr 89030 702-799-7103
Amy Negrete, prin. Fax 799-0406
Cozine ES 800/K-5
5335 Coleman St 89031 702-799-0690
Samuel Rado, prin. Fax 799-0665
Craig ES 800/K-5
2637 E Gowan Rd 89030 702-799-4910
Randy Cheung, prin. Fax 799-4942
Cram MS 1,600/6-8
1900 W Deer Springs Way 89084 702-799-7020
Gary Bugash, prin. Fax 799-8346
Dickens ES 700/K-5
5550 Milan Peak St, 702-799-3878
Carolyn King, prin. Fax 799-3871
Duncan ES 600/K-5
250 W Rome Blvd 89084 702-799-7100
Amy Manning, prin. Fax 799-7094

Elizondo ES 800/K-5
4865 Goldfield St 89031 702-799-1730
Keith France, prin. Fax 799-1722
Findlay MS 1,500/6-8
333 W Tropical Pkwy 89031 702-799-3160
Brenda Caszatt, prin. Fax 799-3169
Fitzgerald ES 400/K-5
2651 Revere St 89030 702-799-0600
Frederick Watson, prin. Fax 799-7045
Gilbert ES 500/K-5
2101 W Cartier Ave 89032 702-799-4730
Kimberly Daniels, prin. Fax 799-4728
Goynes ES 900/K-5
3409 W Deer Springs Way 89084 702-799-1770
Stacie Nelson, prin. Fax 799-1721
Guy ES 600/K-5
4028 W La Madre Way 89031 702-799-3150
Wendy Garrett, prin. Fax 799-3156
Hayden ES 700/K-5
150 W Rome Blvd 89084 702-799-3870
Jason Schrock, prin. Fax 799-3877
Herron ES 900/K-5
2421 Kenneth Rd 89030 702-799-7123
Judy Jordahl, prin. Fax 799-8337
Johnston MS 1,400/6-8
5855 Lawrence St, 702-799-7001
Demetrius Johnson, prin. Fax 799-7010
Lincoln ES 700/K-5
3010 Berg St 89030 702-799-7133
Jennifer Newton, prin. Fax 799-1724
Mackey ES 500/K-5
2726 Englestad St 89030 702-799-7139
Kemala Conley-Washington, prin. Fax 799-7132
Martinez ES 600/PK-5
350 Judson Ave 89030 702-799-3800
Timothy Adams, prin. Fax 799-3804
McCall ES 400/K-5
800 E Carey Ave 89030 702-799-7149
Ana De Beauvernet, prin. Fax 799-7043
Perkins ES 700/K-5
3700 Shadow Tree St 89032 702-799-1805
Rene Cazier, prin. Fax 799-1814
Priest ES 800/K-5
4150 Fuselier Dr 89032 702-799-6200
Pam Hays, prin. Fax 799-4787
Scott ES 900/K-5
5700 N Bruce St, 702-799-1766
Dana Roseman, prin. Fax 799-1769
Sedway MS 1,500/6-8
3465 Engelstad St 89032 702-799-3880
Chareece Sheppard, prin. Fax 799-1785
Simmons ES 700/K-5
2328 Silver Clouds Dr 89031 702-799-1891
Elizabeth Katten, prin. Fax 799-1812
Smith MS 900/6-8
1301 E Tonopah Ave 89030 702-799-7080
Henry Rodda, prin. Fax 799-7195
Squires ES 800/K-5
1312 E Tonopah Ave 89030 702-799-7169
Barry Bonsacker, prin. Fax 799-7109
Swainston MS 1,100/6-8
3500 W Gilmore Ave 89032 702-799-4860
Lori Desiderato, prin. Fax 799-4806
Tartan ES 600/K-5
3030 E Tropical Pkwy, 702-799-4701
Pedro Garcia, prin. Fax 799-4707
Triggs ES 800/K-5
4470 W Rome Blvd 89084 702-799-1890
Sheila Cooper, prin. Fax 799-1865
Watson ES 700/K-5
5845 N Commerce St 89031 702-799-7040
Traci Holloway, prin. Fax 799-7028
Wilhelm ES 600/K-5
609 W Alexander Rd 89032 702-799-1750
Debra Jones, prin. Fax 799-1756
Williams ES 900/K-5
3000 E Tonopah Ave 89030 702-799-7179
Kristie Cole, prin. Fax 799-8341
Wolfe ES 600/K-5
4027 W Washburn Rd 89031 702-799-1860
Jennifer French, prin. Fax 799-1869

St. Christopher S 200/K-8
1840 N Bruce St 89030 702-657-8008
Christopher Zunno, prin. Fax 642-2461
University Baptist Academy 100/K-12
3770 W Washburn Rd 89031 702-732-3385

Orovada, Humboldt, Pop. 152
Humboldt County SD
Supt. — See Winnemucca
Kings River S 50/K-8
134 Kings River Rd 89425 775-859-0352
Michelle Garrison, prin. Fax 859-0352
Orovada S 50/K-8
PO Box 85 89425 775-272-3333
Lisa Weber, prin. Fax 272-3333

Overton, Clark
Clark County SD
Supt. — See Las Vegas
Lyon MS 400/6-8
179 S Andersen St 89040 702-397-8610
Kenneth Paul, prin. Fax 397-2754

Owyhee, Elko, Pop. 941
Elko County SD
Supt. — See Elko
Owyhee S 100/K-12
PO Box 100 89832 775-757-3400
Steve Cook, prin. Fax 757-3663

Pahrump, Nye, Pop. 35,299
Nye County SD
Supt. — See Tonopah
Clarke MS 900/6-8
4201 N Blagg Rd 89060 775-727-5546
Tim Wombaker, prin. Fax 727-7104

Floyd ES 400/PK-5
6181 Jane Ave 89061 775-751-4889
Jeff Skelton, prin. Fax 751-5904
Hafen ES 400/K-5
7120 Hafen Ranch Rd 89061 775-751-4688
Ken Weaver, prin. Fax 751-4686
Johnson ES 500/PK-5
900 Jack Rabbit St 89048 775-727-6619
Charles O'Connor, prin. Fax 727-7885
Manse ES 500/PK-5
4881 N Lola Ln 89060 775-727-5252
Kyle Lindberg, prin. Fax 727-1526

Community Christian Academy 100/K-9
PO Box 280 89041 775-751-9777
Renee Bell, admin. Fax 727-7548

Panaca, Lincoln, Pop. 955
Lincoln County SD 900/PK-12
PO Box 118 89042 775-728-8000
Pam Teel, supt. Fax 728-4435
lcsdnv.com
Meadow Valley MS 100/7-8
PO Box 567 89042 775-728-4655
Cody Christensen, prin. Fax 728-4302
Panaca ES 100/PK-6
PO Box 307 89042 775-728-4446
Pete Peterson, prin. Fax 728-4470
Other Schools – See Alamo, Caliente, Pioche

Paradise Valley, Humboldt, Pop. 109
Humboldt County SD
Supt. — See Winnemucca
Paradise Valley S 50/K-8
PO Box 33 89426 775-578-3382
Robert Lindsay, prin. Fax 578-3385

Pioche, Lincoln, Pop. 989
Lincoln County SD
Supt. — See Panaca
Pioche ES 100/PK-6
PO Box 30 89043 775-962-5832
Stephanie Vincent, prin. Fax 962-5257

Reno, Washoe, Pop. 217,361
Washoe County SD 63,900/PK-12
PO Box 30425 89520 775-348-0200
Traci Davis, supt. Fax 348-0304
www.washoeschools.net
Anderson ES 400/K-6
1055 Berrum Ln 89509 775-689-2500
Michael Martindale, prin. Fax 689-2622
Beck ES 600/K-6
1900 Sharon Way 89509 775-689-2520
Erin Lane, prin. Fax 689-2598
Billinghurst MS 700/7-8
6685 Chesterfield Ln 89523 775-746-5870
M. Hutchinson, prin. Fax 746-5875
Booth ES 400/K-6
1450 Stewart St 89502 775-333-5140
Yuen Fong, prin. Fax 333-6053
Brown ES 800/K-6
13815 Spelling Ct, 775-851-5600
Angie Bryan, prin. Fax 851-5605
Cannan ES 800/K-6
2450 Cannan St 89512 775-353-5750
Dr. Kelly Humphreys, prin. Fax 353-5752
Caughlin Ranch ES 600/K-6
4885 Village Green Pkwy, 775-689-2600
Melissa Thoroughman, prin. Fax 689-2535
Clayton Pre-AP Academy 600/7-8
1295 Wyoming Ave 89503 775-746-5860
Bruce Meissner, prin. Fax 746-5864
Cold Springs MS 700/5-8
18235 Cody Ct, 775-677-5433
Roberta Duval, prin. Fax 677-5439
Corbett ES 500/K-6
1901 Villanova Dr 89502 775-333-5180
Denise Dufrene, prin. Fax 333-5184
Depoali MS 1,100/6-8
9300 Wilbur May Pkwy, 775-852-6700
Joye Ancina, prin. Fax 852-6701
Desert Heights ES 400/K-6
13948 Mount Bismark St 89506 775-677-5444
Vickie Duty, prin. Fax 677-5448
Dodson ES 400/K-6
4355 Houston Dr 89502 775-689-2530
Don McHenry, prin. Fax 689-2531
Donner Springs ES 600/K-6
5125 Escuela Way 89502 775-689-2626
Sara Cunningham, prin. Fax 689-2628
Doublo Diamond ES 800/K-6
1200 S Meadows Pkwy, 775-850-6212
Mike Dixon, prin. Fax 850-6215
Duncan STEM Academy 400/K-5
1200 Montello St 89512 775-333-5190
Dave Keller, prin. Fax 333-5193
Echo Loder ES 600/K-6
600 Apple St 89502 775-689-2540
Dina Ciaramella, prin. Fax 689-2542
Elmcrest ES 400/K-6
855 McDonald Dr 89503 775-746-5850
Ann Dickson, prin. Fax 746-5852
Gomes ES 500/K-4
3870 Limkin St, 775-677-5440
Sean Whisler, prin. Fax 677-5435
Gomm ES 400/K-6
4000 Mayberry Dr, 775-333-5000
John Sutherland, prin. Fax 333-5002
Hidden Valley ES 500/K-6
2115 Alphabet Dr 89502 775-857-3150
Dr. Robin Olson, prin. Fax 857-3153
Huffaker ES 500/K-6
980 Wheatland Rd 89511 775-689-2510
Susan Novelli, prin. Fax 689-2623
Hunsburger ES 800/K-6
2505 Crossbow Ct 89511 775-851-7095
Molly Lauf, prin. Fax 850-6204

Hunter Lake ES 300/K-6
909 Hunter Lake Dr 89509 775-333-5040
Amanda McWilliams, prin. Fax 333-5098
Lemelson ES 400/K-6
2001 Soaring Eagle Dr 89512 775-333-5080
Jonna AuCoin, prin. Fax 333-5008
Lemmon Valley ES 600/K-6
255 W Patrician Dr 89506 775-677-5460
Michael Lansing, prin. Fax 677-5462
Lenz ES 500/K-6
2500 Homeland Dr 89511 775-851-5620
Bill Burt, prin. Fax 851-7080
Loder ES K-6
600 Apple St 89502 775-689-2540
Dina Ciaramella, prin. Fax 689-2542
Mathews ES 600/K-6
2750 Elementary Dr 89512 775-353-5950
Heidi Gavrilles, prin. Fax 353-5954
Melton ES 600/K-5
6575 Archimedes Ln 89523 775-746-7440
Kathy Gage, prin. Fax 746-7443
Mount Rose ES 300/K-6
915 Lander St 89509 775-333-5030
Kristen Brown, prin. Fax 333-5032
O'Brien STEM Academy 700/7-8
10500 Stead Blvd 89506 775-677-5420
Mary Basso, prin. Fax 677-5423
Peavine ES 400/PK-5
1601 Grandview Ave 89503 775-746-5840
Alan Holmes, prin. Fax 746-5841
Pine MS 900/7-8
4800 Neil Rd 89502 775-689-2550
Brad Boudreau, prin. Fax 689-2539
Pleasant Valley ES 400/K-6
405 Surrey Dr, 775-849-0255
Derek Cordell, prin. Fax 849-2761
Silver Lake ES 600/K-5
8719 Red Baron Blvd 89506 775-677-5400
Angela Flora, prin. Fax 677-5406
Smith ES 700/K-6
1070 Beckwourth Dr 89506 775-677-5410
Arch Ruth, prin. Fax 677-5413
Smithridge STEM Academy 700/K-5
4801 Neil Rd 89502 775-689-2560
Tom Wortman, prin. Fax 689-2507
Stead ES 700/K-6
10580 Stead Blvd 89506 775-677-5480
Dr. Sue Egloff, prin. Fax 677-5483
Swope MS 700/7-8
901 Keele Dr 89509 775-333-5330
Desiree Mandeville, prin. Fax 333-5083
Towles ES 400/K-6
2800 Kings Row 89503 775-746-5820
Rhonda Van Deusen, prin. Fax 746-5822
Traner MS 600/7-8
1700 Carville Dr 89512 775-333-5130
Tiffany McMaster, prin Fax 333-5135
Vaughn MS 600/7-8
1200 Bresson Ave 89502 775-333-5160
Dr. Victoria Roybal, prin. Fax 333-5118
Veterans Memorial STEM Academy 400/K-6
1200 Locust St 89502 775-333-5090
Jenni Anderson, prin. Fax 333-5092
Warner ES 400/K-6
3075 Heights Dr 89503 775-746-5830
Don Angotti, prin. Fax 746-5899
Westergard ES 700/K-5
1785 Ambassador Dr 89523 775-746-5800
Katie Weir, prin. Fax 746-5803
Winnemucca ES 600/K-6
1349 Backer Way 89523 775-746-5810
Dr. Susan Frank, prin. Fax 746-5813
Other Schools – See Gerlach, Incline Village, Sparks, Sun Valley, Verdi, Wadsworth

---

Brookfield S 200/PK-8
6800 S McCarran Blvd 89509 775-825-0257
Katie Johnson, dir. Fax 825-3463
Church Academy 50/1-12
1205 N McCarran Blvd 89512 775-329-5848
Dan Moriarty, admin. Fax 329-3360
Holy Child Early Learning Center K-K
440 Reno Ave 89509 775-329-2979
Marie Short, prin. Fax 329-8537
King's Academy 100/K-7
3195 Everett Dr 89503 775-747-1217
Little Flower S 300/K-8
1300 Casazza Dr 89502 775-323-2931
Vicki Rossolo, prin. Fax 323-2997
Mountain View Montessori S 200/PK-6
565 Zolezzi Ln 89511 775-852-6162
Nevada Sage Waldorf S 50/PK-6
565 Reactor Way 89502 775-348-6622
Our Lady of the Snows S 300/K-8
1125 Lander St 89509 775-322-2773
Tim Fuetsch, prin. Fax 322-0827
Riverview Christian Academy 50/K-8
7125 W 4th St 89523 775-322-0714
St. Albert the Great S 300/K-8
1255 Saint Alberts Dr 89503 775-747-3392
Pat Perry, prin. Fax 747-6296

Round Mountain, Nye
Nye County SD
Supt. — See Tonopah
Round Mountain ES 200/PK-5
PO Box 1429 89045 775-377-2236
James Fitch, prin. Fax 377-2354

Ruby Valley, Elko, Pop. 37
Elko County SD
Supt. — See Elko
Ruby Valley S 50/1-8
HC 60 Box 620 89833 775-779-2289
Gary Kimber, prin. Fax 779-2289

Sandy Valley, Clark, Pop. 1,978
Clark County SD
Supt. — See Las Vegas
Sandy Valley S 100/K-12
HC 31 Box 111 89019 702-799-0935
Dawna O'Dea-Alexander, prin. Fax 723-1802

Schurz, Mineral, Pop. 639
Mineral County SD
Supt. — See Hawthorne
Schurz ES 100/PK-6
PO Box 70 89427 775-773-2323
Mike Domagala, prin. Fax 773-2275

Searchlight, Clark, Pop. 525
Clark County SD
Supt. — See Las Vegas
Reid ES 50/K-5
300 Michael Wendell Way 89046 702-297-1224
Benjamin Day, prin. Fax 297-1767

Silverpeak, Esmeralda, Pop. 106
Esmeralda County SD
Supt. — See Goldfield
Silverpeak ES 50/K-8
PO Box 218 89047 775-937-2261
Rob Valentine, lead tchr. Fax 937-2308

Silver Springs, Lyon, Pop. 5,112
Lyon County SD
Supt. — See Yerington
Silver Stage ES 600/PK-8
3900 W Spruce Ave 89429 775-577-5050
Mindi Hammill, prin. Fax 577-5053
Silver Stage MS 5-8
3800 W Spruce St 89429 775-577-5050
Amber Taylor, prin.

Smith, Lyon, Pop. 1,033
Lyon County SD
Supt. — See Yerington
Smith Valley S 200/K-12
20 Day Ln 89430 775-465-2332
Kathy Bomba-Edgerton, prin. Fax 465-2681

Sparks, Washoe, Pop. 87,304
Storey County SD
Supt. — See Virginia City
Hillside ES 100/PK-5
1250 Peri Ranch Rd 89434 775-342-0400
Rick Taylor, prin. Fax 342-0785

Washoe County SD
Supt. — See Reno
Beasley ES 700/K-6
2100 Canyon Pkwy 89436 775-626-5250
MaryEllen Arrascada, prin. Fax 626-5254
Diedrichsen ES 400/K-6
1735 Del Rosa Way 89434 775-353-5730
Megan Waugh, prin. Fax 353-5719
Dilworth MS 600/7-8
255 Prater Way 89431 775-353-5740
Laura Petersen, prin. Fax 353-5584
Drake ES 300/K-6
2755 4th St 89431 775-353-5510
Dr. Nichole Truax, prin. Fax 353-5512
Dunn ES 500/K-6
1135 O Callaghan Dr 89434 775-353-5520
Allison Fannin, prin. Fax 353-5522
Greenbrae ES 400/K-6
1840 4th St 89431 775-353-5530
Dr. Rose Kane, prin. Fax 353-5596
Hall ES 700/K-6
185 Shelby Dr 89436 775-425-7755
Lea Anderson, prin. Fax 425-7756
Juniper ES 500/K-6
225 Queen Way 89431 775-353-5540
Kim Polson, prin. Fax 353-5759
Lincoln Park ES 400/K-6
201 Lincoln Way 89431 775-353-5570
Tracy Fisher, prin. Fax 353-5797
Maxwell ES 600/K-6
2300 Rock Blvd 89431 775-353-5580
Tierney Cahill, prin. Fax 353-5763
Mendive MS 1,000/7-8
1900 Whitewood Dr 89434 775-353-5990
Brandon Bringhurst, prin. Fax 353-5994
Mitchell ES 400/K-6
1216 Prater Way 89431 775-353-5590
Teri Vaughn, prin. Fax 353-5739
Moss ES 500/K-6
2200 Primio Way 89434 775-353-5507
Colbee Riordan, prin. Fax 353-5905
Risley ES 500/K-6
1900 Sullivan Ln 89431 775-353-5760
Amy Wright, prin. Fax 353-5762
Sepulveda ES 700/K-6
5075 Ion Dr 89436 775-626-5257
Dr. Doug Parry, prin. Fax 626-5258
Shaw MS 1,000/7-8
600 Eagle Canyon Dr, 775-425-7777
Gina Leonhard, prin. Fax 425-7779
Smith ES 300/K-6
1925 F St 89431 775-353-5720
Debbie O'Gorman, prin. Fax 353-5927
Spanish Springs ES 700/K-6
100 Marilyn Mae Dr, 775-425-7710
James Verdi, prin. Fax 425-7707
Sparks MS 700/7-8
2275 18th St 89431 775-353-5770
Stacey Ting-Senini, prin. Fax 353-5585
Taylor ES 700/K-6
252 Egyptian Dr, 775-425-7700
Karen Wallis, prin. Fax 425-7704
Van Gorder ES 800/K-6
7650 Campello Dr 89436 775-425-7722
Jennifer Van Tress, prin. Fax 425-7725
Whitehead ES 500/K-6
3570 Waterfall Dr 89434 775-626-5200
Kelly Dominguez, prin. Fax 626-5202

Excel Christian S 100/PK-12
850 Baring Blvd 89434 775-356-9995
Lisa Cross, prin. Fax 356-9527

Spring Creek, Elko, Pop. 12,111
Elko County SD
Supt. — See Elko
Mound Valley S 50/1-8
HC 30 Box 348 89815 775-744-4382
Gary Kimber, prin.
Sage ES 600/K-5
208 Boyd Kennedy Rd 89815 775-738-4711
Ray Smith, prin. Fax 753-4154
Spring Creek ES 800/K-5
7 Licht Pkwy 89815 775-753-6881
Candice Tournahu, prin. Fax 753-1074
Spring Creek MS 700/6-8
14650 Lamoille Hwy 89815 775-777-1688
Jon Foss, prin. Fax 777-1738

Sun Valley, Washoe, Pop. 18,768
Washoe County SD
Supt. — See Reno
Allen ES 600/K-6
5155 McGuffey Rd 89433 775-674-4430
Mischelle Bain, prin. Fax 674-4433
Bennett ES 500/K-6
5900 Sidehill Dr 89433 775-674-4444
Gladis Diaz, prin. Fax 674-4451
Palmer ES 500/K-6
5890 Klondike Dr 89433 775-674-4400
Reagan Virgil, prin. Fax 674-4417
Sun Valley ES 600/K-6
5490 Leon Dr 89433 775-674-4420
Prim Walters, prin. Fax 674-4423

Tonopah, Nye, Pop. 2,418
Nye County SD 4,800/PK-12
PO Box 113 89049 775-482-6258
Dale Norton, supt. Fax 482-8573
www.nye.k12.nv.us
Tonopah Elementary MS 100/PK-8
PO Box 1749 89049 775-482-6644
Scott Moore, prin. Fax 482-5717
Other Schools – See Amargosa Valley, Beatty, Duckwater, Gabbs, Pahrump, Round Mountain

Tuscarora, Elko
Elko County SD
Supt. — See Elko
Independence Valley S 50/1-8
HC 32 Box 110 89834 775-756-6508
Gary Kimber, prin. Fax 756-5598

Verdi, Washoe, Pop. 1,384
Washoe County SD
Supt. — See Reno
Verdi ES 200/K-6
PO Box 309 89439 775-345-8100
Susan Kehoe, prin. Fax 345-7277

Virginia City, Storey, Pop. 832
Storey County SD 400/PK-12
PO Box C 89440 775-847-0983
Todd Hess, supt. Fax 847-0989
www.storey.k12.nv.us
Gallagher ES 100/PK-5
PO Box C 89440 775-847-0977
Patrick Beckwith, prin. Fax 847-0938
Virginia City MS 100/6-8
PO Box C 89440 775-847-0980
Rick Taylor, prin. Fax 847-0913
Other Schools – See Sparks

Wadsworth, Washoe, Pop. 819
Washoe County SD
Supt. — See Reno
Natchez ES 200/K-6
PO Box 130 89442 775-351-1902
Rick Taylor, prin. Fax 575-1888

Wells, Elko, Pop. 1,257
Elko County SD
Supt. — See Elko
Wells S 100/K-12
PO Box 338 89835 775-752-3837
Shaun Taylor, prin. Fax 752-2470

West Wendover, Elko, Pop. 4,333
Elko County SD
Supt. — See Elko
West Wendover ES 600/K-6
PO Box 2400 89883 775-664-3100
Patrick DiSpirito, prin. Fax 664-2343
West Wendover MS 200/7-8
PO Box 5100 89883 775-664-4406
Michael Condie, prin. Fax 664-4408

Winnemucca, Humboldt, Pop. 7,277
Humboldt County SD 3,400/K-12
310 E 4th St 89445 775-623-8100
Dr. David Jensen, supt. Fax 623-8102
www.hcsdnv.com
French Ford MS 500/5-6
5495 Palisade Dr 89445 775-623-8200
Robert Lindsay, prin. Fax 623-8210
Grass Valley ES 400/K-4
6465 Grass Valley Rd 89445 775-623-8150
Byron Jeppsen, prin. Fax 623-8152
Sonoma Heights ES 500/K-4
1500 Melarkey St 89445 775-623-8165
Amy Nelson, prin. Fax 623-8194
Winnemucca Grammer S 400/K-4
522 Lay St 89445 775-623-8160
Jonathan Reynolds, prin. Fax 623-8176
Winnemucca JHS 500/7-8
451 Reinhart St 89445 775-623-8120
Janet Kennedy, prin. Fax 623-8208
Other Schools – See Denio, Mc Dermitt, Orovada, Paradise Valley

Yerington, Lyon, Pop. 2,993
Lyon County SD 8,100/PK-12
25 E Goldfield Ave 89447 775-463-6800
Wayne Workman, supt. Fax 463-6808
www.lyoncsd.org
Yerington ES 500/PK-4
112 N California St 89447 775-463-6844
Heather Moyle, prin. Fax 463-6850
Yerington IS 400/5-8
215 Pearl St 89447 775-463-6833
Sean Moyle, prin. Fax 463-6840
Other Schools – See Dayton, Fernley, Silver Springs, Smith

Zephyr Cove, Douglas, Pop. 557
Douglas County SD
Supt. — See Minden
Zephyr Cove ES 200/K-6
PO Box 7 89448 775-588-4574
Nancy Cauley, prin. Fax 588-4572

NEW HAMPSHIRE

NEW HAMPSHIRE DEPT. OF EDUCATION
101 Pleasant St, Concord 03301-3860
Telephone 603-271-3494
Fax 603-271-1953
Website http://www.education.nh.gov/

Commissioner of Education Frank Edelblut

NEW HAMPSHIRE BOARD OF EDUCATION
101 Pleasant St, Concord 03301-3860

Chairperson vacant

SCHOOL ADMINISTRATIVE UNITS (SAU)

SAU 1
Kimberly Saunders, supt. 603-924-3336
106 Hancock Rd Fax 924-6707
Peterborough 03458
convalsd.net

SAU 2
Mary Moriarty, supt. 603-279-7947
103 Main St Ste 2, Meredith 03253 Fax 279-3044
www.sau2.k12.nh.us/

SAU 3
Corinne Cascadden, supt. 603-752-6500
183 Hillside Ave, Berlin 03570 Fax 752-2528
www.sau3.org/

SAU 4
Stacy Buckley, supt. 603-744-5555
20 N Main St, Bristol 03222 Fax 744-6659
www.sau4.org

SAU 5
Dr. James Morse, supt. 603-868-5100
36 Coe Dr, Durham 03824 Fax 868-6668
www.orcsd.org

SAU 6
Dr. Middleton McGoodwin Ed.D., supt 603-543-4200
165 Broad St, Claremont 03743 Fax 543-4244
www.sau6.org

SAU 7
Bruce Beasley, supt. 603-237-5571
21 Academy St, Colebrook 03576 Fax 237-5126
www.sau7.org

SAU 8
Terri Forsten, supt. 603-225-0811
38 Liberty St, Concord 03301 Fax 226-2187
www.sau8.org

SAU 9
Kevin Richard, supt. 603-447-8368
176A Main St, Conway 03818 Fax 447-8497
www.sau9.org

SAU 10
Dr. MaryAnn Krikorian, supt. 603-432-1210
18 S Main St, Derry 03038 Fax 432-1264
www.sau10.org

SAU 11
Dr. William Harbron, supt. 603-516-6800
61 Locust St Ste 409, Dover 03820 Fax 516-6809
www.dover.k12.nh.us

SAU 12
Scott Laliberte, supt. 603-432-6920
268C Mammoth Rd Fax 425-1049
Londonderry 03053
www.londonderry.org

SAU 13
Louis Goscinski, supt. 603-323-5088
881A Tamworth Rd Fax 323-5093
Tamworth 03886
sau13.weebly.com

SAU 14
Valerie McKenney, supt. 603-679-5402
213 Main St, Epping 03042 Fax 679-1237
www.sau14.org

SAU 15
Dr. Charles Littlefield, supt. 603-622-3731
90 Farmer Rd, Hooksett 03106 Fax 669-4352
www.sau15.net

SAU 16
Dr. Christine Rath, supt. 603-775-8653
30 Linden St, Exeter 03833 Fax 775-8673
www.sau16.org

SAU 17
Thomas Ambrose, supt. 603-642-3688
178 Main St, Kingston 03848 Fax 642 7885
web.sau17.org

SAU 18
Daniel LeGallo, supt. 603-934-3108
119 Central St, Franklin 03235 Fax 934-3462
www.franklin.k12.nh.us

SAU 19
Brian Balke, supt. 603-497-4818
11 School St, Goffstown 03045 Fax 497-8425
www.goffstown.k12.nh.us

SAU 20
Paul Bousquet, supt. 603-466-3632
123 Main St, Gorham 03581 Fax 466-3870
www.sau20.org/

SAU 21
Robert Sullivan Ed.D., supt. 603-926-8992
2 Alumni Dr, Hampton 03842 Fax 926-5157
www.sau21.org/sau

SAU 23
Laurie Melanson, supt. 603-787-2113
2975 Dartmouth College Hwy Fax 787-2118
North Haverhill 03774
www.sau23.org

SAU 24
Dr. Lorraine Tacconi-Moore, supt. 603-428-3269
258 Western Ave, Henniker 03242 Fax 428-6545
www.sau24.org

SAU 25
Eric McGee, supt. 603-472-3755
103 County Rd, Bedford 03110 Fax 472-2567
www.sau25.net/

SAU 26
Marjorie Chiafery, supt. 603-424-6200
36 McElwain St, Merrimack 03054 Fax 424-6229
www.sau26.org

SAU 27
James O'Neill, supt. 603-578-3570
1 Highlander Ct, Litchfield 03052 Fax 578-1267
www.litchfieldsd.org

SAU 28
William Furbush, supt. 603-635-1145
59A Marsh Rd, Pelham 03076 Fax 635-1283
www.pelhamsd.org

SAU 29
Robert Malay, supt. 603-357-9002
193 Maple Ave, Keene 03431 Fax 357-9012
www.sau29.org

SAU 30
Dr. Brendan Minnihan, supt. 603-524-5710
PO Box 309, Laconia 03247 Fax 528-8442
laconiaschools.weebly.com

SAU 31
Meredith Nadeau, supt. 603-659-5020
186A Main St, Newmarket 03857 Fax 659-5022
www.newmarket.k12.nh.us

SAU 32
Frank Perotti, supt. 603-469-3442
92 Bonner Rd, Meriden 03770 Fax 469-3259
www.plainfieldschool.org

SAU 33
Tina McCoy, supt. 603-895-4299
43 Harriman Hill Rd Fax 895 0147
Raymond 03077
www.sau33.com

SAU 34
Dr. Robert Hassett, supt. 603-464-4466
PO Box 2190, Deering 03244 Fax 464-4053
www.hdsd.org

SAU 35
Pierre Couture, supt. 603-444-3925
260 Cottage St Ste C Fax 444 6299
Littleton 03561
www.sau35.k12.nh.us

SAU 36
Marion Anastasia, supt. 603-837-9363
14 King Sq, Whitefield 03598 Fax 837-2326
www.sau36.org

SAU 37
Dr. Bolgen Vargas, supt. 603-624-6300
195 McGregor St Ste 201 Fax 624-6337
Manchester 03102
www.mansd.org

SAU 39
Peter Warburton, supt. 603-673-2690
PO Box 849, Amherst 03031 Fax 672-1786
www.sau39.org

SAU 40
Robert Marquis, supt 603-673-2202
100 West St, Milford 03055 Fax 673-2237
milfordk12.org

SAU 41
Andrew Corey, supt. 603-324-5999
4 Lund Ln, Hollis 03049 Fax 465-3933
www.sau41.org

SAU 42
Dr. Jahmal Mosley Ed.D., supt. 603-966-1000
PO Box 687, Nashua 03061 Fax 594-4350
www.nashua.edu

SAU 43
Dr. Cynthia Gallagher, supt. 603-865-9701
247 N Main St, Newport 03773 Fax 865-9707
www.sau43.org

SAU 44
Robert Gadomski, supt. 603-942-1290
23 Mountain Ave Unit A Fax 942-1295
Northwood 03261
www.sau44.org

SAU 45
Susan Noyes M.Ed., supt. 603-476-5247
PO Box 419 Fax 476-8009
Moultonborough 03254
sau45.org

SAU 46
Mark MacLean, supt. 603-753-6561
105 Community Dr Fax 753-6023
Penacook 03303
www.mvsdpride.org/school-administrative-unit-46

SAU 47
Reuben Duncan, supt. 603-532-8100
81 Fitzgerald Dr Unit 2 Fax 532-8165
Jaffrey 03452
www.sau47.org

SAU 48
Mark Halloran, supt. 603-536-1254
47 Old Ward Bridge Rd Fax 536-3545
Plymouth 03264
sau48.org

SAU 49
Kathleen Cuddy-Egbert, supt. 603-569-1658
PO Box 190, Wolfeboro Falls 03896 Fax 569 6983
www.gwrsd.org

SAU 50
Salvatore Petralia, supt. 603-422-9572
48 Post Rd, Greenland 03840 Fax 422-9575
www.sau50.org

SAU 51
Dr. John Freeman, supt. 603-435-5526
23 Oneida St Unit 1 Fax 435-5331
Pittsfield 03263
www.pittsfieldnhschools.org

SAU 52
Stephen Zadravec, supt. 603-431-5080
1 Junkins Ave Unit 402 Fax 431-6753
Portsmouth 03801
www.cityofportsmouth.com/school/

SAU 53
Patricia Sherman, supt. 603-485-5188
267 Pembroke St, Pembroke 03275 Fax 485-9529
www.sau53.org

SAU 54
Michael Hopkins, supt. 603-332-3678
150 Wakefield St Ste 8 Fax 335-7367
Rochester 03867
www.rochesterschools.com

SAU 55
Dr. Earl Metzler, supt. 603-382-6119
30 Greenough Rd, Plaistow 03865 Fax 382-3334
www.timberlane.net/sau/

SAU 56
Lori Lane, supt. 603-692-4450
51 W High St, Somersworth 03878 Fax 692-9100
www.sau56.org

SAU 57
Michael Delahanty, supt. 603-893-7040
38 Geremonty Dr, Salem 03079 Fax 893-7080
www.sau57.org

SAU 58
Michael Kelley, supt. 603-636-1437
15 Preble St, Groveton 03582 Fax 636-6102
www.sau58.org

SAU 59
Dr. Tammy Davis, supt. 603-286-4116
433 W Main St, Northfield 03276 Fax 286-7402
www.winnisquam.k12.nh.us/Sau/index.htm

SAU 60
Lorraine Landry, supt. 603-835-0006
159 East St, Charlestown 03603 Fax 835-0007
www.sau60.org

SAU 61
Ruth Vaughn, supt. 603-755-2627
35 School St, Farmington 03835 Fax 755-9334
www.sau61.org

SAU 62
Patrick Andrew, supt. 603-632 5563
PO Box 789, Enfield 03748 Fax 632-4181
www.mascoma.k12.nh.us

SAU 63
Bryan Lane, supt., 192 Forest Rd 603-654-8088
Lyndeborough 03082 Fax 654-6691
www.sau63.org

SAU 64
Earl Sussman, supt. 603-652-0262
20 School St, Milton 03851 Fax 652-0250
www.sau64.org
SAU 65
Winfried Feneberg, supt. 603-526-2051
114 Cougar Ct, New London 03257 Fax 526-2145
www.kearsarge.org
SAU 66
Steven Chamberlin, supt. 603-746-5186
204 Maple St, Contoocook 03229 Fax 746-5714
www.hopkintonschools.org
SAU 67
Dr. Dean Cascadden, supt. 603-224-4728
32 White Rock Hill Rd, Bow 03304 Fax 224-4111
www.bownet.org
SAU 68
Judith McGann, supt. 603-745-2051
PO Box 846, Lincoln 03251 Fax 745-2352
www.lin-wood.org
SAU 70
Dr. Jay Badams, supt. 603-643-6050
41 Lebanon St Ste 2 Fax 643-3073
Hanover 03755
www.sau70.org/
SAU 71
Dr. Michele Munson, supt. 603-863-2420
29 School Rd, Lempster 03605 Fax 863-2451
www.sau71.org
SAU 72
Dr. Pamela Stiles, supt. 603-875-7890
252 Suncook Valley Rd Fax 875-0391
Alton 03809
www.myacs.org/domain/8
SAU 73
Kirk Beitler, supt. 603-527-9215
2 Belknap Mountain Rd Fax 527-9216
Gilford 03249
www.sau73.org/
SAU 74
Daniel Moulis, supt. 603-664-2715
572 Calef Hwy, Barrington 03825 Fax 664-2609
www.sau74.org
SAU 75
Sydney Leggett, supt. 603-863-9689
300 Route 10 S, Grantham 03753 Fax 863-9684
www.gvshawks.org/sau-75
SAU 76
Jeffrey Valence, supt. 603-795-4431
PO Box 117, Lyme 03768 Fax 795-9407
www.lymeschool.org
SAU 77
Susan Hodgdon, admin. 603-638-2800
PO Box 130, Monroe 03771 Fax 638-2031
www.monroeschool77.com

SAU 78
Elaine Arbour, supt. 603-353-2170
10 School Dr, Orford 03777 Fax 353-2189
SAU 79
John Fauci, supt. 603-267-9097
9 Currier Hill Rd, Gilmanton 03237 Fax 267-9498
www.sau79.org
SAU 80
Michael Tursi, supt. 603-267-9223
58 School St, Belmont 03220 Fax 267-9225
www.sau80.org
SAU 81
Lawrence Russell, supt. 603-886-1235
20 Library St, Hudson 03051 Fax 886-1236
www.sau81.org
SAU 82
Dr. Darrell Lockwood, supt. 603-887-1401
22 Murphy Dr, Chester 03036 Fax 887-4961
www.chesteracademy.org
SAU 83
Allyn Hutton, supt. 603-895-6903
432 Main St, Fremont 03044 Fax 895-6905
www.sau83.org
SAU 83
Allyn Hutton, supt. 603-895-6903
432 Main St, Fremont Fax 895-6905
SAU 84
Dr. Steven Nilhas, supt. 603-444-5215
65 Maple St, Littleton 03561 Fax 444-3015
www.littletonschools.org/
SAU 85
Russell Holden, supt. 603-763-4627
70 Lower Main St, Sunapee 03782 Fax 763-4718
www.sunapeeschools.org
SAU 86
Dr. Brian Cochrane, supt. 603-435-1510
PO Box 250 Fax 435-1511
Center Barnstead 03225
www.barnstead.k12.nh.us/sau-86.html
SAU 87
Dr. Stephen Russell, supt. 603-721-0160
16 School St, Greenville 03048 Fax 721-0175
www.mascenic.org
SAU 88
Joanne Roberts, supt. 603-790-8500
20 Seminary Hl Fax 790-8310
West Lebanon 03784
www.sau88.net
SAU 89
Kristen Kivela, supt. 603-878-2962
13 Darling Hill Rd, Mason 03048 Fax 878-3439
mason.sau89.org
SAU 90
Kathleen Murphy, supt. 603-926-4560
7 Scott Rd, Hampton 03842 Fax 926-5070
www.sau90.org/

SAU 91
Kenneth Dassau, supt. 603-209-3315
1 Village Rd, Surry 03431
SAU 92
Wayne Woolridge, supt. 603-336-5728
PO Box 27, Hinsdale 03451 Fax 336-5731
www.hnhsd.org
SAU 93
Lisa Witte, supt. 603-352-6955
600 Old Homestead Hwy Fax 358-6708
Swanzey 03446
www.mrsd.org
SAU 94
Alan Genovese, supt. 603-239-8061
PO Box 46, Winchester 03470 Fax 239-7593
www.wnhsd.org
SAU 95
Richard Langlois, supt. 603-425-1976
19 Haverhill Rd, Windham 03087 Fax 425-1719
www.sau95.org
SAU 96
Kenneth Dassau, supt. 603-209-3315
PO Box 111, Sullivan 03445
SAU 97
Kathleen Vizard, supt. 603-356-5535
91 Samuel Hale Dr Fax 356-5535
Hales Location 03860
SAU 98
Jennifer Fish, supt. 603-246-3321
136 County Farm Rd Fax 246-8117
West Stewartstown 03597
SAU 100
Frank Perotti, supt. 603-675-5891
274 Town House Rd Fax 675-6279
Cornish 03745
SAU 101
Christine Tyrie, supt. 603-871-8502
76 Taylor Way, Sanbornville 03872 Fax 871-8608
SAU 102
Gail Paludi, supt., 54 Mill Village Rd 603-495-1293
!!UNKNOWN!! 03752
SAU 103
Michele Munson, supt. 603-934-2245
32 Crescent St, Hill 03243 Fax 934-3079
SAU 201
David Smith, hdmstr. 603-942-5531
907 1st NH Tpke Fax 942-7537
Northwood 03261
www.coebrown.org
SAU 202
Griffin Morse, hdmstr. 603-437-5200
5 Pinkerton St, Derry 03038 Fax 432-5328
www.pinkertonacademy.net
SAU 301
Robert Cullison, supt. 603-875-8600
242 Suncook Valley Rd Fax 875-8200
Alton 03809
www.pmhschool.com

PUBLIC, PRIVATE AND CATHOLIC ELEMENTARY SCHOOLS

Acworth, Sullivan
Fall Mountain Regional SD
Supt. — See Langdon
Acworth Center S 50/1-4
PO Box 69 03601 603-835-2270
Gail Rowe, prin. Fax 835-6218

Albany, Carroll

White Mountain Waldorf S 100/PK-8
1371 NH Route 16 03818 603-447-3168
Karen Albert, admin. Fax 617-3413

Allenstown, Merrimack
Allenstown SD
Supt. — See Pembroke
Allenstown ES 200/PK-4
30 Main St 03275 603-485-9574
Anthony Blinn, prin. Fax 485-1805
Dupont MS 100/5-8
10 1/2 School St 03275 603-485-4474
Mark Dangora, prin. Fax 485-1806

Alstead, Cheshire
Fall Mountain Regional SD
Supt. — See Langdon
Alstead PS 100/PK-4
58 Mechanic St 03602 603-835-2482
Gail Rowe, prin. Fax 835-9096
Vilas MS 100/5-8
82 Mechanic St 03602 603-835-6351
Gail Rowe, prin. Fax 835-2052

Alton, Belknap, Pop. 499
Alton SD 500/PK-8
252 Suncook Valley Rd 03809 603-875-7890
Pamela Stiles M.Ed., supt. Fax 875-0391
www.myacs.org
Alton Central S 500/PK-8
41 School St 03809 603-875-7500
John W. MacArthur, prin. Fax 875-0380

Amherst, Hillsborough, Pop. 612
Amherst SD 1,400/K-8
PO Box 849 03031 603-673-2690
Peter Warburton, supt. Fax 672-1786
www.sau39.org
Amherst MS 700/5-8
PO Box 966 03031 603-673-8944
Porter Dodge, prin. Fax 673-6774
Clark ES 200/K-1
PO Box 420 03031 603-673-2343
Gerry St. Amand, prin. Fax 673-5114
Wilkins ES 500/1-4
PO Box 420 03031 603-673-4411
Gerry St. Amand, prin. Fax 672-0968

Mont Vernon SD 200/K-6
PO Box 849 03031 603-673-2690
Peter Warburton, supt. Fax 672-1786
www.sau39.org
Other Schools – See Mont Vernon

Country Village Montessori S 50/PK-6
2 Overlook Dr 03031 603-672-3882
Claire Doody M.Ed., head sch

Andover, Merrimack
Andover SD
Supt. — See Penacook
Andover ES 200/K-8
20 School St 03216 603-735-5494
Jane Slayton, prin. Fax 735-6108

Antrim, Hillsborough, Pop. 1,376
Contoocook Valley SD
Supt. — See Peterborough
Antrim ES 200/PK-4
10 School St 03440 603-588-6371
Stefanie Syre-Hager, prin. Fax 588-6972
Great Brook MS 300/5-8
16 School St 03440 603-588-6630
James Elder, prin. Fax 588-3207

Ashland, Grafton, Pop. 1,228
Ashland SD
Supt. — See Meredith
Ashland ES 200/K-8
16 Education Dr 03217 603-968-7622
Shannon Bartlett, prin. Fax 968-3167

Atkinson, Rockingham
Timberlane Regional SD
Supt. — See Plaistow
Atkinson Academy 400/PK-5
17 Academy Ave 03811 603-362-5521
Kathie Dayotis, prin. Fax 362-5842

Auburn, Rockingham
Auburn SD
Supt. — See Hooksett
Auburn Village S 600/K-8
11 Eaton Hill Rd 03032 603-483-2769
Lori Collins Ed.D., prin. Fax 483-5144

Barrington, Strafford
Barrington SD 1,000/PK-8
572 Calef Hwy 03825 603-664-2715
Daniel Moulis, supt. Fax 664-2609
www.sau74.org
Barrington ES 400/1-4
570 Calef Hwy 03825 603-664-2641
Mary Maxfield, prin. Fax 664-5271
Barrington MS 400/5-8
51 Haley Dr 03825 603-664-2127
Terrence Leatherman, prin. Fax 664-5739

Early Childhood Learning Center 100/PK-K
77 Ramsdell Ln 03825 603-664-5586
Laura Deely, prin. Fax 664-5589

Bartlett, Carroll, Pop. 362
Bartlett SD
Supt. — See Conway
Bartlett ES 200/K-8
PO Box 396 03812 603-374-2331
Joseph Voci, prin. Fax 374-1941

Bath, Grafton
Bath SD
Supt. — See North Haverhill
Bath Village ES 100/K-6
61 Lisbon Rd 03740 603-747-2004
Bernice Buroughs, prin. Fax 747-3260

Bedford, Hillsborough
Bedford SD 4,400/PK-12
103 County Rd 03110 603-472-3755
Eric McGee, supt. Fax 472-2567
www.sau25.net/
Lurgio MS 800/7-8
47 Nashua Rd Unit A 03110 603-310-9100
Edward Joyce, prin. Fax 472-5090
McKelvie IS 700/5-6
108 Liberty Hill Rd 03110 603-472-3951
Michael Fournier, prin. Fax 472-4503
Memorial ES 400/PK-4
55 Old Bedford Rd 03110 603-627-1776
Philip Schappler, prin. Fax 644-5122
Riddle Brook ES 500/K-4
230 New Boston Rd 03110 603-471-1082
Molly McCarthy, prin. Fax 472-7879
Woodbury ES 500/K-4
180 County Rd 03110 603-622-0431
Cheryl Daley, prin. Fax 644-5128

Belmont, Belknap, Pop. 1,272
Shaker Regional SD 1,400/PK-12
58 School St 03220 603-267-9223
Michael Tursi, supt. Fax 267-9225
www.sau80.org
Belmont ES 500/PK-4
26 Best St 03220 603-267-6568
Benjamin Hill, prin. Fax 267-6136
Belmont MS 400/5-8
38 School St 03220 603-267-9220
Aaron Pope, prin. Fax 267-9228
Other Schools – See Canterbury

Bennington, Hillsborough, Pop. 370
Contoocook Valley SD
Supt. — See Peterborough
Pierce ES 100/K-4
19 Main St 03442 603-588-2131
Stefanie Syre-Hager, prin. Fax 588-3802

Berlin, Coos, Pop. 9,890
Berlin SD 1,300/K-12
183 Hillside Ave 03570 603-752-6500
Corinne Cascadden, supt. Fax 752-2528
www.sau3.org/
Berlin MS 300/6-8
200 State St 03570 603-752-5311
Tammy Fauteux, prin. Fax 752-8580
Brown ES 300/K-2
190 Norway St 03570 603-752-1471
Amy Huter, prin. Fax 752-8581
Hillside ES 200/3-5
183 Hillside Ave 03570 603-752-5328
Julie King, prin. Fax 752-2528

Bethlehem, Grafton, Pop. 962
Bethlehem SD
Supt. — See Littleton
Bethlehem ES 200/K-6
2297 Main St 03574 603-869-5842
Shelli Roberts, prin. Fax 869-2482

Profile SD
Supt. — See Littleton
Profile JHS 100/7-8
691 Profile Rd 03574 603-823-7411
Benjamin Jellison, prin. Fax 823-7490

Boscawen, Merrimack
Merrimack Valley SD
Supt. — See Penacook
Boscawen ES 300/PK-5
1 Best Ave 03303 603-753-6512
Jeffrey Drouin, prin. Fax 753-8140

Bow, Merrimack
Bow SD 1,600/PK-12
55 Falcon Way 03304 603-224-4728
Dr. Dean Cascadden, supt. Fax 224-4111
www.bownet.org
Bow ES 400/PK-4
22 Bow Center Rd 03304 603-225-3049
Kurt Gergler, prin. Fax 228-2205
Bow Memorial S 500/5-8
20 Bow Center Rd 03304 603-225-3212
Adam Osburn, prin. Fax 228-2228
Other Schools – See Dunbarton

Meeting House Montessori S 50/PK-5
28 Logging Hill Rd 03304 603-224-0004
Susan Bradley, dir.

Bradford, Merrimack, Pop. 353
Kearsarge Regional SD
Supt. — See New London
Kearsarge Regional ES - Bradford 200/K-5
PO Box 435 03221 603-938-5959
James Spadaro, prin.

Brentwood, Rockingham
Brentwood SD
Supt. — See Exeter
Swasey ES 300/PK-5
355 Middle Rd 03833 603-642-3487
Ron Kew, prin. Fax 642-6825

Bridgewater, Grafton
Newfound Area SD
Supt. — See Bristol
Bridgewater-Hebron Village ES 200/PK-5
25 School House Ln, 603-744-6969
Dana Andrews, prin. Fax 744-9747

Bristol, Grafton, Pop. 1,657
Newfound Area SD 1,200/PK-12
20 N Main St 03222 603-744-5555
Stacy Buckley, supt. Fax 744-6659
www.sau4.org
Bristol ES 200/K-5
55 School St 03222 603-744-2761
Sarah Rollins, prin. Fax 744-2520
Newfound Memorial MS 300/6-8
155 N Main St 03222 603-744-8162
Jay Lewis, prin. Fax 744-8037
Other Schools – See Bridgewater, Danbury, New Hampton

Brookline, Hillsborough
Brookline SD
Supt. — See Hollis
Douglass Academy 300/4-6
PO Box 480 03033 603-673-0122
Dennis Dobe, prin. Fax 673-7384
Maghakian Memorial S 300/PK-3
PO Box 68 03033 603-673-4640
Daniel Molinari, prin. Fax 673-4785

Campton, Grafton
Campton SD
Supt. — See Plymouth
Campton ES 300/PK-8
1110 NH Route 175 03223 603-726-3931
James George, prin. Fax 726-8081

Canaan, Grafton, Pop. 511
Mascoma Valley Regional SD
Supt. — See Enfield
Canaan ES 300/PK-4
PO Box 18 03741 603-523-4312
Amanda Isabelle, prin. Fax 523-8872
Indian River S 400/5-8
45 Royal Rd 03741 603-632-4357
Kevin Towle, prin. Fax 632-4262

Candia, Rockingham
Candia SD
Supt. — See Hooksett
Moore S 400/K-8
12 Deerfield Rd 03034 603-483-2251
Robert St. Cyr Ed.D., prin. Fax 483-2536

Canterbury, Merrimack
Shaker Regional SD
Supt. — See Belmont
Canterbury ES 100/K-5
15 Baptist Hill Rd 03224 603-783-9944
Mary Morrison, prin. Fax 783-4981

Center Barnstead, Belknap
Barnstead SD 500/PK-8
PO Box 250 03225 603-435-1510
Dr. Brian Cochrane, supt. Fax 435-1511
www.barnstead.k12.nh.us
Barnstead ES 500/PK-8
91 Maple St 03225 603-269-5161
Timothy Rice, prin. Fax 269-2632

Center Conway, Carroll
Conway SD
Supt. — See Conway
Pine Tree ES 200/K-6
183 Mill St 03813 603-447-2882
Aimee Frechette, prin. Fax 447-6838

Cady Memorial S 50/K-8
PO Box 126 03813 603-447-6298

Center Ossipee, Carroll, Pop. 555
Governor Wentworth Regional SD
Supt. — See Wolfeboro
Ossipee Central ES 300/PK-6
PO Box 68 03814 603-539-4589
Elizabeth Hertzfeld, prin. Fax 539-4390

Center Sandwich, Carroll, Pop. 121
Inter-Lakes Cooperative SD
Supt. — See Meredith
Sandwich Central ES 100/K-6
28 Squam Lake Rd 03227 603-284-7712
Jeremy Hillger, prin. Fax 284-6104

Center Tuftonboro, Carroll
Governor Wentworth Regional SD
Supt. — See Wolfeboro
Tuftonboro Central ES 100/K-6
PO Box 118 03816 603-569-2050
Andrea. Fournier, prin. Fax 569-8276

Charlestown, Sullivan, Pop. 1,173
Fall Mountain Regional SD
Supt. — See Langdon
Charlestown ES 200/PK-5
84 E Street Ext 03603 603-826-3694
Christopher Young, prin. Fax 826-3905
Charlestown MS 100/6-8
307 Main St 03603 603-826-7711
Aaron Cinquemani, prin. Fax 826-3102
North Charlestown Community ES 100/1-5
509 River Rd 03603 603-826-3986
Aaron Cinquemani, prin. Fax 826-3186

Chester, Rockingham
Chester SD 500/PK-8
22 Murphy Dr 03036 603-887-1401
Dr. Darrell Lockwood, supt. Fax 887-4961
www.chesteracademy.org
Chester Academy 500/PK-8
22 Murphy Dr 03036 603-887-3621
Karen Lacroix, prin. Fax 887-4961

Chesterfield, Cheshire
Chesterfield SD
Supt. — See Keene
Chesterfield Central S 300/K-8
PO Box 205 03443 603-363-8301
Sharyn D'Eon, prin. Fax 363-8406

Chichester, Merrimack
Chichester SD
Supt. — See Pembroke
Chichester Central S 200/K-8
219 Main St 03258 603-798-5651
Brian Beaverstock, prin. Fax 798-3230

Claremont, Sullivan, Pop. 13,132
Claremont SD 1,800/PK-12
165 Broad St 03743 603-543-4200
Dr. Middleton McGoodwin Ed.D., supt. Fax 543-4244
www.sau6.org
Bluff ES 200/K-5
1 Summit Rd 03743 603-543-4273
Dale Chenette, prin. Fax 542-3703
Claremont MS 400/6-8
107 South St 03743 603-543-4250
Paulette Fitzgerald, prin. Fax 543-4289
Claremont Preschool Center PK-PK
111 South St 03743 603-543-4220
Diane Edwards, prin.
Disnard ES 300/K-5
160 Hanover St 03743 603-543-4260
Melissa Lewis, prin. Fax 543-4262
Maple Avenue ES 400/PK-5
210 Maple Ave 03743 603-543-4270
Dan Cherry, prin. Fax 543-4235

Cornish SD 100/PK-8
165 Broad St 03743 603-543-4200
Dr. Middleton McGoodwin Ed.D., supt. Fax 543-4244
www.sau6.org
Other Schools – See Cornish

Unity SD 100/PK-8
165 Broad St 03743 603-543-4200
Dr. Middleton McGoodwin Ed.D., supt. Fax 543-4244
www.sau6.org
Other Schools – See Newport

Claremont Christian Academy 100/K-12
97 Maple Ave 03743 603-542-8759
Mark Pomeroy, dir. Fax 542-8759

Colebrook, Coos, Pop. 1,376
Colebrook SD 400/PK-12
21 Academy St 03576 603-237-5571
Bruce Beasley, supt. Fax 237-5126
www.sau7.org
Colebrook ES 300/PK-8
27 Dumont St 03576 603-237-4801
Dan Gorham, prin. Fax 237-5246

Pittsburg SD 100/PK-12
21 Academy St 03576 603-237-5571
Bruce Beasley, supt. Fax 237-5126
www.sau7.org
Other Schools – See Pittsburg

Stewartstown SD 100/K-8
21 Academy St 03576 603-237-5571
Bruce Beasley, supt. Fax 237-5571
www.sau7.org
Other Schools – See West Stewartstown

Concord, Merrimack, Pop. 41,988
Concord SD 4,800/PK-12
38 Liberty St 03301 603-225-0811
Terri Forsten, supt. Fax 226-2187
www.sau8.org
Abbot-Downing ES 400/K-5
152 South St 03301 603-225-0827
Kathleen Riordan, prin. Fax 225-0829
Beaver Meadow ES 400/K-5
40 Sewalls Falls Rd 03301 603-225-0854
Michele Vance, prin. Fax 225-0857
Broken Ground ES 400/3-5
51 S Curtisville Rd 03301 603-225-0855
Susan Lauze, prin. Fax 225-0869
McAuliffe ES 400/K-5
17 N Spring St 03301 603-225-0840
Kristen Gallo, prin. Fax 225-0839
Mill Brook PS 500/PK-2
53 S Curtisville Rd 03301 603-225-0830
Philip Callanan, prin. Fax 225-0851
Rundlett MS 1,000/6-8
144 South St 03301 603-225-0862
James McCollum, prin. Fax 226-3288

Capital Christian S 50/K-8
PO Box 4087 03302 603-224-3641
William Snow M.A., prin.
Concord Christian Academy 200/PK-12
37 Regional Dr 03301 603-228-8888
Dr. David Johnson, hdmstr. Fax 226-9696
St. John Regional S 200/PK-8
61 S State St 03301 603-225-3222
Stephen Donohue, prin. Fax 225-0195
Shaker Road S 300/PK-8
131 Shaker Rd 03301 603-224-0161
Patricia Hicks, head sch Fax 226-0257
Trinity Christian S 200/PK-12
80 Clinton St 03301 603-225-5410
Michael Kingsley, prin. Fax 225-3235

Contoocook, Merrimack, Pop. 1,432
Hopkinton SD 900/PK-12
204 Maple St 03229 603-746-5186
Steven Chamberlin, supt. Fax 746-5714
www.hopkintonschools.org
Hopkinton MS 100/7-8
297 Park Ave 03229 603-746-4167
Christopher Kelley, prin. Fax 746-5109
Maple Street S 200/4-6
194 Maple St 03229 603-746-4195
William Carozza, prin. Fax 746-6863
Other Schools – See Hopkinton

Conway, Carroll, Pop. 1,799
Bartlett SD 200/K-8
176A Main St 03818 603-447-8368
Kevin Richard, supt. Fax 447-8497
www.sau9.org
Other Schools – See Bartlett

Conway SD 1,800/K-12
176A Main St 03818 603-447-8368
Kevin Richard, supt. Fax 447-8497
www.sau9.org
Conway ES 200/K-6
160 Main St 03818 603-447-3369
Brian Hastings, prin. Fax 447-6981
Kennett MS 300/7-8
176 Main St 03818 603-447-6364
Richard Biche, prin. Fax 447-6842
Other Schools – See Center Conway, North Conway

Jackson SD 50/K-6
176A Main St 03818 603-447-8368
Kevin Richard, supt. Fax 447-8497
www.sau9.org
Other Schools – See Jackson

Cornish, Sullivan
Cornish SD
Supt. — See Claremont
Cornish ES 100/PK-8
274 Town House Rd 03745 603-675-5891
Jennifer Prileson, prin. Fax 675-6279

Croydon, Sullivan
Croydon SD 50/PK-4
889 NH Rt 10 03773 603-865-9500
Dr. Cynthia Gallagher, supt. Fax 865-9707
www.sau43.org
Croydon Village S 50/PK-4
889 NH Route 10 03773 603-863-2080
Kelly George, prin. Fax 863-7178

Danbury, Merrimack
Newfound Area SD
Supt. — See Bristol
Danbury ES 100/K-5
20 Daffodil Ln 03230 603-768-3434
Alison Roberts, prin. Fax 768-9802

Danville, Rockingham
Timberlane Regional SD
Supt. — See Plaistow
Danville ES 300/PK-5
23 School St 03819 603-382-5554
Nancy Barcelos, prin. Fax 382-1680

Deerfield, Rockingham
Deerfield SD
Supt. — See Pembroke

Deerfield Community S — 500/PK-8
66 North Rd 03037 — 603-463-7422
Christopher Smith, prin. — Fax 463-2839

Derry, Rockingham, Pop. 21,640
Derry Cooperative SD — 3,600/PK-8
18 S Main St 03038 — 603-432-1210
Dr. MaryAnn Krikorian, supt. — Fax 432-1264
www.sau10.org
Barka ES — 600/K-5
21 Eastgate Rd 03038 — 603-434-2430
Daniel LaFleur, prin. — Fax 432-2305
Derry Early Education Program — 100/PK-PK
5 Hood Rd 03038 — 603-845-1202
Jayne Boyle, dir. — Fax 432-1227
Derry Village ES — 400/K-5
28 S Main St 03038 — 603-432-1233
Christopher McCallum, prin. — Fax 432-1235
East Derry Memorial ES — 400/K-5
18 Dubeau Dr 03038 — 603-432-1260
Kim Carpentino, prin. — Fax 437-3575
Grinnell ES — 500/K-5
6 Grinnell Rd 03038 — 603-432-1238
Mary Hill, prin. — Fax 432-8717
Hood MS — 700/6-8
5 Hood Rd 03038 — 603-432-1224
William Fox, prin. — Fax 432-1227
South Range ES — 400/K-5
1 Drury Ln 03038 — 603-432-1219
Matthew Olsen, prin. — Fax 432-1221
West Running Brook MS — 600/6-8
1 W Running Brook Ln 03038 — 603-432-1250
Justin Krieger, prin. — Fax 432-1243

St. Thomas Aquinas S — 200/PK-8
3 Moody St 03038 — 603-432-2712
Patricia Berthiaume, prin. — Fax 432-2179

Dover, Strafford, Pop. 29,321
Dover SD — 4,000/PK-12
61 Locust St Ste 409 03820 — 603-516-6800
Dr. William Harbron, supt. — Fax 516-6809
www.dover.k12.nh.us
Dover MS — 1,100/5-8
16 Daley Dr 03820 — 603-516-7200
Kimberly Lyndes, prin. — Fax 516-5747
Garrison ES — 500/K-4
50 Garrison Rd 03820 — 603-516-6752
Elizabeth Dunton, prin. — Fax 516-6742
Horne Street ES — 500/K-4
78 Horne St 03820 — 603-516-6756
Patricia Driscoll, prin. — Fax 516-6766
Woodman Park ES — 600/PK-4
11 Towle Ave 03820 — 603-516-6700
Patrick Boodey, prin. — Fax 516-6703

Portsmouth Christian Academy — 600/PK-12
20 Seaborne Dr 03820 — 603-742-3617
Dr. John Engstrom, head sch — Fax 750-0490
St. Mary Academy — 300/PK-8
222 Central Ave 03820 — 603-742-3299
Blake McGurty, prin. — Fax 743-3483

Dublin, Cheshire
Contoocook Valley SD
Supt. — See Peterborough
Dublin Consolidated ES — 100/K-5
1177 Main St 03444 — 603-563-8332
Nicole Pease, prin. — Fax 563-3465

Dunbarton, Merrimack, Pop. 1,759
Bow SD
Supt. — See Bow
Dunbarton ES — 200/PK-6
20 Robert Rogers Rd 03046 — 603-774-3181
Owen Harrington, admin. — Fax 774-3186

Durham, Strafford, Pop. 10,187
Oyster River Cooperative SD — 2,000/K-12
36 Coe Dr 03824 — 603-868-5100
Dr. James Morse Ed.D., supt. — Fax 868-6668
www.orcsd.org
Oyster River MS — 700/5-8
1 Coe Dr 03824 — 603-868-2155
Jay Richard, prin. — Fax 868-3469
Other Schools – See Lee, Madbury

East Kingston, Rockingham
East Kingston SD
Supt. — See Exeter
East Kingston ES — 200/K-5
5 Andrews Ln 03827 — 603-642-3511
Steve Tullar, prin. — Fax 642-6338

East Lempster, Sullivan
Goshen-Lempster Cooperative SD
Supt. — See Lempster
Goshen-Lempster Coop S — 200/K-8
29 School Rd 03605 — 603-863-1080
Ralph Peterson, prin. — Fax 863-2451

East Rochester, See Rochester
Rochester SD
Supt. — See Rochester
East Rochester ES — 300/PK-5
773 Portland St 03868 — 603-332-2146
Christine Hebert, prin. — Fax 335-7368
Loud ES — 100/K-4
5 Cocheco Ave 03868 — 603-332-6486
Erin Mahoney, prin. — Fax 335-7367

Effingham, Carroll
Governor Wentworth Regional SD
Supt. — See Wolfeboro
Effingham ES — 100/K-6
6 Partridge Cove Rd 03882 — 603-539-6032
Patricia Morrissey, prin. — Fax 539-4511

Enfield, Grafton, Pop. 1,510
Mascoma Valley Regional SD — 1,200/PK-12
PO Box 789 03748 — 603-632-5563
Patrick Andrew, supt. — Fax 632-4181
sites.google.com/a/mvrsd.org/home/
Enfield Village S — 200/PK-4
PO Box 329 03748 — 603-632-4231
Cynthia Collea, prin. — Fax 632-5482
Other Schools – See Canaan

Epping, Rockingham, Pop. 1,654
Epping SD — 1,000/PK-12
213 Main St 03042 — 603-679-5402
Valerie McKenney, supt. — Fax 679-1237
www.sau14.org
Epping ES — 500/PK-5
17 Prospect St 03042 — 603-679-8018
Justin Benna, prin. — Fax 679-9822
Epping MS — 200/6-8
33 Prescott Rd 03042 — 603-679-2544
Coby Troidl, prin. — Fax 679-5514

Epsom, Merrimack
Epsom SD
Supt. — See Pembroke
Epsom Central S — 400/K-8
282 Black Hall Rd 03234 — 603-736-9331
Patrick Connors, prin. — Fax 736-8703

Errol, Coos
Errol SD
Supt. — See Gorham
Errol Consolidated ES — 50/K-8
PO Box 129 03579 — 603-482-3341
Kathleen Urso, prin. — Fax 482-3722

Exeter, Rockingham, Pop. 9,087
Brentwood SD — 300/PK-5
30 Linden St 03833 — 603-775-8653
Dr. Christine Rath, supt. — Fax 775-8673
www.sau16.org
Other Schools – See Brentwood

East Kingston SD — 200/K-5
30 Linden St 03833 — 603-775-8653
Dr. Christine Rath, supt. — Fax 775-8673
www.sau16.org
Other Schools – See East Kingston

Exeter Region Cooperative SD — 3,100/6-12
30 Linden St 03833 — 603-775-8653
Dr. Christine Rath, supt. — Fax 775-8673
www.sau16.org
Other Schools – See Stratham

Exeter SD — 1,000/PK-5
30 Linden St 03833 — 603-775-8653
Dr. Christine Rath, supt. — Fax 775-8673
www.sau16.org
Lincoln Street ES — 500/3-5
25 Lincoln St 03833 — 603-775-8860
Drew Bairstow, prin. — Fax 775-8968
Main Street ES — 500/PK-2
40 Main St 03833 — 603-775-8946
Steve Adler, prin. — Fax 775-8964

Kensington SD — 100/K-5
30 Linden St 03833 — 603-775-8653
Dr. Christine Rath, supt. — Fax 775-8673
www.sau16.org
Other Schools – See Kensington

Newfields SD — 100/K-5
30 Linden St 03833 — 603-775-8653
Dr. Christine Rath, supt. — Fax 775-8673
www.sau16.org
Other Schools – See Newfields

Stratham SD — 600/PK-5
30 Linden St 03833 — 603-775-8653
Dr. Christine Rath, supt. — Fax 775-8673
www.sau16.org
Other Schools – See Stratham

Farmington, Strafford, Pop. 3,815
Farmington SD — 1,200/PK-12
35 School St 03835 — 603-755-2627
Ruth Vaughn, supt. — Fax 755-9334
www.sau61.org
Valley View ES — 400/PK-3
79 Thayer Dr 03835 — 603-755-4757
Rebecca Fredette, prin. — Fax 755-4738
Wilson Memorial MS — 400/4-8
51 School St 03835 — 603-755-2181
Jessica Richardson, prin. — Fax 755-9473

Fitzwilliam, Cheshire
Monadnock Regional SD
Supt. — See Swanzey
Emerson ES — 200/PK-6
27 Rhododendron Rd 03447 — 603-585-6611
Kevin Stone, prin. — Fax 585-9287

Francestown, Hillsborough
Contoocook Valley SD
Supt. — See Peterborough
Francestown ES — 100/K-4
PO Box 179 03043 — 603-547-2976
Katherine Foecking, prin. — Fax 547-2636

Franconia, Grafton
Lafayette Regional SD
Supt. — See Littleton
Lafayette Regional ES — 100/K-6
149 Main St 03580 — 603-823-7741
Gordon Johnk, prin. — Fax 823-5452

Franklin, Merrimack, Pop. 8,346
Franklin SD — 1,100/PK-12
119 Central St 03235 — 603-934-3108
Daniel LeGallo, supt. — Fax 934-3462
www.sau18.org
Franklin MS — 300/4-8
200 Sanborn St 03235 — 603-934-5828
Kevin Barbour, prin. — Fax 934-2432
Other Schools – See West Franklin

Hill SD — 100/K-6
119 Central St 03235 — 603-934-3108
Daniel LeGallo, supt. — Fax 934-3462
www.franklin.k12.nh.us
Other Schools – See Hill

Freedom, Carroll
Freedom SD
Supt. — See Tamworth
Freedom ES — 100/PK-6
40 Loon Lake Rd 03836 — 603-539-2077
Patricia Stone, prin. — Fax 539-5782

Fremont, Rockingham
Fremont SD — 400/PK-8
432 Main St 03044 — 603-895-6903
Allyn Hutton, supt. — Fax 895-6905
www.sau83.org
Ellis ES — 400/PK-8
432 Main St 03044 — 603-895-2511
Andrew Haas, prin. — Fax 895-1106

Gilford, Belknap
Gilford SD — 1,200/K-12
2 Belknap Mountain Rd 03249 — 603-527-9215
Kirk Beitler, supt. — Fax 527-9216
www.sau73.org/
Gilford ES — 300/K-4
76 Belknap Mountain Rd 03249 — 603-524-1661
Danielle Bolduc, prin. — Fax 528-0041
Gilford MS — 300/5-8
72 Alvah Wilson Rd 03249 — 603-527-2460
Peter Sawyer, prin. — Fax 527-2461

Gilmanton, Belknap
Gilmanton SD — 400/K-8
9 Currier Hill Rd 03237 — 603-267-9097
John Fauci, supt. — Fax 267-9498
www.sau79.org
Gilmanton ES — 400/K-8
1386 NH Route 140, — 603-364-5681
Carol Locke, prin. — Fax 364-7311

Gilsum, Cheshire
Monadnock Regional SD
Supt. — See Swanzey
Gilsum ES — 50/K-6
PO Box 38 03448 — 603-352-2226
Adrienne Noel, prin. — Fax 352-2901

Goffstown, Hillsborough, Pop. 14,621
Goffstown SD — 2,900/PK-12
11 School St 03045 — 603-497-4818
Brian Balke, supt. — Fax 497-8425
www.goffstown.k12.nh.us
Glen Lake S — 200/PK-K
251 Elm St 03045 — 603-497-3550
Kathryn Stoyle, prin. — Fax 497-3660
Maple Avenue ES — 400/1-4
16 Maple Ave 03045 — 603-497-3330
Suzanne Pyszka, prin. — Fax 497-5624
Mountain View MS — 900/5-8
41 Lauren Ln 03045 — 603-497-8288
Wendy Hastings, prin. — Fax 497-4987
Other Schools – See Manchester

New Boston SD — 500/PK-6
11 School St 03045 — 603-497-4818
Brian Balke, supt. — Fax 497-8425
www.goffstown.k12.nh.us
Other Schools – See New Boston

Gonic, Strafford
Rochester SD
Supt. — See Rochester
Gonic ES — 200/K-5
10 Railroad Ave 03839 — 603-332-6487
Dr. Maureen Oakman, prin. — Fax 332-2004

Gorham, Coos, Pop. 1,579
Errol SD — 50/K-8
123 Main St 03581 — 603-466-3632
Paul Bousquet, supt. — Fax 466-3870
www.sau20.org/
Other Schools – See Errol

Gorham Randolph Shelburne Cooperative SD — 400/K-12
123 Main St 03581 — 603-466-3632
Paul Bousquet, supt. — Fax 466-3870
www.sau20.org/
Fenn ES — 200/K-5
169 Main St 03581 — 603-466-3334
Christina Binette, prin. — Fax 466-3109
Gorham MS — 100/6-8
120 Main St 03581 — 603-466-2776
David Backler, prin. — Fax 466-3111

Milan SD — 100/PK-6
123 Main St 03581 — 603-466-3632
Paul Bousquet, supt. — Fax 466-3870
www.sau20.org/
Other Schools – See Milan

Grantham, Sullivan
Grantham SD — 200/K-6
300 Route 10 S 03753 — 603-863-9689
Sydney Leggett, supt. — Fax 863-9684
www.gvshawks.org
Grantham Village ES — 200/K-6
75 Learning Dr 03753 — 603-863-1681
Heather Cantagallo, prin. — Fax 863-8377

Greenfield, Hillsborough
Contoocook Valley SD
Supt. — See Peterborough
Greenfield ES — 100/PK-4
860 Forest Rd 03047 — 603-547-3334
Colleen Roy, prin. — Fax 547-2647

Greenland, Rockingham
Greenland SD — 400/K-8
48 Post Rd 03840 — 603-422-9572
Salvatore Petralia, supt. — Fax 422-9575
www.sau50.org
Greenland Central S — 400/K-8
70 Post Rd 03840 — 603-431-6723
Tamara Hallee, prin. — Fax 430-7683

New Castle SD — 50/K-6
48 Post Rd 03840 — 603-422-9572
Salvatore Petralia, supt. — Fax 422-9575
www.sau50.org
Other Schools – See New Castle

Newington SD 50/K-6
48 Post Rd 03840 603-422-9572
Salvatore Petralia, supt. Fax 422-9575
www.sau50.org
Other Schools – See Newington

Rye SD 500/K-8
48 Post Rd 03840 603-422-9572
Salvatore Petralia, supt. Fax 422-9575
www.sau50.org
Other Schools – See Rye

Greenville, Hillsborough, Pop. 1,101
Mascenic Regional SD 1,100/PK-12
16 School St 03048 603-721-0160
Dr. Stephen Russell, supt. Fax 721-0175
www.mascenic.org
Other Schools – See New Ipswich

Groveton, Coos, Pop. 1,110
Northumberland SD 300/K-12
15 Preble St 03582 603-636-1437
Michael Kelley, supt. Fax 636-6102
www.sau58.org
Groveton ES 100/K-5
36 Church St 03582 603-636-1806
Patricia Peel, prin. Fax 636-6253

Stark SD 50/K-6
15 Preble St 03582 603-636-1437
Michael Kelley, supt. Fax 636-6102
www.sau58.org
Other Schools – See Stark

Stratford SD 100/K-8
15 Preble St 03582 603-636-1437
Michael Kelley, supt. Fax 636-6102
www.sau58.org
Other Schools – See North Stratford

Hampstead, Rockingham
Hampstead SD
Supt. — See Plaistow
Hampstead Central ES 500/PK-4
21 Emerson Ave 03841 603-329-6326
Dillard Collins, prin. Fax 329-4323
Hampstead MS 400/5-8
28 School St 03841 603-329-6743
Maria Di Nola, prin. Fax 329-4120

Hampstead Academy 200/PK-9
320 East Rd 03841 603-329-4406
Lyn Kutzelman M.A., dir. Fax 329-7124

Hampton, Rockingham, Pop. 9,556
Hampton Falls SD 300/K-8
2 Alumni Dr 03842 603-926-8992
Robert Sullivan Ed.D., supt. Fax 926-5157
www.sau21.org/sau
Other Schools – See Hampton Falls

Hampton SD 1,200/PK-8
7 Scott Rd 03842 603-926-4560
Kathleen Murphy, supt. Fax 926-5070
www.sau90.org
Hampton Academy 400/6-8
29 Academy Ave 03842 603-926-2000
David O'Connor, prin. Fax 926-1855
Hampton Centre ES 400/PK-2
53 Winnacunnet Rd 03842 603-926-8706
Timothy Lannan, prin. Fax 926-1177
Marston IS 400/3-5
4 Marston Way 03842 603-926-8708
Dr. Lois Costa, prin. Fax 926-7896

North Hampton SD 400/PK-8
2 Alumni Dr 03842 603-926-8992
Robert Sullivan Ed.D., supt. Fax 926-5157
www.sau21.org/sau
Other Schools – See North Hampton

Seabrook SD 700/PK-8
2 Alumni Dr 03842 603-926-8992
Robert Sullivan Ed.D., supt. Fax 926-5157
www.sau21.org/sau
Other Schools – See Seabrook

South Hampton SD 100/K-8
2 Alumni Dr 03842 603-926-8992
Robert Sullivan Ed.D., supt. Fax 926-5157
www.sau21.org/sau
Other Schools – See South Hampton

Sacred Heart S 200/PK-8
289 Lafayette Rd 03842 603-926-3254
Teresa Morin Bailey, prin. Fax 929-1109

Hampton Falls, Rockingham
Hampton Falls SD
Supt. — See Hampton
Akerman S 300/K-8
8 Exeter Rd 03844 603-926-2539
Mark Deblois, prin. Fax 929-3708

Heronfield Academy 100/6-8
356 Exeter Rd 03844 603-772-9093
Martha Shepardson-Killam, head sch

Hancock, Hillsborough, Pop. 200
Contoocook Valley SD
Supt. — See Peterborough
Hancock ES 100/K-4
10 Elementary Ln 03449 603-525-3303
Amy Janoch, prin. Fax 525-3864

Hanover, Grafton, Pop. 8,321
Dresden SD 1,100/6-12
41 Lebanon St Ste 2 03755 603-643-6050
Dr. Jay Badams, supt. Fax 643-3073
www.sau70.org/
Richmond MS 400/6-8
63 Lyme Rd 03755 603-643-6040
Michael Lepene, prin. Fax 643-0662

Hanover SD 800/K-6
41 Lebanon St Ste 2 03755 603-643-6050
Dr. Jay Badams, supt. Fax 643-3073
sau70.hanovernorwichschools.org
Ray ES 500/K-5
26 Reservoir Rd 03755 603-643-6655
Kevin Cotter, prin. Fax 643-0658

Harrisville, Cheshire, Pop. 981
Harrisville SD
Supt. — See Keene
Wells Memorial ES 50/K-6
235 Chesham Rd 03450 603-827-3272
Cheryl McDaniel-Thomas, prin. Fax 827-3073

Henniker, Merrimack, Pop. 1,723
Henniker SD 400/PK-8
258 Western Ave 03242 603-428-3269
Dr. Lorraine Tacconi-Moore, supt. Fax 428-6545
www.sau24.org
Henniker Community S 400/PK-8
51 Western Ave 03242 603-428-3476
Karen Raymond, prin. Fax 428-8271

Stoddard SD 100/K-5
258 Western Ave 03242 603-428-3269
Dr. Lorraine Tacconi-Moore, supt. Fax 428-6545
www.sau24.org
Other Schools – See Stoddard

Weare SD 1,000/PK-8
258 Western Ave 03242 603-428-3269
Dr. Lorraine Tacconi-Moore, supt. Fax 428-6545
www.sau24.org
Other Schools – See Weare

Hill, Merrimack
Hill SD
Supt. — See Franklin
Blake ES 100/K-6
32 Crescent St 03243 603-934-2245
Brian Connelly, prin. Fax 934-5582

Hillsborough, Hillsborough, Pop. 1,929
Hillsboro-Deering Cooperative SD 1,200/PK-12
PO Box 2190 03244 603-464-4466
Dr. Robert Hassett, supt. Fax 464-4053
www.hdsd.org
Hillsboro-Deering ES 600/PK-5
4 Hillcat Dr 03244 603-464-1110
Daniel Record, prin. Fax 464-4385
Hillsboro-Deering MS 300/6-8
6 Hillcat Dr 03244 603-464-1120
Marc Peterson, prin. Fax 464-5759

Washington SD 50/K-5
PO Box 2190 03244 603-464-4466
Dr. Robert Hassett, supt. Fax 464-4053
www.hdsd.org
Other Schools – See Washington

Hinsdale, Cheshire, Pop. 1,534
Hinsdale SD 500/PK-12
PO Box 27 03451 603-336-5728
Wayne Woolridge, supt. Fax 336-5731
www.hnhsd.org
Hinsdale ES 300/PK-5
12 School St 03451 603-336-5332
Joseph Boggio, prin. Fax 336-7522
Hinsdale MS 100/6-8
49 School St 03451 603-336-5984
Ann Freitag, prin. Fax 336-7497

Holderness, Grafton
Holderness SD
Supt. — See Plymouth
Holderness Central S 200/K-8
19 School Rd 03245 603-536-2538
William Van Bennekum, prin. Fax 536-1772

Hollis, Hillsborough
Brookline SD 600/PK-6
4 Lund Ln 03049 603-324-5999
Andrew Corey, supt. Fax 465-3933
www.sau41.org
Other Schools – See Brookline

Hollis SD 600/PK-6
4 Lund Ln 03049 603-324-5999
Andrew Corey, supt. Fax 465-3933
www.sau41.org
Hollis PS 400/PK-3
36 Silver Lake Rd 03049 603-465-2260
Paula Izbicki, prin. Fax 465-3243
Hollis Upper ES 300/4-6
12 Drury Ln 03049 603-465-9182
Candice Fowler, prin. Fax 465-9068

Hollis-Brookline Cooperative SD 1,300/7-12
4 Lund Ln 03049 603-324-5999
Andrew Corey, supt. Fax 465-3933
www.sau41.org
Hollis-Brookline MS 400/7-8
25 Main St 03049 603-324-5997
Robert Thompson, prin. Fax 465-7523

Hooksett, Merrimack, Pop. 4,079
Auburn SD 600/K-8
90 Farmer Rd 03106 603-622-3731
Dr. Charles Littlefield Ed.D., supt. Fax 669-4352
www.sau15.net
Other Schools – See Auburn

Candia SD 400/K-8
90 Farmer Rd 03106 603-622-3731
Dr. Charles Littlefield Ed.D., supt. Fax 669-4352
www.sau15.net
Other Schools – See Candia

Hooksett SD 1,400/PK-8
90 Farmer Rd 03106 603-622-3731
Dr. Charles Littlefield, supt. Fax 669-4352
www.sau15.net
Cawley MS 500/6-8
89 Whitehall Rd 03106 603-518-5047
Matthew Benson, prin. Fax 518-5086

Hooksett Memorial S 500/3-5
5 Memorial Dr 03106 603-485-9890
Stephen Harrises, prin. Fax 485-8574
Underhill ES 400/PK-2
2 Sherwood Dr 03106 603-623-7233
Benjamin Loi, prin. Fax 623-5896

Hopkinton, Merrimack
Hopkinton SD
Supt. — See Contoocook
Martin S 300/PK-3
271 Main St 03229 603-746-3473
William Carozza, prin. Fax 746-6803

Beech Hill S, 20 Beech Hill Rd 03229 50/6-8
Rick Johnson, head sch 603-715-5129

Hudson, Hillsborough, Pop. 7,236
Hudson SD 3,900/PK-12
20 Library St 03051 603-883-7765
Lawrence Russell, supt. Fax 886-1236
www.sau81.org
Hills Garrison S 500/2-5
190 Derry Rd 03051 603-881-3930
Lois Connors, prin. Fax 881-3933
Hudson Memorial S 900/6-8
1 Memorial Dr 03051 603-886-1240
Keith Bowen, prin. Fax 883-1252
Library Street S 200/PK-K
22 Library St 03051 603-886-1255
Mary-Ellen Labrie, prin. Fax 595-1514
Nottingham West ES 600/2-5
10 Pelham Rd 03051 603-595-1570
Fax 595-1515
Smith S 300/1-1
33 School St 03051 603-886-1248
Mary-Ellen Labrie, prin. Fax 886-1239

Presentation of Mary Academy 500/PK-8
182 Lowell Rd 03051 603-889-6054
Sr. Maria Rosa, prin. Fax 595-8504

Jackson, Carroll
Jackson SD
Supt. — See Conway
Jackson ES 50/K-6
PO Box J 03846 603-383-6861
Gayle Dembowski, prin. Fax 383-0827

Jaffrey, Cheshire, Pop. 2,700
Jaffrey-Rindge Cooperative SD 1,500/PK-12
81 Fitzgerald Dr Unit 2 03452 603-532-8100
Reuben Duncan, supt. Fax 532-8165
www.sau47.org
Jaffrey Grade S 300/PK-5
18 School St 03452 603-532-8355
Susan Shaw Sarles, prin. Fax 532-4091
Jaffrey-Rindge MS 400/6-8
1 Conant Way 03452 603-532-8122
Robert Clark, prin. Fax 532-8124
Other Schools – See Rindge

Jefferson, Coos
White Mountains Regional SD
Supt. — See Whitefield
Jefferson ES 100/K-6
PO Box 100 03583 603-586-4363
Sherri Gregory, prin. Fax 586-4540

Keene, Cheshire, Pop. 23,106
Chesterfield SD 300/K-8
193 Maple Ave 03431 603-357-9002
Robert Malay, supt. Fax 357-9012
www.sau29.org
Other Schools – See Chesterfield

Harrisville SD 50/K-6
193 Maple Ave 03431 603-357-9002
Robert Malay, supt. Fax 357-9012
www.sau29.org
Other Schools – See Harrisville

Keene SD 3,400/PK-12
193 Maple Ave 03431 603-357-9002
Robert Malay, supt. Fax 357-9012
www.sau29.org
Daniels Pre-School 200/PK-PK
227 Maple Ave 03431 603-354-2106
Joanne Mulligan, admin.
Franklin ES 200/K-5
217 Washington St 03431 603-352-1712
Erik Kress, prin. Fax 357-9015
Fuller ES 300/K-5
422 Elm St 03431 603-352-1245
Emily Hartshorne, prin. Fax 357-9031
Keene MS 700/6-8
167 Maple Ave 03431 603-357-9020
Deanna Zilske, prin. Fax 357-9045
Symonds ES 400/K-5
79 Park Ave 03431 603-352-3405
Richard Cate, prin. Fax 357-9018
Wheelock ES 200/PK-5
24 Adams St 03431 603-352-2244
Patricia Yoerger, prin. Fax 357-9028

Marlborough SD 200/K-8
193 Maple Ave 03431 603-357-9002
Robert Malay, supt. Fax 357-9012
www.sau29.org
Other Schools – See Marlborough

Marlow SD 50/PK-6
193 Maple Ave 03431 603-357-9002
Robert Malay, supt. Fax 357-9012
www.sau29.org
Other Schools – See Marlow

Nelson SD 100/K-6
193 Maple Ave 03431 603-357-9002
Robert Malay, supt. Fax 357-9012
www.sau29.org
Other Schools – See Nelson

Westmoreland SD 200/K-8
193 Maple Ave 03431 603-357-9002
Robert Malay, supt. Fax 357-9012
www.sau29.org
Other Schools – See Westmoreland

Monadnock Waldorf S 200/PK-12
98 S Lincoln St 03431 603-357-4442
Tiffany Nichols, admin. Fax 357-2955
St. Joseph Regional S 100/PK-8
92 Wilson St 03431 603-355-2720
Christopher Smith, prin. Fax 358-5465
Trinity Christian S 100/PK-8
100 Maple Ave 03431 603-352-9403
Markus Konig, prin. Fax 358-3405

Kensington, Rockingham
Kensington SD
Supt. — See Exeter
Kensington ES 100/K-5
122 Amesbury Rd 03833 603-772-5705
Jennifer Ruel, prin. Fax 775-0502

Kingston, Rockingham
Sanborn Regional SD 1,800/PK-12
17 Danville Rd 03848 603-642-3688
Tom Ambrose, supt. Fax 642-7885
sau17.org
Bakie ES 400/PK-5
179 Main St 03848 603-642-5272
Christopher Snyder, prin. Fax 642-8906
Other Schools – See Newton

Laconia, Belknap, Pop. 15,741
Laconia SD 2,000/PK-12
PO Box 309 03247 603-524-5710
Brendan Minnihan, supt. Fax 528-8442
laconiaschools.weebly.com
Elm Street ES 300/PK-5
478 Elm St 03246 603-524-4113
Tara Beauchemin, prin. Fax 528-1249
Laconia MS 500/6-8
150 McGrath St 03246 603-524-4632
Dr. Alison Bryant, prin. Fax 528-8675
Pleasant Street ES 300/PK-5
350 Pleasant St 03246 603-524-2168
David Levesque, prin. Fax 528-8452
Woodland Heights ES 400/PK-5
225 Winter St 03246 603-524-8733
Eric Johnson, prin. Fax 528-8688

Holy Trinity Catholic S 100/PK-8
50 Church St 03246 603-524-3156
Mary Jane Cooney, prin. Fax 524-4454
Laconia Christian Academy 100/PK-12
1386 Meredith Center Rd 03246 603-524-3250
Rick Duba, head sch Fax 524-3285

Lancaster, Coos, Pop. 1,709
White Mountains Regional SD
Supt. — See Whitefield
Lancaster ES 400/PK-8
34 Ice Pond Rd 03584 603-788-4924
Todd Lamarque, prin. Fax 788-2216

Landaff, Grafton
Landaff SD
Supt. — See Littleton
Landaff Blue ES 50/K-3
813 Mill Brook Rd 03585 603-838-6416
Molly Culver, lead tchr.

Langdon, Sullivan
Fall Mountain Regional SD 1,600/PK-12
PO Box 720 03602 603-835-0006
Lorraine Landry, supt. Fax 835-0007
www.sau60.org
Fall Mountain Early Learning Center 50/PK-PK
134 Fmrhs Rd 03602 603-835-6314
Tammy Vittum, coord. Fax 835-6314
Porter ES 50/1-4
111 Village Rd 03602 603-835-2260
Gail Rowe, prin. Fax 835-9097
Other Schools – See Acworth, Alstead, Charlestown, North Walpole, Walpole

Lebanon, Grafton, Pop. 12,877
Lebanon SD
Supt. — See West Lebanon
Hanover Street ES 300/K-4
193 Hanover St 03766 603-448-2945
Ken Rosser, prin. Fax 448-0615
Lebanon MS 400/5-8
3 Moulton Ave 03766 603-448-3056
John D'Entremont, prin. Fax 448-0616

Lee, Strafford
Oyster River Cooperative SD
Supt. — See Durham
Mast Way ES 300/K-4
23 Mast Rd, 603-659-3001
Carrie Vaich, prin. Fax 659-8612

Lempster, Sullivan
Goshen-Lempster Cooperative SD 200/K-8
29 School Rd 03605 603-863-2420
Dr. Michele Munson, supt. Fax 863-2451
www.sau71.org
Other Schools – See East Lempster

Lincoln, Grafton, Pop. 991
Lincoln-Woodstock Cooperative SD 100/K-12
PO Box 846 03251 603-745-2051
Judith McGann, supt. Fax 745-2351
www.lin-wood.org
Lin-Wood S 100/K-12
72 Linwood Dr 03251 603-745-2214
Scott Currier, prin. Fax 745-6797

Lisbon, Grafton, Pop. 967
Lisbon Regional SD
Supt. — See Littleton
Lisbon Regional S 100/K-12
24 Highland Ave 03585 603-838-5506
Jacqueline Daniels, prin. Fax 838-5012

Litchfield, Hillsborough
Litchfield SD 1,400/PK-12
1 Highlander Ct 03052 603-578-3570
James O'Neill, supt. Fax 578-1267
www.litchfieldsd.org
Griffin Memorial ES 500/PK-4
229 Charles Bancroft Hwy 03052 603-424-0078
Scott Thompson, prin. Fax 424-2677
Litchfield MS 500/5-8
19 McElwain Dr 03052 603-424-0566
Thomas Lecklider, prin. Fax 424-1296

St. Francis of Assisi S 100/PK-6
9 Saint Francis Way 03052 603-424-3312
Dr. Steven O'Brien, prin. Fax 424-9128

Littleton, Grafton, Pop. 4,350
Bethlehem SD 200/K-6
260 Cottage St Ste C 03561 603-444-3925
Pierre Couture, supt. Fax 444-6299
www.sau35.k12.nh.us
Other Schools – See Bethlehem

Lafayette Regional SD 100/K-6
260 Cottage St Ste C 03561 603-444-3925
Pierre Couture, supt. Fax 444-6299
www.sau35.k12.nh.us
Other Schools – See Franconia

Landaff SD 50/K-3
260 Cottage St Ste C 03561 603-444-3925
Pierre Couture, supt. Fax 444-6299
www.sau35.k12.nh.us
Other Schools – See Landaff

Lisbon Regional SD 100/K-12
260 Cottage St Ste C 03561 603-444-3925
Pierre Couture, supt. Fax 444-6299
www.sau35.k12.nh.us
Other Schools – See Lisbon

Littleton SD 800/K-12
65 Maple St 03561 603-444-5215
Dr. Steven Nilhas, supt. Fax 444-3015
www.littletonschools.org
Bronson JHS 100/7-8
159 Oak Hill Ave 03561 603-444-5601
Jennifer Carbonneau, prin. Fax 444-3009
Lakeway ES 400/K-6
325 Union St 03561 603-444-2831
Crystal Martin, prin. Fax 444-2716

Profile SD 300/7-12
260 Cottage St Ste C 03561 603-444-3925
Pierre Couture, supt. Fax 444-6299
www.sau35.k12.nh.us
Other Schools – See Bethlehem

Londonderry, Rockingham, Pop. 10,903
Londonderry SD 4,500/PK-12
268C Mammoth Rd 03053 603-432-6920
Scott Laliberte, supt. Fax 425-1049
www.londonderry.org
Londonderry MS 1,100/6-8
313 Mammoth Rd 03053 603-432-6925
Richard Zacchilli, prin. Fax 432-0714
Moose Hill S 300/PK-K
150 Pillsbury Rd 03053 603-437-5855
Bonnie Breithaupt, prin. Fax 437-3709
North Londonderry ES 400/1-5
19 Sanborn Rd 03053 603-432-6933
Paul Dutton, prin. Fax 425-1006
South Londonderry ES 500/1-5
88 South Rd 03053 603-432-6956
Linda Boyd, prin. Fax 425-1004
Thornton ES 600/1-5
275 Mammoth Rd 03053 603-432-6937
Sharon Putney, prin. Fax 425-1005

Loudon, Merrimack, Pop. 552
Merrimack Valley SD
Supt. — See Penacook
Loudon ES 300/K-5
7039 School St 03307 603-783-4400
Catherine Inman Masterso, prin. Fax 783-4222

Lyme, Grafton
Lyme SD 200/K-8
PO Box 117 03768 603-795-4431
Jeffrey Valence, supt. Fax 795-9407
www.lymeschool.org
Lyme S 200/K-8
PO Box 60 03768 603-795-2125
Jeffrey Valence, prin. Fax 795-4719

Crossroads Academy 100/K-8
95 Dartmouth College Hwy 03768 603-795-3111

Lyndeborough, Hillsborough
Wilton-Lyndeborough Cooperative SD 400/PK-12
192 Forest Rd 03082 603-654-8088
Bryan Lane, supt. Fax 654-6691
www.sau63.org
Lyndeborough Central ES 50/PK-K
192 Forest Rd 03082 603-654-9381
Timothy O'Connell, prin. Fax 654-6884
Other Schools – See Wilton

Madbury, Strafford
Oyster River Cooperative SD
Supt. — See Durham
Moharimet ES 400/K-4
11 Lee Rd, 603-742-2900
David Goldsmith, prin. Fax 742-7569

Madison, Carroll
Madison SD
Supt. — See Tamworth
Madison ES 100/K-6
2069 Village Rd 03849 603-367-4642
Heather Woodward, prin. Fax 367-8784

Manchester, Hillsborough, Pop. 107,082
Goffstown SD
Supt. — See Goffstown

Bartlett ES 200/1-4
689 Mast Rd 03102 603-623-8088
Geraldine St. Gelais, prin. Fax 644-8488

Manchester SD 14,700/PK-12
195 McGregor St Ste 201 03102 603-624-6300
Dr. Bolgen Vargas, supt. Fax 624-6337
www.mansd.org
Bakersville ES 400/PK-5
20 Elm St 03101 603-624-6312
Kate Josef, prin. Fax 624-6431
Beech Street ES 600/K-5
333 Beech St 03103 603-624-6314
Dr. Christine Martin, prin. Fax 624-6572
Gossler Park ES 400/K-5
99 Sullivan St 03102 603-624-6327
Lori Upham, prin. Fax 624-6392
Green Acres ES 600/PK-5
100 Aurore Ave 03109 603-624-6330
Richard Norton, prin. Fax 624-6284
Hallsville ES 300/K-5
275 Jewett St 03103 603-624-6332
Bonnie Skogsholm, prin. Fax 665-6869
Highland/Goffes Falls ES 500/K-5
2021 Goffs Falls Rd 03103 603-624-6334
Susan Matthews, prin. Fax 665-6699
Hillside MS 800/6-8
112 Reservoir Ave 03104 603-624-6352
Brendan McCafferty, prin. Fax 628-6049
Jewett Street ES 400/PK-5
130 S Jewett St 03103 603-624-6336
Peter Lubelczyk, prin. Fax 665-6840
McDonough ES 600/K-5
550 Lowell St 03104 603-624-6373
Kenneth DiBenedetto, prin. Fax 665-6692
McLaughlin MS 800/6-8
290 S Mammoth Rd 03109 603-628-6247
William Krantz, prin. Fax 628-6274
Northwest ES 700/K-5
300 Youville St 03102 603-624-6321
Shelly Larochelle, prin. Fax 624-6319
Parker-Varney ES 500/PK-5
223 James A Pollock Dr 03102 603-624-6338
Amy Allen, prin. Fax 624-6399
Parkside MS 700/6-8
75 Parkside Ave 03102 603-624-6356
Forrest Ransdell, prin. Fax 624-6355
Smyth Road ES 400/PK-5
245 Bruce Rd 03104 603-624-6340
Jennifer Briggs, prin. Fax 665-6839
Southside MS 800/6-8
140 S Jewett St 03103 603-624-6359
Jennifer Gillis, prin. Fax 624-6361
Webster ES 400/K-5
2519 Elm St 03104 603-624-6344
Sarah Lynch, prin. Fax 628-6059
Weston ES 600/PK-5
1066 Hanover St 03104 603-624-6347
Lizabeth MacDonald, prin. Fax 624-6375
Wilson ES 500/K-5
401 Wilson St 03103 603-624-6350
Polly Golden, prin. Fax 624-6395

Holy Cross ECC PK-K
420 Island Pond Rd 03109 603-668-0510
Betty Mulrey, dir. Fax 668-0510
Mt. St. Mary Academy 200/PK-6
2291 Elm St 03104 603-623-3155
Kate Segal, prin. Fax 621-9254
Mount Zion Christian S 100/PK-12
132 Titus Ave 03103 603-606-7930
North End Montessori S PK-3
698 Beech St 03104 603-621-9011
Susan Bradley, prin. Fax 621-9866
St. Anthony of Padua S 200/PK-6
148 Belmont St 03103 603-622-0414
Betty Beebe, prin. Fax 669-5212
St. Augustine Preschool & K 50/PK-K
251 Merrimack St 03103 603-623-8800
Crystal Elie, dir. Fax 626-1517
St. Benedict Academy 100/PK-6
85 3rd St 03102 603-669-3932
Heather Silveira, prin. Fax 669-3932
St. Casimir S 100/K-8
456 Union St 03103 603-623-6411
Richard Flagg, prin. Fax 623-3236
St. Catherine of Siena S 300/PK-6
206 North St 03104 603-622-1711
Jocelyn Bergeron, prin. Fax 624-4935
St. Joseph Regional JHS 100/7-8
148 Belmont St 03103 603-624-4811
Denis Mailloux, prin. Fax 624-6670
Ste. Marie Child Care Center 100/PK-K
133 Wayne St 03102 603-668-2356
Therese Cody, dir. Fax 666-4732

Marlborough, Cheshire, Pop. 1,076
Marlborough SD
Supt. — See Keene
Marlborough ES 200/K-8
41 Fitch Ct 03455 603-876-4465
RobinWhitney, prin. Fax 876-4302

Marlow, Cheshire
Marlow SD
Supt. — See Keene
Perkins Academy of Marlow 50/PK-6
919 NH Route 10 03456 603-446-3307
Walter Huston, prin. Fax 446-7323

Mason, Hillsborough, Pop. 1,212
Mason SD 100/PK-5
13 Darling Hill Rd 03048 603-878-2962
Kristen Kivela, supt. Fax 878-3439
mason.sau89.org
Mason ES 100/PK-5
13 Darling Hill Rd 03048 603-878-2962
Kristen Kivela, prin. Fax 878-3439

Meredith, Belknap, Pop. 1,695
Ashland SD 200/K-8
103 Main St Ste 2 03253 603-279-7947
Mary A. Moriarty, supt. Fax 279-3044
sau2.k12.nh.us/

Other Schools – See Ashland

Inter-Lakes Cooperative SD 1,100/PK-12
103 Main St Ste 2 03253 603-279-7947
Mary Moriarty, supt. Fax 279-3044
www.interlakes.org/
Inter-Lakes ES 400/PK-4
21 Laker Ln 03253 603-279-7968
Jennifer Wrath, prin. Fax 279-6344
Inter-Lakes MS 300/5-8
1 Laker Ln 03253 603-279-5312
Everett Bennett, prin. Fax 279-5310
Other Schools – See Center Sandwich

Meriden, Sullivan
Plainfield SD 200/K-8
92 Bonner Rd 03770 603-469-3442
Frank Perotti, supt. Fax 469-3259
www.plainfieldschool.org
Plainfield ES 200/K-8
92 Bonner Rd 03770 603-469-3250
Sondra Brake, prin. Fax 469-3259

Merrimack, Hillsborough, Pop. 22,156
Merrimack SD 3,900/PK-12
36 McElwain St 03054 603-424-6200
Marjorie Chiafery, supt. Fax 424-6229
www.sau26.org
Mastricola ES 500/PK-4
7 School St 03054 603-424-6218
Michelle Romein, prin. Fax 424-6239
Mastricola Upper ES 600/5-6
26 Baboosic Lake Rd 03054 603-424-6221
Marsha McGill, prin. Fax 424-6323
Merrimack MS 600/7-8
31 Madeline Bennett Ln 03054 603-424-6289
Adam Caragher, prin. Fax 423-1109
Reeds Ferry ES 500/PK-4
15 Lyons Rd 03054 603-424-6215
Kimberly Yarlott, prin. Fax 424-6238
Thorntons Ferry ES 500/PK-4
134 Camp Sargent Rd 03054 603-889-1577
Bridey Bellemare, prin. Fax 598-9821

South Merrimack Christian Academy 300/PK-12
517 Boston Post Rd 03054 603-880-6832
Brian Burbach, hdmstr. Fax 598-7085

Middleton, Strafford
SAU 49
Supt. — See Wolfeboro Falls
Middleton ES K-5
116 Kings Hwy 03887 603-473-5000
Kathleen Crosby, prin. Fax 473-2225

Milan, Coos
Milan SD
Supt. — See Gorham
Milan Village ES 100/PK-6
11 Bridge St 03588 603-449-3306
Matthew Underwood, prin. Fax 449-2509

Milford, Hillsborough, Pop. 8,681
Milford SD 2,600/PK-12
100 West St 03055 603-673-2202
Robert Marquis, supt. Fax 673-2237
milfordk12.org
Heron Pond ES 700/2-5
80 Heron Pond Rd 03055 603-673-1811
Chantal Alcox, prin. Fax 459-0814
Jacques Memorial ES 300/PK-1
9 Elm St 03055 603-673-4434
Nancy Maguire, prin. Fax 459-0814
Milford MS 700/6-8
33 Osgood Rd 03055 603-673-5221
Anthony DeMarco, prin. Fax 673-5221

Milton, Strafford, Pop. 560
Milton SD 600/K-12
18 Commerce Way 03851 603-652-0262
Earl Sussman, supt. Fax 652-0250
www.sau64.org
Milton ES 300/K-5
8 School St 03851 603-652-4539
Frank Safina, prin. Fax 652-9431
Nute JHS 100/6-8
22 Elm St 03851 603-652-4591
Janette Radowicz, prin. Fax 652-9926

Wakefield SD 400/PK-8
18 Commerce Way 03851 603-652-0262
Earl Sussman, supt. Fax 652-0250
www.sau101.org/
Other Schools – See Sanbornville

Monroe, Grafton
Monroe SD 100/PK-8
PO Box 130 03771 603-638-2800
Susan Hodgdon, supt. Fax 638-2031
www.monroeschool77.com
Monroe Consolidated S 100/PK-8
PO Box 130 03771 603-638-2800
Leah Holz, prin. Fax 638-2031

Mont Vernon, Hillsborough
Mont Vernon SD
Supt. — See Amherst
Mont Vernon Village ES 200/K-6
PO Box 98 03057 603-673-5141
John Schuttinger, prin. Fax 672-1924

Moultonborough, Carroll
Moultonborough SD 500/PK-12
PO Box 419 03254 603-476-5247
Susan Noyes M.Ed., supt. Fax 476-8009
sau45.org
Moultonborough Academy 100/7-8
PO Box 228 03254 603-476-5517
Andrew Coppinger, prin. Fax 476-5153
Moultonborough Central S 300/PK-6
PO Box 149 03254 603-476-5535
Kathleen D'Haene, prin. Fax 476-2409

Nashua, Hillsborough, Pop. 84,540
Nashua SD 11,600/PK-12
PO Box 687 03061 603-966-1000
Dr. Jahmal Mosley Ed.D., supt. Fax 594-4350
www.nashua.edu
Amherst Street ES 300/K-5
71 Amherst St 03064 603-594-4385
Jennifer Scarpati, prin. Fax 594-4470
Bicentennial ES 600/PK-5
296 E Dunstable Rd 03062 603-594-4382
Michael Mahoney, prin. Fax 594-4389
Birch Hill ES 500/K-5
17 Birch Hill Dr 03063 603-594-4340
Mark Lucas, prin. Fax 594-4342
Broad Street ES 400/PK-5
390 Broad St 03063 603-594-4404
Stacy Bachelder, prin. Fax 882-2332
Charlotte Avenue ES 500/K-5
48 Charlotte Ave 03064 603-594-4334
Patricia Beaulieu, prin. Fax 594-4336
Crisp ES 400/PK-5
50 Arlington St 03060 603-594-4390
Cherrie Fulton, prin. Fax 594-4395
Elm Street MS 1,100/6-8
117 Elm St 03060 603-594-4322
Ian Atwell, prin. Fax 594-4370
Fairgrounds ES 500/K-5
37 Blanchard St 03060 603-594-4318
Michael Harrington, prin. Fax 594-4348
Fairgrounds MS 700/6-8
27 Cleveland St 03060 603-594-4393
Sharon Coffey, prin. Fax 594-4355
Ledge Street ES 500/K-5
139 Ledge St 03060 603-966-2280
Fax 594-4344
Main Dunstable ES 500/K-5
20 Whitford Rd 03062 603-594-4400
Kelley Paradis, prin. Fax 594-4369
Mt. Pleasant ES 400/PK-5
10 Manchester St 03064 603-594-4331
Patricia Snow, prin. Fax 594-4417
New Searles ES 500/PK-5
39 Shady Ln 03062 603-594-4409
Jay Harding, prin. Fax 891-5504
Pennichuck MS 700/6-8
207 Manchester St 03064 603-594-4308
Lynne Joseph, prin. Fax 594-4413
Purple Panthers Preschool 50/PK-PK
36 Riverside Dr 03062 603-589-8561
Nicole Robinson, dir. Fax 589-0722
Sunset Heights ES 400/K-5
15 Osgood Rd 03060 603-594-4387
Marie Alsup, prin. Fax 594-4349

Infant Jesus S 200/PK-6
3 Crown St 03060 603-889-2649
Kelly Veilleux, prin. Fax 594-9117
Nashua Catholic Regional JHS 200/7-8
6 Bartlett Ave 03064 603-883-6707
Glenda McFadden, prin. Fax 594-8955
Nashua Christian Academy 200/PK-12
55 Franklin St 03064 603-889-8892
Christine Urban, hdmstr. Fax 821-7451
St. Christopher S 300/PK-6
20 Cushing Ave 03064 603-882-7442
Cynthia Clarke, prin. Fax 594-9253
World Academy 300/PK-8
138 Spit Brook Rd 03062 603-888-1982
Kathleen Nelson, pres. Fax 888-5880

Nelson, Cheshire
Nelson SD
Supt. — See Keene
Nelson ES 100/K-6
441 Granite Lake Rd 03457 603-847-3408
Ron Upton, prin. Fax 847-9612

New Boston, Hillsborough
New Boston SD
Supt. — See Goffstown
New Boston Central ES 500/PK-6
15 Central School Rd 03070 603-487-2211
Tori Underwood, prin. Fax 487-2215

New Castle, Rockingham
New Castle SD
Supt. — See Greenland
Trefethen ES 50/K-6
PO Box 228 03854 603-436-5416
David Latchaw, prin. Fax 427-1918

New Durham, Strafford
Governor Wentworth Regional SD
Supt. — See Wolfeboro
New Durham ES 200/PK-6
PO Box 212 03855 603-859-2061
Kelly Colby-Seavey, prin. Fax 859-5308

Newfields, Rockingham, Pop. 301
Newfields SD
Supt. — See Exeter
Newfields ES 100/K-5
9 Piscassic Rd 03856 603-772-5555
David Foster, prin. Fax 658-0401

New Hampton, Belknap, Pop. 350
Newfound Area SD
Supt. — See Bristol
New Hampton Community ES 100/K-5
191 Main St 03256 603-744-3221
Ann Holloran, prin. Fax 744-3450

Newington, Rockingham, Pop. 990
Newington SD
Supt. — See Greenland
Newington ES 50/K-6
133 Nimble Hill Rd 03801 603-436-1482
Peter Latchaw, prin. Fax 427-0692

New Ipswich, Hillsborough
Mascenic Regional SD
Supt. — See Greenville
Boynton MS 300/5-8
500 Turnpike Rd 03071 603-878-4800
Elizabeth Pogorzelski, prin. Fax 878-0525

Highbridge Hill ES 400/PK-4
171 Turnpike Rd 03071 603-878-4387
Marion Saari, prin.

New London, Merrimack, Pop. 1,397
Kearsarge Regional SD 1,800/PK-12
114 Cougar Ct 03257 603-526-2051
Winfried Feneberg, supt.
www.kearsarge.org
James House Preschool 50/PK-PK
114 Cougar Ct 03257 603-526-8604
Nicole Gagnon, prin. Fax 526-2145
Kearsarge Regional ES - New London 300/K-5
64 Cougar Ct 03257 603-526-4737
Kelly Collins, prin.
Other Schools – See Bradford, North Sutton, Sutton Mills, Warner

Newmarket, Rockingham, Pop. 5,181
Newmarket SD 800/PK-12
186A Main St 03857 603-659-5020
Dr. Meredith Nadeau, supt. Fax 659-5022
www.newmarket.k12.nh.us
Newmarket ES 600/PK-5
243 S Main St 03857 603-659-2192
Sean Pine, prin. Fax 659-4716

Newport, Sullivan, Pop. 4,688
Newport SD 1,000/PK-12
247 N Main St 03773 603-865-9701
Dr. Cynthia Gallagher, supt. Fax 865-9707
www.sau43.org
Newport MS 100/6-8
245 N Main St 03773 603-863-2414
Shannon Martin, prin. Fax 863-0887
Richards ES 300/PK-5
21 School St 03773 603-863-3710
Susan Schroeter, prin. Fax 863-3895

Unity SD
Supt. — See Claremont
Unity ES 100/PK-8
864 2nd NH Tpke 03773 603-542-5888
Maynard Baldwin, prin. Fax 543-4211

Newton, Rockingham
Sanborn Regional SD
Supt. — See Kingston
Sanborn Regional Memorial ES 300/PK-5
31 W Main St 03858 603-382-5251
Patricia Haynes, prin. Fax 382-1466
Sanborn Regional MS 400/6-8
31A W Main St 03858 603-382-6226
Alexander Rutherford, prin. Fax 382-9771

North Conway, Carroll, Pop. 2,311
Conway SD
Supt. — See Conway
Fuller ES 200/K-6
51 Pine St 03860 603-356-5381
Danielle Nutting, prin. Fax 356-9382

Northfield, Merrimack
Winnisquam Regional SD
Supt. — See Tilton
Southwick S 200/3-5
50 Zion Hill Rd 03276 603-286-3611
Eric Keck, prin. Fax 286-3526
Union Sanborn S 300/PK-2
5 Elm St 03276 603-286-4332
Lori Krueger, prin. Fax 286-2153

North Hampton, Rockingham
North Hampton SD
Supt. — See Hampton
North Hampton S 400/PK-8
201 Atlantic Ave 03862 603-964-5501
Erik Anderson, prin. Fax 964-9018

North Haverhill, Grafton
Bath SD 100/K-6
2975 Dartmouth College Hwy 03774 603-787-2113
Laurie Melanson, supt. Fax 787-2118
www.sau23.org
Other Schools – See Bath

Haverhill Cooperative SD 700/PK-12
2975 Dartmouth College Hwy 03774 603-787-2113
Laurie Melanson, supt. Fax 787-2118
www.sau23.org
Haverhill Cooperative MS 300/4-8
175 Morrill Dr 03774 603-787-2100
Robert Phillips, prin. Fax 787-6117
Other Schools – See Woodsville

Piermont SD 100/PK-8
2975 Dartmouth College Hwy 03774 603-787-2113
Laurie Melanson, supt. Fax 787-2118
www.sau23.org
Other Schools – See Piermont

Warren SD 100/PK-8
2975 Dartmouth College Hwy 03774 603-787-2113
Laurie Melanson, supt. Fax 787-2118
www.sau23.org
Other Schools – See Warren

North Stratford, Coos
Stratford SD
Supt. — See Groveton
Stratford S 100/K-8
19 School St 03590 603-922-3387
Sandra Adams, prin. Fax 922-3303

North Sutton, Merrimack
Kearsarge Regional SD
Supt. — See New London
Kearsarge Regional MS 500/6-8
PO Box 269 03260 603-927-2100
Stephen Paterson, prin.

North Walpole, Cheshire, Pop. 808
Fall Mountain Regional SD
Supt. — See Langdon
North Walpole ES 100/2-4
17 Cray Rd 03609 603-445-5450
Samuel Jacobs, prin. Fax 445-1955

Northwood, Rockingham
Northwood SD 400/K-8
23 Mountain Ave Unit A 03261 603-942-1290
Dr. Robert Gadomski, supt. Fax 942-1295
www.northwood.k12.nh.us
Northwood ES 400/K-8
511 1st NH Tpke 03261 603-942-5488
Jocelyn Young, prin. Fax 942-5746

Nottingham SD 500/K-8
23 Mountain Ave Unit A 03261 603-942-1290
Dr. Robert Gadomski Ph.D., supt. Fax 942-1295
www.nottingham.k12.nh.us
Other Schools – See Nottingham

Strafford SD 400/K-8
23 Mountain Ave Unit A 03261 603-942-1290
Dr. Robert Gadomski, supt. Fax 942-1295
www.strafford.k12.nh.us
Other Schools – See Strafford

Nottingham, Rockingham
Nottingham SD
Supt. — See Northwood
Nottingham ES 500/K-8
245 Stage Rd 03290 603-679-5632
Christopher Sousa, prin. Fax 679-1617

Ossipee, Carroll

Cornerstone Christian Academy 100/PK-8
129 Route 28 03864 603-539-8636
Cindy Hyatt, hdmstr. Fax 539-8637

Pelham, Hillsborough
Pelham SD 2,000/PK-12
59A Marsh Rd 03076 603-635-1145
Dr. Betsey Cox-Buteau, supt. Fax 635-1283
www.pelhamsd.org
Pelham ES 800/K-5
61 Marsh Rd 03076 603-635-8875
Thomas Adamakos, prin. Fax 635-8922
Pelham Memorial S 500/6-8
59 Marsh Rd 03076 603-635-2321
Stacy Maghakian, prin. Fax 635-2369
Pelham Preschool 50/PK-PK
61 Marsh Rd 03076 603-635-1145
Trisha Kaufmann, dir. Fax 635-1283

Pembroke, Merrimack, Pop. 6,561
Allenstown SD 400/PK-8
267 Pembroke St 03275 603-485-5188
David Ryan, supt. Fax 485-9529
www.sau53.org
Other Schools – See Allenstown

Chichester SD 200/K-8
267 Pembroke St 03275 603-485-5188
David Ryan, supt. Fax 485-9529
www.sau53.org
Other Schools – See Chichester

Deerfield SD 500/PK-8
267 Pembroke St 03275 603-485-5188
Patricia Sherman, supt. Fax 485-9529
www.sau53.org
Other Schools – See Deerfield

Epsom SD 400/K-8
267 Pembroke St 03275 603-485-5188
David Ryan, supt. Fax 485-9529
www.sau53.org
Other Schools – See Epsom

Pembroke SD 1,600/K-12
267 Pembroke St 03275 603-485-5188
Patricia Sherman, supt. Fax 485-9529
www.sau53.org
Pembroke Hill ES 200/2-4
300 Belanger Dr 03275 603-485-9000
Susan Griffith, prin. Fax 485-8872
Pembroke Village ES 200/K-1
30 High St 03275 603-485-1807
Mona Sandberg, prin. Fax 485-1811
Three Rivers MS 300/5-8
243 Academy Rd 03275 603-485-9539
Jonathan Marston, prin. Fax 485-1829

Penacook, See Concord
Andover SD 200/K-8
105 Community Dr 03303 603-753-6561
Mark MacLean, supt. Fax 753-6023
www.aemseagles.org
Other Schools – See Andover

Merrimack Valley SD 2,600/PK-12
105 Community Dr 03303 603-753-6561
Mark MacLean, supt. Fax 753-6023
www.mvsdpride.org
Merrimack Valley MS 600/6-8
14 Allen St 03303 603-753-6336
Kara Lamontagne, prin. Fax 753-8107
Penacook ES 400/PK-5
60 Village St 03303 603-753-4891
Jennifer Moore, prin. Fax 753-6419
Other Schools – See Boscawen, Loudon, Salisbury, Webster

Peterborough, Hillsborough, Pop. 3,075
Contoocook Valley SD 2,400/PK-12
106 Hancock Rd 03458 603-924-3336
Kimberly Rizzo Saunders, supt. Fax 924-6707
www.conval.edu
Peterborough ES 200/PK-4
17 High St 03458 603-924-3828
Helena Bates, prin. Fax 924-4193
South Meadow MS 400/5-8
108 Hancock Rd 03458 603-924-7105
Anne O'Bryant, prin. Fax 924-2064
Other Schools – See Antrim, Bennington, Dublin, Francestown, Greenfield, Hancock, Temple

---

Well S 100/PK-8
36 Well School Rd 03458 603-924-6908
Margaret Williams M.Ed., head sch Fax 924-2141

Piermont, Grafton
Piermont SD
Supt. — See North Haverhill
Piermont Village S 100/PK-8
PO Box 98 03779 603-272-5881
Debra Norwood, prin. Fax 272-9203

Pittsburg, Coos
Pittsburg SD
Supt. — See Colebrook
Pittsburg ES 100/PK-8
12 School St 03592 603-538-6536
Elaine Sherry, prin. Fax 538-6996

Pittsfield, Merrimack, Pop. 1,547
Pittsfield SD 500/PK-12
23 Oneida St Unit 1 03263 603-435-5526
Dr. John Freeman, supt. Fax 435-5331
www.pittsfieldnhschools.org
Pittsfield ES 300/PK-6
34 Bow St 03263 603-435-8432
Danielle Harvey, prin. Fax 435-7358
Pittsfield MS 100/7-8
23 Oneida St 03263 603-435-6701
Danielle Harvey, prin. Fax 435-7087

Plainfield, Sullivan, Pop. 204

Estabrook Christian S 50/1-10
1050 Route 12A 03781 603-675-2455
Ellen Busl M.Ed., prin.

Plaistow, Rockingham
Hampstead SD 900/PK-8
30 Greenough Rd 03865 603-382-6119
Dr. Earl Metzler, supt. Fax 382-3334
www.hampstead.k12.nh.us
Other Schools – See Hampstead

Timberlane Regional SD 3,900/PK-12
30 Greenough Rd 03865 603-382-6119
Dr. Earl Metzler, supt. Fax 382-3334
www.timberlane.net/
Pollard ES 500/PK-5
120 Main St 03865 603-382-7146
Michelle Auger, prin. Fax 382-2782
Timberlane Regional MS 900/6-8
44 Greenough Rd 03865 603-382-7131
Michael Flynn, prin. Fax 382-2781
Other Schools – See Atkinson, Danville, Sandown

Holy Angels Preschool & K 100/PK-K
8 Atkinson Depot Rd 03865 603-382-9783
Jean Lanctot, prin. Fax 382-1113

Plymouth, Grafton, Pop. 4,412
Campton SD 300/PK-8
47 Old Ward Bridge Rd 03264 603-536-1254
Mark Halloran, supt. Fax 536-3545
www.sau48.org
Other Schools – See Campton

Holderness SD 200/K-8
47 Old Ward Bridge Rd 03264 603-536-1254
Mark Halloran, supt. Fax 536-3545
www.sau48.org
Other Schools – See Holderness

Plymouth SD 400/PK-8
47 Old Ward Bridge Rd 03264 603-536-1254
Mark Halloran, supt. Fax 536-3545
www.sau48.org
Plymouth ES 400/PK-8
43 Old Ward Bridge Rd 03264 603-536-1152
Julie Flynn, prin. Fax 536-9085

Rumney SD 100/K-8
47 Old Ward Bridge Rd 03264 603-536-1254
Mark Halloran, supt. Fax 536-3545
www.sau48.org
Other Schools – See Rumney

Thornton SD 200/K-8
47 Old Ward Bridge Rd 03264 603-536-1254
Mark Halloran, supt. Fax 536-3545
www.sau48.org
Other Schools – See Thornton

Waterville Valley SD 50/K-8
47 Old Ward Bridge Rd 03264 603-536-1254
Mark Halloran, supt. Fax 536-3545
www.sau48.org
Other Schools – See Waterville Valley

Wentworth SD 100/K-8
47 Old Ward Bridge Rd 03264 603-536-1254
Mark Halloran, supt. Fax 536-3545
www.sau48.org
Other Schools – See Wentworth

Portsmouth, Rockingham, Pop. 20,315
Portsmouth SD 2,700/PK-12
1 Junkins Ave Unit 402 03801 603-431-5080
Steve Zadravec, supt. Fax 431-6753
www.cityofportsmouth.com/school/
Dondero ES 300/PK-5
32 Van Buren Ave 03801 603-436-2231
Katherine Callahan, prin. Fax 427-2329
Little Harbour ES 500/K-5
50 Clough Dr 03801 603-436-1708
Charlie Grossman, prin. Fax 436-8235
New Franklin ES 300/K-5
1 Franklin Dr 03801 603-436-0910
Joanne Simons, prin. Fax 427-2335
Portsmouth Early Education Program 50/PK-PK
100 Campus Dr 03801 603-422-8228
Elizabeth Setear, dir. Fax 422-8230
Portsmouth MS 500/6-8
155 Parrott Ave 03801 603-436-5781
Phillip Davis, prin. Fax 427-2326

St. Patrick Academy 200/PK-8
125 Austin St 03801 603-436-0739
Mark Schwerdt, head sch Fax 436-1569

Raymond, Rockingham, Pop. 2,815
Raymond SD 1,400/PK-12
43 Harriman Hill Rd 03077 603-895-4299
Tina McCoy, supt. Fax 895-0147
www.sau33.com/
Gove MS 400/5-8
1 Stephen K Batchelder Pkwy 03077 603-895-3394
Robert Bickford, prin. Fax 895-9856
Lamprey River ES 600/PK-4
33 Old Manchester Rd 03077 603-895-3117
Bryan Belanger, prin. Fax 895-9627

Rindge, Cheshire
Jaffrey-Rindge Cooperative SD
Supt. — See Jaffrey
Rindge Memorial S 400/PK-5
58 School St 03461 603-899-3363
Kelly Marcotte, prin. Fax 899-9816

Rochester, Strafford, Pop. 29,277
Rochester SD 4,400/PK-12
150 Wakefield St Ste 8 03867 603-332-3678
Michael Hopkins, supt. Fax 335-7367
www.rochesterschools.com
Allen ES 400/K-5
23 Granite St 03867 603-332-2280
Lynn Allen, prin. Fax 335-7381
Chamberlain Street ES 400/K-5
65 Chamberlain St 03867 603-332-5258
Mark Campbell, prin. Fax 335-3098
Maple Street Magnet S 100/K-5
27 Maple St 03867 603-332-6481
Robin Brown, prin. Fax 335-7367
McClelland ES 400/K-5
59 Brock St 03867 603-332-2180
Michelle McAlister, prin. Fax 335-7369
Rochester MS 900/6-8
47 Brock St 03867 603-332-4090
Adam Houghton, prin. Fax 332-9384
School Street ES 100/K-4
13 School St 03867 603-332-6483
Jennifer Hersom, prin. Fax 335-7367
Other Schools – See East Rochester, Gonic

St. Elizabeth Seton S 100/PK-8
16 Bridge St 03867 603-332-4803
Suzanne Boutin, prin. Fax 332-2915

Rollinsford, Strafford
Rollinsford SD
Supt. — See Somersworth
Rollinsford ES 200/K-6
487 Locust St 03869 603-742-2358
Kate Lucas, prin. Fax 749-5629

Rumney, Grafton
Rumney SD
Supt. — See Plymouth
Russell ES 100/K-8
195 School St 03266 603-786-9591
Jonann Torsey, prin. Fax 786-9626

Rye, Rockingham
Rye SD
Supt. — See Greenland
Rye ES 300/K-5
461 Sagamore Rd 03870 603-436-4731
Suzanne Lull, prin. Fax 431-6702
Rye JHS 200/6-8
501 Washington Rd 03870 603-964-5591
Marie Soucy, prin. Fax 964-3881

Salem, Rockingham, Pop. 27,400
Salem SD 3,700/PK-12
38 Geremonty Dr 03079 603-893-7040
Dr. Michael Delahanty, supt. Fax 893-7080
www.sau57.org
Barron ES 300/K-5
55 Butler St 03079 603-893-7067
Anna Parrill, prin. Fax 893-7068
Fisk ES 200/PK-5
14 Main St 03079 603-893-7051
George Murray, prin. Fax 893-7052
Lancaster ES 300/K-5
54 Millville St 03079 603-893-7059
Adam Pagliarulo, prin. Fax 893-7059
North Salem ES 400/K-5
140 Zion Hill Rd 03079 603-893-7062
Janice Wilkins, prin. Fax 893-7062
Soule ES 200/K-5
173 S Policy St 03079 603-893-7053
Christine Honey-Nadeau, prin. Fax 898-0218
Woodbury MS 900/6-8
206 Main St 03079 603-893-7055
Brad St. Laurent, prin. Fax 898-0634

St. Joseph Regional Catholic S 200/PK-8
40 Main St 03079 603-893-6811
Mary Croteau, prin. Fax 893-6811

Salisbury, Merrimack
Merrimack Valley SD
Supt. — See Penacook
Salisbury ES 100/K-5
6 Whittemore Rd 03268 603-648-2206
Stephanie Wheeler, prin. Fax 648-2529

Sanbornton, Belknap
Winnisquam Regional SD
Supt. — See Tilton
Sanbornton Central ES 200/K-5
16 Hunkins Pond Rd 03269 603-286-8223
Kathy Pope, prin. Fax 286-2151

Sant Bani S 200/K-8
19 Ashram Rd 03269 603-934-4240

Sanbornville, Carroll, Pop. 1,046
Wakefield SD
Supt. — See Milton
Paul ES 400/PK-8
60 Taylor Way 03872 603-522-8891
Jerry Gregoire, prin. Fax 522-6143

Sandown, Rockingham
Timberlane Regional SD
Supt. — See Plaistow
Sandown North ES 200/1-5
23 Stagecoach Rd 03873 603-887-8505
Jo Ann Georgian, prin. Fax 887-8509
TLC at Sandown Central 200/PK-K
295 Main St 03873 603-887-3648
Jennifer Marino, prin. Fax 887-3635

Seabrook, Rockingham
Seabrook SD
Supt. — See Hampton
Seabrook ES 400/PK-4
256 Walton Rd 03874 603-474-2252
Stephanie Lafreniere, prin. Fax 474-3504
Seabrook MS 300/5-8
236 Walton Rd 03874 603-474-9221
Leslie Shepard, prin. Fax 474-8020

Somersworth, Strafford, Pop. 11,470
Rollinsford SD 200/K-6
51 W High St 03878 603-692-4450
Lori Lane, supt. Fax 692-9100
www.sau56.org/rollinsford-school-district/
Other Schools – See Rollinsford

Somersworth SD 1,800/PK-12
51 W High St 03878 603-692-4450
Lori Lane, supt. Fax 692-9100
www.sau56.org/somersworth-school-district/home
Idlehurst ES 500/PK-5
46 Stackpole Rd 03878 603-692-2435
Eris Hersey, prin. Fax 692-9115
Maple Wood ES 300/PK-5
184 Maple Street Ext 03878 603-692-3331
Devin McNelly, prin. Fax 692-4600
Somersworth MS 400/6-8
7 Memorial Dr 03878 603-692-2126
Dana Hilliard, prin. Fax 692-9101

Tri-City Christian Academy 300/PK-12
150 W High St 03878 603-692-2093
Paul Edgar, admin. Fax 692-6305

South Hampton, Rockingham, Pop. 740
South Hampton SD
Supt. — See Hampton
South Hampton Barnard S 100/K-8
219 Main Ave 03827 603-394-7744
Kenneth Darsney, prin. Fax 394-0267

Amesbury SDA S 50/K-8
285 Main Ave 03827 603-394-9970

Stark, Coos
Stark SD
Supt. — See Groveton
Stark Village S 50/K-6
1192 Stark Hwy 03582 603-636-1092
Erin Messer, prin. Fax 636-1081

Stoddard, Cheshire
Stoddard SD
Supt. — See Henniker
Faulkner ES 100/K-5
200 School St 03464 603-446-3348
Martha LeMahieu, prin. Fax 446-3638

Strafford, Strafford
Strafford SD
Supt. — See Northwood
Strafford ES 400/K-8
22 Roller Coaster Rd Unit 1 03884 603-664-2842
Dr. Scott Young, prin. Fax 664-5269

Stratham, Rockingham
Exeter Region Cooperative SD
Supt. — See Exeter
Cooperative MS 1,400/6-8
100 Academic Way 03885 603-775-8700
Patricia Wons, prin. Fax 775-0151

Stratham SD
Supt. — See Exeter
Stratham Memorial S 600/PK-5
39 Gifford Farm Rd 03885 603-772-5413
Thomas Fosher, prin. Fax 772-0021

Cornerstone S 200/PK-8
146 High St 03885 603-772-4349
Lee Anne Robertson, head sch Fax 772-4349

Sunapee, Sullivan
Sunapee SD 400/K-12
70 Lower Main St 03782 603-763-4627
Russell Holden, supt. Fax 763-4718
www.sunapeeschools.org
Sunapee Central ES 200/K-5
22 School St 03782 603-763-5675
Jodi Bergen, prin. Fax 763-9627
Sunapee MS 100/6-8
10 North Rd 03782 603-763-5615
Sean Moynihan, prin. Fax 763-3055

Mount Royal Academy 100/PK-12
PO Box 362 03782 603-763-9010
Derek Tremblay, hdmstr. Fax 763-5390

Sutton Mills, Merrimack
Kearsarge Regional SD
Supt. — See New London
Sutton Central ES 100/K-5
28 Newbury Rd, 603-927-4215
Steven Potoczak, prin.

Swanzey, Cheshire
Monadnock Regional SD 1,800/PK-12
600 Old Homestead Hwy 03446 603-352-6955
Lisa Witte, supt. Fax 358-6708
www.mrsd.org
Cutler ES 300/3-6
31 S Winchester St 03446 603-352-3383
Audrey Salzmann, prin. Fax 352-0815
Monadnock Regional MS 300/7-8
580 Old Homestead Hwy 03446 603-352-6575
Lisa Spencer, prin. Fax 357-6520
Mt. Caesar ES 300/PK-2
585 Old Homestead Hwy 03446 603-352-4797
Dr. Melissa Suarez, prin. Fax 352-1713
Other Schools – See Fitzwilliam, Gilsum, Troy

Tamworth, Carroll
Freedom SD 100/PK-6
881A Tamworth Rd 03886 603-323-5088
Louis Goscinski, supt. Fax 323-5093
sau13.weebly.com
Other Schools – See Freedom

Madison SD 100/K-6
881A Tamworth Rd 03886 603-323-5088
Louis Goscinski, supt. Fax 323-5093
sau13.weebly.com
Other Schools – See Madison

Tamworth SD 200/K-8
881A Tamworth Rd 03886 603-323-5088
Louis Goscinski, supt. Fax 323-5093
sau13.weebly.com
Brett ES 200/K-8
881 Tamworth Rd 03886 603-323-7271
Kenneth Hawkins, prin. Fax 323-7454

Temple, Hillsborough
Contoocook Valley SD
Supt. — See Peterborough
Temple ES 100/K-4
830 NH Route 45 03084 603-878-1955
Fabiola Woods, prin. Fax 878-2506

Thornton, Grafton
Thornton SD
Supt. — See Plymouth
Thornton Central S 200/K-8
1886 NH Route 175, 603-726-8904
Jonathan Bownes, prin. Fax 726-3801

Tilton, Belknap, Pop. 3,081
Winnisquam Regional SD 1,500/PK-12
433 W Main St 03276 603-286-4116
Dr. Tammy Davis, supt. Fax 286-7402
www.winnisquam.k12.nh.us
Winnisquam Regional MS 300/6-8
76 Winter St 03276 603-286-7143
Robert Seaward, prin. Fax 286-7410
Other Schools – See Northfield, Sanbornton

Troy, Cheshire, Pop. 1,217
Monadnock Regional SD
Supt. — See Swanzey
Troy ES 100/K-6
44 School St 03465 603-242-7741
Keith Stone, prin. Fax 242-9710

Walpole, Cheshire, Pop. 595
Fall Mountain Regional SD
Supt. — See Langdon
Walpole MS 100/5-8
PO Box 549 03608 603-756-4728
Samuel Jacobs, prin. Fax 756-3343
Walpole PS 100/PK-1
PO Box 549 03608 603-756-4241
Samuel Jacobs, prin. Fax 756-4131

Warner, Merrimack, Pop. 440
Kearsarge Regional SD
Supt. — See New London
Simonds ES, PO Box 250 03278 100/K-5
Laura Stoneking, prin. 603-456-2241

Warren, Grafton
Warren SD
Supt. — See North Haverhill
Warren Village ES 100/PK-8
11 School St 03279 603-764-5538
Patricia Parsons, prin. Fax 764-9382

Washington, Sullivan
Washington SD
Supt. — See Hillsborough
Washington ES 50/K-5
62 Wolf Way 03280 603-495-3463
Dr. Kevin Johnson, prin. Fax 495-0140

Waterville Valley, Grafton
Waterville Valley SD
Supt. — See Plymouth
Waterville Valley S 50/K-8
PO Box 275 03215 603-236-4700
Gale Adams Davis, prin. Fax 236-2018

Weare, Hillsborough
Weare SD
Supt. — See Henniker
Center Woods ES 500/PK-4
14 Center Rd 03281 603-529-4500
Jess Potter, prin. Fax 529-0446
Weare MS 500/5-8
16 East Rd 03281 603-529-7555
Mark Willis, prin. Fax 529-0464

Webster, Merrimack
Merrimack Valley SD
Supt. — See Penacook
Webster ES 100/K-5
936 Battle St 03303 603-648-2467
Stephanie Wheeler, prin. Fax 648-2439

Wentworth, Grafton
Wentworth SD
Supt. — See Plymouth
Wentworth ES 100/K-8
PO Box 139 03282 603-764-5811
Joseph Sampson, prin. Fax 764-9973

West Franklin, Merrimack
Franklin SD
Supt. — See Franklin
Smith ES 400/PK-3
41 Daniel Webster Dr 03235 603-934-4144
Susan Blair, prin. Fax 934-7449

West Lebanon, See Lebanon
Lebanon SD 1,700/PK-12
20 Seminary Hl 03784 603-790-8500
Dr. Joanne Roberts, supt. Fax 790-8310
www.sau88.net
Mt. Lebanon ES 300/PK-4
5 White Ave 03784 603-298-8202
Eloise Ginty, prin. Fax 298-6433
Other Schools – See Lebanon

Westmoreland, Cheshire
Westmoreland SD
Supt. — See Keene
Westmoreland S 200/K-8
40 Glebe Rd 03467 603-399-4421
Mark Hayward, prin. Fax 399-7107

Pioneer Junior Academy 50/1-8
13 Mount Gilboa Rd 03467 603-399-4803
Karina Pimentel, prin. Fax 399-4803

West Stewartstown, Coos, Pop. 383
Stewartstown SD
Supt. — See Colebrook
Stewartstown Community S 100/K-8
PO Box 120 03597 603-246-7082
Jennifer Mathieu, prin. Fax 246-3311

Whitefield, Coos, Pop. 1,128
White Mountains Regional SD 1,200/PK-12
14 King Sq 03598 603-837-9363
Dr. Marion Anastasia, supt. Fax 837-2326
www.sau36.org
Whitefield ES 300/PK-8
PO Box 128 03598 603-837-3088
Michael Cronin, prin. Fax 837-9161
Other Schools – See Jefferson, Lancaster

Wilton, Hillsborough, Pop. 1,150
Wilton-Lyndeborough Cooperative SD
Supt. — See Lyndeborough
Rideout ES 200/1-5
18 Tremont St 03086 603-654-6714
Timothy O'Connell, prin. Fax 654-3490

High Mowing S 100/PK-12
222 Isaac Frye Hwy 03086 603-654-2391
Geraldine Kline, head sch Fax 654-6588

Winchester, Cheshire, Pop. 1,700
Winchester SD 400/PK-8
85A Parker St 03470 603-239-4381
Alan Genovese, supt. Fax 239-4968
www.wnhsd.org
Winchester S 400/PK-8
85A Parker St 03470 603-239-4721
Fax 239-4968

Windham, Rockingham
Windham SD 2,700/PK-12
19 Haverhill Rd 03087 603-425-1976
Richard Langlois, supt. Fax 425-1719
www.sau95.org
Golden Brook ES 600/PK-2
112 Lowell Rd Ste B 03087 603-898-9586
Christopher Hunt, prin. Fax 870-9030
Windham Center ES 600/3-5
2 Lowell Rd 03087 603-432-7312
Rory O'Connor, prin. Fax 432-1189
Windham MS 700/6-8
112 Lowell Rd Ste A 03087 603-893-2636
Brenda Morrow, prin. Fax 870-9007

Wolfeboro, Carroll, Pop. 2,811
Governor Wentworth Regional SD 2,300/PK-12
140 Pine Hill Rd 03894 603-569-1658
Kathleen Cuddy-Egbert, supt. Fax 569-6983
www.gwrsd.org
Carpenter ES 200/K-3
PO Box 659 03894 603-569-3457
Janice Brooks, prin. Fax 569-8111
Crescent Lake S 200/4-6
75 McManus Rd 03894 603-569-0223
James Reilly, prin. Fax 569-4839
Kingswood Regional MS 400/7-8
404 S Main St 03894 603-569-3689
Aaron Bronson, prin. Fax 569-8113
Other Schools – See Center Ossipee, Center Tuftonboro, Effingham, New Durham

Wolfeboro Falls, Carroll
SAU 49
PO Box 190 03896 603-569-1658
Kathleen Cuddy-Egbert, supt. Fax 569-6983
www.gwrsd.org
Other Schools – See Middleton

Woodsville, Grafton, Pop. 1,115
Haverhill Cooperative SD
Supt. — See North Haverhill
Woodsville ES 200/PK-3
206 Central St 03785 603-747-3363
Jay Marshall, admin. Fax 747-3247

NEW JERSEY

NEW JERSEY DEPARTMENT OF EDUCATION
PO Box 500, Trenton 08625
Telephone 609-292-4469
Fax 609-777-4099
Website http://www.state.nj.us/education

Commissioner of Education Lamont Repollet

NEW JERSEY BOARD OF EDUCATION
PO Box 500, Trenton 08625

President Mark Biedron

COUNTY SUPERINTENDENTS OF SCHOOLS

Atlantic County Office of Education
Dr. Richard Stepura, supt. 609-625-0004
6260 Old Harding Hwy Ste 1 Fax 625-6539
Mays Landing 08330
www.atlantic-county.org/education/

Bergen County Office of Education
Joseph Zarra, supt. 201-336-6875
1 Bergen County Plz Rm 350 Fax 336-6880
Hackensack 07601

Burlington County Office of Education
Darryl Minus-Vincent, supt. 609-265-5060
PO Box 6000, Westampton 08060 Fax 265-5922
www.co.burlington.nj.us/553/Superintendent-of-School

Camden County Office of Education
Dr. Lovell Pugh-Bassett, supt. 856-401-2400
PO Box 200, Blackwood 08012 Fax 401-2410
www.camdencounty.com/education

Cape May County Office of Education
Dr. Richard Stepura, supt. 609-465-1283
4 Moore Rd Fax 465-2094
Cape May Court House
www.capemaycountygov.net/

Cumberland County Office of Education
Peggy Nicolosi, supt. 856-451-0211
43 Fayette St, Bridgeton 08302 Fax 455-9523
www.co.cumberland.nj.us/

Essex County Office of Education
Joseph Zarra, supt. 973-621-2750
60 Nelson Pl, Newark 07102 Fax 621-1603

Gloucester County Office of Education
Ave Altersitz, supt. 856-686-8370
115 Budd Blvd, West Deptford Fax 686-8387
www.gloucestercountynj.gov/depts/s/sos/default.asp

Hudson County Office of Education
Melissa Pearce, supt. 201-369-5290
830 Bergen Ave Ste 7B Fax 369-5288
Jersey City 07306
www.hcstonline.org/main/hcdoe/Home.aspx

Hunterdon County Office of Education
Juan Torres, supt. 908-788-1414
PO Box 2900, Flemington 08822 Fax 788-1457
www.co.hunterdon.nj.us/schools.htm

Mercer County Office of Education
Yasmin Hernndez-Manno, supt. 609-588-5877
1075 Old Trenton Rd Fax 588-5878
Trenton 08690
nj.gov/counties/mercer/departments/schools/index

Middlesex County Office of Education
Yasmin Hernandez-Manno, supt. 732-249-2900
13 Kennedy Blvd Fax 296-0683
East Brunswick 08816
www.middlesexcountynj.gov

Monmouth County Office of Education
Dr. Lester Richens, supt. 732-431-7810
PO Box 1264, Freehold 07728 Fax 776-7237
co.monmouth.nj.us/page.aspx?ID=172

Morris County Office of Education
Roger Jinks, supt. 973-285-8332
PO Box 900, Morristown 07963 Fax 285-8341

Ocean County Office of Education
Judith DeStefano-Anen Ed.D., supt. 732-929-2078
212 Washington St Fax 506-5336
Toms River 08753
www.co.ocean.nj.us/ocschools/

Passaic County Office of Education
Robert Davis, supt. 973-569-2110
501 River St, Paterson 07524 Fax 754-0241
www.passaiccountynj.org

Salem County Office of Education
Peggy Nicolosi, supt. 856-339-8611
110 5th St Ste 900, Salem 08079 Fax 935-6290
www.salemcountynj.gov/departments/schools/

Somerset County Office of Education
Roger Jinks, supt. 908-541-5700
PO Box 3000, Somerville 08876 Fax 722-6902
www.co.somerset.nj.us/schools/

Sussex County Office of Education
Dr. Rosalie Lamonte, supt. 973-579-6996
262 White Lake Rd, Sparta 07871 Fax 579-6476
www.sussex.nj.us/Cit-e-Access/webpage.cfm?TID=7&
TPID=1560

Union County Office of Education
Juan Torres, supt. 908-654-9860
300 North Ave E, Westfield 07090 Fax 654-9869
ucnj.org

Warren County Office of Education
Dr. Rosalie Lamonte, supt. 908-689-0497
1501 State Route 57 W Fax 689-1457
Washington 07882
www.co.warren.nj.us/edu.html

PUBLIC, PRIVATE AND CATHOLIC ELEMENTARY SCHOOLS

Aberdeen, Monmouth, Pop. 17,038
Matawan-Aberdeen Regional SD 3,700/PK-12
1 Crest Way 07747 732-705-4000
Joseph Majka J.D., supt.
www.marsd.org
Cambridge Park S 100/PK-PK
1 Crest Way 07747 732-705-4000
Fax 290-7938
Lloyd Road ES 600/4-5
401 Lloyd Rd 07747 732-705-5700
Joseph Jerabek, prin. Fax 566-2975
Strathmore ES 500/K-3
282 Church St 07747 732-705-5900
Kelly Bera, prin. Fax 290-8463
Other Schools – See Cliffwood, Matawan

Absecon, Atlantic, Pop. 8,239
Absecon CSD 800/K-8
800 Irelan Ave 08201 609-641-5375
Dr. Theresa DeFranco, supt. Fax 641-8692
www.abseconschools.org
Attales MS 300/5-8
800 Irelan Ave Ste 1 08201 609-641-5375
Steven Deo, prin. Fax 641-8692
Marsh ES 500/K-4
800 Irelan Ave 08201 609-641-5375
Joseph Giardina, prin. Fax 641-8692

Allamuchy, Warren, Pop. 77
Allamuchy Township SD 400/PK-8
PO Box J 07820 908-852-1894
Joseph Flynn, supt. Fax 852-9816
www.aes.k12.nj.us
Allamuchy S 300/3-8
PO Box J 07820 908-852-1894
Jennifer Chickey, prin. Fax 852-9816
Mountain Villa ES 50/PK-2
1686 County Road 517 07820 908-852-1894
Joseph Flynn, admin. Fax 850-1213

Allendale, Bergen, Pop. 6,407
Allendale SD 900/PK-8
100 Brookside Ave 07401 201-327-2020
Michael Barcadepone Ed.D., supt. Fax 785-9735
www.allendalek8.com
Brookside MS 500/4-8
100 Brookside Ave 07401 201-327-2020
Bruce Winkelstein, prin. Fax 825-6553
Hillside ES 400/PK-3
89 Hillside Ave 07401 201-327-2020
Anastasia Maroulis, prin. Fax 327-8120

Allentown, Monmouth, Pop. 1,798
Upper Freehold Regional SD 2,300/PK-12
27 High St 08501 609-259-7292
Dr. Richard Fitzpatrick, supt. Fax 259-0881
www.ufrsd.net
Newell ES 500/PK-4
27 High St 08501 609-259-7292
Kelly Huggins, prin. Fax 208-1411
Stone Bridge MS 500/5-8
27 High St 08501 609-259-7292
Stefanie Negro, prin. Fax 208-1411

Allenwood, Monmouth, Pop. 919
Wall Township SD
Supt. — See Wall
Allenwood ES 300/K-5
3301 Allenwood Lakewood Rd 08720 732-556-2150
Erin O'Connell, prin. Fax 223-6259

Alloway, Salem, Pop. 1,378
Alloway Township SD 400/PK-8
PO Box 327 08001 856-935-1622
Dr. Kristin Schell, supt. Fax 935-3017
www.allowayschool.org
Alloway Township S 400/PK-8
PO Box 327 08001 856-935-1622
Fax 935-3017

Alpha, Warren, Pop. 2,331
Alpha SD 200/K-8
817 North Blvd 08865 908-454-5000
Seth Cohen, supt. Fax 454-4347
www.apsedu.org
Alpha S 200/K-8
817 North Blvd 08865 908-454-5000
Seth Cohen, supt. Fax 454-4347

Alpine, Bergen, Pop. 1,813
Alpine SD 200/K-8
500 Hillside Ave 07620 201-768-8255
Dr. Tali Axelrod, supt. Fax 768-7855
www.alpineschool.org
Alpine S 200/K-8
500 Hillside Ave 07620 201-768-8255
Maureen McCann M.A., prin. Fax 768-7855

Andover, Sussex, Pop. 595

Tranquility Adventist S 50/PK-9
2 Pond View Cir 07821 908-852-1391

Annandale, Hunterdon, Pop. 1,653

Immaculate Conception S 500/PK-8
314 Old Allerton Rd 08801 908-735-6334
Cynthia Casciola Kitts, prin. Fax 238-0724

Asbury, Hunterdon, Pop. 273
Bethlehem Township SD 400/K-8
940 Iron Bridge Rd 08802 908-537-4044
Dr. Gregory Farley, admin. Fax 537-4309
www.btschools.org
Conley ES 200/K-5
940 Iron Bridge Rd 08802 908-537-4044
Jane Smith, prin. Fax 537-7224
Hoppock MS 200/6-8
280 Asbury West Portal Rd 08802 908-479-6336
Dr. Gregory Farley, prin. Fax 479-1021

Asbury Park, Monmouth, Pop. 15,693
Asbury Park SD 2,000/PK-12
910 4th Ave 07712 732-776-2606
Dr. Lamont Repollet, supt. Fax 774-8067
www.asburypark.k12.nj.us
Bradley ES 500/PK-5
1100 3rd Ave 07712 732-776-3100
Edwin Ruiz, prin. Fax 776-2284
King MS 300/6-8
1200 Bangs Ave 07712 732-776-2559
Dr. Mark Gerbino, prin. Fax 776-7503
Marshall ES 500/PK-5
600 Monroe Ave 07712 732-776-2660
Thea Jackson-Byers, prin. Fax 775-5067
Obama ES 400/PK-5
1300 Bangs Ave 07712 732-776-2545
Reginald Mirthil, prin. Fax 775-1428

Our Lady of Mt. Carmel S 200/K-8
Pine St & 1st Ave 07712 732-775-8989
Sr. Jude Boyce, prin. Fax 775-0108
Sisters Academy of New Jersey 5-8
1416 Springwood Ave 07712 732-774-9056
Sr. Mary Louise Miller, prin. Fax 774-5552

Atco, Camden
Waterford Township SD
Supt. — See Waterford Works
Atco ES 200/K-1
2162 Cooper Rd 08004 856-767-4200
Dr. Brenda Harring, prin. Fax 768-5497
Richards ES 200/PK-PK, 2-
934 Lincoln Ave 08004 856-767-2421
Richard Czyz, prin. Fax 753-1032

Winslow Township SD 4,700/PK-12
40 Cooper Folly Rd 08004 856-767-2850
Dr. H. Major Poteat, supt. Fax 767-4782
www.winslow-schools.com
Winslow Township MS 800/7-8
30 Cooper Folly Rd 08004 856-767-7222
Stella Nwanguma, prin. Fax 767-5411
Other Schools – See Berlin, Blue Anchor, Sicklerville

Atlantic City, Atlantic, Pop. 38,716
Atlantic City SD 7,200/PK-12
1300 Atlantic Ave 08401 609-343-7200
Barry Caldwell, supt. Fax 345-3268
www.acboe.org
Brighton Avenue S 300/PK-5
30 N Brighton Ave 08401 609-343-7200
Dorothy Bullock-Fernande, admin.
Chelsea Heights S 300/K-8
4101 Filbert Ave 08401 609-343-7272
Kenneth Flood, prin. Fax 344-7668
King S 700/PK-8
1700 Marmora Ave 08401 609-343-7380
Jodi Burroughs, prin. Fax 343-1647
New York Ave S 700/PK-8
411 N New York Ave 08401 609-343-7280
James Knox, prin. Fax 345-2603
Pennsylvania Avenue ES 600/K-8
201 N Pennsylvania Ave 08401 609-343-7290
Dr. LaQuetta Small, prin. Fax 441-0405
Richmond Ave S 600/PK-8
4115 Ventnor Ave 08401 609-343-7250
Shelley Williams, prin. Fax 344-0974
Sovereign Avenue S 700/PK-8
111 N Sovereign Ave 08401 609-343-7260
Medina Peyton, prin. Fax 343-1583
Texas Avenue S 600/K-8
2523 Arctic Ave 08401 609-343-7350
LaKecia Hyman, prin. Fax 343-0016
Uptown S Complex 600/K-8
323 Madison Ave 08401 609-344-8809
Atiba Rose, prin. Fax 449-0346
Venice Park S 100/PK-PK
1601 Penrose Ave 08401 609-343-7270
Jodi Burroughs, prin. Fax 347-9598

Our Lady Star of the Sea S 200/PK-8
15 N California Ave 08401 609-345-0648
Susan Tarrant, prin. Fax 344-6784

Atlantic Highlands, Monmouth, Pop. 4,320
Atlantic Highlands SD 300/PK-6
140 1st Ave 07716 732-291-2020
Dr. Susan Compton, supt. Fax 872-9117
www.ahes.k12.nj.us
Atlantic Highlands ES 300/PK-6
140 1st Ave 07716 732-291-2020
Dr. Susan Compton, supt. Fax 872-9117

Middletown Township SD
Supt. — See Leonardo
Navesink ES 300/K-5
151 Monmouth Ave 07716 732-291-0289
James Altobello, prin.

Audubon, Camden, Pop. 8,746
Audubon SD 1,500/PK-12
350 Edgewood Ave 08106 856-547-7695
Robert Goldschmidt, supt. Fax 546-8550
www.audubonschools.org/
Haviland Avenue ES 300/PK-2
240 S Haviland Ave 08106 856-546-4922
Dr. Carleene Slowik, prin. Fax 547-1248
Mansion Avenue ES 300/3-6
300 Mansion Ave 08106 856-546-4926
Bonnie Smeltzer, prin. Fax 547-1483

Avalon, Cape May, Pop. 1,326
Avalon SD 100/PK-PK, 5-
235 32nd St 08202 609-967-7544
Stacey Tracy, supt. Fax 967-3109
www.avesnj.org/
Avalon ES 100/PK-PK, 5-
235 32nd St 08202 609-967-7544
Stacey Tracy, supt. Fax 967-3109

Avenel, Middlesex, Pop. 16,588
Woodbridge Township SD
Supt. — See Woodbridge
Avenel MS 600/6-8
85 Woodbine Ave 07001 732-586-5622
Joseph Short, prin. Fax 574-0573
Avenel Street ES 500/K-5
230 Avenel St 07001 732-602-8504
Dr. Maria Gencarelli, prin. Fax 855-9586
Woodbine Avenue ES 500/K-5
89 Woodbine Ave 07001 732-602-8523
June Puskuldjian, prin. Fax 855-0650

Avon by the Sea, Monmouth, Pop. 1,883
Avon Borough SD 200/K-8
505 Lincoln Ave 07717 732-775-4328
Christopher Albrizio, supt. Fax 775-0761
www.avonschool.com
Avon S 200/K-8
505 Lincoln Ave 07717 732-775-4328
Christopher Albrizio, prin. Fax 775-0761

Barnegat, Ocean, Pop. 2,775
Barnegat Township SD 3,200/PK-12
550 Barnegat Blvd N 08005 609-698-5800
Karen Wood, supt. Fax 698-6638
www.barnegatschools.com
Brackman MS 700/6-8
600 Barnegat Blvd N 08005 609-698-5880
John Fiorentino, prin. Fax 698-7965
Collins ES 400/K-5
570 Barnegat Blvd N 08005 609-698-5832
Patrick Magee, prin. Fax 698-5843
Donahue ES 300/K-5
200 Bengal Blvd 08005 609-660-8900
Josh Toddings, prin. Fax 698-7389
Dunfee ES 400/K-5
128 Barnegat Blvd S 08005 609-698-5826
Katherine Makela, prin. Fax 698-2083
Horbelt ES 400/K-5
104 Burr St 08005 609-660-7500
Joseph Saxton, prin. Fax 660-7501

Barrington, Camden, Pop. 6,884
Barrington Borough SD 600/PK-8
311 Reading Ave 08007 856-547-8467
Anthony Arcodia, supt. Fax 547-5533
www.barringtonschools.net/
Woodland MS 200/5-8
1 School Ln 08007 856-547-8402
Michael Silvestri, prin. Fax 522-1248
Other Schools – See Haddonfield

Castle Academy 200/PK-12
500 Clements Bridge Rd 08007 856-546-5901

Basking Ridge, Somerset, Pop. 4,000
Bernards Township SD 5,600/K-12
101 Peachtree Rd 07920 908-204-2600
Nick Markarian, supt. Fax 766-7641
www.bernardsboe.com/
Annin MS 1,300/6-8
70 Quincy Rd 07920 908-204-2610
Karen Hudock, prin. Fax 204-0244
Cedar Hill ES 600/K-5
100 Peachtree Rd 07920 908-204-2633
Paul Ciempola, prin. Fax 204-1956
Mount Prospect ES 600/K-5
111 Hansom Rd 07920 908-470-1600
Joanne Hozeny, prin. Fax 470-1610
Oak Street ES 600/K-5
70 W Oak St 07920 908-204-2565
Dr. Jane Costa, prin. Fax 204-9289
Other Schools – See Liberty Corner

Bridgewater-Raritan Regional SD
Supt. — See Martinsville
Hamilton PS 500/K-4
9 Hamilton Ln 07920 908-575-0050
Daniel Fonder, prin. Fax 658-3431

Albrook S 100/PK-6
361 Somerville Rd 07920 908-580-0661
Jean Hicks, head sch Fax 580-0785
Mendham Country Day S 200/PK-6
PO Box 167 07920 908-766-3323
St. James S 400/PK-8
PO Box 310 07920 908-766-4774
Vincent Parisi, prin. Fax 766-4432

Bay Head, Ocean, Pop. 966
Bay Head SD 100/K-8
145 Grove St 08742 732-892-0668
Fax 892-6427
www.bayheadschool.org
Bay Head S 100/K-8
145 Grove St 08742 732-892-0668
Frank Camardo, prin. Fax 892-6427

Bayonne, Hudson, Pop. 61,671
Bayonne SD 9,100/PK-12
669 Avenue A 07002 201-858-5800
Dr. Michael Wanko, supt. Fax 858-6289
www.bboed.org
Bailey Community S 600/PK-8
75 W 10th St 07002 201-858-5824
Albert McCormick, prin. Fax 339-5618
Donohoe Community S 500/PK-8
38 Dodge St 07002 201-858-5969
Philip Baccarella, prin. Fax 858-3720
Harris Community S 700/PK-8
135 Avenue C 07002 201-858-5945
Maria Kazimir, prin. Fax 436-5169
Lincoln Community S 400/PK-8
208 Prospect Ave 07002 201-858-5973
Keith Makowski, prin. Fax 339-0943
Mann Community S 500/PK-8
25 W 38th St 07002 201-858-5979
Dr. Catherine Quinn Ed.D., prin. Fax 243-4288
Midtown Community S 1,100/PK-8
550 Avenue A 07002 201-858-5984
Christina Mercun, prin. Fax 858-4584
Oresko Community S 500/PK-8
33 E 24th St 07002 201-858-6281
Charles Costello, prin. Fax 436-5079
Robinson Community S 800/PK-8
95 W 31st St 07002 201-858-5964
Maryann Connelly, prin. Fax 858-5845
Vroom Community S 400/PK-8
18 W 26th St 07002 201-858-5956
Stacey Janeczko, prin. Fax 858-5562
Washington Community S 500/PK-8
191 Avenue B 07002 201-858-5990
George Becker, prin. Fax 436-0256
Wilson Community S 600/PK-8
101 W 56th St 07002 201-858-5996
Maureen Brown, prin. Fax 339-8513

All Saints Academy 500/PK-8
19 W 13th St 07002 201-443-8384
Sr. Rita Marie Fritzen, prin. Fax 437-6084
Beacon Christian Academy 100/PK-8
30 Prospect Ave 07002 201-437-5056
Rev. Donna Kelly, admin. Fax 437-5059

Bayville, Ocean
Berkeley Township SD 1,900/PK-6
53 Central Pkwy 08721 732-269-2321
Dr. James D. Roselli, supt. Fax 269-4487
www.btboe.org
Bayville ES 400/PK-4
356 Atlantic City Blvd 08721 732-269-1300
Steve Rieder, prin. Fax 237-2142
Berkeley Township ES 500/5-6
10 Emory Ave 08721 732-269-2909
Daniel Prima, prin. Fax 606-0228
Potter ES 400/PK-4
60 Veeder Ln 08721 732-269-5700
Andrea Cimino, prin. Fax 269-3041
Worth ES 600/PK-4
57 Central Pkwy 08721 732-269-1700
Cara Burton, prin. Fax 237-2159

Central Regional SD 1,900/7-12
509 Forest Hills Pkwy 08721 732-269-1100
Dr. Trian Parlapanides Ed.D., supt. Fax 237-8872
www.centralreg.k12.nj.us
Central Regional MS 600/7-8
509 Forest Hills Pkwy 08721 732-269-1100
Joseph Firetto, prin. Fax 269-7723

Beach Haven, Ocean, Pop. 1,166
Beach Haven Borough SD 100/PK-6
700 N Beach Ave 08008 609-492-7411
Evamarie Raleigh, supt. Fax 492-7459
www.beachhavenschool.com/
Beach Haven ES 100/PK-6
700 N Beach Ave 08008 609-492-7411
Carl Krushinski, admin. Fax 492-7459

Beachwood, Ocean, Pop. 10,934
Toms River Regional SD
Supt. — See Toms River
Beachwood ES 500/K-5
901 Berkeley Ave 08722 732-505-5820
Kimberly Muir, prin. Fax 341-1659
Toms River IS South 900/6-8
1675 Pinewald Rd 08722 732-505-3900
Paul Gluck, prin. Fax 818-7512

Bedminster, Somerset
Bedminster Township SD 500/PK-8
234 Somerville Rd 07921 908-234-0768
Jennifer Giordano, supt. Fax 234-2318
www.bedminsterschool.org
Bedminster Township S 500/PK-8
234 Somerville Rd 07921 908-234-0768
Corby Swan, prin. Fax 234-2318

Belford, Monmouth, Pop. 1,742
Middletown Township SD
Supt. — See Leonardo
Bayview ES 400/K-5
300 Leonardville Rd 07718 732-787-3590
Tara Raspanti, prin.

Belleville, Essex, Pop. 36,300
Belleville SD 4,400/PK-12
102 Passaic Ave 07109 973-450-3500
Dr. Richard Tomko, supt. Fax 450-3504
www.bellevilleschools.org
Belleville ES 3 300/PK-5
230 Joralemon St 07109 973-450-3530
Ricardo Acosta, prin. Fax 450-3084
Belleville ES 4 300/PK-5
30 Magnolia St 07109 973-450-3540
Dora Cavallo, prin. Fax 450-5463
Belleville ES 5 300/K-5
149 Adelaide St 07109 973-450-3450
Nanatte Rotonda, prin. Fax 844-1424
Belleville ES 7 300/PK-5
20 Passaic Ave 07109 973-450-3470
Lucy Demikoff, prin. Fax 844-1421
Belleville ES 8 400/K-5
183 Union Ave 07109 973-450-3480
Robert Silvera, prin. Fax 844-1428
Belleville ES 9 100/K-5
301 Ralph St 07109 973-450-3490
Joseph Rotonda, prin. Fax 450-3488
Belleville ES 10 100/K-5
527 Belleville Ave 07109 973-450-3510
Joseph Rotonda, prin. Fax 844-1433
Belleville MS 900/6-8
279 Washington Ave 07109 973-450-3500
Romain Royal, prin. Fax 450-5001

St. Peter S 200/PK-8
152 William St 07109 973-759-3143
Phyllis Sisco, prin. Fax 759-4160

Bellmawr, Camden, Pop. 11,414
Bellmawr Borough SD 1,000/PK-8
256 Anderson Ave 08031 856-931-3620
Annette Castiglione, supt. Fax 931-9326
bellmawrschools.org
Bellmawr Park ES 400/PK-4
29 Peach Rd 08031 856-931-6272
Elizabeth Calabria, prin. Fax 931-1322
Bell Oaks MS 400/5-8
256 Anderson Ave 08031 856-931-6273
Anthony Farinelli, prin. Fax 931-9326
Burke ES 300/K-4
112 S Black Horse Pike 08031 856-931-6362
Frank Jankowski, prin. Fax 931-1417

Belmar, Monmouth, Pop. 5,731
Belmar SD 500/PK-8
1101 Main St 07719 732-681-2388
David Hallman, supt. Fax 681-8709
www.belmar.k12.nj.us/
Belmar ES 500/PK-8
1101 Main St 07719 732-681-2388
Lisa Hannah, prin. Fax 681-5334

St. Rose S 300/PK-8
605 6th Ave 07719 732-681-5555
Gregory Guito, prin. Fax 681-5890

Belvidere, Warren, Pop. 2,652
Belvidere SD 700/K-12
809 Oxford St 07823 908-475-6600
Christopher Carrubba, supt. Fax 475-6619
www.belviderеsd.org
Oxford Street MS 200/4-8
807 Oxford St 07823 908-475-4001
Chris Karabinus, prin. Fax 475-6619
Third Street ES 100/K-3
300 3rd St 07823 908-475-0104
Brian Staples, prin. Fax 475-3521

White Township SD 300/K-8
565 County Road 519 07823 908-475-4773
Michael Slattery, admin. Fax 475-3627
www.whitetwpsd.org
White Township S 300/K-8
565 County Road 519 07823 908-475-4773
Dawn Werkheiser, prin. Fax 475-3627

Bergenfield, Bergen, Pop. 26,177
Bergenfield SD 3,400/PK-12
225 W Clinton Ave 07621 201-385-8801
Dr. Christopher Tully, supt. Fax 384-2914
www.bergenfield.org/
Brown MS 800/6-8
130 S Washington Ave 07621 201-385-8847
Shane Biggins, prin. Fax 385-0219
Franklin ES 300/K-5
2 N Franklin Ave 07621 201-385-8581
Everett Thompson, prin. Fax 385-9708
Hoover ES 200/K-5
273 Murray Hill Ter 07621 201-385-8582
William Fleming, prin. Fax 385-0946
Jefferson ES 300/K-5
200 Hickory Ave 07621 201-385-8804
Craig Vogt, prin. Fax 385-9389
Lincoln ES 300/PK-5
115 Highview Ave 07621 201-385-8759
James Mitchel, prin. Fax 385-9838
Washington ES 300/K-5
49 S Summit St 07621 201-385-8771
Thomas Lawrence, prin. Fax 385-3703

Transfiguration Academy 300/PK-8
10 Bradley Ave 07621 201-384-3627
James Carlo, prin. Fax 384-0293

Berkeley Heights, Union, Pop. 11,980
Berkeley Heights SD 2,700/PK-12
345 Plainfield Ave 07922 908-464-1718
Judith Rattner, supt. Fax 464-1728
www.bhpsnj.org/
Columbia MS 600/6-8
345 Plainfield Ave 07922 908-464-1600
Frank Geiger, prin. Fax 464-0017
Hughes ES 300/2-5
446 Snyder Ave 07922 908-464-1717
Jessica Nardi, prin. Fax 464-1783
McMillin ECC 300/PK-1
651 Mountain Ave 07922 908-464-5583
Anne Corley-Hand, prin. Fax 464-5398
Mountain Park ES 300/2-5
55 Fairfax Dr 07922 908-464-1713
Jonathan Morisseau, prin. Fax 665-0969
Woodruff ES 200/2-5
55 Briarwood Dr W 07922 908-464-1723
Patricia Gasparini, prin. Fax 464-3369

Berlin, Camden, Pop. 7,476
Berlin Borough SD 800/PK-8
215 S Franklin Ave 08009 856-767-0129
Kristen Martello, supt. Fax 767-2465
www.bcsberlin.k12.nj.us
Berlin Community S 800/PK-8
215 S Franklin Ave 08009 856-767-0129
Dr. Shelly Ward Richards, prin. Fax 767-2465

Winslow Township SD
Supt. — See Atco
Winslow Township Upper ES 5 600/4-6
130 Oak Leaf Rd 08009 856-728-9445
Nython Carter, prin. Fax 875-5402

Our Lady of Mt. Carmel Regional S 200/K-8
1 N Cedar Ave 08009 856-767-1751
Alice Malloy, prin. Fax 767-1293

Bernardsville, Somerset, Pop. 7,613
Somerset Hills SD 2,000/PK-12
25 Olcott Ave 07924 908-204-1930
Dr. Frances Wood, supt. Fax 953-0699
www.shsd.org/
Bedwell ES 600/PK-4
141 Seney Dr 07924 908-204-1920
Amy Phelan, prin. Fax 204-0481
Bernardsville MS 600/5-8
141 Seney Dr 07924 908-204-1916
Gretchen Dempsey, prin. Fax 953-2184

St. Elizabeth S 200/PK-8
30 Seney Dr 07924 908-766-0244
William Venezia, prin. Fax 766-5273

Beverly, Burlington, Pop. 2,484
Beverly CSD 300/PK-8
601 Bentley Ave 08010 609-387-2200
Elizabeth Giacobbe, supt. Fax 387-4447
www.beverlycityschool.org
Beverly S 300/PK-8
601 Bentley Ave 08010 609-387-2200
Elizabeth Giacobbe, prin. Fax 387-4447

Blackwood, Camden, Pop. 4,485
Gloucester Township SD 6,500/PK-8
17 Erial Rd 08012 856-227-1400
John Bilodeau, supt. Fax 228-1422
www.gloucestertownshipschools.org
Blackwood ES 600/PK-5
260 Erial Rd 08012 856-227-9510
Andrea Stubbs, prin. Fax 228-2005
Chews ES 700/PK-5
600 Somerdale Rd 08012 856-783-6607
David Hinlicky, prin. Fax 783-8696
Glen Landing MS 800/6-8
85 Little Gloucester Rd 08012 856-227-3534
Suzanne Schultes, prin. Fax 228-5260
Gloucester Township ES 300/K-5
270 S Black Horse Pike 08012 856-227-8845
Joseph Gentile, prin. Fax 228-4366
Lewis MS 700/6-8
875 Erial Rd 08012 856-227-8400
Theodore Otten, prin. Fax 228-5130
Loring-Flemming ES 700/K-5
135 Little Gloucester Rd 08012 856-227-4045
Aaron Rose, prin. Fax 228-4666
Other Schools – See Erial, Glendora, Sicklerville

Our Lady of Hope Regional S 500/PK-8
420 S Black Horse Pike 08012 856-227-4442
Sr. Paula Randow, prin. Fax 228-7527

Blairstown, Warren
Blairstown Township SD 500/K-6
PO Box E 07825 908-362-6111
Mark Saalfield, supt. Fax 362-9638
www.blairstownelem.net
Blairstown ES 500/K-6
PO Box E 07825 908-362-6111
Bruce Leal, prin. Fax 362-9638

Bloomfield, Essex, Pop. 48,200
Bloomfield Township SD 6,100/PK-12
155 Broad St 07003 973-680-8500
Salvatore Goncalves, supt. Fax 680-8274
www.bloomfield.k12.nj.us
Berkeley ES 400/K-6
351 Bloomfield Ave 07003 973-680-8540
Natashia Baxter, prin. Fax 743-0307
Bloomfield MS 900/7-8
60 Huck Rd 07003 973-680-8620
Alla Vayda-Manzo, prin. Fax 338-6523
Brookdale ES 400/K-6
1230 Broad St 07003 973-680-8520
Lauren Barton, prin. Fax 338-0704
Carteret ES 400/K-6
158 Grove St 07003 973-680-8580
John Baltz, prin. Fax 743-5310
Demarest ES 500/K-6
465 Broughton Ave 07003 973-680-8510
Mary Todaro, prin. Fax 893-9547
Early Childhood @ Forest Glen 200/PK-PK
280 Davey St 07003 973-680-8686
Fax 429-7960
Fairview ES 500/K-6
376 Berkeley Ave 07003 973-680-8550
Ginamarie Mignone, prin. Fax 743-9782
Franklin ES 400/K-6
85 Curtis St 07003 973-680-8560
Marianne Abbasso, prin. Fax 743-0249
Oak View ES 300/PK-6
150 Garrabrant Ave 07003 973-680-8590
Mary DiTrani, prin. Fax 893-0534
Watsessing ES 300/K-6
71 Prospect St 07003 973-680-8570
Dr. Gina Rosamilia, prin. Fax 566-9135

St. Thomas the Apostle S 200/PK-8
50 Byrd Ave 07003 973-338-8505
Michael Petrillo, prin. Fax 338-9565

Bloomingdale, Passaic, Pop. 7,587
Bloomingdale SD 500/PK-8
225 Glenwild Ave 07403 973-838-3282
Elaine Baldwin, supt. Fax 838-8898
www.bloomingdaleschools.org
Bergen MS 300/5-8
225 Glenwild Ave 07403 973-838-4835
Frank Verducci, prin. Fax 283-1893
Day ES 100/PK-1
225 Rafkind Rd 07403 973-838-1311
Cheryl Mallen, prin. Fax 283-1476
Donald ES 200/2-4
29 Captolene Ave 07403 973-838-5353
Elaine Baldwin, prin. Fax 838-3195

Bloomsbury, Hunterdon, Pop. 859
Bloomsbury SD 100/PK-8
20 Main St 08804 908-479-4414
Dr. Jenniffer Marycz, supt. Fax 479-1631
www.bburyes.com
Bloomsbury ES 100/PK-8
20 Main St 08804 908-479-4414
Dr. Jenniffer Marycz, admin. Fax 479-1631

Blue Anchor, Camden
Winslow Township SD
Supt. — See Atco
Winslow Township ES 1 400/PK-3
413 Inskip Rd 08037 609-561-8300
Sharon Thomas-Galloway, prin. Fax 704-1032

Bogota, Bergen, Pop. 7,987
Bogota SD 1,100/PK-12
1 Henry C Luthin Pl 07603 201-441-4800
Dr. Vincent Varcadipane, supt. Fax 489-5759
www.bogotaboe.com
Bixby ES 300/PK-6
25 Fischer Ave 07603 201-441-4834
Damon Englese, prin. Fax 441-9186
Steen ES 300/K-6
134 W Main St 07603 201-342-6446
Dayle Santoro, prin. Fax 441-9184

St. Joseph Academy 200/K-8
131 E Fort Lee Rd 07603 201-487-8641
Stella Scarano, prin. Fax 487-7405
Trinity Lutheran S 100/PK-K
167 Palisade Ave 07603 201-487-3580
Cynthia Keohane, dir. Fax 487-1748

Boonton, Morris, Pop. 8,097
Boonton SD 1,200/PK-12
434 Lathrop Ave 07005 973-335-9700
Robert Presuto, supt. Fax 335-8281
www.boontonschools.org
Hill ES 600/1-8
435 Lathrop Ave 07005 973-335-9700
Dr. Louis Caruso, prin. Fax 402-9375
School Street ES 50/PK-K
730 Birch St 07005 973-335-9700
Christine Muench, prin. Fax 402-9283

Boonton Township SD 500/PK-8
11 Valley Rd 07005 973-334-4162
Dr. Christian Angelillo, supt. Fax 316-6956
www.rvsnj.org
Rockaway Valley S 500/PK-8
11 Valley Rd 07005 973-334-4162
Dr. Christian Angelillo, prin. Fax 316-6956

Parsippany-Troy Hills Township SD
Supt. — See Parsippany
Intervale ES 300/K-5
60 Pitt Rd 07005 973-263-7075
Christopher Waack, prin. Fax 331-7150

Our Lady of Mt. Carmel S 100/PK-8
205 Oak St 07005 973-334-2777
Douglas Minson, prin. Fax 334-0975

Bordentown, Burlington, Pop. 3,853
Bordentown Regional SD 2,400/PK-12
318 Ward Ave 08505 609-298-0025
Dr. Edward Forsthoffer, supt. Fax 298-2515
www.bordentown.k12.nj.us
Barton ES 200/PK-3
100 Crosswicks St 08505 609-298-0676
Louisa Kenny, prin. Fax 324-2898
Bordentown Regional MS 600/6-8
50 Dunns Mill Rd 08505 609-298-0674
Joseph Sprague, prin. Fax 291-1929
McFarland IS 400/4-5
87 Crosswicks St 08505 609-291-7192
Megan Geibel, prin. Fax 291-7199
Muschal ES 600/PK-3
323 Ward Ave 08505 609-298-2600
Daniel Riether, prin. Fax 324-1788

Bound Brook, Somerset, Pop. 10,250
Bound Brook Borough SD 1,600/PK-12
111 W Union Ave 08805 732-652-7920
Dr. Daniel Gallagher, supt. Fax 271-9097
www.bbrook.org
Community MS, 120 E 2nd St 08805 6-8
Dr. Joseph Santicerma, prin. 732-852-1130
Lafayette ES 300/3-5
60 W High St 08805 732-652-7930
Priscila Weber, prin. Fax 271-5783
LaMonte ES 200/PK-K
337 W 2nd St 08805 732-652-7960
Aldo Russo, prin. Fax 748-8524
LaMonte ES Annex 300/PK-PK, 1-
330 W 2nd St 08805 732-652-7934
Aldo Russo, prin.
Smalley ES 300/4-6
163 Cherry Ave 08805 732-652-7940
Sheena Delgaizo, prin. Fax 271-4879

Bradley Beach, Monmouth, Pop. 4,229
Bradley Beach SD 300/PK-8
515 Brinley Ave 07720 732-775-4413
Dr. Stephen Wisniewski Ed.D., supt. Fax 775-2463
www.bbesnj.org
Bradley Beach ES 300/PK-8
515 Brinley Ave 07720 732-775-4413
Dr. Stephen Wisniewski Ed.D., admin. Fax 775-2463

Branchburg, Somerset
Branchburg Township SD 1,600/PK-8
240 Baird Rd 08876 908-722-3335
Rebecca Gensel, supt. Fax 526-6144
www.branchburg.k12.nj.us
Branchburg Central MS 600/6-8
220 Baird Rd 08876 908-526-1415
Matthew Barbosa, prin. Fax 526-7486
Stony Brook ES 400/4-5
136 Cedar Grove Rd 08876 908-722-2400
Frank Altmire, prin. Fax 722-4201
Other Schools – See Neshanic Station

Branchville, Sussex, Pop. 834
Frankford Township SD 500/PK-8
4 Pines Rd 07826 973-948-3727
Braden Hirsch, supt. Fax 948-2907
www.frankfordschool.org
Frankford Township S 500/PK-8
2 Pines Rd 07826 973-948-3727
Thomas Valle, prin. Fax 948-6593

Brick, Ocean, Pop. 78,300
Brick Township SD 8,500/PK-12
101 Hendrickson Ave 08724 732-785-3000
Dennis Filippone, supt. Fax 840-9089
www.brickschools.org/
Drum Point Road ES 500/K-5
41 Drum Point Rd 08723 732-785-3000
Colleen Kerr, prin. Fax 262-2795
Herbertsville ES 200/K-5
2282 Lanes Mill Rd 08724 732-785-3000
Bonnie Giles, prin. Fax 785-5252
Lake Riviera MS 900/6-8
171 Beaverson Blvd 08723 732-785-3000
Dr. Alyce Anderson, prin. Fax 477-0392

Lanes Mill ES 500/1-5
1891 Lanes Mill Rd 08724 732-785-3000
Jeffrey Luckenbach, prin. Fax 458-3830
Midstreams ES 400/1-5
500 Midstreams Rd 08724 732-785-3070
Dr. John Billen, prin. Fax 899-9528
Osbornville ES 300/1-5
218 Drum Point Rd 08723 732-785-3000
Kathleen DiGrigoli, prin. Fax 262-3813
Veteran's Memorial ES 500/1-5
103 Hendrickson Ave 08724 732-785-3000
Dr. Lynn Coddington, prin. Fax 785-5654
Veteran's Memorial MS 1,100/6-8
105 Hendrickson Ave 08724 732-785-3000
Renee Kotsianas, prin. Fax 458-9777
Wolf ES 100/PK-5
224 Chambersbridge Rd 08723 732-262-2590
Theresa Goodfellow, prin. Fax 920-3417
Young ES 900/K-5
43 Drum Point Rd 08723 732-785-3000
David Kasyan, admin. Fax 477-0390

St. Dominic S 600/PK-8
250 Old Squan Rd 08724 732-840-1412
Carol Bathmann, prin. Fax 840-6457

Bridgeton, Cumberland, Pop. 24,883
Bridgeton SD 5,300/PK-12
PO Box 657 08302 856-455-8030
Dr. Thomasina Jones Ed.D., supt. Fax 455-0176
www.bridgeton.k12.nj.us/
Broad Street S 1,100/K-8
251 W Broad St 08302 856-455-8030
Rebecca Guess, prin. Fax 453-7684
Buckshutem Road S 500/K-8
550 Buckshutem Rd 08302 856-455-8030
Derek Macchia, prin. Fax 453-8225
Cherry Street S 700/K-8
20 Cherry St 08302 856-455-8030
Terrence Spencer, prin. Fax 453-2851
ExCEL Program 6-8
398 N Pearl St 08302 856-455-8030
Isaias Garza, lead tchr. Fax 451-0328
Foster ECC 400/PK-PK
550 Buckshutem Rd 08302 856-455-8030
Deionne ThrBak, prin. Fax 453-8476
Indian Avenue S 600/K-8
399 Indian Ave 08302 856-455-8030
Carl Dolente, prin. Fax 455-7706
Quarter Mile Lane S 300/PK-8
300 Quarter Mile Ln 08302 856-455-8030
Dr. Roy Dawson, prin. Fax 453-5644
West Avenue S 700/K-8
51 N West Ave 08302 856-455-8030
Sam Hull, prin. Fax 451-4935

Fairfield Township SD 600/PK-8
375 Gouldtown Woodruff Rd 08302 856-453-1882
Dr. Michael Knox, supt. Fax 453-7148
www.fairfield.k12.nj.us
Fairfield Township S 600/PK-8
375 Gouldtown Woodruff Rd 08302 856-453-1882
Dr. Michael Knox, prin. Fax 453-7148

Hopewell Township SD 500/K-8
122 Sewall Rd 08302 856-451-9203
Meghan E. Lammersen, supt. Fax 451-9420
www.hopewellcrest.org
Hopewell Crest S 500/K-8
122 Sewall Rd 08302 856-451-9203
Meghan E. Lammersen, admin. Fax 451-9420

Stow Creek Township SD 100/K-8
11 Gum Tree Corner Rd 08302 856-455-1717
John Klug, supt. Fax 455-0833
www.stowcreekschool.com/
Stow Creek Township S 100/K-8
11 Gum Tree Corner Rd 08302 856-455-1717
John Klug, supt. Fax 455-0833

Bridgeton Christian S 100/PK-8
27 Central Ave 08302 856-455-1733
Glenn Clement, admin. Fax 453-7729
Woodland Country Day S 100/PK-8
1216 Roadstown Rd 08302 856-453-8499
Cosmo Terrigno, hdmstr. Fax 453-1648

Bridgewater, Somerset, Pop. 36,400
Bridgewater-Raritan Regional SD
Supt. — See Martinsville
Adamsville PS 500/PK-4
400 Union Ave 08807 908-526-6440
Dr. James Singagliese, prin. Fax 725-0610
Bradley Gardens PS 300/K-4
148 Pine St 08807 908-725-8444
Barbara Binford, prin Fax 725-0614
Bridgewater-Raritan MS 1,500/7-8
PO Box 6933 08807 908-231-8661
Nancy Iatesta, prin. Fax 575-0847
Crim PS 400/K-4
1300 Crim Rd 08807 908-231-1022
Margaret Kerr, prin. Fax 725-0640
Eisenhower IS 800/5-6
791 Eisenhower Ave 08807 908-231-0230
Joseph Diskin, prin. Fax 231-1079
Hillside IS 600/5-6
844 Brown Rd 08807 908-231-1905
William Ferry, prin. Fax 231-1083
Milltown ES 400/K-4
611 Milltown Rd 08807 908-927-9510
Matthew Lembo, prin. Fax 927-9524
Van Holten PS 400/K-4
360 Van Holten Rd 08807 908-231-1220
George Rauh, prin. Fax 231-1065

Raritan Valley Montessori Academy 100/PK-6
120 Finderne Ave 08807 908-595-2900
St. Bernard Preschool and K 100/PK-K
500 US Highway 22 08807 908-725-0552
Barbara Turse, prin. Fax 725-4524

Brielle, Monmouth, Pop. 4,717
Brielle Borough SD 600/PK-8
605 Union Ln 08730 732-528-6400
Christine Carlson, supt. Fax 528-0810
www.brielleschool.org
Brielle S 600/PK-8
605 Union Ln 08730 732-528-6400
Christine Carlson, prin. Fax 528-0810

Brigantine, Atlantic, Pop. 9,281
Brigantine SD 700/PK-8
PO Box 947 08203 609-266-7671
Brian M. Pruitt, supt. Fax 266-4748
www.brigantineschools.org/
Brigantine ES 400/PK-4
PO Box 947 08203 609-264-9501
Dr. Jennifer Luff, prin. Fax 264-0767
Brigantine North MS 300/5-8
PO Box 947 08203 609-266-3603
Kathleen Fox, prin. Fax 266-7062

Brooklawn, Camden, Pop. 1,923
Brooklawn SD 300/PK-8
301 Haakon Rd 08030 856-456-4039
Sam Rosetti, admin. Fax 456-2797
www.alicecostello.com
Costello S 300/PK-8
301 Haakon Rd 08030 856-456-4039
Sam Rosetti, admin. Fax 456-2797

Brookside, Morris
Mendham Township SD 700/PK-8
PO Box 510 07926 973-543-7107
Dr. Salvatore Constantino, supt. Fax 543-5537
www.mendhamtwp.org
Mendham Township ES 300/PK-4
PO Box 510 07926 973-543-7107
Julianne Kotcho, prin. Fax 543-4631
Mendham Township MS 400/5-8
PO Box 510 07926 973-543-2505
Dr. Patrick Ciccone, prin. Fax 543-0701

Browns Mills, Burlington, Pop. 10,677
Pemberton Township SD
Supt. — See Pemberton
Denbo ES 300/3-5
2 Learning Way 08015 609-893-8141
Brett Thorp, prin. Fax 893-8256
Haines ES 100/K-2
125 Trenton Rd Bldg B 08015 609-893-8141
Norman Adams, prin. Fax 893-0676
Harker Wylie ES 300/K-2
125C Trenton Rd 08015 609-893-8141
Robin Blue, prin. Fax 735-0118
Stackhouse ES 300/3-5
125A Trenton Rd 08015 609-893-8141
Keith Swaney, prin. Fax 735-0083

Budd Lake, Morris, Pop. 8,814
Mt. Olive Township SD
Supt. — See Flanders
Mt. Olive MS 1,200/6-8
160 Wolfe Rd 07828 973-691-4006
Susan Breton, prin. Fax 691-4029
Sandshore Road ES 400/K-5
498 Sand Shore Rd 07828 973-691-4003
Nicole Musarra, prin. Fax 691-4027
Stephens ES 600/K-5
99 Sunset Dr 07828 973-691-4002
Kevin Moore, prin. Fax 691-4030

Buena, Atlantic, Pop. 4,524
Buena Regional SD
Supt. — See Richland
Buena Regional MS 400/6-8
175 Weymouth Rd 08310 856-697-0100
Karen Santoro, prin. Fax 697-9580
Milanesi ES 300/PK-3
880 Harding Hwy 08310 856-697-0605
Anna Bettini, prin. Fax 697-3412

Burlington, Burlington, Pop. 9,602
Burlington CSD 1,700/PK-12
518 Locust Ave 08016 609-387-5874
Dr. Patricia Doloughty, supt. Fax 386-6971
www.burlington-nj.net
Boudinot ES 100/K-2
213 Ellis St 08016 609-387-5867
Sherry Knight, prin. Fax 387-3162
Lawrence ES 100/PK-2
316 Barclay St 08016 609-387-5859
Sherry Knight, prin. Fax 387-3096
Smith ES 300/PK-2
250 Farner Ave 08016 609-387-5854
Marilyn Dunham, prin. Fax 747-0758
Watts IS 400/3-6
550 High St 08016 609-387-5834
Robert Shappell, prin. Fax 387-8509

Burlington Township SD 3,900/PK-12
PO Box 428 08016 609-387-3955
Dr. Mary Ann Bell, supt. Fax 239-2192
www.burltwpsch.org
BTMS @ Springside 1,000/6-8
1600 Burlington Byp 08016 609-699-4021
Lawrence Penny, prin. Fax 699-4022
Fountain Woods ES 800/3-5
601 Fountain Ave 08016 609-387-1799
John Johnson, prin. Fax 387-1735
Young ES 800/PK-2
1203 Neck Rd 08016 609-386-3520
Dr. Denise King, prin. Fax 239-3532

Doane Academy 200/PK-12
350 Riverbank 08016 609-386-3500
George Sanderson, hdmstr. Fax 386-5878
Life Center Academy 300/PK-12
2045 Columbus Rd 08016 609-499-2100
St. Paul S 200/K-8
250 James St 08016 609-386-1645
Fax 386-1345

Butler, Morris, Pop. 7,440
Butler SD 1,100/K-12
38 Bartholdi Ave 07405 973-492-2025
Dr. Mario Cardinale, supt. Fax 492-1016
www.butlerboe.org
Butler MS 300/5-8
30 Pearl Pl 07405 973-492-2079
Jamie Manco, prin. Fax 492-9774
Decker ES 400/K-4
98 Decker Rd 07405 973-492-2037
Virginia Scala, prin. Fax 492-8679

Caldwell, Essex, Pop. 7,489
Caldwell-West Caldwell SD
Supt. — See West Caldwell
Cleveland MS 600/6-8
36 Academy Rd 07006 973-228-9115
James Brown, prin. Fax 228-7471
Lincoln ES, 18 Crane St 07006 300/K-5
Adam Geher, prin. 973-228-3987

North Caldwell SD
Supt. — See North Caldwell
Grandview ES 400/K-3
35 Hamilton Dr E 07006 973-712-4400
Michael Stefanelli, prin.

Trinity Academy 300/PK-8
235 Bloomfield Ave 07006 973-226-3386
Linda Payonzeck, prin. Fax 226-6548

Califon, Hunterdon, Pop. 1,050
Califon SD 100/K-8
6 School St 07830 908-832-2828
Jason Kornegay, supt. Fax 832-6719
www.califonschool.org
Califon S 100/K-8
6 School St 07830 908-832-2828
Daniel Patton, prin. Fax 832-6719

Lebanon Township SD 700/PK-8
70 Bunnvale Rd 07830 908-638-4521
Jason R. Kornegay, supt. Fax 638-5511
www.lebtwpk8.org
Valley View ES 300/PK-4
400 County Road 513 07830 908-832-2175
Patricia Bell, prin. Fax 832-6280
Woodglen MS 400/5-8
70 Bunnvale Rd 07830 908-638-4111
Michael Rubright, prin. Fax 638-8418

Tewksbury Township SD 700/PK-8
173 County Road 517 07830 908-439-2010
Monica Rowland, supt. Fax 439-2655
www.tewksburyschools.org
Old Turnpike MS 300/5-8
171 County Road 517 07830 908-439-2010
Monica Rowland, prin. Fax 439-3160
Tewksbury ES 300/PK-4
109 Fairmount Rd E 07830 908-832-2594
James Miller, prin. Fax 832-6296

Camden, Camden, Pop. 76,282
Camden CSD 8,800/PK-12
201 N Front St 08102 856-966-2000
Paymon Rouhanifard, supt. Fax 966-2161
www.camden.k12.nj.us
Catto Family S 500/PK-8
3100 Westfield Ave 08105 856-966-4097
Byron Dixon, prin. Fax 756-0273
Cooper's Poynt Family S 400/PK-8
201 State St 08102 856-966-5370
Stephen Bournes, prin. Fax 756-0334
Cramer ES 500/PK-6
2800 Mickle St 08105 856-966-8910
Danielle Phillips, prin. Fax 756-0328
Cream Family S 400/PK-8
1875 Mulford St 08104 856-966-4760
LaTane Bradley, prin. Fax 963-8274
Davis Family S 500/PK-8
3425 Cramer St 08105 856-966-8920
Sharon Woodridge, prin. Fax 963-8379
Dudley Family S 500/PK-8
2250 Berwick St 08105 856-966-2000
Gloria Martinez-Vega, prin. Fax 365-0520
Early Childhood Developement Center 400/PK-K
1602 Pine St 08103 856-966-8901
Loray Dobson, prin. Fax 963-8267
Forest Hill ES 200/K-5
1625 Wildwood Ave 08103 856-966-8930
David Corvi, prin. Fax 963-8609
Sharp ES 300/PK-8
928 N 32nd St 08105 856-966-8988
Evelyn Ruiz, prin. Fax 342-8103
Veterans Memorial Family S 500/PK-8
800 N 26th St 08105 856-966-5090
Danette Sapowsky, prin. Fax 541-5141
Wiggins Family S 600/PK-8
400 Mount Vernon St 08103 856-966-5120
Lana Murray, prin. Fax 964-9782
Wilson Family S 600/PK-8
2250 S 8th St 08104 856-966-3961
Janna Johnson, prin. Fax 964-9560
Yorkship ES 500/PK-8
1200 Collings Rd 08104 856-966-5110
Tracey Reed-Thompson, prin. Fax 964-9650

NJ Charter Schools
Supt. — See Trenton
McGraw ES 300/K-5
3051 Fremont Ave 08105 856-966-8960
LaQuanda Jackson, prin. Fax 963-8065

Camden Forward S 100/K-8
PO Box 1479 08105 856-382-1010
Holy Name S 200/K-8
700 N 5th St 08102 856-365-7930
Patricia Quinter, prin. Fax 365-8041
Sacred Heart S 300/K-8
404 Jasper St 08104 856-963-1341
Janet Williams, prin. Fax 963-3551

St. Anthony of Padua S 200/K-8
2824 River Rd 08105 856-966-6791
Dr. Mary Burke, prin. Fax 966-1616
St. Joseph Pro-Cathedral S 300/K-8
2907 Federal St 08105 856-964-4336
Frances Montgomery, prin. Fax 964-1080

Cape May, Cape May, Pop. 3,525
Cape May CSD 200/PK-6
921 Lafayette St 08204 609-884-8485
Victoria Zelenak, supt. Fax 884-7037
www.cmcboe.org
Cape May City ES 200/PK-6
921 Lafayette St 08204 609-884-8485
Victoria Zelenak, admin. Fax 884-7037

Lower Cape May Regional SD 1,400/7-12
687 Route 9 08204 609-884-3475
Chris Kobik, supt. Fax 884-0546
lcmrschooldistrict.com
Teitelman MS 500/7-8
687 Route 9 08204 609-884-3475
Greg Lasher, prin. Fax 884-0546

Lower Township ESD 1,700/PK-6
905 Seashore Rd 08204 609-884-9400
Jeff Samaniego, supt. Fax 884-1821
www.lowertwpschools.com
Abrams ES 400/3-4
714 Town Bank Rd 08204 609-884-9420
John King, prin. Fax 884-9421
Mitnick PS 400/1-2
905 Seashore Rd 08204 609-884-9470
Christopher Shivers, prin. Fax 898-9481
Sandman Consolidated ES 500/5-6
838 Seashore Rd 08204 609-884-9410
Van Cathcart, prin. Fax 884-9412
Other Schools – See Villas

Cape May Court House, Cape May, Pop. 5,227
Dennis Township SD 500/PK-8
601 Hagan Rd, 609-861-2821
MARK MILLER, supt. Fax 861-1833
www.dtschools.org
Dennis Township PS 200/PK-3
601 Hagan Rd, 609-861-2821
Jamie VanArtsdalen, prin. Fax 861-1567
Other Schools – See Dennisville

Middle Township SD 2,500/PK-12
216 S Main St, 609-465-1800
Dr. David Salvo, supt. Fax 463-1979
www.middletwp.k12.nj.us
Middle Township ES 1 600/PK-2
215 Eldredge Rd, 609-463-1900
Christian Paskalides, prin. Fax 463-1901
Middle Township ES 2 500/3-5
101 W Pacific Ave, 609-465-1828
Doug Penkethman, prin. Fax 463-1909
Middle Township MS 4 500/6-8
300 E Pacific Ave, 609-465-1834
Jeff Ortman, prin. Fax 465-5524

Bishop McHugh Regional S 200/PK-8
2221 N Route 9, 609-624-1900
Thomas McGuire, prin. Fax 624-9696

Carlstadt, Bergen, Pop. 6,042
Carlstadt SD 600/PK-8
550 Washington St 07072 201-672-3000
Stephen Kollinok, supt. Fax 672-9845
www.carlstadt.org
Carlstadt ES 600/PK-8
550 Washington St 07072 201-672-3000
Kenneth Foy, prin. Fax 939-2085

Carneys Point, Salem, Pop. 7,250
Penns Grove-Carneys Point Regional SD
Supt. — See Penns Grove
Field Street ES 500/1-3
144 Field St 08069 856-299-0170
Mary Kwiatkowski, prin. Fax 299-1833
Lafayette-Pershing ES 400/PK-K
237 Shell Rd 08069 856-299-3230
Christopher Meyrick, prin. Fax 299-2180

Carteret, Middlesex, Pop. 22,279
Carteret Borough SD 3,700/PK-12
599 Roosevelt Ave 07008 732-541-8960
Rosa Diaz, supt. Fax 541-0433
www.carteretschools.org
Carteret MS 900/6-8
300 Carteret Ave 07008 732-541-8960
Mary Spiga, prin. Fax 541-0483
Columbus ES 600/PK-5
1 Carteret Ave 07008 732-541-8960
Stephen Peters, prin. Fax 541-4245
Hale ES 500/PK-5
678 Roosevelt Ave 07008 732-541-8960
Christian Zimmer, prin. Fax 969-8694
Minue ES 700/PK-5
83 Post Blvd 07008 732-541-8960
Cheryl Bolinger, prin. Fax 969-3902

St. Joseph S 200/PK-8
865 Roosevelt Ave 07008 732-541-7111
Roseann Johnson, prin. Fax 541-0676

Cedar Grove, Essex, Pop. 12,053
Cedar Grove Township SD 1,700/PK-12
520 Pompton Ave 07009 973-239-1550
Michael Fetherman, supt. Fax 239-2994
www.cgschools.org
Cedar Grove Memorial MS 600/5-8
500 Ridge Rd 07009 973-239-5233
Nicholas DeCorte, prin.
North End ES 300/PK-4
122 Stevens Ave 07009 973-256-1454
Traci Dyer, prin. Fax 256-8224
South End ES 300/PK-4
16 Harper Ter 07009 973-239-2116
Lynn DiMatteo, prin. Fax 239-5419

St. Catherine of Siena S 300/PK-8
39 E Bradford Ave 07009 973-239-6968
Celine Kerwin, prin. Fax 239-1008

Cedarville, Cumberland, Pop. 761
Lawrence Township SD 500/PK-8
225 Main St 08311 856-447-4237
Dr. Shelleymarie Magan, supt. Fax 447-3446
www.myronlpowell.org
Powell S 500/PK-8
225 Main St 08311 856-447-4237
Shellymarie Magan, prin. Fax 447-3446

Chatham, Morris, Pop. 8,814
School District of the Chathams 4,100/K-12
58 Meyersville Rd 07928 973-457-2520
Dr. Michael LaSusa, supt. Fax 457-2481
www.chatham-nj.org
Chatham MS 900/6-8
480 Main St 07928 973-457-2506
Jill Gihorski, prin. Fax 457-2492
Lafayette ES 700/4-5
221 Lafayette Ave 07928 973-457-2507
Cheryl Russo, prin. Fax 701-9153
Milton Avenue ES 300/K-3
16 Milton Ave 07928 973-457-2508
Nicholas Andreazza, prin. Fax 635-2116
Southern Boulevard ES 400/K-3
192 Southern Blvd 07928 973-457-2509
Robert Gardella, prin. Fax 635-4022
Washington Avenue ES 400/K-3
102 Washington Ave 07928 973-457-2510
Kristine Dudlo, prin. Fax 635-9062

Chatham Day S 100/PK-8
700 Shunpike Rd 07928 973-410-0400
Dr. David Lowry, head sch Fax 410-0401
St. Patrick S 300/PK-8
45 Chatham St 07928 973-635-4623
Christine Ross, prin. Fax 635-2311

Chatsworth, Burlington
Woodland Township SD 100/PK-8
PO Box 477 08019 609-726-1230
Misty Weiss, supt. Fax 726-9037
www.woodlandboe.org
Chatsworth S 100/PK-8
PO Box 477 08019 609-726-1230
Misty Weiss, prin. Fax 726-9037

Cherry Hill, Camden, Pop. 70,100
Cherry Hill SD 10,900/K-12
PO Box 5015 08034 856-429-5600
Dr. Joseph Meloche, supt. Fax 354-1864
www.chclc.org
Barton ES 500/K-5
223 Rhode Island Ave 08002 856-667-3303
Sean Sweeney, prin. Fax 667-7968
Beck MS 900/6-8
950 Cropwell Rd 08003 856-424-4505
Dr. Bernie O'Connor, prin. Fax 424-8602
Carusi MS 900/6-8
315 Roosevelt Dr 08002 856-667-1220
John Cafagna, prin. Fax 779-0613
Cooper ES 200/K-5
1960 Greentree Rd 08003 856-424-4554
Rebecca Tiernan, prin. Fax 751-0974
Harte ES 400/K-5
1909 Queen Ann Rd 08003 856-795-0515
Neil Burti, prin. Fax 795-7090
Johnson ES 400/K-5
500 Kresson Rd 08034 856-428-8848
Jared Peltzman, prin. Fax 795-7132
Kilmer ES 500/K-5
2900 Chapel Ave W 08002 856-667-3903
Eloisa DeJesus-Woodruff, prin. Fax 667-8516
Kingston ES 500/K-5
320 Kingston Rd 08034 856-667-0986
William Marble, prin. Fax 667-0343
Knight ES 300/K-5
140 Old Carriage Rd 08034 856-428-0830
Eugene Park, prin. Fax 428-0972
Mann ES 300/K-5
150 Walt Whitman Blvd 08003 856-428-1144
Shilpa Dave, prin. Fax 428-7168
Paine ES 400/K-5
4001 Church Rd 08034 856-667-1350
Kirk Rickansrud, prin. Fax 755-1491
Rosa International MS 800/6-8
485 Browning Ln 08003 856-616-8787
George Guy, prin. Fax 616-0904
Sharp ES 300/K-5
300 Old Orchard Rd 08003 856-424-1550
Ric Miscioscia, prin. Fax 424-6577
Stockton ES 400/K-5
200 Wexford Dr 08003 856-424-1505
James Riordan, prin. Fax 761-0367
Woodcrest ES 400/K-5
400 Cranford Rd 08003 856-429-2058
Dr. Jonathan Cohen, prin. Fax 216-9073

Kings Christian S 300/PK-12
5 Carnegie Plz 08003 856-489-6720
Meg McHale, prin. Fax 489-6727
Politz Day S of Cherry Hill 200/PK-8
720 Cooper Landing Rd 08002 856-667-1013
Resurrection Regional Catholic S 400/PK-8
402 Kings Hwy N Ste A 08034 856-667-3034
Molly Webb, prin. Fax 667-9160

Chesilhurst, Camden, Pop. 1,593

Legacy Classical Christian Academy K-6
511 Edwards Ave 08089 856-335-5015

Chester, Morris, Pop. 1,618
Chester SD 1,200/K-8
50 North Rd 07930 908-879-7373
Dr. Christina Van Woert, supt. Fax 879-5887
www.chester-nj.org
Black River MS 500/6-8
133 North Rd 07930 908-879-6363
Andrew White, prin. Fax 879-9085
Bragg IS 400/3-5
250 State Route 24 07930 908-879-5324
Michele Stanton, prin. Fax 879-5438
Dickerson ES 300/K-2
250 State Route 24 07930 908-879-5313
Melissa Fair, prin. Fax 879-7018

Chesterfield, Burlington
Chesterfield Township SD 700/K-6
30 Saddle Way, 609-298-6900
Scott Heino, supt. Fax 298-7884
www.chesterfieldschool.com
Chesterfield ES 700/K-6
30 Saddle Way, 609-298-6900
Michael Mazzoni, prin. Fax 298-7884

Meadow View Junior Academy 50/K-10
241 Bordentown Chstrfeld Rd, 609-298-1122

Cinnaminson, Burlington, Pop. 14,583
Cinnaminson Township SD 2,300/PK-12
PO Box 224 08077 856-829-7600
Stephen Cappello, supt. Fax 786-9618
www.cinnaminson.com
Cinnaminson MS 600/6-8
312 N Fork Landing Rd 08077 856-786-8012
Frank Goulburn, prin. Fax 786-1860
New Albany ES 500/PK-2
2701 New Albany Rd 08077 856-786-2284
John Layden, prin. Fax 786-3763
Rush IS 500/3-5
1200 Wynwood Dr 08077 856-829-7778
Deborah Banecker, prin. Fax 303-0218

St. Charles Borromeo S 300/PK-8
2500 Branch Pike 08077 856-829-2778
Kathy Chesnut, prin. Fax 829-2159
Westfield Friends S 200/PK-8
2201 Riverton Rd 08077 856-829-0895
Jon Hall Ed.D., head sch Fax 829-9320

Clark, Union, Pop. 14,629
Clark Township SD 2,200/PK-12
365 Westfield Ave 07066 732-574-9600
Edward Grande, supt. Fax 574-1456
www.clarkschools.org
Clark Preschool PK-PK
430 Westfield Ave 07066 732-428-8408
Fax 388-0456
Hehnly ES 500/K-5
590 Raritan Rd 07066 732-381-8100
Shirley Bergin, prin. Fax 381-9359
Kumpf MS 500/6-8
59 Mildred Ter 07066 732-381-0400
Richard Delmonaco, prin. Fax 381-0262
Valley Road ES 400/K-5
150 Valley Rd 07066 732-388-7900
Joseph Beltramba, prin. Fax 388-6209

Featherbed Lane S 100/PK-K
801 Featherbed Ln 07066 732-388-7063
St. John the Apostle S 500/PK-8
541 Valley Rd 07066 732-388-1360
Dr. Deborah Egan, prin. Fax 388-0775

Clayton, Gloucester, Pop. 7,923
Clayton SD 1,400/PK-12
350 E Clinton St 08312 856-881-8700
Nick Koutsogiannis, supt. Fax 863-8196
claytonps.org
Clayton MS 300/6-8
55 Pop Kramer Blvd 08312 856-881-8701
Marvin Tucker, prin. Fax 881-8623
Simmons ES 700/PK-5
300 W Chestnut St 08312 856-881-8704
Scott Uribe, prin. Fax 307-0924

St. Michael the Archangel Regional S 300/PK-8
51 W North St 08312 856-881-0067
Janice Bruni, prin. Fax 881-4064

Clementon, Camden, Pop. 4,875
Clementon SD 400/PK-8
4 Audubon Ave 08021 856-783-2300
Kathleen Haines, supt. Fax 783-8929
www.clementon.k12.nj.us
Clementon S 400/PK-8
4 Audubon Ave 08021 856-783-2300
Adrienne McManis, prin. Fax 783-8929

Cliffside Park, Bergen, Pop. 22,965
Cliffside Park SD 2,500/PK-12
525 Palisade Ave 07010 201-313-2310
Michael Romagnino, supt. Fax 943-7050
www.cliffsidepark.edu
Cliffside Park ES 3 300/1-6
397 Palisade Ave 07010 201-313-2330
Donna Calabrese, prin. Fax 313-9488
Cliffside Park ES 4 300/K-6
279 Columbia Ave 07010 201-313-2340
Jaclyn Roussos, prin. Fax 313-0397
Cliffside Park ES 5 200/PK-PK, 1-
214 Day Ave 07010 201-313-2350
Dana Martinotti, prin. Fax 313-5642
Cliffside Park S 6 600/1-8
440 Oakdene Ave 07010 201-313-2360
Robert Bargna, prin. Fax 941-2012

Cliffwood, Monmouth, Pop. 1,500
Matawan-Aberdeen Regional SD
Supt. — See Aberdeen

Cliffwood ES 300/PK-3
422 Cliffwood Ave 07721 732-705-5600
Mark Van Horn, prin. Fax 566-2837
Matawan Aberdeen MS 800/6-8
469 Matawan Ave 07721 732-705-5400
Aaron Eyler, prin. Fax 765-0894

Cliffwood Beach, Middlesex, Pop. 3,115
Old Bridge Township SD
Supt. — See Matawan
Cooper ES 200/K-5
160 Birchwood Dr 07735 732-290-3881
Dr. Cathy Gramata, prin. Fax 583-7109

Clifton, Passaic, Pop. 82,465
Clifton SD, 745 Clifton Ave 07013 10,300/PK-12
Richard Tardalo, supt. 973-470-2300
www.clifton.k12.nj.us
Columbus MS 1,200/6-8
350 Piaget Ave 07011 973-470-2360
Francine Parker, prin. Fax 470-2365
Public S 1 300/K-5
158 Park Slope 07011 973-470-2370
Theresa Evans, prin. Fax 253-3237
Public S 2 400/K-5
1270 Van Houten Ave 07013 973-470-2380
Jennifer Lucas, prin. Fax 458-8325
Public S 3 300/K-5
365 Washington Ave 07011 973-470-2390
Linette Shyers, prin. Fax 478-2576
Public S 4 200/K-5
194 W 2nd St 07011 973-470-2382
Joelle Rosetti, prin. Fax 253-3286
Public S 5 300/K-5
136 Valley Rd 07013 973-470-2386
Dr. Steven Anderson, prin. Fax 357-2184
Public S 8 200/PK-5
41 Oak St 07014 973-470-2393
Nancy Latzoni, prin. Fax 458-9249
Public S 9 300/K-5
25 Brighton Rd 07012 973-470-2396
Michele DeVita, prin. Fax 458-8416
Public S 11 500/K-5
147 Merselis Ave 07011 973-470-2401
Luca Puzzo, prin. Fax 340-7205
Public S 12, 165 Clifton Ave 07011 700/PK-5
Maria Parham-Talley, prin. 973-470-2404
Public S 13 500/K-5
782 Van Houten Ave 07013 973-470-2410
Dr. Rachel Capizzi, prin. Fax 458-9253
Public S 14 200/K-5
99 Saint Andrews Blvd 07012 973-470-2411
Jason Habedank, prin. Fax 458-9216
Public S 15 400/PK-5
700 Gregory Ave 07011 973-470-2418
Dr. Luginda Batten-Walker, prin. Fax 458-9238
Public S 16 100/K-5
755 Grove St 07013 973-470-2420
Joanna Juarbe, prin. Fax 773-7834
Public S 17, 361 Lexington Ave 07011 500/PK-5
Laura Zagorski, prin. 973-458-6017
Wilson MS 1,200/6-8
1400 Van Houten Ave 07013 973-470-2348
Maria Caiafa-Romeo, prin. Fax 470-2607

Clifton Cheder 200/PK-8
123 Industrial St E 07012 973-472-0011
Rabbi Yonah Lazar, dean Fax 518-5682
New Hope S 100/K-8
780 Clifton Ave 07013 973-473-4144
St. Andrew the Apostle S 200/PK-8
418 Mount Prospect Ave 07012 973-473-3711
Cynthia Schirm, prin. Fax 473-6611
St. Brendan S 400/PK-8
154 E 1st St 07011 973-772-1149
Rev. Robert Mitchell, prin. Fax 772-5547
St. Philip the Apostle S 400/PK-8
797 Valley Rd 07013 973-779-4700
Barbara Zito, prin. Fax 779-2959

Clinton, Hunterdon, Pop. 2,686
Clinton Township SD
Supt. — See Lebanon
Clinton Township MS 400/7-8
34 Grayrock Rd 08809 908-238-9141
Judith Hammond, prin. Fax 238-9376
Spruce Run S 300/PK-1
27 Belvidere Ave 08809 908-735-7916
Melissa Goad, prin. Fax 735-2213

Clinton-Glen Gardner SD 500/K-8
10 School St 08809 908-735-8512
Dr. Seth Cohen, supt. Fax 735-5895
www.cpsnj.org
Clinton Public S 500/K-8
10 School St 08809 908-735-8512
Dr. Seth Cohen, prin. Fax 735-5895

Crossroads Christian Academy 100/PK-8
9 Pittstown Rd 08809 908-735-5501
David Homa, prin. Fax 735-7517

Closter, Bergen, Pop. 8,270
Closter SD 1,100/PK-8
340 Homans Ave 07624 201-768-3001
Joanne Newberry, supt. Fax 768-1903
www.closterschools.org
Hillside ES 500/PK-4
340 Homans Ave 07624 201-768-3860
Alfred Baffa, prin. Fax 768-6770
Tenakill MS 600/5-8
275 High St 07624 201-768-1332
William Tantum, prin. Fax 784-0726

Collingswood, Camden, Pop. 13,647
Collingswood Borough SD 1,800/PK-12
200 Lees Ave 08108 856-962-5700
Dr. Scott Oswald, supt. Fax 962-5723
www.collingswood.k12.nj.us/
Collingswood MS 300/6-8
414 W Collings Ave 08108 856-962-5702
Dr. John McMullin, prin. Fax 962-5751
Garfield ES 100/PK-5
480 Haddon Ave 08108 856-962-5705
Mark Wiltsey, prin. Fax 962-5705
Newbie ES 100/K-5
2 E Browning Rd 08108 856-962-5706
Steven Smith, prin. Fax 962-5719
Tatem ES 200/K-5
265 Lincoln Ave 08108 856-962-5704
Jennifer McPartland, prin. Fax 962-5574
Zane North ES 200/PK-5
801 Stokes Ave 08108 856-962-5703
Thomas Santo, prin. Fax 962-5712
Other Schools – See West Collingswood

Good Shepherd Regional S 200/PK-8
100 Lees Ave 08108 856-858-1562
Donald Garecht, prin. Fax 854-2943

Colonia, Middlesex, Pop. 17,529
Woodbridge Township SD
Supt. — See Woodbridge
Claremont Avenue ES 300/K-5
90 Claremont Ave 07067 732-596-5628
Dr. Joseph Massimino, prin. Fax 574-1634
Colonia MS 600/6-8
100 Delaware Ave 07067 732-396-7000
Cynthia Lagunovich, prin. Fax 574-0772
Lynn Crest ES 300/PK-5
98 Ira Ave 07067 732-499-6558
Matthew Connelly, prin. Fax 396-1874
Oak Ridge Heights ES 300/K-5
720 Inman Ave 07067 732-499-6553
Scott Osborne, prin. Fax 574-1746
Pennsylvania Avenue ES 300/K-5
80 N Pennsylvania Ave 07067 732-499-6566
Dr. Samuel Fancera, prin. Fax 574-1841

St. John Vianney S 400/PK-8
420 Inman Ave 07067 732-388-1662
Sr. Eileen Jude Wust, prin. Fax 388-1003

Colts Neck, Monmouth
Colts Neck Township SD 1,000/PK-8
70 Conover Rd 07722 732-946-0055
MaryJane Garibay Ed.D., supt. Fax 858-8583
www.coltsneckschools.org
Cedar Drive MS 400/6-8
73 Cedar Dr 07722 732-946-0055
Colin Rigby, prin. Fax 462-4108
Conover PS 300/PK-2
56 Conover Rd 07722 732-946-0055
Tricia Barr, prin. Fax 332-9501
Conover Road ES 300/3-5
76 Conover Rd 07722 732-946-0055
James Osmond, prin. Fax 858-8682

Columbus, Burlington
Mansfield Township SD 700/K-6
200 Mansfield Rd E 08022 609-298-2037
Tiffany Moutis, supt. Fax 298-5365
www.mansfieldschool.com
Hydock ES 200/K-2
19 Locust Ave 08022 609-298-0308
Stacy Cullari, prin. Fax 298-1341
Mansfield Township ES 400/3-6
200 Mansfield Rd E 08022 609-298-2037
Glenn Kershner, prin. Fax 298-5812

Northern Burlington County Regional SD 2,100/7-12
160 Mansfield Rd E 08022 609-298-3900
Dr. James Sarruda, supt. Fax 298-3154
www.nburlington.com
Northern Burlington County Regional JHS 800/7-8
180 Mansfield Rd E 08022 609-298-3900
Andrew Kearns Ed.D., prin. Fax 291-1563

Cranbury, Middlesex, Pop. 2,142
Cranbury Township SD 500/K-8
23 N Main St 08512 609-395-1700
Dr. Susan Genco, admin. Fax 860-9655
www.cranburyschool.org
Cranbury S 500/K-8
23 N Main St 08512 609-395-1700
Dr. Susan Genco, prin. Fax 860-9655

Cranford, Union, Pop. 22,624
Cranford Township SD 3,700/K-12
132 Thomas St 07016 908-709-6202
Dr. Scott Rubin, supt. Fax 272-7735
www.cranfordschools.org
Bloomingdale Avenue ES 200/K-2
200 Bloomingdale Ave 07016 908-709-6969
Lourdes Murphy, prin. Fax 709-9138
Brookside Place ES 400/K-5
700 Brookside Pl 07016 908-709-6244
Michael Klimko, prin. Fax 709-6724
Hillside Avenue S 700/K-8
125 Hillside Ave 07016 908-709-6229
Curt Fogas Ed.D., prin. Fax 709-6752
Livingston Avenue ES 300/3-5
75 Livingston Ave 07016 908-709-6248
Kevin Deacon, prin. Fax 709-6748
Orange Avenue S 800/3-8
901 Orange Ave 07016 908-709-6257
Kevin Deacon, prin. Fax 272-3025
Walnut Avenue ES 200/K-2
370 Walnut Ave 07016 908-709-6253
Angelo Paternoster, prin. Fax 709-6754

St. Michael S 300/PK-8
100 Alden St 07016 908-276-9425
Sandy Miragliotta, prin. Fax 276-4371

Cresskill, Bergen, Pop. 8,463
Cresskill SD 1,700/K-12
1 Lincoln Dr 07626 201-227-7791
Michael Burke, supt. Fax 567-7976
www.cboek12.org
Bryan ES 400/K-5
51 Brookside Ave 07626 201-569-1191
Erik Roth, prin. Fax 569-3367
Cresskill MS 400/6-8
1 Lincoln Dr 07626 201-227-7791
John Massaro, prin. Fax 567-0028
Merritt Memorial ES 300/K-5
91 Dogwood Ln 07626 201-569-8381
Paul Diverio, prin. Fax 569-3862

Academy of St. Therese of Lisieux 200/PK-8
220 Jefferson Ave 07626 201-568-4296
Glenn Clark, prin. Fax 568-3179

Dayton, Middlesex, Pop. 6,871
South Brunswick Township SD
Supt. — See North Brunswick
Dayton ES PK-K
310 Georges Rd 08810 732-329-1043
April Gonzalez, prin. Fax 329-1891
Indian Fields ES 500/1-5
359 Ridge Rd 08810 732-329-1043
April Gonzalez, prin. Fax 274-1234

Deal, Monmouth, Pop. 741
Deal Borough SD 200/K-8
201 Roseld Ave 07723 732-531-0480
Dr. Donato Saponaro, supt. Fax 531-1908
www.dealschool.org
Deal S 200/K-8
201 Roseld Ave 07723 732-531-0480
Donato Saponaro, prin. Fax 531-1908

Yeshiva at the Jersey Shore 300/K-8
100 Grant Ave 07723 732-663-2929
Rabbi Elie Tuchman Ed.D., head sch Fax 663-0033

Delair, Camden
Pennsauken Township SD
Supt. — See Pennsauken
Delair ES 400/K-4
850 Derousse Ave 08110 856-662-6164
Roslyn Lawrence, prin. Fax 317-0362

Delanco, Burlington, Pop. 3,316
Delanco Township SD 400/K-8
1301 Burlington Ave 08075 856-461-1905
Joseph Mersinger, supt. Fax 461-1627
www.delanco.com
Pearson ES 300/K-5
1301 Burlington Ave 08075 856-461-1976
Louis Conti, prin. Fax 461-4419
Walnut Street MS 100/6-8
411 Walnut St 08075 856-461-0874
Joseph Mersinger, admin. Fax 461-6903

Delaware, Warren, Pop. 144
Knowlton Township SD 200/K-6
PO Box 227 07833 908-475-5118
Jeannine DeFalco, supt. Fax 475-1141
www.knowltonschool.com
Knowlton Township ES 200/K-6
PO Box 227 07833 908-475-5118
Jeannine DeFalco, supt. Fax 475-1141

Delran, Burlington, Pop. 13,178
Delran Township SD 2,800/PK-12
52 Hartford Rd 08075 856-461-6800
Dr. Brian Brotschul, supt. Fax 461-6125
www.delranschools.org/
Delran IS 700/3-5
20 Creek Rd 08075 856-764-5100
Kimberly Hickson, prin. Fax 764-5315
Delran MS 700/6-8
905 S Chester Ave 08075 856-461-8822
Wendy DeVicaris, prin. Fax 461-0311
Millbridge ES 700/PK-2
282 Conrow Rd 08075 856-461-2900
Jennifer Lowe, prin. Fax 461-0866

Montessori Academy Delran 100/PK-9
28 Conrow Rd 08075 856-461-2121

Demarest, Bergen, Pop. 4,792
Demarest SD 700/PK-8
568 Piermont Rd 07627 201-768-6060
Michael Fox, supt. Fax 767-9122
demarestsd.schoolwires.net/
County Road ES 100/PK-1
130 County Rd 07627 201-768-6060
Frank Mazzini, prin. Fax 768-1285
Demarest MS 300/5-8
568 Piermont Rd 07627 201-768-6060
Jonathon Regan, prin. Fax 768-9122
Emerson ES 200/2-4
15 Columbus Rd 07627 201-784-6060
Frank Mazzini, prin. Fax 784-6093

Dennisville, Cape May
Dennis Township SD
Supt. — See Cape May Court House
Dennis Township ES 400/4-8
165 Academy Rd 08214 609-861-2821
Jamie VanArtsdalen, prin. Fax 861-5229

Denville, Morris, Pop. 13,812
Denville Township SD 1,700/PK-8
400 Morris Ave Ste 279 07834 973-983-6530
Steven Forte, supt. Fax 784-4778
www.denville.org
Lakeview ES 700/PK-5
44 Cooper Rd 07834 973-983-6540
Elizabeth Baisley, prin. Fax 366-4345
Riverview ES 400/K-5
33 Saint Marys Pl 07834 973-983-6545
Christina Theodoropoulos, prin. Fax 627-3681

Valleyview MS 700/6-8
320 Diamond Spring Rd 07834 973-983-6535
Paul Iantosca, prin. Fax 627-0632

St. Marys S 300/PK-8
100 US Highway 46 07834 973-627-2606
Dr. Margaret McCluskey, prin. Fax 627-9316

Deptford, Gloucester
Deptford Township SD 4,200/PK-12
2022 Good Intent Rd 08096 856-232-2700
Dr. Charles Ford Jr, supt. Fax 227-7473
www.deptford.k12.nj.us
Central ECC 600/PK-1
1040 Monmouth Rd 08096 856-384-8750
Maria Gioffre, prin. Fax 686-9829
Good Intent ES 400/2-6
1555 Good Intent Rd 08096 856-232-2737
Kimberly Matthews, prin. Fax 227-8014
Lake Tract ES 500/2-6
690 Iszard Rd 08096 856-686-2240
Cheryl Battee, prin. Fax 845-3057
Other Schools – See Sewell, Wenonah, Westville

Dorothy, Atlantic
Weymouth Township SD 200/PK-8
1202 11th Ave 08317 609-476-2412
Dr. John Alfieri, supt. Fax 476-3966
www.weymouthtownshipschool.org
Weymouth Township S 200/PK-8
1202 11th Ave 08317 609-476-2412
Dr. John Alfieri, supt. Fax 476-3966

Dover, Morris, Pop. 17,974
Dover Town SD 2,900/PK-12
100 Grace St 07801 973-989-2000
Robert Becker, supt. Fax 989-1662
district.dover-nj.org
Academy Street ES 500/K-6
14 Academy St 07801 973-989-2030
David Marion, prin. Fax 989-6270
Dover MS 400/7-8
302 E McFarlan St 07801 973-989-2040
Tawana Clarrett, prin. Fax 361-2117
East Dover ES 500/K-6
302 E McFarlan St 07801 973-989-2055
Tawana Clarrett, prin. Fax 361-2117
North Dover ES 700/PK-6
51 Highland Ave 07801 973-989-2020
Patrick Pandolfo, prin. Fax 361-1841

Rockaway Township SD
Supt. — See Hibernia
Birchwood ES 300/K-5
1 Art St 07801 973-361-7080
Alison Schessler, prin. Fax 361-8739
O'Brien ES 300/K-5
418 Mineral Springs Rd 07801 973-361-7330
Christopher Marangon, prin. Fax 361-8537

Dumont, Bergen, Pop. 17,212
Dumont SD 2,600/PK-12
25 Depew St 07628 201-387-1600
Emanuele Triggiano, supt. Fax 387-0259
www.dumontnj.org
Grant ES 300/K-5
100 Grant Ave 07628 201-387-3050
Richard Gronda, prin. Fax 384-7148
Honiss S 700/K-8
31 Depew St 07628 201-387-3020
Dr. Karen Bennett, prin. Fax 387-8109
Lincoln ES 200/K-5
80 Prospect Ave 07628 201-387-3040
Luis Lopez, prin. Fax 384-0422
Selzer S 500/PK-8
435 Prospect Ave 07628 201-387-3030
John Podesta, prin. Fax 384-1005

Dunellen, Middlesex, Pop. 7,100
Dunellen SD 1,100/PK-12
400 High St 08812 732-968-3226
Gene Mosley, supt. Fax 968-3513
www.dunellenschools.org
Faber ES 500/PK-5
400 High St 08812 732-968-5311
Gary Lubisco, prin. Fax 968-4243
Lincoln MS 300/6-8
400 Dunellen Ave 08812 732-968-0885
Robert Altmire, prin. Fax 424-1359

Eastampton, Burlington
Eastampton Township SD 600/K-8
1 Student Dr 08060 609-267-9172
Ambrose Duckett Ed.D., supt. Fax 702-9625
www.eastampton.k12.nj.us
Eastampton Township S 600/K-8
1 Student Dr 08060 609-267-9172
Ambrose Duckett Ed.D., prin. Fax 261-3338

Timothy Christian Academy 100/PK-8
1341 Woodlane Rd 08060 609-261-9578
Dawn Adams, prin. Fax 261-7122

East Brunswick, Middlesex, Pop. 47,400
East Brunswick Township SD 8,100/PK-12
760 State Route 18 08816 732-613-6700
Victor Valeski, supt. Fax 698-9871
www.ebnet.org
Bowne-Munro ES 200/K-5
120 Main St 08816 732-613-6810
Ronald Lieberman, prin. Fax 257-0029
Brook ES 400/PK-5
48 Sullivan Way 08816 732-613-6870
Elizabeth Dunn, prin. Fax 249-5913
Central ES 400/K-5
371 Cranbury Rd 08816 732-613-6820
Danielle DiNinno, prin. Fax 254-2624
Chittick ES 400/PK-5
5 Flagler St 08816 732-613-6830
Megan Manetta, prin. Fax 390-0172
Frost ES 400/PK-5
65 Frost Ave 08816 732-613-6850
Loretta Payette, prin. Fax 257-2034
Hammarskjold MS 1,300/6-7
200 Rues Ln 08816 732-613-6892
Michael Gaskell, prin. Fax 651-7135
Irwin ES 500/K-5
71 Race Track Rd 08816 732-613-6840
JoAnn Chmielowicz, prin. Fax 257-7021
Memorial ES 500/PK-5
14 Innes Rd 08816 732-613-6860
Cheryl Jones, prin. Fax 698-0930
Warnsdorfer ES 400/K-5
9 Hardenburg Ln 08816 732-613-6880
Joseph Csatari, prin. Fax 613-1548

St. Bartholomew S 300/PK-8
470 Ryders Ln 08816 732-254-7105
Ann Wierzbicki, prin. Fax 254-6352
Yeshivat Netivot Montessori 100/PK-8
511 Ryders Ln 08816 732-985-4626

East Hanover, Morris, Pop. 9,926
East Hanover Township SD 1,000/PK-8
20 School Ave 07936 973-887-2112
Natalee Bartlett, supt. Fax 887-2773
www.easthanoverschools.org/
Central ES 300/3-5
400 Ridgedale Ave 07936 973-887-0358
Melissa Falcone, prin. Fax 887-6565
East Hanover MS 400/6-8
477 Ridgedale Ave 07936 973-887-8810
Stacie Costello, prin. Fax 887-5079
Smith ES 300/PK-2
27 Green Dr 07936 973-887-5650
Kerry Quinn, prin. Fax 887-6406

East Newark, Hudson, Pop. 2,352
East Newark SD 300/PK-8
501 N 3rd St 07029 973-481-6800
Dr. Patrick Martin, supt. Fax 485-1344
eastnewarkschool.org/
East Newark S 300/PK-8
501 N 3rd St 07029 973-481-6800
Dr. Patrick Martin, prin. Fax 485-1344

East Orange, Essex, Pop. 62,841
East Orange SD 8,100/PK-12
199 4th Ave 07017 973-266-5760
Dr. Kevin West, supt. Fax 678-4865
www.eastorange.k12.nj.us
Banneker Academy 400/PK-5
500 S Clinton St 07018 973-266-4320
Sharon Vincent, prin. Fax 672-2891
Barry-Garvin MicroSociety S 200/1-5
1 Grove Pl 07017 973-673-5410
Fidelia Sturdivant, prin. Fax 266-5815
Bowser S of Excellence 700/PK-5
180 Lincoln St 07017 973-414-4170
Brian Heaphy, prin. Fax 414-4182
Carver Institute 300/PK-5
135 Glenwood Ave 07017 973-266-5860
Sharon Alsbrook-Davis, prin. Fax 266-2495
Cochran Academy 200/K-5
190 Midland Ave 07017 973-395-5975
Ralph Jacob, prin. Fax 395-5980
Costley MS 400/6-6
116 Hamilton St 07017 973-266-5660
Amaila Trono, prin. Fax 266-2956
Gibson ECC 200/PK-K
490 William St 07017 973-266-7017
Crystal Davis, prin. Fax 395-5990
Healy MS 300/6-6
116 Hamilton St 07017 973-266-5670
Dr. Howard Walker, prin. Fax 266-5693
Houston Academy 300/K-8
215 Dodd St 07017 973-266-5880
Henry Hamilton, prin. Fax 673-1466
Hughes ES 600/PK-5
160 Rhode Island Ave 07018 973-266-5870
Vincent Stallings, prin. Fax 414-4196
Jackson Academy 300/K-5
106 Prospect St 07017 973-266-5895
Yvy Joseph, prin. Fax 266-5569
Louverture ES 300/PK-5
330 Central Ave 07018 973-266-5940
David Johnson, prin. Fax 677-2470
Parks Academy 200/K-6
98 Greenwood Ave 07017 973-266-5950
Leslie Shults, prin. Fax 414-4197
Truth MS 400/7-8
116 Hamilton St 07017 973-266-5665
Dr. Monica Burton, prin. Fax 395-3586
Tyson Community ES 400/K-5
45 N Arlington Ave 07017 973-414-9222
Passion Moss-Hasan, prin. Fax 395-3883
Wahlstrom ECC 200/PK-K
340 Prospect St 07017 973-395-1210
Annie Jackson, prin. Fax 395-1215
Warwick Institute 400/PK-5
120 Central Ave 07018 973-266-5930
Flore Lovett, prin. Fax 266-3459

Ahlus Sunnah S 100/PK-12
215 N Oraton Pkwy 07017 973-672-4121
Jamas Children's University 100/PK-12
141 Hoffman Blvd 07017 973-678-7033
Our Lady Help of Christian S 200/PK-8
23 N Clinton St 07017 973-677-1546
Sr. Patricia Hogan, prin. Fax 677-3939
St. Joseph S 400/PK-8
115 Telford St 07018 973-674-2326
Karen Cavaness, prin. Fax 674-7718

East Rutherford, Bergen, Pop. 8,757
East Rutherford SD 800/PK-8
100 Uhland St 07073 201-804-3100
Giovanni A. Giancaspro, supt. Fax 804-3131
www.erboe.net/
Faust MS 300/5-8
100 Uhland St 07073 201-804-3100
Regina Barrale, prin. Fax 804-3131
McKenzie ES 500/PK-4
125 Carlton Ave 07073 201-804-3100
Brian Barrow, prin. Fax 531-1491

East Windsor, Mercer, Pop. 22,353
East Windsor Regional SD
Supt. — See Hightstown
Drew ES 600/K-5
70 Twin Rivers Dr N 08520 609-443-7820
Robert Dias, prin. Fax 443-7891
Kreps MS 1,100/6-8
5 Kent Ln 08520 609-443-7767
Lori Emmerson, prin. Fax 443-8972
McKnight ES 600/K-5
58 Twin Rivers Dr 08520 609-443-7800
Nicole Foulks, prin. Fax 443-7852

Eatontown, Monmouth, Pop. 12,304
Eatontown SD 500/PK-8
5 Grant Ave 07724 732-542-1055
Scott T. McCue, supt. Fax 578-0017
www.eatontown.org
Meadowbrook ES 100/K-2
65 Wyckoff Rd 07724 732-542-2777
Valerie Cioffi, prin. Fax 935-0813
Memorial MS 200/7-8
7 Grant Ave 07724 732-542-5013
Jay Medlin, prin. Fax 389-1364
Vetter ES 100/5-6
3 Grant Ave 07724 732-542-4644
Kevin Iozzi, prin. Fax 389-2205
Woodmere ES 50/PK-PK, 3-
65 Raleigh Ct 07724 732-542-3388
Kristoffer Brogna, prin. Fax 544-1560

Voyagers' Community S 100/PK-12
215 Broad St 07724 732-842-1660
Karen Giuffre, dir.

Edgewater, Bergen, Pop. 11,224
Edgewater SD 600/PK-6
251 Undercliff Ave 07020 201-945-4106
Kerry Postma, supt. Fax 945-4104
www.edgewaterschools.org
Van Gelder ES 200/3-6
251 Undercliff Ave 07020 201-945-4106
Raul Sandoval, prin. Fax 945-4104
Washington ES 300/PK-2
801 Undercliff Ave 07020 201-886-3480
Chris Kirkby, prin.

Edgewater Park, Burlington, Pop. 8,388
Edgewater Park Township SD 800/PK-8
25 Washington Ave 08010 609-877-2124
Dr. Roy Rakszawski, supt. Fax 877-4235
edgewaterparksd.org
Magowan ES 500/PK-4
405 Cherrix Ave 08010 609-877-1430
Raymond Marini, prin. Fax 877-8956
Ridgeway MS 300/5-8
300 Delanco Rd 08010 609-871-3434
Ronald Trampe, prin. Fax 871-2434

Edison, Middlesex, Pop. 99,500
Edison Township SD 14,100/PK-12
312 Pierson Ave 08837 732-452-4900
Dr. Richard O'Malley, supt. Fax 452-4993
www.edison.k12.nj.us
Adams MS 800/6-8
1081 New Dover Rd 08820 732-452-2920
Joan Valentine, prin. Fax 452-2922
Edison Early Learning Center PK-PK
10 Boulevard of Eagles 08817 732-650-5200
Christopher Conklin, admin.
Franklin ES 600/K-5
2485 Woodbridge Ave 08817 732-650-5300
Steven Preville, prin. Fax 650-5302
Hoover MS 800/6-8
174 Jackson Ave 08837 732-452-2940
Brian McGrath, prin. Fax 452-2950
Jefferson MS 700/6-8
450 Division St 08817 732-650-5290
Antoinette Emden, prin. Fax 652-5295
King ES 600/K-5
285 Tingley Ln 08820 732-452-2980
Diane Wilton, prin. Fax 452-2982
Lincoln ES 700/K-5
53 Brookville Rd 08817 732-650-5270
Timothy Hart, prin. Fax 650-5275
Lindeneau ES 400/K-5
50 Blossom St 08817 732-650-5320
Sara Bright, prin. Fax 650-5322
Madison IS 600/3-5
838 New Dover Rd 08820 732-452-2960
Kathleen Miller, prin. Fax 452-2964
Madison PS 500/PK-2
840 New Dover Rd 08820 732-452-2990
Michael Seiler, prin. Fax 452-2994
Marshall ES 600/K-5
15 Cornell St 08817 732-650-5370
Ami Hoffman, prin. Fax 650-5376
Menlo Park ES 800/K-5
155 Monroe Ave 08820 732-452-2910
Michael Duggan, prin. Fax 452-2911
Monroe ES 500/K-5
45 Wilus Way 08837 732-452-2970
Lynda Zapoticzny, prin. Fax 452-2975
Roosevelt Preschool PK-PK
838 New Dover Rd 08820 732-452-2939
Christopher Conklin, admin.
Washington ES 600/K-5
153 Winthrop Rd 08817 732-650-5280
Sandra Schlatter, prin. Fax 650-5283
Wilson MS 1,000/6-8
50 Woodrow Wilson Dr 08820 732-452-2870
Patricia Cotoia, prin. Fax 452-2876

Woodbrook ES 900/K-5
15 Robin Rd 08820 732-452-2901
Nicole Cirillo, prin. Fax 452-2904

Perth Amboy SD
Supt. — See Perth Amboy
Dual Language S 2-5
630 Amboy Ave 08837 732-376-6090
Jose Santos, prin. Fax 347-8947

Rabbi Pesach Raymon Yeshiva 400/PK-8
2 Harrison St 08817 732-572-5052
St. Helena S 300/PK-8
930 Grove Ave 08820 732-549-6234
Sr. Mary Charles Wienckoski, prin. Fax 549-6205
St. Matthew S 200/PK-8
100 Seymour Ave 08817 732-985-6633
Joan Sullivan, prin. Fax 985-7748
Wardlaw-Hartridge S 400/PK-12
1295 Inman Ave 08820 908-754-1882
Andrew Webster, head sch Fax 754-9678

Egg Harbor City, Atlantic, Pop. 4,134
Egg Harbor City SD 400/PK-8
730 Havana Ave 08215 609-965-1034
Adrienne Shulby, supt. Fax 965-6719
www.ehcs.k12.nj.us
Egg Harbor City Community S 200/4-8
730 Havana Ave 08215 609-965-1034
Jack Griffith, prin. Fax 965-4742
Spragg ES 200/PK-3
601 Buffalo Ave 08215 609-965-1034
Adrienne Shulby, prin. Fax 965-3651

Galloway Township SD
Supt. — See Galloway
Pomona Preschool 50/PK-PK
400 S Genoa Ave 08215 609-748-1250
Dr. Donald Gross, prin. Fax 965-4267

Pilgrim Academy 300/PK-12
PO Box 322 08215 609-965-2866

Egg Harbor Township, Atlantic
Egg Harbor Township SD 7,500/PK-12
13 Swift Ave 08234 609-646-7911
Dr. Kimberly Gruccio, supt. Fax 383-8749
www.eht.k12.nj.us
Alder Avenue MS 900/6-8
25 Alder Ave 08234 609-383-3366
Joseph Marinelli, prin. Fax 383-1492
Davenport ES 800/PK-3
2499 Spruce Ave 08234 609-645-3550
Maryann Giardina, prin. Fax 645-1116
Fernwood Avenue MS 900/6-8
4034 Fernwood Ave 08234 609-383-3355
James Battersby, prin. Fax 383-0628
Miller ES 1,100/4-5
2 Alder Ave 08234 609-407-2500
Latifah Potter, prin. Fax 383-3297
Slaybaugh ES 900/PK-3
11 Swift Ave 08234 609-927-8222
Kevin Fricke, prin. Fax 927-0038
Swift ES 500/PK-3
5 Swift Ave 08234 609-927-4141
Patricia Connor, prin. Fax 927-9099

Atlantic Christian S 400/PK-12
391 Zion Rd 08234 609-653-1199
Karen Oblen M.Ed., head sch Fax 653-1435
Trocki Hebrew Academy 50/PK-12
6814 Black Horse Pike 08234 609-383-8484

Elizabeth, Union, Pop. 122,789
Elizabeth SD 23,900/PK-12
500 N Broad St 07208 908-436-5000
Olga Hugelmeyer, supt. Fax 436-6133
www.epsnj.org
Battin S 700/K-8
300 S Broad St 07202 908-436-6300
Hollis Mendes, prin. Fax 436-6293
Butler S 700/PK-8
631-657 Westminster Ave 07208 908-436-5900
B. Harmon-Carolina, prin. Fax 436-5886
Columbus S 700/K-8
511 3rd Ave 07202 908-436-5730
Gina Dalton, prin. Fax 436-5718
Duarte - Marti S 900/PK-8
25 1st St 07206 908-436-3950
Evelyn Rodriguez-Salcedo, prin. Fax 436-3987
Dunn Academy K-8
125 3rd St 07206 908-436-5580
Yalitza Torres, prin. Fax 436-5586
Edreira Academy 500/PK-8
1014 S Elmora Ave 07208 908-436-5950
Howard Teitelbaum, prin. Fax 436-5954
Einstein Academy 800/PK-8
919 N Broad St 07208 908-436-6900
Maria Labrador, prin. Fax 436-6920
Elmora S 700/PK-8
638 Magie Ave 07208 908-436-5650
Dr. Mari Celi Sanchez, prin. Fax 436-5645
Franklin S 400/K-8
248 Ripley Pl 07206 908-436-5700
Dr. Alina Stewart, prin. Fax 436-5678
Halloran S 900/PK-PK, 2-
612 Pulaski St 07202 908-436-4860
Chihui Alfaro, prin. Fax 436-4880
Holmes S 900/PK-8
650 Bayway Ave 07202 908-436-6270
Yvonne McGovern, prin. Fax 436-6263
Hudson S 600/K-8
525 1st Ave 07206 908-436-5930
Christina Silveira, prin. Fax 436-5921
iPrep Academy School No 8 400/K-8
227 Court St 07206 908-275-6902
Lawrence Roodenburg, prin. Fax 275-6910
King ECC 300/PK-PK
130 Trumbull St 07206 908-436-6450
Gladys Castellanos, prin. Fax 436-6449

LaCorte-Peterstown S 600/K-8
700 2nd Ave 07202 908-436-6230
Jennifer Campel, prin. Fax 436-6220
Lincoln S 700/K-8
50 Grove St 07202 908-436-5828
Kathy Badalis, prin. Fax 436-5810
L'ouverture-Marquis de Lafayette S 800/PK-8
1071 Julia St 07201 908-436-5600
James Mondesir, prin. Fax 436-5595
Madison-Monroe S 800/PK-8
1091 North Ave 07201 908-436-5770
Antonio DiFonzo, prin. Fax 436-5756
Marshall S 400/K-8
521 Magnolia Ave 07206 908-436-5800
Nichol Comas, prin. Fax 436-5781
Morris S 500/K-8
860 Cross Ave 07208 908-436-6000
Oscar Crespo, prin. Fax 436-5987
Mravlag S, 132 Shelley Ave 07208 400/PK-8
Dr. Michael Wansaw, prin. 908-436-5850
Pantoja S 900/PK-8
505 Morris Ave 07208 908-436-3900
Sulisnet Jimenez, prin. Fax 436-3945
Reagan Academy 700/PK-8
730 Pennsylvania Ave 07208 908-436-6950
Arlene Campbell, prin. Fax 436-6959
Reilly S 1,000/PK-PK, 2-
436 1st Ave 07206 908-436-6030
Theodore Panagopoulos, prin. Fax 436-6012
Scott S 700/PK-8
125 Madison Ave 07201 908-436-6150
Samuel Etienne, prin. Fax 436-6141
Smith ECC 300/PK-PK
1000 S Elmora Ave 07202 908-436-6380
Kathy DiProfio, prin. Fax 436-6364
Stewart ECC 300/PK-PK
544 Pennsylvania Ave 07201 908-436-6410
Jocelyn Rodriguez, prin. Fax 436-6442
Washington Academy 1,300/PK-8
250 Broadway 07206 908-436-5555
Anthony Ziobro, prin. Fax 436-5538
Wilson S 700/PK-8
529 Edgar Rd 07202 908-436-6200
Carolina Cespedes, prin. Fax 436-6191

Our Lady of Guadalupe Academy 200/PK-8
227 Center St 07202 908-352-7419
Patricia Cymbaluk, prin. Fax 352-7062
St. Genevieve S 200/PK-8
209 Princeton Rd 07208 908-355-3355
Anika Logan, prin. Fax 355-1460
Yeshiva of Elizabeth 300/PK-6
330 Elmora Ave 07208 908-355-4850

Elmer, Salem, Pop. 1,381
Pittsgrove Township SD
Supt. — See Pittsgrove
Elmer ES 200/1-2
207 Front St 08318 856-358-6761
Daniel Bruce, prin. Fax 358-7550

Elmwood Park, Bergen, Pop. 19,032
Elmwood Park SD 2,400/PK-12
60 E 53rd St 07407 201-796-8700
Anthony Grieco, supt. Fax 625-6359
www.elmwoodparkschools.org
Gantner Avenue ES 300/K-5
99 Roosevelt Ave 07407 201-796-8700
Allison Jackter, prin. Fax 625-6427
Gilbert Avenue ES 400/PK-5
151 Gilbert Ave 07407 201-796-8700
David Saper, prin. Fax 625-6424
Memorial MS 500/6-8
375 River Dr 07407 201-796-8700
Corinne DiMartino, prin. Fax 625-6379
Sixteenth Avenue ES 400/PK-5
73 16th Ave 07407 201-796-8700
Dominick Silla, prin. Fax 625-6417

St. Leo S 300/PK-8
300 Market St 07407 201-796-5156
Traci Koval, prin. Fax 796-2092

Elwood, Atlantic, Pop. 1,395
Mullica Township SD 700/PK-8
PO Box 318 08217 609-561-3868
Andrew Weber, supt. Fax 561-7133
www.mullicaschools.com
Mullica Township ES 400/PK-4
PO Box 318 08217 609-561-3868
Matt Mazzoni, prin. Fax 561-7133
Mullica Township MS 300/5-8
PO Box 318 08217 609-561-3868
Matt Mazzoni, prin. Fax 561-7133

Emerson, Bergen, Pop. 7,299
Emerson SD 1,200/PK-12
131 Main St 07630 201-262-3875
Brian Gatens, supt. Fax 599-4160
www.emersonschools.org
Emerson Memorial ES 300/PK-2
1 Haines Ave 07630 201-599-7580
Jessica Espinoza, prin. Fax 262-1400
Villano ES 300/3-6
175 Linwood Ave 07630 201-262-4049
Jessica Espinoza, prin. Fax 599-7579

Assumption Academy 200/PK-8
35 Jefferson Ave 07630 201-262-0300
Susan Jurevich, prin. Fax 262-5910

Englewood, Bergen, Pop. 26,555
Englewood CSD 2,900/PK-12
274 Knickerbocker Rd 07631 201-862-6000
Robert Kravitz, supt. Fax 569-6099
www.epsd.org
Dismus MS 400/7-8
325 Tryon Ave 07631 201-862-6025
Lamarr Thomas, prin. Fax 833-9103

Grieco ES 500/1-3
50 Durie Ave 07631 201-862-6167
Daniela Small-Bailey, prin. Fax 871-9278
McCloud ES 500/4-6
325 Tenafly Rd 07631 201-862-6155
Carroll Milla-Sanchez, prin. Fax 871-8573
Quarles K 400/PK-K
155 Davison Pl 07631 201-862-6113
Arlene Ng, prin. Fax 871-4751

Dwight-Englewood S 900/PK-12
315 E Palisade Ave 07631 201-569-9500
Dr. Rodney DeJarnett, head sch Fax 569-1676
Moriah S 800/PK-8
53 S Woodland St 07631 201-567-0208
Morrow S 400/PK-8
435 Lydecker St 07631 201-568-5566
Aaron Cooper, head sch Fax 568-1209

Englewood Cliffs, Bergen, Pop. 5,175
Englewood Cliffs SD 500/PK-8
143 Charlotte Pl 07632 201-567-7292
Jennifer Brower, supt. Fax 567-2738
www.englewoodcliffs.org
North Cliff ES 200/PK-2
700 Floyd St 07632 201-567-6151
Siobhan Tauchert, prin. Fax 568-9874
Upper S 300/3-8
143 Charlotte Pl 07632 201-567-6151
Siobhan Tauchert, prin. Fax 541-8672

Englishtown, Monmouth, Pop. 1,825
Manalapan-Englishtown Regional SD 4,900/PK-8
54 Main St 07726 732-786-2500
John Marciante Ph.D., supt. Fax 786-2542
www.mers.k12.nj.us
Other Schools – See Manalapan

Erial, Camden, Pop. 2,500
Gloucester Township SD
Supt. — See Blackwood
Erial ES 600/PK-5
20 Essex Ave 08081 856-627-5415
Patrick McCarthy, prin. Fax 783-6003

Erial Community Church Christian S 200/PK-8
1725 New Brooklyn Rd 08081 856-346-0105

Essex Fells, Essex, Pop. 2,081
Essex Fells SD 200/PK-6
102 Hawthorne Rd 07021 973-226-0505
Michelle Gadaleta, supt. Fax 226-0451
www.efsk-6.org
Essex Fells ES 200/PK-6
102 Hawthorne Rd 07021 973-226-0505
Michelle Gadaleta, prin. Fax 226-0451

Estell Manor, Atlantic, Pop. 1,723
Estell Manor CSD 200/K-8
128 Cape May Ave 08319 609-476-2267
Robert Garguilo, supt. Fax 476-4205
www.estellmanorschool.com
Estell Manor S 200/K-8
128 Cape May Ave 08319 609-476-2267
Robert Garguilo, admin. Fax 476-4205

Ewing, Mercer, Pop. 36,000
Ewing Township SD 3,400/PK-12
2099 Pennington Rd 08618 609-538-9800
Michael Nitti, supt. Fax 538-0041
www.ewing.k12.nj.us
Antheil ES 600/K-5
339 Ewingville Rd 08638 609-538-9800
Jennifer Whitner, prin. Fax 883-4604
Fisher MS 800/6-8
1325 Lower Ferry Rd 08618 609-538-9800
Dr. Maggy Hanna, prin. Fax 637-9753
Lore ES 500/PK-5
13 Westwood Dr 08628 609-538-9800
Charles Welsh, prin. Fax 883-1027
Parkway ES 400/PK-5
446 Parkway Ave 08618 609-538-9800
Nicole Harris, prin. Fax 637-9721

Fairfield, Essex, Pop. 7,615
Fairfield Township SD 600/PK-6
15 Knoll Rd 07004 973-227-5586
Susan Ciccotelli, supt. Fax 227-2964
www.fpsk6.org/
Churchill ES 300/4-6
233 Fairfield Rd 07004 973-227-2638
Ray Santana, prin. Fax 227-8994
Stevenson ES 300/PK-3
15 Knoll Rd 07004 973-227-2120
Dr. Michael Trabucco, prin. Fax 227-3676

Fair Haven, Monmouth, Pop. 6,047
Fair Haven Borough SD 1,000/PK-8
224 Hance Rd 07704 732-747-2294
Sean McNeil, supt. Fax 747-7441
www.fairhaven.edu
Knollwood S 600/4-8
224 Hance Rd 07704 732-747-0320
Amy Romano, prin. Fax 747-7441
Sickles ES 400/PK-3
25 Willow St 07704 732-741-6151
Cheryl Cuddihy, prin. Fax 741-1397

Fair Lawn, Bergen, Pop. 32,055
Fair Lawn SD 4,400/PK-12
37-01 Fair Lawn Ave 07410 201-794-5500
Dr. Ernest Palestis, supt. Fax 797-9296
www.fairlawnschools.org
Forrest ES 300/K-5
10-00 Hopper Ave 07410 201-794-5565
Michael Weaver, prin. Fax 791-4427
Jefferson MS 600/6-8
35-01 Morlot Ave 07410 201-703-2240
Sherrie Galofaro, prin. Fax 475-9185
Lyncrest ES 200/K-5
9-04 Morlot Ave 07410 201-794-5555
Kelly Diee, prin. Fax 796-0536

Memorial MS 400/6-8
12-00 1st St 07410 201-794-5470
Scott Helfand, prin. Fax 703-2237
Milnes ES 400/K-5
8-01 Philip St 07410 201-794-5550
Joseph Fulco, prin. Fax 791-4608
Radburn ES 400/K-5
18-00 Radburn Rd 07410 201-794-5480
Jill Lindsay, prin. Fax 797-7398
Warren Point ES 400/K-5
30-07 Broadway 07410 201-794-5570
Nancy Schwindt, prin. Fax 475-0614
Westmoreland ES 300/PK-5
16-50 Parmelee Ave 07410 201-794-5490
Christine Dell'Aglio, prin. Fax 794-8621

St. Anne S 300/K-8
1-30 Summit Ave 07410 201-796-3353
Loretta Stachiotti, prin. Fax 796-9058

Fairton, Cumberland, Pop. 1,193

Fairton Christian Center Academy 100/K-12
199 Fairton-Millville Rd 08320 856-455-0408
Woodson Moore, head sch Fax 455-6783

Fairview, Bergen, Pop. 13,423
Fairview SD 1,200/PK-8
130 Hamilton Ave 07022 201-943-0564
Dr. David Sleppin, supt. Fax 840-7754
www.fairviewps.org
Fairview ES 3 300/2-3
Cliff & 6th Sts 07022 201-943-0563
Maria Kushi, prin. Fax 943-8753
Fairview ES 3 Annex 100/K-3
240 4th St 07022 201-313-0249
Lucille Juliano, prin. Fax 313-9958
Lincoln S 600/4-8
140 Anderson Ave 07022 201-943-0560
Lea Turro, prin. Fax 943-7154
Lincoln S Annex 200/PK-K
130 Hamilton Ave 07022 201-943-4809
Veronica Scerbo, prin. Fax 840-7754

Academy of Our Lady of Grace 300/PK-8
400 Kamena St 07022 201-945-8300
Filomena D'Amico, prin. Fax 945-4580

Far Hills, Somerset, Pop. 910

Far Hills Country Day S 400/PK-8
PO Box 8 07931 908-766-0622
Thomas Woelper, head sch Fax 766-6705

Farmingdale, Monmouth, Pop. 1,307
Farmingdale SD 100/PK-8
49 Academy St 07727 732-938-9611
Edith Conroy, supt. Fax 938-2317
www.farmingdaleschool.com
Farmingdale S 100/PK-8
49 Academy St 07727 732-938-9611
Edith Conroy, admin. Fax 938-2317

Howell Township SD 4,000/PK-8
200 Squankum Yellowbrook Rd 07727 732-751-2480
Joseph Isola, supt. Fax 919-1060
www.howell.k12.nj.us
Ardena ES 200/3-5
355 Adelphia Rd 07727 732-751-2485
Dr. Deborah Pennell, prin. Fax 938-5947
Griebling ES 300/K-2
130 Havens Bridge Rd 07727 732-751-2487
Nancy Rupp, prin. Fax 462-2985
Howell Township MS North 800/6-8
501 Squankum Yellowbrook Rd 07727 732-919-0095
Paul Farley, prin. Fax 919-1008
Other Schools – See Freehold, Howell

Flagtown, Somerset

Cherry Blossom Montessori S 100/PK-6
20 Equator Ave 08821 908-369-4436

Flanders, Morris, Pop. 1,200
Mt. Olive Township SD 4,400/K-12
227 US Highway 206 Ste 10 07836 973-691-4000
Larrie Reynolds Ph.D., supt. Fax 691-4022
www.mtoliveboe.org
Mountain View ES 400/K-5
118 Clover Hill Dr 07836 973-927-2201
Frank Fischel Ph.D., prin. Fax 927-2202
Tinc Road ES 400/K-5
24 Tinc Rd 07836 973-927-2203
Dr. Scott Lipson, prin. Fax 927-2200
Other Schools – See Budd Lake

Flemington, Hunterdon, Pop. 4,482
Flemington-Raritan Regional SD 3,300/PK-8
50 Court St 08822 908-284-7561
Maryrose Caulfield, supt. Fax 284-7514
www.frsd.k12.nj.us/
Barley Sheaf ES 400/K-4
80 Barley Sheaf Rd 08822 908-284-7584
Karen Gabruk, prin. Fax 284-7587
Case MS 800/7-8
301 Case Blvd 08822 908-284-5100
Robert Castellano, prin. Fax 284-5144
Desmares ES 500/K-4
16 Old Clinton Rd 08822 908-284-7540
Carol Howell, prin. Fax 284-7548
Hunter ES 400/K-4
8 Dayton Rd 08822 908-284-7620
Dr. Kathy Suchorsky, prin. Fax 284-7630
Reading-Fleming IS 800/5-6
50 Court St 08822 908-284-7504
Anthony DeMarco, prin. Fax 284-7518
Other Schools – See Ringoes

Florence, Burlington, Pop. 4,260
Florence Township SD 1,500/K-12
201 Cedar St 08518 609-499-4600
Donna Ambrosius, supt. Fax 499-9679
www.florence.k12.nj.us
Riverfront S 700/4-8
500 E Front St 08518 609-499-4647
Jaime Mungo, prin. Fax 499-8356
Other Schools – See Roebling

Florham Park, Morris, Pop. 11,496
Florham Park SD 1,000/PK-8
PO Box 39 07932 973-822-3880
Dr. Melissa Varley, supt. Fax 822-0716
www.fpks.org
Briarwood ES 300/PK-2
150 Briarwood Rd Ste A 07932 973-822-3884
Sherri Glaab, prin. Fax 822-0289
Brooklake ES 300/3-5
235 Brooklake Rd 07932 973-822-3888
Dr. Stephen Caponegro, prin. Fax 822-1158
Ridgedale MS 300/6-8
71 Ridgedale Ave 07932 973-822-3855
Peter Christ, prin. Fax 822-7963

Holy Family S 200/PK-K
17 Lloyd Ave 07932 973-377-4181
Mary Denis Smith, dir. Fax 377-0273

Folsom, Atlantic, Pop. 1,856
Folsom SD 400/PK-8
1357 Mays Landing Rd 08037 609-561-8666
Dr. Evelyn Browne, supt. Fax 567-8751
www.folsomschool.org
Folsom S 400/PK-8
1357 Mays Landing Rd 08037 609-561-8666
Dr. Evelyn Browne, prin. Fax 567-3021

Fords, Middlesex, Pop. 14,870
Woodbridge Township SD
Supt. — See Woodbridge
Ford Avenue ES 200/K-5
186 Ford Ave 08863 732-568-5414
Catherine Wehrle, prin. Fax 417-2156
Fords MS 700/6-8
100 Fanning St 08863 732-596-4200
Dr. James Parry, prin. Fax 417-2159
Lafayette Estates ES 600/K-5
500 Ford Ave 08863 732-596-4143
Stephanie West, prin. Fax 346-0708

Our Redeemer Lutheran S 100/PK-8
28 S 4th St 08863 732-738-7470
Carol Johnson, prin. Fax 738-6547

Forked River, Ocean, Pop. 5,199
Lacey Township SD
Supt. — See Lanoka Harbor
Forked River ES 500/PK-4
110 Lacey Rd 08731 609-971-2080
Eric Fiedler, prin. Fax 242-1081
Lacey Township MS 600/7-8
660 Denton Ave 08731 609-242-2100
Jason King, prin. Fax 242-2114

Fort Dix, Burlington, Pop. 7,518
Pemberton Township SD
Supt. — See Pemberton
Fort Dix ES 400/PK-5
1199 Fort Dix-Juliustown Rd 08640 609-893-8141
Tamara Garbutt, prin. Fax 723-5213

Fort Lee, Bergen, Pop. 34,777
Fort Lee SD 3,700/PK-12
2175 Lemoine Ave Fl 6 07024 201-585-4612
Kenneth Rota, supt. Fax 585-7997
www.flboe.com
Cole MS 600/7-8
467 Stillwell Ave 07024 201-585-4660
Robert Daniello, prin. Fax 585-1688
Fort Lee ES 1 700/K-6
250 Hoym St 07024 201-585-4620
Rosemary Giacomelli, prin. Fax 585-8082
Fort Lee ES 2 400/PK-6
2047 Jones Rd 07024 201-585-4630
Marianela Martin, prin. Fax 585-8972
Fort Lee ES 3 500/K-6
2405 2nd St 07024 201-585-4640
Jay Berman, prin. Fax 585-1488
Fort Lee ES 4 500/K-6
1193 Anderson Ave 07024 201-585-4650
Patrick Ambrosio, prin. Fax 585-1546

Christ the Teacher S 300/PK-8
359 Whiteman St 07024 201-944-0421
Frances Lacinak, prin. Fax 944-6293

Franklin, Sussex, Pop. 4,952
Franklin Borough SD 400/K-8
50 Washington Ave 07416 973-827-9775
J. R. Giacchi, supt. Fax 827-6522
www.fboe.org
Franklin S 400/K-8
50 Washington Ave 07416 973-827-9775
Dr. Patricia Pfeil, prin. Fax 827-6522

Hardyston Township SD
Supt. — See Hamburg
Hardyston ES 400/PK-4
50 State Rt 23 07416 973-823-7000
Jennifer Cimaglia, prin. Fax 827-6845

Franklin Lakes, Bergen, Pop. 10,458
Franklin Lakes SD 1,200/PK-8
490 Pulis Ave 07417 201-891-1856
Dr. Lydia Furnari, supt. Fax 891-9333
district.franklinlakes.k12.nj.us
Colonial Road ES 300/K-5
749 Colonial Rd 07417 201-337-0336
Christine Gagliardo, prin. Fax 337-1512
Franklin Avenue MS 500/6-8
755 Franklin Ave 07417 201-891-0202
Joseph Keiser, prin. Fax 848-5190
High Mountain Road ES 200/PK-5
765 High Mountain Rd 07417 201-891-4433
Jaclyn Bajzath, prin. Fax 891-1689
Woodside Avenue ES 300/K-5
305 Woodside Ave 07417 201-891-5600
Ann Jameson, prin. Fax 891-1483

Academy of the Most Blessed Sacrament 200/PK-8
785 Franklin Lakes Rd 07417 201-891-4250
Dr. Thomas Altonjy, prin. Fax 847-9227

Franklin Park, Somerset, Pop. 12,866
Franklin Township SD
Supt. — See Somerset
Franklin Park ES 800/PK-4
30 Eden St 08823 732-297-5666
Nicole Scott, prin. Fax 297-5834

Franklinville, Gloucester
Delsea Regional SD 1,700/7-12
242 Fries Mill Rd 08322 856-694-0100
Dr. Piera Gravenor, supt. Fax 694-4417
www.delsearegional.us/
Delsea Regional MS 600/7-8
PO Box 405 08322 856-694-0100
Jill Bryfogle, prin. Fax 694-4417

Franklin Township SD 1,300/PK-6
3228 Coles Mill Rd 08322 856-629-9500
Troy Walton, supt. Fax 629-1486
www.franklintwpschools.org
Janvier ES 600/PK-2
1532 Pennsylvania Ave 08322 856-629-0431
Henry Kobik, prin. Fax 629-1486
Reutter ES 400/3-6
2150 Delsea Dr 08322 856-694-0223
Theodore Peters, prin. Fax 629-1486
Other Schools – See Newfield

Freehold, Monmouth, Pop. 11,870
Freehold Borough SD 1,400/PK-8
280 Park Ave 07728 732-761-2100
Rocco Tomazic Ed.D., supt. Fax 462-8954
www.freeholdboro.k12.nj.us
Freehold IS 400/6-8
280 Park Ave 07728 732-761-2156
Ronnie Dougherty, prin. Fax 761-2181
Freehold Learning Center 500/PK-4
30 Dutch Lane Rd 07728 732-761-2239
William Smith, prin. Fax 577-7029
Park Avenue ES 500/K-5
280 Park Ave 07728 732-761-2124
Patrick Mulhern, prin. Fax 761-2161

Freehold Township SD 4,000/PK-8
384 W Main St 07728 732-866-8400
Ross Kasun Ed.D., supt. Fax 761-1809
www.freeholdtwp.k12.nj.us/
Applegate ES 500/K-5
47 Jean Brennan Dr 07728 732-431-5460
Bradley Millaway, prin. Fax 294-4853
Barkalow MS 700/6-8
498 Stillwells Corner Rd 07728 732-431-4403
John Soviero, prin. Fax 294-5560
Catena ES 500/K-5
275 Burlington Rd 07728 732-431-4430
Dr. Jeffery Huguenin, prin. Fax 294-5684
Donovan ES 500/K-5
237 Stonehurst Blvd 07728 732-431-3321
Jennifer Benbrook, prin. Fax 308-9238
Early Childhood Learning Center 100/PK-PK
510 Stillwells Corner Rd 07728 732-866-6858
Rebecca Montgomery, prin. Fax 308-9204
Eisenhower MS 700/6-8
279 Burlington Rd 07728 732-431-3910
Dr. Dianne Brethauer, prin. Fax 294-7180
Errickson ES 500/K-5
271 Elton Adelphia Rd 07728 732-431-8022
Cathleen Areman, prin. Fax 308-4541
West Freehold ES 500/K-5
100 Castranova Way 07728 732-431-5101
Dr. Edward Aldarelli, prin. Fax 308-9627

Howell Township SD
Supt. — See Farmingdale
Adelphia ES 200/K-2
495 Adelphia Rd 07728 732-919-1553
Danielle Palazzolo, prin. Fax 780-7714
Memorial ES 600/3-5
485 Adelphia Rd 07728 732-919-1085
Alysson Keelen, prin. Fax 751-0325

St. Rose of Lima S 400/PK-8
51 Lincoln Pl 07728 732-462-2646
Sr. Patricia Doyle, prin. Fax 462-0331

Frenchtown, Hunterdon, Pop. 1,362
Frenchtown Borough SD 100/PK-8
902 Harrison St 08825 908-996-2751
Daria Wasserbach, supt. Fax 996-3599
www.frenchtownschool.org/
Frenchtown S 100/PK-8
902 Harrison St 08825 908-996-2751
Christina Lauck, prin. Fax 996-3599

Kingwood Township SD 400/PK-8
880 County Road 519 08825 908-996-2941
Dr. Rick Falkenstein, supt. Fax 996-7268
www.kingwoodschool.org
Kingwood Township S 400/PK-8
880 County Road 519 08825 908-996-2941
Rick Falkenstein, admin. Fax 996-7268

Galloway, Atlantic
Galloway Township SD 3,100/PK-8
101 S Reeds Rd 08205 609-748-1250
Annette Giaquinto Ed.D., supt. Fax 748-1796
www.gtps.k12.nj.us

Galloway Township MS 800/7-8
100 S Reeds Rd 08205 609-748-1250
Paula Junker, prin. Fax 748-8926
Rann ES 600/K-6
515 8th Ave 08205 609-748-1250
Kevin McGloin, prin. Fax 652-1740
Reeds Road ES 600/K-6
103 S Reeds Rd 08205 609-748-1250
Dr. William Zipparo, prin. Fax 748-6564
Rogers ES 500/K-6
105 S Reeds Rd 08205 609-748-1250
Dr. Robin Moore, prin. Fax 748-6563
Smithville ES 600/PK-6
37 Old Port Republic Rd 08205 609-748-1250
David Ragazzi, prin. Fax 748-6566
Other Schools – See Egg Harbor City

Assumption Regional S 400/PK-8
146 S Pitney Rd 08205 609-652-7134
Mary Schurtz, prin. Fax 652-2544

Garfield, Bergen, Pop. 30,041
Garfield SD 4,400/PK-12
34 Outwater Ln 07026 973-340-5000
Nicholas Perrapato, supt. Fax 340-4620
www.garfield.k12.nj.us/
Columbus ES 400/PK-5
147 Cedar St 07026 973-340-5038
Ann Taylor, prin. Fax 340-6851
Garfield ECC 300/PK-PK
241 Ray St 07026 973-253-6600
Frank D'Amico, prin. Fax 478-0976
Garfield ECC Annex #3 PK-PK
541 Midland Ave 07026 973-772-0016
Valerie Stewart, prin. Fax 772-1915
Garfield ECC Annex 100/PK-PK
464 Outwater Ln 07026 973-272-7470
Bea Mendez, prin. Fax 272-7475
Garfield MS 900/6-8
175 Lanza Ave 07026 973-272-7020
Anna Sciacca, prin. Fax 340-1767
Irving ES 200/PK-5
12 Madonna Pl 07026 973-340-5034
Jeffrey Wilson, prin. Fax 340-4028
Lincoln ES 400/PK-5
111 Palisade Ave 07026 973-340-5036
Christopher Annibal, prin. Fax 365-1194
Madison ES 300/PK-5
62 Alpine St 07026 973-340-5039
Sally Bulger, prin. Fax 340-1963
Roosevelt ES 300/PK-5
225 Lincoln Pl 07026 973-340-5037
Jennifer Alfonso, prin. Fax 340-6645
Wilson ES 300/PK-5
205 Outwater Ln 07026 973-340-5035
Charles Bonanno, prin. Fax 340-2463

Garwood, Union, Pop. 4,160
Garwood SD 400/PK-8
400 2nd Ave 07027 908-789-0331
Dr. Teresa Quigley, supt. Fax 789-2970
www.garwoodschools.org
Lincoln S 400/PK-8
400 2nd Ave 07027 908-789-0331
Mary Emmons, prin. Fax 789-2970

Gibbsboro, Camden, Pop. 2,245
Gibbsboro SD 300/PK-8
37 Kirkwood Rd 08026 856-783-1140
Jack Marcellus, supt. Fax 783-9155
www.gibbsboroschool.org
Gibbsboro S 300/PK-8
37 Kirkwood Rd 08026 856-783-1140
Jack Marcellus, prin. Fax 783-9155

Gibbstown, Gloucester, Pop. 3,693
Greenwich Township SD 400/PK-8
415 Swedesboro Rd 08027 856-224-4920
Dr. Jennifer Foley-Hindman, supt. Fax 224-5761
www.greenwich.k12.nj.us
Greenwich Township ES 200/PK-5
255 W Broad St 08027 856-224-4900
Alisa Whitcraft, prin. Fax 423-7945
Nehaunsey MS 100/6-8
415 Swedesboro Rd 08027 856-224-4920
Dr. Jennifer Foley-Hindman, prin. Fax 224-5765

Guardian Angels Regional S 300/PK-8
150 S School St 08027 856-423-9440
Sr. Jerilyn Einstein, prin. Fax 423-9445

Gillette, Morris
Long Hill Township SD 800/PK-8
759 Valley Rd 07933 908-647-1200
Dr. Edwin Acevedo, supt. Fax 647-1200
www.longhill.org
Gillette ES 200/PK-1
759 Valley Rd 07933 908-647-2313
Dr. Lori Jones, prin. Fax 647-4969
Other Schools – See Millington, Stirling

Gladstone, Somerset, Pop. 2,086

Gill St. Bernard's S 700/PK-12
PO Box 604 07934 908-234-1611
Sid Rowell, hdmstr. Fax 234-1712
Willow S 100/PK-8
1150 Pottersville Rd 07934 908-470-9500
Jerry Loewen, head sch Fax 470-9545

Glassboro, Gloucester, Pop. 18,158
Elk Township SD 400/PK-6
900 Clems Run 08028 856-881-4551
Dr. Piera Gravenor, supt. Fax 881-3674
www.auraelementary.us/pages/aura
Aura ES 400/PK-6
900 Clems Run 08028 856-881-4551
Wayne Murschell, prin. Fax 881-3674

Glassboro SD 2,100/PK-12
560 Bowe Blvd 08028 856-652-2700
Dr. Mark Silverstein, supt. Fax 881-0884
www.gpsd.us
Bowe ES 400/4-6
7 Ruth H Mancuso Ln 08028 856-652-2700
Ryan Caltabiano, prin. Fax 589-0869
Bullock ES 500/1-3
370 New St E 08028 856-652-2700
Richard Taibi, prin. Fax 881-7587
Glassboro IS 300/7-8
202 Delsea Dr N 08028 856-652-2700
Kriston Matthews, prin. Fax 881-3751
Rodgers S 300/PK-K
301 Georgetown Rd 08028 856-652-2700
Aaron Edwards, prin. Fax 881-1670

Ambassador Christian Academy 100/PK-8
535 Mullica Hill Rd 08028 856-881-3009
Sharon Civile, prin. Fax 881-3827

Glendora, Camden, Pop. 4,693
Gloucester Township SD
Supt. — See Blackwood
Glendora ES 300/K-5
201 Station Ave 08029 856-939-4704
Patricia Ferrier, prin. Fax 939-6552

Glen Ridge, Essex, Pop. 7,336
Glen Ridge SD 1,900/PK-12
12 High St 07028 973-429-8302
Dirk Phillips, supt. Fax 429-5750
www.glenridge.org
Forest Avenue S 200/PK-2
287 Forest Ave 07028 973-429-8308
Matthew Murphy, prin. Fax 429-2908
Linden Avenue S 300/PK-2
205 Linden Ave 07028 973-429-8301
Joseph Caravela, prin. Fax 429-3243
Ridgewood Avenue S 600/3-6
235 Ridgewood Ave 07028 973-429-8306
Michael Donovan, prin. Fax 743-7181

Glen Rock, Bergen, Pop. 11,424
Glen Rock SD 2,400/PK-12
620 Harristown Rd 07452 201-445-7700
Bruce Watson, supt. Fax 389-5019
www.glenrocknj.org
Byrd ES 200/K-5
640 Doremus Ave 07452 201-445-7700
Linda Weber, prin. Fax 389-5025
Central ES 300/K-5
600 S Maple Ave 07452 201-445-7700
Krista La Croix, prin. Fax 389-5030
Coleman ES 300/PK-5
100 Pinelynn Rd 07452 201-445-7700
Edward Thompson, prin. Fax 389-5039
Glen Rock MS 600/6-8
400 Hamilton Ave 07452 201-445-7700
Dr. Jennifer Wirt, prin. Fax 389-5042
Hamilton ES 300/K-5
380 Harristown Rd 07452 201-445-7700
Irene Pierides, prin. Fax 670-6529

Academy of Our Lady S 400/PK-8
180 Rodney St 07452 201-445-0622
James Newman, prin. Fax 445-8345

Gloucester City, Camden, Pop. 11,306
Gloucester City SD 1,900/PK-12
520 Cumberland St 08030 856-456-7000
Dr. Dennis Vespe, supt. Fax 742-8815
www.gcsd.k12.nj.us
Cold Springs ES 800/PK-3
1194 Market St 08030 856-456-7000
Karen Kessler, prin. Fax 456-2160
Gloucester City MS 4-8
500 Market St 08030 856-456-7000
William O'Kane, prin. Fax 456-1254

Great Meadows, Warren, Pop. 303
Great Meadows Regional SD 700/PK-8
PO Box 74 07838 908-637-6576
David C. Mango, supt. Fax 637-6356
www.gmrsd.com
Great Meadows Regional MS 300/6-8
273 US Highway 46 07838 908-637-4584
Israel Marmolejos, prin. Fax 637-4492
Independence Central ES 200/PK-2
281 US Highway 46 07838 908-637-4351
Michael Mai, prin. Fax 637-8935
Liberty Township ES 300/3-5
334 Mountain Lake Rd 07838 908-637-4115
Jennifer Macones, prin. Fax 637-6008

Green Brook, Somerset
Green Brook Township SD 900/PK-8
132 Jefferson Ave 08812 732-968-1171
Kevin Carroll, supt. Fax 968-1869
www.gbtps.org
Feldkirchner ES 500/PK-4
105 Andrew St 08812 732-968-1052
Susan Wardell, prin. Fax 968-0791
Green Brook MS 400/5-8
132 Jefferson Ave 08812 732-968-1051
Dr. James Bigsby, prin. Fax 752-1086

Greendell, Sussex
Green Township SD 500/PK-8
PO Box 14 07839 973-300-3800
John Nittolo, supt. Fax 383-5705
www.greenhills.org
Green Hills S 500/PK-8
PO Box 14 07839 973-300-3800
Jennifer Thompson, prin. Fax 383-5705

Greenwich, Cumberland, Pop. 2,090
Greenwich Township SD 100/K-8
839 Ye Greate St 08323 856-451-5513
John Klug, supt. Fax 451-4476
www.morrisgoodwinschool.org/

Goodwin S 100/K-8
839 Ye Greate St 08323 856-451-5513
John Klug, admin. Fax 451-4476

Guttenberg, Hudson, Pop. 11,013
Guttenberg SD 1,000/PK-8
301 69th St 07093 201-861-3100
Michelle Rosenberg, supt. Fax 861-1348
www.edlinesites.net/pages/Anna_L_Klein
Klein S 1,000/PK-8
301 69th St 07093 201-861-3100
Keith Petry, admin. Fax 861-1348

Hackensack, Bergen, Pop. 42,163
Hackensack SD 5,300/PK-12
191 2nd St 07601 201-646-8000
Rosemary Marks, supt. Fax 646-7827
www.hackensackschools.org
Fairmount ES 600/PK-4
105 Grand Ave 07601 201-646-7890
Joseph Cicchelli, prin. Fax 342-7249
Hackensack MS 1,400/5-8
360 Union St 07601 201-646-7842
Celso King, prin. Fax 646-7840
Hillers ES 500/PK-4
56 Longview Ave 07601 201-646-7870
Joy Dorsey-Whiting, prin. Fax 646-0114
Jackson Avenue ES 400/PK-4
421 Jackson Ave 07601 201-646-7991
Christopher Moran, prin. Fax 931-0135
Parker ES 600/PK-4
261 Maple Hill Dr 07601 201-646-8020
Lillian Whitaker, prin. Fax 457-9573

Bergen County Christian Academy 200/PK-12
15 Conklin Pl 07601 201-487-7212

Hackettstown, Warren, Pop. 9,581
Hackettstown SD 1,800/PK-12
PO Box 465 07840 908-852-2800
David C. Mango, supt. Fax 852-0286
www.hackettstown.org
Hackettstown MS 400/5-8
500 Washington St 07840 908-852-8554
William Thompson, prin. Fax 850-6544
Hatchery Hill ES 200/PK-4
398 5th Ave 07840 908-852-8550
Marie Griffin, prin. Fax 850-1286
Willow Grove ES 300/PK-4
601 Willow Grove St 07840 908-852-2805
Patrick McQueeney, prin. Fax 852-7431

Haddonfield, Camden, Pop. 11,436
Barrington Borough SD
Supt. — See Barrington
Avon ES 400/PK-4
862 Mercer Dr 08033 856-547-6632
Anthony Arcodia, prin. Fax 522-1125

Haddon Township SD
Supt. — See Westmont
Stoy ES 200/PK-5
206 Briarwood Ave 08033 856-869-7725
Charles Warfield, prin. Fax 869-7728
Van Sciver ES 300/PK-5
625 Rhoads Ave 08033 856-869-7730
Don Pullano, prin.

Haddonfield Borough SD 2,500/PK-12
1 Lincoln Ave 08033 856-429-7510
Dr. Richard Perry, supt. Fax 429-6015
www.haddonfield.k12.nj.us
Central ES 400/K-5
3 Lincoln Ave 08033 856-429-5851
Shannon Simkus, prin. Fax 429-2006
Haddon ES 300/K-5
501 W Redman Ave 08033 856-429-0811
Gerry Bissinger, prin. Fax 429-8906
Haddonfield MS 600/6-8
5 Lincoln Ave 08033 856-429-5851
Dennis Moroldo, prin. Fax 429-2006
Tatem ES 400/K-5
1 Glover Ave 08033 856-429-0902
Karen-Joy Schultz, prin. Fax 427-2844

Christ the King Regional S 300/K-8
164 Hopkins Ave 08033 856-429-2084
Anne Hartman, prin. Fax 429-4959
Haddonfield Friends S 200/PK-8
47 N Haddon Ave 08033 856-429-6786
Matthew Sharp, head sch Fax 429-6376

Haddon Heights, Camden, Pop. 7,379
Haddon Heights SD 1,200/PK-12
316A 7th Ave 08035 856-547-1412
Michael Adams, supt. Fax 547-3868
hhsd.k12.nj.us
Atlantic Avenue ES 100/PK-6
21 E Atlantic Ave 08035 856-547-0630
Christopher Ormsby, prin. Fax 546-4657
Glenview Avenue ES 200/K-6
1700 Sycamore St 08035 856-547-7647
Samuel Sassano, prin. Fax 546-9566
Seventh Avenue ES 100/K-6
316 7th Ave 08035 856-547-0610
Christopher Ormsby, prin. Fax 546-2891

Baptist Regional S 200/K-12
300 Station Ave 08035 856-547-2996
Lynn Conahan, admin. Fax 547-6584
St. Rose of Lima S 400/PK-8
300 Kings Hwy 08035 856-546-6166
Willliam Stonis, prin. Fax 546-6601

Hainesport, Burlington
Hainesport Township SD 600/PK-8
211 Broad St 08036 609-267-1316
Joseph Corn, supt. Fax 702-0142
www.hainesport.k12.nj.us

Hainesport Township S 600/PK-8
211 Broad St 08036 609-267-1316
Joseph Corn, prin. Fax 702-0142

Haledon, Passaic, Pop. 8,172
Haledon SD 1,000/PK-8
70 Church St 07508 973-389-2841
Dr. Miguel Hernandez, supt. Fax 956-0781
www.haledon.org
Haledon S 1,000/PK-8
91 Henry St 07508 973-790-9000
Chris Wacha, prin. Fax 790-3506

Hamburg, Sussex, Pop. 3,209
Hamburg Borough SD 300/K-8
30 Linwood Ave 07419 973-827-7570
Roger Jinks, supt. Fax 827-3624
www.hamburgschool.com/
Hamburg S 300/K-8
30 Linwood Ave 07419 973-827-7570
Roger Jinks, admin. Fax 827-3624

Hardyston Township SD 700/PK-8
183 Wheatsworth Rd 07419 973-823-7000
Michael Ryder, supt. Fax 823-7010
www.htps.org
Hardyston MS 300/5-8
183 Wheatsworth Rd 07419 973-823-7000
Michael Ryder, admin. Fax 823-7011
Other Schools – See Franklin

Hamilton, Mercer
Hamilton Township SD 11,500/PK-12
90 Park Ave 08690 609-631-4100
Scott Rocco Ed.D., supt. Fax 631-4103
www.hamilton.k12.nj.us
Crockett MS 800/6-8
2631 Kuser Rd 08691 609-631-4149
Roxann Clarke-Holmes, prin. Fax 631-4116
Greenwood ES 300/PK-5
2069 Greenwood Ave 08609 609-631-4151
Nicole Dickens-Simons, prin. Fax 631-4118
Grice MS 900/6-8
901 Whitehorse Hamilton Sq 08610 609-631-4152
David Innocenzi, prin. Fax 631-4119
Kisthardt ES 200/PK-5
215 Harcourt Dr 08610 609-631-4153
Earl Tankard, prin. Fax 631-4120
Klockner ES 200/PK-5
830 Klockner Rd 08619 609-631-4154
Dr. LaShawn Gibson, prin. Fax 631-4121
Kuser ES 400/K-5
70 Newkirk Ave 08629 609-631-4155
Roberto Kesting, prin. Fax 631-4123
Lalor ES 300/K-5
25 Barnt Deklyn Rd 08610 609-631-4156
Joanna Giuliano, prin. Fax 631-4124
Langtree ES 300/PK-5
2080 Whatley Rd 08690 609-631-4157
Joyce Gallo, prin. Fax 631-4125
McGalliard ES 300/K-5
1600 Arena Dr 08610 609-631-4158
Barbara Morales, prin. Fax 631-4126
Mercerville ES 400/K-5
60 Regina Ave 08619 609-631-4159
John Byrne, prin. Fax 631-4127
Morgan ES 300/PK-5
38 Stamford Rd 08619 609-631-4160
Regina McIntyre, prin. Fax 631-4128
Reynolds MS 1,000/6-8
2145 Yrdvll Hamilton Squ Rd 08690 609-631-4162
P. Landolfi-Collins, prin. Fax 631-4130
Robinson ES 300/K-5
495 Gropp Ave 08610 609-631-4163
Kelli Eppley, prin. Fax 631-4131
Sayen ES 300/K-5
3333 Nottingham Way 08690 609-631-4164
Nancy Whalen, prin. Fax 631-4132
Sunnybrae ES 300/K-5
166 Elton Ave 08620 609-631-4166
Josephine Arcaro, prin. Fax 631-4135
University Heights/Morrison ES 300/K-5
645 Paxson Ave 08619 609-631-4167
Suzanne Diszler, prin. Fax 631-4136
Wilson ES 400/PK-5
600 E Park Ave 08610 609-631-4169
Barbara Panfili, prin. Fax 631-4139
Yardville ES 200/K-5
450 Yardville Allentown Rd 08620 609-631-4170
Elena Manning, prin. Fax 631-4140
Yardville Heights ES 200/K-5
3880 S Broad St 08620 609-631-4171
James Sterenczak, prin. Fax 631-4141
Other Schools – See Hamilton Square

Our Lady of Sorrows S 200/PK-8
3800 E State Street Ext 08619 609-587-4140
Maureen Tuohy, prin. Fax 584-8853
Trenton Catholic Academy - Lower 300/PK-8
177 Leonard Ave 08610 609-586-5888
Anne Reap, prin. Fax 631-9295

Hamilton Square, Mercer, Pop. 12,662
Hamilton Township SD
Supt. — See Hamilton
Alexander ES 300/K-5
20 Robert Frost Dr 08690 609-631-4148
Joseph Bookholdt, prin. Fax 631-4112

Faith Christian S 400/PK-8
2111 Kuser Rd 08690 609-585-3353
Lance Walker, admin. Fax 581-2038
St. Gregory the Great Academy 500/PK-8
4680 Nottingham Way 08690 609-587-1131
Dr. Jason Briggs, prin. Fax 587-0322

Hammonton, Atlantic, Pop. 14,622
Hammonton SD 3,300/PK-12
566 Old Forks Rd 08037 609-567-7000
Robin Chieco, supt. Fax 561-3567
www.hammontonps.org/
Hammonton ECC 400/PK-1
601 N 4th St 08037 609-567-6693
Darla Salay, prin. Fax 567-6399
Hammonton MS 800/6-8
75 N Liberty St 08037 609-567-7007
Dr. Michael Nolan, prin. Fax 561-3974
Sooy ES 800/2-5
601 N 4th St 08037 609-567-7070
Dr. Kristina Erman, prin. Fax 704-1201

St. Joseph Regional S 300/PK-8
133 N 3rd St 08037 609-704-2400
Sr. Betty Jean Takacs, prin. Fax 561-4940

Hampton, Hunterdon, Pop. 1,385
Hampton Borough SD 100/PK-8
32-41 South St 08827 908-537-4101
Michael Jones, admin. Fax 537-6871
hampton.nhvweb.net
Hampton S 100/PK-8
32-41 South St 08827 908-537-4101
Michael Jones, admin. Fax 537-6871

Union Township SD 500/PK-8
165 Perryville Rd 08827 908-735-5511
Nicholas Diaz, supt. Fax 735-6657
www.uniontwpschool.org
Union Township ES 200/PK-4
149 Perryville Rd 08827 908-735-5511
Nicholas Diaz, prin. Fax 730-7591
Union Township MS 200/5-8
165 Perryville Rd 08827 908-735-5511
Frances Suchovic, prin. Fax 735-6657

Harrington Park, Bergen, Pop. 4,599
Harrington Park SD 600/PK-8
191 Harriot Ave 07640 201-768-5700
Dr. Adam Fried Ed.D., supt. Fax 768-1487
www.hpsd.org
Harrington Park S 600/PK-8
191 Harriot Ave 07640 201-768-5700
Jessica Nitzberg, prin. Fax 768-1487

Harrison, Hudson, Pop. 13,212
Harrison SD 2,000/K-12
501 Hamilton St 07029 973-483-4627
Dr. Cynthia Baumgartner Ed.D., supt. Fax 484-7484
www.harrisonschools.org
Hamilton IS 300/4-5
223 Hamilton St 07029 973-483-6400
Kevin Stahl, prin. Fax 482-2054
Lincoln ES 600/K-3
221 Cross St 07029 973-483-6400
Amy Heberling, prin. Fax 483-2455
Washington MS 400/6-8
1 N 5th St 07029 973-483-2285
Michael Landy, prin. Fax 482-3625

Harrisonville, Gloucester
South Harrison Township SD 300/K-6
PO Box 112 08039 856-769-0855
Corinne Mesmer, prin. Fax 769-5426
www.southharrison.k12.nj.us
South Harrison ES 300/K-6
PO Box 112 08039 856-769-0855
Corinne Mesmer, prin. Fax 769-5426

Hasbrouck Heights, Bergen, Pop. 11,674
Hasbrouck Heights SD 1,800/PK-12
379 Boulevard 07604 201-288-6150
Dr. Matthew Helfant, supt. Fax 288-0289
www.hhschools.org
Euclid ES, 1 Burton Ave 07604 400/PK-5
Michael Sickels, prin. 201-393-8176
Hasbrouck Heights MS 400/6-8
365 Boulevard 07604 201-393-8170
Joseph Mastropietro, prin. Fax 288-2083
Lincoln ES 400/K-5
302 Burton Ave 07604 201-393-8182
Joseph Colangelo, prin. Fax 393-8183

Corpus Christi S 500/PK-8
215 Kipp Ave 07604 201-288-0614
Elizabeth Pinto, prin. Fax 288-5956

Haskell, See Wanaque
Wanaque SD 900/PK-8
973A Ringwood Ave 07420 973-835-8200
Donna Cardiello, supt. Fax 835-1316
www.wanaqueps.org
Haskell S, 973 Ringwood Ave 07420 400/PK-8
Celia Pino-Morales, prin. 973-835-8200
Other Schools – See Wanaque

Haworth, Bergen, Pop. 3,317
Haworth SD 400/K-8
205 Valley Rd 07641 201-384-5526
Herbert Ammerman, supt. Fax 384-8619
www.haworth.org
Haworth S 400/K-8
205 Valley Rd 07641 201-384-5526
John Smatla, prin. Fax 384-8619

Hawthorne, Passaic, Pop. 18,585
Hawthorne SD 2,200/PK-12
445 Lafayette Ave 07506 973-427-1300
Richard Spirito, supt. Fax 427-1757
www.hawthorne.k12.nj.us
Jefferson ES 200/PK-5
233 Goffle Hill Rd 07506 973-423-6480
Stephen Droske, prin. Fax 423-6429
Lincoln MS 500/6-8
230 Hawthorne Ave 07506 973-423-6460
Erin Devor, prin. Fax 427-5393
Roosevelt ES 500/K-5
50 Roosevelt Ave 07506 973-423-6485
Joseph Pisacane, prin. Fax 427-9335
Washington ES 300/K-5
176 Mohawk Ave 07506 973-423-6495
Susan Spinelli, prin. Fax 636-2094

Hawthorne Christian Academy 400/PK-12
2000 State Rt 208 07506 973-423-3331
David Seidman, head sch Fax 238-1718
St. Anthony S 200/PK-8
270 Diamond Bridge Ave 07506 973-423-1818
Sr. Colleen Clair, prin. Fax 423-6065

Hazlet, Monmouth, Pop. 21,976
Hazlet Township SD 3,100/PK-12
421 Middle Rd 07730 732-264-8402
Renae LapRete, supt. Fax 264-1599
www.hazlet.org
Beers Street ES 300/5-6
610 Beers St 07730 732-264-1107
Joseph Krouse, prin. Fax 264-1081
Cove Road ES 200/5-6
8 Cove Rd 07730 732-264-5050
Wayne Ramsey, prin. Fax 264-5826
Hazlet MS 500/7-8
1639 Union Ave 07730 732-264-0940
Christine McCoid, prin. Fax 264-0571
Lillian Drive ES 300/1-4
28 Lillian Dr 07730 732-787-2332
Kathleen Matsutani, prin. Fax 495-9332
Middle Road ES 300/1-4
305 Middle Rd 07730 732-264-9012
Loretta Zimmer, prin. Fax 203-2146
Raritan Valley ES 300/1-4
37 Cresci Blvd 07730 732-264-1333
John Verderosa, prin. Fax 264-6600
Sycamore Drive Early Childhood Lrng Ctr 300/PK-K
37 Sycamore Dr 07730 732-264-2180
Susan Galbraith, prin. Fax 264-0182

Hewitt, Passaic
West Milford Township SD
Supt. — See West Milford
Upper Greenwood Lake ES 300/K-6
41 Henry Rd 07421 973-853-4466
Gregory Matlosz, prin. Fax 853-1233

Hibernia, Morris, Pop. 200
Rockaway Township SD 2,300/K-8
PO Box 500 07842 973-627-8200
Dr. Greg McGann, supt. Fax 627-7968
www.rocktwp.org
Other Schools – See Dover, Rockaway, Wharton

High Bridge, Hunterdon, Pop. 3,609
High Bridge SD 300/PK-8
50 Thomas St 08829 908-638-4103
Dr. Gregory Hobaugh, supt. Fax 638-4211
www.hbschools.org
High Bridge ES 200/PK-4
40 Fairview Ave 08829 908-638-4105
Dr. Gregory Hobaugh, admin. Fax 638-5260
High Bridge MS 100/5-8
50 Thomas St 08829 908-638-4101
Rich Kolton, prin. Fax 638-4211

Highland Park, Middlesex, Pop. 13,661
Highland Park SD 1,600/PK-12
435 Mansfield St 08904 732-572-2400
Fax 393-1174
www.hpschools.net
Bartle ES 400/2-5
435 Mansfield St 08904 732-572-4100
Anthony Benjamin, prin. Fax 572-6446
Highland Park MS 300/6-8
330 Wayne St 08904 732-572-2400
Jennifer Minaya-Osemwegi, prin. Fax 819-7041
Irving PS 300/PK-1
121 S 11th Ave 08904 732-572-1205
Kelly Freeborn, prin. Fax 572-3709

Highlands, Monmouth, Pop. 4,929
Highlands Borough SD 200/PK-6
360 State Route 36 07732 732-872-1476
Dr. Susan Compton, supt. Fax 872-0973
www.highlandselementary.org
Highlands ES 200/PK-6
360 State Route 36 07732 732-872-1476
Rosemary Schutz, prin. Fax 872-0973

Hightstown, Mercer, Pop. 5,390
East Windsor Regional SD 5,000/PK-12
25A Leshin Ln 08520 609-443-7717
Dr. Richard Katz, supt. Fax 443-7704
www.eastwindsorregionalschools.com
Black ES 500/K-5
371 Stockton St 08520 609-443-7816
Samantha Felicetta, prin. Fax 443-7809
Rogers ES 700/PK-5
380 Stockton St 08520 609-443-7833
Heather Gladkowski, prin. Fax 443-7835
Other Schools – See East Windsor

SciCore Academy PK-12
156 Maxwell Ave 08520 609-448-8950

Hillsborough, Somerset
Hillsborough Township SD 6,900/PK-12
379 S Branch Rd 08844 908-431-6600
Dr. Jorden Schiff, supt. Fax 369-8286
www.htps.us
Amsterdam ES 500/K-4
301 Amsterdam Dr 08844 908-431-6600
Dr. Mary Ann Mullady, prin. Fax 874-6101
Auten Road IS 1,100/5-6
281 Auten Rd 08844 908-431-6600
Christopher Carey, prin. Fax 371-1614
Hillsborough ES 500/K-4
435 US Highway 206 08844 908-431-6600
Susan Eckstein, prin. Fax 874-3693
Hillsborough MS 1,100/7-8
260 Triangle Rd 08844 908-431-6600
Dr. Joseph Trybulski, prin. Fax 874-3492
Sunnymead ES 400/PK-4
55 Sunnymeade Rd 08844 908-431-6600
Dr. Tammy Jenkins, prin. Fax 575-1459

Triangle ES 400/K-4
156 S Triangle Rd 08844 908-431-6600
Lisa Heisel, prin. Fax 874-8563
Woodfern ES 400/K-4
425 Woodfern Rd 08844 908-431-6600
Steven Kerrigan, prin. Fax 369-0781
Woods Road ES 400/PK-4
401 South Woods Rd 08844 908-431-6600
Jodi Howe, prin. Fax 874-6298

Hillsdale, Bergen, Pop. 10,123
Hillsdale SD 1,300/PK-8
32 Ruckman Rd 07642 201-664-4512
Dr. Jeffrey Feifer Ed.D., supt. Fax 664-9049
www.hillsdaleschools.com
Meadowbrook ES 300/PK-4
50 Piermont Ave 07642 201-664-8088
Christopher Bell, prin. Fax 664-6132
Smith ES 300/K-4
1000 Hillsdale Ave 07642 201-664-1188
Angela Iskenderian, prin. Fax 664-6354
White MS 600/5-8
120 Magnolia Ave 07642 201-664-0286
Donald Bergamini, prin. Fax 664-2715

St. John Academy 400/PK-8
460 Hillsdale Ave 07642 201-664-6364
Suzanne Socha, prin. Fax 664-8096

Hillside, Union, Pop. 21,044
Hillside Township SD 2,800/PK-12
195 Virginia St 07205 908-352-7664
Dr. Antoine Gayles, supt. Fax 282-5831
www.hillsidek12.org
Coolidge ES 200/2-2
614 Tillman St 07205 908-352-7664
Rahim Graham, prin. Fax 282-5835
Hurden-Looker ES 400/3-4
1261 Liberty Ave 07205 908-352-7664
Tracey Wolff, prin. Fax 282-5845
Krumbiegel MS 700/7-8
145 Hillside Ave 07205 908-352-7664
Joyce Caine, prin. Fax 282-5840
Morris ECC 600/PK-1
143 Coe Ave 07205 908-352-7664
April Lowe, prin. Fax 282-5850
Washington ES 200/5-6
1530 Leslie St 07205 908-352-7664
Dr. Sharon Festante, prin. Fax 282-5855

Trinity Temple Academy 100/PK-8
1500 Maple Ave 07205 973-923-7568

Hoboken, Hudson, Pop. 49,047
Hoboken SD, 158 4th St 07030 1,700/PK-12
Dr. Christine Johnson, supt. 201-356-3600
www.hoboken.k12.nj.us
Brandt PS 300/PK-2
215 9th St 07030 201-356-3695
Sandra Rodriguez, prin. Fax 356-3697
Calabro ES, 524 Park Ave 07030 100/K-6
Joseph Vespignani, prin. 201-356-3670
Connors ES 200/K-6
201 Monroe St 07030 201-356-3680
Dr. Tamika Pollins, prin. Fax 356-3686
Hoboken MS 7-8
158 4th St 07030 201-356-3700
Dr. Sharon Davis, prin. Fax 356-3704
Wallace ES 600/PK-6
1100 Willow Ave 07030 201-356-3650
Martin Shannon, prin. Fax 356-3655

All Saints Episcopal Day S 200/PK-8
707 Washington St 07030 201-792-0736
Jill Singleton, head sch Fax 792-1595
Hoboken Catholic Academy 400/PK-8
555 7th St 07030 201-963-9535
Matthew McGrath, prin. Fax 963-1256
Mustard Seed S 200/PK-8
422 Willow Ave 07030 201-653-5548
Thomas Postema, hdmstr. Fax 653-4751
Stevens Cooperative S - Hoboken 400/PK-8
301 Garden St Ste 4 07030 201-792-3688
Sergio Alati Ed.D., head sch Fax 792-0826

Ho Ho Kus, Bergen, Pop. 4,015
Ho-Ho-Kus SD 700/PK-8
70 Lloyd Rd 07423 201-652-4555
Dr. Diane Mardy, supt. Fax 652-2824
www.hohokus.org
Ho Ho Kus S 700/PK-8
70 Lloyd Rd 07423 201-652-4555
Dr. Alexis Eckert, prin. Fax 652-2824

Holmdel, Monmouth
Holmdel Township SD 3,000/K-12
65 McCampbell Rd 07733 732-946-1800
Dr. Robert McGarry, supt. Fax 946-1875
www.holmdelschools.org
Indian Hill ES 700/4-6
735 Holmdel Rd 07733 732-946-1045
Lisa Marino, prin. Fax 946-7610
Satz MS 500/7-8
24 Crawfords Corner Rd 07733 732-946-1808
Arthur Howard, prin. Fax 834-0089
Village ES 800/K-3
67 McCampbell Rd 07733 732-946-1820
Brian Schillaci, prin. Fax 946-1831

St. Benedict S 500/K-8
165 Bethany Rd 07733 732-264-5578
Candace Wallace, prin. Fax 264-8679

Hopatcong, Sussex, Pop. 14,950
Hopatcong Borough SD 1,600/K-12
PO Box 1029 07843 973-398-8800
Cynthia Randina, supt. Fax 398-1961
www.hopatcongschools.org/
Durban Avenue ES 200/4-5
PO Box 1029 07843 973-398-8805
Tracey Hensz, prin. Fax 398-0971
Hopatcong MS 400/6-8
PO Box 1029 07843 973-398-8804
Emil Binotto, prin. Fax 398-4184
Maxim ES 200/K-1
PO Box 1029 07843 973-398-8807
Katherine McFadden, prin. Fax 398-7408
Tulsa Trail ES 200/2-3
PO Box 1029 07843 973-398-8806
Brian Byrne, prin. Fax 398-0970

Hope, Warren, Pop. 195
Hope Township SD 200/PK-8
PO Box 293 07844 908-459-4242
Michael Slattery, supt. Fax 459-5553
www.hope-elem.org
Hope Township S 200/PK-8
PO Box 293 07844 908-459-4242
Pat Orsini, prin. Fax 459-5553

Hopewell, Mercer, Pop. 1,901
Hopewell Valley Regional SD
Supt. — See Pennington
Hopewell ES 400/PK-5
35 Princeton Ave 08525 609-737-4007
David Friedrich, prin. Fax 466-8095

Howell, Monmouth
Howell Township SD
Supt. — See Farmingdale
Aldrich ES 300/3-5
615 Aldrich Rd 07731 732-751-2483
Drew Smith, prin. Fax 363-9164
Greenville ES 100/K-2
210 Ramtown Greenville Rd 07731 732-202-1745
Lynn Coco, prin. Fax 458-5456
Howell Township MS South 700/6-8
1 Kuzminski Way 07731 732-836-1327
Dr. Robert Henig, prin. Fax 836-0698
Land O Pines ES 200/PK-2
1 Thompson Way 07731 732-751-2489
Dheranie Suarez, prin. Fax 905-8505
Newbury ES 100/3-5
179 Newbury Rd 07731 732-751-2491
Dr. James Quinn, prin. Fax 364-0866
Ramtown ES 200/3-5
216 Ramtown Greenville Rd 07731 732-751-2493
Albert Bohrer, prin. Fax 458-6773
Taunton ES 200/K-2
41 Taunton Dr 07731 732-751-2497
Diana Rochon, prin. Fax 364-4678

St. Veronica S 300/PK-8
4219 US Highway 9 07731 732-364-4130
Sr. Cherree Ann Power, prin. Fax 363-4932

Irvington, Essex, Pop. 60,600
Irvington Township SD 6,100/PK-12
1 University Pl 07111 973-399-6800
Dr. Neely Hackett, supt. Fax 372-3724
www.irvington.k12.nj.us
Augusta Preschool Academy 300/PK-PK
97 Augusta St 07111 973-399-6868
Rose Gordon, prin. Fax 399-0527
Berkeley Terrace ES 400/PK-5
787 Grove St 07111 973-399-6852
Stacey Love, prin. Fax 372-5244
Chancellor Avenue ES 500/K-5
844 Chancellor Ave 07111 973-399-6858
Dr. Winston Jackson, prin. Fax 375-2488
Florence Avenue ES 600/K-5
1324 Springfield Ave 07111 973-399-6800
April Magee, prin. Fax 399-6965
Grove Street ES 400/PK-5
602 Grove St 07111 973-399-6867
Dr. Denisee Cooper, prin. Fax 399-2442
Madison Avenue ES 500/PK-5
36 Mount Vernon Ave 07111 973-399-6871
Alexis Osterhoudt, prin. Fax 399-7768
Marshall ES 400/PK-5
141 Montgomery Ave 07111 973-399-6800
Wanda Warren, prin. Fax 416-3807
Mt. Vernon Avenue S PK-5
54 Mount Vernon Ave 07111 973-399-6875
Nicole Gilmore, prin. Fax 371-6875
Union Avenue MS 600/6-8
427 Union Ave 07111 973-399-6885
Muller Pierre, prin. Fax 371-0957
University ES 600/K-5
1 University Pl 07111 973-399-6826
Sandra Boone-Gibbs, prin. Fax 373-0734
University MS 700/6-8
255 Myrtle Ave 07111 973-399-6879
Andrea Tucker, prin. Fax 351-1025

Good Shepherd Academy 200/PK-8
285 Nesbit Ter 07111 973-375-0659
Thomas Scalea, prin. Fax 373-4882

Iselin, Middlesex, Pop. 18,174
Woodbridge Township SD
Supt. — See Woodbridge
Indiana Avenue ES 500/K-5
256 Indiana Ave 08830 732-602-8518
Sharon McGreevey, prin. Fax 283-2637
Iselin MS 700/6-8
900 Woodruff St 08830 732-602-8450
Kelly Cilento, prin. Fax 750-4861
Kennedy Park ES 400/K-5
150 Goodrich St 08830 732-602-8424
Jill Osborne, prin. Fax 283-2864
Mascenik ES 300/K-5
300 Benjamin Ave 08830 732-602-8526
Judith Martino, prin. Fax 283-2665

Island Heights, Ocean, Pop. 1,642
Island Heights SD 100/K-6
PO Box 329 08732 732-929-1222
Tim Rehm, supt. Fax 929-9563
www.islandheights.k12.nj.us
Island Heights ES 100/K-6
PO Box 329 08732 732-929-1222
Timothy Rehm, prin. Fax 929-9563

Jackson, Ocean, Pop. 800
Jackson Township SD 8,800/PK-12
151 Don Connor Blvd 08527 732-833-4600
Dr. Stephen Genco, supt. Fax 833-4609
www.jacksonsd.org
Crawford-Rodriguez ES 800/PK-5
1025 Larsen Rd 08527 732-833-4690
Adriann Jean-Denis, prin. Fax 833-4759
Elms ES 600/PK-5
780 Patterson Rd 08527 732-833-4680
Michael Burgos, prin. Fax 833-4139
Goetz MS 1,200/6-8
835 Patterson Rd 08527 732-833-4610
Carl Perino, prin. Fax 833-4749
Holman ES 600/K-5
125 Manhattan St 08527 732-833-4620
Richard Karas, prin. Fax 833-4789
Johnson ES 500/K-5
1021 Larsen Rd 08527 732-833-4640
Dr. Michael Raymond, prin. Fax 833-4769
McAuliffe MS 900/6-8
35 S Hope Chapel Rd 08527 732-833-4701
Debra Phillips, prin. Fax 833-4729
Rosenauer ES 300/PK-5
60 Citadel Dr 08527 732-833-4630
Ronald Polakowski, prin. Fax 833-4779
Switlik ES 800/K-5
75 W Veterans Hwy 08527 732-833-4650
Kathleen McKiernan, prin. Fax 833-4672

St. Aloysius S 400/PK-8
935 Bennetts Mills Rd 08527 732-370-1515
Elizabeth O'Connor, prin. Fax 370-3555

Jamesburg, Middlesex, Pop. 5,804
Jamesburg SD 700/PK-8
13 Augusta St 08831 732-521-0303
Brian Betze, supt. Fax 521-1267
www.jamesburg.org
Breckwedel MS 200/6-8
13 Augusta St 08831 732-521-0303
Chad Donahue, prin. Fax 521-1267
Kennedy ES 500/PK-5
28 Front St 08831 732-521-0400
Pamela Hernandez, prin. Fax 605-0571

Jersey City, Hudson, Pop. 239,244
Jersey City SD 26,300/PK-12
346 Claremont Ave 07305 201-915-6202
Dr. Marcia Lyles, supt. Fax 915-6084
www.jcboe.org/
Angelou S 600/PK-5
160 Danforth Ave 07305 201-915-6470
Maritza Dortrait, prin. Fax 332-7898
Barnes S 300/PK-8
91 Astor Pl 07304 201-915-6420
Annie Graham, prin. Fax 333-7316
Bradford ES 300/PK-5
96 Sussex St 07302 201-915-6450
Terry Watkins-Williams, prin. Fax 915-0724
Brensinger S 1,200/PK-8
600 Bergen Ave 07304 201-915-6120
Robert Brower, prin. Fax 434-2824
Conti S 600/PK-8
182 Merseles St 07302 201-714-4300
John Rivero, prin. Fax 659-5717
Conwell ES 600/PK-5
111 Bright St 07302 201-915-6100
Darren Micchol, prin. Fax 413-5118
Conwell MS 800/6-8
107 Bright St 07302 201-946-5740
Joanna Veloz, prin. Fax 209-1293
Copernicus ES 800/PK-5
3385 John F Kennedy Blvd 07307 201-714-4340
Diane Pistilli, prin. Fax 222-0949
Cordero S 700/PK-8
158 Erie St 07302 201-714-4390
Marvin Strynar, prin. Fax 222-9055
Culbreth ES 500/PK-8
153 Union St 07304 201-915-6430
Sharon Abbruscato, prin. Fax 333-7255
DeFuccio S 400/PK-8
214 Plainfield Ave 07306 201-915-6560
Dawn Reynolds, prin. Fax 915-6563
Gandhi S 1,400/PK-8
143 Romaine Ave 07306 201-915-6490
Peter Mattaliano, prin. Fax 435-8514
King S 800/PK-8
886 Bergen Ave 07306 201-915-6521
Dr. Cleopatra Wingard, prin. Fax 418-8582
Martin Center for the Arts 400/PK-8
59 Wilkinson Ave 07305 201-915-6590
Glenda Jennings, prin. Fax 915-6596
McAuliffe S 1,000/PK-8
167 Hancock Ave 07307 201-714-4360
Dr. Janet Elder, prin. Fax 656-0225
Murray S 900/PK-8
339 Stegman Pkwy 07305 201-915-6620
Sandra Jones, prin. Fax 333-6044
Nolan MS 200/6-8
88 Gates Ave 07305 201-915-6570
Francine Luce, prin. Fax 369-3749
Noonan S PK-5
164 Laidlaw Ave 07306 201-963-7160
Ann Beirne, prin. Fax 222-8620
Nunnery ES 400/PK-5
123 Claremont Ave 07305 201-915-6520
Cara Szeles, prin. Fax 433-2920
Public S 34 600/PK-8
1830 John F Kennedy Blvd 07305 201-915-6550
Shante Jones, prin. Fax 915-6553

Rafalides ES 400/PK-4
362 Union St 07304 201-915-6540
Frank Piccillo, prin. Fax 433-4232
Sullivan ES 800/PK-5
171 Seaview Ave 07305 201-915-6530
Fax 332-7147
Trefurt ES 800/PK-5
96 Franklin St 07307 201-714-4320
Marissa Migliozzi, prin. Fax 653-7274
Wakeman ES 800/PK-5
100 Saint Pauls Ave 07306 201-714-4310
Nicholas Capodice, prin. Fax 659-5992
Watters S 900/PK-8
220 Virginia Ave 07304 201-915-6510
Rosalyn Barnes, prin. Fax 433-3150
Webb ES 600/PK-5
264 Van Horne St 07304 201-915-6480
Oscar Velez, prin. Fax 521-0909
Williams MS 900/6-8
222 Laidlaw Ave 07306 201-714-8342
Edwin Rivera, prin. Fax 659-6457
Young ES 800/PK-8
135 Stegman St 07305 201-369-3724
Michelle West, prin. Fax 433-6939
Zampella S 1,000/K-8
201 North St 07307 201-714-4350
Dr. Joseph Galano, prin. Fax 420-9082

Genesis Educational Center 100/PK-K
317 3rd St 07302 201-798-0642
Ruby Armooh, dir. Fax 798-1408
Hamilton Park Montessori S 300/PK-8
1 McWilliams Pl 07302 201-533-1910
Alexa Huxel, head sch Fax 533-1920
Hudson Montessori S 100/PK-6
10 Regent St 07302 201-516-0700
Our Lady of Czestochowa S 400/PK-8
248 Marin Blvd 07302 201-434-2405
Anna Mae Stefanelli, prin. Fax 434-6068
Sacred Heart S 200/K-8
183 Bayview Ave 07305 201-332-7111
Sr. Frances Salemi, prin. Fax 332-7160
St. Aloysius Elementary Academy 300/PK-8
721 W Side Ave 07306 201-433-4270
Helen O'Connell, prin. Fax 433-6916
St. Joseph S 200/PK-8
509 Pavonia Ave 07306 201-653-0128
John Richards, prin. Fax 222-5324
St. Nicholas S 200/PK-8
118 Ferry St 07307 201-659-5948
Bernadette Miglin, prin. Fax 798-6868
Stevens Cooperative S - Newport PK-8
100 River Dr S 07302 201-626-4020
Sergio Alati Ed.D., head sch Fax 626-4021
Waterfront Montessori 200/PK-8
150 Warren St Ste 108 07302 201-333-5600

Jobstown, Burlington
Springfield Township SD 200/PK-6
2146 Jacksonville Jobstown 08041 609-723-2479
Craig Vaughn, supt. Fax 723-6112
www.springfieldschool.org/
Springfield Township ES 200/PK-6
2146 Jacksonville Jobstown 08041 609-723-2479
Craig Vaughn, prin. Fax 723-6112

Keansburg, Monmouth, Pop. 9,873
Keansburg Borough SD 1,100/PK-12
100 Palmer Pl 07734 732-787-2007
John Niesz, supt. Fax 495-6714
www.keansburg.k12.nj.us
Bolger MS 400/5-8
100 Palmer Pl 07734 732-787-2007
Joseph LaRocca, prin. Fax 495-7906
Caruso ES 200/K-4
81 Frances Pl 07734 732-787-2007
Kathleen Flanzbaum, prin. Fax 787-5791
Port Monmouth Road Preschool 200/PK-PK
142 Port Monmouth Rd 07734 732-787-2007
Anne Hazeldine, head sch Fax 787-7536

Kearny, Hudson, Pop. 39,579
Kearny SD 5,000/PK-12
172 Midland Ave 07032 201-955-5000
Patricia Blood, supt. Fax 955-0544
www.kearnyschools.com
Franklin ES 900/PK-6
100 Davis Ave 07032 201-955-5020
Yvonne Cali, prin. Fax 955-0139
Garfield ES 600/PK-6
360 Belgrove Dr 07032 201-955-5090
Curtis Brack, prin. Fax 246-1340
Lincoln MS 400/7-8
121 Beech St 07032 201-955-5095
Robert Zika, prin. Fax 997-2590
Roosevelt ES 400/PK-6
733 Kearny Ave 07032 201-955-5100
Steven Way, prin. Fax 991-7523
Schuyler ES 400/PK-6
644 Forest St 07032 201-955-5105
Valerie Iacono, prin. Fax 997-4875
Washington ES 500/PK-6
80 Belgrove Dr 07032 201-955-5110
Jon Zimmerman, prin. Fax 246-1129

Kearny Christian Academy 100/PK-12
22 Wilson Ave 07032 201-998-0788
Helena DiSarro, admin. Fax 998-1102

Kendall Park, Middlesex, Pop. 9,153
South Brunswick Township SD
Supt. — See North Brunswick
Brunswick Acres ES 500/K-5
41 Kory Dr 08824 732-297-6621
Stacey Ta, prin. Fax 940-2014
Cambridge ES 600/K-5
35 Cambridge Rd 08824 732-297-2941
Christi Pemberton, prin. Fax 940-2030
Constable ES 500/K-5
29 Constable Rd 08824 732-297-2488
Peter Rattien, prin. Fax 297-7807
Greenbrook ES 400/K-5
23 Roberts St 08824 732-297-2480
Jodi Mahoney, prin. Fax 940-2028

St. Augustine of Canterbury S 500/PK-8
45 Henderson Rd 08824 732-297-6042
Sr. Mary Louise Shulas, prin. Fax 297-7062

Kenilworth, Union, Pop. 7,800
Kenilworth SD 1,400/PK-12
426 Boulevard 07033 908-276-5936
Dr. Thomas Tramaglini, supt. Fax 709-7315
www.kenilworthschools.com
Harding ES 700/PK-6
426 Boulevard 07033 908-276-5936
Kathleen Murphy, prin. Fax 276-1993

St. Theresa S 300/PK-8
540 Washington Ave 07033 908-276-7220
Joseph Caporaso, prin. Fax 709-1103

Keyport, Monmouth, Pop. 7,124
Keyport SD 1,100/PK-12
370 Broad St 07735 732-212-6100
Dr. Lisa Savoia, supt. Fax 212-6125
www.kpsdschools.org
Central ES 700/PK-8
335 Broad St 07735 732-212-6100
Erik Mammano, prin. Fax 212-6135

Kingston, Somerset, Pop. 1,467

YingHua International S 100/PK-8
25 Laurel Ave 08528 609-375-8015
Joy Zhao, head sch

Kinnelon, Morris, Pop. 10,145
Kinnelon Borough SD 2,000/PK-12
109 Kiel Ave 07405 973-838-1418
Diane DiGiuseppe, supt. Fax 838-5527
kinnelonpublicschools.org/
Kiel ES 300/PK-2
115 Kiel Ave 07405 973-838-0611
Ivonne Ciresi, prin. Fax 838-6338
Miller MS 500/6-8
117 Kiel Ave 07405 973-838-5250
Mark Mongon, prin. Fax 283-0390
Stonybrook ES 500/K-K, 3-5
118 Boonton Ave 07405 973-838-1881
Jodi Mulholland, prin. Fax 838-7575

Lafayette, Sussex
Lafayette Township SD 200/PK-8
178 Beaver Run Rd 07848 973-875-3344
Jennifer Cenatiempo, supt. Fax 875-3066
www.ltes.org
Lafayette Township S 200/PK-8
178 Beaver Run Rd 07848 973-875-3344
Jennifer Cenatiempo, supt. Fax 875-3066

Lake Hiawatha, Morris
Parsippany-Troy Hills Township SD
Supt. — See Parsippany
Knollwood ES 300/K-5
445 Knoll Rd 07034 973-263-7060
Merisa Rosa, prin. Fax 331-7153
Lake Hiawatha ES 400/PK-5
1 Lincoln Ave 07034 973-263-4344
Angelina Finnegan, prin. Fax 263-4346

Lake Hopatcong, Morris, Pop. 3,000
Jefferson Township SD 3,100/PK-12
31 State Route 181 07849 973-663-5780
Dr. Joseph Kraemer, supt. Fax 663-2790
www.jefftwp.org/
Briggs ES 300/K-2
1 Jefferson Dr 07849 973-663-0900
Dr. Michael Valenti, prin. Fax 663-7853
Other Schools – See Oak Ridge, Wharton

Lakehurst, Ocean, Pop. 2,552
Lakehurst SD 400/PK-8
301 Union Ave 08733 732-657-5741
Loren Fuhring, supt. Fax 408-0681
www.lakehurstschool.org/
Lakehurst S 400/PK-8
301 Union Ave 08733 732-657-5741
Loren Fuhring, admin. Fax 408-0681

Lakewood, Ocean, Pop. 53,516
Lakewood Township SD 5,400/PK-12
1771 Madison Ave Ste B 08701 732-364-2400
Laura Winters, supt. Fax 905-3687
www.lakewoodpiners.org
Clarke ES 500/1-5
455 Manetta Ave 08701 732-905-3620
Ebony Rivera, prin. Fax 905-3623
Clifton Avenue ES 800/1-5
625 Clifton Ave 08701 732-905-3650
Debra Long, prin. Fax 905-3653
Lakewood ECC 200/PK-PK
100 Linden Ave 08701 732-886-3775
Heni Mozes, admin.
Lakewood MS 1,000/6-8
755 Somerset Ave 08701 732-905-3600
Richard Goldstein, prin. Fax 905-3695
Oak Street ES 800/1-5
75 Oak St 08701 732-905-3670
Joseph Schroepfer, prin. Fax 901-2703
Piner ES PK-1
1143 E County Line Rd 08701 732-363-4771
James Sterenczak, prin.
Spruce Street ES 1,000/PK-1
90 Spruce St 08701 732-905-3660
Aleida Salguerdo, prin. Fax 905-3663

Ateres Tzipora PK-8
150 Oberlin Ave N 08701 732-886-8860
Bais Faiga S Gratter Building 700/PK-1
100 Park Ave S 08701 732-370-6420
Bais Reuven Kamenitz 300/PK-8
41 Henry St 08701 732-363-0579
Bais Rivka Rochel 900/PK-8
285 River Ave 08701 732-367-4855
Bais Rochel 500/K-8
115 Carey St 08701 732-905-1251
Bais Tova 500/PK-8
555 Oak St 08701 732-901-3913
Bnos Bina 200/K-8
1 E 13th St 08701 732-730-1259
Bnos Bracha 500/K-8
1665 Corporate Rd W 08701 732-905-3030
Bnos Melech of Lakewood 400/K-8
550 James St 08701 732-364-5911
Bnos Penina / Jewish Education for Girls K-8
501 Prospect St Ste 117A 08701 732-987-6868
Bnos Rivka 200/PK-8
961 E County Line Rd 08701 732-370-0100
Bnos Yaakov S 600/PK-8
2 Kent Rd 08701 732-363-1400
Bnot Yisroel K-5
17 High St 08701 732-730-0819
Calvary Academy 300/PK-12
1133 E County Line Rd 08701 732-363-3633
Dr. Stephanie Cruz M.Ed., prin. Fax 363-7337
Lakewood Cheder S PK-4
PO Box 838 08701 732-370-6480
Lakewood Cheder S 5-6
520 James St 08701 732-370-6460
Lakewood Cheder S Bais Faga 1,300/3-8
350 Courtney Rd 08701 732-370-6450
Talmud Torah Bais Avrohom 500/PK-8
915 New Hampshire Ave 08701 732-363-0040
Talmud Torah Ohr Elchonon 200/PK-8
805 Cross St 08701 732-730-2820
Tashbar S of Lakewood 400/PK-8
655 Princeton Ave 08701 732-905-1111
Tiferes Bais Yaakov S 600/PK-8
613 Oak St 08701 732-364-0466
Shulamith Rozsansky, prin. Fax 364-3655
Tiferes Chaya 100/K-8
431 Joe Parker Rd 08701 732-367-9255
I. Iskowitz, prin. Fax 994-7718
United Talmudical Academy/Satmar Chedar 200/K-9
800 Princeton Ave 08701 732-370-8757
Yeshiva Ketanah of Lakewood 700/K-8
120 2nd St 08701 732-363-0303
Yeshiva Masoras Avos 300/PK-8
23 Congress St S 08701 732-942-7522
Rabbi Pesach M. Grossman, dean Fax 960-2384
Yeshiva Orchos Chaim 800/PK-8
PO Box 963 08701 732-370-0799
Yeshiva Tiferes Torah 400/PK-8
PO Box 420 08701 732-370-9889

Lambertville, Hunterdon, Pop. 3,873
South Hunterdon Regional SD 900/PK-12
301 Mt Airy Harbourton Rd 08530 609-397-2060
Dr. Louis Muenker, supt. Fax 397-2366
shrsd.org
Lambertville ES 200/PK-6
200 N Main St 08530 609-397-0183
Wanda Quinones, prin. Fax 397-4607
West Amwell Township ES 200/K-6
1417 Route 179 08530 609-397-0819
David Miller, prin. Fax 397-4350
Other Schools – See Stockton

Landing, Morris, Pop. 3,000
Roxbury Township SD
Supt. — See Succasunna
Nixon ES 300/PK-4
275 Mount Arlington Blvd 07850 973-398-2564
Danielle Lynch, prin. Fax 398-3341

Lanoka Harbor, Ocean
Lacey Township SD 4,100/PK-12
200 Western Blvd 08734 609-971-2000
Craig Wigley, supt. Fax 242-9406
www.laceyschools.org
Cedar Creek ES 500/PK-4
220 Western Blvd 08734 609-971-5850
Jacqueline Ranuska, prin. Fax 971-2846
Lanoka Harbor ES 500/PK-4
281 Manchester Ave 08734 609-971-2090
Jeffrey Brewer, prin. Fax 971-0968
Mill Pond ES PK-6
210 Western Blvd 08734 609-971-2070
Edward Subokow, prin. Fax 971-2057
Other Schools – See Forked River

Laurel Springs, Camden, Pop. 1,884
Laurel Springs SD 200/K-6
623 Grand Ave 08021 856-783-1086
Thomas Attanasi, supt. Fax 784-0474
www.laurelspringschool.org
Laurel Springs ES 200/K-6
623 Grand Ave 08021 856-783-1086
Kathleen Westerby, prin.

Laurence Harbor, Middlesex, Pop. 6,425
Old Bridge Township SD
Supt. — See Matawan
Memorial ES 400/K-5
11 Ely Ave 08879 732-290-3876
Raymond Payton, prin. Fax 583-9431

Lavallette, Ocean, Pop. 1,868
Lavallette Borough SD 100/K-8
105 Brooklyn Ave 08735 732-793-7722
Dr. Peter Morris, supt. Fax 830-1604
www.lavallettek12.org/
Lavallette S 100/K-8
105 Brooklyn Ave 08735 732-793-7722
Dr. Peter Morris, prin. Fax 830-1604

Lawnside, Camden, Pop. 2,850
Lawnside Borough SD 300/PK-8
426 E Charleston Ave 08045 856-546-4850
Dr. Ronn Johnson, supt. Fax 310-0901
www.lawnside.k12.nj.us
Lawnside S 300/PK-8
426 E Charleston Ave 08045 856-546-4850
Dr. Ronn Johnson, admin. Fax 310-0901

Lawrenceville, Mercer, Pop. 3,814
Lawrence Township SD 3,900/PK-12
2565 Princeton Pike 08648 609-671-5500
Crystal Edwards Ed.D., supt. Fax 883-4225
www.ltps.org
Eldridge Park ES 300/K-3
55 Lawn Park Ave 08648 609-671-5560
Kathy Robbins, prin. Fax 671-3431
Franklin ES 400/PK-3
2939 Princeton Pike 08648 609-671-5540
William Meurer, prin. Fax 671-3441
Lawrence IS 900/4-6
66 Eggerts Crossing Rd 08648 609-671-5530
Cynthia Westhead, prin. Fax 637-3431
Lawrence MS 600/7-8
2455 Princeton Pike 08648 609-671-5520
Mindy Milavsky, prin. Fax 671-3421
Lawrenceville ES 300/PK-3
40 Craven Ln 08648 609-671-5570
Melissa Lockett, prin. Fax 671-3471
Slackwood ES 300/PK-3
2060 Princeton Ave 08648 609-671-5580
Jay Billy, prin. Fax 671-3481

Princeton Junior S 100/PK-5
90 Fackler Rd 08648 609-924-8126
Silvana Clark M.A., head sch Fax 924-7456
St. Ann S 300/PK-8
34 Rossa Ave 08648 609-882-8077
John McKenna, prin. Fax 882-0327

Layton, Sussex
Sandyston-Walpack Consolidated SD 100/K-6
PO Box 128 07851 973-948-4450
Dr. Jeanne Apryasz, supt. Fax 948-4492
www.sandystonwalpack.org
Sandyston-Walpack Consolidated S 100/K-6
PO Box 128 07851 973-948-4450
Dr. Jeanne Apryasz, supt. Fax 948-4492

Lebanon, Hunterdon, Pop. 1,334
Clinton Township SD 1,500/PK-8
128 Cokesbury Rd 08833 908-236-7235
Pamela Fiander, supt. Fax 236-7645
www.ctsdnj.org
McGaheran S 300/2-3
63 Allerton Rd 08833 908-735-5151
Mary Postma, prin. Fax 730-7744
Round Valley S 500/4-6
128 Cokesbury Rd 08833 908-236-6341
Sue High, prin. Fax 236-2847
Other Schools – See Clinton

Lebanon Borough SD 100/PK-6
6 Maple St 08833 908-236-2448
Bruce Arcurio, supt. Fax 236-7645
www.lebanonschool.org
Lebanon Borough ES 100/PK-6
6 Maple St 08833 908-236-2448
Bruce Arcurio, admin. Fax 236-7670

Acorn Montessori S 50/PK-6
1222 State Route 31 08833 908-730-8986

Leonardo, Monmouth, Pop. 2,725
Middletown Township SD 9,500/PK-12
834 Leonardville Rd Fl 2 07737 732-671-3850
Dr. William George, supt. Fax 615-9351
mtps.schoolwires.net
Bayshore MS 600/6-8
834 Leonardville Rd 07737 732-291-1380
Michael Scarano, prin.
Leonardo ES, 14 Hosford Ave 07737 200/K-5
Peter Smith, prin. 732-291-1330
Other Schools – See Atlantic Highlands, Belford, Lincroft, Middletown, New Monmouth, Port Monmouth, Red Bank

Leonia, Bergen, Pop. 8,727
Leonia SD 1,700/PK-12
570 Grand Ave 07605 201-302-5200
Joanne Megargee, supt. Fax 947-4782
www.leoniaschools.org
Leonia MS 500/6-8
500 Broad Ave 07605 201-302-5200
David Saco, prin. Fax 461-1510
Scott ES 600/PK-5
100 Highland St 07605 201-302-5200
Maria Martinez, prin. Fax 592-8915

Liberty Corner, Somerset
Bernards Township SD
Supt. — See Basking Ridge
Liberty Corner ES 500/K-5
61 Church St 07938 908-204-2550
Dr. James Oliver, prin. Fax 647-2425

Lincoln Park, Morris, Pop. 10,363
Lincoln Park Borough SD 900/PK-8
92 Ryerson Rd 07035 973-696-5500
James Grube, supt. Fax 696-9273
www.lincolnparkboe.org
Lincoln Park ES 500/PK-4
274 Pine Brook Rd 07035 973-696-5530
Melissa Flach-Bammer, prin. Fax 696-5321
Lincoln Park MS 400/5-8
90 Ryerson Rd 07035 973-696-5520
Michael Meyer, prin. Fax 872-8930

Lincroft, Monmouth, Pop. 6,069
Middletown Township SD
Supt. — See Leonardo
Lincroft ES 500/K-5
729 Newman Springs Rd 07738 732-741-5838
Daniel Imbimbo, prin. Fax 741-3382

Oak Hill Academy 400/PK-8
347 Middletown Lincroft Rd 07738 732-530-1343
Joseph Pacelli, hdmstr. Fax 530-0045
St. Leo the Great S 600/PK-8
550 Newman Springs Rd 07738 732-741-3133
Cornelius Begley, prin. Fax 741-2241

Linden, Union, Pop. 39,711
Linden SD 5,400/PK-12
2 E Gibbons St 07036 908-486-2800
Danny Robertozzi Ed.D., supt. Fax 486-6331
www.linden.k12.nj.us
McManus MS 600/6-8
300 Edgewood Rd 07036 908-486-7751
Peter Fingerlin, prin. Fax 587-0607
Public S 1 100/3-5
728 N Wood Ave 07036 908-486-2668
Dona Preston, prin. Fax 925-7287
Public S 2 500/PK-5
1700 S Wood Ave 07036 908-862-3287
Atiya Perkins, prin. Fax 862-3856
Public S 4 400/PK-5
1602 Dill Ave 07036 908-486-3286
Anthony Cataline, prin. Fax 925-7284
Public S 5 200/PK-2
1014 Bower St 07036 908-486-2666
Laura Scamardella, prin. Fax 925-7335
Public S 6 400/PK-5
19 E Morris Ave 07036 908-862-3003
William Mastriano, prin. Fax 862-3862
Public S 8 300/PK-5
500 W Blancke St 07036 908-862-4397
Michelle Rodriguez, prin. Fax 862-3868
Public S 9 400/PK-5
1401 Deerfield Ter 07036 908-486-5164
Dr. Larry Plummer, prin. Fax 925-7281
Public S 10 300/PK-5
2801 Highland Ave 07036 908-486-2043
Sandra Coglianese, prin. Fax 925-7369
Soehl MS 600/6-8
300 E Henry St 07036 908-486-0550
Richard Molinaro, prin. Fax 486-3478

Sinai Christian Academy 100/PK-12
2301 Grier Ave 07036 908-486-2006

Lindenwold, Camden, Pop. 17,154
Lindenwold SD 2,300/PK-12
801 Egg Harbor Rd 08021 856-783-0276
Lori Moore, supt. Fax 435-5887
www.lindenwold.k12.nj.us/
Lindenwold ES 4 500/K-4
900 E Gibbsboro Rd 08021 856-783-0405
Dana Lawrence, prin. Fax 782-2299
Lindenwold ES 5 600/K-4
550 Chews Landing Rd 08021 856-784-4063
Sandra Martinez-Preyor, prin. Fax 782-2293
Lindenwold MS 700/5-8
40 White Horse Ave 08021 856-346-3330
Theodore Pugliese, prin. Fax 346-0554
Lindenwold Preschool PK-PK
100 South Ave 08021 856-605-0119
Fax 685-4112

Linwood, Atlantic, Pop. 6,996
Linwood CSD 800/PK-8
51 Belhaven Ave 08221 609-926-6700
Dr. Michelle Cappellutti Ed.D., supt. Fax 926-6705
www.linwoodschools.org
Belhaven MS 400/5-8
51 Belhaven Ave 08221 609-926-6700
Susan Speirs, prin. Fax 926-6705
Seaview ES 400/PK-4
2015 Wabash Ave 08221 609-926-6700
Georgette Meister Ed.D., prin. Fax 926-6729

Little Egg Harbor Township, Ocean, Pop. 13,333
Little Egg Harbor Township SD 1,600/PK-6
307 Frog Pond Rd 08087 609-296-1719
Melissa A. McCooley, supt. Fax 296-3225
www.lehsd.k12.nj.us
Frog Pond ES 700/K-6
305 Frog Pond Rd 08087 609-296-1719
Troy Henderson, prin. Fax 296-4156
Mitchell ES 600/K-6
950 N Green St 08087 609-296-7131
Deborah Giannuzzi, prin. Fax 296-0849
Wood ECC 300/PK-PK
950 Route 539 08087 609-296-7131
Anne L. Flynn, prin. Fax 296-0849

Little Falls, Passaic, Pop. 11,294
Little Falls Township SD 800/K-8
32 Stevens Ave 07424 973-256-1034
Dr. Tracey Marinelli, supt. Fax 812-2107
www.lfnjschools.org
Little Falls ES 2 300/K-2
78 Long Hill Rd 07424 973-256-1386
Jill Castaldo, prin. Fax 256-1610
Little Falls ES 3 200/3-4
560 Main St 07424 973-812-9512
Nicole Dilkes, prin. Fax 256-6542
Little Falls MS 1 400/5-8
32 Stevens Ave 07424 973-256-1033
Philip Ligus, prin. Fax 785-4857

Little Ferry, Bergen, Pop. 10,396
Little Ferry SD 1,000/PK-8
130 Liberty St 07643 201-641-6192
Dr. Frank Scarafile, supt. Fax 641-6604
www.littleferry.k12.nj.us
Memorial ES 800/PK-PK, 2-
130 Liberty St 07643 201-641-6186
Robert Porfido, prin. Fax 641-3245
Washington ES 200/K-1
123 Liberty St 07643 201-641-6760
Tonilyn Peragallo, prin. Fax 641-4072

Little Silver, Monmouth, Pop. 5,876
Little Silver Borough SD 900/PK-8
124 Willow Dr 07739 732-741-2188
Dr. Carolyn Kossack, supt. Fax 741-3644
www.littlesilverschools.org
Markham Place MS 400/5-8
95 Markham Pl 07739 732-741-7112
Eric Platt, prin. Fax 741-3562
Point Road ES 500/PK-4
357 Little Silver Point Rd 07739 732-741-4022
Dr. Pamela Albert-Devine, prin. Fax 741-2384

Livingston, Essex, Pop. 27,500
Livingston SD 5,700/PK-12
11 Foxcroft Dr 07039 973-535-8000
Christina Steffner, supt. Fax 535-1254
www.livingston.org
Burnet Hill ES, 25 Byron Pl 07039 400/PK-5
Sara Bright, prin. 973-535-8000
Collins ES 400/K-5
67 Martin Rd 07039 973-535-8000
Tim Hart, prin. Fax 535-9586
Harrison ES 500/K-5
148 N Livingston Ave 07039 973-535-8000
Cynthia Healy, prin. Fax 716-9138
Heritage MS 900/7-8
20 Foxcroft Dr 07039 973-535-8000
Shawn Kelly, prin. Fax 597-9492
Hillside ES 400/K-5
98 Belmont Dr 07039 973-535-8000
Carlos Gramata, prin. Fax 535-8747
Mt. Pleasant ES 400/K-5
11 Broadlawn Dr 07039 973-535-8000
Emily Sortino, prin. Fax 535-8791
Mt. Pleasant MS 500/6-6
11 Broadlawn Dr 07039 973-535-8000
Debra Ostrowski, prin. Fax 535-8742
Riker Hill ES 400/K-5
31 Blackstone Dr 07039 973-535-8000
Jo Tandler, prin. Fax 740-1356

Aquinas Academy 300/PK-8
388 S Livingston Ave 07039 973-992-1587
John Cohrs, prin. Fax 992-1742
Kushner Hebrew Academy 600/PK-8
110 S Orange Ave 07039 973-437-8000

Lodi, Bergen, Pop. 23,608
Lodi SD 3,200/PK-12
8 Hunter St 07644 973-778-4620
Frank Quatrone, supt. Fax 778-6393
www.lodi.k12.nj.us
Columbus ES 300/K-5
370 Westervelt Pl 07644 973-478-0514
Vincent DiChiara, prin. Fax 478-7753
Hilltop ES 400/PK-5
200 Woodside Ave 07644 973-778-1213
Glenn Focarino, prin. Fax 471-5729
Jefferson MS 700/6-8
75 1st St 07644 973-478-8662
Robert Sciolaro, prin. Fax 478-0358
Roosevelt ES 200/PK-5
435 Passaic Ave 07644 973-777-8511
Michael Cardone, prin. Fax 249-0840
Washington ES 400/PK-5
310 Main St 07644 973-777-8513
Emil Carafa, prin. Fax 777-2075
Wilson ES 300/PK-5
80 Union St 07644 973-473-8189
Christie Vanderhook, prin. Fax 471-7345

Logan, Gloucester
Logan Township SD 1,000/PK-8
110 School Ln 08085 856-467-5133
Patricia Haney, supt. Fax 467-9012
www.logan.k12.nj.us
Center Square S 200/PK-1
100 Peachwood Dr 08085 856-294-0145
Beverly Green, prin. Fax 294-0151
Logan MS 400/6-8
110 School Ln 08085 856-467-5133
Heather Moran, prin. Fax 467-9012
Logan S 300/2-5
110 School Ln 08085 856-467-5133
Catherine Kelly, prin. Fax 467-9012

Long Branch, Monmouth, Pop. 29,197
Long Branch SD 4,900/PK-12
540 Broadway 07740 732-571-2868
Michael Salvatore, supt. Fax 229-0797
www.longbranch.k12.nj.us
Anastasia ES 700/PK-5
92 7th Ave 07740 732-571-3396
Francisco Rodriguez, prin. Fax 222-8469
Catrambone ES PK-5
240 Park Ave 07740 732-222-3215
Chris Volpe, prin. Fax 222-6953
Clark ES 400/PK-PK, 3-
192 Garfield Ave 07740 732-571-4677
Kristine Villano, prin. Fax 571-1693
Conrow Preschool 400/PK-K
335 Long Branch Ave 07740 732-222-4539
Bonita Potter-Brown, prin. Fax 222-2001
Ferraina ECC 300/PK-K
80 Avenel Blvd 07740 732-571-4150
Loretta Johnson, prin. Fax 483-0239
Gregory ES 700/K-5
201 Monmouth Ave 07740 732-222-7048
Beth McCarthy, prin. Fax 222-2807
Long Branch MS 1,000/6-8
350 Indiana Ave 07740 732-229-5533
Michael Viturello, prin. Fax 229-4894
Morris Avenue ES 400/PK-2
318 Morris Ave 07740 732-571-3139
Matthew Johnson, prin. Fax 870-1911

Seashore S 200/PK-8
345 2nd Ave 07740 732-222-6464

Long Valley, Morris, Pop. 1,859
Washington Township SD 2,300/PK-8
53 W Mill Rd 07853 908-876-4172
Jeffrey Mohre, supt. Fax 876-9392
www.wtschools.org
Cucinella ES 500/PK-5
470 Naughright Rd 07853 908-850-3161
Monica Whitmore, prin. Fax 684-4874
Flocktown-Kossman ES 500/PK-5
90 Flocktown Rd 07853 908-852-1376
Michael Craver, prin. Fax 850-0853
Long Valley MS 900/6-8
51 W Mill Rd 07853 908-876-3434
Mark Ippolito, prin. Fax 876-3436
Old Farmers Road ES 300/PK-5
51 Old Farmers Rd 07853 908-876-3865
Joseph Ciulla, prin. Fax 876-9506

Lumberton, Burlington
Lumberton Township SD 1,400/K-8
33 Municipal Dr 08048 609-267-1406
Joseph Langowski, supt. Fax 267-0002
www.lumberton.k12.nj.us/
Ashbrook ES 300/2-3
33 Municipal Dr 08048 609-518-0030
Heather Wawrzyniak, prin. Fax 784-5101
Bobby's Run ES 300/4-5
32 Dimsdale Dr 08048 609-702-5555
Tracy Hofstrom, prin. Fax 702-1463
Lumberton MS 500/6-8
30 Dimsdale Dr 08048 609-265-0123
Pete DeFeo, prin. Fax 265-0476
Walther ES 300/K-1
56 Chestnut St 08048 609-267-1404
Coletta Black, prin. Fax 267-6038

Lyndhurst, Bergen, Pop. 18,262
Lyndhurst Township SD 2,100/PK-12
420 Fern Ave 07071 201-438-5683
Shauna DeMarco, supt. Fax 896-2118
www.lyndhurstschools.net
Columbus ES 200/PK-2
640 Lake Ave 07071 201-896-2074
Robert Giangeruso, prin. Fax 933-3078
Franklin S 200/K-2
360 Stuyvesant Ave 07071 201-896-2077
Jennifer Scardino, prin. Fax 933-3106
Jefferson S 200/4-8
336 Lake Ave 07071 201-896-2065
Joseph Vastola, prin. Fax 933-3112
Lincoln S 200/4-8
281 Ridge Rd 07071 201-438-5683
Michael Rizzo, prin. Fax 438-5786
Memorial Campus 3-3
319 New York Ave 07071 201-438-6390
Michael Rizzo, prin. Fax 438-6366
Roosevelt S 400/4-8
530 Stuyvesant Ave 07071 201-896-2068
Peter Strumolo, prin. Fax 933-3143
Washington S 200/K-2
709 Ridge Rd 07071 201-896-2072
Christina Bernardo, prin. Fax 933-3173

Sacred Heart S 300/PK-8
620 Valley Brook Ave 07071 201-939-4277
Linda Durocher, prin. Fax 939-0534

Mc Guire AFB, Burlington, Pop. 3,478
North Hanover Township SD
Supt. — See Wrightstown
Atlantis ES 200/1-2
3 School House Rd 08641 609-738-2653
Michelle Stecchini, prin. Fax 723-5586
Discovery K 300/PK-K
2 School House Rd 08641 609-738-2652
Robert Scranton, prin. Fax 723-2196

Madison, Morris, Pop. 15,563
Madison SD 2,500/PK-12
359 Woodland Rd 07940 973-593-3100
Mark Schwarz, supt. Fax 301-2170
www.madisonpublicschools.org
Central Avenue ES 500/PK-5
50 Central Ave 07940 973-593-3173
Thomas Liss, prin. Fax 514-2070
Kings Road ES 300/K-5
215 Kings Rd 07940 973-593-3178
Kathleen Koop, prin. Fax 966-1927
Madison JHS 500/6-8
160 Main St 07940 973-593-3149
Fax 966-1908
Sabatini ES 300/K-5
359 Woodland Rd 07940 973-593-3182
Allison Stager, prin. Fax 966-1925

St. Vincent the Martyr S 400/PK-8
26 Green Village Rd 07940 973-377-1104
Sr. Noreen Holly, prin. Fax 377-2632

Magnolia, Camden, Pop. 4,260
Magnolia Borough SD 400/PK-8
420 N Warwick Rd 08049 856-783-4763
Dr. Warren Pross, supt. Fax 566-9736
www.magnoliaschools.org/
Magnolia S 400/PK-8
420 N Warwick Rd 08049 856-783-4763
Ralph Johnson, prin. Fax 566-9736

Mahwah, Bergen, Pop. 17,905
Mahwah Township SD 3,100/PK-12
60 Ridge Rd 07430 201-762-2400
C. Lauren Schoen, supt. Fax 529-1287
www.mahwah.k12.nj.us
Kilmer ES 500/4-5
80 Ridge Rd 07430 201-762-2270
Michael DeTuro, prin. Fax 529-4754
Lenape Meadows ES 400/PK-3
160 Ridge Rd 07430 201-762-2260
Dawn Uttel, prin. Fax 529-6821
Ramapo Ridge MS 800/6-8
150 Ridge Rd 07430 201-762-2380
Daniel Vander Molen, prin. Fax 529-6790
Ross ES 200/K-3
20 Malcolm Rd 07430 201-762-2250
Linda Bovino-Romeo, prin. Fax 529-4150
Washington ES 200/K-3
39 Fardale Ave 07430 201-762-2240
Kevin Ulmer, prin. Fax 529-2759

Young World Day S 100/PK-6
585 Wyckoff Ave 07430 201-327-3888

Manahawkin, Ocean, Pop. 2,289
Southern Regional SD 3,000/7-12
105 Cedar Bridge Rd 08050 609-597-9481
Craig Henry, supt. Fax 978-0298
www.srsd.net
Southern Regional MS 1,000/7-8
75 Cedar Bridge Rd 08050 609-597-9481
Lorraine Airey, prin. Fax 978-8209

Stafford Township SD 2,100/PK-6
250 N Main St 08050 609-978-5700
George Chidiac, supt. Fax 978-0807
www.staffordschools.org
McKinley Avenue ES 600/3-4
1000 McKinley Ave 08050 609-978-5700
Margaret Hoffman, prin. Fax 978-5737
Meinders Primary Learning Ctr 200/K-K
1000 McKinley Ave 08050 609-978-5700
Lori Coyne, prin. Fax 978-8393
Ocean Acres ES 500/1-2
489 Nautilus Dr 08050 609-978-5700
Susan D'Alessandro, prin. Fax 607-1983
Oxycocus S 100/PK-PK
250 N Main St 08050 609-978-5700
William Wilkinson, prin. Fax 978-5739
Stafford IS 600/5-6
1000 Mckinley Ave 08050 609-978-5700
Stephanie Bush, prin. Fax 978-5738

All Saints Regional S 400/PK-8
400 Doc Cramer Blvd 08050 609-597-3800
Kathleen Blazewicz, prin. Fax 597-2223
Lighthouse Christian Academy 100/PK-8
400 Beach Ave 08050 609-597-3915
Lorraine Sherman, admin. Fax 597-9659

Manalapan, Monmouth
Manalapan-Englishtown Regional SD
Supt. — See Englishtown
Clark Mills ES 500/K-5
34 Gordons Corner Rd 07726 732-786-2720
Jayme Orlando, prin. Fax 786-2730
Dawes Early Learning Center 300/PK-K
38 Gordons Corner Rd 07726 732-786-2830
Melissa Foy, prin. Fax 786-2840
Lafayette Mills ES 500/1-5
66 Maxwell Ln 07726 732-786-2700
Gregory Duffy, prin. Fax 786-2710
Manalapan-Englishtown MS 1,200/7-8
155 Millhurst Rd 07726 732-786-2650
Robert Williams, prin. Fax 786-2660
Milford Brook ES 500/K-5
20 Glo Bar Ter 07726 732-786-2780
Jodi Pepchinski, prin. Fax 786-2790
Pine Brook ES 600/6-6
155 Pease Rd 07726 732-786-2800
Julie Szustowicz, prin. Fax 786-2810
Taylor Mills ES 500/K-5
77 Gordons Corner Rd 07726 732-786-2760
Kerry Marsala, prin. Fax 786-2770
Wemrock Brook ES 700/1-5
118 Millhurst Rd 07726 732-786-2600
Beverly Wilpon, prin. Fax 786-2610

Manasquan, Monmouth, Pop. 5,870
Manasquan SD 1,600/PK-12
169 Broad St 08736 732-528-8800
Dr. Frank Kasyan, supt. Fax 223-6286
www.manasquanschools.org
Manasquan ES 700/PK-8
168 Broad St 08736 732-528-8810
Colleen Graziano, prin. Fax 223-9736

Atlantis Preparatory S 300/PK-K
1904 Atlantic Ave 08736 732-528-5437

Manchester, Ocean
Manchester Township SD
Supt. — See Whiting
Manchester Township ES 600/PK-5
101 N Colonial Dr 08759 732-323-9600
Linda Waldron, prin. Fax 323-9820
Manchester Township MS 700/6-8
2759 Ridgeway Rd 08759 732-657-1717
Nancy Driber, prin. Fax 657-0326
Ridgeway ES 500/PK-5
2861 Ridgeway Rd 08759 732-323-0800
Nikki Mazur, prin. Fax 323-9812

Mantua, Gloucester
Mantua Township SD
Supt. — See Sewell
Centre City ES 400/PK-3
301 Columbus Dr 08051 856-468-2100
Jennifer Cavalieri, prin. Fax 468-7530
Tomlin ES 600/4-6
393 Main St 08051 856-468-0818
Robert Miles, prin. Fax 468-7174

Manville, Somerset, Pop. 10,188
Manville Borough SD 1,300/K-12
410 Brooks Blvd 08835 908-231-8500
Robert Beers, supt. Fax 707-3963
www.manvilleschools.org
Batcho IS, 100 N 13th Ave 08835 300/6-8
Michael Magliacano, prin. 908-231-8521
Roosevelt ES, 410 Brooks Blvd 08835 200/4-5
Jamil Maroun, prin. 908-231-6809
Weston ES, 600 Newark Ave 08835 500/K-3
Melissa Keiser, prin. 908-231-8548

Maple Shade, Burlington, Pop. 19,211
Maple Shade Township SD 1,900/PK-12
170 Frederick Ave 08052 856-779-1750
Beth Norcia, supt. Fax 779-1054
www.mapleshade.org
Steinhauer ES 300/5-6
25 N Fellowship Rd 08052 856-779-7323
Cathy Quattrone, prin. Fax 779-2921
Wilkins ES 300/PK-PK, 3-
34 W Mill Rd 08052 856-779-1129
Steve Ormsby, prin. Fax 321-9217
Yocum ES 600/K-2
748 N Forklanding Rd 08052 856-779-7423
Yvonne Reitz, prin. Fax 779-7598

Our Lady of Perpetual Help S 200/PK-8
236 E Main St 08052 856-779-7526
Carl Jankowski, prin. Fax 667-3083

Maplewood, Essex, Pop. 21,756
South Orange-Maplewood SD 6,600/PK-12
525 Academy St 07040 973-762-5600
Dr. Thomas Ficarra, supt. Fax 378-9464
www.somsd.k12.nj.us
Boyden ES 500/K-5
274 Boyden Ave 07040 973-378-5209
Damion Frye, prin. Fax 378-5244
Clinton ES 500/K-5
27 Berkshire Rd 07040 973-378-7686
Ann Bodnar, prin. Fax 378-5241
Jefferson ES 500/3-5
518 Ridgewood Rd 07040 973-378-7696
Kimberly Hutchinson, prin. Fax 378-7692
Maplewood MS 800/6-8
7 Burnett St 07040 973-378-7660
Dara Gronau, prin. Fax 378-5247
Tuscan ES 600/K-5
25 Harvard Ave 07040 973-378-5221
Malikah Majeed, prin. Fax 378-7626
Other Schools – See South Orange

Margate City, Atlantic, Pop. 6,302
Margate City SD 400/PK-8
8103 Winchester Ave 08402 609-822-1686
John DiNicola, supt. Fax 822-3399
www.margateschools.org
Ross ES 200/PK-4
101 N Haverford Ave 08402 609-822-2080
Michelle CarneyRay-Yoder, prin. Fax 822-3489
Tighe MS 200/5-8
7804 Amherst Ave 08402 609-822-2353
Audrey Becker, prin. Fax 822-8456

Marlboro, Monmouth
Marlboro Township SD 5,100/PK-8
1980 Township Dr 07746 732-972-2000
Dr. Eric Hibbs, supt. Fax 972-2003
www.mtps.org
Defino Central ES 500/1-5
175 State Route 79 N 07746 732-972-2099
Jill Green, prin. Fax 332-0521
Dugan ES 600/1-5
48 Topanemus Rd 07746 732-972-2110
Samuel Hendrickson, prin. Fax 617-9736
Marlboro ES 500/1-5
100 School Rd W 07746 732-972-2095
Mitchell Shatz, prin. Fax 972-3429
Marlboro MS 1,100/6-8
355 County Road 520 07746 732-972-2100
Patricia Nieliwocki, prin. Fax 972-6765
Other Schools – See Morganville

Solomon Schecter Day S 200/PK-8
PO Box 203 07746 732-431-5525

Marlton, Burlington, Pop. 9,983
Evesham Township SD 4,400/PK-8
25 S Maple Ave 08053 856-983-1800
John Scavelli, supt. Fax 983-2939
www.evesham.k12.nj.us
Beeler ES 400/K-5
60 Caldwell Ave 08053 856-988-0619
Gerard Boland, prin. Fax 988-0495
DeMasi ES 300/K-5
199 Evesboro Medford Rd 08053 856-988-0777
Irene Romanelli, prin. Fax 988-1691
DeMasi MS 800/6-8
199 Evesboro Medford Rd 08053 856-988-0777
Irene Romanelli, prin. Fax 596-1571
Jaggard ES 300/K-5
2 Wescott Rd 08053 856-988-0679
Maria Sobel, prin. Fax 988-7788
Marlton ES 500/K-5
190 Tomlinson Mill Rd 08053 856-988-9811
Julio Feldman, prin. Fax 988-9812
Marlton MS 800/6-8
150 Tomlinson Mill Rd 08053 856-988-0684
Gary Hoffman, prin. Fax 988-9327
Rice ES 400/PK-5
50 Crown Royale Pkwy 08053 856-988-0685
Tami Aronow, prin. Fax 988-7799
Van Zant ES 400/K-5
270 Conestoga Dr 08053 856-988-0687
Nicholas DiBlasi, prin. Fax 988-8989

Joyful Noise Christian S 100/PK-K
55 E Main St 08053 856-983-1630
Laura Dolan, dir. Fax 983-1814
Marlton Christian Academy 100/PK-5
625 E Main St 08053 856-988-8503
Miriam Wegner, prin. Fax 596-3382
St. Joan of Arc S 400/K-8
101 Evans Rd 08053 856-983-0774
Sr. Patricia Pycik, prin. Fax 983-3278

Marmora, Cape May
Upper Township SD
Supt. — See Petersburg
Upper Township ES 400/3-5
50 N Old Tuckahoe Rd 08223 609-628-3500
Andrea Urbano, prin. Fax 390-3003
Upper Township PS 500/PK-2
130 N Old Tuckahoe Rd 08223 609-628-3500
Jamie Gillespie, prin. Fax 390-2390

Martinsville, Somerset, Pop. 11,795
Bridgewater-Raritan Regional SD 8,500/PK-12
836 Newmans Ln 08836 908-685-2777
Russell Lazovick, supt. Fax 231-8496
www.brrsd.org
Other Schools – See Basking Ridge, Bridgewater, Raritan

Matawan, Monmouth, Pop. 8,609
Matawan-Aberdeen Regional SD
Supt. — See Aberdeen
Ravine Drive ES 400/K-3
170 Ravine Dr 07747 732-705-5800
Patricia Janover, prin. Fax 566-6423

Old Bridge Township SD 8,600/K-12
4207 Highway 516 07747 732-566-1000
David Cittadino, supt.
www.oldbridgeadmin.org
Cheesequake ES 300/K-5
111 State Route 34 07747 732-360-4552
Dr. Thomas Ferry, prin. Fax 316-9353
Other Schools – See Cliffwood Beach, Laurence Harbor, Old Bridge, Parlin

Mays Landing, Atlantic, Pop. 2,098
Hamilton Township SD 3,000/PK-8
1876 Dr Dennis Foreman Dr 08330 609-476-6300
Frank Vogel, supt. Fax 625-4847
www.hamiltonschools.org
Davies MS 1,000/6-8
1876 Dr Dennis Foreman Dr 08330 609-476-6242
Stephen Santilli, prin.
Hess S, 700 Babcock Rd 08330 1,400/PK-PK, 2-
Melanie Lamanteer, prin. 609-476-6100
Shaner Memorial ES 600/PK-1
5801 3rd St 08330 609-476-6141
Daniel Cartwright, prin.

St. Vincent DePaul S 200/PK-8
5809 Main St 08330 609-625-1565
Linda Pirolli, prin. Fax 625-4703

Maywood, Bergen, Pop. 9,373
Maywood SD 900/PK-8
452 Maywood Ave 07607 201-845-9114
Michael Jordan, supt. Fax 845-7146
www.maywoodschools.org
Maywood Avenue MS 500/4-8
452 Maywood Ave 07607 201-845-9110
Michael Jordan, prin. Fax 291-1917
Memorial ES 400/PK-3
764 Grant Ave 07607 201-845-9113
Raymond Bauer, prin. Fax 845-0657

Medford, Burlington
Medford Township SD 2,800/PK-8
137 Hartford Rd 08055 609-654-6416
Joseph Del Rossi Ed.D., supt. Fax 654-7436
www.medford.k12.nj.us/
Allen ES, 24 Allen Ave 08055 400/K-5
Christopher Clarke, prin. 609-654-4203
Chairville ES, 36 Chairville Rd 08055 400/K-5
Jared Fudurich, prin. 609-654-9610
Cranberry Pines ES 300/K-5
400 Fairview Rd 08055 856-983-2861
Lucas Coesfeld, prin.
Haines S 300/6-6
162 Stokes Rd 08055 609-654-4056
Brooke Farrow, prin. Fax 654-4717
Kirby's Mill ES, 151 Hartford Rd 08055 300/PK-5
Helen Saul, prin. 609-953-7014
Medford Township Memorial MS 700/7-8
55 Mill St 08055 609-654-7707
Shawn Ryan, prin. Fax 654-7297
Taunton Forge ES 300/K-5
32 Evergreen Trl 08055 609-654-6723
Richard Lacovara, prin.

St. Mary of the Lakes S 400/PK-8
196 Route 70 08055 609-654-2546
Amy Rash, prin. Fax 654-8125

Medford Lakes, Burlington, Pop. 4,117
Medford Lakes Borough SD 500/PK-8
44 Neeta Trl 08055 609-654-5155
Anthony V. Dent, supt. Fax 714-0235
www.medford-lakes.k12.nj.us
Neeta S 300/3-8
44 Neeta Trl 08055 609-654-5155
Anthony Dent, admin. Fax 953-8258
Nokomis S 200/PK-2
135 Mudjekeewis Trl 08055 609-654-0991
Carole Ramage, prin. Fax 654-7629

Mendham, Morris, Pop. 4,930
Mendham Borough SD 600/PK-8
12 Hilltop Rd 07945 973-543-4251
Dr. Mitzi N. Morillo, supt. Fax 543-2805
www.mendhamboro.org
Hilltop ES 300/PK-4
12 Hilltop Rd 07945 973-543-4251
David Heller, prin. Fax 543-2805
Mountain View MS 300/5-8
100 Dean Rd 07945 973-543-7075
Aimee Toth, prin. Fax 543-7993

St. Joseph S 200/K-8
8 W Main St 07945 973-543-7474
Lori Arends, prin. Fax 543-7817

Merchantville, Camden, Pop. 3,729
Merchantville SD 400/PK-8
130 S Centre St 08109 856-663-1091
Scott Strong, supt. Fax 486-9755
www.merchantvilleschool.org
Merchantville S 400/PK-8
130 S Centre St 08109 856-663-1091
Scott Strong, supt. Fax 486-9755

St. Peter S 300/PK-8
51 W Maple Ave 08109 856-665-5879
Joseph Saffioti, prin. Fax 665-4943

Metuchen, Middlesex, Pop. 13,256
Metuchen SD 2,000/PK-12
16 Simpson Pl 08840 732-321-8700
Vincent Caputo, supt. Fax 321-6567
www.metuchenschools.org
Campbell S 700/1-4
24 Durham Ave 08840 732-321-8777
Edward Porowski, prin. Fax 767-9324
Edgar MS 700/5-8
49 Brunswick Ave 08840 732-321-8770
Kevin McPeek, prin. Fax 452-0571
Moss S 100/PK-K
16 Simpson Pl 08840 732-321-8700
Richard Cohen, prin. Fax 321-1285

Woodbridge Township SD
Supt. — See Woodbridge
Menlo Park Terrace ES 400/K-5
19 Maryknoll Rd 08840 732-596-4147
Margaret Truppa, prin. Fax 549-8329

Metuchen Christian Academy 200/K-8
130 Whitman Ave 08840 732-549-7854
Susan Howarth, prin. Fax 549-4434
St. Francis Cathedral S 500/PK-8
528 Main St 08840 732-548-3107
Barbara Stevens, prin. Fax 548-5760

Mickleton, Gloucester
East Greenwich Township SD 1,200/PK-6
559 Kings Hwy 08056 856-423-0412
Dr. James Lynch, supt. Fax 224-0144
www.eastgreenwich.k12.nj.us
Clark ES 500/PK-2
7 Quaker Rd 08056 856-423-0613
Jessica Mahoney, prin. Fax 423-9186
Mickle ES 600/3-6
559 Kings Hwy 08056 856-423-0412
Andrea Evans, prin. Fax 423-9337

Middlesex, Middlesex, Pop. 13,451
Middlesex Borough SD 2,000/PK-12
300 John F Kennedy Dr 08846 732-317-6000
Dr. Linda A. Madison Ed.D., supt. Fax 317-6006
www.middlesex.k12.nj.us
Hazelwood ES 200/PK-3
800 Hazelwood Ave 08846 732-317-6000
Richard Gianchiglia, prin. Fax 317-6003
Mauger MS 800/4-8
Fisher Ave 08846 732-317-6000
Jason Sirna, prin. Fax 317-6002
Parker ES 200/K-3
150 S Lincoln Ave 08846 732-317-6000
Dr. Remi Christofferson Ed.D., prin. Fax 317-6001
Watchung ES 200/K-3
1 Fisher Ave 08846 732-317-6000
Richard Rampolla, prin. Fax 317-6004

Middletown, Monmouth, Pop. 24,000
Middletown Township SD
Supt. — See Leonardo
Middletown Village ES 400/K-5
147 Kings Hwy 07748 732-671-0267
Karen Zupancic, prin.
New Monmouth ES 400/PK-5
121 New Monmouth Rd 07748 732-671-5317
Matthew Ferri, prin.
Nut Swamp ES 600/K-5
925 Nutswamp Rd 07748 732-671-5795
Neil Leone, prin. Fax 671-3529
Ocean Avenue ES 300/PK-5
235 Ocean Ave 07748 732-787-0092
Cynthia Wilson, prin.
Thompson MS 900/6-8
1001 Middletown Lincroft Rd 07748 732-671-2212
Brian Currie, prin.

St. Mary S 800/PK-8
538 Church St 07748 732-671-0129
Craig Palmer, prin. Fax 671-2653

Midland Park, Bergen, Pop. 7,021
Midland Park Borough SD 1,000/PK-12
250 Prospect St 07432 201-444-1400
Dr. Marie C. Cirasella Ed.D., supt. Fax 444-3051
www.mpsnj.org
Godwin ES 200/PK-2
41 E Center St 07432 201-445-5350
Danielle Bache, prin. Fax 652-5709
Highland Avenue ES 300/3-6
31 Highland Ave 07432 201-445-3880
Peter Galasso, prin. Fax 447-0826

Eastern Christian ES 200/PK-4
25 Baldin Dr 07432 201-445-6150
Sandra Bottge, prin. Fax 445-0488

Milford, Hunterdon, Pop. 1,220
Holland Township SD 600/PK-8
710 Milford Warren Glen Rd 08848 908-995-2401
Dave Bailey, supt. Fax 995-2805
www.hollandschool.org/
Holland Township S 600/PK-8
710 Milford Warren Glen Rd 08848 908-995-2401
Dr. Nancy Yard, prin. Fax 995-7138

Milford Borough SD 100/K-8
7 Hillside Ave 08848 908-995-4349
Edward Stoloski, supt. Fax 995-4310
www.milfordpublicschool.com
Milford S 100/K-8
7 Hillside Ave 08848 908-995-4349
Dr. Todd Fay, prin. Fax 995-4310

Millburn, Essex, Pop. 18,630
Millburn Township SD 4,900/PK-12
434 Millburn Ave 07041 973-376-3600
Dr. Christine Burton, supt. Fax 912-9396
www.millburn.org
Millburn MS 1,100/6-8
25 Old Short Hills Rd 07041 973-379-2600
John Connolly, prin. Fax 912-0939
South Mountain ES 300/PK-4
2 Southern Slope Dr 07041 973-921-1394
Scott Wolfe, prin. Fax 921-1365
Washington IS, 70 Spring St 07041 5-5
Peter Mercurio, prin.
Wyoming ES 300/K-4
55 Myrtle Ave 07041 973-761-1619
Kristin Mueller, prin. Fax 763-4128
Other Schools – See Short Hills

Millington, Morris
Long Hill Township SD
Supt. — See Gillette
Millington S 300/2-5
91 Northfield Rd 07946 908-647-2312
Jennifer Dawson, prin. Fax 647-4917

Millstone Township, Monmouth
Millstone Township SD 1,300/PK-8
5 Dawson Ct, 732-786-0950
Dr. Christopher Huss, supt. Fax 792-0951
www.millstone.k12.nj.us
Millstone Township ES 400/3-5
308 Millstone Rd, 732-786-0950
Suzanne Guidry, prin. Fax 792-9754
Millstone Township MS 500/6-8
5 Dawson Ct, 732-786-0950
Trish Bogusz, prin. Fax 786-0953
Millstone Township PS 300/PK-2
18 Schoolhouse Rd, 732-786-0950
Paul Baker, prin. Fax 446-5342

Milltown, Middlesex, Pop. 6,830
Milltown SD 600/K-8
80 Violet Ter 08850 732-214-2365
Dr. Stephanie Brown, supt. Fax 214-2376
www.milltownps.org
Kilmer S 300/4-8
21 W Church St 08850 732-214-2370
William Veit, prin. Fax 214-2378
Parkview ES 300/K-3
80 Violet Ter 08850 732-214-2360
Eric Siegel, prin. Fax 214-2376

Millville, Cumberland, Pop. 27,693
Millville SD 5,600/PK-12
PO Box 5010 08332 856-293-2000
Dr. David Gentile, supt. Fax 293-9852
www.millville.org
Bacon ES 300/K-5
501 S 3rd St 08332 856-327-6101
Michael Coyle, prin. Fax 327-7964
Child Family Center 600/PK-PK
1100 Coombs Rd 08332 856-293-2170
JoAnn Burns, prin. Fax 293-2174
Holly Heights ES 400/K-5
2509 E Main St 08332 856-293-2195
Stephen Saul, prin. Fax 327-8738
Lakeside MS 1,100/6-8
2 Sharp St N 08332 856-293-2420
Dr. Spike Cook, prin. Fax 825-7588
Mt. Pleasant ES 200/K-5
100 Carmel Rd 08332 856-293-2220
Arlene Jenkins, prin. Fax 327-3913
Rieck Avenue ES 400/K-5
339 Rieck Ave 08332 856-327-6093
Dr. Brian Robinson, prin. Fax 327-6088
Silver Run ES 500/K-5
301 Silver Run Rd 08332 856-327-6121
Eric Reissek, prin. Fax 327-3598

Mine Hill, Morris, Pop. 3,333
Mine Hill Township SD 400/PK-6
42 Canfield Ave 07803 973-366-0590
Lee S. Nittel, supt. Fax 366-3881
www.minehillcas.org
Canfield Avenue ES 400/PK-6
42 Canfield Ave 07803 973-366-0590
Adam Zygmunt, prin. Fax 366-3881

Minotola, See Buena
Buena Regional SD
Supt. — See Richland
Cleary ES 300/3-5
1501 Central Ave 08341 856-697-0800
Richard Lawrence, prin. Fax 697-8085

Monmouth Beach, Monmouth, Pop. 3,249
Monmouth Beach Borough SD 300/PK-8
7 Hastings Pl 07750 732-222-6139
Michael Ettore, supt. Fax 222-2395
www.mbschool.org
Monmouth Beach S 300/PK-8
7 Hastings Pl 07750 732-222-6139
Michael Ettore, supt. Fax 222-2395

Monmouth Junction, Middlesex, Pop. 2,829
South Brunswick Township SD
Supt. — See North Brunswick
Brooks Crossing ES 700/K-5
50 Deans Rhode Hall Rd 08852 732-821-7478
W Glenn Famous, prin. Fax 821-7429
Crossroads North MS 1,000/6-8
635 Georges Rd 08852 732-329-4191
Mark Daniels, prin. Fax 329-1905

Crossroads South MS 1,000/6-8
195 Major Rd 08852 732-329-4633
Bonnie Capes, prin. Fax 329-1906
Deans ES K-1
848 Georges Rd 08852 732-821-7478
Glenn Famous, prin. Fax 940-8430
Monmouth Junction ES 400/PK-5
630 Ridge Rd 08852 732-329-6981
Cristina Vildostegui-Cer Ed.D., prin. Fax 329-1892

Noor-Ul-Iman S 500/PK-12
4137 US Highway 1 08852 732-329-1800

Monroe Township, Middlesex
Monroe Township SD 5,900/PK-12
423 Buckelew Ave 08831 732-521-2111
Dr. Michael Kozak, supt. Fax 521-2719
www.monroe.k12.nj.us
Applegarth ES 300/4-5
227 Applegarth Rd 08831 609-655-0604
Dennis Ventrello, prin.
Barclay Brook ES 400/PK-2
358 Buckelew Ave 08831 732-521-1000
Erinn Mahoney M.Ed., prin. Fax 656-9082
Brookside ES 500/3-5
370 Buckelew Ave 08831 732-521-1101
Antonio Pepe, prin. Fax 521-6022
Mill Lake ES 400/PK-3
115 Monmouth Rd 08831 732-251-5336
Kristen Mignoi, prin. Fax 251-0886
Monroe Township MS 1,400/6-8
1629 Perrineville Rd 08831 732-521-6042
Chari Chanley, prin. Fax 521-2846
Oak Tree ES 600/PK-3
226 Applegarth Rd 08831 609-655-7642
Patricia Dinsmore M.Ed., prin. Fax 655-7612
Woodland ES 300/4-5
42 Harrison Ave 08831 732-251-1177
Adam Layman M.Ed., prin. Fax 251-1563

Monroeville, Salem
Upper Pittsgrove Township SD 400/PK-8
235 Pine Tavern Rd 08343 856-358-8116
Dr. Scott Eckstein, supt. Fax 358-1024
upperpitts.org/wordpress/
Upper Pittsgrove S 400/PK-8
235 Pine Tavern Rd 08343 856-358-8163
Scott Eckstein, prin. Fax 358-0319

Montague, Sussex
Montague SD 200/K-7
475 US Highway 206 07827 973-293-7131
Timothy Capone, supt. Fax 293-3391
montagueschool.org/
Montague ES 200/K-7
475 US Highway 206 07827 973-293-7131
Timothy Capone, supt. Fax 293-3391

Montclair, Essex, Pop. 39,200
Montclair SD 6,700/K-12
22 Valley Rd 07042 973-509-4000
Barbara Pinsak, supt. Fax 509-0586
www.montclair.k12.nj.us
Bradford ES 400/K-5
87 Mount Hebron Rd 07043 973-509-4155
Naomi Kirkman, prin. Fax 509-9523
Bullock ES 500/K-5
55 Washington St 07042 973-509-4255
Nami Kuwabara, prin. Fax 509-4247
Edgemont ES 300/K-5
20 Edgemont Rd 07042 973-509-4162
Cheryl Hopper, prin. Fax 655-0489
Glenfield MS 700/6-8
25 Maple Ave 07042 973-509-4172
Dr. Joseph Putrino, prin. Fax 509-4179
Hillside ES 500/3-5
54 Orange Rd 07042 973-509-4200
Dr. Samanthaa Anglin, prin. Fax 509-1448
Nishuane ES 500/K-2
32 Cedar Ave 07042 973-509-4222
Jill McLaughlin, prin. Fax 746-8865
Renaissance MS 300/6-8
176 N Fullerton Ave 07042 973-509-5741
Edward Wilson, prin. Fax 509-5752
Watchung ES 500/K-5
14 Garden St 07042 973-509-4259
Anthony Grosso, prin. Fax 509-1344
Other Schools – See Upper Montclair

Lacordaire Academy 100/PK-12
155 Lorraine Ave 07043 973-744-1156
Dr. William Hambleton, head sch Fax 783-9521
Montclair Cooperative S 200/PK-8
65 Chestnut St 07042 973-783-4955
Namita Tolia, head sch Fax 783-1316
Montclair Kimberley Academy 200/PK-3
201 Valley Rd 07042 973-746-9800
Thomas Nammack, hdmstr. Fax 783-8800
Montclair Kimberley Academy 400/4-8
201 Valley Rd 07042 973-746-9800
Thomas Nammack, hdmstr. Fax 509-7950
St. Cassian S 200/PK-8
190 Lorraine Ave 07043 973-746-1636
Maria Llanes, prin. Fax 746-3271

Montvale, Bergen, Pop. 7,749
Montvale SD 1,000/PK-8
47 Spring Valley Rd 07645 201-391-1662
Dr. Darren Petersen, supt. Fax 391-8935
www.montvalek8.org
Fieldstone MS 500/5-8
47 Spring Valley Rd 07645 201-391-9000
Gina McCormack, prin. Fax 391-8935
Memorial ES 500/PK-4
53 W Grand Ave 07645 201-391-2900
David Collier, prin. Fax 391-1330

Montville, Morris, Pop. 15,600
Montville Township SD 3,900/K-12
86 River Rd 07045 973-331-7100
Dr. Rene Rovtar, supt. Fax 316-4640
montville.net
Lazar MS 1,000/6-8
123 Changebridge Rd 07045 973-331-7100
Michael Pasciuto, prin. Fax 331-9279
Mason ES 300/K-5
5 Shawnee Trl 07045 973-331-7100
David Melucci, prin. Fax 331-9425
Valley View ES 300/K-5
30 Montgomery Ave 07045 973-331-7100
Dr. Patricia Kennedy, prin. Fax 336-4645
Other Schools – See Pine Brook, Towaco

St. Pius X S 200/PK-8
24 Changebridge Rd 07045 973-335-1253
John Galka, prin. Fax 335-2392
Trinity Christian S 200/K-12
160 Changebridge Rd 07045 973-334-1785
Douglas Prol, head sch Fax 334-9282

Moonachie, Bergen, Pop. 2,658
Moonachie SD 300/PK-8
20 W Park St 07074 201-641-5833
Dr. Jonathan Ponds, supt. Fax 641-3723
www.moonachieschool.org
Craig S 300/PK-8
20 W Park St 07074 201-641-5833
Dr. Jonathan Ponds, admin. Fax 641-3723

Moorestown, Burlington, Pop. 13,242
Moorestown Township SD 3,900/PK-12
803 N Stanwick Rd 08057 856-778-6600
Dr. Scott McCartney, supt. Fax 235-0961
www.mtps.com
Allen III MS 700/7-8
801 N Stanwick Rd 08057 856-778-6620
Matthew Keith, prin. Fax 727-9309
Baker ES 400/K-3
139 W Maple Ave 08057 856-778-6630
Michelle Rowe, prin. Fax 778-4412
Moorestown Upper ES 900/4-6
325 Bortons Landing Rd 08057 856-793-0333
Susan Powell, prin. Fax 793-0363
Roberts ES 300/PK-3
290 Crescent Ave 08057 856-778-6635
Brian Carter, prin. Fax 778-4426
South Valley ES 300/K-3
210 S Stanwick Rd 08057 856-778-6640
Dr. Leisa Karanjia, prin. Fax 727-4357

Moorestown Friends S 700/PK-12
110 E Main St 08057 856-235-2900
Laurence Van Meter, head sch Fax 235-6684
Our Lady of Good Counsel S 500/PK-8
23 W Prospect Ave 08057 856-235-7885
Dr. Carla Chiarelli, prin. Fax 235-2570

Morganville, Monmouth, Pop. 4,962
Marlboro Township SD
Supt. — See Marlboro
Abbott Early Learning Center 300/PK-K
171 Tennent Rd 07751 732-972-7100
Albert Perno, prin. Fax 972-2493
Holmes ES 600/1-5
48 Menzel Ln 07751 732-972-2080
JoAnn Cilmi, prin. Fax 617-1361
Marlboro Memorial MS 1,000/6-8
71 Nolan Rd 07751 732-972-7115
John Pacifico, prin. Fax 972-7118
Robertsville ES 500/1-5
36 Menzel Ln 07751 732-972-2044
David Stratuik, prin. Fax 617-0275

Shalom Torah Academy 100/PK-8
70 Amboy Rd 07751 732-536-0911

Morris Plains, Morris, Pop. 5,456
Hanover Township SD
Supt. — See Whippany
Mountview Road ES 300/K-5
30 Mountview Rd 07950 973-637-1550
Carmen Bellino, prin. Fax 539-0628

Morris Plains SD 600/PK-8
520 Speedwell Ave 07950 973-538-1650
Mark Maire, supt. Fax 540-1983
morrisplains.schoolwires.net
Borough MS 400/3-8
500 Speedwell Ave 07950 973-538-1650
Andrew Kramar, prin. Fax 538-8367
Mountain Way ES 200/PK-2
205 Mountain Way 07950 973-538-0339
Lindsay Vieira, prin. Fax 538-0405

Morris SD
Supt. — See Morristown
Vail ES, 125 Speedwell Ave 07950 300/K-2
Janet Kellman, prin. 973-292-2080

Parsippany-Troy Hills Township SD
Supt. — See Parsippany
Littleton ES 300/K-5
51 Brooklawn Dr 07950 973-682-2847
Michele Hoffman, prin. Fax 984-2980

Morristown, Morris, Pop. 18,125
Morris SD 5,000/K-12
31 Hazel St 07960 973-292-2300
Mackey Pendergrast, supt. Fax 292-2057
www.morrisschooldistrict.org
Frelinghuysen MS 1,100/6-8
10 Jean St 07960 973-292-2200
Joseph Uglialoro, prin. Fax 292-2458
Hamilton ES 300/3-5
34 Mills St 07960 973-292-2190
Edward Cisneros, prin. Fax 292-2194
Hillcrest ES 300/K-2
160 Hillcrest Ave 07960 973-292-2240
Gregory Sumski, prin. Fax 292-2236
Jefferson ES 300/3-5
101 James St 07960 973-292-2090
Cristina Frazzano, prin. Fax 292-2069
Normandy Park ES 400/K-5
19A Normandy Pkwy 07960 973-889-7690
Lora Clark, prin.
Sussex Avenue ES 300/3-5
125 Sussex Ave 07960 973-292-2250
Peter Frazzano, prin.
Woodland Avenue ES 300/K-2
15 Johnston Dr 07960 973-292-2230
Marie Hardenberg, prin.
Other Schools – See Morris Plains

Assumption of the BVM S 500/PK-8
63 MacCulloch Ave 07960 973-538-0590
Sr. Merris Larkin, prin. Fax 984-3632
Cheder Lubavitch S 200/PK-8
PO Box 1996 07962 973-455-0168
Peck S 300/K-8
247 South St 07960 973-539-8660
Andrew Delinsky, head sch Fax 539-6894
Red Oaks S 200/PK-8
21 Cutler St 07960 973-539-7853
Marilyn E. Stewart, head sch Fax 539-5182

Mountain Lakes, Morris, Pop. 4,079
Mountain Lakes SD 1,400/K-12
400 Boulevard 07046 973-334-8280
Dr. Anne Mucci, supt. Fax 334-2316
www.mlschools.org
Briarcliff MS 300/6-8
93 Briarcliff Rd 07046 973-334-0342
Fran Schlenoff Ed.D., prin. Fax 334-6857
Wildwood ES 500/K-5
51 Glen Rd 07046 973-334-3609
Beth Azar, prin. Fax 334-4905

Mountainside, Union, Pop. 6,605
Mountainside SD 800/PK-8
1497 Woodacres Dr 07092 908-232-3232
Dr. Nancy Lubarsky, admin. Fax 232-1743
www.mountainsideschools.org
Beechwood S 300/PK-2
1497 Woodacres Dr 07092 908-301-9104
Joy Blom, prin. Fax 301-1249
Deerfield ES 500/3-8
302 Central Ave 07092 908-232-8828
Kimberly Richards, prin. Fax 232-7338

Holy Trinity Interparochial S 100/PK-K
304 Central Ave 07092 908-233-1899
Sr. Maureen Fichner, dir. Fax 654-6680

Mount Arlington, Morris, Pop. 4,979
Mount Arlington SD 300/PK-8
446 Howard Blvd 07856 973-770-7140
Monica Rowland, supt. Fax 398-3614
www.mtarlingtonk8.org
Decker ES 100/PK-2
446 Howard Blvd 07856 973-398-6400
Jeff Grillo, admin. Fax 398-4687
Mount Arlington MS 200/3-8
235 Howard Blvd 07856 973-398-4400
Jeffrey Grillo, prin. Fax 398-5726

Mount Ephraim, Camden, Pop. 4,636
Mount Ephraim Borough SD 400/PK-8
225 W Kings Hwy 08059 856-931-7807
Leslie Koller, supt. Fax 931-5831
mtephraimschools.org/
Bray ES 300/PK-4
225 W Kings Hwy 08059 856-931-7807
Michael Hunter, prin. Fax 931-5831
Kershaw MS 200/5-8
125 S Black Horse Pike 08059 856-931-1634
Michael Hunter, prin. Fax 931-5831

Mount Holly, Burlington, Pop. 10,639
Mount Holly Township SD 1,000/PK-8
331 Levis Dr 08060 609-267-7108
James DiDonato, supt. Fax 702-9082
www.mtholly.k12.nj.us
Brainerd ES 400/PK-2
100 Wollner Dr 08060 609-267-3600
Joseph Convery, prin. Fax 702-0569
Folwell ES 300/3-5
455 Jacksonville Rd 08060 609-267-0071
Robert Mungo, prin. Fax 267-0062
Holbein MS 300/6-8
333 Levis Dr 08060 609-267-7200
Carolyn McDonald, prin. Fax 702-9775

Sacred Heart S 300/PK-8
250 High St 08060 609-267-1728
Kathryn Besheer, prin. Fax 267-4476

Mount Laurel, Burlington
Mount Laurel Township SD 4,000/K-8
330 Mount Laurel Rd 08054 856-235-3387
Dr. George Rafferty, supt. Fax 235-1837
www.mtlaurelschools.org
Countryside ES 300/K-4
115 Schoolhouse Ln 08054 856-234-2750
Lori Zataveski, prin. Fax 222-9755
Fleetwood ES 300/K-4
231 Fleetwood Ave 08054 856-235-3004
Michael Profico, prin. Fax 222-9756
Harrington MS 900/7-8
514 Mount Laurel Rd 08054 856-234-1610
Keith Land, prin. Fax 222-9754
Hartford S 1,000/5-6
397 Hartford Rd 08054 856-231-5899
Marques Stanard, prin. Fax 222-1221
Hillside ES 300/K-4
1370 Hanesport Mt Laurel Rd 08054 856-235-1341
Dr. Briean Madden, prin. Fax 222-9757

Larchmont ES 300/K-4
301 Larchmont Blvd 08054 856-273-3700
Dr. George Jackson, prin. Fax 222-9759
Parkway ES 400/K-4
142 Ramblewood Pkwy 08054 856-235-3364
Donna Kinn, prin. Fax 222-9758
Springville ES 400/K-4
520 Hartford Rd 08054 856-231-4140
Dr. Gailen Mitchell, prin. Fax 231-4146

Mount Tabor, Morris
Parsippany-Troy Hills Township SD
Supt. — See Parsippany
Mt. Tabor ES 400/K-5
PO Box 509 07878 973-889-3361
Marlene Toomey, prin. Fax 451-1958

Mullica Hill, Gloucester, Pop. 3,933
Clearview Regional HSD 2,500/7-12
420 Cedar Rd 08062 856-223-2765
John Horchak, supt. Fax 478-0409
www.clearviewregional.edu
Clearview Regional MS 900/7-8
595 Jefferson Rd 08062 856-223-2740
Peter DeFeo, prin. Fax 223-9068

Harrison Township SD 1,400/PK-6
120 N Main St 08062 856-478-2016
Dr. Margaret Quinn-Peretti, supt. Fax 478-4825
www.harrisontwp.k12.nj.us
Harrison Township ES 800/PK-3
120 N Main St 08062 856-478-2016
Renee Ingiosi, prin. Fax 223-1672
Pleasant Valley IS 600/4-6
401 Cedar Rd 08062 856-223-5120
Lisa Heenan, prin. Fax 223-2692

Friends S Mullica Hill 200/PK-8
15 High St 08062 856-478-2908
Matt Bradley, head sch Fax 478-0263

National Park, Gloucester, Pop. 3,003
National Park Borough SD 300/PK-6
516 Lakehurst Ave 08063 856-845-6876
Dr. Shannon Whalen, supt. Fax 848-6710
www.npelem.com/
National Park ES 300/PK-6
516 Lakehurst Ave 08063 856-845-6876
Carla Bittner, prin. Fax 848-6710

Neptune, Monmouth, Pop. 4,773
Neptune CSD 400/K-8
210 W Sylvania Ave 07753 732-775-5319
Debra Mercora Ed.D., admin. Fax 775-4335
www.neptunecityschool.org/
Wilson S 400/K-8
210 W Sylvania Ave 07753 732-775-5319
Debra Mercora Ed.D., admin. Fax 775-4335

Neptune Township SD 4,200/PK-12
60 Neptune Blvd 07753 732-776-2000
Tami Crader, supt. Fax 897-7595
www.neptune.k12.nj.us/
ECC 200/PK-PK
11 Memorial Dr 07753 732-776-2200
Lori Burns, prin. Fax 897-0878
Gables ES 300/PK-5
1 Gables Ct 07753 732-776-2200
Dr. Sally Millaway, prin. Fax 776-2260
Green Grove ES 400/PK-5
909 Green Grove Rd 07753 732-776-2200
James Nulle, prin. Fax 776-2257
Midtown Community ES 500/PK-5
1155 Corlies Ave 07753 732-776-2200
Dr. Mark Alfone, prin. Fax 897-9703
Neptune MS 800/6-8
2300 Heck Ave 07753 732-776-2200
Dr. Arlene Rogo, prin. Fax 776-2254
Shark River Hills ES 400/PK-5
312 Brighton Ave 07753 732-776-2200
Lakeda Demery, prin. Fax 776-2259
Summerfield ES 400/PK-5
1 Summerfield Ln 07753 732-776-2200
Dr. Jerard Terrell, prin. Fax 643-8695

Holy Innocents S 200/PK-8
3455 W Bangs Ave 07753 732-922-3141
Cynthia Reimer, prin. Fax 922-6531

Neshanic Station, Somerset
Branchburg Township SD
Supt. — See Branchburg
Whiton ES 700/PK-3
470 Whiton Rd 08853 908-371-0842
Dee Shober, prin. Fax 369-1582

Netcong, Morris, Pop. 3,192
Netcong SD 300/PK-8
26 College Rd 07857 973-347-0020
Dr. Kathleen Walsh, admin. Fax 347-3676
www.netcongschool.org
Netcong S 300/PK-8
26 College Rd 07857 973-347-0020
Dr. Gina Cinotti, admin. Fax 347-3676

Newark, Essex, Pop. 268,973
Newark SD 30,100/PK-12
2 Cedar St 07102 973-733-7333
Christopher Cerf, supt. Fax 733-6834
www.nps.k12.nj.us
Abington Avenue S 700/PK-8
209 Abington Ave 07107 973-268-5230
Nelson Ruiz, prin. Fax 350-5819
Ann Street S 1,300/PK-8
30 Ann St 07105 973-465-4890
Linda Richardson, prin. Fax 465-4185
Belmont-Runyon ES 300/PK-4
1 Belmont Runyon Way 07108 973-733-6920
Shawn Oxendine-Walter, prin. Fax 424-4447
B.R.I.C.K. Avon Academy 600/PK-8
219 Avon Ave 07108 973-733-6750
Charity Haygood, prin. Fax 733-6841
B.R.I.C.K. Peshine Academy 400/PK-8
433 Peshine Ave 07112 973-705-3890
Chaleeta Barnes, prin. Fax 705-3898
Camden Street ES 400/PK-8
281 Camden St 07103 973-733-6994
Samuel Garrison, prin. Fax 733-8452
Carver S 400/PK-8
333 Clinton Pl 07112 973-705-3800
Kyle Thomas, prin. Fax 705-3818
Chancellor Avenue ES 200/PK-8
321 Chancellor Ave 07112 973-705-3870
Sakina Pitts, prin. Fax 733-6841
Clemente ES 500/K-4
257 Summer Ave 07104 973-268-5290
Claudio Barbaran, prin. Fax 350-5719
Cleveland S 300/PK-8
388 Bergen St 07103 973-733-6944
Derrick Davis, prin. Fax 733-7021
Early Childhood S - Central PK-PK
70 Montgomery St 07103 973-733-7257
Marialana Juliano, dir. Fax 733-8216
Early Childhood S - North PK-PK
24 Crane St 07104 973-268-5112
Alisha Lee, prin. Fax 268-5113
Early Childhood S - South PK-PK
255 Chancellor Ave 07112 973-705-3860
Jamie Juliano, dir.
Early Childhood S - West 200/PK-PK
26 Speedway Ave 07106 973-351-2118
Marshel Perkins, dir. Fax 351-2346
Elliott Street ES 400/PK-5
721 Summer Ave 07104 973-268-5360
Nicole Johnson, prin. Fax 350-5816
First Avenue S 1,000/PK-8
214 1st Ave W 07107 973-268-5240
Jose Fuentes, prin. Fax 268-5333
Flagg S 400/PK-8
150 3rd St 07107 973-268-5190
Ganiat Rufai, prin. Fax 483-5916
Fourteenth Avenue ES 100/PK-5
186 14th Ave 07103 973-733-6940
Alyson Barillarri, prin. Fax 733-8675
Franklin ES 400/K-4
42 Park Ave 07104 973-268-5250
Marisol Diaz, prin. Fax 483-5824
Hawkins Street S 500/PK-8
8 Hawkins St 07105 973-465-4920
Alejandro Lopez, prin. Fax 465-4222
Hawthorne Avenue S 300/PK-8
428 Hawthorne Ave 07112 973-705-3960
Grady James, prin. Fax 705-3962
Hernandez S 200/PK-5
345 Broadway 07104 973-481-5004
Patricia Gois, prin. Fax 497-5703
Horton S 600/PK-8
291 N 7th St 07107 973-268-5260
Ginamarie Mignone, prin. Fax 268-5261
Ivy Hill ES 500/PK-8
107 Ivy St 07106 973-351-2121
Dorrice Rayam-Johnson, prin. Fax 374-2102
Lafayette Street S 1,000/PK-8
205 Lafayette St 07105 973-465-4860
Maria Merlo, prin. Fax 465-4863
Lincoln S 400/PK-8
87 Richelieu Ter 07106 973-374-2290
Debora Weaver, prin. Fax 374-2223
Marin S 700/K-8
663 Broadway 07104 973-268-5330
Maria Ortiz, prin. Fax 268-5972
McKinley S 700/PK-8
1 Colonnade Pl 07104 973-268-5270
Jessica Silva, prin. Fax 350-5719
Mt. Vernon S 600/PK-8
142 Mount Vernon Pl 07106 973-374-2090
Bertha Dyer, prin. Fax 374-2102
Oliver Street S 900/PK-8
86 Oliver St 07105 973-465-4870
Douglas Petty, prin. Fax 465-4873
Park S 700/PK-8
120 Manchester Pl 07104 973-268-5999
Sylvia Esteves, prin. Fax 497-5703
Quitman Street S 500/PK-8
21 Quitman St 07103 973-733-6947
Evelyn Vargas, prin. Fax 733-6636
Ridge Street S 600/PK-8
735 Ridge St 07104 973-268-5210
David DeOliveira, prin. Fax 268-5283
South Seventeenth Street S 400/PK-8
619 S 17th St 07103 973-374-2570
Clarence Allen, prin. Fax 374-2345
South Street ES 300/PK-5
104 Oliver St 07105 973-465-4880
Havier Nazario, prin. Fax 465-4024
Speedway S 400/PK-8
701 S Orange Ave 07106 973-374-2740
Atiba Buckman, prin. Fax 374-2152
Spencer - Miller S 300/PK-8
66 Muhammad Ali Ave 07108 973-733-6931
Jennifer Pellegrine, prin. Fax 424-4371
Sussex Avenue S 500/PK-8
307 Sussex Ave 07107 973-268-5200
Darleen Gearhart, prin. Fax 268-5282
Thirteenth Avenue/Dr MLK S 600/PK-8
359 13th Ave 07103 973-733-7045
Simone Rose, prin. Fax 733-7926
Tubman ES 300/PK-6
504 S 10th St 07103 973-733-6934
Fax 733-8628
Wilson Avenue S 900/PK-8
19 Wilson Ave 07105 973-465-4910
Margarita Hernandez, prin. Fax 465-4911

Alpha & Omega Christian S 100/PK-12
4 Fleming Ave 07105 973-465-5333
Dr. Jose Torres, dir. Fax 465-5335
Ironbound Catholic Academy 200/PK-8
366 E Kinney St 07105 973-589-0108
Egle Sausaitiene, prin. Fax 589-0239
Newark Boys Chorus S 100/3-8
1016 Broad St 07102 973-621-8900
Richard Willett, head sch Fax 621-1343
New Testament S 50/PK-12
511 Orange St 07107 973-268-1310
Lisa Billow, head sch Fax 268-1310
St. Benedict Preparatory S 600/K-12
520 Martin Luther King Jr 07102 973-643-4800
Rev. Edwin Leahy, hdmstr. Fax 643-6922
St. Francis Xavier S 200/PK-8
594 N 7th St 07107 973-482-9410
Lisa Perez, prin. Fax 482-2466
St. Michael S 500/K-8
27 Crittenden St 07104 973-482-7400
Dr. Linda Cerino, prin. Fax 482-1833

New Brunswick, Middlesex, Pop. 54,229
New Brunswick SD 7,600/PK-12
PO Box 2683 08903 732-745-5300
Dr. Aubrey Johnson, supt. Fax 745-5459
www.nbpschools.net
Lincoln Annex S 3-7
165 Somerset St 08901 732-745-5300
Sally Dobson, prin. Fax 448-1080
Lincoln ES 600/PK-5
66 Bartlett St 08901 732-745-5300
Joann Kocis, prin. Fax 937-7574
Livingston ES 600/K-5
206 Delavan St 08901 732-745-5300
Jose Negron, prin. Fax 937-7575
Lord Stirling ES 600/PK-5
101 Redmond St 08901 732-745-5300
Cesar Cabrera, prin. Fax 937-7576
McKinley Community S 600/PK-8
15 Van Dyke Ave 08901 732-745-5300
Janene Rodriguez, prin. Fax 937-7577
New Brunswick MS 1,300/6-8
1125 Livingston Ave 08901 732-745-5300
Jeremiah Clifford, prin. Fax 565-7630
Redshaw ES 700/PK-5
216 Livingston Ave 08901 732-745-5300
Vikki Abdus-Salaam, prin. Fax 937-7578
Robeson Community S for the Arts 500/K-6
40 Van Dyke Ave 08901 732-745-5300
Kelly Mooring, prin. Fax 937-7570
Roosevelt ES 800/K-5
83 Livingston Ave 08901 732-745-5300
Georgette Gonzalez, prin. Fax 937-7562
Wilson S 400/PK-8
133 Tunison Rd 08901 732-745-5300
William Smith, prin. Fax 937-7579

New Egypt, Ocean, Pop. 2,476
Plumsted Township SD 1,400/PK-12
117 Evergreen Rd 08533 609-758-6800
Gerald North, supt. Fax 758-6808
www.newegypt.us
New Egypt MS 400/6-8
115 Evergreen Rd 08533 609-758-6800
Richard DeMarco, prin. Fax 758-5538
New Egypt PS 100/PK-PK
131 Evergreen Rd 08533 609-758-6800
Andrea Caldes, prin. Fax 758-0912
Woehr ES 400/K-5
44 N Main St 08533 609-758-6800
Walter Therien, prin. Fax 758-6868

Newfield, Gloucester, Pop. 1,534
Franklin Township SD
Supt. — See Franklinville
Main Road ES 400/PK-PK, 3-
1452 Main Rd 08344 856-697-0220
Amy Morley, prin. Fax 629-1486

Edgarton Christian S PK-8
PO Box 646 08344 856-697-7300

New Gretna, Burlington
Bass River Township SD 100/PK-6
PO Box 304 08224 609-296-4230
Detlef Kern Ed.D., supt. Fax 296-4953
www.bassriverschooldistrict.org
Bass River Township ES 100/PK-6
PO Box 304 08224 609-296-4230
Detlef Kern Ed.D., admin. Fax 296-4953

New Milford, Bergen, Pop. 16,071
New Milford SD 1,900/PK-12
145 Madison Ave 07646 201-261-2952
Michael Polizzi M.Ed., supt. Fax 261-8018
www.newmilfordschools.org
Berkley Street ES 400/K-5
812 Berkley St 07646 201-262-0191
Caridad Chrisomalis, prin. Fax 967-8947
Gibbs ES 400/PK-5
195 Sutton Pl 07646 201-261-0939
Scott Davies, prin. Fax 967-8952
Owens MS 500/6-8
470 Marion Ave 07646 201-265-8661
James DeLalla, prin. Fax 265-5680

French American Academy 200/PK-6
1092 Carnation Dr 07646 201-338-8320
Hovnanian S 200/PK-8
817 River Rd 07646 201-967-5940
Shakeh Tashjian, prin. Fax 967-0249
Solomon Schecter Day S 400/PK-8
275 Mckinley Ave 07646 201-262-9898

New Monmouth, Monmouth
Middletown Township SD
Supt. — See Leonardo
Harmony ES, 100 Murphy Rd 07748 500/PK-5
Erik Paulson, prin. 732-671-2111

Newport, Cumberland
Downe Township SD 200/PK-8
220 Main St 08345 856-447-4673
Sherri Miller, supt. Fax 447-3005
www.downeschool.org
Downe Township S 200/PK-8
220 Main St 08345 856-447-4673
Sherri Miller, prin. Fax 447-3005

New Providence, Union, Pop. 12,002
New Providence SD 2,300/PK-12
356 Elkwood Ave 07974 908-464-9050
David Miceli Ed.D., supt. Fax 464-9041
www.npsd.k12.nj.us
New Providence MS 400/7-8
35 Pioneer Dr 07974 908-464-9161
Karin Kidd, prin. Fax 464-5927
Roberts ES 600/PK-6
80 Jones Dr 07974 908-464-4707
Gina Hansen, prin. Fax 464-4144
Salt Brook ES 700/K-6
40 Maple St 07974 908-464-7100
Jean Drexinger, prin. Fax 464-0786

Academy of Our Lady of Peace 200/PK-8
99 South St 07974 908-464-8657
Joel Castillo, prin. Fax 464-3377
St. Andrew's Preschool & K 200/PK-K
419 South St 07974 908-464-4878
Deborah V.H. Cook, dir. Fax 464-2439

Newton, Sussex, Pop. 7,865
Andover Regional SD 600/K-8
707 Limecrest Rd 07860 973-383-3746
Matthew L. Beck, supt. Fax 579-3972
www.andoverregional.org
Burd S 300/K-4
219 Newton Sparta Rd 07860 973-940-1234
Cindy Mizelle, prin. Fax 383-3778
Long Pond S 300/5-8
707 Limecrest Rd 07860 973-940-1234
Bryan Fleming, prin. Fax 579-2690

Fredon Township SD 300/PK-6
459 State Route 94 S 07860 973-383-4151
Dr. Gayle Carrick, supt. Fax 383-3644
www.fredon.org
Fredon Township ES 300/PK-6
459 State Route 94 S 07860 973-383-4151
Fax 383-3644

Frelinghuysen Township SD 200/PK-6
780 State Route 94 S 07860 908-362-6319
Stephanie Bonaparte, admin. Fax 362-5730
www.frelinghuysenschool.org
Frelinghuysen Township ES 200/PK-6
780 State Route 94 S 07860 908-362-6319
Stephanie Bonaparte, admin. Fax 362-5730

Hampton Township SD 300/K-6
1 School Rd 07860 973-383-5300
Craig M. Hutcheson, supt. Fax 383-3835
www.mckeown.org
McKeown ES 300/K-6
1 School Rd 07860 973-383-5300
Dr. Janet Goodwin Ed.D., prin. Fax 383-3835

Newton SD 1,500/PK-12
57 Trinity St 07860 973-383-1900
Dr. G. Kennedy Greene, supt. Fax 383-5378
www.newtonnj.org
Halsted Street MS 200/6-8
59 Halsted St 07860 973-383-7440
Kristi Greene, prin. Fax 383-7432
Merriam Avenue ES 500/PK-5
81 Merriam Ave 07860 973-383-7202
Kevin Stanton, prin. Fax 383-7276

Auxillium S 200/PK-K
14 Old Swartswood Rd 07860 973-383-2621
Sr. Isabel Garza, prin. Fax 383-3214
Northwest Christian S 200/PK-8
92 County Road 519 07860 973-383-9713
Joseph Cottrell, prin. Fax 383-6141

New Vernon, Morris
Harding Township SD 300/PK-8
34 Lees Hill Rd 07976 973-267-6398
Matthew Spelker, supt. Fax 267-7133
www.hardingtwp.org
Harding Township S 300/PK-8
34 Lees Hill Rd 07976 973-267-6398
Mary Donohue, prin. Fax 292-1318

North Arlington, Bergen, Pop. 15,146
North Arlington SD 1,700/PK-12
222 Ridge Rd 07031 201-991-6800
Dr. Stephen Yurchak, supt. Fax 991-1656
www.narlington.k12.nj.us
Jefferson ES 300/PK-5
100 Prospect Ave 07031 201-991-6800
Jennifer Rodriguez, prin. Fax 955-5254
North Arlington MS 300/6-8
45 Beech St 07031 201-991-6800
Nicole Russo, prin. Fax 246-0703
Roosevelt ES, 50 Webster St 07031 300/PK-5
Marie Griggs, prin. 201-991-6800
Washington ES 300/PK-5
175 Albert St 07031 201-991-6800
Elaine Jaume, prin. Fax 246-0135

Queen of Peace S 300/PK-8
21 Church Pl 07031 201-998-8222
Ellen Naughton, prin. Fax 997-7930

North Bergen, Hudson, Pop. 59,000
North Bergen SD 7,300/PK-12
7317 Kennedy Blvd 07047 201-868-1000
Dr. George Solter, supt. Fax 295-2747
www.northbergen.k12.nj.us/
Franklin S 600/1-8
5211 Columbia Ave 07047 201-974-7007
Janet Sandstrom, prin. Fax 866-3697
Fulton S 1,200/1-8
7407 Hudson Ave 07047 201-295-2900
Noreen Garcia, prin. Fax 868-7656
Kennedy S 500/PK-8
1210 11th St 07047 201-974-7000
Francis Bafumi, prin. Fax 974-1288
Lincoln S 1,100/K-8
1206 63rd St 07047 201-295-2850
Nicolas Sacco, prin. Fax 295-2857
Mann S 1,100/1-8
1215 83rd St 07047 201-295-2880
Richard Locricchio, prin. Fax 868-1243
McKinley S 400/PK-8
3110 Liberty Ave 07047 201-974-7020
Peter Clark, prin. Fax 974-7003

North Brunswick, Middlesex, Pop. 37,400
North Brunswick Township SD 5,900/PK-12
PO Box 6016 08902 732-289-3000
Dr. Brian Zychowski, supt. Fax 297-8567
www.nbtschools.org
Adams ES 600/K-5
1450 Redmond St 08902 732-289-3100
Dr. Frederick Johnson, prin. Fax 249-4521
Judd ES 700/PK-5
1601 Roosevelt Ave 08902 732-289-3200
Joseph Schmidt, prin. Fax 297-0036
Linwood MS 1,300/6-8
25 Linwood Pl 08902 732-289-3600
Roy Wilson, prin. Fax 247-7033
Livingston Park ES 700/K-5
1128 Livingston Ave 08902 732-289-3300
Sidney Dawson, prin. Fax 249-5283
Parsons ES 700/K-5
899 Hollywood St 08902 732-289-3400
Dianna Whalen, prin. Fax 435-1709

South Brunswick Township SD 8,500/PK-12
231 Black Horse Ln 08902 732-297-7800
Scott Feder, supt. Fax 297-8456
www.sbschools.org
Other Schools – See Dayton, Kendall Park, Monmouth Junction

North Caldwell, Essex, Pop. 6,124
North Caldwell SD 600/K-6
132A Gould Ave 07006 973-712-4400
Dr. Linda Freda, supt.
www.ncboe.org/
Gould S, 132 Gould Ave 07006 300/4-6
Chris Checchetto, prin. 973-712-4400
Other Schools – See Caldwell

West Essex Regional SD 1,600/7-12
65 W Greenbrook Rd 07006 973-228-1200
Barbara Longo, supt. Fax 228-0559
www.westex.org
West Essex MS 600/7-8
65 W Greenbrook Rd 07006 973-228-1200
Vee Popat, prin. Fax 228-5852

Northfield, Atlantic, Pop. 8,484
Northfield CSD 1,000/K-8
2000 New Rd 08225 609-407-4000
Pedro Bretones, supt. Fax 646-0608
northfield.groupfusion.net
Northfield Community ES 500/K-4
2000 New Rd 08225 609-407-4005
Maureen Vaccaro, prin. Fax 646-0608
Northfield Community MS 500/5-8
2000 New Rd 08225 609-407-4008
Kevin Morrison, prin. Fax 641-2646

North Haledon, Passaic, Pop. 8,332
North Haledon SD 700/PK-8
201 Squaw Brook Rd 07508 973-427-8993
Nicholas Coffaro M.A., supt. Fax 427-4357
www.nhschools.net
High Mountain MS 300/5-8
515 High Mountain Rd 07508 973-427-1220
Michele Mazzola, prin. Fax 427-7685
Memorial ES 400/PK-4
201 Squaw Brook Rd 07508 973-427-8993
Melissa Tait M.A., prin. Fax 427-4357

North Plainfield, Somerset, Pop. 21,559
North Plainfield Borough SD 2,700/PK-12
33 Mountain Ave 07060 908-769-6000
Dr. James McLaughlin, supt. Fax 755-5490
www.nplainfield.org
East End ES 500/PK-4
170 Oneida Ave 07060 908-769-6070
John Ferguson, prin. Fax 668-5536
North Plainfield MS 7-8
34 Wilson Ave 07060 908-769-6065
Luis Jaime, prin.
Somerset IS 400/5-6
303 Somerset St 07060 908-769-6080
Reginald Sainte-Rose, prin. Fax 769-6077
Stony Brook ES 200/K-4
269 Grove St 07060 908-769-6063
Catherine Kobylarz, prin. Fax 668-5535
West End ES 600/PK-4
447 Greenbrook Rd 07063 908-769-6083
Filipe Luis, prin. Fax 668-5538

Sundance S 300/PK-5
401 Greenbrook Rd 07063 973-868-0051

Northvale, Bergen, Pop. 4,576
Northvale SD 500/K-8
441 Tappan Rd 07647 201-768-8484
Michael Pinajian, supt. Fax 768-4948
www.northvaleschool.org
Northvale S 500/K-8
441 Tappan Rd 07647 201-768-8484
Dianne Smith, prin. Fax 768-4948

North Wildwood, Cape May, Pop. 3,978
North Wildwood CSD 300/PK-8
1201 Atlantic Ave 08260 609-522-1454
Christopher Armstrong, supt. Fax 522-2308
www.mmace.com
Mace S 300/PK-8
1201 Atlantic Ave 08260 609-522-1454
Christopher Armstrong, prin. Fax 522-2308

Norwood, Bergen, Pop. 5,641
Norwood SD 600/K-8
177 Summit St 07648 201-768-6363
Lisa Gross, supt. Fax 768-4916
www.wearenorwood.org
Norwood S 600/K-8
177 Summit St 07648 201-768-6363
Vito DeLaura, supt. Fax 768-4916

Nutley, Essex, Pop. 27,400
Nutley SD 3,900/K-12
315 Franklin Ave 07110 973-661-8798
Dr. Julie Glazer, supt. Fax 320-8476
www.nutleyschools.org
Lincoln ES 400/K-6
301 Harrison St 07110 973-661-8883
Lorraine Restel, prin. Fax 661-4392
Radcliffe ES 300/K-6
379 Bloomfield Ave 07110 973-661-8820
Michael Kearney, prin. Fax 661-4395
Spring Garden ES 300/K-6
59 S Spring Garden Ave 07110 973-661-8983
Laurie LaGuardia, prin. Fax 661-5138
Walker MS 600/7-8
325 Franklin Ave 07110 973-661-8871
Tracy Egan, prin. Fax 661-3775
Washington ES 500/K-6
155 Washington Ave 07110 973-661-8888
Douglas Jones, prin. Fax 661-1369
Yantacaw ES 500/K-6
20 Yantacaw Pl 07110 973-661-8892
Frank Francia, prin. Fax 661-5289

Abundant Life Academy 400/PK-12
390 Washington Ave 07110 973-667-9700
John Kuebler, head sch Fax 667-1278
Good Shepherd Academy 200/K-8
24 Brookline Ave 07110 973-667-2049
Sr. Jane Feltz, prin. Fax 661-9259

Oakhurst, Monmouth, Pop. 3,965
Ocean Township SD 3,600/PK-12
163 Monmouth Rd 07755 732-531-5600
Dr. James Stefankiewicz, supt. Fax 531-3874
www.oceanschools.org
Ocean Township ES 400/PK-4
555 Dow Ave 07755 732-531-5690
Dr. Doreen Ryan, prin. Fax 531-3682
Other Schools – See Ocean, Wanamassa

Oakland, Bergen, Pop. 12,608
Oakland SD 1,600/PK-8
315 Ramapo Valley Rd 07436 201-337-6156
Dr. Gina Coffaro, supt. Fax 405-1237
www.oaklandschoolsnj.org
Dogwood Hill ES 300/K-5
25 Dogwood Dr 07436 201-337-5822
Glenn Clark, prin. Fax 337-3268
Heights ES 400/PK-5
114 Seminole Ave 07436 201-337-4147
Barbara Ciambra, prin. Fax 337-5694
Manito ES 300/K-5
111 Manito Ave 07436 201-337-6106
Adam Silverstein, prin. Fax 337-3571
Valley MS 600/6-8
71 Oak St 07436 201-337-8185
Gregg Desiderio, prin. Fax 337-7089

Academies at Gerrard Berman Day S 100/PK-8
45 Spruce St 07436 201-337-1111

Oaklyn, Camden, Pop. 3,984
Haddon Township SD
Supt. — See Westmont
Jennings ES 100/K-5
100 E Cedar Ave 08107 856-869-7720
Charles Warfield, prin. Fax 869-7722

Oaklyn Borough SD 400/PK-9
136 Kendall Blvd 08107 856-858-0335
Dr. Scott Oswald, supt. Fax 869-3474
oaklynschool.org/
Oaklyn S 400/PK-9
136 Kendall Blvd 08107 856-858-0335
Jennifer Boulden, prin. Fax 858-1623

Oak Ridge, Passaic
Jefferson Township SD
Supt. — See Lake Hopatcong
Cozy Lake ES 200/1-2
205 Cozy Lake Rd 07438 973-697-4777
Karl Mundi, prin. Fax 697-3569
Jefferson Township MS 800/6-8
1000 Weldon Rd 07438 973-697-1980
Dr. Kelly Cooke, prin. Fax 697-1348
Milton K 100/PK-K
52 School House Rd 07438 973-697-4742
Karl Mundi, prin. Fax 697-8623
White Rock ES 400/3-5
2 Francine Pl 07438 973-697-2414
Dr. Randi DeBrito, prin. Fax 697-2049

West Milford Township SD
Supt. — See West Milford
Paradise Knoll ES 300/K-6
103 Paradise Rd 07438 973-697-7142
Jennifer Miller, prin. Fax 697-9444

Ocean, Monmouth, Pop. 26,700
Ocean Township SD
Supt. — See Oakhurst

Ocean Township IS 1,200/5-8
1200 W Park Ave 07712 732-531-5630
Larry Kostula, prin. Fax 493-1891
Wayside ES, 733 Bowne Rd 07712 600/PK-4
Denise Palaia, prin. 732-531-5710

Hillel Yeshiva S 500/PK-8
1025 Deal Rd 07712 732-493-9300

Ocean City, Cape May, Pop. 11,545
Ocean City SD 2,100/K-12
501 Atlantic Ave Ste 1 08226 609-399-5150
Dr. Kathleen Taylor, supt. Fax 399-4656
www.oceancityschools.org/
Ocean City IS 500/4-8
1801 Bay Ave 08226 609-399-5611
Geoffrey Haines, prin. Fax 398-7089
Ocean City PS 400/K-3
550 West Ave 08226 609-399-3191
Cathleen Smith, prin. Fax 399-8257

Ocean Gate, Ocean, Pop. 1,995
Ocean Gate SD 100/PK-6
PO Box 478 08740 732-269-3023
Frank Vanalesti, supt. Fax 269-9777
www.oceangateschool.net
Ocean Gate ES 100/PK-6
PO Box 478 08740 732-269-3023
Frank Vanalesti, admin. Fax 269-9777

Oceanport, Monmouth, Pop. 5,763
Oceanport Borough SD 600/PK-8
29 Wolfhill Ave 07757 732-542-0683
Thomas Farrell, supt.
www.oceanport.k12.nj.us
Maple Place MS 300/5-8
2 Maple Pl 07757 732-229-0267
Matthew Howell, prin. Fax 229-0961
Wolf Hill ES 300/PK-4
29 Wolfhill Ave 07757 732-542-0683
Melanie Lipinski, prin. Fax 578-0719

Ogdensburg, Sussex, Pop. 2,388
Ogdensburg Borough SD 300/PK-8
100 Main St 07439 973-827-7126
David Astor, supt. Fax 827-0134
www.obboe.org
Ogdensburg S 300/PK-8
100 Main St 07439 973-827-7126
David Astor, admin. Fax 827-0134

Old Bridge, Middlesex, Pop. 23,304
Old Bridge Township SD
Supt. — See Matawan
Carpenter ES 300/K-5
1 Par Ave 08857 732-360-4452
Christopher McCue, prin. Fax 360-2964
Grissom ES 200/K-5
1 Sims Ave 08857 732-360-4481
Dr. Anthony Arico, prin. Fax 360-0725
McDivitt ES 500/K-5
1 Manny Martin Way 08857 732-360-4512
Laurie Coletti, prin. Fax 721-5706
Miller S 300/K-5
2 Old Matawan Rd 08857 732-360-4589
Dr. Kimberly Giles, prin. Fax 698-0448
Salk MS 1,000/6-8
155 W Greystone Rd 08857 732-360-4519
William Rezes, prin. Fax 251-1690
Sandburg MS 1,200/6-8
3439 Highway 516 08857 732-360-4400
Martha Simon, prin. Fax 360-9676
Schirra ES 300/K-5
1 Awn St 08857 732-360-4495
Tricia Barrett, prin. Fax 360-0736
Shepard ES 200/K-5
33 Bushnell Rd 08857 732-360-4499
Joseph Marinzoli, prin. Fax 679-5112
Southwood ES 300/K-5
64 Southwood Dr 08857 732-360-4539
Karen Foley, prin. Fax 257-2356
Voorhees ES 300/K-5
11 Liberty St 08857 732-360-4544
Courtney Lowery, prin. Fax 251-8549

Calvary Christian S 300/PK-12
123 White Oak Ln 08857 732-479-0700
Jim Dunne, prin. Fax 679-1948
St. Ambrose S 400/PK-8
81 Throckmorton Ln 08857 732-679-4700
Dr. Theodore Kadela, prin. Fax 679-6062
St. Thomas the Apostle S 400/PK-8
333 State Route 18 08857 732-251-4000
Joanne Kowit, prin. Fax 251-5315

Old Tappan, Bergen, Pop. 5,680
Old Tappan SD 800/K-8
277 Old Tappan Rd 07675 201-664-1421
Danielle DaGiau, supt. Fax 664-4418
oldtappanschools.org
DeMarest ES 400/K-4
1 School St 07675 201-664-7176
Angela Connelly, prin. Fax 664-7167
DeWolf MS 400/5-8
275 Old Tappan Rd 07675 201-664-1475
Justin O'Neill, prin. Fax 664-8101

Oradell, Bergen, Pop. 7,880
Oradell SD 800/K-6
350 Prospect Ave 07649 201-261-1180
Dr. John Anzul, supt. Fax 261-1167
www.oradellschool.org
Oradell S 800/K-6
350 Prospect Ave 07649 201-261-1180
Megan Bozios, supt. Fax 261-1167

St. Joseph S 300/PK-8
305 Elm St 07649 201-261-2388
Dr. Paula Valenti, prin. Fax 261-0830

Orange, Essex, Pop. 33,300
Orange SD 4,300/PK-12
451 Lincoln Ave 07050 973-677-4000
Paula Howard, supt. Fax 677-0486
www.orange.k12.nj.us
Cleveland Street ES 300/K-7
355 Cleveland St 07050 973-677-4100
Dr. Cayce Cummins, prin. Fax 676-8492
Forest Street ES 300/K-7
651 Forest St 07050 973-677-4120
Yancisca Cooke, prin. Fax 676-5387
Heywood Avenue ES 300/K-7
421 Heywood Ave 07050 973-677-4105
Faith Alcantara, prin. Fax 672-2107
Lincoln Avenue ES 600/K-7
216 Lincoln Ave 07050 973-677-4130
Denise White, prin. Fax 673-6669
Oakwood Avenue ES 200/K-7
135 Oakwood Ave 07050 973-677-4095
Robert Pettit, prin. Fax 674-8015
Orange ECC PK-PK
397 Park Ave 07050 973-677-4000
Jacquelyn Blanton, prin. Fax 414-0201
Park Avenue ES 400/PK-8
231 Park Ave 07050 973-677-4124
Dr. Myron Hackett, prin. Fax 675-1291
Parks S 900/K-7
369 Main St 07050 973-677-4515
Debra Joseph-Charles, prin. Fax 675-0925

Oxford, Warren, Pop. 1,081
Oxford Township SD 300/PK-8
17 Kent St 07863 908-453-4101
Bob Magnuson, admin. Fax 453-0022
www.oxfordcentral.org/
Oxford Central S 300/PK-8
17 Kent St 07863 908-453-4101
Robert Magnuson, admin. Fax 453-0022

Palisades Park, Bergen, Pop. 19,390
Palisades Park SD 1,300/PK-12
410 2nd St 07650 201-947-3550
Dr. Joseph Cirillo, supt. Fax 947-4079
www.palpkschools.org
Lindbergh ES 600/1-6
401 Glen Ave 07650 201-947-3556
Toni Bongard, prin. Fax 947-2721
Smith ECC 200/PK-K
271 2nd St 07650 201-947-2761
Jillian Vivanco, admin. Fax 947-0945

Notre Dame Academy 300/PK-8
312 1st St 07650 201-947-5262
Mark Valvano, prin. Fax 947-8319

Palmyra, Burlington, Pop. 7,223
Palmyra Borough SD 900/PK-12
301 Delaware Ave 08065 856-786-9300
Brian McBride, supt. Fax 829-9638
palmyraschools.com
Charles Street ES 500/PK-6
100 W Charles St 08065 856-786-9300
Mark Pease, prin. Fax 303-0481

Paramus, Bergen, Pop. 25,735
Paramus SD 3,700/K-12
145 Spring Valley Rd 07652 201-261-7800
Michele Robinson, supt. Fax 261-5861
www.paramusschools.org/ppsd/
East Brook MS 600/5-8
190 Spring Valley Rd 07652 201-261-7800
Thomas LoBue, prin. Fax 262-1541
Memorial ES 300/K-4
203 E Midland Ave 07652 201-261-7800
Laverne O'Boyle, prin. Fax 262-5619
Midland ES 200/K-4
241 W Midland Ave 07652 201-261-7800
Cynthia Hulse, prin. Fax 262-1541
Parkway ES 200/K-4
145 E Ridgewood Ave 07652 201-261-7800
Suzanne Barbi, prin. Fax 262-8214
Ridge Ranch ES 300/K-4
345 Lockwood Dr 07652 201-261-7800
Jeanine Nostrame, prin. Fax 262-2998
Stony Lane ES 200/K-4
110 W Ridgewood Ave 07652 201-261-7800
Thomas Marshall, prin. Fax 445-8971
West Brook MS 600/5-8
560 Roosevelt Blvd 07652 201-261-7800
Dr. Deirdre Spollen-LaRaia, prin. Fax 652-0376

Visitation Academy 300/PK-8
222 N Farview Ave 07652 201-262-6067
Kimberly Harrigan, prin. Fax 261-4613
Yavneh Academy 700/PK-8
PO Box 428 07653 201-262-8494
Yeshivat Noam PK-8
70 W Century Rd 07652 201-261-1919

Park Ridge, Bergen, Pop. 8,566
Park Ridge SD 1,300/PK-12
85 Pascack Rd 07656 201-573-6000
Dr. Robert Gamper, supt. Fax 391-6511
www.parkridge.k12.nj.us
East Brook ES 300/K-6
167 Sibbald Dr 07656 201-573-6000
Kevin Stokes, prin. Fax 930-1650
West Ridge ES 300/K-6
18 S 1st St 07656 201-573-6000
Christine McCaffery, prin. Fax 573-8658

Our Lady of Mercy Academy 400/PK-8
25 Fremont Ave 07656 201-391-3838
Laraine Meehan, prin. Fax 391-3080

Parlin, Middlesex
Old Bridge Township SD
Supt. — See Matawan

Madison Park ES 200/K-5
33 Harvard Rd 08859 732-360-4485
John Daly, prin. Fax 721-4924

Sayreville SD
Supt. — See South Amboy
Arleth ES 400/K-3
3198 Washington Rd 08859 732-525-5244
Robert Preston, prin. Fax 525-5554
Eisenhower ES 500/K-3
601 Ernston Rd 08859 732-525-5229
Dr. Edward Aguiles, prin. Fax 525-5234
Samsel Upper ES 800/4-5
298 Ernston Rd 08859 732-316-4050
Stacey Maher, prin. Fax 727-3716
Sayreville MS 1,300/6-8
800 Washington Rd 08859 732-525-5290
Donna Jakubik, prin. Fax 727-5621
Truman ES 500/K-3
1 Taft Pl 08859 732-525-5214
Timothy Byrne, prin. Fax 727-5563

Parsippany, Morris, Pop. 51,000
Parsippany-Troy Hills Township SD 6,800/PK-12
PO Box 52 07054 973-263-7200
Barbara Sargent, supt. Fax 263-7230
www.pthsd.k12.nj.us
Brooklawn MS 900/6-8
250 Beachwood Rd 07054 973-428-7551
Dr. Natalie Betz, prin. Fax 781-0309
Central MS 700/6-8
1620 US Highway 46 07054 973-263-7125
Mark Gray, prin. Fax 402-1579
Eastlake ES 300/PK-5
40 Eba Rd 07054 973-428-7583
Bryan Hershkowitz, prin. Fax 428-3352
Lake Parsippany ES 300/K-5
225 Kingston Rd 07054 973-428-7572
Steven Linzenbold, prin. Fax 781-0307
Northvail ES 400/K-5
10 Eileen Ct 07054 973-263-7070
Jeff Martens, prin. Fax 316-1086
Rockaway Meadow ES 200/K-5
160 Edwards Rd 07054 973-263-7308
Keith Cortright, prin. Fax 402-1478
Troy Hills ES 300/K-5
509 S Beverwyck Rd 07054 973-428-7588
Renee Brandler, prin. Fax 781-0308
Other Schools – See Boonton, Lake Hiawatha, Morris Plains, Mount Tabor

All Saints Academy 200/PK-8
189 Baldwin Rd 07054 973-334-4704
Judith Berg, prin. Fax 334-0622
Parsippany Christian S 200/PK-12
PO Box 5365 07054 973-539-7012
David Detwiler, admin. Fax 539-2527
St. Elizabeth S 300/PK-K
499 Park Rd 07054 973-540-0721
Sr. Cathy Lynn Cummings, prin. Fax 540-9186

Passaic, Passaic, Pop. 69,000
Passaic CSD 12,700/PK-12
PO Box 388 07055 973-470-5500
Pablo Munoz, supt. Fax 470-8984
www.passaicschools.org/
Capuana K 15 200/PK-K
374 Broadway 07055 973-815-8563
Janet Drago, prin. Fax 815-8568
Cruise Memorial ES 11 1,300/1-6
390 Gregory Ave 07055 973-470-5511
Manuel Negron, prin. Fax 470-5134
Drago ES 3 1,000/PK-6
155 Van Houten Ave 07055 973-470-5503
Diana Kattak, prin. Fax 470-5127
Gero ES 9 700/3-6
140 1st St 07055 973-470-5509
Jason Marx, prin. Fax 470-5132
Grant ES 7 300/PK-1
155 Summer St 07055 973-470-5507
Corey McKinney, prin. Fax 470-5130
Jefferson ES 1 800/PK-6
390 Van Houten Ave 07055 973-470-5501
Karen Fragale, prin. Fax 470-5125
King ES 6 1,300/PK-6
85 Hamilton Ave 07055 973-470-5506
Stacey Barbetta, prin. Fax 470-5129
Lincoln MS 1,800/7-8
291 Lafayette Ave 07055 973-470-5504
Fawzi Naji, prin. Fax 470-5128
Passaic City ES 5 300/K-6
168 Monroe St 07055 973-591-6747
Stefania Portelli, prin. Fax 591-6751
Passaic City K 16 500/PK-K
657 Main Ave 07055 973-815-8516
Dr. Terrence Love, prin. Fax 574-2145
Passaic Gifted & Talented Academy 20 2-8
19 Henry St 07055 973-815-8520
John Mellody, prin.
Pulaski ES 8 500/PK-2
100 4th St 07055 973-470-5508
Rafael Fraguela, prin. Fax 470-8828
Roosevelt ES 10 500/2-6
151 Harrison St 07055 973-470-5510
Steven Cruz, prin. Fax 470-5133
Ryan ES 19 400/2-6
320 Highland Ave 07055 973-779-4019
Gulamhussein Janoowalla, prin. Fax 249-8019
Washington PS 2 200/K-2
48 Bergen St 07055 973-470-5578
Luis Lobello, prin. Fax 470-5126

Noble Leadership Academy 300/PK-12
123 Jefferson St 07055 973-685-2550
St. Nicholas Ukranian Catholic S 100/PK-8
223 President St 07055 973-779-0249
Sr. Eliane Ilnitski, prin. Fax 779-6309
Yeshiva Bais Hillel 500/PK-8
270 Passaic Ave 07055 973-777-0735
Rabbi Berel Leiner, prin. Fax 777-9477

Yeshiva Ktana of Passaic Boys Division 1,000/PK-8
1 Main Ave 07055 973-916-1555
Yeshiva Ktana of Passaic Girls Division 900/PK-8
181 Pennington Ave 07055 973-365-0100
Sharon Schloss, prin. Fax 365-1445

Paterson, Passaic, Pop. 143,991
Paterson SD 23,700/PK-12
90 Delaware Ave 07503 973-321-1000
Dr. Donnie Evans, supt. Fax 321-0470
www.paterson.k12.nj.us
Academy of Gifted & Talented 2-8
200 Presidential Blvd 07522 973-321-0280
Nancy Castro, prin. Fax 321-0287
Awadallah S, 515 Marshall St 07503 K-8
Christine Johnson, prin. 973-413-2600
Bosco Technology Academy 300/7-8
764 11th Ave 07514 973-321-0580
Cecilia O'Toole-Frederic, prin. Fax 321-0587
Clemente ES 300/K-5
434 Rosa Parks Blvd 07501 973-321-0340
Lourdes Rodriguez, prin. Fax 321-0347
Dale Avenue ES 400/PK-2
21 Dale Ave 07505 973-321-0410
Richele Neal, prin. Fax 321-0417
Early Learning Center 100/K-K
660 14th Ave 07504 973-321-0660
Richard Sanducci, admin. Fax 321-0667
Hamilton Academy 500/K-8
11-27 16th Ave 07501 973-321-0320
Virginia Galizia, prin. Fax 321-0327
Kilpatrick ES 300/PK-3
295 Ellison St 07501 973-321-0330
Derrick Hoff, prin. Fax 321-0337
King S 800/K-8
851 E 28th St 07513 973-321-0300
Monica Florez, prin. Fax 321-0307
Madison Early Learning Center PK-PK
512 Market St 07501 973-321-2480
Ramona Garcia, prin.
Napier S of Technology 400/2-8
55 Clinton St 07522 973-321-0040
Marc Medley, prin. Fax 321-0047
Newcomers 100/4-8
482-506 Market Street 07501 973-321-0110
Carlos Ortiz, prin. Fax 321-0117
New Roberto Clemente S 600/6-8
482 Market St 07501 973-321-0240
Hector Montes, prin. Fax 321-0247
Paterson City S 1 300/PK-5
589 11th Ave 07514 973-321-0490
JoAnn Barca, prin. Fax 321-0496
Paterson City S 2 600/K-8
22 Passaic St 07501 973-321-0020
Felisa VanLiew, prin. Fax 321-0027
Paterson City S 3 400/K-8
448 Main St 07501 973-321-0030
Steven Rodriguez, prin. Fax 321-0037
Paterson City S 5 700/K-5
430 Totowa Ave 07502 973-321-0050
Annette Romaniello, prin. Fax 321-0057
Paterson City S 6 400/K-8
137 Carroll St 07501 973-321-0060
Boblyn Dobbs, prin. Fax 321-0067
Paterson City S 7 200/5-8
106 Ramsey St 07501 973-321-0070
Rebecca Cecala, prin. Fax 321-0077
Paterson City S 8 500/K-8
35 Chadwick St 07503 973-321-0080
Sham Bacchus, prin. Fax 321-0087
Paterson City S 9 1,300/PK-8
6 Timothy St 07503 973-321-0090
Domenico Carriero, prin. Fax 321-0097
Paterson City S 10 600/K-8
48 Mercer St 07524 973-321-0100
Lolita Vaughan, prin. Fax 321-0107
Paterson City S 12 600/K-8
121 N 2nd St 07522 973-321-0120
Andre McCollum, prin. Fax 321-0127
Paterson City S 13 600/K-8
690 E 23rd St 07504 973-321-0130
Nicole Booker, prin. Fax 321-0137
Paterson City S 14 200/K-4
522 Union Ave 07522 973-321-0140
Hilburn Sparrow, prin. Fax 321-0147
Paterson City S 15 700/PK-5
98 Oak St 07501 973-321-0150
Ramona Garcia, prin. Fax 321-0157
Paterson City S 16 PK-8
11 22nd Ave 07513
Olga Reyes, prin.
Paterson City S 18 1,100/PK-8
51 E 18th St 07524 973-321-0180
Deyanira Cartegena, prin. Fax 321-0187
Paterson City S 19 400/K-4
31 James St 07502 973-321-0190
Rosalie Bespalko, prin. Fax 321-0197
Paterson City S 20 500/K-8
500 E 37th St 07504 973-321-0200
Boris Simon, prin. Fax 321-0207
Paterson City S 21 700/PK-8
322 10th Ave 07514 973-321-0210
Dr. JoAnne Riviello, prin. Fax 321-0217
Paterson City S 24 900/PK-8
50 19th Ave 07513 973-321-0160
Florita Cotto, prin. Fax 321-0167
Paterson City S 25 700/K-8
287 Trenton Ave 07503 973-321-0250
Dr. Sandra Mickens, prin. Fax 321-0257
Paterson City S 26 600/K-8
1 E 32nd St 07514 973-321-0260
Courtney Glover, prin. Fax 321-0267
Paterson City S 27 700/PK-6
250 Richmond Ave 07502 973-321-0270
Frank Puglise, prin. Fax 321-0277
Paterson City S 28 300/PK-3
200 Presidential Blvd 07522 973-321-0280
Nancy Castro, prin. Fax 321-0287
Paterson City S 29 300/K-4
88 Danforth Ave 07501 973-321-0290
Jorge Ventura, prin. Fax 321-0297
Urban Leadership Academy 100/K-4
112 N 5th St 07522 973-321-2520
Petra Liz-Morel, prin. Fax 321-0178
Weir S 200/K-8
152 College Blvd 07505 973-321-0750
Grace Giglio, prin. Fax 321-0757
Young Men's Leadership Academy 3-6
45 Smith St 07501 973-321-0310
Vernon Maynor, prin.

Madison Avenue Baptist Academy 100/K-12
900 Madison Ave 07501 973-279-5800
St. Gerard Majella S 200/PK-8
10 Carrelton Dr 07522 973-595-5640
Sr. Joann Pompa, prin. Fax 595-5475
Treader Christian S 50/K-8
1 Market St 07501 973-345-9830
Charles Salinas, admin. Fax 345-6668

Paulsboro, Gloucester, Pop. 5,820
Paulsboro SD 1,100/PK-12
662 N Delaware St 08066 856-423-2222
Dr. Laurie Bandlow, supt. Fax 423-4602
www.paulsboro.k12.nj.us
Billingsport ES 300/PK-2
441 Nassau Ave 08066 856-423-2226
Paul Bracciante, prin. Fax 423-8912
Loudenslager ES 300/3-6
100 Baird Ave 08066 856-423-2228
Matthew Browne, prin. Fax 423-8914
Paulsboro JHS 200/7-8
670 N Delaware St 08066 856-423-2222
Mildred Tolbert, prin. Fax 423-8915

Pedricktown, Salem, Pop. 518
Oldmans Township SD 300/PK-8
10 Freed Rd 08067 856-299-4240
Alicia Smith, supt. Fax 299-8182
www.oldmans.org/
Oldmans Township S 300/PK-8
10 Freed Rd 08067 856-299-4240
Alicia Smith, admin. Fax 299-8182

Pemberton, Burlington, Pop. 1,373
Pemberton Township SD 4,900/PK-12
1 Egbert St 08068 609-893-8141
Tony Trongone, supt. Fax 894-0933
www.pemberton.k12.nj.us
Busansky ES 300/3-5
16 Scrapetown Rd 08068 609-893-8141
Maureen DiBella, prin. Fax 894-0545
Emmons ES 400/K-2
14 Scrapetown Rd 08068 609-893-8141
John Schmidt, prin. Fax 894-0544
Fort MS 1,000/7-8
301 Fort Dix Rd 08068 609-893-8141
Tami Strege, prin. Fax 894-9287
Newcomb ES 600/6-6
300 Fort Dix Rd 08068 609-893-8141
Ashley Walulak, prin. Fax 726-1597
Pemberton ECC 500/PK-PK
100 Arneys Mount Rd 08068 609-893-8141
Deb Ceplo, prin. Fax 894-3100
Other Schools – See Browns Mills, Fort Dix

Pennington, Mercer, Pop. 2,560
Hopewell Valley Regional SD 3,600/PK-12
425 S Main St 08534 609-737-4000
Dr. Thomas A. Smith, supt. Fax 737-1418
www.hvrsd.org/
Stony Brook ES 400/PK-5
20 Stephenson Rd 08534 609-737-4006
Steve Wilfing, prin. Fax 730-3888
Timberlane MS 900/6-8
51 Timberlane Dr 08534 609-737-4004
Nicole Gianfredi, prin. Fax 737-2718
Toll Gate Grammar S 300/PK-5
275 S Main St 08534 609-737-4008
Dr. Faye Lewis, prin. Fax 737-7348
Other Schools – See Hopewell, Titusville

Pennsauken, Camden, Pop. 35,900
Pennsauken Township SD 4,600/PK-12
1695 Hylton Rd 08110 856-662-8505
Ronnie Tarchichi Ed.D., supt. Fax 663-5865
www.pennsauken.net
Baldwin Preschool 100/PK-PK
3901 Sharon Ter 08110 856-662-8464
Diane Joyce, prin. Fax 665-4134
Burling ES 100/K-4
3600 Harris Ave 08110 856-662-1923
Christopher Harris, prin. Fax 662-3609
Carson ES 300/PK-4
4150 Garfield Ave 08109 856-662-5751
Diane Joyce, prin. Fax 486-7992
Fine ES 300/PK-4
3800 Gladwyn Ave 08109 856-662-8568
Tonya Harmon, prin. Fax 317-0363
Franklin ES 400/PK-4
7201 Irving Ave 08109 856-662-6455
Landrus Lewis, prin. Fax 662-8469
Longfellow ES 200/K-4
1400 Forrest Ave 08110 856-662-9037
Dana Gery, prin. Fax 317-0366
Pennsauken IS 600/5-6
8125 Park Ave 08109 856-662-8501
Richard Bonkowski, prin. Fax 662-5387
Phifer MS 700/7-8
8201 Park Ave 08109 856-662-8511
Thomas Honeyman, prin. Fax 486-1422
Roosevelt ES 200/K-4
5526 Wisteria Ave 08109 856-662-8141
Lori Massey, prin. Fax 317-0365
Other Schools – See Delair

Luther Christian S 100/PK-8
4106 Terrace Ave 08109 856-665-0231
Elizabeth Mauro, prin. Fax 665-5312
St. Cecilia S 200/K-8
4851 Camden Ave 08110 856-662-0149
Sr. Alicia Perna, prin. Fax 662-7460

Penns Grove, Salem, Pop. 4,982
Penns Grove-Carneys Point Regional SD 2,300/PK-12
100 Iona Ave 08069 856-299-4250
Dr. Zenaida Cobian, supt. Fax 299-5226
pgcpschools.org
Carleton ES 300/4-5
251 E Maple Ave 08069 856-299-1706
Emma Shockley, prin. Fax 299-1545
Penns Grove MS 500/6-8
351 E Maple Ave 08069 856-299-0576
Dr. Luis Amberths, prin. Fax 299-4378
Other Schools – See Carneys Point

Pennsville, Salem, Pop. 11,771
Pennsville Township SD 1,700/PK-12
30 Church St 08070 856-540-6200
Dr. Michael Brodzik, supt. Fax 678-7565
www.psdnet.org
Central Park ES 300/2-3
43 Oliver Ave 08070 856-540-6260
Steve Hindman, prin. Fax 678-4728
Penn Beach ES 300/4-5
96 Kansas Rd 08070 856-540-6250
Mark Zoppina, prin. Fax 678-3924
Pennsville MS 400/6-8
4 William Penn Ave 08070 856-540-6240
Sheila Burris, prin. Fax 678-2908
Valley Park ES 300/PK-1
63 Mahoney Rd 08070 856-540-6255
Bobbie-Ann Jordan, prin. Fax 540-6218

Salem County Christian Academy 200/PK-12
104 Sparks Ave 08070 856-678-9464
Mike Tardive, admin. Fax 678-3696

Pequannock, Morris, Pop. 12,844
Pequannock Township SD
Supt. — See Pompton Plains
Gerace ES 300/K-5
59 Boulevard 07440 973-305-5615
Matthew Reiner, prin. Fax 305-5831

Holy Spirit S 300/PK-8
330 Newark Pompton Tpke 07440 973-835-5680
Sr. Marie Antonelli, prin. Fax 835-1757

Perth Amboy, Middlesex, Pop. 50,388
Perth Amboy SD 9,800/PK-12
178 Barracks St 08861 732-376-6200
Dr. David Roman, supt. Fax 826-1644
www.paps.net
Ceres ES 700/K-4
445 State St 08861 732-376-6020
Derrick Kyriacou, prin. Fax 376-6025
Cruz ECC 700/PK-PK
601 Cortlandt St 08861 732-376-6250
Susan Roque, prin. Fax 376-6255
Flynn ES 900/K-4
850 Chamberlain Ave 08861 732-376-6080
Regina Postogna, prin. Fax 376-6087
Hmieleski ECC 400/PK-PK
925 Amboy Ave 08861 732-376-5460
Dr. Gerarda Mast, prin.
McGinnis MS 1,400/5-8
271 State St 08861 732-376-6040
Dr. Melissa Espana-Rodriguez, prin. Fax 376-6047
Patten ES 900/K-4
500 Charles St 08861 732-376-6050
Michelle Velez-Jonte, prin. Fax 376-6057
Richardson 21st Century S 800/K-4
318 Stockton St 08861 732-376-6010
Edwin Nieves, prin. Fax 376-6016
Shull MS 1,400/5-8
380 Hall Ave 08861 732-376-6060
Dr. Rosario Casiano, prin. Fax 376-6067
Wilentz ES 900/K-4
51 1st St 08861 732-376-6070
Ronald Anderson, prin. Fax 376-6077
Other Schools – See Edison

Assumption Catholic S 200/PK-8
380 Meredith St 08861 732-826-8721
Michael Szpyhulsky, prin. Fax 826-5013
Perth Amboy Catholic PS 100/PK-3
613 Carlock Ave 08861 732-826-5747
Sr. Beverly Policastro, prin. Fax 826-6096
Perth Amboy Catholic Upper S 100/4-8
500 State St 08861 732-826-1598
Sr. Mary Rebecca Piatek, prin. Fax 826-7063

Petersburg, See Woodbine
Upper Township SD 1,300/PK-8
525 Perry Rd 08270 609-628-3500
Vincent Palmieri, supt. Fax 628-2002
upperschools.org
Upper Township MS 500/6-8
525 Perry Rd 08270 609-628-3500
Jeffery Leek, prin. Fax 628-3506
Other Schools – See Marmora

Phillipsburg, Warren, Pop. 14,597
Harmony Township SD 300/PK-8
2551 Belvidere Rd 08865 908-859-1001
Christopher Carrubba, supt. Fax 859-2277
www.htesd.org
Harmony Township S 300/PK-8
2551 Belvidere Rd 08865 908-859-1001
Ryan Bigelli, prin. Fax 859-2277

Lopatcong SD 800/PK-8
321 Stonehenge Dr 08865 908-213-2995
Rainie Roncoroni, supt. Fax 213-1339
www.lopatcongschool.org
Lopatcong ES 400/PK-4
263 State Route 57 08865 908-859-0800
Noelle Kondikoff, prin. Fax 213-1339
Lopatcong MS 400/5-8
321 Stonehenge Dr 08865 908-213-2955
Rick Bonney, prin. Fax 213-0373

Phillipsburg SD 3,100/PK-12
50 Sargent Ave 08865 908-454-3400
Gregory Troxell, supt. Fax 213-2424
www.pburgsd.net/
Phillipsburg Early Childhood Learng Ctr 500/PK-K
459 Center St 08865 908-213-2700
Amy Russo-Farina, prin. Fax 213-2821
Phillipsburg ES, 525 Warren St 08865 300/3-5
John Finken, prin. 908-454-3400
Phillipsburg MS 500/6-8
200 Hillcrest Blvd 08865 908-454-3400
Raffaele LaForgia, prin. Fax 213-2546
Phillipsburg PS, 1000 Green St 08865 200/PK-2
Amy Fontana, prin. 908-454-3400

Pohatcong Township SD 300/K-8
240 County Road 519 08865 908-859-8155
Diane Mandry, supt. Fax 859-8067
www.pohatcong.org/
Pohatcong Township S 300/K-8
240 County Road 519 08865 908-859-8155
Keith Kullman, prin. Fax 859-8067

SS. Philip & James S 200/PK-8
137 Roseberry St 08865 908-859-1244
Donna Kucinski, prin. Fax 859-1202

Pilesgrove, Salem
Woodstown-Pilesgrove Regional SD
Supt. — See Woodstown
Roper ECC, 211 E Lake Rd 08098 100/PK-K
Diane Cioffi, admin. 856-769-0144

Pine Beach, Ocean, Pop. 2,111
Toms River Regional SD
Supt. — See Toms River
Pine Beach ES 400/K-5
101 Pennsylvania Ave 08741 732-505-5870
Tricia Tutzauer, prin. Fax 286-2132

Pine Brook, Morris
Montville Township SD
Supt. — See Montville
Hilldale ES 400/K-5
123 Konner Ave 07058 973-331-3100
Jill Cisneros, prin. Fax 331-4655
Woodmont ES 300/K-5
39 Woodmont Rd 07058 973-331-7100
Dominic Esposito, prin. Fax 882-8361

Pine Hill, Camden, Pop. 9,944
Pine Hill Borough SD 1,800/PK-12
1003 Turnerville Rd 08021 856-783-6900
Dr. Kenneth Koczur, supt. Fax 783-2955
www.pinehill.k12.nj.us
Bean ES 400/PK-5
70 E 3rd Ave 08021 856-783-5300
Daniel Schuster, prin. Fax 741-0377
Glenn ES 400/PK-5
1005 Turnerville Rd 08021 856-783-4100
James Vacca, prin. Fax 741-0347
Pine Hill MS 300/6-8
1100 Turnerville Rd 08021 856-210-0200
Kathleen Klemick, prin. Fax 210-0195

Piscataway, Middlesex, Pop. 48,900
Piscataway Township SD 7,100/PK-12
1515 Stelton Rd 08854 732-572-2289
Teresa Rafferty, supt. Fax 777-1361
www.piscatawayschools.org/
Arbor ES 600/4-5
1717 Lester Pl 08854 732-752-8652
Janelle Williams, prin. Fax 752-8102
Conackamack MS 400/6-8
5205 Witherspoon St 08854 732-699-1577
Donna White, prin. Fax 699-0118
Eisenhower ES 500/K-3
360 Stelton Rd 08854 732-752-1801
Colleen Pongratz, prin. Fax 752-7670
Grandview ES 700/PK-3
130 N Randolphville Rd 08854 732-752-2501
William Baskerville, prin. Fax 752-8101
King ES 500/4-5
5205 Ludlow St 08854 732-699-1563
Dr. Alex Gray, prin. Fax 699-1677
Knollwood ES 500/K-3
333 Willow Ave 08854 732-885-1528
Lisa Parker, prin. Fax 885-5831
Quibbletown MS 500/6-8
99 Academy St 08854 732-752-0444
William Gonzalez, prin. Fax 752-5798
Randolphville ES 600/K-3
1 Suttie Ave 08854 732-699-1573
Dr. Avi Slivko, prin. Fax 699-1985
Schor MS 600/6-8
243 N Randolphville Rd 08854 732-752-4457
Richard Hueston, prin. Fax 424-9445

An-Noor Academy 300/PK-12
1000 Hoes Ln 08854 732-667-5300
Lake Nelson SDA S 100/K-12
555 S Randolphville Rd 08854 732-981-0626
Timothy Christian S 500/PK-12
2008 Ethel Rd 08854 732-985-0300
Dr. Hubert Hartzler, head sch Fax 985-8008
Yeshiva Shaarei Tzion Boys Division 200/K-8
71 Ethel Rd W 08854 732-777-0029
Yeshiva Shaarei Tzion Girls Division 300/PK-8
51 Park Ave 08854 732-235-0042

Pitman, Gloucester, Pop. 8,890
Pitman SD 1,400/PK-12
420 Hudson Ave 08071 856-589-2145
Dr. Patrick McAleer, supt. Fax 582-5465
www.pitman.k12.nj.us
Elwood Kindle ES 200/K-5
211 Washington Ave 08071 856-589-2628
Karolyn Mason, prin.
Memorial ES, 400 Hudson Ave 08071 200/PK-5
Deborah Calabree, prin. 856-589-2526
Pitman MS 300/6-8
138 E Holly Ave 08071 856-589-0636
Kristen Stewart, prin. Fax 589-2289
Walls ES, 320 Grant Ave 08071 200/PK-5
Chris Morris, prin. 856-589-1316

Pittsgrove, Salem
Pittsgrove Township SD 1,700/PK-12
1076 Almond Rd 08318 856-358-3094
Henry Bermann, supt. Fax 358-6020
www.pittsgrove.org
Norma K 200/PK-K
873 Gershal Ave 08318 856-358-6904
Daniel Bruce, prin. Fax 691-2285
Olivet ES 400/3-5
235 Sheep Pen Rd 08318 856-358-2081
Tino Monti, prin. Fax 358-0231
Pittsgrove Township MS 400/6-8
1082 Almond Rd 08318 856-358-8529
Dr. Priscilla Ocasio-Jimenez, prin. Fax 358-2686
Other Schools – See Elmer

Pittstown, Hunterdon
Alexandria Township SD 500/PK-8
557 County Road 513 08867 908-996-6811
Dr. Matthew Jennings, supt. Fax 996-7029
www.alexandriaschools.org
Alexandria MS 300/4-8
557 County Road 513 08867 908-996-6811
Joy Dominic, prin. Fax 996-7963
Wilson ES 200/PK-3
525 County Road 513 08867 908-996-6812
Sandra Kacedon, prin. Fax 996-3163

Plainfield, Union, Pop. 48,849
Plainfield SD 6,800/PK-12
1200 Myrtle Ave 07063 908-731-4335
Dr. Caryn Cooper, supt. Fax 731-4336
www.plainfieldnjk12.org
Barlow ES 400/K-5
2 Farragut Rd 07062 908-731-4300
Wilson Aponte, prin. Fax 731-4294
Cedarbrook S 600/K-8
1049 Central Ave 07060 908-731-4280
Gwynetta Joe, prin. Fax 731-4277
Clinton S 400/PK-8
1302 W 4th St 07063 908-731-4220
Dion Roach, prin. Fax 731-4222
Cook S 300/K-7
739 Leland Ave 07062 908-731-4215
Johan Rojas, prin. Fax 731-4213
Emerson ES 500/PK-5
305 Emerson Ave 07062 908-731-4205
Frank Asante, prin. Fax 731-4206
Evergreen ES 600/K-5
1033 Evergreen Ave 07060 908-731-4260
B.J. Brown, prin. Fax 731-4259
Hubbard MS 400/6-8
661 W 8th St 07060 908-731-4320
Kwame Asante, prin. Fax 731-4315
Jefferson ES 400/PK-5
1750 W Front St 07063 908-731-4250
Telaya Parham, prin. Fax 731-4249
Maxson MS 400/6-8
920 E 7th St 07062 908-731-4310
Dr. Janet Grooms, prin. Fax 731-4306
Stillman ES 300/K-5
201 W 4th St 07060 908-731-4240
Mark Williams, prin. Fax 731-4239
Washington ES 600/PK-5
427 Darrow Ave 07060 908-731-4230
Anthony Jenkins, prin.
Woodland ES 200/PK-5
730 Central St 07062 908-731-4290
Lisa Armstead, prin. Fax 731-4286

Koinonia Academy 200/PK-12
1040 Plainfield Ave 07060 908-668-9002
Lelia Pappas, prin. Fax 668-9883

Plainsboro, Middlesex
West Windsor-Plainsboro Regional SD
Supt. — See West Windsor
Community MS 1,100/6-8
95 Grovers Mill Rd 08536 609-716-5300
Dr. Shauna Carter, prin. Fax 716-5333
Millstone River S 800/4-5
75 Grovers Mill Rd 08536 609-716-5500
Roseann Bonino, prin. Fax 716-5544
Town Center ES 500/PK-2
700 Wyndhurst Dr 08536 609-716-8330
Janet Bowes, prin. Fax 716-5089
Wicoff ES 400/K-3
510 Plainsboro Rd 08536 609-716-5450
Dr. Michael Welborn, prin. Fax 716-5462

Montessori Corner at Princeton Meadows 100/PK-K
666 Plainsboro Rd Bldg 2100 08536 877-959-4105
Montessori Country Day S 100/PK-6
72 Grovers Mill Rd 08536 609-799-7990

Pleasantville, Atlantic, Pop. 19,789
Pleasantville SD 3,800/PK-12
PO Box 960 08232 609-383-6800
Dr. Clarence Alston, supt. Fax 677-8101
www.pps-nj.us/
Decatur Avenue ECC 200/PK-PK
115 W Decatur Ave 08232 609-383-6800
Nanette Stuart, prin.

Leeds Avenue ES 600/PK-5
100 W Leeds Ave 08232 609-383-6800
Howard Johnson, prin. Fax 383-1260
North Main Street ES 400/PK-5
215 N Main St 08232 609-383-6800
Teresa McGaneyGuy, prin. Fax 569-0182
Pleasantville MS 800/6-8
801 Mill Rd 08232 609-383-6800
Rayna Hendricks, prin. Fax 677-0852
South Main Street ES 600/PK-5
701 S Main St 08232 609-383-6800
Felicia Hyman, prin. Fax 407-9125
Washington Avenue ES 400/K-5
225 W Washington Ave 08232 609-383-6800
Cynthia Ruis-Cooper, prin. Fax 383-1796

Point Pleasant, Ocean, Pop. 18,265
Point Pleasant Borough SD 2,900/PK-12
2100 Panther Path 08742 732-701-1900
Vincent Smith, supt. Fax 892-8403
www.pointpleasant.k12.nj.us/
Bennett ES 700/PK-5
2000 Riviera Pkwy 08742 732-701-1900
James Karaba, prin. Fax 892-0981
Memorial MS 700/6-8
808 Laura Herbert Dr 08742 732-701-1900
Gary Floyd, prin. Fax 892-0984
Ocean Road ES 500/PK-5
Benedict St 08742 732-701-1900
Sheila Buck, prin. Fax 892-1056

Pt Pleas Bch, Ocean, Pop. 4,621
Point Pleasant Beach SD 800/PK-12
299 Cooks Ln 08742 732-899-8840
William Smith, supt. Fax 899-1730
ptbeach.com
Antrim S 500/PK-8
401 Niblick St 08742 732-899-3737
Thomas O'Hara, prin. Fax 892-1081

St. Peter S 200/K-8
415 Atlantic Ave 08742 732-892-1260
Tracey Kobrin, prin. Fax 892-3488

Pompton Lakes, Passaic, Pop. 10,956
Pompton Lakes SD 1,600/K-12
237 Van Ave 07442 973-835-1700
Dr. Paul Amoroso, supt. Fax 835-1748
www.plps-k12.org
Lakeside MS 400/6-8
316 Lakeside Ave 07442 973-835-2221
Jake Herninko, prin. Fax 835-8088
Lenox ES 300/K-5
35 Lenox Ave 07442 973-839-3777
Helen Tardif, prin. Fax 839-0793
Lincoln ES 300/K-5
40 Mill St 07442 973-835-1910
Louis Shadiack, prin. Fax 835-2369

St. Mary S 200/PK-8
25 Pompton Ave 07442 973-835-2010
Carol LaSalle, prin. Fax 835-7529

Pompton Plains, Morris
Pequannock Township SD 2,200/PK-12
538 Newark Pompton Tpke 07444 973-616-6040
Brett Charleston, supt. Fax 616-6043
www.pequannock.org
Hillview ES 300/K-5
206 Boulevard 07444 973-616-6080
Michael Portas, prin. Fax 616-5997
North Boulevard ES 300/PK-5
363 Boulevard 07444 973-616-6070
Ted Loeffler, prin. Fax 616-5309
Pequannock Valley MS 600/6-8
493 Newark Pompton Tpke 07444 973-616-6050
Richard Hayzler, prin. Fax 616-8370
Other Schools – See Poquannock

Netherlands Reformed Christian S 200/PK-12
164 Jacksonville Rd 07444 973-628-7400
John VanDerBrink, prin. Fax 628-0461

Port Elizabeth, Cumberland
Maurice River Township SD 400/PK-8
PO Box 464 08348 856-825-7411
Walter Kappeler M.Ed., supt. Fax 825-1248
www.mrtes.com
Maurice River Township S 400/PK-8
PO Box 464 08348 856-825-7411
Walter Kappeler M.Ed., admin. Fax 825-1248

Port Monmouth, Monmouth, Pop. 3,791
Middletown Township SD
Supt. — See Leonardo
Port Monmouth ES, 202 Main St 07758 300/K-5
Maureen McCormack, prin. 732-787-0441
Thorne MS, 70 Murphy Rd 07758 700/6-8
Thomas Olausen, prin. 732-787-1220

Port Murray, Warren, Pop. 128
Mansfield Township SD 700/K-6
50 Port Murray Rd 07865 908-689-3212
Edward Kemp, supt. Fax 689-6576
www.mansfieldelementary.org
Mansfield Township ES 700/K-6
50 Port Murray Rd 07865 908-689-3212
John Melitsky, prin. Fax 689-6576

Port Norris, Cumberland, Pop. 1,319
Commercial Township SD 600/PK-8
1308 North Ave 08349 856-785-0840
Daniel Dooley Ed.D., supt. Fax 785-2354
www.commercial.k12.nj.us
Haleyville-Mauricetown ES 400/PK-5
1308 North Ave 08349 856-785-2333
Daniel Dooley, prin. Fax 785-8120
Port Norris MS 200/6-8
6812 Brown St 08349 856-785-1611
Daniel Dooley, prin. Fax 785-2556

Port Reading, Middlesex, Pop. 3,662
Woodbridge Township SD
Supt. — See Woodbridge
Port Reading ES 400/K-5
77 Turner St 07064 732-602-8409
Patricia Fitzgerald, prin. Fax 541-0195

Port Republic, Atlantic, Pop. 1,107
Port Republic SD 100/K-8
137 Pomona Ave 08241 609-652-7377
Carmine Bonanni, supt. Fax 652-3664
www.portnj.org
Port Republic S 100/K-8
137 Pomona Ave 08241 609-652-7377
John Davis, admin. Fax 652-3664

Princeton, Mercer, Pop. 11,896
Princeton SD 3,400/PK-12
25 Valley Rd 08540 609-806-4220
Stephen Cochrane, supt. Fax 806-4221
www.princetonk12.org
Community Park ES 300/K-5
372 Witherspoon St 08542 609-806-4230
Dineen Gruchacz, prin. Fax 806-4231
Johnson Park ES 300/PK-5
285 Rosedale Rd 08540 609-806-4240
Robert Ginsberg, prin. Fax 806-4241
Littlebrook ES 300/K-5
39 Magnolia Ln 08540 609-806-4250
Annie Kosek, prin. Fax 806-4251
Riverside ES 300/PK-5
58 Riverside Dr 08540 609-806-4260
Valerie Ulrich, prin. Fax 806-4261
Witherspoon MS 700/6-8
217 Walnut Ln 08540 609-806-4270
Jason Burr, prin. Fax 806-4271

Chapin S 300/PK-8
4101 Princeton Pike 08540 609-924-2449
Barbara Pasteris, head sch Fax 924-2364
French American S of Princeton 100/PK-8
75 Mapleton Rd 08540 609-430-3001
Corinne Gungor, head sch Fax 430-0370
Princeton Academy of the Sacred Heart 200/K-8
1128 Great Rd 08540 609-921-6499
Alfred Dugan, hdmstr. Fax 921-9198
Princeton Day S 900/PK-12
PO Box 75 08542 609-924-6700
Paul Stellato, head sch Fax 924-8944
Princeton Friends S 100/PK-8
470 Quaker Rd 08540 609-683-1194
Jane Fremon, head sch Fax 252-0686
Princeton Montessori S 200/PK-8
487 Cherry Valley Rd 08540 609-924-4594
Michelle Morrison, head sch Fax 924-2216
St. Paul S 400/PK-8
218 Nassau St 08542 609-921-7587
Dr. Ryan Killeen, prin. Fax 921-0264
Stuart Country Day S 400/K-12
1200 Stuart Rd 08540 609-921-2330
Dr. Patty Fagin, hdmstr. Fax 497-0784
Waldorf S of Princeton 200/PK-8
1062 Cherry Hill Rd 08540 609-466-1970

Princeton Junction, Mercer, Pop. 2,407
West Windsor-Plainsboro Regional SD
Supt. — See West Windsor
Grover MS 1,200/6-8
10 Southfield Rd 08550 609-716-5250
Lamont Thomas, prin. Fax 716-5270

Wilberforce S 100/PK-12
99 Clarksville Rd 08550 609-924-6111
Howe Whitman, head sch Fax 924-6995

Prospect Park, Passaic, Pop. 5,739
Prospect Park SD 900/PK-8
290 N 8th St 07508 973-720-1981
Allison Angermeyer M.Ed., supt. Fax 720-1992
www.prospectparknj.com/
Prospect Park S 1 900/PK-8
94 Brown Ave 07508 973-790-7909
Catherine D'Arrigo, prin. Fax 790-3635

Al-Hikmah ES 300/PK-6
278 N 8th St 07508 973-790-4700

Quakertown, Hunterdon
Franklin Township SD 300/K-8
PO Box 368 08868 908-735-7929
Dr. Carol Fredericks, supt. Fax 735-0368
www.ftschool.org/
Franklin Township S 300/K-8
PO Box 368 08868 908-735-7929
Carol Fredericks, prin. Fax 735-0368

Quinton, Salem, Pop. 561
Quinton Township SD 300/PK-8
PO Box 365 08072 856-935-2379
Margaret M. Delia, supt. Fax 935-1978
quinton.nj.schoolwebpages.com
Quinton Township S 300/PK-8
PO Box 365 08072 856-935-2379
Stewart Potter, prin. Fax 935-1978

Rahway, Union, Pop. 26,740
Rahway SD 3,600/PK-12
1138 Kline Pl 07065 732-396-1000
Patricia Camp Ph.D., supt. Fax 396-1391
www.rahway.net
Cleveland ES 500/PK-6
486 E Milton Ave 07065 732-396-1040
Al Giambrone, prin. Fax 396-2636
Franklin ES 600/PK-6
1809 Saint Georges Ave 07065 732-396-1050
Fran Gavin, prin. Fax 396-2638
Madison ES 300/PK-6
944 Madison Ave 07065 732-396-1070
Arina Robinson, prin. Fax 396-2641
Rahway 7th & 8th Grade Academy 500/7-8
1138 Kline Pl 07065 732-396-1025
Alan Johnson, prin. Fax 396-2633
Roosevelt ES 500/PK-6
811 Saint Georges Ave 07065 732-396-1060
Dr. Cary Fields, prin. Fax 396-2643

Ramsey, Bergen, Pop. 14,315
Ramsey SD 2,900/PK-12
266 E Main St 07446 201-785-2300
Dr. Matthew Murphy Ed.D., supt. Fax 934-6623
www.ramsey.k12.nj.us
Dater IS 400/4-5
35 School St 07446 201-785-2325
Dr. Molly Dinning, prin. Fax 785-2333
Hubbard ES 400/PK-3
10 Hubbard Ln 07446 201-785-2301
Kathy Pina, prin. Fax 785-2311
Smith MS 700/6-8
2 Monroe St 07446 201-785-2313
Andrew Herre, prin. Fax 785-2320
Tisdale ES 400/PK-3
200 Island Ave 07446 201-785-2336
Gina Aliano, prin. Fax 785-2344

Academy of St. Paul 200/K-8
187 Wyckoff Ave 07446 201-327-1108
Gail Ritchie, prin. Fax 236-1318

Randolph, Morris, Pop. 19,974
Randolph Township SD 4,900/PK-12
25 Schoolhouse Rd 07869 973-361-0808
Jennifer Fano, supt. Fax 361-2405
www.rtnj.org
Center Grove ES 500/PK-5
25 Schoolhouse Rd 07869 973-361-7835
Mario Rodas, prin. Fax 328-4705
Fernbrook ES 600/K-5
206 Quaker Church Rd 07869 973-361-0660
Dr. Michele Telischak, prin. Fax 328-4707
Ironia ES 500/K-5
303 Dover Chester Rd 07869 973-584-8588
David Kricheff, prin. Fax 927-5791
Randolph MS 1,300/6-8
507 Millbrook Ave 07869 973-366-8700
Dr. Dennis Copeland Ed.D., prin. Fax 361-6501
Shongum ES 500/K-5
9 Arrow Pl 07869 973-895-2322
Dr. Clifford Burns, prin. Fax 328-4708

Gottesman RTW Academy 200/PK-8
146 Dover Chester Rd 07869 973-584-5530

Raritan, Somerset, Pop. 6,746
Bridgewater-Raritan Regional SD
Supt. — See Martinsville
Kennedy PS 400/K-4
255 Woodmere St 08869 908-231-1179
Joseph Walsh, prin. Fax 231-1050

St. Ann S 200/PK-8
29 2nd Ave 08869 908-725-7787
Sr. Mary Klersey, prin. Fax 541-9335

Red Bank, Monmouth, Pop. 11,983
Middletown Township SD
Supt. — See Leonardo
Fairview ES, 230 Cooper Rd 07701 300/K-5
Michael Melando, prin. 732-747-3308
River Plaza ES 300/K-5
155 Hubbard Ave 07701 732-747-3679
David Whitman, prin.

Red Bank Borough SD 1,100/PK-8
76 Branch Ave 07701 732-758-1507
Dr. Jared Rumage, supt. Fax 212-1356
www.rbb.k12.nj.us
Red Bank MS 500/4-8
101 Harding Rd 07701 732-758-1500
Maria Iozzi, prin. Fax 758-1518
Red Bank PS 600/PK-3
222 River St 07701 732-758-1500
Luigi Laugelli, prin. Fax 758-0172

St. James S 600/PK-8
30 Peters Pl 07701 732-741-3363
JoAnn Giordano, prin. Fax 933-4960

Richland, Atlantic
Buena Regional SD 2,000/PK-12
914 Main Ave 08350 856-697-0800
Mary Lou DeFrancisco, supt. Fax 697-4963
www.buena.k12.nj.us
Other Schools – See Buena, Minotola, Williamstown

Ridgefield, Bergen, Pop. 10,875
Ridgefield SD 1,500/1-12
555 Chestnut St 07657 201-945-9236
Dr. Frank Romano, supt. Fax 945-7830
www.ridgefieldschools.com
Bergen Boulevard ES 200/1-2
635 Bergen Blvd 07657 201-943-1909
Dr. Tamika DePass, prin. Fax 943-8397
Slocum/Skewes ES 700/3-8
650 Prospect Ave 07657 201-943-4299
Gerard Bellizzi, prin. Fax 943-9527

Ridgefield Park, Bergen, Pop. 12,530
Ridgefield Park SD 1,900/PK-12
712 Lincoln Ave 07660 201-641-0800
Eric Koenig, supt. Fax 641-2203
www.rpps.net
Grant ES 200/2-6
104 Henry St 07660 201-641-0441
Angela Bender, prin. Fax 440-9579
Jefferson ECC PK-1
110 Mount Vernon St 07660 201-336-9855
Matthew Perrapato, prin. Fax 336-9858
Lincoln ES 300/2-6
712 Lincoln Ave 07660 201-994-1830
Tom Kraljic, prin. Fax 994-1626
Roosevelt ES 300/2-6
508 Teaneck Rd 07660 201-440-0808
Mike Alberque, prin. Fax 440-9573

Ridgewood, Bergen, Pop. 24,497
Ridgewood Village SD 5,600/PK-12
49 Cottage Pl 07450 201-670-2700
Dr. Daniel Fishbein, supt. Fax 670-2668
www.ridgewood.k12.nj.us
Franklin MS 700/6-8
335 N Van Dien Ave 07450 201-670-2780
Anthony Orsini, prin. Fax 670-3382
Glen ECC, 865 E Glen Ave 07450 50/PK-PK
Karen Price, prin. 201-251-3140
Hawes ES, 531 Stevens Ave 07450 400/K-5
Dr. Paul Semendinger, prin. 201-670-2720
Orchard ES 300/K-5
230 Demarest St 07450 201-670-2730
Mary Ferreri, prin. Fax 670-2879
Ridge ES 500/K-5
325 W Ridgewood Ave 07450 201-670-2740
Jean Schoenlank, prin. Fax 670-2877
Somerville ES 500/K-5
45 S Pleasant Ave 07450 201-670-2750
Dr. Lorna Oates-Santos, prin. Fax 670-3381
Travell ES, 340 Bogert Ave 07450 300/K-5
Dr. Margy Leininger, prin. 201-670-2760
Washington MS 700/6-8
155 Washington Pl 07450 201-670-2790
Dr. Katie Kashmanian, prin. Fax 670-3290
Willard ES 500/K-5
601 Morningside Rd 07450 201-670-2770
Caroline Hoffman, prin. Fax 670-3207

Ringoes, Hunterdon
East Amwell Township SD 400/PK-8
PO Box 680 08551 908-782-6464
Edward Stoloski, supt. Fax 782-8529
www.eastamwell.org
East Amwell Township S 400/PK-8
PO Box 680 08551 908-782-6464
John Capuano, prin. Fax 782-8529

Flemington-Raritan Regional SD
Supt. — See Flemington
Copper Hill ES 500/PK-4
100 Everitts Rd 08551 908-284-7660
Kevin McPeek, prin. Fax 284-7671

Ringwood, Passaic, Pop. 11,996
Ringwood SD 1,200/K-8
121 Carletondale Rd 07456 973-962-7028
Dr. Nicholas Bernice, supt. Fax 962-9211
www.ringwoodschools.org/
Cooper ES 200/K-3
54 Roger Ct 07456 973-835-5844
Timothy Johnson, prin. Fax 835-0986
Erskine ES 200/K-3
88 Erskine Rd 07456 973-962-7026
Gregg Festa, prin. Fax 962-9186
Hewitt IS 300/4-5
266 Sloatsburg Rd 07456 973-962-7015
Nancy Dondero, prin. Fax 962-6963
Ryerson MS 400/6-8
130 Valley Rd 07456 973-962-7063
Paul Scutti, prin. Fax 962-6905

St. Catherine of Bologna S 300/PK-8
112 Erskine Rd 07456 973-962-7131
Sr. Theresa Firenze, prin. Fax 962-0585

Riverdale, Morris, Pop. 3,501
Riverdale Borough SD 300/PK-8
52 Newark Pompton Tpke 07457 973-839-1300
Vicki Pede, supt. Fax 839-8856
www.rpsnj.org
Riverdale S 300/PK-8
52 Newark Pompton Tpke 07457 973-839-1300
Sean Bowe, prin. Fax 839-8856

River Edge, Bergen, Pop. 11,204
River Dell Regional SD 1,600/7-12
230 Woodland Ave 07661 201-599-7200
Patrick Fletcher, supt. Fax 261-3809
www.riverdell.org/
River Dell MS 600/7-8
230 Woodland Ave 07661 201-599-7250
Richard Freedman, prin. Fax 599-2202

River Edge SD 1,200/PK-6
410 Bogert Rd 07661 201-261-3404
Dr. Tova Ben-Dov, supt. Fax 261-0698
www.riveredgeschools.org
Cherry Hill ES 500/1-6
410 Bogert Rd 07661 201-261-3405
Denise Heitman, prin. Fax 986-1256
New Bridge Center 200/PK-K
101 Greene Ave 07661 201-261-5620
Fax 261-1052
Roosevelt ES 400/1-6
711 Summit Ave 07661 201-261-1546
Michael Henzel, prin. Fax 261-0798

Rosenbaum Yeshiva of North Jersey 900/PK-8
666 Kinderkamack Rd 07661 201-986-1414
St. Peter Academy 200/PK-8
431 5th Ave 07661 201-261-3468
James McCarthy, prin. Fax 261-4316

Riverside, Burlington, Pop. 7,974
Riverside Township SD 1,400/PK-12
112 E Washington St 08075 856-461-1255
Robin A. Ehrich, supt. Fax 461-5168
www.riverside.k12.nj.us
Riverside ES 700/PK-5
112 E Washington St 08075 856-461-1255
Scott Shumway, prin. Fax 461-1674

Riverside MS 300/6-8
112 E Washington St 08075 856-461-1255
Michael W. Mongon, prin. Fax 461-0182

Riverton, Burlington, Pop. 2,729
Riverton Borough SD 300/PK-8
600 5th St 08077 856-829-0087
Mary Ellen Eck, supt. Fax 829-5317
www.riverton.k12.nj.us
Riverton S 300/PK-8
600 5th St 08077 856-829-0087
Mary Ellen Eck, prin. Fax 829-5317

River Vale, Bergen, Pop. 9,410
River Vale SD 1,200/K-8
609 Westwood Ave 07675 201-358-4000
Rory McCourt, supt. Fax 358-8319
www.rivervaleschools.com/
Holdrum MS 500/6-8
393 Rivervale Rd 07675 201-358-4016
James Cody, prin. Fax 358-8427
Roberge ES 400/K-5
617 Westwood Ave 07675 201-358-4006
Stephen Wren, prin.
Woodside ES 400/K-5
801 Rivervale Rd 07675 201-358-4028
Melissa Signore, prin. Fax 358-8335

Robbinsville, Mercer, Pop. 2,974
Robbinsville SD 2,600/PK-12
155 Robbinsville Edinburg 08691 609-632-0910
Dr. Kathleen Foster, supt. Fax 371-7964
www.robbinsville.k12.nj.us
Pond Road MS 900/5-8
150 Pond Rd 08691 609-632-0940
Paul Gizzo, prin. Fax 918-9011
Sharon ES 800/PK-4
234 Sharon Rd 08691 609-632-0960
Janet Sinkewicz, prin. Fax 259-7506

Rochelle Park, Bergen, Pop. 5,587
Rochelle Park SD 500/PK-8
300 Rochelle Ave 07662 201-843-3120
Geoffrey Zoeller, supt. Fax 843-5358
rp.bergen.org
Midland S 1 500/PK-8
300 Rochelle Ave 07662 201-843-3120
Brian Cannici, prin. Fax 843-5358

Rockaway, Morris, Pop. 6,360
Rockaway Borough SD 600/PK-8
103 E Main St 07866 973-625-8600
Phyllis Alpaugh, supt. Fax 625-7355
www.rockboro.org/
Jefferson MS, 95 E Main St 07866 400/4-8
David Waxman, prin. 973-625-8603
Lincoln ES, 37 Keller Ave 07866 300/PK-3
Milissa Dachisen, prin. 973-625-8602

Rockaway Township SD
Supt. — See Hibernia
Copeland MS 900/6-8
100 Lake Shore Dr 07866 973-627-2465
Alfonso Gonnella, prin. Fax 983-1843
Malone ES 200/K-5
524 Green Pond Rd 07866 973-627-7512
Melissa Lewis, prin. Fax 627-1729
Stony Brook ES 300/K-5
44 Stony Brook Rd 07866 973-627-2411
Stephen J. Wisniewski, prin. Fax 627-1689

Divine Mercy Academy 200/PK-8
87 Halsey Ave 07866 973-627-6003
Ann Mitchell, prin. Fax 627-5217

Roebling, Burlington, Pop. 3,618
Florence Township SD
Supt. — See Florence
Roebling ES 500/K-3
1330 Hornberger Ave 08554 609-499-4640
Christopher Butler, prin. Fax 499-4664

Roosevelt, Monmouth, Pop. 864
Roosevelt Borough SD 100/PK-6
PO Box 160 08555 609-448-2798
Mary Cohen, supt. Fax 448-2681
www.rps1.org
Roosevelt ES 100/PK-6
PO Box 160 08555 609-448-2798
Mary Cohen, prin. Fax 448-2681

Roseland, Essex, Pop. 5,768
Roseland SD 400/K-6
100 Passaic Ave 07068 973-226-7644
Dr. Deanne Somers, supt. Fax 226-7630
www.roselandnjboe.org
Noecker ES 400/K-6
100 Passaic Ave 07068 973-226-7644
Robyn Greenwald, prin. Fax 226-7630

Roselle, Union, Pop. 20,670
Roselle SD 2,600/PK-12
710 Locust St 07203 908-298-2040
Richard Corbett, supt. Fax 298-3353
www.roselleschools.org
Harrison ES 300/1-4
310 Harrison Ave 07203 908-298-2052
Dr. Lissette Gonzalez-Perez, prin. Fax 298-3371
Kindergarten Success Academy 200/K-K
150 E 3rd Ave 07203 908-298-2040
Dr. Nathan Fisher, prin. Fax 259-5602
Moore MS 400/5-6
720 Locust St 07203 908-298-2047
Craig Messmer, prin. Fax 298-3333
Polk ES 300/1-4
1100 Warren St 07203 908-298-2061
Andreea Harry, prin. Fax 298-3381
Roselle Preschool Annex 100/PK-PK
1305 Saint George Ave 07203 908-298-2040
Angela Robinson, supt. Fax 241-4530

Washington ES 300/1-4
501 W 5th Ave 07203 908-298-2072
Marianne Tankard, prin. Fax 298-9450
Wilday JHS 400/7-8
400 Brooklawn Ave 07203 908-298-2066
Erik Leite, prin. Fax 298-2068

St. Joseph the Carpenter S 300/PK-8
140 E 3rd Ave 07203 908-245-6560
Patrick Mullen, prin. Fax 245-3342

Roselle Park, Union, Pop. 13,111
Roselle Park SD 1,900/K-12
510 Chestnut St 07204 908-245-1197
Pedro Garrido, supt. Fax 245-1226
www.rpsd.org/
Finizio-Aldene ES 200/K-5
339 W Webster Ave 07204 908-245-1521
Sloan Scully, prin. Fax 245-5168
Gordon ES 200/K-5
59 W Grant Ave 07204 908-245-2285
Frances Kenny, prin. Fax 245-4574
Roselle Park MS 500/6-8
57 W Grant Ave 07204 908-245-1634
Kathleen Carlin, prin. Fax 245-7491
Sherman ES 300/K-5
375 E Grant Ave 07204 908-245-1886
Donna Glomb, prin. Fax 245-4741

Rosenhayn, Cumberland, Pop. 1,051
Deerfield Township SD 300/PK-8
PO Box 375 08352 856-451-6610
Mary Steinhauer-Kula, supt. Fax 451-6720
www.deerfield.k12.nj.us
Deerfield Township S 300/PK-8
PO Box 375 08352 856-451-6610
Mary Steinhauer-Kula, admin. Fax 451-6720

Rumson, Monmouth, Pop. 7,054
Rumson Borough SD 1,000/PK-8
60 Forrest Ave 07760 732-842-4747
Dr. John Bormann, supt. Fax 842-4877
www.rumsonschool.org/
Deane-Porter ES 400/PK-3
50 Black Point Rd 07760 732-842-0330
Shari Feeney, prin. Fax 212-0843
Forrestdale MS 600/4-8
60 Forrest Ave 07760 732-842-0383
Jennifer Gibbons, prin. Fax 219-9458

Holy Cross S 400/PK-8
40 Rumson Rd 07760 732-842-0348
Dr. Mark DeMareo, prin. Fax 741-3134
Rumson Country Day S 400/PK-8
35 Bellevue Ave 07760 732-842-0527
Jayne Geiger, head sch Fax 758-6528

Runnemede, Camden, Pop. 8,357
Runnemede Borough SD 800/PK-8
505 W 3rd Ave 08078 856-931-5365
Mark Iannucci, supt. Fax 931-4446
www.runnemedeschools.org/
Bingham ES, 100 Orchard Ave 08078 200/K-3
Jade Yezzi, prin. 856-939-3192
Downing ES, 100 E 3rd Ave 08078 200/K-3
Jade Yezzi, prin. 856-939-4036
Volz MS 500/PK-PK, 4-
505 W 3rd Ave 08078 856-931-5353
Steve Pili, prin. Fax 931-1827

St. Teresa Regional S 200/PK-8
27 E Evesham Rd 08078 856-939-0333
Sr. Nancy Kindelan, prin. Fax 939-1204

Rutherford, Bergen, Pop. 17,647
Rutherford SD, 176 Park Ave 07070 2,000/PK-12
John Hurley, supt. 201-438-7675
www.rutherfordschools.org
Lincoln ES 400/PK-3
414 Montross Ave 07070 201-438-7675
Jeanna Velechko, prin. Fax 438-4915
Pierrepont S 300/4-6
70 E Pierrepont Ave 07070 201-438-7675
Joan Carrion, prin. Fax 842-0452
Union MS 200/7-8
359 Union Ave 07070 201-438-7675
Kurt Schweitzer, prin. Fax 804-8248
Washington ES 300/PK-PK, 1-
89 Wood St 07070 201-438-7675
William Mulcahy, prin. Fax 438-5386

Academy at St. Mary 300/PK-8
72 Chestnut St 07070 201-933-8410
Ana Castaneda, prin. Fax 531-9020

Saddle Brook, Bergen, Pop. 13,296
Saddle Brook Township SD 1,600/K-12
355 Mayhill St 07663 201-843-2880
Anthony Riscica, supt. Fax 843-0216
www.saddlebrookschools.org
Franklin ES 300/K-6
95 Caldwell Ave 07663 201-843-8664
Toni Violetti, prin. Fax 843-3231
Long Memorial ES 300/K-6
260 Floral Ln 07663 201-796-6250
Jaynellen Jenkins, prin. Fax 796-1671
Smith ES 300/K-6
30 Cambridge Ave 07663 201-796-6650
Deborah Wunder, prin. Fax 796-0665

Saddle River, Bergen, Pop. 3,086
Saddle River SD 200/PK-5
97 E Allendale Rd 07458 201-327-0727
Louis DeLisio, supt. Fax 327-0704
www.wandellschool.org
Wandell ES 200/PK-5
97 E Allendale Rd 07458 201-327-0727
Louis DeLisio, prin. Fax 327-0704

Saddle River Day S 300/PK-12
147 Chestnut Ridge Rd 07458 201-327-4050
Eileen Lambert, head sch Fax 327-6161

Salem, Salem, Pop. 4,985
Elsinboro Township SD 100/K-8
631 Salem Fort Elfsborg Rd 08079 856-935-3817
Constance McAllister, admin. Fax 935-6944
www.elsinboroschool.org
Elsinboro Township S 100/K-8
631 Salem Fort Elfsborg Rd 08079 856-935-3817
Constance McAllister, prin. Fax 935-6944

Lower Alloways Creek SD 200/PK-8
967 Main St 08079 856-935-2707
Dr. Phillip Neff, supt. Fax 935-9673
lacschool.org
Lower Alloways Creek S 200/PK-8
967 Main St 08079 856-935-2707
Dr. Philli Neff, admin. Fax 935-9673

Mannington Township SD 200/PK-8
495 Route 45 08079 856-935-1078
Kristin Williams, supt. Fax 935-3747
www.manningtonschool.org/
Mannington Township S 200/PK-8
495 Route 45 08079 856-935-1078
Kristin Williams, admin. Fax 935-3747

Salem CSD 1,200/PK-12
205 Walnut St 08079 856-935-3800
Dr. Amiot Michel, supt. Fax 935-6977
www.salemnj.org
Fenwick ES 400/PK-2
183 Smith St 08079 856-935-4100
Syeda Woods, prin. Fax 935-1252
Salem MS 400/3-8
51 New Market St 08079 856-935-2700
Pascale DeVilme, prin. Fax 935-2284

Sayreville, Middlesex, Pop. 41,808
Sayreville SD
Supt. — See South Amboy
Wilson ES 400/K-3
65 Dane St 08872 732-525-5239
Carmen Davis, prin. Fax 698-9529

Our Lady of Victories S 200/PK-8
36 Main St 08872 732-254-1676
Rosalind Esemplare, prin. Fax 254-5066
St. Stanislaus Kostka S 200/PK-8
221 MacArthur Ave 08872 732-254-5819
Elena Malinconico, prin. Fax 254-7220

Scotch Plains, Union, Pop. 21,160
Scotch Plains-Fanwood SD 5,400/PK-12
2280 Evergreen Ave 07076 908-232-6161
Dr. Margaret Hayes, supt. Fax 889-1769
www.spfk12.org
Brunner ES 400/PK-4
721 Westfield Rd 07076 908-889-2148
Scott Bortnick, prin. Fax 889-4718
Coles ES 500/PK-4
16 Kevin Rd 07076 908-757-7555
Dr. Karen Wetherell, prin. Fax 561-1840
Evergreen ES 400/PK-4
2280 Evergreen Ave 07076 908-889-5331
Colleen Haubert, prin. Fax 889-9332
McGinn ES 500/K-4
1100 Roosevelt Ave 07076 908-233-7950
Dr. Sasha Slocum, prin. Fax 233-6766
Park MS 900/5-8
580 Park Ave 07076 908-322-4445
Dr. Jocelyn Dumaresq, prin. Fax 561-5929
School One 400/PK-4
563 Willow Ave 07076 908-322-7731
Justin Fiory, prin. Fax 322-7142
Terrill MS 800/5-8
1301 Terrill Rd 07076 908-322-5215
Dr. Kevin Holloway, prin. Fax 322-6813

St. Bartholomew Academy 200/PK-8
2032 Westfield Ave 07076 908-322-4265
Sr. Elizabeth Calello, prin. Fax 322-7065

Seabrook, Cumberland, Pop. 1,405
Upper Deerfield Township SD 900/PK-8
1385 Highway 77 08302 856-455-2267
Dr. Peter Koza Ed.D., supt. Fax 453-7077
www.udts.org
Moore ES 200/4-5
1361 Highway 77 08302 856-455-2267
Dr. Lindsay McCarron, prin. Fax 451-0670
Seabrook ES 400/PK-3
1373 Highway 77 08302 856-455-2267
Stephen Wilchensky, prin. Fax 451-1930
Woodruff MS 300/6-8
1385 Highway 77 08302 856-455-2267
Harold Hill, prin. Fax 453-7077

Sea Girt, Monmouth, Pop. 1,820
Sea Girt Borough SD 200/PK-8
451 Bell Pl 08750 732-449-3422
Rick Papera, supt. Fax 449-1204
www.seagirt.k12.nj.us
Sea Girt S 200/PK-8
451 Bell Pl 08750 732-449-3422
Rick Papera, prin. Fax 449-1204

Wall Township SD
Supt. — See Wall
Old Mill ES 400/K-5
2119 Old Mill Rd 08750 732-556-2140
Eric Laughlin, prin. Fax 449-4260

Brookside S 200/PK-8
2135 Highway 35 08750 732-449-4747

Seaside Heights, Ocean, Pop. 2,804
Seaside Heights Borough SD 200/PK-6
1200 Bay Blvd 08751 732-793-8485
Dr. Tom Parlapanides, supt. Fax 793-5874
www.sshschool.org
Boyd ES 200/PK-6
1200 Bay Blvd 08751 732-793-8485
Chris Raichle, prin. Fax 793-5874

Secaucus, Hudson, Pop. 15,983
Secaucus SD 1,900/PK-12
PO Box 1496 07096 201-974-2000
Kenneth Knops, supt. Fax 614-0197
www.sboe.org
Clarendon ES 500/K-5
685 5th St 07094 201-974-2010
Steve Viggiani, prin. Fax 974-0530
Huber Street ES 600/PK-5
1520 Paterson Plank Rd 07094 201-974-2053
Linda Wilhelm, prin. Fax 974-0626
Secaucus MS 300/6-8
11 Millridge Rd 07094 201-974-2025
Robert Valente, prin. Fax 974-0275

Sergeantsville, Hunterdon
Delaware Township SD 400/PK-8
PO Box 1000 08557 609-397-3179
Dr. Richard Wiener, supt. Fax 397-0057
www.dtsk8.org
Delaware Township S 400/PK-8
PO Box 1000 08557 609-397-3179
Dr. Richard Weiner, supt. Fax 397-1485

Sewaren, Middlesex, Pop. 2,718
Woodbridge Township SD
Supt. — See Woodbridge
Jago ES 300/K-5
99 Central Ave 07077 732-602-8428
Robert Patten, prin. Fax 855-0826

Sewell, Gloucester
Deptford Township SD
Supt. — See Deptford
Monongahela MS 600/7-8
890 Bankbridge Rd 08080 856-415-9540
Arthur Dietz, prin. Fax 464-9284

Mantua Township SD 1,200/PK-6
684 Main St 08080 856-468-2225
Dr. Robert Fisicaro, supt. Fax 468-5563
www.mantuaschools.com
Sewell ES 200/K-3
40 McAnally Dr 08080 856-468-0626
Jennifer Connell, prin. Fax 468-7130
Other Schools – See Mantua

Washington Township SD 7,400/PK-12
206 E Holly Ave 08080 856-589-6644
Joseph Bollendorf, supt. Fax 582-1918
www.wtps.org
Bunker Hill MS 700/6-8
372 Pitman Downer Rd 08080 856-881-7007
Dr. Joseph Vandenberg, prin. Fax 881-5414
Chestnut Ridge MS 600/6-8
641 Hurffville Crosskeys Rd 08080 856-582-3535
James Barnes, prin. Fax 589-0683
Grenloch Terrace ECC 400/PK-K
251 Woodbury Turnersville 08080 856-227-1303
Wendy Crawford, prin. Fax 227-8207
Hurffville ES 500/1-5
200 Hurffville Grenloch Rd 08080 856-589-7459
Jeffery Pollock, prin. Fax 589-6909
Orchard Valley MS 600/6-8
238 Pitman Downer Rd 08080 856-582-5353
Colleen McLaughlin, prin. Fax 589-0197
Wedgwood ES 400/1-5
236 Hurffville Rd 08080 856-227-8110
Charles Zimmerman, prin. Fax 227-8163
Other Schools – See Turnersville

Gloucester County Christian S 400/PK-12
151 Golf Club Rd 08080 856-589-1665

Shamong Township, Burlington, Pop. 5,765
Shamong Township SD 800/PK-8
295 Indian Mills Rd 08088 609-268-0120
Christine Vespe Ed.D., supt. Fax 268-1229
www.shamongschools.org
Indian Mills ES 400/PK-4
112 Indian Mills Rd 08088 609-268-0220
Nicole Moore, prin. Fax 268-9535
Indian Mills Memorial MS 400/5-8
295 Indian Mills Rd 08088 609-268-0440
Timothy Carroll, prin. Fax 268-1229

Ship Bottom, Ocean, Pop. 1,151
Long Beach Island SD 200/PK-6
201 20th St 08008 609-494-8851
Megan Gally, admin. Fax 494-2921
www.lbischools.org
Long Beach Island ES 100/3-6
201 20th St 08008 609-494-8851
Peter Kopack, prin. Fax 494-8035
Other Schools – See Surf City

Short Hills, Essex, Pop. 12,919
Millburn Township SD
Supt. — See Millburn
Deerfield ES 600/PK-4
26 Troy Ln 07078 973-379-4843
Kelly Salazar, prin. Fax 912-4456
Glenwood ES 500/K-4
325 Taylor Rd S 07078 973-379-7576
Dr. David Jasin, prin. Fax 912-4497
Hartshorn ES 500/K-4
400 Hartshorn Dr 07078 973-379-7550
Kenneth Frattini, prin. Fax 912-5205

Far Brook S 200/PK-8
52 Great Hills Rd 07078 973-379-3442
Amy Ziebarth, hdmstr. Fax 379-9237

Montessori Children's Academy 200/PK-8
200 Hartshorn Dr 07078 973-258-1400
Jessica DeJong, dir. Fax 258-1430
Pingry S 300/K-5
50 Country Day Dr 07078 973-379-4550
Nathaniel Conard, hdmstr. Fax 379-1861
St. Rose of Lima Academy 200/PK-8
52 Short Hills Ave 07078 973-379-3973
Tina Underwood, prin. Fax 379-3722

Shrewsbury, Monmouth, Pop. 3,774
Shrewsbury Borough SD 500/K-8
20 Obre Pl 07702 732-747-0882
Brent MacConnell, supt. Fax 747-7510
www.sbs.k12.nj.us
Shrewsbury S 500/K-8
20 Obre Pl 07702 732-747-0882
Brent MacConnell, prin. Fax 747-7510

Mastro Montessori 100/PK-6
35 White Rd 07702 732-219-5400

Sicklerville, Camden
Gloucester Township SD
Supt. — See Blackwood
Lilley ES 500/PK-5
1275 Williamstown Erial Rd 08081 856-875-0991
Angela Rose-Bounds, prin. Fax 728-3028
Mullen MS 900/6-8
1400 Sicklerville Rd 08081 856-875-8777
Edmund Cetrullo, prin. Fax 875-0902
Union Valley ES 500/PK-5
1300 Jarvis Rd 08081 856-309-5031
Tracey Elwell, prin. Fax 309-5193

Winslow Township SD
Supt. — See Atco
Winslow Township ES 2 300/PK-3
125 1st Ave 08081 609-561-8450
Kimara Ramsey, prin. Fax 704-1024
Winslow Township ES 3 400/PK-3
131 Sicklerville Rd 08081 856-728-1080
Tamika Floyd, prin. Fax 875-5147
Winslow Township ES 4 500/PK-3
541 Kali Rd 08081 856-728-2440
Sheresa Clement, prin. Fax 875-5401
Winslow Township Upper ES 6 500/4-6
617 Sickler Ave 08081 856-875-4110
Glen Jackson, prin. Fax 875-8052

Skillman, Somerset, Pop. 236
Montgomery Township SD 4,700/PK-12
1014 Route 601 08558 609-466-7600
Nancy Gartenberg, supt. Fax 466-0944
www.mtsd.k12.nj.us
Montgomery Lower MS 800/5-6
373 Burnt Hill Rd 08558 609-466-7604
Michael Richards, prin. Fax 874-4857
Montgomery Upper MS 800/7-8
375 Burnt Hill Rd 08558 609-466-7604
Cory Delgado, prin. Fax 874-7045
Orchard Hill ES 800/PK-2
244 Orchard Rd 08558 609-466-7605
Kathleen Scotti, prin. Fax 359-1126
Village ES 600/3-4
100 Main Blvd 08558 609-466-7606
Susan Lacy, prin. Fax 466-7196

Somerdale, Camden, Pop. 5,010
Somerdale Borough SD 500/PK-8
301 Grace St 08083 856-783-6261
Dr. Dennis M. Vespe, supt. Fax 783-2607
www.somerdale-park.org
Somerdale Park S 500/PK-8
301 Grace St 08083 856-783-6261
Dr. Dennis M. Vespe, prin. Fax 783-2607

Somerset, Somerset, Pop. 21,468
Franklin Township SD 7,400/PK-12
1755 Amwell Rd 08873 732-873-2400
Dr. John Ravally, supt.
www.franklinboe.org
Conerly Road ES 400/PK-4
35 Conerly Rd 08873 732-249-9362
Dr. Donna Silva-Burnett, prin. Fax 247-7076
Elizabeth Avenue ES 600/PK-4
363 Elizabeth Ave 08873 732-356-0113
John Haney, prin. Fax 271-2534
Franklin MS 1,100/7-8
415 Francis St 08873 732-249-6410
Nicholas Solomon, prin. Fax 246-0770
Hillcrest ES 400/PK-4
500 Franklin Blvd 08873 732-246-0170
Albert Fico M.Ed., prin. Fax 247-8405
MacAfee Road ES 400/PK-4
53 MacAfee Rd 08873 732-249-9097
William Grippo, prin. Fax 247-1408
Pine Grove Manor ES 400/PK-4
130 Highland Ave 08873 732-246-2424
Miguel Rivera, prin. Fax 843-5572
Smith Upper ES 1,100/5-6
1649 Amwell Rd 08873 732-873-2800
Evelyn Rutledge, prin. Fax 873-0451
Other Schools – See Franklin Park

Cedar Hill Prep S 300/PK-8
152 Cedar Grove Ln 08873 732-356-5400
Community Christian Academy & Preschool 50/PK-3
211 Demott Ln 08873 732-246-9383
LaShonda Gittens, dir. Fax 246-1884
Rutgers Preparatory S 700/PK-12
1345 Easton Ave 08873 732-545-5600
Dr. Steven Loy, hdmstr. Fax 214-1819
St. Matthias S 500/PK-8
170 John F Kennedy Blvd 08873 732-828-1402
Sr. Jean Laurich, prin. Fax 846-3099

Somers Point, Atlantic, Pop. 10,546
Somers Point SD 1,000/PK-8
121 W New York Ave 08244 609-927-2053
Dr. Thomas Baruffi, supt. Fax 927-7351
www.somersptschools.org
Dawes Avenue ES 400/K-6
22 W Dawes Ave 08244 609-653-1027
Doreen Lee, prin. Fax 653-6143
Jordan Road S 600/K-8
129 Jordan Rd 08244 609-927-7161
Susan Dugan, prin. Fax 927-9648
New York Avenue S 100/PK-PK
121 W New York Ave 08244 609-927-2053
Kimberly Tucker, prin. Fax 927-7351

St. Joseph Regional S 500/PK-8
11 Harbor Ln 08244 609-927-2228
Theodore Pugliese, prin. Fax 927-7834

Somerville, Somerset, Pop. 11,787
Somerville Borough SD 2,100/PK-12
51 W Cliff St 08876 908-218-4100
Timothy Teehan, supt. Fax 526-9668
www.somervillenjk12.org
Somerville MS 300/6-8
51 W Cliff St 08876 908-218-4107
Georgette Boulegeris, prin. Fax 575-9526
Van Derveer ES 500/PK-2
51 Union Ave 08876 908-218-4105
Susan Moran, prin. Fax 218-4185
Van Derveer ES 100/3-5
51 Union Ave 08876 908-218-4106
Robert Reavey, prin. Fax 526-9668

Immaculate Conception S 500/PK-8
41 Mountain Ave 08876 908-725-6516
Sr. Mary Chapman, prin. Fax 725-3172

South Amboy, Middlesex, Pop. 8,493
Sayreville SD 5,700/K-12
150 Lincoln St 08879 732-525-5200
Dr. Richard Labbe, supt. Fax 727-5769
www.sayrevillek12.net/
Other Schools – See Parlin, Sayreville

South Amboy SD 900/PK-12
240 John St 08879 732-525-2100
Jorge Diaz, supt. Fax 727-0730
www.sapublicschools.com
South Amboy ES 500/PK-5
249 John St 08879 732-525-2118
Sean Dunphy, prin. Fax 316-1588

Southampton, Burlington
Southampton Township SD 700/K-8
177 Main St 08088 609-859-2256
Michael Harris, supt. Fax 859-1542
www.southampton.k12.nj.us
Southampton Township IS 2 200/3-5
100 Miss Mabel Dr 08088 609-859-2256
Jennifer Horner, prin. Fax 859-3048
Southampton Township MS 3 200/6-8
100 Warrior Way 08088 609-859-2256
Jennifer Horner, prin. Fax 801-0754
Southampton Township PS 1 200/K-2
26 Pleasant St 08088 609-859-2256
James Winkelspetch, prin. Fax 859-0142

South Bound Brook, Somerset, Pop. 4,427
South Bound Brook Borough SD 400/PK-8
122 Elizabeth St 08880 732-356-3018
Dr. Lorise Goeke, supt. Fax 356-0621
www.southboundbrookk8.org
Morris S 400/PK-8
122 Elizabeth St 08880 732-356-3018
Dr. Lorise Goeke, prin. Fax 356-0621

South Hackensack, Bergen
South Hackensack SD 300/PK-8
1 Dyer Ave 07606 201-440-2782
Gregorio Maceri, supt. Fax 440-9156
www.shmemorial.org/
Memorial S 300/PK-8
1 Dyer Ave 07606 201-440-2782
Gregorio Maceri, prin. Fax 440-9156

South Orange, Essex, Pop. 16,390
South Orange-Maplewood SD
Supt. — See Maplewood
Marshall ES 500/K-2
262 Grove Rd 07079 973-378-7698
Bonita Samuels, prin. Fax 378-5243
Montrose ECC PK-PK
356 Clark St 07079 973-378-2086
Renee Joyce, dir. Fax 378-2085
South Mountain ES 400/2-5
444 W South Orange Ave 07079 973-378-5216
Alyna Jacobs, prin. Fax 763-5620
South Mountain ES Annex 200/K-1
112 Glenview Rd 07079 973-378-2801
Alyna Jacobs, prin. Fax 378-2033
South Orange MS 800/6-8
70 N Ridgewood Rd 07079 973-378-2772
Lynn Irby, prin. Fax 378-2775

Our Lady of Sorrows S 200/PK-8
172 Academy St 07079 973-762-5169
Judith Foley, prin. Fax 378-9781

South Plainfield, Middlesex, Pop. 22,711
South Plainfield SD 3,400/K-12
125 Jackson Ave 07080 908-754-4620
Dr. Noreen Lishak, supt. Fax 822-2453
www.spboe.org
Franklin ES 300/K-4
1000 Franklin Ave 07080 908-754-4620
Ralph Errico, prin. Fax 754-8819
Grant ES 500/5-6
305 Cromwell Pl 07080 908-754-4620
Patrick Sarullo, prin. Fax 755-5895

Kennedy ES 300/K-4
2900 Norwood Ave 07080 908-754-4620
Kevin Hajduk, prin. Fax 754-8659
Riley ES 300/K-4
100 Morris Ave 07080 908-754-4620
Leo Whalen, prin. Fax 754-8591
Roosevelt ES 400/K-4
135 Jackson Ave 07080 908-754-4620
Robert Diehl, prin. Fax 822-9375
South Plainfield MS 500/7-8
2201 Plainfield Ave 07080 908-754-4620
Roger Vroom, admin. Fax 791-1152

Holy Savior Academy 100/PK-8
149 S Plainfield Ave 07080 908-822-5890
Kristen Kiernan, prin. Fax 822-5891

South River, Middlesex, Pop. 15,456
South River SD 2,300/PK-12
15 Montgomery St 08882 732-613-4000
Sylvia Zircher, supt. Fax 613-4756
www.srivernj.org
South River ES 600/PK-PK, 3-
81 Johnson Pl 08882 732-613-4073
Lisa Wargo, prin. Fax 698-9269
South River MS 500/6-8
3 Montgomery St 08882 732-613-4073
Lisa Wargo, prin. Fax 698-9305
South River PS 500/K-2
22 David St 08882 732-613-4006
Kevin Kidney, prin. Fax 613-4020

Sparta, Sussex, Pop. 15,157
Sparta Township SD 3,400/PK-12
18 Mohawk Ave 07871 973-729-7886
Michael Rossi, supt. Fax 729-0576
www.sparta.org
Mohawk Avenue S 200/PK-K
18 Mohawk Ave 07871 973-729-1289
Laura Trent, prin. Fax 729-5574
Morgan ES 500/4-5
100 Stanhope Rd 07871 973-729-5770
Douglas Layman, prin. Fax 729-0245
Sparta Alpine ES 700/1-3
151 Andover Rd 07871 973-729-3107
Giuseppe Leone, prin. Fax 729-0483
Sparta MS 800/6-8
350 Main St 07871 973-729-3151
Michael Gregory, prin. Fax 729-0573

Brown Memorial S 500/PK-4
294 Sparta Ave 07871 973-729-9174
Patricia Klebez, prin. Fax 729-0318
Hilltop Country Day S 100/PK-8
32 Lafayette Rd 07871 973-729-5485
Kevin Folan, head sch Fax 729-9057
Pope St. John XXIII MS 300/5-7
28 Andover Rd 07871 973-729-1967
Susan Santore, prin.

Spotswood, Middlesex, Pop. 8,141
Spotswood SD 1,700/PK-12
105 Summerhill Rd 08884 732-723-2200
Graham Peabody, supt. Fax 251-7666
www.spotswood.k12.nj.us
Appleby ES 400/2-5
23 Vliet St 08884 732-723-2213
Nancy Torchiano, prin. Fax 251-7666
Schoenly ES 200/PK-1
80 Kane Ave 08884 732-723-2220
Jennifer Asprocolas, prin. Fax 251-7666
Spotswood Memorial MS 300/6-8
115 Summerhill Rd 08884 732-723-2227
Brian Kitchin, prin. Fax 251-7666

Immaculate Conception S 400/PK-8
23 Manalapan Rd 08884 732-251-3090
Mary Erath, prin. Fax 251-8270

Springfield, Union, Pop. 13,420
Springfield SD 2,200/PK-12
PO Box 210 07081 973-376-1025
Michael Davino, supt. Fax 912-9229
www.springfieldschools.com
Caldwell ES 300/3-5
36 Caldwell Pl 07081 973-376-1025
David Rennie, prin. Fax 379-8372
Gaudineer MS 400/6-8
75 S Springfield Ave 07081 973-376-1025
Timothy Kielty, prin. Fax 376-3259
Sandmeier ES 200/3-5
666 S Springfield Ave 07081 973-376-1025
Michael Plias, prin. Fax 379-8371
Walton ES 700/PK-2
601 Mountain Ave 07081 973-376-1025
Dr. Suzy Hung, prin. Fax 258-0753

St. James the Apostle S 200/PK-8
41 S Springfield Ave 07081 973-376-5194
Caroline Ponterio, prin. Fax 376-5228

Spring Lake, Monmouth, Pop. 2,971
Spring Lake Borough SD 200/PK-8
411 Tuttle Ave 07762 732-449-6380
Dr. Raymond J. Boccuti, supt. Fax 449-3178
www.hwmountz.k12.nj.us
Mountz S 200/PK-8
411 Tuttle Ave 07762 732-449-6380
Dr. Raymond J. Boccuti, supt. Fax 449-3178

St. Catharine S 400/K-8
301 2nd Ave 07762 732-449-4424
Robert Dougherty, prin. Fax 449-7876

Spring Lake Heights, Monmouth, Pop. 4,680
Spring Lake Heights SD 300/K-8
1110 Highway 71 07762 732-449-6149
John Spalthoff, supt. Fax 449-9492
www.slheights.org
Spring Lake Heights S 300/K-8
1110 Highway 71 07762 732-449-6149
John Spalthoff, admin. Fax 449-9492

Monmouth Montessori Academy 50/PK-8
2307 Railroad Ave 07762 732-449-0500

Stanhope, Sussex, Pop. 3,550
Byram Township SD 900/K-8
12 Mansfield Dr 07874 973-347-1047
Bryan Hensz, supt. Fax 347-9001
www.byramschools.org
Byram IS 400/5-8
12 Mansfield Dr 07874 973-347-1047
John Fritzky, prin. Fax 691-7780
Byram Lakes ES 400/K-4
11 Mansfield Dr 07874 973-347-1047
Edward Abato, prin. Fax 691-7771

Stanhope Borough SD 300/K-8
24 Valley Rd 07874 973-347-0008
Timothy Nicinski, supt. Fax 347-8368
www.stanhopeschools.org
Valley Road S 300/K-8
24 Valley Rd 07874 973-347-0008
Steven Hagemann, prin. Fax 347-8368

Stewartsville, Warren, Pop. 346
Greenwich Township SD 800/PK-8
101 Wyndham Farm Blvd 08886 908-859-2022
Maria Eppolite, supt. Fax 859-4522
www.gtsd.net
Greenwich S 500/PK-5
101 Wyndham Farm Blvd 08886 908-859-2022
Nichole Hutnik, prin. Fax 859-4522
Stewartsville MS 300/6-8
642 S Main St 08886 908-859-2023
Stephanie Snyder, prin. Fax 859-4522

Stillwater, Sussex
Stillwater Township SD 300/K-6
PO Box 12 07875 973-383-6171
Matthew Robinson, admin. Fax 383-7021
www.stillwaterschool.net
Stillwater Township ES 300/K-6
PO Box 12 07875 973-383-6171
Matthew Robinson, prin. Fax 383-1895

Stirling, Morris
Long Hill Township SD
Supt. — See Gillette
Central MS 300/6-8
90 Central Ave 07980 908-647-2311
Michael Viturello, prin. Fax 647-0610

Stockton, Hunterdon, Pop. 535
South Hunterdon Regional SD
Supt. — See Lambertville
Stockton Borough S 50/5-6
19 S Main St 08559 609-397-2012
Geoff Hewitt, prin. Fax 397-2602

Stone Harbor, Cape May, Pop. 863
Stone Harbor SD 100/K-4
275 93rd St 08247 609-368-4413
Stacey Tracy, supt. Fax 368-6545
www.avalonstoneharborschools.org/
Stone Harbor S 100/K-4
275 93rd St 08247 609-368-4413
Stacey Tracy, supt. Fax 368-6545

Stratford, Camden, Pop. 6,903
Stratford Borough SD 800/PK-8
111 Warwick Rd 08084 856-783-2555
Thomas Attanasi, supt. Fax 784-8486
www.stratford.k12.nj.us
Parkview ES 400/PK-3
123 Parkview Rd 08084 856-783-2876
Michele Taylor, prin. Fax 783-3468
Yellin MS 500/4-8
111 Warwick Rd 08084 856-783-1094
David Ricci, prin. Fax 309-0304

St. John Paul II Regional S 400/PK-8
55 Warwick Rd 08084 856-783-3088
Helen Persing, prin. Fax 783-9302

Succasunna, Morris, Pop. 9,054
Roxbury Township SD 3,600/PK-12
42 N Hillside Ave 07876 973-584-6099
Loretta Radulic, supt. Fax 252-1434
www.roxbury.org
Eisenhower MS 600/7-8
47 Eyland Ave 07876 973-584-2973
Dominick Miller, prin. Fax 584-4529
Franklin ES 300/K-4
8 Meeker St 07876 973-584-5549
Lisa Ferrare, prin. Fax 252-1151
Jefferson ES 300/PK-4
35 Cornhollow Rd 07876 973-584-8955
Melissa Cosgrove, prin. Fax 584-4380
Kennedy ES 200/K-4
20 Pleasant Hill Rd 07876 973-584-3938
Eric Renfors, prin. Fax 584-8098
Lincoln/Roosevelt ES 500/5-6
34 N Hillside Ave 07876 973-584-4331
Christopher Argenziano, prin. Fax 584-4257
Other Schools – See Landing

American Christian S 200/PK-12
126 S Hillside Ave 07876 973-584-6616
Kristen Brennan, head sch Fax 584-0686
St. Therese S 300/PK-8
135 Main St 07876 973-584-0812
Timothy Dunnigan, prin. Fax 584-2029

Summit, Union, Pop. 21,055
Summit CSD 4,100/PK-12
14 Beekman Ter 07901 908-918-2100
Mr. June Chang, supt. Fax 273-3656
www.summit.k12.nj.us
Brayton ES 400/1-5
89 Tulip St 07901 908-273-1276
Dr. Cheryl Moretz, prin. Fax 918-2112
Franklin ES 400/1-5
136 Blackburn Rd 07901 908-277-2613
Dalia Mirrione, prin. Fax 918-2114
Jefferson ES 200/1-5
110 Ashwood Ave 07901 908-273-3807
Joseph Cordero, prin. Fax 918-2116
Jefferson Primary Center 100/PK-K
110 Ashwood Ave 07901 908-918-2160
Janice Tierney, prin. Fax 918-2133
Lincoln-Hubbard ES 300/1-5
52 Woodland Ave 07901 908-273-1333
Matthew Carlin, prin. Fax 918-2118
Summit MS 1,000/6-8
272 Morris Ave 07901 908-273-1190
Damen Cooper, prin. Fax 273-8320
Washington ES 300/1-5
507 Morris Ave 07901 908-273-0817
Lauren Banker, prin. Fax 918-2120
Wilson Primary Center 100/PK-K
14 Beekman Ter 07901 908-918-2175
Janice Tierney, prin. Fax 918-2134

Kent Place S 600/PK-12
42 Norwood Ave 07901 908-273-0900
Dr. Jennifer Galambos Ed.D., head sch Fax 273-9390
Oak Knoll S of the Holy Child 600/K-12
44 Blackburn Rd 07901 908-522-8100
Timothy Saburn, head sch Fax 277-1838
St. Theresa of Avila S 200/PK-K
306 Morris Ave 07901 908-277-6043
Christine Monaco, prin. Fax 273-1770

Surf City, Ocean, Pop. 1,196
Long Beach Island SD
Supt. — See Ship Bottom
Jacobsen ES 100/PK-2
200 S Barnegat Ave 08008 609-494-2341
Frank Birney, prin. Fax 494-0362

Sussex, Sussex, Pop. 2,089
Sussex-Wantage Regional SD 1,100/PK-8
27 Bank St 07461 973-875-3175
Robert Mooney, supt. Fax 875-7175
www.swregional.org
Lawrence ES 300/PK-2
31 Ryan Rd 07461 973-875-8820
Jennifer Connors, prin. Fax 875-8933
Sussex MS 400/6-8
10 Loomis Ave 07461 973-875-4138
Shane Schwarz, prin. Fax 875-6790
Wantage ES 400/3-5
815 State Rt 23 07461 973-875-4589
Michael Gall, prin. Fax 875-2184

Sussex Christian S 100/K-8
51 Unionville Ave 07461 973-875-5595
Trish King, admin. Fax 875-5420

Swedesboro, Gloucester, Pop. 2,503
Swedesboro-Woolwich SD 1,600/PK-6
15 Fredrick Blvd 08085 856-241-1552
Dr. Kristin O'Neil, supt. Fax 467-7041
www.swedesboro-woolwich.com
Clifford S 200/PK-K
601 Auburn Ave 08085 856-241-1552
Jamie Flick, prin. Fax 241-9285
Hill ES 200/6-6
1815 Kings Hwy 08085 856-241-1552
Leigh Donato, prin. Fax 467-4016
Other Schools – See Woolwich

Tabernacle, Burlington
Tabernacle Township SD 700/K-8
132 New Rd 08088 609-268-0153
Glenn Robbins, supt. Fax 268-1006
www.tabschools.org
Olson MS 400/5-8
132 New Rd 08088 609-268-0153
Susan Grosser, prin. Fax 268-1006
Tabernacle ES 400/K-4
141 New Rd 08088 609-268-0150
Dr. Gerald Paterson, prin. Fax 268-3233

Teaneck, Bergen, Pop. 39,500
Teaneck SD 3,400/PK-12
1 Merrison St 07666 201-833-5510
Vincent McHale, supt. Fax 837-9468
www.teaneckschools.org
Bryant K 200/PK-K
1 E Tryon Ave 07666 201-833-5545
Leslie Abrew, prin. Fax 862-2348
Franklin MS 500/5-8
1315 Taft Rd 07666 201-833-5450
Natasha Pitt, prin. Fax 862-2465
Hawthorne ES 300/1-4
201 Fycke Ln 07666 201-833-5540
Emilio Jennette, prin. Fax 862-2350
Jefferson MS 500/5-8
655 Teaneck Rd 07666 201-833-5471
Angela Davis, prin. Fax 833-3083
Lowell ES 300/1-4
1025 Lincoln Pl 07666 201-833-5550
Antoine Green, prin. Fax 862-2358
Whittier ES 300/1-4
491 W Englewood Ave 07666 201-833-5535
Pedro Valdes, prin. Fax 862-2354

Mays SDA S 50/PK-8
405 Englewood Ave 07666 201-837-6655

Tenafly, Bergen, Pop. 14,170
Tenafly SD 3,500/K-12
500 Tenafly Rd 07670 201-816-4500
Geoffrey Gordon, supt. Fax 816-4521
www.tenafly.k12.nj.us

Mackay ES 400/K-5
111 Jefferson Ave 07670 201-816-7700
Brenda Yoo, prin. Fax 568-7687
Maugham ES 400/K-5
111 Magnolia Ave 07670 201-816-7705
Jennifer Ferrara, prin. Fax 871-9641
Smith ES 400/K-5
101 Downey Dr 07670 201-816-7715
Brian Ross, prin. Fax 568-7801
Stillman ES 400/K-5
75 Tenafly Rd 07670 201-816-7710
Gayle Lander, prin. Fax 568-7760
Tenafly MS 800/6-8
10 Sunset Ln 07670 201-816-4900
Dr. John Fabbo, prin. Fax 569-0327

Academy of Our Lady of Mt. Carmel 300/PK-8
10 County Rd 07670 201-567-6491
Kelly Koval, prin. Fax 568-1402
Spring S 300/PK-8
67 N Summit St 07670 201-541-5780
Dr. Deborah Knapp, dir. Fax 541-5782

Three Bridges, Hunterdon
Readington Township SD
Supt. — See White House Station
Three Bridges ES 300/PK-3
PO Box 443 08887 908-782-2141
Kristen Higgins, prin. Fax 349-3059

Tinton Falls, Monmouth, Pop. 17,575
Tinton Falls SD 1,300/K-8
658 Tinton Ave 07724 732-460-2400
John Russo, supt. Fax 542-1158
www.tfs.k12.nj.us
Atchison ES 400/K-2
961 Sycamore Ave 07724 732-542-2500
Jessica Black, prin. Fax 542-4905
Swimming River ES 300/3-5
220 Hance Ave 07724 732-460-2416
Dr. Marion Lamberti, prin. Fax 530-8684
Tinton Falls MS 500/6-8
674 Tinton Ave 07724 732-542-0775
Mary Ehid, prin. Fax 542-8723

Ranney S 800/PK-12
235 Hope Rd 07724 732-542-4777
Dr. John Griffith, head sch Fax 544-1629

Titusville, Mercer
Hopewell Valley Regional SD
Supt. — See Pennington
Bear Tavern ES 400/PK-5
1162 Bear Tavern Rd 08560 609 737 4005
Christopher Turnbull, prin. Fax 737-7351

Toms River, Ocean, Pop. 87,576
Toms River Regional SD 15,300/PK-12
1144 Hooper Ave 08753 732-505-5510
David Healy, supt. Fax 505-9330
www.trschools.com
Cedar Grove ES 700/PK-5
173 Cedar Grove Rd 08753 732-505-5830
Jeffrey Ryan, prin. Fax 914-1350
Citta ES 600/K-5
2050 Route 9 08755 732-818-8550
Gary Azzolini, prin. Fax 240-0156
East Dover ES 700/K-5
725 Vaughn Ave 08753 732-505-5840
Matthew Gray, prin. Fax 270-4757
Hooper Avenue ES 700/K-5
1517 Hooper Ave 08753 732-505-5850
Michael Citta, prin. Fax 914-1253
North Dover ES 600/K-5
1759 New Hampshire Ave 08755 732-505-5860
Colleen McGrath, prin. Fax 914-9706
Silver Bay ES 600/PK-5
100 Silver Bay Rd 08753 732-505-5880
Michael DeVita, prin. Fax 255-0649
South Toms River ES 300/K-5
419 Dover Rd 08757 732-505-5890
Dennis Holzapfel, prin. Fax 914-1861
Toms River IS East 1,400/6-8
1519 Hooper Ave 08753 732-505-5777
Bryan Madigan, prin. Fax 286-1290
Toms River IS North 1,200/6-8
150 Intermediate North Way 08753 732-505-5800
Lynn Fronzak, prin. Fax 286-1291
Walnut Street ES 800/K-5
60 Walnut St 08753 732-505-5900
Richard Fastnacht, prin. Fax 914-9724
Washington Street ES 400/K-5
500 W Earl Ct 08753 732-505-5910
Kelly Kernasovic, prin. Fax 914-9715
West Dover ES 400/K-5
50 Blue Jay Dr 08755 732-505-5920
Michael Pallen, prin. Fax 914-2174
Other Schools – See Beachwood, Pine Beach

Ambassador Christian Academy 100/PK-8
700 Main St 08753 732-341-0860
Christina Hutchings, head sch Fax 349-0731
St. Joseph S 600/K-8
711 Hooper Ave 08753 732-349-2355
Madeline Kinloch, prin. Fax 349-1064

Totowa, Passaic, Pop. 10,662
Totowa SD 1,000/PK-8
10 Crews St 07512 973-956-0010
Patricia Capitelli, supt. Fax 956-9859
www.totowa.k12.nj.us
Memorial ES 400/PK-2
294 Totowa Rd 07512 973-956-0010
Joseph Compel, prin. Fax 904-1082
Washington Park MS 600/3-8
10 Crews St 07512 973-956-0010
Michael O'Brien, prin. Fax 389-2270

Academy of St. James of the Marches 300/PK-8
400 Totowa Rd 07512 973-956-8824
Leslie Dreps, prin. Fax 956-8824

Towaco, Morris
Montville Township SD
Supt. — See Montville
Cedar Hill ES 300/K-5
46 Pine Brook Rd 07082 973-331-7100
Dr. Michael Raj, prin. Fax 331-3430

Trenton, Mercer, Pop. 83,491
NJ Charter Schools 17,900/PK-12
100 Riverview Pl CN 500 08611 609-292-5850
Fax 633-9825
www.state.nj.us/education
Other Schools – See Camden

Trenton SD 9,300/PK-12
108 N Clinton Ave 08609 609-656-4900
Dr. Fredrick McDowell, supt. Fax 989-2682
www.trenton.k12.nj.us
Columbus ES 300/K-5
1200 Brunswick Ave 08638 609-656-4690
Deward Wood, prin. Fax 392-7061
Dunn MS 800/6-8
401 Dayton St 08611 609-656-4700
Madeline Roman, prin. Fax 989-1478
Franklin ES 300/K-5
200 William St 08610 609-656-4720
Nicole Bethea, prin. Fax 421-6386
Grant ES 500/PK-5
159 N Clinton Ave 08609 609-656-4730
Alfonso Llano, prin. Fax 777-5359
Gregory ES 400/K-5
500 Rutherford Ave 08618 609-656-4740
Michael Rosenberg, prin. Fax 278-3004
Hedgepeth-Williams MS 400/6-8
301 Gladstone Ave 08629 609-656-4760
Adrienne Hill, prin. Fax 989-2544
Hill ES 400/PK-5
1010 E State St 08609 609-656-4980
Talaya Stoddard-Wilson, prin. Fax 989-2544
Jefferson ES 400/PK-5
1 Whittlesey Rd 08618 609-656-4660
Gedeon Wadner, prin. Fax 599-9519
Kilmer MS 400/6-8
1300 Stuyvesant Ave 08618 609-656-4800
Paula Bethea, prin. Fax 989-2927
King ES, 401 Brunswick Ave 08638 500/K-5
Kim Page, prin. 609-656-4690
Mott ES 300/K-5
45 Stokely Ave 08611 609-656-4830
Dr. Channing Conway, prin. Fax 989-2900
Munoz-Rivera MS 500/6-8
400 N Montgomery St 08618 609-656-4840
Bernadette Trapp, prin. Fax 656-2149
Parker ES 400/K-5
117 Ferry St 08611 609-656-4880
Jeannette Harris, prin. Fax 396-6049
Robbins ES 300/K-5
283 Tyler St 08609 609-656-4910
Christopher DeJesus, prin. Fax 989-2918
Washington ES 200/K-5
331 Emory Ave 08611 609-656-4960
Yolanda Armstrong, prin. Fax 989-2532
Wilson ES 300/PK-5
175 Girard Ave 08638 609-656-4970
Janet Nicodemus, prin. Fax 656-4966

Christina Seix Academy 100/PK-8
1550 Stuyvesant Ave 08618 609-643-0424
Rob Connor Ph.D., head sch Fax 643-5555
St. Raphael S 300/PK-8
151 Gropp Ave 08610 609-585-7733
Ann Cwirko, prin. Fax 581-8436

Tuckerton, Ocean, Pop. 3,315
Tuckerton Borough SD 300/PK-6
PO Box 217 08087 609-295-2858
Janet Gangemi, supt. Fax 296-1480
www.tuckerton.k12.nj.us
Tuckerton ES 300/PK-6
PO Box 217 08087 609-296-2858
Siobhan Grayson, prin. Fax 296-1480

Turnersville, Gloucester, Pop. 3,705
Washington Township SD
Supt. — See Sewell
Bells ES 500/1-5
227 Greentree Rd 08012 856-589-8441
Virginia Grier, prin. Fax 589-6607
Birches ES 500/1-5
416 Westminster Blvd 08012 856-232-1290
Jessica Rose, prin. Fax 232-7963
Jefferson ES 400/K-5
95 Altair Dr 08012 856-589-8248
Gary Breen, prin. Fax 589-6919
Whitman ES 500/K-5
827 Whitman School Rd 08012 856-227-1103
Raymond Anderson, prin. Fax 227-0965

Union, Union, Pop. 55,000
Township of Union SD 7,300/PK-12
2369 Morris Ave 07083 908-851-3000
Gregory Tatum, supt. Fax 851-9688
www.twpunionschools.org
Battle Hill ES 400/PK-4
2600 Killian Pl 07083 908-851-6480
Mark Hoyt, prin. Fax 851-4687
Burnet MS 1,000/6-8
1000 Caldwell Ave 07083 908-851-6490
Raymond Salvatore, prin. Fax 687-2645
Caldwell ES 600/PK-4
1120 Commerce Ave 07083 908-206-6100
Dr. Kathy DiGiovanni, prin. Fax 206-9282
Connecticut Farms ES 400/PK-4
875 Stuyvesant Ave 07083 908-851-6470
Michelle Osborne-Warren, prin. Fax 687-7332
Franklin ES 400/PK-4
1500 Lindy Ter 07083 908-851-6450
Latee Walton-McCleod, prin. Fax 810-0710
Kawameeh MS 600/6-8
490 David Ter 07083 908-851-6570
Jason Malanda, prin. Fax 687-5741
Livingston ES 400/PK-4
960 Midland Blvd 07083 908-851-6440
Benjamin Kloc, prin. Fax 810-0417
Washington ES 600/PK-4
301 Washington Ave 07083 908-851-6460
Thomas Matthews, prin. Fax 810-1012
Other Schools – See Vauxhall

Holy Spirit S 200/PK-8
970 Suburban Rd 07083 908-687-8415
Armand Lamberti, prin. Fax 687-3996
St. Michael S 400/PK-8
1212 Kelly St 07083 908-688-1063
Antoinette Telle, prin. Fax 687-7927

Union Beach, Monmouth, Pop. 6,114
Union Beach SD 700/PK-8
221 Morningside Ave 07735 732-264-5405
Dr. Scott Ridley Ed.D., supt. Fax 264-6109
www.unionbeachschools.org
Memorial S 700/PK-8
221 Morningside Ave 07735 732-264-5400
Kelly Savicky, prin. Fax 264-0964

Union City, Hudson, Pop. 65,896
Union City SD 10,700/PK-12
3912 32nd St 07087 201-348-5851
Silvia Abbato, supt. Fax 330-1736
www.ucboe.us
de Hostos ECC 300/PK-K
2200 Kennedy Blvd 07087 201-271-2310
Adriana Birne, prin. Fax 271-2314
Edison ES 1,100/PK-6
507 West St 07087 201-348-5965
Eliseo Aleman, prin. Fax 348-4306
Emerson MS 900/6-8
318 18th St 07087 201-348-5900
Mike Cirone, prin. Fax 864-2262
Gilmore Academy 1-8
1600 Kerrigan Ave 07087 201-299-9855
Geri Perez, prin.
Hudson ES PK-2
166 18th St 07087 201-624-9800
Barbara McNerney, prin. Fax 223-5091
Jefferson ES 300/PK-4
3400 Palisade Ave 07087 201-348-5960
Michael Celebrano, prin. Fax 601-2396
Powell ES, 1500 New York Ave 07087 900/K-5
Teresita Diaz, prin. 201-351-5165
Roosevelt ES 900/K-6
4507 Hudson Ave 07087 201-348-5971
Martha O'Connell, prin. Fax 348-3337
Union Hill MS 700/7-8
3808 Hudson Ave 07087 201-348-5808
Victoria Dickson, prin. Fax 867-4205
Veteran's Memorial ES 600/PK-5
1401 Central Ave 07087 201-348-2737
Catalina Tamargo, prin. Fax 583-0656
Washington ES 700/PK-6
3905 New York Ave 07087 201-348-5954
Les Hanna, prin. Fax 974-8937
Waters ES 1,000/PK-6
2800 Summit Ave 07087 201-348-5925
Faith Tieri, prin. Fax 866-6598

Learning Institute of Union City - Boys 300/K-12
3400 New York Ave 07087 201-867-9107
Learning Institute of Union City - Girls 100/PK-8
3300 New York Ave 07087 201-867-9107
Miftaahul Uloom Academy 200/PK-12
501 15th St 07087 201-223-9920
Msgr. Saima Sanaullah, prin. Fax 223-9921
Mother Seton S 300/PK-8
1501 New York Ave 07087 201-863-8433
Mary McErlaine, prin. Fax 863-8145
Rising Star Academy 100/PK-12
4613 Cottage Pl 07087 201-758-5590
St. Augustine S 200/PK-8
3920 New York Ave 07087 201-865-5319
Sr. Lillian Sharrock, prin. Fax 865-2567
St. Francis Academy 300/PK-8
1601 Central Ave 07087 201-863-4112
Deborah Savage, prin. Fax 601-5905

Upper Montclair, Essex, Pop. 11,116
Montclair SD
Supt. — See Montclair
Aldrin MS 600/6-8
173 Bellevue Ave 07043 973-509-4220
Dr. Jill Sack, prin. Fax 509-4218
Northeast ES 400/K-5
603 Grove St 07043 973-509-4242
Gail Clarke, prin. Fax 509-1386

Upper Saddle River, Bergen, Pop. 8,104
Upper Saddle River SD 1,300/PK-8
395 W Saddle River Rd 07458 201-961-6500
Dr. Richard Brockel, supt. Fax 934-4923
www.usrschoolsk8.com
Bogert ES 500/3-5
391 W Saddle River Rd 07458 201-961-6350
David Kaplan, prin. Fax 825-9101
Cavallini MS 500/6-8
392 W Saddle River Rd 07458 201-961-6400
James McCusker, prin. Fax 236-9662
Reynolds PS 400/PK-2
391 W Saddle River Rd 07458 201-961-6300
Devin Severs, prin. Fax 236-8432

Vauxhall, Union
Township of Union SD
Supt. — See Union

Jefferson ES 500/5-5
155 Hilton Ave 07088 908-851-6560
Laura Damato, prin. Fax 687-8464

Ventnor City, Atlantic, Pop. 10,474
Ventnor City SD 800/PK-8
400 N Lafayette Ave 08406 609-487-7900
Eileen Johnson, supt. Fax 822-0150
www.veccnj.org/
Ventnor ES 500/PK-4
400 N Lafayette Ave 08406 609-487-7900
Carmella Somershoe, prin. Fax 823-4036
Ventnor MS 400/5-8
400 N Lafayette Ave 08406 609-487-7900
Robert Baker, prin. Fax 823-4036

Vernon, Sussex
Vernon Township SD 3,500/PK-12
PO Box 99 07462 973-764-2900
Arthur DiBenedetto, supt. Fax 764-0033
www.vtsd.com
Cedar Mountain PS 400/K-1
PO Box 420 07462 973-764-2890
Rosemay Gebhardt, prin. Fax 764-3294
Glen Meadow MS 600/6-8
PO Box 516 07462 973-764-8981
Edwina Piszczek, prin. Fax 764-3295
Lounsberry Hollow MS 500/4-5
PO Box 219 07462 973-764-8745
Dennis Mudrick, prin. Fax 764-0101
Rolling Hills PS 400/2-3
PO Box 769 07462 973-764-2784
Dr. Stewart Stumper, prin. Fax 764-3284
Walnut Ridge PS 500/PK-PK
PO Box 190 07462 973-764-2801
Joseph Piccirillo, prin. Fax 764-0066

Verona, Essex, Pop. 13,597
Verona SD 2,100/K-12
121 Fairview Ave 07044 973-571-2029
Dr. Rui Dionisio, supt. Fax 571-6779
www.veronaschools.org
Brookdale Avenue ES 100/K-4
14 Brookdale Ct 07044 973-571-6752
Nicole Stuto, prin. Fax 571-6768
Brown ES 200/K-4
125 Grove Ave 07044 973-571-6753
Dr. Anthony Lanzo, prin. Fax 571-6769
Forest Avenue ES 200/K-4
118 Forest Ave 07044 973-571-6754
Jeffrey Monacelli, prin. Fax 571-6770
Laning Avenue ES 200/K-4
18 Lanning Rd 07044 973-571-6755
Howard Freund, prin. Fax 571-6764
Whitehorne MS 700/5-8
600 Bloomfield Ave 07044 973-571-6751
Yvette McNeal, prin. Fax 571-6767

Our Lady of the Lake S 200/PK-8
26 Lakeside Ave 07044 973-239-1160
Benjamin Ronquillo, prin. Fax 239-6496

Villas, Cape May, Pop. 9,312
Lower Township ESD
Supt. — See Cape May
Douglas Veterans Memorial S 400/PK-K
2600 Bayshore Rd Ste 3 08251 609-884-9430
Nicholas Bailey, prin. Fax 886-0515

Vineland, Cumberland, Pop. 59,740
Vineland CSD 9,400/PK-12
625 E Plum St 08360 856-794-6700
Dr. Mary Gruccio, supt. Fax 794-9464
www.vineland.org
Barse ES 300/K-5
240 S Orchard Rd 08360 856-794-6940
Joseph Camardo, prin. Fax 507-8743
Dallago Preschool 200/PK-PK
240 S 6th St 08360 856-641-8502
Lynn Monteleone, prin. Fax 362-8978
D'Ippolito ES 600/K-5
1578 N Valley Ave 08360 856-794-6934
Renee Braxton, prin. Fax 507-8757
Durand ES 500/K-5
371 W Forest Grove Rd 08360 856-794-6929
Dan Greco, prin. Fax 507-8745
Johnstone ES 300/K-5
165 S Brewster Rd 08361 856-794-6967
Sylvia Morano, prin. Fax 507-8746
Leuchter ES 200/K-5
519 N West Ave 08360 856-794-6922
Carmella Heer, prin. Fax 507-8738
Mennies ES 600/K-5
361 E Grant Ave 08360 856-794-6957
Lisa Arena, prin. Fax 507-8742
Petway ES 500/K-5
1115 S Lincoln Ave 08361 856-362-8855
Jennifer Frederico, prin. Fax 362-8981
Rossi MS 500/6-8
2572 Palermo Ave 08361 856-794-6961
Tammy Monahan, prin. Fax 507-8786
Sabater ES 800/K-5
301 S East Blvd 08360 856-641-8502
Jeff DuBois, prin. Fax 362-8979
Veterans Memorial MS 500/6-8
424 S Main Rd 08360 856-794-6918
Hope Johnson, prin. Fax 507-8759
Wallace MS 500/6-8
688 N Mill Rd 08360 856-362-8887
Dr. Juanita Davis, prin. Fax 362-8980
Winslow ES 500/K-5
1335 Magnolia Rd 08361 856-794-6973
Debra Quinn, prin. Fax 507-8739

Bishop Schad Regional S 300/PK-8
922 E Landis Ave 08360 856-691-4490
Sr. Rosa Ojeda, prin. Fax 691-5579
Cumberland Christian S 400/PK-12
1100 W Sherman Ave 08360 856-696-1600
Ken Howard, hdmstr. Fax 696-0631
Ellison S 100/PK-8
1017 S Spring Rd 08361 856-691-1734
St. Mary Regional S 200/PK-8
735 Union Rd 08360 856-692-8537
Steven Hogan, prin. Fax 692-5034
Vine Haven Adventist S 50/K-8
1155 E Landis Ave 08360 856-691-9393

Voorhees, Camden, Pop. 946
Voorhees Township SD 2,900/PK-8
329 Route 73 08043 856-751-8446
Raymond Brosel, supt. Fax 751-3666
www.voorhees.k12.nj.us/
Hamilton ES 400/K-5
23 Northgate Dr 08043 856-767-4888
Andrew Moskowitz, prin. Fax 753-2894
Kresson ES 300/K-5
7 School Ln 08043 856-424-1816
Stacey Morris, prin. Fax 424-2728
Osage ES 700/K-5
112 Somerdale Rd 08043 856-428-2990
Robert Cranmer, prin. Fax 427-0296
Signal Hill ES 500/PK-5
33 Signal Hill Dr 08043 856-767-6749
Sharon Stallings, prin. Fax 767-6221
Voorhees MS 1,100/6-8
1000 Holly Oak Dr 08043 856-795-2025
Kristine Calabria, prin. Fax 795-4611

Kellman Brown Academy 200/PK-8
1007 Laurel Oak Rd 08043 856-679-2929
Rachel Zivic, prin. Fax 679-2928
Trinity Preparatory S 100/K-12
1801 S Burnt Mill Rd 08043 856-282-3800
Matt Williams, hdmstr.

Waldwick, Bergen, Pop. 9,513
Waldwick SD 1,500/PK-12
155 Summit Ave 07463 201-445-3131
Dr. Paul Casarico, supt. Fax 445-0584
www.waldwickschools.org
Crescent ES 300/K-5
165 Crescent Ave 07463 201-445-0690
Marisa Kossoy, prin. Fax 445-6955
Traphagen ES 400/K-5
153 Summit Ave 07463 201-445-0730
Robert Sileo, prin. Fax 445-7196
Waldwick MS 400/6-8
155 Wyckoff Ave 07463 201-652-9000
Michael Meyers, prin. Fax 652-5053

Village S for Children 300/PK-8
100 W Prospect St 07463 201-445-6160
Waldwick SDA S 100/PK-12
70 Wyckoff Ave 07463 201-652-6078

Wall, Monmouth, Pop. 5,201
Wall Township SD 3,700/PK-12
1620 18th Ave 07719 732-556-2000
Cheryl Dyer, supt. Fax 556-2101
www.wall.k12.nj.us
Central ES 500/K-5
2007 Allenwood Rd 07719 732-556-2540
Jill Antoniello, prin. Fax 556-2551
Wall IS 900/6-8
2801 Allaire Rd 07719 732-556-2500
Erin Embon, prin. Fax 556-2535
Wall PS 50/PK-PK
2500 Bedford Corner Ln 07719 732-556-2114
Carol Duffy, prin. Fax 556-2115
West Belmar ES 200/K-5
925 17th Ave 07719 732-556-2560
Anthony Abeal, prin. Fax 556-2571
Other Schools – See Allenwood, Sea Girt

Wallington, Bergen, Pop. 11,200
Wallington SD 1,100/K-12
32 Pine St 07057 973-777-4421
James Albro, supt. Fax 614-9391
www.wboe.org
Gavlak ES 400/K-6
106 King St 07057 973-777-4420
Nancy Giambrone, prin. Fax 574-9517
Jefferson Annex ES 200/K-3
6 Bond St 07057 973-836-4700
Nancy Giambrone, prin. Fax 777-4609

Wanamassa, Monmouth, Pop. 4,434
Ocean Township SD
Supt. — See Oakhurst
Wanamassa ES 300/PK-4
901 Bendermere Ave 07712 732-531-5700
Victor Milano, prin. Fax 531-3720

Wanaque, Passaic, Pop. 10,935
Wanaque SD
Supt. — See Haskell
Wanaque S, 1 1st St 07465 500/PK-8
Charles Frick, prin. 973-835-8200

Waretown, Ocean, Pop. 1,552
Ocean Township SD 500/PK-6
64 Railroad Ave 08758 609-693-3131
Dr. Christopher Lommerin, supt. Fax 693-5833
www.otsdk6.org
Priff ES 200/4-6
139 Wells Mill Rd 08758 609-693-3131
Ariane Phillips, prin. Fax 693-6972
Waretown ES 300/PK-3
64 Railroad Ave 08758 609-693-3131
Sarah Reinhold, prin. Fax 242-2190

Warren, Somerset
Warren Township SD 1,900/PK-8
213 Mount Horeb Rd 07059 732-753-5300
Dr. Matthew Mingle, supt. Fax 560-8801
www.warrentboe.org
Central ES 300/K-5
109 Mount Bethel Rd 07059 908-753-5300
Alison Tugya, prin. Fax 757-3930
Mt. Horeb ES 200/PK-5
80 Mount Horeb Rd 07059 732-753-5300
Scott Cook, prin. Fax 356-3753
Tomaso ES 300/K-5
46 Washington Valley Rd 07059 732-753-5300
Christine Smith, prin. Fax 302-9140
Warren MS 700/6-8
100 Old Stirling Rd 07059 908-753-5300
George Villar, prin. Fax 753-4789
Woodland ES 300/K-5
114 Stirling Rd 07059 908-753-5300
Jeff Heaney, prin. Fax 604-6633

Washington, Warren, Pop. 6,336
Franklin Township SD 300/PK-6
52 Asbury Broadway Rd 07882 908-689-2958
Matt Eagleburger, supt. Fax 689-1786
www.franklinschool.org
Franklin Township ES 300/PK-6
52 Asbury Broadway Rd 07882 908-689-2958
Matt Eagleburger, prin. Fax 689-1786

Warren Hills Regional HSD 1,800/7-12
89 Bowerstown Rd 07882 908-689-3143
Earl Clymer, supt. Fax 689-4814
www.warrenhills.org
Warren Hills Regional MS 600/7-8
64 Carlton Ave 07882 908-689-0750
Lee Turkowski, prin. Fax 689-3663

Washington Borough SD 500/PK-6
300 W Stewart St 07882 908-689-0241
Lance Rozsa, supt. Fax 689-8269
www.washboroschools.org/
Taylor Street ES 200/PK-2
16 Taylor St 07882 908-689-0091
Jacqueline Nassry, prin. Fax 689-8273
Washington Memorial ES 300/3-6
300 W Stewart St 07882 908-689-0241
Lance Rozsa, prin. Fax 689-8269

Washington Township SD 500/PK-6
1 E Front St 07882 908-689-1119
Keith Neuhs, supt. Fax 689-3748
www.washtwpsd.org/
Brass Castle ES 300/PK-K, 4-6
16 Castle St 07882 908-689-1188
Jessica Garcia, prin. Fax 689-2356
Port Colden ES 200/1-3
30 Port Colden Rd 07882 908-689-0681
Michael Neu, prin. Fax 689-8584

Good Shepherd Christian Academy 200/PK-12
490 State Route 57 W 07882 908-835-1399
Cindy Weaver, admin. Fax 835-1398

Washington Township, Bergen, Pop. 9,245
Westwood Regional SD 2,600/K-12
701 Ridgewood Rd 07676 201-664-0880
Dr. Raymond Gonzalez, supt. Fax 664-7642
www.wwrsd.org
George ES 200/K-5
1 Palm St 07676 201-664-3033
Victoria Hickey, prin. Fax 722-0670
Washington ES 300/K-5
600 School St 07676 201-664-6440
Melissa Palianto, prin. Fax 722-0793
Other Schools – See Westwood

Watchung, Somerset, Pop. 5,662
Watchung Borough SD 700/PK-8
1 Dr Parenty Way 07069 908-755-8121
Dr. Barbara Resko, supt. Fax 755-6946
www.watchungschools.com
Bayberry ES 400/PK-4
113 Bayberry Ln 07069 908-755-8184
Michael Vignola, prin. Fax 755-0366
Valley View MS 300/5-8
50 Valleyview Rd 07069 908-755-4422
Mary Nunn, prin. Fax 755-4035

Waterford Works, Camden
Waterford Township SD 800/PK-6
1106 Old White Horse Pike 08089 856-767-8293
Dr. Brenda Harring, supt. Fax 767-4159
www.wtsd.org
Waterford ES 400/4-6
1106 Old White Horse Pike 08089 856-767-8293
Patrick Davidson, prin. Fax 768-8086
Other Schools – See Atco

Wayne, Passaic, Pop. 55,000
Wayne Township SD 8,100/PK-12
50 Nellis Dr 07470 973-633-3000
Dr. Mark Toback, supt. Fax 628-8058
www.wayneschools.com
Carter ES 300/K-5
531 Alps Rd 07470 973-633-3145
Scot Burkholder, prin. Fax 694-4370
Dey ES 400/PK-5
55 Webster Dr 07470 973-633-3155
Necole Jadick, prin. Fax 633-6916
Fallon ES 400/K-5
51 Clifford Dr 07470 973-633-3125
Ethan Maayan, prin. Fax 633-0601
Kennedy ES 400/K-5
1310 Ratzer Rd 07470 973-633-3160
Kolleen Myers, prin. Fax 942-1711
Lafayette ES 400/PK-5
100 Laauwe Ave 07470 973-633-3165
Matthew Kriley, prin. Fax 942-1457
Packanack ES 500/PK-5
190 Oakwood Dr 07470 973-633-3170
Roger Rogalin, prin. Fax 872-1215
Pines Lake ES 400/K-5
511 Pines Lake Dr E 07470 973-633-3175
Jose Celis, prin. Fax 839-7885
Ryerson ES 200/PK-5
30 McClelland Ave 07470 973-633-3180
Debora Foti, prin. Fax 633-2595

Schuyler-Colfax MS 700/6-8
1500 Hamburg Tpke 07470 973-633-3130
Matthew Mignanelli, prin. Fax 633-3195
Terhune ES 400/PK-5
40 Geoffrey Way 07470 973-633-3150
Dawn Auerbach, prin. Fax 831-7450
Washington MS 600/6-8
68 Lenox Rd 07470 973-633-3140
Jack Leonard, prin. Fax 633-7590
Wayne MS 700/6-8
201 Garside Ave 07470 973-389-2120
David Aulenbach, prin. Fax 389-2130

Apple Montessori of Wayne 300/PK-6
25 Nevins Rd 07470 973-696-9750
Immaculate Heart of Mary S 200/PK-8
580 Ratzer Rd 07470 973-694-1225
Frances Alberta, prin. Fax 872-9043
Pioneer Academy 300/PK-12
164 Totowa Rd 07470 973-405-5169
Tufan Aydin M.Ed., prin. Fax 405-5176

Weehawken, Hudson, Pop. 12,385
Weehawken Township SD 1,300/PK-12
53 Liberty Pl 07086 201-422-6120
Dr. Robert Zywicki, supt.
www.weehawken.k12.nj.us
Roosevelt ES, 1 Louisa Pl 07086 400/3-6
Suzanne Mera, prin. 201-422-6140
Webster ES, 2700 Palisade Ave 07086 400/PK-2
Anna Rudowsky, prin. 201-422-6150

Wenonah, Gloucester, Pop. 2,254
Deptford Township SD
Supt. — See Deptford
Oak Valley ES 400/2-6
525 College Blvd 08090 856-415-9218
John Schilling, prin. Fax 464-1794
Pine Acres ECC 300/PK-1
720 Purdue Ave 08090 856-464-1260
Shelli Jones, prin. Fax 464-1788

Wenonah SD 200/PK-6
200 N Clinton Ave 08090 856-468-6000
Kristine Height, admin. Fax 468-9674
www.wenonahsd.org
Wenonah ES 200/PK-6
200 N Clinton Ave 08090 856-468-6000
Kristine Height, admin. Fax 468-9674

Westampton, Burlington, Pop. 60,004
Westampton Township SD 1,000/PK-8
700 Rancocas Rd 08060 609-267-2053
Dr. Anthony Petruzzelli, supt. Fax 267-2760
www.westamptonschools.org
Holly Hills ES 500/K-4
500 Ogden Dr 08060 609-267-8565
Dr. Rachel Feldman, prin. Fax 702-9744
Westampton MS 500/PK-PK, 5-
700 Rancocas Rd 08060 609-267-2722
Matthew Andris, prin. Fax 702-9017

West Berlin, Camden, Pop. 3,000
Berlin Township SD 600/PK-8
225 Grove Ave 08091 856-767-9480
Dr. Edythe Austermuhl Ed.D., supt. Fax 767-8235
www.btwpschools.org
Eisenhower MS 300/4-8
235 Grove Ave 08091 856-767-9480
Marilyn Bright, prin. Fax 767-7992
Kennedy Memorial ES 300/PK-3
228 Mount Vernon Ave 08091 856-767-9164
Michael Murphy, prin. Fax 768-9066

West Caldwell, Essex, Pop. 10,422
Caldwell-West Caldwell SD 2,600/PK-12
104 Gray St 07006 973-228-6979
Dr. James Heinegg, supt. Fax 228-8716
www.cwcboe.org/
Harrison Preschool PK-PK
104 Gray St 07006 973-228-6979
Jefferson ES, 85 Prospect St 07006 300/K-5
Timothy Ayers, prin. 973-228-5994
Washington ES 400/K-5
201 Central Ave 07006 973-228-8941
Barbara Adams, prin.
Wilson ES, Orton Rd 07006 300/K-5
Scott Keena, prin. 973-228-7173
Other Schools – See Caldwell

West Cape May, Cape May, Pop. 1,011
West Cape May SD 100/PK-6
301 Moore St 08204 609-884-4614
Dr. Alfred Savio, supt. Fax 884-0932
westcape.nj.schoolwebpages.com
West Cape May ES 100/PK-6
301 Moore St 08204 609-884-4614
Dr. Alfred Savio, supt. Fax 884-0932

West Collingswood, See Collingswood
Collingswood Borough SD
Supt. — See Collingswood
Sharp ES 100/PK-5
400 Comly Ave 08107 856-962-5707
Dr. Karen Principato, prin. Fax 962-5569

West Creek, Ocean
Eagleswood Township SD 100/PK-6
511 Main St 08092 609-597-3663
Deborah Snyder, supt. Fax 978-0949
www.eagleswood.org
Eagleswood Township ES 100/PK-6
511 Main St 08092 609-597-3663
Deborah Snyder, supt. Fax 978-0949

West Deptford, Gloucester, Pop. 19,380
West Deptford Township SD 2,800/PK-12
675 Grove Rd 08066 856-848-4300
Steve Crispin, supt. Fax 845-5743
www.wdeptford.k12.nj.us/
Green-Fields ES 500/K-K, 3-4
15 Hill Ln, 856-845-7929
Karry Corbitt, prin. Fax 384-6505
Oakview ES 200/PK-2
350 Dubois Ave, 856-845-1856
Ryan Dougherty, prin. Fax 845-3241
Red Bank ES 200/K-2
192 Philadelphia Ave, 856-845-2727
Jill Scheetz, prin. Fax 251-1927
West Deptford MS 900/5-8
675 Grove Rd 08066 856-848-1200
Christine Trampe, prin. Fax 848-2325

Westfield, Union, Pop. 29,789
Westfield SD 6,100/PK-12
302 Elm St 07090 908-789-4400
Dr. Margaret Dolan, supt. Fax 789-4192
www.westfieldnjk12.org
Edison IS 800/6-8
800 Rahway Ave 07090 908-789-4470
Dr. Matthew Bolton, prin. Fax 789-1506
Franklin ES 600/1-5
700 Prospect St 07090 908-789-4590
Dr. Eileen Cambria, prin. Fax 789-0263
Jefferson ES 500/1-5
1200 Boulevard 07090 908-789-4490
Dr. Susie Hung, prin. Fax 789-0939
Lincoln Early Childhood Learning Center 200/PK-K
728 Westfield Ave 07090 908-789-4455
Audrey Zavetz, prin. Fax 232-1734
McKinley ES 300/1-5
500 1st St 07090 908-789-4555
Marc Biunno, prin. Fax 789-6116
Roosevelt IS 700/6-8
301 Clark St 07090 908-789-4560
Mary Asfendis, prin. Fax 789-4193
Tamaques ES 400/1-5
641 Willow Grove Rd 07090 908-789-4580
David Duelks, prin. Fax 789-2566
Washington ES 300/1-5
900 Saint Marks Ave 07090 908-789-4600
Dr. Andrew Perry, prin. Fax 789-2597
Wilson ES 400/1-5
301 Linden Ave 07090 908-789-4605
Joseph Malanga, prin. Fax 789-2890

Holy Trinity Interparochial S 200/1-8
336 1st St 07090 908-233-0484
Sr. Maureen Fichner, prin. Fax 233-6204
Redeemer Lutheran S 50/PK-K
229 Cowperthwaite Pl 07090 908-232-1592
Kathy Calello, dir. Fax 317-9301

West Long Branch, Monmouth, Pop. 8,009
West Long Branch SD 500/PK-8
135 Locust Ave 07764 732-222-5900
Thomas Farrell, supt. Fax 222-9325
www.wlbschools.com
Antonides S 300/5-8
135 Locust Ave 07764 732-222-5900
Dr. Michael Fiorillo, prin. Fax 222-8154
McElmon ES 200/PK-4
20 Parker Rd 07764 732-222-5900
James Erhardt, prin. Fax 483-0845

St. Jerome S 300/PK-8
250 Wall St 07764 732-222-8686
Sr. Angelina Pelliccia, prin. Fax 263-0343

West Milford, Passaic, Pop. 26,600
West Milford Township SD 3,500/PK-12
46 Highlander Dr 07480 973-697-1700
Dr. Alex Anemone, supt. Fax 697-8351
www.wmtps.org
Apshawa ES 300/K-6
140 High Crest Dr 07480 973-838-6515
Stephanie Primavera, prin. Fax 838-6896
Macopin MS 600/7-8
70 Highlander Dr 07480 973-697-5691
Marc Citro, prin. Fax 697-0301
Maple Road ES 300/K-6
36 Maple Rd 07480 973-697-3606
William Kane, prin. Fax 208-0257
Marshall Hill ES 300/K-6
210 Marshall Hill Rd 07480 973-728-3430
Janet Cash, prin. Fax 728-1444
Westbrook ES 400/PK-6
55 Nosenzo Pond Rd 07480 973-697-5700
Dr. Dana Swarts, prin. Fax 208-0136
Other Schools – See Hewitt, Oak Ridge

Westmont, Camden, Pop. 5,500
Haddon Township SD 1,700/PK-12
500 Rhoads Ave 08108 856-869-7700
Bonnie J. Edwards, supt. Fax 854-7792
www.haddontwpschools.com/
Edison ES, 205 Melrose Ave 08108 100/PK-5
Eileen Loffredo, prin. 856-869-7715
Rohrer MS 400/6-8
101 MacArthur Blvd 08108 856-869-7750
Dr. Patricia Schwab, prin. Fax 869-7772
Strawbridge ES 200/K-5
307 Strawbridge Ave 08108 856-869-7735
Eileen Loffredo, prin.
Other Schools – See Haddonfield, Oaklyn

West New York, Hudson, Pop. 49,199
West New York SD 8,000/PK-12
6028 Broadway 07093 201-553-4000
Clara Herrera, supt. Fax 865-2725
www.wnyschools.net
Bain ES 700/PK-6
6200 Broadway 07093 201-553-4095
Tara Mantineo, prin. Fax 758-0366
Early Childhood S 1,300/PK-PK
5204 Hudson Ave 07093 201-553-4035
Cara Zebrowski, prin. Fax 330-2945
Menendez ES 500/PK-6
600 55th St 07093 201-553-4060
Robert Reiman, prin. Fax 583-6633
Public S 1 800/K-6
6129 Madison St 07093 201-553-4025
Alexander Calderone, prin. Fax 861-6998
Public S 2 700/PK-6
5200 Broadway 07093 201-553-4040
Christian Cardenas, prin. Fax 553-7432
Public S 5 700/PK-6
5401 Hudson Ave 07093 201-553-4080
Nelson Lopez, prin. Fax 330-7828
Sires ES 700/PK-6
6300 Palisade Ave 07093 201-553-4070
Brian Cooney, prin. Fax 553-4050
West New York MS 900/7-8
201 57th St 07093 201-563-4160
Patrick Gagliardi, prin. Fax 863-6698

Academy of St. Joseph of the Palisades S 200/K-8
6408 Palisade Ave 07093 201-861-3227
Lauren Lytle, prin. Fax 861-5744

West Orange, Essex, Pop. 45,500
West Orange SD 6,500/PK-12
179 Eagle Rock Ave 07052 973-669-5400
Jeffrey Rutzky, supt. Fax 669-1432
www.woboe.org
Edison MS 400/6-6
75 William St 07052 973-669-5360
Xavier Fitzgerald, prin. Fax 243-9802
Gregory ES 500/K-5
301 Gregory Ave 07052 973-669-5397
Michele Thompson, prin. Fax 243-0251
Hazel Avenue ES 400/K-5
45 Hazel Ave 07052 973-669-5448
William Kochis, prin. Fax 243-0696
Kelly ES 400/PK-5
555 Pleasant Valley Way 07052 973-669-5452
Joanne Pollara, prin. Fax 669-5455
Liberty MS 500/7-8
1 Kelly Dr 07052 973-243-2007
Robert Klemt, prin. Fax 243-2743
Maddalena Early Learning Center PK-PK
747 Northfield Ave 07052 973-435-9630
Mt. Pleasant ES 400/K-5
9 Manger Rd 07052 973-669-5480
Julie DiGiacomo, prin. Fax 669-5496
Redwood ES 600/K-5
75 Redwood Ave 07052 973-669-5457
Bruce Arcurio, prin. Fax 324-9224
Roosevelt MS 500/7-8
36 Gilbert Pl 07052 973-669-5373
Lionel Hush, prin. Fax 243-9807
St. Cloud ES 400/K-5
71 Sheridan Ave 07052 973-669-5393
Eric Price, prin. Fax 325-1685
Washington ES 400/K-5
289 Main St 07052 973-669-5385
Marie DeMaio, prin. Fax 669-5462

Golda Och Academy - Lower S 300/PK-5
122 Gregory Ave 07052 973-602-3700
Adam Shapiro, head sch Fax 669-8689

Westville, Gloucester, Pop. 4,234
Deptford Township SD
Supt. — See Deptford
Shady Lane ES 400/2-6
130 Peach St 08093 856-384-6046
Jackie Scerbo, prin. Fax 845-3459

Westville SD 300/PK-6
101 Birch Ave 08093 856-456-0235
Dr. Shannon Whalen, supt. Fax 456-0484
www.westvillesd.com
Parkview ES 300/PK-6
101 Birch Ave 08093 856-456-0235
Renee Egan, prin. Fax 456-5974

Holy Trinity Regional S 200/PK-8
1215 Delsea Dr 08093 856-848-6826
Elsie Tedeski, prin. Fax 251-0344

West Windsor, Mercer
West Windsor-Plainsboro Regional SD 9,300/PK-12
PO Box 505 08550 609-716-5000
David Aderhold Ed.D., supt. Fax 716-5012
www.ww-p.org
Dutch Neck ES 600/K-3
392 Village Rd E 08550 609-716-5400
David Argese, prin. Fax 716-5409
Hawk ES 800/K-3
303 Clarksville Rd 08550 609-716-5425
Patricia Buell, prin. Fax 716-5439
Village S 700/PK-PK, 4-
601 New Village Rd 08550 609-716-5200
Barbara Gould, prin. Fax 716-5206
Other Schools – See Plainsboro, Princeton Junction

Westwood, Bergen, Pop. 10,781
Westwood Regional SD
Supt. — See Washington Township
Berkeley Avenue ES 300/K-5
47 Berkeley Ave 07675 201-664-7760
Michael Fiorello, prin. Fax 664-1168
Brookside ES 400/K-5
20 Lake Dr 07675 201-664-9000
Thomas Conroy, prin. Fax 722-0661
Westwood Regional MS 400/6-7
23 3rd Ave 07675 201-664-5560
Shelley LaForgia, prin.

Wharton, Morris, Pop. 6,390
Jefferson Township SD
Supt. — See Lake Hopatcong
Stanlick ES 400/3-5
121B E Shawnee Trl 07885 973-663-0520
Kevin Lipton, prin. Fax 663-7854

Rockaway Township SD
Supt. — See Hibernia
Dwyer ES 300/K-5
665 Mount Hope Ave 07885 973-361-7450
Michael McGovern, prin. Fax 361-8751

Wharton Borough SD 700/K-8
137 E Central Ave 07885 973-361-2592
Christopher Herdman, supt. Fax 895-2187
www.wbps.org/
Duffy ES 500/K-5
137 E Central Ave 07885 973-361-2506
Pamela Blalock, prin. Fax 361-4917
MacKinnon MS 300/6-8
137 E Central Ave 07885 973-361-1253
Patrick Ketch, prin. Fax 361-4805

Whippany, Morris
Hanover Township SD 1,500/K-8
61 Highland Ave 07981 973-515-2404
Michael Wasko, supt. Fax 540-1023
www.hanovertwpschools.com/
Bee Meadow ES 300/K-5
120 Reynolds Ave 07981 973-515-2419
Darrin Stark, prin. Fax 515-7528
Memorial JHS 500/6-8
61 Highland Ave 07981 973-515-2427
Michael Anderson, prin. Fax 515-2481
Salem Drive ES 300/K-5
29 Salem Dr N 07981 973-515-2440
Rob Camean, prin. Fax 515-5097
Other Schools – See Morris Plains

Abundant Life Christian S 100/PK-8
90 Whippany Rd 07981 973-888-2083
Jessica Jaruczyk, prin. Fax 463-9677

White House Station, Hunterdon, Pop. 2,066
Readington Township SD 1,800/PK-8
PO Box 807 08889 908-534-2195
Dr. William DeFabiis, supt. Fax 349-3042
www.readington.k12.nj.us
Holland Brook ES 400/4-5
PO Box 1500 08889 908-823-0454
Paul Nigro, prin. Fax 349-3021
Readington MS 700/6-8
PO Box 700 08889 908-534-2113
Sharon Moffat, prin. Fax 534-6802
Whitehouse ES 300/K-3
PO Box 157 08889 908-534-4411
Dr. Ann DeRosa, prin. Fax 349-3057
Other Schools – See Three Bridges

Whiting, Ocean
Manchester Township SD 2,000/PK-12
121 Route 539 08759 732-350-5900
David Trethaway, supt. Fax 350-0436
www.manchestertwp.org
Whiting ES 200/PK-5
412 Manchester Blvd 08759 732-350-4994
Evelyn Swift, prin. Fax 350-4476
Other Schools – See Manchester

Wildwood, Cape May, Pop. 5,246
Wildwood CSD 800/PK-12
4300 Pacific Ave 08260 609-522-7922
J. Kenyon Kummings, supt. Fax 523-1014
www.edline.net/pages/Wildwood_PSD
Glenwood Avenue ES 400/PK-5
2900 New York Ave 08260 609-522-1630
Travis LaFerriere, prin. Fax 729-5243
Wildwood MS 200/6-8
4300 Pacific Ave 08260 609-522-7922
Philip Schaffer, prin. Fax 522-7914

Wildwood Crest SD 200/PK-8
9100 Pacific Ave 08260 609-522-1522
David DelConte, supt.
www.crestmem.edu
Crest Memorial S 200/PK-8
9100 Pacific Ave 08260 609-522-1522
Dave DelConte, prin.

Cape Trinity Catholic S 200/PK-8
1500 Central Ave 08260 609-522-2704
Sr. Sheila Murphy, dir. Fax 522-5329

Williamstown, Gloucester, Pop. 15,255
Buena Regional SD
Supt. — See Richland
Collings Lake ES 200/K-3
620 Cains Mill Rd 08094 856-885-4994
Daniel Benedetto, prin. Fax 561-5646

Monroe Township SD 5,800/PK-12
75 E Academy St 08094 856-629-6400
Charles Earling, supt. Fax 262-2499
www.monroetwp.k12.nj.us
Holly Glen ES 500/PK-4
900 N Main St 08094 856-728-8706
Karen Crossley, prin. Fax 262-4732
Oak Knoll ES 500/K-4
23 Bodine Ave 08094 856-728-3944
Kristy Baker, prin. Fax 728-6791
Radix ES 600/PK-4
363 Radix Rd 08094 856-728-8650
Dr. JILL DELCONTE, prin. Fax 262-7491
Whitehall ES 400/K-4
161 Whitehall Rd 08094 856-728-8782
Joanne Rumpf, prin. Fax 262-7923
Williamstown MS 1,900/5-8
561 Clayton Rd 08094 856-629-7444
Dana Mericle, prin. Fax 875-6757

St. Mary S 600/PK-8
32 Carroll Ave 08094 856-629-6190
Patricia Mancuso, prin. Fax 728-1437

Willingboro, Burlington, Pop. 32,400
Willingboro Township SD 3,600/PK-12
440 Beverly Rancocas Rd 08046 609-835-8600
Dr. Ronald G. Taylor, supt. Fax 835-3880
www.willingboroschools.org/
Garfield East ES 400/PK-5
150 Evergreen Dr 08046 609-835-8990
Phillip Crisostomo, prin. Fax 835-8999
Hawthorne ES 500/PK-5
84 Hampshire Ln 08046 609-835-8960
Dumar Burgess, prin. Fax 835-8969
James ES 400/PK-5
41 Pinetree Ln 08046 609-835-8940
Sylvia Miles-Wright, prin. Fax 835-8929
Memorial MS 6th Grade Academy 6-6
50 Martin Luther King Blvd 08046 609-835-8930
Ellis Brown, prin. Fax 835-8600
Memorial MS 700/7-8
451 Van Sciver Pkwy 08046 609-835-8700
Ellis Brown, prin. Fax 835-1457
Stuart ES 400/PK-5
70 Sunset Rd 08046 609-835-3881
Nadine Tribbett, prin. Fax 835-3889
Twin Hills ES 400/PK-5
110 Twin Hill Dr 08046 609-835-8980
Sonya Nock-Lemons, prin. Fax 835-8989

Pope John Paul II Regional S 200/PK-8
11 S Sunset Rd 08046 609-877-2144
Catherine Zagola, prin. Fax 877-3153

Winfield Park, Union, Pop. 1,576
Winfield Township SD 100/PK-8
7 1/2 Gulfstream Ave 07036 908-486-7410
Ross LeBrun, supt. Fax 486-4571
www.winfieldschool.org
Winfield Township S 100/PK-8
7 1/2 Gulfstream Ave 07036 908-486-7410
Ross LeBrun, prin. Fax 486-4571

Woodbine, Cape May, Pop. 2,422
Woodbine SD 200/PK-8
801 Webster St 08270 609-861-5174
Anthony DeVico, supt. Fax 861-0723
Woodbine ES 200/PK-8
801 Webster St 08270 609-861-5174
Anthony DeVico, supt. Fax 861-0723

Woodbridge, Middlesex, Pop. 18,933
Woodbridge Township SD 12,800/PK-12
PO Box 428 07095 732-750-3200
Dr. Robert Zega, supt. Fax 750-3493
www.woodbridge.k12.nj.us
Mawbey Street ES 400/K-5
275 Mawbey St 07095 732-602-8401
Barbara Balog, prin. Fax 855-7654
Ross Street ES 400/K-5
110 Ross St 07095 732-602-8511
Tammy Giordano, prin. Fax 855-0597
Woodbridge MS 400/6-8
525 Barron Ave 07095 732-602-8690
Dr. John Crowe, prin. Fax 855-0326
Other Schools – See Avenel, Colonia, Fords, Iselin, Metuchen, Port Reading, Sewaren

---

St. James S 300/PK-8
341 Amboy Ave 07095 732-634-2090
Fran Comiskey, prin. Fax 634-4390

Woodbury, Gloucester, Pop. 9,869
Woodbury SD 1,400/PK-12
25 N Broad St 08096 856-853-0123
Lynn DiPietropolo, supt. Fax 853-0704
www.woodburysch.com
Evergreen Avenue ES 300/PK-5
160 N Evergreen Ave 08096 856-853-0125
Thomas Braddock, prin. Fax 853-2867
Walnut Street ES 100/K-5
60 Walnut St 08096 856-853-0126
Dr. Jeffrey Adams, prin. Fax 384-1040
West End Memorial ES 400/PK-5
215 Queen St 08096 856-853-0124
Vincent Myers, prin. Fax 853-2667

Woodbury Heights, Gloucester, Pop. 3,021
Woodbury Heights SD 200/PK-6
100 Academy Ave 08097 856-848-2610
Janis Gansert, admin. Fax 848-8739
www.woodburyhtselem.com/
Woodbury Heights ES 200/PK-6
100 Academy Ave 08097 856-848-2610
Janis Gansert, admin. Fax 848-8739

St. Margaret Regional S 600/PK-8
773 Third St 08097 856-845-5200
Sr. Michele DeGregorio, prin. Fax 845-2405

Woodcliff Lake, Bergen, Pop. 5,674
Woodcliff Lake SD 800/PK-8
134 Woodcliff Ave 07677 201-930-5600
Lauren Barbelet, supt. Fax 930-0488
www.woodcliff-lake.com
Dorchester ES 500/PK-5
100 Dorchester Rd 07677 201-930-5600
Stefanie Marsich, prin. Fax 930-0488
Woodcliff MS 300/6-8
134 Woodcliff Ave 07677 201-930-5600
Robert Lombardy, prin. Fax 391-7932

Woodland Park, Passaic
Woodland Park SD 1,000/K-8
853 McBride Ave, 973-317-7700
Dr. Michele R. Pillari, supt. Fax 317-7773
wpschools.org
Gilmore ES 200/3-4
1075 McBride Ave, 973-317-7740
Sharon Tomback, prin. Fax 317-7743
Memorial MS 500/5-8
15 Memorial Dr, 973-317-7750
Charles Silverstein, prin. Fax 317-7753
Olbon ES 400/K-2
50 Lincoln Ln, 973-317-7730
Giovanna Irizarry, prin. Fax 317-7733

Woodlynne, Camden, Pop. 2,895
Woodlynne Borough SD 400/PK-8
131 Elm Ave 08107 856-962-8822
Dr. Jack McCulley, supt. Fax 962-0191
www.woodlynne.k12.nj.us
Woodlynne S 400/PK-8
131 Elm Ave 08107 856-962-8822
Dr. Jack McCulley, admin. Fax 962-0191

Wood Ridge, Bergen, Pop. 7,540
Wood-Ridge SD 800/PK-12
540 Windsor Rd 07075 201-933-6777
Nicholas Cipriano, supt. Fax 804-9204
www.wood-ridgeschools.org
Doyle ES 300/PK-3
250 Wood Ridge Ave 07075 201-933-6777
Anthony Albro, prin. Fax 939-6049
Wood-Ridge IS 100/4-6
151 1st St 07075 201-933-6777
Keith Lisa, prin. Fax 939-0259

Woodstown, Salem, Pop. 3,420
Woodstown-Pilesgrove Regional SD 1,500/PK-12
135 East Ave 08098 856-769-0144
Virginia Grossman, supt. Fax 769-4549
www.woodstown.org
Shoemaker ES 400/1-5
201 E Millbrooke Ave 08098 856-769-0144
Diane Cioffi, prin. Fax 769-9388
Woodstown MS 300/6-8
15 Lincoln Ave 08098 856-769-0144
Allison Pessolano, prin. Fax 769-3872
Other Schools – See Pilesgrove

Woolwich, Gloucester
Kingsway Regional SD 2,400/7-12
213 Kings Hwy 08085 856-467-3300
Dr. James Lavender, supt. Fax 467-5382
www.krsd.org
Kingsway Regional MS 900/7-8
203 Kings Hwy 08085 856-467-3300
Brian Tonelli, prin. Fax 467-2703

Swedesboro-Woolwich SD
Supt. — See Swedesboro
Harker ES 700/3-5
1771 Oldmans Creek Rd 08085 856-241-1552
Carolynne Sandy, prin. Fax 241-2365
Stratton S 500/1-2
15 Fredrick Blvd 08085 856-241-1552
Rob Titus, prin. Fax 467-4379

Wrightstown, Burlington, Pop. 764
New Hanover Township SD 200/K-8
122 Fort Dix St 08562 609-723-2139
Dr. Richard Wiener, supt. Fax 723-6694
www.newhanover.k12.nj.us
New Hanover Township S 200/K-8
122 Fort Dix St 08562 609-723-2139
Scott Larkin, prin. Fax 723-6694

North Hanover Township SD 1,200/PK-6
331 Monmouth Rd 08562 609-738-2600
Helen Payne, supt. Fax 738-2659
nhanover.com
Lamb ES 400/1-4
46 Schoolhouse Rd 08562 609-738-2630
Dennis Morolda Ed.D., prin. Fax 738-4993
North Hanover Township Upper ES 300/5-6
351 Monmouth Rd 08562 609-738-2622
James Alvarez, prin. Fax 738-2658
Other Schools – See Mc Guire AFB

Wyckoff, Bergen, Pop. 15,372
Wyckoff Township SD 2,100/PK-8
241 Morse Ave 07481 201-848-5700
Dr. Richard Kuder, supt. Fax 848-5695
www.wyckoffps.org
Coolidge ES 300/K-5
420 Grandview Ave 07481 201-848-5710
Robert Famularo, prin. Fax 652-0860
Eisenhower MS 800/6-8
344 Calvin Ct 07481 201-848-5750
Christopher Iasiello, prin. Fax 848-5682
Lincoln ES 300/K-5
325 Mason Ave 07481 201-848-5720
Patrick Lee, prin. Fax 848-1607
Sicomac ES 300/PK-5
356 Sicomac Ave 07481 201-848-5730
Stephen Raimo, prin. Fax 848-5739
Washington ES 400/K-5
270 Woodland Ave 07481 201-848-5740
Scott Blake, prin. Fax 848-0630

Eastern Christian MS 200/5-8
518 Sicomac Ave 07481 201-891-3663
Daniel Lazor, prin.
St. Elizabeth S 300/PK-8
100 Greenwood Ave 07481 201-891-1481
Karen Lewis, prin. Fax 891-8669

NEW MEXICO

NEW MEXICO PUBLIC EDUCATION DEPARTMENT
300 Don Gaspar Ave, Santa Fe 87501-2744
Telephone 505-827-5800
Fax 505-827-6696
Website http://www.sde.state.nm.us

Secretary of Education Hanna Skandara

NEW MEXICO PUBLIC EDUCATION COMMISSION
300 Don Gaspar Ave, Santa Fe 87501-2744

Chairperson Patricia Gipson

REGIONAL EDUCATION COOPS (REC) & REGIONAL CENTER COOPS (RCC)

Central REC 5
Maria Jaramillo, dir. 505-889-3412
PO Box 37440, Albuquerque 87176 Fax 889-3422
www.crecnm.org
High Plains REC 3
R. Stephen Aguirre, dir. 575-445-7090
101 N 2nd St, Raton 87740 Fax 445-7663
www.hprec.com
Northeast REC 4
Dr. Jim Abreu, dir. 505-426-2262
PO Box 927, Las Vegas 87701 Fax 454-1473
www.rec4.com
Northwest REC 2
Adan Delgado, dir. 575-756-1274
PO Box 113, Chama 87520 Fax 756-1278
www.nwrec2.org
Pecos Valley REC 8
David Willden, dir. 575-748-6100
PO Box 155, Artesia 88211 Fax 748-6160
www.pvrec8.com
REC 6
Scott McMath, dir. 575-562-4455
1500 S Avenue K, Portales 88130 Fax 562-4460
www.rec6.net
REC 7
Belinda Morris, dir. 575-393-0755
315 E Clinton St, Hobbs 88240 Fax 393-0249
hobbsschools.net/department/regional_education_cooperative_7
REC 9
Bryan Dooley, dir. 575-257-2368
143 El Paso Rd, Ruidoso 88345 Fax 257-2141
www.rec9nm.org
Southwest REC 10
Vicki Chavez, dir. 575-546-5951
1321 E Poplar St, Deming 88030 Fax 546-5994
www.swrecnm.org

PUBLIC, PRIVATE AND CATHOLIC ELEMENTARY SCHOOLS

Abiquiu, Rio Arriba, Pop. 229
Espanola SD 55
Supt. — See Espanola
Abiquiu ES 100/K-6
SR 84/285 #1911 Gate 21342 87510 505-685-4457
Fanny Castillo de Gonzal, prin. Fax 685-4644

Alamogordo, Otero, Pop. 29,463
Alamogordo SD 6,000/PK-12
PO Box 650 88311 575-812-6000
Adrianne Salas, supt. Fax 812-6003
www.aps4kids.org
Buena Vista ES 300/K-5
PO Box 650 88311 575-812-5100
Tena Spitsberg, prin. Fax 812-5103
Chaparral MS 700/6-8
PO Box 650 88311 575-812-6300
Robbi Coker, prin. Fax 812-6303
Desert Star ES K-5
PO Box 650 88311 575-812-5750
Victor Gonzales, prin. Fax 812-5753
Heights ES 300/K-5
PO Box 650 88311 575-812-5200
Cathy Jackson, prin. Fax 812-5203
Mountain View MS 400/6-8
PO Box 650 88311 575-812-6400
Moises Cardiel, prin. Fax 812-6403
North ES 300/PK-5
PO Box 650 88311 575-812-5400
Manuela Sanchez, prin. Fax 812-5403
Oregon ES 300/K-5
PO Box 650 88311 575-812-5600
Teresa Bruederle, prin. Fax 812-5603
Sierra ES 400/K-5
PO Box 650 88311 575-812-5800
Melissa Cole, prin. Fax 812-5803
Yucca ES 500/K-5
PO Box 650 88311 575-812-5900
Catherine Diaz, prin. Fax 812-5903
Other Schools – See High Rolls Mountain Park, Holloman AFB, La Luz

---

Fr. James B Hay S 100/PK-8
1000 8th St 88310 575-437-7821
Julia Fracker, prin. Fax 443-6129
Imago Dei Academy 100/K-12
1100 Michigan Ave 88310 575-434-3903
Legacy Christian Academy 100/PK-12
3001 Thunder Rd 88310 575-434-0352
Cindy McKee, dir. Fax 434-0352

Albuquerque, Bernalillo, Pop. 534,167
Albuquerque SD 90,500/PK-12
PO Box 25704 87125 505-880-3700
Raquel Reedy, supt. Fax 872-8855
www.aps.edu
Adams MS 700/6-8
5401 Glenrio Rd NW 87105 505-831-0400
Modesta Hernandez, prin. Fax 836-7760
Adobe Acres ES 600/PK-5
1724 Camino Del Valle SW 87105 505-877-4799
Denise Balderas, prin. Fax 873-8533
Alameda ES 300/K-5
412 Alameda Blvd NW 87114 505-898-0070
David Bunch, prin. Fax 898-7430
Alamosa ES 700/PK-5
6500 Sunset Gardens Rd SW 87121 505-836-0288
Dr. Ulrike Kerstges, prin. Fax 831-5643
Alvarado ES 400/K-5
1100 Solar Rd NW 87107 505-344-4412
Caitlin Robinson, prin. Fax 761-8405
Anaya ES 900/K-5
2800 Vermejo Park Dr SW 87121 505-452-3137
Gionna Jaramillo, prin. Fax 873-1360
Apache ES 400/PK-5
12800 Copper Ave NE 87123 505-292-7735
Stephanie Lovato, prin. Fax 296-2669
Armijo ES 500/K-5
1440 Gatewood Ave SW 87105 505-877-2920
Julieta Contreras, prin. Fax 877-5613
Arroyo Del Oso ES 400/PK-5
6504 Harper Dr NE 87109 505-821-9393
Deb Henley, prin. Fax 821-9060
Atrisco ES 400/PK-5
1201 Atrisco Dr SW 87105 505-877-2772
Tina Martinez, prin. Fax 873-8542
Baker ES 500/K-5
12015 Tivoli Ave NE 87111 505-298-7486
Jill Vice, prin. Fax 299-1495
Bandelier ES 600/K-6
3309 Pershing Ave SE 87106 505-255-8744
Ann McCoy, prin. Fax 260-2035
Barcelona ES 500/PK-5
2311 Barcelona Rd SW 87105 505-877-0400
Katherine Trujillo, prin. Fax 873-8531
Bel-Air ES 400/PK-5
4725 Candelaria Rd NE 87110 505-888-4033
Kathy Casaus, prin. Fax 880-3950
Bellehaven ES 300/K-5
8701 Princess Jeanne Ave NE 87112 505-298-7489
Kim Baiamonte, prin. Fax 291-6871
Bent ES 500/K-5
5700 Hendrix Rd NE 87110 505-881-9797
Jonathan Saiz, prin. Fax 881-8885
Binford ES 900/K-5
1400 Corriz Dr SW 87121 505-836-0623
Katrina Cisneros, prin. Fax 836-7734
Carson ES 500/PK-8
1921 Byron St SW 87105 505-877-2724
Cindy Rael, prin. Fax 877-1191
Carter MS 1,200/6-8
8901 Bluewater Rd NW 87121 505-833-7540
Amy Mahr, prin. Fax 833-7559
Chamiza ES 500/K-5
5401 Homestead Cir NW 87120 505-897-5174
Lisa Gutierrez, prin. Fax 897-5176
Chaparral ES 900/PK-5
6325 Milne Rd NW 87120 505-831-3301
Valerie Hoose, prin. Fax 831-6314
Chavez ES 600/PK-5
7500 Barstow St NE 87109 505-821-1810
Jessica Kettler, prin. Fax 857-0171
Chavez ES 300/K-5
2700 Mountain Rd NW 87104 505-764-2008
Loretta Huerta, prin. Fax 764-2010
Chelwood ES 600/K-5
12701 Constitution Ave NE 87112 505-296-5655
Roawn Lee, prin. Fax 291-6872
Cleveland MS 700/6-8
6910 Natalie Ave NE 87110 505-881-9227
Susan Labarge, prin. Fax 881-9441
Cochiti ES 300/K-5
3100 San Isidro St NW 87107 505-345-1432
Lesley Cummings, prin. Fax 761-8406
Collet Park ES 400/PK-5
2100 Morris St NE 87112 505-298-3010
Stephani Treadwell, prin. Fax 291-6868
Comanche ES 400/K-5
3505 Pennsylvania St NE 87110 505-884-5275
Cheryl Wheeler, prin. Fax 880-3988
Cordero PS 800/PK-2
8800 Eucariz Ave SW 87121 505-833-5830
Phyllis Muhovich, prin. Fax 831-5229
Coronado ES 300/K-5
601 4th St SW 87102 505-843-8283
Anna Ulibarri, prin. Fax 242-4636
Coyote Willow Family S K-8
7125 Irving Blvd NW 87114 505-253-0050
Adrianne Lytle, prin. Fax 897-7724
Desert Ridge MS 1,000/6-8
8400 Barstow St NE 87122 505-857-9282
Kathy Alexander, prin. Fax 857-0201
Double Eagle ES 500/K-5
8901 Lowell Dr NE 87122 505-857-0187
Crystal Friedman, prin. Fax 857-0188
Duranes ES 300/K-6
2436 Zickert Rd NW 87104 505-764-2017
Gabe Garcia, prin. Fax 764-2019
East San Jose ES 500/K-5
415 Thaxton Ave SE 87102 505-764-2005
Anna Rodriguez, prin. Fax 764-2007
Eisenhower MS 900/6-8
11001 Camero Ave NE 87111 505-292-2530
Victor Sanchez, prin. Fax 291-6884
Emerson ES 500/K-5
620 Georgia St SE 87108 505-255-9091
Antonio Medina, prin. Fax 260-2036
Field ES 300/PK-5
700 Edith Blvd SE 87102 505-764-2014
Fred March, prin. Fax 764-2016
Garfield STEM MS 300/6-8
3501 6th St NW 87107 505-344-1647
Daniel Gutierrez, prin. Fax 344-6562
Gonzales ES 400/K-5
900 Atlantic Ave SW 87102 505-764-2020
Lorinda Stuit, prin. Fax 243-5440
Gonzales ES 600/3-5
554 90th St SW 87121 505-831-6214
Shayne Goesling, prin. Fax 831-3036
Grant MS 600/6-8
1111 Easterday Dr NE 87112 505-299-2113
Paul Roney, prin. Fax 291-6881
Griegos ES 400/K-5
4040 San Isidro St NW 87107 505-345-3661
Rita Martinez, prin. Fax 344-2565
Harrison MS 900/6-8
3912 Isleta Blvd SW 87105 505-877-1279
Kevin Cummings, prin. Fax 877-6797
Hawthorne ES 500/PK-5
420 General Somervell St NE 87123 505-299-4424
Penelope Buschardt, prin. Fax 291-6836
Hayes STEM MS 400/6-8
1100 Texas St NE 87110 505-265-7741
Antoinette Valenzuela, prin. Fax 260-6108
Hillerman MS 1,000/6-8
8101 Rainbow Blvd NW 87114 505-792-0698
Michelle Armijo, prin. Fax 792-2322

Hodgin ES 600/PK-5
3801 Morningside Dr NE 87110 505-881-9855
Kimberly Woodley, prin. Fax 881-0706
Hoover MS 700/6-8
12015 Tivoli Ave NE Ste A 87111 505-298-6896
Robert Abney, prin. Fax 291-6883
Hughes ES 600/K-5
5701 Mojave St NW 87120 505-897-3080
June Pederson, prin. Fax 898-2894
Humphrey ES 400/PK-5
9801 Academy Hills Dr NE 87111 505-821-4981
Paula Miller, prin. Fax 857-0185
Inez ES 400/PK-5
1700 Pennsylvania St NE 87110 505-299-9010
Cindy Bazner, prin. Fax 299-5311
Jackson ES 600/K-5
4720 Cairo Dr NE 87111 505-296-9536
Jack Vermillion, prin. Fax 292-2346
Jackson MS 600/6-8
10600 Indian School Rd NE 87112 505-299-7377
Tracy Straub, prin. Fax 291-6877
Jefferson MS 900/6-8
712 Girard Blvd NE 87106 505-255-8691
Anthony Fairley, prin. Fax 268-2334
Johnson MS 900/6-8
6811 Taylor Ranch Rd NW 87120 505-898-1492
Mike Bachicha, prin. Fax 898-7150
Kahn S of Integrated Arts 500/K-5
9717 Indian School Rd NE 87112 505-299-4483
Christy Sigmon, prin. Fax 298-3088
Kennedy MS 500/6-8
721 Tomasita St NE 87123 505-298-6701
Ed Bortot, prin. Fax 291-6879
Kirtland ES 300/K-5
3530 Gibson Blvd SE 87116 505-255-3131
Rayetta Baty, prin. Fax 255-1255
La Luz ES 200/PK-5
225 Griegos Rd NW 87107 505-761-8415
Agnes LeDoux, prin. Fax 344-2890
La Mesa ES 700/PK-5
7500 Copper Ave NE 87108 505-262-1581
Bernadette Hall-Cuaron, prin. Fax 260-2033
Lavaland ES 700/PK-5
501 57th St NW 87105 505-836-4911
Susan Neddeau, prin. Fax 833-1332
Longfellow ES 300/K-5
400 Edith Blvd NE 87102 505-764-2024
Richard Ulibarri, prin. Fax 766-5243
Los Padillas ES 300/K-6
2525 Los Padillas Rd SW 87105 505-877-0108
Mary Farrelly, prin. Fax 873-8527
Lowell ES 400/PK-5
1700 Sunshine Ter SE 87106 505-764-2011
Danielle Calvillo, prin. Fax 764-2013
MacArthur ES 200/PK-5
1100 Douglas MacArthur NW 87107 505-344-1482
Agnes LeDoux, prin. Fax 344-3927
Madison MS 700/6-8
3501 Moon St NE 87111 505-299-4735
Debora Garrison, prin. Fax 323-9512
Manzano Mesa ES 700/K-5
801 Elizabeth St SE 87123 505-292-6707
Peggy Candelaria, prin. Fax 292-6719
Marmon ES 800/K-5
1800 72nd St NW 87120 505-831-5400
Sandra Fernandez, prin. Fax 833-1565
Matheson Park ES 300/K-5
10809 Lexington Ave NE 87112 505-291-6837
Jacqueline Lovato, prin. Fax 298-4302
McCollum ES 400/PK-5
10900 San Jacinto Ave NE 87112 505-298-5009
Carrie McGill, prin. Fax 298-3840
McKinley MS 500/6-8
4500 Comanche Rd NE 87110 505-881-9390
Daniel Bonsell, prin. Fax 880-3968
Mission Avenue ES 400/PK-5
725 Mission Ave NE 87107 505-344-5269
Frances Garcia, prin. Fax 761-8413
Mitchell ES 400/K-5
10121 Comanche Rd NE 87111 505-299-1937
Ana Sanchez, prin. Fax 296-0012
Monroe MS 1,000/6-8
6100 Paradise Blvd NW 87114 505-897-0101
Jane Sichler, prin. Fax 897-2371
Monte Vista ES 500/K-5
3211 Monte Vista Blvd NE 87106 505-268-3520
Leith Page, prin. Fax 255-4680
Montezuma ES 500/K-5
3100 Indian School Rd NE 87106 505-260-2040
Mark Woodard, prin. Fax 268-7731
Mountain View ES 400/K-5
5317 2nd St SW 87105 505-877-3800
Anthony Lovato, prin. Fax 873-8511
Navajo ES 700/K-5
2936 Hughes Rd SW 87105 505-873-8512
Elias Casaus, prin. Fax 873-8513
North Star ES 600/K-5
9301 Ventura St NE 87122 505-856-6578
Misty Jaquez-Smith, prin. Fax 856-7486
O'Keefe ES 600/K-5
11701 San Victorio Ave NE 87111 505-293-4259
Gwendolyn Maldonado, prin. Fax 293-4586
Onate ES 200/PK-5
12415 Brntwod Hills Blvd NE 87112 505-291-6819
Theresa Fullerton, prin. Fax 275-0648
Osuna ES 400/K-5
4715 Moon St NE 87111 505-296-4811
Hanna Myers, prin. Fax 291-6840
Painted Sky ES 1,100/K-5
8101 Gavin Dr NW 87120 505-836-7763
Stacia Duarte, prin. Fax 836-7765
Pajarito ES 500/K-8
2701 Don Felipe Rd SW 87105 505-877-9718
Debra Larribas, prin. Fax 873-8539
Petroglyph ES 700/PK-5
5100 Marna Lynn Ave NW 87114 505-898-0923
Francesca VerPlough, prin. Fax 898-0949

Polk MS 400/6-8
2220 Raymac Rd SW 87105 505-877-6444
Ben Bustos, prin. Fax 877-1618
Pyle MS 600/6-8
1820 Valdora Rd SW 87105 505-877-3770
Ryan Homistek, prin. Fax 873-8540
Rey ES 800/PK-5
1215 Cerrillos Rd SW 87121 505-836-7738
Judith Touloumis, prin. Fax 831-4401
Ross ES 500/K-5
6700 Palomas Ave NE 87109 505-821-0185
Amanda Stavig, prin. Fax 821-8688
Sanchez Collaborative Comm S K-8
4050 118th St SW 87121 505-253-0300
Sara Carrillo, prin. Fax 873-1723
Sandia Base ES 500/K-6
21001 Wyoming Blvd SE 87116 505-268-4356
Jude Garcia, prin. Fax 260-2028
Seven Bar ES 800/K-5
4501 Seven Bar Loop Rd NW 87114 505-899-2797
Roberta Montoya, prin. Fax 899-4376
Sierra Vista ES 800/K-5
10220 Paseo Del Norte NW 87114 505-898-0272
Monica Garciasalas, prin. Fax 898-1796
Sombra Del Monte ES 400/PK-5
9110 Shoshone Rd NE 87111 505-291-6842
Jennifer Peak, prin. Fax 292-8237
Sunset View ES 600/K-5
6121 Paradise Blvd NW 87114 505-792-3254
Linda Townsend-Johnson Ph.D., prin. Fax 898-9233
Taylor MS 500/6-8
8200 Guadalupe Trl NW 87114 505-898-3666
Sandra Patterson, prin. Fax 897-5165
Tierra Antigua ES 800/K-5
8121 Rainbow Blvd NW 87114 505-792-3262
Frank Telge, prin. Fax 898-9234
Tomasita ES 400/K-5
701 Tomasita St NE 87123 505-291-6844
Valerie Webb-Jaramillo, prin. Fax 275-0224
Truman MS 1,400/6-8
9400 Benavides Rd SW 87121 505-836-3030
Michele Torres, prin. Fax 836-7745
Twain ES 400/K-5
6316 Constitution Ave NE 87110 505-255-8337
Amanda Walker, prin. Fax 268-3220
Valle Vista ES 600/K-5
1700 Mae Ave SW 87105 505-836-7739
Paloma Aranda, prin. Fax 831-2222
Van Buren MS 500/6-8
700 Louisiana Blvd SE 87108 505-268-3833
Shawn Morris, prin. Fax 260-6104
Ventana Ranch ES 700/K-5
6801 Ventana Village Rd NW 87114 505-890-7375
Vernadette Norman-Chavez, prin. Fax 890-4124
Wallace ES 300/K-5
513 6th St NW 87102 505-848-9409
Anne Marie Strangio, prin. Fax 848-9411
Washington MS 500/6-8
1101 Park Ave SW 87102 505-764-2000
Angela Rodriguez, prin. Fax 764-2022
Whittier ES 400/K-5
1110 Quincy St SE 87108 505-255-2008
Misti Miller, prin. Fax 260-2026
Wilson MS 500/6-8
1138 Cardenas Dr SE 87108 505-268-3961
Teise Reiser, prin. Fax 260-2000
Zia ES 400/K-5
440 Jefferson St NE 87108 505-260-2020
Alyssa Agranat, prin. Fax 255-1014
Zuni ES 400/K-5
6300 Claremont Ave NE 87110 505-881-8313
Glenn Wilcox, prin. Fax 889-8621
Other Schools – See Corrales, Kirtland AFB, Los Ranchos, Sandia Park, Tijeras

---

Albuquerque Christian S 300/PK-8
7201 Montgomery Blvd NE # B 87109 505-872-0777
Regina Santo, prin. Fax 830-3889
Annunciation Catholic S 400/PK-8
2610 Utah St NE 87110 505-299-6783
Cindy Shields, prin. Fax 299-2182
Calvary Christian Academy 100/PK-12
12820 Indian School Rd NE 87112 505-842-8681
Nicole Craner, admin. Fax 292-4782
Christ Lutheran S 200/PK-8
7701 Candelaria Rd NE 87110 505-884-3876
Kimberly Rasmussen, prin. Fax 888-0655
Crestview Christian Academy 50/PK-8
6000 Ouray Rd NW 87120 505-836-0536
Liliana Graf, prin. Fax 836-0538
Cross of Hope ES 100/PK-5
6104 Taylor Ranch Rd NW 87120 505-897-1832
Matt Powell, dir. Fax 897-9455
Eastern Hills Christian Academy 400/PK-8
3100 Morris St NE 87111 505-294-3373
Camille Miller, prin. Fax 298-8564
Escuela del Sol Montessori 200/PK-8
1114 7th St NW 87102 505-242-3033
Evangel Christian Academy 200/PK-12
4501 Montgomery Blvd NE 87109 505-883-4674
Rev. Brenton Franks, supt. Fax 883-1229
Holy Ghost Catholic S 200/PK-8
6201 Ross Ave SE 87108 505-256-1563
Dr. Noreen Copeland, prin. Fax 262-9635
Hope Christian S 1,400/PK-12
8005 Louisiana Blvd NE 87109 505-822-2513
Terry Heisey, head sch Fax 822-8260
Immanuel Lutheran S 200/PK-8
300 Gold Ave SE 87102 505-243-2589
Mark Angell, prin. Fax 554-1428
Legacy Academy 200/PK-9
7201 Central Ave NW 87121 505-923-3659
Brandee Cruse, prin. Fax 923-3668
Manzano Day S 500/PK-5
1801 Central Ave NW 87104 505-243-6659
Neal Piltch, head sch Fax 243-4711

Montessori One Academy PK-6
9360 Holly Ave NE 87122 505-822-5150
Tina Patel, dir. Fax 822-5120
Mountain View Private School 50/K-5
4100 New Vistas Ct NW 87114 505-898-1500
Oak Grove Classical Academy 100/PK-9
PO Box 91314 87199 505-269-2696
Stephen Collins, hdmstr. Fax 830-9684
Our Lady of Fatima S 200/PK-8
4020 Lomas Blvd NE 87110 505-255-6391
Paula DeHaas, prin. Fax 268-3279
Our Lady of the Assumption S 200/PK-8
815 Guaymas Pl NE 87108 505-256-3167
Robert Kaiser, prin. Fax 232-0282
Queen of Heaven Catholic S 200/PK-8
5303 Phoenix Ave NE 87110 505-881-2484
Mary Catherine Keating, prin. Fax 837-1123
Rio Grande Christian Academy K-12
2121 Gun Club Rd 87105 505-877-0535
Risen Savior 50/PK-PK
7701 Wyoming Blvd NE 87120 505-821-1571
Mary Parker, dir.
St. Charles Borromeo Catholic S 300/PK-8
1801 Hazeldine Ave SE 87106 505-243-5788
Paul Horton, prin. Fax 764-8842
St. Mary's Catholic S 500/PK-8
224 7th St NW 87102 505-243-5470
Carissa Cantrell, prin. Fax 242-4837
St. Therese Catholic S 100/PK-8
311 Shropshire Ave NW 87107 505-344-4479
Donna Illerbrun, prin. Fax 344-4486
Salam Academy 100/PK-8
8015 Mountain Road Pl NE 87110 505-888-7688
Sandia Montessori S 100/PK-5
3240 Juan Tabo Blvd NE # A 87111 505-293-6614
San Felipe Del Neri S 200/PK-8
2000 Lomas Blvd NW 87104 505-242-2411
Kathleen Riccio, prin. Fax 242-7355
Shepherd Lutheran S 100/K-8
3900 Wyoming Blvd NE 87111 505-292-6622
Paul Schultz, prin. Fax 323-6766
Sunset Mesa S 400/PK-5
3020 Morris St NE 87111 505-298-7626
Michelle Clark, prin. Fax 298-6132
Victory Christian S 100/K-12
220 El Pueblo Rd NW 87114 505-898-3060
Glenn Frey, supt. Fax 898-6690

Alcalde, Rio Arriba, Pop. 280
Espanola SD 55
Supt. — See Espanola
Alcalde ES 100/PK-6
35 County Road 138A 87511 505-852-4253
Kiva Duckworth-Moulton, prin. Fax 852-2523

Algodones, Sandoval, Pop. 804
Bernalillo SD
Supt. — See Bernalillo
Algodones ES 200/PK-5
1399 Highway 313 87001 505-867-2803
Stephen Pino, prin. Fax 867-7853

Animas, Hidalgo, Pop. 225
Animas SD 200/PK-12
PO Box 85 88020 575-548-2299
Loren Cushman, supt. Fax 548-2388
www.animask12.net
Animas ES 100/PK-4
PO Box 85 88020 575-548-2297
Loren Cushman, prin. Fax 548-2388
Animas MS 50/5-6
PO Box 85 88020 575-548-2296
Loren Cushman, prin. Fax 548-2388

Anthony, Dona Ana, Pop. 9,342
Gadsden ISD
Supt. — See Sunland Park
Anthony ES 400/K-6
600 N Fourth St 88021 575-882-4561
Linda Perez, prin. Fax 882-4696
Anthony Pre K Center PK-PK
609 Church St 88021 575-882-1904
Sandy Silvas, admin. Fax 575-2379
Berino ES 500/K-6
92 Shrode Rd 88021 575-882-2242
Vicki Arnold, prin. Fax 882-7249
Gadsden ES 500/K-6
1440 Highway 478 88021 575-882-3050
Grace Marquez, prin. Fax 882-3415
Gadsden MS 800/7-8
1301 Washington St 88021 575-882-2372
Veronica Quinones, prin. Fax 882-5227
Loma Linda ES 500/K-8
1451 Donaldson Ave 88021 575-882-6000
Cresencio Cardona, prin. Fax 882-4718

Anton Chico, Guadalupe, Pop. 188
Santa Rosa Consolidated SD
Supt. — See Santa Rosa
Anton Chico MS 50/6-8
PO Box 169 87711 575-427-6038
Erica Padilla, prin. Fax 427-4246
Marquez ES 100/K-5
PO Box 169 87711 575-427-6038
Erica Padilla, prin. Fax 427-4246

Arrey, Sierra, Pop. 229
Truth or Consequences Municipal SD
Supt. — See Truth or Consequences
Arrey ES 100/PK-5
7 Arrey Rd 87930 575-267-4778
Serjio Cardona, dean Fax 267-5865

Arroyo Seco, Taos, Pop. 1,759
Taos Municipal SD
Supt. — See Taos
Arroyo Del Norte ES 100/K-5
PO Box 279 87514 575-737-6175
Jim Ivanovich, prin. Fax 776-3853

Artesia, Eddy, Pop. 11,178
Artesia SD 3,800/PK-12
1106 W Quay Ave 88210 575-746-3585
Dr. Crit Caton, supt. Fax 746-6232
www.bulldogs.org
Artesia Zia IS 600/6-7
1100 W Bullock Ave 88210 575-746-2766
Larry Combs, prin. Fax 746-4097
Central ES 200/1-5
405 S 6th St 88210 575-746-4811
Tammy Davis, prin. Fax 746-8765
Grand Heights ECC 400/PK-K
2302 W Grand Ave 88210 575-746-6282
Mitzi McCaleb, prin. Fax 746-1291
Hermosa ES 300/1-5
601 W Hermosa Dr 88210 575-746-3812
Michael Worley, prin. Fax 736-1483
Roselawn ES 200/1-5
600 N Roselawn Ave 88210 575-746-2812
Tina Perez, prin. Fax 746-4790
Yeso ES 500/1-5
1812 W Centre Ave 88210 575-748-2755
Liz Ironmonger, prin. Fax 748-2334
Yucca ES 300/1-5
1106 W Quay Ave 88210 575-746-3711
Christy Takacs, prin. Fax 746-2075
Other Schools – See Hope

Aztec, San Juan, Pop. 6,640
Aztec Municipal SD 3,200/PK-12
1118 W Aztec Blvd 87410 505-334-9474
Kirk Carpenter, supt. Fax 334-9861
www.aztecschools.com
Koogler MS 700/6-8
455 N Light Plant Rd 87410 505-334-6102
Jessica Sledzinski, prin. Fax 599-4385
McCoy Avenue ES 500/PK-3
901 McCoy Ave 87410 505-334-6831
Troy Webb, prin. Fax 599-4384
Park Avenue ES 500/4-5
507 S Park Ave 87410 505-334-9469
Fax 599-4336
Rippey ES 500/PK-3
401 Rio Pecos Rd 87410 505-334-2621
Dana Stanley, prin. Fax 599-4391

Bayard, Grant, Pop. 2,310
Cobre Consolidated SD 1,300/PK-12
PO Box 1000 88023 575-537-4010
Robert Mendoza, supt. Fax 537-5455
www.cobre.k12.nm.us
Bayard ES 200/PK-6
PO Box 1040 88023 575-537-4040
Virginia Chavez, prin. Fax 537-3335
Snell MS 200/7-8
PO Box 729 88023 575-537-4030
Patrick Abalos, prin. Fax 537-3022
Other Schools – See Hurley, San Lorenzo,

Belen, Valencia, Pop. 7,165
Belen Consolidated SD 4,200/PK-12
520 N Main St 87002 505-966-1000
Max Perez, supt. Fax 966-1050
www.beleneagles.org
Belen MS 600/7-8
520 N Main St 87002 505-966-1600
Lawrence Sanchez, prin. Fax 966-1650
Central ES 200/4-6
520 N Main St 87002 505-966-1200
Emily Sisk-Layman, prin. Fax 966-1250
Chavez ES 400/PK-6
520 N Main St 87002 505-966-1800
Kelli Williams-Page, prin. Fax 966-1850
Jaramillo Community S 300/PK-3
520 N Main St 87002 505-966-2000
Jennifer Martinez, prin. Fax 966-2050
La Merced ES 500/K-6
520 N Main St 87002 505-966-2100
Denise Gutierrez, prin. Fax 966-2150
Rio Grande ES 300/PK-6
520 N Main St 87002 505-966-2200
Margaret Manning, prin. Fax 966-2250
Other Schools – See Jarales, Veguita

Canon Christian Academy 200/K-12
19381 Highway 314 87002 505-859-4041
St. Mary's Catholic S 100/PK-8
101 N 10th St 87002 505-864-4724
Melodie Good, prin. Fax 864-2414

Bernalillo, Sandoval, Pop. 8,231
Bernalillo SD 2,700/PK-12
560 S Camino Del Pueblo 87004 505-867-2317
Allan Tapia, supt. Fax 867-7850
www.bernalillo-schools.org
Bernalillo ES 400/3-5
480 Calle Del Norte 87004 505-404-5400
Dr. Elisabeth Valenzuela, prin.
Bernalillo MS 400/6-8
485 Camino don Tomas 87004 505-867-3309
Albert Martinez, prin. Fax 867-7819
Carroll ES 500/PK-2
301 Calle Del Escuela 87004 505-867-5472
Demetria Navarrette, prin. Fax 867-7872
La Escuelita Preschool PK-PK
301 Calle Del Escuela 87004 505-404-5585
Sarah Armstrong, prin.
Other Schools – See Algodones, Pena Blanca, Placitas, Santo Domingo Pueblo

Blanco, San Juan, Pop. 383
Bloomfield SD
Supt. — See Bloomfield
Blanco ES 300/1-6
7313 US 64 87412 505-634-3900
Lynda Spencer, prin. Fax 634-3902

Bloomfield, San Juan, Pop. 7,953
Bloomfield SD 3,000/PK-12
325 N Bergin Ln 87413 505-632-4300
Dr. Kimberly Mizell, supt. Fax 632-4371
www.bsin.k12.nm.us
Bloomfield ECC 200/PK-K
310 La Jara St 87413 505-634-3883
Veronica Olivas, prin. Fax 634-3856
Central PS 600/1-3
310 W Sycamore Ave 87413 505-632-2121
Eddie Ramirez, prin. Fax 634-3675
Mesa Alta JHS 400/7-8
329 N Bergin Ln 87413 505-632-8021
Elvira Crockett, prin. Fax 634-3872
Naaba Ani ES 500/4-6
1201 N 1st St 87413 505-634-3500
Sharon Jensen, prin. Fax 634-3584
Other Schools – See Blanco

Bluewater, Cibola
Grants-Cibola County SD
Supt. — See Grants
Bluewater ES 100/K-6
PO Box 310 87005 505-285-2694
Rosemary Calvert, prin. Fax 285-2698

Bosque Farms, Valencia, Pop. 3,878
Los Lunas SD
Supt. — See Los Lunas
Bosque Farms ES 500/PK-6
1390 W Bosque Loop 87068 505-869-2646
Kaua Matthews, prin. Fax 869-5146

Capitan, Lincoln, Pop. 1,465
Capitan Municipal SD 500/K-12
PO Box 278 88316 575-354-8500
Sean Wootton, supt. Fax 354-8505
www.capitantigers.org
Capitan ES 200/K-5
PO Box 278 88316 575-354-8520
Jim Nesbitt, prin. Fax 354-8505
Capitan MS 100/6-8
PO Box 278 88316 575-354-8550
Patti Nesbitt, prin. Fax 354-8507

Carlsbad, Eddy, Pop. 25,808
Carlsbad Municipal SD 4,600/PK-12
408 N Canyon St 88220 575-234-3300
Fax 234-3367
www.carlsbadnmschools.com
Carlsbad 6th Grade Academy @ Alta Vista 200/6-6
408 N Canyon St 88220 575-234-3316
Lynn Strickland, prin. Fax 234-3478
Carlsbad IS @ P.R. Leyva Campus 600/7-8
408 N Canyon St 88220 575 234 3318
Stephanie West, prin. Fax 234-3452
Craft ES 300/1-5
408 N Canyon St 88220 575-234-3304
Carlos Carrillo, prin. Fax 234-3492
Desert Willow ES 1-5
408 N Canyon St 88220 575-234-3310
Deborah Beard, prin. Fax 234-3543
Early Childhood Education Center 600/K-K
408 N Canyon St 88220 575-234-3303
Joyce Lindauer, prin. Fax 234-3445
Monterrey ES 300/1-5
408 N Canyon St 88220 575-234-3309
Fran McCarthy, prin. Fax 234-3531
Ocotillo ES 1-5
408 N Canyon St 88220 575-234-3312
Allison Hervol, prin. Fax 234-3561
Smith ES 300/1-5
408 N Canyon St 88220 575-234-3314
Misti Fernandez, prin. Fax 234-3581
Smith Preschool 100/PK-PK
408 N Canyon St 88220 575-234-3313
Julie Volpato, prin. Fax 234-3570
Sunset ES 400/1-5
408 N Canyon St 88220 575-234-3315
Yolanda Pirtle, prin. Fax 234-3593

St. Edward S 100/PK-5
805 Walter St 88220 575-885-4620
Abel Montoya, prin. Fax 885-7706

Carrizozo, Lincoln, Pop. 975
Carrizozo Municipal SD 100/K-12
PO Box 99 88301 575-648-2346
Ricky Espinoza, supt. Fax 648-2216
www.carrizozoschools.org
Carrizozo ES 100/K-6
PO Box 99 88301 575-648-2346
Trampus Pierson, prin. Fax 648-3255

Cedar Crest, Bernalillo, Pop. 929

Prince of Peace Lutheran S 100/PK-8
12121 State Highway 14 N 87008 505-281-6833
Felicia Barnum, admin. Fax 281-5372

Chama, Rio Arriba, Pop. 1,005
Chama Valley ISD
Supt. — See Tierra Amarilla
Chama S 100/PK-8
PO Box 337 87520 575-756-2161
Kathy Kegel, prin. Fax 756-2538

Chaparral, Dona Ana, Pop. 14,528
Gadsden ISD
Supt. — See Sunland Park
Chaparral ES 700/K-6
300 E Lisa Dr, 575-824-4722
Fax 824-4034
Chaparral MS 600/7-8
290 E Lisa Dr, 575-824-4847
Marti Muela, prin. Fax 824-4045
Chaparral Pre K Center 200/PK-PK
800 S County Line Dr, 575-824-5382
Nancy Bellagamba, admin. Fax 824-5431

Desert Trail ES 900/K-6
310 E Lisa Dr, 575-824-6500
Sonia Barajas, prin. Fax 824-3390
Sunrise ES 500/K-6
1000 S County Line Dr, 575-824-0060
Cecilia Doran, prin. Fax 824-3136
Yucca Heights ES 400/K-6
580 Angelinda Blvd, 575-824-8210
Laura Pargas, prin. Fax 824-8207

Chimayo, Rio Arriba, Pop. 3,154
Espanola SD 55
Supt. — See Espanola
Chimayo ES 100/K-6
State Road 76 Co Rd 93 #31 87522 505-351-4207
Janet Malcom, lead tchr. Fax 351-2153

Church Rock, McKinley, Pop. 1,123
Gallup-McKinley County SD
Supt. — See Gallup
Church Rock Academy 300/PK-5
PO Box 40 87311 505-488-5273
Joel Copley, prin. Fax 488-5986

Cimarron, Colfax, Pop. 1,000
Cimarron Municipal SD 400/K-12
125 N Collison Ave 87714 575-376-2445
Adan Estrada, supt. Fax 376-2442
cimarronschools.org
Cimarron ES 100/K-4
125 N Collison Ave 87714 575-376-2512
Letitia Martinez, prin. Fax 376-2217
Cimarron MS 100/5-8
125 N Collison Ave 87714 575-376-2512
Letitia Martinez, prin. Fax 376-2217
Other Schools – See Eagle Nest

Clayton, Union, Pop. 2,951
Clayton Municipal SD 500/PK-12
323 S 5th St 88415 575-374-9611
Stacy Diller, supt. Fax 374-9881
www.claytonschools.us
Alvis ES 200/PK-4
323 S 5th St 88415 575-374-2321
Jeanette Walker, prin. Fax 374-2322
Clayton JHS 100/7-8
323 S 5th St 88415 575-374-9543
John Brooks, prin. Fax 374-9469
Kiser ES, 323 S 5th St 88415 100/5-6
John Brooks, prin. 575-374-9543

Cliff, Grant, Pop. 288
Silver Consolidated SD
Supt. — See Silver City
Cliff ES 100/K-6
PO Box 9 88028 575-535-2051
Dean Spurgeon, prin. Fax 535-2054

Cloudcroft, Otero, Pop. 659
Cloudcroft Municipal SD 200/PK-12
PO Box 198 88317 575-601-4416
Travis Dempsey, supt. Fax 235-1668
www.cmsbears.org
Cloudcroft S 100/PK-8
PO Box 198 88317 575-601-4416
Robyn Cook, prin. Fax 805-6335

Clovis, Curry, Pop. 36,950
Clovis Municipal SD 8,600/PK-12
PO Box 19000 88102 575-769-4300
Jody Balch, supt. Fax 769-4333
www.clovis-schools.org
Arts Academy at Bella Vista 400/K-5
2900 Cesar Chavez Dr 88101 575-769-4435
Dr. Shelly Norris, prin. Fax 769-4437
Barry ES 200/K-5
3401 N Thornton St 88101 575-769-4430
Kari Lemke, prin. Fax 769-4433
Bickley ES 400/K-5
500 W 14th St 88101 575-769-4450
Laura Adkins, prin. Fax 769-4826
Cameo ES 300/PK-5
1500 Cameo St 88101 575-769-4440
Mike Read, prin. Fax 769-4444
Gattis MS, 5100 N Thornton St 88101 800/6-8
Gloria Christiansen, prin. 575-769-4305
Highland ES 300/K-5
100 E Plains Ave 88101 575-769-4445
Brenda Benfield, prin. Fax 769-4449
La Casita ES 300/K-5
400 N Davis St 88101 575-769-4455
Dr. Sylvia Martinez, prin. Fax 769-4454
Lincoln-Jackson Family Center 100/PK-PK
206 Alphon St 88101 575-769-4460
Jeremy Martin, prin. Fax 769-4464
Lockwood ES 300/PK-5
1113 S Oak St 88101 575-769-4465
Deborah Westbrook, prin. Fax 769-4467
Marshall MS 500/6-8
100 Commerce Way 88101 575-769-4410
Jennifer Longley, prin. Fax 769-4413
Mesa ES 500/K-5
4801 N Norris St 88101 575-769-4470
Julie Howell, prin. Fax 769-4472
Parkview ES 400/K-5
1121 Maple St 88101 575-769-4475
Shelly Flygare, prin. Fax 769-4478
Sandia ES 400/K-5
2801 Lore St 88101 575-769-4480
Dr. Matthew Vetterly, prin. Fax 769-4482
Yucca MS 600/6-8
1500 Sycamore St 88101 575-769-4420
Loran Hill, prin. Fax 769-4421
Zia ES 400/K-5
2400 N Norris St 88101 575-769-4485
Shalei Bennett, prin. Fax 769-4487

Clovis Christian S PK-12
PO Box 608 88102 575-935-2279
Dr. Ladona Clayton, supt. Fax 935-2281

Columbus, Luna, Pop. 1,643
Deming SD
Supt. — See Deming
Columbus ES 600/PK-5
PO Box 210 88029 575-531-2710
Armando Chavez, prin. Fax 531-2303

Corona, Lincoln, Pop. 169
Corona SD 100/PK-12
PO Box 258 88318 575-849-1911
Travis Lightfoot, supt. Fax 849-2026
www.cpscardinals.org
Corona ES 50/PK-6
PO Box 258 88318 575-849-1911
Rick Cogdill, prin. Fax 849-2026

Corrales, Sandoval, Pop. 8,197
Albuquerque SD
Supt. — See Albuquerque
Corrales ES 400/K-5
200 Target Rd 87048 505-792-7400
Kimberly Finke, prin. Fax 897-5167

Cottonwood S 200/PK-6
3896 Corrales Rd 87048 505-897-8375
Trish Nickerson, head sch Fax 890-1533
Sandia View Christian S 100/PK-8
24 Academy Dr 87048 505-897-4805

Costilla, Taos, Pop. 205
Questa ISD
Supt. — See Questa
Rio Costilla Southwest Learning Academy 50/PK-6
PO Box 99 87524 575-586-0089
Michelle Gonzales, prin. Fax 586-2154

Counselor, Sandoval, Pop. 25
Jemez Mountain SD
Supt. — See Gallina
Lybrook S 100/K-8
PO Box 135 87018 575-568-4491
Jeorj Moralez, prin. Fax 568-0088

Crownpoint, McKinley, Pop. 2,253
Gallup-McKinley County SD
Supt. — See Gallup
Crownpoint ES 300/PK-5
PO Box 709 87313 505-786-5323
Cindy Arsenault, prin. Fax 721-1599
Crownpoint MS 100/6-8
PO Box 1110 87313 505-786-5663
Michael Cubacub, prin. Fax 721-5499

Cuba, Sandoval, Pop. 717
Cuba ISD 500/PK-12
PO Box 70 87013 575-289-3211
Tony Archuleta, supt. Fax 289-3314
cuba.k12.nm.us
Cuba ES 200/PK-5
PO Box 70 87013 575-289-3211
Shirley Hurford, prin. Fax 289-0436
Cuba MS 100/6-8
PO Box 70 87013 575-289-3211
Shirley Hurford, prin. Fax 289-0436

Cubero, Cibola, Pop. 283
Grants-Cibola County SD
Supt. — See Grants
Cubero ES 300/K-6
PO Box 8128 87014 505-552-9441
Milton Head, prin. Fax 285-2709

Datil, Catron, Pop. 53
Quemado ISD
Supt. — See Quemado
Datil ES 50/K-6
PO Box 200 87821 575-772-5574
Don Goodman, prin. Fax 772-5575

Deming, Luna, Pop. 14,749
Deming SD 5,400/PK-12
1001 S Diamond Ave 88030 575-546-8841
Dr. Arsenio Romero, supt. Fax 546-8517
www.demingps.org
Bataan ES 500/PK-5
2200 Highway 418 SW 88030 575-544-0900
Marlene Padron, prin. Fax 544-0829
Bell ES 200/PK-5
1000 E Maple St 88030 575-546-9712
Fax 544-0152
Chaparral ES 400/K-5
1400 E Holly St 88030 575-546-2047
Nasa Speer, prin. Fax 546-6062
Deming IS 400/6-6
500 W Ash St 88030 575-546-6560
Fax 544-3656
Memorial ES 400/K-5
1000 S 10th St 88030 575-546-2502
Fax 546-6013
My Little S 100/PK-PK
905 S Zinc St 88030 575-543-1014
Roxi Acosta, prin. Fax 546-6786
Red Mountain MS 800/7-8
2100 Highway 418 SW 88030 575-546-0668
Robin Parnell, prin. Fax 546-9263
Torres ES 500/K-5
1910 8th St NW 88030 575-544-2723
Connie Maag, prin. Fax 544-2726
Other Schools – See Columbus

Des Moines, Union, Pop. 140
Des Moines Municipal SD 100/K-12
PO Box 38 88418 575-278-2611
Kodi Sumpter, supt. Fax 278-2617
www.desmoines.k12.nm.us/
Des Moines ES 100/K-6
PO Box 38 88418 575-278-2611
Kamau Turner, prin. Fax 278-2617

Dexter, Chaves, Pop. 1,260
Dexter Consolidated SD 1,000/PK-12
PO Box 159 88230 575-734-5420
Lesa Dodd, supt. Fax 734-6810
www.dexterdemons.org
Dexter ES 500/PK-5
PO Box 159 88230 575-734-5420
Bernadette Aragon, prin. Fax 734-5424
Dexter MS 200/6-8
PO Box 159 88230 575-734-5420
Chanda Crandall, prin. Fax 734-6811

Dixon, Rio Arriba, Pop. 913
Espanola SD 55
Supt. — See Espanola
Dixon ES 100/K-6
State Road 75 # 220 87527 505-579-4325
Alice Gonzales, lead tchr. Fax 579-4049

Dora, Roosevelt, Pop. 133
Dora Consolidated SD 200/PK-12
PO Box 327 88115 575-477-2211
Brandon Hays, supt. Fax 477-2464
www.doraschools.com
Dora ES 100/PK-6
PO Box 327 88115 575-477-2211
Brandon Hays, prin. Fax 477-2464

Dulce, Rio Arriba, Pop. 2,716
Dulce ISD 500/K-12
PO Box 547 87528 575-759-3225
Manuel Valdez, supt. Fax 759-3533
www.dulceschools.com
Dulce ES 300/K-6
PO Box 547 87528 575-759-3225
Marcella Maddux, prin. Fax 759-3533

Good News Christian Academy 50/K-6
PO Box 211 87528 575-759-1390

Eagle Nest, Colfax, Pop. 289
Cimarron Municipal SD
Supt. — See Cimarron
Eagle Nest ES 100/K-4
225 Lake St 87718 575-377-6991
Lee Mills, prin. Fax 377-3646
Eagle Nest MS 100/5-8
225 Lake St 87718 575-377-6991
Lee Mills, prin. Fax 377-3646

Edgewood, Santa Fe, Pop. 3,663
Moriarty-Edgewood SD
Supt. — See Moriarty
Edgewood MS 300/6-8
17 Venus Rd W 87015 505-832-5880
Todd Bibiano, prin. Fax 281-7210
Route 66 ES 200/K-5
805 Barton Rd 87015 505-832-5760
Dr. Laraun Harrison, prin. Fax 281-0980
South Mountain ES 200/K-5
577 State Road 344 87015 505-832-5700
Amie Duran, prin. Fax 286-8017

Elida, Roosevelt, Pop. 195
Elida Municipal SD 100/K-12
PO Box 8 88116 575-274-6211
Tandee Delk, supt. Fax 274-6213
www.elidaschools.net
Elida ES 100/K-6
PO Box 8 88116 575-274-6211
Tandee Delk, prin. Fax 274-6213

El Pueblo, San Miguel
West Las Vegas SD
Supt. — See Las Vegas
Valley ES 100/K-5
85 NM Highway 484 87560 505-426-2581
Becky Gallegos, prin. Fax 426-2582
Valley MS 50/6-8
85 NM Highway 484 87560 505-426-2581
Becky Gallegos, prin. Fax 426-2582

El Rito, Rio Arriba, Pop. 781
Mesa Vista Consolidated SD
Supt. — See Ojo Caliente
El Rito ES 100/PK-3
PO Box 267 87530 575-581-4723
Elaine Romero, prin. Fax 581-4403

Espanola, Rio Arriba, Pop. 10,179
Espanola SD 55 3,800/PK-12
1260 Industrial Park Rd 87532 505-753-2254
Bobbie J. Gutierrez, supt. Fax 747-3514
www.k12espanola.org
Los Ninos K 100/PK-K
1260 Industrial Park Rd 87532 505-753-6819
LaDonna Phillips, prin. Fax 753-3477
Quintana Sombrillo ES 300/K-6
1260 Industrial Park Rd 87532 505-753-3213
Sherri Rodriguez, lead tchr. Fax 747-3772
Rodriguez ES 400/1-6
1260 Industrial Park Rd 87532 505-753-2256
Lori Utley, prin. Fax 753-2257
Salazar ES 300/PK-6
1260 Industrial Park Rd 87532 505-753-2391
Roberto Archuleta, prin. Fax 753-0510
Vigil MS 500/7-8
1260 Industrial Park Rd 87532 505-753-1348
Julie Gutierrez, prin. Fax 747-3083
Other Schools – See Abiquiu, Alcalde, Chimayo, Dixon, Hernandez, San Juan Pueblo, Velarde

---

Victory Christian Academy 50/K-12
PO Box 540 87532 505-753-5873

Estancia, Torrance, Pop. 1,626
Estancia Municipal SD 500/K-12
PO Box 68 87016 505-384-2000
Joel Shirley, supt. Fax 384-2015
www.estancia.k12.nm.us
Estancia ES 200/K-5
PO Box 68 87016 505-384-2005
Denise Smythe, prin. Fax 384-2027
Estancia MS 100/6-8
PO Box 68 87016 505-384-2003
Martha Ward, prin. Fax 384-2015

Eunice, Lea, Pop. 2,893
Eunice SD 700/PK-12
PO Box 129 88231 575-394-2524
Dwain Haynes, supt. Fax 394-3006
www.eunice.org
Caton MS 200/6-8
PO Box 129 88231 575-394-3338
Christy Boyd, prin. Fax 394-3661
Jordan ES 400/PK-5
PO Box 129 88231 575-394-2440
Tracy Davis, prin. Fax 394-2084

Farmington, San Juan, Pop. 44,787
Farmington Municipal SD 10,900/PK-12
PO Box 5850 87499 505-324-9840
Dr. Eugene Schmidt, supt. Fax 599-8806
district.fms.k12.nm.us
Animas ES 400/K-5
1612 Hutton Ave 87402 505-599-8601
Emily Foose, prin. Fax 599-8632
Apache ES 500/K-5
700 W Apache St 87401 505-599-8602
Jennifer Bowles, prin. Fax 599-8635
Bluffview ES 500/K-5
1204 Camino Real 87401 505-599-8603
Luanne Davis, prin. Fax 599-8696
Cate Pre K, 301 N Court Ave 87401 PK-PK
Andrea Garcia, prin. 505-599-8744
Country Club ES 500/K-5
5300 Foothills Dr 87402 505-599-8604
Shannon Waller, prin. Fax 599-8645
Esperanza ES 600/PK-5
4501 Wildflower Mesa Dr 87401 505-599-8676
Dr. Virginia Hedges, prin. Fax 599-8679
Heights MS 700/6-8
3700 College Blvd 87402 505-599-8611
Dave Gardner, prin. Fax 599-8673
Hermosa MS 600/6-8
1500 E 25th St 87401 505-599-8612
Mark Harris, prin. Fax 599-8681
Ladera Del Norte ES 600/K-5
308 E 35th St 87401 505-599-8605
Phyllis Maestas, prin. Fax 599-8649
McCormick ES 500/K-5
701 McCormick School Rd 87401 505-599-8606
Lyn White, prin. Fax 599-8653
McKinley ES 600/K-5
1201 N Butler Ave 87401 505-599-8607
Marilee Dexel, prin. Fax 599-8657
Mesa Verde ES 600/K-5
3801 College Blvd 87402 505-599-8608
Pam Schritter, prin. Fax 599-8661
Mesa View MS 600/6-8
4451 Wildflower Mesa Dr 87401 505-599-8622
Jay Gardenhire, prin. Fax 599-8646
Northeast ES 600/K-5
1400 E 23rd St 87401 505-599-8609
Candace Young, prin. Fax 599-8664
Tibbetts MS 600/6-8
3500 Twin Peaks Blvd 87401 505-599-8613
Tammie Hanson, prin. Fax 599-8675

Discover Christian S 50/K-8
5509 Sagebrush Dr 87402 505-325-5875
Emmanuel Baptist Academy 200/PK-8
211 W 20th St 87401 505-325-0090
Grace Baptist Academy 100/PK-12
2200 Sullivan Ave 87401 505-325-7802
Pinon Hills Academy 100/K-4
5101 N Dustin Ave 87401 505-327-2395
Cindy Morphis, dir. Fax 325-4366
Sacred Heart S 100/PK-8
404 N Allen Ave 87401 505-325-7152
Rosalia Beyhan, prin. Fax 325-6157

Floyd, Roosevelt, Pop. 133
Floyd Municipal SD 200/PK-12
PO Box 65 88118 575-478-2211
Damon Terry, supt. Fax 478-2811
www.floydbroncos.com
Floyd ES 100/PK-4
PO Box 65 88118 575-478-2211
Damon Terry, admin. Fax 478-2811
Floyd MS 100/5-8
PO Box 65 88118 575-478-2211
Damon Terry, admin. Fax 478-2811

Fort Sumner, DeBaca, Pop. 1,008
Fort Sumner Municipal SD 300/PK-12
PO Box 387 88119 575-355-7734
Matt Moyer, supt. Fax 355-7663
www.ftsumnerk12.com
Fort Sumner ES 100/PK-5
PO Box 387 88119 575-355-7766
Steve Dimitroff, prin. Fax 355-7716
Fort Sumner MS 100/6-8
PO Box 387 88119 575-355-2231
Sharon Rowley, prin. Fax 355-7663

Fruitland, San Juan
Central Consolidated SD
Supt. — See Shiprock
Ojo Amarillo ES 500/PK-6
PO Box 768 87416 505-960-5271
Dr. Pandora Mike, prin. Fax 960-6324

Gallina, Rio Arriba, Pop. 280
Jemez Mountain SD 200/K-12
PO Box 230 87017 575-638-5419
Fax 638-5571
www.jmsk12.com

Gallina ES 100/K-5
PO Box 230 87017 575-638-5491
Buddy Dillow, prin. Fax 638-0131
Other Schools – See Counselor

Gallup, McKinley, Pop. 21,028
Gallup-McKinley County SD 11,700/PK-12
PO Box 1318 87305 505-721-1000
Frank Chiapetti, supt. Fax 721-1199
www.gmcs.k12.nm.us
Chief Manuelito MS 600/6-8
1325 Rico St 87301 505-721-5600
Steve Wargo, prin. Fax 721-5699
Del Norte ES 300/K-5
700 W Wilson Ave 87301 505-721-5200
Kristen Bischoff, prin. Fax 722-5299
Gallup MS 400/6-8
1001 S Grandview Dr 87301 505-721-2700
Carrie Lovato, prin. Fax 721-2799
Indian Hills ES 300/PK-5
3604 Ciniza Dr 87301 505-721-2900
Ryan Dashner, prin. Fax 721-2999
Jefferson ES 300/PK-5
300 Mollica Dr 87301 505-721-3000
Jessica Landavazo-Guille, prin. Fax 721-3099
Kennedy MS 700/6-8
600 S Boardman Ave 87301 505-721-3100
Roberta Tayah, prin. Fax 721-3199
Lincoln ES 300/PK-5
502 Old Zuni Rd 87301 505-721-3400
Mary Washburn, prin. Fax 721-3499
Red Rock ES 400/PK-5
1305 Red Rock Dr 87301 505-721-3900
Sharmyn Munoz, prin. Fax 721-3999
Rocky View ES 300/K-5
345 Basillio Dr 87301 505-721-4000
Debra Arthur, prin. Fax 721-4099
Roosevelt ES 300/PK-5
400 E Logan Ave 87301 505-721-4100
Vickie Blackburn, prin. Fax 721-4199
Stagecoach ES 300/PK-5
725 Freedom Dr 87301 505-721-4300
Shannon McFarland, prin. Fax 721-4399
Turpen ES 400/PK-5
3310 Manuelito Dr 87301 505-721-5000
Cynthia Mowrer, prin. Fax 721-5099
Washington ES 200/PK-5
700 W Wilson Ave 87301 505-721-5200
Kristen Bischoff, prin. Fax 721-5299
Other Schools – See Church Rock, Crownpoint, Navajo, Ramah, Thoreau, Tohatchi, Twin Lakes, Vanderwagen, Yatahey

---

Hilltop Christian S 100/PK-7
02A Deerfield Street 87301 505-371-5726
Bill Naas, dir. Fax 371-5773
Sacred Heart S 100/PK-8
515 Park Ave 87301 505-863-6652
Linda Gasparich Padilla, prin. Fax 726-8142
St. Francis of Assisi S 100/PK-PK
PO Box 4060 87305 505-863-3145
Jodi Thomas, dir. Fax 863-7452

Garfield, Dona Ana, Pop. 137
Hatch Valley SD
Supt. — See Hatch
Garfield ES 100/PK-3
8820 Highway 187 87936 575-267-8280
Linda Hale, admin. Fax 267-8282

Glenwood, Catron, Pop. 143
Reserve ISD
Supt. — See Reserve
Glenwood ES 50/K-3
PO Box 98 88039 575-539-2341
Cindy Shellhorn, prin. Fax 539-2341

Grady, Curry, Pop. 103
Grady Municipal SD 100/PK-12
PO Box 71 88120 575-357-2192
Ted Trice, supt. Fax 357-2000
www.gradyschool.com
Grady ES 50/PK-5
PO Box 71 88120 575-357-2192
Michell Edwards B.S., prin. Fax 357-2000
Grady MS 50/6-8
PO Box 71 88120 575-357-2192
Michell Edwards B.S., prin. Fax 357-2000

Grants, Cibola, Pop. 9,030
Grants-Cibola County SD 3,500/PK-12
413 Roosevelt 87020 505-285-2600
Dr. Marc Space, supt. Fax 285-2628
www.gccs.cc/
Los Alamitos MS 400/7-8
1100 Mount Taylor Ave 87020 505-285-2683
Joan Gilmore, prin. Fax 285-2628
Mesa View ES 400/PK-6
400 Washington Ave 87020 505-285-2717
Jennifer Griego, prin. Fax 285-2725
Mt. Taylor ES 500/PK-6
1670 Del Norte Blvd 87020 505-285-2740
Benny Gallegos, prin. Fax 285-2747
Other Schools – See Bluewater, Cubero, Milan, San Rafael, Seboyeta

---

St. Teresa of Avila S 100/PK-8
PO Box 729 87020 505-287-2261
Angela Brunson, prin. Fax 285-4350

Hagerman, Chaves, Pop. 1,250
Hagerman Municipal SD 400/PK-12
PO Box B 88232 575-752-3254
Ricky Williams, supt. Fax 752-3255
bobcat.net
Hagerman ES 200/PK-5
PO Box B 88232 575-752-3279
Belia Reyes, prin. Fax 752-0207
Hagerman MS 100/6-8
PO Box B 88232 575-752-2002
Brian Shea, prin. Fax 752-0241

Hatch, Dona Ana, Pop. 1,642
Hatch Valley SD 1,300/PK-12
PO Box 790 87937 575-267-8200
Linda Hale, supt. Fax 267-8202
www.hatchschools.net
Hatch Valley ES 200/PK-2
PO Box 790 87937 575-267-8270
Richard Marquez, prin. Fax 267-8275
Hatch Valley MS 300/6-8
PO Box 790 87937 575-267-8250
Daniel Montoya, prin. Fax 267-8255
Rio Grande ES 300/3-5
PO Box 790 87937 575-267-8260
Rey Gonzalez, prin. Fax 267-8265
Other Schools – See Garfield

Hernandez, Rio Arriba, Pop. 944
Espanola SD 55
Supt. — See Espanola
Hernandez ES 200/K-6
State Road 84/285 #1934B 87537 505-753-4008
Isabel Jarmillo-Terrazas, lead tchr. Fax 753-8381

High Rolls Mountain Park, Otero, Pop. 812
Alamogordo SD
Supt. — See Alamogordo
High Rolls Mountain Park ES 50/K-5
23 Karr Canyon Rd 88325 575-812-5275
Victor Gonzales, prin. Fax 812-5278

Hobbs, Lea, Pop. 33,769
Hobbs Municipal SD 9,700/PK-12
PO Box 1030 88241 575-433-0100
T.J. Parks, supt. Fax 433-0140
www.hobbsschools.net
Broadmoor ES 400/K-5
1500 N Houston St 88240 575-433-1500
Galinda Everhart, prin. Fax 433-1520
College Lane ES 500/K-5
2000 W College Ln 88242 575-433-2600
Susan Flowers, prin. Fax 433-2628
Coronado ES 400/K-5
2600 N Brazos Ave 88240 575-433-2300
Melony Turner, prin. Fax 433-2327
Edison ES 300/K-5
501 E Gypsy St 88240 575-433-1600
Patricia Duran, prin. Fax 433-1626
Heizer MS 700/6-8
101 E Stanolind Rd 88240 575-433-1100
Freddie Salgado, prin. Fax 433-1101
Highland MS 700/6-8
2500 N Jefferson St 88240 575-433-1200
Ron Haggerton, prin. Fax 433-1203
Houston MS 700/6-8
300 N Houston St 88240 575-433-1300
Jon Gilcrease, prin. Fax 433-1304
Jefferson ES 400/K-5
1200 W Park St 88240 575-433-1700
Pam Randall, prin. Fax 433-1727
Mills ES 400/K-5
200 W Copper Ave 88240 575-433-2400
Jennifer Carlson, prin. Fax 433-2428
Murray ES 500/PK-5
510 N Dal Paso St 88240 575-433-0100
Nick Bartlett, prin. Fax 433-2701
Rogers ES 400/K-5
300 E Clinton St 88240 575-433-2200
Andi Engle, prin. Fax 433-2229
Sanger ES 400/K-5
1500 N Houston St 88240 575-433-1800
Pam Hightower, prin. Fax 433-1828
Southern Heights ES 400/K-5
101 E Texas St 88240 575-433-1900
Diana Salinas, prin. Fax 433-1938
Stone ES 400/K-5
1015 W Calle Sur St 88240 575-433-2500
Chaundra Jarrett, prin. Fax 433-2527
Taylor ES 400/K-5
1520 N Breckon Dr 88240 575-433-2000
Lisa Richards, prin. Fax 433-2032
Washington Center 300/PK-2
1200 E Humble St 88240 575-433-2100
LaToshia Thomas, prin. Fax 433-2120

Junction Christian Academy 100/PK-5
9924 N Catchings 88242 575-631-2435
Crill Watson, dir. Fax 446-4168
St. Helena S 50/PK-6
105 E Saint Anne Pl 88240 575-392-5405
Silbia Molina, prin. Fax 392-0128
Veritas Classical Christian Academy PK-12
PO Box 2844 88241 575-942-4664
Lori Bova, admin.

Holloman AFB, Otero, Pop. 2,857
Alamogordo SD
Supt. — See Alamogordo
Holloman ES 500/PK-5
750 Arnold Ave 88330 575-812-6100
Denia Burkhardt, prin. Fax 812-6103
Holloman MS 200/6-8
381 1st St 88330 575-812-6200
Steven Starkovich, prin. Fax 812-6203

Hondo, Lincoln
Hondo Valley SD 100/K-12
PO Box 55 88336 575-653-4411
Marvin Martin, supt. Fax 653-4414
www.hondoschools.org
Hondo ES 100/K-6
PO Box 55 88336 575-653-4411
Marvin Martin, prin. Fax 653-4414

Hope, Chaves, Pop. 105
Artesia SD
Supt. — See Artesia
Penasco S 50/K-8
12 Dunken Rte 88250 575-687-3360
Tami Elkins, lead tchr. Fax 687-2149

House, Quay, Pop. 68
House Municipal SD 100/K-12
PO Box 673 88121 575-279-7353
Lecil Richards, supt. Fax 279-6133
www.houseschools.net
House ES 50/K-6
PO Box 673 88121 575-279-7353
Lecil Richards, prin. Fax 279-6201

Hurley, Grant, Pop. 1,290
Cobre Consolidated SD
Supt. — See Bayard
Hurley ES 100/PK-6
PO Box 39 88043 575-537-4060
Joyce Barela, prin. Fax 537-3300

Jal, Lea, Pop. 2,030
Jal SD 400/PK-12
PO Box 1386 88252 575-395-2101
Brian Snider, supt. Fax 395-2146
www.jalnm.org
Jal ES 300/PK-5
PO Box 1386 88252 575-395-2840
Betty Robinson, prin. Fax 395-2419

Jarales, Valencia, Pop. 2,461
Belen Consolidated SD
Supt. — See Belen
Sanchez ES 300/PK-6
376 Jarales Rd 87023 505-966-1900
E. Renee Sanchez, prin. Fax 966-1950

Jemez Pueblo, Sandoval, Pop. 1,783
Jemez Valley SD 400/PK-12
8501 Highway 4 87024 575-834-7393
Dr. Susan Wilkinson-Davis, supt. Fax 834-7130
www.jvps.org
Jemez Valley ES 100/PK-5
8501 Highway 4 87024 575-834-7393
Dana Pino, prin. Fax 834-7130
Jemez Valley MS 100/6-8
8501 Highway 4 87024 575-834-7393
Dana Pino, prin. Fax 834-7130

Kirtland, San Juan, Pop. 7,619
Central Consolidated SD
Supt. — See Shiprock
Kirtland ES 600/K-6
30 Road 6446 87417 505-598-5893
Melissa Roberts, prin. Fax 598-5894
Kirtland MS 500/7-8
538 Road 6100 87417 505-598-6114
Randy Mason, prin. Fax 598-9562
Nelson ES 200/K-6
40 Road 6580 87417 505-598-6285
Steve Carlson, prin. Fax 598-9495

Kirtland AFB, Bernalillo
Albuquerque SD
Supt. — See Albuquerque
Wherry ES 500/PK-5
Bldg 25000 87117 505-268-2434
Aimee Sewell, prin. Fax 260-2025

Lake Arthur, Chaves, Pop. 422
Lake Arthur Municipal SD 100/PK-12
PO Box 98 88253 575-365-2000
Michael Grossman, supt. Fax 365-2002
www.la-panthers.org
Lake Arthur ES 100/PK-5
PO Box 98 88253 575-365-2000
Jose Porras, prin. Fax 365-2002
Lake Arthur MS 50/6-8
PO Box 98 88253 575-365-2000
Jose Porras, prin. Fax 365-2002

La Luz, Otero, Pop. 1,684
Alamogordo SD
Supt. — See Alamogordo
La Luz ES 300/K-5
99 Alamo St 88337 575-812-5300
Bertha Garza, prin. Fax 812-5303

La Mesa, Dona Ana, Pop. 716
Gadsden ISD
Supt. — See Sunland Park
La Mesa Pre K Center PK-PK
253 E Chimuri St 88044 575-233-3475
Angelic Ramos, admin. Fax 233-0903

Las Cruces, Dona Ana, Pop. 96,217
Las Cruces SD 24,900/PK-12
505 S Main St Ste 249 88001 575-527-5800
Dr. Greg Ewing, supt. Fax 527-5972
www.lcps.k12.nm.us
Alameda ES 500/K-5
505 S Main St Ste 249 88001 575-527-9486
Aine Garcia-Post, prin. Fax 527-9472
Camino Real MS 700/6-8
505 S Main St Ste 249 88001 575-527-6030
Ralph Ramos, prin. Fax 527-6031
Central ES 300/K-5
505 S Main St Ste 249 88001 575-527-9496
Eloisa Solis, prin. Fax 527-9713
Chavez ES 600/PK-2
505 S Main St Ste 249 88001 575-527-6022
Jeannette Martinez, prin. Fax 527-6036
Columbia ES 500/PK-5
505 S Main St Ste 249 88001 575-527-1561
Michael Chaires, prin. Fax 527-5621
Conlee ES 500/K-5
505 S Main St Ste 249 88001 575-527-9656
George Schumpelt, prin. Fax 527-9664

Desert Hills ES 600/PK-5
505 S Main St Ste 249 88001 575-527-9619
Jamie Vance, prin. Fax 527-9785
Dona Ana ES 400/PK-5
505 S Main St Ste 249 88001 575-527-9506
Cherie Love, prin. Fax 527-9716
East Picacho ES 500/K-5
505 S Main St Ste 249 88001 575-527-9516
Nubia Tarazona, prin. Fax 527-9717
Fairacres ES 400/K-5
505 S Main St Ste 249 88001 575-527-9606
Kathy Norris, prin. Fax 527-9612
Hermosa Heights ES 500/PK-5
505 S Main St Ste 249 88001 575-527-9530
Theresa Garcia, prin. Fax 527-9528
Highland ES 800/PK-5
505 S Main St Ste 249 88001 575-527-9636
Karin Hite, prin. Fax 527-9711
Hillrise ES 600/K-5
505 S Main St Ste 249 88001 575-527-9666
Michael Kleczka, prin. Fax 527-9668
Jornada ES 500/K-5
505 S Main St Ste 249 88001 575-527-9536
Julio Martinez, prin. Fax 527-9762
Loma Heights ES 500/PK-5
505 S Main St Ste 249 88001 575-527-9546
Carla Ragan, prin. Fax 527-9553
Lynn MS 800/6-8
505 S Main St Ste 249 88001 575-527-9445
Reynaldo Gomez, prin. Fax 527-9454
MacArthur ES 500/PK-5
505 S Main St Ste 249 88001 575-527-9556
Dr. Roberto Lozano, prin. Fax 527-6029
Mesa MS 600/6-8
505 S Main St Ste 249 88001 575-527-9510
Steven Rodriguez, prin. Fax 527-9511
Monte Vista ES 500/K-5
505 S Main St Ste 249 88001 575-527-9490
Theresa Jones, prin. Fax 527-9511
Picacho MS 800/6-8
505 S Main St Ste 249 88001 575-527-9455
Fred Montalvo, prin. Fax 527-9459
Sierra MS 800/6-8
505 S Main St Ste 249 88001 575-527-9640
Maryester Garza, prin. Fax 527-9768
Sonoma ES 700/PK-5
505 S Main St Ste 249 88001 575-541-7320
Melissa Galaz, prin. Fax 541-7321
Sunrise ES 500/3-5
505 S Main St Ste 249 88001 575-527-9626
Dora Solis, prin. Fax 527-9633
Tombaugh ES 700/K-5
505 S Main St Ste 249 88001 575-527-9575
Guillermo Carmona, prin. Fax 527-9746
University Hills ES 400/PK-5
505 S Main St Ste 249 88001 575-527-9649
Kelly Marires, prin. Fax 527-9460
Valley View ES 400/PK-5
505 S Main St Ste 249 88001 575-527-9586
Ricardo Rincon, prin. Fax 527-9731
Vista MS 700/6-8
505 S Main St Ste 249 88001 575-527-9465
Mike Brewer, prin. Fax 527-9470
Washington ES 400/PK-5
505 S Main St Ste 249 88001 575-527-9595
Mari Rincon, prin. Fax 527-9520
Zia MS 800/6-8
505 S Main St Ste 249 88001 575-527-9475
Heather Kingery, prin. Fax 527-9479
Other Schools – See Mesilla, Mesilla Park, White Sands

College Heights K 100/PK-K
1210 Wofford Dr 88001 575-522-6922
Cyndy Moon, dir. Fax 522-6392
Las Cruces Catholic S 300/PK-12
1331 N Miranda St 88005 575-526-2617
Connie Limon, prin. Fax 524-0544
Mesilla Valley Christian S 400/PK-12
3850 Stern Dr 88001 575-525-8515
Dr. John Foreman, head sch Fax 526-2713
Mission Lutheran S 100/PK-5
2752 N Roadrunner Pkwy 88011 575-532-5489
Mary Martin, admin.

Las Vegas, San Miguel, Pop. 13,609
Las Vegas City SD 1,800/PK-12
901 Douglas Ave 87701 505-454-5700
Kelt Cooper, supt. Fax 454-5712
cybercardinal.com
ECC 100/K-K
901 Douglas Ave 87701 505-454-5780
Cathy Gallegos, prin. Fax 454-2738
Los Ninos ES 200/PK-3
901 Douglas Ave 87701 505-454-5720
L. Carla Pacheco, prin. Fax 454-2745
Memorial MS 400/7-8
901 Douglas Ave 87701 505-454-5710
Juan Carlos Fulgenzi, prin. Fax 454-2753
Sierra Vista ES 200/4-6
901 Douglas Ave 87701 505-454-5740
Cathy Gallegos, prin. Fax 454-2733
Other Schools – See Sapello

West Las Vegas SD 1,500/K-12
179 Bridge St 87701 505-426-2300
Christopher Gutierrez, supt. Fax 426-2318
wlvs.schooldesk.net
Armijo ES 100/K-1
179 Bridge St 87701 505-426-2661
Rosemarie Salinas, prin. Fax 426-2662
Martinez ES 200/2-5
179 Bridge St 87701 505-426-2861
Thomas Sanchez, prin. Fax 426-2862
Serna ES 100/3-5
179 Bridge St 87701 505-426-2621
Rosemarie Salinas, prin. Fax 426-2622
Union Street ES 100/3-5
179 Bridge St 87701 505-426-2701
Thomas Sanchez, prin. Fax 426-2702
West Las Vegas MS 300/6-8
179 Bridge St 87701 505-426-2541
Anna Valdez, prin. Fax 426-2542
Other Schools – See El Pueblo

La Union, Dona Ana, Pop. 1,103
Gadsden ISD
Supt. — See Sunland Park
La Union ES 300/K-6
875 Mercantil Ave 88021 575-874-3592
Vicente Sanchez, prin. Fax 874-8335

Calvary West Christian S 50/K-12
7048 McNutt Rd 88021 575-589-1433
Ryan Smith, prin.

Logan, Quay, Pop. 1,034
Logan Municipal SD 300/PK-12
PO Box 67 88426 575-487-2252
Dennis Roch, supt. Fax 487-9479
www.loganschool.net
Logan ES 100/PK-5
PO Box 67 88426 575-487-2252
Tommy Thompson, prin. Fax 487-9479
Logan MS 100/6-8
PO Box 67 88426 575-487-2252
Tommy Thompson, prin. Fax 487-9479

Lordsburg, Hidalgo, Pop. 2,787
Lordsburg Municipal SD 400/PK-12
PO Box 430 88045 575-542-9361
Randy Piper, supt. Fax 542-9364
www.lmsed.org
Central ES 100/5-6
207 High St 88045 575-542-9222
Jonell Conway, prin. Fax 542-9223
Dugan-Tarango MS 100/7-8
1352 Hardin St 88045 575-542-9806
Jonell Conway, prin. Fax 542-9811
Traylor ES 200/PK-4
500 Ownby St 88045 575-542-3252
Steven Lucas, prin. Fax 542-3239

Los Alamos, Los Alamos, Pop. 11,762
Los Alamos SD 3,500/PK-12
PO Box 90 87544 505-663-2222
Dr. Kurt Steinhaus, supt. Fax 663-2243
www.laschools.net
Aspen ES 400/K-6
2182 33rd St 87544 505-663-2275
Kathryn Vandenkieboom, prin. Fax 662-4398
Barranca Mesa ES 400/PK-6
57 Loma Del Escolar St 87544 505-663-2730
Virginia Terrazas, prin. Fax 662-6645
Los Alamos MS 500/7-8
2101 Hawk Dr 87544 505-663-2375
Michael Johnson, prin. Fax 662-4270
Mountain ES 500/K-6
2280 North Rd 87544 505-663-2325
Jennifer Guy, prin. Fax 661-4059
Other Schools – See White Rock

Ponderosa Montessori S 50/PK-6
304 Rover Blvd 87544 505-672-9211

Los Lunas, Valencia, Pop. 14,610
Los Lunas SD 8,400/PK-12
PO Box 1300 87031 505-865-9636
Dana Sanders, supt. Fax 865-7766
www.llschools.net
Desert View ES 400/PK-6
PO Box 1300 87031 505-866-2488
Diedra Martinez Munos, prin. Fax 866-2485
Gabaldon ES 400/PK-6
PO Box 1300 87031 505-866-0456
Catharine Campbell, prin. Fax 866-2166
Gallegos ES 500/PK-6
PO Box 1300 87031 505-865-6223
Victoria Baca, prin. Fax 866-2159
Los Lunas ES 500/PK-6
PO Box 1300 87031 505-865-9313
Laura Tabet, prin. Fax 866-2151
Los Lunas MS 700/7-8
PO Box 1300 87031 505-865-7273
Lawrence Sosa, prin. Fax 865-9742
Parish ES 500/PK-6
PO Box 1300 87031 505-865-9652
Melissa Contreras, prin. Fax 865-7364
Sundance ES 600/PK-6
PO Box 1300 87031 505-866-0185
Mildred Chavez, prin. Fax 866-0302
Tome ES 500/PK-6
PO Box 1300 87031 505-865-1102
Casey Ahner, prin. Fax 865-8995
Valencia ES 400/PK-6
PO Box 1300 87031 505-865-3017
Sonia Allen, prin. Fax 866-2169
Valencia MS 500/7-8
PO Box 1300 87031 505-865-1750
Barbara Neumann, prin. Fax 866-8921
Other Schools – See Bosque Farms, Peralta

Los Ranchos, Bernalillo
Albuquerque SD
Supt. — See Albuquerque
Los Ranchos ES 300/K-5
7609 4th St NW, 505-898-0704
Craig Robinson, prin. Fax 898-2080
Taft MS 500/6-8
620 Schulte Rd NW, 505-344-4389
Steve Scully, prin. Fax 761-8440

Loving, Eddy, Pop. 1,402
Loving Municipal SD 600/PK-12
PO Box 98 88256 575-745-2000
Dr. Ann Lynn McIlroy, supt. Fax 745-2002
www.lovingschools.com
Loving ES 300/PK-5
PO Box 98 88256 575-745-2070
John Cook, prin. Fax 745-2072
Loving MS 100/6-8
PO Box 98 88256 575-745-2050
Vince Taylor, prin. Fax 745-2040

Lovington, Lea, Pop. 10,904
Lovington Municipal SD 3,700/PK-12
18 W Washington Ave 88260 575-739-2200
LeAnne Gandy, supt. Fax 739-2205
www.lovingtonschools.net/
Alexander ES 300/2-2
1400 S 6th St 88260 575-739-2580
Stefanie Stephens, prin. Fax 739-2584
Jefferson ES 300/3-3
300 W Jefferson Ave 88260 575-739-2540
Lori Brattain, prin. Fax 739-2584
Lea ES 300/1-1
1202 W Birch Ave 88260 575-739-2625
Kelli Ann Moore, prin. Fax 739-2631
Llano ES 500/PK-K
1000 S 1st St 88260 575-739-2670
Alfredo Turrubiates, prin. Fax 739-2672
Sixth Grade Academy 300/6-6
500 W Jefferson Ave 88260 575-739-2330
Mark Mapes, prin. Fax 739-2330
Taylor MS 500/7-8
700 S 11th St 88260 575-739-2435
Ivan DeAnda, prin. Fax 739-2438
Yarbro ES 500/4-5
700 W Jefferson Ave 88260 575-739-2490
Pam Quinones, prin. Fax 739-2493

Lumberton, Rio Arriba, Pop. 70

St. Francis S 100/K-8
21 County Road 356 87528 575-759-3252
Madeline Lyon, prin. Fax 759-3844

Magdalena, Socorro, Pop. 910
Magdalena Municipal SD 400/PK-12
PO Box 24 87825 575-854-2241
Dr. Glenn Haven, supt. Fax 854-2531
www.magdalena.k12.nm.us
Magdalena ES 100/PK-5
PO Box 629 87825 575-854-2241
Dr. Glenn Haven, prin. Fax 854-2294
Magdalena MS 100/6-8
PO Box 629 87825 575-854-8014
Leslie Clark, prin. Fax 854-2294

Maxwell, Colfax, Pop. 243
Maxwell Municipal SD 100/PK-12
PO Box 275 87728 575-375-2371
Kristen Forrester, supt. Fax 375-2375
www.maxwellp12.com
Maxwell ES 100/PK-6
PO Box 275 87728 575-375-2371
John Ward, prin. Fax 375-2375
Maxwell MS 50/7-8
PO Box 275 87728 575-375-2371
John Ward, prin. Fax 375-2375

Melrose, Curry, Pop. 637
Melrose SD 200/PK-12
PO Box 275 88124 575-253-4269
Jamie Widner, supt. Fax 253-4291
www.melroseschools.org
Melrose ES 100/PK-6
PO Box 275 88124 575-253-4266
Brian Stacy, prin. Fax 253-4291

Mesilla, Dona Ana, Pop. 2,164
Las Cruces SD
Supt. — See Las Cruces
Mesilla ES 300/PK-5
2363 Calle del Sur 88046 575-527-9566
Lydia Polanco, prin. Fax 527-9756

Acton Academy Las Cruces 50/K-8
1730 Tierra de Mesilla 88046 575-449-4796

Mesilla Park, See Las Cruces
Las Cruces SD
Supt. — See Las Cruces
Mesilla Park ES 400/K-5
955 W Union Ave 88047 575-527-9615
Diane Barela, prin. Fax 527-9720

Mesquite, Dona Ana, Pop. 1,109
Gadsden ISD
Supt. — See Sunland Park
Mesquite ES 400/K-6
PO Box 320 88048 575-233-3925
Angela Silvaggio, prin. Fax 233-0905

Milan, Cibola, Pop. 3,223
Grants-Cibola County SD
Supt. — See Grants
Milan ES 500/PK-6
404 Sand St 87021 505-285-2727
Clara DeArmond, prin. Fax 285-2731

Mora, Mora, Pop. 656
Mora ISD 400/K-12
PO Box 179 87732 575-387-3101
Ella Arellano, supt. Fax 387-3111
mora.k12.nm.us
Garcia MS 100/6-8
PO Box 687 87732 575-387-3127
Angelo Archuleta, prin. Fax 387-3126
Mora & Holman ES 200/K-5
PO Box 140 87732 575-387-3132
John Maldonado, prin. Fax 387-3131

Moriarty, Torrance, Pop. 1,873
Moriarty-Edgewood SD 2,100/PK-12
PO Box 2000 87035 505-832-4471
Tom Sullivan, supt. Fax 832-4472
www.mesd.us
Moriarty ES 300/PK-5
PO Box 2000 87035 505-832-4927
Lane Widner, prin. Fax 832-2474
Moriarty MS 200/6-8
PO Box 2000 87035 505-832-6200
Amanda Wilson, prin. Fax 832-5919
Other Schools – See Edgewood

Mosquero, Harding, Pop. 93
Mosquero Municipal SD 50/K-12
PO Box 258 87733 575-673-2271
Tommy Turner, supt. Fax 673-2305
www.mosquero.net
Mosquero ES 50/K-6
PO Box 258 87733 575-673-2271
Tommy Turner, prin. Fax 673-2305

Mountainair, Torrance, Pop. 908
Mountainair SD 200/PK-12
PO Box 456 87036 505-847-2333
Dawn Apodaca, supt. Fax 847-2843
mps-nm.schoolloop.com
Mountainair ES 100/PK-5
PO Box 456 87036 505-847-2231
Dr. Deborah Mitchell, prin. Fax 847-2727

Navajo, McKinley, Pop. 1,626
Gallup-McKinley County SD
Supt. — See Gallup
Navajo ES 300/PK-5
PO Box 1012 87328 505-777-2381
Pandora Watchman, prin. Fax 721-3599
Navajo MS 100/6-8
PO Box 1287 87328 505-777-2390
Mary Ann Sherman, prin. Fax 721-5399

Newcomb, San Juan, Pop. 335
Central Consolidated SD
Supt. — See Shiprock
Newcomb ES 300/PK-5
PO Box 7917 87455 505-696-3415
Deborah Belone, prin. Fax 696-3419
Newcomb MS 200/6-8
PO Box 7927 87455 505-696-3434
Ethel Manuelito, prin. Fax 696-3430

Ojo Caliente, Taos
Mesa Vista Consolidated SD 300/PK-12
PO Box 309 87549 505-583-2645
Ernesto Valdez, supt. Fax 583-2815
www.mesavista.org
Ojo Caliente ES 100/4-6
PO Box 369 87549 505-583-2316
Robert Mata, prin. Fax 583-2105
Other Schools – See El Rito

Pecos, San Miguel, Pop. 1,378
Pecos ISD 700/PK-12
PO Box 368 87552 505-757-4700
Fred Trujillo, supt. Fax 757-8721
www.pecos.k12.nm.us
Pecos ES 300/PK-5
PO Box 368 87552 505-757-4770
Debra Sena-Holton, prin. Fax 757-2165
Pecos MS 100/6-8
PO Box 368 87552 505-757-4620
Mike Lister, prin. Fax 757-2561

Pena Blanca, Sandoval, Pop. 704
Bernalillo SD
Supt. — See Bernalillo
Cochiti S 100/K-8
800 Quail Hill Trl 87041 505-867-5547
Shauna Branch, prin. Fax 867-7846

Penasco, Taos, Pop. 584
Penasco ISD 400/K-12
PO Box 520 87553 575-587-2502
Darlene Ulibarri, supt. Fax 587-2513
www.penascoisd.com
Penasco ES 200/K-6
PO Box 520 87553 575-587-2502
Marvin MacAuley, prin. Fax 587-1845
Penasco MS 100/7-8
PO Box 520 87553 575-587-2502
Marina Lopez, prin. Fax 587-9910

Peralta, Valencia, Pop. 3,612
Los Lunas SD
Supt. — See Los Lunas
Peralta ES 400/PK-6
3645 State Highway 47 87042 505-869-2679
Monica Arguello, prin. Fax 869-5428

Placitas, Sandoval, Pop. 4,920
Bernalillo SD
Supt. — See Bernalillo
Placitas ES 100/K-5
5 Calle De Carbon 87043 505-867-2488
James Telles, prin. Fax 867-7812

Polvadera, Socorro, Pop. 267
Socorro Consolidated SD
Supt. — See Socorro
Midway ES 100/K-5
9 Midway Rd 87828 575-835-1098
Gilbert Peralta, prin. Fax 838-3101

Portales, Roosevelt, Pop. 12,080
Portales Municipal SD 2,900/PK-12
501 S Abilene Ave 88130 575-356-7000
Johnnie S. Cain, supt. Fax 356-4377
www.portalesschools.com
Brown ECC 300/PK-K
520 W 5th St 88130 575-356-7075
Becky Flen, prin. Fax 356-4839
James ES 500/1-2
701 W 18th St 88130 575-359-3675
Deanne McKinney, prin. Fax 356-4852
Lindsey-Steiner ES 400/5-6
1000 N Avenue M 88130 575-356-7060
Rick Segovia, prin. Fax 356-4461
Portales JHS 400/7-8
700 E 3rd St 88130 575-356-7045
Steve Harris, prin. Fax 359-0826
Valencia ES 500/3-4
1415 S Globe Ave 88130 575-356-7090
Sandra Harris, prin. Fax 356-2846

Quemado, Catron, Pop. 224
Quemado ISD 200/K-12
PO Box 128 87829 575-773-4700
David Lackey, supt. Fax 773-4717
www.quemadoschools.org
Quemado ES 100/K-6
PO Box 128 87829 575-773-4700
Don Goodman, prin. Fax 773-4717
Other Schools – See Datil

Questa, Taos, Pop. 1,751
Questa ISD 300/PK-12
PO Box 440 87556 575-586-0421
Valerie Trujillo, supt. Fax 586-0531
www.qisd-nm.schoolloop.com
Alta Vista ES 100/K-3
PO Box 829 87556 575-586-0032
Michellle Gonzales, prin. Fax 586-2061
Alta Vista IS 100/4-6
PO Box 829 87556 575-586-0032
Michelle Gonzales, prin. Fax 586-2061
Other Schools – See Costilla

Ramah, McKinley, Pop. 354
Gallup-McKinley County SD
Supt. — See Gallup
Ramah ES 200/K-5
PO Box 869 87321 505-783-4219
Stephanie Vicenti, prin. Fax 721-3799

Ranchos de Taos, Taos, Pop. 2,481
Taos Municipal SD
Supt. — See Taos
Ranchos ES 500/PK-5
200 Ranchos Elementary Rd 87557 575-737-6150
Lourdes Cordova, prin. Fax 737-6151

Raton, Colfax, Pop. 6,809
Raton SD 600/PK-12
1550 Tiger Cir 87740 575-445-9111
Andy Ortiz, supt. Fax 445-5641
www.ratonschools.com
Longfellow ES 200/PK-2
700 E 4th St 87740 575-445-9261
Kim Sanchez, prin. Fax 445-5306
Raton IS 100/3-6
500 S 3rd St 87740 575-445-9881
Kristie Medina, prin. Fax 445-3682

Rehoboth, McKinley

Rehoboth Christian S 400/PK-12
PO Box 41 87322 505-863-4412
Chris VanSlooten, prin. Fax 726-9635

Reserve, Catron, Pop. 285
Reserve ISD 100/K-12
PO Box 350 87830 575-533-6242
Bill Green, supt. Fax 533-6900
www.reserveschools.com
Reserve ES 100/K-6
PO Box 350 87830 575-533-6241
Cindy Shellhorn, prin. Fax 533-6647
Other Schools – See Glenwood

Rio Rancho, Sandoval, Pop. 85,293
Rio Rancho SD 17,200/PK-12
500 Laser Rd NE 87124 505-896-0667
Dr. Sue Cleveland, supt. Fax 896-0662
www.rrps.net
Cielo Azul ES 800/K-5
3804 Shiloh Rd NE, 505-338-2320
Alicia Banes, prin. Fax 896-0302
Colinas del Norte ES 700/K-5
1001 Night Sky Ave NE, 505-896-3378
Laura Moore, prin. Fax 896-3387
Cordova ES 1,000/K-5
1500 Veranda Rd SE 87124 505-994-0229
Katherine House, prin. Fax 994-2684
Eagle Ridge MS 800/6-8
800 Fruta Rd NE 87124 505-892-6630
Catherine Rodriguez, prin. Fax 892-6909
Enchanted Hills ES 700/K-5
5400 Obregon Rd NE, 505-891-8526
Cathy Baehr, prin. Fax 892-9809
King ES 900/K-5
1301 Nicklaus Dr SE 87124 505-892-2575
Janna Chenault, prin. Fax 892-9862
Lincoln MS 1,000/6-8
2287 Lema Rd SE 87124 505-892-1100
Veronica Sanders, prin. Fax 892-9728
Mountain View MS 900/6-8
4101 Montreal Loop NE, 505-867-0711
Julie Arnold, prin. Fax 867-7901
Puesta Del Sol ES 700/K-5
450 Southern Blvd SE 87124 505-994-3305
G. Bryan Garcia, prin. Fax 994-3316
Rio Rancho ES 600/K-5
4601 Pepe Ortiz Rd SE 87124 505-892-0220
Sarah Poutsch, prin. Fax 892-5724
Rio Rancho MS 1,200/6-8
1600 Loma Colorado Blvd NE, 505-891-5335
Lynda Kitts, prin. Fax 896-6761
Sandia Vista ES 600/K-5
6800 Franklin NE, 505-338-2526
Patricia DiVasto, prin. Fax 771-0956
Shining Stars Preschool 500/PK-PK
4477 9th Ave NE 87124 505-892-7735
Kimberly Johns, prin. Fax 892-6166
Stapleton ES 900/K-5
3100 Stapleton Ave NE 87124 505-891-8473
Cheryl Clark, prin. Fax 891-8498
Vista Grande ES 700/K-5
7001 Chayote Rd NE, 505-771-2366
Trent Heffner, prin. Fax 771-2369

Gospel Light Baptist Academy 100/1-12
1500 Southern Blvd SE 87124 505-892-9463
Mark Lenentine, prin.
St. Thomas Aquinas Catholic S 400/K-8
1100 Hood Rd SE 87124 505-892-3221
Sr. Anne Louise Abascal, prin. Fax 892-3350

Roswell, Chaves, Pop. 47,742
Roswell ISD 10,300/PK-12
PO Box 1437 88202 575-627-2500
Susan Sanchez, supt. Fax 627-2512
www.risd.k12.nm.us
Berrendo ES 400/PK-5
505 W Pine Lodge Rd 88201 575-627-2875
Brittany Griffin, prin. Fax 625-8292
Berrendo MS 600/6-8
800 Marion Richards Rd 88201 575-627-2775
Licia HIllman, prin. Fax 625-8248
Del Norte ES 600/K-5
2701 N Garden Ave 88201 575-637-3325
Andrea Edmonson, prin. Fax 625-8227
East Grand Plains ES 300/PK-5
3773 East Grand Plains Rd 88203 575-637-3350
Kathleen Galloway, prin. Fax 622-2844
El Capitan ES 400/PK-5
2807 W Bland St 88203 575-637-3400
Stacey Damon, prin. Fax 625-8243
Lopez ES 300/PK-5
1208 E Bland St 88203 575-637-3500
Andrea Nieto-Walker, prin. Fax 625-8282
Mesa MS 500/6-8
1601 E Bland St 88203 575-627-2800
LaShawn Byrd, prin. Fax 625-8263
Military Heights ES 500/K-5
1900 N Michigan Ave 88201 575-637-3425
Heidi Shanor, prin. Fax 625-8272
Missouri Avenue ES 400/K-5
700 W Deming St 88203 575-637-3450
Kirk DeSoto, prin. Fax 625-8222
Monterrey ES 500/K-5
910 W Gayle St 88203 575-637-3477
Greg Torres, prin. Fax 625-8302
Mountain View MS 500/6-8
312 E Mountain View Rd 88203 575-627-2825
Glenda Leonard, prin. Fax 625-8260
Parkview Early Literacy Center 300/PK-K
1700 W Alameda St 88203 575-637-3525
Kathy Macha, prin. Fax 625-8247
Pecos ES 400/K-5
600 E Hobbs St 88203 575-637-3550
Dr. Barbara Ryan, prin. Fax 625-8293
Sierra MS 600/6-8
615 S Sycamore Ave 88203 575-627-2850
Ralph Matta, prin. Fax 625-8283
Sunset ES 400/K-5
606 O Connor Rd 88203 575-637-3575
Mireya Trujillo, prin. Fax 627-2589
Valley View ES 500/K-5
1400 S Washington Ave 88203 575-637-3600
Karla Stinehart, prin. Fax 625-8297
Washington Avenue ES 500/K-5
408 N Washington Ave 88201 575-637-3625
Amanda Arnold, prin. Fax 625-8249

All Saints Catholic S 100/PK-8
2700 N Kentucky Ave 88201 575-627-5744
Kendra Mathison, prin. Fax 623-3906
Gateway Christian S 300/PK-12
PO Box 1642 88202 575-622-9710
Rick Rapp, admin. Fax 622-9739
Immanuel Lutheran S 100/K-8
1405 N Sycamore Ave 88201 575-622-2853
Fax 622-3723

Roy, Harding, Pop. 234
Roy Municipal SD 50/PK-12
PO Box 430 87743 575-485-2242
Dr. Jim Holloway, supt. Fax 485-2497
www.royschools.org
Roy ES 50/PK-6
PO Box 430 87743 575-485-2242
Dr. Jim Holloway, admin. Fax 485-2497

Ruidoso, Lincoln, Pop. 7,928
Ruidoso Municipal SD 2,100/PK-12
200 Horton Cir 88345 575-630-7000
Dr. George Bickert, supt. Fax 257-4150
www.ruidososchools.org/
Nob Hill ECC 200/PK-K
200 Horton Cir 88345 575-258-6420
Jeremy Green, prin. Fax 257-3689
Ruidoso MS 500/6-8
200 Horton Cir 88345 575-630-7800
Anna Addis, prin. Fax 258-5809
Sierra Vista PS 300/1-2
200 Horton Cir 88345 575-258-6400
Jeremy Green, prin. Fax 258-1300
White Mountain ES 500/3-5
200 Horton Cir 88345 575-258-6300
Jason Edmister, prin. Fax 258-5578

San Antonio, Socorro, Pop. 165
Socorro Consolidated SD
Supt. — See Socorro
San Antonio ES 100/K-5
PO Box 277 87832 575-835-1758
John Dennis, head sch Fax 838-0310

Sandia Park, Bernalillo, Pop. 234
Albuquerque SD
Supt. — See Albuquerque
San Antonito ES 300/K-5
12555 State Highway 14 N 87047 505-281-3931
Patricia Gallegos, prin. Fax 281-5864

San Fidel, Cibola, Pop. 132

St. Joseph S 50/PK-8
PO Box 370 87049 505-552-6362
Antonio Trujillo, prin. Fax 552-0168

San Jon, Quay, Pop. 209
San Jon Municipal SD 100/PK-12
PO Box 5 88434 575-576-2466
Colin Taylor, supt. Fax 576-2772
www.sanjonschools.com
San Jon ES 100/PK-5
PO Box 5 88434 575-576-2466
Fax 576-2772
San Jon MS 50/6-8
PO Box 5 88434 575-576-2466
Fax 576-2772

San Juan Pueblo, Rio Arriba
Espanola SD 55
Supt. — See Espanola
San Juan ES 400/K-6
State Road 74 # 411 87566 505-852-4225
Candice Harrison, prin. Fax 367-2340

San Lorenzo, Grant, Pop. 95
Cobre Consolidated SD
Supt. — See Bayard
San Lorenzo ES 100/PK-6
PO Box 315 88041 575-536-9348
Michael Koury, prin. Fax 536-9490

San Miguel, Dona Ana, Pop. 1,152
Gadsden ISD
Supt. — See Sunland Park
North Valley ES 400/K-6
PO Box C 88058 575-233-1092
Maria Hernandez, prin. Fax 233-3772

,
Cobre Consolidated SD
Supt. — See Bayard
Central ES 400/PK-6
PO Box 315 88026 575-537-4050
Margaret Kesler, prin. Fax 537-5382

San Rafael, Cibola, Pop. 925
Grants-Cibola County SD
Supt. — See Grants
San Rafael ES 100/K-6
27 Mesa View St 87051 505-285-2749
Rosemary Calvert, prin. Fax 285-2753

Santa Cruz, Santa Fe, Pop. 368

Holy Cross Catholic S 100/PK-6
PO Box 1260 87567 505-753-4644
Terri Lopez, prin. Fax 216-0653

Santa Fe, Santa Fe, Pop. 66,849

Pojoaque Valley SD 1,900/PK-12
1574 State Road 502 87506 505-455-2282
Dr. Melville Morgan, supt. Fax 455-7152
www.pvs.k12.nm.us
Pojoaque Valley IS 300/4-5
1574 State Road 502 87506 505-455-2910
Staci Mascarenas, prin. Fax 455-3003
Pojoaque Valley MS 300/7-8
1574 State Road 502 87506 505-455-2238
Vera Trujillo, prin. Fax 455-3392
Pojoaque Valley Sixth Grade Academy 100/6-6
1574 State Road 502 87506 505-819-2300
Mario Vigil, prin. Fax 819-2305
Roybal ES 600/PK-3
1574 State Road 502 87506 505-455-7603
Lillian Griego, prin. Fax 455-3940

Santa Fe SD 13,400/PK-12
610 Alta Vista St 87505 505-467-2000
Dr. Veronica Garcia, supt. Fax 995-3300
www.sfps.info
Acequia Madre ES 200/K-6
700 Acequia Madre 87505 505-467-4000
Ahlum Scarola, prin. Fax 982-0224
Aspen Community S 600/K-8
450 La Madera St 87501 505-467-4500
Gary DeSanctis, prin. Fax 820-3138
Atalaya ES 200/PK-6
721 Camino Cabra 87505 505-467-4400
Katherine Diaz, prin. Fax 982-4079
Biehl Community S 500/K-6
310 Avenida Del Sur 87508 505-467-2100
Deanna Ocampo-Moore, prin. Fax 471-3659
Chaparral ES 400/PK-6
2451 Avenida Chaparral 87505 505-467-1400
Colleen Korce, prin. Fax 471-4308
Chavez ES 600/PK-5
6251 Jaguar Dr 87507 505-467-3200
Tammy Hall, prin. Fax 471-9290
El Camino Real Academy PK-8
2500 S Meadows Rd 87507 505-467-1300
Jakob Lain, prin. Fax 471-3754
El Dorado Community S 600/K-8
2 Avenida Torreon 87508 505-467-4900
Anne Darnton, prin. Fax 466-3094
Gilbert ES 300/K-6
300 Griffin St 87501 505-467-4700
Kim Pietrocci, prin. Fax 982-4016
Gonzales Community S 500/K-8
851 W Alameda St 87501 505-467-3100
Michael Lee, prin. Fax 983-0007
Kearny ES 500/K-6
901 Avenida De Las Campanas 87507 505-467-1800
Stephanie Hubley, prin. Fax 471-0266
Mandela International Magnet S 50/7-8
1604 Agua Fria 87505 505-467-1901
Benjamin Hairgrove, prin. Fax 471-9287
Martinez ES 300/PK-6
401 W San Mateo Rd 87505 505-467-3800
Jill Lee, prin.
Milagro MS 400/7-8
351 W Zia Rd 87505 505-467-3300
Marc DuCharme, prin. Fax 471-3793
Nava ES 300/K-6
2655 Siringo Rd 87505 505-467-1200
Brenda Korting, prin. Fax 473-3555
Nye ECC 100/PK-PK
3200 Calle Po Ae Pi 87507 505-467-4600
Jennifer Thompson, prin. Fax 471-1536
Ortiz MS 700/6-8
4164 S Meadows Rd 87507 505-467-2300
Felicia Sena, prin. Fax 471-0610
Otero Community S PK-8
5901 Herrera Dr 87507 505-467-4200
Pamela Hyde, prin. Fax 471-3714
Pinon ES 500/PK-6
2921 Camino De Los Caballos 87507 505-467-1600
Janis DeVoti, prin. Fax 471-9002
Ramirez Thomas ES 500/K-5
3200 Calle Po Ae Pi 87507 505-467-3000
Loretta Booker, prin. Fax 471-1535
Salazar ES, 1231 Apache Ave 87505 400/K-6
Jule Skoglund, prin. 505-467-3900
Sweeney ES 600/PK-5
501 Airport Rd 87507 505-467-1500
Theresa Liebert, prin. Fax 471-0118
Wood-Gormley ES 400/K-6
141 E Booth St 87505 505-467-4800
Laura Jeffrey, prin. Fax 982-0182
Other Schools – See Tesuque

Adventist Academy of Santa Fe K-9
PO Box 28327 87592 505-954-1845
Rio Grande S 200/PK-6
715 Camino Cabra 87505 505-983-1621
Nigel Taplin, head sch Fax 986-0012
Sante Fe Waldorf S 200/PK-12
26 Puesta Del Sol 87508 505-983-9727
Santo Nino Regional S 300/PK-6
23 College Dr 87508 505-424-1766
Theresa Vaisa, prin. Fax 473-1441

Santa Rosa, Guadalupe, Pop. 2,827
Santa Rosa Consolidated SD 600/PK-12
344 S 4th St 88435 575-472-3171
Richard Perea, supt. Fax 472-5609
www.srlions.com
Santa Rosa ES 200/PK-5
658 S 5th St 88435 575-472-3172
Julie Sanchez, prin. Fax 472-5638
Santa Rosa MS 100/6-8
116 Camino de Vida 88435 575-472-3633
Mario Trujillo, dean Fax 472-0663
Other Schools – See Anton Chico

Santa Teresa, Dona Ana, Pop. 4,240
Gadsden ISD
Supt. — See Sunland Park
Santa Teresa ES 700/K-6
201 Comerciantes Blvd 88008 575-589-3445
Leon Smith, prin. Fax 589-3429
Santa Teresa MS 600/7-8
4800 McNutt Rd 88008 575-874-7200
Rosa Lovelace, prin. Fax 589-2780

Santo Domingo Pueblo, Sandoval, Pop. 2,446
Bernalillo SD
Supt. — See Bernalillo
Santo Domingo S 200/K-8
PO Box 459 87052 505-867-4441
Larryssa Archuleta, prin. Fax 867-7862

Sapello, San Miguel
Las Vegas City SD
Supt. — See Las Vegas
Sena ES 100/K-6
12 County Rd A-1 87745 505-454-5750
Kelt Cooper, prin. Fax 454-2777

Seboyeta, Cibola, Pop. 177
Grants-Cibola County SD
Supt. — See Grants
Seboyeta ES 100/K-6
HC 77 Box 43 87014 505-552-6384
Milton Head, prin. Fax 285-2670

Sheep Springs, San Juan, Pop. 238
Central Consolidated SD
Supt. — See Shiprock
Naschitti ES 100/K-6
PO Box F 87364 505-732-4204
Dr. Dave Goldtooth, prin. Fax 732-4203

Shiprock, San Juan, Pop. 8,162
Central Consolidated SD 6,100/PK-12
PO Box 1199 87420 505-368-4984
Dr. Colleen Bowman, supt. Fax 368-5232
www.ccsdnm.org
Mesa ES 400/K-5
PO Box 1803 87420 505-368-4529
Dr. Louisa Lopez-Martinez, prin. Fax 368-5765
Nizhoni ES 500/PK-5
PO Box 3567 87420 505-368-4565
Tamara Allison, prin. Fax 368-4814
Stokely ES 400/K-5
PO Box 3568 87420 505-368-5109
Terri Denn, prin. Fax 368-5158
Tse' Bit'ai MS 500/6-8
PO Box 1703 87420 505-368-4741
Rick Edwards, prin. Fax 368-5105
Other Schools – See Fruitland, Kirtland, Newcomb, Sheep Springs

Silver City, Grant, Pop. 10,166
Silver Consolidated SD 3,000/PK-12
2810 N Swan St 88061 575-956-2000
Audie Brown, supt. Fax 956-2039
www.silverschools.org
Barrios ES 200/K-5
1625 Little Walnut Rd 88061 575-956-2120
Travis Yurcic, prin. Fax 956-2134
La Plata MS 600/6-8
3500 N Silver St 88061 575-956-2060
Beth Lougee, prin. Fax 956-2098
Schmitt ES 500/K-5
4042 Highway 90 S 88061 575-956-2170
Leslie Ormand, prin. Fax 956-2182
Sixth Street ES 100/PK-5
405 W 6th St 88061 575-956-2150
Louis Alvarez, prin. Fax 956-2169
Stout ES 400/1-6
2601 N Silver St 88061 575-956-2100
Jason Ping, prin. Fax 956-2119
Other Schools – See Cliff

Calvary Christian Academy 100/PK-12
PO Box 29 88062 575-388-4478
Guadalupe Montessori S 100/PK-6
1731 N Alabama St 88061 575-388-3343

Socorro, Socorro, Pop. 8,907
Socorro Consolidated SD 1,800/K-12
700 Franklin St 87801 575-835-0300
Ron Hendrix, supt. Fax 835-1682
www.socorro.k12.nm.us
Parkview ES 400/K-3
107 Francisco De Avando St 87801 575-835-1086
Rey Carrejo, prin. Fax 835-2962
Sarracino MS 400/6-8
1425 El Camino Real St 87801 575-835-0283
Rhonda Martinez, prin. Fax 835-0360
Zimmerly ES 200/4-5
511 El Camino Real St 87801 575-835-1436
Gilbert Peralta, prin. Fax 838-2028
Other Schools – See Polvadera, San Antonio

Springer, Colfax, Pop. 1,037
Springer Municipal SD 200/K-12
PO Box 308 87747 575-483-3432
Eddie King, supt. Fax 483-2387
www.springerschools.org
Forrester ES 50/K-2
PO Box 308 87747 575-483-3485
Laura Cordova, prin. Fax 483-5012
Wilferth IS 100/3-6
PO Box 308 87747 575-483-3485
Laura Cordova, prin. Fax 483-5012

Sunland Park, Dona Ana, Pop. 14,071
Gadsden ISD 14,800/PK-12
4950 McNutt Rd 88063 575-882-6200
Efren Yturralde, supt. Fax 882-6229
www.gisd.k12.nm.us
Desert View ES 500/K-6
1105 Valle Vista Dr 88063 575-589-1180
Jorge Araujo, prin. Fax 589-2212
On Track Pre K Center 200/PK-PK
4950 McNutt Rd 88008 575-882-6740
Amanda Flores, admin. Fax 882-6257
Riverside ES 700/K-6
4085 McNutt Rd 88063 575-589-1663
Teresa Navarro, prin. Fax 874-3611
Sunland Park ES 300/K-6
305 Alto Vista Dr 88063 575-589-1114
Rosa Kahoe, prin. Fax 874-9442
Other Schools – See Anthony, Chaparral, La Mesa, La Union, Mesquite, San Miguel, Santa Teresa, Vado

Taos, Taos, Pop. 5,592
Taos Municipal SD 2,900/PK-12
310 Camino De La Placita 87571 575-758-5202
Dr. Lillian Torrez, supt. Fax 758-5250
www.taosschools.org
Garcia ES 600/PK-5
305 Don Fernando St 87571 575-737-6070
Dr. Gladys Herrera-Gurule, prin. Fax 737-6091
Taos MS 500/6-8
235 Paseo Del Canon E 87571 575-737-6000
Alfred Cordova, prin. Fax 737-6001
Other Schools – See Arroyo Seco, Ranchos de Taos

Tatum, Lea, Pop. 793
Tatum Municipal SD 300/PK-12
PO Box 685 88267 575-398-4455
Buddy Little, supt. Fax 398-8220
www.tatumschools.org
Tatum ES 200/PK-6
PO Box 685 88267 575-398-4191
Fax 398-8220

Tesuque, Santa Fe, Pop. 912
Santa Fe SD
Supt. — See Santa Fe
Tesuque ES 100/PK-6
PO Box 440 87574 505-467-4100
Tina Morris, prin. Fax 982-4193

Texico, Curry, Pop. 1,118
Texico Municipal SD 600/PK-12
PO Box 237 88135 575-482-3801
Robert Brown, supt. Fax 482-3650
www.texicoschools.com
Texico ES 300/PK-5
PO Box 237 88135 575-482-3492
Kayla Pipkin, prin. Fax 482-3650
Texico MS 100/6-8
PO Box 237 88135 575-482-9520
Dee Rae Timberlake, prin. Fax 482-3650

Thoreau, McKinley, Pop. 1,831
Gallup-McKinley County SD
Supt. — See Gallup
Thoreau ES 300/PK-5
PO Box 839 87323 505-721-4400
K'Dawn Montano, prin. Fax 721-4499
Thoreau MS 300/6-8
PO Box 787 87323 505-721-4600
Moni Short, prin. Fax 721-4699

St. Bonaventure S 200/PK-8
PO Box 610 87323 505-862-7465
Tracie Lee, prin. Fax 862-7790

Tierra Amarilla, Rio Arriba, Pop. 379
Chama Valley ISD 300/PK-12
PO Box 10 87575 575-588-7285
Anthony Casados, supt. Fax 588-7860
www.chamaschools.org
Tierra Amarilla ES 100/PK-6
PO Box 66 87575 575-588-7294
Dawn Salazar, prin. Fax 588-7360
Other Schools – See Chama

Tijeras, Bernalillo, Pop. 534
Albuquerque SD
Supt. — See Albuquerque
Montoya ES 400/PK-5
24 Public School Rd 87059 505-281-0880
Cee Nation, prin. Fax 281-1905
Roosevelt MS 300/6-8
11799 State Highway 14 S 87059 505-281-3316
Cee Nation, prin. Fax 281-5120

Holy Child Catholic S 50/PK-8
PO Box 130 87059 505-281-3077
Janice Martinez, prin. Fax 281-3744

Tohatchi, McKinley, Pop. 799
Gallup-McKinley County SD
Supt. — See Gallup
Tohatchi ES 200/PK-5
PO Box 31 87325 505-733-2297
Dan Fruchey, prin. Fax 271-4799
Tohatchi MS 200/6-8
PO Box 322 87325 505-721-4900
Anthony Morrison, prin. Fax 721-4999

Truth or Consequences, Sierra, Pop. 6,359
Truth or Consequences Municipal SD 1,300/PK-12
180 N Date St 87901 575-894-8166
Dr. Craig Cummins, supt. Fax 894-7532
www.torcschools.net
Sierra ES 200/4-5
180 N Date St 87901 575-894-8362
Stephanie Brownfield, prin. Fax 894-5503
Truth or Consequences ES 400/PK-3
180 N Date St 87901 575-894-8372
Stephanie Brownfield, prin. Fax 894-5503
Truth or Consequences MS 300/6-8
180 N Date St 87901 575-894-8380
Dr. Renee Garcia, prin. Fax 894-0606
Other Schools – See Arrey

Manzano Christian S 50/K-12
1300 S Broadway St 87901 505-894-5646
Rebecca Dow, admin. Fax 894-0132

Tucumcari, Quay, Pop. 5,279
Tucumcari SD 1,000/PK-12
PO Box 1046 88401 575-461-3910
Aaron McKinney, supt. Fax 461-3554
tucumcarischools.com
Tucumcari ES 500/PK-5
1623 S 9th St 88401 575-461-8460
Tonya Hodges, prin. Fax 461-8005
Tucumcari MS 200/6-8
1000 S 5th St 88401 575-461-2310
Lendy Borden, prin. Fax 461-8610

Tularosa, Otero, Pop. 2,782
Tularosa Municipal SD 900/K-12
504 1st St 88352 575-585-8800
Brenda Vigil, supt. Fax 585-4439
www.tularosak12.us
Tularosa ES 200/K-2
504 1st St 88352 575-585-8801
Melva Dusek, prin. Fax 585-2332
Tularosa IS 300/3-6
504 1st St 88352 575-585-8802
Anisa Kasuboski, prin. Fax 585-2345
Tularosa MS 100/7-8
504 1st St 88352 575-585-8803
Bobbie Grace, prin. Fax 585-4739

Twin Lakes, McKinley, Pop. 1,044
Gallup-McKinley County SD
Supt. — See Gallup
Twin Lakes ES 200/PK-5
N Highway 491 87301 505-735-2211
Sandra Freeland, prin. Fax 735-2460

Vado, Dona Ana, Pop. 3,193
Gadsden ISD
Supt. — See Sunland Park
Vado ES 500/K-6
330 Holguin Rd 88072 575-233-2861
Cheryl Coyle, prin. Fax 233-3400

Vanderwagen, McKinley
Gallup-McKinley County SD
Supt. — See Gallup
Skeet ES 200/PK-5
PO Box 128 87326 505-778-5571
Wade Bell, prin. Fax 721-1799

Vaughn, Guadalupe, Pop. 444
Vaughn Municipal SD 100/PK-12
PO Box 489 88353 575-584-2283
Jack Props, supt. Fax 584-2355
www.vaughn.k12.nm.us/
Vaughn ES 50/PK-6
PO Box 489 88353 575-584-2283
Lyndsey Padill, prin. Fax 584-2355

Veguita, Socorro, Pop. 227
Belen Consolidated SD
Supt. — See Belen

La Promesa ES 200/PK-6
898 Highway 304 87062 505-966-2400
Sheila Armijo, prin. Fax 966-2450

Velarde, Rio Arriba, Pop. 486
Espanola SD 55
Supt. — See Espanola
Velarde ES 100/K-6
State Road 68 Co Rd 51 # 14 87582 505-852-4331
Dorothy Valdez, lead tchr. Fax 852-2993

Wagon Mound, Mora, Pop. 312
Wagon Mound SD 100/K-12
PO Box 158 87752 575-666-3000
Sheryl Martinez, supt. Fax 666-9001
www.wm.k12.nm.us
Wagon Mound ES 50/K-6
PO Box 158 87752 575-666-3000
Nicea Chavez, lead tchr. Fax 666-9001

White Rock, Los Alamos, Pop. 5,639
Los Alamos SD
Supt. — See Los Alamos
Chamisa ES 300/K-6
301 Meadow Ln, Los Alamos NM 87544
505-663-2470
Suzanne Lynne, prin. Fax 672-0170
Pinon ES 400/PK-6
90 Grand Canyon Dr, Los Alamos NM 87544
505-663-2680
Jill Gonzales, prin. Fax 672-3807

White Sands, Dona Ana, Pop. 1,564
Las Cruces SD
Supt. — See Las Cruces
White Sands ES 300/PK-8
1 Viking St 88002 575-674-1241
Kathy Vigil, prin. Fax 678-8515

Yatahey, McKinley, Pop. 563
Gallup-McKinley County SD
Supt. — See Gallup
Chee Dodge ES 400/PK-5
PO Box 4039 87375 505-721-1300
Amy Hyatt, prin. Fax 721-1399

Zuni, McKinley, Pop. 5,857
Zuni SD 1,300/PK-12
12 Twin Buttes Dr 87327 505-782-5511
Daniel Benavidez, supt. Fax 782-5870
www.zpsd.org
Shiwi Ts'ana ES 300/PK-5
PO Box D 87327 505-782-4441
Leslie Damon, prin. Fax 782-5879
Zuni MS 200/6-8
PO Box E 87327 505-782-5561
Zeno Kheine, prin. Fax 782-5563

St. Anthony S 100/PK-8
PO Box 486 87327 505-782-4596
Sr. Marsha Moon, prin. Fax 782-2013
Zuni Christian Mission S 100/K-8
PO Box 445 87327 505-782-4546
Timothy Becksvoort, prin. Fax 782-4546

NEW YORK

NEW YORK EDUCATION DEPARTMENT

89 Washington Ave, Albany 12234
Telephone 518-474-3852
Fax 518-473-4909
Website http://www.nysed.gov

Commissioner of Education MaryEllen Elia

NEW YORK BOARD OF REGENTS

89 Washington Ave, Albany 12234

Chancellor Betty Rosa

BOARDS OF COOPERATIVE EDUCATIONAL SERVICES (BOCES)

Broome-Deleware-Tioga BOCES
Allen Buyck, supt. 607-766-3802
435 Glenwood Rd Fax 763-3691
Binghamton 13905
www.btboces.org

Capital Region BOCES
John Yagielski, supt. 518-862-4900
900 Watervliet Shaker Rd Fax 862-4903
Albany 12205
www.capregboces.org

Cattaraugus/Allegany/Erie/Wyoming BOCES
Lynda Quick, supt. 585-376-8246
1825 Windfall Rd, Olean 14760 Fax 376-8452
www.caboces.org

Cayuga/Onondaga BOCES
Denise Dzikowski, supt. 315-253-0361
1879 W Genesee Street Rd Fax 252-6493
Auburn 13021
cayboces.org

Champlain Valley Educational Services
Dr. Mark Davey, supt. 518-561-0100
PO Box 455, Plattsburgh 12901 Fax 562-1471
www.cves.org/

Ctr for Instruction Technology & Innovtn
Christopher Todd, supt. 315-963-4222
179 County Route 64 Fax 963-4475
Mexico 13114
citiboces.org/citi

Delaware/Chenango/Madison/Otsego BOCES
Perry Dewey, supt. 607-335-1233
6678 County Road 32 Fax 334-9848
Norwich 13815
www.dcmoboces.com

Dutchess BOCES
Dr. Richard Hooley, supt. 845-486-4800
5 Boces Rd, Poughkeepsie 12601 Fax 486-4981
www.dcboces.org

Eastern Suffolk BOCES
David Wicks, supt. 631-687-3006
201 S Service Rd Fax 289-2529
Patchogue 11772
www.esboces.org

Erie 1 BOCES
Dr. Lynn Fusco, supt. 716-821-7001
355 Harlem Rd Fax 821-7242
West Seneca 14224
www.e1b.org

Erie 2-Chautauqua-Cattaraugus BOCES
Dr. David O'Rourke, supt. 716-549-4454
8685 Erie Rd, Angola 14006 Fax 549-5181
www.e2ccb.org

Franklin-Essex-Hamilton BOCES
Stephen Shafer, supt. 518-483-6420
PO Box 28, Malone 12953 Fax 483-2178
www.fehb.org/

Genesee Valley BOCES
Kevin MacDonald, supt. 585-658-7900
80 Munson St, Le Roy 14482 Fax 344-7910
www.gvboces.org

Greater Southern Tier BOCES
James Frame, supt. 607-654-2283
9579 Vocational Dr Fax 654-2302
Painted Post 14870
www.gstboces.org

Hamilton-Fulton-Montgomery BOCES
Dr. Patrick Michel, supt. 518-736-4300
2755 State Highway 67 Fax 736-4301
Johnstown 12095
www.hfmboces.org

Herkimer-Fulton-Hamilton-Otsego BOCES
Jacklin Starks, supt. 315-867-2023
352 Gros Blvd, Herkimer 13350 Fax 867-2002
www.herkimer-boces.org

Jefferson-Lewis-Hmltn-Hrkmr-Oneida BOCES
Stephen Todd, supt. 315-779-7010
20104 State Route 3 Fax 779-7009
Watertown 13601
www.boces.com

Madison-Oneida BOCES
Jacklin Starks, supt. 315-361-5510
PO Box 168, Verona 13478 Fax 361-5517
www.moboces.org

Monroe 1 BOCES
Daniel White, supt. 585-383-2200
41 OConnor Rd, Fairport 14450 Fax 383-6404
www.monroe.edu/

Monroe 2 BOCES
JoAnne Antonacci, supt. 585-352-2400
3599 Big Ridge Rd Fax 352-2442
Spencerport 14559
www.monroe2boces.org

Nassau BOCES
Dr. Robert Dillon, supt. 516-396-2200
PO Box 9195, Garden City 11530 Fax 997-8742
www.nassauboces.org

Oneida-Herkimer-Madison BOCES
Howard Mettelman, supt. 315-793-8561
PO Box 70, New Hartford 13413 Fax 793-8541
www.oneida-boces.org/

Onondaga-Cortland-Madison BOCES
Jody Manning, supt. 315-433-2602
PO Box 4754, Syracuse 13221 Fax 434-9347
www.ocmboces.org

Orange-Ulster BOCES
William Hecht, supt. 845-291-0100
53 Gibson Rd, Goshen 10924 Fax 291-0118
www.ouboces.org/

Orleans-Niagara BOCES
Dr. Clark Godshall, supt. 716-731-6800
4232 Shelby Basin Rd
Medina 14103
www.onboces.org

Otsego-Northern Catskills BOCES
Nicholas Savin, supt. 607-588-6291
PO Box 382, Stamford 12167 Fax 588-6098
www.oncboces.org

Putnam Northern Westchester BOCES
Dr. James Ryan, supt. 914-245-2700
200 BOCES Dr Fax 248-2308
Yorktown Heights 10598
www.pnwboces.org

Questar III BOCES
Dr. Gladys Cruz, supt. 518-477-8771
10 Empire State Blvd Fax 477-9833
Castleton on Hudson 12033
www.questar.org

Rockland BOCES
Dr. Charlene Jordan, supt. 845-627-4700
65 Parrott Rd, West Nyack 10994 Fax 624-1764
www.rocklandboces.org

St. Lawrence-Lewis BOCES
Thomas Burns, supt. 315-386-4504
PO Box 231, Canton 13617 Fax 386-2099
www.sllboces.org

Southern Westchester BOCES
Dr. Harold Coles, supt. 914-937-3820
17 Berkley Dr, Rye Brook 10573 Fax 937-7850
www.swboces.org

Sullivan County BOCES
Dr. Charles Khoury, supt. 845-295-4000
6 Wierk Ave, Liberty 12754 Fax 292-8694
www.scboces.org

Tompkins-Seneca-Tioga BOCES
Dr. Jeffrey Matteson, supt. 607-257-1551
555 Warren Rd, Ithaca 14850 Fax 257-2825
tstboces.org

Ulster BOCES
Dr. Charles Khoury, supt. 845-255-3040
175 State Route 32 N Fax 255-7942
New Paltz 12561
www.ulsterboces.org/

Washington-Srtg-Warren-Hmltn-Essex BOCES
James Dexter, supt. 518-746-3310
1153 Burgoyne Ave Ste 2 Fax 746-3319
Fort Edward 12828
wswheboces.org

Wayne-Finger Lakes BOCES
Scott Bischoping, supt. 315-332-7284
131 Drumlin Ct, Newark 14513 Fax 332-7425
www.wflboces.org

Western Suffolk BOCES
Angelique Johnson-Dingle, admin. 631-549-4900
507 Deer Park Rd, Dix Hills 11746 Fax 623-4996
www.wsboces.org

PUBLIC, PRIVATE AND CATHOLIC ELEMENTARY SCHOOLS

Accord, Ulster, Pop. 551
Rondout Valley Central SD 2,000/K-12
PO Box 9 12404 845-687-2400
Rosario Agostaro, supt. Fax 687-9577
www.rondout.k12.ny.us

Rondout Valley JHS 300/7-8
PO Box 9 12404 845-687-2400
Charles Tadduni, prin. Fax 687-8980

Roundout Valley IS 500/4-6
PO Box 9 12404 845-687-2400
Lee Cutler, prin. Fax 687-8980

Other Schools – See Kerhonkson, Stone Ridge

Adams, Jefferson, Pop. 1,752
South Jefferson Central SD
Supt. — See Adams Center

Clarke MS 400/6-8
11060 US Route 11 13605 315-232-4531
Jonathan Christopher, prin. Fax 232-4620

Adams Center, Jefferson, Pop. 1,533
South Jefferson Central SD 1,900/K-12
13180 US Route 11 13606 315-583-6104
Mary Beth Denny, supt. Fax 583-6381
www.spartanpride.org

Wilson ES 500/K-5
13180 US Route 11 13606 315-583-5418
Rebecca Dalrymple, prin. Fax 583-6381

Other Schools – See Adams, Mannsville

Addison, Steuben, Pop. 1,744
Addison Central SD 1,000/PK-12
7 Cleveland Dr 14801 607-359-2244
Joseph DioGuardi, supt. Fax 359-2246
www.addisoncsd.org/

Tuscarora ES 600/PK-5
7 Cleveland Dr 14801 607-359-2261
Georgia Weed, prin. Fax 359-3443

Other Schools – See Cameron Mills

Afton, Chenango, Pop. 818
Afton Central SD 500/K-12
PO Box 5 13730 607-639-8229
Timothy McNamara, supt. Fax 639-1801
www.aftoncsd.org

Afton ES 300/K-6
PO Box 5 13730 607-639-8234
Beth Carsello, prin. Fax 639-8257

Airmont, Rockland, Pop. 8,483

Cheder Ateres Tzvi 200/K-8
4 Campbell Ave 10901 845-369-1515
Fax 369-9595

Akron, Erie, Pop. 2,833
Akron Central SD 1,400/K-12
47 Bloomingdale Ave 14001 716-542-5010
Kevin Shanley, supt. Fax 542-5018
www.akronschools.org

Akron ES 600/K-5
47 Bloomingdale Ave 14001 716-542-5050
Todd Esposito, prin. Fax 542-5018
Akron MS 400/6-8
47 Bloomingdale Ave 14001 716-542-5040
Joseph Caprio, prin. Fax 542-5018

Albany, Albany, Pop. 94,773
CSD of Albany 8,200/PK-12
1 Academy Park 12207 518-475-6000
Kaweeda Adams, supt. Fax 475-6009
www.albanyschools.org
Albany S of Humanities 500/PK-6
108 Whitehall Rd 12209 518-475-6575
Marie Culihan, prin. Fax 475-6577
Arbor Hill ES 300/PK-6
1 Arbor Dr 12207 518-475-6625
Rosalind Gaines-Harrell, prin. Fax 475-6627
Delaware Community S 400/PK-5
43 Bertha St 12209 518-475-6750
Kenneth Lein Ed.D., prin. Fax 475-6754
Eagle Point ES 300/PK-6
1044 Western Ave 12203 518-475-6825
Gabriele Barbato, prin. Fax 475-6827
Giffen Memorial ES 400/PK-6
274 S Pearl St 12202 518-475-6650
John Powell, prin. Fax 475-6652
Hackett MS 700/6-8
45 Delaware Ave 12202 518-475-6475
Michael Paolino, prin. Fax 475-6477
Montessori Magnet S 300/PK-5
45 Tremont St 12205 518-475-6675
John Powell, prin. Fax 475-6677
Myers MS 700/6-8
100 Elbel Ct 12209 518-475-6425
Jennifer Chatain, prin. Fax 475-6427
New Scotland ES 500/PK-5
369 New Scotland Ave 12208 518-475-6775
David Amodeo, prin. Fax 475-6777
North Albany Academy 400/PK-8
570 N Pearl St 12204 518-475-6800
Lesley Buff, prin. Fax 475-6802
O'Brien Academy of Science/Tech. 400/PK-6
Lincoln Park 12202 518-475-6875
Teresa Brown, prin. Fax 475-6877
O'Neal MS 6-8
50 N Lark St 12210 518-475-6600
Malik Jones, prin. Fax 475-6602
Pine Hills ES 400/PK-6
41 N Allen St 12203 518-475-6725
Vibetta Sanders, prin. Fax 475-6729
Schuyler Achievement Academy 300/PK-5
676 Clinton Ave 12206 518-475-6700
Kendra Chaires-Francis, prin. Fax 475-6704
Sheridan Preparatory Academy 400/PK-5
400 Sheridan Ave 12206 518-475-6850
Zuleika Sanchez-Gayle, prin. Fax 475-6852

Guilderland Central SD
Supt. — See Guilderland Center
Westmere ES 400/K-5
6270 Johnston Rd 12203 518-456-3771
Beth Bini, prin. Fax 464-6443

South Colonie Central SD 5,000/PK-12
102 Loralee Dr 12205 518-869-3576
Jonathan Buhner, supt. Fax 869-6517
www.southcolonieschools.org
Forest Park ES 300/K-4
100 Forest Dr 12205 518-869-3006
Jill Penn, prin. Fax 869-5891
Lisha Kill MS 700/5-8
68 Waterman Ave 12205 518-456-2306
David Wetzel, prin. Fax 452-8165
Roessleville ES 400/PK-4
100 California Ave 12205 518-459-2157
Marybeth Tedisco, prin. Fax 459-0268
Saddlewood ES 400/PK-4
100 Loralee Dr 12205 518-456-2608
Stacey Wranesh-Roberts, prin. Fax 862-0271
Sand Creek MS 800/5-8
329 Sand Creek Rd 12205 518-459-1333
Thomas Nicholson, prin. Fax 459-1404
Shaker Road ES 300/K-4
512 Albany Shaker Rd 12211 518-458-1440
William Dollard, prin. Fax 459-1283
Veeder ES 400/K-4
25 Veeder Dr 12205 518-869-4661
Nora Sullivan, prin. Fax 869-4495

Albany Academy 500/PK-12
135 Academy Rd 12208 518-429-2300
Dr. Douglas North Ph.D., head sch Fax 427-7016
Albany Academy for Girls 400/PK-12
140 Academy Rd 12208 518-429-2300
Dr. Douglas North Ph.D., head sch Fax 463-5096
All Saints Catholic Academy 200/PK-8
10 Rosemont St 12203 518-438-0066
Traci Johnson, prin. Fax 512-4049
Bet Shraga Hebrew Acad of Capital Dist 100/K-8
54 Sand Creek Rd 12205 518-482-0464
Julie Pollack, head sch Fax 482-0129
Blessed Sacrament S 200/PK-8
605 Central Ave 12206 518-438-5854
Sr. Patricia Lynch, prin. Fax 438-1532
Castle Island Bilingual Montessori PK-5
10 N Main Ave 12203 518-533-9838
Maimonides Hebrew Day S 100/PK-12
404 Partridge St 12208 518-453-9363
Mater Christi S 200/PK-8
35 Hurst Ave 12208 518-489-3111
Theresa Ewell, prin. Fax 489-5865
Our Savior's Lutheran S 200/PK-8
63 Mountain View Ave 12205 518-459-2273
John March, prin. Fax 689-1394
St. Matthew Lutheran S 50/PK-K
75 Whitehall Rd 12209 518-463-6495
Rebecca Martin, dir. Fax 463-9417

Albertson, Nassau, Pop. 5,037
Herricks UFD
Supt. — See New Hyde Park
Herricks MS 1,000/6-8
7 Hilldale Dr 11507 516-305-8600
Joan Keegan, prin. Fax 739-4738
Searingtown ES 500/K-5
106 Beverly Dr 11507 516-305-8500
Robert Neufeld, prin. Fax 248-3277

Mineola UFD
Supt. — See Mineola
Meadow Drive ES 400/PK-2
25 Meadow Dr 11507 516-237-2400
Sue Caryl Fleischmann, prin. Fax 237-2408

Albion, Orleans, Pop. 5,876
Albion Central SD 2,000/PK-12
324 East Ave 14411 585-589-2056
Michael Bonnewell, supt. Fax 589-2059
www.albionk12.org/
Bergerson MS, 254 East Ave 14411 500/6-8
Bradley Pritchard, prin. 585-589-2020
Sodoma ES, 324 East Ave 14411 900/PK-5
Rachel Curtin, prin. 585-589-2030

Alden, Erie, Pop. 2,590
Alden Central SD 1,700/K-12
13190 Park St 14004 716-937-9116
Adam Stoltman, supt. Fax 937-7132
www.aldenschools.org
Alden IS 400/3-5
1648 Crittenden Rd 14004 716-937-9116
Melanie Monacelli, admin. Fax 937-3376
Alden MS 400/6-8
13250 Park St 14004 716-937-9116
Steven Smith, prin. Fax 937-3563
Alden PS at Townline 300/K-2
11197 Broadway St 14004 716-937-9116
Thomas Lyons, prin. Fax 937-9839

St. John the Baptist S 200/PK-8
2028 Sandridge Rd 14004 585-937-9483
Jonna Johnson, prin. Fax 937-9794

Alexander, Genesee, Pop. 501
Alexander Central SD 900/PK-12
3314 Buffalo St 14005 585-591-1551
Catherine Huber, supt. Fax 591-2257
www.alexandercsd.org
Alexander ES 400/PK-5
3314 Buffalo St 14005 585-591-1551
Matthew Stroud, prin. Fax 591-4713

Alexandria Bay, Jefferson, Pop. 1,066
Alexandria Central SD 600/PK-12
34 Bolton Ave 13607 315-482-9971
Christopher Clapper, supt. Fax 482-9973
www.alexandriacentral.org
Alexandria Central ES 300/PK-6
34 Bolton Ave 13607 315-482-9971
Amy St. Croix, prin. Fax 482-9973

Allegany, Cattaraugus, Pop. 1,807
Allegany-Limestone Central SD 800/PK-12
3131 Five Mile Rd 14706 716-375-6600
Dr. Karen Geelan, supt. Fax 375-6629
alcsny.org
Allegany-Limestone ES 500/PK-5
120 Maple Ave 14706 716-375-6600
Kimberly Moore, prin. Fax 375-6628

Almond, Allegany, Pop. 460
Alfred-Almond Central SD 700/PK-12
6795 State Route 21 14804 607-276-6500
Richard Calkins, supt. Fax 276-6556
www.aacs.wnyric.org
Alfred-Almond ES 400/PK-6
6795 State Route 21 14804 607-276-6526
Robert Woughter, prin. Fax 276-6556

Altamont, Albany, Pop. 1,711
Guilderland Central SD
Supt. — See Guilderland Center
Altamont ES 300/K-5
PO Box 648 12009 518-861-8528
Peter Brabant, prin. Fax 861-5189

Amagansett, Suffolk, Pop. 1,160
Amagansett UFD 100/PK-6
PO Box 7062 11930 631-267-3572
Eleanor Tritt, supt. Fax 267-7504
www.aufsd.org
Amagansett ES 100/PK-6
PO Box 7062 11930 631-267-3572
Mari Dorr, prin. Fax 267-7504

Amenia, Dutchess, Pop. 935
Webutuck Central SD 800/PK-12
PO Box 405 12501 845-373-4100
Raymond Castellani, supt. Fax 373-4102
www.webutuckschools.org
Brooks IS 300/4-8
PO Box 405 12501 845-373-4114
Erik Lynch, prin. Fax 373-4126
Webutuck ES 300/PK-3
PO Box 400 12501 845-373-4122
Jennifer Hengen, prin. Fax 373-4125

Kildonan S 100/2-12
425 Morse Hill Rd 12501 845-373-8111
Kevin Pendergast, hdmstr. Fax 373-9793

Amherst, Erie, Pop. 45,800
Amherst Central SD 2,800/K-12
55 Kings Hwy 14226 716-362-3000
Anthony J. Panella, supt. Fax 362-3022
amherstschools.org
Amherst MS 700/6-8
55 Kings Hwy 14226 716-362-7100
John Griesmer, prin. Fax 836-0193
Smallwood Drive S 700/K-5
300 Smallwood Dr 14226 716-362-2100
Daniel Lewis, prin. Fax 839-3578
Windermere Boulevard S 700/K-5
291 Windermere Blvd 14226 716-362-4100
Julie Flanagan, prin. Fax 838-3764

Sweet Home Central SD 3,200/PK-12
1901 Sweet Home Rd 14228 716-250-1402
Anthony Day, supt. Fax 250-1374
www.sweethomeschools.org
Heritage Heights ES 300/PK-5
2545 Sweet Home Rd 14228 716-250-1525
Gregory Smorol, prin. Fax 250-1531
Maplemere ES 400/PK-5
236 E Maplemere Rd 14221 716-250-1550
Ann Laudisio, prin. Fax 250-1555
Sweet Home MS 800/6-8
4150 Maple Rd 14226 716-250-1450
Marty Pizur, prin. Fax 250-1490
Willow Ridge ES 300/PK-5
480 Willow Ridge Dr 14228 716-250-1575
Robert Polino, prin. Fax 250-1585
Other Schools – See Tonawanda

Kadimah Academy 100/K-8
1085 Eggert Rd 14226 716-836-6903
Einav Symons, hdmstr. Fax 837-7322
Ohr Temimim S 100/PK-8
411 John James Audubon Pkwy 14228
716-568-0226
Rabbi Shmuel Shanowitz, prin. Fax 636-1899
St. Benedict S 200/PK-8
3980 Main St 14226 716-835-2518
Laurie Wojtaszczyk, prin. Fax 834-4932

Amityville, Suffolk, Pop. 9,408
Amityville UFD, 150 Park Ave 11701 2,900/PK-12
Dr. Mary Kelly, supt. 631-565-6019
www.amityvilleufsd.org/
Northeast S, 420 Albany Ave 11701 400/PK-K
Pauline Collins, prin. 631-565-6400
Northwest ES 500/1-2
450 County Line Rd 11701 631-565-6500
Kathleen Hyland, prin.
Park Avenue ES, 140 Park Ave 11701 700/3-6
Robyn Shockley-Santiago, prin. 631-565-6300

Bethesda SDA Junior Academy 50/PK-10
76 Parkway Ave 11701 631-842-3321
Sherwin James, prin. Fax 842-1623
St. Martin of Tours S 400/PK-8
30 Union Ave 11701 631-264-7166
Maria Martinez, prin. Fax 264-0136

Amsterdam, Montgomery, Pop. 18,256
Broadalbin-Perth Central SD
Supt. — See Broadalbin
Broadalbin-Perth IS 400/3-5
1870 County Highway 107 12010 518-954-2750
Daniel Casey, prin. Fax 954-2759
Broadalbin-Perth MS 400/6-8
1870 County Highway 107 12010 518-954-2700
Wayne Bell, prin. Fax 954-2709

Greater Amsterdam SD 3,700/PK-12
PO Box 309 12010 518-843-3180
Dr. Vicky Ramos, supt. Fax 842-0012
www.gasd.org
Barkley ES 400/PK-5
66 Destefano Pl 12010 518-843-1850
Donna Decker, prin. Fax 843-6183
Curie ES 500/PK-5
9 Brice St 12010 518-843-2871
John Penman, prin. Fax 843-6290
Lynch Literacy Academy 800/6-8
55 Brandt Pl 12010 518-843-3716
Elizabeth Hanan, prin. Fax 843-6287
McNulty Academy 500/PK-5
60 Brandt Pl 12010 518-843-4773
Todd Giagni, prin. Fax 843-5475
Tecler ES 500/PK-5
210 Northern Blvd 12010 518-843-4805
John Miller, prin. Fax 843-6184

St. Mary's Institute 200/PK-8
10 Kopernick Blvd 12010 518-842-4100
Maureen Daurio, prin. Fax 842-0217

Andes, Delaware, Pop. 250
Andes Central SD 100/PK-12
PO Box 248 13731 845-676-3167
Dr. Robert Chakar M.Ed., supt. Fax 676-3181
www.andescentralschool.org
Andes Central S 100/PK-12
PO Box 248 13731 845-676-3166
Dr. Robert Chakar M.Ed., supt. Fax 676-3181

Andover, Allegany, Pop. 1,032
Andover Central SD 300/PK-12
PO Box G 14806 607-478-8491
Lawrence Spangenburg, supt. Fax 478-8833
www.andovercsd.org/
Andover S 300/PK-12
PO Box G 14806 607-478-8491
Jon Morris, prin. Fax 478-8833

Angola, Erie, Pop. 2,096
Lake Shore Central SD 2,500/K-12
959 Beach Rd 14006 716-549-2300
James E. Przepasniak, supt. Fax 549-6407
www.lakeshorecsd.org
Lake Shore MS 600/6-8
8855 Erie Rd 14006 716-926-2400
Erich Reidell, prin. Fax 549-4374
Schmidt ES 300/K-5
9455 Lake Shore Rd 14006 716-549-2303
Jill Clark, prin. Fax 549-4428

Waugh ES 400/K-5
100 High St 14006 716-549-2305
Paula Eastman, prin. Fax 549-2380
Other Schools – See Derby

Antwerp, Jefferson, Pop. 677
Indian River Central SD
Supt. — See Philadelphia
Antwerp PS 200/K-3
PO Box 10 13608 315-659-8386
Elizabeth Culbertson, prin. Fax 659-8944

Apalachin, Tioga, Pop. 1,119
Owego-Apalachin Central SD
Supt. — See Owego
Apalachin ES 500/PK-5
405 Pennsylvania Ave 13732 607-687-6289
Ryan Hallenbeck, prin. Fax 625-5811

Vestal Central SD
Supt. — See Vestal
Tioga Hills ES 300/K-5
48 Glann Rd 13732 607-757-2366
Hayley Crimmins, prin. Fax 757-2344

Aquebogue, Suffolk, Pop. 2,425
Riverhead Central SD
Supt. — See Riverhead
Aquebogue ES 500/K-4
PO Box 1200 11931 631-369-6780
Philip Kent, prin. Fax 369-0543

Arcade, Wyoming, Pop. 2,044
Yorkshire-Pioneer Central SD
Supt. — See Yorkshire
Arcade ES 600/PK-4
PO Box 9 14009 716-492-9424
Mellisa Devitt, prin. Fax 492-9433

Ardsley, Westchester, Pop. 4,379
Ardsley UFD 2,000/K-12
500 Farm Rd 10502 914-295-5500
Dr. Lauren Allan, supt. Fax 295-5976
www.ardsleyschools.org
Ardsley MS 600/5-8
700 Ashford Ave 10502 914-295-5600
Dr. Stu Horlacher, prin. Fax 295-5676
Concord Road ES 700/K-4
2 Concord Rd 10502 914-231-0800
Melissa Szymanski, prin. Fax 231-0877

Argyle, Washington, Pop. 303
Argyle Central SD 500/PK-12
5023 State Route 40 12809 518-638-8243
Michael Healey, supt. Fax 638-6373
www.argylecsd.org
Argyle Central ES 300/PK-6
5023 State Route 40 12809 518-638-8243
Dawn Wood, prin. Fax 638-6373

Arkport, Steuben, Pop. 839
Arkport Central SD 500/K-12
35 East Ave 14807 607-295-7471
Jesse Harper, supt. Fax 295-7473
www.arkportcsd.org
Arkport Central S 500/K-12
35 East Ave 14807 607-295-7471
Caitlin Dewey, prin. Fax 295-7473

Armonk, Westchester, Pop. 4,278
Byram Hills Central SD 2,600/K-12
10 Tripp Ln 10504 914-273-4082
Jen Lamia, supt. Fax 273-2516
www.byramhills.org
Coman Hill ES 500/K-2
558 Bedford Rd Ste 1 10504 914-273-4183
Marybeth Crupi, prin. Fax 273-3257
Crittenden MS 600/6-8
10 MacDonald Ave 10504 914-273-4250
Kim Lapple, prin. Fax 273-4618
Wampus ES 500/3-5
41 Wampus Ave Ste 1 10504 914-273-4190
Debra Cagliostro, prin. Fax 273-3608

Arverne, See New York
NYC Department of Education
Supt. — See New York
Maple Academy 500/PK-8
365 Beach 56th St 11692 718-945-3300
Angela Logan-Smith, prin. Fax 945-3303
Public S 42 700/PK-8
488 Beach 66th St 11692 718-634-7914
Patricia Finn, prin. Fax 474-7591

Astoria, See New York
NYC Department of Education
Supt. — See New York
Academy for New Americans 100/6-8
3014 30th St 11102 718-956-4140
Betty Cartagena, prin. Fax 932-5990
IS 10 900/6-8
4511 31st Ave 11103 718-278-7054
Clemente Lopes, prin. Fax 274-1578
Public S 234 600/PK-5
3015 29th St 11102 718-956-2760
Dora Danner, prin. Fax 932-5398

Astoria Lutheran S 100/PK-8
3120 21st Ave 11105 718-721-4313
Mary-Elaine Leake, prin. Fax 721-7662
Immaculate Conception Academy 200/K-8
2163 29th St 11105 718-728-1969
Eileen Harnischfeger, prin. Fax 728-3374
St. Francis of Assisi Academy 300/PK-8
2118 46th St 11105 718-726-9405
Anne Stefano, prin. Fax 721-2577

Athens, Greene, Pop. 1,651
Coxsackie-Athens Central SD
Supt. — See Coxsackie

Arthur ES 200/K-4
51 3rd St 12015 518-731-1750
James Martino, prin. Fax 731-1765

Attica, Wyoming, Pop. 2,513
Attica Central SD 1,300/K-12
3338 E Main Street Rd 14011 585-591-0400
Bryce Thompson, supt. Fax 591-2681
www.atticacsd.org
Attica ES 400/K-4
31 Prospect St 14011 585-591-0400
Kelly Bietz, prin. Fax 591-4497
Attica MS 400/5-8
3338 E Main Street Rd 14011 585-591-0400
Paul Clark, prin. Fax 591-4496

Auburn, Cayuga, Pop. 26,874
Auburn CSD 4,200/K-12
78 Thornton Ave 13021 315-255-8800
Jeffrey Pirozzolo, supt. Fax 255-8855
district.auburn.cnyric.org
Auburn JHS 600/7-8
191 Franklin St 13021 315-255-8480
David Oliver, prin. Fax 255-8495
Casey Park ES 500/K-6
101 Pulaski St 13021 315-255-8760
Kelly Garback, prin. Fax 255-8790
Genesee ES 400/K-6
244 Genesee St 13021 315-255-8640
Amanda Simmons, prin. Fax 255-8675
Herman Avenue ES 500/K-6
2 N Herman Ave 13021 315-255-8680
Cynthia Lattimore, prin. Fax 255-8693
Owasco ES 400/K-6
66 Letchworth St 13021 315-255-8720
Abigail Adams Snell, prin. Fax 255-8750
Seward ES 500/K-6
52 Metcalf Dr 13021 315-255-8600
Amy Mahunik, prin. Fax 255-8611

St. Joseph S 200/PK-8
89 E Genesee St 13021 315-253-8327
Michael Carney, prin. Fax 253-2401

Aurora, Cayuga, Pop. 708
Southern Cayuga Central SD 700/PK-12
2384 State Route 34B 13026 315-364-7211
Patrick Jensen, supt. Fax 364-7863
www.southerncayuga.org
Howland ES 400/PK-6
2384 State Route 34B 13026 315-364-7098
Christopher Clapper, prin. Fax 364-7590

Au Sable Forks, Clinton, Pop. 554
Au Sable Valley Central SD
Supt. — See Clintonville
Au Sable Forks ES 200/K-6
PO Box 727 12912 518-647-5503
Ginene Mason, prin. Fax 647-8471

Averill Park, Rensselaer, Pop. 1,668
Averill Park Central SD 3,000/K-12
146 Gettle Rd Ste 1 12018 518-674-7050
Dr. James R. Franchini, supt. Fax 674-3802
www.averillpark.k12.ny.us
Algonquin MS 700/6-8
333 NY Highway 351 12018 518-674-7100
Robert Messia, prin. Fax 674-0671
Miller Hill/Sand Lake ES 400/K-5
8439 Miller Hill Rd 12018 518-674-7075
Denis Sibson, prin. Fax 674-7096
Other Schools – See Poestenkill, West Sand Lake

Avoca, Steuben, Pop. 933
Avoca Central SD 400/K-12
PO Box G 14809 607-566-2221
Stephen Saxton, supt. Fax 566-2398
www.avocacsd.org/
Avoca Central S 400/K-12
PO Box G 14809 607-566-2221
Matthew Pfleegor, prin. Fax 566-8384

Avon, Livingston, Pop. 3,354
Avon Central SD 1,000/K-12
191 Clinton St 14414 585-226-2455
Dr. Aaron Johnson, supt. Fax 226-8202
www.avoncsd.org
Avon Central ES 400/K-4
161 Clinton St 14414 585-226-2455
Robert Lupisella, prin. Fax 226-8202
Avon MS 300/5-8
191 Clinton St 14414 585-226-2455
Jennifer Miller, prin. Fax 226-8202

St. Agnes S 100/PK-6
60 Park Pl 14414 585-226-8500
Elizabeth Jensen, prin. Fax 226-8500

Babylon, Suffolk, Pop. 11,970
Babylon UFD 1,600/K-12
50 Railroad Ave 11702 631-893-7925
Linda J. Rozzi, supt. Fax 893-7935
www.babylonschools.org
Babylon ES 300/K-2
171 Ralph Ave 11702 631-893-7960
Travis Davey, prin. Fax 893-7967
Babylon Memorial Grade S 500/3-6
169 Park Ave 11702 631-893-7980
Steven Goldberg, prin. Fax 893-7990

South Bay Jr Academy of SDA 50/K-8
150 Fire Island Ave 11702 631-321-0857
Maria Thomas, prin. Fax 321-0821

Bainbridge, Chenango, Pop. 1,346
Bainbridge-Guilford Central SD 800/PK-12
18 Julland St 13733 607-967-6321
Timothy R. Ryan, supt. Fax 967-4231
www.bgcsd.org

Greenlawn ES 300/2-6
43 Greenlawn Ave 13733 607-967-6301
Jennifer Henderson, prin. Fax 967-3080
Other Schools – See Guilford

Baldwin, Nassau, Pop. 23,329
Baldwin UFD 4,700/K-12
960 Hastings St 11510 516-434-6010
Dr. Shari Camhi, supt. Fax 434-6308
www.baldwinschools.org/
Baldwin MS 1,100/6-8
3211 Schreiber Pl 11510 516-434-6200
Timothy Maher, prin. Fax 377-9432
Brookside ES 300/K-5
940 Stanton Ave 11510 516-434-6300
Jennifer Bumford, prin. Fax 377-9425
Lenox ES 300/K-5
551 Lenox Rd 11510 516-434-6400
Bernice Acevedo, prin. Fax 377-9426
Meadow ES 600/K-5
880 Jackson St 11510 516-434-6500
Echele May, prin. Fax 377-9427
Plaza ES 500/K-5
501 Seaman Ave 11510 516-434-6600
Mark Gray, prin. Fax 377-9429
Steele ES 300/K-5
860 Church St 11510 516-434-6700
Lori Presti, prin. Fax 377-9431

Uniondale UFD
Supt. — See Uniondale
Union Pre K S PK-PK
835 De Mott Ave 11510 516-405-8303
Elaine DeBono, prin.

St. Christopher S 300/K-8
15 Pershing Blvd 11510 516-223-4404
Anne Lederer, prin. Fax 223-1409

Baldwinsville, Onondaga, Pop. 7,290
Baldwinsville Central SD 5,500/K-12
29 E Oneida St 13027 315-638-6043
Matthew J. McDonald, supt. Fax 638-6041
www.bville.org
Elden ES 500/K-5
29 E Oneida St 13027 315-638-6118
Thomas Coughlin, prin. Fax 638-6171
McNamara ES 500/K-5
29 E Oneida St 13027 315-638-6130
Jane Nadolski, prin. Fax 638-5049
Palmer ES 400/K-5
29 E Oneida St 13027 315-638-6127
Alexander Ewing, prin. Fax 638-6275
Ray MS 900/6-7
29 E Oneida St 13027 315-638-6106
Fax 638-6157
Reynolds ES 400/K-5
29 E Oneida St 13027 315-638-6124
Melissa Chiodo, prin. Fax 638-6169
Van Buren ES 400/K-5
29 E Oneida St 13027 315-638-6121
Danielle Nahorney, prin. Fax 638-6170

Baldwinsville Christian Academy 100/PK-12
7312 Van Buren Rd 13027 315-638-1069
Dave Grey, admin. Fax 293-2012
St. Mary's Academy 100/PK-6
49 Syracuse St 13027 315-635-3977
Renae Henderson, prin. Fax 635-8137
Word of Life Christian Academy 100/PK-6
PO Box 86 13027 315-849-1187
Carmen Durst, admin.

Ballston Lake, Saratoga
Burnt Hills-Ballston Lake Central SD
Supt. — See Burnt Hills
Charlton Heights ES 500/K-5
170 Stage Rd 12019 518-399-9141
Tim Sinnenberg, prin. Fax 399-0227
Stevens ES 400/K-5
25 Lakehill Rd 12019 518-399-9141
Dr. Richard Evans, prin. Fax 399-0343

Shenendehowa Central SD
Supt. — See Clifton Park
Chango ES 500/K-5
100 Chango Dr 12019 518-881-0520
Karin Skarka, prin. Fax 899-5971

Ballston Spa, Saratoga, Pop. 5,283
Ballston Spa Central SD 4,100/K-12
70 Malta Ave 12020 518-884-7195
Joseph Dragone Ph.D., supt. Fax 884-7101
www.bscsd.org
Ballston Spa MS 1,000/6-8
210 Ballston Ave 12020 518-884-7200
Pamela Motler, prin. Fax 884-7234
Gordon Creek ES 500/K-5
50 Wood Rd 12020 518-884-7270
Celeste Keane, prin. Fax 884-7268
Malta Avenue ES 400/K-5
70 Malta Ave 12020 518-884-7250
Sharon D'Agostino, prin. Fax 884-7258
Milton Terrace ES 400/K-5
200 Wood Rd 12020 518-884-7210
Dr. Kathleen Chaucer, prin. Fax 884-7219
Wood Road ES 600/K-5
300 Wood Rd 12020 518-884-7290
Valarie Karas, prin. Fax 884-7286

Malta Montessori S 100/PK-6
100 Saratoga Vill Blvd #34A 12020 518-633-1971
Kerry Brader, head sch Fax 402-6824
St. Mary's S 200/PK-5
40 Thompson St 12020 518-885-7300
Lynn Fitzgerald, prin. Fax 885-7378

Spa Christian S 100/PK-8
206 Greenfield Ave 12020 518-885-0508
Mandy Kergel, admin. Fax 885-0508

Bardonia, Rockland, Pop. 4,047
Clarkstown Central SD
Supt. — See New City
Bardonia ES, 31 Bardonia Rd 10954 400/K-5
Christine Arlt, prin. 845-639-6460

Barker, Niagara, Pop. 527
Barker Central SD 900/PK-12
1628 Quaker Rd 14012 716-795-3832
Dr. Roger Klatt, supt. Fax 795-3394
barkercsd.net
Pratt ES 400/PK-6
1628 Quaker Rd 14012 716-795-3237
John Hoar, prin. Fax 795-9330

Batavia, Genesee, Pop. 15,019
Batavia CSD 2,300/PK-12
260 State St 14020 585-343-2480
Christopher J. Dailey, supt. Fax 344-8204
www.bataviacsd.org
Batavia MS 700/5-8
96 Ross St 14020 585-343-2480
Ashley John Grillo, prin. Fax 344-8626
Jackson PS 400/PK-1
411 S Jackson St 14020 585-343-2480
Kia Evans, prin. Fax 344-8621
Kennedy IS 500/2-4
166 Vine St 14020 585-343-2480
Paul Kesler, prin. Fax 344-8617

St. Joseph S 200/PK-8
2 Summit St 14020 585-343-6154
Karen Green, prin. Fax 343-8911
St. Paul Lutheran S 100/PK-5
31 Washington Ave 14020 585-343-0488
Ann Werk M.Ed., prin. Fax 344-0470

Bath, Steuben, Pop. 5,678
Bath Central SD 1,600/PK-12
25 Ellas Ave 14810 607-776-3301
Joseph L. Rumsey, supt. Fax 776-5021
www.bathcsd.org
Lyon MS 500/4-8
25 Ellas Ave 14810 607-776-2170
Jennifer D'Abbracci, prin. Fax 776-1470
Wightman PS 500/PK-3
216 Maple Hts 14810 607-776-4123
Deborah Barlow, prin. Fax 776-4124

Bayport, Suffolk, Pop. 8,813
Bayport-Blue Point UFD 2,400/K-12
189 Academy St 11705 631-472-7860
Timothy Hearney Ed.D., supt. Fax 472-7873
www.bbpschools.org
Academy Street ES 400/K-5
150 Academy St 11705 631-472-7850
Kerry Vann, prin. Fax 472-7858
Sylvan Avenue ES 400/K-5
600 Sylvan Ave 11705 631-472-7840
Alane Dugan, prin. Fax 472-7857
Young MS 600/6-8
602 Sylvan Ave 11705 631-472-7820
Robert Haas, prin. Fax 472-7849
Other Schools – See Blue Point

Bay Shore, Suffolk, Pop. 25,685
Bay Shore UFD 5,800/K-12
75 Perkal St 11706 631-968-1100
Joseph Bond, supt. Fax 968-4131
www.bayshoreschools.org
Bay Shore MS 1,400/6-8
393 Brook Ave 11706 631-968-1210
Dr. LaQuita Outlaw, prin. Fax 968-2342
Brook Avenue ES 400/K-2
45 Brook Ave 11706 631-968-1130
Regina Vorwald, prin. Fax 968-2439
Clarkson ES 500/K-2
1415 E 3rd Ave 11706 631-968-1205
Leticia Garcia, prin. Fax 968-2461
Fifth Avenue ES 400/K-2
217 5th Ave 11706 631-968-1140
Charlotte Wilson, prin. Fax 968-2463
Gardiner Manor ES 700/3-5
125 Wohseepee Dr 11706 631-968-1150
Carlton Brown, prin. Fax 968-2487
South Country ES 600/3-5
885 Hampshire Rd 11706 631-968-1250
Johnna Grasso, prin. Fax 968-2499

Brentwood UFD
Supt. — See Brentwood
Hemlock Park ES 700/PK-PK, 1-
19 Hemlock Dr 11706 631-434-2451
Dr. Christopher Dalley, prin. Fax 434-2191
Oak Park ES 800/1-5
775 Wisconsin Ave 11706 631-434-2255
Lisa Catandella, prin. Fax 434-2183
Southwest ES 1,200/PK-5
1095 Joselson Ave 11706 631-434-2261
Michelle Rogers, prin. Fax 434-2196
West MS 800/6-8
2030 Udall Rd 11706 631-434-2371
Felicia Thomas-Williams, prin. Fax 242-3992

Fire Island UFD 50/PK-6
99 Maple Ave 11706 631-583-5626
Loretta Ferraro, supt. Fax 583-5167
www.fi.k12.ny.us
Woodhull ES 50/PK-6
99 Maple Ave 11706 631-583-5626
Loretta Ferraro, prin. Fax 583-5167

Bay Shore Christian S 200/PK-6
211 Bay Shore Rd 11706 631-665-5241
Ann-Marie DeAngelis, admin. Fax 665-1066

St. Patrick S 400/PK-8
Montauk Hwy 11706 631-665-0569
Roseann Petruccio, prin. Fax 968-6007

Bayside, See New York
NYC Department of Education
Supt. — See New York
MS 158 1,100/6-8
4635 Oceania St 11361 718-423-8100
Henry Schandel, prin. Fax 423-8135
Bell Academy 400/6-8
1825 212th St 11360 718-428-0587
David Abbott, prin. Fax 428-0237
Public S 31 500/PK-5
21145 46th Rd 11361 718-423-8288
Terri Graybow, prin. Fax 423-8303
Public S 41 600/K-5
21443 35th Ave 11361 718-423-8333
Joseph Ferrara, prin. Fax 423-8362
Public S 130 300/PK-3
20001 42nd Ave 11361 718-357-6606
Michelle Contratti, prin. Fax 428-5927
Public S 159 600/PK-5
20501 33rd Ave 11361 718-423-8553
Paul Di Dio, prin. Fax 423-8583
Public S 169 400/PK-5
1825 212th St 11360 718-428-6160
Vanessa Rosa, prin. Fax 224-1013

Lutheran S of Flushing & Bayside 100/PK-8
3601 Bell Blvd 11361 718-225-5502
Marian Pia Haselbach, prin. Fax 225-7446
Our Lady of the Blessed Sacrament Acad 400/PK-8
3445 202nd St 11361 718-229-4434
Joan Kane, prin. Fax 229-5820
Sacred Heart Academy of Bayside 500/PK-8
21601 38th Ave 11361 718-631-4804
Mary-Anne Cooke, prin. Fax 631-5738

Bayside Hills, Queens
NYC Department of Education
Supt. — See New York
PS 376 PK-K
21021 48th Ave, 929-267-5900
Clara Kang, prin. Fax 267-5910

Divine Wisdom Catholic Academy 200/PK-8
5610 214th St, 718-225-8795
Margaret McGlynn Ed.D., prin. Fax 631-3945

Bayville, Nassau, Pop. 6,592
Locust Valley Central SD
Supt. — See Locust Valley
Bayville ES 400/K-5
50 Mountain Ave 11709 516-277-5400
Scott McElhiney, prin. Fax 277-5408

Beacon, Dutchess, Pop. 15,060
Beacon CSD 3,200/PK-12
10 Education Dr 12508 845-838-6900
Dr. Matthew Landahl, supt. Fax 838-6905
www.beaconcityk12.org
Forrestal ES 300/PK-5
125 Liberty St 12508 845-838-6900
Asheena Baez, prin. Fax 838-0792
Rombout MS 700/6-8
84 Matteawan Rd 12508 845-838-6900
Brian Soltish, prin. Fax 231-0474
Sargent ES 400/PK-5
29 Education Dr 12508 845-838-6900
Brian Archer, prin. Fax 838-6978
South Avenue ES 400/PK-5
60 South Ave 12508 845-838-6900
Laura Cahill, prin. Fax 838-6922
Other Schools – See Fishkill

Beaver Falls, Lewis
Beaver River Central SD 900/K-12
9508 Artz Rd 13305 315-346-1211
Todd Green, supt. Fax 346-6775
www.brcsd.org
Beaver River ES 400/K-5
9508 Artz Rd 13305 315-346-1211
Kimberly Lyman-Wright, prin. Fax 346-6775
Beaver River MS 200/6-8
9508 Artz Rd 13305 315-346-1211
Christine LaBare, prin. Fax 346-6775

Bedford, Westchester, Pop. 1,810
Bedford Central SD 4,300/K-12
632 S Bedford Rd 10506 914-241-6000
Dr. Christopher Manno, supt. Fax 241-6004
www.bcsdny.org
Bedford Village ES 300/K-5
45 Court Rd 10506 914-234-4178
Gina Smith, prin. Fax 234-6071
Other Schools – See Bedford Hills, Mount Kisco, Pound Ridge

St. Patrick S 200/PK-8
483 Old Post Rd 10506 914-234-7914
Sharyn O'Leary, prin. Fax 234-0773

Bedford Hills, Westchester, Pop. 2,942
Bedford Central SD
Supt. — See Bedford
Bedford Hills ES 300/K-5
123 Babbitt Rd 10507 914-666-2708
C. Zbynek Gold, prin. Fax 864-3492
West Patent ES 300/K-5
80 W Patent Rd 10507 914-666-2190
Vera Berezowsky, prin. Fax 666-3819

Belfast, Allegany, Pop. 823
Belfast Central SD 400/PK-12
1 King St 14711 585-365-9940
Dr. Wendy Butler, supt. Fax 365-2648
www.belfast.wnyric.org

Belfast Central S 400/PK-12
1 King St 14711 585-365-8285
Michael Roche, prin. Fax 365-2648

Belle Harbor, Queens

St. Francis De Sales Catholic Academy 500/PK-8
219 Beach 129th St, 718-634-2775
Christopher Scharbach, prin. Fax 634-6673

Bellerose, Queens, Pop. 1,168
NYC Department of Education
Supt. — See New York
Public S 133 400/PK-5
24805 86th Ave 11426 718-831-4016
Nicole Colon, prin. Fax 831-4020
Public S 186 400/PK-5
25212 72nd Ave 11426 718-831-4021
Melissa Haidary, prin. Fax 831-4029
Public S 208 700/K-8
7430 Commonwealth Blvd 11426 718-468-6420
James Philemy, prin. Fax 468-5054
Public S 266 700/PK-8
7410 Commonwealth Blvd 11426 718-479-3920
Ayanna Greenidge, prin. Fax 479-2482

St. Gregory the Great S 300/K-8
24444 87th Ave 11426 718-343-5053
Lynn Alaimo, prin. Fax 347-1142
Yeshiva Har Torah 500/PK-8
25010 Grand Central Pkwy 11426 718-343-2533

Belleville, Jefferson, Pop. 225
Belleville Henderson Central SD 500/PK-12
8372 County Route 75 13611 315-846-5826
Jane Collins, supt. Fax 846-5617
www.bhpanthers.org
Belleville Henderson Central S 500/PK-12
PO Box 158 13611 315-846-5121
Scott Storey, prin. Fax 846-5617

Bellmore, Nassau, Pop. 16,044
Bellmore UFD 1,000/PK-6
580 Winthrop Ave 11710 516-679-2900
Dr. Joseph Famularo Ed.D., supt.
www.bellmoreschools.org
Reinhard ECC 400/PK-2
2750 S Saint Marks Ave 11710 516-679-2930
Patricia Castine, prin. Fax 679-2936
Shore Road S 300/5-6
2801 Shore Rd 11710 516-679-2950
Patrice Matthews, prin. Fax 679-5637
Winthrop Avenue S 300/3-4
580 Winthrop Ave 11710 516-679-2919
Sally Curto, prin. Fax 679-5643

Bellmore-Merrick Central HSD
Supt. — See North Merrick
Grand Avenue MS 1,000/7-8
2301 Grand Ave 11710 516-992-1100
Carlo Conte, prin. Fax 679-5068

St. Elizabeth Ann Seton Regional S 300/PK-8
2341 Washington Ave 11710 516-785-5709
Leeann Graziose, prin. Fax 785-4468

Bellport, Suffolk, Pop. 2,050
South Country Central SD
Supt. — See East Patchogue
Bellport MS 1,000/6-8
35 Kreamer St 11713 631-730-1657
Dr. M. Jamal Colson, prin. Fax 286-4460
Kreamer Street ES 400/K-3
37 Kreamer St 11713 631-730-1651
Sean Clark, prin. Fax 776-0903
Long IS 700/4-5
599 Brookhaven Ave 11713 631-730-1726
Stefanie Rucinski, prin. Fax 286-4412

Belmont, Allegany, Pop. 950
Genesee Valley Central SD 500/PK-12
1 Jaguar Dr 14813 585-268-7900
Dr. Brian Schmitt, supt. Fax 268-7990
www.genvalley.org
Genesee Valley ES 300/PK-6
1 Jaguar Dr 14813 585-268-7900
Brian Edmister, prin. Fax 268-7990

Bemus Point, Chautauqua, Pop. 360
Bemus Point Central SD 700/PK-12
PO Box 468 14712 716-386-2375
Michael Mansfield, supt. Fax 386-2376
www.bemusptcsd.org
Bemus Point ES 300/PK-5
PO Box 468 14712 716-386-3795
Fax 386-4293

Bergen, Genesee, Pop. 1,158
Byron-Bergen Central SD 1,000/PK-12
6917 W Bergen Rd 14416 585-494-1220
Mickey Edwards, supt. Fax 494-2613
www.bbschools.org/
Byron-Bergen ES 500/PK-6
6917 W Bergen Rd 14416 585-494-1220
Brian Meister, prin. Fax 494-2433

Berlin, Rensselaer
Berlin Central SD
Supt. — See Cherryplain
Berlin ES 300/PK-5
53 School St 12022 518-658-2127
Tracy Kent, prin. Fax 658-0482

Berne, Albany
Berne-Knox-Westerlo Central SD 900/K-12
1738 Helderberg Trl 12023 518-872-1293
Dr. Timothy Mundell, supt. Fax 872-2031
www.bkwschools.org

Berne-Knox-Westerlo ES 400/K-6
1738 Helderberg Trl 12023 518-872-2030
Annette Landry, prin. Fax 872-2031

Bethpage, Nassau, Pop. 16,246
Bethpage UFD 2,900/K-12
10 Cherry Ave 11714 516-644-4000
Terrence Clark, supt. Fax 931-8783
www.bethpagecommunity.com
Campagne ES 400/K-5
601 Plainview Rd 11714 516-644-4400
Erin Lindsay-Difiglia, prin. Fax 827-5486
Central Boulevard ES 500/K-5
60 Central Blvd 11714 516-644-4300
Steven Furrey, prin. Fax 827-3178
Kennedy MS 700/6-8
500 Broadway 11714 516-644-4200
Kevin Fullerton, prin. Fax 937-0540
Other Schools – See Plainview

Plainedge UFD
Supt. — See North Massapequa
Plainedge MS 800/6-8
200 Stewart Ave 11714 516-992-7650
Anthony DeRiso, prin. Fax 992-7645
West ES 500/K-5
499 Boundary Ave 11714 516-992-7500
Carol Muscarella, prin. Fax 992-7505

Big Flats, Chemung, Pop. 5,220
Horseheads Central SD
Supt. — See Horseheads
Big Flats ES 400/PK-4
543 Maple St 14814 607-739-6373
Elizabeth Scaptura, prin. Fax 795-2555

Binghamton, Broome, Pop. 45,574
Binghamton CSD 5,600/PK-12
PO Box 2126 13902 607-762-8100
Dr. Tonia Thompson, supt. Fax 762-8112
www.binghamtonschools.org
Coolidge ES 300/K-5
261 Robinson St 13904 607-762-8290
Mary Kay Ryan, prin. Fax 762-8396
East MS 600/6-8
167 E Frederick St 13904 607-762-8300
Tim Simonds, prin. Fax 762-8398
Franklin ES 500/PK-5
262 Conklin Ave 13903 607-762-8340
Suzanne Thomas, prin. Fax 762-8393
Jefferson ES 300/K-5
151 Helen St 13905 607-763-8430
Kristine Battaglino, prin. Fax 763-8436
MacArthur ES, 1123 Vestal Ave 13903 500/PK-5
Maria McIver, prin. 607-762-8119
Mann ES 300/K-5
30 College St 13905 607-762-8270
Peter Stewart, prin. Fax 762-8394
Roosevelt ES 400/PK-5
9 Ogden St 13901 607-762-8280
David Chilson, prin. Fax 762-8395
West MS 600/6-8
W Middle Ave 13905 607-763-8400
Fax 763-8429
Wilson ES 400/K-5
287 Prospect St 13905 607-763-8440
Daniel Miller, prin. Fax 763-8448

Chenango Forks Central SD 1,600/PK-12
1 Gordon Dr 13901 607-648-7543
Dr. Lloyd Peck, supt. Fax 648-7560
www.cforks.org
Chenango Forks ES 700/PK-5
6 Patch Rd 13901 607-648-7580
Catherine Kacyvenski, prin. Fax 648-7595
Chenango Forks MS 400/6-8
1 Gordon Dr 13901 607-648-7576
Andrew Rullo, prin. Fax 648-2767

Chenango Valley Central SD 1,800/PK-12
221 Chenango Bridge Rd 13901 607-762-6800
David Gill, supt. Fax 762-6890
www.cvcsd.stier.org/
Chenango Bridge ES 400/3-5
221 Chenango Bridge Rd 13901 607-762-6950
Timothy Ryan, prin. Fax 648-8959
Chenango Valley MS 300/6-8
221 Chenango Bridge Rd 13901 607-762-6902
Eric Attleson, prin. Fax 779-4784
Port Dickinson ES 600/PK-2
221 Chenango Bridge Rd 13901 607-762-6970
James Pritchard, prin. Fax 779-7830

Susquehanna Valley Central SD
Supt. — See Conklin
Brookside ES 400/K-5
3849 Saddlemire Rd 13903 607-669-4105
Erin Eckert, prin. Fax 669-4811

St. John the Evangelist S 200/PK-6
9 Livingston St 13903 607-723-0703
James Fountaine, prin. Fax 772-6210

Black River, Jefferson, Pop. 1,304
Carthage Central SD
Supt. — See Carthage
Black River ES 500/PK-4
160 Leray St 13612 315-773-5911
Jennifer Premo, prin. Fax 773-3747

Blasdell, Erie, Pop. 2,518
Frontier Central SD
Supt. — See Hamburg
Blasdell ES 400/K-5
3780 S Park Ave 14219 716-926-1750
Linda Dansa, prin. Fax 823-6153

Blauvelt, Rockland, Pop. 5,591
South Orangetown Central SD 3,300/K-12
160 Van Wyck Rd 10913 845-680-1050
Dr. Robert Pritchard, supt. Fax 680-1900
www.socsd.org
Cottage Lane ES 500/3-5
120 Cottage Ln 10913 845-680-1500
Karen Ramirez, prin. Fax 680-1940
South Orangetown MS 800/6-8
160 Van Wyck Rd 10913 845-680-1100
Karen Tesik, prin. Fax 680-1905
Other Schools – See Tappan

Bloomfield, Ontario, Pop. 1,335
Bloomfield Central SD 1,000/PK-12
45 Maple Ave Ste A 14469 585-657-6121
Andrew Doell, supt. Fax 657-6060
www.bloomfieldcsd.org
Bloomfield ES 400/PK-5
45 Maple Ave Ste B 14469 585-657-6121
Scott Donnelly, prin. Fax 657-6926
Bloomfield MS 200/6-8
1 Oakmount Ave 14469 585-657-6121
Daniel McAlpin, prin. Fax 657-4771

Bloomingdale, Essex
Saranac Lake Central SD
Supt. — See Saranac Lake
Bloomingdale ES 200/K-5
93 Main St 12913 518-891-3198
Patricia Kenyon, prin. Fax 891-4675

Blossvale, Oneida, Pop. 300
Camden Central SD
Supt. — See Camden
Mc Connellsville ES 200/PK-4
8564 State Route 13 13308 315-245-3412
Craig Ferretti, prin. Fax 245-4193

Blue Point, Suffolk, Pop. 4,721
Bayport-Blue Point UFD
Supt. — See Bayport
Blue Point ES 200/K-5
212 Blue Point Ave 11715 631-472-6100
Tara Falasco, prin. Fax 472-6110

Bohemia, Suffolk, Pop. 10,114
Connetquot Central SD 6,200/K-12
780 Ocean Ave 11716 631-244-2215
Lynda Adams, supt. Fax 589-0683
www.ccsdli.org
Bosti ES 300/K-5
50 Bourne Blvd 11716 631-244-2291
Laura Kimball, prin. Fax 244-2290
Pearl ES 200/K-5
1070 Smithtown Ave 11716 631-244-2300
Susan White, prin. Fax 244-2282
Sycamore Avenue ES 400/K-5
745 Sycamore Ave 11716 631-244-2261
Stuart Pollak, prin. Fax 244-2260
Other Schools – See Oakdale, Ronkonkoma

Boiceville, Ulster
Onteora Central SD 1,400/K-12
PO Box 300 12412 845-657-6383
Victoria McLaren, supt. Fax 657-8742
onteora.schoolwires.com
Bennett ES 300/K-6
PO Box 300 12412 845-657-2354
Gabriel Buono, prin. Fax 657-8504
Onteora MS 200/7-8
PO Box 300 12412 845-657-2373
Jennifer O'Connor, prin. Fax 657-7763
Other Schools – See Phoenicia, Woodstock

Bolivar, Allegany, Pop. 1,040
Bolivar-Richburg Central SD 800/PK-12
100 School St 14715 585-928-2561
Michael A. Hetzlatt, supt. Fax 928-2411
www.brcs.wnyric.org
Bolivar-Richburg ES 400/PK-5
422 Main St 14715 585-928-1919
Brett Dusinberre, prin. Fax 928-2159

Bolton Landing, Warren, Pop. 501
Bolton Central SD 200/PK-12
PO Box 120 12814 518-644-2400
Michael Graney, supt. Fax 644-2124
www.boltoncsd.org
Bolton Central S 200/PK-12
PO Box 120 12814 518-644-2400
Chad Shippee, prin. Fax 644-2124

Boonville, Oneida, Pop. 2,065
Adirondack Central SD 1,300/PK-12
110 Ford St 13309 315-942-9200
Edward Niznik, supt. Fax 942-5522
www.adirondackcsd.org
Adirondack MS 300/6-8
8181 State Route 294 13309 315-942-9202
Cynthia Lauzon, prin. Fax 942-9211
Boonville ES 300/PK-5
110 Ford St 13309 315-942-9220
Wendy Keehfus-Jones, prin. Fax 942-6162
Other Schools – See Forestport, West Leyden

Bradford, Schuyler
Bradford Central SD 300/PK-12
2820 State Route 226 14815 607-583-4616
John Marshall, supt. Fax 583-4013
www.bradfordcsd.org
Bradford Central S 300/PK-12
2820 State Route 226 14815 607-583-4616
Steve Kiley, prin. Fax 583-4013

Brasher Falls, Saint Lawrence, Pop. 656
Brasher Falls Central SD 1,000/PK-12
PO Box 307 13613 315-389-5131
Robert Stewart, supt. Fax 389-5245
bfcsd.org

St. Lawrence Central ES 400/PK-4
PO Box 307 13613 315-389-5131
Johnathan Hirschey, prin. Fax 389-4651
St. Lawrence Central MS 300/5-8
PO Box 307 13613 315-389-5131
Christoper Rose, prin. Fax 389-4185

Brentwood, Suffolk, Pop. 59,660
Brentwood UFD 17,500/PK-12
52 3rd Ave 11717 631-434-2123
Richard Loeschner, supt. Fax 273-6575
www.bufsd.org
Cannon Southeast ES 700/1-5
1 Melody Ln 11717 631-434-2265
Lisa Calderaro, prin. Fax 434-2175
East K 700/PK-K
50 Timberline Dr 11717 631-434-2525
Minerva Feliciano, prin. Fax 434-2186
East MS 1,000/6-8
75 Hilltop Dr 11717 631-434-2473
Barry Mohammed, prin. Fax 434-2171
Laurel Park ES 600/1-5
48 Swan Ln 11717 631-434-2464
Eric Snell, prin. Fax 434-2190
Loretta Park ES 700/1-5
77 Stahley St 11717 631-434-2246
Robert McCarthy, prin. Fax 434-2189
Northeast ES 1,000/1-5
2 Devon Rd 11717 631-434-2435
Marilyn Friend-Ituarte, prin. Fax 434-2188
North ES 800/1-5
50 W White St 11717 631-434-2275
Patrick Morris, prin. Fax 434-2181
North MS 1,000/6-8
350 Wicks Rd 11717 631-434-2356
Matthew Gengler, prin. Fax 952-9249
Pine Park K 600/K-K
1 Mur Pl 11717 631-434-2251
Ann Weishahn, prin. Fax 434-2168
South MS 900/6-8
785 Candlewood Rd 11717 631-434-2341
Bergre Escobores Ed.D., prin. Fax 434-2560
Twin Pines ES 900/1-5
2 Mur Pl 11717 631-434-2457
Dr. Gloria Jackson, prin. Fax 434-2187
Other Schools – See Bay Shore

Brewerton, Onondaga, Pop. 3,965
Central Square Central SD
Supt. — See Central Square
Brewerton ES 500/PK-5
9530 Brewerton Rd 13029 315-668-4201
Brent Bowden, prin. Fax 668-8175

Brewster, Putnam, Pop. 2,362
Brewster Central SD 3,200/K-12
30 Farm To Market Rd 10509 845-279-8000
Dr. Valerie Henning-Piedmont, supt. Fax 279-3510
www.brewsterschools.org
Kennedy ES 600/K-2
31 Foggintown Rd 10509 845-279-2087
Dr. Frank Zamperlin, prin. Fax 279-7638
Starr IS 700/3-5
20 Farm to Market Rd 10509 845-279-4018
Theresa Cherry, prin. Fax 279-8154
Wells MS 700/6-8
570 Route 312 10509 845-279-3702
John Clark, prin. Fax 279-7634

Briarcliff Manor, Westchester, Pop. 7,748
Briarcliff Manor UFD 1,600/K-12
45 Ingham Rd 10510 914-941-8880
Dr. James Kaishian, supt. Fax 941-2177
www.briarcliffschools.org
Briarcliff MS 400/6-8
444 Pleasantville Rd 10510 914-769-6343
Susan Howard, prin. Fax 769-6375
Todd ES 600/K-5
45 Ingham Rd 10510 914-941-8300
Nadine McDermott, prin. Fax 941-2603

Bridgehampton, Suffolk, Pop. 1,736
Bridgehampton UFD 200/PK-12
PO Box 3021 11932 631-537-0271
Robert Hauser, supt. Fax 537-9038
www.bridgehampton.k12.ny.us
Bridgehampton S 200/PK-12
PO Box 3021 11932 631-537-0271
Michael Miller, prin. Fax 537-0443

Ross Lower S 100/PK-6
PO Box 604 11932 631-537-1240
Jeanette Tyndall, head sch Fax 537-5183

Bridgeport, Madison, Pop. 1,465
Chittenango Central SD
Supt. — See Chittenango
Bridgeport ES 200/K-4
9076 North Rd 13030 315-687-2280
Jamie Durgey, prin. Fax 687-2281

Broadalbin, Fulton, Pop. 1,305
Broadalbin-Perth Central SD 1,800/PK-12
20 Pine St 12025 518-954-2500
Stephen Tomlinson, supt. Fax 954-2509
www.bpcsd.org
Learning Community S 400/PK-2
100 Bridge St 12025 518-954-2650
Bradley Strait, prin. Fax 954-2659
Other Schools – See Amsterdam

Broad Channel, See New York
NYC Department of Education
Supt. — See New York
Public S 47 200/PK-8
9 Power Rd 11693 718-634-7167
Heather Lorenz, prin. Fax 945-5394

Brockport, Monroe, Pop. 8,227
Brockport Central SD — 3,500/K-12
40 Allen St 14420 — 585-637-1810
Dr. Lesli Myers Ed.D., supt. — Fax 637-0165
www.bcs1.org
Barclay ES — 500/2-3
40 Allen St 14420 — 585-637-1840
Scott Morrison, prin. — Fax 637-1845
Ginther ES — 500/K-1
40 Allen St 14420 — 585-637-1830
Debra Waye, prin. — Fax 637-1835
Hill ES — 500/4-5
40 Allen St 14420 — 585-637-1850
Brandon Broughton, prin. — Fax 637-1855
Oliver MS — 800/6-8
40 Allen St 14420 — 585-637-1860
Melody Martinez-Davis, prin. — Fax 637-1869

Cornerstone Christian Academy — 50/PK-12
60 Holley St 14420 — 585-637-4540
Rev. Christopher Johnson, admin. — Fax 637-4518

Brocton, Chautauqua, Pop. 1,467
Brocton Central SD — 500/PK-12
138 W Main St 14716 — 716-792-9121
Jason Delcamp, supt. — Fax 792-9965
www.broctoncsd.org
Brocton ES — 300/PK-5
138 W Main St 14716 — 716-792-2100
Sandra Kopiczak, prin. — Fax 792-2260

Bronx, See New York
NYC Department of Education
Supt. — See New York
Academy for Personal Leadership — 300/6-8
120 E 184th St 10468 — 718-220-3139
Angelo Ledda, prin. — Fax 220-6018
Academy of Applied Math & Technology — 300/6-8
345 Brook Ave 10454 — 718-292-3883
Vincent Gassetto, prin. — Fax 292-4473
Academy of Public Relations — 300/6-8
778 Forest Ave 10456 — 718-665-8866
Amy Andino-Flohr, prin. — Fax 401-0051
Academy of the Arts — 300/PK-5
888 Rev James A Polite Ave 10459 — 718-860-3401
Glorimer Lopez, prin. — Fax 860-4290
Accion Academy — 200/6-8
1825 Prospect Ave 10457 — 718-294-0514
Rajendra Jailall, prin. — Fax 294-3869
Ampark Neighborhood S — 300/K-5
3961 Hillman Ave 10463 — 718-548-3451
Kelly Lennon, prin.
Archer ES — 400/PK-6
1827 Archer St 10460 — 718-828-3791
Zakariah Havlland, prin. — Fax 828-3989
Bassett S — 1,000/PK-5
1075 Pugsley Ave 10472 — 718-822-5198
Michele Montana, prin. — Fax 239-3112
Baychester Academy — 400/PK-5
3500 Edson Ave 10466 — 718-325-1138
Cristine Vaughan, prin. — Fax 325-1558
Baychester MS — 300/6-8
3750 Baychester Ave 10466 — 718-547-1890
Shawn Mangar, prin. — Fax 547-1895
Bedford Park ES — PK-K
3177 Webster Ave 10467 — 718-696-6400
Carolyn Heredia, prin.
Blueprint MS — 100/6-8
1111 Pugsley Ave 10472 — 718-822-2780
Tyneka Harrington, prin. — Fax 822-2279
Bronck Academy — 300/6-8
400 E Fordham Rd 10458 — 718-365-2502
Brenda Gonzalez, prin. — Fax 365-3892
Bronx Alliance MS — 100/6-8
3750 Baychester Ave 10466 — 718-652-2060
Steven Cobb, prin. — Fax 652-3682
Bronx Dance Academy — 200/6-8
3617 Bainbridge Ave 10467 — 718-515-0410
Sandra Sanchez, prin. — Fax 515-0345
Bronx Delta S — PK-5
650 Hollywood Ave 10465 — 718-319-7147
Maria Rogalle, prin.
ES for Math Science and Technology — 300/K-5
125 E 181st St 10453 — 718-933-8061
Avon Connell-Cowell, prin. — Fax 933-8157
Bronx Green MS — 400/6-8
2441 Wallace Ave 10467 — 718-325-6593
Charles Johnson, prin. — Fax 325-3625
IS 117 — 600/6-8
1865 Morris Ave 10453 — 718-583-7750
Delise Jones, prin. — Fax 583-7658
IS 129 — 500/6-8
2055 Mapes Ave 10460 — 718-933-5976
Raymond Granda, prin. — Fax 933-8132
IS 181 — 900/6-8
800 Baychester Ave 10475 — 718-904-5600
Christopher Warnock, prin. — Fax 904-5620
IS 190 — 300/6-8
1550 Crotona Park E 10460 — 718-620-9423
Castella McKenzie, prin. — Fax 620-9927
IS 206 — 300/5-8
2280 Aqueduct Ave 10468 — 718-584-1570
Rafael Cabral, prin. — Fax 584-7928
IS 219 — 400/6-8
3630 3rd Ave 10456 — 718-681-7093
Dominic Cipollone, prin. — Fax 681-7324
IS 224 — 300/6-8
345 Brook Ave 10454 — 718-665-9804
Patricia Catania, prin. — Fax 665-0078
IS 229 — 200/6-8
275 Harlem River Park Brg 10453 — 718-583-6266
Dr. Ezra Matthias, prin. — Fax 583-6325
IS 232 — 500/6-8
1700 Macombs Rd 10453 — 718-583-7007
Desiree Resto, prin. — Fax 583-4864
IS 254 — 400/6-8
2452 Washington Ave 10458 — 718-220-8700
Alexis Marrero, prin. — Fax 220-4881
IS 303 — 300/6-8
1700 Macombs Rd 10453 — 718-583-5466
Patricia Bentley, prin. — Fax 583-2463
IS 318 — 300/6-8
1919 Prospect Ave 10457 — 718-294-8504
Uchechukwu Nioku, prin. — Fax 901-0778
IS 339 — 600/6-8
1600 Webster Ave 10457 — 718-583-6767
Kim Outerbridge, prin. — Fax 583-0281
JHS 22 — 600/6-8
270 E 167th St 10456 — 718-681-6850
Edgar Lin, prin. — Fax 681-6895
JHS 80 — 600/6-8
149 E Mosholu Pkwy N 10467 — 718-405-6300
Emmanuel Polanco, prin. — Fax 405-6324
JHS 98 — 300/6-8
1619 Boston Rd 10460 — 718-589-8200
Mark Turcotte, prin. — Fax 589-8179
JHS 118 — 1,200/6-8
577 E 179th St 10457 — 718-584-2330
Giulia Cox, prin. — Fax 584-7763
JHS 123 — 500/6-8
1025 Morrison Ave 10472 — 718-328-2105
Richard Hallenbeck, prin. — Fax 328-8561
JHS 125 — 400/6-8
1111 Pugsley Ave 10472 — 718-822-5186
Michael Collins, prin. — Fax 239-3121
JHS 127 — 700/6-8
1560 Purdy St 10462 — 718-892-8600
Harry Sherman, prin. — Fax 892-8300
JHS 131 — 700/6-8
885 Bolton Ave 10473 — 718-991-7490
Monique Mason, prin. — Fax 328-6705
JHS 144 — 700/6-8
2545 Gunther Ave 10469 — 718-794-9749
Ellen Barrett-Kelly, prin. — Fax 320-7135
JHS 151 — 300/6-8
250 E 156th St 10451 — 718-292-0260
Socorro Rivera, prin. — Fax 292-5704
Bronx Little S — 400/PK-5
1827 Archer St 10460 — 718-792-2650
Beverly Urquiza, prin. — Fax 792-4149
Bronx Mathematics Preparatory S — 300/6-8
456 White Plains Rd 10473 — 718-542-5063
Dyon Rozier, prin. — Fax 542-5236
MS 101 — 500/6-8
2750 Lafayette Ave 10465 — 718-829-6372
Jared Rosoff, prin. — Fax 829-6594
MS 180 — 800/6-8
700 Baychester Ave 10475 — 718-904-5650
Marlon Williams, prin. — Fax 904-5655
MS 301 — 200/6-8
890 Cauldwell Ave 10456 — 718-585-2950
Hasham Farid, prin. — Fax 401-2567
MS 302 — 600/6-8
681 Kelly St 10455 — 718-292-6070
Liza Ortiz, prin. — Fax 401-2958
MS 390 — 400/6-8
1930 Andrews Ave 10453 — 718-583-5501
Robert Mercedes, prin. — Fax 583-5556
Bronx Park MS — 6-8
2441 Wallace Ave 10467 — 718-652-6090
Renee Rinaldi, prin.
PS 583 — PK-K
1028 White Plains Rd 10472 — 718-348-4960
Glorimer Lopez, prin. — Fax 348-4964
Bronx S for Continuous Learners — 200/1-5
3177 Webster Ave 10467 — 718-696-6440
Janine Tubiolo, prin. — Fax 696-6441
Bronx S of Young Leaders — 400/6-8
40 W Tremont Ave 10453 — 718-583-4146
Serapha Cruz, prin. — Fax 583-4292
Bronx Writing Academy — 500/6-8
270 E 167th St 10456 — 718-293-9048
Lauren Hasson, prin. — Fax 293-9748
Concourse Village ES — 50/PK-5
750 Concourse Vlg W 10451 — 718-402-7503
Alexa Sorden, prin. — Fax 402-7509
Cornerstone Academy for Social Action — 400/PK-5
3441 Steenwick Ave 10475 — 718-794-6160
James Bellon, prin. — Fax 794-6170
Cornerstone Academy for Social Action MS — 200/6-8
3441 Steenwick Ave 10475 — 718-794-7970
Jamaal Bowman, prin. — Fax 794-7981
Creston Academy — 500/6-8
125 E 181st St 10453 — 718-367-5035
Mellissa Miller, prin. — Fax 367-5176
Douglas Academy V — 300/6-8
2111 Crotona Ave 10457 — 718-561-1617
Sayi Neufeld, prin. — Fax 561-2184
East Fordham Academy for the Arts — 400/6-8
120 E 184th St 10468 — 718-220-4185
Francisco De La Cruz, prin. — Fax 220-5976
Emolior Academy — 200/6-8
1970 W Farms Rd 10460 — 718-842-2670
Michael Abbey, prin. — Fax 842-2857
Entrada Academy — 300/6-8
977 Fox St 10459 — 718-378-1649
Victor Frias, prin. — Fax 378-4707
Fairmont Neighborhood S — 200/PK-5
1550 Vyse Ave 10460 — 718-860-5210
Scott Wolfson, prin. — Fax 860-5215
Family S — 500/K-5
1116 Sheridan Ave 10456 — 718-538-3266
Rowena Penn, prin. — Fax 538-3364
Fuentes S of Science & Discovery — 400/PK-5
124 Eames Pl 10468 — 718-601-2632
Yolanda Valez, prin. — Fax 796-7490
Giordano MS — 800/6-8
2502 Lorillard Pl 10458 — 718-584-1660
Anna Maria Perrotta, prin. — Fax 584-7968
Grant Avenue ES — 400/K-5
250 E 164th St 10456 — 718-681-6288
Kristin Erat, prin. — Fax 681-6687
Hamer MS — 300/6-8
1001 Jennings St 10460 — 718-860-2707
Abbey Wilson, prin. — Fax 860-3212
Highbridge Green S — 100/6-8
200 W 167th St 10452 — 718-410-5770
Kyle Brillante, prin. — Fax 410-5779
Hunts Point S — 400/6-8
730 Bryant Ave 10474 — 718-328-1972
David Vazquez, prin. — Fax 328-7330
KAPPA — 300/5-8
3630 3rd Ave 10456 — 718-590-5455
Sheri Warren, prin. — Fax 681-4266
KAPPA III S — 200/6-8
2055 Mapes Ave 10460 — 718-561-3580
Jean Colon, prin. — Fax 561-3719
Leaders of Tomorrow S — 300/6-8
3710 Barnes Ave 10467 — 718-994-1028
Sean Licata, prin.
Linden Tree ES, 1560 Purdy St 10462 — K-5
Lisa DeBonis, prin. — 718-239-7401
Lucero ES — 200/K-5
1425 Walton Ave 10452 — 718-681-8701
Kattia Cuba, prin. — Fax 681-8707
Matilda Avenue S — 100/K-1
4520 Matilda Ave 10470 — 718-325-4360
Miriam Cioffiu, prin. — Fax 325-4365
Mott Hall Community S — 300/6-8
650 Hollywood Ave 10465 — 718-829-3254
Benjamin Basile, prin. — Fax 829-3859
Mott Hall III — 400/6-8
580 Crotona Park S 10456 — 718-842-6138
Jorisis Stupart, prin. — Fax 842-6348
Mount Eden Childrens Academy — PK-5
1501 Jerome Ave 10452 — 718-294-8155
Jacqueline Radoslovich, prin.
New American Academy — 100/PK-5
275 Harlem River Park Brg 10453 — 718-901-9703
Pepe Gutierrez, prin. — Fax 901-9709
New Millenium Business Academy — 200/6-8
1000 Teller Ave 10456 — 718-588-8308
Dorald Bastian, prin. — Fax 681-6913
New S for Leadership and Journalism — 800/6-8
120 W 231st St 10463 — 718-601-2869
Eduardo Mora, prin. — Fax 601-2867
North Bronx S of Empowerment — 300/6-8
3710 Barnes Ave 10467 — 718-652-0519
Magdalen Neyra, prin. — Fax 652-0428
One World MS — 300/6-8
3750 Baychester Ave 10466 — 718-515-6780
Patricia Wynne, prin. — Fax 515-6785
Patri MS — 600/6-8
2225 Webster Ave 10457 — 718-584-1295
Giselle Ocampo, prin. — Fax 584-1358
Pelham Academy of Academics — 300/6-8
2441 Wallace Ave 10467 — 718-881-3136
Anthony Rivera, prin. — Fax 881-3413
Pelham Gardens MS — 6-8
2545 Gunther Ave 10469 — 718-794-9750
Public S 1 — 700/PK-5
335 E 152nd St 10451 — 718-292-9191
Jorge Perdomo, prin. — Fax 292-2227
Public S 3 — 400/PK-8
2100 Lafontaine Ave 10457 — 718-584-1899
Denise Brown, prin. — Fax 584-3590
Public S 4 — 500/K-8
1701 Fulton Ave 10457 — 718-583-6655
Vincent Resto, prin. — Fax 583-6668
Public S 5 — 700/PK-8
564 Jackson Ave 10455 — 718-292-2683
Danielle Keane, prin. — Fax 292-2495
Public S 6 — 600/PK-5
1000 E Tremont Ave 10460 — 718-542-7676
Tiawana Perez, prin. — Fax 589-7278
Public S 7 — 700/K-5
3201 Kingsbridge Ave 10463 — 718-796-8695
Miosotis Ramos, prin. — Fax 796-7204
Public S 8 — 1,200/K-5
3010 Briggs Ave 10458 — 718-584-3043
Claudia Tahiraj-Sadrija, prin. — Fax 584-7376
Public S 9 — 800/PK-5
230 E 183rd St 10458 — 718-584-3291
Jacqueline Bailey, prin. — Fax 584-7579
Public S 11 — 800/K-5
1257 Ogden Ave 10452 — 718-681-7553
Joan Kong, prin. — Fax 681-7711
Public S 14X — 600/K-5
3041 Bruckner Blvd 10461 — 718-822-5341
Ira Schulman, prin. — Fax 239-6386
Public S 15X — 500/K-8
2195 Andrews Ave 10453 — 718-563-0473
Tera Edmonds, prin. — Fax 563-1568
Public S 16 — 600/PK-5
4550 Carpenter Ave 10470 — 718-324-1262
Eduardo Calderon, prin. — Fax 324-8370
Public S 18 — 500/PK-5
502 Morris Ave 10451 — 718-292-2868
Lauren Sewell Walker, prin. — Fax 292-2862
Public S 19 — 500/K-8
4318 Katonah Ave 10470 — 718-324-1924
Timothy Sullivan, prin. — Fax 994-9132
Public S 20 — 1,100/PK-8
3050 Webster Ave 10467 — 718-515-9370
Carla Ling, prin. — Fax 515-9378
Public S 21 — 700/K-5
715 E 225th St 10466 — 718-652-3903
Joyce Coleman, prin. — Fax 231-2556
Public S 23 — 500/PK-4
2151 Washington Ave 10457 — 718-584-3992
Shirley Torres, prin. — Fax 584-7252
Public S 24 — 900/K-5
660 W 236th St 10463 — 718-796-8845
Steven Schwartz, prin. — Fax 796-7243
Public S 25 — 500/PK-5
811 E 149th St 10455 — 718-292-2995
Carmen Toledo-Guerrero, prin. — Fax 292-2997
Public S 28 — 700/PK-5
1861 Anthony Ave 10457 — 718-583-6444
Stephen Beckles, prin. — Fax 583-6537
Public S 29 — 700/PK-8
758 Courtlandt Ave 10451 — 718-292-3785
Deborah Sanabria, prin. — Fax 292-3784

Public S 30 600/PK-5
510 E 141st St 10454 718-292-8817
Debra Michaux, prin. Fax 292-3962
Public S 31 700/PK-8
250 E 156th St 10451 718-292-4397
William Hewlet, prin. Fax 292-4399
Public S 32 800/K-5
690 E 183rd St 10458 718-584-3645
Rebecca Lew, prin. Fax 584-7927
Public S 33 1,100/PK-5
2424 Jerome Ave 10468 718-584-3926
Lynette Santos, prin. Fax 584-7004
Public S 35 700/K-5
261 E 163rd St 10451 718-681-7214
Graciela Navarro, prin. Fax 681-7264
Public S 36 700/PK-5
1070 Castle Hill Ave 10472 718-822-5345
Elvira Maresca, prin. Fax 239-6390
Public S 37X 600/K-8
360 W 230th St 10463 718-796-0360
Kenneth Petriccione, prin. Fax 796-0054
Public S 41 900/K-5
3352 Olinville Ave 10467 718-652-3461
Erika Tobia, prin. Fax 231-2668
Public S 42 500/PK-5
1537 Washington Ave 10457 718-583-7366
Lucia Orduz-Castillo, prin. Fax 583-7345
Public S 43 500/PK-5
165 Brown Pl 10454 718-292-4502
Dr. Giovanna Delucchi, prin. Fax 292-4504
Public S 44 300/PK-5
1825 Prospect Ave 10457 718-583-2360
Melissa Harrow, prin. Fax 901-4068
Public S 46 1,300/K-5
279 E 196th St 10458 718-584-4450
Jennifer Alexander-Ade, prin. Fax 584-7402
Public S 47 1,100/K-5
1794 E 172nd St 10472 718-824-0950
Thomas Guarnieri, prin. Fax 904-1166
Public S 48 800/PK-5
1290 Spofford Ave 10474 718-589-4312
Dwayne D'Avilar, prin. Fax 842-6993
Public S 49 700/PK-5
383 E 139th St 10454 718-292-4623
Frank Hernandez, prin. Fax 292-4568
Public S 51 200/K-5
695 E 182nd St 10457 718-733-0347
Dr. Min Hong, prin. Fax 733-5142
Public S 53 1,300/PK-5
360 E 168th St 10456 718-681-7276
Dr. Collin Wolfe, prin. Fax 681-7298
Public S 54 500/PK-5
2703 Webster Ave 10458 718-584-4203
Marybelle Ferreira, prin. Fax 584-4326
Public S 55 700/PK-5
450 Saint Pauls Pl 10456 718-681-6227
Luis Torres, prin. Fax 681-6247
Public S 56 700/K-5
341 E 207th St 10467 718-920-1100
Maureen O'Neill, prin. Fax 920-1105
Public S 57 600/PK-5
2111 Crotona Ave 10457 718-367-9446
Mary Blandino-Sanchez, prin. Fax 584-1937
Public S 58 500/K-5
459 E 176th St 10457 718-583-6866
Velma Gunn, prin. Fax 583-6895
Public S 59 600/PK-5
2185 Bathgate Ave 10457 718-584-4730
Sita Basu, prin. Fax 584-7518
Public S 61 400/PK-5
1550 Crotona Park E 10460 718-542-7230
Marjorie Sanchez, prin. Fax 589-7361
Public S 62 700/PK-5
660 Fox St 10455 718-585-1617
Lisa Manfredonia, prin. Fax 292-6327
Public S 63 600/PK-5
1260 Franklin Ave 10456 718-589-3058
Reinaldo Diaz-Lens, prin. Fax 589-4917
Public S 65 500/PK-5
677 E 141st St 10454 718-292-4628
Jasmine Gonzalez, prin. Fax 292-4695
Public S 66 700/PK-5
1001 Jennings St 10460 718-318-2820
Kevin Goodman, prin. Fax 589-7375
Public S 67 700/PK-5
2024 Mohegan Ave 10460 718-823-4101
Jeffrey Santiago, prin. Fax 589-7399
Public S 68 800/PK-5
4011 Monticello Ave 10466 718-324-2854
Aidimaris Soler, prin. Fax 324-3852
Public S 69 600/PK-5
560 Thieriot Ave 10473 718-378-4736
Sheila Durant, prin. Fax 328-0925
Public S 70 1,400/K-5
1691 Weeks Ave 10457 718-583-6000
Kerry Castellano, prin. Fax 583-6006
Public S 71 1,700/K-8
3040 Roberts Ave 10461 718-822-5351
Margaret Mirando, prin. Fax 239-3111
Public S 72 900/PK-5
2951 Dewey Ave 10465 718-822-5311
Margarita Colon, prin. Fax 828-4459
Public S 73 900/PK-5
1020 Anderson Ave 10452 718-681-6776
Vivian Bueno, prin. Fax 681-6749
Public S 75 600/PK-5
984 Faile St 10459 718-860-1630
Marines Arrieta-Cruz, prin. Fax 860-4480
Public S 76 1,000/K-5
900 Adee Ave 10469 718-882-8865
Darlene Toron, prin. Fax 882-8870
Public S 78 800/K-5
1400 Needham Ave 10469 718-652-1244
Claudina Skerritt, prin. Fax 231-2756
Public S 81 600/K-5
5550 Riverdale Ave 10471 718-796-8965
Anna Kirrane, prin. Fax 796-7242

Public S 83 1,700/K-8
950 Rhinelander Ave 10462 718-863-1993
Brandon Muccino, prin. Fax 863-5525
Public S 85 1,000/K-5
2400 Marion Ave 10458 718-584-5275
Ted Husted, prin. Fax 584-7765
Public S 86 1,600/PK-6
2756 Reservoir Ave 10468 718-584-5585
Fiona Tyson, prin. Fax 584-7027
Public S 87 600/K-5
1935 Bussing Ave 10466 718-324-5188
Donna Anaman, prin. Fax 325-1148
Public S 88 200/K-3
1340 Sheridan Ave 10456 718-681-6220
Melinda Hyer, prin. Fax 681-6224
Public S 89 1,400/PK-8
980 Mace Ave 10469 718-653-0835
Ralph Martinez, prin. Fax 231-2863
Public S 91 700/K-5
2200 Aqueduct Ave E 10453 718-584-5805
Meridith Struhl Nasjlett, prin. Fax 584-7495
Public S 92 500/PK-5
700 E 179th St 10457 718-731-7900
Yasmin Lugo, prin. Fax 294-1561
Public S 93 400/PK-5
1535 Story Ave 10473 718-430-1700
Jonathan Kaplan, prin. Fax 328-5506
Public S 94 1,200/K-5
3530 Kings College Pl 10467 718-405-6345
Diane DaProcida-Sesin, prin. Fax 405-6358
Public S 95 1,300/PK-8
3961 Hillman Ave 10463 718-796-9200
Serge Davis, prin. Fax 796-7330
Public S 96 1,000/K-5
650 Waring Ave 10467 718-652-4959
Marta Garcia, prin. Fax 231-2889
Public S 97 700/PK-5
1375 Mace Ave 10469 718-655-4446
Kathleen Bornkamp, prin. Fax 655-6063
Public S 100 600/PK-5
800 Taylor Ave 10473 718-842-1461
Chad Altman, prin. Fax 328-5520
Public S 103 1,100/K-5
4125 Carpenter Ave 10466 718-655-0261
Farid Reyes, prin. Fax 654-7930
Public S 105 1,400/K-5
725 Brady Ave 10462 718-824-7350
Christopher Eustace, prin. Fax 828-4531
Public S 106 1,200/PK-5
2120 Saint Raymonds Ave 10462 718-892-1006
Eugenia Montalvo, prin. Fax 823-8008
Public S 107 500/PK-5
1695 Seward Ave 10473 718-860-2596
Katherine Hamm, prin. Fax 328-5799
Public S 108 600/K-5
1166 Neill Ave 10461 718-863-9829
Charles Sperrazza, prin. Fax 828-1712
Public S 109 800/PK-5
1771 Popham Ave 10453 718-583-8878
Josette Claudio, prin Fax 583-7618
Public S 110 500/PK-5
580 Crotona Park S 10456 718-861-0759
Daisy Perez, prin. Fax 861-2750
Public S 111 700/PK-5
3740 Baychester Ave 10466 718-881-2418
Celina Gutierrez, prin. Fax 405-5927
Public S 112 400/PK-5
1925 Schieffelin Ave 10466 718-654-6377
Andrea Tucci, prin. Fax 654-7931
Public S 114X 900/K-5
1155 Cromwell Ave 10452 718-681-7507
Olivia Webber, prin. Fax 681-7519
Public S 121 1,000/PK-5
2750 Throop Ave 10469 718-654-2055
Gloria Martinez, prin. Fax 519-2613
Public S 126 700/PK-6
175 W 166th St 10452 718-681-6120
Nadine Kee-Foster, prin. Fax 681-6131
Public S 130 500/PK-5
750 Prospect Ave 10455 718-665-0962
Lourdes Velazquez, prin. Fax 292-0417
Public S 132 500/PK-5
1245 Washington Ave 10456 718-681-6455
Anissa Reilly, prin. Fax 681-6466
Public S 134 700/PK-5
1330 Bristow St 10459 718-328-3351
Alison King, prin. Fax 589-7581
Public S 138 800/PK-5
2060 Lafayette Ave 10473 718-822-5325
Jeanna Dickerson, prin. Fax 239-3114
Public S 140 600/PK-5
916 Eagle Ave 10456 718-585-1205
Paul Cannon, prin. Fax 292-1349
Public S 146 500/PK-5
968 Cauldwell Ave 10456 718-378-9664
Ronald Laurent, prin. Fax 328-5858
Public S 150 900/PK-5
920 E 167th St 10459 718-328-7729
Norma Sanchez, prin. Fax 589-7590
Public S 152 1,000/PK-5
1007 Evergreen Ave 10472 718 589 4560
Sharon Weissbrot, prin. Fax 328-5867
Public S 153 700/K-5
650 Baychester Ave 10475 718-904-5550
Meghan Kelley, prin. Fax 904-5564
Public S 154 400/PK-5
333 E 135th St 10454 718-292-4742
Dr. Alison Coviello, prin. Fax 292-4721
Public S 157 700/PK-5
757 Cauldwell Ave 10456 718-292-5255
Ramona Duran, prin. Fax 292-5258
Public S 159 200/K-5
2315 Washington Ave 10458 718-584-6140
Luis Liz, prin. Fax 584-7794
Public S 160 300/K-5
4140 Hutchinson River Pky E 10475 718-379-5951
Lori Baker, prin. Fax 320-0392

Public S 161 500/PK-5
628 Tinton Ave 10455 718-292-5478
Elia Marie Soto, prin. Fax 292-5476
Public S 163 600/K-5
2075 Webster Ave 10457 718-584-3045
Dilsia Martinez, prin. Fax 584-3276
Public S 170 300/K-2
1598 Townsend Ave 10452 718-583-0662
Sonia Acevedo Suarez, prin. Fax 583-0685
Public S 175 300/K-8
200 City Island Ave 10464 718-885-1093
Amy Ellis, prin. Fax 885-2315
Public S 178 500/K-5
850 Baychester Ave 10475 718-904-5570
Deborah Levine, prin. Fax 904-5575
Public S 179 400/PK-5
468 E 140th St 10454 718-292-2237
Sherry Williams, prin. Fax 292-3623
Public S 182 1,000/PK-5
601 Stickball Blvd 10473 718-828-6607
Anne O'Grady, prin. Fax 409-8152
Public S 194 1,400/K-8
2365 Waterbury Ave 10462 718-892-5270
Rosa Sifuentes-Rosado, prin. Fax 892-2495
Public S 195 900/PK-5
1250 Ward Ave 10472 718-861-4461
Unal Karakas, prin. Fax 861-7935
Public S 196 900/PK-5
1250 Ward Ave 10472 718-328-7187
Lizzette Graciani, prin. Fax 861-8401
Public S 199 800/PK-5
1449 Shakespeare Ave 10452 718-681-7172
Yasmin Quezada, prin. Fax 681-7176
Public S 204 600/PK-5
1780 MLK Jr Blvd 10453 718-960-9520
Amanda Blatter, prin. Fax 960-9529
Public S 205 1,000/K-5
2475 Southern Blvd 10458 718-584-6390
Jenneth Santiago, prin. Fax 584-7941
Public S 207 400/PK-2
3030 Godwin Ter 10463 718-796-9645
Tara O'Brien, prin. Fax 796-7206
Public S 209 200/PK-2
313 E 183rd St 10458 718-364-0085
Anne Keagan, prin. Fax 364-9548
Public S 211 600/PK-8
1919 Prospect Ave 10457 718-901-0436
Tanya Drummond, prin. Fax 901-4681
Public S 212 500/PK-8
1180 Tinton Ave 10456 718-842-2331
Fatimah Ali, prin. Fax 842-8677
Public S 214 1,000/PK-8
1970 W Farms Rd 10460 718-589-6728
David Cintron, prin. Fax 328-7762
Public S 218 900/K-8
1220 Gerard Ave 10452 718-410-7230
Sergio Caceres, prin. Fax 410-8933
Public S 226 500/PK-5
1950 Sedgwick Ave 10453 718-583-5560
Gloria Darden, prin. Fax 583-5557
Public S 236 300/PK-5
1871 Walton Ave 10453 718-299-6128
Afrina Talukdar, prin. Fax 299-6503
Public S 246 800/K-5
2641 Grand Concourse 10468 718-584-6764
Andrea Johnson, prin. Fax 584-7005
Public S 277 400/PK-5
519 Saint Anns Ave 10455 718-292-3594
Natasha Bracey-Ferguson, prin. Fax 292-3630
Public S 279 1,000/K-8
2100 Walton Ave 10453 718-584-6004
Jean Encke, prin. Fax 584-7220
Public S 280 900/K-8
3202 Steuben Ave 10467 718-405-6360
James Weeks, prin. Fax 405-6329
Public S 291 600/K-5
2195 Andrews Ave 10453 718-563-0776
Carlos Velez, prin. Fax 563-1499
Public S 304 600/PK-5
2750 Lafayette Ave 10465 718-822-5307
Joseph Nobile, prin. Fax 904-0956
Public S 306 800/K-5
40 W Tremont Ave 10453 718-583-5355
Darryl Harrington, prin. Fax 583-5885
Public S 310 800/PK-5
260 W Kingsbridge Rd 10463 718-796-9434
Elizabeth Cardona, prin. Fax 796-9528
Public S 315 300/K-8
2246 Jerome Ave 10453 718-584-7441
Gaby Florez, prin. Fax 584-7433
Public S 333 400/PK-5
888 Rev James A Polite Ave 10459 718-860-3313
Robert German, prin. Fax 842-8734
Public S 340 700/PK-6
25 W 195th St 10468 718-220-1830
Alexei Nichols, prin. Fax 220-1866
Public S 360 500/PK-6
2880 Kingsbridge Ter 10463 718-548-1511
Iris Aldea-Pollack, prin. Fax 548-1536
Public S 396 400/PK-5
1930 Andrews Ave 10453 718-294-0862
Nicole Tine, prin. Fax 583-5556
Public S 536 300/PK-5
1827 Archer St 10460 718-931-4270
Jesse Yarbrough, prin. Fax 931-4275
Samara Community S PK-5
1550 Vyse Ave 10460 718-860-5332
Danielle Derrig, prin.
School for Environmental Citizenship 500/PK-5
125 E 181st St 10453 718-563-3292
Lynnann Fox, prin. Fax 563-3453
School for Inquiry & Social Justice 300/6-8
1025 Morrison Ave 10472 718-860-4181
Andrea Cyprys, prin. Fax 860-4163
School of Performing Arts 400/6-8
977 Fox St 10459 718-589-4844
Dionne Williams, prin. Fax 589-7998

School of Science & Applied Learning 600/PK-5
2050 Prospect Ave 10457 718-584-6310
Venessa Singleton, prin. Fax 220-1370
Science and Technology Academy 400/6-8
250 E 164th St 10456 718-293-4017
Dr. Patrick Awosogba, prin. Fax 293-7396
Sheridan Academy for Young Leaders 600/K-5
1116 Sheridan Ave 10456 718-538-3411
Lisette Febus, prin. Fax 538-3499
Soundview Acad for Culture & Scholarship 300/6-8
885 Bolton Ave 10473 718-991-4027
William Frackelton, prin. Fax 991-4807
South Bronx Academy for Applied Media 400/6-8
778 Forest Ave 10456 718-401-0059
Roshone Ault-Lee, prin. Fax 401-0577
STEAM Bridge S K-1
1684 White Plains Rd 10462 718-239-5660
Katiria Rojas, prin. Fax 239-5665
Urban Institute of Mathematics 300/6-8
650 Hollywood Ave 10465 718-823-6042
Joshua Partridge, prin. Fax 823-6347
Urban Scholars Community S 300/PK-5
1180 Tinton Ave 10456 718-842-8133
Debra Jones, prin. Fax 842-8442
Urban Science Academy 400/5-8
1000 Teller Ave 10456 718-588-8221
Patrick Kelly, prin. Fax 588-8263
Van Nest Academy 500/K-8
1640 Bronxdale Ave 10462 718-409-3001
Carol Gilligan, prin. Fax 409-3002
Walton Avenue S 300/K-5
1425 Walton Ave 10452 718-293-5970
Daniel Russo, prin. Fax 293-2091
Young Leaders ES 300/PK-5
468 E 140th St 10454 718-292-7391
Jaleelah Cooke, prin. Fax 292-8535
Young Scholars Academy 300/6-8
3710 Barnes Ave 10467 718-325-5834
Jeanette Vargas, prin. Fax 325-5676
Young Voices Academy of the Bronx 100/PK-3
800 Lydig Ave 10462 718-794-4080
Nadia Cruz-Perez, prin. Fax 794-4089
Young Womens Leadership S of the Bronx 6-8
1865 Morris Ave 10453 718-731-2590
Devon Eisenberg, prin.

Bronx-Manhattan SDA S 200/K-8
1440 Plimpton Ave 10452 718-588-7598
Marlene Romeo, prin. Fax 588-1052
Christ the King S 500/K-8
1345 Grand Concourse 10452 718-538-5959
Steven Iuso, prin. Fax 538-6369
City of Faith Christian S 100/PK-5
3453 White Plains Rd 10467 718-798-3052
Claudette Reid, admin. Fax 654-4452
Ethical Culture Fieldston S 300/PK-5
3901 Fieldston Rd 10471 718-329-7300
Jessica Bagby, head sch Fax 329-7304
Greek American Institute 200/PK-8
3573 Bruckner Blvd 10461 718-823-2393
Anne Prokop, admin. Fax 823-0790
Holy Cross S 400/PK-8
1846 Randall Ave 10473 718-842-4492
Ernie Zalamea, prin. Fax 842-4052
Holy Family S 300/PK-8
2169 Blackrock Ave 10472 718-863-7280
Claire LaTempa, prin. Fax 931-8690
Holy Rosary S 600/PK-8
1500 Arnow Ave 10469 718-652-1838
Maryann Fusco, prin. Fax 515-9872
Hudson SDA ES 100/PK-8
1122 Forest Ave 10456 718-328-3322
Raymond Dixon, prin. Fax 328-5922
Immaculate Conception S 500/PK-8
378 E 151st St 10455 718-585-4843
Sr. Patrice Owens, prin. Fax 585-6846
Immaculate Conception S 600/PK-8
760 E Gun Hill Rd 10467 718-547-3346
Lawrence Cooke, prin. Fax 547-5505
Kinneret Day S 300/PK-8
2600 Netherland Ave 10463 718-548-0900
Asher Abramovitz, prin. Fax 548-0901
Learning Tree Preparatory S 300/PK-8
801 Bartholdi St 10467 718-944-0958
Lois Gregory, prin. Fax 944-8909
Mann S 1,700/PK-12
231 W 246th St 10471 718-432-4000
Dr. Thomas M. Kelly, head sch Fax 548-2089
Nativity of Our Blessed Lady S 200/PK-8
3893 Dyre Ave 10466 718-324-2188
Douglas Klice, prin. Fax 324-1128
New Covenant Christian S 200/PK-5
1497 Needham Ave 10469 718-519-8884
Verna Blake, prin. Fax 519-8691
Our Lady of Grace S 300/PK-8
3981 Bronxwood Ave 10466 718-547-9918
Richard Helmrich, prin. Fax 547-7602
Our Lady of Mt. Carmel S 200/PK-8
2465 Bathgate Ave 10458 718-295-6080
Valerie Savino, prin. Fax 561-5205
Our Lady of Refuge S 300/PK-8
2708 Briggs Ave 10458 718-367-3081
Robert Billings, prin. Fax 367-0741
Our Lady of the Assumption S 300/PK-8
1617 Parkview Ave 10461 718-829-1706
John Barnaba, prin. Fax 931-2693
Our Saviour Lutheran S 200/PK-12
1734 Williamsbridge Rd 10461 718-792-5665
Ken Famulare, prin. Fax 409-3877
Regent S 200/K-6
719 E 216th St 10467 718-653-2900
Howard Sterling, dir. Fax 653-1166
Riverdale Country S - River Campus 400/PK-5
5250 Fieldston Rd 10471 718-549-7780
Sacred Heart S 500/PK-8
1248 Nelson Ave 10452 718-293-4288
Abigail Akano, prin. Fax 293-4886

St. Angela Merici S 300/PK-8
266 E 163rd St 10451 718-293-3365
John Bellocchio, prin. Fax 293-6617
St. Anselm S 500/PK-8
685 Tinton Ave 10455 718-993-9464
Teresa Lopes, prin. Fax 292-3496
St. Athanasius S 300/PK-8
830 Southern Blvd 10459 718-542-5161
Marianne Kraft, prin. Fax 542-7584
St. Barnabas S 400/PK-8
413 E 241st St 10470 718-324-1088
Jonathan Morano, prin. Fax 324-2397
St. Benedict S 300/K-8
1016 Edison Ave 10465 718-829-9557
Ray Vitiello, prin. Fax 319-1898
St. Brendan S 300/PK-8
268 E 207th St 10467 718-653-2292
Michele Pasquale, prin. Fax 653-3234
St. Clare of Assisi S 400/PK-8
1911 Hone Ave 10461 718-892-4080
Theresa Bivona, prin. Fax 239-1007
St. Frances De Chantal S 300/PK-8
2962 Harding Ave 10465 718-892-5359
Patricia Brito, prin. Fax 892-6937
St. Francis of Assisi S 300/PK-8
4300 Baychester Ave 10466 718-994-4650
Marc Silva, prin. Fax 994-6990
St. Francis Xavier S 500/PK-8
1711 Haight Ave 10461 718-863-0531
Angela Deegan, prin. Fax 319-1152
St. Gabriel S 200/PK-8
590 W 235th St 10463 718-548-0444
Anthony Naccari, prin. Fax 796-2638
St. Helena S 400/PK-8
2050 Benedict Ave 10462 718-892-3234
Richard Meller, prin. Fax 892-3924
St. Ignatius Academy 100/6-8
740 Manida St 10474 718-861-9084
Richard Darrell, prin. Fax 861-9096
St. John Chrysostom S 400/PK-8
1144 Hoe Ave 10459 718-328-7226
Sr. Mary Mooney, prin. Fax 378-5368
St. John S 200/PK-8
3143 Kingsbridge Ave 10463 718-548-0255
Melissa Moore, prin. Fax 548-0864
St. Joseph S 500/PK-8
1946 Bathgate Ave 10457 718-583-9432
Carmen Lopez, prin. Fax 299-0780
St. Lucy S 400/PK-8
830 Mace Ave 10467 718-882-2203
Jane Stefanini, prin. Fax 547-8351
St. Luke S 300/PK-8
608 E 139th St 10454 718-585-0380
Tracey Coleman, prin. Fax 665-3407
St. Margaret Mary S 400/PK-8
121 E 177th St 10453 718-731-5905
Sr. Ann Bivona, prin. Fax 731-8924
St. Margaret of Cortona S 300/PK-8
452 W 260th St 10471 718-549-8580
Hugh Keenan, prin. Fax 884-3298
St. Nicholas of Tolentine S 300/K-8
2336 Andrews Ave 10468 718-364-5110
Raymond Lomupo, prin. Fax 561-3964
St. Philip Neri S 300/PK-8
3031 Grand Concourse 10468 718-365-8806
Ajeia Beebe, prin. Fax 365-1482
St. Raymond S 900/PK-8
2380 E Tremont Ave 10462 718-597-3232
Sr. Eugene Scanlon, prin. Fax 892-4449
St. Simon Stock S 200/K-8
2195 Valentine Ave 10457 718-367-0453
Kinsley Jabouin, prin. Fax 733-1441
St. Theresa S 400/PK-8
2872 Saint Theresa Ave 10461 718-792-3688
Josephine Fanelli, prin. Fax 892-9441
St. Thomas Aquinas S 200/PK-8
1909 Daly Ave 10460 718-893-7600
Jessica Maldonado, prin. Fax 378-5531
Santa Maria S 400/PK-8
1510 Zerega Ave 10462 718-823-3636
Sr. Maureen Flynn, prin. Fax 823-7008
SS. Peter & Paul S PK-PK
838 Brook Ave 10451 718-665-2056
Jacquelyn Alvarez, prin. Fax 665-2725
SS. Philip & James S 200/PK-8
1160 E 213th St 10469 718-882-4576
James O'Connell, prin. Fax 653-6167
Villa Maria Academy 400/PK-8
3335 Country Club Rd 10465 718-824-3260
Sr. Theresa Barton, prin. Fax 824-7315

Bronxville, Westchester, Pop. 6,193
Bronxville UFD 1,700/K-12
177 Pondfield Rd 10708 914-395-0500
Roy Montesano, supt. Fax 337-7109
www.bronxville.k12.ny.us
Bronxville ES 800/K-5
177 Pondfield Rd 10708 914-395-0500
Patricia Murray, prin. Fax 337-6827
Bronxville MS 400/6-8
177 Pondfield Rd 10708 914-395-0500
Dr. Thomas Wilson, prin. Fax 771-6223

Chapel S 400/PK-8
172 White Plains Rd 10708 914-337-3202
Michael Schultz, prin. Fax 771-9711
St. Joseph S 200/K-8
30 Meadow Ave 10708 914-337-0261
Margaret Kazan, prin. Fax 395-1192

Brookfield, Madison
Brookfield Central SD 200/PK-12
PO Box 60 13314 315-899-3323
James Plows, supt. Fax 899-8902
www.brookfieldcsd.org
Brookfield Central S 200/PK-12
PO Box 60 13314 315-899-3323
Carrie Smith, prin. Fax 899-8902

Brookhaven, Suffolk, Pop. 3,414
South Country Central SD
Supt. — See East Patchogue
Brookhaven ES 700/PK-3
101 Fireplace Neck Rd 11719 631-730-1700
Dr. Kathleen Munisteri, prin. Fax 286-6210

Brooklyn, See New York
NYC Department of Education
Supt. — See New York
Academy of Arts and Letters 500/K-8
225 Adelphi St 11205 718-222-1605
John O'Reilly, prin. Fax 852-6020
Academy of Talented Scholars 200/K-5
50 Avenue P 11204 718-621-2730
J. Sportella-Giusto, prin. Fax 621-2735
Brighter Choice Community S 100/PK-5
280 Hart St 11206 718-574-2378
Fabayo McIntosh, prin. Fax 443-0639
Brooklyn Arbor ES K-5
325 S 3rd St 11211 718-963-0393
Eva Irizarry, prin.
Brooklyn Arts & Sciences ES PK-5
443 Saint Marks Ave 11238 718-230-0851
Sandra Beauvoir Soto, prin.
Brooklyn Brownstone S 200/K-5
272 MacDonough St 11233 718-573-2307
Nakia Haskins, prin. Fax 573-2434
Brooklyn Environmental Exploration S 100/6-7
251 MacDougal St 11233 718-453-3039
Craig Garber, prin. Fax 453-3508
Brooklyn Gardens ES 200/PK-5
574 Dumont Ave 11207 718-495-7012
Irene Spence, prin. Fax 495-7018
IS 30 400/6-8
7002 4th Ave 11209 718-491-8440
Carol Heeraman, prin. Fax 491-0071
IS 68 800/6-8
956 E 82nd St 11236 718-241-4800
Merve Williams, prin. Fax 241-5582
IS 96 700/6-8
99 Avenue P 11204 718-236-1344
Erin Lynch, prin. Fax 236-2397
IS 98 1,400/6-8
1401 Emmons Ave 11235 718-891-9005
Maria Timo, prin. Fax 646-7250
IS 136 500/6-8
4004 4th Ave 11232 718-840-1950
Eric Sackler, prin. Fax 965-9567
IS 171 800/5-8
528 Ridgewood Ave 11208 718-647-0111
Indira Mota, prin. Fax 827-5834
IS 211 700/6-8
1001 E 100th St 11236 718-251-4411
Carolyn James, prin. Fax 241-2503
IS 228 1,000/6-8
228 Avenue S 11223 718-375-7635
Dominick D'Angelo, prin. Fax 376-1209
IS 281 1,200/6-8
8787 24th Ave 11214 718-996-6706
Maria Bender, prin. Fax 996-4186
IS 285 900/6-8
5909 Beverley Rd 11203 718-451-2200
George Patterson, prin. Fax 451-0229
IS 303 600/6-8
501 West Ave 11224 718-996-0100
Carmen Amador, prin. Fax 996-3785
IS 318 1,600/6-8
101 Walton St 11206 718-782-0589
Leander Windley, prin. Fax 384-7715
IS 340 200/6-8
227 Sterling Pl 11238 718-857-5516
Tamara Johnson, prin. Fax 230-5479
IS 347 400/5-8
35 Starr St 11221 718-821-4248
John Barbella, prin. Fax 821-1332
IS 349 400/6-8
35 Starr St 11221 718-418-6389
Michael Loughren, prin. Fax 418-6146
IS 364 400/6-8
1426 Freeport Loop 11239 718-642-3007
Nicole Edmund, prin. Fax 642-8516
IS 381 400/6-8
1599 E 22nd St 11210 718-252-0058
Victoria Agard, prin. Fax 252-0035
IS 392 300/5-8
104 Sutter Ave 11212 718-498-2491
Ingrid Joseph, prin. Fax 346-2804
JHS 14 500/6-8
2424 Batchelder St 11235 718-743-0220
Teri Ahearn, prin. Fax 769-8632
JHS 50 300/6-8
183 S 3rd St 11211 718-387-4184
Benjamin Honoroff, prin. Fax 302-2320
JHS 57 200/6-8
125 Stuyvesant Ave 11221 718-574-2357
Anthony Lett, prin. Fax 453-0577
JHS 62 1,300/6-8
700 Cortelyou Rd 11218 718-941-5450
Barry Kevorkian, prin. Fax 693-7433
JHS 78 900/6-8
1420 E 68th St 11234 718-763-4701
Anthony Cusumano, prin. Fax 251-3439
JHS 88 1,200/6-8
544 7th Ave 11215 718-788-4482
Ailene Mitchell, prin. Fax 768-0213
JHS 162 500/6-8
1390 Willoughby Ave 11237 718-821-4860
Amanda Lazerson, prin. Fax 821-1728
JHS 201 1,400/6-8
8010 12th Ave 11228 718-833-9363
Robert Ciulla, prin. Fax 836-1786
JHS 218 500/6-8
370 Fountain Ave 11208 718-647-9050
Lisa Ann Hermann, prin. Fax 827-5839
JHS 220 1,400/6-8
4812 9th Ave 11220 718-633-8200
Sheldon Dempster, prin. Fax 871-7466

JHS 223 900/6-8
4200 16th Ave 11204 718-438-0155
Andrew Frank, prin. Fax 871-7477

JHS 227 1,300/6-8
6500 16th Ave 11204 718-256-8218
Dr. Edwin Hernandez, prin. Fax 234-6204

JHS 234 1,900/6-8
1875 E 17th St 11229 718-645-1334
Tami Flynn, prin. Fax 645-7759

JHS 259 1,400/6-8
7305 Fort Hamilton Pkwy 11228 718-833-1000
Janice Geary, prin. Fax 833-3419

JHS 278 1,100/6-8
1925 Stuart St 11229 718-375-3523
Debra Garofalo, prin. Fax 998-7324

JHS 291 500/6-8
231 Palmetto St 11221 718-574-0361
Janice Bruce, prin. Fax 574-1360

JHS 292 700/6-8
301 Vermont St 11207 718-498-6562
Ahmed Edwards, prin. Fax 345-3327

JHS 383 900/5-8
1300 Greene Ave 11237 718-574-0390
Jeanette Smith, prin. Fax 574-1366

Brooklyn Landmark ES 100/PK-3
251 MacDougal St 11233 718-443-2747
Robin Davson, prin. Fax 443-4365

MS 35 200/6-8
272 MacDonough St 11233 718-574-2345
Jackie Charles, prin. Fax 452-1273

MS 51 1,100/6-8
350 5th Ave 11215 718-369-7603
Lenore Dileo-Berner, prin. Fax 499-4948

MS 61 800/6-8
400 Empire Blvd 11225 718-774-1002
Dewana Daids, prin. Fax 467-4335

MS 113 700/6-8
300 Adelphi St 11205 718-834-6734
Dawnique Daughtry, prin. Fax 596-2802

MS 246 600/6-8
72 Veronica Pl 11226 718-282-5230
Bently Warrington, prin. Fax 284-6429

MS 266 100/6-8
31 New York Ave 11216 718-245-8766
Glenda Esperance, prin. Fax 245-8769

MS 267 300/6-8
800 Gates Ave 11221 718-574-2318
Patricia King, prin. Fax 574-2320

MS 582 300/6-8
207 Bushwick Ave 11206 718-456-8218
Brian Walsh, prin. Fax 456-8220

MS 839 200/6-7
713 Caton Ave 11218 718-686-2730
Michael Perlberg, prin. Fax 686-2735

MS for Art and Philosophy 300/6-8
1084 Lenox Rd 11212 718-342-7563
Neil McNeill, prin. Fax 342-8131

MS of Marketing & Legal Studies 300/6-8
905 Winthrop St 11203 718-773-7343
Jameela Horton, prin. Fax 773-7946

Brooklyn New S 700/PK-5
610 Henry St 11231 718-923-4750
Anna Allanbrook, prin. Fax 923-4780

PS 338 K-5
510 Coney Island Ave 11218 929-397-9200

PS 889, 21 Hinckley Pl 11218 PK-K
Kathryn Anderson, prin. 929-397-9171

S of Science & Technology 900/PK-5
725 E 23rd St 11210 718-434-5222
Gina Smalley, prin. Fax 859-5965

Brooklyn Science and Engineering Academy 6-8
5404 Tilden Ave 11203 718-240-3790
Angela Defilippis, prin.

Brownsville Collaborative MS 6-8
85 Watkins St 11212 718-495-1202
Gregory Jackson, prin.

Christopher Avenue Community S 200/PK-5
51 Christopher Ave 11212 718-495-5761
Deon Mitchell, prin. Fax 495-5764

Clemons Academy 700/K-5
43 Snyder Ave 11226 718-856-6560
Sharon Porter, prin. Fax 856-7493

Conselyea Preparatory S 500/6-8
208 N 5th St 11211 718-486-6211
Maria Masullo, prin. Fax 486-6771

Dock Street S for STEAM Studies 100/6-8
19 Dock St 11201 718-780-7660
Melissa Vaughan, prin. Fax 780-7675

Douglass Academy VIII MS 300/6-8
1400 Pennsylvania Ave 11239 718-348-2465
Chantal Grandchamps, prin. Fax 642-4537

East Flatbush Community Research S 200/6-8
905 Winthrop St 11203 718-773-3059
Daveida Daniel, prin. Fax 773-3827

East New York ES of Excellence 600/PK-5
605 Shepherd Ave 11208 718-272-6075
Janet Huger, prin. Fax 272-6257

East New York MS of Excellence 200/6-8
605 Shepherd Ave 11208 718-257-4061
Malik Small, prin. Fax 257-4738

Ebbets Field MS 300/6-8
46 McKeever Pl 11225 718-941-5097
Jeanne Rowe, prin. Fax 284-7973

Edmonds Learning Center II 100/6-8
430 Howard Ave 11233 718-467-0306
Michele Luard, prin. Fax 953-0682

Ericsson MS 300/6-8
424 Leonard St 11222 718-782-2527
Maria Ortega, prin. Fax 302-2319

Essence MS 100/6-8
590 Sheffield Ave 11207 718-272-8371
Jermaine Lewis, prin. Fax 272-8372

Evergreen MS for Urban Exploration 200/6-8
125 Covert St 11207 718-455-0180
Lauren Reiss, prin. Fax 455-4381

Fabrizio S 900/K-5
7109 6th Ave 11209 718-748-0333
Zhen Wu, prin. Fax 921-6351

Fort Greene Preparatory Academy 300/6-8
100 Clermont Ave 11205 718-254-9401
Paula Lettiere, prin. Fax 254-9407

Fresh Creek S 200/PK-5
875 Williams Ave 11207 718-272-1843
Lisa Goodson, prin. Fax 272-2813

Highland Park Community S 6-8
528 Ridgewood Ave 11208 718-235-1785
Jamilah Seifullah, prin.

Hudde IS 900/6-8
2500 Nostrand Ave 11210 718-253-3700
Gina Votinelli, prin. Fax 253-0356

Jackson S of Sports Art & Technology 600/PK-8
213 Osborn St 11212 718-495-7791
Keva Girard, prin. Fax 495-7839

KAPPA V S, 985 Rockaway Ave 11212 200/6-8
Ronda Phillips, prin. 718-922-4690

Liberty Avenue MS 100/6-8
350 Linwood St 11208 718-647-1301
Kaia Nordtvedt, prin. Fax 647-1307

Madiba Prep MS 6-8
1014 Lafayette Ave 11221 718-574-2804
Anne Marie Malcolm, prin.

Magnet S of Math/Sci/Design Tech 900/PK-5
511 7th Ave 11215 718-965-1190
Laura Scott, prin. Fax 369-1736

Math & Science Exploratory S 500/6-8
345 Dean St 11217 718-330-9328
Arin Rusch, prin. Fax 330-0944

McAuliffe S 900/6-8
1171 65th St 11219 718-236-3394
Justin Berman, prin. Fax 236-3638

Mott Hall Bridges MS 200/6-8
210 Chester St 11212 718-345-6912
Nadia Lopez, prin. Fax 345-6918

Mott Hall IV, 1137 Herkimer St 11233 200/6-8
Dellie Edwards, prin. 718-485-5240

New Bridges ES 200/PK-5
1025 Eastern Pkwy 11213 718-363-8200
Kevin Bowles, prin. Fax 363-8202

New Heights MS 6-8
790 E New York Ave 11203 718-467-4501
Ativia Sandusky, prin.

New Horizons S 200/6-8
317 Hoyt St 11231 718-330-9227
Noreen Mills, dir. Fax 330-9251

New Voices S of Academic & Creative Arts 500/6-8
330 18th St 11215 718-965-0390
Frank Giordano, prin. Fax 965-0603

Parkside Preparatory Academy 500/6-8
655 Parkside Ave 11226 718-462-6992
Adrienne Spencer, prin. Fax 284-7717

Peek-Davis ES 200/PK-5
430 Howard Ave 11233 718-953-4569
Nyree Dixon, prin. Fax 953-4428

Public S 1 1,300/PK-5
309 47th St 11220 718-567-7661
Arlene Ramos, prin. Fax 567-9771

Public S 3 500/PK-5
50 Jefferson Ave 11216 718-622-2960
Kristina Beecher, prin. Fax 623-3193

Public S 5 300/PK-5
820 Hancock St 11233 718-574-2333
Lena Gates, prin. Fax 574-3925

Public S 7 1,100/PK-5
858 Jamaica Ave 11208 718-647-3600
Carolyn Noel, prin. Fax 827-4004

Public S 8 800/PK-8
37 Hicks St 11201 718-834-6740
Patricia Peterson, prin. Fax 834-7690

Public S 9 700/PK-5
80 Underhill Ave 11238 718-638-3260
Denita D'Avilar, prin. Fax 622-2961

Public S 11 700/PK-5
419 Waverly Ave 11238 718-638-2661
Abidemi Hope, prin. Fax 622-3028

Public S 13 500/PK-5
557 Pennsylvania Ave 11207 718-498-3717
Maxine Cameron, prin. Fax 345-2396

Public S 15 400/PK-5
71 Sullivan St 11231 718-330-9280
Peggy Wyns-Madison, prin. Fax 596-2576

Public S 16 200/PK-5
157 Wilson St 11211 718-782-5352
Mary Renny, prin. Fax 486-8447

Public S 17 300/PK-5
208 N 5th St 11211 718-387-2929
Dr. Robert Marchi, prin. Fax 302-2311

Public S 18 200/PK-5
101 Maujer St 11206 718-387-3241
Alison Alexander, prin. Fax 599-7744

Public S 20 300/PK-5
225 Adelphi St 11205 718-834-6744
L. Barbera, prin. Fax 243-0712

Public S 21 600/PK-5
180 Chauncey St 11233 718-493-9681
Leslie Frazier, prin. Fax 953-3980

Public S 23 300/PK-5
545 Willoughby Ave 11206 718-387-0375
Joseph Mattina, prin. Fax 302-2312

Public S 24 700/PK-5
427 38th St 11232 718-832-9366
Jacqueline Nikovic, prin. Fax 832-9360

Public S 25 200/PK-5
787 Lafayette Ave 11221 718-574-2336
Anita Coley, prin. Fax 455-5838

Public S 26 300/PK-5
1014 Lafayette Ave 11221 718-919-5707
Dr. Cynthia Celestine, prin. Fax 574-2803

Public S 28 200/PK-5
1001 Herkimer St 11233 718-467-2865
Judith James, prin. Fax 953-4189

Public S 29 800/PK-5
425 Henry St 11201 718-330-9277
Rebecca Fagin, prin. Fax 596-1887

Public S 31 600/PK-5
75 Meserole Ave 11222 718-383-8998
Mary Scarlato, prin. Fax 383-5652

Public S 32 400/PK-5
317 Hoyt St 11231 718-222-6400
Denise Watson, prin. Fax 797-4362

Public S 34 600/PK-5
131 Norman Ave 11222 718-389-5842
Carmen Asselta, prin. Fax 389-0356

Public S 38 500/PK-5
450 Pacific St 11217 718-330-9305
Yolanda Ramirez, prin. Fax 802-9542

Public S 39 400/PK-5
417 6th Ave 11215 718-330-9310
Anita DePaz, prin. Fax 832-2010

Public S 40 300/PK-5
265 Ralph Ave 11233 718-574-2353
Louise Antoine, prin. Fax 453-0686

Public S 41 500/K-8
411 Thatford Ave 11212 718-495-7732
Shonelle Hall, prin. Fax 346-2141

Public S 44 300/PK-5
432 Monroe St 11221 718-834-6939
Roxanne James, prin. Fax 574-8501

Public S 45 800/PK-7
84 Schaefer St 11207 718-642-5360
Tracy Lott-Davis, prin. Fax 574-1043

Public S 46 400/PK-5
100 Clermont Ave 11205 718-834-7694
Karyn Nicholson, prin. Fax 243-0726

Public S 48 600/PK-5
6015 18th Ave 11204 718-232-3873
Diane Picucci, prin. Fax 232-3451

Public S 52 800/PK-5
2675 E 29th St 11235 718-648-0882
Kristin Hurley, prin. Fax 648-4636

Public S 54 200/PK-5
195 Sandford St 11205 718-834-6752
Anthony Pirro, prin. Fax 852-8129

Public S 56 200/PK-5
170 Gates Ave 11238 718-857-3149
Eric Grande, prin. Fax 783-7379

Public S 58 900/PK-5
330 Smith St 11231 718-330-9322
Katherine Dellostritto, prin. Fax 596-2969

Public S 59 400/PK-5
211 Throop Ave 11206 718-443-3600
Cherry Hislop, prin. Fax 574-6634

Public S 65 600/K-5
696 Jamaica Ave 11208 718-235-2223
Daysi Garcia, prin. Fax 235-2033

Public S 66 800/PK-8
845 E 96th St 11236 718-922-3505
Lucille Jackson, prin. Fax 922-3105

Public S 67 300/PK-5
51 Saint Edwards St 11205 718-834-6756
Kyesha Jackson, prin. Fax 834-6719

Public S 69 900/K-5
6302 9th Ave 11220 718-630-3899
Jaynemarie Capetanakis, prin. Fax 833-9781

Public S 75 600/PK-5
95 Grove St 11221 718-574-0244
Dr. Yolanda Williams, prin. Fax 574-1051

Public S 81 400/PK-5
990 Dekalb Ave 11221 718-574-2365
Cheryl Ault-Barker, prin. Fax 919-9872

Public S 84 600/PK-8
250 Berry St 11249 718-384-8063
Sereida Rodriguez, prin. Fax 302-2313

Public S 86 500/K-5
220 Irving Ave 11237 718-574-0252
Dr. Tina Moschella-Andresen, prin. Fax 919-1839

Public S 89 400/PK-8
265 Warwick St 11207 718-964-1180
Irene Leon, prin. Fax 964-1185

Public S 90 600/PK-5
2840 W 12th St 11224 718-787-3333
Greta Hawkins, prin. Fax 266-7018

Public S 91 500/PK-5
532 Albany Ave 11203 718-756-0243
Tessa Alleyne, prin. Fax 221-1316

Public S 92 500/PK-5
601 Parkside Ave 11226 718-462-2087
John Samerson, prin. Fax 284-8289

Public S 93 300/PK-5
31 New York Ave 11216 718-604-7363
Janeice Bailey, prin. Fax 771-1369

Public S 94 1,500/PK-5
5010 6th Ave 11220 718-435-6034
Jeanette Caban, prin. Fax 871-6251

Public S 95 1,000/PK-8
345 Van Sicklen St 11223 718-449-5050
Janet Ndzibah, prin. Fax 449-3047

Public S 97 800/PK-5
1855 Stillwell Ave 11223 718-627-2550
Irina Cabello, prin. Fax 372-3842

Public S 99 800/PK-8
1120 E 10th St 11230 718-338-9201
Gregory Pirraglia, prin. Fax 951-0418

Public S 100 700/PK-5
2951 W 3rd St 11224 718-266-9477
Chiara Spagnolo, prin. Fax 266-7112

Public S 101 900/PK-5
2360 Benson Ave 11214 718-372-0221
Greg Korrol, prin. Fax 372-1873

Public S 102 1,300/K-5
211 72nd St 11209 718-748-7404
Cornelia Sichenze, prin. Fax 836-9265

Public S 104 1,200/K-8
9115 5th Ave 11209 718-836-4630
Marie Dibella, prin. Fax 836-9412

Public S 105 1,800/K-5
1031 59th St 11219 718-438-3230
Johanna Castronovo, prin. Fax 853-9633

Public S 106 600/PK-5
1328 Putnam Ave 11221 718-574-0261
Magaly Moncayo, prin. Fax 574-1054

Public S 107 600/K-5
1301 8th Ave 11215 718-499-2054
Eve Litwack, prin. Fax 965-6479

Public S 108 900/PK-5
200 Linwood St 11208 718-277-7010
Constance Hahn, prin. Fax 827-4137

Public S 109 500/K-8
1001 E 45th St 11203 718-693-3426
Kerdy Bertra, prin. Fax 693-3072

Public S 110 400/PK-5
124 Monitor St 11222 718-383-7600
Anna Amato, prin. Fax 383-5053

Public S 112 500/K-5
7115 15th Ave 11228 718-232-0685
Louise Alfano, prin. Fax 232-3609

Public S 114 600/PK-5
1077 Remsen Ave 11236 718-257-4428
Darwin Smith, prin. Fax 649-5216

Public S 115 1,200/PK-5
1500 E 92nd St 11236 718-241-1000
Loren Borgese, prin. Fax 209-1714

Public S 116 500/K-5
515 Knickerbocker Ave 11237 718-821-4623
Antoinette Tucci, prin. Fax 821-0363

Public S 119 400/K-5
3829 Avenue K 11210 718-377-7696
Lisa Fernandez, prin. Fax 338-0694

Public S 120 500/PK-5
18 Beaver St 11206 718-455-1000
Liza Caraballo, prin. Fax 574-6637

Public S 121 400/PK-8
5301 20th Ave 11204 718-377-8845
Anthony Mungioli, prin. Fax 252-4075

Public S 123 800/K-5
100 Irving Ave 11237 718-821-4810
Arelis Parache, prin. Fax 821-0858

Public S 124 300/PK-5
515 4th Ave 11215 718-788-0246
Annabelle Burrell, prin. Fax 965-9558

Public S 127 500/K-5
7805 7th Ave 11228 718-833-2323
Agatha Alicandro, prin. Fax 836-9427

Public S 128 400/PK-5
2075 84th St 11214 718-373-5900
Jessica Drzewucki, prin. Fax 266-6254

Public S 130 700/PK-5
70 Ocean Pkwy 11218 718-686-1940
Maria Nunziata, prin. Fax 854-9756

Public S 131 1,100/PK-5
4305 Fort Hamilton Pkwy 11219 718-431-1960
Ruth Quiles, prin. Fax 853-5952

Public S 132 800/PK-5
320 Manhattan Ave 11211 718-599-7301
Beth Lubeck, prin. Fax 599-7417

Public S 133, 610 Baltic St 11217 500/PK-5
Heather Foster-Mann, prin. 718-398-5320

Public S 134 500/PK-5
4001 18th Ave 11218 718-436-7200
Debra Ramsaran, prin. Fax 854-4115

Public S 135 700/PK-5
684 Linden Blvd 11203 718-693-4363
Trevlyn McRae, prin. Fax 941-0847

Public S 137 300/PK-8
121 Saratoga Ave 11233 718-453-2926
Suzette Rose, prin. Fax 453-5363

Public S 138 700/PK-8
760 Prospect Pl 11216 718-467-0800
Marie Chauvet-Monchik, prin. Fax 953-3422

Public S 139 1,000/PK-5
330 Rugby Rd 11226 718-282-5254
Mary McDonald, prin. Fax 940-1205

Public S 145 800/PK-5
100 Noll St 11206 718-821-4823
Linda Malloy, prin. Fax 417-3453

Public S 147 300/PK-5
325 Bushwick Ave 11206 718-497-0326
Sandra Noyola, prin. Fax 628-4988

Public S 149 700/PK-5
700 Sutter Ave 11207 718-385-8666
Yvette Donald, prin. Fax 345-8118

Public S 150 200/K-5
364 Sackman St 11212 718-495-7746
Tracey Quarles, prin. Fax 922-3785

Public S 151 400/PK-5
763 Knickerbocker Ave 11207 718-326-6360
Jayne Hunt, prin. Fax 821-0166

Public S 153 500/PK-5
1970 Homecrest Ave 11229 718-375-4484
Carl Santamaria, prin. Fax 375-4439

Public S 155 500/PK-8
1355 Herkimer St 11233 718-240-4340
Michelle Manns, prin. Fax 345-9064

Public S 156 800/PK-5
104 Sutter Ave 11212 718-498-2811
Naiyma Moore, prin. Fax 346-2804

Public S 157 500/PK-8
850 Kent Ave 11205 718-622-9285
Kourtney Boyd, prin. Fax 398-4155

Public S 158 600/PK-5
400 Ashford St 11207 718-277-6116
Audrey Wilson, prin. Fax 827-4300

Public S 159 800/K-5
2781 Pitkin Ave 11208 718-277-4828
Monica Duncan, prin. Fax 827-4531

Public S 160 1,300/K-5
5105 Fort Hamilton Pkwy 11219 718-438-0337
Margaret Russo, prin. Fax 871-7920

Public S 161 500/K-8
330 Crown St 11225 718-756-3100
Michael Johnson, prin. Fax 953-3605

Public S 163 600/K-8
109 Bay 14th St 11214 718-236-9003
Jessica Riccio, prin. Fax 259-3042

Public S 164 500/PK-5
4211 14th Ave 11219 718-854-4100
Erica Steinberg, prin. Fax 853-9306

Public S 165 500/PK-8
76 Lott Ave 11212 718-495-7759
Jason Rivers, prin. Fax 345-8255

Public S 169 1,600/K-5
4305 7th Ave 11232 718-853-3224
Eujin Tang, prin. Fax 633-9621

Public S 172 600/PK-5
825 4th Ave 11232 718-965-4200
Giacomo Spatola, prin. Fax 965-2468

Public S 176 1,400/K-5
1225 69th St 11219 718-236-7755
Elizabeth Culkin, prin. Fax 331-9188

Public S 177 900/PK-5
346 Avenue P 11204 718-375-9506
Ann Marie Lettieri-Baker, prin. Fax 375-4450

Public S 178 500/PK-8
2163 Dean St 11233 718-495-7768
Joseph Henry, prin. Fax 495-2304

Public S 179 1,000/PK-5
202 Avenue C 11218 718-438-4010
Bernal Thomas, prin. Fax 871-7484

Public S 181 1,000/PK-8
1023 New York Ave 11203 718-462-5298
Victor Esannason, prin. Fax 284-5053

Public S 184 600/PK-8
273 Newport St 11212 718-495-7775
Lisa Caldwell-Linder, prin. Fax 385-4655

Public S 185 700/K-5
8601 Ridge Blvd 11209 718-745-6610
Rena Goudelias, prin. Fax 836-9631

Public S 186 1,000/PK-5
7601 19th Ave 11214 718-236-7071
Bayan Cadotte, prin. Fax 331-9181

Public S 188 500/PK-5
3314 Neptune Ave 11224 718-265-7580
Janice Dalton, prin. Fax 266-7103

Public S 189 1,200/K-8
1100 E New York Ave 11212 718-756-0210
Berthe Faustin, prin. Fax 604-1865

Public S 190 200/PK-5
590 Sheffield Ave 11207 718-346-8780
Stephaun Hill, prin. Fax 345-8765

Public S 191 200/PK-5
1600 Park Pl 11233 718-756-1206
Elsi Capolongo, prin. Fax 756-5417

Public S 192 600/PK-8
4715 18th Ave 11204 718-633-3061
Liset Isaac, prin. Fax 871-8721

Public S 193 900/PK-5
2515 Avenue L 11210 718-338-9011
Shelia Phillip, prin. Fax 338-9074

Public S 194 500/PK-5
3117 Avenue W 11229 718-648-8804
Joy Mendelsohn, prin. Fax 934-0244

Public S 195 500/PK-5
131 Irwin St 11235 718-648-9102
Bernadette Toomey, prin. Fax 934-0625

Public S 196 400/PK-5
207 Bushwick Ave 11206 718-497-0139
Janine Santaromita, prin. Fax 628-5134

Public S 197 500/PK-5
1599 E 22nd St 11210 718-377-7890
Rosemarie Nicoletti, prin. Fax 377-7505

Public S 198 500/PK-5
4105 Farragut Rd 11210 718-282-4920
Joy-Ann Morgan, prin. Fax 940-0821

Public S 199 500/PK-5
1100 Elm Ave 11230 718-339-1422
Rosalia Bacarella, prin. Fax 336-5562

Public S 200 1,300/PK-5
1940 Benson Ave 11214 718-236-5466
Javier Muniz, prin. Fax 232-3428

Public S 202 700/PK-8
982 Hegeman Ave 11208 718-649-7880
Ronald James, prin. Fax 927-2173

Public S 203 800/PK-5
5101 Avenue M 11234 718-241-8488
Yocasta Dominguez-Miller, prin. Fax 209-9641

Public S 204 1,200/PK-5
8101 15th Ave 11228 718-236-2906
Nancy Tomasuolo, prin. Fax 232-9265

Public S 205 1,000/PK-5
6701 20th Ave 11204 718-236-2380
Beth Grater, prin. Fax 331-7299

Public S 206 1,400/PK-8
2200 Gravesend Neck Rd 11229 718-743-5598
Ellen Quigley, prin. Fax 332-4986

Public S 207 1,300/PK-8
4011 Fillmore Ave 11234 718-645-8667
Terri Contursi, prin. Fax 645-8139

Public S 208 500/PK-5
4801 Avenue D 11203 718-629-1670
Nakoley Renville, prin. Fax 451-0185

Public S 209 700/PK-8
2609 E 7th St 11235 718-743-1954
Frances Locurcio, prin. Fax 743-6361

Public S 212 700/PK-5
87 Bay 49th St 11214 718-266-4841
Rina Horne, prin. Fax 266-7080

Public S 213 400/PK-5
580 Hegeman Ave 11207 718-257-4034
Stanley Moise, prin. Fax 272-3446

Public S 214 1,000/PK-5
2944 Pitkin Ave 11208 718-647-1740
Sharon Mahabi, prin. Fax 827-5838

Public S 215 900/PK-5
415 Avenue S 11223 718-339-2464
Antonella Bove, prin. Fax 998-7235

Public S 216 600/PK-5
350 Avenue X 11223 718-645-2862
Donna Neglia, prin. Fax 645-2610

Public S 217 1,300/PK-5
1100 Newkirk Ave 11230 718-434-6960
Robert Bonilla, prin. Fax 434-8170

Public S 219 600/PK-5
1060 Clarkson Ave 11212 718-342-0493
Winsome Smith, prin. Fax 345-3065

Public S 221 400/PK-5
791 Empire Blvd 11213 718-756-0122
Stephanie Martin, prin. Fax 953-2657

Public S 222 900/PK-5
3301 Quentin Rd 11234 718-998-4298
Theresa Olivieri, prin. Fax 339-2107

Public S 224 600/PK-6
757 Wortman Ave 11208 718-235-3600
Rochelle Hinds, prin. Fax 827-5840

Public S 225 900/PK-8
1075 Ocean View Ave 11235 718-743-9793
Michael Cosmai, prin. Fax 743-7096

Public S 226 1,000/PK-8
6006 23rd Ave 11204 718-234-4940
Evan Klein, prin. Fax 256-0384

Public S 229 1,100/PK-8
1400 Benson Ave 11228 718-236-5447
Robert Zappulla, prin. Fax 331-8173

Public S 230 1,300/PK-5
1 Albemarle Rd 11218 718-437-6135
Maria Della Ragione, prin. Fax 871-2624

Public S 233 500/PK-5
9301 Avenue B 11236 718-346-8103
Denean Stephens-Spellman, prin. Fax 345-3078

Public S 235 1,200/PK-8
525 Lenox Rd 11203 718-773-4869
Laurence Lord, prin. Fax 773-0048

Public S 236 600/PK-5
6302 Avenue U 11234 718-444-6969
Salil Paingankar, prin. Fax 241-6630

Public S 238 500/PK-8
1633 E 8th St 11223 718-339-4355
Harla Musoff-Weiss, prin. Fax 998-4351

Public S 241 700/PK-5
976 President St 11225 718-636-4725
Frantz Lucius, prin. Fax 230-5468

Public S 243 300/PK-5
1580 Dean St 11213 718-604-6909
Karen Glover, prin. Fax 778-0492

Public S 244 700/PK-5
5404 Tilden Ave 11203 718-346-6240
Deon Edwards, prin. Fax 345-3083

Public S 245 300/PK-5
249 E 17th St 11226 718-284-2330
Erica Williams, prin. Fax 856-0646

Public S 247 800/PK-5
7000 21st Ave 11204 718-236-4205
Christopher Ogno, prin. Fax 331-8563

Public S 249 800/PK-5
18 Marlborough Rd 11226 718-282-8828
Elisa Brown, prin. Fax 284-5146

Public S 250 800/PK-5
108 Montrose Ave 11206 718-384-0889
Roseann Lacioppa, prin. Fax 302-2314

Public S 251 600/PK-5
1037 E 54th St 11234 718-251-4110
Sheldon Noel, prin. Fax 241-3200

Public S 253 800/PK-5
601 Ocean View Ave 11235 718-332-3331
Lisa Speroni, prin. Fax 743-7194

Public S 254 700/PK-5
1801 Avenue Y 11235 718-743-0890
John Norton, prin. Fax 332-4477

Public S 255 900/PK-5
1866 E 17th St 11229 718-376-8494
Kelly McCann, prin. Fax 627-0626

Public S 256 400/PK-5
114 Kosciuszko St 11216 718-857-9820
Sharyn Hemphill, prin. Fax 783-7384

Public S 257 700/PK-5
60 Cook St 11206 718-384-7128
Brian DeVale, prin. Fax 387-8115

Public S 261 800/PK-6
314 Pacific St 11201 718-330-9275
Jackie Allen, prin. Fax 875-9503

Public S 262 500/PK-8
500 Macon St 11233 718-453-0780
Joeletha Ferguson, prin. Fax 453-0679

Public S 264 100/PK-5
371 89th St 11209 718-630-1650
Patrice Edison, prin. Fax 630-1655

Public S 268 500/PK-5
133 E 53rd St 11203 718-773-5332
Sylvia Fairclough, prin. Fax 493-7448

Public S 269 400/3-5
1957 Nostrand Ave 11210 718-941-2800
Jazmine Santiago, prin. Fax 940-3098

Public S 270 200/PK-5
241 Emerson Pl 11205 718-623-5280
Alyssa Roye, prin. Fax 622-3370

Public S 272 600/PK-5
10124 Seaview Ave 11236 718-241-1300
Dakota Keyes, prin. Fax 241-5549

Public S 273 300/K-5
923 Jerome St 11207 718-649-5739
Melissa Avery, prin. Fax 927-2230

Public S 274 600/PK-5
800 Bushwick Ave 11221 718-574-0273
Maritza Jones, prin. Fax 574-1059

Public S 276 800/PK-5
1070 E 83rd St 11236 718-241-5757
Yasmine Fidelia, prin. Fax 241-5560

Public S 277 500/PK-5
2529 Gerritsen Ave 11229 718-743-6689
Theresa Vlantis, prin. Fax 368-0920

Public S 279 500/PK-5
1070 E 104th St 11236 718-444-4316
Lorenzo Chambers, prin. Fax 241-5581

Public S 282 1,000/PK-8
180 6th Ave 11217 718-622-1626
Rashan Hoke, prin. Fax 622-3471

Public S 287 200/PK-5
50 Navy St 11201 718-834-4745
Michele Rawlins, prin. Fax 834-6766

Public S 288 500/PK-8
2950 W 25th St 11224 718-382-2100
Qadir Dixon, prin. Fax 449-7682

Public S 289 500/PK-5
900 Saint Marks Ave 11213 718-493-3824
Marc Mardy, prin. Fax 467-3735

Public S 290 600/PK-5
135 Schenck Ave 11207 718-647-1113
Brigitte Newell, prin. Fax 827-5842

Public S 295 500/PK-5
330 18th St 11215 718-965-0390
Deanna Marco, prin. Fax 965-0603

Public S 297 300/PK-5
700 Park Ave 11206 718-388-4581
James Brown, prin. Fax 302-2315

Public S 298 300/PK-8
85 Watkins St 11212 718-495-7793
Jonathan Dill, prin. Fax 566-8770

Public S 299 400/PK-5
88 Woodbine St 11221 718-473-8230
Wilma Kirk, prin. Fax 574-1080

Public S 305 200/PK-5
344 Monroe St 11216 718-789-3962
Dr. Julia Mortley, prin. Fax 622-3474

Public S 306 700/PK-8
970 Vermont St 11207 718-649-3155
Lenika Vane, prin. Fax 927-2243

Public S 307 400/PK-5
209 York St 11201 718-834-4748
Stephanie Carroll, prin. Fax 855-4181

Public S 308 400/PK-8
616 Quincy St 11221 718-574-2373
Sharon Odwin, prin. Fax 453-0663

Public S 309 300/PK-5
794 Monroe St 11221 718-574-2381
Tanya Bryant, prin. Fax 453-0643

Public S 310 100/PK-3
942 62nd St 11219 718-491-7670
Yuqing Hong, prin. Fax 765-4635

Public S 312 900/PK-5
7103 Avenue T 11234 718-763-4015
Sungmin Yoo, prin. Fax 531-2796

Public S 315 800/PK-5
2310 Glenwood Rd 11210 718-421-9560
Judith Ranft, prin. Fax 421-9561

Public S 316 300/PK-5
750 Classon Ave 11238 718-638-4043
Olga Maluf, prin. Fax 230-5366

Public S 319 200/PK-1
360 Keap St 11211 718-388-1588
Aleyda Zamora-Martinez, prin. Fax 302-2316

Public S 321 1,500/PK-5
180 7th Ave 11215 718-499-2412
Elizabeth Phillips, prin. Fax 965-9605

Public S 323 400/PK-8
210 Chester St 11212 718-495-7781
Linda Harris, prin. Fax 346-4614

Public S 326 200/PK-2
1000 Utica Ave 11234 718-241-4828
Colleen Ducey, prin. Fax 763-5567

Public S 327 600/PK-8
111 Bristol St 11212 718-495-7801
Georgette Malcolm, prin. Fax 495-7828

Public S 328 400/PK-8
330 Alabama Ave 11207 718-345-9393
Marie Desforges, prin. Fax 345-6566

Public S 329 400/PK-5
2929 W 30th St 11224 718-996-3800
Selema Marbury, prin. Fax 265-1525

Public S 335 400/PK-5
130 Rochester Ave 11213 718-493-7736
Karena Thompson, prin. Fax 953-4697

Public S 345 700/PK-5
111 Berriman St 11208 718-647-8387
Wanda Holt, prin. Fax 827-5884

Public S 346 700/PK-5
1400 Pennsylvania Ave 11239 718-642-3000
Kevin Caifa, prin. Fax 642-8498

Public S 361 700/PK-2
3109 Newkirk Ave 11226 718-856-0600
Tiffany Frazier, prin. Fax 856-0300

Public S 375 500/PK-5
46 McKeever Pl 11225 718-693-6655
Schwanna Ellman, prin. Fax 284-6433

Public S 376 600/K-5
194 Harman St 11237 718-573-0781
Maria Vera, prin. Fax 573-0769

Public S 377 500/PK-8
200 Woodbine St 11221 718-574-0325
Dominic Zagarni, prin. Fax 574-1082

Public S 380 600/PK-5
370 Marcy Ave 11206 718-388-0607
Victoria Prisinzano, prin. Fax 599-3231

Public S 384 700/PK-8
242 Cooper St 11207 718-574-0382
Claudia Harris, prin. Fax 574-1364

Public S 394 600/PK-8
188 Rochester Ave 11213 718-756-3164
Sojourner Welch-David, prin. Fax 756-3177

Public S 397 300/K-5
490 Fenimore St 11203 718-774-5200
Marie Casseus Monteau, prin. Fax 953-4856

Public S 398 400/PK-5
60 E 94th St 11212 718-774-4466
Tammy Brown, prin. Fax 467-4018

Public S 399 500/K-5
2707 Albemarle Rd 11226 718-693-3023
Marion Brown, prin. Fax 940-0702

Public S 503 1,000/K-5
330 59th St 11220 718-439-5962
Nina Demos, prin. Fax 439-0948

Public S 506, 330 59th St 11220 800/PK-5
Dana Parentini, prin. 718-492-0087

Public S 748 400/PK-3
1664 Benson Ave 11214 718-382-3130
Ursula Annio, prin. Fax 382-3140

Public S 770 200/K-5
60 E 94th St 11212 718-221-5837
Jessica Saratovsky, prin. Fax 221-5947

Public S 971 200/PK-2
6214 4th Ave 11220 718-765-2200
Ruth Stanislaus, prin. Fax 765-2205

Red Hook Neighborhood S 200/PK-5
27 Huntington St 11231 718-330-2238
Priscilla Figueroa, prin. Fax 596-6446

Riverdale Avenue Community S PK-2
76 Riverdale Ave 11212 718-485-1679
Meghan Dunn, prin.

Riverdale Avenue MS 50/6-7
76 Riverdale Ave 11212 718-346-0764
Yolanda Lawrence, prin. Fax 346-1783

Satellite East 200/6-8
344 Monroe St 11216 718-789-4251
Kim McPherson, prin. Fax 789-4823

School of Integrated Learning 200/6-8
1224 Park Pl 11213 718-774-0362
Monique Campbell, prin. Fax 774-0521

School of the Future Brooklyn 100/6-8
574 Dumont Ave 11207 718-345-5190
Sarah Kaufmann, prin. Fax 345-5196

Science and Medicine MS 400/6-8
965 E 107th St 11236 718-688-6400
Dennis Herring, prin. Fax 688-6401

Seeall Academy 1,100/PK-8
5601 16th Ave 11204 718-851-8070
Gary Williams, prin. Fax 853-9308

Sendak Community S 100/PK-3
211 8th St 11215 718-840-5660
W. Elizabet Garraway, prin. Fax 840-5666

Stroud MS 300/6-8
750 Classon Ave 11238 718-638-3067
Tricia Delauney, prin. Fax 638-3515

Sunset Park Avenues ES 100/PK-3
4222 4th Ave 11232 718-369-8330
Jill Smith, prin. Fax 840-1982

Sunset Park Prep MS 500/6-8
4004 4th Ave 11232 718-840-1951
Jennifer Spalding, prin. Fax 965-3330

Twain Gifted & Talented S 1,300/6-8
2401 Neptune Ave 11224 718-266-0814
Karen Ditolla, prin. Fax 266-1693

Urban Assembly Unison S 6-8
170 Gates Ave 11238 718-399-1061
Emily Paige, prin.

Van Siclen Community MS 100/6-8
800 Van Siclen Ave 11207 718-927-4701
Adonna Mcfarland, prin. Fax 927-4707

Vista Academy 100/6-8
350 Linwood St 11208 718-647-0913
Bernard Addo, prin. Fax 647-0919

Windsor Terrace ES 500/PK-5
1625 11th Ave 11215 718-768-0057
Michael Buckley, prin. Fax 832-2573

Adelphi Academy of Brooklyn 100/PK-12
8515 Ridge Blvd 11209 718-238-3308
Iphigenia Romanos, head sch Fax 238-2894

Ahi Ezer Yeshiva 200/PK-8
2433 Ocean Pkwy 11235 718-648-6100
Emily Setton, admin. Fax 648-5521

Al Madrasa Al Islamiya S 200/PK-8
5224 3rd Ave 11220 718-567-3334
Amateka Morgan, admin. Fax 567-7383

Al-Noor S 600/PK-12
675 4th Ave 11232 718-768-7181
Abdulhakeem Alhasel, prin. Fax 768-7088

Arista Prep Academy 100/PK-8
221 Kingston Ave 11213 718-756-5550
Artemas Julien Ph.D., prin. Fax 493-0299

Bais Brocha Stolin Karlin 500/PK-12
4314 10th Ave 11219 718-853-1222
Rabbi Ephraim Scherman, admin. Fax 851-0112

Bais Esther S 300/PK-12
1353 50th St 11219 718-436-1234
Mindy Klein, dir. Fax 436-1320

Bais Isaac Zvi 200/PK-1
1019 46th St 11219 718-854-7777
Sally Rosen, prin. Fax 854-6642

Bais Rochel S for Girls 50/1-8
241 Keap St 11211 718-963-9292
Rabbi Hertz Frankel, prin. Fax 387-9216

Bais Rochel S of Boro Park 400/K-12
5301 14th Ave 11219 718-438-7822
Mindy Margulies, prin. Fax 438-3153

Bais Ruchel D'Satmar 3-12
84 Sandford St 11205 718-422-0375
F. Mittelman, prin. Fax 624-2819

Bais Sarah Girls S 900/PK-12
6101 16th Ave 11204 718-871-7571
Nuchem Klein, dean Fax 871-3615

Bais Tziporah S 400/PK-12
1449 39th St 11218 718-436-0336
Moshe Melamed, dir. Fax 436-1201

Bais Yaakov Academy 900/PK-12
1213 Elm Ave 11230 718-339-4747
Bais Yaakov Adas Yereim 500/PK-12
563 Bedford Ave 11211 718-302-7500
D. Ausch, prin. Fax 384-5885

Bais Yaakov Adas Yereim 300/PK-12
1169 43rd St 11219 718-435-5111
Esther Loewy, prin. Fax 435-0968

Bais Yaakov D'Chassidei Gur 500/PK-12
1975 51st St 11204 718-338-5600
Chanie Wosner, prin. Fax 338-5974

Bais Yaakov of 18th Avenue 300/PK-8
4419 18th Ave 11204 718-633-6050
Rabbi D. Pitterman, admin. Fax 633-6052

Bais Yaakov of Bensonhurst 50/PK-8
3901 14th Ave 11218 718-871-6400
Sarah Reit, prin. Fax 431-0770

Bais Yaakov Sara Dabah 100/PK-9
2221 Avenue R 11229 718-513-1931

Barkai Yeshivah 400/PK-8
5302 21st Ave 11204 718-998-7473
Ahuva Halberstam, head sch Fax 758-3551

BASIS Independent Brooklyn PK-12
556 Columbia St 11231 917-473-1615
Hadley Ruggles, head sch

Battalion Christian Academy 200/PK-5
661 Linden Blvd 11203 718-774-5447
Dr. Alfred Cockfield, dir. Fax 774-4295

Bay Ridge Christian Academy 200/PK-8
6324 7th Ave 11220 718-238-4000
Judith Vega, prin. Fax 560-2980

Bay Ridge Preparatory S 400/K-12
8101 Ridge Blvd 11209 718-833-9090
Dr. Charles Fasano, head sch Fax 833-6680

Be'er Hagolah Institutes 500/PK-12
671 Louisiana Ave 11239 718-642-6800
Sheila Taub, prin. Fax 642-4740

Beikvei Hatzoin S 200/PK-12
31 Division Ave 11249 718-486-6363
Shaindy Gross, prin. Fax 486-6639

Beis Chaya Mushka 200/PK-12
1505 Carroll St 11213 718-756-0770
Rabbi Levi Plotkin, prin. Fax 493-9336

Beis Frima Chinuch Ctr 300/PK-10
1377 42nd St 11219 718-438-3061
Rabbi Steve Frankel, dir.

Belz Girls S 1,100/PK-12
600 McDonald Ave 11218 718-871-0500
Berel Hecht, dir. Fax 435-4456

Berkeley Carroll S 300/PK-4
701 Carroll St 11215 718-534-6601
Robert Vitalo, head sch Fax 568-4378

Beth Chana S PK-K
204 Keap St 11211 718-388-5491

Beth Chana S 300/1-12
712 Bedford Ave 11206 718-935-1845
Fishel Taub, prin. Fax 935-1863

Bethel ES 50/PK-8
457 Grand Ave 11238 718-789-3630

Beth Jacob of Boro Park 1,800/PK-8
PO Box 199036 11219 718-436-7300
Basya Weinstein, prin. Fax 436-7358

Beth Jacob S 500/PK-8
85 Parkville Ave 11230 718-633-6555
Rabbi Michael Levi, prin. Fax 633-2930

Beth Rivka Girls S 1,000/K-8
470 Lefferts Ave 11225 718-735-0770
Leah Jacobson, prin. Fax 735-4712

Bet Yaakov Ateret Torah S 600/PK-8
2166 Coney Island Ave 11223 718-732-7770
Joanna Levi, prin. Fax 732-7766

Big Apple Academy 900/K-8
2937 86th St 11223 718-333-0300
Dr. Vlad Gorny, prin. Fax 333-1311

Blessed Sacrament Catholic Academy 300/PK-8
187 Euclid Ave 11208 718-235-4863
Marylou Celmer, prin. Fax 235-1132

Bnei Shimon Yisroel of Sopron 300/PK-9
18 Warsoff Pl 11205 718-855-4092
Rosa Friedman, admin. Fax 855-8479

Bnos Chayil S 600/PK-6
345 Hewes St 11211 718-388-6201
Moses Markowitz, prin. Fax 486-5059

Bnos Margulia Viznitz 200/PK-11
1824 53rd St 11204 718-234-2050
Taub Mayer, prin. Fax 232-2844

Bnos Menachem S for Girls 600/PK-12
739 E New York Ave 11203 718-493-1100
Rabbi Zalman Wilhelm, admin. Fax 493-4836

Bnos Yaakov Educational Center 600/1-12
62 Harrison Ave 11211 718-387-7905

Bnos Yaakov Educational Kindervelt 50/PK-K
274 Keap St 11211 718-387-6880

Bnos Yaakov Pupa 900/PK-12
1402 40th St 11218 718-851-0316

Bnos Yisroel S 300/K-8
1629 E 15th St 11229 718-339-4229
Rabbi Boruch Barnetsky, dean Fax 339-4229

Bnos Yisroel Viznitz S 500/PK-12
12 Franklin Ave 11249 718-330-0222
Eva Rozman, prin. Fax 858-7387

Bnos Zion of Bobov PK-8
1462 62nd St 11219 718-438-0060

Bnos Zion of Bobov 1,400/PK-12
5000 14th Ave 11219 718-438-3080
Benzion Stiel, admin. Fax 438-3144

Bobover Yeshiva Bnei Zion 1,200/K-10
4206 15th Ave 11219 718-851-4000
Heshie Dembitzer, admin. Fax 972-5305

Brooklyn Amity S 200/PK-12
3867 Shore Pkwy 11235 718-891-6100
Eljasa Jashar, prin. Fax 891-6841

Brooklyn Friends S 800/PK-12
375 Pearl St 11201 718-852-1029
Dr. Larry Weiss, head sch Fax 643-4868

Brooklyn Heights Montessori S 200/PK-8
185 Court St 11201 718-858-5100
Martha Haakmat, head sch Fax 858-0500

Brooklyn Jesuit Prep S 100/5-8
560 Sterling Pl 11238 718-638-5884
Gregory Arte, prin. Fax 228-6324

Brooklyn SDA S 100/PK-8
1260 Ocean Ave 11230 718-859-1313
Laura Mayne, prin. Fax 859-8105

Brooklyn Waldorf S 200/PK-8
11 Jefferson Ave 11238 718-783-3270
Christna Pantazis-Blade, admin.

Chatzar Hakodesh Sanz-Klausenberg 700/PK-12
945 39th St 11219 718-436-1248

Cheder S 400/PK-8
129 Elmwood Ave 11230 718-252-6333
Rabbi Meir Gutfreund, prin. Fax 252-4574

Christian Heritage Academy 300/PK-12
1100 E 42nd St 11210 718-377-5682
Rev. Paul Meyerend, dir. Fax 338-9870

Congregation Khal Chasidei Skwer 500/1-8
4500 9th Ave 11220 718-853-9400
Esther Twersky, prin Fax 853-3042

East Midwood Hebrew Day S 200/PK-8
1256 E 21st St 11210 718-253-1555
Shirley Weichselbaum, prin. Fax 338-3934

Ebenezer Prep S 200/PK-8
5464 Kings Hwy 11203 718-629-4231

Epiphany Lutheran ES 200/PK-8
721 Lincoln Pl 11216 718-773-7200
Judy Evans-Gayle, prin. Fax 773-1244
Ericson S 200/PK-8
1037 72nd St 11228 718-748-9023
Christine Hauge, prin. Fax 748-0473
Excelsior S, 418 E 45th St 11203 100/K-8
Ivanhoe Douglas, prin. 718-693-5502
Fantis Parochial S 200/PK-8
195 State St 11201 718-624-0501
Maria Perdik-Zolotas, head sch Fax 624-6868
Flatbush SDA S 100/PK-5
5810 Snyder Ave 11203 718-922-6390
Followers of Jesus S 50/1-12
3065 Atlantic Ave 11208 718-235-5493
Richard Schwartz, prin. Fax 484-1477
Gan Yisroel S 200/PK-K
3909 15th Ave 11218 718-853-9853
Rabbi Aron Ginsberg, dir. Fax 853-9854
Gan Yisroel S PK-8
13 Church Ave 11218 718-435-0101
Gan Yisroel S 100/1-9
1581 52nd St 11219 718-436-9130
Good Shepherd Catholic Academy 300/PK-8
1943 Brown St 11229 718-339-2745
John O'Brien, prin. Fax 645-4513
Great Oaks ES 100/PK-8
4718 Farragut Rd 11203 718-282-6210
Jasmin Hoyt, prin. Fax 282-5615
Greene Hill S 100/PK-8
39 Adelphi St 11205 718-230-3608
Diana Schlesinger, dir. Fax 222-1971
Hanson Place SDA S 100/PK-8
38 Lafayette Ave 11217 718-625-3030
Pauline Evans, prin. Fax 625-1727
Ha'or Beacon S 50/PK-8
2884 Nostrand Ave 11229 718-951-3650
Hebron SDA Bilingual Union S 200/PK-8
920 Park Pl 11213 718-533-4923
Gladly Grant, prin. Fax 533-4926
Holy Angels Catholic Academy 200/PK-8
337 74th St 11209 718-238-5045
Rosemarie McGoldrick, prin. Fax 748-9775
International S of Brooklyn PK-8
477 Court St 11231 718-369-3023
Rebecca Skinner, prin. Fax 795-1998
Kaloidis Parochial S 200/PK-8
8502 Ridge Blvd 11209 718-836-8096
Lefferts Gardens Montessori S 50/PK-4
527 Rogers Ave 11225 718-773-0287
Micaela Almeda, prin. Fax 693-1696
Lev Bais Yaakov S 400/PK-12
3574 Nostrand Ave 11229 718-332-6000
Lubavitcher S 100/PK-12
841 Ocean Pkwy 11230 718-735-6601
Rabbi Dov Baron, prin.
Lubavitcher Yeshiva S 400/K-8
570 Crown St 11213 718-774-4131
Joseph Simpson, prin. Fax 756-5324
Lutheran ES of Bay Ridge 200/PK-8
440 Ovington Ave 11209 718-748-9502
Lorraine Tuccillo, prin. Fax 748-0818
Magen David Yeshivah 1,600/PK-8
2130 McDonald Ave 11223 718-954-3305
Alan Berkowitz, prin. Fax 954-3315
Mary Queen of Heaven Catholic Academy 300/PK-8
1326 E 57th St 11234 718-763-2360
Mary Bellone, prin. Fax 763-7540
Masores Bais Yaakov S 800/PK-12
1395 Ocean Ave 11230 718-692-2424
Shaindy Pinter, prin. Fax 692-3162
Me'orot Beit Yaakov S 50/PK-12
1123 Avenue N 11230 718-627-8758
Rabbi David Maslaton, prin. Fax 336-0149
Mercaz Gan/Yeshiva Ohel Sarah 100/PK-8
2221 Avenue R 11229 718-513-1931
Fax 462-4169
Midwood Catholic Academy 300/K-8
1501 Hendrickson St 11234 718-377-1800
Elena Heimbach, prin. Fax 377-6374
Mill Basin Yeshiva Academy 300/PK-8
6363 Avenue U 11234 718-444-5800
Rabbi Refael Farhi, prin. Fax 444-5851
Mirrer Yeshiva Educational Institute 500/PK-8
1791 Ocean Pkwy 11223 718-375-4321
Maita Rosenblum, admin. Fax 375-6501
Mosdos Chasidei Square 300/K-12
1373 43rd St 11219 718-436-2550
Nefesh Academy 100/PK-12
2005 E 17th St 11229 718-627-4463
Sandra Newhouse, prin.
Nesivos Bais Yaakov 300/PK-12
1021 45th St 11219 718-972-5858
New Grace Education Center 200/PK-8
650 Livonia Ave 11207 718-498-7175
Denaro Liverpool, prin. Fax 498-1656
Oholei Torah - Oholei Menachem 1,000/PK-8
667 Eastern Pkwy 11213 718-774-5050
Joseph Rosenfeld, dir.
Our Lady of Grace Catholic Academy 300/PK-8
385 Avenue W 11223 718-375-2081
Kelly Wolf, prin. Fax 376-7685
Our Lady of Guadalupe Academy 300/PK-8
1514 72nd St 11228 718-331-2070
Muriel Wilkinson, prin. Fax 331-2070
Our Lady of Perpetual Help Academy 200/PK-8
5902 6th Ave 11220 718-439-8067
Margaret Tyndall, prin. Fax 439-8081
Our Lady of Trust School at Saint Jude 300/PK-8
1696 Canarsie Rd 11236 718-241-6633
Arlene Barcia, prin. Fax 531-8012
Packer Collegiate Institute 1,000/PK-12
170 Joralemon St 11201 718-250-0200
Dr. Bruce Dennis, head sch Fax 875-1363
Phyl's Academy 400/PK-5
3520 Tilden Ave 11203 718-469-9400
Abenaa Frempong, prin. Fax 284-1438

Poly Prep Country Day S 200/PK-4
50 Prospect Park W 11215 718-768-1103
Audrius Barzdukas, hdmstr. Fax 768-1687
Prospect Park Yeshiva 500/1-8
1784 E 17th St 11229 718-376-4446
Arlene Klestzick, prin. Fax 382-9185
Prospect Park Yeshiva ECC 200/PK-K
1784 E 17th St 11229 718-376-5959
Queen of All Saints Catholic Academy 200/K-8
300 Vanderbilt Ave 11205 718-857-3114
Manuela Adsuar-Pizzi, prin. Fax 857-0632
Queen of the Rosary Academy 200/PK-8
11 Catherine St 11211 718-388-7992
James Daino, prin. Fax 388-7543
St. Agatha S 200/PK-8
736 48th St 11220 718-435-3137
Maximo Catala, prin. Fax 437-7505
St. Ann's S 1,100/PK-12
129 Pierrepont St 11201 718-522-1660
Vincent Tompkins, hdmstr. Fax 522-2599
St. Anselm S 400/PK-8
365 83rd St 11209 718-745-7643
James McKeown, prin. Fax 745-0086
St. Athanasius Academy 300/PK-8
6120 Bay Pkwy 11204 718-236-4791
Diane Competello, prin. Fax 621-1423
St. Bernadette Academy 400/PK-8
1313 83rd St 11228 718-236-1560
Sr. Joan DiRienzo, prin. Fax 236-3364
St. Bernard Catholic Academy 300/PK-8
2030 E 69th St 11234 718-241-6040
Kathleen Buscemi, prin. Fax 241-7258
St. Brigid Catholic Academy 200/PK-8
438 Grove St 11237 718-821-1477
Marcia Soria, prin. Fax 821-1079
St. Catherine-St. Therese Catholic Acad 300/PK-8
4410 Avenue D 11203 718-629-9330
Sr. Jeannette Charles, prin. Fax 629-6854
St. Edmund S 300/PK-8
1902 Avenue T 11229 718-648-9229
Andrea D'Emic, prin. Fax 743-6402
St. Ephrem S 300/PK-8
924 74th St 11228 718-833-1440
Craig Mercado, prin. Fax 745-5301
St. Frances Cabrini Catholic Academy 300/PK-8
181 Suydam St 11221 718-386-9277
Allison Murphy, prin. Fax 386-9064
St. Francis of Assisi Catholic Academy 300/K-8
400 Lincoln Rd 11225 718-778-3700
Danielle Gonzalez, prin. Fax 778-7877
St. Francis Xavier S 200/K-8
763 President St 11215 718-857-2559
Dorothy Taylor, prin. Fax 857-5391
St. Gregory the Great Catholic Academy 200/PK-8
2520 Church Ave 11226 718-774-3330
Rudolph Cyrus-Charles, prin. Fax 774-3332
St. Joseph the Worker Catholic Academy PK-8
241 Prospect Park W 11215 718-768-7629
Kathleen Schneck, prin. Fax 768-3007
St. Mark Catholic Academy 200/PK-8
2602 E 19th St 11235 718-332-9304
Caroline Donnelly, prin. Fax 274-0575
St. Mark S 300/PK-8
1346 President St 11213 718-756-6602
Derick Smith, prin. Fax 467-4655
St. Patrick Catholic Academy 300/PK-8
401 97th St 11209 718-833-0124
Kathleen Curatolo, prin. Fax 238-6480
St. Peter Catholic Academy 300/PK-8
8401 23rd Ave 11214 718-372-0025
Danielle Alfeo, prin. Fax 265-6498
St. Saviour S 400/PK-8
701 8th Ave 11215 718-768-8000
Susan Walsh, prin. Fax 768-0373
St. Stanislaus Kostka Academy 200/PK-8
12 Newell St 11222 718-383-1970
Christina Cieloszczyk, prin. Fax 383-1711
Salve Regina Catholic Academy 300/PK-8
237 Jerome St 11207 718-277-6766
Michelle Donato, prin. Fax 348-0513
Senesh Community Day S 200/K-8
342 Smith St 11231 718-858-8663
Nicole Nash, head sch Fax 858-7190
Shalsheles Bais Yaakov S 100/1-12
1681 42nd St 11204 718-436-1122
Esti Goodstein, prin. Fax 436-9073
Talmud Torah Bnei Zion D'Bobov PK-K
1362 49th St 11219 718-851-3937
Talmud Torah Bnei Zion D'Bobov 1-9
1315 43rd St 11219 718-431-9595
Talmud Torah D'Rabinu Yoel S 1,200/K-6
5411 Fort Hamilton Pkwy 11219 718-854-2476
Talmud Torah Imrei Chaim 600/PK-8
1824 53rd St 11204 718-234-2000
Rabbi Mayer Taub, admin. Fax 236-0970
Talmud Torah Ohr Moshe 200/PK-12
1774 58th St 11204 718-234-6100
Talmud Torah Tiferes Bunim Munkacs 200/PK-8
5202 13th Ave 11219 718-436-6868
Yehoshua Gelb, dir. Fax 854-1879
Talmud Torah Toldos Yakov Yosef 200/K-8
105 Heyward St 11206 718-852-0502
Rabbi Mordechai Friesel, prin. Fax 852-0512
United Talmudical Academy 500/PK-12
82 Lee Ave 11211 718-963-9260
C.Y. Mandel, prin. Fax 963-9498
United Talmudical Academy 1,200/PK-6
5411 Fort Hamilton Pkwy 11219 718-438-7822
Visitation Academy 200/PK-8
8902 Ridge Blvd 11209 718-680-9452
Arlene Figaro, prin. Fax 680-4441
Whitfield S 600/PK-8
PO Box 384 11208 718-342-7722
Janie Whitney, prin. Fax 342-7775
WIlliamsburg Northside S 100/PK-8
299 N 7th St 11211 718-599-9600
Elie Deu Ph.D., prin. Fax 599-2177

Windmill Montessori S 100/PK-8
1317 Avenue T 11229 718-375-4277
Liza Herzberg, dir. Fax 375-6701
Yeshiva Ahaba Ve Ahava 100/PK-8
2001 E 7th St 11223 718-376-3140
Rabbi Jacob Israel, prin. Fax 376-6097
Yeshiva Ahavas Torah 200/K-8
2961 Nostrand Ave 11229 718-339-9656
Rabbi Alter Obermeister, prin. Fax 336-5885
Yeshiva & Mesivta of Brooklyn 200/PK-8
1200 Ocean Pkwy 11230 718-252-9500
Yeshiva & Mesivta Torah Temimah 600/PK-12
555 Ocean Pkwy 11218 718-853-8500
Avi Pearl, prin. Fax 438-5779
Yeshiva Beth Hillel of Krasna 400/K-7
1371 42nd St 11219 718-438-3535
Rabbi David Vogel, admin. Fax 438-9434
Yeshiva Beth Hillel of Williamsburg 200/K-8
35 Hewes St 11249 718-802-9567
Rabbi Leib Tabak, admin. Fax 802-0499
Yeshiva Bnos Ahavas Yisroel 600/PK-9
2 Lee Ave 11211 718-388-0848
Yeshiva Bnos Spinka 200/PK-3
127 Wallabout St 11206 718-254-8006
Yeshiva Chasdei Torah 50/K-12
54 Avenue O 11204 718-234-1600
Rabbi Aaron Katz, prin.
Yeshiva Ch'san Sofer - Mesivta M'shmuel 500/PK-12
1876 50th St 11204 718-236-1171
Mordechai Stuhl, prin. Fax 236-1119
Yeshiva Derech HaTorah 300/PK-10
2810 Nostrand Ave 11229 718-258-4441
Joel Weisblum, dir. Fax 677-8230
Yeshiva Farm Settlement S 400/K-12
194 Division Ave 11211 914-387-0422
Ernest Schwarz, admin.
Yeshivah of Flatbush 1,500/PK-8
919 E 10th St 11230 718-377-4466
Yeshivah Ohel Moshe 100/PK-8
7914 Bay Pkwy 11214 718-236-4003
Shifra Stone, prin. Fax 236-4923
Yeshiva Imrei Yoseph Spinka 200/K-12
5801 15th Ave 11219 718-851-1600
Yehuda Kornreich, prin. Fax 851-0148
Yeshiva Kehilath Yaakov 50/PK-8
206 Wilson St 11211 718-963-3050
Yeshiva Ketana of Bensonhurst 200/PK-10
2025 67th St 11204 718-236-4100
Zorach Shain, admin. Fax 236-1909
Yeshiva Machzikei Hadas Belz 1,100/PK-8
1601 42nd St 11204 718-436-4445
Rabbi Aron Friedman, admin. Fax 435-9046
Yeshiva Mesivta Arugath Habosem 400/K-12
40 Lynch St 11206 718-237-4500
Joseph Doppelt, prin. Fax 237-6064
Yeshiva Mesivta Karlin Stolin 600/PK-12
1818 54th St 11204 718-232-7800
Rabbi Dovid Stein, admin. Fax 331-4833
Yeshiva Mesivta Tiferes Yisroel S 700/K-12
1271 E 35th St 11210 718-258-9006
David Schonbrun, prin. Fax 258-9055
Yeshiva of Brooklyn-Girls 700/PK-12
1470 Ocean Pkwy 11230 718-376-3775
Shaindee Gornish, prin. Fax 376-4280
Yeshiva of Kings Bay 200/PK-8
2611 Avenue Z 11235 718-646-8500
Rabbi Simcha Klor, prin. Fax 646-8223
Yeshiva Ohr Shraga Veretzky 300/PK-12
1102 Avenue L 11230 718-252-7777
Rabbi Sholom Landau, prin. Fax 252-7797
Yeshiva Rabbi Chaim Berlin 700/PK-8
1310 Avenue I 11230 718-377-5800
Rabbi Moshe Monczyk, prin. Fax 377-6991
Yeshiva Ruach Chaim 200/PK-8
2611 Avenue Z 11235 718-646-8500
Yeshivas Boyan Tiferes Mordechai Shlomo 200/PK-12
1205 44th St 11219 718-435-6060
Rabbi Yakov Fishman, dir. Fax 435-4060
Yeshiva Shaarei Hayosher S 50/PK-PK
PO Box 190295 11219 718-376-4555
Yeshivat Ateret Torah 1,600/PK-12
901 Quentin Rd 11223 718-375-7100
Boruch Manela, prin. Fax 645-5097
Yeshiva Tiferes Elimelech 400/PK-8
1650 56th St 11204 718-438-1177
Malkla David, prin. Fax 438-1779
Yeshivat Lev Torah 200/PK-9
3300 Kings Hwy 11234 718-891-8644
Yeshivat Ohel Torah 200/PK-8
2600 Ocean Ave 11229 718-332-2600
Yeshiva Toldos Yitzchok Bnei Mordechai 500/PK-8
1413 45th St 11219 718-633-4802
Shlomo Kolodny, prin. Fax 633-1063
Yeshiva Torah Vodaath 400/PK-8
452 E 9th St 11218 718-941-8000
Yeshiva Toras Emes Kamenitz 500/PK-12
1904 Avenue N 11230 718-375-0900
Rabbi Chaim Block, prin. Fax 376-4661
Yeshivat Or Hatorah K-8
2959 Avenue Y 11235 718-252-8308
Yeshivat Shaare Torah Boys ES 1-8
1680 Coney Island Ave 11230 718-339-9752
Yeshivat Shaare Torah Girls ES 300/1-8
222 Ocean Pkwy 11218 718-437-6120
Yona Krieser, prin. Fax 437-6119
Yeshiva Tzemach Tzadik Viznitz 200/PK-8
186 Ross St 11211 718-782-6383
Rabbi Yosef Katz, admin.
Yeshiva Yagdil Torah 200/PK-8
5110 18th Ave 11204 718-871-9100
Joseph Segal, prin. Fax 436-0549
Yeshiva Yesode Hatorah 200/K-8
620 Bedford Ave 11249 718-802-1613
Fishel Taub, prin. Fax 852-4364
Yeshiva Yesode Hatorah Adas Yereim 400/PK-9
505 Bedford Ave 11211 718-302-7500
Sam Fisher, admin. Fax 384-5530

Yeshiva Yesode Hatorah Adas Yereim 300/PK-8
1350 50th St 11219 718-851-6462
Chaim Framoitz, admin. Fax 851-7298
Zichron Yehuda-Bais Simcha 100/PK-2
1051 59th St 11219 718-438-9275
Rabbi C.M. Pollack, admin.

Brownville, Jefferson, Pop. 1,107
General Brown Central SD
Supt. — See Dexter
Brownville/Glen Park ES 500/K-6
PO Box 10 13615 315-779-2300
Joseph O'Donnell, prin. Fax 788-6976

Brushton, Franklin, Pop. 466
Brushton-Moira Central SD 700/PK-12
758 County Route 7 12916 518-529-8942
Donna Andre, supt. Fax 529-6062
www.bmcsd.org
Brushton-Moira Central ES 300/PK-6
758 County Route 7 12916 518-529-7324
Dean Yando, prin. Fax 529-6644

Buchanan, Westchester, Pop. 2,203
Hendrick Hudson Central SD
Supt. — See Montrose
Buchanan-Verplanck ES 300/K-5
160 Westchester Ave 10511 914-257-5400
Joshua Cohen, prin. Fax 257-5401

Buffalo, Erie, Pop. 254,867
Buffalo CSD 32,500/PK-12
712 City Hall 14202 716-816-3500
Dr. Kriner Cash, supt. Fax 851-3535
www.buffaloschools.org
Public MS 66 300/5-8
780 Parkside Ave 14216 716-816-3440
Anibal Soler, prin. Fax 838-7448
Public MS 79 500/PK-8
225 Lawn Ave 14207 716-816-4040
Marlon Lee, prin. Fax 871-6115
Public S 3 700/PK-8
255 Porter Ave 14201 716-816-3120
Freddy Barrera, prin. Fax 888-7004
Public S 6 600/PK-8
414 S Division St 14204 716-816-3767
Karen Piotrowski, prin. Fax 851-3770
Public S 17 @ #77 400/PK-4
370 Normal Ave 14213 716-816-3150
Karen Murray, prin. Fax 897-7119
Public S 18 300/PK-8
750 West Ave 14215 716-816-3160
Aakta Patel, prin. Fax 888-7119
Public S 19 500/PK-8
97 W Delavan Ave 14213 716-816-3180
Michael Suwala, prin. Fax 888-7042
Public S 27 700/PK-8
73 Pawnee Pkwy 14210 716-816-4770
Vincent Vanderlip, prin. Fax 828-4771
Public S 30 800/PK-8
21 Lowell Pl 14213 716-816-3220
Rafael Perez, prin. Fax 888-2032
Public S 31 400/PK-8
212 Stanton St 14212 716-816-3780
Heather Short-English, prin. Fax 851-3787
Public S 32 1,200/PK-8
342 Clinton St 14204 716-816-4603
Marianna Cecchini, prin. Fax 851-3895
Public S 33 500/PK-8
157 Elk St 14210 716-816-4783
Miguel Medina, prin. Fax 828-4786
Public S 37 500/PK-8
295 Carlton St 14204 716-816-3800
Linda Marszalek, prin. Fax 851-3796
Public S 43 600/PK-8
161 Benzinger St 14206 716-816-3260
Orniece Hill, prin. Fax 897-8012
Public S 45 700/PK-8
141 Hoyt St 14213 716-816-3300
Lynn Piccirillo, prin. Fax 888-7074
Public S 53 400/PK-8
425 S Park Ave 14204 716-816-3330
Denisca Thompson, prin. Fax 851-3762
Public S 54 500/PK-4
2358 Main St 14214 716-816-3340
Gregory Johnson, prin. Fax 838-7403
Public S 59 800/PK-8
100 Poplar Ave 14211 716-816-3370
Mirlene Dere, prin. Fax 897-8049
Public S 61 300/PK-4
453 Leroy Ave 14215 716-816-3400
Parette Walker, prin. Fax 897-8150
Public S 64 600/PK-4
874 Amherst St 14216 716-816-3420
Marquita Bryant, prin. Fax 816-7430
Public S 65 400/PK-4
249 Skillen St 14207 716-816-3430
Michelle Hope-Barnes, prin. Fax 871-6031
Public S 67 600/PK-8
911 Abbott Rd 14220 716-816-4922
David Thomas, prin. Fax 828-4925
Public S 69 500/PK-8
1725 Clinton St 14206 716-816-4794
Elaine Vandi-Kirkland, prin. Fax 828-4797
Public S 72 700/PK-8
71 Lorraine Ave 14220 716-816-4809
Jeff Banks, prin. Fax 828-4811
Public S 74 500/PK-8
126 Donaldson Rd 14208 716-816-3490
Patrick Cook, prin. Fax 888-7109
Public S 76 700/PK-8
315 Carolina St 14201 716-816-3848
Kathryn Foy, prin. Fax 851-3853
Public S 80 500/PK-8
600 Highgate Ave 14215 716-816-4050
Gayle Irving-White, prin. Fax 838-7475
Public S 81 800/PK-8
167 E Utica St 14208 716-816-4060
Denise Cobbs, prin. Fax 888-7010
Public S 82 500/PK-4
230 Easton Ave 14215 716-816-4070
Tanika Shedrick, prin. Fax 816-4076
Public S 89 800/PK-8
106 Appenheimer Ave 14214 716-816-4110
Contann Dabney, prin. Fax 897-8093
Public S 91 500/PK-8
340 Fougeron St 14211 716-816-4140
Kevin Garcia, prin. Fax 816-4205
Public S 93 1,100/PK-8
430 Southside Pkwy 14210 716-816-4818
Darlene Jesonowski, prin. Fax 828-4820
Public S 94 800/PK-8
489 Hertel Ave 14207 716-816-4150
Cecelie Owens, prin. Fax 816-4151
Public S 95 900/PK-8
95 4th St 14202 716-816-3900
Terence Jenkins, prin. Fax 851-3861
Public S 97 500/PK-8
1405 Sycamore St 14211 716-816-4460
Demario Strickland, prin. Fax 897-8162
Public S 99 700/PK-4
1095 Jefferson Ave 14208 716-816-4180
Tracie-Michele Lewis, prin. Fax 888-2012

Cheektowaga Central SD
Supt. — See Cheektowaga
Pine Hill PS 300/PK-1
1635 E Delavan Ave 14215 716-686-3680
Steven Wright, prin. Fax 892-0634

Kenmore-Town of Tonawanda UFSD 5,100/K-12
1500 Colvin Blvd 14223 716-874-8400
Stephen Bovino, supt. Fax 874-8621
www.ktufsd.org
Franklin ES 500/K-4
500 Parkhurst Blvd 14223 716-874-8415
Pat Kosis, prin. Fax 874-8520
Franklin MS 300/5-7
540 Parkhurst Blvd 14223 716-874-8404
Christopher Ginestre, prin. Fax 874-8480
Hoover ES 500/K-4
199 Thorncliff Rd 14223 716-874-8414
Michael Huff, prin. Fax 874-8460
Hoover MS 400/5-7
249 Thorncliff Rd 14223 716-874-8405
Carmelina Persico, prin. Fax 874-8470
Lindbergh ES 400/K-4
184 Irving Ter 14223 716-874-8410
Michael Muscarella, prin. Fax 874-8570
Other Schools – See Tonawanda

Catholic Academy of West Buffalo 200/PK-8
1069 Delaware Ave 14209 716-885-6111
Sr. Gail Glenn, prin. Fax 885-6452
Darul-Uloom Al Madania 200/PK-10
182 Sobieski St 14212 716-892-2606
Faisal Ansari, prin. Fax 892-6621
Elmwood Franklin S 300/PK-8
104 New Amsterdam Ave 14216 716-877-5035
Andrew Deyell, head sch Fax 877-9680
Nardin Academy 900/K-12
135 Cleveland Ave 14222 716-881-6262
Adrienne Forgette, pres. Fax 881-0086
Nardin Montessori S 200/PK-3
700 W Ferry St 14222 716-881-6565
Kristin Whitlock, prin. Fax 886-5931
Nativity Miguel MS 100/5-8
21 Davidson Ave 14215 716-836-5188
Fr. Edward Durkin, prin. Fax 836-5189
Notre Dame Academy 400/PK-8
1125 Abbott Rd 14220 716-824-0726
Tristan D'Angelo, prin. Fax 825-7685
Our Lady of Black Rock S 100/K-8
16 Peter St 14207 716-873-7497
Martha Eadie, prin. Fax 447-9926
St. Joseph University S 200/PK-8
3275 Main St 14214 716-835-7395
Mark Mattle, prin. Fax 833-6550
St. Mark S 400/K-8
399 Woodward Ave 14214 716-836-1191
Robert Clemens, prin. Fax 836-0391
Universal S PK-8
1957 Genesee St 14211 716-597-0102
Asiyah Teruel, prin. Fax 594-0280

Burnt Hills, Saratoga
Burnt Hills-Ballston Lake Central SD 3,200/K-12
173 Lakehill Rd 12027 518-399-9141
Dr. Patrick McGrath, supt. Fax 399-1882
www.bhbl.org
O'Rourke MS 700/6-8
173 Lake Hill Rd 12027 518-399-9141
Colleen Wolff, prin. Fax 384-2588
Other Schools – See Ballston Lake, Scotia

Burt, Niagara
Newfane Central SD 1,500/PK-12
6048 Godfrey Rd 14028 716-778-6850
Michael Baumann, supt. Fax 778-6852
www.newfane.wnyric.org
Newfane ECC 50/PK-PK
6048 Godfrey Rd 14028 716-778-6351
Bart Schuler, prin. Fax 778-6868
Other Schools – See Newfane

Cairo, Greene, Pop. 1,375
Cairo-Durham Central SD 1,000/PK-12
PO Box 780 12413 518-622-8534
Anthony Taibi, supt. Fax 622-9566
www.cairodurham.org
Cairo-Durham ES 300/PK-5
PO Box 1090 12413 518-622-3231
Mario Culihan, prin. Fax 622-9060
Cairo-Durham MS 300/6-8
PO Box 1139 12413 518-622-0490
Michael Mitchell, prin. Fax 622-0493

Calcium, Jefferson, Pop. 3,352
Indian River Central SD
Supt. — See Philadelphia
Calcium PS 700/PK-3
25440 Indian River Dr 13616 315-629-1100
Wanda Reardon, prin. Fax 629-5254

Caledonia, Livingston, Pop. 2,169
Caledonia-Mumford Central SD 900/PK-12
PO Box 150 14423 585-538-3400
Robert Molisani, supt. Fax 538-3450
www.cal-mum.org
Caledonia-Mumford ES 400/PK-5
PO Box 150 14423 585-538-3481
David Bulter, prin. Fax 538-3460
Caledonia-Mumford MS 200/6-8
PO Box 150 14423 585-538-3482
Paul Estabrooks, prin. Fax 538-3430

Calverton, Suffolk, Pop. 6,430
Riverhead Central SD
Supt. — See Riverhead
Riley Avenue ES 600/K-4
374 Riley Ave 11933 631-369-6804
David Enos, prin. Fax 369-6807

Cambria Heights, See New York
NYC Department of Education
Supt. — See New York
Public S 147 700/PK-8
21801 116th Ave 11411 718-528-2420
Afua Hill, prin. Fax 723-7819
Public S 176 700/PK-5
12045 235th St 11411 718-525-4057
Arlene Bartlett, prin. Fax 276-3458

Cambria Center for the Gifted Child 300/PK-5
23310 Linden Blvd 11411 718-341-1991
Cheder at the Ohel 50/PK-8
22420 Francis Lewis Blvd 11411 718-528-8989
Bassie Shemtov, admin. Fax 483-9529
Sacred Heart Catholic Academy 300/PK-8
11530 221st St 11411 718-527-0123
Yvonne Russell-Smith, prin.
Word Christian Academy 100/K-8
23001 Linden Blvd 11411 718-276-3669
Bridget Fontanelle, prin. Fax 978-9673

Cambridge, Washington, Pop. 1,844
Cambridge Central SD 900/K-12
58 S Park St 12816 518-677-8527
Vincent Canini, supt. Fax 677-3889
www.cambridgecsd.org
Cambridge ES 400/K-6
24 S Park St 12816 518-677-8527
Colleen Lester, prin. Fax 677-3031

Camden, Oneida, Pop. 2,211
Camden Central SD 1,900/PK-12
51 3rd St 13316 315-245-4075
Mary Lynne Szczerba, supt. Fax 245-1622
www.camdenschools.org
Camden ES 400/PK-4
1 Oswego St 13316 315-245-2616
Sharon Kirch, prin. Fax 245-4194
Camden MS 500/5-8
32 Union St 13316 315-245-0080
Mary Walker, prin. Fax 245-0083
Other Schools – See Blossvale, Taberg

Cameron Mills, Steuben
Addison Central SD
Supt. — See Addison
Valley Early Childhood S 50/PK-K
6786 County Route 119 14820 607-359-2261
Tanya Loomis, prin. Fax 359-3443

Camillus, Onondaga, Pop. 1,196
West Genesee Central SD 4,800/K-12
300 Sanderson Dr 13031 315-487-4562
Dr. Christopher Brown, supt. Fax 487-2999
www.westgenesee.org
Camillus MS 500/6-8
5525 Ike Dixon Rd 13031 315-672-3159
Beth Lozier, prin. Fax 672-3309
East Hill ES, 401 Blackmore Rd 13031 400/K-5
Lisa Craig Ph.D., prin. 315-487-4648
Split Rock ES 400/K-5
4151 Split Rock Rd 13031 315-487-4656
Todd Freeman, prin. Fax 488-2250
Stonehedge ES - Blue 400/K-2
400 Sanderson Dr 13031 315-487-4633
Lori Keevil, prin. Fax 487-4599
Stonehedge ES - Gold 400/3-5
400 Sanderson Dr 13031 315-487-4631
Brent Suddaby, prin. Fax 487-4599
West Genesee MS 700/6-8
500 Sanderson Dr 13031 315-487-4615
Stephen Dunham, prin. Fax 487-4618
Other Schools – See Syracuse

Campbell, Steuben, Pop. 695
Campbell-Savona Central SD 800/PK-12
8455 County Route 125 14821 607-527-9800
Kathleen Hagenbuch, supt. Fax 527-9863
www.cscsd.org
Other Schools – See Savona

Canajoharie, Montgomery, Pop. 2,208
Canajoharie Central SD 1,000/PK-12
136 Scholastic Way 13317 518-673-6302
Deborah Grimshaw, supt. Fax 673-3177
www.canajoharieschools.org
Canajoharie MS 200/6-8
25 School District Rd 13317 518-673-6320
Christopher DePaolo, prin. Fax 673-5557
East Hill ES 400/PK-5
25 School District Rd 13317 518-673-6310
Stacy Ward, prin. Fax 673-3887

Canandaigua, Ontario, Pop. 10,383
Canandaigua CSD 2,900/PK-12
143 N Pearl St 14424 585-396-3700
Jamie Farr, supt. Fax 396-7306
www.canandaiguaschools.org
Canandaigua ES 900/PK-5
96 W Gibson St 14424 585-396-3930
Brian Amesbury, prin. Fax 396-3938
Canandaigua MS 800/6-8
215 Granger St 14424 585-396-3850
John Arthur, prin. Fax 396-3863

St. Mary S 200/PK-8
16 Gibson St 14424 585-394-4300
Ann Marie Deutsch, prin. Fax 394-3954

Canaseraga, Allegany, Pop. 544
Canaseraga Central SD 200/PK-12
PO Box 230 14822 607-545-6421
Chad Groff, supt. Fax 545-6265
www.ccsdny.org/
Canaseraga S 200/PK-12
PO Box 230 14822 607-545-6421
Chad Groff, supt. Fax 545-6265

Canastota, Madison, Pop. 4,723
Canastota Central SD 1,400/K-12
120 Roberts St 13032 315-697-2025
June Clarke, supt. Fax 697-6368
www.canastotacsd.org
Peterboro Street ES 200/K-1
220 N Peterboro St 13032 315-697-2027
Jennifer Carnahan, prin. Fax 697-6368
Roberts Street MS 300/4-6
120 Roberts St 13032 315-697-2029
Melissa Stanek, prin. Fax 697-6368
South Side ES 200/2-3
200 High St 13032 315-697-6372
Jennifer Carnahan, prin. Fax 697-6368

Candor, Tioga, Pop. 840
Candor Central SD 800/K-12
PO Box 145 13743 607-659-5010
Jeffrey Kisloski, supt. Fax 659-7112
candor.org
Candor ES 400/K-6
PO Box 145 13743 607-659-3935
Katie Volpicelli, prin. Fax 659-4688

Canisteo, Steuben, Pop. 2,260
Canisteo-Greenwood Central SD 900/PK-12
84 Greenwood St 14823 607-698-4225
Christopher Roser, supt. Fax 698-2833
www.cg.wnyric.org
Canisteo-Greenwood ES 400/PK-4
120 Greenwood St 14823 607-698-4225
Colleen Brownell, prin. Fax 698-2345
Canisteo-Greenwood MS 300/5-7
120 Greenwood St 14823 607-698-4225
Paul Cone, prin. Fax 698-2244

Canton, Saint Lawrence, Pop. 6,213
Canton Central SD 1,300/PK-12
99 State St 13617 315-386-8561
William Gregory, supt. Fax 386-1323
www.ccsdk12.org/
Banford ES 500/PK-4
99 State St 13617 315-386-8561
Joseph McDonough, prin. Fax 386-1323
McKenney MS 400/5-8
99 State St 13617 315-386-8561
Viola Schmid-Doyle, prin. Fax 386-1323

St. Mary S 50/PK-6
2 Powers St 13617 315-386-3572
Michele Meyers, prin. Fax 386-8870

Cape Vincent, Jefferson, Pop. 717
Thousand Islands Central SD
Supt. — See Clayton
Cape Vincent ES 100/K-5
PO Box 282 13618 315-654-2142
Brenda Leddy, prin. Fax 654-4599

Carle Place, Nassau, Pop. 4,914
Carle Place UFD 1,400/K-12
168 Cherry Ln 11514 516-622-6442
David J. Flatley, supt. Fax 622-6447
www.cps.k12.ny.us
Cherry Lane ES 300/K-2
475 Roslyn Ave 11514 516-622-6402
Susan Folkson, prin. Fax 622-6586
Rushmore Avenue S 400/3-6
251 Rushmore Ave 11514 516-622-6421
Catherine Silletti, prin. Fax 622-6588

Carmel, Putnam, Pop. 4,800
Carmel Central SD
Supt. — See Patterson
Fischer MS 1,400/5-8
281 Fair St 10512 845-228-2300
John Piscitella, prin. Fax 228-2304
Kent ES 500/K-4
1091 Route 52 10512 845-225-5029
Deborah Weisel, prin. Fax 225-1849
Kent PS 400/K-4
1065 Route 52 10512 845-225-5025
Daniel Brown, prin. Fax 228-4824

St. James the Apostle S 300/PK-8
12 Gleneida Ave 10512 845-225-9365
Valerie Crocco, prin. Fax 228-2859

Caroga Lake, Fulton, Pop. 511
Wheelerville UFD 100/K-8
PO Box 756 12032 518-835-2171
Richard Ruberti, supt. Fax 835-3551
www.wufsk8.com
Wheelerville S 100/K-8
PO Box 756 12032 518-835-2171
Nicole Dettenrieder, supt. Fax 835-3551

Carthage, Jefferson, Pop. 3,663
Carthage Central SD 3,400/PK-12
25059 Woolworth St 13619 315-493-5000
Peter Turner, supt. Fax 493-5069
www.carthagecsd.org
Carthage ES 400/PK-4
900 Beaver Ln 13619 315-493-1570
Richard Weber, prin. Fax 493-6028
Carthage MS 1,000/5-8
21986 Cole Rd 13619 315-493-5020
Emily Remington, prin. Fax 493-5029
West Carthage ES 500/PK-4
21568 Cole Rd 13619 315-493-2400
Jamie Sweeney, prin. Fax 493-6536
Other Schools – See Black River

Augustinian Academy 200/PK-8
317 West St 13619 315-493-1301
Mary Ann Margrey, prin. Fax 493-0632

Castleton on Hudson, Rensselaer, Pop. 1,464
East Greenbush Central SD
Supt. — See East Greenbush
Green Meadow ES 400/K-5
234 Schuurman Rd 12033 518-207-2640
Daniel Garab, prin. Fax 479-7954

Schodack Central SD 900/K-12
1477 S Schodack Rd 12033 518-732-2297
Jason Chevrier, supt. Fax 732-7710
www.schodack.k12.ny.us
Castleton ES 400/K-5
80 Scott Ave 12033 518-732-7755
James Derby, prin. Fax 732-0495
Maple Hill MS 200/6-8
1477 S Schodack Rd 12033 518-732-7736
Jacqueline Hill, prin. Fax 732-0493

Cato, Cayuga, Pop. 516
Cato-Meridian Central SD 1,000/PK-12
2851 State Route 370 13033 315-626-3439
W. Noel Patterson, supt. Fax 626-2888
www.catomeridian.org/
Cato-Meridian ES 400/PK-4
2851 State Route 370 13033 315-626-3320
Robert Wren, prin. Fax 626-2293
Cato-Meridian MS 300/5-8
2851 State Route 370 13033 315-626-3319
Sean Gleason, prin. Fax 626-2327

Catskill, Greene, Pop. 3,926
Catskill Central SD 1,600/PK-12
343 W Main St 12414 518-943-4696
Dr. Ronel Cook, supt. Fax 943-7116
www.catskillcsd.org
Catskill ES 800/PK-5
770 Embought Rd 12414 518-943-0574
John Rivers, prin. Fax 943-5396
Catskill MS 300/6-8
345 W Main St 12414 518-943-5665
Kerry Overbaugh, prin. Fax 943-3001

Cattaraugus, Cattaraugus, Pop. 997
Cattaraugus-Little Valley Central SD 900/PK-12
25 N Franklin St 14719 716-257-5293
Dr. Sharon Huff, supt. Fax 257-5298
www.cattlv.wnyric.org
Cattaraugus-Little Valley ES 300/PK-4
25 N Franklin St 14719 716-257-3436
Micah Oldham, prin. Fax 257-5237
Cattaraugus-Little Valley MS 200/5-8
25 N Franklin St 14719 716-257-3483
April Preston, prin. Fax 257-5108

Cayuga, Cayuga, Pop. 540
Union Springs Central SD
Supt. — See Union Springs
Cayuga ES 200/K-3
255 Wheat St 13034 315-889-4170
Sheila LaDouce, prin. Fax 889-4175

Cazenovia, Madison, Pop. 2,807
Cazenovia Central SD 1,500/K-12
31 Emory Ave 13035 315-655-1317
Matthew Reilly, supt. Fax 655-1375
cazenoviacsd.com
Burton Street ES 500/K-4
37 Burton St 13035 315-655-1325
Mary Ann Macintosh, prin. Fax 655-1353
Cazenovia MS 400/5-7
31 Emory Ave 13035 315-655-1324
Dr. Jean Regan, prin. Fax 655-1305

Cedarhurst, Nassau, Pop. 6,500
Lawrence UFD
Supt. — See Lawrence
Public S 5 400/1-4
305 Cedarhurst Ave 11516 516-295-6500
Rina Beach, prin. Fax 295-6509

Shulamith S for Girls 500/PK-12
305 Cedarhurst Ave 11516 516-564-1500
Malka Fishman, dir. Fax 977-3159

Centereach, Suffolk, Pop. 31,131
Middle Country Central SD 10,100/PK-12
8 43rd St 11720 631-285-8005
Dr. Roberta Gerold Ed.D., supt. Fax 738-2719
www.mccsd.net
Dawnwood MS 1,200/6-8
10 43rd St 11720 631-285-8200
Kristine Leonard, prin. Fax 285-8201
Holbrook Road ES 400/1-5
170 Holbrook Rd 11720 631-285-8560
Dr. Craig Unkenholz Ed.D., prin. Fax 285-8561
Jericho ES 400/1-5
34 N Coleman Rd 11720 631-285-8600
Glen Rogers, prin. Fax 285-8601
North Coleman Road ES 300/1-5
197 N Coleman Rd 11720 631-285-8660
Gretchen Rodney, prin. Fax 285-8661
Oxhead Road ES 400/1-5
144 Oxhead Rd 11720 631-285-8700
Corinne Seeh, prin. Fax 285-8701
Selden MS 1,100/6-8
22 Jefferson Ave 11720 631-285-8400
Andrew Bennett, prin. Fax 285-8401
Unity Drive Pre-K/K Center 600/PK-K
11 Unity Dr 11720 631-285-8760
Deborah Wolfe, prin. Fax 285-8761
Other Schools – See Lake Grove, Selden

Our Savior New American S 200/PK-12
140 Mark Tree Rd 11720 631-588-2757
Rev. Ronald Stelzer, hdmstr. Fax 588-2617

Center Moriches, Suffolk, Pop. 7,447
Center Moriches UFD 1,600/K-12
529 Main St 11934 631-878-0052
Russell Stewart, supt. Fax 878-4326
www.cmschools.org
Center Moriches MS 400/6-8
311 Frowein Rd 11934 631-878-2519
Melissa Bates, prin. Fax 878-0362
Huey ES 700/K-5
511 Main St 11934 631-878-0052
Kim Hardwick, prin. Fax 878-0238

Our Lady Queen of Apostles Regional S 200/PK-8
2 Saint Johns Pl 11934 631-878-1033
David Erlanger, prin. Fax 878-1059

Centerport, Suffolk, Pop. 5,450
Harborfields Central SD
Supt. — See Greenlawn
Washington Drive PS 600/K-2
95 Washington Dr 11721 631-754-5592
Maureen Kelly, prin. Fax 754-3346

Love of Learning Montessori S 100/PK-6
PO Box 628 11721 631-754-4109
Sheldon Thompson, dir. Fax 754-4109

Central Islip, Suffolk, Pop. 33,583
Central Islip UFD 6,500/PK-12
50 Wheeler Rd 11722 631-348-5112
Dr. Howard Koenig, supt. Fax 348-0366
www.cischools.org
Central Islip ECC 800/PK-K
50 Wheeler Rd 11722 631-348-5139
Ann Bucco, prin. Fax 348-5184
Cordello Avenue ES 700/1-5
51 Cordello Ave 11722 631-348-4191
Brenda Jackson, prin. Fax 348-7712
Mulligan MS 700/6-8
1 Broadway Ave 11722 631-348-5042
Dr. Tracy Hudson, prin. Fax 348-5164
Mulvey ES 600/1-5
44 E Cherry St 11722 631-348-5053
Jessica Iafrate, prin. Fax 348-1532
O'Neill ES 700/1-5
545 Clayton St 11722 631-348-5061
Kristine LoCascio, prin. Fax 348-5162
Reed MS 500/7-8
200 Half Mile Rd 11722 631-348-5066
Matthew Matera, prin. Fax 348-5159
Other Schools – See Islandia

Our Lady of Providence Regional S 300/PK-8
82 Carleton Ave 11722 631-234-6324
Sharon Swift Imperati, prin. Fax 234-6360

Central Square, Oswego, Pop. 1,828
Central Square Central SD 3,900/PK-12
44 School Dr 13036 315-668-4220
Thomas Colabufo, supt. Fax 676-4437
www.cssd.org
Central Square MS 1,000/6-8
248 US Route 11 13036 315-668-4216
Mathew Penrod, prin. Fax 668-8410
Hastings-Mallory ES 200/PK-5
93 Barker Rd 13036 315-668-4252
Lawrence Wink, prin. Fax 668-4299
Hawk ES 400/PK-5
74 School Dr 13036 315-668-4310
Amanda Viel, prin. Fax 668-4356
Other Schools – See Brewerton, Constantia

Central Valley, Orange, Pop. 1,929
Monroe-Woodbury Central SD 6,900/K-12
278 Route 32 10917 845-460-6200
Elsie Rodriguez, supt. Fax 460-6080
www.mw.k12.ny.us
Central Valley ES 600/2-5
45 Route 32 10917 845-460-6700
Rebecca Aviles-Rodriguez, prin. Fax 460-6047
Monroe-Woodbury MS 1,700/6-8
199 Dunderberg Rd 10917 845-460-6400
Michael Maesano, prin. Fax 460-6044
Smith Clove ES 600/K-1
21 Smith Clove Rd 10917 845-460-6300
Chris Berger, prin. Fax 460-6043
Other Schools – See Harriman, Monroe

Champlain, Clinton, Pop. 1,086
Northeastern Clinton Central SD 1,300/K-12
103 State Route 276 12919 518-298-8242
Robin Garrand, supt. Fax 298-4293
www.nccscougar.org
Northeastern Clinton MS 300/6-8
103 State Route 276 12919 518-298-8681
Thomas Brandell, prin. Fax 298-4293
Other Schools – See Mooers, Rouses Point

Chappaqua, Westchester, Pop. 1,404
Chappaqua Central SD 4,000/K-12
PO Box 21 10514 914-238-7200
Christine Ackerman, supt. Fax 238-7231
www.ccsd.ws
Bell MS 700/5-8
50 Senter St 10514 914-238-7202
Martin Fitzgerald, prin. Fax 238-2085
Grafflin ES, 650 King St 10514 400/K-4
Jamie Edelman, prin. 914-238-7204
Roaring Brook ES 500/K-4
530 Quaker Rd 10514 914-238-7205
Alison Porcelli, prin. Fax 238-4716
Seven Bridges MS 600/5-8
PO Box 22 10514 914-238-7203
Andrew Corsilia, prin. Fax 666-7306
Westorchard ES 500/K-4
25 Granite Rd 10514 914-238-7206
James Skoog, prin. Fax 238-6885

Chateaugay, Franklin, Pop. 824
Chateaugay Central SD 500/PK-12
PO Box 904 12920 518-497-6420
Loretta Fowler, supt. Fax 497-3170
www.chateaugaycsd.org
Chateaugay ES 300/PK-6
PO Box 904 12920 518-497-6611
Nicole Calnon, prin. Fax 497-3170

Chatham, Columbia, Pop. 1,720
Chatham Central SD 1,200/K-12
50 Woodbridge Ave 12037 518-392-1501
Dr. Salvatore DeAngelo, supt. Fax 392-2413
www.chathamcentralschools.com
Chatham MS 300/6-8
50 Woodbridge Ave 12037 518-392-1560
Michael Burns, prin. Fax 392-1559
Dardess ES 500/K-5
50 Woodbridge Ave 12037 518-392-2255
Kristen Reno, prin. Fax 392-2795

Chaumont, Jefferson, Pop. 611
Lyme Central SD 400/PK-12
PO Box 219 13622 315-649-2417
Cammy Morrison, supt. Fax 649-2663
www.lymecsd.org
Lyme Central S 400/PK-12
PO Box 219 13622 315-649-2417
Barry Davis, prin. Fax 649-2663

Chazy, Clinton, Pop. 555
Chazy Central UFD 500/K-12
609 Miner Farm Rd 12921 518-846-7135
John Fairchild, supt. Fax 846-8322
www.chazy.org
Chazy Central Rural ES 200/K-6
609 Miner Farm Rd 12921 518-846-7212
Robert McAuliffe, prin. Fax 846-8515

Cheektowaga, Erie, Pop. 74,096
Cheektowaga Central SD 1,900/PK-12
3600 Union Rd 14225 716-686-3606
Mary Morris, supt. Fax 681-5232
www.cheektowagak12.org
Cheektowaga Central MS 500/5-8
3600 Union Rd 14225 716-686-3660
Micah Hanford, prin. Fax 686-3669
Union East ES 400/2-5
3550 Union Rd 14225 716-686-3620
Melissa Mitchell, prin. Fax 686-3666
Other Schools – See Buffalo

Cheektowaga-Maryvale UFD 2,200/PK-12
1050 Maryvale Dr 14225 716-631-7407
Joseph D'Angelo, supt. Fax 635-4699
www.maryvaleufsd.org
Maryvale IS 500/3-5
1050 Maryvale Dr 14225 716-631-7423
Eileen Crumb, prin. Fax 631-4858
Maryvale MS 500/6-8
1050 Maryvale Dr 14225 716-631-7425
Peter Frank, prin. Fax 631-7499
Maryvale PS 600/PK-2
1 Nagel Dr 14225 716-685-5800
Elizabeth Giangreco, prin. Fax 651-0031

Cheektowago-Sloan UFD
Supt. — See Sloan
Kennedy MS 300/6-8
305 Cayuga Creek Rd 14227 716-897-7300
Gretchen Cercone, prin. Fax 892-2624
Roosevelt ES 300/PK-2
2495 William St 14206 716-891-6424
Jeffrey Mochrie, prin. Fax 892-2537

Cleveland Hill UFD 1,300/PK-12
105 Mapleview Dr 14225 716-836-7200
Jon MacSwan, supt. Fax 836-0675
www.clevehill.wnyric.org/
Cleveland Hill ES 600/PK-5
105 Mapleview Dr 14225 716-836-7200
Patrick McCabe, prin. Fax 836-3700
Cleveland Hill MS 300/6-8
105 Mapleview Dr 14225 716-836-7200
Andrea Kersten, prin. Fax 836-7741

Cherryplain, Rensselaer
Berlin Central SD 700/PK-12
17400 Route 22 12040 518-658-2690
Dr. Stephen Young, supt. Fax 658-3822
www.berlincentral.org/
Other Schools – See Berlin

Cherry Valley, Otsego, Pop. 511
Cherry Valley-Springfield Central SD 500/PK-12
PO Box 485 13320 607-264-3265
TheriJo Climenhaga, supt. Fax 264-3458
www.cvscs.org
Cherry Valley-Springfield ES 200/PK-5
PO Box 485 13320 607-264-3265
Nicole Knapp, prin. Fax 264-3458

Chester, Orange, Pop. 3,852
Chester UFD 1,000/K-12
64 Hambletonian Ave 10918 845-469-5052
Sean Michel, supt. Fax 469-2377
chesterufsd.org
Chester ES 500/K-5
2 Herbert Dr 10918 845-469-2178
Cindy Walsh, prin. Fax 469-2794

Chestertown, Warren, Pop. 671
North Warren Central SD 500/PK-12
6110 State Route 8 12817 518-494-3015
Michele French, supt. Fax 494-2929
www.northwarrencsd.org
North Warren Central S 500/PK-12
6110 State Route 8 12817 518-494-3015
Theresa Andrew, prin. Fax 494-2323

Chestnut Ridge, Rockland, Pop. 7,763
East Ramapo Central SD
Supt. — See Spring Valley
Chestnut Ridge MS 500/7-8
892 Chestnut Ridge Rd 10977 845-577-6300
Maria Vergez, prin. Fax 426-1063
Eldorado IS 400/4-6
5 Eldorado Dr 10977 845-577-6150
Astrid Johnson, prin. Fax 426-0850
Fleetwood ES 500/K-3
22 Fleetwood Ave 10977 845-577-6170
Carolyn Partridge, prin. Fax 426-1807

Green Meadow Waldorf S 400/PK-12
307 Hungry Hollow Rd 10977 845-356-2514
TreeAnne McEnery, admin. Fax 356-2921

Chittenango, Madison, Pop. 5,016
Chittenango Central SD 1,500/K-12
1732 Fyler Rd 13037 315-687-2850
Michael Eiffe, supt. Fax 687-2841
www.chittenangoschools.org
Bolivar Road ES 200/K-4
6983 Bolivar Rd 13037 315-687-2880
Renee Burgess, prin. Fax 687-2881
Chittenango MS 500/5-8
1732 Fyler Rd 13037 315-687-2800
Arnold Merola, prin. Fax 687-2801
Other Schools – See Bridgeport

Churchville, Monroe, Pop. 1,935
Churchville-Chili Central SD 3,900/K-12
139 Fairbanks Rd 14428 585-293-1800
Loretta Orologio, supt. Fax 293-1013
www.cccsd.org
Churchville-Chili MS 1,300/5-8
139 Fairbanks Rd 14428 585-293-4541
Carl Christensen, prin. Fax 293-4516
Churchville ES 400/K-4
36 W Buffalo St 14428 585-293-2022
David Johnson, prin. Fax 293-4504
Fairbanks Road ES 500/K-4
175 Fairbanks Rd 14428 585-293-4543
Todd Yunker, prin. Fax 293-4510
Other Schools – See Rochester

Cicero, Onondaga
North Syracuse Central SD
Supt. — See North Syracuse
Cicero ES 600/K-4
5979 State Route 31 13039 315-218-2500
Kathleen Wheeler, prin. Fax 218-2585
Gillette Road MS 1,200/5-7
6150 S Bay Rd 13039 315-218-3000
Christopher Leahey, prin. Fax 218-3085
Lakeshore Road ES 600/K-4
7180 Lakeshore Rd 13039 315-218-2600
John Lawrence, prin. Fax 218-2685

Cincinnatus, Cortland
Cincinnatus Central SD 400/K-12
2809 Cincinnatus Rd 13040 607-863-4069
Steven Hubbard, supt. Fax 863-4109
www.cc.cnyric.org/
Cincinnatus ES 200/K-6
2809 Cincinnatus Rd 13040 607-863-3200
Thomas Durkot, prin. Fax 863-4559

Circleville, Orange, Pop. 1,350
Pine Bush Central SD
Supt. — See Pine Bush
Circleville ES 600/PK-5
PO Box 43 10919 845-744-2031
Amy Brockner, prin. Fax 361-2136
Circleville MS 600/6-8
PO Box 143 10919 845-744-2031
Lisa Hankinson, prin. Fax 361-3811
Pakanasink ES 500/PK-5
PO Box 148 10919 845-744-2031
Brian Breheny, prin. Fax 361-3816

Clarence, Erie, Pop. 2,634
Clarence Central SD 4,700/K-12
9625 Main St 14031 716-407-9100
Dr. Geoffrey Hicks, supt. Fax 407-9126
www.clarenceschools.org
Clarence MS 1,200/6-8
10150 Greiner Rd 14031 716-407-9200
Robert Moore, prin. Fax 407-9229
Ledgeview ES 500/K-5
5150 Old Goodrich Rd 14031 716-407-9275
Keith Kuwik, prin. Fax 407-9279
Other Schools – See Clarence Center, Williamsville

Clarence Center, Erie, Pop. 2,214
Clarence Central SD
Supt. — See Clarence
Clarence Center ES 400/K-5
9600 Clarence Center Rd 14032 716-407-9150
Colleen Coggins, prin. Fax 407-9157

Clayton, Jefferson, Pop. 1,959
Thousand Islands Central SD 1,000/K-12
PO Box 100 13624 315-686-5594
Michael Bashaw, supt. Fax 686-5511
www.1000islandsschools.org
Guardino ES 300/K-5
600 High St 13624 315-686-5594
Lisa Freitag, prin. Fax 686-2874
Thousand Islands MS 200/6-8
8487 County Route 9 13624 315-686-5594
Andrea Lomber, prin. Fax 654-5038
Other Schools – See Cape Vincent

Clifton Park, Saratoga
Shenendehowa Central SD 9,700/K-12
5 Chelsea Pl 12065 518-881-0600
Dr. L. Oliver Robinson, supt. Fax 371-9393
www.shenet.org/
Acadia MS 800/6-8
970 Route 146 Ste 54 12065 518-881-0450
Jonathan Burns, prin. Fax 371-3981
Arongen ES 700/K-5
489 Clifton Park Ctr Rd 12065 518-881-0510
Andrew Hills, prin. Fax 371-8177
Gowana MS 800/6-8
970 Route 146 Ste 55 12065 518-881-0460
Robin Gawrys, prin. Fax 383-1490
Karigon ES 500/K-5
970 Route 146 Ste 50 12065 518-881-0530
Gregory Wing, prin. Fax 383-1176
Koda MS 800/6-8
970 Route 146 Ste 59 12065 518-881-0470
Sean Gnat, prin. Fax 383-1532
Okte ES 500/K-5
1581 Crescent Rd 12065 518-881-0540
Lisa Mickle, prin. Fax 383-1964
Orenda ES 600/K-5
970 Route 146 Ste 51 12065 518-881-0550
Michael Smith, prin. Fax 383-1219
Shatekon ES 600/K-5
35 Maxwell Dr 12065 518-881-0580
Erica Ryan, prin. Fax 371-1762
Skano ES 500/K-5
970 Route 146 Ste 52 12065 518-881-0560
Jill Florio, prin. Fax 383-1260
Tesago ES 500/K-5
970 Route 146 Ste 53 12065 518-881-0570
Gregory Pace, prin. Fax 383-1486
Other Schools – See Ballston Lake

St. George's S 50/PK-2
912 Route 146 12065 518-280-7196
Phyllis Aldrich, head sch Fax 371-7414

Clifton Springs, Ontario, Pop. 2,111
Phelps-Clifton Springs Central SD 1,300/K-12
1490 State Route 488 14432 315-548-6420
Matthew Sickles, supt. Fax 548-6429
www.midlakes.org
Midlakes IS 500/3-6
1510 State Route 488 14432 315-548-6900
Christopher Moyer, prin. Fax 548-6909
Midlakes PS 400/K-2
1500 State Route 488 14432 315-548-6700
Karen Cameron, prin. Fax 548-6709

Climax, Greene

Grapeville Christian S 100/K-12
2416 County Route 26 12042 518-966-5037
Marianne DeDeo B.S., prin. Fax 966-5498

Clinton, Oneida, Pop. 1,917
Clinton Central SD 1,300/K-12
75 Chenango Ave 13323 315-557-2253
Dr. Stephen Grimm, supt. Fax 853-8727
www.ccs.edu
Clinton ES 600/K-5
75 Chenango Ave 13323 315-557-2255
Ellen Leuthauser, prin. Fax 557-2331
Clinton MS 300/6-8
75 Chenango Ave 13323 315-557-2260
Dr. Shaun Carney, prin. Fax 853-8727

Clinton Corners, Dutchess

Upton Lake Christian S 100/K-12
PO Box 63 12514 845-266-3497
Barbara Marrine, prin. Fax 266-3828

Clintonville, Clinton
Au Sable Valley Central SD 1,200/K-12
1273 Route 9N 12924 518-834-2845
Paul Savage, supt. Fax 834-2843
www.avcs.org
Au Sable Valley MS 200/7-8
1490 Route 9N 12924 518-834-2800
Philip Mero, prin. Fax 834-2847
Other Schools – See Au Sable Forks, Keeseville

Clyde, Wayne, Pop. 2,017
Clyde-Savannah Central SD 900/PK-12
215 Glasgow St 14433 315-902-3000
Michael Hayden, supt. Fax 923-2560
www.clydesavannah.org
Clyde-Savannah ES 400/PK-5
212 E Dezeng St 14433 315-902-3100
Kathyrn Lumb, prin. Fax 923-2560
Clyde-Savannah MS 200/6-8
215 Glasgow St 14433 315-902-3200
Jennifer Kelly, prin. Fax 923-2560

Clymer, Chautauqua
Clymer Central SD 400/PK-12
8672 E Main St 14724 716-355-4444
Bert Lictus, supt. Fax 355-2200
www.clymercsd.org

Clymer Central S 400/PK-12
8672 E Main St 14724 716-355-4444
Edward Bailey, prin. Fax 355-4467

Cobleskill, Schoharie, Pop. 4,593
Cobleskill-Richmondville Central SD 1,800/K-12
155 Washington Ave 12043 518-234-4032
Carl Mummenthey, supt. Fax 234-7721
www.crcs.k12.ny.us
Golding MS 400/6-8
193 Golding Dr 12043 518-234-8368
Scott McDonald, prin. Fax 234-1018
Ryder ES 400/K-5
143 Golding Dr 12043 518-234-2585
Kevin Kelly, prin. Fax 234-1018
Other Schools – See Richmondville

Coeymans, Albany
Ravena-Coeymans-Selkirk Central SD
Supt. — See Ravena
Coeymans ES 400/K-5
66 Church St 12045 518-756-5200
Hakim Jones, prin. Fax 756-9162

Cohocton, Steuben, Pop. 826
Wayland-Cohocton Central SD
Supt. — See Wayland
Cohocton ES 200/PK-4
30 Park Ave 14826 585-384-5234
Jason Oliver, prin. Fax 384-5677

Cohoes, Albany, Pop. 15,737
Cohoes CSD 1,900/K-12
7 Bevan St 12047 518-237-0100
Dr. Jennifer Spring Ed.D., supt. Fax 237-2912
www.cohoes.org
Cohoes MS 400/6-8
7 Bevan St 12047 518-237-4131
Daniel Martinelli, prin. Fax 237-2253
Harmony Hill ES 400/K-5
1 Madalon Hickey Way 12047 518-233-1900
Mark Perry, prin. Fax 237-1964
Lansing ES 400/K-5
26 James St 12047 518-237-5044
Clifford Bird, prin. Fax 237-1879
Van Schaick ES 100/K-5
150 Continental Ave 12047 518-237-2828
Jacqueline DeChiaro, prin. Fax 237-3597

North Colonie Central SD
Supt. — See Latham
Boght Hills ES 500/K-6
38 Dunsbach Ferry Rd 12047 518-785-0222
Kimberly Greiner, prin. Fax 785-8801

Colden, Erie
Springville-Griffith Inst. Central SD
Supt. — See Springville
Colden ES 200/K-5
8263 Boston Colden Rd 14033 716-592-3217
Marcole Feuz, prin. Fax 592-3254

Cold Spring, Putnam, Pop. 1,981
Haldane Central SD 900/K-12
15 Craigside Dr 10516 845-265-9254
Diana Bowers, supt. Fax 265-9213
www.haldaneschool.org
Haldane S 600/K-8
15 Craigside Dr 10516 845-265-9254
Brent Harrington, prin. Fax 265-2674

Cold Spring Harbor, Suffolk, Pop. 5,024
Cold Spring Harbor Central SD 1,900/K-12
75 Goose Hill Rd 11724 631-367-5900
Robert Fenter, supt. Fax 367-3108
www.csh.k12.ny.us
Goose Hill PS 200/K-1
75 Goose Hill Rd 11724 631-367-5941
Lynn Herschlein, prin. Fax 367-2157
Other Schools – See Huntington, Syosset

College Point, See New York
NYC Department of Education
Supt. — See New York
Public S 29 800/PK-5
12510 23rd Ave 11356 718-886-5111
Jill Leakey, prin. Fax 461-6812
Public S 129 1,100/PK-5
12802 7th Ave 11356 718-353-3150
Marilyn Alesi, prin. Fax 321-2476

Colton, Saint Lawrence, Pop. 343
Colton-Pierrepont Central SD 300/PK-12
4921 State Highway 56 13625 315-262-2100
Joseph Kardash, supt. Fax 262-2644
www.cpcs.us/
Colton-Pierrepont Central S 300/PK-12
4921 State Highway 56 13625 315-262-2100
James Nee, prin. Fax 262-2644

Commack, Suffolk, Pop. 35,739
Commack UFD
Supt. — See East Northport
Burr IS, 235 Burr Rd 11725 800/3-5
Paul Schmelter, prin. 631-858-3636
Commack MS 1,700/6-8
700 Vanderbilt Pkwy 11725 631-858-3500
Anthony Davidson, prin.
Indian Hollow ES 300/K-2
151 Kings Park Rd 11725 631-858-3590
Brian Simpson, prin.
Mandracchia/Sawmill IS 700/3-5
103 New Hwy 11725 631-858-3650
Michelle Tancredi, prin.
North Ridge ES 400/K-2
300 Townline Rd 11725 631-912-2190
Katherine Rihm, prin.
Wood Park ES, 15 New Hwy 11725 300/K-2
Michelle Collison, prin. 631-858-3680

Holy Family Regional S 300/PK-8
2 Indian Head Rd 11725 631-543-0202
Brian Caltabiano, prin. Fax 543-2818
Jewish Academy 100/K-8
74 Hauppauge Rd 11725 631-368-2600
Dr. Shimon Waronker, dean Fax 368-2384

Congers, Rockland, Pop. 8,213
Clarkstown Central SD
Supt. — See New City
Lakewood ES, 77 Lakeland Ave 10920 400/K-5
Dr. Joan Taylor Ed.D., prin. 845-639-6320

Rockland Country Day S 100/PK-12
34 Kings Hwy 10920 845-268-6802
Kimberly Morcate, head sch Fax 268-4644

Conklin, Broome
Susquehanna Valley Central SD 1,600/K-12
PO Box 200 13748 607-775-0170
Roland Doig, supt. Fax 775-4575
www.svsabers.org
Donnelly ES 300/K-5
PO Box 250 13748 607-775-0176
Jill Rich, prin. Fax 775-9313
Stank MS 400/6-8
PO Box 225 13748 607-775-0303
Donald Gerlach, prin. Fax 775-9142
Other Schools – See Binghamton

Constantia, Oswego, Pop. 1,168
Central Square Central SD
Supt. — See Central Square
Cole ES 200/PK-5
1683 State Route 49 13044 315-623-9823
Michael Smolnik, prin. Fax 623-7209

Cooperstown, Otsego, Pop. 1,834
Cooperstown Central SD 900/K-12
39 Linden Ave 13326 607-547-8181
Dr. William Crankshaw, supt. Fax 547-5100
www.cooperstowncs.org
Cooperstown ES 500/K-6
21 Walnut St 13326 607-547-9976
Ann Meccariello, prin. Fax 547-4427

Copenhagen, Lewis, Pop. 796
Copenhagen Central SD 500/PK-12
PO Box 30 13626 315-688-4411
Scott Connell, supt. Fax 688-2001
www.ccsknights.org/
Copenhagen Central S 500/PK-12
PO Box 30 13626 315-688-4411
Nadine O'Shaughnessy, prin Fax 688-2001

Copiague, Suffolk, Pop. 22,652
Copiague UFD 4,900/K-12
2650 Great Neck Rd 11726 631-842-4015
Dr. Kathleen Bannon, supt. Fax 841-4614
www.copiague.k12.ny.us/
Copiague MS 1,100/6-8
2650 Great Neck Rd 11726 631-842-4011
Andrew Lagnado, prin. Fax 841-4630
Deauville Gardens ES East 500/K-5
100 Deauville Blvd 11726 631-842-3320
Joseph Buccello, prin. Fax 841-4656
Deauville Gardens ES West 500/K-5
100 Deauville Blvd 11726 631-842-4012
Michael Kelly, prin. Fax 841-4656
Great Neck Road ES 500/K-5
1400 Great Neck Rd 11726 631-842-4013
Karla Cangelosi, prin. Fax 842-4676
Wiley ES 800/K-5
365 Scudder Ave 11726 631-842-4014
Cynthia Florio, prin. Fax 841-4670

Coram, Suffolk, Pop. 38,225
Longwood Central SD
Supt. — See Middle Island
Coram ES 1,100/K-4
61 Mount Sinai Coram Rd 11727 631-698-0077
Susan Connolly, prin. Fax 698-0807

Corfu, Genesee, Pop. 702
Pembroke Central SD 900/PK-12
PO Box 308 14036 585-599-4525
Matthew Calderon, supt. Fax 599-4213
www.pembrokecsd.org
Pembroke IS 300/3-6
58 Alleghany Rd 14036 585-599-4531
Norman Foster, prin. Fax 599-4213
Other Schools – See East Pembroke

Corinth, Saratoga, Pop. 2,505
Corinth Central SD 1,200/K-12
105 Oak St 12822 518-654-2601
Mark Stratton, supt. Fax 654-6266
www.corinthcsd.com
Corinth ES 500/K-5
105 Oak St 12822 518-654-2960
Jennifer Ross-Steimle, prin. Fax 654-6235
Corinth MS 300/6-8
105 Oak St 12822 518-654-9005
Eric Schenone, prin. Fax 654-2129

Corning, Steuben, Pop. 10,950
Corning CSD
Supt. — See Painted Post
Carder ES 500/K-5
289 State St 14830 607-962-2454
Dan Davis, prin. Fax 654-2829
Gregg ES 200/K-5
164 Flint Ave 14830 607-962-1514
Ann Collins, prin. Fax 654-2815
Severn ES 400/K-5
36 McMahon Ave 14830 607-962-6844
John Whaley, prin. Fax 654-2869
Winfield Street ES 300/K-5
193 Winfield St 14830 607-962-6706
Michele Wright, prin. Fax 654-2848

All Saints Academy 100/PK-8
158 State St 14830 607-936-9234
T.J. Verzillo, prin. Fax 936-1797
Alternative S for Math & Science 100/6-8
PO Box 114 14830 607-962-0011
Linda Cole, head sch Fax 962-4866
Corning Christian Academy 200/PK-12
11 Aisne St 14830 607-962-4220
Keila Underwood, admin. Fax 962-4410

Cornwall, Orange, Pop. 11,270
Cornwall Central SD
Supt. — See Cornwall on Hudson
Cornwall Central MS 1,100/5-8
122 Main St 12518 845-534-8009
Kate Polumbo, prin. Fax 534-7809
Cornwall ES 500/K-4
99 Lee Rd 12518 845-534-8009
Megan Argenio, prin. Fax 534-0569
Willow Avenue ES 300/K-4
67 Willow Ave 12518 845-534-8009
Greg Schmalz, prin. Fax 534-3474

Cornwall on Hudson, Orange, Pop. 2,955
Cornwall Central SD 3,300/K-12
24 Idlewild Ave 12520 845-534-8009
Neal S. Miller, supt. Fax 534-9032
www.cornwallschools.com
Cornwall on Hudson ES 300/K-4
234 Hudson St 12520 845-534-8009
Darren Corsetti, prin. Fax 534-2284
Other Schools – See Cornwall

Corona, See New York
NYC Department of Education
Supt. — See New York
Corona Arts and Sciences Academy 100/6-8
98-11 44th Ave 11368 718-507-3820
Beth Hert, prin. Fax 507-3828
IS 61 2,300/6-8
9850 50th Ave 11368 718-760-3233
Joseph Lisa, prin. Fax 760-5220
Pioneer Academy 1,000/K-5
4020 100th St 11368 718-779-5068
Cecilia Jackson, prin. Fax 779-5109
Public S 14 1,700/K-5
10701 Otis Ave 11368 718-699-6071
Heather Benson, prin. Fax 699-3224
Public S 16Q 1,700/K-5
4115 104th St 11368 718-505-0140
Elaine Iodice, prin. Fax 505-0141
Public S 19 1,900/K-5
9802 Roosevelt Ave 11368 718-424-5859
Genie Calibar, prin. Fax 424-7953
Public S 28 600/PK-2
10910 47th Ave 11368 718-271-4971
Laura Pessutti, prin. Fax 271-2576
Public S 92 900/PK-5
9901 34th Ave 11368 718-533-1013
Pasquale Baratta, prin. Fax 533-1083
Public S 143 1,800/K-5
3474 113th St 11368 718-429-5700
Jerry Brito, prin. Fax 478-8306
Public S 330 100/K-2
11008 Northern Blvd 11368 718-505-5110
Debra Rudolph, prin.

Our Lady of Sorrows Academy 300/PK-8
3534 105th St 11368 718-426-5517
Dr. Cristina Cruz, prin. Fax 651-5585
St. Leo Catholic Academy 400/PK-8
10419 49th Ave 11368 718-592-7050
Jennifer Hernandez, prin. Fax 592-0787

Cortland, Cortland, Pop. 18,830
Cortland Enlarged CSD 2,600/K-12
1 Valley View Dr 13045 607-758-4100
Michael Hoose, supt. Fax 758-4128
www.cortlandschools.org
Barry ES 400/K-6
20 Raymond Ave 13045 607-758-4100
Douglas Pasquerella, prin. Fax 758-4159
Parker ES 300/K-6
89 Madison St 13045 607-758-4160
Joshua Bacigalupi, prin. Fax 758-4169
Randall ES 300/K-6
31 Randall St 13045 607-758-4170
Clifford Kostuk, prin. Fax 758-4179
Smith ES 300/K-6
33 Wheeler Ave 13045 607-758-4180
Angela Wanish, prin. Fax 758-4189
Virgil ES 100/K-6
1208 Church St 13045 607-758-4130
Lisa Kaup, prin. Fax 758-4139

Cortland Christian Academy 100/PK-12
15 West Rd 13045 607-756-5838
Craig Miller, head sch Fax 756-7716
St. Mary's S 200/PK-6
61 N Main St 13045 607-756-5614
Denise Hall, prin. Fax 753-3444

Cortlandt Manor, See Peekskill
Hendrick Hudson Central SD
Supt. — See Montrose
Blue Mountain MS 600/6-8
7 Furnace Woods Rd 10567 914-257-5700
John Owens, prin. Fax 257-5701
Furnace Woods ES 300/K-5
239 Watch Hill Rd 10567 914-257-5600
Dr. Cynthia Kramer, prin. Fax 257-5601

St. Columbanus S 200/PK-8
122 Oregon Rd 10567 914-739-1200
Carole Arbolino, prin. Fax 739-1109

Coxsackie, Greene, Pop. 2,765
Coxsackie-Athens Central SD 1,400/K-12
24 Sunset Blvd 12051 518-731-1710
Randall Squier, supt. Fax 731-1729
www.cacsd.org
Coxsackie-Athens MS 400/5-8
24 Sunset Blvd 12051 518-731-1850
David Proper, prin. Fax 731-1859
Coxsackie ES 300/K-4
24 Sunset Blvd 12051 518-731-1770
Karen Miller, prin. Fax 731-1785
Other Schools – See Athens

Craryville, Columbia
Taconic Hills Central SD 1,500/PK-12
73 County Route 11A 12521 518-325-2800
Dr. Neil Howard, supt.
www.taconichills.k12.ny.us/
Taconic Hills ES 800/PK-6
73 County Route 11A 12521 518-325-2820
John Gulisane, prin. Fax 325-2825

Crompond, Westchester, Pop. 2,267
Lakeland Central SD
Supt. — See Shrub Oak
Lincoln-Titus ES 400/K-5
10 Lincoln Ave 10517 914-528-2519
Elizabeth McGowan, prin. Fax 528-1471

Cross River, Westchester
Katonah-Lewisboro UFD 3,000/K-12
60 N Salem Rd 10518 914-763-7000
Andrew Selesnick, supt. Fax 763-7035
www.klschooldistrict.org
Jay MS 800/6-8
40 N Salem Rd 10518 914-763-7500
Rich Leprine, prin. Fax 763-7665
Other Schools – See Goldens Bridge, Katonah, South Salem

Croton on Hudson, Westchester, Pop. 7,883
Croton-Harmon UFD 1,700/K-12
10 Gerstein St 10520 914-271-4713
Dr. Edward Fuhrman, supt. Fax 271-8685
www.chufsd.org
Tompkins ES 600/K-4
8 Gerstein St 10520 914-271-5184
Kelly Maloney, prin. Fax 271-5337
Van Cortlandt MS 500/5-8
3 Glen Pl 10520 914-271-2191
Dr. Barbara Ulm, prin. Fax 271-6618

Holy Name of Mary Montessori S PK-K
114 Grand St 10520 914-271-5182
Jeanne Gagnon, dir. Fax 271-6841

Crown Point, Essex
Crown Point Central SD 300/PK-12
PO Box 35 12928 518-597-4200
Shari Brannock, supt. Fax 597-4121
cpcsteam.org/
Crown Point Central S 300/PK-12
PO Box 35 12928 518-597-3285
Tara Celotti, prin. Fax 597-4121

Cuba, Allegany, Pop. 1,561
Cuba-Rushford Central SD 800/K-12
5476 Route 305 14727 585-968-2650
Carlos Gildemeister, supt. Fax 968-2651
www.crcs.wnyric.org/
Cuba-Rushford ES 300/K-5
15 Elm St 14727 585-968-1760
Kevin Erickson, prin. Fax 968-3181
Cuba-Rushford MS 200/6-8
5476 Route 305 14727 585-968-2650
Katie Ralston, prin. Fax 968-2651

Cuddebackville, Orange
Port Jervis CSD
Supt. — See Port Jervis
Hamilton Bicentennial ES 500/K-6
929 US Route 209 12729 845-858-3100
Jared Kahmar, prin. Fax 754-7355

Cutchogue, Suffolk, Pop. 3,330
Mattituck-Cutchogue UFD 1,300/K-12
385 Depot Ln 11935 631-298-4242
Dr. Anne Smith, supt. Fax 298-8573
www.mufsd.com/cms/
Cutchogue East ES 600/K-6
34900 Main Rd 11935 631-734-6049
Dr. Kathleen Devine, prin. Fax 734-4299

Our Lady of Mercy Regional S 100/PK-6
PO Box 970 11935 631-734-5166
Alexandra Conlan, prin. Fax 734-4266

Dalton, Livingston, Pop. 356
Keshequa Central SD
Supt. — See Nunda
Keshequa ES 200/PK-3
1716 Church St 14836 585-468-2900
Kristina Mileham, prin. Fax 476-5606

Dannemora, Clinton, Pop. 3,874
Saranac Central SD 1,500/K-12
32 Emmons St 12929 518-565-5600
Jonathan Parks, supt. Fax 565-5617
www.saranac.org
Other Schools – See Morrisonville, Saranac

Dansville, Livingston, Pop. 4,671
Dansville Central SD 1,500/K-12
284 Main St 14437 585-335-4000
Dr. Paul Alioto, supt. Fax 335-4002
www.dansvillecsd.org
Dansville PS 300/K-2
284 Main St 14437 585-335-4040
Dan Dixon, prin. Fax 335-8181

Hyde ES 500/3-6
280 Main St 14437 585-335-4030
Lisa Johnson, prin. Fax 335-4056

Davenport, Delaware
Charlotte Valley Central SD 400/PK-12
15611 State Highway 23 13750 607-278-5511
James Harter, supt. Fax 278-5900
www.charlottevalleycs.org
Charlotte Valley S 400/PK-12
15611 State Highway 23 13750 607-278-5511
James Harter, supt. Fax 278-5900

Deerfield, Oneida
Whitesboro Central SD
Supt. — See Whitesboro
Deerfield ES 300/K-5
115 Schoolhouse Rd 13502 315-266-3410
Kelli McGowan, prin. Fax 797-7145

Deer Park, Suffolk, Pop. 27,209
Deer Park UFD 4,300/PK-12
1881 Deer Park Ave 11729 631-274-4000
Eva Demyen, supt. Fax 242-6762
www.deerparkschools.org/
Adams ES 500/PK-2
172 Old Country Rd 11729 631-274-4400
Christopher Molinelli, prin. Fax 274-4439
Frost MS 1,000/6-8
450 Half Hollow Rd 11729 631-274-4200
Dr. Eliana Levey, prin. Fax 242-0035
Kennedy IS 900/3-5
101 Lake Ave 11729 631-274-4300
Susan Bonner, prin. Fax 274-4301
Moore ES 500/PK-2
239 Central Ave 11729 631-274-4450
Alicia Konecny, prin. Fax 242-6575

SS. Cyril & Methodius S 200/PK-8
105 Half Hollow Rd 11729 631-667-6229
Sr. Susan Snyder, prin. Fax 667-0093

De Kalb Junction, Saint Lawrence, Pop. 515
Hermon-DeKalb Central SD 400/PK-12
709 E DeKalb Rd 13630 315-347-3442
Mark White, supt. Fax 347-3817
www.hdcsk12.org
Hermon-DeKalb Central S 400/PK-12
709 E DeKalb Rd 13630 315-347-3442
Megan Foster, prin. Fax 347-3817

Delanson, Schenectady, Pop. 371
Duanesburg Central SD 600/K-12
133 School Rd 12053 518-895-2279
Christine Crowley, supt. Fax 895-2626
www.duanesburg.org/
Duanesburg ES 300/K-6
165 Chadwick Rd 12053 518-895-2580
Andrea Conover, prin. Fax 895-2957

Delevan, Cattaraugus, Pop. 1,080
Yorkshire-Pioneer Central SD
Supt. — See Yorkshire
Delevan ES 400/PK-4
PO Box 217 14042 716-492-9463
Tiffany Giannicchi, prin. Fax 492-9477

Delhi, Delaware, Pop. 3,025
Delaware Academy Central SD at Delhi 600/K-12
2 Sheldon Dr 13753 607-746-1300
Jason D. Thomson, supt. Fax 746-6028
www.delhischools.org
Delaware Academy ES 400/K-5
2 Sheldon Dr 13753 607-746-2105
Julie Mable, prin. Fax 746-6223

Delmar, Albany, Pop. 8,360
Bethlehem Central SD 4,700/K-12
700 Delaware Ave 12054 518-439-7098
Jody Monroe, supt. Fax 475-0352
bcsd.k12.ny.us
Bethlehem Central MS 1,200/6-8
332 Kenwood Ave 12054 518-439-7460
Michael Klugman, prin. Fax 475-0092
Eagle ES, 27 Van Dyke Rd 12054 400/K-5
Dianna Reagan, prin. 518-694-8825
Elsmere ES 300/K-5
247 Delaware Ave 12054 518-439-4996
Katherine Kloss, prin. Fax 439-7546
Hamagrael ES 400/K-5
1 McGuffey Ln 12054 518-439-4905
Dave Ksanznak, prin. Fax 475-9659
Slingerlands ES 500/K-5
25 Union Ave 12054 518-439-7681
Heidi Bonacquist, prin. Fax 475-1931
Other Schools – See Glenmont

St. Thomas the Apostle S 200/PK-8
42 Adams Pl 12054 518-439-5573
Thomas Kane, prin. Fax 478-9773

Depew, Erie, Pop. 15,147
Depew UFD 1,800/K-12
5201 Transit Rd 14043 716-686-5105
Dr. Jeffrey Rabey, supt. Fax 686-5101
www.depewschools.org
Cayuga Heights ES 800/K-5
1780 Como Park Blvd 14043 716-686-5005
Michelle Kudla, prin. Fax 686-5016
Depew MS 400/6-8
5201 Transit Rd 14043 716-686-5050
James Lupini, prin. Fax 686-5057

Lancaster Central SD
Supt. — See Lancaster
Sciole ES 400/K-3
86 Alys Dr E 14043 716-686-3285
Carrie Greene, prin. Fax 686-3309

Our Lady of the Blessed Sacrament S 200/PK-8
20 French Rd 14043 716-685-2544
Debbie Szczepanski, prin. Fax 685-9103

Deposit, Delaware, Pop. 1,641
Deposit Central SD 600/PK-12
171 2nd St 13754 607-467-5380
Denise Cook, supt. Fax 467-5535
www.depositcsd.org
Deposit ES 300/PK-6
171 2nd St 13754 607-467-2198
Kelli Parsons, prin. Fax 467-4495

Derby, Erie
Lake Shore Central SD
Supt. — See Angola
Highland ES 400/K-5
6745 Erie Rd 14047 716-549-4397
Christopher Walsh, prin. Fax 549-2337

DeRuyter, Madison, Pop. 552
De Ruyter Central SD 400/K-12
711 Railroad St 13052 315-852-3400
Charles Walters, supt. Fax 852-3446
www.deruytercentral.org/
De Ruyter Central ES 200/K-5
711 Railroad St 13052 315-852-3400
Kimberly O'Brien, prin. Fax 852-9600

De Witt, Onondaga, Pop. 8,244
Jamesville-DeWitt Central SD 2,900/K-12
PO Box 606 13214 315-445-8304
Dr. Alice Kendrick, supt. Fax 445-8477
www.jamesvilledewitt.org
Moses-De Witt ES 300/K-4
201 Jamesville Rd 13214 315-445-8370
Mary Sylvester, prin. Fax 445-2274
Other Schools – See Jamesville

Holy Cross S 200/PK-6
4200 E Genesee St 13214 315-446-4890
Martha O'Leary, prin. Fax 446-4799
Syracuse Hebrew S 100/K-6
5655 Thompson Rd 13214 315-446-1900
Lori Tenenbaum, head sch Fax 446-3714

Dexter, Jefferson, Pop. 1,036
General Brown Central SD 1,500/K-12
PO Box 500 13634 315-779-2300
Barbara Case, supt. Fax 639-6916
www.gblions.org
Dexter ES 300/K-6
415 E Grove St 13634 315-779-2300
David Ramie, prin. Fax 639-6845
Other Schools – See Brownville

Dix Hills, Suffolk, Pop. 26,364
Commack UFD
Supt. — See East Northport
Rolling Hills ES 200/K-2
25 McCulloch Dr 11746 631-858-3570
Janet Studley, prin.

Half Hollow Hills Central SD 8,100/K-12
525 Half Hollow Rd 11746 631-592-3000
Dr. Patrick Harrigan, supt. Fax 592-3900
www.hhh.k12.ny.us
Candlewood MS 1,000/6-8
1200 Carlls Straight Path 11746 631-592-3300
Pamela Higgins, prin. Fax 592-3921
Otsego ES 500/K-5
55 Otsego Ave 11746 631-592-3600
Dr. Stacey Gillespie, prin. Fax 592-3915
Paumanok ES 600/K-5
1 Seaman Neck Rd 11746 631-592-3650
Kendra Cooper, prin. Fax 592-3916
Signal Hill ES 600/K-5
670 Caledonia Rd 11746 631-592-3700
Maryann Fasciana, prin. Fax 592-3917
Vanderbilt ES 400/K-5
350 Deer Park Rd 11746 631-592-3800
Martin Boettcher, prin. Fax 592-3918
Other Schools – See Melville

Upper Room Christian S 200/K-12
722 Deer Park Rd 11746 631-242-5359

Dobbs Ferry, Westchester, Pop. 10,650
Dobbs Ferry UFD 1,500/K-12
505 Broadway 10522 914-693-1506
Dr. Lisa Brady, supt. Fax 693-1787
www.dfsd.org
Dobbs Ferry MS 400/6-8
505 Broadway 10522 914-693-7640
Patrick Mussolini, prin. Fax 693-5229
Springhurst ES 700/K-5
175 Walgrove Ave 10522 914-693-1503
Julia Drake, prin. Fax 693-3188

Dolgeville, Herkimer, Pop. 2,188
Dolgeville Central SD 900/PK-12
38 Slawson St 13329 315-429-3155
Christine Reynolds, supt. Fax 429-8473
www.dolgeville.org
Dolgeville Central ES 400/PK-4
38 Slawson St 13329 315-429-3155
Crystal Chrisman, prin. Fax 429-9328
Dolgeville Central MS 300/5-8
38 Slawson St 13329 315-429-3155
Ruth Leavitt, prin. Fax 429-8473

Douglaston, See New York
NYC Department of Education
Supt. — See New York
Public S 98 200/K-5
4020 235th St 11363 718-423-8535
Lena Kim, prin. Fax 423-8550

Divine Wisdom Catholic Academy 300/PK-8
4511 245th St 11362 718-631-3153
Miriam Bonici, prin. Fax 631-3945

Dover Plains, Dutchess, Pop. 1,293
Dover UFD 1,400/K-12
2368 Route 22 12522 845-877-5700
Michael Tierney, supt. Fax 877-5766
www.doverschools.org
Dover ES 300/3-5
9 School St 12522 845-877-5730
Herman Harmelink, prin. Fax 877-5739
Dover MS 300/6-8
2368 Route 22 12522 845-877-5740
Patricia Rizzo, prin. Fax 877-5749
Other Schools – See Wingdale

Downsville, Delaware, Pop. 606
Downsville Central SD 300/PK-12
PO Box J 13755 607-363-2100
John Evans, supt. Fax 363-2105
www.dcseagles.org
Downsville Central S 300/PK-12
PO Box J 13755 607-363-2111
Timothy McNamara, prin. Fax 363-2105

Dryden, Tompkins, Pop. 1,854
Dryden Central SD 1,600/PK-12
PO Box 88 13053 607-844-5361
William Locke, supt. Fax 844-4733
dcsd-ny.schoolloop.com
Dryden ES 600/PK-5
PO Box 88 13053 607-844-8694
Patricia Wilson, prin. Fax 844-4641
Dryden MS 400/6-8
PO Box 88 13053 607-844-8694
Michael Farney, prin. Fax 844-5174
Other Schools – See Freeville, Mc Lean

Dundee, Yates, Pop. 1,714
Dundee Central SD 700/PK-12
55 Water St 14837 607-243-5533
Kelly Houck, supt. Fax 243-7912
www.dundeecs.org
Dundee ES 300/PK-6
55 Water St 14837 607-243-5535
Laurie Hopkins-Halbert, prin. Fax 243-7912

Dunkirk, Chautauqua, Pop. 12,328
Dunkirk CSD 2,000/K-12
620 Marauder Dr 14048 716-366-9300
Dr. James Tracy, supt. Fax 366-9399
www.dunkirkcsd.org
Dunkirk MS 500/6-8
525 Eagle St 14048 716-366-9300
Rebecca Farwell, prin. Fax 366-9357
Public S 3 200/K-5
742 Lamphere St 14048 716-366-9300
Daniel Genovese, prin. Fax 366-0565
Public S 4 200/K-5
752 Central Ave 14048 716-366-9300
Kimberlee Texter, prin. Fax 366-0548
Public S 5 200/K-5
117 Brigham Rd 14048 716-366-9300
David Boyda, prin. Fax 366-9355
Public S 7 300/K-5
348 Lake Shore Dr E 14048 716-366-9300
Michele Heenan, prin. Fax 366-9426

Northern Chautauqua Catholic S 200/PK-8
336 Washington Ave 14048 716-366-0630
Jennie Tilaro, prin. Fax 366-5101

Durhamville, Oneida, Pop. 575
Oneida CSD
Supt. — See Oneida
Durhamville ES 300/K-6
5462 Main St 13054 315-363-8065
Margaret Visalli, prin. Fax 366-0615

East Amherst, Erie
Williamsville Central SD 10,200/K-12
PO Box 5000 14051 716-626-8000
Dr. Scott Martzloff, supt. Fax 626-8089
www.williamsvillek12.org
Casey MS 700/5-8
105 Casey Rd 14051 716-626-8585
Peter Dobmeier, prin. Fax 626-8562
Dodge ES 600/K-4
1900 Dodge Rd 14051 716-626-9821
Charles Smilinich, prin. Fax 626-9849
Transit MS 1,000/5-8
8730 Transit Rd 14051 716-626-8701
Daniel Walh, prin. Fax 626-8796
Other Schools – See Williamsville

East Aurora, Erie, Pop. 6,180
East Aurora UFD 1,800/K-12
430 Main St 14052 716-687-2302
Brian Russ, supt. Fax 652-8581
eastauroraschools.org/
East Aurora MS 600/5-8
430 Main St 14052 716-687-2453
Matthew Brown, prin. Fax 652-8581
Parkdale ES 600/K-4
141 Girard Ave 14052 716-687-2352
Jessica Lyons, prin. Fax 687-2350

Iroquois Central SD
Supt. — See Elma
Wales PS 200/K-4
4650 Woodchuck Rd 14052 716-652-3000
Kimberly Morrison, prin. Fax 995-2340

Immaculate Conception S 200/K-8
510 Oakwood Ave 14052 585-652-5855
Scott Kapperman, prin. Fax 805-0192

East Berne, Albany

Helderberg Christian S 50/K-12
PO Box 225 12059 518-499-5416
Michael Collins, admin. Fax 499-5416

Eastchester, Westchester, Pop. 19,285
Eastchester UFD 3,100/K-12
580 White Plains Rd 10709 914-793-6130
Dr. Walter Moran Ed.D., supt. Fax 793-9006
district.eastchesterschools.org
Eastchester MS 700/6-8
550 White Plains Rd 10709 914-793-6130
Josh Elder, prin. Fax 793-1699
Hutchinson ES 500/2-5
60 Mill Rd 10709 914-793-6130
Dr. Annette Keane, prin. Fax 793-9006
Waverly PS 500/K-1
45 Hall Ave 10709 914-793-6130
Mari Doyle, prin. Fax 793-9006
Other Schools – See Scarsdale

Tuckahoe UFD 1,000/K-12
65 Siwanoy Blvd 10709 914-337-6600
Carl Albano, supt. Fax 337-3072
www.tuckahoeschools.org
Cottle ES 500/K-5
2 Siwanoy Blvd 10709 914-337-5376
Louis Cuglietto, prin. Fax 337-5334
Tuckahoe MS 200/6-8
65 Siwanoy Blvd 10709 914-337-5376
Mark Barnett, prin. Fax 337-5236

East Elmhurst, See New York
NYC Department of Education
Supt. — See New York
East Elmhurst Community S 100/K-1
2625 97th St 11369 718-505-6050
Rachel Hallenbeck, prin. Fax 505-6055
IS 227 1,700/5-8
3202 Junction Blvd 11369 718-335-7500
Helen Ponella, prin. Fax 779-7186
Public S 127 1,500/PK-8
9801 25th Ave 11369 718-446-4700
Avita Sanavria, prin. Fax 397-7645
Public S 148 1,000/PK-5
8902 32nd Ave 11369 718-898-8181
Yolanda Harvey, prin. Fax 476-2992
Public S 228 400/PK-2
3263 93rd St 11369 718-899-5799
Olga Guzman, prin. Fax 899-7323

East Greenbush, Rensselaer, Pop. 4,416
East Greenbush Central SD 4,100/K-12
29 Englewood Ave 12061 518-207-2500
Jeffrey Simons, supt. Fax 477-4833
www.egcsd.org
Genet ES 400/K-5
29 Englewood Ave 12061 518-207-2680
Ana Yeomans, prin. Fax 477-4466
Goff MS 900/6-8
35 Gilligan Rd 12061 518-207-2430
Wayne Grignon, prin. Fax 477-2667
Other Schools – See Castleton on Hudson, Nassau, Rensselaer, Troy

---

Holy Spirit S 200/PK-8
54 Highland Dr 12061 518-477-5739
Michael Kosar, prin. Fax 477-5743

East Hampton, Suffolk, Pop. 1,079
East Hampton UFD 1,800/K-12
4 Long Ln 11937 631-329-4100
Richard Burns, supt. Fax 324-0109
www.ehufsd.org
East Hampton MS 400/6-8
76 Newtown Ln 11937 631-329-4116
Dr. Charles Soriano, prin. Fax 329-4187
Marshall ES 600/K-5
3 Gingerbread Ln 11937 631-329-4205
Elizabeth Doyle, prin. Fax 329-4157

Springs UFD 700/PK-8
48 School St 11937 631-324-0144
Debra Winter, supt. Fax 324-0269
www.springsschool.org
Springs S 700/PK-8
48 School St 11937 631-324-0144
Eric Casale, prin. Fax 324-0269

East Islip, Suffolk, Pop. 14,328
East Islip UFD
Supt. — See Islip Terrace
Kennedy ES 200/3-5
94 Woodland Dr 11730 631-581-1608
Dr. Deborah Smith, prin. Fax 581-1354
Timber Point ES 200/PK-2
200 Timberpoint Rd 11730 631-581-1887
Danielle Naccara, prin. Fax 581-4078

St. Mary S 400/PK-8
16 Harrison Ave 11730 631-581-3423
Biagio Arpino, prin. Fax 581-7509

East Meadow, Nassau, Pop. 37,572
East Meadow UFD
Supt. — See Westbury
Barnum Woods ES 700/K-5
500 May Ln 11554 516-564-6500
Gregory Bottari, prin. Fax 564-6507
McVey ES 700/K-5
2201 Devon St 11554 516-228-5300
Kerry Dunne, prin. Fax 228-5317
Meadowbrook ES 400/K-5
241 Old Westbury Rd 11554 516-520-4400
Kelly O'Brien, prin. Fax 520-4403
Parkway ES 500/K-5
465 Bellmore Rd 11554 516-679-3500
Jamie Mack, prin. Fax 679-3507

Woodland MS 1,100/6-8
690 Wenwood Dr 11554 516-564-6523
James Lethbridge, prin. Fax 564-6519

East Moriches, Suffolk, Pop. 5,179
East Moriches UFD 700/K-8
9 Adelaide Ave 11940 631-878-0162
Dr. Charles Russo, supt. Fax 878-0186
emoschools.org/
East Moriches ES 400/K-4
523 Montauk Hwy 11940 631-878-0162
Edward Schneyer, prin. Fax 878-1097
East Moriches MS 300/5-8
9 Adelaide Ave 11940 631-878-0162
Michael Carlson, prin. Fax 874-0096

East Northport, Suffolk, Pop. 19,969
Commack UFD 6,900/K-12
480 Clay Pitts Rd 11731 631-912-2000
Dr. Donald James, supt. Fax 912-2240
www.commack.k12.ny.us
Other Schools – See Commack, Dix Hills

Northport-East Northport UFD
Supt. — See Northport
Bellerose ES 400/K-5
253 Bellerose Ave 11731 631-262-6800
Lori Beekman, prin. Fax 262-6805
Dickinson Avenue ES 400/K-5
120 Dickinson Ave 11731 631-262-6810
Patricia Essenfeld, prin. Fax 262-6815
East Northport MS 700/6-8
1075 5th Ave 11731 631-262-6770
Pasquale DeStefano, prin. Fax 262-6773
Fifth Avenue ES 400/K-5
1157 5th Ave 11731 631-262-6820
Thomas Harrison, prin. Fax 262-6825
Pulaski Road ES 400/K-5
623 9th Ave 11731 631-262-6850
Jeffrey Haubrich, prin. Fax 262-6855

Long Island Lutheran Day S at St. Paul's 300/PK-5
106 Vernon Valley Rd 11731 631-754-4424
John Buck, head sch Fax 754-4427
Trinity Regional S 500/PK-8
1025 5th Ave 11731 631-261-5130
Jeanne Morcone, prin. Fax 266-5345

East Norwich, Nassau, Pop. 2,682
Oyster Bay-East Norwich Central SD
Supt. — See Oyster Bay
Vernon S 500/3-6
880 Oyster Bay Rd 11732 516-624-6562
Nancy Gaiman, prin. Fax 624-6522

East Patchogue, Suffolk, Pop. 22,129
South Country Central SD 4,500/PK-12
189 N Dunton Ave 11772 631-730-1500
Dr. Joseph Giani, supt. Fax 286-6394
www.southcountry.org
Critz ES 400/K-3
185 N Dunton Ave 11772 631-730-1675
Brian Ginty, prin. Fax 286-5518
Other Schools – See Bellport, Brookhaven

Victory Christian Academy 100/PK-12
1343 Montauk Hwy 11772 631-654-9284
Barbara Seaton, prin. Fax 654-9297

East Pembroke, Genesee
Pembroke Central SD
Supt. — See Corfu
Pembroke PS 200/PK-2
PO Box 190 14056 585-762-8713
Lisa Blake, prin. Fax 599-4213

Eastport, Suffolk, Pop. 1,814
Eastport-South Manor Central SD
Supt. — See Manorville
Eastport ES 600/3-6
390 Montauk Hwy 11941 631-801-3170
Joseph Steimel, prin. Fax 325-1066
Tuttle Avenue S K-2
1 Tuttle Ave 11941 631-801-3058
Karen Koliadko, prin. Fax 325-1952

East Quogue, Suffolk, Pop. 4,715
East Quogue UFD 400/K-6
6 Central Ave 11942 631-653-5210
Robert J. Long, supt. Fax 653-8644
www.eastquogue.k12.ny.us
East Quogue ES 400/K-6
6 Central Ave 11942 631-653-5210
Robert J. Long, prin. Fax 653-8644

East Rochester, Monroe, Pop. 6,434
East Rochester UFD 1,000/PK-12
222 Woodbine Ave 14445 585-248-6302
Dr. Mark Linton Ed.D., supt. Fax 586-3254
www.erschools.org
East Rochester ES 500/PK-5
400 Woodbine Ave 14445 585-248-6311
Marisa Philp, prin. Fax 248-6318

St. John Bosco S 100/PK-8
501 Garfield St 14445 585-348-9401
Colleen Richards, hdmstr. Fax 348-9403

East Rockaway, Nassau, Pop. 9,736
East Rockaway UFD 1,200/K-12
443 Ocean Ave 11518 516-887-8300
Lisa J. Ruiz, supt. Fax 887-8308
www.eastrockawayschools.org
Centre Avenue ES 400/K-6
55 Centre Ave 11518 516-887-8300
Sherry Ma, prin. Fax 599-5727
Rhame Avenue ES 300/K-6
100 Rhame Ave 11518 516-887-8300
Erik Walter, prin. Fax 887-8332

Lynbrook UFD
Supt. — See Lynbrook
Waverly Park ES 200/1-5
320 Waverly Ave 11518 516-887-6590
Lucille McAssey, prin. Fax 887-8262

St. Raymond S 300/PK-8
263 Atlantic Ave 11518 516-593-9010
Sr. Ruthanne Gypalo, prin. Fax 593-0986

East Setauket, See Setauket
Three Village Central SD
Supt. — See Stony Brook
Arrowhead ES 600/K-6
62 Arrowhead Ln 11733 631-730-4100
Marisa Redden, prin. Fax 730-4104
Minnesauke ES 700/K-6
21 High Gate Dr 11733 631-730-4200
Dr. Brian Biscari Ed.D., prin. Fax 730-4202

Laurel Hill S 400/PK-8
201 Old Town Rd 11733 631-751-1154
Robert Stark, hdmstr. Fax 751-2421

East Syracuse, Onondaga, Pop. 2,961
East Syracuse Minoa Central SD 3,300/PK-12
407 Fremont Rd 13057 315-434-3000
Dr. Donna DeSiato, supt. Fax 434-3020
www.esmschools.org
East Syracuse ES 400/K-5
230 Kinne St 13057 315-434-3850
Ron Perry, prin. Fax 434-3855
Fremont ES 300/K-5
115 W Richmond Rd 13057 315-434-3480
Shane Hacker, prin. Fax 434-3490
Park Hill Preschool 300/PK-PK
303 Roby Ave 13057 315-434-3800
Pamela Buddendeck, prin. Fax 434-3820
Pine Grove MS 500/6-8
6318 Fremont Rd 13057 315-434-3050
Doug Mohorter, prin. Fax 434-3070
Woodland ES 400/K-5
6316 Fremont Rd 13057 315-434-3440
Gina Terzini, prin. Fax 434-3450
Other Schools – See Minoa

East Williston, Nassau, Pop. 2,533
East Williston UFD
Supt. — See Old Westbury
North Side ES 600/K-4
110 E Williston Ave 11596 516-333-6860
James Bloomgarden, prin.

Eden, Erie, Pop. 3,494
Eden Central SD 1,500/PK-12
3150 Schoolview Rd 14057 716-992-3630
Sandra Anzalone, supt. Fax 992-3656
www.edencsd.org/
Eden ES 400/3-6
8289 N Main St 14057 716-992-3610
Kelly Morgan-LaRosa, prin. Fax 992-3658
Preiss PS 300/PK-2
3000 Schoolview Rd 14057 716-992-3638
Loran Carter, prin. Fax 992-3631

Edinburg, Fulton
Edinburg Common SD 100/PK-6
4 Johnson Rd 12134 518-863-8412
Kimberly Hromada, supt. Fax 863-2564
www.edinburgcs.org
Edinburg Common ES 100/PK-6
4 Johnson Rd 12134 518-863-8412
Kimberly Hromada, admin. Fax 863-2564

Edmeston, Otsego, Pop. 650
Edmeston Central SD 400/PK-12
PO Box 5129 13335 607-965-8931
Dr. Gary Furman, supt. Fax 965-8942
edmestoncentralschool.net
Edmeston Central S 400/PK-12
PO Box 5129 13335 607-965-8931
Christine Nichols, prin. Fax 965-8942

Elba, Genesee, Pop. 668
Elba Central SD 400/PK-12
PO Box 370 14058 585-757-9967
Keith Palmer, supt. Fax 757-2713
www.elbacsd.org
Elba ES 200/PK-6
PO Box 370 14058 585-757-9967
Carol Bush, prin. Fax 757-2979

Elbridge, Onondaga, Pop. 1,048
Jordan-Elbridge Central SD
Supt. — See Jordan
Elbridge ES 500/PK-4
PO Box 170 13060 315-689-8540
R.J. Hartwell, prin. Fax 689-3320

Eldred, Sullivan
Eldred Central SD 600/PK-12
PO Box 249 12732 845-456-1100
Dr. John Morgano, supt. Fax 557-3672
www.eldred.k12.ny.us
Other Schools – See Glen Spey

Elizabethtown, Essex
Elizabethtown-Lewis Central SD 300/K-12
PO Box 158 12932 518-873-6371
Scott Osborne, supt. Fax 873-9552
www.elcsd.org
Elizabethtown-Lewis Central S 300/K-12
PO Box 158 12932 518-873-6371
Robert Witkiewicz, prin. Fax 873-9552

Ellenburg Depot, Clinton
Northern Adirondack Central SD 800/K-12
PO Box 164 12935 518-594-7060
Laura Marlow, supt. Fax 594-7255
www.nacs1.org/
Northern Adirondack ES 400/K-5
PO Box 164 12935 518-594-3986
Lisa Silver, prin. Fax 594-7255

Ellenville, Ulster, Pop. 3,954
Ellenville Central SD 1,700/PK-12
28 Maple Ave 12428 845-647-0100
Lisa Wiles, supt. Fax 647-0105
www.ecs.k12.ny.us
Ellenville ES 800/PK-5
28 Maple Ave 12428 845-647-0133
Deborah Fox, prin. Fax 647-7090
Ellenville MS 400/6-8
28 Maple Ave 12428 845-647-0126
Andre Spinelli, prin. Fax 647-0230

Ellicottville, Cattaraugus, Pop. 371
Ellicottville Central SD 600/PK-12
5873 Route 219 S 14731 716-699-2368
Robert Miller, supt. Fax 699-6017
www.ellicottvillecentral.com
Ellicottville ES 300/PK-6
5873 Route 219 S 14731 716-699-2318
Connie Poulin, prin. Fax 699-5635

Elma, Erie
Iroquois Central SD 2,200/K-12
PO Box 32 14059 716-652-3000
Douglas Scofield, supt. Fax 652-9305
www.iroquoiscsd.org
Elma PS 200/K-4
PO Box 32 14059 716-652-3000
Darcy Walker, prin. Fax 995-2321
Iroquois IS 200/5-5
PO Box 32 14059 716-652-3000
Ross Esslinger, prin. Fax 995-2346
Iroquois MS 600/6-8
PO Box 32 14059 716-652-3000
Ross Esslinger, prin. Fax 995-2335
Other Schools – See East Aurora, Marilla

Elmhurst, See New York
NYC Department of Education
Supt. — See New York
Elm Tree ES 100/K-1
8637 53rd Ave 11373 718-457-0370
Kristen Niven, prin. Fax 457-0376
51st Avenue Academy 500/4-5
7605 51st Ave 11373 718-429-5287
Jason Chin, prin. Fax 429-7344
Public S 7 1,100/K-3
8055 Cornish Ave 11373 718-446-2726
Bridget Ruggiero, prin. Fax 397-7916
Public S 13 1,600/K-5
5501 94th St 11373 718-271-1021
Evelin Velez, prin. Fax 699-3008
Public S 89 2,000/K-5
8528 Britton Ave 11373 718-898-2230
Laura LaSala, prin. Fax 672-3066
Public S 102 1,200/K-8
5524 Van Horn St 11373 718-446-3308
William Ko, prin. Fax 672-3101

Jewish Institute of Queens 400/PK-12
6005 Woodhaven Blvd 11373 718-426-9369
Rabbi Zalman Zvulonov, prin. Fax 446-2071
St. Adalbert Academy 400/PK-8
5217 83rd St 11373 718-424-2376
Sr. Kathleen Maciej, prin. Fax 898-7852
St. Bartholomew Catholic Academy 300/PK-8
4415 Judge St 11373 718-446-7575
Denise Gonzalez, prin. Fax 446-7743

Elmira, Chemung, Pop. 27,883
Elmira CSD 5,900/PK-12
951 Hoffman St 14905 607-735-3000
Hillary Austin, supt. Fax 735-3009
www.elmiracityschools.com
Beecher ES 400/3-6
310 Sullivan St 14901 607-735-3500
Michael Lanning, prin. Fax 735-3509
Broadway Academy 300/7-7
1000 Broadway St 14904 607-735-3300
Robert Bailey, prin. Fax 735-3309
Broadway ES 500/3-6
1000 Broadway St 14904 607-735-3600
Rebecca Kiley, prin. Fax 735-3609
Coburn ES 500/3-6
216 Mount Zoar St 14904 607-735-3650
Jason Johnston, prin. Fax 735-3659
Diven ES 500/PK-2
1115 Hall St 14901 607-735-3700
Pam Davis-Webb, prin. Fax 735-3709
Fassett ES 400/PK-2
309 W Thurston St 14901 607-735-3900
Mary Cox, prin. Fax 735-3909
Hendy Avenue ES 500/3-6
110 Hendy Ave 14905 607-735-3750
Marc Vesci, prin. Fax 735-3759
Riverside ES 500/PK-2
409 Riverside Ave 14904 607-735-3850
Heather Donovan, prin. Fax 735-3859
Other Schools – See Pine City

Chemung Valley Montessori S 200/PK-8
23 Winters Rd 14903 607-562-8754
Marcy Cathey, head sch Fax 562-3655
Holy Family ES 200/PK-6
421 Fulton St 14904 607-732-3588
Lorie Brink, prin. Fax 732-1850

Elmira Heights, Chemung, Pop. 4,011
Elmira Heights Central SD 1,100/K-12
2083 College Ave 14903 607-734-7114
Mary Beth Fiore, supt. Fax 734-7134
www.heightsschools.com
Cohen ES 500/K-5
100 Robinwood Ave 14903 607-734-7132
Andy Lutz, prin. Fax 734-9574
Cohen MS 200/6-8
100 Robinwood Ave 14903 607-734-5078
Dawn Hanrahan, prin. Fax 734-9382

Elmont, Nassau, Pop. 32,024
Elmont UFD 3,900/PK-6
135 Elmont Rd 11003 516-326-5500
Al Harper, supt. Fax 326-5574
www.elmontschools.org
Carlson ES 800/PK-6
235 Belmont Blvd 11003 516-326-5570
Stacia Walfall, prin. Fax 326-0349
Covert Avenue ES 800/PK-6
144 Covert Ave 11003 516-326-5560
Mary Natoli, prin. Fax 326-0547
Dutch Broadway ES 800/PK-6
1880 Dutch Broadway 11003 516-326-5550
Amy Buchanan, prin. Fax 326-0519
Gotham Avenue ES 600/PK-6
181 Gotham Ave 11003 516-326-5540
Marshall Zucker, prin. Fax 326-0563
Other Schools – See Stewart Manor, Valley Stream

Elmsford, Westchester, Pop. 4,549
Elmsford UFD 1,000/PK-12
98 S Goodwin Ave 10523 914-592-6632
Dr. Marc Baiocco, supt. Fax 592-2181
www.eufsd.org
Dixson PS 200/PK-1
22 S Hillside Ave 10523 914-592-2092
Jeffery Olender, prin. Fax 592-2163
Grady ES 400/2-6
45 Cobb Ln 10523 914-592-8962
Doug Doller, prin. Fax 592-5439

Our Lady of Mt. Carmel S 200/PK-8
59 E Main St 10523 914-592-7575
Sr. Mary Healy, prin. Fax 345-1591

Elwood, Suffolk, Pop. 11,032
Elwood UFD
Supt. — See Greenlawn
Elwood MS 600/6-8
478 Elwood Rd 11731 631-266-5420
Dr. Christina Sapienza, prin. Fax 266-3987
Harley Avenue PS 400/K-2
30 Harley Ave 11731 631-266-5445
Elissa Millan, prin. Fax 266-3985

Endicott, Broome, Pop. 12,995
Union-Endicott Central SD 4,000/K-12
1100 E Main St 13760 607-757-2111
Dr. Suzanne McLeod, supt. Fax 757-2809
www.uek12.org
Johnson ES 400/K-5
715 Paden St 13760 607-757-2137
Alicia Boyce, prin. Fax 757-2878
Johnson ES 600/K-5
999 Taft Ave 13760 607-757-2143
Johanna Hickey, prin. Fax 658-7119
McGuinness ES 400/K-5
1301 Union Center Maine Hwy 13760 607-757-2131
Elaine Taylor, prin. Fax 757-2127
Snapp MS 900/6-8
101 S Loder Ave 13760 607-757-2156
Timothy Lowie, prin. Fax 658-7117
Watson ES 300/K-5
263 Ridgefield Rd 13760 607-757-2152
Emily Regan, prin. Fax 757-2864
West S 200/K-12
1201 Union Center Maine Hwy 13760
Michaelene Cardell, admin. 607-757-2149

All Saints Catholic S 200/PK-6
1112 Broad St 13760 607-748-7423
Angela Tierno-Sherwood, prin. Fax 484-9576

Endwell, Broome, Pop. 11,248
Maine-Endwell Central SD 2,400/K-12
712 Farm To Market Rd 13760 607-754-1400
Jason R. Van Fossen, supt. Fax 754-1650
www.me.stier.org/
Brink ES 700/K-5
3618 Briar Ln 13760 607-786-8244
William Dundon, prin. Fax 786-8213
Maine-Endwell MS 500/6-8
1119 Farm To Market Rd 13760 607-786-8271
Richard Otis, prin. Fax 786-5137
Other Schools – See Maine

Essex, Essex

Lakeside S, 6 Leaning Rd 12936 PK-3
Maeve Taylor, prin. 518-963-7385

Evans Mills, Jefferson, Pop. 605
Indian River Central SD
Supt. — See Philadelphia
Evans Mills PS 500/PK-3
8442 S Main St 13637 315-629-4331
Pamela Knight, prin. Fax 629-5257

Fabius, Onondaga, Pop. 352
Fabius-Pompey Central SD 700/K-12
1211 Mill St 13063 315-683-5301
Timothy Ryan, supt. Fax 683-5827
www.fabiuspompey.org
Fabius-Pompey ES 300/K-5
7800 Main St 13063 315-683-5857
Chantal Corbin, prin. Fax 683-5680

Fairport, Monroe, Pop. 5,283
Fairport Central SD 6,100/K-12
38 W Church St 14450 585-421-2000
Brett Provenzano, supt. Fax 421-3421
www.fairport.org
Brooks Hill ES 600/K-5
181 Hulburt Ave 14450 585-421-2170
Meredith Klus, prin. Fax 421-2173

Brown MS 800/6-8
665 Ayrault Rd 14450 585-421-2065
David Dunn, prin. Fax 421-2136
Dudley ES 600/K-2
211 Hamilton Rd 14450 585-421-2155
Karen Fingar, prin. Fax 421-2328
Jefferson Avenue ES 600/K-5
303 Jefferson Ave 14450 585-421-2185
Richard Greene, prin. Fax 377-3320
Northside IS 700/3-5
181 Hamilton Rd 14450 585-421-2140
Carolyn Shea, prin. Fax 421-2162
Perrin MS 700/6-8
85 Potter Pl 14450 585-421-2080
Patrick Grow, prin. Fax 421-2097

Falconer, Chautauqua, Pop. 2,402
Falconer Central SD 1,200/PK-12
2 East Ave N 14733 716-665-6624
Stephen Penhollow, supt. Fax 665-9265
www.falconercsd.org
Fenner ES 200/3-5
2 East Ave N 14733 716-665-6627
Gary Gilbert, prin. Fax 665-6668
Other Schools – See Kennedy

Fallsburg, Sullivan
Fallsburg Central SD 1,400/PK-12
PO Box 124 12733 845-434-6800
Dr. Ivan Katz, supt. Fax 434-8346
www.fallsburgcsd.net/
Cosor ES 800/PK-6
PO Box 123 12733 845-434-4110
Mary Kate Stinehour, prin. Fax 434-0871

Fallsburg Cheder S 300/PK-8
PO Box 400 12733 845-434-5240

Farmingdale, Nassau, Pop. 8,087
Farmingdale UFD 5,900/K-12
50 Van Cott Ave 11735 516-434-5100
John Lorentz, supt.
www.farmingdaleschools.org
Howitt MS, 70 Van Cott Ave 11735 1,400/6-8
Luis Pena, prin. 516-434-5410
Northside ES, 55 Powell Pl 11735 500/K-5
Michael Febbraro, prin. 516-434-5610
Saltzman East Memorial ES 600/K-5
25 Mill Ln 11735 516-434-5710
Patricia O'Regan, prin. Fax 752-7038
Woodward Parkway ES 900/K-5
95 Woodward Pkwy 11735 516-434-5810
John Klocek, prin.
Other Schools – See North Massapequa

Farmingville, Suffolk, Pop. 15,238
Sachem Central SD
Supt. — See Ronkonkoma
Lynwood Avenue ES 500/K-5
50 Lynwood Ave 11738 631-696-8652
Danielle DeLorenzo, prin. Fax 736-9478

Far Rockaway, See New York
NYC Department of Education
Supt. — See New York
MS 53 300/6-8
1045 Nameoke St 11691 718-471-6900
Andrea Majied, prin. Fax 471-6955
KAPPA VI 300/6-8
821 Bay 25th St 11691 718-471-6934
Gary Dumornay, prin. Fax 471-6938
Lighthouse ES 200/PK-5
180 Beach 35th St 11691 718-327-5828
Rachelle Legions, prin. Fax 327-5956
Public S 43 1,000/PK-8
160 Beach 29th St 11691 718-327-5860
Simone Nicholas, prin. Fax 327-6925
Public S 104 600/PK-5
2601 Mott Ave 11691 718-327-1910
Katie Grady, prin. Fax 337-2146
Public S 105 800/PK-8
420 Beach 51st St 11691 718-474-8615
Laurie Shapiro, prin. Fax 474-8841
Public S 197 500/PK-5
825 Hicksville Rd 11691 718-327-1083
Christina Villavicencio, prin. Fax 327-3518
Public S 253 500/PK-5
1307 Central Ave 11691 718-327-0895
Phoebe Robinson, prin. Fax 327-3964
Village Academy 300/6-8
1045 Nameoke St 11691 718-471-6042
Doris Lee, prin. Fax 471-6243
Wave Preparatory ES PK-2
535 Briar Pl 11691 718-327-7091
Gemma Ferguson, prin.

Bnos Bais Yaakov 700/PK-8
613 Beach 9th St 11691 718-337-6000
Rabbi Ephraim Blumenkrantz, dir. Fax 337-9160
St. Camillus Academy 200/K-8
185 Beach 99th St 11694 718-634-5260
Sheila Smith-Gonzalez, prin. Fax 634-8353
Talmud Torah Siach Yitzchok S 300/PK-8
1513 Central Ave 11691 718-327-6247
Moshe Goodman, admin. Fax 471-0925
Torah Academy for Girls 1,100/PK-8
444 Beach 6th St 11691 718-471-8444
Temima Feldman, prin. Fax 868-4612
Yeshiva Darchei Torah S 1,600/PK-12
257 Beach 17th St 11691 718-868-2300

Fayetteville, Onondaga, Pop. 4,326
Fayetteville-Manlius Central SD
Supt. — See Manlius
Fayetteville ES 400/K-4
704 S Manlius St 13066 315-692-1600
Eileen Lux, prin. Fax 692-1055
Mott Road ES 400/K-4
7173 Mott Rd 13066 315-692-1700
Jonna Johnson, prin. Fax 692-1054
Wellwood MS 700/5-8
700 S Manlius St 13066 315-692-1300
Melissa Corbin, prin. Fax 692-1049

Immaculate Conception S 300/PK-6
400 Salt Springs St 13066 315-637-3961
Donald Mills, prin. Fax 637-2672

Fillmore, Allegany, Pop. 603
Fillmore Central SD 700/K-12
104 W Main St 14735 585-567-2251
Dr. Ravo Root Ed.D., supt. Fax 567-2541
www.fillmorecsd.org
Fillmore Central S 700/K-12
104 W Main St 14735 585-567-2289
Michael Dodge, prin. Fax 567-2541

Fishers Island, Suffolk, Pop. 231
Fishers Island UFD 100/PK-12
PO Box 600 06390 631-788-7444
Karen Goodwin, supt. Fax 788-5562
www.fischool.com
Fishers Island S 100/PK-12
PO Box 600 06390 631-788-7444
Christian Arsenault, prin. Fax 788-5532

Fishkill, Dutchess, Pop. 2,136
Beacon CSD
Supt. — See Beacon
Glenham ES 500/PK-5
20 Chase Dr 12524 845-838-6900
Cassandra Orser, prin. Fax 838-6976

Wappingers Central SD
Supt. — See Hopewell Junction
Brinckerhoff ES 500/K-6
16 Wedgewood Rd 12524 845-897-6800
Ursula Platz, prin. Fax 897-6802
Fishkill ES 500/K-6
20 Church St 12524 845-897-6780
Dr. Andy McNally, prin. Fax 897-6788

St. Mary Mother of the Church S 300/K-8
106 Jackson St 12524 845-896-9561
Barbara Schwiebert, prin. Fax 896-8477

Floral Park, Nassau, Pop. 15,623
Floral Park-Bellerose UFD 1,400/PK-6
1 Poppy Pl 11001 516-434-2735
Dr. Michael Dantona, supt. Fax 327-9304
www.floralpark.k12.ny.us
Childs ES 600/PK-6
10 Elizabeth St 11001 516-434-2780
Susan Fazio, prin. Fax 327-9321
Floral Park-Bellerose ES 800/PK-6
2 Larch Ave 11001 516-434-2750
Jamie Adams, prin. Fax 327-9304

NYC Department of Education
Supt. — See New York
Altman MS 1,000/6-8
8114 257th St 11004 718-831-4000
Jeffrey Slivko, prin. Fax 831-4008
Ambrose S 600/PK-5
8051 261st St 11004 718-831-4010
Danielle LaPorte, prin. Fax 831-4014
Public S 191 400/PK-5
8515 258th St 11001 718-831-4032
Michael Ranieri, prin. Fax 831-4036

Our Lady of the Snows Academy 500/PK-8
7933 258th St 11004 718-343-1346
Joseph Venticinque, prin. Fax 343-7303
Our Lady of Victory S 400/PK-8
2 Bellmore St 11001 516-352-4466
Margaret Augello, prin. Fax 352-2998

Florida, Orange, Pop. 2,798
Florida UFD 800/K-12
PO Box 757 10921 845-651-3095
Jan Jehring, supt. Fax 651-6801
www.floridaufsd.org
Golden Hill ES 400/K-5
PO Box 757 10921 845-651-4407
Deborah Lisack, prin. Fax 651-7460

Flushing, See New York
NYC Department of Education
Supt. — See New York
Active Learning ES 400/PK-3
13720 Franklin Ave 11355 718-445-5730
Robert Groff, prin. Fax 445-5856
IS 25 800/6-8
3465 192nd St 11358 718-961-3480
Maryellen Beirne, prin. Fax 358-1563
IS 237 1,200/6-8
4621 Colden St 11355 718-353-6464
Judith Freidman, prin. Fax 460-6427
IS 250 300/6-8
15840 76th Rd 11366 718-591-9000
Tara Mrwik, prin. Fax 591-2340
JHS 185 1,500/6-8
14726 25th Dr 11354 718-445-3232
Theresa Mshar, prin. Fax 359-5352
JHS 189 700/6-8
14480 Barclay Ave 11355 718-359-6676
Magdalen Radovich, prin. Fax 358-0155
JHS 216 1,400/6-8
6420 175th St 11365 718-358-2005
Reginald Landeau, prin. Fax 358-2070
Public S 20 1,400/PK-5
14230 Barclay Ave 11355 718-359-0321
Victoria Rice, prin. Fax 358-0762
Public S 21 1,300/PK-5
14736 26th Ave 11354 718-445-8833
Michael Swirsky, prin. Fax 358-0891
Public S 22 800/PK-5
15333 Sanford Ave 11355 718-762-4141
Jennifer Meyer, prin. Fax 358-1260
Public S 24 900/K-5
14111 Holly Ave 11355 718-359-2288
Debra Cassidy, prin. Fax 460-3251
Public S 26 700/PK-5
19502 69th Ave 11365 718-464-4505
Andrew Pecorella, prin. Fax 464-4644
Public S 32 900/PK-5
17111 35th Ave 11358 718-463-3747
Debra Errico, prin. Fax 358-1622
Public S 107 1,000/PK-5
16702 45th Ave 11358 718-762-5995
Lori Cummings, prin. Fax 461-4989
Public S 120 1,000/PK-5
5801 136th St 11355 718-359-3390
Robert Marino, prin. Fax 460-4513
Public S 154 700/PK-5
7502 162nd St 11366 718-591-1500
Pamela Bullard, prin. Fax 591-8751
Public S 163 600/PK-5
15901 59th Ave 11365 718-353-2514
Francine Marsaggi, prin. Fax 460-4244
Public S 164 600/PK-8
13801 77th Ave 11367 718-544-1083
Lisa Liatto, prin. Fax 544-2042
Public S 165 800/PK-5
7035 150th St 11367 718-263-4004
Tiffany Davis, prin. Fax 793-9812
Public S 173 900/PK-5
17410 67th Ave 11365 718-358-2243
Molly Wang, prin. Fax 358-2989
Public S 200 500/PK-8
7010 164th St 11365 718-969-7780
Kevin McAuliffe, prin. Fax 380-2615
Public S 201 500/PK-5
6511 155th St 11367 718-359-0620
Rebecca Lozada, prin. Fax 321-2081
Public S 214 500/PK-5
3115 140th St 11354 718-461-4055
Denise Fuccillo, prin. Fax 460-6841
Public S 219 600/PK-8
14439 Gravett Rd 11367 718-793-2130
Frederick Wright, prin. Fax 793-1039
Public S 242 400/PK-3
2966 137th St 11354 718-445-2902
Jill Pritchard, prin. Fax 939-7751
Queens College S for Math/Sci/Tech 500/PK-8
14820 Reeves Ave 11367 718-461-7462
Simi Minhas, prin. Fax 461-7244
Woodside Community S 200/PK-1
39-07 57th St 11377 718-592-3300
Nayeon Hwang, prin. Fax 592-3310

Flushing Christian S 100/K-8
4154 Murray St 11355 718-445-3533
Karen Blatt, head sch Fax 445-7546
Holy Family Catholic Academy 200/PK-8
7415 175th St 11366 718-969-2124
Mary Scheer, prin. Fax 380-2183
Most Holy Redeemer Catholic Academy 200/PK-8
13658 41st Ave 11355 718-961-0246
Maureen Rogone, prin. Fax 961-1403
New Highland S 200/K-8
19310 Peck Ave 11365 718-357-4747
Robin Korn, dir. Fax 357-4323
Promise Christian Academy 100/PK-8
13030 31st Ave 11354 718-461-4409
John Kim, dir. Fax 461-7368
St. Andrew Avellino Catholic Academy 300/PK-8
3550 158th St 11358 718-359-7887
Debora Hanna, prin. Fax 359-2295
St. Kevin Catholic Academy 200/PK-8
4550 195th St 11358 718-357-8110
Dr. Thomas Piro, prin. Fax 357-2519
St. Mel Catholic Academy 400/PK-8
15424 26th Ave 11354 718-539-8211
Christopher Stein, prin. Fax 539-6563
Solomon Schechter S of Queens 400/PK-8
7616 Parsons Blvd 11366 718-591-9800
Sheldon Naparstek, hdmstr. Fax 591-3946
Spyropoulos S 400/K-8
4315 196th St 11358 718-357-5583
Athena Kromidas, prin. Fax 428-3051
Yeshiva Ketana of Queens 400/PK-8
7815 Parsons Blvd 11366 718-969-1000
Rasha Grossman, prin. Fax 969-9600
Yeshiva of Central Queens 900/PK-8
14737 70th Rd 11367 718-793-8500
Rabbi Mark Landsman, prin. Fax 793-8504

Fonda, Montgomery, Pop. 787
Fonda-Fultonville Central SD 1,400/PK-12
PO Box 1501 12068 518-853-4415
Thomas Ciaccio, supt. Fax 853-4461
www.fondafultonvilleschools.org
Fonda-Fultonville ES 600/PK-4
PO Box 1501 12068 518-853-3332
Darcy Williams, prin. Fax 853-1455
Fonda-Fultonville MS 400/5-8
PO Box 1501 12068 518-853-4747
David Zadoorian, prin. Fax 853-4498

Forest Hills, See New York
NYC Department of Education
Supt. — See New York
Academy for Excellence through the Arts 200/PK-3
10855 69th Ave 11375 718-459-1358
Barbara Leto, prin.
JHS 190 1,000/6-8
6817 Austin St 11375 718-830-4970
John Greggo, prin. Fax 830-3566
Public S 101 600/PK-6
2 Russell Pl 11375 718-268-7231
Monique Lopez-Paniagua, prin. Fax 575-3571

Public S 144 800/PK-6
9302 69th Ave 11375 718-268-2775
Reva Schneider, prin. Fax 575-3734
Public S 196 700/K-5
7125 113th St 11375 718-263-9770
Susan Migliano, prin. Fax 575-3934
Public S 220 700/PK-5
6210 108th St 11375 718-592-3030
Josette Pizarro, prin. Fax 271-7642

Bnos Malka Academy 300/PK-8
7102 113th St 11375 718-268-2667
Michael Weichselbaum, prin. Fax 228-9159
Forest Hills Montessori S 100/PK-6
6704 Austin St 11375 718-275-0173
Sunila Tejpaul, dir. Fax 275-0176
Kew-Forest S 200/PK-12
11917 Union Tpke 11375 718-268-4667
Carla MacMullen, head sch Fax 268-9121
Our Lady of Mercy S 400/PK-8
7025 Kessel St 11375 718-793-2086
Dana McCann, prin. Fax 897-2144
Our Lady Queen of Martyrs Catholic Acad 300/PK-8
7255 Austin St 11375 718-263-2622
Anne Zuschlag, prin. Fax 263-0063
Yeshiva Sha'arei Zion Ohel Bracha - Boys 300/PK-8
7524 Grand Central Pkwy 11375 718-268-3444
Rabbi Hy Geller, dir. Fax 268-3447
Yeshiva Sha'arei Zion Ohel Bracha -Girls 200/PK-8
7524 Grand Central Pkwy 11375 718-897-6771

Forestport, Oneida
Adirondack Central SD
Supt. — See Boonville
Forestport ES 100/PK-5
10275 State Route 28 13338 315-392-2700
Linda Guernsey, prin. Fax 392-2707

Forestville, Chautauqua, Pop. 686
Forestville Central SD 500/K-12
12 Water St 14062 716-965-2742
Renee Garrett, supt. Fax 965-2117
www.forestville.com
Forestville ES 300/K-6
12 Water St 14062 716-965-2742
Lindsay Marcinelli, prin. Fax 965-2117

Fort Ann, Washington, Pop. 482
Fort Ann Central SD 400/K-12
1 Catherine St 12827 518-639-5594
Kevin Froats, supt. Fax 639-8911
www.fortannschool.org
Fort Ann S 400/K-12
1 Catherine St 12827 518-639-5594
Justin Hoskins, prin. Fax 639-8911

Fort Covington, Franklin
Salmon River Central SD 1,500/PK-12
637 County Route 1 12937 518-358-6610
Dr. Stanley Harper, supt. Fax 358-3492
www.srk12.org
Salmon River ES 400/PK-6
637 County Route 1 12937 518-358-6670
Ben Barkley, prin. Fax 358-3492
Salmon River MS 300/6-8
637 County Route 1 12937 518-358-6650
Tammy Russell, prin. Fax 358-6510
Other Schools – See Hogansburg

Fort Edward, Washington, Pop. 3,335
Fort Edward UFD 500/PK-12
220 Broadway 12828 518-747-4594
Daniel Ward, supt. Fax 747-6543
www.fortedward.org
Fort Edward S 500/PK-12
220 Broadway 12828 518-747-4529
Karen Jones, prin. Fax 747-6543

Hudson Falls Central SD 2,400/PK-12
1153 Burgoyne Ave 12828 518-747-2121
Linda Goewey, supt. Fax 747-0951
www.hfcsd.org
Other Schools – See Hudson Falls

Fort Montgomery, Orange, Pop. 1,512
Highland Falls Ft. Montgomery Central SD
Supt. — See Highland Falls
Fort Montgomery ES 100/PK-2
895 Route 9W 10922 845-446-9575
Michael McElduff, prin. Fax 446-6608

Fort Plain, Montgomery, Pop. 2,284
Fort Plain Central SD 800/PK-12
25 High St 13339 518-993-4000
David Ziskin, supt. Fax 993-3393
www.fortplain.org
Hoag ES 500/PK-6
25 High St 13339 518-993-4000
Lauren Crisman, prin. Fax 993-4501

Frankfort, Herkimer, Pop. 2,561
Frankfort-Schuyler Central SD 800/K-12
605 Palmer St 13340 315-894-5083
Robert Reina, supt. Fax 895-7011
www.frankfort-schuyler.org
Frankfort-Schuyler ES 400/K-5
610 Reese Rd 13340 315-895-7491
Melanie Welch, prin. Fax 895-4102

Franklin, Delaware, Pop. 368
Franklin Central SD 300/PK-12
PO Box 888 13775 607-829-3551
Brad Zilliox, supt. Fax 829-2101
www.franklincsd.org
Franklin Central S 300/PK-12
PO Box 888 13775 607-829-3551
Julie Bergman, prin. Fax 829-2101

Franklin Square, Nassau, Pop. 28,887
Franklin Square UFD 2,000/PK-6
760 Washington St 11010 516-481-4100
Patrick Manley, supt. Fax 505-6972
www.franklinsquare.k12.ny.us
John Street ES 500/PK-6
560 Nassau Blvd 11010 516-505-6955
Thomas Riccobono, prin. Fax 505-6988
Polk Street ES 700/PK-6
960 Polk Ave 11010 516-326-3785
Gil Torossian, prin. Fax 326-3794
Washington Street ES 800/PK-6
760 Washington St 11010 516-505-6995
Valerie Mazzone, prin. Fax 505-6991

Valley Stream 13 UFD
Supt. — See Valley Stream
Willow Road ES 500/K-6
880 Catalpa Dr 11010 516-568-6640
Rosalie Ambrosio, prin. Fax 292-2095

Franklinville, Cattaraugus, Pop. 1,715
Franklinville Central SD 700/PK-12
31 N Main St 14737 716-676-8029
Michelle Spasiano, supt. Fax 676-8041
tbafcs.org
Franklinville ES 400/PK-6
32 N Main St 14737 716-676-8020
J. Schirrmacher-Smith, prin. Fax 676-2797

Fredonia, Chautauqua, Pop. 11,103
Fredonia Central SD 1,500/PK-12
425 E Main St 14063 716-679-1581
Jeffrey Sortisio, supt. Fax 679-1555
www.fredonia.wnyric.org
Fredonia ES 600/PK-4
425 E Main St 14063 716-679-1581
Amy Piper, prin. Fax 679-9043
Fredonia MS 500/5-8
425 E Main St 14063 716-679-1581
Andrew Ludwig, prin. Fax 672-2686

Freeport, Nassau, Pop. 41,960
Freeport UFD 6,500/PK-12
235 N Ocean Ave 11520 516-867-5200
Dr. Kishore Kuncham, supt. Fax 623-4759
www.freeportschools.org
Archer St ES Language Arts Math & Tech 600/K-4
255 Archer St 11520 516-867-5250
Paula Lein, prin. Fax 379-6577
Atkinson ES 900/5-6
58 W Seaman Ave 11520 516-867-5270
Connie Velez, prin. Fax 379-7678
Bayview Avenue ES 600/K-4
325 W Merrick Rd 11520 516-867-5255
Mary Garguilo, prin. Fax 379-6906
Columbus Ave S 200/PK-K
150 N Columbus Ave 11520 516-867-5240
Cleopatra Panagiosoulis, prin. Fax 379-6793
Dodd MS 1,000/7-8
25 Pine St 11520 516-867-5280
Johane Ligonde, prin. Fax 379-6794
Giblyn ES 600/K-4
450 S Ocean Ave 11520 516-867-5260
Amanda Muldowney, prin. Fax 379-6887
New Visions Museum ES 500/K-4
80 Raynor St 11520 516-867-5390
Renee Crump, prin. Fax 867-0392

De LaSalle S 100/5-8
87 Pine St 11520 516-379-8660
William Gault, prin. Fax 379-8806
Freeport Christian Academy 100/PK-8
50 N Main St 11520 516-546-2020
Denise Panucci, prin. Fax 546-8394

Freeville, Tompkins, Pop. 511
Dryden Central SD
Supt. — See Dryden
Freeville ES 100/K-3
43 Main St 13068 607-844-9251
Audrey Ryan, prin. Fax 844-3826

Covenant Love Community S 50/PK-8
1768 Drydon Rd 13068 607-347-4413
Pamela Bateman, prin. Fax 347-4466

Frewsburg, Chautauqua, Pop. 1,879
Frewsburg Central SD 900/PK-12
PO Box 690 14738 716-569-7000
Shelly O'Boyle, supt. Fax 569-7050
www.frewsburgcsd.org
Jackson ES 500/PK-6
PO Box 690 14738 716-569-7031
Ann Morrison, prin. Fax 569-7006

Friendship, Allegany, Pop. 1,208
Friendship Central SD 400/PK-12
46 W Main St 14739 585-973-3534
Judy May, supt. Fax 973-2023
www.friendship.wnyric.org/
Friendship Central S 400/PK-12
46 W Main St 14739 585-973-3311
Judy May, supt. Fax 973-2023

Fulton, Oswego, Pop. 11,719
Fulton CSD 3,600/K-12
167 S 4th St 13069 315-593-5510
Brian Pulvino, supt. Fax 598-6351
www.fulton.cnyric.org/
Fairgrieve ES 500/K-6
716 Academy St 13069 315-593-5550
Jean Sampsell, prin. Fax 593-5561
Fulton JHS 600/7-8
129 Curtis St 13069 315-593-5440
Chris Leece, prin. Fax 593-5459
Granby ES 500/K-6
400 W 7th St N 13069 315-593-5480
Heather Perry-Witter, prin. Fax 598-2835

Lanigan ES 400/K-6
59 Bakeman St 13069 315-593-5470
Jeff Hendrickson, prin. Fax 593-5479
Volney ES 400/K-6
2592 State Route 3 13069 315-593-5570
Todd Terpening, prin. Fax 593-5579

Mexico Central SD
Supt. — See Mexico
Palermo ES 300/PK-4
1638 County Route 45 13069 315-963-8400
Margaret Scorzelli, prin. Fax 963-3199

Dexterville SDA S 50/1-8
783 County Route 3 13069 315-593-8674

Gainesville, Wyoming, Pop. 228
Letchworth Central SD 900/PK-12
5550 School Rd 14066 585-493-5450
Todd Campbell, supt. Fax 493-2762
www.letchworth.k12.ny.us
Letchworth ES 400/PK-4
5550 School Rd 14066 585-493-2581
William Bean, prin. Fax 493-2762
Letchworth MS 300/5-8
5550 School Rd 14066 585-493-2592
Amy Leone, prin. Fax 493-2762

Galway, Saratoga, Pop. 200
Galway Central SD 900/K-12
5317 Sacandaga Rd 12074 518-882-1033
Shannon Shine, supt. Fax 882-5250
www.galwaycsd.org
Henry ES 400/K-6
5317 Sacandaga Rd 12074 518-882-1033
Michelle McDougall, prin. Fax 882-5250

Garden City, Nassau, Pop. 22,129
Garden City UFD 3,900/K-12
56 Cathedral Ave 11530 516-478-1000
Dr. Alan Groveman, supt. Fax 294-8348
www.gardencity.k12.ny.us
Garden City MS 900/6-8
98 Cherry Valley Ave 11530 516-478-3000
Dr. Peter Osroff, prin. Fax 294-0732
Hemlock ES 200/K-1
78 Bayberry Ave 11530 516-478-1600
Audrey Bellovin, prin. Fax 747-4767
Homestead ES 200/K-1
2 Homestead Ave 11530 516-478-1700
Dr. Suzanne Viscovich, prin. Fax 616-0906
Locust ES 100/K-1
220 Boylston St 11530 516-478-1800
Dr. Jean Ricotta, prin. Fax 747-4586
Stewart ES 600/2-5
501 Stewart Ave 11530 516-478-1400
Linda Norton, prin. Fax 294-5781
Stratford Avenue ES 600/2-5
97 Stratford Ave 11530 516-478-1500
Eileen Vota, prin. Fax 294-9061

St. Anne S 500/PK-8
25 Dartmouth St 11530 516-352-1205
Gene Fennell, prin. Fax 352-5969
St. Joseph S 300/PK-8
450 Franklin Ave 11530 516-747-2730
Brian Columban, prin. Fax 747-2854
Waldorf S of Garden City 300/PK-12
225 Cambridge Ave 11530 516-742-3434
Susan Braun, admin. Fax 742-3457

Garnerville, See West Haverstraw
North Rockland Central SD 7,800/K-12
65 Chapel St 10923 845-942-3000
Ileana Eckert, supt. Fax 942-3175
www.nrcsd.org
Other Schools – See Haverstraw, Stony Point, Thiells, West Haverstraw

---

St. Gregory Barbarigo S 300/PK-8
29 Cinder Rd 10923 845-947-1330
Dana Spicer, prin. Fax 947-4392

Garrison, Putnam
Garrison UFD 200/K-8
PO Box 193 10524 845-424-3689
Laura Mitchell, supt. Fax 424-4733
www.gufs.org
Garrison Union Free S 200/K-8
PO Box 193 10524 845-424-3689
John Griffiths, prin. Fax 424-4733

Gasport, Niagara, Pop. 1,229
Royalton-Hartland Central SD
Supt. — See Middleport
Royalton-Hartland ES 500/PK-4
4500 Orchard Pl 14067 716-735-2000
Donna VanSlyke, prin. Fax 735-2066

Geneseo, Livingston, Pop. 7,881
Geneseo Central SD 900/K-12
4050 Avon Rd 14454 585-243-3450
Timothy Hayes, supt. Fax 243-9481
www.geneseocsd.org/
Geneseo ES 400/K-5
4050 Avon Rd 14454 585-243-3450
Ronald Chesterton, prin. Fax 243-9481

Genesee Country Christian S 100/PK-8
4120 Long Point Rd 14454 585-243-9580
Betsy Flickner, prin. Fax 243-5604

Geneva, Ontario, Pop. 12,783
Geneva CSD 2,200/PK-12
400 W North St 14456 315-781-0400
Trina Smith Newton, supt. Fax 781-4193
www.genevacsd.org

Geneva MS 500/6-8
101 Carter Rd 14456 315-781-0404
Robert Smith, prin. Fax 781-0694
North Street ES 500/3-5
400 W North St 14456 315-781-0489
Eric Vaillancourt, prin. Fax 781-4195
West Street ES 600/PK-2
30 West St 14456 315-781-0406
Tricia Budgar, prin. Fax 781-0599

St. Francis De Sales - St. Stephen S 200/PK-8
17 Elmwood Ave 14456 315-789-1828
Mary Mantelli, prin. Fax 789-9179

Germantown, Columbia
Germantown Central SD 600/K-12
123 Main St 12526 518-537-6280
Susan Brown, supt. Fax 537-6283
www.germantowncsd.org
Germantown Central ES 300/K-6
123 Main St 12526 518-537-6281
Robert Hess, prin. Fax 537-6893

Ghent, Columbia, Pop. 556

Hawthorne Valley Waldorf S 200/PK-12
330 County Route 21C 12075 518-672-7092
Michael Frosch, dir. Fax 672-8006

Gilbertsville, Otsego, Pop. 397
Gilbertsville-Mount Upton Central SD 400/PK-12
693 State Highway 51 13776 607-783-2207
Annette Hammond, supt. Fax 783-2254
www.gmucsd.org
Gilbertsville-Mount Upton ES 200/PK-5
693 State Highway 51 13776 607-783-2207
Heather Wilcox, prin. Fax 783-2254

Gilboa, Schoharie
Gilboa-Conesville Central SD 300/PK-12
132 Wyckoff Rd 12076 607-588-7541
Ruth Reeve, supt. Fax 588-6820
www.gilboa-conesville.k12.ny.us/
Gilboa-Conesville Central S 300/PK-12
132 Wyckoff Rd 12076 607-588-7541
Tom Santacrose, supt. Fax 588-6820

Glasco, Ulster, Pop. 2,055
Saugerties Central SD
Supt. — See Saugerties
Riccardi ES 300/K-6
70 Plenty 12432 845-247-6870
Susan Osterhoudt, prin. Fax 246-2582

Glen Cove, Nassau, Pop. 26,520
Glen Cove CSD 3,200/PK-12
150 Dosoris Ln 11542 516-801-7010
Dr. Maria Rianna, supt. Fax 801-7019
www.glencove.k12.ny.us
Connolly ES 300/3-5
100 Ridge Dr 11542 516-801-7310
Julie Mullan, prin. Fax 801-7319
Deasy ES 500/PK-2
2 Dosoris Ln 11542 516-801-7110
Melanie Arfman, prin. Fax 801-7119
Finley MS 700/6-8
1 Forest Ave 11542 516-801-7510
Nelson Iocolano, prin. Fax 801-7519
Gribbin ES 400/K-2
100 Walnut Rd 11542 516-801-7210
Francine Santoro, prin. Fax 801-7219
Landing ES 400/3-5
60 McLoughlin St 11542 516-801-7410
Benjamin Roberts, prin. Fax 801-7419

All Saints Regional S 200/PK-8
12 Pearsall Ave 11542 516-676-0762
Rev. Elias Carr, hdmstr. Fax 676-0660

Glendale, See New York
NYC Department of Education
Supt. — See New York
IS 119 800/6-8
7401 78th Ave 11385 718-326-8261
Dr. Jeanne Fagan, prin. Fax 456-9523
Public S 91 800/K-5
6810 Central Ave 11385 718-821-6880
Gregory Filippi, prin. Fax 386-0216
Public S 113 1,000/K-8
7823 87th St 11385 718-847-0724
Alejandro Megias, prin. Fax 805-0737

Redeemer Lutheran S 200/PK-8
6926 Cooper Ave 11385 718-821-6670
Michael Williams, prin. Fax 366-0338
Sacred Heart Academy 300/PK-8
8405 78th Ave 11385 718-456-6636
Joanne Gangi, prin. Fax 456-0286
St. Pancras S 200/PK-8
6820 Myrtle Ave 11385 718-821-6721
Diana Soto, prin. Fax 418-8991

Glenfield, Lewis
South Lewis Central SD
Supt. — See Turin
Glenfield ES 200/PK-4
PO Box 66 13343 315-348-2620
Christine Flansburg, prin. Fax 348-2510

Glen Head, Nassau, Pop. 4,626
North Shore Central SD
Supt. — See Sea Cliff
Glen Head ES 400/K-5
7 School St 11545 516-277-7700
Lori Nimmo, prin. Fax 277-7701
Glenwood Landing ES 400/K-5
60 Cody Ave 11545 516-277-7600
Bridget Finder, prin. Fax 277-7601
North Shore MS 700/6-8
505 Glen Cove Ave 11545 516-277-7300
Robert Dennis, prin. Fax 277-7301

Glenmont, Albany
Bethlehem Central SD
Supt. — See Delmar
Glenmont ES 300/K-5
328 Route 9W 12077 518-463-1154
Laura Heffernan, prin. Fax 432-5209

Glens Falls, Warren, Pop. 14,415
Glens Falls CSD 2,000/PK-12
15 Quade St 12801 518-792-1212
Paul Jenkins, supt. Fax 792-1538
www.gfsd.org
Big Cross Street ES 300/K-4
15 Big Cross St 12801 518-792-2619
Debbie Hall, prin. Fax 792-2668
Glens Falls MS 600/5-8
20 Quade St 12801 518-793-3418
Christopher Reed, prin. Fax 793-4888
Jackson Heights ES 300/PK-4
24 Jackson Ave 12801 518-792-1071
Carrie Mauro, prin. Fax 798-6501
Kensington Road ES 300/K-4
43 Kensington Rd 12801 518-793-5151
Jennifer Hayes, prin. Fax 793-5404

Glens Falls Common SD 200/K-6
120 Lawrence St 12801 518-792-3231
John Godfrey, supt. Fax 792-2557
www.abewing.org
Wing ES 200/K-6
120 Lawrence St 12801 518-792-3231
John Godfrey, prin. Fax 792-2557

St. Mary's/St. Alphonsus Regional S 300/PK-8
10-12 Church St 12801 518-792-3178
Fax 792-6056

Glen Spey, Sullivan
Eldred Central SD
Supt. — See Eldred
MacKenzie ES 300/PK-6
1045 Proctor Rd 12737 845-456-1100
Virginia Keegan, prin. Fax 557-8579

Homestead S 200/PK-6
428 Hollow Rd 12737 845-856-6359
Peter Comstock, dir. Fax 858-4145

Gloversville, Fulton, Pop. 15,362
Gloversville CSD 2,900/PK-12
234 Lincoln St 12078 518-775-5791
Robert DeLilli, supt. Fax 773-7280
www.gesdk12.org
Boulevard ES 400/PK-5
56 East Blvd 12078 518-775-5740
Tom Komp, prin. Fax 725-9216
Gloversville MS 600/6-8
234 Lincoln St 12078 518-775-5720
Mark Batty, prin. Fax 773-0628
Kingsborough ES 300/PK-5
24 W 11th Ave 12078 518-775-5730
Kimberly Ross, prin. Fax 773-7357
Park Terrace ES 300/PK-5
40 Bloomingdale Ave 12078 518-775-5750
Brian DiPasquale, prin. Fax 725-7156

Goldens Bridge, Westchester, Pop. 1,609
Katonah-Lewisboro UFD
Supt. — See Cross River
Increase Miller ES 300/K-5
186 Waccabuc Rd 10526 914-763-7100
Kerry Ford, prin. Fax 763-7173

Goshen, Orange, Pop. 5,361
Goshen Central SD 2,900/K-12
227 Main St 10924 845-615-6720
Daniel Connor, supt. Fax 615-6725
www.gcsny.org
Goshen IS 600/3-5
13 McNally St 10924 845-615-6500
Jason Carter, prin. Fax 615-6505
Hooker MS 700/6-8
41 Lincoln Ave 10924 845-615-6300
William Rolon, prin. Fax 615-6310
Scotchtown Avenue ES 600/K-2
120 Scotchtown Ave 10924 845-615-6600
Gregory Voloshin, prin. Fax 615-6610

St. John ES 200/K-8
77 Murray Ave 10924 845-294-6434
Lisa Ferraro, prin. Fax 294-7303

Gouverneur, Saint Lawrence, Pop. 3,883
Gouverneur Central SD 1,200/PK-12
133 E Barney St 13642 315-287-4870
Lauren French, supt. Fax 287-4736
www.gcsk12.org
Gouverneur MS 400/5-8
113 E Barney St 13642 315-287-1903
Steven Coffin, prin. Fax 287-2666
Gouvernuer ES 300/PK-4
111 Gleason St 13642 315-287-2260
Charity Zawatski, prin. Fax 287-2410

St. James S 100/PK-6
20 S Gordon St 13642 315-287-0130
Michele Lallier, prin. Fax 287-0054

Gowanda, Cattaraugus, Pop. 2,660
Gowanda Central SD 1,000/PK-12
10674 Prospect St 14070 716-532-3325
James Klubek, supt. Fax 995-2154
www.gowcsd.com
Gowanda ES 400/PK-4
10674 Prospect St 14070 716-532-3325
Carrie Dzierba, prin. Fax 532-0287
Gowanda MS 200/5-8
10674 Prospect St 14070 716-532-3325
Todd Miklas, prin. Fax 995-2127

Grahamsville, Sullivan
Tri-Valley Central SD 1,100/PK-12
34 Moore Hill Rd 12740 845-985-2296
Ron Musson, supt. Fax 985-0310
www.trivalleycsd.org
Tri-Valley ES 600/PK-6
34 Moore Hill Rd 12740 845-985-2296
Jennifer Williams, prin. Fax 985-0046

Grand Island, Erie
Grand Island Central SD 3,000/PK-12
1100 Ransom Rd 14072 716-773-8800
Dr. Brian Graham Ed.D., supt.
www.grandislandschools.org
Connor MS 700/6-8
1100 Ransom Rd 14072 716-773-8830
John Fitzpatrick, prin. Fax 773-8983
Huth Road ES 500/2-5
1773 Huth Rd 14072 716-773-8850
Ami Alderman, prin. Fax 773-8984
Kaegebein ES 400/2-5
1690 Love Rd 14072 716-773-8840
Mary Haggerty, prin. Fax 773-8991
Sidway ES 400/PK-1
2451 Baseline Rd 14072 716-773-8870
Denise Dunbar, prin. Fax 773-8985

St. Stephen S 200/PK-8
2080 Baseline Rd 14072 716-773-4347
Scott Gruenauer, prin. Fax 773-1438

Granville, Washington, Pop. 2,523
Granville Central SD 1,100/PK-12
58 Quaker St 12832 518-642-1051
Thomas McGurl, supt. Fax 642-2491
www.granvillecsd.org
Granville ES 200/4-6
61 Quaker St 12832 518-642-9357
Cara Talmadge, prin. Fax 642-0771
Other Schools – See Middle Granville

Great Neck, Nassau, Pop. 9,663
Great Neck UFD 6,600/PK-12
345 Lakeville Rd 11020 516-441-4001
Dr. Teresa Prendergast, supt. Fax 441-4994
www.greatneck.k12.ny.us
Baker ES 600/K-5
69 Baker Hill Rd 11023 516-441-4100
Sharon Fougner, prin. Fax 441-4190
Great Neck South MS 800/6-8
349 Lakeville Rd 11020 516-441-4600
Dr. James Welsch, prin. Fax 441-4690
Kennedy ES 500/K-5
1A Grassfield Rd 11024 516-441-4200
Ronald Gimondo, prin. Fax 441-4290
Lakeville ES 800/1-5
4727 Jayson Ave 11020 516-441-4300
Emily Zucal, prin. Fax 441-4316
Saddle Rock ES 600/K-5
10 Hawthorne Ln 11023 516-441-4400
Fax 441-4993
Sherman Great Neck North MS 700/6-8
77 Polo Rd 11023 516-441-4500
Gerald Cozine, prin. Fax 441-4594
Other Schools – See New Hyde Park

Countryside Montessori S 100/PK-1
354 Lakeville Rd 11020 516-466-8422
Mary Ann Pastorelli, prin. Fax 466-8421
Long Island Hebrew Academy 100/PK-4
122 Cuttermill Rd 11021 516-466-3656
Dalia Shabatian, prin. Fax 466-0774
North Shore Hebrew Academy 400/PK-5
16 Cherry Ln 11024 516-487-8687
North Shore Hebrew Academy 200/6-8
26 Old Mill Rd 11023 516-487-9163

Greene, Chenango, Pop. 1,564
Greene Central SD 1,000/PK-12
40 S Canal St 13778 607-656-4161
Gordie Daniels, supt. Fax 656-9362
www.greenecsd.org
Greene IS 200/3-5
105 Elementary Ln 13778 607-656-9891
Bryan Ayres, prin. Fax 656-8092
Greene MS 200/6-8
40 S Canal St 13778 607-656-4161
Timothy Calice, prin. Fax 656-4520
Greene PS 200/PK-2
127 Elementary Ln 13778 607-656-5174
January Pratt, prin. Fax 656-4044

Greenfield Center, Saratoga
Saratoga Springs CSD
Supt. — See Saratoga Springs
Greenfield ES 400/K-5
3180 Route 9N 12833 518-893-7402
Tina Davis, prin. Fax 893-7408

Green Island, Albany, Pop. 2,545
Green Island UFD 300/K-12
171 Hudson Ave 12183 518-273-1422
Dr. Teresa Snyder, supt. Fax 270-0818
www.greenisland.org
Heatly S 300/K-12
171 Hudson Ave 12183 518-273-1422
Erin Peteani, prin. Fax 270-0818

Greenlawn, Suffolk, Pop. 13,492
Elwood UFD 2,400/K-12
100 Kenneth Ave 11740 631-266-5400
Dr. Kenneth Bossert, supt. Fax 368-2338
www.elwood.k12.ny.us
Other Schools – See Elwood, Huntington

Harborfields Central SD 3,300/K-12
2 Oldfield Rd 11740 631-754-5320
Dr. Francesco Ianni, supt. Fax 261-0068
www.harborfieldscsd.net
Lahey ES 800/3-5
625 Pulaski Rd 11740 631-754-5400
Susan Kenny, prin. Fax 754-5412
Oldfield MS 800/6-8
2 Oldfield Rd 11740 631-754-5310
Joanne Giordano, prin. Fax 754-2677
Other Schools – See Centerport

Greenport, Suffolk, Pop. 2,155
Greenport UFD 600/K-12
720 Front St 11944 631-477-1950
David Gamberg, supt. Fax 593-8951
www.gufsd.org/
Greenport ES 300/K-6
720 Front St 11944 631-477-1950
Joseph Tsaveras, prin. Fax 593-8952

Greenvale, Nassau, Pop. 1,063
Roslyn UFD
Supt. — See Roslyn
Harbor Hill ES 500/1-5
3 Glen Cove Rd 11548 516-801-5400
Jessica Kemler, prin. Fax 801-5408

Greenville, Greene, Pop. 9,528
Greenville Central SD 1,200/K-12
4982 State Route 81 12083 518-966-5070
Tammy Sutherland, supt.
www.greenville.k12.ny.us
Ellis ES, 11219 State Route 32 12083 500/K-5
Peter Mahan, prin. 518-966-5070
Greenville MS 300/6-8
4976 State Route 81 12083 518-966-5070
Brian Reeve, prin.

Greenwich, Washington, Pop. 1,754
Greenwich Central SD 1,000/K-12
10 Gray Ave 12834 518-692-9542
Mark Fish, supt. Fax 692-9547
www.greenwichcsd.org
Greenwich ES 500/K-6
10 Gray Ave 12834 518-692-9542
Jennie Mueller, prin. Fax 692-7658

Greenwood Lake, Orange, Pop. 3,105
Greenwood Lake UFD
Supt. — See Monroe
Greenwood Lake ES 200/K-3
PO Box 8 10925 845-477-2411
Maria Boller, prin. Fax 477-3180

Groton, Tompkins, Pop. 2,324
Groton Central SD 800/PK-12
400 Peru Rd 13073 607-898-5301
Margo Martin, supt. Fax 898-4647
www.grotoncs.org
Groton ES 400/PK-5
516 Elm St 13073 607-898-5853
Kent Maslin, prin. Fax 898-5886

Guilderland, Albany
Guilderland Central SD
Supt. — See Guilderland Center
Farnsworth MS 1,100/6-8
6072 State Farm Rd 12084 518-456-6010
Mary Summermatter, prin. Fax 456-3747
Guilderland ES 600/K-5
2225 Western Ave 12084 518-869-0293
Allan Lockwood, prin. Fax 464-6458

Guilderland Center, Albany
Guilderland Central SD 4,900/K-12
PO Box 18 12085 518-456-6200
Dr. Marie Wiles, supt. Fax 456-1152
www.guilderlandschools.org
Other Schools – See Albany, Altamont, Guilderland, Schenectady

Guilford, Chenango, Pop. 361
Bainbridge-Guilford Central SD
Supt. — See Bainbridge
Guilford ES 200/PK-1
130 School St 13780 607-895-6700
Linda Maynard, prin. Fax 895-6713

Hadley, Saratoga, Pop. 1,003

King's S 200/PK-12
6087 State Route 9N 12835 518-654-6230
Kellie Girling, prin. Fax 654-7310

Hamburg, Erie, Pop. 9,357
Frontier Central SD 4,900/K-12
5120 Orchard Ave 14075 716-926-1700
Dr. Bret Apthorpe, supt. Fax 926-1778
www.frontier.wnyric.org
Big Tree ES 500/K-5
4460 Bay View Rd 14075 716-926-1740
Julia Bermingham, prin. Fax 646-2111
Cloverbank ES 600/K-5
2761 Cloverbank Rd 14075 716-926-1760
Renee Kumiega, prin. Fax 627-7959
Frontier MS 1,100/6-8
2751 Amsdell Rd 14075 716-926-1730
Ryan Sikorski, prin. Fax 646-2207
Other Schools – See Blasdell, Lake View

Hamburg Central SD 3,700/PK-12
5305 Abbott Rd 14075 716-646-3220
Michael Cornell, supt. Fax 646-3209
www.hamburgschools.org
Armor ES 400/K-5
5301 Abbott Rd 14075 716-646-3350
Leslie Bennett, prin. Fax 646-3368
Boston Valley ES 300/K-5
7476 Back Creek Rd 14075 716-646-3240
James Martinez, prin. Fax 646-3244
Charlotte Avenue ES 400/PK-5
301 Charlotte Ave 14075 716-646-3370
Danielle Lango, prin. Fax 646-6396
Hamburg MS 900/6-8
360 Division St 14075 716-646-3250
Jennifer Giallella, prin. Fax 646-6380
Union Pleasant Avenue ES 600/K-5
150 Pleasant Ave 14075 716-646-3280
Jacqueline Peffer, prin. Fax 646-3237

SS. Peter & Paul S 300/PK-8
68 E Main St 14075 716-649-7030
Sr. Marilyn Ann Dudek, prin. Fax 312-9313

Hamilton, Madison, Pop. 4,131
Hamilton Central SD 600/PK-12
47 W Kendrick Ave 13346 315-824-6300
Dr. Anael Alston, supt. Fax 824-6314
www.hamiltoncentral.org
Hamilton ES 300/PK-5
47 W Kendrick Ave 13346 315-824-6330
Kevin Ellis, prin. Fax 824-6334

New Life Christian S 100/PK-12
1528 River Rd 13346 315-824-2625
Todd Slabaugh, prin. Fax 824-5102

Hammond, Saint Lawrence, Pop. 278
Hammond Central SD 300/PK-12
PO Box 185 13646 315-324-5931
Karen Carswell, supt. Fax 324-6057
ny01913694.schoolwires.net
Hammond Central S 300/PK-12
PO Box 185 13646 315-324-5931
Kathleen Cruikshank, prin. Fax 324-6057

Hammondsport, Steuben, Pop. 654
Hammondsport Central SD 500/K-12
8272 Main St 14840 607-569-5200
Kyle Bower, supt. Fax 569-5212
www.hammondsportcsd.org
Curtiss Memorial ES 200/K-6
8272 Main Str 14840 607-569-5200
Joseph Koehler, prin. Fax 569-5212

Hampton Bays, Suffolk, Pop. 13,462
Hampton Bays UFD 2,000/PK-12
86 Argonne Rd E 11946 631-723-2100
Lars Clemensen, supt. Fax 723-2109
www.hbschools.us
Hampton Bays ES 800/PK-4
72 Ponquogue Ave 11946 631-723-2121
Marc Meyer, prin. Fax 723-2840
Hampton Bays MS 600/5-8
70 Ponquogue Ave 11946 631-723-4700
Dennis Schug, prin. Fax 723-4900

Hancock, Delaware, Pop. 1,014
Hancock Central SD 400/PK-12
67 Education Ln 13783 607-637-1301
Dr. Terrance Dougherty, supt. Fax 637-2512
www.hancock.stier.org
Hancock ES 100/PK-4
206 Wildcat Dr 13783 607-637-1219
Lori Asquith, prin. Fax 637-2512

Hannibal, Oswego, Pop. 547
Hannibal Central SD 1,400/PK-12
928 Cayuga St 13074 315-564-8100
Christopher A. Staats, supt. Fax 564-7263
www.hannibalcsd.org
Fairley ES 600/PK-4
928 Cayuga St 13074 315-564-8110
Joseph Musa, prin. Fax 564-7951
Kenney MS 400/5-8
928 Cayuga St 13074 315-564-8120
Shawn Morgan, prin. Fax 564-7509

Harpursville, Broome
Harpursville Central SD 800/PK-12
PO Box 147 13787 607-693-8101
Michael Rullo, supt. Fax 693-1480
www.hcs.stier.org/
Olmsted ES 400/PK-6
PO Box 147 13787 607-693-8115
Pamela Horton, prin. Fax 693-1480

Harriman, Orange, Pop. 2,360
Monroe-Woodbury Central SD
Supt. — See Central Valley
Sapphire ES 300/K-1
159 Harriman Heights Rd 10926 845-460-6500
Karen Brock, prin. Fax 460-6045

Harrison, Westchester, Pop. 26,975
Harrison Central SD 3,500/K-12
50 Union Ave 10528 914-630-3021
Dr. Louis Wool, supt. Fax 835-5893
www.harrisoncsd.org
Harrison Avenue ES 500/K-5
480 Harrison Ave 10528 914-630-3192
Valerie Hymes, prin. Fax 835-4311
Klein MS 800/6-8
50 Union Ave 10528 914-630-3033
Scott Fried, prin. Fax 777-1346
Parsons Memorial ES 500/K-5
200 Halstead Ave 10528 914-630-3222
Mark Woodard, prin. Fax 835-4657
Other Schools – See Purchase, West Harrison

Harrisville, Lewis, Pop. 623
Harrisville Central SD 400/PK-12
14371 Pirate Ln 13648 315-543-2707
Robert Finster, supt. Fax 543-2360
www.hcsk12.org
Harrisville ES 200/PK-6
14371 Pirate Ln 13648 315-543-2707
Amy Bird, prin. Fax 543-2360

Hartford, Washington
Hartford Central SD 500/PK-12
4704 State Route 149 12838 518-632-5222
Andrew Cook, supt. Fax 632-5231
www.hartfordcsd.org
Harwood ES 200/PK-5
4704 State Route 149 12838 518-632-5222
Bethellen Mannix, prin. Fax 632-5231

Hartsdale, Westchester, Pop. 5,198
Greenburgh Central SD 1,800/PK-12
475 W Hartsdale Ave 10530 914-761-6000
Dr. Tahira DuPree Chase, supt. Fax 761-2354
www.greenburghcsd.org
Early Childhood Program 100/PK-PK
475 W Hartsdale Ave 10530 914-949-2745
Dawn Male, dir. Fax 949-1548
Highview ES 300/2-3
200 N Central Ave 10530 914-946-6946
Gary Mastrangelo, prin. Fax 946-0397
Other Schools – See White Plains

Sacred Heart S 200/PK-8
59 Wilson St 10530 914-946-7242
Dr. Judith Johnston, prin. Fax 946-7323

Hastings on Hudson, Westchester, Pop. 7,663
Greenburgh-Graham UFD 300/1-12
1 S Broadway 10706 914-478-1106
Oliver Levy, supt. Fax 478-0904
www.greenburgh-graham.org
Ziccolella S 100/1-8
1 S Broadway 10706 914-478-1106
Paul Tobin, prin. Fax 478-8028

Hastings-on-Hudson UFD 1,600/K-12
27 Farragut Ave 10706 914-478-2900
Dr. Antony Sinanis, supt. Fax 478-6209
www.hohschools.org
Farragut MS 500/5-8
27 Farragut Ave 10706 914-478-6230
Gail Kipper, prin. Fax 478-6314
Hillside ES 600/K-4
120 Lefurgy Ave 10706 914-478-6270
Amy Cazes, prin. Fax 478-6279

Hauppauge, Suffolk, Pop. 20,653
Hauppauge UFD 3,900/K-12
PO Box 6006 11788 631-265-3630
Dr. Dennis O'Hara, supt. Fax 265-9546
www.hauppauge.k12.ny.us
Bretton Woods ES 700/K-5
PO Box 6006 11788 631-582-6633
George Gagliardi, prin. Fax 582-1136
Hauppauge MS 900/6-8
PO Box 6006 11788 631-761-8230
Maryann Fletcher, prin. Fax 265-9546
Other Schools – See Smithtown

Haverstraw, Rockland, Pop. 11,732
North Rockland Central SD
Supt. — See Garnerville
Haverstraw ES 500/4-6
16 Grant St 10927 845-942-3400
Benito Herrero, prin. Fax 942-3403

Hawthorne, Westchester, Pop. 4,555
Mount Pleasant Central SD
Supt. — See Thornwood
Hawthorne ES 400/K-2
225 Memorial Dr 10532 914-769-8536
Anne Stern, prin. Fax 769-8527

Hempstead, Nassau, Pop. 52,895
Hempstead UFD 7,200/PK-12
185 Peninsula Blvd 11550 516-434-4000
Regina Armstrong, supt. Fax 292-9471
www.hempsteadschools.org
Franklin ES 700/1-5
335 S Franklin St 11550 516-434-4500
Sandra Powell, prin. Fax 292-7008
Front Street ES 300/1-5
436 Front St 11550 516-434-4550
Arlise Carson, prin. Fax 489-5701
Jackson Annex ES 400/1-5
380 Jackson St 11550 516-434-4600
Sheena Burke, prin. Fax 564-3040
Jackson ES 400/1-5
451 Jackson St 11550 516-434-4650
Richard Brown, prin. Fax 292-0933
Marshall Pre/Kindergarten 300/PK-K
15 E Marshall St 11550 516-434-4750
Juanita Diaz, prin. Fax 292-1433
Obama ES 400/1-5
176 William St 11550 516-434-4400
Kelly Fairclough, prin. Fax 489-1107
Paterson ES 400/1-5
40 Fulton Ave 11550 516-434-4700
Gary Rush, prin. Fax 489-6492
Prospect ES 700/K-K
265 Peninsula Blvd 11550 516-481-5360
Carol Eason, prin.
Schultz MS 1,400/6-8
70 Greenwich St 11550 516-434-4300
Dr. Adrian Manuel, prin. Fax 483-2549

Uniondale UFD
Supt. — See Uniondale
Lawrence Road MS 700/6-8
50 Lawrence Rd 11550 516-918-1500
Dexter Hodge, prin. Fax 565-5023

Crescent S 200/PK-12
130 Front St 11550 516-292-1787
Sr. Iffat Ahmed, prin. Fax 292-1788

Henrietta, Monroe
Rush-Henrietta Central SD 5,300/K-12
2034 Lehigh Station Rd 14467 585-359-5000
Dr. J. Kenneth Graham, supt. Fax 359-5022
www.rhnet.org
Sherman ES 400/4-6
50 Authors Ave 14467 585-359-5498
Jeffrey Pollard, prin. Fax 359-5493
Vollmer ES 4-6
150 Telephone Rd, 585-359-5550
Lisa Farina, prin. Fax 359-5559
Winslow ES 500/K-3
755 Pinnacle Rd 14467 585-359-5098
Rob Hathaway, prin. Fax 359-5073
Other Schools – See Rochester, Rush

Herkimer, Herkimer, Pop. 7,636
Herkimer Central SD 1,200/K-12
801 W German St 13350 315-866-2230
Robert Miller, supt. Fax 866-2234
www.herkimercsd.org
Herkimer ES 600/K-6
255 Gros Blvd 13350 315-866-8562
Renee Vogt, prin. Fax 866-8568

St. Francis deSales Regional S 100/PK-6
220 Henry St 13350 315-866-4831
Kathleen Coye, prin. Fax 866-9043

Hermon, Saint Lawrence, Pop. 418
Edwards-Knox Central SD 600/PK-12
2512 County Route 24 13652 315-562-8130
Ronald Burke, supt. Fax 562-2477
www.ekcsk12.org
Edwards-Knox ES 300/PK-6
2512 County Route 24 13652 315-562-8132
Lura Hughes, prin. Fax 562-2477

Heuvelton, Saint Lawrence, Pop. 711
Heuvelton Central SD 500/PK-12
PO Box 375 13654 315-344-2414
Jesse Coburn, supt. Fax 344-2349
heuvelton.schoolfusion.us
Heuvelton Central S 500/PK-12
PO Box 375 13654 315-344-2414
Shannon Jordan, prin. Fax 344-2349

Hewlett, Nassau, Pop. 6,722
Hewlett-Woodmere UFD
Supt. — See Woodmere
Franklin ECC, 1180 Henrietta Pl 11557 500/PK-1
Lorraine Smyth, prin. 516-792-4600
Hewlett ES, 1570 Broadway 11557 400/2-5
Christopher Uccellini, prin. 516-792-4500
Woodmere MS 700/6-8
1170 Peninsula Blvd 11557 516-792-4368
Albert Bauer, prin.

Hebrew Academy of Long Beach ECC PK-K
291 Meadowview Ave 11557 516-374-7195
Yeshiva Toras Chaim at South Shore 500/PK-8
1170 William St 11557 516-374-7363
Rabbi Chanina Herzberg, hdmstr. Fax 374-2024

Hicksville, Nassau, Pop. 40,674
Hicksville UFD 5,100/PK-12
200 Division Ave 11801 516-733-2105
Dr. Carl Bonuso, supt. Fax 733-6584
www.hicksvillepublicschools.com
Burns Avenue ES 300/K-5
40 Burns Ave 11801 516-733-2311
Michael Dunn, prin. Fax 733-6694
Dutch Lane ES 200/PK-5
50 Stewart Ave 11801 516-733-2361
Susan Strauss, prin. Fax 733-3520
East Street ES 400/K-5
50 East St 11801 516-733-2321
Jean-Marie Serra, prin. Fax 733-3533
Fork Lane ES 200/K-5
4 Fork Ln 11801 516-733-2341
Christopher Scardino, prin. Fax 733-3521
Hicksville MS 1,200/6-8
215 Jerusalem Ave 11801 516-733-2261
Mara Jorisch, prin. Fax 733-6528
Lee Avenue ES 500/K-5
1 7th St 11801 516-733-2351
Stephanie Stam, prin. Fax 733-3522
Old Country Road ES 300/K-5
49 Rhodes Ln 11801 516-733-2301
Anthony Lubrano, prin. Fax 733-3523
Woodland Avenue ES 300/K-5
85 Ketcham Rd 11801 516-733-2331
Diana Ketcham, prin. Fax 733-3524

Holy Family S 300/PK-8
17 Fordham Ave 11801 516-938-3846
Maryalice Doherty, prin. Fax 938-5041
Our Lady of Mercy S 400/PK-8
520 S Oyster Bay Rd 11801 516-433-7040
Jane Harrigan, prin. Fax 433-8286
Trinity Lutheran S 400/PK-8
40 W Nicholai St 11801 516-931-2225
Tammy Mazza, prin. Fax 931-6345

Highland, Ulster, Pop. 5,534
Highland Central SD 1,800/K-12
320 Pancake Hollow Rd 12528 845-691-1000
Thomas Bongiovi, supt. Fax 691-1039
www.highland-k12.org
Highland ES 800/K-5
16 Lockhart Ln 12528 845-691-1072
Joel Freer, prin. Fax 691-1073
Highland MS 400/6-8
71 Main St 12528 845-691-1080
Daniel Wetzel, prin. Fax 691-1083

Highland Falls, Orange, Pop. 3,773
Highland Falls Ft. Montgomery Central SD 900/PK-12
PO Box 287 10928 845-446-9575
Dr. Frank Sheboy, supt. Fax 446-3321
www.hffmcsd.org
Highland Falls IS 300/3-8
PO Box 287 10928 845-446-9575
Chris Fiorentino, prin. Fax 446-0858
Other Schools – See Fort Montgomery

Hillburn, Rockland, Pop. 844
Suffern Central SD 4,500/K-12
45 Mountain Ave 10931 845-357-7783
Dr. Douglas Adams, supt. Fax 357-5707
www.sufferncentral.org/
Other Schools – See Sloatsburg, Suffern

Hilton, Monroe, Pop. 5,826
Hilton Central SD 4,500/PK-12
225 West Ave 14468 585-392-1000
Dr. Casey Kosiorek, supt. Fax 392-1038
www.hilton.k12.ny.us
Northwood ES 900/K-6
433 N Greece Rd 14468 585-392-1000
Kirk Ashton, prin. Fax 392-1026
Quest ES 500/PK-6
225 West Ave 14468 585-392-1000
Derek Warren, prin. Fax 392-1033
Village ES 1,000/PK-6
100 School Ln 14468 585-392-1000
Dr. Benjamin Rudd, prin. Fax 392-1012
Williams MS 700/7-8
200 School Ln 14468 585-392-1000
Tracie Czebatol, prin. Fax 392-1054

St. Paul Lutheran S 100/PK-8
158 East Ave 14468 585-392-4000
Mark Ball, prin. Fax 392-4001

Hinsdale, Cattaraugus
Hinsdale Central SD 400/PK-12
3701 Main St 14743 716-557-2227
Larry Ljungberg, supt. Fax 557-2259
www.hinsdalebobcats.org
Hinsdale Central S 400/PK-12
3701 Main St 14743 716-557-2227
Laurie Cuddy, prin. Fax 557-2259

Hogansburg, Franklin
Salmon River Central SD
Supt. — See Fort Covington
St. Regis Mohawk ES 400/PK-6
385 Church St 13655 518-358-2763
Kevin Walbridge, prin. Fax 358-9275

Holbrook, Suffolk, Pop. 26,920
Sachem Central SD
Supt. — See Ronkonkoma
Grundy Avenue ES 500/K-5
950 Grundy Ave 11741 631-471-1820
Laura Amato, prin. Fax 467-3867
Merrimac ES 400/K-5
1090 Broadway Ave 11741 631-244-5670
Veronica DeCicco, prin. Fax 563-3369
Nokomis ES 500/K-5
151 Holbrook Rd 11741 631-471-1840
Denise Kleinman, prin. Fax 467-3894
Seneca MS 800/6-8
850 Main St 11741 631-471-1850
Gemma Salvia, prin. Fax 471-1849

Holland, Erie, Pop. 1,197
Holland Central SD 900/PK-12
103 Canada St 14080 716-537-8200
Cathy Fabiatos, supt. Fax 537-8203
www.holland.wnyric.org
Brumsted ES 500/PK-6
173 Canada St 14080 716-537-8250
Jason Smith, prin. Fax 537-8252

Holland Patent, Oneida, Pop. 456
Holland Patent Central SD 1,200/PK-12
9601 Main St 13354 315-865-7200
Jason Evangelist, supt. Fax 865-4057
www.hpschools.org
Floyd ES 200/PK-2
9601 Main St 13354 315-865-5721
Kristin Casab, prin. Fax 865-7284
Holland Patent ES 200/3-5
9601 Main St 13354 315-865-8151
Sarah Vergis, prin. Fax 865-7265
Holland Patent MS 300/6-8
9601 Main St 13354 315-865-8152
Lisa Gentile, prin. Fax 865-7243

Holley, Orleans, Pop. 1,790
Holley Central SD 1,200/PK-12
3800 N Main Street Rd 14470 585-638-6316
Robert D'Angelo, supt. Fax 638-7409
www.holleycsd.org
Holley ES 600/PK-6
3800 N Main Street Rd 14470 585-638-6318
Karri Schiavone, prin. Fax 638-0706

Hollis, See New York
NYC Department of Education
Supt. — See New York
IS 238 1,500/6-8
8815 182nd St 11423 718-297-9821
Peter Leddy, prin. Fax 658-5288
Public S 35 700/PK-5
19102 90th Ave 11423 718-465-6820
Mark Dempsey, prin. Fax 217-4314

Holtsville, Suffolk, Pop. 19,502
Sachem Central SD
Supt. — See Ronkonkoma
Chippewa ES 500/K-5
31 Morris Ave 11742 631-696-8640
Patricia Aubrey, prin. Fax 696-8645
Sagamore MS 800/6-8
57 Division St 11742 631-696-8600
Frank Panasci, prin. Fax 696-8620
Tamarac ES 600/K-5
50 Spence Ave 11742 631-244-5680
Michael Saidens, prin. Fax 244-5685
Waverly Avenue ES 600/K-5
1111 Waverly Ave 11742 631-654-8690
John Ruggero, prin. Fax 475-3970

Homer, Cortland, Pop. 3,225
Homer Central SD 1,900/K-12
PO Box 500 13077 607-749-7241
Nancy Ruscio, supt. Fax 749-2312
www.homercentral.org
Homer ES 400/K-2
PO Box 500 13077 607-749-1250
Jim McGory, prin. Fax 749-1261
Homer IS 400/3-5
PO Box 500 13077 607-749-1240
Stephanie Falls, prin. Fax 749-1238
Homer JHS 500/6-8
PO Box 500 13077 607-749-1230
Tom Turck, prin. Fax 749-1238

Honeoye, Ontario, Pop. 571
Honeoye Central SD 600/K-12
PO Box 170 14471 585-229-4125
David C. Bills, supt. Fax 229-5633
www.honeoye.org
Honeoye ES 300/K-5
PO Box 170 14471 585-229-5171
Michael Bastian, prin. Fax 229-4187

Honeoye Falls, Monroe, Pop. 2,631
Honeoye Falls-Lima Central SD 2,300/K-12
20 Church St 14472 585-624-7000
Gene Mancuso, supt. Fax 624-7003
www.hflcsd.org/
Honeoye Falls-Lima MS 600/6-8
619 Quaker Meeting House Rd 14472 585-624-7100
Shawn Williams, prin. Fax 624-7121
Manor IS 700/2-5
147 East St 14472 585-624-7160
Jeanine Lupisella, prin. Fax 624-3722
Other Schools – See Lima

Hoosick Falls, Rensselaer, Pop. 3,451
Hoosick Falls Central SD 1,200/PK-12
PO Box 192 12090 518-686-7012
Kenneth Facin, supt. Fax 686-9060
www.hoosickfallscsd.org/
Hoosick Falls ES 600/PK-6
PO Box 192 12090 518-686-9492
Amy Netti, prin. Fax 686-7496

St. Mary's Academy 100/PK-8
4 Parsons Ave 12090 518-686-4314
Amanda Goyer, prin. Fax 686-5957

Hopewell Junction, Dutchess, Pop. 354
Wappingers Central SD 11,100/K-12
PO Box 396 12533 845-298-5000
Jose Carrion, supt. Fax 298-5041
www.wappingersschools.org
Gayhead ES 900/K-6
15 Entry Rd 12533 845-227-1756
Adam Gerson, prin. Fax 227-1764
Other Schools – See Fishkill, Poughkeepsie, Wappingers Falls

SS. Denis & Columba S 400/1-8
PO Box 368 12533 845-227-7777
Sr. Kathleen Gerritse, prin. Fax 226-8470

Hornell, Steuben, Pop. 8,357
Hornell CSD 1,700/K-12
25 Pearl St 14843 607-324-1302
Jeremy Palotti, supt. Fax 324-4060
www.hornellcityschools.com
Bryant ES 200/2-3
173 Terry St 14843 607-324-2171
Jennifer Sorochin, prin. Fax 324-5588
Hornell IS 400/4-6
71 Buffalo St 14843 607-324-1304
Sean Gaffney, prin. Fax 324-1301
North Hornell ES 300/K-1
Avondale Avenue 14843 607-324-0014
Barbara Kramer, prin. Fax 324-7478

Horseheads, Chemung, Pop. 6,375
Horseheads Central SD 4,100/PK-12
1 Raider Ln 14845 607-739-5601
Dr. Thomas J. Douglas, supt. Fax 795-2405
www.horseheadsdistrict.com/
Center Street ES 300/PK-4
812 Center St 14845 607-739-5601
Patricia Sotero, prin. Fax 795-2585
Gardner Road ES 400/PK-4
541 Gardner Rd 14845 607-739-6347
Patrick Patterson, prin. Fax 795-2545
Horseheads IS 700/5-6
952 Sing Sing Rd 14845 607-739-6366
Michael Bostwick, prin. Fax 795-2495
Horseheads MS 700/7-8
950 Sing Sing Rd 14845 607-739-6357
Ronald Holloway, prin. Fax 795-2525
Ridge Road ES 400/PK-4
112 Ridge Rd 14845 607-739-6351
Anne Marie Bailey, prin. Fax 795-2485
Other Schools – See Big Flats

St. Mary Our Mother S 100/PK-6
811 Westlake St 14845 607-739-9157
Jean Yorio, prin. Fax 739-2532

Howard Beach, See New York
NYC Department of Education
Supt. — See New York
Public S 146 700/PK-8
9801 159th Ave 11414 718-843-4880
Mary Keegan, prin. Fax 641-0901
Public S 207 800/PK-8
15915 88th St 11414 718-848-2700
Eileen Davies, prin. Fax 848-4226
Public S 232 1,100/K-8
15323 83rd St 11414 718-848-9247
Lisa Josephson, prin. Fax 738-8505

Ave Maria Catholic Academy 200/K-8
15820 101st St 11414 718-848-7440
Marybeth McManus, prin. Fax 641-3464
St. Helen Academy 200/PK-8
8309 157th Ave 11414 718-835-4155
Dr. Christine Zerillo, prin. Fax 738-0580

Hudson, Columbia, Pop. 6,373
Hudson CSD 1,900/PK-12
215 Harry Howard Ave 12534 518-828-4360
Maria J. Suttmeier, supt. Fax 697-8777
www.hudsoncityschooldistrict.com
Edwards PS 500/PK-2
360 State St 12534 518-828-9493
Steven Spicer, prin. Fax 697-8516
Hudson JHS 300/7-8
215 Harry Howard Ave 12534 518-828-4360
Derek Reardon, prin. Fax 697-8522
Smith IS 500/3-6
102 Harry Howard Ave 12534 518-828-4650
Mark Brenneman, prin. Fax 697-8434

Hudson Falls, Washington, Pop. 7,173
Hudson Falls Central SD
Supt. — See Fort Edward
Hudson Falls IS 300/4-5
139 Maple St 12839 518-747-2121
Michael McTague, prin. Fax 747-2774
Hudson Falls MS 500/6-8
131 Notre Dame St 12839 518-747-2121
Todd Gonyeau, prin. Fax 746-2790
Hudson Falls PS 600/1-3
47 Vaughn Rd 12839 518-747-2121
April Struwing, prin. Fax 747-3502
Murphy K 300/PK-K
2 Clark St 12839 518-747-2121
Michael McTague, prin. Fax 747-3853

Kingsbury Junior Academy 50/1-8
PO Box 185 12839 518-747-4424
Alicia Bick, prin. Fax 746-1750

Hunter, Greene, Pop. 494
Hunter-Tannersville Central SD
Supt. — See Tannersville
Hunter ES 200/PK-6
7794 Main St 12442 518-263-4256
Nathan Jones, prin. Fax 263-4086

Huntington, Suffolk, Pop. 17,836
Cold Spring Harbor Central SD
Supt. — See Cold Spring Harbor
Lloyd Harbor ES 400/2-6
7 School Ln 11743 631-367-8800
Valerie Massimo, prin. Fax 421-4229

Elwood UFD
Supt. — See Greenlawn
Boyd IS 600/3-5
286 Cuba Hill Rd 11743 631-266-5430
Dr. Denise Toscano, prin. Fax 266-6265

Huntington UFD
Supt. — See Huntington Station
Finley MS 700/7-8
20 Greenlawn Rd 11743 631-673-2020
John Amato, prin. Fax 425-4746
Flower Hill PS 400/K-4
98 Flower Hill Rd 11743 631-673-2050
Marlon Small, prin. Fax 425-6255
Jefferson PS 400/K-4
253 Oakwood Rd 11743 631-673-2070
Valerie Capitulo-Saide, prin. Fax 425-6257
Southdown PS 400/K-4
125 Browns Rd 11743 631-673-2080
Scott Oshrin, prin. Fax 425-6258
Woodhull IS 600/5-6
140 Woodhull Rd 11743 631-673-2030
Traci Roethel, prin. Fax 425-4718

South Huntington UFD
Supt. — See Huntington Station
Oakwood Primary Center 700/K-2
264 W 22nd St 11743 631-812-3500
Eileen Kerrigan, prin. Fax 812-3535

St. Patrick S 800/PK-8
360 Main St 11743 631-385-3311
Sr. Maureen McDade, prin. Fax 673-4609

Huntington Station, Suffolk, Pop. 32,344
Huntington UFD 4,300/K-12
50 Tower St 11746 631-673-2038
James W.Polansky, supt. Fax 423-3447
www.hufsd.edu/
Abrams STEM Magnet S 100/4-6
155 Lowndes Ave 11746 631-673-2060
Donna Moro, prin.
Washington PS 400/K-4
78 Whitson Rd 11746 631-673-2090
Marsha Neville, prin. Fax 425-6259
Other Schools – See Huntington

South Huntington UFD 5,900/K-12
60 Weston St 11746 631-812-3070
Dr. David P. Bennardo, supt. Fax 812-3075
www.shufsd.org
Countrywood Primary Center 700/K-2
499 Old Country Rd 11746 631-812-3300
Barbara Kenney, prin. Fax 812-3344
Maplewood IS 700/3-5
19 School Ln 11746 631-812-3400
Dr. Vito D'Elia, prin. Fax 812-3434
Stimson MS 900/7-8
401 Oakwood Rd 11746 631-812-3700
Edwin Smith, prin. Fax 812-3737
Wood 6th Grade S 500/6-6
23 Harding Pl 11746 631-812-3600
Stephen Toto, prin. Fax 812-3636
Other Schools – See Huntington, Melville

Hurley, Ulster, Pop. 3,401
Kingston CSD
Supt. — See Kingston
Myer ES 200/K-5
Millbrook Ave 12443 845-331-6905
Wanda Lobianco, prin. Fax 331-1520

Hyde Park, Dutchess, Pop. 1,897
Hyde Park Central SD 3,600/K-12
PO Box 2033 12538 845-229-4000
Dr. Greer Rychcik, supt. Fax 229-4056
www.hpcsd.org
Haviland MS 900/6-8
PO Box 721 12538 845-229-4030
Eric Shaw, prin. Fax 229-2475
Netherwood ES 300/K-5
648 Netherwood Rd 12538 845-229-4055
Christine Jamin, prin. Fax 229-2797
North Park ES 500/K-5
PO Box 722 12538 845-229-4040
Lynette Williams, prin. Fax 229-5655
Smith ES 300/K-5
16 Smith Ct 12538 845-229-4060
Melissa Lawson, prin. Fax 229-2828
Other Schools – See Poughkeepsie

Ilion, Herkimer, Pop. 7,948
Central Valley Central SD 1,200/PK-12
111 Frederick St 13357 315-894-9934
Jeremy Rich, supt. Fax 894-2716
www.cvalleycsd.org
Barringer Road ES 300/2-4
326 Barringer Rd 13357 315-894-8420
Aaron Carey, prin. Fax 894-0153
Other Schools – See Mohawk

Indian Lake, Hamilton
Indian Lake Central SD 100/PK-12
6345 Nys Route 30 12842 518-648-5024
David Snide, supt. Fax 648-6346
www.ilcsd.org
Indian Lake Central S 100/PK-12
6345 Nys Route 30 12842 518-648-5024
David Snide, prin. Fax 648-6346

Inlet, Hamilton
Inlet Common SD 50/PK-6
PO Box 207 13360 315-357-3305
Christine Holt, supt. Fax 357-2177
inletcommonschool.wordpress.com/
Inlet ES 50/PK-6
PO Box 207 13360 315-357-3305
Christine Holt, prin. Fax 357-2177

Interlaken, Seneca, Pop. 594
South Seneca Central SD
Supt. — See Ovid
South Seneca ES 300/PK-5
8326 Main St 14847 607-869-9636
Adam Rundell, prin. Fax 532-8540

Inwood, Nassau, Pop. 9,567
Lawrence UFD
Supt. — See Lawrence
Public K 4 300/PK-K
87 Wanser Ave 11096 516-295-6400
Frank Zangari, prin. Fax 295-6416
Public S 2 400/1-4
1 Donahue Ave 11096 516-295-6200
Christine Moore, prin. Fax 239-6603

Yeshiva Ketana of Long Island 400/PK-8
321 Doughty Blvd 11096 516-791-2800
Rabbi Ari Ginian, dir. Fax 791-3901

Irvington, Westchester, Pop. 6,319
Irvington UFD 1,800/K-12
6 Dows Ln 10533 914-591-8500
Dr. Kristopher Harrison, supt. Fax 591-3064
www.irvingtonschools.org
Dows Lane ES 500/K-3
6 Dows Ln 10533 914-591-6012
Deborah Mariniello, prin. Fax 591-6863
Irvington MS 400/6-8
40 N Broadway 10533 914-591-9494
David Sottile, prin. Fax 591-8535
Main Street IS 300/4-5
101 Main St 10533 914-591-1961
Joyce Chapnick, prin. Fax 591-6863

Islandia, Suffolk, Pop. 3,274
Central Islip UFD
Supt. — See Central Islip
Morrow ES 700/1-5
299 Sycamore Ln 11749 631-348-5037
Dr. Neema Coker, prin. Fax 348-5163

Island Park, Nassau, Pop. 4,586
Island Park UFD 700/PK-8
99 Radcliffe Rd 11558 516-434-2600
Dr. Rosmarie Bovino, supt. Fax 431-7550
www.ips.k12.ny.us
Hegarty ES 400/K-4
100 Radcliffe Rd 11558 516-434-2670
Jacob Russum, prin. Fax 431-7550
Island Park/Lincoln Orens MS 300/PK-PK, 5-
150 Trafalgar Blvd 11558 516-434-2630
Dr. Bruce Hoffman, prin. Fax 431-7550

Islip, Suffolk, Pop. 18,391
Islip UFD 3,100/K-12
215 Main St 11751 631-650-8210
Susan Schnebel, supt. Fax 650-8218
www.islipufsd.org
Commack Road ES 500/2-5
300 Commack Rd 11751 631-650-8605
James Cameron, prin. Fax 650-8608
Islip MS 700/6-8
211 Main St 11751 631-650-8505
Dr. Timothy Martin, prin. Fax 650-8508
Sherwood ES 400/2-5
301 Smith Ave 11751 631-650-8655
Chad Walerstein, prin. Fax 650-8658
Wing ES 400/K-1
1 Winganhauppauge Rd 11751 631-650-8455
Christopher Smalley, prin. Fax 650-8458

Islip Terrace, Suffolk, Pop. 5,327
East Islip UFD 3,200/PK-12
1 Craig B Gariepy Ave 11752 631-224-2000
John Dolan, supt. Fax 581-1617
www.eischools.org
Connetquot ES 200/PK-2
1 Merrick St 11752 631-581-1778
Danielle Flaumenhaft, prin. Fax 581-5315
East Islip MS 900/6-8
100 Redmen St 11752 631-224-2170
Mark Bernard, prin. Fax 859-3745
Kinney ES 200/3-5
1 Spur Dr S 11752 631-581-1862
Hillary Bromberg, prin. Fax 581-0969
Other Schools – See East Islip

Ithaca, Tompkins, Pop. 28,833
Ithaca CSD 5,400/PK-12
400 Lake St 14850 607-274-2101
Dr. Luvelle Brown, supt. Fax 274-2271
www.icsd.k12.ny.us
Belle Sherman ES 400/K-5
501 Mitchell St 14850 607-274-2206
Daniel Breiman, prin. Fax 272-4059
Boynton MS 500/6-8
1601 N Cayuga St 14850 607-274-2241
Jeffery Tomasik, prin. Fax 274-2357
Cayuga Heights ES 400/PK-5
110 E Upland Rd 14850 607-257-8557
Brad Pollack, prin. Fax 257-8142
De Witt MS 500/6-8
560 Warren Rd 14850 607-257-3222
Mac Knight, prin. Fax 266-3502
Enfield ES 300/PK-5
20 Enfield Main Rd 14850 607-274-2221
Lisa Rieger, prin. Fax 274-6810
Fall Creek ES 200/PK-5
202 King St 14850 607-274-2214
Caitlin Bram, prin. Fax 274-2339
Martin ES 300/PK-5
302 W Buffalo St 14850 607-274-2209
Susan Eschbach, prin. Fax 274-2196
Northeast ES 400/K-5
425 Winthrop Dr 14850 607-257-2121
Lily Talcott, prin. Fax 257-8157
South Hill ES 300/PK-5
520 Hudson St 14850 607-274-2129
Perry Gorgen, prin. Fax 274-2379
Other Schools – See Slaterville Springs

Clune Montessori S 200/PK-8
120 E King Rd 14850 607-277-7335
Laura Gottfried, prin. Fax 277-0251
Ithaca Waldorf S 100/PK-8
20 Nelson Rd 14850 607-256-2020
Dr. Emily Butler D.V.M., dir. Fax 256-2020

Jackson Heights, See New York
NYC Department of Education
Supt. — See New York
IS 145 2,100/6-8
3334 80th St 11372 718-457-1242
Ivan Rodriguez, prin. Fax 335-0601
IS 230 1,000/6-8
7310 34th Ave 11372 718-335-7648
Ronald Zirin, prin. Fax 335-7513
Public S 2 700/K-5
7510 21st Ave, East Elmhurst NY 11370 718-728-1459
Amy Goldman, prin. Fax 274-4332
Public S 69 1,200/PK-5
7702 37th Ave 11372 718-424-7700
Martha Vazquez, prin. Fax 458-6567
Public S 149 1,300/K-5
9311 34th Ave 11372 718-898-3630
Onalis Hernandez, prin. Fax 476-1976
Public S 212 800/K-5
3425 82nd St 11372 718-898-6973
Carin Ellis, prin. Fax 898-7068
Public S 222Q 300/PK-2
8615 37th Ave 11372 718-429-2563
Yvonne Marrero, prin. Fax 429-3484
Public S 280 100/K-2
3420 94th St 11372 718-424-9031
Lisa Hidalgo, prin. Fax 424-9093

Garden S 300/PK-12
3316 79th St 11372 718-335-6363
Dr. Richard Marotta, hdmstr. Fax 565-1169
Our Lady of Fatima S 500/K-8
2538 80th St, East Elmhurst NY 11370 718-429-7031
Cassie Zelic, prin. Fax 899-2811

St. Joan of Arc S 600/PK-8
3527 82nd St 11372 718-639-9020
John Fruner, prin. Fax 639-5428

Jamaica, See New York
NYC Department of Education
Supt. — See New York
Basie MS 900/6-8
13325 Guy R Brewer Blvd 11434 718-723-6200
Omotayo Cineus, prin. Fax 527-1675
Emerson S 100/6-8
10835 167th St 11433 718-657-4801
Jakub Lau, prin. Fax 657-4807
Green STEM Institute of Queens PK-3
12610 Bedell St 11434 718-276-1348
Raevan Askew, prin. Fax 276-2498
Jamaica Children's S K-5
10920 Union Hall St 11433 718-526-0160
Suzanne Schatz, prin.
JHS 8 600/6-8
10835 167th St 11433 718-739-6883
Katiana Louissaint, prin. Fax 526-2727
JHS 217 1,600/6-8
8505 144th St 11435 718-657-1120
Patrick Burns, prin. Fax 291-3668
MS 358 300/6-7
88-08 164th St 11432 718-558-6240
Brendan Mims, prin. Fax 558-6245
Jenkins S 500/PK-5
17937 137th Ave 11434 718-528-5399
Pascale Benjaminpereira, prin. Fax 949-0887
Public S 40 600/PK-5
10920 Union Hall St 11433 718-526-1906
Alison Branker, prin. Fax 526-1209
Public S 48 500/PK-5
10829 155th St 11433 718-558-6700
Patricia Mitchell, prin. Fax 558-6710
Public S 50 800/PK-5
14326 101st Ave 11435 718-526-5336
Rina Manjarrez, prin. Fax 526-7261
Public S 52 500/PK-5
17837 146th Ter 11434 718-528-2238
Linda Pough, prin. Fax 276-2854
Public S 55 500/PK-5
13110 97th Ave 11419 718-849-3845
Ralph Honore, prin. Fax 847-5473
Public S 80 500/K-5
17105 137th Ave 11434 718-528-7070
Kersandra Cox, prin. Fax 949-0963
Public S 82 600/K-5
8802 144th St 11435 718-526-4139
Grisel Rodriguez, prin. Fax 297-0290
Public S 86Q 900/PK-5
8741 Parsons Blvd 11432 718-291-6264
Rosita Rivera, prin. Fax 297-0298
Public S 95 1,500/K-5
17901 90th Ave 11432 718-739-0007
Kim Hill, prin. Fax 658-5271
Public S 116 700/PK-8
10725 Wren Pl 11433 718-526-4884
Debra Farrow, prin. Fax 658-5663
Public S 117 1,000/PK-5
8515 143rd St 11435 718-526-4780
Paula Cunningham, prin. Fax 297-1796
Public S 118 600/PK-5
19020 109th Rd 11412 718-465-5538
Michelle Soussoudis, prin. Fax 264-9178
Public S 131 800/K-5
17045 84th Ave 11432 718-739-4229
Veronica DePaolo, prin. Fax 658-5690
Public S 140 600/PK-5
11601 116th St 11434 718-657-4760
David Norment, prin. Fax 526-1051
Public S 160 700/PK-5
10959 Inwood St 11435 718-526-5523
Tiffany Hicks, prin. Fax 526-8191
Public S 178 500/PK-8
18910 Radnor Rd 11423 718-464-5763
Jessica Cruz, prin. Fax 464-5766
Public S 182 800/K-4
15327 88th Ave 11432 718-298-7700
Andrew Topol, prin. Fax 298-7706
Public S 223 600/PK-5
12520 Sutphin Blvd 11434 718-322-9012
Deborah Otto, prin. Fax 925-9020
Public S 268 600/K-8
9207 175th St 11433 718-206-3240
Lissa Stewart, admin. Fax 206-2938
Queens S for Leadership and Excellence 600/PK-1
88-08 164th St 11432 718-558-6220
Tanya Howell, prin. Fax 558-6225
Redwood MS 6-8
13325 Guy R Brewer Blvd 11434 718-276-4540
Judson Hamilton, prin.

Al-Iman S 100/PK-12
8989 Van Wyck Expy 11435 718-297-6520
Nassir Aliakber, prin. Fax 785-4226
Ideal Montessori S 200/PK-8
8741 165th St 11432 718-523-6237
Dr. K.P. Chandu, prin.
Immaculate Conception Catholic Academy 500/PK-8
17914 Dalny Rd 11432 718-739-5933
Dori Breen, prin. Fax 523-7436
Jamaica SDA S 100/PK-8
8828 163rd St 11432 718-297-3491
Dorette Francis, prin. Fax 297-3491
St. Nicholas of Tolentine Catholic Acad 300/PK-8
8022 Parsons Blvd 11432 718-380-1900
Robert Lowenberg, prin. Fax 591-6977

Jamestown, Chautauqua, Pop. 30,116
Jamestown CSD 4,900/PK-12
197 Martin Rd 14701 716-483-4420
Bret Apthorpe, supt. Fax 483-4421
ww2.jamestownpublicschools.org
Bush ES 300/PK-4
150 Pardee Ave 14701 716-483-4401
Daniel Bracey, prin. Fax 483-7100
Fletcher ES 500/PK-4
301 Cole Ave 14701 716-483-4404
Maria DeJoy, prin. Fax 483-4210
Jefferson MS 500/5-8
195 Martin Rd 14701 716-483-4411
Chad Bongiovanni, prin. Fax 483-4273
Lincoln ES 500/PK-4
301 Front St 14701 716-483-4412
Katie Russo, prin. Fax 483-4435
Love ES 300/PK-4
50 E 8th St 14701 716-483-4405
Renee Hartling, prin. Fax 483-4291
Persell MS 500/5-8
375 Baker St 14701 716-483-4406
Philip Cammarata, prin. Fax 483-4417
Ring ES 400/PK-4
333 Buffalo St 14701 716-483-4407
Connie Foster, prin. Fax 483-4232
Washington MS 500/5-8
159 Buffalo St 14701 716-483-4413
Melissa Emerson, prin. Fax 483-4268

Southwestern Central SD 1,400/PK-12
600 Hunt Rd 14701 716-484-1136
Maureen Donahue, supt. Fax 484-1139
www.swcsk12.org
Southwestern ES 600/PK-5
600 Hunt Rd 14701 716-664-1881
Matthew Langworthy, prin. Fax 487-3170
Southwestern MS 300/6-8
600 Hunt Rd 14701 716-664-6270
Richard Rybicki, prin. Fax 487-0855

Bethel Baptist Christian Academy 100/K-12
200 Hunt Rd 14701 716-484-7420
Mike Stormont, chrpsn. Fax 484-0087

Jamesville, Onondaga
Jamesville-DeWitt Central SD
Supt. — See De Witt
Jamesville-DeWitt MS 900/5-8
6280 Randall Rd 13078 315-445-8360
Thomas A. Eldridge, prin. Fax 445-8421
Jamesville ES 400/K-4
6409 E Seneca Tpke 13078 315-445-8460
Peter Reyes, prin. Fax 445-8444
Tecumseh ES 400/K-4
901 Nottingham Rd 13078 315-445-8320
Jill Zerrillo, prin. Fax 445-9872

Jasper, Steuben
Jasper-Troupsburg Central SD 500/PK-12
3769 State Route 417 14855 607-792-3675
Michael A. Mead, supt. Fax 792-3749
www.jtcsd.org
Other Schools – See Troupsburg

Jefferson, Schoharie
Jefferson Central SD 300/K-12
1332 State Route 10 12093 607-652-7821
Brian Corey, supt. Fax 652-7806
www.jeffersoncs.org
Jefferson Central S 300/K-12
1332 State Route 10 12093 607-652-7821
Thomas Abraham, admin. Fax 652-7806

Jeffersonville, Sullivan, Pop. 355
Sullivan West Central SD 1,100/PK-12
PO Box 308 12748 845-482-4610
Dr. Nancy Hackett, supt. Fax 482-3022
www.swcsd.org/
Sullivan West ES 600/PK-6
PO Box 308 12748 845-482-4610
Rod McLaughlin, prin. Fax 482-4720

Jericho, Nassau, Pop. 13,391
Jericho UFD 3,000/PK-12
99 Old Cedar Swamp Rd 11753 516-203-3600
Henry Grishman, supt. Fax 933-2047
www.jerichoschools.org
Cantiague ES 400/K-5
678 Cantiague Rock Rd 11753 516-203-3650
Gina Faust, prin. Fax 681-0341
Jackson ES 400/PK-5
58 Maytime Dr 11753 516-203-3640
Berardino D'Aquila, prin. Fax 681-2891
Jericho MS 700/6-8
99 Old Cedar Swamp Rd 11753 516-203-3620
Donald Gately, prin. Fax 681-8984
Seaman ES 300/K-5
137 Leahy St 11753 516-203-3630
Ivy Sherman, prin. Fax 681-9493

Solomon Schechter S of Long Island 200/K-5
1 Barbara Ln 11753 516-935-1441
Sandi Swerdloff, prin. Fax 935-8280

Johnson City, Broome, Pop. 14,676
Johnson City Central SD 2,500/K-12
666 Reynolds Rd 13790 607-763-1230
Mary Roland, supt. Fax 729-2767
www.jcschools.com
Johnson City IS 600/3-5
601 Columbia Dr 13790 607-763-1254
Denise Riley, prin. Fax 763-1284
Johnson City MS 600/6-8
601 Columbia Dr 13790 607-763-1240
Daniel Erickson, prin. Fax 763-1297
Johnson City PS 600/K-2
601 Columbia Dr 13790 607-763-1243
Adam Bauchner, prin. Fax 763-1280

St. James ES 100/PK-6
143 Main St 13790 607-797-5444
Susan Kitchen, prin. Fax 797-6794

Johnstown, Fulton, Pop. 8,615
Johnstown CSD 1,100/PK-12
1 Sir Bills Cir Ste 101 12095 518-762-4611
Patricia Kilburn, supt. Fax 762-6379
www.johnstownschools.org
Glebe Street ES 100/2-3
502 Glebe St 12095 518-762-3714
Abbey North, prin. Fax 762-3756
Knox JHS 300/7-8
400 S Perry St 12095 518-762-3711
Michael Satterlee, prin. Fax 762-2775
Pleasant Avenue ES 100/PK-1
235 Pleasant Ave 12095 518-762-8610
Michelle Gabree-Huba, prin. Fax 762-1217
Warren Street ES 100/4-6
110 Warren St 12095 518-762-3715
Nicole Lent, prin. Fax 762-8805

Jordan, Onondaga, Pop. 1,356
Jordan-Elbridge Central SD 1,400/PK-12
PO Box 902 13080 315-689-8500
James Froio, supt. Fax 689-0084
www.jecsd.org
Jordan-Elbridge MS 400/5-8
PO Box 1150 13080 315-689-8520
David Shafer, prin. Fax 689-6524
Other Schools – See Elbridge

Katonah, Westchester, Pop. 1,654
Katonah-Lewisboro UFD
Supt. — See Cross River
Katonah ES 400/K-5
106 Huntville Rd 10536 914-763-7700
Cristy Harris, prin. Fax 763-7789

Keene Valley, Essex
Keene Central SD 200/K-12
PO Box 67 12943 518-576-4555
Daniel Mayberry, supt. Fax 576-4599
www.keenecentralschool.org
Keene Central S 200/K-12
PO Box 67 12943 518-576-4555
Daniel Mayberry, supt. Fax 576-4599

Keeseville, Clinton, Pop. 1,787
Au Sable Valley Central SD
Supt. — See Clintonville
Keeseville ES 400/K-6
1825 Main St 12944 518-834-2839
Kevin Hulbert, prin. Fax 834-2857

Kendall, Orleans
Kendall Central SD 700/K-12
1932 Kendall Rd 14476 585-659-2741
Julie Christensen, supt. Fax 659-8903
www.kendallschools.org
Kendall ES 400/K-6
1932 Kendall Rd 14476 585-659-8317
Sharon Smith, prin. Fax 659-2952

Kenmore, Erie, Pop. 15,148

St. Andrew's Country Day S 200/PK-8
1545 Sheridan Dr 14217 716-877-0422
Colleen Politowski, prin. Fax 877-3973
St. John the Baptist S 300/PK-8
1085 Englewood Ave 14223 716-877-6401
JennyBainbridge, prin. Fax 877-9139

Kennedy, Chautauqua, Pop. 464
Falconer Central SD
Supt. — See Falconer
Temple ES 300/PK-2
3470 Cemetery St 14747 716-267-3255
Holly Hannon, prin. Fax 267-9420

Kerhonkson, Ulster, Pop. 1,661
Rondout Valley Central SD
Supt. — See Accord
Kerhonkson ES 200/K-3
30 Academy St 12446 845-626-2451
Jacqueline Vannosdall, prin. Fax 626-5767

Kew Gardens, See New York
NYC Department of Education
Supt. — See New York
Public S 99 800/K-6
8237 Kew Gardens Rd 11415 718-544-4343
Paulette Foglio, prin. Fax 544-5992

Bais Yaakov Academy for Girls 700/PK-8
12450 Metropolitan Ave 11415 718-847-5352
Sarah Bergman, prin. Fax 847-2912
Yeshiva Tifereth Moshe 500/PK-8
8306 Abingdon Rd 11415 718-846-7300
Rabbi Yaakov May, prin. Fax 441-3962

Kiamesha Lake, Sullivan

Hebrew Day S 50/PK-12
PO Box 239 12751 845-794-7890
Rabbi Menachem Fruchter, prin. Fax 794-0859

Kings Park, Suffolk, Pop. 17,098
Kings Park Central SD 3,600/K-12
180 Lawrence Rd 11754 631-269-3310
Dr. Timothy Eagen, supt. Fax 269-0750
www.kpcsd.org
Parkview ES 400/K-3
23 Roundtree Dr 11754 631-269-3770
Kevin Storch, prin. Fax 361-6590
RJO IS 600/4-5
99 Old Dock Rd 11754 631-269-3798
Rudy Massimo, prin. Fax 269-3222
Rogers MS 900/6-8
97 Old Dock Rd 11754 631-269-3369
Carlo Spinola, prin. Fax 269-3282
Other Schools – See Northport

Kingston, Ulster, Pop. 22,973
Kingston CSD 5,900/PK-12
61 Crown St 12401 845-339-3000
Dr. Paul Padalino, supt. Fax 339-2249
www.kingstoncityschools.org/
Bailey MS 800/6-8
118 Merilina Ave 12401 845-943-3940
Debra Fitzgerald, prin. Fax 338-6312
Chambers ES 300/K-5
945 Morton Blvd 12401 845-336-5995
Kate Petrie, prin. Fax 336-5616
Edson ES 500/K-5
116 Merilina Ave 12401 845-338-6990
Brian Martin, prin. Fax 331-9034
Kennedy ES 300/K-5
107 Gross St 12401 845-943-3100
Paula Perez, prin. Fax 331-2477
Washington ES 400/PK-5
67 Wall St 12401 845-338-1978
Valerie Hannum, prin. Fax 338-3041
Other Schools – See Hurley, Lake Katrine, Port Ewen

Kingston Catholic S 200/PK-8
159 Broadway 12401 845-331-9318
Jill Albert, prin. Fax 331-2674

Kirkwood, Broome
Windsor Central SD
Supt. — See Windsor
Bell ES 300/PK-5
15 Golden St 13795 607-775-2730
Lorraine Hulbert, prin. Fax 775-4834

Lackawanna, Erie, Pop. 17,629
Lackawanna CSD 1,700/PK-12
245 S Shore Blvd 14218 716-827-6767
Anne Spadone, supt. Fax 827-6710
www.lackawannaschools.org
Lackawanna MS 200/6-8
550 Martin Rd 14218 716-827-6704
Bethany Schill, prin. Fax 827-6784
Martin Road ES 500/K-5
135 Martin Rd 14218 716-827-6734
Julie Andreozzi, prin. Fax 827-6715
Truman ES 500/PK-1
15 Inner Dr 14218 716-827-6741
Angela McCaffrey, prin. Fax 827-6779

Our Lady of Victory S 200/PK-8
2760 S Park Ave 14218 716-828-9434
Carolyn Kraus, prin. Fax 828-7728

La Fargeville, Jefferson, Pop. 577
La Fargeville Central SD 600/PK-12
PO Box 138 13656 315-658-2241
Travis Hoover, supt. Fax 658-4223
www.lafargevillecsd.org
La Fargeville Central ES 300/PK-6
PO Box 138 13656 315-658-2241
Jaycee Welsh, prin. Fax 658-4223

La Fayette, Onondaga
La Fayette Central SD 900/PK-12
5955 US Route 20 13084 315-677-9728
Jeremy Belfield, supt. Fax 677-3372
www.lafayetteschools.org
Grimshaw ES 400/PK-6
5957 US Route 20 13084 315-677-3152
Jennifer Blossey, prin. Fax 677-3154
Other Schools – See Nedrow

Lagrangeville, Dutchess
Arlington Central SD 8,500/K-12
144 Todd Hill Rd 12540 845-486-4460
Dr. Brendan Lyons, supt. Fax 486-4457
www.arlingtonschools.org
Lagrange MS 800/6-8
110 Stringham Rd 12540 845-486-4880
Eric Schetter, prin. Fax 486-8863
Union Vale MS 900/6-8
1657 E Noxon Rd 12540 845-223-8600
Scott Wood, prin. Fax 223-8610
Vail Farm ES 700/K-5
1659 E Noxon Rd 12540 845-223-8030
Claudine Khare, prin. Fax 227-1940
Other Schools – See Pleasant Valley, Poughkeepsie, Poughquag

Lake George, Warren, Pop. 894
Lake George Central SD 800/K-12
381 Canada St 12845 518-668-5456
Lynne C. Rutnik, supt. Fax 668-2285
www.lkgeorge.org
Lake George ES 400/K-6
69 Sun Valley Dr 12845 518-668-5714
James Conway, prin. Fax 668-5876

Lake Grove, Suffolk, Pop. 11,039
Middle Country Central SD
Supt. — See Centereach
Auer Memorial ES 400/1-5
17 Wing St 11755 631-285-8500
Kenneth Gutmann, prin. Fax 285-8501

Sachem Central SD
Supt. — See Ronkonkoma
Cayuga ES 500/K-5
865 Hawkins Ave 11755 631-471-1800
Matthew Wells, prin. Fax 467-2486
Wenonah ES 500/K-5
251 Hudson Ave 11755 631-471-1880
Christine DiPaola, prin. Fax 471-1886

Maimonides Day S 50/PK-6
821 Hawkins Ave 11755 631-585-0521
Rivkie Grossbaum, prin. Fax 585-0570

Lake Katrine, Ulster, Pop. 2,330
Kingston CSD
Supt. — See Kingston
Crosby ES 400/K-5
767 Neighborhood Rd 12449 845-382-2633
Marie Anderson, prin. Fax 382-2668
Miller MS 700/6-8
65 Fording Place Rd 12449 845-943-3941
Andrew Sheber, prin. Fax 382-6069

Lake Luzerne, Warren, Pop. 1,220
Hadley-Luzerne Central SD 400/PK-12
PO Box 200 12846 518-696-2378
Beecher Baker, supt. Fax 696-5884
www.hlcs.org
Townsend ES 200/PK-5
PO Box 200 12846 518-696-2378
Patrick Cronin, prin. Fax 696-2485

Lake Placid, Essex, Pop. 2,496
Lake Placid Central SD 700/K-12
50 Cummings Rd 12946 518-523-2475
Dr. Roger Carania, supt. Fax 523-4971
www.lpcsd.org
Lake Placid ES 300/K-5
318 Old Military Rd 12946 518-523-3640
Sonja Franklin, prin. Fax 523-4314

North Country S 100/4-9
4382 Cascade Rd 12946 518-523-9329
David Hochschartner, head sch Fax 523-4858
St. Agnes S 100/PK-3
2322 Saranac Ave 12946 518-523-3771
Catherine Bemis, prin. Fax 523-2203

Lake Ronkonkoma, Suffolk, Pop. 19,855
Sachem Central SD
Supt. — See Ronkonkoma
Hiawatha ES 500/K-5
97 Patchogue Holbrook Rd 11779 631-471-1830
Kathleen O'Farrell, prin. Fax 467-3861
Samoset MS 900/6-8
51 School St 11779 631-471-1700
James Horan, prin. Fax 471-1706

Lake View, Erie
Frontier Central SD
Supt. — See Hamburg
Pinehurst ES 700/K-5
6050 Fairway Ct 14085 716-926-1770
Jennifer Makowski, prin. Fax 627-3132

Southtowns Catholic S 200/PK-8
2052 Lakeview Rd 14085 716-627-5011
Marc Bandelian, prin. Fax 627-5335

Lancaster, Erie, Pop. 10,243
Lancaster Central SD 5,700/K-12
177 Central Ave 14086 716-686-3201
Dr. Michael Vallely, supt. Fax 686-3350
www.lancasterschools.org
Como Park ES 400/K-3
1985 Como Park Blvd 14086 716-686-3235
Mary Marcinelli, prin. Fax 686-3303
Court Street ES 300/K-3
91 Court St 14086 716-686-3240
Jacqueline Clinard, prin. Fax 686-3284
Hillview ES 400/K-3
11 Pleasant View Dr 14086 716-686-3280
Amy Moeller, prin. Fax 686-3307
Lancaster MS 900/7-8
148 Aurora St 14086 716-686-3220
Peter Kruszynski, prin. Fax 686-3223
William Street ES 1,300/4-6
5201 William St 14086 716-686-3800
Jacqueline Bull, prin. Fax 686-3822
Other Schools – See Depew

Buffalo Suburban Christian Academy 50/1-8
5580 Genesee St 14086 716-684-2943
Jeffrey Locke, prin.
St. Mary S 300/PK-8
2 Saint Marys Hl 14086 716-683-2112
Kim Kwitowski, prin. Fax 683-2134

Lansing, Tompkins, Pop. 3,411
Lansing Central SD 1,100/K-12
284 Ridge Rd 14882 607-533-3020
Chris Pettograsso, supt. Fax 533-3602
www.lcsd.k12.ny.us/
Buckley ES 400/K-4
284 Ridge Rd 14882 607-533-3020
Lorri Whiteman, prin. Fax 533-4684
Lansing MS 300/5-8
6 Ludlowville Rd 14882 607-533-3020
Christine Rebera, prin. Fax 533-3543

Larchmont, Westchester, Pop. 5,760
Mamaroneck UFD
Supt. — See Mamaroneck
Central ES 500/PK-5
1100 Palmer Ave 10538 914-220-3400
Joanne Hindley, prin. Fax 220-3415
Chatsworth Avenue ES 600/K-5
34 Chatsworth Ave 10538 914-220-3500
Katie Andersen, prin. Fax 220-3515
Hommocks MS 1,200/6-8
10 Hommocks Rd 10538 914-220-3300
Seth Weitzman, prin. Fax 220-3315
Murray Avenue ES 700/K-5
250 Murray Ave 10538 914-220-3700
Alison Hazut, prin. Fax 220-3715

French-American S of New York 900/PK-12
111 Larchmont Ave 10538 914-250-0401
Joel Peinado, hdmstr.

SS. John & Paul S 300/K-8
280 Weaver St Ste 2 10538 914-834-6332
Fatima Carvalho-Gianni, prin. Fax 834-8242

Latham, Albany, Pop. 10,131
North Colonie Central SD 5,300/K-12
91 Fiddlers Ln 12110 518-785-8591
D. Joseph Corr, supt. Fax 785-5504
www.northcolonie.org
Blue Creek ES 500/K-6
100 Clinton Rd 12110 518-785-7451
Annette Trapini, prin. Fax 785-3273
Forts Ferry ES 500/K-6
95 Forts Ferry Rd 12110 518-785-9203
Dr. Candace Lobdell, prin. Fax 783-8874
Latham Ridge ES 400/K-6
6 Mercer Ave 12110 518-785-3211
Aaron Thiell, prin. Fax 783-8875
Shaker JHS 900/7-8
475 Watervliet Shaker Rd 12110 518-785-1341
Dr. Russell Moore, prin. Fax 783-8877
Other Schools – See Cohoes, Loudonville

St. Ambrose S 200/PK-8
347 Old Loudon Rd 12110 518-785-6453
Fax 785-8370

Laurelton, See New York
NYC Department of Education
Supt. — See New York
Collaborative Arts MS 500/6-8
14500 Springfield Blvd 11413 718-977-6181
Tammy Holloway, prin.
Community Voices MS 500/6-8
14500 Springfield Blvd 11413 718-977-6180
Ryan Branch, prin. Fax 977-6182
Public S 132 300/PK-5
13215 218th St 11413 718-528-5734
Alicia Hawkins-Davis, prin. Fax 723-6931

Linden SDA ES 100/1-8
13701 228th St 11413 718-527-6868
Dr. Laurene Richards-Usher, prin. Fax 527-6650

Laurens, Otsego, Pop. 259
Laurens Central SD 300/K-12
PO Box 301 13796 607-432-2050
Romona Wenck, supt. Fax 432-4388
laurenscs.org
Laurens Central S 300/K-12
PO Box 301 13796 607-432-2050
William Dorritie, prin. Fax 432-4388

Lawrence, Nassau, Pop. 6,454
Lawrence UFD 2,800/PK-12
PO Box 477 11559 516-295-7030
Dr. Ann Pedersen, supt. Fax 239-7164
www.lawrence.org
Lawrence MS 800/5-8
195 Broadway 11559 516-295-7000
Willis Perry, prin. Fax 295-7196
Other Schools – See Cedarhurst, Inwood

Brandeis S 200/PK-8
25 Frost Ln 11559 516-371-4747
Raz Levin, head sch Fax 371-1572
Hebrew Academy of Five Towns & Rockaway 700/PK-5
33 Washington Ave 11559 516-569-3043
Joy Hammer, prin. Fax 569-3014
Hebrew Academy of Five Towns Rockaway MS 300/6-8
44 Frost Ln 11559 516-569-6352

Le Roy, Genesee, Pop. 4,322
Le Roy Central SD 1,300/PK-12
2 Trigon Park 14482 585-768-8133
Merritt Holly, supt. Fax 768-8929
www.leroycsd.org
Wolcott Street ES 700/PK-6
2 Trigon Park 14482 585-768-7115
Carol Messura, prin. Fax 768-8929

Levittown, Nassau, Pop. 51,176
Island Trees UFD 2,300/K-12
74 Farmedge Rd 11756 516-520-2100
Dr. Charles Murphy, supt. Fax 520-2113
www.islandtrees.org
Island Trees Memorial MS 700/5-8
45 Wantagh Ave 11756 516-520-2157
Daniel Keegan, prin. Fax 520-2168
Sparke ES 300/K-1
100 Robin Pl 11756 516-520-2126
Dr. Penny Fisher, prin Fax 520-0987
Stokes ES 500/2-4
101 Owl Pl 11756 516-520-2103
Allison Ackerman, prin. Fax 520-0984

Levittown UFD 7,200/K-12
150 Abbey Ln 11756 516-434-7020
Dr. Tonie McDonald, supt. Fax 520-8314
www.levittownschools.com
Abbey Lane ES 700/K-5
239 Gardiners Ave 11756 516-434-7400
Dr. George Maurer, prin. Fax 520-8494
Gardiners Avenue ES 500/K-5
610 Gardiners Ave 11756 516-434-7450
Susan Hendler, prin. Fax 520-8490
Northside ES 600/K-5
35 Pelican Rd 11756 516-434-7500
Frank Mortillaro, prin. Fax 520-8394
Salk MS 900/6-8
3359 N Jerusalem Rd 11756 516-434-7350
John Zampaglione, prin. Fax 520-8479
Summit Lane ES 400/K-5
4 Summit Ln 11756 516-434-7525
Keith Squillacioti, prin. Fax 520-8390
Wisdom Lane MS 700/6-8
120 Center Ln 11756 516-434-7300
John Avena, prin. Fax 520-8380
Other Schools – See Seaford, Wantagh

Maria Montessori S 50/PK-8
5 N Village Grn 11756 516-520-0301
Carolyn Larcy, admin. Fax 520-2935

Lewiston, Niagara, Pop. 2,675
Niagara-Wheatfield Central SD
Supt. — See Niagara Falls
Tuscarora Indian S 100/PK-5
2015 Mount Hope Rd 14092 716-215-3670
Elizabeth Corieri, prin. Fax 215-3685

Sacred Heart Villa S 50/PK-5
5269 Lewiston Rd 14092 716-284-8273
Sr. Elizabeth Domin, prin. Fax 284-8273
St. Peter S 100/PK-8
140 N 6th St 14092 716-754-4470
Maureen Ingham, prin. Fax 754-0167

Liberty, Sullivan, Pop. 4,273
Liberty Central SD 1,600/PK-12
115 Buckley St 12754 845-292-6990
Carol Napolitano, supt. Fax 292-1164
www.libertyk12.org
Liberty ES 700/PK-4
201 N Main St 12754 845-292-5400
Jacqueline Harris, prin. Fax 295-9201
Liberty MS 400/5-8
145 Buckley St 12754 845-292-5400
Jack Strassman, prin. Fax 292-5691

St. Peter's Regional S 100/PK-5
121 Lincoln Pl 12754 845-292-7270
Lisa Layman, prin. Fax 292-2891

Lido Beach, Nassau, Pop. 2,865
Long Beach CSD 3,500/PK-12
235 Lido Blvd 11561 516-897-2000
David Weiss, supt. Fax 897-2107
www.lbeach.org
Lido ES 400/PK-5
237 Lido Blvd 11561 516-897-2140
Brenda Young, prin. Fax 771-3783
Long Beach MS 700/6-8
239 Lido Blvd 11561 516-897-2166
Paul Romanelli, prin. Fax 897-2145
Other Schools – See Long Beach

Lima, Livingston, Pop. 2,111
Honeoye Falls-Lima Central SD
Supt. — See Honeoye Falls
Lima ES 300/K-1
7342 College St 14485 585-624-7140
Lisa Moosbrugger, prin. Fax 624-7003

Lima Christian S 200/K-12
1574 Rochester St 14485 585-624-3841
Todd Steltz, prin. Fax 624-8293

Lincolndale, Westchester, Pop. 1,500
Somers Central SD
Supt. — See Somers
Primrose ES 600/K-2
PO Box 630 10540 914-248-8888
Catherine Winter, prin. Fax 248-5384

Lindenhurst, Suffolk, Pop. 26,920
Lindenhurst UFD 6,200/K-12
PO Box 621 11757 631-867-3000
Daniel Giordano, supt. Fax 867-3008
www.lindenhurstschools.org
Albany Avenue ES 400/K-5
180 Albany Ave 11757 631-867-3150
Marcy Miller, prin. Fax 867-3158
Alleghany Avenue ES 300/K-5
250 S Alleghany Ave 11757 631-867-3200
Laura Newman, prin. Fax 867-3208
Daniel Street ES 600/K-5
289 Daniel St 11757 631-867-3300
Linda Domanico, prin. Fax 867-3308
Harding Avenue ES 400/K-5
2 Harding Ave 11757 631-867-3350
Brian Chamberlin, prin. Fax 867-3358
Lindenhurst MS 1,400/6-8
350 S Wellwood Ave 11757 631-867-3500
Frank Naccarato, prin. Fax 867-3508
Rall ES 600/K-5
761 Wellwood Ave 11757 631-867-3450
Farrah Mckenna, prin. Fax 867-3458
West Gates Avenue ES 400/K-5
175 W Gates Ave 11757 631-867-3400
Donna Smawley, prin. Fax 867-3408

Lisbon, Saint Lawrence
Lisbon Central SD 600/PK-12
6866 County Route 10 13658 315-393-4951
Patrick Farrand, supt. Fax 393-7666
lisboncs.schoolwires.com
Lisbon Central S 600/PK-12
6866 County Route 10 13658 315-393-4951
C. Lauren Morley, prin. Fax 393-7666

Little Falls, Herkimer, Pop. 4,870
Little Falls CSD 1,100/K-12
15 Petrie St 13365 315-823-1470
Dr. Keith Levatino, supt. Fax 823-0321
www.lfcsd.org
Benton Hall Academy 500/K-5
1 Ward Sq 13365 315-823-1400
John Long, prin. Fax 823-4407
Little Falls MS 300/6-8
1 High School Rd 13365 315-823-4300
Maria Lindsay, prin. Fax 823-3920

Little Neck, See New York
NYC Department of Education
Supt. — See New York
JHS 67 900/6-8
5160 Marathon Pkwy 11362 718-423-8138
Brian Annello, prin. Fax 423-8281
Public S 94 400/K-5
4177 Little Neck Pkwy 11363 718-423-8491
Laura Avakians, prin. Fax 423-8531
Public S 221 600/PK-5
5740 Marathon Pkwy 11362 718-423-8825
Patricia Bullard, prin. Fax 423-8841

Liverpool, Onondaga, Pop. 2,310
Liverpool Central SD 6,500/K-12
195 Blackberry Rd 13090 315-622-7900
Dr. Mark Potter, supt. Fax 622-7115
www.liverpool.k12.ny.us
Chestnut Hill ES 300/K-6
200 Saslon Park Dr 13088 315-453-0242
Todd Bourcy, prin. Fax 453-0283
Chestnut Hill MS 300/7-8
204 Saslon Park Dr 13088 315-453-0245
Michael Baroody, prin. Fax 453-0278
Donlin Drive ES 500/K-6
299 Donlin Dr 13088 315-453-0249
Heather Silvia, prin. Fax 453-0253
Elmcrest ES 500/K-6
350 Woodspath Rd 13090 315-453-1252
Daphne Valentine, prin. Fax 453-1258
Liverpool ES 300/K-6
910 2nd St 13088 315-453-0254
Darcy Woodcock, prin. Fax 453-0286
Liverpool MS 300/7-8
720 7th St 13088 315-453-0258
Joseph Mussi, prin. Fax 453-0281
Long Branch ES 400/K-6
4035 Long Branch Rd 13090 315-453-0261
Robert McCrone, prin. Fax 453-0269
Morgan Road ES 500/K-6
7795 Morgan Rd 13090 315-453-1268
Brett Woodcock, prin. Fax 453-0275
Perry ES 400/K-6
7053 Buckley Rd 13088 315-453-0272
Dana Ziegler, prin. Fax 453-0281
Soule Road ES 400/K-6
8338 Soule Rd 13090 315-453-1280
Jeanne Brown, prin. Fax 453-1286
Soule Road MS 500/7-8
8340 Soule Rd 13090 315-453-1283
Amanda Caldwell, prin. Fax 453-1286
Willow Field ES 500/K-6
3900 State Route 31 13090 315-453-1196
Susan Lohret, prin. Fax 453-1255

Livingston Manor, Sullivan, Pop. 1,201
Livingston Manor Central SD 400/PK-12
PO Box 947 12758 845-439-4400
John Evans, supt. Fax 439-4717
lmcs.k12.ny.us
Livingston Manor ES 200/PK-6
PO Box 947 12758 845-439-4400
Christopher Hubert, prin. Fax 439-4717

Livonia, Livingston, Pop. 1,405
Livonia Central SD 1,700/PK-12
PO Box E 14487 585-346-4000
Matthew Cole, supt. Fax 346-6145
www.livoniacsd.org
Livonia ES 800/PK-5
PO Box E 14487 585-346-4020
Charles Whittel, prin. Fax 346-4082
Livonia MS 400/6-8
PO Box E 14487 585-346-4050
Chuck D'Imperio, prin. Fax 346-6835

Lockport, Niagara, Pop. 20,480
Lockport CSD 4,600/K-12
130 Beattie Ave 14094 716-478-4800
Michelle T. Bradley, supt. Fax 478-4832
www.lockportschools.org
Belknap IS 700/5-6
491 High St 14094 716-478-4550
Gary Wilson, prin. Fax 478-4535
Kelley ES 400/K-5
610 E High St 14094 716-478-4670
Heather Walton, prin. Fax 478-4685
Merritt ES 400/K-5
389 Green St 14094 716-478-4725
Michael Sobieraski, prin. Fax 478-4730
North Park JHS 700/7-8
160 Passaic Ave 14094 716-478-4700
James Snyder, prin. Fax 478-4705
Southard ES 400/K-5
6385 Locust Street Ext 14094 716-478-4770
Christopher Arnold, prin. Fax 478-4775
Upson ES, 28 Harding Ave 14094 500/K-5
Jennifer Gilson, prin. 716-478-4400

Starpoint Central SD 2,600/K-12
4363 Mapleton Rd 14094 716-210-2352
Dr. Sean M. Croft, supt. Fax 210-2355
www.starpointcsd.org/
Fricano PS 600/K-2
4363 Mapleton Rd 14094 716-210-2100
Kathleen Brachmann, prin. Fax 210-2112
Regan IS 600/3-5
4363 Mapleton Rd 14094 716-210-2150
Monica Daigler, prin. Fax 210-2158
Starpoint MS 600/6-8
4363 Mapleton Rd 14094 716-210-2200
James Bryer, prin. Fax 210-2233

Desales Catholic S 400/PK-8
6914 Chestnut Ridge Rd 14094 716-433-6422
Regina Granchelli, prin. Fax 434-4002

Locust Valley, Nassau, Pop. 3,370
Locust Valley Central SD 2,200/K-12
22 Horse Hollow Rd 11560 516-277-5000
Dr. Anna Hunderfund, supt. Fax 277-5098
www.lvcsd.k12.ny.us/
Locust Valley ES 500/K-5
119 Ryefield Rd 11560 516-277-5350
Dr. Sophia Gary, prin. Fax 277-5358
Locust Valley MS 600/6-8
99 Horse Hollow Rd 11560 516-277-5200
H. Thomas Hogan, prin. Fax 277-5208
Other Schools – See Bayville

Friends Academy 700/PK-12
270 Duck Pond Rd 11560 516-676-0393
Andrea Kelly, head sch Fax 393-4276
Portledge S 400/PK-12
355 Duck Pond Rd 11560 516-750-3100
Simon Owen-Williams, head sch Fax 674-7063

Long Beach, Nassau, Pop. 32,689
Long Beach CSD
Supt. — See Lido Beach
East ES 400/K-5
456 Neptune Blvd 11561 516-897-2184
Kathleen Connolly, prin. Fax 897-2291
Lindell Boulevard ES 400/K-5
601 Lindell Blvd 11561 516-897-2198
Karen Sauter, prin. Fax 897-2288
West ES 400/K-5
91 Maryland Ave 11561 516-897-2215
Patrick McKinney, prin. Fax 897-2290

Long Beach Catholic S 500/PK-8
735 W Broadway 11561 516-432-8900
Kerry Kahn, prin. Fax 432-3841

Long Island City, See New York
NYC Department of Education
Supt. — See New York
Children's Lab S, 4545 42nd St 11104 PK-K
Brooke Barr, prin. 718-361-3300
Hunters Point Community MS 100/6-8
150 51st Ave 11101 718-609-3300
Sarah Goodman, prin. Fax 609-3319
IS 141 1,200/6-8
3711 21st Ave 11105 718-278-6403
Miranda Pavlou, prin. Fax 278-2884
IS 204 700/6-8
3641 28th St 11106 718-937-1463
Faye Kotzer, prin. Fax 937-7964
Public S 17 500/PK-5
2837 29th St 11102 718-278-1220
Rebecca Heyward, prin. Fax 278-8257
Public S 70 1,000/PK-5
3045 42nd St 11103 718-728-4646
Donna Geller, prin. Fax 728-5817
Public S 76 600/PK-5
3636 10th St 11106 718-361-7464
Timothy Miller, prin. Fax 361-8014
Public S 78 300/PK-5
4809 Center Blvd 11109 718-392-5402
Luis Pavone, prin. Fax 392-5434
Public S 84 300/PK-8
2245 41st St 11105 718-278-1915
John Buffa, prin. Fax 932-4649
Public S 85 600/PK-5
2370 31st St 11105 718-278-3630
Ann Gordon-Chang, prin. Fax 278-8312
Public S 110, 4829 37th St 11101 K-5
Elisa Gomez, prin. 718-472-2490
Public S 111 400/PK-8
3715 13th St 11101 718-786-2073
Dionne Jaggon, prin. Fax 729-7102
Public S 112 400/K-5
2505 37th Ave 11101 718-784-5250
Rafael Campos-Gatjens, prin. Fax 784-5681
Public S 122 1,400/PK-8
2121 Ditmars Blvd 11105 718-721-6410
Anna Aprea, prin. Fax 726-0016
Public S 150 1,200/PK-6
4001 43rd Ave 11104 718-784-2252
Carmen Parache, prin. Fax 729-7823
Public S 166 1,200/PK-5
3309 35th Ave 11106 718-786-6703
Jessica Geller, prin. Fax 729-7443
Public S 171 600/PK-5
1414 29th Ave 11102 718-932-0909
Lisa Stone, prin. Fax 932-6749
Public S 199 1,000/K-4
3920 48th Ave 11104 718-784-3431
Anthony Inzerillo, prin. Fax 786-1375
Riverview S K-12
1-50 51st Ave 11101 718-609-3320
Annette Beale, prin. Fax 609-3322
Shanker S for Visual & Performing Arts 500/6-8
3151 21st St 11106 718-274-8316
Alexander Angueira, prin. Fax 278-6512
30th Avenue S, 2837 29th St 11102 K-8
Vasilios Biniaris, prin. 718-626-8502

Evangel Christian S 500/PK-12
3921 Crescent St 11101 718-937-9600
Carolyn Marko, hdmstr. Fax 706-8669
St. Joseph Catholic Academy 400/PK-8
2846 44th St 11103 718-728-0724
Luke Nawrocki, prin. Fax 728-6142

Long Lake, Hamilton, Pop. 541
Long Lake Central SD 100/PK-12
PO Box 217 12847 518-624-2147
Noelle Short, supt. Fax 624-3896
www.longlakecsd.org
Long Lake Central S 100/PK-12
PO Box 217 12847 518-624-2147
Noelle Short, prin. Fax 624-3896

Loudonville, Albany, Pop. 10,822
North Colonie Central SD
Supt. — See Latham
Loudonville ES 300/K-6
349 Osborne Rd 12211 518-434-1960
Kerry Flynn, prin. Fax 434-0739
Southgate ES 400/K-6
30 Southgate Rd 12211 518-785-6607
Jerri Lynne Dedrick, prin. Fax 783-8878

Loudonville Christian S 300/PK-12
374 Loudon Rd 12211 518-434-6051
Kathryn Hills M.Ed., head sch Fax 935-2258
St. Gregory's S 100/PK-8
121 Old Niskayuna Rd 12211 518-785-6621
Alan Barr, head sch Fax 782-1364
St. Pius X S 700/PK-8
75 Upper Loudon Rd 12211 518-465-4539
Dennis Mullaly, prin. Fax 465-4895

Lowville, Lewis, Pop. 3,442
Lowville Central SD 1,300/K-12
7668 N State St 13367 315-376-9000
Cheryl Steckly, supt. Fax 376-1933
www.lowvilleacademy.org
Lowville ES 600/K-5
7668 N State St 13367 315-376-9005
Philomena Goss, prin. Fax 376-1933
Lowville MS 300/6-8
7668 N State St 13367 315-376-9010
Scott Exford, prin. Fax 376-9011

Lynbrook, Nassau, Pop. 19,147
Lynbrook UFD 2,800/K-12
111 Atlantic Ave 11563 516-887-0253
Melissa Burak, supt. Fax 887-3263
www.lynbrookschools.org
Atlantic Avenue K 200/K-K
111 Atlantic Ave 11563 516-887-8065
Ellen Postman, prin. Fax 887-8264
Lynbrook North MS 300/6-8
529 Merrick Rd 11563 516-887-0282
Sean Fallon, prin. Fax 887-0286
Lynbrook South MS 400/6-8
333 Union Ave 11563 516-887-0266
Caryn Blum, prin. Fax 887-0268
Marion Street ES 400/1-5
100 Marion St 11563 516-887-0295
Theresa Macchia, prin. Fax 887-3350
West End ES 400/1-5
30 Clark Ave 11563 516-887-0288
Cindy Lee, prin. Fax 887-8269
Other Schools – See East Rockaway

Malverne UFD
Supt. — See Malverne
Davison Avenue IS 400/3-5
49 Davison Ave 11563 516-887-6462
Rachel Gross, prin. Fax 887-6468

Our Lady of Peace S 300/PK-8
21 Fowler Ave 11563 516-593-4884
Jineen Leach, prin. Fax 593-9861

Lyndonville, Orleans, Pop. 823
Lyndonville Central SD 600/PK-12
PO Box 540 14098 585-765-3101
Jason Smith, supt. Fax 765-2106
www.lyndonvillecsd.org/
Lyndonville ES 300/PK-6
PO Box 540 14098 585-765-3122
Dr. Elissa Smith, prin. Fax 765-3190

Lyons, Wayne, Pop. 3,527
Lyons Central SD 700/K-12
10 Clyde Rd 14489 315-946-2200
Donald Putnam, supt. Fax 946-2205
www.lyonscsd.org
Lyons ES 500/K-6
98 William St 14489 315-946-2200
Erin Long, prin. Fax 946-2254

Macedon, Wayne, Pop. 1,496
Palmyra-Macedon Central SD
Supt. — See Palmyra
Palmyra-Macedon IS 400/3-5
4 West St 14502 315-597-3400
Marcia Liberatore, prin. Fax 986-8223

Mc Graw, Cortland, Pop. 1,031
Mc Graw Central SD 500/K-12
10 W Academy St 13101 607-836-3636
Melinda McCool, supt. Fax 836-3635
www.mcgrawschools.org
Mc Graw ES 200/K-5
50 W Academy St 13101 607-836-3650
Susan Prince, prin. Fax 836-3609

Mc Lean, Tompkins
Dryden Central SD
Supt. — See Dryden
Cassavant ES 100/K-3
36 School St 13102 607-838-3522
Audrey Ryan, prin. Fax 838-8907

Madison, Madison, Pop. 304
Madison Central SD 500/PK-12
7303 State Route 20 13402 315-893-1878
Michael Davis, supt. Fax 893-7111
www.madisoncentralny.org
Madison Central S 500/PK-12
7303 State Route 20 13402 315-893-1878
Larry Nichols, prin. Fax 893-7111

Madrid, Saint Lawrence, Pop. 751
Madrid-Waddington Central SD 700/PK-12
PO Box 67 13660 315-322-5746
Eric Burke, supt. Fax 322-4462
www.mwcsk12.org
Madrid-Waddington ES 300/PK-5
PO Box 67 13660 315-322-5746
Matthew Daley, prin. Fax 322-0030

Mahopac, Putnam, Pop. 8,268
Mahopac Central SD 4,600/K-12
179 E Lake Blvd 10541 845-628-3415
Anthony DiCarlo, supt. Fax 628-5502
www.mahopac.k12.ny.us
Austin Road ES 700/K-5
390 Austin Rd 10541 845-628-1346
James Gardineer, prin. Fax 628-5521
Fulmar Road ES 500/K-5
55 Fulmar Rd 10541 845-628-0440
Gary Chadwick, prin. Fax 628-5714
Lakeview ES 600/K-5
112 Lakeview Dr 10541 845-628-3331
Jennifer Pontillo, prin. Fax 628-5849
Mahopac Falls Academy 200/8-8
100 Myrtle Ave 10541 845-621-0656
Fax 628-4819
Mahopac MS 1,200/6-8
425 Baldwin Place Rd 10541 845-621-1330
Tom Cozzocrea, prin. Fax 628-5847

Mahopac Falls, Putnam

Hudson Valley Christian Academy 50/PK-5
PO Box 135 10542 845-628-2775
Maija Murry, prin. Fax 621-9135

Maine, Broome
Maine-Endwell Central SD
Supt. — See Endwell
Maine Memorial ES 400/K-5
PO Box 218 13802 607-862-3263
Linda Kelly, prin. Fax 862-3323

Malone, Franklin, Pop. 5,853
Malone Central SD 2,300/PK-12
PO Box 847 12953 518-483-7800
Jerry Griffin, supt. Fax 483-3071
www.malonecsd.org
Davis ES 600/PK-5
179 Webster St 12953 518-483-7802
Michelle Bailey, prin. Fax 483-6390
Flanders ES 200/PK-5
524 E Main St 12953 518-483-7803
Joseph Coakley, prin. Fax 483-9491
Malone MS 500/6-8
15 Francis St 12953 518-483-7801
James Knight, prin. Fax 483-9497
St. Josephs ES 300/PK-5
99 Elm St 12953 518-483-7806
Lisa Dupree, prin. Fax 483-9567

Holy Family S 200/PK-8
12 Homestead Park 12953 518-483-4443
Marianne Jadlos, prin. Fax 481-6762

Malverne, Nassau, Pop. 8,420
Malverne UFD 1,700/K-12
301 Wicks Ln 11565 516-887-6405
Dr. James Hunderfund, supt. Fax 590-2910
www.malverne.k12.ny.us
Downing PS 400/K-2
55 Lindner Pl 11565 516-887-6469
Edward Tallon, prin. Fax 887-8620
Herber MS 400/6-8
75 Ocean Ave 11565 516-887-6444
Daniel Nehlsen, prin. Fax 596-0525
Other Schools – See Lynbrook

Grace Lutheran S 300/PK-6
400 Hempstead Ave 11565 516-599-6557
Wanda Walters, prin. Fax 599-6151
Our Lady of Lourdes S 300/PK-8
76 Park Blvd 11565 516-599-7328
Mary Murphy, prin. Fax 599-3813

Mamaroneck, Westchester, Pop. 18,587
Mamaroneck UFD 5,200/PK-12
1000 W Boston Post Rd 10543 914-220-3000
Dr. Robert Shaps Ed.D., supt. Fax 220-3010
www.mamkschools.org
Mamaroneck Avenue ES 700/K-5
850 Mamaroneck Ave 10543 914-220-3600
Virginia Lockwood Zisa, prin. Fax 220-3615
Other Schools – See Larchmont

Rye Neck UFD 1,300/K-12
310 Hornidge Rd 10543 914-777-5200
Dr. Barbara Ferraro, supt. Fax 777-5201
www.ryeneck.org
Bellows ES 300/2-4
200 Carroll Ave 10543 914-777-5200
Michael Scarantino, prin. Fax 777-4601
Rye Neck MS 300/5-8
300 Hornidge Rd 10543 914-777-5200
Dr. Eric Lutinski, prin. Fax 777-4701
Warren ES 300/K-1
1310 Harrison Ave 10543 914-777-5200
Tara Napoleoni-Goldberg, prin. Fax 777-4201

Little Flower Nursery S PK-PK
310 E Boston Post Rd 10543 914-777-1281
Leila Marie Badran, prin. Fax 698-5274
Westchester Day S 400/PK-8
856 Orienta Ave 10543 914-698-8900
Rachel Goldman, dir. Fax 777-2146

Manhasset, Nassau, Pop. 7,968
Manhasset UFD 3,300/K-12
200 Memorial Pl 11030 516-267-7700
Dr. Vincent Butera, supt. Fax 627-1618
www.manhassetschools.org
Manhasset MS 600/7-8
200 Memorial Pl 11030 516-267-7500
Dean Schlanger, prin. Fax 627-8157
Munsey Park ES 900/K-6
1 Hunt Ln 11030 516-267-7400
Dr. Jean Kendall, prin. Fax 869-8244
Shelter Rock ES 800/K-6
27 Shelter Rock Rd 11030 516-267-7450
Robert Geczik, prin. Fax 365-3937

Our Lady of Grace Montessori S 200/PK-3
29 Shelter Rock Rd 11030 516-365-9832
Sr. Kelly Quinn, prin. Fax 365-9329
St. Mary's ES 400/PK-8
1340 Northern Blvd 11030 516-627-0184
Dr. Sarah de Venoge, prin. Fax 627-3795

Manlius, Onondaga, Pop. 4,642
Fayetteville-Manlius Central SD 4,200/K-12
8199 E Seneca Tpke 13104 315-692-1234
Dr. Craig Tice, supt. Fax 692-1227
www.fmschools.org
Eagle Hill MS 700/5-8
4645 Enders Rd 13104 315-692-1400
Maureen McCrystal, prin. Fax 692-1046
Enders Road ES 500/K-4
4725 Enders Rd 13104 315-692-1500
Deborah Capri, prin. Fax 692-1053
Other Schools – See Fayetteville

Mannsville, Jefferson, Pop. 353
South Jefferson Central SD
Supt. — See Adams Center
Mannsville Manor ES 300/K-5
423 N Main St 13661 315-465-4281
Jeffery Ginger, prin. Fax 465-4088

Manorville, Suffolk, Pop. 14,172
Eastport-South Manor Central SD 3,300/K-12
149 Dayton Ave 11949 631-801-3013
Dr. Patrick Brimstein, supt. Fax 874-6750
www.esmonline.org
Dayton Avenue S 600/3-6
151 Dayton Ave 11949 631-801-3080
Dr. John Christie, prin. Fax 878-6404
South Street ES 300/K-2
130 South St 11949 631-801-3140
Jane Ruthkowski, prin. Fax 878-4954
Other Schools – See Eastport

Marathon, Cortland, Pop. 912
Marathon Central SD 700/PK-12
PO Box 339 13803 607-849-3117
Rebecca Stone, supt. Fax 849-3305
www.marathonschools.org/
Appleby ES 400/PK-6
PO Box 339 13803 607-849-3282
Jonathan Hillis, prin. Fax 849-3305

Marcellus, Onondaga, Pop. 1,781
Marcellus Central SD 1,700/K-12
2 Reed Pkwy 13108 315-673-6000
Michelle Brantner, supt. Fax 673-1727
marcellusschools.org
Driver MS 700/4-8
2 Reed Pkwy 13108 315-673-6200
Janet O'Mara, prin. Fax 673-1727
Hoffernan ES 500/K-3
2 Learners Ldg 13108 315-673-6100
Robert Montgomery, prin. Fax 673-1117

Marcy, Oneida, Pop. 8,685
Whitesboro Central SD
Supt. — See Whitesboro
Marcy ES 300/K-5
9479 Maynard Dr 13403 315-266-3420
Kimberly Newton, prin. Fax 735-3358

Margaretville, Delaware, Pop. 595
Margaretville Central SD 300/K-12
PO Box 319 12455 845-586-2647
Robert Chakar Ed.D., supt. Fax 586-2949
www.margaretvillecs.org
Margaretville Central S 300/K-12
PO Box 319 12455 845-586-2647
Laura Norris, prin. Fax 586-2949

Catskill Mountain Christian Academy 50/K-12
PO Box 26 12455 845-586-1955
Robert Engelhardt, head sch Fax 586-3492

Marilla, Erie
Iroquois Central SD
Supt. — See Elma
Marilla PS 200/K-4
11683 Bullis Rd 14102 716-652-3000
Amy Stanfield, prin. Fax 995-2330

Marion, Wayne, Pop. 1,490
Marion Central SD 800/PK-12
4034 Warner Rd 14505 315-926-2300
Donald Bavis, supt. Fax 926-5797
www.marioncs.org/
Marion ES 400/PK-6
3863 N Main St 14505 315-926-4256
Dr. Ellen Lloyd, prin. Fax 926-3115

Marlboro, Ulster, Pop. 3,611
Marlboro Central SD
Supt. — See Milton
Marlboro ES 900/K-5
1380 Route 9W 12542 845-236-1636
Patricia Walsh, prin. Fax 236-1639
Marlboro MS 400/6-8
1375 Route 9W 12542 845-236-5840
Debra Clinton, prin. Fax 236-3634

Maspeth, See New York
NYC Department of Education
Supt. — See New York
IS 73 1,700/6-8
7002 54th Ave 11378 718-639-3817
Michael Casale, prin. Fax 429-5162
Public S 58 1,000/K-6
7224 Grand Ave 11378 718-533-6712
Adelina Tripoli, prin. Fax 533-6794
Public S 153 1,400/PK-6
6002 60th Ln 11378 718-821-7850
David Berkowitz, prin. Fax 386-7392

St. Stanislaus Kostka S 200/PK-8
6117 Grand Ave 11378 718-326-1585
Barbara DeMaio, prin. Fax 326-1745

Massapequa, Nassau, Pop. 21,527
Massapequa UFD 7,400/K-12
4925 Merrick Rd 11758 516-308-5000
Lucille Iconis, supt.
www.msd.k12.ny.us
Berner MS, 50 Carman Mill Rd 11758 1,200/6-8
Jason Esposito, prin. 516-308-5700
Fairfield ES 600/K-5
330 Massapequa Ave 11758 516-308-5300
Lori Dano, prin.
Lockhart ES 500/K-5
199 Pittsburgh Ave 11758 516-308-5400
Steve Scarallo, prin.
Unqua ES, 350 Unqua Rd 11758 700/K-5
Deanna Catapano, prin. 516-308-5600
Other Schools – See Massapequa Park

Plainedge UFD
Supt. — See North Massapequa
Schwarting ES 500/K-5
1 Flower Rd 11758 516-992-7400
Jennifer Thearle, prin. Fax 992-7405

Grace Day ECC 300/PK-K
23 Cedar Shore Dr 11758 516-798-1122
Rev. Walter Hillebrand, head sch Fax 799-0711
Montessori Children's S 100/PK-K
PO Box 1609 11758 516-541-6365
Diane Beatty, dir.
St. Rose of Lima S 500/PK-8
4704 Merrick Rd 11758 516-541-1546
Sr. Kathleen Gallina, prin. Fax 797-0351

Massapequa Park, Nassau, Pop. 16,923
Massapequa UFD
Supt. — See Massapequa
Birch Lane ES, 41 Birch Ln 11762 800/K-5
Stephen Aspetti, prin. 516-308-5100
East Lake ES, 154 Eastlake Ave 11762 600/K-5
Thomas McKillop, prin. 516-308-5200
McKenna ES, 210 Spruce St 11762 500/K-5
Dr. Amanda Lowry, prin. 516-308-5500

Massena, Saint Lawrence, Pop. 10,748
Massena Central SD 2,900/PK-12
84 Nightengale Ave 13662 315-764-3700
Patrick Brady, supt. Fax 764-3701
www.mcs.k12.ny.us
Jefferson ES 500/PK-6
84 Nightengale Ave 13662 315-764-3730
Duane Richards, prin. Fax 764-3739
Leary JHS 400/7-8
84 Nightengale Ave 13662 315-764-3720
Alan Oliver, prin. Fax 764-3723
Madison ES 500/PK-6
84 Nightengale Ave 13662 315-764-3740
Danielle Chapman, prin. Fax 764-3743
Nightengale ES 500/PK-6
84 Nightengale Ave 13662 315-764-3750
Amy Hornung, prin. Fax 764-3753

Trinity Catholic S 200/PK-6
188 Main St 13662 315-769-5911
Kathleen Behrens, prin. Fax 769-1185

Mastic Beach, Suffolk, Pop. 12,605
William Floyd UFD 8,700/K-12
240 Mastic Beach Rd 11951 631-874-1100
Kevin Coster, supt. Fax 281-3047
www.wfsd.k12.ny.us
Paca MS 900/6-8
338 Blanco Dr 11951 631-874-1414
Dr. Michele Gode, prin. Fax 874-1561
Tangier Smith ES 800/K-5
336 Blanco Dr 11951 631-874-1341
Toni Komorowski, prin. Fax 874-1416
Other Schools – See Moriches, Shirley

Mattydale, Onondaga, Pop. 6,274

St. Margaret's S 200/PK-6
201 Roxboro Rd 13211 315-455-5791
Amanda Hopkins, prin. Fax 455-1250

Mayfield, Fulton, Pop. 827
Mayfield Central SD 900/PK-12
27 School St 12117 518-661-8207
Jon Peterson, supt. Fax 661-7666
www.mayfieldcsd.org
Mayfield ES 500/PK-6
80 N Main St 12117 518-661-8251
Nicholas Criscone, prin. Fax 661-6590

Mayville, Chautauqua, Pop. 1,698
Chautauqua Lake Central SD 900/PK-12
100 N Erie St 14757 716-753-5808
Benjamin Spitzer, supt. Fax 753-5813
www.clake.org
Chautauqua Lake Central ES 400/PK-6
100 N Erie St 14757 716-753-5842
Ella Ames, prin. Fax 753-5850

Mechanicville, Saratoga, Pop. 5,096
Mechanicville CSD 1,400/K-12
25 Kniskern Ave 12118 518-664-5727
Dr. Michael J. McCarthy, supt. Fax 514-2101
www.mechanicville.org
Mechanicville ES 700/K-5
25 Kniskern Ave 12118 518-664-7336
Stephen Marra, prin. Fax 514-2119
Mechanicville JHS 300/6-8
25 Kniskern Ave 12118 518-664-5727
Craig Forth, prin. Fax 664-5727

Augustine Classical Academy 100/K-12
7 N Main St 12118 518-541-2089
Matt Hopkins, head sch

Medford, Suffolk, Pop. 23,778
Patchogue-Medford UFD
Supt. — See Patchogue
Eagle ES, 1000 Wave Ave 11763 600/K-5
Erin Skahill, prin. 631-687-8150
Tremont ES, 143 Tremont Ave 11763 500/K-5
Lori Koerner, prin. 631-687-8700

Medina, Orleans, Pop. 5,905
Medina Central SD 1,700/PK-12
1 Mustang Dr 14103 585-798-2700
Mark B. Kruzynski, supt. Fax 798-5676
www.medinacsd.org
Oak Orchard ES 500/PK-3
335 W Oak Orchard St 14103 585-798-2700
Julie Webber, prin. Fax 798-2352
Wise Intermediate/Middle S 500/4-7
1016 Gwinn St 14103 585-798-2700
Christopher Hughes, prin. Fax 798-1062

Melville, Suffolk, Pop. 18,680
Half Hollow Hills Central SD
Supt. — See Dix Hills
Sunquam ES 500/K-5
515 Sweet Hollow Rd 11747 631-592-3750
Karen Littell, prin. Fax 592-3920
West Hollow MS 1,300/6-8
250 Old East Neck Rd 11747 631-592-3400
Steven Hauk, prin. Fax 592-3922

South Huntington UFD
Supt. — See Huntington Station
Birchwood IS 700/3-5
121 Wolf Hill Rd 11747 631-812-3200
Anthony Ciccarelli, prin. Fax 812-3232

Menands, Albany, Pop. 3,901
Menands UFD 300/K-8
19 Wards Ln 12204 518-465-4561
Dr. Maureen Long, supt. Fax 465-4572
www.menands.org
Menands S 300/K-8
19 Wards Ln 12204 518-465-4561
Antoinetta Schroeder, prin. Fax 465-4572

Merrick, Nassau, Pop. 21,879
Bellmore-Merrick Central HSD
Supt. — See North Merrick
Merrick Avenue MS 900/7-8
1870 Merrick Ave 11566 516-992-1200
Taryn Johnson, prin. Fax 867-6391

Merrick UFD 1,500/K-6
21 Babylon Rd 11566 516-992-7200
Dr. Dominick Palma, supt. Fax 378-3904
merrick.k12.ny.us
Birch ES 500/K-6
2400 Central Pkwy 11566 516-992-7249
Kerri Galante, prin. Fax 546-1723
Chatterton ES 400/K-6
108 Merrick Ave 11566 516-992-7270
Dana Bermas, prin. Fax 546-1718
Levy Lakeside ES 500/K-6
21 Babylon Rd 11566 516-992-7230
Elizabeth Trencheny, prin. Fax 546-6592

Grace Christian Academy 100/K-12
36 Smith St 11566 516-379-2223
Stephen Schultz, hdmstr. Fax 771-8063
Progressive S of Long Island 100/K-8
1425 Merrick Ave 11566 516-868-6835
Eric Jacobson, dir. Fax 868-7033

Mexico, Oswego, Pop. 1,597
Mexico Central SD 2,100/PK-12
16 Fravor Rd Ste A 13114 315-963-8400
Sean Bruno, supt. Fax 963-5801
www.mexicocsd.org
Mexico ES 300/PK-4
26 Academy St 13114 315-963-8400
Robert Briggs, prin. Fax 963-8992
Mexico MS 600/5-8
16 Fravor Rd 13114 315-963-8400
Kim Holliday, prin. Fax 963-3848
Other Schools – See Fulton, New Haven

Middleburgh, Schoharie, Pop. 1,471
Middleburgh Central SD 600/PK-12
PO Box 606 12122 518-827-3625
Michele Weaver, supt. Fax 827-6632
www.middleburghcsd.org
Middleburgh ES 400/PK-6
245 Main St 12122 518-827-3600
Michael Teator, prin. Fax 827-5321

Middle Granville, Washington
Granville Central SD
Supt. — See Granville
Tanner PS 300/PK-3
PO Box 200 12849 518-642-9460
Keith LaLone, prin. Fax 642-9594

Middle Island, Suffolk, Pop. 10,280
Longwood Central SD 8,900/K-12
35 Yaphank Middle Island Rd 11953 631-345-2172
Dr. Michael Lonergan, supt. Fax 345-2166
www.longwood.k12.ny.us
Longwood JHS 1,300/7-8
198 Longwood Rd 11953 631-345-2701
Adam Dewitt, prin. Fax 345-9281
Longwood MS 1,400/5-6
41 Yaphank Middle Island Rd 11953 631-345-2735
Dr. Tracy Adams, prin. Fax 345-9296
West Middle Island ES 900/K-4
30 Swezey Ln 11953 631-345-2160
Gretchen Schaentzler, prin. Fax 345-2193

Other Schools – See Coram, Ridge, Yaphank

Middleport, Niagara, Pop. 1,807
Royalton-Hartland Central SD 1,400/PK-12
54 State St 14105 716-735-2000
Dr. Roger Klatt, supt. Fax 735-2036
www.royhart.org
Royalton-Hartland MS 500/5-8
78 State St 14105 716-735-2000
John Fisgus, prin. Fax 735-2056
Other Schools – See Gasport

Middletown, Orange, Pop. 27,256
Middletown CSD 6,700/K-12
223 Wisner Ave 10940 845-326-1193
Dr. Kenneth Eastwood, supt. Fax 326-1225
www.middletowncityschools.org/
Carter ES 600/K-5
435 E Main St 10940 845-326-1711
Kathleen Jensen, prin. Fax 326-1723
Maple Hill ES 1,100/K-5
491 County Highway 78 10940 845-326-1740
Amy Creeden, prin. Fax 326-1795
Monhagen MS 800/6-8
555 County Highway 78 10940 845-326-1700
Dominick Radogna, prin. Fax 326-1701
Presidential Park ES 1,300/K-5
50 Roosevelt Ave 10940 845-326-1850
Susan Short, prin. Fax 326-1851
Twin Towers MS 800/6-8
112 Grand Ave 10940 845-326-1650
Gordon Dean, prin. Fax 326-1651

Harmony Christian S 200/PK-12
1790 Route 211 E 10941 845-692-5353
Kevin Barry, admin. Fax 692-7140
Middletown SDA Christian S 50/PK-8
70 Highland Ave 10940 845-343-3775
Lionel Jacques, prin. Fax 343-6633
Our Lady of Mt. Carmel S 200/PK-8
205 Wawayanda Ave 10940 845-343-8836
Jennifer Langford, prin. Fax 342-1404

Middle Village, See New York
NYC Department of Education
Supt. — See New York
Public S 49 1,100/K-8
6360 80th St 11379 718-326-2111
Thomas Carty, prin. Fax 894-3026
Public S 87 600/K-8
6754 80th St 11379 718-326-8243
Caryn Michaeli, prin. Fax 894-3797
Public S 128 900/K-8
6910 65th Dr 11379 718-326-6210
Camillo Turriciano, prin. Fax 326-6080

Our Lady of Hope Academy 600/PK-8
6121 71st St 11379 718-458-3535
Giuseppe Campailla, prin. Fax 458-9031
St. Margaret Academy 300/PK-8
6610 80th St 11379 718-326-0922
Victoria Richardson, prin. Fax 326-3308

Milford, Otsego, Pop. 406
Milford Central SD 400/PK-12
PO Box 237 13807 607-286-7721
Mark Place, supt. Fax 286-7879
www.web.milfordcentral.org
Milford Central S 400/PK-12
PO Box 237 13807 607-286-3349
Teresa Glavin, prin. Fax 286-7879

Millbrook, Dutchess, Pop. 1,439
Millbrook Central SD 1,000/K-12
PO Box AA 12545 845-677-4200
Philip D'Angelo, supt. Fax 677-4206
www.millbrookcsd.org/
Alden Place ES 200/3-5
PO Box AA 12545 845-677-4220
Thomas Libka, prin. Fax 677-4213
Elm Drive ES 200/K-2
PO Box AA 12545 845-677-4225
Karen Ferguson, prin. Fax 677-4224
Millbrook MS 200/6-8
PO Box AA 12545 845-677-4210
Dr. Phyllis Amori, prin. Fax 677-6913

Dutchess Day S 100/PK-8
415 Route 343 12545 845-677-5014
Matthew Heard, hdmstr. Fax 677-6722

Miller Place, Suffolk, Pop. 12,218
Miller Place UFD 2,800/K-12
7 Memorial Dr 11764 631-474-2700
Dr. Marianne Cartisano, supt. Fax 474-0686
www.millerplace.k12.ny.us
Muller PS 600/K-2
65 Lower Rocky Point Rd 11764 631-474-2715
Laura Gewurz, prin. Fax 474-4738
North Country Road MS 700/6-8
191 N Country Rd 11764 631-474-2710
Matthew Clark, prin. Fax 474-5178
Sound Beach ES 700/3-5
197 N Country Rd 11764 631-474-2719
Catherine Honeyman, prin. Fax 474-2497

Milton, Ulster, Pop. 1,389
Marlboro Central SD 1,900/K-12
21 Milton Tpke Ste 100 12547 845-236-8000
Michael Brooks, supt. Fax 795-5904
www.marlboroschools.org
Other Schools – See Marlboro

Mineola, Nassau, Pop. 18,445
Mineola UFD 2,500/PK-12
121 Jackson Ave 11501 516-237-2000
Dr. Michael Nagler, supt. Fax 237-2008
www.mineola.k12.ny.us

Hampton Street ES — 400/PK-2
10 Hampton St 11501 — 516-237-2200
Margarita Maravel, prin. — Fax 237-2208
Jackson Avenue ES — 400/3-5
300 Jackson Ave 11501 — 516-237-2300
Janet Gonzalez, prin. — Fax 237-2308
Mineola MS — 400/6-7
200 Emory Rd 11501 — 516-237-2500
Andrew Casale, prin. — Fax 237-2508
Other Schools – See Albertson

Minetto, Oswego, Pop. 1,056
Oswego CSD
Supt. — See Oswego
Minetto ES — 400/K-6
2411 County Route 8 13115 — 315-341-2600
Jennifer Sullivan, prin. — Fax 341-2960

Minoa, Onondaga, Pop. 3,415
East Syracuse Minoa Central SD
Supt. — See East Syracuse
Minoa ES — 400/K-5
501 N Main St 13116 — 315-434-3420
Amy Fiedler-Horack, prin. — Fax 434-3430

Mohawk, Herkimer, Pop. 2,697
Central Valley Central SD
Supt. — See Ilion
Fisher ES — 300/PK-1
10 Fisher Ave 13407 — 315-866-4851
Michele Pilla, prin. — Fax 866-0055
Jarvis MS — 100/5-8
28 Grove St 13407 — 315-866-2620
Melissa Hoskey, prin. — Fax 867-2909

Mohegan Lake, Westchester, Pop. 3,600
Lakeland Central SD
Supt. — See Shrub Oak
Van Cortlandtville ES — 600/K-5
3100 E Main St 10547 — 914-528-1354
Jacqueline Woodruff, prin. — Fax 528-1376
Washington ES — 500/K-5
3634 Lexington Ave 10547 — 914-528-2021
Tracy Norman, prin. — Fax 528-2134

Monroe, Orange, Pop. 8,240
Greenwood Lake UFD — 500/K-8
1247 Lakes Rd 10950 — 845-782-8678
Dr. Steven Cohen, supt. — Fax 782-8582
www.gwlufsd.org/
Greenwood Lake MS — 300/4-8
1247 Lakes Rd 10950 — 845-782-8678
Jeffrey Golubchick, prin. — Fax 782-2004
Other Schools – See Greenwood Lake

Kiryas Joel Village UFSD — 50/PK-12
48 Bakertown Rd Ste 401 10950 — 845-782-2300
Joel Petlin, supt. — Fax 782-4176
Kiryas Joel Village S — 50/PK-12
1 Dinev Ct 10950 — 845-782-7510
Jehuda Halpern, prin. — Fax 782-5849

Monroe-Woodbury Central SD
Supt. — See Central Valley
North Main Street ES — 600/2-5
212 N Main St 10950 — 845-460-6800
Joseph Coto, prin. — Fax 460-6048
Pine Tree ES — 900/2-5
156 Pine Tree Rd 10950 — 845-460-6900
Bryan Giudice, prin. — Fax 460-6049

Bnei Yoel S — 300/PK-12
PO Box 255, — 845-783-8036
Yitchok Tyrnauer, prin. — Fax 782-7039
Sacred Heart S — 300/PK-8
26 Still Rd 10950 — 845-783-0365
Catherine Muenkel, prin. — Fax 782-0354
St. Paul Christian Education Center — 200/PK-2
21 Still Rd 10950 — 845-783-1068
Ramona Adams, dir. — Fax 783-7593
UTA of Kiryas Joel — 5,800/PK-12
13 Riminev Ct 10950 — 845-783-5800
Shloma Weiss, admin. — Fax 782-1922

Monsey, Rockland, Pop. 18,318
East Ramapo Central SD
Supt. — See Spring Valley
Elmwood IS — 400/4-6
43 Robert Pitt Dr 10952 — 845-577-6160
Ellen Adriello, prin. — Fax 426-0852
Grandview ES — 400/K-3
151 Grandview Ave 10952 — 845-577-6260
Patricia Smith, prin. — Fax 362-0646
Margetts ES — 500/K-3
25 Margetts Rd 10952 — 845-577-6190
Barbara Grieco, prin. — Fax 426-0958

Bais Malka Girls S of Belz — 500/PK-12
PO Box 977 10952 — 845-354-9500
Rabbi Aron Grossman, dir. — Fax 425-2629
Bais Mikroh — 500/PK-8
221 Viola Rd 10952 — 845-425-4880
Yaakov Horowitz, admin. — Fax 425-1062
Bais Shifra Miriam S — 300/K-12
PO Box 682 10952 — 845-356-0061
Gabriel Kramarsky, admin. — Fax 356-0223
Bais Trany, PO Box 870 10952 — 50/PK-3
Moishe Silberman, prin. — 845-371-6900
Beth Rochel School for Girls — 1,000/K-12
145 Saddle River Rd 10952 — 845-352-5000
Rabbi M. Zenwirth, prin. — Fax 352-6571
Bnos Yisroel Girls S of Viznitz — 50/PK-K
20 Ashel Ln 10952 — 845-731-3777
Bnos Yisroel Girls S of Viznitz — 1,400/1-12
1 School Ter 10952 — 845-731-3700
Bernard Rosenfeld, prin. — Fax 731-3751
Talmud Torah Me'or Hachaim Viznitz — K-9
15 Elyon Rd 10952 — 845-731-3700

Yeshiva Beth David S — 600/PK-12
PO Box 136 10952 — 845-352-3100
Rabbi Aron Bayer, prin. — Fax 352-0153
Yeshiva Derech Emes — 50/PK-12
133 Route 59 10952 — 845-426-2130
Yeshiva of Spring Valley — 1,600/PK-8
230 Maple Ave 10952 — 845-356-1400
Rabbi Eliezer Stern, prin. — Fax 356-8551
Yeshiva of Spring Valley Girls Div — K-8
142 Grandview Ave 10952 — 845-356-1400
Eliezer Stern, prin. — Fax 356-8551

Montauk, Suffolk, Pop. 3,289
Montauk UFD — 400/PK-8
50 S Dorset Dr 11954 — 631-668-2474
J. Philip Perna, supt. — Fax 668-1107
www.montaukschool.org
Montauk ES — 400/PK-8
50 S Dorset Dr 11954 — 631-668-2474
J. Philip Perna, supt. — Fax 668-1107

Montgomery, Orange, Pop. 3,752
Valley Central SD — 4,300/K-12
944 State Route 17K 12549 — 845-457-2400
John P. Xanthis, supt. — Fax 457-4319
www.vcsd.k12.ny.us
Berea ES — 400/K-5
946 State Route 17K 12549 — 845-457-2400
John Solimando, prin. — Fax 457-4442
Montgomery ES — 600/K-5
141 Union St 12549 — 845-457-2400
Matthew Canino, prin. — Fax 457-9120
Valley Central MS — 1,000/6-8
1189 State Route 17K 12549 — 845-457-2400
Ned Hayes, prin. — Fax 457-4008
Other Schools – See Newburgh, Walden

Montgomery Montessori S — 50/PK-8
136 Clinton St 12549 — 845-401-9232
Parinaz Mokhtari, dir. — Fax 457-4440

Monticello, Sullivan, Pop. 6,485
Monticello Central SD — 3,000/K-12
237 Forestburgh Rd 12701 — 845-794-7700
Tammy Mangus, supt. — Fax 794-7710
www.monticelloschools.net
Cooke ES — 500/K-5
69 Richardson Ave 12701 — 845-794-8830
Rosemary Romano, prin. — Fax 794-8854
Kaiser MS — 700/6-8
45 Breakey Ave 12701 — 845-796-3058
Nicholas Millas, prin. — Fax 796-3099
Rutherford ES — 500/K-5
26 Patricia Pl 12701 — 845-794-4240
Michelle Knowlton, prin. — Fax 794-5137
Other Schools – See Wurtsboro

Montour Falls, Schuyler, Pop. 1,693
Odessa-Montour Central SD
Supt. — See Odessa
Cate ES — 200/PK-2
262 Canal St 14865 — 607-535-7267
Veronica Lewis, prin. — Fax 535-7802

Montrose, Westchester, Pop. 2,689
Hendrick Hudson Central SD — 2,400/K-12
61 Trolley Rd 10548 — 914-257-5100
Joseph Hochreiter, supt. — Fax 257-5121
www.henhudschools.org/
Lindsey ES — 400/K-5
57 Trolley Rd 10548 — 914-257-5500
Donna Torrisi, prin. — Fax 257-5501
Other Schools – See Buchanan, Cortlandt Manor

Mooers, Clinton, Pop. 441
Northeastern Clinton Central SD
Supt. — See Champlain
Mooers ES — 300/K-5
16 School St 12958 — 518-236-7373
Dennis Rasco, prin. — Fax 298-4293

Moravia, Cayuga, Pop. 1,274
Moravia Central SD — 1,000/PK-12
PO Box 1189 13118 — 315-497-2670
John Birmingham, supt. — Fax 497-2260
www.moraviaschool.org
Fillmore ES — 500/PK-5
PO Box 1188 13118 — 315-497-2670
Howard Seamans, prin. — Fax 497-3961

Moriches, Suffolk, Pop. 2,802
William Floyd UFD
Supt. — See Mastic Beach
Floyd MS — 1,000/6-8
630 Moriches Middle Island 11955 — 631-874-5505
Carolyn Schick, prin. — Fax 878-7690
Moriches ES — 900/K-5
16 Louis Ave 11955 — 631-874-1397
Eileen Filippone, prin. — Fax 874-1890

Morris, Otsego, Pop. 573
Morris Central SD — 400/PK-12
PO Box 40 13808 — 607-263-6102
Matthew Sheldon, supt. — Fax 263-2483
www.morriscsd.org
Morris Central S — 400/PK-12
PO Box 40 13808 — 607-263-6100
Katharine Smith, prin. — Fax 263-2483

Morrisonville, Clinton, Pop. 1,525
Saranac Central SD
Supt. — See Dannemora
Morrisonville ES — 300/K-5
47 Sand Rd 12962 — 518-565-5980
Kathleen Moore, prin. — Fax 565-5972

Morristown, Saint Lawrence, Pop. 395
Morristown Central SD — 300/PK-12
PO Box 217 13664 — 315-375-8814
Douglas H. McQueer, supt. — Fax 375-8604
www.greenrockets.org
Morristown Central S — 300/PK-12
PO Box 217 13664 — 315-375-8814
David L. Doe, prin. — Fax 375-8604

Morrisville, Madison, Pop. 2,159
Morrisville-Eaton Central SD — 700/PK-12
PO Box 990 13408 — 315-684-9300
Gregory Molloy, supt. — Fax 684-9399
www.m-ecs.org
Andrews ES — 400/PK-5
PO Box 990 13408 — 315-684-9288
Debra Dushko, prin. — Fax 684-7252

Mount Kisco, Westchester, Pop. 10,701
Bedford Central SD
Supt. — See Bedford
Fox Lane MS — 1,000/6-8
S Bedford Rd 10549 — 914-241-6126
Susan Ostrofsky, prin. — Fax 241-6129
Mount Kisco ES — 600/K-5
47 W Hyatt Ave 10549 — 914-666-2677
Inas Morsi Hogans, prin. — Fax 666-8245

Rippowam Cisqua S — 300/PK-4
325 W Patent Rd 10549 — 914-244-1200
Colm MacMahon, head sch — Fax 244-1234
Talmud Torah Bais Yechiel-Nitra — 200/K-9
PO Box 241 10549 — 914-666-2929

Mount Morris, Livingston, Pop. 2,942
Mount Morris Central SD — 500/PK-12
30 Bonadonna Ave 14510 — 585-658-2568
Gregory Bump, supt. — Fax 658-4814
www.mtmorriscsd.org
Mount Morris ES — 300/PK-6
30 Bonadonna Ave 14510 — 585-658-3333
Rachael Greene, prin. — Fax 658-4814

Mount Sinai, Suffolk, Pop. 11,989
Mount Sinai UFD — 2,400/K-12
118 N Country Rd 11766 — 631-870-2550
Gordon Brosdal, supt. — Fax 473-0905
www.mtsinai.k12.ny.us
Mount Sinai ES — 800/K-4
118 N Country Rd 11766 — 631-870-2600
Rob Catlin, prin. — Fax 928-3860
Mount Sinai MS — 800/5-8
114 N Country Rd 11766 — 631-870-2700
Peter Pramataris, prin. — Fax 928-3129

Mount Vernon, Westchester, Pop. 64,673
Mount Vernon CSD — 7,800/PK-12
165 N Columbus Ave 10553 — 914-358-2400
Dr. Kenneth R. Hamilton, supt. — Fax 665-6077
www.mtvernoncsd.org
Columbus ES at Franko — 500/K-6
455 N High St 10552 — 914-358-2700
Dr. Colleen Crawford, prin. — Fax 665-0481
Davis MS — 700/7-8
350 Gramatan Ave 10552 — 914-665-5120
Jennifer Wesolowski, prin. — Fax 665-5128
Graham S — 400/K-8
421 E 5th St 10553 — 914-358-2800
Dr. Natasha Hunter-McGregor, prin. — Fax 665-1230
Grimes ES — 400/K-6
58 S 10th Ave 10550 — 914-665-5020
Erik VanGunten, prin. — Fax 665-5016
Hamilton ES — 400/K-6
20 Oak St 10550 — 914-665-5050
Alan Gonzalez, prin. — Fax 665-5052
Holmes ES — 400/PK-6
195 N Columbus Ave 10553 — 914-665-5110
Danielle Davis-Marrow, prin. — Fax 665-5116
Lincoln ES — 700/K-6
170 E Lincoln Ave 10552 — 914-665-5039
Rebecca Jones, prin. — Fax 665-5378
Parker ES — 300/PK-6
461 S 6th Ave 10550 — 914-665-5040
Natalie Dweck, prin. — Fax 665-5353
Pennington S — 400/PK-8
20 Fairway St 10552 — 914-665-5105
Ilene Bichler, prin. — Fax 665-5107
Traphagen ES — 200/K-6
72 Lexington Ave 10552 — 914-665-5060
Carol Quinones, prin. — Fax 665-5062
Turner ES — 400/K-6
625 S 4th Ave 10550 — 914-665-5100
Jamal Doggett, prin. — Fax 665-5096
Turner MS — 400/6-8
624 S 3rd Ave 10550 — 914-665-5150
Dr. Jonathan Brown, prin. — Fax 665-5152
Williams ES — 500/K-6
9 Union Ln 10553 — 914-665-5070
Dr. Crystal Waterman, prin. — Fax 665-5237

Emmanuel Children's Mission S — 300/PK-6
32 S 5th Ave 10550 — 914-664-1810
R. Richards, dir.
Our Lady of Victory S — 300/PK-8
38 N 5th Ave 10550 — 914-667-4063
Helena Castilla-Byrne, prin. — Fax 665-3135

Munnsville, Madison, Pop. 470
Stockbridge Valley Central SD — 400/K-12
PO Box 732 13409 — 315-495-4400
Cindy Stocker, supt. — Fax 495-4492
www.stockbridgevalley.org
Stockbridge Valley Central S — 400/K-12
PO Box 732 13409 — 315-495-4400
Jonathan Kilian, admin. — Fax 495-4492

Nanuet, Rockland, Pop. 17,600
Nanuet UFD — 2,200/K-12
101 Church St 10954 — 845-627-9888
Dr. Mark McNeill, supt. — Fax 624-5338
www.nanuetsd.org
Barr 5-6 Academy for Excellence — 400/5-6
143 Church St 10954 — 845-627-4040
Anne Chen, prin. — Fax 624-3138

Barr MS 400/7-8
143 Church St 10954 845-627-4040
Roger Guccione, prin. Fax 624-3138
Highview ES 300/3-4
24 Highview Ave 10954 845-627-3460
Nancy Bonner, prin. Fax 627-0340
Miller ES 500/K-2
50 Blauvelt Rd 10954 845-627-4860
Maryellen Griffin, prin. Fax 624-1534

St. Anthony S 200/PK-8
34 W Nyack Rd 10954 845-623-2311
Sr. Patricia Howell, prin. Fax 623-0055

Naples, Ontario, Pop. 1,024
Naples Central SD 700/PK-12
136 N Main St 14512 585-374-7900
Matthew Frahm, supt. Fax 374-5859
www.naplescsd.org
Naples ES 400/PK-6
2 Academy St 14512 585-374-7952
Kristina Saucke, prin. Fax 374-7955

Nassau, Rensselaer, Pop. 1,110
East Greenbush Central SD
Supt. — See East Greenbush
Sutherland ES 300/K-5
PO Box 429 12123 518-207-2620
John Alvey, prin. Fax 766-9548

Nedrow, Onondaga, Pop. 2,167
La Fayette Central SD
Supt. — See La Fayette
Onondaga Nation S 100/PK-8
RR 1 Box 270 13120 315-469-6991
Fax 469-0994

Onondaga Central SD 900/PK-12
4466 S Onondaga Rd 13120 315-552-5000
Robin Price, supt. Fax 492-4650
www.ocs.cnyric.org
Rockwell ES 200/PK-2
208 Rockwell Rd 13120 315-552-5070
Margaret Hart, prin. Fax 469-7732
Wheeler ES 300/3-6
4543 S Onondaga Rd 13120 315-552-5050
Timothy H. Cowin, prin. Fax 552-5054

Nesconset, Suffolk, Pop. 13,284
Smithtown Central SD
Supt. — See Smithtown
Great Hollow MS 1,000/6-8
150 Southern Blvd 11767 631-382-2800
John Scomillio, prin. Fax 382-2807
Tackan ES 500/K-5
99 Midwood Ave 11767 631-382-2670
Dr. Allyn Leeds, prin. Fax 382-2676

Newark, Wayne, Pop. 8,894
Newark Central SD 2,100/PK-12
100 E Miller St Ste 5 14513 315-332-3217
Matthew Cook, supt. Fax 332-3523
www.newarkcsd.org
Kelley IS 500/3-5
316 W Miller St 14513 315-332-3326
Jeffrey Hamelinck, prin. Fax 332-3624
Lincoln ES 300/PK-2
1014 N Main St 14513 315-332-3342
Stephanie Miller, prin. Fax 332-3604
Newark MS 500/6-8
701 Peirson Ave 14513 315-332-3295
Teresa Prinzi, prin. Fax 332-3584
Perkins ES 300/PK-2
439 W Maple Ave 14513 315-332-3315
Susan Achille, prin. Fax 332-3614

Newark Valley, Tioga, Pop. 980
Newark Valley Central SD 1,200/K-12
PO Box 547 13811 607-642-3221
Ryan Dougherty, supt. Fax 642-8821
www.nvcs.stier.org/
Hall ES 400/K-3
86 Whig St 13811 607-642-3340
Robert Rodgers, prin. Fax 642-5004
Newark Valley MS 300/4-7
88 Whig St 13811 607-642-5524
Todd Schaffer, prin. Fax 642-8494

New Berlin, Chenango, Pop. 1,014
Unadilla Valley Central SD 900/PK-12
PO Box F 13411 607-847-7500
Robert Mackey, admin. Fax 847-6924
www.uvstorm.org
Unadilla Valley ES 400/PK-5
PO Box F 13411 607-847-7500
Christopher Harper, prin. Fax 847-9988

Newburgh, Orange, Pop. 28,122
Newburgh Enlarged CSD 11,900/PK-12
124 Grand St 12550 845-563-3500
Dr. Roberto Padilla, supt. Fax 563-3501
www.newburghschools.org
Balmville ES 500/PK-5
5144 Route 9W 12550 845-563-8550
Danny Dottin, prin. Fax 563-8554
Fostertown E.T.C. Magnet ES 600/K-5
364 Fostertown Rd 12550 845-568-6425
Maritza Ramos, prin. Fax 568-6430
GAMS Tech Magnet ES 600/K-5
300 Gidney Ave 12550 845-563-8450
Marsha Sobel, prin. Fax 563-8459
Gardnertown Fundamental Magnet ES 600/PK-5
6 Plattekill Tpke 12550 845-568-6400
Lillian Torres, prin. Fax 568-6408
Horizons-on-the-Hudson Magnet ES 500/PK-5
137 Montgomery St 12550 845-563-3725
Terry Lucas, prin. Fax 563-3730
Meadow Hill Global Explortns Magnet ES 1,000/K-8
124 Meadow Hill Rd 12550 845-568-6600
Dennis Camt, prin. Fax 568-6609

South MS 800/6-8
33 Monument St 12550 845-563-7000
Lisa Buon, prin. Fax 563-7019
Other Schools – See New Windsor

Valley Central SD
Supt. — See Montgomery
East Coldenham ES 300/K-5
286 Route 17K 12550 845-457-2400
Marianne Serratore, prin. Fax 564-1554

Bishop Dunn Memorial S 300/PK-8
50 Gidney Ave 12550 845-569-3494
Nancy Benfer, prin. Fax 569-3303
Cronin Presentation Academy 100/5-8
69 Bay View Ter 12550 845-567-0708
Sr. Yliana Hernandez, prin. Fax 567-0709
Sacred Heart S 200/PK-8
24 S Robinson Ave 12550 845-561-1433
Lori Anne Evanko, prin. Fax 561-4383

New City, Rockland, Pop. 32,957
Clarkstown Central SD 8,400/K-12
62 Old Middletown Rd 10956 845-639-6418
Martin Cox, supt. Fax 639-6488
www.ccsd.edu
Laurel Plains ES 400/K-5
14 Teakwood Ln 10956 845-639-6350
Carol Pilla, prin. Fax 639-4206
Link ES, 55 Red Hill Rd 10956 400/K-5
Francine Cuccia, prin. 845-624-3494
Little Tor ES 300/K-5
56 Gregory St 10956 845-624-3471
Matthew Younghans, prin. Fax 638-0807
New City ES, 60 Crestwood Dr 10956 300/K-5
Debra Forman, prin. 845-624-3467
Woodglen ES 500/K-5
121 Phillips Hill Rd 10956 845-624-3417
Lisa Maher, prin.
Other Schools – See Bardonia, Congers, West Nyack

East Ramapo Central SD
Supt. — See Spring Valley
Summit Park ES 400/K-3
925 Route 45 10956 845-577-6290
Kim A. Hewlett, prin. Fax 362-0920

Cornerstone Christian S 100/K-8
384 New Hempstead Rd 10956 845-634-7977
Jeannette Rosa-Sanchez, prin. Fax 634-7979
Hebrew Academy 100/PK-8
315 N Main St 10956 845-634-0951
Rabbi Avremel Kotlarsky, prin. Fax 634-7704
Schreiber Hebrew Academy 300/PK-8
360 New Hempstead Rd 10956 845-357-1515
Rabbi Ari Jacobson, prin. Fax 357-1516

Newcomb, Essex
Newcomb Central SD 100/PK-12
PO Box 418 12852 518-582-3341
Clark Hults, supt. Fax 582-2163
www.newcombcsd.org
Newcomb Central S 100/PK-12
PO Box 418 12852 518-582-3341
Clark Hults, prin. Fax 582-2163

Newfane, Niagara, Pop. 3,772
Newfane Central SD
Supt. — See Burt
Newfane ES 400/K-4
2909 Transit Rd 14108 716-778-6376
Jenna Arroyo, prin. Fax 778-6377
Newfane MS 500/5-8
2700 Transit Rd 14108 716-778-6452
Thomas Adams, prin. Fax 778-6460

Newfield, Tompkins
Newfield Central SD 800/PK-12
247 Main St 14867 607-564-9955
Dr. Cheryl Thomas, supt. Fax 564-0055
www.newfieldschools.org
Newfield ES 400/PK-5
247 Main St 14867 607-564-9955
Vicky Volpicelli, prin. Fax 564-0055
Newfield MS 200/6-8
247 Main St 14867 607-564-9955
Eric Hartz, prin. Fax 564-3403

New Hartford, Oneida, Pop. 1,828
New Hartford Central SD 2,600/K-12
33 Oxford Rd 13413 315-624-1218
Robert Nole, supt. Fax 724-8940
www.newhartfordschools.org
Bradley ES 500/K-6
33 Oxford Rd 13413 315-624-1220
Maureen Futscher, prin. Fax 735-1873
Hughes ES 500/K-6
340 Higby Rd 13413 315-738-9350
Kathleen Carney, prin. Fax 724-1899
Myles ES 400/K-6
100 Clinton Rd 13413 315-738-9600
Cindy Langone, prin. Fax 724-2653

New Haven, Oswego, Pop. 2,778
Mexico Central SD
Supt. — See Mexico
New Haven ES 200/PK-4
4320 State Route 104 13121 315-963-8400
Jennifer Granholm, prin. Fax 963-8813

New Hempstead, Rockland, Pop. 5,051

Ateres Bais Yaakov 300/PK-12
200 Summit Park Rd 10977 845-368-2200
Rabbi Aaron Fink, dean Fax 368-2210

New Hyde Park, Nassau, Pop. 9,473
Great Neck UFD
Supt. — See Great Neck

Parkville S 400/PK-K
10 Campbell St 11040 516-441-4350
Debra Shalom, prin. Fax 441-4367

Herricks UFD 3,900/K-12
999 Herricks Rd 11040 516-305-8900
Dr. Fino Celano, supt. Fax 248-3108
www.herricks.org
Denton Avenue ES 600/K-5
1050 Denton Ave 11040 516-305-8400
Mel Haley, prin. Fax 739-4754
Other Schools – See Albertson, Williston Park

New Hyde Park-Garden City Park UFD 1,700/PK-6
1950 Hillside Ave 11040 516-434-2305
Dr. Jennifer Morrison, supt. Fax 352-6282
nhp-gcp.org
Garden City Park ES 300/PK-6
51 Central Ave 11040 516-434-2390
Amy Sullivan, prin. Fax 873-6368
Hillside ES 500/PK-6
150 Maple Dr W 11040 516-434-2410
Beth Torreano, prin. Fax 352-6081
Manor Oaks/Bowie ES 400/PK-6
1950 Hillside Ave 11040 516-434-2350
Ken Craft, prin. Fax 616-1959
New Hyde Park Road ES 500/PK-6
300 New Hyde Park Rd 11040 516-434-2370
Kim LaRegina, prin. Fax 352-6059

Notre Dame S 400/PK-8
25 Mayfair Rd 11040 516-354-5618
Caryn Durkin, prin. Fax 354-5373

New Lebanon, Columbia
New Lebanon Central SD 400/K-12
14665 State Route 22 12125 518-794-9016
Leslie Whitcomb, supt. Fax 766-5574
www.newlebanoncsd.org
Howard ES 200/K-6
1478 State Route 20 12125 518-794-8554
Andrew Kourt, prin. Fax 766-2220

New Paltz, Ulster, Pop. 6,646
New Paltz Central SD 2,200/K-12
196 Main St 12561 845-256-4020
Maria Rice, supt. Fax 256-4025
www.newpaltz.k12.ny.us
Duzine ES 500/K-2
196 Main St 12561 845-256-4350
Debra Hogencamp, prin. Fax 256-4359
Lenape ES 500/3-5
196 Main St 12561 845-256-4300
Fax 256-4309
New Paltz MS 500/6-8
196 Main St 12561 845-256-4200
Dr. Richard Wiesenthal, prin. Fax 256-4209

Mountain Laurel Waldorf S 200/PK-8
PO Box 939 12561 845-255-0033
Judith Jaeckel, prin. Fax 255-0597

Newport, Herkimer, Pop. 637
West Canada Valley Central SD 700/K-12
PO Box 360 13416 315-845-6800
D.J. Shepardson, supt. Fax 845-8652
www.westcanada.org
West Canada Valley ES 400/K-6
PO Box 360 13416 315-845-6800
Correne Holmes, prin. Fax 845-1640

New Rochelle, Westchester, Pop. 75,662
New Rochelle CSD 10,700/PK-12
515 North Ave 10801 914-576-4300
Dr. Brian G. Osborne, supt. Fax 632-4144
www.nred.org
Barnard ECC 500/PK-2
129 Barnard Rd 10801 914-576-4386
Dr. Nicolas Cracco, prin. Fax 576-4625
Columbus ES 800/K-5
275 Washington Ave 10801 914-576-4401
Michael Galland, prin. Fax 576-4628
Davis ES 700/K-5
80 Iselin Dr 10804 914-576-4420
Anthony Brambola, prin. Fax 576-4225
Jefferson ES 600/K-5
131 Weyman Ave 10805 914-576-4430
Kimmerly Nieves, prin. Fax 576-4631
Leonard MS 1,200/6-8
25 Gerada Ln 10804 914-576-4339
John Barnes, prin. Fax 576-4784
Trinity ES 800/K-5
180 Pelham Rd 10805 914-576-4440
Anthony DiCarlo, prin. Fax 576-4266
Ward ES 1,000/K-5
311 Broadfield Rd 10804 914-576-4450
Franco Miele, prin. Fax 576-4263
Webster ES 500/K-5
95 Glenmore Dr 10801 914-576-4460
Melissa Passarelli, prin. Fax 576-4479
Young MS 1,100/6-8
270 Centre Ave 10805 914-576-4360
Dr. Anthony Bongo, prin. Fax 632-2738

Holy Name of Jesus S 200/PK-8
70 Petersville Rd 10801 914-576-6672
Joanne Kelly, prin. Fax 576-6676
Hudson Country Montessori S 200/PK-8
340 Quaker Ridge Rd 10804 914-636-6202
Mark Meyer, hdmstr. Fax 636-5139
Iona Prep Lower S 200/PK-8
173 Stratton Rd 10804 914-633-7744
Joseph Blanco, prin. Fax 235-6338
Thornton-Donovan S 200/K-12
100 Overlook Cir 10804 914-632-8836
Douglas Fleming, hdmstr. Fax 576-7936

Westchester Area S 100/PK-8
456 Webster Ave 10801 914-235-5799
Rosalind Aaron, prin. Fax 235-4332

New Square, Rockland, Pop. 6,907

Avir Yaakov Girl's S 1,200/K-12
15 Roosevelt Ave 10977 845-354-0874

New Suffolk, Suffolk, Pop. 349

New Suffolk Common SD 50/PK-6
PO Box 111 11956 631-734-6940
Dr. Christopher Gallagher, admin. Fax 734-6940
www.newsuffolkschool.com/

New Suffolk ES 50/PK-6
PO Box 111 11956 631-734-6940
Dr. Christopher Gallagher, prin. Fax 734-6940

New Windsor, Orange, Pop. 8,717

Newburgh Enlarged CSD
Supt. — See Newburgh

Heritage MS 900/6-8
405 Union Ave 12553 845-563-3750
Lynnette Brunger, prin. Fax 563-3759

New Windsor ES 700/PK-5
175 Quassaick Ave 12553 845-563-3700
Dr. Lisamarie Spindler, prin. Fax 563-3709

Temple Hill Academy 1,000/K-8
525 Union Ave 12553 845-568-6450
Ventura Lopez, prin. Fax 568-6470

Vails Gate High Tech Magnet ES 600/K-5
400 Old Forge Hill Rd 12553 845-563-7900
Ciria Briscoe-Perez, prin. Fax 563-7909

Washingtonville Central SD
Supt. — See Washingtonville

Little Britain ES 500/1-5
1160 Little Britain Rd 12553 845-497-4000
Sagrario O'Neill, prin. Fax 497-4003

New York, New York, Pop. 7,965,821

NYC Department of Education 940,300/PK-12
52 Chambers St 10007 718-935-2000
Carmen Farina, chncllr.
schools.nyc.gov/

Amistad Dual Language S 400/K-8
4862 Broadway 10034 212-544-8021
Robin Edmonds, prin. Fax 569-7765

Anderson S 600/K-8
100 W 77th St 10024 212-595-7193
Jodi Hyde, prin. Fax 496-2854

Baker S 300/PK-8
317 E 67th St, 212-717-8809
Joshua Satin, prin. Fax 717-8807

Ballet Tech / S for Dance 100/4-8
890 Broadway Fl 3 10003 212-254-1803
Roy O'Neill, prin. Fax 477-5048

Battery Park City S 900/PK-8
55 Battery Pl 10280 212-266-5800
Terri Ruyter, prin.

Bilingual Bicultural ES 400/K-5
219 E 109th St 10029 212-860-6031
Yazmin Perez, prin. Fax 860-4536

Castle Bridge ES K-1
560 W 169th St 10032 212-740-4701
Julia Zuckerman, prin.

Central Park East S I 200/PK-5
1573 Madison Ave 10029 212-860-5821
Gabriel Feldberg, prin. Fax 860-6017

Central Park East S II 300/PK-8
19 E 103rd St 10029 212-860-5992
Naomi Smith, prin. Fax 410-6041

Children's Workshop S 300/PK-5
610 E 12th St 10009 212-614-9531
Maria Velez-Clarke, prin. Fax 614-9462

City Knoll MS, 525 W 44th St 10036 6-8
Kaye Kerr, prin. 718-935-3649

Community Action S - MS 258 200/6-8
154 W 93rd St 10025 212-678-5888
Andrew Sullivan, prin. Fax 961-1613

Dos Puentes ES 100/K-5
185 Wadsworth Ave 10033 212-781-1803
Victoria Hunt, prin.

Eagle Academy for Young Men of Harlem 100/6-7
6 Edgecombe Ave 10030 212-694-6051
Mahaliel Bethea, prin. Fax 694-6053

Earth S 300/PK-5
600 E 6th St 10009 212-477-1735
Abbe Futterman, prin. Fax 477-2396

East Side ES, 213 E 63rd St, 100/K-5
Medea Mcevoy, prin. 212-888-7848

East Side MS 400/6-8
331 E 91st St 10128 212-360-0114
David Getz, prin. Fax 360-0121

East Village Community S 300/PK-5
610 E 12th St 10009 212-982-0682
Bradley Goodman, prin. Fax 260-4012

Esperanza Preparatory Academy 200/6-8
240 E 109th St 10029 212-722-6507
Luisa Morales, prin. Fax 722-6717

Global Technology Preparatory S 200/6-8
160 E 120th St 10035 212-722-1395
Robert Perales, prin. Fax 722-5864

Grange MS 6-8
500 W 138th St 10031 212-281-6184
Benjamin Lev, prin. Fax 234-4903

Hamilton Heights ES 200/K-5
1750 Amsterdam Ave 10031 212-862-9940
Deirdre Budd, prin. Fax 862-9946

Harbor Heights MS 200/6-8
306 Fort Washington Ave 10033 212-568-6052
Monica Klehr, prin. Fax 568-7959

Hedbavny S 500/K-8
421 W 219th St 10034 212-942-3440
Lillian Reyes, prin. Fax 942-8177

Johnson S 800/PK-8
176 E 115th St 10029 212-876-5522
Nancy Diaz, prin. Fax 860-6072

KAPPA IV S 200/6-8
6 Edgecombe Ave 10030 212-694-6040
Juan Vives, prin. Fax 690-8056

Lafayette Academy 200/6-8
154 W 93rd St 10025 212-222-2857
Brian Zager, prin. Fax 531-0586

Lexington Academy 500/PK-5
131 E 104th St 10029 212-860-5831
Antonio Hernandez, prin. Fax 860-6094

Lower Manhattan Community MS 400/6-8
26 Broadway 10004 646-826-8100
Kelly McGuire, prin. Fax 826-8101

Marshall Academy Lower S 200/K-5
276 W 151st St 10039 212-368-8731
Dawn Decosta, prin. Fax 368-8641

Mosaic Preparatory Academy 300/PK-6
141 E 111th St 10029 212-722-3109
Lisette Caesar, prin. Fax 722-3167

Mott Hall II 300/6-8
234 W 109th St 10025 212-678-2960
Marlon Lowe, prin. Fax 222-0560

Mott Hall S 300/6-8
71 Convent Ave 10027 212-281-5028
Judith De Los Santos, prin. Fax 491-3451

Muscota S 300/K-5
4862 Broadway 10034 212-544-0614
Camille Wallin, prin. Fax 544-2678

Neighborhood S - Public S 363 300/PK-5
121 E 3rd St 10009 212-387-0195
Dyanthe Spielberg, prin. Fax 387-0198

New Design MS 6-8
625 W 133rd St 10027 212-281-6339
Jeanine Benitez, prin. Fax 281-6674

New Explorations Science Tech/Math S 1,700/K-12
111 Columbia St 10002 212-677-5190
Mark Berkowitz, prin. Fax 260-8124

Newton MS for Science Math Tech 300/6-8
260 Pleasant Ave 10029 212-860-6006
Florin Purice, prin. Fax 987-4197

IS 218 200/6-8
4600 Broadway 10040 212-567-2322
June Barnett, prin. Fax 569-7421

IS 289 300/6-8
201 Warren St 10282 212-571-9268
Zeynep Ozkan, prin. Fax 587-6610

IS 528 200/6-8
180 Wadsworth Ave 10033 212-740-4900
Carlos Pichardo, prin. Fax 781-7302

JHS 52 500/6-8
650 Academy St 10034 212-567-9162
Lupe Leon, prin. Fax 942-4952

JHS 54 800/6-8
103 W 107th St 10025 212-678-2861
Dr. Elana Elstor, prin. Fax 316-0883

JHS 104 1,000/6-8
330 E 21st St 10010 212-674-4545
Rocco Macri, prin. Fax 477-2205

JHS 143 400/6-8
511 W 182nd St 10033 212-927-7739
Lakisha Luke, prin. Fax 781-5539

JHS 167 1,300/6-8
220 E 76th St 10021 212-535-8610
Jennifer Rehn, prin. Fax 472-9385

MS 131 400/6-8
100 Hester St 10002 212-219-1204
Phyllis Tam, prin. Fax 925-6386

MS 224 200/6-8
410 E 100th St 10029 212-860-6047
Luis Genao, prin. Fax 410-0678

MS 243 200/5-8
100 W 84th St 10024 212-799-1477
Elaine Schwartz, prin. Fax 579-9728

MS 245 The Computer S 400/6-8
100 W 77th St 10024 917-441-0873
Henry Zymeck, prin. Fax 678-5908

MS 247 200/6-8
32 W 92nd St 10025 212-799-2653
Kristina Jelinek, prin. Fax 579-2407

MS 250 200/6-8
735 W End Ave 10025 212-866-6313
Novella Bailey, dir. Fax 678-5295

MS 255 400/6-8
319 E 19th St 10003 212-614-8785
Rhonda Perry, prin. Fax 614-0095

MS 297, 75 Morton St 10003 6-8
Jacqueline Getz, prin. 212-678-8367

MS 319 600/6-8
21 Jumel Pl 10032 212-923-3827
Ysidro Abreu, prin. Fax 923-3676

MS 322 400/6-8
4600 Broadway 10040 212-304-0853
Erica Zigelman, prin. Fax 567-3016

MS 324 400/6-8
21 Jumel Pl 10032 212-923-4057
Carlos Guzman, prin. Fax 923-4626

MS 328 300/6-8
401 W 164th St 10032 917-521-2508
Olga Quiles, prin. Fax 521-7797

NYC Lab MS for Collaborative Studies 600/6-8
333 W 17th St 10011 212-691-6119
Megan Adams, prin. Fax 691-6219

Peck Slip S K-5
1 Peck Slip 10038 212-345-5210
Maggie Siena, prin. Fax 964-3507

Professor Bosch S 200/K-5
12 Ellwood St 10040 212-569-0327
Dierdre Budd, prin. Fax 569-0389

Public S 1 500/PK-5
8 Henry St 10038 212-267-4133
Amy Hom, prin. Fax 267-4469

Public S 2 800/PK-5
122 Henry St 10002 212-964-0350
Silvana Ng, prin. Fax 608-4080

Public S 3 800/K-5
490 Hudson St 10014 212-691-1183
Lisa Siegman, prin. Fax 675-5306

Public S 4 700/PK-5
500 W 160th St 10032 212-928-0739
Adam Stevens, prin. Fax 928-2532

Public S 5 700/K-5
3703 10th Ave 10034 212-567-8109
Christopher Anest, prin. Fax 567-6526

Public S 6 800/K-5
45 E 81st St 10028 212-737-9774
Lauren Fontana, prin. Fax 772-8669

Public S 7 400/PK-8
160 E 120th St 10035 212-860-5827
David Graeber, prin. Fax 860-6070

Public S 8 600/K-5
465 W 167th St 10032 212-928-4364
Washington Hernandez, prin. Fax 928-4072

Public S 9 600/PK-5
100 W 84th St 10024 212-678-2812
Katherine Witzke, prin. Fax 873-4681

Public S 11 800/PK-5
320 W 21st St 10011 212-929-1743
Robert Bender, prin. Fax 989-7816

Public S 15 200/PK-5
333 E 4th St 10009 212-228-8730
Irene Sanchez, prin. Fax 477-0931

Public S 18 400/K-8
4124 9th Ave 10034 212-521-2220
Connie Majia, prin. Fax 304-1423

Public S 19 300/PK-5
185 1st Ave 10003 212-533-5340
Jacqueline Flanagan, prin. Fax 673-1477

Public S 20 600/PK-5
166 Essex St 10002 212-254-9577
Sarah Viagran, prin. Fax 254-3526

Public S 28 800/PK-5
475 W 155th St 10032 212-690-3014
Awilda Baez, prin. Fax 368-5978

Public S 30 300/PK-5
144 E 128th St 10035 212-876-1825
Teri Stinson, prin. Fax 876-4034

Public S 33 600/PK-5
281 9th Ave 10001 212-244-6426
Chingchien Wang, prin. Fax 629-6893

Public S 34 400/PK-8
730 E 12th St 10009 212-228-4433
Angeliki Loukatos, prin. Fax 353-1973

Public S 36 500/PK-5
123 Morningside Dr 10027 212-690-5807
Heather Baptist, prin. Fax 690-5811

Public S 38 300/PK-5
232 E 103rd St 10029 212-860-5882
Carlina Santos-Barton, prin. Fax 860-6093

Public S 40 600/PK-5
319 E 19th St 10003 212-475-5500
Susan Felder, prin. Fax 533-5388

Public S 41 800/PK-5
116 W 11th St 10011 212-675-2756
Kelly Shannon, prin. Fax 924-0910

Public S 42 800/PK-5
71 Hester St 10002 212-226-8410
May Lee, prin. Fax 431-7384

Public S 46 800/PK-8
2987 Frederick Douglass 10039 212-360-1519
Kerry Ann Hazell, prin. Fax 690-5913

Public S 48 600/PK-5
4360 Broadway 10033 917-521-3800
Tracy Walsh, prin. Fax 521-3805

Public S 50 300/K-8
433 E 100th St 10029 212-860-5976
Ellen Johnson, prin. Fax 860-6071

Public S 51, 525 W 44th St 10036 300/K-5
Ryan Bourke, prin. 212-315-7160

Public S 59 600/K-5
231 E 56th St 10022 212-888-7870
Adele Schroeter, prin. Fax 888-7872

Public S 64 300/PK-5
600 E 6th St 10009 212-673-6510
Marlon Hosang, prin. Fax 477-2369

Public S 75 600/K-5
735 W End Ave 10025 212-866-5400
Robert O'Brien, prin. Fax 866-5543

Public S 76 500/PK-8
220 W 121st St 10027 212-678-2865
Charles DeBerry, prin. Fax 678-2867

Public S 77 300/K-5
1700 3rd Ave 10128 212-427-2798
Sandra Miller, prin. Fax 423-0634

Public S 83 500/PK-5
219 E 109th St 10029 212-860-5847
Frances Castillo, prin. Fax 860-6073

Public S 84 500/PK-5
32 W 92nd St 10025 212-799-2534
Dr. Evelyn Lolis, prin. Fax 501-9071

Public S 87 900/PK-5
160 W 78th St 10024 212-678-2826
Monica Berry, prin. Fax 678-5886

Public S 89 500/PK-5
201 Warren St 10282 212-571-5659
Veronica Najjar, prin. Fax 571-0739

Public S 92 300/PK-5
222 W 134th St 10030 212-690-5915
Rosa Davila, prin. Fax 690-5920

Public S 96 500/PK-8
216 E 120th St 10035 212-860-5851
David Pretto, prin. Fax 860-6074

Public S 98 600/PK-5
512 W 212th St 10034 212-927-7870
Maritza Rodriguez, prin. Fax 569-1827

Public S 102 300/PK-5
315 E 113th St 10029 212-860-5834
Gaynell Taylor, prin. Fax 860-6076

Public S 108 700/PK-8
1615 Madison Ave 10029 212-860-5803
William Gladstone, prin. Fax 860-6095

Public S 110 400/PK-5
285 Delancey St 10002 212-674-2690
Karen Feuer, prin. Fax 475-5835

Public S 111 500/PK-8
440 W 53rd St 10019 212-582-7420
Edward Gilligan, prin. Fax 245-7236
Public S 112 400/PK-2
535 E 119th St 10035 212-860-5868
Eileen Reiter, prin. Fax 860-6077
Public S 115 600/PK-5
586 W 177th St 10033 212-927-9233
Boris Consuegra, prin. Fax 795-4051
Public S 116 700/K-5
210 E 33rd St 10016 212-685-4366
Jane Hsu, prin. Fax 696-1009
Public S 123 600/PK-8
301 W 140th St 10030 212-342-6200
Melitina Hernandez, prin. Fax 690-5930
Public S 124 900/PK-5
40 Division St 10002 212-966-7237
Alice Hom, prin. Fax 219-3069
Public S 125 200/PK-5
425 W 123rd St 10027 212-666-6400
Reginald Higgins, prin. Fax 749-1291
Public S 126 800/PK-8
80 Catherine St 10038 212-962-2188
Carlos Romero, prin. Fax 349-7342
Public S 128 600/PK-5
560 W 169th St 10032 212-927-0607
Cary Pantaleon, prin. Fax 781-8002
Public S 129 600/PK-8
425 W 130th St 10027 212-690-5932
Odelphia Pierre, prin. Fax 690-5934
Public S 130 1,000/PK-5
143 Baxter St 10013 212-226-8072
Renny Fong, prin. Fax 431-5524
Public S 132 600/K-5
185 Wadsworth Ave 10033 212-927-7857
Jessica Torres-Maheia, prin. Fax 568-8163
Public S 133 300/PK-5
2121 5th Ave 10037 212-690-5936
Patricia Balbuena, prin. Fax 690-5939
Public S 134 300/PK-5
293 E Broadway 10002 212-673-4470
Daniel Kim, prin. Fax 475-6142
Public S 140 400/PK-8
123 Ridge St 10002 212-677-4680
Melissa Rodriguez, prin. Fax 677-3907
Public S 142 400/PK-5
100 Attorney St 10002 212-598-3800
Daphna Gutman, prin. Fax 598-3810
Public S 145 400/PK-5
150 W 105th St 10025 212-678-2857
Dr. Natalie Russo, prin. Fax 222-4610
Public S 146 400/PK-5
421 E 106th St 10029 212-860-5877
Mona Silfen, prin. Fax 860-6078
Public S 149 300/PK-8
41 W 117th St 10026 646-672-9020
Claudia Aguirre, prin. Fax 672-9302
Public S 150 200/PK-5
334 Greenwich St 10013 212-732-4392
Jennifer Bonnet, prin. Fax 766-5895
Public S 152 700/PK-5
93 Nagle Ave 10040 212-567-5456
Julie Pietri, prin. Fax 942-6319
Public S 153 900/PK-5
1750 Amsterdam Ave 10031 212-927-8611
Karen Bailey, prin. Fax 234-4616
Public S 154 300/PK-5
250 W 127th St 10027 212-864-2400
Elizabeth Jarrett, prin. Fax 864-3933
Public S 155 400/PK-5
319 E 117th St 10035 212-860-5885
Avionne Cummings, prin. Fax 828-3587
Public S 158 700/PK-5
1458 York Ave, 212-744-6562
Dina Ercolano, prin. Fax 772-8424
Public S 161 900/K-8
499 W 133rd St 10027 212-690-5945
Pamela Haynes, prin. Fax 507-0524
Public S 163 600/PK-5
163 W 97th St 10025 212-678-2854
Donny Lopez, prin. Fax 678-2856
Public S 165 900/PK-8
234 W 109th St 10025 212-678-2873
Aracelis Castellano-Folk, prin. Fax 222-6700
Public S 166 600/K-5
132 W 89th St 10024 212-678-2829
Debra Mastriano, prin. Fax 579-4542
Public S 171 700/PK-8
19 E 103rd St 10029 212-860-5801
Dimitres Pantelides, prin. Fax 860-6079
Public S 173 700/PK-5
306 Fort Washington Ave 10033 212-927-7850
Rachael Garcia, prin. Fax 740-0905
Public S 175 400/PK-5
175 W 134th St 10030 212-283-0426
Kavita Pereira, prin. Fax 286-6319
Public S 180 600/PK-8
370 W 120th St 10027 212-678-2849
Jeneca Parker, prin. Fax 665-1572
Public S 183 600/K-5
419 E 66th St, 212-734-7719
Martin Woodard, prin. Fax 861-8314
Public S 184 700/PK-8
327 Cherry St 10002 212-602-9700
Iris Chiu, prin. Fax 602-9710
Public S 185 200/PK-3
20 W 112th St 10026 212-534-7490
Jane Murphy, prin. Fax 831-8613
Public S 187 800/K-8
349 Cabrini Blvd 10040 212-927-8218
Cynthia Chory, prin. Fax 795-9119
Public S 188 500/PK-8
442 E Houston St 10002 212-677-5710
Suany Ramos, prin. Fax 228-3007
Public S 189 1,100/PK-5
2580 Amsterdam Ave 10040 212-927-8303
Rosalina Perez, prin. Fax 928-7733

Public S 191 500/PK-8
210 W 61st St 10023 212-757-4343
Lauren Keville, prin. Fax 757-1022
Public S 192 300/PK-5
500 W 138th St 10031 212-281-8395
Hilduara Abreu, prin. Fax 862-7129
Public S 194 200/PK-5
244 W 144th St 10030 212-690-5954
Mieasia Harris, prin. Fax 862-5743
Public S 197 300/PK-5
2230 5th Ave 10037 212-690-5960
Natasha Spann, prin. Fax 690-5959
Public S 198 500/PK-5
1700 3rd Ave 10128 212-289-3702
Katharine MacManus, prin. Fax 410-1731
Public S 199 800/K-5
270 W 70th St 10023 212-799-1033
Louise Xerri, prin. Fax 799-1179
Public S 200 500/PK-5
2589 7th Ave 10039 212-491-6636
Renee Belton, prin. Fax 491-6925
Public S 206 400/3-8
508 E 120th St 10035 212-860-5809
Camille Forbes, prin. Fax 860-6080
Public S 208 200/3-5
21 W 111th St 10026 212-534-9580
Susan Green, prin. Fax 534-8227
Public S 210 21st Century Academy 500/PK-8
501 W 152nd St 10031 212-283-0012
Evelyn Linares, prin. Fax 283-0017
Public S 212 300/K-5
328 W 48th St 10036 212-247-0208
Kathleen Loua, prin. Fax 757-4933
Public S 217 500/PK-8
645 Main St 10044 212-980-0294
Mandana Beckman, prin. Fax 980-1192
Public S 234 800/K-5
292 Greenwich St 10007 212-233-6034
Lisa Ripperger, prin. Fax 374-1719
Public S 242 200/PK-5
134 W 122nd St 10027 212-678-2908
Denise Gomez, prin. Fax 678-2927
Public S 290 700/K-5
311 E 82nd St 10028 212-734-7127
Doreen Esposito, prin. Fax 772-8879
Public S 325 300/K-5
500 W 138th St 10031 212-234-1335
Gary Cruz, prin. Fax 234-2022
Public S 333 800/K-8
154 W 93rd St 10025 212-222-1450
Claire Lowenstein, prin. Fax 222-1828
Public S 452 200/K-2
100 W 77th St 10024 212-496-1050
David Parker, prin. Fax 505-1636
Public S 527, 323 E 91st St 10128 K-5
Daniel McCormick, prin. 212-828-2710
Renaissance School of the Arts 200/6-8
319 E 117th St 10035 212-534-6072
Brian Bradley, prin. Fax 534-7418
River S 100/PK-5
425 E 35th St 10016 212-251-6640
Jessica Orleans, prin. Fax 251-6645
School for Global Leaders 200/6-8
145 Stanton St 10002 212-260-5375
Keri Ricks, prin. Fax 260-7386
Sixth Avenue ES, 590 6th Ave 10011 200/PK-5
Patricia Carney, prin. 718-935-3440
Special Music School of America 100/K-8
129 W 67th St 10023 212-501-3318
Katherine Banucci-Smith, prin. Fax 501-3339
Spruce Street ES 50/PK-8
12 Spruce St 10038 212-266-4800
Nancy Harris, prin. Fax 266-4805
Star Academy 200/PK-5
121 E 3rd St 10009 212-674-3180
Darlene Cameron, prin. Fax 420-9018
STEM Institute of Manhanttan 100/K-5
240 W 113th St 10026 212-678-2898
Marcia Hendricks, prin. Fax 678-2975
TAG Young Scholars 500/K-8
240 E 109th St 10029 212-860-6003
Janette Cesar, prin. Fax 831-1842
Teachers College Community S PK-5
168 Morningside Ave 10027 212-316-8080
Michelle Verdiner, prin. Fax 316-8085
Technology Arts & Sciences Studio 200/6-8
185 1st Ave 10003 212-982-1836
George Morgan, prin. Fax 982-0528
Tompkins Square MS 400/6-8
600 E 6th St 10009 212-995-1430
Sonhando Estwick, prin. Fax 979-1341
University Nieghborhood MS 100/6-8
220 Henry St 10002 212-267-5701
Laura Peynado Castro, prin. Fax 349-8224
Urban Assembly Acad for Future Leaders 200/6-8
509 W 129th St 10027 212-543-4960
Joseph Gates, prin. Fax 694-4124
Washington Heights Academy 400/PK-5
202 Sherman Ave 10034 212-304-3320
Renzo Martinez, prin. Fax 304-3322
West End Secondary S 200/6-7
227 W 61st St 10023 212-245-1506
Jessica Jenkins, prin. Fax 245-1291
West Prep Academy 200/6-8
150 W 105th St 10025 212-280-8502
Carland Washington, prin. Fax 362-2794
Yorkville Community S 400/K-3
421 E 88th St 10128 212-722-5240
Samantha Kaplan, prin. Fax 427-8069
Yorkville East MS 6-8
1458 York Ave, 917-432-5413
Christina Riggio, prin. Fax 432-5418

Other Schools – See Arverne, Astoria, Bayside, Bayside Hills, Bellerose, Broad Channel, Bronx, Brooklyn, Cambria Heights, College Point, Corona, Douglaston, East Elmhurst, Elmhurst, Far Rockaway, Floral Park, Flushing, Forest Hills, Glendale, Hollis, Howard Beach, Jackson Heights, Jamaica, Kew Gardens, Laurelton, Little Neck, Long Island City, Maspeth, Middle Village, Oakland Gardens, Ozone Park, Queens Village, Rego Park, Richmond Hill, Ridgewood, Rockaway Beach, Rockaway Park, Rosedale, Saint Albans, South Ozone Park, Springfield Gardens, Staten Island, Whitestone, Wood Haven, Woodside

---

Academy of St. Joseph 100/PK-5
111 Washington Pl 10014 212-243-5420
Angela Coombs, hdmstr. Fax 414-4526
Allen-Stevenson S 400/K-9
132 E 78th St, 212-288-6710
David Trower, hdmstr. Fax 288-6802
Ascension S 300/PK-8
220 W 108th St 10025 212-222-5161
Donna Gabella, prin. Fax 280-4690
Avenues: The World S 700/PK-12
259 10th Ave 10001 212-524-9000
Evan Glazer, head sch Fax 664-0701
Bank Street S for Children 400/PK-8
610 W 112th St 10025 212-875-4420
Jed Lippard Ed.D., head sch Fax 875-4454
Beth Jacob S 200/PK-8
142 Broome St 10002 212-473-4500
Rochel Kahn, prin. Fax 460-5317
Birch Wathen Lenox S 600/K-12
210 E 77th St, 212-861-0404
Frank J. Carnabuci, hdmstr. Fax 879-3388
Blessed Sacrament S 300/PK-8
147 W 70th St 10023 212-724-7561
Caroline Sliney, prin. Fax 724-0735
Blue S 100/PK-8
241 Water St 10038 212-228-6341
Gina Farrar Ph.D., head sch Fax 260-3824
Brearley S 700/K-12
610 E 83rd St 10028 212-744-8582
Jane Fried, head sch Fax 472-8020
Brick Church S 200/PK-K
62 E 92nd St 10128 212-289-5683
Dr. Lydia Spinelli Ed.D., dir. Fax 289-5372
Browning S 400/K-12
52 E 62nd St, 212-838-6280
John Botti, head sch Fax 355-5602
Buckley S, 113 E 73rd St 10021 400/K-9
Gregory O'Melia, hdmstr. 212-535-8787
Caedmon S 300/PK-5
416 E 80th St, 212-879-2296
Matthew Stuart, head sch Fax 879-0627
Calhoun Lower S 200/PK-2
160 W 74th St 10023 212-497-6550
Steven Solnick, hdmstr. Fax 497-6540
Calhoun S 500/3-12
433 W End Ave 10024 212-497-6500
Steven Solnick, admin. Fax 497-6530
Cathedral S PK-8
319 E 74th St 10021 212-249-2840
Kristine Cecere, head sch Fax 249-2847
Cathedral S of St. John Devine 300/K-8
1047 Amsterdam Ave 10025 212-316-7500
Marsha Nelson, head sch Fax 316-7558
Chapin S 700/K-12
100 E End Ave 10028 212-744-2335
Patricia Hayot Ph.D., head sch Fax 535-8138
City & Country S 300/PK-8
146 W 13th St 10011 212-242-7802
Scott Moran, prin. Fax 242-7996
Collegiate S 600/K-12
260 W 78th St 10024 212-812-8500
Dr. Lee Levison, hdmstr. Fax 812-8524
Columbia Grammar & Preparatory S 1,300/PK-12
5 W 93rd St 10025 212-749-6200
Dr. William Donohue, head sch Fax 865-4278
Connelly Center for Education 100/4-8
220 E 4th St 10009 212-982-2287
Shalonda Gutierrez, prin. Fax 982-0547
Convent of the Sacred Heart S 700/PK-12
1 E 91st St 10128 212-722-4745
Dr. Joseph Ciancaglini, head sch Fax 996-1784
Corlears S 200/PK-5
324 W 15th St 10011 212-741-2800
David Egolf, head sch Fax 807-1550
Corpus Christi S 200/PK-8
535 W 121st St 10027 212-662-9344
Matthew Bull, prin. Fax 662-2725
Dalton S 1,300/K-12
108 E 89th St 10128 212-423-5200
Ellen Stein, head sch Fax 423-5259
De La Salle Academy 100/6-8
332 W 43rd St 10036 212-316-5840
Br. Brian Carty, pres. Fax 316-5998
Dwight S 800/PK-12
291 Central Park W 10024 212-724-6360
Dianne Drew, head sch Fax 874-4232
East Harlem S 200/4-8
309 E 103rd St 10029 212-876-8775
Donald Albert, supt. Fax 876-8776
Ecole Internationale de New York 100/PK-8
111 E 22nd St 10010 646-410-2238
Yves Rivaud, head sch
Epiphany S 500/PK-8
234 E 22nd St 10010 212-473-4128
Kate McHugh, prin. Fax 473-4392
Ethical Culture Fieldston S 400/PK-5
33 Central Park W 10023 212-712-6220
Jessica Bagby, head sch Fax 712-8444
Family S 200/PK-6
323 E 47th St 10017 212-688-5950
Lesley Haberman, hdmstr. Fax 980-2475
Friends Seminary 700/K-12
222 E 16th St 10003 212-979-5030
Robert Lauder, prin. Fax 979-5034

Gateway S 100/K-8
211 W 61st St 10023 212-777-5966
Carolyn Salzman, head sch Fax 777-5794
Geneva S of Manhattan 200/PK-8
593 Park Ave, 212-754-9988
Rim Hinckley, head sch Fax 754-9987
Good Shepherd S 200/PK-8
620 Isham St 10034 212-567-5800
Geraldine Lavery, prin. Fax 567-5839
Grace Church S 400/PK-8
86 4th Ave 10003 212-475-5609
George Davison, head sch Fax 475-5015
Guardian Angel S 200/PK-8
193 10th Ave 10011 212-989-8280
Christie Acosta-Perez, prin. Fax 352-1467
Harlem Academy 100/1-8
1330 5th Ave 10026 212-348-2600
Vincent Dotoli, head sch Fax 348-3500
Heschel Lower S 800/PK-5
30 W End Ave 10023 212-784-1234
Ariela Dubler, head sch Fax 595-7252
Heschel MS 100/6-8
30 W End Ave 10023 212-784-1234
Ariela Dubler, head sch Fax 595-7252
Hewitt S 500/K-12
45 E 75th St 10021 212-288-1919
Dr. Tara Kinsey, head sch Fax 472-7531
Hunter College Campus S 300/K-12
71 E 94th St 10128 646-963-6341
Lisa Siegmann, dir. Fax 722-6693
IDEAL S and Academy 100/PK-12
314 W 91st St 10024 212-769-1699
Janet Wolfe, head sch Fax 769-1698
Immaculate Conception S 200/PK-8
419 E 13th St 10009 212-475-2590
Mary Barry, prin. Fax 777-2818
Incarnation S 500/K-8
570 W 175th St 10033 212-795-1030
Nick Green, prin. Fax 795-1564
La Scuola d'Italia Guglielmo Marconi 200/PK-12
12 E 96th St 10128 212-369-3290
Leman Manhattan Preparatory S 500/PK-12
41 Broad St 10004 212-232-0266
Maria Castelluccio, head sch Fax 232-0284
Lookstein MS 200/5-8
114 E 85th St 10028 212-774-8040
Jennifer Bernstein, head sch Fax 774-8069
LREI Little Red S House & Irwin HS 400/PK-12
272 6th Ave 10014 212-477-5316
Philip Kassen, dir. Fax 677-9159
Lycee Francais De New York 1,300/PK-12
505 E 75th St 10021 212-369-1400
Sean Lynch, head sch Fax 439-4200
Lyceum Kennedy French American S 200/PK-12
225 E 43rd St 10017 212-681-1877
Bolek Poniatowski, head sch Fax 681-1299
Manhattan Christian Academy 300/PK-8
401 W 205th St 10034 212-567-5521
Bianca Mercedes, prin. Fax 567-2815
Manhattan Country S 200/PK-8
150 W 85th St 10024 212-348-0952
Michele Sola, dir. Fax 348-1621
Manhattan Day S 500/PK-8
310 W 75th St 10023 212-376-6800
Rabbi Raizi Chechik, prin. Fax 376-6389
Marymount S 600/PK-12
1026 5th Ave 10028 212-744-4486
Concepcion Alvar, hdmstr. Fax 744-0163
Mesivta Tifereth Jerusalem S 200/K-12
145 E Broadway 10002 212-964-2830
Rabbi Ginzberg, prin. Fax 349-5213
Metropolitan Montessori S 200/PK-6
325 W 85th St 10024 212-579-5525
Brenda Mizel, head sch Fax 579-5526
Mt. Carmel-Holy Rosary S 300/PK-8
371 Pleasant Ave 10035 212-876-7555
Molly Smith, prin. Fax 876-0152
Nightingale-Bamford S 600/K-12
20 E 92nd St 10128 212-289-5020
Paul Burke, head sch Fax 876-1045
Our Lady of Lourdes S 300/PK-8
468 W 143rd St 10031 212-926-5820
Cathy Hufnagel, prin. Fax 491-6034
Our Lady of Pompeii S 200/PK-8
240 Bleecker St 10014 212-242-4147
Sr. Diane Mastroianni, prin. Fax 691-2361
Our Lady Queen of Angels S 300/PK-8
232 E 113th St 10029 212-722-9277
Stephanie Becker, prin. Fax 987-8837
Our Lady Queen of Martyrs S 300/PK-8
71 Arden St 10040 212-567-3190
Andrew Woods, prin. Fax 304-8587
Pine Street S 100/PK-5
25 Pine St 10005 212-913-9704
Eileen Baker, head sch Fax 591-0254
Portfolio S, 27 N Moore St 10013 K-5
Shira Leibowitz Ph.D., dir. 212-226-8252
Quad Preparatory S, 25 Pine St 10005 K-12
Kimberly Busi M.D., dir. 646-649-3913
Ramaz Lower S 400/PK-4
125 E 85th St 10028 212-774-8010
Rabbi Tavi Koslowe, head sch Fax 774-8039
Resurrection Episcopal Day S 100/PK-K
119 E 74th St 10021 212-535-9666
Rodeph Sholom S 700/PK-8
10 W 84th St 10024 646-438-8500
Danny Karpf, head sch Fax 874-0117
Sacred Heart of Jesus S 200/PK-8
456 W 52nd St 10019 212-246-4784
Kelly Burke, prin. Fax 707-8382
St. Albans S, 317 E 50th St 10022 100/PK-8
M.P. Harrington, hdmstr. 212-755-0997
St. Ann S 300/PK-8
314 E 110th St 10029 212-722-1295
Hope Mueller, prin. Fax 722-8267

St. Bernard's S 400/K-9
4 E 98th St 10029 212-289-2878
Stuart Johnson, hdmstr. Fax 410-6628
St. Brigid S 100/PK-8
185 E 7th St 10009 212-677-5210
Molly Carone, prin. Fax 260-2262
St. Charles Borromeo S 200/K-8
214 W 142nd St 10030 212-368-6666
Dan Faas, prin. Fax 281-1323
St. David's S 400/PK-8
12 E 89th St 10128 212-369-0058
Dr. P. David O'Halloran, hdmstr. Fax 722-6127
St. Elizabeth S 300/PK-8
612 W 187th St 10033 212-568-7291
Dr. ANNA RAMIREZ-ADAM, prin. Fax 928-2515
St. Hilda's & St. Hugh's S 400/PK-8
619 W 114th St 10025 212-932-1980
Virginia Connor, head sch Fax 749-7174
St. Ignatius Loyola S 500/K-8
48 E 84th St 10028 212-861-3820
Mary Larkin, prin. Fax 879-8248
St. Joseph of Yorkville S 300/PK-8
420 E 87th St 10128 212-289-3057
Theresa Bernero, prin. Fax 289-7239
St. Luke's S 200/PK-8
487 Hudson St 10014 212-924-5960
Bart Baldwin, head sch Fax 924-1352
St. Mark the Evangelist S 200/PK-8
55 W 138th St 10037 212-283-4848
Dominic Fanelli, prin. Fax 926-0419
St. Paul S 300/K-8
114 E 118th St 10035 212-534-0619
Dr. Joseph Muscente, prin. Fax 534-3990
St. Rose of Lima S 300/PK-8
517 W 164th St 10032 212-927-1619
Joseph De Bona, prin. Fax 927-0648
St. Stephen of Hungary S 200/PK-8
408 E 82nd St 10028 212-288-1989
Caroline Walker, head sch Fax 517-5877
St. Thomas Choir S 50/3-8
202 W 58th St 10019 212-247-3311
Fr. Charles Wallace, hdmstr. Fax 247-3393
Schneier Park East Day S 300/PK-8
164 E 68th St, 212-737-7330
Barbara Etra, prin. Fax 639-1568
School At Columbia University 500/K-8
556 W 110th St 10025 212-851-4215
Amani Reed, head sch Fax 851-4270
Solomon Schechter S of Manhattan 100/K-8
805 Columbus Ave 10025 212-427-9500
Spence S, 22 E 91st St 10128 700/K-12
Bodie Brizendine, head sch 212-289-5940
Speyer Legacy S 100/K-8
925 9th Ave 10019 212-581-4000
Dr. Barbara Tischler, head sch Fax 603-2560
Steiner Lower S 200/PK-6
15 E 79th St, 212-535-2130
Dr. William Macatee Ed.D., admin. Fax 744-4497
Studio S, 117 W 95th St 10025 100/PK-8
Christine Bochar, admin. 212-678-2416
Town S 100/PK-8
540 E 76th St 10021 212-288-4383
Anthony Featherston, head sch Fax 988-5846
Transfiguration ECC 200/PK-PK
10 Confucius Plz 10002 212-431-8769
Dr. Patrick Taharally, prin. Fax 431-8917
Transfiguration ES 200/4-8
37 Saint James Pl 10038 212-267-9289
Dr. Patrick Taharally, prin. Fax 227-0065
Transfiguration S 200/K-3
29 Mott St 10013 212-962-5265
Dr. Patrick Taharally, prin. Fax 964-8965
Trevor Day S 400/PK-5
1 W 88th St 10024 212-426-3300
Scott Reisinger, head sch Fax 873-8520
Trinity S 1,000/K-12
139 W 91st St 10024 212-873-1650
John Allman, head sch Fax 799-3417
United Nations International S 1,500/PK-12
2450 FDR Dr 10010 212-684-7400
Jane Camblin, dir. Fax 684-1382
Village Community S 300/K-8
272 W 10th St 10014 212-691-5146
Eve Kleger, head sch Fax 691-9767
Yeshiva Ketana of Manhattan 200/PK-8
346 W 89th St 10024 212-769-1790
Ethel Salomon, prin. Fax 874-5706
Yeshiva Rabbi S.R. Hirsch 400/PK-12
91 Bennett Ave 10033 212-568-6200
Diane Lanzkron, prin. Fax 928-4422

New York Mills, Oneida, Pop. 3,298
New York Mills UFD 600/K-12
1 Marauder Blvd 13417 315-768-8127
Dr. Joanne Shelmidine, supt. Fax 768-3521
www.newyorkmills.org
New York Mills ES 300/K-6
1 Marauder Blvd 13417 315-768-8129
Brent Dodge, prin. Fax 768-3396

Niagara Falls, Niagara, Pop. 48,343
Niagara Falls CSD 6,900/PK-12
630 66th St 14304 716-286-4253
Mark Laurrie, supt. Fax 286-4283
www.nfschools.net
Abate ES 600/PK-6
1625 Lockport St 14305 716-278-7960
Cynthia Jones, prin. Fax 278-7979
Cataract ES 500/PK-6
6431 Girard Ave 14304 716-278-9120
Jeffrey Showers, prin. Fax 278-9122
Gaskill Preparatory S 500/7-8
910 Hyde Park Blvd 14301 716-278-5820
Sheila Smith, prin. Fax 278-5829
Hyde Park ES 500/PK-6
1620 Hyde Park Blvd 14305 716-278-7980
Mary Kerins, prin. Fax 278-7988

Kalfas Magnet ES 500/PK-6
1880 Beech Ave 14305 716-278-9180
Italo Baldassarre, prin. Fax 278-9173
La Salle Preparatory S 500/7-8
7436 Buffalo Ave 14304 716-278-5880
James Spanbauer, prin. Fax 278-5899
Mann ES 500/PK-6
1330 95th St 14304 716-278-7940
Tina Smeal, prin. Fax 278-7946
Maple Avenue ES 400/PK-6
952 Maple Ave 14305 716-278-9140
Maria Chille-Zafuto, prin. Fax 278-9156
Niagara Street ES 600/PK-6
2513 Niagara St 14303 716-278-5860
Rocco Merino, prin. Fax 278-5876
Seventy Ninth Street ES 500/PK-6
551 79th St 14304 716-278-7900
Diane Coty, prin. Fax 278-7901

Niagara-Wheatfield Central SD 4,100/PK-12
6700 Schultz St 14304 716-215-3003
Daniel Ljiljanich, supt. Fax 215-3039
www.nwcsd.k12.ny.us
Colonial Village ES 400/K-5
1456 Saunders Settlement Rd 14305 716-215-3270
Marissa Vuich, prin. Fax 215-3290
Other Schools – See Lewiston, North Tonawanda, Sanborn

Catholic Academy of Niagara Falls 100/PK-6
1055 N Military Rd 14304 716-283-1455
Jeannine Fortunate, prin. Fax 283-1355
Holy Ghost Lutheran S 100/PK-8
6630 Luther St 14304 716-731-3030
Kevin Gundell, prin. Fax 731-9449

North Babylon, Suffolk, Pop. 17,252
North Babylon UFD 4,700/K-12
5 Jardine Pl 11703 631-620-7000
Glen Eschbach, supt. Fax 321-3295
www.northbabylonschools.net
Belmont ES 400/K-5
108 Barnum St, 631-620-7500
Valerie Jackson, prin. Fax 376-0278
Deluca ES 400/K-5
223 Phelps Ln 11703 631-620-7700
Vincent Fantauzzi, prin. Fax 321-3331
Moses MS 1,100/6-8
250 Phelps Ln 11703 631-620-7300
Elizabeth Walsh-Bulger, prin. Fax 587-2619
Parliament Place ES 400/K-5
80 Parliament Pl 11703 631-620-7900
Drew Olson, prin. Fax 254-2318
Vedder ES 400/K-5
794 Deer Park Ave 11703 631-620-7600
Kerry Larke, prin. Fax 587-2480
Woods Road ES 400/K-5
110 Woods Rd 11703 631-620-7800
Celeste Archer, prin. Fax 243-5492

North Baldwin, See Baldwin
Uniondale UFD
Supt. — See Uniondale
Grand Avenue ES 300/K-5
711 School Dr 11510 516-918-2100
Juanita Bryant-Bell, prin. Fax 483-4345

North Bellmore, Nassau, Pop. 19,654
North Bellmore UFD 2,100/K-6
2616 Martin Ave 11710 516-992-3000
Marie Testa, supt. Fax 992-3020
www.northbellmoreschools.org
Dinkelmeyer ES 400/K-6
2100 Waltoffer Ave 11710 516-992-3000
Faith Skelos, prin. Fax 992-3054
Martin Avenue ES 300/K-6
2616 Martin Ave 11710 516-992-3000
Leyna Malone, prin. Fax 992-3164
Newbridge Road ES 400/K-6
1601 Newbridge Rd 11710 516-992-3000
Denise Fisher, prin. Fax 992-3214
Saw Mill Road ES 700/K-6
2801 Sawmill Rd 11710 516-992-3000
Jeffrey Rosof, prin. Fax 992-3324
Other Schools – See North Merrick

North Collins, Erie, Pop. 1,203
North Collins Central SD 600/PK-12
2045 School St 14111 716-337-0101
Scott Taylor, supt. Fax 337-3457
www.northcollins.com
North Collins ES 300/PK-6
10469 Bantle Rd 14111 716-337-0166
John Cataldo, prin. Fax 337-0598

North Creek, Warren, Pop. 613
Johnsburg Central SD 300/K-12
165 Main St 12853 518-251-2814
Michael Markwica, supt. Fax 251-2562
www.johnsburgcsd.org
Johnsburg Central S 300/K-12
165 Main St 12853 518-251-3504
Heather Flanagan, prin. Fax 251-2562

North Massapequa, Nassau, Pop. 17,762
Farmingdale UFD
Supt. — See Farmingdale
Albany Avenue ES 600/K-5
101 N Albany Ave 11758 516-434-5510
Joseph Valentine, prin.

Plainedge UFD 3,200/K-12
241 Wyngate Dr 11758 516-992-7455
Dr. Edward Salina, supt. Fax 992-7446
www.plainedgeschools.org
Eastplain ES 300/K-5
301 N Delaware Ave 11758 516-992-7600
Emily O'Brien, prin. Fax 992-7605
Other Schools – See Bethpage, Massapequa

North Merrick, Nassau, Pop. 12,143
Bellmore-Merrick Central HSD 5,600/7-12
1260 Meadowbrook Rd 11566 516-992-1000
John DeTommaso, supt. Fax 623-0151
www.bellmore-merrick.k12.ny.us
Other Schools – See Bellmore, Merrick

North Bellmore UFD
Supt. — See North Bellmore
Park Avenue ES 300/K-6
1599 Park Ave 11566 516-992-3000
Eileen Speidel, prin. Fax 992-3274

North Merrick UFD 1,200/K-6
1057 Merrick Ave 11566 516-292-3694
Dr. Cynthia Seniuk, supt. Fax 292-3097
nmerrickschools.org
Camp Avenue ES 500/K-6
1712 Merrick Ave 11566 516-379-3732
Ronald Reinken, prin. Fax 292-3097
Fayette ES 300/K-6
1057 Merrick Ave 11566 516-489-3090
Howard Merims, prin. Fax 292-3097
Old Mill Road ES 500/K-6
1775 Old Mill Rd 11566 516-379-0945
Laura Leudesdorff, prin. Fax 379-1695

Northport, Suffolk, Pop. 7,346
Kings Park Central SD
Supt. — See Kings Park
Ft. Salonga ES 400/K-3
39 Sunken Meadow Rd 11768 631-269-3364
Stephanie Montecalvo, prin. Fax 269-2190

Northport-East Northport UFD 5,900/K-12
PO Box 210 11768 631-262-6604
Robert L. Banzer, supt. Fax 262-6607
web.northport.k12.ny.us/
Northport MS 800/6-8
11 Middleville Rd 11768 631-262-6750
Timothy Hoss, prin. Fax 262-6793
Norwood Avenue ES 400/K-5
25 Norwood Rd 11768 631-262-6830
Michael Genovese, prin. Fax 262-6835
Ocean Avenue ES 400/K-5
100 Ocean Ave 11768 631-262-6840
Sabina Larkin, prin. Fax 262-6845
Other Schools – See East Northport

North Rose, Wayne, Pop. 616
North Rose-Wolcott Central SD
Supt. — See Wolcott
North Rose-Wolcott ES 500/PK-4
10456 Salter Rd 14516 315-594-3141
Melissa Pietricola, prin. Fax 587-2432

North Salem, Westchester
North Salem Central SD 1,200/K-12
230 June Rd 10560 914-669-5414
Dr. Kenneth Freeston, supt. Fax 669-8753
www.northsalemschools.org
Pequenakonck ES 500/K-5
173 June Rd 10560 914-669-5317
Mary Johnson, prin. Fax 669-4326

North Syracuse, Onondaga, Pop. 6,697
North Syracuse Central SD 9,000/PK-12
5355 W Taft Rd 13212 315-218-2100
Annette Speach, supt. Fax 218-2185
www.nscsd.org
Allen Road ES 400/K-4
803 Allen Rd 13212 315-218-2300
David Lunden, prin. Fax 218-2385
Main Street Preschool 100/PK-PK
205 S Main St 13212 315-218-2200
Dawn Hussein, prin. Fax 218-2285
Saile Bear Road ES 600/K-4
5590 Bear Rd 13212 315-218-2400
John Cole, prin. Fax 218-2485
Smith Road ES 600/K-4
5959 Smith Rd 13212 315-218-2800
Gregory Stone, prin. Fax 218-2885
Other Schools – See Cicero, Syracuse

St. Rose of Lima S 400/PK-6
411 S Main St 13212 315-458-6036
Mary Crysler, prin. Fax 458-6038

North Tonawanda, Niagara, Pop. 31,199
Niagara-Wheatfield Central SD
Supt. — See Niagara Falls
Errick Road ES 600/K-5
6839 Errick Rd 14120 716-215-3240
Nora O'Bryan, prin. Fax 215-3260

North Tonawanda CSD 3,600/K-12
176 Walck Rd 14120 716-807-3655
Gregory Woytila, supt. Fax 807-3525
www.ntschools.org
Drake ES 300/K-6
380 Drake Dr 14120 716-807-3725
Katie Smith, prin. Fax 807-3726
Meadow ES 600/K-6
455 Meadow Dr 14120 716-807-3825
Janet Matyevich, prin. Fax 807-3835
North Tonawanda MS 600/7-8
1500 Vanderbilt Ave 14120 716-807-3700
Gregory Burgess, prin. Fax 807-3701
Ohio ES 500/K-6
625 Ohio Ave 14120 716-807-3800
Michael Hiller, prin. Fax 807-3801
Spruce ES 400/K-6
195 Spruce St 14120 716-807-3850
Patricia Adler, prin. Fax 807-3858

Christian Academy of Western New York 100/PK-12
789 Gilmore Ave 14120 716-433-1652
Patricia Poeller, admin.

St. John Lutheran S 200/PK-8
6950 Ward Rd 14120 716-693-9677
Katie Gundell, prin. Fax 693-2686

Northville, Fulton, Pop. 1,084
Northville Central SD 500/PK-12
PO Box 608 12134 518-863-7000
Dr. Leslie Ford, supt. Fax 863-7011
northvillecsd.org
Northville ES 200/PK-5
PO Box 608 12134 518-863-7000
Tammy Reidell, prin. Fax 863-7011

North White Plains, See White Plains
Valhalla UFD
Supt. — See Valhalla
Virginia Road ES 300/K-2
86 Virginia Rd 10603 914-683-5035
Haidee Anaya, prin. Fax 683-5291

Norwich, Chenango, Pop. 7,042
Norwich CSD 1,900/PK-12
89 Midland Dr 13815 607-334-1600
Gerard O'Sullivan, supt. Fax 336-8652
www.norwichcsd.org
Browne IS 400/3-5
89 Midland Dr 13815 607-334-1600
Jennifer Post, prin. Fax 334-6201
Gibson PS 500/PK-2
89 Midland Dr 13815 607-334-1600
Kisten Giglio, prin. Fax 334-4193
Norwich MS 400/6-8
89 Midland Dr 13815 607-334-1600
Scott Ryan, prin. Fax 334-6210

Holy Family S 100/PK-6
17 Prospect St 13815 607-337-2207
Lydia Brenner, admin. Fax 337-2210

Norwood, Saint Lawrence, Pop. 1,621
Norwood-Norfolk Central SD 1,000/PK-12
7852 State Highway 56 13668 315-353-6631
James Cruikshank, supt. Fax 353-2467
www.nncsk12.org/
Norwood-Norfolk ES 500/PK-4
7852 State Highway 56 13668 315-353-6674
Rebecca Kingsley, prin. Fax 353-2408
Norwood-Norfolk MS 300/5-8
7852 State Highway 56 13668 315-353-6631
Jon Sovay, prin.

Nunda, Livingston, Pop. 1,354
Keshequa Central SD 600/PK-12
PO Box 517 14517 585-468-2900
Thomas Kopp, supt. Fax 468-3814
www.keshequa.org
Keshequa IS 4-6
PO Box 517 14517 585-468-2900
Ami Hunt, prin. Fax 468-3814
Keshequa MS 100/7-8
PO Box 517 14517 585-468-2900
Peter Reynolds, prin. Fax 468-5493
Other Schools – See Dalton

Nyack, Rockland, Pop. 6,636
Nyack UFD 2,900/K-12
13A Dickinson Ave 10960 845-353-7000
James Montesano Ed.D., supt. Fax 353-7019
www.nyackschools.org
Nyack MS 700/6-8
98 S Highland Ave 10960 845-353-7200
David Johnson, prin. Fax 353-0506
Other Schools – See Upper Nyack, Valley Cottage

Oakdale, Suffolk, Pop. 7,925
Connetquot Central SD
Supt. — See Bohemia
Idle Hour ES 300/K-5
334 Idle Hour Blvd 11769 631-244-2306
Sandra Rubin, prin. Fax 244-2305
Oakdale-Bohemia Road MS 800/6-8
60 Oakdale Bohemia Rd 11769 631-244-2268
Susanne Bailey, prin. Fax 563-6167

Oakfield, Genesee, Pop. 1,789
Oakfield-Alabama Central SD 900/PK-12
7001 Lewiston Rd 14125 585-948-5211
Mark Alexander, supt. Fax 948-9362
www.oahornets.org
Oakfield-Alabama ES 500/PK-6
7001 Lewiston Rd 14125 585-948-5211
Kelly Santora, prin. Fax 948-8913

Oakland Gardens, See New York
NYC Department of Education
Supt. — See New York
JHS 74 1,000/6-8
6115 Oceania St 11364 718-631-6800
Anthony Armstrong, prin. Fax 631-6899
Public S 46 600/K-5
6445 218th St 11364 718-423-8395
Stamo Karalazarides, prin. Fax 423-8472
Public S 162 700/K-5
20102 53rd Ave 11364 718-423-8621
Pamela Lee, prin. Fax 423-8647
Public S 188 600/PK-5
21812 Hartland Ave 11364 718-464-5768
Janet Caraisco, prin. Fax 464-5771
Public S 203 900/PK-5
5311 Springfield Blvd 11364 718-423-8652
Deborah Florio, prin. Fax 423-8713
Public S 205 300/PK-5
7525 Bell Blvd 11364 718-464-5773
Karen Piazza, prin. Fax 464-5875
Public S 213 400/PK-5
23102 67th Ave 11364 718-423-8747
Megan McCauley, prin. Fax 423-8805

Oceanside, Nassau, Pop. 31,810
Oceanside UFD 5,600/PK-12
145 Merle Ave 11572 516-678-1215
Dr. Phyllis Harrington, supt. Fax 678-7503
www.oceansideschools.org
Boardman ES 300/1-6
170 Beatrice Ave 11572 516-678-8510
Joslyn McPherson, prin. Fax 678-7336
Fulton Ave ES 400/1-6
3252 Fulton Ave 11572 516-678-8503
Laurie Storch, prin. Fax 678-6591
North Oceanside Rd ES 500/1-6
2440 Oceanside Rd 11572 516-678-7585
Scott Bullis, prin. Fax 678-6597
Oaks ES 500/1-6
2852 Fortesque Ave 11572 516-678-7564
Beth-Ann Castiello, prin. Fax 678-6568
Oceanside MS 900/7-8
186 Alice Ave 11572 516-678-8518
Allison Glickman-Rogers, prin. Fax 594-2365
Public K 6 400/PK-K
25 Castleton Ct 11572 516-594-2345
Julie McGahan, prin. Fax 678-7347
Smith ES 400/1-6
2745 Terrell Ave 11572 516-678-7557
Thomas Capone, prin. Fax 678-6513
South Oceanside Road ES 300/1-6
3210 Oceanside Rd 11572 516-678-7581
Joanna Kletter, prin. Fax 678-6583

Odessa, Schuyler, Pop. 582
Odessa-Montour Central SD 800/PK-12
300 College Ave 14869 607-594-3341
Christopher Wood, supt. Fax 594-3976
www.omschools.org
Hanlon ES 200/3-6
300 College Ave 14869 607-594-3341
Robert Francischelli, prin. Fax 594-3434
Other Schools – See Montour Falls

Ogdensburg, Saint Lawrence, Pop. 10,977
Ogdensburg CSD 1,500/PK-12
1100 State St 13669 315-393-0900
Timothy Vernsey, supt. Fax 393-2767
www.ogdensburgk12.org/
Kennedy ES 500/PK-6
900 Park St 13669 315-393-4264
Susan Jacobs, prin. Fax 394-0480
Madill ES 300/PK-6
800 Jefferson Ave 13669 315-393-7729
Paula Scott, prin. Fax 393-0419

Old Bethpage, Nassau, Pop. 5,469
Plainview-Old Bethpage Central SD
Supt. — See Plainview
Old Bethpage ES 400/K-4
1191 Round Swamp Rd 11804 516-434-3419
Suzanne Gray, prin. Fax 756-3204

Old Brookville, Nassau, Pop. 2,097

Green Vale S 400/PK-8
250 Valentines Ln 11545 516-621-2420
Jesse Dougherty Ed.D., head sch Fax 621-1317

Old Forge, Herkimer, Pop. 747
Town of Webb UFD 300/K-12
PO Box 38 13420 315-369-3222
Rex Germer, supt. Fax 369-6216
www.towschool.org
Town of Webb S 300/K-12
PO Box 38 13420 315-369-3222
John Swick, prin. Fax 369-6216

Old Westbury, Nassau, Pop. 4,556
East Williston UFD 1,700/K-12
11 Bacon Rd 11568 516-333-1630
Dr. Elaine Kanas, supt. Fax 333-1937
www.ewsdonline.org
Other Schools – See East Williston, Roslyn Heights

Westbury UFD 4,700/PK-12
2 Hitchcock Ln 11568 516-876-5016
Eudes Budhai, supt. Fax 876-5181
www.westburyschools.org
Other Schools – See Westbury

Holy Child Academy 200/PK-8
25 Store Hill Rd 11568 516-626-9300
Michael O'Donoghue, prin. Fax 626-7914
Whispering Pines SDA S 50/PK-8
211 Jericho Tpke 11568 516-997-5177
Maurice Grant, prin. Fax 997-2138

Olean, Cattaraugus, Pop. 14,023
Olean CSD 2,200/PK-12
410 W Sullivan St 14760 716-375-8001
Dr. Rick Moore, supt. Fax 375-8047
www.oleanschools.org
East View ES 400/PK-3
690 E Spring St 14760 716-375-8920
Brian Crawford, prin. Fax 375-8929
Olean IS 300/4-5
401 Wayne St 14760 716-375-8060
Joel Whitcher, prin. Fax 375-8070
Olean MS 300/6-7
401 Wayne St 14760 716-375-8060
Gerald Trietley, prin. Fax 375-8070
Washington West ES 300/PK-3
1626 Washington St 14760 716-375-8960
Lauren Stuff, prin. Fax 375-8970

Southern Tier Catholic S 200/PK-8
208 N 24th St 14760 585-372-8122
Thomas Manko, prin. Fax 372-6707

Olmstedville, Essex
Minerva Central SD 100/K-12
PO Box 39 12857 518-251-2000
Timothy Farrell, supt. Fax 251-2395
www.minervasd.org/
Minerva Central S 100/K-12
PO Box 39 12857 518-251-2000
Timothy Farrell, prin. Fax 251-2395

Oneida, Madison, Pop. 11,232
Oneida CSD 2,100/PK-12
PO Box 327 13421 315-363-2550
Mary-Margaret Zehr, supt. Fax 363-6728
www.oneidacsd.org
North Broad Street ES 200/K-6
230 N Broad St 13421 315-363-3650
Eric Coriale, prin. Fax 366-0617
Prior ES 300/PK-5
205 East Ave 13421 315-363-2190
Moira Yardley, prin. Fax 366-0616
Seneca Street ES 200/K-6
436 Seneca St 13421 315-363-3930
Molly Hagan, prin. Fax 363-0618
Other Schools – See Durhamville, Wampsville

St. Patrick S 100/K-6
354 Elizabeth St 13421 315-363-3620
Kristin Healt, prin. Fax 363-5075

Oneonta, Otsego, Pop. 13,601
Oneonta CSD 1,600/PK-12
31 Center St 13820 607-433-8200
Joseph Yelich, supt. Fax 433-8290
oneontacsd.org
Greater Plains ES 300/PK-6
60 W End Ave 13820 607-433-8272
Nancy Osborn, prin. Fax 433-8207
Oneonta MS 300/7-8
130 East St 13820 607-433-8262
Colleen Lewis, prin. Fax 433-8203
Riverside ES 300/K-6
39 House St 13820 607-433-8273
Melinda Murdock, prin. Fax 433-8210
Valleyview ES 300/K-6
40 Valleyview St 13820 607-433-8252
Walter Baskin, prin. Fax 433-8211

Lighthouse Christian Academy 50/PK-12
12 Grove St 13820 607-432-2031
Chris Cleveland, admin. Fax 432-3403
Oneonta Community Christian S 100/PK-12
158 River St 13820 607-432-0383
David Pritchard, prin. Fax 436-9137

Ontario Center, Wayne
Wayne Central SD 2,300/K-12
PO Box 155 14520 315-524-1000
Dr. Mathis Calvin, supt. Fax 524-1049
www.wayne.k12.ny.us
Armstrong MS 500/6-8
PO Box 155 14520 315-524-1080
Derek Demass, prin. Fax 524-1119
Wayne Central ES 300/3-5
PO Box 155 14520 315-524-1130
Donna Rizzo, prin. Fax 524-1149
Wayne Central PS 400/K-2
PO Box 155 14520 315-524-1150
Pamela Tatro, prin. Fax 524-1169

Orchard Park, Erie, Pop. 3,209
Orchard Park Central SD
Supt. — See West Seneca
Eggert Road ES 600/K-5
3580 Eggert Rd 14127 716-209-6215
Terry Tryon, prin. Fax 209-6371
Ellicott Road ES 600/K-5
5180 Ellicott Rd 14127 716-209-6278
Paul Pietrantone, prin. Fax 209-6203
Orchard Park MS 1,300/6-8
60 S Lincoln Ave 14127 716-209-6227
Aaron Grupka, prin. Fax 209-6338
South Davis ES 400/K-5
51 S Davis St 14127 716-209-6246
Christine Rassow, prin. Fax 209-8195
Windom ES 600/K-5
3870 Sheldon Rd 14127 716-209-6279
Philip Johnson, prin. Fax 209-6490

Nativity of Our Lord S 200/PK-8
4414 S Buffalo St 14127 716-662-7572
Chris Gardon, prin. Fax 662-3483
St. John Vianney S 200/PK-8
2950 Southwestern Blvd 14127 716-674-9232
Glenn Olejniczak, prin. Fax 674-9248

Orient, Suffolk, Pop. 735
Oysterponds UFD 100/K-6
23405 Main Rd 11957 631-323-2410
Richard Malone, supt. Fax 323-3713
www.oysterponds.org
Oysterponds ES 100/K-6
23405 Main Rd 11957 631-323-2410
Jennifer Wissemann, prin. Fax 323-3713

Oriskany, Oneida, Pop. 1,381
Oriskany Central SD 600/K-12
PO Box 539 13424 315-768-2058
Timothy Gaffney, supt. Fax 768-1733
www.oriskanycsd.org
Walbran ES 300/K-6
PO Box 539 13424 315-768-2149
Karen Hinderling, prin. Fax 768-2137

Ossining, Westchester, Pop. 24,636
Ossining UFD 4,700/PK-12
190 Croton Ave 10562 914-941-7700
Raymond Sanchez, supt. Fax 941-7291
www.ossiningufsd.org/
Brookside S 800/1-2
30 Ryder Rd 10562 914-762-5780
Ann Dealy, prin. Fax 941-4674
Claremont S 700/3-4
2 Claremont Rd 10562 914-762-5830
Kate Mathews, prin. Fax 941-4964
Dorner MS 1,000/6-8
Van Cortlandt Ave 10562 914-762-5740
Regina Cellio, prin. Fax 762-5246
Park ECC 600/PK-K
22 Edward St 10562 914-762-5850
Cynthia Bardwell, prin. Fax 941-4335
Roosevelt S 400/5-5
190 Croton Ave 10562 914-762-2682
Michelle Grier, prin. Fax 941-5341

St. Augustine S 500/PK-8
381 N Highland Ave 10562 914-941-3849
Sr. Mary Donoghue, prin. Fax 941-4342

Oswego, Oswego, Pop. 17,912
Oswego CSD 3,700/K-12
120 E 1st St Ste 1 13126 315-341-2000
Dr. Dean Goewey, supt. Fax 341-2910
www.oswego.org
Fitzhugh Park ES 500/K-6
195 E Bridge St 13126 315-341-2400
Donna Simmons, prin. Fax 341-2940
Kingsford Park ES 400/K-6
275 W 5th St 13126 315-341-2500
Dr. Mary Volkomer, prin. Fax 341-2950
Leighton ES 300/K-6
1 Buccaneer Blvd 13126 315-341-2700
Kara Shore, prin. Fax 341-2970
Oswego MS 600/7-8
100 Mark Fitzgibbons Dr 13126 315-341-2300
Mary Fierro, prin. Fax 341-2390
Riley ES 400/K-6
269 E 8th St 13126 315-341-2800
Dr. Linda Doty, prin. Fax 341-2980
Other Schools – See Minetto

Oswego Community Christian S 100/PK-8
400 E Albany St 13126 315-342-9322
David Proietti, prin. Fax 342-0268
Trinity Catholic S 200/PK-6
115 E 5th St 13126 315-343-6700
Barbara Sugar, prin. Fax 342-9471

Otego, Otsego, Pop. 991
Unatego Central SD 900/K-12
2641 State Highway 7 13825 607-988-5038
Dr. David S. Richards, supt. Fax 988-1039
www.unatego.org
Unatego MS 200/6-8
2641 State Highway 7 13825 607-988-5036
Patricia Hoyt, prin. Fax 988-5050
Other Schools – See Unadilla

Otisville, Orange, Pop. 1,058
Minisink Valley Central SD
Supt. — See Slate Hill
Otisville ES 600/K-5
2525 Mt Hope Rd 10963 845-355-5850
Vinnie Biele, prin. Fax 355-5853

Ovid, Seneca, Pop. 592
South Seneca Central SD 700/PK-12
7263 Main St 14521 607-869-9636
Stephen Zielinski, supt. Fax 532-8540
www.southseneca.com
South Seneca MS 200/6-8
7263 Main St 14521 607-869-9636
Tim Houseknecht, prin. Fax 532-9553
Other Schools – See Interlaken

Owego, Tioga, Pop. 3,824
Owego-Apalachin Central SD 2,200/PK-12
36 Talcott St 13827 607-687-6224
Corey Green, supt. Fax 687-6313
www.oacsd.org
Owego-Apalachin MS 500/5-8
3 Sheldon Guile Blvd 13827 607-687-7302
Thomas Beatty, prin. Fax 687-6593
Owego ES 500/PK-5
2 Sheldon Guile Blvd 13827 607-687-7303
Laurie McKeveny, prin. Fax 687-6268
Other Schools – See Apalachin

Zion Lutheran S 50/PK-5
3917 Waverly Rd 13827 607-687-6376
Fax 687-6376

Oxford, Chenango, Pop. 1,425
Oxford Academy & Central SD 800/PK-12
PO Box 192 13830 607-843-2025
Shawn Bissetta, supt. Fax 843-3241
www.oxac.org
Oxford Academy MS 200/5-8
PO Box 192 13830 607-843-2025
Heather Fredenburg, prin. Fax 843-3241
Oxford Academy PS 300/PK-4
PO Box 192 13830 607-843-2025
Kathleen Hansen, prin. Fax 843-7030

Oyster Bay, Nassau, Pop. 6,598
Oyster Bay-East Norwich Central SD 1,600/PK-12
1 McCouns Ln 11771 516-624-6505
Dr. Laura Seinfeld, supt. Fax 624-6520
obenschools.org
Roosevelt ES 400/PK-2
150 W Main St 11771 516-624-6572
Tami McElwee, prin. Fax 624-6591
Other Schools – See East Norwich

East Woods S 200/PK-8
31 Yellow Cote Rd 11771 516-922-4400
Laura Kang, head sch Fax 922-2589
St. Dominic S 300/PK-8
35 School St 11771 516-922-4233
Ron Martorelli, prin. Fax 624-7613

Ozone Park, See New York
NYC Department of Education
Supt. — See New York
JHS 202 1,000/6-8
13830 Lafayette St 11417 718-848-0001
William Fitzgerald, prin. Fax 848-8082
JHS 210 1,900/6-8
9311 101st Ave 11416 718-845-5942
Bonnie Butcher, prin. Fax 845-4037
MS 137 1,900/6-8
10915 98th St 11417 718-659-0471
Laura Mastrogiovanni, prin. Fax 659-4594
PS 377 PK-K
15015 Raleigh St 11417 929-398-3215
Tracy Keane, prin. Fax 398-3218
Public S 63 1,300/K-5
9015 Sutter Ave 11417 718-845-7560
Diane Colman, prin. Fax 845-7269
Public S 64 600/K-5
8201 101st Ave 11416 718-845-8290
Elizabeth Mitchell, prin. Fax 848-0052
Public S 65 500/K-5
10322 99th St 11417 718-323-1685
Rafael Morales, prin. Fax 323-1785
Queens Explorers ES PK-5
9007 101st Ave 11416 718-558-7088
Melissa Compson, prin.

Divine Mercy Catholic Academy 300/PK-8
10160 92nd St 11416 718-845-3074
Sr. Francis Wystepek, prin. Fax 845-5068
St. Elizabeth Catholic Academy 300/PK-8
9401 85th St 11416 718-641-6990
William Ferguson, prin. Fax 323-5010
St. Mary Gate of Heaven Catholic Academy 500/K-8
10406 101st Ave 11416 718-846-0689
Philip Heide, prin. Fax 846-1059

Painted Post, Steuben, Pop. 1,780
Corning CSD 4,000/K-12
165 Charles St 14870 607-936-3704
Michael Ginalski, supt. Fax 654-2735
www.corningareaschools.com
Corning Painted Post MS 1,100/6-8
35 Victory Hwy 14870 607-654-2966
Richard Kimble, prin. Fax 654-2908
Erwin Valley ES 400/K-5
16 Beartown Rd 14870 607-936-6514
Kate Merrill, prin. Fax 654-2878
Smith ES 300/K-5
3414 Stanton St 14870 607-936-4156
Jeffrey Marchionda, prin. Fax 654-2859
Other Schools – See Corning

Palmyra, Wayne, Pop. 3,491
Palmyra-Macedon Central SD 1,900/K-12
151 Hyde Pkwy 14522 315-597-3400
Dr. Robert Ike, supt. Fax 597-3898
www.palmaccsd.org
Palmyra-Macedon MS 400/6-8
163 Hyde Pkwy 14522 315-597-3400
Darcy Smith, prin. Fax 597-3460
Palmyra-Macedon PS 500/K-2
120 Canandaigua St 14522 315-597-3400
Brian Brooks, prin. Fax 597-6903
Other Schools – See Macedon

East Palmyra Christian S 100/PK-12
2023 E Palmyra Port Gibson 14522 315-597-4400
Keith Vanderzwan, prin. Fax 597-9717

Panama, Chautauqua, Pop. 475
Panama Central SD 500/PK-12
41 North St 14767 716-782-2455
Bert Lictus, supt. Fax 782-4674
www.pancent.org
Panama Central ES 300/PK-6
41 North St 14767 716-782-2455
Frances Frey, prin. Fax 782-4674

Parish, Oswego, Pop. 445
Altmar-Parish-Williamstown Central SD 1,300/PK-12
PO Box 97 13131 315-625-5251
Dr. Jeffrey Bryant, supt. Fax 625-7952
www.apw.cnyric.org
Altmar-Parish-Williamstown ES 700/PK-6
640 County Route 22 13131 315-625-5260
Julie Woolson, prin. Fax 625-4937

Parishville, Saint Lawrence, Pop. 641
Parishville-Hopkinton Central SD 500/PK-12
PO Box 187 13672 315-265-4642
Dr. William Collins Ed.D., supt. Fax 268-1309
phcs.neric.org
Parishville-Hopkinton ES 300/PK-6
PO Box 187 13672 315-265-4642
Brooke Reid, prin. Fax 268-1309

Patchogue, Suffolk, Pop. 11,620
Patchogue-Medford UFD 7,100/PK-12
241 S Ocean Ave 11772 631-687-6300
Michael Hynes Ph.D., supt.
www.pmschools.org
Barton ES, 199 Barton Ave 11772 500/PK-5
Judith Soltner, prin. 631-687-6900
Bay ES 400/K-5
114 Bay Ave 11772 631-687-6950
Rui Mendes, prin. Fax 758-1126
Canaan ES, 59 Fry Blvd 11772 500/K-5
Robert Epstein, prin. 631-687-8100
Medford ES, 281 Medford Ave 11772 600/K-5
Margherita Proscia, prin. 631-687-8300
River ES, 46 River Ave 11772 400/K-5
Tania Dalley, prin. 631-687-8350
Other Schools – See Medford

Emanuel Lutheran S 100/PK-8
179 E Main St 11772 631-758-2250
Denise Norman, prin. Fax 758-2418
Holy Angels Regional S 300/K-8
1 Division St 11772 631-475-0422
Michael Connell, prin. Fax 475-2036

Patterson, Putnam
Carmel Central SD 4,300/K-12
PO Box 296 12563 845-878-2094
Andy Irvin, supt. Fax 878-2566
www.carmelschools.org
Paterson ES 600/K-4
100 South St 12563 845-878-3211
Joseph Keenan, prin. Fax 878-3964
Other Schools – See Carmel

Pavilion, Genesee, Pop. 644
Pavilion Central SD 700/PK-12
7014 Big Tree Rd 14525 585-584-3115
Kenneth Ellison, supt. Fax 584-3421
www.pavilioncsd.org
Bunce ES 300/PK-5
7071 York Rd 14525 585-584-3011
Jon Wilson, prin. Fax 584-3421

Pawling, Dutchess, Pop. 2,332
Pawling Central SD 1,200/K-12
515 Route 22 12564 845-855-4600
Dr. William M. Ward, supt. Fax 855-4659
www.pawlingschools.org
Pawling ES 400/K-4
7 Haight St 12564 845-855-4630
Dr. Debra Kirkhus, prin. Fax 855-4636
Pawling MS 400/5-8
80 Wagner Dr 12564 845-855-4653
Allan Lipsky, prin. Fax 855-4131

Mizzentop Day S 100/PK-8
64 E Main St 12564 845-855-7338

Pearl River, Rockland, Pop. 15,720
Pearl River UFD 2,600/K-12
135 W Crooked Hill Rd 10965 845-620-3900
Marco Pochintesta, supt. Fax 620-3927
www.pearlriver.org
Evans Park ES 300/K-4
40 Marion Pl 10965 845-620-3950
Peggy Lynch, prin. Fax 620-7570
Franklin Avenue ES 300/K-4
48 Franklin Ave 10965 845-620-3965
Maureen Alaimo, prin. Fax 620-3981
Lincoln Ave ES 200/K-4
115 Lincoln Ave 10965 845-620-3850
Kathleenanne Cool, prin. Fax 620-3975
Pearl River MS 600/5-7
520 Gilbert Ave 10965 845-620-3870
Maria Paese, prin. Fax 620-3894

St. Margaret S 200/PK-8
34 N Magnolia St 10965 845-735-2855
Patricia Maldonado, prin. Fax 735-0131

Peekskill, Westchester, Pop. 22,929
Peekskill CSD 3,200/PK-12
1031 Elm St 10566 914-737-3300
Mary Keenan Foster, supt. Fax 737-3912
www.peekskillcsd.org
Hillcrest ES 500/4-5
99 Horton Dr 10566 914-739-2284
Randy Lichtenwalner, prin. Fax 737-9053
Hill Jr. ECC 100/PK-PK
980 Pemart Ave 10566 914-739-0682
Carmen Vargas, prin. Fax 739-8795
Oakside ES 500/2-3
200 Decatur Ave 10566 914-737-1591
Staci Woodley, prin. Fax 737-1530
Peekskill MS 700/6-8
212 Ringgold St 10566 914-737-4542
Jamal Lewis, prin. Fax 737-3253
Woodside ES 500/K-1
702 Depew St 10566 914-739-0093
Colleen Hardiman, prin. Fax 737-9039

Pelham, Westchester, Pop. 6,710
Pelham UFD 2,800/K-12
18 Franklin Pl 10803 914-738-3434
Dr. Cheryl H. Champ, supt. Fax 738-7223
www.pelhamschools.org
Colonial ES 300/K-5
315 Highbrook Ave 10803 914-738-2680
Tonya Wilson, prin. Fax 738-8187
Hutchinson ES 300/K-5
301 Third Ave 10803 914-738-3640
Trisha Fitzgerald, prin. Fax 738-8198
Pelham MS 700/6-8
28 Franklin Pl 10803 914-738-8190
Dr. Robert Roelle, prin. Fax 738-8132
Prospect Hill ES 300/K-5
1000 Washington Ave 10803 914-738-6690
Jeannine Carr, prin. Fax 738-8258
Siwanoy ES 300/K-5
489 Siwanoy Pl 10803 914-738-7650
Susan Gilbert, prin. Fax 738-8199

Our Lady of Perpetual Help S 200/PK-8
575 Fowler Ave 10803 914-738-5158
Paul Henshaw, prin. Fax 738-8974

Penfield, Monroe, Pop. 30,219
Penfield Central SD
Supt. — See Rochester
Bay Trail MS 1,100/6-8
1760 Scribner Rd 14526 585-249-6450
Winton Buddington, prin. Fax 248-0735
Cobbles ES 500/K-5
140 Gebhardt Rd 14526 585-249-6500
Dr. Stephen Kenny, prin. Fax 248-2108
Harris Hill ES 500/K-5
2126 Penfield Rd 14526 585-249-6600
Marc Nelson, prin. Fax 249-6616
Scribner Road ES 500/K-5
1750 Scribner Rd 14526 585-249-6400
Scott Hirschler, prin. Fax 249-6411

Finney S 200/K-12
2070 Five Mile Line Rd 14526 585-387-3770
Michael VanLeeuwen, pres. Fax 387-3771
St. Joseph S 400/PK-6
39 Gebhardt Rd 14526 585-586-6968
Amy Johnson, prin. Fax 586-4619

Penn Yan, Yates, Pop. 5,081
Penn Yan Central SD 1,500/PK-12
1 School Dr 14527 315-536-3371
Howard Dennis, supt. Fax 536-0068
www.pycsd.org
Penn Yan ES 600/PK-5
3 School Dr 14527 315-536-3346
Edward Foote, prin. Fax 536-7162
Penn Yan MS 300/6-8
515 Liberty St 14527 315-536-3366
Kelley Johnson, prin. Fax 536-7769

St. Michael S 100/PK-5
214 Keuka St 14527 315-536-6112
Thomas Flood, prin. Fax 536-6112

Perry, Wyoming, Pop. 3,633
Perry Central SD 600/PK-12
33 Watkins Ave 14530 585-237-0270
Daryl McLaughlin, supt. Fax 237-6172
www.perry.k12.ny.us
Perry ES 300/PK-6
50 Olin Ave 14530 585-237-0270
Stephen Haynes, admin. Fax 237-3483

Peru, Clinton, Pop. 1,580
Peru Central SD 1,900/K-12
PO Box 68 12972 518-643-6000
Cynthia Ford-Johnston, supt. Fax 643-2043
www.perucsd.org
Peru ES 1,000/K-6
PO Box 68 12972 518-643-6100
Matthew Slattery, prin. Fax 643-6126

Philadelphia, Jefferson, Pop. 1,192
Indian River Central SD 4,200/PK-12
32735 County Route 29 Ste B 13673 315-642-3441
James Kettrick, supt. Fax 642-3738
www.ircsd.org
Indian River IS 700/4-5
32430 US Route 11 13673 315-642-0405
Brian Moore, prin. Fax 642-3180
Indian River MS 900/6-8
32735 County Route 29 Ste A 13673 315-642-0125
Nancy Taylor-Schmitt, prin. Fax 642-0802
Philadelphia PS 100/K-3
3 Sand St 13673 315-642-3432
Barbara Zehr, prin. Fax 642-5650
Other Schools – See Antwerp, Calcium, Evans Mills, Theresa

Phoenicia, Ulster, Pop. 303
Onteora Central SD
Supt. — See Boiceville
Phoenicia ES 100/K-6
PO Box 599 12464 845-688-5580
Linda Sella, prin. Fax 688-2324

Phoenix, Oswego, Pop. 2,343
Phoenix Central SD 1,700/K-12
116 Volney St 13135 315-695-1555
Christopher Byrne, supt. Fax 695-1201
www.phoenixcsd.org
Dillon MS 400/6-8
116 Volney St 13135 315-695-1521
Susan Anderson, prin. Fax 695-1523
Maroun ES 600/K-5
11 Elm St 13135 315-695-1561
Brett Doody, prin. Fax 695-1528

Pine Bush, Orange, Pop. 1,744
Pine Bush Central SD 5,500/PK-12
PO Box 700 12566 845-744-2031
Ti m O. Mains, supt. Fax 744-6189
www.pinebushschools.org
Crispell MS 700/6-8
PO Box 780 12566 845-744-2031
John Boyle, prin. Fax 744-2261
Pine Bush ES 700/PK-5
PO Box 899 12566 845-744-2031
Eric Winter, prin. Fax 744-8092
Russell ES 600/PK-5
PO Box 730 12566 845-744-2031
Elizabeth Sproul, prin. Fax 744-3308
Other Schools – See Circleville

AEF Chapel Field S 100/PK-12
211 Fleury Rd 12566 845-778-1881
William Spanjer, pres. Fax 778-5841

Pine City, Chemung
Elmira CSD
Supt. — See Elmira
Pine City ES 400/PK-2
1551 Pennsylvania Ave 14871 607-735-3800
Rhonda Baran, prin. Fax 735-3809

Pine Plains, Dutchess, Pop. 1,324
Pine Plains Central SD 900/PK-12
2829 Church St 12567 518-398-7181
Dr. Martin Handler Ed.D., supt. Fax 398-6592
www.ppcsd.org
Smith Intermediate Learning Ctr 200/2-5
41 Academy St 12567 518-398-3000
Julie Roberts, prin. Fax 398-1141
Other Schools – See Stanfordville

Pittsford, Monroe, Pop. 1,344
Pittsford Central SD 5,800/K-12
75 Barker Rd 14534 585-267-1000
Michael Pero, supt. Fax 267-1088
www.pittsfordschools.org
Barker Road MS 800/6-8
75 Barker Rd 14534 585-267-1800
Shana Cutaia, prin. Fax 385-5960
Calkins Road MS 700/6-8
1899 Calkins Rd 14534 585-267-1900
Joshua Walker, prin. Fax 264-0053
Jefferson Road ES 400/K-5
15 School Ln 14534 585-267-1300
Shawn Clark, prin. Fax 385-6426
Mendon Center ES 800/K-5
110 Mendon Center Rd 14534 585-267-1400
Heather Clayton, prin. Fax 218-1430
Park Road ES 500/K-5
50 Park Rd 14534 585-267-1500
Dr. Mark Balsamo, prin. Fax 385-6356
Thornell Road ES 400/K-5
431 Thornell Rd 14534 585-267-1700
Roger DeBell, prin. Fax 385-2099
Other Schools – See Rochester

St. Louis S 400/PK-5
11 Rand Pl 14534 585-586-5200
Fran Barr, prin. Fax 586-4561

Plainview, Nassau, Pop. 25,853
Bethpage UFD
Supt. — See Bethpage
Kramer Lane ES 300/K-5
1 Kramer Ln 11803 516-644-4500
Kerri McCarthy, prin. Fax 933-9819

Plainview-Old Bethpage Central SD 4,800/K-12
106 Washington Ave 11803 516-434-3000
Dr. Lorna R. Lewis, supt. Fax 937-6303
www.pobschools.org
Mattlin MS 800/5-8
100 Washington Ave 11803 516-434-3250
Joseph Coladonato, prin. Fax 937-6431
Parkway ES 300/K-4
300 Manetto Hill Rd 11803 516-434-3358
Gregory Scesney, prin. Fax 349-4780
Pasadena ES 300/K-4
3 Richard Ct 11803 516-434-3451
Karen Heitner, prin. Fax 937-7291
Plainview-Old Bethpage MS 800/5-8
121 Central Park Rd 11803 516-434-3308
Alice Bowman, prin. Fax 349-4777
Stratford Road ES 400/1-4
33 Bedford Rd 11803 516-434-3389
Alison Clark, prin. Fax 937-6347
Other Schools – See Old Bethpage

Syosset Central SD
Supt. — See Syosset
Baylis ES, 580 Woodbury Rd 11803 400/K-5
Lisa Greiner, prin. 516-364-5798

Hebrew Academy of Nassau County 200/PK-6
25 Country Dr 11803 516-681-5922

Plattekill, Ulster, Pop. 1,232
Wallkill Central SD
Supt. — See Wallkill
Plattekill ES 500/K-6
1270 Route 32 12568 845-895-7250
Monica Hasbrouck, prin. Fax 564-5103

Plattsburgh, Clinton, Pop. 19,572
Beekmantown Central SD
Supt. — See West Chazy
Cumberland Head ES 500/PK-5
1187 Cumberland Head Rd 12901 518-563-8321
Darcy Stoutenger, prin. Fax 563-8343

Plattsburgh CSD 1,800/PK-12
49 Broad St 12901 518-957-6002
John Lebrun, supt. Fax 561-6605
www.plattscsd.org
Bailey Avenue ES 200/PK-2
50 Bailey Ave 12901 518-563-2410
Claudine Selzer-Clark, prin. Fax 566-7663
Momot ES 500/PK-5
60 Monty St 12901 518-563-1140
Susan Wilson, prin. Fax 566-7739
Oak Street IS 200/3-5
108 Oak St 12901 518-563-4950
Jayson Barnhart, prin. Fax 561-5828
Stafford MS 400/6-8
15 Broad St 12901 518-563-6800
Jamie Labarge, prin. Fax 563-8520

Seton Academy 200/PK-5
23 St Charles St 12901 518-825-7386
Sr. Helen Hermann, prin. Fax 563-4553

Pleasant Valley, Dutchess, Pop. 1,128
Arlington Central SD
Supt. — See Lagrangeville
Traver Road PS 300/K-2
801 Traver Rd 12569 845-635-4300
Cara Conrad, prin. Fax 635-4316
West Road/D'Aquanni IS 300/3-5
181 West Rd 12569 845-635-4310
Heather Ogborn, prin. Fax 635-4317

Pleasantville, Westchester, Pop. 6,927
Pleasantville UFD 1,700/K-12
60 Romer Ave 10570 914-741-1400
Mary Fox-Alter, supt. Fax 741-1499
www.pleasantvilleschools.com

Bedford Road PS — 600/K-4
289 Bedford Rd 10570 — 914-741-1440
Margaret Galotti, prin. — Fax 741-1468
Pleasantville MS — 500/5-8
40 Romer Ave 10570 — 914-741-1450
Donald Marra, prin. — Fax 741-1476

Poestenkill, Rensselaer, Pop. 1,050
Averill Park Central SD
Supt. — See Averill Park
Poestenkill ES — 400/K-5
1 School Rd 12140 — 518-674-7125
John Bishop, prin. — Fax 286-1971

Poland, Herkimer, Pop. 505
Poland Central SD — 600/PK-12
PO Box 8 13431 — 315-826-7900
Laura Dutton, supt. — Fax 826-7516
www.polandcs.org
Poland ES — 300/PK-5
PO Box 8 13431 — 315-826-7000
Gregory Cuthbertson, prin. — Fax 826-7516

Pomona, Rockland, Pop. 3,013

Bais Yaakov Chofetz Chaim of Pomona — 400/PK-8
44 Camp Hill Rd 10970 — 845-362-3166
Rabbi Henoch Zaks, prin. — Fax 354-6682

Port Byron, Cayuga, Pop. 1,272
Port Byron Central SD — 1,000/K-12
30 Maple Ave 13140 — 315-776-5728
Neil O'Brien, supt. — Fax 776-4050
pbcschools.org
Gates ES — 500/K-6
30 Maple Ave 13140 — 315-776-5728
Julie Podolak, prin. — Fax 776-4050

Port Chester, Westchester, Pop. 28,517
Port Chester Rye UFD — 4,400/K-12
PO Box 246 10573 — 914-934-7900
Dr. Edward Kliszus, supt. — Fax 934-0727
www.portchesterschools.org
Edison ES — 400/K-5
132 Rectory St 10573 — 914-934-7980
Ivan Tolentino, prin. — Fax 934-7879
Kennedy ES — 900/K-5
40 Olivia St 10573 — 914-934-7990
Judy Diaz, prin. — Fax 939-6625
King Street ES — 400/K-5
697 King St 10573 — 914-934-7995
Samuel Ortiz, prin. — Fax 939-9351
Park Avenue ES — 400/K-5
75 Park Ave 10573 — 914-934-7895
Rosa Taylor, prin. — Fax 939-9243
Port Chester MS — 1,000/6-8
113 Bowman Ave 10573 — 914-934-7930
Patrick Swift, prin. — Fax 934-7886

Corpus Christi - Holy Rosary S — 300/PK-8
135 S Regent St 10573 — 914-937-4407
Deirdre McDermott, prin. — Fax 937-6904

Port Ewen, Ulster, Pop. 3,446
Kingston CSD
Supt. — See Kingston
Graves ES — 400/K-5
345 Mountain View Ave 12466 — 845-943-3915
Errin Parese, prin. — Fax 338-3049

Port Henry, Essex, Pop. 1,181
Moriah Central SD — 700/PK-12
39 Viking Ln 12974 — 518-546-3301
William Larrow, supt. — Fax 546-7895
www.moriahk12.org
Moriah ES — 400/PK-6
39 Viking Ln 12974 — 518-546-3301
Valerie Stahl, prin. — Fax 546-7895

Port Jefferson, Suffolk, Pop. 7,650
Port Jefferson UFD — 1,200/PK-12
550 Scraggy Hill Rd 11777 — 631-791-4500
Paul Casciano Ed.D., supt. — Fax 476-4409
www.portjeffschools.org
Port Jefferson MS — 300/6-8
350 Old Post Rd 11777 — 631-791-4400
Robert Neidig, prin. — Fax 476-4430
Spear ES — 500/PK-5
500 Scraggy Hill Rd 11777 — 631-791-4300
Thomas Meehan, prin. — Fax 476-4419

Our Lady of Wisdom Regional S — 200/K-8
114 Myrtle Ave 11777 — 631-473-1211
John Piropato, prin. — Fax 473-1064

Port Jefferson Station, Suffolk, Pop. 7,762
Comsewogue SD — 3,700/K-12
290 Norwood Ave 11776 — 631-474-8100
Joseph Rella Ed.D., supt. — Fax 474-3568
www.comsewogue.k12.ny.us
Boyle Road ES — 400/3-5
424 Boyle Rd 11776 — 631-474-8140
Robert Pearl, prin. — Fax 474-8498
Clinton Avenue ES — 500/K-5
140 Clinton Ave 11776 — 631-474-8150
Toni Bifalco, prin. — Fax 474-8499
Kennedy MS — 900/6-8
200 Jayne Blvd 11776 — 631-474-8160
Michael Fama, prin. — Fax 474-8176
Norwood Avenue ES — 400/K-5
290 Norwood Ave 11776 — 631-474-8130
Annemarie Sciove, prin. — Fax 474-8385
Terryville Road ES — 500/K-5
401 Terryville Rd 11776 — 631-474-2834
April Victor, prin. — Fax 474-2846

Port Jervis, Orange, Pop. 8,515
Port Jervis CSD — 2,700/K-12
9 Thompson St 12771 — 845-858-3100
Ruth Zuclich, supt. — Fax 856-1885
www.pjschools.org
Kuhl ES — 900/K-6
10 Route 209 12771 — 845-858-3100
Brett Cancredi, prin. — Fax 858-2894
Port Jervis MS — 500/7-8
118 E Main St 12771 — 845-858-3100
Jean Fazzino-Lain, prin. — Fax 858-2893
Other Schools – See Cuddebackville

Port Leyden, Lewis, Pop. 667
South Lewis Central SD
Supt. — See Turin
Port Leyden ES — 200/PK-4
PO Box 68 13433 — 315-348-2660
Christopher Villiere, prin. — Fax 348-2570

Portville, Cattaraugus, Pop. 993
Portville Central SD — 1,000/PK-12
PO Box 790 14770 — 585-933-6000
Mr. Thomas Simon, supt. — Fax 933-6774
www.portville.wnyric.org/
Portville ES — 600/PK-6
PO Box 790 14770 — 585-933-6045
Mr. Lynn Corder, prin. — Fax 933-6037

Port Washington, Nassau, Pop. 15,596
Port Washington UFD — 5,100/K-12
100 Campus Dr 11050 — 516-767-5000
Dr. Kathleen Mooney, supt. — Fax 767-5007
www.portnet.org
Daly ES — 400/K-5
36 Rockwood Ave 11050 — 516-767-5200
Sheri Suzzan, prin. — Fax 767-5207
Guggenheim ES — 500/K-5
38 Poplar Pl 11050 — 516-767-5250
Barbara Giebel, prin. — Fax 767-5257
Manorhaven ES — 400/K-5
1N Morewood Oaks 11050 — 516-767-5300
Bonni Cohen, prin. — Fax 767-5303
Sousa ES — 600/K-5
101 Sands Point Rd 11050 — 516-767-5350
Dr. David Meoli, prin. — Fax 767-5356
South Salem ES — 400/K-5
10 Newbury Rd 11050 — 516-767-5400
Pia Sanchez-Ferrante, prin. — Fax 767-5407
Weber MS — 1,200/6-8
52 Campus Dr 11050 — 516-767-5500
Christopher Shields, prin. — Fax 767-5507

St. Peter of Alcantara S — 300/PK-8
1321 Port Washington Blvd 11050 — 516-944-3772
Marianne Carberry, prin. — Fax 767-8075

Potsdam, Saint Lawrence, Pop. 9,246
Potsdam Central SD — 1,300/PK-12
29 Leroy St 13676 — 315-265-2000
Joann Chambers, supt. — Fax 265-2048
www.potsdam.k12.ny.us
Kingston MS — 400/5-8
29 Leroy St 13676 — 315-265-2000
Fax 265-8103
Lawrence Avenue ES — 600/PK-4
29 Leroy St 13676 — 315-265-2000
Jennifer Gray, prin. — Fax 265-5458

Poughkeepsie, Dutchess, Pop. 31,635
Arlington Central SD
Supt. — See Lagrangeville
May ES — 400/K-5
601 Dutchess Tpke 12603 — 845-486-4960
Sheri Primeaux, prin. — Fax 486-4777
Noxon Road ES — 400/K-5
4 Old Noxon Rd 12603 — 845-486-4950
Kelly Murray, prin. — Fax 486-4774
Overlook PS — 400/K-2
11 Mapleview Rd 12603 — 845-486-4970
Jessica Wheeler, prin. — Fax 486-7792
Titusville IS — 400/3-5
128 Meadow Ln 12603 — 845-486-4470
Daniel Shornstein, prin. — Fax 486-4475

Hyde Park Central SD
Supt. — See Hyde Park
Violet Avenue ES — 400/K-5
191 Violet Ave 12601 — 845-486-4499
Deanna Gonzalez, prin. — Fax 486-7796

Poughkeepsie CSD — 4,200/PK-12
11 College Ave 12603 — 845-451-4900
Dr. Nicole Williams, supt. — Fax 451-4955
www.poughkeepsieschools.org/
Clinton ES — 400/K-5
100 Montgomery St 12601 — 845-451-4600
David Scott, prin. — Fax 451-4614
Columbus ES — 300/K-5
12 S Perry St 12601 — 845-451-4630
Joseph Mazzetti, prin. — Fax 451-4655
Krieger ES — 600/K-5
265 Hooker Ave 12603 — 845-451-4660
Andrea Moriarty, prin. — Fax 451-4672
Morse Young Child Magnet ES — 200/K-2
101 Mansion St 12601 — 845-451-4690
Nadine Dargan, prin. — Fax 451-4711
Poughkeepsie MS — 1,000/6-8
55 College Ave 12603 — 845-451-4800
Da'Ron Wilson, prin. — Fax 451-4836
Smith Early Learning Center — 200/PK-1
372 Church St 12601 — 845-451-4720
Margaret Pineiro, prin. — Fax 451-4741
Warring Academy — 300/K-5
283 Mansion St 12601 — 845-451-4750
Jason Gerard, prin. — Fax 451-4769

Spackenkill UFD — 1,500/K-12
15 Croft Rd 12603 — 845-463-7800
Dr. Mark Villanti, supt. — Fax 463-7804
www.sufsdny.org
Hagan ES — 300/3-5
42 Hagan Dr 12603 — 845-463-7840
John Farrell, prin. — Fax 463-7881
Nassau ES — 300/K-2
7 Nassau Rd 12601 — 845-463-7844
Nancy Ferrarone, prin. — Fax 463-7842
Todd MS — 400/6-8
11 Croft Rd 12603 — 845-463-7830
Daniel Doherty, prin. — Fax 463-7832

Wappingers Central SD
Supt. — See Hopewell Junction
Kinry Road ES — 400/4-6
58 Kinry Rd 12603 — 845-463-7322
Mary Bish, prin. — Fax 463-7327
Oak Grove ES — 400/K-6
40 Kerr Rd 12601 — 845-298-5280
Angelina Alvarez-Rooney, prin. — Fax 298-5270
Vassar Road ES — 300/K-3
174 Vassar Rd 12603 — 845-463-7860
Richard Dominick, prin. — Fax 463-7859

Faith Christian Academy — 300/PK-12
25 Golf Club Ln 12601 — 845-462-0266
Alexander Averin, hdmstr. — Fax 462-1561
Hawk Meadow Montessori S — 100/PK-8
110 Overlook Rd 12603 — 845-223-3783
Erin Castle, dir. — Fax 214-0261
Holy Trinity S — 200/PK-8
20 Springside Ave 12603 — 845-471-0520
Kathleen Spina, prin. — Fax 471-0309
Poughkeepsie Day S — 300/PK-12
260 Boardman Rd 12603 — 845-462-7600
Benedict Chant, head sch — Fax 462-7603
Poughkeepsie SDA ES — 50/PK-8
71 Mitchell Ave 12603 — 845-454-1781
Carol Ashe, prin. — Fax 790-5223
St. Martin DePorres S — 400/PK-8
122 Cedar Valley Rd 12603 — 845-452-4428
Kathleen Leahy, prin. — Fax 452-9013
St. Peter S — 200/PK-8
12 Father Cody Dr 12601 — 845-471-6600
Susan Traudt, prin. — Fax 454-1674
Tabernacle Christian Academy — 100/K-12
155 Academy St 12601 — 845-454-2792
Timothy Hostetter, prin. — Fax 483-0926

Poughquag, Dutchess
Arlington Central SD
Supt. — See Lagrangeville
Beekman ES — 600/K-5
201 Lime Ridge Rd 12570 — 845-227-1834
Matt Latvis, prin. — Fax 227-1822

Pound Ridge, Westchester
Bedford Central SD
Supt. — See Bedford
Pound Ridge ES — 400/K-5
7 Pound Ridge Rd 10576 — 914-764-8133
Amy Beth Fishkin, prin. — Fax 764-4009

Prattsburgh, Steuben, Pop. 649
Prattsburg Central SD — 400/PK-12
1 Academy St 14873 — 607-522-3795
Jeffrey Black, supt. — Fax 522-6221
www.prattsburghcsd.org/
Prattsburg Central S — 400/PK-12
1 Academy St 14873 — 607-522-3795
Thomas Crook, supt. — Fax 522-6221

Pulaski, Oswego, Pop. 2,352
Pulaski Central SD — 1,100/PK-12
2 Hinman Rd 13142 — 315-298-5188
Dr. Brian Hartwell, supt. — Fax 298-4390
www.pulaskicsd.org
Pulaski MS — 300/6-8
4624 Salina St 13142 — 315-298-6001
Paula Brillo, prin. — Fax 298-2371
Sharp ES — 500/PK-5
2 Hinman Rd 13142 — 315-298-2412
Joelle Hendry, prin. — Fax 298-7464

Purchase, See Harrison
Harrison Central SD
Supt. — See Harrison
Purchase ES — 400/K-5
2995 Purchase St 10577 — 914-630-3172
Adam Gutterman, prin. — Fax 946-0286

Putnam Station, Washington
Putnam Central SD — 50/PK-6
PO Box 91 12861 — 518-547-8266
Matthew Boucher, supt. — Fax 547-9567
www.putnamcsd.org/
Putnam Central ES — 50/PK-6
PO Box 91 12861 — 518-547-8266
Matthew Boucher, prin. — Fax 547-9567

Putnam Valley, Putnam
Putnam Valley Central SD — 1,000/K-12
146 Peekskill Hollow Rd 10579 — 845-528-8143
Dr. Frances Wills, supt. — Fax 528-8386
www.pvcsd.org
Putnam Valley ES — 600/K-4
171 Oscawana Lake Rd 10579 — 845-528-8092
Margaret Podesta, prin. — Fax 528-8171
Putnam Valley MS — 500/5-8
142 Peekskill Hollow Rd 10579 — 845-528-8101
Travis McCarty, prin. — Fax 528-8145

Queensbury, Warren
Queensbury UFD — 3,400/K-12
429 Aviation Rd 12804 — 518-824-5600
Douglas Huntley Ed.D., supt. — Fax 793-4476
www.queensburyschool.org/

Barton IS 500/4-5
425 Aviation Rd 12804 518-824-2609
John Luthringer, prin. Fax 824-2681
Queensbury ES 900/K-3
431 Aviation Rd 12804 518-824-1604
Jessica Rossetti, prin. Fax 824-1680
Queensbury MS 800/6-8
455 Aviation Rd 12804 518-824-3610
Michael Brannigan, prin. Fax 824-3682

Queens Village, See New York
NYC Department of Education
Supt. — See New York
Bellaire S 1,000/K-5
20711 89th Ave 11427 718-464-2119
Diana Lagnese, prin. Fax 464-8448
Nuzzi IS 1,100/6-8
21310 92nd Ave 11428 718-465-0651
Karleen Comrie, prin. Fax 264-1246
Public S 18 600/PK-5
8635 235th Ct 11427 718-464-4167
Laurie Careddu, prin. Fax 464-4273
Public S 33 1,000/K-5
9137 222nd St 11428 718-465-6283
Vincent Gatto, prin. Fax 464-7588
Public S 34 600/PK-5
10412 Springfield Blvd 11429 718-465-6818
Pauline Shakespeare, prin. Fax 464-9073
Public S 295 500/PK-8
22214 Jamaica Ave 11428 718-464-1433
Deon Lavigne-Jones, prin.

Incarnation Academy 300/K-8
8915 Francis Lewis Blvd 11427 718-465-5066
Sati Marchan, prin. Fax 464-4128
Our Lady of Lourdes Catholic Academy 300/PK-8
9280 220th St 11428 718-464-1480
Debra Molloy, prin. Fax 740-4091
SS. Joachim & Anne S 500/PK-8
21819 105th Ave 11429 718-465-2230
Linda Freebes, prin. Fax 468-5698

Quogue, Suffolk, Pop. 946
Quogue UFD 100/PK-6
PO Box 957 11959 631-653-4285
Jeffrey Ryvicker, supt. Fax 996-4600
www.quogueschool.com
Quogue ES 100/PK-6
PO Box 957 11959 631-653-4285
Jefrey Ryvicker, prin. Fax 996-4600

Randolph, Cattaraugus, Pop. 1,268
Randolph Central SD 900/PK-12
18 Main St 14772 716-358-7005
Kaine Kelly, supt. Fax 358-7072
www.randolphcsd.org
Chapman ES 500/PK-6
22 Main St 14772 716-358-7030
Kristy Carlson, prin. Fax 358-7060

Ravena, Albany, Pop. 3,205
Ravena-Coeymans-Selkirk Central SD 1,900/PK-12
15 Mountain Rd 12143 518-756-5200
Dr. Brian Bailey, supt. Fax 767-2644
www.rcscsd.org
Ravena-Coeymans-Selkirk MS 400/5-8
2025 US Route 9W 12143 518-756-5200
Pam Black, prin. Fax 756-1988
Other Schools – See Coeymans, Selkirk

Red Creek, Wayne, Pop. 530
Red Creek Central SD 900/K-12
PO Box 190 13143 315-754-2010
David Sholes, supt. Fax 754-8169
www.rccsd.org
Cuyler ES 400/K-5
PO Box 190 13143 315-754-2100
Bridgette Barr, prin. Fax 754-2192
Red Creek MS 200/6-8
PO Box 190 13143 315-754-2070
Matthew Vanorman, prin. Fax 754-2077

Red Hook, Dutchess, Pop. 1,942
Red Hook Central SD 2,000/K-12
9 Mill Rd 12571 845-758-2241
Paul Finch Ed.D., supt. Fax 758-3366
www.redhookcentralschools.org/
Linden Avenue MS 500/6-8
65 W Market St 12571 845-758-2241
Dr. Katie Zahedi, prin. Fax 758-0688
Mill Road ES 400/K-2
9 Mill Rd 12571 845-758-2241
Erin Hayes, prin. Fax 758-0385
Mill Road IS 400/3-5
9 Mill Rd 12571 845-758-2241
Brian Boyd, prin. Fax 758-0289

Rego Park, See New York
NYC Department of Education
Supt. — See New York
Public S 139 900/K-5
9306 63rd Dr 11374 718-459-1044
Natalie Perez-Hernandez, prin. Fax 997-8639
Public S 174 700/PK-5
6510 Dieterle Cres 11374 718-897-7006
Karin Kelly, prin. Fax 897-7254
Public S 175 700/PK-5
6435 102nd St 11374 718-897-8600
Patricia Cooper, prin. Fax 997-8644
Public S 206 600/PK-5
6102 98th St 11374 718-592-0300
Joan Thomas, prin. Fax 271-7011

Our Lady of the Angelus Academy 200/PK-8
9805 63rd Dr 11374 718-896-7220
Ligoria Berkeley-Cummins, prin. Fax 896-5723
Resurrection Ascension Academy 300/PK-8
8525 61st Rd 11374 718-426-4963
JoAnn Heppt, prin. Fax 426-0940

Remsen, Oneida, Pop. 502
Remsen Central SD 400/PK-12
PO Box 406 13438 315-205-4300
Rebecca Dunckel-King, supt. Fax 831-2172
www.remsencsd.org
Remsen ES 200/PK-6
PO Box 406 13438 315-205-4300
Rebecca Dunckel-King, admin. Fax 831-2172

Remsenburg, Suffolk, Pop. 1,851
Remsenburg-Speonk UFD 200/K-6
PO Box 900 11960 631-325-0203
Dr. Ronald Masera, supt. Fax 325-8439
rsufsd.weebly.com
Remsenburg-Speonk ES 200/K-6
PO Box 900 11960 631-325-0203
Dr. Ronald Masera, admin. Fax 325-8439

Rensselaer, Rensselaer, Pop. 9,055
East Greenbush Central SD
Supt. — See East Greenbush
Red Mill ES 400/K-5
225 McCullough Pl 12144 518-207-2660
John Caporta, prin. Fax 449-2480

Rensselaer CSD 1,100/PK-12
25 Van Rensselaer Dr 12144 518-465-7509
Sally Ann Shields, supt. Fax 436-0479
www.rcsd.k12.ny.us
Van Rensselaer ES 700/PK-6
25 Van Rensselaer Dr 12144 518-436-4618
Jeffrey Palmer, prin. Fax 436-4692

Doane Stuart S 300/PK-12
199 Washington Ave 12144 518-465-5222
Pamela Clarke, head sch Fax 465-5230
Woodland Hill Montessori S 200/PK-8
100 Montessori Pl 12144 518-283-5400
Susan Kambrich, head sch Fax 283-4861

Retsof, Livingston, Pop. 330
York Central SD 700/K-12
PO Box 102 14539 585-243-1730
David Furleetti, supt. Fax 243-5269
www.yorkcsd.org
York Central ES 300/K-6
PO Box 102 14539 585-243-1730
Mary Kate Noble, prin. Fax 243-5269

Rexford, Saratoga
Niskayuna Central SD
Supt. — See Schenectady
Glencliff ES 300/K-5
961 Riverview Rd 12148 518-399-2323
Dr. Shelley Baldwin-Nye, prin. Fax 399-4072

Rhinebeck, Dutchess, Pop. 2,623
Rhinebeck Central SD 1,100/K-12
PO Box 351 12572 845-871-5520
Joseph Phelan, supt. Fax 876-4276
www.rhinebeckcsd.org/
Bulkeley MS 300/6-8
PO Box 351 12572 845-871-5500
John Kemnitzer, prin. Fax 871-5553
Livingston ES 400/K-5
PO Box 351 12572 845-871-5570
Brett King, prin. Fax 876-4174

Richfield Springs, Otsego, Pop. 1,252
Richfield Springs Central SD 500/PK-12
PO Box 631 13439 315-858-0610
Tom Piatti, supt. Fax 858-2440
www.richfieldcsd.org
Richfield Springs Central S 500/PK-12
PO Box 631 13439 315-858-0610
Joseph D'Apice, prin. Fax 858-2440

Richmond Hill, See New York
NYC Department of Education
Supt. — See New York
Public S 51 300/PK-1
8745 117th St 11418 718-850-0738
Magdaly St. Juste, prin. Fax 850-0830
Public S 54 600/K-5
8602 127th St 11418 718-849-0962
Anita Prashav, prin. Fax 847-4629
Public S 56 400/2-5
8610 114th St 11418 718-441-4448
Ann Leiter, prin. Fax 805-1538
Public S 62 900/K-5
9725 108th St, S Richmond Hl NY 11419
718-286-4460
Angela O'Dowd, prin. Fax 850-5521
Public S 66 500/PK-5
8511 102nd St 11418 718-849-0184
Helen Desario, prin. Fax 846-6889
Public S 90 900/PK-5
8650 109th St 11418 718-847-3370
Adrienne Ubertini, prin. Fax 847-2965
Public S 161 700/K-5
10133 124th St, S Richmond Hl NY 11419
718-441-5493
Jill Hoder, prin. Fax 441-6202
Public S 254 600/PK-5
8440 101st St 11418 718-846-1840
Pamela Markham, prin. Fax 846-7404
Public S 273, 8807 102nd St 11418 100/PK-2
Brenda Ward, prin. 718-286-8300

Holy Child Jesus Catholic Academy 400/PK-8
11102 86th Ave 11418 718-849-3988
Patricia Winters, prin. Fax 850-2842
Yeshivat Ohr Haiim S 300/PK-8
8606 135th St 11418 718-658-7066
Mordechai Kashani, prin. Fax 658-1022

Richmondville, Schoharie, Pop. 910
Cobleskill-Richmondville Central SD
Supt. — See Cobleskill

Radez ES 400/K-5
319 Main St 12149 518-294-6621
Eric Whipple, prin. Fax 234-3165

Ridge, Suffolk, Pop. 13,175
Longwood Central SD
Supt. — See Middle Island
Ridge ES 700/K-4
105 Ridge Rd 11961 631-345-2765
Janine Rozycki, prin. Fax 345-9289

Ridgewood, See New York
NYC Department of Education
Supt. — See New York
ACE Academy for Scholars 100/K-2
5520 Metropolitan Ave 11385 718-571-6900
Jose Jimenez, prin. Fax 571-6920
Learners and Leaders S 400/PK-3
378 Seneca Ave 11385 718-366-1061
Lynn Botfeld, prin. Fax 366-4301
Public S 68 800/PK-5
5909 Saint Felix Ave 11385 718-821-7246
Ann Marie Snadecky, prin. Fax 497-8945
Public S 71 900/K-5
6285 Forest Ave 11385 718-821-7772
Indiana Soto, prin. Fax 386-7088
Public S 81 1,000/K-5
559 Cypress Ave 11385 718-821-9800
Romy Diamond, prin. Fax 386-7203
Public S 88 1,100/PK-5
6085 Catalpa Ave 11385 718-821-8121
Robert Quintana, prin. Fax 386-7214
Public S 239 700/PK-5
1715 Weirfield St 11385 718-417-2840
Michele Dzwonek, prin. Fax 381-0592
IS 77 1,100/6-8
976 Seneca Ave 11385 718-366-7120
Joseph Miller, prin. Fax 456-9512
IS 93 1,200/6-8
6656 Forest Ave 11385 718-821-4882
Edward Santos, prin. Fax 456-9521

Notre Dame Catholic Academy of Ridgewood 300/PK-8
6222 61st St 11385 718-821-2221
Maria Cuomo, prin. Fax 821-1058
St. Matthias Academy 400/PK-8
5825 Catalpa Ave 11385 718-381-8003
Barbara Wehnes, prin. Fax 381-3519

Ripley, Chautauqua, Pop. 862
Ripley Central SD 200/PK-6
PO Box 688 14775 716-736-2631
Dr. Lauren Ormsby, supt. Fax 736-2010
ripleyelementary.weebly.com
Ripley Central ES 200/PK-6
PO Box 688 14775 716-736-2631
Dr. Lauren Ormsby, admin. Fax 736-2010

Riverdale, See New York

Salanter Akiba Riverdale Academy 800/PK-8
655 W 254th St 10471 718-548-1717
Rabbi Binyamin Krauss, prin. Fax 601-0082

Riverhead, Suffolk, Pop. 12,979
Riverhead Central SD 5,000/K-12
700 Osborn Ave 11901 631-369-6700
Dr. Aurelia Henriquez, supt. Fax 369-6816
www.riverhead.net
Phillips Avenue PS 600/K-4
141 Phillips Ave 11901 631-369-6787
Debra Rodgers, prin. Fax 369-6833
Pulaski Street MS 700/5-6
300 Pulaski St 11901 631-369-6794
David Densieski, prin. Fax 369-7795
Riverhead MS 700/7-8
600 Harrison Ave 11901 631-369-6759
Andrea Pekar, prin. Fax 369-6829
Roanoke Avenue ES 400/K-4
549 Roanoke Ave 11901 631-369-6813
Thomas Payton, prin. Fax 369-6830
Other Schools – See Aquebogue, Calverton

St. Isidore S 200/PK-8
515 Marcy Ave 11901 631-727-1650
Helen Anne Livingston, prin. Fax 727-3945

Rochester, Monroe, Pop. 203,996
Brighton Central SD 3,500/K-12
2035 Monroe Ave 14618 585-242-5200
Dr. Kevin McGowan, supt. Fax 242-5164
www.bcsd.org
Council Rock PS 700/K-2
600 Grosvenor Rd 14610 585-242-5170
Matthew Tappon, prin. Fax 242-5186
French Road ES 800/3-5
488 French Rd 14618 585-242-5140
Allison Rioux, prin. Fax 242-5156
Twelve Corners MS 800/6-8
2643 Elmwood Ave 14618 585-242-5100
Rob Thomas, prin. Fax 242-2540

Churchville-Chili Central SD
Supt. — See Churchville
Chestnut Ridge ES 500/K-4
3560 Chili Ave 14624 585-889-2188
Kimberly Hale, prin. Fax 293-4512

East Irondequoit Central SD 2,900/K-12
600 Pardee Rd 14609 585-339-1210
Susan Allen, supt. Fax 339-1219
www.eastiron.org
Durand-Eastman IS 300/3-5
95 Point Pleasant Rd 14622 585-339-1350
Timothy Roach, prin. Fax 339-1359
East Irondequoit MS 700/6-8
155 Densmore Rd 14609 585-339-1400
Lori Garsin, prin. Fax 339-1409

Green ES 400/K-2
800 Brown Rd 14622 585-339-1310
Teralyn Strauss, prin. Fax 339-1319
Helendale Road PS 400/K-2
220 Helendale Rd 14609 585-339-1330
Eric Daniels, prin. Fax 339-1339
Laurelton/Pardee IS 300/3-5
600 Pardee Rd 14609 585-339-1370
Lucas Hiley, prin. Fax 339-1379

Gates-Chili Central SD 4,100/K-12
3 Spartan Way 14624 585-247-5050
Kimberle Ward, supt. Fax 340-1072
www.gateschili.org
Armstrong ES 500/K-5
3273 Lyell Rd 14606 585-247-3190
Lisa McGary, prin. Fax 340-5550
Brasser ES 300/K-5
1000 Coldwater Rd 14624 585-247-1880
Timothy Young, prin. Fax 340-5577
Disney ES 400/K-5
175 Coldwater Rd 14624 585-247-3151
Elaine Damelio, prin. Fax 340-5567
Gates-Chili MS 1,000/6-8
2 Spartan Way 14624 585-247-5050
Dr. Lisa Buckshaw, prin. Fax 340-5532
Paul Road ES 500/K-5
571 Paul Rd 14624 585-247-2144
Peter Hens, prin. Fax 340-5571

Greece Central SD 10,400/PK-12
750 Maiden Ln 14615 585-966-2000
Kathleen Graupman, supt. Fax 581-8203
www.greececsd.org
Arcadia MS 800/6-8
130 Island Cottage Rd 14612 585-966-3300
Brian Lumb, prin. Fax 966-3339
Athena MS 800/6-8
800 Long Pond Rd 14612 585-966-8800
Jason Fulkerson, prin. Fax 966-4039
Autumn Lane ES 400/PK-2
2089 Maiden Ln 14626 585-966-4700
Tasha Potter, prin. Fax 966-4739
Brookside ES 200/K-5
1144 Long Pond Rd 14626 585-966-4800
Anthony Reale, prin. Fax 966-4839
Buckman Heights ES 300/3-5
550 Buckman Rd 14615 585-966-5900
Anitra Huchzermeier, prin. Fax 966-5939
Craig Hill ES 300/3-5
320 W Craig Hill Dr 14626 585-966-4500
Melissa Pacelli, prin. Fax 966-4539
English Village ES 500/PK-2
800 Tait Ave 14616 585-966-3800
Cheryl Hurst, prin. Fax 966-3839
Holmes Road ES 400/PK-2
300 Holmes Rd 14626 585-966-4900
Kristin Tsang, prin. Fax 966-4939
Lakeshore ES 400/3-5
1200 Latta Rd 14612 585-966-3900
James Palermo, prin. Fax 966-3939
Longridge ES 900/K-5
190 Longridge Ave 14616 585-966-5800
Jason Juszczak, prin. Fax 966-5839
Paddy Hill ES 300/PK-5
1801 Latta Rd 14612 585-966-3700
Susan Streicher, prin. Fax 966-3739
Pine Brook ES 600/K-5
2300 English Rd 14616 585-966-4600
Elizabeth Bolly, prin. Fax 966-4639
West Ridge ES 400/PK-5
1010 English Rd 14616 585-966-3600
Kenneth Merkey, prin. Fax 966-3639

Penfield Central SD 4,400/K-12
2590 Atlantic Ave 14625 585-249-5700
Dr. Thomas K. Putnam Ed.D., supt. Fax 248-8412
www.penfield.edu
Indian Landing ES 400/K-5
702 Landing Rd N 14625 585-249-6900
Marcie Ware, prin. Fax 387-9276
Other Schools – See Penfield

Pittsford Central SD
Supt. — See Pittsford
Allen Creek ES 400/K-5
3188 East Ave 14618 585-267-1200
Michael Biondi, prin. Fax 381-9217

Rochester CSD 28,000/PK-12
131 W Broad St 14614 585-262-8100
Barbara Deane-Williams, supt. Fax 262-8381
www.rcsdk12.org
Northwest JHS at Douglass 300/7-8
940 Fernwood Park 14609 585-324-9289
Barbara Fagan-Zelazny, prin.
Public S 2 400/PK-6
190 Reynolds St 14608 585-235-2820
Sharon Murrell-Dilbert, prin. Fax 464-6174
Public S 3 700/K-8
85 Adams St 14608 585-454-3525
Rodney Moore, prin. Fax 262-8938
Public S 4 400/K-8
198 Dr Samuel McCree Way 14611 585-235-7848
Karon Jackson, prin. Fax 464-6194
Public S 5 600/PK-8
1 Edgerton Park 14608 585-325-2255
Terrilyn Hammond, prin. Fax 262-8959
Public S 7 600/PK-6
31 Bryan St 14613 585-254-3110
David Lincoln, prin. Fax 277-0104
Public S 8 600/PK-8
1180 Saint Paul St 14621 585-262-8888
Laurel Avery-DeToy, prin. Fax 262-8990
Public S 9 700/PK-6
485 Clinton Ave N 14605 585-325-7828
Sharon Jackson, prin. Fax 262-8962
Public S 10, 353 Congress Ave 14619 300/PK-6
Camaron Clyburn, prin. 585-324-2010

Public S 12 700/K-6
999 South Ave 14620 585-461-3280
Dr. Jennifer Gkourlias, prin. Fax 256-8987
Public S 15 300/K-6
595 Upper Falls Blvd 14605 585-262-8830
Jay Piper, prin. Fax 262-8834
Public S 16 500/PK-8
625 Scio St 14605 585-235-1272
Carla Roberts, prin. Fax 464-6188
Public S 17 700/PK-8
158 Orchard St 14611 585-436-2560
Caterina Leone-Mannino, prin. Fax 464-6100
Public S 19 400/PK-8
465 Seward St 14608 585-328-7454
Moniek Silas-Lee, prin. Fax 464-6195
Public S 20 400/PK-6
54 Oakman St 14605 585-325-2920
D'Onnarae Johnson, prin. Fax 262-8885
Public S 22 500/PK-6
950 Norton St 14621 585-467-7160
Clinton Bell, prin. Fax 336-5573
Public S 23 300/PK-6
170 Barrington St 14607 585-473-5099
John Gonzalez, prin. Fax 256-8994
Public S 25 300/PK-6
965 Goodman St N 14609 585-288-3654
Deborah Lazio, prin. Fax 654-1074
Public S 28 500/K-7
595 Upper Falls Blvd 14605 585-482-4836
Susan Ladd, prin. Fax 324-2103
Public S 29 300/PK-6
88 Kirkland Rd 14611 585-328-8228
Joseph Baldino, prin. Fax 464-6196
Public S 33 1,200/PK-6
500 Webster Ave 14609 585-482-9290
Dr. Larry Ellison, prin. Fax 654-1077
Public S 34 500/PK-6
530 Lexington Ave 14613 585-458-3210
Dr. Carmine Peluso, prin. Fax 277-0106
Public S 35 400/K-6
194 Field St 14620 585-271-4583
Anaida Gonzalez-Fortiche, prin. Fax 473-7131
Public S 39 600/PK-6
145 Midland Ave 14621 585-467-8816
Jacquelyn Cox, prin. Fax 336-5575
Public S 41 600/PK-6
279 W Ridge Rd 14615 585-254-4472
Lisa Whitlow, prin. Fax 277-0107
Public S 42 500/PK-6
3330 Lake Ave 14612 585-663-4330
Beverley Pringle, prin. Fax 621-0276
Public S 43 500/PK-6
1305 Lyell Ave 14606 585-458-4200
Richard Smith, prin. Fax 277-0102
Public S 44 400/PK-8
820 Chili Ave 14611 585-328-5272
Donna Andersen, prin. Fax 464-6197
Public S 45 700/PK-8
1445 Clifford Ave 14621 585-325-6945
Rhonda Morien, prin. Fax 262-8037
Public S 46 300/K-6
250 Newcastle Rd 14610 585-288-8008
T'Hani Pantoja, prin. Fax 654-1078
Public S 50 600/PK-8
301 Seneca Ave 14621 585-266-0331
Connie Wehner, prin. Fax 336-5576
Public S 52 400/PK-6
100 Farmington Rd 14609 585-482-9614
Mary Aronson, prin. Fax 654-1079
Public S 53 200/PK-6
625 Scio St 14605 585-325-0935
Dr. Kimberly Harris-Pappin, prin. Fax 324-3709
Public S 54, 36 Otis St 14606 500/K-6
Lessie Hamilton-Rose, prin. 585-254-2080
Public S 57 200/PK-2
15 Costar St 14608 585-277-0190
Roshon Bradley, prin. Fax 277-0108
Wilson Foundation Academy 400/PK-8
200 Genesee St 14611 585-463-4100
Dr. Deasure Matthew, prin. Fax 463-4103
World of Inquiry S 58 700/K-12
200 University Ave 14605 585-325-6170
Sheelarani Webster, prin. Fax 262-8964

Rush-Henrietta Central SD
Supt. — See Henrietta
Crane ES 400/K-3
85 Shell Edge Dr 14623 585-359-5408
Brian Hill, prin. Fax 359-5403
Fyle ES 500/K-3
133 Vollmer Pkwy 14623 585-359-5438
Gina Diesenberg, prin. Fax 359-5433

West Irondequoit Central SD 3,600/K-12
321 List Ave 14617 585-342-5500
Jeffrey Crane, supt. Fax 266-1556
www.westirondequoit.org
Briarwood ES 200/K-3
215 Briarwood Dr 14617 585-336-1610
Kathleen Bush, prin. Fax 336-1611
Brookview ES 200/K-3
300 Brookview Dr 14617 585-336-1630
Alicia Spitz, prin. Fax 336-1631
Colebrook ES 200/K-3
210 Colebrook Dr 14617 585-336-1600
Kathleen Bush, prin. Fax 336-1601
Dake JHS 600/7-8
350 Cooper Rd 14617 585-342-2140
Michelle Cramer, prin. Fax 336-3034
Iroquois MS 400/4-6
150 Colebrook Dr 14617 585-342-3450
Charles Miller, prin. Fax 336-3042
Listwood ES 100/K-3
325 List Ave 14617 585-336-1640
Joyce Nagle, prin. Fax 336-1666
Rogers MS 400/4-6
219 Northfield Rd 14617 585-342-1330
Michelle Flood, prin. Fax 336-3097

Seneca ES 200/K-3
4143 Saint Paul Blvd 14617 585-336-1620
Alicia Spitz, prin. Fax 336-1621
Southlawn ES 200/K-3
455 Rawlinson Rd 14617 585-266-5070
Joyce Nagle, prin. Fax 336-3097

Allendale Columbia S 300/PK-12
519 Allens Creek Rd 14618 585-381-4560
Michael Gee, head sch Fax 383-1191
Bay Knoll S 50/K-8
2639 E Ridge Rd 14622 585-467-2722
Sue Kingman, prin. Fax 467-9722
Derech HaTorah 100/K-8
71 Maiden Ln 14616 585-266-2920
Lea Goldstein, prin. Fax 486-1089
Destiny Christian S 100/PK-12
1876 Elmwood Ave 14620 585-473-1680
Lavonda Lofton, prin. Fax 473-2112
Greece Christian S 200/PK-8
750 Long Pond Rd 14612 585-723-1165
Dr. Herbert Parker, prin. Fax 723-8241
Harley S 500/PK-12
1981 Clover St 14618 585-442-1770
Larry Frye, head sch Fax 442-5758
Hillel Community Day S 100/K-8
191 Fairfield Dr 14620 585-271-6877
Tracie Glazer, head sch Fax 473-8039
Holy Cross S 300/PK-6
4488 Lake Ave 14612 585-663-6533
Mary Martell, prin. Fax 621-4630
Montessori S of Rochester 100/PK-K
220 Idlewood Rd 14618 585-256-2520
Julia Payne-Lewis, head sch Fax 256-3279
Nativity Preparatory Academy 5-8
15 Whalin St 14620 585-271-1633
Maria Cahill, prin. Fax 271-1633
Nazareth ES 200/PK-6
311 Flower City Park 14615 585-458-3786
Sr. Margaret Mancuso, prin. Fax 647-8717
Northstar Christian Academy 300/PK-12
332 Spencerport Rd 14606 585-429-5530
Chris Boshnack, lead tchr. Fax 429-7913
Rochester Christian S 100/PK-8
260 Embury Rd 14625 585-671-4910
Michelle Selvaggio, prin. Fax 671-3676
St. John Neumann S 200/PK-5
31 Empire Blvd 14609 585-288-0580
Jackie Senecal, prin. Fax 288-2612
St. Kateri School 200/PK-5
445 Kings Hwy S 14617 585-467-8730
Sr. Kathleen Lurz, prin. Fax 467-5392
St. Lawrence S 300/PK-5
1000 N Greece Rd 14626 585-225-3870
Frank Arvizzigno, prin. Fax 225-1336
St. Pius X S 300/PK-5
3000 Chili Ave 14624 585-247-5650
Daniel Pitnell, prin. Fax 247-7409
Seton Catholic S 400/PK-6
165 Rhinecliff Dr 14618 585-473-6604
Patty Selig, prin. Fax 473-3347
Siena Catholic Academy 300/6-8
2617 East Ave 14610 585-381-1220
Martin Kilbridge, prin. Fax 381-1223
Trinity Montessori S 200/PK-6
100 Golden Flyer Dr 14618 585-586-1044
Lorraine Scarafile, head sch Fax 586-1821

Rockaway Beach, See New York
NYC Department of Education
Supt. — See New York
Public S 183 500/PK-8
245 Beach 79th St 11693 718-634-9459
Jessica Romero, prin. Fax 634-9458

St. Rose of Lima S 500/PK-8
154 Beach 84th St 11693 718-474-7079
Theresa Andersen, prin. Fax 634-0524

Rockaway Park, See New York
NYC Department of Education
Supt. — See New York
Public S 114 700/K-8
13401 Cronston Ave 11694 718-634-3382
Elizabeth Wolcome, prin. Fax 945-4510
Waterside Children's Studio S 400/PK-5
190 Beach 110th St 11694 718-634-1344
Dana Gerendasi, prin. Fax 634-3884
Waterside S for Leadership 200/6-8
190 Beach 110th St 11694 718-634-1128
Linda Munro, prin. Fax 634-1185

Rockville Centre, Nassau, Pop. 23,734
Rockville Centre UFD 3,500/K-12
128 Shepherd St 11570 516-255-8957
Dr. William H. Johnson, supt. Fax 255-8810
www.rvcschools.org
Hewitt ES 400/K-5
446 Hempstead Ave 11570 516-255-8913
Elizabeth Pryke, prin. Fax 763-1817
Riverside ES 200/K-5
110 Riverside Dr 11570 516-255-8902
Patricia Bock, prin. Fax 763-1812
South Side MS 800/6-8
67 Hillside Ave 11570 516-255-8976
Shelagh McGinn, prin. Fax 763-0914
Watson ES 300/K-5
277 N Centre Ave 11570 516-255-8904
Joan Waldman, prin. Fax 763-1808
Wilson ES 400/K-5
25 Buckingham Rd 11570 516-255-8910
Thomas Ricupero, prin. Fax 763-1806
Other Schools – See South Hempstead

St. Agnes Cathedral S 800/K-8
70 Clinton Ave 11570 516-678-5550
Cecilia St. John, prin. Fax 678-0437

Rocky Point, Suffolk, Pop. 13,836
Rocky Point UFD 3,300/K-12
90 Rocky Point Yaphank Rd 11778 631-744-1600
Dr. Michael Ring, supt. Fax 849-7557
www.rockypointschools.org
Carasiti ES 700/K-2
90 Rocky Point Yaphank Rd 11778 631-744-1601
Virginia Gibbons, prin. Fax 744-1396
Edgar IS 700/3-5
525 Route 25A 11778 631-744-1602
Linda Towlen, prin. Fax 744-4898
Rocky Point MS 800/6-8
76 Rocky Point Yaphank Rd 11778 631-744-1603
Dr. Scott O'Brien Ed.D., prin. Fax 886-0000

Rome, Oneida, Pop. 32,943
Rome CSD 5,400/PK-12
409 Bell Rd S 13440 315-338-6500
Peter Blake, supt. Fax 334-7409
www.romecsd.org
Bellamy ES 500/K-4
7118 Brennon Ave 13440 315-338-5261
Nancy Opperman, prin. Fax 334-7472
Denti ES 500/K-4
1001 Ruby St 13440 315-338-5371
Sherry Lubey, prin. Fax 334-7528
Gansevoort ES 400/K-4
758 W Liberty St 13440 315-334-5181
Wendy Waters, prin. Fax 334-7352
Joy ES 200/K-4
110 W Linden St 13440 315-334-1261
Andria Lacey, prin. Fax 334-7362
Ridge Mills ES 200/K-4
7841 Ridge Mills Rd 13440 315-334-1281
Sheila Spencer, prin. Fax 334-7382
Rome ECC 200/PK-PK
409 Bell Rd S 13440 315-334-1250
Nancy Kristl, dir. Fax 334-7371
Staley Upper ES 800/5-6
620 E Bloomfield St 13440 315-338-5302
Julie Kimmel-Gorman, prin. Fax 338-5306
Stokes ES 300/K-4
9095 Turin Rd 13440 315-334-1221
Karen Miller, prin. Fax 334-7399
Strough MS 700/7-8
801 Laurel St 13440 315-338-5201
Tracy O'Rourke, prin. Fax 334-7465

Rome Catholic S 300/PK-6
400 Floyd Ave 13440 315-336-6190
Patty Bliss, prin. Fax 336-6194

Romulus, Seneca, Pop. 400
Romulus Central SD 400/PK-12
5705 State Route 96 14541 866-810-0345
Martin Rotz, supt. Fax 869-5961
www.romuluscsd.org
Romulus Central ES 200/PK-6
5705 State Route 96 14541 866-810-0345
Christopher Puylara, prin. Fax 869-5961

Ronkonkoma, Suffolk, Pop. 18,816
Connetquot Central SD
Supt. — See Bohemia
Cherokee Street ES 600/K-5
130 Cherokee St 11779 631-467-6027
Jill Lahey, prin. Fax 467-6166
Duffield ES 400/K-5
600 1st St 11779 631-467-6010
Lisa Farrell, prin. Fax 467-6326
Ronkonkoma MS 700/6-8
501 Peconic St 11779 631-467-6000
Charles Morea, prin. Fax 467-6003
Slocum ES 400/K-5
2460 Sycamore Ave 11779 631-467-6040
John Delio, prin. Fax 467-6446

Sachem Central SD 12,100/K-12
51 School St 11779 631-471-1336
Dr. Kenneth Graham, supt. Fax 471-1341
www.sachem.edu
Other Schools – See Farmingville, Holbrook, Holtsville, Lake Grove, Lake Ronkonkoma

---

St. Joseph S 300/PK-8
25 Church St 11779 631-588-4760
Richard Kuntzler, prin. Fax 588-0543

Roosevelt, Nassau, Pop. 15,891
Roosevelt UFD 3,000/PK-12
240 Denton Pl 11575 516-345-7000
Dr. Marnie Hazelton, supt. Fax 345-7326
www.rooseveltufsd.org
Byas ES 500/PK-6
60 Underhill Ave 11575 516-345-7500
Angela Hudson, prin. Fax 345-7590
Centennial Avenue ES 600/PK-6
140 W Centennial Ave 11575 516-345-7400
Dr. Barbara Solomon, prin. Fax 345-7490
Roosevelt MS 400/7-8
335 E Clinton Ave 11575 516-345-7700
Dr. Jeremiah Sumter, prin. Fax 345-7791
Washington Rose ES 700/PK-6
2 Rose Ave 11575 516-345-7600
Clyde Braswell, prin. Fax 345-7690

Roscoe, Sullivan, Pop. 539
Roscoe Central SD 300/PK-12
PO Box 429 12776 607-498-4126
John Evans, supt. Fax 498-5609
www.roscoe.k12.ny.us
Roscoe Central S 300/PK-12
PO Box 429 12776 607-498-4126
Janice Phillips, prin. Fax 498-6015

Rosedale, See New York
NYC Department of Education
Supt. — See New York
Parks S 700/K-8
23315 Merrick Blvd 11422 718-341-8280
Chaybonne Harper, prin. Fax 341-5589
Public S 38 200/K-5
13521 241st St 11422 718-528-2276
Julia Soussis, prin. Fax 712-1598
Public S 138 800/PK-8
25111 Weller Ave 11422 718-528-9053
James McEnaney, prin. Fax 723-5670
Public S 195 700/PK-5
25350 149th Ave 11422 718-723-0313
Beryl Bailey, prin. Fax 723-7826

St. Clare S 300/PK-8
13725 Brookville Blvd 11422 718-528-7174
Mary Rafferty-Basile, prin. Fax 528-4389

Roslyn, Nassau, Pop. 2,718
Roslyn UFD 3,100/PK-12
PO Box 367 11576 516-801-5000
Allison Brown, supt. Fax 801-5008
www.roslynschools.org
Other Schools – See Greenvale, Roslyn Heights

Buckley Country Day S 300/PK-8
2 I U Willets Rd 11576 516-627-1910
Dr. Jean-Marc Juhel Ph.D., hdmstr. Fax 627-8627

Roslyn Heights, Nassau, Pop. 6,383
East Williston UFD
Supt. — See Old Westbury
Willets Road MS 400/5-7
455 I U Willets Rd 11577 516-333-8797
Stephen Kimmel, prin. Fax 333-8915

Roslyn UFD
Supt. — See Roslyn
East Hills ES 500/2-5
400 Round Hill Rd 11577 516-801-5300
Melissa Krieger, prin. Fax 801-5308
Heights S 300/PK-1
240 Willow St 11577 516-801-5500
Regina Colardi, prin. Fax 801-5508
Roslyn MS 800/6-8
375 Locust Ln 11577 516-801-5200
Craig Johanson, prin. Fax 801-5208

Rouses Point, Clinton, Pop. 2,191
Northeastern Clinton Central SD
Supt. — See Champlain
Rouses Point ES 200/K-5
80 Maple St 12979 518-297-7211
Heidi Sample, prin. Fax 298-4293

Roxbury, Delaware
Roxbury Central SD 300/PK-12
53729 State Highway 30 12474 607-326-4151
Thomas O'Brien, supt. Fax 326-4154
www.roxburycs.org
Roxbury Central S 300/PK-12
53729 State Highway 30 12474 607-326-4151
Jill Ten Eyck, prin. Fax 326-4154

Rush, Monroe
Rush-Henrietta Central SD
Supt. — See Henrietta
Leary ES 600/K-3
5509 E Henrietta Rd 14543 585-359-5468
Jennifer Tomalty, prin. Fax 359-5463

Rushville, Ontario, Pop. 661
Marcus Whitman Central SD 1,200/K-12
4100 Baldwin Rd 14544 585-554-4848
Jeramy Clingerman, supt. Fax 554-4882
www.mwcsd.org
Middlesex Valley PS 200/K-2
149 State Route 245 14544 585-554-3115
Bonnie Cazer, prin. Fax 554-6172
Whitman MS 300/6-8
4100 Baldwin Rd 14544 585-554-6442
Dr. Clayton Cole, prin. Fax 554-3414
Other Schools – See Stanley

Rye, Westchester, Pop. 15,489
Rye CSD 3,300/K-12
411 Theodore Fremd Ste 100S 10580 914-967-6100
Dr. Eric Byrne, supt. Fax 967-6957
www.ryeschools.org
Midland ES 600/K-5
312 Midland Ave 10580 914-967-6100
James Boylan, prin. Fax 921-6848
Milton ES 400/K-5
12 Hewlett St 10580 914-967-6100
Dr. JoAnne Nardone, prin. Fax 921-2796
Osborn ES 600/K-5
10 Osborn Rd 10580 914-967-6100
Angela Garcia, prin. Fax 921-3842
Rye MS 700/6-8
3 Parsons St 10580 914-967-6100
Dr. Ann Edwards, prin. Fax 921-6189

Resurrection S 500/PK-8
116 Milton Rd 10580 914-967-1218
Sr. Anne Massell, prin. Fax 925-3511
Rye Country Day S 900/PK-12
3 Cedar St 10580 914-967-1417
Scott Nelson, hdmstr. Fax 967-1418

Rye Brook, Westchester, Pop. 9,207
Blind Brook-Rye UFD 1,500/K-12
390 N Ridge St 10573 914-937-3600
Dr. Jonathan Ross, supt. Fax 937-5871
www.blindbrook.org
Blind Brook MS 400/6-8
840 King St 10573 914-937-3600
Todd Richard, prin. Fax 937-4509
Ponterio Ridge Street ES 600/K-5
390 N Ridge St 10573 914-937-3600
Tracy Taylor, prin. Fax 937-1265

Sackets Harbor, Jefferson, Pop. 1,431
Sackets Harbor Central SD 500/K-12
PO Box 290 13685 315-646-3575
Jennifer Gaffney, supt. Fax 646-1038
www.sacketspatriots.org
Sackets Harbor Central S 500/K-12
PO Box 290 13685 315-646-3575
Carrie Tibbles, prin. Fax 646-1038

Sagaponack, Suffolk, Pop. 308
Sagaponack Common SD 50/K-3
PO Box 1500 11962 631-537-0651
Alan Van Cott, supt. Fax 537-2342
www.sagaponackschool.com
Sagaponack S 50/K-3
PO Box 1500 11962 631-537-0651
Alan Van Cott, admin. Fax 537-2342

Sag Harbor, Suffolk, Pop. 2,139
Sag Harbor UFD 1,100/PK-12
200 Jermain Ave 11963 631-725-5300
Catherine Barber-Graves, supt. Fax 725-5330
www.sagharborschools.org
Sag Harbor ES 500/PK-5
68 Hampton St 11963 631-725-5301
Matthew Malone, prin. Fax 899-3744

Saint Albans, See New York
NYC Department of Education
Supt. — See New York
Public S 36 500/K-5
18701 Foch Blvd 11412 718-528-1862
Lynn Staton, prin. Fax 723-6928
Public S 134 500/PK-5
20302 109th Ave 11412 718-464-5544
Randi Marino, prin. Fax 464-7779
Public S 136 600/PK-5
20115 115th Ave 11412 718-465-2286
Tanya Walker, prin. Fax 464-0040
IS 192 500/6-8
10989 204th St 11412 718-479-5540
Harriett Diaz, prin. Fax 217-4645
PS 360 100/PK-1
199-10 112th Ave 11412 718-776-7370
Rachel Thomas, prin. Fax 776-7380

Saint James, Suffolk, Pop. 13,215
Smithtown Central SD
Supt. — See Smithtown
Mills Pond ES 500/K-5
246 Moriches Rd 11780 631-382-4300
Ireen Westrack, prin. Fax 382-4304
Nesaquake MS 800/6-8
479 Edgewood Ave 11780 631-382-5100
Daniel McCabe, prin. Fax 382-5107
Saint James ES 700/K-5
580 Lake Ave 11780 631-382-4450
Mary Grace Lynch, prin. Fax 382-4456

Harbor Country Day S 100/PK-8
17 Three Sisters Rd 11780 631-584-5555
John Cissel, head sch Fax 862-7664
SS. Philip & James S 300/PK-8
359 Clinton Ave 11780 631-584-7896
Ruth Ellen Testa, prin. Fax 584-3258

Saint Johnsville, Montgomery, Pop. 1,719
Oppenheim-Ephratah-St. Jhnsvll Cntrl SD 400/PK-12
44 Center St 13452 518-568-2011
David Halloran, supt. Fax 568-2797
www.oesj.org
Oppenheim-Ephratah-St. Johnsville ES 200/PK-6
6486 State Highway 29 13452 518-568-2014
Jeanine Kawryga, prin. Fax 568-2941

Saint Regis Falls, Franklin, Pop. 456
Saint Regis Falls Central SD 300/PK-12
PO Box 309 12980 518-856-9421
Wayne Walbridge, supt. Fax 856-0142
stregisfallscsd.org
Saint Regis Falls S 300/PK-12
PO Box 309 12980 518-856-9421
Lorraine Childs, prin. Fax 856-0142

Salamanca, Cattaraugus, Pop. 5,605
Salamanca City Central SD 1,300/PK-12
50 Iroquois Dr 14779 716-945-2400
Robert Breidenstein, supt. Fax 945-3964
www.salamancany.org/
Prospect ES 500/PK-3
300 Prospect Ave 14779 716-945-5170
Gayle Pavone, prin. Fax 945-2374
Seneca ES 300/4-6
25 Center St 14779 716-945-5140
Michelle Siebert, prin. Fax 945-3567

Salem, Washington, Pop. 930
Salem Central SD 500/K-12
PO Box 517 12865 518-854-7855
Dr. David Glover, supt. Fax 854-3957
salemcsd.org
Salem ES 200/K-6
PO Box 517 12865 518-854-9505
Sharon Varney, prin. Fax 854-3957

Sanborn, Niagara, Pop. 1,620
Niagara-Wheatfield Central SD
Supt. — See Niagara Falls
Town MS 900/6-8
2292 Saunders Settlement Rd 14132 716-215-3150
Jordan Schmidt, prin. Fax 215-3160
West Street ES 500/K-5
5700 West St 14132 716-215-3200
Theron Mong, prin. Fax 215-3216

Sandy Creek, Oswego, Pop. 769
Sandy Creek Central SD 800/PK-12
PO Box 248 13145 315-387-3445
Kyle Faulkner, supt. Fax 387-2196
www.sccs.cnyric.org/

Sandy Creek ES 400/PK-5
PO Box 248 13145 315-387-3445
Timothy Filiatrault, prin. Fax 387-2196
Sandy Creek MS 200/6-8
PO Box 248 13145 315-387-3445
Carolyn Shirley, prin. Fax 387-2196

Saranac, Clinton
Saranac Central SD
Supt. — See Dannemora
Saranac ES 400/K-5
PO Box 8 12981 518-565-5900
Tracy Manor, prin. Fax 565-5890
Saranac MS 300/6-8
PO Box 8 12981 518-565-5700
Katie Francisco, prin. Fax 565-5706

Saranac Lake, Franklin, Pop. 5,317
Saranac Lake Central SD 1,300/K-12
79 Canaras Ave 12983 518-891-5460
Diane Fox, supt. Fax 891-5140
saranaclakecs.org
Petrova ES 400/K-5
79 Canaras Ave 12983 518-891-4221
Bryan Munn, prin. Fax 891-6548
Saranac Lake MS 300/6-8
79 Canaras Ave 12983 518-891-4221
Bruce VanWeelden, prin. Fax 891-6615
Other Schools – See Bloomingdale

St. Bernard S 50/K-5
63 River St 12983 518-891-2830
Raymond Dora, prin. Fax 891-4619

Saratoga Springs, Saratoga, Pop. 26,062
Saratoga Springs CSD 6,500/K-12
3 Blue Streak Blvd 12866 518-583-4700
Dr. Michael Piccirillo, supt. Fax 584-6624
www.saratogaschools.org
Caroline Street ES 400/K-5
310 Caroline St 12866 518-584-7612
Dr. Daniel Packard, prin. Fax 583-3696
Division Street ES 400/K-5
220 Division St 12866 518-583-4794
Dr. Greer Miller, prin. Fax 583-4722
Geyser Road ES 400/K-5
61 Geyser Rd 12866 518-584-7699
Kristy Moore, prin. Fax 583-4733
Lake Avenue ES 400/K-5
126 Lake Ave 12866 518-584-3678
Dr. Barbara Messier, prin. Fax 583-4778
Maple Ave MS 1,600/6-8
515 Maple Ave 12866 518-587-4551
Dr. Jeffrey Palmer, prin Fax 587-5759
Nolan ES 800/K-5
221 Jones Rd 12866 518-584-7383
Dana Bush, prin. Fax 583-4726
Other Schools – See Greenfield Center

St. Clement's Regional Catholic S 300/PK-5
231 Lake Ave 12866 518-584-7350
Jane Kromm, prin. Fax 587-2623
Waldorf S of Saratoga Springs 200/PK-12
122 Regent St 12866 518-587-0549
Anne Maguire, admin. Fax 581-1682

Saugerties, Ulster, Pop. 3,876
Saugerties Central SD 2,200/K-12
PO Box A 12477 845-247-6550
Seth Turner, supt. Fax 246-8364
www.saugerties.k12.ny.us
Cahill ES 300/K-6
PO Box A 12477 845-247-6800
Dawn Scannapieco, prin. Fax 246-4302
Morse ES 300/K-6
PO Box A 12477 845-247-6960
Donald Dieckmann, prin. Fax 246-4184
Mount Marion ES 300/K-6
PO Box A 12477 845-247-6920
Carole Kelder, prin. Fax 246-4103
Other Schools – See Glasco

Woodstock Day S 200/PK-12
1430 Glasco Tpke 12477 845-246-3744
Kara Stern, head sch Fax 246-0053

Sauquoit, Oneida
Sauquoit Valley Central SD 900/K-12
2601 Oneida St 13456 315-839-6311
Ronald Wheelock, supt. Fax 839-5352
www.svcsd.org
Sauquoit Valley ES 400/K-5
2601 Oneida St 13456 315-839-6339
Mark Putnam, prin. Fax 839-6366
Sauquoit Valley MS 200/6-8
2601 Oneida St 13456 315-839-6371
Peter Madden, prin. Fax 839-6390

Savona, Steuben, Pop. 819
Campbell-Savona Central SD
Supt. — See Campbell
Campbell-Savona ES 500/PK-6
64 E Lamoka Ave 14879 607-527-9800
James Anderson, prin. Fax 527-9866

Sayville, Suffolk, Pop. 16,715
Sayville UFD 3,100/K-12
99 Greeley Ave 11782 631-244-6510
Dr. John Stimmel, supt. Fax 244-6504
www.sayvilleschools.org
Lincoln Avenue ES 500/K-5
440 Lincoln Ave 11782 631-244-6725
Dr. Michele LeBlanc, prin. Fax 244-6507
Sayville MS 700/6-8
291 Johnson Ave 11782 631-244-6650
Thomas Murray, prin. Fax 244-6655
Sunrise Drive ES 400/K-5
320 Sunrise Dr 11782 631-244-6750
Dr. James Foy, prin. Fax 244-6509

Other Schools – See West Sayville

Scarsdale, Westchester, Pop. 16,786
Eastchester UFD
Supt. — See Eastchester
Greenvale ES 600/2-5
1 Gabriel Resicgno Dr 10583 914-793-6130
Darrell Stinchcomb, prin. Fax 793-9006

Edgemont UFD 1,900/K-12
300 White Oak Ln 10583 914-472-7768
Dr. Victoria S. Kniewel, supt. Fax 472-6846
www.edgemont.org
Greenville ES 500/K-6
100 Glendale Rd 10583 914-472-7760
Jennifer Allen, prin. Fax 472-7785
Seely Place ES 500/K-6
51 Seely Pl 10583 914-472-8040
Carol Bartlik, prin. Fax 472-3512

Scarsdale UFD 4,800/K-12
2 Brewster Rd Ste 2 10583 914-721-2410
Dr. Thomas Hagerman, supt. Fax 722-2822
www.scarsdaleschools.k12.ny.us
Edgewood ES 400/K-5
1 Roosevelt Pl 10583 914-721-2700
Dr. Scott Houseknecht, prin. Fax 721-2717
Fox Meadow ES 500/K-5
59 Brewster Rd 10583 914-721-2720
Duncan Wilson, prin. Fax 721-2730
Greenacres ES 400/K-5
41 Huntington Rd 10583 914-721-2740
Sharon Hill, prin. Fax 721-2755
Heathcote ES 400/K-5
26 Palmer Ave 10583 914-721-2760
Maria Stile, prin. Fax 721-2777
Quaker Ridge ES 400/K-5
125 Weaver St 10583 914-721-2780
Dr. Felix Gil, prin. Fax 721-2784
Scarsdale MS 1,100/6-8
134 Mamaroneck Rd 10583 914-721-2600
Meghan Troy, prin. Fax 721-2655

Immaculate Heart of Mary S 300/PK-8
201 Boulevard 10583 914-723-5608
Teresa Sopot, prin. Fax 723-8004

Schaghticoke, Rensselaer, Pop. 588
Hoosic Valley Central SD 700/K-12
2 Pleasant Ave 12154 518-753-4450
Amy Goodell, supt. Fax 753-7665
www.hoosicvalley.k12.ny.us
Hoosic Valley ES 300/K-6
22 Pleasant Ave 12154 518-753-4491
Mark Foti, prin. Fax 753-7576

Schenectady, Schenectady, Pop. 59,889
Guilderland Central SD
Supt. — See Guilderland Center
Lynnwood ES 400/K-5
8 Regina Dr 12303 518-355-7930
Alicia Rizzo, prin. Fax 356-3087
Pine Bush ES 400/K-5
3437 Carman Rd 12303 518-357-2770
Christopher Sanita, prin. Fax 356-3172

Mohonasen Central SD 2,800/K-12
2072 Curry Rd 12303 518-356-8200
Dr. Kathleen Spring, supt. Fax 356-8247
www.mohonasen.org
Bradt PS 600/K-2
2719 Hamburg St 12303 518-356-8400
Leslie Smith, prin. Fax 356-8404
Draper MS 700/6-8
2070 Curry Rd 12303 518-356-8350
Rick Arket, prin. Fax 356-8359
Pinewood IS 600/3-5
901 Kings Rd 12303 518-356-8430
Jason Thompson, prin. Fax 356-8434

Niskayuna Central SD 4,100/K-12
1239 Van Antwerp Rd 12309 518-377-4666
Dr. Cosimo Tangorra Ed.D., supt. Fax 377-4074
www.niskyschools.org
Birchwood ES 300/K-5
897 Birchwood Ln 12309 518-344-2910
Debra Berndt, prin. Fax 785-3776
Craig ES 400/K-5
2566 Balltown Rd 12309 518-377-0156
Dr. William Anders, prin. Fax 377-1075
Hillside ES 300/K-5
1100 Cornelius Ave 12309 518-377-1856
Dr. Shireen Fasciglione, prin. Fax 377-1099
Iroquois MS 600/6-8
2495 Rosendale Rd 12309 518-377-2233
Vicki Wyld, prin. Fax 377-2219
Rosendale ES 400/K-5
2445 Rosendale Rd 12309 518-377-3123
Joseph Dicaprio, prin. Fax 377-1098
Van Antwerp MS 400/6-8
2253 Story Ave 12309 518-370-1243
Luke Rakoczy, prin. Fax 370-4610
Other Schools – See Rexford

Schalmont Central SD 1,800/K-12
4 Sabre Dr 12306 518-355-9200
Carol Pallas, supt. Fax 355-9203
www.schalmont.org
Jefferson ES 600/K-4
100 Princetown Rd 12306 518-355-1342
Joby Gifford, prin. Fax 357-0293
Schalmont MS 600/5-8
2 Sabre Dr 12306 518-355-6255
Scott Ziomek, prin. Fax 355-5329

Schenectady CSD 8,400/PK-12
108 Education Dr 12303 518-370-8100
Laurence Spring, supt. Fax 370-8173
www.schenectady.k12.ny.us
Central Park MS 300/6-8
421 Elm St 12304 518-370-8250
Tamara Thorpe-Odom, prin. Fax 881-3602
Hamilton ES 500/PK-6
1091 Webster St 12303 518-881-3720
Michelle Vanderlinden, prin. Fax 881-3722
Howe ES 300/PK-5
90 Elmer Ave 12308 518-370-8295
Susan Gorman, admin. Fax 881-3542
Keane ES 300/PK-5
1252 Albany St 12304 518-881-3960
John Sardos, prin. Fax 881-3961
King ES 400/PK-5
918 Stanley St 12307 518-370-8360
Nicola DiLeva, prin. Fax 370-8363
Lincoln ES 300/PK-5
2 Robinson St 12304 518-370-8355
Laura Buzas, prin. Fax 395-3576
Mont Pleasant MS 800/6-8
1121 Forest Rd 12303 518-370-8160
Jeffery Bennett, prin. Fax 881-3562
Oneida MS 700/6-8
1529 Oneida St 12308 518-370-8260
Tony Farina, admin. Fax 370-8277
Paige ES 300/PK-5
104 Elliott Ave 12304 518-370-8300
Deborah MacDerment, prin. Fax 881-3522
Pleasant Valley ES 400/PK-5
1097 Forest Rd 12303 518-881-3640
Sean Inglee, prin. Fax 881-3642
Van Corlaer ES 400/PK-5
2310 Guilderland Ave 12306 518-370-8270
Mariann Bellai, prin. Fax 881-3742
Woodlawn ES 400/PK-5
3311 Wells Ave 12304 518-370-8280
John Perreault, prin. Fax 370-8283
Yates ES 300/PK-5
725 Salina St 12308 518-370-8320
Robert Flanders, prin. Fax 881-3862
Zoller ES 300/PK-5
1880 Lancaster St 12308 518-370-8290
Patricia Doyle, prin. Fax 370-8291

Brown S 200/PK-8
150 Corlaer Ave 12304 518-370-0366
Patti Vitale, head sch Fax 370-1514
St. Kateri Tekakwitha Parish S 300/PK-5
1801 Union St 12309 518-382-8225
Tosha Burnie-Grimmer, prin. Fax 374-8522
St. Madeleine Sophie S 200/PK-5
3510 Carman Rd 12303 518-355-3080
Kelly Sloan, prin. Fax 355-3106

Schenevus, Otsego, Pop. 543
Schenevus Central SD 300/K-12
159 Main St 12155 607-638-5881
Thomas Jennings, supt. Fax 638-5600
www.schenevuscs.org/
Schenevus Central S 300/K-12
159 Main St 12155 607-638-5881
Thomas Jennings, prin. Fax 638-5600

Schoharie, Schoharie, Pop. 912
Schoharie Central SD 800/K-12
PO Box 430 12157 518-295-6600
David Blanchard, supt. Fax 295-8178
www.schoharie.k12.ny.us
Schoharie ES 400/K-6
PO Box 430 12157 518-295-6652
Andrea Polikoski, prin. Fax 295-9506

Schroon Lake, Essex, Pop. 817
Schroon Lake Central SD 200/PK-12
PO Box 338 12870 518-532-7164
Stephen Gratto, supt. Fax 532-0284
www.schroonschool.org
Schroon Lake Central S 200/PK-12
PO Box 338 12870 518-532-7164
Stephen Gratto, admin. Fax 532-0284

Schuylerville, Saratoga, Pop. 1,376
Schuylerville Central SD 1,700/K-12
14 Spring St 12871 518-695-3255
Ryan Sherman Ed.D., supt. Fax 695-6491
www.schuylervilleschools.org
Schuylerville ES 700/K-5
14 Spring St 12871 518-695-3255
Gregg Barthelmas, prin. Fax 695-6405
Schuylerville MS 400/6-8
14 Spring St 12871 518-695-3255
Mary Kate Elsworth, prin. Fax 695-6491

Scio, Allegany, Pop. 604
Scio Central SD 400/PK-12
3968 Washington St 14880 585-593-5076
Gregory L. Hardy, supt. Fax 593-3468
www.scio.wnyric.org
Scio Central S 400/PK-12
3968 Washington St 14880 585-593-5510
Dawn Race, prin. Fax 593-0653

Scotia, Schenectady, Pop. 7,607
Burnt Hills-Ballston Lake Central SD
Supt. — See Burnt Hills
Pashley ES 400/K-5
30 Pashley Rd 12302 518-399-9141
Jill Bonacio, prin. Fax 399-0534

Scotia-Glenville Central SD 2,500/K-12
900 Preddice Pkwy 12302 518-382-1215
Susan Swartz, supt. Fax 386-4336
www.sgcsd.net
Glendaal ES 200/K-5
774 Sacandaga Rd 12302 518-382-1201
Thomas Eagan, prin. Fax 382-1203

Glen-Worden ES — 200/K-5
30 Worden Rd 12302 — 518-346-0469
Mark McCarthy, prin. — Fax 346-0855
Lincoln ES — 300/K-5
40 Albion St 12302 — 518-382-1296
John Geniti, prin. — Fax 386-2808
Sacandaga ES — 400/K-5
300 Wren St 12302 — 518-382-1282
Tonya Federico, prin. — Fax 386-4311
Scotia-Glenville MS — 600/6-8
10 Prestige Pkwy 12302 — 518-382-1263
Robert Cosmer, prin. — Fax 386-4303

Mekeel Christian Academy — 300/PK-12
36-38 Sacandaga Rd 12302 — 518-370-4272
W. Chad Bowman, head sch — Fax 370-4778

Scottsville, Monroe, Pop. 1,964
Wheatland-Chili Central SD — 700/K-12
13 Beckwith Ave 14546 — 585-889-6246
Dr. Deborah Leh, supt. — Fax 889-6284
www.wheatland.k12.ny.us
Connor ES — 300/K-5
13 Beckwith Ave 14546 — 585-889-6298
Margaret Wright, prin. — Fax 889-8227

Sea Cliff, Nassau, Pop. 4,948
North Shore Central SD — 2,700/K-12
112 Franklin Ave 11579 — 516-277-7800
Dr. Peter Giarrizzo, supt. — Fax 277-7801
www.northshoreschools.org
Sea Cliff ES — 300/K-5
280 Carpenter Ave 11579 — 516-277-7500
Christopher Zublionis, prin. — Fax 277-7501
Other Schools – See Glen Head

Seaford, Nassau, Pop. 15,154
Levittown UFD
Supt. — See Levittown
East Broadway ES — 700/K-5
751 Seamans Neck Rd 11783 — 516-434-7425
Jeanmarie Wink, prin. — Fax 785-5186

Seaford UFD — 2,300/K-12
1600 Washington Ave 11783 — 516-592-4010
Dr. Adele Pecora, supt. — Fax 592-4049
www.seaford.k12.ny.us
Seaford Harbor ES — 600/K-5
3500 Bayview St 11783 — 516-592-4180
Thomas Burke, prin. — Fax 592-4101
Seaford Manor ES — 400/K-5
1590 Washington Ave 11783 — 516-592-4080
Debra Emmerich, prin. — Fax 592-4051
Seaford MS — 500/6-8
3940 Sunset Ave 11783 — 516-592-4280
Dan Smith, prin. — Fax 592-4201

Maria Regina S — 400/PK-8
4045 Jerusalem Ave 11783 — 516-541-1229
Leona Arpino, prin. — Fax 541-1235
St. William the Abbot S — 600/PK-8
2001 Jackson Ave 11783 — 516-785-6784
Elizabeth Bricker, prin. — Fax 785-2752

Selden, Suffolk, Pop. 19,540
Middle Country Central SD
Supt. — See Centereach
Bicycle Path Pre-K/K Center — 500/PK-K
27 N Bicycle Path 11784 — 631-285-8800
Lisa Contarino, prin. — Fax 285-8801
Hawkins Path ES — 300/1-5
485 Hawkins Rd 11784 — 631-285-8530
Adam Frankel, prin. — Fax 285-8531
New Lane Memorial ES — 900/1-5
15 New Ln 11784 — 631-285-8900
Dr. Brian Doelger Ed.D., prin. — Fax 285-8901
Stagecoach ES — 400/1-5
205 Dare Rd 11784 — 631-285-8730
Shaun Rothberg, prin. — Fax 285-8731

Selkirk, Albany
Ravena-Coeymans-Selkirk Central SD
Supt. — See Ravena
Becker ES — 500/PK-5
1146 US Route 9W 12158 — 518-756-5200
Debra Neubart, prin. — Fax 767-2512

Seneca Falls, Seneca, Pop. 6,593
Seneca Falls Central SD — 1,200/K-12
PO Box 268 13148 — 315-568-5500
Robert McKeveny, supt. — Fax 712-0535
www.sfcs.k12.ny.us/
Knight ES — 300/K-2
98 Clinton St 13148 — 315-568-5500
Janet Clendenen, prin. — Fax 712-0527
Seneca Falls MS — 300/6-8
95 Troy St 13148 — 315-568-5500
Kevin Rhinehart, prin. — Fax 712-0524
Stanton ES — 300/3-5
38 Garden St 13148 — 315-568-5500
Amy Hibbard, prin. — Fax 712-0526

Setauket, Suffolk, Pop. 15,248
Three Village Central SD
Supt. — See Stony Brook
Nassakeag ES — 600/K-6
490 Pond Path 11733 — 631-730-4400
Gail Casciano, prin. — Fax 730-4403
Setauket ES — 700/K-6
134 Main St 11733 — 631-730-4600
Kristin Rimmer, prin. — Fax 730-4604

Sharon Springs, Schoharie, Pop. 550
Sharon Springs Central SD — 300/K-12
PO Box 218 13459 — 518-284-2266
Patterson Green, supt. — Fax 284-9033
www.sharonsprings.org/
Sharon Springs Central S — 300/K-12
PO Box 218 13459 — 518-284-2267
Patterson Green, prin. — Fax 284-9075

Shelter Island, Suffolk, Pop. 1,316
Shelter Island UFD — 200/PK-12
PO Box 2015 11964 — 631-749-0302
Dr. Christine Finn, supt. — Fax 749-1262
www.shelterisland.k12.ny.us
Shelter Island S — 200/PK-12
PO Box 2015 11964 — 631-749-0302
Dr. Christine Finn, supt. — Fax 749-1262

Sherburne, Chenango, Pop. 1,358
Sherburne-Earlville Central SD — 1,300/K-12
15 School St 13460 — 607-674-7300
Eric Schnabl, supt. — Fax 674-9742
www.secsd.org
Sherburne-Earlville ES — 600/K-5
15 School St 13460 — 607-674-7336
Antoinette Halliday, prin. — Fax 674-9742
Sherburne-Earlville MS — 300/6-8
13 School St 13460 — 607-674-7350
Jolene Emhof, prin. — Fax 674-7392

Sherman, Chautauqua, Pop. 717
Sherman Central SD — 400/PK-12
PO Box 950 14781 — 716-761-6122
Michael V. Ginestre, supt. — Fax 761-6119
shermancsd.org
Sherman ES — 200/PK-6
PO Box 950 14781 — 716-761-6121
Bryna Booth, prin. — Fax 761-6119

Sherrill, Oneida, Pop. 3,051
Vernon-Verona-Sherrill Central SD
Supt. — See Verona
McAllister ES — 300/PK-6
217 Kinsley St 13461 — 315-363-3080
James Rozwod, prin. — Fax 361-4783

Shirley, Suffolk, Pop. 27,288
William Floyd UFD
Supt. — See Mastic Beach
Floyd ES — 700/K-5
111 Lexington Rd 11967 — 631-874-1258
Dr. Keith Fasciana, prin. — Fax 874-1637
Hobart ES — 800/K-5
230 Van Buren St 11967 — 631-874-1295
James Westcott, prin. — Fax 874-1618
Woodhull ES — 700/K-5
6 Francis Landau Pl 11967 — 631-874-1301
Monica Corona, prin. — Fax 874-1804

Shoreham, Suffolk, Pop. 528
Shoreham-Wading River Central SD — 1,800/K-12
250B Route 25A 11786 — 631-821-8100
Gerard Poole, supt. — Fax 929-3001
www.swrschools.org
Miller Avenue ES — 100/K-2
3 Miller Ave 11786 — 631-821-8232
Christine Carlson, prin. — Fax 821-8249
Prodell MS — 600/6-8
100 Randall Rd 11786 — 631-821-8212
Kevin Vann, prin. — Fax 821-8275
Other Schools – See Wading River

Shortsville, Ontario, Pop. 1,429
Manchester-Shortsville Central SD — 800/PK-12
1506 State Route 21 14548 — 585-289-3964
Charlene Dehn, supt. — Fax 289-6660
www.redjacket.org
Red Jacket ES — 400/PK-5
1506 State Route 21 14548 — 585-289-9647
Jeffrey McCarthy, prin. — Fax 289-4499
Red Jacket MS — 200/6-8
1506 State Route 21 14548 — 585-289-3967
Karen Hall, prin. — Fax 289-8715

Shrub Oak, Westchester, Pop. 1,970
Lakeland Central SD — 5,900/K-12
1086 E Main St 10588 — 914-245-1700
Dr. George Stone, supt. — Fax 245-1589
www.lakelandschools.org
Other Schools – See Crompond, Mohegan Lake, Yorktown Heights

St. Elizabeth Ann Seton S — 300/PK-8
1375 E Main St 10588 — 914-528-3563
Sr. Brian Donahue, prin. — Fax 528-0341

Sidney, Delaware, Pop. 3,846
Sidney Central SD — 900/K-12
95 W Main St 13838 — 607-563-2135
William Christensen, supt. — Fax 563-2386
www.sidneycsd.org
Sidney ES — 500/K-6
15 Pearl St E 13838 — 607-561-7701
Robert Hanson, prin. — Fax 563-9257

Silver Creek, Chautauqua, Pop. 2,618
Silver Creek Central SD — 1,100/PK-12
1 Dickinson St 14136 — 716-934-2603
Todd Crandall, admin. — Fax 934-7983
www.silvercreekschools.org
Silver Creek ES — 500/PK-5
1 Dickinson St 14136 — 716-934-2603
Merrie Maxon, prin. — Fax 934-2173
Silver Creek MS — 200/6-8
1 Dickinson St 14136 — 716-934-2603
Eleanor Payne, prin. — Fax 934-3760

Sinclairville, Chautauqua, Pop. 578
Cassadaga Valley Central SD — 1,000/PK-12
PO Box 540 14782 — 716-962-5155
Charles Leichner, supt. — Fax 962-5976
cvweb.wnyric.org
Sinclairville ES — 400/PK-5
PO Box 540 14782 — 716-962-5195
Joshua Gilevski, prin. — Fax 962-5468

Skaneateles, Onondaga, Pop. 2,428
Skaneateles Central SD — 1,500/K-12
55 East St 13152 — 315-291-2221
Kenneth Slentz, supt. — Fax 685-0347
www.skanschools.org
Skaneateles MS — 300/6-8
35 East St 13152 — 315-291-2241
Michael Caraccio, prin. — Fax 291-2267
State Street IS — 300/3-5
72 State St 13152 — 315-291-2261
Christopher Goncalves, prin. — Fax 291-2256
Waterman PS — 300/K-2
55 East St 13152 — 315-291-2351
Christopher Goncalves, prin. — Fax 291-2302

Slate Hill, Orange
Minisink Valley Central SD — 4,000/K-12
PO Box 217 10973 — 845-355-5100
Brian Monahan, supt. — Fax 355-5119
www.minisink.com
Minisink Valley ES — 500/K-2
PO Box 217 10973 — 845-355-5270
Colleen Fitzgerald, prin. — Fax 355-5147
Minisink Valley IS — 500/3-5
PO Box 217 10973 — 845-355-5250
Paul Dombal, prin. — Fax 355-5252
Minisink Valley MS — 1,000/6-8
PO Box 217 10973 — 845-355-5200
Michael Larsen, prin. — Fax 355-5205
Other Schools – See Otisville

Slaterville Springs, Tompkins
Ithaca CSD
Supt. — See Ithaca
Caroline ES — 300/PK-5
2439 Slaterville Rd 14881 — 607-539-7155
Mary Grover, prin. — Fax 539-6966

Sleepy Hollow, Westchester, Pop. 9,977
Pocantico Hills Central SD — 300/PK-8
599 Bedford Rd 10591 — 914-631-2440
Carol Conklin-Spillane, supt. — Fax 631-3280
www.pocanticohills.org
Pocantico Hills Central S — 300/PK-8
599 Bedford Rd 10591 — 914-631-2440
Brent Harrington, prin. — Fax 631-3280

Tarrytown UFD — 2,700/PK-12
200 N Broadway 10591 — 914-631-9404
Christopher Borsari, supt. — Fax 332-6283
www.tufsd.org
Morse ES — 400/1-2
30 Pocantico St 10591 — 914-631-4144
Thomas Holland, prin. — Fax 332-4267
Sleepy Hollow MS — 600/6-8
210 N Broadway 10591 — 914-332-6275
Joshua Whitham, prin. — Fax 332-6546
Other Schools – See Tarrytown

Sloan, Erie, Pop. 3,611
Cheektowaga-Sloan UFD — 1,400/PK-12
166 Halstead Ave 14212 — 716-891-6402
Andrea Galenski, supt. — Fax 891-6435
www.sloanschools.org
Wilson ES — 300/3-5
166 Halstead Ave 14212 — 716-891-6418
Carolyn Segal, prin. — Fax 892-6956
Other Schools – See Cheektowaga

Sloatsburg, Rockland, Pop. 2,991
Suffern Central SD
Supt. — See Hillburn
Sloatsburg ES — 200/K-5
11 2nd St 10974 — 845-753-2720
Joseph Lloyd, prin. — Fax 753-6636

Smithtown, Suffolk, Pop. 27,100
Hauppauge UFD
Supt. — See Hauppauge
Forest Brook ES — 400/K-5
299 Lilac Ln 11787 — 631-265-3265
Kristen Reingold, prin. — Fax 265-3673
Pines ES — 500/K-5
22 Holly Dr 11787 — 631-543-8700
Dr. Claudine DiMuzio, prin. — Fax 543-3632

Smithtown Central SD — 10,000/K-12
26 New York Ave 11787 — 631-382-2000
James J. Grossane Ed.D., supt. — Fax 382-2010
www.smithtown.k12.ny.us
Accompsett ES — 600/K-5
1 Lincoln St 11787 — 631-382-4155
Jeanne Kull-Minarik, prin. — Fax 382-4157
Accompsett MS — 700/6-8
660 Meadow Rd 11787 — 631-382-2300
Paul McNeil, prin. — Fax 382-2307
Dogwood ES — 400/K-5
50 Dogwood Dr 11787 — 631-382-4250
Renee Carpenter, prin. — Fax 382-4256
Mt. Pleasant ES — 500/K-5
33 Plaisted Ave 11787 — 631-382-4350
Joseph Ierano, prin. — Fax 382-4356
Smithtown ES — 500/K-5
51 Lawrence Ave 11787 — 631-382-4500
Janine Lavery, prin. — Fax 382-4507
Other Schools – See Nesconset, Saint James

Ivy League S — 200/PK-8
211 Brooksite Dr 11787 — 631-265-4177
Ismael Colon, prin. — Fax 265-4698
St. Patrick S — 500/PK-8
284 E Main St 11787 — 631-724-0285
Barbara Pelireto, prin. — Fax 265-4841
Smithtown Christian S — 500/PK-12
1 Higbie Dr 11787 — 631-265-3334
Rev. Larry Falco M.A., supt. — Fax 265-1079

Snyder, Erie

Christ the King S 300/PK-8
2 Lamarck Dr 14226 716-839-0473
Samuel Zalacca, prin. Fax 568-8198
Park S of Buffalo 300/PK-12
4625 Harlem Rd 14226 716-839-1242
Christopher Lauricella, head sch Fax 839-2014

Sodus, Wayne, Pop. 1,754
Sodus Central SD 800/PK-12
PO Box 220 14551 315-483-5201
Nelson Kise, supt. Fax 483-4755
www.soduscsd.org
Sodus ES 300/PK-3
PO Box 220 14551 315-483-5282
Michael Sereno, prin. Fax 483-5292
Sodus IS 200/4-6
PO Box 220 14551 315-483-5281
Dr. Ellen Lloyd, prin. Fax 483-5291

Solvay, Onondaga, Pop. 6,416
Solvay UFD 1,500/K-12
PO Box 980 13209 315-468-1111
Jay Tinklepaugh, supt. Fax 468-2755
www.solvayschools.org
Solvay ES 400/K-3
701 Woods Rd 13209 315-488-5422
Matthew Carpenter, prin. Fax 484-1417
Other Schools – See Syracuse

Somers, Westchester
Somers Central SD 3,300/K-12
250 Route 202 10589 914-277-2400
Dr. Raymond Blanch, supt. Fax 277-2409
www.somersschools.org/
Somers IS 800/3-5
240 Route 202 10589 914-277-4344
Stacey Elconin, prin. Fax 277-3168
Somers MS 800/6-8
250 Route 202 10589 914-277-3399
Jeffrey Getman, prin. Fax 277-2236
Other Schools – See Lincolndale

Southampton, Suffolk, Pop. 3,057
Southampton UFD 1,600/PK-12
70 Leland Ln 11968 631-591-4500
Nicholas Dyno Ed.D., supt. Fax 287-2870
www.southamptonschools.org
Southampton ES 600/PK-4
30 Pine St 11968 631-591-4800
Dr. Jamie Bottcher, prin. Fax 283-6891
Southampton IS 400/5-8
70 Leland Ln 11968 631-591-4700
Timothy Frazier, prin. Fax 283-0899

Tuckahoe Common SD 400/PK-8
468 Magee St 11968 631-283-3550
Dr. Allan Gerstenlauer, supt. Fax 283-3469
www.tuckahoecommonsd.com
Tuckahoe S 400/PK-8
468 Magee St 11968 631-283-3550
Arlette Sicari, prin. Fax 283-3469

Our Lady of the Hamptons Regional S 400/PK-8
160 N Main St 11968 631-283-9140
Sr. Kathryn Schlueter, prin. Fax 287-3958

South Dayton, Chautauqua, Pop. 607
Pine Valley Central SD 600/PK-12
7755 Route 83 14138 716-988-3293
Scott Payne, supt. Fax 988-3243
www.pval.org
Pine Valley ES 300/PK-6
7755 Route 83 14138 716-988-3291
Kelly Zimmerman, prin. Fax 988-3864

South Fallsburg, Sullivan, Pop. 2,810

Zichron Moshe S 50/PK-12
PO Box 580 12779 845-434-5240
Rabbi Ephraim Sher, prin. Fax 434-1009

South Glens Falls, Saratoga, Pop. 3,492
South Glens Falls Central SD 3,100/PK-12
6 Bluebird Rd 12803 518-793-9617
Michael Patton Ed.D., supt. Fax 761-0723
www.sgfcsd.org
Harrison Avenue ES 400/K-5
76 Harrison Ave 12803 518-793-9048
Carla Biviano, prin. Fax 793-9095
Moreau ES 300/PK-5
76 Bluebird Rd 12803 518-793-9044
Rebecca Toleman, prin. Fax 793-9561
Tanglewood ES 400/K-5
60 Tanglewood Dr 12803 518-793-5631
Matt Conrick, prin. Fax 793-9241
Winch MS 700/6-8
99 Hudson St 12803 518-792-5891
Tim Dawkins, prin. Fax 793-9505
Other Schools – See Wilton

South Hempstead, Nassau, Pop. 3,194
Rockville Centre UFD
Supt. — See Rockville Centre
Covert ES 300/K-5
379 Willow St 11550 516-255-8916
Darren Raymar, prin. Fax 538-3165

South Huntington, Suffolk, Pop. 9,264

Long Island S for the Gifted 300/PK-9
165 Pidgeon Hill Rd 11746 631-423-3557
Dr. Patricia Geyer, head sch Fax 423-4368

South Kortright, Delaware
South Kortright Central SD 400/PK-12
PO Box 113 13842 607-538-9111
Patricia Norton-White, supt. Fax 538-9205
www.skcs.org/pages/South_Kortright_Central_School
South Kortright Central S 400/PK-12
PO Box 113 13842 607-538-9111
Krislynn Dengler, prin. Fax 538-9205

Southold, Suffolk, Pop. 5,696
Southold UFD 800/K-12
PO Box 470 11971 631-765-5400
David Gamberg, supt. Fax 765-5086
www.southoldufsd.com
Southold ES 400/K-6
PO Box 470 11971 631-765-5208
Ellen Waldron-O'Neill, prin. Fax 765-6893

South Otselic, Chenango
Otselic Valley Central SD 300/PK-12
PO Box 161 13155 315-653-7218
Daniel Henner, supt. Fax 653-7500
www.ovcs.org
Otselic Valley S 300/PK-12
PO Box 161 13155 315-653-7218
Warren Smith, prin. Fax 653-7500

South Ozone Park, See New York
NYC Department of Education
Supt. — See New York
Hawtree Creek MS 100/6-8
12110 Rockaway Blvd 11420 718-659-3792
Dr. Maureen Hussey, prin. Fax 659-3798
Public S 45 400/PK-6
12628 150th St, Jamaica NY 11436 718-529-1885
Samantha Severin, prin. Fax 322-8287
Public S 96 300/PK-5
13001 Rockaway Blvd 11420 718-529-2547
Vivian Eweka, prin. Fax 659-0113
Public S 100 1,000/K-5
11111 118th St 11420 718-843-8390
Laureen Fromberg, prin. Fax 641-2474
Public S 108 1,500/PK-5
10810 109th Ave 11420 718-558-2700
Jennifer Iovine, prin. Fax 558-2701
Public S 121 800/PK-5
12610 109th Ave 11420 718-738-5126
Evelyn Vadi, prin. Fax 843-5584
Public S 123 700/PK-5
14501 119th Ave, Jamaica NY 11436 718-529-4300
Anthony Hooks, prin. Fax 529-4290
Public S 124 1,300/K-8
12915 150th Ave 11420 718-529-2580
Maritza Jones, prin. Fax 322-4039
Public S 155 600/PK-5
13002 115th Ave 11420 718-529-0767
Gregory Jacobs, prin. Fax 529-0773
JHS 226 1,200/6-8
12110 Rockaway Blvd 11420 718-843-2260
Rushell White, prin. Fax 835-6317

Al-Ihsan Academy 400/PK-12
PO Box 200215 11420 718-322-3154
Br. Refeek Mohamed, prin. Fax 322-7069
Our Lady of Perpetual Help S 600/PK-8
11110 115th St 11420 718-843-4184
Frances DeLuca, prin. Fax 843-6838
Our Lady's Catholic Academy 300/K-8
12518 Rockaway Blvd 11420 718-641-0212
Kevin Coyne, prin. Fax 641-8079
Our Lady's Catholic Academy 200/K-8
10955 128th St 11420 718-641-1316
Kevin Coyne, prin. Fax 843-0769

South Salem, Westchester
Katonah-Lewisboro UFD
Supt. — See Cross River
Meadow Pond ES 300/K-5
185 Smith Ridge Rd 10590 914-763-7900
Carolann Castellono, prin. Fax 763-7986

Speculator, Hamilton, Pop. 321
Lake Pleasant Central SD 100/PK-9
PO Box 140 12164 518-548-7571
Heather Philo, supt. Fax 548-3230
lpschool.com
Lake Pleasant Central S 100/PK-9
PO Box 140 12164 518-548-7571
Heather Philo, admin. Fax 548-3230

Spencer, Tioga, Pop. 744
Spencer-Van Etten Central SD 900/PK-12
16 Dartts Xrd 14883 607-589-7100
Dr. Joseph Morgan, supt. Fax 589-3010
www.svecsd.org/
Spencer-Van Etten MS 300/5-8
1 Center St 14883 607-589-7120
Eric Knolles, prin. Fax 589-3020
Other Schools – See Van Etten

North Spencer Christian Academy 100/PK-12
721 Ithaca Rd 14883 607-589-6366
Fax 589-4455

Spencerport, Monroe, Pop. 3,553
Spencerport Central SD 3,700/K-12
71 Lyell Ave 14559 585-349-5000
Daniel Milgate, supt. Fax 349-5011
www.spencerportschools.org
Bernabi ES 400/K-5
1 Bernabi Rd 14559 585-349-5400
David Caiazza, prin. Fax 349-5466
Canal View ES 500/K-5
1 Ranger Rd 14559 585-349-5700
Carol Robinson, prin. Fax 349-5766
Cosgrove MS 800/6-8
2749 Spencerport Rd 14559 585-349-5300
Ned Dale, prin. Fax 349-5346
Munn ES 300/K-5
2333 Manitou Rd 14559 585-349-5500
Michael Canny, prin. Fax 349-5566
Taylor ES 400/K-5
399 Ogden Parma Town Line 14559 585-349-5600
Monica Macaluso, prin. Fax 349-5666

Springfield Gardens, See New York
NYC Department of Education
Supt. — See New York
Public S 15 500/PK-5
12115 Lucas St 11413 718-525-1670
Antonio K'Tori, prin. Fax 723-7613
Public S 156 500/K-8
22902 137th Ave 11413 718-528-9173
Estelle Moore, prin. Fax 723-7720
Public S 181 400/PK-5
14815 230th St 11413 718-528-5807
Dina Wheeler, prin. Fax 723-7825
Public S 251 300/K-3
14451 Arthur St 11413 718-276-2745
Relda Grant, prin. Fax 723-7822
Queens United MS 100/6-8
22902 137th Ave 11413 718-723-3501
Richard Roder, prin. Fax 723-3507
IS 59 600/6-8
13255 Ridgedale St 11413 718-527-3501
Carleton Gordon, prin. Fax 276-1364

Spring Valley, Rockland, Pop. 30,786
East Ramapo Central SD 7,900/K-12
105 S Madison Ave 10977 845-577-6000
Deborah Wortham, supt. Fax 577-6168
www.ercsd.org/pages/East_Ramapo_CSD
ECC 700/K-K
465 Viola Rd 10977 845-577-6585
Jacqueline Polanco, prin. Fax 577-6370
Hempstead ES 300/K-4
80 Brick Church Rd 10977 845-577-6270
Hazel Ortiz, prin. Fax 362-0627
Kakiat ES 400/4-8
465 Viola Rd 10977 845-577-6100
Jennifer Wilmoth, prin. Fax 426-1059
Other Schools – See Chestnut Ridge, Monsey, New City, Suffern

---

Bas Mikroh Girls S 300/PK-8
381 Viola Rd 10977 845-352-5296
Bnos Esther Pupa 300/PK-12
246 N Main St 10977 845-371-1220
Rabbi Ernest Schwartz, prin.
Cheder Chabad of Monsey 10977 300/PK-8
Libby Steiner, admin. 845-356-1213
Fax 290-9616
Cheder Chabad of Monsey - Boys 1-8
15 Widman Ct 10977 845-356-1213
Cong Machzikei Hadas of Beltz S 300/K-8
PO Box 57 10977 845-425-0909
Eliyohu Grossman, admin. Fax 425-5590
Talmud Torah Khal Adas Yereim 200/K-8
33 Union Rd 10977 845-425-5678
Lazar Katz, admin. Fax 425-5725
United Talmudical Academy 1,700/K-12
89 S Main St 10977 845-425-0392
Yidel Spitzer, admin. Fax 352-7253
Yeshiva Avir Yaakov 3,100/PK-12
766 N Main St 10977 845-362-6600
Rabbi Eluzer Moschel, admin. Fax 354-6809
Yeshiva Bais Hachinuch 100/3-8
50A S Main St Ste 8 10977 845-354-3805
Jordan Most, dir. Fax 354-3806
Yeshiva Degel Hatorah 300/K-12
PO Box 213 10977 845-356-4610
Rabbi Moshe Schwab, prin. Fax 356-4507
Yeshiva Eitz Chaim 50/PK-8
15 Widman Ct 10977 845-425-3623
Sarah Eidlitz, dir. Fax 548-2117
Yeshiva Machzikei Hadas Belz 300/K-9
3 N Cole Ave 10977 845-425-0909
Yeshiva Tzoin Yosef-Pupa 400/PK-12
15 Widman Ct 10977 845-371-1220
Ernest Schwartz, prin. Fax 371-1237

Springville, Erie, Pop. 4,257
Springville-Griffith Inst. Central SD 1,800/K-12
307 Newman St 14141 716-592-3230
Kimberly Moritz, supt. Fax 592-3209
www.springvillegi.org
Griffith Institute MS 500/6-8
267 Newman St 14141 716-592-3203
Shanda Duclon, prin. Fax 592-3268
Springville ES 600/K-5
283 North St 14141 716-592-3204
Christopher Scarpine, prin. Fax 592-3264
Other Schools – See Colden

St. Aloysius Regional S 100/PK-8
186 Franklin St 14141 716-592-7002
Mary Beth Webster, prin. Fax 592-4032

Stamford, Delaware, Pop. 1,103
Stamford Central SD 300/K-12
1 River St 12167 607-652-7301
Dr. Glen Huot, supt. Fax 652-3446
www.stamfordcs.org
Stamford Central S 300/K-12
1 River St 12167 607-652-7301
Dr. Patrick Sweeney, prin. Fax 652-3446

Stanfordville, Dutchess
Pine Plains Central SD
Supt. — See Pine Plains
Cold Spring Early Learning Center 100/PK-1
358 Homan Rd 12581 845-868-7451
James Glynn, prin. Fax 868-1105

Stanley, Ontario
Marcus Whitman Central SD
Supt. — See Rushville
Gorham IS 300/3-5
2705 State Route 245 14561 585-526-6351
Dr. Susan Wissick, prin. Fax 526-4435

Star Lake, Saint Lawrence, Pop. 799
Clifton-Fine Central SD 300/PK-12
11 Hall Ave 13690 315-848-3333
Regina Yeo, supt. Fax 848-3350
www.cliftonfine.org
Clifton-Fine ES 200/PK-6
11 Hall Ave 13690 315-848-3333
Rebecca Bascom, prin. Fax 848-3350

Staten Island, See New York
NYC Department of Education
Supt. — See New York
Eagle Academy for Young Men 6-8
101 Warren St 10304 718-727-6201
Jermaine Cameron, prin.
Esselborn S 700/PK-5
330 Durant Ave 10308 718-987-8020
Beth Albano, prin. Fax 987-3675
Fort Hill Collaborative ES K-5
80 Monroe Ave 10301 718-420-5115
Jennifer Gonzalez Funes, prin.
Grimm S for Leadership & Sustainability 100/PK-1
644 Bloomingdale Rd 10309 718-668-8640
Lisa Sarnicola, prin. Fax 668-8645
Harbor View S 100/PK-1
300 Richmond Ter 10301 718-390-2190
Carol Mongiello, prin. Fax 390-2195
Marsh Ave S for Expeditionary Learning 400/6-8
100 Essex Dr 10314 718-370-6850
Cara DeAngelo, prin. Fax 370-6860
Naples Street ES 100/PK-1
1055 Targee St 10304 718-876-4610
Deanna Marco, prin.
Petrides S 1,300/K-12
715 Ocean Ter 10301 718-815-0186
Joanne Buckheit, prin. Fax 815-9638
Public S 1 500/PK-5
58 Summit St 10307 718-984-0960
Grace Silverstein, prin. Fax 984-3389
Public S 3 1,000/PK-5
80 S Goff Ave 10309 718-984-1021
Elmer Myers, prin. Fax 984-3628
Public S 4 800/PK-5
200 Nedra Pl 10312 718-984-1197
Suzanne Dimitri, prin. Fax 984-2324
Public S 5 200/K-5
348 Deisius St 10312 718-984-2233
Lisa Arcuri, prin. Fax 984-4761
Public S 6 800/PK-5
555 Page Ave 10307 718-697-3760
Elizabeth Waters, prin. Fax 697-3761
Public S 8 500/PK-5
112 Lindenwood Rd 10308 718-356-2800
Lisa Esposito, prin. Fax 356-2065
Public S 11 300/PK-5
50 Jefferson St 10304 718-979-1030
Erica Mattera, prin. Fax 979-0259
Public S 13 900/PK-5
191 Vermont Ave 10305 718-447-1462
Paul Martuccio, prin. Fax 447-8681
Public S 16 700/PK-5
80 Monroe Ave 10301 718-447-0124
Michele Ramos, prin. Fax 447-5398
Public S 18 600/PK-5
221 Broadway 10310 718-442-0216
Robert Rodriguez, prin. Fax 720-1558
Public S 19 600/K-5
780 Post Ave 10310 718-442-3860
Lynette Cartagena, prin. Fax 815-2862
Public S 20 500/K-5
161 Park Ave 10302 718-442-4110
Marie Munoz, prin. Fax 815-2228
Public S 21 400/K-5
168 Hooker Pl 10302 718-442-1520
Anthony Cosentino, prin. Fax 815-3149
Public S 22 1,000/PK-5
1860 Forest Ave 10303 718-442-2219
Melissa Donath, prin. Fax 815-3104
Public S 23 500/PK-5
30 Natick St 10306 718-351-1155
Paul Proscia, prin. Fax 667-4958
Public S 26 200/PK-5
4108 Victory Blvd 10314 718-698-1530
Laura Kump, prin. Fax 494-2907
Public S 29 800/PK-5
1581 Victory Blvd 10314 718-556-4400
Linda Manfredi, prin. Fax 556-4429
Public S 30 800/PK-5
200 Wardwell Ave 10314 718-442-0462
Alan Ihne, prin. Fax 442-4265
Public S 31 500/PK-5
55 Layton Ave 10301 718-273-3500
Daniel Singleton, prin. Fax 815-4826
Public S 32 800/PK-5
32 Elverton Ave 10308 718-984-1688
Nancy Spataro-Bellocch, prin. Fax 227-5736
Public S 35 400/K-5
60 Foote Ave 10301 718-442-3037
Melissa Garofalo, prin. Fax 815-4855
Public S 36 900/PK-5
255 Ionia Ave 10312 718-984-1422
Barbara Bellafatto, prin. Fax 227-6354
Public S 38 300/PK-5
421 Lincoln Ave 10306 718-351-1225
Nancy Murillo, prin. Fax 979-2487
Public S 39 600/PK-5
71 Sand Ln 10305 718-447-4543
Tracey Wright, prin. Fax 447-0500
Public S 42 900/PK-5
380 Genesee Ave 10312 718-984-3800
Brian Sharkey, prin. Fax 227-6358
Public S 44 900/PK-5
80 Maple Pkwy 10303 718-442-0433
Kasandra Garcia, prin. Fax 442-2323
Public S 45 900/K-5
58 Lawrence Ave 10310 718-442-6123
Christine Chavez, prin. Fax 442-4141
Public S 46 300/PK-5
41 Reid Ave 10305 718-987-5155
Andrea Maffeo, prin. Fax 987-1703
Public S 48 600/K-5
1055 Targee St 10304 718-447-8323
Jacqueline Mammolito, prin. Fax 815-3956
Public S 50 900/PK-5
200 Adelaide Ave 10306 718-987-0396
Joseph Santello, prin. Fax 987-1925
Public S 52 500/PK-5
450 Buel Ave 10305 718-351-5454
Jane McCord, prin. Fax 667-8900
Public S 54 800/PK-5
1060 Willowbrook Rd 10314 718-698-0600
Karen Catanzarolarosa, prin. Fax 698-1736
Public S 55 700/PK-5
54 Osborne St 10312 718-356-2211
Sharon Fishman, prin. Fax 356-0114
Public S 56 700/PK-5
250 Kramer Ave 10309 718-605-1189
Philip Carollo, prin. Fax 605-1195
Public S 57 700/PK-5
140 Palma Dr 10304 718-447-1191
Karyn Lind, prin. Fax 720-0747
Public S 60 900/PK-5
55 Merrill Ave 10314 718-761-3325
Donna Bonanno, prin. Fax 983-8534
Public S 65 400/PK-5
98 Grant St 10301 718-981-5034
Sophie Scarmadella, prin. Fax 981-6109
Public S 69 900/K-5
144 Keating Pl 10314 718-698-6661
Doreen Murphy, prin. Fax 698-1903
Public S 74 300/PK-3
211 Daniel Low Ter 10301 718-727-5380
Nicole Reid-Christopher, prin. Fax 727-5386
Public S 78, 100 Tompkins Ave 10304 PK-2
Louis Bruschi, prin. 718-442-3064
Space Shuttle Columbia S 800/PK-5
77 Marsh Ave 10314 718-761-2155
Michael LaMorte, prin. Fax 761-7384
IS 2 900/6-8
333 Midland Ave 10306 718-987-5336
Adrienne Stallone, prin. Fax 987-6937
IS 7 1,200/6-8
1270 Huguenot Ave 10312 718-697-8488
Dr. Nora DeRosa, prin. Fax 967-0809
IS 24 1,400/6-8
225 Cleveland Ave 10308 718-982-4700
Lenny Santamaria, prin. Fax 356-5834
IS 27 1,100/6-8
11 Clove Lake Pl 10310 718-981-8800
Matthew Barone, prin. Fax 815-4677
IS 34 1,100/6-8
528 Academy Ave 10307 718-477-4500
John Boyle, prin. Fax 227-4074
IS 49 800/6-8
101 Warren St 10304 718-727-6040
James DeFrancesco, prin. Fax 876-8207
IS 51 1,100/6-8
20 Houston St 10302 718-981-0502
Nicholas Mele, prin. Fax 815-3957
IS 61 1,200/6-8
445 Castleton Ave 10301 718-727-8481
Susan Tronolone, prin. Fax 447-2112
IS 72 1,200/6-8
33 Ferndale Ave 10314 718-698-5757
Peter Macellari, prin. Fax 761-5928
IS 75 1,300/6-8
455 Huguenot Ave 10312 718-356-0130
Kenneth Zapata, prin. Fax 984-5302
PS 68 PK-2
1625 Forest Ave 10302 718-816-3377
Lorrie Morgan, prin. Fax 816-3378
Staten Island S for Civic Leadership 800/PK-8
280 Regis Dr 10314 718-697-5250
Donna Nilsen, prin. Fax 697-5260
Vierno ES 700/PK-5
216 Clawson St 10306 718-351-6777
Jennifer Logan, prin. Fax 667-8200

Academy of St. Dorothy S 300/PK-8
1305 Hylan Blvd 10305 718-351-0939
Sr. Sharon McCarthy, prin. Fax 351-0661
Blessed Sacrament S 500/PK-8
830 Delafield Ave 10310 718-442-3090
Joseph Cocozello, prin. Fax 442-9654
Eltingville Lutheran S 100/PK-8
300 Genesee Ave 10312 718-356-7811
Deborah Cortez, prin. Fax 967-8892
Gateway Academy 100/PK-8
200 Boscombe Ave 10309 718-966-8695
Christopher DeSanctis, head sch Fax 948-2241
Holy Rosary S 300/PK-8
100 Jerome Ave 10305 718-447-1195
Ann Major, prin. Fax 815-5862
Jewish Foundation S of Staten Island 400/PK-8
400 Caswell Ave 10314 718-983-6042
Rabbi Netanel Gralla, dean Fax 370-2591
New Dorp Christian Academy 100/PK-8
259 Rose Ave 10306 718-351-4442
Mark Rawnsley, prin. Fax 351-1765
Notre Dame Academy 200/PK-8
78 Howard Ave 10301 718-273-9096
Rebecca Signorelli, prin. Fax 273-1093
Oakdale Academy 200/2-5
366 Oakdale St 10312 718-948-4220
Deborah Wallach, dir. Fax 356-0221
Our Lady Help of Christians S 300/PK-8
23 Summit St 10307 718-984-1360
Nicholas Fargione, prin. Fax 966-9356
Our Lady of Good Counsel S 300/PK-8
42 Austin Pl 10304 718-447-7260
Tara Hynes, prin. Fax 447-8639
Our Lady of Mt. Carmel St. Benedicta S 200/PK-8
285 Clove Rd 10310 718-981-5131
Stephen Sanchez, prin. Fax 981-0027
Our Lady Queen of Peace S 600/PK-8
22 Steele Ave 10306 718-351-0970
Theresa Signorile, prin. Fax 351-0950
Our Lady Star of the Sea S 800/PK-8
5411 Amboy Rd 10312 718-984-5750
Jeannine Roland, prin. Fax 984-1346
Rabbi Jacob Joseph S for Boys 200/PK-8
3495 Richmond Rd 10306 718-979-6333
Rabbi Sharir Yablonsky, admin. Fax 979-5152
Rabbi Jacob Joseph S for Girls 200/PK-8
400 Caswell Ave 10314 718-982-8745
Esther Akerman, prin. Fax 982-8796
Sacred Heart S 200/PK-8
301 N Burgher Ave 10310 718-442-0347
Celeste Catalano, prin. Fax 442-6978
St. Adalbert S 300/PK-8
355 Morningstar Rd 10303 718-442-2020
Diane Hesterhagen, prin. Fax 447-2012
St. Ann S 200/K-8
125 Cromwell Ave 10304 718-351-4343
Bernadette Ficchi, prin. Fax 987-3117
St. Charles S 700/PK-8
200 Penn Ave 10306 718-987-0200
John Kiernan, prin. Fax 987-8158
St. Christopher S 200/PK-8
15 Lisbon Pl 10306 718-351-0902
Catherine Falabella, prin. Fax 351-0975
St. Clare S 600/K-8
151 Lindenwood Rd 10308 718-984-7091
Theresa Signorile, prin. Fax 227-5052
St. John's Lutheran S 200/PK-8
663 Manor Rd 10314 718-761-1858
Kelly Speiser, prin. Fax 761-4962
St. John Villa Academy 200/PK-8
57 Cleveland Pl 10305 718-447-2668
James Smith, prin. Fax 447-2079
St. Joseph Hill Academy 500/PK-8
850 Hylan Blvd 10305 718-981-1187
Lawrence Hansen, prin. Fax 448-7016
St. Patrick S 500/K-8
3560 Richmond Rd 10306 718-979-8815
Vincent Sadowski, prin. Fax 979-4984
St. Peter-St. Paul S 200/PK-8
129 Clinton Ave 10301 718-447-1796
Jennifer Olivera, prin. Fax 447-4240
St. Rita S 300/PK-8
30 Wellbrook Ave 10314 718-761-2504
Nicole Fresca, prin. Fax 761-0014
St. Teresa S 300/PK-8
1632 Victory Blvd 10314 718-448-9650
Anna Simione, prin. Fax 447-6426
SS. Joseph & Thomas S 300/PK-8
50 Maguire Ave 10309 718-356-3344
Joanne DelGeorge, prin. Fax 227-9531
Staten Island Academy 300/PK-12
715 Todt Hill Rd 10304 718-987-8100
Albert Cauz, head sch Fax 979-7641

Stella Niagara, Niagara

Stella Niagara Education Park 200/PK-8
4421 Lower River Rd 14144 716-754-4314
Sr. Margaret Sullivan, prin. Fax 754-2964

Stewart Manor, Nassau, Pop. 1,876
Elmont UFD
Supt. — See Elmont
Stewart Manor ES 400/PK-6
38 Stewart Ave 11530 516-326-5530
Hope Kranidis, prin. Fax 326-0548

Stillwater, Saratoga, Pop. 1,707
Stillwater Central SD 1,200/PK-12
1068 Hudson Ave 12170 518-373-6100
Patricia Morris, supt. Fax 664-9134
www.scsd.org
Stillwater ES 500/PK-5
1068 Hudson Ave 12170 518-373-6100
Paul Morcone, prin. Fax 664-1805
Stillwater MS 300/6-8
1068 Hudson Ave 12170 518-373-6100
Timothy Hulihan, prin. Fax 664-1832

Stone Ridge, Ulster, Pop. 1,136
Rondout Valley Central SD
Supt. — See Accord
Marbletown ES 300/K-3
12 Pine Bush Rd 12484 845-687-0284
Andrew Davenport, prin. Fax 687-7691

High Meadow S 200/PK-8
3643 Main St 12484 845-687-4855
Dr. Susan Paynter, head sch Fax 687-5151

Stony Brook, Suffolk, Pop. 13,574
Three Village Central SD 6,900/K-12
100 Suffolk Ave 11790 631-730-4000
Cheryl Pedisich, supt. Fax 474-7784
www.threevillagecsd.org
Mount ES 700/K-6
50 Dean Ln 11790 631-730-4300
Kathryn White, prin. Fax 730-4309
Other Schools – See East Setauket, Setauket

North Shore Montessori S 100/PK-K
218 Christian Ave 11790 631-689-8273

Stony Point, Rockland, Pop. 11,981
North Rockland Central SD
Supt. — See Garnerville
Farley ES 500/4-6
140 Route 210 10980 845-942-3200
Avis Shelby, prin. Fax 942-3207
Stony Point ES 700/K-3
7 Gurnee Dr 10980 845-942-3140
Farid Johnson, prin. Fax 942-3083

Suffern, Rockland, Pop. 10,548
East Ramapo Central SD
Supt. — See Spring Valley
Lime Kiln IS 400/4-6
35 Lime Kiln Rd 10901 845-577-6280
Lori Grant, prin. Fax 362-3570
Pomona MS 700/7-8
101 Pomona Rd 10901 845-577-6200
Christine Alfonso, prin. Fax 577-6245

Suffern Central SD
Supt. — See Hillburn
Cherry Lane ES 400/K-5
1 Heather Dr 10901 845-357-3988
Eric Baird, prin. Fax 357-2191
Connor ES 500/K-5
13 Cypress Rd 10901 845-357-2858
Kelly Dowd, prin. Fax 357-8657
Montebello Road ES 400/K-5
50 Montebello Rd 10901 845-357-4466
Dr. Teresa Ivey, prin. Fax 368-4161
Suffern MS 1,000/6-8
80 Hemion Rd 10901 845-357-7400
Brian Fox, prin. Fax 357-4563
Viola ES 400/K-5
557 Haverstraw Rd 10901 845-357-8315
Christine Druss, prin. Fax 357-2230

Sacred Heart S 200/PK-8
60 Washington Ave 10901 845-357-1684
Kathleen Grande, prin. Fax 357-0318
Yeshiva Darchei Noam 300/PK-8
257 Grandview Ave 10901 845-352-7100
Rabbi Yisroel Gottlieb, prin. Fax 352-9593

Swormville, Erie

St. Mary S 200/PK-8
6919 Transit Rd 14051 716-689-8424
Mary Jo Aiken, prin. Fax 689-8424

Syosset, Nassau, Pop. 18,544
Cold Spring Harbor Central SD
Supt. — See Cold Spring Harbor
West Side ES 200/2-6
1597 Laurel Hollow Rd 11791 516-692-7900
Kurt Simon, prin. Fax 692-4845

Syosset Central SD, 99 Pell Ln 11791 6,400/K-12
Dr. Thomas Rogers, supt. 516-364-5600
www.syossetschools.org
Berry Hill ES 400/K-5
181 Cold Spring Rd 11791 516-364-5790
Mary Kolkhorst, prin.
Robbins Lane ES 500/K-5
157 Robbins Ln 11791 516-364-5804
Thea Pallos, prin.
South Grove ES, 60 Colony Ln 11791 400/K-5
Mi Jung An, prin. 516-364-5810
South Woods MS, 99 Pell Ln 11791 700/6-8
Michelle Burget, prin. 516-364-5621
Thompson MS, 98 Ann Dr 11791 800/6-8
James Kassebaum, prin. 516-364-5760
Village ES, 90 Convent Rd 11791 400/K-5
Jeffery Kasper, prin. 516-364-5817
Willits ES, 99 Nana Pl 11791 300/K-5
James Connolly, prin. 516-364-5829
Other Schools – See Plainview, Woodbury

St. Edward Confessor S 200/PK-8
2 Teibrook Ave 11791 516-921-7767
Vincent Albrecht, prin. Fax 496-0001

Syracuse, Onondaga, Pop. 138,722
Lyncourt UFD 300/PK-8
2707 Court St 13208 315-455-7571
James Austin, supt. Fax 455-7573
www.lyncourtschool.org
Lyncourt S 300/PK-8
2709 Court St 13208 315-455-7571
Kimberly Davis, prin. Fax 455-7573

North Syracuse Central SD
Supt. — See North Syracuse
Roxboro Road ES 500/K-4
200 Bernard St 13211 315-218-2700
Matthew Motala, prin. Fax 218-2785
Roxboro Road MS 900/5-7
300 Bernard St 13211 315-218-3300
David Shaw, prin. Fax 218-3385

Solvay UFD
Supt. — See Solvay
Solvay MS 500/4-8
299 Bury Dr 13209 315-487-7061
Neil Gottlieb, prin. Fax 484-1444

Syracuse CSD 20,100/PK-12
725 Harrison St 13210 315-435-4499
Jaime Alicea, supt. Fax 435-4015
www.syracusecityschools.com
Bellevue ES 500/K-5
530 Stolp Ave 13207 315-435-4520
Sarah Cupelli, prin. Fax 435-6207
Clary MS 400/6-8
100 Amidon Dr 13205 315-435-4411
Charina Johnson-Turner, prin. Fax 435-5832
Danforth MS 400/6-8
309 W Brighton Ave 13205 315-435-4535
Katrina Allen, prin. Fax 435-6208
Delaware Academy 500/K-5
900 S Geddes St 13204 315-435-4540
Margaret Wilson, prin. Fax 435-4544
Delaware PS, 900 S Geddes St 13204 PK-2
Eliezer Hernandez, prin. 315-435-4540
Expeditionary Learning MS 100/6-8
4942 S Salina St 13205 315-435-6416
Kevin Burns, prin. Fax 435-4880
Franklin ES 700/K-5
428 S Alvord St 13208 315-435-4550
Kimberly Coyne, prin. Fax 435-6211
Frazer S 900/K-8
741 Park Ave 13204 315-435-4555
William Mecum, prin. Fax 435-4820
Grant MS 600/6-8
2400 Grant Blvd 13208 315-435-4433
Bruno Primerano, prin. Fax 435-4856
Hughes S 300/K-8
345 Jamesville Ave 13210 315-435-4404
Robert DiFlorio, prin. Fax 435-6552
Huntington S 900/K-8
400 Sunnycrest Rd 13206 315-435-4565
Joanne Harlow, prin. Fax 435-6206
Hyde ES 500/K-6
450 Durston Ave 13203 315-435-4570
Patricia Floyd-Echols, prin. Fax 435-6212
King ES 600/K-5
416 E Raynor Ave 13202 315-435-4580
Andrea Ellis-Smith, prin. Fax 435-6213
LeMoyne ES 500/K-5
1528 LeMoyne Ave 13208 315-435-4590
Jason Armstrong, prin. Fax 435-4591
Lincoln MS 600/6-8
1613 James St 13203 315-435-4450
LaJuan White, prin. Fax 435-4455
McKinley-Brighton ES 500/K-5
141 W Newell St 13205 315-435-4605
Mayra Ortiz, prin. Fax 435-4603
Meachem ES 500/K-5
171 Spaulding Ave 13205 315-435-4610
Kathryne Moulton, prin. Fax 435-6216
Porter ES 500/K-6
512 Emerson Ave 13204 315-435-4625
Jennifer King-Reese, prin. Fax 435-4897
Roberts S 800/PK-8
715 Glenwood Ave 13207 315-435-4635
John Devendorf, prin. Fax 435-6217
Seymour Dual Language Academy 500/K-5
108 Shonnard St 13204 315-435-4645
Stephen Polera, prin. Fax 435-4646
Smith S 700/PK-8
1106 Lancaster Ave 13210 315-435-4650
Samuel Barber, prin. Fax 435-6219
Smith S 800/PK-8
1130 Salt Springs Rd 13224 315-435-4490
Theresa Haley, prin. Fax 435-6220
Syracuse Latin S K-3
345 Jamesville Ave 13210 315-435-4606
Kelly Manard, prin.
Van Duyn ES 300/K-5
401 Loomis Ave 13207 315-435-4660
Eva Williams, prin Fax 435-6221
Webster ES 600/K-5
500 Wadsworth St 13208 315-435-4670
Iverna Minor, prin. Fax 435-4021
Weeks ES 700/K-5
710 Hawley Ave 13203 315-435-4097
Carin Reeve-Larham, prin. Fax 435-6222
Westside Academy at Blodgett 400/6-8
312 Oswego St 13204 315-435-4386
Vanessa Hopkins, prin. Fax 435-4539

West Genesee Central SD
Supt. — See Camillus
Onondaga Road ES 400/K-5
703 S Onondaga Rd 13219 315-487-4653
Jeannette Clark, prin. Fax 487-2999

Westhill Central SD 1,800/K-12
400 Walberta Rd 13219 315-426-3218
Casey Barduhn, supt. Fax 488-6411
www.westhillschools.org/
Cherry Road ES 400/2-4
201 Cherry Rd 13219 315-426-3300
Maureen Mulderig, prin. Fax 468-0623
Onondaga Hill MS 600/5-8
4860 Onondaga Rd 13215 315-426-3400
Mark Bednarski, prin. Fax 492-0156
Walberta Park PS 200/K-1
400 Walberta Rd 13219 315-426-3200
Beth Kramer, prin. Fax 484-9056

Blessed Sacrament S 300/PK-6
3129 James St 13206 315-463-1261
Andrea Polcaro, prin. Fax 463-0253
Cathedral Academy at Pompei 100/PK-6
923 N McBride St 13208 315-422-8548
Sr. Helen Charlebois, prin. Fax 472-0754
Faith Heritage S 300/PK-12
3740 Midland Ave 13205 315-469-7777
Neal Capone, head sch Fax 492-7440
Holy Family S 300/PK-6
130 Chapel Dr 13219 315-487-8515
Sr. Christina Mari Luczynski, prin. Fax 487-2086
Living Word Academy 200/PK-12
6101 Court Street Rd 13206 315-437-6744
Isaiah Rocine, prin. Fax 437-6766
Manlius Pebble Hill S 500/PK-12
5300 Jamesville Rd 13214 315-446-2452
Jim Dunaway, head sch Fax 446-2620
Montessori S of Syracuse 100/PK-6
155 Waldorf Pkwy 13224 315-449-9033
Mary O'Connor, head sch Fax 449-9867
Most Holy Rosary S 200/PK-6
1031 Bellevue Ave 13207 315-476-6035
Jennifer Petosa, prin.
Parkview Junior Academy 100/PK-9
412 S Avery Ave 13219 315-468-0117
Kim Kaiser, prin. Fax 487-1732

Taberg, Oneida
Camden Central SD
Supt. — See Camden
Annsville Area ES 200/PK-4
9374 Main St 13471 315-334-8030
Patricia Fallon, prin. Fax 334-8032

Tannersville, Greene, Pop. 531
Hunter-Tannersville Central SD 400/PK-12
PO Box 1018 12485 518-589-5400
Dr. Susan Vickers, supt. Fax 589-5403
www.htcsd.org
Other Schools – See Hunter

Tappan, Rockland, Pop. 6,517
South Orangetown Central SD
Supt. — See Blauvelt
Schaefer ES 400/K-2
140 Lester Dr 10983 845-680-1300
Nora Polansky, prin. Fax 680-1920

Tarrytown, Westchester, Pop. 11,035
Tarrytown UFD
Supt. — See Sleepy Hollow
Irving IS 600/3-5
103 S Broadway 10591 914-631-4442
Susan Bretti, prin. Fax 332-4077
Paulding S 200/PK-K
154 N Broadway 10591 914-631-5526
Maureen Barnett, prin. Fax 332-4265

Hackley S 800/K-12
293 Benedict Ave 10591 914-366-2642
Michael Wirtz, hdmstr. Fax 366-2636
Transfiguration S 200/PK-8
40 Prospect Ave 10591 914-631-3737
Gina Marie Fonte, prin. Fax 631-6640

Theresa, Jefferson, Pop. 842
Indian River Central SD
Supt. — See Philadelphia
Theresa PS 200/PK-3
125 Bridge St 13691 315-628-4432
Marlene Durgin, prin. Fax 628-5890

Thiells, Rockland, Pop. 4,970
North Rockland Central SD
Supt. — See Garnerville
Fieldstone MS 1,300/7-8
100 Fieldstone Dr 10984 845-942-7900
Anthony Zollo, prin. Fax 942-7910
Thiells ES 800/K-3
78 Rosman Rd 10984 845-942-3160
Peter DiBernardi, prin. Fax 942-3251
Willow Grove ES 700/4-6
153 Storrs Rd 10984 845-942-8000
Michael Roth, prin. Fax 942-8009

Thornwood, Westchester, Pop. 3,718
Mount Pleasant Central SD 1,900/K-12
825 Westlake Dr 10594 914-769-5500
Dr. Susan Guiney, supt. Fax 769-3733
www.mtplcsd.org
Columbus ES 500/3-5
580 Columbus Ave 10594 914-769-8538
Michael Cunzio, prin. Fax 769-8512
Westlake MS 500/6-8
825 Westlake Dr 10594 914-769-8540
Dr. Adam Bronstein, prin. Fax 769-8550
Other Schools – See Hawthorne

Ticonderoga, Essex, Pop. 3,342
Ticonderoga Central SD 800/PK-12
5 Calkins Pl 12883 518-585-7400
Dr. John McDonald Ed.D., supt. Fax 585-2682
www.ticonderogak12.org
Ticonderoga ES 300/PK-5
116 Alexandria Ave 12883 518-585-7400
Elizabeth Hayes, prin. Fax 585-9065
Ticonderoga MS 200/6-8
116 Alexandria Ave 12883 518-585-7400
Herbert Tedford, prin. Fax 585-2716

St. Mary S 100/PK-8
64 Amherst Ave 12883 518-585-7433
Sr. Sharon Dalton, prin. Fax 585-7505

Tioga Center, Tioga
Tioga Central SD 1,000/K-12
PO Box 241 13845 607-687-8000
Scot Taylor, supt. Fax 687-8007
www.tiogacentral.org
Tioga ES 400/K-4
PO Box 241 13845 607-687-8002
LuEllen Hoyt, prin. Fax 687-6945
Tioga MS 300/5-8
PO Box 241 13845 607-687-8004
Willard Cook, prin. Fax 687-6910

Tonawanda, Erie, Pop. 14,988
Kenmore-Town of Tonawanda UFSD
Supt. — See Buffalo
Edison ES 400/K-4
236 Grayton Rd 14150 716-874-8416
David King, prin. Fax 874-8526
Holmes ES 300/K-4
365 Dupont Ave 14150 716-874-8423
Lisa Cross, prin. Fax 874-8560

Sweet Home Central SD
Supt. — See Amherst
Glendale ES 400/PK-5
101 Glendale Dr 14150 716-250-1500
Joleen Dimitroff, prin. Fax 250-1510

Tonawanda CSD 1,800/PK-12
100 Hinds St 14150 716-694-7784
Dr. Timothy Oldenburg, supt. Fax 695-8738
www.tonawandacsd.org
Fletcher ES 300/4-5
555 Fletcher St 14150 716-694-7694
Barbara Partell, prin. Fax 694-3449
Mullen ES 300/PK-3
130 Syracuse St 14150 716-694-6805
Larry Badgley, prin. Fax 694-5897

Riverview ES 300/K-3
55 Taylor Dr 14150 716-694-7697
Claudia Panaro, prin. Fax 694-7172

St. Amelia S 500/PK-8
2999 Eggert Rd 14150 716-836-2230
James Mule, prin. Fax 832-9700
St. Christopher S 500/PK-8
2660 Niagara Falls Blvd 14150 716-693-5604
Cindy Bryk, prin. Fax 693-5127

Troupsburg, Steuben
Jasper-Troupsburg Central SD
Supt. — See Jasper
Jasper-Troupsburg ES 300/PK-6
PO Box 98 14885 607-525-6301
LeeAnne C. Herold, prin. Fax 525-6309

Troy, Rensselaer, Pop. 48,315
Brunswick Central SD 1,200/PK-12
3992 State Highway 2 12180 518-279-4600
Dr. Angelina Maloney, supt. Fax 279-1918
www.brittonkill.k12.ny.us
Tamarac ES 500/PK-5
3992 State Highway 2 12180 518-279-4600
Lindsay Morris, prin. Fax 279-0612

East Greenbush Central SD
Supt. — See East Greenbush
Bell Top ES 300/K-5
39 Reynolds Rd 12180 518-207-2600
Martin Mahar, prin. Fax 283-1184

Lansingburgh Central SD 2,400/PK-12
576 5th Ave 12182 518-233-6850
Cynthia DeDominick, supt. Fax 235-7436
www.lansingburgh.org
Knickerbacker MS 600/6-8
320 7th Ave 12182 518-233-6811
Michael Harkin, prin. Fax 238-2518
Rensselaer Park ES 500/3-5
70 110th St 12182 518-233-6823
Rebecca McGrouty, prin. Fax 238-1708
Turnpike ES 600/PK-2
55 New Turnpike Rd 12182 518-233-6822
Tina O'Brien, prin. Fax 235-3593

North Greenbush Common SD 50/K-1
52 N Greenbush Rd Unit B 12180 518-283-6748
Christine Hamill, supt. Fax 283-6609
www.northgreenbushcommon.org
Little Red School House 50/K-1
49 N Greenbush Rd 12180 518-283-6748
Christine Hamill, supt. Fax 283-6609

Troy CSD, 475 1st St 12180 4,400/PK-12
John Carmello, supt. 518-328-5052
www.troycsd.org
Carroll Hill ES 400/PK-5
112 Delaware Ave 12180 518-328-5701
Roy Stiles, prin. Fax 274-4587
Public S 2 300/PK-5
470 10th St 12180 518-328-5603
Natelege Turner-Hassell, prin. Fax 271-5205
Public S 14 500/PK-5
1700 Tibbits Ave 12180 518-328-5801
Karen Cloutier, prin. Fax 274-0371
Public S 16 300/K-5
40 Collins Ave 12180 518-328-5101
Tracy Ford, prin. Fax 274-4585
Public S 18 300/K-5
412 Hoosick St 12180 518-328-5501
Virginia DonVito-MacPhee, prin. Fax 274-4374
Troy MS 800/6-8
1976 Burdett Ave 12180 518-328-5301
Brian Dunn, prin. Fax 274-8160

Wynantskill UFD 300/K-8
25 East Ave 12180 518-283-4600
Thomas Reardon, supt. Fax 283-3684
www.wynantskillufsd.org
Gardner-Dickinson S 300/K-8
25 East Ave 12180 518-283-4600
Thomas Reardon, admin. Fax 283-3684

Redemption Christian Academy 100/PK-12
PO Box 753 12181 518-272-6679
John Massey, hdmstr. Fax 270-8039
Sacred Heart S 100/PK-6
308 Spring Ave 12180 518-274-3655
Devon Camenga, prin. Fax 274-8720

Trumansburg, Tompkins, Pop. 1,761
Trumansburg Central SD 1,100/K-12
100 Whig St 14886 607-387-7551
Kimberly Bell, supt. Fax 387-2807
www.tburgschools.org
Doig MS 300/5-8
100 Whig St 14886 607-387-7551
Joshua Hunkele, prin. Fax 387-2807
Trumansburg ES 400/K-4
100 Whig St 14886 607-387-7551
Jean Wiggins, prin. Fax 387-2807

Tuckahoe, Westchester, Pop. 6,361

Annunciation S 500/PK-8
465 Westchester Ave 10707 914-337-8760
Maureen Noonan, prin. Fax 337-8878
Immaculate Conception S 300/PK-8
53 Winter Hill Rd 10707 914-961-3785
Maureen Harten, prin. Fax 961-6054

Tully, Onondaga, Pop. 852
Tully Central SD 900/K-12
20 State St 13159 315-696-6204
Robert Hughes, supt. Fax 883-1343
www.tullyschools.org
Tully ES 400/K-6
20 State St 13159 315-696-6213
Edward Kupiec, prin. Fax 696-6220

Tupper Lake, Franklin, Pop. 3,639
Tupper Lake Central SD 800/PK-12
294 Hosley Ave 12986 518-359-3371
Seth McGowan, supt. Fax 359-7862
www.tupperlakecsd.net/
Quinn ES 400/PK-6
294 Hosley Ave 12986 518-359-2981
Michele Pinard, prin. Fax 359-3415

Turin, Lewis, Pop. 232
South Lewis Central SD 1,000/PK-12
PO Box 10 13473 315-348-2500
Douglas Premo, supt. Fax 348-2510
www.southlewis.org
South Lewis MS 300/5-8
PO Box 70 13473 315-348-2570
Judith Duppert, prin. Fax 348-2510
Other Schools – See Glenfield, Port Leyden

Tuxedo Park, Orange, Pop. 598
Tuxedo UFD 500/K-12
PO Box 2002 10987 845-351-4799
Nancy Teed, supt. Fax 351-5296
www.tuxedoufsd.org
Mason ES 100/K-6
PO Box 2002 10987 845-351-4797
Jason Schrammel, prin. Fax 351-3402

Tuxedo Park S 200/PK-9
Mountain Farm Rd 10987 845-351-4737
Todd Stansbery, hdmstr. Fax 351-4219

Unadilla, Otsego, Pop. 1,114
Unatego Central SD
Supt. — See Otego
Unatego ES 200/K-5
265 Main St 13849 607-369-6200
Katherine Mazourek, prin. Fax 369-6222

Uniondale, Nassau, Pop. 24,253
Uniondale UFD 6,400/PK-12
933 Goodrich St 11553 516-560-8800
Dr. William Lloyd, supt. Fax 292-2659
district.uniondaleschools.org
California Avenue ES 800/K-5
236 California Ave 11553 516-918-1850
Bryan Bruno, prin. Fax 505-9763
Northern Parkway ES 800/K-5
440 Northern Pkwy 11553 516-918-1700
Dr. Bilal Polson, prin. Fax 481-0541
Smith Street ES 400/K-5
780 Smith St 11553 516-918-2000
Dr. Lynnda Nadien, prin. Fax 486-2441
Turtle Hook MS 700/6-8
975 Jerusalem Ave 11553 516-918-1300
Dr. Donald Humphrey, prin. Fax 505-2533
Walnut Street ES 600/K-5
1270 Walnut St 11553 516-918-2200
Kevin Bracht, prin. Fax 485-9724
Other Schools – See Baldwin, Hempstead, North Baldwin

Pat-Kam S & ECC 200/PK-5
705 Nassau Rd 11553 516-486-7887
Ronald Clahar, prin. Fax 486-7905
St. Martin DePorres Marianist S 400/PK-8
530 Hempstead Blvd 11553 516-481-3303
John Holian, hdmstr. Fax 483-4138

Union Springs, Cayuga, Pop. 1,182
Union Springs Central SD 800/K-12
239 Cayuga St 13160 315-889-4101
Jarett Powers, supt. Fax 889-4108
www.unionspringscsd.org
Smith ES 200/4-6
26 Homer St 13160 315-889-7102
Karen Burcroff, prin. Fax 889-4165
Union Springs MS 100/6-8
239 Cayuga St 13160 315-889-4112
Michael Wurster, prin. Fax 889-4133
Other Schools – See Cayuga

Frontenac S 50/K-8
963 Spring Street Rd 13160 315-889-5094
Rebecca Runnals, prin.

Upper Nyack, Rockland, Pop. 2,003
Nyack UFD
Supt. — See Nyack
Upper Nyack ES 400/K-5
336 N Broadway 10960 845-353-7260
Joseph Mercora, prin. Fax 353-7262

Utica, Oneida, Pop. 60,287
Utica CSD 9,000/K-12
106 Memorial Pkwy 13501 315-792-2210
Bruce Karam, supt. Fax 792-2200
www.uticacsd.org/
Albany ES 500/K-5
1151 Albany St 13501 315-792-2150
Tania Kalavazoff, prin. Fax 792-2152
Columbus ES 600/K-5
934 Armory Dr 13501 315-792-2011
Elizabeth Gerling, prin. Fax 792-2014
Conkling ES 500/K-5
1115 Mohawk St 13501 315-368-6800
Mary Belden, prin. Fax 724-7242
Donovan MS 700/6-8
1701 Noyes St 13502 315-792-2006
Ann Marie Palladino, prin. Fax 792-2077
Herkimer ES 600/K-5
420 Keyes Rd 13502 315-792-2160
Alicia D'Ambrosio, prin. Fax 792-2034
Hughes ES 400/K-5
24 Prospect St 13501 315-792-2165
Michele Lagase, prin. Fax 792-2271
Jefferson ES 500/K-5
190 Booth St 13502 315-792-2163
Vanessa Rejrat, prin. Fax 732-5902
Jones ES 400/K-5
2630 Remington Rd 13501 315-792-2171
Alaine Canestrari, prin. Fax 792-2154
Kennedy MS 600/6-8
500 Deerfield Dr E 13502 315-792-2088
Joshua Gifford, prin. Fax 792-2084
Kernan ES 600/K-5
929 York St 13502 315-792-2185
Denise Dispirito, prin. Fax 792-2187
King ES 300/K-5
211 Square St 13501 315-792-2175
Kimberly VandUren, prin. Fax 368-6733
Watson Williams ES 600/K-5
107 Elmwood Pl 13501 315-792-2167
Cheryl Beckett-Minor, prin. Fax 792-1133

Notre Dame ES 300/PK-6
11 Barton Ave 13502 315-732-4374
Mary Rossi, prin. Fax 738-9720

Valatie, Columbia, Pop. 1,798
Ichabod Crane Central SD 1,800/K-12
PO Box 820 12184 518-758-7575
Mike Vanyo, supt. Fax 758-7579
www.ichabodcrane.org/
Crane ES 300/4-5
PO Box 820 12184 518-758-7575
Timothy Farley, prin. Fax 758-7579
Crane MS 400/6-8
PO Box 820 12184 518-758-7575
Tim Farley, prin. Fax 758-1405
Crane PS 600/K-3
PO Box 820 12184 518-758-7575
Andrea Williams, prin. Fax 758-2199

Valhalla, Westchester, Pop. 3,081
Valhalla UFD 1,500/K-12
316 Columbus Ave 10595 914-683-5040
Dr. Karen Geelan, supt. Fax 683-5075
www.valhallaschools.org
Kensico S 300/3-5
320 Columbus Ave 10595 914-683-5030
Matt Curran, prin. Fax 683-5304
Valhalla MS 400/6-8
300 Columbus Ave 10595 914-683-5011
Roberto Trigosso, prin. Fax 683-5003
Other Schools – See North White Plains

Valley Cottage, Rockland, Pop. 8,908
Nyack UFD
Supt. — See Nyack
Liberty ES 400/K-5
142 Lake Rd 10989 845-353-7240
Ellen Rechenberger, prin. Fax 353-7243
Valley Cottage ES 400/K-5
26 Lake Rd 10989 845-353-7280
Gina Cappiello, prin. Fax 353-7287

St. Paul S 200/PK-8
365 Kings Hwy 10989 845-268-6506
Sr. Stephen Gerard, prin. Fax 268-1809

Valley Stream, Nassau, Pop. 36,423
Elmont UFD
Supt. — See Elmont
Alden Terrace ES 400/PK-6
1835 N Central Ave 11580 516-285-8310
Shawnee Warfield, prin. Fax 285-8610

Hewlett-Woodmere UFD
Supt. — See Woodmere
Ogden ES, 875 Longview Ave 11581 400/2-5
Dina Anzalone, prin. 516-792-4700

Valley Stream 13 UFD 2,100/K-6
585 N Corona Ave 11580 516-568-6100
Constance Evelyn, supt. Fax 825-2537
www.valleystream13.com
Dever ES 500/K-6
585 N Corona Ave 11580 516-568-6120
Darren Gruen, prin. Fax 568-6119
Howell Road ES 500/K-6
1475 Howell Rd 11580 516-568-6130
Frank Huplosky, prin. Fax 568-6107
Wheeler Avenue ES 600/1-6
1 Wheeler Ave W 11580 516-568-6140
Dr. Gayle Steele, prin. Fax 568-0061
Other Schools – See Franklin Square

Valley Stream 24 UFD 1,100/K-6
75 Horton Ave 11581 516-434-2825
Dr. Edward Fale, supt. Fax 256-0163
www.valleystreamschooldistrict24.org/
Brooklyn Avenue ES 300/K-6
24 Brooklyn Ave 11581 516-434-2850
Dr. Scott Comis, prin. Fax 256-0169
Buck ES 300/K-6
75 Horton Ave 11581 516-434-2840
Susan Leggett, prin. Fax 256-0157
Carbonaro ES 400/K-6
50 Hungry Harbor Rd 11581 516-434-2860
Rosario Iacono, prin. Fax 791-4573

Valley Stream UFD 30 1,500/K-6
175 N Central Ave 11580 516-434-3600
Dr. Nicholas Stirling, supt. Fax 706-1177
www.valleystream30.com
Clearstream Avenue ES 400/K-6
60 Clearstream Ave 11580 516-434-3550
John Singleton, prin. Fax 872-1205
Forest Road ES 300/K-6
16 Forest Rd 11581 516-434-3800
Erin Malone, prin. Fax 792-2931

Shaw Avenue ES 700/K-6
99 Shaw Ave 11580 516-434-3700
Alejandro Rivera, prin. Fax 568-2436

Holy Name of Mary S 300/PK-8
90 S Grove St 11580 516-825-4009
Pamela Sanders, prin. Fax 825-2710
Valley Stream Christian Academy 200/K-12
12 E Fairview Ave 11580 516-561-6122
Rev. Leslie Fowley, supt. Fax 284-7191

Van Etten, Chemung, Pop. 523
Spencer-Van Etten Central SD
Supt. — See Spencer
Spencer-Van Etten ES 400/PK-4
7 Langford St 14889 607-589-7110
Matthew Stroup, prin. Fax 589-3017

Van Hornesville, Herkimer
Van Hornesville-Owen D. Young Central SD 200/K-12
PO Box 125 13475 315-858-0729
Brennan Fahey, supt. Fax 858-2019
www.odyoungcsd.org
Young Central S 200/K-12
PO Box 125 13475 315-858-0729
Brennan Fahey, supt. Fax 858-2019

Vernon, Oneida, Pop. 1,156
Vernon-Verona-Sherrill Central SD
Supt. — See Verona
Wettel ES 300/PK-6
PO Box 990 13476 315-829-3615
Vincent Pompo, prin. Fax 829-4326

Verona, Oneida, Pop. 837
Vernon-Verona-Sherrill Central SD 2,000/PK-12
PO Box 128 13478 315-829-2520
Martha Group, supt. Fax 829-4949
www.vvsschools.org
George ES 500/PK-6
PO Box 108 13478 315-363-2580
Gary Bissaillon, prin. Fax 361-5895
Vernon-Verona-Sherrill MS 300/7-8
PO Box 128 13478 315-829-7444
Carrie Hodkinson, prin. Fax 829-5966
Other Schools – See Sherrill, Vernon

Vestal, Broome, Pop. 5,000
Vestal Central SD 3,400/K-12
201 Main St 13850 607-757-2241
Jeffrey Ahearn, supt. Fax 757-2227
www.vestal.k12.ny.us
African Road ES 300/K-5
600 S Benita Blvd 13850 607-757-2311
Meghan Stenta, prin. Fax 757-2705
Clayton Avenue ES 300/K-5
209 Clayton Ave 13850 607-757-2271
Bradley Bruce, prin. Fax 757-2372
Glenwood ES 300/K-5
337 Jones Rd 13850 607-757-2391
Doreen McSain, prin. Fax 757-2233
Vestal Hills ES 300/K-5
709 Country Club Rd 13850 607-757-2357
Therese Mastro, prin. Fax 757-2347
Vestal MS 800/6-8
600 S Benita Blvd 13850 607-757-2331
Ann Marie Loose, prin. Fax 757-2229
Other Schools – See Apalachin

Hillel Academy 50/PK-8
4737 Deerfield Pl 13850 607-304-4544
Julie Piaker, admin.
Ross Corners Christian Academy 100/PK-12
2101 Owego Rd 13850 607-748-3301
Toby Wyse, admin. Fax 748-3301

Victor, Ontario, Pop. 2,645
Victor Central SD 4,300/PK-12
953 High St 14564 585-924-3252
Dr. Dawn Santiago-Marullo, supt. Fax 742-7090
www.victorschools.org
Victor Early Childhood S 700/PK-1
953 High St 14564 585-924-3252
Dorothy DiAngelo, prin. Fax 742-7033
Victor IS 1,000/4-6
953 High St 14564 585-924-3252
Kevin Swartz, prin. Fax 742-7055
Victor JHS 700/7-8
953 High St 14564 585-924-3252
Brian Gee, prin. Fax 924-9535
Victor PS 700/1-3
953 High St 14564 585-924-3252
Jennifer Check, prin. Fax 742-7031

Voorheesville, Albany, Pop. 2,770
Voorheesville Central SD 1,200/K-12
432 New Salem Rd 12186 518-765-3313
Brian Hunt, supt. Fax 765-2751
www.voorheesville.org
Voorheesville ES 500/K-5
129 Maple Ave 12186 518-765-2382
Jeffrey Vivenzio, prin. Fax 765-3842
Voorheesville MS 300/6-8
432 New Salem Rd 12186 518-765-3314
Jennifer Drautz, prin. Fax 765-3842

Wading River, Suffolk, Pop. 7,603
Shoreham-Wading River Central SD
Supt. — See Shoreham
Wading River ES 300/3-5
1900 Wading River Manor Rd 11792 631-821-8254
Louis Parrinello, prin. Fax 821-8256

Wainscott, Suffolk, Pop. 640
Wainscott Common SD 50/K-3
PO Box 79 11975 631-537-1080
Deborah Haab, supt. Fax 537-6977
www.wainscottschool.org
Wainscott Common S 50/K-3
PO Box 79 11975 631-537-1080
Fax 537-6977

Walden, Orange, Pop. 6,814
Valley Central SD
Supt. — See Montgomery
Walden ES 500/K-5
75 Orchard St 12586 845-457-2400
Gregory Heidemann, prin. Fax 778-7110

Most Precious Blood S 200/PK-8
180 Ulster Ave 12586 845-778-3028
Woodrow Hallaway, prin. Fax 778-3785

Wallkill, Ulster, Pop. 2,258
Wallkill Central SD 3,100/K-12
PO Box 310 12589 845-895-7100
Kevin Castle, supt. Fax 895-3630
www.wallkillcsd.k12.ny.us
Borden MS 500/7-8
PO Box 310 12589 845-895-7175
Marjorie Anderson, prin. Fax 895-8036
Leptondale ES 500/K-6
PO Box 310 12589 845-895-7200
Scott Brown, prin. Fax 564-8098
Ostrander ES 500/K-6
PO Box 310 12589 845-895-7225
Nicholas Pantaleone, prin. Fax 895-8043
Other Schools – See Plattekill

Walton, Delaware, Pop. 3,059
Walton Central SD 1,000/PK-12
47-49 Stockton Ave 13856 607-865-4116
Roger Clough, supt. Fax 865-8568
www.waltoncsd.org
Mack MS 200/6-8
47-49 Stockton Ave 13856 607-865-4116
Andy Gates, prin. Fax 865-8568
Townsend ES 500/PK 5
42 North St 13856 607-865-4116
Mike Snider, prin. Fax 865-8568

Walworth, Wayne
Gananda Central SD 1,000/K-12
1500 Dayspring Rdg 14568 315-986-3521
Dr. Shawn Van Scoy, supt. Fax 986-2003
www.gananda.org
Gananda MS 300/6-8
1500 Dayspring Rdg 14568 315-986-3521
Tracie Douglas, prin. Fax 986-1927
Gananda / Richard Mann ES 400/K-5
1500 Dayspring Rdg 14568 315-986-3521
Kim Ernstberger, prin. Fax 986-3506

Wampsville, Madison, Pop. 531
Oneida CSD
Supt. — See Oneida
Shortell MS 300/7-8
PO Box 716 13163 315-363-1050
Todd Widrick, prin. Fax 366-0622

Wantagh, Nassau, Pop. 18,699
Levittown UFD
Supt. — See Levittown
Lee Road ES 300/K-5
901 Lee Rd 11793 516-434-7475
Anthony Goss, prin. Fax 783-5194

Wantagh UFD 3,200/K-12
3301 Beltagh Ave 11793 516-781-8000
John McNamara, supt. Fax 781-6076
www.wantaghschools.org
Forest Lake ES 400/K-5
3100 Beltagh Ave 11793 516-679-6470
Anthony Ciuffo, prin. Fax 679-6478
Mandalay ES 300/K-5
2667 Bayview Ave 11793 516-679-6390
Marie Pisicchio, prin. Fax 679-6484
Wantagh ES 700/K-5
1765 Beech St 11793 516-679-6480
Dr. Randee Bonagura, prin. Fax 679-6365
Wantagh MS 800/6-8
3299 Beltagh Ave 11793 516-679-6350
Dawn Matrochano, prin. Fax 679-6311

Maplewood S 200/PK-K
2166 Wantagh Ave 11793 516-221-2121
Dr. Joseph Holden, dir. Fax 221-9303

Wappingers Falls, Dutchess, Pop. 5,339
Wappingers Central SD
Supt. — See Hopewell Junction
Evans ES 400/K-6
747 Sergeant Palmateer Way 12590 845-298-5240
Lauren Hernandez, prin. Fax 298-5232
Fishkill Plains ES 600/K-6
17 Lake Walton Rd 12590 845-227-1770
Eric Seipp, prin. Fax 227-1747
Myers Corners ES 700/K-6
156 Myers Corners Rd 12590 845-298-5260
Sydnie Goldstein, prin. Fax 298-5250
Sheafe Road ES 500/K-6
287 Sheafe Rd 12590 845-298-5290
James Daley, prin. Fax 298-5282
Van Wyck JHS 1,000/7-8
6 Hillside Lake Rd 12590 845-227-1700
Dr. Steve Shuchat, prin. Fax 227-1748
Wappingers JHS 800/7-8
30 Major MacDonald Way 12590 845-298-5200
Terrence Thompson, prin. Fax 298-5156

St. Mary S 200/PK-8
2 Convent Ave 12590 845-297-7500
Thomas Hamilton, prin. Fax 297-0886

Blessed Virgin Mary Mother of God Acad 200/K-12
2656 Warners Rd 13164 315-320-4085
Fr. Richard Boyle, prin. Fax 320-4093

Warrensburg, Warren, Pop. 3,071
Warrensburg Central SD 800/K-12
103 Schroon River Rd 12885 518-623-2861
John Goralski, supt. Fax 623-2436
www.wcsd.org
Warrensburg ES 400/K-6
1 James St 12885 518-623-9747
Amy Langworthy, prin. Fax 623-3336

Warsaw, Wyoming, Pop. 3,438
Warsaw Central SD 900/K-12
153 W Buffalo St 14569 585-786-8000
Joseph Englebert, supt. Fax 786-8008
www.warsaw.k12.ny.us
Warsaw ES 400/K-5
153 W Buffalo St 14569 585-786-8000
Kimberly Monahan, prin. Fax 786-2537

Warwick, Orange, Pop. 6,603
Warwick Valley Central SD 3,700/K-12
PO Box 595 10990 845-987-3000
Dr. David Leach, supt. Fax 986-1408
www.warwickvalleyschools.com
Park Avenue ES 500/K-4
PO Box 595 10990 845-987-3170
Sandra Wood, prin. Fax 988-5893
Sanfordville ES 700/K-5
PO Box 595 10990 845-987-3300
Johnna Maraia, prin. Fax 986-7287
Warwick Valley MS 1,100/5-8
PO Box 595 10990 845-987-3100
Georgianna Diopoulos, prin. Fax 986-6942

SS. Stephen & Edward S 200/PK-8
75 Sanfordville Rd 10990 845-986-3533
Bethany Negersmith, prin. Fax 987-7023

Washingtonville, Orange, Pop. 5,806
Washingtonville Central SD 4,300/PK-12
52 W Main St 10992 845-497-4000
Roy Reese, supt. Fax 497-4030
www.ws.k12.ny.us
Round Hill ES 600/PK-PK, 1-
1314 Route 208 10992 845-497-4000
Steven Kiel, prin. Fax 497-4005
Taft ES 800/K-5
20 Toleman Rd 10992 845-497-4000
Barbara Quinn, prin. Fax 497-4002
Washingtonville MS 1,000/6-8
38 W Main St 10992 845-497-4000
Teresa Thompson, prin. Fax 497-4001
Other Schools – See New Windsor

Waterford, Saratoga, Pop. 1,958
Waterford-Halfmoon UFD 800/K-12
125 Middletown Rd 12188 518-237-0800
Patrick Pomerville, supt. Fax 237-7335
www.whufsd.org
Waterford-Halfmoon ES 400/K-6
125 Middletown Rd 12188 518-237-0800
Joseph Siracuse, prin. Fax 237-7083

St. Mary's S 300/PK-8
12 6th St 12188 518-237-0652
Mary Rushkoski, prin. Fax 233-0898

Waterloo, Seneca, Pop. 5,097
Waterloo Central SD 1,700/K-12
109 Washington St 13165 315-539-1500
Terri Bavis, supt. Fax 539-1504
www.waterloocsd.org
La Fayette IS 400/3-5
71 Inslee St 13165 315-539-1530
Shaun Merrill, prin. Fax 539-1529
Skoi-Yase ES 300/K-2
65 Fayette St 13165 315-539-1520
Elizabeth Springer, prin. Fax 539-1527
Waterloo MS 400/6-8
65 Center St 13165 315-539-1540
Vincent Vitale, prin. Fax 539-1534

Watertown, Jefferson, Pop. 26,112
Watertown CSD 3,900/K-12
1351 Washington St 13601 315-785-3700
Patricia LaBarr, supt. Fax 785-6855
www.watertowncsd.org
Case MS 600/7-8
1237 Washington St 13601 315-785-3870
Thomas Nabinger, prin. Fax 785-3731
Knickerbocker ES 400/K-4
739 Knickerbocker Dr 13601 315-785-3740
Janelle Dupee, prin. Fax 779-5654
North ES 500/K-4
171 E Hoard St 13601 315-785-3750
Sandra Cain, prin. Fax 785-3752
Ohio Street ES 300/K-4
1537 Ohio St 13601 315-785-3755
Mark Taylor, prin. Fax 785-9742
Sherman ES 300/K-4
832 Sherman St 13601 315-785-3760
Terrance Gonseth, prin. Fax 785-0152
Starbuck ES 200/K-4
430 E Hoard St 13601 315-785-3765
Chad Fairchild, prin. Fax 785-0919
Wiley IS 600/5-6
1351 Washington St 13601 315-785-3780
Lynn Gaffney, prin. Fax 785-3764

Faith Fellowship Christian S 200/PK-12
131 Moore Ave 13601 315-782-9342

Immaculate Heart S 200/PK-6
122 Winthrop St 13601 315-788-7011
Kari Conklin, prin. Fax 788-7011

Waterville, Oneida, Pop. 1,551
Waterville Central SD 800/PK-12
381 Madison St 13480 315-841-3900
Charles Chafee, supt. Fax 841-3939
www.watervillecsd.org
Memorial Park ES 400/PK-6
145 E Bacon St 13480 315-841-3700
Maureen Gray, prin. Fax 841-3718

Watervliet, Albany, Pop. 9,992
Watervliet CSD 1,300/K-12
1245 Hillside Dr 12189 518-629-3200
Dr. Lori Caplan, supt. Fax 629-3265
vliet.neric.org
Watervliet ES 700/K-6
2557 10th Ave 12189 518-629-3400
Loida Lewinter, prin. Fax 629-3250

Watkins Glen, Schuyler, Pop. 1,826
Watkins Glen Central SD 1,000/PK-12
303 12th St 14891 607-535-3220
Gregory Kelahan, supt. Fax 535-4629
www.wgcsd.org
Watkins Glen ES 600/PK-6
612 S Decatur St 14891 607-535-3250
Rebecca Trank, prin. Fax 535-7012

Waverly, Tioga, Pop. 4,388
Waverly Central SD 1,500/PK-12
15 Frederick St 14892 607-565-2841
Dr. Randy Richards, supt. Fax 565-4997
www.waverlyschools.com
Elm Street ES 400/2-4
145 Elm St 14892 607-565-8186
John Cheresnowsky, prin. Fax 565-4997
Lincoln Street ES 300/PK-1
45 Lincoln St 14892 607-565-8176
Colleen Hall, prin. Fax 565-4997
Waverly MS 400/5-8
1 Frederick St 14892 607-565-3410
Paul Vesci, prin. Fax 565-4997

Wayland, Steuben, Pop. 1,852
Wayland-Cohocton Central SD 1,400/PK-12
2350 State Route 63 14572 585-728-2211
Michael Wetherbee, supt. Fax 728-3566
www.wccsk12.org
Wayland-Cohocton MS 400/5-8
2350 State Route 63 14572 585-728-2551
Jeremy Lonneville, prin. Fax 728-3556
Wayland ES 400/PK-4
2350 State Route 63 14572 585-728-3547
Theresa Carhart, prin. Fax 728-3566
Other Schools – See Cohocton

Webster, Monroe, Pop. 5,251
Webster Central SD 8,500/K-12
119 South Ave 14580 585-216-0000
Carmen Gumina, supt. Fax 265-6561
www.websterschools.org
Dewitt Road ES 500/K-5
722 Dewitt Rd 14580 585-671-0710
Debra Reed, prin. Fax 671-4366
Klem Road North ES 500/K-5
1015 Klem Rd 14580 585-872-1770
Laura Ballou, prin. Fax 872-2763
Klem Road South ES 600/K-5
1025 Klem Rd 14580 585-872-1320
Erin Land, prin. Fax 872-2067
Plank Road North ES 500/K-5
705 Plank Rd 14580 585-671-8858
Craig Bodensteiner, prin. Fax 787-9009
Plank Road South ES 600/K-5
715 Plank Rd 14580 585-671-3190
Scott Wilcox, prin. Fax 671-4574
Schlegel Road ES 500/K-5
1548 Schlegel Rd 14580 585-265-2500
Francine Leggett, prin. Fax 265-0716
Spry MS 1,000/6-8
119 South Ave 14580 585-265-6500
James Baehr, prin. Fax 265-6512
State Road ES 500/K-5
1401 State Rd 14580 585-872-4200
Christine Noeth-Abele, prin. Fax 872-5834
Willink MS 1,000/6-8
900 Publishers Pkwy 14580 585-670-1030
Jim Gindling, prin. Fax 671-1978

St. Rita S 400/PK-5
1008 Maple Dr 14580 585-671-3132
Mary Ellen Wagner, prin. Fax 671-4562
Webster Montessori S 100/PK-6
1310 Five Mile Line Rd 14580 585-347-0055
Jacqueline Griebel, head sch Fax 347-0057

Weedsport, Cayuga, Pop. 1,803
Weedsport Central SD 800/K-12
2821 E Brutus Street Rd 13166 315-834-6637
Shaun O'Connor, supt.
www.weedsport.org
Weedsport ES 400/K-5
8954 Jackson St 13166 315-834-6685
Melinda Ervay, prin. Fax 834-8693

Wells, Hamilton
Wells Central SD 100/PK-12
PO Box 300 12190 518-924-6000
Thomas Sincavage, supt. Fax 924-9246
www.wellscsd.org
Wells Central S 100/PK-12
PO Box 300 12190 518-924-6000
Thomas Sincavage, supt. Fax 924-9246

Wellsville, Allegany, Pop. 4,622
Wellsville Central SD 1,300/PK-12
126 W State St 14895 585-596-2170
David Foster, supt. Fax 596-2177
www.wellsvilleschools.org
Wellsville ES 600/PK-5
50 School St 14895 585-596-2122
Elizabeth Sinski, prin. Fax 596-2120

Immaculate Conception S 200/PK-8
24 Maple Ave 14895 585-593-5840
Nora Burdick, prin. Fax 593-5846

West Babylon, Suffolk, Pop. 42,432
West Babylon UFD 4,100/K-12
10 Farmingdale Rd 11704 631-376-7000
Dr. Yiendhy Farrelly, supt. Fax 376-7019
www.wbschools.org
Forest Avenue ES 300/K-5
200 Forest Ave 11704 631-376-7301
Patrick Acocella, prin. Fax 376-7309
Kennedy ES 400/K-5
175 Brookvale Ave 11704 631-376-7801
Gregg Cunningham, prin. Fax 376-7809
Santapogue ES 400/K-5
1130 Herzel Blvd 11704 631-376-7401
Jennifer Carere, prin. Fax 376-7409
South Bay ES 300/K-5
160 Great East Neck Rd 11704 631-376-7501
JoAnn Scott, prin. Fax 376-7509
Tooker Avenue ES 300/K-5
855 Tooker Ave 11704 631-376-7601
Charles Germano, prin. Fax 376-7609
West Babylon JHS 900/6-8
200 Old Farmingdale Rd 11704 631-376-7201
Daniel McKeon, prin. Fax 376-7209

Westbury, Nassau, Pop. 14,820
East Meadow UFD 7,100/K-12
718 The Plain Rd 11590 516-478-5776
Dr. Kenneth A. Card Ed.D., supt. Fax 478-5779
www.eastmeadow.k12.ny.us
Bowling Green ES 700/K-5
2340 Stewart Ave 11590 516-876-7480
Maria Ciarametaro, prin. Fax 876-8458
Clarke MS 600/6-8
740 Edgewood Dr 11590 516-876-7401
Stacy Breslin, prin. Fax 876-7407
Other Schools – See East Meadow

Westbury UFD
Supt. — See Old Westbury
Drexel Avenue ES 500/1-5
161 Drexel Ave 11590 516-876-5030
Dr. Wanda Toledo, prin. Fax 876-5032
Dryden Street S 400/PK-K
545 Dryden St 11590 516-876-5039
Gloria Dingwall, prin. Fax 876-5172
Park Ave ES 900/1-5
955 Park Ave 11590 516-876-5109
Robert Chambers, prin. Fax 876-5190
Powells Lane ES 500/1-5
603 Powells Ln 11590 516-876-5124
Claudia Germain, prin. Fax 876-5160
Westbury MS 1,000/6-8
455 Rockland St 11590 516-876-5082
David Zimbler, prin. Fax 876-5141

St. Brigid/Our Lady of Hope Regional S 300/PK-8
101 Maple Ave 11590 516-333-0580
Paul Clagnaz, prin. Fax 333-0590
Westbury Friends S 100/PK-3
550 Post Ave 11590 516-333-3178
Eve Nealy, head sch Fax 333-1353

West Chazy, Clinton, Pop. 516
Beekmantown Central SD 1,900/PK-12
37 Eagle Way 12992 518-563-8250
Daniel W. Mannix, supt. Fax 563-8132
www.bcsdk12.org
Beekmantown ES 400/PK-5
37 Eagle Way 12992 518-563-8035
Sarah Paquette, prin. Fax 563-8087
Beekmantown MS 500/6-8
37 Eagle Way 12992 518-563-8690
Amy Campbell, prin. Fax 563-8691
Other Schools – See Plattsburgh

West Falls, Erie

Aurora Waldorf S 200/PK-8
525 W Falls Rd 14170 716-655-2029
Anna Harp, admin. Fax 655-2029

Westfield, Chautauqua, Pop. 3,195
Westfield Central SD 700/PK-12
203 E Main St 14787 716-326-2151
David Davison, supt. Fax 326-2195
www.wacs.wnyric.org/
Westfield ES 300/PK-5
203 E Main St 14787 716-326-2151
Dr. Mary Rockey, prin. Fax 326-2157
Westfield MS 100/6-8
203 E Main St 14787 716-326-2151
Ivana Hite, prin. Fax 326-2157

Westhampton, Suffolk, Pop. 3,035

Raynor Country Day S PK-6
PO Box 380 11977 631-288-4658
Kerry Coonan, prin. Fax 288-4654

Westhampton Beach, Suffolk, Pop. 1,702
Westhampton Beach UFD 1,800/K-12
340 Mill Rd 11978 631-288-3800
Mike Radday, supt. Fax 288-8351
www.westhamptonbeach.k12.ny.us
Westhampton Beach ES 400/K-5
379 Mill Rd 11978 631-288-3800
Lisa Slover, prin. Fax 288-7867
Westhampton Beach MS 400/6-8
340 Mill Rd 11978 631-288-3800
Charisse Miller, prin. Fax 288-5496

West Harrison, Westchester
Harrison Central SD
Supt. — See Harrison
Preston ES 300/K-5
50 Taylor Ave 10604 914-630-3152
Dennis Kortright, prin. Fax 761-7166

West Haverstraw, Rockland, Pop. 9,957
North Rockland Central SD
Supt. — See Garnerville
West Haverstraw ES 700/K-3
71 Blauvelt Ave 10993 845-942-3180
Mary Esposito, prin. Fax 942-3084

West Hempstead, Nassau, Pop. 18,467
West Hempstead UFD 2,100/K-12
252 Chestnut St 11552 516-390-3100
Patricia Sullivan-Kriss, supt. Fax 489-1776
www.whufsd.com
Chestnut Street S 200/K-K
252 Chestnut St 11552 516-390-3150
Faith Tripp, prin. Fax 390-3152
Cornwell Avenue ES 300/1-5
250 Cornwell Ave 11552 516-390-3140
Deanna Sinito, prin. Fax 489-0365
Washington ES 300/1-5
347 William St 11552 516-390-3130
Michelle Notti, prin. Fax 489-0068
West Hempstead MS 500/6-8
450 Nassau Blvd 11552 516-390-3160
Dina Reilly, prin. Fax 489-8946

HANC - Samuel & Eliz Bass Golding Schl 300/K-6
609 Hempstead Ave 11552 516-485-7786
St. Thomas the Apostle S 400/PK-8
12 Westminster Rd 11552 516-481-9310
Valerie Gigante, prin. Fax 481-8769

West Islip, Suffolk, Pop. 28,075
West Islip UFD 4,800/K-12
100 Sherman Ave 11795 631-893-3200
Bernadette Burns, supt. Fax 893-3212
www.wi.k12.ny.us
Bayview ES 500/K-5
165 Snedecor Ave 11795 631-893-3330
John Mullins, prin. Fax 893-3335
Beach Street MS 600/6-8
17 Beach St 11795 631-893-3310
Andrew O'Farrell, prin. Fax 893-3318
Bellew ES 500/K-5
25 Higbie Ln 11795 631-893-3340
Rhonda Pratt, prin. Fax 893-3346
Manetuck ES 500/K-5
800 Van Buren Ave 11795 631-893-3350
Dawn Morrison, prin. Fax 893-3356
Oquenock ES 500/K-5
425 Spruce Ave 11795 631-893-3360
Jack Maniscalco, prin. Fax 893-3367
Udall Road MS 600/6-8
900 Udall Rd 11795 631-893-3290
Dr. Daniel Marquardt, prin. Fax 893-3301

Our Lady of Lourdes S 400/PK-8
44 Toomey Rd 11795 631-587-7200
Louise Krol, prin. Fax 587-4531

West Leyden, Lewis
Adirondack Central SD
Supt. — See Boonville
West Leyden ES 200/PK-5
PO Box 304 13489 315-942-9280
Daniel Roberts, prin. Fax 942-9212

Westmoreland, Oneida, Pop. 420
Westmoreland Central SD 900/K-12
PO Box 430 13490 315-557-2614
Rocco Migliori, supt. Fax 853-4602
www.westmorelandschool.org
Westmoreland ES 400/K-4
PO Box 430 13490 315-557-2637
Mary Anne O'Connell, prin. Fax 853-6597
Westmoreland MS 300/5-8
PO Box 430 13490 315-557-2618
David Langone, prin. Fax 557-2760

West Nyack, Rockland, Pop. 3,385
Clarkstown Central SD
Supt. — See New City
Festa MS, 30 Parrott Rd 10994 2,200/6-8
Dr. Michael St. John, prin. 845-624-3970
Strawtown ES 300/K-5
413 Strawtown Rd 10994 845-624-3473
Martha Ryan, prin.
West Nyack ES 300/K-5
661 W Nyack Rd 10994 845-624-3474
Annie Streiff, prin.

Westport, Essex, Pop. 508
Westport Central SD 200/K-12
25 Sisco St 12993 518-962-8244
A. Paul Scott, supt. Fax 962-4571
www.westportcs.org
Westport Central S 200/K-12
25 Sisco St 12993 518-962-8244
Joshua Meyer, prin. Fax 962-4571

West Sand Lake, Rensselaer, Pop. 2,619
Averill Park Central SD
Supt. — See Averill Park
West Sand Lake ES 400/K-5
24 Meeler Rd 12196 518-674-7175
Laura Kyer, prin. Fax 674-3225

West Sayville, Suffolk, Pop. 4,972
Sayville UFD
Supt. — See Sayville
Cherry Avenue ES 400/K-5
155 Cherry Ave 11796 631-244-6700
Dr. Lisa Ihne, prin. Fax 244-6506

West Sayville Christian S 100/K-8
37 Rollstone Ave 11796 631-589-2180
Jill Golden, prin. Fax 589-2143

West Seneca, Erie, Pop. 44,393
Orchard Park Central SD 4,900/K-12
2240 Southwestern Blvd 14224 716-209-6200
Matthew McGarrity, supt. Fax 209-6353
www.opschools.org
Other Schools – See Orchard Park

West Seneca Central SD 6,300/PK-12
675 Potters Rd 14224 716-677-3100
Fax 677-3104
www.wscschools.org
Allendale ES 400/K-5
1399 Orchard Park Rd 14224 716-677-3660
Dr. Holly Quinn, prin. Fax 675-3104
Clinton Street ES 600/K-4
4100 Clinton St 14224 716-677-3620
Kimberly McCartan, prin. Fax 674-7821
East MS 900/5-8
1445 Center Rd 14224 716-677-3530
Sharon Loughran, prin. Fax 674-1046
Northwood ES 400/PK-4
250 Northwood Ave 14224 716-677-3640
Angela Ferri, prin. Fax 674-3505
West ES 600/K-5
1397 Orchard Park Rd 14224 716-677-3250
Kristen Frawley, prin. Fax 677-3123
West MS 900/6-8
395 Center Rd 14224 716-677-3500
Dave Kean, prin. Fax 675-6134
Winchester ES 200/1-5
650 Harlem Rd 14224 716-677-3580
Tracy Spagnono, prin. Fax 822-2670

Queen of Heaven S 200/PK-8
839 Mill Rd 14224 716-674-5206
Mary Damico, prin. Fax 674-2793
Trinity Lutheran S 100/PK-8
146 Reserve Rd 14224 716-674-5353
Kathleen Fretthold, prin. Fax 674-4910
West Seneca Christian S 100/PK-12
511 Union Rd 14224 716-674-1820
Joshua Sexton, admin. Fax 674-4894

West Valley, Cattaraugus, Pop. 518
West Valley Central SD 300/PK-12
PO Box 290 14171 716-942-3293
Eric Lawton, supt. Fax 942-3440
www.wvalley.wnyric.org
West Valley Central S 300/PK-12
PO Box 290 14171 716-942-3293
Daniel Amodeo, prin. Fax 942-3440

West Winfield, Herkimer, Pop. 820
Mount Markham CSD 1,100/K-12
500 Fairground Rd 13491 315-822-2824
Dr. Paul Berry, supt. Fax 822-6162
www.mmcsd.org
Mount Markham ES 400/K-4
500 Fairground Rd 13491 315-822-2840
Jennifer McDonald, prin. Fax 822-3436
Mount Markham MS 300/5-8
500 Fairground Rd 13491 315-822-2870
Dawn Yerkie, prin. Fax 822-6125

Whitehall, Washington, Pop. 2,580
Whitehall Central SD 700/K-12
87 Buckley Rd 12887 518-499-1772
Patrick Dee, supt. Fax 499-1759
www.railroaders.net
Whitehall ES 300/K-6
99 Buckley Rd 12887 518-499-0330
Rich Trowbridge, prin. Fax 499-1752

White Plains, Westchester, Pop. 55,780
Greenburgh Central SD
Supt. — See Hartsdale
Bailey ES 300/4-6
33 Hillside Ave S 10607 914-948-8107
Kiana Washington, prin. Fax 948-2934
Jackson ES 300/K-1
2 Saratoga Rd 10607 914-948-2992
Patricia Simone, prin. Fax 681-0038

White Plains CSD 7,000/K-12
5 Homeside Ln 10605 914-422-2000
Dr. Joseph Ricca Ed.D., supt. Fax 422-2024
www.whiteplainspublicschools.org
Church Street ES 700/K-5
295 Church St 10603 914-422-2400
Myra Castillo, prin. Fax 422-2409
Mamaroneck Avenue ES 700/K-5
7 Nosband Ave 10605 914-422-2286
Eileen McGuire, prin. Fax 422-2109
Post Road ES 600/K-5
175 W Post Rd 10606 914-422-2320
Jesimae Ossorio, prin. Fax 422-2097
Ridgeway ES 700/K-5
225 Ridgeway 10605 914-422-2081
Tashia Brown, prin. Fax 422-2366
Washington ES 700/K-5
100 Orchard St 10604 914-422-2380
Laura Mungin, prin. Fax 422-2105
White Plains MS - Eastview Campus 6-8
350 Main St 10601 914-422-2223
Joseph Cloherty, prin. Fax 422-2222
White Plains MS - Highlands Campus 1,500/6-8
128 Grandview Ave 10605 914-422-2092
Ernest Spatafore, prin. Fax 422-2273

German International S New York 300/PK-12
50 Partridge Rd 10605 914-948-6513
Our Lady of Sorrows S 200/K-8
888 Mamaroneck Ave 10605 914-761-0124
Sr. Marie Cecile Larizza, prin. Fax 761-0176
Solomon Schechter S of Westchester 400/K-5
30 Dellwood Rd 10605 914-948-3111
Michael Kay Ph.D., head sch Fax 948-4356

Whitesboro, Oneida, Pop. 3,727
Whitesboro Central SD 3,200/K-12
65 Oriskany Blvd 13492 315-266-3300
Brian Bellair, supt. Fax 768-9730
www.wboro.org
Harts Hill ES 400/K-5
8551 Clark Mills Rd 13492 315-266-3430
Lisa Putnam, prin. Fax 768-9855
Parkway MS 200/6-6
65 Oriskany Blvd 13492 315-266-3175
Christopher Staats, prin. Fax 768-9882
Westmoreland Road ES 400/K-5
8596 Westmoreland Rd 13492 315-266-3440
Andrea Centro, prin. Fax 768-9789
Whitesboro MS 500/7-8
75 Oriskany Blvd 13492 315-266-3100
John Egresits, prin. Fax 768-9770
Other Schools – See Deerfield, Marcy

Whitestone, See New York
NYC Department of Education
Supt. — See New York
Public S 79 1,000/PK-5
14727 15th Dr 11357 718-746-0396
George Carter, prin. Fax 746-3103
Public S 184 500/PK-5
16315 21st Ave 11357 718-352-7800
Anna Dimilta, prin. Fax 352-0311
Public S 193 500/PK-5
15220 11th Ave 11357 718-767-8810
Diane Tratner, prin. Fax 746-7617
Public S 209 600/PK-5
1610 Utopia Pkwy 11357 718-352-3939
Mary McDonnell, prin. Fax 352-0367
JHS 194 1,000/6-8
15460 17th Ave 11357 718-746-0818
Jennifer Miller, prin. Fax 746-7618

Holy Trinity Academy 300/PK-8
1445 143rd St 11357 718-746-1479
Barbara Kavanagh, prin. Fax 746-4793
St. Luke S 500/PK-8
1601 150th Pl 11357 718-746-3833
Jan Brunswick, prin. Fax 747-2101

Whitesville, Allegany
Whitesville Central SD 200/K-12
692 Main St 14097 607-356-3301
Laurie Sanders, supt. Fax 356-3598
www.whitesvillesd.org
Whitesville Central S 200/K-12
692 Main St 14897 607-356-3301
Tammy Emery, prin. Fax 356-3598

Whitney Point, Broome, Pop. 945
Whitney Point Central SD 1,500/PK-12
PO Box 249 13862 607-692-8202
Patricia Follette, supt. Fax 692-4434
www.wpcsd.org
Adams PS 500/PK-3
PO Box 249 13862 607-692-8241
JoAnne Knapp, prin. Fax 692-8297
Tioughnioga Riverside Academy 600/4-8
PO Box 249 13862 607-692-8232
Laura Chestnut, prin. Fax 692-8283

Williamson, Wayne, Pop. 2,435
Williamson Central SD 1,100/K-12
PO Box 900 14589 315-589-9661
Dr. Gregory Macaluso, supt. Fax 589-7611
www.williamsoncentral.org
Williamson ES 400/K-4
PO Box 900 14589 315-589-9668
Ellen Saxby, prin. Fax 589-8315
Williamson MS 300/5-8
PO Box 900 14589 315-589-9665
John Fulmer, prin. Fax 589-8314

Williamsville, Erie, Pop. 5,229
Clarence Central SD
Supt. — See Clarence
Harris Hill ES 500/K-5
4260 Harris Hill Rd 14221 716-407-9175
Margaret Aldrich, prin. Fax 407-9182
Sheridan Hill ES 500/K-5
4560 Boncrest Dr E 14221 716-407-9250
Lee Pierce, prin. Fax 407-9258

Williamsville Central SD
Supt. — See East Amherst
Country Parkway ES 600/K-4
35 Hollybrook Dr 14221 716-626-9860
Andrew Bowen, prin. Fax 626-9879
Forest ES 500/K-4
250 N Forest Rd 14221 716-626-9800
Keith Wing, prin. Fax 626-9819
Heim ES 700/K-4
155 Heim Rd 14221 716-626-8697
Bonnie Stafford, prin. Fax 626-8679
Heim MS 700/5-8
175 Heim Rd 14221 716-626-8603
Jeffrey Jachlewski, prin. Fax 626-8626
Maple East ES 600/K-4
1500 Maple Rd 14221 716-626-8801
Cathy Mihalic, prin. Fax 626-8808
Maple West ES 600/K-4
851 Maple Rd 14221 716-626-8843
Dr. Charles Galluzzo, prin. Fax 626-8859
Mill MS 900/5-8
505 Mill St 14221 716-626-8329
Michael Calandra, prin. Fax 626-8326

Christian Central Academy 400/K-12
39 Academy St 14221 716-634-4821
Thad Gaebelein, hdmstr. Fax 634-5851
Nativity of BVM S 200/PK-8
8550 Main St 14221 716-633-7441
Joseph Roaldi, prin. Fax 626-1637
St. Gregory the Great S 600/PK-8
250 Saint Gregory Ct 14221 716-688-5323
Julie Gajewski, prin. Fax 688-6629
SS. Peter & Paul S 400/PK-8
5480 Main St 14221 716-632-6146
Deborah Lester, prin. Fax 626-0971

Williston Park, Nassau, Pop. 7,170
Herricks UFD
Supt. — See New Hyde Park
Center Street ES 500/K-5
240 Center St 11596 516-305-8300
Brennen Bierwiler, prin. Fax 739-4739

St. Aidan S 600/PK-8
510 Willis Ave 11596 516-746-6585
Eileen Oliver, prin. Fax 746-3086

Willsboro, Essex, Pop. 740
Willsboro Central SD 300/PK-12
PO Box 180 12996 518-963-4456
Stephen Broadwell, supt. Fax 963-7577
www.willsborocsd.org/
Willsboro Central S 300/PK-12
PO Box 180 12996 518-963-4456
Stephen Broadwell, prin. Fax 963-7577

Wilson, Niagara, Pop. 1,249
Wilson Central SD 1,000/K-12
PO Box 648 14172 716-751-9341
Timothy Carter, supt. Fax 751-6556
www.wilson.wnyric.org
Wilson ES 300/K-5
PO Box 648 14172 716-751-9341
John Diodate, prin. Fax 751-1269
Wilson MS 300/6-8
PO Box 648 14172 716-751-9341
Scott Benton, prin. Fax 751-9597

Wilton, Saratoga
South Glens Falls Central SD
Supt. — See South Glens Falls
Ballard ES 400/K-5
300 Ballard Rd 12831 518-587-0600
Mike Huchro, prin. Fax 587-2248

Windham, Greene, Pop. 359
Windham-Ashland-Jewett Central SD 300/K-12
PO Box 429 12496 518-734-3400
John Wiktorko, supt. Fax 734-6050
www.wajcs.org/
Windham-Ashland Central S 300/K-12
PO Box 429 12496 518-734-3400
David Donner, prin. Fax 734-6050

Windsor, Broome, Pop. 903
Windsor Central SD 1,700/PK-12
1191 State Route 79 13865 607-655-8216
Jason Andrews Ed.D., supt. Fax 655-3553
www.windsor-csd.org
Palmer ES 200/PK-5
213 Main St 13865 607-655-8225
Jamie Bernard, prin. Fax 655-8309
Weeks ES 300/PK-5
440 Foley Rd 13865 607-775-3226
Kristin Beriman, prin. Fax 775-4835
Windsor MS 400/6-8
215 Main St 13865 607-655-8247
Kevin Strahley, prin. Fax 655-3760
Other Schools – See Kirkwood

Wingdale, Dutchess
Dover UFD
Supt. — See Dover Plains
Wingdale ES 300/K-2
6413 Route 55 12594 845-877-5720
Catherine Alvarez, prin. Fax 877-5729

Wolcott, Wayne, Pop. 1,683
North Rose-Wolcott Central SD 1,200/PK-12
11631 Salter Colvin Rd 14590 315-594-3141
Stephan Vigliotti, supt. Fax 594-2352
www.nrwcs.org
North Rose-Wolcott MS 400/5-8
5957 New Hartford St 14590 315-594-3141
Mark Mathews, prin. Fax 594-3120
Other Schools – See North Rose

Woodbury, Nassau, Pop. 8,811
Syosset Central SD
Supt. — See Syosset
Whitman ES, 482 Woodbury Rd 11797 200/K-5
Chad Synder, prin. 516-364-5823

Wood Haven, See New York
NYC Department of Education
Supt. — See New York
New York City Academy for Discovery 500/PK-5
9516 89th Ave, 718-441-2165
Cheryl Ann Leone, prin. Fax 441-5923
Public S 60 1,300/PK-5
9102 88th Ave, 718-441-5046
Frank Desario, prin. Fax 805-1487
Public S 97 700/PK-5
8552 85th St, 718-849-4870
Marilyn Custodio, prin. Fax 849-5356

St. Thomas Apostle Catholic Academy 200/PK-8
8749 87th St, 718-847-3904
Dr. Phyllis Reggio, prin. Fax 847-3513

Woodmere, Nassau, Pop. 17,006
Hewlett-Woodmere UFD 3,100/PK-12
1 Johnson Pl 11598 516-792-4800
Dr. Ralph Marino, supt. Fax 374-8185
www.hewlett-woodmere.net
Other Schools – See Hewlett, Valley Stream

Hebrew Academy Long Beach 800/1-8
523 Church Ave 11598 516-432-8285
Lawrence Woodmere Academy 300/PK-12
336 Woodmere Blvd 11598 516-374-9000
Alan Bernstein, hdmstr. Fax 374-4707

Woodside, See New York
NYC Department of Education
Supt. — See New York
Public S 11 1,400/K-6
5425 Skillman Ave 11377 718-779-2090
Elizabeth Pena Jorge, prin. Fax 458-6362
Public S 12 1,300/K-5
4200 72nd St 11377 718-424-5905
Stephanie Moskos, prin. Fax 424-0207
Public S 151 500/PK-5
5005 31st Ave 11377 718-728-2676
Samantha Maisonet, prin. Fax 545-2028
Public S 152 1,400/PK-6
3352 62nd St 11377 718-429-3141
Vincent Vitolo, prin. Fax 779-7532
Public S 229 1,500/PK-6
6725 51st Rd 11377 718-446-2120
Seth Berger, prin. Fax 672-3117
IS 125 1,700/5-8
4602 47th Ave 11377 718-937-0320
Judy Mittler, prin. Fax 361-2451

Jackson Heights SDA S 100/K-8
7225 Woodside Ave 11377 718-426-5729
Veronica Quinones, prin. Fax 426-0079
Rainbow Christian Preschool & K 100/PK-K
7201 43rd Ave 11377 718-335-3361
Carla Olmez, dir. Fax 335-2931
Razi S 300/PK-12
5511 Queens Blvd 11377 718-779-0711
Dr. Ghassan Elcheikhali, prin. Fax 779-0103
St. Sebastian Academy 400/PK-8
3976 58th St 11377 718-429-1982
JoAnn Dolan, prin. Fax 446-7225

Woodstock, Ulster, Pop. 2,034
Onteora Central SD
Supt. — See Boiceville
Woodstock ES 300/K-6
8 W Hurley Rd 12498 845-679-2316
Scott Richards, prin. Fax 679-1207

Worcester, Otsego, Pop. 1,097
Worcester Central SD 400/PK-12
198 Main St 12197 607-397-8785
Edmund Shultis, supt. Fax 397-8464
www.worcestercs.org
Worcester Central S 400/PK-12
198 Main St 12197 607-397-8785
Jessie Westfall, prin. Fax 397-9454

Wurtsboro, Sullivan, Pop. 1,229
Monticello Central SD
Supt. — See Monticello
Chase ES 400/K-5
28 Pennsylvania Ave 12790 845-888-2471
William Frandino, prin. Fax 888-2029

Wyandanch, Suffolk, Pop. 11,382
Wyandanch UFD 2,200/PK-12
1445 Straight Path 11798 631-870-0400
Dr. Mary Jones, supt. Fax 870-0404
www.wufsd.net/
Hardiman ES 700/PK-2
792 Mount Ave 11798 631-870-0580
Shamika Simpson, prin. Fax 870-0584
King ES 500/3-4
792 Mount Ave 11798 631-870-0556
Shamika Simpson, prin. Fax 870-0564
Olive MS 400/5-8
140 Garden City Ave 11798 631-870-0525
Kenya Vanterpool, prin. Fax 870-0533

Wynantskill, Rensselaer, Pop. 3,234

Parker S PK-8
4254 NY Route 43 12198 518-286-3449
Laura Graceffa, head sch Fax 286-3452
St. Jude the Apostle S 300/PK-6
42 Dana Ave 12198 518-283-0333
Danielle Cox, prin. Fax 283-0475

Wyoming, Wyoming, Pop. 427
Wyoming Central SD 100/K-8
PO Box 244 14591 585-495-6222
Kathleen Schuessler, supt. Fax 495-6341
www.wyomingcsd.org
Wyoming Central S 100/K-8
PO Box 244 14591 585-495-6222
Kathleen Schuessler, admin. Fax 495-6341

Yaphank, Suffolk, Pop. 5,884
Longwood Central SD
Supt. — See Middle Island
Walters ES 800/K-4
15 Everett Dr 11980 631-345-2758
Yvette Tilley, prin. Fax 345-2849

Yonkers, Westchester, Pop. 192,139
Yonkers CSD 25,500/PK-12
1 Larkin Ctr 10701 914-376-8000
Dr. Edwin Quezada, supt. Fax 376-8584
www.yonkerspublicschools.org
Cedar Place S 600/PK-8
20 Cedar Pl 10705 914-376-8969
Magdaline Delany, prin. Fax 376-8972
Cornell Academy 300/PK-6
15 Saint Marys St 10701 914-376-8315
Dr. Edward Beglane, prin. Fax 968-5790
Cross Hill Academy 700/PK-8
160 Bolmer Ave 10703 914-376-8300
Brian Gray, prin. Fax 376-8499
de Hostos MicroSociety S 600/PK-8
75 Morris St 10705 914-376-8430
Elda Perez-Mejia, prin. Fax 376-8432
Dichiaro S 600/PK-8
373 Bronxville Rd 10708 914-376-8565
Patricia Langan, prin. Fax 376-8567
Dodson S 800/PK-8
105 Avondale Rd 10710 914-376-8159
Evelina Medina, prin. Fax 337-5207
Family S 32 600/PK-8
1 Montclair Pl 10710 914-376-8595
Dr. Miriam Digneo, prin. Fax 376-8597
Fermi S 900/PK-8
27 Poplar St 10701 914-376-8460
Mark Ametrano, prin. Fax 376-8468
Gibran S 600/PK-8
18 Rosedale Rd 10710 914-376-8580
Dianne White, prin. Fax 376-8583
King Jr. Academy 600/PK-8
135 Locust Hill Ave 10701 914-376-8470
Natalie Davy, prin. Fax 376-8472
Montessori S 27 400/PK-6
132 Valentine Ln 10705 914-376-8455
Moira Gleeson, prin. Fax 376-8457
Montessori S 31 300/PK-6
7 Ravenswood Rd 10710 914-376-8623
Dr. Sharon Banks-Williams, prin. Fax 376-8626
Museum S 25 400/PK-5
579 Warburton Ave 10701 914-376-8450
JoAnn DiMaria, prin. Fax 376-8452
Paideia S 15 600/PK-8
175 Westchester Ave 10707 914-376-8645
Jane Wermuth, prin Fax 376-8630
Paideia S 24 500/PK-6
50 Colin St 10701 914-376-8640
Kim Davis, prin. Fax 376-8642
PEARLS Hawthorne S 1,100/PK-8
350 Hawthorne Ave 10705 914-376-8250
Marwan Sayegh, prin. Fax 376-8257
Pulaski S 600/PK-8
150 Kings Cross, 914-376-8575
Christine Montero, prin. Fax 722-7697
Scholastic Acad for Academic Excellence 600/PK-8
77 Park Hill Ave 10701 914-376-8420
Dr. Valencia Brown-Wyatt, prin. Fax 376-8423
Siragusa S 600/PK-6
60 Crescent Pl 10704 914-376-8570
Anthony Cioffi, prin. Fax 776-7041
Thompson S 600/PK-8
1061 N Broadway 10701 914-376-8563
Dr. Taren Washington, prin. Fax 376-8578
Westchester Hills S 29 500/PK-8
47 Croydon Rd 10710 914-376-8585
Steven Murphy, prin. Fax 961-1287
Yonkers Early Childhood Academy 100/PK-1
160 Bolmer Ave 10703 914-376-8500
Brian Curtis, admin. Fax 376-8499
Yonkers Montessori Academy 1,300/PK-12
160 Woodlawn Ave 10704 914-376-8540
Dr. Eileen Rivera-Shapiro, prin. Fax 376-8499
S 5 700/PK-8
118 Lockwood Ave 10701 914-376-8320
Dr. Geraldine Pisacreta, prin. Fax 376-8322
S 9 400/PK-6
53 Fairview St 10703 914-376-8325
Tracie Creighton-Thiam, prin. Fax 376-8327
S 13 700/PK-8
195 McLean Ave 10705 914-376-8335
Isabel Hernandez, prin. Fax 965-2870
S 16 600/PK-8
759 N Broadway 10701 914-376-8340
Cynthia Eisner, prin. Fax 376-8342
S 17 600/PK-5
745 Midland Ave 10704 914-376-8345
Robert Riccuti, prin. Fax 376-8347
S 21 500/PK-6
100 Lee Ave 10705 914-376-8435
Leslie Powell-Grant, prin. Fax 375-3907
S 22 500/PK-6
1408 Nepperhan Ave 10703 914-376-8440
Leslie Dildy, prin. Fax 376-8442
S 23 600/PK-8
56 Van Cortlandt Pk Ave 10701 914-376-8445
Michael Walpole, prin. Fax 376-8448
S 30 600/PK-8
30 Nevada Pl 10708 914-376-8590
Dr. Majorie Brown-Anfelouss, prin. Fax 376-8592

New Testament Church S 50/PK-8
306 Rumsey Rd 10705 914-966-1766
Sr. Mary Zachariah M.Ed., admin. Fax 966-1767
Oakview Preparatory S of SDA 200/PK-8
29 Chestnut St 10701 914-423-7369
Jean Imbert, prin. Fax 423-0813
Sacred Heart S 300/PK-8
34 Convent Ave 10703 914-965-3114
Karen Valenti-DeCecco, prin. Fax 965-4510
St. Ann S 200/PK-8
40 Brewster Ave 10701 914-965-4333
Michael Vicario, prin. Fax 965-1778
St. Anthony S 300/PK-8
1395 Nepperhan Ave 10703 914-476-8489
Elizabeth Carney, prin. Fax 965-7939
St. Eugene S 300/PK-8
707 Tuckahoe Rd 10710 914-779-2956
Joan Fox, prin. Fax 779-7668
St. John the Baptist Catholic S 300/PK-8
670 Yonkers Ave 10704 914-965-2356
Sr. Maryalice Reamer, prin. Fax 375-1115
St. Mark's Lutheran S 100/PK-8
7 Saint Marks Pl 10704 914-237-4944
Debra Masiello, prin. Fax 237-4480
St. Paul the Apostle S 200/PK-8
77 Lee Ave 10705 914-965-2165
Grace Mallardi, prin. Fax 965-5792
St. Peter S 200/PK-8
204 Hawthorne Ave 10705 914-963-2314
Sheila Alagia, prin. Fax 966-8822
Stein Yeshiva of Lincoln Park 100/PK-8
287 Central Park Ave 10704 914-965-7082
Rabbi Joseph Cherns, prin. Fax 965-1902

Yorkshire, Cattaraugus, Pop. 1,167
Yorkshire-Pioneer Central SD 2,500/PK-12
PO Box 579 14173 716-492-9300
Ben Halsey, supt. Fax 492-9360
www.pioneerschools.org
Pioneer MS 700/5-8
PO Box 619 14173 716-492-9371
Melissa Prorok, prin. Fax 492-9417
Other Schools – See Arcade, Delevan

Yorktown Heights, Westchester, Pop. 1,760
Lakeland Central SD
Supt. — See Shrub Oak
Franklin ES 600/K-5
3477 Kamhi Dr 10598 914-245-7444
Patricia Moore, prin. Fax 245-7668
Jefferson ES 500/K-5
3636 Gomer St 10598 914-245-4802
Dr. Karen Gagliardi, prin. Fax 245-0511
Lakeland-Copper Beech MS 1,300/6-8
3401 Old Yorktown Rd 10598 914-245-1885
Robert Bergmann, prin. Fax 245-1259

Yorktown Central SD 3,500/K-12
2725 Crompond Rd 10598 914-243-8000
Dr. Ron Hattar, supt. Fax 243-8002
www.yorktown.org
Brookside IS 500/K-3
2285 Broad St 10598 914-243-8130
Deirdre Amerling, prin. Fax 243-0017
Crompond IS 500/4-5
2901 Manor St 10598 914-243-8140
Lori Roberts, prin. Fax 243-0018
Mohansic ES 400/K-3
704 Locksley Rd 10598 914-243-8160
Susan Berry, prin. Fax 243-0019
Strang MS 900/6-8
2701 Crompond Rd 10598 914-243-8100
Marie Horowitz, prin. Fax 243-0016

Our Montessori S 200/PK-6
PO Box 72 10598 914-962-9466
St. Patrick S 300/PK-8
117 Moseman Rd 10598 914-962-2211
Darlene Delvecchio, prin. Fax 243-4814

Youngstown, Niagara, Pop. 1,918
Lewiston-Porter Central SD 2,000/K-12
4061 Creek Rd 14174 716-754-8281
Paul Casseri, supt. Fax 754-2755
www.lew-port.com
Lewiston-Porter Intermediate Educ Ctr 400/3-5
4061 Creek Rd 14174 716-286-7254
Tina Rodriguez, prin. Fax 286-7854
Lewiston-Porter MS 500/6-8
4061 Creek Rd 14174 716-286-7201
Andrew Auer, prin. Fax 286-7204
Lewiston-Porter Primary Education Center 400/K-2
4061 Creek Rd 14174 716-286-7222
Tamara Larson, prin. Fax 286-7855

NORTH CAROLINA

NORTH CAROLINA DEPT. PUBLIC INSTRUCTION

301 N Wilmington St, Raleigh 27601-1058
Telephone 919-807-3300
Fax 919-807-3445
Website http://www.dpi.state.nc.us

Superintendent of Public Instruction Mark Johnson

NORTH CAROLINA BOARD OF EDUCATION

301 N Wilmington St, Raleigh 27601-1058

Chairperson William Cobey

PUBLIC, PRIVATE AND CATHOLIC ELEMENTARY SCHOOLS

Aberdeen, Moore, Pop. 6,182
Moore County SD
Supt. — See Carthage
Aberdeen ES 300/3-5
503 N Sandhills Blvd 28315 910-944-1124
Dante Poole, prin. Fax 944-3597
Aberdeen PS 300/PK-2
310 Keyser St 28315 910-944-1523
Molly Capps, prin. Fax 944-3171
Southern MS 800/6-8
717 Johnson St 28315 910-693-1550
Marcy Cooper, prin. Fax 693-1544

Advance, Davie, Pop. 1,117
Davie County SD
Supt. — See Mocksville
Ellis MS 500/6-8
144 William Ellis Dr 27006 336-998-2007
Leigh Walters, prin. Fax 998-6249
Shady Grove ES 600/K-5
3179 Cornatzer Rd 27006 336-998-4719
Mary Margaret Sullivan, prin. Fax 998-7024

Ahoskie, Hertford, Pop. 4,982
Hertford County SD
Supt. — See Winton
Ahoskie ES 500/4-5
200 Talmage Ave N 27910 252-332-2588
Keisha Peele, prin. Fax 332-2017
Bearfield PS 800/PK-3
145 Hertford County High Rd 27910 252-209-6140
Julie Shields, prin. Fax 209-6148

Ahoskie Christian S 200/PK-12
500 Kiwanis St 27910 252-332-2764
Ridgecroft S 300/PK-12
PO Box 1008 27910 252-332-2964

Albemarle, Stanly, Pop. 15,632
Stanly County SD 8,300/PK-12
1000 N 1st St Ste 4 28001 704-961-3000
Georgia Harvey, supt. Fax 961-3099
www.stanlycountyschools.org
Albemarle MS 400/6-8
1811 Badin Rd 28001 704-961-3400
Beverly Pennington, prin. Fax 961-3499
Central ES 600/K-5
250 N 3rd St 28001 704-961-3200
Melissa Smith, prin. Fax 961-3299
East Albemarle ES 400/K-5
1813 E Main St 28001 704-961-3500
Jonathan Brooks, prin. Fax 961-3599
Endy ES 300/PK-5
27670 Betty Rd 28001 704-961-3300
Karen Nixon, prin. Fax 961-3399
Millingport ES 300/PK-5
24198 NC 73 Hwy 28001 704-961-4300
Shelby Lawson, prin. Fax 961-4399
Other Schools – See Badin, Locust, New London, Norwood, Oakboro, Richfield, Stanfield

---

Park Ridge Christian S 200/K-8
312 Park Ridge Rd 28001 704-982-9798

Albertson, Duplin
Duplin County SD
Supt. — See Kenansville
Grady ES 900/PK-8
2627 N NC 11 903 Hwy 28508 252-568-3487
Amy Wallace, prin. Fax 568-6238

Andrews, Cherokee, Pop. 1,715
Cherokee County SD
Supt. — See Murphy
Andrews ES 400/PK-4
205 Jean Christy Ave 28901 828-321-4415
Melissa Godfrey, prin. Fax 321-0401
Andrews MS 200/5-8
2750 Business 19 28901 828-321-5762
Julie Higdon, prin. Fax 321-2009

Angier, Harnett, Pop. 4,289
Harnett County SD
Supt. — See Lillington
Angier ES 400/3-5
130 E Mciver St 27501 919-639-2635
Elizabeth Hodge, prin. Fax 639-9583
Harnett Central MS 1,300/6-8
2529 Harnett Central Rd 27501 919-639-6000
Lynn Herring, prin. Fax 639-9617
North Harnett PS 500/K-2
282 North Harnett School Rd 27501 919-639-4480
Lisa Williams, prin. Fax 639-7064

Johnston County SD
Supt. — See Smithfield
McGee's Crossroads ES 900/PK-5
10330 NC 50 Hwy N 27501 919-894-7161
Christie Turner, prin. Fax 894-1960

Apex, Wake, Pop. 36,623
Wake County SD
Supt. — See Cary
Apex ES 700/K-5
700 Tingen Rd 27502 919-387-2150
Keith Faison, prin. Fax 387-2152
Apex MS 1,100/6-8
400 E Moore St 27502 919-387-2181
Monica Yllanes, prin. Fax 387-2203
Baucom ES 900/K-5
400 Hunter St 27502 919-387-2168
Suzanne Owen, prin. Fax 387-2170
Laurel Park ES 1,000/K-5
2450 Laura Duncan Rd, 919-290-2333
Raleigh Bame, prin. Fax 290-2334
Lufkin Road MS 1,000/6-8
1002 Lufkin Rd, 919-387-4465
Karen Sinders, prin. Fax 363-1095
Middle Creek ES 900/K-5
110 Middle Creek Park Ave, 919-773-9555
Wiladean Thomas, prin. Fax 773-9568
Oakview ES PK-5
11500 Holly Springs New Hl, 919-694-8885
Steven Moore, prin. Fax 589-6460
Olive Chapel ES 1,000/K-5
1751 Olive Chapel Rd 27502 919-387-4440
Dr. Ruth Steidinger, prin. Fax 387-4447
Salem ES 800/K-5
6116 Old Jenks Rd, 919-363-2865
Derrick Evans, prin. Fax 363-2973
Salem MS 1,200/6-8
6150 Old Jenks Rd, 919-363-1870
Elaine Hofmann, prin. Fax 363-1876
Scotts Ridge ES K-5
6601 Apex Barbecue Rd 27502 919-694-0300
Mel Leach, prin. Fax 694-0310
West Lake ES 900/PK-5
4500 W Lake Rd, 919-662-2300
Daniel Simons, prin. Fax 704-2003
West Lake MS 1,300/6-8
4600 W Lake Rd, 919-662-2900
Anne Adkins, prin. Fax 662-2906
White Oak ES PK-5
1512 White Oak Church Rd, 919-694-0202
Robin Swaim, prin. Fax 363-2969

St. Andrew ECC 100/PK-PK
3008 Old Raleigh Rd 27502 919-387-8656
Nancy Wujek, dir. Fax 362-5778
St. Mary Magdalene S 700/PK-8
625 Magdala Pl 27502 919-657-4800
Robert Cadran, prin. Fax 657-4805
Thales Academy Apex 300/K-5
1177 Ambergate Sta 27502 919-303-3108
Rachael Bradley, admin. Fax 367-9630

Archdale, Randolph, Pop. 11,273
Randolph County SD
Supt. — See Asheboro
Archdale ES 400/K-5
207 Trindale Rd 27263 336-431-9121
Lisa Thompson, prin. Fax 431-5943
Lawrence ES 500/K-5
6068 Suits Rd 27263 336-861-8100
Anthony Warden, prin. Fax 861-8101
Trindale ES 300/PK-5
400 Balfour Dr 27263 336-434-1516
Todd Henderson, prin. Fax 434-2508

Arden, Buncombe
Buncombe County SD
Supt. — See Asheville
Avery's Creek ES 700/K-4
15 Park South Rd 28704 828-654-1810
Denise Montgomery, prin. Fax 654-9801
Glen Arden ES 500/K-4
50 Pinehurst Cir 28704 828-654-1800
Kristina Specht, prin. Fax 654-1801
Valley Springs MS 600/6-8
224 Long Shoals Rd 28704 828-654-1785
Eddie Burchfiel, prin. Fax 654-1789

Ash, Brunswick
Brunswick County SD
Supt. — See Bolivia
Monroe ES 400/PK-5
250 Pea Landing Rd NW 28420 910-287-4014
Alecia Williams, prin. Fax 287-4027
Waccamaw S 600/K-8
5901 Waccamaw School Rd NW 28420 910-287-6437
Roman Kelley, prin. Fax 287-5123

Asheboro, Randolph, Pop. 24,567
Asheboro CSD 4,700/PK-12
PO Box 1103 27204 336-625-5104
Dr. Terry Worrell, supt. Fax 625-9238
www.asheboro.k12.nc.us
Balfour ES 600/K-5
2097 N Asheboro School Rd 27203 336-672-0322
Dr. Penny Crooks, prin. Fax 672-0328
Lindley Park ES 400/K-5
312 Cliff Rd 27203 336-625-6226
Nikia Domally, prin. Fax 629-5895
Loflin ES 400/K-5
405 S Park St 27203 336-625-1685
Jordi Roman, prin. Fax 625-1688
McCrary ES 400/K-5
400 Ross St 27203 336-629-1817
Julie Brady, prin. Fax 629-1327
North Asheboro MS 500/6-8
1861 N Asheboro School Rd 27203 336-672-1900
Candace Call, prin. Fax 672-6267
South Asheboro MS 600/6-8
523 W Walker Ave 27203 336-629-4141
Ronald Dixon, prin. Fax 629-3761
Teachey ES 500/PK-5
294 Newbern Ave 27205 336-625-4163
Amy Day, prin. Fax 629-6178

Randolph County SD 18,100/PK-12
2222 S Fayetteville St # C 27205 336-318-6100
Dr. Stephen Gainey, supt. Fax 318-6155
www.randolph.k12.nc.us
Farmer ES 400/K-5
3557 Grange Hall Rd 27205 336-857-3400
Nathan Gray, prin. Fax 857-3409
Southmont ES 600/PK-5
2497 Southmont Dr 27205 336-625-1558
Penny Baber, prin. Fax 625-5693
Southwestern Randolph MS 600/6-8
1509 Hopewell Friends Rd 27205 336-381-3900
Michael Crider, prin. Fax 381-3905
Tabernacle ES 400/PK-5
4901 Tabernacle School Rd 27205 336-629-3533
Ceretha Mitchell, prin. Fax 629-4463
Other Schools – See Archdale, Franklinville, Liberty, Ramseur, Randleman, Seagrove, Sophia, Trinity

---

Fayetteville Street Christian S 200/PK-12
151 W Pritchard St 27203 336-629-1383
Neighbors Grove Christian Academy 100/PK-12
1928 N Fayetteville St 27203 336-672-1147
Randy Haithcock, admin. Fax 672-5500

Asheville, Buncombe, Pop. 81,334
Asheville CSD 4,200/PK-12
85 Mountain St 28801 828-350-7000
Dr. Denise Patterson, supt. Fax 255-5131
www.ashevillecityschools.net
Asheville MS 800/6-8
211 S French Broad Ave 28801 828-350-6200
April Dockery, prin. Fax 255-5311

Asheville PS, 441 Haywood Rd 28806 PK-3
Dr. Dawn Meskil, prin. 828-350-2900
Claxton ES 400/K-5
241 Merrimon Ave 28801 828-350-6500
Derek Edwards, prin. Fax 255-5239
Dickson ES 500/PK-5
125 Hill St 28801 828-350-6800
Brad Johnson, prin. Fax 255-5589
Fletcher ES 300/PK-5
60 Ridgelawn Rd 28806 828-350-6400
Cynthia Sellinger, prin. Fax 255-5070
Jones ES 400/PK-5
544 Kimberly Ave 28804 828-350-6700
Sarah Cain, prin. Fax 251-4914
Montford North Star Academy 6-7
90 Montford Ave 28801 828-350-6900
Shannon Baggett, prin.
Vance ES 500/K-5
98 Sulphur Springs Rd 28806 828-350-6600
Ruletta Hughes, prin. Fax 251-4952

Buncombe County SD 25,500/K-12
175 Bingham Rd 28806 828-255-5921
Dr. Tony Baldwin, supt. Fax 255-5923
www.buncombe.k12.nc.us
Bell ES 300/K-5
90 Maple Springs Rd 28805 828-298-3789
Jenny Klein, prin. Fax 299-0685
Eblen IS 800/5-6
59 Lees Creek Rd 28806 828-255-5757
Christopher Cody, prin. Fax 255-5759
Emma ES 400/K-4
37 Brickyard Rd 28806 828-232-4272
Jeremy Stowe, prin. Fax 232-4275
Erwin MS 900/7-8
20 Erwin Hills Rd 28806 828-232-4264
Chris Thompson, prin. Fax 253-4267
Estes ES 800/K-5
275 Overlook Rd 28803 828-654-1795
Paula Pinkerton, prin. Fax 654-1798
Haw Creek ES 400/K-5
21 Trinity Chapel Rd 28805 828-298-4022
Jay Dale, prin. Fax 299-8117
Johnston ES 300/K-4
230 Johnston Blvd 28806 828-232-4291
Danna Grimes, prin. Fax 252-7653
Koontz IS 800/5-6
305 Overlook Rd 28803 828-684-1295
Reginald Bright, prin. Fax 684-1290
Oakley ES 500/K-5
753 Fairview Rd 28803 828-274-7515
Danny Fusco, prin. Fax 274-1721
Reynolds MS 600/6-8
2 Rocket Dr 28803 828-298-7484
Stanley Wheless, prin. Fax 298-7503
Sand Hill-Venable ES 700/K-5
154 Sand Hill School Rd 28806 828-670-5028
Amy Dupree, prin. Fax 670-5034
West Buncombe ES 600/K-4
175 Erwin Hills Rd 28806 828-232-4282
Brian Chandler, prin. Fax 232-1316
Woodfin ES 100/K-4
108 Elk Mountain Rd 28804 828-232-4287
April Wright, prin. Fax 232-4288
Other Schools – See Arden, Barnardsville, Black Mountain, Candler, Fairview, Fletcher, Leicester, Swannanoa, Weaverville

---

Asheville Catholic S 200/PK-8
12 Culvern St 28804 828-252-7896
Michael Miller, prin. Fax 252-5708
Carolina Day S 700/PK-12
1345 Hendersonville Rd 28803 828-274-0757
Kirk Duncan, head sch Fax 274-0756
Emmanuel Lutheran S 200/PK-8
51 Wilburn Pl 28806 828-281-8182
Elizabeth Meschke, prin. Fax 254-3940
New City Christian S 100/K-5
PO Box 6412 28816 828-252-8173
Matthew Fuller, prin.
Providence Christian Academy 100/PK-6
48 Woodland Hills Rd 28804 828-658-8964
Larry Basinger, prin. Fax 370-1462
Rainbow Community S 200/PK-8
574 Haywood Rd 28806 828-258-9264
Renee Owen, prin. Fax 348-5492
Reynolds Mountain Christian Academy 100/PK-12
20 Reynolds Mountain Blvd 28804 828-645-8053
Susie Hepler, admin. Fax 645-4542
Temple Baptist S 100/PK-12
985 1/2 Patton Ave 28806 828-252-3712
William Spence, admin. Fax 254-5119

Atlantic, Carteret, Pop. 541
Carteret County SD
Supt. — See Beaufort
Atlantic S 100/PK-5
PO Box 98 28511 252-225-3961
Greg Guthrie, prin. Fax 225-1077

Aulander, Bertie, Pop. 885
Bertie County SD
Supt. — See Windsor
Aulander ES 200/PK-5
2515 NC Highway 305 27805 252-345-3211
Clara Lee, prin. Fax 345-0066

Aurora, Beaufort, Pop. 503
Beaufort County SD
Supt. — See Washington
Snowden ES 200/PK-8
693 N 7th St 27806 252-322-5351
Debra Windley, prin. Fax 322-4372

Autryville, Sampson, Pop. 185
Sampson County SD
Supt. — See Clinton

Clement ES 400/PK-5
3220 Maxwell Rd 28318 910-567-2112
James Mullins, prin. Fax 567-5910

Ayden, Pitt, Pop. 4,853
Pitt County SD
Supt. — See Greenville
Ayden ES 700/PK-5
187 3rd St 28513 252-746-2121
Cornelia Cox, prin. Fax 746-6470
Ayden MS 400/6-8
192 3rd St 28513 252-746-3672
Dr. Jeff Theus, prin. Fax 746-9923

Badin, Stanly, Pop. 1,956
Stanly County SD
Supt. — See Albemarle
Badin ES 400/K-5
47 Henderson St 28009 704-961-3900
Damon Rhodes, prin. Fax 961-3999

Bahama, Durham
Durham County SD
Supt. — See Durham
Mangum ES 400/K-5
9008 Quail Roost Rd 27503 919-560-3948
Karen Kellett, prin. Fax 560-2204

Bailey, Nash, Pop. 561
Nash-Rocky Mount SD
Supt. — See Nashville
Bailey ES 600/PK-5
PO Box 39 27807 252-451-2892
Mary Jones, prin. Fax 235-6028

Bakersville, Mitchell, Pop. 450
Mitchell County SD 1,900/K-12
72 Ledger School Rd 28705 828-766-2220
Chad Calhoun, supt. Fax 766-2221
www.mcsnc.org
Bowman MS 300/5-8
410 S Mitchell Ave 28705 828-766-3370
Paula Holder, prin. Fax 688-6002
Gouge ES 300/K-4
134 Laurel St 28705 828-766-2260
Colby Calhoun, prin. Fax 688-9344
Other Schools – See Spruce Pine

Banner Elk, Avery, Pop. 1,011
Avery County SD
Supt. — See Newland
Banner Elk ES 200/PK-5
PO Box 218 28604 828-737-5700
Justin Carver, prin. Fax 898-6036

Barco, Currituck
Currituck County SD
Supt. — See Currituck
Central ES 200/PK-5
504 Shortcut Rd 27917 252-453-0010
Karrie Chappell, prin. Fax 453-0011
Currituck County MS 300/6-8
4263 Caratoke Hwy 27917 252-453-2171
Dr. Matt Lutz, prin. Fax 453-0019

Barnardsville, Buncombe
Buncombe County SD
Supt. — See Asheville
Barnardsville ES 200/K-4
20 Hillcrest Dr 28709 828-626-2290
Jason Miller, prin. Fax 626-3750

Bath, Beaufort, Pop. 248
Beaufort County SD
Supt. — See Washington
Bath ES 600/K-8
110 S King St 27808 252-923-3251
Spencer Pake, prin. Fax 923-0202

Battleboro, Edgecombe, Pop. 559
Edgecombe County SD
Supt. — See Tarboro
Coker-Wimberly ES 400/PK-5
1619 NC 97 W 27809 252-823-4446
Katelin Row, prin. Fax 641-5704
Phillips MS 200/6-8
4371 Battleboro Leggett Rd 27809 252-446-2031
Jennifer O'Meara, prin. Fax 446-1629

Nash-Rocky Mount SD
Supt. — See Nashville
Hubbard ES 400/K-5
7921 Red Oak Battleboro Rd 27809 252-451-8515
D. Tiffany Hopkins, prin. Fax 985-4326
Red Oak MS 900/6-8
3170 Red Oak Battleboro Rd 27809 252-462-2000
Timothy Mudd, prin. Fax 451-5510

Bayboro, Pamlico, Pop. 1,250
Pamlico County SD 1,300/PK-12
507 Anderson Dr 28515 252-745-4171
Lisa Jackson, supt. Fax 745-4172
www.pamlicoschools.org
Anderson ES 300/3-5
515 Anderson Dr 28515 252-745-4611
Tunmorya Bennett, prin. Fax 745-5021
Pamlico County MS 300/6-8
15526 NC Highway 55 28515 252-745-4061
Jeremy Johnson, prin. Fax 745-5583
Pamlico County PS 300/PK-2
323 Neals Creek Rd 28515 252-745-3404
Crystal Dixon, prin. Fax 745-3118

Beaufort, Carteret, Pop. 3,948
Carteret County SD 8,500/PK-12
107 Safrit Dr 28516 252-728-4583
Dr. Mat Bottoms, supt. Fax 728-3028
www.carteretcountyschools.org
Beaufort ES 400/PK-5
110 Carraway Dr 28516 252-728-3316
DeAnne Rosen, prin. Fax 728-2753

Beaufort MS 300/6-8
100 Carraway Dr 28516 252-728-4520
Dr. Cathy Tomon, prin. Fax 728-3392
Other Schools – See Atlantic, Cape Carteret, Harkers Island, Morehead City, Newport, Smyrna

Belhaven, Beaufort, Pop. 1,666

Pungo Christian Academy 200/PK-12
983 W Main St 27810 252-943-2678
Marcy Morgan, head sch Fax 943-3292

Belmont, Gaston, Pop. 9,916
Gaston County SD
Supt. — See Gastonia
Belmont Central ES 700/2-5
310 Eagle Rd 28012 704-825-8479
Phyllis Whitworth, prin. Fax 825-8080
Belmont MS 800/6-8
110 N Central Ave 28012 704-825-9619
Susan Redmond, prin. Fax 825-6951
Catawba Heights ES 400/PK-5
101 Ivey St 28012 704-827-3221
Cindy Stroupe, prin. Fax 827-2419
North Belmont ES 400/PK-5
210 School St 28012 704-836-9135
Justin Beam, prin. Fax 827-0423
Page PS 400/PK-1
215 Ewing Dr 28012 704-836-9116
Bill Kessler, prin. Fax 825-4883

Bennett, Chatham, Pop. 277
Chatham County SD
Supt. — See Pittsboro
Bennett S 200/K-8
PO Box 107 27208 336-581-3586
Dan Barnwell, prin. Fax 581-4054

Moore County SD
Supt. — See Carthage
Highfalls ES 300/K-8
1220 NC Highway 22 27208 910-464-3600
Dyan Pope, prin. Fax 464-5404

Benson, Johnston, Pop. 3,270
Johnston County SD
Supt. — See Smithfield
Benson ES 600/PK-4
2040 NC Highway 50 N 27504 919-894-4233
Takicey Dunston, prin. Fax 894-7133
Benson MS 400/5-8
1600 N Wall St 27504 919-894-3889
Ron Anthony, prin. Fax 894-1551
McGee's Crossroads MS 900/6-8
13353 NC Highway 210 27504 919-894-6003
Dorlisa Johnson-Cowart, prin. Fax 894-6007
Meadow ES 700/PK-8
7507 NC Highway 50 S 27504 919-894-4226
Sonya Grice, prin. Fax 894-1804

Bessemer City, Gaston, Pop. 5,262
Gaston County SD
Supt. — See Gastonia
Bessemer City Central ES 300/3-5
1400 Puetts Chapel Rd 28016 704-836-9108
Caroline Black, prin. Fax 629-6320
Bessemer City MS 500/6-8
525 Ed Wilson Rd 28016 704-836-9602
Dr. Fran DaCanal, prin. Fax 629-4501
Bessemer City PS 400/PK-2
1320 N 12th St 28016 704-629-4181
Kristie Gornto, prin. Fax 629-6119
Tryon ES 400/PK-5
2620 Tryon Courthouse Rd 28016 704-836-9107
Todd Dellinger, prin. Fax 629-5967

Community Christian Academy 100/K-12
616 Athenia Pl 28016 704-629-2391

Bethel, Pitt, Pop. 1,573
Pitt County SD
Supt. — See Greenville
Bethel S 300/PK-8
152 E Washington St 27812 252-825-3801
Jeremiah Miller, prin. Fax 825-1203

Beulaville, Duplin, Pop. 1,278
Duplin County SD
Supt. — See Kenansville
Beulaville ES 1,000/PK-8
138 Lyman Rd 28518 910-298-3171
Jackie Arthur, prin. Fax 298-3342

Biscoe, Montgomery, Pop. 1,683
Montgomery County SD
Supt. — See Troy
East MS 500/6-8
1834 US Highway 220 Alt S 27209 910-428-3278
Della Ingram, prin. Fax 428-1279
Green Ridge ES 500/PK-5
129 McCaskill Rd 27209 910-428-4196
Craig Wright, prin. Fax 428-4708

Black Creek, Wilson, Pop. 760
Wilson County SD
Supt. — See Wilson
Woodard ES 200/K-5
PO Box 26 27813 252-399-7940
Corey Walker, prin. Fax 399-7898

Black Mountain, Buncombe, Pop. 7,683
Buncombe County SD
Supt. — See Asheville
Black Mountain ES 200/4-5
100 Flat Creek Rd 28711 828-669-5217
Nicole Roberts, prin. Fax 669-5529
Black Mountain PS 500/K-3
301 E State St 28711 828-669-2645
Mallorie McGinnis, prin. Fax 669-1616

Swannanoa Valley Montessori S 100/PK-6
101 Carver Ave 28711 828-669-8571
Katie Hanning, dir.

Bladenboro, Bladen, Pop. 1,726
Bladen County SD
Supt. — See Elizabethtown
Bladenboro MS 400/5-8
910 S Main St 28320 910-863-3232
Randi Harrelson, prin. Fax 418-3594
Bladenboro PS 500/PK-4
PO Box 820 28320 910-863-3387
Deborah Guyton, prin. Fax 589-5068

Blowing Rock, Watauga, Pop. 1,217
Watauga County SD
Supt. — See Boone
Blowing Rock ES 300/K-8
PO Box 228 28605 828-295-3204
Patrick Sukow, prin. Fax 295-4977

Bolivia, Brunswick, Pop. 139
Brunswick County SD 12,500/PK-12
35 Referendum Dr NE 28422 910-253-2900
Leslie K. Tubb, supt. Fax 253-2983
www.bcswan.net
Bolivia ES 500/PK-5
4036 Business 17 E 28422 910-253-6516
Kelly Andrews, prin. Fax 253-8162
Williamson ES 600/K-5
1020 Zion Hill Rd SE 28422 910-754-8660
Helen Otto, prin. Fax 754-8661
Other Schools – See Ash, Leland, Shallotte, Southport, Supply, Winnabow

Bonlee, Chatham
Chatham County SD
Supt. — See Pittsboro
Bonlee S 400/K-8
PO Box 168 27213 919-837-5316
Kim Taylor, prin. Fax 837-5583

Boomer, Wilkes
Wilkes County SD
Supt. — See North Wilkesboro
Boomer-Ferguson ES 200/PK-5
556 Boomer Frgson School Rd 28606 336-651-8900
Beth Hubbard, prin. Fax 921-4290

Boone, Watauga, Pop. 16,843
Watauga County SD 4,400/PK-12
PO Box 1790 28607 828-264-7190
Dr. Scott Elliott, supt. Fax 264-7196
www.wataugaschools.org
Green Valley ES 400/PK-8
189 Big Hill Rd 28607 828-264-3606
Philip Norman, prin. Fax 264-8108
Hardin Park ES 800/PK-8
361 Jefferson Rd 28607 828-264-8481
Mary Smalling, prin. Fax 265-3609
Parkway ES 500/PK-8
160 Parkway School Dr 28607 828-264-3032
Patricia Buckner, prin. Fax 264-7999
Other Schools – See Blowing Rock, Sugar Grove, Vilas, Zionville

Boonville, Yadkin, Pop. 1,215
Yadkin County SD
Supt. — See Yadkinville
Boonville ES 300/PK-6
232 E Main St 27011 336-367-7021
Annette Johnson, prin. Fax 367-5172
Starmount MS 400/7-8
2626 Longtown Rd 27011 336-468-6833
Dr. Jed Cockrell, prin. Fax 468-6838

Bostic, Rutherford, Pop. 382
Rutherford County SD
Supt. — See Forest City
East Rutherford MS 600/6-8
259 E Church St 28018 828-245-3750
Jo Oliver, prin. Fax 245-1491
Sunshine ES 200/K-5
231 Toney Rd 28018 828-245-0658
Neil Higgins, prin. Fax 248-2407

Brevard, Transylvania, Pop. 7,401
Transylvania County SD 3,600/PK-12
225 Rosenwald Ln 28712 828-884-6173
Dr. Jeff McDaris, supt. Fax 884-9524
www.tcsnc.org
Brevard ES 500/PK-5
399 Greenville Hwy 28712 828-884-2001
April Gaydosh, prin. Fax 884-3304
Brevard MS 500/6-8
400 Fisher Rd 28712 828-884-2091
Jeff Bailey, prin. Fax 883-3150
Pisgah Forest ES 500/K-5
1076 Ecusta Rd 28712 828-877-4481
Tonya Treadway, prin. Fax 884-2551
Other Schools – See Lake Toxaway, Rosman

Broadway, Lee, Pop. 1,211
Lee County SD
Supt. — See Sanford
Broadway ES 600/K-5
307 S Main St 27505 919-258-3828
Ricky Secor, prin. Fax 258-6954

Browns Summit, Guilford
Guilford County SD
Supt. — See Greensboro
Brown Summit MS 200/6-8
4720 E NC Highway 150 27214 336-656-0432
Dr. Kimberly Robertson, prin. Fax 656-0439
McNair ES 500/PK-5
4603 Yanceyville Rd 27214 336-691-5460
George Boschini, prin. Fax 375-5420
Monticello-Brown Summit ES 400/PK-5
5006 E NC Highway 150 27214 336-656-4010
Christopher Scott, prin. Fax 656-4616

Bryson City, Swain, Pop. 1,399
Swain County SD 2,000/PK-12
PO Box 2340 28713 828-488-3129
Sam Pattillo, supt. Fax 488-8510
www.swain.k12.nc.us
Swain County East ES 400/K-5
4747 Ela Rd 28713 828-488-0939
Tommy Dills, prin. Fax 488-6635
Swain County MS 500/PK-PK, 6-
135 Arlington Ave 28713 828-488-3480
Brandon Sutton, prin. Fax 488-0949
Swain County West ES 500/K-5
4142 Highway 19 W 28713 828-488-2119
Vicki Davis, prin. Fax 488-0797

Buies Creek, Harnett, Pop. 2,881
Harnett County SD
Supt. — See Lillington
Buies Creek ES 300/K-5
PO Box 68 27506 910-893-3505
Tracey Lubawski, prin. Fax 893-6979

Bunn, Franklin, Pop. 340
Franklin County SD
Supt. — See Louisburg
Bunn ES 700/K-5
PO Box 143 27508 919-496-4015
Geoffrey Hawthorne, prin. Fax 496-0301
Bunn MS 700/6-8
4742 NC 39 Hwy S 27508 919-496-7700
Dr. Danielle Jones, prin. Fax 496-1404

Bunnlevel, Harnett, Pop. 530
Harnett County SD
Supt. — See Lillington
Anderson Creek PS 600/K-2
914 Anderson Creek Sch Rd 28323 910-893-4523
Leanne O'Quinn, prin. Fax 893-6752
South Harnett ES 500/3-5
8335 NC Highway 210 S 28323 910-893-9153
Trinity Kelly, prin. Fax 893-5726

Burgaw, Pender, Pop. 3,819
Pender County SD 9,000/PK-12
925 Penderlea Hwy 28425 910-259-2187
Dr. Terri Cobb, supt. Fax 259-0133
www.pendercountyschools.net/
Burgaw ES 500/PK-5
400 N Wright St 28425 910-259-0145
Dr. Quinetta Hall, prin. Fax 259-0148
Burgaw MS 200/6-8
500 S Wright St 28425 910-259-0149
Caroline Godwin, prin. Fax 259-0150
Malpass Corner ES 500/PK-5
4992 Malpass Corner Rd 28425 910-283-5889
Avery Horrell, prin. Fax 283-5868
West Pender MS 200/6-8
10750 NC Highway 53 W 28425 910-283-5626
Cassandra Morrison, prin. Fax 283-9537
Other Schools – See Hampstead, Rocky Point, Willard

Burlington, Alamance, Pop. 49,060
Alamance-Burlington SD 22,900/PK-12
1712 Vaughn Rd 27217 336-570-6060
Dr. William Harrison, supt. Fax 570-6218
www.abss.k12.nc.us
Andrews ES 600/PK-5
2630 Buckingham Rd 27217 336-570-6170
Sabre Robinson, prin. Fax 570-6201
Broadview MS 800/6-8
2229 Broadview Dr 27217 336-570-6195
Yolanda Anderson, prin. Fax 570-6202
Eastlawn ES 500/PK-5
502 N Graham Hopedale Rd 27217 336-570-6180
Daniel McInnis, prin. Fax 570-6204
Grove Park ES 600/PK-5
141 Trail One 27215 336-570-6115
Traci Horton, prin. Fax 570-6205
Highland ES 700/K-5
3720 Bonnar Bridge Rd 27215 336-538-8700
Hollis Wroblewski, prin. Fax 538-8705
Hillcrest ES 600/PK-5
1714 W Davis St 27215 336-570-6120
Jeremy Wells, prin. Fax 570-6206
Holt ES 600/K-5
4751 S NC Highway 62 27215 336-570-6420
Mariah Vignali, prin. Fax 570-6429
Newlin ES 700/PK-5
316 Carden St 27215 336-570-6125
Lawrence Conte, prin. Fax 570-6207
Pleasant Grove ES 300/PK-5
2847 Pleasant Grove Un Sch 27217 336-421-3701
Scott Lewis, prin Fax 421-9844
Smith ES 500/PK-5
2235 Delaney Dr 27215 336-570-6140
Julie Hancock, prin. Fax 570-6209
Turrentine MS 900/6-8
1710 Edgewood Ave 27215 336-570-6150
Fredrick Sellars, prin. Fax 570-6210
Other Schools – See Elon, Graham, Haw River, Mebane, Snow Camp

Blessed Sacrament S 200/PK-8
515 Hillcrest Ave 27215 336-570-0019
Maria Gomez, prin. Fax 570-9623
Burlington Christian Academy 700/PK-12
621 E 6th St 27215 336-227-0288
Michael Brown, head sch Fax 570-1314
Burlington S 200/PK-12
1615 Greenwood Ter 27215 336-228-0296
Ronnie Wall, head sch Fax 226-6249

Burnsville, Yancey, Pop. 1,680
Yancey County SD 2,300/K-12
PO Box 190 28714 828-682-6101
Dr. Tony Tipton Ed.D., supt. Fax 682-7110
www.yanceync.net
Bald Creek ES 200/K-5
100 Bald Creek School Rd 28714 828-682-2535
Sherry Robinson, prin. Fax 682-3575
Bee Log ES 100/K-5
55 Bee Log Rd 28714 828-682-3271
Andrea Allen, prin. Fax 682-3790
Burnsville ES 400/K-5
395 Burnsville School Rd 28714 828-682-4515
Dr. Barbara Tipton Ed.D., prin. Fax 682-3566
Cane River MS 300/6-8
1128 Cane River School Rd 28714 828-682-2202
Miranda Elkins, prin. Fax 682-3754
East Yancey MS 300/6-8
285 Georges Fork Rd 28714 828-682-2281
Tamara Presnell, prin. Fax 682-3513
South Toe ES 100/K-5
139 S Toe School Rd 28714 828-675-4321
Holly Houchard, prin. Fax 675-0098
Other Schools – See Green Mountain, Micaville

Butner, Granville, Pop. 7,466
Granville County SD
Supt. — See Oxford
Butner-Stem ES 400/PK-5
201 E D St 27509 919-575-6947
Courtney Currin, prin. Fax 575-6130
Butner-Stem MS 400/6-8
501 E D St 27509 919-575-9429
Lauren Curtis, prin. Fax 575-5894

Buxton, Dare, Pop. 1,259
Dare County SD
Supt. — See Nags Head
Cape Hatteras ES 300/PK-5
PO Box 989 27920 252-995-6196
Sherry Couch, prin. Fax 995-3950

Camden, Camden, Pop. 580
Camden County SD 1,900/PK-12
174 NC Highway 343 N 27921 252-335-0831
Joe Ferrell Ed.D., supt. Fax 331-2300
ccsnc.org
Camden IS 500/4-6
123 Noblitt Dr 27921 252-335-7808
Monique Hicks, prin. Fax 335-4327
Camden MS 300/7-8
248 Scotland Rd 27921 252-335-3349
Francesca Gantt, prin. Fax 331-2253
Grandy PS 600/PK-3
175 NC Highway 343 N 27921 252-331-4838
Timothy Lazar, prin. Fax 338-5449

Cameron, Moore, Pop. 274
Harnett County SD
Supt. — See Lillington
Johnsonville ES 600/K-5
18495 NC Highway 27 W 28326 919-499-4912
Jeane Pope, prin. Fax 499-1402

Moore County SD
Supt. — See Carthage
Cameron ES 300/K-5
2636 NC Highway 24 27 28326 910-245-7814
Robert Breyer, prin. Fax 245-2760
New Century MS 600/6-8
1577 Union Church Rd 28326 910-947-1301
Tracy Metcalf, prin. Fax 947-1227

Candler, Buncombe
Buncombe County SD
Supt. — See Asheville
Candler ES 600/K-5
121 Candler School Rd 28715 828-670-5018
Charlotte Hipps, prin. Fax 667-2439
Enka IS 5-6
125 Asheville Commerce Pkwy 28715 828-255-1380
Carleene Finger, prin. Fax 255-1383
Enka MS 1,000/7-8
390 Asbury Rd 28715 828-670-5010
Leland Blankenship, prin. Fax 670-5015
Hominy Valley ES 500/K-5
450 Enka Lake Rd 28715 828-665-0619
JoAnne Walker, prin. Fax 667-3770
Pisgah ES 200/K-5
1495 Pisgah Hwy 28715 828-670-5023
Jeanann Yates, prin. Fax 667-9357

Asheville-Pisgah Christian S 100/PK-8
90 Academy Dr 28715 828-667-3255
Erin Miller, prin. Fax 667-8465

Candor, Montgomery, Pop. 835
Montgomery County SD
Supt. — See Troy
Candor ES 400/PK-5
414 S Main St 27229 910-974-4582
Laurie Brown, prin. Fax 974-4315

Canton, Haywood, Pop. 4,165
Haywood County SD
Supt. — See Waynesville
Bethel ES 500/K-5
4700 Old River Rd 28716 828-646-3448
Kim Shipman, prin. Fax 646-3470
Canton MS 600/6-8
60 Penland St 28716 828-646-3467
Todd Barbee, prin. Fax 646-3478
Meadowbrook ES 400/PK-5
85 Morning Star Rd 28716 828-646-3445
Stephanie Mancini, prin. Fax 648-8506
North Canton ES 400/PK-5
60 Thompson St 28716 828-646-3444
Jill Mann, prin. Fax 648-6668

Cape Carteret, Carteret, Pop. 1,900
Carteret County SD
Supt. — See Beaufort
White Oak ES 800/PK-5
555 WB McLean Dr 28584 252-393-3990
Terri Brett, prin. Fax 393-2773

Carolina Beach, New Hanover, Pop. 5,629
New Hanover County SD
Supt. — See Wilmington
Carolina Beach ES 400/K-5
400 4th St S 28428 910-458-4340
Cynthia Wartel, prin. Fax 458-0459

Carrboro, Orange, Pop. 19,067
Chapel Hill-Carrboro CSD
Supt. — See Chapel Hill
Carrboro ES 500/PK-5
400 Shelton St 27510 919-968-3652
Jillian LaSerna, prin. Fax 969-2476

Carthage, Moore, Pop. 2,154
Moore County SD 13,000/PK-12
PO Box 1180 28327 910-947-2976
Robert Grimesey, supt. Fax 947-3011
www.ncmcs.org
Carthage ES 400/K-5
312 Rockingham St 28327 910-947-2781
Debbie Warren, prin. Fax 947-5670
Crain's Creek MS 400/6-8
4631 Union Church Rd 28327 910-245-3796
William Chisholm, prin. Fax 245-7312
Sandhills Farm Life ES 600/K-5
2201 Farm Life School Rd 28327 910-949-2501
Nora McNeill, prin. Fax 949-2927
Other Schools – See Aberdeen, Bennett, Cameron, Pinehurst, Robbins, Seagrove, Southern Pines, Vass, West End

Cary, Wake, Pop. 131,955
Wake County SD 153,500/PK-12
5625 Dillard Dr 27518 919-431-7400
Dr. Jim Merrill, supt.
www.wcpss.net
Adams ES 800/K-5
805 Cary Towne Blvd 27511 919-460-3431
Douglas Hooper, prin. Fax 460-3439
Alston Ridge ES 1,000/K-5
11555 Green Level Church Rd 27519 919-544-2474
Teresa Caswell, prin. Fax 544-6545
Briarcliff ES 600/K-5
1220 Pond St 27511 919-460-3443
Stephanie Raiford, prin. Fax 460-3420
Carpenter ES 700/K-5
2100 Morrisville Pkwy 27519 919-462-6780
Fay Jones, prin. Fax 462-6809
Cary ES 600/PK-5
400 Kildaire Farm Rd 27511 919-460-3455
Rodney Stanton, prin. Fax 460-3550
Davis Drive ES 1,000/K-5
2151 Davis Dr 27519 919-387-2130
James Mack, prin. Fax 387-2132
Davis Drive MS 1,200/6-8
2101 Davis Dr 27519 919-387-3033
Rick Williams, prin. Fax 387-3039
East Cary MS 800/6-8
1111 SE Maynard Rd 27511 919-466-4377
Nikia Davis, prin. Fax 466-4388
Farmington Woods ES 800/K-5
1413 Hampton Valley Rd 27511 919-460-3469
Anne Winston Pierce, prin. Fax 460-3423
Green Hope ES 800/K-5
2700 Louis Stephens Dr 27519 919-388-5270
Kristin Walker, prin. Fax 388-5294
Highcroft Drive ES 900/K-5
5415 Highcroft Dr 27519 919-460-3527
Dr. Tanner Gamble, prin. Fax 463-8626
Hortons Creek ES PK-5
7615 O'Kelly Chapel Rd 27519 919-694-8660
Dr. Sandy Chambers, prin. Fax 704-2078
Kingswood ES 300/K-5
200 E Johnson St 27513 919-460-3481
Sherry Schliesser, prin. Fax 460-3387
Mills Park ES 1,000/K-5
509 Mills Park Dr 27519 919-466-1466
Michael Regan, prin. Fax 466-1478
Mills Park MS 1,700/6-8
441 Mills Park Dr 27519 919-466-1500
Robert Smith, prin. Fax 466-1522
Northwoods ES 600/PK-5
8850 Chapel Hill Rd 27513 919-460-3491
Robin Wahl, prin. Fax 460-3493
Penny Road ES 700/K-5
10900 Penny Rd 27518 919-387-2136
Mary Bohr, prin. Fax 387-4403
Reedy Creek ES 700/K-5
940 Reedy Creek Rd 27513 919-380-3660
Catherine Yanello, prin. Fax 380-3678
Reedy Creek MS 800/6-8
930 Reedy Creek Rd 27513 919-460-3504
Hilton Evans, prin. Fax 460-3391
Turner Creek ES 800/K-5
6801 Turner Creek Rd 27519 919-363-1391
Lisa Spalding, prin. Fax 290-2011
Weatherstone ES 900/PK-5
1000 Olde Weatherstone Way 27513 919-380-6988
Timothy Chadwick, prin. Fax 380-6967
West Cary MS 800/6-8
1000 Evans Rd 27513 919-460-3528
Robert James, prin. Fax 460-3540
Other Schools – See Apex, Fuquay Varina, Garner, Holly Springs, Knightdale, Morrisville, Raleigh, Rolesville, Wake Forest, Wendell, Willow Spring, Zebulon

---

Cary Christian S 800/K-12
1330 Old Apex Rd 27513 919-303-2560
Chesterbrook Academy 200/PK-5
130 Towne Village Dr 27513 919-319-9622
Resurrection Lutheran S 200/K-8
100 W Lochmere Dr 27518 919-851-7270
Tom Kolb, prin. Fax 851-6411
St. Michael Preschool 200/PK-K
804 High House Rd 27513 919-468-6110
Marianna Toscano, dir. Fax 468-6130
St. Michael the Archangel S 500/PK-8
810 High House Rd 27513 919-468-6150
Tara Navarro, prin. Fax 468-6160

Casar, Cleveland, Pop. 292
Cleveland County SD
Supt. — See Shelby
Casar ES 300/PK-5
436 School House Rd 28020 704-538-9982
Dr. David Walker, prin. Fax 538-5601

Cashiers, Jackson, Pop. 156
Jackson County SD
Supt. — See Sylva
Blue Ridge S 200/K-6
95 Bobcat Dr 28717 828-743-2646
Teri Walawender, prin. Fax 743-5320

Castle Hayne, New Hanover, Pop. 1,182
New Hanover County SD
Supt. — See Wilmington
Castle Hayne ES 500/PK-5
3925 Roger Haynes Dr 28429 910-602-4970
Sam Highsmith, prin. Fax 602-4979
College Park ES 500/K-5
5301 Sidbury Rd 28429 910-350-2058
Maria Madison, prin. Fax 350-2162
Holly Shelter MS 800/6-8
3921 Roger Haynes Dr 28429 910-602-4046
Jayne Kiker, prin. Fax 602-4045

Catawba, Catawba, Pop. 599
Catawba County SD
Supt. — See Newton
Catawba ES 500/PK-6
5415 Hudson Chapel Rd 28609 828-241-3131
J.R. Sigmon, prin. Fax 241-2332

Cerro Gordo, Columbus, Pop. 201
Columbus County SD
Supt. — See Whiteville
Cerro Gordo S 400/PK-8
PO Box 280 28430 910-654-4250
Leslie Faulk, prin. Fax 654-6155

Chadbourn, Columbus, Pop. 1,832
Columbus County SD
Supt. — See Whiteville
Chadbourn ES 300/PK-5
409 E 3rd Ave 28431 910-654-3825
Deanna Shuman, prin. Fax 654-5366
Chadbourn MS 200/6-8
801 W Smith St 28431 910-654-4300
Michael Powell, prin. Fax 654-6809

Chapel Hill, Orange, Pop. 55,802
Chapel Hill-Carrboro CSD 12,100/PK-12
750 S Merritt Mill Rd 27516 919-967-8211
Dr. Pam Bakdwin, supt. Fax 933-4560
www.chccs.k12.nc.us
Ephesus Road ES 400/K-5
1495 Ephesus Church Rd 27517 919-929-8715
Victoria Creamer, prin. Fax 969-2366
Estes Hills ES 500/K-5
500 N Estes Dr 27514 919-942-4753
Pamela McCann, prin. Fax 969-2475
Glenwood ES 500/PK-5
2 Prestwick Rd 27517 919-968-3473
Katie Caggia, prin. Fax 969-2387
Graham Bilingue ES 500/K-5
101 Smith Level Rd 27516 919-942-6491
Emily Bivins, prin. Fax 942-5405
Grey Culbreth MS 700/6-8
225 Culbreth Rd 27516 919-929-7161
Monica Bintz, prin. Fax 969-2412
McDougle ES 500/PK-5
890 Old Fayetteville Rd 27516 919-969-2435
Patrenia McDowell, prin. Fax 969-2454
McDougle MS 700/6-8
900 Old Fayetteville Rd 27516 919-933-1556
Bob Bales, prin. Fax 969-2433
Morris Grove ES 600/K-5
215 Eubanks Rd 27516 919-918-4800
Amy Rickard, prin. Fax 969-2592
Northside ES 500/K-5
350 Caldwell Ext 27516 919-918-2220
Coretta Sharpless, prin. Fax 918-2210
Phillips MS 700/6-8
606 N Estes Dr 27514 919-929-2188
Drew Ware, prin. Fax 969-2477
Rashkis ES 500/K-5
601 Meadowmont Ln 27517 919-918-2160
Janice Crossmun, prin. Fax 918-7085
Scroggs ES 600/PK-5
501 Kildaire Rd 27516 919-918-7165
Crystal Epps, prin. Fax 918-7173
Seawell ES 500/PK-5
9115 Seawell School Rd 27516 919-967-4343
Arrica Dubose, prin. Fax 969-2404
Smith MS 800/6-8
9201 Seawell School Rd 27516 919-918-2145
Stephon Goode, prin. Fax 918-2079
Other Schools – See Carrboro

Chatham County SD
Supt. — See Pittsboro
North Chatham S 500/K-5
3380 Lystra Rd 27517 919-967-3094
Carla Murray, prin. Fax 968-6216
Pollard MS 600/6-8
185 Granite Mill Blvd 27516 919-969-0070
LaShonda Hester, prin. Fax 918-4790

Orange County SD
Supt. — See Hillsborough
New Hope ES 600/K-5
1900 New Hope Church Rd 27514 919-942-9696
Ambra Wilson, prin. Fax 942-2493

Emerson Waldorf S 200/PK-12
6211 New Jericho Rd 27516 919-967-1858
Christina Wise, admin. Fax 967-2732
St. Thomas More S 400/PK-8
920 Carmichael St 27514 919-929-1546
Darrell Fulford, prin. Fax 929-1783

Charlotte, Mecklenburg, Pop. 715,605
Charlotte/Mecklenburg County SD 142,700/PK-12
PO Box 30035 28230 980-343-6270
Dr. Clayton Wilcox, supt. Fax 343-7135
www.cms.k12.nc.us/
Albemarle Road ES 1,200/K-5
7800 Riding Trail Rd 28212 980-343-6414
Phillip Steffes, prin. Fax 343-6503
Albemarle Road MS 1,200/6-8
6900 Democracy Dr 28212 980-343-6420
Toni Perry, prin. Fax 343-6501
Alexander ES 900/PK-5
7910 Neal Rd 28262 980-343-5268
Bridget Wilson, prin. Fax 343-5190
Allenbrook ES 500/K-5
1430 Allenbrook Dr 28208 980-343-6004
Katharine Bonasera, prin. Fax 343-6115
Ashley Park ES 600/PK-8
2401 Belfast Dr 28208 980-343-6018
Meaghan Loftus, prin. Fax 343-6120
Ballantyne ES 800/K-5
15425 Scholastic Dr 28277 980-343-0413
Summer Rogers, prin. Fax 343-1828
Barringer Academic Center 600/PK-5
1546 Walton Rd 28208 980-343-5533
Stephanie Range, prin. Fax 343-5603
Berewick ES 700/PK-5
5910 Dixie River Rd 28278 980-344-1010
Mojdeh Henderson, prin. Fax 343-1837
Berryhill ES 600/PK-8
10501 Windy Grove Rd 28278 980-343-6100
Cara Heath, prin. Fax 343-6146
Beverly Woods ES 700/K-5
6001 Quail Hollow Rd 28210 980-343-3627
Caroline Horne, prin. Fax 343-3733
Billingsville ES 600/PK-5
124 Skyland Ave 28205 980-343-5520
Cheryl Turner, prin. Fax 343-5583
Briarwood ES 700/K-5
1001 Wilann Dr 28215 980-343-6475
Beth Marshall, prin. Fax 343-6525
Bruns Academy 800/K-8
501 S Bruns Ave 28208 980-343-5495
Marc Angerer, prin. Fax 343-5598
Byers S 500/PK-8
1415 Hamilton St 28206 980-343-6940
Anthony Calloway, prin. Fax 343-6943
Carmel MS 1,000/6-8
5001 Camilla Dr 28226 980-343-6705
LeDuan Pratt, prin. Fax 343-6749
Chantilly Montessori S 300/PK-6
701 Briar Creek Rd 28205 980-343-0692
Ivy Gill, prin. Fax 343-0694
Clear Creek ES 700/K-5
13501 Albemarle Rd 28227 980-343-6922
Michelle Johnson, prin. Fax 343-6156
Collinswood Language Academy 700/K-8
4000 Applegate Rd 28209 980-343-5820
Jennifer Pearsall, prin. Fax 343-5850
Community House MS 1,600/6-8
9500 Community House Rd 28277 980-343-0689
Jamie Brooks, prin. Fax 343-0691
Cotswold ES 800/K-5
300 Greenwich Rd 28211 980-343-6720
Alicia Hash, prin. Fax 343-6739
Coulwood MS 700/6-8
500 Kentberry Dr 28214 980-343-6090
Janet Moss, prin. Fax 343-6142
Croft Community S 700/K-5
4911 Hucks Rd 28269 980-343-0370
Megan Cahill Morris, prin. Fax 343-1793
David Cox Road ES 800/K-5
4215 David Cox Rd 28269 980-343-6540
Celeste Spears-Ellis, prin. Fax 343-6566
Davis S K-8
3351 W Griffith St 28203 980-343-0006
Ann Laszewski, prin. Fax 343-1735
Devonshire ES 600/K-5
6500 Barrington Dr 28215 980-343-6445
Dr. Brookyln Hough, prin. Fax 343-6519
Dilworth ES 500/K-5
405 E Park Ave 28203 980-343-2240
Terry Hall, prin. Fax 343-2241
Druid Hills Academy 600/PK-8
2801 Lucena St 28206 980-343-5515
Raymond Barnes, prin. Fax 343-5581
Eastover ES 500/K-5
500 Cherokee Rd 28207 980-343-5505
Susan Nichols, prin. Fax 343-5524
Eastway MS 900/6-8
1501 Norland Rd 28205 980-343-6410
Mary Webb, prin. Fax 343-6406
Elizabeth Traditional Classical ES 500/K-5
1601 Park Dr 28204 980-343-5475
Susan Spencer-Smith, prin. Fax 343-5474
Elon Park ES 1,100/K-5
11425 Ardrey Kell Rd 28277 980-343-1440
Kelly Dowdy, prin. Fax 343-1439
Endhaven ES 700/K-5
6815 Endhaven Ln 28277 980-343-5436
Brian Slattery, prin. Fax 343-5437
First Ward Creative Arts Academy 400/K-5
715 N Caldwell St 28202 980-343-5485
Selestine Adams, prin. Fax 343-5587
Graham MS 1,400/6-8
1800 Runnymede Ln 28211 980-343-5810
Robert Folk, prin. Fax 343-5868
Greenway Park ES 600/K-5
8301 Monroe Rd 28212 980-343-5060
Anna Kuykendall, prin. Fax 343-5064

Grier Academy 800/K-5
8330 Grier Rd 28215 980-343-5671
Theresa Townsend, prin. Fax 343-5394
Gunn ES 700/K-5
7400 Harrisburg Rd 28215 980-343-6477
Monique Davis, prin. Fax 343-6527
Hawk Ridge ES 900/K-5
9201 Bryant Farms Rd 28277 980-343-5927
Mike Drye, prin. Fax 343-5933
Hickory Grove ES 1,000/K-5
6709 Pence Rd 28215 980-343-6464
Dr. Jessie Becker, prin. Fax 343-6517
Hidden Valley ES 900/K-5
5100 Snow White Ln 28213 980-343-6810
Michael Lungarini, prin. Fax 343-6798
Highland Creek ES 1,200/K-5
7242 Highland Creek Pkwy 28269 980-343-1065
Ernest Saxton, prin. Fax 343-1066
Highland Mill Montessori S 300/PK-6
3201 Clemson Ave 28205 980-343-5525
Dr. Patricia Riska, prin. Fax 343-5589
Highland Renaissance Academy 500/K-5
125 W Craighead Rd 28206 980-343-5511
Charles Fortuna, prin. Fax 343-5579
Hornets Nest ES 600/K-5
6700 Beatties Ford Rd 28216 980-343-6110
Susan Wilson, prin. Fax 343-6148
Huntingtowne Farms ES 900/K-5
2520 Huntingtowne Farms Ln 28210 980-343-3625
Carolyn Rodd, prin. Fax 343-3731
Idlewild ES 800/K-5
7101 Idlewild Rd 28212 980-343-6411
Larenda Denien, prin. Fax 343-6499
Irwin Academic Center 600/K-5
329 N Irwin Ave 28202 980-343-5480
Dr. Vanessa Ashford, prin. Fax 343-5574
Kennedy MS 700/6-8
4000 Gallant Ln 28273 980-343-5540
Kevin Sudimack, prin. Fax 343-5412
King MS 900/6-8
500 Bilmark Ave 28213 980-343-0698
Jennifer Dean, prin. Fax 343-0700
Lake Wylie ES 600/PK-5
13620 Erwin Rd 28273 980-343-3680
Earl French, prin. Fax 343-3719
Lansdowne ES 600/K-5
6400 Prett Ct 28270 980-343-6733
Penelope Crisp, prin. Fax 343-6747
Mallard Creek ES 900/K-5
9801 Mallard Creek Rd 28262 980-343-3980
Shalinda Williams, prin. Fax 343-3984
Martin MS 1,100/6-8
6301 University Pointe Blvd 28262 980-343-5382
Tonya Faison, prin Fax 343-5135
McAlpine ES 500/PK-5
9100 Carswell Ln 28277 980-343-3750
Dina Modine, prin. Fax 343-3759
McClintock MS 800/6-8
1925 Rama Rd 28212 980-343-6425
Mark McHugh, prin. Fax 343-6509
McKee Road ES 500/K-5
4101 McKee Rd 28270 980-343-3970
Lane Price, prin. Fax 343-3976
Merry Oaks International Academy 700/K-5
3508 Draper Ave 28205 980-343-6422
Michael Turner, prin. Fax 343-6505
Montclaire ES 600/K-5
5801 Farmbrook Dr 28210 980-343-3635
Leora Itzhaki, prin. Fax 343-3737
Morehead STEM Academy 1,100/K-8
7810 Neal Rd 28262 980-343-5775
Dr. Kevin Woods, prin. Fax 343-5781
Mountain Island ES 700/PK-8
7905 Pleasant Grove Rd 28216 980-343-6948
Tanya Branham, prin. Fax 343-6954
Myers Park Traditional ES 700/K-5
2132 Radcliffe Ave 28207 980-343-5522
Lauren Fowler, prin. Fax 343-5518
Nations Ford ES 600/K-5
7050 Nations Ford Rd 28217 980-343-5838
Alejandra Garcia, prin. Fax 343-5870
Newell ES 700/K-5
325 Rocky River Rd W 28213 980-343-6820
Lydia Fergison, prin. Fax 343-6792
Northridge MS 800/6-8
7601 The Plaza 28215 980-343-5015
Vince Golden, prin. Fax 343-5174
Oakdale ES 700/K-5
1825 Oakdale Rd 28216 980-343-6076
Mary Weston, prin. Fax 343-6134
Oakhurst STEAM Academy 600/K-5
4511 Monroe Rd 28205 980-343-6482
Dr. Tisha Greene, prin. Fax 343-6507
Oaklawn Language Academy 500/K-8
1810 Oaklawn Ave 28216 980-343-0400
Carmen Concepcion, prin. Fax 343-0410
Olde Providence ES 700/K-5
3800 Rea Rd 28226 980-343-3755
Patti Johanson, prin. Fax 343-3722
Orr ES PK-5
4835 Shamrock Dr 28215 980-343-9919
Kimberly Vayght, prin. Fax 343-9917
Palisades Park ES K-5
15321 York Rd 28278 980-343-9895
Gina O'Hare, prin. Fax 343-2453
Park Road Montessori S 500/PK-6
3701 Haven Dr 28209 980-343-5830
Melanie Francis, prin. Fax 343-5858
Parkside ES K-5
2945 Johnston-Oehler Rd 28269 980-343-9915
Dianna Newman, prin. Fax 343-9913
Paw Creek ES 500/PK-5
1300 Cathey Rd 28214 980-343-6088
Danielle Belton, prin. Fax 343-6140
Piedmont IB MS 1,000/6-8
1241 E 10th St 28204 980-343-5435
Jackie Barone, prin. Fax 343-5557

Pinewood ES 600/PK-5
805 Seneca Pl 28210 980-343-5825
Natashia Pegram, prin. Fax 343-5852
Piney Grove ES 800/K-5
8801 Eaglewind Dr 28212 980-343-6470
William Campbell, prin. Fax 343-6523
Polo Ridge ES 1,000/K-5
11830 Tom Short Rd 28277 980-343-0749
Jovana Edwards, prin. Fax 343-0785
Providence Spring ES 800/K-5
10045 Providence Church Ln 28277 980-343-6935
Ran Barnes, prin. Fax 343-6939
Quail Hollow MS 1,000/6-8
2901 Smithfield Church Rd 28210 980-343-3620
Rachael Neill, prin. Fax 343-3622
Rama Road ES 700/PK-5
1035 Rama Rd 28211 980-343-6730
Patricia Denny, prin. Fax 343-6745
Randolph MS 1,200/6-8
4400 Water Oak Rd 28211 980-343-6700
Brian Bambauer, prin. Fax 343-6741
Ranson MS 1,100/6-8
5850 Statesville Rd 28269 980-343-6800
Erica Jordan-Thomas, prin. Fax 343-6796
Reedy Creek ES 700/PK-5
10801 Plaza Road Ext 28215 980-343-6480
Orlando Robinson, prin. Fax 343-6529
Reid Park Academy 800/PK-8
4108 W Tyvola Rd 28208 980-343-5035
James Garvin, prin. Fax 343-3826
Renaissance West STEAM Academy PK-5
3241 New Renaissance Way 28208 980-343-0049
Erin Barksdale, prin. Fax 343-0053
Ridge Road MS 1,400/6-8
7260 Highland Creek Pkwy 28269 980-344-3410
Leah Davis, prin. Fax 343-1835
River Gate ES 900/K-5
15340 Smith Rd 28273 980-344-1000
Terri Cooper, prin. Fax 343-1836
River Oaks Academy 600/K-5
1015 Mt Holly Hntrsvl Rd 28214 980-344-1020
Marilyn Osborne, prin. Fax 343-1816
Robinson MS 1,100/6-8
5925 Ballantyne Commons Pky 28277 980-343-6944
Mike Miliote, prin. Fax 343-6947
Sedgefield ES 400/PK-5
715 Hartford Ave 28209 980-343-5826
Stacey Clark, prin. Fax 343-5856
Sedgefield MS 700/6-8
2700 Dorchester Pl 28209 980-343-5840
Erik Turner, prin. Fax 343-5862
Selwyn ES 800/K-5
2840 Colony Rd 28211 980-343-5835
Shane Lis, prin. Fax 343-5864
Shamrock Gardens ES 400/K-5
3301 Country Club Dr 28205 980-343-6440
Sarah Reeves, prin. Fax 343-6513
Sharon ES 800/K-5
4330 Foxcroft Rd 28211 980-343-6725
Catherine Phelan, prin. Fax 343-6743
Smithfield ES 700/PK-5
3200 Smithfield Church Rd 28210 980-343-6550
Dr. Allison Plunkett, prin. Fax 343-6555
South Charlotte MS 900/6-8
8040 Strawberry Ln 28277 980-343-3670
Lisa Bailes, prin. Fax 343-3725
Southwest MS 1,400/6-8
13624 Steele Creek Rd 28273 980-343-5006
Barry Blair, prin. Fax 343-3239
Starmount Academy of Excellence K-5
1600 Brookdale Ave 28210 980-343-3630
Nancy Martinez, prin. Fax 343-3735
Statesville Road ES 500/K-5
5833 Milhaven Ln 28269 980-343-6815
Jeanette Reber, prin. Fax 343-6794
Steele Creek ES 700/K-5
4100 Gallant Ln 28273 980-343-3810
Merita Brown-Little, prin. Fax 343-3814
Stoney Creek ES 900/K-5
14015 Mallard Roost Rd 28262 980-344-1030
Susannah Barr, prin. Fax 343-1833
Thomasboro Academy 800/K-8
538 Bradford Dr 28208 980-343-6000
Janette McIver, prin. Fax 343-6017
Tuckaseegee ES 800/K-5
2028 Little Rock Rd 28214 980-343-6055
Dr. Rhonda Gomez, prin. Fax 343-6128
University Meadows ES 700/PK-6
1600 Pavilion Blvd 28262 980-343-3685
Christopher Bernard, prin. Fax 343-3728
University Park Creative Arts ES 400/K-5
2400 Hildebrand St 28216 980-343-5178
Dr. Regina Boyd, prin. Fax 343-5182
Vaughn Academy of Technology K-5
8601 Old Concord Rd 28213 980-343-0030
Toyia Matthews, prin. Fax 343-0034
Waddell Language Academy 1,400/K-8
7030 Nations Ford Rd 28217 980-343-5815
Dr. Felicia Eybl, prin. Fax 343-5854
Westerly Hills Academy 600/K-8
4420 Denver Ave 28208 980-343-6021
Malacy Williams, prin. Fax 343-6122
Whitewater Academy 700/K-5
11600 White Rapids Rd 28214 980-343-0003
Laura Bloom, prin. Fax 343-1773
Whitewater MS 900/6-8
10201 Running Rapids Rd 28214 980-344-3400
Beth Thompson, prin. Fax 344-1814
Winding Springs ES 800/PK-5
6601 Horace Mann Rd 28269 980-343-5140
Courtney Wall, prin. Fax 343-5144
Windsor Park ES 900/K-5
3910 Sudbury Rd 28205 980-343-6405
Dr. Lauren Finley, prin. Fax 343-6495
Winget Park ES 1,000/PK-5
12235 Winget Rd 28278 980-343-1063
Rick Mohrien, prin. Fax 343-1062

Winterfield ES 700/PK-5
3100 Winterfield Pl 28205 980-343-6400
Angela Grant, prin. Fax 343-6493
Other Schools – See Cornelius, Davidson, Huntersville, Matthews, Mint Hill, Pineville

---

Adventist Christian Academy 100/K-8
4601 Emory Ln 28211 704-366-4351
Terry Tryon, lead tchr. Fax 367-1872
Anami Montessori S 100/PK-6
2901 Archdale Dr 28210 704-556-0042
Back Creek Christian Academy 200/PK-12
1827 Back Creek Church Rd 28213 704-549-4101
Janet Ballard, head sch Fax 548-1152
Berean Junior Academy 50/K-8
3748 Beatties Ford Rd 28216 704-391-7800
Brisbane Academy ES 100/PK-4
5901 Statesville Rd 28269 704-598-5208
Christopher Crooks, dir. Fax 597-0792
British International S of Charlotte 100/PK-12
7000 Endhaven Ln 28277 704-341-3236
Adam Stevens, prin. Fax 341-3258
Brookstone S 100/K-8
PO Box 667890 28266 704-392-6330
Charlotte Christian S 1,000/PK-12
7301 Sardis Rd 28270 704-366-5657
Barry Giller, head sch Fax 366-5678
Charlotte Country Day S 1,600/PK-12
1440 Carmel Rd 28226 704-943-4500
Mark Reed, hdmstr. Fax 943-4536
Charlotte Jewish Day S 100/K-5
5007 Providence Rd Bldg E 28226 704-366-4558
Mariashi Groner, prin. Fax 364-0443
Charlotte Latin S 1,400/PK-12
9502 Providence Rd 28277 704-846-1100
Arch McIntosh, hdmstr. Fax 846-1712
Charlotte Preparatory S 300/PK-8
212 Boyce Rd 28211 704-366-5994
Eddie Mensah, head sch Fax 366-0221
Cornerstone Adventist Academy 1-8
11431 University City Blvd 28213 704-549-8007
Sandra Greenleaf, lead tchr. Fax 549-8013
Hickory Grove Christian S 1,000/PK-12
7200 E WT Harris Blvd 28215 704-531-4198
Dr. Jimmie Quesinberry, head sch Fax 531-3509
Holy Trinity Catholic MS 900/6-8
3100 Park Rd 28209 704-527-7822
Kevin Parks, prin. Fax 525-7288
Mountain Island Day S 100/PK-12
1209 Little Rock Rd 28214 704-391-5516
Rev. Tom Winstead, head sch Fax 391-2540
Northside Christian Academy 500/PK-12
333 Jeremiah Blvd 28262 704-596-4074
J. Van Wade, head sch Fax 921-1384
Omni Montessori S 200/PK-9
9536 Blakeney Heath Rd 28277 704-541-1326
Diane McCalmont, head sch Fax 541-1326
Our Lady of the Assumption S 100/PK-8
4225 Shamrock Dr 28215 704-531-0067
Allana-Rae Ramkissoon, prin. Fax 531-7633
Palisades Episcopal S 200/PK-8
13120 Grand Palisades Pkwy 28278 704-583-1825
Kerin Hughes, head sch Fax 583-1885
Prosperity Guidepost Montessori S 200/PK-3
4755 Prosperity Church Rd 28269 704-503-6000
Providence Day S 1,500/PK-12
5800 Sardis Rd 28270 704-887-6000
Dr. Glyn Cowlishaw, head sch Fax 887-7042
St. Ann S 200/PK-5
600 Hillside Ave 28209 704-525-4938
Kathy McKinney, prin. Fax 525-2640
St. Gabriel S 600/K-5
3028 Providence Rd 28211 704-366-2409
Michele Snoke, prin. Fax 362-5063
St. Matthew S 600/K-5
11525 Elm Ln 28277 704-544-2070
Kevin O'Herron, prin. Fax 544-2184
St. Patrick S 300/K-5
1125 Buchanan St 28203 704-333-3174
Debbie Mixer, prin. Fax 333-3178
Trinity Episcopal S 400/K-8
750 E 9th St 28202 704-358-8101
Thomas J. Franz, head sch Fax 358-9908
United Faith Christian Academy 300/PK-12
8617 Providence Rd 28277 704-541-1742
Victory Christian Center S 300/PK-12
1501 Carrier Dr 28216 704-391-7339
Cheryl Riley, prin. Fax 391-0494

Cherokee, Swain, Pop. 2,018

New Kituwah Academy 100/PK-6
60 Water Dam Rd 28719 828-554-6401

Cherryville, Gaston, Pop. 5,683
Gaston County SD
Supt. — See Gastonia
Beam IS 200/4-5
401 E 1st St 28021 704-435-8330
Chad Hovis, prin. Fax 435-6056
Chavis MS 400/6-8
103 S Chavis Dr 28021 704-836-9606
Ryan Smith, prin. Fax 435-6168
Cherryville ES 400/PK-3
700 E Academy St 28021 704-836-9115
Shawn Hubers, prin. Fax 435-9611

China Grove, Rowan, Pop. 3,516
Rowan-Salisbury County SD
Supt. — See Salisbury
Bostian ES 300/K-5
4245 Old Beatty Ford Rd 28023 704-857-2322
Lisa Sigmon, prin. Fax 857-8800
China Grove ES 600/K-5
514 S Franklin St 28023 704-857-7708
LeaAnn Thomas, prin. Fax 857-7710

China Grove MS 600/6-8
1013 N Main St 28023 704-857-7038
Ben Crawford, prin. Fax 857-6650
Enochville ES 400/K-5
925 N Enochville Ave 28023 704-933-2534
Kelly Street, prin. Fax 933-6253
Millbridge ES 600/K-5
155 Ed Deal Rd 28023 704-855-5591
Jordan Baker, prin. Fax 855-5597

Chinquapin, Duplin
Duplin County SD
Supt. — See Kenansville
Chinquapin ES 600/PK-8
3894 S NC 50 Hwy 28521 910-285-3476
Tracy Mintz, prin. Fax 285-6879

Chocowinity, Beaufort, Pop. 806
Beaufort County SD
Supt. — See Washington
Chocowinity MS 400/5-8
3831 US Highway 17 S 27817 252-946-6191
KImberly Gibbs, prin. Fax 975-3812
Chocowinity PS 600/PK-4
606 Gray Rd 27817 252-946-3881
Alicia Vosburgh, prin. Fax 946-4869

Unity Christian Academy 100/K-12
1501 Haw Branch Rd 27817 252-946-5083
Jessica Crocker, admin. Fax 946-2707

Claremont, Catawba, Pop. 1,328
Catawba County SD
Supt. — See Newton
Claremont ES 400/PK-6
3384 E Main St 28610 828-459-7921
Dr. Jessica Mays, prin. Fax 459-1734
Mill Creek MS 500/7-8
1041 Shiloh Rd 28610 828-241-2711
Amy Rucker, prin. Fax 241-2743
Oxford ES 700/PK-6
5915 Oxford School Rd 28610 828-459-7220
Kelly Nicholson, prin. Fax 459-1122
River Bend MS 500/7-8
4670 Oxford School Rd 28610 828-241-2754
Chip Cathey, prin. Fax 241-2820

Clarkton, Bladen, Pop. 821
Bladen County SD
Supt. — See Elizabethtown
Clarkton MS of Discovery 300/6-8
PO Box 127 28433 910-647-6531
Stephanie Ensminger, prin. Fax 707-0814
Washington ES 200/PK-5
66 Booker T Washington Rd 28433 910-647-4161
Elizabeth Brown, prin. Fax 618-0532

Clayton, Johnston, Pop. 15,821
Johnston County SD
Supt. — See Smithfield
Clayton MS 800/6-8
490 Guy Rd 27520 919-553-5811
Catherine Trudell, prin. Fax 553-6978
Cleveland ES 900/PK-5
10225 Cleveland Rd 27520 919-550-2700
Maureen Hanahue, prin. Fax 553-2920
Cooper Academy 600/PK-5
849 Mial St 27520 919-553-0256
Jocell Flores, prin. Fax 553-0723
East Clayton ES 600/PK-5
2075 NC Highway 42 E, 919-550-5311
Jamie Tyler, prin. Fax 550-5266
Powhatan ES 600/PK-5
3145 Vinson Rd, 919-553-3259
Dan Kerwin, prin. Fax 553-6349
River Dell ES 800/PK-5
12100 Buffalo Rd, 919-553-1977
Chad Jewett, prin. Fax 553-1774
Riverwood ES 800/PK-5
108 Athletic Club Blvd, 919-359-6300
Leigh White, prin. Fax 359-6301
Riverwood MS 1,100/6-8
204 Athletic Club Blvd, 919-359-2769
Jamie Stoke, prin. Fax 359-1519
Swift Creek MS 6-8
325 Norris Rd 27520 919-262-0750
Kerri Evans, prin. Fax 262-0751
West Clayton ES 900/PK-5
1012 S Lombard St 27520 919-553-7113
Paige Barnes, prin. Fax 553-0930

LifeSpring Academy 100/K-12
PO Box 1567, 919-359-9959
Southside Christian S 100/PK-12
299 Carlton St 27520 919-553-7652
Dr. Daniel Patton, supt. Fax 553-5077

Clemmons, Forsyth, Pop. 18,375
Winston-Salem/Forsyth SD
Supt. — See Winston Salem
Clemmons ES 700/K-5
6200 Bingham Ave 27012 336-703-4210
Wendy Brewington, prin. Fax 712-4420
Morgan ES 800/K-5
3210 Village Point Dr 27012 336-703-4148
Ramona Warren, prin. Fax 712-1540
Southwest ES 400/K-5
1631 SW School Rd 27012 336-703-4195
Summer Jackson, prin. Fax 712-4425

Montessori S of Winston-Salem 200/PK-6
6050 Holder Rd 27012 336-766-5550

Cleveland, Rowan, Pop. 847
Iredell-Statesville SD
Supt. — See Statesville
Cool Spring ES 400/K-5
1969 Mocksville Hwy 27013 704-873-4949
Judy Hix, prin. Fax 873-2661

Rowan-Salisbury County SD
Supt. — See Salisbury
Cleveland ES 300/K-5
107 School St 27013 704-278-2131
Kristine Wolfe, prin. Fax 278-2507

Cliffside, Rutherford, Pop. 605
Rutherford County SD
Supt. — See Forest City
Cliffside ES 400/K-5
PO Box 338 28024 828-288-2235
Shannon Henson, prin. Fax 657-6680

Clinton, Sampson, Pop. 8,488
Clinton CSD 3,200/PK-12
300 Westover Rd 28328 910-592-3132
Dr. Stuart Blount, supt. Fax 592-2011
www.clinton.k12.nc.us
Butler Avenue ES 500/2-3
301 W Butler Ave 28328 910-592-2629
Robert Turlington, prin. Fax 592-2183
Kerr ES 700/PK-1
112 Kimbrough Rd 28328 910-592-3066
Jennifer Pope, prin. Fax 592-0404
Sampson MS 800/6-8
1201 W Elizabeth St 28328 910-592-3327
Greg Dirks, prin. Fax 592-6185
Sunset Avenue ES 400/4-5
505 Sunset Ave 28328 910-592-5623
Vanessa Brown, prin. Fax 592-2292

Sampson County SD 8,700/PK-12
PO Box 439 28329 910-592-1401
Dr. Eric Bracy, supt. Fax 590-2445
www.sampson.k12.nc.us
Union ES 600/PK-3
10400 Taylors Bridge Hwy 28328 910-532-2104
Dr. Linda Carr, prin. Fax 532-4434
Union IS 300/4-5
1190 Edmond Matthis Rd 28328 910-592-2287
Jim Workman, prin. Fax 592-7382
Union MS 500/6-8
455 River Rd 28328 910-592-4547
Dr. Theresa Melenas, prin. Fax 592-4211
Other Schools – See Autryville, Dunn, Faison, Newton Grove, Roseboro, Salemburg

Clyde, Haywood, Pop. 1,216
Haywood County SD
Supt. — See Waynesville
Clyde ES 500/PK-5
4182 Old Clyde Rd 28721 828-627-2206
Clint Conner, prin. Fax 627-1471
Riverbend ES 200/K-5
71 Learning Ln 28721 828-627-6565
Jill Chambers, prin. Fax 627-3269

Haywood Christian Academy 100/PK-12
1400 Old Clyde Rd 28721 828-627-0229
Kelli Herbert, head sch Fax 880-8447

Coats, Harnett, Pop. 2,068
Harnett County SD
Supt. — See Lillington
Coats ES 700/PK-5
585 Brick Mill Rd 27521 910-897-8353
Sandy Howard, prin. Fax 897-4737

Colerain, Bertie, Pop. 203
Bertie County SD
Supt. — See Windsor
Colerain ES 300/PK-5
202 N Academy St 27924 252-356-4714
Carol Mizelle, prin. Fax 356-4522

Colfax, Guilford
Guilford County SD
Supt. — See Greensboro
Colfax ES 600/PK-5
9112 W Market St 27235 336-992-6060
Michelle Thigpen, prin. Fax 993-0172

Collettsville, Caldwell
Caldwell County SD
Supt. — See Lenoir
Collettsville S 300/K-8
4690 Collettsville School 28611 828-754-6913
Craig Styron, prin. Fax 758-5800

Columbia, Tyrrell, Pop. 886
Tyrrell County SD 600/PK-12
PO Box 328 27925 252-796-1121
Dr. Will Hoffman, supt. Fax 796-1492
www.tyrrell.k12.nc.us
Columbia MS 100/6-8
PO Box 839 27925 252-796-0369
Stephanie Horton, prin. Fax 796-3639
Tyrrell ES 300/PK-5
486 Elementary School Rd 27925 252-796-3881
Wayne Price, prin. Fax 796-0544

Columbus, Polk, Pop. 981
Polk County SD 2,400/PK-12
PO Box 638 28722 828-894-3051
Aaron Greene, supt. Fax 894-8153
www.polkschools.org
Other Schools – See Mill Spring, Saluda, Tryon

Concord, Cabarrus, Pop. 77,521
Cabarrus County SD 30,200/PK-12
PO Box 388 28026 704-786-6191
Dr. Chris Lowder, supt. Fax 786-6141
www.cabarrus.k12.nc.us
Allen ES 900/K-5
3939 Abilene Rd 28025 704-788-2182
Susann Nash, prin. Fax 782-0645
Beverly Hills ES 400/K-6
87 Palaside Dr NE 28025 704-782-0115
Aimy Steele, prin. Fax 782-0954
Coltrane-Webb STEM ES 500/PK-6
61 Spring St NW 28025 704-782-5912
Julie Barbee, prin. Fax 784-1965
Concord MS 900/6-8
1500 Gold Rush Dr 28025 704-786-4121
Carrie Tulbert, prin. Fax 782-8632
Cox Mill ES 1,200/K-6
1450 Cox Mill Rd 28027 704-795-6519
Alison Moore, prin. Fax 795-1011
Furr ES 700/K-6
2725 Clover Rd NW 28027 704-788-4300
Darin Roberts, prin. Fax 795-9332
Harris Road MS 1,100/6-8
1251 Patriot Plantation 28027 704-782-2002
Steven Bookhart, prin. Fax 262-4298
Irvin ES 900/PK-8
1400 Gold Rush Dr 28025 704-782-8864
Tonya Williams, prin. Fax 795-4376
McAllister ES 300/K-5
541 Sunnyside Dr SE 28025 704-788-3165
Sandy Ward, prin. Fax 782-1539
Northwest Cabarrus MS 900/6-8
5140 NW Cabarrus Dr 28027 704-788-4135
Anna Blessington, prin. Fax 784-2649
Odell ES 3-5
1885 Odell School Rd 28027 704-260-6030
Sandy Ward, prin. Fax 260-6049
Odell PS 900/K-2
1 Dragon Pride Dr 28027 704-782-0601
Dr. Jim Helf, prin. Fax 782-2057
Patriots STEM ES 900/K-5
1510 Holden Ave 28025 704-455-1882
Steven Bookhardt, prin. Fax 455-1886
Pitts School Road ES 900/K-6
720 Pitts School Rd SW 28027 704-788-3430
William Davis, prin. Fax 788-3448
Rocky River ES 800/K-5
5454 Rocky River Rd 28025 704-795-4505
Adrian Parry, prin. Fax 795-4555
Weddington Hills ES 800/K-5
4401 Weddington Rd NW 28027 704-795-9385
Chasity Dolan, prin. Fax 795-9388
Winecoff ES 900/PK-6
375 Winecoff School Rd 28027 704-782-4322
Trisha Scardina, prin. Fax 784-8512
Wolf Meadow ES 600/K-6
150 Wolfmeadow Dr SW 28027 704-786-9173
Jennifer Brinson, prin. Fax 782-7011
Other Schools – See Harrisburg, Kannapolis, Midland, Mount Pleasant

---

Cannon S 900/PK-12
5801 Poplar Tent Rd 28027 704-786-8171
Matthew Gossage, head sch Fax 788-7779
CFA Academy 600/PK-12
154 Warren C Coleman Blvd N 28027 704-793-4750
Covenant Classical S 200/PK-12
3200 Patrick Henry Dr NW 28027 704-792-1854
Hope Academy 100/K-12
7655 Bruton Smith Blvd 28027 704-999-2436
Courtney Elliott, head sch Fax 706-9160

Connelly Sprngs, Burke
Burke County SD
Supt. — See Morganton
East Burke MS 800/6-8
3519 Miller Bridge Rd, 828-397-7446
Terry Penland, prin. Fax 397-1086
Hildebrand ES 400/PK-5
8078 George Hildebrand Sch, 828-879-9595
Jeanne Jandrew, prin. Fax 879-1184
Icard ES 300/PK-5
3087 Icard School Rd, 828-397-3491
Daniel Wall, prin. Fax 397-7296

Conover, Catawba, Pop. 8,005
Catawba County SD
Supt. — See Newton
Lyle Creek ES 500/PK-6
1845 Edgewater Dr NW 28613 828-464-0299
Angela Garcia, prin. Fax 464-3397
St. Stephens ES 700/PK-6
684 30th St NE 28613 828-256-2570
Dr. Kathy Keane, prin. Fax 256-5641

Newton-Conover CSD
Supt. — See Newton
Newton-Conover MS 700/6-8
873 Northern Dr NW 28613 828-464-4221
Rosanna Whisnant, prin. Fax 464-5238
Shuford ES 500/PK-5
810 Hunsucker Dr NE 28613 828-464-1973
Yakisha Clemons, prin. Fax 464-1405

Concordia Christian Day S 300/PK-8
215 5th Ave SE 28613 828-464-3011
Dave Beringer, prin. Fax 464-9899
Tri-City Christian S 200/PK-12
PO Box 1690 28613 828-465-0475
Keith Thomas, admin. Fax 466-3749

Conway, Northampton, Pop. 825
Northampton County SD
Supt. — See Jackson
Conway MS 400/5-8
400 E Main St 27820 252-585-0312
Mark Long, prin. Fax 585-0335

Cooleemee, Davie, Pop. 932
Davie County SD
Supt. — See Mocksville
Cooleemee ES 500/K-5
136 Marginal St 27014 336-284-2581
Cindy Stone, prin. Fax 284-6618

Cordova, Richmond, Pop. 1,748
Richmond County SD
Supt. — See Hamlet

Cordova MS 300/6-8
PO Box 149 28330 910-997-9839
Robert Ransom, prin. Fax 997-8172

Cornelius, Mecklenburg, Pop. 24,533
Charlotte/Mecklenburg County SD
Supt. — See Charlotte
Bailey MS 1,600/6-8
11900 Bailey Rd 28031 980-343-1068
Chad Thomas, prin. Fax 343-1069
Cornelius ES 600/K-5
21126 Catawba Ave 28031 980-343-3905
Jessica Holbrook, prin. Fax 343-3907
Washam ES 1,100/K-5
9611 Westmoreland Rd 28031 980-343-1071
Jaime Tecza, prin. Fax 343-1072

Grace Covenant Academy 100/PK-6
17301 Statesville Rd 28031 704-892-5601
Kim Goodwin, dir. Fax 892-7206

Cove City, Craven, Pop. 397
Craven County SD
Supt. — See New Bern
Smith ES 600/PK-5
150 Koonce Town Rd 28523 252-514-6466
Renee Whitford, prin. Fax 514-6469

Cramerton, Gaston, Pop. 4,105
Gaston County SD
Supt. — See Gastonia
Cramerton MS 900/6-8
601 Cramer Mountain Rd 28032 704-836-9603
Bryan Denton, prin. Fax 824-0228

Cramerton Christian Academy 300/K-12
426 Woodlawn Ave 28032 704-824-2840

Creedmoor, Granville, Pop. 4,037
Granville County SD
Supt. — See Oxford
Creedmoor ES 400/PK-5
PO Box 725 27522 919-528-2313
Latisa McKnight, prin. Fax 528-9523
Hawley MS 600/6-8
2173 Brassfield Rd 27522 919-528-0091
Frank Wiggins, prin. Fax 528-0051
Mt. Energy ES 400/PK-5
2652 NC Highway 56 27522 919-529-0586
Mary Ann Crews, prin. Fax 529-0238

Creswell, Washington, Pop. 268
Washington County SD
Supt. — See Plymouth
Creswell ES 200/PK-5
PO Box 327 27928 252-797-7474
Tracy Peele, prin. Fax 797-7343

Crossnore, Avery, Pop. 189
Avery County SD
Supt. — See Newland
Crossnore ES 200/PK-5
PO Box 566 28616 828-737-7204
Matthew Bentley, prin. Fax 737-7209

Cullowhee, Jackson, Pop. 6,135
Jackson County SD
Supt. — See Sylva
Cullowhee Valley ES 600/K-8
240 Wisdom Dr 28723 828-293-5667
Kathryn Kantz, prin. Fax 293-5845

Currituck, Currituck
Currituck County SD 3,900/PK-12
2958 Caratoke Hwy 27929 252-232-2223
Mark Stefanik, supt. Fax 232-3655
www.currituck.k12.nc.us
Other Schools – See Barco, Jarvisburg, Knotts Island, Moyock, Poplar Branch, Shawboro

Dallas, Gaston, Pop. 4,415
Gaston County SD
Supt. — See Gastonia
Carr ES 700/PK-5
307 S Pine St 28034 704-922-3636
Rebekah Duncan, prin. Fax 922-7992
Costner ES 600/PK-5
PO Box 980 28034 704-922-3522
Lonnia Beam, prin. Fax 922-7503
Friday MS 700/6-8
1221 Ratchford Dr 28034 704-922-5297
Andrea Meyer, prin. Fax 922-9841

Dana, Henderson, Pop. 3,275
Henderson County SD
Supt. — See Hendersonville
Dana ES 500/K-5
PO Box 37 28724 828-685-7743
Kimberly Morgan, prin. Fax 685-4004

Danbury, Stokes, Pop. 189
Stokes County SD 6,500/PK-12
PO Box 50 27016 336-593-8146
Dr. Brad Rice, supt. Fax 593-2041
www.stokes.k12.nc.us
Other Schools – See Germanton, King, Lawsonville, Pine Hall, Pinnacle, Sandy Ridge, Walnut Cove, Westfield

Davidson, Mecklenburg, Pop. 10,776
Charlotte/Mecklenburg County SD
Supt. — See Charlotte
Davidson ES 700/K-5
635 South St 28036 980-343-3900
Dana Jarrett, prin. Fax 343-3909

Davidson Day S 500/PK-12
750 Jetton St 28036 704-237-5200
Dr. Latta Baucom, head sch Fax 896-5535

Lake Norman Christian S 100/K-12
PO Box 4267 28036 704-987-9811
Dr. Wes Johnston, head sch Fax 896-5875

Delco, Columbus, Pop. 332
Columbus County SD
Supt. — See Whiteville
Acme-Delco MS 200/6-8
26133 Andrew Jackson Hwy E 28436 910-655-3200
Kevin Toman, prin. Fax 655-6865

Denton, Davidson, Pop. 1,618
Davidson County SD
Supt. — See Lexington
Denton ES 400/PK-5
305 W Salisbury St 27239 336-242-5708
Kelsey Greer, prin. Fax 242-5713
South Davidson MS 400/6-8
14954 S NC Highway 109 27239 336-242-5705
Crystal Sexton, prin. Fax 242-5707

Denver, Lincoln, Pop. 2,276
Lincoln County SD
Supt. — See Lincolnton
Catawba Springs ES 500/K-5
206 N Little Egypt Rd 28037 704-736-1895
Kristi Smith, prin. Fax 736-1893
North Lincoln MS 700/6-8
1503 Amity Church Rd 28037 704-736-0262
Kqisha Dagenhart, prin. Fax 736-9812
Rock Springs ES 700/K-5
3633 N Highway 16 28037 704-483-2281
Dr. Melia Neale, prin. Fax 483-1633
St. James ES 600/K-5
1774 Saint James Church Rd 28037 704-736-1958
Shanti Clancy, prin. Fax 736-1947

Dobson, Surry, Pop. 1,569
Surry County SD 8,400/PK-12
PO Box 364 27017 336-386-8211
Dr. Travis Reeves, supt. Fax 386-4279
www.surry.k12.nc.us/
Central MS 700/6-8
PO Box 768 27017 336-386-4018
Bill Goins, prin. Fax 386-4371
Copeland ES 400/PK-5
948 Copeland School Rd 27017 336-374-2572
Margaret Spicer, prin. Fax 374-4700
Dobson ES 400/PK-5
PO Box 248 27017 336-386-8913
Sharia Templeton, prin. Fax 386-4347
Rockford ES 400/PK-5
719 Rockford Rd 27017 336-374-6300
Molly Anderson, prin. Fax 374-6302
Other Schools – See Lowgap, Mount Airy, Pilot Mountain, Pinnacle, State Road

---

Salem Christian Academy 50/PK-2
430 Rockford Rd 27017 336-374-4419
Jennifer Freeman, prin.

Dublin, Bladen, Pop. 329
Bladen County SD
Supt. — See Elizabethtown
Dublin PS 300/PK-4
PO Box 307 28332 910-862-2202
Susan Cheshire, prin. Fax 740-0618

Dudley, Wayne
Wayne County SD
Supt. — See Goldsboro
Brogden MS 500/5-8
3761 US 117 Alt 28333 919-705-6010
Dr. Damesha Smith, prin. Fax 705-6000
Brogden PS 800/PK-4
2253 Old Mt Olive Hwy 28333 919-705-6020
Youlanda Wynn, prin. Fax 731-5956

Dunn, Harnett, Pop. 9,078
Harnett County SD
Supt. — See Lillington
Coats-Erwin MS 700/6-8
2833 NC Highway 55 E 28334 910-230-0300
Sharon Johnson, prin. Fax 230-0306
Dunn MS 400/6-8
1301 Meadow Lark Rd 28334 910-892-1017
Dr. Janet Doffermyre, prin. Fax 892-7923
Harnett PS 600/PK-3
800 W Harnett St 28334 910-892-0126
Dr. Sylvia Wilkins, prin. Fax 892-5561
Wayne Avenue ES 300/4-5
910 W Harnett St 28334 910-892-1059
Steven McLean, prin. Fax 892-2257

Sampson County SD
Supt. — See Clinton
Midway ES 500/PK-5
15375 Spiveys Corner Hwy 28334 910-567-2244
Robbin Cooper, prin. Fax 567-4003
Midway MS 700/6-8
1115 Roberts Grove Church 28334 910-567-5879
Kevin Hunter, prin. Fax 567-5131
Plain View ES 400/K-5
4140 Plain View Hwy 28334 910-891-4354
Nicole Peterson, prin. Fax 891-4868

Durham, Durham, Pop. 223,352
Durham County SD 33,100/PK-12
PO Box 30002 27702 919-560-2000
Aaron Beaulieu, supt. Fax 560-2422
www.dpsnc.net
Bethesda ES 700/K-5
2009 S Miami Blvd 27703 919-560-3904
Shaneeka Moore-Lawrence, prin. Fax 560-3482
Brogden MS 700/6-8
1001 Leon St 27704 919-560-3906
Latonya Smith, prin. Fax 560-3957
Burton ES 400/K-5
1500 Mathison St 27701 919-560-3908
Dr. Kimberly Ferrell, prin. Fax 560-2087
Carrington MS 1,200/6-8
227 Milton Rd 27712 919-560-3916
Holly Emmanuel, prin. Fax 560-3522
Club Boulevard ES 500/K-5
400 W Club Blvd 27704 919-560-3918
Terry Phillips, prin. Fax 560-2525
Creekside ES 900/K-5
5321 Ephesus Church Rd 27707 919-560-3919
Arrica Dubose, prin. Fax 560-2355
Easley ES 600/K-5
302 Lebanon Cir 27712 919-560-3913
Jennifer Hauser, prin. Fax 560-3523
Eastway ES 600/K-5
610 N Alston Ave 27701 919-560-3910
Shayla Holeman, prin. Fax 560-3421
Eno Valley ES 600/K-5
117 Milton Rd 27712 919-560-3915
Rodney Berry, prin. Fax 560-3922
Fayetteville Street ES 200/K-5
2905 Fayetteville St 27707 919-560-3944
Ebony Hopkins, prin. Fax 560-3489
Forest View ES 700/K-5
3007 Mount Sinai Rd 27705 919-560-3932
Neil Clay, prin. Fax 560-3735
Githens MS 1,000/6-8
4800 Old Chapel Hill Rd 27707 919-560-3966
Crystal Isom, prin. Fax 560-3454
Glenn ES 700/K-5
2415 E Geer St 27704 919-560-3920
Cornelius Redfearn, prin. Fax 560-2101
Harris ES 400/K-5
1520 Cooper St 27703 919-560-3967
Carolyn Pugh, prin. Fax 560-3951
Hillandale ES 700/K-5
2730 Hillandale Rd 27705 919-560-3924
Shannon Gill, prin. Fax 560-3644
Holt ES 600/K-5
4019 Holt School Rd 27704 919-560-3928
Donya Jones, prin. Fax 560-3759
Hope Valley ES 600/K-5
3005 Dixon Rd 27707 919-560-3980
Kristin Tate, prin. Fax 560-2616
Lakewood ES 500/K-5
2520 Vesson Ave 27707 919-560-3939
James Hopkins, prin. Fax 560-2398
Lakewood Montessori S 300/6-8
2119 Chapel Hill Rd 27707 919-560-2894
Dr. W. Renee Carmon, prin. Fax 237-7388
Little River ES 400/K-8
2315 Snow Hill Rd 27712 919-560-3940
Dr. Cory Hogans, prin. Fax 560-3427
Lowes Grove MS 700/6-8
4418 S Alston Ave 27713 919-560-3946
Dr. Tekeisha Mitchell, prin. Fax 560-2102
Lucas MS 600/6-8
923 Snow Hill Rd 27712 919-560-3843
Michael Somers, prin. Fax 471-0072
Merrick-Moore ES 700/K-5
2325 Cheek Rd 27704 919-560-3952
Matthew Hunt, prin. Fax 560-2128
Morehead Montessori S 300/PK-5
909 Cobb St 27707 919-560-3954
Cynthia Webb, prin. Fax 560-2527
Neal MS 900/6-8
201 Baptist Rd 27704 919-560-3955
Michael Fuga, prin. Fax 560-3451
Oak Grove ES 600/K-5
3810 Wake Forest Rd 27703 919-560-3960
Aisha Howard, prin. Fax 596-4145
Parkwood ES 600/K-5
5207 Revere Rd 27713 919-560-3962
Michelle Bell, prin. Fax 560-3768
Pearson ES 600/K-5
3501 Fayetteville St 27707 919-560-3988
Christy Boykin, prin. Fax 560-2661
Pearsontown ES 800/K-5
4915 Barbee Rd 27713 919-560-3964
Rodriguez Teal, prin. Fax 560-2103
Powe ES 400/K-5
913 9th St 27705 919-560-3963
Dr. Meg Goodhand, prin. Fax 560-2315
Rogers-Herr MS 600/6-8
911 W Cornwallis Rd 27707 919-560-3970
Kecia Rogers, prin. Fax 560-2439
Sandy Ridge ES 600/K-5
1417 Old Oxford Rd 27704 919-560-2695
Keri Pitchford, prin. Fax 595-4222
Shepard MS 500/6-8
2401 Dakota St 27707 919-560-3938
Micah Copeland, prin. Fax 560-3945
Smith ES 400/PK-5
2410 E Main St 27703 919-560-3900
Letisha Judd, prin. Fax 560-3909
Southwest ES 600/K-5
2320 Cook Rd 27713 919-560-3972
Nicholas Rotosky, prin. Fax 544-1112
Spaulding ES 300/PK-5
1531 S Roxboro St 27707 919-560-3974
Jamie Carr, prin. Fax 560-3878
Spring Valley ES 600/K-5
2051 Northern Durham Pkwy 27703 919-560-2890
Sarah Sanchez, prin. Fax 560-2106
Watts ES 400/PK-5
700 Watts St 27701 919-560-3947
Patti Crum, prin. Fax 560-3949
Other Schools – See Bahama

Bethesda Christian Academy 200/K-8
1914 S Miami Blvd 27703 919-598-0190
Tony Manning, admin. Fax 596-3760
Camelot Academy 100/K-12
809 Proctor St 27707 919-688-3040
Thelma DeCarlo-Glynn, dir. Fax 682-4320
Carolina Friends S 500/PK-12
4809 Friends School Rd 27705 919-383-6602
Karen Cumberbatch, prin. Fax 383-6009

Cresset Christian Academy 200/PK-12
3707 Garrett Rd 27707 919-354-8000
Greg Hardy, admin. Fax 354-8009
Duke S 500/PK-8
3716 Erwin Rd 27705 919-493-1827
Dave Michelman, head sch Fax 419-1185
Durham Academy 400/PK-4
3501 Ridge Rd 27705 919-489-3400
Michael Ulku-Steiner, head sch Fax 489-4893
Durham Academy 400/5-8
3116 Academy Rd 27707 919-489-9118
Michael Ulku-Steiner, head sch Fax 489-9110
Fellowship Baptist Academy 100/PK-12
515 Southerland St 27703 919-596-9331
Five Oaks Adventist Christian S 50/K-8
4124 Farrington Rd 27707 919-489-5555
Gorman Christian Academy 200/PK-8
3311 E Geer St 27704 919-688-2567
Terry Chambers, prin. Fax 688-6948
Immaculata Catholic S 400/PK-8
721 Burch Ave 27701 919-682-5847
Dana Corcoran, prin. Fax 956-7073
International Montessori S 100/PK-5
3001 Academy Rd Ste 300 27707 919-401-4343
Lerner Jewish Community Day S 100/PK-5
1935 W Cornwallis Rd 27705 919-286-5517
Liberty Christian S 200/K-12
3864 Guess Rd 27705 919-471-5522
Montessori Children's House of Durham 100/PK-6
2800 Pickett Rd 27705 919-489-9045
Tammy Squires, head sch Fax 490-1572
Montessori Community S 200/PK-8
4512 Pope Rd 27707 919-493-8541
Tim Daniel, head sch Fax 493-8165
Mt. Zion Christian Academy 200/K-12
3519 Fayetteville St 27707 919-688-4245
Peggy McIlwain, prin. Fax 688-2201
Quality Education Institute 50/K-6
800 Elmira Ave 27707 919-680-6544
Triangle Day S 200/PK-8
4911 Neal Rd 27705 919-383-8800
Douglas Norry, head sch Fax 383-7157
Trinity S of Durham & Chapel Hill 500/PK-12
4011 Pickett Rd 27705 919-402-8262
Dr. Peter Denton, head sch Fax 402-0762

East Bend, Yadkin, Pop. 604
Yadkin County SD
Supt. — See Yadkinville
East Bend ES 300/PK-6
205 School St 27018 336-699-3989
Lavonne Fortner, prin. Fax 699-2607
Fall Creek ES 300/PK-6
2720 Smithtown Rd 27018 336-699-8257
Kelly Byrd-Johnson, prin. Fax 699-2136
Forbush ES 300/PK-6
1400 Bloomtown Rd 27018 336-699-8447
Jeffrey Maglio, prin. Fax 699-2793
Forbush MS 500/7-8
1431 Falcon Rd 27018 336-961-6360
Anthony Davis, prin. Fax 961-6370

East Flat Rock, Henderson, Pop. 4,872
Henderson County SD
Supt. — See Hendersonville
Flat Rock MS 700/6-8
191 Preston Ln 28726 828-697-4775
Melonie Adams, prin. Fax 698-6124
Hillandale ES 600/K-5
40 Preston Ln 28726 828-697-4782
Jenny Moreno, prin. Fax 697-4661

Eastover, Cumberland, Pop. 3,565
Cumberland County SD
Supt. — See Fayetteville
Armstrong ES 400/PK-5
3395 Dunn Rd, 910-483-2425
Ardry Adams, prin. Fax 483-1842
Eastover Central ES 500/PK-5
5174 Dunn Rd, 910-483-8997
Ashley Porter, prin. Fax 483-6177

Eden, Rockingham, Pop. 15,244
Rockingham County SD 13,200/PK-12
511 Harrington Hwy 27288 336-627-2600
Dr. Rodney Shotwell, supt. Fax 627-2660
www.rock.k12.nc.us
Central ES 500/K-5
435 E Stadium Dr 27288 336-623-8378
Elizabeth Covell, prin. Fax 623-8405
Douglass ES 400/PK-5
408 Price St 27288 336-623-6521
Dr. Nancy Mark, prin. Fax 627-0348
Draper ES 200/PK-5
1719 E Stadium Dr 27288 336-635-6541
Christy Bailey, prin. Fax 635-3203
Holmes MS 800/6-8
211 N Pierce St 27288 336-623-9791
Nicole Lancaster, prin. Fax 627-0075
Leaksville-Spray ES 500/PK-5
415 Highland Dr 27288 336-627-7068
Madison Hester, prin. Fax 627-8823
Other Schools – See Madison, Reidsville, Ruffin, Stoneville

Edenton, Chowan, Pop. 4,952
Edenton-Chowan SD 2,300/PK-12
PO Box 206 27932 252-482-4436
Dr. Rob Jackson, supt. Fax 482-7309
www.ecps.k12.nc.us
Walker ES 500/3-5
125 Sandy Ridge Rd 27932 252-221-4151
Michelle White, prin. Fax 221-4386
White Oak ES 600/PK-2
111 Sandy Ridge Rd 27932 252-221-4078
Sheila Evans, prin. Fax 221-4552
Other Schools – See Tyner

Efland, Orange, Pop. 722
Orange County SD
Supt. — See Hillsborough
Efland-Cheeks Global ES 500/K-5
4401 Fuller Rd 27243 919-563-5112
Kiley Brown, prin. Fax 563-3137
Gravelly Hill MS 500/6-8
4819 W Ten Rd 27243 919-245-4050
Dr. Chris Gammon, prin. Fax 245-4055

Elizabeth City, Pasquotank, Pop. 18,282
Elizabeth City/Pasquotank County SD 5,800/PK-12
PO Box 2247 27906 252-335-2981
Dr. Larry Cartner, supt. Fax 335-0974
www.ecpps.k12.nc.us
Central ES 400/K-5
1059 US Highway 17 S 27909 252-335-4305
Michael Drew, prin. Fax 337-6601
Elizabeth City MS 600/6-8
1066 Northside Rd 27909 252-335-2974
Timothy Worrell, prin. Fax 335-1751
Moore ES 400/K-5
606 Roanoke Ave 27909 252-338-5000
Sara English, prin. Fax 338-6554
Northside ES 600/K-5
1062 Northside Rd 27909 252-335-2033
Simona White, prin. Fax 331-1322
Pasquotank ES 300/K-5
1407 Peartree Rd 27909 252-335-4205
Antoinette Reid, prin. Fax 335-4966
River Road MS 600/6-8
1701 River Rd 27909 252-333-1454
Adrian Fonville, prin. Fax 331-1339
Sawyer ES 400/K-5
1007 Park St 27909 252-338-1012
Chris Paullet, prin. Fax 338-2388
Sheep-Harney ES 500/PK-5
200 W Elizabeth St 27909 252-335-4303
Katina Waples, prin. Fax 335-4738
Weeksville ES 300/K-5
1170 Salem Church Rd 27909 252-330-2606
Angela Cobb, prin. Fax 330-5700

Albemarle S 200/PK-12
1210 US Highway 17 S 27909 252-338-0883
Dr. Holly Glenn, hdmstr. Fax 338-1222
Victory Christian S 200/PK-12
684 Old Hertford Hwy 27909 252-264-2011

Elizabethtown, Bladen, Pop. 3,534
Bladen County SD 5,000/PK-12
PO Box 37 28337 910-862-4136
Robert Taylor, supt. Fax 860-6170
www.bladen.k12.nc.us/
Bladen Lakes PS 300/PK-4
9554 Johnsontown Rd 28337 910-247-4608
Dia Collins-Thomas, prin. Fax 347-8109
Elizabethtown MS 400/5-8
PO Box 639 28337 910-862-4071
Elizabeth Cole, prin. Fax 819-0429
Elizabethtown PS 500/PK-4
PO Box 2649 28337 910-862-3380
Priscilla Brayboy, prin. Fax 829-5496
Other Schools – See Bladenboro, Clarkton, Dublin, Riegelwood, Tar Heel

---

Elizabethtown Christian Academy 100/K-8
1800 W Broad St 28337 910-862-3427
Beverly Bridgers, head sch Fax 554-2099

Elkin, Surry, Pop. 3,953
Elkin CSD 1,200/PK-12
202 W Spring St 28621 336-835-3135
Dr. Myra Cox, supt. Fax 835-3376
www.elkin.k12.nc.us
Elkin ES 700/PK-6
135 Old Virginia Rd 28621 336-835-2756
Pam Colbert, prin. Fax 835-6042
Elkin MS 200/7-8
300 Elk Spur St 28621 336-835-3175
Cassundra Morrison, prin. Fax 835-1427

Wilkes County SD
Supt. — See North Wilkesboro
Eller ES 300/PK-5
1288 CB Eller School Rd 28621 336-903-6100
Chad Mann, prin. Fax 526-2220

Elk Park, Avery, Pop. 449
Avery County SD
Supt. — See Newland
Cranberry MS 200/6-8
6230 N US Highway 19E 28622 828-733-2932
Ricky Ward, prin. Fax 733-6863
Freedom Trail ES 200/PK-5
6110 N US Highway 19E 28622 828-733-4744
Ricky Ward, prin. Fax 733-6863

Ellenboro, Rutherford, Pop. 856
Rutherford County SD
Supt. — See Forest City
Ellenboro ES 600/K-5
PO Box 1419 28040 828-453-8185
Bill Bass, prin. Fax 453-0231

Ellerbe, Richmond, Pop. 1,027
Richmond County SD
Supt. — See Hamlet
Ellerbe MS 200/6-8
128 W Ballard St 28338 910-652-3231
Melvin Ingram, prin. Fax 652-3106
Mineral Springs ES 500/PK-5
1426 Greenlake Rd 28338 910-652-2931
Kate Smith, prin. Fax 652-7750

Elm City, Wilson, Pop. 1,289
Nash-Rocky Mount SD
Supt. — See Nashville
Coopers ES 600/PK-5
6833 NC 58 S 27822 252-937-9035
Allison Williams, prin. Fax 937-5648

Wilson County SD
Supt. — See Wilson
Elm City ES 400/K-5
5544 Lake Wilson Rd 27822 252-236-4574
Claudia Spencer, prin. Fax 236-3666
Elm City MS 500/6-8
215 Church St E 27822 252-236-4148
Robert Pope, prin. Fax 236-3754
Gardners ES 300/K-5
5404 NC 42 27822 252-399-7920
Cheryl Baggett, prin. Fax 399-7895

Elon, Alamance, Pop. 9,262
Alamance-Burlington SD
Supt. — See Burlington
Altamahaw Ossipee ES 500/K-5
2832 N NC Highway 87 27244 336-538-6030
Kristen Gravely, prin. Fax 538-6032
Elon ES 600/PK-5
510 E Haggard Ave 27244 336-538-6000
Jack Davern, prin. Fax 538-6003
Western Alamance MS 900/6-8
2100 Eldon Dr 27244 336-538-6010
Gregory Holland, prin. Fax 538-6012

Enfield, Halifax, Pop. 2,522
Halifax County SD
Supt. — See Halifax
Enfield Middle S.T.E.A.M. Academy 300/6-8
13723 NC Highway 481 27823 252-445-5455
Teicher Patterson, prin. Fax 445-3866
Inborden Elementary S.T.E.A.M. Academy 400/PK-5
13587 NC Highway 481 27823 252-445-5455
Chastity Kinsey, prin. Fax 445-3885
Pittman Elementary Leadership Academy 200/PK-5
25041 NC Highway 561 27823 252-445-5268
Jacqueline Williams, prin. Fax 445-2511

Ennice, Alleghany
Alleghany County SD
Supt. — See Sparta
Glade Creek ES 300/PK-8
32 Glade Creek School Rd 28623 336-657-3388
Dr. Gerald Miller, prin. Fax 657-3435

Erwin, Harnett, Pop. 4,318
Harnett County SD
Supt. — See Lillington
Erwin ES 300/3-5
301 S 10th St 28339 910-897-7178
Thomas Backus, prin. Fax 897-3460
Gentry PS 300/K-2
114 Porter Dr 28339 910-897-5711
Steven Murphy, prin. Fax 897-4543

Cape Fear Christian Academy 300/PK-12
138 Erwin Chapel Rd 28339 910-897-5423
Karen Parker, hdmstr. Fax 897-2150

Etowah, Henderson, Pop. 6,826
Henderson County SD
Supt. — See Hendersonville
Etowah ES 400/K-5
320 Etowah School Rd 28729 828-891-6560
Matthew Haney, prin. Fax 891-6579

Evergreen, Columbus, Pop. 417
Columbus County SD
Supt. — See Whiteville
Evergreen ES 300/PK-8
7211 Old Highway 74 28438 910-654-3502
Georgia Spaulding, prin. Fax 654-7168

Fairmont, Robeson, Pop. 2,595
Robeson County SD
Supt. — See Lumberton
Fairgrove MS 300/4-8
1953 Fairgrove Rd 28340 910-628-8290
Hawhana Locklear, prin. Fax 628-6181
Fairmont MS 400/5-8
402 Iona St 28340 910-628-4363
Darlene Cummings, prin. Fax 628-0335
Green Grove ES 300/PK-3
1850 School Rd 28340 910-628-7433
Tawanna Curry, prin. Fax 628-8715
Rosenwald ES 500/PK-4
301 Martin Luther King Dr 28340 910-628-9786
Isabel Jones, prin. Fax 628-4361

Fairview, Buncombe, Pop. 2,619
Buncombe County SD
Supt. — See Asheville
Fairview ES 700/K-5
1355 Charlotte Hwy 28730 828-628-2732
Dr. Angie Jackson, prin. Fax 628-4950

Faison, Sampson, Pop. 954
Sampson County SD
Supt. — See Clinton
Hargrove ES 400/PK-5
7725 Faison Hwy 28341 910-533-3444
Edward Holmes, prin. Fax 533-2121

Faith, Rowan, Pop. 803
Rowan-Salisbury County SD
Supt. — See Salisbury
Faith ES 400/PK-5
PO Box 161 28041 704-279-3195
Denita Reavis, prin. Fax 279-2469

Fallston, Cleveland, Pop. 598
Cleveland County SD
Supt. — See Shelby
Fallston ES 600/PK-5
112 Gary St 28042 704-476-8240
David Mitchell, prin. Fax 538-5347

Farmville, Pitt, Pop. 4,617
Pitt County SD
Supt. — See Greenville
Bundy ES 400/3-5
3994 Grimmersburg St 27828 252-753-2013
Allison Setser, prin. Fax 753-2812
Farmville MS 600/6-8
3914 Grimmersburg St 27828 252-753-2116
Paul Briney, prin. Fax 753-7995
Sugg ES 500/PK-2
3992 Grimmersburg St 27828 252-753-2671
Allison Setser, prin. Fax 753-7997

Fayetteville, Cumberland, Pop. 191,875
Cumberland County SD 51,700/PK-12
PO Box 2357 28302 910-678-2300
Dr. Tim Kinlaw, supt. Fax 678-2339
ccs.k12.nc.us
Abbott MS 900/6-8
590 Winding Creek Rd 28305 910-323-2201
Carla Crenshaw, prin. Fax 485-0841
Alderman Road ES 600/PK-5
2860 Alderman Rd 28306 910-321-0398
Charla Trogdon, prin. Fax 321-0744
Ashley ES 200/3-5
810 Trainer Dr 28304 910-484-4156
Tiffany Fogelquist, prin. Fax 484-3175
Auman ES 600/PK-5
6882 Raeford Rd 28304 910-868-8153
Tara Bratcher, prin. Fax 868-0712
Berrien ES 200/K-5
800 North St 28301 910-483-8288
Brenda Winfrey-Knox, prin. Fax 483-3634
Brentwood ES 500/PK-5
1115 Bingham Dr 28304 910-864-5310
Anne McFadyen, prin. Fax 864-2266
Byrd MS 700/7-8
1616 Ireland Dr 28304 910-483-3101
Meshonda Williams, prin. Fax 483-3741
Cashwell ES 700/PK-5
2970 Legion Rd 28306 910-424-2312
Kim Robertson, prin. Fax 423-9673
Chesnutt MS 600/6-8
2121 Skibo Rd 28314 910-867-9147
Phyllis Jackson, prin. Fax 868-3695
Cliffdale ES 600/PK-5
6450 Cliffdale Rd 28314 910-864-3442
Michael Tucker, prin. Fax 867-2940
College Lakes ES 400/K-5
4963 Rosehill Rd 28311 910-488-6650
Jackie White, prin. Fax 630-0221
Coon ES 300/PK-5
905 Hope Mills Rd 28304 910-425-6141
Regina Blanding, prin. Fax 425-0878
Cumberland Mills ES 700/PK-5
2576 Hope Mills Rd 28306 910-424-4536
Shannon Booth, prin. Fax 423-6359
Cumberland Road ES 400/PK-5
2700 Cumberland Rd 28306 910-485-7171
Dr. Michele Cain, prin. Fax 484-5616
Easom PS 300/K-1
1610 Westlawn Ave 28305 910-484-0194
Rebecca McAlister, prin. Fax 484-4486
Ferguson-Easley ES 300/PK-5
1857 Seabrook Rd 28301 910-483-4883
Dr. Mary Hales, prin. Fax 323-5286
Glendale Acres ES 200/K-2
2915 Skycrest Dr 28304 910-484-9031
Dr. Julie Dees, prin. Fax 486-8750
Griffin MS 1,000/6-8
5551 Fisher Rd 28304 910-424-7678
Tommy Dent, prin. Fax 424-7002
Hall ES 600/PK-5
526 Andrews Rd 28311 910-822-5100
Erica Fenner-McAdoo, prin. Fax 822-8413
Hefner ES 800/K-5
7059 Calamar Dr 28314 910-860-7058
Dr. Don Cahill, prin. Fax 860-7062
Honeycutt ES 800/PK-5
4665 Lakewood Dr 28306 910-426-2020
Lori Bostrom-Mueller, prin. Fax 426-2024
Howard Learning Academy 200/6-8
1608 Camden Rd 28306 910-483-5434
Allen Hines, prin. Fax 323-3159
Ireland Drive MS 400/6-6
1606 Ireland Dr 28304 910-483-4037
Christina DiGuadio, prin. Fax 483-4885
Jeralds MS 500/6-8
2517 Ramsey St 28301 910-822-2570
Joy Williams, prin. Fax 822-1534
Lake Rim ES 700/PK-5
1455 Hoke Loop Rd 28314 910-867-1133
Debora McPhaul, prin. Fax 867-0819
Lewis Chapel MS 600/6-8
2150 Skibo Rd 28314 910-864-1407
Dr. Sheldon Harvey, prin. Fax 864-8298
Long Hill ES 500/2-5
6490 Ramsey St 28311 910-488-0012
Monica Carter, prin. Fax 488-0014
Martin ES 500/PK-5
430 N Reilly Rd 28303 910-864-4843
Donald Caudle, prin. Fax 867-3777
McArthur ES 400/PK-5
3809 Village Dr 28304 910-424-2206
Tanya Higgins, prin. Fax 424-3451
Miller ES 600/PK-5
1361 Rim Rd 28314 910-868-2800
Gerald Hernandez, prin. Fax 867-1960
Montclair ES 500/PK-5
555 Glensford Dr 28314 910-868-5124
Stephanie Walls-Rivers, prin. Fax 487-2179
Morganton Road ES 500/K-5
102 Bonanza Dr 28303 910-867-4137
Chad McLamb, prin. Fax 867-1030
New Century International ES 700/K-5
7465 Century Cir 28306 910-487-2340
Brady Davis, prin. Fax 487-2344
New Century International MS 400/6-8
7455 Century Cir 28306 910-487-2001
Lavette McMillan, prin. Fax 487-2009
Owen ES 500/PK-5
4533 Raeford Rd 28304 910-425-6163
Gemette McEachern, prin. Fax 425-6165
Pine Forest MS 800/6-8
6901 Ramsey St 28311 910-488-2711
Bill Starks, prin. Fax 630-2357
Ponderosa ES 400/PK-5
311 Bonanza Dr 28303 910-864-0148
Christina Tucker, prin. Fax 867-8902
Seabrook ES 300/PK-5
4619 NC Highway 210 S, 910-323-2930
Antoine McGill, prin. Fax 486-8872
Seventy-First Classical MS 500/6-8
6830 Raeford Rd 28304 910-864-0092
Patricia Ramos, prin. Fax 487-8547
Sherwood Park ES 400/PK-5
2115 Hope Mills Rd 28304 910-424-4797
Melvetta Wright, prin. Fax 424-2087
Souders ES 500/PK-5
128 Hillview Ave 28301 910-488-6705
Rhonda McNatt, prin. Fax 630-2010
Stoney Point ES 800/K-5
7411 Rockfish Rd 28306 910-424-3945
Cynthia Anderson, prin. Fax 424-6924
Sunnyside ES 400/K-5
3876 Sunnyside School Rd, 910-483-4319
Sheri Bain, prin. Fax 483-5711
Vanstory Hills ES 500/2-5
400 Foxhall Rd 28303 910-483-0809
James Mask, prin. Fax 483-6679
Walker-Spivey ES 300/K-5
500 Fisher St 28301 910-483-5656
Larry Parker, prin. Fax 483-3706
Warrenwood ES 500/PK-5
4618 Rosehill Rd 28311 910-488-6609
Margaret Goodwin, prin. Fax 488-1722
Westarea ES 500/PK-5
941 Country Club Dr 28301 910-488-1705
Dr. Zakiyyah Backman, prin. Fax 488-9484
Westover MS 800/6-8
275 Bonanza Dr 28303 910-864-0813
La'Shanda Carver-Moore, prin. Fax 864-7906
Williams MS 1,200/6-8
4644 Clinton Rd, 910-483-8222
Steven Morris, prin. Fax 483-4831
Willis ES 300/PK-5
1412 Belvedere Ave 28305 910-484-9064
Kacey Northrop, prin. Fax 484-9065
Other Schools – See Eastover, Hope Mills, Linden, Roseboro, Spring Lake, Stedman, Wade

---

Bal-Perazim Christian Academy 50/PK-12
4921 Bragg Blvd 28303 910-487-4220
Morris Braxton, prin. Fax 864-3451
Berean Baptist Academy 400/PK-12
518 Glensford Dr 28314 910-868-2511
Jack Farmer, head sch Fax 868-1550
Cornerstone Christian Academy 200/PK-12
3000 Scotty Hill Rd 28303 910-867-1166
Fayetteville Academy 400/PK-12
3200 Cliffdale Rd 28303 910-868-5131
Ray Quesnel, head sch Fax 868-7351
Fayetteville Adventist Christian S 50/K-8
2601 Lone Pine Dr 28306 910-484-6091
Fayetteville Christian S 600/PK-12
1422 Ireland Dr 28304 910-483-3905
Tammi Potoro, head sch Fax 483-0906
Freedom Christian Academy 300/PK-12
3130 Gillespie St 28306 910-485-7777
Paul Williams, head sch Fax 485-7757
Harvest Preparatory Academy 50/PK-8
PO Box 2391 28302 910-483-6838
Dr. Rosa Herman, head sch Fax 433-2364
Liberty Christian Academy 300/PK-12
6548 Rockfish Rd 28306 910-424-1205
Duncan Edge, prin. Fax 424-8049
Northwood Temple Academy 400/PK-12
4200 Ramsey St 28311 910-822-7711
Renee McLamb, head sch Fax 488-7299
Renaissance Classical Christian Academy 100/PK-11
6427 Cliffdale Rd 28314 910-221-0400
Ray Hendrickson, hdmstr. Fax 864-5476
Riverside Christian Academy 50/PK-8
2010 Middle River Loop, 910-323-4026
Dr. Lin Wheeler, supt. Fax 323-2843
St. Ann S 200/PK-8
365 N Cool Spring St 28301 910-483-3902
N. Rone Cordero, prin. Fax 483-3195
St. Patrick S 200/PK-8
1620 Marlborough Rd 28304 910-323-1865
Laura Abboud, prin. Fax 484-1573
Trinity Christian S of Academics 200/K-12
3727 Rosehill Rd 28311 910-488-6779
Dennis Vandevender, prin. Fax 488-2729
Village Christian Academy 800/K-12
908 S McPherson Church Rd 28303 910-483-5500
Tom Rider, supt. Fax 483-5335

Ferguson, Wilkes
Wilkes County SD
Supt. — See North Wilkesboro
Mt. Pleasant ES 300/PK-5
532 Champion Mt Pleasant Rd 28624 336-651-7600
Kristine Kennington, prin. Fax 973-7099

Flat Rock, Henderson, Pop. 3,091
Henderson County SD
Supt. — See Hendersonville
Upward ES 500/K-5
45 Education Dr 28731 828-697-4764
Jason Joyce, prin. Fax 698-6131

Faith Christian Academy 50/PK-12
127 Boyd Dr 28731 828-435-0670
Dr. Paul Cates, prin. Fax 435-0670
Upward SDA S 50/1-8
957 Upward Rd 28731 828-693-6532

Fletcher, Henderson, Pop. 7,049
Buncombe County SD
Supt. — See Asheville
Cane Creek MS 700/6-8
570 Lower Brush Creek Rd 28732 828-628-0824
Karen Barnhill, prin. Fax 628-9833

Henderson County SD
Supt. — See Hendersonville
Fletcher ES 500/K-5
500 Howard Gap Rd 28732 828-684-0580
Jennifer Shelton, prin. Fax 687-1217

Gilmer Christian S 100/K-8
PO Box 5338 28732 828-684-8221
Veritas Christian Academy 400/PK-12
17 Cane Creek Rd 28732 828-681-0546
Fax 681-0547

Forest City, Rutherford, Pop. 7,281
Rutherford County SD 8,500/PK-12
382 W Main St 28043 828-288-2200
Dr. Janet Mason, supt. Fax 288-2490
www.rcsnc.org/
Chase MS 700/6-8
840 Chase High Rd 28043 828-247-1043
Dr. Jason Byrd, prin. Fax 247-0551
Forest City - Dunbar ES 400/K-5
286 Learning Pkwy 28043 828-245-4978
Brad Richardson, prin. Fax 245-4444
Harris ES 500/K-5
3330 US Highway 221 S 28043 828-248-2354
Don Ingle, prin. Fax 248-9471
Hunt ES 400/K-5
100 Forrest W Hunt Dr 28043 828-245-2161
Tammie Ash, prin. Fax 248-3286
Mt. Vernon-Ruth ES 300/K-5
2785 Hudlow Rd 28043 828-287-4792
Keith Ezell, prin. Fax 287-5253
Other Schools – See Bostic, Cliffside, Ellenboro, Rutherfordton, Spindale

Four Oaks, Johnston, Pop. 1,883
Johnston County SD
Supt. — See Smithfield
Four Oaks ES 1,100/PK-5
180 W Hatcher St 27524 919-963-2166
Kathy Parrish, prin. Fax 963-3851
Four Oaks MS 500/6-8
1475 Boyette Rd 27524 919-963-4022
Tol Avery, prin. Fax 963-4123

Franklin, Macon, Pop. 3,786
Macon County SD 4,300/K-12
1202 Old Murphy Rd 28734 828-524-3314
Dr. Chris Baldwin, supt. Fax 369-7240
www.macon.k12.nc.us
Cartoogechaye ES 300/K-4
3295 Old Murphy Rd 28734 828-524-2845
Josh Lynch, prin. Fax 369-3263
East Franklin ES 400/K-4
100 Watauga St 28734 828-524-3216
Landon Holland, prin. Fax 369-6779
Iotla Valley ES 400/K-4
1166 Iotla Church Rd 28734 828-524-2938
Michelle Bell, prin. Fax 369-8403
Macon MS 600/7-8
1345 Wells Grove Rd 28734 828-524-3766
Scot Maslin, prin. Fax 349-3900
Mountain View IS 600/5-6
161 Clarks Chapel Rd 28734 828-349-1325
Kristen Lynch, prin. Fax 349-0761
South Macon ES 500/K-4
855 Addington Bridge Rd 28734 828-369-0796
Allison Guynn, prin. Fax 369-0947
Other Schools – See Highlands, Topton

Trimont Christian Academy 200/PK-12
98 Promise Ln 28734 828-369-6756

Franklinton, Franklin, Pop. 1,988
Franklin County SD
Supt. — See Louisburg
Franklinton ES 500/K-5
431 S Hillsborough St 27525 919-494-2479
Melissa Richardson, prin. Fax 494-7115
Franklinton MS 300/6-8
3 N Main St 27525 919-494-2971
David Brown-Averette, prin. Fax 494-1625

Granville County SD
Supt. — See Oxford
Tar River ES 500/PK-5
2642 Philo White Rd 27525 919-528-2767
Erin Robbins, prin. Fax 528-2774
Wilton ES 300/PK-5
2555 NC Highway 96 27525 919-528-0033
Shelia Atkins, prin. Fax 528-9852

Franklinville, Randolph, Pop. 1,143
Randolph County SD
Supt. — See Asheboro
Franklinville ES 500/K-5
162 Pine St 27248 336-824-2306
Debbie Sheron, prin. Fax 824-1427
Grays Chapel ES 500/K-5
5322 NC Highway 22 N 27248 336-824-8620
Ross Reaves, prin. Fax 824-3992

Fremont, Wayne, Pop. 1,228
Wayne County SD
Supt. — See Goldsboro

Fremont STARS ES 300/PK-5
101 N Pine St 27830 919-242-3410
Kelly Langston, prin. Fax 242-3359
Norwayne MS 1,000/6-8
1394 Norwayne School Rd 27830 919-242-3414
Lisa Tart, prin. Fax 242-3418

Fuquay Varina, Wake, Pop. 17,531
Harnett County SD
Supt. — See Lillington
LaFayette ES 700/K-5
108 Lafayette School Rd 27526 919-552-4353
Sonya Pearce, prin. Fax 557-3066

Wake County SD
Supt. — See Cary
Ballentine ES 500/K-5
1651 N McLaurin Ln 27526 919-557-1120
Kimberly Short, prin. Fax 557-1144
Fuquay-Varina ES 700/K-5
6600 Johnson Pond Rd 27526 919-557-2566
Heather Johnson, prin. Fax 670-4210
Fuquay-Varina MS 800/6-8
109 N Ennis St 27526 919-557-2727
Terrance McCotter, prin. Fax 557-2754
Herbert Akins Road ES 900/K-5
2255 Herbert Akins Rd 27526 919-567-4100
Kendra Culberson, prin. Fax 567-4109
Lincoln Heights ES 500/K-5
307 Bridge St 27526 919-557-2587
Kimberly Grant, prin. Fax 694-8627

Hilltop Christian S 300/K-12
10212 Fayetteville Rd 27526 919-552-5612

Garner, Wake, Pop. 25,256
Johnston County SD
Supt. — See Smithfield
Cleveland MS 1,100/6-8
2323 Cornwallis Rd 27529 919-553-7500
Sarah Reynolds, prin. Fax 553-7798
Polenta ES 1,000/PK-5
105 Josephine Rd 27529 919-989-6039
Kristina Benson, prin. Fax 989-6272
West View ES 900/PK-5
11755 Cleveland Rd 27529 919-661-6184
Brayton Leonhardt, prin. Fax 661-6192

Wake County SD
Supt. — See Cary
Aversboro ES 600/PK-5
1605 Aversboro Rd 27529 919-662-2325
Tiffany Stuart, prin. Fax 662-2329
Creech Road ES 600/K-5
450 Creech Rd 27529 919-662-2359
Margie Fowler, prin. Fax 662-2372
East Garner ES 600/K-5
5545 Jones Sausage Rd 27529 919-773-7411
Carmen Graf, prin. Fax 773-7415
East Garner MS 1,300/6-8
6301 Jones Sausage Rd 27529 919-662-2339
James Sposato, prin. Fax 662-2357
North Garner MS 1,100/6-8
720 Powell Dr 27529 919-662-2434
Gregory Butler, prin. Fax 662-5637
Rand Road ES 500/PK-5
300 Arbor Greene Dr 27529 919-662-2275
Rhonda Jones, prin. Fax 704-2134
Timber Drive ES 700/K-5
1601 Timber Dr 27529 919-773-9500
Brady Kocher, prin. Fax 773-9507
Vandora Springs ES 600/PK-5
8317 Bryan Rd 27529 919-662-2486
Troy Peuler, prin. Fax 662-5626

Gaston, Northampton, Pop. 1,141
Northampton County SD
Supt. — See Jackson
Gaston ES 300/PK-4
PO Box J 27832 252-537-2520
Barbara Stephenson, prin. Fax 535-5692
Gaston MS 200/5-8
PO Box J 27832 252-537-1910
Monte Freeman, prin. Fax 537-9028

Gastonia, Gaston, Pop. 70,333
Gaston County SD 31,300/PK-12
PO Box 1397 28053 704-866-6100
Jeffrey Booker, supt. Fax 866-6321
www.gaston.k12.nc.us/
Beam ES 600/PK-5
200 Davis Park Rd 28052 704-866-6618
Leigh Smith, prin. Fax 866-6320
Bess ES 600/K-5
4340 Beaty Rd 28056 704-866-6075
Laura Dixon, prin. Fax 866-6102
Brookside ES 600/PK-5
1925 Auten Rd 28054 704-866-6283
Logan McGuire, prin. Fax 866-6294
Chapel Grove ES 400/K-5
5201 Lewis Rd 28052 704-866-6077
Chad Carper, prin. Fax 861-1204
Gardner Park ES 600/K-5
738 Armstrong Park Rd 28054 704-866-6082
Jaime Wallace, prin. Fax 396-6879
Grier MS 700/6-8
1622 E Garrison Blvd 28054 704-836-9604
Loretta Reed, prin. Fax 866-6116
Hawks Nest STEAM Academy 100/K-5
3430 Robinwood Rd 28054 704-866-8467
Jill Payne, prin. Fax 866-8470
Lingerfeldt ES 500/PK-5
1601 Madison St 28052 704-866-6094
Staci Bradley, prin. Fax 866-6311
New Hope ES 500/PK-5
137 Stowe Rd 28056 704-836-9112
Lynn Whiteside, prin. Fax 824-4715
Pleasant Ridge ES 300/PK-5
1260 Floyd Ln 28052 704-866-6096
Glenn Cook, prin. Fax 866-6097
Robinson ES 400/K-5
3122 Union Rd 28056 704-866-6607
Torben Ross, prin. Fax 866-6314
Sadler ES 500/PK-5
3950 W Franklin Blvd 28052 704-862-5895
James Ramere, prin. Fax 862-5899
Sherwood ES 700/PK-5
1744 Dixon Rd 28054 704-866-6609
Tyler West, prin. Fax 866-6617
Southwest MS 800/6-8
1 Roadrunner Dr 28052 704-866-6290
Cindy Hester, prin. Fax 866-6293
Woodhill ES 400/PK-5
1027 Woodhill Dr 28054 704-866-6295
Amy Hord, prin. Fax 866-6170
York Chester MS 400/6-8
601 S Clay St 28052 704-866-6297
Amy Holbrook, prin. Fax 866-6319
Other Schools – See Belmont, Bessemer City, Cherryville, Cramerton, Dallas, Lowell, Mc Adenville, Mount Holly, Stanley

---

First Wesleyan Christian S 300/PK-8
208A S Church St 28054 704-865-9823
John Wilfong, admin. Fax 852-4219
Gaston Christian S 800/PK-12
1625 Lowell Bethesda Rd 28056 704-349-5020
Gaston Day S 500/PK-12
2001 Gaston Day School Rd 28056 704-864-7744
Dr. Richard Rankin, hdmstr. Fax 865-3813
St. Michael S 200/PK-8
704 Saint Michaels Ln 28052 704-865-4382
Shelia Levesque, prin. Fax 867-6379

Gates, Gates
Gates County SD
Supt. — See Gatesville
Buckland ES 200/K-5
448 NC Highway 37 N 27937 252-357-1611
Gail Hawkins, prin. Fax 357-1106

Gatesville, Gates, Pop. 318
Gates County SD 1,700/PK-12
PO Box 125 27938 252-357-1113
Dr. Barry Williams, supt. Fax 357-0207
coserver.gates.k12.nc.us/
Central MS 400/6-8
362 US Highway 158 W 27938 252-357-0470
Steve Hunter, prin. Fax 357-1319
Gatesville ES 300/PK-5
709 Main St 27938 252-357-0613
Scott Corrente, prin. Fax 357-2809
Other Schools – See Gates, Sunbury

Germanton, Stokes, Pop. 824
Stokes County SD
Supt. — See Danbury
Germanton ES 200/K-5
6085 NC 8 Hwy S 27019 336-591-4021
Kim Dixon, prin. Fax 591-7013

Gibsonville, Guilford, Pop. 6,318
Guilford County SD
Supt. — See Greensboro
Eastern MS 900/6-8
435 Peeden Dr 27249 336-449-4255
Kathy Kirkpatrick, prin. Fax 449-0728
Gibsonville ES 500/K-5
401 E Joyner St 27249 336-449-4214
Marcy Roan, prin. Fax 449-6745

Glade Valley, Alleghany

Blue Ridge Christian S 50/K-8
PO Box 518 28627 336-372-6900
Christine Choate, lead tchr. Fax 372-2530

Gold Hill, Rowan
Rowan-Salisbury County SD
Supt. — See Salisbury
Morgan ES 400/PK-5
3860 Liberty Rd 28071 704-636-0169
Derek DiStefano, prin. Fax 633-8689

Goldsboro, Wayne, Pop. 35,562
Wayne County SD 18,600/PK-12
PO Box 1797 27533 919-731-5900
Dr. Michael Dunsmore, supt. Fax 705-6199
www.waynecountyschools.org
Carver Heights ES 300/PK-4
411 Bunche Dr 27530 919-731-7222
Cortrina Smith, prin. Fax 731-4503
Dillard MS 600/5-8
1101 Devereaux St 27530 919-580-9360
Theresa Cox, prin. Fax 736-1121
Eastern Wayne ES 800/PK-5
1271 E New Hope Rd 27534 919-751-7130
Robert Yelverton, prin. Fax 751-7146
Eastern Wayne MS 600/6-8
3518 Central Heights Rd 27534 919-751-7110
Catherine Fulcher, prin. Fax 751-7114
Grantham ES 500/K-4
174 Grantham School Rd 27530 919-689-5000
Antoinette Ward, prin. Fax 689-5004
Grantham MS 5-8
3093 US Highway 13 S 27530 919-689-9999
Makita Jenkins, prin.
Greenwood MS 500/5-8
3209 E Ash St 27534 919-751-7100
Ryan Nelson, prin. Fax 751-7201
Meadow Lane ES 700/PK-4
3500 E Ash St 27534 919-751-7150
Wendy Hooks, prin. Fax 751-7108
North Drive ES 500/PK-4
1108 North Dr 27534 919-731-5950
Charlenna Bennett-Carter, prin. Fax 705-6029
Rosewood ES 700/PK-5
126 Charlie Braswell Rd 27530 919-705-6040
Charles Smith, prin. Fax 705-6003
Rosewood MS 400/6-8
541 NC 581 Hwy S 27530 919-736-5050
Brian Weeks, prin. Fax 736-5055
School Street Early Learning Center 200/PK-PK
415 S Virginia St 27530 919-731-5960
Karen Wellington, coord. Fax 731-5963
Spring Creek ES 1,000/PK-5
1050 Saint John Church Rd 27534 919-751-7155
Nicole Barrett, prin. Fax 751-7165
Tommys Road ES 600/PK-5
1150 Tommys Rd 27534 919-736-5040
Tameka Allen, prin. Fax 736-5039
Other Schools – See Dudley, Fremont, Mount Olive, Pikeville, Seven Springs

---

Faith Christian Academy 300/PK-12
1200 W Grantham St 27530 919-734-8701
Micah Conlon, admin. Fax 734-9658
St. Mary S 200/PK-8
1601 Edgerton St 27530 919-735-1931
Lynn Magoon, prin. Fax 735-1917
Wayne Christian S 500/PK-12
1201 Patetown Rd 27530 919-735-5605
Dr. Ashley Shook, admin. Fax 735-5229
Wayne Country Day S 300/PK-12
480 Country Day Rd 27530 919-736-1045
Wayne Montessori S 100/PK-5
PO Box 10646 27532 919-734-0051

Goldston, Chatham, Pop. 264
Chatham County SD
Supt. — See Pittsboro
Waters S 300/K-8
55 JS Waters School Rd 27252 919-898-2259
Beverly Browne, prin. Fax 898-4160

Graham, Alamance, Pop. 13,906
Alamance-Burlington SD
Supt. — See Burlington
Graham MS 700/6-8
311 E Pine St 27253 336-570-6460
Lee Williams, prin. Fax 570-6464
Jordan ES 400/K-5
5827 Church Rd 27253 336-376-3673
Terri Drummond, prin. Fax 376-6243
North Graham ES 400/PK-5
1025 Trollinger Rd 27253 336-578-2272
Nancy Cothren, prin. Fax 578-8335
Southern Alamance MS 800/6-8
771 Southern High School Rd 27253 336-570-6500
Heather Ward, prin. Fax 570-6504
South Graham ES 700/PK-5
320 Ivey Rd 27253 336-570-6520
Elizabeth Price, prin. Fax 570-6521
Wilson ES 600/PK-5
2518 S NC Highway 54 27253 336-578-1366
Ashley Westmorland, prin. Fax 578-8092

Alamance Christian S 300/PK-12
PO Box 838 27253 336-578-0318
Michael Lofin, admin. Fax 578-7200

Granite Falls, Caldwell, Pop. 4,669
Caldwell County SD
Supt. — See Lenoir
Baton ES 400/K-5
1400 Baton School Rd 28630 828-728-9531
Jason Teffeteller, prin. Fax 728-7548
Dudley Shoals ES 500/K-5
1500 Dudley Shoals Rd 28630 828-396-3457
Gwyn Roop, prin. Fax 396-3461
Granite Falls ES 700/K-5
60 N Highland Ave 28630 828-396-2222
Chris Greene, prin. Fax 396-7796
Granite Falls MS 600/6-8
90 N Main St 28630 828-396-2341
Melissa Costin, prin. Fax 396-7072
Sawmills ES 300/K-5
4436 Sawmills School Rd 28630 828-396-2610
Courtney Wright, prin. Fax 396-2232

Green Mountain, Yancey
Yancey County SD
Supt. — See Burnsville
Clearmont ES 100/K-5
1175 Clearmont School Rd 28740 828-682-2337
Stuart Jolley, prin. Fax 682-3656

Greensboro, Guilford, Pop. 263,264
Guilford County SD 73,500/PK-12
PO Box 880 27402 336-370-8100
Sharon Contreras Ph.D., supt. Fax 370-8299
www.gcsnc.com
Academy at Lincoln 700/4-8
1016 Lincoln St 27401 336-370-3471
Anita Stewart, prin. Fax 370-3480
Alamance ES 800/PK-5
3600 Williams Dairy Rd 27406 336-697-3177
Eric Taylor, prin. Fax 697-3175
Alderman ES 400/PK-5
4211 Chateau Dr 27407 336-294-7320
Jeffrey Uhlenberg, prin. Fax 294-7330
Allen MS 700/6-8
1108 Glendale Dr 27406 336-294-7325
Sheila Gorham, prin. Fax 294-7315
Archer ES 400/PK-5
2610 Four Seasons Blvd 27407 336-294-7335
Sophia Roberts, prin. Fax 294-7359
Aycock MS 600/6-8
811 Cypress St 27405 336-370-8110
Keisha Brown, prin. Fax 370-8044
Bessemer ES 500/PK-5
918 Huffine Mill Rd 27405 336-375-2585
Catina Chestnut, prin. Fax 375-2588

Bluford STEM Academy 300/K-5
1901 Tuscaloosa St 27401 336-370-8120
Gradesa Lockhart, prin. Fax 370-8124
Brightwood ES 600/PK-5
2001 Brightwood School Rd 27405 336-375-2565
Latrice Stokes, prin. Fax 375-2570
Brooks Global ES 400/K-5
1215 Westover Ter 27408 336-370-8228
Dr. Darcy Kemp, prin. Fax 370-8173
Claxton ES 600/K-5
3720 Pinetop Rd 27410 336-545-2010
Anessa Burgman, prin. Fax 545-2025
Cone ES 500/PK-5
2501 N Church St 27405 336-375-2595
Christopher Weikart, prin. Fax 375-2597
Erwin Montessori ES 300/K-5
3012 E Bessemer Ave 27405 336-370-8152
Deborah Parker, prin. Fax 574-3855
Falkener ES 600/PK-5
3931 Naco Rd 27401 336-370-8150
Dr. Angela Draper, prin. Fax 370-8025
Foust ES 400/PK-5
2610 Floyd St 27406 336-370-8155
Merrie Conaway, prin. Fax 370-8057
Frazier ES 300/PK-5
4215 Galway Dr 27406 336-294-7340
Nicole Hill, prin. Fax 294-7364
Gillespie Park ES 300/PK-5
1900 Martin Luther King Dr 27406 336-370-8640
Lei Washington, prin. Fax 574-1608
Greene ES 500/K-5
1501 Benjamin Pkwy 27408 336-545-2015
Stephanie Harris, prin. Fax 545-2037
Guilford ES 600/PK-5
920 Stage Coach Trl 27410 336-316-5844
Lamont McMillan, prin. Fax 316-5841
Guilford MS 700/6-8
320 Lindley Rd 27410 336-316-5833
Patrice Brown, prin. Fax 316-5837
Hairston MS 700/6-8
3911 Naco Rd 27401 336-370-8250
Calvin Freeman, prin. Fax 370-8153
Hampton Magnet ES 300/PK-5
2301 Trade St 27401 336-370-8220
Dr. LaToy Kennedy, prin. Fax 370-8192
Hunter ES 500/PK-5
1305 Merritt Dr 27407 336-294-7345
Michelle Wolverton, prin. Fax 294-7379
Irving Park ES 600/PK-5
1310 Sunset Dr 27408 336-370-8225
Cynthia McKee, prin. Fax 370-8105
Jackson MS 500/6-8
2200 Ontario St 27403 336-294-7350
Katrinka Brown, prin. Fax 294-7316
Jefferson ES 700/PK-5
1400 New Garden Rd 27410 336-316-5870
Susan Villarrubia, prin. Fax 316-5878
Jones ES 700/PK-5
502 South St 27406 336-370-8230
William Luciano, prin. Fax 370-8034
Joyner ES 300/K-5
3300 Normandy Rd 27408 336-545-2020
Denise Ebbs, prin. Fax 545-2029
Kernodle MS 900/6-8
3600 Drawbridge Pkwy 27410 336-545-3717
Thea McHam, prin. Fax 545-3714
Kiser MS 800/6-8
716 Benjamin Pkwy 27408 336-370-8240
Gerald O'Donnell, prin. Fax 370-8248
Lindley ES 500/PK-5
2700 Camden Rd 27403 336-294-7360
Tracy Roof, prin. Fax 294-7363
Mendenhall MS 900/6-8
205 Willoughby Blvd 27408 336-545-2000
Kris Vecchione, prin. Fax 545-2004
Morehead ES 600/K-5
4630 Tower Rd 27410 336-294-7370
Shirley Stipe-Zendle, prin. Fax 294-7368
Murphey Traditional Academy 300/K-5
2306 Ontario St 27403 336-294-7380
Cynthia Brown, prin. Fax 294-7450
Northern ES 600/K-5
3801 NC Highway 150 E 27455 336-656-4032
Teresa Kennedy, prin. Fax 643-4043
Northern MS 1,000/6-8
616 Simpson Calhoun Rd 27455 336-605-3342
Karen Ellis, prin. Fax 643-8435
Northwest MS 1,000/6-8
5300 NW School Rd 27409 336-605-3333
Erik Naglee, prin. Fax 605-3325
Pearce ES 700/K-5
2006 Pleasant Ridge Rd 27410 336-605-5480
Richard Thomae, prin. Fax 605-5488
Peck ES 400/PK-5
1601 W Florida St 27403 336-370-8235
Ashley Triplett, prin. Fax 370-8237
Peeler Open ES 400/K-5
2200 Randall St 27401 336-370-8270
Andrew Gann, prin. Fax 370-8039
Pilot ES 800/PK-5
4701 Chimney Springs Dr 27407 336-316-5820
Kimberly Fleming, prin. Fax 316-5818
Rankin ES 800/PK-5
1501 Spry St 27405 336-375-2545
Patricia Kirkpatrick, prin. Fax 375-2542
Reedy Fork ES 400/K-5
4571 Reedy Fork Pkwy 27405 336-656-3723
Denise Schroeder, prin. Fax 656-3488
Sedgefield ES 500/PK-5
2905 Groometown Rd 27407 336-316-5858
Michele Simmons, prin. Fax 316-5855
Simpkins ES K-5
3511 E Lee St 27406 336-697-3070
Lisa Jordan, prin. Fax 697-3837
Southeast MS 1,000/6-8
4825 Woody Mill Rd 27406 336-674-4280
Karen Burress, prin. Fax 674-4276
Southern ES 300/PK-5
5720 Drake Rd 27406 336-674-4325
Carole Ashby, prin. Fax 674-4330
Southern MS 800/6-8
5747 Drake Rd 27406 336-674-4266
Jusmar Maness, prin. Fax 674-4278
Sternberger ES 400/PK-5
518 N Holden Rd 27410 336-294-7390
Lisa Williams, prin. Fax 294-7394
Sumner ES 600/PK-5
1915 Harris Dr 27406 336-316-5888
Johnita Readus, prin. Fax 316-5880
Vandalia ES 300/PK-5
407 E Vandalia Rd 27406 336-370-8275
Stephanie Rakes, prin. Fax 370-8053
Washington Montessori S 400/PK-5
1110 E Washington St 27401 336-370-8290
Sharon Jacobs, prin. Fax 370-8963
Wharton ES 500/K-5
5813 Lake Brandt Rd 27455 336-545-3700
Dr. Angella Hauser, prin. Fax 545-3703
Wiley ES 300/PK-5
600 W Terrell St 27406 336-370-8295
Tavy Fields, prin. Fax 370-8040
Other Schools – See Browns Summit, Colfax, Gibsonville, High Point, Jamestown, Liberty, Mc Leansville, Oak Ridge, Pleasant Garden, Sedalia, Stokesdale, Summerfield

---

B'nai Shalom Day S 100/PK-8
804 Winview Dr Ste A 27410 336-855-5091
Susan Siegel, head sch Fax 855-1018
Caldwell Academy 700/PK-12
2900 Horse Pen Creek Rd 27410 336-665-1161
Sam Cox, head sch Fax 665-1178
Canterbury S 400/PK-8
5400 Old Lake Jeanette Rd 27455 336-288-2007
Phil Spears, head sch Fax 288-1933
Greensboro Day S 900/PK-12
5401 Lawndale Dr 27455 336-288-8590
Mark Hale, head sch Fax 282-2905
Greensboro Islamic Academy 100/PK-8
2023 16th St 27405 336-285-7766
Greensboro Montessori S 300/PK-9
2856 Horse Pen Creek Rd 27410 336-668-0119
Dr. Kevin Navarro, head sch Fax 665-9531
Hope Academy 50/5-8
PO Box 10616 27404 336-907-7155
Josh Mullins, head sch Fax 907-7155
New Garden Friends S 300/PK-12
1128 New Garden Rd 27410 336-299-0964
Kim Freedman, head sch Fax 346-3169
Our Lady of Grace S 300/PK-8
201 S Chapman St 27403 336-275-1522
Amy Pagano, prin. Fax 279-8824
St. Pius X S 500/K-8
2200 N Elm St 27408 336-273-9865
Ann Flynt, prin. Fax 273-0199
Shining Light Academy 200/PK-12
4530 W Wendover Ave 27409 336-299-9688
Vandalia Christian S 700/PK-12
3919 Pleasant Garden Rd 27406 336-379-8380
Dr. Mark Weatherford, admin. Fax 379-8671

Greenville, Pitt, Pop. 82,822
Pitt County SD 24,000/PK-12
1717 W 5th St 27834 252-830-4200
Dr. Ethan Lenker, supt. Fax 830-4239
www.pitt.k12.nc.us/
Aycock MS 700/6-8
1325 Red Banks Rd 27858 252-756-4181
Darryl Thomas, prin. Fax 756-2408
Belvoir ES 500/PK-5
2568 NC Highway 33 W 27834 252-752-6365
Alison Covington, prin. Fax 752-5008
Chicod S 1,000/PK-8
7557 NC Highway 43 S 27858 252-746-6742
Mike Pollard, prin. Fax 746-4751
Eastern ES 600/K-5
1700 Cedar Ln 27858 252-758-4813
Robert Johnson, prin. Fax 758-7508
Elmhurst ES 400/PK-5
1815 W Berkley Rd 27858 252-756-0180
Colleen Burt, prin. Fax 756-0513
Eppes MS 600/6-8
1100 S Elm St 27858 252-757-2160
Charlie Langley, prin. Fax 757-2163
Falkland ES 400/K-5
503 NC Highway 121 27834 252-752-7820
Ferdonia Stewart, prin. Fax 752-3017
Hope MS 700/6-8
2995 Mills Rd 27858 252-355-7071
Jennifer Poplin, prin. Fax 355-6055
Lakeforest ES 800/K-5
3300 Briarcliff Dr 27834 252-756-3941
Lavette Ford, prin. Fax 756-3946
Northwest ES 400/PK-5
1471 Holland Rd 27834 252-752-6329
Catina Moore, prin. Fax 752-6906
Pactolus S 600/PK-8
3405 Yankee Hall Rd 27834 252-752-6941
Juan Castillo, prin. Fax 758-5817
Saulter Preschool 50/PK-PK
400 Spruce St 27834 252-758-4621
Victor Coffenberry, prin. Fax 758-5893
South Greenville ES 500/PK-5
811 Howell St 27834 252-756-7004
Lakeesha Lynch, prin. Fax 756-3285
Wahl-Coates ES 400/PK-5
2200 E 5th St 27858 252-752-2514
Marty Baker, prin. Fax 758-6205
Wellcome MS 500/6-8
3101 N Memorial Dr 27834 252-752-5938
Kim Harris, prin. Fax 752-1685
Wintergreen IS 700/3-5
4720 County Home Rd 27858 252-355-2411
Cathy Kirkland, prin. Fax 355-0284
Wintergreen PS 800/PK-2
4710 County Home Rd 27858 252-353-5270
Cathy Kirkland, prin. Fax 353-5275
Other Schools – See Ayden, Bethel, Farmville, Grifton, Grimesland, Stokes, Winterville

---

Greenville Christian Academy 300/PK-12
1621 Greenville Blvd SW 27834 252-756-0939
Oakwood S 300/PK-12
4000 MacGregor Downs Rd 27834 252-931-0760
Robert Peterson, hdmstr. Fax 931-0964
St. Peter S 600/PK-8
2606 E 5th St 27858 252-752-3529
Douglas Jones, prin. Fax 752-7604
Trinity Christian S 400/PK-12
3111 Golden Rd 27858 252-758-0037

Grifton, Lenoir, Pop. 2,568
Pitt County SD
Supt. — See Greenville
Grifton S 600/PK-8
PO Box 219 28530 252-524-5141
Kevin Smith, prin. Fax 524-4505

Grimesland, Pitt, Pop. 436
Pitt County SD
Supt. — See Greenville
Whitfield S 500/PK-8
PO Box 129 27837 252-752-6614
Tracy Gibbs, prin. Fax 752-7484

Grover, Cleveland, Pop. 687
Cleveland County SD
Supt. — See Shelby
Grover ES 400/PK-4
206 Carolina Ave 28073 704-476-8351
Linda King, prin. Fax 734-5616

Halifax, Halifax, Pop. 232
Halifax County SD 2,900/PK-12
PO Box 468 27839 252-583-5111
Dr. Eric Cunningham, supt. Fax 583-1474
www.halifax.k12.nc.us/
Other Schools – See Enfield, Hollister, Littleton, Roanoke Rapids, Scotland Neck

Weldon CSD
Supt. — See Weldon
Weldon MS 300/5-8
4489 US Highway 301 27839 252-536-2571
Andre Stewart, prin. Fax 536-3485

Hallsboro, Columbus, Pop. 457
Columbus County SD
Supt. — See Whiteville
Hallsboro Artesia ES 400/PK-5
1337 Giles Byrd Rd 28442 910-646-3510
Josephine Spaulding, prin. Fax 646-5048
Hallsboro MS 200/6-8
89 School Rd 28442 910-646-4192
Derrick Boyd, prin. Fax 646-5072

Hamilton, Martin, Pop. 403
Martin County SD
Supt. — See Williamston
Andrews ES 100/K-5
PO Box 239 27840 252-798-5631
Rana Beach, prin. Fax 798-2726

Hamlet, Richmond, Pop. 6,381
Richmond County SD 7,800/PK-12
PO Box 1259 28345 910-582-5860
Cindy Goodman Ed.D., supt. Fax 582-7921
www.richmond.k12.nc.us
Fairview Heights ES 600/PK-5
104 Hamilton St 28345 910-582-7900
Joyce McRae, prin. Fax 582-7901
Hamlet MS 500/6-8
1406 Mcdonald Ave 28345 910-582-7903
Karen Allen, prin. Fax 582-5730
Monroe Avenue ES 400/PK-5
400 Monroe Ave 28345 910-582-7907
Dawn Terry, prin. Fax 582-7913
Other Schools – See Cordova, Ellerbe, Rockingham

Second Baptist Church Day S 100/K-6
518 4th St 28345 910-205-0055

Hampstead, Pender, Pop. 4,028
Pender County SD
Supt. — See Burgaw
North Topsail ES 600/PK-5
1310 Sloop Point Loop Rd 28443 910-270-0694
Peter Wildeboer, prin. Fax 270-9533
South Topsail ES 600/PK-5
997 Hoover Rd 28443 910-270-2756
Jennifer Angel, prin. Fax 270-4056
Topsail ES 500/PK-5
17385 US Highway 17 N 28443 910-270-1977
Melissa Wilson, prin. Fax 270-1936
Topsail MS 900/6-8
17445 US Highway 17 N 28443 910-270-2612
AnnaMaria Romero-Lehrer, prin. Fax 270-3190

Topsail Montessori 50/PK-6
301 Whitebridge Rd 28443 910-319-0813

Hamptonville, Yadkin
Yadkin County SD
Supt. — See Yadkinville
West Yadkin ES 600/PK-6
4432 W Old US 421 Hwy 27020 336-468-2526
Jill Logan, prin. Fax 468-1178

Harkers Island, Carteret, Pop. 1,195
Carteret County SD
Supt. — See Beaufort
Harkers Island ES 100/K-5
1163 Island Rd 28531 252-728-3755
Jessica Emory, prin. Fax 728-6399

Harmony, Iredell, Pop. 529
Iredell-Statesville SD
Supt. — See Statesville
Harmony ES 400/K-5
139 Harmony School Rd 28634 704-546-2643
Andy Mehall, prin. Fax 546-3074

Harrells, Sampson, Pop. 202

Harrells Christian Academy 400/K-12
PO Box 88 28444 910-532-4575

Harrisburg, Cabarrus, Pop. 11,315
Cabarrus County SD
Supt. — See Concord
Harrisburg ES 900/K-6
3900 Stallings Rd 28075 704-455-5118
Erin Anderson, prin. Fax 455-5414
Hickory Ridge MS 1,100/6-8
7336 Raging Ridge Rd 28075 704-455-1331
Elizabeth Snyder, prin. Fax 455-1338

Charlotte Islamic Academy 200/PK-12
8810 Hickory Ridge Rd 28075 704-537-1772

Havelock, Craven, Pop. 19,878
Craven County SD
Supt. — See New Bern
Barden ES 400/PK-5
200 Cedar Dr 28532 252-444-5100
Marilyn Brown, prin. Fax 444-5103
Bell ES 400/K-5
804 Fontana Blvd 28532 252-444-5133
Benjamin Barnes, prin. Fax 444-5136
Edwards ES 500/K-5
200 Education Ln 28532 252-444-5140
Kathleen Leffler, prin. Fax 444-5145
Gurganus ES 500/K-5
535 US Highway 70 W 28532 252-444-5150
Debra Hurst, prin. Fax 444-5154
Havelock ES 400/K-5
201 Cunningham Blvd 28532 252-444-5106
Kathy Barber, prin. Fax 444-5109
Havelock MS 500/6-8
102 High School Dr 28532 252-444-5125
William Byland, prin. Fax 444-5129
Tucker Creek MS 400/6-8
200 Sermons Blvd 28532 252-444-7200
Claudia Casey, prin. Fax 444-7206

Annunciation S 100/PK-8
246 E Main St 28532 252-447-3137
Anna Bragg, prin. Fax 447-3138

Haw River, Alamance, Pop. 2,271
Alamance-Burlington SD
Supt. — See Burlington
Haw River ES 600/PK-5
701 E Main St 27258 336-578-0177
Jennifer Reed, prin. Fax 578-8336

Hayesville, Clay, Pop. 309
Clay County SD 1,400/PK-12
154 Yellow Jacket Dr 28904 828-389-8513
Dr. Mark Leek, supt. Fax 389-3437
www.clayschools.org/
Hayesville ES 600/PK-4
72 Elementary Dr 28904 828-389-8586
Tommy Hollingsworth, prin. Fax 389-3243
Hayesville MS 500/5-8
135 School Dr 28904 828-389-9924
Dr. Cathy Andrews, prin. Fax 389-1706

Hays, Wilkes, Pop. 1,835
Wilkes County SD
Supt. — See North Wilkesboro
Mountain View ES 600/PK-5
5464 Mountain View Rd 28635 336-696-5512
Rebecca Mastin, prin. Fax 696-7216

Henderson, Vance, Pop. 15,184
Vance County SD 7,200/PK-12
PO Box 7001 27536 252-492-2127
Dr. Anthony D. Jackson, supt. Fax 438-6119
www.vcs.k12.nc.us
Aycock ES 400/PK-5
305 Carey Chapel Rd 27537 252-492-1516
Kristen Boyd, prin. Fax 492-7038
Carver ES 200/PK-5
987 Carver School Rd 27537 252-438-6955
David Westbrook, prin. Fax 438-7323
Clarke ES 500/PK-5
309 Mount Carmel Church Rd 27537 252-438-8415
Crystal Richardson, prin. Fax 438-6193
Dabney ES 500/PK-5
150 Lanning Rd 27537 252-438-6918
Dr. Michael Putney, prin. Fax 438-2604
Eaton-Johnson MS 700/6-8
500 N Beckford Dr 27536 252-438-5017
Travis Taylor, prin. Fax 738-0250
Henderson MS 700/6-8
219 Charles St 27536 252-492-0054
Dr. John Hargrove, prin. Fax 430-8588
New Hope ES 200/PK-5
10199 NC 39 Hwy N 27537 252-438-6549
Dr. Harold Thompson, prin. Fax 438-7389
Pinkston Street ES 300/PK-5
855 Adams St 27536 252-438-3441
Heddie Somerville, prin. Fax 438-5524
Rollins ES 500/PK-5
1600 S Garnett Street Ext 27536 252-438-2189
Stephanie Alston, prin. Fax 438-2180
STEM Early HS 300/6-8
925 Garrett Rd 27537 252-738-2260
Iris Dethmers, prin. Fax 738-2261
Yancey ES 300/PK-5
311 Hawkins Dr 27536 252-438-8336
Carnetta Thomas, prin. Fax 438-2541
Young ES 300/PK-5
6655 Broad St 27537 252-438-6423
Marylaura McKoon, prin. Fax 433-0215
Other Schools – See Kittrell

Crossroads Christian S 200/PK-12
PO Box 249 27536 252-431-1333
Jonathan Capps, hdmstr. Fax 431-0333
Kerr-Vance Academy 500/PK-12
700 Vance Academy Rd 27537 252-492-0018
Victory Christian S 100/K-12
PO Box 592 27536 252-492-6079

Hendersonville, Henderson, Pop. 12,877
Henderson County SD 13,500/K-12
414 4th Ave W 28739 828-697-4733
Bo Caldwell, supt. Fax 697-5541
www.hendersoncountypublicschoolsnc.org
Apple Valley MS 900/6-8
43 Fruitland Rd 28792 828-697-4545
Peggy Marshall, prin. Fax 698-6119
Atkinson ES 400/K-5
2510 Old Kanuga Rd 28739 828-697-4755
Mark Page, prin. Fax 698-6120
Clear Creek ES 500/K-5
737 N Clear Creek Rd 28792 828-697-4760
Marcie Wilson, prin. Fax 698-6121
Drysdale ES 400/K-5
271 Bearcat Blvd 28792 828-697-5568
Dr. William Laughter, prin. Fax 698-6122
Edneyville ES 500/K-5
2875 Pace Rd 28792 828-685-7600
Donna Brackett, prin. Fax 685-4006
Hendersonville ES 400/K-5
1039 Randall Cir 28791 828-697-4752
Kerry Stewart, prin. Fax 698-6125
Hendersonville MS 600/6-8
825 N Whitted St 28791 828-697-4800
Luke Manuel, prin. Fax 698-6127
Rugby MS 900/6-8
3345 Haywood Rd 28791 828-891-6566
Scott Moore, prin. Fax 891-6589
Sugarloaf ES 400/K-5
2270 Sugarloaf Rd 28792 828-697-4600
Jennifer Newcomer, prin. Fax 697-4632
Other Schools – See Dana, East Flat Rock, Etowah, Flat Rock, Fletcher, Mills River

---

Immaculata S 200/PK-8
711 Buncombe St 28791 828-693-3277
Meredith Canning, prin. Fax 696-3677

Hertford, Perquimans, Pop. 2,119
Perquimans County SD 1,800/PK-12
PO Box 337 27944 252-426-5741
Matthew Cheeseman, supt. Fax 426-4913
www.pqschools.org
Hertford Grammar S 400/3-5
PO Box 397 27944 252-426-7166
Jason Griffin, prin. Fax 426-7293
Other Schools – See Winfall

Hickory, Catawba, Pop. 39,263
Burke County SD
Supt. — See Morganton
Childers ES 400/PK-5
1183 Cape Hickory Rd 28601 828-324-1340
Heidi Bristol, prin. Fax 324-1390

Catawba County SD
Supt. — See Newton
Arndt MS 700/7-8
3350 34th Street Dr NE 28601 828-256-9545
Lee Miller, prin. Fax 256-6748
Campbell ES 500/K-6
2121 35th Avenue Dr NE 28601 828-256-2769
Adrienne Dula, prin. Fax 256-2846
Mountain View ES 800/PK-6
5911 Dwayne Starnes Dr 28602 828-294-2020
Dyanne Sherrill, prin. Fax 294-3239
Murray ES 400/K-6
3901 Section House Rd 28601 828-256-2196
Dr. Robin Honeycutt, prin. Fax 256-2197
Snow Creek ES 500/K-6
3238 Snow Creek Rd NE 28601 828-256-2335
Nichole Ijames, prin. Fax 256-2187

Hickory CSD 4,300/PK-12
432 4th Ave SW 28602 828-322-2855
Robbie Adell Ed.D., supt. Fax 322-1834
www.hickoryschools.net
Grandview MS 500/6-8
451 Catawba Valley Blvd 28602 828-328-2289
Dr. Aaron Joplin, prin. Fax 328-2992
Jenkins ES 400/PK-5
3750 N Center St 28601 828-327-3491
Ryan McCreary, prin. Fax 327-3590
Longview ES 300/3-5
737 12th St SW 28602 828-485-0975
Judy Jolly, prin. Fax 485-0981
Northview MS 600/6-8
302 28th Ave NE 28601 828-327-6300
Nala Sadler-Sherrill, prin. Fax 327-6367
Oakwood ES 400/PK-5
366 4th St NW 28601 828-322-1340
Jennifer Griffin, prin. Fax 322-4980
Southwest PS 400/PK-2
1580 32nd St SW 28602 828-324-8884
Stephanie Dischiavi, prin. Fax 345-6226
Viewmont ES 600/PK-5
21 16th Ave NW 28601 828-324-7049
Jeffrey Hodakowski, prin. Fax 327-4619

Alexander Christian Academy 100/PK-11
3919 Icard Ridge Rd 28601 828-471-7826
Angela Gettler, dir. Fax 632-3397
Hickory Christian Academy 400/K-12
3260 6th Street Dr NW 28601 828-324-5405
Johnston SDA S 50/K-8
174 23rd St NW 28601 828-327-4005
St. Stephens Lutheran S 200/PK-8
2304 Springs Rd NE 28601 828-256-2166
Ross Chiles, prin. Fax 256-7994
Tabernacle Christian S 100/PK-12
1225 29th Avenue Dr NE 28601 828-324-9936

Hiddenite, Alexander, Pop. 532
Alexander County SD
Supt. — See Taylorsville
East Alexander MS 700/6-8
1285 White Plains Rd 28636 828-632-7565
Dr. Lisa Harrington, prin. Fax 632-4508
Hiddenite ES 500/PK-5
374 Sulphur Springs Rd 28636 828-632-2503
Rene Stilwell, prin. Fax 635-0656

Highlands, Macon, Pop. 908
Macon County SD
Supt. — See Franklin
Highlands S 400/K-12
PO Box 940 28741 828-526-2147
Brian Jetter, prin. Fax 526-0615

High Point, Guilford, Pop. 102,180
Guilford County SD
Supt. — See Greensboro
Fairview ES 400/PK-5
608 Fairview St 27260 336-819-2890
Angela Dawson, prin. Fax 819-2892
Ferndale MS 900/6-8
701 Ferndale Blvd 27262 336-819-2855
Quincy Williams, prin. Fax 885-2854
Florence ES 700/K-5
7605 Florence School Dr 27265 336-819-2120
Edward Wohlgemuth, prin. Fax 454-5579
Jay ES 400/PK-5
1311 E Springfield Rd 27263 336-434-8490
Carla Flores-Ballesteros, prin. Fax 431-6555
Jay MS 100/5-5
1201 E Fairfield Rd 27263 336-819-2164
Kevin Wheat, prin. Fax 882-0069
Johnson Street Global Studies S 400/K-8
1601 Johnson St 27262 336-819-2900
Kristina Wheat, prin. Fax 819-2899
Kirkman Park ES 300/PK-5
1101 N Centennial St 27262 336-819-2905
Dr. Jamal Crawford, prin. Fax 889-6218
Montlieu Academy of Technology 600/PK-5
1105 Montlieu Ave 27262 336-819-2910
Kimberly Scott, prin. Fax 819-2915
Northwood ES 600/PK-5
818 W Lexington Ave 27262 336-819-2920
Scott Winslow, prin. Fax 819-2921
Oak Hill ES 400/PK-5
320 Wrightenberry St 27260 336-819-2925
Dr. Candice Bailey, prin. Fax 819-2931
Oak View ES 500/PK-5
614 Oakview Rd 27265 336-819-2935
Heather Bare, prin. Fax 869-6856
Parkview Village ES 400/K-5
325 Gordon St 27260 336-819-2945
Crystal Gregory, prin. Fax 819-2943
Shadybrook ES 500/K-5
503 Shadybrook Rd 27265 336-819-2950
George Green, prin. Fax 869-1575
Southwest ES 700/K-5
4372 SW School Rd 27265 336-819-2992
Dr. Sandra Culmer, prin. Fax 454-8372
Southwest MS 1,200/6-8
4368 Barrow Rd 27265 336-819-2985
Kerrie Douglas, prin. Fax 454-4015
Triangle Lake Montessori ES 600/PK-5
2401 Triangle Lake Rd 27260 336-819-2883
Pamela Ford, prin. Fax 819-2754
Union Hill ES 500/PK-5
3523 Triangle Lake Rd 27260 336-819-2130
Shayla Savage, prin. Fax 882-7162
Welborn Academy of Science & Technology 500/6-8
1710 McGuinn Dr 27265 336-819-2880
Ashauna Harris, prin. Fax 819-2879

Hayworth Christian S 100/PK-12
1696 Westchester Dr 27262 336-882-3126
Vicki Beale, admin.
High Point Christian Academy 700/PK-12
800 Phillips Ave 27262 336-841-8702
Keith Curlee, head sch Fax 841-8850
High Point Friends S 100/PK-8
800 Quaker Ln Ste A 27262 336-886-5516
Immaculate Heart of Mary Catholic S 300/PK-8
4145 Johnson St 27265 336-887-2613
Greg Roberts, prin. Fax 884-1849
Tri-City Christian Academy 100/PK-12
8000 Clinard Farms Rd 27265 336-665-9822
Wesleyan Christian Academy 1,000/PK-12
1917 N Centennial St 27262 336-884-3333
Dr. Rob Brown, head sch Fax 884-8232
Westchester Country Day S 400/PK-12
2045 N Old Greensboro Rd 27265 336-869-2128
Cobb Atkinson, head sch Fax 869-6685

Hildebran, Burke, Pop. 2,008
Burke County SD
Supt. — See Morganton
Hildebran ES 300/PK-5
703 US Highway 70 W 28637 828-397-3181
Randy Sain, prin. Fax 397-5330

Hillsborough, Orange, Pop. 5,962
Orange County SD 7,600/K-12
200 E King St 27278 919-732-8126
Dr. Todd Wirt, supt. Fax 732-8120
www.orangecountyfirst.com
Brown ES 500/K-5
1100 New Grady Brown School 27278 919-732-6138
Leslie Armistad Bryant, prin. Fax 644-2800

Cameron Park ES 700/K-5
240 Saint Marys Rd 27278 919-732-9326
Cindy Daniels, prin. Fax 732-9736
Central ES 300/K-5
154 Hayes St 27278 919-732-3622
Myron Wilson, prin. Fax 732-2352
Hillsborough ES 500/K-5
402 N Nash St 27278 919-732-6137
Ashley Slaughterbeck, prin. Fax 732-7791
Pathways ES 400/K-5
431 Strouds Creek Rd 27278 919-732-9136
Lynn Brown, prin. Fax 732-9142
Stanback MS 600/6-8
3700 NC Highway 86 S 27278 919-644-3200
Jeff Rachlin, prin. Fax 644-3226
Stanford MS 600/6-8
308 Orange High School Rd 27278 919-732-6121
Anne Purcell, prin. Fax 732-6910
Other Schools – See Chapel Hill, Efland

Hillsborough Christian Academy 50/PK-6
121 Orange High School Rd 27278 919-732-0888
Bryan Turner M.A., head sch
Pinewoods Montessori S 100/PK-6
109 Millstone Dr 27278 919-644-2090

Hobgood, Halifax, Pop. 346

Hobgood Academy 200/PK-12
201 S Beech St 27843 252-826-4116

Hollister, Halifax, Pop. 662
Halifax County SD
Supt. — See Halifax
Hollister Elementary Leadership Academy 200/PK-5
37432 NC Highway 561 27844 252-586-4344
Amy Boyette, prin. Fax 586-6124

Holly Ridge, Onslow, Pop. 1,230
Onslow County SD
Supt. — See Jacksonville
Dixon ES 900/PK-4
130 Betty Dixon Rd 28445 910-327-2104
Glenn Reed, prin. Fax 327-3336

Holly Springs, Wake, Pop. 24,092
Wake County SD
Supt. — See Cary
Holly Grove ES 1,100/K-5
1451 Avent Ferry Rd 27540 919-577-1700
Kathy Knezevic, prin. Fax 577-1706
Holly Grove MS 1,400/6-8
1401 Avent Ferry Rd 27540 919-567-4177
Kenneth Proulx, prin Fax 567-4159
Holly Ridge ES 900/K-5
900 Holly Springs Rd 27540 919-577-1300
Joy Gorman, prin. Fax 577-1311
Holly Ridge MS 1,200/6-8
950 Holly Springs Rd 27540 919-577-1335
Emily Mountford, prin. Fax 577-1379
Holly Springs ES 1,100/K-5
401 Holly Springs Rd 27540 919-557-2660
Mary Warren, prin. Fax 557-2666

New S Montessori Center 100/PK-8
5617 Sunset Lake Rd 27540 919-303-3636

Hope Mills, Cumberland, Pop. 14,573
Cumberland County SD
Supt. — See Fayetteville
Baldwin ES 700/PK-5
4441 Legion Rd 28348 910-424-0145
Todd Yardis, prin. Fax 424-7359
Collier ES 600/PK-5
3522 Sturbridge Dr 28348 910-424-7200
Ann-Marie Palmer, prin. Fax 424-1684
Galberry Farm ES 900/PK-5
8019 Byerly Dr 28348 910-424-1490
Dawn Collins, prin. Fax 424-1173
Grays Creek ES 400/PK-5
2964 School Rd 28348 910-483-3352
Katrina McKinnon, prin. Fax 483-7945
Grays Creek MS 1,100/6-8
5151 Celebration Dr 28348 910-483-4124
Mark Pepper, prin. Fax 483-5296
Hope Mills MS 700/6-8
4975 Cameron Rd 28348 910-425-5106
Yolanda Epps, prin. Fax 423-5887
Rockfish ES 800/K-5
5763 Rockfish Rd 28348 910-424-5313
Lisa Crawford, prin. Fax 424-5338
South View MS 700/6-8
4100 Elk Rd 28348 910-424-3131
Christian Qually, prin. Fax 424-2402

Hot Springs, Madison, Pop. 554
Madison County SD
Supt. — See Marshall
Hot Springs ES 100/K-5
63 N Serpentine Ave 28743 828-622-3292
Kristin Dillon, prin. Fax 622-3685

Hubert, Onslow
Onslow County SD
Supt. — See Jacksonville
Sand Ridge ES 500/K-5
868 Sandridge Rd 28539 910-326-5190
Denise Gartner, prin. Fax 326-5622

Hudson, Caldwell, Pop. 3,744
Caldwell County SD
Supt. — See Lenoir
Hudson ES 700/K-5
200 Roy E Coffey Dr 28638 828-728-3712
Adam Windmillor, prin. Fax 726-8214
Hudson MS 800/6-8
291 Pine Mountain Rd 28638 828-728-4281
Julia Knight, prin. Fax 726-8157

Heritage Christian S 100/K-12
239 Mount Herman Rd 28638 828-726-0055

Huntersville, Mecklenburg, Pop. 45,893
Charlotte/Mecklenburg County SD
Supt. — See Charlotte
Alexander MS 900/6-8
12010 Hambright Rd 28078 980-343-3830
Angela Richardson, prin. Fax 343-3851
Barnette ES 600/K-5
13659 Beatties Ford Rd 28078 980-343-0372
Lynanne Gabriel, prin. Fax 343-1711
Blythe ES 1,100/K-5
12202 Hambright Rd 28078 980-343-5770
Felisa Simpson, prin. Fax 343-5766
Bradley MS 1,100/6-8
13345 Beatties Ford Rd 28078 980-343-5750
Amy Mims, prin. Fax 343-5743
Grand Oak ES 600/K-5
15410 Stumptown Rd 28078 980-343-2063
Raymond Giovanelli, prin. Fax 343-0672
Huntersville ES 800/K-5
200 Gilead Rd 28078 980-343-3835
Jeff Ruppenthal, prin. Fax 343-3849
Long Creek ES 500/PK-5
9213 Beatties Ford Rd 28078 980-343-6095
Kim Alexander, prin. Fax 343-6144
Torrence Creek ES 500/K-5
14550 Ranson Rd 28078 980-343-0695
Jason Bissinger, prin. Fax 343-0697
Trillium Springs Montessori ES PK-6
9213 Beatties Ford Rd 28078 980-343-9442
Rachel McKenzie, prin. Fax 343-9901

St. Mark S 800/K-8
14750 Stumptown Rd 28078 704-766-5000
Debbie Butler, prin. Fax 875-6377
SouthLake Christian Academy 900/PK-12
13820 Hagers Ferry Rd 28078 704-949-2200
David Rowles, head sch Fax 949-2203

Hurdle Mills, Person
Person County SD
Supt. — See Roxboro
Oak Lane ES 300/K-5
2076 Jim Morton Rd 27541 336-364-2204
Heather Bowling, prin. Fax 364-1036

Indian Trail, Union, Pop. 32,854
Union County SD
Supt. — See Monroe
Hemby Bridge ES 500/K-5
6701 Indian Trail Fairview 28079 704-882-1191
Stephanie Burris, prin. Fax 882-1192
Indian Trail ES 700/PK-5
200 Education St 28079 704-296-3095
Gina Chisum, prin. Fax 821-7712
Poplin ES 700/K-5
5627 Poplin Rd 28079 704-296-0320
Scott Broome, prin. Fax 882-4853
Porter Ridge ES 600/K-5
2843 Ridge Rd 28079 704-289-1965
Lisa Taylor, prin. Fax 289-6523
Porter Ridge MS 1,400/6-8
2827 Ridge Rd 28079 704-225-7555
Brian Patience, prin. Fax 226-9844
Sun Valley MS 1,300/6-8
1409 Wesley Chapel Rd 28079 704-296-3009
Vicki Merritt, prin. Fax 296-3045

Metrolina Christian Academy 1,200/PK-12
PO Box 1460 28079 704-882-3375
Richard Calloway, head sch Fax 882-0631

Iron Station, Lincoln, Pop. 736
Lincoln County SD
Supt. — See Lincolnton
East Lincoln MS 700/6-8
4137 Highway 73 28080 704-732-0761
Heather Myers, prin. Fax 732-4456
Iron Station ES 500/PK-5
4207 E Highway 27 28080 704-736-4292
Audrey Benton, prin. Fax 735-8336

Jackson, Northampton, Pop. 512
Northampton County SD 2,100/PK-12
PO Box 158 27845 252-534-1371
Dr. Monica Smith-Woofter Ed.D., supt. Fax 534-4631
www.northampton.k12.nc.us
Central ES 300/PK-4
9742 NC Highway 305 27845 252-534-3381
Danny McCaw, prin. Fax 534-0591
Other Schools – See Conway, Gaston, Pendleton

Jacksonville, Onslow, Pop. 67,399
Onslow County SD 25,300/PK-12
PO Box 99 28541 910-455-2211
Rick Stout, supt. Fax 455-3027
www.onslow.k12.nc.us
Bell Fork ES 500/PK-5
500 Bell Fork Rd 28540 910-347-4459
Dr. Gregory Williams, prin. Fax 347-6555
Blue Creek ES 500/PK-5
1260 Burgaw Hwy 28540 910-347-1717
Tim Joines, prin. Fax 347-0095
Carolina Forest ES 1,000/K-5
141 Carolina Forest Blvd 28546 910-346-1778
Leanne Ervin, prin. Fax 347-2108
Erwin ES 500/PK-5
323 New River Dr 28540 910-347-1261
Tara Patterson, prin. Fax 989-2034
Hunters Creek ES 500/PK-5
3450 Hunters Trl 28546 910-353-4443
Teah Bulris, prin. Fax 353-4425
Hunters Creek MS 800/6-8
4040 Hunters Trl 28546 910-353-2147
Jocelyn Cassidy, prin. Fax 353-7939

Jacksonville Commons ES 600/PK-5
1121 Commons Dr N 28546 910-347-1056
Deborah Hoffman, prin. Fax 347-2007
Jacksonville Commons MS 800/6-8
315 Commons Dr S 28546 910-346-6888
Curtis Ehmann, prin. Fax 938-1682
Meadow View ES 800/K-5
1026 Fire Tower Rd 28540 910-478-3522
Kelly Clarke, prin. Fax 478-3422
Morton ES 600/PK-5
485 Old 30 Rd 28546 910-353-0930
Allene Batchelor, prin. Fax 353-0103
New Bridge MS 500/6-8
401 New Bridge St 28540 910-346-5144
Jane Dennis, prin. Fax 346-5402
Northwoods ES 500/PK-5
617 Henderson Dr 28540 910-347-2808
Gail Pylant, prin. Fax 347-2939
Northwoods Park MS 500/6-8
904 Sioux Dr 28540 910-347-1202
Angela Garland, prin. Fax 347-0713
Parkwood ES 500/PK-5
2900 Northwoods Dr 28540 910-347-6711
Linda Kopec, prin. Fax 347-2745
Southwest ES 800/PK-5
2601 Burgaw Hwy 28540 910-347-0900
Elizabeth Castle, prin. Fax 347-0909
Southwest MS 500/6-8
3000 Furia Dr 28540 910-455-1105
Jerome Gidrey, prin. Fax 455-4082
Stateside ES 700/K-5
132 Stateside Blvd 28546 910-478-3460
Kristie Bracy, prin. Fax 478-3454
Summersill ES 600/PK-5
250 Summersill School Rd 28540 910-455-2672
Willie Jarman, prin. Fax 455-2129
Thompson ECC PK-PK
440 College St 28540 910-346-6222
James Lanier, dir. Fax 346-6636
Other Schools – See Holly Ridge, Hubert, Maysville, Richlands, Sneads Ferry, Swansboro

Grace Classical S 50/K-9
PO Box 12034 28546 910-526-0718
Katie Martin, head sch
Infant of Prague Catholic S 100/PK-8
501 Bordeaux St 28540 910-455-0838
Jennifer Cupsta, prin. Fax 455-0270
Jacksonville Christian Academy 300/K-12
919 Gum Branch Rd 28540 910-347-2358
Living Water Christian S 200/PK-12
3980 Gum Branch Rd 28540 910-938-7017
Montessori Children's S 100/PK-6
714 Dates St 28540 910-938-3826
St. Annes Parish Day S 200/PK-2
711 Henderson Dr 28540 910-347-0755

Jamestown, Guilford, Pop. 3,331
Guilford County SD
Supt. — See Greensboro
Jamestown ES 500/PK-5
108 Potter Dr 27282 336-819-2110
Dwayne Jordan, prin. Fax 454-6588
Jamestown MS 1,200/6-8
301 Haynes Rd 27282 336-819-2100
Dwayne Jordan, prin. Fax 454-6734
Millis Road ES 500/PK-5
4310 Millis Rd 27282 336-819-2125
Russell Harper, prin. Fax 819-2127

Jamesville, Martin, Pop. 479
Martin County SD
Supt. — See Williamston
Jamesville ES 200/PK-5
PO Box 190 27846 252-792-8304
Jim Lammert, prin. Fax 809-4813

Jarvisburg, Currituck
Currituck County SD
Supt. — See Currituck
Jarvisburg ES 200/K-5
110 Jarvisburg Rd 27947 252-491-2050
Kelly Flora, prin. Fax 491-2085

Jefferson, Ashe, Pop. 1,599
Ashe County SD 3,300/PK-12
PO Box 604 28640 336-246-7175
Phyllis Yates, supt. Fax 246-7609
www.ashe.k12.nc.us/
Mountain View ES 700/PK-6
2789 US Highway 221 N 28640 336-982-4200
David Blackburn, prin. Fax 982-4203
Other Schools – See Warrensville, West Jefferson

Jonesville, Yadkin, Pop. 2,229
Yadkin County SD
Supt. — See Yadkinville
Jonesville ES 300/PK-6
101 Cedarbrook Rd 28642 336-835-3201
Ida Weisner, prin. Fax 835-1882

Kannapolis, Cabarrus, Pop. 41,850
Cabarrus County SD
Supt. — See Concord
Boger ES 800/PK-5
5150 Dovefield Ln 28081 704-788-1600
Rick Seaford, prin. Fax 794-6232
Royal Oaks ES 300/K-5
5150 Dovefield Ln 28081 704-788-1600
Melody Marsh, prin. Fax 794-6232

Kannapolis CSD 5,400/PK-12
100 Denver St 28083 704-938-1131
Dr. Chip Buckwell, supt. Fax 933-6370
www.kcs.k12.nc.us
Carver ES 900/K-5
525 E C St 28083 704-932-4161
Erik Johnson, prin. Fax 938-4010

Forest Park ES 600/K-5
1333 Forest Park Dr 28083 704-932-8121
Josh Sain, prin. Fax 932-4889
Jackson Park ES 500/K-5
1400 Jackson St 28083 704-933-2831
Deana Lewis, prin. Fax 932-1677
Kannapolis MS 800/6-8
1445 Oakwood Ave 28081 704-932-4102
Nick Carlascio, prin. Fax 932-4104
Shady Brook ES 400/K-5
903 Rogers Lake Rd 28081 704-933-2434
Will Gibson, prin. Fax 933-9571
Wilson ES 400/K-5
1401 Pine St 28081 704-932-8656
Mandi Campbell, prin. Fax 933-7798
Wilson ES 500/PK-5
800 N Walnut St 28081 704-933-2935
Jason Irving, prin. Fax 932-5502

Kelford, Bertie, Pop. 248
Bertie County SD
Supt. — See Windsor
West Bertie ES 400/PK-5
3734 Governors Rd 27847 252-344-7621
Cynthia Byrd, prin. Fax 344-2828

Kenansville, Duplin, Pop. 849
Duplin County SD 9,900/PK-12
315 N Main St 28349 910-296-1521
Dr. Austin Obasohan, supt. Fax 296-1396
www.duplinschools.net
Kenansville ES 400/PK-8
PO Box 98 28349 910-296-1647
Debra Hunter, prin. Fax 296-0022
Other Schools – See Albertson, Beulaville, Chinquapin, Mount Olive, Rose Hill, Wallace, Warsaw

Kenly, Johnston, Pop. 1,330
Johnston County SD
Supt. — See Smithfield
Glendale-Kenly ES 600/PK-5
2001 Bay Valley Rd 27542 919-284-2821
Cole Yarborough, prin. Fax 284-5087

Kernersville, Forsyth, Pop. 22,718
Winston-Salem/Forsyth SD
Supt. — See Winston Salem
Caleb's Creek ES 800/K-5
1109 Salem Crossing Rd 27284 336-703-6757
Rita McPhatter, prin. Fax 993-2439
Cash ES 700/K-5
4700 Old Hollow Rd 27284 336-703-4174
Alicia Bailey, prin. Fax 996-2809
East Forsyth MS 800/6-8
810 Bagley Rd 27284 336-703-6765
Dossie Poteat, prin. Fax 607-8531
Kernersville ES 900/K-5
512 W Mountain St 27284 336-703-4100
Lora Tiano, prin. Fax 996-8664
Kernersville MS 800/6-8
110 Brown Rd 27284 336-703-4255
Lisa Duggins, prin. Fax 996-1966
Piney Grove ES 600/K-5
1500 Piney Grove Rd 27284 336-703-4122
Robert Vorbroker, prin. Fax 993-9429
Sedge Garden ES 800/K-5
475 Sedge Garden Rd 27284 336-771-4545
Donald Wyatt, prin. Fax 771-4784
Southeast MS 1,200/6-8
1200 Old Salem Rd 27284 336-703-4219
Stephanie Gentry, prin. Fax 996-0148
Union Cross ES 800/K-5
4300 High Point Rd 27284 336-703-4233
Trish Spencer, prin. Fax 769-3311

Triad Baptist Christian Academy 200/PK-12
1175 S Main St 27284 336-996-7573
Dennis Roberts, admin. Fax 996-9791

Kill Devil Hills, Dare, Pop. 6,558
Dare County SD
Supt. — See Nags Head
First Flight ES 400/PK-5
107 Veterans Dr 27948 252-441-1111
Drew Sawyer, prin. Fax 441-5832
First Flight MS 600/6-8
109 Veterans Dr 27948 252-441-8888
Dave Guiley, prin. Fax 441-7694

King, Stokes, Pop. 6,843
Stokes County SD
Supt. — See Danbury
Chestnut Grove MS 800/6-8
2185 Chestnut Grove Rd 27021 336-983-2106
David Durham, prin. Fax 983-2725
King ES 500/PK-5
152 E School St 27021 336-983-5824
Karen Boles Nunn, prin. Fax 985-0432
Mt. Olive ES 300/K-5
2145 Chestnut Grove Rd 27021 336-983-4351
Robin Layman, prin. Fax 983-9428
Poplar Springs ES 500/K-5
223 Hobe Kiser Rd 27021 336-985-0234
David Priddy, prin. Fax 983-3882

Calvary Christian S 200/PK-12
748 Spainhour Rd 27021 336-983-3743
Sid Main, prin. Fax 983-8426

Kings Mountain, Cleveland, Pop. 10,130
Cleveland County SD
Supt. — See Shelby
Bethware ES 400/PK-4
115 Bethware Dr 28086 704-476-8346
Dr. Amy Jones, prin. Fax 734-5606
East ES 300/K-4
600 N Cleveland Ave 28086 704-476-8356
Becky Bailey, prin. Fax 734-5617
Kings Mountain IS 600/5-6
227 Kings Mountain Blvd 28086 704-476-8366
Amy Moss, prin. Fax 734-5682
Kings Mountain MS 700/7-8
1000 Phifer Rd 28086 704-476-8340
Dr. Anita Ware, prin. Fax 734-5615
North ES 300/PK-4
900 Ramseur St 28086 704-476-8225
Amy Allen, prin. Fax 734-5607
West ES 300/PK-4
500 W Mountain St 28086 704-476-8345
Heather Pagan, prin. Fax 734-5618

Grace Christian Academy 100/PK-12
260 Range Rd 28086 704-734-0509

Kinston, Lenoir, Pop. 21,394
Lenoir County SD 9,300/PK-12
PO Box 729 28502 252-527-1109
Dr. Brent Williams, supt. Fax 527-6884
www.lenoir.k12.nc.us
Banks ES 500/K-5
2148 Falling Creek Rd 28504 252-527-9470
Melissa Lynch, prin. Fax 522-9714
Contentnea-Savannah S 800/PK-8
3400 Ferrell Rd 28501 252-527-8591
Rhonda Greene, prin. Fax 527-9014
Moss Hill ES 500/K-5
6040 Hwy 55 W 28504 252-569-5071
Stacy Cauley, prin. Fax 569-1405
Northeast ES 600/PK-5
1002 E Highland Ave 28501 252-527-4166
Kendra Woods, prin. Fax 527-3040
Northwest ES 500/K-5
1701 Old Well Rd 28504 252-527-5143
Heather Walston, prin. Fax 527-9375
Rochelle MS 500/6-8
301 N Rochelle Blvd 28501 252-527-4290
Felicia Solomon, prin. Fax 527-6498
Southeast ES 300/K-5
201 McDaniels St 28501 252-527-4210
Janet Blaebaum, prin. Fax 527-5965
Southwood ES 400/K-5
1245 Hwy 58 S 28504 252-527-9081
Jerry Walton, prin. Fax 527-6417
Woodington MS 700/6-8
4939 Hwy 258 S 28504 252-527-9570
Pam Heath, prin. Fax 527-3883
Other Schools – See La Grange, Pink Hill

Arendell Parrott Academy 800/PK-12
PO Box 1297 28503 252-522-4222
Bert S. Bright Ed.D., hdmstr. Fax 208-0090
Bethel Christian Academy 300/PK-12
1936 Banks School Rd 28504 252-522-4636

Kittrell, Vance, Pop. 462
Vance County SD
Supt. — See Henderson
Vance ES 300/PK-5
4800 Raleigh Rd 27544 252-438-8492
Kristian Herring, prin. Fax 431-0570

Kitty Hawk, Dare, Pop. 3,234
Dare County SD
Supt. — See Nags Head
Kitty Hawk ES 500/K-5
16 S Dogwood Trl 27949 252-261-2313
Dr. Gregory Florence, prin. Fax 261-3400

Knightdale, Wake, Pop. 11,083
Wake County SD
Supt. — See Cary
Forestville Road ES 700/K-5
100 Lawson Ridge Rd 27545 919-266-8487
Jesenia Hafner, prin. Fax 266-8494
Hodge Road ES 600/K-5
2128 Mingo Bluff Blvd 27545 919-266-8599
Feliz Keyes, prin. Fax 266-8558
Knightdale ES 800/PK-5
PO Box 309 27545 919-266-8540
Teresa James, prin. Fax 670-4286
Lockhart ES 700/K-5
1320 N Smithfield Rd 27545 919-266-8525
Daniel Zoller, prin. Fax 266-8537

Knotts Island, Currituck
Currituck County SD
Supt. — See Currituck
Knotts Island ES 100/K-5
PO Box 40 27950 252-429-3327
Deborah Gorza, prin. Fax 429-3172

La Grange, Lenoir, Pop. 2,845
Lenoir County SD
Supt. — See Kinston
Frink MS 600/6-8
102 Martin Luther King Jr 28551 252-566-3326
Elizabeth Pierce, prin. Fax 566-4027
La Grange ES 600/PK-5
402 W Railroad St 28551 252-566-4036
Lorene Bell, prin. Fax 566-9055

Lake Toxaway, Transylvania
Transylvania County SD
Supt. — See Brevard
Henderson S of Science & Technology 100/K-5
11839 Rosman Hwy 28747 828-862-4463
Audrey Reneau, prin. Fax 862-4621

Landis, Rowan, Pop. 3,094
Rowan-Salisbury County SD
Supt. — See Salisbury
Corriher-Lipe MS 500/6-8
214 W Rice St 28088 704-857-7946
Justin James, prin. Fax 855-2670
Landis ES 600/PK-5
801 W Ryder Ave 28088 704-857-3111
Brooke Zehmer, prin. Fax 857-3131

Lasker, Northampton, Pop. 119

Northeast Academy 200/PK-12
210 E Church St 27845 252-539-2461

Laurel Hill, Scotland, Pop. 1,230
Scotland County SD
Supt. — See Laurinburg
Carver MS 400/6-8
18601 Fieldcrest Rd 28351 910-462-4669
Dr. Mary Hemphill, prin. Fax 462-4674
Laurel Hill ES 500/PK-5
11340 Old Wire Rd 28351 910-462-2111
Kesha Hood, prin. Fax 462-3502

Laurinburg, Scotland, Pop. 15,644
Scotland County SD 5,600/PK-12
322 S Main St 28352 910-276-1138
Dr. Ronald Hargrave, supt. Fax 277-4310
www.scotland.k12.nc.us
Covington Street ES 300/K-5
615 W Covington St 28352 910-277-4312
Amy Sloop, prin. Fax 277-4315
Johnson ES 400/PK-5
815 McGirts Bridge Rd 28352 910-277-4308
LaTonya McLean, prin. Fax 277-4314
North Laurinburg ES 300/PK-5
831 N Gill St 28352 910-277-4336
Kachina Singletary, prin. Fax 277-4317
South Scotland ES 500/PK-5
17200 Barnes Bridge Rd 28352 910-277-4356
Laura Bailey, prin. Fax 276-4154
Spring Hill MS 400/6-8
22801 Airbase Rd 28352 910-369-0590
Pam Lewis, prin. Fax 369-0595
Sycamore Lane ES 600/K-5
2100 Sycamore Ln 28352 910-277-4350
Kristin Broadbelt, prin. Fax 277-4321
Other Schools – See Laurel Hill, Wagram

Christ the Cornerstone Academy 50/K-12
10401 McColl Rd 28352 910-277-0077
Emily Baines, prin. Fax 277-8682
Scotland Christian Academy 200/PK-12
10300 McColl Rd 28352 910-276-7722

Lawndale, Cleveland, Pop. 596
Cleveland County SD
Supt. — See Shelby
Burns MS 900/6-8
215 Shady Grove Rd 28090 704-476-8223
Dr. Chris Bennett, prin. Fax 538-3944

Lawsonville, Stokes
Stokes County SD
Supt. — See Danbury
Lawsonville ES 200/K-5
4611 NC 8 Hwy N 27022 336-593-8284
Greg Ottaway, prin. Fax 593-2290
Piney Grove MS 300/6-8
3415 Piney Grove Church Rd 27022 336-593-4000
Heather Pendleton, prin. Fax 593-4003

Leicester, Buncombe
Buncombe County SD
Supt. — See Asheville
Leicester ES 500/K-4
31 Gilbert Rd 28748 828-683-2341
Chad Upton, prin. Fax 683-9179

Leland, Brunswick, Pop. 13,291
Brunswick County SD
Supt. — See Bolivia
Belville ES 700/K-5
575 River Rd SE 28451 910-371-0601
Dr. Rick Hessman, prin. Fax 371-0063
Leland MS 800/6-8
927 Old Fayetteville Rd NE 28451 910-371-3030
Patricia Underwood, prin. Fax 371-0647
Lincoln ES 500/PK-5
1664 Lincoln Rd NE 28451 910-371-3597
Molly White, prin. Fax 371-6149

Lenoir, Caldwell, Pop. 17,882
Caldwell County SD 12,100/PK-12
1914 Hickory Blvd SW 28645 828-728-8407
Dr. Steve Stone, supt. Fax 728-0012
www.caldwellschools.com
Davenport ES 500/K-5
901 College Ave SW 28645 828-754-6941
Kelly Smith, prin. Fax 758-5034
Gamewell ES 500/K-5
2904 Morganton Blvd SW 28645 828-758-1193
Andy Berry, prin. Fax 754-3503
Gamewell MS 600/6-8
3210 Gamewell School Rd 28645 828-754-6204
Anna Crooke, prin. Fax 754-6278
Happy Valley S 300/K-8
1350 Yadkin River Rd 28645 828-754-3496
Meredith Griffin, prin. Fax 758-1044
Kings Creek S 200/K-8
3680 Wilkesboro Blvd 28645 828-754-6039
Jeni McNulty, prin. Fax 754-9477
Lenoir MS 500/6-8
1366 Wildcat Trl SE 28645 828-758-2500
Lisa Vaughn, prin. Fax 758-1570
Lower Creek ES 400/K-5
630 Lower Creek Dr NE 28645 828-754-4022
Leigh Anne Frye, prin. Fax 754-8758
Oak Hill S 100/K-8
4603 Oakhill School Rd 28645 828-754-6128
Chris Ackerman, prin. Fax 758-1884
Valmead ES 200/K-5
111 Elizabeth St NW 28645 828-754-9612
Carol Sturgis, prin. Fax 758-4936
West Lenoir ES 200/K-5
125 Maple Dr NW 28645 828-754-5161
Travis Gillespie, prin. Fax 754-8379

Whitnel Four Seasons ES 300/PK-5
1425 Berkley St SW 28645 828-728-6423
Kim Case, prin. Fax 728-2204
Other Schools – See Collettsville, Granite Falls, Hudson

Lewisville, Forsyth, Pop. 12,465
Winston-Salem/Forsyth SD
Supt. — See Winston Salem
Lewisville ES 600/K-5
150 Lucy Ln 27023 336-703-4224
Angela Choplin, prin. Fax 945-3915

Forsyth Country Day S 800/PK-12
5501 Shallowford Rd 27023 336-945-3151
Gardner Barrier, head sch Fax 945-2907

Lexington, Davidson, Pop. 18,479
Davidson County SD 20,000/PK-12
PO Box 2057 27293 336-249-8181
Dr. Emily Lipe, supt. Fax 249-1062
www.davidson.k12.nc.us
Central Davidson MS 800/6-8
2591 NC Highway 47 27292 336-357-2310
Sloan Denny, prin. Fax 357-5965
Churchland ES 500/PK-5
7571 S NC Highway 150 27295 336-242-5690
Casey Milstead, prin. Fax 242-5691
Davis-Townsend ES 500/PK-5
975 Heath Church Rd 27292 336-249-9880
Lydia Hedrick, prin. Fax 249-8565
Midway ES 500/PK-5
318 Midway School Rd 27295 336-764-0064
April Willard, prin. Fax 764-2313
North Davidson MS 800/6-8
333 Critcher Dr 27295 336-731-2331
Amy Hyatt, prin. Fax 731-2328
Northwest ES 500/K-5
400 NW Elementary Rd 27295 336-764-0360
Marivee Miles, prin. Fax 764-3398
Reeds ES 400/K-5
791 S NC Highway 150 27295 336-242-5620
Christie Weatherly, prin. Fax 242-5621
Silver Valley ES 300/K-5
11161 E Old US Highway 64 27292 336-472-1576
Christy Slate, prin. Fax 472-3250
Southmont ES 400/PK-5
398 Owen Rd 27292 336-242-5800
Tammy Bush, prin. Fax 242-5801
Southwood ES 600/K-5
5850 NC Highway 8 27292 336-357-2777
Ashley Lemley, prin. Fax 357-5227
Tyro ES 400/K-5
450 Cow Palace Rd 27295 336-242-5760
Leah Leonard, prin. Fax 242-5761
Tyro MS 700/6-8
2946 Michael Rd 27295 336-853-7795
Russ Snyder, prin. Fax 853-7357
Welcome ES 600/PK-5
5701 Old US Highway 52 27295 336-731-3361
Cheryl Rich, prin. Fax 731-2799
Other Schools – See Denton, Thomasville, Winston Salem

Lexington CSD 3,200/PK-12
1010 Fair St 27292 336-242-1527
Richard Kriesky, supt. Fax 249-3206
lexcs.org
England ES 600/1-5
111 Cornelia St 27292 336-242-1552
Jackie Miller, prin. Fax 242-1252
Lexington MS 700/6-8
100 W Hemstead St 27292 336-242-1557
Sean Gaillard, prin. Fax 242-1372
Pickett ES 400/1-5
200 Biesecker Rd 27295 336-242-1546
Gina Spencer, prin. Fax 249-3969
South Lexington S PK-K
1000 Cotton Grove Rd 27292 336-242-1544
Sharolyn Harry-Clark, prin.
Southwest ES 300/1-5
434 Central Ave 27292 336-242-1548
Kim Britt, prin. Fax 249-7684

Sheets Memorial Christian S 300/PK-12
307 Holt St 27292 336-249-4224
Steven Weer, admin. Fax 249-6985
Union Grove Christian S 400/PK-12
2295 Union Grove Rd 27295 336-764-3105

Liberty, Randolph, Pop. 2,592
Guilford County SD
Supt. — See Greensboro
Greene ES 300/K-5
2717 NC Highway 62 E 27298 336-685-5000
Brian McCain, prin. Fax 685-5006

Randolph County SD
Supt. — See Asheboro
Liberty ES 500/PK-5
206 N Fayetteville St 27298 336-622-2253
Kelli Harrell, prin. Fax 622-2255
Northeastern Randolph MS 700/6-8
3493 Ramseur Julian Rd 27298 336-622-5808
Dana Albright-Johnson, prin. Fax 622-5868

Lilesville, Anson, Pop. 528
Anson County SD
Supt. — See Wadesboro
Lilesville ES 300/PK-6
121 Camden St 28091 704-848-4975
Dr. Joshua McLaurin, prin. Fax 848-4205

Lillington, Harnett, Pop. 3,141
Harnett County SD 20,600/PK-12
PO Box 1029 27546 910-893-8151
Dr. Aaron Fleming, supt. Fax 893-4279
www.harnett.k12.nc.us
Boone Trail ES 900/K-5
1425 Adcock Rd 27546 910-893-4013
Scott Avery, prin. Fax 893-6865
Lillington-Shawtown ES 600/PK-5
855 Old US 421 27546 910-893-3483
Clara Clinton, prin. Fax 893-8243
Western Harnett MS 1,100/6-8
11135 NC 27 W 27546 919-499-4497
Jennifer Smith, prin. Fax 499-1788
Other Schools – See Angier, Buies Creek, Bunnlevel, Cameron, Coats, Dunn, Erwin, Fuquay Varina, Olivia, Sanford, Spring Lake

Lincolnton, Lincoln, Pop. 10,295
Lincoln County SD 11,700/PK-12
PO Box 400 28093 704-732-2261
Dr. Lory Morrow, supt. Fax 736-4321
www.lcsnc.org
Battleground ES 300/PK-2
201 Jeb Seagle Dr 28092 704-735-3146
Donald Welch, prin. Fax 736-4262
Childers ES 500/PK-5
2595 Rock Dam Rd 28092 704-736-9610
Holly Skibo, prin. Fax 736-9612
Kiser IS 300/3-5
301 Jeb Seagle Dr 28092 704-736-1626
Tracy Eley, prin. Fax 736-1628
Lincolnton MS 700/6-8
2361 Startown Rd 28092 704-735-1120
Dr. Dana Ayers, prin. Fax 732-6811
Love Memorial ES 300/PK-5
1463 Love Memorial School 28092 704-735-5649
Chris Kolasinski, prin. Fax 736-4265
Lowder ES 200/PK-3
350 Kennedy Dr 28092 704-735-2741
Scott Carpenter, prin. Fax 736-4267
Massey ES 300/PK-4
130 Newbold St 28092 704-735-2322
Marty Helton, prin. Fax 732-0968
Pumpkin Center IS 300/3-5
3980 King Wilkinson Rd 28092 704-736-1504
Marie Ashford, prin. Fax 736-1177
Pumpkin Center PS 200/K-2
3970 King Wilkinson Rd 28092 704-736-1394
Anita Robinson, prin. Fax 736-4914
West Lincoln MS 700/6-8
260 Shoal Rd 28092 704-276-1760
Kristie Ballard, prin. Fax 276 2293
Other Schools – See Denver, Iron Station, Vale

Linden, Cumberland, Pop. 128
Cumberland County SD
Supt. — See Fayetteville
Raleigh Road ES 200/K-1
0330 Ramsey St 28356 910 488 0850
Alyson Beavers, prin. Fax 822-5663

Littleton, Halifax, Pop. 660
Halifax County SD
Supt. — See Halifax
Aurelian Springs Inst. Global Learning 400/PK-5
10536 NC Highway 48 27850 252-586-4944
Marcus Jones, prin. Fax 586-2707

Locust, Stanly, Pop. 2,907
Stanly County SD
Supt. — See Albemarle
Locust ES 400/K-5
103 School Rd 28097 704-961-5500
David Grice, prin. Fax 961-5599
West Stanly MS 700/6-8
339 Running Creek Church Rd 28097 704-961-3600
Jennnifer Huneycutt, prin. Fax 961-3699

Carolina Christian S 300/PK-12
PO Box 399 28097 704-888-4332
Erica Stroup, head sch Fax 888-4492

Louisburg, Franklin, Pop. 3,311
Franklin County SD 8,800/PK-12
53 West River Rd 27549 919-496-2600
Dr. Rhonda Schuhler, supt. Fax 496-2104
www.fcschools.net
Best ES 500/PK-5
4011 NC 56 Hwy E 27549 919-853-2347
Stephanie Brooks, prin. Fax 853-6759
Laurel Mill ES 300/PK-5
730 Laurel Mill Rd 27549 919-853-3577
Genie Faulkner, prin. Fax 853-3579
Louisburg ES 500/PK-5
50 Stone Southerland Rd 27549 919-496-3676
Trenace Gilmore, prin. Fax 496-2460
Royal ES 600/PK-5
308 Flat Rock Church Rd 27549 919-496-7377
Dominique Teasley, prin. Fax 496-7343
Terrell Lane MS 500/6-8
101 Terrell Ln 27549 919-496-1855
Eric Betheil, prin. Fax 496-1370
Other Schools – See Bunn, Franklinton, Youngsville

Lowell, Gaston, Pop. 3,488
Gaston County SD
Supt. — See Gastonia
Holbrook MS 700/6-8
418 S Church St 28098 704-836-9607
Jessica Steiner, prin. Fax 824-4529
Lowell ES 600/K-5
1500 Power Dr 28098 704-824-2264
Kristin Kiser, prin. Fax 824-7427

Lowgap, Surry, Pop. 321
Surry County SD
Supt. — See Dobson
Cedar Ridge ES 400/PK-5
734 Flippin Rd 27024 336-352-4320
Donna Bledsoe, prin. Fax 352-4347

Lucama, Wilson, Pop. 1,093
Wilson County SD
Supt. — See Wilson
Lucama ES 400/K-5
6260 Blalock Rd 27851 252-239-1257
Fax 239-1943
Springfield MS 500/6-8
5551 Wiggins Mill Rd 27851 252-237-4250
Marquis Spell, prin. Fax 239-1686

Lumber Bridge, Robeson, Pop. 94
Hoke County SD
Supt. — See Raeford
Sandy Grove ES 600/PK-5
8452 N Old Wire Rd 28357 910-875-6008
Kimberly Foley, prin. Fax 875-8498
Sandy Grove MS 600/6-8
300 Chason Rd 28357 910-875-3559
Tommy Jacobs, prin. Fax 875-3632

Lumberton, Robeson, Pop. 21,026
Robeson County SD 24,100/PK-12
410 Caton Rd 28360 910-671-6000
Dr. Shanita Wooten, supt. Fax 671-6024
www.robeson.k12.nc.us
Carroll MS 700/4-6
300 Bailey Rd 28358 910-671-6098
Anthony Britt, prin. Fax 671-6033
Deep Branch ES 400/PK-6
4045 Deep Branch Rd 28360 910-738-2514
James Hunt, prin. Fax 738-6811
East Robeson PS 700/PK-3
4840 7th Street Rd 28358 910-671-6055
Kristy West, prin. Fax 738-6639
Hargrave ES 200/PK-4
100 Hargrave St 28358 910-671-6060
Amy Baker, prin. Fax 671-4388
Knuckles ES 300/PK-4
1520 Martin Luther King Jr 28358 910-671-6020
Eric Sanderson, prin. Fax 671-4380
Littlefield MS 700/4-8
9674 NC Highway 41 N 28358 910-671-6065
Kendall Hamilton, prin. Fax 671-6068
Long Branch ES 500/PK-4
10218 NC Highway 72 E 28358 910-739-3864
Billy Tyner, prin. Fax 739-8710
Lumberton JHS 500/7-8
82 Marion Rd 28358 910-735-2108
Angela Faulkner, prin. Fax 671-4350
Magnolia S 900/PK-8
10928 US Highway 301 N 28360 910-671-6070
Dacia Bullard, prin. Fax 738-4182
Piney Grove ES 700/PK-6
1680 Piney Grove Rd 28360 910-671-6025
Nikki Brooks, prin. Fax 671-6010
Rowland-Norment ES 500/PK-4
701 Godwin Ave 28358 910-671-6030
Shawn Fooko, prin. Fax 671-4390
Shining Stars Preschool PK-PK
430 Caton Rd 28360 910-671-4343
Mary Schultz, prin. Fax 671-4345
Tanglewood ES 400/K-3
400 W 29th St 28358 910-671-6035
Joanna Hunt, prin. Fax 671-6036
West Lumberton ES 100/PK-4
82 Marion Rd 28358 910-671-6045
Tara Bullard, prin. Fax 671-6046
Other Schools – See Fairmont, Maxton, Orrum, Parkton, Pembroke, Red Springs, Rowland, Saint Pauls, Shannon

Antioch Christian Academy 300/K-12
5071 Old Whiteville Rd 28358 910-735-1011

Mc Adenville, Gaston, Pop. 641
Gaston County SD
Supt. — See Gastonia
Mc Adenville ES 200/PK-5
PO Box 129 28101 704-824-2236
Lucretia Rice, prin. Fax 824-8192

Mc Leansville, Guilford, Pop. 1,014
Guilford County SD
Supt. — See Greensboro
Madison ES 200/K-5
3600 Hines Chapel Rd 27301 336-375-2555
Penny Loschin, prin. Fax 375-2560
McLeansville ES 500/PK-5
5315 Frieden Church Rd 27301 336-698-0144
Shervawn Sockwell, prin. Fax 698-0266
Northeast MS 900/6-8
6720 Mcleansville Rd 27301 336-375-2525
Jamie King, prin. Fax 375-2534

Macon, Warren, Pop. 118
Warren County SD
Supt. — See Warrenton
Vaughan ES 300/PK-5
2936 US Highway 158 E 27551 252-257-6802
Brian Biles, prin. Fax 586-7350

Madison, Rockingham, Pop. 2,190
Rockingham County SD
Supt. — See Eden
Dillard ES 300/PK-5
810 Cure Dr 27025 336-548-2472
Trina McCoy, prin. Fax 548-6442
Huntsville ES 500/PK-5
2020 Sardis Church Rd 27025 336-427-3266
Russell Vernon, prin. Fax 427-4089
New Vision S of Math Science Technology 300/K-5
705 Ayersville Rd 27025 336-548-4780
Jane Frazier, prin. Fax 548-4779
Western Rockingham MS 800/6-8
915 Ayersville Rd 27025 336-548-2168
Stephanie Wray, prin. Fax 548-1799

Maiden, Catawba, Pop. 3,281
Catawba County SD
Supt. — See Newton
Maiden ES 500/K-6
201 N Main Ave 28650 828-428-8769
Lori Reed, prin. Fax 428-4374

Maiden MS 500/7-8
518 N C Ave 28650 828-428-2326
Brian Hefner, prin. Fax 428-5389
Tuttle ES 500/K-6
2872 Water Plant Rd 28650 828-428-3080
Mitzi Story, prin. Fax 428-0675

Manteo, Dare, Pop. 1,400
Dare County SD
Supt. — See Nags Head
Manteo ES 800/PK-5
701 US Highway 64 and 264 27954 252-473-2742
Steve Blackstock, prin. Fax 473-2496
Manteo MS 400/6-8
1000 US Highway 64 and 264 27954 252-473-5549
Dr. Michael Sasscer, prin. Fax 473-2612

Marion, McDowell, Pop. 7,708
McDowell County SD 5,400/PK-12
PO Box 130 28752 828-652-4535
Mark Garrett, supt. Fax 659-2238
www.mcdowell.k12.nc.us/
Eastfield Global Magnet ES 400/PK-5
170 Eastfield School Rd 28752 828-652-3730
Michelle Baker, prin. Fax 652-6312
East McDowell MS 500/6-8
676 State St 28752 828-652-7711
Jennifer Croymans, prin. Fax 652-1469
Glenwood ES 400/PK-5
1545 Old US 221 S 28752 828-738-4220
Amy Dowdle, prin. Fax 738-3828
Marion ES 400/PK-5
209 Robert St 28752 828-652-2141
Dr. Ashley McCartha, prin. Fax 652-7301
North Cove ES 300/PK-5
401 American Thread Rd 28752 828-756-4342
Rodney Slagle, prin. Fax 756-7316
Pleasant Gardens ES 400/PK-5
100 John Roach Dr 28752 828-724-4422
Mark Robertson, prin. Fax 724-4217
West Marion ES 400/PK-5
820 Marler Rd 28752 828-738-3353
Nakia Carson, prin. Fax 738-3592
West McDowell MS 500/6-8
346 W McDowell Jr High Sch 28752 828-652-3390
Dr. Donna Gardner, prin. Fax 659-1964
Other Schools – See Nebo, Old Fort

New Manna Christian S 100/K-12
PO Box 1085 28752 828-652-7729

Marshall, Madison, Pop. 859
Madison County SD 2,400/K-12
5738 US 25/70 Hwy 28753 828-649-9276
Dr. Jim Causby, supt. Fax 649-9334
www.madisonk12.net
Brush Creek ES 400/K-5
265 Upper Brush Creek Rd 28753 828-649-1547
Monica Ponder, prin. Fax 649-1528
Madison MS 600/6-8
95 Upper Brush Creek Rd 28753 828-649-2269
Nicholas Honeycutt, prin. Fax 649-9015
Other Schools – See Hot Springs, Mars Hill

Mars Hill, Madison, Pop. 1,829
Madison County SD
Supt. — See Marshall
Mars Hill ES 500/K-5
200 School House Ln 28754 828-689-2922
Daniel Metcalf, prin. Fax 689-5536

Marshville, Union, Pop. 2,366
Union County SD
Supt. — See Monroe
East Union MS 800/6-8
6010 W Marshville Blvd 28103 704-290-1540
Terrance Sanders, prin. Fax 624-9302
Marshville ES 500/PK-5
515 N Elm St 28103 704-296-6340
Janna Licata, prin. Fax 624-6946
New Salem ES 300/K-5
6106 Highway 205 28103 704-385-9430
Bryan Lynip, prin. Fax 385-8205

Marvin, Union, Pop. 5,469
Union County SD
Supt. — See Monroe
Marvin ES 700/PK-5
9700 Marvin School Rd, 704-843-5399
Vera Woodard, prin. Fax 843-6911

Matthews, Mecklenburg, Pop. 26,705
Charlotte/Mecklenburg County SD
Supt. — See Charlotte
Crestdale MS 800/6-8
940 Sam Newell Rd 28105 980-343-5755
Jennifer Schroeder, prin. Fax 343-5761
Crown Point ES 700/K-5
3335 Sam Newell Rd 28105 980-343-6535
Mark Anderson, prin. Fax 343-6539
Elizabeth Lane ES 1,000/K-5
121 Elizabeth Ln 28105 980-343-5700
Crystal Lail, prin. Fax 343-5704
Matthews ES 1,000/K-5
200 Mcdowell St 28105 980-343-3940
Jessica Blanchard, prin. Fax 343-3944
Mint Hill MS 1,200/6-8
11501 Idlewild Rd 28105 980-343-5439
Steve Drye, prin. Fax 343-5442

Union County SD
Supt. — See Monroe
Antioch ES 800/K-5
3101 Antioch Church Rd 28104 704-841-2505
Tom Childers, prin. Fax 841-2578
Weddington ES 700/K-5
3927 Twelve Mile Creek Rd 28104 704-849-7238
Kristen Sebek, prin. Fax 849-2238
Weddington MS 1,200/6-8
5903 Deal Rd 28104 704-814-9772
Marcus Leake, prin. Fax 814-9775

Arborbrook Christian Academy 100/K-12
4823 Waxhaw Indian Trail Rd 28104 704-821-9952
Andy Zawacki, head sch
Bible Baptist Christian S 200/PK-12
2724 Margaret Wallace Rd 28105 704-535-1694
Carmel Christian S 600/K-12
1145 Pineville Matthews Rd 28105 704-849-9723
Michael Long, head sch Fax 847-9908
Covenant Day S 800/PK-12
800 Fullwood Rd 28105 704-847-2385
Mark Davis, hdmstr. Fax 708-6137
Grace Academy 300/K-12
PO Box 2553 28106 704-234-0292

Maxton, Robeson, Pop. 2,397
Robeson County SD
Supt. — See Lumberton
Dean ES 300/PK-4
202 S Hooper St 28364 910-844-5982
Sherry Park, prin. Fax 844-9419
Oxendine ES 400/PK-6
5599 Oxendine School Rd 28364 910-843-4243
Paul Locklear, prin. Fax 843-9144
Prospect ES 1,000/PK-8
4024 Missouri Rd 28364 910-521-4766
Johnathan Blue, prin. Fax 521-8638
Townsend MS 200/5-8
105 Carolina St 28364 910-844-5086
Andre Ramseur, prin. Fax 844-4292

Maysville, Onslow, Pop. 990
Jones County SD
Supt. — See Trenton
Maysville ES 200/PK-6
814 6th St 28555 910-743-3631
Bryce Marquis, prin. Fax 743-2319

Onslow County SD
Supt. — See Jacksonville
Silverdale ES 400/PK-5
841 Smith Rd 28555 910-326-5146
Crystal Howard, prin. Fax 326-5976

Mebane, Alamance, Pop. 11,146
Alamance-Burlington SD
Supt. — See Burlington
Garrett ES 700/PK-5
3224 Old Hillsborough Rd 27302 919-563-2088
Michelle Ammann, prin. Fax 304-5384
Hawfields MS 700/6-8
1951 S NC Highway 119 27302 919-563-5303
Greg Hook, prin. Fax 563-1351
South Mebane ES 600/PK-5
600 S Third St 27302 919-563-6905
Rebecca Royal, prin. Fax 563-4616
Woodlawn MS 600/6-8
3970 Mebane Rogers Rd 27302 919-563-3222
Brian Williams, prin. Fax 563-6807
Yoder ES 300/PK-5
301 N Charles St 27302 919-563-3722
Leslie Eldreth, prin. Fax 563-9079

Caswell County SD
Supt. — See Yanceyville
South ES 300/PK-5
8925 NC Highway 86 S 27302 336-694-1212
Stephen Evans, prin. Fax 694-1249

Bradford Academy 100/K-10
939 S 3rd St 27302 919-563-9001
Jeff Johnston, hdmstr.

Merry Hill, Bertie

Lawrence Academy 300/PK-12
PO Box 70 27957 252-482-4748

Micaville, Yancey
Yancey County SD
Supt. — See Burnsville
Micaville ES 200/K-5
112 State Highway 80 S, 828-675-4161
Michele Laws, prin. Fax 675-0370

Micro, Johnston, Pop. 438
Johnston County SD
Supt. — See Smithfield
Micro ES K-5
301 E Main St 27555 919-588-4300
T.J. Parrish, prin. Fax 588-4302
North Johnston MS 600/6-8
PO Box 69 27555 919-284-3374
Brian Johnson, prin. Fax 284-3399

Middlesex, Nash, Pop. 801
Nash-Rocky Mount SD
Supt. — See Nashville
Middlesex ES 400/PK-5
13081 W Hanes Ave 27557 252-462-2815
Sherri Wells, prin. Fax 235-5216

Midland, Cabarrus, Pop. 3,028
Cabarrus County SD
Supt. — See Concord
Bethel ES 600/K-5
2425 Midland Rd 28107 704-888-5811
Kevin Blackburn, prin. Fax 888-1550

Millers Creek, Wilkes, Pop. 2,085
Wilkes County SD
Supt. — See North Wilkesboro
Millers Creek ES 900/PK-5
4320 N NC Highway 16 28651 336-667-2379
Cynthia Price, prin. Fax 667-2937

Millers Creek Christian S 200/PK-12
PO Box 559 28651 336-838-2517
Roy Putman, prin. Fax 838-2546

Mill Spring, Polk
Polk County SD
Supt. — See Columbus
Polk Central ES 400/PK-5
2141 Highway 9 S 28756 828-894-8233
Jan Crump, prin. Fax 894-3916
Polk County MS 500/6-8
321 Wolverine Trl 28756 828-894-2215
Hank Utz, prin. Fax 894-0191
Sunny View ES 200/PK-5
86 Sunny View School Rd 28756 828-625-4530
Kevin Weis, prin. Fax 625-8409

Mills River, Henderson, Pop. 6,729
Henderson County SD
Supt. — See Hendersonville
Marlow ES 500/K-5
1985 Butler Bridge Rd, 828-654-3225
John Hart, prin. Fax 687-1214
Mills River ES 500/K-5
94 School House Rd, 828-891-6563
Chad Auten, prin. Fax 891-6584

Mills River SDA S K-8
2142 Jeffress Rd, 828-785-2319

Mint Hill, Mecklenburg, Pop. 22,306
Charlotte/Mecklenburg County SD
Supt. — See Charlotte
Bain ES 900/K-5
11540 Bain School Rd 28227 980-343-6915
Tracey Hayes, prin. Fax 343-6150
Lebanon Road ES 800/K-5
7300 Lebanon Rd 28227 980-343-3640
Janelle Styons, prin. Fax 343-3717
Northeast MS 800/6-8
5960 Brickstone Dr 28227 980-343-6920
Deborah Heath, prin. Fax 343-3264

Mocksville, Davie, Pop. 4,904
Davie County SD 6,400/PK-12
220 Cherry St 27028 336-751-5921
Dr. Darrin Hartness, supt. Fax 751-9013
www.davie.k12.nc.us
Cornatzer ES 400/K-5
552 Cornatzer Rd 27028 336-940-5097
Catherine Moreland, prin. Fax 940-5647
Davie ES 400/PK-5
3437 US Highway 601 N 27028 336-492-5421
Karen Stephens, prin. Fax 492-2699
Mocksville ES 600/K-5
295 Cemetery St 27028 336-751-2740
Jennifer Swofford, prin. Fax 751-4883
North Davie MS 500/6-8
497 Farmington Rd 27028 336-998-5555
Mary Foster, prin. Fax 998-7233
Pinebrook ES 500/K-5
477 Pinebrook School Rd 27028 336-998-3868
Brooke Preslar, prin. Fax 940-5663
South Davie MS 600/6-8
197 S Davie Dr 27028 336-751-5941
Melissa Lynch, prin. Fax 751-5656
Other Schools – See Advance, Cooleemee

Moncure, Chatham, Pop. 701
Chatham County SD
Supt. — See Pittsboro
Moncure S 300/K-8
600 Moncure School Rd 27559 919-542-3725
Justin Sudol, prin. Fax 542-2035

Monroe, Union, Pop. 32,321
Union County SD 41,300/PK-12
400 N Church St 28112 704-296-0766
Dr. Andrew Houlihan, supt. Fax 282-2171
www.ucps.k12.nc.us
Benton Heights ES 700/PK-5
1200 Concord Ave 28110 704-296-3100
Candice Boatright, prin. Fax 296-3106
Bickett Education Center PK-PK
501 Lancaster Ave 28112 704-289-7497
Ken Roess, admin. Fax 296-3066
Bickett ES 700/PK-5
830 M L King Jr Blvd S 28112 704-283-8520
Dr. Jamie Benfield, prin. Fax 225-9543
East ES 500/PK-5
515 Elizabeth Ave 28112 704-296-3110
Camilla Brothers, prin. Fax 296-3112
Fairview ES 500/K-5
110 Clontz Rd 28110 704-753-2800
Kelly Thomas, prin. Fax 753-2804
Monroe MS 1,000/6-8
601 E Sunset Dr 28112 704-296-3120
Denny Ferguson, prin. Fax 296-3122
Parkwood MS 700/6-8
3219 Parkwood School Rd 28112 704-764-2910
Dr. Jeff Kraftson, prin. Fax 764-2914
Piedmont MS 1,000/6-8
2816 Sikes Mill Rd 28110 704-753-2840
Tracy Strickland, prin. Fax 753-2846
Prospect ES 500/K-5
3005 Ruben Rd 28112 704-764-2920
Dr. Kim Chinnis, prin. Fax 764-2923
Rock Rest ES 700/PK-5
814 Old Pageland Monroe Rd 28112 704-290-1513
Kristy Thomas, prin. Fax 283-6528
Rocky River ES 800/PK-5
500 N Rocky River Rd 28110 704-290-1523
Sherry Richardson, prin. Fax 292-1395
Sardis ES 500/PK-5
4416 Sardis Church Rd 28110 704-882-4303
Theresa Benson, prin. Fax 882-4305

Shiloh ES 600/PK-5
5210 Rogers Rd 28110 704-296-3035
Scott Spencer, prin. Fax 296-3039
Sun Valley ES 600/K-5
5200 Rogers Rd 28110 704-290-1559
Susan Rodgers, prin. Fax 291-2217
Unionville ES 700/PK-5
4511 Unionville Rd 28110 704-296-3055
Dr. Sharyn Von Cannon, prin. Fax 296-3057
Wesley Chapel ES 500/K-5
110 S Potter Rd 28110 704-296-3081
Mike Henderson, prin. Fax 296-3080
Other Schools – See Indian Trail, Marshville, Marvin, Matthews, Stallings, Waxhaw, Wingate

---

Shining Light Baptist Academy 100/PK-12
2541 Old Charlotte Hwy 28110 704-283-1480
Tabernacle Christian S 200/K-12
2900 Walkup Ave 28110 704-283-4395

Mooresville, Iredell, Pop. 32,023
Iredell-Statesville SD
Supt. — See Statesville
Brawley MS 700/6-8
132 Swift Arrow Dr 28117 704-664-4430
Jimmie Dancy, prin. Fax 664-9846
Coddle Creek ES 500/K-5
141 Franks Crossing Loop 28115 704-439-1550
Susan Fail, prin. Fax 439-1554
Lake Norman ES 500/K-5
255 Oak Tree Rd 28117 704-662-8261
Mark Shinkaruk, prin. Fax 662-8264
Lakeshore ES 600/K-5
252 Lakeshore School Dr 28117 704-660-5970
Christopher Grace, prin. Fax 660-7809
Lakeshore MS 500/6-8
244 Lakeshore School Dr 28117 704-799-0187
Brian Foster, prin. Fax 663-6431
Shepherd ES 500/K-5
1748 Charlotte Hwy 28115 704-664-2582
Kim Mitchell, prin. Fax 660-1642
Woodland Heights ES 800/K-5
288 Forest Lake Blvd 28117 704-663-1370
Kristie Franco, prin. Fax 663-1383

Mooresville Graded SD 5,900/PK-12
305 N Main St 28115 704-658-2530
Dr. Stephen Mauney, supt. Fax 663-3005
www.mgsd.k12.nc.us
East Mooresville IS 700/4-6
1711 Landis Hwy 28115 704-658-2700
Meghan McGrath, prin. Fax 799-2580
Mooresville IS 700/4-6
1438 Coddle Creek Rd 28115 704-658-2680
Tammy Russ, prin. Fax 799-2965
Mooresville MS 1,000/7-8
233 Kistler Farm Rd 28115 704-658-2720
Dr. Ayana Robinson, prin. Fax 664-5101
Park View ES 700/PK-3
217 W McNeely Ave 28115 704-658-2550
Dr. Misha Rogers, prin. Fax 664-7935
Rocky River ES 600/PK-3
483 Rocky River Rd 28115 704-658-2740
Dr. Chuck LaRusso, prin. Fax 658-2759
South ES 600/PK-3
839 S Magnolia St 28115 704-658-2650
Dr. Mark Cottone, prin. Fax 664-5103

Liberty Preparatory Christian Academy 100/K-12
246 Blume Rd 28117 704-660-3933
Amie Weir, admin. Fax 288-1750
Woodlawn S 200/K-12
135 Woodlawn School Loop 28115 704-895-8653
Adam Schapiro, head sch Fax 782-1836

Moravian Falls, Wilkes, Pop. 1,870
Wilkes County SD
Supt. — See North Wilkesboro
Central Wilkes MS 700/6-8
3541 S NC Highway 16 28654 336-667-7453
Jeffrey Johnson, prin. Fax 667-5825
Moravian Falls ES 200/PK-5
2001 Moravian Falls Rd 28654 336-838-4077
Shanda Adkins, prin. Fax 838-8450

Morehead City, Carteret, Pop. 8,439
Carteret County SD
Supt. — See Beaufort
Morehead City ES at Camp Glenn 300/4-5
3316 Arendell St 28557 252-726-1131
Adam Olander, prin. Fax 726-5896
Morehead City MS 500/6-8
400 Barbour Rd 28557 252-726-1126
Al Roberson, prin. Fax 726-4980
Morehead City PS 600/PK-3
4409 Country Club Rd 28557 252-247-2448
Dr. Jeanne Smith, prin. Fax 247-3127

St. Egbert S 100/PK-5
1705 Evans St 28557 252-726-3418
Kimberlee Felix, prin. Fax 727-0150

Morganton, Burke, Pop. 16,462
Burke County SD 13,200/PK-12
PO Box 989 28680 828-439-4312
Larry Putnam Ed.D., supt. Fax 439-4314
www.burke.k12.nc.us
Chesterfield ES 200/PK-5
2142 Pax Hill Rd 28655 828-437-3026
Charles Williams, prin. Fax 433-4806
Drexel ES 500/PK-5
100 Alta Vista St 28655 828-437-3160
Keith Hecker, prin. Fax 437-1227
Forest Hill ES 500/PK-5
304 Ann St 28655 828-437-5906
Sara LeCroy, prin. Fax 430-9323
Glen Alpine ES 400/PK-5
302 London St 28655 828-584-0661
Caroline Howard, prin. Fax 584-6669
Hillcrest ES 500/PK-5
201 Tennessee St 28655 828-437-4258
Lora Austin, prin. Fax 437-6311
Johnson MS 400/6-8
701 Lenoir Rd 28655 828-430-7340
Brett Wilson, prin. Fax 430-4801
Liberty MS 600/6-8
529 Enola Rd 28655 828-437-1330
Christie Abernathy, prin. Fax 432-2124
Mull ES 300/PK-5
1140 Old NC 18 28655 828-437-5785
Shirley Fore, prin. Fax 437-7988
Oak Hill ES 400/PK-5
2363 NC 181 28655 828-433-1533
Rob Gregory, prin. Fax 430-9356
Salem ES 600/PK-5
1329 Salem Rd 28655 828-437-5901
Shane Gardner, prin. Fax 437-8419
Table Rock MS 600/6-8
1585 NC 126 28655 828-437-5212
Jennifer Hawkins, prin. Fax 439-5702
Young ES 400/PK-5
325 Conley Rd 28655 828-584-0632
Christie McMahon, prin. Fax 584-1463
Other Schools – See Connelly Sprngs, Hickory, Hildebran, Rutherford College, Valdese

---

Morganton Day S 100/PK-8
305 W Concord St 28655 828-437-6782
Silver Creek Adventist S 50/K-8
2195 Jamestown Rd 28655 828-584-3010

Morrisville, Wake, Pop. 17,983
Wake County SD
Supt. — See Cary
Cedar Fork ES 900/K-5
1050 Town Hall Dr 27560 919-388-5240
Che-Von Stone, prin. Fax 462-6824
Morrisville ES 800/K-5
1519 Morrisville Pkwy 27560 919-460-3400
Michael Matthews, prin. Fax 460-3410
Pleasant Grove ES PK-5
3605 Pleasant Grove Church 27560 919-694-8770
Burt Batten, prin. Fax 589-6461

Morven, Anson, Pop. 499
Anson County SD
Supt. — See Wadesboro
Morven ES 200/PK-6
6715 US Highway 52 S 28119 704-851-9306
Dr. Dionnya Pratt, prin. Fax 851-9308

Mount Airy, Surry, Pop. 10,205
Mt. Airy CSD 1,700/PK-12
130 Rawley Ave 27030 336-786-8355
Dr. Kim Morrison, supt. Fax 786-7553
www.mtairy.k12.nc.us
Jones IS 300/3-5
2170 Riverside Dr 27030 336-786-4131
Sherry Cox, prin. Fax 719-2339
Mount Airy MS 400/6-8
249 Hamburg St 27030 336-789-9021
Olivia Byerly, prin. Fax 789-6074
Tharrington PS 400/PK-2
315 Culbert St 27030 336-789-9046
Emily Niston, prin. Fax 789-6068

Surry County SD
Supt. — See Dobson
Flat Rock ES 300/PK-5
1539 E Pine St 27030 336-786-2910
Dana Draughn, prin. Fax 786-5058
Franklin ES 600/PK-5
519 S Franklin Rd 27030 336-786-2459
Jodi Southern, prin. Fax 786-2835
Gentry MS 400/6-8
1915 W Pine St 27030 336-786-4155
Brandon Whitaker, prin. Fax 786-6863
Meadowview MS 400/6-8
1282 Mckinney Rd 27030 336-789-0276
Dr. Shelley Goins, prin. Fax 789-0449
White Plains ES 400/PK-5
710 Cadle Ford Rd 27030 336-320-3434
Nicole Hazelwood, prin. Fax 320-3090

Mount Gilead, Montgomery, Pop. 1,163
Montgomery County SD
Supt. — See Troy
Mount Gilead ES 300/PK-5
PO Box 308 27306 910-439-5411
Sloan Browning, prin. Fax 439-1074
West MS 500/6-8
129 NC Highway 109 S 27306 910-572-9378
Chris Jonassen, prin. Fax 572-2114

Mount Holly, Gaston, Pop. 13,424
Gaston County SD
Supt. — See Gastonia
Mount Holly MS 800/6-8
124 S Hawthorne St 28120 704-827-4811
Jamie Peoples, prin. Fax 822-1049
Pinewood ES 600/PK-5
1925 N Main St 28120 704-836-9138
Kathi Withers, prin. Fax 822-0227
Rankin ES 600/PK-5
301 W Central Ave 28120 704-827-7266
Donna Kelly, prin. Fax 827-9116

Mount Olive, Wayne, Pop. 4,528
Duplin County SD
Supt. — See Kenansville
North Duplin ES 700/PK-6
157 N Duplin School Rd 28365 919-658-2931
Ann Hardy, prin. Fax 658-2983

Wayne County SD
Supt. — See Goldsboro
Carver ES 600/PK-4
400 Old 7 Springs Rd 28365 919-658-7330
Lori Goodman, prin. Fax 658-7326
Mount Olive MS 500/5-8
309 Wooten St 28365 919-658-7320
NaTale Nelson, prin. Fax 658-7325

Mount Pleasant, Cabarrus, Pop. 1,645
Cabarrus County SD
Supt. — See Concord
Mount Pleasant ES 700/K-6
8555 North Dr 28124 704-436-6534
Corey Cochran, prin. Fax 436-2710

Mount Ulla, Rowan
Rowan-Salisbury County SD
Supt. — See Salisbury
Mount Ulla ES 300/K-5
13155 NC Highway 801 28125 704-278-2750
Brenda Sokolowski, prin. Fax 278-1901

Moyock, Currituck, Pop. 3,696
Currituck County SD
Supt. — See Currituck
Moyock ES 500/K-5
255 Shingle Landing Rd 27958 252-435-6521
Brandi Kelly, prin. Fax 435-6351
Moyock MS 600/6-8
216 Survey Rd 27958 252-435-2566
Dr. Abram Davenport, prin. Fax 435-2576

Murfreesboro, Hertford, Pop. 2,786
Hertford County SD
Supt. — See Winton
Hertford County MS 500/6-8
1850 NC Highway 11 27855 252-398-4091
Crystal Phillips, prin. Fax 398-5570
Riverview ES 500/PK-5
236 US Highway 158 Bus 27855 252-398-4862
Lee Ford, prin. Fax 398-3600

Murphy, Cherokee, Pop. 1,590
Cherokee County SD 3,500/PK-12
911 Andrews Rd 28906 828-837-2722
Dr. Jeana Conley, supt. Fax 837-5799
www.cherokee.k12.nc.us
Hiwassee Dam Union S 200/PK-8
337 Blue Eagle Cir 28906 828-644-5115
Kami Tipton, prin. Fax 644-9463
Martins Creek ES 300/PK-8
1459 Tobe Stalcup Rd 28906 828-837-2831
Paul Wilson, prin. Fax 837-0023
Murphy ES 500/PK-5
315 Valley River Ave 28906 828-837-2424
C.J. Rummler, prin. Fax 837-3887
Murphy MS 400/6-8
65 Middle School Dr 28906 828-837-0160
Tiffany Clapsaddle, prin. Fax 837-5814
Peachtree ES 100/PK-5
30 Upper Peachtree Rd 28906 828-837-2479
Kimberly Worley, prin. Fax 837-6494
Ranger S 300/PK-8
101 Hardy Truett Rd 28906 828-644-5111
Kelley McDonald, prin. Fax 644-9828
Other Schools – See Andrews

Murphy Adventist Christian S 50/PK-8
1584 Old Ranger Rd 28906 828-837-5857

Nags Head, Dare, Pop. 2,716
Dare County SD 5,100/PK-12
PO Box 1508 27959 252-480-8888
Dr. John Farrelly, supt. Fax 480-8889
www.daretolearn.org
Nags Head ES 600/PK-5
3100 S Wrightsville Ave 27959 252-480-8880
Dr. Adrienne Palma, prin. Fax 480-8881
Other Schools – See Buxton, Kill Devil Hills, Kitty Hawk, Manteo

Nakina, Columbus
Columbus County SD
Supt. — See Whiteville
Nakina MS 200/6-8
9822 Seven Creeks Hwy 28455 910-642-8301
Wendell Duncan, prin. Fax 641-3287

Nashville, Nash, Pop. 5,285
Nash-Rocky Mount SD 15,900/PK-12
930 Eastern Ave 27856 252-459-5220
Dr. Shelton Jefferies, supt. Fax 459-6403
www.nrms.k12.nc.us
Cedar Grove ES 200/PK-5
8967 Cedar Grove School Rd 27856 252-462-2830
Aaron Jones, prin. Fax 459-5347
Nash Central MS 600/6-8
1638 S 1st St 27856 252-937-9065
Eric Mitchell, prin. Fax 459-5297
Nashville ES 800/PK-5
209 E Virginia Ave 27856 252-451-2877
Quintin Mangano, prin. Fax 459-1135
Other Schools – See Bailey, Battleboro, Elm City, Middlesex, Red Oak, Rocky Mount, Spring Hope, Whitakers

Nebo, McDowell
McDowell County SD
Supt. — See Marion
Nebo ES 400/PK-5
254 Nebo School Rd 28761 828-652-4737
Desarae Kirkpatrick, prin. Fax 652-8404

New Bern, Craven, Pop. 28,922
Craven County SD 14,600/PK-12
3600 Trent Rd 28562 252-514-6300
Dr. Meghan Doyle, supt. Fax 514-6351
www.cravenk12.org

Bangert ES 400/K-5
3712 Canterbury Rd 28562 252-514-6415
Catherine Alligood, prin. Fax 514-6418
Barber ES 400/PK-5
1700 Cobb St 28560 252-514-6460
Erica Phillips, prin. Fax 514-6464
Bridgeton ES 500/PK-5
230 Branch Canal Rd 28560 252-514-6425
Melisa Thompson, prin. Fax 514-6428
Brinson Memorial ES 700/K-5
319 Neuse Forrest Ave 28560 252-514-6431
Christopher Germain, prin. Fax 514-6434
Creekside ES 600/K-5
2790 Landscape Dr 28562 252-514-4360
Angie Franks, prin. Fax 514-4365
Fields MS 600/6-8
2000 Dr M L King Jr Blvd 28560 252-514-6438
Shawn McCarthy, prin. Fax 514-6443
MacDonald MS 900/6-8
3127 Elizabeth Ave 28562 252-514-6450
Pamie Reese, prin. Fax 514-6456
Oaks Road ES 400/K-5
2811 Oaks Rd 28560 252-514-6475
Dr. Eleanor Patrick, prin. Fax 514-6478
Quinn ES 500/PK-5
4275 Dr M L King Jr Blvd 28562 252-514-6420
Curtis Gatlin, prin. Fax 514-6423
Trent Park ES 400/K-5
2500 Educational Dr 28562 252-514-6481
Ashley Faulkenberry, prin. Fax 514-6485
West Craven MS 900/6-8
515 NW Craven Middle School 28562 252-514-6488
Thomas Wilson, prin. Fax 514-6491
Other Schools – See Cove City, Havelock, Vanceboro

Calvary Baptist Church S 200/PK-12
PO Box 1089 28563 252-633-5410
Epiphany S of Global Studies 300/K-12
2301 Trent Rd 28562 252-638-0122
New Bern Christian Academy 200/K-12
2911 Old Cherry Point Rd 28560 252-637-2704
St. Paul Catholic S 100/PK-8
3007 Country Club Rd 28562 252-633-0100
David Kierski, prin. Fax 633-4457

Newland, Avery, Pop. 690
Avery County SD 1,700/PK-12
PO Box 1360 28657 828-733-6006
Bill Miller, supt. Fax 733-8943
www.averyschools.net
Avery MS 300/6-8
PO Box 729 28657 828-733-0145
Ruth Shirley, prin. Fax 733-3506
Newland ES 300/PK-5
750 Linville St 28657 828-733-4911
Jamie Johnson, prin. Fax 733-1402
Riverside ES 100/PK-5
8020 S US 19E Hwy 28657 828-737-5600
Dr. Monet Samuelson, prin. Fax 765-0922
Other Schools – See Banner Elk, Crossnore, Elk Park

New London, Stanly, Pop. 599
Stanly County SD
Supt. — See Albemarle
North Stanly MS 600/6-8
36605 Old Salisbury Rd 28127 704-961-3700
Anne Watson, prin. Fax 961-3799

Newport, Carteret, Pop. 4,038
Carteret County SD
Supt. — See Beaufort
Bogue Sound ES 400/K-5
3323 Highway 24 28570 252-393-1279
Jenny Bell, prin. Fax 393-1379
Broad Creek MS 700/6-8
2382 Highway 24 28570 252-247-3135
Sarah Weinhold, prin. Fax 247-5114
Newport ES 800/PK-5
219 Chatham St 28570 252-223-4201
Jody McClenny, prin. Fax 223-4107
Newport MS 500/6-8
500 E Chatham St 28570 252-223-3482
Christopher Yeomans, prin. Fax 223-4914

Gramercy Christian S 200/K-12
8170 Highway 70 28570 252-223-5199
Kara Withee, dir. Fax 223-2359

Newton, Catawba, Pop. 12,714
Catawba County SD 17,000/PK-12
PO Box 1010 28658 828-464-8333
Dr. Matt Stover, supt. Fax 464-0925
www.catawbaschools.net
Balls Creek ES 600/PK-6
2620 Balls Creek Rd 28658 828-464-4766
Rita Lail, prin. Fax 464-5396
Blackburn ES 700/K-6
4377 W NC 10 Hwy 28658 704-462-1344
Jessica Minton-Cable, prin. Fax 462-4496
Jacobs Fork MS 500/7-8
3431 Plateau Rd 28658 704-462-1827
Thomas Howell, prin. Fax 462-1600
Startown ES 600/PK-6
4119 Startown Rd 28658 828-464-1257
Dr. Kim Jordan, prin. Fax 465-6568
Other Schools – See Catawba, Claremont, Conover, Hickory, Maiden, Sherrills Ford, Vale

Newton-Conover CSD 3,100/PK-12
605 N Ashe Ave 28658 828-464-3191
Dr. David Stegall, supt. Fax 466-0063
www.newton-conover.org
North Newton ES 500/PK-5
221 W 26th St 28658 828-464-2631
Shane Whitener, prin. Fax 464-5891
South Newton ES 400/PK-5
306 W I St 28658 828-464-4061
Amber Humphrey, prin. Fax 464-7528

Other Schools – See Conover

Newton Grove, Sampson, Pop. 561
Sampson County SD
Supt. — See Clinton
Hobbton ES 500/PK-5
12361 Hobbton Hwy 28366 910-594-0392
Dawn Wilkes, prin. Fax 594-1610
Hobbton MS 500/6-8
12081 Hobbton Hwy 28366 910-594-1420
Jeff Bradshaw, prin. Fax 594-0049

Norlina, Warren, Pop. 1,094
Warren County SD
Supt. — See Warrenton
Northside K-8 S 400/PK-8
164 Elementary Ave 27563 252-456-2656
Medicus Riddick, prin. Fax 257-6814

Norlina Christian S 50/PK-8
PO Box 757 27563 252-456-3385
Rev. Seth Miller, admin. Fax 456-3354

North Wilkesboro, Wilkes, Pop. 4,150
Wilkes County SD 10,300/PK-12
613 Cherry St 28659 336-667-1121
D. Mark Byrd, supt. Fax 667-5971
www.wilkescountyschools.org
Mulberry ES 500/PK-5
190 Mulberry School Rd 28659 336-667-4641
Ritchie Cornette, prin. Fax 670-9783
North Wilkesboro ES 300/PK-5
200 Flint Hill Rd 28659 336-838-2872
Delaina Smith, prin. Fax 667-6863
North Wilkes MS 600/6-8
2776 Yellow Banks Rd 28659 336-903-6224
Heather Freeman, prin. Fax 696-4183
Wright ES 500/PK-5
200 CC Wright School Rd 28659 336-838-5513
Dr. Kimberlee Stone, prin. Fax 667-6099
Other Schools – See Boomer, Elkin, Ferguson, Hays, Millers Creek, Moravian Falls, Roaring River, Ronda, Traphill, Wilkesboro

Norwood, Stanly, Pop. 2,351
Stanly County SD
Supt. — See Albemarle
Aquadale ES 300/PK-5
11707 NC 138 Hwy 28128 704-961-5600
Devron Furr, prin. Fax 961-5699
Norwood ES 400/K-5
PO Box 636 28128 704-961-4000
Emily Shaw, prin. Fax 961-4099
South Stanly MS 400/6-8
12492 Cottonville Rd 28128 704-961-5700
Terri Crocker, prin. Fax 961-5799

Oakboro, Stanly, Pop. 1,840
Stanly County SD
Supt. — See Albemarle
Oakboro Choice STEM S 300/K-8
1244 N Main St 28129 704-961-4700
Kelly Dombrowski, prin. Fax 961-4799

Oak Ridge, Guilford, Pop. 6,114
Guilford County SD
Supt. — See Greensboro
Oak Ridge ES 700/PK-5
2050 Oak Ridge Rd 27310 336-643-8410
Denise Francisco, prin. Fax 643-8415

Ocracoke, Hyde, Pop. 942
Hyde County SD
Supt. — See Swanquarter
Ocracoke S 200/PK-12
PO Box 189 27960 252-928-3251
Leslie Cole, prin. Fax 928-5380

Old Fort, McDowell, Pop. 899
McDowell County SD
Supt. — See Marion
Old Fort ES 400/PK-5
128 Mauney Ave 28762 828-668-7646
Lisa Thompson, prin. Fax 668-4939

Olin, Iredell
Iredell-Statesville SD
Supt. — See Statesville
North Iredell MS 600/6-8
2467 Jennings Rd 28660 704-876-4802
Robert Sipes, prin. Fax 876-6190

Olivia, Harnett
Harnett County SD
Supt. — See Lillington
Benhaven ES 500/K-5
PO Box 9 28368 919-499-4811
Lora Street, prin. Fax 499-1401

Orrum, Robeson, Pop. 91
Robeson County SD
Supt. — See Lumberton
Orrum MS 400/5-8
PO Box 129 28369 910-628-6285
Cynthia Lewis, prin. Fax 628-8408

Oxford, Granville, Pop. 8,335
Granville County SD 7,700/PK-12
PO Box 927 27565 919-693-4613
Dr. Alisa McLean, supt. Fax 693-7391
www.gcs.k12.nc.us/
Credle ES 500/PK-5
223 College St 27565 919-693-9191
Julie Finch, prin. Fax 603-0047
Northern Granville MS 400/6-8
3144 Webb School Rd 27565 919-693-1483
Ashley Lewis, prin. Fax 693-1716
Potter MS 400/6-8
200 Taylor St 27565 919-693-3914
Dr. Chris Ham, prin. Fax 693-2896

Toler-Oak Hill ES 200/PK-5
8176 NC Highway 96 27565 919-693-8935
Michael Allen, prin. Fax 693-4040
West Oxford ES 600/PK-5
412 Ivey Day Rd 27565 919-693-9161
Shelby Hunt, prin. Fax 693-9163
Other Schools – See Butner, Creedmoor, Franklinton, Stovall

Pantego, Beaufort, Pop. 178

Terra Ceia Christian S 100/K-12
4428 Christian School Rd 27860 252-943-2485
Vern Parsons, prin. Fax 944-0458

Parkton, Robeson, Pop. 436
Robeson County SD
Supt. — See Lumberton
Parkton ES 600/PK-8
400 Green St 28371 910-858-3951
Kendra Deese, prin. Fax 858-0009

Peachland, Anson, Pop. 428
Anson County SD
Supt. — See Wadesboro
Peachland-Polkton ES 500/PK-6
9633 US Highway 74 W 28133 704-272-8061
Travis Steagall, prin. Fax 272-9278

Pembroke, Robeson, Pop. 2,870
Robeson County SD
Supt. — See Lumberton
Pembroke ES 800/PK-5
PO Box 878 28372 910-521-4204
Tona Jacobs, prin. Fax 521-3510
Pembroke MS 700/6-8
PO Box 1148 28372 910-522-5013
Anthony Barton, prin. Fax 522-1562
Shining Stars Preschool PK-PK
818 W 3rd St 28372 910-521-0559
Mary Schultz, prin. Fax 521-1784
Union Chapel ES 600/PK-6
4271 Union Chapel Rd 28372 910-521-4456
Antonio Wilkins, prin. Fax 521-4991

Pendleton, Northampton
Northampton County SD
Supt. — See Jackson
Hare ES 300/PK-4
479 Willis Hare Rd 27862 252-585-1900
Kimberly Scott, prin. Fax 585-1616

Pfafftown, Forsyth
Winston-Salem/Forsyth SD
Supt. — See Winston Salem
Vienna ES 600/K-5
1975 Chickasha Dr 27040 336-703-4178
Lee Koch, prin. Fax 945-9506

Pikeville, Wayne, Pop. 673
Wayne County SD
Supt. — See Goldsboro
Northeast ES 700/PK-5
4665 NC Highway 111 N 27863 919-705-6030
Julie West, prin. Fax 731-5957
Northwest ES 900/K-5
1769 Pikeville Princeton NW 27863 919-242-3419
Shelia Wolfe, prin. Fax 242-3714

Pilot Mountain, Surry, Pop. 1,458
Surry County SD
Supt. — See Dobson
Pilot Mountain ES 400/PK-5
218 Friends St 27041 336-444-8200
Alison York, prin. Fax 444-8205
Pilot Mountain MS 500/6-8
543 Old Westfield Rd 27041 336-368-2641
Dr. Tracey Lewis, prin. Fax 368-3935
Westfield ES 200/PK-5
273 Jessup Grove Church Rd 27041 336-351-2745
Holly Whitaker, prin. Fax 351-4467

Pine Hall, Stokes
Stokes County SD
Supt. — See Danbury
Pine Hall ES 200/K-5
1400 Pine Hall Rd 27042 336-427-3689
Amy Musten, prin. Fax 427-4944

Pinehurst, Moore, Pop. 12,981
Moore County SD
Supt. — See Carthage
Pinehurst ES 500/K-5
PO Box 729 28370 910-295-6969
Ashlee Ciccone, prin. Fax 295-1027

Sacred Heart Preschool 50/PK-PK
300 Dundee Rd 28374 910-295-3514
Stephanie Hinds, dir. Fax 255-0299

Pine Level, Johnston, Pop. 1,681
Johnston County SD
Supt. — See Smithfield
Pine Level ES 600/K-5
PO Box 69 27568 919-965-3323
Allen Sasser, prin. Fax 965-6723

Pinetops, Edgecombe, Pop. 1,369
Edgecombe County SD
Supt. — See Tarboro
Carver ES 800/PK-5
PO Box 48 27864 252-827-2116
Snannon Castillo, prin. Fax 827-2814
South Edgecombe MS 400/6-8
230 Pinetops Crisp Rd 27864 252-827-5083
Billy Strother, prin. Fax 827-2811

Pinetown, Beaufort, Pop. 155
Beaufort County SD
Supt. — See Washington

Northeast ES 600/PK-8
21000 US Highway 264 E 27865 252-943-6545
Mark Clinkscales, prin. Fax 943-9160

Pineville, Mecklenburg, Pop. 7,318
Charlotte/Mecklenburg County SD
Supt. — See Charlotte
Pineville ES 800/K-5
204 Lowry St 28134 980-343-3920
Brian Doerer, prin. Fax 343-3925
Sterling ES 600/PK-5
9601 China Grove Church Rd 28134 980-343-3636
Emily Miles, prin. Fax 343-3743

Piney Creek, Alleghany
Alleghany County SD
Supt. — See Sparta
Piney Creek ES 200/PK-8
559 Piney Creek School Rd 28663 336-359-2988
Steve Hall, prin. Fax 359-8246

Pink Hill, Lenoir, Pop. 550
Lenoir County SD
Supt. — See Kinston
Pink Hill ES 500/PK-5
2666 HC Turner Rd 28572 252-568-4176
Lee Anne Hardy, prin. Fax 568-6144

Pinnacle, Stokes, Pop. 887
Stokes County SD
Supt. — See Danbury
Pinnacle ES 200/PK-5
1095 Surry Line Rd 27043 336-368-2990
Shannon Boles, prin. Fax 368-5107

Surry County SD
Supt. — See Dobson
Shoals ES 300/PK-5
1800 Shoals Rd 27043 336-325-2518
Jared Jones, prin. Fax 325-2143

Pittsboro, Chatham, Pop. 3,666
Chatham County SD 8,300/PK-12
PO Box 128 27312 919-542-3626
Dr. Derrick D. Jordan, supt. Fax 542-1380
www.chatham.k12.nc.us
Harrison S 600/K-5
2655 Hamlet Chapel Rd 27312 919-967-9925
Freda Hicks, prin. Fax 967-5844
Horton MS 400/5-8
PO Box 639 27312 919-542-2303
Valencia Toomer, prin. Fax 542-7099
Pittsboro ES 500/K-4
375 Pittsboro School Rd 27312 919-542-3987
Chris Poston, prin Fax 542-1146
Other Schools – See Bennett, Bonlee, Chapel Hill, Goldston, Moncure, Siler City

---

Haw River Christian Academy 100/PK-12
2428 Silk Hope Gum Springs 27312 919-533-4139
Larry Robinson, hdmstr.

Pleasant Garden, Guilford, Pop. 4,413
Guilford County SD
Supt. — See Greensboro
Pleasant Garden ES 500/PK-5
4833 Pleasant Garden Rd 27313 336-674-4321
Brian Lehman, prin. Fax 674-4320

Plymouth, Washington, Pop. 3,841
Washington County SD 1,700/PK-12
802 Washington St 27962 252-793-5171
Fannie Williams, supt. Fax 793-5062
www.wcsnc.org
Pines ES 700/PK-5
3177 US Highway 64 E 27962 252-793-1137
Jacqueline Maloney, prin. Fax 793-1105
Other Schools – See Creswell, Roper

Pollocksville, Jones, Pop. 308
Jones County SD
Supt. — See Trenton
Pollocksville ES 200/PK-6
300 Trent St 28573 252-224-8071
Steven Howard, prin. Fax 224-0290

Poplar Branch, Currituck
Currituck County SD
Supt. — See Currituck
Griggs ES 300/PK-5
261 Poplar Branch Rd 27965 252-453-2700
Angela Lasher, prin. Fax 453-2132

Princeton, Johnston, Pop. 1,179
Johnston County SD
Supt. — See Smithfield
Princeton ES 800/PK-5
650 Holts Pond Rd 27569 919-936-0755
Rhonda Ward, prin. Fax 936-0750

Providence, Caswell
Caswell County SD
Supt. — See Yanceyville
North ES 400/PK-5
10390 NC Highway 86 N 27315 336-388-2222
Carla Murray, prin. Fax 388-5522

Raeford, Hoke, Pop. 4,467
Hoke County SD 8,500/PK-12
PO Box 370 28376 910-875-4106
Dr. Freddie Williamson, supt. Fax 875-3362
www.hcs.k12.nc.us
East Hoke MS 700/6-8
4702 Fayetteville Rd 28376 910-875-5048
Michelle Creammer, prin. Fax 875-9307
McLauchlin ES 300/PK-5
326 N Main St 28376 910-875-8721
Laurie Ashley, prin. Fax 904-6868
Rockfish Hoke ES 700/PK-5
6251 Rockfish Rd 28376 910-875-9343
Shawn O'Connor, prin. Fax 875-3761
Scurlock ES 600/PK-5
775 Rockfish Rd 28376 910-875-4182
Jennifer Damin, prin. Fax 875-0292
Steed ES 700/K-5
800 Philippi Church Rd 28376 910-875-1125
Kimberly Gray, prin. Fax 875-2274
Upchurch ES 600/PK-5
730 Turnpike Rd 28376 910-875-1574
Shannon Southerland, prin. Fax 904-0624
West Hoke ES 400/PK-5
6050 Turnpike Rd 28376 910-875-2584
Alfred Hammond, prin. Fax 875-7312
West Hoke MS 700/6-8
200 NC Highway 211 28376 910-875-3411
Mary McLeod, prin. Fax 875-0332
Other Schools – See Lumber Bridge, Red Springs

Raleigh, Wake, Pop. 395,376
Wake County SD
Supt. — See Cary
Abbotts Creek ES PK-5
9900 Durant Rd 27614 919-694-0555
Paula Trantham, prin. Fax 694-0571
Baileywick Road ES 400/K-5
9425 Baileywick Rd 27615 919-518-0090
Kendall Grigg, prin. Fax 518-0101
Banks Road ES 700/K-5
10225 Chambers Rd 27603 919-890-7333
Tracy Purvis, prin. Fax 890-7328
Barwell Road ES 800/K-5
3925 Barwell Rd 27610 919-661-5405
Tammy Carey, prin. Fax 662-2111
Beaverdam ES PK-5
3591 Tarheel Club Rd 27604 919-694-0222
Marion Evans, prin. Fax 589-6427
Brassfield ES 800/K-5
2001 Brassfield Rd 27614 919-870-4080
Teresa Winstead, prin. Fax 676-5022
Brentwood ES 400/K-5
3426 Ingram Dr 27604 919-850-8720
Robert Epler, prin. Fax 850-8728
Brier Creek ES 900/K-5
9801 Brier Creek Pkwy 27617 919-484-4747
Dr. Kathy Livengood, prin. Fax 484-4724
Brooks ES 600/K-5
700 Northbrook Dr 27609 919-881-1350
Felecia Locklear, prin. Fax 881-1349
Bugg ES 600/PK-5
825 Cooper Rd 27610 919-250-4750
Chris Lassiter, prin. Fax 250-4753
Carnage MS 1,200/6-8
1425 Carnage Dr 27610 919-856-7600
Teresa Abron, prin. Fax 856-7619
Carroll MS 800/6-8
4520 Six Forks Rd 27609 919-881-1370
Elizabeth MacWilliams, prin. Fax 881-1381
Centennial MS 600/6-8
1900 Main Campus Dr 27606 919-233-4217
Kathryn Hutchinson, prin. Fax 670-4302
Combs ES 900/K-5
2001 Lorimer Rd 27606 919-233-4300
Muriel Summers, prin. Fax 233-4042
Conn ES 600/PK-5
1220 Brookside Dr 27604 919-856-7637
Gary Duvall, prin. Fax 856-7643
Daniels MS 1,100/6-8
2816 Oberlin Rd 27608 919-881-4860
Dr. David Gaudet, prin. Fax 881-1418
Dillard Drive ES 700/K-5
5018 Dillard Dr 27606 919-233-4200
James Douglas, prin. Fax 854-1631
Dillard Drive MS 1,100/6-8
5200 Dillard Dr 27606 919-233-4228
Luther Thomas, prin. Fax 854-1615
Douglas ES 700/K-5
600 Ortega Rd 27609 919-881-4894
Derek Burns, prin. Fax 881-4896
Durant Road ES 1,000/PK-5
9901 Durant Rd 27614 919-870-4220
Janet Kehoe, prin. Fax 870-4218
Durant Road MS 1,400/6-8
10401 Durant Rd 27614 919-870-4098
Michael Chappell, prin. Fax 518-0021
East Millbrook MS 1,000/6-8
3801 Spring Forest Rd 27616 919-850-8755
Eric Fitts, prin. Fax 704-2333
East Wake MS 900/6-8
2700 Old Milburnie Rd 27604 919-266-8500
Rebecca Beaulieu, prin. Fax 266-8506
Forest Pines Drive ES 700/PK-5
11455 Forest Pines Dr 27614 919-562-6262
Dr. Carl Grant, prin. Fax 562-6260
Fox Road ES 800/K-5
7101 Fox Rd 27616 919-850-8845
Dr. Robert Lewis, prin. Fax 850-8854
Fuller ES 600/K-5
806 Calloway Dr 27610 919-856-7625
Cheryl Fenner, prin. Fax 856-7633
Green ES 600/K-5
5307 Six Forks Rd 27609 919-431-8141
Dr. Lisa Brown, prin. Fax 431-2277
Harris Creek ES 1,000/K-5
3829 Forestville Rd 27616 919-217-5100
Tracie Sanchez, prin. Fax 217-3273
Hilburn Academy 600/K-8
7100 Hilburn Dr 27613 919-571-6800
Katherine White, prin. Fax 571-6804
Hunter ES 700/K-5
1018 E Davie St 27601 919-856-7676
Jan Hargrove, prin. Fax 856-7680
Jeffreys Grove ES 500/PK-5
6119 Creedmoor Rd 27612 919-881-4910
Lisa Cruz, prin. Fax 881-4911
Joyner ES 700/PK-5
2300 Lowden St 27608 919-856-7650
Jennifer Zezza, prin. Fax 856-7661
Lacy ES 800/K-5
2001 Lake Boone Trl 27607 919-881-4920
Candace Watson, prin. Fax 881-1434
Lead Mine ES 600/K-5
8301 Old Lead Mine Rd 27615 919-870-4120
Aaron Marcin, prin. Fax 670-4244
Leesville Road ES 1,000/K-5
8402 Pride Way 27613 919-870-4200
Ari Cohen, prin. Fax 870-4188
Leesville Road MS 1,200/6-8
8406 Pride Way 27613 919-870-4141
Cynthia Kremer, prin. Fax 589-6608
Ligon MS 1,200/6-8
706 E Lenoir St 27601 919-856-7929
Gretta Dula, prin. Fax 856-3745
Lynn Road ES 500/K-5
1601 Lynn Rd 27612 919-870-4074
Victoria Privott, prin. Fax 670-4226
Martin MS 1,100/6-8
1701 Ridge Rd 27607 919-881-4970
Lacey Peckham, prin. Fax 881-5017
Millbrook ES 800/PK-5
1520 E Millbrook Rd 27609 919-850-8700
Dr. Jamee Lynch, prin. Fax 850-8709
Moore Square Museums MS 500/6-8
301 S Person St 27601 919-664-5737
Dr. Jackie Jordan, prin. Fax 856-8194
North Forest Pines ES 800/K-5
11501 Forest Pines Dr 27614 919-570-2220
Freda Cole, prin. Fax 570-2219
North Ridge ES 800/K-5
7120 Harps Mill Rd 27615 919-870-4100
Robert Soutter, prin. Fax 870-4107
Oak Grove ES 800/K-5
10401 Penny Rd 27606 919-387-4490
Beth Jarman, prin. Fax 387-4496
Olds ES 400/K-5
204 Dixie Trl 27607 919-856-7699
Dr. Mary Wheeler, prin. Fax 856-2989
Partnership ES 300/K-5
601 Devereux St 27605 919-856-8200
Dr. Mark Kenjarski, prin. Fax 670-4393
Pine Hollow MS 6-8
5365 Bartram Pl 27617 919-694-8880
Andrew Livengood, prin. Fax 589-6350
Pleasant Union ES 600/K-5
1900 Plsant Union Church Rd 27614 919-870-4230
Kevin Biles, prin. Fax 589-6650
Poe ES 400/PK-5
400 Peyton St 27610 919-250-4777
Dr. Annice Williams, prin. Fax 250-4774
Powell ES 400/PK-5
1130 Marlborough Rd 27610 919-856-7737
Curtis Brower, prin. Fax 856-7749
River Bend ES 900/K-5
6710 Perry Creek Rd 27616 919-431-8010
Gary Major, prin. Fax 431-8047
River Bend MS 6-8
5601 Wallace Martin Way 27616 919-694-8690
Stacey Weddle, prin. Fax 704-2073
Rogers Lane ES PK-5
201 N Rogers Ln 27610 919-694-8670
Shane Barham, prin. Fax 704-2084
Root ES 500/K-5
3202 Northampton St 27609 919-881-4940
Blaine Clark, prin. Fax 881-1427
Smith ES 700/PK-5
1101 Maxwell Dr 27603 919-662-2458
Kimberly Mitchell, prin. Fax 662-2948
Stough ES 600/K-5
4210 Edwards Mill Rd 27612 919-881-4950
Christopher Cox, prin. Fax 881-1422
Swift Creek ES 500/K-5
5601 Tryon Rd 27606 919-233-4320
Jan Hargrove, prin. Fax 670-4229
Sycamore Creek ES 1,100/K-5
10921 Leesville Rd 27613 919-841-4333
Melody Brunson, prin. Fax 841-4337
Underwood ES 500/K-5
1614 Glenwood Ave 27608 919-856-7663
Travis Shillings, prin. Fax 856-7981
Vance ES 500/K-5
8808 Old Stage Rd 27603 919-662-2472
Sarah Simmons, prin. Fax 662-2498
Wakefield ES 700/K-5
2400 Wakefield Pines Dr 27614 919-562-3555
Cynthia Keech, prin. Fax 562-3553
Wakefield MS 1,200/6-8
2300 Wakefield Pines Dr 27614 919-562-3500
Alison Cleveland, prin. Fax 670-4322
Walnut Creek ES 700/K-5
2600 Sunnybrook Rd 27610 919-857-9500
Vonda Martin, prin. Fax 857-9519
Washington ES 600/PK-5
1000 Fayetteville St 27601 919-856-7960
Robert Grant, prin. Fax 856-7985
West Millbrook MS 1,000/6-8
8115 Strickland Rd 27615 919-870-4050
Kelly Aman, prin. Fax 870-4064
Wilburn ES 700/K-5
3707 Marsh Creek Rd 27604 919-850-8738
Lutashia Dove, prin. Fax 850-8780
Wildwood Forest ES 800/K-5
8401 Wild Wood Forest Dr 27616 919-713-0600
Holly Shaw, prin. Fax 713-0615
Wiley ES 500/K-5
301 Saint Marys St 27605 919-856-7723
Leslie Taylor, prin. Fax 856-2956
Yates Mill ES 600/K-5
5993 Yates Mill Pond Rd 27606 919-233-4244
Barry Richburg, prin. Fax 233-4029
York ES 500/K-5
5201 Brookhaven Dr 27612 919-881-4960
Kate Williams, prin. Fax 881-1338

Adventist Christian Academy of Raleigh 50/K-10
4805 Dillard Dr 27606 919-233-1300

Al-Iman S 300/PK-8
3020 Ligon St 27607 919-821-1699
Sr. Mussarut Jabeen, prin. Fax 821-2988
Cathedral S 300/PK-8
204 Hillsborough St 27603 919-832-4711
Donna Moss, prin. Fax 832-8329
Chesterbrook Academy North Raleigh 100/PK-5
10200 Strickland Rd 27615 919-847-3120
Mike Williams, prin. Fax 847-2120
Follow the Child Montessori S 100/PK-6
3601 Harden Rd 27607 919-755-1150
Dominique Mouthon, head sch
Franciscan S 700/K-8
10000 Saint Francis Dr 27613 919-847-8205
Michael Watson, prin. Fax 847-9558
Friendship Christian S 300/PK-12
5510 Falls of Neuse Rd 27609 919-872-2133
Ric Nelson, head sch Fax 872-7451
Gethsemane Christian S 50/K-8
PO Box 14663 27620 919-833-1844
GRACE Christian S 300/PK-6
801 Buck Jones Rd 27606 919-747-2020
Eric Bradley, hdmstr. Fax 783-0856
Montessori S of Raleigh 300/PK-12
7005 Lead Mine Rd 27615 919-848-1545
Dr. Nancy Errichetti, head sch Fax 848-9611
Neuse Christian Academy 200/K-12
7600 Falls of Neuse Rd 27615 919-844-6496
Penny Hill, admin. Fax 861-6819
North Raleigh Christian Academy 1,500/PK-12
7300 Perry Creek Rd 27616 919-573-7900
Dr. S.L. Sherrill, supt. Fax 573-7901
Our Lady of Lourdes S 500/K-8
2710 Overbrook Dr 27608 919-782-1670
Sr. Therese Bauer, prin. Fax 420-2188
Raleigh Christian Academy 300/PK-12
2110 Trawick Rd 27604 919-872-2215
Raleigh S 400/PK-5
1141 Raleigh School Dr 27607 919-546-0788
Bud Lichtenstein, head sch Fax 546-9045
Ravenscroft S 1,200/PK-12
7409 Falls of Neuse Rd 27615 919-847-0900
Doreen Kelly, head sch Fax 847-7952
St. David's S 600/PK-12
3400 White Oak Rd 27609 919-782-3331
Jonathan Yonan, hdmstr. Fax 571-3330
St. Francis of Assisi Preschool 200/PK-PK
11401 Leesville Rd 27613 919-847-8205
Dawn Eagan, dir. Fax 865-2852
St. Raphael Catholic S 400/K-8
5815 Falls of Neuse Rd 27609 919-865-5750
John Mihalyo, prin. Fax 865-5751
St. Raphael Preschool 200/PK-K
5801 Falls of Neuse Rd 27609 919-865-5728
Molly DeAngelo, dir. Fax 865-5701
St. Timothy's S 500/PK-8
4523 Six Forks Rd 27609 919-787-3011
Thales Academy Raleigh 300/PK-5
8151 Town Dr 27616 919-882-2320
Trinity Academy of Raleigh 400/PK-12
10224 Baileywick Rd 27613 919-786-0114
Matthew Breazeale, prin. Fax 786-0621
Wake Christian Academy 900/K-12
5500 Wake Academy Dr 27603 919-772-6264
Mike Woods M.A., head sch Fax 779-0948
Word of God Christian Academy 200/K-12
3000 Rock Quarry Rd 27610 919-834-8200
Anesha Pittman M.Ed., prin. Fax 899-3640

Ramseur, Randolph, Pop. 1,657
Randolph County SD
Supt. — See Asheboro
Coleridge ES 400/K-5
4528 NC Hwy 22 S 27316 336-879-3348
Jo Glidewell, prin. Fax 879-4199
Ramseur ES 500/PK-5
6755 Jordan Rd 27316 336-824-4106
Tammie Abernethy, prin. Fax 824-7174
Southeastern Randolph MS 700/6-8
5302 Foushee Rd 27316 336-824-6700
Gail Powers, prin. Fax 824-6705

Faith Christian S 300/PK-12
5449 Brookhaven Rd 27316 336-824-4156

Randleman, Randolph, Pop. 4,054
Randolph County SD
Supt. — See Asheboro
Level Cross ES 500/PK-5
5417 Old Greensboro Rd 27317 336-495-5915
Cindy Walker, prin. Fax 495-6216
Randleman ES 700/K-4
100 Swaim St 27317 336-495-1322
Dr. James Johnson, prin. Fax 495-6447
Randleman MS 800/5-8
800 High Point St 27317 336-498-2606
Tracy Dawes, prin. Fax 498-8015

Red Oak, Nash, Pop. 3,398
Nash-Rocky Mount SD
Supt. — See Nashville
Red Oak ES 300/K-2
PO Box 70 27868 252-462-2496
Courtney Bissette, prin. Fax 937-2746

Red Springs, Robeson, Pop. 3,362
Hoke County SD
Supt. — See Raeford
Hawk Eye ES 400/PK-5
4321 Old Maxton Rd 28377 910-875-2470
Bridget Parnell-Hayes, prin. Fax 875-1702

Robeson County SD
Supt. — See Lumberton
Peterson ES 600/PK-4
102 Phillips Ave 28377 910-843-4125
Melinda Sellers, prin. Fax 843-2414
Red Springs MS 600/5-8
302 W 2nd Ave 28377 910-843-3883
Karen Brooks-Floyd, prin. Fax 843-3765

Highlander Academy 100/PK-12
200 N College St 28377 910-843-4995
Debra Duncan M.A., head sch Fax 843-8102

Reidsville, Rockingham, Pop. 14,244
Caswell County SD
Supt. — See Yanceyville
Stoney Creek ES 200/K-5
1803 Stoney Creek School Rd 27320 336-694-6222
Edgar Zimmerman, prin. Fax 694-5840

Rockingham County SD
Supt. — See Eden
Bethany ES 400/PK-5
271 Bethany Rd 27320 336-951-2710
Josh Eanes, prin. Fax 951-3788
Monroeton ES 500/PK-5
8081 US 158 27320 336-634-3280
Roy Weaver, prin. Fax 634-3043
Moss Street ES 400/K-5
419 Moss St 27320 336-349-5370
Leslie Coleman, prin. Fax 342-3145
Reidsville MS 600/6-8
1903 South Park Dr 27320 336-342-4726
Erica Blackwell, prin. Fax 342-9434
Rockingham County MS 800/6-8
182 High School Rd 27320 336-616-0073
Moriah Dollarhite, prin. Fax 616-0870
South End ES 300/PK-5
1307 South Park Dr 27320 336-349-6085
Matthew Smothers, prin. Fax 349-5119
Wentworth ES 500/PK-5
8806 NC Highway 87 27320 336-634-3250
Jennifer Hardin, prin. Fax 342-9380
Williamsburg ES 500/PK-5
2830 NC Highway 87 27320 336-349-4632
Gary Pyrtle, prin. Fax 342-2699

Community Baptist S 200/PK-12
509 Triangle Rd 27320 336-342-5991
Gene Carwile, admin. Fax 342-7180

Richfield, Stanly, Pop. 605
Stanly County SD
Supt. — See Albemarle
Richfield ES 300/K-5
120 Morgan St 28137 704-961-4800
Ellen Blue, prin. Fax 961-4899

Richlands, Onslow, Pop. 1,464
Onslow County SD
Supt. — See Jacksonville
Richlands ES 700/3-5
PO Box 67 28574 910-324-4142
Laurie Strope, prin. Fax 324-4879
Richlands PS 900/K-2
7444 Richlands Hwy 28574 910-324-3139
Gena Misciagno, prin. Fax 324-7801
Trexler MS 900/6-8
112 E Foy St 28574 910-324-4414
Lynn Jackson, prin. Fax 324-3963

Liberty Christian Academy 300/PK-12
215 Kinston Hwy 28574 910-430-0741
Cheryl Cavanaugh, head sch Fax 430-0394

Riegelwood, Columbus, Pop. 566
Bladen County SD
Supt. — See Elizabethtown
East Arcadia S 100/PK-8
21451 NC Highway 87 E 28456 910-247-4609
Victoria Clark, prin. Fax 788-6033

Columbus County SD
Supt. — See Whiteville
Acme-Delco ES 400/PK-5
PO Box 704 28456 910-655-2957
Janet Hedrick, prin. Fax 268-1568

Roanoke Rapids, Halifax, Pop. 15,565
Halifax County SD
Supt. — See Halifax
Davie STEM Academy 500/6-8
4391 US Highway 158 27870 252-519-0300
Dr. Pamela Chamblee, prin. Fax 519-0222

Roanoke Rapids CSD 3,100/PK-12
536 Hamilton St 27870 252-519-7100
Dr. Dain Butler, supt. Fax 519-7195
www.rrgsd.org
Belmont ES 800/PK-5
1517 Bolling Rd 27870 252-519-7500
Terrell Jones, prin. Fax 519-7595
Chaloner MS 700/6-8
2100 Virginia Ave 27870 252-519-7600
Jeff White, prin. Fax 519-7695
Manning ES 700/PK-5
1102 Barrett St 27870 252-519-7400
Lauren Hinnant, prin. Fax 519-7495

Halifax Academy 400/PK-12
1400 Three Bridges Rd 27870 252-537-8527

Roaring River, Wilkes
Wilkes County SD
Supt. — See North Wilkesboro
Roaring River ES 200/PK-5
283 White Plains Rd 28669 336-696-4628
Craig Tidline, prin. Fax 696-7839

Robbins, Moore, Pop. 1,085
Moore County SD
Supt. — See Carthage
Elise MS 200/6-8
180 W Elm St 27325 910-948-2421
Jeni Wiley, prin. Fax 948-4112
Robbins ES 500/PK-5
268 Rushwood Rd 27325 910-948-2411
Kim Bullard, prin. Fax 948-3264

Robbinsville, Graham, Pop. 615
Graham County SD 1,200/PK-12
52 Moose Branch Rd 28771 828-479-3413
Angela Knight, supt. Fax 479-9844
www.graham.k12.nc.us
Robbinsville ES 700/PK-6
54 Moose Branch Rd 28771 828-479-9850
Jaime Hooper, prin. Fax 479-9845
Robbinsville MS 200/7-8
301 Sweetwater Rd Ste B 28771 828-479-9840
Cullin Buchanan, prin. Fax 479-9847

Robersonville, Martin, Pop. 1,478
Martin County SD
Supt. — See Williamston
East End ES 300/PK-5
1121 3rd Street Ext 27871 252-795-4775
Jan Wagner, prin. Fax 795-4220
South Creek MS 200/6-8
21230 NC Highway 903 27871 252-795-3910
Angela Cross, prin. Fax 795-3890

Rockingham, Richmond, Pop. 9,384
Richmond County SD
Supt. — See Hamlet
Bell ES 600/PK-5
442 Hawthorne Ave 28379 910-997-9834
Yvonne Gilmer, prin. Fax 997-9848
East Rockingham ES 600/PK-5
154 Chalk Rd 28379 910-557-0900
Jamie Greene, prin.
Rockingham MS 700/6-8
415 Wall St 28379 910-997-9827
Theresa Gardner, prin. Fax 997-9859
Washington Street ES 600/PK-5
566 E Washington Street Ext 28379 910-997-9836
Angela Watkins, prin. Fax 895-0208
West Rockingham ES 400/PK-5
271 W US Highway 74 28379 910-997-9802
Willette Surgeon, prin. Fax 997-9803

Rockwell, Rowan, Pop. 2,077
Rowan-Salisbury County SD
Supt. — See Salisbury
Rockwell ES 500/K-5
114 Link St 28138 704-279-3145
Jennifer Warden, prin. Fax 279-8657
Shive ES, 655 Holshouser Rd 28138 500/PK-5
Zebbie Bondurant, prin. 704-279-2899

Grace Academy 200/PK-5
6725 Highway 152 E 28138 704-279-6683
Joey Phillips, admin. Fax 233-3334
Rockwell Christian S 100/PK-12
PO Box 609 28138 704-279-8854

Rocky Mount, Edgecombe, Pop. 56,654
Edgecombe County SD
Supt. — See Tarboro
Bulluck ES 700/PK-5
3090 Bulluck School Rd 27801 252-985-3456
Hillary Boutwell, prin. Fax 442-2370
West Edgecombe MS 400/6-8
6301 Nobles Mill Pond Rd 27801 252-446-2030
Claude Archer, prin. Fax 446-1592

Nash-Rocky Mount SD
Supt. — See Nashville
Baskerville ES 400/K-5
1100 Stokes St 27801 252-451-2880
Roderick Tillery, prin. Fax 977-0714
Benvenue ES 700/K-5
2700 Nicodemus Mile 27804 252-462-2835
Angela Ward, prin. Fax 937-5650
Edwards MS 600/6-8
720 Edwards St 27803 252-937-9025
Chris Sivills, prin. Fax 446-5527
Englewood ES 500/3-5
101 S Englewood Dr 27804 252-462-2501
Michelle Griffin, prin. Fax 937-5652
Fairview ES 300/PK-2
720 N Fairview Rd 27801 252-462-2005
Monique-Hargrove Jones, prin. Fax 985-4342
Johnson ES 200/K-5
600 N Fairview Rd 27801 252-451-2895
Michelle Royster, prin. Fax 446-5703
Parker MS 300/6-8
1500 E Virginia St 27801 252-937-9060
John Milliner-Williams, prin. Fax 446-5756
Rocky Mount MS 400/6-8
841 Nash St 27804 252-462-2010
Michael Girouard, prin. Fax 459-5220
Williford ES 400/K-5
801 Williford St 27803 252-937-9030
Kendrick Alston, prin. Fax 985-4331
Winstead Avenue ES 600/K-2
991 S Winstead Ave 27803 252-462-2845
Yolanda Wiggins, prin. Fax 451-5540

Faith Christian S 400/PK-12
1333 Faith Christian Dr 27803 252-443-3700
Dr. Edward Bunn, head sch Fax 443-2456
New Life Christian Academy 200/K-12
PO Box 8761 27804 252-443-6560
Our Lady of Perpetual Help S 100/PK-8
315 Hammond St 27804 252-972-1971
Debbie Haggerty, prin. Fax 972-0538
Rocky Mount Academy 400/PK-12
1313 Avondale Ave 27803 252-443-4126
Beth Covolo, head sch Fax 937-7922

Rocky Point, Pender, Pop. 1,566
Pender County SD
Supt. — See Burgaw
Cape Fear ES 500/K-5
1882 NC Highway 133 28457 910-602-3767
Charles Chestnut, prin. Fax 602-7828
Cape Fear MS 500/6-8
1886 NC Highway 133 28457 910-602-3334
Christie Brown, prin. Fax 602-3036
Rocky Point ES 500/PK-5
255 Elementary School Rd 28457 910-675-2309
Dr. Dawn McKernan, prin. Fax 675-8730

Rolesville, Wake, Pop. 3,697
Wake County SD
Supt. — See Cary
Rolesville ES 700/PK-5
307 S Main St 27571 919-554-8686
Dana Dougherty-Primiano, prin. Fax 554-8601
Rolesville MS 1,000/6-8
4700 Burlington Mills Rd 27571 919-570-2260
Michael Chappell, prin. Fax 570-2270
Sanford Creek ES 700/K-5
701 Granite Falls Blvd 27571 919-570-2100
Tiffany Rich, prin. Fax 570-2168

Ronda, Wilkes, Pop. 410
Wilkes County SD
Supt. — See North Wilkesboro
East Wilkes MS 400/6-8
2202 Macedonia Church Rd 28670 336-651-4300
Sandra Burchette, prin. Fax 957-8734
Ronda-Clingman ES 300/PK-5
316 Ronda Clingman School 28670 336-651-4200
Penny Grit, prin. Fax 984-3201

Roper, Washington, Pop. 608
Washington County SD
Supt. — See Plymouth
Washington County Union MS 300/6-8
37 E Mill Pond Rd 27970 252-793-2835
Dianne Stokes, prin. Fax 793-4411

Roseboro, Sampson, Pop. 1,167
Cumberland County SD
Supt. — See Fayetteville
Beaver Dam ES 100/PK-5
12059 NC Highway 210 S 28382 910-531-3378
Jeanna Daniels, prin. Fax 531-4353

Sampson County SD
Supt. — See Clinton
Roseboro ES 400/PK-5
180 Butler Island Rd 28382 910-525-4538
Tonya Colwell, prin. Fax 525-3032
Roseboro-Salemburg MS 400/6-8
PO Box 976 28382 910-525-4764
Shajuana Sellers, prin. Fax 525-3471

Mintz Christian Academy 100/K-12
2741 Mintz Rd 28382 910-564-6221
Dr. Winnie White, prin. Fax 564-6510

Rose Hill, Duplin, Pop. 1,619
Duplin County SD
Supt. — See Kenansville
Rose Hill-Magnolia ES 900/PK-8
PO Box 340 28458 910-289-3667
Janice Wynn, prin. Fax 289-3378

Rosman, Transylvania, Pop. 567
Transylvania County SD
Supt. — See Brevard
Rosman ES 400/K-5
167 Rosman School Rd 28772 828-862-4431
Scott Strickler, prin. Fax 862-4281
Rosman MS 300/6-8
2770 Old Rosman Hwy 28772 828-862-4286
Greg Carter, prin. Fax 885-5573

Rowland, Robeson, Pop. 1,020
Robeson County SD
Supt. — See Lumberton
Rowland MS 200/6-8
408 W Chapel St 28383 910-422-3983
Adrian Sinclair-Davis, prin. Fax 422-8369
Southside/Ashpole ES 300/PK-5
607 S Martin Luther King Jr 28383 910-422-3791
Lisa Washington, prin. Fax 422-3105
Union ES 400/PK-6
2547 NC Highway 710 S 28383 910-521-4272
Dr. Sheri Herndon, prin. Fax 521-0167

Roxboro, Person, Pop. 8,217
Person County SD 4,600/PK-12
304 S Morgan St Ste 25 27573 336-599-2191
Dr. Rodney Peterson, supt. Fax 599-0844
www.person.k12.nc.us
Bradsher Preschool Center PK-PK
404 S Morgan St 27573 336-599-7585
Treco Lea-Jeffers, dir. Fax 599-3484
North ES 300/K-5
260 Henderson Rd 27573 336-599-7262
Patti Barnes, prin. Fax 599-0128
North End ES 200/K-5
378 Mill Creek Rd, 336-599-3313
Sherita Fuller, prin. Fax 597-8700
Northern MS 500/6-8
1935 Carver Dr, 336-599-6344
Ashley Warren, prin. Fax 598-9207
South ES 300/K-5
1333 Hurdle Mills Rd 27573 336-599-7133
Patrick Holmes, prin. Fax 597-4611
Southern MS 600/6-8
209 Southern Middle School 27573 336-599-6995
Dr. Jonte Hill, prin. Fax 503-0587
Stories Creek ES 400/K-5
133 Stories Creek School Rd, 336-503-8071
Dustin Martin, prin. Fax 503-8083
Other Schools – See Hurdle Mills, Semora, Timberlake

Ruffin, Rockingham, Pop. 367
Rockingham County SD
Supt. — See Eden
Lincoln ES 300/PK-5
2660 Oregon Hill Rd 27326 336-348-2929
Karen Hester, prin. Fax 939-7779

Rural Hall, Forsyth, Pop. 2,885
Winston-Salem/Forsyth SD
Supt. — See Winston Salem
Rural Hall ES 600/K-5
275 College St 27045 336-703-6789
Diamond Cotton, prin. Fax 969-5994

Rutherford College, Burke, Pop. 1,336
Burke County SD
Supt. — See Morganton
Rutherford College ES 200/PK-5
PO Box 247 28671 828-879-8870
Lisa Dale, prin. Fax 879-9470

Rutherfordton, Rutherford, Pop. 4,144
Rutherford County SD
Supt. — See Forest City
Pinnacle ES 300/K-5
1204 Painters Gap Rd 28139 828-287-3440
Jennifer McBrayer, prin. Fax 287-0950
R-S MS 700/6-8
545 Charlotte Rd 28139 828-286-4461
Dr. Keith Silver, prin. Fax 286-4882
Rutherfordton ES 300/K-5
201 Bob Hardin Rd 28139 828-287-3778
Kelly Sisk, prin. Fax 286-0346

Trinity Christian S 100/PK-8
299 Deter St 28139 828-286-3900
Tiffany Walker, head sch Fax 286-3816

Saint Pauls, Robeson, Pop. 1,997
Robeson County SD
Supt. — See Lumberton
Saint Pauls ES 1,000/PK-5
222 Martin Luther King Dr 28384 910-865-4103
Dr. Jill Hathaway, prin. Fax 865-3951
Saint Pauls MS 500/6-8
526 W Shaw St 28384 910-865-4070
Avery Brooks, prin. Fax 865-1599

Salemburg, Sampson, Pop. 427
Sampson County SD
Supt. — See Clinton
Salemburg ES 500/PK-5
PO Box 9 28385 910-525-5547
Gerald Johnson, prin. Fax 525-4002

Salisbury, Rowan, Pop. 33,082
Rowan-Salisbury County SD 20,000/PK-12
PO Box 2349 28145 704-636-7500
Lynn Moody, supt.
www.rss.k12.nc.us
Dole ES 500/PK-5
465 Choate Rd 28146 704-639-3046
Lauren Raper, prin. Fax 639-3073
Erwin MS 900/6-8
170 Saint Luke Church Rd 28146 704-279-7265
Daniel Herring, prin. Fax 279-7954
Granite Quarry ES 500/K-5
118 S Walnut Gq St 28146 704-279-2154
Catherine Hampton, prin. Fax 279-4625
Hurley ES 600/PK-5
625 Hurley School Rd 28147 704-639-3038
Ryan Disseler, prin. Fax 639-3111
Isenberg ES 400/PK-5
2800 Jake Alexander Blvd N 28147 704-639-3009
Marvin Moore, prin. Fax 639-3113
Knollwood ES 700/K-5
3075 Shue Rd 28147 704-857-3400
Shonda Hairston, prin. Fax 855-1703
Knox MS 600/6-8
1625 W Park Rd 28144 704-633-2922
Michael Courtwright, prin. Fax 638-3538
Koontz ES 600/K-5
685 E Ritchie Rd 28146 704-216-0273
Lori Marrero, prin. Fax 216-0294
Overton ES 400/PK-5
1825 W Park Rd 28144 704-639-3000
Candice Austin, prin. Fax 638-3534
Southeast MS 700/6-8
1570 Peeler Rd 28146 704-638-5561
Jennifer Lentz, prin. Fax 638-5719
West Rowan MS 700/6-8
5925 Statesville Blvd 28147 704-633-4775
Derek McCoy, prin. Fax 633-3157
Other Schools – See China Grove, Cleveland, Faith, Gold Hill, Landis, Mount Ulla, Rockwell, Spencer, Woodleaf

---

North Hills Christian S 300/PK-12
2970 W Innes St 28144 704-636-3005
Maria Lowder, dir. Fax 636-3597
Sacred Heart S 200/PK-8
385 Lumen Christie Ln 28147 704-633-2841
Frank Cardelle, prin. Fax 633-6033
Salisbury Academy 200/PK-8
2210 Jake Alexander Blvd N 28147 704-636-3002
Beverly Fowler, head sch Fax 636-0778
Salisbury Adventist S 50/K-8
305 Rudolph Rd 28146 704-633-1282
Misty Stein, head sch

Saluda, Polk, Pop. 708
Polk County SD
Supt. — See Columbus
Saluda ES 200/PK-5
214 Main St 28773 828-749-5571
Cari Maneen, prin. Fax 749-1106

Sandy Ridge, Stokes
Stokes County SD
Supt. — See Danbury
Sandy Ridge ES 200/K-5
1070 Amostown Rd 27046 336-871-2400
Jeff Boyles, prin. Fax 871-8415

Sanford, Lee, Pop. 27,645
Harnett County SD
Supt. — See Lillington
Highland MS 300/6-8
345 Highland School Rd 27332
Brian Graham, prin.
Highlands ES 800/K-5
1915 Buffalo Lake Rd 27332 919-499-2200
Jennifer Spivey, prin. Fax 499-2524

Lee County SD 10,100/PK-12
PO Box 1010 27331 919-774-6226
Andy Bryan Ed.D., supt. Fax 776-0443
www.lee.k12.nc.us
Bullock ES 700/K-5
1410 McNeill Rd 27330 919-718-0160
Stefanie Clarke, prin. Fax 708-7347
Deep River ES 600/K-5
4000 Deep River Rd 27330 919-776-2722
Amy Lundy, prin. Fax 776-0737
East Lee MS 700/6-8
1337 Broadway Rd 27332 919-776-8441
Sharron Williams, prin. Fax 774-7451
Edwards ES 800/K-5
3115 Cemetery Rd 27332 919-774-3733
Natalie Kelly, prin. Fax 776-8689
Greenwood ES 700/K-5
1127 Greenwood Rd 27332 919-776-0506
Aimee Petrarca, prin. Fax 776-5574
Ingram Jr. ES 700/K-5
3309 Wicker St 27330 919-774-3772
Lisa Duffey, prin. Fax 774-7090
SanLee MS 800/6-8
2309 Tramway Rd 27332 919-708-7227
Betsy Bridges, prin. Fax 718-2875
Tramway ES 700/K-5
360 Center Church Rd 27330 919-718-0170
Andrea Sloan, prin. Fax 774-1325
West Lee MS 700/6-8
3301 Wicker St 27330 919-775-7351
Fax 776-3604
Other Schools – See Broadway

Grace Christian S 300/K-12
PO Box 1408 27331 919-774-4415
Stuart Shumway, admin. Fax 718-6777
Lee Christian S 400/PK-12
3220 Keller Andrews Rd 27330 919-708-5115
Don Payne, head sch Fax 708-6933

Scotland Neck, Halifax, Pop. 2,054
Halifax County SD
Supt. — See Halifax
Scotland Neck Leadership Academy 200/PK-5
901 Jr High School Rd 27874 252-826-4413
Christina Williams, prin. Fax 826-4309

Seagrove, Randolph, Pop. 221
Moore County SD
Supt. — See Carthage
Westmoore ES 400/K-8
2159 S NC Highway 705 27341 910-464-3401
Lisa Scott, prin. Fax 464-5293

Randolph County SD
Supt. — See Asheboro
Seagrove ES 500/K-5
528 Old Plank Rd 27341 336-873-7321
Jamie Armfield, prin. Fax 873-8745

Sedalia, Guilford, Pop. 612
Guilford County SD
Supt. — See Greensboro
Sedalia ES 500/PK-5
6120 Burlington Rd 27342 336-449-4711
Pamela Moore, prin. Fax 449-6523

Selma, Johnston, Pop. 5,974
Johnston County SD
Supt. — See Smithfield
Selma ES 900/PK-4
311 W Richardson St 27576 919-965-3361
Suzanne Mitchell, prin. Fax 965-0639
Selma MS 400/5-8
1533 US Highway 301 N 27576 919-965-2555
Christopher Germanoski, prin. Fax 202-0116

Semora, Person
Person County SD
Supt. — See Roxboro
Woodland ES 200/K-5
7391 Semora Rd 27343 336-599-7442
Joey Warren, prin. Fax 599-8730

Seven Springs, Wayne, Pop. 109
Wayne County SD
Supt. — See Goldsboro
Spring Creek MS 5-8
3579 NC Highway 111 S 28578 919-751-7125
Cheryll Price, prin. Fax 751-7126

Shallotte, Brunswick, Pop. 3,616
Brunswick County SD
Supt. — See Bolivia
Shallotte MS 600/6-8
225 Village Rd SW 28470 910-754-6882
Marie Laboy, prin. Fax 754-3108
Union ES 600/K-5
180 Union School Rd NW 28470 910-579-3591
Vickie Smith, prin. Fax 579-5542

Academy of Coastal Carolina 50/PK-12
PO Box 1988 28459 910-754-9637
Theresa Cox, head sch Fax 754-9630
Southeastern Christian Academy 100/PK-12
PO Box 2328 28459 910-754-2389
Kim Lancaster, admin. Fax 754-4895

Shannon, Robeson, Pop. 263
Robeson County SD
Supt. — See Lumberton
Rex-Rennert ES 500/PK-5
11780 Rennert Rd 28386 910-843-5298
Sandra Oxendine, prin. Fax 843-8533

Shawboro, Currituck
Currituck County SD
Supt. — See Currituck
Shawboro ES 500/K-5
370 Shawboro Rd 27973 252-232-2237
Greta Nelson, prin. Fax 232-2287

Shelby, Cleveland, Pop. 19,999
Cleveland County SD 15,600/PK-12
400 W Marion St 28150 704-476-8000
Dr. Stephen Fisher, supt. Fax 476-8300
www.clevelandcountyschools.org
Boiling Springs ES 600/PK-5
1522 Patrick Ave 28152 704-476-8361
Paula Peeler, prin. Fax 434-5286
Crest MS 900/6-8
315 Beaver Dam Church Rd 28152 704-476-8221
Jeremy Shields, prin. Fax 487-0378
Graham ES 300/PK-4
1100 Blanton St 28150 704-476-8386
Nelsa Feaster, prin. Fax 487-2868
Jefferson ES 400/PK-4
1166 Wyke Rd 28150 704-476-8390
Katie Barbee, prin. Fax 487-2880
Love ES 400/PK-4
309 James Love School Rd 28152 704-476-8385
Kim Kepner, prin. Fax 487-2882
Marion ES 400/PK-4
410 Forest Hill Dr 28150 704-476-8381
Heather Self, prin. Fax 487-2864
Shelby IS 500/5-6
220 S Post Rd 28152 704-476-8371
Dr. Kim Greene, prin. Fax 480-0856
Shelby MS 500/7-8
1480 S DeKalb St 28152 704-476-8328
Dr. Dustin Bridges, prin. Fax 487-2889
Springmore ES 700/K-5
616 McBrayer Homestead Rd 28152 704-476-8235
Laura McGill, prin. Fax 434-2216
Township Three ES 700/PK-5
526 Davis Rd 28152 704-487-7809
Molly Blanton, prin. Fax 487-0460
Union ES 400/PK-5
1440 Union Church Rd 28150 704-481-8001
Jake Wilson, prin. Fax 481-1940
Washington ES 400/PK-5
1907 Stony Point Rd 28150 704-435-9521
Chris Hall, prin. Fax 435-5777
Other Schools – See Casar, Fallston, Grover, Kings Mountain, Lawndale

Sherrills Ford, Catawba, Pop. 3,185
Catawba County SD
Supt. — See Newton
Sherrills Ford ES 600/K-6
8103 Sherrills Ford Rd 28673 828-478-2662
Lathan Fowler, prin. Fax 478-5927

Siler City, Chatham, Pop. 7,749
Chatham County SD
Supt. — See Pittsboro
Chatham MS 500/5-8
2025 S 2nd Avenue Ext 27344 919-663-2414
Chad Morgan, prin. Fax 663-2871
Cross ES 500/PK-5
234 Cross School Rd 27344 919-742-4279
Allison Buckner, prin. Fax 742-5266
Siler City ES 700/PK-5
671 Ellington Rd 27344 919-663-2032
Dr. Larry Savage, prin. Fax 742-5591
Silk Hope S 400/PK-8
7945 Silk Hope Gum Springs 27344 919-742-3911
Angie Brady-Andrew, prin. Fax 742-5032

Smithfield, Johnston, Pop. 10,815
Johnston County SD 33,900/PK-12
PO Box 1336 27577 919-934-6031
Dr. Ross Renfrow, supt. Fax 934-2586
www.johnston.k12.nc.us
Smithfield MS 800/6-8
1455 Buffalo Rd 27577 919-934-4696
Heather Anders, prin. Fax 934-7552
South Smithfield ES 600/PK-5
201 W Sanders St 27577 919-934-8979
Laura Makey, prin. Fax 934-1739
West Smithfield ES 600/PK-5
2665 Galilee Rd 27577 919-989-6418
Sharon Bryant, prin. Fax 989-3470
Other Schools – See Angier, Benson, Clayton, Four Oaks, Garner, Kenly, Micro, Pine Level, Princeton, Selma, Wendell, Willow Spring, Wilsons Mills, Zebulon

Smyrna, Carteret
Carteret County SD
Supt. — See Beaufort
Down East MS 200/6-8
174 Marshallberg Rd 28579 252-729-2301
Rolanda Golden, prin.
Smyrna ES 200/PK-5
174 Marshallberg Rd 28579 252-729-2301
Rolanda Golden, prin. Fax 729-1015

Sneads Ferry, Onslow, Pop. 2,600
Onslow County SD
Supt. — See Jacksonville

Dixon MS 700/5-8
118 Ridgefield Ave 28460 910-347-2738
Leigh Bizzell, prin. Fax 347-4399

Snow Camp, Alamance
Alamance-Burlington SD
Supt. — See Burlington
Sylvan ES 300/K-5
7718 Sylvan Rd 27349 336-376-3350
Mark Gould, prin. Fax 376-3318

Snow Hill, Greene, Pop. 1,577
Greene County SD 3,100/PK-12
301 Kingold Blvd 28580 252-747-3425
Dr. Patrick Miller, supt. Fax 747-5942
www.gcsedu.org/
Greene County IS 400/4-5
614 Middle School Rd 28580 252-747-0182
Jada Mumford, prin. Fax 747-0164
Greene County MS 700/6-8
485 Middle School Rd 28580 252-747-8191
Diane Blackman, prin. Fax 747-2484
Snow Hill PS 500/PK-1
502 SE 2nd St 28580 252-747-8113
Emery Smith, prin. Fax 747-4656
West Greene ES 500/2-3
303 Kingold Blvd 28580 252-747-3955
JoAnn Pennington, prin. Fax 747-7591

Sophia, Randolph
Randolph County SD
Supt. — See Asheboro
New Market ES 500/K-5
6096 US Highway 311 27350 336-495-3340
Kimberly Bowie, prin. Fax 495-3343

Southern Pines, Moore, Pop. 12,175
Moore County SD
Supt. — See Carthage
Southern Pines ES 400/3-5
255 S May St 28387 910-692-2357
Dale Buie, prin. Fax 693-1745
Southern Pines PS 500/PK-2
1250 W New York Ave 28387 910-692-8659
Tonya Wagner, prin. Fax 692-8259

Calvary Christian S 100/PK-12
400 S Bennett St 28387 910-692-8311
Episcopal Day S 200/PK-5
340 E Massachusetts Ave 28387 910-692-3492
Thomas Brereton, head sch Fax 692-7914
O'Neal S 400/PK-12
PO Box 290 28388 910-692-6920
John Elmore, head sch Fax 692-6930
St. John Paul II S 200/PK-8
2922 Camp Easter Rd 28387 910-692-6241
John Donohue, prin. Fax 692-2286
Sandhills Classical Christian S 100/PK-10
PO Box 2600 28388 910-695-1874
Dr. Alan Marshall, head sch Fax 401-1335

Southport, Brunswick, Pop. 2,791
Brunswick County SD
Supt. — See Bolivia
South Brunswick MS 800/6-8
100 Cougar Rd 28461 910-845-2771
David Ruth, prin. Fax 845-8972
Southport ES 700/K-5
701 W 9th St 28461 910-457-6036
Beverly Eury, prin. Fax 457-6042

Southport Christian S 100/PK-12
4457 Flagship Ave SE 28461 910-457-5060
Lisa Kjome, prin. Fax 457-5017

Sparta, Alleghany, Pop. 1,751
Alleghany County SD 1,500/PK-12
85 Peachtree St 28675 336-372-4345
Chad Beasley, supt. Fax 372-4204
www.alleghany.k12.nc.us
Sparta ES 600/PK-8
450 N Main St 28675 336-372-8546
Dustin Webb, prin. Fax 372-8732
Other Schools – See Ennice, Piney Creek

Spencer, Rowan, Pop. 3,207
Rowan-Salisbury County SD
Supt. — See Salisbury
North Rowan ES 500/PK-5
600 Charles St 28159 704-639-3042
Katherine Bryant, prin. Fax 639-3080
North Rowan MS 500/6-8
512 Charles St 28159 704-639-3018
Carl Snider, prin. Fax 639-3099

Spindale, Rutherford, Pop. 4,228
Rutherford County SD
Supt. — See Forest City
Carver Center PK-PK
141 Carver St 28160 828-286-3901
Paula Lewis, dir. Fax 287-5585
Spindale ES 400/K-5
161 N Oak St 28160 828-286-2861
Brandon Hill, prin. Fax 287-1026

Word of Faith Christian S 100/K-12
207 Old Flynn Rd 28160 828-286-3772

Spring Hope, Nash, Pop. 1,294
Nash-Rocky Mount SD
Supt. — See Nashville
Southern Nash MS 900/6-8
5301 S NC Highway 581 27882 252-937-9020
Carina Bryant, prin. Fax 478-4861
Spring Hope ES 500/PK-5
401 McLean St 27882 252-451-8530
Kelly Mudd, prin. Fax 478-4859

Spring Lake, Cumberland, Pop. 11,305
Cumberland County SD
Supt. — See Fayetteville
Black ES 200/K-5
125 S 3rd St 28390 910-497-7147
Brenda McAllister, prin. Fax 497-3817
Brown ES 600/PK-5
2522 Andrews Church Rd 28390 910-497-1258
Dr. Shanessa Fenner, prin. Fax 497-0882
Manchester ES 400/K-5
611 Spring Ave 28390 910-436-2151
Kailey Hill, prin. Fax 436-6034
Spring Lake MS 500/6-8
612 Spring Ave 28390 910-497-1175
Masa Kinsey-Shipp, prin. Fax 497-1598

Harnett County SD
Supt. — See Lillington
Overhills ES 800/K-5
2626 Ray Rd 28390 910-436-3545
Sue Polumbo, prin. Fax 436-3686
Overhills MS 1,300/6-8
2711 Ray Rd 28390 910-436-0009
Tina Tasker, prin. Fax 436-0948

Spruce Pine, Mitchell, Pop. 2,151
Mitchell County SD
Supt. — See Bakersville
Deyton ES 300/3-5
308 Harris St 28777 828-766-2070
Brandon Birchfield, prin. Fax 765-0052
Greenlee PS 300/K-2
2206 Carters Ridge Rd 28777 828-766-9562
Julie Weatherman, prin. Fax 766-9566
Harris MS 300/6-8
121 Harris St 28777 828-766-3340
Michael Tountasakis, prin. Fax 765-1595

Altapass Christian S 50/PK-12
3631 Altapass Hwy 28777 828-765-0660
Tri County Christian S 50/K-12
207 Pinebridge Ave 28777 828-765-2969
Teresa Young, prin. Fax 520-1034

Stallings, Union, Pop. 13,604
Union County SD
Supt. — See Monroe
Stallings ES 600/K-5
3501 Stallings Rd 28104 704-290-1558
Laura Gaddy, prin. Fax 893-0825

Stanfield, Stanly, Pop. 1,471
Stanly County SD
Supt. — See Albemarle
Stanfield ES 300/PK-5
101 Montgomery Ave 28163 704-961-5800
Jessie Morton, prin. Fax 961-5899

Stanley, Gaston, Pop. 3,517
Gaston County SD
Supt. — See Gastonia
Kiser ES 400/3-5
311 E College St 28164 704-836-9105
Lorinda Brusie, prin. Fax 263-9372
Springfield PS 500/PK-2
900 S Main St 28164 704-836-9106
Emily Poag, prin. Fax 263-1890
Stanley MS 500/6-8
317 Hovis Rd 28164 704-836-9600
Rebecca Huffstetler, prin. Fax 263-0993

Stantonsburg, Wilson, Pop. 782
Wilson County SD
Supt. — See Wilson
Speight MS 400/6-8
5514 Old Stantonsburg Rd 27883 252-238-3983
Valerie Budd, prin. Fax 238-2104
Stantonsburg ES 300/K-5
PO Box 160 27883 252-238-3639
Jenny Hayes, prin. Fax 238-2290

Star, Montgomery, Pop. 866
Montgomery County SD
Supt. — See Troy
Star ES 200/K-5
302 S Main St 27356 910-428-4333
Jennifer Beck, prin. Fax 428-1439

State Road, Surry
Surry County SD
Supt. — See Dobson
Mountain Park ES 200/PK-5
505 Mountain Park Rd 28676 336-874-3933
Janet Sutphin, prin. Fax 874-7963

Statesville, Iredell, Pop. 24,072
Iredell-Statesville SD 20,800/K-12
PO Box 911 28687 704-924-2029
Brady Johnson, supt. Fax 871-2834
www.iss.k12.nc.us
Central ES 300/K-5
4083 Wilkesboro Hwy 28625 704-876-0746
Diana Jones, prin. Fax 876-6226
Cloverleaf ES 800/K-5
300 James Farm Rd 28625 704-978-2110
Dr. Alisha Cloer, prin. Fax 978-2117
East Iredell ES 800/K-5
400 East Elementary Rd 28625 704-872-9541
Amy Rhyne, prin. Fax 872-1085
East Iredell MS 500/6-8
590 Chestnut Grove Rd 28625 704-872-4666
Dr. Tonya Houpe, prin. Fax 873-6602
Henkel ES 600/K-5
1503 Old Mountain Rd 28677 704-873-7333
Keeley Ward, prin. Fax 871-0153
Mills ES 500/K-5
1410 Pearl St 28677 704-873-8498
Sheliah Burnette, prin. Fax 872-3755

Scotts ES 400/K-5
4743 Taylorsville Hwy 28625 704-585-6526
LeAnne Hall, prin. Fax 585-6971
Sharon ES 300/K-5
880 Sharon School Rd 28625 704-872-3401
Jason Humphrey, prin. Fax 924-9963
Statesville MS 400/6-8
321 Clegg St 28677 704-872-2135
Kelly Campbell, prin. Fax 871-9279
Third Creek ES 600/K-5
361 E Barkley Rd 28677 704-873-3002
Jonathan Nicastro, prin. Fax 871-0755
West Iredell MS 700/6-8
303 Watermelon Rd 28625 704-873-2887
David Ivey, prin. Fax 881-0582
Other Schools – See Cleveland, Harmony, Mooresville, Olin, Troutman, Union Grove

---

Cornerstone Christian Academy 100/PK-12
650 Glover St 28625 704-873-0032
Crossroads Christian S of Statesville 50/K-12
2200 E Broad St 28625 704-871-1515
Anne W. Wooten, admin. Fax 871-1515
Southview Christian S 100/K-12
625 Wallace Springs Rd 28677 704-872-9554
Statesville Christian S 200/K-12
1210 Museum Rd 28625 704-873-9511
Dr. Barry Redmond, head sch Fax 873-0841
Statesville Montessori S 100/PK-8
1012 Harmony Dr 28677 704-873-1092

Stedman, Cumberland, Pop. 1,004
Cumberland County SD
Supt. — See Fayetteville
Stedman ES 300/2-5
7370 Clinton Rd 28391 910-483-3886
Stanley Douglas, prin. Fax 483-0519
Stedman PS 200/PK-1
155 E First St 28391 910-484-6954
April Thomas, prin. Fax 484-1604

Stokes, Pitt, Pop. 372
Pitt County SD
Supt. — See Greenville
Stokes S 300/PK-8
2683 NC Highway 903 N 27884 252-752-6907
Jennifer James, prin. Fax 752-2956

Stokesdale, Guilford, Pop. 4,986
Guilford County SD
Supt. — See Greensboro
Stokesdale ES 500/PK-5
8025 US Highway 158 27357 336-643-8420
Meredith Chandler, prin. Fax 643-8425

Stoneville, Rockingham, Pop. 1,031
Rockingham County SD
Supt. — See Eden
Stoneville ES 400/PK-5
PO Box 7 27048 336-573-4000
Kasie Pruitt, prin. Fax 573-4002

Stony Point, Alexander, Pop. 1,289
Alexander County SD
Supt. — See Taylorsville
Stony Point ES 300/PK-5
311 Stony Point School Rd 28678 704-585-6981
Andy Palmer, prin. Fax 585-6812

Stovall, Granville, Pop. 415
Granville County SD
Supt. — See Oxford
Stovall-Shaw ES 300/PK-5
PO Box 39 27582 919-693-3478
Amy Rice, prin. Fax 693-4959

Sugar Grove, Watauga
Watauga County SD
Supt. — See Boone
Bethel ES 200/K-8
138 Bethel School Rd 28679 828-297-2240
Fax 297-5182
Valle Crucis ES 400/PK-8
2998 Broadstone Rd 28679 828-963-4712
Preston Clarke, prin. Fax 963-8185

Summerfield, Guilford, Pop. 10,091
Guilford County SD
Supt. — See Greensboro
Summerfield ES 600/K-5
7501 Summerfield Rd 27358 336-643-8444
Jill Walsh, prin. Fax 643-8447

Sunbury, Gates, Pop. 287
Gates County SD
Supt. — See Gatesville
Cooper ES 200/K-5
PO Box 58 27979 252-465-4091
Jeremy Wright, prin. Fax 465-4238

Supply, Brunswick
Brunswick County SD
Supt. — See Bolivia
Cedar Grove MS 500/6-8
750 Grove Trl SW 28462 910-846-3400
Michael Hobbs, prin. Fax 846-3401
Supply ES 700/PK-5
51 Benton Rd SE 28462 910-754-7644
Askia Kirby, prin. Fax 754-3112

Swannanoa, Buncombe, Pop. 4,465
Buncombe County SD
Supt. — See Asheville
Owen MS 600/6-8
730 Old US 70 Hwy 28778 828-686-7739
Jim Lewis, prin. Fax 686-7938
Williams ES 400/K-5
161 Bee Tree Rd 28778 828-686-3856
Caroline Lynch, prin. Fax 686-3075

Asheville Christian Academy 500/PK-12
PO Box 1089 28778 828-581-2200
Dr. William George, head sch Fax 581-2218

Swanquarter, Hyde, Pop. 313
Hyde County SD 600/PK-12
PO Box 217 27885 252-926-3281
Dr. Randolph Latimore, supt. Fax 926-3083
www.hyde.k12.nc.us/
Mattamuskeet ES 200/PK-5
60 Juniper Bay Rd 27885 252-926-0240
Allison Etheridge, prin. Fax 926-0243
Other Schools – See Ocracoke

Swansboro, Onslow, Pop. 2,580
Onslow County SD
Supt. — See Jacksonville
Queens Creek ES 600/K-5
159 Queens Creek Rd 28584 910-326-5115
Elaine Justice, prin. Fax 326-5235
Swansboro ES 600/PK-5
118 School Rd 28584 910-326-1501
Page Highsmith, prin. Fax 326-6170
Swansboro MS 800/6-8
1240 W Corbett Ave 28584 910-326-3601
Helen Gross, prin. Fax 326-5848

Sylva, Jackson, Pop. 2,551
Jackson County SD 3,600/PK-12
398 Hospital Rd 28779 828-586-2311
Dr. Kimberly Elliott, supt. Fax 586-5450
www.jcps.k12.nc.us
Fairview ES 800/K-8
251 Big Orange Way 28779 828-586-2819
Fred Osborn, prin. Fax 586-3462
Scotts Creek ES 500/PK-8
516 Parris Branch Rd 28779 828-631-2740
Dr. Wanda Fernandez, prin. Fax 631-2478
Other Schools – See Cashiers, Cullowhee, Whittier

Tabor City, Columbus, Pop. 2,463
Columbus County SD
Supt. — See Whiteville
Guideway ES 200/PK-5
11570 Swamp Fox Hwy E 28463 910-653-2723
Dale Norris, prin. Fax 653-3744
Tabor City ES 400/PK-5
203 Stake Rd 28463 910-653-3618
Theresa Brown, prin. Fax 653-4274
Tabor City MS 200/6-8
701 W 6th St 28463 910-653-3637
Kelly Bullard, prin. Fax 653-2093

Tarboro, Edgecombe, Pop. 11,342
Edgecombe County SD 6,100/PK-12
2311 N Main St 27886 252-641-2600
Dr. Valerie Bridges, supt. Fax 641-5714
www.ecps.us
Martin Millenium Academy 400/K-8
400 E Johnston St 27886 252-641-5710
Keith Parker, prin. Fax 641-5713
Pattillo MS 100/6-8
PO Box 609 27886 252-823-3812
Lauren Lampron, prin. Fax 641-5706
Princeville ES 300/PK-5
710 Panola St 27886 252-823-4718
Annette Walker, prin. Fax 641-5702
Stocks ES 500/PK-5
400 W Hope Lodge St 27886 252-823-2632
Lois Glass, prin. Fax 823-7834
Other Schools – See Battleboro, Pinetops, Rocky Mount

Tar Heel, Bladen, Pop. 115
Bladen County SD
Supt. — See Elizabethtown
Plain View PS 200/PK-4
1963 Chicken Foot Rd 28392 910-862-2371
Vanessa Huffin, prin. Fax 835-2139
Tar Heel MS 300/5-8
PO Box 128 28392 910-862-2475
Teresa Coleman, prin. Fax 878-9323

Taylorsville, Alexander, Pop. 2,066
Alexander County SD 5,400/PK-12
700 Liledoun Rd 28681 828-632-7001
Dr. Jennifer Hefner, supt. Fax 632-8862
www.alexander.k12.nc.us
Bethlehem ES 500/PK-5
7900 NC Highway 127 28681 828-495-8198
Jill Peek, prin. Fax 495-2580
Ellendale ES 300/PK-5
175 Ellendale Park Ln 28681 828-632-4866
Crystal Hoke, prin. Fax 632-4912
Sugar Loaf ES 300/K-5
3600 NC Highway 16 N 28681 828-632-2192
Cary Cash, prin. Fax 635-1742
Taylorsville ES 300/K-5
100 7th St SW 28681 828-632-3072
Janel Lingle, prin. Fax 632-0276
West Alexander MS 600/6-8
85 Bulldog Ln 28681 828-495-4611
Dr. Chad Maynor, prin. Fax 495-3527
Wittenburg ES 300/PK-5
7300 Church Rd 28681 828-632-2395
Mary Brown, prin. Fax 635-0405
Other Schools – See Hiddenite, Stony Point

Thomasville, Davidson, Pop. 26,312
Davidson County SD
Supt. — See Lexington
Brier Creek ES 300/K-5
175 Watford Rd 27360 336-474-8200
Aaron Barr, prin. Fax 474-8201
Brown MS 800/6-8
1140 Kendall Mill Rd 27360 336-475-8845
Christa DiBonaventura, prin. Fax 475-3842
Fair Grove ES 500/PK-5
217 Cedar Lodge Rd 27360 336-472-7020
Ashley Barr, prin. Fax 472-3462
Hasty ES 600/K-5
325 Hasty School Rd 27360 336-475-1924
Beth Goins, prin. Fax 475-3723
Ledford MS 700/6-8
3954 N NC Highway 109 27360 336-476-4816
Bruce Carroll, prin. Fax 476-1479
Pilot ES 400/PK-5
145 Pilot School Rd 27360 336-472-7965
Stephanie Hall, prin. Fax 472-3323

Thomasville CSD 2,400/PK-12
400 Turner St 27360 336-474-4200
Dr. Catherine Gentry, supt. Fax 475-0356
www.tcs.k12.nc.us
Liberty Drive ES 300/4-5
401 Liberty Dr 27360 336-474-4186
Krystal Sanders, prin. Fax 472-3723
Thomasville MS 500/6-8
400 Unity St 27360 336-474-4120
Kevin Leake, prin. Fax 472-5081
Thomasville PS 900/PK-3
915 E Sunrise Ave 27360 336-474-4160
Dr. Angela Moore, prin. Fax 472-5020

New Hope Christian Academy 50/K-12
105 Pineywood St 27360 336-475-5654

Timberlake, Person
Person County SD
Supt. — See Roxboro
Helena ES 600/K-5
355 Helena Moriah Rd 27583 336-364-7715
Chrystal Clayton, prin. Fax 364-2501

Tobaccoville, Forsyth, Pop. 2,429
Winston-Salem/Forsyth SD
Supt. — See Winston Salem
Old Richmond ES 500/K-5
6315 Tobaccoville Rd 27050 336-703-4287
Brian Brookshire, prin. Fax 924-2442

Topton, Macon
Macon County SD
Supt. — See Franklin
Nantahala S 100/K-12
213 Winding Stairs Rd 28781 828-321-4388
James Bryan, prin. Fax 321-4834

Traphill, Wilkes
Wilkes County SD
Supt. — See North Wilkesboro
Traphill ES 200/PK-5
9794 Traphill Rd 28685 336-651-7160
Joey Ortiz, prin. Fax 957-4032

Trenton, Jones, Pop. 270
Jones County SD 1,200/PK-12
320 W Jones St 28585 252-448-2531
Dr. Michael Bracy, supt. Fax 448-1394
www.jonesnc.net
Comfort ES 200/PK-6
4384 NC Highway 41 W 28585 910-324-4249
David Moody, prin. Fax 324-6729
Jones MS 200/7-8
190 Old New Bern Rd 28585 252-448-3956
Tremaine Young, prin. Fax 448-1044
Trenton ES 200/PK-6
188 Elementary School Ln 28585 252-448-3441
Stella Downs, prin. Fax 448-1449
Other Schools – See Maysville, Pollocksville

Trinity, Randolph, Pop. 6,568
Randolph County SD
Supt. — See Asheboro
Archdale-Trinity MS 900/7-8
PO Box 232 27370 336-431-2589
Brian Hodgin, prin. Fax 431-1809
Braxton Craven IS 400/6-6
7037 NC Highway 62 27370 336-431-4078
David Cross, prin. Fax 431-0145
Hopewell ES 600/K-5
6294 Welborn Rd 27370 336-861-2030
Sharon Harper, prin. Fax 861-7040
Trinity ES 500/PK-5
5457 Braxton Craven Rd 27370 336-431-1027
Ginger Crites, prin. Fax 431-9088

Troutman, Iredell, Pop. 2,323
Iredell-Statesville SD
Supt. — See Statesville
Troutman ES 700/K-5
220 S Main St 28166 704-528-4526
Kimberly Cressman, prin. Fax 528-0988
Troutman MS 400/6-8
305 Rumple St 28166 704-528-5137
Bryan Paslay, prin. Fax 528-4006

Troy, Montgomery, Pop. 3,135
Montgomery County SD 4,300/PK-12
PO Box 427 27371 910-576-6511
Dr. Dale Ellis, supt. Fax 576-2044
www.montgomery.k12.nc.us
Page Street ES 300/3-5
897 Page St 27371 910-576-1307
Teresa Dunn, prin. Fax 576-1310
Troy ES 300/PK-2
310 N Russell St 27371 910-576-3651
Maxine Brown, prin. Fax 572-2082
Other Schools – See Biscoe, Candor, Mount Gilead, Star

Wescare Christian Academy 100/K-8
1368 NC Hwy 134 N 27371 910-572-2270
Queen Faulkner, prin. Fax 572-2257

Tryon, Polk, Pop. 1,626
Polk County SD
Supt. — See Columbus
Tryon ES 500/PK-5
100 School Pl 28782 828-859-6584
Todd Murphy, prin. Fax 859-6170

Tryon SDA S 50/K-8
2820 Lynn Rd 28782 828-859-6889

Tyner, Chowan
Edenton-Chowan SD
Supt. — See Edenton
Chowan MS 500/6-8
2845 Virginia Rd 27980 252-221-4131
John Lassiter, prin. Fax 221-8033

Union Grove, Iredell
Iredell-Statesville SD
Supt. — See Statesville
Union Grove ES 300/K-5
1314 Sloans Mill Rd 28689 704-539-4354
Kelley James, prin. Fax 539-5500

Valdese, Burke, Pop. 4,425
Burke County SD
Supt. — See Morganton
Heritage MS 600/6-8
1951 Enon Rd 28690 828-874-0731
Katie Moore, prin. Fax 879-6330
Valdese ES 400/K-5
298 Praley St NW 28690 828-874-0704
Teresa Dale, prin. Fax 874-1571

Vale, Lincoln
Catawba County SD
Supt. — See Newton
Banoak ES 300/K-6
7651 W NC 10 Hwy 28168 704-462-2849
Regina Bumgarner, prin. Fax 462-4125

Lincoln County SD
Supt. — See Lincolnton
North Brook ES 400/PK-5
642 Highway 274 28168 704-276-2479
Kim Davis, prin. Fax 276-3378
Union ES 300/K-5
4875 Reepsville Rd 28168 704-276-1493
Heather Houser, prin. Fax 276-3072

Vanceboro, Craven, Pop. 972
Craven County SD
Supt. — See New Bern
Vanceboro-Farm Life ES 700/PK-5
2000 Farm Life Ave 28586 252-244-3215
Daniel Palimetakis, prin. Fax 244-3219

Vass, Moore, Pop. 708
Moore County SD
Supt. — See Carthage
Vass-Lakeview ES 700/PK-5
141 James St 28394 910-245-3444
Bridget Johnson, prin. Fax 245-1301

Vilas, Watauga
Watauga County SD
Supt. — See Boone
Cove Creek ES 300/PK-8
930 Vanderpool Rd 28692 828-297-2781
Kelly Walker, prin. Fax 297-1311

Wade, Cumberland, Pop. 550
Cumberland County SD
Supt. — See Fayetteville
District 7 ES 300/PK-5
5721 Smithfield Rd 28395 910-483-0001
Cathryn Helms, prin. Fax 483-6047

Wadesboro, Anson, Pop. 5,742
Anson County SD 3,600/PK-12
320 Camden Rd 28170 704-694-4417
Michael Freeman, supt. Fax 694-7479
www.ansonschools.org/
Anson MS 600/7-8
832 US Highway 52 N 28170 704-694-3945
Danielle Blount, prin. Fax 694-5209
Ansonville ES 200/PK-6
9104 US Highway 52 N 28170 704-826-8337
Michael Vetter, prin. Fax 826-6136
Wadesboro ES 200/5-6
321 Camden Rd 28170 704-694-9383
Linda McCormick, prin. Fax 694-5816
Wadesboro PS 500/PK-4
1542 US Highway 52 S 28170 704-694-4423
Fred Davis, prin. Fax 695-1490
Other Schools – See Lilesville, Morven, Peachland

Wagram, Scotland, Pop. 822
Scotland County SD
Supt. — See Laurinburg
Wagram PS 500/PK-5
24081 Main St 28396 910-369-2252
Dr. Bobbie Mills, prin. Fax 369-2438

Wake Forest, Wake, Pop. 29,480
Wake County SD
Supt. — See Cary
Heritage ES 900/K-5
3500 Rogers Rd 27587 919-562-6000
Jennifer Abraham, prin. Fax 562-6006
Heritage MS 1,400/6-8
3400 Rogers Rd 27587 919-562-6204
Christopher McCabe, prin. Fax 562-6227
Jones Dairy ES 900/K-5
1100 Jones Dairy Rd 27587 919-562-6181
Robert Bendel, prin. Fax 562-6186
Richland Creek ES 200/K-5
840 Wallridge Dr 27587 919-554-6333
Dr. Tammie Sexton, prin. Fax 670-4206
Wake Forest ES 600/K-5
136 W Sycamore Ave 27587 919-554-8655
Julia Smith, prin. Fax 554-8660
Wake Forest MS 1,100/6-8
1800 S Main St 27587 919-554-8440
Christopher Bradford, prin. Fax 554-8435

St. Catherine of Siena Catholic S 100/PK-8
520 W Holding Ave 27587 919-556-7613
Carl Bilotta, prin. Fax 570-0071
Thales Academy Wake Forest 400/PK-5
3106 Heritage Trade Dr 27587 919-453-6415
Suzanne Lambert M.Ed., admin. Fax 453-6418

Walkertown, Forsyth, Pop. 4,605
Winston-Salem/Forsyth SD
Supt. — See Winston Salem
Middle Fork ES 300/K-5
3125 Williston Rd 27051 336-748-4090
Tasha Powell, prin. Fax 727-2942
Walkertown ES 800/PK-5
2971 Main St 27051 336-703-4252
Trina Bethea, prin. Fax 595-3964
Walkertown MS 700/6-8
5240 Sullivantown Rd 27051 336-703-4154
Scott Munsie, prin. Fax 595-1372

Wallace, Duplin, Pop. 3,853
Duplin County SD
Supt. — See Kenansville
Wallace ES 800/PK-5
4266 S NC Highway 11 28466 910-285-7183
Angelo Cavallaro, prin. Fax 285-4340

Walnut Cove, Stokes, Pop. 1,407
Stokes County SD
Supt. — See Danbury
London ES 200/K-5
609 School St 27052 336-591-7204
Kristine Mitchell, prin. Fax 591-7032
Southeastern Stokes MS 400/6-8
1044 N Main St 27052 336-591-4371
Rhonda Jackson, prin. Fax 591-8164
Walnut Cove ES 300/PK-5
1211 Walnut Cove School Rd 27052 336-591-4408
Samuel Jones, prin. Fax 591-8068

Warrensville, Ashe
Ashe County SD
Supt. — See Jefferson
Ashe County MS 500/7-8
PO Box 259 28693 336-384-3591
Dustin Farmer, prin. Fax 384-2112
Blue Ridge ES 500/PK-6
PO Box 229 28693 336-384-4500
Callie Grubb, prin. Fax 384-4512

Warrenton, Warren, Pop. 855
Warren County SD 2,500/PK-12
PO Box 110 27589 252-257-3184
Dr. Ray Spain, supt. Fax 257-5357
www.warrenk12nc.org/
Boyd ES 400/PK-5
203 Cousin Lucys Ln 27589 252-257-3695
Katrinka Brewer, prin. Fax 257-0163
South Warren ES 200/PK-5
216 Shocco Springs Rd 27589 252-257-4606
Michelle Dunbar, prin. Fax 257-7123
Warren County MS 500/6-8
118 Campus Dr 27589 252-257-3751
Noland Hicks, prin. Fax 257-4532
Other Schools – See Macon, Norlina

Warsaw, Duplin, Pop. 3,022
Duplin County SD
Supt. — See Kenansville
Warsaw ES 600/PK-8
158 Lanefield Rd 28398 910-293-3121
Pamela Murray, prin. Fax 293-4096

Washington, Beaufort, Pop. 9,614
Beaufort County SD 7,200/PK-12
321 Smaw Rd 27889 252-946-6593
Dr. Don Phipps, supt. Fax 946-3255
www.beaufort.k12.nc.us
Eastern ES 700/PK-1
947 Hudnell St 27889 252-946-1611
Seth Smith, prin. Fax 974-1228
Jones MS 900/6-8
4105 Market Street Ext 27889 252-946-0874
Tracey Nixon, prin. Fax 946-7604
Small ES 500/4-5
4103 Market Street Ext 27889 252-946-3941
Kelly Makepeace, prin. Fax 946-0260
Tayloe ES 600/2-3
910 Tarboro St 27889 252-946-3350
Keith Mitchell, prin. Fax 975-7712
Other Schools – See Aurora, Bath, Chocowinity, Pinetown

Waxhaw, Union, Pop. 9,622
Union County SD
Supt. — See Monroe
Cuthbertson MS 1,300/6-8
1520 Cuthbertson Rd 28173 704-296-0107
Michael Murray, prin. Fax 243-1673
Kensington ES 1,000/K-5
8701 Kensington Dr 28173 704-290-1500
Dr. Rachel Clarke, prin. Fax 243-3821
Marvin Ridge MS 1,400/6-8
2831 Crane Rd 28173 704-290-1510
James Eversole, prin. Fax 243-0153
New Town ES 900/PK-5
1100 Waxhaw Indian Trail S 28173 704-290-1525
Catherine Perry, prin. Fax 843-8422
Rea View ES 700/K-5
320 Reid Dairy Rd 28173 704-290-1524
Jennifer Hoover, prin. Fax 845-1653
Sandy Ridge ES 900/K-5
10101 Waxhaw Manor Dr 28173 704-290-1505
Emily Kraftson, prin. Fax 243-3812
Waxhaw ES 600/PK-5
1101 Old Providence Rd 28173 704-290-1590
Eric Doan, prin. Fax 843-4259
Western Union ES 400/K-5
4111 Western Union School 28173 704-843-2153
Kristi Williford, prin. Fax 843-9019

Waynesville, Haywood, Pop. 9,753
Haywood County SD 7,200/PK-12
1230 N Main St 28786 828-456-2400
Dr. Anne Garrett, supt. Fax 456-2438
www.haywood.k12.nc.us
Bethel MS 300/6-8
630 Sonoma Rd 28786 828-646-3442
Shawn Parris, prin. Fax 648-6259
Hazelwood ES 500/PK-5
1111 Plott Creek Rd 28786 828-456-2406
Wendy Rogers, prin. Fax 456-5438
Jonathan Valley ES 400/PK-5
410 Hall Dr 28785 828-926-3207
Heather Hollingsworth, prin. Fax 926-2678
Junaluska ES 300/K-5
2238 Asheville Rd 28786 828-456-2407
Sherri Arrington, prin. Fax 456-2446
Waynesville MS 900/6-8
495 Brown Ave 28786 828-456-2403
Trevor Putnam, prin. Fax 452-7905
Other Schools – See Canton, Clyde

Blue Ridge Adventist Christian S K-8
119 Hampshire Dr 28786 828-400-8681

Weaverville, Buncombe, Pop. 3,037
Buncombe County SD
Supt. — See Asheville
North Buncombe ES 700/K-4
251 Flat Creek Church Rd 28787 828-645-6054
Deborah Devane, prin. Fax 658-3059
North Buncombe MS 600/6-8
51 N Buncombe School Rd 28787 828-645-7944
Dr. Jamie Johnson, prin. Fax 645-2509
North Windy Ridge IS 600/5-6
20 Doan Rd 28787 828-658-1892
Brent Wise, prin. Fax 658-1983
Weaverville ES 400/2-4
129 S Main St 28787 828-645-3127
Heidi Allison, prin. Fax 645-5129
Weaverville PS 200/K-1
39 S Main Street Ext 28787 828-645-4275
Steve Chandler, prin. Fax 658-0121

Weddington, Mecklenburg, Pop. 9,325

Weddington Christian Academy 100/K-8
13901 Providence Rd 28104 704-846-1039
Adell Keen, prin.

Weldon, Halifax, Pop. 1,616
Weldon CSD 1,200/PK-12
301 Mulberry St 27890 252-536-4821
Dr. Anitra Wells, supt. Fax 536-3062
district.weldoncityschools.org
Weldon ES 500/PK-4
805 Washington Ave 27890 252-536-4815
Keedra Whitaker, prin. Fax 536-3633
Other Schools – See Halifax

Wendell, Wake, Pop. 5,709
Johnston County SD
Supt. — See Smithfield
Archer Lodge MS 1,100/6-8
740 Wendell Rd 27591 919-553-0714
Melissa Hubbard, prin. Fax 553-8540

Wake County SD
Supt. — See Cary
Carver ES 500/K-5
291 Liles Dean Rd 27591 919-365-2680
Katherine Faison, prin. Fax 365-2622
Lake Myra ES 600/K-5
1300 Elk Falls Dr 27591 919-365-8990
Tina Zarzecki, prin. Fax 365-8968
Wendell ES 500/K-5
3355 Wendell Blvd 27591 919-365-2660
Jack Zellmer, prin. Fax 365-2666
Wendell MS 1,000/6-8
3409 NC 97 Hwy 27591 919-365-1667
Robert Morrison, prin. Fax 365-1686

West End, Moore
Moore County SD
Supt. — See Carthage
West End ES 400/PK-5
4483 NC Highway 211 27376 910-673-6691
Antigone Peek, prin. Fax 673-7640
West Pine ES 500/K-5
272 Archie Rd 27376 910-673-2004
Mary-Frances Tintle, prin. Fax 673-2023
West Pine MS 900/6-8
144 Archie Rd 27376 910-673-1464
Doug Massengill, prin. Fax 673-1272

Westfield, Surry
Stokes County SD
Supt. — See Danbury
Reynolds ES 100/K-5
1585 NC Highway 66 N 27053 336-351-2480
Nichole Rose, prin. Fax 351-6130

West Jefferson, Ashe, Pop. 1,280
Ashe County SD
Supt. — See Jefferson
Westwood ES 600/PK-6
4083 US Highway 221 S 28694 336-877-2921
Jennifer Robinson, prin. Fax 877-2932

Whitakers, Nash, Pop. 726
Nash-Rocky Mount SD
Supt. — See Nashville
Swift Creek ES 300/PK-PK, 3-
2420 Swift Creek School Rd 27891 252-462-2840
Kristen Tedford, prin. Fax 937-1817

Whiteville, Columbus, Pop. 5,303
Columbus County SD 6,200/PK-12
PO Box 729 28472 910-642-5168
Alan Faulk, supt. Fax 640-1010
www.columbus.k12.nc.us/
Old Dock ES 300/PK-8
12489 New Britton Hwy E 28472 910-642-2084
Ronna Gore, prin. Fax 642-7872
Williams Township S 700/PK-8
10400 James B White Hwy S 28472 910-653-3791
Thomas McLam, prin. Fax 653-6459
Other Schools – See Cerro Gordo, Chadbourn, Delco, Evergreen, Hallsboro, Nakina, Riegelwood, Tabor City

Whiteville CSD 2,300/PK-12
107 W Walter St 28472 910-642-4116
Charles Garland, supt. Fax 642-0564
www.whiteville.k12.nc.us
Central MS 500/6-8
310 S Martin Luther King Jr 28472 910-642-3546
Chris Kelly, prin. Fax 642-7484
Edgewood ES 500/3-5
317 E Calhoun St 28472 910-642-3121
Jared Worthington, prin. Fax 642-2284
Whiteville PS 600/PK-2
805 Barbcrest Ave 28472 910-642-4119
Kimberly Ward, prin. Fax 642-4506

Carolina Adventist Academy 50/PK-10
PO Box 1937 28472 910-640-0855
Columbus Christian Academy 200/K-12
PO Box 1100 28472 910-642-6196

Whittier, Jackson
Jackson County SD
Supt. — See Sylva
Smokey Mountain ES 400/K-8
884 US 441 N 28789 828-497-5535
Dr. Tracie Metz, prin. Fax 497-4907

Wilkesboro, Wilkes, Pop. 3,340
Wilkes County SD
Supt. — See North Wilkesboro
West Wilkes MS 700/6-8
1677 N NC Highway 16 28697 336-651-4381
Pam Huffman, prin. Fax 973-7423
Wilkesboro ES 400/PK-5
1248 School St 28697 336-838-4261
Rodney Graham, prin. Fax 667-8611

Willard, Pender
Pender County SD
Supt. — See Burgaw
Penderlea S 600/K-8
82 Penderlea School Rd 28478 910-285-2761
George Humphrey, prin. Fax 285-2990

Williamston, Martin, Pop. 5,452
Martin County SD 3,400/PK-12
300 N Watts St 27892 252-792-1575
Dr. Chris Mansfield, supt. Fax 792-1965
martin.sharpschool.net/
Hayes ES 400/3-5
201 Andrews St 27892 252-792-3678
Dr. Larry Hodgkins, prin. Fax 792-5510
Riverside MS 400/6-8
2920 US Highway 17 27892 252-792-1111
Serena Paschal, prin. Fax 792-6644
Rodgers ES 300/K-5
2277 Rodgers School Rd 27892 252-792-3834
Shannon Cecil, prin. Fax 809-4900
Williamston PS 500/PK-2
400 West Blvd 27892 252-792-3253
Nancy Greene, prin. Fax 792-7470
Other Schools – See Hamilton, Jamesville, Robersonville

Willow Spring, Wake
Johnston County SD
Supt. — See Smithfield
Dixon Road ES 500/PK-5
835 Dixon Rd 27592 919-894-7771
Kenneth Bennett, prin. Fax 894-3642

Wake County SD
Supt. — See Cary
Willow Springs ES 900/K-5
6800 Dwight Rowland Rd 27592 919-557-2770
Camille Miller, prin. Fax 557-2953

Wilmington, New Hanover, Pop. 104,394
New Hanover County SD 25,600/PK-12
6410 Carolina Beach Rd 28412 910-254-4200
Dr. Tim Markley, supt. Fax 254-4479
www.nhcs.net
Alderman ES 300/K-5
2025 Independence Blvd 28403 910-350-2031
Kate Tayloe, prin. Fax 350-2035
Anderson ES 600/K-5
455 Halyburton Memorial Pky 28412 910-798-3311
Krista Holland, prin. Fax 798-3358
Bellamy ES 700/K-5
70 Sanders Rd 28412 910-350-2039
Burt Kilpatrick, prin. Fax 350-2036
Blair ES 600/K-5
416 Edgewater Club Rd 28411 910-350-2045
Rebecca Higgins-Opgrand, prin. Fax 350-2049
Bradley Creek ES 500/K-5
6211 Greenville Loop Rd 28409 910-350-2051
Dr. Lauren Kefalonitis, prin. Fax 350-2053
Codington ES 600/K-5
4321 Carolina Beach Rd 28412 910-790-2236
Eric Pfirman, prin. Fax 790-2238
College Road ECC PK-K
4905 S College Rd 28412 910-350-7860
Karen McCarty, admin. Fax 397-7091
Eaton ES 600/K-5
6701 Gordon Rd 28411 910-397-1544
Heather Byers, prin. Fax 397-1546
Forest Hills Global ES 400/K-5
602 Colonial Dr 28403 910-251-6190
Boni Hall, prin. Fax 251-6054
Freeman S of Engineering 400/K-5
2601 Princess Place Dr 28405 910-251-6011
Susan Sellers, prin. Fax 251-6013
Holly Tree ES 500/K-5
3020 Web Trce 28409 910-790-2250
Laura Holliday, prin. Fax 790-2252
Howe Pre K Center PK-PK
1020 Meares St 28401 910-251-6195
Dionne Sturdivant, prin. Fax 251-6040
International S at Gregory 400/K-8
1106 Ann St 28401 910-251-6185
Leigh Ann Lampley, prin. Fax 251-6023
Johnson Pre K Center 100/PK-PK
1100 McRae St 28401 910-251-6155
Rachel Greer, prin. Fax 251-6050
Murray MS 900/6-8
655 Halyburton Memorial Pky 28412 910-790-2363
Philip Sutton, prin. Fax 790-2351
Murrayville ES 700/K-5
225 Mabee Way 28411 910-790-5067
Tim Dominowski, prin. Fax 790-5068
Myrtle Grove MS 800/6-8
901 Piner Rd 28409 910-350-2100
Cyndy Bliss, prin. Fax 350-2104
Noble MS 800/6-8
6520 Market St 28405 910-350-2112
Wade Smith, prin. Fax 350-2109
Ogden ES 700/K-5
3637 Middle Sound Loop Rd 28411 910-686-6464
Tammy Bruestle, prin. Fax 686-2096
Parsley ES 600/K-5
3518 Masonboro Loop Rd 28409 910-790-2355
Dr. Robin Hamilton, prin. Fax 790-2362
Pine Valley ES 500/K-5
440 John S Mosby Dr 28412 910-350-2121
Samuel Kantrowitz, prin. Fax 350-2116
Roland-Grise MS 800/6-8
4412 Lake Ave 28403 910-350-2136
Dr. Charlie Broadfoot, prin. Fax 350-2133
Snipes Academy of Arts & Design 500/K-5
2150 Chestnut St 28405 910-251-6175
Rachel Manning, prin. Fax 815-6974
Sunset Park ES 500/K-5
613 Alabama Ave 28401 910-815-6948
Dr. Diego LeHockey, prin. Fax 815-6901
Trask MS 800/6-8
2900 N College Rd 28405 910-350-2142
Dr. Maggie Rollison, prin. Fax 350-2144
Virgo MS 200/6-8
813 Nixon St 28401 910-251-6150
Dr. Sabrina Hill-Black, prin. Fax 251-6055
Williams ES 500/PK-5
801 Silver Lake Rd 28412 910-350-2150
Amy Oots, prin. Fax 350-2108
Williston MS 800/6-8
401 S 10th St 28401 910-815-6906
Ronald Villines, prin. Fax 815-6904
Winter Park ES 400/K-5
204 S MacMillan Ave 28403 910-350-2159
Paul Slovik, prin. Fax 350-2155
Wrightsboro ES 500/K-5
2716 Castle Hayne Rd 28401 910-815-6909
Delores Overby, prin. Fax 815-6915
Other Schools – See Carolina Beach, Castle Hayne, Wrightsville Beach

---

Calvary Christian S 100/PK-10
423 N 23rd St 28405 910-343-1565
Dr. Donnie Lovette, prin. Fax 762-5847
Cape Fear Academy 600/PK-12
3900 S College Rd 28412 910-791-0287
Donald Berger, head sch Fax 791-0290
Children's Schoolhouse Montessori S 100/PK-K
612 S College Rd 28403 910-799-1531
Lucy Hieronymus, dir.
Friends S of Wilmington 200/PK-8
350 Peiffer Ave 28409 910-792-1811
Brenda Esch, head sch Fax 792-9274
Myrtle Grove Christian S 400/PK-8
806 Piner Rd 28409 910-392-2067
Glenn Pleasant, head sch Fax 792-0016
Peace Rose Montessori S 50/PK-5
2173 Wrightsville Ave 28403 910-769-2812
St. Mark Catholic S 400/PK-8
1013 Eastwood Rd 28403 910-452-2800
Dennis Fleck, prin. Fax 332-6505
St. Mary S 300/PK-8
217 S 4th St 28401 910-762-5491
Joyce Price, prin. Fax 772-8034
Wilmington Adventist S 50/K-8
2833 Market St 28403 910-762-4224
Wilmington Christian Academy 800/PK-12
1401 N College Rd 28405 910-791-4248

Wilson, Wilson, Pop. 48,488
Wilson County SD 12,400/PK-12
PO Box 2048 27894 252-399-7700
Dr. Lane Mills, supt. Fax 399-2776
www.wilsonschoolsnc.net
Barnes ES 400/K-5
1913 Martin Luther King Jr 27893 252-399-7875
Khari Grant, prin. Fax 399-7833
Darden MS 400/6-8
1665 Lipscomb Rd E 27893 252-206-4973
Jagtar Singh, prin. Fax 206-1508
Forest Hills MS 600/6-8
1210 Forest Hills Rd NW 27896 252-399-7913
Jonathan Tribula, prin. Fax 399-7894
Hearne ES 500/PK-5
300 W Gold St 27893 252-399-7925
Thomas Holland, prin. Fax 399-7896
Jones ES 600/K-5
4028 NC Highway 42 W 27893 252-265-4020
Elizabeth Jenkins, prin. Fax 237-4233
New Hope ES 600/K-5
4826 Packhouse Rd 27896 252-399-7950
Kendral Flowers, prin. Fax 399-7899
Rock Ridge ES 500/K-5
6605 Rock Ridge School Rd 27893 252-399-7955
Jennifer Lewis, prin. Fax 399-7995
Toisnot MS 500/6-8
1301 Corbett Ave N 27893 252-399-7973
Wendy Sullivan, prin. Fax 399-7749
Vick ES 300/PK-5
504 Carroll St N 27893 252-399-7886
Pamela Walthall, prin. Fax 399-7873
Vinson-Bynum ES 400/K-5
1601 Tarboro St SW 27893 252-399-7981
Daniel Barnes, prin. Fax 399-7758
Wells ES 500/K-5
1400 Grove St N 27893 252-399-7986
Sharon Huneycutt, prin. Fax 399-7771
Winstead ES 400/K-5
1713 Downing St SW 27893 252-399-7990
Tracy Joyner, prin. Fax 399-7772
Other Schools – See Black Creek, Elm City, Lucama, Stantonsburg

---

Community Christian S 300/PK-12
5160 Packhouse Rd 27896 252-399-1376
Greenfield S 300/PK-12
3351 NC Highway 42 W 27893 252-237-8046
Wilson Christian Academy 500/PK-12
1820 Airport Blvd W 27893 252-237-8064

Wilsons Mills, Johnston
Johnston County SD
Supt. — See Smithfield
Wilsons Mills ES 500/K-5
4654 Wilsons Mills Rd 27593 919-934-2978
Andrea Jones, prin. Fax 934-5640

Windsor, Bertie, Pop. 3,573
Bertie County SD 2,800/PK-12
PO Box 10 27983 252-794-6000
Dr. Steven Hill, supt. Fax 794-9727
www.bertie.k12.nc.us
Bertie MS 600/6-8
652 US Highway 13 N 27983 252-794-2143
William Peele, prin. Fax 794-4024
Windsor ES 500/PK-5
104 Cooper Hill Rd 27983 252-794-5221
Tracy Gregory M.Ed., admin. Fax 794-5218
Other Schools – See Aulander, Colerain, Kelford

Bethel Assembly Christian Academy 200/PK-12
105 Askewville Bryant St 27983 252-794-4034

Winfall, Perquimans, Pop. 587
Perquimans County SD
Supt. — See Hertford
Perquimans Central S 500/PK-2
PO Box 129 27985 252-426-5332
Melissa Fields, prin. Fax 426-5480
Perquimans County MS 400/6-8
PO Box 39 27985 252-426-7355
Laura Moreland, prin. Fax 426-1424

Wingate, Union, Pop. 3,424
Union County SD
Supt. — See Monroe
Union ES 400/PK-5
5320 White Store Rd 28174 704-624-5400
Jennifer Deaton, prin. Fax 624-5406
Wingate ES 600/PK-5
301 Bivens St 28174 704-296-0635
Maxie Johnson, prin. Fax 233-9415

Winnabow, Brunswick
Brunswick County SD
Supt. — See Bolivia
Town Creek ES 500/PK-5
6330 Lake Park Dr SE 28479 910-253-6500
Walker Constantinesco, prin. Fax 253-6501

Winston Salem, Forsyth, Pop. 225,143
Davidson County SD
Supt. — See Lexington
Friedberg ES 500/K-5
1131 Friedberg Church Rd 27127 336-764-2050
Sarah Maier, prin. Fax 775-4722
Friendship ES 500/K-5
1490 Friendship Ledford Rd 27107 336-231-8744
Steve Reynolds, prin. Fax 231-8746
Oak Grove MS 700/6-8
1771 Hoy Long Rd 27107 336-474-8250
Dan Shamblen, prin. Fax 474-8257
Wallburg ES 900/PK-5
205 Motsinger Rd 27107 336-769-2921
James Sparks, prin. Fax 769-0967

Winston-Salem/Forsyth SD 53,600/PK-12
PO Box 2513 27102 336-727-2816
Dr. Beverly Emory, supt. Fax 661-6572
wsfcs.k12.nc.us
Ashley Academy Global Studies 500/PK-5
1047 NE Ashley School Cir 27105 336-703-4203
Scarlet Linville, prin. Fax 727-2344
Bolton ES 500/PK-5
1250 Bolton St 27103 336-703-4247
Cheryl Frazier, prin. Fax 774-4618
Brunson ES 600/K-5
155 N Hawthorne Rd 27104 336-703-4206
Jeff Faullin, prin. Fax 748-3233
Clemmons MS 900/6-8
3785 Fraternity Church Rd 27127 336-703-4217
Sandra Hunter, prin. Fax 774-4678
Cook Literacy Model S 300/PK-5
920 W 11th St 27105 336-703-4201
Paula Wilkins, prin. Fax 727-8160
Diggs-Latham ES 500/PK-5
986 Hutton St 27101 336-703-4102
Ted Burcaw, prin. Fax 727-2073

Downtown ES 300/PK-5
601 N Cherry St 27101 336-703-4125
Andy Lester-Niles, prin. Fax 748-3361
Easton ES 600/PK-5
734 Clemmonsville Cir 27107 336-748-4063
Colin Tribby, prin. Fax 771-4733
Flat Rock MS, 4648 Ebert Rd 27127 900/6-8
Becky Hodges, prin. 336-703-6762
Forest Park ES 600/PK-5
2019 Milford St 27107 336-703-4291
Trent Watkins, prin. Fax 771-4726
Gibson ES 800/K-5
2020 Walker Rd 27106 336-703-4212
Glenn Starnes, prin. Fax 922-7335
Griffith ES 500/K-5
1385 W Clemmonsville Rd 27127 336-703-4245
Alesia Hilton, prin. Fax 771-4735
Hall-Woodward ES 700/PK-5
125 Nicholson Rd 27107 336-703-4238
Kenneth Jordan, prin. Fax 771-4727
Hanes Magnet MS 900/6-8
2355 Pleasant St 27107 336-703-4171
Robin Willard, prin. Fax 727-3207
Ibraham ES 500/PK-5
5036 Old Walkertown Rd 27105 336-703-6771
Tabitha Hamilton, prin. Fax 661-4852
Jefferson ES 600/K-5
4000 Jefferson School Ln 27106 336-703-4215
Debbie McIntyre, prin. Fax 923-2111
Jefferson MS 1,300/6-8
3500 Sally Kirk Rd 27106 336-703-4222
Shane O'Neal, prin. Fax 774-4635
Kimberley Park ES 300/PK-5
1701 Cherry St 27105 336-703-6731
Amber Baker, prin. Fax 727-8245
Kimmel Farm ES 800/K-5
4672 Ebert Rd 27127 336-703-6760
Celena Tribby, prin. Fax 784-4427
Konnoak ES 700/K-5
3200 Renon Rd 27127 336-703-4163
Sheila Burnette, prin. Fax 771-4565
Meadowlark ES 900/K-5
401 Meadowlark Dr 27106 336-703-4208
Neil Raymer, prin. Fax 924-8419
Meadowlark MS 1,200/6-8
301 Meadowlark Dr 27106 336-703-4228
Joey Hearl, prin. Fax 922-1745
Mineral Springs ES 600/K-5
4527 Ogburn Ave 27105 336-703-6788
Deborah Gladstone, prin. Fax 661-4865
Mineral Springs MS 400/6-8
4559 Ogburn Ave 27105 336-703-6733
Debra Gladstone, prin. Fax 661-4857
Moore Magnet ES 600/K-5
451 Knollwood St 27103 336-727-2860
Adam Dovico, prin. Fax 748-3233
North Hills ES 500/PK-5
340 Alspaugh Dr 27105 336-703-4176
Tiffany Krafft, prin. Fax 661-4943
Northwest MS 900/6-8
5501 Murray Rd 27106 336-703-4161
Alfreda Smith, prin. Fax 924-5128
Old Town ES 600/PK-5
3930 Reynolda Rd 27106 336-703-4283
Kimberly Kelley, prin. Fax 924-5610
Petree ES 400/PK-5
3815 Old Greensboro Rd 27101 336-703-4141
Heather Horton, prin. Fax 748-3455
Philo-Hill Magnet MS 500/6-8
410 Haverhill St 27127 336-703-4165
Essie McCoy, prin. Fax 771-4737
Sherwood Forest ES 600/K-5
1055 Yorkshire Rd 27106 336-774-4646
Jacob Lowther, prin. Fax 774-4693
Smith Farm ES 200/K-5
4250 Johnny Knoll Ln 27107 336-703-4188
Cynthia Rash, prin.
South Fork ES 500/PK-5
4332 Country Club Rd 27104 336-703-4231
Joanell Gatling, prin. Fax 774-4666
Speas ES 400/PK-5
2000 Polo Rd 27106 336-703-4135
Robert Ash, prin. Fax 774-4697
Ward ES 700/K-5
3775 Fraternity Church Rd 27127 336-703-4235
Angela McHam, prin. Fax 774-4687
Whitaker ES 600/PK-5
2600 Buena Vista Rd 27104 336-703-6740
Sharon Creasy, prin. Fax 727-2303
Wiley Magnet MS 500/6-8
1400 W Northwest Blvd 27104 336-727-2378
Lisa Bodenheimer, prin. Fax 727-8412
ES Academy, 920 W 11th St 27105 K-5
David Jarmon, prin. 336-703-4290
Other Schools – See Clemmons, Kernersville, Lewisville, Pfafftown, Rural Hall, Tobaccoville, Walkertown

---

Calvary Day S 700/PK-12
5000 Country Club Rd 27104 336-765-5546
Richard Hardee, head sch Fax 714-5577
Ephesus Junior Academy 50/K-8
1225 N Cleveland Ave 27101 336-723-3140
Gospel Light Christian S 400/PK-12
4940 Gospel Light Church Rd 27101 336-722-6100
Our Lady of Mercy S 200/PK-8
1730 Link Rd 27103 336-722-7204
Sr. Geri Rogers, prin. Fax 725-2294
Redeemer S 200/PK-8
1046 Miller St 27103 336-724-9460
Billy Creech, admin. Fax 724-9555
St. John's Lutheran S 100/PK-8
2415 Silas Creek Pkwy 27103 336-725-1651
Mark Edmiston, prin. Fax 725-1603
St. Leo S 300/PK-8
333 Springdale Ave 27104 336-748-8252
Joanne Brown, prin. Fax 748-9005
Salem Baptist Christian S 300/PK-12
429 S Broad St 27101 336-725-6113
Martha Drake, hdmstr. Fax 725-8455
Summit S 500/PK-9
2100 Reynolda Rd 27106 336-722-2777
Dr. Michael Ebeling, head sch Fax 724-0099
Winston Salem Christian S 300/PK-12
3730 University Pkwy 27106 336-759-7762
Dr. Bryan Wolfe, head sch Fax 896-7667
Woodland Baptist Christian S 200/PK-12
1175 Bethania Rural Hall Rd 27106 336-969-2088

Winterville, Pitt, Pop. 9,094
Pitt County SD
Supt. — See Greenville
Cox MS 800/6-8
2657 Church St 28590 252-756-3105
Norman McDuffie, prin. Fax 756-1081
Creekside ES 700/PK-5
431 Forlines Rd 28590 252-353-5253
Carla Frinsko, prin. Fax 353-8107
Ridgewood ES 700/PK-5
3601 South Bend Rd 28590 252-355-7879
Leslie Hayes, prin. Fax 355-3349
Robinson ES 600/PK-5
2439 Railroad St 28590 252-756-3707
Kamara Roach, prin. Fax 756-5072

Brookhaven SDA S 50/K-8
4658 Reedy Branch Rd 28590 252-756-5777
Christ Covenant S 200/K-12
4889 Old Tar Rd 28590 252-756-3002
Greenville Montessori S 100/PK-6
822 Laurie Ellis Rd 28590 252-355-6268
Suellen Biel, hdmstr.

Winton, Hertford, Pop. 760
Hertford County SD 3,200/PK-12
PO Box 158 27986 252-358-1761
Dr. William Wright, supt. Fax 358-4745
www.hertford.k12.nc.us
Other Schools – See Ahoskie, Murfreesboro

Woodleaf, Rowan
Rowan-Salisbury County SD
Supt. — See Salisbury
Woodleaf ES 400/K-5
PO Box 10 27054 704-278-2203
Kris Wolfe, prin. Fax 278-2204

Wrightsville Beach, New Hanover, Pop. 2,457
New Hanover County SD
Supt. — See Wilmington
Wrightsville Beach ES 300/K-5
220 Coral Dr 28480 910-256-3171
Jackson Norvell, prin. Fax 256-4386

Yadkinville, Yadkin, Pop. 2,941
Yadkin County SD 5,700/PK-12
121 Washington St 27055 336-679-2051
Dr. Todd Martin, supt. Fax 679-4013
www.yadkin.k12.nc.us
Courtney ES 300/PK-6
2529 Courtney Huntsville Rd 27055 336-463-5510
Amy Rankin, prin. Fax 463-2883
Yadkinville ES 600/PK-6
305 N State St 27055 336-679-8921
Dr. Kelly Kirkland, prin. Fax 679-2909
Other Schools – See Boonville, East Bend, Hamptonville, Jonesville

Yanceyville, Caswell, Pop. 1,971
Caswell County SD 2,800/PK-12
PO Box 160 27379 336-694-4116
Dr. Sandra Carter, supt. Fax 694-5154
www.caswell.k12.nc.us/
Dillard MS 700/6-8
255 Hatchett Rd 27379 336-694-4941
Terri Gullick, prin. Fax 694-6353
Oakwood ES 400/PK-5
PO Box 640 27379 336-694-4221
Jennifer Coeburn, prin. Fax 694-4376
Other Schools – See Mebane, Providence, Reidsville

Youngsville, Franklin, Pop. 1,142
Franklin County SD
Supt. — See Louisburg
Cedar Creek MS 600/6-8
2228 Cedar Creek Rd 27596 919-554-4848
James Elliott, prin. Fax 570-5143
Long Mill ES 600/PK-5
1753 Long Mill Rd 27596 919-554-0667
Dr. Monica Headen, prin. Fax 554-1765
Youngsville ES 500/K-5
PO Box 338 27596 919-556-5250
Caroline Linker, prin. Fax 556-3962

Zebulon, Wake, Pop. 4,340
Johnston County SD
Supt. — See Smithfield
Corinth Holder ES 600/PK-5
3976 NC Highway 231 27597 919-365-7560
Christopher Kennedy, prin. Fax 365-7717

Wake County SD
Supt. — See Cary
Wakelon ES 600/K-5
8921 Pippin Rd 27597 919-404-3844
Angela Cooper, prin. Fax 404-3829
Zebulon ES 500/PK-5
700 Proctor St 27597 919-404-3680
David Newkirk, prin. Fax 404-3676
Zebulon MS 600/6-8
1000 Shepard School Rd 27597 919-404-3630
Candis Jones, prin. Fax 404-3651

Zionville, Watauga
Watauga County SD
Supt. — See Boone
Mabel ES 200/K-8
404 Mabel School Rd 28698 828-297-2512
Mark Hagaman, prin. Fax 297-4109

NORTH DAKOTA

NORTH DAKOTA DEPT. OF PUBLIC INSTRUCTION
600 E Boulevard Ave, Bismarck 58505-0601
Telephone 701-328-2260
Fax 701-328-2461
Website http://www.dpi.state.nd.us

Superintendent of Public Instruction Kirsten Baesler

NORTH DAKOTA BOARD OF EDUCATION
600 E Boulevard Ave, Bismarck 58505-0602

EDUCATION COOPERATIVES

Great Northwest Education Cooperative
David Richter, supt. 701-609-5681
PO Box 1964, Williston 58802
www.gnwec.k12.nd.us

Mid-Dakota Education Cooperative
Luke Schaefer, dir. 701-838-3025
900 N Broadway Ste 300
Minot 58707
www.ndmdec.org

Missouri River Educational Cooperative
Lyle Krueger, dir. 701-751-4041
3001 Memorial Hwy Ste B
Mandan 58554
www.mrecnd.org

North Central Education Cooperative
Cynthia Jelleberg, dir. 701-228-2090
514 Thompson St, Bottineau 58318
www.ncecnorthdakota.org

Northeast Education Services Cooperative
Jennifer Carlson, dir. 701-662-7650
205 16th St NW, Devils Lake 58301 Fax 662-7658
www.nesc.k12.nd.us

Red River Valley Education Cooperative
Janet O'Hara, dir. 218-779-5121
4201 James Ray Dr
Grand Forks 58202
sites.google.com/a/rrvecnd.org/rrvec/

Roughrider Education Services Program
Riley Mattson, dir. 701-483-0999
300 13th Ave W Ste 6C Fax 483-0998
Dickinson 58601
www.resp-k12-education.org

South East Educational Cooperative
Kyle Davison, dir. 701-446-3170
1305 9th Ave S, Fargo 58103 Fax 446-3176
www.ndseec.com

PUBLIC, PRIVATE AND CATHOLIC ELEMENTARY SCHOOLS

Abercrombie, Richland, Pop. 263
Richland SD 44
Supt. — See Colfax
Richland ES 100/K-6
PO Box 139 58001 701-553-8321
Cindy Erbes, prin. Fax 553-8850

Alexander, McKenzie, Pop. 220
Alexander SD 2 200/PK-12
PO Box 63 58831 701-828-3334
Leslie Bieber, supt. Fax 828-3134
Alexander ES 100/PK-6
PO Box 66 58831 701-828-3334
Karen Shaide, prin. Fax 828-3134

Amidon, Slope, Pop. 20
Central Elementary SD 32 50/K-8
206 Main St 58620 701-879-6231
Jackie Kathrein, supt. Fax 879-6278
Amidon ES 50/K-8
206 Main St 58620 701-879-6231
JoDee Foreman, prin. Fax 879-6278

Anamoose, McHenry, Pop. 227
Anamoose SD 14 100/PK-6
706 3rd St W 58710 701-465-3258
Steven Heim, supt. Fax 465-3259
www.anamoose-drake.k12.nd.us
Anamoose-Drake ES 100/PK-6
706 3rd St W 58710 701-465-3258
Melissa Melaas, prin. Fax 465-3259

Ashley, McIntosh, Pop. 736
Ashley SD 9 100/PK-12
703 W Main St 58413 701-288-3456
Jason Schmidt, supt. Fax 288-3457
www.ashley.k12.nd.us
Ashley ES 100/PK-6
703 W Main St 58413 701-288-3456
Cary Hauth, prin. Fax 288-3457

Beach, Golden Valley, Pop. 1,013
Beach SD 3 300/PK-12
PO Box 368 58621 701-872-4161
David Wegner, supt. Fax 872-3801
www.beach.k12.nd.us
Lincoln ES 100/PK-6
PO Box 639 58621 701-872-4253
Lynn Swanson-Puckett, prin. Fax 872-3805

Belcourt, Rolette, Pop. 2,055
Belcourt SD 7 1,600/K-12
PO Box 440 58316 701-477-6471
Dr. Lana DeCoteau, supt. Fax 477-6470
www.belcourt.k12.nd.us
Turtle Mountain Community ES 700/K-5
PO Box 440 58316 701-477-6471
Fax 477-8006
Turtle Mountain Community MS 400/6-8
PO Box 440 58316 701-477-6471
Cary Morin, prin. Fax 477-3973

St. Ann S 50/PK-5
PO Box 2020 58316 701-477-2667
Allen Mehrer, prin. Fax 477-0602

Belfield, Stark, Pop. 793
Belfield SD 13 200/K-12
PO Box 97 58622 701-575-4275
Wade Northrop, supt. Fax 575-8533
www.belfield.k12.nd.us/
Belfield ES, PO Box 97 58622 100/K-6
Louise Lorge, prin. 701-575-4275

Billings County SD 1
Supt. — See Medora
Prairie S 50/PK-8
12793 20th St 58622 701-575-4773
Shae Peplinski, prin. Fax 575-4110

Berthold, Ward, Pop. 449
Lewis and Clark SD 161 300/PK-12
PO Box 185 58718 701-453-3484
Marc Ritteman, supt. Fax 453-3488
www.lewisandclark.k12.nd.us/
Berthold ES 100/PK-6
PO Box 185 58718 701-453-3484
Melissa Lahti, prin. Fax 453-3488
Other Schools – See Plaza

Beulah, Mercer, Pop. 3,078
Beulah SD 27 700/K-12
204 5th St NW 58523 701-873-2237
Travis Jordan, supt. Fax 873-5273
www.beulah.k12.nd.us
Beulah ES 300/K-4
200 7th St NW 58523 701-873-2298
Amber Skalsky, prin. Fax 873-2842
Beulah MS 200/5-8
1700 Central Ave N 58523 701-873-4325
Stacy Murschel, prin. Fax 873-2844

Binford, Griggs, Pop. 183
Midkota SD 7 100/K-12
PO Box 38 58416 701-676-2511
Les Dale, supt. Fax 676-2510
www.midkotaschools.com
Midkota ES 100/K-6
PO Box 38 58416 701-676-2511
Linn Dockter, prin. Fax 676-2510

Bismarck, Burleigh, Pop. 60,375
Apple Creek SD 39 100/K-6
2000 93rd St SE 58504 701-223-7349
Fax 223-1991
www.applecreekschool.org
Apple Creek ES 100/K-6
2000 93rd St SE 58504 701-223-7349
Sonya Miller, prin. Fax 223-1991

Bismarck SD 1 11,800/PK-12
806 N Washington St 58501 701-323-4000
Tamara Uselman, supt. Fax 355-4001
www.bismarckschools.org
Bismarck ECC 300/PK-PK
720 N 14th St 58501 701-323-4400
Michelle Hougen, prin. Fax 323-4405
Centennial ES 500/K-5
2800 Ithica Dr 58503 701-323-4290
Michele Svihovec, prin. Fax 323-4295
Grimsrud ES 200/K-5
716 W Saint Benedict Dr 58501 701-323-4150
Wilda Nelson, prin. Fax 323-4155
Highland Acres ES 100/K-5
1200 Prairie Dr 58501 701-323-4160
Shawn Oban, prin. Fax 323-4165
Horizon MS 900/6-8
500 Ash Coulee Dr 58503 701-323-4550
Tabby Rabenberg, prin. Fax 323-4555
Liberty ES 400/K-5
5400 Onyx Dr 58503 701-323-4320
Linnett Schmidkunz, prin. Fax 323-4325
Miller ES 400/K-5
1989 N 20th St 58501 701-323-4170
John Alstad, prin. Fax 323-4175
Moses ES 400/K-5
1312 Columbia Dr 58504 701-323-4180
Dr. Jason Hornbacher, prin. Fax 323-4185
Murphy ES 400/K-5
611 N 31st St 58501 701-323-4190
Matt Fricke, prin. Fax 323-4195
Myhre ES 300/K-5
919 S 12th St 58504 701-323-4200
Alivia Wamboldt, prin. Fax 323-4205
Northridge ES 500/K-5
1727 N 3rd St 58501 701-323-4210
Yvonne Engelhart, prin. Fax 323-4215
Pioneer ES 300/K-5
1400 Braman Ave 58501 701-323-4220
Jim Jeske, prin. Fax 323-4225
Prairie Rose ES 200/K-5
2200 Oahe Bnd 58504 701-323-4280
Brenda Beiswenger, prin. Fax 323-4285
Roosevelt ES 100/K-5
613 W Avenue B 58501 701-323-4240
Shawn Oban, prin. Fax 323-4245
Simle MS 800/6-8
1215 N 19th St 58501 701-323-4600
Russ Riehl, prin. Fax 323-4605
Solheim ES 500/K-5
325 Munich Dr 58504 701-323-4260
Charles Dalusong, prin. Fax 323-4265
Sunrise ES 600/K-5
3800 Nickerson Ave 58503 701-323-4300
Sarah Jordan, prin. Fax 323-4305
Wachter MS 800/6-8
1107 S 7th St 58504 701-323-4650
Lee Ziegler, prin. Fax 323-4655
Will-Moore ES 300/K-5
400 E Avenue E 58501 701-323-4270
Brad Barnhardt, prin. Fax 323-4275
Other Schools – See Lincoln

Manning SD 45 50/K-8
10500 Highway 1804 S 58504 701-223-0082
Manning S 50/K-8
10500 Highway 1804 S 58504 701-223-0082
Rachel Steffen, prin.

Naughton SD 25 50/K-8
9101 123rd Ave NE 58503 701-673-3119
Fax 673-3349
Naughton S 50/K-8
9101 123rd Ave NE 58503 701-258-6034
Kathy Schlabach, prin.

Brentwood SDA S 50/1-8
9111 Wentworth Dr 58503 701-258-1579
Cathedral of the Holy Spirit S 200/K-8
508 Raymond St 58501 701-223-5484
Matt Strinden, prin. Fax 223-5485
Luther S 200/PK-8
413 E Avenue D 58501 701-224-9070
Denise Wolfgram, prin. Fax 250-9487
St. Anne S 300/PK-8
1315 N 13th St 58501 701-223-3373
Cori Hilzendeger, prin. Fax 250-9214
St. Mary's Academy 200/6-8
1025 N 2nd St 58501 701-223-4114
Michael Bichler, prin. Fax 223-8629
St. Marys S 200/PK-8
807 E Thayer Ave 58501 701-223-0225
Tony Fladeland, prin. Fax 250-9918
Shiloh Christian S 400/PK-12
1915 Shiloh Dr 58503 701-221-2104
Mike Dwyer, admin. Fax 224-8221

Bottineau, Bottineau, Pop. 2,163
Bottineau SD 1 600/K-12
301 Brander St 58318 701-228-2266
Pat Brenden, supt. Fax 228-2021
www.bottineau.k12.nd.us/
Bottineau ES 400/K-6
301 Brander St 58318 701-228-3718
Brian Palmer, prin. Fax 228-2021

Bowbells, Burke, Pop. 335
Bowbells SD 14 100/K-12
PO Box 279 58721 701-377-2396
Celeste Thingvold, supt. Fax 377-2399
www.bowbells.k12.nd.us
Bowbells ES 50/K-6
PO Box 279 58721 701-377-2396
Celeste thingvold, supt. Fax 377-2399

Bowman, Bowman, Pop. 1,641
Bowman County SD 1 500/K-12
PO Box H 58623 701-523-3283
David Mahon, supt. Fax 523-3849
www.bowman.k12.nd.us
Bowman S 300/K-8
PO Box H 58623 701-523-3358
Tracy Lecoe, prin. Fax 523-3849
Other Schools – See Rhame

Buchanan, Stutsman, Pop. 90
Pingree-Buchanan SD 10
Supt. — See Pingree
Pingree Buchanan ES 100/K-6
PO Box 99 58420 701-252-4653
Terrie Neys, prin. Fax 252-4660

Buffalo, Cass, Pop. 179
Maple Valley SD 4
Supt. — See Tower City
Buffalo ES 100/K-3
PO Box 165 58011 701-633-5183
Jayson Kocka, prin. Fax 633-5193

Burlington, Ward, Pop. 1,041
United SD 7
Supt. — See Des Lacs
Burlington Des Lacs S 400/PK-8
PO Box 158 58722 701-839-7135
Sue Kranz, prin. Fax 838-1573

Buxton, Traill, Pop. 323
Central Valley SD 3 100/K-12
1556 Highway 81 NE 58218 701-847-2220
Jeremy Brandt, supt. Fax 847-2407
www.centralvalleynd.com
Central Valley S 100/K-12
1556 Highway 81 NE 58218 701-847-2220
Frank Justin, prin. Fax 847-2407

Cando, Towner, Pop. 1,101
North Star SD 10 300/PK-12
PO Box 489 58324 701-968-4416
Jeff Hagler, supt. Fax 968-4418
www.northstar.k12.nd.us
North Star S 200/PK-8
PO Box 489 58324 701-968-4416
Vicki Held, prin. Fax 968-4418

Cannon Ball, Sioux, Pop. 856
Solen SD 3
Supt. — See Solen
Cannon Ball ES 100/K-6
PO Box 218 58528 701-854-3341
Amber James, prin. Fax 854-3342

Carrington, Foster, Pop. 2,050
Carrington SD 49 500/PK-12
PO Box 48 58421 701-652-3136
Dr. Brian Duchscherer, supt. Fax 652-1243
www.carrington.k12.nd.us/
Carrington ES 300/PK-6
232 9th Ave N 58421 701-652-2739
Jenna Helseth, prin. Fax 652-2740

Carson, Grant, Pop. 292
Roosevelt SD 18 100/K-8
PO Box 197 58529 701-622-3263
Judy Zins, admin. Fax 622-3236
www.roosevelt.k12.nd.us
Roosevelt S 100/K-8
PO Box 197 58529 701-622-3263
Cody Miller-Kraft, prin. Fax 622-3236

Cartwright, McKenzie
Horse Creek SD 32 50/K-8
1812 Horse Creek Rd 58838 701-481-1373
Fax 481-1373
Horse Creek S 50/K-8
1812 Horse Creek Rd 58838 701-481-1373
Katie Tosch, prin. Fax 481-1373

Casselton, Cass, Pop. 2,310
Central Cass SD 17 800/K-12
802 5th St N 58012 701-347-5352
Morgan Forness, supt. Fax 347-5354
www.central-cass.k12.nd.us
Central Cass ES 400/K-5
802 5th St N 58012 701-347-5353
Christopher Bastian, prin. Fax 347-5354
Central Cass MS 200/6-8
802 5th St N 58012 701-347-5352
Lisa Narum, lead tchr. Fax 347-5354

Cavalier, Pembina, Pop. 1,278
Cavalier SD 6 400/K-12
PO Box 410 58220 701-265-8417
Jeff Manley, supt. Fax 265-8106
www.cavalierschool.org
Cavalier S 300/K-8
PO Box 410 58220 701-265-8417
Matt Ford, prin. Fax 265-8106

Center, Oliver, Pop. 569
Center-Stanton SD 1 200/K-12
PO Box 248 58530 701-794-8778
Tracy Peterson, supt. Fax 794-3659
www.center.k12.nd.us
Center S 100/K-6
PO Box 248 58530 701-794-8731
Kathleen Bullinger, prin. Fax 794-3659

Colfax, Richland, Pop. 121
Richland SD 44 300/K-12
PO Box 49 58018 701-372-3713
Tim Godfrey, supt. Fax 372-3718
www.richland.k12.nd.us
Other Schools – See Abercrombie

Cooperstown, Griggs, Pop. 983
Griggs County Central SD 18 200/K-12
1207 Foster Ave NE 58425 701-797-3114
Meghan Brown, supt. Fax 797-3130
www.griggs-co.k12.nd.us/
Griggs County Central ES 100/K-6
1207 Foster Ave NE 58425 701-797-3114
Audrey Faul, prin. Fax 797-3130

Crosby, Divide, Pop. 1,064
Divide County SD 1 400/PK-12
PO Box G 58730 701-965-6313
Fax 965-6004
www.divide-co.k12.nd.us
Divide County ES 200/PK-6
PO Box G 58730 701-965-6324
Tanja Brown, prin. Fax 965-6004

Crystal, Pembina, Pop. 137
Valley-Edinburg SD 118 200/K-12
PO Box 129 58222 701-657-2163
Mitch Jorgensen, supt. Fax 657-2150
www.edinburg.k12.nd.us
Valley-Edinburg MS 100/5-8
PO Box 129 58222 701-657-2163
Andrew Currie, prin. Fax 657-2150
Other Schools – See Hoople

Des Lacs, Ward, Pop. 201
United SD 7 600/PK-12
PO Box 117 58733 701-725-4334
Christopher Bachmeier, supt. Fax 725-4375
www.dbhs.united.k12.nd.us
Other Schools – See Burlington

Devils Lake, Ramsey, Pop. 6,910
Devils Lake SD 1 1,500/PK-12
1601 College Dr N 58301 701-662-7640
Scott Privratsky, supt. Fax 662-7646
www.dlschools.org/
Central MS 500/5-8
325 7th St NE 58301 701-662-7664
Dan Kaffar, prin. Fax 662-7649
Minnie H K Center 50/PK-K
210 College Dr S 58301 701-662-7670
Kimberly Krogfoss, prin. Fax 662-7677
Prairie View ES 200/1-4
200 12th Ave NE 58301 701-662-7626
Lynn Goodwill, prin. Fax 662-7629
Sweetwater ES 200/1-4
1304 2nd Ave NE 58301 701-662-7630
Dr. Debra Follman, prin. Fax 662-7637

St. Joseph ES 100/PK-6
824 10th Ave NE 58301 701-477-5016
Michelle Clouse, prin. Fax 477-5017

Dickinson, Stark, Pop. 17,565
Dickinson SD 1 3,100/PK-12
444 4th St W 58601 701-456-0002
Dr. Douglas Sullivan, supt. Fax 456-0035
www.dickinson.k12.nd.us
Dickinson MS 500/6-8
2675 21st St W 58601 701-456-0021
Dr. Marcus Lewton, prin. Fax 456-0044
ECC 50/PK-PK
107 3rd Ave SE 58601 701-227-3010
Dr. Julie Jahner, dir. Fax 225-1968
Heart River ES 300/K-5
720 7th St SW 58601 701-456-0012
Susan Cook, prin. Fax 456-0005
Jefferson ES 300/K-5
599 11th Ave W 58601 701-456-0013
Sara Streeter, prin. Fax 456-0025
Lincoln ES 400/K-5
102 10th St W 58601 701-456-0014
Tammy Praus, prin. Fax 456-0029
Prairie Rose ES 300/K-5
2785 10th Ave W 58601 701-456-0016
Sherry Libis, prin. Fax 456-0045
Roosevelt ES 300/K-5
230 3rd Ave E 58601 701-456-0015
Henry Mack, prin. Fax 456-0001

Hope Christian Academy 100/PK-12
2891 5th Ave W 58601 701-225-3919
Shane Bradley, prin. Fax 227-1464
Invitation Hill Adventist S K-8
10730 Highway 10 58601 701-783-2050
Trinity East ES 100/PK-6
515 3rd St E 58601 701-225-9463
JoLyn Tessier, prin. Fax 225-0474
Trinity North ES, 810 Empire Rd 58601 5-6
JoLyn Tessier, prin. 701-483-6081
Trinity West ES 200/PK-4
145 3rd Ave W 58601 701-225-8094
JoLyn Tessier, prin. Fax 225-8831

Drayton, Pembina, Pop. 819
Drayton SD 19 200/PK-12
108 S 5th St 58225 701-454-3324
Dean Ralston, supt. Fax 454-3485
www.drayton.k12.nd.us
Drayton ES 100/PK-6
108 S 5th St 58225 701-454-3324
Jennifer Olson, prin. Fax 454-3485

Dunseith, Rolette, Pop. 742
Dunseith SD 1 400/K-12
PO Box 789 58329 701-244-0480
David Sjol, supt. Fax 244-5129
www.dunseith.k12.nd.us/
Dunseith ES 200/K-6
PO Box 789 58329 701-244-5792
Rebecca Ward, prin. Fax 244-5183

Edgeley, LaMoure, Pop. 562
Edgeley SD 3 200/K-12
PO Box 37 58433 701-493-2292
Tyler Hanson, supt. Fax 493-2411
www.edgeley.k12.nd.us/
Edgeley ES 100/K-6
PO Box 37 58433 701-493-2292
Mary Beth Carlson, prin. Fax 493-2411
Willow Bank Colony S 50/K-8
PO Box 37 58433 701-493-2292
Mary Beth Carlson, prin. Fax 493-2411

Edmore, Ramsey, Pop. 179
Edmore SD 2 100/K-12
PO Box 188 58330 701-644-2281
Francis Schill, supt. Fax 644-2222
www.edmore.k12.nd.us
Edmore ES 50/K-8
PO Box 188 58330 701-644-2281
Diane Martinson, prin. Fax 644-2222

Elgin, Grant, Pop. 638
Elgin - New Leipzig SD 49 100/K-12
PO Box 70 58533 701-584-2374
Daniel Ludvigson, supt. Fax 584-3018
www.gcs.k12.nd.us
Elgin - New Leipzig ES 100/K-6
PO Box 70 58533 701-584-2374
Daniel Ludvigson, prin. Fax 584-3018

Ellendale, Dickey, Pop. 1,371
Ellendale SD 40 300/K-12
PO Box 400 58436 701-349-3232
Jeff Fastnacht, supt. Fax 349-3447
www.ellendale.k12.nd.us
Ellendale ES 100/K-6
PO Box 400 58436 701-349-3232
Dan Girard, prin. Fax 349-3447
Other Schools – See Fullerton

Emerado, Grand Forks, Pop. 397
Emerado SD 127 100/PK-8
PO Box 69 58228 701-594-5125
Sara Bilden, supt. Fax 594-8180
www.emeradok8.com
Emerado S 100/PK-8
PO Box 69 58228 701-594-5125
Sara Bilden, prin. Fax 594-8180

Enderlin, Ransom, Pop. 884
Enderlin Area SD 24 300/K-12
410 Bluff St 58027 701-437-2240
Tom Rettig, supt. Fax 437-2242
www.enderlin.k12.nd.us/
Enderlin Area ES 200/K-6
410 Bluff St 58027 701-437-2240
Brian Midthun, prin. Fax 437-2242

Fairmount, Richland, Pop. 360
Fairmount SD 18 100/K-12
PO Box 228 58030 701-474-5469
Brian Nelson, supt. Fax 474-5862
www.fairmount.k12.nd.us/
Fairmount ES 100/K-6
PO Box 228 58030 701-474-5469
Jay Townsend, prin. Fax 474-5862

Fargo, Cass, Pop. 103,464
Fargo SD 1 11,900/K-12
415 4th St N 58102 701-446-1000
Dr. Jeff Schatz, supt. Fax 446-1200
www.fargo.k12.nd.us
Barton ES 200/3-5
1417 6th St S 58103 701-446-4400
Rebecca Folden, prin. Fax 446-4499
Bennett ES 600/K-5
2000 58th Ave S 58104 701-446-4000
Sara Schafer, prin. Fax 446-4099
Centennial ES 600/K-5
4201 25th St S 58104 701-446-4300
Jeff Reznecheck, prin. Fax 446-4399
Clapp ES 500/K-5
3131 28th St S 58103 701-446-2900
Jennifer Schuldheisz, prin. Fax 446-2999
Discovery MS 900/6-8
1717 40th Ave S 58104 701-446-3300
Vincent Williams, prin. Fax 446-3599

Eagles ES 400/K-5
3502 University Dr S 58104 701-446-3900
Rebecca Campbell, admin. Fax 446-3999
Eielson MS 800/6-8
1601 13th Ave S 58103 701-446-1700
Brad Larson, prin. Fax 446-1799
Franklin MS 700/6-8
1420 8th St N 58102 701-446-3600
John Nelson, prin. Fax 446-3899
Hawthorne ES 200/K-2
555 8th Ave S 58103 701-446-4500
Rebecca Folden, prin. Fax 446-4599
Jefferson ES 300/K-5
1701 4th Ave S 58103 701-446-4700
Brad Franklin, prin. Fax 446-4799
Kennedy ES 700/K-5
4401 42nd St S 58104 701-446-4200
Karrie Rage, prin. Fax 446-4299
Lewis & Clark ES 600/K-5
1729 16th St S 58103 701-446-4800
Jason Cresap, prin. Fax 446-4899
Lincoln ES 500/K-5
2120 9th St S 58103 701-446-4900
Megan Kiser, prin. Fax 446-4999
Longfellow ES 400/K-5
20 29th Ave NE 58102 701-446-5000
Eric Henrickson, prin. Fax 446-5099
Madison ES 200/K-5
1040 29th St N 58102 701-446-5100
Bobby Olson, prin. Fax 446-5199
Mann ES 200/K-2
1025 3rd St N 58102 701-446-4600
Leandra Ostrom, prin. Fax 446-4699
McKinley ES 200/K-5
2930 8th St N 58102 701-446-5200
Cheryl Janssen, prin. Fax 446-5299
Roosevelt ES 200/3-5
1026 10th St N 58102 701-446-5300
Kim Colwell, prin. Fax 446-5399
Washington ES 300/K-5
1725 Broadway N 58102 701-446-5400
Cathy Selberg, prin. Fax 446-5499

West Fargo SD 6
Supt. — See West Fargo
Independence ES 200/1-5
3700 54th St S 58104 701-356-5890
Michael Shea, prin. Fax 356-5899
Osgood ES 500/PK-2
5550 44th Ave S 58104 701-356-2190
Kristi Toy, prin. Fax 356-2199

Dakota Montessori S 100/PK-6
1134 Westrac Dr S 58103 701-235-9184
Julia Jones, prin. Fax 235-6303
Grace Lutheran S 100/PK-8
1025 14th Ave S 58103 701-232-7747
John Hagge, prin. Fax 237-0618
Holy Spirit ES 200/PK-5
1441 8th St N 58102 701-232-4087
Jason Kotrba, prin. Fax 232-8240
Nativity ES 300/PK-5
1825 11th St S 58103 701-232-7461
Kimbra Amerman, prin. Fax 298-8981
Oak Grove Lutheran S 200/PK-5
2720 32nd Ave S 58103 701-893-3073
Josh Kading, prin. Fax 893-3076
Red River Adventist ES K-8
3000 Elm St N 58102 701-630-3183
Kimberly Clarke, prin.
Sullivan MS 200/6-8
5600 25th St S 58104 701-893-3200
Leon Knodel, prin. Fax 893-3277

Fessenden, Wells, Pop. 475
Fessenden-Bowdon SD 25 100/PK-12
PO Box 67 58438 701-547-3296
Nancy Bollingberg, supt.
www.fessenden-bowdon.org
Fessenden-Bowdon S 100/PK-8
PO Box 67 58438 701-547-3296
Warren Strand, prin.

Finley, Steele, Pop. 440
Finley-Sharon SD 19 100/K-12
PO Box 448 58230 701-524-2420
Jeff Larson, supt. Fax 524-2588
www.finleysharonschool.com
Finley-Sharon ES 50/K-6
PO Box 448 58230 701-524-2420
Jeff Larson, prin. Fax 524-2588

Flasher, Morton, Pop. 229
Flasher SD 39 200/K-12
PO Box 267 58535 701-597-3355
Judy Zins, supt. Fax 597-3781
www.flasher.k12.nd.us
Flasher ES 100/K-6
PO Box 267 58535 701-597-3355
Christina Reynolds, prin. Fax 597-3781

Forbes, Dickey, Pop. 53
Leola SD 44-2
Supt. — See Leola, SD
Spring Creek Colony S 50/K-8
36562 102nd St 58439 605-439-3477
Beverly Myer, prin. Fax 439-3206

Fordville, Walsh, Pop. 211
Fordville-Lankin SD 5 50/K-12
PO Box 127 58231 701-229-3297
Michael O'Brien, supt. Fax 229-3231
www.fordville-lankin.k12.nd.us/
Fordville Lankin S 50/K-6
PO Box 127 58231 701-229-3297
Darlene Christianson, prin. Fax 229-3231

Forman, Sargent, Pop. 501
Sargent Central SD 6 200/PK-12
575 5th St SW 58032 701-724-3205
Daniel Warcken, supt. Fax 724-3559
www.sargent.k12.nd.us
Sargent Central ES 100/PK-6
575 5th St SW 58032 701-724-3205
Terry Buringrud, prin. Fax 724-3559

Fort Ransom, Ransom, Pop. 77
Fort Ransom SD 6, 135 Mill Rd 58033 50/K-6
Steven Johnson, supt. 701-683-4106
www.ft-ransom.k12.nd.us/?file=kop1.php
Fort Ransom ES, 135 Mill Rd 58033 50/K-6
Elinor Meckle, prin. 701-683-4108

Fort Yates, Sioux, Pop. 181
Fort Yates SD 4 200/6-8
9189 Highway 24 58538 701-854-2142
Robyn Baker, admin. Fax 854-7488
www.fort-yates.k12.nd.us
Fort Yates MS 200/6-8
9189 Highway 24 58538 701-854-3819
Lisa Taken Alive, prin. Fax 854-7467

St. Bernards Mission S 100/1-6
PO Box 394 58538 701-854-7413
Gayleen Yellow Fat, prin. Fax 854-3474

Fullerton, Dickey, Pop. 54
Ellendale SD 40
Supt. — See Ellendale
Maple River S 50/K-8
9262 93rd Ave SE 58441 701-349-3232
Dan Girard, prin. Fax 349-3447

Gackle, Logan, Pop. 308
Gackle-Streeter SD 56 100/K-12
PO Box 375 58442 701-485-3692
David Larson, supt. Fax 485-3620
www.gacklestreeter.k12.nd.us/
Gackle-Streeter ES 100/K-6
PO Box 375 58442 701-485-3692
Mark Berg, prin. Fax 485-3620

Garrison, McLean, Pop. 1,428
Garrison SD 51 400/PK-12
PO Box 249 58540 701-463-2818
Nicholas Klemisch, supt. Fax 463-2067
www.garrison.k12.nd.us/
Callies ES 200/PK-6
PO Box 369 58540 701-463-2213
Michelle Fuller, prin. Fax 463-2214

Glenburn, Renville, Pop. 368
Glenburn SD 26 300/PK-12
PO Box 138 58740 701-362-7426
Jerry Erdahl, supt. Fax 362-7349
www.glenburn.k12.nd.us/
Glenburn ES 100/PK-6
PO Box 138 58740 701-362-7426
Christopher Doane, prin. Fax 362-7349

Glen Ullin, Morton, Pop. 794
Glen Ullin SD 48 200/K-12
PO Box 548 58631 701-348-3590
John Barry, supt. Fax 348-3084
www.glen-ullin.k12.nd.us
Glen Ullin ES 100/K-8
PO Box 548 58631 701-348-3590
John Barry, prin. Fax 348-3084

Golva, Golden Valley, Pop. 61
Lone Tree SD 6 50/K-8
PO Box 170 58632 701-872-3674
Janine Olson, admin. Fax 872-3004
www.golva.k12.nd.us
Golva S 50/K-8
PO Box 170 58632 701-872-3674
Janine Olson, prin. Fax 872-3004

Goodrich, Sheridan, Pop. 98
Goodrich SD 16 50/K-12
PO Box 159 58444 701-884-2469
Rodney Scherbenske, supt. Fax 884-2496
Goodrich ES 50/K-6
PO Box 159 58444 701-884-2469
Rodney Scherbenske, prin. Fax 884-2496

Grafton, Walsh, Pop. 4,231
Grafton SD 3 900/K-12
1548 School Rd 58237 701-352-1930
Darren Albrecht, supt. Fax 352-1943
www.grafton.k12.nd.us
Century ES 400/K-4
1542 School Rd 58237 701-352-1739
Stephanie Nilson, prin. Fax 352-0163
Grafton Central MS 300/5-8
1556 School Rd 58237 701-352-1469
Mike Kaiser, prin. Fax 352-1120

Grand Forks, Grand Forks, Pop. 51,662
Grand Forks SD 1 6,900/K-12
PO Box 6000 58206 701-746-2200
Dr. Larry P. Nybladh, supt. Fax 772-7739
www.gfschools.org
Century ES 600/K-5
3351 17th Ave S 58201 701-746-2440
Dr. David Saxberg, prin. Fax 787-4079
Discovery ES K-5
3300 43rd Ave S 58201 701-787-4359
Allison Parkinson, prin. Fax 787-5053
Franklin ES 300/K-5
1016 S 20th St 58201 701-746-2250
Leslie Bjelde, prin. Fax 746-2255
Kelly ES 500/K-5
3000 Cherry St 58201 701-746-2265
Mike LaMoine, prin. Fax 746-2266
Lake Agassiz ES 400/K-5
605 Stanford Rd 58203 701-746-2275
Amy Bartsch, prin. Fax 746-2274
Lewis & Clark ES 200/K-5
1100 13th Ave S 58201 701-746-2285
Kelli Tannahill, prin. Fax 746-2288
Phoenix ES 300/K-5
351 4th Ave S 58201 701-746-2240
Kevin Ohnstad, prin. Fax 746-2244
Schroeder MS 500/6-8
800 32nd Ave S 58201 701-746-2330
Catherine Gillach, prin. Fax 746-2332
South MS 600/6-8
1999 47th Ave S 58201 701-746-2345
Nancy Dutot, prin. Fax 746-2355
Valley MS 400/6-8
2100 5th Ave N 58203 701-746-2360
Todd Selk, prin. Fax 746-2363
Viking ES 300/K-5
809 22nd Ave S 58201 701-746-2300
Jolyn Bergstrom, prin. Fax 746-2303
West ES 200/K-5
615 N 25th St 58203 701-746-2310
Angie Jonasson, prin. Fax 746-2454
Wilder ES 100/K-5
1009 N 3rd St 58203 701-746-2320
Leslie Wiegandt, prin. Fax 746-2322
Winship ES 200/K-5
1412 5th Ave N 58203 701-746-2325
Travis Thorvilson, prin. Fax 746-2374
Other Schools – See Grand Forks AFB

Holy Family - St. Mary ES 100/PK-6
1001 17th Ave S 58201 701-775-9886
Ken Schill, prin. Fax 775-0221
Prairie Voyager Adventist S 50/K-8
3610 Cherry St 58201 701-775-5936
Leanne Erickson, lead tchr.
St. Michael ES 100/PK-5
504 5th Ave N 58203 701-772-1822
Sara Dudley, prin. Fax 772-0211

Grand Forks AFB, Grand Forks, Pop. 2,246
Grand Forks SD 1
Supt. — See Grand Forks
Twining S 100/K-8
1422 Louisiana St 58204 701-787-5100
Shari Bilden, prin. Fax 787-5143

Granville, McHenry, Pop. 241
TGU SD 60
Supt. — See Towner
TGU Granville ES 100/PK-6
210 6th St SW 58741 701-728-6641
Tonya Hunskor, prin. Fax 728-6386

Grenora, Williams, Pop. 241
Grenora SD 99 200/K-12
PO Box 38 58845 701-694-2711
Troy Walters, supt. Fax 694-2717
www.grenora.k12.nd.us/
Grenora ES 100/K-6
PO Box 38 58845 701-694-2711
Joseph Paine, prin. Fax 694-2717

Gwinner, Sargent, Pop. 749
North Sargent SD 3 200/K-12
PO Box 289 58040 701-678-2492
Randall Cale, supt. Fax 678-2311
www.northsargent.k12.nd.us
North Sargent ES 100/K-6
PO Box 289 58040 701-678-2492
Michael Sorlie, prin. Fax 678-2311

Hague, Emmons, Pop. 71
Bakker SD 10 50/PK-8
880 96th St SE 58542 701-336-7284
Fax 336-4600
Bakker S 50/PK-8
880 96th St SE 58542 701-336-7284
Joy Dykema, prin. Fax 336-4600

Halliday, Dunn, Pop. 185
Halliday SD 19 50/K-12
PO Box 188 58636 701-938-4391
Anthony Duletski, supt. Fax 938-4373
www.halliday.k12.nd.us
Halliday S 50/K-12
PO Box 188 58636 701-938-4391
Anthony Duletski, prin. Fax 938-4373

Hankinson, Richland, Pop. 903
Hankinson SD 8 300/K-12
PO Box 220 58041 701-242-7516
Chad Benson, supt. Fax 242-7434
www.hankinson.k12.nd.us
Hankinson ES 100/K-6
PO Box 220 58041 701-242-8336
Anne Biewer, prin. Fax 242-7434

Harvey, Wells, Pop. 1,771
Harvey SD 38 300/K-12
200 North St E 58341 701-324-2267
Daniel Stutlien, supt. Fax 324-2424
www.harvey.k12.nd.us/
Hanson ES 200/K-6
811 Burke Ave 58341 701-324-2265
Laurie Pranke, prin. Fax 324-4414

Harwood, Cass, Pop. 715
West Fargo SD 6
Supt. — See West Fargo
Harwood ES 100/K-5
110 Freedland Dr 58042 701-356-2040
Jerry Standifer, prin. Fax 356-2049

Hatton, Traill, Pop. 763
Hatton Eielson SD 7 200/K-12
PO Box 200 58240 701-543-3455
Kevin Rogers, supt. Fax 543-3459
www.hattonk12.com
Hatton Eielson ES 100/K-6
PO Box 200 58240 701-543-3455
Lucas Soine, prin. Fax 543-3459

Hazelton, Emmons, Pop. 234
Hazelton-Moffit-Braddock SD 6 100/K-12
PO Box 209 58544 701-782-6231
Tracy Hanzal, supt. Fax 782-6245
www.hmb.k12.nd.us
Hazelton-Moffit-Braddock ES 100/K-6
PO Box 209 58544 701-782-4226
Tad Larson, prin. Fax 782-4263

Hazen, Mercer, Pop. 2,396
Hazen SD 3 600/PK-12
PO Box 487 58545 701-748-2345
Ken Miller, supt. Fax 748-2342
www.hazen.k12.nd.us
Hazen ES 300/PK-6
PO Box 487 58545 701-748-6120
Trevor Sinclair, prin. Fax 748-6647
Hazen JHS 100/7-8
PO Box 487 58545 701-748-6649
Ed Boger, prin. Fax 748-6650

Hebron, Morton, Pop. 732
Hebron SD 13 200/K-12
PO Box Q 58638 701-878-4442
Myron Schaff, supt. Fax 878-4345
www.hebron.k12.nd.us/
Hebron ES 100/K-6
PO Box Q 58638 701-878-4442
Jenifer Hosman, prin. Fax 878-4345

Hettinger, Adams, Pop. 1,214
Hettinger SD 13 300/PK-12
PO Box 1188 58639 701-567-4502
Ryan Moser, supt. Fax 567-5094
www.hettinger.k12.nd.us
Hettinger ES 200/PK-6
PO Box 1188 58639 701-567-4501
Ryan Moser, prin. Fax 567-5094

Hillsboro, Traill, Pop. 1,587
Hillsboro SD 9 400/PK-12
PO Box 579 58045 701-636-4360
Paula Suda, supt. Fax 636-4362
www.hillsborok12.com
Hillsboro ES 200/PK-6
PO Box 579 58045 701-636-4711
Jon Dryburgh, prin. Fax 636-4712

Hoople, Walsh, Pop. 242
Valley-Edinburg SD 118
Supt. — See Crystal
Valley-Edinburg ES 100/K-4
PO Box 150 58243 701-894-6226
Andrew Currie, prin. Fax 894-6146

Horace, Cass, Pop. 2,418
West Fargo SD 6
Supt. — See West Fargo
Horace ES 200/K-5
110 3rd Ave N 58047 701-356-2080
Carol Zent, prin. Fax 356-2089

Hunter, Cass, Pop. 255
Northern Cass SD 97 500/PK-12
16021 18th St SE 58048 701-874-2322
Dr. Cory Steiner, supt. Fax 874-2422
www.northerncass.k12.nd.us
Northern Cass ES 300/PK-6
16021 18th St SE 58048 701-874-2322
Crysta Wagner, prin. Fax 874-2422

Inkster, Grand Forks, Pop. 47
Midway SD 128 200/PK-12
3202 33rd Ave NE, 701-869-2432
Dr. Roger Abbe Ed.D., supt. Fax 869-2688
www.midwayk12.org
Midway S 100/PK-8
3202 33rd Ave NE, 701-869-2432
Kristine Dale, prin. Fax 869-2688

Jamestown, Stutsman, Pop. 15,252
Jamestown SD 1 2,100/PK-12
PO Box 269 58402 701-252-1950
Robert Lech, supt. Fax 251-2011
www.jamestown.k12.nd.us
Gussner ES 300/K-5
PO Box 269 58402 701-252-3846
Luke Anderson, prin. Fax 952-3845
Jamestown MS 500/6-8
PO Box 269 58402 701-252-0317
Ryan Harty, prin. Fax 252-3310
L'Amour ES 100/K-5
PO Box 269 58402 701-251-2102
Vikki Coombs, prin. Fax 952-2734
Lincoln ES 200/K-5
PO Box 269 58402 701-252-0867
Sherry Schmidt, prin. Fax 952-0868
Roosevelt ES 200/K-5
PO Box 269 58402 701-252-1679
Pat Smith, prin. Fax 251-2011
Washington ES 100/PK-5
PO Box 269 58402 701-252-0468
Phyllis Clemens, prin. Fax 251-2011

Hillcrest SDA S 50/K-8
116 15th Ave NE 58401 701-252-5409
RaeLea Frishman, lead tchr.
St. Johns Academy 200/PK-6
215 5th St SE 58401 701-252-3397
Lawrie Paulson, prin. Fax 952-2434

Kenmare, Ward, Pop. 1,084
Kenmare SD 28 300/K-12
PO Box 667 58746 701-385-4996
Duane Mueller, supt. Fax 385-4390
www.kenmare.k12.nd.us/
Kenmare ES 200/K-6
PO Box 667 58746 701-385-4688
Janis Gerding, prin. Fax 385-4390

Kensal, Stutsman, Pop. 163
Kensal SD 19 50/K-6
803 1st Ave 58455 701-435-2484
Les Dale, supt. Fax 435-2486
www.kensalschool.org
Kensal ES 50/K-6
803 1st Ave 58455 701-435-2484
Matt Lokemoen, prin. Fax 435-2486

Killdeer, Dunn, Pop. 734
Killdeer SD 16 400/PK-12
PO Box 579 58640 701-764-5877
Gary Wilz, supt. Fax 764-5648
www.killdeer.k12.nd.us
Killdeer ES 200/PK-6
PO Box 579 58640 701-764-5877
Andrew Cook, prin. Fax 764-5648

Kindred, Cass, Pop. 678
Kindred SD 2 700/K-12
255 Dakota St 58051 701-428-3177
Steven Hall, supt. Fax 428-3149
www.kindred.k12.nd.us/
Kindred ES 400/K-6
55 1st Ave S 58051 701-428-3388
Nancy Kochmann, prin. Fax 428-3736

Kulm, LaMoure, Pop. 352
Kulm SD 7 100/PK-12
PO Box G 58456 701-647-2303
Tami Kramlich, supt. Fax 647-2304
www.kulmschool.com
Kulm ES 100/PK-6
PO Box G 58456 701-647-2303
Amy Johnson, prin. Fax 647-2304

Lakota, Nelson, Pop. 665
Lakota SD 66 200/K-12
PO Box 388 58344 701-247-2992
Joseph Harder, supt. Fax 247-2910
www.lakota.k12.nd.us
Lakota ES 100/K-6
PO Box 388 58344 701-247-2955
Alyson Parsley, prin. Fax 247-2995

LaMoure, LaMoure, Pop. 884
La Moure SD 8 300/K-12
PO Box 656 58458 701-883-5396
Andrew DelaBarre, supt. Fax 883-5144
www.lamoure.k12.nd.us/
La Moure Colony S 50/K-8
PO Box 656 58458 701-883-5397
Denise Musland, prin. Fax 883-5144
La Moure ES 200/K-6
PO Box 656 58458 701-883-5397
Denise Musland, prin. Fax 883-5144

Langdon, Cavalier, Pop. 1,855
Langdon Area SD 23 400/PK-12
715 14th Ave 58249 701-256-5291
Daren Christianson, supt. Fax 256-2606
www.langdon.k12.nd.us
Langdon Area ES 200/PK-6
721 11th Ave 58249 701-256-3270
Todd Hetler, prin. Fax 256-3291

St. Alphonsus ES 100/PK-8
209 10th Ave 58249 701-256-2354
Derek Simonsen, prin. Fax 256-2358

Larimore, Grand Forks, Pop. 1,320
Larimore SD 44 400/PK-12
PO Box 769 58251 701-343-2366
Dr. Steve Swiontek, supt. Fax 343-2908
www.larimorek12.org
Larimore ES 200/PK-6
PO Box 769 58251 701-343-2249
Kylie Swanson, prin. Fax 343-2463

Leeds, Benson, Pop. 425
Leeds SD 6 200/PK-12
PO Box 189 58346 701-466-2461
Robert Bubach M.Ed., supt. Fax 466-2422
leedsps.ss8.sharpschool.com
Leeds ES 100/PK-8
PO Box 189 58346 701-466-2461
Roger Jensen M.Ed., prin. Fax 466-2422

Lidgerwood, Richland, Pop. 649
Lidgerwood SD 28 200/PK-12
PO Box 468 58053 701-538-7341
Mark Weston, supt. Fax 538-4483
www.lidgerwoodk12.com
Lidgerwood ES 100/PK-6
PO Box 468 58053 701-538-7341
Doug Margerum, prin. Fax 538-4483

Lignite, Burke, Pop. 154
Burke Central SD 36 100/K-12
PO Box 91 58752 701-933-2821
Sherry Lalum, supt. Fax 933-2823
www.burkecentral.k12.nd.us
Burke Central ES 100/K-6
PO Box 91 58752 701-933-2821
John Bruce, prin. Fax 933-2823

Lincoln, Burleigh, Pop. 2,357
Bismarck SD 1
Supt. — See Bismarck
Lincoln ES 400/K-5
3320 McCurry Way 58504 701-323-4310
Shelly Swanson, prin. Fax 323-4315

Linton, Emmons, Pop. 1,084
Linton SD 36 300/PK-12
PO Box 970 58552 701-254-4717
Paul Keeney, supt. Fax 254-4313
www.linton.k12.nd.us
Linton ES 200/PK-8
PO Box 970 58552 701-254-4173
Brian Flyberg, prin. Fax 254-0159

Lisbon, Ransom, Pop. 2,132
Lisbon SD 19 600/K-12
PO Box 593 58054 701-683-4106
Steven Johnson, supt. Fax 683-4414
www.lisbon.k12.nd.us/
Lisbon ES 200/K-4
PO Box 593 58054 701-683-4107
Elinor Meckle, prin. Fax 683-4111
Lisbon MS 200/5-8
PO Box 593 58054 701-683-4108
Jared Hoff, prin. Fax 683-4111

Litchville, Barnes, Pop. 166
Litchville-Marion SD 46
Supt. — See Marion
Litchville-Marion ES 100/PK-6
304 6th Ave 58461 701-762-4234
Renee Bowen, prin. Fax 762-4233

Mc Clusky, Sheridan, Pop. 368
McClusky SD 19 100/K-12
PO Box 499 58463 701-363-2470
Dale Ekstrom, supt. Fax 363-2239
www.mcclusky.k12.nd.us
McClusky ES 50/K-6
PO Box 499 58463 701-363-2647
Sarah Beck, prin. Fax 363-2239

Mc Ville, Nelson, Pop. 344
Dakota Prairie SD 1
Supt. — See Petersburg
Dakota Prairie ES 200/K-6
PO Box 337 58254 701-322-4771
Jackie Bye, prin. Fax 322-5128

Maddock, Benson, Pop. 380
Maddock SD 9 200/K-12
PO Box 398 58348 701-438-2531
Robert Thom, supt. Fax 438-2620
maddock-school.com
Maddock S 100/K-8
PO Box 398 58348 701-438-2531
Jennifer Sundby, prin. Fax 438-2620

Mandan, Morton, Pop. 18,009
Mandan SD 1 3,500/K-12
901 Division St NW 58554 701-751-6500
Dr. Mike Bitz, supt. Fax 751-6674
www.mandan.k12.nd.us
Custer ES 100/K-5
205 8th Ave NE 58554 701-751-6503
Jean Schafer, prin. Fax 751-6677
Fort Lincoln ES 500/K-5
2007 8th Ave SE 58554 701-751-6504
Pat Beckman, prin. Fax 751-6679
Lewis & Clark ES 500/K-5
600 14th St NW 58554 701-751-6505
Susie Atkinson, prin. Fax 751-6681
Mandan MS 800/6-8
2901 12th Ave NW 58554 701-751-6502
Ryan Leingang, prin. Fax 751-6682
Red Trail ES K-5
4801 37th Ave NW 58554 701-751-6508
Dave Steckler, admin. Fax 751-6693
Roosevelt ES 300/K-5
305 10th Ave NW 58554 701-751-6507
Wade Meschke, prin. Fax 751-6680
Stark ES 300/K-5
405 8th Ave SW 58554 701-751-6506
Chad Radke, prin. Fax 751-6678

Marmot SD 100/K-12
701 16th Ave SW 58554 701-328-6707
Penny Veit-Hetletved, supt. Fax 328-6651
Marmot ES, 701 16th Ave SW 58554 50/K-8
Michelle Pfaff, prin. 701-667-1445

Sweet Briar SD 17 50/K-8
4060 County Road 83 58554 701-663-7453
Sweet Briar S 50/K-8
4060 County Road 83 58554 701-663-7453
Sherilyn Johnson, prin.

Christ the King S 100/PK-8
505 10th Ave NW 58554 701-663-6200
Derrick Nagel, prin. Fax 667-1730
St. Joseph S 100/PK-6
410 Collins Ave 58554 701-663-9563
Valerie Vogel, prin. Fax 663-0183

Mandaree, McKenzie, Pop. 592
Mandaree SD 36 200/PK-12
PO Box 488 58757 701-759-3311
Ann Longie, supt. Fax 759-3112
www.mandaree.k12.nd.us
Mandaree ES 100/PK-8
PO Box 488 58757 701-759-3311
Dr. Alfred Taylor, prin. Fax 759-3112

Manvel, Grand Forks, Pop. 358
Manvel SD 125 100/PK-8
801 Oldham Ave 58256 701-696-2212
Mark Mindt, supt. Fax 696-8217
www.manvel.k12.nd.us
Manvel S 100/PK-8
801 Oldham Ave 58256 701-696-2212
Melissa Hiltner, prin. Fax 696-8217

Mapleton, Cass, Pop. 759
Mapleton SD 7 100/PK-6
PO Box 39 58059 701-282-3833
Fax 282-3855
www.mapleton.k12.nd.us
Mapleton ES 100/PK-6
PO Box 39 58059 701-282-3833
Tim Jacobson, prin. Fax 282-3855

Marion, LaMoure, Pop. 131
Litchville-Marion SD 46 100/PK-12
PO Box 159 58466 701-669-2262
Mitch Carlson, supt. Fax 669-2316
www.litchville-marion.k12.nd.us/
Other Schools – See Litchville

Marmarth, Slope, Pop. 135
Marmarth SD 12 50/PK-8
PO Box 70 58643 701-279-5521
Jackie Kathrein, supt. Fax 279-5521
Marmarth S 50/PK-8
PO Box 70 58643 701-279-5521
Joaine Heggem, prin. Fax 279-5521

Max, McLean, Pop. 324
Max SD 50 200/K-12
PO Box 297 58759 701-679-2685
Pat Windish, supt. Fax 679-2245
www.max.k12.nd.us/
Max ES 100/K-6
PO Box 297 58759 701-679-2685
Robert Randel, prin. Fax 679-2245

Mayville, Traill, Pop. 1,819
May-Port CG SD 14 500/K-12
900 Main St W 58257 701-788-2281
Michael Bradner, supt. Fax 788-2959
www.mayportcg.com
Boe ES 200/K-5
20 2nd St NW 58257 701-788-2116
Jeffrey Houdek, prin. Fax 788-9115
Mayville-Portland CG MS 100/6-8
900 Main St W 58257 701-788-2281
Scott Ulland, prin. Fax 788-2959

Medina, Stutsman, Pop. 298
Medina SD 3 200/PK-12
PO Box 547 58467 701-486-3121
Brian Christopherson, supt. Fax 486-3138
www.medina.k12.nd.us/
Medina ES 100/PK-6
PO Box 547 58467 701-486-3121
Damon Bosche, prin. Fax 486-3138

Medora, Billings, Pop. 111
Billings County SD 1 100/PK-8
PO Box 307 58645 701-623-4363
Fax 623-4941
www.billingscounty.k12.nd.us
Demores S 50/PK-8
PO Box 307 58645 701-623-4868
Shae Peplinski, prin. Fax 623-4941
Other Schools – See Belfield

Menoken, Burleigh, Pop. 70
Menoken SD 33 50/PK-8
412 Bismarck St N 58558 701-673-3175
Fax 673-3075
www.menoken.k12.nd.us
Menoken S 50/PK-8
412 Bismarck St N 58558 701-673-3175
Amanda Zabel, prin. Fax 673-3075

Milnor, Sargent, Pop. 648
Milnor SD 2 200/K-12
PO Box 369 58060 701-427-5237
Chris Larson M.Ed., supt. Fax 427-5304
www.milnor.k12.nd.us/
Milnor ES 100/K-6
PO Box 369 58060 701-427-5237
Lyndsy Lynch, prin. Fax 427-5304
Sundale Colony S 50/K-12
PO Box 369 58060 701-427-5237
Lyndsy Lynch, prin. Fax 427-5304

Minnewaukan, Benson, Pop. 217
Minnewaukan SD 5 200/PK-12
4675 Highway 281 58351 701-473-5306
Jean Callahan, supt. Fax 473-5420
www.minnewaukan.k12.nd.us
Minnewaukan S 200/PK-12
4675 Highway 281 58351 701-473-5306
Jean Callahan, admin. Fax 473-5420

Minot, Ward, Pop. 39,893
Minot SD 1 7,500/PK-12
215 2nd St SE 58701 701-857-4400
Dr. Mark Vollmer, supt. Fax 857-4432
www.minot.k12.nd.us/
Bel Air ES 400/K-5
501 25th St NW 58703 701-857-4590
Corey Thorson, prin. Fax 857-8762
Bell ES 100/K-6
5901 Highway 52 S 58701 701-420-1880
Karen Gullicks, prin. Fax 838-7048
Edison ES 400/K-5
701 17th Ave SW 58701 701-857-4595
Dale Roed, prin. Fax 857-8752
Hill MS 800/6-8
1000 6th St SW 58701 701-857-4477
Michael Arlien, prin. Fax 857-4479
Hoeven ES K-5
3400 13th St SE 58701 701-418-1600
Joy Walker, prin. Fax 418-1669
Lewis and Clark ES 400/PK-5
2215 8th St NW 58703 701-857-4665
Patrick Slotsve, prin. Fax 857-8757
Longfellow ES 400/K-5
600 16th St NW 58703 701-857-4610
Jenn Arlien, prin. Fax 857-8755
McKinley ES 100/PK-5
5 5th Ave NE 58703 701-857-4615
Karen Gullicks, prin. Fax 857-8756
Perkett ES 300/PK-5
2000 5th Ave SW 58701 701-857-4680
Renae Rudolph, prin. Fax 857-8758
Ramstad MS 600/6-8
1215 36th Ave NW 58703 701-857-4466
Bryn Iverson, prin. Fax 857-4464
Roosevelt ES 100/K-5
715 8th St NE 58703 701-857-4685
Todd Kaylor, prin. Fax 857-8759
Sunnyside ES 300/K-5
1000 5th Ave SE 58701 701-857-4690
Cynthia Cook, prin. Fax 857-8760
Washington ES 500/K-5
600 17th Ave SE 58701 701-857-4695
Kendo Carlson, prin. Fax 857-8761
Other Schools – See Minot AFB

Nedrose SD 4 200/K-12
6900 Highway 2 E 58701 701-838-5552
Charles Miller, admin. Fax 852-6971
www.tinyurl.com/nedrose
Nedrose ES 200/K-5
6900 Highway 2 E 58701 701-838-5552
Charles Miller, admin. Fax 852-6971

South Prairie SD 70 200/K-8
100 177th Ave SW 58701 701-722-3537
Darwin Routledge, supt. Fax 722-3280
www.south-prairie.k12.nd.us
South Prairie S 200/K-8
100 177th Ave SW 58701 701-722-3537
Delwyn Groninger, admin. Fax 722-3280

Bishop Ryan S 400/PK-12
316 11th Ave NW 58703 701-852-4004
Chase Lee, prin. Fax 839-4651
Our Redeemer's Christian S 300/PK-12
700 16th Ave SE 58701 701-839-0772
Charles Strand, admin.

Minot AFB, Ward, Pop. 5,179
Minot SD 1
Supt. — See Minot
Dakota ES 400/PK-6
101 Eagle Way 58704 701-727-3310
Kathryn Lenertz, prin. Fax 727-3318
Memorial MS 100/7-8
1 Rocket Rd 58704 701-727-3300
Ed Sehn, prin. Fax 727-3303
North Plains ES 400/PK-6
101 C St 58704 701-727-3320
Ned Strand, prin. Fax 727-3328

Minto, Walsh, Pop. 603
Minto SD 20 200/PK-12
200 4th St 58261 701-248-3479
Linda Lutovsky, supt. Fax 248-3001
sites.google.com/mintoschools.com/website/home
Minto ES 100/PK-6
200 4th St 58261 701-248-3479
Linda Lutovsky, prin. Fax 248-3001

Mohall, Renville, Pop. 775
Mohall-Lansford-Sherwood SD 1 300/K-12
PO Box 187 58761 701-756-6660
Robby Voigt, supt. Fax 756-6549
www.mls.k12.nd.us
Mohall ES 100/K-6
PO Box 187 58761 701-756-6660
Janet Asheim, prin. Fax 756-6549

Montpelier, Stutsman, Pop. 87
Montpelier SD 14 100/PK-12
214 7th Ave 58472 701-489-3348
Jerry Waagen, supt. Fax 489-3349
www.montpelier.k12.nd.us
Montpelier ES 50/PK-6
214 7th Ave 58472 701-489-3348
Jerry Waagen, admin. Fax 489-3349

Mott, Hettinger, Pop. 709
Mott-Regent SD 1 200/K-12
205 Dakota Ave 58646 701-824-2795
Dr. Viola Lafontaine Ed.D., supt. Fax 824-2249
mott.nd.schoolwebpages.com
Mott / Regent ES 100/K-6
205 Dakota Ave 58646 701-824-2247
Deb Bohn, prin. Fax 824-2249

Munich, Cavalier, Pop. 209
Munich SD 19 100/PK-12
PO Box 39 58352 701-682-5321
Gerald Krenzke, supt. Fax 682-5323
www.munich.k12.nd.us
Munich ES 100/PK-8
PO Box 39 58352 701-682-5321
Jean Klein, prin. Fax 682-5323

Napoleon, Logan, Pop. 791
Napoleon SD 2 300/K-12
PO Box 69 58561 701-754-2244
Richard Bjerklie, supt. Fax 754-2233
www.napoleon.k12.nd.us/
Napoleon ES 100/K-6
PO Box 69 58561 701-754-2244
Cindy Weigel, prin. Fax 754-2233

Newburg, Bottineau, Pop. 110
Newburg - United SD 54 100/PK-12
PO Box 427 58762 701-272-6151
Jason Kersten, supt. Fax 272-6117
www.newburg.k12.nd.us/
Newburg United ES 50/PK-6
PO Box 427 58762 701-272-6151
Bob Beaudrie, prin. Fax 272-6117

New England, Hettinger, Pop. 588
New England SD 9 200/PK-12
PO Box 307 58647 701-579-4160
Kelly Koppinger, supt. Fax 579-4462
www.new-england.k12.nd.us
New England ES 100/PK-6
PO Box 307 58647 701-579-4160
Kelly Koppinger, prin. Fax 579-4462

New Rockford, Eddy, Pop. 1,375
New Rockford-Sheyenne SD 2 300/K-12
437 1st Ave N 58356 701-947-5036
Jill Louters, supt. Fax 947-2195
www.newrockford-sheyenne.k12.nd.us
New Rockford-Sheyenne ES 200/K-6
437 1st Ave N 58356 701-947-5036
Natalie Becker, prin. Fax 947-2195

New Salem, Morton, Pop. 936
New Salem-Almont SD 49 300/PK-12
PO Box 378 58563 701-843-7610
Andrew Jordan, supt. Fax 843-7011
www.newsalem.k12.nd.us/
Prairie View ES 200/PK-6
PO Box 29 58563 701-843-7823
Haley Haugen, prin. Fax 843-8493

New Town, Mountrail, Pop. 1,853
New Town SD 1 700/K-12
PO Box 700 58763 701-627-3650
Marc Bluestone, supt. Fax 627-3689
www.new-town.k12.nd.us
Loe ES 400/K-5
PO Box 700 58763 701-627-3718
Rick Lindblad, prin. Fax 627-4100
New Town MS 200/6-8
PO Box 700 58763 701-627-3660
Kara Four Bear, prin. Fax 627-3689

Northwood, Grand Forks, Pop. 931
Northwood SD 129 200/K-12
420 Trojan Rd 58267 701-587-5221
Keith Arneson, supt. Fax 587-5423
www.northwoodk12.com
Northwood ES 100/K-6
420 Trojan Rd 58267 701-587-5221
Cydnee Strand, prin. Fax 587-5423

Oakes, Dickey, Pop. 1,836
Oakes SD 41 500/PK-12
804 Main Ave 58474 701-742-3234
Kraig Steinhoff, supt. Fax 742-2812
www.oakes.k12.nd.us
Oakes ES 300/PK-6
804 Main Ave 58474 701-742-3204
Anna Sell, prin. Fax 742-2812

Oberon, Benson, Pop. 99
Oberon SD 16 100/K-6
PO Box 2 58357 701-798-2231
Dr. Lane Azure, admin. Fax 798-2091
Oberon ES 100/K-6
PO Box 2 58357 701-798-2231
Dr. Lane Azure, prin. Fax 798-2091

Oriska, Barnes, Pop. 117
Maple Valley SD 4
Supt. — See Tower City
Oriska ES 50/4-6
PO Box 337 58063 701-845-2846
Jayson Kocka, prin. Fax 845-5830

Page, Cass, Pop. 230
Page SD 80 100/PK-6
PO Box 26 58064 701-668-2520
Dr. Hy Schlieve, supt. Fax 668-2292
Page ES 100/PK-6
PO Box 26 58064 701-668-2520
Heidi Kingston, prin. Fax 668-2292

Park River, Walsh, Pop. 1,393
Park River Area SD 8 300/K-12
PO Box 240 58270 701-284-7164
Kirk Ham, supt. Fax 284-7936
www.parkriver.k12.nd.us/
Park River ES 200/K-6
PO Box 240 58270 701-284-6550
Brenda Nilson, prin. Fax 284-7936

Parshall, Mountrail, Pop. 852
Parshall SD 3 300/PK-12
PO Box 158 58770 701-862-3129
Beth Schwarz, supt. Fax 862-3801
www.parshall.k12.nd.us
Parshall ES 200/PK-6
PO Box 69 58770 701-862-3417
Anthony Esquibel, prin. Fax 862-3419

Pembina, Pembina, Pop. 576
North Border SD 100
Supt. — See Walhalla
North Border Pembina ES 50/PK-8
155 S 3rd St 58271 701-825-6261
Justine Gruenberg, prin. Fax 825-6645

Petersburg, Nelson, Pop. 192
Dakota Prairie SD 1 300/K-12
PO Box 37 58272 701-345-8233
Jay Slade, supt. Fax 345-8251
www.dakotaprairiek12nd.org
Other Schools – See Mc Ville

Pingree, Stutsman, Pop. 59
Pingree-Buchanan SD 10 100/K-12
111 Lincoln Ave 58476 701-252-5563
Denise Harrington, supt. Fax 252-2245
www.pingree.k12.nd.us/
Other Schools – See Buchanan

Plaza, Mountrail, Pop. 170
Lewis and Clark SD 161
Supt. — See Berthold
North Shore Plaza S 100/PK-12
PO Box 38 58771 701-497-3734
Todd Lee, prin. Fax 497-3401

Powers Lake, Burke, Pop. 279
Powers Lake SD 27 100/K-12
PO Box 346 58773 701-464-5432
John Gruenberg, supt. Fax 464-5435
www.powerslake.k12.nd.us

Powers Lake ES 100/K-5
PO Box 346 58773 701-464-5431
John Gruenberg, prin. Fax 464-5435

Ray, Williams, Pop. 585
Nesson SD 2 200/K-12
PO Box 564 58849 701-568-3301
Benjamin Schafer, supt. Fax 568-3302
www.ray.k12.nd.us
Ray ES 100/K-6
PO Box 564 58849 701-568-3301
Angela Cancade, prin. Fax 568-3302

Rhame, Bowman, Pop. 166
Bowman County SD 1
Supt. — See Bowman
Rhame S 50/K-6
PO Box 250 58651 701-279-5523
Tracy Lecoe, prin. Fax 279-5750

Richardton, Stark, Pop. 528
Richardton-Taylor SD 34 300/K-12
320 Raider Rd 58652 701-974-2111
Brent Bautz, supt. Fax 974-2161
www.richardton-taylor.k12.nd.us
Other Schools – See Taylor

Rolette, Rolette, Pop. 566
Rolette SD 29 100/K-12
PO Box 97 58366 701-246-3595
Wade Sherwin, supt. Fax 246-3452
www.rolettepublicschools.com
Rolette ES 100/K-6
PO Box 97 58366 701-246-3595
Wade Sherwin, prin. Fax 246-3452

Rolla, Rolette, Pop. 1,226
Mt. Pleasant SD 4 300/PK-12
201 5th St NE 58367 701-477-3151
Kevin Baumgarn, supt. Fax 477-5001
www.rolla.k12.nd.us
Mt. Pleasant ES 200/PK-6
201 5th St NE 58367 701-477-3151
Kristin Mitchell, prin. Fax 477-5001

Rugby, Pierce, Pop. 2,841
Rugby SD 5 500/PK-12
1123 S Main Ave 58368 701-776-5201
Dr. Michael McNeff, supt. Fax 776-5091
www.rugby.k12.nd.us/
Rugby Ely ES 300/PK-6
207 2nd St SW 58368 701-776-5757
Jason Gullickson, prin. Fax 776-5759

Little Flower S 100/PK-6
306 3rd Ave SE 58368 701-776-6258
Jorgen Knutson, prin. Fax 776-6740

Saint Anthony, Morton
Little Heart SD 4 50/K-8
2354 County Road 136 58566 701-445-7331
Fax 445-7331
Little Heart S 50/K-8
2354 County Road 136 58566 701-445-7331
Jennifer Vetter, prin. Fax 445-7331

Saint John, Rolette, Pop. 309
Saint John SD 3 400/K-12
PO Box 200 58369 701-477-5651
Donald Davis, supt. Fax 477-8195
www3.stjohn.k12.nd.us
Saint John S 300/K-8
PO Box 200 58369 701-477-5651
Paul Frydenlund, prin. Fax 477-8195

Saint Thomas, Pembina, Pop. 330
Saint Thomas SD 43 100/K-12
PO Box 150 58276 701-257-6424
Jack Maus, supt. Fax 257-6461
sites.google.com/a/goblueknights.org/st-thomas-public-school
Saint Thomas ES 50/K-6
PO Box 150 58276 701-257-6424
Kevin Beaudoin, prin. Fax 257-6461

Sawyer, Ward, Pop. 354
Sawyer SD 16 100/K-8
25 1st Ave SW 58781 701-624-5167
Dr. Wayne Trottier, supt. Fax 624-5482
www.sawyer.k12.nd.us
Sawyer S 100/K-8
25 1st Ave SW 58781 701-624-5167
Thomas Warman, prin. Fax 624-5482

Scranton, Bowman, Pop. 279
Scranton SD 33 100/K-12
PO Box 126 58653 701-275-8897
John Pretzer, supt. Fax 275-6221
www.scrantonpublicschool.homestead.com/
Scranton ES 100/K-6
PO Box 126 58653 701-275-8266
Kelly Pierce, prin. Fax 275-6221

Selfridge, Sioux, Pop. 151
Selfridge SD 8 100/K-12
PO Box 45 58568 701-422-3353
James Gross, supt. Fax 422-3348
www.selfridge.k12.nd.us
Selfridge ES 50/K-6
PO Box 45 58568 701-422-3353
Kristi Miller M.Ed., prin. Fax 422-3348

Solen, Sioux, Pop. 73
Solen SD 3 200/K-12
PO Box 128 58570 701-445-3331
Justin Fryer, supt. Fax 445-3323
www.solen.k12.nd.us/
Other Schools – See Cannon Ball

South Heart, Stark, Pop. 298
South Heart SD 9 200/PK-12
PO Box 159 58655 701-677-5671
Calvin Dean, supt. Fax 677-5616
www.southheart.k12.nd.us/
South Heart ES 100/PK-6
PO Box 159 58655 701-677-5671
Jessica Geis, prin. Fax 677-5616

Stanley, Mountrail, Pop. 1,448
Stanley SD 2 600/K-12
PO Box 10 58784 701-628-3811
Tim Holte, supt. Fax 628-3358
www.stanley.k12.nd.us/
Stanley ES 300/K-6
PO Box 10 58784 701-628-2422
Mark Morgan, prin. Fax 628-2279

Starkweather, Ramsey, Pop. 114
Starkweather SD 44 100/PK-12
PO Box 45 58377 701-292-4381
Larry Volk M.Ed., supt. Fax 292-5714
www.starkweather.k12.nd.us
Starkweather ES 50/PK-6
PO Box 45 58377 701-292-4381
Alysson Groves, prin. Fax 292-5714

Steele, Kidder, Pop. 715
Kidder County SD 1 400/K-12
PO Box 380 58482 701-475-2243
Rick Diegel, supt. Fax 475-2737
www.kiddercounty.k12.nd.us
Steele-Dawson ES 100/K-6
PO Box 380 58482 701-475-2243
Ryan Larson, prin. Fax 475-2737
Other Schools – See Tappen

Sterling, Burleigh
Sterling SD 35 50/K-8
PO Box 68 58572 701-387-4413
www.sterling.k12.nd.us
Sterling S 50/K-8
PO Box 68 58572 701-387-4413
Danielle Stoppler, prin. Fax 387-4413

Strasburg, Emmons, Pop. 408
Strasburg SD 15 100/PK-12
PO Box 308 58573 701-336-2667
Larry Sebastian, supt. Fax 336-7490
www.strasburg.k12.nd.us/
Strasburg ES 100/PK-6
PO Box 308 58573 701-336-2667
Gloria Odden, admin. Fax 336-7490

Surrey, Ward, Pop. 914
Surrey SD 41 400/PK-12
PO Box 40 58785 701-838-1262
Terry Voiles, supt. Fax 838-8822
www.surrey.k12.nd.us
Surrey ES 200/PK-6
PO Box 40 58785 701-838-3282
Debbie Hansen, prin. Fax 838-1262

Tappen, Kidder, Pop. 197
Kidder County SD 1
Supt. — See Steele
Tappen S 50/K-8
PO Box 127 58487 701-327-4256
Ryan Larson, prin. Fax 327-4255

Taylor, Stark, Pop. 148
Richardton-Taylor SD 34
Supt. — See Richardton
Taylor Richardton ES 200/K-6
PO Box 157 58656 701-974-3585
Scott Bohn, prin. Fax 974-3520

Thompson, Grand Forks, Pop. 982
Thompson SD 61 500/K-12
424 3rd St 58278 701-599-2765
John Maus, supt. Fax 599-2819
www.tps-k12.org
Thompson ES 300/K-6
424 3rd St 58278 701-599-2765
John Maus, prin. Fax 599-2819

Tioga, Williams, Pop. 1,208
Tioga SD 15 500/K-12
PO Box 279 58852 701-664-2333
Carolyn Eide, supt. Fax 664-3356
www.tioga.k12.nd.us
Central ES 300/K-6
PO Box 69 58852 701-664-3441
Timothy Schaffer, prin. Fax 664-4441

Tower City, Cass, Pop. 251
Maple Valley SD 4 200/K-12
PO Box 168 58071 701-749-2570
Dr. Brian Wolf, supt. Fax 749-2313
www.maple-valley.k12.nd.us/
Wheatland Colony S 50/K-8
3361 134th Ave SE 58071 701-749-5310
Jayson Kocka, prin.
Other Schools – See Buffalo, Oriska

Towner, McHenry, Pop. 528
TGU SD 60 300/PK-12
PO Box 270 58788 701-537-5414
Erik Sveet, supt. Fax 537-5413
www.tgu.k12.nd.us
TGU Towner ES 100/PK-6
PO Box 270 58788 701-537-5414
Scott Thorson, prin. Fax 537-5413
Other Schools – See Granville

Trenton, Williams
Eight Mile SD 6 200/K-12
PO Box 239 58853 701-774-8221
Matt Schriver, supt. Fax 774-8040
www.eight-mile.k12.nd.us
Eight Mile ES 100/K-6
PO Box 239 58853 701-774-8221
Kay Cavanaugh, prin. Fax 774-8040

Turtle Lake, McLean, Pop. 570
Turtle Lake - Mercer SD 72 200/K-12
PO Box 160 58575 701-448-2365
Shane Sagert, supt. Fax 448-2368
www.tlm.k12.nd.us/
Turtle Lake Mercer ES 100/K-6
PO Box 160 58575 701-448-2365
Sheila Schlafmann, prin. Fax 448-2368

Underwood, McLean, Pop. 762
Underwood SD 8 200/PK-12
PO Box 100 58576 701-442-3201
Brandt Dick, supt. Fax 442-3274
sites.google.com/a/underwoodschool.org/ups/
Underwood ES 100/PK-6
PO Box 100 58576 701-442-3201
Lee Weisgarber, prin. Fax 442-3274

Valley City, Barnes, Pop. 6,490
Valley City SD 2 1,100/PK-12
460 Central Ave N 58072 701-845-0483
Joshua Johnson, supt. Fax 845-4109
www.valley-city.k12.nd.us
Jefferson ES 300/PK-3
1150 Central Ave N 58072 701-845-0622
Troy Miller, prin. Fax 845-5497
Valley City JHS 200/7-8
460 Central Ave N 58072 701-845-0483
Daniel Larson, prin. Fax 845-2762
Washington ES 200/4-6
510 8th Ave SW 58072 701-845-0849
Chad Lueck, prin. Fax 845-3560

St. Catherine ES 100/PK-6
540 3rd Ave NE 58072 701-845-1453
Dawn Ihry, dean Fax 845-0556

Velva, McHenry, Pop. 1,077
Velva SD 1 400/K-12
PO Box 179 58790 701-338-2022
Dave Schoch, supt. Fax 338-2023
www.velva.k12.nd.us
Velva ES 300/K-6
PO Box 179 58790 701-338-2022
Nancy Dockter, prin. Fax 338-2023

Wahpeton, Richland, Pop. 7,637
Wahpeton SD 37 1,200/PK-12
PO Box 10 58074 701-642-6741
Rick Jacobson, supt. Fax 642-4908
www.wahpeton.k12.nd.us
Wahpeton ES 500/1-5
PO Box 10 58074 701-642-8328
Carmen Tubbs, prin. Fax 642-2420
Wahpeton MS 300/6-8
PO Box 10 58074 701-642-6687
Steve Hockert, prin. Fax 642-5622
Zimmerman ES 100/PK-K
PO Box 10 58074 701-642-3050
Rosemary Hardie, prin. Fax 642-5499

St. John ES 100/PK-6
212 Dakota Ave 58075 701-642-6116
Renee Langenwalter, prin. Fax 642-9134

Walhalla, Pembina, Pop. 969
North Border SD 100 300/PK-12
PO Box 558 58282 701-549-3751
Dr. Paul Stremick, supt. Fax 549-3753
www.northborder.k12.nd.us
North Border Walhalla ES 100/K-8
PO Box 558 58282 701-549-3751
Jana Carson, prin. Fax 549-3753
Other Schools – See Pembina

Warwick, Benson, Pop. 65
Warwick SD 29 300/PK-12
210 4th Ave 58381 701-294-2561
Dean Dauphinais, supt. Fax 294-2626
www.warwick.k12.nd.us
Warwick ES 200/PK-6
210 4th Ave 58381 701-294-2561
Angela Brandt, prin. Fax 294-2626

Washburn, McLean, Pop. 1,238
Washburn SD 4 300/K-12
PO Box 280 58577 701-462-3221
Brad Rinas, supt. Fax 462-3561
sites.google.com/site/washburnk12
Washburn ES 200/K-6
PO Box 280 58577 701-462-3261
Jerad Voglewede, prin. Fax 462-3561

Watford City, McKenzie, Pop. 1,714
McKenzie County SD 1 1,000/K-12
PO Box 589 58854 701-444-3626
Dr. Steven Holen, supt. Fax 444-6345
www.watford-city.k12.nd.us/
Watford City ES 600/K-6
PO Box 589 58854 701-444-2985
Brad Foss, prin. Fax 444-2986

Johnson Corners Christian Academy 50/K-12
11008 Highway 23 58854 701-675-2359
David Combs, admin. Fax 675-2357

West Fargo, Cass, Pop. 25,407
West Fargo SD 6 8,500/PK-12
207 Main Ave W 58078 701-356-2000
Dr. David Flowers, supt. Fax 356-2009
www.west-fargo.k12.nd.us
Aurora ES 500/K-5
3420 9th St W 58078 701-356-2130
Lynn Bormann, prin. Fax 356-2139

Berger ES 400/1-5
631 4th Ave E 58078 701-356-2010
Chad Clark, prin. Fax 356-2019
Brooks Harbor ES 200/K-5
801 22nd Ave W 58078 701-356-8310
Manix Zepeda, prin. Fax 356-8319
Cheney MS 1,100/6-8
825 17th Ave E 58078 701-356-2090
Don Lennon, prin. Fax 356-2099
Eastwood ES 500/1-5
500 10th Ave E 58078 701-356-2030
Dr. Paula Henry, prin. Fax 356-2039
Freedom ES 500/1-5
401 26th Ave E 58078 701-356-5221
Dr. Jeffry Johnson, prin. Fax 356-5229
Legacy ES, 5150 9th St W 58078 K-5
Jason Markusen, prin. 701-356-2000
Liberty MS 800/6-8
801 36th Ave E 58078 701-356-2671
Michelle Weber, prin. Fax 356-2679
Lodoen K Center 500/PK-K
330 3rd Ave E 58078 701-356-2020
Ethan Ehlert, prin. Fax 356-2029
South ES 400/1-5
117 6th Ave W 58078 701-356-2100
Jody Sjolin-Nelson, prin. Fax 356-2109
Westside ES 500/1-5
945 7th Ave W 58078 701-356-2110
Tabatha Joyce, prin. Fax 356-2119
Other Schools – See Fargo, Harwood, Horace

Trinity ES 200/PK-5
2811 7th St E 58078 701-356-0793
Davonne Eldredge, prin. Fax 356-0796

Westhope, Bottineau, Pop. 415
Westhope SD 17 100/K-12
PO Box 406 58793 701-245-6444
Martin Bratrud, supt. Fax 245-6418
www.westhopeschool.com
Westhope ES 100/K-6
PO Box 406 58793 701-245-6444
Terri Lundberg, prin. Fax 245-6418

Williston, Williams, Pop. 14,321
New SD 8 200/K-8
111 7th Ave W 58801 701-572-6359
Robert Turner, supt. Fax 572-9311
www.district8.k12.nd.us/
Garden Valley ES 100/K-5
111 7th Ave W 58801 701-826-4261
Brenda Herland, prin. Fax 826-4531
Round Prairie ES 100/K-5
111 7th Ave W 58801 701-875-4346
Dr. Robert Smith, prin. Fax 875-4344
Stoney Creek MS 50/6-8
111 7th Ave W 58801 701-572-3579
Steven Guglich, prin. Fax 572-2731

Williston SD 1 3,200/K-12
PO Box 1407 58802 701-572-1580
Michael Campbell, supt. Fax 572-3547
www.williston.k12.nd.us
Bakken ES 5-6
PO Box 1407 58802 701-713-7300
Jeremy Mehlhoff, prin. Fax 713-7319
Hagan ES 400/K-6
PO Box 1407 58802 701-572-4960
Darla Ratzak, prin. Fax 572-3147
Lewis & Clark ES 300/K-6
PO Box 1407 58802 701-572-6331
Meridith Johnson, prin. Fax 572-0171
McVay ES 300/K-5
PO Box 1407 58802 701-572-9140
Keith Leintz, admin. Fax 572-9114
Rickard ES 300/K-6
PO Box 1407 58802 701-572-5412
Kevin Klassen, prin. Fax 572-0347
Wilkinson ES 300/K-6
PO Box 1407 58802 701-572-6532
Laura Benz, prin. Fax 572-0384
Williston MS 400/7-8
PO Box 1407 58802 701-572-5618
Duane Noeske, prin. Fax 774-3109

St. Joseph S 100/K-6
124 6th St W 58801 701-572-6384
Julie Quamme, prin. Fax 774-0998
Williston Trinity Christian S 200/PK-12
2419 9th Ave W 58801 701-774-9056
Cory Fleck, prin. Fax 774-3158

Wilton, McLean, Pop. 705
Wilton SD 1 200/PK-12
PO Box 249 58579 701-734-6559
Amanda Meier, supt. Fax 734-6944
www.wilton.k12.nd.us
Wilton ES 100/PK-6
PO Box 249 58579 701-734-6331
Courtney Seiler, prin. Fax 734-6944

Wimbledon, Barnes, Pop. 210
Barnes County North SD 7 300/PK-12
2192 101st Ave SE 58492 701-646-6202
Mike Severson, supt. Fax 646-6566
www.barnescountynorth.k12.nd.us/
Barnes County North S 200/PK-6
2192 101st Ave SE 58492 701-646-6202
Lloyd Wilson, prin. Fax 646-6566

Wing, Burleigh, Pop. 148
Wing SD 28 100/K-12
PO Box 130 58494 701-943-2319
David Goetz, supt. Fax 943-2318
www.wing.k12.nd.us
Wing ES 100/K-6
PO Box 130 58494 701-943-2319
David Goetz, prin. Fax 943-2318

Wishek, McIntosh, Pop. 999
Wishek SD 19 200/PK-12
PO Box 247 58495 701-452-2892
Shawn Kuntz, supt. Fax 452-4273
www.wishek.k12.nd.us
Wishek ES 100/PK-6
PO Box 247 58495 701-452-2892
Yvonne Engelhart, prin. Fax 452-4273

Wolford, Pierce, Pop. 36
Wolford SD 1 50/K-12
401 3rd Ave SW 58385 701-583-2387
Larry Zavada, supt. Fax 583-2519
www.wolford.k12.nd.us/
Wolford ES 50/K-6
401 3rd Ave SW 58385 701-583-2387
Carol Braaten, prin. Fax 583-2519

Wyndmere, Richland, Pop. 423
Wyndmere SD 42 200/K-12
PO Box 190 58081 701-439-2287
Dan Dalchow, supt. Fax 439-2804
wyndmere.schoolinsites.com
Wyndmere ES 100/K-6
PO Box 190 58081 701-439-2287
Mikal Kern, prin. Fax 439-2804

Zeeland, McIntosh, Pop. 86
Zeeland SD 4 50/K-12
PO Box 2 58581 701-423-5429
Corbley Ogren, supt. Fax 423-5465
www.zeeland.k12.nd.us/
Zeeland ES 50/K-6
PO Box 2 58581 701-423-5429
Trudy Fraase Wolf, prin. Fax 423-5465

OHIO

OHIO DEPARTMENT OF EDUCATION
25 S Front St, Columbus 43215-4183
Telephone 877-644-6338
Website http://www.ode.state.oh.us

Superintendent of Public Instruction Paolo DeMaria

OHIO BOARD OF EDUCATION
25 S Front St, Columbus 43215-4183

President Tess Elshoff

EDUCATIONAL SERVICE CENTERS (ESC)

Allen County ESC
Steve Arnold, supt. 419-222-1836
1920 Slabtown Rd, Lima 45801 Fax 224-0718
www.allencountyesc.org

Ashtabula County ESC
John Rubesich, supt. 440-576-9023
4200 State Rd, Ashtabula 44004 Fax 576-3065
www.acesc.k12.oh.us

Athens-Meigs Counties ESC
Ricky Edwards, supt. 740-797-0064
PO Box 40, Chauncey 45719 Fax 797-0070
www.athensmeigs.org

Auglaize County ESC
Shawn Brown, supt. 419-738-3422
1045 Dearbaugh Ave Ste 2 Fax 738-1267
Wapakoneta 45895
www.auglaizeesc.org

Brown County ESC
James Frazier, supt. 937-378-6118
9231 Hamer Rd Fax 378-4286
Georgetown 45121
brown.k12.oh.us

Butler County ESC
, 400 N Erie Hwy Ste A 513-887-3710
Hamilton 45011 Fax 887-3709
www.bcesc.org

Clark County ESC
Dan Bennett Ph.D., supt. 937-325-7671
25 W Pleasant St Fax 717-0518
Springfield 45506
www.clarkesc.org

Clermont County ESC
Jeff Weir, supt. 513-735-8300
2400 Clermont Center Dr Fax 735-8371
Batavia 45103
www.ccesc.org

Columbiana County ESC
Anna Vaughn, supt. 330-424-9591
38720 Saltwell Rd, Lisbon 44432 Fax 424-9481
www.ccesc.k12.oh.us/

Darke County ESC
Michael Gray, supt. 937-548-4915
5279 Education Dr Fax 548-8920
Greenville 45331
darkeesc.org

East Central Ohio ESC
Randy Lucas, supt., 834 E High Ave 330-308-9939
New Philadelphia 44663 Fax 422-3216
www.ecoesc.org

ESC of Central Ohio
Dr. Tom Goodney, supt. 614-445-3750
2080 Citygate Dr, Columbus 43219 Fax 445-3767
www.escco.org

ESC of Cuyahoga County
Dr. Robert Mengerink, supt. 216-524-3000
6393 Oak Tree Blvd Fax 524-3683
Independence 44131
www.esc-cc.org/

ESC of Lake Erie West
Sandra C. Frisch, supt. 419-245-4150
2275 Collingwood Blvd Fax 245-4186
Toledo 43620
www.esclakeeriewest.org

ESC of Lorain County
Greg Ring, supt. 440-324-5777
1885 Lake Ave, Elyria 44035 Fax 324-7355
www.loraincountyesc.org

ESC of Medina County
William Koran, supt. 330-723-6393
124 W Washington St Fax 723-0573
Medina 44256
www.medina-esc.org/

Fairfield County ESC
Marie Ward, supt. 740-653-3193
955 Liberty Dr, Lancaster 43130 Fax 653-4053
faircoesc.org/

Gallia-Vinton Counties ESC
Dr. Denise Shockley, supt. 740-245-0593
PO Box 178, Rio Grande 45674 Fax 245-0596
www.galliavintonesc.org

Geauga County ESC
Jennifer Felker, supt. 440-279-1700
470 Center St Bldg 2 Fax 286-7106
Chardon 44024
www.geaugaesc.org

Greene County ESC
Terry Graves-Strieter, supt. 937-767-1303
360 E Enon Rd Fax 767-1025
Yellow Springs 45387
www.greeneesc.org

Hamilton County ESC
David Distel, supt. 513-674-4200
11083 Hamilton Ave Fax 742-8339
Cincinnati 45231
www.hcesc.org

Hancock County ESC
Larry Busdeker, supt. 419-422-7525
7746 County Road 140 Fax 422-8766
Findlay 45840
hancockesc.org

Jefferson County ESC
Dr. Chuck Kokiko, supt. 740-283-3347
2023 Sunset Blvd Fax 283-2709
Steubenville 43952
www.jcesc.k12.oh.us

Knox County ESC
Timm Mackley, supt. 740-393-6767
308 Martinsburg Rd Fax 393-6812
Mount Vernon 43050
www.knoxesc.org

Lake County ESC
Dr. Brian Bontempo, supt. 440-350-2563
8221 Auburn Rd, Concord 44077 Fax 350-2566
www.esc-lc.org

Lawrence County ESC
Jeff Saunders, supt. 740-532-4223
111 S 4th St, Ironton 45638 Fax 532-7226
www.lawrencecountyesc.com

Licking County ESC
Dale Lewellen, supt. 740-349-6084
145 N Quentin Rd, Newark 43055 Fax 349-6107
www.lcesc.org

Madison-Champaign ESC
Dr. Daniel Kaffenbarger, supt. 937-484-1557
2200 S US Highway 68 Fax 652-2221
Urbana 43078
www.mccesc.org

Mahoning County ESC
Dr. Ronald Iarussi, supt. 330-533-8755
7320 N Palmyra Rd Fax 533-8777
Canfield 44406
www.mahoningesc.org

Mercer County ESC
Shelly Vaughn, supt. 419-586-6628
441 E Market St, Celina 45822 Fax 586-3377
www.mercercountyesc.org

Miami County ESC
Tom Dunn, supt. 937-339-5100
2000 W Stanfield Rd, Troy 45373 Fax 339-3256
www.miami.k12.oh.us

Mid-Ohio ESC
Linda Keller, supt. 419-774-5520
890 W 4th St Ste 100 Fax 774-5523
Mansfield 44906
www.moesc.net/

Midwest Regional ESC
Scott Howell, supt., 121 S Opera St 937-599-5195
Bellefontaine 43311 Fax 599-1959
www.mresc.org

Montgomery County ESC
Frank DePalma, supt. 937-225-4598
200 S Keowee St, Dayton 45402 Fax 496-7426
www.mcesc.org

Muskingum Valley ESC
David Branch, supt. 740-452-4518
205 N 7th St, Zanesville 43701 Fax 455-6702
www.mvesc.org

North Central Ohio ESC
Dr. James Lahoski, supt. 419-447-2927
928 W Market St Ste A, Tiffin 44883 Fax 447-2825
www.ncoesc.org/

North Point ESC
Doug Crooks, supt. 419-627-3900
1210 E Bogart Rd, Sandusky 44870 Fax 627-3999
www.npesc.org

Northwest Ohio ESC
Kerri Gearhart, supt. 567-444-4800
205 Nolan Pkwy, Archbold 43502 Fax 444-4802
www.nwoesc.org

Ohio Valley ESC
Chris Keylor, supt. 740-439-3558
128 E 8th St, Cambridge 43725 Fax 439-0012
www.ovesc.k12.oh.us

Pickaway County ESC
Tyrus Ankrom, supt. 740 474 7529
2050 Stoneridge Dr Fax 474-7251
Circleville 43113
pickawayesc.org/

Portage County ESC
Joseph Iacano, supt. 330-297-1436
326 E Main St, Ravenna 44266 Fax 297-1113
www.portage-esc.org

Preble County ESC
Mike Gray, supt. 937-456-1187
597 Hillcrest Dr, Eaton 45320 Fax 456-3253
www.preblecountyesc.org

Putnam County ESC
Dr. Jan Osborn, supt. 419-523-5951
124 Putnam Pkwy, Ottawa 45875 Fax 523-6126
www.putnamcountyesc.org

Ross-Pike Counties ESC
Steve Martin, supt. 740-702-3120
475 Western Ave Ste E Fax 702-3123
Chillicothe 45601
rpesd.org

South Central Ohio ESC
Sandy Mers, supt. 740-354-7761
522 Glenwood Ave Fax 353-1882
New Boston 45662
www.scoesc.org

Southern Ohio ESC
Beth Justice, supt. 937-382-6921
3321 Airborne Rd Fax 383-3171
Wilmington 45177
www.southernohioesc.org

Stark County ESC
Joe Chaddock, supt. 330-492-8136
2100 38th St NW, Canton 44709 Fax 492-6381
www.starkcountyesc.org

Summit County ESC
Joseph Iacano, supt. 330-945-5600
420 Washington Ave Ste 200 Fax 945-6222
Cuyahoga Falls 44221
www.cybersummit.org

Tri-County ESC
James Ritchie, supt. 330-345-6771
741 Winkler Dr, Wooster 44691 Fax 345-7622
www.youresc.k12.oh.us

Trumbull County ESC
Michael Hanshaw, supt. 330-505-2800
6000 Youngstown Warren Rd Fax 505-2814
Niles 44446
www.trumbullesc.org

Warren County ESC
Tom Isaacs, supt. 513-695-2900
1879 Deerfield Rd, Lebanon 45036 Fax 695-2961
www.warrencountyesc.com/

Western Buckeye ESC
Steve Arnold, supt. 419-399-4711
PO Box 176, Paulding 45879 Fax 399-3346
www.wbesc.org

Wood County ESC
Kyle Kanuckel, supt. 419-354-9010
1867 N Research Dr Fax 354-1146
Bowling Green 43402
www.wcesc.org/

PUBLIC, PRIVATE AND CATHOLIC ELEMENTARY SCHOOLS

Aberdeen, Brown, Pop. 1,615
Ripley-Union-Lewis-Huntington Local SD
Supt. — See Ripley
Ripley-Union-Lewis-Huntington MS 300/5-8
2300 Rains Eitel Rd 45101 937-795-8001
Jerod Michael, prin. Fax 795-8035

Ada, Hardin, Pop. 5,849
Ada EVD 900/K-12
725 W North Ave 45810 419-634-6421
Meri Skilliter, supt. Fax 634-0311
www.adabulldogs.org
Ada ES 500/K-6
725 W North Ave 45810 419-634-2341
Robin Vanbuskirk, prin. Fax 634-3948

Adamsville, Muskingum, Pop. 113
Tri-Valley Local SD
Supt. — See Dresden
Adamsville ES 300/K-6
7950 East St 43802 740-796-2153
Michael Smith, prin. Fax 796-4781

Adena, Jefferson, Pop. 745
Buckeye Local SD
Supt. — See Dillonvale
Buckeye West ES 300/PK-6
243 N Mill St 43901 740-546-3413
Lucas Parsons, prin. Fax 546-3815

Akron, Summit, Pop. 192,922
Akron CSD 21,000/PK-12
70 N Broadway St 44308 330-761-1661
David James, supt. Fax 761-3225
www.akronschools.com
Arnold Community Learning Center 300/K-6
450 Vernon Odom Blvd 44307 330-376-0153
Lamonica Davis, prin. Fax 376-7765
Barber Community Learning Center 300/K-6
665 Garry Rd 44305 330-761-7911
Ranae Williams, prin. Fax 784-0451
Case ES 400/K-5
400 W Market St 44303 330-873-3350
Danjile Henderson, prin. Fax 873-3326
Crouse Community Learning Center 400/K-6
1000 Diagonal Rd 44320 330-761-1625
Tara Bruce, prin. Fax 761-1371
Essex Preschool PK-PK
1160 Winhurst Dr 44313 330-873-3390
Pat Cronin, prin. Fax 873-3300
Findley Community Learning Center 500/K-5
65 W Tallmadge Ave 44310 330-761-7909
Sherry Bennington, prin. Fax 761-1327
Firestone Park ES 500/K-5
1479 Girard St 44301 330-773-1308
Sharon Hill-Jones, prin. Fax 773-1025
Forest Hill Community Learning Center 300/K-5
850 Damon St 44310 330-761-1645
Gregory Blondheim, prin. Fax 761-3175
Glover Community Learning Center 400/K-5
935 Hammel St 44306 330-773-1245
Nancy Ritch, prin. Fax 773-1065
Harris-Jackson Community Learning Center 300/K-5
1085 Clifton Ave 44310 330-761-1315
Andrea Aller, prin. Fax 761-1519
Hatton Community Learning Center 500/K-5
1933 Baker Ave 44312 330-761-7980
Darcy Forshee, prin. Fax 794-4208
Hill Community Learning Center 300/K-6
1060 E Archwood Ave 44306 330-773-1129
Tina McIntyre, prin. Fax 773-7308
Hyre Community Learning Center 800/6-8
2385 Wedgewood Dr 44312 330-761-7930
Larry Bender, prin. Fax 761-7932
Innes Community Learning Center 400/6-8
1999 East Ave 44314 330-761-7900
Kathryn Rodocker, prin. Fax 848-5212
Jane Community Learning Center 500/K-5
444 Darrow Rd 44305 330-794-4117
Jennifer Lucas, prin. Fax 794-6970
Jennings Community Learning Center 600/6-8
227 E Tallmadge Ave 44310 330-761-2002
Charles Jones, prin. Fax 761-2611
King Community Learning Center 400/K-5
805 Memorial Pkwy 44303 330-873-3375
Mary Dean, prin. Fax 761-3197
Leggett Community Learning Center 400/K-5
333 E Thornton St 44311 330-761-1735
Philomena Vincente, prin. Fax 761-1351
Litchfield MS 600/6-8
470 Castle Blvd 44313 330-873-3330
Dyan Floyd, prin. Fax 873-3347
Mason Community Learning Center 300/K-6
700 E Exchange St 44306 330-761-2237
Angela Harper, prin. Fax 761-3309
McEbright Community Learning Center 300/K-5
349 Cole Ave 44301 330-761-7940
Deborah Musiek, prin. Fax 761-7942
Miller South S for Visual & Perform Arts 500/4-8
1055 East Ave 44307 330-761-1765
Dawn Wilson, prin. Fax 761-1764
National Inventors Hall of Fame S - STEM 400/5-8
199 S Broadway St 44308 330-761-3195
Amanda Morgan, prin. Fax 761-5576
Pfeiffer ES 200/K-5
2081 9th St SW 44314 330-848-5244
Regina Llewellyn, prin. Fax 848-5249
Portage Path Community Learning Center 400/K-5
55 S Portage Path 44303 330-761-2795
Kimberly Summers, prin. Fax 761 1383
Resnik Community Learning Center 400/K-5
65 N Meadowcroft Dr 44313 330-873-3370
Kristen Booth, prin. Fax 873-3325
Rimer Community Learning Center 300/K-5
2370 Manchester Rd 44314 330-761-7905
Becca Cacioppo, prin. Fax 848-3614
Ritzman Community Learning Center 400/K-5
629 Canton Rd 44312 330-761-7903
Ione McIntosh, prin. Fax 794-4106
Robinson Community Learning Center 300/K-6
1156 4th Ave 44306 330-761-2785
Anthony Lane, prin. Fax 761-5566
Salem Community Learning Center 200/K-5
1222 W Waterloo Rd 44314 330-848-5231
Anna Panning, prin. Fax 848-5213
Schumacher Community Learning Center 400/K-6
1020 Hartford Ave 44320 330-761-7934
Brandi Davis, prin. Fax 761-7936
Seiberling Community Learning Center 400/K-6
400 Brittain Rd 44305 330-761-7956
Jennifer Moff, prin. Fax 761-4142
Voris Community Learning Center 300/K-5
1885 Glenmount Ave 44301 330-773-6926
Jennifer Douglas, prin. Fax 773-8073
Windemere Community Learning Center 400/K-5
2283 Windemere Ave 44312 330-761-7937
Megan Lee-Wilfong, prin. Fax 761-7939

Coventry Local SD 1,800/PK-12
2910 S Main St 44319 330-644-8489
Russell Chaboudy, supt. Fax 644-0159
www.coventryschools.org/
Coventry ES 600/PK-4
3089 Manchester Rd 44319 330-644-8469
Timothy Bryan, prin. Fax 644-1142
Coventry MS 500/5-8
3257 Cormany Rd 44319 330-644-2232
Tina Norris, prin. Fax 644-0331

Manchester Local SD 1,300/K-12
6075 Manchester Rd 44319 330-882-6926
Dr. James Robinson, supt. Fax 882-0013
www.panthercountry.org
Manchester MS 400/5-8
760 W Nimisila Rd 44319 330-882-3812
James Miller, prin. Fax 882-2013
Nolley ES 400/K-4
6285 Renninger Rd 44319 330-882-4133
Christina Pappas, prin. Fax 882-2001

Springfield Local SD 2,500/PK-12
2410 Massillon Rd 44312 330-798-1111
Chuck Sincere, supt. Fax 798-1161
www.springfieldspartans.org/
Schrop IS 500/4-6
2215 Pickle Rd 44312 330-798-1007
Lisa Vardon, prin. Fax 798-1167
Spring Hill ES 400/PK-3
660 Lessig Ave 44312 330-798-1006
Dave Jurmanovich, prin. Fax 798-1166
Young ES 300/K-3
3258 Nidover Dr 44312 330-798-1008
Jennifer Ganzer, prin. Fax 798-1168

Arlington Christian Academy 100/K 8
539 S Arlington St 44306 330-785-9116
Lawrence Swoope, prin. Fax 785-9361
Billiart S of St. Sebastian Parish PK-PK
380 Mineola Ave 44320 330-206-0941
Jason Wojnicz, prin.
Chapel Hill Christian S South Campus 200/PK-6
1639 Killian Rd 44312 330-896-0852
John Wilson, admin. Fax 896-9918
Emmanuel Christian Academy 200/PK-8
350 S Portage Path 44320 330-836-7182
Veronica Suber, prin. Fax 836-7274
Lippman S 100/K-8
750 White Pond Dr 44320 330-836-0419
Sam Chestnut, hdmstr. Fax 869-2514
Old Trail S 500/PK-8
2315 Ira Rd 44333 330-666-1118
Sarah Johnston, head sch Fax 666-2187
Our Lady of the Elms S 200/PK-6
1290 W Market St 44313 330-864-7210
Deborah Farquhar Jones, pres. Fax 867-1262
St. Anthony of Padua S 100/PK-5
80 E York St 44310 330-253-6918
Sr. Elizabeth Szilvasi, prin. Fax 762-2229
St. Bernard - St. Mary S 200/K-8
750 S Main St 44311 330-253-1233
Dr. Patricia Nugent, prin. Fax 253-1472
St. Francis De Sales S 300/K-8
4009 Manchester Rd 44319 330-644-0638
Kathryn Buzzelli, prin. Fax 644-2663
St. Matthew S 300/PK-8
2580 Benton Ave 44312 330-784-1711
John Czaplicki, prin. Fax 733-1004
St. Paul S 200/PK-8
1580 Brown St 44301 330-724-1253
William DiBacco, prin. Fax 724-1253
St. Sebastian S 500/PK-8
352 Elmdale Ave 44320 330-836-9107
Anthony Rohr, prin. Fax 836-7690
St. Vincent De Paul S 200/PK-8
17 S Maple St 44303 330-762-5912
Maria Meeker, prin. Fax 535-2515

Albany, Athens, Pop. 825
Alexander Local SD 1,400/PK-12
6091 Ayers Rd 45710 740-698-8831
Lindy Douglas, supt. Fax 698-2038
www.alexanderschools.org/
Alexander ES 700/PK-5
6105 School Rd 45710 740-698-8831
Melissa Guffey, prin. Fax 698-2137

Alexandria, Licking, Pop. 512
Northridge Local SD
Supt. — See Johnstown
Northridge PS 300/K-3
PO Box 68 43001 740-924-2691
Brian Blum, prin. Fax 924-6013

Alliance, Stark, Pop. 21,573
Alliance CSD 2,500/PK-12
200 Glamorgan St 44601 330-821-2100
Jeffery Talbert, supt. Fax 821-0202
www.alliancecityschools.org
Alliance Early Learning S 400/PK-K
285 W Oxford St 44601 330-829-2266
Tim Calfee, prin. Fax 823-8106
Alliance MS 600/6-8
3205 S Union Ave 44601 330-829-2254
Troy Russell, prin. Fax 823-0872
Northside IS 100/4-5
701 Johnson Ave 44601 330-829-2269
Stephanie Garren, prin. Fax 823-0761
Parkway ES 200/1-3
1490 Parkway Blvd 44601 330-829-2264
Cory Muller, prin. Fax 829-0559
Rockhill ES 300/1-3
2400 S Rockhill Ave 44601 330-829-2260
Michelle Balderson, prin. Fax 829-8829

Marlington Local SD 2,400/K-12
10320 Moulin Ave NE 44601 330-823-7458
Joe Knoll, supt. Fax 823-7759
www.marlingtonlocal.org
Lexington ES 400/K-5
12333 Atwater Ave NE 44601 330-823-7570
David Rogers, prin. Fax 829-1980
Marlington MS 600/6-8
10325 Moulin Ave NE 44601 330-823-7566
Nick Evanich, prin. Fax 823-7594
Washington ES 300/K-5
5786 Beechwood Ave 44601 330-823-7586
Dan Swisher, prin. Fax 823-7465
Other Schools – See Louisville

West Branch Local SD
Supt. — See Beloit
Knox ES 400/K-4
2900 Knox School Rd 44601 330-938-1122
Stephen Fowler, prin. Fax 938-1121

Regina Coeli / St. Joseph S 100/PK-5
733 Fernwood Blvd 44601 330-823-9239
Marcella Watry, prin. Fax 823-1877

Amanda, Fairfield, Pop. 725
Amanda-Clearcreek Local SD 1,600/K-12
328 E Main St 43102 740-969-7250
J.B. Dick, supt. Fax 969-7620
www.amanda.k12.oh.us
Amanda-Clearcreek ES 400/3-5
328 E Main St 43102 740-969-7253
Theresa Pinstock, prin. Fax 969-4764
Amanda-Clearcreek MS 400/6-8
328 E Main St 43102 740-969-7252
Patricia Haughn, prin. Fax 969-4764
Amanda-Clearcreek PS 400/K-2
414 N School St 43102 740-969-7254
Rebecca Wagner, prin. Fax 969-3086

Amelia, Clermont, Pop. 4,729
West Clermont Local SD
Supt. — See Cincinnati
Amelia ES 700/K-5
5 E Main St 45102 513-943-3800
Jeffrey Riel, prin. Fax 943-3642
Holly Hill ES 400/K-5
3520 State Route 132 45102 513-943-8900
Shane Short, prin. Fax 797-5604

St. Bernadette S 200/PK-8
1453 Locust Lake Rd 45102 513-753-4744
Lizanne Ingram, prin. Fax 753-9018

Amesville, Athens, Pop. 149
Federal Hocking Local SD
Supt. — See Stewart
Amesville ES 300/PK-6
PO Box 189 45711 740-448-2501
Cathe Blower, prin. Fax 448-3500

Amherst, Lorain, Pop. 11,868
Amherst EVD 3,800/PK-12
185 Forest St 44001 440-988-4406
Steven Sayers, supt. Fax 988-4413
www.amherst.k12.oh.us
Amherst JHS 700/6-8
548 Milan Ave 44001 440-988-0324
Andrew Gibson, prin. Fax 988-0328
Nord MS 600/3-5
501 Lincoln St 44001 440-988-4441
Jill Jiovanazzo, prin. Fax 988-2371
Powers ES 700/PK-2
401 Washington St 44001 440-988-8670
Elizabeth Schwartz, prin. Fax 988-8674

St. Joseph S 200/PK-8
175 Saint Joseph Dr 44001 440-988-4244
Amy Makruski, prin. Fax 988-5249

Andover, Ashtabula, Pop. 1,129
Pymatuning Valley Local SD 1,300/K-12
PO Box 1180 44003 440-293-6488
Mike Candela, supt. Fax 293-7654
pvschools.org
Pymatuning Valley MS 400/5 8
PO Box 1180 44003 440-293-6981
Hendrik Wolfert, prin. Fax 293-7237
Pymatuning Valley PS 500/K-4
PO Box 1180 44003 440-293-6206
Lori Slekar, prin. Fax 293-5152

Anna, Shelby, Pop. 1,544
Anna Local SD 1,200/K-12
1 McRill Way 45302 937-394-2011
Andrew Bixler, supt. Fax 394-7658
www.anna.k12.oh.us
Anna ES 600/K-5
607 N Pike St 45302 937-394-2011
John Holtzapple, prin. Fax 394-3119
Anna MS 300/6-8
1 McRill Way 45302 937-394-2011
Cynthia Endsley, prin. Fax 394-7658

Ansonia, Darke, Pop. 1,168
Ansonia Local SD 700/K-12
PO Box 279 45303 937-337-4000
James Atchley, supt. Fax 337-9520
www.ansonia.k12.oh.us/
Ansonia ES 400/K-6
PO Box 279 45303 937-337-5141
Ashlee Fourman M.Ed., prin. Fax 337-9520
Ansonia MS 100/7-8
PO Box 279 45303 937-337-5591
Jim Robson M.Ed., prin. Fax 337-9520

Antwerp, Paulding, Pop. 1,725
Antwerp Local SD 600/PK-12
303 S Harrmann Rd 45813 419-258-5421
Martin Miller, supt. Fax 258-4041
www.antwerpschools.org
Antwerp Local ES 300/PK-5
303 S Harrmann Rd 45813 419-258-5421
Amy Hammer, prin. Fax 258-4041
Antwerp Local MS 200/6-8
303 S Harrmann Rd 45813 419-258-5421
Travis Lichty, prin. Fax 258-4041

Apple Creek, Wayne, Pop. 1,169
Southeast Local SD 1,400/PK-12
9048 Dover Rd 44606 330-698-3001
James Ritchie, supt. Fax 698-5000
www.southeast.k12.oh.us
Apple Creek ES 400/PK-6
173 W Main St 44606 330-698-3111
Matt Karolewski, prin. Fax 698-2922
Lea MS 200/7-8
9130 Dover Rd 44606 330-698-3151
Erich Riebe, prin. Fax 698-1922
Other Schools – See Fredericksburg, Holmesville, Mount Eaton

Arcadia, Hancock, Pop. 583
Arcadia Local SD 500/K-12
19033 State Route 12 44804 419-894-6431
Bruce Kidder, supt. Fax 894-6970
www.arcadia.noacsc.org
Arcadia ES 300/K-6
19033 State Route 12 44804 419-894-6431
David Golden, prin. Fax 894-6970

Arcanum, Darke, Pop. 2,116
Arcanum Butler Local SD 1,100/PK-12
2011 Trojan Ave 45304 937-692-5174
John Stephens, supt. Fax 692-5959
www.arcanum-butler.k12.oh.us
Arcanum Early Learning Center PK-PK
310 N Main St 45304 937-692-5092
Joni Pechie, prin.
Arcanum ES 400/K-4
2011 Trojan Ave 45304 937-692-5174
Joni Pechie, prin. Fax 692-8865
Butler MS 400/5-8
2011 Trojan Ave 45304 937-692-5174
Marcus Bixler, prin. Fax 692-8865

Franklin Monroe Local SD 600/K-12
8639 Oakes Rd 45304 937-947-1212
Jeffrey Patrick, supt. Fax 947-1372
www.franklin-monroe.k12.oh.us
Franklin Monroe ES 300/K-5
8591 Oakes Rd 45304 937-947-1327
Jeremy Pequignot, prin. Fax 947-1370

Archbold, Fulton, Pop. 4,305
Archbold Area Local SD 1,200/PK-12
600 Lafayette St 43502 419-446-2728
Aaron Rex, supt. Fax 445-8536
www.archbold.k12.oh.us
Archbold ES 500/PK-4
500 Lafayette St 43502 419-446-2727
Dorothy Lambert, prin. Fax 446-4627
Archbold MS 400/5-8
306 Stryker St 43502 419-446-2726
Matthew Shields, prin. Fax 445-8402

Arlington, Hancock, Pop. 1,451
Arlington Local SD 600/PK-12
336 S Main St 45814 419-365-5121
Kevin Haught, supt. Fax 365-1282
www.arlingtonlocalschools.com
Arlington Local ES 300/PK-6
336 S Main St 45814 419-365-5123
Scott Marcum, prin. Fax 365-1282

Ashland, Ashland, Pop. 20,088
Ashland CSD 2,500/K-12
1407 Claremont Ave 44805 419-289-1117
Douglas Marrah, supt. Fax 289-9534
ashlandcityschools.org/
Ashland MS 500/7-8
1520 King Rd 44805 419-289-7966
Matthew White, prin. Fax 289-2303
Edison ES 500/K-3
1202 Masters Ave 44805 419-289-7965
Krist Manley, prin. Fax 281-3947
Reagan ES 100/K-3
850 Jackson Dr 44805 419-289-7967
Nicole Brodie, prin. Fax 289-4571
Taft IS 300/4-6
825 Smith Rd 44805 419-289-7969
Tim Keller, prin. Fax 281-4516

Crestview Local SD 1,100/PK-12
1575 State Route 96 44805 419-895-1700
L. Randall Dunlap, supt. Fax 895-1733
www.crestviewschools.net
Crestview ES 300/PK-3
1575 State Route 96 44805 419-895-1700
Kate Hamilton, prin. Fax 895-1733
Crestview MS 500/4-8
1575 State Route 96 44805 419-895-1700
Eric Yetter, prin. Fax 895-1733

Mapleton Local SD 900/K-12
635 County Road 801 44805 419-945-2188
Rodney Hopton, supt. Fax 945-8133
www.mapleton.k12.oh.us/
Mapleton ES 400/K-5
2 Mountie Dr 44805 419-945-2188
LuAnn Kunisch, prin. Fax 945-8199
Mapleton MS 200/6-8
1 Mountie Dr 44805 419-945-2188
Corey Kline, prin. Fax 945-8167

Ashland Christian S 200/PK-8
1144 W Main St 44805 419-289-6617
St. Edward S 100/K-8
433 Cottage St 44805 419-289-7456
Sue Valentine, prin. Fax 289-9474

Ashley, Delaware, Pop. 1,303
Buckeye Valley Local SD
Supt. — See Delaware
Buckeye Valley East ES 300/PK-4
522 E High St 43003 740-363-2253
Kathryn Karacson, prin. Fax 747-3510

Ashtabula, Ashtabula, Pop. 18,304
Ashtabula Area CSD 3,700/PK-12
2630 W 13th St 44004 440-992-1200
Dr. Melissa Watson, supt. Fax 992-1209
www.aacs.net
AACS Early Learning Center 200/PK-PK
2630 W 13th St 44004 440-992-1280
Lisa Newsome, dir. Fax 964-0485
Erie IS 400/4-6
2306 Wade Ave 44004 440-992-1260
Julie Fulton, prin. Fax 992-1262
Huron PS 400/K-3
2300 Wade Ave 44004 440-992-1230
Valerie Harper, prin. Fax 992-1232
Lakeside JHS 500/7-8
6620 Sanborn Rd 44004 440-993-2618
Scott Anservitz, prin. Fax 992-2647
Michigan PS 400/K-3
2304 Wade Ave 44004 440-992-1250
Janie Carey, prin. Fax 992-1252
Ontario PS 400/K-3
2302 Wade Ave 44004 440-992-1240
Rebecca Evanson, prin. Fax 992-1242
Superior IS 400/4-6
2308 Wade Ave 44004 440-992-1270
Cristine Rutz, prin. Fax 992-1272

Buckeye Local SD 1,800/K-12
3436 Edgewood Dr 44004 440-998-4411
Patrick Colucci, supt. Fax 992-8369
www.buckeyeschools.info/
Braden MS 400/6-8
3436 Edgewood Dr 44004 440-998-0550
Bill Billington, prin.
Ridgeview ES, 3456 Liberty St 44004 400/K-5
Danyel Ryan, prin. 440-997-7321
Other Schools – See Kingsville

Christian Faith Academy 50/K-8
4322 Park Ave 44004 440-998-3887
Dawn Schaubert, admin. Fax 998-3887
St. John S 200/K-12
7911 Depot Rd 44004 440-997-5531
Scott Plescia, prin. Fax 998-1661

Ashville, Pickaway, Pop. 4,045
Teays Valley Local SD 3,700/PK-12
385 Circleville Ave 43103 740-983-5000
Robin Halley, supt. Fax 983-4158
www.tvsd.us/
Ashville ES 300/PK-5
90 Walnut St 43103 740-983-5000
Gretchen Weiler, prin. Fax 983-5073
Teays Valley East MS 500/6-8
655 Viking Way 43103 740-983-5000
Shannon Helser, prin. Fax 983-5037
Walnut ES 400/PK-5
7150 Ashville Fairfield Rd 43103 740-983-5000
Greg Kovack, prin. Fax 983-5049
Other Schools – See Commercial Point, South Bloomfield

Athens, Athens, Pop. 23,284
Athens CSD
Supt. — See The Plains
Athens MS 400/7-8
51 W State St 45701 740-593-7107
Kara Bolin, prin. Fax 594-6506
East ES 400/K-6
3 Wallace Dr 45701 740-593-6901
Andrea Bobo, prin. Fax 593-3631
Morrison ES 400/K-6
793 W Union St 45701 740-593-5445
Penny McDowell, prin. Fax 594-5362
West ES 300/K-6
41 Central Ave 45701 740-593-6866
Jeanna Sycks, prin. Fax 594-3178

Attica, Seneca, Pop. 880
Seneca East Local SD 700/K-12
13343 E US Highway 224 44807 419-426-7041
Laura Kagy, supt. Fax 426-5514
www.seneca-east.k12.oh.us/
Seneca East ES 400/K-6
13343 E US Highway 224 44807 419-426-3344
Bradley Powers, prin. Fax 426-5400

Atwater, Portage, Pop. 754
Waterloo Local SD 1,100/K-12
1464 Industry Rd 44201 330-947-2664
Shawn Braman, supt. Fax 947-2847
www.viking.portage.k12.oh.us
Waterloo ES 500/K-5
1464 Industry Rd 44201 330-947-2153
Aaron Walker, prin. Fax 947-3331
Waterloo MS 300/6-8
1464 Industry Rd 44201 330-947-0033
Lauren Hutchinson, prin. Fax 947-4073

Aurora, Portage, Pop. 15,422
Aurora CSD 2,900/PK-12
102 E Garfield Rd 44202 330-562-6106
Pat Ciccantelli, supt. Fax 562-4892
www.aurora-schools.org
Craddock ES 600/1-2
105 Hurd Rd 44202 330-562-3175
Julie Troman, prin. Fax 954-2087
Harmon MS 700/6-8
130 Aurora Hudson Rd 44202 330-562-3375
Mark Abramovich, prin. Fax 562-4796
Leighton ES 600/3-5
121 Aurora Hudson Rd 44202 330-562-2209
Mike Janatovich, prin. Fax 562-2265
Miller ES PK-K
646 S Chillicothe Rd 44202 330-562-6199
Julie Troman, prin. Fax 954-2272

Valley Christian Academy 300/PK-8
1037 East Blvd 44202 330-562-8191
Dale Moncrief, admin. Fax 562-9257

Austinburg, Ashtabula, Pop. 512
Geneva CSD
Supt. — See Geneva
Austinburg ES 300/PK-5
3030 State Route 307 44010 440-466-4831
Amy Burzanko, prin. Fax 275-3195

Austintown, Mahoning, Pop. 31,500
Austintown Local SD
Supt. — See Youngstown
Austintown ES, 245 Idaho Rd 44515 1,100/K-2
Thomas Lenton, prin.
Austintown IS, 225 Idaho Rd 44515 1,100/3-5
Jeffrey Swavel, prin.

Avon, Lorain, Pop. 20,897
Avon Local SD 3,400/PK-12
36600 Detroit Rd 44011 440-937-4680
Michael Laub, supt. Fax 937-4688
www.avonlocalschools.org
Avon Early Learning Center 300/PK-K
3075 Stoney Ridge Rd 44011 440-934-5124
Colleen Mudore, prin. Fax 934-5147
Avon East ES 700/1-2
3100 Nagel Rd 44011 440-937-6015
Krista Kotecki, prin. Fax 937-5525
Avon Heritage ES 400/3-5
35575 Bentley Dr 44011 440-937-3055
Jason Call, prin. Fax 937-3054
Avon MS 700/6-8
3445 Long Rd 44011 440-934-3800
Dr. Craig Koehler, prin. Fax 934-3803

Avon Montessori Academy 50/PK-6
37701 Colorado Ave Ste C 44011 440-934-1774
Holy Trinity S 500/PK-8
2610 Nagel Rd 44011 440-937-6420
Kimberly Kuchta, prin. Fax 937-1029
St. Mary Immaculate Conception S 200/K-8
2680 Stoney Ridge Rd 44011 440-934-6246
Colleen Schager, prin. Fax 934-6250

Avon Lake, Lorain, Pop. 22,318
Avon Lake CSD 3,700/PK-12
175 Avon Belden Rd 44012 440-933-6210
Robert Scott, supt. Fax 933-6711
www.avonlakecityschools.org
Eastview ES 400/K-4
230 Lear Rd 44012 440-933-6283
Jamie Franko, prin. Fax 930-7012
Erieview ES 300/K-4
32630 Electric Blvd 44012 440-933-6282
David Schindler, prin. Fax 933-6381
Learwood MS 600/7-8
340 Lear Rd 44012 440-933-8142
Dr. Vishtasp Nuggud Ph.D., prin. Fax 933-8406
Redwood ES 400/PK-4
32967 Redwood Blvd 44012 440-933-5145
T.J. Ebert, prin. Fax 933-6230
Troy IS 600/5-6
237 Belmar Blvd 44012 440-933-2701
Andrew Peltz, prin. Fax 930-7005
Westview ES 200/K-4
155 Moore Rd 44012 440-933-8131
Nick Moore, prin. Fax 933-7025

St. Joseph S 300/K-8
32946 Electric Blvd 44012 440-933-6233
Joan Hazen, prin. Fax 933-2463

Bainbridge, Ross, Pop. 838
Paint Valley Local SD 900/K-12
7454 US Highway 50 W 45612 740-634-2826
Timothy Winland, supt. Fax 634-2890
paintvalleylocalschools.org
Paint Valley ES 500/K-5
7454 US Highway 50 W 45612 740-634-3454
Heather Bowles, prin. Fax 634-3459
Paint Valley MS 200/6-8
7454 US Highway 50 W 45612 740-634-3512
Lewis Ewry, prin. Fax 634-3459

Baltic, Holmes, Pop. 789
Garaway Local SD
Supt. — See Sugarcreek
Baltic ES 100/K-6
300 E Main St 43804 330-897-7261
Jeffery Williams, prin. Fax 897-3201

Baltimore, Fairfield, Pop. 2,921
Liberty Union-Thurston Local SD 1,300/PK-12
1108 S Main St 43105 740-862-4171
Todd Osborn, supt. Fax 862-2015
www.libertyunion.org
Liberty Union ES 500/PK-4
1000 S Main St 43105 740-862-4143
Linda Rainey, prin. Fax 862-0253
Liberty Union MS 400/5-8
994 S Main St 43105 740-862-4126
Tim Turner, prin. Fax 862-0239

Barberton, Summit, Pop. 25,978
Barberton CSD 3,900/PK-12
479 Norton Ave 44203 330-753-1025
Jeffrey Ramnytz, supt. Fax 848-0884
www.barbertonschools.org
Barberton ES East 700/K-4
292 Robinson Ave 44203 330-745-5492
Kenneth Lasky, prin.
Barberton ES West 700/K-4
1151 Shannon Ave 44203 330-825-2183
Brenda Wiles, prin.
Barberton MS 1,200/5-8
477 4th St NW 44203 330-745-9950
Michael Andric, prin. Fax 745-9962
Barberton Preschool PK-PK
633 Brady Ave 44203 330-780-3208
Jennifer Sutton, dir.

St. Augustine S 200/PK-8
195 7th St NW 44203 330-753-6435
Elaine Faessel, prin. Fax 753-4095

Barnesville, Belmont, Pop. 4,130
Barnesville EVD 1,200/PK-12
210 W Church St 43713 740-425-3615
Angela Hannahs, supt. Fax 425-5000
www.barnesville.k12.oh.us/
Barnesville ES 600/PK-4
210 W Church St 43713 740-425-3639
Clinton Abbott, prin. Fax 425-1136
Barnesville MS 400/5-8
970 Shamrock Dr 43713 740-425-3116
Casey Mayo, prin. Fax 425-9204

Bascom, Seneca, Pop. 390
Hopewell-Loudon Local SD 900/K-12
181 N County Rd 7 44809 419-937-2216
David Alvarado, supt. Fax 937-2516
www.hlschool.org
Hopewell-Loudon Local ES 500/K-6
290 N County Rd 7 44809 419-937-2804
Kendra Nelson, prin. Fax 937-2516

Batavia, Clermont, Pop. 1,482
Batavia Local SD 2,000/PK-12
2400 Clermont Center Dr 45103 513-732-2343
Keith Millard, supt. Fax 732-3221
www.bataviaschools.org
Batavia ES 1,000/PK-5
3 Bulldog Pl 45103 513-732-0780
Renee Filiater, prin. Fax 732-1863
Batavia MS 500/6-8
800 Bauer Ave 45103 513-732-9534
Steve Brokamp, prin. Fax 732-3696

Clermont Northeastern Local SD 1,500/PK-12
2792 US Highway 50 45103 513-625-5478
Michael Brandt, supt. Fax 625-6080
www.cneschools.org
Clermont Northeastern ES 700/K-5
5347 Hutchinson Rd 45103 513-625-1211
Tonya Schmidt, prin. Fax 732-0285
Clermont Northeastern MS 400/6-8
2792 US Highway 50 45103 513-625-1211
Laura Nazzarine, prin. Fax 625-3325
Other Schools – See Owensville

West Clermont Local SD
Supt. — See Cincinnati
West Clermont MS 1,000/6-8
1341 Clough Pike 45103 513-947-7400
Lori Crowe, prin. Fax 753-1070
Willowville ES 400/K-5
4529 Schoolhouse Rd 45103 513-943-6800
Michelle Kennedy, prin. Fax 752-9181

Bath, Summit
Revere Local SD
Supt. — See Richfield
Bath ES 400/PK-PK, 4-
1246 N Cleveland Massillon 44210 330-666-4155
Dan Fry, prin. Fax 666-3058
Revere MS 600/6-8
PO Box 330 44210 330-666-4155
Bill Conley, prin. Fax 659-3795

Bay Village, Cuyahoga, Pop. 15,468
Bay Village CSD 2,500/K-12
377 Dover Center Rd 44140 440-617-7300
Clinton Keener, supt. Fax 617-7301
www.bayvillageschools.com
Bay MS 800/5-8
27725 Wolf Rd 44140 440-617-7600
Sean McAndrews, prin. Fax 617-7601
Normandy ES 500/K-2
26920 Normandy Rd 44140 440-617-7350
Dan Sebring, prin. Fax 617-7351
Westerly ES 400/3-4
30301 Wolf Rd 44140 440-617-7550
Josie Sanfillippo, prin. Fax 617-7551

St. Raphael S 800/K-8
525 Dover Center Rd 44140 440-871-6760
Ann Miller, prin. Fax 871-1358

Beachwood, Cuyahoga, Pop. 11,798
Beachwood CSD 1,500/PK-12
24601 Fairmount Blvd 44122 216-464-2600
Robert Hardis, supt. Fax 292-2340
www.beachwoodschools.org/
Beachwood MS 300/6-8
2860 Richmond Rd 44122 216-831-0355
Paul Chase, prin. Fax 831-1891
Bryden ES 200/K-2
25501 Bryden Rd 44122 216-831-3933
Sherry Miller, prin. Fax 292-2375
Fairmount ECC 50/PK-PK
24601 Fairmount Blvd 44122 216-292-2344
Karen Leeds, dir. Fax 292-4174
Hilltop ES 300/3-5
24524 Hilltop Dr 44122 216-831-7144
Rebecca Holthaus, prin. Fax 292-4236

Fuchs Mizrachi S 400/PK-12
26600 Shaker Blvd 44122 216-932-0220
Lauren Ginsburg, head sch Fax 932-0345
Mandel Jewish Day S 300/PK-8
26500 Shaker Blvd 44122 216-464-4055
Jerry Isaak-Shapiro, head sch Fax 464-3229

Beallsville, Monroe, Pop. 400
Switzerland of Ohio Local SD
Supt. — See Woodsfield
Beallsville ES 200/PK-6
PO Box 262 43716 740-926-1309
Kellie Hayden, prin. Fax 926-2487

Beaver, Pike, Pop. 431
Eastern Local SD 800/PK-12
1170 Tile Mill Rd 45613 740-226-4851
Neil Leist, supt. Fax 226-1331
www.ep.k12.oh.us
Eastern IS 200/3-5
1170 Tile Mill Rd 45613 740-226-6402
Matt Hines, prin. Fax 226-6122
Eastern MS 200/6-8
1170 Tile Mill Rd 45613 740-226-1544
Lance Allen, prin. Fax 226-6322
Eastern PS 200/PK-2
1170 Tile Mill Rd 45613 740-226-6402
Matt Hines, prin. Fax 226-6122

Beavercreek, Greene, Pop. 44,171
Beavercreek CSD 7,500/PK-12
3040 Kemp Rd 45431 937-426-1522
Dr. Paul Otten, supt. Fax 429-7517
www.beavercreek.k12.oh.us/
Ankeney MS 800/6-8
4085 Shakertown Rd 45430 937-429-7567
Dale Wren, prin. Fax 429-7685
Beavercreek Preschool Center PK-PK
3038 Kemp Rd 45431 937-458-2360
Bobbie Fiori, prin. Fax 458-2361
Fairbrook ES 500/K-5
260 N Fairfield Rd 45430 937-429-7616
Joell Mangan, prin. Fax 429-7687
Main ES 600/K-5
2942 Dayton Xenia Rd 45434 937-429-7588
Sharma Nachlinger, prin. Fax 429-7688
Parkwood ES 600/PK-5
1791 Wilene Dr 45432 937-429-7604
Susan Bamford, prin. Fax 429-7684
Shaw ES 700/K-5
3560 Kemp Rd 45431 937-429-7610
Susan Peveler, prin. Fax 429-7690
Valley ES 500/K-5
3601 Jonathon Dr 45434 937-429-7597
Daniel Schwieterman, prin. Fax 429-7691
Other Schools – See Xenia

St. Luke S 400/K-8
1442 N Fairfield Rd 45432 937-426-8551
Leslie Vondrell, prin. Fax 426-6435

Bedford, Cuyahoga, Pop. 12,768
Bedford CSD 3,500/PK-12
475 Northfield Rd 44146 440-439-1500
Dr. Andrea Celico Ph.D., supt. Fax 439-4850
www.bedford.k12.oh.us
Carylwood IS 400/4-6
1387 Caryl Dr 44146 440-439-4509
Mary Catherine Ratkocky, prin. Fax 439-0366
Central PS 500/K-3
799 Washington St 44146 440-439-4225
Monique Winston, prin. Fax 439-4361
Glendale ES 500/PK-3
400 W Glendale St 44146 440-439-4227
Nora Beach, prin. Fax 439-3487
Other Schools – See Bedford Heights

Bedford Heights, Cuyahoga, Pop. 10,538
Bedford CSD
Supt. — See Bedford
Columbus IS 400/4-6
23600 Columbus Rd 44146 440-786-3322
Karla Robinson, prin. Fax 439-0495
Heskett MS 500/7-8
5771 Perkins Rd 44146 440-439-4450
Virginia Golden, prin. Fax 786-3572

Bellaire, Belmont, Pop. 4,190
Bellaire Local SD 1,200/K-12
340 34th St 43906 740-676-1826
Darren Jenkins Ed.D., supt. Fax 676-1826
www.bellaire.k12.oh.us
Bellaire ES 500/K-4
53299 Pike St 43906 740-676-1272
Derek Ault, prin. Fax 676-2334

Bellaire MS 400/5-8
54555 Neffs Bellaire Rd 43906 740-676-1635
Derrick McAfee, prin. Fax 676-3014

St. John Central S 100/PK-8
350 37th St 43906 740-676-2620
Jarett Kuhns, prin. Fax 676-8502

Bellbrook, Greene, Pop. 6,854
Bellbrook-Sugarcreek Local SD 2,500/K-12
3757 Upper Bellbrook Rd 45305 937-848-5001
Dr. Keith St. Pierre, supt. Fax 848-5018
www.sugarcreek.k12.oh.us
Bellbrook MS 600/6-8
3600 Feedwire Rd 45305 937-848-2141
Jenness Sigman, prin. Fax 848-2152
Bell Creek IS 600/3-5
3777 Upper Bellbrook Rd 45305 937-848-5001
Jill Adams, prin. Fax 848-5078
Bell ES 500/K-2
4122 N Linda Dr 45305 937-848-7831
Ginger Keeton, prin. Fax 848-5007

Bellefontaine, Logan, Pop. 12,899
Bellefontaine CSD 2,500/K-12
820 Ludlow Rd 43311 937-593-9060
Brad Hall, supt. Fax 599-1346
www.bellefontaine.k12.oh.us/
Bellefontaine IS 600/3-5
509 N Park St 43311 937-592-5646
Krista Adelsberger, prin. Fax 599-3327
Bellefontaine MS 600/6-8
1201 Ludlow Rd 43311 937-593-9010
Lynda Holycross, prin. Fax 593-9030
Bellfontaine ES 600/K-2
1001 Ludlow Rd 43311 937-599-4431
Pat Martz, prin. Fax 599-3262

Benjamin Logan Local SD 1,700/K-12
4740 County Road 26 43311 937-593-9211
David Harmon, supt. Fax 599-4059
www.benjaminlogan.org
Logan ES 700/K-4
4560 County Road 26 43311 937-592-4838
Colleen Bodin, prin. Fax 592-4063
Logan MS 500/5-8
4626 County Road 26 43311 937-599-2386
Rob Walter, prin. Fax 599-4062

Calvary Christian S 200/PK-12
1140 Rush Ave 43311 937-599-6847
Ryan Hyde, admin. Fax 599-4879

Bellevue, Huron, Pop. 8,079
Bellevue CSD 2,100/PK-12
125 North St 44811 419-484-5000
Kim Schubert, supt. Fax 483-0723
www.bellevueschools.org
Bellevue ES 900/PK-5
1150 Castalia St 44811 419-484-5050
Shannon Turner, prin. Fax 484-5105
Bellevue MS 500/6-8
1035 Castalia St 44811 419-484-5060
John Bollinger, prin. Fax 484-5096

Immaculate Conception S 200/PK-8
304 E Main St 44811 419-483-6066
Pamela Griebel, prin. Fax 483-2736

Bellville, Richland, Pop. 1,888
Clear Fork Valley Local SD 1,700/K-12
92 Hines Ave 44813 419-886-3855
Janice Wyckoff, supt. Fax 886-2237
www.clearfork.k12.oh.us
Bellville ES 400/K-5
195 School St 44813 419-886-3244
Kirsten DeVito, prin. Fax 886-3851
Clear Fork MS 400/6-8
987 State Route 97 E 44813 419-886-3111
Jennifer Klaus, prin. Fax 886-4749
Other Schools – See Butler

Belmont, Belmont, Pop. 449
Union Local SD 1,500/PK-12
66779 Belmont Morristown Rd 43718 740-782-1978
Robert Porter, supt. Fax 782-1212
www.ulschools.com
Union Local ES 700/PK-5
66699 Belmont Morristown Rd 43718 740-782-1384
Dana Kendziorski, prin. Fax 782-0181
Union Local MS 300/6-8
66859 Belmont Morristown Rd 43718 740-782-1388
Rick Barnhouse, prin. Fax 782-1474

Beloit, Mahoning, Pop. 960
West Branch Local SD 2,100/K-12
14277 S Main St 44609 330-938-9324
Dr. Timothy Saxton, supt. Fax 938-6815
www.westbranch.k12.oh.us
West Branch MS 700/5-8
14409 Beloit Snodes Rd 44609 330-938-4300
Roger Kitzmiller, prin. Fax 938-4301
Other Schools – See Alliance, Salem

Belpre, Washington, Pop. 6,292
Belpre CSD 1,000/K-12
2014 Rockland Ave 45714 740-423-9511
Dwight Dunn, supt. Fax 423-3050
www.belpre.k12.oh.us
Belpre ES 600/K-6
2000 Rockland Ave 45714 740-423-3010
Joy Edgell, prin. Fax 423-3012

Berea, Cuyahoga, Pop. 18,699
Berea CSD 7,000/PK-12
390 Fair St 44017 216-898-8300
Michael Sheppard, supt. Fax 898-8551
www.berea.k12.oh.us

Grindstone ES 900/PK-4
191 Race St 44017 216-898-8305
Theresa Grimm, prin. Fax 898-8563
Other Schools – See Brook Park, Middleburg Heights

Academy of St. Adalbert 100/PK-8
56 Adelbert St 44017 440-234-5529
Susan Herman, prin. Fax 234-2881
St. Mary S 400/PK-8
265 Baker St 44017 440-243-4555
Andrew Carner, prin. Fax 243-6214

Bergholz, Jefferson, Pop. 660
Edison Local SD
Supt. — See Hammondsville
Gregg ES 400/PK-6
212 County Road 75A 43908 740-768-2100
Tammy Burchfield, prin. Fax 768-2616

Berlin, Holmes, Pop. 892
East Holmes Local SD
Supt. — See Millersburg
Berlin ES 300/K-6
4978 W Main St 44610 330-893-2817
Darren Blochlinger, prin. Fax 893-3503
Chestnut Ridge S 300/K-8
5088 TR 401 44610 330-893-2413
James Luneborg, prin. Fax 893-2827

Berlin Center, Mahoning
Western Reserve Local SD 300/K-12
13850 W Akron Canfield Rd 44401 330-547-4100
Douglas McGlynn, supt. Fax 547-9302
www.westernreserve.k12.oh.us
Western Reserve S 300/K-12
13850 W Akron Canfield Rd 44401 330-547-4100
Dallas Saunders, prin. Fax 547-9302

Berlin Heights, Erie, Pop. 698
Edison Local SD
Supt. — See Milan
Edison MS 600/4-8
20 Center St 44814 419-588-2078
Cory Smith, prin. Fax 588-3212

Bethel, Clermont, Pop. 2,658
Bethel-Tate Local SD 1,600/K-12
675 W Plane St 45106 513-734-2271
Melissa Kircher, supt. Fax 734-4792
www.betheltate.org
Bethel-Tate MS 400/6-8
649 W Plane St 45106 513-734-2271
Christen Davis, prin. Fax 734-0888
Bick PS 400/K-2
101 Fossyl Dr 45106 513-734-2271
Kay Nau, prin. Fax 734-0444
Hill IS 400/3-5
150 Fossyl Dr 45106 513-734-2271
Matthew Wagner, prin. Fax 734-3013

Bettsville, Seneca, Pop. 659
Old Fort Local SD
Supt. — See Old Fort
Old Fort ES 200/K-6
118 Washington St 44815 419-986-5166
Michelle Dantuono, prin. Fax 986-6039

Beverly, Washington, Pop. 1,285
Fort Frye Local SD 900/K-12
PO Box 1149 45715 740-984-2497
Stephanie Starcher, supt. Fax 984-8784
www.fortfrye.k12.oh.us
Beverly-Center ES 200/K-6
510 5th St 45715 740-984-2371
Megan Miller, prin. Fax 984-8167
Other Schools – See Lowell, Lower Salem

Bexley, Franklin, Pop. 12,740
Bexley CSD 2,200/K-12
348 S Cassingham Rd 43209 614-231-7611
Dr. Kimberly Miller, supt. Fax 231-8448
www.bexleyschools.org
Bexley MS 400/7-8
300 S Cassingham Rd 43209 614-237-4277
Dr. Jason Caudill, prin. Fax 338-2090
Cassingham ES 400/K-6
250 S Cassingham Rd 43209 614-237-4266
Jeannine Hetzler, prin. Fax 338-2092
Maryland ES 300/K-6
2754 Maryland Ave 43209 614-237-3280
Jon Hood, prin. Fax 338-2080
Montrose ES 400/K-6
2555 E Main St 43209 614-237-4226
Dr. Quint Gage, prin. Fax 338-2088

Bidwell, Gallia
Gallia County Local SD
Supt. — See Patriot
River Valley MS 400/6-8
8779 State Route 160 45614 740-446-8399
O. Ed Moore, prin. Fax 441-3038

Big Prairie, Holmes
West Holmes Local SD
Supt. — See Millersburg
Nashville ES 100/K-2
13495 State Route 39 44611 330-378-2111
Brian Zimmerly, prin. Fax 378-2323

Blacklick, Franklin
Gahanna-Jefferson CSD
Supt. — See Gahanna
Blacklick ES 500/PK-5
6540 Havens Corners Rd 43004 614-759-5100
Kristen Groves, prin. Fax 759-5110

Licking Heights Local SD
Supt. — See Pataskala
Licking Heights West ES 900/K-4
1490 Climbing Fig Dr 43004 614-864-9089
Belinda Hohman, prin. Fax 501-4672

Grace Christian S 400/K-8
7510 E Broad St 43004 614-861-0724
Cynthia Phillips, supt. Fax 863-8509

Blanchester, Clinton, Pop. 4,195
Blanchester Local SD 1,700/PK-12
951 Cherry St 45107 937-783-3523
Dean D. Lynch, supt. Fax 783-2990
www.blan.org
Blanchester IS 200/4-5
955 Cherry St 45107 937-783-2040
Marci Goodrich, prin. Fax 783-3477
Blanchester MS 400/6-8
955 Cherry St 45107 937-783-3642
Amy Schaljo, prin. Fax 783-3477
Putman ES 600/PK-3
327 E Baldwin St 45107 937-783-2681
Michael Snider, prin. Fax 783-5192

Little Miami Local SD
Supt. — See Maineville
Harlan-Butlerville PS 100/1-2
8276 State Route 132 45107 513-899-5200
Maryann Duffy, prin. Fax 877-3200

Bloomdale, Wood, Pop. 675
Elmwood Local SD 1,200/PK-12
7650 Jerry City Rd 44817 419-655-2583
Tony Borton, supt. Fax 655-3995
www.elmwood.k12.oh.us
Elmwood ES 500/PK-4
7650 Jerry City Rd 44817 419-655-2583
Gary Dulle, prin. Fax 655-3995
Elmwood MS 400/5-8
7650 Jerry City Rd 44817 419-655-2583
Roger Frank, prin. Fax 655-3995

Bluffton, Allen, Pop. 4,072
Bluffton EVD 1,100/K-12
102 S Jackson St 45817 419-358-5901
Dr. Gregory Denecker, supt. Fax 358-4871
www.blufftonschools.org
Bluffton ES 500/K-5
102 S Jackson St 45817 419-358-7951
Timothy Closson, prin. Fax 358-4871
Bluffton MS 200/6-8
116 S Jackson St 45817 419-358-7961
Kyle Leatherman, prin. Fax 358-4871

Boardman, Mahoning, Pop. 34,850

St. Charles S 400/PK-8
7325 Westview Dr 44512 330-758-6689
Mary Welsh, prin. Fax 758-7404

Bolivar, Tuscarawas, Pop. 990
Tuscarawas Valley Local SD
Supt. — See Zoarville
Tuscarawas Valley IS 300/2-4
216 Park Ave NW 44612 330-874-3234
Diana Flickinger, prin. Fax 859-8875

Botkins, Shelby, Pop. 1,145
Botkins Local SD 300/K-12
404 E State St 45306 937-693-4241
Jeff McPheron, supt. Fax 693-2557
www.botkins.k12.oh.us
Botkins S 300/K-12
404 E State St 45306 937-693-4241
Jeff McPheron, admin. Fax 693-2557

Bowerston, Harrison, Pop. 397
Conotton Valley Union Local SD
Supt. — See Sherrodsville
Conotton Valley ES 100/PK-5
7205 Cumberland Rd SW 44695 740-269-2141
Mike Wright, prin. Fax 269-4405

Bowling Green, Wood, Pop. 29,467
Bowling Green CSD 3,000/PK-12
137 Clough St 43402 419-352-3576
Francis Scruci, supt. Fax 352-1701
www.bgcs.k12.oh.us
Bowling Green MS 700/6-8
1079 Fairview Ave 43402 419-354-0200
Eric Radabaugh, prin. Fax 353-1958
Bowling Green Preschool 100/PK-PK
1020 Scott Hamilton Ave 43402 419-354-0400
Melanie Garbig, prin. Fax 352-7675
Conneaut ES 500/K-5
542 Haskins Rd 43402 419-354-0300
James Lang, prin. Fax 352-6661
Crim ES 500/K-5
1020 Scott Hamilton Ave 43402 419-354-0400
Alyssa Karaffa, prin. Fax 352-7675
Kenwood ES 500/K-5
710 Kenwood Ave 43402 419-354-0500
Kathleen Daney, prin. Fax 352-8261

Otsego Local SD 1,500/PK-12
18505 Tontogany Creek Rd 43402 419-823-4381
Adam Koch, supt. Fax 823-3035
www.otsegoknights.org
Otsego ES 700/PK-5
18505 Tontogany Creek Rd 43402 419-823-4381
Katrina Baughman, prin. Fax 823-1703
Otsego JHS 400/6-8
18505 Tontogany Creek Rd 43402 419-823-4381
Jon Rife, prin. Fax 823-0944

Bowling Green Christian Academy 200/PK-12
1165 Haskins Rd 43402 419-354-2422
Daniel Kessler, prin. Fax 354-0232
Montessori S Bowling Green 100/PK-8
515 Sand Ridge Rd 43402 419-352-4203
Bev Bechstein, admin. Fax 353-1914
St. Aloysius S 200/PK-8
PO Box 485 43402 419-352-8614
Andrea Puhl, prin. Fax 352-4738

Bradford, Darke, Pop. 1,831
Bradford EVD 500/K-12
760 Railroad Ave 45308 937-448-2770
Joseph Hurst, supt. Fax 448-2493
www.bradford.k12.oh.us
Bradford ES 300/K-5
740 Railroad Ave 45308 937-448-2811
Michelle Lavey, prin. Fax 448-2742

Brecksville, Cuyahoga, Pop. 13,500
Brecksville-Broadview Heights CSD 4,100/PK-12
6638 Mill Rd 44141 440-740-4000
Joelle Magyar, supt. Fax 740-4004
www.bbhcsd.org
Central ES 600/4-5
27 Public Sq 44141 440-740-4100
Christopher Hartland, prin. Fax 740-4104
Chippewa ES 300/K-3
8611 Wiese Rd 44141 440-740-4200
Beverly Chambers, prin. Fax 740-4204
Highland Drive ES 300/K-3
9457 Highland Dr 44141 440-740-4300
Eva O'Mara, prin. Fax 740-4304
Hilton ES 400/PK-3
6812 Mill Rd 44141 440-740-4600
David Martin, prin. Fax 740-4604
Other Schools – See Broadview Heights

South Suburban Montessori S 100/PK-8
4450 Oakes Rd Bldg 6 44141 440-526-1966
Amy Mackie-Barr, head sch Fax 526-6026

Bremen, Fairfield, Pop. 1,407
Fairfield Union Local SD
Supt. — See Lancaster
Bremen ES 300/K-4
210 Strayer Ave 43107 740-569-4135
Dawn Rice, prin. Fax 569-9605

Brice, Franklin, Pop. 103

Brice Christian Academy 200/K-8
PO Box 370 43109 614-866-6789
Margaret McCoy, admin. Fax 861-4217

Bridgeport, Belmont, Pop. 1,773
Bridgeport EVD 800/PK-12
55781 National Rd 43912 740-635-1713
Zachary Shutler, supt. Fax 635-6003
www.bevs.k12.oh.us/
Bridgeport ES 400/PK-4
55707 Industrial Dr 43912 740-635-0853
Kamaron Sabinski, prin. Fax 635-6006
Bridgeport MS 200/5-8
55707 Industrial Dr 43912 740-635-0853
Anne Haverty, prin. Fax 635-6003

Brilliant, Jefferson, Pop. 1,469
Buckeye Local SD
Supt. — See Dillonvale
Buckeye North ES 400/PK-6
1004 3rd St 43913 740-598-4589
Susan Nolan, prin. Fax 598-3909

Bristolville, Trumbull
Bristol Local SD 700/K-12
PO Box 260 44402 330-889-3882
Christopher Dray, supt. Fax 889-2529
www.bristol.k12.oh.us
Bristol ES 400/K-6
PO Box 260 44402 330-889-2700
Ryan Stowell, prin. Fax 889-2529

Broadview Heights, Cuyahoga, Pop. 19,168
Brecksville-Broadview Heights CSD
Supt. — See Brecksville
Brecksville-Broadview Heights MS 1,000/6-8
6376 Mill Rd 44147 440-740-4400
Todd Rings, prin. Fax 740-4404

Assumption Academy 300/PK-8
9183 Broadview Rd 44147 440-526-4877
Joanne Lopresti, prin. Fax 526-3752

Brookfield, Trumbull
Brookfield Local SD 1,100/K-12
614 Bedford Rd SE 44403 330-448-4930
Velina Taylor, supt. Fax 448-5026
www.brookfield.k12.oh.us
Brookfield ES 400/K-4
614 Bedford Rd SE 44403 330-619-5240
Stacey Filicky, prin. Fax 619-5240
Brookfield MS 300/5-8
614 Bedford Rd SE 44403 330-448-3003
William Gibson, prin. Fax 448-5028

Brooklyn, Cuyahoga, Pop. 10,955
Brooklyn CSD 1,300/PK-12
9200 Biddulph Rd 44144 216-485-8100
Dr. Mark Gleichauf, supt. Fax 485-8118
www.brooklyn.k12.oh.us
Brooklyn ES 400/PK-3
9200 Biddulph Rd 44144 216-485-8176
Patrick Yarman, prin. Fax 485-8120
Brooklyn IS 300/4-7
9200 Biddulph Rd 44144 216-485-8127
Mark Tanski, prin. Fax 485-8130

St. Thomas More S 400/PK-8
4180 N Amber Dr 44144 216-749-1660
Jennifer Francis, prin. Fax 398-4265

Brook Park, Cuyahoga, Pop. 18,877
Berea CSD
Supt. — See Berea
Brookpark Memorial ES 700/PK-4
16900 Holland Rd 44142 216-433-1350
Michael Kostyack, prin. Fax 676-2073

Brookview ES 400/PK-4
14105 Snow Rd 44142 216-676-4334
Tracy Schneid, prin. Fax 676-2074

Ford IS 900/5-6
17001 Holland Rd 44142 216-433-1133
Mark Mucha, prin. Fax 676-2072

Brookville, Montgomery, Pop. 5,844

Brookville Local SD 1,400/K-12
75 June Pl 45309 937-833-2181
Timothy Hopkins, supt. Fax 833-2787
www.brookvilleschools.org

Brookville ES 400/K-3
3 Blue Pride Dr 45309 937-833-6796
Stephanie Hinds, prin. Fax 833-5354

Brookville IS 600/4-8
2 Blue Pride Dr 45309 937-833-6731
Erin Wheat, prin. Fax 833-6756

Brunswick, Medina, Pop. 33,855

Brunswick CSD 7,200/PK-12
3643 Center Rd 44212 330-225-7731
Michael Mayell, supt. Fax 273-0507
www.bcsoh.org

Applewood ES 500/K-5
3891 Applewood Dr 44212 330-225-7731
Amren Fowler, prin. Fax 273-0507

Brunswick Memorial ES 400/K-5
3845 Magnolia Dr 44212 330-225-7731
Kati Mann, prin. Fax 273-0507

Crestview ES 400/K-5
300 W 130th St 44212 330-225-7731
Jamie Schulke, prin. Fax 273-0507

Edwards MS 500/6-8
1497 Pearl Rd 44212 330-225-7731
Heidi Armentrout, prin. Fax 273-0507

Hickory Ridge ES 500/K-5
4628 Hickory Ridge Ave 44212 330-225-7731
Marisa Bavaro, prin. Fax 273-0507

Huntington ES 400/K-5
1931 Huntington Cir 44212 330-225-7731
Kesh Boodheshwar, prin. Fax 273-0507

Kidder ES 500/PK-5
3650 Grafton Rd 44212 330-225-7731
Bonnie Kubec, prin. Fax 273-0507

Towslee ES 500/K-5
3555 Center Rd 44212 330-225-7731
Lisa Mayle, prin. Fax 273-0507

Visintainer MS 600/6-8
1459 Pearl Rd 44212 330-225-7731
Brian Sharosky, prin. Fax 273-0507

Willetts MS 700/6-8
1045 Hadcock Rd 44212 330-225-7731
Brian Miller, prin. Fax 273-0507

St. Ambrose S 500/PK-8
923 Pearl Rd 44212 330-225-2116
Lisa Cinadr, prin. Fax 225-5425

Bryan, Williams, Pop. 8,426

Bryan CSD 800/PK-12
1350 Fountain Grove Dr 43506 419-636-6973
Diana Savage, supt. Fax 633-6280
www.bryan.k12.oh.us

Bryan ES 300/PK-5
1301 Center St 43506 419-636-6931
Karyn Cox, prin. Fax 633-6282

Fountain City Christian S 100/K-12
120 S Beech St 43506 419-636-2333
Troy Cummins, admin. Fax 636-2888

St. Patrick S 200/PK-8
610 S Portland St 43506 419-636-3592
Connie Niese, prin. Fax 633-9112

Bucyrus, Crawford, Pop. 12,227

Bucyrus CSD 1,400/PK-12
170 Plymouth St 44820 419-562-4045
Kevin Kimmel, supt. Fax 562-3990
bucyrusschools.org

Bucyrus ES 700/PK-5
245 Woodlawn Ave 44820 419-562-6089
Tim Souder, prin. Fax 562-2367

Bucyrus MS 300/6-8
455 Redman Way 44820 419-562-0003
Jay Dennison, admin. Fax 562-1773

Wynford Local SD 1,100/PK-12
3288 Holmes Center Rd 44820 419-562-7828
Frederick Fox, supt. Fax 562-7825
www.wynfordroyals.org

Wynford ES 700/PK-6
3300 Holmes Center Rd 44820 419-562-4619
Nelle Nutter, prin. Fax 563-2905

Wynford JHS 200/7-8
3288 Holmes Center Rd 44820 419-562-7828
Chris Solis, prin. Fax 562-7825

Burton, Geauga, Pop. 1,446

Berkshire Local SD 1,100/PK-12
14259 Claridon Troy Rd 44021 440-834-3380
John Stoddard, supt.
www.berkshireschools.org

Burton ES, 13724 Carlton St 44021 400/PK-6
Amanda Randles, prin. 440-834-3380
Other Schools – See Thompson

Agape Christian Academy 100/PK-4
14220 Claridon Troy Rd 44021 440-834-8022
Susan Gifford, pres. Fax 834-4931

Butler, Richland, Pop. 926

Clear Fork Valley Local SD
Supt. — See Bellville

Butler ES 400/K-5
125 College St 44822 419-883-3451
Libby Nickoli, prin. Fax 883-3395

Byesville, Guernsey, Pop. 2,409

Rolling Hills Local SD
Supt. — See Cambridge

Brook IS 400/3-5
58601 Marietta Rd 43723 740-685-2526
Shelly Sowers, prin. Fax 685-5230

Byesville ES 200/K-2
212 Main St 43723 740-685-3113
Gail Thomas, prin. Fax 685-5410

Meadowbrook MS 400/6-8
58607 Marietta Rd 43723 740-685-2561
William Spence, admin. Fax 685-2628

Cadiz, Harrison, Pop. 3,237

Harrison Hills CSD 1,600/PK-12
730 Peppard Ave 43907 740-942-7800
Dana Snider, supt. Fax 942-7812
www.hhcsd.org/
Other Schools – See Hopedale, Scio

Caldwell, Noble, Pop. 1,727

Caldwell EVD 800/PK-12
516 Fairground St 43724 740-732-5637
Kacey Cottrill, supt. Fax 732-7303
www.caldwell.k12.oh.us

Caldwell S 600/PK-8
44350 Fairground Rd 43724 740-732-4614
Rebecca Johnson, prin.

Caledonia, Marion, Pop. 572

River Valley Local SD 1,900/K-12
197 Brocklesby Rd 43314 740-725-5400
James Peterson, supt. Fax 725-5499
www.rvk12.org

Liberty ES 400/K-5
1932 Whetstone River Rd N 43314 740-725-5600
Sandra Richards, prin. Fax 725-5699

River Valley MS 500/6-8
4334 Marion Mount Gilead Rd 43314 740-725-5700
Donald Gliebe, prin. Fax 725-5799
Other Schools – See Marion

Cambridge, Guernsey, Pop. 10,324

Cambridge CSD 2,100/K-12
518 S 8th St 43725 740-439-5021
Dan Coffman, supt. Fax 439-3796
www.cambridge.k12.oh.us/

Cambridge IS 400/3-5
1451 Deerpath Dr 43725 740-435-1180
Laurie Goggin, prin. Fax 435-1181

Cambridge MS 500/6-8
1400 Deerpath Dr 43725 740-435-1140
Heath Hayes, prin. Fax 435-1141

Cambridge PS 400/K-2
1115 Clairmont Ave 43725 740-439-7547
Leslie Leppla, prin. Fax 439-7590

East Muskingum Local SD
Supt. — See New Concord

Pike ES 100/K-2
4533 Peters Creek Rd 43725 740-439-1645
Anne Troendly, prin. Fax 432-3201

Rolling Hills Local SD 1,600/K-12
60851 Southgate Rd 43725 740-432-5370
Ryan Caldwell, supt. Fax 432-6523
www.rhcolts.org
Other Schools – See Byesville, Senecaville

St. Benedict S 100/K-8
220 N 7th St 43725 740-432-6751
Jane Rush, prin. Fax 432-4511

Camden, Preble, Pop. 2,033

Preble Shawnee Local SD 1,400/PK-12
124 Bloomfield St 45311 937-452-1283
Matt Bishop, supt. Fax 452-3926
www.preble-shawnee.k12.oh.us

Camden PS 500/PK-3
120 Bloomfield St 45311 937-452-1204
Heather Campbell, prin. Fax 452-3787
Other Schools – See West Elkton

Campbell, Mahoning, Pop. 8,033

Campbell CSD 900/K-12
280 6th St 44405 330-799-8777
Matthew Bowen, supt. Fax 799-0875
www.campbell.k12.oh.us

Campbell K-7 S 500/K-7
2002 Community Cir 44405 330-799-0054
James Klingensmith, prin. Fax 799-8259

Canal Fulton, Stark, Pop. 5,390

Northwest Local SD 1,900/K-12
2309 Locust St S 44614 330-854-2291
Dr. Michael Shreffler, supt. Fax 854-3591
www.northwest.sparcc.org/

Northwest MS 500/6-8
8614 Erie Ave NW 44614 330-854-3303
Gregory Ramos, prin. Fax 854-5883

Northwest PS 400/K-2
8436 Erie Ave NW 44614 330-854-5405
James Lariccia, prin. Fax 854-5809

Stinson ES 400/3-5
8454 Erie Ave NW 44614 330-854-4646
Lori Mariani, prin. Fax 854-7136

SS. Philip & James S 200/PK-8
532 High St NE 44614 330-854-2823
Daniel Mitchell, prin. Fax 854-1109

Canal Winchester, Franklin, Pop. 6,995

Canal Winchester Local SD 3,600/K-12
100 Washington St 43110 614-837-4533
James Sotlar, supt. Fax 833-2165
www.cwls.us

Canal Winchester MS 900/6-8
7155 Parkview Dr 43110 614-833-2151
Kelly Zywczyk, prin. Fax 833-2173

Indian Trail ES 800/K-2
6767 Gender Rd 43110 614-833-2154
Eric Riddle, prin. Fax 833-2167

Winchester Trail ES 800/3-5
6865 Gender Rd 43110 614-833-2150
Dr. Lori Green, prin. Fax 833-2161

Harvest Preparatory S 500/PK-12
PO Box 400 43110 614-382-1111
Dr. Kenneth Grunden, prin. Fax 837-9591

Canfield, Mahoning, Pop. 7,448

Canfield Local SD 2,800/K-12
100 Wadsworth St 44406 330-533-3303
Alex Geordan, supt. Fax 533-6827
www.canfieldschools.net/

Campbell ES 400/K-4
300 Moreland Dr 44406 330-533-5959
Travis Lavery, prin. Fax 702-7061

Canfield Village MS 900/5-8
42 Wadsworth St 44406 330-533-4019
Judd Rubin, prin. Fax 702-7064

Hilltop ES 500/K-4
400 Hilltop Blvd 44406 330-533-9806
Joe Maroni, prin. Fax 702-7051

South Range Local SD 1,200/K-12
11300 Columbiana Canfield 44406 330-549-5226
Dennis J. Dunham, supt. Fax 549-4740
www.southrange.k12.oh.us/

South Range ES 400/K-4
11300 Columbiana Canfield 44406 330-549-5578
Steven Matos, prin. Fax 549-3430

South Range MS 400/5-8
11300 Columbiana Canfield 44406 330-549-4071
Daniel Szolek, prin. Fax 549-4073

Canton, Stark, Pop. 69,508

Canton CSD 7,300/PK-12
305 McKinley Ave NW 44702 330-438-2500
Adrian Allison, supt. Fax 430-4230
www.ccsdistrict.org

Allen ES 200/PK-2
1326 Sherrick Rd SE 44707 330-453-2782
Christen Sedmock, prin. Fax 588-2127

Altitude Academy @ Crenshaw 500/6-8
2525 19th St NE 44705 330-454-7717
Tiffany Hardwick, prin. Fax 588-2120

Arts Academy @ Summit 300/K-8
1100 10th St NW 44703 330-452-6537
Chet Lenartowicz, prin. Fax 580-3190

Belden ES 100/3-5
2115 Georgetown Rd NE 44704 330-453-6902
Angela Seders, prin. Fax 588-2128

Cedar ES 200/3-5
2823 9th St SW 44710 330-580-3502
Kathryn Kisha-Wise, prin. Fax 580-3165

Clarendon ES 200/3-5
412 Clarendon Ave NW 44708 330-453-7681
Nicole Herberghs, prin. Fax 438-2773

College and Career Readiness Academy 600/6-8
1400 Broad Ave NW 44708 330-456-1963
Shawn Monahan, prin. Fax 456-8121

Dueber ES 200/PK-2
815 Dueber Ave SW 44706 330-580-3517
Jolinda Seiple, prin. Fax 580-3163

Early College Academy @ Souers 400/6-8
2800 13th St SW 44710 330-438-2736
Amy Conn, prin. Fax 580-3540

Gibbs ES 100/3-5
1320 Gibbs Ave NE 44705 330-456-1521
Myra Watkins, prin. Fax 580-3164

Harter ES 300/PK-2
317 Raff Rd NW 44708 330-456-1001
Debbie Wensel, prin. Fax 588-2132

Mason ES 100/3-5
316 30th St NW 44709 330-588-2156
Renee Brown, prin. Fax 580-3038

McGregor ES 200/PK-2
2339 17th St SW 44706 330-452-7069
Marianna Arvidson, prin. Fax 588-2133

Schreiber ES 100/PK-2
1503 Woodland Ave NW 44703 330-452-1672
Aaron Bouie, prin. Fax 580-3031

STEAMM Academy @ Hartford 400/6-8
1824 3rd St SE 44707 330-453-6012
David Thompson, prin. Fax 453-5096

Stone ES 200/PK-2
2100 Rowland Ave NE 44714 330-452-6521
Charla Malone, prin. Fax 452-6858

Worley ES 200/PK-2
1340 23rd St NW 44709 330-452-5748
Elena Monahan, prin. Fax 588-2150

Youtz ES 100/3-5
1901 Midway Ave NE 44705 330-452-7601
Michael Black, prin. Fax 588-2159
Other Schools – See North Canton

Canton Local SD 2,200/PK-12
800 Faircrest Ave SE 44707 330-484-8010
Stephen Milano M.Ed., supt. Fax 484-8032
www.cantonlocal.org

Faircrest Memorial MS 600/5-8
616 Faircrest St SW 44706 330-484-8015
Gay Welker, prin. Fax 484-8033

Walker ES 700/PK-4
3525 Sandy Ave SE 44707 330-484-8020
Frank Kruger, prin. Fax 484-8134

Jackson Local SD
Supt. — See Massillon

Lake Cable ES 500/K-5
5335 Villa Padova Dr NW 44718 330-494-8171
Angela Leggett, prin. Fax 494-3040

Perry Local SD
Supt. — See Massillon
Knapp ES 400/PK-4
5151 Oakcliff St SW 44706 330-478-6174
Tricia Self, prin. Fax 477-4542
Whipple Heights ES 400/K-4
4800 12th St NW 44708 330-478-6177
Joseph Hug, prin. Fax 478-6179

Plain Local SD 6,100/K-12
901 44th St NW 44709 330-492-3500
Brent May, supt. Fax 493-5542
www.plainlocal.org/
Avondale ES 300/K-4
3933 Eaton Rd NW 44708 330-491-3720
Maria Smith, prin. Fax 491-3721
Barr ES 400/K-4
2000 47th St NE 44705 330-491-3730
Trisha Williams, prin. Fax 491-3731
Frazer ES 300/K-4
3900 Frazer Ave NW 44709 330-491-3740
James Easterling, prin. Fax 491-3741
Glenwood IS 900/5-6
1015 44th St NW 44709 330-491-3780
Brett Niarchos, prin. Fax 491-3781
Middlebranch ES 500/K-4
7500 Middlebranch Ave NE 44721 330-491-3750
Jill Downing, prin. Fax 491-3751
Oakwood MS 900/7-8
2300 Schneider St NE 44721 330-491-3790
Jeanne McNeal, prin. Fax 491-3791
Taft ES 400/K-4
3829 Guilford Ave NW 44718 330-491-3760
Ann Bartley, prin. Fax 491-3761
Warstler ES 300/K-4
2500 Schneider St NE 44721 330-491-3770
Mark Yocum, prin. Fax 491-3771

Canton Country Day S 200/PK-8
3000 Demington Ave NW 44718 330-453-8279
Mike Brown, head sch Fax 453-6038
Heritage Christian S 300/PK-12
2107 6th St SW 44706 330-452-8271
Sharla Elton, supt. Fax 452-0672
Holy Cross Preschool & K 100/PK-K
7707 Market Ave N 44721 330-494-6478
Marjorie James, prin. Fax 499-2319
Our Lady of Peace S 200/PK-5
1001 39th St NW 44709 330-492-0622
Richard Hull, prin. Fax 492-0959
St. Joan of Arc S 300/PK-8
120 Bordner Ave SW 44710 330-477-2972
Christopher Pollard, prin Fax 478-2606
St. Michael S 300/PK-8
3431 Saint Michaels Blvd NW 44718 330-492-2657
Claire Gatti, prin. Fax 492-9618
St. Peter S 200/PK-5
702 Cleveland Ave NW 44702 330-452-0125
Sandra Fusillo, prin. Fax 453-8083

Cardington, Morrow, Pop. 2,023
Cardington-Lincoln Local SD 1,000/K-12
121 Nichols St 43315 419-864-3691
Brian Petrie, supt. Fax 864-0946
www.cardington.k12.oh.us
Cardington-Lincoln ES 400/K-4
121 Nichols St 43315 419-864-6692
Lealon Hardwick, prin. Fax 864-8701
Cardington-Lincoln JHS 200/5-8
349 Chesterville Ave 43315 419-864-0609
Jennifer Zierden, prin. Fax 864-3168

Carey, Wyandot, Pop. 3,640
Carey EVD 800/K-12
2016 Blue Devil Dr 43316 419-396-7922
Michael Wank, supt. Fax 396-3158
careyevs.schoolwires.com/
Carey ES 400/K-6
2016 Blue Devil Dr 43316 419-396-6767
Tammy Wagner, prin. Fax 396-3158

Our Lady of Consolation S 200/PK-8
401 Clay St 43316 419-396-6166
Brian Gerber, prin. Fax 396-3355

Carlisle, Warren, Pop. 4,885
Carlisle Local SD 1,600/K-12
724 Fairview Dr 45005 937-746-0710
Larry Hook, supt. Fax 746-0438
www.carlisleindians.org
Brown ES 400/K-2
310 Jamaica Rd 45005 937-746-7610
Michael Milner, prin. Fax 746-0511
Chamberlain MS 400/6-8
720 Fairview Dr 45005 937-746-3227
Daniel Turner, prin. Fax 746-0519
Grigsby IS 400/3-5
100 Jamaica Rd 45005 937-746-8969
Shane Estep, prin. Fax 746-0512

Carroll, Fairfield, Pop. 510
Bloom-Carroll Local SD 1,800/K-12
PO Box 338 43112 614-837-6560
Shawn Haughn, supt. Fax 756-4221
www.bloomcarroll.net
Bloom-Carroll MS 600/5-8
PO Box 338 43112 740-756-9231
Chad Young, prin. Fax 756-7466
Bloom-Carroll PS 400/K-2
PO Box 338 43112 740-756-4326
Vicky Pease, prin. Fax 756-7551
Other Schools – See Lithopolis

Carrollton, Carroll, Pop. 3,218
Carrollton EVD 2,200/PK-12
252 3rd St NE 44615 330-627-2181
David Quattrochi, supt. Fax 627-2182
www.carrolltonschools.org
Augusta ES 200/PK-5
3117 Aurora Rd NE 44615 330-627-2442
Darin Abel, prin. Fax 627-2442
Bell-Herron MS 500/6-8
252 3rd St NE 44615 330-627-7188
Matthew Nicholas, prin. Fax 627-8429
Carrollton ES 600/PK-5
252 3rd St NE 44615 330-627-4592
Timothy Albrecht, prin. Fax 627-8433
Other Schools – See Dellroy

Casstown, Miami, Pop. 267
Miami East Local SD 1,200/K-12
3825 N State Route 589 45312 937-335-7505
Dr. Todd Rappold, supt. Fax 335-6309
www.miamieast.k12.oh.us
Miami East ES 600/K-5
4025 N State Route 589 45312 937-335-5439
Brian Rohrer, prin. Fax 332-9488
Miami East JHS 300/6-8
4025 N State Route 589 45312 937-335-5439
Allen Mack, prin. Fax 332-7927

Castalia, Erie, Pop. 846
Margaretta Local SD 1,500/PK-12
305 S Washington St 44824 419-684-5322
Dennis Mock, supt. Fax 684-9003
www.margarettaschooldistrict.com
Margaretta ES 600/PK-5
5906 Bogart Rd W 44824 419-684-5357
Christine Opelt, prin. Fax 684-6001

Firelands Christian Academy 50/K-12
3809 Maple Ave 44824 419-684-8642
Rusty Yost, prin. Fax 684-5378

Cedarville, Greene, Pop. 3,956
Cedar Cliff Local SD 500/K-12
248 N Main St 45314 937-766-6000
Dr. Chad Mason, supt. Fax 766-4717
www.cedarcliffschools.org
Cedarville ES 300/K-6
194 Walnut St 45314 937-766-3811
Mark Gainer, prin. Fax 766-4717

Celina, Mercer, Pop. 10,225
Celina CSD 2,700/K-12
585 E Livingston St 45822 419-586-8300
Dr. Ken Schmiesing, supt. Fax 586-7046
www.celinaschools.org
Celina ES 400/3-4
1225 W Logan St 45822 419-586-8300
Cory Ahrens, prin. Fax 586-6541
Celina IS 400/5-6
227 Portland St 45822 419-586-8300
Derek Wenning, prin. Fax 584-0353
Celina MS 400/7-8
615 Holly St 45822 419-586-8300
Ann Esselstein, prin. Fax 586-9166
Celina PS 600/K-2
615 E Wayne St 45822 419-586-8300
Michelle Duncan, prin. Fax 584-0215

Immaculate Conception S 200/PK-6
200 W Wayne St 45822 419-586-2379
Pauline Muhlenkamp, prin. Fax 586-6649

Centerburg, Knox, Pop. 1,748
Centerburg Local SD 1,100/K-12
119 S Preston St 43011 740-625-6346
Mike Hebenthal, supt. Fax 625-9939
www.centerburgschools.org/
Centerburg ES 500/K-5
207 S Preston St 43011 740-625-6488
John Morgan, prin. Fax 625-5894
Centerburg MS 300/6-8
3782 Columbus Rd 43011 740-625-6055
Ryan Gallwitz, prin. Fax 625-5799

Centerville, Montgomery, Pop. 23,528
Centerville CSD 8,300/PK-12
111 Virginia Ave 45458 937-433-8841
Dr. Tom Henderson Ph.D., supt. Fax 438-6057
www.centerville.k12.oh.us
Centerville PS Village North 500/PK-1
6450 Marshall Rd 45459 937-438-6062
Mindy Cline, prin. Fax 438-6076
Centerville PS Village South 700/PK-1
8388 Paragon Rd 45458 937-312-1273
Amy Allen, prin. Fax 312-1274
Cline ES 400/2-5
99 Virginia Ave 45458 937-435-1315
Sherley Kurtz, prin. Fax 435-3893
Magsig MS 600/6-8
192 W Franklin St 45459 937-433-0965
Stacey Westendorf, prin. Fax 433-5256
Stingley ES 300/2-5
95 Linden Dr 45459 937-434-1054
Diana Keller, prin. Fax 438-6049
Tower Heights MS 500/6-8
195 N Johanna Dr 45459 937-434-0383
Clint Freese, prin. Fax 434-3033
Weller ES 500/2-5
9600 Sheehan Rd 45458 937-885-3273
Andrew Boeke, prin. Fax 885-5092
Other Schools – See Dayton

Springboro Community CSD
Supt. — See Springboro
Five Points ES 1,200/2-5
650 E Lytle 5 Points Rd 45458 937-748-6090
Traci Griffen, prin. Fax 748-6069

Incarnation S 800/PK-8
45 Williamsburg Ln 45459 937-433-1051
Dr. Cheryl Reichel, prin. Fax 433-9796
Spring Valley Academy 300/K-12
1461 E Spring Valley Pike 45458 937-433-0790
Darren Wilkins, prin. Fax 433-0914

Chagrin Falls, Cuyahoga, Pop. 4,089
Chagrin Falls EVD 2,000/PK-12
400 E Washington St 44022 440-247-4363
Robert Hunt, supt. Fax 247-5883
www.chagrinschools.org
Chagrin Falls IS 500/4-6
77 E Washington St 44022 440-893-7690
Sarah Read, prin. Fax 893-7694
Chagrin Falls MS 300/7-8
342 E Washington St 44022 440-247-4746
Laila Discenza, prin. Fax 247-4855
Gurney ES 500/PK-3
1155 Bell Rd 44022 440-893-4030
Dr. Rachel Jones, prin. Fax 338-4272

Kenston Local SD 3,000/PK-12
17419 Snyder Rd 44023 440-543-9677
Nancy Santilli, supt. Fax 543-8634
www.kenstonlocal.org
Kenston IS 500/4-5
17419 Snyder Rd 44023 440-543-9722
Adam Fender, prin. Fax 543-3159
Kenston MS 700/6-8
17425 Snyder Rd 44023 440-543-8241
Patricia Brockway, prin. Fax 543-4851
Timmons ES 800/PK-3
9595 Washington St 44023 440-543-9380
David Rogaliner, prin. Fax 543-9163

Heritage Classical Academy K-8
7100 Pettibone Rd 44023 330-998-0554
St. Joan of Arc S 200/K-8
498 E Washington St 44022 440-247-6530
Shelley DiBacco, prin. Fax 247-2045

Chardon, Geauga, Pop. 5,091
Chardon Local SD 3,000/K-12
428 North St 44024 440-285-4052
Michael Hanlon, supt. Fax 285-7229
www.chardon.k12.oh.us
Chardon MS 700/6-8
424 North St 44024 440-285-4062
Timothy Velotta, prin. Fax 286-0461
Hambden ES 300/K-5
13871 Gar Hwy 44024 440-286-7503
Mat Prezioso, prin. Fax 286-0507
Maple ES 300/K-5
308 Maple Ave 44024 440-285-4065
Kelly Moran, prin. Fax 286-0469
Munson ES 400/K-5
12687 Bass Lake Rd 44024 440-286-5901
Louise Henry, prin. Fax 286-3460
Park ES 300/K-5
111 Goodrich Ct 44024 440-285-4067
Rhonda Garrett, prin. Fax 286-0515

Notre Dame S 500/PK-8
13000 Auburn Rd 44024 440-279-1127
Barbara Doering, prin. Fax 286-1235
St. Mary S 300/PK-8
401 North St 44024 440-286-3590
Sr. Mary Petelin, prin. Fax 285-2818

Charm, Holmes
East Holmes Local SD
Supt. — See Millersburg
Charm ES, 4416 SR 557 44617 50/K-1
Casey Travis, prin. 330-893-2300
Flat Ridge S, 2609 CR 600 44617 100/2-4
Casey Travis, prin. 330-893-3156
Wise ES 100/5-8
4579 CR 120 44617 330-893-2505
Casey Travis, prin. Fax 893-3041

Chauncey, Athens, Pop. 1,029
Athens CSD
Supt. — See The Plains
Chauncey Early-Learning Center 100/PK-PK
21 Birge Dr 45719 740-797-4544
Nathan Young, admin.

Chesapeake, Lawrence, Pop. 736
Chesapeake Union EVD 1,300/K-12
10183 County Road 1 45619 740-867-3135
Jerry McConnell, supt. Fax 867-3136
www.peake.k12.oh.us
Chesapeake ES 500/K-4
11359 County Road 1 45619 740-867-3448
Trisha Harris, prin. Fax 867-3136
Chesapeake MS 500/5-8
10335 County Road 1 45619 740-867-3972
Ty Johnson, prin. Fax 867-1120

Chesterland, Geauga, Pop. 2,498
West Geauga Local SD 2,200/K-12
8615 Cedar Rd 44026 440-729-5900
Dr. Richard Markwardt, supt. Fax 729-5939
www.westg.org
Lindsey ES 400/K-5
11844 Caves Rd 44026 440-729-5980
Kim Menta, prin. Fax 729-5989
West Geauga MS 500/6-8
8611 Cedar Rd 44026 440-729-5940
James Kish, prin. Fax 729-5909
Other Schools – See Novelty

St. Anselm S 300/PK-8
13013 Chillicothe Rd 44026 440-729-7806
Joan Agresta, prin. Fax 729-3524

Chillicothe, Ross, Pop. 21,171
Chillicothe CSD 2,800/K-12
425 Yoctangee Pkwy 45601 740-775-4250
Jon Saxton, supt. Fax 775-4270
www.ccsd.us/
Allen ES 400/K-6
174 Plyleys Ln 45601 740-774-1119
Joanna Bradley, prin. Fax 774-9460

Chillicothe MS Site 1 400/7-8
381 Yoctangee Pkwy 45601 740-773-2241
Matthew Ballentine, prin. Fax 774-9482

Mt. Logan ES 400/K-6
841 E Main St 45601 740-773-2638
Aaron Brown, prin. Fax 774-9480

Tiffin ES 300/K-6
145 S Bridge St 45601 740-774-2123
Michael Shoemaker, prin. Fax 774-9465

Worthington ES 400/K-6
450 Allen Ave 45601 740-774-3307
David Bennett, prin. Fax 774-9466

Huntington Local SD 1,200/K-12
188 Huntsman Rd 45601 740-663-5892
Peter Ruby, supt. Fax 663-6078
www.huntsmen.org

Huntington ES 600/K-4
188 Huntsman Rd 45601 740-663-2191
Matt Murphy, prin. Fax 663-4584

Huntington MS 300/5-8
188 Huntsman Rd 45601 740-663-6079
Alice Kellough, prin. Fax 663-6080

Southeastern Local SD 1,200/K-12
2003 Lancaster Rd 45601 740-774-2003
Brian Justice, supt. Fax 774-1687
www.sepanthers.org

Southeastern ES 500/K-4
2003 Lancaster Rd 45601 740-774-2003
Nicole Wills, prin. Fax 774-1673

Southeastern MS 400/5-8
2003 Lancaster Rd 45601 740-774-2003
Zachary Pfeifer, prin. Fax 774-1684

Union-Scioto Local SD 2,200/PK-12
1565 Egypt Pike 45601 740-773-4102
Matt Thornsberry, supt. Fax 775-2852
www.unioto.org

Unioto ES 1,100/PK-5
138 Sandusky Rd 45601 740-773-4103
Karen Mercer, prin. Fax 775-4074

Unioto MS 500/6-8
160 Moundsville Rd 45601 740-773-5211
Wilma Gillott, prin. Fax 772-2974

Zane Trace Local SD 1,500/K-12
946 State Route 180 45601 740-775-1355
Jerry Mowery, supt. Fax 773-0249
www.zanetrace.org

Zane Trace ES 600/K-4
946 State Route 180 45601 740-775-1304
Susan Congrove, prin. Fax 775-1301

Zane Trace MS 500/5-8
946 State Route 180 45601 740-773-5842
Bret Mavis, prin. Fax 773-9998

Bishop Flaget S 100/PK-8
570 Parsons Ave 45601 740-774-2970
Laura Corcoran, prin. Fax 774-2998

Ross County Christian Academy 200/PK-10
2215 Egypt Pike 45601 740-772-4532
Jake Grooms, head sch Fax 422-1622

Cincinnati, Hamilton, Pop. 289,429

Cincinnati CSD 31,600/PK-12
2651 Burnet Ave 45219 513-363-0000
Laura Mitchell, supt.
www.cps-k12.org

Academy Multilingual Immersion Studies 400/PK-8
1908 Seymour Ave 45237 513-363-1800
Sherwin Ealy, prin. Fax 363-1820

Academy of World Languages S 500/PK-8
2030 Fairfax Ave 45207 513-363-7800
Jacquelyn Rowedder, prin. Fax 363-7820

Bond Hill Academy 300/PK-6
1510 California Ave 45237 513-363-7900
Sharon Johnson, prin. Fax 363-7920

Carson ES 700/PK-6
4323 Glenway Ave 45205 513-363-9800
Ruthenia Jackson, prin. Fax 363-9820

Carthage Preschool PK-PK
125 W North Bend Rd 45216 513-363-1100
Ruthenia Jackson, prin. Fax 363-1120

Chase ES 300/PK-6
4151 Turrill St 45223 513-363-1300
Lynsa Davie, prin. Fax 363-1320

Cheviot ES 500/PK-6
4040 Harrison Ave 45211 513-363-1400
Tammy Gray, prin. Fax 363-1420

College Hill Fundamental Academy 500/PK-6
1625 Cedar Ave 45224 513-363-1600
Monica Battle, prin. Fax 363-1620

Covedale ES 500/K-6
5130 Sidney Rd 45238 513-363-1700
Michele Kipp, prin. Fax 363-1720

Dater Montessori S 800/PK-6
2840 Boudinot Ave 45238 513-363-0900
Anthony Greco, prin. Fax 363-0920

Douglass ES 300/PK-6
2627 Park Ave 45206 513-363-1900
Jeffery Hall, prin. Fax 363-1920

Evanston Academy 300/PK-6
1835 Fairfax Ave 45207 513-363-2700
Stacey Hill-Simmons, prin. Fax 363-2720

Fairview-Clifton German Language ES 800/PK-6
3689 Clifton Ave 45220 513-363-2100
Monisha House, prin. Fax 363-2120

Hartwell S 600/PK-8
8320 Vine St 45216 513-363-2300
Antwan Lewis, prin. Fax 363-2320

Hays-Porter ES 300/PK-6
1030 Cutter St 45203 513-363-1000
Nedrla McClain, prin. Fax 363-1020

Hyde Park ES 200/PK-6
3401 Edwards Rd 45208 513-363-2800
Jill Sunderman, prin. Fax 363-2820

Kilgour ES 700/K-6
1339 Herschel Ave 45208 513-363-3000
Angela Cook-Frazier, prin. Fax 363-3020

Leap Academy PK-PK
2240 Baltimore Ave 45225 513-363-1200
Priya Sonty, prin. Fax 363-1220

Midway ES 600/PK-6
3156 Glenmore Ave 45211 513-363-3500
Cathy Lutts, prin. Fax 363-3520

Mt. Airy ES 500/PK-6
5730 Colerain Ave 45239 513-363-3700
Angel Roddy, prin. Fax 363-3720

Mt. Washington ES 400/PK-6
1730 Mears Ave 45230 513-363-3800
Debra Klein, prin. Fax 363-3820

North Avondale Montessori ES 600/PK-6
615 Clinton Springs Ave 45229 513-363-3900
Roger Lewis, prin. Fax 363-3920

Oyler S 700/PK-12
2121 Hatmaker St 45204 513-363-4100
Amy Randolph, prin. Fax 363-4120

Parker ES 300/PK-6
5051 Anderson Pl 45227 513-363-2900
Kimberly Mack, prin. Fax 363-2920

Parker Woods Montessori S 500/PK-6
4370 Beech Hill Ave 45223 513-363-6200
Whitney Simmons, prin. Fax 363-6220

Pleasant Hill Academy 400/PK-6
1350 W North Bend Rd 45224 513-363-4300
Shauna McDowell, prin. Fax 363-4320

Pleasant Ridge Montessori S 600/PK-6
5945 Montgomery Rd 45213 513-363-4400
Jennifer Mauch, prin. Fax 363-4420

Price Academy 500/PK-6
1228 Considine Ave 45204 513-363-6000
Jennifer Myree, prin. Fax 363-6020

Rising Stars Academy at Glennmore PK-PK
3420 Glenmore Ave 45211 513-389-0301
Jaren Finney, prin. Fax 389-1596

Rising Stars Academy at Vine PK-PK
2120 Vine St 45210 513-363-6500
Jaren Finney, prin. Fax 363-6520

Rising Stars Academy at Westwood PK-PK
3011 Harrison Ave 45211 513-363-6500
Chris Grant, prin. Fax 363-6520

Riverview East Academy 600/PK-12
3555 Kellogg Ave 45226 513-363-3400
Charlene Myers, prin. Fax 363-3420

Roberts Paideia Academy 600/PK-8
1702 Grand Ave 45214 513-363-4600
Vera Brooks, prin. Fax 363-4620

Rockdale Academy 300/PK-6
335 Rockdale Ave 45229 513-363-4700
Belinda Wallace, prin. Fax 363-4720

Roll Hill Academy 400/PK-6
2411 Baltimore Ave 45225 513-363-4000
Vicki Graves-Hill, prin. Fax 363-4020

Roselawn-Condon S 300/PK-8
1594 Summit Rd 45237 513-363-4800
Harry Voll, prin. Fax 363-4820

Rothenberg Preparatory Academy 400/PK-6
241 E Clifton Ave 45202 513-363-5700
Amber Simpson, prin. Fax 363-5720

Sands Montessori ES 700/PK-6
6421 Corbly Rd 45230 513-363-5000
Sarah Lord, prin. Fax 363-5020

Sayler Park S 400/PK-8
6700 Home City Ave 45233 513-363-5100
Jerry Sowders, prin. Fax 363-5120

School for Creative & Performing Arts 1,500/K-12
108 W Central Pkwy 45202 513-363-8000
Michael Owens, prin. Fax 363-8020

Silverton Paideia Academy 400/PK-6
7451 Montgomery Rd 45236 513-363-5400
Leniese Fuqua, prin. Fax 363-5420

South Avondale ES 400/PK-6
636 Prospect Pl 45229 513-363-5500
Michael Allison, prin. Fax 363-5520

Spencer Center for Gifted & Exceptional 3-8
2825 Alms Pl 45206 513-363-5800
Nina Ginocchio, prin. Fax 363-5820

Taft ES 300/PK-6
270 Southern Ave 45219 513-363-5600
Jonathan Brown, prin. Fax 363-5620

Taylor Academy 300/PK-6
1930 Fricke Rd 45225 513-363-3600
Ceair Baggett, prin. Fax 363-3620

Westwood ES 400/PK-6
2981 Montana Ave 45211 513-363-5900
Christopher Grant, prin. Fax 363-5920

Winton Hills Academy 400/PK-6
5300 Winneste Ave 45232 513-363-6300
Benjamin Fulton, prin. Fax 363-6320

Woodford Paideia Academy 400/PK-6
3716 Woodford Rd 45213 513-363-6400
Dewolfe Turpeau, prin. Fax 363-6420

Deer Park Community CSD 1,200/K-12
4131 Matson Ave 45236 513-891-0222
Jay Phillips, supt. Fax 891-2930
www.deerparkcityschools.org

Amity IS 300/3-6
4320 E Galbraith Rd 45236 513-891-5995
M. Smiley, prin. Fax 891-3508

Holmes ES 300/K-2
8688 Donna Ln 45236 513-891-6662
Sonny Tudor, prin. Fax 891-3519

Finneytown Local SD 1,400/K-12
8916 Fontainebleau Ter 45231 513-728-3700
Theresa Noe, supt. Fax 931-0986
www.finneytown.org

Brent ES 300/K-2
8791 Brent Dr 45231 513-728-3720
Lana Gerber, prin. Fax 728-7243

Whitaker ES 500/3-6
7400 Winton Rd 45224 513-728-3737
Dr. Ljuana Booker, prin. Fax 728-3725

Forest Hills SD 7,400/PK-12
7946 Beechmont Ave 45255 513-231-3600
Scot T. Prebles, supt. Fax 231-3830
www.foresthills.edu

Ayer ES 700/K-6
8471 Forest Rd 45255 513-474-3811
Todd Hartman, prin. Fax 474-7228

Maddux ES 600/K-6
943 Rosetree Ln 45230 513-231-0780
Steve Troehler, prin. Fax 231-5308

Mercer ES 700/K-6
2600 Bartels Rd 45244 513-232-7000
Jodi Davidson, prin. Fax 232-3156

Nagel MS 1,300/7-8
1500 Nagel Rd 45255 513-474-5407
John Vander Meer, prin. Fax 474-5584

Sherwood ES 500/PK-6
7080 Grantham Way 45230 513-231-7565
Dan Hamilton, prin. Fax 231-3666

Summit ES 600/PK-6
8400 Northport Dr 45255 513-474-2270
Michele Sulfsted, prin. Fax 474-1525

Wilson ES 700/K-6
2465 Little Dry Run Rd 45244 513-231-3240
Bob Buck, prin. Fax 231-3202

Indian Hill EVD 1,900/K-12
6855 Drake Rd 45243 513-272-4500
Dr. Mark Miles, supt. Fax 272-4756
indianhillschools.org

Indian Hill ES 400/3-5
6100 Drake Rd 45243 513-272-4703
Whitney Buell, prin. Fax 272-4708

Indian Hill MS 500/6-8
6845 Drake Rd 45243 513-272-4642
Jen Ulland, prin. Fax 272-4690

Indian Hill PS 400/K-2
6207 Drake Rd 45243 513-272-4754
James Nichols, prin. Fax 272-4759

Lakota Local SD
Supt. — See Liberty Twp

Shawnee Early Childhood S 600/PK-1
9394 Sterling Dr 45241 513-779-3014
Theresa Brock, prin. Fax 779-3494

Madeira CSD 1,400/PK-12
7465 Loannes Dr 45243 513-985-6070
Kenji Matsudo, supt. Fax 985-6072
www.madeiracityschools.org

Madeira ES 600/PK-4
7840 Thomas Dr 45243 513-985-6080
Chris Flanagan, prin. Fax 985-6082

Madeira MS 400/5-8
6612 Miami Ave 45243 513-561-5555
Tom Olson, prin. Fax 272-4145

Mariemont CSD 1,700/K-12
2 Warrior Way 45227 513-272-7500
Steven E. Estepp, supt. Fax 527-3436
www.mariemontschools.org

Mariemont ES 600/K-6
6750 Wooster Pike 45227 513-272-7400
Ericka Simmons, prin. Fax 527-3411

Mariemont JHS 300/7-8
3847 Southern Ave 45227 513-272-7300
Molly Connaughton, prin. Fax 527-3432

Other Schools – See Terrace Park

Mt. Healthy CSD
Supt. — See Mount Healthy

North ES 900/K-6
2170 Struble Rd 45231 513-742-6004
Felecia Dorsey, prin. Fax 742-3460

South ES 900/K-6
1743 Adams Rd 45231 513-728-4683
Yzvetta Macon, prin. Fax 521-0796

New Richmond EVD
Supt. — See New Richmond

Locust Corner ES 500/K-6
3431 Locust Corner Rd 45245 513-752-1432
Joseph Roach, prin. Fax 752-0611

North College Hill CSD 1,600/PK-12
1731 Goodman Ave 45239 513-931-8181
Eugene Blalock, supt. Fax 728-4774
www.nchcityschools.org

North College Hill ES 700/PK-4
6955 Grace Ave 45239 513-728-4787
Sheri Renneker, prin. Fax 728-4788

North College Hill MS 500/5-8
1624 W Galbraith Rd 45239 513-728-4785
Tim Sica, prin. Fax 728-4786

Northwest Local SD 9,200/PK-12
3240 Banning Rd 45239 513-923-1000
Todd Bowling, supt. Fax 923-3644
www.nwlsd.org

Colerain ES 900/K-5
4850 Poole Rd 45251 513-385-8740
Collin Climer, prin. Fax 385-8770

Colerain MS 600/6-8
4700 Poole Rd 45251 513-385-8490
Elizabeth Styles, prin. Fax 385-6685

Houston Early Learning Center 200/PK-PK
3308 Compton Rd 45251 513-385-8000
Emily Stepaniak, prin. Fax 385-8090

Monfort Heights ES 700/K-5
3711 W Fork Rd 45247 513-389-1570
Kevin Gale, prin. Fax 389-1572

Pleasant Run ES 500/4-5
11765 Hamilton Ave 45231 513-825-7070
Casey Scherz, prin. Fax 825-1076

Pleasant Run MS 700/6-8
11770 Pippin Rd 45231 513-851-2400
Eric Dunn, prin. Fax 851-7071

Struble ES 400/K-2
2760 Jonrose Ave 45239 513-522-2700
Karen Grayson, prin. Fax 522-2711

Taylor ES 600/K-3
3173 Springdale Rd 45251 513-825-3000
Trey Rischmann, prin. Fax 825-2983
Weigel ES 500/3-5
3242 Banning Rd 45239 513-923-4040
Lori Riehle, prin. Fax 923-1376
Welch ES 500/K-3
12084 Deerhorn Dr 45240 513-742-1240
Jemel Weathers, prin. Fax 742-8632
White Oak MS 800/6-8
3130 Jessup Rd 45239 513-741-4300
Dustin Gehring, prin. Fax 741-0717

Oak Hills Local SD 7,800/K-12
6325 Rapid Run Rd 45233 513-574-3200
Jeffrey Brandt, supt. Fax 598-2947
ohlsd.us
Bridgetown MS 600/6-8
3900 Race Rd 45211 513-574-3511
Adam Taylor, prin. Fax 574-6689
Delhi MS 600/6-8
5280 Foley Rd 45238 513-922-8400
Scott Toon, prin. Fax 922-8472
Delshire ES 500/K-5
4402 Glenhaven Rd 45238 513-471-1766
Tara Willig, prin. Fax 471-1767
Dulles ES 700/K-5
6481 Bridgetown Rd 45248 513-574-3443
Beth Riesenberger, prin. Fax 574-3182
Harrison ES 1,000/K-5
585 Neeb Rd 45233 513-922-1485
Brian Conners, prin. Fax 922-3330
Oakdale ES 700/K-5
3850 Virginia Ct 45248 513-574-1100
Emily Winkle, prin. Fax 574-5116
Rapid Run MS 700/6-8
6345 Rapid Run Rd 45233 513-467-0300
Geoff Harold, prin. Fax 467-0333
Springmyer ES 500/K-5
4179 Ebenezer Rd 45248 513-574-1205
Mark Winters, prin. Fax 574-1206

Princeton CSD 5,400/PK-12
3900 Cottingham Dr 45241 513-864-1000
Dr. Thomas Tucker, supt. Fax 864-1008
www.princetonschools.net
Evendale ES 300/PK-5
3940 Glendale Milford Rd 45241 513-864-1200
Joycelyn Senter, prin. Fax 864-1291
Glendale ES 300/PK-5
930 Congress Ave 45246 513-864-1300
Ronald Fausnaugh, prin. Fax 864-1391
Heritage Hill ES 400/PK-5
11961 Chesterdale Rd 45246 513-864-1400
Shari Hoskins, prin. Fax 864-1491
Lincoln Heights ES 200/PK-5
1113 Adams St 45215 513-864-2400
Dawn Bailey, prin. Fax 864-2491
Princeton Community MS 1,200/6-8
200 Viking Way 45246 513-864-2000
Ali Moore, prin. Fax 864-2091
Sharonville ES 500/PK-5
11150 Maple St 45241 513-864-2600
Kasi Jordan, prin. Fax 864-2691
Springdale ES 500/PK-5
350 W Kemper Rd 45246 513-864-2700
Lisa Tenbarge, prin. Fax 864-2791
Stewart ES 500/PK-5
11850 Conrey Rd 45249 513-864-2800
Kathleen McFadden, prin. Fax 864-2891
Woodlawn ES 200/PK-5
31 Riddle Rd 45215 513-864-2900
Sherry Thompson, prin. Fax 864-2991

Sycamore Community CSD 5,300/PK-12
5959 Hagewa Dr 45242 513-686-1700
Frank Forsthoefel, supt. Fax 791-4873
www.sycamoreschools.org
Blue Ash ES 500/K-4
9541 Plainfield Rd 45236 513-686-1710
Leslie Combs, prin. Fax 792-0305
Greene IS 800/5-6
5200 Aldine Dr 45242 513-686-1750
Matt Tudor, prin. Fax 792-6172
Maple Dale ES 400/K-4
6100 Hagewa Dr 45242 513-686-1720
Anne Marie Reinke, prin. Fax 792-6112
Montgomery ES 600/K-4
9609 Montgomery Rd 45242 513-686-1730
Linda Overbeck, prin. Fax 792-6131
Sycamore JHS 900/7-8
5757 Cooper Rd 45242 513-686-1760
Traci Rea, prin. Fax 891-3162
Other Schools – See Loveland

West Clermont Local SD 8,000/K-12
4350 Aicholtz Rd 45245 513-943-5000
Dr. Keith Kline, supt. Fax 752-6158
www.westcler.k12.oh.us
Brantner Lane ES 400/K-5
609 Brantner Ln 45244 513-943-6400
Dr. Lisa Courtney, prin. Fax 528-0179
Clough Pike ES 500/K-5
808 Clough Pike 45245 513-943-6700
Kevin Thacker, prin. Fax 752-7347
Merwin ES 600/K-5
1040 Gaskins Rd 45245 513-947-7800
Cheryl Turner, prin. Fax 752-5629
Summerside ES 500/K-5
4639 Vermona Dr 45245 513-947-7900
Robert Winterberger, prin. Fax 528-3520
Withamsville-Tobasco ES 500/K-5
3950 Britton Blvd 45245 513-943-6900
Suelee Litman-Hall, prin. Fax 752-6571
Other Schools – See Amelia, Batavia

Winton Woods CSD 3,600/PK-12
1215 W Kemper Rd 45240 513-619-2300
Anthony G. Smith, supt. Fax 619-2309
www.wintonwoods.org
Winton Woods ES 500/3-4
1501 Kingsbury Dr 45240 513-619-2490
Adrienne Martin, prin. Fax 619-2497
Winton Woods IS 500/5-6
825 Waycross Rd 45240 513-619-2450
Jeremy Day, prin. Fax 619-2451
Winton Woods MS 500/7-8
147 Farragut Rd 45218 513-619-2440
Doug Sanker, prin. Fax 619-2452
Winton Woods North PS 500/PK-2
73 Junefield Ave 45218 513-619-2390
Kevin Jones, prin. Fax 619-2398
Winton Woods Preschool 100/PK-PK
73 Junefield Ave 45218 513-619-2390
Elizabeth Styles, prin.
Winton Woods South PS 400/K-2
825 Lakeridge Dr 45231 513-619-2470
Danielle Wallace, prin. Fax 619-2479

Aldersgate Christian Academy 100/K-12
1810 Young St 45202 513-763-6655
Tim Makcen, prin. Fax 763-6643
All Saints S 400/K-8
8939 Montgomery Rd 45236 513-792-4732
Kevan Hartman, prin. Fax 792-7990
Annunciation S 200/PK-8
3545 Clifton Ave 45220 513-221-1230
Anthony Ertel, prin. Fax 281-8009
Beautiful Savior Lutheran S 100/PK-8
11981 Pippin Rd 45231 513-825-2290
Daniel Markgraf, prin. Fax 825-2172
Bethany S 200/K-8
555 Albion Ave 45246 513-771-7462
Cheryl Pez M.Ed., hdmstr. Fax 771-2292
Cardinal Pacelli S 400/PK-8
927 Ellison Ave 45226 513-321-1048
Terri Cento, prin. Fax 533-6113
Central Baptist Academy 100/K-8
7645 Winton Rd 45224 513-521-5481
Richard Voiles, admin. Fax 728-3682
Central Montessori Academy 100/PK-6
1904 Springdale Rd 45231 513-742-5800
Kristin Patterson, head sch Fax 742-5870
Cincinnati Country Day S 800/PK-12
6905 Given Rd 45243 513-561-7298
Anthony Jaccaci, head sch Fax 527-7600
Cincinnati Hebrew Day S 200/PK-8
2222 Losantiville Ave 45237 513-351-7777
Rabbi Yitzchak Goldstein, prin. Fax 351-7794
Cincinnati Hills Christian Academy 600/PK-3
8283 E Kemper Rd 45249 513-247-0900
Randy Brunk, head sch Fax 247-0125
Cincinnati Hills Christian Academy 400/4-8
11300 Snider Rd 45249 513-247-0900
Randy Brunk, head sch Fax 247-9362
Cincinnati Hills Chrstn Acad - Armleder 200/PK-6
140 W 9th St 45202 513-721-2422
Cammie Montgomery, prin. Fax 721-3300
Cincinnati Junior Academy 100/K-8
3798 Clifton Ave 45220 513-751-1255
Jeanier Howard, prin. Fax 751-1224
Cincinnati Waldorf S 200/PK-8
6743 Chestnut St 45227 513-541-0220
Stephen Mergner, dir. Fax 541-3586
Corryville Catholic S 200/PK-8
108 Calhoun St 45219 513-281-4856
Sr. Linda Westendorf, prin. Fax 281-6497
Eden Grove Academy 100/PK-8
6277 Collegevue Pl 45224 513-542-0643
Chad Harville, prin. Fax 681-3450
Good Shepherd Montessori S 200/PK-8
4460 Berwick St 45227 513-271-4171
Anne Vega, prin. Fax 271-4680
Guardian Angels S 600/K-8
6539 Beechmont Ave 45230 513-624-3141
Corey Stoops, prin. Fax 624-3150
Holy Family S 200/K-8
3001 Price Ave 45205 513-921-8483
Jennifer O'Brien, prin. Fax 921-2460
Immaculate Heart of Mary S 600/K-8
7800 Beechmont Ave 45255 513-388-4086
Krista Devine, prin. Fax 388-4097
John Paul II S 400/K-8
9375 Winton Rd 45231 513-521-0860
Leanora Roach, prin. Fax 728-3101
Mercy Montessori Center 300/PK-8
2335 Grandview Ave 45206 513-475-6700
Patricia Normile, prin. Fax 475-6755
Miami Valley Christian Academy 300/PK-12
6830 School St 45244 513-272-6822
Greg Beasley, head sch Fax 272-3711
Nativity of Our Lord S 400/K-8
5936 Ridge Ave 45213 513-458-6767
Christopher Shisler, prin. Fax 458-6769
New S 100/PK-6
3 Burton Woods Ln 45229 513-281-7999
Jeffrey Groh, prin. Fax 281-7996
Our Lady of Grace S 600/K-8
2940 W Galbraith Rd 45239 513-931-3070
Mandy Kirk, prin. Fax 931-3707
Our Lady of Lourdes S 300/K-8
5835 Glenway Ave 45238 513-347-2660
Heather Bessler, prin. Fax 347-2663
Our Lady of Victory S 500/K-8
808 Neeb Rd 45233 513-347-2072
Amy Borgman, prin. Fax 922-5476
Our Lady of Visitation S 900/1-8
3180 South Rd 45248 513-347-2222
Holly Aug, prin. Fax 347-2225
Resurrection of Our Lord Academy 200/K-8
1740 Iliff Ave 45205 513-471-6600
Delores Heffner, prin. Fax 471-2610

Rockwern Academy 100/K-8
8401 Montgomery Rd 45236 513-984-3770
Dr. Elaine Kaplan, hdmstr. Fax 984-3974
St. Aloysius Gonzaga S 200/PK-8
4390 Bridgetown Rd 45211 513-574-4035
Sandra Staud, prin. Fax 574-5421
St. Aloysius on the Ohio S 100/PK-8
6207 Portage St 45233 513-941-7831
Kristin Penley, prin. Fax 941-5418
St. Antoninus S 500/K-8
5425 Julmar Dr 45238 513-922-2500
Michelle Kahny, prin. Fax 922-5519
St. Bernard S 200/K-8
7115 Springdale Rd 45247 513-353-4224
Courtney Brown, prin. Fax 353-3958
St. Boniface S 200/K-8
4305 Pitts Ave 45223 513-541-5122
Sr. Miriam Kaeser, prin. Fax 541-3939
St. Catherine of Siena S 200/K-8
3324 Wunder Ave 45211 513-481-7683
Jerome Metz, prin. Fax 481-9438
St. Cecilia S 200/K-8
4115 Taylor Ave 45209 513-533-6060
Michael Goedde, prin. Fax 533-6068
St. Dominic S 500/K-8
371 Pedretti Ave 45238 513-251-1276
William Cavanaugh, prin. Fax 251-6428
St. Francis De Sales S 200/K-8
1602 Madison Rd Unit 1 45206 513-961-1953
Dr. Joanne Browarsky, prin. Fax 961-2900
St. Francis Seraph S 100/K-8
14 E Liberty St 45202 513-721-7778
Halsey Mabry, prin. Fax 721-5445
St. Gabriel Consolidated S 400/K-8
18 W Sharon Rd 45246 513-771-5220
Nicole Brainard, prin. Fax 771-5133
St. Gertrude S 400/K-8
6543 Miami Ave 45243 513-561-8020
Sr. Mary Halbmaier, prin. Fax 561-7184
St. Ignatius Loyola S 1,000/K-8
5222 N Bend Rd Ste 1 45247 513-389-3242
Timothy Reilly, prin. Fax 389-3255
St. James the Greater S 700/K-8
6111 Cheviot Rd 45247 513-741-5333
Jeffrey Fulmer, prin. Fax 741-5312
St. John the Baptist S 500/PK-8
5375 Dry Ridge Rd 45252 513-385-7970
Al Grote, prin. Fax 699-6964
St. Joseph S 200/K-8
745 Ezzard Charles Dr 45203 513-381-2126
Dionne Partee, prin. Fax 381-6513
St. Jude S 500/K-8
5940 Bridgetown Rd 45248 513-598-2100
Louis Eichhold, prin. Fax 598-2118
St. Lawrence S 300/PK-8
1020 Carson Ave 45205 513-921-4996
Richard Klus, prin. Fax 921-5108
St. Martin of Tours S 200/K-8
3729 Harding Ave 45211 513-661-7609
Jason Fightmaster, prin. Fax 661-8102
St. Mary S 500/K-8
2845 Erie Ave 45208 513-321-0703
Marianne Rosemond, prin. Fax 533-5517
St. Nicholas Academy 300/PK-8
170 Siebenthaler Ave 45215 513-686-2727
Aideen Briggs, prin. Fax 686-2729
St. Teresa of Avila S 300/K-8
1194 Rulison Ave 45238 513-471-4530
Sharon Willmes, prin. Fax 471-1254
St. Ursula Villa S 500/PK-8
3660 Vineyard Pl 45226 513-871-7218
Polly Duplace, prin. Fax 871-0082
St. Veronica S 500/K-8
4475 Mount Carmel Tobasco 45244 513-528-0442
Sharon Bresler, prin. Fax 528-0513
St. Vincent Ferrer S 200/K-8
7754 Montgomery Rd 45236 513-791-6320
Kimberly Roy, prin. Fax 791-3332
St. Vivian S 400/PK-8
885 Denier Pl 45224 513-522-6858
Jane Brack, prin. Fax 728-4336
St. William S 200/PK-8
4125 Saint Williams Ave 45205 513-471-2989
Jarrod Zeiser, prin. Fax 471-8226
Seven Hills S 500/PK-12
5400 Red Bank Rd 45227 513-728-2400
Christopher Garten, hdmstr. Fax 728-2409
Summit Country Day S 1,100/PK-12
2161 Grandin Rd 45208 513-871-4700
Richard Wilson, head sch Fax 533-5373
Xavier University Montessori Lab S 50/PK-6
3800 Victory Pkwy 45207 513-745-3424
Rosemary Quaranta, prin. Fax 745-4378

Circleville, Pickaway, Pop. 13,083
Circleville CSD 1,000/PK-12
388 Clark Dr 43113 740-474-4340
Jonathan Davis, supt. Fax 474-6600
www.circlevillecityschools.org/
Circleville ES PK-5
100 Tiger Dr 43113 740-474-2495
Karen Bullock, prin. Fax 477-6681
Circleville MS 500/6-8
360 Clark Dr 43113 740-474-2345
Kevin Fox, prin. Fax 477-6684

Logan Elm Local SD 2,000/PK-12
9579 Tarlton Rd 43113 740-474-7501
Tim Williams, supt. Fax 477-6525
www.loganelmschools.com/
McDowell-Exchange JHS 300/7-8
9579 Tarlton Rd 43113 740-474-7538
Marsha Waidelich, prin. Fax 474-8539
Pickaway ES 200/K-4
28158 Kingston Pike 43113 740-474-3877
James Wolfe, prin. Fax 477-1324

Washington ES 200/K-4
7990 Stoutsville Pike 43113 740-474-2851
James Wolfe, prin. Fax 474-7693
Other Schools – See Kingston, Laurelville

New Hope Christian Academy 300/PK-12
2264 Walnut Creek Pike 43113 740-477-6427
Rev. Wendell Brown, head sch Fax 420-3910

Clarksville, Clinton, Pop. 544

Clinton-Massie Local SD 1,900/K-12
2556 Lebanon Rd 45113 937-289-2471
Dr. Matthew Baker, supt. Fax 289-3313
www.clinton-massie.k12.oh.us

Clinton-Massie ES 800/K-5
2380 Lebanon Rd 45113 937-289-2515
Jennifer Updike, prin. Fax 289-3313

Clinton-Massie MS 500/6-8
2556 Lebanon Rd 45113 937-289-2932
Joseph Hollon, prin. Fax 289-3313

Clayton, Montgomery, Pop. 12,864

Northmont CSD
Supt. — See Englewood

Kleptz Early Learning Center PK-1
1100 W National Rd 45315 937-832-6750
Dr. Beth Wyandt, prin. Fax 832-6751

Northmont MS 800/7-8
4810 National Rd 45315 937-832-6500
Jarrod Brumbaugh, prin. Fax 832-6501

Salem Christian Academy 100/K-6
PO Box 309 45315 937-836-9910
Karen Tanto, prin. Fax 836-7630

Cleveland, Cuyahoga, Pop. 388,662

Cleveland Municipal SD 35,900/PK-12
1111 Superior Ave E 44114 216-838-0000
Eric Gordon, admin. Fax 436-5144
clevelandmetroschools.org

Agassiz S 300/K-8
3595 Bosworth Rd 44111 216-838-6450
Angela Boie, prin. Fax 251-4735

Alcott ES, 10308 Baltic Rd 44102 200/K-5
Eileen Stull, prin. 216-838-6500

Almira ES, 3375 W 99th St 44102 300/K-8
James Greene, prin. 216-838-6150

Baker S of Arts 400/PK-8
3690 W 159th St 44111 216-838-6650
Wendy Rose-Geiling, prin. Fax 889-4040

Benesch S 400/PK-8
5393 Quincy Ave 44104 216-838-1300
Erin Murphy, prin. Fax 432-4527

Bethune S 300/K-8
11815 Moulton Ave 44106 216-838-2250
Melanie Nakonachny, prin. Fax 231-0110

Bolton S 300/PK-8
9803 Quebec Ave 44106 216-838-1200
Juliet King, prin. Fax 795-2948

Booker S 400/K-8
2121 W 67th St 44102 216-838-6350
Nicholas Scheibelhood, prin. Fax 634-2225

Bryant S 400/K-8
3121 Oak Park Ave 44109 216-838-3350
Amy Mobley, prin. Fax 749-8139

Buhrer Dual Language S 400/PK-8
1600 Buhrer Ave 44109 216-838-8350
michele sanchez, prin. Fax 621-8461

Campus International S @ CSU 400/K-6
2160 Payne Ave 44115 216-838-8000
Ameer El-Mallawany, prin.

Carver STEM S 400/PK-8
2200 E 55th St 44103 216-838-1450
Susan Harvey, prin. Fax 391-5041

Case S, 4050 Superior Ave 44103 300/K-8
Janet McDowell, prin. 216-838-1350

Clark S, 5550 Clark Ave 44102 600/K-8
Amanda Rodriguez, prin. 216-838-7300

Clement Boys Leadership Academy 200/PK-8
14311 Woodworth Rd 44112 216-838-8800
John Story, prin. Fax 541-7562

Cleveland S of the Arts - Lower Campus 300/PK-5
2501 E 61st St 44104 216-838-9150
Alisha Starks, prin.

Denison S, 3799 W 33rd St 44109 500/K-8
Sonja Thornton-Clark, prin. 216-838-3250

Dickens S, 13013 Corlett Ave 44105 300/K-8
Vanessa Moore, prin. 216-838-4200

Dunbar S, 2159 W 29th St 44113 200/PK-8
Sofia Piperis, prin. 216-838-7400

East Clark S, 885 E 146th St 44110 300/PK-8
Charlene Hilliard, prin. 216-838-0650

Eliot S, 15700 Lotus Dr 44128 400/PK-8
Ivy Wheeler, prin. 216-838-5350

Euclid Park ES 300/K-8
17914 Euclid Ave 44112 216-838-0700
Jennifer Woody, prin.

Franklin S 600/PK-8
1905 Spring Rd 44109 216-838-3150
Rachel Snider, prin. Fax 778-6575

Fullerton S 300/K-8
5920 Fullerton Ave 44105 216-838-4400
Kevin Payton, prin. Fax 441-8049

Gallagher S 700/PK-8
6601 Franklin Blvd 44102 216-838-6400
Thomas Kubiak, prin. Fax 634-2353

Garfield ES 500/K-8
3800 W 140th St 44111 216-838-6300
Dawn Imler, prin. Fax 476-4223

Gibbons STEM S 300/PK-8
1401 Larchmont Rd 44110 216-838-0750
Dr. Gregory Adkins, prin. Fax 383-4556

Gridina S 300/PK-8
2955 E 71st St 44104 216-838-1150
Harold Booker, prin. Fax 341-6895

Hale S 300/K-8
3588 Martin Luther King Jr 44105 216-838-4250
Joelle McIntosh, prin. Fax 441-8034

Henry S 400/PK-8
11901 Durant Ave 44108 216-838-2350
Brittany Anderson, prin. Fax 268-6089

Iowa-Maple S 400/PK-8
12510 Maple Ave 44108 216-838-0800
Natalie Smith-Benson, prin. Fax 541-7669

Jamison S 400/PK-8
4092 E 146th St 44128 216-838-5400
Sharon Cooper, prin. Fax 295-3512

Jefferson Intl Newcomers Academy 300/PK-12
3145 W 46th St 44102 216-838-7150
Marisol Burgos, prin. Fax 404-5492

Jones S 400/PK-8
4550 W 150th St 44135 216-838-6750
Melissa Watts, prin. Fax 433-7249

MacArthur S 300/PK-8
4401 Valleyside Rd 44135 216-838-8400
Victoria King, admin.

Marin S 600/K-8
1701 Castle Ave 44113 216-838-3300
Ricardo Torres, prin. Fax 685-5177

Marion-Sterling S 300/PK-8
3033 Central Ave 44115 216-838-1550
Kelly Gibbs, prin. Fax 694-4746

Martin S 400/K-8
8200 Brookline Ave 44103 216-838-1600
Gary McPherson, prin. Fax 229-2052

McKinley S 200/K-8
3349 W 125th St 44111 216-251-4175
Victoria Mousty, prin. Fax 476-6847

Memorial S 400/PK-8
410 E 152nd St 44110 216-838-0850
Maria Dinkins, prin. Fax 692-4181

Miles Park S 500/K-8
4090 E 93rd St 44105 216-838-4450
Dr. Tamika Taylor-Ivory, prin. Fax 641-2819

Miles S 200/PK-8
11918 Miles Ave 44105 216-838-5250
Roy James, prin. Fax 518-3873

Mooney S, 3213 Montclair Ave 44109 500/K-8
Michelle Person, prin. 216-838-3200

Morgan S, 8912 Morris Ct 44106 300/PK-8
Dessie Sanders, prin. 216-838-1400

Mound STEM 400/K-8
5935 Ackley Rd 44105 216-838-1650
Velma McNeil, prin. Fax 441-8092

Orchard STEM S 300/PK-8
4200 Bailey Ave 44113 216-838-7350
Kathryn Francis, prin. Fax 281-1005

Perry S 300/PK-8
18400 Schenely Ave 44119 216-838-0900
Brittani Irvin, prin. Fax 383-5164

Rice S 400/K-8
2730 E 116th St 44120 216-838-1500
Jason Tidmore, prin. Fax 472-5348

Rickoff S 500/PK-8
3500 E 147th St 44120 216-838-4150
Shelby Schutt, prin. Fax 295-4606

Riverside S 500/K-8
14601 Montrose Ave 44111 216-838-6700
Neil Murphy, prin. Fax 688-3603

Roosevelt Academy 400/PK-8
800 Linn Dr 44108 216-838-2200
Sherie Turner, prin. Fax 268-6954

Scranton S 300/K-8
1991 Barber Ave 44113 216-838-7450
Troy Beadling, prin. Fax 363-5034

Seltzer S 400/K-8
1468 W 98th St 44102 216-838-6550
Caitlin Kilbane, prin. Fax 634-8733

Stevenson S 400/PK-8
18300 Woda Ave 44122 216-838-5300
Christopher Wyland, prin. Fax 921-1212

Sunbeam S 300/PK-8
11731 Mount Overlook Ave 44120 216-838-1700
Katrinka Dean, prin. Fax 229-5308

Tremont Montessori 600/PK-8
2409 W 10th St 44113 216-838-9850
Natalie Celeste, prin. Fax 621-2066

Valley View Boys Leadership Academy 200/PK-8
17200 Valleyview Ave 44135 216-838-8900
Dr. Terrance Mitchell, prin. Fax 889-4093

Wade Park S 400/PK-8
7600 Wade Park Ave 44103 216-838-1750
Lee Buddy, prin. Fax 920 6979

Walton S 300/K-8
3409 Walton Ave 44113 216-838-7500
Gretchen Liggens, prin. Fax 634-8790

Ward S 500/PK-8
4315 W 140th St 44135 216-838-6200
Chris Myslenski, prin. Fax 476-4467

Warner Girls Leadership Academy 400/PK-8
8315 Jeffries Ave 44105 216-838-8950
Audrey Staton-Thompson, prin. Fax 206-4621

Waverly S 300/K-8
1422 W 74th St 44102 216-838-7550
Sommer Edwards, prin. Fax 634-8746

Westropp S, 19101 Puritas Ave 44135 400/PK-8
Krystle George, prin. 216-838-6250

White STEM 300/K-8
1000 E 92nd St 44108 216-838-2300
Gretchen Liggens, prin. Fax 451-4692

Willow S 200/K-8
5004 Glazier Ave 44127 216-838-1800
Lisa Williams-Locklear, prin. Fax 429-3294

Willson S 300/K-8
1126 Ansel Rd 44108 216-838-1850
Dawn Hayden, prin. Fax 920-1284

Wright S 400/PK-8
11005 Parkhurst Dr 44111 216-838-6800
Virmeal Finley, prin. Fax 476-4206

Young Academy 300/2-12
17900 Harvard Ave 44128 216-838-5500
Karen Byron-Johnson, prin. Fax 295-3547

Archbishop Lyke S 200/K-8
18230 Harvard Ave 44128 216-991-9644
Margarete Smith, prin. Fax 991-9470

Birchwood S of Hawken 100/PK-8
4400 W 140th St 44135 216-251-2321
Charles Debelak, hdmstr. Fax 251-2787

Cleveland Montessori 100/PK-8
12510 Mayfield Rd 44106 216-421-0700

Holy Name S 100/K-8
8328 Broadway Ave 44105 216-341-0084
Lorenzo Jones, prin. Fax 341-1122

Luther Memorial Lutheran S 50/PK-8
4464 Pearl Rd 44109 216-749-5300
Nicole Creutz, prin. Fax 749-4270

Mary Queen of Peace S 200/PK-8
4419 Pearl Rd 44109 216-741-3685
Jessica Robertson, prin. Fax 741-5534

Metro Catholic S 600/PK-8
1910 W 54th St 44102 216-281-4044
Sr. Ann Maline, dir. Fax 634-2853

Our Lady of Angels S 400/K-8
3644 Rocky River Dr 44111 216-251-6841
Kathleen Krupar, prin. Fax 251-7831

Our Lady of Mt. Carmel S 200/PK-8
1355 W 70th St 44102 216-281-7146
Sr. Mary Vega, prin. Fax 281-7001

Ramah Junior Academy 100/PK-8
4770 Lee Rd 44128 216-581-2626
Celeste Giles, prin. Fax 581-4128

St. Adalbert S 200/PK-8
2345 E 83rd St 44104 216-881-6250
James Smith, prin. Fax 881-9030

St. Francis S 200/PK-8
7206 Myron Ave 44103 216-361-4858
Scott Embacher, prin. Fax 361-1673

St. Ignatius of Antioch S 300/K-8
10205 Lorain Ave 44111 216-671-0535
Margaret Ricksecker, prin. Fax 671-0536

St. Jerome S 200/K-8
15100 Lake Shore Blvd 44110 216-486-3587
Susan Coan, prin. Fax 486-4288

St. John Lutheran S 100/K-8
1027 E 176th St 44119 216-531-8204
David Peck, prin. Fax 531-8204

St. Leo the Great S 300/PK-8
4900 Broadview Rd 44109 216-661-2120
Sr. Denise Burns, prin. Fax 661-7125

St. Mark S 400/K-8
15724 Montrose Ave 44111 216-521-4115
Karen Cocita, prin. Fax 221-8664

St. Mary Byzantine S 200/PK-8
4600 State Rd 44109 216-749-7980
Rita Basalla, prin.

St. Rocco S 200/K-8
3205 Fulton Rd 44109 216-961-8557
Sr. Matthew Daniels, prin. Fax 961-1112

St. Stanislaus S 300/K-8
6615 Forman Ave 44105 216-883-3307
Deborah Martin, prin. Fax 883-0514

St. Thomas Aquinas S 200/K-8
9101 Superior Ave 44106 216-421-4668
Nancy Lynch, prin. Fax 721-8444

SS. Agatha & Aloysius S 100/K-8
640 Lakeview Rd 44108 216-451-2050
Sr. Dennis Kless, prin. Fax 451-1601

Urban Community S 400/PK-8
4909 Lorain Ave 44102 216-939-8330
Lisa DeCore, prin. Fax 939-8324

West Park Lutheran S 50/K-8
4260 Rocky River Dr 44135 216-941-2770
Nancy Clark, prin. Fax 941-3035

Cleveland Heights, Cuyahoga, Pop. 44,828

Cleveland Hts - University Hts CSD
Supt. — See University Heights

Boulevard ES 300/K-5
1749 Lee Rd 44118 216-371-7140
Michael Jenkins, prin. Fax 397-5955

Canterbury ES 400/K-5
2530 Canterbury Rd 44118 216-371-7470
Erica Wigton, prin. Fax 397-5956

Fairfax ES 400/K-5
3150 Fairfax Rd 44118 216-371-7480
Quatrice James, prin. Fax 397-5958

Heights MS 400/6-8
2181 Miramar Blvd 44118 216-371-6520
Jeff Johnston, prin. Fax 397-5967

Noble ES 400/K-5
1293 Ardoon St 44121 216-371-6535
Rachael Coleman, prin. Fax 397-5960

Oxford ES 300/K-5
939 Quilliams Rd 44121 216-371-6525
Brigitte Pronty, prin. Fax 397-5961

Roxboro ES 400/K-5
2405 Roxboro Rd 44106 216-371-7115
Michele Pulling, prin. Fax 397-5962

East Cleveland CSD
Supt. — See East Cleveland

Caledonia ES 200/K-6
914 Caledonia Ave 44112 216-268-6690
Charles McCants, prin. Fax 268-6463

Communion of Saints S 300/K-8
2160 Stillman Rd 44118 216-932-4177
Gertrude Whiteley, prin. Fax 932-7439

Hebrew Academy of Cleveland 600/PK-12
1860 S Taylor Rd 44118 216-321-5838
Rabbi Simcha Dessler, dir. Fax 932-4597

Mosdos Ohr HaTorah S - Girls 400/PK-12
1700 S Taylor Rd 44118 216-321-1547

Ruffing Montessori S 300/PK-8
3380 Fairmount Blvd 44118 216-321-7571

Yeshiva Derech Hatorah 200/PK-12
1508 Warrensville Center Rd 44121 216-382-6248
Susan Freund, admin. Fax 382-4585

Cleves, Hamilton, Pop. 3,191
Three Rivers Local SD 1,400/PK-12
401 N Miami Ave 45002 513-941-6400
Craig Hockenberry, supt. Fax 941-1102
www.threeriversschools.org
Taylor MS 5-8
56 Cooper Ave 45002 513-467-3500
Holly Simms, prin. Fax 467-0053
Three Rivers ES 900/PK-4
56 Cooper Ave 45002 513-467-3210
Adam Biedenbach, prin. Fax 467-0138

Clyde, Sandusky, Pop. 6,212
Clyde-Green Springs EVD 2,200/K-12
106 S Main St 43410 419-547-0588
Dennis Haft, supt. Fax 547-8644
www.clyde.k12.oh.us
Clyde ES 500/K-3
821 S Main St 43410 419-547-9868
Jackie Davis, prin. Fax 547-4885
McPherson MS 600/6-8
4230 Limerick Rd 43410 419-547-9150
Brian Cannon, prin. Fax 547-9173
Other Schools – See Green Springs

Coal Grove, Lawrence, Pop. 2,141
Dawson-Bryant Local SD 1,200/K-12
222 Lane St 45638 740-532-6451
Steve Easterling, supt. Fax 533-6019
db.k12.oh.us
Dawson-Bryant MS 300/6-8
1 Hornet Ln 45638 740-533-6008
Rick Roach, prin. Fax 533-6002
Other Schools – See Ironton

Coldwater, Mercer, Pop. 4,401
Coldwater EVD 1,400/K-12
310 N 2nd St 45828 419-678-2611
Jason Wood, supt. Fax 678-3100
cw.noacsc.org
Coldwater ES 500/K-4
310 N 2nd St 45828 419-678-2613
Mike Etzler, prin. Fax 678-3100
Coldwater MS 400/5-8
310 N 2nd St 45828 419-678-3331
Dan Pohlman, prin. Fax 678-3100

College Corner, Preble, Pop. 402
College Corner Local SD 50/PK-5
230 Ramsey St 45003 765-732-3183
Lynn Sheets, supt. Fax 732-3574
www.uc.k12.in.us/
College Corner Union ES 50/PK-5
230 Ramsey St 45003 765-732-3183
Ryan Simmons, prin. Fax 732-3574

Collins, Huron, Pop. 625
Western Reserve Local SD 1,100/PK-12
3765 State Route 20 44826 419-660-8508
Rodge Wilson, supt. Fax 660-8429
www.western-reserve.org
Western Reserve ES 600/K-6
3851 State Route 20 44826 419-660-9824
Melanie Conaway, prin. Fax 660-8566
Western Reserve MS 200/7-8
3841 State Route 20 44826 419-668-1924
Lisa Border, prin. Fax 663-2521
Other Schools – See Wakeman

Columbiana, Columbiana, Pop. 6,337
Columbiana EVD 1,000/PK-12
700 Columbiana Waterford Rd 44408 330-482-5352
Donald Mook, supt. Fax 482-5361
www.columbiana.k12.oh.us
Dixon ES 400/PK-4
333 N Middle St 44408 330-482-5355
Kimberly Sharshan, prin. Fax 482-5358
South Side MS 200/5-8
720 Columbiana Waterford Rd 44408 330-482-5354
Jason Martin, prin. Fax 482-6332

Crestview Local SD 1,200/K-12
44100 Crestview Rd Ste A 44408 330-482-5526
Matthew Manley, supt. Fax 482-5367
www.crestviewrebels.org
Crestview ES 500/K-4
3407 Middleton Rd 44408 330-482-5370
Marian Dangerfield, prin. Fax 482-5373
Crestview MS 400/5-8
44100 Crestview Rd Ste C 44408 330-482-4648
Allison Lemaster, prin. Fax 482-5374

Heartland Christian S 300/PK-12
28 Pittsburgh St 44408 330-482-2331
Eric Hosler, admin. Fax 482-2413

Columbia Station, Lorain
Columbia Local SD 900/K-12
25796 Royalton Rd 44028 440-236-5008
Graig Bansek, supt. Fax 236-8817
www.columbia.k12.oh.us/
Columbia MS 300/5-8
13646 W River Rd 44028 440-236-5741
Robert Magyar, prin. Fax 236-9274
Copopa ES 300/K-4
13644 W River Rd 44028 440-236-5020
Troy Bunner, prin. Fax 236-1220

Columbus, Franklin, Pop. 762,045
Columbus CSD 48,500/PK-12
270 E State St 43215 614-365-5000
Dan Good Ph.D., supt. Fax 365-5689
www.ccsoh.us
Africentric Early College ES 300/K-5
3223 Allegheny Ave 43209 614-365-6517
Sherri Edwards, prin. Fax 365-6520
Alpine ES 500/K-5
1590 Alpine Dr 43229 614-365-5359
Dr. Tawanna Williams, prin. Fax 365-5358
Arts Impact MS at Everett 500/6-8
680 Jack Gibbs Blvd 43215 614-365-5558
Leon Leavell, prin. Fax 365-5561
Avalon ES 600/K-5
5220 Avalon Ave 43229 614-365-5361
Lenelle Taylor, prin. Fax 365-8221
Avondale ES 300/PK-5
141 Hawkes Ave 43222 614-365-6511
April Knight, prin. Fax 365-8205
Berwick Alternative ES 700/PK-8
2655 Scottwood Rd 43209 614-365-6140
Kyla Mitchell, prin. Fax 365-6142
Binns ES 300/K-5
1080 Binns Blvd 43204 614-365-5911
Joel Grant, prin. Fax 365-5910
Broadleigh ES 300/PK-5
3039 Maryland Ave 43209 614-365-6144
Jennifer Vargo, prin. Fax 365-6143
Buckeye MS 500/6-8
2950 Parsons Ave 43207 614-365-5417
Derick Vickroy, prin. Fax 365-5895
Burroughs ES 400/PK-5
551 S Richardson Ave 43204 614-365-5923
Laura Schnebelen, prin. Fax 365-5424
Cassady Alternative ES 300/K-5
2500 N Cassady Ave 43219 614-365-5456
Natosha Schafer, prin. Fax 365-8700
Cedarwood Alternative ES 400/PK-5
775 Bartfield Dr 43207 614-365-5421
Latasha Turner, prin. Fax 365-5420
Champion MS 300/6-8
284 N 22nd St 43203 614-365-6082
Stephanie Bland, prin. Fax 365-6080
Clinton ES 400/K-5
10 Clinton Heights Ave 43202 614-365-6532
Carmen Suarez Graff, prin. Fax 365-6530
Colerain ES 200/PK-5
499 E Weisheimer Rd 43214 614-365-6001
Sherri Berridge, prin. Fax 365-6706
Columbus City Prep S for Boys 200/6-8
3450 Medway Ave 43213 614-365-6166
Kyle Gibson, prin. Fax 365-6164
Columbus City Prep S for Girls 400/6-8
1390 Bryden Rd 43205 614-365-6113
Stephanie Patton, prin. Fax 365-6112
Columbus Spanish Immersion Academy 300/K-8
3940 Karl Rd 43224 614-365-8129
Kathryn Myers, prin. Fax 365-8130
Como ES 400/PK-5
2989 Reis Ave 43224 614-365-6013
Anthony Summer, prin. Fax 365-6011
Cranbrook ES 300/K-5
908 Bricker Blvd 43221 614-365-5497
Stanley Embry, prin. Fax 365-5496
Devonshire Alternative ES 500/PK-5
6286 Ambleside Dr 43229 614-365-5335
Patricia Price, prin. Fax 365-8094
Dominion MS 500/6-8
330 E Dominion Blvd 43214 614-365-6020
Dorothy Flanagan, prin. Fax 365-6018
Duxberry Park Alternative ES 300/PK-5
1779 E Maynard Ave 43219 614-365-6023
Nicole Henry, prin. Fax 365-6022
Eakin ES 300/PK-5
3774 Eakin Rd 43228 614-365-5928
Theresa Eraybar, prin. Fax 365-5930
East Columbus ES 500/PK-5
3100 E 7th Ave 43219 614-365-6147
Jaime Spreen, prin. Fax 365-6146
Eastgate ES 300/PK-6
1925 Stratford Way 43219 614-365-6132
India Wilson, prin. Fax 365-6131
Easthaven ES 400/PK-5
2360 Garnet Pl 43232 614-365-6149
Verniedo Miller, prin. Fax 365-6721
East Linden ES 300/PK-5
2505 Brentnell Ave 43211 614-365-5459
Cheryl Jones, prin. Fax 365-5458
Ecole Kenwood French Immersion S 300/K-6
3770 Shattuck Ave 43220 614-365-5502
Emily Corbin, prin. Fax 365-5504
Fairmoor ES 400/K-5
3281 Mayfair Park Pl 43213 614-365-6169
Linda Willis, prin. Fax 365-6171
Fairwood Alternative ES 400/PK-6
726 Fairwood Ave 43205 614-365-6111
DeWayne Davis, prin. Fax 365-6110
Fifth Avenue International S 300/K-8
100 W 4th Ave 43201 614-365-5564
Susan McGeean, prin. Fax 365-5562
Forest Park ES 500/K-5
5535 Sandalwood Blvd 43229 614-365-5337
Rhonna McKibbin, prin. Fax 365-8219
Gables ES 400/K-5
1680 Becket Ave 43235 614-365-5499
Gene Smith, prin. Fax 365-6451
Georgian Heights Alternative ES 500/K-5
784 Georgian Dr 43228 614-365-5931
Nakita Smoot, prin. Fax 365-6885
Hamilton STEM Academy 500/PK-6
2047 Hamilton Ave 43211 614-365-5568
Christopher Brady, prin. Fax 365-5570
Highland ES 300/PK-5
40 S Highland Ave 43223 614-365-5935
Elizabeth McNally, prin. Fax 365-8726
Hilltonia MS 500/6-8
2345 W Mound St 43204 614-365-5937
Joyce Albright, prin. Fax 365-8015
Huy/A.G. Bell ES 500/PK-5
1545 Huy Rd 43224 614-365-5977
Denyse Woods, prin. Fax 365-5941
Indianola S 600/K-8
251 E Weber Rd 43202 614-365-5579
Brandy Koeth, prin. Fax 365-8324
Indian Springs ES 400/K-5
50 E Henderson Rd 43214 614-365-6032
Lisa Adams, prin. Fax 365-6031
Innis ES 300/K-5
3399 Kohr Blvd 43224 614-365-5462
Amber Hatcher, prin. Fax 365-5461
Johnson Park MS 400/6-8
1130 S Waverly St 43227 614-365-6501
David Walker, prin. Fax 365-8698
Leawood ES 300/PK-5
1677 S Hamilton Rd 43227 614-365-6504
Maria Malik, prin. Fax 365-6506
Liberty ES 300/K-5
2901 Whitlow Rd 43232 614-365-6482
Shalonda Likely-Roach, prin. Fax 365-5698
Lincoln Park ES 400/PK-6
579 E Markison Ave 43207 614-365-5524
Karla Case, prin. Fax 365-5523
Lindbergh ES 200/K-5
2541 Lindbergh Dr 43223 614-365-6727
Annette Tooman, prin. Fax 365-5598
Linden Park Neighborhood ECC PK-PK
1400 Myrtle Ave 43211 614-365-7963
Candace Nespeca, prin.
Linden STEM Academy 500/PK-6
2626 Cleveland Ave 43211 614-365-6537
Adrean Winfrey, prin. Fax 365-6536
Livingston ES 400/PK-5
825 E Livingston Ave 43205 614-365-5527
Stacy Macarthy, prin. Fax 365-5526
Maize Road ES 300/PK-5
4360 Maize Rd 43224 614-365-6040
Nichole Cavinee, prin. Fax 365-6039
Medina MS 500/6-8
1425 Huy Rd 43224 614-365-6050
Charmaine Tinker, prin. Fax 365-8136
Mifflin MS 400/6-8
3000 Agler Rd 43219 614-365-5474
Tracey Colson, prin. Fax 365-5477
Moler ES 400/PK-6
1201 Moler Rd 43207 614-365-5529
Jameica Shoultz, prin. Fax 365-5531
Northgate IS 4-5
6655 Sharon Woods Blvd 43229 614-365-8815
Andre Jones, prin.
North Linden ES 400/K-5
1718 E Cooke Rd 43224 614-365-6055
Sarah Foster, prin. Fax 365-6054
Northtowne ES 300/PK-5
4767 Northtowne Blvd 43229 614-365-5488
Germaine Wells, prin. Fax 365-5487
Oakland Park Alternative ES 400/PK-5
3392 Atwood Ter 43224 614-365-6058
Robert Losee, prin. Fax 365-6057
Oakmont ES 300/K-5
5666 Oakmont Dr 43232 614-365-5385
Shawyna McFadden, prin. Fax 365-5384
Ohio Avenue ES 300/PK-5
505 S Ohio Ave 43205 614-365-6130
Olympia Della Flora, prin. Fax 365-6128
Olde Orchard Alternative ES 500/K-5
800 McNaughten Rd 43213 614-365-5388
Joan Bucy, prin. Fax 365-5387
Parkmoor ES 300/PK-5
1711 Penworth Dr 43229 614-365-5349
Charmaine Campbell, prin. Fax 365-5348
Parsons ES 500/PK-5
3231 Lee Ellen Pl 43207 614-365-5099
Melinda Dixon, prin. Fax 365-5115
Ridgeview MS 500/6-8
4241 Rudy Rd 43214 614-365-5506
Natalie James, prin. Fax 365-5505
Salem ES 300/K-5
1040 Garvey Rd 43229 614-365-5351
Nikki Myers, prin. Fax 365-5353
Scottwood ES 500/PK-5
3392 Scottwood Rd 43227 614-365-6507
Kerri Myers, prin. Fax 365-6509
Shady Lane ES 400/K-5
1444 Shady Lane Rd 43227 614-365-5391
Kevin Hainer, prin. Fax 365-5390
Sherwood MS 400/6-8
1400 Shady Lane Rd 43227 614-365-5393
Kevin Freeman, prin. Fax 365-8351
Siebert ES 300/PK-6
385 Reinhard Ave 43206 614-365-6613
Debra Archie-Wilkerson, prin. Fax 365-6612
South Mifflin STEM Academy 300/PK-6
2365 Middlehurst Dr 43219 614-365-6135
Pamela Eberhardt-Horton, prin. Fax 365-6134
Southwood ES 400/PK-6
1500 S 4th St 43207 614-365-5553
Danita Turner, prin. Fax 365-8071
Starling K-8 STEM 600/PK-8
145 S Central Ave 43222 614-365-5945
Angela Tyler, prin. Fax 365-5942
Stewart Alternative ES 300/K-6
40 Stewart Ave 43206 614-365-5556
Ebone Johnson, prin. Fax 365-6704
Sullivant ES 300/PK-5
791 Griggs Ave 43223 614-365-6524
Lisa Stamos, prin. Fax 365-6522
Trevitt ES 400/PK-5
519 Trevitt St 43203 614-365-6137
Patrese Mason, prin. Fax 365-6139
Valley Forge ES 300/PK-5
1321 Urban Dr 43229 614-365-5648
Andrew Smith, prin. Fax 365-5779
Valleyview ES 300/PK-5
2989 Valleyview Dr 43204 614-365-6312
Amy Morris, prin. Fax 365-6768
Watkins ES 400/PK-5
1520 Watkins Rd 43207 614-365-6411
Tom Revou, prin. Fax 365-6415
Wedgewood MS 500/6-8
3800 Briggs Rd 43228 614-365-5947
Diane Campbell, prin. Fax 365-5950
Weinland Park ES 400/PK-5
211 E 7th Ave 43201 614-365-5321
Rhonda Peeples, prin. Fax 365-5431

West Broad Street ES 500/PK-5
2744 W Broad St 43204 614-365-5964
James Eslinger, prin. Fax 365-5966
Westgate Alternative ES 400/PK-5
3080 Wicklow Rd 43204 614-365-5971
Angela Sweeney, prin. Fax 365-5149
Westmoor MS 500/6-8
3001 Valleyview Dr 43204 614-365-5974
Paul Bailey, prin. Fax 365-6705
West Mound ES 500/PK-5
2051 W Mound St 43223 614-365-5968
Angela Tyler, prin. Fax 365-6937
Windsor STEM Academy 500/PK-6
1219 E 12th Ave 43211 614-365-5906
Latasha Bah, prin. Fax 365-6939
Winterset ES 300/PK-5
4776 Winterset Dr 43220 614-365-5510
Audra Pearson, prin. Fax 365-5509
Woodcrest ES 400/PK-5
5321 E Livingston Ave 43232 614-365-6747
Brianne Pannell, prin. Fax 365-6751
Woodward Park MS 900/6-8
5151 Karl Rd 43229 614-365-5354
Diane Agnes, prin. Fax 365-5357
Yorktown MS 400/6-8
5600 E Livingston Ave 43232 614-365-5408
Shannon Tucker, prin. Fax 365-5411

Dublin CSD
Supt. — See Dublin
Wright ES 600/PK-5
2335 West Case Rd 43235 614-538-0464
Lucas Bauer, prin. Fax 761-5874

Grandview Heights CSD 800/PK-12
1587 W 3rd Ave 43212 614-485-4015
Andy Culp, supt. Fax 481-3648
www.ghcsd.org
Edison Intermediate/Larson MS 200/4-8
1240 Oakland Ave 43212 614-481-4100
Tracie Lees, prin. Fax 481-3628
Stevenson ES 300/PK-3
1065 Oxley Rd 43212 614-485-4200
Angela Ullum, prin. Fax 429-6083

Groveport Madison Local SD
Supt. — See Groveport
Asbury ES 400/K-5
5127 Harbor Blvd 43232 614-833-2000
Staci Peters, prin. Fax 833-2004
Dunloe ES 400/K-5
3200 Dunloe Rd 43232 614-833-2008
Naim Sanders, prin. Fax 833-2007
Groveport Madison MS North 400/6-8
5474 Sedalia Dr 43232 614-837-5508
Brandy Grieves, prin. Fax 833-2033
Madison ES 500/K-5
4600 Madison School Dr 43232 614-833-2011
Tricia Faulkner, prin. Fax 836-4683
Sedalia ES 500/K-5
5400 Sedalia Dr 43232 614-833-2014
Matthew Decastro, prin. Fax 833-2429

Hamilton Local SD 3,100/PK-12
775 Rathmell Rd 43207 614-491-8044
William J. Morrison, supt. Fax 491-8323
www.hamiltonrangers.org
Hamilton ES 900/K-3
745 Rathmell Rd 43207 614-491-8044
Dr. Joshua Conley, prin. Fax 492-1499
Hamilton IS 700/4-6
765 Rathmell Rd 43207 614-492-8044
Kelly Buxton, prin. Fax 492-1059
Hamilton MS 500/7-8
755 Rathmell Rd 43207 614-491-8044
Jeffrey Endres, prin. Fax 491-0260
Hamilton Preschool PK-PK
775 Rathmell Rd 43207 614-491-8044
Jan Strahm, coord. Fax 491-8323

Hilliard CSD 15,600/K-12
2140 Atlas St 43228 614-921-7000
John Marschhausen Ph.D., supt. Fax 921-7001
www.hilliardschools.org
Hilliard Horizon ES 600/K-5
6000 Renner Rd 43228 614-921-5800
Hilary Sloat, prin. Fax 921-5801
Other Schools – See Dublin, Hilliard

South-Western CSD
Supt. — See Grove City
Alton Hall ES 500/K-4
982 Alton Ave 43219 614-801-8000
Jamie Clark, prin. Fax 851-5379
Finland ES 400/K-4
1835 Finland Ave 43223 614-801-8125
Sean Flynn, prin. Fax 279-3241
Finland MS 700/7-8
1825 Finland Ave 43223 614-801-3600
Lori Balough, prin. Fax 278-6334
Franklin Woods IS 600/5-6
1831 Finland Ave 43223 614-801-8600
Andy Stolz, prin. Fax 801-8601
Norton MS 500/7-8
215 Norton Rd 43228 614-801-3700
Tresa Davis, prin. Fax 870-5528
Prairie Lincoln ES 500/K-4
4900 Amesbury Way 43228 614-801-8300
Julie Kenney, prin. Fax 853-2268
Prairie Norton ES 600/PK-4
105 Norton Rd 43228 614-801-8450
Michael Gosztyla, prin. Fax 851-0298
Stiles ES 700/PK-4
4700 Stiles Ave 43228 614-801-8375
Jessica Cahill, prin. Fax 853-0798
West Franklin ES 500/K-4
3501 Briggs Rd 43223 614-801-8400
Dr. Dawn Lauridsen, prin. Fax 351-4911

Westerville CSD
Supt. — See Westerville
Hawthorne ES 600/K-5
5001 Farview Dr 43231 614-797-7130
Angela Ervin, prin. Fax 797-7131

Worthington CSD
Supt. — See Worthington
Bluffsview ES 400/K-6
7111 Linworth Rd 43235 614-450-5100
Cindy Fox, prin. Fax 883-2710
Brookside ES 300/K-6
6700 Mcvey Blvd 43235 614-450-5300
Jenny Wielinski, prin. Fax 883-2760
Granby ES 400/K-6
1490 Hard Rd 43235 614-450-4500
Patricia Schlaegel, prin. Fax 883-2910
McCord MS 500/7-8
1500 Hard Rd 43235 614-450-4000
Michael Kuri, prin. Fax 883-3560
Worthington Hills ES 500/K-6
1221 Candlewood Dr 43235 614-450-4700
Alexandra Seiling, prin. Fax 883-3410

All Saints Academy 300/PK-8
2855 E Livingston Ave 43209 614-231-3391
Laura Miller, prin. Fax 338-2170
Calumet Christian S 300/PK-8
2774 Calumet St 43202 614-261-8136
James Fulford, prin. Fax 261-9086
Clintonville Academy 100/PK-8
3916 Indianola Ave 43214 614-267-4799
Sally Lindsay, prin. Fax 267-1723
Columbus Adventist Academy 100/K-8
3650B Sunbury Rd 43219 614-471-2083
Brenda Arthurs, prin. Fax 471-5035
Columbus Montessori Education Center 200/PK-6
979 S James Rd 43227 614-231-3790
Columbus School for Girls 600/PK-12
65 S Drexel Ave 43209 614-252-0781
Jennifer Ciccarelli, hdmstr. Fax 252-0571
Columbus Torah Academy 200/K-12
181 Noe Bixby Rd 43213 614-864-0299
Rabbi Avrohom Drandoff, head sch Fax 864-2119
Friend Christian Academy 50/K-6
428 E Main St 43215 614-221-1518
Nadia Reed, admin. Fax 221-8470
Harambee Christian S 100/K-8
1000 Bonham Ave 43211 614-291-0885
Alexander Steinman, prin. Fax 298-7776
Holy Spirit S 300/PK-8
4382 Duchene Ln 43213 614-861-0475
Amy Chessler, prin. Fax 861-8608
Immaculate Conception S 500/K-8
366 E North Broadway St 43214 614-267-6579
Colleen Kent, prin. Fax 267-2549
Mansion Day S 100/PK-5
72 Woodland Ave 43203 614-258-4449
Dee James, head sch Fax 258-7001
Our Lady of Bethlehem S 100/PK-K
4567 Olentangy River Rd 43214 614-459-8285
Lori Dulin, prin. Fax 451-3706
Our Lady of Peace S 300/K-8
40 E Dominion Blvd 43214 614-267-4535
Jim Silcott, prin. Fax 267-2333
St. Agatha S 300/K-8
1880 Northam Rd 43221 614-488-9000
Luna Alsharaiah, prin. Fax 488-5783
St. Andrew S 500/PK-8
4081 Reed Rd 43220 614-451-1626
Joel Wichtman, prin. Fax 451-0272
St. Anthony S 200/K-8
1300 Urban Dr 43229 614-888-4268
Chris Iaconis, prin. Fax 888-4435
St. Catharine S 300/PK-8
2865 Fair Ave 43209 614-235-1396
Janet Weisner, prin. Fax 235-9708
St. Cecilia S 300/PK-8
440 Norton Rd 43228 614-878-3555
Deborah Adamczak, prin. Fax 878-6852
St. James the Less S 500/K-8
1628 Oakland Park Ave 43224 614-268-3311
Samary Cecchetti, prin. Fax 268-1808
St. Joseph Montessori S 300/PK-8
933 Hamlet St 43201 614-291-8601
Matt Brenner, hdmstr. Fax 291-7411
St. Mary Magdalene S 200/PK-8
2940 Parkside Rd 43204 614-279-9935
Rocco Fumi, prin. Fax 279-9575
St. Mary S 300/PK-8
700 S 3rd St 43206 614-444-8994
Kayla Walton, prin. Fax 449-2853
St. Matthias S 300/K-8
1566 Ferris Rd 43224 614-268-3030
Dan Kinley, prin. Fax 268-4681
St. Paul's Lutheran S 100/K-8
322 Stewart Ave 43206 614-444-4216
Philip Glende, prin. Fax 444-4216
St. Timothy S 300/K-8
1070 Thomas Ln 43220 614-451-1405
George Mosholder, prin. Fax 451-3108
Sonshine Christian Academy 200/PK-8
1965 Gladstone Ave 43211 614-291-6840
Carol Parron, prin. Fax 291-6841
Tree of Life Christian S - Indianola 100/PK-5
2141 Indianola Ave 43201 614-299-4906
Colleen Hoffman, prin. Fax 299-3047
Trinity S 200/PK-8
1440 Grandview Ave 43212 614-488-7650
Kimber Moehrrman, prin. Fax 488-7885
Wellington S 700/PK-12
3650 Reed Rd 43220 614-457-7883
Robert Brisk, head sch Fax 442-3286
Worthington Christian ES 000/1-5
50 Westview Ave 43214 614-431-8240
James Parrish, prin. Fax 438-5581

Columbus Grove, Putnam, Pop. 2,103
Columbus Grove Local SD 800/K-12
201 W Cross St 45830 419-659-2639
George Verhoff, supt. Fax 659-5134
cg.noacsc.org
Columbus Grove ES 300/K-4
201 W Cross St 45830 419-659-2631
Brad Calvelage, prin. Fax 659-5134
Columbus Grove MS 200/5-8
201 W Cross St 45830 419-659-2631
Brad Calvelage, prin. Fax 659-5134

St. Anthony of Padua S 100/PK-8
520 W Sycamore St 45830 419-659-2103
Scott Hummel, prin. Fax 659-4194

Commercial Point, Pickaway, Pop. 1,557
Teays Valley Local SD
Supt. — See Ashville
Scioto ES 600/PK-5
20 W Scioto St 43116 740-983-5000
Devin Anderson, prin. Fax 983-5088
Teays Valley West MS 400/6-8
200 Grove Run Rd 43116 740-983-5000
Michael Kauffeld, prin. Fax 983-5040

Concord, Lake

Hershey Montessori S 200/PK-8
10229 Prouty Rd 44077 440-357-0918
Paula Leigh-Doyle, head sch Fax 357-9096

Conesville, Coshocton, Pop. 347
River View Local SD
Supt. — See Warsaw
Conesville ES 300/PK-6
199 State St 43811 740-829-2334
Joel Moore, prin. Fax 829-2856

Conneaut, Ashtabula, Pop. 12,629
Conneaut Area CSD 1,700/PK-12
230 Gateway Ave Ste B 44030 440-593-7200
Lori Riley, supt. Fax 593-6253
www.cacsk12.org
Conneaut MS 400/6-8
230 Gateway Ave 44030 440-593-7240
James Kennedy, prin. Fax 593-6289
Gateway ES 400/3-5
229 Gateway Ave 44030 440-593-7280
Dawn Zappitelli, prin. Fax 599-2703
Lakeshore PS 500/PK-2
755 Chestnut St 44030 440-593-7250
Wendy Tisch, prin. Fax 599-7149

Continental, Putnam, Pop. 1,147
Continental Local SD 500/K-12
5211 State Route 634 45831 419-596-3671
Danny Kissell, supt. Fax 596-3861
www.continentalpirates.org
Continental ES 300/K-6
5211 State Route 634 45831 419-596-3860
Tracy Potts, prin. Fax 596-2652

Convoy, Van Wert, Pop. 1,077
Crestview Local SD 800/K-12
531 E Tully St 45832 419-749-9100
Michael Estes, supt. Fax 749-4235
www.crestviewknights.com/
Crestview ES 400/K-6
531 E Tully St 45832 419-749-9100
Kathleen Mollenkopf, prin. Fax 749-2026
Crestview MS 100/7-8
531 E Tully St 45832 419-749-9100
David Bowen, prin. Fax 749-2484

Coolville, Athens, Pop. 488
Federal Hocking Local SD
Supt. — See Stewart
Coolville ES 300/PK-6
26461 Main St 45723 740-667-3121
Mary Mitchell, prin. Fax 667-6183

Copley, Summit, Pop. 11,130
Copley-Fairlawn CSD 3,100/PK-12
3797 Ridgewood Rd 44321 330-664-4800
Brian Poe, supt. Fax 664-4811
www.copley-fairlawn.org
Arrowhead PS 300/K-4
1600 Raleigh Blvd 44321 330-664-4885
Roman Capper, prin. Fax 664-4927
Copley-Fairlawn MS 1,000/5-8
1531 S Cleveland Massillon 44321 330-664-4875
Kathleen Ashcroft, prin. Fax 664-4912
Other Schools – See Fairlawn

Spring Garden Waldorf S 200/PK-8
1791 Jacoby Rd 44321 330-666-0574
Tracy Edwards, prin. Fax 666-9210

Corning, Perry, Pop. 572
Southern Local SD 700/K-12
10397 State Route 155 SE 43730 740-394-2426
Greg Holbert, supt. Fax 394-2083
www.spsd.k12.oh.us
Millcreek ES 400/K-6
10397 State Route 155 SE 43730 740-721-0520
Mary Lou Wycinski, prin. Fax 394-2083

Cortland, Trumbull, Pop. 7,046
Lakeview Local SD 1,800/K-12
300 Hillman Dr 44410 330-637-8741
Robert Wilson, supt. Fax 282-4260
www.lakeviewlocal.org
Lakeview MS 600/4-7
640 Wakefield Dr 44410 330-637-4360
Ashley Handrych, prin. Fax 638-1913
Other Schools – See Warren

Maplewood Local SD 800/K-12
2414 Greenville Rd 44410 330-637-7506
Perry Nicholas, supt. Fax 637-6616
www.maplewood.k12.oh.us/
Maplewood ES 300/K-6
4174 Greenville Rd 44410 330-924-2431
Elizabeth Goerig, prin. Fax 924-5151

Mathews Local SD 600/K-12
4096 Cadwallader Sonk Rd 44410 330-637-7000
Lew Lowery, supt. Fax 637-1930
www.mathews.k12.oh.us
Currie ES, 3306 Ridge Rd 44410 200/K-2
Michael King, prin. 330-637-2976
Other Schools – See Vienna

Coshocton, Coshocton, Pop. 11,049
Coshocton CSD 1,600/PK-12
1207 Cambridge Rd 43812 740-622-1901
Dr. David Hire, supt. Fax 623-5803
www.coshoctonredskins.com/
Coshocton ES 900/PK-6
1203 Cambridge Rd 43812 740-622-5514
Dave Skelton, prin. Fax 295-7716

River View Local SD
Supt. — See Warsaw
Keene ES 200/K-6
27052 County Road 1 43812 740-622-5884
Beth Hamersley, prin. Fax 622-5458

Coshocton Christian S 100/PK-12
23891 Airport Rd 43812 740-622-5052
Stanley Zurowski, prin. Fax 622-9244
Sacred Heart S 100/PK-6
39 Burt Ave 43812 740-622-3728
Mary Kobel, prin. Fax 622-9151

Covington, Miami, Pop. 2,556
Covington EVD 800/K-12
807 Chestnut St 45318 937-473-2249
Gene Gooding, supt. Fax 473-3730
www.covington.k12.oh.us
Covington ES 400/K-6
807 Chestnut St Ste B 45318 937-473-2252
Josh Long, prin. Fax 473-3685
Covington JHS 200/7-8
807 Chestnut St Ste A 45318 937-473-3746
Jo DeMotte, prin. Fax 473-3730

Crestline, Crawford, Pop. 4,534
Colonel Crawford Local SD
Supt. — See North Robinson
Crawford ES 200/PK-5
5444 Crestline Rd 44827 419-562-5753
Cindy Voss, prin. Fax 562-2983
Crawford IS 200/6-8
5444 Crestline Rd 44827 419-562-7529
April Bond, prin. Fax 562-3319

Crestline EVD 600/PK-12
401 Heiser Ct 44827 419-683-3647
Noreen Mullens, supt. Fax 683-4984
www.crestline.k12.oh.us
Crestline ES 300/K-5
435 Oldfield Rd 44827 419-683-5351
Julie Murphy-Theodore, prin. Fax 683-0341
Crestline Preschool 100/PK-PK
435 Oldfield Rd 44827 419-683-3647
Julie Murphy-Theodore, prin.

St. Joseph S 100/PK-8
333 N Thoman St 44827 419-683-1284
Daniel Salvati, prin. Fax 683-8957

Creston, Wayne, Pop. 2,138
Norwayne Local SD 1,400/PK-12
350 S Main St 44217 330-435-6382
Karen O'Hare, supt. Fax 435-4633
www.norwayne.net
Norwayne ES 700/PK-5
286 S Main St 44217 330-435-6383
David Dreher, prin. Fax 435-4633
Norwayne MS 400/6-8
350 S Main St 44217 330-435-1195
Kevin Leatherman, prin. Fax 435-4633

Cridersville, Allen, Pop. 1,838
Wapakoneta CSD
Supt. — See Wapakoneta
Cridersville ES 400/PK-4
501 Reichelderfer Rd 45806 419-645-3000
Jason Wolke, prin. Fax 645-3003

Crooksville, Perry, Pop. 2,512
Crooksville EVD 900/PK-12
4065 Ceramic Way 43731 740-982-7040
Matt Sheridan, supt. Fax 982-3551
www.crooksville.k12.oh.us
Crooksville ES 400/PK-4
12400 Tunnel Hill Rd 43731 740-982-7010
John Toeller, prin. Fax 982-5087
Crooksville MS 300/5-8
12400 Tunnel Hill Rd 43731 740-982-7010
John Toeller, prin. Fax 982-5087

Crown City, Gallia, Pop. 412
Gallia County Local SD
Supt. — See Patriot
Hannan Trace ES 200/PK-5
9345 State Route 218 45623 740-256-6468
Dr. Edie Bostic, prin. Fax 256-1803

Curtice, Lucas, Pop. 1,519
Oregon CSD
Supt. — See Oregon
Jerusalem ES 500/K-4
535 S Yondota Rd 43412 419-836-6111
Jeffrey Straka, prin. Fax 836-1501

Custar, Wood, Pop. 178

St. Louis S 50/PK-6
PO Box 125 43511 419-669-1875
Elizabeth Panning, prin. Fax 669-2878

Cuyahoga Falls, Summit, Pop. 48,868
Cuyahoga Falls CSD 5,000/K-12
431 Stow Ave 44221 330-926-3800
Dr. Todd Nichols, supt. Fax 920-1074
www.cfalls.org
Bolich MS 600/6-8
2630 13th St 44223 330-926-3801
Ryan Huch, prin. Fax 920-3737
Dewitt ES 400/K-5
425 Falls Ave 44221 330-926-3802
Catherine Perrow, prin. Fax 916-6016
Lincoln ES 500/K-5
3131 Bailey Rd 44221 330-926-3803
Tracy Early, prin. Fax 916-6024
Preston ES 300/K-5
800 Tallmadge Rd 44221 330-926-3805
Tamara Brown, prin. Fax 916-6027
Price ES 300/K-5
2610 Delmore St 44221 330-926-3806
John Musat, prin. Fax 929-3171
Richardson ES 400/K-5
2226 23rd St 44223 330-926-3807
Julie Wilson, prin. Fax 916-6022
Roberts MS 500/6-8
3333 Charles St 44221 330-926-3809
James Holzapfel, prin. Fax 920-3748
Other Schools – See Silver Lake

Woodridge Local SD
Supt. — See Peninsula
Woodridge PS 400/K-2
3313 Northampton Rd 44223 330-928-1223
Beth Harrington, prin. Fax 928-2050

Chapel Hill Christian S North Campus 300/PK-6
1090 Howe Ave 44221 330-929-1901
John Wilson, admin. Fax 929-1737
Immaculate Heart of Mary S 400/K-8
2859 Lillis Dr 44223 330-923-1220
Kathleen Friess, prin. Fax 929-4373
Redeemer Christian S 200/PK-8
2141 5th St 44221 330-923-1280
Kenneth Krueger, prin. Fax 923-4517
St. Joseph S 300/K-8
1909 3rd St 44221 330-928-2151
Carrie DePasquale, prin. Fax 928-3139
Summit Christian S 100/K-8
2800 13th St 44223 330-762-3382
Stephanie Fleser, prin. Fax 926-9058

Cuyahoga Heights, Cuyahoga, Pop. 635
Cuyahoga Heights Local SD 900/PK-12
4820 E 71st St 44125 216-429-5700
Thomas Evans, supt. Fax 341-3737
www.cuyhts.org
Cuyahoga Heights ES 400/PK-5
4880 E 71st St 44125 216-429-5880
Joy Houchen, prin. Fax 429-5883
Cuyahoga Heights MS 200/6-8
4840 E 71st St 44125 216-429-5757
William Young, prin. Fax 429-5735

Dalton, Wayne, Pop. 1,798
Dalton Local SD 500/PK-12
PO Box 514 44618 330-828-2267
James R. Saxer, supt. Fax 828-2800
www.dalton.k12.oh.us
Dalton ES, 250 N Church St 44618 300/PK-8
Joseph Petrak, prin. 330-828-2405

Danville, Knox, Pop. 1,035
Danville Local SD 600/K-12
PO Box 30 43014 740-599-6116
Jason Snively, supt. Fax 599-5417
www.danvilleschools.org
Danville ES 300/K-5
PO Box 30 43014 740-599-6116
Tara Bond, prin. Fax 599-5904
Danville MS 100/6-8
PO Box 30 43014 740-599-6116
Matthew Proper, dir. Fax 599-5904

Darbydale, Franklin, Pop. 781
South-Western CSD
Supt. — See Grove City
Darbydale ES 300/PK-4
7000 London Groveport Rd 43123 614-801-8050
James Micciulla, prin. Fax 877-9553

Dayton, Montgomery, Pop. 137,548
Centerville CSD
Supt. — See Centerville
Driscoll ES 300/2-5
5767 Marshall Rd 45429 937-434-0562
Cherie Colopy, prin. Fax 434-0393
Hole ES 300/2-5
180 W Whipp Rd 45459 937-434-0725
Lisa May, prin. Fax 434-0557
Normandy ES 500/2-5
401 Normandy Ridge Rd 45459 937-434-0917
Rebecca O'Neil, prin. Fax 434-0953
Watts MS 800/6-8
7056 McEwen Rd 45459 937-434-0370
Brian Miller, prin. Fax 434-2907

Dayton CSD 14,300/PK-12
115 S Ludlow St 45402 937-542-3000
Dr. Rhonda Corr, supt. Fax 542-3188
www.dps.k12.oh.us
Adams Earley Academy for Girls 400/K-8
444 Shoup Mill Rd 45415 937-542-5840
Shirlette Burks, prin. Fax 542-5841
Belle Haven S 500/PK-8
4401 Free Pike 45416 937-542-4220
Joy Stokes, prin. Fax 542-4221
Brown S 400/PK-8
31 Willowwood Dr 45405 937-542-5740
Channey Goode, prin. Fax 542-5741
Cleveland ES 400/PK-6
1102 Pursell Ave 45420 937-542-4340
Laura Hormann, prin. Fax 542-4341
Dayton Boys Prep Academy 400/PK-8
1923 W 3rd St 45417 937-542-5340
Horace Lovelace, prin. Fax 542-5341
Eastmont S 500/PK-8
1480 Edendale Rd 45432 937-542-4490
Celeste Hoerner, prin. Fax 542-4491
Edison S 500/PK-8
228 N Broadway St 45402 937-542-4540
Basharus Simmons, prin. Fax 542-4541
Fairview S 500/PK-8
2314 Elsmere Ave 45406 937-542-4590
Monica Utley, prin. Fax 542-4591
Kemp S 400/PK-6
1923 Gondert Ave 45403 937-542-5090
Stacy Maney, prin. Fax 542-5091
Kiser S 500/PK-8
1401 Leo St 45404 937-542-6130
James Fowler, prin. Fax 542-6131
Mann S 500/PK-8
715 Krebs Ave 45419 937-542-4890
Sheri Moss, prin. Fax 542-4891
Meadowdale S 500/PK-6
3871 Yellowstone Ave 45416 937-542-5390
Therman Sampson, prin. Fax 542-5391
Parks Early Learning Center 50/PK-PK
3705 Lori Sue Ave 45406 937-542-4390
Michelle Fulcher, prin. Fax 542-4391
River's Edge Montessori ES 500/PK-6
108 Linwood St 45405 937-542-4640
Lisa Keane, prin. Fax 542-4641
Ruskin S 500/PK-8
407 Ambrose Ct 45410 937-542-5680
Jennifer Dearwester, prin. Fax 542-5681
Troy ES 400/PK-4
1630 Miami Chapel Rd 45417 937-542-4290
Karla Goins, prin. Fax 542-4291
Valerie ES 400/PK-6
4020 Bradwood Dr 45405 937-542-5690
Shawnkeida Whitlow, prin. Fax 542-5691
Westwood S 400/PK-8
2805 Oakridge Dr 45417 937-542-4990
Akisha Shehee, prin. Fax 542-4991
Wogaman MS 300/7-8
920 McArthur Ave 45417 937-542-5890
Karl Perkins, prin. Fax 542-5891
World of Wonder S 500/PK-8
4411 Oakridge Dr 45417 937-542-3600
LaDawn Mims, prin. Fax 542-3601
Wright Brothers MS 500/7-8
1361 Huffman Ave 45403 937-542-5940
Shawna Welch, prin. Fax 542-5941

Jefferson Township Local SD 400/K-12
2625 S Union Rd 45417 937-835-5682
Dr. Richard Gates, supt. Fax 835-5955
www.jeffersontwp.k12.oh.us/
Blairwood ES 200/K-6
1241 Blairwood Ave 45417 937-263-3504
Semone Epps, prin. Fax 262-3450

Mad River Local SD 3,900/PK-12
801 Old Harshman Rd 45431 937-259-6606
Chad Wyen, supt. Fax 259-6607
www.madriverschools.org
Beverly Gardens ES 400/K-4
5555 Enright Ave 45431 937-259-6620
Cristal Fields, prin. Fax 259-6614
Brantwood ES 400/K-4
4350 Schwinn Dr 45404 937-237-4270
Andrea Rastatter, prin. Fax 237-4277
Mad River ECC 100/PK-PK
801 Old Harshman Rd 45431 937-259-6640
Pam Roberts, prin. Fax 259-6612
Mad River MS 600/7-8
1801 Harshman Rd 45424 937-237-4265
Laurie Plank, prin. Fax 237-4273
Saville ES 400/K-4
5800 Burkhardt Rd 45431 937-259-6625
Steven Kandel, prin. Fax 259-6648
Spinning Hills MS 600/5-6
5001 Eastman Ave 45432 937-259-6635
Mike Combs, prin. Fax 259-6644
Stevenson ES 300/K-4
805 Old Harshman Rd 45431 937-259-6630
Cory Miller, prin. Fax 259-6628

Miamisburg CSD
Supt. — See Miamisburg
Bauer ES 400/K-5
701 Springboro Pike 45449 937-434-9191
Tammy Sundermann, prin. Fax 434-8879

Northmont CSD
Supt. — See Englewood
Northwood ES 300/2-6
6200 Noranda Dr 45415 937-832-6240
Sally Moore, prin. Fax 832-6241

Northridge Local SD 1,700/K-12
2008 Timber Ln 45414 937-278-5885
David Jackson, supt. Fax 276-8351
www.northridgeschools.org
Dennis MS 400/4-6
2655 Wagoner Ford Rd 45414 937-275-6833
Tim Whitestone, prin. Fax 276-8357
Morrison ES 400/1-3
2235 Arthur Ave 45414 937-276-8341
Tabitha Hardin, prin. Fax 276-8343

Timberlane Learning Center 200/K-K
2131 Timber Ln 45414 937-278-0689
Tabitha Hardin, prin. Fax 278-4029

Vandalia-Butler CSD
Supt. — See Vandalia
Smith MS 100/4-5
3625 Little York Rd 45414 937-415-7000
Ryan Rogers, prin. Fax 415-7051

West Carrollton CSD
Supt. — See West Carrollton
Holliday ES 400/1-5
4100 S Dixie Dr 45439 937-859-5121
Janet Schieman, prin. Fax 643-5460
Nicholas ES 200/1-5
3846 Vance Rd 45439 937-859-5121
Dorian Glover, prin. Fax 859-2765

Bishop Leibold Consolidated S East 300/4-8
6666 Springboro Pike 45449 937-434-9343
Dr. Theodore Wallace, prin. Fax 436-3048
East Dayton Christian S 500/PK-12
999 Spinning Rd 45431 937-252-5400
Stacie Auvil, prin. Fax 258-4099
Gloria Dei Montessori S 100/PK-8
615 Shiloh Dr 45415 937-274-7195
Laurie Kemp, head sch
Hillel Academy of Dayton 50/K-6
305 Sugar Camp Cir 45409 937-277-8966
Holy Angels S 300/PK-8
223 L St 45409 937-229-5959
Jacob LaForge, prin. Fax 229-5960
Immaculate Conception S 200/K-8
2268 S Smithville Rd 45420 937-253-8831
Daniel Stringer, prin. Fax 252-1992
Miami Valley S 500/PK-12
5151 Denise Dr 45429 937-434-4444
Jay Scheurle, hdmstr. Fax 434-1033
Mother Maria Anna Brunner Catholic S 400/PK-8
4870 Denlinger Rd 45426 937-277-2291
Robin Johnson, prin. Fax 277-2217
Our Lady of the Rosary S 200/K-8
40 Notre Dame Ave 45404 937-222-7231
Jacki Loffer, prin. Fax 222-7393
St. Anthony S 200/PK-8
1824 Saint Charles Ave 45410 937-253-6251
Alana Campion, prin. Fax 253-1541
St. Benedict the Moor Catholic S 200/K-8
138 Gramont Ave 45417 937-268-6391
Marianne Pitts, prin. Fax 268-9775
St. Helen S 300/PK-8
5086 Burkhardt Rd 45431 937-256-1761
Christine Buschur, prin. Fax 254-4614

Defiance, Defiance, Pop. 16,265
Ayersville Local SD 800/K-12
28046 Watson Rd 43512 419-395-1111
Don Diglia, supt. Fax 395-9990
www.ayersville.org
Ayersville ES 400/K-6
28046 Watson Rd 43512 419-395-1111
Beth Hench, prin. Fax 395-9990

Defiance CSD 2,500/K-12
629 Arabella St 43512 419-782-0070
Michael Struble, supt. Fax 782-4395
www.defiancecityschools.org
Defiance ES 1,200/K-5
400 Carter Rd 43512 419-785-2260
Deanne Held, prin. Fax 785-2262
Defiance MS 600/6-8
629 Arabella St 43512 419-782-0050
Richard Peters, prin. Fax 782-0060

Northeastern Local SD 1,100/K-12
5921 Domersville Rd 43512 419-497-3461
James Roach, supt. Fax 497-3401
www.tinora.org
Noble ES 200/K-1
10553 Haller St 43512 419-782-7941
Denise Wright, prin. Fax 784-3788
Tinora ES 500/2-6
5751 Domersville Rd 43512 419-497-1022
Nicole Wells, prin. Fax 497-1024
Tinora JHS 200/7-8
5921 Domersville Rd 43512 419-497-2361
Lisa Maxwell, prin. Fax 497-3401

Holy Cross Catholic S of Defiance 100/PK-6
1745 S Clinton St 43512 419-784-2021
Sr. Rose Reinhart, prin.
St. John Lutheran S 200/PK-8
655 Wayne Ave 43512 419-782-1751
Shellie Kosmerchock, prin. Fax 782-0954

De Graff, Logan, Pop. 1,275
Riverside Local SD 700/K-12
2096 County Road 24 S 43318 937-585-5981
Scott Mann, supt. Fax 585-4599
www.riverside.k12.oh.us
Riverside ES 400/K-6
2096 County Road 24 S 43318 937-585-5981
Mason Bryan, prin. Fax 585-4599

Delaware, Delaware, Pop. 33,899
Buckeye Valley Local SD 2,200/PK-12
679 Coover Rd 43015 740-369-8735
Andrew Miller, supt. Fax 363-7654
www.buckeyevalley.k12.oh.us
Buckeye Valley MS 800/5-8
683 Coover Rd 43015 740-363-6626
Brian Baker, prin. Fax 363-4483
Other Schools – See Ashley, Ostrander

Delaware CSD 4,500/PK-12
74 W William St 43015 740-833-1100
Paul Craft, supt. Fax 833-1149
www.dcs.k12.oh.us
Carlisle ES 500/K-5
746 State Route 37 W 43015 740-833-1450
Paula Vertikoff, prin. Fax 833-1499
Conger ES 400/K-5
10 Channing St 43015 740-833-1300
Josh Page, prin. Fax 833-1349
Dempsey MS 800/6-8
599 Pennsylvania Ave 43015 740-833-1800
Dan Bartha, prin. Fax 833-1899
Schultz ES 600/K-5
499 Applegate Ln 43015 740-833-1400
Travis Woodworth, prin. Fax 833-1449
Smith ES 400/K-5
355 N Liberty St 43015 740-833-1350
Rochelle Thompson, prin. Fax 833-1399
Woodward ES 400/PK-5
200 S Washington St 43015 740-833-1600
Ryan Malany, prin. Fax 833-1649

Olentangy Local SD
Supt. — See Lewis Center
Cheshire ES 600/PK-5
2681 Gregory Rd 43015 740-657-5750
Justin Syroka, prin. Fax 657-5799

Delaware Christian S 300/PK-12
45 Belle Ave 43015 740-363-8425
John Stubblefield, admin. Fax 203-2117
Grace Community S 100/PK-8
PO Box 358 43015 740-363-5800
Phil Mears, admin. Fax 363-5800
St. Mary S 400/PK-8
66 E William St 43015 740-362-8961
Gina Stull, prin. Fax 362-3733

Dellroy, Carroll, Pop. 355
Carrollton EVD
Supt. — See Carrollton
Dellroy ES 200/K-5
34 E Main St 44620 330-735-2850
Darin Abel, prin. Fax 735-3202

Delphos, Allen, Pop. 7,017
Delphos CSD 1,100/K-12
234 N Jefferson St 45833 419-692-2509
Kevin Wolfe, supt. Fax 692-2653
www.delphoscityschools.org
Franklin ES 400/K-5
310 E 4th St 45833 419-692-8766
Robert Hohlbein, prin. Fax 692-2766
Jefferson MS 200/6-8
227 N Jefferson St 45833 419-695-2523
Doug Westrick, prin. Fax 692-2302
Landeck ES 100/1-5
14750 Landeck Rd 45833 419-695-3185
Robert Hohlbein, prin. Fax 692-3428

St. John ES 500/PK-6
110 N Pierce St 45833 419-692-8561
Dr. Nathan Stant, prin. Fax 692-4501

Delta, Fulton, Pop. 3,070
Pike-Delta-York Local SD 1,300/K-12
504 Fernwood St 43515 419-822-3391
Dr. Ted Haselman Ed.D., supt. Fax 822-4478
www.pdys.org
Delta ES 500/K-4
1099 Panther Pride Dr 43515 419-822-5630
Ellen Bernal, prin. Fax 822-2828
Pike-Delta-York MS 400/5-8
1101 Panther Pride Dr 43515 419-822-9118
Douglas Ford, prin. Fax 822-8490

Dennison, Tuscarawas, Pop. 2,624
Claymont CSD 1,500/PK-12
201 N 3rd St 44621 740-922-5478
John Rocchi, supt. Fax 922-7325
www.claymontschools.org
Claymont IS 200/4-5
220 N 3rd St 44621 740-922-1901
Richard Page, prin. Fax 922-6302
Claymont Preschool 100/PK-PK
200 Jewett Ave 44621 740-922-2930
Holly Hall, prin. Fax 922-7425
Other Schools – See Uhrichsville

Immaculate Conception S 100/PK-8
100 Sherman St 44621 740-922-3539
Matt Ritzert, prin. Fax 922-2486

Diamond, Portage
Southeast Local SD
Supt. — See Ravenna
Southeast MS 400/6-8
8540 Tallmadge Rd 44412 330-654-1950
Craig Nettleton, prin. Fax 654-9110

Dillonvale, Jefferson, Pop. 660
Buckeye Local SD 1,900/PK-12
6899 State Route 150 43917 740-769-7395
Kimberly Leonard, supt. Fax 769-2361
buckeye.omeresa.net/
Other Schools – See Adena, Brilliant, Rayland, Tiltonsville

Dola, Hardin, Pop. 136
Hardin Northern Local SD 400/K-12
11589 State Route 81 45835 419-759-2331
Dr. Jeffrey Price Ed.D., supt. Fax 759-2581
www.hardinnorthern.org
Hardin Northern ES 200/K-6
11589 State Route 81 45835 419-759-3158
Brett Halsey, prin. Fax 759-2581

Donnelsville, Clark, Pop. 303
Tecumseh Local SD
Supt. — See New Carlisle
Donnelsville ES 50/2-3
PO Box 130 45319 937-845-4540
Jay Burkholder, prin. Fax 845-4504

Dover, Tuscarawas, Pop. 12,639
Dover CSD 2,800/PK-12
219 W 6th St 44622 330-364-1906
Carla Birney, supt. Fax 343-7070
www.dovertornadoes.com
Dover Avenue ES 400/K-5
125 W 13th St 44622 330-364-7117
Renee Sattler, prin. Fax 343-7636
Dover MS 700/6-8
2131 N Wooster Ave 44622 330-364-7121
Jack Edwards, prin. Fax 364-7127
East ES 500/K-5
325 Betscher Ave 44622 330-364-7114
Brooke Grafe, prin. Fax 343-8526
South ES 400/PK-5
280 E Shafer Ave 44622 330-364-7111
Tracie Murphy, prin. Fax 343-3976

Tuscarawas Central Catholic ES 200/PK-6
600 N Tuscarawas Ave 44622 330-343-9134
Matt Ritzert, prin. Fax 364-6509

Doylestown, Wayne, Pop. 3,018
Chippewa Local SD 1,400/K-12
56 N Portage St 44230 330-658-6368
Sandy Stebly, supt. Fax 658-5842
www.chippewa.k12.oh.us
Chippewa MS 400/5-8
257 High St 44230 330-658-2214
Steven Watkins, prin. Fax 658-5842
Harvey ES 500/K-4
165 Brooklyn Ave 44230 330-658-2522
Jodie Hughes, prin. Fax 658-4255

SS. Peter & Paul S 100/K-8
169 W Clinton St 44230 330-658-2804
Andrew Richards, prin. Fax 658-2287

Dresden, Muskingum, Pop. 1,503
Tri-Valley Local SD 3,000/K-12
36 E Muskingum Ave 43821 740-754-1442
Mark Neal, supt. Fax 754-6400
www.tvschools.org
Dresden ES 500/K-6
1318 Main St 43821 740-754-4001
Heather Welch, prin. Fax 754-6405
Tri-Valley MS 500/7-8
1360 Main St 43821 740-754-3531
Patrick Hopkins, prin. Fax 754-1879
Other Schools – See Adamsville, Frazeysburg, Nashport

Dublin, Franklin, Pop. 40,967
Dublin CSD 14,700/PK-12
7030 Coffman Rd 43017 614-764-5913
Dr. Todd Hoadley, supt. Fax 761-5856
www.dublinschools.net
Bailey ES 500/PK-5
4900 Brandonway Dr 43017 614-717-6611
Tyler Wolfe, prin. Fax 717-6610
Chapman ES 600/PK-5
8450 Sawmill Rd, 614-761-5864
Scott Zeoli, prin. Fax 761-5867
Davis MS 900/6-8
2400 Sutter Pkwy 43016 614-761-5820
Tracey Deagle, prin. Fax 761-5893
Deer Run ES 500/K-5
8815 Avery Rd 43017 614-764-5932
Susann Wittig, prin. Fax 718-8759
Glacier Ridge ES 600/K-5
7175 Glacier Ridge Blvd 43017 614-733-0012
Peter Kurty, prin. Fax 733-0785
Griffith Thomas ES 700/PK-5
4671 Tuttle Crossing Blvd 43017 614-764-5970
Jennifer Davis, prin. Fax 718-8879
Grizzell MS 700/6-8
8705 Avery Rd 43017 614-798-3569
Corinne Evans, prin. Fax 761-6514
Indian Run ES 700/K-5
80 W Bridge St 43017 614-764-5928
Jennifer Schwanke, prin. Fax 764-5998
Karrer MS 800/6-8
7245 Tullymore Dr 43016 614-873-0459
Mark Mousa, prin. Fax 873-1492
Olde Sawmill ES 400/K-5
2485 Olde Sawmill Blvd 43016 614-764-5936
Martha Barley, prin. Fax 764-5988
Pinney ES 600/PK-5
9989 Concord Rd 43017 614-798-3570
Troy Ehrsam, prin. Fax 718-8961
Riverside ES 500/K-5
3260 Riverside Green Dr 43017 614-764-5940
Staci Lutz, prin. Fax 764-5987
Scottish Corners ES 600/K-5
5950 Sells Mill Dr 43017 614-764-5963
Janet Rinefierd, prin. Fax 761-5814
Sells MS 900/6-8
150 W Bridge St 43017 614-764-5919
Matthew Sachtleben, prin. Fax 764-5923
Wyandot ES 600/PK-5
5620 Dublinshire Dr 43017 614-761-5840
Renae Schwartz, prin. Fax 718-8929
Other Schools – See Columbus

Hilliard CSD
Supt. — See Columbus
Washington ES 400/K-5
5675 Eiterman Rd 43016 614-921-6200
Samantha Althouse, prin. Fax 921-6201

St. Brigid of Kildare S 600/PK-8
7175 Avery Rd 43017 614-718-5825
Kathleen O'Reilly, prin. Fax 718-5831
Tree of Life Christian S - Dublin 100/PK-5
2900 Martin Rd 43017 614-792-2671
Lydia Seevers M.Ed., prin. Fax 588-0236

Duncan Falls, Muskingum, Pop. 873
Franklin Local SD 2,000/PK-12
PO Box 428 43734 740-674-5203
Sharon McDermott, supt. Fax 674-5214
www.franklinlocalschools.org
Duncan Falls ES 800/PK-5
PO Box 398 43734 740-674-5211
Dustan Henderson, prin. Fax 674-5216
Other Schools – See Philo, Roseville

Dundee, Tuscarawas, Pop. 296
Garaway Local SD
Supt. — See Sugarcreek
Dundee ES 200/K-6
PO Box 146 44624 330-852-2022
Curtis Fisher, prin. Fax 852-9952

East Canton, Stark, Pop. 1,566
Osnaburg Local SD 900/PK-12
310 Browning Ct N 44730 330-488-1609
Todd Boggs, supt. Fax 488-4001
ecweb.sparcc.org
East Canton ES 400/PK-5
310 Browning Ct N 44730 330-488-0392
Rebecca Carter, prin. Fax 488-4014
East Canton MS 200/6-8
310 Browning Ct N 44730 330-488-0334
Gregory Dente, prin. Fax 488-4015

East Cleveland, Cuyahoga, Pop. 17,585
East Cleveland CSD 2,500/PK-12
1843 Stanwood Rd 44112 216-268-6600
Myrna Corley, supt. Fax 268-6676
www.east-cleveland.k12.oh.us
Chambers ES 300/K-6
14305 Shaw Ave 44112 216-268-6640
Crystal Cash, prin. Fax 268-6272
Heritage MS 300/7-8
14410 Terrace Rd 44112 216-268-6610
Gilda Roberts, prin. Fax 268-6617
Mayfair ES 300/K-6
13916 Mayfair Ave 44112 216-268-6650
Sabrina Worthy-Gibson, prin. Fax 268-6496
Superior ES 300/PK-6
1865 Garfield Rd 44112 216-268-6670
Shawna LeSure, prin. Fax 268-6497
Other Schools – See Cleveland Heights

Eastlake, Lake, Pop. 18,364
Willoughby-Eastlake CSD
Supt. — See Willoughby Hills
Eastlake MS 400/6-8
35972 Lake Shore Blvd 44095 440-942-5696
Michael Chokshi, prin. Fax 918-8973
Jefferson ES 400/K-5
35980 Lake Shore Blvd 44095 440-942-7244
Lisa George, prin. Fax 954-3550
Longfellow ES 400/K-5
35200 Stevens Blvd 44095 440-975-3720
Allison Aber, prin. Fax 269-3022
Willoughby-Eastlake Preschool PK-PK
34050 Glen Dr 44095 440-283-2220
Camille Ritt, prin.

East Liverpool, Columbiana, Pop. 10,871
Beaver Local SD 1,600/K-12
46088 Bell School Rd 43920 330-385-6831
Eric Lowe, supt. Fax 386-8711
www.beaver.k12.oh.us/
Beaver Local ES 400/K-4
46090 Bell School Rd 43920 330-386-8700
Ashley Weber, prin. Fax 386-8720
Beaver Local MS 600/5-8
46088 Bell School Rd 43920 330-386-8700
Connie Shive, prin. Fax 382-0317

East Liverpool CSD 2,200/K-12
810 W 8th St 43920 330-385-7132
Randy Taylor, supt. Fax 382-7673
www.elcsd.k12.oh.us
East Liverpool JHS 300/7-8
100 Maine Blvd 43920 330-386-8750
Jonathan Ludwig, prin. Fax 386-8753
La Croft ES 500/K-4
2460 Boring Ln 43920 330-386-8774
Jake Walgate, prin. Fax 382-1867
North ES 400/K-4
90 Maine Blvd 43920 330-386-8772
Jack Cunningham, prin. Fax 386-4228
Westgate MS 300/5-6
810 W 8th St 43920 330-386-8765
Bryian Burson, prin. Fax 382-7670

East Liverpool Christian S 100/PK-12
46682 Florence St 43920 330-385-5588
Susan Mackall, hdmstr. Fax 385-1267

East Palestine, Columbiana, Pop. 4,696
East Palestine CSD 1,100/PK-12
200 W North Ave 44413 330-426-4191
Traci Hostetler, supt. Fax 426-9592
www.myepschools.org
East Palestine ES 400/PK-4
195 W Grant St 44413 330-426-3638
Kimberly Russo, prin. Fax 426-5109
East Palestine MS 400/5-8
320 W Grant St 44413 330-426-9451
James Rook, prin. Fax 426-5118

Eaton, Preble, Pop. 8,276
Eaton Community SD 2,100/K-12
306 Eaton Lewisburg Rd 45320 937-456-1107
Barbara Curry, supt. Fax 472-1057
www.eaton.k12.oh.us
Bruce ES 500/3-5
506B Aukerman St 45320 937-456-3874
Kipling Powell, prin. Fax 472-2092
Eaton MS 500/6-8
814 Camden Rd 45320 937-456-2286
Derek Flatter, prin. Fax 456-9687
Hollingsworth East ES 500/K-2
506 Aukerman St 45320 937-456-5173
Pamela Friesel, prin. Fax 456-4656

Edgerton, Williams, Pop. 1,997
Edgerton Local SD 600/PK-12
111 E River St 43517 419-298-2112
Kermit Riehle, supt. Fax 298-1322
www.edgerton.k12.oh.us
Edgerton ES 300/PK-6
111 E River St 43517 419-298-2332
Kermit Riehle, prin. Fax 298-3466

St. Mary S 100/1-6
314 S Locust St 43517 419-298-2531
Juliana Taylor, prin. Fax 298-3123

Edon, Williams, Pop. 823
Edon Northwest Local SD 500/K-12
802 W Indiana St 43518 419-272-3213
Dr. Anthony Stevens, supt. Fax 272-2240
www.edon.k12.oh.us/
Edon Northwest ES 300/K-6
802 W Indiana St 43518 419-272-3213
Jennifer Ripke, prin. Fax 272-2240

Elida, Allen, Pop. 1,868
Elida Local SD 2,500/K-12
4380 Sunnydale St 45807 419-331-4155
Joel Mengerink, supt. Fax 331-1656
home.elida.k12.oh.us
Elida ES 1,000/K-4
300 Pioneer Rd 45807 419-331-7901
Melanie Nixon, prin. Fax 331-2706
Elida MS 800/5-8
4500 Sunnydale St 45807 419-331-2505
Douglas Drury, prin. Fax 331-6822

Elmore, Ottawa, Pop. 1,392
Woodmore Local SD 800/PK-12
349 Rice St 43416 419-862-1060
Timothy Rettig, supt. Fax 862-1951
www.woodmoreschools.com
Other Schools – See Woodville

Elmwood Place, Hamilton, Pop. 2,100
St. Bernard-Elmwood Place CSD
Supt. — See Saint Bernard
Elmwood Place ES 300/PK-6
400 Maple St, 513-482-7115
Sherry Peters, prin. Fax 641-5502

Elyria, Lorain, Pop. 52,588
Elyria CSD 6,400/PK-12
42101 Griswold Rd 44035 440-284-8000
Dr. Thomas Jama, supt. Fax 284-0678
www.elyriaschools.org
Crestwood ES 400/K-5
42331 Griswold Rd 44035 440-284-8002
Steven Grossman, prin.
Eastern Heights MS 500/6-8
528 Garford Ave 44035 440-284-8015
Dr. Kimberly Benetto, prin. Fax 323-0827
Ely ES 400/K-5
312 Gulf Rd 44035 440-284-8005
Dr. Jack Dibee, prin. Fax 284-8148
Elyria Early Childhood Village 300/PK-K
42101 Griswold Rd 44035 440-284-8250
Jacqueline Plantner, prin. Fax 284-8162
Franklin ES 400/K-5
446 11th St 44035 440-284-8007
Lisa Licht, prin. Fax 284-8371
McKinley ES 400/K-5
620 E River St 44035 440-284-8009
Vriginia Fitch, prin. Fax 284-8382
Northwood MS 500/6-8
700 Gulf Rd 44035 440-284-8016
Michael Basinski, prin. Fax 284-1546
Oakwood ES 300/1-5
925 Spruce St 44035 440-284-8010
Joy Jones, prin. Fax 284-8181
Prospect ES 400/K-5
1410 Prospect St 44035 440-284-8011
Jessica Barwacz, prin. Fax 284-8051
Westwood MS 400/6-8
42350 Adelbert St 44035 440-284-8017
Theresa Lengel, prin. Fax 284-1055
Windsor ES 400/K-5
264 Windsor Dr 44035 440-284-8014
Miranda Roscoe, prin. Fax 284-8199

First Baptist Christian S 100/PK-12
11400 Lagrange Rd 44035 440-458-5185
Tim Spickler, admin. Fax 458-8717
Open Door Christian S 500/PK-12
8287 W Ridge Rd 44035 440-322-6386
Denver Daniel, pres. Fax 284-6033
St. Jude S 400/PK-8
594 Poplar St 44035 440-366-1681
Molly Takacs-Hibler, prin. Fax 366-5238
St. Mary S 200/PK-8
237 4th St 44035 440-322-2808
Sharon Urig, prin. Fax 323-0886

Englewood, Montgomery, Pop. 13,133
Northmont CSD 4,000/PK-12
4001 Old Salem Rd 45322 937-832-5000
Tony Thomas, supt. Fax 832-5001
www.northmontschools.com/
Englewood ES 200/2-6
702 Albert St 45322 937-832-5900
Joe Johnston, prin. Fax 832-5901
Englewood Hills ES 300/2-6
508 Durst Dr 45322 937-832-5950
Katie Grothaus, prin. Fax 832-5951
Northmoor ES 400/2-6
4421 Old Salem Rd 45322 937-832-6800
Shannon Williamson, prin. Fax 832-6801
Other Schools – See Clayton, Dayton, Union

Enon, Clark, Pop. 2,391
Greenon Local SD 1,000/PK-12
500 S Xenia Dr 45323 937-864-1202
Bradley Silvus, supt. Fax 864-2470
www.greenon.k12.oh.us
Enon ES 100/PK-1
120 S Xenia Dr 45323 937-864-7361
Darrin Knapke, prin. Fax 864-6014
Indian Valley IS 300/2-6
510 S Xenia Dr 45323 937-864-7348
Michael Tighe, prin. Fax 864-6009

Etna, Licking, Pop. 1,187
Southwest Licking Local SD
Supt. — See Pataskala
Etna ES 200/4-5
8500 Columbia Rd SW, 740-927-5906
Tanya Moore, prin. Fax 964-0129
Watkins MS 900/6-8
8808 Watkins Rd SW, 740-927-5767
Ryan Brown, prin. Fax 927-2337

Euclid, Cuyahoga, Pop. 47,840
Euclid CSD 4,400/PK-12
651 E 222nd St 44123 216-261-2900
Dr. Charles Smialek, supt. Fax 261-3120
www.euclidschools.org
Arbor ES 600/K-5
20400 Arbor Ave 44123 216-797-6200
Lawanda Johnson, prin. Fax 383-1912
Bluestone ES 500/K-5
1455 E 260th St 44132 216-797-6300
Christopher Papouras, prin. Fax 289-6619
Chardon Hills Magnet S 300/K-5
1750 E 234th St 44117 216-797-6400
Christopher Papouras, prin. Fax 692-9239
Early Learning Center 200/PK-PK
22800 Fox Ave 44123 216-732-2700
Sanya Henley, prin. Fax 732-2705
Euclid Central MS 400/6-7
20701 Euclid Ave 44117 216-797-5300
Michael Mennel, prin. Fax 797-5333
Shoreview ES 500/K-5
490 E 260th St 44132 216-797-6500
Mary Thomas, prin. Fax 797-1252

Our Lady of the Lake S 300/K-8
175 E 200th St 44119 216-481-6824
Rita Kingsbury, prin. Fax 481-9841
SS. Robert and William S 400/PK-8
351 E 260th St 44132 216-731-3060
Meg Cosgriff, prin. Fax 731-0300

Fairborn, Greene, Pop. 31,321
Fairborn CSD 4,400/PK-12
306 E Whittier Ave 45324 937-878-3961
Mark North, supt. Fax 879-8180
www.fairborn.k12.oh.us
Baker MS 900/6-8
200 Lincoln Dr 45324 937-878-4681
Deborah Hauberg, prin. Fax 879-8193
Fairborn IS 700/4-5
25 Dellwood Dr 45324 937-878-3969
Betsy Wyatt, prin. Fax 879-8191
Fairborn PS 1,700/PK-3
4 W Dayton Yellow Springs 45324 937-878-8668
Susan Riegle, prin. Fax 879-8181

Bethlehem Lutheran S 100/PK-8
1240 S Maple Ave 45324 937-878-7050
Beth Landon, prin. Fax 878-8794

Fairfield, Butler, Pop. 41,547
Fairfield CSD 9,700/PK-12
4641 Bach Ln 45014 513-829-6300
Billy Smith, supt. Fax 829-0148
www.fairfieldcityschools.com
Creekside MS 1,600/6-8
1111 Nilles Rd 45014 513-829-4433
Kari Franchini, prin. Fax 829-6480
Crossroads MS 1,500/6-8
255 Donald Dr 45014 513-829-4504
David Maine, prin. Fax 829-7447
Fairfield Central ES 900/K-5
5054 Dixie Hwy 45014 513-829-7979
Karrie Gallo, prin. Fax 829-7830
Fairfield Compass ES 700/K-5
8801 Holden Blvd 45014 513-829-6300
Kim Wotring, prin.
Fairfield South ES 800/PK-5
5460 Bibury Rd 45014 513-829-3078
Jason Hussel, prin. Fax 829-8350
Fairfield West ES 800/PK-5
4700 River Rd 45014 513-868-3021
Missy Muller, prin. Fax 868-3624
Other Schools – See Hamilton

Cincinnati Christian Schools - ES Campus 300/PK-6
7350 Dixie Hwy 45014 513-874-8500
Donna Hempelmann, prin. Fax 874-9718

Sacred Heart S 400/1-8
400 Nilles Rd 45014 513-858-4215
Joseph Nagle, prin. Fax 858-4218

Fairlawn, Summit, Pop. 7,299
Copley-Fairlawn CSD
Supt. — See Copley
Ft. Island PS 400/K-4
496 Trunko Rd 44333 330-664-4890
Robert Whitaker, prin. Fax 664-4921
Herberich PS 300/PK-4
2645 Smith Rd 44333 330-664-4991
William Kerrigan, prin. Fax 664-4989

St. Hilary S 600/K-8
645 Moorfield Rd 44333 330-867-8720
Tracey Arnone, prin. Fax 867-5081

Fairport Harbor, Lake, Pop. 3,058
Fairport Harbor EVD 600/K-12
329 Vine St 44077 440-354-5400
Domenic Paolo, supt. Fax 357-1478
www.fhevs.org
McKinley ES 300/K-5
602 Plum St 44077 440-354-4982
Jennifer Polak, prin. Fax 354-4012

Fairview Park, Cuyahoga, Pop. 16,640
Fairview Park CSD 1,800/PK-12
21620 Mastick Rd 44126 440-331-5500
William Wagner, supt. Fax 356-3545
www.fairviewparkschools.org
Fairview Park Early Education Ctr 100/PK-K
21620 Mastick Rd 44126 440-356-3515
Patricia Moran, dir.
Gilles-Sweet ES 700/K-5
4320 W 220th St 44126 440-356-3525
Barbara Brady, prin. Fax 356-3701
Mayer MS 400/6-8
21200 Campus Dr 44126 440-356-3510
Raymond Mohr, prin. Fax 895-2191

Messiah Lutheran S 200/PK-8
4401 W 215th St 44126 440-331-6553
Helen Casselberry, prin. Fax 331-1604
St. Angela Merici S 500/PK-8
20830 Lorain Rd 44126 440-333-2126
Elizabeth Andrachik, prin. Fax 333-8480

Farmersville, Montgomery, Pop. 991
Valley View Local SD
Supt. — See Germantown
Valley View JHS 300/7-8
202 Jackson St 45325 937-696-2591
Nichole Thomas, prin. Fax 696-1007

Fayette, Fulton, Pop. 1,278
Fayette Local SD 400/PK-12
400 E Gamble Rd 43521 419-237-2573
Erik Belcher, supt. Fax 237-3125
www.fayettesch.org
Fayette ES 200/PK-6
400 E Gamble Rd 43521 419-237-2776
Allie Reucher, prin. Fax 237-4306

Fayetteville, Brown, Pop. 329
Fayetteville-Perry Local SD 800/PK-12
551 S Apple St 45118 513-875-2423
James Brady, supt. Fax 875-2703
www.fp.k12.oh.us
Fayetteville-Perry ES 400/PK-5
601 S Apple St 45118 513-875-2083
Jeri Earley, prin. Fax 875-4511
Fayetteville-Perry MS 200/6-8
521 S Apple St 45118 513-875-2829
Ryan Briggs, prin. Fax 875-4200

Felicity, Clermont, Pop. 815
Felicity-Franklin Local SD 900/PK-12
105 Market St 45120 513-876-2113
David Gibson, supt. Fax 876-2519
www.felicityschools.org
Felicity-Franklin Local ES 400/PK-4
105 Market St 45120 513-876-2113
Jennifer Keller, prin. Fax 876-2051
Felicity-Franklin Local MS 300/5-8
415 Market St 45120 513-876-2662
Joe Pfeffer, prin. Fax 876-2848

Findlay, Hancock, Pop. 40,536
Findlay CSD 5,800/PK-12
2019 Broad Ave 45840 419-425-8212
Edward Kurt, supt. Fax 425-8203
www.findlaycityschools.org
Bigelow Hill ES 300/4-5
300 Hillcrest Ave 45840 419-425-8317
Dr. Jennifer Theis, prin. Fax 427-5456
Chamberlin Hill ES 200/3-5
600 W Yates Ave 45840 419-425-8328
Lyndsey Stephenson, prin. Fax 427-5457
Donnell MS, 301 Baldwin Ave 45840 600/6-8
Don Williams, prin. 419-425-8370
Glenwood MS 600/6-8
1715 N Main St 45840 419-425-8373
Janice Panuto, prin. Fax 427-5455
Jacobs ES 300/K-3
600 Jacobs Ave 45840 419-425-8299
Krista Miller, prin. Fax 427-5458
Jefferson ES 200/K-2
204 Fairlawn Pl 45840 419-425-8298
Kim Plesec, prin. Fax 427-5459
Lincoln ES 300/K-5
200 W Lincoln St 45840 419-425-8310
Dr. Mike Scoles, prin. Fax 427-5460
Northview ES 300/K-3
133 Lexington Ave 45840 419-425-8290
Eric Payne, prin. Fax 427-5462
Vance ES 400/3-5
610 Bristol Dr 45840 419-425-8332
David Barnhill, prin. Fax 427-5465
Washington Preschool 100/PK-PK
1100 Broad Ave 45840 419-425-8231
Kathleen Young, prin.
Whittier ES 400/K-2
733 Wyandot St 45840 419-425-8358
Kelly Stahl, prin. Fax 427-5464

Liberty-Benton Local SD 1,300/K-12
9190 County Road 9 45840 419-422-8526
Ronald Kowalski, supt. Fax 422-5108
www.liberty-benton.org
Liberty-Benton ES 600/K-5
9050 W State Route 12 45840 419-422-9161
Brian Burkett, prin. Fax 420-9237
Liberty Benton MS 300/6-8
9050 W State Route 12 45840 419-422-9166
Bruce Otley, prin. Fax 420-9237

St. Michael the Archangel S 500/PK-8
723 Sutton Pl 45840 419-423-2738
Amy Holzwart, prin. Fax 423-2720

Fort Jennings, Putnam, Pop. 485
Jennings Local SD 400/K-12
1 Musketeer Dr 45844 419-286-2238
Nicholas Langhals, supt. Fax 286-2240
www.jenningslocal.org
Fort Jennings ES 200/K-6
1 Musketeer Dr 45844 419-286-2762
Matthew Dube, prin. Fax 286-2240

Fort Loramie, Shelby, Pop. 1,478
Fort Loramie Local SD 800/K-12
575 Greenback Rd 45845 937-295-3931
Daniel Holland, supt. Fax 295-2758
www.loramie.k12.oh.us/
Fort Loramie ES 500/K-6
35 Elm St 45845 937-295-2931
Scott Rodeheffer, prin. Fax 295-2758

Fort Recovery, Mercer, Pop. 1,410
Fort Recovery Local SD 900/PK-12
PO Box 604 45846 419-375-4139
Justin Firks, supt. Fax 375-1058
www.fortrecoveryschools.org
Fort Recovery ES 400/PK-5
865 Sharpsburg Rd 45846 419-375-2768
Tracy Evers Westgerdes, prin. Fax 375-4231
Fort Recovery MS 200/6-8
865 Sharpsburg Rd 45846 419-375-2815
Anthony Stahl, prin. Fax 375-4231

Fostoria, Seneca, Pop. 12,940
Fostoria CSD 1,800/PK-12
1001 Park Ave 44830 419-435-8163
Andrew Sprang, supt. Fax 436-4109
www.fostoriaschools.org/
Fostoria IS 500/3-6
1202 H L Ford Dr 44830 419-436-4125
Kori Bernal, prin. Fax 436-4169
Longfellow K 300/PK-K
619 Sandusky St 44830 419-436-4135
Kelli Bauman, prin. Fax 436-4155
Riley ES 300/1-2
1324 Walnut St 44830 419-436-4145
Kelli Bauman, prin. Fax 436-4158

St. Wendelin S 300/PK-12
533 N Countyline St 44830 419-435-8144
Teresa Kitchen, prin. Fax 436-4042

Frankfort, Ross, Pop. 1,038
Adena Local SD 1,300/PK-12
3367 County Road 550 45628 740-998-4633
John Balzer, supt. Fax 998-4632
www.adenalocalschools.com
Adena ES 600/K-4
3367 County Road 550 45628 740-998-5293
Lisa Wayland, prin. Fax 998-2359
Adena MS 300/5-8
3367 County Road 550 45628 740-998-2313
Dustin England, prin. Fax 998-2317
Adena Preschool 50/PK-PK
3367 County Road 550 45628 740-998-5293
Lisa Wayland, prin.

Franklin, Warren, Pop. 11,585
Franklin CSD 2,900/K-12
150 E 6th St 45005 937-746-1699
Michael Sander, supt. Fax 743-8620
www.franklincityschools.com
Bennett ECC, 150 E 6th St 45005 200/K-K
Timothy Crowe, prin. 937-743-5290
Franklin JHS 500/7-8
136 E 6th St 45005 937-743-8630
Jeremy Ward, prin. Fax 743-8635
Gerke ES 300/1-6
312 Sherman Dr 45005 937-743-8650
Steven Greenwood, prin. Fax 743-8649
Hunter ES 300/1-6
4418 State Route 122 45005 937-743-8655
Kevin Sizemore, prin. Fax 743-8608
Pennyroyal ES 300/1-6
4203 Pennyroyal Rd 45005 937-743-8660
Kelli Fromm, prin. Fax 743-8609
Schenck ES 200/1-6
350 Arlington Ave 45005 937-743-8665
Deborah Kienle, prin. Fax 743-8644
Wayne ES 300/1-6
16 Farm Ave 45005 937-743-8640
James Rhoades, prin. Fax 743-8642

Middletown Christian S 500/PK-12
3011 Union Rd 45005 513-423-4542
Brian Williams, supt. Fax 261-6841

Franklin Furnace, Scioto, Pop. 1,641
Green Local SD 400/PK-12
4070 Gallia Pike 45629 740-354-9221
Jodi Armstrong, supt. Fax 355-8975
www.green.k12.oh.us
Green ES 200/PK-6
46 Braunlin Rd 45629 740-354-9290
John Biggs, prin. Fax 354-9904

Frazeysburg, Muskingum, Pop. 1,302
Tri-Valley Local SD
Supt. — See Dresden
Frazeysburg ES 300/K-6
120 E 3rd St 43822 740-828-2781
Rebecca Norris, prin. Fax 828-3666

Fredericksburg, Wayne, Pop. 422
Southeast Local SD
Supt. — See Apple Creek
Fredericksburg ES 200/K-8
PO Box 249 44627 330-695-2741
Shawn Snyder, prin. Fax 695-2116

Fredericktown, Knox, Pop. 2,475
Fredericktown Local SD 900/K-12
117 Columbus Rd 43019 740-694-2956
Matthew W. Chrispin, supt. Fax 694-0956
www.fredericktownschools.com
Fredericktown ES 600/K-5
111 Stadium Dr 43019 740-694-2781
Miguel Thompson, prin. Fax 694-1294

Freeport, Harrison, Pop. 360

Antrim Mennonite S 50/K-12
20360 Cadiz Rd 43973 740-489-5161
Titus Lapp, prin.

Fremont, Sandusky, Pop. 16,145
Fremont CSD 4,100/K-12
500 W State St Ste A 43420 419-332-6454
Jon Detwiler, supt. Fax 334-5454
www.fremontschools.net
Atkinson ES 300/K-5
1100 Delaware Ave 43420 419-332-5361
Christopher Ward, prin. Fax 334-6749
Croghan ES 300/K-5
1110 Chestnut St 43420 419-332-1511
Lori Pierce, prin. Fax 332-4314
Fremont MS 1,000/6-8
1250 North St 43420 419-332-5569
Marjoe Cooper, prin. Fax 334-5494
Hayes ES 300/K-5
916 Hayes Ave 43420 419-332-6371
Joshua Matz, prin. Fax 334-6761
Lutz ES 300/K-5
1929 Buckland Ave 43420 419-332-0091
Randall Macko, prin. Fax 334-5499
Otis ES 300/K-5
718 N Brush St 43420 419-332-8964
Laura Bryant, prin. Fax 334-6788
Stamm ES 400/K-5
1038 Miller St 43420 419-332-5538
Bridget Smith, prin. Fax 334-6746
Other Schools – See Lindsey

Bishop Hoffman S - Sacred Heart Campus 200/PK-6
500 Smith Rd 43420 419-332-7102
Dave Perin, head sch Fax 332-1542

Gahanna, Franklin, Pop. 32,425
Gahanna Jefferson CSD 7,100/PK-12
160 S Hamilton Rd 43230 614-471-7065
Stephen Barrett, supt. Fax 478-5568
www.gahannaschools.org
Chapelfield ES 400/PK-5
280 Chapelfield Rd 43230 614-478-5575
Shea Reed, prin. Fax 337-3755
Gahanna MS East 600/6-8
730 Clotts Rd 43230 614-478-5550
Brad Barboza, prin. Fax 478-5544
Gahanna MS South 600/6-8
349 Shady Spring Dr 43230 614-337-3730
Robin Murdock, prin. Fax 337-3734
Gahanna MS West 600/6-8
350 N Stygler Rd 43230 614-478-5570
Aaron Winner, prin. Fax 337-3771
Goshen Lane ES 400/K-5
370 Goshen Ln 43230 614-478-5580
Melanie McGue, prin. Fax 337-3757
High Point ES 500/K-5
700 Venetian Way 43230 614-478-5545
Kathleen Erhard, prin. Fax 337-3762
Jefferson ES 500/K-5
136 Carpenter Rd 43230 614-478-5560
Roben Frentzel, prin. Fax 337-3766
Lincoln ES 400/K-5
515 Havens Corners Rd 43230 614-478-5555
Claire Giardino, prin. Fax 337-3750
Royal Manor ES 400/PK-5
299 Empire Dr 43230 614-478-5585
Rick Oxley, prin. Fax 337-2160
Other Schools – See Blacklick

Columbus Academy 1,100/PK-12
4300 Cherry Bottom Rd 43230 614-475-2311
Melissa Soderberg, head sch Fax 475-0396
Gahanna Christian Academy 500/PK-12
817 N Hamilton Rd 43230 614-471-9270
Anitra Simmons, prin. Fax 471-9201
St. Matthew S 600/K-8
795 Havens Corners Rd 43230 614-471-4930
Susan Maloy, prin. Fax 471-1673
Shepherd Christian S 100/PK-5
425 S Hamilton Rd 43230 614-471-0859
Ken Pease, prin. Fax 471-3466

Galena, Delaware, Pop. 644
Big Walnut Local SD
Supt. — See Sunbury
Hylen Souders ES 300/PK-4
4121 Miller Paul Rd 43021 740-965-3200
Andrew Hoffman, prin. Fax 965-3986

Olentangy Local SD
Supt. — See Lewis Center
Berkshire MS 900/6-8
2869 S 3 Bs and K Rd 43021 740-657-5200
Carla Baker, prin. Fax 657-5299
Johnnycake Corners ES 600/PK-5
6783 Falling Meadows Dr 43021 740-657-5650
Peter Stern, prin. Fax 657-5699
Walnut Creek ES 600/K-5
5600 Grand Oak Blvd 43021 740-657-4750
Michelle Seitz, prin. Fax 657-4799

Galion, Crawford, Pop. 10,395
Galion CSD 1,900/PK-12
470 Portland Way N 44833 419-468-3432
Dr. James Grubbs, supt. Fax 468-4333
www.galionschools.org
Galion IS 500/3-5
476 Portland Way N 44833 419-468-3676
Alexander Sharick, prin. Fax 468-4333
Galion MS 500/6-8
474 Portland Way N 44833 419-468-3134
Joseph Morabito, prin. Fax 468-4333
Galion PS 500/PK-2
478 Portland Way N 44833 419-468-4010
Melisa Watters, prin. Fax 468-4333

Northmor Local SD 1,100/PK-12
5247 County Road 29 44833 419-946-8861
Chad Redmon, supt. Fax 947-6255
www.northmor.k12.oh.us
Northmor ES 600/PK-6
7819 State Route 19 44833 419-947-1900
Amanda Albert, prin. Fax 946-2397

St. Joseph S 100/PK-8
138 N Liberty St 44833 419-468-5436
Kate Holzer, prin. Fax 468-3611

Gallipolis, Gallia, Pop. 3,534
Gallia County Local SD
Supt. — See Patriot
Addaville ES 300/PK-5
1333 Brick School Rd 45631 740-367-7283
Brandon Mitchem, prin. Fax 367-5004

Gallipolis CSD 2,100/PK-12
61 State 45631 740-446-3211
Roger Mace, supt. Fax 446-6433
www.gc.k12.oh.us
Gallia Academy MS 500/6-8
340 4th Ave 45631 740-446-3214
Craig Wright, prin. Fax 446-2493
Green ES 300/PK-5
113 Centenary Church Rd 45631 740-446-3236
Corey Luce, prin. Fax 446-0482
Washington ES 500/PK-5
450 4th Ave 45631 740-446-3213
Helenlu Morgan, prin. Fax 446-0355
Other Schools – See Rio Grande

Ohio Valley Christian S 100/PK-12
1100 4th Ave 45631 740-446-0374
Patrick O'Donnell, admin. Fax 446-3961

Galloway, Franklin
South-Western CSD
Supt. — See Grove City
Darby Woods ES 700/K-4
255 Westwoods Blvd 43119 614-801-8075
Brian Novar, prin. Fax 853-1047
Galloway Ridge IS 700/5-6
122 Galloway Rd 43119 614-801-8850
Timothy Barton, prin. Fax 801-8851

Cypress Christian S 300/K-8
375 Alton Darby Creek Rd 43119 614-870-1181
Lori Guffey, prin. Fax 878-5866

Gambier, Knox, Pop. 2,300
Mt. Vernon CSD
Supt. — See Mount Vernon
Wiggin Street ES 200/K-5
207 Wiggin St 43022 740-427-4262
Deanna Lowers, prin. Fax 427-3926

Garfield Heights, Cuyahoga, Pop. 28,281
Garfield Heights CSD 3,700/K-12
5640 Briarcliff Dr 44125 216-475-8100
Terrance Olszewski, supt. Fax 475-1824
www.garfieldheightscityschools.com
Elmwood ES 400/K-5
5275 Turney Rd 44125 216-475-8110
Gwen Abraham, prin. Fax 475-8371
Foster ES 600/K-5
12801 Bangor Ave 44125 216-475-8123
Sean Patton, prin. Fax 475-8080
Garfield Heights MS 900/6-8
12000 Maple Leaf Dr 44125 216-475-8105
Christopher Sauer, prin. Fax 475-8146
Maple Leaf ES 500/K-5
5764 Turney Rd 44125 216-662-3800
Jean Rizi, prin. Fax 663-9217

St. Benedict S 300/K-8
13633 Rockside Rd 44125 216-662-9380
Lisa Oriti, prin. Fax 662-3137

Garrettsville, Portage, Pop. 2,303
James A. Garfield Local SD 1,200/PK-12
10235 State Route 88 44231 330-527-4336
Ted A. Lysiak, supt. Fax 527-5941
www.jagschools.org
Garfield ES 600/PK-6
10207 State Route 88 44231 330-527-2184
Dr. Keri Leindecker, prin. Fax 527-3015
Garfield MS 200/7-8
10231 State Route 88 44231 330-527-2151
Jennifer Mulhern, prin. Fax 527-2601

Gates Mills, Cuyahoga, Pop. 2,236
Mayfield CSD
Supt. — See Mayfield Heights
Gates Mills ES 100/K-5
7639 Colvin Rd 44040 440-995-7500
Tammi Bender, prin. Fax 995-7505

Gilmour Academy 700/PK-12
34001 Cedar Rd 44040 440-473-8090
Kathleen Kenny, head sch Fax 473-8010
St. Francis of Assisi S 400/PK-8
6850 Mayfield Rd 44040 440-442-7450
Adrienne Publicover, prin. Fax 446-1132

Geneva, Ashtabula, Pop. 6,134
Geneva CSD 2,500/PK-12
135 S Eagle St 44041 440-466-4831
Eric Kujala, supt. Fax 466-0908
www.genevaschools.org/
Cork ES 300/K-5
341 State Route 534 S 44041 440-466-4831
Melissa Doherty, prin. Fax 466-0715
Geneva MS 600/6-8
839 Sherman St 44041 440-466-4831
Alex Anderson, prin. Fax 466-5692
Geneva Platt R. Spencer ES 500/K-5
755 Austin Rd 44041 440-415-9325
Michael Penzenik, prin. Fax 466-0206
Other Schools – See Austinburg

Genoa, Ottawa, Pop. 2,309
Genoa Area Local SD 1,300/K-12
2810 N Genoa Clay Center Rd 43430 419-855-7741
Michael Ferguson, supt. Fax 855-4030
www.genoaschools.com
Genoa Area MS 300/6-8
2950 N Genoa Clay Center Rd 43430 419-855-7741
Kevin Katafias, prin. Fax 855-7784
Genoa ES 600/K-5
2820 N Genoa Clay Center Rd 43430 419-855-7741
Brenda Murphy, prin. Fax 855-9027

Georgetown, Brown, Pop. 4,266
Georgetown EVD 1,000/PK-12
1043 Mount Orab Pike 45121 937-378-3730
Christopher Burrows, supt. Fax 378-2219
www.gtown.k12.oh.us/
Georgetown ES 500/PK-6
935 Mount Orab Pike 45121 937-378-6235
Nina Miller, prin. Fax 378-3489

Germantown, Montgomery, Pop. 5,508
Valley View Local SD 1,900/PK-12
59 Peffley St 45327 937-855-6581
Richard Earley, supt. Fax 855-0266
www.valleyview.k12.oh.us
Valley View IS 500/PK-PK, 4-
64 Comstock St 45327 937-855-4203
William Lauson, prin. Fax 855-0267
Valley View PS 500/K-3
110 Comstock St 45327 937-855-6571
Bill Lauson, prin. Fax 855-6283
Other Schools – See Farmersville

Germantown Christian S 100/PK-12
9440 Eby Rd 45327 937-855-7334
Jeremiah Collins, prin. Fax 855-7746

Gibsonburg, Sandusky, Pop. 2,557
Gibsonburg EVD 1,100/PK-12
301 S Sunset Ave 43431 419-637-2479
Tim Murray, supt. Fax 637-3029
www.gibsonburg.k12.oh.us/
Gibsonburg MS 200/6-8
740 S Main St 43431 419-637-2873
Sonia Herman, prin. Fax 637-2873
Hilfiker ES 500/PK-5
301 S Sunset Ave 43431 419-637-7249
Emily Sisco, prin. Fax 637-2478

Girard, Trumbull, Pop. 9,767
Girard CSD 1,700/K-12
100 W Main St Ste 2 44420 330-545-2596
David Cappuzzello, supt. Fax 545-2597
www.girardcityschools.org/
Girard IS 400/4-6
702 E Prospect St 44420 330-545-5219
Gregory Bonamase, prin. Fax 545-2597
Girard JHS 300/7-8
1244 Shannon Rd 44420 330-545-5431
Jennifer Santangelo, prin. Fax 545-5440
Prospect ES 500/K-3
700 E Prospect St 44420 330-545-3854
Dr. Debra Gratz, prin. Fax 545-7149

St. Rose S 300/K-8
61 E Main St 44420 330-545-1163
Linda Borton, prin. Fax 545-0119

Glandorf, Putnam, Pop. 997
Ottawa-Glandorf Local SD
Supt. — See Ottawa
Glandorf ES 600/K-8
140 Church St 45848 419-538-6880
Scott Ketner, prin. Fax 538-6115

Glenford, Perry, Pop. 172
Northern Local SD
Supt. — See Thornville
Glenford ES 300/K-5
128 High St 43739 740-659-2209
Sherri Lawrence, prin. Fax 659-2228

Glouster, Athens, Pop. 1,756
Trimble Local SD 800/PK-12
1 Tomcat Dr 45732 740-767-4444
Scott Christman, supt. Fax 767-4901
trimble.k12.oh.us
Trimble ES 400/PK-5
18500 Jacksonville Rd 45732 740-767-2810
Jamie Starrett, prin. Fax 767-9523
Trimble MS 100/6-8
18500 Jacksonville Rd 45732 740-767-2810
Jamie Starrett, prin. Fax 767-9523

Gnadenhutten, Tuscarawas, Pop. 1,282
Indian Valley Local SD 1,800/K-12
100 N Walnut St 44629 740-254-4334
Gary Wentworth, supt. Fax 254-9271
www.ivschools.org/
Other Schools – See Midvale, Port Washington, Tuscarawas

Goshen, Clermont
Goshen Local SD 2,700/PK-12
6694 Goshen Rd 45122 513-722-2222
Darrell Edwards, supt. Fax 722-3767
www.goshenlocalschools.org
Goshen MS 600/6-8
6692 Goshen Rd 45122 513-722-2226
Wendy Flynn, prin. Fax 722-2246
Marr/Cook ES 700/PK-2
6696 Goshen Rd 45122 513-722-2224
Troy Smith, prin. Fax 722-2244
Spaulding ES 600/3-5
6755 Linton Rd 45122 513-722-2225
Tom Turner, prin. Fax 722-2245

Grafton, Lorain, Pop. 6,573
Midview Local SD 3,000/PK-12
13050 Durkee Rd 44044 440-748-5353
Dr. Bruce Willingham, supt. Fax 748-5395
www.midviewk12.org
Midview East IS 500/5-6
13060 Durkee Rd 44044 440-748-1851
Shane Sullivan, prin. Fax 748-7016
Midview MS 500/7-8
12865 Grafton Rd 44044 440-748-2122
John Brown, prin. Fax 748-0411
Midview North ES 500/K-2
13070 Durkee Rd 44044 440-748-6869
Carla Molnar, prin. Fax 748-7056
Midview West ES 500/PK-K, 3-4
13080 Durkee Rd 44044 440-748-2305
Patricia Hamilton, prin. Fax 748-4032

Granville, Licking, Pop. 5,563
Granville EVD 2,500/K-12
PO Box 417 43023 740-587-8101
Jeffrey Brown, supt. Fax 683-7730
www.granvilleschools.org
Granville ES 600/K-3
310 N Granger St 43023 740-587-8102
Travis Morris, prin. Fax 587-2374
Granville IS 600/4-6
2025 Burg St 43023 740-587-8103
Gayle Burris, prin. Fax 587-1138
Granville MS 400/7-8
210 New Burg St 43023 740-587-8104
Lisa Sealover-Ormond, prin. Fax 587-8194

Granville Christian Academy 300/K-12
1820 Newark Granville Rd 43023 740-587-4423
Tim Barrett, supt. Fax 587-4776
Welsh Hills S 100/PK-10
2610 Newark Granville Rd 43023 740-522-2020
Michelle Lerner, head sch Fax 920-4326

Graysville, Monroe, Pop. 68
Switzerland of Ohio Local SD
Supt. — See Woodsfield
Skyvue S 200/PK-8
33329 Hartshorn Ridge Rd 45734 740-567-3312
Christopher Caldwell, prin. Fax 567-3498

Greenfield, Highland, Pop. 4,562
Greenfield EVD 2,000/PK-12
200 N 5th St 45123 937-981-2152
James Wills, supt. Fax 981-4395
greenfield.k12.oh.us
Greenfield ES 400/PK-5
200 N 5th St 45123 937-981-3241
Robert Schumm, prin. Fax 981-2521
Greenfield MS 500/6-8
200 N 5th St 45123 937-981-2197
Wendy Callewaert, prin. Fax 981-0417
Rainsboro ES 200/PK-5
12916 Barretts Mill Rd 45123 937-365-1271
Quincey Gray, prin. Fax 365-2006
Other Schools – See South Salem

Green Springs, Sandusky, Pop. 1,354
Clyde-Green Springs EVD
Supt. — See Clyde
Green Springs ES 500/K-5
420 N Broadway St 44836 419-547-4902
Randall Stockmaster, prin. Fax 547-4906

Greenville, Darke, Pop. 13,080
Greenville CSD 2,600/K-12
215 W 4th St 45331 937-548-3185
Douglas Fries, supt. Fax 548-6943
www.greenville.k12.oh.us
Greenville ES 600/K-4
1111 N Ohio St 45331 937-548-3185
Jody Harter, prin. Fax 548-2175

Greenville MS 400/5-8
1111 N Ohio St 45331 937-548-3185
Christian Mortensen, prin. Fax 548-3315

St. Mary S 100/PK-8
238 W 3rd St 45331 937-548-2345
Vernon Rosenbeck, prin. Fax 548-0878

Greenwich, Huron, Pop. 1,472
South Central Local SD 800/PK-12
3305 Greenwich Angling Rd 44837 419-752-3815
Dr. Benjamin Chaffee, supt. Fax 752-0182
www.south-central.org
South Central ES 400/PK-4
3291 Greenwich Angling Rd 44837 419-752-0011
Nathan Richards, prin. Fax 752-8705
South Central JHS 200/5-8
3291 Greenwich Angling Rd 44837 419-752-0011
Alicia McKee, prin. Fax 752-8705

Grove City, Franklin, Pop. 34,836
South-Western CSD 20,600/PK-12
3805 Marlane Dr 43123 614-801-3000
Dr. Bill Wise, supt. Fax 871-2781
www.swcsd.us
Bolton Crossing ES 300/K-4
2695 Holt Rd 43123 614-801-8275
Michele Harkins, prin. Fax 878-4037
Brookpark MS 600/7-8
2803 Southwest Blvd 43123 614-801-3500
Holly Carr, prin. Fax 871-6512
Buckeye Woods ES 800/K-4
2525 Holton Rd 43123 614-801-8025
Jenniffer Kauffeld, prin. Fax 871-1131
Harmon ES 500/K-4
1861 Gantz Rd 43123 614-801-8150
Michael Wang, prin. Fax 272-1249
Hayes IS 400/5-6
4436 Haughn Rd 43123 614-801-6200
Michael Nesler, prin. Fax 801-6201
Highland Park ES 500/K-4
2600 Cameron St 43123 614-801-8200
Stephanie Baker, prin. Fax 871-0585
Holt Crossing IS 700/5-6
2706 Holt Rd 43123 614-801-8700
Tyler Winner, prin. Fax 801-8701
Jackson MS 600/7-8
2271 Holton Rd 43123 614-801-3800
Daniel Boland, prin. Fax 801-3818
Monterey ES 400/K-4
3811 Hoover Rd 43123 614-801-8250
Margaret Moretti, prin. Fax 871-3805
Park Street IS 600/5-6
3205 Park St 43123 614-801-8800
Clinton Rardon, prin. Fax 801-8801
Pleasant View MS 800/7-8
7255 Kropp Rd 43123 614-801-3900
Brett Harmon, prin. Fax 870-5530
Richard Avenue ES 500/K-4
3646 Richard Ave 43123 614-801-8325
Catherine Moore, prin. Fax 871-0712
Sommer ES 600/K-4
3055 Kingston Ave 43123 614-801-8350
Elaine McLaughlin, prin. Fax 875-0089
South-Western Preschool Center 200/PK-PK
4324 Haughn Rd 43123 614-801-8448
Dawn Brewer, coord. Fax 871-9568
Other Schools – See Columbus, Darbydale, Galloway

Beautiful Savior Lutheran S 100/PK-8
2213 White Rd 43123 614-875-1147
David Knittel, prin. Fax 875-9637
Grove City Christian S 600/K-12
4750 Hoover Rd 43123 614-875-3000
David Arrell, dir. Fax 875-8933
Our Lady of Perpetual Help S 400/PK-8
3752 Broadway 43123 614-875-6779
Julie Freeman, prin. Fax 539-5719

Groveport, Franklin, Pop. 5,240
Groveport Madison Local SD 5,300/K-12
4400 Marketing Pl 43125 614-492-2520
Bruce Hoover, supt. Fax 492-2532
www.gocruisers.org
Glendening ES 500/K-5
4200 Glendenning Dr 43125 614-836-4972
Curt Brogan, prin. Fax 836-4974
Groveport ES 400/K-5
715 Main St 43125 614-836-4975
April Bray, prin. Fax 836-4680
Groveport Madison MS Central 500/6-8
751 Main St 43125 614-836-4957
Neil Britton, prin. Fax 836-4999
Groveport Madison MS South 400/6-8
4400 Glendenning Dr 43125 614-836-4953
Darren Fillman, prin. Fax 836-4956
Other Schools – See Columbus

Madison Christian S 500/PK-12
3565 Bixby Rd 43125 614-497-3456
Ray Kochis, prin. Fax 497-3057

Grover Hill, Paulding, Pop. 398
Wayne Trace Local SD
Supt. — See Haviland
Grover Hill ES 200/PK-6
PO Box 125 45849 419-587-3414
Kevin Wilson, prin. Fax 587-3415

Hamden, Vinton, Pop. 879
Vinton County Local SD
Supt. — See Mc Arthur
South ES 400/PK-5
38234 State Route 93 45634 740-384-2731
Miranda Smith, prin. Fax 384-4001

Hamersville, Brown, Pop. 540
Western Brown Local SD
Supt. — See Mount Orab
Hamersville S 700/PK-8
PO Box 205 45130 937-379-1144
Melinda Pride, prin. Fax 379-1676

Hamilton, Butler, Pop. 60,903
Fairfield CSD
Supt. — See Fairfield
Fairfield East ES 700/PK-5
6711 Morris Rd 45011 513-737-5000
Paige Gillespie, prin. Fax 737-5225
Fairfield North ES 800/K-5
6116 Morris Rd 45011 513-868-0070
Denise Hayes, prin. Fax 868-3621

Hamilton CSD 10,000/PK-12
533 Dayton St 45011 513-887-5000
Tony Orr, supt. Fax 868-4473
hamiltoncityschools.com
Bridgeport ES 800/PK-6
2171 Bridgeport Dr 45013 513-868-5580
Victoria Kowalk, prin. Fax 868-5585
Brookwood ES 700/K-6
1325 Stahlheber Rd 45013 513-868-5590
Jesse Weisbrod, prin. Fax 868-5595
Crawford Woods ES 700/K-6
2200 Hensley Ave 45011 513-868-5600
Aaron Hopkins, prin. Fax 868-5605
Fairwood ES 700/PK-6
281 N Fair Ave 45011 513-868-5610
Paige Patton-Radel, prin. Fax 868-5615
Garfield MS 800/7-8
250 N Fair Ave 45011 513-887-5035
Brandon Stanfill, prin. Fax 887-4700
Highland ES 700/K-6
1125 Main St 45013 513-868-5620
Ty Smallwood, prin. Fax 868-5625
Linden ES 800/K-6
801 Hoadley Ave 45015 513-868-5630
Katherine Huber, prin. Fax 868-5639
Ridgeway ES 700/PK-6
267 Wasserman Rd 45013 513-868-5640
Katherine Wagonfield, prin. Fax 868-5645
Riverview ES 700/PK-6
250 Knightsbridge Dr 45011 513-868-5650
Mary Anne Hazlett, prin. Fax 868 5655
Wilson MS 700/7-8
714 Eaton Ave 45013 513-887-5170
Jonathan Szary, prin. Fax 887-5068

New Miami Local SD 700/K-12
600 Seven Mile Ave 45011 513-863-0833
Rhonda Parker, supt. Fax 863-0497
www.new-miami.k12.oh.us
New Miami ES 300/K-5
606 Seven Mile Ave 45011 513-896-7153
Tabatha Class, prin. Fax 896-9313
New Miami MS 200/6-8
600 Seven Mile Ave 45011 513-863-4917
Kara Hanges, prin. Fax 863-3956

Ross Local SD 2,700/PK-12
3371 Hamilton Cleves Rd 45013 513-863-1253
Scott Gates, supt. Fax 863-6250
www.rossrams.com
Elda ES 700/K-4
3980 Hamilton Cleves Rd 45013 513-738-1972
Jesse Kohls, prin. Fax 738-0163
Morgan ES 300/PK-4
3427 Chapel Rd 45013 513-738-1980
Tom Perry, prin. Fax 738-4887
Ross MS 900/5-8
3425 Hamilton Cleves Rd 45013 513-863-1251
Christopher Saylor, prin. Fax 863-0066

Immanuel Lutheran S 100/PK-8
1285 Main St 45013 513-895-9212
Lukas Bickel, prin. Fax 863-2502
Queen of Peace S 200/PK-8
2550 Millville Ave 45013 513-863-8705
Christina Conners, prin. Fax 863-4310
St. Ann S 100/K-8
3064 Pleasant Ave 45015 513-863-0604
Sarah Bitzer, prin. Fax 863-2017
St. Joseph Consolidated S 200/K-8
925 S 2nd St 45011 513-863-8758
William Hicks, prin. Fax 863-5772
St. Peter in Chains S 200/K-8
451 Ridgelawn Ave 45013 513-863-0685
Michael Collins, prin. Fax 863-1859

Hamler, Henry, Pop. 573
Patrick Henry Local SD 600/PK-12
6900 State Route 18 43524 419-274-3015
Thomas L. Taylor, supt. Fax 274-1641
www.phpatriots.org
Henry ES PK-4
E076 County Road 7 43524 419-274-3015
Bryan Hieber, prin. Fax 274-1641
Henry MS 300/5-8
E050 County Road 7 43524 419-274-3015
Jordan LeFevre, prin. Fax 274-1641

Hammondsville, Jefferson
Edison Local SD 1,300/PK-12
14890 State Route 213 43930 330-532-3199
Bill Beattie, supt. Fax 532-2860
www.edisonlocal.k12.oh.us
Stanton ES 400/PK-6
14890 State Route 213 43930 330-532-1594
Julie Kireta, prin. Fax 532-1594
Other Schools – See Bergholz

Hannibal, Monroe, Pop. 405
Switzerland of Ohio Local SD
Supt. — See Woodsfield

River ES 100/K-8
PO Box 56 43931 740-483-1624
Becky Hall, prin. Fax 483-1630

Hanoverton, Columbiana, Pop. 408
United Local SD 1,200/K-12
8143 State Route 9 44423 330-223-1521
Lance Hostetler, supt. Fax 223-2363
www.united.k12.oh.us
United ES 600/K-6
8143 State Route 9 44423 330-223-8001
Christina Hughes, prin. Fax 223-2363

Harrison, Hamilton, Pop. 9,812
Southwest Local SD 3,500/K-12
230 S Elm St 45030 513-367-4139
John Hamstra, supt. Fax 367-2287
www.southwestschools.org
Crosby ES 400/K-6
8382 New Haven Rd 45030 513-738-1717
Kiersten Rogers, prin. Fax 738-1718
Harrison ES 600/K-6
600 E Broadway St 45030 513-367-4161
Ron Mangus, prin. Fax 367-1856
Harrison MS 500/7-8
9830 West Rd 45030 513-367-4831
Christian Tracy, prin. Fax 367-0370
Whitewater Valley ES 600/K-6
10800 Campbell Rd 45030 513-367-5577
Fax 367-5594
Other Schools – See Miamitown

St. John the Baptist S 300/K-8
508 Park Ave 45030 513-367-6826
Susan Meymann, prin. Fax 367-6864

Harrod, Allen, Pop. 415
Allen East Local SD 1,100/PK-12
9105 Harding Hwy 45850 419-648-3333
Mel Rentschler, supt. Fax 648-5282
www.ae.k12.oh.us
Allen East ES 600/PK-5
9105 Harding Hwy 45850 419-648-3333
Larry Altenburger, prin. Fax 648-5282
Allen East MS 400/6-8
9105 Harding Hwy 45850 419-648-3333
Jarrod Wehri, prin.

Hartville, Stark, Pop. 2,894
Lake Local SD
Supt. — See Uniontown
Hartville ES 500/K-3
245 Belle St SW 44632 330-877-4278
Julie Lyberger, prin. Fax 877-4758
Lake ES 500/4-5
225 Lincoln St SW 44632 330-877-4276
Donna Bruner, prin. Fax 877-4738
Lake MS 800/6-8
511 Market Ave SW 44632 330-877-4290
Brian Reed, prin. Fax 877-1384

Lake Center Christian S 600/PK-12
12893 Kaufman Ave NW 44632 330-877-2049
Dr. Joseph Beeson, supt. Fax 877-2040

Haviland, Paulding, Pop. 213
Wayne Trace Local SD 900/PK-12
4915 US Route 127 45851 419-263-2415
Benjamin A. Winans, supt. Fax 263-2377
www.waynetrace.org
Other Schools – See Grover Hill, Payne

Hayesville, Ashland, Pop. 442
Hillsdale Local SD
Supt. — See Jeromesville
Hillsdale ES 300/K-4
W Main St 44838 419-368-4364
Tom Williams, prin. Fax 368-3701

Heath, Licking, Pop. 10,088
Heath CSD 1,600/K-12
107 Lancaster Dr 43056 740-522-2816
Trevor Thomas, supt. Fax 522-4697
www.heath.k12.oh.us
Garfield ES 400/K-2
680 S 30th St 43056 740-522-4810
Andra Kisner, prin. Fax 522-8830
Heath MS 400/6-8
310 Licking View Dr 43056 740-788-3200
Jeffrey Hempleman, prin. Fax 788-3209
Stevenson ES 400/3-5
152 Cynthia St 43056 740-522-8442
Andra Kisner, prin. Fax 522-6241

Hebron, Licking, Pop. 2,293
Lakewood Local SD 1,900/K-12
525 E Main St 43025 740-928-5878
Mary Andrews, supt. Fax 928-3152
www.lakewoodlocal.k12.oh.us/
Hebron ES 400/K-2
709 Deacon St 43025 740-928-2661
Deanna Martindale, prin. Fax 928-7510
Jackson IS 400/3-5
9370 Lancer Rd 43025 740-928-1915
Carol Field, prin. Fax 928-3756
Lakewood MS 400/6-8
5222 National Rd SE 43025 740-928-8330
Jessica Fry, prin. Fax 928-5627

Hicksville, Defiance, Pop. 3,540
Hicksville EVD 900/PK-12
958 E High St 43526 419-542-7665
Keith Countryman, supt. Fax 542-8534
www.hicksvilleschools.org/
Hicksville ES 500/PK-6
958 E High St 43526 419-542-7475
Kirsten Coffman, prin. Fax 542-8711

Highland Heights, Cuyahoga, Pop. 8,256
Mayfield CSD
Supt. — See Mayfield Heights
Millridge ES 600/K-5
962 Millridge Rd 44143 440-995-7250
Craig Caroff, prin. Fax 995-7255

St. Paschal Baylon S 500/PK-8
5360 Wilson Mills Rd 44143 440-442-6766
Carol Jansky, prin. Fax 446-9037

Hilliard, Franklin, Pop. 27,909
Hilliard CSD
Supt. — See Columbus
Avery ES 400/K-5
4388 Avery Rd 43026 614-921-5100
Kevin Landon, prin. Fax 921-5101
Beacon ES 500/K-5
3600 Lacon Rd 43026 614-921-5200
Matthew Sparks, prin. Fax 921-5201
Britton ES 400/K-5
4501 Britton Pkwy 43026 614-921-5300
Stephanie Borlaza, prin. Fax 921-5301
Brown ES 600/K-5
2494 Walker Rd 43026 614-921-5400
Kathryn Miller, prin. Fax 921-5401
Darby Creek ES 500/K-5
6305 Pinefield Dr 43026 614-921-5500
Cindy Teske, prin. Fax 921-5501
Darby ES 400/K-5
2730 Alton Darby Creek Rd 43026 614-921-5000
Herb Higginbotham, prin. Fax 921-5001
Hilliard Crossing ES 500/K-5
3340 Hilliard Rome Rd 43026 614-921-5600
Kayla Pinnick, prin. Fax 921-5601
Hilliard Heritage MS 800/7-8
5670 Scioto Darby Rd 43026 614-921-7500
Matthew Trombitas, prin. Fax 921-7501
Hilliard Memorial MS 800/7-8
5600 Scioto Darby Rd 43026 614-921-7600
Barry Bay, prin. Fax 921-7601
Hilliard Station Sixth Grade S 600/6-6
3859 Main St 43026 614-921-6800
Lauren Schmidt, prin. Fax 921-6801
Hilliard Weaver MS 800/7-8
4600 Avery Rd 43026 614-921-7700
Craig Vroom, prin. Fax 921-7701
Hoffman Trails ES 500/K-5
4301 Hoffman Farms Dr 43026 614-921-5700
Katie Windham, prin. Fax 921-5701
Norwich ES 500/K-5
4454 Davidson Rd 43026 614-921-6000
Michael Heitzman, prin. Fax 921-6001
Reason ES 500/K-5
4790 Cemetery Rd 43026 614-921-5900
Jacki Prati, prin. Fax 921-5901
Ridgewood ES 600/K-5
4237 Dublin Rd 43026 614-921-6100
Kevin Buchman, prin. Fax 921-6101
Scioto Darby ES 500/K-5
5380 Scioto Darby Rd 43026 614-921-6300
Deborah Campbell-Sauer, prin. Fax 921-6301
Tharp Sixth Grade S 700/6-6
4681 Leap Rd 43026 614-921-6900
Cori Kindl, prin. Fax 921-6901

St. Brendan S 500/K-8
4475 Dublin Rd 43026 614-876-6132
Will Gruber, prin. Fax 529-8929
Sunrise Academy 300/K-8
5657 Scioto Darby Rd 43026 614-527-0465

Hillsboro, Highland, Pop. 6,439
Bright Local SD
Supt. — See Mowrystown
Bright ES 400/PK-6
6100 Fair Ridge Rd 45133 937-927-7010
Mike Bick, prin. Fax 927-7015

Hillsboro CSD 2,600/PK-12
39 Willetsville Pike 45133 937-393-3475
Brian Davis, supt. Fax 393-5841
www.hcs-k12.org
Hillsboro ECC 400/PK-1
500 US Highway 62 45133 937-393-3132
Pamela Hollon, prin. Fax 393-3077
Hillsboro IS 400/4-5
500 US Highway 62 45133 937-393-3132
James Rhoades, prin. Fax 393-3077
Hillsboro MS 600/6-8
550 US Highway 62 45133 937-393-9877
Kimberly Beam, prin. Fax 393-5843
Hillsboro PS 400/2-3
500 US Highway 62 45133 937-393-3132
Jacob Zink, prin. Fax 393-3077

Hillsboro Christian Academy 100/K-12
849 S High St 45133 937-393-8422
Connie Sears, admin. Fax 393-4963
St. Mary S 50/PK-6
119 E Walnut St 45133 937-840-9932
Darlene Smith, prin. Fax 840-9932

Hinckley, Medina
Highland Local SD
Supt. — See Medina
Hinckley ES 400/K-5
1586 Center Rd 44233 330-239-1901
James Carpenter, prin. Fax 239-7390

Holgate, Henry, Pop. 1,102
Holgate Local SD 500/K-12
801 Joe E Brown Ave 43527 419-264-5141
Kelly Meyers, supt. Fax 264-1965
www.holgateschools.org
Holgate ES 200/K-5
801 Joe E Brown Ave 43527 419-264-5231
Laura Young, prin. Fax 264-1965

Holland, Lucas, Pop. 1,746
Springfield Local SD 3,900/K-12
6900 Hall St 43528 419-867-5600
Matt Geha, supt. Fax 867-5700
www.springfieldlocalschools.net
Crissey ES 400/K-5
9220 Geiser Rd 43528 419-867-5677
Oatis Amick, prin. Fax 867-5739
Holland ES 600/K-5
7001 Madison Ave 43528 419-867-5655
Hilary Steinmiller, prin. Fax 867-5738
Holloway ES 500/K-5
6611 Pilliod Rd 43528 419-867-5703
Robb Brown, prin. Fax 867-5707
Springfield MS 900/6-8
7001 Madison Ave 43528 419-867-5644
Jeffrey Pendry, prin. Fax 867-5732
Other Schools – See Toledo

Holmesville, Holmes, Pop. 369
Southeast Local SD
Supt. — See Apple Creek
Holmesville ES 100/K-6
PO Box 8 44633 330-279-2341
Shawn Snyder, prin. Fax 279-2023

Hopedale, Harrison, Pop. 936
Harrison Hills CSD
Supt. — See Cadiz
Harrison East ES 600/PK-6
410 Normal St 43976 740-942-7550
Jennifer Birney, prin. Fax 942-7554

Houston, Shelby
Hardin-Houston Local SD 900/PK-12
5300 Houston Rd 45333 937-295-3010
Larry Claypool, supt. Fax 295-3737
www.houston.k12.oh.us
Hardin-Houston ES 500/PK-6
5300 Houston Rd 45333 937-295-3010
Sara Roseberry, prin. Fax 295-3737

Howard, Knox, Pop. 239
East Knox Local SD 1,000/K-12
23201 Coshocton Rd 43028 740-599-7493
Stephen Larcomb, supt. Fax 599-5863
www.ekschools.com
East Knox ES 600/K-6
23081 Coshocton Rd 43028 740-599-7000
Cody Reese, prin. Fax 599-6397

Hubbard, Trumbull, Pop. 7,784
Hubbard EVD 1,900/K-12
108 Orchard Ave 44425 330-534-1921
Raymond W. Soloman, supt. Fax 534-0522
www.hubbard.k12.oh.us/
Hubbard ES 700/K-4
150 Hall Ave 44425 330-534-1921
Shawn Marcello, prin. Fax 534-6197
Hubbard MS 600/5-8
250 Hall Ave 44425 330-534-1921
Brian Hoffman, prin. Fax 534-6191

Huber Heights, Montgomery, Pop. 36,793
Huber Heights CSD 5,900/PK-12
5954 Longford Rd 45424 937-237-6300
Susan Gunnell, supt. Fax 237-6307
www.huberheightscityschools.org
Huber ES 600/K-6
8895 Emeraldgate Dr 45424 937-237-6375
Tamara Granata, prin. Fax 669-3529
Monticello ES 600/K-6
6523 Alter Rd 45424 937-237-6360
Dwon Bush, prin. Fax 237-8833
Rushmore ES 600/K-6
7701 Berchman Dr 45424 937-237-6365
Fax 237-8585
Studebaker Preschool 100/PK-PK
5950 Longford Rd 45424 937-237-6345
Pamela Bitsko, prin. Fax 237-2178
Valley Forge ES 600/K-6
7191 Troy Manor Rd 45424 937-237-6380
Rebecca Molfenter, prin. Fax 237-8679
Weisenborn JHS 900/7-8
6061 Troy Pike 45424 937-237-6350
Brent Carey, prin. Fax 237-7491
Wright Brothers ES 700/K-6
5758 Harshmanville Rd 45424 937-237-6392
Chip Holloway, prin. Fax 237-2741

St. Peter S 500/PK-8
6185 Chambersburg Rd 45424 937-233-8710
Ronald Albino, prin. Fax 237-3974

Hudson, Summit, Pop. 21,988
Hudson CSD 4,600/PK-12
2400 Hudson Aurora Rd 44236 330-653-1200
Phillip Herman, supt. Fax 653-1474
www.hudson.k12.oh.us
East Woods ES 700/4-5
120 N Hayden Pkwy 44236 330-653-1256
Michael Sedlak, prin. Fax 653-1269
Ellsworth Hill ES 300/PK-PK, 2-
7750 Stow Rd 44236 330-653-1236
Jennifer Filomena, prin. Fax 653-1236
Evamere ES 600/K-1
76 N Hayden Pkwy 44236 330-653-1226
Beth Trivelli, prin. Fax 653-1234
Hudson MS 1,100/6-8
77 N Oviatt St 44236 330-653-1316
Dr. Kim Cockley, prin. Fax 653-1368
McDowell ES 300/3-3
280 N Hayden Pkwy 44236 330-653-1246
Natalie Wininger, prin. Fax 653-1238

Heritage Classical Academy K-8
190 W Streetsboro St 44236 330-998-0554

Hudson Montessori S 200/PK-8
7545 Darrow Rd 44236 330-650-0424
Matt Virgil, head sch Fax 656-1870
Seton Catholic S 400/K-8
6923 Stow Rd 44236 330-342-4200
Karen Alestock, prin. Fax 342-4276

Huron, Erie, Pop. 7,058
Huron CSD 1,400/PK-12
712 Cleveland Rd E 44839 419-433-1234
Dennis Muratori, supt. Fax 433-7095
www.huron-city.k12.oh.us
McCormick JHS 200/7-8
325 Ohio St 44839 419-433-1234
Chad Carter, prin. Fax 433-8427
Shawnee ES 300/PK-2
712 Cleveland Rd E 44839 419-433-1234
Brian Kucbel, prin. Fax 616-0054
Woodlands ES 400/3-6
1810 Maple Ave 44839 419-433-1234
Mark Doughty, prin. Fax 433-9619

Firelands Montessori Academy 100/PK-5
329 Ohio St 44839 419-433-6181
Kathryn Hayden, dir. Fax 433-8199
St. Peter S 200/PK-8
429 Huron St 44839 419-433-4640
Anne Asher, prin. Fax 433-2118

Independence, Cuyahoga, Pop. 7,078
Independence Local SD 1,100/PK-12
7733 Stone Rd 44131 216-642-5850
Benjamin Hegedish, supt. Fax 642-3482
www.independence.k12.oh.us
Independence MS 300/5-8
6111 Archwood Rd 44131 216-642-5865
Kevin Jakub, prin. Fax 520-7002
Independence PS 400/PK-4
7600 Hillside Rd 44131 216-642-5870
Cynthia Ipsaro, prin. Fax 642-1318

St. Michael S 400/PK-8
6906 Chestnut Rd 44131 216-524-6405
Margaret Campisi, prin. Fax 524-7538

Ironton, Lawrence, Pop. 10,894
Dawson-Bryant Local SD
Supt. — See Coal Grove
Dawson-Bryant ES 600/K-5
4503 State Route 243 45638 740-532-6898
Angela Lafon, prin. Fax 534-5581

Ironton CSD 1,500/K-12
105 S 5th St 45638 740-532-4133
William Nance, supt. Fax 532-2314
www.tigertown.com
Ironton ES 700/K-5
302 Delaware St 45638 740-532-2209
John Maynard, prin. Fax 532-3077
Ironton MS 300/6-8
302 Delaware St 45638 740-532-3347
Toben Schreck, prin. Fax 532-3077

Rock Hill Local SD 1,400/PK-12
2325 County Road 26 Unit A 45638 740-532-7030
Wesley Hairston, supt. Fax 532-7043
rockhill.org
Rock Hill ES 700/PK-5
2676 County Road 26 45638 740-532-7016
Fred Evans, prin. Fax 532-7020
Rock Hill MS 300/6-8
2171 County Road 26 45638 740-532-7026
Jason Owen, prin. Fax 532-7028

St. Lawrence S 100/PK-6
315 S 6th St 45638 740-532-5052
Paul Mollett, prin. Fax 532-5082

Jackson, Jackson, Pop. 6,292
Jackson CSD 2,500/PK-12
450 Vaughn St 45640 740-286-6442
Phil Howard, supt. Fax 286-6445
www.jcs.k12.oh.us
Jackson MS 600/6-8
21 Tropic St 45640 740-286-7586
Mark Broermann, prin. Fax 286-8637
Jackson Northview ES 400/K-5
11507 Chillicothe Pike 45640 740-286-2390
Melissa Ball, prin. Fax 286-7845
Jackson Southview ES 400/PK-5
13842 State Route 93 45640 740-286-1831
Phillip Kuhn, prin. Fax 286-7834
Jackson Westview ES 400/PK-5
16349 Beaver Pike 45640 740-286-2790
Karen Ochsenbein, prin. Fax 286-7831

Christian Life Academy 100/PK-12
10595 Chillicothe Pike 45640 740-286-1234
Melissa Boggs, admin. Fax 286-0234

Jackson Center, Shelby, Pop. 1,444
Jackson Center Local SD 400/PK-12
204 S Linden St 45334 937-596-6053
William Reichert, supt. Fax 596-6490
www.jackson-center.k12.oh.us
Jackson Center ES 200/PK-3
204 S Linden St 45334 937-596-6053
Ginger Heuker, prin. Fax 596-6490

Jamestown, Greene, Pop. 1,954
Greeneview Local SD 1,400/PK-12
4 S Charleston Rd 45335 937-675-2728
Isaac Seevers, supt. Fax 675-6807
www.greeneview.k12.oh.us
Greeneview ES 500/PK-4
53 N Limestone St 45335 937-675-6867
William Hayes, prin. Fax 675-2438

Greeneview MS 500/5-8
4990 Cottonville Rd 45335 937-675-9391
Dennis Morrison, prin. Fax 675-6866

Jefferson, Ashtabula, Pop. 3,086
Jefferson Area Local SD 1,700/K-12
121 S Poplar St 44047 440-576-9180
John Montanaro, supt. Fax 576-9876
www.jalsd.org
Jefferson Area JHS 300/7-8
207 W Mulberry St 44047 440-576-1736
Richard Hoyson, prin. Fax 576-3082
Jefferson ES 600/K-6
204 W Mulberry St 44047 440-576-2646
Steve Candela, prin. Fax 576-0179
Other Schools – See Rock Creek

Jenera, Hancock, Pop. 219

Trinity Lutheran S 100/PK-8
PO Box 25 45841 419-326-4685
Steven Strong, prin. Fax 326-9001

Jeromesville, Ashland, Pop. 562
Hillsdale Local SD 900/K-12
485 Township Road 1902 44840 419-368-8231
Steve Dickerson, supt. Fax 368-7504
www.hillsdale.k12.oh.us/
Hillsdale MS 300/5-8
144 N High St 44840 419-368-4911
Tim Keib, prin. Fax 368-3613
Other Schools – See Hayesville

Johnstown, Licking, Pop. 4,591
Johnstown-Monroe Local SD 1,600/K-12
441 S Main St 43031 740-967-6846
Dale Dickson, supt. Fax 967-1106
www.johnstown.k12.oh.us/
Adams MS 400/6-8
80 W Maple St 43031 740-967-8766
Kris Almendinger, prin. Fax 967-0051
Johnstown ES 400/K-5
200 Leafy Dell Rd 43031 740-967-5461
Marcie Wilson, prin.

Northridge Local SD 1,200/K-12
6097 Johnstown Utica Rd 43031 740-967-6631
Scott Schmidt, supt. Fax 967-5022
www.northridge.k12.oh.us
Northridge IS 200/4-5
6066 Johnstown Utica Rd 43031 740-967-1401
John Rathburn, prin. Fax 967-2140
Northridge MS 300/6-8
6066 Johnstown Utica Rd 43031 740-967-6671
John Rathburn, prin. Fax 967-7083
Other Schools – See Alexandria

Junction City, Perry, Pop. 805
New Lexington CSD
Supt. — See New Lexington
Junction City ES 400/K-5
307 Poplar St 43748 740-987-3751
Elizabeth Halaiko, prin. Fax 987-3752

Kalida, Putnam, Pop. 1,534
Kalida Local SD 600/K-12
PO Box 269 45853 419-532-3534
Karl Lammers, supt. Fax 532-2277
kalidaschools.org
Kalida ES 200/K-4
PO Box 358 45853 419-532-3845
Kathy Verhoff, prin. Fax 532-3541

Kansas, Sandusky, Pop. 179
Lakota Local SD 1,000/PK-12
5200 County Road 13 44841 419-986-6650
Dr. Chad Coffman, supt. Fax 986-6651
www.lakota-sandusky.k12.oh.us
Lakota ES 400/PK-4
5200 County Road 13 44841 419-986-6640
Dana Ward, prin. Fax 986-6631
Lakota MS 300/5-8
5200 County Road 13 44841 419-986-6630
Patrick Flanagan, prin. Fax 986-6631

Kelleys Island, Erie, Pop. 311
Kelleys Island Local SD 50/PK-12
PO Box 349 43438 419-746-2730
Phillip Thiede, supt. Fax 746-2271
www.kelleys.k12.oh.us/
Kelleys Island S 50/PK-12
PO Box 349 43438 419-746-2730
Phillip Thiede, supt. Fax 746-2271

Kent, Portage, Pop. 28,086
Field Local SD
Supt. — See Mogadore
Brimfield ES 600/K-5
4170 State Route 43 44240 330-673-8581
Barbara Werstler, prin. Fax 677-2514

Kent CSD 3,300/PK-12
321 N Depeyster St 44240 330-676-7600
George Joseph, supt. Fax 677-6166
www.kentschools.net
Davey ES 500/PK-5
196 N Prospect St 44240 330-673-6703
Abbey Bolton, prin. Fax 677-6190
Holden ES 200/K-5
132 W School St 44240 330-673-6737
Todd Poole, prin. Fax 677-6192
Longcoy ES 300/K-5
1069 Elno Ave 44240 330-673-6772
Janice Swan, prin. Fax 677-6198
Stanton MS 800/6-8
1175 Hudson Rd 44240 330-676-8600
Anthony Horton, prin. Fax 673-1561
Walls ES 200/K-5
900 Doramor St 44240 330-676-8300
Heidi Singer, prin. Fax 677-6196

St. Patrick S 300/K-8
127 Portage St 44240 330-673-7232
Howard Mancini, prin. Fax 678-6612

Kenton, Hardin, Pop. 8,149
Kenton CSD 900/PK-12
222 W Carrol St 43326 419-673-0775
Jennifer Penczarski, supt. Fax 673-3180
www.kentoncityschools.org
Kenton ES PK-6
631 Silver St 43326 419-673-7248
Angela Butterman, prin. Fax 675-0681
Kenton MS 300/7-8
300 Oriental St 43326 419-673-1237
Kirk Cameron, prin. Fax 673-1626

Kettering, Montgomery, Pop. 55,018
Kettering CSD 7,700/PK-12
3750 Far Hills Ave 45429 937-499-1400
Scott Inskeep, supt. Fax 499-1465
www.ketteringschools.org
Beavertown ES 400/PK-5
2700 Wilmington Pike 45419 937-499-1740
Michael Kozarec, prin. Fax 499-1779
Greenmont ES 400/PK-5
1 E Wren Cir 45420 937-499-1850
Brian Zawodny, prin. Fax 499-1859
Indian Riffle ES 500/PK-5
3090 Glengarry Dr 45420 937-499-1720
Debbie Beiter, prin. Fax 499-1739
Kennedy ES 600/PK-5
5030 Polen Dr 45440 937-499-1830
Monica Butcher, prin. Fax 499-1839
Kettering MS 1,000/6-8
3000 Glengarry Dr 45420 937-499-1550
Brian Snyder, prin. Fax 499-1598
Oakview ES 400/K-5
4001 Ackerman Blvd 45429 937-499-1870
Aaron Smith, prin. Fax 499-1885
Orchard Park ES 300/K-5
600 E Dorothy Ln 45419 937-499-1910
Micki Ambrose, prin. Fax 499-1929
Prass ES 400/K-5
2601 Parklawn Dr 45440 937-499-1780
Valerie Dupler, prin. Fax 499-1799
Southdale ES 600/K-5
1200 W Dorothy Ln 45409 937-499-1890
Jay Borchers, prin. Fax 499-1909
Van Buren MS 700/6-8
3775 Shroyer Rd 45429 937-499-1800
Sarah Adams, prin. Fax 499-1820
Other Schools – See Moraine

Oakwood CSD
Supt. — See Oakwood
Lange S 100/K-K
219 W Dorothy Ln 45429 937-299-8730
Frank Eaton, prin. Fax 299-8734

Ascension S 400/K-8
2001 Woodman Dr 45420 937-254-5411
Susan DiGiorgio, prin. Fax 254-1150
Montessori S of Dayton 200/PK-8
2900 Acosta St 45420 937-293-8986
Toby Meixner, prin. Fax 293-8996
St. Albert the Great S 400/PK-8
104 W Dorothy Ln 45429 937-293-9452
Sherry Gabert, prin. Fax 293-7525
St. Charles Borromeo S 400/K-8
4600 Ackerman Blvd 45429 937-434-4933
David Bogle, prin. Fax 434-6692

Kidron, Wayne, Pop. 938

Central Christian S 300/PK-12
PO Box 9 44636 330-857-7311

Killbuck, Holmes, Pop. 812
West Holmes Local SD
Supt. — See Millersburg
Killbuck ES 300/K-5
299 School St 44637 330-276-2891
Carrie Maltarich, prin. Fax 276-1382

Kings Mills, Warren, Pop. 1,300
Kings Local SD 4,000/PK-12
1797 King Ave 45034 513-398-8050
Tim Ackermann, supt. Fax 229-7590
www.kingslocal.net/
Burns ES 600/K-4
8471 Columbia Rd 45034 513-398-8050
Cheryl Montag, prin. Fax 683-8367
Columbia IS 600/5-6
8263 Columbia Rd 45034 513-398-8050
Shelley Detmer-Bogaert, prin. Fax 459-2961
Kings JHS 600/7-8
5620 Columbia Rd 45034 513-398-8050
Nicole Huelsman, prin. Fax 459-2951
Kings Mills ES 500/K-4
1780 King Ave 45034 513-398-8050
Shawn Rosekrans, prin. Fax 398-4863
Kings Preschool PK-PK
1797 King Ave 45034 513-398-8050
Susan Guckert, prin.
Other Schools – See Maineville

Kingston, Ross, Pop. 1,029
Logan Elm Local SD
Supt. — See Circleville
Saltcreek IS 300/5-6
13190 State Route 56 45644 740-332-4212
Ted Dille, prin. Fax 332-1751

Kingsville, Ashtabula
Buckeye Local SD
Supt. — See Ashtabula
Kingsville ES 400/K-5
5875 State Route 193 44048 440-224-0281
Traci Landis, prin. Fax 224-2452

Kinsman, Trumbull
Joseph Badger Local SD 800/PK-12
7119 State Route 7 44428 330-876-2800
Dr. David Bair, supt. Fax 876-2811
badgerbraves.org
Badger ES 300/PK-4
7119 State Route 7 44428 330-876-2860
Dr. Mary Williams, prin. Fax 876-2861
Badger MS 300/5-8
7119 State Route 7 44428 330-876-2840
Steven Kochemba, prin. Fax 876-2841

Kirkersville, Licking, Pop. 519
Southwest Licking Local SD
Supt. — See Pataskala
Kirkersville ES 400/K-1
PO Box 401 43033 740-927-7281
Brad Wehrman, prin. Fax 927-4720

Kirtland, Lake, Pop. 6,804
Kirtland Local SD 1,200/K-12
9252 Chillicothe Rd 44094 440-256-3311
William R. Wade, supt. Fax 256-3831
www.kirtlandschools.org
Kirtland ES 500/K-5
9140 Chillicothe Rd 44094 440-256-3344
Chad VanArnhem, prin. Fax 256-1045
Kirtland MS 300/6-8
9152 Chillicothe Rd 44094 440-256-3358
Scott A. Amstutz, prin. Fax 256-3928

LaGrange, Lorain, Pop. 2,072
Keystone Local SD 1,600/K-12
531 Opportunity Way 44050 440-355-2424
Franco Gallo, supt. Fax 355-4465
www.keystonelocalschools.org/
Keystone ES 700/K-5
531 Opportunity Way 44050 440-355-2300
Maura Neville, prin. Fax 355-4242
Keystone MS 400/6-8
501 Opportunity Way 44050 440-355-2200
Toni Filut, prin. Fax 355-6678

Lakeside, Ottawa, Pop. 691
Danbury Local SD 500/PK-12
9451 East Harbor Rd 43440 419-798-5185
Daniel Parent, supt. Fax 798-2260
www.danbury.k12.oh.us
Danbury ES 200/PK-4
9451 East Harbor Rd 43440 419-798-4081
Daniel Humphrey, prin. Fax 798-2261
Danbury MS 200/5-8
9451 East Harbor Rd 43440 419-798-2258
Joseph Miller, prin. Fax 798-2259

Lakeville, Holmes
West Holmes Local SD
Supt. — See Millersburg
Lakeville ES 100/3-5
PO Box 68 44638 419-827-2006
Rick Mullins, prin. Fax 827-2352

Lakewood, Cuyahoga, Pop. 50,830
Lakewood CSD 5,600/K-12
1470 Warren Rd 44107 216-529-4000
Jeffrey Patterson, supt. Fax 228-8327
www.lakewoodcityschools.org
Emerson ES 500/K-5
13439 Clifton Blvd 44107 216-529-4254
Denice Leddy, prin. Fax 227-5752
Garfield MS 600/6-8
13114 Detroit Ave 44107 216-529-4241
Mark Walter, prin. Fax 529-4146
Grant ES 200/K-5
1470 Victoria Ave 44107 216-529-4217
Kaitlyn Turner, prin. Fax 227-5535
Harding MS 600/6-8
16601 Madison Ave 44107 216-529-4261
Joseph Niemantsverdriet, prin. Fax 529-4708
Harrison ES 400/K-5
2080 Quail St 44107 216-529-4230
Sabrina Crawford, prin. Fax 227-5556
Hayes ES 400/K-5
16401 Delaware Ave 44107 216-529-4228
Sandra Powers, prin. Fax 227-5575
Lincoln ES 400/K-5
15615 Clifton Blvd 44107 216-529-4232
Sandra Kozelka, prin. Fax 529-4305
Mann ES 300/K-5
1215 W Clifton Blvd 44107 216-529-4257
Dr. Merritt Waters, prin. Fax 227-5828
Roosevelt ES 300/K-5
14237 Athens Ave 44107 216-529-4224
Eileen Griffiths, prin. Fax 529-4308

Lakewood Catholic Academy 600/PK-8
14808 Lake Ave 44107 216-521-0559
Brian Sinchak, pres. Fax 521-0515
Lakewood Lutheran S 50/K-8
14560 Madison Ave 44107 216-221-6941
Carolyn Potantus, prin. Fax 226-4082

Lancaster, Fairfield, Pop. 38,140
Fairfield Union Local SD 2,000/K-12
6417 Cincinnati Zanesvll NE 43130 740-536-7384
Chad Belville, supt. Fax 536-9132
www.fairfieldunion.org
Rushville MS 600/5-8
6409 Cincinnati Zanesvll NE 43130 740-536-7249
Chris Walton, prin. Fax 536-7211
Other Schools – See Bremen, Pleasantville

Lancaster CSD 5,000/PK-12
345 E Mulberry St 43130 740-687-7300
Steven Wigton, supt. Fax 687-7303
www.lancaster.k12.oh.us
ECC 2 PK-PK
1450 Marietta Rd 43130 740-687-7354
Brenda Zeiders, prin. Fax 687-7206

Ewing JHS 700/6-8
825 E Fair Ave 43130 740-687-7347
Steve Poston, prin. Fax 687-3446
Gorsuch West ES K-5
440 Trace Dr 43130 740-687-7300
Fax 687-6202
Lancaster Preschool 400/PK-PK
425 Whittier Dr N 43130 740-687-7340
Dustin Knight, prin. Fax 687-7208
Medill ES 400/K-5
1160 Sheridan Dr 43130 740-687-7352
Dr. Jennifer Woods, prin. Fax 687-7205
Mt. Pleasant ES K-5
712 N Broad St 43130 740-687-7300
Shannon Burke, prin. Fax 687-7207
Sherman JHS 700/6-8
701 Union St 43130 740-687-7344
Charles Page, prin. Fax 687-3443
Tallmadge ES 300/K-5
694 Talmadge Ave 43130 740-687-7336
Dr. Jacob Campbell, prin. Fax 687-7204
Tarhe Trails ES 400/K-5
2141 Greencrest Way 43130 740-687-7300
Dustin Knight, prin. Fax 687-7201

Fairfield Christian Academy 600/PK-12
1965 N Columbus St 43130 740-654-2889
Craig Carpenter, supt. Fax 654-7689
St. Bernadette S 200/PK-5
1325 Wheeling Rd NE 43130 740-654-3137
Pamela Eltringham, prin. Fax 654-1602
St. Mary S 300/K-8
309 E Chestnut St 43130 740-654-1632
Erin Schornack, prin. Fax 654-0877

Latham, Pike
Western Local SD 500/K-12
7959 State Route 124 45646 740-493-3113
Brock Brewster, supt. Fax 493-2065
www.westernlocalschools.com/
Western ES 200/K-6
7959 State Route 124 45646 740-493-2881
Bethany Whitt, prin. Fax 493-1059

Laurelville, Hocking, Pop. 518
Logan Elm Local SD
Supt. — See Circleville
Laurelville ES 300/PK-4
16138 Pike St 43135 740-332-2021
Bret King, prin. Fax 332-1401

Leavittsburg, Trumbull, Pop. 1,932
LaBrae Local SD 1,400/K-12
1001 N Leavitt Rd 44430 330-898-0800
Anthony J. Calderone, supt. Fax 898-6112
www.labrae.school
Bascom ES 300/K-2
1015 N Leavitt Rd 44430 330-898-0800
Margaret Kowach, prin. Fax 898-1448
LaBrae IS 300/3-5
1001 N Leavitt Rd 44430 330-898-0800
Milajean Harkabus, prin. Fax 898-7808
LaBrae MS 300/6-8
1001 N Leavitt Rd 44430 330-898-0800
Martin Kelly, prin. Fax 898-7808

Lebanon, Warren, Pop. 19,670
Lebanon CSD 5,000/PK-12
700 Holbrook Ave 45036 513-934-5770
Todd Yohey, supt. Fax 932-5906
www.lebanonschools.org
Berry IS 900/5-6
160 Miller Rd 45036 513-934-5700
Elizabeth Kletzly, prin. Fax 228-1944
Bowman PS 800/PK-2
825 Hart Rd 45036 513-934-5800
Sheri McHenry, prin. Fax 934-2466
Donovan ES 900/3-4
401 Justice Dr 45036 513-934-5400
Clifton Franz, prin. Fax 934-2467
Lebanon JHS 900/7-8
160 Miller Rd 45036 513-934-5300
Brian Dalton, prin. Fax 932-9436

Lebanon Christian S 400/PK-8
1436 Deerfield Rd 45036 513-932-5590
Kent Jurgenson, prin. Fax 934-5698
St. Francis De Sales S 200/K-8
20 DeSales Ave Ste A 45036 513-932-6501
Paul McLaughlin, prin. Fax 932-9919

Leesburg, Highland, Pop. 1,294
Fairfield Local SD 900/K-12
11611 State Route 771 45135 937-780-2221
William Garrett, supt. Fax 780-6900
www.fairfield-highland.k12.oh.us
Fairfield ES 400/K-4
11611 State Route 771 45135 937-780-2988
Deanne Miller, prin. Fax 780-2841
Fairfield MS 300/5-8
11611 State Route 771 45135 937-780-2977
Stephen Hackett, prin. Fax 780-2841

Leetonia, Columbiana, Pop. 1,931
Leetonia EVD 700/K-12
450 Walnut St 44431 330-427-6594
Robert Mehno, supt. Fax 427-1136
www.leetonia.k12.oh.us
Leetonia ES 300/K-4
450 Walnut St 44431 330-427-6129
Jackie Dunnigan, prin. Fax 427-2549
Leetonia MS 200/5-8
450 Walnut St 44431 330-427-2444
Troy Radinsky, prin. Fax 427-2549

Leipsic, Putnam, Pop. 2,076
Leipsic Local SD 600/K-12
232 Oak St 45856 419-943-2165
Greg Williamson, supt. Fax 943-4331
llsdk12.org/
Leipsic ES 300/K-5
232 Oak St 45856 419-943-2163
Darren Henry, prin. Fax 943-2185

St. Mary S 100/1-8
129 Saint Marys St 45856 419-943-2801
Sr. Nancy Schroeder, prin. Fax 943-3555

Lewisburg, Preble, Pop. 1,788
Tri-County North Local SD 800/K-12
436 N Commerce St 45338 937-962-2671
William Derringer, supt. Fax 962-4731
www.tcnschools.org
Tri-County North ES 400/K-5
570 Panther Way 45338 937-962-2673
Joe Finkbine, prin. Fax 833-4330
Tri-County North MS 200/6-8
530 Panther Way 45338 937-962-2631
Joe Hoelzle, prin. Fax 833-4860

Lewis Center, Delaware, Pop. 300
Olentangy Local SD 18,000/PK-12
7840 Graphics Way 43035 740-657-4050
Dr. Mark Raiff, supt. Fax 657-4099
www.olentangy.k12.oh.us
Alum Creek ES 600/PK-5
2515 Parklawn Dr 43035 740-657-4600
Brandy Worth, prin. Fax 657-4649
Arrowhead ES 400/PK-5
2385 Hollenback Rd 43035 740-657-4650
Bridget McMillen, prin. Fax 657-4699
Freedom Trail ES 600/K-5
6743 Bale Kenyon Rd 43035 740-657-5700
Stephen Sargent, prin. Fax 657-5749
Glen Oak ES 600/PK-5
7300 Blue Holly Dr 43035 740-657-5500
Jaclyn Roscoe, prin. Fax 657-5549
Heritage ES 600/PK-5
679 Lewis Center Rd 43035 740-657-5000
Susan Staum, prin. Fax 657-5049
Oak Creek ES 600/K-5
1256 Westwood Dr 43035 740-657-4700
Julie Lather, prin. Fax 657-4749
Olentangy Meadows ES 600/K-5
8950 Emerald Hill Dr 43035 740-657-5550
Kristin Baker, prin. Fax 657-5599
Olentangy Orange MS 900/6-8
2680 E Orange Rd 43035 740-657-5300
Scott Cunningham, prin. Fax 657-5399
Olentangy Shanahan MS 1,000/6-8
814 Shanahan Rd 43035 740-657-4300
Joshua McDaniels, prin. Fax 657-4398
Other Schools – See Delaware, Galena, Powell

Polaris Christian Academy 100/K-8
2150 E Powell Rd 43035 614-431-6888
Judith Hoban, prin. Fax 431-0137

Lewistown, Logan, Pop. 220
Indian Lake Local SD 1,700/K-12
6210 State Route 235 N 43333 937-686-8601
Robert Underwood, supt. Fax 686-8421
www.ils-k12.org
Indian Lake ES 700/K-4
8770 County Road 91 43333 937-686-7323
Molly Hall, prin. Fax 686-0049
Indian Lake MS 500/5-8
8920 County Road 91 43333 937-686-8833
Melissa Mefford, prin. Fax 686-8993

Lexington, Richland, Pop. 4,768
Lexington Local SD 2,400/PK-12
103 Clever Ln 44904 419-884-2132
J. Michael Ziegelhofer, supt. Fax 884-3129
www.lexington.k12.oh.us
Central ES 400/K-4
124 Frederick St 44904 419-884-1308
Kathleen Weidig, prin. Fax 884-6154
Eastern ES 500/4-6
155 Castor Rd 44904 419-884-3610
Buddy Miller, prin. Fax 884-2987
Lexington JHS 400/7-8
90 Frederick St 44904 419-884-2112
Taylor Gerhardt, prin. Fax 884-0134
Western ES 300/PK-3
385 W Main St 44904 419-884-2765
Genelle Eggerton, prin. Fax 884-2221

Liberty Center, Henry, Pop. 1,169
Liberty Center Local SD 1,000/PK-12
PO Box 434 43532 419-533-5011
Dr. Tod Hug, supt. Fax 533-5036
www.libertycenterschools.org
Liberty Center ES 400/PK-4
PO Box 434 43532 419-533-2604
Kelly Hartbarger, prin. Fax 533-5036
Liberty Center MS 400/5-8
PO Box 434 43532 419-533-0020
Fax 533-1021

Liberty Twp, Butler
Lakota Local SD 15,500/PK-12
5572 Princeton Rd 45011 513-874-5505
Matthew Miller, supt. Fax 644-1167
www.lakotaonline.com
Cherokee ES 700/2-6
5345 Kyles Station Rd 45011 513-755-8200
Valerie Montgomery, prin. Fax 755-8067
Heritage ES 500/2-6
5052 Hamilton Mason Rd 45011 513-863-7060
Missy Alexander, prin. Fax 887-5483
Independence ES 700/2-6
7480 Princeton Rd 45044 513-755-8300
Greg Finke, prin. Fax 755-6941
Lakota Plains JHS 700/7-8
5500 Princeton Rd 45011 513-644-1130
Kim Wade, prin. Fax 644-1135
Liberty Early Childhood S 400/PK-1
6040 Princeton Rd 45011 513-777-6194
Carrie Montgomery, prin. Fax 759-2672
Liberty JHS 800/7-8
7055 Dutchland Pkwy 45044 513-777-4420
Eric Bauman, prin. Fax 777-7950
VanGorden ES 600/2-6
6475 Lesourdsville Rd 45011 513-644-1150
Gail Allshouse, prin. Fax 644-1160
Woodland ES 500/2-6
6923 Dutchland Blvd 45044 513-779-7775
John Wise, prin. Fax 779-7389
Wyandot Early Childhood S 700/K-1
7667 Summerlin Blvd 45044 513-759-8100
Mary Brophy, prin. Fax 759-8105
Other Schools – See Cincinnati, West Chester

Mother Teresa S 400/K-8
7197 Mother Teresa Ln 45044 513-779-6585
Sr. Anne Schulz, prin. Fax 779-6468

Lima, Allen, Pop. 37,107
Bath Local SD 1,600/K-12
2650 Bible Rd 45801 419-221-0807
Richard Dackin, supt. Fax 221-0983
www.bathwildcats.org
Bath ES 700/K-5
2450 Bible Rd 45801 419-221-1837
Christopher Renner, prin. Fax 221-3937
Bath MS 400/6-8
2700 Bible Rd 45801 419-221-1839
Bradley Clark, prin. Fax 221-2431

Lima CSD 3,800/PK-12
755 Saint Johns Ave 45804 419-996-3400
Jill Ackerman, supt. Fax 996-3401
www.limacityschools.org
Freedom ES 400/PK-4
575 Calumet Ave 45804 419-996-3380
Chandra Nuveman, prin. Fax 996-3381
Heritage ES 500/PK-4
816 College Ave 45805 419-996-3390
Stacy Barker, prin. Fax 996-3391
Independence ES 300/K-4
615 Tremont Ave 45801 419-996-3330
Matt Quatman, prin. Fax 996-3331
Liberty Arts Magnet K-8 400/K-8
338 W Kibby St 45804 419-996-3320
Angela Heffner, prin. Fax 996-3321
Lima North MS 400/5-6
1135 N West St 45801 419-996-3100
Julie Stewart, prin. Fax 996-3101
Lima South Science & Technology Magnet S 200/K-8
755 Saint Johns Ave 45804 419-996-3190
Chad Fallis, prin. Fax 996-3191
Lima West MS 400/7-8
503 N Cable Rd 45805 419-996-3150
Thomas Winkler, prin. Fax 996-3151
Unity ES 200/K-4
925 E 3rd St 45804 419-996-3300
Tricia Winkler, prin. Fax 996-3301

Perry Local SD 800/K-12
2770 E Breese Rd 45806 419-221-2770
Alison Van Gorder, supt. Fax 224-6215
mycommodores.org
Perry ES 500/K-6
2770 E Breese Rd 45806 419-221-2771
Kelly Schooler, prin. Fax 224-6312

Shawnee Local SD 2,500/K-12
3255 Zurmehly Rd 45806 419-998-8031
James Kanable, supt. Fax 998-8050
www.limashawnee.com
Elmwood ES 600/K-2
4295 Shawnee Rd 45806 419-998-8090
Leigh Daily, prin. Fax 998-8110
Maplewood ES 400/3-4
1670 Wonderlick Rd 45805 419-998-8076
Larry Foos, prin. Fax 998-8085
Shawnee MS 800/5-8
3235 Zurmehly Rd 45806 419-998-8057
Judy Gephart, prin. Fax 222-6572

St. Charles S 400/PK-8
2175 W Elm St 45805 419-222-2536
Megan Scheid, prin. Fax 222-8720
St. Gerard S 200/PK-8
1311 N Main St 45801 419-222-0431
Rev. Natalie Schoonover, prin. Fax 224-6580
St. Rose of Lima S 100/K-8
523 N West St 45801 419-223-6361
Donna Judy, prin. Fax 222-2032
Temple Christian S 200/PK-12
982 Brower Rd 45801 419-227-1644
Bruce Bowman, prin. Fax 227-6635

Lindsey, Sandusky, Pop. 444
Fremont CSD
Supt. — See Fremont
Washington ES 100/K-5
109 W Lincoln St 43442 419-665-2327
Susan Gray, prin. Fax 665-2241

Lisbon, Columbiana, Pop. 2,802
Lisbon EVD 900/PK-12
317 N Market St 44432 330-424-7714
Joseph Siefke, supt. Fax 424-0135
www.lisbon.k12.oh.us/
McKinley ES 400/PK-5
441 E Chestnut St 44432 330-424-9869
Daniel Kemats, prin. Fax 424-9860

Lithopolis, Fairfield, Pop. 1,092
Bloom-Carroll Local SD
Supt. — See Carroll

Bloom-Carroll IS 300/3-4
200 S Market St 43136 614-837-4044
Stephen Rozeski, prin. Fax 837-8144

Little Hocking, Washington, Pop. 257
Warren Local SD
Supt. — See Vincent
Little Hocking ES 200/K-4
95 Federal Rd 45742 740-989-2000
Robin Carter, prin. Fax 989-2585

Lockland, Hamilton, Pop. 3,333
Lockland Local SD 500/PK-12
210 N Cooper Ave 45215 513-563-5000
Ted Jebens, supt. Fax 563-9611
www.locklandschools.org
Lockland ES 300/PK-6
200 N Cooper Ave 45215 513-563-5000
Anthony Comer, prin. Fax 563-9611
Lockland MS 100/7-8
249 W Forrer St 45215 513-563-5000
Anthony Comer, prin. Fax 563-9611

Lodi, Medina, Pop. 2,720
Cloverleaf Local SD 2,500/PK-12
8525 Friendsville Rd 44254 330-948-2500
Daryl Kubilus, supt. Fax 948-1034
www.cloverleaflocal.org/
Other Schools – See Seville

Logan, Hocking, Pop. 7,087
Logan-Hocking Local SD 3,900/PK-12
2019 E Front St 43138 740-385-8517
Monte Bainter, supt. Fax 385-3683
www.lhsd.k12.oh.us
Central ES 500/PK-4
445 N Market St 43138 740-380-4664
Lisa Van Horn, prin. Fax 521-8209
Chieftain ES 400/K-4
28296 Chieftain Dr 43138 740-385-1171
Debra Heath, prin. Fax 521-8212
Green ES 300/PK-4
13495 Maysville Williams Rd 43138 740-385-7789
Rebecca Osburn, prin. Fax 521-8214
Hocking Hills ES 200/PK-4
19197 State Route 664 S 43138 740-385-7071
Kevin Rice, prin. Fax 521-8217
Logan-Hocking MS 1,300/5-8
1 Middleschool Dr 43138 740-385-8764
Chad Grow, prin. Fax 385-9547
Other Schools – See Union Furnace

St. John S 100/PK-6
321 N Market St 43138 740-385-2767
Andy Potter, prin. Fax 385-9727

London, Madison, Pop. 9,615
Jonathan Alder Local SD
Supt. — See Plain City
Monroe ES 300/PK-4
5000 State Route 38 NW 43140 614-873-8503
Michelle Hughes, prin. Fax 873-0685

London CSD 2,200/PK-12
380 Elm St 43140 740-852-5700
Dr. Louis Kramer, supt. Fax 845-3282
www.london.k12.oh.us/
London ES 1,000/PK-5
380 Elm St 43140 740-845-3272
Tabatha Wilburn, prin. Fax 845-3283
London MS 500/6-8
270 Keny Blvd 43140 740-852-5701
Michael Belmont, prin. Fax 845-1279

Madison-Plains Local SD 1,200/K-12
55 Linson Rd 43140 740-852-0290
Tim Dettwiller, supt. Fax 852-5895
www.mplsd.org/
Madison-Plains IS 300/4-6
9940 State Route 38 SW 43140 740-490-0610
Brad Miller, prin. Fax 490-0612
Madison-Plains JHS 200/6-8
803 Linson Rd 43140 740-852-1707
Dr. Matt Unger, prin. Fax 852-6351
Madison-Plains Local ES 400/K-3
47 Linson Rd 43140 740-874-3310
Brad Miller, prin. Fax 874-3104

St. Patrick S 200/PK-8
226 Elm St 43140 740-852-0161
Jacob Froning Ph.D., prin. Fax 852-0602

Lorain, Lorain, Pop. 62,074
Clearview Local SD 1,700/K-12
4700 Broadway 44052 440-233-5412
Jerome M. Davis M.Ed., supt. Fax 233-6034
www.clearviewschools.org
Durling MS 500/5-8
100 N Ridge Rd W 44053 440-233-6869
Laura Manning, prin. Fax 233-6204
Vincent ES 600/K-4
2303 N Ridge Rd E 44055 440-233-7113
Wesley Davies, prin. Fax 233-7114

Lorain CSD 6,700/PK-12
2601 Pole Ave 44052 440-233-2271
Jeffrey Graham, supt. Fax 282-9151
www.lorainschools.org
Dohanos ES 400/K-6
1625 E 32nd St 44055 440-277-1008
Sean Wolanin, prin. Fax 277-1014
Garfield ES 300/PK-6
200 W 31st St 44055 440-246-1114
Michelle Spotts-Hayes, prin. Fax 246-1121
Hawthorne ES 300/K-6
610 W 20th St 44052 440-246-1080
Stephanie Johnson, prin. Fax 246-1083
Jacinto ES 300/PK-6
2515 Marshall Ave 44052 440-960-5800
Leila Flores, prin. Fax 960-5810

King ES 400/K-6
720 Washington Ave 44052 440-245-6315
Jay Keefer, prin. Fax 245-4251
Larkmoor ES 400/PK-6
1201 Nebraska Ave 44052 440-288-3203
Chantelle Lewis, prin. Fax 288-5017
Longfellow MS 500/7-8
305 Louisiana Ave 44052 440-830-4220
Christine Miller, prin. Fax 288-1149
Morrison ES 300/PK-6
1830 W 40th St 44053 440-960-7008
Megan Young, prin. Fax 960-7015
Palm ES 300/K-6
2319 E 34th St 44055 440-277-1240
Deborah Pustulka, prin. Fax 277-1225
Rice ES 300/PK-6
4500 Tacoma Ave 44055 440-240-1220
Brandon Easton, prin. Fax 240-1221
Southview MS 6-8
2321 Fairless Dr 44055 440-830-4280
Rae Bastock, prin. Fax 277-5566
Washington ES 400/K-6
1025 W 23rd St 44052 440-246-2187
Marie Deshuk, prin. Fax 246-4920
Wilson MS 400/7-8
2700 Washington Ave 44052 440-830-4240
Fax 246-1016

St. Anthony of Padua S 300/PK-8
1339 E Erie Ave 44052 440-288-2155
Joseph Akosi, prin. Fax 288-2159
St. Peter S 400/PK-8
3601 Oberlin Ave 44053 440-282-9909
Rebecca Brown, prin. Fax 282-9490

Lore City, Guernsey, Pop. 322
East Guernsey Local SD
Supt. — See Old Washington
Buckeye Trail ES 500/K-5
65553 Wintergreen Rd 43755 740-489-5100
Casey Tolzda, prin. Fax 489-9049
Buckeye Trail MS 300/6-8
65553 Wintergreen Rd 43755 740-489-5100
William Hartmeyer, prin. Fax 489-9049

Loudonville, Ashland, Pop. 2,623
Loudonville-Perrysville EVD 900/PK-12
210 E Main St 44842 419-994-3912
Catherine M. Puster M.Ed., supt. Fax 994-5528
www.lpschools.k12.oh.us
Budd ES 300/4-6
210 E Main St 44842 419-994-3327
Lisa Gonzalez, prin. Fax 994-7003
McMullen ES 300/PK-3
224 E Bustle St 44842 419-994-3913
Annette Gorrell, prin. Fax 994-5116

Louisville, Stark, Pop. 9,114
Louisville CSD 3,000/PK-12
407 E Main St 44641 330-875-1666
Michele Shaffer, supt. Fax 875-7603
www.louisvillecityschools.org
Louisville ES 1,100/K-5
415 N Nickelplate St 44641 330-875-1177
Michael Norris, prin. Fax 875-7608
Louisville MS 700/6-8
1300 S Chapel St 44641 330-875-5597
Jason Orin, prin. Fax 875-7620
North Nimishillen ES 300/PK-2
7337 Easton St 44641 330-875-2661
Melanie Davis, prin. Fax 875-7614

Marlington Local SD
Supt. — See Alliance
Marlboro ES 300/K-5
8131 Edison St 44641 330-935-2469
Michael Groholy, prin. Fax 935-2155

Good Shepherd S 50/1-12
PO Box 169 44641 330-935-0623
Rev. Gary Spencer, admin. Fax 935-0700
St. Louis S 100/PK-5
214 N Chapel St 44641 330-875-1467
Mario Calandros, prin. Fax 875-2511

Loveland, Hamilton, Pop. 11,848
Loveland CSD 4,700/PK-12
757 S Lebanon Rd 45140 513-683-5600
Amy Crouse Ph.D., supt. Fax 683-5697
www.lovelandschools.org/
Loveland ECC 500/PK-1
6740 Loveland Miamiville Rd 45140 513-683-4200
Kyle Bush, prin. Fax 677-7960
Loveland ES 700/3-4
600 Loveland Madeira Rd 45140 513-683-4333
Jennifer Forren, prin. Fax 677-7932
Loveland IS 800/5-6
757 S Lebanon Rd 45140 513-774-7000
Garth Carlier, prin. Fax 677-7978
Loveland MS 800/7-8
801 S Lebanon Rd 45140 513-683-3100
Christopher Burke, prin. Fax 677-7986
Loveland PS 500/1-2
550 Loveland Madeira Rd 45140 513-683-3101
Kevin Fancher, prin. Fax 677-7922

Milford EVD
Supt. — See Milford
McCormick ES 600/K-6
751 Loveland Miamiville Rd 45140 513-575-0190
Donald Baker, prin. Fax 575-4019

Sycamore Community CSD
Supt. — See Cincinnati
Symmes ES 500/PK-4
11820 Enyart Rd 45140 513-686-1740
Anne Van Kirk, prin. Fax 677-7861

Childrens Meeting House Montessori S 100/PK-6
927 OBannonville Rd 45140 513-683-4757
St. Columban S 700/K-8
896 Oakland Rd 45140 513-683-7903
Joann Rhoten, prin. Fax 683-7904
St. Margaret of York S 700/K-8
9495 Columbia Rd 45140 513-697-3100
Dr. Kevin Vance, prin. Fax 683-8949

Lowell, Washington, Pop. 545
Fort Frye Local SD
Supt. — See Beverly
Lowell ES 100/K-6
305 Market St 45744 740-896-2523
Krista Ross, prin. Fax 896-3425

Lowellville, Mahoning, Pop. 1,148
Lowellville Local SD 600/K-12
52 Rocket Pl 44436 330-536-6318
Dr. Eugene Thomas, supt. Fax 536-8221
www.lowellville.k12.oh.us/
Lowellville ES 300/K-6
52 Rocket Pl 44436 330-536-8426
Dennis Hynes, prin. Fax 536-8468

Lower Salem, Washington, Pop. 86
Fort Frye Local SD
Supt. — See Beverly
Salem-Liberty ES 100/K-6
10930 State Route 821 45745 740-585-2252
Krista Ross, prin. Fax 585-2252

Lucas, Richland, Pop. 605
Lucas Local SD 600/PK-12
84 Lucas North Rd 44843 419-892-2338
Bradley Herman, supt. Fax 892-1138
www.lucascubs.org
Lucas ES 300/PK-5
84 Lucas North Rd 44843 419-892-2338
Kari Case, prin. Fax 892-1138
Lucas Heritage MS 100/6-7
80 Lucas North Rd 44843 419-892-2338
Kari Case, prin. Fax 892-1138

Lucasville, Scioto, Pop. 2,738
Valley Local SD 1,000/PK-12
1821 State Route 728 45648 740-259-3115
Jeffrey Rolfe, supt. Fax 259-2314
www.valleyindians.net
Valley ES 400/PK-4
1821A State Route 728 45648 740-259-2611
Jeremy Clark, prin. Fax 259-3822
Valley MS, 393 Indian Dr 45648 300/5-8
Aaron Franke, prin. 740-259-2651

Lynchburg, Highland, Pop. 1,486
Lynchburg-Clay Local SD 1,200/PK-12
PO Box 515 45142 937-364-2338
Brett Justice, supt. Fax 364-2339
www.lynchclay.k12.oh.us
Lynchburg-Clay ES 500/PK-5
6760 State Route 134 45142 937-364-9119
Angela Godby, prin. Fax 364-8119
Lynchburg-Clay MS 300/6-8
8250 State Route 134 45142 937-364-2811
Dr. Casey Smith, prin. Fax 364-2159

Lyndhurst, Cuyahoga, Pop. 13,838
South Euclid-Lyndhurst CSD 3,800/K-12
5044 Mayfield Rd 44124 216-691-2000
Linda Reid, supt. Fax 691-2298
www.sel.k12.oh.us
Memorial JHS 600/7-8
1250 Professor Rd 44124 216-691-2141
Dominick Kaple, prin. Fax 691-2159
Sunview ES 400/K-3
5520 Meadow Wood Blvd 44124 216-691-2225
Arika Taylor, prin. Fax 691-2226
Other Schools – See South Euclid

Corpus Christi Academy 200/PK-8
5655 Mayfield Rd 44124 440-449-4242
Kenneth Mitskavich, prin. Fax 449-1497
Hawken S 200/PK-8
5000 Clubside Rd 44124 440-423-4446
D. Scott Looney, head sch Fax 423-2960

Mc Arthur, Vinton, Pop. 1,685
Vinton County Local SD 2,300/PK-12
307 W High St 45651 740-596-5218
Rick Brooks, supt. Fax 596-3142
www.vinton.k12.oh.us/
Central ES 400/PK-5
507 Jefferson Ave 45651 740-596-4386
Terri Snider, prin. Fax 596-4027
Vinton County MS 500/6-8
63780 Locker Plant Rd 45651 740-596-5243
Jeremy Ward, prin. Fax 596-3815
West ES 400/PK-5
57772 US Highway 50 45651 740-596-5236
Mary Ann Hale, prin. Fax 596-5237
Other Schools – See Hamden

Mc Comb, Hancock, Pop. 1,624
Mc Comb Local SD 700/PK-12
328 S Todd St 45858 419-293-3979
Tony Fenstermaker, supt. Fax 293-2412
mccomblocalschools.org
Mc Comb Local ES 400/PK-6
328 S Todd St 45858 419-293-3286
Matt Harp, prin. Fax 293-3107
Mc Comb Local MS 100/7-8
328 S Todd St 45858 419-293-3853
Jeremy Herr, prin. Fax 293-3107

Mc Connelsville, Morgan, Pop. 1,738
Morgan Local SD 2,000/PK-12
PO Box 509 43756 740-962-2782
Lori Snyder-Lowe, supt. Fax 962-4931
www.mlsd.k12.oh.us/

East ES 400/PK-6
4265 N State Route 376 NW 43756 740-962-3361
Lynn Copeland, prin. Fax 962-6804
Morgan JHS 300/7-8
820 Junior Raider Dr 43756 740-962-2833
Timothy Hopkins, prin. Fax 962-3389
Other Schools – See Malta, Stockport

Mc Dermott, Scioto, Pop. 428
Northwest Local SD 1,600/PK-12
800 Mohawk Dr 45652 740-259-5558
Todd Jenkins, supt. Fax 259-3476
www.nwmohawks.org
Northwest ES 800/PK-5
4738 Henley Deemer Rd 45652 740-259-2250
Brian Martin, prin. Fax 259-2337
Northwest MS 400/6-8
692 Mohawk Dr 45652 740-259-2528
Michael Armstrong, prin. Fax 259-5731

Mc Donald, Trumbull, Pop. 3,227
McDonald Local SD 800/K-12
600 Iowa Ave 44437 330-530-8051
Robert Rostan, supt. Fax 530-7041
www.mcdonald.k12.oh.us
Roosevelt ES 400/K-6
410 W 7th St 44437 330-530-8051
David Vecchione, prin. Fax 530-7033

Macedonia, Summit, Pop. 11,001
Nordonia Hills CSD
Supt. — See Northfield
Ledgeview ES 500/K-4
9130 Shepard Rd 44056 330-467-0583
Kristen Cottrell, prin. Fax 468-4647

Mc Guffey, Hardin, Pop. 491
Upper Scioto Valley Local SD 500/K-12
PO Box 305 45859 419-757-3231
Miklos Kis, supt. Fax 757-0135
usv.k12.oh.us
Upper Scioto Valley ES 300/K-6
PO Box 305 45859 419-757-3231
Wayne Schneider, prin. Fax 757-0135
Upper Scioto Valley MS 100/7-8
PO Box 305 45859 419-757-3231
Adam Baumgartner, prin. Fax 757-0135

Madison, Lake, Pop. 3,130
Madison Local SD 3,300/PK-12
1956 Red Bird Rd 44057 440-428-2166
Angela Smith, supt. Fax 428-9379
www.madisonschools.net
Madison MS 700/6-8
6079 Middle Ridge Rd 44057 440-428-1196
Thomas Brady, prin. Fax 428-9389
Madison Preschool 200/PK-PK
1956 Red Bird Rd 44057 440-428-5111
Jovette Hiltunen, dir. Fax 428-9384
North ES 700/K-5
1941 Red Bird Rd 44057 440-428-2155
Sally Rogus, prin. Fax 428-9384
South ES 700/K-5
92 E Main St 44057 440-428-5121
Shannon Kriegmont, prin. Fax 428-8438

Magnolia, Stark, Pop. 965
Sandy Valley Local SD 1,100/PK-12
5362 State Route 183 NE 44643 330-866-3339
David Fischer, supt. Fax 866-5238
www.sandyvalleylocal.org
Sandy Valley ES 600/PK-5
5018 State Route 183 NE 44643 330-866-9225
Victor Johnson, prin. Fax 866-2572

Maineville, Warren, Pop. 962
Kings Local SD
Supt. — See Kings Mills
South Lebanon ES 400/K-4
50 Ridgeview Ln 45039 513-398-8050
Dave Winebrenner, prin. Fax 494-1469

Little Miami Local SD 3,400/PK-12
7247 Zoar Rd 45039 513-899-2264
Gregory Power, supt. Fax 899-3244
www.littlemiamischools.com
Hamilton-Maineville ES 300/1-2
373 E Fosters Maineville Rd 45039 513-899-4760
Teresa Reynolds, prin. Fax 683-3879
Little Miami IS 700/5-6
7247 Zoar Rd 45039 513-899-2334
Dan Distel, prin. Fax 899-4020
Other Schools – See Blanchester, Morrow

Malta, Morgan, Pop. 639
Morgan Local SD
Supt. — See Mc Connelsville
West ES 300/PK-6
9675 State Route 37 43758 740-342-4873
Greg Gifford, prin. Fax 342-7326

Malvern, Carroll, Pop. 1,175
Brown Local SD 600/K-12
3242 Coral Rd NW 44644 330-863-1170
Scott Bowling, supt. Fax 863-1172
www.brownlocalschools.com
Malvern ES 300/K-5
3242 Coral Rd NW 44644 330-863-1355
Ashley Weber, prin. Fax 863-1366
Malvern MS 200/6-8
3242 Coral Rd NW 44644 330-863-1355
Timothy Babiczuk, prin. Fax 863-1366

Manchester, Adams, Pop. 1,976
Manchester Local SD 900/PK-12
130 Wayne Frye Dr 45144 937-549-4777
Dr. Brian Rau, supt. Fax 549-4744
www.mlsd.us
Manchester ES 500/PK-6
130 Wayne Frye Dr 45144 937-549-4777
Nick Roberts, prin. Fax 549-1289

Mansfield, Richland, Pop. 46,379
Madison Local SD 2,600/PK-12
1379 Grace St 44905 419-589-2600
Shelley Hilderbrand, supt. Fax 589-3653
www.mlsd.net/
Eastview ES 300/K-4
1262 Eastview Dr 44905 419-589-7335
Melissa Wigton, prin. Fax 589-3031
Madison MS 500/5-8
1419 Grace St 44905 419-522-0471
Jonathan Muro, prin. Fax 522-1463
Madison South ES 600/PK-4
700 S Illinois Ave 44907 419-522-4319
Chris Scholl, prin. Fax 526-2911
Mifflin ES 300/K-4
441 Reed Rd 44903 419-589-6517
Nathan Stump, prin. Fax 589-6659

Mansfield CSD 3,300/PK-12
856 W Cook Rd 44907 419-525-6400
Brian Garverick, supt. Fax 525-6415
www.tygerpride.com
Malabar IS 700/3-6
205 W Cook Rd 44907 419-525-6374
Andrea Moyer, prin. Fax 525-6376
Mansfield MS 500/7-8
124 N Linden Rd 44906 419-525-6307
Robert McQuate, prin. Fax 525-6306
Mansfield Spanish Immersion S 200/PK-6
240 Euclid Ave 44903 419-525-6321
Carmen Costa, prin. Fax 525-6386
Prospect ES 300/K-3
485 Gilbert Ave 44907 419-525-6313
Jason Douglas, prin. Fax 525-6312
Sherman ES 500/K-3
1138 Springmill St 44906 419-525-6337
Michael Wallace, prin. Fax 525-6340
Springmill STEM ES K-K
1200 Nestor Dr 44906 419-525-6348
David Gilbert, prin.
Woodland ES 300/K-3
460 Davis Rd 44907 419-525-6325
Kimberly Johnson, prin. Fax 525-6392

Discovery S 100/PK-6
855 Millsboro Rd 44903 419-756-8880
Mansfield Adventist S 50/K-8
1040 W Cook Rd 44906 419-756-9947
Christina Dotson, prin. Fax 756-8977
Mansfield Christian S 500/PK-12
500 Logan Rd 44907 419-756-5651
Dr. Cy Smith, supt. Fax 756-7470
St. Mary S 100/PK-8
1630 Ashland Rd 44905 419-589-2114
Susan Sanders, prin. Fax 589-7085
St. Peter S 300/PK-6
63 S Mulberry St 44902 419-524-3351
Madalyn Bauer, prin. Fax 524-3366
Temple Christian S 200/PK-12
752 Stewart Rd N 44905 419-589-9707
Jessica Day, prin. Fax 589-7213

Mantua, Portage, Pop. 1,029
Crestwood Local SD 1,900/PK-12
11260 Bowen Rd 44255 330-357-8206
David Toth, supt. Fax 274-3710
www.crestwoodschools.org
Crestwood IS 400/3-5
11260 Bowen Rd 44255 330-357-8203
Michelle Gerbrick, prin. Fax 274-3825
Crestwood MS 400/6-8
10880 John Edward Dr 44255 330-357-8202
Julie Schmidt, prin. Fax 274-3705
Crestwood PS 400/PK-2
11256 Bowen Rd 44255 330-357-8204
Cynthia Ducca, prin. Fax 274-3824

Maple Heights, Cuyahoga, Pop. 22,680
Maple Heights CSD 3,700/PK-12
5740 Lawn Ave 44137 216-587-6100
Dr. Charles Keenan, supt. Fax 518-2674
www.mapleschools.com/
Kennedy ES 600/2-3
5933 Dunham Rd 44137 216-438-6010
Zelina Pames, prin. Fax 587-4187
Lincoln ES 600/PK-1
6009 Dunham Rd 44137 216-438-6030
Dawn Besteder, prin. Fax 587-4376
Milkovich MS 900/6-8
19800 Stafford Ave 44137 216-438-6000
Loretta Rodman, prin. Fax 587-4523
Obama ES 600/4-5
5800 Glenwood Ave 44137 216-438-6020
Matthew Bryan, prin. Fax 587-4269

Marengo, Morrow, Pop. 330
Highland Local SD 1,800/K-12
6506 State Route 229 43334 419-768-2206
Daniel Freund, supt. Fax 768-3115
www.highland.k12.oh.us/
Highland ES 800/K-5
1250 Township Road 16 43334 419-768-3040
Shawn Winkelfoos, prin. Fax 768-2127
Highland MS 500/6-8
6506 State Route 229 43334 419-768-2781
Matthew Bradley, prin. Fax 768-2742

Maria Stein, Mercer
Marion Local SD 900/K-12
7956 State Route 119 45860 419-925-4294
Michael Pohlman, supt. Fax 925-0212
marionlocal.org
Marion Local S 600/K-8
7956 State Route 119 45860 419-925-4595
Nicholas Wilker, prin. Fax 925-5199

Marietta, Washington, Pop. 13,848
Marietta CSD 2,700/K-12
111 Academy Dr 45750 740-374-6500
William Hampton, supt. Fax 374-6506
mariettacityschools.k12.oh.us
Harmar ES 300/K-5
100 Fort Sq 45750 740-374-6510
Cheryl Cook, prin. Fax 376-2465
Marietta MS 600/6-8
242 N 7th St 45750 740-374-6530
Brittany Schob, prin. Fax 374-6531
Phillips ES 400/K-5
300 Pike St 45750 740-374-6514
Kristi Lantz, prin. Fax 374-6515
Putnam ES 300/K-5
598 Masonic Park Rd 45750 740-374-6516
D.Scott Kratche, prin. Fax 374-6517
Washington ES 300/K-5
401 Washington St 45750 740-374-6520
Alicia McIntire, prin. Fax 374-6521

Warren Local SD
Supt. — See Vincent
Warren ES 200/K-4
16855 State Route 550 45750 740-445-5300
Robin Carter, prin. Fax 373-0517

St. John S 200/PK-8
17654 State Route 676 45750 740-896-2697
Dr. Larry A. Moegling, prin. Fax 896-2555
St. Mary S 200/PK-8
320 Marion St 45750 740-374-8181
Susan Rauch, prin. Fax 374-8602

Marion, Marion, Pop. 36,113
Elgin Local SD 900/K-12
1239 Keener Rd S 43302 740-382-1101
Bruce Gast, supt. Fax 382-1672
www.elginschools.org
Elgin ES 200/K-5
1250 Keener Rd S 43302 740-223-4301
Kristen Dyer, prin. Fax 223-4311
Elgin MS 300/6-8
1200 Keener Rd S 43302 740-223-4300
Michael Malcom, prin. Fax 223-4310

Marion CSD 4,400/PK-12
420 Presidential Dr Ste B 43302 740-387-3300
Stephen Fujii, supt. Fax 223-4400
www.marioncityschools.org
Garfield ES 300/PK-5
1170 Brookside Rd 43302 740-223-4444
Marianne Bailey, prin. Fax 223-4485
Grant MS 1,000/6-8
420 Presidential Dr 43302 740-223-4900
Kirk Ballinger, prin. Fax 223-4820
Harrison ES 400/PK-5
625 Brightwood Dr 43302 740-223-4999
Leah Filliater, prin. Fax 223-4990
Hayes ES 300/PK-5
750 Silver St 43302 740-223-4950
William Glenn, prin. Fax 223-4960
McKinley ES 400/K-5
925 Chatfield Rd 43302 740-223-4600
Matthew Holsinger, prin. Fax 223-4574
Taft ES 500/PK-5
1000 Robinson St 43302 740-223-4500
Samanta Chatman, prin. Fax 223-4499
Washington ES 400/PK-5
400 Pennsylvania Ave 43302 740-223-3883
Scott Curtis, prin. Fax 223-3726

Pleasant Local SD 1,200/K-12
1107 Owens Rd W 43302 740-389-4476
Jennier Adams, supt. Fax 389-6985
www.pleasantlocalschools.org
Pleasant ES 500/K-5
1105 Owens Rd W 43302 740-389-4815
Dr. Shelly Dason, prin. Fax 389-5063
Pleasant MS 300/6-8
3507 Smeltzer Rd 43302 740-389-5167
Lane Warner, prin. Fax 389-5111

River Valley Local SD
Supt. — See Caledonia
Heritage ES 500/K-5
720 Columbus Sandusky Rd S 43302 740-725-5500
Melanie Comstock, prin. Fax 725-5599

St. Mary S 200/K-8
274 N Prospect St 43302 740-382-1607
Jack Mental, prin. Fax 382-6577

Martins Ferry, Belmont, Pop. 6,765
Martins Ferry CSD 1,400/K-12
5001 Ayers Lime Stone Rd 43935 740-633-1732
Jim Fogle, supt. Fax 633-5666
www.mfcsd.k12.oh.us
Ayers ES 600/K-4
5002 Ayers Lime Stone Rd 43935 740-635-2444
Nick Stankovich, prin. Fax 635-3108
Martins Ferry MS 400/5-8
5000 Ayers Lime Stone Rd 43935 740-633-9741
Michael Delatore, prin. Fax 635-6107

Martins Ferry Christian S 100/K-7
710 S Zane Hwy 43935 740-633-0199
Becky Hill, admin. Fax 738-0516
St. Mary Central S 100/PK-8
24 N 4th St 43935 740-633-5424
Mary Nichelson, prin. Fax 633-5462
Speiro Academy, 500 N 5th St 43935 50/K-11
Susan Cline, prin. 740-738-0203

Marysville, Union, Pop. 21,701
Marysville EVD 5,100/K-12
1000 Edgewood Dr 43040 937-578-6100
Diane Mankins, supt. Fax 578-6113
www.marysville.k12.oh.us

Bunsold MS 900/7-8
14198 State Route 4 43040 937-578-6400
Michelle Kaffenbarger, prin. Fax 578-6413
Creekview IS 800/5-6
2000 Creekview Dr 43040 937-578-6600
Timothy Kannally, prin. Fax 578-6613
Edgewood ES 400/K-4
203 Grove St 43040 937-578-6800
David Hensinger, prin. Fax 578-6813
Mill Valley ES 400/K-4
633 Mill Wood Blvd 43040 937-578-6900
Amey McGlenn, prin. Fax 578-6913
Navin ES 400/K-4
16265 County Home Rd 43040 937-578-7000
Lynette Lewis, prin. Fax 578-7013
Northwood ES 500/K-4
2100 Creekview Dr 43040 937-578-7100
Karen Wells, prin. Fax 578-7113
Other Schools – See Raymond

St. John Lutheran S 200/K-8
12809 State Route 736 43040 937-644-5540
Cyndi Cathcart, prin. Fax 644-1086
Trinity Lutheran S 300/PK-6
220 S Walnut St 43040 937-642-1726
Lori Poling, prin.

Mason, Warren, Pop. 30,202
Mason CSD 10,300/PK-12
211 N East St 45040 513-398-0474
Dr. Gail Kist-Kline, supt. Fax 398-4554
www.masonohioschools.com
Mason ECC 1,400/PK-1
4631 Hickory Woods Ln 45040 513-398-3741
Melissa Bly, prin. Fax 398-2169
Mason IS Campus 2,600/4-6
6307 S Mason Montgomery Rd 45040 513-459-2850
Gregory Sears, prin. Fax 459-2874
Mason MS 1,800/7-8
6370 S Mason Montgomery Rd 45040 513-398-9035
Tonya Mccall, prin. Fax 459-0904
Western Row ES 1,000/2-3
755 Western Row Rd 45040 513-398-5821
James Messer, prin. Fax 398-1072

King of Kings Lutheran ECC 100/PK-K
3621 Socialville Foster Rd 45040 513-398-6089
Diane Horvath, dir. Fax 459-9896
Liberty Bible Academy 200/PK-12
4900 Old Irwin Simpson Rd 45040 513-754-1234
Dana Garwood, prin. Fax 754-1237
Mars Hill Academy 300/K-12
4230 Aero Dr 45040 513 770-3223
Montessori Academy of Cincinnati 200/PK-8
8293 Duke Blvd 45040 513-398-7773
Megan Ball, head sch Fax 398-1031
Royalmont Academy 200/PK-8
200 Northcrest Dr 45040 513-754-0555
Veronica Murphy, dir. Fax 754-0009
St. Susanna S 600/K-8
500 Reading Rd 45040 513-398-3821
Daniel Albrinck, prin. Fax 398-1657

Massillon, Stark, Pop. 31,305
Jackson Local SD 5,900/K-12
7602 Fulton Dr NW 44646 330-830-8000
Chris DiLoreto, supt. Fax 830-8008
jackson.stark.k12.oh.us
Amherst ES 600/K-5
8750 Jane St NW 44646 330-830-8024
William Hayden, prin. Fax 830-8071
Jackson Memorial MS 1,400/6-8
7355 Mudbrook St NW 44646 330-830-8034
Kacy Carter, prin. Fax 830-8068
Sauder ES 800/K-5
7503 Mudbrook St NW 44646 330-830-8028
J.R. Reindel, prin. Fax 830-8032
Strausser ES 700/K-5
8646 Strausser St NW 44646 330-830-8056
Susanne Waltman, prin. Fax 834-4656
Other Schools – See Canton

Massillon CSD 4,100/PK-12
930 17th St NE 44646 330-830-3900
Richard Goodright, supt. Fax 830-3901
www.massillonschools.org
Franklin ES 500/PK-3
1237 16th St SE 44646 330-830-3907
Mike Medure, prin. Fax 830-6532
Gorrell ES 400/K-3
2420 Schuler Ave NW 44647 330-830-3905
Alyssia Kappas, prin. Fax 830-6533
Massillon IS 900/4-6
250 29th St NW 44647 330-830-3902
Jarred Zapolnik, prin. Fax 830-3952
Massillon JHS 600/7-8
250 29th St NW 44647 330-830-3902
Vincent Lindsey, prin. Fax 830-3952
Massillon Preschool PK-PK
930 17th St NE 44646 330-830-3900
Kristi Muzi, coord.
Whittier ES 400/K-3
1212 10th St NE 44646 330-830-3904
Matthew Plybon, prin. Fax 830-6592

Perry Local SD 5,000/PK 12
4201 13th St SW 44646 330-477-8121
Scott Beatty, supt. Fax 478-6184
www.perrylocal.org
Edison MS 800/7-8
4201 13th St SW 44646 330-478-6167
Diane Kittelberger, prin. Fax 477 4612
Genoa ES 400/K-4
519 Genoa Ave SW 44646 330-478-6171
DaNita Berry, prin. Fax 478-6173
Pfeiffer IS 700/5-6
4315 13th St SW 44646 330-478-6163
William Hildebrand, prin. Fax 478-6800

Watson ES 300/K-4
515 Marion Ave NW 44646 330-832-8100
Stacy Daugherty, prin. Fax 832-1427
Other Schools – See Canton, Navarre

Tuslaw Local SD 1,400/PK-12
1835 Manchester Ave NW 44647 330-837-7813
Melissa Marconi, supt. Fax 837-7804
www.tuslaw.sparcc.org/
Tuslaw ES 400/PK-4
1920 Manchester Ave NW 44647 330-837-7809
Shelly Menuez, prin. Fax 837-7810
Tuslaw MS 500/5-8
1723 Manchester Ave NW 44647 330-837-7807
Mike Hamm, prin. Fax 837-6015

St. Barbara S 100/PK-5
2809 Lincoln Way NW 44647 330-833-9510
Jackie Thomas, prin. Fax 833-3297
St. Mary S 200/PK-8
640 1st St NE 44646 330-832-9355
Jennifer Fischer, prin. Fax 832-9030

Maumee, Lucas, Pop. 14,100
Maumee CSD 2,500/PK-12
716 Askin St 43537 419-893-3200
Todd Cramer, supt. Fax 891-5387
www.maumee.k12.oh.us
Fairfield ES 400/K-3
1313 Eastfield Dr 43537 419-893-9821
Michele Loboschefski, prin. Fax 891-5377
Fort Miami ES 300/K-3
2501 River Rd 43537 419-893-2201
Joel Hefner, prin. Fax 891-5380
Gateway MS 600/6-8
900 Gibbs St 43537 419-893-3386
Angela Wojcik, prin. Fax 893-2263
Wayne Trail ES 400/PK-PK, 4-
1147 7th St 43537 419-893-2851
Nick Neiderhouse, prin. Fax 891-5378

Perrysburg SD
Supt. — See Perrysburg
Perrysburg Preschool PK-PK
102 E Broadway St 43537 419-893-2221
Kristin Koester, prin.

St. Joseph S 200/PK-8
112 W Broadway St 43537 419-893-3304
David Nichols, prin. Fax 891-6969

Mayfield Heights, Cuyahoga, Pop. 18,836
Mayfield CSD 4,500/K-12
1101 SOM Center Rd 44124 440-995-6800
Dr. Keith Kelly, supt. Fax 995-7205
www.mayfieldschools.org
Center ES 400/K-5
6625 Wilson Mills Rd 44143 440-995-7400
Katharine Rateno, prin. Fax 995-7405
Lander ES 500/K-5
1714 Lander Rd 44124 440-995-7350
Felecia Evans, prin. Fax 995-7355
Mayfield MS 900/6-8
1123 SOM Center Rd 44124 440-995-7800
Paul Destino, prin. Fax 449-1413
Other Schools – See Gates Mills, Highland Heights

Mechanicsburg, Champaign, Pop. 1,610
Mechanicsburg EVD 900/K-12
60 High St 43044 937-834-2453
Danielle Prohaska, supt. Fax 834-3954
www.mechanicsburg.k12.oh.us
Mechanicsburg MS, 60 High St 43044 200/6-8
Marlo Schipfer, prin. 937-834-2453
Wilson ES 400/K-5
60 High St 43044 937-834-2453
Christy Garver, prin. Fax 834-3954

Medina, Medina, Pop. 26,154
Buckeye Local SD 2,200/PK-12
3044 Columbia Rd 44256 330-722-8257
Kent Morgan, supt. Fax 722-5793
www.buckeyeschools.org
Buckeye IS 600/PK-PK, 4-
3140 Columbia Rd 44256 330-722-8257
Kelli Knapp, prin. Fax 725-0164
Buckeye JHS 400/7-8
3024 Columbia Rd 44256 330-722-8257
Daniel Flood, prin. Fax 725-2413
Buckeye PS 700/K-3
3180 Columbia Rd 44256 330-722-8257
Dawn Hartwell, prin. Fax 723-0651

Highland Local SD 3,200/PK-12
3880 Ridge Rd 44256 330-239-1901
Catherine Aukerman, supt. Fax 239-2456
www.highlandschools.org
Granger ES 500/PK-5
3940 Ridge Rd 44256 330-239-1901
LeAnn Gausman, prin. Fax 239-7379
Highland MS 800/6-8
3880 Ridge Rd 44256 330-239-1901
Jonathan Henry, prin. Fax 239-7388
Sharon ES 400/K-5
6335 Ridge Rd 44256 330-239-1901
Kathryn Kowza, prin. Fax 239-7391
Other Schools – See Hinckley

Medina CSD 7,000/PK-12
739 Weymouth Rd 44256 330-725-8831
Aaron Sable, supt. Fax 636-3006
www.medinabees.org
Blake ES 500/K-5
4704 Lexington Ridge Dr 44256 330 636 3900
Eldora Lavdas, prin. Fax 764-3569
Canavan ES 400/K-5
825 Lawrence St 44256 330-636-4000
Brian Condit, prin. Fax 725-9379

Claggett MS 900/6-8
420 E Union St 44256 330-636-3600
Paul Worsencroft, prin. Fax 725-9349
Fenn ES 500/K-5
320 N Spring Grove St 44256 330-636-4100
Craig Komar, prin. Fax 725-9397
Garfield ES 300/K-5
234 S Broadway St 44256 330-636-4200
Karen McGinty, prin. Fax 725-9396
Heritage ES 400/K-5
833 Guilford Blvd 44256 330-636-4400
Shannon Federinko, prin. Fax 725-9394
Northrop ES 500/PK-5
950 E Reagan Pkwy 44256 330-636-4600
Kimberly Hallock, prin. Fax 722-2098
Root MS 800/6-8
333 W Sturbridge Dr 44256 330-636-3500
Bryan Farson, prin. Fax 764-1471
Waite ES 500/K-5
4765 Cobblestone Park Dr 44256 330-636-4500
Cindy Grice, prin. Fax 722-8010

Medina Christian Academy 200/PK-8
3646 Medina Rd 44256 330-725-3227
Paige Donahoe, prin. Fax 725-7762
St. Francis Xavier S 500/PK-8
612 E Washington St 44256 330-725-3345
Bibiana Seislove, prin. Fax 721-8626

Mentor, Lake, Pop. 46,722
Mentor EVD 7,500/K-12
6451 Center St 44060 440-255-4444
William Porter, supt. Fax 255-4622
www.mentorschools.net
Bellflower ES 400/K-5
6655 Reynolds Rd 44060 440-255-4212
Heather Hardy, prin. Fax 255-1602
Brentmoor ES 300/K-5
7671 Johnnycake Ridge Rd 44060 440-255-7813
Pam Hutto, prin. Fax 974-5272
Fairfax ES 300/K-5
6465 Curtiss Ct 44060 440-255-7223
Melanie Pearn, prin. Fax 974-5294
Garfield ES 400/K-5
7090 Hopkins Rd 44060 440-255-6609
Marc Kaminicki, prin. Fax 974-5283
Hopkins ES 500/K-5
7565 Hopkins Rd 44060 440-255-6179
Christine Riley, prin. Fax 974-5419
Lake ES 300/K-5
7625 Pinehurst Dr 44060 440-257-5953
Jodi Poremba, prin. Fax 257-8773
Memorial MS 700/6-8
8979 Mentor Ave 44060 440-974-2250
Adam Dudziak, prin. Fax 974-2259
Morton ES 300/K-5
9292 Jordan Dr 44060 440-257-5954
Jacqueline Sturm, prin. Fax 257-8799
Orchard Hollow ES 400/K-5
8700 Hendricks Rd 44060 440-257-5955
Karen Trunk, prin. Fax 257-8779
Ridge MS 500/6-8
7860 Johnnycake Ridge Rd 44060 440-974-5400
Ericka Blackburn, prin. Fax 974-5285
Shore MS 600/6-8
5670 Hopkins Rd 44060 440-257-8750
Michael Sears, prin. Fax 257-8761

St. Gabriel S 900/PK-8
9935 Johnnycake Ridge Rd 44060 440-352-6169
Donna Saladino, prin. Fax 639-0143
St. Mary of the Assumption S 500/PK-8
8540 Mentor Ave 44060 440-255-9781
Mary Benns, prin. Fax 974-8107

Mesopotamia, Trumbull
Bloomfield-Mespo Local SD
Supt. — See North Bloomfield
Mesopotamia ES 200/K-5
4466 Kinsman Rd 44439 440-693-4125
Russell McQuaide, prin. Fax 693-4656

Metamora, Fulton, Pop. 623
Evergreen Local SD 1,100/PK-12
14544 County Road 6 43540 419-644-3521
James Wyse, supt. Fax 644-6070
www.evergreen.k12.oh.us
Evergreen ES 500/PK-5
14844 County Road 6 43540 419-644-9221
Jane Draheim, prin. Fax 644-9226
Evergreen MS 300/6-8
14544 County Road 6 43540 419-644-2331
Joseph Zabowski, prin. Fax 644-9203

Miamisburg, Montgomery, Pop. 19,876
Miamisburg CSD 5,600/PK-12
540 Park Ave 45342 937-866-3381
Dr. David Vail, supt. Fax 865-5250
www.miamisburgcityschools.org
Bear ES 200/K-5
545 School St 45342 937-866-4691
Shannon Ruppert, prin. Fax 866-4065
Chance ES 400/K-5
10661 Wood Rd 45342 937-866-4461
Dale Geyer, prin. Fax 384-0560
Kinder ES, 536 E Central Ave 45342 400/K-5
Jeremy Saylor, prin. 937-866-4461
Maddux-Lang PS 100/PK-PK
4010 Crains Run Rd 45342 937-847-2766
Sarah Buzek, prin. Fax 847-8349
Medlar View ES 400/K-5
4400 Medlar Rd 45342 937-865-5257
Susan Woods, prin. Fax 865-5295
Miamisburg MS 1,300/6-8
8668 Miamisburg Springboro 45342 937-865-0011
Kelly Thomas, prin. Fax 865-0114

Mound ES 400/K-5
1108 Range Ave 45342 937-866-4641
Michael Black, prin. Fax 866-6767
Twain ES 400/K-5
822 N 9th St 45342 937-866-2581
Kelly Lee-Marker, prin. Fax 866-4085
Other Schools – See Dayton

Bishop Leibold Consolidated S West 200/PK-3
24 S 3rd St 45342 937-866-3021
Dr. Theodore Wallace, prin. Fax 866-5680
Dayton Christian S 1,000/PK-12
9391 Washington Church Rd 45342 937-291-7201
Dr. John Gredy, prin. Fax 291-7202

Miamitown, Hamilton, Pop. 1,242
Southwest Local SD
Supt. — See Harrison
Miamitown ES 300/K-6
6578 State Route 128 45041 513-353-1416
Dave Kelly, prin. Fax 353-9026

Middleburg Heights, Cuyahoga, Pop. 15,799
Berea CSD
Supt. — See Berea
Big Creek ES 600/PK-4
7247 Big Creek Pkwy 44130 216-898-8303
Katie Rolland, prin. Fax 898-8562

Academy of St. Bartholomew 400/PK-8
14875 Bagley Rd 44130 440-845-6660
Elizabeth Palascak, prin. Fax 845-6672

Middlefield, Geauga, Pop. 2,651
Cardinal Local SD 1,000/K-12
PO Box 188 44062 440-632-0261
Dr. Scott J. Hunt Ed.D., supt. Fax 632-5886
www.cardinalschools.org
Cardinal MS 300/5-8
PO Box 879 44062 440-632-0261
Andy Cardinal, prin. Fax 632-0294
Jordak ES 300/K-4
PO Box 188 44062 440-632-0261
Kelly Bearer, prin. Fax 632-5192

Middleport, Meigs, Pop. 2,488
Meigs Local SD
Supt. — See Pomeroy
Meigs IS 400/3-5
36871 State Route 124 45760 740-742-2666
Jody Howard, prin. Fax 742-2825
Meigs PS 400/K-2
36871 State Route 124 45760 740-742-3000
Kristin Baer, prin. Fax 742-2651

Mid Valley Christian S 100/PK-12
500 N 2nd Ave 45760 740-992-6249
Melissa Dailey, admin. Fax 992-6249

Middletown, Butler, Pop. 47,397
Madison Local SD 1,300/PK-12
1324 Middletown Eaton Rd 45042 513-420-4750
Curtis Philpot, supt. Fax 420-4781
www.madisonmohawks.org/
Madison ES 800/PK-6
5795 W Alexandria Rd 45042 513-420-4755
Jason Jackson, prin. Fax 420-4990

Middletown CSD 6,200/PK-12
1 Donham Plz Fl 4 45042 513-423-0781
Marlon Styles, supt. Fax 420-4579
www.middletowncityschools.com
Amanda ES 500/PK-5
1300 Oxford State Rd 45044 513-420-4542
Dr. Beth Hendricks, prin. Fax 420-4632
Central Academy 300/K-6
4601 Sophie Ave 45042 513-420-4537
Misha Monnin, prin. Fax 420-4589
Creekview ES 500/PK-5
4800 Timber Trail Dr 45044 513-420-4544
Kelly Wilham, prin. Fax 420-4587
Highview 6th Grade Center 400/6-6
106 S Highview Rd 45044 513-420-4566
Jennifer Dennis, prin. Fax 420-4647
Mayfield ES 500/K-5
3325 Burbank Ave 45044 513-420-4549
Heather Keal, prin. Fax 420-4551
Middleton MS 800/7-8
1415 Girard Ave 45044 513-420-4528
Michael Valenti, prin. Fax 420-4527
Miller Ridge ES 500/K-5
4704 Miller Rd 45042 513-420-4559
Kee Edwards, prin. Fax 420-4560
Parks ES 600/PK-5
1210 S Verity Pkwy 45044 513-420-4552
Fax 420-4553
Wildwood ES 500/PK-5
3300 Wildwood Rd 45042 513-420-4564
Keri Hensley, prin. Fax 420-4627

St John XXIII Consolidated S 400/K-8
3806 Manchester Rd 45042 513-424-1196
Dawn Pickerill, prin. Fax 420-8480

Midvale, Tuscarawas, Pop. 748
Indian Valley Local SD
Supt. — See Gnadenhutten
Midvale ES 500/K-5
4259 W State St 44653 330-339-1191
Ryan Wells, prin. Fax 339-1194

Milan, Erie, Pop. 1,356
Edison Local SD 1,600/PK-12
140 S Main St 44846 419-499-3000
Thomas Roth, supt. Fax 499-4859
www.edisonchargers.org/
Edison ES 500/PK-3
140 S Main St 44846 419-499-2471
David Hermes, prin. Fax 499-4859

Other Schools – See Berlin Heights

Milford, Clermont, Pop. 6,599
Milford EVD 6,600/PK-12
777 Garfield Ave 45150 513-831-1314
Nancy C. House, supt. Fax 831-3208
www.milfordschools.org
Meadowview ES 700/K-6
5556 Mount Zion Rd 45150 513-831-9170
Kelli Ellison, prin. Fax 831-9340
Milford JHS 1,000/7-8
5735 Pleasant Hill Rd 45150 513-831-1900
Rob Dunn, prin. Fax 248-3451
Milford Preschool 100/PK-PK
1039 State Route 28 45150 513-831-9690
Minna Espy, dir. Fax 831-8764
Mulberry ES 700/K-6
5950 Buckwheat Rd 45150 513-722-3588
Sarah Sloan, prin. Fax 722-4584
Pattison ES 700/K-6
5330 S Milford Rd 45150 513-831-6570
Melissa Borger, prin. Fax 831-9693
Seipelt ES 400/K-6
900 State Route 131 45150 513-831-9460
Sarah Greb, prin. Fax 248-5443
Smith ES 500/K-6
1052 Jer Les St 45150 513-575-1643
Douglas Savage, prin. Fax 575-2835
Other Schools – See Loveland

St. Andrew/St. Elizabeth Ann Seton S 200/PK-5
5900 Buckwheat Rd 45150 513-575-0093
Mark Wilburn, prin. Fax 575-1078
St. Andrew/St. Elizabeth Ann Seton S 200/6-8
555 Main St 45150 513-831-5277
Mark Wilburn, prin. Fax 831-8436
St. Mark's Lutheran S 200/PK-8
5849 Buckwheat Rd 45150 513-575-3354
Timothy Kollmorgen, prin. Fax 575-2472

Milford Center, Union, Pop. 776
Fairbanks Local SD 1,000/K-12
11158 State Route 38 43045 937-349-3731
Robert Humble, supt. Fax 349-8885
www.fairbanks.k12.oh.us
Fairbanks ES 400/K-5
11140 State Route 38 43045 937-349-9000
Mark Lotycz, prin. Fax 349-9001
Fairbanks MS 300/6-8
11158 State Route 38 43045 937-349-6841
Thomas Montgomery, prin. Fax 349-2013

Millbury, Wood, Pop. 1,191
Lake Local SD 1,600/PK 12
28090 Lemoyne Rd 43447 419-661-6690
Jim Witt, supt. Fax 661-6678
www.lakeschools.org
Lake ES 600/PK-4
28150 Lemoyne Rd 43447 419-661-6680
Melissa Dimmerling, prin. Fax 661-6683
Lake MS 300/5-7
28100 Lemoyne Rd 43447 419-661-6660
Katie Beard, prin. Fax 661-6664

Miller City, Putnam, Pop. 137
Miller City-New Cleveland Local SD 500/K-12
200 N Main St 45864 419-876-3172
Kerry Johnson, supt. Fax 876-3849
www.mcncschools.org
Miller City-New Cleveland ES 200/K-5
5195 SR 108 45864 419-876-3174
Dustin Pester, prin. Fax 876-2020
Miller City-New Cleveland MS 100/6-8
5195 SR 108 45864 419-876-3174
Dustin Pester, prin. Fax 876-2020

Millersburg, Holmes, Pop. 2,985
East Holmes Local SD 1,800/K-12
6108 County Road 77 44654 330-893-2610
Erik Beun, supt. Fax 893-2838
www.eastholmes.k12.oh.us
Other Schools – See Berlin, Charm, Mount Hope, Walnut Creek, Winesburg

West Holmes Local SD 2,400/K-12
28 W Jackson St 44654 330-674-3546
William Sterling, supt. Fax 674-6833
www.westholmes.k12.oh.us
Clark ES 100/K-5
1390 State Route 83 44654 330-674-7936
Diana McMillen, prin. Fax 674-3246
Millersburg ES 400/K-5
430 E Jackson St 44654 330-674-5681
Renee Woods, prin. Fax 674-2506
West Holmes MS 600/6-8
10901 State Route 39 44654 330-674-4761
Jeff Woods, prin. Fax 674-2311
Other Schools – See Big Prairie, Killbuck, Lakeville

Gospel Haven Academy 100/K-12
6871 State Route 241 44654 330-674-0752
Kendrick Miller, prin. Fax 674-0752

Millersport, Fairfield, Pop. 1,033
Walnut Township Local SD 600/K-12
11850 Lancaster St 43046 740-467-2802
Randall Cotner, supt. Fax 467-3494
www.walnuttsd.org
Millersport ES 300/K-6
11850 Lancaster St 43046 740-467-2216
Kim Yenni, prin. Fax 467-3494

Mineral City, Tuscarawas, Pop. 717
Tuscarawas Valley Local SD
Supt. — See Zoarville
Tuscarawas Valley PS 200/PK-1
PO Box 428 44656 330-859-2461
Andrea Clements, prin. Fax 859-8885

Mineral Ridge, Trumbull, Pop. 3,840
Weathersfield Local SD 900/K-12
1334 Seaborn St 44440 330-652-0287
Damon Dohar, supt. Fax 544-7476
www.weathersfield.k12.oh.us
Seaborn ES 500/K-6
3800 Niles Carver Rd 44440 330-652-9695
Thomas Koniowsky, prin. Fax 544-7482

Minerva, Stark, Pop. 3,671
Minerva Local SD 1,800/K-12
406 East St 44657 330-868-4332
Gary Chaddock, supt. Fax 868-4731
www.mlsd.sparcc.org
Minerva ES 800/K-5
130 Bonnieview Ave 44657 330-868-4011
Mark Scott, prin. Fax 868-3681
Minerva MS 500/6-8
600 E Line St 44657 330-868-4497
Scott Cassidy, prin. Fax 868-3144

Minerva Area Christian S 100/PK-12
300 W Lincolnway 44657 330-868-5728
Beverly Kennedy, admin. Fax 868-5834

Minford, Scioto, Pop. 684
Minford Local SD 1,400/K-12
491 Bond Rd 45653 740-820-3896
Jeremy Litteral, supt. Fax 820-3334
www.minfordfalcons.net
Minford MS 600/4-8
135 Falcon Rd 45653 740-820-2181
Dennis Evans, prin. Fax 820-2191
Minford PS 400/K-3
215 Falcon Rd 45653 740-820-2287
Cecil Mcgraw, prin. Fax 820-2466

Mingo Junction, Jefferson, Pop. 3,405
Indian Creek Local SD
Supt. — See Wintersville
Hills ES 300/PK-4
2281 Wilson Ave 43938 740-283-2479
Michele Minto, prin. Fax 283-2286
Indian Creek MS 300/5-8
2379 Wilson Ave 43938 740-282-0834
Dr. Holly Minch-Hick, prin. Fax 282-3092

Minster, Auglaize, Pop. 2,793
Minster Local SD 900/K-12
50 E 7th St 45865 419-628-3397
Brenda Boeke, supt. Fax 628-2482
www.minsterschools.org
Minster ES 500/K-6
50 E 7th St 45865 419-628-4174
Leanne Keller, prin. Fax 628-2482

Mogadore, Summit, Pop. 3,799
Field Local SD 2,000/K-12
2900 State Route 43 44260 330-673-2659
David Heflinger, supt. Fax 673-0270
www.fieldlocalschools.org
Field MS, 1379 Saxe Rd 44260 500/6-8
Susan Blake, prin. 330-673-4176
Other Schools – See Kent, Suffield

Mogadore Local SD 700/K-12
1 S Cleveland Ave 44260 330-628-9946
Dr. John Knapp, supt. Fax 628-6661
www.mogadore.net
Somers ES 500/K-6
3600 Herbert St 44260 330-628-9947
John Knapp, prin. Fax 628-6662

St. Joseph S 100/PK-8
2617 Waterloo Rd Ste 1 44260 330-628-9555
Beth Frank, prin. Fax 628-9942

Monclova, Lucas
Anthony Wayne Local SD
Supt. — See Whitehouse
Monclova ES 600/K-4
8035 Monclova Rd 43542 419-865-9408
Betsey Murry, prin. Fax 865-1397

Monclova Christian Academy 200/K-12
7819 Monclova Rd 43542 419-866-7630
Neil Black, supt. Fax 868-1062

Monroe, Butler, Pop. 12,294
Monroe Local SD 2,500/PK-12
500 Yankee Rd 45050 513-539-2536
Dr. Philip Cagwin, supt. Fax 539-2648
www.monroelocalschools.com/
Monroe ES 1,000/2-6
230 Yankee Rd 45050 513-539-8101
Nancy Stratton, prin. Fax 539-8151
Monroe PS 500/PK-1
225 Macready Ave 45050 513-360-0700
Kathy Gall, prin. Fax 360-0720

Monroeville, Huron, Pop. 1,379
Monroeville Local SD 600/K-12
101 West St 44847 419-465-2610
G. Ralph Moore, supt. Fax 465-4263
www.monroevilleschools.org/
Monroeville ES 300/K-6
101 West St 44847 419-465-2533
William Butler, prin. Fax 465-3549

St. Joseph S 100/PK-8
79 Chapel St 44847 419-465-2625
David McDowell, prin. Fax 465-2170

Montpelier, Williams, Pop. 4,026
Montpelier EVD 900/PK-12
1015 E Brown Rd 43543 419-485-6700
Jamison Grime, supt. Fax 485-3487
www.montpelier-k12.org

Montpelier ES 500/PK-6
1015 E Brown Rd 43543 419-485-6701
Lance Thorp, prin. Fax 485-3487

Moraine, Montgomery, Pop. 6,134
Kettering CSD
Supt. — See Kettering
Kettering ECC 100/PK-PK
2600 Holman St 45439 937-499-1450
Cindy Smith, admin. Fax 499-1517

Morral, Marion, Pop. 394
Ridgedale Local SD 700/K-12
3103 Hillman Ford Rd 43337 740-382-6065
Robert Britton, supt. Fax 383-6538
www.ridgedale.k12.oh.us/
Ridgedale ES 300/K-5
3105 Hillman Ford Rd 43337 740-382-6065
Samuel Staton, prin. Fax 383-6538

Morrow, Warren, Pop. 1,164
Little Miami Local SD
Supt. — See Maineville
Little Miami JHS 600/7-8
5290 Morrow Cozaddale Rd 45152 513-899-3408
Ryan Cherry, prin. Fax 899-2048
Little Miami Preschool PK-PK
605 Welch Rd 45152 513-899-5275
Erin Losey, dir. Fax 899-3196
Salem Township ES 800/PK-K, 3-4
605 Welch Rd 45152 513-899-5275
Lisa Smith, prin. Fax 899-2891

Mount Blanchard, Hancock, Pop. 482
Riverdale Local SD 800/K-12
20613 State Route 37 45867 419-694-4994
Jeffrey Young, supt. Fax 694-6465
www.riverdale.k12.oh.us
Riverdale ES 200/K-5
20613 State Route 37 45867 419-694-2211
Dr. Julie Greer, prin. Fax 694-8005
Riverdale MS 200/6-8
20613 State Route 37 45867 419-694-2211
Dan Evans, prin. Fax 694-5008

Mount Eaton, Wayne, Pop. 239
Southeast Local SD
Supt. — See Apple Creek
Mount Eaton ES 200/K-8
PO Box 268 44659 330-359-5519
Patti Arnold, prin. Fax 857-3703

Mount Gilead, Morrow, Pop. 3,594
Mt. Gilead EVD 1,200/PK-12
145 N Cherry St 43338 419-946-1646
Jeffrey Thompson, supt. Fax 946-3651
www.mgschools.org
Mount Gilead MS 300/6-8
324 W Park Ave 43338 419-947-9517
Jon Grega, prin. Fax 947-9518
Park Avenue ES 600/PK-5
335 W Park Ave 43338 419-946-5736
Chris Kamenski, prin. Fax 946-2336

Gilead Christian S North Campus 200/K-5
220 S Main St 43338 419-947-5739
Bryan Potteiger, admin. Fax 947-5010

Mount Healthy, Hamilton, Pop. 5,926
Mt. Healthy CSD 3,200/K-12
7615 Harrison Ave 45231 513-729-0077
Reva Cosby, supt. Fax 728-4692
www.mthcs.org
Other Schools – See Cincinnati

Mount Hope, Holmes
East Holmes Local SD
Supt. — See Millersburg
Mount Hope S 100/K-8
8242 SR 241 44660 330-674-0418
James Luneborg, prin. Fax 674-4647

Mount Orab, Brown, Pop. 3,635
Western Brown Local SD 3,100/PK-12
524 W Main St 45154 937-444-2044
Raegan White, supt. Fax 444-4303
www.wb.k12.oh.us
Mount Orab ES 900/PK-4
474 W Main St 45154 937-444-2528
Marty Paeltz, prin. Fax 444-4183
Mount Orab MS 800/5-8
472 W Main St 45154 937-444-2529
Sabrina Armstrong, prin. Fax 444-4268
Other Schools – See Hamersville

Mount Vernon, Knox, Pop. 16,729
Mt. Vernon CSD 3,800/PK-12
300 Newark Rd 43050 740-397-7422
William Seder, supt. Fax 393-5949
www.mvcsd.us/
Columbia ES 200/K-5
150 Columbus Rd 43050 740-393-5975
Dr. Matthew Dill, prin. Fax 393-5976
East ES 300/K-5
714 E Vine St 43050 740-393-5985
Dr. Teresa Weaver, prin. Fax 393-5987
Emmett ES 300/K-5
108 Mansfield Ave 43050 740-393-5950
Margaret Arck, prin. Fax 393-5953
Mount Vernon MS 900/6-8
298 Martinsburg Rd 43050 740-392-6867
Gary Hankins, prin. Fax 392-3369
Pleasant Street ES 500/PK-5
305 E Pleasant St 43050 740-393-5990
Karen Boylan, prin. Fax 393-3175
Twin Oak ES 400/K-5
8888 Martinsburg Rd 43050 740-393-5970
Suzanne Miller, prin. Fax 397-2598
Other Schools – See Gambier

Christian Star Academy 50/K-12
7 E Sugar St 43050 740-393-0251
Suzanne Feasel, admin. Fax 393-0067
Mount Vernon SDA ES 50/K-8
PO Box 891 43050 740-393-7060
Kimberly Myers, prin. Fax 393-7060
St. Vincent de Paul S 200/PK-8
206 E Chestnut St 43050 740-393-3611
Martha Downs, prin. Fax 393-0236

Mount Victory, Hardin, Pop. 626
Ridgemont Local SD 500/PK-12
560 Taylor St W 43340 937-354-2441
Dr. Suzanne Darmer, supt. Fax 354-2194
www.ridgemont.k12.oh.us
Ridgemont ES 300/PK-6
560 Taylor St W 43340 937-354-2141
Sally Henrick, prin. Fax 354-5099

Mowrystown, Highland, Pop. 359
Bright Local SD 600/PK-12
PO Box 299 45155 937-442-3114
Ted Downing, supt. Fax 442-6655
www.brightlocalschools.com
Other Schools – See Hillsboro

Munroe Falls, Summit, Pop. 4,951
Stow-Munroe Falls CSD
Supt. — See Stow
Kimpton MS 900/7-8
380 N River Rd 44262 330-689-5288
Susan Palchesko, prin. Fax 686-4718
Riverview ES 200/K-4
240 N River Rd 44262 330-689-5310
Traci Kosmach, prin. Fax 686-4713

Napoleon, Henry, Pop. 8,677
Napoleon Area CSD 1,500/PK-12
701 Briarheath Ave Ste 108 43545 419-599-7015
Dr. Stephen R. Fogo, supt. Fax 599-7035
www.napoleonareaschools.org/
Napoleon ES 3-6
725 Westmoreland Ave 43545 419-592-6991
Adam Niese, prin. Fax 599-7638
Napoleon PS PK-2
725 Westmoreland Ave 43545 419-592-6991
Matthew Dietrich, prin. Fax 599-7638

St. Augustine S 100/PK-8
722 Monroe St 43545 419-592-3641
James George, prin. Fax 592-6316
St. John Lutheran S 100/PK-8
16035 County Road U 43545 419-598-8702
Charles Kramer, prin. Fax 598-8518
St. Paul Lutheran S 200/PK-8
1075 Glenwood Ave 43545 419-592-5536
Christine Spohn, prin. Fax 592-0652

Nashport, Muskingum
Tri-Valley Local SD
Supt. — See Dresden
Nashport ES 500/K-6
3775 Creamery Rd 43830 740-452-3977
Larry Bevard, prin. Fax 452-7101

Navarre, Stark, Pop. 1,939
Fairless Local SD 1,500/K-12
11885 Navarre Rd SW 44662 330-767-3577
Broc Bidlack, supt. Fax 767-3298
www.fairlesslocalschools.org
Fairless ES 700/K-5
12000 Navarre Rd SW 44662 330-767-3913
Colleen Kornish, prin. Fax 767-4398
Fairless MS 400/6-8
11836 Navarre Rd SW 44662 330-767-4293
Cindy Class, prin. Fax 767-3807

Perry Local SD
Supt. — See Massillon
Lohr ES 300/K-4
5300 Richville Dr SW 44662 330-484-3924
Nicholas Huskins, prin. Fax 484-4987

Nelsonville, Athens, Pop. 5,295
Nelsonville-York CSD 1,300/PK-12
2 Buckeye Dr 45764 740-753-4441
Charles McClelland, supt. Fax 753-1968
www.nelsonvilleyork.k12.oh.us/
Nelsonville-York ES 700/PK-6
4 Buckeye Dr 45764 740-753-4441
Rebecca Dalton, prin. Fax 753-6207
Nelsonville-York MS 200/7-8
3 Buckeye Dr 45764 740-753-4441
Thomas Taggart, prin. Fax 753-9450

New Albany, Franklin, Pop. 7,553
New Albany - Plain Local SD 5,400/PK-12
55 N High St 43054 614-855-2040
Michael Sawyers, supt. Fax 855-2043
www.napls.us
New Albany Early Learning Center 700/PK-K
5101 Swickard Woods Blvd 43054 614-413-8700
Michelle Unger, prin. Fax 413-8701
New Albany IS 1,500/4-6
87 N High St 43054 614-413-8600
Katherine Nowak, prin. Fax 413-8601
New Albany MS 1,200/7-8
6600 E Dublin Granville Rd 43054 614-413-8500
Donna LeBeau, prin. Fax 413-8501
New Albany PS 700/1-3
87 N High St 43054 614-413-8600
Teresa Smith, prin. Fax 413-8601

Newark, Licking, Pop. 46,372
Licking Valley Local SD 2,000/K-12
1379 Licking Valley Rd 43055 740-763-3525
David Hile, supt. Fax 763-0471
www.lickingvalley.k12.oh.us/
Licking Valley ES 900/K-5
1510 Licking Valley Rd 43055 740-763-2031
Sherry Crum, prin. Fax 763-3227
Licking Valley MS 500/6-8
1379 Licking Valley Rd 43055 740-763-3396
Scott Beery, prin. Fax 763-2612

Newark CSD 6,200/PK-12
621 Mount Vernon Rd 43055 740-670-7000
Douglas Ute, supt. Fax 670-7009
www.newarkcityschools.org
Carson ES 500/K-5
549 E Main St 43055 740-670-7300
Julie Elwell, prin. Fax 670-7309
Cherry Valley ES 500/PK-5
1040 W Main St 43055 740-670-7330
Chester Coleman, prin. Fax 670-7339
Clem ES 500/PK-5
475 Jefferson Rd 43055 740-670-7130
Lynda Nabors, prin. Fax 670-7139
Franklin ES 400/K-5
533 Beacon Rd 43055 740-670-7340
Dena Cable-Miller, prin. Fax 670-7349
Heritage MS 500/6-8
600 Arlington Ave 43055 740-670-7110
Brent Fickes, prin. Fax 670-7119
Hillview ES 500/PK-5
1927 Horns Hill Rd 43055 740-670-7310
Nick Myers, prin. Fax 670-7319
Legend ES 500/PK-5
1075 Evans Blvd 43055 740-670-7100
Ellen Cooper, prin. Fax 670-7109
Liberty MS 500/6-8
1055 Evans Blvd 43055 740-670-7320
Diane Henry, prin. Fax 670-7329
McGuffey ES 500/K-5
130 Green Wave Dr 43055 740-670-7140
Cynthia Baker, prin. Fax 670-7149
Wilson MS 400/6-8
805 W Church St 43055 740-670-7120
John Davis, prin. Fax 670-7129

North Fork Local SD
Supt. — See Utica
Newton ES 400/K-5
6645 Mount Vernon Rd 43055 740-745-5982
Michele Gorius, prin. Fax 745-5524

Blessed Sacrament S 200/K-8
394 E Main St 43055 740-345-4125
Mary Packham, prin. Fax 345-6168
St. Francis De Sales S 400/PK-8
38 Granville St 43055 740-345-4049
Sally Mummey, prin. Fax 345-9768

New Boston, Scioto, Pop. 2,223
New Boston Local SD 500/PK-12
1 Glenwood Tiger Trl 45662 740-456-4559
Melinda Burnside, supt. Fax 456-6402
www.newboston.k12.oh.us
Oak IS 100/4-6
1 Glenwood Tiger Trl 45662 740-456-5225
Christina Dever, prin. Fax 456-6402
Stanton PS 200/PK-3
1 Glenwood Tiger Trl 45662 740-456-4637
Christina Dever, prin. Fax 456-6402

New Bremen, Auglaize, Pop. 2,950
New Bremen Local SD 800/K-12
901 E Monroe St 45869 419-629-8606
Jason Schrader, supt. Fax 629-0115
www.newbremenschools.org
New Bremen ES 600/K-8
202 S Walnut St 45869 419-629-3244
Diane Kramer, prin. Fax 629-8113

Newbury, Geauga
Newbury Local SD 500/K-12
14775 Auburn Rd 44065 440-564-5501
Michelle Mrakovich, supt. Fax 564-9460
www.newburyschools.org/
Newbury ES 200/K-5
14775 Auburn Rd 44065 440-564-2282
Cynthia Tomassetti, prin. Fax 564-9788

St. Helen S 200/PK-8
12060 Kinsman Rd 44065 440-564-7125
Sr. Margaret Hartman, prin. Fax 564-7969

New Carlisle, Clark, Pop. 5,735
Tecumseh Local SD 2,600/K-12
9760 W National Rd 45344 937-845-3576
Norm Glicmann, supt. Fax 845-4453
www.tecumseh.k12.oh.us
New Carlisle ES 500/4-5
1203 Kennison Ave 45344 937-845-4480
Kathryn Randenburg, prin. Fax 845-4482
Park Layne ES 500/K-1
12355 Dille Rd 45344 937-845-4470
Karyl Strader, prin. Fax 845-4458
Tecumseh MS 800/6-8
10000 W National Rd 45344 937-845-4465
Brian Dixon, prin. Fax 845-4484
Other Schools – See Donnelsville

Newcomerstown, Tuscarawas, Pop. 3,763
Newcomerstown EVD 1,000/PK-12
702 S River St 43832 740-498-8373
Jeffrey Staggs, supt. Fax 498-8375
www.nctschools.org
Newcomerstown East ES 200/K-1
137 S College St 43832 740-498-6601
Brian Collins, prin. Fax 498-4997
Newcomerstown MS 200/6-8
325 W State St 43832 740-498-8151
Jason Peoples, prin. Fax 498-4991
Newcomerstown West ES 300/PK-5
517 Beaver St 43832 740-498-4151
Erin Peoples, prin. Fax 498-4998

New Concord, Muskingum, Pop. 2,459
East Muskingum Local SD 2,100/K-12
13505 John Glenn School Rd 43762 740-826-7655
Jill Sheridan, supt. Fax 826-7194
www.east-muskingum.k12.oh.us
East Muskingum MS 500/6-8
13120 John Glenn School Rd 43762 740-826-7631
Trent Cubbison, prin. Fax 826-4392
Miller IS 500/3-5
13125 John Glenn School Rd 43762 740-826-2271
Mike House, prin. Fax 826-7443
New Concord ES 300/K-2
4 Stormont St 43762 740-826-4453
Chad Briggs, prin. Fax 826-1332
Other Schools – See Cambridge, Zanesville

New Knoxville, Auglaize, Pop. 875
New Knoxville Local SD 300/K-12
PO Box 476 45871 419-753-2431
Kim Waterman, supt. Fax 753-2333
www.nkrangers.org
New Knoxville ES 200/K-3
PO Box 476 45871 419-753-2431
Kim Waterman, prin. Fax 753-2333

New Lebanon, Montgomery, Pop. 3,918
New Lebanon Local SD 1,100/K-12
320 S Fuls Rd 45345 937-687-1301
Dr. Greg Williams, supt. Fax 687-7321
www.newlebanonschools.org
Dixie ES 400/K-4
1150 W Main St 45345 937-687-3511
Holly Keadle, prin. Fax 687-3579
Dixie MS 300/5-8
200 S Fuls Rd 45345 937-687-3508
Thom Maxwell, prin. Fax 687-7705

New Lexington, Perry, Pop. 4,679
New Lexington CSD 1,800/K-12
2549 Panther Dr 43764 740-342-4133
Casey Coffey, supt. Fax 342-6051
www.nlpanthers.org
New Lexington ES 500/K-5
2550 Panther Dr NE 43764 740-342-2556
Greg Grant, prin. Fax 342-6062
New Lexington MS 400/6-8
2549 Panther Dr NE 43764 740-342-4128
Fax 342-6071
Other Schools – See Junction City

St. Rose of Lima S 100/K-8
119 W Water St 43764 740-342-3043
Michael Lollo, prin. Fax 342-1082

New London, Huron, Pop. 2,415
New London Local SD 900/PK-12
2 Wildcat Dr 44851 419-929-8433
Bradley Romano, supt. Fax 929-4108
www.nlschools.org
New London ES 500/PK-5
1 Wildcat Dr 44851 419-929-8117
Amanda Accavallo, prin. Fax 929-9512
New London MS 200/6-8
1 Wildcat Dr 44851 419-929-5409
Christopher Dulka, prin. Fax 929-9513

New Madison, Darke, Pop. 886
Tri-Village Local SD 700/K-12
315 S Main St 45346 937-996-6261
Joshua Sagester, supt. Fax 996-5537
www.tri-village.k12.oh.us
Tri-Village ES 400/K-6
315 S Main St 45346 937-996-1511
Shane Mead, prin. Fax 996-0307

New Matamoras, Washington, Pop. 879
Frontier Local SD 500/K-12
44870 State Route 7 45767 740-865-3473
Brian Rentsch, supt. Fax 865-2010
www.frontierlocalschools.com
Matamoras ES 100/K-6
PO Box 339 45767 740-865-3422
William Creighton, prin. Fax 865-3423
Other Schools – See Newport

New Middletown, Mahoning, Pop. 1,611
Springfield Local SD 1,100/K-12
11335 Yngstwn Pittsburgh Rd 44442 330-542-2929
Thomas Yazvac, supt. Fax 542-9453
www.springfieldlocal.us
Springfield ES 400/K-4
11419 Yngstwn Pittsburgh Rd 44442 330-542-3722
Anthony Albanese, prin. Fax 542-2488
Springfield IS 400/5-8
11333 Youngstown Pittsburgh 44442 330-542-3624
David Malone, prin. Fax 542-2159

New Paris, Preble, Pop. 1,607
National Trail Local SD 1,000/K-12
6940 Oxford Gettysburg Rd 45347 937-437-3333
Jeff Parker, supt. Fax 437-7865
www.nationaltrail.k12.oh.us/
National Trail ES 400/K-4
6940 Oxford Gettysburg Rd 45347 937-437-3333
Ed Eales, prin. Fax 437-7306
National Trail MS 300/5-8
6940 Oxford Gettysburg Rd 45347 937-437-3333
Michael Eyler, prin. Fax 437-7306

New Philadelphia, Tuscarawas, Pop. 17,008
New Philadelphia CSD 3,000/PK-12
248 Front Ave SW 44663 330-364-0600
David Brand, supt. Fax 364-9310
www.npschools.org
Central ES 300/K-5
145 Ray Ave NW 44663 330-364-0700
John Zucal, prin. Fax 364-0611
East ES 300/PK-5
470 Fair Ave NE 44663 330-364-0715
Ryan Holmes, prin. Fax 343-6891
South ES 500/PK-5
132 Providence Ave SW 44663 330-364-0725
Jacklyn Triplett, prin. Fax 364-0730
Welty MS 700/6-8
315 4th St NW 44663 330-364-0645
Carl McCrory, prin. Fax 364-0677
West ES 300/PK-5
232 Tuscarawas Ave NW 44663 330-364-0755
Christa Frantz, prin. Fax 364-0758
York ES 200/K-5
938 Stonecreek Rd SW 44663 330-364-0770
Jaclyn Smolinski, prin. Fax 364-0773

Newport, Washington
Frontier Local SD
Supt. — See New Matamoras
Newport ES 200/K-6
100 Harrison St 45768 740-473-2667
Brian Williams, prin. Fax 473-2963

New Richmond, Clermont, Pop. 2,535
New Richmond EVD 2,400/K-12
212 Market St 45157 513-553-2616
Adam Bird, supt. Fax 553-6431
www.nrschools.org
Monroe ES 400/K-6
2117 Laurel Lindale Rd 45157 513-553-3183
William Horn, prin. Fax 553-6033
New Richmond ES 400/K-6
1141 Bethel New Richmond Rd 45157 513-553-3181
Jamie Kunz, prin. Fax 553-2604
New Richmond MS 400/7-8
1135 Bethel New Richmond Rd 45157 513-553-3161
Courtney Lilly, prin. Fax 553-6412
Other Schools – See Cincinnati

New Riegel, Seneca, Pop. 248
New Riegel Local SD 400/K-12
44 N Perry St 44853 419-595-2256
David Rombach, supt. Fax 595-2901
newriegelschools.org
New Riegel ES 200/K-4
44 N Perry St 44853 419-595-2256
David Rombach, prin. Fax 595-2901

Newton Falls, Trumbull, Pop. 4,737
Newton Falls EVD 1,200/K-12
909 1/2 Milton Blvd 44444 330-872-5445
Paul Woodard, supt. Fax 872-3351
www.newton-falls.k12.oh.us/
Newton Falls ES 300/K-3
909 Milton Blvd 44444 330-872-5225
Ron Purnell, prin. Fax 872-0228
Newton Falls MS 300/4-6
905 Milton Blvd 44444 330-872-0695
Thomas Sullivan, prin. Fax 872-8327

New Vienna, Clinton, Pop. 1,211
East Clinton Local SD
Supt. — See Sabina
New Vienna ES 300/PK-5
301 E Church St 45159 937-987-2448
Jason Jones, prin. Fax 987-2485

New Washington, Crawford, Pop. 962
Buckeye Central Local SD 700/K-12
938 S Kibler St 44854 419-492-2864
Mark Robinson, supt. Fax 492-2039
www.buckeye-central.k12.oh.us
Buckeye Central ES 300/K-4
938 S Kibler St 44854 419-492-1022
Matthew Millinger, prin. Fax 492-2039
Buckeye Central MS 200/5-8
938 S Kibler St 44854 419-492-1035
Deborah Daniel, prin. Fax 492-2039

St. Bernard S 100/PK-8
320 W Mansfield St 44854 419-492-2693
Mary Obringer, prin. Fax 492-2604

Niles, Trumbull, Pop. 18,878
Niles CSD 2,400/K-12
309 N Rhodes Ave 44446 330-989-5095
Ann Marie Thigpen, supt. Fax 989-5096
www.nilescityschools.org/
Niles IS 600/3-5
120 E Margaret Ave 44446 330-989-5093
Christopher Staph, prin. Fax 989-5094
Niles MS 600/6-8
411 Brown St 44446 330-652-5656
Samuel Reigle, prin. Fax 652-9158
Niles PS 500/K-2
960 Frederick St 44446 330-989-5091
Joanna Gatta, prin. Fax 989-5092

Victory Christian S 100/K-12
2053 Pleasant Valley Rd 44446 330-539-9827
Colleen McCullough, prin. Fax 539-9828

North Baltimore, Wood, Pop. 3,396
North Baltimore Local SD 600/PK-12
201 S Main St 45872 419-257-3531
Ryan Delaney, supt. Fax 257-2008
www.nbls.org
North Baltimore MS 100/7-8
2012 Tiger Dr 45872 419-257-3464
Dr. Bob Falkenstein Ph.D., prin. Fax 257-0084
Powell ES 400/PK-6
500 N Main St 45872 419-257-2124
Dr. Mark Lange M.D., prin. Fax 257-3044

North Bloomfield, Trumbull
Bloomfield-Mespo Local SD 300/K-12
2077 Park West Rd 44450 440-685-4711
John Sheets, supt. Fax 685-4751
www.bloomfieldmesposchools.org
Other Schools – See Mesopotamia

North Canton, Stark, Pop. 17,236
Canton CSD
Supt. — See Canton
Portage Montessori S 200/K-8
1000 55th St NE, Canton OH 44721 330-966-1912
Kim Rimmele, prin. Fax 966-0737

North Canton CSD 4,600/PK-12
525 7th St NE 44720 330-497-5600
Jeff Wendorf, supt. Fax 497-5618
www.northcantonschools.org
Clearmount ES 400/K-2
150 Clearmount Ave SE 44720 330-497-5640
Matthew Ile, prin. Fax 966-0801
Evans ECC 50/PK-K
301 Portage St NW 44720 330-497-5608
Michael Coppa, prin. Fax 966-0703
Greentown IS 500/3-5
3330 State St NW 44720 330-497-5645
Ryan Kumpf, prin. Fax 966-1603
North Canton MS 1,100/6-8
605 Fair Oaks Ave SW 44720 330-497-5635
David Eby, prin. Fax 497-5659
Northwood ES 500/K-2
1500 School Ave NE 44720 330-497-5650
Matthew Donaldson, prin. Fax 966-1503
Orchard Hill ES 400/3-5
1305 Jonathan Ave SW 44720 330-497-5655
Renee Manse, prin. Fax 966-1701

St. Paul S 400/PK-8
303 S Main St 44720 330-494-0223
Amie Hale, prin. Fax 494-3226

North Eaton, Lorain

Christian Community S 100/PK-12
35716 Royalton Rd 44044 440-748-6224
Joel Brickner, hdmstr. Fax 748-1007

Northfield, Summit, Pop. 3,593
Nordonia Hills CSD 3,700/K-12
9370 Olde 8 Rd 44067 330-467-0580
Joseph Clark, supt. Fax 468-0152
www.nordoniaschools.org
Eaton ES 600/5-6
115 Ledge Rd 44067 330-467-0582
Robert Schrembeck, prin. Fax 468-5218
Nordonia MS 600/7-8
73 Leonard Ave 44067 330-467-0584
Ryan Durr, prin. Fax 468-6719
Northfield ES 400/K-4
9370 Olde 8 Rd 44067 330-467-2010
Staci Albanese, prin. Fax 468-0152
Rushwood ES 400/K-4
8200 Rushwood Ln 44067 330-467-0581
Jacqueline O'Connor, prin. Fax 468-4631
Other Schools – See Macedonia

Northfield Baptist Christian S 100/PK-6
311 W Aurora Rd 44067 330-467-8918
Terry Mencarini, admin. Fax 467-4248
St. Barnabas S 700/PK-8
9200 Olde 8 Rd 44067 330-467-7921
Erin Faetanini, prin. Fax 468-1926

North Jackson, Mahoning
Jackson-Milton Local SD 800/K-12
13910 Mahoning Ave 44451 330-538-3232
Kirk Baker, supt. Fax 538-6297
www.jacksonmilton.k12.oh.us/
Jackson-Milton ES 400/K-6
14110 Mahoning Ave 44451 330-538-2257
Kimberly Fisk, prin. Fax 538-2259
Jackson-Milton MS 100/7-8
13910 Mahoning Ave 44451 330-538-3308
David Vega, prin. Fax 538-0821

North Lewisburg, Union, Pop. 1,449
Triad Local SD 900/K-12
7920 Brush Lake Rd 43060 937-826-4961
Chris Piper, supt. Fax 826-3281
www.triad.k12.oh.us
Triad ES 300/K-4
7920 Brush Lake Rd 43060 937-826-3102
Lee Claypool, prin. Fax 826-0111
Triad MS 300/5-8
7941 Brush Lake Rd 43060 937-826-3071
Duane Caudill, prin. Fax 826-1000

North Olmsted, Cuyahoga, Pop. 32,229
North Olmsted CSD 3,600/PK-12
26669 Butternut Ridge Rd 44070 440-779-3576
Michael Zalar Ph.D., supt. Fax 779-3505
www.northolmstedschools.org
Birch ES 300/K-2
24100 Palm Dr 44070 440-779-3570
Frank Samerigo, prin. Fax 779-3521
Chestnut IS 300/3-6
30395 Lorain Rd 44070 440-779-3641
Brent Monnin, prin. Fax 779-3645
Forest PS 200/PK-2
28963 Tudor Dr 44070 440-779-3526
Denise Ressler, prin. Fax 779-3529
Maple IS 400/3-6
24101 Maple Ridge Rd 44070 440-779-3533
Jim Alexandrou, prin. Fax 779-3617
North Olmsted MS 600/7-8
26855 Lorain Rd 44070 440-779-8503
Bryan Busold, prin. Fax 779-8510
Pine S 300/3-6
4267 Dover Center Rd 44070 440-779-3536
Terese D'Amico, prin. Fax 779-3618
Spruce PS 200/PK-2
28590 Windsor Dr 44070 440-779-3541
Mary K. McDade, prin. Fax 779-3542

St. Brendan S 200/PK-8
4242 Brendan Ln 44070 440-777-8433
Julie Onacila, prin. Fax 779-7997

North Ridgeville, Lorain, Pop. 29,069
North Ridgeville CSD 4,100/PK-12
34620 Bainbridge Rd 44039 440-327-4444
James Powell, supt. Fax 327-9774
www.nrcs.k12.oh.us
Early Childhood Learning Center 200/PK-K
5490 Mills Creek Ln 44039 440-353-1100
Andrea Vance, prin. Fax 353-1155
Liberty ES 700/1-3
5700 Jaycox Rd 44039 440-327-6767
Mitch Heffron, prin. Fax 353-3683
North Ridgeville Academic Center 3-8
34620 Bainbridge Rd 44039 440-353-1180
Lee Armbruster, prin.
Ranger High-Tech Academy 300/4-8
5580 Lear Nagle Rd 44039 440-353-1178
Mitchell Heffron, prin. Fax 353-1172

Lake Ridge Academy 400/K-12
37501 Center Ridge Rd 44039 440-327-1175
Carol Klimas, pres. Fax 327-3641
St. Peter S 300/K-8
35749 Center Ridge Rd 44039 440-327-3212
Roger Brooks, prin. Fax 327-6843

North Robinson, Crawford, Pop. 201
Colonel Crawford Local SD 700/PK-12
2303 State Route 602 44827 419-562-4666
Todd Martin, supt. Fax 562-3304
www.cck12.org
Other Schools – See Crestline

North Royalton, Cuyahoga, Pop. 30,115
North Royalton CSD 4,300/1-12
6579 Royalton Rd 44133 440-237-8800
Greg Gurka, supt. Fax 582-7336
www.northroyaltonsd.org
Albion ES 400/1-4
9360 Albion Rd 44133 440-582-9060
Vince Ketterer, prin. Fax 582-7237
North Royalton MS 1,500/5-8
14709 Ridge Rd 44133 440-582-9120
Jeffrey Cicerchi, prin. Fax 582-7229
Royal View ES 400/1-4
13220 Ridge Rd 44133 440-582-9080
Kirk Pavelich, prin. Fax 582-7254
Valley Vista ES 400/1-4
4049 Wallings Rd 44133 440-582-9101
Jeff Hill, prin. Fax 582-7239

Royal Redeemer Lutheran S 500/PK-8
11680 Royalton Rd 44133 440-237-7988
Heidi Malone, prin. Fax 237-7713
St. Albert the Great S 600/K-8
6667 Wallings Rd 44133 440-237-1032
Edward Vittardi, prin. Fax 237-3308

Northwood, Wood, Pop. 5,174
Northwood Local SD 900/PK-12
600 Lemoyne Rd 43619 419-691-3888
Greg Clark, supt. Fax 697-2470
www.northwoodschools.org
Northwood ES 300/PK-6
600 Lemoyne Rd 43619 419-691-3888
Lindsey Krontz, prin. Fax 697-2470

Norton, Summit, Pop. 11,968
Norton CSD 2,600/K-12
4128 Cleveland Massillon Rd 44203 330-825-0863
Dana Addis, supt. Fax 825-0929
www.norton.k12.oh.us
Norton ES 400/K-4
4138 Cleveland Massillon Rd 44203 330-825-3828
Brady Sackett, prin. Fax 825-3817
Norton MS 800/5-8
4108 Cleveland Massillon Rd 44203 330-825-5607
Joyce Gerber, prin. Fax 825-1461
Norton PS 400/K-4
3163 Greenwich Rd 44203 330-825-5133
Wendy Minne, prin. Fax 825-0794

Norwalk, Huron, Pop. 16,729
Norwalk CSD 2,800/PK-12
134 Benedict Ave 44857 419-668-2779
George Fisk, supt. Fax 663-3302
www.norwalktruckers.net
League ES 200/4-4
16 E League St 44857 419-668-2450
Adam Kreischer, prin. Fax 668-6794
Main Street S 400/5-6
80 E Main St 44857 419-660-1957
Dan Bauman, prin. Fax 668-0354
Maplehurst ES 500/PK-1
195 Saint Marys St 44857 419-668-6035
Ken Moore, prin. Fax 668-5895
Norwalk MS 500/7-8
64 Christie Ave 44857 419-660-0370
Gary Swartz, prin. Fax 668-6622
Pleasant ES 500/2-3
16 S Pleasant St 44857 419-668-4134
V. Janice Smith, prin. Fax 668-4964

Norwalk Catholic ES 300/1-6
31 Milan Ave 44857 419-668-6091
Melissa Englert, prin. Fax 668-5584
Norwalk Catholic S - Early Childhood Ctr 100/PK-K
77 State St 44857 419-668-8480
Angie Smith, dir. Fax 668-3269

Norwood, Hamilton, Pop. 18,788
Norwood CSD 1,800/PK-12
2132 Williams Ave 45212 513-924-2500
Katherine Sabo, supt. Fax 396-6420
www.norwoodschools.org
Norwood MS 300/7-8
2060 Sherman Ave 45212 513-924-2700
Katherine Sabo, prin. Fax 396-5537
Norwood View ES 400/K-6
5328 Carthage Ave 45212 513-924-2610
Linville Yates, prin. Fax 396-5527
Sharpsburg ES 300/PK-6
4400 Smith Rd 45212 513-924-2600
Joseph Westendorf, prin. Fax 396-5528
Williams Avenue ES 300/PK-6
2132 Williams Ave Ste 2 45212 513-924-2520
Mark Gabbard, prin. Fax 396-5593

Novelty, Geauga
West Geauga Local SD
Supt. — See Chesterland
Westwood ES 400/K-5
13738 Caves Rd 44072 440-729-5990
Deborah Nanney, prin. Fax 729-5924

Oak Harbor, Ottawa, Pop. 2,732
Benton Carroll Salem Local SD 1,600/K-12
11685 W State Route 163 43449 419-898-6210
Dr. Guy Parmigian, supt. Fax 898-4303
www.bcssd.com
Oak Harbor MS 500/4-7
315 N Church St 43449 419-898-6217
Laramie Spurlock, prin. Fax 898-1613
Waters ES 500/K-3
220 E Ottawa St 43449 419-898-6219
Dawn Bryant, prin. Fax 898-1412

St. Boniface S 50/K-5
215 W Oak St 43449 419-898-1340
Millie Greggila, prin. Fax 898-4193

Oak Hill, Jackson, Pop. 1,527
Oak Hill Union Local SD 1,300/PK-12
205 Western Ave 45656 740-682-7595
Michael A. McCoy, supt. Fax 682-6998
www.oakhill.k12.oh.us
Oak Hill ES 600/PK-5
401 Evans St 45656 740-682-7096
Adam Michael, prin. Fax 682-7065

Oakwood, Paulding, Pop. 604
Oakwood CSD 2,100/PK-12
20 Rubicon Rd 45409 937-297-5332
Kyle Ramey Ed.D., supt. Fax 297-5345
www.oakwoodschools.org
Harman ES 400/1-6
735 Harman Ave 45419 937-297-5338
Sarah Patterson, prin. Fax 297-1514
Oakwood JHS 400/7-8
1200 Far Hills Ave 45419 937-297-5328
Tim Badenhop, prin. Fax 297-7807
Smith ES 500/PK-PK, 1-
1701 Shafor Blvd 45419 937-297-5335
Lynn Cowell, prin. Fax 297-1841
Other Schools – See Kettering

Paulding EVD
Supt. — See Paulding
Oakwood ES 300/PK-6
PO Box 37 45873 419-594-3346
Jennifer Manz, prin. Fax 594-3929

Oberlin, Lorain, Pop. 7,787
Firelands Local SD
Supt. — See South Amherst
Firelands ES 700/K-5
10779 Vermilion Rd 44074 440-965-5381
Sun Choe, prin. Fax 965-8849

Oberlin CSD 1,000/PK-12
153 N Main St 44074 440-774-1458
Dr. David H. Hall, supt. Fax 774-4492
www.oberlinschools.net
Eastwood ES 200/PK-2
198 E College St 44074 440-775-3473
Susan Alig, prin. Fax 774-7209
Langston MS 200/6-8
150 N Pleasant St 44074 440-775-7961
Christopher Frank, prin. Fax 776-4520
Prospect ES 200/3-5
36 S Prospect St 44074 440-774-4421
James Eibel, prin. Fax 775-2609

Old Fort, Seneca, Pop. 185
Old Fort Local SD 400/K-12
7635 N County Rd 51 44861 419-992-4291
Stephen Anway, supt. Fax 992-4293
www.old fort.k12.oh.us/
Other Schools – See Bettsville

Old Washington, Guernsey, Pop. 277
East Guernsey Local SD 1,000/K-12
237 Beymer Rd 43768 740-489-5190
Adam Pittis, supt. Fax 489-9813
www.eguernsey.k12.oh.us
Other Schools – See Lore City

Olmsted Falls, Cuyahoga, Pop. 8,919
Olmsted Falls CSD 3,800/PK-12
PO Box 38010 44138 440-427-6000
Dr. Jim Lloyd, supt. Fax 427-6010
www.ofcs.net
Falls-Lenox PS 800/1-3
26450 Bagley Rd 44138 440-427-6400
Lisa Barrett, prin. Fax 427-6410
Olmsted Falls ECC 300/PK-K
7105 Fitch Rd 44138 440-427-6360
Melinda Brunner, prin. Fax 427-6370
Olmsted Falls IS 600/4-5
27043 Bagley Rd 44138 440-427-6500
Don Svec, prin. Fax 427-6510
Olmsted Falls MS 1,000/6-8
27045 Bagley Rd 44138 440-427-6200
Mark Kurz, prin. Fax 427-6210

St. Mary of the Falls S 300/PK-8
8262 Columbia Rd 44138 440-235-4580
Annemarie Rajnicek, prin. Fax 235-6833

Ontario, Richland, Pop. 6,103
Ontario Local SD 1,400/PK-12
457 Shelby Ontario Rd, 419-747-4311
Lisa Carmichael, supt. Fax 747-6859
www.ontarioschools.org
Ontario MS 400/6-8
447 Shelby Ontario Rd, 419-529-5507
Sue Weirich, prin. Fax 747-6859
Stingel ES 400/PK-5
426 Shelby Ontario Rd, 419-529-4955
Mike Ream, prin. Fax 747-6859

Orange Village, Cuyahoga, Pop. 3,252

Bethlehem Christian Academy 100/PK-8
27250 Emery Rd 44128 216-292-4685
Christine Warner, hdmstr. Fax 360-9995

Oregon, Lucas, Pop. 20,036
Oregon CSD 3,600/K-12
5721 Seaman Rd 43616 419-693-0661
Hal Gregory, supt. Fax 698-6016
www.oregoncityschools.org
Coy ES 400/K-4
3604 Pickle Rd 43616 419-693-0624
Amy Molnar, prin. Fax 698-6018
Eisenhower IS 400/5-6
331 N Curtice Rd S 43616 419-836-8498
Timothy Holcombe, prin. Fax 836-2005
Fassett JHS 600/7-8
3025 Starr Ave 43616 419-693-0455
Paul Gibbs, prin. Fax 698-6048
Starr ES 500/K-4
3230 Starr Ave 43616 419-693-0589
Tricia Soltesz, prin. Fax 698-6019
Other Schools – See Curtice

Cardinal Stritch Catholic Academy 300/PK-8
3225 Pickle Rd 43616 419-693-0465
Kevin Parkins, prin. Fax 697-2816

Orrville, Wayne, Pop. 8,182
Orrville CSD 1,500/PK-12
815 N Ella St 44667 330-682-4651
James Ritchie, supt. Fax 682-0073
www.orrville.k12.oh.us
Orrville ES 600/PK-4
605 Mineral Springs St 44667 330-682-1851
Beverly Waseman, prin. Fax 682-2143
Orrville MS 500/5-8
801 Mineral Springs St 44667 330-682-1791
David Sovacool, prin. Fax 682-2743

Kingsway Christian S 100/PK-12
11138 Old Lincoln Way E 44667 330-683-0012
Keith Fuller M.Ed., prin. Fax 683-0017

Orwell, Ashtabula, Pop. 1,614
Grand Valley Local SD 1,300/K-12
111 W Grand Valley Ave # A 44076 440-437-6260
Dr. William Nye, supt. Fax 437-1025
www.grandvalley.school
Grand Valley ES 500/K-4
111 W Grand Valley Ave # B 44076 440-437-6260
Ellen Winer, prin. Fax 437-2050
Grand Valley MS 400/5-8
111 W Grand Valley Ave # D 44076 440-437-6260
Roberta Cozad, prin. Fax 437-6156

Ostrander, Delaware, Pop. 635
Buckeye Valley Local SD
Supt. — See Delaware
Buckeye Valley West ES 400/PK-4
61 N 3rd St 43061 740-666-2731
Barry Lyons, prin. Fax 666-2221

Ottawa, Putnam, Pop. 4,436
Ottawa-Glandorf Local SD 1,500/K-12
630 Glendale Ave 45875 419-523-5261
Don Horstman, supt. Fax 523-5978
www.ottawaglandorf.org
Ottawa ES 400/K-8
123 Putnam Pkwy 45875 419-523-4290
Audrey Beining, prin. Fax 523-6032
Other Schools – See Glandorf

SS. Peter & Paul S 200/1-8
320 N Locust St 45875 419-523-3697
Nate Lanwehr, prin.

Ottawa Hills, Lucas, Pop. 4,439
Ottawa Hills Local SD 900/K-12
3600 Indian Rd, 419-536-6371
Dr. Kevin Miller, supt. Fax 534-5380
www.ottawahillsschools.org/
Ottawa Hills ES 500/K-6
3602 Indian Rd, 419-536-8329
Kori Kawczynski, prin. Fax 536-6932

Ottoville, Putnam, Pop. 974
Ottoville Local SD 400/K-12
650 W Third St 45876 419-453-3356
Scott Mangas, supt. Fax 453-3367
www.ottovilleschools.org
Ottoville ES 200/K-6
650 W Third St 45876 419-453-3357
Scott Mangas, prin. Fax 453-3367

Owensville, Clermont, Pop. 781
Clermont Northeastern Local SD
Supt. — See Batavia
Clermont Northeastern Preschool PK-PK
463 S Broadway 45160 513-685-5374
Wayne Johnson, prin. Fax 625-3328

St. Louis S 200/K-8
PO Box 85 45160 513-732-0636
Elizabeth Leu, prin. Fax 732-1748

Oxford, Butler, Pop. 20,904
Talawanda CSD 3,000/PK-12
131 W Chestnut St 45056 513-273-3333
Kelly Spivey, supt. Fax 273-3113
www.talawanda.net/
Bogan ES 400/PK-5
5200 Hamilton Richmond Rd 45056 513-273-3400
Jeffrey Winslow, prin. Fax 273-3405
Kramer ES 500/PK-5
400 W Sycamore St 45056 513-273-3500
Jason Merz, prin. Fax 273-3505
Marshall ES 400/PK-5
3260 Oxford Millville Rd 45056 513-273-3600
Chad Hinton, prin. Fax 273-3606
Talawanda MS 700/6-8
4030 Oxford Reily Rd 45056 513-273-3300
Mike Malone, prin. Fax 273-3303

Painesville, Lake, Pop. 18,851
Painesville City Local SD 3,100/PK-12
58 Jefferson St 44077 440-392-5060
John Shepard, supt. Fax 392-5089
www.pcls.net
Chestnut ES, 341 Chestnut St 44077 500/K-5
Jamie Smith, prin. 440-392-5350
Elm Street ES, 585 Elm St 44077 500/K-5
Cynthia Urbic, prin. 440-392-5520
Heritage MS 600/6-8
135 Cedarbrook Dr 44077 440-392-5250
Melissa DeAngelis, prin.
Maple ES, 560 W Jackson St 44077 500/K-5
Zachary Cousins, prin. 440-392-5440
Red Raider Preschool 100/PK-PK
350 Cedarbrook Dr 44077 440-392-5610
Karen Capretta, dir.

Riverside Local SD 4,500/K-12
585 Riverside Dr 44077 440-352-0668
James Kalis, supt. Fax 639-1959
www.riversidelocalschools.com
Buckeye ES 400/K-5
175 Buckeye Rd 44077 440-352-2191
Cassandre Smolen, prin. Fax 352-1087
Hadden ES 200/K-5
1800 Mentor Ave 44077 440-354-4414
Michelle Walker, prin. Fax 354-8246
Hale Road ES 500/K-5
56 Hale Rd 44077 440-352-2300
Tim St. Clair, prin. Fax 352-0665
LaMuth MS 700/6-7
6700 Auburn Rd 44077 440-354-4394
Nick Orlando, prin. Fax 354-8218
Leroy ES 200/K-5
13613 Painesville Warren Rd 44077 440-358-8750
Greg Miller, prin. Fax 254-0503
Madison Avenue ES 300/K-5
845 Madison Ave 44077 440-357-6171
Traci Shantery, prin. Fax 357-5690
Melridge ES 400/K-5
6689 Melridge Dr 44077 440-352-3854
Julie Weber, prin. Fax 352-2076

Our Shepherd Lutheran S 100/K-8
508 Mentor Ave 44077 440-357-7776
Barb Riley, prin. Fax 358-1149

Pandora, Putnam, Pop. 1,146
Pandora-Gilboa Local SD 500/K-12
410 Rocket Rdg 45877 419-384-3227
Todd Schmutz, supt. Fax 384-3230
www.pgrockets.org
Pandora-Gilboa ES 200/K-4
410 Rocket Rdg 45877 419-384-3225
Jodi Schroeder, prin. Fax 384-3230
Pandora-Gilboa MS 200/5-8
410 Rocket Rdg 45877 419-384-3225
Jodi Schroeder, prin. Fax 384-3230

Parma, Cuyahoga, Pop. 80,516
Parma CSD 11,100/PK-12
5311 Longwood Ave 44134 440-842-5300
Carl Hilling, supt. Fax 885-8304
www.parmacityschools.org
Dentzler ES 500/K-4
3600 Dentzler Rd 44134 440-885-2430
Renee Dzurnak, prin. Fax 885-3704
Greenbriar MS 900/5-7
11810 Huffman Rd 44130 440-885-2370
Jill Schissler, prin. Fax 885-8353
Green Valley ES 400/K-4
2401 W Pleasant Valley Rd 44134 440-885-2431
Jacqueline Marconi, prin. Fax 885-3705
Muir ES 500/K-4
5531 W 24th St 44134 440-885-2424
Karl Schneider, prin. Fax 885-2472
Pleasant Valley ES 800/K-4
9906 W Pleasant Valley Rd 44130 440-885-2380
Stephanie Boka, prin. Fax 885-8664
Pleasantview Preschool 200/PK-PK
7700 Malibu Dr 44134 440-885-8665
Dana Massimino, prin.
Renwood ES 300/K-4
8020 Deerfield Dr 44129 440-885-2338
Lashonda Abdussatar, prin. Fax 885-3716
Ridge-Brook ES 400/K-4
7915 Manhattan Ave 44129 440-885-2350
Steve Perry, prin. Fax 885-3717
Shiloh MS 800/5-7
2303 Grantwood Dr 44134 440-885-8485
Nicola Discenza, prin. Fax 885-8486
Thoreau Park ES 500/K-4
5401 W 54th St 44129 440-885-2351
Theodore Bickley, prin. Fax 885-2460
Other Schools – See Parma Heights, Seven Hills

Bethany Lutheran S 300/PK-8
6041 Ridge Rd 44129 440-884-1010
William Moses, prin. Fax 884-9834
Bethel Christian Academy 100/PK-8
12901 W Pleasant Valley Rd 44130 440-842-8575
Rev. Jeremy Burnett, prin. Fax 842-3226
Holy Family S 200/PK-8
7367 York Rd 44130 440-842-7785
Thomas Brownfield, prin. Fax 842-3634
St. Anthony of Padua S 300/K-8
6800 State Rd 44134 440-845-3444
Sr. Patrick Klimkewicz, prin. Fax 884-4548
St. Bridget of Kildare S 300/PK-8
5620 Hauserman Rd 44130 440-886-1468
Heather Hawk Frank, prin. Fax 886-5121
St. Charles Borromeo S 600/PK-8
7107 Wilber Ave 44129 440-886-5546
Eileen Updegrove, prin. Fax 886-1163
St. Columbkille S 400/PK-8
6740 Broadview Rd 44134 216-524-4816
Renee Cerny, prin. Fax 524-4153

Parma Heights, Cuyahoga, Pop. 20,381
Parma CSD
Supt. — See Parma
Parma Park ES 300/K-4
6800 Commonwealth Blvd 44130 440-885-2390
Wendy Jewell, prin. Fax 885-3707

Incarnate Word Academy 500/K-8
6620 Pearl Rd 44130 440-842-6818
Janette Cicerchi, prin. Fax 888-1377
Parma Heights Christian Academy 200/K-6
8971 W Ridgewood Dr 44130 440-845-8668
David Griffey, admin. Fax 886-5748

Pataskala, Licking, Pop. 14,629
Licking Heights Local SD 3,700/PK-12
6539 Summit Rd SW 43062 740-927-6926
Dr. Philip Wagner, supt. Fax 927-9043
www.licking-heights.k12.oh.us/
Licking Heights Central MS 900/6-8
6565 Summit Rd SW 43062 740-927-3365
Tiffane Warren, prin. Fax 927-5845
Licking Heights North ES 300/5-5
6507 Summit Rd SW 43062 740-927-3268
Tiffane Warren, prin. Fax 927-5736
Licking Heights South ES 600/K-4
6623 Summit Rd SW 43062 740-964-1674
Kurt Scheiderer, prin. Fax 964-1625
Summit Station Preschool PK-PK
6626 Summit Rd SW 43062 740-927-6926
Other Schools – See Blacklick

Southwest Licking Local SD 2,900/PK-12
927 South St Unit A 43062 740-927-3941
Robert Jennell, supt. Fax 927-4648
www.swl.k12.oh.us
Pataskala ES 200/2-3
395 S High St 43062 740-927-3861
Joseph Pratt, prin. Fax 927-7259
Southwest Licking Early Learning Center 300/PK-PK
927B South St 43062 740-927-5437
Alissa Horstman, admin.
Other Schools – See Etna, Kirkersville

Liberty Christian Academy 300/PK-12
10447 Refugee Rd SW 43062 740-964-2211
LaVonne McIlrath, head sch Fax 964-2311

Patriot, Gallia
Gallia County Local SD 1,900/PK-12
4836 State Route 325 45658 740-379-9085
Jude Meyers, supt. Fax 379-9135
gallialocal.org
Southwestern ES 100/PK-5
4834 State Route 325 45658 740-379-2532
Larry Carter, prin. Fax 379-2000
Other Schools – See Bidwell, Crown City, Gallipolis, Vinton

Paulding, Paulding, Pop. 3,557
Paulding EVD 1,400/PK-12
405 N Water St 45879 419-399-4656
Kenneth Amstutz, supt. Fax 399-2404
www.pauldingschools.org/
Paulding ES 500/PK-5
405 N Water St 45879 419-399-4656
Greg Puthoff, prin. Fax 399-2404
Paulding MS 300/6-8
405 N Water St 45879 419-399-4656
Chris Etzler, prin. Fax 399-2404
Other Schools – See Oakwood

Payne, Paulding, Pop. 1,180
Wayne Trace Local SD
Supt. — See Haviland
Payne ES 300/PK-6
501 W Townline St 45880 419-263-2512
Jody Dunham, prin. Fax 263-1313

Divine Mercy Catholic S 100/PK-6
120 Arturus St 45880 419-263-2114
Joseph Linder, prin. Fax 263-2114

Peebles, Adams, Pop. 1,762
Adams County/Ohio Valley Local SD
Supt. — See West Union
Peebles ES 700/PK-6
700 Peebles Indian Rd 45660 937-587-2611
Amanda Lamb, prin. Fax 587-5240

Pemberville, Wood, Pop. 1,357
Eastwood Local SD 1,400/K-12
120 E College Ave 43450 419-833-6411
William Welker, supt. Fax 833-4915
www.eastwoodschools.org
Eastwood ES 200/K-4
4700 Sugar Ridge Rd 43450 419-833-2821
Joe Wank, prin. Fax 833-2660
Eastwood MS 500/5-8
4800 Sugar Ridge Rd 43450 419-833-6011
Edward Eding, prin. Fax 833-7454

Peninsula, Summit, Pop. 560
Woodridge Local SD 2,000/K-12
4411 Quick Rd 44264 330-928-9074
Walter Davis, supt. Fax 928-1542
www.woodridge.k12.oh.us/
Woodridge IS 400/3-5
1930 Bronson St 44264 330-928-8974
Kristin Jagger, prin. Fax 657-2353
Woodridge MS 500/6-8
4451 Quick Rd 44264 330-928-7420
Jesse Hosford, prin. Fax 928-5645
Other Schools – See Cuyahoga Falls

Pepper Pike, Cuyahoga, Pop. 5,884
Orange CSD 2,100/PK-12
32000 Chagrin Blvd 44124 216-831-8600
Dr. Edwin Holland, supt. Fax 831-8029
www.orangeschools.org
Brady MS 500/6-8
32000 Chagrin Blvd 44124 216-831-8600
Brian Frank, prin. Fax 839-1335
Moreland Hills ES 900/K-5
32000 Chagrin Blvd 44124 216-831-8600
Renee Tuttle, prin. Fax 831-4298
Orange Inclusive Preschool 100/PK-PK
32000 Chagrin Blvd 44124 216-831-8600
Christine Goudy, admin. Fax 831-0963

Gross Schechter Day S 300/PK-8
27601 Fairmount Blvd 44124 216-763-1400
Randy Boroff, head sch Fax 763-1106
Ratner S 200/PK-8
27575 Shaker Blvd 44124 216-464-0033
Michael Griffith, head sch Fax 464-0031

Perry, Lake, Pop. 1,647
Perry Local SD 1,800/K-12
4325 Manchester Rd 44081 440-259-9200
Jack Thompson Ph.D., supt. Fax 259-3607
www.perry-lake.org
Perry ES 600/K-4
1 Learning Ln 44081 440-259-9600
Arianna Neading, prin. Fax 259-9649
Perry MS 600/5-8
2 Learning Ln 44081 440-259-9500
Robert Knisely, prin. Fax 259-5149

Perrysburg, Wood, Pop. 20,359
Perrysburg SD 4,700/PK-12
140 E Indiana Ave 43551 419-874-9131
Thomas Hosler, supt. Fax 872-8820
www.perrysburgschools.net
Fort Meigs ES 600/K-4
26431 Fort Meigs Rd 43551 419-872-8822
Kellie Johnson, prin. Fax 872-8825
Frank ES 500/K-4
401 W South Boundary St 43551 419-874-8721
Chad Warnimont, prin. Fax 874-1808
Hull Prairie IS 5-6
25480 Hull Prairie Rd 43551 419-873-6293
Scott Best, prin. Fax 873-6294
Perrysburg JHS 1,100/7-8
550 E South Boundary St 43551 419-874-9193
Donald Christie, prin. Fax 872-8812
Toth ES 500/K-4
200 E 7th St 43551 419-874-3123
Dr. Beth Christoff, prin. Fax 872-8828
Woodland ES 600/K-4
27979 White Rd 43551 419-874-8736
Brook Price, prin. Fax 874-2964
Other Schools – See Maumee

Rossford EVD
Supt. — See Rossford
Glenwood ES 200/PK-2
8950 Avenue Rd 43551 419-666-8130
Megan Spangler, prin. Fax 661-2848

Islamic S of Greater Toledo 50/PK-2
25877 Scheider Rd 43551 419-874-8820
Catherine Hammoud, prin. Fax 874-9123
St. Rose S 400/PK-8
217 E Front St 43551 419-874-5631
Bryon Borgelt, prin. Fax 874-1002

Pettisville, Fulton, Pop. 497
Pettisville Local SD 500/PK-12
PO Box 53001 43553 419-446-2705
Dr. Stephen Switzer, supt. Fax 445-2992
pettisvilleschools.org
Pettisville ES 300/PK-6
PO Box 53001 43553 419-446-2705
Jason Waldvogel, prin. Fax 445-2992

Philo, Muskingum, Pop. 726
Franklin Local SD
Supt. — See Duncan Falls
Philo JHS 400/6-8
PO Box 178 43771 740-674-5210
Robert Preston, prin. Fax 674-5217

Pickerington, Fairfield, Pop. 17,708
Pickerington Local SD 10,200/K-12
90 N East St 43147 614-833-2110
Chris Briggs Ed.D., supt. Fax 833-2143
www.pickerington.k12.oh.us
Diley MS 600/5-6
750 Preston Trails Dr 43147 614-830-2900
Heather Hedgepeth, prin. Fax 830-2910
Fairfield ES 500/K-4
13000 Coventry Ave 43147 614-834-7600
Ruth Stickel, prin. Fax 834-7610

Harmon MS 600/5-6
12410 Harmon Rd 43147 614-835-2000
Jared Moore, prin. Fax 835-2010
Heritage ES 400/K-4
100 N East St 43147 614-833-6385
Chad Rice, prin. Fax 833-6415
Pickerington ES 600/K-4
775 Long Rd 43147 614-548-1400
Melissa Moriarty, prin. Fax 548-1410
Pickerington Lakeview JHS 900/7-8
12445 Ault Rd 43147 614-830-2200
Pam Bertke, prin. Fax 834-3267
Pickerington Ridgeview STEM JHS 900/7-8
130 Hill Rd S 43147 614-548-1700
Eric Koch, prin. Fax 548-1710
Sycamore Creek ES 700/K-4
500 Sycamore Creek St 43147 614-834-6200
Nikki Arnold, prin. Fax 834-6210
Toll Gate ES 500/K-4
12183 Tollgate Rd 43147 614-834-6300
Kristi Motsch, prin. Fax 834-6310
Toll Gate MS 500/5-6
12089 Tollgate Rd 43147 614-834-6400
Kara Jackson, prin. Fax 834-6410
Violet ES 400/K-4
8855 Education Dr 43147 614-548-1500
Dorethia Copas, prin. Fax 548-1510
Other Schools – See Reynoldsburg

Piketon, Pike, Pop. 2,150
Scioto Valley Local SD 1,300/K-12
PO Box 600 45661 740-289-4456
Dr. Todd Burkitt, supt. Fax 289-3065
www.piketon.k12.oh.us/
Jasper ES 500/K-3
3185 Jasper Rd 45661 740-289-2425
Krista Conley, prin. Fax 289-4437
Zahn's MS 300/4-6
13806 State Route 220 45661 740-289-2871
Jason Mantell, prin. Fax 289-2291

Pioneer, Williams, Pop. 1,360
North Central Local SD 600/PK-12
400 E Baubice St 43554 419-737-2392
William Hanak, supt. Fax 737-3361
www.northcentralschool.org
North Central ES 300/PK-6
400 E Baubice St 43554 419-737-2293
Andrew Morr, prin. Fax 737-3361

Piqua, Miami, Pop. 19,922
Piqua CSD 2,300/K-12
719 E Ash St 45356 937-773-4321
Dwayne A. Thompson, supt. Fax 773-4518
www.piqua.org
Piqua Central IS 300/4-6
807 Nicklin Ave 45356 937-773-2017
Joshua Kauffman, prin.
Piqua JHS 500/7-8
1 Tomahawk Trl 45356 937-778-2997
William Clark, prin. Fax 773-3574
Springcreek PS 300/K-3
145 E US Route 36 45356 937-773-6540
Connie Strehle, prin. Fax 778-2995
Washington PS 300/K-3
800 N Sunset Dr 45356 937-773-8472
Tracy Trogdlon, prin. Fax 778-2996

Piqua Catholic S 200/K-8
503 W North St 45356 937-773-1564
Bradley Zimmerman, prin. Fax 773-0380
Piqua SDA S 50/1-8
4020 W State Route 185 45356 937-778-0223
Anita Brown, prin. Fax 773-0848

Plain City, Madison, Pop. 4,160
Jonathan Alder Local SD 2,200/PK-12
9200 US Highway 42 S 43064 614-873-5621
Gary Chapman, supt. Fax 873-8462
www.alder.k12.oh.us
Alder JHS 300/7-8
6440 Kilbury Huber Rd 43064 614-873-4635
Jonathan Hayes, prin. Fax 873-0845
Canaan MS 400/5-6
7055 US Highway 42 S 43064 614-733-3975
Matthew Keller, prin. Fax 733-3972
Plain City ES 700/PK-4
580 S Chillicothe St 43064 614-873-4608
Kelly Hicks, prin. Fax 873-2559
Other Schools – See London

Shekinah Christian S 100/K-12
10040 Lafayette Plain City 43064 614-873-3130
Brice Kaufmann, dir. Fax 873-3699

Pleasant Hill, Miami, Pop. 1,191
Newton Local SD 600/K-12
201 N Long St 45359 937-676-2002
Pat McBride, supt. Fax 676-2054
www.newton.k12.oh.us/
Newton ES 300/K-6
201 N Long St 45359 937-676-2002
Danielle Davis, prin. Fax 676-2054

Pleasantville, Fairfield, Pop. 928
Fairfield Union Local SD
Supt. — See Lancaster
Pleasantville ES 400/K-4
300 W Columbus St 43148 740-468-2181
Michael Myers, prin. Fax 468-3539

Plymouth, Huron, Pop. 1,844
Plymouth-Shiloh Local SD 600/K-12
365 Sandusky St 44865 419-687-4733
James Metcalf, supt. Fax 687-1541
www.plymouth.k12.oh.us
Plymouth-Shiloh ES 200/K-5
420 Trux St 44865 419-687-8200
Laura Kanney, prin. Fax 687-9040
Shiloh MS 200/6-8
400 Trux St 44865 419-687-8200
Bradley Turson, prin. Fax 687-8175

Poland, Mahoning, Pop. 2,537
Poland Local SD 1,600/K-12
3199 Dobbins Rd 44514 330-757-7000
David Janofa, supt. Fax 757-2390
www.polandbulldogs.com/
Dobbins ES 100/3-4
3030 Dobbins Rd 44514 330-757-7011
Michael Daley, prin. Fax 757-2390
McKinley ES 300/5-6
7 Elm St 44514 330-757-7015
Lisa Iberis, prin. Fax 757-2390
Poland MS 400/7-8
47 College St 44514 330-757-7003
Mark Covell, prin. Fax 757-2390
Poland Union ES 200/K-2
30 Riverside Dr 44514 330-757-7014
Michael Masucci, prin. Fax 757-2390

Holy Family S 300/K-8
2731 Center Rd 44514 330-757-3713
Kathleen Stoops, prin. Fax 757-7648

Pomeroy, Meigs, Pop. 1,809
Meigs Local SD 1,800/K-12
41765 Pomeroy Pike 45769 740-992-2153
Scot Gheen, supt. Fax 992-7814
www.ml.k12.oh.us
Meigs MS 400/6-8
42353 Charles Chancey Dr 45769 740-992-3058
Vickie Jones, prin. Fax 992-6952
Other Schools – See Middleport

Port Clinton, Ottawa, Pop. 5,954
Port Clinton CSD 1,700/K-12
811 Jefferson St 43452 419-732-2102
Patrick Adkins, supt. Fax 734-4527
www.pccsd.net/
Bataan Memorial IS 400/3-5
525 W 6th St 43452 419-734-3931
Geoff Halsey, prin. Fax 734-3705
Bataan Memorial PS 400/K-2
575 W 6th St 43452 419-734-2815
Kendra Van Doren, prin. Fax 960-7672
Port Clinton MS 400/6-8
807 Jefferson St 43452 419-734-4448
Carrie Sanchez, prin. Fax 734-4440

Immaculate Conception S 100/PK-6
109 W 4th St 43452 419-734-3315
Constance Snyder, prin. Fax 734-6172

Portsmouth, Scioto, Pop. 19,655
Clay Local SD 500/PK-12
44 Clay High St 45662 740-354-6645
William Warnock, supt. Fax 354-5746
clay.k12.oh.us/
Clay ES 400/PK-5
44 Clay High St 45662 740-354-6644
Larry Piguet, prin. Fax 354-6105

Portsmouth CSD 1,800/PK-12
724 Findlay St 45662 740-354-5663
Gary Dutey, supt. Fax 355-4496
www.portsmouthtrojans.org
East Portsmouth ES 200/PK-6
5929 Harding Ave 45662 740-776-6444
Kristi Toppins, prin. Fax 776-6296
Portsmouth ES 1,000/PK-6
514 Union St 45662 740-353-6719
Beth Born, prin. Fax 353-1778

Notre Dame S 300/PK-6
1401 Gallia St 45662 740-353-2354
Josh McMackin, prin. Fax 353-6769

Port Washington, Tuscarawas, Pop. 567
Indian Valley Local SD
Supt. — See Gnadenhutten
Port Washington ES 400/K-5
304 W Arch St 43837 740-498-8389
Troy Page, prin. Fax 498-6312

Powell, Delaware, Pop. 11,313
Olentangy Local SD
Supt. — See Lewis Center
Indian Springs ES 700/K-5
3828 Home Rd 43065 740-657-4950
Chris Heuser, prin. Fax 657-4999
Liberty Tree ES 600/K-5
6877 Sawmill Pkwy 43065 740-657-5600
Teresa Caton, prin. Fax 657-5649
Olentangy Hyatts MS 800/6-8
6885 Sawmill Pkwy 43065 740-657-5400
Derrick Gilliam, prin. Fax 657-5499
Olentangy Liberty MS 800/6-8
7940 Liberty Rd N 43065 740-657-4400
Nichole Crothers, prin. Fax 657-4499
Scioto Ridge ES 600/K-5
8715 Big Bear Ave 43065 740-657-4800
Melany Ondrus, prin. Fax 657-4849
Tyler Run ES 600/PK-5
580 Salisbury Dr 43065 740-657-4900
Jennifer Mazza, prin. Fax 657-4949
Wyandot Run ES 500/PK-5
2800 Carriage Rd 43065 740-657-4850
Jeremy Ross, prin. Fax 657-4899

Worthington CSD
Supt. — See Worthington
Liberty ES 500/K-6
8081 Saddle Run 43065 614-450-5200
Susan Drake, prin. Fax 883-2960
Sutter Park Preschool 200/PK-PK
1850 Sutter Pkwy 43065 614-450-4900
Patricia Hosking, prin. Fax 883-3260

Village Academy 300/PK-12
284 S Liberty St 43065 614-841-0050
Tres Marangoni, head sch Fax 841-0501

Powhatan Point, Belmont, Pop. 1,582
Switzerland of Ohio Local SD
Supt. — See Woodsfield
Powhatan Point S 300/PK-8
54685 Mount Victory Rd 43942 740-795-5665
Zac Housley, prin. Fax 795-5830

Proctorville, Lawrence, Pop. 565
Fairland Local SD 1,600/K-12
228 Private Drive 10010 45669 740-886-3100
Roni Hayes, supt. Fax 886-7253
www.fairland.k12.oh.us
Fairland East ES 400/K-2
10732 County Road 107 45669 740-886-3120
Abbie Lewis Pannell, prin. Fax 886-7630
Fairland MS 400/6-8
7875 County Road 107 45669 740-886-3200
Aaron Lewis, prin. Fax 886-5125
Fairland West ES 400/3-5
110 Township Road 1125 45669 740-886-3150
Mary Johnson, prin. Fax 886-5259

Put in Bay, Ottawa, Pop. 138
Put-in-Bay Local SD 100/K-12
PO Box 659 43456 419-285-3614
Steven Poe, supt. Fax 285-2137
www.put-in-bay.k12.oh.us
Put-in-Bay ES 50/K-6
PO Box 659 43456 419-285-3614
Steven Poe, supt. Fax 285-2137

Racine, Meigs, Pop. 665
Southern Local SD 700/PK-12
920 Elm St 45771 740-949-2669
Anthony Deem, supt. Fax 949-3309
www.southernlocalmeigs.org/
Southern ES 500/PK-8
906 Elm St 45771 740-949-4222
Tricia McNickle, prin. Fax 949-1101

Ravenna, Portage, Pop. 11,455
Ravenna CSD 2,700/PK-12
507 E Main St 44266 330-296-9679
Dennis Honkala, supt. Fax 297-4158
www.ravennaschools.us
Brown MS 600/6-8
228 S Scranton St 44266 330-296-3849
Jonathan Lane, prin. Fax 297-4146
Carlin ES 300/1-5
531 Washington Ave 44266 330-296-6622
Robert Mittiga, prin. Fax 297-4144
Early Childhood Education Preschool 50/PK-PK
3590 State Route 59 44266 330-297-4139
Lori Slattery, prin. Fax 297-7605
West Main ES 400/1-5
639 W Main St 44266 330-296-6522
Lee Smith, prin. Fax 297-4149
West Park S 200/K-K
1071 Jones St 44266 330-297-1744
Frank Sciarabba, prin. Fax 297-4167
Willyard ES 300/1-5
680 Summit Rd 44266 330-296-6481
Joseph Kuzior, prin. Fax 297-4151

Southeast Local SD 1,400/K-12
8245 Tallmadge Rd 44266 330-654-5841
Robert Dunn, supt. Fax 654-9110
www.sepirates.org
Southeast IS 400/3-5
8301 Tallmadge Rd 44266 330-654-1940
Jamie Brawley, prin. Fax 654-9110
Southeast PS 100/K-2
8301 Tallmadge Rd 44266 330-654-1930
David Fesemyer, prin. Fax 654-9110
Other Schools – See Diamond

Rawson, Hancock, Pop. 564
Cory-Rawson Local SD 600/PK-12
3930 County Road 26 45881 419-963-3415
Dr. Robert Hlasko, supt. Fax 963-4400
cory-rawson.k12.oh.us
Cory-Rawson ES 300/PK-6
3930 County Road 26 45881 419-963-7017
Rebecca Rosenbauer, prin. Fax 963-4400

Rayland, Jefferson, Pop. 413
Buckeye Local SD
Supt. — See Dillonvale
Buckeye JHS 300/7-8
10692 State Route 150 43943 740-859-2196
Jason Kovalski, prin. Fax 859-2857

Raymond, Union, Pop. 257
Marysville EVD
Supt. — See Marysville
Raymond ES 200/K-4
21511 Main St 43067 937-578-7200
Carol Lentz, prin. Fax 578-7213

Reading, Hamilton, Pop. 10,188
Reading Community CSD 1,600/K-12
1301 Bonnell St 45215 513-554-1800
Chuck LaFata, supt. Fax 483-6754
www.readingschools.org
Central Community ES 300/K-5
416 W Vine St 45215 513-554-1001
Susan Fraley, prin. Fax 483-6766
Hilltop Community ES 500/K-5
2236 Bolser Dr 45215 513-733-4322
Dennis Ramsey, prin. Fax 483-6772
Reading Community MS 400/6-8
230 Halker Ave 45215 513-842-5151
Damon Davis, prin. Fax 842-5146

SS. Peter & Paul Academy 100/K-8
231 Clark Rd 45215 513-761-7772
Glenda Donnelly, prin. Fax 761-0652

Reedsville, Meigs
Eastern Local SD 800/K-12
50008 State Route 681 45772 740-667-6079
Steven Ohlinger, supt. Fax 667-3978
www.easternlocal.com
Eastern ES 300/K-4
38850 State Route 7 45772 740-985-3304
Robin Burrow, prin. Fax 985-4318
Eastern MS 300/5-8
38850 State Route 7 45772 740-985-3304
William Francis, prin. Fax 985-4318

Reynoldsburg, Franklin, Pop. 34,685
Pickerington Local SD
Supt. — See Pickerington
Tussing ES 600/K-4
7117 Tussing Rd 43068 614-834-2600
Matt Dansby, prin. Fax 834-2610

Reynoldsburg CSD 5,800/PK-12
7244 E Main St 43068 614-501-1020
Melvin Brown, supt. Fax 501-1050
www.reyn.org/
Ashton MS 200/5-6
1482 Jackson St 43068 614-367-1530
Jamie Wilson, prin. Fax 367-1549
Baldwin Road JHS 300/7-8
2300 Baldwin Pl 43068 614-367-1600
Brian Coffey, prin. Fax 367-1625
French Run ES 400/PK-4
1200 Epworth Ave 43068 614-367-1950
Terra Baker, prin. Fax 367-1958
Mills ES 400/K-4
6826 Retton Rd 43068 614-367-2160
Mary Weeks, prin. Fax 367-2168
Rose Hill ES 300/PK-4
760 Rosehill Rd 43068 614-367-2380
Kim Lewis, prin. Fax 367-2386
Slate Ridge ES 500/PK-4
10466 Taylor Rd SW 43068 614-501-5500
Micca Conley, prin. Fax 501-5520
Summit ES, 8591 Summit Rd 43068 500/K-4
Melissa Drury, prin. 614-501-5530
Taylor Road ES 400/PK-4
8200 Taylor Rd SW 43068 614-367-2930
Jeremy Miller, prin. Fax 367-2933
Waggoner Road JHS 400/7-8
360 Waggoner Rd 43068 614-501-5700
Breen Slauter, prin. Fax 501-5700
Waggoner Road MS 400/5-6
340 Waggoner Rd 43068 614-501-5600
Christopher Brooks, prin. Fax 501-5622

St. Pius X S 700/PK-8
1061 Waggoner Rd 43068 614-866-6050
Darren Smith, prin. Fax 866-6187

Richfield, Summit, Pop. 3,610
Revere Local SD 2,600/PK-12
3496 Everett Rd 44286 330-666-4155
Matthew Montgomery, supt. Fax 659-3127
www.revereschools.org
Hillcrest ES 700/K-3
3080 Revere Rd 44286 330-659-6111
Julie Gulley, prin. Fax 659-6701
Other Schools – See Bath

Richmond Heights, Cuyahoga, Pop. 10,347
Richmond Heights Local SD 800/PK-12
447 Richmond Rd 44143 216-692-0086
Renee Willis Ph.D., supt. Fax 692-8487
www.richmondheightsschools.org
Richmond Heights ES 400/PK-6
447 Richmond Rd 44143 216-692-0099
Elizabeth Boyd, prin. Fax 692-8499

Richwood, Union, Pop. 2,209
North Union Local SD 1,500/PK-12
12920 State Route 739 43344 740-943-2509
Richard Baird, supt. Fax 943-2534
www.n-union.k12.oh.us
North Union ES 700/PK-5
420 Grove St 43344 740-943-3113
Dar Allison, prin. Fax 943-1010
North Union MS 400/6-8
12555 Mulvane Rd 43344 740-943-2369
Matt Burggraf, prin. Fax 943-9279

Rio Grande, Gallia, Pop. 808
Gallipolis CSD
Supt. — See Gallipolis
Rio Grande ES 300/PK-5
PO Box 197 45674 740-245-5333
Julie Bays, prin. Fax 245-9152

Ripley, Brown, Pop. 1,713
Ripley-Union-Lewis-Huntington Local SD 1,000/PK-12
PO Box 85 45167 937-392-4396
James Wilkins, supt. Fax 392-7003
www.rulh.us
Ripley-Union-Lewis-Huntington ES 400/PK-4
502 S 2nd St 45167 937-392-1141
Aric Fiscus, prin. Fax 392-7027
Other Schools – See Aberdeen

St. Michael S 100/PK-8
300 Market St 45167 937-392-4202
Andrew Arn, prin. Fax 392-4248

Rittman, Wayne, Pop. 6,392
Rittman EVD 1,100/K-12
100 Saurer St 44270 330-927-7401
James Ritchie, supt. Fax 927-7405
www.rittman.k12.oh.us/
Rittman ES 500/K-5
131 N Metzger Ave 44270 330-927-7461
Dr. Shawna DeVoe, prin. Fax 927-7465
Rittman MS 300/6-8
50 Saurer St 44270 330-927-7101
Keri Hamsher, prin. Fax 927-7145

Rock Creek, Ashtabula, Pop. 525
Jefferson Area Local SD
Supt. — See Jefferson
Rock Creek ES 300/K-6
3134 N Main St 44084 440-563-3820
Christopher Edison, prin. Fax 563-5609

Rockford, Mercer, Pop. 1,102
Parkway Local SD 1,100/PK-12
400 Buckeye St 45882 419-363-3045
Jeanne Osterfeld, supt. Fax 363-2595
www.parkwayschools.org/
Parkway ES 500/PK-4
400 Buckeye St 45882 419-363-3045
Mark Esselstein, prin. Fax 363-2598
Parkway MS 300/5-8
400 Buckeye St 45882 419-363-3045
Brian Woods, prin. Fax 363-2597

Rocky River, Cuyahoga, Pop. 19,974
Rocky River CSD 2,600/PK-12
1101 Morewood Pkwy 44116 440-333-6000
Dr. Michael Shoaf, supt. Fax 356-6014
www.rrcs.org
Beach S PK-PK
1101 Morewood Pkwy 44116 440-356-6000
Tara Marley, prin. Fax 356-6008
Goldwood PS 600/K-2
21600 Center Ridge Rd 44116 440-356-6720
Dr. Carol Rosiak, prin. Fax 356-6044
Kensington IS 600/3-5
20140 Lake Rd 44116 440-356-6770
Todd Murphy, prin. Fax 356-6040
Rocky River MS 600/6-8
1631 Lakeview Ave 44116 440-356-6870
Megan Rose, prin. Fax 356-6881

Ruffing Montessori S 300/K-8
1285 Orchard Park Dr 44116 440-333-2250
John McNamara, prin. Fax 333-2540
St. Christopher S 500/K-8
1610 Lakeview Ave 44116 440-331-3075
Scott Raiff, prin. Fax 331-0674
St. Thomas Lutheran S 50/PK-K
21211 Detroit Rd 44116 440-331-4426
Allyson Cipollo, prin. Fax 331-2681

Rootstown, Portage
Rootstown Local SD 1,200/K-12
4140 State Route 44 44272 330-325-9911
Andrew Hawkins, supt. Fax 325-4105
rootstown.sparcc.org
Rootstown ES 600/K-5
4140 State Route 44 44272 330-325-7971
Jeffrey Turner, prin. Fax 325-2683
Rootstown MS 300/6-8
4140 State Route 44 44272 330-325-9956
Robert Campbell, prin. Fax 325-8505

Roseville, Perry, Pop. 1,833
Franklin Local SD
Supt. — See Duncan Falls
Roseville ES 300/PK-6
PO Box 96 43777 740-697-7216
Frank VanKirk, prin. Fax 697-7143

Rossford, Wood, Pop. 6,225
Rossford EVD 1,100/PK-12
601 Superior St 43460 419-666-2010
Daniel Creps, supt. Fax 661-5432
www.rossfordschools.org/
Eagle Point ES 100/3-5
203 Eagle Point Rd 43460 419-666-1174
Jeffrey Taylor, prin. Fax 662-3050
Rossford JHS 300/6-8
651 Superior St 43460 419-666-5254
Bryan Skrzyniecki, prin. Fax 661-2890
Other Schools – See Perrysburg

All Saints S 200/PK-8
630 Lime City Rd 43460 419-661-2070
Sr. Teresa Fischer, prin. Fax 661-2077

Russellville, Brown, Pop. 559
Eastern Local SD
Supt. — See Winchester
Russellville ES 300/K-5
239 W Main St 45168 937-377-4771
Katrina Wagoner, prin. Fax 377-9110

Russia, Shelby, Pop. 636
Russia Local SD 400/K-12
100 School St 45363 937-526-3156
Steven Rose, supt. Fax 526-0045
www.russiaschool.org
Russia ES 200/K-6
100 School St 45363 937-295-3454
Brian Hogan, prin. Fax 526-9519

Sabina, Clinton, Pop. 2,532
East Clinton Local SD 1,400/PK-12
97 Astro Way 45169 937-584-2461
Eric Magee, supt. Fax 584-2817
www.eastclinton.org
East Clinton MS 300/6-8
174 Larrick Rd 45169 937-584-9267
Robbin Luck, prin. Fax 584-9558
Sabina ES 400/PK-5
246 W Washington St 45169 937-584-5421
Jennifer Pierson, prin. Fax 584-5232
Other Schools – See New Vienna

Saint Bernard, Hamilton, Pop. 4,269
St. Bernard-Elmwood Place CSD 1,000/PK-12
105 Washington Ave 45217 513-482-7121
Dr. Mimi Webb, supt. Fax 641-0066
www.sbepschools.org
Saint Bernard ES 300/K-6
4515 Tower Ave 45217 513-482-7110
Karen Clemons, prin. Fax 641-0278
Other Schools – See Elmwood Place

St. Clement S 200/PK-8
4534 Vine St 45217 513-641-2137
Jeffrey Eiser, prin. Fax 242-6036

Saint Clairsville, Belmont, Pop. 5,119
St. Clairsville-Richland CSD 1,700/PK-12
108 Woodrow Ave 43950 740-695-1624
Dr. Walter Skaggs, supt. Fax 695-1627
www.stcschools.com
St. Clairsville ES 600/PK-4
120 Norris St 43950 740-695-2753
Amber Shepherd-Smith, prin. Fax 695-2753
St. Clairsville MS 500/5-8
104 Woodrow Ave 43950 740-695-1591
Michael Mckeever, prin. Fax 695-2317

East Richland Christian S 100/PK-12
67888 Friends Church Rd 43950 740-695-2005
April Woods, admin. Fax 296-5219
St. Mary S 200/PK-8
226 W Main St 43950 740-695-3189
Nannette Kennedy, prin. Fax 695-3851

Saint Henry, Mercer, Pop. 2,423
St. Henry Consolidated Local SD 1,000/K-12
391 E Columbus St 45883 419-678-4834
Julie Garke, supt. Fax 678-1724
sthenryschools.org
Saint Henry ES 400/K-4
251 E Columbus St 45883 419-678-4834
Adam Puthoff, prin. Fax 678-2544
Saint Henry MS 300/5-8
381 E Columbus St 45883 419-678-4834
Kyle Kunk, prin. Fax 678-1724

Saint Marys, Auglaize, Pop. 8,208
St. Marys CSD 2,100/K-12
100 W Spring St 45885 419-394-4312
Shawn Brown, supt. Fax 394-5638
sm.k12.oh.us
St. Marys East PS 400/K-2
650 Armstrong St 45885 419-394-2616
Sue Sherman, prin. Fax 394-1149
St. Marys MS 500/6-8
2250 State Route 66 45885 419-394-2112
Mary Miller, prin. Fax 394-1932
St. Marys West IS 400/3-5
1301 W High St 45885 419-394-2016
Lisa Elson, prin. Fax 394-1881

Holy Rosary S 100/PK-8
128 S Pine St 45885 419-394-5291
Lora Krugh, prin. Fax 394-0184

Saint Paris, Champaign, Pop. 2,056
Graham Local SD 2,000/PK-12
7790 US Highway 36 43072 937-663-4123
Kirk Koennecke, supt. Fax 663-4670
www.grahamlocalschools.org
Graham ES 1,000/PK-5
9464 US Highway 36 43072 937-663-4449
Chad Miller, prin. Fax 663-0257
Graham MS 500/6-8
9644 US Highway 36 43072 937-663-5339
Adam Kunkle, prin. Fax 663-4674

Salem, Columbiana, Pop. 12,168
Salem CSD 2,100/K-12
1226 E State St 44460 330-332-0316
Dr. Joseph Shivers, supt. Fax 332-8936
www.salemquakers.org
Buckeye ES 500/K-2
1200 Buckeye Ave 44460 330-332-8917
John Lundin, prin. Fax 332-2137
Reilly ES 300/3-4
491 Reilly Ave 44460 330-332-8921
Cindy Viscounte, prin. Fax 332-2138
Salem JHS 300/7-8
1200 E 6th St 44460 330-332-8914
Sean Kirkland, prin. Fax 332-8923
Southeast ES 300/5-6
2200 Merle Rd 44460 330-332-8925
Lisa Whitacre, prin. Fax 332-8953

West Branch Local SD
Supt. — See Beloit
Damascus ES 400/K-4
14405 Pricetown Rd 44460 330-938-4500
Caitlin Reash, prin. Fax 938-4501

St. Paul S 100/PK-7
925 E State St 44460 330-337-3451
David Pancurak, prin. Fax 337-3607
Salem Wesleyan Academy 100/K-12
1095 Newgarden Ave 44460 330-332-4819
Dan Forrider, prin. Fax 332-4819

Salineville, Columbiana, Pop. 1,294
Southern Local SD 900/K-12
38095 State Route 39 43945 330-679-2343
John Wilson, supt. Fax 679-0193
www.southern.k12.oh.us
Southern Local ES 500/K-6
38095E State Route 39 43945 330-679-0281
Anita Romeo, prin. Fax 679-3005

Sandusky, Erie, Pop. 24,586
Perkins Local SD 2,300/K-12
3714 Campbell St Ste B 44870 419-625-0484
Jodie Hausmann Ed.D., supt. Fax 621-2052
www.perkinsschools.org
Briar MS 500/6-8
3700 South Ave 44870 419-625-0132
Scott Matheny, prin. Fax 625-0523
Furry ES 500/K-2
310 Douglas Dr 44870 419-625-4352
Jennifer Long, prin. Fax 625-6211
Meadowlawn ES 500/2-5
1313 E Strub Rd 44870 419-625-0214
Cristin Cicco, prin. Fax 625-6459

Sandusky CSD 3,300/PK-12
407 Decatur St 44870 419-626-6940
Eugene Sanders Ph.D., supt. Fax 621-2784
www.scs-k12.net
Hancock ES 400/PK-6
2314 Hancock St 44870 419-984-1210
Kathleen Pace-Sanders, prin. Fax 621-2854
Mills ES 400/PK-6
1918 Mills St 44870 419-984-1230
Jude Andres, prin. Fax 621-2855
Ontario ES 400/K-6
924 Ontario St 44870 419-984-1250
Timothy Kozak, prin. Fax 621-2852
Osborne ES 400/K-6
920 W Osborne St 44870 419-984-1270
Rebecca Muratori, prin. Fax 626-9435
Sandusky MS 400/7-8
2130 Hayes Ave 44870 419-984-1182
Marie Prieto, prin. Fax 621-2849
Venice Heights ES 400/K-6
4501 Venice Heights Blvd 44870 419-984-1290
Donna Brown, prin. Fax 621-2850

Sandusky Central Catholic S 600/PK-12
410 W Jefferson St 44870 419-626-1892
Dennis Antonelli, prin. Fax 621-2252

Sarahsville, Noble, Pop. 166
Noble Local SD 900/PK-12
20977 Zep Rd E 43779 740-732-2084
Daniel Leffingwell, supt. Fax 732-7669
www.gozeps.org/
Shenandoah S 700/PK-8
20977 Zep Rd E 43779 740-732-5661
Frank Wesson, prin.

Sardinia, Brown, Pop. 978
Eastern Local SD
Supt. — See Winchester
Sardinia ES 300/K-6
PO Box 67 45171 937-446-2250
Joshua Michael, prin. Fax 446-3518

Brown County Christian Academy 50/K-6
PO Box 48 45171 937-446-1220

Scio, Harrison, Pop. 750
Harrison Hills CSD
Supt. — See Cadiz
Harrison North ES 400/PK-6
322 W Main St 43988 740-942-7500
Michael Saffell, prin. Fax 942-7504

Seaman, Adams, Pop. 934
Adams County/Ohio Valley Local SD
Supt. — See West Union
North Adams ES 700/PK-6
2295 Moores Rd 45679 937-386-2516
Deirdre Mills, prin. Fax 386-2032

Sebring, Mahoning, Pop. 4,362
Sebring Local SD 600/K-12
510 N 14th St 44672 330-938-6165
Toni Viscounte M.Ed., supt. Fax 938-4701
www.sebring.k12.oh.us/
Miller ES 300/K-6
506 W Virginia Ave 44672 330-938-2025
Heather Whipkey, prin. Fax 938-4703

Senecaville, Guernsey, Pop. 454
Rolling Hills Local SD
Supt. — See Cambridge
Secrest ES 200/K-2
58860 Wintergreen Rd 43780 740-685-2504
Jude Black, prin. Fax 685-6220

Seven Hills, Cuyahoga, Pop. 11,709
Parma CSD
Supt. — See Parma
Hillside MS 700/5-7
1 Educational Park Dr 44131 440-885-2373
Michelle Cook, prin. Fax 885-8448

Seven Mile, Butler, Pop. 743
Edgewood CSD
Supt. — See Trenton
Seven Mile ES 200/K-5
200 W Ritter St 45062 513-726-6234
Lori Harrison, prin. Fax 726-6239

Seville, Medina, Pop. 2,268
Cloverleaf Local SD
Supt. — See Lodi
Cloverleaf ES 1,100/PK-5
8337 Friendsville Rd 44273 330-721-3841
Karen Martin, prin.
Cloverleaf MS 600/6-8
7500 Buffham Rd 44273 330-721-3606
Brian Madigan, prin. Fax 721-3619

Shadyside, Belmont, Pop. 3,765
Shadyside Local SD 800/PK-12
3890 Lincoln Ave 43947 740-676-3235
John Haswell, supt. Fax 676-6616
www.shadyside.k12.oh.us
Jefferson Avenue ES 200/PK-2
4895 Jefferson Ave 43947 740-676-9669
Cynthia Caldwell, prin. Fax 671-5002
Leona Avenue MS 200/3-6
3795 Leona Ave 43947 740-676-9220
Kevin Roseberry, prin. Fax 676-6616

Shaker Heights, Cuyahoga, Pop. 27,675
Shaker Heights CSD 5,300/PK-12
15600 Parkland Dr 44120 216-295-1400
Gregory C. Hutchings Ed.D., supt. Fax 295-4340
www.shaker.org
Boulevard ES 400/K-4
14900 Drexmore Rd 44120 216-295-4020
Neal Robinson, prin. Fax 295-4019
Fernway ES 300/K-4
17420 Fernway Rd 44120 216-295-4040
Christopher Hayward, prin. Fax 295-4036
Lomond ES 400/K-4
17917 Lomond Blvd 44122 216-295-4050
Carina Freeman, prin. Fax 295-4016
Mercer ES 300/PK-4
23325 Wimbledon Rd 44122 216-295-4070
J. Lindsay Florence, prin. Fax 295-4017
Onaway ES 400/PK-4
3115 Woodbury Rd 44120 216-295-4080
Eric Forman, prin. Fax 295-4018
Shaker Heights MS 900/7-8
20600 Shaker Blvd 44122 216-295-4100
David Glasner, prin. Fax 295-4129
Woodbury ES 800/5-6
15400 S Woodland Rd 44120 216-295-4150
H. Danny Young, prin. Fax 295-4032

Hathaway Brown S 800/PK-12
19600 N Park Blvd 44122 216-932-4214
Dr. Fran Bisselle, head sch Fax 397-0991
Laurel S 700/PK-12
1 Lyman Cir 44122 216-464-1441
Ann V. Klotz, head sch Fax 464-8996
St. Dominic S 200/PK-8
3455 Norwood Rd 44122 216-561-4400
Susan Biggs, prin. Fax 561-1573
University S 500/K-8
20701 Brantley Rd 44122 216-321-8260
Stephen Murray, hdmstr. Fax 321-4074

Sharonville, Hamilton, Pop. 13,127

St. Michael S 400/K-8
11136 Oak St 45241 513-554-3555
Carolyn Murphy, prin. Fax 554-3551

Sheffield Lake, Lorain, Pop. 8,902
Sheffield-Sheffield Lake CSD 1,300/PK-12
1824 Harris Rd 44054 440-949-6181
Michael Cook, supt. Fax 949-4204
www.sheffield.k12.oh.us
Brookside IS 100/3-6
1812 Harris Rd 44054 440-949-4237
Daniel Rahm, prin. Fax 949-4279
Forestlawn ES 100/2-2
3975 Forestlawn Ave 44054 440-949-4238
Gretchen Loper, prin. Fax 949-4204
Knollwood ES 300/PK-1
4975 Oster Rd 44054 440-949-4234
Gretchen Loper, prin. Fax 949-4204
Other Schools – See Sheffield Vlg

Northern Ohio Adventist Academy K-12
555 Kenilworth Ave 44054 440-830-2043
Leona Bange, prin.

Sheffield Vlg, Lorain
Sheffield-Sheffield Lake CSD
Supt. — See Sheffield Lake
Brookside MS 300/7-8
1662 Harris Rd 44054 440-949-4228
Brent Schremp, prin. Fax 949-4204

Shelby, Richland, Pop. 9,228
Shelby CSD 1,800/K-12
PO Box 31 44875 419-342-3520
Tim Tarvin, supt. Fax 347-3586
www.shelbyk12.org
Auburn ES 400/K-4
109 Auburn Ave 44875 419-342-5456
Kelly Kuhn, prin. Fax 342-3023
Dowds ES 300/K-4
18 Seneca Dr 44875 419-342-4641
Kristin Kaple-Jones, prin. Fax 342-2825
Shelby MS 600/5-8
109 W Smiley Ave 44875 419-347-5451
Jeff Eichorn, prin. Fax 347-2095

Sacred Heart S 100/PK-8
5754 State Route 61 S 44875 419-683-1697
Lisa Myers, prin. Fax 342-2797
St. Mary S 100/PK-7
26 West St 44875 419-342-2626
Lisa Rhodes, prin. Fax 347-2763

Sherrodsville, Carroll, Pop. 303
Conotton Valley Union Local SD 400/PK-12
PO Box 187 44675 740-269-2000
Jerry T. Herman, supt. Fax 269-7901
www.cvul.org
Other Schools – See Bowerston

Sherwood, Defiance, Pop. 819
Central Local SD 1,100/K-12
6289 US Highway 127 43556 419-658-2808
Vicki L. Brunn, supt. Fax 658-4010
www.centrallocal.org
Fairview ES 500/K-5
14060 Blosser Rd 43556 419-658-2511
Sheryl Brown, prin. Fax 658-2302
Fairview MS 300/6-8
6289 US Highway 127 43556 419-658-2331
Suzanne Geis, prin. Fax 658-4010

Shreve, Wayne, Pop. 1,500
Triway Local SD
Supt. — See Wooster
Shreve ES 400/K-6
598 N Market St 44676 330-567-2837
Adam Stein, prin. Fax 567-9107

Sidney, Shelby, Pop. 20,551
Fairlawn Local SD 600/PK-12
18800 Johnston Rd 45365 937-492-1974
Jeffrey Hobbs, supt. Fax 492-8613
www.fairlawn.k12.oh.us
Fairlawn ES 300/PK-6
18800 Johnston Rd 45365 937-492-5930
Karen McRill, prin. Fax 492-5225

Sidney CSD 3,300/K-12
750 S 4th Ave 45365 937-497-2200
John Scheu, supt. Fax 497-2211
www.sidneycityschools.org
Emerson ES 400/K-4
901 Campbell Rd 45365 937-497-2261
Michael Moore, prin. Fax 497-2262
Longfellow ES 300/K-5
1250 Park St 45365 937-497-2264
Fran Dembski, prin. Fax 497-2263
Northwood ES 600/K-5
1152 Saint Marys Rd 45365 937-497-2231
Eric Barr, prin. Fax 497-2232
Sidney MS 900/5-8
980 Fair Rd 45365 937-497-2225
Diane Voress, prin. Fax 497-2204
Whittier ES 300/K-5
425 Belmont St 45365 937-497-2275
Keith Helmlinger, prin. Fax 497-2276

Christian Academy S 100/K-12
2151 W Russell Rd 45365 937-492-7556
Mary Smith, supt. Fax 492-5399
Holy Angels S 200/K-8
120 E Water St 45365 937-492-9293
Beth Spicer, prin. Fax 492-8578

Silver Lake, Summit, Pop. 2,502
Cuyahoga Falls CSD
Supt. — See Cuyahoga Falls
Silver Lake ES 200/K-5
2970 Overlook Rd 44224 330-926-3811
Rachael Seifert, prin. Fax 916-6023

Smithville, Wayne, Pop. 1,248
Green Local SD 1,000/K-12
PO Box 438 44677 330-669-3921
Doan Frank, supt. Fax 669-2121
www.green-local.k12.oh.us/
Green ES 300/K-4
200 Smithie Dr 44677 330-669-3501
Christine Miller, prin. Fax 669-2974
Green MS 400/5-8
200 Smithie Dr 44677 330-669-3165
Jason DeMassimo, prin. Fax 669-2069

Solon, Cuyahoga, Pop. 23,009
Solon CSD 4,400/PK-12
33800 Inwood Dr 44139 440-248-1600
Joseph Regano, supt. Fax 248-7665
www.solonschools.org
Arthur Road ES 100/PK-PK
33425 Arthur Rd 44139 440-349-6210
Carla Rodenbucher, prin. Fax 349-8018
Lewis ES 300/K-4
32345 Cannon Rd 44139 440-349-6225
Michael Acomb, prin. Fax 349-8012
Orchard MS 800/5-6
6800 Som Center Rd 44139 440-349-6215
Cariann Mineard, prin. Fax 349-8054
Parkside ES 400/K-4
6845 Som Center Rd 44139 440-349-2175
Amanda Sullen, prin. Fax 349-8055
Roxbury ES 400/K-4
6795 Solon Blvd 44139 440-349-6220
Mariann Moeschberger, prin. Fax 349-8048
Solon MS 800/7-8
6835 Som Center Rd 44139 440-349-3848
Scott Hatteberg, prin. Fax 349-8034

St. Rita S 400/PK-8
33200 Baldwin Rd 44139 440-248-1350
Deborah Grgic, prin. Fax 248-0442

Somerset, Perry, Pop. 1,577
Northern Local SD
Supt. — See Thornville
Somerset ES 300/K-5
100 High St 43783 740-743-1454
Ed Wolfel, prin. Fax 743-3324

Holy Trinity S 100/K-8
225 S Columbus St 43783 740-743-1324
Bill Noll, prin. Fax 743-1324

South Amherst, Lorain, Pop. 1,662
Firelands Local SD 1,700/K-12
112 N Lake St 44001 440-965-5821
Dr. Michael Von Gunten, supt. Fax 986-5990
www.firelandsschools.org/
South Amherst MS 400/6-8
152 W Main St 44001 440-986-7021
Cara Gomez, prin. Fax 986-7022
Other Schools – See Oberlin

South Bloomfield, Pickaway, Pop. 1,723
Teays Valley Local SD
Supt. — See Ashville

South Bloomfield ES 400/PK-5
194 Dowler Dr 43103 740-983-5000
Bruce Bryant, prin. Fax 983-5004

South Charleston, Clark, Pop. 1,672
Southeastern Local SD 700/PK-12
226 Clifton Rd 45368 888-627-6745
David Shea, supt. Fax 650-9129
www.sels.us
Miami View ES 400/PK-6
230 Clifton Rd 45368 937-462-8364
David Shea, prin. Fax 462-7914
Southeastern JHS 100/7-8
PO Box Z 45368 937-462-8308
P.J. Bertemes, prin. Fax 462-8394

South Euclid, Cuyahoga, Pop. 21,751
South Euclid-Lyndhurst CSD
Supt. — See Lyndhurst
Adrian ES 300/K-3
1071 Homestead Rd 44121 216-691-2170
Dr. Mark Woodby, prin. Fax 691-2295
Greenview Upper ES 800/4-6
1825 S Green Rd 44121 216-691-2245
Kelly Murphy, prin. Fax 691-3482
Rowland ES 400/K-3
4300 Bayard Rd 44121 216-691-2200
Maleeka Bussey, prin. Fax 691-2206

St. John Lutheran S 100/K-7
4386 Mayfield Rd 44121 216-381-8595
Tammy Szoyka, prin. Fax 381-1564

Southington, Trumbull
Southington Local SD 500/PK-12
2482 State Route 534 44470 330-898-7480
Rocco Nero, supt. Fax 898-4828
www.southington.k12.oh.us/
Southington ES 200/PK-5
2482 State Route 534 44470 330-898-7480
Lori Hall, prin. Fax 898-4828
Southington MS 200/6-8
2482 State Route 534 44470 330-898-1781
Robert Kujala, prin. Fax 898-4828

South Point, Lawrence, Pop. 3,885
South Point Local SD 1,600/K-12
302 High St 45680 740-377-4315
Mark Christian, supt. Fax 377-9735
www.southpoint.k12.oh.us
Burlington ES 400/K-5
8781 County Road 1 45680 740-894-4230
Michael Clay, prin. Fax 894-4201
South Point ES 400/K-5
201 Park Ave 45680 740-377-2756
Chris Mathes, prin. Fax 377-3229
South Point MS 400/6-8
983 County Road 60 45680 740-377-4343
Mylissa Bentley, prin. Fax 377-3228

South Salem, Ross, Pop. 203
Greenfield EVD
Supt. — See Greenfield
Buckskin ES 300/K-5
PO Box 69 45681 937-981-2673
Michael Shumate, prin. Fax 981-1924

South Vienna, Clark, Pop. 375
Northeastern Local SD
Supt. — See Springfield
South Vienna ES 600/K-5
140 W Main St 45369 937-346-0840
Denise Jones, prin. Fax 346-0842
South Vienna MS 300/6-8
140 W Main St 45369 937-346-0880
Belinda Banks, prin. Fax 568-4988

South Webster, Scioto, Pop. 856
Bloom-Vernon Local SD 900/PK-12
PO Box 237 45682 740-778-2281
Marc Kreischer, supt. Fax 778-2526
www.bv.k12.oh.us
Bloom-Vernon ES 600/PK-6
PO Box 479 45682 740-778-2339
Sandy Smith, prin. Fax 778-7600

Spencerville, Allen, Pop. 2,168
Spencerville Local SD 1,000/K-12
600 School St 45887 419-647-4111
Dennis Fuge, supt. Fax 647-6498
www.spencervillebearcats.com
Spencerville ES 400/K-4
2500 Wisher Dr 45887 419-647-4113
Susan Wagner, prin. Fax 647-5124
Spencerville MS 300/5-8
2500 Wisher Dr 45887 419-647-4112
Susan Wagner, prin. Fax 647-5124

Springboro, Warren, Pop. 17,124
Springboro Community CSD 5,800/PK-12
1685 S Main St 45066 937-748-3960
Daniel Schroer, supt. Fax 748-3956
www.springboro.org
Clearcreek ES 300/PK-1
750 S Main St 45066 937-748-3958
Carrie Corder, prin. Fax 748-3980
Dennis ES 1,100/2-5
1695 S Main St 45066 937-748-6070
Terrah Hunter, prin. Fax 748-6067
Springboro IS 500/6-6
705 S Main St 45066 937-748-4113
Diane Stacy, prin. Fax 748-8498
Springboro JHS 1,000/7-8
1605 S Main St 45066 937-748-3953
Jonathan Franks, prin. Fax 748-3964
Other Schools – See Centerville

CinDay Academy 300/PK-12
11 Sycamore Creek Dr 45066 937-748-1991
Gina Pangalangan, prin. Fax 748-2091

Springfield, Clark, Pop. 58,259
Clark-Shawnee Local SD 1,500/PK-12
3680 Selma Rd 45502 937-328-5378
Gregg Morris, supt. Fax 328-5379
www.clark-shawnee.k12.oh.us
Possum ES 300/K-6
2589 S Yellow Springs St 45506 937-328-5383
Michelle Heims, prin. Fax 328-5390
Reid ES 400/K-6
3640 E High St 45505 937-328-5380
Christina Elliott, prin. Fax 328-5392
Rockway ES 200/PK-6
3500 W National Rd 45504 937-328-5385
Amanda Shaffer, prin. Fax 328-5399
Shawnee MS 7-8
1675 E Possum Rd 45502 937-325-9296
Amanda Ike, admin. Fax 328-5389

Northeastern Local SD 3,400/K-12
1414 Bowman Rd 45502 937-325-7615
John Kronour, supt. Fax 328-6592
www.nelsd.org/
Northridge ES 400/K-5
4445 Ridgewood Rd E 45503 937-342-4627
Rob Shaffer, prin. Fax 342-4631
Northridge MS 500/6-8
4445 Ridgewood Rd E 45503 937-399-2852
Gary Miller, prin. Fax 342-4631
Rolling Hills ES 500/K-5
2613 Moorefield Rd 45502 937-399-2250
Scott Blackburn, prin. Fax 399-3454
Other Schools – See South Vienna

Northwestern Local SD 1,700/PK-12
5610 Troy Rd 45502 937-964-1318
Jesse Steiner, supt. Fax 964-6019
www.northwestern.k12.oh.us
Northwestern ES 1,000/PK-6
5610 Troy Rd 45502 937-964-3240
Luke Everhart, prin. Fax 964-3244

Springfield CSD 7,500/PK-12
1500 W Jefferson St 45506 937-505-2800
Dr. Robert F. Hill Ed.D., supt. Fax 505-2978
www.scsdoh.org
Clark Center Preschool 200/PK-PK
1500 W Jefferson St 45506 937-505-4170
Debra Accurso, prin. Fax 325-9358
Fulton ES 400/K-6
631 S Yellow Springs St 45506 937-505-4150
Dr. Sherry Cross, prin. Fax 322-5246
Hayward MS 400/7-8
1700 Clifton Ave 45505 937-505-4190
Susie Samuels, prin. Fax 323-9812
Kenton ES 400/K-6
731 E Home Rd 45503 937-505-4210
Amy Paul, prin. Fax 342-8528
Kenwood Heights ES 400/K-6
1421 Nagley St 45505 937-505-4220
Allyson Thurman, prin. Fax 324-9721
Lagonda ES 400/K-6
800 E McCreight Ave 45503 937-505-4240
Cathie Scott, prin. Fax 342-8954
Lincoln ES 400/K-6
1500 Tibbetts Ave 45505 937-505-4260
Michael Wilson, prin. Fax 324-8684
Mann ES 400/K-6
521 Mount Joy St 45505 937-505-4280
Kevin Schalnat, prin. Fax 323-7646
Perrin Woods ES 400/K-6
431 W John St 45506 937-505-4310
Dr. Nena Dorsey, prin. Fax 322-7576
Roosevelt MS 400/7-8
721 E Home Rd 45503 937-505-4370
Monte Brigham, prin. Fax 342-0280
Schaefer MS 300/7-8
147 S Fostoria Ave 45505 937-505-4390
Kimberly Watkins, prin. Fax 325-8974
Snowhill ES 500/K-6
531 W Harding Rd 45504 937-505-4410
Jennifer Paxson, prin. Fax 399-2585
Snyder Park ES 400/K-6
1600 Maiden Ln 45504 937-505-4430
Cheryl Farnbaugh, prin. Fax 324-2246
Warder Park - Wayne ES 400/K-6
2820 Hillside Ave 45503 937-505-4450
Roy Swanson, prin. Fax 323-7924

Catholic Central ES Lagonda Campus 3-8
1200 E High St 45505 937-324-4551
Shannon DeWeese, prin. Fax 327-4070
Catholic Central ES Limestone Campus 300/PK-2
1200 E High St 45505 937-399-5451
Shannon DeWeese, prin. Fax 342-0042
Emmanuel Christian Academy 500/PK-12
2177 Emmanuel Way 45502 937-390-3777
Kirk Peterson, supt. Fax 390-0966
Nightingale Montessori S 50/PK-12
1106 E High St 45505 937-324-0336
Maria Taylor, prin. Fax 398-0086
Ridgewood S 100/K-8
2420 Saint Paris Pike 45504 937-399-8900
Aliya Ranginwala, head sch Fax 399-8173
Risen Christ Lutheran S 100/PK-6
41 E Possum Rd 45502 937-323-3688
Rebecca Reid, prin. Fax 323-3746
Springfield Christian S 100/PK-8
311 W High St 45506 937-325-3113
Judy Loy, prin. Fax 325-9302

Steubenville, Jefferson, Pop. 18,007
Steubenville CSD 2,400/PK-12
PO Box 189 43952 740-283-3767
Melinda Young, supt. Fax 283-8930
scs.steubenville.k12.oh.us
East Garfield ES 400/PK-4
936 N 5th St 43952 740-282-4912
Thomas Kotsanis, prin. Fax 283-8935
Harding MS 700/5-8
2002 Sunset Blvd 43952 740-282-3481
Bryan Mills, prin. Fax 283-8949
Wells Academy 300/PK-4
420 N 4th St 43952 740-282-1651
Michael Crosier, prin. Fax 283-8945
West Pugliese ES 500/PK-4
435 John Scott Connector 43952 740-264-1590
Lynnett Gorman, prin. Fax 264-2190

Bishop John King Mussio Central JHS 7-8
320 Westview Ave Ste 2 43952 740-346-0028
Theresa Danaher, prin. Fax 346-0070
Bishop John King Mussio Central S 400/PK-8
100 Etta Ave 43952 740-264-2550
Theresa Danaher, prin. Fax 266-2843

Stewart, Athens, Pop. 244
Federal Hocking Local SD 1,000/PK-12
8461 State Route 144 45778 740-662-6691
Dr. George Wood, supt. Fax 662-5065
www.fedhock.com
Federal Hocking MS 100/7-8
8461 State Route 144 45778 740-662-6691
Cliff Bonner, prin. Fax 662-3805
Other Schools – See Amesville, Coolville

Stockport, Morgan, Pop. 476
Morgan Local SD
Supt. — See Mc Connelsville
South ES 400/PK-6
3555 State Route 792 43787 740-559-2377
Sherry Poling, prin. Fax 559-2864

Stow, Summit, Pop. 34,347
Stow-Munroe Falls CSD 5,300/PK-12
4350 Allen Rd 44224 330-689-5445
Thomas Bratten, supt. Fax 689-5448
www.smfschools.org
Echo Hills ES 300/K-4
4405 Stow Rd 44224 330-689-5450
David Ulbricht, prin. Fax 686-3129
Fishcreek ES 400/K-4
5080 Fishcreek Rd 44224 330-689-5460
Joanne Bratten, prin. Fax 686-3126
Highland ES 300/K-4
1843 Graham Rd 44224 330-689-5330
Meghan Graziano, prin. Fax 686-4711
Indian Trail ES 300/PK-4
3512 Kent Rd 44224 330-689-5320
John Lacoste, prin. Fax 686-4716
Lakeview IS 800/5-6
1819 Graham Rd 44224 330-689-5250
Andy Yanchunas, prin. Fax 686-4708
Woodland ES 300/K-4
2908 Graham Rd 44224 330-689-5470
Mary Lou Muckleroy, prin. Fax 686-4712
Other Schools – See Munroe Falls

Heritage Classical Academy K-8
4460 Stow Rd 44224 330-998-0554
Holy Family S 700/PK-8
3163 Kent Rd 44224 330-688-3816
Sharon Fournier, prin. Fax 688-3474

Strasburg, Tuscarawas, Pop. 2,588
Strasburg-Franklin Local SD 600/K-12
140 N Bodmer Ave 44680 330-878-5571
Cynthia Brown, supt. Fax 878-7900
www.strasburg.k12.oh.us/
Strasburg-Franklin ES 300/K-5
140 N Bodmer Ave 44680 330-878-6503
Sheila Doerschuk, prin. Fax 878-5983

Streetsboro, Portage, Pop. 15,768
Streetsboro CSD 2,200/PK-12
9000 Kirby Ln 44241 330-626-4900
R. Michael Daulbaugh, supt. Fax 626-8102
www.streetsboroschools.com
Defer IS 500/4-6
1895 Annalane Dr 44241 330-422-2480
Jeff Keruski, prin. Fax 626-4192
Streetsboro ES 300/PK-3
8955 Kirby Ln 44241 330-626-4907
Amy Cruse, prin. Fax 626-8106
Streetsboro MS 300/7-8
1951 Annalane Dr 44241 330-626-4905
Vincent Suber, prin. Fax 626-8104

Strongsville, Cuyahoga, Pop. 44,134
Strongsville CSD 4,700/PK-12
18199 Cook Ave 44136 440-572-7000
Cameron Ryba, supt. Fax 572-7041
strongnet.org
Chapman ES 400/K-6
13883 Drake Rd 44136 440-572-7140
Gregory Pollock, prin. Fax 572-7146
Kinsner ES 400/K-6
19091 Waterford Pkwy 44149 440-572-7120
Adam Marino, prin. Fax 572-7125
Muraski ES 500/K-6
20270 Royalton Rd 44149 440-572-7160
Justina Peters, prin. Fax 572-7165
Strongsville Early Learning Preschool 100/PK-PK
19543 Lunn Rd 44149 440-572-7046
Megan Surso, dir. Fax 846-3227
Strongsville MS 500/7-8
13200 Pearl Rd 44136 440-572-7090
Steve Deitrick, prin. Fax 572-7094
Surrarrer ES 300/K-6
9306 Priem Rd 44149 440-572-7170
Dr. Sally Wierzbicki, prin. Fax 572-7175
Whitney ES 300/K-6
13548 Whitney Rd 44136 440-572-7180
Glen Stacho, prin. Fax 572-7185

SS. Joseph & John S 600/K-8
12580 Pearl Rd 44136 440-238-4877
Darlene Thomas, prin. Fax 238-8745

Struthers, Mahoning, Pop. 10,554
Struthers CSD 1,900/K-12
99 Euclid Ave 44471 330-750-1061
Pete Pirone, supt. Fax 750-5516
www.strutherscityschools.org
Struthers ES 700/K-4
520 9th St 44471 330-750-1065
Bethany Carlson, prin. Fax 750-1489
Struthers MS 600/5-8
800 5th St 44471 330-750-1064
Dave Vecchione, prin. Fax 755-4749

St. Nicholas S 200/K-8
762 5th St 44471 330-755-2128
Elizabeth McCullough, prin. Fax 755-9949

Stryker, Williams, Pop. 1,320
Stryker Local SD 400/K-12
400 S Defiance St 43557 419-682-6961
Nate Johnson, supt. Fax 682-2646
www.stryker.k12.oh.us
Stryker ES 200/K-6
400 S Defiance St 43557 419-682-2841
Denise Meyer, prin. Fax 682-3508

Suffield, Portage
Field Local SD
Supt. — See Mogadore
Suffield ES 400/K-5
1128 Waterloo Rd 44260 330-552-5252
Shawn Bookman, prin. Fax 628-9160

Sugarcreek, Tuscarawas, Pop. 2,197
Garaway Local SD 1,200/K-12
146 Dover Rd NW 44681 330-852-2421
Dr. James Millet, supt. Fax 852-2991
www.garaway.org
Miller Avenue ES 200/K-6
840 Miller Ave SW 44681 330-852-2441
Curtis Fisher, prin. Fax 852-7702
Ragersville ES 100/K-6
2405 Ragersville Rd SW 44681 330-897-5021
Joffery Williams, prin. Fax 897-9941
Other Schools – See Baltic, Dundee

Sugar Grove, Fairfield, Pop. 424
Berne Union Local SD 900/PK-12
PO Box 187 43155 740-746-8341
Richard Spindler, supt. Fax 746-9824
www.buschools.com
Berne Union ES 500/PK-6
PO Box 187 43155 740-746-9668
Steven Templin, prin. Fax 746-9824

Sullivan, Ashland
Black River Local SD 1,100/PK-12
257A County Road 40 44880 419-736-3300
Chris Clark, supt. Fax 736-3308
www.blackriver.k12.oh.us/
Black River ES 500/PK-5
257 County Road 40 44880 419-736-2161
Becky Luth, prin. Fax 736-2165
Black River MS 300/6-8
257 County Road 40 44880 419-736-3304
Cathy Aviles, prin. Fax 736-3309

Sunbury, Delaware, Pop. 4,313
Big Walnut Local SD 3,400/PK-12
110 Tippett Ct 43074 740-965-3010
Angela Pollock, supt. Fax 965-4688
www.bwls.net
Big Walnut ES 500/PK-4
940 S Old 3C Rd 43074 740-965-3902
Andrea Clark, prin. Fax 965-3168
Big Walnut IS 500/5-6
105 Baughman St 43074 740-965-7800
Ryan McLane, prin.
Big Walnut MS 500/6-8
777 Cheshire Rd 43074 740-965-3006
Joshua Frame, prin. Fax 965-6471
Harrison Street ES 300/K-5
70 Harrison St 43074 740-965-7850
Kim Castiglione, prin. Fax 965-7851
Rosecrans ES 500/PK-4
301 S Miller Dr 43074 740-965-8900
Megan Forman, prin. Fax 965-8993
Other Schools – See Galena

Swanton, Fulton, Pop. 3,658
Swanton Local SD 1,300/PK-12
108 N Main St 43558 419-826-7085
Jay LeFevre, supt. Fax 825-1197
www.swantonschools.org
Swanton ES 300/K-4
111 Crestwood Dr 43558 419-826-8991
Kristi Molter, prin. Fax 826-8646
Swanton MS 300/5-8
101 Elton Pkwy 43558 419-826-3766
Matt Smith, prin. Fax 826-2965

Holy Trinity S 200/PK-8
2639 US Highway 20 43558 419-644-3971
Brandon Kulka, prin. Fax 644-9372
St. Richard S 100/PK-8
333 Brookside Dr 43558 419-826-5041
Sr. Jean Walczak, prin. Fax 826-7256

Sycamore, Wyandot, Pop. 857
Mohawk Local SD 1,000/PK-12
605 State Highway 231 44882 419-927-2414
Kenneth Ratliff, supt. Fax 927-2393
www.mohawklocal.org
Mohawk ES 500/PK-6
605 State Highway 231 44882 419-927-2595
Tamara Wallace, prin. Fax 927-6139

Sylvania, Lucas, Pop. 18,670
Sylvania SD 7,400/K-12
4747 N Holland Sylvania Rd 43560 419-824-8500
Adam Fineske, supt. Fax 824-8503
www.sylvaniaschools.org
Arbor Hills JHS 500/6-8
5334 Whiteford Rd 43560 419-824-8640
Mellisa McDonald, prin. Fax 824-8659
Central Trail ES 600/K-5
4321 Mitchaw Rd 43560 419-824-8610
Amanda Ogren, prin. Fax 824-8606
Highland ES 600/K-5
7720 Erie St 43560 419-824-8611
Mark Pugh, prin. Fax 824-8635
Hill View ES 400/K-5
5424 Whiteford Rd 43560 419-824-8612
Chad Kolebuck, prin. Fax 824-8639
Maplewood ES 400/K-5
6769 Maplewood Ave 43560 419-824-8613
John Duwve, prin. Fax 824-8649
McCord JHS 700/6-8
4304 N McCord Rd 43560 419-824-8650
Joshua Tyburski, prin. Fax 824-8619
Sylvan ES 300/K-5
4830 Wickford Dr E 43560 419-824-8615
Juliane Gault, prin. Fax 824-8679
Timberstone JHS 500/6-8
9000 Sylvania Ave 43560 419-824-8680
Mike Bader, prin. Fax 824-8690
Other Schools – See Toledo

St. Joseph S 700/PK-8
5411 Main St 43560 419-882-6670
Sally Koppinger, prin. Fax 885-1990
Toledo Islamic Academy 200/PK-12
5225 Alexis Rd 43560 419-882-3339
Dr. Nabila Gomaa Ph.D., prin. Fax 882-3334

Tallmadge, Summit, Pop. 17,273
Tallmadge CSD 2,400/K-12
486 East Ave 44278 330-633-3291
Jeffrey Ferguson, supt. Fax 633-5331
www.tallmadgeschools.org
Dunbar ES 500/K-2
731 Dunbar Rd 44278 330-633-4515
Courtney Davis, prin. Fax 630-5981
Munroe ES 500/3-5
230 N Munroe Rd 44278 330-633-5427
Shelley Monachino, prin. Fax 630-5983
Tallmadge MS 600/6-8
484 East Ave 44278 330-633-4994
Jeff Manion, prin. Fax 630-5984

Cornerstone Community S 100/PK-6
90 W Overdale Dr 44278 330-686-8900
David Smith, hdmstr. Fax 686-8224
Fact Academy/Tallmadge Kiddie Kollege 100/PK-6
199 South Ave 44278 330-633-9049
Teresa Hymes, admin. Fax 630-1792

Terrace Park, Hamilton, Pop. 2,238
Mariemont CSD
Supt. — See Cincinnati
Terrace Park ES 300/K-6
723 Elm Ave 45174 513-272-7700
Linda Lee, prin. Fax 831-1249

The Plains, Athens, Pop. 2,987
Athens CSD 2,700/PK-12
25 S Plains Rd 45780 740-797-4544
Dr. Thomas J. Gibbs, supt. Fax 797-2486
www.athenscsd.org
The Plains ES 400/K-6
90 Connett Rd 45780 740-797-4572
Heather Skinner, prin. Fax 797-4432
Other Schools – See Athens, Chauncey

Thompson, Geauga
Berkshire Local SD
Supt. — See Burton
Ledgemont ES 200/PK-6
16200 Burrows Rd 44086 440-298-3341
Kelly Timmons, prin. Fax 298-3342

Thornville, Perry, Pop. 982
Northern Local SD 2,100/K-12
8700 Sheridan Dr 43076 740-743-1303
Thomas Perkins, supt. Fax 743-3301
nlsd.k12.oh.us
Sheridan MS 500/6-8
8660 Sheridan Dr 43076 740-743-1315
Jay Hickman, prin. Fax 743-3319
Thornville ES 300/K-5
70 E Columbus St 43076 740-246-6636
Clinton Rhodes, prin. Fax 246-5399
Other Schools – See Glenford, Somerset

Tiffin, Seneca, Pop. 17,722
Tiffin CSD 2,800/PK-12
244 S Monroe St 44883 419-447-2515
Dr. Gary Barber Ed.D., supt. Fax 448-5202
www.tiffin.k12.oh.us
Krout ES 400/2-3
20 Glenn St 44883 419-447-2652
William Beaston, prin. Fax 448-5223
Lincoln Pre-Kindergarten 100/PK-PK
124 Ohio Ave 44883 419-455-9102
Michelle Tuite, prin.
Noble ES 400/4-5
130 Minerva St 44883 419-447-1566
Michael Newlove, prin. Fax 448-5219
Tiffin MS 700/6-8
103 Shepherd Dr 44883 419-447-3358
Shawn Murphy, prin. Fax 448-5250
Washington ES 400/K-1
151 Elmer St 44883 419-447-1072
Nichole Jiran, prin. Fax 448-5217

Calvert ES 400/PK-6
357 S Washington St 44883 419-447-5790
Michael Kaucher, prin. Fax 447-5798

Tiltonsville, Jefferson, Pop. 1,354
Buckeye Local SD
Supt. — See Dillonvale
Buckeye South ES 400/PK-6
100 Walden Ave 43963 740-859-2800
Julie Packer, prin. Fax 859-4004

Tipp City, Miami, Pop. 9,564
Bethel Local SD 900/K-12
7490 State Route 201 45371 937-845-9414
Virginia Potter, supt. Fax 845-5007
www.bethel.k12.oh.us
Bethel ES 500/K-5
7490 State Route 201 45371 937-845-9439
Jodi Petty, prin. Fax 845-5007
Bethel MS 200/6-8
7490 State Route 201 45371 937-845-9430
Alexis Dedrick, prin. Fax 845-5007

Tipp City EVD 2,500/K-12
90 S Tippecanoe Dr 45371 937-667-8444
Dr. Gretta Kumpf, supt. Fax 667-6886
www.tippcityschools.com/
Ball IS 400/4-5
575 N Hyatt St 45371 937-667-8454
Michael Vagedes, prin. Fax 667-0874
Broadway ES 400/2-3
223 W Broadway St 45371 937-667-6216
Tina Smith, prin. Fax 669-9405
Coppock ES 400/K-1
525 N Hyatt St 45371 937-667-2275
Katy Barker, prin. Fax 669-5508
Tippecanoe MS 600/6-8
555 N Hyatt St 45371 937-667-8454
Greg Southers, prin. Fax 667-0874

Toledo, Lucas, Pop. 278,478
Springfield Local SD
Supt. — See Holland
Dorr Street ES 400/K-5
1205 King Rd 43617 419-867-5666
Cheri Copeland-Shull, prin. Fax 867-5734

Sylvania SD
Supt. — See Sylvania
Stranahan ES 400/K-5
3840 N Holland Sylvania Rd 43615 419-824-8614
Jeremy Bauer, prin. Fax 824-8665
Whiteford ES 400/K-5
4708 Whiteford Rd 43623 419-824-8616
Andrew Duncan, prin. Fax 824-8697

Toledo CSD 21,200/PK-12
1609 N Summit St 43604 419-671-0001
Dr. Romules Durant, supt. Fax 671-8425
www.tps.org
Arlington ES 400/K-8
707 Woodsdale Ave 43609 419-671-2550
Dr. Melisa Viers, prin. Fax 671-2595
Beverly ES 700/K-8
3548 S Detroit Ave 43614 419-671-2600
Matthew Rowley, prin. Fax 671-2645
Birmingham ES 400/K-8
2222 Bakewell St 43605 419-671-7700
Stacey Scharf, prin. Fax 671-7745
Burroughs ES 400/K-8
2420 South Ave 43609 419-671-2350
Arlene Tucker, prin. Fax 671-2395
Byrnedale ES 400/K-8
3635 Glendale Ave 43614 419-671-2200
Christina Ramsey, prin. Fax 671-2260
Chase STEM Academy 200/K-8
600 Bassett St 43611 419-671-6650
Jack Hunter, prin. Fax 671-6695
Crossgates Preschool 200/PK-PK
3901 Shadylawn Dr 43614 419-671-2750
Lynn Pearson, prin. Fax 671-2795
DeVeaux ES 400/K-8
2620 W Sylvania Ave 43613 419-671-3200
Shaun Mitchell, prin. Fax 671-3260
East Broadway ES 500/K-8
1755 E Broadway St 43605 419-671-7200
Craig Otterson, prin. Fax 671-7260
Edgewater ES 200/K-8
5549 Edgewater Dr 43611 419-726-2254
Elizabeth Bethany, prin. Fax 729-8596
Elmhurst ES 500/K-8
4530 Elmhurst Rd 43613 419-671-3550
Lynn Moran, prin. Fax 671-3595
Garfield ES 400/K-8
1103 N Ravine Pkwy 43605 419-671-7550
Janice Richardson, prin. Fax 671-7595
Glendale-Feilbach ES 400/PK-8
2317 Cass Rd 43614 419-671-2650
Susan Chorba, prin. Fax 671-2695
Glenwood ES 200/K-8
2800 Glenwood Ave 43610 419-671-4600
Michael Carr, prin. Fax 671-4645
Grove Patterson Academy 400/K-8
3020 Marvin Ave 43606 419-671-3350
Herneika Johnson, prin. Fax 671-3395
Harvard ES 400/K-8
1949 Glendale Ave 43614 419-671-2700
Dr. John Jordan, prin. Fax 671-2745
Hawkins ES 400/K-8
5550 W Bancroft St 43615 419-671-1550
Jeffrey Hanthorn, prin. Fax 671-1595
Keyser ES 200/K-8
3900 Hill Ave 43607 419-671-1450
Natasha Allen, prin. Fax 671-1495
King Academy for Boys 300/K-8
1300 Forest Ave 43607 419-671-4550
Willie Ward, prin. Fax 671-4595

Larchmont ES 500/K-8
1515 Slater St 43612 419-671-3650
Kari Sharp, prin. Fax 671-3695
Leverette ES 400/K-8
445 E Manhattan Blvd 43608 419-671-6200
Kimberly Sams, prin. Fax 671-6260
Longfellow ES 600/K-8
1955 W Laskey Rd 43613 419-671-3800
Yolanda Johnson, prin. Fax 671-3845
Marshall ES 300/K-8
415 Colburn St 43609 419-671-5700
Marsha Jackisch, prin. Fax 671-5745
McKinley ES 300/K-8
3344 Westland Ave 43613 419-671-3750
John Korenowsky, prin. Fax 671-3795
McTigue ES 400/K-8
5555 Nebraska Ave 43615 419-671-1200
Tiffany Turner, prin. Fax 671-1260
Navarre ES 500/K-8
800 Kingston Ave 43605 419-671-7600
Katherine Taylor, prin. Fax 671-7645
Oakdale ES 400/K-8
1620 E Broadway St 43605 419-671-7350
Robert Yenrick, prin. Fax 671-7395
Old Orchard ES 300/PK-8
2402 Cheltenham Rd 43606 419-671-3700
Valerie Dreier, prin. Fax 671-3745
Old West End Academy 300/PK-8
3131 Cambridge St 43610 419-242-1050
Kathy Gregory, prin. Fax 242-1041
Ottawa River ES 500/K-8
4747 290th St 43611 419-671-6350
Tamra Bacon, prin. Fax 671-6395
Parks ES 200/K-8
3350 Cherry St 43608 419-671-4350
Angela Hickman-Richburg, prin. Fax 671-4395
Pickett Academy 200/K-8
1144 Blum St 43607 419-671-5600
Martha Jude, prin. Fax 671-5645
Raymer ES 600/K-8
550 Raymer Blvd 43605 419-671-7650
Barbara Ferguson, prin. Fax 671-7695
Reynolds ES 300/K-8
5000 Norwich Rd 43615 419-671-1500
Monica Clark Eagle, prin. Fax 671-1545
Riverside ES 400/K-8
500 Chicago St 43611 419-671-6700
Nathan Mollenhauer, prin. Fax 671-6745
Robinson ES 300/K-8
1075 Horace St 43606 419-671-4200
James Jones, prin. Fax 671-4260
Sherman ES 300/K-8
817 Sherman St 43608 419-671-6550
Kelli Williams, prin. Fax 671-6595
Spring ES 300/K-8
730 Spring St 43608 419-671-6600
Victoria Dipman, prin. Fax 671-6645
Stewart Academy for Girls 300/K-8
707 Avondale Ave 43604 419-671-5350
Teresa Quinn, prin. Fax 671-5395
Walbridge ES 400/K-8
1245 Walbridge Ave 43609 419-671-5650
Monica DeBerg-Peace, prin. Fax 671-5695
Whittier ES 600/K-8
4221 Walker Ave 43612 419-671-3600
Eric Remley, prin. Fax 671-3645

Washington Local SD 6,800/PK-12
3505 W Lincolnshire Blvd 43606 419-473-8220
Dr. Susan Hayward, supt. Fax 473-8200
www.wls4kids.org
Greenwood ES 400/K-6
760 Northlawn Dr 43612 419-473-8263
William Colon, prin. Fax 473-8264
Hiawatha ES 400/K-6
3020 Photos Dr 43613 419-473-8268
Albert Bernhardt, prin. Fax 473-8269
Jackman ES 400/K-6
2010 Northover Rd 43613 419-473-8274
Dr. Amy Franco, prin. Fax 473-8275
Jefferson JHS 500/8-8
5530 Whitmer Dr 43613 419-473-8482
Lisa Morse, prin. Fax 473-8393
McGregor ES 400/K-6
3535 McGregor Ln 43623 419-473-8279
Gerald Bell, prin. Fax 473-8280
Meadowvale ES 600/K-6
2755 Edgebrook Dr 43613 419-473-8284
Christine Williams, prin. Fax 473-8285
Monac ES 500/K-6
3845 Clawson Ave 43623 419-473-8289
Sean Flemmings, prin. Fax 473-8290
Shoreland ES 600/K-6
5650 Suder Ave 43611 419-473-8294
Kim Dedo, prin. Fax 473-8295
Washington JHS 500/7-7
5700 Whitmer Dr 43613 419-473-8449
Jennifer Bronikowski, prin. Fax 473-8340
Wernert ES 400/PK-6
5050 Douglas Rd 43613 419-473-8218
Scott Scharf, prin. Fax 473-8219

Blessed Sacrament S 300/PK-8
4255 Bellevue Rd 43613 419-472-1121
Gregory Sattler, prin. Fax 472-1679
CCMT-Queen of Apostles S 200/K-8
235 Courtland Ave 43609 419-241-7829
Sr. Joselyn Weeman M.Ed., prin. Fax 241-4180
CCMT-Rosary Cathedral S 200/PK-8
2535 Collingwood Blvd 43610 419-243-4396
Joselyn Weeman, prin. Fax 243-6049
Christ the King S 500/PK-8
4100 Harvest Ln 43623 419-475-0909
Joseph Carroll, prin. Fax 475-4050
Emmanuel Christian S 400/K-12
4607 W Laskey Rd 43623 419-885-3558
Warren Aldrich, admin. Fax 885-0139
Gesu S 400/PK-8
2045 Parkside Blvd 43607 419-536-5634
Manuel Gonzales, prin. Fax 531-8932
Maumee Valley Country Day S 500/PK-12
1715 S Reynolds Rd 43614 419-381-1313
Gary Boehm, head sch Fax 381-1314
Our Lady of Perpetual Help S 200/PK-8
2255 Central Grv 43614 419-382-5696
Kari Bonnell, prin. Fax 382-7360
Regina Coeli S 300/PK-8
600 Regina Pkwy 43612 419-476-0920
Dr. Debra Bloomquist, prin. Fax 476-6792
St. Benedict Catholic S 300/PK-8
5522 Dorr St 43615 419-536-1194
Martha Hartman, prin. Fax 531-5140
St. Joan of Arc S 400/PK-8
5950 Heatherdowns Blvd 43614 419-866-6177
Jennifer Guzman, prin. Fax 866-4107
St. Patrick of Heatherdowns S 500/PK-8
4201 Heatherdowns Blvd 43614 419-381-1775
Tina Abel, prin. Fax 389-1161
St. Pius X S 300/PK-8
2950 Ilger Ave 43606 419-535-7688
Susan Richardson, prin. Fax 535-7829
Toledo Christian S 600/PK-12
2303 Brookford Dr 43614 419-389-8700
Scott Gibson, supt. Fax 389-8703
Toledo Junior Academy 100/K-8
4909 W Sylvania Ave 43623 419-841-0082
Trinity Lutheran S 200/PK-8
4560 Glendale Ave 43614 419-385-2301
Jim Landskroener, prin. Fax 385-2636
West Side Montessori - Toledo Campus 400/PK-8
7115 W Bancroft St 43615 419-866-1931
Zion Lutheran S 50/K-8
630 Cuthbert Rd 43607 419-531-1507
Luke Scherschel, prin. Fax 531-1507

Toronto, Jefferson, Pop. 5,027
Toronto CSD 1,000/PK-12
1307 Dennis Way 43964 740-537-2456
Maureen Taggart, supt. Fax 537-1102
www.torontocsd.org
Karaffa MS 500/PK-5
1307 Dennis Way 43964 740-537-2471
Christopher Dopp, prin. Fax 537-1102

Trenton, Butler, Pop. 11,671
Edgewood CSD 3,600/PK-12
3500 Busenbark Rd 45067 513-863-4692
Simon Fussnecker, supt. Fax 867-7421
www.edgewoodschools.com
Babeck Early Learning Center 600/PK-1
100 Maple Ave 45067 513-988-0111
Jeffrey Banks, prin. Fax 988-5561
Edgewood ES 900/2-5
3440 Busenbark Rd 45067 513-867-7430
Jenny Halsey, prin. Fax 867-7571
Edgewood MS 900/6-8
5005 State Route 73 45067 513-867-7425
David Slamer, prin. Fax 867-7428
Other Schools – See Seven Mile

Trotwood, Montgomery, Pop. 23,764
Trotwood-Madison CSD 2,500/PK-12
3594 N Snyder Rd 45426 937-854-3050
Kevin Bell, supt. Fax 854-3057
www.trotwood.k12.oh.us/
Madison Park ES 400/2-4
301 S Broadway St 45426 937-854-4456
Tamara Rizzo-Sterner, prin. Fax 854-4493
Trotwood-Madison Early Learning Center 500/PK-2
4400 N Union Rd 45426 937-854-4511
Nicole Davis, prin. Fax 854-4624
Trotwood-Madison MS 700/5-8
4420 N Union Rd 45426 937-854-0017
Nathan Warner, prin. Fax 854-8433
Westbrooke Village ES 100/PK-PK
6500 Westford Rd 45426 937-854-3196
Tracey Mallory, prin. Fax 854-8704

Troy, Miami, Pop. 24,463
Troy CSD 4,300/K-12
500 N Market St 45373 937-332-6700
Eric Herman, supt. Fax 332-6771
www.troy.k12.oh.us
Concord ES 600/K-5
3145 State Route 718 45373 937-332-6730
Dan Hake, prin. Fax 332-3840
Cookson ES 400/K-5
921 Mystic Ln 45373 937-332-6740
Stephanie Johnson, prin. Fax 332-3980
Forest ES 300/K-5
413 E Canal St 45373 937-332-6746
Paul Hohlbein, prin. Fax 332-3976
Heywood ES 300/K-5
260 S Ridge Ave 45373 937-332-6750
Maurice Sadler, prin. Fax 332-3891
Hook ES 300/K-5
729 Trade Sq W 45373 937-332-6760
Penny Johnson, prin. Fax 332-3911
Kyle ES 200/K-5
501 S Plum St 45373 937-332-6770
Matt Dillon, prin. Fax 335-9585
Troy JHS 700/7-8
556 Adams St 45373 937-332-6720
Dave Dilbone, prin. Fax 332-3812
Van Cleve 6th Grade S 300/6-6
617 E Main St 45373 937-332-6780
Matt Siefring, prin. Fax 332-3951

Miami Montessori S 100/PK-6
86 Troy Town Dr 45373 937-339-0025
Sharon Prais, head sch Fax 302-8586
St. Patrick S 200/PK-6
420 E Water St 45373 937-339-3705
Cynthia Cathcart, prin. Fax 339-1158
Troy Christian ES 200/PK-6
1586 McKaig Rd 45373 937-339-5692
Dr. Gary Wilber, supt. Fax 335-6258

Tuscarawas, Tuscarawas, Pop. 1,051
Indian Valley Local SD
Supt. — See Gnadenhutten
Indian Valley MS 500/6-8
261 School St 44682 740-922-4226
Brent Carter, prin. Fax 922-2493

Twinsburg, Summit, Pop. 18,443
Twinsburg CSD 4,200/PK-12
11136 Ravenna Rd 44087 330-486-2000
Kathryn Powers, supt. Fax 425-7216
www.twinsburg.k12.oh.us
Bissell ES 600/2-3
1811 Glenwood Dr 44087 330-486-2100
Misty Johnson, prin. Fax 963-8333
Chamberlin MS 700/7-8
10270 Ravenna Rd 44087 330-486-2281
James Ries, prin. Fax 963-8313
Dodge IS 900/4-6
10225 Ravenna Rd 44087 330-486-2200
Reginald Holland, prin. Fax 963-8323
Wilcox PS 600/PK-1
9198 Darrow Rd 44087 330-486-2030
Lynn Villa, prin. Fax 963-8332

Uhrichsville, Tuscarawas, Pop. 5,330
Claymont CSD
Supt. — See Dennison
Claymont ES 100/2-3
1200 Eastport Ave 44683 740-922-4641
Elizabeth DiDonato, prin. Fax 922-7428
Claymont MS 300/6-8
215 E 6th St 44683 740-922-5241
Brian Watkins, prin. Fax 922-7330
Claymont PS 200/K-1
320 Trenton Ave 44683 740-922-5641
Eric Seibert, prin. Fax 922-7427

Union, Montgomery, Pop. 6,304
Northmont CSD
Supt. — See Englewood
Union ES 300/2-6
418 W Martindale Rd 45322 937-832-6700
Kevin Grone, prin. Fax 832-6701

Union City, Darke, Pop. 1,628
Mississinawa Valley Local SD 700/PK-12
1469 State Road 47 E 45390 937-968-5656
Douglas Dunham, supt. Fax 968-6731
www.mississinawa.k12.oh.us
Mississinawa Valley ES 400/K-6
10480 Staudt Rd 45390 937-968-4464
Stephanie Klingshirn, prin. Fax 968-6731
Mississinawa Valley Preschool PK-PK
1469 State Road 47 E 45390 937-968-3284

Union Furnace, Hocking
Logan-Hocking Local SD
Supt. — See Logan
Union Furnace ES 300/PK-4
PO Box 172 43158 740-380-6881
Roger Nott, prin. Fax 545-1553

Uniontown, Stark, Pop. 3,274
Green Local SD 4,200/PK-12
1755 Town Park Blvd 44685 330-896-7500
Jeffrey Miller, supt. Fax 896-7580
www.greenlocalschools.org
Green IS 1,000/4-6
1737 Steese Rd 44685 330-896-7700
Mark Booth, prin. Fax 896-7725
Green MS 700/7-8
1711 Steese Rd 44685 330-896-7710
Jeff Wells, prin. Fax 896-7760
Green PS 900/1-3
2300 Graybill Rd 44685 330-899-8700
Carrie Marochino, prin. Fax 899-8799
Greenwood Early Learning Center 400/PK-K
2250 Graybill Rd 44685 330-896-7474
Scott Shank, prin. Fax 896-7492

Lake Local SD 3,500/K-12
436 King Church Ave SW 44685 330-877-9383
Kevin Tobin, supt. Fax 877-4754
www.lakelocal.org
Uniontown ES 500/K-3
13244 Cleveland Ave NW 44685 330-877-4298
Frank Gant, prin. Fax 699-3101
Other Schools – See Hartville

Mayfair Christian S 50/K-9
2350 Graybill Rd 44685 330-896-3184
H. Clifford Reynolds, prin. Fax 896-0703

University Heights, Cuyahoga, Pop. 13,323
Cleveland Hts - University Hts CSD 5,300/PK-12
2155 Miramar Blvd 44118 216-371-7171
Dr. Talisa Dixon, supt. Fax 397-3880
www.chuh.org
Gearity Professional Development S 400/PK-5
2323 Wrenford Rd 44118 216-371-6515
Katrina Hicks, prin. Fax 397-5959
Other Schools – See Cleveland Heights

Gesu S 700/PK-8
2450 Miramar Blvd 44118 216-932-0620
Sr. Lucy Iemmolo, prin. Fax 932-8326

Upper Arlington, Franklin, Pop. 33,225
Upper Arlington CSD 5,800/K-12
1950 N Mallway Dr 43221 614-487-5000
Paul Imhoff, supt. Fax 487-5012
www.uaschools.org
Barrington ES 700/K-5
1780 Barrington Rd 43221 614-487-5180
Carla Wilson, prin. Fax 487-5189

Greensview ES 400/K-5
4301 Greensview Dr 43220 614-487-5050
Jason Wulf, prin. Fax 487-5190
Hastings MS 700/6-8
1850 Hastings Ln 43220 614-487-5100
Robb Gonda, prin. Fax 487-5116
Jones MS 700/6-8
2100 Arlington Ave 43221 614-487-5080
Jason Fine, prin. Fax 487-5307
Tremont ES 600/K-5
2900 Tremont Rd 43221 614-487-5170
Jim Buffer, prin. Fax 487-5746
Wickliffe ES 500/K-5
2405 Wickliffe Rd 43221 614-487-5150
Chris Collaros, prin. Fax 487-5161
Windermere ES 400/K-5
4101 Windermere Rd 43220 614-487-5060
Julie Nolan, prin. Fax 487-5378

Upper Sandusky, Wyandot, Pop. 6,540
Upper Sandusky EVD 1,600/K-12
800 N Sandusky Ave 43351 419-294-2307
Laurie Vent, supt. Fax 294-6891
www.usevs.org
East ES 100/K-5
401 N 3rd St 43351 419-294-2396
Angela Murphy, prin. Fax 294-6895
South ES 100/K-5
444 S 8th St 43351 419-294-2304
Angela Murphy, prin. Fax 294-6892
Union ES 300/K-3
390 W Walker St 43351 419-294-5721
Janine McMillan, prin. Fax 294-2586
Union MS 500/4-8
390 W Walker St 43351 419-294-5721
James Wheeler, prin. Fax 294-2586

St. Peter S 100/K-6
310 N 8th St 43351 419-294-1395
Patricia Anderson, prin. Fax 209-0295

Urbana, Champaign, Pop. 11,459
Urbana CSD 2,000/K-12
711 Wood St 43078 937-653-1402
Charles Thiel, supt. Fax 652-3845
www.urbana.k12.oh.us
East ES 300/4-5
630 Washington Ave 43078 937-653-1453
Jill Weimer, prin. Fax 652-3845
North ES 400/K-1
626 N Russell St 43078 937-653-1445
Julie Willoughby, prin. Fax 653-1447
South ES 300/2-3
725 S Main St 43078 937-653-1449
Cheryl Carter, prin. Fax 652-0233
Urbana JHS 400/6-8
500 Washington Ave 43078 937-653-1439
Joanne Petty, prin. Fax 658-1487

Utica, Licking, Pop. 2,106
North Fork Local SD 1,600/K-12
312 Maple Ave 43080 740-892-3666
Scott Hartley, supt. Fax 892-2937
www.northfork.k12.oh.us
Utica ES 500/K-5
367 Church St 43080 740-892-2551
Brett Ballinger, prin. Fax 892-2138
Utica MS 300/6-8
260 N Jefferson St 43080 740-892-2691
Marcia Rutherford, prin. Fax 892-2203
Other Schools – See Newark

Van Buren, Hancock, Pop. 327
Van Buren Local SD 1,000/PK-12
217 S Main St 45889 419-299-3578
Timothy Myers, supt. Fax 299-3668
www.vbschools.net
Van Buren ES 500/PK-5
301 S Main St 45889 419-299-3416
Michael Newcomer, prin. Fax 299-3566
Van Buren MS 200/6-8
217 S Main St 45889 419-299-3385
Jason Clark, prin. Fax 299-3340

Vandalia, Montgomery, Pop. 14,921
Vandalia-Butler CSD 2,800/PK-12
500 S Dixie Dr 45377 937-415-6400
Robert O'Leary, supt. Fax 415-6429
www.vbcsd.com
Demmitt ES 500/PK-3
1010 E National Rd 45377 937-415-6500
Garry Martin, prin. Fax 415-6538
Helke ES 400/K-3
611 Randler Ave 45377 937-415-3000
Brian Tregoning, prin. Fax 415-3031
Morton MS 700/6-8
8555 Peters Pike 45377 937-415-6600
Shannon White, prin. Fax 415-6648
Other Schools – See Dayton

St. Christopher S 400/PK-8
405 E National Rd 45377 937-898-5104
Mary Kincaid, prin. Fax 454-4790

Vanlue, Hancock, Pop. 358
Vanlue Local SD 300/K-12
PO Box 250 45890 419-387-7724
Traci Conley, supt. Fax 387-7722
vanlueschool.org
Vanlue ES 100/K-5
PO Box 250 45890 419-387-7724
Robyn Hoadley, prin. Fax 387-7722

Van Wert, Van Wert, Pop. 10,671
Lincolnview Local SD 900/K-12
15945 Middle Point Rd 45891 419-968-2226
Jeffrey Synder, supt. Fax 968-2227
www.lincolnview.k12.oh.us
Lincolnview ES 500/K-6
15945 Middle Point Rd 45891 419-968-2351
Nita Meyer, prin. Fax 968-2227

Van Wert CSD 2,000/PK-12
205 W Crawford St 45891 419-238-0648
Staci Kaufman, supt. Fax 238-3974
vwcs.net
Van Wert ECC 300/PK-K
1120 Buckeye Dr 45891 419-238-0384
Lori Bittner, prin. Fax 238-2137
Van Wert ES 800/1-5
10992 State Route 118 45891 419-238-1761
Justin Krogman, prin. Fax 238-5055
Van Wert MS 500/6-8
10694 State Route 118 45891 419-238-0727
Mark Bagley, prin. Fax 238-7166

St. Mary of the Assumption S 100/K-6
611 Jennings Rd 45891 419-238-5186
Daniel Metzger, prin. Fax 238-5842

Vermilion, Erie, Pop. 10,413
Vermilion Local SD 1,900/K-12
1250 Sanford St 44089 440-204-1700
Philip Pempin, supt. Fax 204-1771
vermilionschools.org
Sailorway MS 600/4-7
5355 Sailorway Dr 44089 440-204-1702
Beth Bartlome, prin. Fax 204-1757
Vermilion ES 500/K-3
1285 Douglas St 44089 440-204-1703
Bonnie Meyer, prin. Fax 204-1747

St. Mary S 100/PK-6
5450 Ohio St 44089 440-967-7911
Barbara Bialko, prin. Fax 967-8287

Versailles, Darke, Pop. 2,673
Versailles EVD 1,400/K-12
PO Box 313 45380 937-526-4773
Aaron Moran, supt. Fax 526-5745
www.versailles.k12.oh.us
Versailles ES 500/K-4
PO Box 313 45380 937-526-4681
Brenda Braun, prin. Fax 526-3480
Versailles MS 400/5-8
PO Box 313 45380 937-526-4426
Jon Hemmelgarn, prin. Fax 526-3085

Vienna, Trumbull, Pop. 1,067
Mathews Local SD
Supt. — See Cortland
Baker ES, 4095 Sheridan Dr 44473 200/3-6
Michael King, prin. 330-539-5042

Vincent, Washington, Pop. 337
Warren Local SD 1,400/K-12
220 Sweetapple Rd 45784 740-678-2366
Kyle R. Newton, supt. Fax 678-8275
www.warrenlocal.org
Warren MS 400/5-8
70 Warrior Dr 45784 740-678-2395
Brent Taylor, prin. Fax 678-0118
Other Schools – See Little Hocking, Marietta

Vinton, Gallia, Pop. 222
Gallia County Local SD
Supt. — See Patriot
Vinton ES 300/PK-5
123 Keystone Rd 45686 740-388-8261
Leslie Henry, prin. Fax 388-4000

Wadsworth, Medina, Pop. 21,350
Wadsworth CSD 4,900/PK-12
524 Broad St 44281 330-336-3571
Andrew Hill Ed.D., supt. Fax 335-1313
www.wadsworthschools.org
Central IS 700/5-6
151 Main St 44281 330-335-1480
Joanne Gahan, prin. Fax 335-1484
Franklin ES 300/K-4
200 Takacs Dr 44281 330-335-1470
Roger Havens, prin. Fax 335-1468
Isham Memorial ES 400/K-4
325 Sunset Blvd 44281 330-335-1440
Nance Watts, prin. Fax 335-1330
Lincoln ES 300/K-4
280 N Lyman St 44281 330-335-1460
Steve Brady, prin. Fax 335-1462
Overlook ES 400/PK-4
650 Broad St 44281 330-335-1420
Erin Simpson, prin. Fax 335-1425
Valley View ES 400/K-4
625 Orchard St 44281 330-335-1430
Christopher Roberts, prin. Fax 335-1428
Wadsworth MS 700/7-8
150 Silvercreek Rd 44281 330-335-1410
Eric Jackson, prin. Fax 336-3820

Northside Christian Academy 300/PK-8
7615 Ridge Rd 44281 330-336-4622
Wendy Turocy, dir. Fax 334-7729
Sacred Heart of Jesus S 300/K-8
110 Humbolt Ave 44281 330-334-6272
William Adams, prin. Fax 334-3236

Wakeman, Huron, Pop. 1,042
Western Reserve Local SD
Supt. — See Collins
Western Preserve Preschool PK-PK
28 River St 44889 419-839-5086

Walnut Creek, Holmes, Pop. 874
East Holmes Local SD
Supt. — See Millersburg
Walnut Creek ES 200/K-6
4840 Olde Pump St 44687 330-893-2213
Darrell Haven, prin. Fax 893-2564

Wapakoneta, Auglaize, Pop. 9,743
Wapakoneta CSD 2,800/PK-12
1102 Gardenia Dr 45895 419-739-2900
Keith Horner, supt. Fax 739-2918
www.wapak.org/
Wapakoneta ES 1,000/PK-4
900 N Blackhoof St 45895 419-739-5000
Mark Selvaggio, prin. Fax 739-5051
Wapakoneta MS 700/5-7
400 W Harrison St 45895 419-739-5100
William Snyder, prin. Fax 739-5165
Other Schools – See Cridersville

Warren, Trumbull, Pop. 40,148
Champion Local SD 1,500/K-12
5976 Mahoning Ave NW 44483 330-847-2330
Pamela Hood, supt. Fax 847-2336
championlocal.org
Champion Central ES 500/K-4
5759 Mahoning Ave NW 44483 330-847-2328
Alexandra Nannicola, prin. Fax 847-2322
Champion MS 500/5-8
5435 Kuszmaul Ave NW 44483 330-847-2340
Heather Campbell, prin. Fax 847-2355

Howland Local SD 2,900/K-12
8200 South St SE 44484 330-856-8200
Kevin Spicher, supt. Fax 856-8214
www.howlandschools.com
Howland Glen ES 300/K-2
8000 Bridle Ln NE 44484 330-856-8275
Carl Clark, prin. Fax 856-8289
Howland MS 700/6-8
8100 South St SE 44484 330-856-8250
Stephen Kovach, prin. Fax 856-2157
Howland Springs ES 300/K-2
9500 Howland Springs Rd SE 44484 330-856-8280
Joseph Simko, prin. Fax 856-2475
Mines ES 300/3-5
850 Howland Wilson Rd NE 44484 330-856-8270
Jennifer Stephenson, prin. Fax 856-8288
North Road ES 300/3-5
863 North Rd SE 44484 330-856-8265
Stephen Kovach, prin. Fax 856-8287

Lakeview Local SD
Supt. — See Cortland
Lakeview ES 500/K-3
2755 Bazetta Rd NE 44481 330-638-2145
Scott Taylor, prin. Fax 637-6727

Lordstown Local SD 500/K-12
1824 Salt Springs Rd W 44481 330-824-2534
Terry Armstrong, supt. Fax 824-2847
www.lordstown.k12.oh.us
Lordstown ES 300/K-6
1776 Salt Springs Rd 44481 330-824-2572
Rich Zigarovich, prin. Fax 824-2568

Warren CSD 5,100/PK-12
105 High St NE 44481 330-841-2321
Stephen Chiaro, supt. Fax 841-2434
www.warrenschools.k12.oh.us
Jefferson S 700/PK-8
1543 Tod Ave SW 44485 330-675-6960
Carrie Boyer, prin. Fax 675-6961
Lincoln S 1,300/PK-8
2253 Atlantic St NE 44483 330-373-4500
Dani Burns, prin. Fax 373-4510
McGuffey S 800/PK-8
3465 Tod Ave NW 44485 330-675-6980
Holly Welch, prin. Fax 675-6981
Willard Avenue S 900/PK-8
2020 Willard Ave SE 44484 330-675-8700
Michelle Chiaro, prin. Fax 675-8710

Kennedy Lower S 300/PK-6
3000 Reeves Rd NE 44483 330-372-2375
Jacquelyn Venzeio, prin. Fax 372-2465

Warrensville Heights, Cuyahoga, Pop. 13,282
Warrensville Heights CSD 1,300/PK-12
4500 Warrensville Center Rd 44128 216-865-4717
Donald J. Jolly, supt. Fax 921-5942
www.warrensville.k12.oh.us
Dewey ES 400/PK-1
23401 Emery Rd 44128 216-755-8743
Takiba Thompson, prin. Fax 921-5905
Eastwood ES 200/4-5
4050 Eastwood Ln 44122 216-336-6546
Andrea Bishop, prin. Fax 921-6463
Warrensville Heights MS 200/6-7
4285 Warrensville Center Rd 44128 216-752-4050
Lisa Hill-Braxton, prin. Fax 752-5813
Westwood ES 300/2-3
19000 Garden Blvd 44128 216-865-4934
Rafiq Vaughn, prin.

Warsaw, Coshocton, Pop. 679
River View Local SD 2,000/PK-12
26496 State Route 60 43844 740-824-3521
Dalton Summers, supt. Fax 824-3760
www.river-view.k12.oh.us
River View MS 300/7-8
26546 State Route 60 43844 740-824-3523
Jerry Olinger, prin. Fax 824-5241
Union ES 200/K-6
19781 State Route 79 43844 740-327-2351
Jarred Renner, prin. Fax 327-2012
Warsaw ES 300/PK-6
PO Box 97 43844 740-824-3727
Tracey Herron, prin. Fax 824-4267
Other Schools – See Conesville, Coshocton

Washington Court House, Fayette, Pop. 13,899
Miami Trace Local SD 2,500/PK-12
3818 State Route 41 NW 43160 740-335-3010
David Lewis, supt. Fax 335-1959
miamitrace.k12.oh.us

Miami Trace ES — 1,200/PK-5
3836 State Route 41 NW 43160 — 740-333-2400
Ryan Davis, prin. — Fax 333-2300
Miami Trace MS — 600/6-8
3800 State Route 41 NW 43160 — 740-333-4900
Jason Binegar, prin. — Fax 333-4901

Washington Court House CSD — 2,200/K-12
306 Highland Ave 43160 — 740-335-6620
Thomas Bailey M.Ed., supt. — Fax 335-1245
www.washingtonch.k12.oh.us
Belle Aire IS — 500/3-5
1120 High St 43160 — 740-335-1810
Jeffrey Conroy, prin. — Fax 335-6432
Cherry Hill PS — 600/K-2
720 W Oakland Ave 43160 — 740-335-3370
Craig Maddux, prin. — Fax 335-2897
Washington MS — 500/6-8
500 S Elm St 43160 — 740-335-0291
Eric Wayne, prin. — Fax 333-3606

Waterford, Washington, Pop. 445
Wolf Creek Local SD — 600/PK-12
PO Box 67 45786 — 740-984-2373
Douglas Baldwin M.A., supt. — Fax 984-4420
www.wolfcreek.k12.oh.us
Waterford ES — 400/PK-8
PO Box 45 45786 — 740-984-2342
Jana Thomas, prin. — Fax 984-4608

Waterville, Lucas, Pop. 5,478
Anthony Wayne Local SD
Supt. — See Whitehouse
Waterville ES — 400/K-4
457 Sycamore Ln 43566 — 419-878-2436
Jamie Hollinger, prin. — Fax 878-4312

Wauseon, Fulton, Pop. 7,227
Wauseon EVD — 1,800/K-12
930 E Oak St 43567 — 419-335-6616
Larry Brown, supt. — Fax 335-3978
www.wauseon.k12.oh.us
Wauseon ES — 400/3-5
950 E Oak St 43567 — 419-335-6581
Theresa Vietmeier, prin. — Fax 335-0045
Wauseon MS — 400/6-8
940 E Oak St 43567 — 419-335-2701
Joe Friess, prin. — Fax 335-0089
Wauseon PS — 400/K-2
940 E Leggett St 43567 — 419-335-4000
Blake Young, prin. — Fax 335-4003

Waverly, Pike, Pop. 5,086
Waverly CSD — 1,900/PK-12
1 Tiger Dr 45690 — 740-947-4770
J. Edward Dickens, supt. — Fax 947-4483
www.waverly.k12.oh.us
Waverly IS — 400/3-5
5 Tiger Dr 45690 — 740-947-5173
Travis Robertson, prin. — Fax 947-0301
Waverly JHS — 500/6-8
3 Tiger Dr 45690 — 740-947-4527
Ferdie Marquez, prin. — Fax 947-8047
Waverly PS — 500/PK-2
7 Tiger Dr 45690 — 740-947-2813
Sarah Turner, prin. — Fax 947-8284

Pike Christian Academy — 100/PK-12
400 Clough St 45690 — 740-947-5700
Keith Smith, prin. — Fax 947-9500

Waynesburg, Stark, Pop. 913

St. James S — 100/PK-6
400 W Lisbon St 44688 — 330-866-9556
Kathy Kettler, prin. — Fax 866-1750

Waynesfield, Auglaize, Pop. 843
Waynesfield-Goshen Local SD — 500/K-12
500 N Westminster St 45896 — 419-568-9100
J. Chris Pfister, supt. — Fax 568-8024
www.wgschools.org
Waynesfield-Goshen ES — 200/K-5
500 N Westminster St 45896 — 419-568-9100
Timothy Pence, prin. — Fax 568-8024

Waynesville, Warren, Pop. 2,780
Wayne Local SD — 1,500/K-12
659 Dayton Rd 45068 — 513-897-6971
Patrick Dubbs, supt. — Fax 897-9605
www.wayne-local.com
Waynesville ES — 700/K-5
659 Dayton Rd 45068 — 513-897-2761
Tammy Burchfield, prin. — Fax 897-3938
Waynesville MS — 300/6-8
723 Dayton Rd 45068 — 513-897-4706
Randy Gebhardt, prin. — Fax 897-2083

Wellington, Lorain, Pop. 4,725
Wellington EVD — 1,200/PK-12
305 Union St 44090 — 440-647-4286
Edward Weber, supt. — Fax 647-4806
www.wellington.k12.oh.us
McCormick MS — 500/4-8
627 N Main St 44090 — 440-647-2342
Nathan Baxendale, prin. — Fax 647-7310
Westwood ES — 300/PK-3
305 Union St 44090 — 440-647-3636
Paul Holland, prin. — Fax 647-1089

Wellston, Jackson, Pop. 5,598
Wellston CSD — 1,500/PK-12
1 E Broadway St 45692 — 740-384-2152
Karen Boch, supt. — Fax 384-3948
www.wcs.k12.oh.us
Bundy ES — 400/PK-2
525 W 7th St 45692 — 740-384-6245
Dana Eberts, prin. — Fax 384-4683
Wellston IS — 300/3-5
225 Golden Rocket Dr 45692 — 740-384-2060
Michelle Kight, prin. — Fax 384-9801
Wellston MS — 300/6-8
227 Golden Rocket Dr 45692 — 740-384-2251
Brandi Cupp, prin. — Fax 384-9801

SS. Peter & Paul S — 100/PK-8
229 S New York Ave 45692 — 740-384-6354
Kristyl Fulton, prin. — Fax 384-2945

Wellsville, Columbiana, Pop. 3,433
Wellsville Local SD — 800/PK-12
929 Center St 43968 — 330-532-2643
Richard Bereschik, supt. — Fax 532-6204
www.wellsville.k12.oh.us
Daw ES — 200/4-7
929 Center St 43968 — 330-532-1372
Burt Stellers, prin. — Fax 532-6204
Garfield ES — 300/PK-3
1600 Lincoln Ave 43968 — 330-532-3301
Lisa Ferguson, prin. — Fax 532-1108

West Alexandria, Preble, Pop. 1,321
Twin Valley Community Local SD — 900/K-12
100 Education Dr 45381 — 937-839-4688
Robert O. Fischer M.Ed., supt. — Fax 839-4898
www.tvs.k12.oh.us
Twin Valley South ES — 500/K-6
100 Education Dr 45381 — 937-839-4315
Patti Holly, prin. — Fax 839-5541
Twin Valley South MS — 100/7-8
100 Education Dr 45381 — 937-839-4165
Scott Cottingim, prin. — Fax 839-4898

West Carrollton, Montgomery, Pop. 12,886
West Carrollton CSD — 3,900/PK-12
430 E Pease Ave 45449 — 937-859-5121
Andrea Townsend Ed.D., supt. — Fax 859-5250
www.westcarrolltonschools.com
Russell ES — 500/1-5
123 Elementary Dr 45449 — 937-859-5121
Pamela Dudley, prin. — Fax 865-5720
Schnell ES — 500/1-5
5995 Student St 45449 — 937-859-5121
Korinne Toadvine, prin. — Fax 859-2775
Shade ECC — 500/PK-K
510 E Pease Ave 45449 — 937-859-5121
Kimberly Hall, prin. — Fax 859-2768
West Carrollton MS — 800/6-8
424 E Main St 45449 — 937-859-5121
Doug Mescher, prin. — Fax 859-2780
Other Schools – See Dayton

West Chester, Butler
Lakota Local SD
Supt. — See Liberty Twp
Adena ES — 600/2-6
9316 Minuteman Way 45069 — 513-777-0100
John Mattingly, prin. — Fax 777-3475
Creekside Early Childhood S — 600/PK-1
5070 Tylersville Rd 45069 — 513-874-0175
Linda Pavlinac, prin. — Fax 682-4213
Endeavor ES — 800/2-6
4400 Smith Rd 45069 — 513-759-8300
Andrea Blevins, prin. — Fax 759-8301
Freedom ES — 600/2-6
6035 Beckett Ridge Blvd 45069 — 513-777-9787
Lance Green, prin. — Fax 777-6014
Hopewell ES — 700/2-6
8300 Cox Rd 45069 — 513-777-6128
Christina French, prin. — Fax 777-3805
Hopewell JHS — 600/7-8
8200 Cox Rd 45069 — 513-777-2258
Jeffrey Rouff, prin. — Fax 777-1908
Lakota Ridge JHS — 600/7-8
6199 Beckett Ridge Blvd 45069 — 513-777-0552
Benjamin Brown, prin. — Fax 777-0919
Union ES — 600/2-6
7672 Lesourdsville W Chestr 45069 — 513-777-2201
Kyle Lichey, prin. — Fax 777-3603

El-Sewedy Intl Academy of Cincinnati — 200/PK-8
8094 Plantation Dr 45069 — 513-755-0169
Marie Marawi M.Ed., prin. — Fax 755-0179

West Elkton, Preble, Pop. 196
Preble Shawnee Local SD
Supt. — See Camden
West Elkton IS — 300/4-6
11751 State Route 503 45070 — 937-787-4102
Robert Morton, prin. — Fax 787-3453

Westerville, Franklin, Pop. 35,380
Westerville CSD — 14,700/PK-12
936 Eastwind Dr 43081 — 614-797-5700
Dr. John R. Kellogg, supt. — Fax 797-5701
www.wcsoh.org
Alcott ES — 600/K-5
7117 Mount Royal Ave 43082 — 614-797-7350
Lauren DeMars, prin. — Fax 797-7351
Annehurst ES — 400/K-5
925 W Main St 43081 — 614-797-7000
Earl Rahm, prin. — Fax 797-7001
Blendon MS — 700/6-8
223 S Otterbein Ave 43081 — 614-797-6400
Kendall Harris, prin. — Fax 797-6401
Cherrington ES — 400/K-5
522 Cherrington Rd 43081 — 614-797-7050
Andrew Heck, prin. — Fax 797-7051
Early Learning Center Preschool — 200/PK-PK
936 Eastwind Dr 43081 — 614-797-7450
Suzanne Kile, dir.
Emerson ES — 200/1-5
44 N Vine St 43081 — 614-797-7080
Chris Doolittle, prin. — Fax 797-7081
Fouse ES — 700/K-5
5800 S Old 3C Hwy 43082 — 614-797-7400
Robert Stranges, prin. — Fax 797-7401
Frost ES — 500/K-5
270 N Spring Rd 43082 — 614-797-7280
Sara Berka, prin. — Fax 797-7281
Genoa MS — 900/6-8
5948 S Old 3C Hwy 43082 — 614-797-6500
Mike Hinze, prin. — Fax 797-6501
Hanby ES — 200/1-5
56 S State St 43081 — 614-797-7100
Monica Brown, prin. — Fax 797-7101
Heritage MS — 900/6-8
390 N Spring Rd 43082 — 614-797-6600
Dr. Dru Tomlin, prin. — Fax 797-6601
Huber Ridge ES — 600/K-5
5757 Buenos Aires Blvd 43081 — 614-797-7150
Tyson Hilkert, prin. — Fax 797-7151
Longfellow ES — 100/K-K
120 Hiawatha Ave 43081 — 614-797-7180
Chris Doolittle, prin.
McVay ES — 500/K-5
270 S Hempstead Rd 43081 — 614-797-7230
Scott May, prin. — Fax 797-7231
Pointview ES — 300/K-5
720 Pointview Dr 43081 — 614-797-7250
Sherry Birchem, prin. — Fax 797-7251
Twain ES — 500/K-5
799 E Walnut St 43081 — 614-797-7200
Vicki Moss, prin. — Fax 797-7201
Walnut Springs MS — 900/6-8
888 E Walnut St 43081 — 614-797-6700
Becca Yanni, prin. — Fax 797-6701
Whittier ES — 300/K-5
130 E Walnut St 43081 — 614-797-7300
Cheryl Relford, prin. — Fax 797-7301
Wilder ES — 500/K-5
6375 Goldfinch Dr 43081 — 614-797-7330
Dr. Victoria Hazlett, prin. — Fax 797-7331
Other Schools – See Columbus

Worthington CSD
Supt. — See Worthington
Worthington Park ES — 400/K-6
500 Park Rd 43081 — 614-450-5500
Asia Armstrong, prin. — Fax 883-3460

Central College Christian Academy — 200/K-8
975 S Sunbury Rd 43081 — 614-794-8146
Howard Baum, prin. — Fax 794-8146
Eastwood SDA Junior Academy — 50/K-8
6350 S Sunbury Rd 43081 — 614-794-6350
Genoa Christian Academy — 300/PK-12
7562 Lewis Center Rd 43082 — 740-965-5433
Craig Bartley, supt. — Fax 965-8214
Northside Christian S — 200/K-12
2655 W Schrock Rd 43081 — 614-882-1493
John Taylor, prin. — Fax 882-5011
St. Paul S — 800/K-8
61 Moss Rd 43082 — 614-882-2710
Kathleen Norris Ph.D., prin. — Fax 882-5998
Worthington Christian MS — 200/6-8
8225 Worthington Galena Rd 43081 — 614-431-8230
Tamara Evans, prin. — Fax 431-8216

West Jefferson, Madison, Pop. 4,287
Jefferson Local SD — 1,200/PK-12
906 W Main St 43162 — 614-879-7654
William Mullett, supt. — Fax 879-5376
www.west-jefferson.k12.oh.us
Norwood ES — 600/PK-5
899 Norwood Dr 43162 — 614-879-7642
Sue Barte, prin. — Fax 879-5377
West Jefferson MS — 300/6-8
2 Roughrider Dr 43162 — 614-879-8345
Deborah Omen, prin. — Fax 879-5399

West Lafayette, Coshocton, Pop. 2,307
Ridgewood Local SD — 1,200/PK-12
301 S Oak St 43845 — 740-545-6354
Michael Masloski, supt. — Fax 545-6336
www.ridgewood.k12.oh.us
Ridgewood ES — 400/PK-3
225 W Union Ave 43845 — 740-545-5312
Lori Cabot, prin. — Fax 545-7015
Ridgewood MS — 400/4-7
517 S Oak St 43845 — 740-545-6335
Trista Claxon, prin. — Fax 545-5300

Westlake, Cuyahoga, Pop. 32,199
Westlake CSD — 3,300/PK-12
24525 Hilliard Blvd 44145 — 440-871-7300
Scott Goggin, supt. — Fax 871-6034
www.wlake.org
Bassett ES — 400/K-4
2155 Bassett Rd 44145 — 440-835-6330
James Sanfilippo, prin. — Fax 899-7409
Burneson MS — 600/7-8
2260 Dover Center Rd 44145 — 440-835-6340
Amanda Musselman, prin. — Fax 808-8964
Dover IS — 300/5-6
2240 Dover Center Rd 44145 — 440-835-6322
Alex Fleming, prin. — Fax 899-7407
Hilliard ES — 300/PK-4
24365 Hilliard Blvd 44145 — 440-835-6343
Kim Tucker, prin. — Fax 835-5698
Holly Lane ES — 300/K-4
3057 Holly Ln 44145 — 440-835-6332
Elizabeth Dagostino, prin. — Fax 734-4312

Montessori Children's S — 100/PK-3
28370 Bassett Rd 44145 — 440-871-8773
Barbara Kincaid, dir. — Fax 871-1799
St. Bernadette S — 500/K-8
2300 Clague Rd 44145 — 440-734-7717
Monica Dietz, prin. — Fax 734-9198
St. Paul Lutheran S — 300/PK-8
27981 Detroit Rd 44145 — 440-835-3051
Dale Lehrke, prin. — Fax 835-8216

Westside Christian Academy 200/K-11
23096 Center Ridge Rd 44145 440-331-1300
Jim Whiteman, prin. Fax 331-1301

West Liberty, Champaign, Pop. 1,773
West Liberty-Salem Local SD 1,200/K-12
7208 US Highway 68 N 43357 937-465-1075
Kraig Hissong, supt. Fax 465-1095
www.wlstigers.org/
West Liberty-Salem ES 500/K-5
7208 US Highway 68 N 43357 937-465-0060
Aaron Hollar, prin. Fax 465-1095

West Milton, Miami, Pop. 4,568
Milton-Union EVD 1,300/PK-12
7610 Milton Potsdam Rd 45383 937-884-7910
Dr. Brad Ritchey, supt. Fax 884-7911
www.milton-union.k12.oh.us
Milton-Union ES 500/PK-5
7620 Milton Potsdam Rd 45383 937-884-7920
Loretta Henderson, prin. Fax 884-7921
Milton-Union MS 400/6-8
7630 Milton Potsdam Rd 45383 937-884-7930
Katie Hartley, prin. Fax 884-7931

West Portsmouth, Scioto, Pop. 3,091
Washington-Nile Local SD 1,400/K-12
15332 US Highway 52 45663 740-858-1111
Jeff Stricklett, supt. Fax 858-1110
www.west.k12.oh.us
Portsmouth West ES 600/K-4
15332 US Highway 52 Unit A 45663 740-858-1116
William Platzer, prin. Fax 858-1118
Portsmouth West MS 500/5-8
15332 US Highway 52 Unit B 45663 740-858-6668
Christopher Jordan, prin. Fax 858-4101

West Salem, Wayne, Pop. 1,452
Northwestern Local SD 1,400/K-12
7571 N Elyria Rd 44287 419-846-3151
Dr. Jeffrey Layton Ed.D., supt. Fax 846 3361
www.northwestern-wayne.k12.oh.us
Northwestern ES 600/K-5
7334 N Elyria Rd 44287 419-846-3519
Julie McCumber, prin. Fax 846-3584
Northwestern MS 300/6-8
7569 N Elyria Rd 44287 419-846-3974
Joseph Brightbill, prin. Fax 846-3750

West Union, Adams, Pop. 3,193
Adams County/Ohio Valley Local SD 3,900/PK-12
141 Lloyd Rd 45693 937-544-5586
Richard Seas, supt. Fax 544-3720
www.ovsd.us
West Union ES 800/PK-6
555 Lloyd Rd 45693 937-544-2951
Ben King, prin. Fax 544-7380
Other Schools – See Peebles, Seaman

Adams County Christian S 100/K-12
187 Willow Dr 45693 937-544-5502
Amy Mason, head sch Fax 544 5503

West Unity, Williams, Pop. 1,653
Millcreek-West Unity Local SD 600/K-12
1401 W Jackson St 43570 419-924-2365
Larry Long, supt. Fax 924-2367
www.hilltop.k12.oh.us
Hilltop ES 300/K-6
1401 W Jackson St 43570 419-924-2365
Laurie Worline, prin. Fax 924-2367

Wheelersburg, Scioto, Pop. 6,353
Wheelersburg Local SD 1,500/PK-12
PO Box 340 45694 740-574-8484
Mark Knapp, supt. Fax 574-6134
www.wheelersburg.net
Wheelersburg ES 600/PK-3
800 Pirate Dr 45694 740-574-8130
Janeen Spradlin, prin. Fax 574-9201
Wheelersburg MS 600/4-8
800 Pirate Dr 45694 740-574-2515
David Rucker, prin. Fax 574-9201

Whitehall, Franklin, Pop. 17,402
Whitehall CSD 3,200/PK-12
625 S Yearling Rd 43213 614-417-5000
Brian Hamler, supt. Fax 417-5023
www.wcsrams.org
Beechwood ES 500/2-5
455 Beechwood Rd 43213 614-417-5300
Kelly Rivers-Golsby, prin. Fax 417-5304
Etna Road ES 500/K-5
4531 Etna Rd 43213 614-417-5400
Jessica Horowitz-Moore, prin. Fax 417-5410
Kae Avenue ES 500/PK-1
4750 Kae Ave 43213 614-417-5600
Kelly Golsby, prin. Fax 417-5607
Rosemore MS 700/6-8
4800 Langley Ave 43213 614-417-5200
Rochelle Rankin, prin. Fax 417-5212
Williams ECC 100/PK-PK
4738 Kae Ave 43213 614-417-5680
Shirley Drake, prin. Fax 417-5606

Whitehouse, Lucas, Pop. 4,098
Anthony Wayne Local SD 4,300/K-12
PO Box 2487 43571 419-877-5377
Jim Fritz, supt. Fax 877-9352
www.anthonywayneschools.org
Fallen Timbers MS 700/5-6
6119 Finzel Rd 43571 419-877-0601
Gary Gardner, prin. Fax 877-4907
Wayne JHS 800/7-8
6035 Finzel Rd 43571 419-877-5342
Brian Bocian, prin. Fax 877-4908
Whitehouse ES 500/K-4
6510 N Texas St 43571 419-877-0543
Brad Rhodes, prin. Fax 877-4905
Other Schools – See Monclova, Waterville

Lial Catholic S 200/PK-8
5700 Davis Rd 43571 419-877-5167
Sr. Patricia McClain, prin. Fax 877-9385

Wickliffe, Lake, Pop. 12,545
Wickliffe CSD 1,500/PK-12
2221 Rockefeller Rd 44092 440-943-6900
Joseph Spiccia, supt. Fax 943-7738
www.wickliffeschools.org
Wickliffe ES 600/PK-4
1821 Lincoln Rd 44092 440-943-0320
Rosemarie Rogers, prin. Fax 943-7738
Wickliffe MS 500/5-8
29240 Euclid Ave 44092 440-943-3220
Dr. Bradley Leyrer, prin. Fax 943-7755

All Saints of St. John Vianney S 300/PK-8
28702 Euclid Ave 44092 440-943-1395
Theresa Armelli, prin. Fax 943-4468
Mater Dei Academy 300/PK-8
29840 Euclid Ave 44092 440-585-0800
Joan Klemens, prin. Fax 585-9391

Willard, Huron, Pop. 6,140
Willard CSD 1,300/PK-12
110 S Myrtle Ave 44890 419-935-1541
Jeffrey Ritz, supt. Fax 935-8491
www.willardschools.org/
Willard ES, 1 Flashes Ave 44890 500/PK-5
Tracy Stephens, prin. 419-935-5341

Celeryville Christian S 100/PK-12
4200 Broadway Rd 44890 419-935-3633
Jacob Bush, admin. Fax 933-6030
St. Francis Xavier S 100/K-6
25 W Perry St 44890 419-935-4744
Donna McDowell, prin. Fax 933-6000

Williamsburg, Clermont, Pop. 2,468
Williamsburg Local SD 1,000/PK-12
549 W Main St Ste A 45176 513-724-3077
Matthew Earley, supt. Fax 724-1504
www.burgschools.org
Williamsburg ES 400/PK-5
839 Spring St 45176 513-724-2241
Kevin Dunn, prin. Fax 724-3902

Williamsport, Pickaway, Pop. 1,007
Westfall Local SD 1,500/PK-12
19463 Pherson Pike 43164 740-986-3671
Lynn Landis Ph.D., supt. Fax 986-8375
www.westfallschools.com
Westfall ES 700/PK-5
9391 State Route 56 43164 740-986-4008
Joseph Patete, prin. Fax 986-4018
Westfall MS 400/6-8
19545 Pherson Pike 43164 740 986 2941
Jason Fife, prin. Fax 986-8882

Willoughby, Lake, Pop. 21,949
Willoughby Eastlake CSD
Supt. — See Willoughby Hills
Edison ES 800/K-5
5288 Karen Isle Dr 44094 440-942-2099
Jatina Threat, prin. Fax 975-3837
Grant ES 600/K-5
38281 Hurricane Dr 44094 440-942-5944
Laurie Hoynes, prin. Fax 918-8980
School of Innovation 200/3-7
32500 Chardon Rd 44094 440-942-1525
Brian Patrick, prin. Fax 347-0273
Willoughby MS 800/6-8
36901 Ridge Rd 44094 440-975-3600
Lawrence Keller, prin. Fax 975-3618

Andrews Osborne Academy 400/PK-12
38588 Mentor Ave 44094 440-942-3600
Larry Goodman Ph.D., head sch Fax 942-3660
Willo-Hill Christian S 100/PK-6
4200 State Route 306 44094 440-951-5391
Mark Tedeschi, prin. Fax 951-5434

Willoughby Hills, Lake, Pop. 9,326
Willoughby-Eastlake CSD 8,000/PK-12
32500 Chardon Rd 44094 440-946-5000
Stephen Thompson, supt. Fax 946-4671
www.weschools.org
Other Schools – See Eastlake, Willoughby, Willowick

Cornerstone Christian Academy 400/PK-12
2846 SOM Center Rd, 440-943-9260
Sandra Ortiz, prin. Fax 943-9262

Willowick, Lake, Pop. 14,003
Willoughby-Eastlake CSD
Supt. — See Willoughby Hills
Royalview ES 900/K-5
31500 Royalview Dr 44095 440-944-3130
Kimberly Cantwell, prin. Fax 943-9965
Willowick MS 600/6-8
31500 Royalview Dr 44095 440-943-2950
Brett McCann, prin. Fax 943-9964

Willow Wood, Lawrence
Symmes Valley Local SD 800/K-12
14778 State Route 141 45696 740-643-2451
Darrell Humphreys, supt. Fax 643-1219
www.svlsd.com
Symmes Valley ES 600/K-8
14860 State Route 141 45696 740-643-0022
Eric Holmes, prin. Fax 643-0033

Wilmington, Clinton, Pop. 12,076
Wilmington CSD 3,000/K-12
341 S Nelson Ave 45177 937-382-1641
Melinda McCarty-Stewart, supt. Fax 382-1645
www.wilmington.k12.oh.us
Borror MS 700/6-8
275 Thorne Ave 45177 937-382-7556
Jeffrey Sherby, prin. Fax 382-3295
Denver Place ES 600/K-5
291 Lorish Ave 45177 937-382-2380
Karen Long, prin. Fax 383-2711
East End ES 300/K-5
769 Rombach Ave 45177 937-382-2443
Jennifer Martin, prin. Fax 382-2872
Holmes ES 500/K-5
1350 W Truesdell St 45177 937-382-2750
Cortney Karshner, prin. Fax 382-2881

Wilmington Christian Academy 100/K-12
642 Davids Dr 45177 937-283-6683
Matt Black, admin. Fax 283-9541

Winchester, Adams, Pop. 1,044
Eastern Local SD 1,300/K-12
11479 US Highway 62 45697 937-378-3981
Michele Filon, supt. Fax 695-9046
www.eb.k12.oh.us
Eastern MS 300/6-8
11479 US Highway 62 45697 937-695-1249
Jordan Michael, prin. Fax 695-1299
Other Schools – See Russellville, Sardinia

Windham, Portage, Pop. 2,132
Windham EVD 600/PK-12
9530 Bauer Ave 44288 330-326-2711
Gregory Isler, supt. Fax 326-2134
www.windham-schools.org
Thomas ES 300/PK-5
9032 Maple Grove Rd 44288 330-326-9800
Sheri Gross, prin. Fax 326-9810
Windham JHS 100/6-8
9530 Bauer Ave 44288 330-326-2711
Laura Amero, prin. Fax 326-3713

Winesburg, Holmes, Pop. 352
East Holmes Local SD
Supt. — See Millersburg
Winesburg ES 200/K-6
2165 US 62 44690 330-359-5059
Darrell Haven, prin. Fax 359-5759

Wintersville, Jefferson, Pop. 3,879
Indian Creek Local SD 1,800/PK-12
587 Bantam Ridge Rd 43953 740-264-3502
Dr. T.C. Chappelear Ed.D., supt. Fax 266-2915
www.iclsd.org
Wintersville ES 600/PK-4
100 Park Dr 43953 740-264-1691
Lorrie Jarrett, prin. Fax 264-1112
Other Schools – See Mingo Junction

Jefferson County Christian S 200/PK-12
125 Fernwood Rd 43953 740-275-4326
Diane Hutchison, prin. Fax 275-4296

Withamsville, Clermont, Pop. 6,918

St. Thomas More S 300/K-8
788 Ohio Pike 45245 513-753-2540
Candace Hurley, prin. Fax 753-2554

Woodsfield, Monroe, Pop. 2,354
Switzerland of Ohio Local SD 2,200/PK-12
304 Mill St 43793 740-472-5801
Jeffrey Greenley, supt. Fax 472-5806
www.swissohio.k12.oh.us
Woodsfield S 500/K-8
473 Lewisville Rd 43793 740-472-0953
Joshua Ischy, prin. Fax 472-1646
Other Schools – See Beallsville, Graysville, Hannibal, Powhatan Point

St. Sylvester S 100/PK-8
119 Wayne St 43793 740-472-0321
Robyn C. Guiler, prin. Fax 472-1994

Woodville, Sandusky, Pop. 2,126
Woodmore Local SD
Supt. — See Elmore
Woodmore ES 500/PK-5
800 W Main St 43469 419-862-1070
Gary Haas, prin. Fax 849-2132
Woodmore MS 6-8
800 W Main St 43469 419-862-1070
Kevin Ball, prin. Fax 849-2132

Solomon Lutheran S 100/PK-6
305 W Main St 43469 419-849-3600
Natalie Schiets, prin. Fax 849-2260

Wooster, Wayne, Pop. 25,513
Triway Local SD 1,700/K-12
3205 Shreve Rd 44691 330-264-9491
Nathan Schindewolf, supt. Fax 262-3955
www.triway.k12.oh.us/
Franklin Township ES 200/K-6
2060 E Moreland Rd 44691 330-264-2378
Claudia Stupi, prin. Fax 263-7057
Triway JHS 300/7-8
3145 Shreve Rd 44691 330-264-2114
Joshua Stutz, prin. Fax 264-6025
Wooster Township ES 400/K-6
1071 Dover Rd 44691 330-264-6252
Angela Carmichael, prin. Fax 263-7078
Other Schools – See Shreve

Wooster CSD 3,700/PK-12
144 N Market St 44691 330-988-1111
Dr. Michael Tefs Ed.D., supt. Fax 262-3407
www.woostercityschools.org
Cornerstone ES 400/PK-4
101 W Bowman St 44691 330-988-1111
Eric Vizzo, prin. Fax 262-7611

Edgewood MS 800/5-7
2695 Graustark Path 44691 330-988-1111
Bradley Warner, prin. Fax 345-8237
Kean ES 300/K-4
432 Oldman Rd 44691 330-988-1111
Brandon Cobb, prin. Fax 345-7845
Littlest Generals Preschool 100/PK-PK
101 W Bowman St 44691 330-988-1111
Karen Arbogast, dir. Fax 262-7611
Melrose ES 300/K-4
1641 Sunset Ln 44691 330-988-1111
Kaylee Harrell, prin. Fax 345-7868
Parkview ES 400/K-4
773 Parkview Dr 44691 330-988-1111
Sara Crooks, prin. Fax 262-4655

Montessori S of Wooster 100/PK-8
1170 Akron Rd 44691 330-264-5222
Joseph Edinger, head sch
St. Mary Immaculate Conception S 200/PK-8
515 Beall Ave 44691 330-262-8671
Laura Marvin, prin. Fax 262-0967
Wooster Christian S 200/PK-8
480B Fry Rd 44691 330-345-6436
Randy Claes, admin.

Worthington, Franklin, Pop. 13,300
Worthington CSD 9,500/PK-12
200 E Wilson Bridge Rd 43085 614-450-6000
Trent Bowers Ph.D., supt. Fax 883-3010
www.worthington.k12.oh.us
Colonial Hills ES 400/K-6
5800 Greenwich St 43085 614-450-5400
Thomas Bates, prin. Fax 883-2810
Evening Street ES 500/K-6
885 Evening St 43085 614-450-4400
Mary Rykowski, prin. Fax 883-2860
Kilbourne MS 400/7-8
50 E Dublin Granville Rd 43085 614-450-4200
James Gaskill, prin. Fax 883-3510
Slate Hill ES 500/K-6
7625 Alta View Blvd 43085 614-450-5000
Elizabeth Audette, prin. Fax 883-3210
Wilson Hill ES 500/K-6
6500 Northland Rd 43085 614-450-4800
Daniel Girard, prin. Fax 883-3310
Worthington Estates ES 600/K-6
6760 Rieber St 43085 614-450-4600
Robert Messenheimer, prin. Fax 883-3360
Worthingway MS 400/7-8
6625 Guyer St 43085 614-450-4300
Nathan Kellenberger, prin. Fax 883-3660
Other Schools – See Columbus, Powell, Westerville

St. Michael S 500/K-8
64 E Selby Blvd 43085 614-885-3149
Patricia Maher, prin. Fax 885-1249
Worthington Adventist Academy 50/K-8
870 Griswold St 43085 614-885-9525
Valerie Green, prin. Fax 885-9501

Wyoming, Hamilton, Pop. 8,224
Wyoming CSD 1,900/K-12
420 Springfield Pike 45215 513-206-7000
Dr. Susan Lang, supt. Fax 672-3355
www.wyomingcityschools.org
Elm Avenue ES 200/K-4
134 Elm Ave 45215 513-206-7315
LaDora Hill, prin. Fax 206-7337
Hilltop ES 200/K-4
425 Oliver Rd 45215 513-206-7270
LaDora Hill, prin. Fax 206-7305
Vermont Avenue ES 200/K-4
33 Vermont Ave 45215 513-206-7345
LaDora Hill, prin. Fax 206-7370
Wyoming MS 600/5-8
17 Wyoming Ave 45215 513-206-7170
Jennifer Klein, prin. Fax 206-7245

Xenia, Greene, Pop. 24,906
Beavercreek CSD
Supt. — See Beavercreek
Coy MS 1,100/6-8
1786 Dayton Xenia Rd 45385 937-429-7577
Shaun Kelly, prin. Fax 429-7686
Trebien ES 600/K-5
1728 Dayton Xenia Rd 45385 937-458-2300
Lisa Walk, prin. Fax 458-2395

Xenia Community SD 4,100/PK-12
819 Colorado Dr 45385 937-376-2961
Gabriel Lofton, supt. Fax 372-4701
www.xenia.k12.oh.us
Arrowood ES 500/K-5
1588 Pawnee Dr 45385 937-372-9251
Travis Yost, prin. Fax 374-4402
Cox ES 300/K-5
506 Dayton Ave 45385 937-372-9201
Lisa Peterson, prin. Fax 374-4723
McKinley ES 400/K-5
829 Colorado Dr 45385 937-372-1251
Garry Hawes, prin. Fax 374-4406
Shawnee ES 400/K-5
92 E Ankeney Mill Rd 45385 937-372-6461
Scott Poole, prin. Fax 374-4230
Tecumseh ES 300/K-5
1058 Old Springfield Pike 45385 937-372-3321
Cathryn Petticrew, prin. Fax 374-4398
Warner MS 600/6-8
600 Buckskin Trl 45385 937-376-9488
Theodore Holop, prin. Fax 374-4228
Xenia Preschool 300/PK-PK
425 Edison Blvd 45385 937-562-9706
Jean Brady, prin. Fax 374-4410

Legacy Christian Academy 400/PK-12
1101 Wesley Ave 45385 937-352-1640
Dr. Dan Bragg, supt. Fax 352-1641
St. Brigid S 200/PK-8
312 Fairground Rd 45385 937-372-3222
Terry Adkins, prin. Fax 374-3622

Yellow Springs, Greene, Pop. 3,226
Yellow Springs EVD 700/K-12
201 S Walnut St 45387 937-767-7381
Mario Basora, supt. Fax 767-6604
www.yellow-springs.k12.oh.us/
Mills Lawn ES 400/K-6
200 S Walnut St 45387 937-767-7217
Matt Housh, prin. Fax 767-6602

Youngstown, Mahoning, Pop. 65,039
Austintown Local SD 5,200/K-12
700 S Raccoon Rd 44515 330-797-3900
Vincent Colauca, supt. Fax 792-8625
www.austintownschools.org
Austintown MS 1,300/6-8
800 S Raccoon Rd 44515 330-797-3900
James Penk, prin. Fax 792-9130
Other Schools – See Austintown

Boardman Local SD 4,400/PK-12
7410 Market St 44512 330-726-3404
Timothy Saxton, supt. Fax 726-3432
www.boardman.k12.oh.us
Boardman Center MS 600/5-6
7410 Market St 44512 330-726-3400
Randall Ebie, prin. Fax 726-3431
Boardman Glenwood MS 800/7-8
7635 Glenwood Ave 44512 330-726-3414
Bart Smith, prin. Fax 758-8067
Market Street ES 400/PK-4
5555 Market St 44512 330-782-3743
BillieJo Johnson, prin. Fax 782-1063
Robinwood Lane ES 400/PK-4
835 Indianola Rd 44512 330-782-3164
Donald Robinson, prin. Fax 782-2405
Stadium Drive ES 400/PK-4
111 Stadium Dr 44512 330-726-3428
Michael Zoccali, prin. Fax 726-0496
West Boulevard ES 500/PK-4
6125 West Blvd 44512 330-726-3427
Alphonse Cervello, prin. Fax 726-0397

Liberty Local SD 1,200/K-12
4115 Shady Rd 44505 330-759-0807
Joseph Nohra, supt. Fax 759-1209
sites.liberty.k12.oh.us
Blott ES 500/K-4
4003 Shady Rd 44505 330-759-1053
Michael Palmer, prin. Fax 759-9151
Guy MS 300/5-8
4115 Shady Rd 44505 330-759-1733
Andrew Scarmack, prin. Fax 759-4507

Youngstown CSD 5,200/PK-12
20 W Wood St 44503 330-744-6900
Krishanjeev Mohip Ph.D., supt. Fax 743-1157
www.youngstown.k12.oh.us
Bunn ES 400/PK-6
1825 Sequoya Dr 44514 330-744-8963
William Baun, prin. Fax 744-8586
Harding ES 500/PK-6
1903 Cordova Ave 44504 330-744-7517
Robert Kearns, admin. Fax 744-8589
King ES 400/PK-6
2724 Mariner Ave 44505 330-744-7823
Artemus Scissum, prin. Fax 480-1907
McGuffey ES 800/PK-6
310 S Schenley Ave 44509 330-744-7999
Catherine Dorbish, prin. Fax 744-8796
Rayen Early College MS 200/6-8
731 S Hazelwood Ave 44509 330-744-7602
Deborah DiFrancesco, prin. Fax 793-9675
Taft ES 400/K-6
730 E Avondale Ave 44502 330-744-7973
Christopher Haynes, prin. Fax 788-6509
Volney ES 400/K-8
2400 S Schenley Ave 44511 330-744-8845
Kelly Weeks, prin. Fax 480-1908
Williamson ES 400/K-6
58 Williamson Ave 44507 330-744-7155
Michelle Payich, prin. Fax 480-1902
Wilson ES K-8
2725 Gibson St 44502 330-744-8002
Jennifer Walker, prin. Fax 788-1326

St. Christine S 400/PK-8
3125 S Schenley Ave 44511 330-792-4544
Walter Carpenter, prin. Fax 792-6888
St. Joseph the Provider S 100/K-8
1145 Turin St 44510 330-259-0353
Cheryl Jablonski, prin. Fax 259-0364
Valley Christian S 500/PK-12
4401 Southern Blvd 44512 330-788-8088
Michael Pecchia, pres. Fax 788-2875

Zanesville, Muskingum, Pop. 24,279
East Muskingum Local SD
Supt. — See New Concord
Perry ES 100/K-2
6975 East Pike 43701 740-872-3436
Leigh Ann Atkins, prin. Fax 872-3372

Maysville Local SD 2,100/PK-12
3715 Panther Dr 43701 740-453-0754
Ruth Zitnik, supt. Fax 455-4081
www.maysville.k12.oh.us
Maysville ES 1,000/K-5
3850 Panther Dr 43701 740-454-4490
Renae Church, prin. Fax 454-2109
Maysville MS 500/6-8
3725 Panther Dr 43701 740-454-7982
Erik Winland, prin. Fax 452-9921
Maysville O'Tags Preschool 200/PK-PK
3715 Panther Dr 43701 740-453-0754
Cindy Miller, admin. Fax 454-2109

West Muskingum Local SD 1,300/K-12
4880 West Pike 43701 740-455-4052
Chad Shawger, supt. Fax 455-4063
www.westm.k12.oh.us
West Muskingum ES 400/K-4
200 Kimes Rd 43701 740-455-4058
Elizabeth Carpenter, prin. Fax 455-2592
West Muskingum MS 500/5-8
100 Kimes Rd 43701 740-455-4055
Lindsay Rayner, prin. Fax 455-9717

Zanesville CSD 3,300/PK-12
956 Moxahala Ave 43701 740-454-9751
Dr. Doug Baker, supt. Fax 455-4325
www.zanesville.k12.oh.us
McIntire ES 700/K-6
1275 Roosevelt Ave 43701 740-453-2851
Michael Emmert, prin. Fax 588-0714
National Road ES 400/K-6
3505 East Pike 43701 740-450-1538
Libby Hitchens, prin. Fax 450-1544
Zane Grey ES 800/PK-6
711 Fess St 43701 740-453-0576
Mark Stallard, prin. Fax 453-3571
Zanesville MS 500/7-8
1429 Blue Ave 43701 740-453-0711
Robert Dalton, prin. Fax 454-7005

Bishop Fenwick S 100/PK-8
139 N 5th St 43701 740-454-9731
Kelly Sagan, prin. Fax 454-0653
Zanesville SDA S 50/K-8
824 Taylor St 43701 740-453-6050
Clare Hoover, prin. Fax 453-6050

Zoarville, Tuscarawas
Tuscarawas Valley Local SD 1,400/PK-12
2637 Tusky Valley Rd NE 44656 330-859-2213
Mark Murphy, supt. Fax 859-2706
www.tvtrojans.org/
Tuscarawas Valley MS 500/5-8
2633 Tusky Valley Rd NE 44656 330-859-2427
Scott Young, prin. Fax 859-8845
Other Schools – See Bolivar, Mineral City

OKLAHOMA

OKLAHOMA DEPARTMENT OF EDUCATION
2500 N Lincoln Blvd Rm 112, Oklahoma City 73105-4503
Telephone 405-521-3301
Fax 405-521-6205
Website sde.ok.gov/sde/

Superintendent of Public Instruction Joy Hofmeister

OKLAHOMA BOARD OF EDUCATION
2500 N Lincoln Blvd Rm 112, Oklahoma City 73105-4503

Chairperson

INTERLOCAL COOPERATIVES (IC)

Choctaw Nation IC
Kenneth Keeling, dir. 580-931-0691
PO Box 602, Durant 74702 Fax 931-0120
choctawinterlocal.org

Five Star IC
Nancy Anderson, dir. 918-225-5600
1405 E Moses St, Cushing 74023 Fax 225-3026
www.fsilc.k12.ok.us

Osage County IC
Jacque Canady, dir. 918-885-2667
207 E Main St, Hominy 74035 Fax 885-6742
www.ocic.k12.ok.us/

Seminole County IC 405-382-6121
, 630 Golf Rd, Seminole 74868 Fax 382-5254

Southeastern Oklahoma IC
Craig Wall, dir. 580-212-0831
103 NE Ave A, Idabel 74745

Tri-County IC
Michelle Taylor, dir. 580-673-2310
100 School St, Fox 73435 Fax 673-2309

PUBLIC, PRIVATE AND CATHOLIC ELEMENTARY SCHOOLS

Achille, Bryan, Pop. 443
Achille ISD 300/PK-12
PO Box 280 74720 580-283-3775
Richard Beene, supt. Fax 283-3787
achilleisd.org
Achille ES 200/PK-8
PO Box 280 74720 580-283-3775
Lora Stanglin, prin. Fax 283-3765

Ada, Pontotoc, Pop. 15,623
Ada ISD 2,700/PK-12
324 W 20th St 74820 580-310-7200
Mike Anderson, supt. Fax 310-7206
www.adapss.com/
Ada ECC 500/PK-K
630 W 33rd St 74820 580-310-7283
Cindy Brady, prin. Fax 310-7284
Hayes ES 400/1-2
500 S Mississippi Ave 74820 580-310-7294
Diana Clampitt, prin. Fax 310-7295
Washington ES 400/3-4
600 S Oak Ave 74820 580-310-7303
Pam Martin, prin. Fax 310-7304
Willard ES 400/5-6
817 E 9th St 74820 580-310-7250
Kevin Mann, prin. Fax 310-7252

Byng ISD 1,800/PK-12
500 S New Bethel Blvd 74820 580-436-3020
Todd Crabtree, supt. Fax 436-3052
www.byngschools.com
Byng ES 300/4-6
500 S New Bethel Blvd 74820 580-310-6720
Dennis Kymes, prin. Fax 310-6721
Francis ES 200/PK-3
18461 County Road 1480 74820 580-332-4114
Johna Hancock, prin. Fax 436-6021
Homer ES 600/PK-5
1400 N Monte Vista St 74820 580-332-4303
Janna Davis, prin. Fax 436-3566

Latta ISD 800/PK-12
13925 County Road 1560 74820 580-332-2092
Cliff Johnson, supt. Fax 332-3116
www.latta.k12.ok.us/
Latta ES 400/PK-4
13925 County Road 1560 74820 580-332-7669
Shawna Lancaster, prin.
Latta MS 200/5-8
13925 County Road 1560 74820 580-332-8100
Terry Painter, prin.

Vanoss ISD 400/PK-12
4665 County Road 1555 74820 580-759-2251
Marjana Tharp, supt. Fax 759-8916
www.vanoss.k12.ok.us
Vanoss ES 200/PK-5
4665 County Road 1555 74820 580-759-2503
Beth Walker, prin. Fax 759-3080

Adair, Mayes, Pop. 736
Adair ISD 1,000/PK-12
PO Box 197 74330 918-785-2424
Mark Lippe, supt. Fax 785-2491
adair.k12.ok.us/APS/
Adair MS 200/6-8
PO Box 197 74330 918-785-2425
Brad Rogers, prin. Fax 785-2491
Hughes ES 500/PK-5
PO Box 197 74330 918-785-2438
Carla Lyons, prin. Fax 785-2491

Afton, Ottawa, Pop. 950
Afton ISD 500/PK-12
PO Box 100 74331 918-257-4470
Randy Gardner, supt. Fax 257-4846
www.aftonschools.net
Afton ES 400/PK-8
PO Box 100 74331 918-257-8304
Kim Johnson, prin. Fax 257-4846

Cleora SD 100/PK-8
451358 E 295 Rd 74331 918-256-6401
Kenny Guthrie, supt. Fax 256-2128
cleora.net
Cleora S 100/PK-8
451358 E 295 Rd 74331 918-256-6401
Kenny Guthrie, supt. Fax 256-2128

Agra, Lincoln, Pop. 313
Agra ISD 400/PK-12
PO Box 279 74824 918-375-2261
Brent Meeks, supt. Fax 375-2263
www.agra.k12.ok.us/
Agra ES 300/PK-6
PO Box 279 74824 918-375-2261
Brent Meeks, supt. Fax 375-2263

Albion, Pushmataha, Pop. 90
Albion SD 100/PK-8
206 S Texas Ave 74521 918-563-4331
C. Lynn Bullard, supt. Fax 563-4330
albion.k12.ok.us
Albion S 100/PK-8
206 S Texas Ave 74521 918-563-4331
C. Lynn Bullard, prin. Fax 563-4330

Alex, Grady, Pop. 528
Alex ISD 300/PK-12
PO Box 188 73002 405-785-2605
Dr. Jason James, supt. Fax 785-2914
www.alex.k12.ok.us
Alex ES 200/PK-8
PO Box 188 73002 405-785-2217
Nicole Bauman, prin. Fax 785-2302

Aline, Alfalfa, Pop. 202
Aline-Cleo ISD 200/PK-12
PO Box 49 73716 580-463-2255
Barry Nault, supt. Fax 463-2256
www.alinecleo.k12.ok.us
Other Schools – See Cleo Springs

Allen, Pontotoc, Pop. 878
Allen ISD 500/PK-12
PO Box 430 74825 580-857-2417
Dr. Bill Caruthers, supt. Fax 857-2636
www.allen.k12.ok.us
Allen ES 300/PK-8
PO Box 430 74825 580-857-2419
Jeff Hiatt, dean Fax 857-2636

Altus, Jackson, Pop. 19,118
Altus ISD 2,700/PK-12
PO Box 558 73522 580-481-2100
Roger Hill, supt. Fax 481-2129
www.altusps.com
Altus ECC 100/PK-K
PO Box 558 73522 580-481-2151
Renee Long, prin. Fax 481-2539
Altus ES 200/3-4
PO Box 558 73522 580-481-2180
Ken Kenner, prin. Fax 481-2534
Altus IS 500/5-6
PO Box 558 73522 580-481-2155
Jay Richeson, prin. Fax 481-2596
Altus JHS 500/7-8
PO Box 558 73522 580-481-2173
Roe Worbes, prin. Fax 481-2547
Altus PS 100/1-2
PO Box 558 73522 580-481-2185
Cheryl Anderson, prin. Fax 477-7617
Rivers ES 400/PK-4
PO Box 558 73522 580-481-2183
Robbie Holder, prin. Fax 481-2124

Navajo ISD 300/PK-12
15695 S County Road 210 73521 580-482-7742
Vicki Nance, supt. Fax 482-7749
www.navajo.k12.ok.us
Navajo ES 200/PK-6
15695 S County Road 210 73521 580-482-7742
Glenn Hasty, prin. Fax 482-7749

Altus Christian Academy 100/PK-6
1220 N Grady St 73521 580-477-2511
Dana Darby, head sch Fax 477-2511

Alva, Woods, Pop. 4,829
Alva ISD 900/PK-12
418 Flynn St 73717 580-327-4823
J. Stephen Parkhurst, supt. Fax 327-2965
www.alvaschools.com
Alva MS 200/6-8
800 Flynn St 73717 580-327-0608
Stephanie Marteney, prin. Fax 327-4255
Lincoln ES 100/4-5
1540 Davis St 73717 580-327-3008
Madison Williams, prin. Fax 327-6785
Longfellow ES 100/2-3
19 Barnes Ave 73717 580-327-3327
Alysson Tucker, prin. Fax 327-4527
Washington ES 200/PK-1
701 Barnes Ave 73717 580-327-3518
Shane Feely, prin. Fax 327-6040

Amber, Grady, Pop. 416
Amber-Pocasset ISD 500/PK-12
PO Box 38 73004 405-224-5768
Jerime Parker, supt. Fax 224-5115
www.amposchools.org
Amber-Pocasset ES 300/PK-6
PO Box 38 73004 405-224-5768
Angie Morrison, prin. Fax 224-5115

Anadarko, Caddo, Pop. 6,230
Anadarko ISD 1,900/PK-12
1400 S Mission St 73005 405-247-6605
Cindy Hackney, supt. Fax 247-6819
www.apswarriors.com
Anadarko MS 400/6-8
900 W College St 73005 405-247-6671
LaVonda Bost, prin. Fax 247-3666
East ES 300/2-3
107 SE 5th St 73005 405-247-2496
Danny Harris, prin. Fax 247-4133
Mission ES 400/PK-PK, 4-
1200 S Mission St 73005 405-247-6607
Jeff Barrett, prin. Fax 247-4142
Sunset ES 300/K-1
508 SW 7th St 73005 405-247-2503
Rhonda Tallent, prin. Fax 247-2504

Antlers, Pushmataha, Pop. 2,335
Antlers ISD 900/K-12
219 NE A St 74523 580-298-5504
Cary Ammons, supt. Fax 298-4006
www.antlers.k12.ok.us

Brantley ES — 500/K-5
219 NE A St 74523 — 580-298-3108
Debbie Brame, prin. — Fax 298-4002
Obuch MS — 200/6-8
219 NE A St 74523 — 580-298-3308
William Neyman, prin. — Fax 298-4012

Apache, Caddo, Pop. 1,370
Boone-Apache ISD — 600/PK-12
PO Box 354 73006 — 580-588-3369
Don Schneberger, supt. — Fax 588-3400
www.apacheps.org
Apache ES — 300/PK-5
PO Box 354 73006 — 580-588-3577
Amber Crow, prin. — Fax 588-2030
Apache MS — 100/6-8
PO Box 354 73006 — 580-588-2122
Steven Base, prin. — Fax 588-3026

Arapaho, Custer, Pop. 774
Arapaho-Butler ISD — 400/PK-12
PO Box 160 73620 — 580-323-3262
James Edelen, supt. — Fax 323-5886
www.arapaho.k12.ok.us
Arapaho-Butler ES — 300/PK-8
PO Box 160 73620 — 580-323-7264
Brad Southall, prin. — Fax 323-3469

Ardmore, Carter, Pop. 22,734
Ardmore ISD — 3,200/PK-12
PO Box 1709 73402 — 580-223-2483
Kim Holland, supt. — Fax 226-2472
www.ardmoreschools.org
Ardmore MS — 600/6-8
PO Box 1709 73402 — 580-223-2475
Cindy Huddleston, prin. — Fax 221-3060
Evans ES — 700/1-5
PO Box 1709 73402 — 580-223-2472
Denise Brunk, prin. — Fax 221-3020
Jefferson ES — 300/1-5
PO Box 1709 73402 — 580-223-2474
Myiesha Antwine, prin. — Fax 221-3022
Lincoln ES — 300/1-5
PO Box 1709 73402 — 580-223-2477
Lacy Mitchell, prin. — Fax 221-3023
Rogers ES — 500/PK-K
PO Box 1709 73402 — 580-223-2482
Johncy Martin, prin. — Fax 224-9864

Dickson ISD — 1,300/PK-12
4762 State Highway 199 73401 — 580-223-9557
Jeff Colclasure, supt. — Fax 490-9152
www.dickson.k12.ok.us
Dickson Lower ES — 400/PK-2
4762 State Highway 199 73401 — 580-223-9509
Debby Custer, prin. — Fax 223-3543
Dickson MS — 300/6-8
4762 State Highway 199 73401 — 580-223-2700
Jason Ward, prin. — Fax 223-3972
Dickson Upper ES — 300/3-5
4762 State Highway 199 73401 — 580-223-1443
David Gardner, prin. — Fax 223-6347

Plainview ISD — 1,500/PK-12
1140 S Plainview Rd 73401 — 580-223-6319
Karl Stricker, supt. — Fax 490-3190
www.plainview.k12.ok.us/
Plainview IS — 300/3-5
1140 S Plainview Rd 73401 — 580-223-6437
Julie Altom, prin. — Fax 490-3193
Plainview MS — 300/6-8
1140 S Plainview Rd 73401 — 580-223-6502
Tim Parham, prin. — Fax 490-3192
Plainview PS — 400/PK-2
1140 S Plainview Rd 73401 — 580-223-5757
Lisa Moore, prin. — Fax 490-3194

Ardmore Adventist Academy — 50/1-10
154 Beaver Academy Rd 73401 — 580-223-4948
Oak Hall Episcopal S — 200/PK-8
2815 Mount Washington Rd 73401 — 580-226-2341
Dr. Ken Willy, hdmstr. — Fax 226-8141

Arkoma, LeFlore, Pop. 1,878
Arkoma ISD — 400/PK-12
PO Box 349 74901 — 918-875-3351
John Turner Ed.D., supt. — Fax 875-3780
sites.google.com/site/arkomak12/
Singleton ES — 300/PK-6
PO Box 349 74901 — 918-875-3835
Shelly Harmon, prin. — Fax 875-3780

Arnett, Ellis, Pop. 514
Arnett ISD — 200/PK-12
PO Box 317 73832 — 580-885-7811
Tracy Kincannon, supt. — Fax 885-7922
www.arnett.k12.ok.us
Arnett ES — 100/PK-6
PO Box 317 73832 — 580-885-7285
Scot Friesen, prin. — Fax 885-7349

Asher, Pottawatomie, Pop. 357
Asher ISD — 300/PK-12
PO Box 168 74826 — 405-784-2332
Terry Grissom, supt. — Fax 784-2306
www.asher.k12.ok.us
Asher ES — 200/PK-8
PO Box 168 74826 — 405-784-2331
Jeremy Frye, prin. — Fax 784-2306

Atoka, Atoka, Pop. 2,819
Atoka ISD — 800/PK-12
801 S Greathouse Dr 74525 — 580-889-6612
Ron Whipkey, supt. — Fax 889-2513
atoka.org
Atoka ES — 400/PK-5
706 Greathouse Dr 74525 — 580-889-3553
Kayla Moore, prin. — Fax 889-4050
McCall MS — 200/6-8
1003 W 11th St 74525 — 580-889-5640
Wesley Burnett, prin. — Fax 889-4064

Harmony SD — 200/PK-8
490 S Bentley Rd 74525 — 580-889-3687
Brian Walker, supt. — Fax 889-4631
www.harmonyps.org
Harmony S — 200/PK-8
490 S Bentley Rd 74525 — 580-889-3687
Brian Walker, prin. — Fax 889-4631

Tushka ISD — 400/PK-12
261 W Boggy Depot Rd 74525 — 580-889-7355
Matthew Simpson, supt. — Fax 889-6144
www.tushka.k12.ok.us
Tushka ES — 300/PK-8
261 W Boggy Depot Rd 74525 — 580-889-7355
Paul Weaver, prin. — Fax 889-6144

Avant, Osage, Pop. 290
Avant SD — 100/K-8
PO Box 9 74001 — 918-263-2135
Cindi Hemm, supt. — Fax 263-2143
www.avant.k12.ok.us/
Avant S — 100/K-8
PO Box 9 74001 — 918-263-2135
Cindi Hemm, admin. — Fax 263-2143

Balko, Beaver
Balko ISD, RR 1 Box 37 73931 — 200/PK-12
Roger Mendell, supt. — 580-646-3385
www.balko.k12.ok.us/
Balko S, RR 1 Box 37 73931 — 100/PK-8
Douglas Davis, prin. — 580-646-3385

Barnsdall, Osage, Pop. 1,134
Barnsdall ISD — 400/PK-12
PO Box 629 74002 — 918-847-2271
Jeff Lay, supt. — Fax 847-3029
www.barnsdallschools.org
Barnsdall ES, PO Box 629 74002 — 200/PK-6
Regiena Henderson, prin. — 918-847-2731
Barnsdall JHS, PO Box 629 74002 — 100/7-8
Sayra Bryant, prin. — 918-847-2721

Bartlesville, Washington, Pop. 33,922
Bartlesville ISD — 5,100/PK-12
1100 SW Jennings Ave 74003 — 918-336-8600
Dr. Chuck McCauley, supt. — Fax 337-3643
www.bps-ok.org
Central MS — 700/6-8
815 SE Deleware Ave 74003 — 918-336-9302
Ryan Huff, prin. — Fax 337-6270
Hoover ES — 400/PK-5
512 SE Madison Blvd 74006 — 918-333-9337
Susan Burns, prin. — Fax 335-6337
Kane ES — 500/PK-5
801 E 13th St 74003 — 918-337-3711
Shelly White, prin. — Fax 337-6221
Madison MS — 600/6-8
5900 Baylor Dr 74006 — 918-333-4444
Joseph Eidson, prin. — Fax 335-6377
Phillips ES — 400/PK-5
1500 S Rogers Ave 74003 — 918-336-9479
David Mueller, prin. — Fax 337-6251
Ranch Heights ES — 600/PK-5
5100 David Dr 74006 — 918-333-3810
Kevin Brown, prin. — Fax 335-6318
Wayside ES — 500/K-5
3000 Wayside Dr 74006 — 918-333-8000
Kenneth Copeland, prin. — Fax 335-6315
Wilson ES — 600/PK-5
245 N Spruce Ave 74006 — 918-335-1177
Tammie Krause, prin. — Fax 335-6313

Osage Hills SD — 200/PK-8
225 County Road 2706 74003 — 918-336-6804
Jeannie O'Daniel, supt. — Fax 336-4238
www.osagehills.k12.ok.us
Osage Hills S — 200/PK-8
225 County Road 2706 74003 — 918-336-6804
Tammy Wilson, prin. — Fax 336-4238

St. John Catholic S — 100/PK-8
816 S Keeler Ave 74003 — 918-336-0603
Traci McKee, prin. — Fax 336-0624
Wesleyan Christian S — 300/PK-12
1780 Silver Lake Rd 74006 — 918-333-8631
Rocky Clark, admin. — Fax 333-8632

Battiest, McCurtain
Battiest ISD — 300/PK-12
PO Box 199 74722 — 580-241-7810
Stace Ebert, supt. — Fax 241-7847
www.battiest.k12.ok.us
Battiest ES — 200/PK-8
PO Box 199 74722 — 580-241-5499
Geovonna Davis, prin. — Fax 241-5499

Beaver, Beaver, Pop. 1,494
Beaver ISD — 400/PK-12
PO Box 580 73932 — 580-625-3444
Scott Kinsey, supt. — Fax 625-3690
www.beaver.k12.ok.us
Beaver ES — 300/PK-8
PO Box 580 73932 — 580-625-3444
Read Cates, prin. — Fax 625-3690

Beggs, Okmulgee, Pop. 1,177
Beggs ISD — 1,000/PK-12
1201 W 9th St 74421 — 918-267-3628
Rondald Martin, supt. — Fax 267-3635
www.beggs.k12.ok.us
Beggs ES — 500/PK-4
1201 W 9th St 74421 — 918-267-3631
Nancy McCune, prin. — Fax 267-3629
Beggs MS — 200/5-8
1201 W 9th St 74421 — 918-267-4916
Kenny Hurst, prin. — Fax 267-4779

Bennington, Bryan, Pop. 304
Bennington ISD — 300/PK-12
729 N Perry St 74723 — 580-847-2310
Pamela Reynolds, supt. — Fax 847-2787
www.benningtonisd.org
Bennington ES — 200/PK-8
729 N Perry St 74723 — 580-847-2310
Scot McCorstin, prin. — Fax 847-2787

Bethany, Oklahoma, Pop. 18,252
Bethany ISD — 1,700/PK-12
6721 NW 42nd St 73008 — 405-789-3801
Drew Eichelberger, supt. — Fax 499-4606
www.bethanyschools.com/
Bethany MS — 400/6-8
6721 NW 42nd St 73008 — 405-787-3240
Trey Keoppel, prin. — Fax 499-4606
Harris ES — 700/PK-5
6721 NW 42nd St 73008 — 405-789-6673
Rueben Bellows, prin. — Fax 499-4625

Putnam City ISD
Supt. — See Oklahoma City
Apollo ES — 400/PK-5
1901 N Peniel Ave 73008 — 405-787-6636
Angela Habben, prin. — Fax 491-7528
Lake Park ES — 300/PK-5
8221 NW 30th St 73008 — 405-789-7068
Lori Freeman, prin. — Fax 491-7590
Overholser ES — 500/PK-5
7900 NW 36th St 73008 — 405-789-7913
Marjorie Iven, prin. — Fax 491-7586
Western Oaks ES — 700/PK-5
7210 NW 23rd St 73008 — 405-789-1711
Stephanie Treadway, prin. — Fax 491-7578
Western Oaks MS — 700/6-8
7200 NW 23rd St 73008 — 405-789-4434
Isaac McCord, prin. — Fax 491-7616

Billings, Noble, Pop. 499
Billings ISD — 100/PK-12
PO Box 39 74630 — 580-725-3271
Rustin Clark, supt. — Fax 725-3278
www.billings.k12.ok.us
Billings ES, PO Box 39 74630 — 50/PK-8
Rustin Clark, prin. — 580-725-3271

Binger, Caddo, Pop. 635
Binger-Oney ISD — 400/PK-12
323 S Apache 73009 — 405-656-2304
Rex Trent, supt. — Fax 656-2267
www.binger-oney.k12.ok.us
Binger-Oney ES — 300/PK-6
323 S Apache 73009 — 405-656-2304
Tanae Rodriguez, prin. — Fax 656-2267

Bixby, Tulsa, Pop. 19,948
Bixby ISD — 5,200/PK-12
109 N Armstrong St 74008 — 918-366-2200
Dr. Kyle Wood, supt. — Fax 366-4241
www.bixbyps.org
Bixby MS — 800/7-8
109 N Armstrong St 74008 — 918-366-2201
Rowland Vernon, prin. — Fax 366-2337
Central ES — 900/PK-3
109 N Armstrong St 74008 — 918-366-2282
Lydia Wilson, prin. — Fax 366-2332
Central IS — 500/4-6
109 N Armstrong St 74008 — 918-366-2248
Brenda Shaw, prin. — Fax 366-2263
North ES — 900/PK-3
109 N Armstrong St 74008 — 918-366-2690
Phil Streets, prin. — Fax 366-2684
North IS — 500/4-6
109 N Armstrong St 74008 — 918-366-2669
Linda Ricks, prin. — Fax 366-1899
Other Schools – See Broken Arrow

Blackwell, Kay, Pop. 6,745
Blackwell ISD — 1,200/PK-12
201 E Blackwell Ave 74631 — 580-363-2570
Richard Riggs, supt. — Fax 363-5513
www.blackwell.k12.ok.us
Blackwell ES — 500/PK-5
2105 W Ferguson Ave 74631 — 580-363-0118
Mellisa Moore, prin. — Fax 363-7013
Blackwell MS — 300/6-8
1041 S 1st St 74631 — 580-363-2100
Preston Kysar, prin. — Fax 363-7010

Blair, Jackson, Pop. 786
Blair ISD — 300/PK-12
PO Box 428 73526 — 580-563-2632
Jimmy Smith, supt. — Fax 563-9166
www.blairschool.org
Blair ES — 200/PK-8
PO Box 428 73526 — 580-563-2235
Lissa Mcmillin, prin. — Fax 563-9166

Blanchard, McClain, Pop. 7,360
Blanchard ISD — 1,900/PK-12
211 N Tyler Ave 73010 — 405-485-3391
Dr. Jim Beckham, supt. — Fax 485-2985
www.blanchard.k12.ok.us/
Blanchard ES — 600/PK-2
211 N Tyler Ave 73010 — 405-485-3394
Donna Edge, prin. — Fax 485-9116
Blanchard IS, 211 N Tyler Ave 73010 — 400/3-5
Paula Floyd, prin. — 405-485-3391
Blanchard MS — 400/6-8
211 N Tyler Ave 73010 — 405-485-3393
Larry McVay, prin. — Fax 485-9103

Bridge Creek ISD — 1,500/PK-12
2209 E Sooner Rd 73010 — 405-387-4880
David Morrow, supt. — Fax 387-4882
www.bridgecreek.k12.ok.us/
Bridge Creek ECC — 700/PK-2
2209 E Sooner Rd 73010 — 405-387-3681
Tina Floyd, prin. — Fax 387-2553
Bridge Creek IS — 3-5
2209 E Sooner Rd 73010 — 405-387-5824
Mandy Byrd, admin. — Fax 387-2419
Bridge Creek MS — 300/6-8
2209 E Sooner Rd 73010 — 405-387-9681
Kenneth Ward, prin. — Fax 387-2552

Middleberg SD 200/PK-8
2130 County Road 1317 73010 405-485-3612
Joel Read, supt. Fax 485-3204
www.middleberg.k12.ok.us
Middleberg S 200/PK-8
2130 County Road 1317 73010 405-485-3612
Joel Read, admin. Fax 485-3204

Bluejacket, Craig, Pop. 318
Bluejacket ISD 200/PK-12
PO Box 29 74333 918-784-2365
Shellie Baker, supt. Fax 784-2130
www.bluejacket.k12.ok.us
Bluejacket ES 100/PK-5
PO Box 29 74333 918-784-2266
Amy Rogers, prin. Fax 784-2130
Bluejacket MS, PO Box 29 74333 100/6-8
Tracy Mendez, prin. 918-784-2133

Boise City, Cimarron, Pop. 1,253
Boise City ISD 300/PK-12
PO Box 1116 73933 580-544-3110
Dr. Ira Harris Ph.D., supt. Fax 544-2972
www.boisecity.k12.ok.us/
Boise City ES 200/PK-8
PO Box 1117 73933 580-544-3161
John Farmer, prin. Fax 544-2146

Bokchito, Bryan, Pop. 591
Rock Creek ISD 500/PK-12
200 E Steakley St 74726 580-295-3137
Preston Burns, supt. Fax 295-3762
www.rockcreekisd.net
Other Schools – See Durant

Bokoshe, LeFlore, Pop. 466
Bokoshe ISD 200/PK-12
PO Box 158 74930 918-969-2341
Grant Ralls, supt. Fax 969-2117
www.bokosheschool.org
Bokoshe ES 100/PK-6
PO Box 158 74930 918-969-2341
Dustin Long, prin. Fax 969-2117

Boswell, Choctaw, Pop. 659
Boswell ISD 400/PK-12
PO Box 839 74727 580-566-2558
Keith Edge, supt. Fax 566-2265
www.boswellschools.org/
Boswell ES 200/PK-6
PO Box 839 74727 580-566-2655
Rick Grimes, prin. Fax 566-2265
Boswell MS 50/7-8
PO Box 839 74727 580-566-2735
Rick Grimes, prin. Fax 566-2265

Bowlegs, Seminole, Pop. 377
Bowlegs ISD 300/PK-12
PO Box 88 74830 405-398-4172
Tommy Eaton, supt. Fax 398-4175
www.bowlegs.k12.ok.us
Bowlegs ES 200/PK-8
PO Box 88 74830 405-398-4322
Becky Roberts, prin. Fax 398-4169

Braggs, Muskogee, Pop. 242
Braggs ISD 200/PK-12
PO Box 59 74423 918-487-5265
Bradley Wade, supt. Fax 487-7171
www.braggs.k12.ok.us
Braggs S 100/PK-8
PO Box 59 74423 918-487-5265
John Pinkston, prin. Fax 487-7171

Bristow, Creek, Pop. 3,811
Bristow ISD 1,700/PK-12
420 N Main St 74010 918-367-5555
Curtis Shelton, supt. Fax 367-5848
www.bristow.k12.ok.us
Bristow MS 400/6-8
420 N Main St 74010 918-367-3551
Brian Burden, prin. Fax 367-1362
Collins ES 300/3-5
420 N Main St 74010 918-367-5551
Teresa Barnett, prin. Fax 367-9177
Edison ES 500/PK-2
420 N Main St 74010 918-367-5521
Debbie Ponder, prin. Fax 367-5081

Bristow Adventist S 50/PK-8
PO Box 496 74010 918-367-6782

Broken Arrow, Tulsa, Pop. 94,005
Bixby ISD
Supt. — See Bixby
Northeast Elementary & IS 500/PK-6
11901 E 131st St S 74011 918-366-2200
Jana Williams, prin. Fax 364-5415

Broken Arrow ISD 15,800/PK-12
701 S Main St 74012 918-259-5700
Janet Dunlop, supt. Fax 258-0399
www.baschools.org/
Arrowhead ES 500/K-5
915 W Norman St 74012 918-259-4390
Nate Hutchings, prin. Fax 251-8183
Arrow Springs ECC PK-PK
101 W Twin Oaks St 74011 918-259-4380
Debbie McClellan, admin. Fax 451-1640
Aspen Creek ECC 300/PK-PK
2700 W Florence St 74011 918-505-5290
Julie Wallace, prin. Fax 505-5299
Aspen Creek ES 600/K-5
2800 W Florence St 74011 918-259-4410
Bridget Powell, prin. Fax 455-1731
Centennial MS 1,000/6-8
225 E Omaha St 74012 918-259-4340
Ashley Bowser, prin. Fax 251-8347
Childers MS 700/6-8
301 E Tucson St 74011 918-259-4350
Stacy Replogle, prin. Fax 451-5465
Country Lane IS 800/3-5
251 E Omaha St 74012 918-449-5600
Todd Greathouse, prin. Fax 355-9275
Country Lane PS 800/K-2
301 E Omaha St 74012 918-259-4400
Karen Morrison, prin. Fax 259-4403
Creekwood ECC 300/PK-PK
1351 E Albany St 74012 918-505-5280
Vicki Beckwith, prin. Fax 505-5289
Creekwood ES 600/K-5
1301 E Albany St 74012 918-259-4500
Rachel Kaiser, prin. Fax 355-1174
Highland Park ES 800/K-5
7200 E Quincy Pl 74014 918-505-5930
Elizabeth Schmidt, prin. Fax 259-7799
Leisure Park ES 500/K-5
4300 S Juniper Pl 74011 918-259-4420
Janet Dotson, prin. Fax 451-0000
Liberty ES 800/K-5
4300 S 209th East Ave 74014 918-259-4470
Elora Orr, prin. Fax 355-0095
Oak Crest ES 500/K-5
405 E Richmond St 74012 918-259-4450
Kristin Henness, prin. Fax 251-8553
Oliver MS 800/6-8
3100 W New Orleans St 74011 918-259-4590
Wendy Johnson, prin. Fax 250-8185
Oneta Ridge MS 700/6-8
6800 E Quincy Pl 74014 918-259-4360
Mickey Replogle, prin. Fax 251-8685
Park Lane ECC 300/PK-PK
7700 S Shelby Ln 74014 918-806-8665
Barbara Jones, prin. Fax 806-8720
Rhoades ES 400/K-5
320 E Midway St 74012 918-259-4440
Lance Crawley, prin. Fax 258-4265
Sequoyah MS 500/6-8
2701 S Elm Pl 74012 918-259-4370
Lindsey Johnson, prin. Fax 451-2167
Spring Creek ES 500/K-5
6801 S 3rd St 74011 918-259-4480
Teresa Bowker, prin. Fax 455-9160
Timber Ridge ES K-5
3500 E Kenosha St 74014 918-505-5260
Tiffany Green, prin. Fax 505-5261
Vandever ES 400/K-5
2200 S Lions Ave 74012 918-259-4490
Leslie Officer, prin. Fax 455-0980
Wolf Creek ES 500/K-5
3000 W New Orleans St 74011 918-259-4510
Stacy Strow, prin. Fax 250-6769
Wood ES 500/K-5
1600 W Quincy St 74012 918-259-4430
Chris England, prin. Fax 258-0596

Union ISD
Supt. — See Tulsa
Anderson ES 500/PK-5
1200 S Willow Ave 74012 918-357-4328
Bethany Harper, prin. Fax 357-8299
McAuliffe ES 700/PK-5
6515 S Garnett Rd 74012 918-357-4336
Jennifer McKnight, prin. Fax 357-6599
Moore ES 500/PK-5
800 N Butternut Pl 74012 918-357-4337
Lindsay Smith, prin. Fax 357-6996
Peters ES 500/PK-5
2900 W College St 74012 918-357-4338
Tracy Weese, prin. Fax 357-6799
Union Eighth Grade Center 1,100/8-8
6501 S Garnett Rd 74012 918-357-4325
Michelle Cundy, prin. Fax 357-7899

All Saints Catholic S 300/PK-8
299 S 9th St 74012 918-251-3000
Anne Scalet, prin. Fax 258-9879
Immanuel Lutheran Christian Academy 100/PK-12
400 N Aspen Ave 74012 918-251-5422
Stephen Zehnder, hdmstr. Fax 251-8365
Kids in Motion Academy 100/PK-3
1700 N Redbud Pl 74012 918-258-5437
Priscilla Godi, prin. Fax 258-2042
Legacy Christian Academy 100/K-6
1201 N Elm Pl 74012 918-286-6794
Tandi Wells, prin. Fax 251-1300
Summit Christian Academy 500/K-12
200 E Broadway St 74012 918-251-1997

Broken Bow, McCurtain, Pop. 3,865
Broken Bow ISD 1,700/PK-12
108 W 5th St 74728 580-584-3306
Carla Ellisor, supt. Fax 584-9482
www.bbisd.org
Bennett ES 300/3-5
108 W 5th St 74728 580-584-6440
Joanna Hall, prin. Fax 584-9576
Dierks ES, 108 W 5th St 74728 500/PK-2
Lindsay Gaston, prin. 580-584-2765
Rector Johnson MS 300/6-8
108 W 5th St 74728 580-584-9603
Belinda Highful, prin. Fax 584-2549

Glover SD 100/K-8
701 Lavender Rd 74728 580-420-3232
Tanya Stuart, supt. Fax 420-3232
www.glover.k12.ok.us
Glover S 100/K-8
701 Lavender Rd 74728 580-420-3232
Tanya Stuart, admin. Fax 420-3232

Holly Creek SD 200/PK-8
401 Holly Creek Rd 74728 580-420-6961
Harvey Brumley, supt. Fax 420-7022
www.hollycreek.org
Holly Creek S 200/PK-8
401 Holly Creek Rd 74728 580-420-6968
Harvey Brumley, prin. Fax 420-7022
Lukfata SD 400/PK-8
1685 Old Broken Bow Hwy 74728 580-584-6834
Kurt Neal, supt. Fax 584-9473
www.lukfata.org
Lukfata S 400/PK-8
1685 Old Broken Bow Hwy 74728 580-584-6834
Kurt Neal, supt. Fax 584-9473

Buffalo, Harper, Pop. 1,288
Buffalo ISD 100/K-12
PO Box 130 73834 580-735-2448
Dale Spradlin, supt. Fax 735-2619
www.buffalo.k12.ok.us
Buffalo S 100/K-12
PO Box 130 73834 580-735-2448
Kenneth Horn, prin. Fax 735-2619

Bunch, Adair
Cave Springs ISD 200/PK-12
PO Box 200 74931 918-775-2364
Dr. Geary Brown Ed.D., supt. Fax 776-2052
www.cavesprings.k12.ok.us
Cave Springs ES 50/PK-4
PO Box 200 74931 918-775-2364
Dr. Geary Brown Ed.D., prin. Fax 776-2052
Cave Springs MS 50/5-8
PO Box 200 74931 918-775-2364
Dr. Geary Brown Ed.D., prin. Fax 776-2052

Greasy SD 100/PK-8
RR 1 Box 1589 74931 918-696-7768
Michael Wolfe, supt. Fax 696-7240
Greasy S 100/PK-8
RR 1 Box 1589 74931 918-696-7768
Michael Wolfe, prin. Fax 696-7240

Marble CSD 100/PK-8
95266 S 4610 Rd 74931 918-775-2135
Bill London, supt. Fax 775-3019
www.mcps.k12.ok.us
Marble City S 100/PK-8
95266 S 4610 Rd 74931 918-775-2135
Bill London, prin. Fax 775-3019

Burlington, Alfalfa, Pop. 145
Burlington ISD 100/PK-12
PO Box 17 73722 580-431-2501
Glen Elliott, supt. Fax 431-2237
www.burlingtonschool.com/
Burlington S 100/PK-8
PO Box 17 73722 580-431-2222
Lane Pruett, prin. Fax 431-2237

Burneyville, Love
Turner ISD 300/PK-12
PO Box 159 73430 580-276-1307
Burl Solie, supt. Fax 276-2006
www.turnerisd.org
Turner ES 200/PK-8
PO Box 159 73430 580-276-2707
Jamie Roberts, prin. Fax 276-1306

Burns Flat, Washita, Pop. 1,998
Burns Flat-Dill City ISD 700/PK-12
PO Box 129 73624 580-562-4844
Larry Johnson, supt. Fax 562-4847
www.bfdc.k12.ok.us
Rogers S, PO Box 449 73624 500/PK-8
Lace Davis, prin. 580-562-4851

Cache, Comanche, Pop. 2,626
Cache ISD 1,700/PK-12
102 E H Ave 73527 580-429-3266
Chad Hance, supt. Fax 429-3271
www.cacheps.org
Cache 5th & 6th Grade Center 300/5-6
102 E H Ave 73527 580-429-0222
Christy Taylor, prin. Fax 429-0223
Cache IS, 102 E H Ave 73527 400/2-4
Rellon Sampler, prin. 580-429-8536
Cache MS, 102 E H Ave 73527 200/7-8
Mitch Ange, prin. 580-429-8489
Cache PS, 102 E H Ave 73527 300/PK-1
Jacqueline Green, prin. 580-429-3542

Caddo, Bryan, Pop. 914
Caddo ISD 500/PK-12
PO Box 128 74729 580-367-2208
Lee Northcutt, supt. Fax 367-2837
www.caddoisd.org
Caddo ES, PO Box 128 74729 300/PK-8
Spencer Phipps, prin. 580-367-2515

Calera, Bryan, Pop. 1,972
Calera ISD 700/PK-12
PO Box 386 74730 580-434-5700
Gerald Parks, supt. Fax 434-5800
www.caleraisd.k12.ok.us
Calera ES 500/PK-8
PO Box 386 74730 580-434-5603
Steve Evans, prin. Fax 434-5800

Calumet, Canadian, Pop. 484
Calumet ISD 300/PK-12
PO Box 10 73014 405-893-2222
Keith Weldon, supt. Fax 893-8019
www.chs.k12.ok.us
Calumet ES 100/PK-8
PO Box 10 73014 405-893-2222
Lindy Renbarger, dean Fax 893-8019

Maple SD 200/PK-8
904 S Maple Rd 73014 405-262-5647
William Derryberry, supt. Fax 262-5651
mapleschool.us
Maple S 200/PK-8
904 S Maple Rd 73014 405-262-5647
Shana Thiel, prin. Fax 262-5651

Calvin, Hughes, Pop. 277
Calvin ISD 200/PK-12
PO Box 127 74531 405-645-2411
Travis Graham, supt. Fax 645-2384
www.calvin.k12.ok.us

Calvin ES 100/PK-8
PO Box 127 74531 405-645-2411
Patricia Marlow, prin. Fax 645-2384

Cameron, LeFlore, Pop. 274
Cameron ISD 300/PK-12
PO Box 190 74932 918-654-3412
Jim Caughern, supt. Fax 654-7387
www.cameronps.org
Cameron ES 200/PK-8
PO Box 190 74932 918-654-3412
Dr. Curtis Curry Ed.D., prin. Fax 654-7387

Canadian, Pittsburg, Pop. 206
Canadian ISD 400/PK-12
PO Box 168 74425 918-339-2705
Michael Broyles, supt. Fax 339-2393
www.canadian.k12.ok.us
Canadian ES 300/PK-8
PO Box 168 74425 918-339-7253
Kristi Lokey, prin. Fax 339-2393

Caney, Atoka, Pop. 176
Caney ISD 300/PK-12
PO Box 60 74533 580-889-1996
Lori Delay, supt. Fax 889-5033
www.caneyisd.org
Caney S 200/PK-8
PO Box 60 74533 580-889-6966
Lori Delay, prin. Fax 889-2008

Canton, Blaine, Pop. 594
Canton ISD 400/PK-12
PO Box 639 73724 580-886-3516
Carl Baker, supt. Fax 886-3501
canton.k12.ok.us
Canton ES 300/PK-8
PO Box 639 73724 580-886-2251
Daniel Ingram, prin. Fax 886-2308

Canute, Washita, Pop. 537
Canute ISD 400/PK-12
PO Box 490 73626 580-472-3295
Larry Parrish, supt. Fax 472-3187
www.canutepublicschool.com
Canute ES 300/PK-8
PO Box 490 73626 580-472-3295
Ronda Mendez, prin. Fax 472-3187

Carnegie, Caddo, Pop. 1,645
Carnegie ISD 600/PK-12
330 W Wildcat Dr 73015 580-654-1470
Mark Batt, supt. Fax 654-1644
www.carnegie.k12.ok.us
Carnegie ES 300/PK-5
330 W Wildcat Dr 73015 580-654-1945
Lori Graham, prin. Fax 654-1807
Carnegie MS 100/6-8
330 W Wildcat Dr 73015 580-654-1766
Kirk Graham, prin. Fax 654-2281

Carney, Lincoln, Pop. 589
Carney ISD 200/PK-12
PO Box 240 74832 405-865-2344
Alicia O'Donnell, supt. Fax 865-2345
www.carney.k12.ok.us/
Carney ES, PO Box 240 74832 200/PK-8
Alicia O'Donnell, prin. 405-865-2344

Cashion, Logan, Pop. 779
Cashion ISD 400/PK-12
101 N Euclid Ave 73016 405-433-2741
Sammy Jackson, supt. Fax 433-2646
www.cashionps.org
Cashion ES 200/PK-5
101 N Euclid Ave 73016 405-433-2614
Julie Moore, prin. Fax 433-2646

Catoosa, Rogers, Pop. 6,601
Catoosa SD 2,100/PK-12
2000 S Cherokee St 74015 918-266-8603
Donna Campo, supt. Fax 266-8647
www.catoosaps.net/
Cherokee ES 300/4-5
2000 S Cherokee St 74015 918-266-8630
Ben Malone, prin. Fax 266-1478
Paul Learning Center 400/PK-1
2000 S Cherokee St 74015 918-266-8643
Sandee Cross, prin. Fax 266-0606
Sam ES 300/2-3
2000 S Cherokee St 74015 918-266-8637
Angela Hobson, prin. Fax 266-1479
Wells MS 500/6-8
2000 S Cherokee St 74015 918-266-8623
Joshua Brown, prin. Fax 266-1282

Cement, Caddo, Pop. 491
Cement ISD 200/PK-12
PO Box 60 73017 405-489-3216
David Davidson, supt. Fax 489-3219
www.cement.k12.ok.us
Cement ES 200/PK-8
PO Box 60 73017 405-489-3216
Steve Pelzer, prin. Fax 489-3219

Chandler, Lincoln, Pop. 2,922
Chandler ISD 1,200/PK-12
901 S CHS 74834 405-258-1450
Wayland Kimble, supt. Fax 258-2657
www.chandler.k12.ok.us
Chandler JHS 200/7-8
901 S CHS 74834 405-258-0183
Kent Barton, prin. Fax 258-1850
East Side ES 400/PK-2
901 S CHS 74834 405-258-1872
Lisa Hart, prin. Fax 240-5717
Park Road Upper ES 300/3-6
901 S CHS 74834 405-258-1828
Melody Toma, prin. Fax 258-1163

Chattanooga, Comanche, Pop. 452
Chattanooga ISD 200/PK-12
PO Box 129 73528 580-597-3347
Jerry Brown, supt. Fax 597-3344
www.chatty.k12.ok.us/
Chattanooga ES, PO Box 129 73528 200/PK-8
Shelli Mahoney, prin. 580-597-6638

Checotah, McIntosh, Pop. 3,060
Checotah ISD 1,600/PK-12
PO Box 289 74426 918-473-5610
Janet Blocker, supt. Fax 473-1020
www.checotah.k12.ok.us/
Checotah IS 300/3-4
PO Box 289 74426 918-473-2384
Ryan Ambrose, prin. Fax 473-1437
Checotah MS 300/5-8
PO Box 289 74426 918-473-2239
Jason Donathan, prin. Fax 473-2532
Marshall ES 500/PK-2
PO Box 289 74426 918-473-5832
Cindy Frame, prin. Fax 473-6654

Chelsea, Rogers, Pop. 1,729
Chelsea ISD 900/PK-12
401 Redbud Ln 74016 918-789-2528
Rich McSpadden, supt. Fax 789-3271
Chelsea MS, 401 Redbud Ln 74016 200/6-8
Howard Hill, prin. 918-789-2521
Goad ES, 401 Redbud Ln 74016 500/PK-5
Zenda Willcut, prin. 918-789-2503

Cherokee, Alfalfa, Pop. 1,474
Cherokee ISD 300/PK-12
PO Box 325 73728 580-596-3391
Donna Anderson, supt. Fax 596-2319
www.cherokee.k12.ok.us
Cherokee ES 200/PK-6
700 S Nebraska Ave 73728 580-596-3277
Ruth Richmond, prin.

Cheyenne, Roger Mills, Pop. 783
Cheyenne ISD 400/PK-12
PO Box 650 73628 580-497-3371
Robert Trammell, supt. Fax 497-3373
www.cheyenne.k12.ok.us
Cheyenne ES 300/PK-8
PO Box 650 73628 580-497-2486
Belinda Chalfant, prin. Fax 497-3373

Chickasha, Grady, Pop. 15,287
Chickasha ISD 2,500/PK-12
900 W Choctaw Ave 73018 405-222-6500
David Cash, supt. Fax 222-6590
www.chickasha.k12.ok.us/
Chickasha MS 300/7-8
1000 S 9th St 73018 405-222-6530
Dan Turner, prin. Fax 222-6594
Grand Avenue ES 500/2-4
1415 W Grand Ave 73018 405-222-6524
Cindy Stone, prin. Fax 222-6565
Lincoln ES 300/5-6
103 E Dakota Ave 73018 405-222-6522
Rashaun Ashant-Alexander, prin. Fax 222-6580
Wallace ECC 600/PK-1
2301 S 16Th St 73018 405-222-6544
Tressia Meeks, prin. Fax 222-6582

Friend SD 200/PK-8
1307 County Road 1350 73018 405-224-3822
Jason Brittain, supt. Fax 222-5416
www.friend.k12.ok.us
Friend S 200/PK-8
1307 County Road 1350 73018 405-224-3822
Jason Brittain, admin. Fax 222-5416

Pioneer SD 400/PK-8
3686 State Highway 92 73018 405-224-2700
Mike Sparks, supt. Fax 224-2755
pioneerk8.k12.ok.us
Pioneer S 400/PK-8
3686 State Highway 92 73018 405-224-2700
Tyler Locke, admin. Fax 224-2755

Caraway Christian S PK-12
730 County Road 1330 73018 405-224-1998
Tracy Caraway, supt. Fax 892-9039

Choctaw, Oklahoma, Pop. 10,497
Choctaw-Nicoma Park ISD 5,500/PK-12
12880 NE 10th St 73020 405-769-4859
Dr. Jim McCharen, supt. Fax 769-9821
www.cnpschools.org
Choctaw ES 400/PK-5
14663 NE 3rd St 73020 405-390-2225
Cheryl Lidia, prin. Fax 390-3101
Choctaw MS 700/6-8
14667 NE 3rd St 73020 405-390-2207
Donna O'Neal, prin. Fax 390-4439
Griffith IS 400/3-5
1861 S Indian Meridian 73020 405-390-2153
Kelli Hosford, prin. Fax 390-4429
Indian Meridian ES 600/PK-2
1865 S Indian Meridian 73020 405-390-8585
Christine Floyd, prin. Fax 390-2218
Nicoma Park ES 500/PK-2
1200 Hickman Ave 73020 405-769-2445
Dorothy Shetley, prin. Fax 769-5067
Nicoma Park IS 400/3-5
1318 Hickman Ave 73020 405-769-4693
Misti Tye, prin. Fax 769-6271
Nicoma Park MS 600/6-8
1321 Hickman Ave 73020 405-769-3106
Brent Ingraham, prin. Fax 769-9355
Westfall ES 500/PK-5
13239 NE 10th St 73020 405-769-3078
Shannon Shay, prin. Fax 769-4365

Life Christian Academy 200/K-12
3200 N Choctaw Rd 73020 405-390-5081
Rodney Burchett, admin. Fax 390-5086

Chouteau, Mayes, Pop. 1,930
Chouteau-Mazie ISD 800/PK-12
PO Box 969 74337 918-476-8376
Kenny Mason, supt. Fax 476-8538
www.chouteauwildcats.com
Chouteau ES 200/2-5
PO Box 969 74337 918-476-8336
Cheryl McCartney, prin. Fax 476-8303
Chouteau-Mazie ECC 200/PK-1
PO Box 969 74337 918-476-6551
Josh Gwartney, prin.
Chouteau-Mazie MS 100/6-8
PO Box 969 74337 918-476-8336
Michelle Middleton, prin. Fax 476-8306
Mazie S 100/PK-8
PO Box 969 74337 918-476-5389
Joanie Gaskins, prin. Fax 476-4833

Claremore, Rogers, Pop. 17,084
Claremore ISD 4,100/PK-12
102 W 10th St 74017 918-923-4200
Bryan Frazier, supt. Fax 341-8447
www.claremore.k12.ok.us
Catalayah ES 400/PK-5
2700 King Rd, 918-923-4260
Kellye Shuck, prin. Fax 923-4329
Claremont ES 500/PK-5
318 E 7th St 74017 918-923-4202
Randa Fay, prin. Fax 923-4332
Rogers JHS 900/6-8
1915 N Florence Ave 74017 918-923-4205
Brian Young, prin. Fax 923-4218
Roosa ES 400/PK-5
2001 N Sioux Ave 74017 918-923-4206
Christine Willard, prin. Fax 343-6337
Westside ES 600/PK-5
2600 Holly Rd 74017 918-923-4201
Glen Abshere, prin. Fax 343-6338

Foyil ISD 600/PK-12
17002 E 4th St 74017 918-341-1113
Rod Carter, supt. Fax 341-1223
www.foyil.k12.ok.us
Foyil ES 300/PK-6
17002 E 4th St 74017 918-342-3310
Brad Jordan, prin. Fax 341-1223

Justus-Tiawah SD 500/PK-8
14902 E School Rd, 918-341-3626
David Garroutte, supt. Fax 341-4920
www.justustiawah.com
Justus-Tiawah ES 300/PK-3
14902 E School Rd, 918-341-3626
Kim Larmon, prin. Fax 342-2635
Justus-Tiawah JHS North Campus 100/7-8
14902 E School Rd, 918-341-1252
David Garroutte, prin. Fax 341-4920
Justus-Tiawah MS South Campus 200/4-6
15011 E 523 Rd, 918-341-1252
Ed Crum, prin. Fax 341-4579

Sequoyah ISD 1,200/PK-12
16441 S 4180 Rd 74017 918-341-5472
Terry Saul, supt. Fax 341-5764
www.sequoyaheagles.net
Sequoyah ES 600/PK-5
16441 S 4180 Rd 74017 918-341-6111
Lisa Tittle, prin. Fax 343-8108
Sequoyah MS 300/6-8
16403 S 4180 Rd 74017 918-343-5105
Barry Bulman, prin. Fax 343-8109

Verdigris ISD 800/PK-12
26501 S 4110 Rd, 918-266-7227
Michael Payne, supt. Fax 266-3910
vps.k12.ok.us
Anderson ECC, 8237 E 540 Rd, PK-K
Amanda May, prin. 918-266-3807
Verdigris Lower ES 300/1-3
8207 E 540 Rd, 918-266-6343
Gregory Kelley, prin. Fax 266-1554
Verdigris Upper ES 300/4-6
8204 E 540 Rd, 918-266-7227
Denton Holland, prin.

Claremore Christian S 100/PK-12
1055 W Blue Starr Dr 74017 918-341-1805
Ryan Mullins, prin. Fax 341-1011
Heritage Adventist S 50/K-8
20555 S 4170 Rd Unit B 74017 918-283-2243
Legacy Christian S 100/PK-6
107 E Will Rogers Blvd 74017 918-342-1450
Pete Jensen, admin. Fax 341-8193

Clayton, Pushmataha, Pop. 740
Clayton ISD 300/PK-12
329 N 1st St 74536 918-569-4492
Randall Erwin, supt. Fax 569-7757
www.clayton.k12.ok.us/
Crain ES 200/PK-8
300 W Pine St 74536 918-569-4158
Keith Milligan, prin. Fax 569-7656

Cleo Springs, Major, Pop. 334
Aline-Cleo ISD
Supt. — See Aline
Aline-Cleo Springs S 100/PK-8
PO Box 38 73729 580-438-2330
Barry Nault, prin. Fax 438-2563

Cleveland, Pawnee, Pop. 3,054
Cleveland ISD 1,700/PK-12
600 N Gilbert Ave 74020 918-358-2210
Aaron Espolt, supt. Fax 358-3071
www.clevelandtigers.com/
Cleveland IS 400/3-5
705 N Swan Dr 74020 918-358-2210
Jeremy McKinney, prin. Fax 358-2550
Cleveland MS 400/6-8
322 N Gilbert Ave 74020 918-358-2210
Sol Bayouth, prin. Fax 358-2534

Cleveland PS 400/PK-2
300 N Gilbert Ave 74020 918-358-2210
Angela Ragland, prin. Fax 358-2532

Clinton, Custer, Pop. 8,804
Clinton ISD 2,300/PK-12
PO Box 729 73601 580-323-1800
Kevin Hime, supt. Fax 323-1804
www.clintonokschools.org/
Clinton MS 300/7-8
PO Box 729 73601 580-323-4228
Kyle Hilterbran, prin. Fax 323-3896
Nance ES 500/PK-1
PO Box 729 73601 580-323-0260
Janalyn Taylor, prin. Fax 323-8672
Southwest ES 500/2-4
PO Box 729 73601 580-323-1290
Nathan Meget, prin. Fax 323-3769
Washington ES 400/5-6
PO Box 729 73601 580-323-0311
Gene Ray, prin. Fax 323-2618

Western Oklahoma Christian S - Clinton 100/PK-6
22381 E 1070 Rd 73601 580-323-9150
Dora Miller, prin. Fax 323-0786

Coalgate, Coal, Pop. 1,800
Coalgate SD 700/PK-12
2 W Cedar Ave 74538 580-927-2351
Greg Davidson, supt. Fax 927-2694
www.coalgateschools.org
Byrd MS 100/7-8
2 W Cedar Ave 74538 580-927-3560
Phillip Wilkinson, prin. Fax 927-4031
Emerson ES 400/PK-6
2 W Cedar Ave 74538 580-927-2350
Charles Canida, prin. Fax 927-3537

Cottonwood SD 200/PK-8
PO Box 347 74538 580-927-2937
John Daniel, supt. Fax 927-2938
www.cottonwoodschool.net
Cottonwood S 200/PK-8
PO Box 347 74538 580-927-3907
John Daniel, prin. Fax 927-2938

Colbert, Bryan, Pop. 1,037
Colbert ISD 900/PK-12
PO Box 310 74733 580-296-2624
Jarvis Dobbs, supt. Fax 296-2219
www.colbertisd.org
Colbert MS 100/7-8
PO Box 310 74733 580-296-2590
Wesley Schreier, prin. Fax 296-2219
East Ward ES 200/4-6
PO Box 310 74733 580-296-2198
Stephanie Carlton, prin. Fax 296-5400
West Ward ES, PO Box 310 74733 400/PK-3
Karen Hedgecock, prin. 580-296-2626

Colcord, Delaware, Pop. 719
Colcord ISD 600/PK-12
433 S Larmon 74338 918-326-4116
Bud Simmons, supt. Fax 326-4471
www.colcordschools.com
Colcord ES 300/PK-6
433 S Larmon 74338 918-326-4117
Misty Winfiled, prin. Fax 326-4511
Colcord MS 100/7-8
433 S Larmon 74338 918-326-4852
Terrill Denny, prin. Fax 326-4468

Moseley SD 200/PK-8
7904 Moseley Rd 74338 918-505-1000
Charlene Carter, supt. Fax 422-5971
www.moseleyschool.com/
Moseley S 200/PK-8
7904 Moseley Rd 74338 918-505-1000
Charlene Carter, admin. Fax 422-5971

Coleman, Johnston
Coleman ISD 200/PK-12
PO Box 188 73432 580-937-4418
John Sheridan, supt. Fax 937-4615
www.coleman.k12.ok.us
Coleman ES 100/PK-8
PO Box 188 73432 580-937-4418
Tina Eldridge, prin. Fax 937-4866

Collinsville, Tulsa, Pop. 5,212
Collinsville ISD 2,100/PK-12
1092 W Maple St 74021 918-371-2386
Lance West, supt. Fax 371-4285
www.collinsville.k12.ok.us
Collinsville MS 400/7-8
1415 W Center St 74021 918-371-2541
Dale Harp, prin. Fax 371-1302
Collinsville Upper ES 4-5
12800 N 129th East Ave 74021 918-371-2202
Jennipher Keim, prin.
Herald ES 200/1-3
12818 N 129th East Ave 74021 918-371-4173
Cheryl Hunt, prin. Fax 371-3832
Pollard ECC 400/PK-K
12936 N 129th East Ave 74021 918-371-6870
Ashley Boomer, prin. Fax 371-4773
Wilson 6th Grade Center 400/6-6
402 N 17th St 74021 918-371-3144
Jennipher Keim, prin. Fax 371-4811

Comanche, Stephens, Pop. 1,590
Comanche ISD 1,000/PK-12
1030 Ash Ave 73529 580-439-2900
Terry Davidson, supt. Fax 439-2907
www.cpsok.org
Comanche ES 500/PK-5
1030 Ash Ave 73529 580-439-2911
Robin Troutman, prin. Fax 439-2947
Comanche MS 200/6-8
1030 Ash Ave 73529 580-439-2922
Brent Crow, prin. Fax 439-2979

Grandview SD 200/PK-8
277062 E 1840 Rd 73529 580-439-2467
Dr. Gary Wade, supt. Fax 439-5589
www.grandviewschool.k12.ok.us
Grandview S 200/PK-8
277062 E 1840 Rd 73529 580-439-2467
Dr. Gary Wade, supt. Fax 439-5589

Commerce, Ottawa, Pop. 2,364
Commerce ISD 900/PK-12
217 Commerce St 74339 918-675-4316
Jimmy R. Haynes, supt. Fax 675-4464
www.commercetigers.net
Alexander ES 500/PK-5
601 6th St 74339 918-675-4336
Kevin Wade, prin. Fax 675-5056
Commerce MS 200/6-8
500 Commerce St 74339 918-675-4101
Jack Kelley, prin. Fax 675-5353

Copan, Washington, Pop. 683
Copan ISD 900/PK-12
PO Box 429 74022 918-532-4344
Chris Smith, supt. Fax 532-4649
www.copan.k12.ok.us/
Copan S 500/PK-8
PO Box 429 74022 918-532-4344
Chris Tanner, prin. Fax 532-4649

Cordell, Washita, Pop. 2,865
Cordell ISD 800/PK-12
606 E 3rd St 73632 580-832-3420
Brad Overton, supt. Fax 832-1090
www.cordell.k12.ok.us
Cordell ES 500/PK-6
419 N Massingale 73632 580-832-3420
Alan Hull, prin. Fax 832-3406

Council Hill, Muskogee, Pop. 140
Midway ISD 300/PK-12
PO Box 127 74428 918-474-3434
Bruce Douglas, supt. Fax 474-3636
www.midway.k12.ok.us
Midway ES 200/PK-8
PO Box 127 74428 918-474-3434
Kurt Scullawl, prin. Fax 474-3636

Covington, Garfield, Pop. 512
Covington-Douglas ISD 300/PK-12
400 E Main St 73730 580-864-7481
Darren Sharp, supt. Fax 864-7644
www.c-d.k12.ok.us
Covington-Douglas S 200/PK-8
400 E Main St 73730 580-864-7849
Brian Smith, prin. Fax 864-7644

Coweta, Wagoner, Pop. 9,182
Coweta ISD 3,300/PK-12
PO Box 550 74429 918-486-6506
Jeff Holmes, supt. Fax 486-4167
www.cowetaps.org
Central ES 300/PK-3
PO Box 550 74429 918-486-2130
Sherri Dotson, prin. Fax 486-7810
Heritage IS 300/4-6
PO Box 550 74429 918-486-8590
Tim Brandt, prin. Fax 486-8599
Mission IS 400/4-6
PO Box 550 74429 918-486-2186
Gentry Pierce, prin. Fax 486-4404
Northwest ES 300/PK-3
PO Box 550 74429 918-486-6559
Richard Lock, prin. Fax 279-1168
Sloat JHS 500/7-8
PO Box 550 74429 918-486-2127
Scott Kempenich, prin. Fax 486-7307
Southside ES 500/PK-3
PO Box 550 74429 918-279-0480
Doug Flanary, prin. Fax 279-1223

Coyle, Logan, Pop. 317
Coyle ISD 300/PK-12
PO Box 287 73027 405-466-2242
Josh Sumrall M.Ed., supt. Fax 466-2448
www.coyle.k12.ok.us
Coyle ES 200/PK-8
PO Box 287 73027 405-466-2242
Patrick Smith, prin. Fax 466-2448

Crescent, Logan, Pop. 1,340
Crescent ISD 700/PK-12
PO Box 719 73028 405-969-3738
Bart Watkins, supt. Fax 969-2003
www.crescentok.com/
Crescent ES 300/PK-5
PO Box 719 73028 405-969-2227
Wayne Owens, prin. Fax 969-2835
Crescent MS 100/6-8
PO Box 719 73028 405-969-2227
Mickey Hart, prin. Fax 969-2003

Cromwell, Seminole, Pop. 270
Butner ISD 200/PK-12
PO Box 157 74837 405-944-5530
Diane Parris, supt. Fax 944-5746
www.butnerpublicschools.com/
Butner ES 200/PK-8
PO Box 157 74837 405-944-5526
Greg Dodson, prin. Fax 944-5746

Crowder, Pittsburg, Pop. 420
Crowder ISD 500/PK-12
PO Box B 74430 918-334-3203
Robert Florenzano, supt. Fax 334-3295
www.crowder.k12.ok.us
Crowder ES, PO Box B 74430 400/PK-8
Anna Killebrew, prin. 918-334-3205

Cushing, Payne, Pop. 7,369
Cushing ISD 1,600/PK-12
PO Box 1609 74023 918-225-3425
Koln Knight, supt. Fax 225-5256
cushing.k12.ok.us
Cushing Lower ES 100/K-1
1601 S Harmony Rd 74023 918-225-4697
Nancy Dowell, prin. Fax 225-2864
Cushing MS 400/5-8
521 S Harmony Rd 74023 918-225-1311
Stacy Weaver, prin.
Cushing Pre-Kindergarten 300/PK-PK
1919 S Kings Hwy 74023 918-225-4683
Sally Wright, prin.
Cushing Upper ES 400/2-4
316 N Steele Ave 74023 918-225-4497
Martha Cackler, prin.

Oak Grove SD 200/PK-8
8409 E 9th St 74023 918-352-2889
Jon Aven, supt. Fax 352-4187
www.oakgrove.k12.ok.us
Oak Grove S 200/PK-8
8409 E 9th St 74023 918-352-2889
Jon Aven, prin. Fax 352-4187

Cyril, Caddo, Pop. 1,013
Cyril ISD 300/PK-12
PO Box 449 73029 580-464-2272
Jamie Mitchell, supt. Fax 464-2445
www.cyrilschools.org
Cyril ES 200/PK-6
PO Box 449 73029 580-464-2437
Tammy Cocheran, prin. Fax 464-3703

Dale, Pottawatomie, Pop. 176
Dale ISD 700/PK-12
300 Smith Ave 74851 405-964-5558
Charles Dickinson, supt. Fax 964-5559
www.dale.k12.ok.us
Dale ES 300/PK-5
300 Smith Ave 74851 405-964-5514
Bruce Throckmorton, prin. Fax 964-5519
Dale MS, 300 Smith Ave 74851 200/6-8
Ky Wilkins, prin. 405-964-2799

Davenport, Lincoln, Pop. 781
Davenport ISD 400/PK-12
PO Box 849 74026 918-377-2277
Daniel Acord, supt. Fax 377-2553
www.davenport.k12.ok.us/
Davenport ES 300/PK-8
PO Box 849 74026 918-377-2279
Misty Emmons, prin. Fax 377-2339

Davidson, Tillman, Pop. 307
Davidson Dependent SD 100/PK-8
PO Box 338 73530 580-568-2423
Phillip Ratcliff, supt. Fax 568-2219
www.davidson.k12.ok.us
Davidson ES 100/PK-8
PO Box 338 73530 580-568-2511
Phillip Ratcliff, prin. Fax 568-2219

Davis, Murray, Pop. 2,557
Davis ISD 1,100/PK-12
400 E Atlanta Ave 73030 580-369-2386
Todd Garrison, supt. Fax 369-3507
www.daviswolves.org
Davis ES 500/PK-4
400 E Atlanta Ave 73030 580-369-5544
Tammie Webb, prin. Fax 369-3983
Davis MS 300/5-8
400 E Atlanta Ave 73030 580-369-5565
Jeff Jennings, prin. Fax 369-3289

Deer Creek, Grant, Pop. 124
Deer Creek-Lamont ISD
Supt. — See Lamont
Deer Creek-Lamont ES 100/PK-8
1643 Main St 74636 580-267-3241
Barbara Hegier, prin. Fax 267-3276

Del City, Oklahoma, Pop. 19,870
Midwest City-Del City ISD
Supt. — See Midwest City
Del City ES 400/PK-5
2400 Epperly Dr 73115 405-671-8640
Rodney Boyer, prin. Fax 671-8642
Del Crest MS 500/6-8
4731 Judy Dr 73115 405-671-8615
Justin Mann, prin. Fax 671-8618
Epperly Heights ES 700/PK-5
3805 Del Rd 73115 405-671-8650
Kevin Hill, prin. Fax 671-8652
Kerr MS 600/6-8
2300 Linda Ln 73115 405-671-8625
Nathan Elliott, prin. Fax 671-8626
Townsend ES 500/PK-5
4000 Epperly Dr 73115 405-671-8680
Michael Becker, prin. Fax 671-8682

Christian Heritage Academy 600/PK-12
4400 SE 27th St 73115 405-672-1787
Josh Bullard, hdmstr. Fax 672-1839
Destiny Christian S 500/PK-12
3801 SE 29th St 73115 405-677-6000
Jim Howard, admin. Fax 677-6066

Depew, Creek, Pop. 440
Depew ISD 400/PK-12
PO Box 257 74028 918-324-5466
Leon Hiett, supt. Fax 324-5336
depew.k12.ok.us
Depew ES 200/PK-8
PO Box 257 74028 918-324-5368
Jayson Larremore, prin. Fax 324-5336

Gypsy SD 100/PK-8
30899 S 417th West Ave 74028 918-324-5365
Rachel Collins, supt. Fax 324-5003
www.gypsy.k12.ok.us/
Gypsy S 100/PK-8
30899 S 417th West Ave 74028 918-324-5365
Rachel Collins, prin. Fax 324-5003

Dewar, Okmulgee, Pop. 790
Dewar ISD 400/PK-12
PO Box 790 74431 918-652-9625
Todd Been, supt. Fax 652-3096
www.dewar.k12.ok.us/
Dewar ES 200/PK-5
PO Box 790 74431 918-652-2184
Brett Thomas, prin. Fax 652-7522
Dewar MS 100/6-8
PO Box 790 74431 918-652-9625
Josh Kilhoffer, prin. Fax 652-3096

Dewey, Washington, Pop. 3,212
Dewey ISD 1,300/PK-12
1 Bulldogger Rd 74029 918-534-2241
Vince Vincent, supt. Fax 534-0149
www.deweyk12.org
Dewey ES 600/PK-5
1 Bulldogger Rd 74029 918-534-2241
Jerri Moore, prin. Fax 534-0149
Dewey MS 300/6-8
1 Bulldogger Rd 74029 918-534-2241
Brent Massey, prin. Fax 534-0934

Dibble, McClain, Pop. 838
Dibble ISD 700/PK-12
PO Box 9 73031 405-344-6375
Chad Clanton, supt. Fax 344-6977
www.dibbleps.org
Dibble ES, PO Box 9 73031 300/PK-5
Mechell Prince, prin. 405-344-6868
Dibble MS 200/6-8
PO Box 9 73031 405-344-6380
Darlene Hayhurst, prin. Fax 344-7275

Dover, Kingfisher, Pop. 461
Dover ISD 200/PK-12
PO Box 195 73734 405-828-4205
Shannon Grimes, supt. Fax 828-7150
www.dover.k12.ok.us
Dover ES 100/PK-8
PO Box 195 73734 405-828-4205
Trilla Cranford, prin. Fax 828-7150

Drummond, Garfield, Pop. 444
Drummond ISD 300/PK-12
PO Box 240 73735 580-493-2216
Brent Rousey, supt. Fax 493-2273
www.drummond.k12.ok.us/
Drummond ES, PO Box 240 73735 200/PK-8
Jarrod Johnson, prin. 580-493-2271

Drumright, Creek, Pop. 2,673
Drumright ISD 600/PK-12
505 W 2nd St 74030 918-352-2492
Robbie Dorsey, supt. Fax 352-4430
www.drumright.k12.ok.us
Bradley ES 300/PK-5
508 S Skinner Ave 74030 918-352-9519
Tara Osterhout, prin. Fax 352-4608
Cooper MS 100/6-8
510 S Skinner Ave 74030 918-352-2318
Kevin Bilyeu, prin. Fax 352-4033

Olive ISD 400/PK-12
9352 S 436th West Ave 74030 918-352-9568
Jimmy Reynolds, supt. Fax 352-4379
www.olive.k12.ok.us
Olive ES 300/PK-8
9352 S 436th West Ave 74030 918-352-9569
Joanna Lobaugh, prin. Fax 352-4379

Duke, Jackson, Pop. 417
Duke ISD 200/PK-12
PO Box 160 73532 580-679-3014
Kevin Brown, supt. Fax 679-3017
www.dukeschools.com/
Duke S, PO Box 160 73532 100/PK-8
Rick Wilson, prin. 580-679-3311

Duncan, Stephens, Pop. 22,474
Duncan ISD 3,800/PK-12
PO Box 1548 73534 580-255-0686
Melonie Hau, supt. Fax 252-2453
www.duncanps.org
Duncan MS 800/6-8
PO Box 1548 73534 580-470-8106
Wade Hampton, prin. Fax 470-8743
Emerson ES 500/K-5
PO Box 1548 73534 580-255-7146
Koree Goldsmith, prin. Fax 252-5413
Mann ES 500/K-5
PO Box 1548 73534 580-255-6530
Vicki Nighswonger, prin. Fax 255-3673
Plato ES 300/K-5
PO Box 1548 73534 580-255-6167
Brandy Peters, prin. Fax 255-3672
Rogers Preschool Center 300/PK-PK
PO Box 1548 73534 580-255-9012
Mona Evans, prin. Fax 255-1074
Twain ES 200/K-5
PO Box 1548 73534 580-255-1324
Bud Conway, prin. Fax 255-3819
Wilson ES 300/K-5
PO Box 1548 73534 580-255-8107
Cassie Berthold, prin. Fax 255-3893

Empire SD 400/PK-12
276803 E 1760 Rd 73533 580-252-5392
Vicki Davison, supt. Fax 252-4231
www.empireschools.org
Empire ES 300/PK-5
276803 E 1760 Rd 73533 580-255-4150
Josh Skiles, prin. Fax 251-9026
Empire MS 6-8
276803 E 1760 Rd 73533 580-255-7515
Jodie Roberts, prin. Fax 255-2971

Durant, Bryan, Pop. 14,924
Durant ISD 3,600/PK-12
1323 Waco St 74701 580-924-1276
Duane Merideth, supt. Fax 924-6019
www.durantisd.org
Durant IS 700/4-6
1314 Waco St 74701 580-924-1397
Aaron McCoy, prin. Fax 920-7940
Durant MS 500/7-8
802 W Walnut St 74701 580-924-1321
John Williamson, prin. Fax 924-8278
Irving ES 600/PK-3
812 W Locust St 74701 580-924-3805
Lisa Whitley, prin. Fax 920-4939
Lee ECC 200/PK-PK
824 W Louisiana St 74701 580-924-3628
Jan Chaffin, prin. Fax 920-4931
Northwest Heights ES 600/PK-3
1715 W University Blvd 74701 580-924-5595
Valerie Crabtree, prin. Fax 924-4748

Rock Creek ISD
Supt. — See Bokchito
Rock Creek ES 300/PK-8
23072 US Highway 70 74701 580-924-9601
Ryan Cordell, prin. Fax 924-1012

Silo ISD 700/PK-12
122 W Bourne St 74701 580-924-7000
Kate McDonald, supt. Fax 920-7988
www.siloisd.org
Silo ES 500/PK-6
122 W Bourne St 74701 580-924-7001
Katie Brister, prin. Fax 924-5771

Victory Life Academy 100/PK-12
3412 W University Blvd 74701 580-920-0850
Sarah Morrison M.Ed., hdmstr. Fax 920-9923

Dustin, Hughes, Pop. 344
Graham-Dustin SD
Supt. — See Weleetka
Dustin ES 50/PK-4
203 Wisdom Ave 74839 918-652-8935
C.J. Buesser, prin. Fax 656-2422

Eagletown, McCurtain, Pop. 515
Eagletown ISD 200/PK-12
PO Box 38 74734 580-835-2242
Brian Armstrong, supt. Fax 835-7420
www.eagletownisd.org
Eagletown ES 100/PK-8
PO Box 38 74734 580-835-2241
Jamie Bean, prin. Fax 835-7420

Earlsboro, Pottawatomie, Pop. 569
Earlsboro ISD 200/PK-12
PO Box 10 74840 405-997-5616
Mark Maloy, supt. Fax 997-3181
www.earlsboro.k12.ok.us
Earlsboro ES 200/PK-8
PO Box 10 74840 405-997-5312
Mike Goats, prin. Fax 997-3181

Edmond, Oklahoma, Pop. 78,271
Deer Creek ISD 4,900/PK-12
20701 N MacArthur Blvd, 405-348-6100
Ranet Tippens, supt. Fax 348-3049
www.deercreekschools.org
Deer Creek ES 500/PK-4
4704 NW 164th St 73013 405-348-9100
Laura Koehn, prin. Fax 359-3164
Deer Creek IS 800/5-6
2601 NW 234th St, 405-348-4830
Sherri Verble, prin.
Deer Creek MS 800/7-8
2601 NW 234th St, 405-348-4830
Kristy VanDorn, prin. Fax 359-2292
Grove Valley ES 500/PK-4
3500 NW 192nd St, 405-359-3195
Dr. Kelly Faught, prin. Fax 359-3198
Prairie Vale ES 600/PK-4
22522 N Pennsylvania Ave, 405-359-3170
Michelle Anderson, prin. Fax 359-1819
Rose Union ES 300/PK-4
5100 NW 220th St, 405-359-3188
Tina Nunn, prin. Fax 359-3191
Other Schools – See Oklahoma City

Edmond ISD 22,900/PK-12
1001 W Danforth Rd 73003 405-340-2800
Dr. Cathey Bugg, supt. Fax 340-2835
www.edmondschools.net/
Centennial ES 800/PK-5
4400 N Coltrane Rd 73034 405-340-2275
Jessele Miller, prin. Fax 340-2255
Central MS 800/6-8
500 E 9th St 73034 405-340-2890
Laura McGee, prin. Fax 340-3961
Cheyenne MS 1,000/6-8
1271 W Covell Rd 73003 405-340-2940
Michelle Grinsteiner, prin. Fax 330-7397
Chisholm ES 700/PK-5
2300 E 33rd St 73013 405-340-2950
Tom Higdon, prin. Fax 330-3352
Cimarron MS 800/6-8
3701 S Bryant Ave 73013 405-340-2935
Cordell Ehrich, prin. Fax 330-3398
Clegern ES 300/K-5
601 S Jackson St 73034 405-340-2955
Teri Cowden-Draper, prin. Fax 330-3345
Cross Timbers ES 1,100/PK-5
4800 N Kelly Ave, 405-340-2200
Jamila Crawford, prin. Fax 330-3355
Debo ES 900/PK-5
16060 N May Ave 73013 405-340-2270
Candice Delcamp, prin. Fax 330-3357
Dougherty ES 300/PK-5
19 N Boulevard 73034 405-340-2985
Penny Dilg, prin. Fax 330-3346
Freeman ES 500/PK-5
501 W Hurd St 73003 405-340-2965
Nicole Marler, prin. Fax 330-3347
Frontier ES 500/PK-5
4901 Explorer Dr, 405-340-2211
Cara Jernigan, prin. Fax 340-2211
Haskell ES 900/PK-5
1701 NW 150th St 73013 405-340-2945
Dayna Hamilton, prin. Fax 330-3354
Heartland MS 6-8
4900 Explorer Dr, 405-340-2972
Jason Galloway, prin.
Heritage ES K-5
400 E Sorghum Mill Rd 73034 405-340-2921
Cathey Bugg, prin.
Howell ECC PK-PK
45 E 12th St 73034 405-340-2960
Teri Cowden-Draper, prin. Fax 330-3344
Irving ES 800/PK-5
18101 N Western Ave, 405-340-2210
Kinberly Frank, prin. Fax 330-3356
Northern Hills ES 700/PK-5
901 E Wayne St 73034 405-340-2975
Michele Milner, prin. Fax 330-3348
Risner ES 600/PK-5
2801 S Rankin St 73013 405-340-2984
Penny Gooch, prin. Fax 330-3349
Rogers ES 700/PK-5
1215 E 9th St 73034 405-340-2995
Dr. Sheron House, prin. Fax 330-3351
Ross ES 900/PK-5
1901 Thomas Dr 73003 405-340-2970
Christa Ellis, prin. Fax 330-3353
Sequoyah MS 1,300/6-8
1125 E Danforth Rd 73034 405-340-2900
Jason Galloway, prin. Fax 340-2909
Summit MS 1,200/6-8
1703 NW 150th St 73013 405-340-2920
Lisa Adams, prin. Fax 340-2933
Sunset ES 700/PK-5
400 W 8th St 73003 405-340-2990
Dr. Kartina McDaniel, prin. Fax 330-3350
West Field ES 800/PK-5
17601 N Pennsylvania Ave, 405-340-2285
Lisa Crosslin, prin. Fax 330-7364

Oakdale SD 600/PK-8
10901 N Sooner Rd 73013 405-771-3373
Kim Lanier, supt. Fax 771-5220
www.oakdale.org
Oakdale ES 600/PK-8
10901 N Sooner Rd 73013 405-771-3373
Susan Honeycutt, prin. Fax 771-5220

Holy Trinity Lutheran S 200/K-5
308 NW 164th St 73013 405-844-4000
Debbie Swanson, prin.
Mercy S Institute PK-12
14001 N Harvey Ave 73013 405-748-5500
Oklahoma Christian Academy 300/PK-12
1101 E 9th St 73034 405-844-6478
Oklahoma Christian S 900/PK-12
PO Box 509 73083 405-341-2265
Dr. Al King, hdmstr. Fax 341-4710
St. Elizabeth Ann Seton S 500/PK-8
PO Box 510 73083 405-348-5364
Laura Gallagher, prin. Fax 340-9627
St. Mary's Episcopal S 200/PK-5
505 E Covell Rd 73034 405-341-9541

Elgin, Comanche, Pop. 2,058
Elgin ISD 1,700/PK-12
PO Box 369 73538 580-492-3663
Nathaniel Meraz, supt. Fax 492-4084
www.elginps.org
Elgin Lower ES 400/PK-1
PO Box 369 73538 580-492-3680
Robert Hughes, prin. Fax 492-3698
Elgin MS 600/5-8
PO Box 369 73538 580-492-3655
Melissa Hitt, prin. Fax 492-3658
Elgin Upper ES 2-4
PO Box 369 73538 580-492-3680
Todd Osborn, prin. Fax 492-4083

Elk City, Beckham, Pop. 11,396
Elk City ISD 2,300/PK-12
222 W Broadway Ave 73644 580-225-0175
Rick Garrison, supt. Fax 225-8644
www.elkcityschools.com
Elk City ES PK-3
222 W Broadway Ave 73644 580-225-7722
Richard Moran, prin.
Elk City IS 300/4-6
222 W Broadway Ave 73644 580-225-2687
Randy Turney, prin. Fax 225-2687
Elk City MS 200/7-8
222 W Broadway Ave 73644 580-225-5043
Richard Moran, prin. Fax 225-5043

Merritt ISD 700/PK-12
19693 E 1130 Rd 73644 580-225-5460
Jeff Daugherty, supt. Fax 225-5469
www.merritt.k12.ok.us
Merritt ES 600/PK-8
19693 E 1130 Rd 73644 580-225-5460
Amy Edler, prin. Fax 225-5469

Western Oklahoma Christian S - Elk City 100/PK-6
2000 S Randall Ave 73644 580-303-4922
Dora Miller, prin. Fax 323-0786

Elmore City, Garvin, Pop. 671
Elmore City-Pernell ISD 400/PK-12
100 N Muse Ave 73433 580-788-2565
Jennifer Cruz, supt. Fax 788-4665
www.ecphs.k12.ok.us
Elmore City-Pernell ES 300/PK-6
100 N Muse Ave 73433 580-788-2869
Sheila Riddle, prin. Fax 788-2860

El Reno, Canadian, Pop. 16,130
Banner SD 200/PK-8
2455 N Banner Rd 73036 405-262-0598
Larry York, supt. Fax 262-0628
www.bannerschool.net

Banner S 200/PK-8
2455 N Banner Rd 73036 405-262-0598
Larry York, prin. Fax 262-0628

Darlington SD 200/PK-8
4408 N Highway 81 73036 405-262-0137
Loren Tackett, supt. Fax 262-3215
www.darlingtonps.org/
Darlington S 200/PK-8
4408 N Highway 81 73036 405-262-0137
Cheryl Garrison, admin. Fax 262-3215

El Reno ISD 2,200/PK-12
PO Box 580 73036 405-262-1703
Craig McVay, supt. Fax 262-8620
www.elrenops.org
Dale JHS 200/7-8
PO Box 580 73036 405-262-3253
Kim Landers, prin. Fax 262-8650
Hillcrest ES 400/PK-K
PO Box 580 73036 405-262-2396
Lanae Goucher, prin. Fax 262-3265
Lincoln ES 300/3-4
PO Box 580 73036 405-262-1941
Robin Holley, prin. Fax 262-8479
Roblyer MS 200/5-6
PO Box 580 73036 405-262-2700
Carmen Holmes, prin. Fax 262-8449
Witcher ES 400/1-2
PO Box 580 73036 405-262-5592
Tiffani Patrick, prin. Fax 262-8439

Riverside SD 200/PK-8
4800 Foreman Rd E 73036 405-262-2907
David Garner, supt. Fax 262-2925
www.riverside.k12.ok.us/
Riverside S 200/PK-8
4800 Foreman Rd E 73036 405-262-2907
David Garner, prin. Fax 262-2925

Sacred Heart S 100/PK-8
210 S Evans Ave 73036 405-262-2284
Shannon Statton, prin. Fax 262-3818

Enid, Garfield, Pop. 46,752
Chisholm ISD 1,000/PK-12
305 Utah 73701 580-237-5512
Roydon Tilley, supt. Fax 234-5494
www.chisholm.k12.ok.us
Chisholm ES 500/PK-5
300 Redwood 73701 580-237-5645
Darla Smith, prin. Fax 234-5334
Chisholm MS 200/6-8
4202 W Carrier Rd 73703 580-234-0234
Crystal Szymanski, prin. Fax 234-0343

Enid ISD 7,700/PK-12
500 S Independence Ave 73701 580-366-7000
Dr. Darrell Floyd, supt. Fax 366-8900
www.enidpublicschools.org
Adams ES 300/K-5
2200 E Randolph Ave 73701 580-366-7600
Reba Gregory, prin. Fax 366-8901
Carver ECC PK-PK
815 S 5th St 73701 580-366-8601
Chris Smith, prin. Fax 366-8918
Coolidge ES 500/PK-5
1515 E Ash Ave 73701 580-366-7550
Sherri Hendrie, prin. Fax 366-8902
Eisenhower ES 200/PK-5
1301 W Fox Dr 73703 580-366-8100
Jamie Jarnagin, prin. Fax 366-8911
Emerson MS 400/6-8
700 W Elm Ave 73701 580-366-7250
Candice Wojciechowsky, prin. Fax 249-3587
Garfield ES 600/K-5
400 N 7th St 73701 580-366-7700
Jane Johnson, prin. Fax 366-8907
Glenwood ES 500/PK-5
824 N Oakwood Rd 73703 580-366-7800
James Rainey, prin. Fax 366-8908
Hayes ES 400/PK-5
2102 Beverly Dr 73703 580-366-7650
Lyntel Murphy, prin. Fax 366-8909
Hoover ES 300/PK-5
2800 W Maine Ave 73703 580-366-7350
Karen Heizer, prin. Fax 366-8910
Longfellow MS 500/6-8
900 E Broadway Ave 73701 580-366-8200
Sam Robinson, prin. Fax 366-8912
McKinley ES 300/PK-5
1701 W Broadway Ave 73703 580-366-7400
Kay Kiner, prin. Fax 366-8913
Monroe ES 500/PK-5
400 W Cottonwood Ave 73701 580-366-7500
M. Scott Allen, prin. Fax 366-8914
Prairie View ES 500/PK-5
4700 W Willow Rd 73703 580-366-8000
Clark Koepping, prin. Fax 366-8915
Taft ES 400/PK-5
1002 Sequoyah Dr 73703 580-366-7450
Peggy Kenaga, prin. Fax 366-8916
Waller MS 600/6-8
2604 W Randolph Ave 73703 580-366-7900
Robb Mills, prin. Fax 366-8917

Pioneer-Pleasant Vale ISD
Supt. — See Waukomis
Pioneer-Pleasant Vale ES 300/PK-6
6020 E Willow Rd 73701 580-234-9628
Larry Coonrod, prin. Fax 232-9694

Emmanuel Christian S 200/PK-5
2505 W Owen K Garriott Rd 73703 580-237-0032
Dr. Stephen Glazier, hdmstr. Fax 237-0662
St. Joseph S 100/PK-5
PO Box 3527 73702 580-242-4449
Wade Laffey, prin. Fax 242-3541
St. Paul's Lutheran S 100/PK-8
1626 E Broadway Ave 73701 580-234-6646
Lois Ancell-Nichols, prin. Fax 234-6692

Erick, Beckham, Pop. 1,034
Erick ISD 200/PK-12
PO Box 9 73645 580-526-3476
Jeff Kelly, supt. Fax 526-3308
www.erickps.k12.ok.us/
Erick ES 100/PK-6
PO Box 9 73645 580-526-3203
Kenneth Hill, prin. Fax 526-3308

Eufaula, McIntosh, Pop. 2,615
Eufaula ISD 1,200/PK-12
1717 J M Bailey Hwy 74432 918-689-2152
Jeanette Smith, supt. Fax 689-1080
eufaula.k12.ok.us
Eufaula ES 600/PK-5
1705 J M Bailey Hwy 74432 918-689-2682
Brenda Lewis, prin. Fax 689-1067
Eufaula MS 200/6-8
1711 J M Bailey Hwy 74432 918-689-2711
Chris Whelan, prin. Fax 689-2874

Stidham SD 100/PK-8
HC 64 Box 2110 74432 918-689-5241
Danny Williams, supt. Fax 689-9163
www.stidham.k12.ok.us
Stidham S 100/PK-8
HC 64 Box 2110 74432 918-689-5241
Danny Williams, prin. Fax 689-9163

Fairfax, Osage, Pop. 1,241
Woodland SD 400/PK-12
100 N 6th St 74637 918-642-3297
Todd Kimrey, supt. Fax 642-5754
www.woodland.k12.ok.us/
Woodland ES 200/PK-4
100 N 6th St 74637 918-642-3295
Claudette Mashburn, prin. Fax 642-3280
Other Schools – See Ralston

Fairland, Ottawa, Pop. 935
Fairland ISD 600/PK-12
202 W Washington Ave 74343 918-676-3811
Mark Alexander, supt. Fax 676-3594
www.fairlandowls.com
Fairland ES 300/PK-5
202 W Washington Ave 74343 918-676-3224
Angie Wade, prin.
Fairland MS 100/6-8
202 W Washington Ave 74343 918-676-3246
Jerry Johnson, prin.

Fairview, Major, Pop. 2,532
Fairview ISD 700/PK-12
408 E Broadway 73737 580-227-2531
Craig Church, supt. Fax 227-2642
www.fairviewschools.net
Chamberlain MS 100/6-8
1000 E Elm St 73737 580-227-2555
Brock Robison, prin. Fax 227-2642
Cornelsen ES 400/PK-5
1200 E Elm St 73737 580-227-2561
Mark VanMeter, prin. Fax 227-2642

Fanshawe, LeFlore, Pop. 382
Fanshawe SD 100/PK-8
PO Box 100 74935 918-659-2341
Wes McGowen, supt. Fax 659-2275
Fanshawe S 100/PK-8
PO Box 100 74935 918-659-2341
Wes McGowen, prin. Fax 659-2275

Fargo, Ellis, Pop. 359
Fargo-Gage SD 200/PK-12
PO Box 200 73840 580-698-2298
Mike Jones, supt. Fax 698-8019
www.fargo.k12.ok.us
Fargo-Gage ES 200/PK-8
PO Box 200 73840 580-698-2298
Bryan Pope, prin. Fax 698-8019

Felt, Cimarron, Pop. 89
Felt ISD 100/PK-12
PO Box 47 73937 580-426-2220
Lewetta Hefley, supt. Fax 426-2799
www.felt.k12.ok.us
Felt ES 100/PK-8
PO Box 47 73937 580-426-2220
Christopher May, prin. Fax 426-2799

Fletcher, Comanche, Pop. 1,123
Fletcher ISD 400/PK-12
PO Box 489 73541 580-549-6027
Shane Gilbreath, supt. Fax 549-6016
www.fletcherschools.org/
Fletcher ES 300/PK-6
PO Box 489 73541 580-549-6020
Sandi Butler, prin. Fax 549-6016

Forgan, Beaver, Pop. 539
Forgan ISD 200/PK-12
PO Box 406 73938 580-487-3366
Travis Smalts, supt. Fax 487-3368
www.forgan.k12.ok.us
Forgan S 100/PK-8
PO Box 406 73938 580-487-3366
Todd Kerr, prin. Fax 487-3368

Fort Cobb, Caddo, Pop. 599
Fort Cobb-Broxton ISD 300/PK-12
PO Box 130 73038 405-643-2336
Kyle Lierle, supt. Fax 643-2547
www.fcbmustangs.com
Fort Cobb-Broxton ES 200/PK-5
PO Box 130 73038 405-643-2334
James Biddy, prin. Fax 643-2547
Fort Cobb-Broxton MS 100/6-8
PO Box 130 73038 405-643-2820
James Biddy, prin. Fax 643-2547

Fort Gibson, Muskogee, Pop. 3,804
Fort Gibson ISD 1,900/PK-12
500 Ross Ave 74434 918-478-2474
Derald Glover, supt. Fax 478-8533
www.ftgibson.k12.ok.us
Fort Gibson Early Learning Center 500/PK-2
500 Ross Ave 74434 918-478-4841
Shelly Holderby, prin. Fax 478-6411
Fort Gibson IS 400/3-5
500 Ross Ave 74434 918-478-2465
Sherry Rybolt, prin. Fax 478-6401
Fort Gibson MS 400/6-8
500 Ross Ave 74434 918-478-2471
Gregory Phares, prin. Fax 478-6412

Fort Sill, Comanche, Pop. 12,107
Lawton ISD
Supt. — See Lawton
Freedom ES PK-5
5720 Geronimo Rd 73503 580-713-0060
Mikel Shanklin, prin.

Fort Supply, Woodward, Pop. 320
Fort Supply ISD 100/PK-12
PO Box 160 73841 580-766-2611
Melva Little, supt. Fax 766-8019
www.fortsupply.k12.ok.us/
Fort Supply S 100/PK-8
PO Box 160 73841 580-766-2611
Melva Little, prin. Fax 766-8019

Fort Towson, Choctaw, Pop. 508
Fort Towson ISD 400/PK-12
PO Box 39 74735 580-873-2712
Charles Caughern, supt. Fax 873-1053
www.forttowson.k12.ok.us/
Fort Towson ES 200/PK-6
PO Box 39 74735 580-873-2780
Ami Payne, prin. Fax 873-2712

Fox, Carter
Fox ISD 300/PK-12
PO Box 248 73435 580-673-2081
Brent Phelps, supt. Fax 673-2389
www.foxps.k12.ok.us
Fox ES 200/PK-8
PO Box 248 73435 580-673-2083
Mark Williams, prin. Fax 673-2389

Frederick, Tillman, Pop. 3,832
Frederick ISD 600/PK-12
817 N 15th St 73542 580-335-5516
Shannon Vanderburg, supt. Fax 335-2324
www.frederickbombers.net
Frederick ES 200/3-5
817 N 15th St 73542 580-335-3513
Kay Cabaniss, prin. Fax 335-5088
Frederick MS 200/6-8
817 N 15th St 73542 580-335-2014
Jeremy Newton, prin. Fax 335-2763
Prather Brown S PK-2
817 N 15th St 73542 580-335-5713
Janice Crume, prin. Fax 335-5630

Freedom, Woods, Pop. 280
Freedom ISD 100/PK-12
PO Box 5 73842 580-621-3271
James Miller, supt. Fax 621-3699
www.freedom.k12.ok.us
Freedom S 100/PK-8
PO Box 5 73842 580-621-3271
James Miller, admin. Fax 621-3699

Gans, Sequoyah, Pop. 289
Gans ISD 400/PK-12
PO Box 70 74936 918-775-2236
Larry Calloway, supt. Fax 775-5145
www.gans.k12.ok.us
Gans S 300/PK-8
PO Box 70 74936 918-775-2236
Regina Brannon, prin. Fax 775-5145

Garber, Garfield, Pop. 806
Garber ISD 400/PK-12
PO Box 539 73738 580-863-2220
Will Jones, supt. Fax 863-2259
www.garber.k12.ok.us
Garber ES, PO Box 539 73738 200/PK-8
Phil Hoopes, prin. 580-863-2232

Garvin, McCurtain, Pop. 246
Forest Grove SD 200/PK-8
PO Box 60 74736 580-286-3961
John Smith, supt. Fax 286-3974
www.forestgrove.k12.ok.us
Forest Grove S 200/PK-8
PO Box 60 74736 580-286-3961
Deena Smith, prin. Fax 286-3974

Geary, Blaine, Pop. 1,213
Geary ISD 400/PK-12
110 SW Embree Dr 73040 405-884-2411
Todd Glasgow, supt. Fax 884-2099
www.gearyschools.org
Geary ES 200/PK-5
110 SW Embree Dr 73040 405-884-5701
Sean Buchanan, prin. Fax 884-2983
Geary MS 100/6-8
110 SW Embree Dr 73040 405-884-2362
Tim Rawls, prin. Fax 884-5487

Geronimo, Comanche, Pop. 1,179
Geronimo ISD 400/PK-12
800 W Main St 73543 580-355-3160
Bill Pascoe, supt. Fax 357-8307
www.geronimo.k12.ok.us
Geronimo ES 200/PK-6
800 W Main St 73543 580-353-0882
Amy Latimer, prin. Fax 355-9670
Geronimo MS 50/7-8
800 W Main St 73543 580-355-3160
Heath Selcer, prin. Fax 357-8307

Glencoe, Payne, Pop. 577
Glencoe ISD 300/PK-12
201 E Lone Chimney Rd 74032 580-669-2261
John Lazenby, supt. Fax 669-2961
www.glencoe.k12.ok.us

Glencoe ES 200/PK-8
201 E Lone Chimney Rd 74032 580-669-2254
Tammy Lane, prin. Fax 669-2254

Glenpool, Tulsa, Pop. 9,951
Glenpool ISD 2,600/PK-12
PO Box 1149 74033 918-322-9500
Jerry Olansen, supt. Fax 322-1529
www.glenpool.k12.ok.us
Glenpool ES 1,300/PK-5
PO Box 1149 74033 918-322-9500
Dr. Deanna Dobbins, prin. Fax 322-6486
Glenpool MS 600/6-8
PO Box 1149 74033 918-322-9500
Matt Fore, prin. Fax 322-6411

Goodwell, Texas, Pop. 1,268
Goodwell ISD 200/PK-12
PO Box 580 73939 580-349-2271
Jerry Birdsong, supt. Fax 349-2531
www.goodwell.k12.ok.us
Goodwell ES 200/PK-8
PO Box 580 73939 580-349-2271
Jason Schreiner, prin. Fax 349-2531

Yarbrough ISD 100/PK-12
RR 1 Box 31 73939 580-545-3329
Jim Wiggin, supt. Fax 545-3392
www.yarbrough.k12.ok.us/
Yarbrough ES 100/PK-8
RR 1 Box 31 73939 580-545-3328
Wade Stafford, prin. Fax 545-3392

Gore, Sequoyah, Pop. 891
Gore ISD 500/PK-12
1200 N Highway 10 74435 918-489-5587
Lucky McCrary, supt. Fax 489-5664
www.gorepublicschools.org
Gore ES 300/PK-5
1200 N Highway 10 74435 918-489-5638
Tonya Pugh, prin. Fax 489-2465
Gore MS 100/6-8
1200 N Highway 10 74435 918-487-5587
James Bliss, prin. Fax 489-5664

Gracemont, Caddo, Pop. 298
Gracemont ISD 200/PK-12
PO Box 5 73042 405-966-2236
Jamie Mitchell, supt. Fax 966-2395
www.gracemont.k12.ok.us
Gracemont ES 100/PK-8
PO Box 5 73042 405-966-2551
Sharon Edelen M.Ed., prin. Fax 966-2100

Grandfield, Tillman, Pop. 1,001
Grandfield ISD 300/PK-12
PO Box 639 73546 580-479-5237
James Higdon, supt. Fax 479-3381
www.grandfield.k12.ok.us/
Grandfield S 200/PK-8
PO Box 639 73546 580-479-3288
Ramiro Longoria, prin. Fax 479-3381

Granite, Greer, Pop. 2,034
Granite ISD 300/PK-12
PO Box 98 73547 580-535-2104
Rodney Calhoun, supt. Fax 535-2106
www.granite.k12.ok.us
Granite ES 200/PK-8
PO Box 98 73547 580-535-2104
Listena Prickett, prin. Fax 535-2106

Grove, Delaware, Pop. 6,167
Grove ISD 2,600/PK-12
PO Box 450789 74345 918-786-3003
Sandy Coaly, supt. Fax 786-9365
www.ridgerunners.net
Grove ECC 400/PK-K
PO Box 450789 74345 918-786-6127
Julie Bloss, prin. Fax 787-2004
Grove Lower ES 600/1-3
PO Box 450789 74345 918-786-5573
Kelly Trumbull, prin. Fax 787-5207
Grove MS 400/7-8
PO Box 450789 74345 918-786-2209
Pat Dodson, prin. Fax 786-6454
Grove Upper ES 500/4-6
PO Box 450789 74345 918-786-2297
Shelly Barnes, prin. Fax 786-5321

Guthrie, Logan, Pop. 9,702
Guthrie ISD 3,500/PK-12
802 E Vilas Ave 73044 405-282-8900
Dr. Mike Simpson, supt. Fax 282-5904
www.guthrieps.net
Central ES 300/1-1
321 E Noble Ave 73044 405-282-0352
Dani Watson, prin. Fax 282-9988
Cotteral ES 400/PK-K
2001 W Noble Ave 73044 405-282-5928
Scot Graham, prin. Fax 282-5322
Fogarty ES 500/2-3
902 N Wentz St 73044 405-282-5932
Marsha Todd, prin. Fax 282-6511
Guthrie JHS 500/7-8
705 E Oklahoma Ave 73044 405-282-5936
Robbie Rainwater, prin. Fax 282-3598
Guthrie Upper ES 700/4-6
702 N Crooks Dr 73044 405-282-5924
Susan Davison, prin. Fax 282-5946

St. Marys S 100/PK-8
502 E Warner Ave 73044 405-282-2071
Jacque Cook, prin. Fax 282-2924

Guymon, Texas, Pop. 11,299
Guymon ISD 2,900/PK-12
PO Box 1307 73942 580-338-4340
Doug Melton, supt. Fax 338-3812
www.guymontigers.com
Academy ES 400/3-4
PO Box 1307 73942 580-338-4370
Melissa Watson, prin. Fax 338-4307
Carrier ES 200/PK-PK
PO Box 1307 73942 580-338-0420
Loire Aubrey, prin. Fax 338-4404
Central JHS 400/7-8
PO Box 1307 73942 580-338-4360
Claudia Winters, prin. Fax 338-0212
Long ES 200/K-2
PO Box 1307 73942 580-338-4380
Kasey Meyer, prin. Fax 338-3812
Northeast ES 200/K-2
PO Box 1307 73942 580-338-4380
Kasey Meyer, prin. Fax 338-3812
North Park ES 400/5-6
PO Box 1307 73942 580-338-4390
Mark Strickland, prin. Fax 338-3812
Prairie ES 200/K-2
PO Box 1307 73942 580-338-0420
Loire Aubrey, prin. Fax 338-4404
Salyer ES 100/K-2
PO Box 1307 73942 580-338-0420
Loire Aubrey, lead tchr. Fax 338-4404

Straight SD 100/PK-6
RR 1 Box 89 73942 580-652-2232
Steve Baird, supt. Fax 652-3299
Straight ES 100/PK-6
RR 1 Box 89 73942 580-652-2232
Steve Baird, prin. Fax 652-3299

Pioneer Adventist Christian S K-8
PO Box 1245 73942 580-338-5093

Haileyville, Pittsburg, Pop. 762
Haileyville ISD 400/PK-12
PO Box 29 74546 918-297-2626
Roger Hemphill, supt. Fax 297-7136
www.haileyville.k12.ok.us
Haileyville ES 300/PK-8
PO Box 29 74546 918-297-2733
Brandie Kirkes, prin. Fax 297-3004

Hammon, Roger Mills, Pop. 547
Hammon ISD 300/PK-12
PO Box 279 73650 580-473-2221
Fax 473-2464
www.hammon.k12.ok.us
Hammon ES 200/PK-8
PO Box 279 73650 580-473-2289
Jeff Morton, prin. Fax 473-2464

Hanna, McIntosh, Pop. 131
Hanna ISD 200/PK-12
PO Box 10 74845 918-657-2523
Michael Parsons, supt. Fax 657-2424
www.hanna.k12.ok.us
Hanna ES 100/PK-8
PO Box 10 74845 918-657-2527
David Dewalt, prin. Fax 657-2424

Hardesty, Texas, Pop. 209
Hardesty ISD 100/PK-12
PO Box 129 73944 580-888-4258
Greg Faris, supt. Fax 888-4560
www.hardesty.k12.ok.us
Hardesty ES 100/PK-8
PO Box 129 73944 580-888-4258
Cheryl Kerr, prin. Fax 888-4560

Harrah, Oklahoma, Pop. 4,831
Harrah ISD 1,800/PK-12
20670 Walker St 73045 405-454-6244
Paul Blessington, supt. Fax 454-0022
www.harrahschools.com
Babb ES 300/4-5
20901 NE 10th St 73045 405-347-2700
Mike McAfee, prin. Fax 454-6844
Harrah MS 300/6-8
1480 N Dobbs 73045 405-347-2700
Steve Keiffer, prin. Fax 347-2799
Reynolds ES 300/2-3
755 Harrison St 73045 405-347-2500
Cheryl Hessman, prin. Fax 347-2599
Smith ES 400/PK-1
20227 NE 10th St 73045 405-347-2400
Dr. Doug Parker, prin. Fax 454-3698

Hartshorne, Pittsburg, Pop. 1,925
Hartshorne ISD 700/PK-12
520 S 5th St 74547 918-297-2534
Jason Lindley, supt. Fax 297-2698
www.hartshorne.k12.ok.us
Hartshorne ES 300/PK-5
520 S 5th St 74547 918-297-2345
Brian Akins, prin. Fax 297-2074

Haskell, Muskogee, Pop. 1,802
Haskell ISD 800/PK-12
900 N Ohio Ave 74436 918-482-5221
Doyle Bates, supt. Fax 482-3346
www.haskellps.org
Beavers MS 200/6-8
900 N Ohio Ave 74436 918-482-5221
Julie Bills, prin. Fax 482-3346
White ES 400/PK-5
408 W Center St 74436 918-482-1402
Scott Bein, prin. Fax 482-3711

Haworth, McCurtain, Pop. 273
Haworth ISD 500/PK-12
300 N Maple St 74740 580-245-1406
Jason Price, supt. Fax 245-2265
www.haworth.k12.ok.us
Haworth ES 300/PK-5
300 N Maple St 74740 580-245-1406
Brent Smith, prin. Fax 245-4912
Haworth MS 100/6-8
300 N Maple St 74740 580-245-1406
Brandy Wall, prin. Fax 245-4911

Healdton, Carter, Pop. 2,670
Healdton ISD 500/PK-12
PO Box 490 73438 580-229-0566
Terry D. Shaw, supt. Fax 229-1522
www.healdtonschools.org/
Healdton ES 300/PK-5
PO Box 490 73438 580-229-1201
Donielle Cantwell, prin. Fax 229-1481
Healdton MS 100/6-8
PO Box 490 73438 580-229-0303
Terry D. Shaw, prin. Fax 229-1475

Heavener, LeFlore, Pop. 3,279
Heavener ISD 1,100/PK-12
PO Box 698 74937 918-653-7223
Edward Wilson, supt. Fax 653-7843
www.heavenerschools.org
Heavener ES, PO Box 698 74937 800/PK-8
Diane Cox, prin. 918-653-4313

Helena, Alfalfa, Pop. 1,366
Timberlake ISD 300/PK-12
PO Box 287 73741 580-852-3307
Mark Newton, supt. Fax 852-8019
tlakeschools.weebly.com
Other Schools – See Jet

Hennessey, Kingfisher, Pop. 2,093
Hennessey ISD 900/PK-12
604 E Oklahoma St 73742 405-853-4321
Dr. Mike Woods, supt. Fax 853-4439
www.hps.k12.ok.us
Hennessey ES 400/PK-4
130 N Mitchell Rd 73742 405-853-4305
Barry Crosswhite, prin. Fax 853-6106
Hennessey MS 300/5-8
120 N Mitchell Rd 73742 405-853-4303
Stacey Schovanec, prin. Fax 853-4848

Henryetta, Okmulgee, Pop. 5,595
Henryetta ISD 1,300/PK-12
1801 W Troy Aikman Dr 74437 918-652-6523
Dwayne Noble, supt. Fax 652-6510
www.henryetta.k12.ok.us
Henryetta ES 700/PK-5
1801 W Troy Aikman Dr 74437 918-652-6587
Kelly Furer, prin. Fax 652-6598
Henryetta MS 300/6-8
1801 W Troy Aikman Dr 74437 918-652-6578
Brad Wion, prin. Fax 652-6506

Ryal SD 100/PK-8
115035 S 3960 Rd 74437 918-652-7461
Lynn Maxwell, admin. Fax 652-7635
www.ryal.k12.ok.us/
Ryal S 100/PK-8
115035 S 3960 Rd 74437 918-652-7461
Lynn Maxwell, admin. Fax 652-7635

Wilson ISD 200/PK-12
8867 Chestnut Rd 74437 918-652-3374
Andrea James, supt. Fax 652-8140
www.wpstigers.k12.ok.us
Wilson ES 100/PK-8
8867 Chestnut Rd 74437 918-652-3375
Tena Medlock, prin. Fax 652-8140

Hillsdale, Garfield, Pop. 118

Hillsdale Christian S 100/PK-8
PO Box 8 73743 580-635-2211
Renae Haymaker, admin. Fax 635-2392

Hinton, Caddo, Pop. 3,079
Hinton ISD 700/PK-12
PO Box 1036 73047 405-542-3257
Richard Brownen, supt. Fax 542-3286
www.hintonschools.org
Hinton ES 400/PK-5
PO Box 1036 73047 405-542-3295
Marcy Derryberry, prin. Fax 542-3286
Hinton MS 100/6-8
PO Box 1036 73047 405-542-3235
Rennie Nickell, prin. Fax 542-3286

Hobart, Kiowa, Pop. 3,599
Hobart ISD 900/PK-12
PO Box 899 73651 580-726-5691
Cathy Hunt, supt. Fax 726-2855
www.hobart.k12.ok.us
Hobart ES, PO Box 899 73651 400/PK-5
Kim Reed, prin. 580-726-5665
Hobart MS, PO Box 899 73651 200/6-8
Mark Harmon, prin. 580-726-5615

Hodgen, LeFlore
Hodgen SD 300/PK-8
PO Box 69 74939 918-653-4476
Ward Brown, supt. Fax 653-2525
www.hodgen.k12.ok.us
Hodgen S 300/PK-8
PO Box 69 74939 918-653-4476
Courtney Altstatt, prin. Fax 653-2525

Holdenville, Hughes, Pop. 5,493
Holdenville ISD 1,100/PK-12
210 Grimes Ave 74848 405-379-5483
Randy Davenport, supt. Fax 379-5874
www.holdenville.k12.ok.us
Reed ES 500/PK-3
210 Grimes Ave 74848 405-379-6618
Danielle Patterson, prin. Fax 379-8100
Thomas MS 300/4-8
210 Grimes Ave 74848 405-379-6661
Mark Turner, prin. Fax 379-8118

Moss ISD 300/PK-12
8087 E 134 Rd 74848 405-379-2273
Brett Hill, supt. Fax 379-2333
www.moss.k12.ok.us
Moss ES 200/PK-8
8087 E 134 Rd 74848 405-379-7251
Tina Cartwright, prin. Fax 379-2333

Hollis, Harmon, Pop. 1,997
Hollis ISD 500/PK-12
PO Box 193 73550 580-688-3450
Jennifer Mcqueen, supt. Fax 688-2532
www.hollis.k12.ok.us
Hollis ES 300/PK-5
PO Box 193 73550 580-688-3616
Amy Estes, prin. Fax 688-2147
Hollis MS, PO Box 193 73550 100/6-8
Roderick Zachary, prin. 580-688-2707

Hominy, Osage, Pop. 3,347
Hominy ISD 600/PK-12
200 S Pettit Ave 74035 918-885-6511
Doyle Edwards, supt. Fax 885-2538
www.hominy.k12.ok.us
Hominy ECC 100/PK-K
200 S Pettit Ave 74035 918-885-6813
Kelly Dyer, prin. Fax 885-2538
Hominy MS 100/6-8
200 S Pettit Ave 74035 918-885-6253
Scott Harmon, prin. Fax 885-6369
Mann ES 200/1-5
200 S Pettit Ave 74035 918-885-6255
Angel Supernaw, prin. Fax 885-2538

Hooker, Texas, Pop. 1,875
Hooker ISD 600/PK-12
220 N Swem St 73945 580-652-2162
Dan Faulkner, supt. Fax 652-3118
www.hookerpublicschools.net
Hooker ES, 502 N Jefferson 73945 500/PK-8
Todd Kerr, prin. 580-652-2463

Howe, LeFlore, Pop. 762
Howe ISD 500/PK-12
PO Box 259 74940 918-658-3666
Scott Parks, supt. Fax 658-2233
www.howeschools.org
Howe ES 400/PK-8
PO Box 259 74940 918-658-3508
Jeremy Dyer, prin. Fax 658-2233

Hugo, Choctaw, Pop. 4,926
Hugo ISD 1,200/PK-12
208 N 2nd St 74743 580-326-6483
Dr. Earl Dalke, supt. Fax 326-2480
www.hugoschools.com
Hugo ES 500/PK-3
208 N 2nd St 74743 580-326-8373
Carey Malone, prin. Fax 326-6312
Hugo IS 200/4-5
208 N 2nd St 74743 580-326-0106
Vivian Shanklin, prin. Fax 326-0109
Hugo MS 200/6-8
208 N 2nd St 74743 580-326-3365
Heather Samis, prin. Fax 326-7352

Hulbert, Cherokee, Pop. 518
Hulbert ISD 500/PK-12
PO Box 188 74441 918-772-2501
Dr. Marilyn Dewoody, supt. Fax 772-2766
www.hulbertriders.com
Hulbert ES 300/PK-6
PO Box 188 74441 918-772-2501
Taf Morphis, prin. Fax 772-1274

Norwood SD 200/PK-8
7966 W 790 Rd 74441 918-478-3092
Diana Garnatz, supt. Fax 478-3833
norwood.k12.ok.us
Norwood S 200/PK-8
7966 W 790 Rd 74441 918-478-3092
Diana Garnatz, prin. Fax 478-3833

Shady Grove SD 100/PK-8
11042 W Shady Grove Rd 74441 918-772-2511
Emmett Thompson, supt. Fax 772-2430
www.shadygrove.k12.ok.us
Shady Grove S 100/PK-8
11042 W Shady Grove Rd 74441 918-772-2511
Emmett Thompson, prin. Fax 772-2430

Hydro, Caddo, Pop. 947
Hydro-Eakly ISD 400/PK-12
407 E 7th St 73048 405-663-2246
Jeremy Bussey, supt. Fax 663-2139
www.hydroeakly.k12.ok.us
Hydro-Eakly ES 200/PK-5
407 E 7th St 73048 405-663-2246
Jeremy Tharp, prin. Fax 663-2449
Hydro-Eakly MS 100/6-8
407 E 7th St 73048 405-663-2246
Jeremy Bussey, prin. Fax 663-2139

Idabel, McCurtain, Pop. 6,641
Denison SD 300/PK-8
3001 E Washington St 74745 580-286-3319
Jordan Hill, supt. Fax 286-5743
www.denison.k12.ok.us
Denison S 300/PK-8
3001 E Washington St 74745 580-286-3319
Toni Butler, prin. Fax 286-5743

Idabel ISD 1,200/PK-12
200 NE Ave C 74745 580-286-7639
Doug Brown, supt. Fax 286-2331
www.idabelps.org
Central ES 200/2-5
206 SE Ave F 74745 580-286-5346
Nancy Copeland, prin. Fax 286-3430
Idabel MS 200/6-8
100 NE Ave D 74745 580-286-6558
Laura Bullock, prin. Fax 286-8272
Idabel PS 300/PK-1
1212 SE Tyler Dr 74745 580-286-4400
Terri Bastible, prin. Fax 286-4443

Indiahoma, Comanche, Pop. 331
Indiahoma ISD 200/PK-12
307 Chebahtah 73552 580-246-3448
Deanna Voegeli, supt. Fax 246-3372
www.indiahomaps.org
Indiahoma ES 100/PK-8
307 Chebahtah 73552 580-246-3333
Deanna Voegeli, admin. Fax 246-3372

Indianola, Pittsburg, Pop. 149
Indianola ISD 200/PK-12
PO Box 119 74442 918-823-4231
Adam Newman, supt. Fax 823-4234
www.indianola.k12.ok.us
Indianola S, PO Box 119 74442 200/PK-8
Adam Newman, prin. 918-823-4244

Inola, Rogers, Pop. 1,643
Inola ISD 1,400/PK-12
PO Box 1149 74036 918-543-1610
Dr. Kent Holbrook, supt. Fax 543-8754
www.inola.k12.ok.us
Inola ES 600/PK-4
PO Box 909 74036 918-543-2271
Rebecca Cutsinger, prin. Fax 543-6866
Inola MS 400/5-8
PO Box 819 74036 918-543-2434
Jeff Unrau, prin. Fax 543-6268

Jay, Delaware, Pop. 2,212
Jay ISD 1,700/PK-12
PO Box 630 74346 918-253-4293
Kenneth Bridges, supt. Fax 253-8970
www.jay.k12.ok.us
Jay ES 700/PK-3
PO Box 630 74346 918-253-4413
Jan Fasano, prin. Fax 253-4391
Jay MS 200/6-8
PO Box 630 74346 918-253-8510
Arlis Henegar, prin. Fax 253-3342
Jay Upper ES, PO Box 630 74346 200/4-5
Marvin Stockton, prin. 918-253-3535

Jenks, Tulsa, Pop. 16,162
Jenks ISD 11,200/PK-12
205 E B St 74037 918-299-4411
Dr. Stacey Butterfield, supt. Fax 299-9197
www.jenksps.org
West ES 2,000/PK-4
205 E B St 74037 918-299-4411
Suzanne Lair, prin. Fax 298-6636
West IS 600/5-6
205 E B St 74037 918-299-4415
Michelle Sumner, prin. Fax 298-0355
Other Schools – See Tulsa

Jennings, Pawnee, Pop. 343
Jennings SD 200/PK-8
475 N Oak St 74038 918-757-2536
Derrick Meador, supt. Fax 549-7011
www.jennings.k12.ok.us
Jennings S 200/PK-8
475 N Oak St 74038 918-757-2536
Derrick Meador, prin. Fax 757-2338

Jet, Alfalfa, Pop. 208
Timberlake ISD
Supt. — See Helena
Timberlake ES 200/PK-8
PO Box 188 73749 580-626-4411
Kale Pierce, prin. Fax 626-4414

Jones, Oklahoma, Pop. 2,585
Jones ISD 1,100/PK-12
9200 N Hiwassee Rd 73049 405-399-9215
Dr. Carl Johnson, supt. Fax 399-9212
www.jones.k12.ok.us
Jones ES 500/PK-5
13145 Montana St 73049 405-399-9118
Cindy Harrison, prin. Fax 399-2897
Jones MS 300/6-8
16011 E Wilshire Blvd 73049 405-399-9114
Mike Watkins, prin. Fax 399-6101

Kansas, Delaware, Pop. 726
Kansas ISD 900/PK-12
PO Box 196 74347 918-868-2562
Jim Burgess, supt. Fax 868-3103
www.kansasps.com/
Kansas ES 400/PK-5
PO Box 196 74347 918-868-2427
Gina Glass, prin. Fax 868-5587
Kansas JHS 200/6-8
PO Box 196 74347 918-868-5308
Bryon Arnold, prin. Fax 868-5582

Kaw City, Kay, Pop. 358
Shidler ISD
Supt. — See Shidler
Shidler MS 100/5-8
904 Washunga Dr 74641 580-269-2911
Janice Finton, prin. Fax 269-2992

Kellyville, Creek, Pop. 1,083
Kellyville ISD 1,100/PK-12
PO Box 99 74039 918-247-6133
Joe Pierce, supt. Fax 247-6120
www.kellyvilleschools.org/
Kellyville ES, PO Box 99 74039 400/PK-3
John Castillo, prin. 918-247-6300
Kellyville MS, PO Box 99 74039 200/7-8
Rod Pitts, prin. 918-247-6134
Kellyville Upper ES, PO Box 99 74039 200/4-6
Marcie Lawley, prin. 918-247-2257

Keota, Haskell, Pop. 531
Keota ISD 400/PK-12
110 NE 6th St 74941 918-966-3950
Twylah Morris, supt. Fax 966-3247
www.keota.k12.ok.us
Keota ES 300/PK-8
110 NE 6th St 74941 918-966-3141
Jimmy Ray, prin. Fax 966-3247

Ketchum, Mayes, Pop. 396
Ketchum ISD 600/PK-12
PO Box 720 74349 918-782-5091
Joy Taylor, supt. Fax 782-9018
www.ketchumwarriors.com
Ketchum ES 300/PK-5
PO Box 720 74349 918-782-9543
Joy Taylor, prin. Fax 782-9018
Ketchum MS 100/6-8
PO Box 720 74349 918-782-3242
Jennifer Turner, prin. Fax 782-3016

Keyes, Cimarron, Pop. 321
Keyes ISD 100/PK-12
PO Box 47 73947 580-546-7231
Sherri Hitchings, supt. Fax 546-7338
www.keyes.k12.ok.us
Keyes ES 50/PK-8
PO Box 47 73947 580-546-7231
Sherri Hitchings, prin. Fax 546-7338

Kiefer, Creek, Pop. 1,550
Kiefer ISD 700/PK-12
4600 W 151st St S 74041 918-321-3421
Mary Murrell, supt. Fax 321-5216
www.kiefer.k12.ok.us/
Kiefer ES 400/PK-6
4600 W 151st St S 74041 918-321-5444
Brent Weaver, prin. Fax 321-4442
Rongey MS 100/7-8
4600 W 151st St S 74041 918-321-3533
Cory Campbell, prin. Fax 321-4443

Kildare, Kay, Pop. 98
Kildare SD 100/PK-6
1265 Church St, Ponca City OK 74604
580-362-2811
Bruce Shelley, supt. Fax 362-3342
www.kildare.k12.ok.us
Kildare ES 100/PK-6
1265 Church St, Ponca City OK 74604
580-362-2811
Bruce Shelley, prin. Fax 362-3342

Kingfisher, Kingfisher, Pop. 4,523
Kingfisher SD 1,400/PK-12
602 W Chisholm Dr 73750 405-375-4194
Jason Sternberger, supt. Fax 375-5565
www.kingfisher.k12.ok.us
Gilmour ES 400/PK-2
1400 S Oak St 73750 405-375-4080
Melissa Slezickey, prin. Fax 375-4456
Kingfisher Heritage S 200/3-4
600 S 9th St 73750 405-375-3018
Shane Hood, prin. Fax 375-4903
Kingfisher MS 400/5-8
601 S 13th St 73750 405-375-6607
Keith Campbell, prin. Fax 375-6410

SS. Peter & Paul S 50/PK-5
309 S Main St 73750 405-375-4616
Steve Lykes, prin. Fax 375-5296

Kingston, Marshall, Pop. 1,514
Kingston ISD 1,200/PK-12
PO Box 370 73439 580-564-9033
Brian Brister, supt. Fax 564-9516
www.kingston.k12.ok.us
Kingston ES 600/PK-5
PO Box 550 73439 580-564-2993
David Gill, prin. Fax 564-0903
Kingston MS 300/6-8
PO Box 370 73439 580-564-2996
Jon Holmes, prin. Fax 564-0902

Kinta, Haskell, Pop. 279
Kinta ISD 200/PK-12
PO Box 219 74552 918-768-3338
Patricia Deville, supt. Fax 768-3321
www.kinta.k12.ok.us
Kinta ES 100/PK-8
PO Box 219 74552 918-768-3338
Patricia Deville, prin. Fax 768-3321

Kiowa, Pittsburg, Pop. 681
Kiowa ISD 300/PK-12
PO Box 6 74553 918-432-5631
Rick Pool, supt. Fax 432-5683
www.kiowa.k12.ok.us
Kiowa ES 200/PK-8
PO Box 6 74553 918-432-5631
Garry Rind, prin. Fax 432-5683

Konawa, Seminole, Pop. 1,168
Konawa ISD 700/PK-12
701 W South St 74849 580-925-3244
Andy Gower, supt. Fax 925-2146
www.konawa.k12.ok.us
Konawa ES 300/PK-5
701 W South St 74849 580-925-3118
Kim Wilson, prin. Fax 925-2146
Konawa MS 200/6-8
701 W South St 74849 580-925-3221
Sean Walker, prin. Fax 925-2146

Krebs, Pittsburg, Pop. 1,869
Krebs SD 400/PK-8
PO Box 67 74554 918-426-4700
Patrick Turner, supt. Fax 423-2909
www.krebs.k12.ok.us
Krebs S 400/PK-8
PO Box 67 74554 918-426-4700
Patrick Turner, supt. Fax 423-2909

Kremlin, Garfield, Pop. 247
Kremlin-Hillsdale ISD 200/PK-12
PO Box 198 73753 580-874-2284
Jim Patton M.Ed., supt. Fax 574-4488
www.kremlin.k12.ok.us/
Kremlin-Hillsdale S 200/PK-5
PO Box 198 73753 580-874-2283
Brad Hawkins B.S., prin.

Lahoma, Garfield, Pop. 597
Cimarron ISD 300/PK-12
PO Box 8 73754 580-796-2204
Charles Anglin, supt. Fax 796-2350
www.cimarron.k12.ok.us

Cimarron ES 200/PK-8
PO Box 8 73754 580-796-2205
Kyle Karns, prin. Fax 796-2350

Lamont, Grant, Pop. 412
Deer Creek-Lamont ISD 200/PK-12
PO Box 10 74643 580-388-4333
Barbara Regier, supt. Fax 388-4341
www.dcla.k12.ok.us/
Other Schools – See Deer Creek

Lane, Atoka, Pop. 376
Lane SD 300/PK-8
601 S West McGee Cr Rd 74555 580-889-2743
Roland Smith, supt. Fax 889-9157
lane.ok.schoolwebpages.com
Lane S 300/PK-8
601 S West McGee Cr Rd 74555 580-889-2743
Cindy Hauff, dean Fax 889-9157

Laverne, Harper, Pop. 1,316
Laverne ISD 500/PK-12
PO Box 40 73848 580-921-3362
Ed Thomas, supt. Fax 921-3636
www.laverne.k12.ok.us
Laverne ES 300/PK-8
PO Box 40 73848 580-921-5025
Tim Allen, prin. Fax 921-3636

Lawton, Comanche, Pop. 91,002
Bishop SD 500/PK-6
2204 SW Bishop Rd 73505 580-353-4870
Howard Hampton, supt. Fax 353-4879
www.bishop.k12.ok.us/
Bishop ES 500/PK-6
2204 SW Bishop Rd 73505 580-353-4870
Howard Hampton, prin. Fax 353-4879

Flower Mound SD 300/PK-8
2805 SE Flower Mound Rd 73501 580-353-4088
Dax Trent, supt. Fax 353-5742
www.flowermound.k12.ok.us
Flower Mound S 300/PK-8
2805 SE Flower Mound Rd 73501 580-353-4088
Dax Trent, prin. Fax 353-5742

Lawton ISD 13,400/PK-12
753 NW Fort Sill Blvd 73507 580-357-6900
Dr. Tom Deighan, supt. Fax 585-6319
www.lawtonps.org
Adams ES 200/K-5
3501 NW Ferris Ave 73505 580-353-7983
Lisa Bell, prin. Fax 585-4670
Almor West ES 400/PK-5
6902 SW Delta Ave 73505 580-536-6006
Stan Melby, prin. Fax 536-2547
Bish ES 300/K-5
5611 NW Alan A Dale Ln 73505 580-248-2244
Sherry Havron, prin. Fax 585 6482
Carriage Hills ES 300/PK-5
215 SE Warwick Way 73501 580-248-6161
Cheryl Scammahorn, prin. Fax 585-4672
Central MS 900/6-8
1201 NW Fort Sill Blvd 73507 580-355-8544
Dr. Blake Thomas, prin. Fax 585-6452
Cleveland ES 300/PK-5
1202 SW 27th St 73505 580-353-8861
Calvin Prince, prin. Fax 585-4632
Crosby Park ES 300/K-5
1602 NW Horton Blvd 73505 580-353-7107
Dana Moore, prin. Fax 585-6493
Edison ES 400/K-5
5801 NW Columbia Ave 73505 580-536-4223
Donna Catlin, prin. Fax 536-0858
Eisenhower ES 300/K-5
315 SW 52nd St 73505 580-355-4599
Lupe Ostruske, prin. Fax 585-4603
Eisenhower MS 900/6-8
5702 W Gore Blvd 73505 580-353-1040
Beverly Mattingly, prin. Fax 585-6436
Henry ES 500/K-5
1401 NW Bessie Ave 73507 580-355-2617
Karen Cooksey, prin. Fax 585-6383
Learning Tree Academy 300/PK-PK
1908 NW 38th St 73505 580-355-6197
Larry Stormer, prin. Fax 585-4684
Lincoln ES 400/PK-5
601 SW Park Ave 73501 580-355-4799
Oscar Castro, prin. Fax 585-4608
MacArthur MS 700/6-8
510 NE 45th St 73507 580-353-5111
Regina Lambert, prin. Fax 585-6435
Pioneer Park ES 300/PK-5
3005 NE Angus Pl 73507 580-355-5844
Gabe Winn, prin. Fax 585-4626
Ridgecrest ES 300/K-5
1614 NW 47th St 73505 580-355-6033
Ora Fitzgerald, prin. Fax 585-4693
Sullivan Village ES 300/PK-5
3802 SE Elmhurst Ln 73501 580-355-0800
Brenda Breeze, prin. Fax 585-4681
Tomlinson MS 700/6-8
702 NW Homestead Dr 73505 580-585-6416
Eddie Williams, prin. Fax 585-6451
Washington ES 200/PK-5
805 NW Columbia Ave 73507 580-353-6299
Phil Smith, prin. Fax 585-4675
Whittier ES 200/K-5
1115 NW Laird Ave 73507 580-355-5238
Melanie Nungesser, prin. Fax 585-4687
Woodland Hills ES 400/PK-5
405 NW Woodland Dr 73505 580-536-7991
Traci Newell, prin. Fax 536-1496
Other Schools – See Fort Sill

Lawton Academy of Arts and Sciences 100/PK-12
1911 NW 72nd St 73505 580-536-1900
Kay Johnson, supt. Fax 536-2972
Lawton Christian S 500/PK-12
1 NW Crusader Dr 73505 580-536-6885
Patti Rhea, supt. Fax 536-5242

St. Mary S 100/PK-8
611 SW A Ave 73501 580-355-5288
Nancy Post, prin. Fax 355-4336
Trinity Christian Academy 100/PK-8
902 SW A Ave 73501 580-250-1900
Shelly McKee, prin. Fax 250-1932

Leedey, Dewey, Pop. 416
Leedey ISD 200/PK-12
505 E 6th St 73654 580-488-3424
Rusty Puffinbarger, supt. Fax 488-3428
www.leedey.k12.ok.us
Leedey ES, 500 E 6th St 73654 100/PK-8
Darren Danielson, prin. 580-488-3377

LeFlore, LeFlore, Pop. 182
LeFlore ISD 200/PK-12
PO Box 147 74942 918-753-2345
Bill Neyman, supt. Fax 753-2604
www.lefloreps.k12.ok.us
LeFlore ES 200/PK-8
PO Box 147 74942 918-753-2345
Diana Hames, prin. Fax 753-2604

Lexington, Cleveland, Pop. 2,050
Lexington ISD 900/PK-12
420 NE 4th St 73051 405-527-7236
Ronda Bass, supt. Fax 527-9517
www.lexington.k12.ok.us/
Lexington ES 400/PK-3
420 NE 4th St 73051 405-527-7236
Julie Malone, prin. Fax 527-8119
Lexington IS 100/4-5
420 NE 4th St 73051 405-527-7236
Julie Malone, prin. Fax 527-5165
Lexington MS 200/6-8
420 NE 4th St 73051 405-527-7236
Dale Berglan, prin. Fax 527-1415

Lindsay, Garvin, Pop. 2,771
Lindsay ISD 1,200/PK-12
800 W Creek St 73052 405-756-3131
Dan Chapman, supt. Fax 756-8819
www.lindsay.k12.ok.us
Lindsay ES 700/PK-5
800 W Creek St 73052 405-756-3134
Kim Boeckman, prin. Fax 756-1179
Lindsay MS, 800 W Creek St 73052 300/6-8
Tommy Ferguson, prin. 405-756-3133

Locust Grove, Mayes, Pop. 1,264
Locust Grove ISD 1,500/PK-12
PO Box 399 74352 918-479-5243
Lori Helton, supt. Fax 479-6468
www.lg.k12.ok.us
Locust Grove Early Learning Center 300/PK-1
PO Box 399 74352 918-479-5233
Shane Holman, prin. Fax 479-6995
Locust Grove MS 300/6-8
PO Box 399 74352 918-479-5244
Jamie Hall, prin. Fax 479-2930
Locust Grove Upper ES 400/2-5
PO Box 399 74352 918-479-5234
Shannon Hall, prin. Fax 479-5277

Lone Grove, Carter, Pop. 4,751
Lone Grove ISD 1,500/PK-12
PO Box 1330 73443 580-657-3131
Meri Jayne Miller, supt. Fax 657-4355
www.lonegrove.k12.ok.us/
Lone Grove IS 300/3-5
PO Box 1330 73443 580-657-3720
Amy Benson, prin. Fax 657-3486
Lone Grove MS 300/6-8
PO Box 1330 73443 580-657-3132
Richie McKee, prin. Fax 657-2691
Lone Grove PS 500/PK-2
PO Box 1330 73443 580-657-4367
Tonya Finnerty, prin. Fax 657-2837

Lone Wolf, Kiowa, Pop. 435
Lone Wolf ISD 100/PK-12
PO Box 158 73655 580-846-9091
James Sutherland, supt. Fax 846-5266
lonewolfschool.com
Lone Wolf ES 100/PK-8
PO Box 158 73655 580-846-9091
Karolyn Koester, prin. Fax 846-5266

Lookeba, Caddo, Pop. 163
Lookeba-Sickles ISD 300/PK-12
10108 County Road 1150 73053 405-457-6623
Mike Davis, supt. Fax 457-6382
www.lookeba.k12.ok.us
Lookeba-Sickles ES 200/PK-8
307 W Sickles Ave 73053 405-457-6300
Mike Davis, supt. Fax 457-6382

Loyal, Kingfisher, Pop. 76
Lomega ISD
Supt. — See Omega
Lomega ES 200/PK-8
409 Main St 73756 405-729-4251
Chad Fox, prin. Fax 729-4252

Luther, Oklahoma, Pop. 1,168
Luther ISD 900/PK-12
PO Box 430 73054 405-277-3233
Dr. Barry Gunn, supt. Fax 277-3498
www.lutherlions.org
Luther ES 400/PK-4
PO Box 430 73054 405-277-3545
Shelia Wilson, prin. Fax 277-3877
Luther MS 300/5-8
PO Box 430 73054 405-277-3264
Barry Gunn, prin. Fax 277-3877

McAlester, Pittsburg, Pop. 17,248
Frink-Chambers SD 400/PK-8
485 Frink Rd 74501 918-423-2434
Charles Peckio, supt. Fax 423-4687
frink.k12.ok.us
Frink-Chambers S 400/PK-8
485 Frink Rd 74501 918-423-2434
Scott Burke, prin. Fax 423-4687

Haywood SD 100/PK-8
11461 W State Highway 31 74501 918-423-6265
Phillip Rattan, supt. Fax 423-8063
www.haywood.k12.ok.us/
Haywood S 100/PK-8
11461 W State Highway 31 74501 918-423-6265
Roger Smith, prin. Fax 423-8063

McAlester ISD 2,800/PK-12
PO Box 1027 74502 918-423-4771
Randy Hughes, supt. Fax 423-8166
www.mcalester.k12.ok.us
Doyle ES 100/1-4
PO Box 1027 74502 918-423-0588
Kathy Hunt, prin. Fax 423-8104
Emerson ES 300/1-4
PO Box 1027 74502 918-423-6465
Jamie Price, prin. Fax 423-8151
Gay ECC 100/K-K
PO Box 1027 74502 918-423-6229
Lisa Mitchell, prin. Fax 423-8201
Jefferson ECC 100/PK-PK
PO Box 1027 74502 918-423-5963
Karen Johnson, prin. Fax 423-8149
Parker IS 400/5-6
PO Box 1027 74502 918-423-4647
Stefanie Norman, prin. Fax 423-8871
Puterbaugh MS 400/7-8
PO Box 1027 74502 918-423-5445
Caroline Miller, prin. Fax 423-7021
Rogers ES 500/1-4
PO Box 1027 74502 918-423-4542
Dawn Testa, prin. Fax 423-8114

Tannehill SD 200/PK-8
9283 Tannehill Rd 74501 918-423-6393
John Wilcox, supt. Fax 423-3068
www.tannehill.k12.ok.us
Tannehill S 200/PK-8
9283 Tannehill Rd 74501 918-423-6393
Memorie Harrell, prin. Fax 423-3068

Lakewood Christian S 200/PK-12
840 S George Nigh Expy 74501 918-426-2000
Amy Shaw, prin. Fax 302-2000

Mc Curtain, Haskell, Pop. 484
McCurtain ISD 300/PK-12
PO Box 189 74944 918-945-7237
Deward Palmer, supt. Fax 945-7064
www.mccurtain.k12.ok.us
McCurtain ES 200/PK-8
PO Box 189 74944 918-945-7236
Janna Blaylock, prin. Fax 945-7384

Mc Loud, Pottawatomie, Pop. 3,818
McLoud ISD 1,800/PK-12
PO Box 240, 405-964-3314
Steve Stanley, supt. Fax 964-2801
www.mcloudschools.us
McLoud ES 1,100/PK-6
PO Box 690, 405-964-3314
Fax 964-2494
McLoud JHS 200/7-8
PO Box 730, 405-964-3314
Angie Drew, prin. Fax 964-7530

White Rock SD 100/PK-8
334998 E 1010 Rd, 405-964-3428
Dr. Bob Gragg, supt. Fax 964-3427
www.whiterock.k12.ok.us/
White Rock S 100/PK-8
334998 E 1010 Rd, 405-964-3428
Dr. Bob Gragg, admin. Fax 964-3427

Macomb, Pottawatomie, Pop. 32
Macomb ISD 300/PK-12
36591 Highway 59B 74852 405-598-3892
Matthew Riggs, supt. Fax 598-8041
www.macomb.k12.ok.us
Macomb ES 200/PK-8
36591 Highway 59B 74852 405-598-2716
Janet Turner, prin. Fax 598-6529

Madill, Marshall, Pop. 3,605
Madill ISD 1,800/PK-12
601 W McArthur St 73446 580-795-3303
Jon Tuck, supt. Fax 795-3210
www.madillok.com
Madill ECC 400/PK-1
701 W Tishomingo St 73446 580-795-3680
Elissa Cox, prin.
Madill ES 500/2-5
701 W Tishomingo St 73446 580-795-3680
Dr. Devin Birdsong, prin. Fax 795-3035
Madill MS 400/6-8
601 W McArthur St 73446 580-795-7373
Gaylynn Smith, prin. Fax 795-6930

Mangum, Greer, Pop. 2,935
Mangum ISD 700/PK-12
400 N Pennsylvania Ave 73554 580-782-3371
Shane Boothe, supt. Fax 782-2313
www.mangum.k12.ok.us/
Edison ES 300/PK-4
201 W Madison St 73554 580-782-2703
Leslie Perry, prin. Fax 782-7908
Mangum JHS 100/7-8
400 N Oklahoma Ave 73554 580-782-2702
Barbara Gahagan, prin. Fax 782-5911
Mangum MS 100/5-6
401 N Oklahoma Ave 73554 580-782-5912
Barbara Gahagan, prin. Fax 782-5914

Mannford, Creek, Pop. 2,901
Mannford ISD 1,600/PK-12
136 Evans Ave 74044 918-865-4062
Dr. Steve Waldvogel, supt. Fax 865-3405
www.mannford.k12.ok.us

Mannford ECC 200/PK-K
211 Hinton Blvd 74044 918-865-5664
Brenda Dorsey, prin. Fax 865-4062
Mannford Lower ES 300/1-3
219 Evans Ave 74044 918-865-4334
Joshua Pierce, prin. Fax 865-2890
Mannford MS 300/6-8
100 Green Valley Rd 74044 918-865-4680
Steve Anderson, prin. Fax 865-2862
Mannford Upper ES 200/4-5
100 Green Valley Rd 74044 918-865-3092
James Norman, prin. Fax 865-6963

Mannsville, Johnston, Pop. 794
Mannsville SD 100/PK-8
PO Box 68 73447 580-371-2892
Brandi Price, supt. Fax 371-9336
Mannsville S 100/PK-8
PO Box 68 73447 580-371-2892
Brandi Price, prin. Fax 371-9336

Marietta, Love, Pop. 2,521
Greenville SD 100/PK-8
4671 Wolfpac Rd 73448 580-276-2968
Gregory Raper, supt. Fax 276-4605
www.greenville.k12.ok.us
Greenville S 100/PK-8
4671 Wolfpac Rd 73448 580-276-2968
Greg Raper, prin. Fax 276-4605

Marietta ISD 1,100/PK-12
800 S 4th Ave 73448 580-276-9444
Chad Broughton, supt. Fax 276-4037
www.mariettaisd.org
Marietta ES 500/PK-5
800 S 4th Ave 73448 580-276-2455
Dana McMillin, prin. Fax 276-4489
Marietta MS 200/6-8
800 S 4th Ave 73448 580-276-3886
Brandi Naylor, prin. Fax 276-1203

Marlow, Stephens, Pop. 4,444
Bray-Doyle ISD 400/PK-12
1205 S Brooks Rd 73055 580-658-5076
David Eads, supt. Fax 658-5888
www.braydoyle.k12.ok.us
Bray-Doyle ES 300/PK-8
1205 S Brooks Rd 73055 580-658-5070
Kelli Heinrich, prin. Fax 658-5888

Central High ISD 300/PK-12
274801 Broncho Rd 73055 580-658-6858
Bennie Newton M.Ed., supt. Fax 658-8006
www.central.k12.ok.us
Central ES 200/PK-6
274801 Broncho Rd 73055 580-658-2970
LeAnn Johnson, prin. Fax 658-8005

Marlow ISD 1,400/PK-12
PO Box 73 73055 580-658-2719
George Coffman, supt. Fax 658-6455
www.marlow.k12.ok.us
Marlow ES 700/PK-5
PO Box 73 73055 580-658-1541
Kim Kizarr, prin. Fax 658-3216
Marlow MS 300/6-8
PO Box 73 73055 580-658-2619
Ross Ridge, prin. Fax 658-1169

Mason, Okfuskee
Mason ISD 300/PK-12
374006 E 1000 Rd 74859 918-623-0231
Cindy Swearingen, supt. Fax 623-0884
www.mason.k12.ok.us/
Mason ES 200/PK-8
374006 E 1000 Rd 74859 918-623-2218
Richard Williams, prin. Fax 623-3020

Maud, Pottawatomie, Pop. 993
Maud ISD 300/PK-12
PO Box 130 74854 405-374-2416
Jerry McCormick, supt. Fax 374-2628
www.maud.k12.ok.us
Maud ES 200/PK-8
PO Box 130 74854 405-374-2421
Ty Harman, prin. Fax 374-1109

Maysville, Garvin, Pop. 1,159
Maysville ISD 400/PK-12
600 1st St 73057 405-867-5595
Dr. Shelly Hildebrand-Beach, supt. Fax 867-4864
maysville.k12.ok.us
Maysville ES 300/PK-8
600 1st St 73057 405-867-5550
John Edwards, prin. Fax 867-4046

Medford, Grant, Pop. 970
Medford ISD 300/PK-12
301 N Main St 73759 580-395-2392
Mickey Geurkink, supt. Fax 395-2391
www.medford.k12.ok.us/
Medford ES 200/PK-8
301 N Main St 73759 580-395-2392
Tyler Locke, prin. Fax 395-2391

Meeker, Lincoln, Pop. 1,096
Meeker ISD 900/PK-12
214 E Carl Hubbell Blvd 74855 405-788-4540
Jeffrey Pruitt, supt. Fax 279-2765
www.meeker.k12.ok.us
Meeker ES 400/PK-5
400 S Culver St 74855 405-788-4540
Mike Mcafee, prin. Fax 279-2765
Meeker MS 200/6-8
214 E Carl Hubbell Blvd 74855 405-788-4540
Virgil Fowler, dean Fax 279-2765

Miami, Ottawa, Pop. 12,277
Miami ISD 1,900/PK-12
26 N Main St 74354 918-542-8455
Jeremy Hogan, supt. Fax 542-1236
www.miami.k12.ok.us

Nichols ES 100/4-5
504 14th Ave NW 74354 918-542-3309
Keni Iverson, prin. Fax 540-7004
Rockdale ES 100/K-3
2116 Rockdale Blvd 74354 918-542-6697
Andrea Berry, prin. Fax 540-7013
Rogers MS 500/6-8
504 Goodrich Blvd 74354 918-542-5588
Justin Chase, prin. Fax 542-4400
Roosevelt ES 200/K-3
129 G St NE 74354 918-542-5576
Melissa Bekemeier, prin. Fax 540-7002
Washington ES 200/K-3
1930 B St NE 74354 918-542-3394
Melissa Turner, prin. Fax 540-7005
Wilson ES 200/PK-3
308 G St NW 74354 918-542-8419
Courtney Murphy, prin. Fax 540-7011

Mt. Olive Lutheran S 50/PK-4
2337 N Main St 74354 918-540-3456
Fax 540-3456

Midwest City, Oklahoma, Pop. 51,213
Midwest City-Del City ISD 13,800/PK-12
7217 SE 15th St 73110 405-737-4461
Dr. Rick Cobb, supt. Fax 739-1615
www.mid-del.net
Albert MS 800/6-8
2515 S Post Rd 73130 405-739-1761
Cindy Anderson, prin. Fax 739-1780
Bailey ES 300/PK-5
3301 Sunvalley Dr 73110 405-739-1656
Danielle Peterson, prin. Fax 739-1658
Country Estates ES 400/PK-5
1609 Felix Pl 73110 405-739-1661
Brooke Guthery, prin. Fax 739-1663
Jarman MS 500/6-8
5 W MacArthur Dr 73110 405-739-1771
Lynette Brown, prin. Fax 739-1773
Midwest City ES 400/PK-5
2211 S Midwest Blvd 73110 405-582-7017
Brandi Skokowski, prin. Fax 582-2919
Monroney MS 600/6-8
7400 E Reno Ave 73110 405-739-1786
Michelle Reeves, prin. Fax 739-1789
Ridgecrest ES 300/PK-5
137 W Ridgewood Dr 73110 405-739-1671
Donna Collier, prin. Fax 739-1670
Soldier Creek ES 600/PK-5
9021 SE 15th St 73130 405-739-1676
Jeff Holland, prin. Fax 739-1679
Steed ES 400/PK-5
2118 Flannery Dr 73110 405-739-1686
Patrice Tucker, prin. Fax 739-1688
Other Schools – See Del City, Oklahoma City

Good Shepherd Lutheran S 100/PK-8
700 N Air Depot Blvd 73110 405-732-0070
Gary Kuschnereit, prin. Fax 732-3977
St. Philip Neri S 200/PK-8
1121 Felix Pl 73110 405-737-4496
Brenda Tener, prin. Fax 732-7823

Milburn, Johnston, Pop. 295
Milburn ISD 200/PK-12
PO Box 429 73450 580-443-5522
Joey McBride, supt. Fax 443-5303
www.milburnps.org
Milburn ES 100/PK-8
PO Box 429 73450 580-443-5522
Shelly Lansdale, prin. Fax 443-5303

Mill Creek, Johnston, Pop. 283
Mill Creek ISD 100/PK-12
602 S Chickasaw Ave 74856 580-384-5514
Lorinda Chancellor, supt. Fax 384-3920
www.millcreek.k12.ok.us/
Mill Creek ES 100/PK-8
602 S Chickasaw Ave 74856 580-384-5514
Lorinda Chancellor, prin. Fax 384-3920

Minco, Grady, Pop. 1,580
Minco ISD 600/PK-12
PO Box 428 73059 405-352-4867
Kevin Sims, supt. Fax 352-4006
www.minco.k12.ok.us
Minco ES, PO Box 428 73059 300/PK-5
Troy Wittrock, prin. 405-352-4234
Minco MS 100/6-8
PO Box 428 73059 405-352-4377
Troy Wittrock, prin. Fax 352-4006

Moffett, Sequoyah, Pop. 118
Moffett SD 400/PK-8
PO Box 180 74946 918-875-3668
Jimmie Owens, supt. Fax 875-3201
www.moffett.k12.ok.us
Moffett S 400/PK-8
PO Box 180 74946 918-875-3668
Lance Stuart, prin. Fax 875-3201

Monroe, LeFlore
Monroe SD 100/PK-8
PO Box 10 74947 918-658-3516
Karen LaRosa, supt. Fax 658-3347
Monroe S 100/PK-8
PO Box 10 74947 918-658-3516
Karen LaRosa, prin. Fax 658-3347

Moore, Cleveland, Pop. 51,925
Moore ISD 23,000/PK-12
1500 SE 4th St 73160 405-735-4200
Dr. Robert Romines, supt. Fax 735-4392
www.mooreschools.com
Apple Creek ES 500/PK-6
1101 SE 14th St 73160 405-735-4100
Pamela Huston, prin. Fax 793-3253
Broadmoore ES 600/PK-6
3401 S Broadway St 73160 405-735-4120
Debra Hendrix, prin. Fax 799-7554

Central ES 500/PK-6
123 NW 2nd St 73160 405-735-4140
Becky Jackson, prin. Fax 793-3289
Central JHS 600/7-8
400 N Broadway St 73160 405-735-4560
Tammy Baker, prin. Fax 895-7398
Heritage Trails ES 800/PK-6
1801 S Bryant Ave 73160 405-735-4520
Shelley Jaques-McMillin, prin. Fax 378-2449
Highland East JHS 700/7-8
1200 SE 4th St 73160 405-735-4580
Mark Archer, prin. Fax 793-3198
Highland West JHS 600/7-8
901 N Santa Fe Ave 73160 405-735-4600
Dan Schwarz, prin. Fax 793-3218
Houchin ES 500/PK-6
3200 Webster St 73160 405-735-4190
Krystal Swindler, prin. Fax 912-5608
Kelley ES 500/PK-6
1900 N Janeway Ave 73160 405-735-4400
Dena Taylor, prin. Fax 793-3238
Northmoor ES 400/PK-6
211 NE 19th St 73160 405-735-4420
Vernona DeCarlo, prin. Fax 912-5514
Oakridge ES 700/PK-6
3201 S Santa Fe Ave 73160 405-735-4530
Seth Meier, prin. Fax 378-2126
Plaza Towers ES 400/PK-6
852 SW 11th St 73160 405-735-4430
Patrick Chase, prin. Fax 793-3232
Santa Fe ES 600/PK-6
501 N Santa Fe Ave 73160 405-735-4450
Jennifer Mankins, prin. Fax 895-6581
Sky Ranch ES 600/PK-6
9501 S Western Ave, Oklahoma City OK 73139
405-735-4460
Amy Braun, prin. Fax 692-5653
Southgate-Rippetoe ES 600/PK-6
500 N Norman Ave 73160 405-735-4480
Kris Johansen, prin. Fax 793-3227
Timber Creek ES PK-6
3501 S Sunnylane Rd 73160 405-735-4670
Kristen Kuepker, prin. Fax 703-1401
Winding Creek ES 600/PK-6
1401 NE 12th St 73160 405-735-4510
Christi Olstad, prin. Fax 793-3273
Other Schools – See Oklahoma City

St. John's Lutheran S 100/PK-8
1032 NW 12th St 73160 405-794-8686
Gina Scroggins M.Ed., prin. Fax 794-1579

Mooreland, Woodward, Pop. 1,172
Mooreland ISD 500/PK-12
PO Box 75 73852 580-994-5388
Terry Kellner M.S., supt. Fax 994-5900
www.mooreland.k12.ok.us
Mooreland ES 400/PK-8
PO Box 75 73852 580-994-5520
Mickey Gregory, prin. Fax 994-5522

Morris, Okmulgee, Pop. 1,388
Morris ISD 1,100/PK-12
307 S 6th St 74445 918-733-9072
Chris Karch, supt. Fax 733-4205
morrisschools.net
Morris ES 500/PK-5
400 S 5th St 74445 918-733-9072
Rebecca Alexander, prin. Fax 733-4205
Morris MS 200/6-8
307 S 6th St 74445 918-733-9072
Monte Womack, prin. Fax 733-4205

Morrison, Noble, Pop. 700
Morrison ISD 400/PK-12
PO Box 176 73061 580-724-3341
Jay Vernon, supt. Fax 724-3004
www.morrisonps.com
Morrison ES, 1225 W Hwy 64 73061 300/PK-6
Christy Williams, prin. 580-724-3620

Mounds, Creek, Pop. 1,107
Liberty ISD 600/PK-12
2727 E 201st St S 74047 918-366-8496
Jim Gilmartin, supt. Fax 366-8497
libertyps.org
Liberty ES, 2727 E 201st St S 74047 400/PK-8
Kim Stewart, prin. 918-366-8311

Mounds ISD 600/PK-12
PO Box 189 74047 918-827-6100
Doran Smith, supt. Fax 827-3704
www.moundsps.com
Mounds ES 400/PK-8
PO Box 189 74047 918-827-6100
Jerry Hurst, prin. Fax 827-6897

Mountain View, Kiowa, Pop. 770
Mountain View-Gotebo ISD 300/PK-12
RR 2 Box 88 73062 580-347-2211
Sam Belcher, supt. Fax 347-2869
www.mvgschools.com
Mountain View-Gotebo ES 200/PK-8
401 W Main St 73062 580-347-2214
Lori Horton, prin. Fax 347-3214

Moyers, Pushmataha
Moyers ISD 200/PK-12
PO Box 88 74557 580-298-5549
Donna Dudley, supt. Fax 298-2022
Moyers ES 200/PK-8
PO Box 88 74557 580-298-5547
Becky Alexander, prin. Fax 298-2022

Muldrow, Sequoyah, Pop. 3,165
Belfonte SD 200/PK-8
475751 State Highway 101 74948 918-427-3522
Paul Pinkerton, supt. Fax 427-1288
www.belfonte.k12.ok.us
Belfonte S 100/PK-8
475751 State Highway 101 74948 918-427-3522
Paul Pinkerton, admin. Fax 427-1288

Other Schools – See Stilwell

Liberty SD 300/PK-8
476490 E 1060 Rd 74948 918-427-3808
Jeff Ransom, supt. Fax 427-4961
www.liberty.seq.k12.ok.us
Liberty S 300/PK-8
476490 E 1060 Rd 74948 918-427-3808
Jeff Neighbors, prin. Fax 427-4961

Muldrow ISD 1,600/PK-12
PO Box 660 74948 918-427-7406
Ron Flanagan, supt. Fax 427-6088
www.muldrowps.org
Muldrow ES 600/PK-4
PO Box 550 74948 918-427-3316
Tammy Hall, prin. Fax 427-1033
Muldrow MS 500/5-8
PO Box 660 74948 918-427-5421
Angela Williams, prin. Fax 427-1034

Mulhall, Logan, Pop. 214
Mulhall-Orlando ISD
Supt. — See Orlando
Mulhall-Orlando ES 200/PK-8
215 S Lewis St 73063 405-649-2000
Rodney Vollmer, prin. Fax 649-2020

Muskogee, Muskogee, Pop. 36,324
Hilldale ISD 1,900/PK-12
500 E Smith Ferry Rd 74403 918-683-0273
Dr. Kaylin Coody, supt. Fax 683-8725
www.hilldale.k12.ok.us
Hilldale Lower ES 500/PK-2
3101 Grandview Park Blvd 74403 918-683-9167
Kair Ridenhour, prin. Fax 683-9204
Hilldale MS 400/6-8
400 E Smith Ferry Rd 74403 918-683-0763
Darren Riddle, prin. Fax 683-0766
Hilldale Upper ES 400/3-5
315 E Peak Blvd 74403 918-683-1101
Kair Ridenhour, prin. Fax 683-0556

Muskogee ISD 6,100/PK-12
202 W Broadway St 74401 918-684-3700
Mike Garde, supt. Fax 684-3838
www.mpsi20.org
Cherokee ES 200/K-6
2400 Estelle Ave 74401 918-684-3890
Lori Jefferson, prin. Fax 684-3891
Creek ES 300/K-6
200 S Country Club Rd 74403 918-684-3880
Rick Hoos, prin. Fax 684-3881
Franklin Science Academy 500/K-8
300 Virgil Matthews Dr 74401 918-684-3870
Donna Pillars, prin. Fax 684-3871
Goetz ES 400/K-6
2412 Haskell Blvd 74403 918 684-3810
P. David Shouse, prin. Fax 684-3811
Grant-Foreman ES 300/K-6
800 S Bacone St 74403 918-684-3860
Justin Walker, prin. Fax 684-3861
Irving ES 400/K-6
1100 N J St 74403 918-684-3840
Debra Dennis, prin. Fax 684-3841
Muskogee ECC 500/PK-PK
901 Emporia St 74401 918-684-3770
Malinda Lindsey, prin. Fax 684-3771
Pershing ES 400/K-6
301 N 54th St 74401 918-684-3830
Karen Watkins, prin. Fax 684-3831
Robertson JHS 700/7-8
402 N S St 74403 918-684-3775
Peggy Jones, prin. Fax 684-3776
Sadler Arts Academy 400/K-8
800 Altamont St 74401 918-684-3820
Ronia Davison, prin. Fax 684-3821
Whittier ES 300/K-6
1705 E Cincinnati Ave 74403 918-684-3800
Lisa Rogers, prin. Fax 684-3801

Muskogee Adventist Academy K-8
170 N Country Club Rd 74403 918-682-5602
St. Joseph Catholic S 100/PK-8
323 N Virginia St 74403 918-683-1291
Sandy Brewer, prin. Fax 682-5374

Mustang, Canadian, Pop. 16,780
Mustang ISD 10,500/PK-12
906 S Heights Dr 73064 405-376-2461
Dr. Sean McDaniel, supt. Fax 376-7333
www.mustangps.org
Canyon Ridge IS 800/5-6
906 S Heights Dr 73064 405-256-6955
Kathy Blackwell, prin. Fax 577-2236
Mustang Centennial ES 500/PK-4
906 S Heights Dr 73064 405-256-6466
Molly Wilson, prin. Fax 256-6661
Mustang ES 500/K-4
906 S Heights Dr 73064 405-376-2491
Leah Anderson, prin. Fax 376-7338
Mustang Horizon IS 700/5-6
906 S Heights Dr 73064 405-256-6282
Holly McKinney, prin. Fax 376-7858
Mustang Lakehoma ES 600/K-4
906 S Heights Dr 73064 405-376-2409
Shawna Carter, prin. Fax 376-7348
Mustang MS 700/7-8
906 S Heights Dr 73064 405-376-2448
Kathy Knowles, prin. Fax 376-7373
Mustang North MS 800/7-8
906 S Heights Dr 73064 405-324-2236
Christy Bradley, prin. Fax 324-2258
Other Schools – See Oklahoma City, Yukon

Mutual, Woodward, Pop. 59
Sharon-Mutual ISD 300/PK-12
210 S Maple St 73853 580-989-3210
Jeff Thompson, supt. Fax 989-8019
www.smps.k12.ok.us
Other Schools – See Sharon

Nashoba, Pushmataha
Nashoba SD 50/PK-8
PO Box 17 74558 918-755-4343
Charles Caughern, supt. Fax 755-4418
www.nashoba.k12.ok.us/
Nashoba S 50/PK-8
PO Box 17 74558 918-755-4343
Charles Caughern, admin. Fax 755-4418

Newcastle, McClain, Pop. 7,304
Newcastle ISD 2,000/PK-12
101 N Main St 73065 405-387-2890
Tony O'Brien, supt. Fax 387-3482
www.newcastle.k12.ok.us
Newcastle ECC 500/PK-1
251 NE 2nd St 73065 405-387-6200
Kristi Ferguson, prin. Fax 387-3441
Newcastle ES 600/2-5
418 NW 10th St 73065 405-387-6474
Terri Scott, prin. Fax 387-5058
Newcastle MS 400/6-8
611 E Fox Ln 73065 405-387-3139
John Harris, prin. Fax 387-5563

Newkirk, Kay, Pop. 2,182
Newkirk ISD 800/PK-12
625 W South St 74647 580-362-2388
Brady Barnes, supt. Fax 362-3413
www.newkirk.k12.ok.us
Newkirk ES 300/PK-4
701 W South St 74647 580-362-2279
Pam Hunter, prin. Fax 362-1151
Newkirk MS 300/5-8
711 S Academy Ave 74647 580-362-2516
Jeff Wilson, prin. Fax 362-1150

Peckham SD 100/PK-8
7175 W School St 74647 580-362-2633
Gary Young, supt. Fax 362-3970
www.peckham.k12.ok.us/
Peckham S 100/PK-8
7175 W School St 74647 580-362-2633
Gary Young, prin. Fax 362-3970

Ninnekah, Grady, Pop. 970
Ninnekah ISD 500/PK-12
PO Box 275 73067 405-224-4092
Todd Bunch, supt. Fax 224-4096
www.ninnekah.k12.ok.us
Ninnekah ES 300/PK-5
PO Box 275 73067 405-222-0420
Vickie Loughridge, prin. Fax 222-3371
Ninnekah MS 100/6-8
PO Box 275 73067 405-224-4299
Glen Shoemake, prin. Fax 224-4665

Noble, Cleveland, Pop. 6,155
Noble ISD 2,900/PK-12
111 S 4th St 73068 405-872-3452
Frank Solomon, supt. Fax 872-3271
www.nobleps.com
Daily ES 600/PK-1
300 S 5th St 73068 405-872-3406
Michael Prior, prin. Fax 872-7699
Hubbard ES 400/2-3
1104 E Maguire Rd 73068 405-872-9201
Nathan Gray, prin. Fax 872-7680
Inge MS 600/6-8
1201 N 8th St 73068 405-872-3495
Ronald Fulks, prin. Fax 872-8670
Pioneer IS 400/4-5
611 Ash St 73068 405-872-3472
Nathan Gray, prin. Fax 872-9135

Norman, Cleveland, Pop. 105,378
Little Axe ISD 1,200/PK-12
2000 168th Ave NE 73026 405-329-7691
Jay Thomas, supt. Fax 579-2929
littleaxeps.org/
Little Axe ES 600/PK-5
2000 168th Ave NE 73026 405-447-0913
Brian Tupper, prin. Fax 579-2976
Little Axe MS 300/6-8
2000 168th Ave NE 73026 405-329-2156
Dalton Griffin, prin. Fax 579-2937

Norman ISD 15,300/PK-12
131 S Flood Ave 73069 405-364-1339
Dr. Nicholas Migliorino, supt. Fax 366-5851
www.norman.k12.ok.us
Adams ES 600/PK-5
817 Denison Dr 73069 405-366-5972
Patricia Thomason, prin. Fax 366-5975
Alcott MS 700/6-8
1919 W Boyd St 73069 405-366-5845
Dr. Dana Morris, prin. Fax 447-6572
Cleveland ES 600/PK-5
500 N Sherry Ave 73069 405-366-5875
Ty Bell, prin. Fax 366-5877
Eisenhower ES 700/PK-5
1415 Fairlawn Dr 73071 405-366-5879
Cheryl Schoonover, prin. Fax 573-3503
Irving MS 900/6-8
125 Vicksburg Ave 73071 405-366-5941
Jonathan Atchley, prin. Fax 366-5944
Jackson ES 500/PK-5
520 Wylie Rd 73069 405-366-5884
Dr. Craig Stevens, prin. Fax 447-6563
Jefferson ES 400/PK-5
250 N Cockrel Ave 73071 405-366-5889
Carla Atkinson, prin. Fax 366-5892
Kennedy ES 500/PK-5
621 Sunrise St 73071 405-366-5894
Montie Koehn, prin. Fax 366-5896
Lakeview ES 200/PK-5
3310 108th Ave NE 73026 405-366-5899
Paula Palermo, prin. Fax 366-5901
Lincoln ES 300/PK-5
915 Classen Blvd 73071 405-366-5904
Olivia Dean, prin. Fax 366-5906
Longfellow MS 700/6-8
215 N Ponca Ave 73071 405-366-5948
Carie Spannagel, prin. Fax 366-5952
Madison ES 400/PK-5
500 James Dr 73072 405-366-5910
Dominic Barone, prin. Fax 366-5912
McKinley ES 300/PK-5
728 S Flood Ave 73069 405-366-5914
Carol Emerson, prin. Fax 366-5916
Monroe ES 400/PK-5
1601 McGee Dr 73072 405-366-5927
Dr. Lori Connery, prin. Fax 366-5930
Reagan ES, 1601 24th Ave SE 73071 500/PK-5
Kelly Otis, prin. 405-364-1339
Roosevelt ES 700/PK-5
4250 W Tecumseh Rd 73072 405-447-6581
Tiffany Dixon, prin. Fax 447-6583
Truman ES 400/3-5
600 Parkside Rd 73072 405-366-5980
Robye Jackson, prin. Fax 366-5988
Truman PS 500/PK-2
601 Meadow Ridge Rd 73072 405-366-5950
Kristie Eselin, prin. Fax 307-6733
Washington ES 500/PK-5
600 48th Ave SE 73026 405-366-5984
Dr. Linda Parsons, prin. Fax 366-5960
Whittier MS 1,100/6-8
2000 W Brooks St 73069 405-366-5956
Kendall Still, prin. Fax 447-6562
Wilson ES 300/PK-5
800 N Peters Ave 73069 405-366-5932
Chris Crelia, prin. Fax 366-5934

Robin Hill SD 300/PK-8
4801 E Franklin Rd 73026 405-321-4186
Brandon Voss, supt. Fax 321-5179
www.robinhillschool.org
Robin Hill S 300/PK-8
4801 E Franklin Rd 73026 405-321-4186
Brandon Voss, supt. Fax 321-5179

All Saints S 500/PK-8
4001 36th Ave NW 73072 405-447-4600
Dana Wade, prin. Fax 447-7227
Children's House of Norman Inc 50/PK-3
606 S Santa Fe Ave 73069 405-321-1275
Community Christian S 700/PK-12
3002 Broce Dr 73072 405-329-2500
Trinity Lutheran S 50/PK-5
603 Classen Blvd 73071 405-329-1503
Cheryl Anderson, admin. Fax 928-2686

Nowata, Nowata, Pop. 3,335
Nowata ISD 1,000/PK-12
707 W Osage Ave 74048 918-273-3425
Leon Ashlock, supt. Fax 273-2105
www.npsok.org
Moore ES 500/PK-5
707 W Osage Ave 74048 918-273-0771
Tana Haas, prin. Fax 273-2105
Nowata MS 200/6-8
707 W Osage Ave 74048 918-273-1346
James Sexson, prin. Fax 273-2105

Oaks, Delaware, Pop. 277
Oaks-Mission ISD 200/PK-12
PO Box 160 74359 918-868-2499
Wyman Thompson, supt. Fax 868-2707
Oaks-Mission ES 100/PK-8
PO Box 160 74359 918-868-2455
Barbara Tucker, dean Fax 868-5013

Ochelata, Washington, Pop. 387
Caney Valley ISD
Supt. — See Ramona
Caney Valley ES 400/PK-5
401 W Main St 74051 918-535-2205
Kelli Longan, prin. Fax 535-2764

Oilton, Creek, Pop. 965
Oilton ISD 300/PK-12
309 E Peterson St 74052 918-862-0389
Matt Posey, supt. Fax 615-9698
www.oilton.k12.ok.us
Kennedy S 200/PK-8
306 E Peterson St 74052 918-862-0389
Matt Posey, prin. Fax 862-3763

Okarche, Kingfisher, Pop. 1,196
Okarche ISD 300/PK-12
PO Box 276 73762 405-263-7300
Robert Friesen, supt. Fax 263-7515
www.okarche.k12.ok.us
Okarche ES 200/PK-6
PO Box 276 73762 405-263-4447
Cinda Schaefer, prin. Fax 263-7515

Holy Trinity S 100/PK-8
PO Box 485 73762 405-263-4422
Steve Lykes, prin. Fax 263-9753

Okay, Wagoner, Pop. 586
Okay ISD 400/PK-12
PO Box 830 74446 918-682-0371
Pete Hiseley, supt. Fax 683-8331
www.okayps.org
Okay ES 300/PK-8
PO Box 830 74446 918-682-7961
Mike Lasater, prin. Fax 682-6532

Okeene, Blaine, Pop. 1,187
Okeene ISD 300/PK-12
PO Box 409 73763 580-822-3268
Ron Pittman, supt. Fax 822-4123
www.okeene.k12.ok.us
Okeene ES 200/PK-6
PO Box 409 73763 580-822-3425
Mike Jinkens, prin. Fax 822-4769

Okemah, Okfuskee, Pop. 3,000
Bearden SD 100/PK-8
372006 Highway 48 74859 918-623-0156
Danielle Deere, supt. Fax 623-9349
www.bearden.k12.ok.us
Bearden S 100/PK-8
372006 Highway 48 74859 918-623-0156
Danielle Deere, prin. Fax 623-9349

Okemah ISD 800/PK-12
107 W Date St 74859 918-623-1874
Tony Dean, supt. Fax 623-1203
www.okemahk12.com
Oakes ES 300/PK-3
101 N 16th St 74859 918-623-1874
Sandra Lambert, prin. Fax 623-2465
Okemah MS 200/4-8
107 W Date St 74859 918-623-1874
Sandra Lambert, prin. Fax 623-9151

Oklahoma City, Oklahoma, Pop. 555,623
Crooked Oak ISD 1,100/PK-12
1450 S Eastern Ave 73129 405-677-5252
Brad Richards, supt. Fax 670-8070
www.crookedoak.org
Central Oak ES 600/PK-5
1450 S Eastern Ave 73129 405-677-6212
Kim Templeman, prin. Fax 677-8411
Crooked Oak MS 300/6-8
1450 S Eastern Ave 73129 405-677-5133
Dennis McCray, prin. Fax 670-2256

Crutcho SD 400/PK-8
2401 N Air Depot Blvd 73141 405-427-3771
Teresa McAfee, supt. Fax 427-3816
www.crutchoesd.org
Crutcho ES 400/PK-8
2401 N Air Depot Blvd 73141 405-427-3771
Teresa McAfee, prin. Fax 427-3816

Deer Creek ISD
Supt. — See Edmond
Spring Creek ES 400/PK-4
15400 N Rockwell Ave, 405-715-9898
Michelle Eidson, prin.

Midwest City-Del City ISD
Supt. — See Midwest City
Barnes ES 400/PK-5
10551 SE 59th St 73150 405-739-1651
Jon Kalsu, prin. Fax 739-1653
Highland Park ES 600/PK-5
5301 S Dimple Dr 73135 405-671-8660
Dr. Donna Cloud, prin. Fax 671-8661
Parkview ES 700/PK-5
5701 Mackelman Dr 73135 405-671-8670
Mike Stiglets, prin. Fax 671-8672
Pleasant Hill ES 200/PK-5
4346 NE 36th St 73121 405-427-6551
Dr. Tamara Roberson, prin. Fax 427-6552
Schwartz ES 300/PK-5
12001 SE 104th St 73165 405-794-4703
Rondall Jones, prin. Fax 794-2178
Tinker ES 500/PK-5
4500 Tinker Rd 73135 405-739-1630
Wendy Eaton, prin. Fax 739-1635

Millwood ISD 37 800/PK-12
6724 N Martin Luther King 73111 405-478-1336
Cecilia Robinson-Woods, supt. Fax 478-4698
millwood.k12.ok.us
Millwood Arts Academy 6-8
6724 N Martin Luther King 73111 405-475-1004
Candice Greene, prin. Fax 478-7134
Millwood ES 500/PK-5
6710 N Martin Luther King 73111 405-475-1004
Susan Baldwin, prin. Fax 475-1009

Moore ISD
Supt. — See Moore
Bonds ES 700/PK-6
14025 S May Ave 73170 405-735-4500
Greg Waggoner, prin. Fax 692-6260
Briarwood ES 600/PK-6
14901 S Hudson Ave 73170 405-735-4110
Valerie Singleton, prin. Fax 793-3283
Brink JHS 1,000/7-8
11420 S Western Ave 73170 405-735-4540
Joseph Ross, prin. Fax 692-5634
Bryant ES 700/PK-6
9400 S Bryant Ave 73160 405-735-4130
Stephanie Gunter, prin. Fax 793-2737
Earlywine ES 500/PK-6
12800 S May Ave 73170 405-735-4150
Ben Randall, prin. Fax 692-5659
Eastlake ES 500/PK-6
1301 SW 134th St 73170 405-735-4160
Charla Uhles, prin. Fax 692-5763
Fairview ES 600/PK-6
2431 SW 89th St 73159 405-735-4170
Tammy Robinson, prin. Fax 682-5521
Fisher ES 500/PK-6
11800 Southwood Dr 73170 405-735-4180
Kathy Massey, prin. Fax 692-5673
Kingsgate ES 500/PK-6
1400 Kingsgate Rd 73159 405-735-4410
Karie Hill, prin. Fax 692-5643
Moore West JHS 600/7-8
9400 S Pennsylvania Ave 73159 405-735-4620
Jeni Dutton, prin. Fax 692-5660
Red Oak ES 600/PK-6
11224 S Pennsylvania Ave 73170 405-735-4440
Amber Balderrama, prin. Fax 692-5678
Sooner ES 600/PK-6
5420 SE 89th St 73135 405-735-4470
Kevin McElroy, prin. Fax 672-6498
South Lake ES PK-6
12701 S Portland Ave 73170 405-735-4660
Amy Simpson, prin. Fax 703-1294
Southridge JHS 7-8
14141 S Pennsylvania 73170 405-735-4680
Melanie Smith, prin.

Mustang ISD
Supt. — See Mustang
Mustang Prairie View ES 600/PK-5
9201 SW 59th St 73179 405-256-6989
Shanda Cummings, prin. Fax 745-6831
Mustang Valley ES 800/K-4
3100 S Morgan Rd 73179 405-324-2541
Jill Mitchell, prin. Fax 324-4578

Oklahoma City ISD 40,800/PK-12
900 N Klein Ave 73106 405-587-0000
Aurora Lora, supt. Fax 587-0443
www.okcps.org
Adams ES 700/PK-6
3416 SW 37th St 73119 405-587-1600
Heather Zacarias, prin. Fax 587-1605
Arthur ES 600/PK-5
5100 S Independence Ave 73119 405-587-7600
Rhonda Schroeder, prin. Fax 587-7605
Belle Isle Enterprise MS 500/6-8
5904 N Villa Ave 73112 405-587-6600
Lynn Kellert, prin. Fax 587-6605
Bodine ES 500/PK-5
5301 S Bryant Ave 73129 405-587-2500
Nikki Coshow, prin. Fax 587-2505
Britton ES 600/PK-5
1215 NW 95th St 73114 405-587-6100
Ronda Hamilton, prin. Fax 587-6105
Buchanan ES 500/PK-6
4126 NW 18th St 73107 405-587-4700
Tonya Brackeen, prin. Fax 587-4705
Capitol Hill ES 500/PK-6
2717 S Robinson Ave 73109 405-587-1800
Angela Houston, prin. Fax 587-1805
Chavez ES 1,000/PK-6
600 SE Grand Blvd 73129 405-587-9800
Dr. Laura Morris, prin. Fax 587-9805
Cleveland ES 400/PK-5
2725 NW 23rd St 73107 405-587-8200
Marsha Stafford, prin. Fax 587-8205
Coolidge ES 800/PK-5
5212 S Villa Ave 73119 405-587-2800
Melissa Brett, prin. Fax 587-2805
Edgemere ES 200/PK-6
3200 N Walker Ave 73118 405-587-5100
Alisa Stieg, prin. Fax 587-5105
Edwards ES 400/PK-6
1123 NE Grand Blvd 73117 405-587-3200
Patrice Allen, prin. Fax 587-3205
Field ES 600/PK-5
1515 N Klein Ave 73106 405-587-5700
Paige Bressman, prin. Fax 587-5705
Fillmore ES 800/PK-5
5200 S Blackwelder Ave 73119 405-587-4800
Susan Martin Rachels, prin. Fax 587-4805
Gatewood ES 200/PK-5
1821 NW 21st St 73106 405-587-2400
Gayla Goff, prin. Fax 587-2405
Greystone ES 400/PK-6
2401 NW 115th Ter 73120 405-587-3100
Debra Thomas, prin. Fax 587-3105
Hawthorne ES 500/PK-5
2300 NW 15th St 73107 405-587-5900
Randy Brewer, prin. Fax 587-5905
Hayes ES 500/PK-6
6900 S Byers Ave 73149 405-587-5800
Shaun Ross, prin. Fax 587-5805
Heronville ES 900/PK-5
1240 SW 29th St 73109 405-587-6000
Leon Hill, prin. Fax 587-6005
Hillcrest ES 400/PK-5
6421 S Miller Blvd 73159 405-587-3800
Shelly Deas, prin. Fax 587-3805
Jackson Enterprise ES PK-6
2601 S Villa Ave 73108 405-587-8700
Patrick Duffy, prin.
Jefferson MS 900/6-8
6800 S Blackwelder Ave 73159 405-587-1300
Heather Messer, prin. Fax 587-1305
Johnson ES 200/PK-5
1810 Sheffield Rd 73120 405-587-6700
Margaret Saunders, prin. Fax 587-6705
Kaiser ES 700/PK-5
3101 Lyon Blvd 73112 405-587-3600
Lana Lewis, prin. Fax 587-3605
King ES 600/PK-6
1201 NE 48th St 73111 405-587-4000
Cherron Ukpaka, prin. Fax 587-4005
Lee ES 700/PK-5
424 SW 29th St 73109 405-587-3400
Amy Daugherty, prin. Fax 587-3405
Linwood ES 500/PK-5
3416 NW 17th St 73107 405-587-1700
Susan Combs, prin. Fax 587-1705
Mann ES 400/PK-5
1105 NW 45th St 73118 405-587-3500
Dr. Mitch Ruzzoli, prin. Fax 587-3505
Monroe ES 500/PK-5
4810 N Linn Ave 73112 405-587-5600
Eric Meador, prin. Fax 587-5605
Moon Academy 400/PK-6
1901 NE 13th St 73117 405-587-8700
Warren Pete, prin. Fax 587-8705
Nichols Hills ES 400/K-5
1301 W Wilshire Blvd 73116 405-587-2583
Kim Iraggi, prin. Fax 587-2602
North Highland ES 400/PK-5
8400 N Robinson Ave 73114 405-587-6250
Anita Jones, prin. Fax 587-6254
Oakridge ES 300/PK-5
4200 Leonhardt Dr 73115 405-587-5500
Ycedra Daughty, prin. Fax 587-5505
Parks ES 200/PK-5
1501 NE 30th St 73111 405-587-4400
Rejeana Payne, prin. Fax 587-4405
Parmelee ES 800/K-5
6700 S Hudson Ave 73139 405-587-6750
Jan Parks, prin. Fax 587-6755
Pierce ES 300/PK-5
2601 S Tulsa Ave 73108 405-587-7400
Paula Pluess, prin. Fax 587-7405

Prairie Queen ES 800/PK-5
6609 S Blackwelder Ave 73159 405-587-7750
Jacqueline Horton, prin. Fax 587-7755
Putnam Heights ES 400/PK-5
1601 NW 36th St 73118 405-587-2700
Susan Carlsen, prin. Fax 587-2705
Quail Creek ES 400/PK-5
11700 Thorn Ridge Rd 73120 405-587-6500
Dr. Jan Matthews, prin. Fax 587-6505
Rancho Village ES 400/PK-5
1401 Johnston Dr 73119 405-587-9700
Carol Perry, prin. Fax 587-9705
Ridgeview ES 300/PK-5
10010 Ridgeview Dr 73120 405-587-6800
Michael Lisenby, prin. Fax 587-6805
Rockwood ES 600/PK-5
3101 SW 24th St 73108 405-587-1500
Dr. Sheryl Barnett, prin. Fax 587-1505
Roosevelt MS 600/6-8
3233 SW 44th St 73119 405-587-8300
David Clark, prin. Fax 587-8305
Sequoyah ES 400/PK-5
2400 NW 36th St 73112 405-587-9200
Kandy Bishop, prin. Fax 587-9205
Shidler ES 300/PK-5
1415 S Byers Ave 73129 405-587-4600
Armando Ayala, prin. Fax 587-4605
Southern Hills ES 500/PK-5
7800 S Kentucky Ave 73159 405-587-2900
Jennifer McKay, prin. Fax 587-2905
Stand Watie ES 700/PK-5
3517 S Linn Ave 73119 405-587-6900
Marcus Macias, prin. Fax 587-6905
Taft MS, 2901 NW 23rd St 73107 600/6-8
Charmaine Johnson, prin. 405-587-8000
Telstar ES 300/PK-5
9521 NE 16th St 73130 405-587-8900
Vanessa Van Trease, prin. Fax 587-8905
Twain ES 300/PK-5
2451 W Main St 73107 405-587-3700
Sandy Phillips, prin. Fax 587-3705
Van Buren ES 400/PK-5
2700 SW 40th St 73119 405-686-4080
Amparo Macias, prin. Fax 686-4083
Webster MS 800/6-8
6708 S Santa Fe Ave 73139 405-587-3900
Joey Slate, prin.
West Nichols Hills ES 300/PK-5
8400 Greystone Ave 73120 405-587-4900
Gloria Anderson, prin. Fax 587-4905
Westwood ES 300/PK-5
1701 Exchange Ave 73108 405-702-1685
Susan Robertson, prin.
Wheeler ES 500/PK-6
501 SE 25th St 73129 405-587-7000
Heather Bullock, prin. Fax 587-7005
Willow Brook ES 500/PK-5
8105 NE 10th St 73110 405-587-7500
Glenna Berry, prin. Fax 587-7505
Wilson ES 400/PK-5
501 NW 21st St 73103 405-587-7100
Susan Marshall-Armstrong, prin. Fax 587-7105
Other Schools – See Spencer

Putnam City ISD 19,300/PK-12
5401 NW 40th St 73122 405-495-5200
Dr. Fred Rhodes, supt. Fax 495-8648
www.putnamcityschools.org
Arbor Grove ES 500/PK-5
4711 N Tulsa Ave 73112 405-789-4985
Brenda Davis, prin. Fax 491-7551
Cooper MS 700/6-8
8001 River Bend Blvd 73132 405-720-9887
Jeff Brown, prin. Fax 728-5632
Coronado Heights ES 500/PK-5
5911 N Sapulpa Ave 73112 405-942-8593
Dr. Nona Burling, prin. Fax 948-9014
Dennis ES 500/PK-5
11800 James L Dennis Dr 73162 405-722-6510
Renita White, prin. Fax 728-5613
Downs ES 500/PK-5
7501 W Hefner Rd 73162 405-721-4431
Stephanie Wallace, prin. Fax 728-5625
Harvest Hills ES 500/PK-5
8201 NW 104th St 73162 405-721-2013
Lynn Johnson, prin. Fax 728-5637
Hefner MS 1,100/6-8
8400 N MacArthur Blvd 73132 405-721-2411
Mark Lebsack, prin. Fax 728-5645
Hilldale ES 700/PK-5
4801 NW 16th St 73127 405-942-8600
Shanda Brody, prin. Fax 948-9009
Kirkland ES 100/PK-2
6020 N Independence Ave 73112 405-842-1491
Ashley Hoggatt, prin. Fax 842-5156
Mayfield MS 700/6-8
1600 N Purdue Ave 73127 405-947-8693
Tracy Sowinski, prin. Fax 948-9000
Northridge ES 700/PK-5
8501 NW 82nd St 73132 405-722-5560
Kim Mclaughlin, prin. Fax 728-5649
Post ES 700/PK-5
6920 W Britton Rd 73132 405-721-8123
Sheryl Rexach, prin. Fax 728-5622
Putnam City ECC 300/PK-PK
12777 N Rockwell Ave 73122 405-717-7799
Ashley Hoggatt, prin.
Rogers ES 500/PK-5
8201 NW 122nd St 73142 405-722-9797
John Lunn, prin. Fax 728-5636
Rollingwood ES 500/PK-5
6301 N Ann Arbor Ave 73122 405-721-3644
Pam Miller, prin. Fax 728-5616
Tulakes ES 600/PK-5
6600 Galaxie Dr 73132 405-721-4360
Danyelle Speight, prin. Fax 728-5618
Windsor Hills ES 700/PK-5
2909 N Ann Arbor Ave 73127 405-942-8673
Shbrone Brookings, prin. Fax 948-9006
Other Schools – See Bethany, Warr Acres

Western Heights ISD 3,800/PK-12
8401 SW 44th St 73179 405-350-3410
Joe Kitchens, supt. Fax 745-6322
www.westernheights.k12.ok.us
Bridgestone IS 600/5-6
1700 S Council Rd 73128 405-350-3420
Jennifer Colvin, prin. Fax 261-6095
Council Grove ES 500/PK-4
7721 Melrose Ln 73127 405-350-3465
Michelle Braisher, prin. Fax 495-6620
Glenn ES 700/PK-4
6501 S Land Ave 73159 405-350-3480
Archie Scott, prin. Fax 681-8632
Greenvale ES 300/PK-4
901 Greenvale Rd 73127 405-350-3470
Diane Klein, prin. Fax 787-6539
Western Heights MS 500/7-8
8435 SW 44th St 73179 405-350-3455
Patricia Stanley, prin. Fax 745-6341
Winds West ES 400/PK-4
8300 SW 37th St 73179 405-350-3475
Nancy Ingle, prin. Fax 745-2580

Academy of Classical Christian Studies 500/PK-12
1120 E Hefner Rd 73131 405-478-2077
Bishop John Carroll S 200/PK-8
1100 NW 32nd St 73118 405-525-0956
Connie Diotte, prin. Fax 523-3053
Casady S 900/PK-12
9500 N Pennsylvania Ave 73120 405-749-3100
Nathan Sheldon, head sch Fax 749-3214
Christ the King S 500/PK-8
1905 Elmhurst Ave 73120 405-843-3909
Amy Feighny, admin. Fax 843-6519
Crossings Christian S 700/PK-12
14400 N Portland Ave 73134 405-842-8495
Paul MacDonald, hdmstr. Fax 767-1520
Heritage Hall S 900/PK-12
1800 NW 122nd St 73120 405-749-3001
Guy Bramble, hdmstr. Fax 751-7372
King's Gate Christian S 100/PK-7
11400 N Portland Ave 73120 405-752-2111
Wyndi Bradley, head sch Fax 755-6946
Messiah Lutheran S 100/PK-8
3600 NW Expressway 73112 405-946-0462
Sharla Haight, admin. Fax 946-0682
Parkview Adventist Academy 100/PK-12
4201 N Martin Luther King 73111 405-427-6525
Rosary S 200/PK-8
1910 NW 19th St 73106 405-525-9272
Christy Harris, prin. Fax 525-5643
Sacred Heart S 200/PK-8
2700 S Shartel Ave 73109 405-634-5673
Adriana Garza, prin. Fax 634-7011
St. Charles Borromeo S 200/PK-8
5000 N Grove Ave 73122 405-789-0224
Todd Gungoll, prin. Fax 789-3583
St. Eugene S 400/PK-8
PO Box 20930 73156 405-751-0067
Jeremy Eaton, prin. Fax 302-4254
St. James the Greater S 200/PK-8
1224 SW 41st St 73109 405-636-6810
Alicia Vazquez, prin. Fax 636-6818
St. John Christian Heritage Academy 100/PK-5
5700 N Kelley Ave 73111 405-478-8607
Janet King, supt. Fax 418-0043
Trinity S K-12
321 NW 36th St 73118 405-525-5600
Jennifer Vaught, prin. Fax 525-5602
Westminster S 500/PK-8
600 NW 44th St 73118 405-524-0631
Bob Vernon, head sch Fax 528-4412

Okmulgee, Okmulgee, Pop. 11,317
Okmulgee ISD 1,500/PK-12
PO Box 1346 74447 918-758-2000
Renee Dove, supt. Fax 758-2088
www.okmulgeeps.com
Dunbar IS 500/5-8
1421 Martin Luther King Dr 74447 918-758-2050
Stephanie Lee, admin. Fax 758-2088
Okmulgee PS 500/PK-4
1003 N Okmulgee St 74447 918-758-2030
Jennifer Neal, prin. Fax 758-2093

Twin Hills SD 400/PK-8
7225 Twin Hills Rd 74447 918-733-2531
Gary McElroy, supt. Fax 733-2861
www.twinhills.k12.ok.us
Twin Hills S 400/PK-8
7225 Twin Hills Rd 74447 918-733-2531
Gary McElroy, supt. Fax 733-2861

Stonebridge Academy PK-8
PO Box 99 74447 918-752-1200

Oktaha, Muskogee, Pop. 343
Oktaha ISD 800/PK-12
PO Box 9 74450 918-687-7556
Jerry Needham M.Ed., supt. Fax 687-0074
www.oktahaschool.com
Oktaha ES 500/PK-8
PO Box 9 74450 918-682-5665
Tanna Kincade B.S., prin. Fax 682-7520

Olustee, Jackson, Pop. 583
Olustee-Eldorado ISD 200/PK-12
PO Box 70 73560 580-648-2243
Gaylene Freeman, supt. Fax 648-2501
www.olustee.k12.ok.us
Olustee-Eldorado ES 100/PK-8
PO Box 70 73560 580-648-2243
Melvin Hazel, prin. Fax 648-2501

Omega, Kingfisher
Lomega ISD 200/PK-12
18319 N 2700 Rd 73764 405-729-4215
Karen Castonguay, supt. Fax 729-4666
www.lomega.k12.ok.us
Other Schools – See Loyal

Oologah, Rogers, Pop. 1,080
Oologah-Talala ISD 1,800/PK-12
PO Box 189 74053 918-443-6000
Max Tanner, supt. Fax 443-9088
www.oologah.k12.ok.us
Oologah Lower ES 500/PK-2
PO Box 189 74053 918-443-6141
Crysti York, prin. Fax 443-6056
Oologah MS 400/6-8
PO Box 189 74053 918-443-6161
Kelli Dixon, prin. Fax 443-2875
Oologah Upper ES 400/3-5
PO Box 189 74053 918-443-6041
Joan Ricks, prin. Fax 443-2672

Optima, Texas, Pop. 348
Optima SD 100/K-6
107 E 5th St 73945 580-338-6712
Freida Burgess, supt. Fax 338-6721
optimawarriors.com
Optima ES 100/K-6
107 E 5th St 73945 580-338-6712
Freida Burgess, prin. Fax 338-6721

Orlando, Logan, Pop. 142
Mulhall-Orlando ISD 200/PK-12
100 E Main 73073 405-649-2000
Rodney Vollmer, supt. Fax 649-2020
www.mulhall-orlando.k12.ok.us
Other Schools – See Mulhall

Owasso, Tulsa, Pop. 27,251
Owasso ISD 9,400/PK-12
1501 N Ash St 74055 918-272-5367
Dr. Clark Ogilvie, supt. Fax 272-8111
www.owassops.org
Ator ES 600/PK-5
1500 N Ash St 74055 918-272-2204
Jennifer Newton, prin. Fax 272-2205
Bailey ES 600/PK-5
10221 E 96th St N 74055 918-272-5399
Ashley Hearn, prin. Fax 272-8437
Barnes ES 600/PK-5
7809 E 76th St N 74055 918-272-1153
Rylee Zaragoza, prin. Fax 272-1154
Hodson ES 500/PK-5
14500 E 86th St N 74055 918-272-8160
Charlene Duncan, prin. Fax 272-8081
Mills ES 500/PK-5
8200 N 124th East Ave 74055 918-272-2288
Gina Metcalf, prin. Fax 272-8406
Northeast ES 600/PK-5
13650 E 103rd St N 74055 918-272-2615
Michelle Million, prin. Fax 272-2853
Owasso Eighth Grade Center 800/8-8
13901 E 86th St N 74055 918-272-6274
Alton Lusk, prin. Fax 272-5562
Owasso Seventh Grade Center 700/7-7
1400 N Main St 74055 918-272-1183
Eric Nantois, prin. Fax 272-8050
Owasso Sixth Grade Center 700/6-6
8101 N 129th East Ave 74055 918-274-3020
Kira Kelsey, prin. Fax 272-3024
Smith ES 500/PK-5
12223 E 91st St N 74055 918-272-5162
Patrick James, prin. Fax 272-5189
Stone Canyon ES 600/PK-5
7305 N 177th East Ave 74055 918-274-1634
George Holderman, prin. Fax 274-1025

Rejoice Christian S 300/PK-12
13407 E 106th St N 74055 918-516-0050
Dr. Craig Shaw, prin. Fax 516-0299

Paden, Okfuskee, Pop. 430
Paden ISD 300/PK-12
PO Box 370 74860 405-932-5053
Michelle Stiles, supt. Fax 932-4132
www.paden.k12.ok.us
Paden ES, PO Box 370 74860 200/PK-8
Frank Jordan, prin. 405-932-4499

Panama, LeFlore, Pop. 1,335
Panama ISD 600/PK-12
401 High School Dr 74951 918-963-2215
Grant Ralls, supt. Fax 963-4860
www.panama.k12.ok.us
Panama ES 200/PK-5
1101 Kentucky 74951 918-963-2218
Dearl Tobey, prin. Fax 963-4866
Panama MS 100/6-8
1102 Kentucky 74951 918-963-4479
James Hoffman, dean Fax 963-4493

Panola, Latimer
Panola ISD 200/PK-12
PO Box 6 74559 918-465-3298
Ben Wadley, supt. Fax 465-3656
panolabearcats.org
Panola ES 100/PK-8
PO Box 6 74559 918-465-0011
Brad Corcoran, prin. Fax 465-3656

Paoli, Garvin, Pop. 587
Paoli ISD 300/PK-12
PO Box 278 73074 405-484-7336
David Morris, supt. Fax 484-7268
www.paoli.k12.ok.us/
Paoli ES 200/PK-8
PO Box 278 73074 405-484-7231
Byron Mooney, prin. Fax 484-7268

Park Hill, Cherokee, Pop. 3,515
Keys ISD 900/PK-12
26622 S 520 Rd 74451 918-458-1835
Vol Woods, supt. Fax 456-1656
www.keys.k12.ok.us
Keys ES 500/PK-8
26622 S 520 Rd 74451 918-456-4501
Tami Woods, prin. Fax 456-7559

Pauls Valley, Garvin, Pop. 5,834
Pauls Valley ISD 1,300/PK-12
PO Box 780 73075 405-238-6453
Mike Martin, supt. Fax 238-9178
www.paulsvalleyschools.com/
Jackson ES 300/1-3
PO Box 780 73075 405-238-2312
Mitzi Winters, prin. Fax 238-1225
Jefferson Early Learning Center 200/PK-K
PO Box 780 73075 405-238-6413
Mialisa Wigley, prin. Fax 238-9370
Lee ES 200/4-6
PO Box 780 73075 405-238-7336
Kristin Holt, prin. Fax 238-1227

Whitebead SD 400/PK-8
16476 N County Road 3200 73075 405-238-3021
Lou Ann Wood, supt. Fax 238-6258
Whitebead S 400/PK-8
16476 N County Road 3200 73075 405-238-3021
Lou Ann Wood, prin. Fax 238-6258

Pawhuska, Osage, Pop. 3,306
Bowring SD 100/PK-8
87 County Road 3304 74056 918-336-6892
Nicole Hinkle, supt. Fax 336-1348
www.bowringps.k12.ok.us
Bowring S 100/PK-8
87 County Road 3304 74056 918-336-6892
Nicole Hinkle, prin. Fax 336-1348

Pawhuska ISD 800/PK-12
1801 McKenzie Rd 74056 918-287-1281
Janet Neufeld, supt. Fax 287-4461
www.pawhuskadistrict.org
Indian Camp ES 200/PK-2
2005 E Boundary Ave 74056 918-287-1967
Kimberly Hester, prin. Fax 287-1244
Pawhuska ES 200/3-7
1700 Lynn Ave 74056 918-287-1977
Bryon Cowan, prin. Fax 287-1163

Pawnee, Pawnee, Pop. 2,051
Pawnee ISD 800/PK-12
615 Denver St 74058 918-762-3676
Ned Williams, supt. Fax 762-2704
www.pawnee.k12.ok.us
Pawnee ES 400/PK-5
602 Forest St 74058 918-762-3618
Tracy Burnett, prin. Fax 762-6436
Pawnee MS 200/6-8
605 Denver St 74058 918-762-3055
Stacy Womack, prin. Fax 762-3585

Peggs, Cherokee, Pop. 692
Peggs SD 300/PK-8
PO Box 119 74452 918-598-3412
Dr. John Cox, supt. Fax 598-3833
Peggs S 300/PK-8
PO Box 119 74452 918-598-3412
Dr. Carolyn Robbins, prin. Fax 598-3833

Perkins, Payne, Pop. 2,678
Perkins-Tryon ISD 1,500/PK-12
PO Box 549 74059 405-547-5703
James Ramsey, supt. Fax 547-2020
www.p-t.k12.ok.us
Perkins-Tryon ES 400/PK-2
PO Box 549 74059 405-547-5741
Bobby Simma, prin. Fax 547-5744
Perkins-Tryon IS 400/3-5
PO Box 549 74059 405-547-5713
Donna Boles, prin. Fax 547-2020
Perkins-Tryon JHS 300/6-8
PO Box 549 74059 405-547-5715
Jerry Burnett, prin. Fax 547-5761

Perry, Noble, Pop. 4,921
Perry ISD 1,200/PK-12
900 Fir St 73077 580-336-4511
Dr. Terry McCarty, supt. Fax 336-5185
www.perry.k12.ok.us
Perry JHS 200/7-8
901 Elm St 73077 580-336-2265
Andrea Rains, prin. Fax 336-4211
Perry Lower ES, 1103 N 15th 73077 PK-2
Kenda Miller, prin. 580-336-4471
Perry Upper ES 700/3-6
1303 N 15th St 73077 580-336-2577
Joe Jacobs, prin. Fax 336-7310

Piedmont, Canadian, Pop. 5,527
Piedmont ISD 3,200/PK-12
713 Piedmont Rd N 73078 405-373-2311
James White, supt. Fax 373-0912
www.piedmontschools.org
Northwood ES 400/K-4
14100 Northwood Dr 73078 405-373-5151
Jennifer Warner, prin. Fax 373-5375
Piedmont ES 400/K-4
1011 Piedmont Rd N 73078 405-373-2353
Andrew Graham, prin. Fax 373-5002
Piedmont IS 500/5-6
977 Washington Ave E 73078 405-373-5155
Kayleen Wichert, prin.
Piedmont MS 500/7-8
823 2nd St NW 73078 405-373-1315
Clay McDonald, prin. Fax 373-5006
Piedmont PS 200/PK-PK
615 Edmond Rd NW 73078 405-373-4848
Jennifer Carver, prin. Fax 373-3688
Other Schools – See Yukon

Pittsburg, Pittsburg, Pop. 206
Pittsburg ISD 100/PK-12
PO Box 200 74560 918-432-5062
Chad Graham, supt. Fax 432-5312
www.pittsburg.k12.ok.us
Pittsburg ES, PO Box 200 74560 100/PK-8
Chad Graham, prin. 918-432-5513

Pocola, LeFlore, Pop. 3,869
Pocola ISD 800/PK-12
600 E Pryor Ave 74902 918-436-2424
Lawrence Barnes, supt. Fax 436-2437
www.pocola.k12.ok.us
Pocola ES 400/PK-5
1000 E Pryor Ave 74902 918-436-2561
James McInerney, prin. Fax 436-2488
Pocola MS 200/6-8
603 E Pryor Ave 74902 918-436-2091
Mark Mckenzie, prin. Fax 436-9880

Ponca City, Kay, Pop. 24,217
McCord SD 200/PK-6
977 S McCord Rd 74604 580-765-8806
Beverly Moore, supt. Fax 765-8552
www.mccord.k12.ok.us
McCord ES 200/PK-6
977 S McCord Rd 74604 580-765-8806
Beverly Moore, prin. Fax 765-8552

Ponca City ISD 5,300/PK-12
613 E Grand Ave 74601 580-767-8000
Dr. Shelley Arrott, supt. Fax 767-8007
www.pcps.us
East MS 400/8-8
612 E Grand Ave 74601 580-767-8010
John Long, prin. Fax 762-5301
Garfield ES 300/PK-5
600 S 8th St 74601 580-767-8030
Lori Cox, prin. Fax 767-9510
Liberty ES 400/PK-5
505 W Liberty Ave 74601 580-767-8040
Jennifer Martinez, prin. Fax 767-8041
Lincoln ES 600/PK-5
1501 W Grand Ave 74601 580-767-8050
Elisabeth Hargraves, prin. Fax 767-8051
Roosevelt ES 400/PK-5
815 E Highland Ave 74601 580-767-8060
Ronda Merrifield, prin. Fax 767-8062
Trout ES 400/PK-5
2109 E Prospect Ave 74604 580-767-8070
Carla Fry, prin. Fax 767-8073
Union ES 400/PK-5
2617 N Union St 74601 580-767-8035
Dr. Trina Resler, prin. Fax 767-8038
Washington Pre K Center PK-PK
1615 N 7th St 74601 580-767-8080
Barbara Davis, prin. Fax 767-8082
West MS 700/6-7
1401 W Grand Ave 74601 580-767-8020
Trenton Murner, prin. Fax 767-8094
Woodlands ES 400/PK-5
2005 E Woodland Rd 74604 580-767-8025
Tim Williams, prin. Fax 767-9525

First Lutheran S 200/PK-8
1104 N 4th St 74601 580-762-9950
Ponca City Christian Academy 100/PK-8
901 Monument Rd Bldg 3 74604 580-765-6038
Michelle Newport, admin. Fax 762-3835
St. Mary's S 100/PK-8
415 S 7th St 74601 580-765-4387
Marilyn Nash, prin. Fax 765-1352

Pond Creek, Grant, Pop. 839
Pond Creek-Hunter ISD 300/PK-12
200 E Broadway St 73766 580-532-4242
Joel Quinn, supt. Fax 532-4965
www.pondcreek-hunter.k12.ok.us
Pond Creek-Hunter ES 200/PK-4
200 E Broadway St 73766 580-532-4240
James Pearce, prin. Fax 532-4965
Pond Creek-Hunter MS 100/5-8
200 E Broadway St 73766 580-532-4262
Jamie Ronck, prin. Fax 532-4965

Porter, Wagoner, Pop. 534
Porter Consolidated ISD 600/PK-12
PO Box 120 74454 918-483-2401
Charles McMahan, supt. Fax 483-2310
www.porter.k12.ok.us
Porter Consolidated ES 400/PK-8
PO Box 120 74454 918-483-5231
Richard Cottle, prin. Fax 483-2310

Porum, Muskogee, Pop. 622
Porum ISD 500/PK-12
PO Box 189 74455 918-484-5121
Dr. Landon Berry, supt. Fax 484-2310
www.porum.k12.ok.us
Porum ES 400/PK-8
PO Box 189 74455 918-484-5123
Cora Fletcher, prin. Fax 484-2310

Poteau, LeFlore, Pop. 8,045
Poteau ISD 2,400/PK-12
100 Mockingbird Ln 74953 918-647-7700
Dr. Don Sjoberg, supt. Fax 647-9357
www.poteau.k12.ok.us
Kidd MS 500/6-8
100 Mockingbird Ln 74953 918-647-7741
Joe Ballard, prin. Fax 647-4286
Poteau PS 800/PK-2
100 Mockingbird Ln 74953 918-647-7780
Kristie Smith, prin. Fax 647-9143
Poteau Upper ES 500/3-5
100 Mockingbird Ln 74953 918-647-7760
Kelly Holton, prin. Fax 647-1029

Prague, Lincoln, Pop. 2,232
Prague ISD 1,000/K-12
3504 NBU 74864 405-567-4455
Vallery Feltman, supt. Fax 567-3095
www.prague.k12.ok.us
Prague ECC 200/K-1
3504 NBU 74864 405-567-2285
Chad Smith, prin. Fax 567-0239
Prague ES 300/2-5
3504 NBU 74864 405-567-2281
Chad Smith, prin. Fax 567-8199
Prague MS 200/6-8
3504 NBU 74864 405-567-2281
Benny Burnett, prin. Fax 567-3095

Preston, Okmulgee
Preston ISD 500/PK-12
PO Box 40 74456 918-756-3388
Mark Hudson, supt. Fax 756-2122
www.preston.k12.ok.us/
Preston ES 400/PK-8
PO Box 40 74456 918-756-8470
Cassie Holleman, prin. Fax 756-2122

Prue, Osage, Pop. 443
Prue ISD 300/PK-12
PO Box 130 74060 918-242-3351
Tom Scully, supt. Fax 242-3392
www.prue.k12.ok.us/
Prue ES 200/PK-8
PO Box 130 74060 918-242-3385
Craig Thurman, prin. Fax 242-3788

Pryor, Mayes, Pop. 8,842
Osage SD 200/PK-8
7960 W 490 74361 918-825-2550
Donald Pullen, supt. Fax 825-1433
www.osageelementary.com
Osage S 200/PK-8
7960 W 490 74361 918-825-2550
Donald Pullen, admin. Fax 825-1433

Pryor ISD 2,600/PK-12
PO Box 548 74362 918-825-1255
Don Raleigh, supt. Fax 825-3938
sites.google.com/a/pryorschools.org/pryorschools-org
Jefferson ES 300/K-6
PO Box 548 74362 918-825-1374
Linda Tincher, prin. Fax 825-3966
Lincoln ES 700/PK-6
PO Box 548 74362 918-825-0653
Karen Cook, prin. Fax 825-3922
Roosevelt ES 400/PK-6
PO Box 548 74362 918-825-3523
Brian Bradshaw, prin. Fax 825-3936

Bradford Christian S 50/K-12
2320 NE 1st St 74361 918-825-7038
Larry Stamper, admin. Fax 825-7037

Purcell, McClain, Pop. 5,558
Purcell ISD 1,500/PK-12
919 1/2 N 9th Ave 73080 405-527-2146
Dr. Jason Midkiff, supt. Fax 527-6366
www.purcellps.org
Purcell ES 500/PK-2
809 N 9th Ave 73080 405-527-2146
Tammy Dillard, prin. Fax 527-9676
Purcell IS 300/3-5
711 N 9th Ave 73080 405-527-2146
Tara White, prin. Fax 527-4454
Purcell JHS 300/6-8
201 Lester Ln 73080 405-527-6591
Jay Solomon, prin. Fax 527-6593

Quapaw, Ottawa, Pop. 859
Quapaw ISD 600/PK-12
305 W 1st St 74363 918-674-2501
Dr. Randy D. Darr Ed.D., supt. Fax 674-2721
www.qpswildcats.com
Quapaw ES 300/PK-5
305 W 1st St 74363 918-674-2236
James Dawson, prin. Fax 674-2688
Quapaw MS 100/6-8
305 W 1st St 74363 918-674-2496
Tamara Bacon, prin. Fax 674-2721

Quinton, Pittsburg, Pop. 953
Quinton ISD 500/PK-12
PO Box 670 74561 918-469-3100
Stacey Henderson, supt. Fax 469-3308
www.quintonschools.com
Quinton ES 400/PK-8
PO Box 670 74561 918-469-3313
Todd Wilson, prin. Fax 469-2710

Ralston, Pawnee, Pop. 314
Woodland SD
Supt. — See Fairfax
Woodland MS 100/5-8
6th & McKinley 74650 918-738-4286
Shelly Doshier, prin. Fax 738-4287

Ramona, Washington, Pop. 498
Caney Valley ISD 800/PK-12
PO Box 410 74061 918-536-2500
Rick Peters, supt. Fax 536-2600
www.caneyvalleyschool.org/
Caney Valley MS 200/6-8
PO Box 410 74061 918-536-2705
Travis Lashbrook, prin. Fax 536-7105
Other Schools – See Ochelata

Randlett, Cotton, Pop. 435
Big Pasture ISD 200/PK-12
PO Box 167 73562 580-281-3831
Danny McCuiston, supt. Fax 281-3299
www.bigpasture.org
Big Pasture ES 200/PK-8
PO Box 167 73562 580-281-3460
Danna Thompson, prin. Fax 281-3299

Rattan, Pushmataha, Pop. 299
Rattan ISD 500/PK-12
PO Box 44 74562 580-587-2546
Shari Pillow, supt. Fax 587-4000
www.rattan.k12.ok.us
Rattan ES 300/PK-6
PO Box 44 74562 580-587-2715
Dana House, prin. Fax 587-4001
Rattan JHS 100/7-8
PO Box 44 74562 580-587-2715
Neil Birchfield, prin. Fax 587-2476

Ravia, Johnston, Pop. 490
Ravia SD 100/K-8
PO Box 299 73455 580-371-9163
David Duncan, supt. Fax 371-3067
www.ravia.k12.ok.us
Ravia S 100/K-8
PO Box 299 73455 580-371-9163
David Duncan, supt. Fax 371-3067

Red Oak, Latimer, Pop. 508
Red Oak ISD 200/PK-12
PO Box 310 74563 918-754-2426
Bryan Deatherage, supt. Fax 754-2898
redoak.k12.ok.us
Red Oak S 200/PK-8
PO Box 310 74563 918-754-2426
Randy Brigance, prin. Fax 754-2898

Red Rock, Noble, Pop. 265
Frontier ISD 400/PK-12
PO Box 130 74651 580-723-4361
Robert Weckstein, supt. Fax 723-4516
www.frontierok.com
Frontier S 300/PK-8
PO Box 130 74651 580-723-4582
Jera Kiespert, prin. Fax 723-4516

Reydon, Roger Mills, Pop. 205
Reydon ISD 100/PK-12
PO Box 10 73660 580-655-4375
Phil Drouhard, supt. Fax 655-4622
www.reydon.k12.ok.us
Reydon ES, PO Box 10 73660 100/PK-8
Ryan Baker, prin. 580-655-4376

Ringling, Jefferson, Pop. 968
Ringling ISD 500/PK-12
PO Box 1010 73456 580-662-2385
Kent Southward, supt. Fax 662-2683
www.ringling.k12.ok.us
Ringling ES 300/PK-6
PO Box 1010 73456 580-662-2388
Barry Benson, prin. Fax 662-2683

Ringwood, Major, Pop. 490
Ringwood ISD 400/PK-12
101 W 5th St 73768 580-883-2201
Wade Detrick, supt. Fax 883-2220
www.ringwood.k12.ok.us
Ringwood ES 300/PK-8
101 W 5th St 73768 580-883-2203
Denise Bowers, prin. Fax 883-2220

Ripley, Payne, Pop. 385
Ripley ISD 500/PK-12
PO Box 97 74062 918-372-4567
Dr. Kenny Beams, supt. Fax 372-4608
www.ripley.k12.ok.us/
Ripley S 300/PK-8
PO Box 97 74062 918-372-4570
Lisa Pitts, prin. Fax 372-4608

Roff, Pontotoc, Pop. 687
Roff ISD 400/PK-12
PO Box 157 74865 580-456-7663
Scott Morgan, supt. Fax 456-7245
www.roff.k12.ok.us
Roff ES 300/PK-8
PO Box 157 74865 580-456-7251
Danny Baldridge, prin. Fax 456-7245

Roland, Sequoyah, Pop. 2,907
Roland ISD 1,200/PK-12
300 Ranger Blvd 74954 918-427-4601
Paul Wood, supt. Fax 427-1785
www.rolandschools.org
Roland Lower ES 400/PK-3
300 Ranger Blvd 74954 918-427-5993
Lori Wiggins, prin. Fax 427-3635
Roland Upper ES 200/4-6
300 Ranger Blvd 74954 918-427-5139
Angie Pena, prin. Fax 427-3635

Rose, Mayes, Pop. 255
Leach SD 200/PK-8
55979 S 530 Rd 74364 918-868-2277
Regiena Henderson, supt. Fax 868-3501
www.leachschool.net
Leach S 200/PK-8
55979 S 530 Rd 74364 918-868-2277
Andrea Shreve, admin. Fax 868-3501

Rush Springs, Grady, Pop. 1,191
Rush Springs ISD 600/PK-12
PO Box 308 73082 580-476-3929
Robbie Burch, supt. Fax 476-2018
www.rushsprings.k12.ok.us
Rush Springs ES 300/PK-5
PO Box 308 73082 580-476-3172
Mickey Seifried, prin. Fax 476-3777
Rush Springs MS 100/6-8
PO Box 308 73082 580-476-3447
Renessa Cramer, prin. Fax 476-2148

Ryan, Jefferson, Pop. 785
Ryan ISD 300/PK-12
1201 Washington St 73565 580-757-2308
Marcus Chapman, supt. Fax 757-2609
www.ryan.k12.ok.us
Ryan ES, 1201 Washington St 73565 200/PK-8
Myra Hamm, prin. 580-757-2296

Salina, Mayes, Pop. 1,257
Kenwood SD 100/K-8
48625 S 502 Rd 74365 918-434-5799
Billy Taylor, supt. Fax 434-6552
Kenwood S 100/K-8
48625 S 502 Rd 74365 918-434-5799
Billy Taylor, prin. Fax 434-6552

Salina ISD 800/PK-12
PO Box 98 74365 918-434-5091
Tony Thomas, supt. Fax 434-5346
www.salina.k12.ok.us
Salina ES 400/PK-5
PO Box 98 74365 918-434-5300
Honesti Williams, prin. Fax 434-6051
Salina MS 200/6-8
PO Box 98 74365 918-434-5311
Debbie Cox, prin. Fax 434-5173

Wickliffe SD 100/PK-8
11176 E 470 74365 918-434-5559
Teresia Knott, supt. Fax 434-3592
wickliffeschool.com
Wickliffe S 100/PK-8
11176 E 470 74365 918-434-5559
Teresia Knott, supt. Fax 434-5515

Sallisaw, Sequoyah, Pop. 7,974

Brushy SD 400/PK-8
100968 S 4650 Rd 74955 918-775-4458
Greg Reynolds, supt. Fax 775-3638
www.brushy.k12.ok.us
Brushy S 400/PK-8
100968 S 4650 Rd 74955 918-775-4458
Greg Reynolds, admin. Fax 775-3638

Central ISD 500/PK-12
108089 S 4670 Rd 74955 918-775-5525
Larry Henson, supt. Fax 775-8557
www.centralps.k12.ok.us
Central S 300/PK-8
108089 S 4670 Rd 74955 918-775-5525
Beverly Cawhorn, prin. Fax 775-5349

Sallisaw ISD 2,000/PK-12
701 S J T Stites St 74955 918-775-5544
Scott Farmer, supt. Fax 775-1257
sallisawps.org
Eastside ES 400/3-5
1206 E Creek Ave 74955 918-775-9491
Chad Jasna, prin. Fax 775-1277
Liberty ES 600/PK-2
136 S Dogwood St 74955 918-775-4741
Toni Jasna, prin. Fax 775-1278
Sallisaw MS 400/6-8
2101 W Ruth Ave 74955 918-775-6561
Greg Cast, prin. Fax 775-1276

Sand Springs, Tulsa, Pop. 17,953

Anderson SD 300/PK-6
2195 Anderson Rd 74063 918-245-0289
Kevin Younger, supt. Fax 245-3281
www.andersontrojans.org
Anderson ES 300/PK-6
2195 Anderson Rd 74063 918-245-0289
Kevin Younger, admin. Fax 245-3281

Keystone SD 300/PK-8
23810 W Highway 51 74063 918-363-8711
Rhett Bynum, supt. Fax 363-8194
www.keystonerangers.org
Keystone S 300/PK-8
23810 W Highway 51 74063 918-363-8298
Rhett Bynum, admin. Fax 363-8194

Sand Springs ISD 5,300/PK-12
11 W Broadway St 74063 918-246-1400
Sherry Durkee, supt. Fax 246-1401
www.sandites.org/
Angus Valley ES 400/K-5
412 W 55th St 74063 918-246-1520
Angelia Noel, prin. Fax 246-1522
Boyd MS 1,200/6-8
305 W 35th St 74063 918-246-1535
Nancy Ogle, prin. Fax 246-1544
Early Childhood Education Center 200/PK-PK
1701 Park Rd 74063 918-246-1570
Renee Plant, prin. Fax 246-1573
Garfield ES 400/3-5
701 N Roosevelt Ave 74063 918-246-1462
Russell Ragland, prin. Fax 246-1465
Limestone ES 200/K-5
4201 S Walnut Creek Dr 74063 918-246-1560
Karen Biggs, prin. Fax 246-1559
Northwoods Fine Arts Academy 500/K-2
1691 E Old North Rd 74063 918-246-1455
Laura Hamilton, prin. Fax 246-1458
Pratt ES 500/K-5
301 W 34th St 74063 918-246-1550
Danese Tanner, prin. Fax 246-1552

Sapulpa, Creek, Pop. 19,322

Lone Star SD 900/PK-8
2945 S Hickory St 74066 918-224-0201
Tracie Hale, supt. Fax 224-3927
lss-k12-ct.schoolloop.com
Lone Star ES 900/PK-8
2945 S Hickory St 74066 918-224-0201
Tracie Hale, admin. Fax 224-3927

Pretty Water SD 300/PK-8
15223 W 81st St S 74066 918-224-4952
Jeff Taylor, supt. Fax 224-4039
www.prettywater.k12.ok.us
Pretty Water S 300/PK-8
15223 W 81st St S 74066 918-224-4952
Jeff Taylor, prin. Fax 224-4039

Sapulpa ISD 4,000/PK-12
511 E Lee Ave 74066 918-224-3400
Robert Armstrong, supt. Fax 227-8347
www.sapulpaps.org
Freedom ES 500/PK-5
9170 Freedom Ave 74066 918-227-7838
Alison Owens, prin. Fax 227-7839
Holmes Park ES 700/PK-5
1231 E Dewey Ave 74066 918-227-6800
Roger Johnson, prin. Fax 227-4204
Jefferson Heights ES 400/PK-5
1521 S Wickham Rd 74066 918-224-2028
Bridget Hailey, prin. Fax 224-0129
Liberty ES 300/PK-5
631 N Brown St 74066 918-224-1492
Tom Walsh, prin. Fax 224-0134
Sapulpa MS 500/6-7
1304 E Cleveland Ave 74066 918-224-8441
Stephanie Kiesau, prin. Fax 224-0184

Eagle Point Christian Academy 100/PK-12
602 S Mounds St 74066 918-227-2441
Jim Pryor, admin. Fax 248-3117

Sasakwa, Seminole, Pop. 141

Sasakwa ISD 200/PK-12
PO Box 323 74867 405-941-3250
Kyle Wilson, supt. Fax 941-3561
www.sasakwaschools.org
Sasakwa ES 100/PK-8
PO Box 323 74867 405-941-3250
Brent Griffin, prin. Fax 941-3561

Savanna, Pittsburg, Pop. 629

Savanna ISD 400/PK-12
PO Box 266 74565 918-548-3777
Gary Reeder, supt. Fax 548-3836
www.savanna.k12.ok.us/
Savanna ES 200/PK-8
PO Box 266 74565 918-548-3777
Brad Kellogg, prin. Fax 548-3914

Sayre, Beckham, Pop. 4,304

Sayre ISD 800/PK-12
716 NE Highway 66 73662 580-928-5531
Danny Crabb, supt. Fax 928-5538
www.sayre.k12.ok.us
Sayre ES 400/PK-5
716 NE Highway 66 73662 580-928-2013
Cody Huckaby, prin. Fax 928-3936
Sayre MS 200/6-8
716 NE Highway 66 73662 580-928-5578
Danny Clifton, prin. Fax 928-3045

Schulter, Okmulgee, Pop. 449

Schulter ISD 200/PK-12
PO Box 203 74460 918-652-8219
Allen Callahan, supt. Fax 652-8474
www.schulter.k12.ok.us/
Schulter ES 100/PK-8
PO Box 203 74460 918-652-8200
Jay Fox, prin. Fax 652-8474

Seiling, Dewey, Pop. 824

Seiling ISD 300/PK-12
PO Box 780 73663 580-922-7383
Randy Seifried, supt. Fax 922-8019
www.seiling.k12.ok.us
Seiling ES 200/PK-6
PO Box 780 73663 580-922-7381
Brandon Nyberg, prin. Fax 922-8019

Seminole, Seminole, Pop. 6,934

Seminole ISD 1,500/PK-12
PO Box 1031 74818 405-382-5085
Alfred Gaches, supt. Fax 382-8281
www.sps.k12.ok.us/
Northwood ES 400/4-6
PO Box 1031 74818 405-382-5800
David Carter, prin. Fax 382-8658
Seminole MS 300/7-8
PO Box 1031 74818 405-382-5065
David Dean, prin. Fax 382-8653
Smith ECC PK-K
PO Box 1031 74818 405-382-5962
Angela Willmett, prin. Fax 382-5995
Wilson ES 400/1-3
PO Box 1031 74818 405-382-1431
Denese Cheatwood, prin. Fax 382-8657

Strother ISD 400/PK-12
36085 EW 1140 74868 405-382-4014
Kolby Johnson, supt. Fax 382-3339
www.strother.k12.ok.us
Strother ES 300/PK-8
36085 EW 1140 74868 405-382-4014
Mechelle Johnson, prin. Fax 382-3339

Varnum ISD 300/PK-12
11929 NS 3550 74868 405-382-1448
David Brewer, supt. Fax 382-8618
www.varnum.k12.ok.us
Varnum ES, 11929 NS 3550 74868 200/PK-8
Brenda Shockley, prin. 405-382-0812

Sentinel, Washita, Pop. 867

Sentinel ISD 300/PK-12
PO Box 640 73664 580-393-2101
Jason Goostree, supt. Fax 393-4334
www.sentinel.k12.ok.us/
McMurray ES 300/PK-8
PO Box 640 73664 580-393-4997
Paula Combs, prin. Fax 393-4334

Shady Point, LeFlore, Pop. 975

Shady Point SD 100/PK-8
22838 Wheelus St 74956 918-963-2595
Bruce Gillham, supt. Fax 963-2605
www.spk12.org
Shady Point S 100/PK-8
22838 Wheelus St 74956 918-963-2595
Bruce Gillham, prin. Fax 963-2605

Sharon, Woodward, Pop. 135

Sharon-Mutual ISD
Supt. — See Mutual
Sharon-Mutual ES 200/PK-8
201 S 3rd St 73857 580-866-3333
Terry Mulbery, prin. Fax 866-3332

Shattuck, Ellis, Pop. 1,338

Shattuck ISD 400/PK-12
PO Box 159 73858 580-938-2586
Tyson Bullard, supt. Fax 938-8019
www.shattuck.k12.ok.us/
Shattuck ES 300/PK-8
PO Box 159 73858 580-938-2222
Camille Holt, prin. Fax 938-8019

Shawnee, Pottawatomie, Pop. 28,106

Bethel ISD 1,300/PK-12
36000 Clearpond Rd 74801 405-273-0385
Tod Harrison M.Ed., supt. Fax 273-5056
bethel.k12.ok.us
Bethel Lower ES 300/PK-2
36000 Clearpond Rd 74801 405-273-7632
Jenny Affentranger M.Ed., prin. Fax 878-5571
Bethel MS 300/6-8
36000 Clearpond Rd 74801 405-273-5944
Tina Moon M.Ed., prin. Fax 273-6025
Bethel Upper ES 300/3-5
36000 Clearpond Rd 74801 405-273-7632
Tammy Cook M.Ed., prin. Fax 878-5574

Grove ESD 400/PK-8
2800 N Bryan Ave 74804 405-275-7435
Mark Bowlan, supt. Fax 273-2541
www.grove.k12.ok.us
Grove S 400/PK-8
2800 N Bryan Ave 74804 405-275-7435
Dr. Rusty Carmichael, prin. Fax 273-2541

North Rock Creek SD 600/PK-8
42400 Garretts Lake Rd 74804 405-275-3473
Blake Moody, supt. Fax 273-7368
www.nrc.k12.ok.us/
North Rock Creek S 600/PK-8
42400 Garretts Lake Rd 74804 405-275-3473
Denise Sims, prin. Fax 273-7368

Pleasant Grove SD 300/PK-8
1927 E Walnut St 74801 405-275-6092
Scott Roper, supt. Fax 275-6094
www.pgs.k12.ok.us
Pleasant Grove S 300/PK-8
1927 E Walnut St 74801 405-275-6092
Scott Roper, prin. Fax 275-6094

Shawnee ISD 4,100/PK-12
326 N Union Ave 74801 405-273-0653
Dr. April Grace Ed.D., supt. Fax 273-6818
www.shawnee.k12.ok.us
Jefferson ES 400/1-5
800 N Louisa Ave 74801 405-273-1846
Vickie Penson, prin. Fax 878-1048
Mann ES 300/1-5
412 N Draper Ave 74801 405-273-1806
Susan Field, prin. Fax 273-1946
Rogers ES 400/1-5
2600 N Union Ave 74804 405-273-1519
Jackie Noble, prin. Fax 878-1041
Sequoyah ES 400/1-5
1401 E Independence St 74804 405-273-1878
Terri Lemos, prin. Fax 273-1048
Shawnee ECC 600/PK-K
1831 Airport Dr 74804 405-273-3388
Ann Worden, prin. Fax 273-3389
Shawnee MS 800/6-8
4300 N Union Ave 74804 405-273-0403
Joey Slate, prin. Fax 275-9651

South Rock Creek SD 400/PK-8
17800 S Rock Creek Rd 74801 405-273-6072
Michael Crawford, supt. Fax 273-8926
www.src.k12.ok.us/
South Rock Creek S 400/PK-8
17800 S Rock Creek Rd 74801 405-273-6072
Ryan Rosser, prin. Fax 273-8926

Family of Faith Christian S 100/K-12
PO Box 1442 74802 405-273-5331
Kathy Matthews, admin. Fax 273-8535
Liberty Academy 300/PK-12
PO Box 1176 74802 405-273-3022
Susan Harmon, supt. Fax 273-3029

Shidler, Osage, Pop. 394

Shidler ISD 300/PK-12
PO Box 85 74652 918-793-2021
Ben West, supt. Fax 793-2061
www.shidlerpublicschools.org
Ward ES 100/PK-4
PO Box 85 74652 918-793-2051
Tonya Lemon, prin. Fax 793-2063
Other Schools – See Kaw City

Skiatook, Tulsa, Pop. 6,871

Skiatook ISD 2,300/PK-12
355 S Osage St 74070 918-396-1792
Rick Thomas, supt. Fax 396-1799
www.skiatookschools.org
Marrs ES 500/PK-1
355 S Osage St 74070 918-396-2295
Steve Mason, prin. Fax 396-1799
Newman MS 600/6-8
355 S Osage St 74070 918-396-2307
Steve Cantrell Ph.D., prin. Fax 396-1799
Skiatook ES 2-2
355 S Osage St 74070 918-396-5737
Tim Buck, prin. Fax 396-1799
Skiatook IS 500/3-5
355 S Osage St 74070 918-396-5745
Tim Buck, prin. Fax 396-1799

Hope Christian Academy 100/PK-12
612 S Broadway St 74070 918-396-4000
Sabrina Miller, prin. Fax 396-4009

Smithville, McCurtain, Pop. 106

Smithville ISD 300/PK-12
PO Box 8 74957 580-244-3333
Delbert McBroom, supt. Fax 244-3101
www.smithville.k12.ok.us
Smithville ES 100/PK-5
PO Box 8 74957 580-244-7212
Stacy Nichols, prin. Fax 244-3651

Smithville MS 100/6-8
PO Box 8 74957 580-244-7212
Stacy Nichols, prin. Fax 244-3651

Snyder, Kiowa, Pop. 1,354
Snyder ISD 400/PK-12
PO Box 368 73566 580-569-2773
Travis Gates, supt. Fax 569-4205
www.snyder.k12.ok.us
Snyder ES 200/PK-3
PO Box 368 73566 580-569-2010
Tamra Phelan, prin. Fax 569-2520
Snyder MS 200/4-8
PO Box 368 73566 580-569-2691
Tamra Phelan, prin. Fax 569-4657

Soper, Choctaw, Pop. 237
Soper ISD 400/PK-12
PO Box 149 74759 580-345-2757
Dr. Scotty Van Worth Ed.D., supt. Fax 345-2222
soperisd.com
Soper ES 300/PK-8
PO Box 149 74759 580-345-2211
Tina Jeffreys M.A., prin. Fax 345-2896

South Coffeyville, Nowata, Pop. 715
Oklahoma Union ISD 700/PK-12
RR 1 Box 377-7 74072 918-255-6550
Kevin Stacy, supt. Fax 255-6817
www.okunion.k12.ok.us/
Oklahoma Union ES 300/PK-5
RR 1 Box 377-7 74072 918-255-6550
Brenda Taylor, prin. Fax 255-6817
Oklahoma Union MS 200/6-8
RR 1 Box 377-7 74072 918-255-6550
David Lovelace, prin. Fax 255-6817

South Coffeyville ISD 300/PK-12
PO Box 190 74072 918-255-6202
Clemo Haddox, supt. Fax 255-6230
www.scps.k12.ok.us
South Coffeyville ES 200/PK-8
PO Box 190 74072 918-255-6087
Steve Johns, prin. Fax 255-6115

Spencer, Oklahoma, Pop. 3,660
Oklahoma City ISD
Supt. — See Oklahoma City
Green Pastures ES 200/PK-5
4300 N Post Rd 73084 405-587-4500
Harry Bryant, prin. Fax 587-4505
Rogers MS, 4000 Spencer Rd 73084 300/6-8
Jahree Herzer, prin. 405-587-4100
Spencer ES 300/PK-5
8900 NE 50th St 73084 405-587-8600
Dr. Sandy Jackson, prin. Fax 587-8605

Sperry, Tulsa, Pop. 1,118
Sperry ISD 1,200/PK-12
400 W Main St 74073 918-288-6258
Brian Beagles Ed.D., supt. Fax 288-7067
www.sperry.k12.ok.us
Sperry ES 600/PK-5
400 W Main St 74073 918-288-7213
Richard Akin, prin. Fax 288-7234
Sperry MS 300/6-8
400 W Main St 74073 918-288-7213
Mike Juby, prin. Fax 288-7231

Cornerstone Christian Academy 100/K-12
7770 Whirlpool Dr 74073 918-274-3918
Karen Linton, prin.

Spiro, LeFlore, Pop. 2,077
Spiro ISD 1,100/K-12
600 W Broadway St 74959 918-962-2463
Richard Haynes, supt. Fax 962-2757
www.spiro.k12.ok.us
Spiro ES, 600 W Broadway St 74959 300/K-2
Karen Tobler, prin. 918-962-2413
Spiro MS, 600 W Broadway St 74959 300/6-8
Rickey McGee, prin. 918-962-2488
Spiro Upper ES 300/3-5
600 W Broadway St 74959 918-962-2414
Kyle House, prin.

Springer, Carter, Pop. 636
Springer ISD 200/PK-12
16624 US Highway 77 73458 580-653-2656
Cynthia Hunter, supt. Fax 653-2666
www.springerschools.com
Springer S 200/PK-8
16624 US Highway 77 73458 580-653-2471
Jason Wright, prin.

Sterling, Comanche, Pop. 758
Sterling ISD 400/PK-12
PO Box 158 73567 580-365-4307
Kent Lemons, supt. Fax 365-4705
www.sterling.k12.ok.us/
Sterling ES 300/PK-8
PO Box 158 73567 580-365-4166
Sandy Fehring, prin. Fax 365-4705

Stigler, Haskell, Pop. 2,525
Stigler ISD 1,400/PK-12
309 NW E St 74462 918-967-2805
Monty Guthrie, supt. Fax 967-4550
www.stiglerps.com
Stigler ES 600/PK-4
309 NW E St 74462 918-967-8835
Lana Mayhall, prin. Fax 967-5124
Stigler MS 400/5-8
309 NW E St 74462 918-967-2521
Tony Gilmore, prin. Fax 967-5125

Stillwater, Payne, Pop. 43,498
Stillwater ISD 6,100/PK-12
314 S Lewis St 74074 405-533-6300
Dr. Marc Moore, supt. Fax 743-6311
www.stillwaterschools.com
Highland Park ES 600/PK-5
400 S Drury St 74074 405-533-6350
Laura Gordon, prin. Fax 743-6354
Richmond ES 500/PK-5
201 W Richmond Rd 74075 405-533-6400
Kendra Rider, prin. Fax 743-6334
Rogers ES 500/PK-5
1211 N Washington St 74075 405-533-6380
Dr. Susan Popplewell, prin. Fax 743-6329
Sangre Ridge ES 600/PK-5
2500 S Sangre Rd 74074 405-533-6360
Ryan Blake, admin. Fax 743-6337
Skyline ES 500/PK-5
1402 E Sunrise Dr 74075 405-533-6390
Fax 743-6388
Stillwater MS 800/6-7
2200 S Sangre Rd 74074 405-533-6430
Bo Gamble, prin. Fax 743-6324
Westwood ES 600/PK-5
502 S Kings St 74074 405-533-6370
Darren Nelson, prin. Fax 743-6328

Stillwater Christian S 100/PK-8
421 E Richmond Rd 74075 405-377-3748
Anita Hauf, head sch Fax 372-2505

Stilwell, Adair, Pop. 3,604
Belfonte SD
Supt. — See Muldrow
Bell ES 100/PK-8
RR 5 Box 4470 74960 918-696-7181
Tony Davidson, prin. Fax 696-2353

Dahlonegah SD 100/PK-8
RR 1 Box 1795 74960 918-696-7807
Jeff Limore, supt. Fax 696-2192
www.dahlonegah.k12.ok.us/
Dahlonegah S 100/PK-8
RR 1 Box 1795 74960 918-696-7807
Jeff Limore, prin. Fax 696-2192

Maryetta SD 700/PK-8
RR 6 Box 2840 74960 918-696-2285
Lori Means, supt. Fax 696-6746
www.maryetta.k12.ok.us
Maryetta S 700/PK-8
RR 6 Box 2840 74960 918-696-2285
Corey Bunch, prin. Fax 696-6746

Peavine SD 100/PK-8
PO Box 389 74960 918-696-7818
Michael Hargis, supt. Fax 696-2199
www.peavinepanthers.net
Peavine S 100/PK-8
PO Box 389 74960 918-696-7818
Michael Hargis, admin. Fax 696-2199

Rocky Mountain SD 200/PK-8
RR 1 Box 665 74960 918-696-7509
Alicia Ketcher, supt. Fax 696-3654
www.rockymtn.k12.ok.us/
Rocky Mountain S 200/PK-8
RR 1 Box 665 74960 918-696-7509
Alicia Ketcher, supt. Fax 696-3654

Stilwell ISD 1,400/PK-12
1801 W Locust St 74960 918-696-7001
Geri Gilstrap, supt. Fax 696-2193
www.stilwellk12.org
Stilwell ES 500/PK-4
10 S 6th St 74960 918-696-7656
Mark Lea, prin. Fax 696-6040
Stilwell MS 300/5-8
12 N 7th St 74960 918-696-2685
Dale Girdner, prin. Fax 696-7761

Zion SD 300/PK-8
PO Box 347 74960 918-696-7866
Charles Benham, supt. Fax 696-6226
www.zionjets.com
Zion S 300/PK-8
PO Box 347 74960 918-696-7866
Joey O'Neal, prin. Fax 696-6226

Stonewall, Pontotoc, Pop. 416
Stonewall ISD 400/PK-12
600 Highschool 74871 580-265-4241
Kevin Flowers, supt. Fax 265-4536
www.stonewall.k12.ok.us
McLish MS 100/5-8
600 Highschool 74871 580-232-1020
Greg Lovelis, prin. Fax 777-2222
Stonewall ES, 600 Highschool 74871 200/PK-4
Larry Rayburn, prin. 580-265-4243

Stratford, Garvin, Pop. 1,461
Stratford ISD 700/PK-12
PO Box 589 74872 580-759-3615
Michael Blackburn, supt. Fax 759-2669
www.stratford.k12.ok.us
Stratford ES 300/PK-5
PO Box 589 74872 580-759-2382
Anglea Martin, prin. Fax 759-8914
Stratford MS 200/6-8
PO Box 589 74872 580-759-3615
Tracy Felan, prin. Fax 759-2513

Stringtown, Atoka, Pop. 364
Stringtown ISD 200/PK-12
PO Box 130 74569 580-346-7423
Tony Potts, supt. Fax 346-7726
www.stringtown.k12.ok.us/
Stringtown ES 100/PK-8
PO Box 130 74569 580-346-7621
Ricky Heard, prin. Fax 346-7726

Stroud, Lincoln, Pop. 2,575
Stroud ISD 800/PK-12
212 W 7th St 74079 918-968-2541
Joe Van Tuyl, supt. Fax 968-2582
www.stroud.k12.ok.us
Parkview ES 400/PK-5
212 W 7th St 74079 918-968-4711
Brenda Gooch, prin. Fax 968-2622
Stroud MS 200/6-8
212 W 7th St 74079 918-968-2200
Bob Hoover, prin. Fax 968-2391

Stuart, Hughes, Pop. 165
Stuart ISD 300/PK-12
8837 4th St 74570 918-546-2476
Tracy Blasengame, supt. Fax 546-2329
www.stuart.k12.ok.us
Stuart ES 200/PK-8
8837 4th St 74570 918-546-2627
Adam Newman, prin. Fax 546-2329

Sulphur, Murray, Pop. 4,613
Sulphur ISD 1,500/PK-12
1021 W 9th St 73086 580-622-2061
Gary Jones, supt. Fax 622-6789
www.sis.sulphurk12.org
Sulphur ES 500/PK-2
1021 W 9th St 73086 580-622-3326
Shannon Muck, prin. Fax 622-2722
Sulphur IS 300/3-5
1021 W 9th St 73086 580-622-6161
John Mann, prin. Fax 622-4373
Sulphur JHS 300/6-8
1021 W 9th St 73086 580-622-4010
Steven Pyle, prin. Fax 622-3900

Veritas Christian S 50/K-10
3320 Charles F Cooper Mem 73086 580-622-9097
Donna Abla, head sch

Sweetwater, Roger Mills, Pop. 86
Sweetwater ISD 100/PK-12
11107 N Highway 30 73666 580-534-2272
Casey Reed, supt. Fax 534-2273
www.sweetwater.k12.ok.us/
Sweetwater ES 100/PK-8
11107 N Highway 30 73666 580-534-2272
Brenda Quinn, prin. Fax 534-2273

Swink, Choctaw, Pop. 62
Swink SD 200/PK-8
PO Box 73 74761 580-873-2695
Mark Bush, supt. Fax 873-9493
www.swink.k12.ok.us
Swink S 200/PK-8
PO Box 73 74761 580-873-2695
Mark Bush, prin. Fax 873-9493

Tahlequah, Cherokee, Pop. 14,483
Briggs SD 500/PK-8
17210 S 569 Rd 74464 918-456-4221
Stephen Haynes, supt. Fax 456-3228
www.briggs.k12.ok.us
Briggs S 500/PK-8
17210 S 569 Rd 74464 918-456-4221
George Ritzhaupt, prin. Fax 456-3228

Grand View SD 600/PK-8
15481 N Jarvis Rd 74464 918-456-5131
Ed Kennedy, supt. Fax 456-1526
www.grandviewchargers.org
Grand View S 600/PK-8
15481 N Jarvis Rd 74464 918-456-5131
Steve Gillman, prin. Fax 456-1526

Lowrey SD 200/PK-8
21132 E 640 Rd 74464 918-456-4053
Cris Wyse, supt. Fax 458-0647
www.lowrey.k12.ok.us
Lowrey S 200/PK-8
21132 E 640 Rd 74464 918-456-4053
Cris Wyse, prin. Fax 458-0647

Tahlequah SD 3,300/PK-12
PO Box 517 74465 918-458-4100
Lisa Presley, supt. Fax 458-4103
www.tahlequahschools.org
Cherokee ES 400/K-5
800 Goingsnake St 74464 918-458-4110
Marissa McCoy, prin. Fax 458-4112
Greenwood ES 500/K-5
400 E Ross St 74464 918-458-4120
Nikki Molloy, prin. Fax 458-4122
Heritage ES 400/K-5
333 Southridge Rd 74464 918-458-4180
Lacie Davenport, prin. Fax 458-4182
Sequoyah Preschool 200/PK-PK
425 S College Ave 74464 918-458-4130
Kristin Stark, prin. Fax 458-4132
Tahlequah MS 600/6-8
871 Pendleton St 74464 918-458-4140
David Bookout, prin. Fax 458-4142

Woodall SD 500/PK-8
14090 W 835 Rd 74464 918-458-5444
Linda Clinkenbeard, supt. Fax 456-5015
www.woodall.k12.ok.us
Woodall S 500/PK-8
14090 W 835 Rd 74464 918-458-5444
Ginger Knight, prin. Fax 456-5015

Shiloh Christian S 50/K-8
1282 Amity Ln 74464 918-458-5041
Hannah Foreman, prin. Fax 458-5047

Talihina, Latimer, Pop. 1,013
Buffalo Valley ISD 200/PK-12
4384 SE Highway 63 74571 918-522-4426
Justin Kennedy, supt. Fax 522-4287
www.buffalovalley.k12.ok.us
Buffalo Valley ES 100/PK-8
4384 SE Highway 63 74571 918-522-4426
Anna Pate, prin. Fax 522-4287

Talihina ISD 600/PK-12
PO Box 38 74571 918-567-2259
Jason Lockhart, supt. Fax 567-3507
www.talihina.k12.ok.us/
Talihina ES 400/PK-6
PO Box 38 74571 918-567-2138
Kathey Anderson, prin. Fax 567-3507
Talihina JHS 100/7-8
PO Box 38 74571 918-567-2266
Kelly Gravitt, prin. Fax 567-3507

Taloga, Dewey, Pop. 290
Taloga ISD 100/PK-12
PO Box 158 73667 580-328-5577
Darci Brown, supt. Fax 328-5237
www.taloga.k12.ok.us
Taloga ES 100/PK-8
PO Box 158 73667 580-328-5586
Lora Burch, prin. Fax 328-5237

Tecumseh, Pottawatomie, Pop. 6,036
Tecumseh ISD 2,200/PK-12
1301 E Highland St 74873 405-598-3739
Tom Wilsie, supt. Fax 598-2861
www.tecumseh.k12.ok.us
Barnard ES 300/1-2
315 E Locust St 74873 405-598-3169
Cindy Horn, prin. Fax 598-5520
Cross Timbers ES 500/3-5
1111 W Highland St 74873 405-598-3771
Brandi Burks, prin. Fax 598-8717
Krouch ECC 300/PK-K
723 W Park St 74873 405-598-2967
Tammy Giaudrone, prin. Fax 598-1633
Tecumseh MS 500/6-8
315 W Park St 74873 405-598-3744
Robert Kinsey, prin. Fax 598-1948

Temple, Cotton, Pop. 952
Temple ISD 200/PK-12
PO Box 400 73568 580-342-6230
Justin Smith, supt. Fax 342-6230
www.temple.k12.ok.us/
Temple ES 100/PK-8
PO Box 400 73568 580-342-6230
Justin Smith, admin. Fax 342-6230

Terral, Jefferson, Pop. 377
Terral SD 100/PK-8
PO Box 340 73569 580-437-2244
Greg Fouse, supt. Fax 437-2246
Terral S 100/PK-8
PO Box 340 73569 580-437-2244
Greg Fouse M.Ed., supt. Fax 437-2246

Texhoma, Texas, Pop. 917
Texhoma ISD 200/5-12
PO Box 648 73949 580-423-7371
Tom Schroeder, supt. Fax 423-7096
www.texhoma61.net
Texhoma ES 100/5-8
PO Box 648 73949 580-423-7371
Connie Miller, prin. Fax 423-7141

Thackerville, Love, Pop. 429
Thackerville ISD 300/PK-12
PO Box 377 73459 580-276-2630
Russell Noland, supt. Fax 276-2638
www.thackervilleschools.org
Thackerville ES 200/PK-5
PO Box 377 73459 580-276-9655
Heather Holland, prin. Fax 276-8315
Thackerville MS, PO Box 377 73459 6-8
Carrie Tucker, prin. 580-276-3610

Thomas, Custer, Pop. 1,152
Thomas-Fay-Custer Unified ISD 500/PK-12
PO Box 190 73669 580-661-3522
Rob Royalty, supt. Fax 661-3589
thomas.k12.ok.us/
Thomas-Fay-Custer ES 300/PK-6
PO Box 190 73669 580-661-3521
Leesa Brandly, prin. Fax 661-3589

Tipton, Tillman, Pop. 830
Tipton ISD 200/K-12
PO Box 340 73570 580-667-5268
Steve Glenn, supt. Fax 667-5267
www.tiptontigers.net
Tipton ES 200/K-8
PO Box 340 73570 580-667-5268
Amy Ferris, prin. Fax 667-5481

Tishomingo, Johnston, Pop. 2,754
Tishomingo ISD 1,000/PK-12
1300 E Main St 73460 580-371-9190
Kevin Duncan, supt. Fax 371-3765
www.tishomingo.k12.ok.us/
Tishomingo ES, 1300 E Main St 73460 400/PK-4
Melissa Ferguson, prin. 580-371-2548
Tishomingo MS, 1300 E Main St 73460 200/5-8
Charles Hook, prin. 580-371-3602

Tonkawa, Kay, Pop. 3,131
Tonkawa ISD 600/PK-12
500 E North Ave 74653 580-628-3597
Lori Simpson, supt. Fax 628-5132
www.tonkawa.k12.ok.us/
Tonkawa ES 400/PK-5
501 N Public St 74653 580-628-2592
Kelly Martin, prin. Fax 628-2594

Tulsa, Tulsa, Pop. 371,916
Allen-Bowden SD 400/PK-8
7049 Frankoma Rd 74131 918-224-4440
Kelly Husted, supt. Fax 224-0617
www.allenbowden.k12.ok.us
Allen-Bowden S 400/PK-8
7049 Frankoma Rd 74131 918-224-4440
Amy Karnes, prin. Fax 224-0617

Berryhill ISD 1,300/PK-12
3128 S 63rd West Ave 74107 918-446-1966
Mike Campbell, supt. Fax 446-6370
www.berryhillschools.org/
Berryhill MS 200/7-8
3128 S 63rd West Ave 74107 918-445-6039
Ronna Taylor, prin. Fax 445-6018
Berryhill North ES 200/4-6
3128 S 63rd West Ave 74107 918-445-6034
Julie Belk, prin. Fax 446-0500
Berryhill South ES 400/PK-3
3128 S 63rd West Ave 74107 918-445-6041
Kye Payne, prin. Fax 445-6021

Jenks ISD
Supt. — See Jenks
East ES 1,900/PK-4
8925 S Harvard Ave 74137 918-299-4411
Ryan Glaze, prin. Fax 298-6628
East IS 900/5-6
3933 E 91st St 74137 918-299-4411
Linda Reid, prin. Fax 298-6610
Jenks MS 1,600/7-8
3019 E 101st St 74137 918-299-4411
Dr. Nick Brown, prin. Fax 298-0652
Northwest ES 1,000/PK-4
7625 S Elwood Ave 74132 918-299-4415
Lynette Talkington, prin.
Southeast ES 900/PK-4
10222 S Yale Ave 74137 918-299-4411
Lindy Risenhoover, prin. Fax 298-6625

Tulsa ISD 35,600/PK-12
PO Box 470208 74147 918-746-6800
Dr. Deborah Gist, supt. Fax 746-6850
www.tulsaschools.org
Academy Central ES 300/PK-5
1789 W Seminole St 74127 918-833-8760
Elizabeth Taylor, prin. Fax 833-8775
Anderson ES, 1921 E 29th St N 74110 300/PK-5
Tracy Thompson, prin. 918-925-1300
Bell ES 500/PK-5
6304 E Admiral Blvd 74115 918-833-8600
Kelly Blakney, prin. Fax 833-8619
Bell PS, 209 S Lakewood Ave 74112 K-2
Kelley Blakney, prin. 918-833-9340
Bunche ECC 600/PK-PK
5402 N ML King Jr Blvd 74106 918-746-9020
Julie Smith, prin.
Burroughs ES 300/PK-5
1924 N Martin Luther King 74106 918-833-8780
Tammy Britton, prin. Fax 833-8795
Carnegie ES 400/K-5
4309 E 56th St 74135 918-833-9440
Robin Emerson, prin. Fax 833-9457
Carver MS 600/6-8
624 E Oklahoma Pl 74106 918-925-1420
Elton Sykes, prin. Fax 925-1450
Chouteau ES 400/PK-5
4132 W Cameron St 74127 918-833-8860
Elaine Buxton, prin. Fax 833-8812
Clinton ES 500/K-5
1740 N Harvard Ave 74115 918-746-9320
Tanya Davis, prin. Fax 746-9332
Clinton West ES K-8
2224 W 41st St 74107 918-745-8860
Phaedra Shipley, prin.
Columbus ES 300/K-5
10620 E 27th St 74129 918-925-1460
Janice Thoumire, prin. Fax 925-1466
Cooper ES 800/PK-5
1808 S 123rd East Ave 74128 918-746-9480
Joy Modenbach, prin. Fax 746-9497
Disney ES 800/PK-5
11702 E 25th St 74129 918-925-1480
Donna Gilford, prin. Fax 925-1495
Dual Language Academy 200/PK-3
2703 N Yorktown Pl 74110 918-925-1400
Irma Sandoval, prin.
East Central JHS 700/7-8
12121 E 21st St 74129 918-746-9500
Joshua Regnier, prin. Fax 746-9519
Eisenhower International ES 400/K-5
3111 E 56th St 74105 918-746-9100
Connie Horner, prin. Fax 746-9103
Eliot ES 400/K-5
1442 E 36th St 74105 918-746-8700
Sharon Holt, prin. Fax 746-8715
Emerson ES 200/K-5
5402 N Martin Luther King 74106 918-925-1320
Tammy States, prin. Fax 925-1333
Field ES 400/PK-5
2249 S Phoenix Ave 74107 918-746-8840
Courtney Selking, prin. Fax 746-8855
Gilcrease ES 300/PK-5
5550 Martin Luther King Jr 74126 918-746-9600
Tasha Johnson, prin. Fax 833-8918
Grimes ES 300/PK-5
3213 E 56th St 74105 918-746-8720
Dawn Henley, prin. Fax 746-8738
Grissom ES 300/PK-5
6646 S 73rd East Ave 74133 918-833-9460
Brent Rowland, prin. Fax 833-9476
Hale JHS 700/7-8
2177 S 67th East Ave 74129 918-746-9260
Jody Parsons, prin. Fax 746-9291
Hamilton ES 600/PK-6
2316 N Norwood Pl 74115 918-746-9440
Tera Carr, prin. Fax 746-9447
Hawthorne ES 400/PK-5
1105 E 33rd St N 74106 918-925-1340
Karesha Solomon, prin. Fax 925-1354
Henry ES 500/PK-5
3820 E 41st St 74135 918-746-9160
Jene Carpenter, prin. Fax 746-9178
Hoover ES 600/PK-5
2327 S Darlington Ave 74114 918-746-9120
Deborah Simpson, prin. Fax 746-9131
Jackson ES 300/PK-5
2137 N Pittsburg Ave 74115 918-746-9340
Elmer Thomas, prin. Fax 746-9356

Jones ES 400/K-5
1515 S 71st East Ave 74112 918-746-9040
Bradley Griffin, prin. Fax 746-9046
Kendall-Whittier ES 900/K-5
2601 E 5th Pl 74104 918-833-9900
Ronda Kesler, prin. Fax 833-9930
Kerr ES 500/K-5
202 S 117th East Ave 74128 918-746-9580
Mollie Miller, prin. Fax 746-9583
Key ES 500/PK-5
5702 S Irvington Ave 74135 918-833-9480
Doug Howard, prin. Fax 833-9493
Lanier ES 300/PK-5
1727 S Harvard Ave 74112 918-833-9380
Betty Adams, prin. Fax 833-9393
Lee ES 400/PK-5
1920 S Cincinnati Ave 74119 918-833-9400
Aubrey Flowers, prin. Fax 833-9415
Lewis & Clark ES 500/PK-5
737 S Garnett Rd 74128 918-746-9540
Scott Griffith, prin. Fax 746-9575
Lindbergh ES 400/PK-5
931 S 89th East Ave 74112 918-833-8700
Deidre Prevett, prin. Fax 833-8716
MacArthur ES 400/K-5
2182 S 73rd East Ave 74129 918-746-9140
Twyla Waterson, prin. Fax 746-9155
Marshall ES 400/PK-5
1142 E 56th St 74105 918-746-8740
Kristy Tatum, prin. Fax 746-8757
Mayo Demonstration S 300/PK-5
1127 S Columbia Ave 74104 918-925-1500
Kenneth Joslin, prin. Fax 925-1516
McClure ES, 1770 E 61st St 74136 500/PK-5
Katy Jimenez, prin. 918-746-8760
McKinley ES 500/PK-5
6703 E King St 74115 918-833-8720
Lynnette Dixon, prin. Fax 833-8737
McLain Seventh Grade Academy 7-7
525 E 46th St N 74126 918-746-9660
Tarsha Guillory, prin.
Memorial JHS 600/7-8
7502 E 57th St 74145 918-833-9520
Ginger Bunnell, prin. Fax 833-9551
Mitchell ES 500/PK-5
733 N 73rd East Ave 74115 918-833-8740
Bryan Gibson, prin. Fax 833-8757
Monroe Demonstration Academy 200/6-8
2010 E 48th St N 74130 918-833-8900
Kiana Smith, prin. Fax 833-8918
Owen ES 500/PK-5
1132 N Vandalia Ave 74115 918-746-9230
Erica Foshee-Moore, prin. Fax 746-9240
Peary ES 300/K-5
10818 E 17th St 74128 918-925-1520
Tessa Cross, prin. Fax 925-1536
Penn ES 300/K-5
2138 E 48th St N 74130 918-833-8940
Shalise Jackson, prin. Fax 833-8955
Robertson ES 400/K-5
2721 W 50th St 74107 918-746-8900
Candace Stine, prin. Fax 746-8917
Salk ES 500/PK-5
7625 E 58th St 74145 918-833-9500
Traci Thomas, prin. Fax 833-9506
Sequoyah ES 500/PK-5
724 N Birmingham Ave 74110 918-746-9360
Raye Nero, prin. Fax 746-9377
Skelly ES 800/1-6
2940 S 90th East Ave 74129 918-925-1540
Ramona Gestland, prin. Fax 925-1555
Skelly K, 2714 S 90th East Ave 74129 200/PK-K
Jennifer Pense, prin. 918-925-1560
Springdale ES 400/K-5
2510 E Pine St 74110 918-746-9380
Rebecca Bacon, prin. Fax 746-9394
Thoreau Demonstration Academy 600/6-8
7370 E 71st St 74133 918-833-9700
Audrey Doctor, prin. Fax 833-9720
Twain ES 400/PK-5
541 S 43rd West Ave 74127 918-833-8820
Angie Teas, prin. Fax 833-8823
Whitman ES 400/K-5
3924 N Lansing Ave 74106 918-925-1380
Jana Rodriguez, prin. Fax 925-1383
Wright ES 400/PK-5
1110 E 45th Pl 74105 918-746-8920
Stephanie Tate, prin. Fax 746-8923
Zarrow International S 400/K-5
3613 S Hudson Ave 74135 918-746-9180
Denise Marquez, prin. Fax 746-9195

Union ISD 15,500/PK-12
8506 E 61st St 74133 918-357-4321
Dr. Kirt Hartzler Ed.D., supt. Fax 357-6019
www.unionps.org
Boevers ES 600/PK-5
3433 S 133rd East Ave 74134 918-357-4329
Amy Smith, prin. Fax 357-8399
Cedar Ridge ES 500/PK-5
9817 S Mingo Rd 74133 918-357-4331
Sherri Fair, prin. Fax 357-8600
Clark ES 600/PK-5
3656 S 103rd East Ave 74146 918-357-4332
Theresa Kiger, prin. Fax 357-8599
Darnaby ES 600/PK-5
7625 E 87th St 74133 918-357-4333
Chris Reynolds, prin. Fax 357-8799
Grove ES 600/PK-5
10202 E 62nd St 74133 918-357-4334
Kim Berns, prin. Fax 357-8899
Jarman ES 600/PK-5
9015 E 79th St 74133 918-357-4335
Shawna Thompson, prin. Fax 357-8999
Jefferson ES 600/PK-5
8418 S 107th East Ave 74133 918-357-4339
Kim Rampey, prin. Fax 357-6699
Ochoa ES K-5
12000 E 31st St 74146 918-357-4330
Rita Long, prin. Fax 357-8499

Parks ES 700/PK-5
13702 E 46th Pl 74134 918-357-2757
Karen Vance, prin. Fax 357-6899
Sixth/Seventh Grade Center 2,300/6-7
10100 E 61st St 74133 918-357-4326
Scott Pennington, prin. Fax 357-8047
Other Schools – See Broken Arrow

Augustine Christian Academy 200/PK-12
6310 E 30th St 74114 918-832-4600
Crossover Preparatory Academy 50/7-8
940 E 36th St N 74106 918-986-7499
Philip Abode, dir. Fax 202-2429
Holland Hall 1,000/PK-12
5666 E 81st St 74137 918-481-1111
J.P. Culley, head sch Fax 481-1145
Holy Family Cathedral S 100/PK-8
820 S Boulder Ave 74119 918-582-0422
Leslie Southerland, prin. Fax 582-9705
Lincoln Christian S 800/PK-12
1003 N 129th East Ave 74116 918-234-8863
Trandy Birch, prin. Fax 234-8864
Marquette Catholic S 500/PK-8
1519 S Quincy Ave 74120 918-584-4631
Pete Theban, prin. Fax 584-4847
Metro Christian Academy 1,000/PK-12
6363 S Trenton Ave 74136 918-745-9868
Mingo Valley Christian S 200/PK-12
8304 S 107th East Ave 74133 918-294-0404
Dr. Boyd Chitwood, supt. Fax 459-0601
Monte Cassino S 900/PK-8
2206 S Lewis Ave 74114 918-742-3364
Kevin Smith M.Ed., head sch Fax 742-5206
Peace Academy PK-12
4620 S Irvington Ave 74135 918-627-1040
Regent Preparatory S of Oklahoma 500/PK-12
8621 S Memorial Dr 74133 918-663-1002
St. Catherine S 100/PK-8
2515 W 46th St 74107 918-446-9756
Michelle Anthamatten, prin. Fax 447-3780
St. Pius X S 400/PK-8
1717 S 75th East Ave 74112 918-627-5367
Lisa Bell, prin. Fax 627-6179
San Miguel MS 100/6-8
2444 E Admiral Blvd 74110 918-728-7337
John Dowdell, pres. Fax 660-2040
School of St. Mary 300/PK-8
1365 E 49th Pl 74105 918-749-9361
Maureen Clements, prin. Fax 712-9604
Solid Foundation Preparatory Academy 100/PK-5
PO Box 481085 74148 918-794-7800
Jayme Broome, admin. Fax 794-7801
SS. Peter & Paul Catholic S 200/PK-8
1428 N 67th East Ave 74115 918-836-2165
Patrick Martin, prin. Fax 836-2597
Tulsa Adventist Academy 100/PK-10
900 S New Haven Ave 74112 918-834-1107
Undercroft Montessori S 200/PK-8
3745 S Hudson Ave 74135 918-622-2890
Victory Christian S 1,100/PK-12
7700 S Lewis Ave 74136 918-491-7720
Jim Cherry, supt. Fax 491-7727
Wright Christian Academy 200/PK-12
11391 E Admiral Pl 74116 918-438-0922
Jeff Brown, supt. Fax 438-0700

Tupelo, Coal, Pop. 308
Tupelo ISD 300/PK-12
200 S 7th Ave 74572 580-845-2460
Jerry Romines, supt. Fax 845-2565
www.tupelo.k12.ok.us
Tupelo ES 200/PK-8
200 S 7th Ave 74572 580-845-2802
Lance Britt, prin. Fax 845-2565

Turpin, Beaver, Pop. 457
Turpin ISD 400/PK-12
PO Box 187 73950 580-778-3333
Keith Custer, supt. Fax 778-3179
www.turpinps.org
Turpin ES 300/PK-6
PO Box 187 73950 580-778-3331
Kim Barnes, prin. Fax 778-3800

Tuskahoma, Pushmataha, Pop. 147
Tuskahoma SD 100/PK-8
PO Box 100 74574 918-569-7737
Barry Simpson, supt. Fax 569-4154
www.tuskahoma.k12.ok.us
Tuskahoma S 100/PK-8
PO Box 100 74574 918-569-7737
Barry Simpson, prin. Fax 569-4154

Tuttle, Grady, Pop. 5,837
Tuttle ISD 1,800/PK-12
PO Box 780 73089 405-381-2605
Bobby Waitman, supt. Fax 381-4008
www.tuttleschools.info/
Tuttle ECC, PO Box 780 73089 PK-PK
Kim Williams, prin. 405-381-2373
Tuttle ES 600/PK-3
PO Box 780 73089 405-381-2486
Tara Norvell, prin. Fax 381-5008
Tuttle IS 300/4-5
PO Box 780 73089 405-381-2368
Cheryl Williams, prin. Fax 381-5028
Tuttle MS 400/6-8
PO Box 780 73089 405-381-2062
Scott Moore, prin. Fax 381-4630

Tyrone, Texas, Pop. 753
Tyrone ISD 300/PK-12
PO Box 168 73951 580-854-6298
Josh Bell, supt. Fax 854-6474
www.tyrone.k12.ok.us/
Tyrone ES 200/PK-8
PO Box 168 73951 580-854-6298
Donovan Smith, prin. Fax 854-6474

Union City, Canadian, Pop. 1,578
Union City ISD 300/PK-12
PO Box 279 73090 405-483-3531
Todd Carel, supt. Fax 483-5599
www.unioncity.k12.ok.us/
Union City ES 200/PK-8
PO Box 279 73090 405-483-5327
Kerri Griggs, prin. Fax 483-5587

Valliant, McCurtain, Pop. 701
Valliant ISD 900/PK-12
604 E Lucas St 74764 580-933-7232
James Eberts, supt. Fax 933-7289
www.vpsd.org
Valliant ES 400/PK-5
604 E Lucas St 74764 580-933-7248
Rickey Bowen, prin. Fax 933-7249
Valliant MS 200/6-8
604 E Lucas St 74764 580-933-4253
Dennis Robberson, prin. Fax 933-4254

Velma, Stephens, Pop. 608
Velma-Alma ISD 400/PK-12
PO Box 8 73491 580-444-3355
Raymond Rice, supt. Fax 444-2554
www.velma-alma.k12.ok.us
Velma-Alma ES 300/PK-5
PO Box 8 73491 580-444-3357
Shannon Williams, prin. Fax 444-2554

Verden, Grady, Pop. 510
Verden ISD 200/PK-12
PO Box 99 73092 405-453-7247
David Davidson, supt. Fax 453-7246
www.verdenschools.org
Verden ES 100/PK-6
PO Box 99 73092 405-453-7104
Roxi Tallent, prin. Fax 453-7246

Vian, Sequoyah, Pop. 1,346
Vian ISD 1,000/PK-12
PO Box 434 74962 918-773-5798
Victor Salcedo, supt. Fax 773-3051
www.vian.k12.ok.us
Vian ES 500/PK-5
PO Box 434 74962 918-773-5311
Kathy Wingo, prin. Fax 773-3051
Vian MS 200/6-8
PO Box 434 74962 918-773-8631
Marilyn Oliver, prin. Fax 773-3051

Vici, Dewey, Pop. 673
Vici ISD 300/PK-12
PO Box 60 73859 580-995-4744
Coby Nelson, supt. Fax 995-3101
www.vicischools.k12.ok.us
Vici ES 300/PK-8
PO Box 60 73859 580-995-4252
Kas Nelson, prin. Fax 995-3101

Vinita, Craig, Pop. 5,215
Vinita ISD 1,600/PK-12
114 S Scraper St 74301 918-256-6778
Kelly Grimmett, supt. Fax 256-5617
www.vinitahornets.com
Hall Halsell ES 400/PK-2
402 W Clyde Ave 74301 918-256-6692
Mary Voith Smith, prin. Fax 256-4199
Rogers ES 300/3-5
101 S Smith St 74301 918-256-5350
Michael Wilson, prin. Fax 256-7137
Vinita MS 300/6-8
226 N Miller St 74301 918-256-2402
Duwayne King, prin. Fax 256-5401

White Oak ISD 100/PK-8
27355 S 4340 Rd 74301 918-256-4484
Richard Mcspadden, supt. Fax 256-4486
White Oak S, 27355 S 4340 Rd 74301 100/PK-8
David Money, prin. 918-256-4484

Ketchum Adventist Academy 50/PK-10
35369 S Highway 82 74301 918-782-2986

Wagoner, Wagoner, Pop. 7,460
Wagoner ISD 2,500/PK-12
707 N Story Ave 74467 918-485-4046
Randy Harris, supt. Fax 485-8710
www.wagonerps.org
Central IS 300/4-5
202 N Casaver Ave 74467 918-485-9543
Shawndy Young, prin. Fax 485-9544
Ellington ES 500/PK-1
601 SE 6th St 74467 918-485-3692
Brian Hummingbird, prin. Fax 485-5162
Teague ES 300/2-3
700 N Story Ave 74467 918-485-2212
Penny Risley, prin. Fax 485-5206
Wagoner MS 500/6-8
500 Bulldog Cir 74467 918-485-9541
Jeremy Holmes, prin. Fax 485-4149

Wainwright, Muskogee, Pop. 135
Wainwright SD 100/PK-8
PO Box 189 74468 918-474-3484
Jim Ogden, supt. Fax 474-3744
Wainwright S 100/PK-8
PO Box 189 74468 918-474-3484
Jim Ogden, admin. Fax 474-3744

Walters, Cotton, Pop. 2,379
Walters ISD 700/PK-12
418 S Broadway St 73572 580-875-2568
Jimmie Dedmon, supt. Fax 875-2831
blued.org
Walters ES 300/PK-5
418 S Broadway St 73572 580-875-3144
Amanda James, prin. Fax 875-2752
Walters MS 200/6-8
418 S Broadway St 73572 580-875-3214
Jimmie Dedmon, prin. Fax 875-3401

Wanette, Pottawatomie, Pop. 331
Wanette ISD 200/PK-12
PO Box 161 74878 405-383-2656
Dr. Silvia McNeely, supt. Fax 383-2449
Wanette ES 100/PK-8
PO Box 161 74878 405-383-2222
Silvia Mcneely, prin. Fax 383-2185

Wapanucka, Johnston, Pop. 399
Wapanucka ISD 200/PK-12
PO Box 188 73461 580-937-4288
Davis Walters, supt. Fax 937-4804
www.wpss.k12.ok.us
Wapanucka ES, PO Box 188 73461 200/PK-8
Davis Walters, prin. 580-937-4288

Warner, Muskogee, Pop. 1,489
Warner ISD 700/PK-12
1012 5th Ave 74469 918-463-5171
David Vinson, supt. Fax 463-2542
www.warner.k12.ok.us
Warner ES 500/PK-8
1012 5th Ave 74469 918-463-2950
Alan Gordon, dean Fax 463-5936

Warr Acres, Oklahoma, Pop. 9,574
Putnam City ISD
Supt. — See Oklahoma City
Capps MS 900/6-8
4020 N Grove Ave 73122 405-787-3660
James Burnett, prin. Fax 491-7536
Central ES 700/PK-5
5721 NW 39th St 73122 405-789-5696
Kimberly Harper, prin. Fax 491-7572
Putnam City ECC PK-PK
6624 NW 63rd St 73122 405-721-1830
Ashley Hoggatt, prin.

Washington, McClain, Pop. 585
Washington ISD 1,000/PK-12
PO Box 98 73093 405-288-6190
A.J. Brewer, supt. Fax 288-6214
www.washington.k12.ok.us/
Washington ES 500/PK-5
PO Box 98 73093 405-288-2353
Rocky Clarke, prin. Fax 288-6214
Washington MS 200/6-8
PO Box 98 73093 405-288-2428
Stuart McPherson, prin. Fax 288-6214

Watonga, Blaine, Pop. 4,947
Watonga ISD 800/PK-12
1200 Eagle Ln 73772 580-623-7364
Bill Seitter, supt. Fax 623-7370
www.watonga.k12.ok.us
Watonga ES 400/PK-5
PO Box 640 73772 580-623-5248
Jeanne Karns, prin. Fax 623-5238

Watts, Adair, Pop. 292
Watts ISD 400/PK-12
616 6th St 74964 918-422-5311
Lisa Weaver, supt. Fax 422-5556
www.wattsschool.com
Watts ES, 616 6th St 74964 300/PK-8
Tony Mitchell, prin. 918-422-5131

Waukomis, Garfield, Pop. 1,254
Pioneer-Pleasant Vale ISD 600/PK-12
6520 E Wood Rd 73773 580-758-3282
Brent Koontz, supt. Fax 758-3504
www.ppv.k12.ok.us/
Pioneer-Pleasant Vale JHS 100/7-8
6520 E Wood Rd 73773 580-758-3282
Tom Betchan, prin. Fax 758-1541
Other Schools – See Enid

Waukomis ISD 300/PK-12
PO Box 729 73773 580-758-3247
Shawn Tennyson, supt. Fax 758-3834
www.waukomis.k12.ok.us
Waukomis ES 200/PK-5
PO Box 729 73773 580-758-3264
Bandon Bookout, prin. Fax 758-3078

Waurika, Jefferson, Pop. 1,993
Waurika ISD 300/PK-12
600 E Florida Ave 73573 580-228-3373
Roxie Terry M.Ed., supt. Fax 228-3428
www.waurikaschools.org
Waurika ES 200/PK-5
600 Educational Ave 73573 580-228-3531
Cody Simmons, prin. Fax 228-3428

Wayne, McClain, Pop. 635
Wayne ISD 500/PK-12
212 S Seifried St 73095 405-449-3646
David Powell, supt. Fax 449-7095
www.wayne.k12.ok.us
Wayne ES 200/PK-5
212 S Seifried St 73095 405-449-3305
Donna Soutee, prin. Fax 449-7095
Wayne MS 100/6-8
212 S Seifried St 73095 405-449-7047
Brandon Sharp, prin. Fax 449-7095

Waynoka, Woods, Pop. 895
Waynoka ISD 300/PK-12
2134 Lincoln St 73860 580-824-4341
Scott Cline, supt. Fax 824-0656
www.waynoka.k12.ok.us/
Waynoka ES 200/PK-8
2134 Lincoln St 73860 580-824-4341
Michael Meriwether, prin. Fax 824-0656

Weatherford, Custer, Pop. 10,475
Weatherford ISD 2,200/PK-12
516 N Broadway St 73096 580-772-3327
Chad Wilson, supt. Fax 774-0821
www.wpsok.org
Burcham ES 600/PK-1
1401 N Lark St 73096 580-774-0812
Marla Pankratz, prin. Fax 774-1910

East ES 300/2-3
701 E Proctor Ave 73096 580-772-3533
Brad Howl, prin. Fax 774-1905
Weatherford MS 500/6-8
509 N Custer St 73096 580-772-2270
Doug Gunselman, prin. Fax 774-1981
West ES 300/4-5
811 W Huber Ave 73096 580-772-5888
Robyn Randol, prin. Fax 774-1903

Western Oklahoma Christian S Weatherford 50/PK-2
1709 Lyle Rd 73096 580-774-8159
Dora Miller, prin. Fax 323-0786

Webbers Falls, Muskogee, Pop. 572
Webbers Falls ISD, PO Box 300 74470 300/PK-12
Dr. Dixie Swearingen Ph.D., supt. 918-464-2580
www.webbersfalls.k12.ok.us
Webbers Falls ES, PO Box 300 74470 200/PK-8
Lisa Ward, prin. 918-464-2334

Welch, Craig, Pop. 576
Welch ISD 300/PK-12
PO Box 189 74369 918-788-3129
Dr. Clark McKeon, supt. Fax 788-3734
welchwildcats.net
Welch ES 200/PK-6
PO Box 189 74369 918-788-3129
Kim Hall, prin. Fax 788-3734
Welch MS 100/7-8
PO Box 189 74369 918-788-3129
Kim Hall, prin. Fax 788-3734

Weleetka, Okfuskee, Pop. 906
Graham-Dustin SD 200/PK-12
116118 Highway 84 74880 918-652-8935
C. J. Buesser, supt. Fax 652-2422
www.graham-dustin.k12.ok.us
Graham MS 50/5-8
116118 Highway 84 74880 918-652-8935
Linda Riddle, prin. Fax 652-2422
Other Schools – See Dustin

Weleetka ISD 400/PK-12
PO Box 278 74880 405-786-2203
Chris Carter, supt. Fax 786-2625
www.weleetka.k12.ok.us
Spence Memorial ES 200/PK-6
PO Box 278 74880 405-786-2346
Courtney Hare, prin.

Welling, Cherokee, Pop. 638
Tenkiller SD 300/PK-8
26106 E 863 Rd 74471 918-457-5996
Bryan Hix, supt. Fax 457-5619
Tenkiller S 300/PK-8
26106 E 863 Rd 74471 918-457-5996
Kenneth Thornton, prin. Fax 457-5619

Wellston, Lincoln, Pop. 751
Wellston ISD 700/PK-12
PO Box 60 74881 405-356-2534
Dwayne Danker, supt. Fax 356-2838
www.wellstonschools.org
Wellston ES 300/PK-5
PO Box 60 74881 405-356-2256
Letha Bauter, prin. Fax 356-4402
Wellston MS 200/6-8
PO Box 60 74881 405-356-2533
Tracy Fredman, prin. Fax 356-2838

Westville, Adair, Pop. 1,479
Westville ISD 1,100/PK-12
PO Box 410 74965 918-723-3181
Terry Heustis, supt. Fax 723-3042
www.westville.k12.ok.us
Westville ES 600/PK-6
PO Box 410 74965 918-723-3351
Ryan Swank, prin. Fax 723-4337

Wetumka, Hughes, Pop. 1,171
Wetumka ISD 500/PK-12
416 S Tiger St 74883 405-452-5150
Donna McGee, supt. Fax 452-3052
www.wetumka.k12.ok.us/
Wetumka S 400/PK-8
416 S Tiger St 74883 405-452-3245
Robin Gann, prin. Fax 452-5809

Wewoka, Seminole, Pop. 3,192
Justice SD 200/PK-8
36507 EW 1310 74884 405-257-2962
Chris Bryan, supt. Fax 257-2963
www.justice.k12.ok.us
Justice S 200/PK-8
36507 EW 1310 74884 405-257-2962
Chris Jones, admin. Fax 257-2963

New Lima ISD 300/PK-12
116 Gross St 74884 405-257-5771
James Mathews, supt. Fax 257-3127
www.newlima.k12.ok.us
New Lima ES 200/PK-8
116 Gross St 74884 405-257-3948
Rebeccah Green, prin. Fax 257-9354

Wewoka ISD 800/PK-12
PO Box 870 74884 405-257-5475
Torrey Gaines, supt. Fax 257-2303
www.wps.k12.ok.us
Wewoka ES 300/PK-4
PO Box 870 74884 405-257-2341
Pat Hensley, prin. Fax 257-2303
Wewoka MS 100/5-8
PO Box 870 74884 405-257-2347
Richard Jasna, prin. Fax 257-2303

Whitefield, Haskell, Pop. 351
Whitefield SD 100/PK-8
PO Box 178 74472 918-967-8572
Scott Shepherd, supt. Fax 967-0007
www.whitefield.k12.ok.us
Whitefield S 100/PK-8
PO Box 178 74472 918-967-8572
Scott Shepherd, prin. Fax 967-0007

Whitesboro, LeFlore, Pop. 244
Whitesboro ISD 200/PK-12
PO Box 150 74577 918-567-2556
Katie Blagg, supt. Fax 567-2842
www.whitesborops.k12.ok.us/
Whitesboro ES, PO Box 150 74577 100/PK-8
Katie Blagg, prin. 918-567-3016

Wilburton, Latimer, Pop. 2,654
Wilburton ISD 900/PK-12
1201 W Blair Ave 74578 918-465-2100
Dr. Trice Butler, supt. Fax 465-3086
wilburtondiggers.org
Wilburton ES 400/PK-5
1201 W Blair Ave 74578 918-465-2245
Jan Gilmore, prin. Fax 465-5616
Wilburton MS 200/6-8
1201 W Blair Ave 74578 918-465-2281
Kyle Vanderburg, prin. Fax 465-3094

Wilson, Carter, Pop. 1,643
Wilson ISD 500/PK-12
1860 Hewitt Rd 73463 580-668-2306
Eric Smith, supt. Fax 668-2170
www.wilson.k12.ok.us
Wilson ES 400/PK-8
1860 Hewitt Rd 73463 580-668-2355
Clifford Benson, prin. Fax 668-2170

Zaneis SD 300/PK-8
30515 US Highway 70 73463 580-668-2955
Ryan Cole, supt. Fax 668-2114
www.zaneis.k12.ok.us
Zaneis S 300/PK-8
30515 US Highway 70 73463 580-668-2955
Ryan Cole, prin. Fax 668-2114

Wister, LeFlore, Pop. 1,038
Wister ISD 600/PK-12
201 Logan St 74966 918-655-7381
Rachel Pugh, supt. Fax 655-7402
www.wisterschools.org
Wister ES 400/PK-8
201 Logan St 74966 918-655-7481
Keli Cartwright, prin. Fax 655-7402

Woodward, Woodward, Pop. 11,818
Woodward ISD 3,000/PK-12
PO Box 668 73802 580-256-6063
Kyle Reynolds, supt. Fax 256-4391
www.woodwardps.net
Cedar Heights ES 300/1-4
PO Box 668 73802 580-256-6521
Bana Bogdahn, prin. Fax 571-6250
Highland Park ES 300/1-4
PO Box 668 73802 580-256-2500
Tara Burnett, prin. Fax 571-6251
Mann ES 300/1-4
PO Box 668 73802 580-256-2660
Dawna Nelson, prin. Fax 571-6252
Woodward ECC 800/PK-K
PO Box 668 73802 580-256-2561
Debbie Jones, prin. Fax 571-3155
Woodward MS North 400/5-6
PO Box 668 73802 580-256-5357
Sarah Hall, prin. Fax 571-3154
Woodward MS South 600/7-8
PO Box 668 73802 580-256-7901
Sarah Hall, prin. Fax 256-8014

Wright City, McCurtain, Pop. 687
Wright City ISD 400/PK-12
PO Box 329 74766 580-981-2824
David Hawkins, supt. Fax 981-2115
www.wcisd.org/
Wright City ES 200/PK-6
PO Box 329 74766 580-981-2248
Frank Partridge, prin. Fax 981-2304
Wright City JHS 100/7-8
PO Box 329 74766 580-981-2558
Mike Converse, prin. Fax 981-2329

Wyandotte, Ottawa, Pop. 310
Turkey Ford SD 100/PK-6
23900 S 670 Rd 74370 918-786-4902
Tamyra Larson, supt. Fax 787-5015
www.turkeyford.net/
Turkey Ford ES 100/PK-6
23900 S 670 Rd 74370 918-786-4902
Tamyra Larson, supt. Fax 787-5015

Wyandotte ISD 800/PK-12
PO Box 360 74370 918-678-2255
Troy Gray M.Ed., supt. Fax 678-2304
www.wyandotte.k12.ok.us
Wyandotte ES 400/PK-5
PO Box 360 74370 918-678-2299
Vicky Lewis, prin. Fax 678-3907
Wyandotte MS 200/6-8
PO Box 360 74370 918-678-2222
Stacy Sloan, prin. Fax 678-3906

Wynnewood, Garvin, Pop. 2,125
Wynnewood ISD 700/PK-12
702 E Robert S Kerr Blvd 73098 405-665-2004
Timothy Simpson, supt. Fax 665-5425
www.wynnewood.k12.ok.us/
Central ES, 301 E Chickasaw St 73098 400/PK-4
Tammy Grove, prin. 405-665-4371
Wynnewood MS 200/5-8
702 E Robert S Kerr Blvd 73098 405-665-4105
Kevin Lynch, prin.

Wynona, Osage, Pop. 396
Wynona ISD 100/PK-12
PO Box 700 74084 918-846-2467
Shelly Shulanberger, supt. Fax 846-2883
www.wynona.k12.ok.us
Wynona ES 100/PK-8
PO Box 700 74084 918-846-2467
Shelly Shulanberger, prin. Fax 846-2883

Yale, Payne, Pop. 1,132
Yale ISD 500/PK-12
315 E Chicago Ave 74085 918-387-2118
Dale Bledsoe, supt. Fax 387-4243
www.yale.k12.ok.us
Yale ES 200/PK-5
800 N C St 74085 918-387-2428
Amber Locke, prin. Fax 387-4243
Yale JHS 100/6-8
315 E Chicago Ave 74085 918-387-2118
Rocky Kennedy, prin. Fax 387-4243

Yukon, Canadian, Pop. 21,966
Mustang ISD
Supt. — See Mustang
Mustang Creek ES 700/PK-4
10821 SW 15th Street 73099 405-324-4567
Susan Dombek, prin. Fax 324-4562
Mustang Trails ES 900/PK-4
12025 SW 15th Ter 73099 405-324-0016
Alisha Suffield, prin. Fax 324-4577

Piedmont ISD
Supt. — See Piedmont
Stone Ridge ES 400/PK-4
10000 W Memorial Rd 73099 405-373-4227
Debbie Caywood, prin. Fax 373-1682

Yukon ISD 8,100/PK-12
600 Maple St 73099 405-354-2587
Dr. Jason Simeroth, supt. Fax 354-4208
www.yukonps.com
Central ES 400/PK-3
300 S 9th St 73099 405-354-2501
Laura Gallagher, prin. Fax 354-2502
Independence ES 600/4-5
500 E Vandament Ave 73099 405-265-1352
Roni McKee, prin. Fax 265-1353
Lakeview ES 600/4-5
872 S Yukon Pkwy 73099 405-265-1342
Scott Hein, prin. Fax 265-1343
Myers ES 300/PK-3
1200 S 1st St 73099 405-354-5252
Ron Brummett, prin. Fax 354-5253
Parkland ES 400/PK-3
2201 Cornwell Dr 73099 405-354-7786
Lance Haggard, prin. Fax 354-2327
Ranchwood ES 400/PK-3
607 Annawood Dr 73099 405-354-6616
Kristin Lipe, prin. Fax 354-4541
Shedeck ES 400/PK-3
2100 Holly Ave 73099 405-354-6601
Diedre Bradley, prin. Fax 354-6602
Skyview ES 600/PK-3
650 S Yukon Pkwy 73099 405-354-4852
Carla Smith, prin. Fax 354-4853
Surrey Hills ES 400/PK-3
10700 Hastings Ave 73099 405-373-1973
Bill Pierce, prin. Fax 373-2021
Yukon MS 1,800/6-8
801 Garth Brooks Blvd 73099 405-354-5274
Diana Lebsack, prin. Fax 354-6640

St. John Nepomuk S 200/PK-8
600 Garth Brooks Blvd 73099 405-354-2509
Natalie Johnson, prin. Fax 354-8192
Southwest Covenant S 300/PK-12
2300 S Yukon Pkwy 73099 405-354-0772
Steve Lessman, hdmstr. Fax 350-2670

OREGON

OREGON DEPARTMENT OF EDUCATION
255 Capitol St NE, Salem 97310-1206
Telephone 503-947-5600
Fax 503-378-5156
Website http://www.oregon.gov/ode/Pages/default.aspx

Superintendent of Public Instruction Colt Gill

OREGON BOARD OF EDUCATION
255 Capitol St NE, Salem 97310-1300

Chairperson Charles Martinez

EDUCATION SERVICE DISTRICTS (ESD)

Clackamas ESD
Jada Rupley, supt. 503-675-4000
13455 SE 97th Ave Fax 675-4200
Clackamas 97015
www.clackesd.k12.or.us

Columbia Gorge ESD
Patricia Sublette, supt. 541-506-5155
400 E Scenic Dr Ste 207 Fax 296-2965
The Dalles 97058
www.cgesd.k12.or.us

Douglas ESD
Michael Lasher, supt. 541-440-4777
1871 NE Stephens St Fax 440-4771
Roseburg 97470
www.douglasesd.k12.or.us

Grant ESD
Robert Waltenburg, supt. 541-575-1349
835 S Canyon Blvd Ste A Fax 575-3601
John Day 97845
www.grantesd.k12.or.us

Harney ESD
Charles Beck, supt. 541-573-2122
25 Fairview Hts, Burns 97720 Fax 573-1822
www.harneyesd.k12.or.us

High Desert ESD
John Rexford, supt. 541-693-5600
2804 SW 6th St, Redmond 97756 Fax 693-5601
www.hdesd.org

InterMountain ESD
Mark Mulvihill Ed.D., supt. 541-276-6616
2001 SW Nye Ave Fax 276-4252
Pendleton 97801
www.imesd.k12.or.us

Jefferson ESD
Rick Molitor, supt. 541-475-2804
295 SE Buff St, Madras 97741 Fax 475-2827
www.jcesd.k12.or.us

Lake ESD
Bob Nash, supt. 541-947-3371
357 N L St, Lakeview 97630 Fax 947-3373
www.lakeesd.k12.or.us

Lane ESD
Larry Sullivan, supt. 541-461-8200
1200 Highway 99 N, Eugene 97402 Fax 461-8298
www.lesd.k12.or.us

Linn-Benton-Lincoln ESD
Mary McKay, supt. 541-812-2600
905 4th Ave SE, Albany 97321 Fax 926-6047
www.lblesd.k12.or.us

Malheur ESD
Mark Redmond, supt. 541-473-3138
363 A St W, Vale 97918 Fax 473-3915
www.malesd.k12.or.us

Multnomah ESD
Sam Breyer, supt. 503-255-1841
PO Box 301039, Portland 97294 Fax 257-1519
www.mesd.k12.or.us

North Central ESD
Robert Waltenberg, supt. 541-384-2732
PO Box 637, Condon 97823 Fax 384-2752
www.ncesd.k12.or.us

Northwest Regional ESD
Rob Saxton, supt. 503-614-1428
5825 NE Ray Cir, Hillsboro 97124 Fax 614-1440
www.nwresd.k12.or.us

Region 18 ESD
Karen Patton, supt. 541-426-7600
107 SW 1st St Ste 105 Fax 426-3732
Enterprise 97828
www.r18esd.org

South Coast ESD
Tenneal Wetherell, supt. 541-269-1611
1350 Teakwood Ave Fax 266-4040
Coos Bay 97420
www.scesd.k12.or.us

Southern Oregon ESD
Scott Beveridge, supt. 541-776-8590
101 N Grape St, Medford 97501 Fax 779-2018
www.soesd.k12.or.us

Willamette ESD
Dave Novotney, supt. 503-588-5330
2611 Pringle Rd SE, Salem 97302 Fax 363-5787
www.wesd.org

PUBLIC, PRIVATE AND CATHOLIC ELEMENTARY SCHOOLS

Adel, Lake
Adel SD 21
Supt. — See Lakeview
Adel ES, PO Box 117 97620 50/4-8
Bob Nash, prin. 541-947-3371

Adrian, Malheur, Pop. 173
Adrian SD 61 200/K-12
PO Box 108 97901 541-372-2335
Gene Mills, supt. Fax 372-5380
www.adriansd.com
Adrian ES 200/K-8
PO Box 108 97901 541-372-2337
Bill Ellsworth, prin. Fax 372-5516

Albany, Linn, Pop. 48,696
Greater Albany SD 8J 9,200/K-12
718 7th Ave SW 97321 541-967-4501
Jim Golden, supt. Fax 967-4587
albany.k12.or.us
Calapooia MS 600/6-8
830 24th Ave SE, 541-967-4555
Gina Ayers, prin. Fax 924-3702
Central ES 100/3-5
336 9th Ave SW 97321 541-967-4561
Lisa Shogren, prin. Fax 924-3625
Clover Ridge PS 300/K-2
2953 Clover Ridge Rd NE, 541-967-4565
Elisa Stephens, prin. Fax 924-3707
Fir Grove PS 100/K-1
5355 NW Scenic Dr 97321 541-967-4570
Jerrie Matuzak, prin.
Lafayette ES 300/K-5
3122 Madison St SE, 541-967-4575
Jodi Smith, prin. Fax 924-3622
Liberty ES 400/K-5
2345 Liberty St SW 97321 541-967-4578
Tracy Day, prin. Fax 924-3710
Memorial MS 600/6-8
1050 Queen Ave SW 97321 541-967-4537
Ken Gilbert, prin. Fax 924-3703
North Albany ES 300/K-5
815 NW Thornton Lake Dr 97321 541-967-4588
Kilee Sowa, prin. Fax 924-3719
North Albany MS 500/6-8
1205 NW North Albany Rd 97321 541-967-4541
Marshall Jackson, prin. Fax 924-3704
Oak ES 300/K-5
3610 Oak St SE, 541-967-4591
Kelly Bussard, prin. Fax 924-3708
Oak Grove ES 200/2-5
1500 NW Oak Grove Dr 97321 541-967-4596
Jerrie Matuzak, prin. Fax 924-3715
Periwinkle ES 400/K-5
2196 21st Ave SE, 541-967-4600
Chaundra Smith, prin. Fax 924-3711
South Shore ES 500/K-5
910 Bain St SE, 541-967-4604
Kraig Sproles, prin. Fax 924-3718
Sunrise ES 400/K-5
730 19th Ave SE, 541-967-4608
Bob Daugherty, prin. Fax 924-3726
Takena ES 100/K-2
1210 12th Ave SW 97321 541-967-4613
Lisa Shogren, prin. Fax 924-3717
Timber Ridge S 700/3-8
373 Timber Ridge St NE, 541-704-1095
Jodi Dedera, prin. Fax 704-1099
Waverly ES 200/K-5
425 Columbus St SE 97321 541-967-4617
Anne Griffith, prin. Fax 924-3620
Other Schools – See Tangent

Albany Christian S 200/PK-8
420 3rd Ave SE 97321 541-928-1110
Doug Tharp, prin. Fax 791-1864
Good Shepherd Lutheran S 100/PK-K
1910 34th Ave SE, 541-926-0246
Fax 926-6057

Aloha, Washington, Pop. 47,267
Beaverton SD 48J
Supt. — See Beaverton
Hassell ES 500/K-5
18100 SW Bany Rd 97007 503-356-2090
Scarlet Valentine, prin. Fax 356-2095
Kinnaman ES 700/K-5
4205 SW 193rd Ave, 503-356-2420
Michael Crandall, prin. Fax 356-2425

Hillsboro SD 1J
Supt. — See Hillsboro
Butternut Creek ES 400/K-6
20395 SW Florence St, 503-844-1390
Danielle Johnson, prin. Fax 844-1397
Indian Hills ES 400/K-6
21260 SW Rock Rd, 503-844-1350
Bruce Bourget, prin. Fax 844-1359
Reedville ES 200/K-6
2695 SW 209th Ave, 503-844-1570
Robin Farup-Romero, prin. Fax 844-1579
Tobias ES 500/K-6
1065 SW 206th Ave, 503-844-1310
Andrew Bekken, prin. Fax 848-1317

Faith Bible Christian S 100/PK-8
16860 SW Blanton St, 503-642-4112
Kevin Rex, supt. Fax 649-4470
Life Christian S 200/PK-12
5585 SW 209th Ave, 503-259-1329
Cary Tyler, prin. Fax 649-5484

Amity, Yamhill, Pop. 1,569
Amity SD 4J 900/K-12
807 S Trade St 97101 503-835-2171
Jeff Clark, supt. Fax 835-5050
www.amity.k12.or.us
Amity ES 400/K-5
807 S Trade St 97101 503-835-3751
Danielle Ludwick, prin. Fax 835-0411
Amity MS 200/6-8
807 S Trade St 97101 503-835-0518
Dave Lund, prin. Fax 835-0418

Perrydale SD 21 500/K-12
7445 Perrydale Rd 97101 503-835-3184
Eric Milburn, supt. Fax 835-0631
www.perrydale.k12.or.us
Perrydale S, 7445 Perrydale Rd 97101 200/K-12
Eric Milburn, admin. 503-835-3184

Applegate, Jackson
Three Rivers SD
Supt. — See Grants Pass
Applegate ES 100/K-8
14188 Highway 238 97530 541-846-6280
Steven Fuller, prin. Fax 846-6055

Arock, Malheur
Arock SD 81 50/K-8
3513 Arock Rd 97902 541-586-2325
Fax 586-2304
www.malesd.k12.or.us/arock-school-district

Jones ES 50/K-8
PO Box 131 97902 541-586-2325
Vicki McConnell, lead tchr. Fax 586-2304

Ashland, Jackson, Pop. 19,339
Ashland SD 5 2,600/K-12
885 Siskiyou Blvd 97520 541-482-2811
Suzanne Cusick, supt. Fax 482-2185
www.ashland.k12.or.us
Ashland MS 600/6-8
100 Walker Ave 97520 541-482-1611
Steve Retzlaff, prin. Fax 482-8112
Bellview ES 300/K-5
1070 Tolman Creek Rd 97520 541-482-1310
Christine McCollom, prin. Fax 482-2591
Helman ES 300/K-5
705 Helman St 97520 541-482-5620
Michelle Cuddeback, prin. Fax 482-2560
Muir S 100/K-8
100 Walker Ave 97520 541-482-8577
Rebecca Gyarmathy, prin. Fax 482-8112
Walker ES 300/K-5
364 Walker Ave 97520 541-482-1516
Tiffany Burns, prin. Fax 482-2671

Pinehurst SD 94 50/K-5
15337 Highway 66 97520 541-482-1910
Holly Amann, admin. Fax 482-7956
www.pinehurst.k12.or.us
Pinehurst S 50/K-5
15337 Highway 66 97520 541-482-1910
Holly Amann, admin. Fax 482-7956

Siskiyou S 200/1-8
631 Clay St 97520 541-482-8223

Ashwood, Jefferson
Ashwood SD 8 50/K-6
18624 NE Main St 97711 541-489-3297
Mary Lewis, contact Fax 489-3388
www.ashwood.k12.or.us
Ashwood ES 50/K-6
18624 NE Main St 97711 541-489-3297
Mary Lewis, contact Fax 489-3388

Astoria, Clatsop, Pop. 9,193
Astoria SD 1 1,900/K-12
785 Alameda Ave 97103 503-325-6441
Craig Hoppes, supt. Fax 325-6524
www.astoria.k12.or.us
Astor ES 500/K-2
3550 Franklin Ave 97103 503-325-6672
Kate Gohr, prin. Fax 325-6335
Astoria MS 400/6-8
1100 Klaskanine Ave 97103 503-325-4331
Linda Berger, prin. Fax 325-3040
Lewis & Clark ES 400/3-5
92179 Lewis and Clark Rd 97103 503-325-2032
Brian Ploghoft, prin. Fax 325-2298

Knappa SD 4 500/K-12
41535 Old Highway 30 97103 503-458-5993
Paulette Johnson, supt. Fax 458-6979
www.knappa.k12.or.us
Lahti ES 400/K-8
41535 Old Highway 30 97103 503-458-5993
Leila Collier, prin. Fax 458-6023

Peace Learning Center 50/PK-PK
565 12th St 97103 503-325-4041
Holly Dornfeld, dir.

Athena, Umatilla, Pop. 1,106
Athena-Weston SD 29RJ 600/K-12
375 S 5th St 97813 541-566-3551
Laure Quaresma, supt. Fax 566-9454
www.athwest.k12.or.us
Athena ES 200/K-3
375 S 5th St 97813 541-566-3581
Laure Quaresma, prin. Fax 566-9454
Other Schools – See Weston

Aumsville, Marion, Pop. 3,437
Cascade SD 5
Supt. — See Turner
Aumsville ES 600/K-5
572 N 11th St 97325 503-749-8040
Cyndi Ganfield, prin. Fax 749-8049

Aurora, Marion, Pop. 900
North Marion SD 15 2,000/PK-12
20256 Grim Rd NE 97002 503-678-7100
Ginger Redlinger, supt. Fax 678-1473
www.nmarion.k12.or.us
North Marion IS 500/3-5
20237 Grim Rd NE 97002 503-678-7114
Cory Gaub, admin. Fax 678-7187
North Marion MS 400/6-8
20246 Grim Rd NE 97002 503-678-7118
Tami Badinger, prin. Fax 678-7185
North Marion PS 500/PK-2
20257 Grim Rd NE 97002 503-678-8555
Andrew Kronser, admin. Fax 678-8510

Baker City, Baker, Pop. 9,619
Baker SD 5J 1,700/PK-12
2090 4th St 97814 541-524-2260
Mark Witty, supt. Fax 524-2564
www.baker.k12.or.us
Baker MS 300/7-8
2320 Washington Ave 97814 541-524-2500
Skye Flanagan, prin. Fax 524-2563
Brooklyn PS 400/K-3
1350 Washington Ave 97814 541-524-2450
Phil Anderson, prin. Fax 524-2477
Keating ES 50/K-6
2090 4th St 97814 541-523-2377
Mark Witty, admin. Fax 524-2564
South Baker IS 300/4-6
1285 3rd St 97814 541-524-2350
Nanette Lehman, prin. Fax 524-2382
Other Schools – See Haines

Baker Valley SDA S 50/K-8
42171 Chico Rd 97814 541-523-4165

Bandon, Coos, Pop. 2,978
Bandon SD 54 700/K-12
455 9th St SW 97411 541-347-4411
Doug Ardiana, supt. Fax 347-3974
www.bandon.k12.or.us
Harbor Lights MS 200/5-8
390 9th St SW 97411 541-347-4415
Deirdre Pearson, prin. Fax 347-1280
Ocean Crest ES 300/K-4
1040 Allegheny Ave SW 97411 541-347-4416
Becky Armistead, prin. Fax 347-1898

Banks, Washington, Pop. 1,714
Banks SD 13 1,000/K-12
12950 NW Main St 97106 503-324-8591
Jeff Leo, supt. Fax 324-6969
www.banks.k12.or.us
Banks ES 500/K-5
42350 NW Trellis Way 97106 503-324-2772
Darla Waite-Larkin, prin. Fax 324-3333
Banks MS 200/6-8
12850 NW Main St 97106 503-324-3111
Shelley Mitchell, prin. Fax 324-7441

St. Francis of Assisi S 100/K-8
39085 NW Harrington Rd 97106 503-324-2182
Diane Ramsperger, prin. Fax 324-7032

Beavercreek, Clackamas, Pop. 4,358
Oregon City SD 62
Supt. — See Oregon City
Beavercreek ES 500/K-5
21944 S Yeoman Rd 97004 503-785-8350
Cori Waufle, prin. Fax 632-8264

Beaverton, Washington, Pop. 86,161
Beaverton SD 48J 39,200/K-12
16550 SW Merlo Rd 97003 503-356-4500
Don Grotting, supt.
www.beaverton.k12.or.us
Aloha-Huber Park S 900/K-8
5000 SW 173rd Ave 97078 503-356-2000
Scott Drue, prin. Fax 356-2005
Barnes ES 800/K-5
13730 SW Walker Rd 97005 503-356-2130
Paul Mariotta, prin. Fax 356-2135
Beaver Acres ES 800/K-5
2125 SW 170th Ave, 503-356-2020
Stacy Geale, prin. Fax 356-2025
Bethany ES 500/K-5
3305 NW 174th Ave 97006 503-356-2030
Casey Lange, prin. Fax 356-2035
Carson Environmental MS 200/6-8
1600 NW 173rd Ave 97006 503-356-2600
Shirley Brock, prin. Fax 356-2605
Chehalem ES 500/K-5
15555 SW Davis Rd 97007 503-356-2060
Angee Silliman, prin. Fax 356-2065
Conestoga MS 900/6-8
12250 SW Conestoga Dr 97008 503-356-2580
Zan Hess, prin. Fax 356-2585
Cooper Mountain ES 500/K-5
7670 SW 170th Ave 97007 503-356-2070
Kristin LeMon, prin. Fax 356-2075
Elmonica ES 600/K-5
16950 SW Lisa Ct 97006 503-356-2080
Cynthia Lam-Moffett, prin. Fax 356-2085
Fir Grove ES 500/K-5
6300 SW Wilson Ave 97008 503-356-2110
Erin Miles, prin. Fax 356-2115
Five Oaks MS 1,100/6-8
1600 NW 173rd Ave 97006 503-356-2600
Shirley Brock, prin. Fax 356-2605
Greenway ES 400/K-5
9150 SW Downing Dr 97008 503-356-2120
Jennifer Bailey, prin. Fax 356-2125
Highland Park MS 800/6-8
7000 SW Wilson Ave 97008 503-356-2620
Curtis Semana, prin. Fax 356-2625
Hiteon ES 700/K-5
13800 SW Brockman St 97008 503-356-2140
Meghan Warren, prin. Fax 356-2145
McKay ES 400/K-5
7485 SW Scholls Ferry Rd 97008 503-356-2170
Erin Kollings, prin. Fax 356-2175
McKinley ES 700/K-5
1500 NW 185th Ave 97006 503-356-2180
Annie Pleau, prin. Fax 356-2185
Meadow Park MS 800/6-8
14100 SW Downing St 97006 503-356-2640
Jared Freeman, prin. Fax 356-2645
Mountain View MS 800/6-8
17500 SW Farmington Rd 97007 503-356-2660
Matt Pedersen, prin. Fax 356-2665
Oak Hills ES 600/K-5
2625 NW 153rd Ave 97006 503-356-2410
Sheila Baumgardner, prin. Fax 356-2415
Ryles ES 500/K-5
10250 SW Cormorant Dr 97007 503-356-2400
Kayla Bell, prin. Fax 356-2405
Scholls Heights ES 600/K-5
16400 SW Loon Dr 97007 503-356-2460
Monique Singleton, prin. Fax 356-2465
Sexton Mountain ES 600/K-5
15645 SW Sexton Mountain Rd 97007 503-356-2470
Teresa Clemens-Brower, prin. Fax 356-2475
Vose ES 700/K-5
11350 SW Denney Rd 97008 503-356-2430
Veronica Galvan, prin. Fax 356-2435
Whitford MS 700/6-8
7935 SW Scholls Ferry Rd 97008 503-356-2700
Brian Peerenboom, prin. Fax 356-2705
Other Schools – See Aloha, Portland

Agia Sophia Academy 100/PK-8
14485 SW Walker Rd 97006 503-641-4600
Holy Trinity S 300/K-8
13755 SW Walker Rd 97005 503-644-5748
Ashley Sheridan, prin. Fax 643-4475
Pilgrim Lutheran Christian S 200/PK-8
5650 SW Hall Blvd 97005 503-644-8697
Sherri Lam, prin. Fax 644-8182
St. Cecilia S 200/K-8
12250 SW 5th St 97005 503-644-2619
Sue Harris, prin. Fax 646-4217
St. Stephen's Academy 200/PK-12
7275 SW Hall Blvd 97008 503-646-4617
John Breckenridge, hdmstr. Fax 459-7715
Valley Catholic ES K-5
4420 SW Saint Marys Dr 97078 503-718-6500
Krista Jacobson, prin. Fax 718-6520
Valley Catholic MS 6-8
4200 SW St Marys Dr 97078 503-626-3745
Jennifer Gfroerer, prin.
Valor Christian S International 200/K-12
3350 SW 182nd Ave 97006 503-642-1593
Angie Taylor, head sch Fax 649-8031

Bend, Deschutes, Pop. 74,904
Bend-LaPine Administrative SD 1 16,500/K-12
520 NW Wall St, 541-355-1000
Shay Mikalson, supt. Fax 355-1009
www.bend.k12.or.us
Amity Creek ES 200/K-5
437 NW Wall St, 541-355-2800
Andrew Slavin, admin. Fax 355-2810
Bear Creek ES 700/K-5
51 SE 13th St 97702 541-355-1400
Anissa Wiseman, prin. Fax 355-1410
Buckingham ES 500/K-5
62560 Hamby Rd 97701 541-355-2600
Sunshine Dandurand, prin. Fax 355-2610
Cascade MS 900/6-8
19619 Mountaineer Way 97702 541-355-7000
Stephen DuVal, prin. Fax 355-7010
Desert Sky Montessori S K-3
150 NE Bend River Mall, 541-350-2090
Jodie Borgia, prin.
Elk Meadow ES 500/K-5
60880 Brookswood Blvd 97702 541-355-1500
Kelle Hildebrant, prin. Fax 355-1510
Ensworth ES 200/K-5
2150 NE Daggett Ln 97701 541-355-1600
Dana Arntson, prin. Fax 355-1610
High Desert MS 800/6-8
61000 Diamondback Ln 97702 541-355-7200
Susan Heberlein, prin. Fax 355-7210
High Lakes ES 600/K-5
2500 NW High Lakes Loop, 541-355-1700
Linda Burley, prin. Fax 355-1710
Highland Magnet ES at Kenwood 400/K-5
701 NW Newport Ave, 541-355-1900
Brian Kissell, prin. Fax 355-1910
Jewell ES 600/K-5
20550 Murphy Rd 97702 541-355-2100
Scott Edmondson, prin. Fax 355-2110
Juniper ES 600/K-5
1300 NE Norton Ave 97701 541-355-1800
Dan Wolnick, prin. Fax 355-1810
Lava Ridge ES 600/K-5
20805 Cooley Rd 97701 541-355-2400
Gary DeFrang, prin. Fax 355-2410
Miller ES 600/K-5
300 Crosby, 541-355-2500
Jen Healy, prin. Fax 355-2510
Pacific Crest MS 6-8
3030 NW Elwood Ln, 541-355-7800
Chris Boyd, prin. Fax 355-7810
Pilot Butte MS 700/6-8
1501 NE Neff Rd 97701 541-355-7400
Steven Stancliff, prin. Fax 355-7410
Pine Ridge ES 600/K-5
19840 Hollygrape St 97702 541-355-2700
Kevin Gehrig, prin. Fax 355-2710
Ponderosa ES 600/K-5
3790 NE Purcell Blvd 97701 541-355-4300
Stephen Austin, prin. Fax 355-4310
REALMS 100/6-8
63175 O B Riley Rd, 541-355-4900
Roger White, dir. Fax 355-4910
Silver Rail ES K-5
61530 SE Stone Creek Ln 97702 541-355-2900
Tammy Doty, prin. Fax 355-2910
Sky View MS 800/6-8
63555 18th St 97701 541-355-7600
Scott Olszewski, prin. Fax 355-7610
Westside Village Magnet S at Kingston 300/K-8
1101 NW 12th St, 541-355-2000
Wendy Winchel, admin. Fax 355-2010
Other Schools – See La Pine, Sunriver

Redmond SD 2J
Supt. — See Redmond
Tumalo Community S 400/K-8
19835 2nd St, 541-382-2853
Justin Nicklous, prin. Fax 389-4197

Cascades Academy 200/PK-12
19860 Tumalo Reservoir Rd, 541-382-0699
Julie Amberg, head sch Fax 382-0225
Eastmont S 100/PK-5
62425 Eagle Rd 97701 541-382-2049
Anthony Parla, prin. Fax 330-4074
Morning Star Christian S 100/PK-8
19741 Baker Rd 97702 541-382-5091
Joe Bales, admin. Fax 382-0268

St. Francis of Assisi S 300/PK-8
2450 NE 27th St 97701 541-382-4701
Crystal Mooney, prin. Fax 312-9111
Three Sisters Adventist Christian S 50/PK-8
21155 Tumalo Rd, 541-389-2091
Trinity Lutheran S 300/PK-12
2550 NE Butler Market Rd 97701 541-382-1850
Hanne Krause, prin. Fax 382-1850
Waldorf S of Bend 50/PK-8
2150 NE Studio Rd Ste 2 97701 541-330-8841

Blodgett, Benton, Pop. 58
Philomath SD 17J
Supt. — See Philomath
Blodgett ES 50/K-4
PO Box 27 97326 541-453-4101
Susan Halliday, prin. Fax 453-4389

Bly, Klamath
Klamath County SD
Supt. — See Klamath Falls
Gearhart ES 50/K-8
PO Box 47 97622 541-353-2363
James Huntsman, prin. Fax 353-2367

Boardman, Morrow, Pop. 3,160
Morrow SD 1
Supt. — See Irrigon
Boardman ES 300/K-3
PO Box 529 97818 541-481-7383
Sarah Kimmell, prin. Fax 481-2046
Windy River ES 200/4-6
500 Tatone St 97818 541-481-2526
Brandon Hammond, prin. Fax 481-3264

Bonanza, Klamath, Pop. 407
Klamath County SD
Supt. — See Klamath Falls
Bonanza S 200/K-12
PO Box 128 97623 541-545-6581
Arthur Ochoa, prin. Fax 545-1719

Boring, Clackamas
Oregon Trail SD 46
Supt. — See Sandy
Boring MS 400/6-8
27801 SE Dee St 97009 503-668-9393
Tim Werner, prin. Fax 668-5291
Kelso ES 300/K-5
34651 SE Kelso Rd 97009 503-668-8020
Garet Luebbert, prin. Fax 668-0883
Naas ES 300/K-5
12240 SE School Ave 97009 503-668-4454
Kimberly Brooks, prin. Fax 668-5428

Good Shepherd S 200/PK-8
28986 SE Haley Rd 97009 503-663-5280
Greg Suminski, prin. Fax 663-7760
Hood View Junior Academy 100/PK-8
PO Box 128 97009 503-663-4568

Brookings, Curry, Pop. 6,146
Brookings-Harbor SD 17C 1,600/K-12
629 Easy St 97443 541-469-7443
Sean Gallagher, supt. Fax 463-6599
www.brookings.k12.or.us
Azalea MS 400/6-8
629 Easy St 97415 541-469-7427
Nicole Medrano, prin. Fax 469-7080
Kalmiopsis ES 700/K-5
629 Easy St 97415 541-469-7417
Helena Chirinian, prin. Fax 469-0413

Brookings Harbor Christian S 100/PK-11
18881 Cornett Rd 97415 541-469-6478
Kari Schultz, dir. Fax 469-6478

Brooks, Marion, Pop. 395

Willamette Valley Christian S 200/PK-12
9075 Pueblo Ave NE 97305 503-393-5236
Debbie Tipton, prin. Fax 485-8203

Brothers, Deschutes
Crook County SD
Supt. — See Prineville
Brothers ES 50/K-8
34396 Highway 20 East 97712 541-903-2819
Mona Boyd, dir.

Burns, Harney, Pop. 2,728
Harney County SD 3 800/K-12
550 N Court Ave 97720 541-573-6811
Steve Quick, supt. Fax 573-7557
www.burnsschools.k12.or.us
Slater ES 400/K-5
800 N Fairview Ave 97720 541-573-7201
Sid Hobgood, prin. Fax 573-7272
Other Schools – See Hines

Buxton, Washington

Faith Bible West S 50/PK-8
22785 NW Fisher Rd 97109 503-324-4500
Kevin Rex, supt.

Camp Sherman, Jefferson, Pop. 225
Black Butte SD 41 50/K-8
PO Box 150 97730 541-595-6203
Delaney Sharp, lead tchr. Fax 595-5016
www.blackbutte.k12.or.us
Black Butte S 50/K-8
PO Box 150 97730 541-595-6203
Delaney Sharp, lead tchr. Fax 595-5016

Canby, Clackamas, Pop. 15,520
Canby SD 86 4,700/K-12
1130 S Ivy St 97013 503-266-7861
Samuel Goodall, supt. Fax 266-0022
www.canby.k12.or.us
Baker Prairie MS 600/7-8
1859 SE Township Rd 97013 503-263-7170
Jennifer Turner, prin. Fax 263-7189
Eccles ES 500/K-6
562 NW 5th Ave 97013 503-263-7120
Andy McKean, prin. Fax 263-3225
Knight ES 400/K-6
501 N Grant St 97013 503-263-7100
Christine Taylor, prin. Fax 263-2459
Lee ES 400/K-6
1110 S Ivy St 97013 503-263-7150
Cherie Switzer, prin. Fax 263-7159
Trost ES 400/K-6
800 S Redwood St 97013 503-263-7130
Angie Navarro, prin. Fax 263-7139
Other Schools – See Hubbard, Oregon City

Canyon City, Grant, Pop. 694
Grant SD 3 600/K-12
401 N Canyon City Blvd 97820 541-575-1280
Curt Shelley, supt. Fax 575-3614
www.grantesd.k12.or.us
Humbolt ES 300/K-6
329 N Humbolt St 97820 541-575-0454
Kim Smith, prin. Fax 575-3609
Other Schools – See Seneca

Canyonville, Douglas, Pop. 1,804
South Umpqua SD 19
Supt. — See Myrtle Creek
Canyonville ES 200/K-8
PO Box 745 97417 541-839-4396
Doug Park, prin. Fax 839-6528

Canyonville SDA S 50/K-8
PO Box 1155 97417 541-839-4053

Carlton, Yamhill, Pop. 1,912
Yamhill-Carlton SD 1
Supt. — See Yamhill
Yamhill-Carlton ES 400/K-4
420 S 3rd St 97111 503-852-7161
Lauren Berg, prin. Fax 852-7364

Cascade Locks, Hood River, Pop. 1,080
Hood River County SD
Supt. — See Hood River
Cascade Locks ES 100/K-5
PO Box 279 97014 541-374-8467
Amy Moreland, prin. Fax 374-8446

Cave Junction, Josephine, Pop. 1,818
Three Rivers SD
Supt. — See Grants Pass
Byrne MS 300/5-8
101 S Junction Ave 97523 541-592-2163
Scott Polen, prin. Fax 592-4851
Evergreen ES 400/K-4
520 W River St 97523 541-592-3136
David Regal, prin. Fax 592-3186

Madrone Adventist ES 50/PK-8
4300 Holland Loop Rd 97523 541-592-3330

Central Point, Jackson, Pop. 16,683
Central Point SD 6 4,400/K-12
300 Ash St 97502 541-494-6200
Samantha Steele, supt. Fax 664-1637
www.district6.org
Central Point ES 500/K-5
450 S 4th St 97502 541-494-6500
Walt Davenport, prin. Fax 664-1147
Jewett ES 500/K-5
1001 Manzanita St 97502 541-494-6600
Tom Rambo, prin. Fax 664-5035
Richardson ES 600/K-5
200 W Pine St 97502 541-494-6700
Lynn Scott, prin. Fax 665-5881
Sams Valley ES 300/K-5
14235 Table Rock Rd 97502 541-494-6870
Christine Beck, prin. Fax 826-2469
Scenic MS 800/6-8
1955 Scenic Ave 97502 541-494-6400
Brad Eaton, prin. Fax 664-8534
Other Schools – See Gold Hill

New Heights Christian S 50/PK-4
305 Oak St 97502 541-664-5016

Chiloquin, Klamath, Pop. 678
Klamath County SD
Supt. — See Klamath Falls
Chiloquin ES 200/K-6
PO Box 375 97624 541-783-2338
Rita Hepper, prin. Fax 783-2410

Christmas Valley, Lake

Solid Rock Christian S 50/K-12
PO Box 745 97641 541-576-2895
Dr. Megan Eide, head sch Fax 576-3554

Clackamas, Clackamas, Pop. 2,578
North Clackamas SD 12
Supt. — See Milwaukie
Oregon Trail ES 400/K-5
13895 SE 152nd Dr 97015 503-353-5540
Kim Kellogg, prin. Fax 353-5555
Rock Creek MS 800/6-8
14897 SE Parklane Dr 97015 503-353-5680
John Brooks, prin. Fax 353-5695
Sunnyside ES 500/K-5
13401 SE 132nd Ave 97015 503-353-5620
Mike Poter, prin. Fax 353-5635

Spring Mountain Christian Academy PK-12
12152 SE Mather Rd 97015 503-454-0319
Dr. Hanna Grishkevich Ph.D., prin. Fax 286-0473

Clatskanie, Columbia, Pop. 1,681
Clatskanie SD 6J 700/K-12
PO Box 678 97016 503-728-0587
Dr. Lloyd Hartley, supt. Fax 728-0608
www.csd.k12.or.us
Clatskanie ES 300/K-6
PO Box 327 97016 503-728-2191
Brad Thorud, prin. Fax 728-2840

Cloverdale, Tillamook, Pop. 245
Nestucca Valley SD 101 500/K-12
PO Box 99 97112 503-392-4892
David Phelps, supt. Fax 392-9061
www.nestucca.k12.or.us
Nestucca Valley ES 200/K-6
36925 Highway 101 S 97112 503-392-3194
Misty Wharton, prin. Fax 392-4948

Colton, Clackamas
Colton SD 53 600/K-12
30429 S Grays Hill Rd 97017 503-824-3535
Koreen Brown, supt. Fax 824-3530
www.colton.k12.or.us
Colton ES 200/K-5
30439 S Grays Hill Rd 97017 503-824-3536
Nathan Meik, prin. Fax 824-3538
Colton MS 100/6-8
21580 S Schieffer Rd 97017 503-824-2319
Grant Hayball, prin. Fax 824-2309

Columbia City, Columbia, Pop. 1,908
Saint Helens SD 502
Supt. — See Saint Helens
Columbia City S 300/K-6
2000 2nd St 97018 503-366-7550
Jennifer Vanderschuere, prin. Fax 366-3215

Condon, Gilliam, Pop. 677
Condon SD 25J 100/K-12
210 E Bayard St 97823 541-384-2441
Michelle Geer, supt. Fax 384-2504
www.condon.k12.or.us
Condon ES 100/K-8
210 E Bayard St 97823 541-384-2581
Michelle Geer, prin. Fax 384-2585

Coos Bay, Coos, Pop. 15,210
Coos Bay SD 9 3,000/K-12
1255 Hemlock Ave 97420 541-267-3104
Bryan Trendell, supt. Fax 269-5366
www.cbd9.net
Blossom Gulch ES 500/K-3
1255 Hemlock Ave 97420 541-267-1340
Linda Vickrey, prin. Fax 267-7109
Madison ES 400/K-3
1255 Hemlock Ave 97420 541-888-1218
Janice Schock, prin. Fax 888-3064
Millicoma IS 500/4-7
1255 Hemlock Ave 97420 541-267-1468
Michelle Inskeep, prin. Fax 267-8225
Sunset IS 500/4-7
1255 Hemlock Ave 97420 541-888-1242
Shelly McKnight, prin. Fax 888-9814

Christ Lutheran S 100/PK-7
1835 N 15th St 97420 541-267-3851
Rev. Brandt Hoffman, admin. Fax 267-3331
Gold Coast Christian S 50/1-8
2175 Newmark Ave 97420 541-756-7413

Coquille, Coos, Pop. 3,760
Coquille SD 8 400/PK-12
1366 N Gould St 97423 541-396-2181
Tim Sweeney, supt. Fax 396-5015
www.coquille.k12.or.us
Coquille Valley ES 100/1-6
1115 N Baxter St 97423 541-396-2914
Geoff Wetherell, prin. Fax 396-4543
Lincoln S of Early Learning 100/PK-K
1366 N Gould St 97423 541-396-2811
Sharon Nelson, prin. Fax 396-7351

United Valley Christian Academy 50/PK-6
1742 N Fir St 97423 541-396-6079
Julee Phelps, dir. Fax 824-0124

Corbett, Multnomah
Corbett SD 39 900/K-12
35800 E Historic Colmb Riv 97019 503-261-4211
Dr. Randy Trani, supt. Fax 695-3641
corbett.k12.or.us
CAPS 100/K-8
35800 E Historic Colmb Riv 97019 503-261-4294
Lori Luna M.Ed., prin. Fax 695-3641
Corbett ES 300/K-5
35800 E Historic Colmb Riv 97019 503-261-4236
DeeDee Hanes M.Ed., prin. Fax 261-4288
Corbett MS 200/6-8
35800 E Historic Colmb Riv 97019 503-261-4226
Randy Trani, prin. Fax 695-3641

Cornelius, Washington, Pop. 11,622
Forest Grove SD 15
Supt. — See Forest Grove
Cornelius ES 500/PK-4
200 N 14th Ave 97113 503-359-2500
Angella Graves, prin. Fax 359-2564
Echo Shaw ES 300/PK-6
914 S Linden St 97113 503-359-2489
Dr. Perla Rodriguez, prin. Fax 359-2567

Hillsboro SD 1J
Supt. — See Hillsboro
Free Orchards ES 500/K-6
2499 S Beech St 97113 503-844-1140
Karen Murphy, prin. Fax 844-1142

Forest Hills Lutheran Christian S 200/PK-8
4221 SW Golf Course Rd 97113 503-359-4853
Mike Schiemann, prin. Fax 357-2213
Swallowtail Waldorf S and Farm 100/PK-8
460 S Heather St 97113 503-846-0336

Corvallis, Benton, Pop. 52,340
Corvallis SD 509J 6,400/K-12
PO Box 3509J 97339 541-757-5811
Ryan Noss, supt. Fax 757-5703
www.csd509j.net/
Adams ES 400/K-5
1615 SW 35th St 97333 541-757-5938
Byron Bethards, prin. Fax 757-4586
Cheldelin MS 500/6-8
987 NE Conifer Blvd 97330 541-757-5971
Darren Bland, prin. Fax 757-4596
Franklin K-8 S 400/K-8
750 NW 18th St 97330 541-757-5747
Craig Harlow, prin. Fax 757-5766
Garfield ES 400/K-5
1205 NW Garfield Ave 97330 541-757-5941
Leigh Santy, prin. Fax 757-4588
Hoover ES 400/K-5
3838 NW Walnut Blvd 97330 541-757-5958
Anna Marie Gosser, prin. Fax 757-4590
Jefferson ES 300/K-5
1825 NW 27th St 97330 541-757-5951
Melissa Harder, prin. Fax 757-4592
Lincoln ES 400/K-5
110 SE Alexander Ave 97333 541-757-5955
Aaron Hale, prin. Fax 757-4593
Mountain View ES 300/K-5
340 NE Granger Ave 97330 541-766-4760
Lisa Krause, prin. Fax 766-4764
Pauling MS 700/6-8
1111 NW Cleveland Ave 97330 541-757-5961
Alicia Ward-Satey, prin. Fax 757-4598
Wilson ES 400/K-5
2701 NW Satinwood St 97330 541-757-5988
Eric Beasley, prin. Fax 757-4595

Ashbrook Independent S 200/PK-8
4045 SW Research Way 97333 541-766-8313
Cindy Roelofs, prin. Fax 766-1066
Corvallis Montessori S 100/PK-2
2730 NW Greeley Ave 97330 541-753-2513
Tamara Basham, head sch
Corvallis Waldorf S 200/PK-8
3855 NE Highway 20 97330 541-758-4674
Peter Zaremba, dir. Fax 758-5091
Santiam Christian S 600/PK-12
7220 NE Arnold Ave 97330 541-745-5524
Lance Villers, supt. Fax 745-6338
Zion Lutheran S 200/PK-8
2800 NW Tyler Ave 97330 541-753-7503
Jonathan Schultz, prin. Fax 754-8254

Cottage Grove, Lane, Pop. 9,371
South Lane SD 45J3 2,900/K-12
PO Box 218 97424 541-942-3381
Dr. Krista Parent, supt. Fax 942-8098
www.slane.k12.or.us
Bohemia ES 500/K-5
721 S R St 97424 541-942-3313
Heather Bridgens, prin. Fax 767-5958
Harrison ES 400/K-5
1000 S 10th St 97424 541-942-3389
Heidi Brown, prin. Fax 942-1316
Latham ES 100/K-5
32112 Latham Rd 97424 541-942-0147
Anne Fisk, prin. Fax 767-2180
Lincoln MS 500/6-8
1565 S 4th St 97424 541-942-3316
Jeremy Smith, prin. Fax 942-9801
London S 100/K-8
73288 London Rd 97424 541-942-0183
Bill Bechen, prin. Fax 942-8849
Other Schools – See Dorena

Crane, Harney, Pop. 128
Harney County SD 4 100/K-8
PO Box 828 97732 541-493-2641
Matt Hawley, supt. Fax 493-2051
www.harneyuh.k12.or.us
Crane S 100/K-8
PO Box 828 97732 541-493-2641
Matt Hawley, supt. Fax 493-2051

Creswell, Lane, Pop. 4,867
Creswell SD 40 1,300/K-12
998 A St 97426 541-895-6000
Todd Hamilton, supt. Fax 895-6019
www.creswell.k12.or.us
Creslane ES 600/K-5
996 A St 97426 541-895-6140
Ryan Beck, prin. Fax 895-6199
Creswell MS 300/6-8
655 W Oregon Ave 97426 541-895-6090
Shirley Burrus, prin. Fax 895-6139

Creswell Christian S 100/PK-12
PO Box 217 97426 541-895-4622
Rebecca Lake, prin. Fax 895-4622

Culver, Jefferson, Pop. 1,338
Culver SD 4 700/K-12
PO Box 259 97734 541-546-2541
Stefanie Garber, supt. Fax 546-7517
www.culver.k12.or.us/
Culver ES 300/K-5
PO Box 259 97734 541-546-6861
Stefanie Garber, prin. Fax 546-7522
Culver MS 200/6-8
PO Box 259 97734 541-546-3090
Brad Kudlac, prin. Fax 546-2137

Dallas, Polk, Pop. 14,264
Dallas SD 2 3,200/K-12
111 SW Ash St 97338 503-623-5594
Dr. Michelle Johnstone, supt. Fax 623-5597
www.dallas.k12.or.us
LaCreole MS 700/6-8
701 SE Lacreole Dr 97338 503-623-6662
Jamie Richardson, prin. Fax 623-8477
Lyle ES 400/K-3
185 SW Levens St 97338 503-623-8367
Amber Eaton, prin. Fax 623-2071
Oakdale Heights ES 400/K-3
1375 SW Maple St 97338 503-623-8316
Todd Baughman, prin. Fax 623-5165
Whitworth ES 400/4-5
1151 SE Miller Ave 97338 503-623-8351
Caleb Harris, prin. Fax 623-6089

Faith Christian S 100/PK-8
2290 E Ellendale Ave 97338 503-623-6632
Michele Stein, prin. Fax 623-4563

Damascus, Clackamas, Pop. 10,286
Gresham-Barlow SD 10J
Supt. — See Gresham
Deep Creek Damascus ES 200/K-8
14151 SE 242nd Ave, 503-658-3171
Lori Walter, prin. Fax 658-6275

Damascus Christian S 200/K-12
14251 SE Rust Way, 503-658-4100
Zachary Davidson, prin. Fax 658-5827

Dayton, Yamhill, Pop. 2,476
Dayton SD 8 1,000/K-12
PO Box 219 97114 503-864-2215
Jason Hay, supt. Fax 864-3927
daytonk12.org
Dayton ES 400/K-5
526 Ferry St 97114 503-864-2217
Stephanie Ewing, prin. Fax 864-3766
Dayton JHS 200/6-8
801 Ferry St 97114 503-864-2246
Jami Fluke, prin. Fax 864-2932

Dayville, Grant, Pop. 148
Dayville SD 16J 100/PK-12
PO Box C 97825 541-987-2412
Kathryn Hedrick, supt. Fax 987-2155
www.dayvilleschools.com
Dayville S 100/PK-12
PO Box C 97825 541-987-2412
Kathryn Hedrick, prin. Fax 987-2155

Diamond, Harney
Diamond SD 7 50/K-8
40524 S Diamond Ln 97722 541-493-2464
Fax 493-2858
www.harneyesd.k12.or.us
Diamond ES 50/K-8
40524 S Diamond Ln 97722 541-493-2464
Rae-Jean Neumann, lead tchr. Fax 493-2858

Dorena, Lane
South Lane SD 45J3
Supt. — See Cottage Grove
Dorena S 100/K-8
37141 Row River Rd 97434 541-946-1506
Linda Pabst, prin. Fax 767-3516

Drain, Douglas, Pop. 1,120
North Douglas SD 22 300/K-12
PO Box 428 97435 541-836-2223
John Lahley, supt. Fax 836-7558
www.northdouglas.k12.or.us
North Douglas ES 200/K-8
PO Box 338 97435 541-836-2213
Jody Cyr, prin. Fax 836-7034

Drewsey, Harney
Drewsey SD 13 50/K-8
PO Box 109 97904 541-493-2367
Fax 493-2401
Drewsey ES 50/K-8
PO Box 109 97904 541-493-2367
Jodi Miller, lead tchr. Fax 493-2401

Pine Creek SD 5 50/K-8
79654 Pine Creek Rd 97904 541-573-3229
Julie Opie, contact Fax 573-3229
Pine Creek S 50/K-8
79654 Pine Creek Rd 97904 541-493-2600
Katherine Tracy, lead tchr. Fax 493-2602

Dufur, Wasco, Pop. 590
Dufur SD 29 300/K-12
802 NE 5th St 97021 541-467-2509
Jack Henderson, supt. Fax 467-2589
www.dufur.k12.or.us
Dufur S 300/K-12
802 NE 5th St 97021 541-467-2509
Leo Baptiste, prin. Fax 467-2589

Dundee, Yamhill, Pop. 3,085
Newberg SD 29J
Supt. — See Newberg
Dundee ES 300/K-5
140 SW 5th St 97115 503-554-4850
Reed Langdon, prin. Fax 538-0729

Eagle Point, Jackson, Pop. 8,245
Jackson County SD 9 3,600/PK-12
PO Box 548 97524 541-830-6551
Cynda Rickert, supt. Fax 830-6550
www.eaglepnt.k12.or.us
Eagle Point MS 500/6-8
PO Box 218 97524 541-830-1250
Heather Marinucci, prin. Fax 830-6086
Eagle Rock ES 300/K-5
1280 Barton Rd 97524 541-830-6162
Joni Parsons, prin. Fax 830-6195
Hillside ES 500/K-5
PO Box 549 97524 541-830-1225
Jodi Salinas, prin. Fax 830-6150
Lake Creek Learning Center 100/K-5
391 Lake Creek Loop 97524 541-830-1540
Joni Parsons, prin. Fax 830-6369
Other Schools – See Shady Cove, White City

St. John Lutheran S 100/PK-5
42 Alta Vista Rd 97524 541-826-4334
Linda Tripp, admin.
Shady Point SDA S 50/1-8
PO Box 216 97524 541-826-2255

Echo, Umatilla, Pop. 686
Echo SD 5 300/PK-12
600 E Gerone St 97826 541-376-8436
Raymon Smith, supt. Fax 376-8473
www.echo.k12.or.us
Echo S 300/PK-12
600 E Gerone St 97826 541-376-8436
Raymon Smith, prin. Fax 376-8473

Elgin, Union, Pop. 1,678
Elgin SD 23 400/PK-12
PO Box 68 97827 541-437-1211
Dianne Greif, supt. Fax 437-1231
www.elgin.k12.or.us
Mayfield S 300/PK-6
PO Box 35 97827 541-437-2321
Dianne Greif, prin. Fax 437-8212

Elmira, Lane
Fern Ridge SD 28J 1,500/K-12
88834 Territorial Rd 97437 541-935-2253
Gary Carpenter, supt. Fax 935-8222
www.fernridge.k12.or.us
Elmira ES 300/K-5
88960 Territorial Rd 97437 541-935-8214
Michelle Marshall, prin. Fax 935-8243
Fern Ridge MS 300/6-8
88831 Territorial Rd 97437 541-935-8230
Olivia Johnson, prin. Fax 935-8234
Other Schools – See Veneta

Enterprise, Wallowa, Pop. 1,904
Enterprise SD 21 400/K-12
201 SE 4th St 97828 541-426-3193
Erika Pinkerton, supt. Fax 426-3504
www.enterprise.k12.or.us
Enterprise ES 200/K-6
201 SE 4th St 97828 541-426-3812
Erika Pinkerton, prin. Fax 426-4485

Troy SD 54 50/K-8
66247 Redmond Grade Ln 97828 541-828-7788
Karen Patton, supt. Fax 426-7748
www.troy.k12.or.us
Troy S 50/K-8
66247 Redmond Grade Ln 97828 541-426-7600
Karen Patton, prin. Fax 426-3732

Enterprise SDA S 50/1-8
PO Box N 97828 541-426-8339

Estacada, Clackamas, Pop. 2,646
Estacada SD 108 2,400/K-12
255 NE 6th Ave 97023 503-630-6871
Marla Stephenson, supt. Fax 630-8513
www.estacada.k12.or.us
Clackamas River ES 500/K-5
301 NE 2nd Ave 97023 503-630-8552
Amy Hudson, prin. Fax 630-8577
Estacada MS 300/6-8
500 NE Main St 97023 503-630-8516
Kristin Turnquist, prin. Fax 630-8693
River Mill ES 300/K-5
850 N Broadway St 97023 503-630-8517
Jennifer Behrman, prin. Fax 630-8676

Eugene, Lane, Pop. 149,658
Bethel SD 52 5,600/K-12
4640 Barger Dr 97402 541-689-3280
Chris Parra, supt. Fax 689-0719
www.bethel.k12.or.us
Cascade MS 300/6-8
1525 Echo Hollow Rd 97402 541-689-0641
Natalie Oliver, prin. Fax 689-9622
Clear Lake ES 300/K-5
4646 Barger Dr 97402 541-689-0511
John Luhman, prin. Fax 689-5617
Danebo ES 300/K-5
1265 Candlelight Dr 97402 541-688-8735
Mari Ford, prin. Fax 607-8186
Fairfield ES 300/K-5
3455 Royal Ave 97402 541-689-3751
Jenny Sink, prin. Fax 689-9956
Irving ES 400/K-5
3200 Hyacinth St 97404 541-688-2620
Nathan Bridgens, prin. Fax 607-9706
Malabon ES 400/K-5
1380 Taney St 97402 541-461-6421
Maureen Spence, prin. Fax 607-9708
Meadow View S 800/K-8
1855 Legacy St 97402 541-607-9700
Erika Case, prin. Fax 607-9702
Prairie Mountain S 700/K-8
5305 Royal Ave 97402 541-607-9849
Carey Killen, prin. Fax 607-9856
Shasta MS 500/6-8
4656 Barger Dr 97402 541-688-9611
Brady Cottle, prin. Fax 689-9382

Crow-Applegate-Lorane SD 66 300/K-12
85955 Territorial Hwy 97402 541-935-2100
Aaron Brown, supt. Fax 935-6107
www.cal.k12.or.us
Applegate ES 100/K-6
85955 Territorial Hwy 97402 541-935-2100
Aaron Brown, prin. Fax 935-6107

Eugene SD 4J 16,400/PK-12
200 N Monroe St 97402 541-790-7700
Dr. Gustavo Balderas, supt. Fax 790-7711
www.4j.lane.edu
Adams ES 400/K-5
950 W 22nd Ave 97405 541-790-5000
Kevin Gordon, prin. Fax 790-5005
Arts and Technology Academy at Jefferson 300/6-8
1650 W 22nd Ave 97405 541-790-5700
Larry Williams, prin. Fax 790-5705
Awbrey Park ES 400/K-5
158 Spring Creek Dr 97404 541-790-4050
Michael Riplinger, prin. Fax 790-4055
Buena Vista Spanish Immersion ES 400/K-5
1500 Queens Way 97401 541-790-6500
Melissa Ibarra, prin. Fax 790-6505
Camas Ridge Community S 400/K-5
1150 E 29th Ave 97403 541-790-8800
Wes Flinn, prin. Fax 790-8805
Charlemagne French Immersion ES 300/K-5
3875 Kincaid St 97405 541-790-7080
Eric Anderson, prin. Fax 790-7085
Chavez ES 400/K-5
1510 W 14th Ave 97402 541-790-5300
Denisa Taylor, prin. Fax 790-5310
Chinese Language Immersion S 50/K-2
155 Crest Dr 97405 541-790-3700
Jennifer Hebard, prin. Fax 790-3705
Corridor ES 300/K-5
250 Silver Ln 97404 541-790-4600
Thomas Piowaty, prin. Fax 790-4605
Edgewood Community ES 400/K-5
577 E 46th Ave 97405 541-790-8700
Jim Moore, prin. Fax 790-8705
Edison ES 400/K-5
1328 E 22nd Ave 97403 541-790-8900
Scott Marsh, prin. Fax 790-8905
Family MS 6-8
1650 W 22nd Ave 97405 541-790-5700
Larry Williams, prin. Fax 790-5705
Family S 200/K-5
1155 Crest Dr 97405 541-790-3700
Jennifer Hebard, prin. Fax 790-3705
Gilham ES 500/K-5
3307 Honeywood St 97408 541-790-6200
Gina Wilde, prin. Fax 790-6205
Holt ES 600/K-5
770 Calvin St 97401 541-790-6100
Joyce Smith-Johnson, prin. Fax 790-6141
Howard ES 300/PK-5
700 Howard Ave 97404 541-790-4900
Allan Chinn, prin. Fax 790-4905
Kelly MS 400/6-8
850 Howard Ave 97404 541-790-4740
Juan Cuadros, prin. Fax 790-4746
Kennedy MS 500/6-8
2200 Bailey Hill Rd 97405 541-790-5500
Morgan Christensen, prin. Fax 790-5505
Madison MS 500/6-8
875 Wilkes Dr 97404 541-790-4300
Peter Barsotti, prin. Fax 790-4320
McCornack ES 300/K-5
1968 Brittany St 97405 541-790-5800
Londa Rochholz, prin. Fax 790-5805
Monroe MS 500/6-8
2800 Bailey Ln 97401 541-790-6300
Mike Johnson, prin. Fax 790-6305
River Road/El Camino del Rio ES 300/K-5
120 W Hilliard Ln 97404 541-790-7200
Joel Lavin, prin. Fax 790-7205
Roosevelt MS 600/6-8
500 E 24th Ave 97405 541-790-8500
Chris Mitchell, prin. Fax 790-8505
Spencer Butte MS 500/6-8
500 E 43rd Ave 97405 541-790-8300
Tasha Katsuda, prin. Fax 790-8305
Spring Creek ES 400/K-5
560 Irvington Dr 97404 541-790-4870
Raquel Gwinn, prin. Fax 790-4880
Twin Oaks ES 200/K-5
85916 Bailey Hill Rd 97405 541-790-3417
Lizette Rodgers, prin. Fax 790-3305
Willagillespie ES 500/K-5
1125 Willagillespie Rd 97401 541-790-7100
David Jacobson, prin. Fax 790-7105
Young MS 500/6-8
2555 Gilham Rd 97408 541-790-6400
Jericho Dunn, prin. Fax 790-6456
Yujin Gakuen Japanese Immersion ES 300/K-5
250 Silver Ln 97404 541-790-4606
Tom Piowaty, prin. Fax 790-4610

Eugene Christian S 100/PK-8
2895 Chad Dr 97408 541-686-9145
Jared Mlynczyk, prin. Fax 686-3190
Eugene Waldorf S 100/PK-8
1350 McLean Blvd 97405 541-683-6951
LIFE! Lutheran S 50/PK-6
710 E 17th Ave 97401 541-342-5433
Shar Heinz M.Ed., prin. Fax 342-2241
Oak Hill S 100/K-12
86397 Eldon Schafer Dr 97405 541-744-0954
Robert Sarkisian, head sch Fax 741-6968
O'Hara Catholic S 500/PK-8
715 W 18th Ave 97402 541-485-5291
Tammy Conway, prin. Fax 484-9138
St. Paul S 300/PK-8
1201 Satre St 97401 541-344-1401
Kelli Braud, prin. Fax 344-2572

Willamette Christian S 200/PK-8
2500 W 18th Ave 97402 541-686-8655
Dr. John Eckelbarger, prin. Fax 686-8747

Fairview, Multnomah, Pop. 8,478
Reynolds SD 7 11,600/PK-12
1204 NE 201st Ave 97024 503-661-7200
Linda Florence, supt. Fax 667-6932
www.reynolds.k12.or.us
Fairview ES 400/K-5
225 Main St 97024 503-667-2954
Jonathan Steinhoff, prin. Fax 262-3787
Reynolds MS 1,000/6-8
1200 NE 201st Ave 97024 503-665-8166
Stacy Talus, prin. Fax 262-3796
Salish Ponds ES 500/K-5
1210 NE 201st Ave 97024 503-492-7260
Henry Ramirez, prin. Fax 491-3469
Woodland ES 500/K-5
21607 NE Glisan St 97024 503-674-8188
Rob Robinson, prin. Fax 262-3794
Other Schools – See Portland, Troutdale

Falls City, Polk, Pop. 925
Falls City SD 57 200/K-12
111 N Main St 97344 503-787-3521
Jack Thompson, supt. Fax 787-5805
www.fallscityschools.org
Falls City ES 100/K-8
177 Prospect Ave 97344 503-787-3521
Art Houghtaling, prin. Fax 787-5805

Fields, Harney
South Harney SD 33 50/K-8
23657 Fields Denio Rd 97710 541-495-2233
Stacey Moser, admin. Fax 495-1910
Fields ES 50/K-8
23657 Fields Denio Rd 97710 541-495-2233
Stacey Moser, admin. Fax 495-1910

Finn Rock, Lane
McKenzie SD 68 200/K-12
51187 Blue River Dr, Vida OR 97488 541-822-3338
Jim Thomas, supt. Fax 822-8014
www.mckenzie.k12.or.us
McKenzie ES 200/K-8
51187 Blue River Dr, Vida OR 97488 541-822-3315
Lane Tompkins, prin. Fax 822-8014

Florence, Lane, Pop. 8,201
Siuslaw SD 97J 1,300/K-12
2111 Oak St 97439 541-997-2651
Andy Grzeskowiak, supt. Fax 997-6748
www.siuslaw.k12.or.us
Siuslaw ES 600/K-5
2221 Oak St 97439 541-997-2514
Michael Harklerode, prin. Fax 997-4163
Siuslaw MS 300/6-8
2525 Oak St 97439 541-997-8241
Andy Marohl, prin. Fax 902-7478

Shoreline Christian S 1-8
4445 Highway 101 97439 541-997-5909

Forest Grove, Washington, Pop. 20,448
Forest Grove SD 15 5,900/PK-12
1728 Main St 97116 503-357-6171
Dr. Yvonne Curtis, supt. Fax 359-2520
www.fgsd.k12.or.us
Armstrong MS 800/7-8
1777 Mountain View Ln 97116 503-359-2465
Osvaldo Garcia-Contreras, prin. Fax 359-2560
Clarke ES 500/K-4
2516 B St 97116 503-359-2478
Pete Moshinsky, prin. Fax 359-2561
Dilley ES 300/K-4
4115 SW Dilley Rd 97116 503-359-2493
Mariela Mireles, prin. Fax 359-2565
Fern Hill ES 400/K-4
4445 Heather St 97116 503-359-2550
Naomi Montelongo, prin. Fax 359-2570
Gale ES 300/K-4
3130 18th Ave 97116 503-359-2482
Gretchen Schlag, prin. Fax 359-2562
McCall Upper ES 800/5-6
1341 Pacific Ave 97116 503-359-2506
Chandra Cooper, prin. Fax 359-2566
Other Schools – See Cornelius

Visitation S 100/K-8
4189 NW Visitation Rd 97116 503-357-6990
Carol Funk, prin. Fax 359-0819

Foster, Linn
Sweet Home SD 55
Supt. — See Sweet Home
Foster ES 300/K-6
PO Box 747 97345 541-367-7180
Luke Augsburger, prin. Fax 367-8902

Frenchglen, Harney
Frenchglen SD 16 100/K-12
39235 Highway 205 97736 541-493-2404
Fax 493-4660
www.frenchglen.k12.or.us
Frenchglen S 50/K-8
39235 Highway 205 97736 541-493-2404
Carolyn Koskela, lead tchr. Fax 493-4660

Garibaldi, Tillamook, Pop. 757
Neah-Kah-Nie SD 56
Supt. — See Rockaway
Garibaldi ES 200/K-5
PO Box 317 97118 503-322-0311
Janmarie Nugent, prin. Fax 322-2193

Gaston, Washington, Pop. 631
Gaston SD 511J 500/K-12
PO Box 68 97119 503-985-0210
Susy McKenzie, supt. Fax 985-3366
www.gaston.k12.or.us
Gaston ES 300/K-6
PO Box 68 97119 503-985-7240
Tim Larkin, prin. Fax 985-7663

Gearhart, Clatsop, Pop. 1,434
Seaside SD 10
Supt. — See Seaside
Gearhart ES 300/K-5
1002 Pacific Way 97138 503-738-8348
Juliann Wozniak, prin. Fax 738-8349

Gervais, Marion, Pop. 2,415
Gervais SD 1 1,100/PK-12
PO Box 100 97026 503-792-3803
Matt Henry, supt. Fax 792-3809
www.gervais.k12.or.us
Gervais ES 500/PK-5
150 Douglas Ave 97026 503-792-3803
Sylvia Valentine-Garcia, prin. Fax 792-3626
Gervais MS 200/6-8
PO Box 176 97026 503-792-3626
Ann O'Connell, prin. Fax 792-3770

Sacred Heart S 100/K-8
PO Box 215 97026 503-792-4541
Lucy Shindler-Shawn, prin. Fax 792-3826

Gilchrist, Klamath
Klamath County SD
Supt. — See Klamath Falls
Gilchrist S 100/K-12
PO Box 668 97737 541-433-2295
Steve Prock, prin. Fax 433-2688

Gladstone, Clackamas, Pop. 11,109
Gladstone SD 115 2,100/PK-12
17789 Webster Rd 97027 503-655-2777
Bob Stewart, supt. Fax 655-5201
www.gladstone.k12.or.us
Gladstone Center for Children 200/PK-K
18905 Portland Ave 97027 503-496-3939
Carol Kemhus, dir. Fax 479-6075
Kraxberger MS 500/6-8
17777 Webster Rd 97027 503-655-3636
John Olson, prin. Fax 650-2596
Wetten ES 700/1-5
250 E Exeter St 97027 503-656-6564
Wendy Wilson, prin. Fax 656-0917

Grace Christian S 100/PK-12
6460 Glen Echo Ave 97027 503-655-3074
Paideia Classical Christian S 50/K-8
6125 Caldwell Rd 97027 503-974-4711
Rivergate Adventist ES 200/PK-8
1505 Rivergate School Rd 97027 503-656-0544

Glendale, Douglas, Pop. 847
Glendale SD 77 300/K-12
PO Box E 97442 541-832-1760
David Hanson, supt. Fax 832-3183
www.glendale.k12.or.us
Glendale ES 200/K-8
PO Box E 97442 541-832-1701
Sean O'Brady, prin. Fax 832-2158

Glide, Douglas, Pop. 1,756
Glide SD 12 600/K-12
301 Glide Loop Dr 97443 541-496-3521
Mike Narkiewicz, supt. Fax 496-4300
www.glide.k12.or.us
Glide ES 300/K-6
1477 Glide Loop Dr 97443 541-496-3524
Jerry Halter, prin. Fax 496-4301
Glide MS 100/7-8
18990 N Umpqua Hwy 97443 541-496-3516
Dr. Kristina Haug, prin. Fax 496-4302

Gold Beach, Curry, Pop. 2,158
Central Curry SD 1 500/K-12
29516 Ellensburg Ave 97444 541-247-2003
Roy Durfee, supt. Fax 247-9717
www.ccsd.k12.or.us
Riley Creek ES 300/K-8
94350 6th St 97444 541-247-6604
Tom Denning, prin. Fax 247-6484

Gold Hill, Jackson, Pop. 1,181
Central Point SD 6
Supt. — See Central Point
Hanby MS 200/6-8
806 6th Ave N 97525 541-494-6800
Scott Dippel, prin. Fax 855-1120
Patrick ES 200/K-5
1500 2nd Ave 97525 541-494-6840
Sara Hanberg, prin. Fax 855-7487

Grants Pass, Josephine, Pop. 33,499
Grants Pass SD 7 5,700/K-12
725 NE Dean Dr 97526 541-474-5700
Kirk Kolb, supt. Fax 474-5705
www.grantspass.k12.or.us
Allen Dale ES 500/K-5
2320 Williams Hwy 97527 541-474-5760
Jake Musser, prin. Fax 474-5762
Highland ES 400/K-5
1845 NW Highland Ave 97526 541-474-5765
George Personius, prin. Fax 474-5767
Lincoln ES 500/K-5
1132 NE 10th St 97526 541-474-5770
Missy Fitzsimmons, prin. Fax 474-5718
North MS 700/6-8
1725 NW Highland Ave 97526 541-474-5740
Tommy Blanchard, prin. Fax 474-5739

Parkside ES 400/K-5
735 SW Wagner Meadows Dr 97526 541-474-5777
Rob Lewis, prin. Fax 474-9579
Redwood ES 500/K-5
3163 Leonard Rd 97527 541-474-5775
Christine Mooney, prin. Fax 474-5768
Riverside ES 400/K-5
1200 SE Harvey Dr 97526 541-474-5780
Rob Henderson, prin. Fax 474-5782
South MS 600/6-8
350 W Harbeck Rd 97527 541-474-5750
Jeff Weiss, prin. Fax 474-9742

Three Rivers SD 4,800/K-12
8550 New Hope Rd 97527 541-862-3111
Dave Valenzuela, supt. Fax 862-3119
www.threerivers.k12.or.us
Fleming MS 400/6-8
6001 Monument Dr 97526 541-476-8284
Lori Conner, prin. Fax 471-2458
Ft. Vannoy ES 300/K-5
5250 Upper River Rd 97526 541-479-4440
Alicia Timbs, prin. Fax 471-2445
Fruitdale ES 400/K-5
1560 Bill Baker Way 97527 541-476-2276
Heather Yount, prin. Fax 471-2447
Lincoln Savage MS 400/6-8
8551 New Hope Rd 97527 541-862-2171
Mark Higgins, prin. Fax 862-2713
Madrona ES 400/K-5
520 Detrick Dr 97527 541-476-6624
Miranda Carpenter, prin. Fax 471-2452
Manzanita ES 400/K-5
310 San Francisco St 97526 541-479-6433
Renee Hults, prin. Fax 471-2450
Other Schools – See Applegate, Cave Junction, Williams

Brighton Academy 100/PK-12
1121 NE 7th St 97526 541-474-6865
Grants Pass Adventist S 100/K-10
2250 NW Heidi Ln 97526 541-479-2293
Richard Rasmussen, prin. Fax 479-8412
New Hope Christian S 200/PK-12
5961 New Hope Rd 97527 541-476-4588
Ron Hanson, admin. Fax 474-7626
St. Anne S 100/PK-6
1131 NE 10th St 97526 541-479-1582
Colleen Kotrba, prin. Fax 479-1582
Vineyard Christian S 100/PK-8
275 Potts Way 97526 541-479-9649
Doug Thomas, prin. Fax 479-3506

Gresham, Multnomah, Pop. 101,317
Centennial SD 28J
Supt. — See Portland
Butler Creek ES 500/K-6
2789 SW Butler Rd 97080 503-762-6100
Andrea Sande, prin. Fax 762-6110
Pleasant Valley ES 500/K-6
17625 SE Foster Rd 97080 503-762-3209
Laura Nixon, prin. Fax 762-3239

Gresham-Barlow SD 10J 11,900/PK-12
1331 NW Eastman Pkwy 97030 503-261-4550
Dr. A. Katrise Perera, supt. Fax 261-4552
www.gresham.k12.or.us
Clear Creek MS 700/6-8
219 NE 219th Ave 97030 503-492-6700
David Atherton, prin. Fax 492-6707
East Gresham ES 500/K-5
900 SE 5th St 97080 503-661-6050
Kimberly Miles, prin. Fax 665-4131
East Orient ES 400/K-5
7431 SE 302nd Ave 97080 503-663-4818
James Milliken, prin. Fax 663-6008
Hall ES 500/K-5
2505 NE 23rd St 97030 503-661-6330
Heidi Lasher, prin. Fax 492-6728
Highland ES 500/K-5
295 NE 24th St 97030 503-665-7158
Shawnda Sewell, prin. Fax 492-6755
Hogan Cedars ES 600/K-5
1770 SE Fleming Ave 97080 503-261-4500
Elaine Luckenbaugh, prin. Fax 261-4546
Hollydale ES 400/K-5
505 SW Birdsdale Dr 97080 503-661-6226
Debra James, prin. Fax 492-6718
Kelly Creek ES 600/K-5
2400 SE Baker Way 97080 503-663-7483
Nancy Torbert, prin. Fax 663-7491
McCarty MS 600/6-8
1400 SE 5th St 97080 503-665-0148
John George, prin. Fax 669-1892
North Gresham ES 500/K-5
1001 SE 217th Ave 97030 503-661-6415
Tracy Klinger, prin. Fax 666-4873
Powell Valley ES 500/K-5
4825 SE Powell Valley Rd 97080 503-661-1510
Michele Cook, prin. Fax 492-6711
Russell MS 800/6-8
3625 SE Powell Valley Rd 97080 503-667-6900
Rolland Hayden, prin. Fax 492-6708
West Gresham ES 300/K-5
330 W Powell Blvd 97030 503-661-0144
Carlynn Capps, prin. Fax 492-6735
West Orient MS 400/6-8
29805 SE Orient Dr 97080 503-663-3323
Elise Cantanese, prin. Fax 663-2504
Other Schools – See Damascus

Phonics Phactory 300/PK-10
PO Box 2128 97030 503-661-5632
Rev. Brian Mayer, admin. Fax 907-5827
Portland Adventist ES 300/PK-8
3990 NW 1st St 97030 503-665-4102
Brandon O'Neal, prin. Fax 665-9486

Haines, Baker, Pop. 402
Baker SD 5J
Supt. — See Baker City
Haines ES 100/PK-6
PO Box 306 97833 541-524-2400
Marilyn McBride, prin. Fax 524-2427

Halsey, Linn, Pop. 874
Central Linn SD 552 700/K-12
PO Box 200 97348 541-369-2813
Brian Gardner, supt. Fax 369-3439
www.centrallinn.k12.or.us
Central Linn ES 400/K-6
239 W 2nd St 97348 541-369-2851
Amanda OBrien, prin. Fax 369-3437

Happy Valley, Clackamas, Pop. 13,434
North Clackamas SD 12
Supt. — See Milwaukie
Duncan ES 500/K-5
14898 SE Parklane Dr 97015 503-353-3270
Mason Branstetter, prin. Fax 353-3285
Happy Valley ES 400/K-5
13865 SE King Rd, 503-353-5420
Dianna Ngai, prin. Fax 353-5435
Happy Valley MS 1,000/6-8
13865 SE King Rd Ste B, 503-353-1920
Emily Behunin, prin. Fax 353-1935
Mt. Scott ES 400/K-5
11201 SE Stevens Rd, 503-353-5500
Cameron Kitchen, prin. Fax 353-5515
Scouters Mountain ES 500/K-5
10811 SE 172nd Ave, 503-353-3250
Kevin Spooner, prin. Fax 353-3265
Spring Mountain ES 400/K-5
11645 SE Masa Ln, 503-353-5600
Curtis Long, prin. Fax 353-5615

Harrisburg, Linn, Pop. 3,472
Harrisburg SD 7 900/K-12
PO Box 208 97446 541-995-6626
Bryan Starr, supt. Fax 995-3453
www.harrisburg.k12.or.us
Harrisburg ES 400/K-5
PO Box 247 97446 541-995-6544
Darrick Bruns, prin. Fax 995-6194
Harrisburg MS 200/6-8
PO Box 317 97446 541-995-6551
Darci Stuller, prin. Fax 995-5120

Helix, Umatilla, Pop. 175
Helix SD 1 200/K-12
PO Box 398 97835 541-457-2175
Darrick Cope, supt. Fax 457-2481
www.helix.k12.or.us
Helix S 200/K-12
PO Box 398 97835 541-457-2175
Darrick Cope, prin. Fax 457-2481

Heppner, Morrow, Pop. 1,251
Morrow SD 1
Supt. — See Irrigon
Heppner ES 200/K-6
PO Box 367 97836 541-676-9128
Matt Combe, prin. Fax 676-5835

Hermiston, Umatilla, Pop. 16,457
Hermiston SD 8 5,200/K-12
305 SW 11th St 97838 541-667-6000
Tricia Mooney, supt. Fax 667-6050
www.hermiston.k12.or.us
Desert View ES 500/K-5
1225 SW 9th St 97838 541-667-6900
Laura Jacobsma-Opdahl, prin. Fax 667-6950
Highland Hills ES 400/K-5
450 SE 10th St 97838 541-667-6500
Jake Bacon, prin. Fax 667-6550
Larive MS 700/6-8
1497 SW 9th St 97838 541-667-6200
Stacie Roberts, prin. Fax 667-6250
Rocky Heights ES 500/K-5
650 W Standard Ave 97838 541-667-6600
Jerad Farley, prin. Fax 667-6650
Sandstone MS 500/6-8
400 NE 10th St 97838 541-667-6300
Lori Mills, prin. Fax 667-6350
Sunset ES 600/K-5
300 E Catherine Ave 97838 541-667-6700
Christie Petersen, prin. Fax 667-6750
West Park ES 600/K-5
555 SW 7th St 97838 541-667-6800
Kevin Headings, prin. Fax 667-6850

Hermiston Junior Academy 50/PK-8
1300 NW Academy Ln 97838 541-567-8523
Jordan Lindsay, prin. Fax 564-0569

Hillsboro, Washington, Pop. 88,100
Hillsboro SD 1J 20,800/K-12
3083 NE 49th Pl 97124 503-844-1500
Mike Scott, supt. Fax 844-1540
www.hsd.k12.or.us
Brookwood ES 400/K-6
3960 SE Cedar St 97123 503-844-1715
Michelle Jensen, prin. Fax 844-1722
Brown MS 800/7-8
1505 SW Cornelius Pass Rd 97123 503-844-1070
Roger Will, prin. Fax 844-1071
Eastwood ES 500/K-6
2100 NE Lincoln St 97124 503-844-1725
Lindsay Garcia, prin. Fax 844-1731
Evergreen MS 800/7-8
456 NE Evergreen Rd 97124 503-844-1400
Otis Gulley, prin. Fax 844-1402
Farmington View ES 200/K-6
8300 SW Hillsboro Hwy 97123 503-844-1735
Nabil Zerizef, prin. Fax 844-1744
Groner K-8 S 100/K-8
23405 SW Scholls Ferry Rd 97123 503-844-1600
Katie Thomas, prin. Fax 844-1609
Henry ES 400/K-6
1060 SE 24th Ave 97123 503-844-1690
Lisa Aguilar, prin. Fax 844-1699
Imlay ES 500/K-6
5900 SE Lois St 97123 503-844-1090
Alano Ciliberto, prin. Fax 844-1098
Jackson ES 500/K-6
675 NE Estate Dr 97124 503-844-1670
Sarah Crane, prin. Fax 844-1678
Ladd Acres ES 500/K-6
2425 SW Cornelius Pass Rd 97123 503-844-1300
Franchesca Sinapi, prin. Fax 844-1308
Lincoln Street ES 600/K-6
801 NE Lincoln St 97124 503-844-1160
Carmen Brodniak, prin. Fax 844-1162
McKinney ES 500/K-6
535 NW Darnielle St 97124 503-844-1660
Justin Welch, prin. Fax 844-1669
Minter Bridge ES 500/K-6
1750 SE Jacquelin Dr 97123 503-844-1650
Erika Pierce, prin. Fax 844-1659
Mooberry ES 500/K-6
1230 NE 10th Ave 97124 503-844-1640
Peter Muilenburg, prin. Fax 844-1644
Orenco ES 600/K-6
7050 NE Birch St 97124 503-844-1370
Allison Combs, prin. Fax 844-1024
Patterson ES 500/K-6
261 NE Lenox St 97124 503-844-1380
Jamie Lentz, prin. Fax 844-1025
Poynter MS 700/7-8
1535 NE Grant St 97124 503-844-1580
Jon Pede, prin. Fax 844-1583
Quatama ES 600/K-6
6905 NE Campus Way 97124 503-844-1180
Christy Walters, prin. Fax 844-1182
Rosedale ES 400/K-6
3901 SW 229th Ave, 503-844-1200
Mike Strande, prin. Fax 844-1201
South Meadows MS 800/7-8
4690 SE Davis Rd 97123 503-844-1220
Mary Mendez, prin. Fax 844-1221
West Union ES 300/K-6
23870 NW West Union Rd 97124 503-844-1620
John Allen, prin. Fax 844-1624
Witch Hazel ES 600/K-6
4950 SE Davis St 97123 503-844-1610
Jennifer Hernandez, prin. Fax 844-1619
Other Schools – See Aloha, Cornelius, North Plains, Portland

St. Matthew S 200/K-8
221 SE Walnut St 97123 503-648-2512
Joanne Smith, prin. Fax 648-4518
Tualatin Valley Academy 200/PK-9
21975 W Baseline Rd 97123 503-649-5518

Hines, Harney, Pop. 1,525
Double O SD 28 50/K-8
PO Box 888 97738 541-493-2400
Fax 493-2782
Double O S, PO Box 888 97738 50/K-8
Karla Neuschwander, lead tchr. 541-493-2400

Harney County SD 3
Supt. — See Burns
Hines MS 200/6-8
PO Box 38 97738 541-573-6436
David Robinson, prin. Fax 573-7255

Suntex SD 10 50/K-8
PO Box 805 97738 541-573-3229
Julie Opie, contact Fax 573-3229
Other Schools – See Riley

Hood River, Hood River, Pop. 7,008
Hood River County SD 4,000/K-12
1011 Eugene St 97031 541-386-2511
Dan Goldman, supt. Fax 387-5099
www.hoodriver.k12.or.us
Hood River MS 500/6-8
1602 May St 97031 541-386-2114
Brent Emmons, prin. Fax 387-5070
May Street ES 500/K-5
911 May St 97031 541-386-2656
Kelly Beard, prin. Fax 387-5068
Westside ES 500/K-5
3685 Belmont Dr 97031 541-386-1535
Bill Newton, prin. Fax 387-5059
Wy'East MS 500/6-8
3000 Wyeast Rd 97031 541-354-1548
Sarah Braman-Smith, prin. Fax 354-5120
Other Schools – See Cascade Locks, Mount Hood Parkdale, Odell

---

Horizon Christian S 200/PK-12
700 Pacific Ave 97031 541-387-3200
Ken Block, supt. Fax 387-3651
Mid-Columbia Adventist Academy 50/K-10
1100 22nd St 97031 541-386-3187

Hubbard, Clackamas, Pop. 3,098
Canby SD 86
Supt. — See Canby
Ninety-One S 400/K-8
5811 S Whiskey Hill Rd 97032 503-263-7110
Skyler Rodolph, prin. Fax 263-7112

Huntington, Baker, Pop. 429
Huntington SD 16J 100/K-12
520 3rd St E 97907 541-869-2204
Scott Bullock, supt. Fax 869-2444
www.huntington.k12.or.us/
Huntington S 100/K-12
520 3rd St E 97907 541-869-2204
Scott Bullock, admin. Fax 869-2444

Imnaha, Wallowa
Joseph SD 6
Supt. — See Joseph
Imnaha S, 78976 Imnaha Hwy 97842 50/K-8
Sherri Kilgore, prin. 541-577-3119

Independence, Polk, Pop. 8,352
Central SD 13J 3,100/K-12
750 S 5th St 97351 503-838-0030
Jennifer Kubista, supt. Fax 838-0033
www.central.k12.or.us
Independence ES 400/K-5
150 S 4th St 97351 503-838-1322
S. Ensminger, prin. Fax 838-6980
Talmadge MS 700/6-8
51 S 16th St 97351 503-606-2252
Perry LaBounty, prin. Fax 606-2436
Other Schools – See Monmouth

Irrigon, Morrow, Pop. 1,788
Morrow SD 1 2,200/K-12
240 Columbia Ln 97844 541-676-9128
Dirk Dirksen, supt. Fax 676-5742
www.morrow.k12.or.us
Houghton ES 300/K-3
1105 NE Main Ave 97844 541-922-3321
Tracey Johnson, prin. Fax 922-2375
Irrigon ES 200/4-6
490 SE Wyoming Ave 97844 541-922-2421
Erin Stocker, prin. Fax 922-5540
Other Schools – See Boardman, Heppner

Jacksonville, Jackson, Pop. 2,731
Medford SD 549C
Supt. — See Medford
Jacksonville ES 400/K-6
655 Hueners Ln 97530 541-842-3790
Fred Kondziela, prin. Fax 842-3155
Ruch S 200/K-8
156 Upper Applegate Rd 97530 541-842-3850
Julie Barry, prin. Fax 842-3480

Jefferson, Marion, Pop. 3,013
Jefferson SD 14J 900/K-12
1328 N 2nd St 97352 541-327-3337
Kent Klewitz, supt. Fax 327-2960
www.jefferson.k12.or.us
Jefferson ES 400/K-5
615 N 2nd St 97352 541-327-3337
Anna Keifer, prin. Fax 327-1216
Jefferson MS 200/6-8
1344 N 2nd St 97352 541-327-3337
Tracy Keuler, prin. Fax 327-7762

Jordan Valley, Malheur, Pop. 179
Jordan Valley SD 3 100/K-12
PO Box 99 97910 541-586-2213
Rusty Bengoa, supt. Fax 586-2568
www.jordanvalley.k12.or.us
Jordan Valley ES 50/K-6
PO Box 99 97910 541-586-2213
Rusty Bengoa, supt. Fax 586-2568
Rockville ES, PO Box 99 97910 50/K-8
Rusty Bengoa, supt. 541-586-2213

Pleasant Valley ESD 364 50/K-8
PO Box 119 97910 208-583-2420
Rene Maestrejuan, admin. Fax 583-2421
pleasantvalleyschools.org
Pleasant Valley S 50/K-8
PO Box 119 97910 208-583-2420
Rene Maestrejuan, admin. Fax 583-2421

Joseph, Wallowa, Pop. 1,054
Joseph SD 6 200/K-12
PO Box 787 97846 541-432-7311
Lance Homan, supt. Fax 432-1100
www.joseph.k12.or.us/
Other Schools – See Imnaha

Junction City, Lane, Pop. 5,249
Junction City SD 69 1,700/K-12
325 Maple St 97448 541-998-6311
Dr. Kathleen Rodden-Nord, supt. Fax 998-3926
www.junctioncity.k12.or.us
Laurel ES 500/K-4
1401 Laurel St 97448 541-998-2386
Nadira Rizkallah, prin. Fax 998-8422
Oaklea MS 500/5-8
1515 Rose St 97448 541-998-3381
Justin Corey, prin. Fax 998-3383
Territorial ES 100/K-5
92609 Territorial Hwy 97448 541-998-8371
Annette Sieler, dean Fax 998-4744

Juntura, Malheur, Pop. 56
Juntura SD 12 50/K-8
PO Box 248 97911 541-277-3261
Fax 277-3261
www.malesd.k12.or.us/juntura
Juntura S 50/K-8
PO Box 248 97911 541-277-3261
Kathleen Schram, lead tchr. Fax 277-3261

Keizer, Marion, Pop. 35,273
Salem-Keizer SD 24J
Supt. — See Salem
Claggett Creek MS 900/6-8
1810 Alder Dr NE 97303 503-399-3701
Aaron Persons, prin. Fax 399-3708
Clear Lake ES 500/K-5
7425 Meadowglen St NE 97303 503-399-3138
Tara Baldridge, prin. Fax 391-4072
Cummings ES 400/K-5
613 Cummings Ln N 97303 503-399-3141
Martina Mangan, prin. Fax 391-4033
Forest Ridge ES 200/K-5
7905 June Reid Pl NE 97303 503-399-5548
Tom Charboneau, prin. Fax 399-3469
Gubser ES 500/K-5
6610 14th Ave NE 97303 503-399-3275
Dave Bertholf, prin. Fax 391-4135
Keizer ES 600/K-5
5600 McClure St N 97303 503-399-3161
Christine Bowlby, prin. Fax 399-3435
Kennedy ES 500/K-5
4912 Noren Ave NE 97303 503-399-3163
Jesse Leonard, prin. Fax 399-3436
Weddle ES 500/K-5
1825 Alder Dr NE 97303 503-399-3604
Stacey Lund, prin. Fax 362-7122
Whiteaker MS 800/6-8
1605 Lockhaven Dr NE 97303 503-399-3224
Julia DeWitt, prin. Fax 375-7872

Crosshill Christian S 100/PK-5
2105 Keizer Rd NE 97303 503-566-8520
Molly Dillon, prin. Fax 304-2014

Keno, Klamath
Klamath County SD
Supt. — See Klamath Falls
Keno ES 200/K-6
PO Box 180 97627 541-883-5055
Sarah Shively, prin. Fax 883-5028

Klamath Falls, Klamath, Pop. 20,019
Klamath County SD 5,800/K-12
2845 Greensprings Dr 97601 541-883-5000
Greg Thede, supt. Fax 883-6677
www.kcsd.k12.or.us
Brixner JHS 300/7-8
4727 Homedale Rd 97603 541-883-5025
Leslie Garrett, prin. Fax 883-5019
Ferguson ES 400/K-6
2901 Homedale Rd 97603 541-883-5036
Kelley Fritz, prin. Fax 885-3357
Henley ES 400/K-6
8227 Highway 39 97603 541-883-5038
Janell Preston, prin. Fax 885-3356
Henley MS 300/7-8
7925 Highway 39 97603 541-883-5050
Kristine Creed, prin. Fax 883-5012
Peterson ES 600/K-6
4856 Clinton Ave 97603 541-883-5058
Jennifer Hawkins-Utley, prin. Fax 883-6679
Shasta ES 500/K-6
1951 Madison St 97603 541-883-5060
David Wehr, prin. Fax 850-3811
Stearns ES 300/K-6
3641 Crest St 97603 541-883-5063
Beth Clark, prin. Fax 883-4542
Other Schools – See Bly, Bonanza, Chiloquin, Gilchrist, Keno, Malin, Merrill

Klamath Falls CSD 3,000/K-12
1336 Avalon St 97603 541-883-4700
Dr. Paul Hillyer, supt. Fax 850-2766
www.kfalls.k12.or.us
Conger ES 400/K-5
1700 California Ave 97601 541-883-4772
Julie Bainbridge, prin. Fax 883-4752
Mills ES 400/K-5
520 E Main St 97601 541-883-4754
Fred Bartels, prin. Fax 883-4775
Pelican ES 300/K-5
501 Mclean St 97601 541-883-4765
Michelle McCabe, prin. Fax 883-4729
Ponderosa JHS 700/6-8
2554 Main St 97601 541-883-4740
Daymond Monteith, prin. Fax 885-4286
Roosevelt ES 400/K-5
1125 N Eldorado Ave 97601 541-883-4750
Joel Sauter, prin. Fax 883-4728

Hosanna Christian S 300/PK-12
5000 Hosanna Way 97603 541-882-7732
Don Wonsley, admin. Fax 882-6940
Klamath Falls Adventist Christian S 50/1-8
2499 Main St 97601 541-882-4151
Triad S 200/PK-12
2450 Summers Ln 97603 541-885-7940
Jim Libby, prin. Fax 885-7945

Lafayette, Yamhill, Pop. 3,638
McMinnville SD 40
Supt. — See Mc Minnville
Wascher ES 400/K-5
PO Box 788 97127 503-565-5400
Kourtney Ferrua, prin. Fax 565-5406

La Grande, Union, Pop. 12,600
La Grande SD 1 2,200/K-12
1305 N Willow St 97850 541-663-3200
George Mendoza, supt. Fax 663-3215
www.lagrandesd.org
Central ES 400/K-5
701 H Ave 97850 541-663-3500
Suzy Mayes, prin. Fax 663-3502
Greenwood ES 200/K-5
2300 N Spruce St 97850 541-663-3580
Ryan Westenskow, prin. Fax 663-3582
Island City ES 300/1-5
10201 W 4th St 97850 541-663-3270
John Tolan, prin. Fax 663-3272
La Grande MS 500/6-8
1108 4th St 97850 541-663-3421
Kyle McKinney, prin. Fax 663-3422

Grande Ronde Academy 50/K-8
507B Palmer Ave 97850 541-975-1147
Don McLean, admin. Fax 963-3398
La Grande Adventist S 50/K-8
PO Box 1025 97850 541-963-6203

Lake Oswego, Clackamas, Pop. 35,589
Lake Oswego SD 7J 6,800/K-12
PO Box 70 97034 503-534-2000
Dr. Heather Beck, supt. Fax 534-2030
www.losdschools.org
Forest Hills ES 400/K-5
1133 Andrews Rd 97034 503-534-2350
Amy Blakey, prin. Fax 534-2234
Hallinan ES 400/K-5
16800 Hawthorne Dr 97034 503-534-2353
Alix Pickett, prin. Fax 534-2251
Lake Grove ES 500/K-5
15777 Boones Ferry Rd 97035 503-534-2357
Scott Schinderle, prin. Fax 534-2388
Lake Oswego JHS 900/6-8
2500 Country Club Rd 97034 503-534-2335
Dr. Sara Deboy, prin. Fax 534-2341
Lakeridge JHS 800/6-8
4700 Jean Rd 97035 503-534-2343
Kurt Schultz, prin. Fax 534-2276
Oak Creek ES 500/K-5
55 Kingsgate Rd 97035 503-534-2323
Lilian Sarlos, prin. Fax 534-2257
River Grove ES 400/K-5
5850 McEwan Rd 97035 503-534-2363
Dan Draper Ed.D., prin. Fax 534-2247
Westridge ES 500/K-5
3400 Royce Way 97034 503-534-2371
Kari Montgomery, prin. Fax 534-2373

International Leadership Academy 100/PK-5
14788 Boones Ferry Rd 97035 503-662-8542
Our Lady of the Lake S 200/K-8
650 A Ave 97034 503-636-2121
Corrine Buich, prin. Fax 635-7760

Lakeview, Lake, Pop. 2,216
Adel SD 21 50/4-8
357 N L St 97630 541-947-5418
Fax 947-3373
www.lakeesd.k12.or.us
Other Schools – See Adel

Lake County SD 7 700/K-12
1341 S 1st St 97630 541-947-3347
Will Cahill, supt. Fax 947-3386
www.lakeview.k12.or.us
Daly MS 100/7-8
906 S 3rd St 97630 541-947-2287
Jesse Hamilton, prin. Fax 947-3601
Fremont/A.D. Hay ES 300/K-6
500 S I St 97630 541-947-2136
Susan Warner, prin. Fax 947-3535
Union ES 50/K-6
92398 Water Users Ln 97630 541-947-2553
Susan Warner, prin. Fax 947-2445

La Pine, Deschutes, Pop. 1,617
Bend-LaPine Administrative SD 1
Supt. — See Bend
La Pine ES 400/K-5
51615 Coach Rd 97739 541-355-8000
Patrick Flanagan, prin. Fax 355-8010
La Pine MS 300/6-8
16360 1st St 97739 541-355-8200
Robi Phinney, prin. Fax 355-8210
Rosland ES 200/K-5
52350 Yaeger Way 97739 541-355-8100
Rochelle Williams, prin. Fax 355-8110

Lebanon, Linn, Pop. 15,042
Lebanon Community SD 9 4,200/K-12
485 S 5th St 97355 541-451-8511
Dr. Rob Hess, supt. Fax 259-6857
www.lebanon.k12.or.us
Cascades ES 400/K-5
2163 S 7th St 97355 541-451-8524
Tami Volz, prin. Fax 451-8439
Green Acres ES 300/K-5
700 S 10th St 97355 541-451-8534
Amanda Plummer, prin. Fax 451-8429
Hamilton Creek S 300/K-8
32135 Berlin Rd 97355 541-451-8574
Geno Bates, prin. Fax 451-8473
Lacomb S 200/K-8
34110 E Lacomb Rd 97355 541-451-8565
Tim Geoghegan, prin. Fax 451-8568
Pioneer S 500/K-6
500 N 5th St 97355 541-451-8487
Tonya Cairo, prin. Fax 451-8488
Riverview ES 400/K-5
1011 Mountain River Dr 97355 541-451-8451
Joe Vore, prin. Fax 451-8452
Seven Oak MS 500/6-8
550 Cascade Dr 97355 541-451-8416
Wayne Raposa, prin. Fax 451-8431

East Linn Christian Academy 300/PK-12
36883 Victory Dr 97355 541-259-2324
Janelle Detweiler M.Ed., supt. Fax 244-9334

Lincoln City, Lincoln, Pop. 7,723
Lincoln County SD
Supt. — See Newport
Oceanlake ES 200/K-6
2420 NE 22nd St 97367 541-994-5296
Sandy Mummey, prin. Fax 994-8102
Taft ES 200/3-6
4040 SE High School Dr 97367 541-996-2136
Nick Lupo, prin. Fax 996-3999

Lincoln City Seventh-day Adventist S 100/1-8
2126 NE Surf Ave 97367 541-994-5181
Karie MacPhee, prin. Fax 994-5181

Long Creek, Grant, Pop. 191
Long Creek SD 17 50/PK-12
PO Box 429 97856 541-421-3896
Del Dykstra, supt. Fax 421-3012
www.longcreekschool.com
Long Creek S 50/PK-12
PO Box 429 97856 541-421-3896
Del Dykstra, prin. Fax 421-3012

Lowell, Lane, Pop. 983
Lowell SD 71 300/K-12
65 S Pioneer St 97452 541-937-8405
Dr. Walt Hanline, supt. Fax 937-2112
www.lowell.k12.or.us
Lundy ES 100/K-6
65 S Pioneer St 97452 541-937-2105
Johnie Matthews, prin. Fax 937-8709

Lyons, Linn, Pop. 1,122
North Santiam SD 29J
Supt. — See Stayton
Mari-Linn S 200/K-8
641 5th St 97358 503-859-2154
Jeri Harbison, prin. Fax 859-2164

Mc Minnville, Yamhill, Pop. 31,337
McMinnville SD 40 6,600/K-12
800 NE Lafayette Ave 97128 503-565-4000
Maryalice Russell, supt. Fax 565-4030
www.msd.k12.or.us
Buel ES 500/K-5
1985 SE Davis St 97128 503-565-5500
Darlene Geddes, prin. Fax 565-5506
Columbus ES 500/K-5
1600 SW Fellows St 97128 503-565-4600
Kathi Fowler, prin. Fax 565-4606
Duniway MS 800/6-8
575 NW Michelbook Ln 97128 503-565-4400
Hilary Brittan Lack, prin. Fax 565-4414
Grandhaven ES 600/K-5
3200 NE Mcdonald Ln 97128 503-565-4700
Marjorie Johnson, prin. Fax 565-4706
Memorial ES 500/K-5
501 NW 14th St 97128 503-565-4800
Dan Sheppard, prin. Fax 565-4806
Newby ES 500/K-5
1125 NW 2nd St 97128 503-565-4900
Davey Altree, prin. Fax 565-4906
Patton MS 800/6-8
1175 NE 19th St 97128 503-565-4500
Brian Crain, prin. Fax 565-4515
Other Schools – See Lafayette

McMinnville Adventist Christian S 50/K-8
1349 NW Elm St 97128 503-472-3336
McMinnville Christian Academy 200/PK-6
325 NW Baker Creek Rd 97128 503-472-6076
Dr. Derrik Graham, admin. Fax 434-5543
St. James S 100/PK-5
206 NE Kirby St 97128 503-472-2661
Shirley Gray, prin. Fax 472-4414

Madras, Jefferson, Pop. 5,846
Jefferson County SD 509J 3,100/K-12
445 SE Buff St 97741 541-475-6192
Rick Molitor, supt. Fax 475-6856
www.jcsd.k12.or.us
Big Muddy K-8 S 50/K-8
445 SE Buff St 97741 541-475-6192
Melinda Boyle, prin.
Buff ES 300/K-5
375 SE Buff St 97741 541-475-2457
Billie White, prin. Fax 325-5444
Jefferson County MS 600/6-8
1180 SE Kemper Way 97741 541-475-7253
Simon White, prin. Fax 475-4825
Madras ES 400/K-5
215 SE 10th St 97741 541-475-3520
Deborah Hunt, prin. Fax 475-9448
Other Schools – See Metolius, Warm Springs

Malin, Klamath, Pop. 795
Klamath County SD
Supt. — See Klamath Falls
Malin ES 100/K-6
PO Box 25 97632 541-723-2261
Larita Ongman, prin. Fax 723-2184

Mapleton, Lane
Mapleton SD 32 200/K-12
10868 E Mapleton Rd 97453 541-268-4312
Jodi O'Mara, supt. Fax 268-4632
www.mapleton.k12.or.us
Mapleton ES 100/K-6
10868 E Mapleton Rd 97453 541-268-4471
Jodi O'Mara, prin. Fax 268-9919

Marcola, Lane
Marcola SD 79J 200/K-12
PO Box 820 97454 541-933-2512
Bill Watkins, supt. Fax 933-2338
www.marcola.k12.or.us
Marcola ES 100/K-6
PO Box 820 97454 541-933-2411
Tami White, prin. Fax 933-1428

Maupin, Wasco, Pop. 405
South Wasco County SD 1 200/PK-12
PO Box 347 97037 541-395-2645
Ryan Wraught, supt. Fax 395-2679
www.swasco.net
Maupin ES 100/PK-6
PO Box 346 97037 541-395-2665
Lynn Cowdrey, prin. Fax 395-2675

Medford, Jackson, Pop. 72,448
Medford SD 549C 13,400/K-12
815 S Oakdale Ave 97501 541-842-3636
Dr. Brian Shumate, supt. Fax 842-1087
www.medford.k12.or.us
Griffin Creek ES 600/K-6
2430 Griffin Creek Rd 97501 541-842-3740
Louis Dix, prin. Fax 842-1818
Hedrick MS 900/7-8
1501 E Jackson St 97504 541-842-3700
Beth Anderson, prin. Fax 842-1548
Hoover ES 600/K-6
2323 Siskiyou Blvd 97504 541-842-3750
Lynn Cataldo, prin. Fax 842-1874
Howard ES 500/K-6
286 Mace Rd 97501 541-842-3760
Javier Del Rio, prin. Fax 842-3010
Jackson ES 400/K-6
713 Summit Ave 97501 541-842-3770
Kelly Soter, prin. Fax 842-3083
Jefferson ES 500/K-6
333 Holmes Ave 97501 541-842-3800
Rick Snyder, prin. Fax 842-3208
Kennedy ES 600/K-6
2860 N Keene Way Dr 97504 541-842-3810
Tom Ettel, prin. Fax 842-3265
Lincoln ES 500/K-6
3101 McLoughlin Dr 97504 541-842-3730
Megan Young, prin. Fax 842-1754
Lone Pine ES 600/K-6
3158 Lone Pine Rd 97504 541-842-3820
Gerry Flock, prin. Fax 842-3319
McLoughlin MS 900/7-8
320 W 2nd St 97501 541-842-3720
Linda White, prin. Fax 842-1652
Oak Grove ES 500/K-6
2838 W Main St 97501 541-842-3830
Elizabeth Landon, prin. Fax 842-3375
Roosevelt ES 400/K-6
1212 Queen Anne Ave 97504 541-842-3840
Kristi Anderson, prin. Fax 842-3430
Washington ES 500/K-6
610 S Peach St 97501 541-842-3860
Sallie Johnson, prin. Fax 842-3520
Wilson ES 500/K-6
1400 Johnson St 97504 541-842-3870
Gerry Flock, prin. Fax 842-3575
Other Schools – See Jacksonville

Phoenix-Talent SD 4
Supt. — See Phoenix
Orchard Hill ES 400/K-5
1011 La Loma Dr 97504 541-779-1766
Shawna Schleif, prin. Fax 770-9037

Grace Christian ES PK-5
649 Crater Lake Ave 97504 541-772-1438
Tim Teterud, prin. Fax 858-7288
Rogue Valley Adventist Academy 100/K-12
3675 S Stage Rd 97501 541-773-2988
Sacred Heart S 300/PK-8
431 S Ivy St 97501 541-772-4105
Leslie Jones, prin. Fax 732-0633

Merrill, Klamath, Pop. 817
Klamath County SD
Supt. — See Klamath Falls
Merrill ES 200/K-6
PO Box 468 97633 541-798-5723
Larita Ongman, prin. Fax 798-5814

Metolius, Jefferson, Pop. 688
Jefferson County SD 509J
Supt. — See Madras
Metolius ES 300/K-5
420 Butte Ave 97741 541-546-3104
Adam Dietrich, prin. Fax 546-3902

Mill City, Linn, Pop. 1,789
Santiam Canyon SD 129J 300/K-12
PO Box 197 97360 503-897-2321
Todd Miller, supt.
www.santiam.k12.or.us
Santiam ES 100/K-6
PO Box 198 97360 503-897-2368
Margo Williams, prin. Fax 897-4034

Milton Freewater, Umatilla, Pop. 6,982
Milton-Freewater USD 7 1,200/K-12
1020 S Mill St 97862 541-938-3551
Dr. Robert Clark, supt. Fax 938-6704
www.miltfree.k12.or.us
Central MS 400/6-8
306 SW 2nd Ave 97862 541-938-5504
Tim Sprenger, prin. Fax 938-6615
Ferndale ES 100/2-3
53445 W Ferndale Rd 97862 541-938-5412
Bruce Neil, prin. Fax 938-0503
Freewater ES 100/4-5
17 NW 8th Ave 97862 541-938-6611
Don Davis, prin. Fax 938-5337
Grove ES 100/K-1
129 SE 15th Ave 97862 541-938-3233
Ami Muilenberg, prin. Fax 938-2100

Milton-Stateline Adventist S 100/PK-8
53565 W Crockett Rd 97862 541-938-7131

Milwaukie, Clackamas, Pop. 19,622
North Clackamas SD 12 16,700/K-12
12400 SE Freeman Way 97222 503-353-6000
Matt Utterback, supt. Fax 353-6007
www.nclack.k12.or.us
Alder Creek MS 1,000/6-8
13801 SE Webster Rd 97267 503-353-5700
Alyson Brant, prin. Fax 353-5715
Ardenwald ES 500/K-5
8950 SE 36th Ave 97222 503-353-5320
Karon Webster, prin. Fax 353-5335
Bilquist ES 400/K-5
15708 SE Webster Rd 97267 503-353-5340
Charles Foote, prin. Fax 353-5355
El Puente ES 200/K-5
11250 SE 27th Ave 97222 503-353-5480
Colleen Sackos, prin. Fax 353-5485
Lewelling ES 400/K-5
5325 SE Logus Rd 97222 503-353-5440
Kristi Weathers, prin. Fax 353-5445
Linwood ES 300/K-5
11909 SE Linwood Ave 97222 503-353-5460
Amy Busch, prin. Fax 353-5475
Milwaukie ES 200/K-5
11250 SE 27th Ave 97222 503-353-5480
Colleen Sackos, prin. Fax 353-5485
Oak Grove ES 400/K-5
2150 SE Torbank Rd 97222 503-353-5520
Sid Ong, prin. Fax 353-5535
Riverside ES 300/K-5
16303 SE River Rd 97267 503-353-5560
Alison Schlicht, prin. Fax 353-5575
Rowe MS 900/6-8
3606 SE Lake Rd 97222 503-353-5725
Greg Harris, prin. Fax 353-5740
Sojourner ES 200/K-5
11909 SE Linwood Ave 97222 503-353-5460
Amy Busch, prin. Fax 353-5595
Whitcomb ES 500/K-5
7400 SE Thompson Rd 97222 503-353-5660
Cathy Lehmann, prin. Fax 353-5675
Other Schools – See Clackamas, Happy Valley, Portland

Oregon City SD 62
Supt. — See Oregon City
Candy Lane ES 300/2-5
5901 SE Hull Ave 97267 503-785-8150
April Albers, prin. Fax 654-2693
Jennings Lodge ES 300/K-2
18521 SE River Rd 97267 503-785-8035
April Albers, prin. Fax 654-9240

Christ the King S 200/K-8
7414 SE Michael Dr 97222 503-785-2411
Patrick Jefferies, prin. Fax 794-9607
Portland Waldorf S 300/PK-12
2300 SE Harrison St 97222 503-654-2200
Mary Beaton, admin. Fax 652-5162
St. John the Baptist S 200/K-8
10956 SE 25th Ave 97222 503-654-0200
Angie Gomez, prin. Fax 654-8419

Mist, Columbia
Vernonia SD 47J
Supt. — See Vernonia
Mist ES 50/K-5
69163 Highway 47 97016 503-755-2486
Aaron Miller, prin. Fax 755-2213

Mitchell, Wheeler, Pop. 123
Mitchell SD 55 100/K-12
PO Box 247 97750 541-462-3311
Nancy Moon, supt. Fax 462-3849
www.mitchell.k12.or.us
Mitchell S 100/K-12
PO Box 247 97750 541-462-3311
Nancy Moon, admin. Fax 462-3849

Molalla, Clackamas, Pop. 7,927
Molalla River SD 35 2,700/K-12
PO Box 188 97038 503-829-2359
Tony Mann, supt. Fax 829-5540
www.molallariv.k12.or.us
Molalla ES 400/K-5
PO Box 206 97038 503-829-4333
Frank Luzaich, prin. Fax 829-2614
Molalla River MS 500/6-8
PO Box 225 97038 503-829-6133
Mike Nelson, prin. Fax 829-5680
Rural Dell ES 200/K-5
10500 S Highway 211 97038 503-651-2128
Larry Conley, prin. Fax 651-2127
Other Schools – See Mulino

Country Christian S 200/K-12
16975 S Highway 211 97038 503-829-5503

Monmouth, Polk, Pop. 9,171
Central SD 13J
Supt. — See Independence
Ash Creek ES 500/K-5
1360 N 16th St 97361 503-606-9016
Ashley Wildfang, prin. Fax 606-3666
Monmouth ES 500/K-5
958 Church St E 97361 503-838-1433
K. Siedel, prin. Fax 606-9797

Mid Valley Christian Academy 100/PK-12
1483 N 16th St 97361 503-838-2818
Gaye Stewart, admin.

Monroe, Benton, Pop. 601
Monroe SD 1J 500/K-12
365 N 5th St 97456 541-847-6292
Randall Crowson, supt. Fax 847-6290
www.monroe.k12.or.us
Monroe Grade S 300/K-8
600 Dragon Dr 97456 541-847-5139
Kathi Holvey, prin. Fax 847-5128

Monument, Grant, Pop. 127
Monument SD 8 50/PK-12
PO Box 127 97864 541-934-2646
Fax 934-2005
monumentschool.com
Monument S 50/PK-12
PO Box 127 97864 541-934-2646
Fax 934-2005

Moro, Sherman, Pop. 321
Sherman County SD 200/PK-12
65912 High School Loop 97039 541-565-3500
Wes Owens, supt. Fax 565-3319
shermancountyschooldistrict.weebly.com
Sherman County S 100/PK-12
65912 High School Loop 97039 541-565-3500
Mike Somnis, prin. Fax 565-3319

Mount Angel, Marion, Pop. 3,231
Mt. Angel SD 91 700/K-12
PO Box 1129 97362 503-845-2345
Troy Stoops, supt. Fax 845-2789
www.masd91.org
Mount Angel MS 200/6-8
460 E Marquam St 97362 503-845-6137
Jennifer McCallum, prin. Fax 845-2856
St. Mary's ES 300/K-5
590 E College St 97362 503-845-2547
Katie Voss, prin. Fax 845-9438

Silver Falls SD 4J
Supt. — See Silverton
Butte Creek ES 300/K-8
37569 S Highway 213 97362 503-829-6803
Therese Gerlits, prin. Fax 829-8701

Mount Hood Parkdale, Hood River, Pop. 250
Hood River County SD
Supt. — See Hood River
Parkdale ES 200/K-5
PO Box 69 97041 541-352-6255
Gus Hedberg, prin. Fax 352-5207

Mulino, Clackamas, Pop. 2,070
Molalla River SD 35
Supt. — See Molalla
Clarkes ES 200/K-5
19100 S Windy City Rd 97042 503-632-3290
Kathleen French, prin. Fax 632-5212
Mulino ES 300/K-5
26660 S Highway 213 97042 503-829-6888
Alan Willey, prin. Fax 829-2037

Myrtle Creek, Douglas, Pop. 3,296
South Umpqua SD 19 1,500/PK-12
558 Chadwick Ln 97457 541-863-3115
Tim Porter, supt. Fax 863-5212
www.sucd.k12.or.us
Coffenberry MS 300/6-8
591 Rice St 97457 541-863-3104
Laurie Collins, prin. Fax 863-5187
Myrtle Creek ES 300/PK-5
651 NE Division St 97457 541-863-3168
Beverly Krystosek, prin. Fax 863-5185
Tri City ES 200/K-5
546 Chadwick Ln 97457 541-863-6887
Lori Dilbeck, prin. Fax 863-5510
Other Schools – See Canyonville

Myrtle Point, Coos, Pop. 2,411
Myrtle Point SD 41 600/PK-12
413 C St 97458 541-572-1220
Nanette Hagen, supt. Fax 572-5401
www.mpsd.k12.or.us
Myrtle Crest ES 300/PK-6
903 Myrtle Crest Ln 97458 541-572-1230
Allyson Backman, prin. Fax 559-0372

Nehalem, Tillamook, Pop. 264
Neah-Kah-Nie SD 56
Supt. — See Rockaway
Nehalem ES 200/K-5
PO Box 190 97131 503-355-3650
Kristi Woika, prin. Fax 368-7721

Newberg, Yamhill, Pop. 21,511
Newberg SD 29J 5,200/K-12
714 E 6th St 97132 503-554-5000
Dr. Kym LeBlanc-Esparza, supt. Fax 538-4374
www.newberg.k12.or.us
Antonia Crater ES 500/K-5
203 W Foothills Dr 97132 503-554-4650
Michele Paton, prin. Fax 537-3251
Austin ES 300/K-5
2200 N Center St 97132 503-554-4550
Alaina Carter, prin. Fax 538-4571
Chehalem Valley MS 700/6-8
403 W Foothills Dr 97132 503-554-4600
Karen Pugsley, prin. Fax 537-3239
Edwards ES 400/K-5
715 E 8th St 97132 503-554-5050
Scott Murphy, prin. Fax 537-3220
Mountain View MS 600/6-8
2015 N Emery Dr 97132 503-554-4500
Terry McElligott, prin. Fax 537-3337
Rush ES 600/K-5
1441 Deborah Rd 97132 503-554-4450
Troy Fisher, prin. Fax 554-1687
Young ES 200/K-5
17600 NE North Valley Rd 97132 503-554-4750
Kevin Milner, prin. Fax 538-7269
Other Schools – See Dundee

Country Faith Christian Academy 50/3-12
26155 NE Bell Rd 97132
Jolaine Davis M.Ed., admin.
Lewis Academy 100/PK-12
PO Box 3250 97132 503-538-0114
Clay Swanson, prin. Fax 538-4113
Veritas S 200/K-12
401 Mission Dr 97132 503-538-1962

New Pine Creek, Lake, Pop. 113
Modoc JUSD
Supt. — See Alturas, CA
State Line ES 50/K-5
PO Box 99 97635 530-946-4127
Kristen Budmark, prin. Fax 946-4127

Newport, Lincoln, Pop. 9,688
Lincoln County SD 3,500/K-12
PO Box 1110 97365 541-265-9211
Tom Rinearson, supt. Fax 265-0511
www.lincoln.k12.or.us
Case ES 100/3-5
459 NE 12th St 97365 541-265-8598
Shelley Moore, prin. Fax 574-2234
Newport MS 100/6-8
825 NE 7th St 97365 541-265-6601
Aaron Belloni, prin. Fax 265-6493
Yaquina View ES 300/K-5
351 SE Harney St 97365 541-265-4637
Kristin Becker, prin. Fax 265-4011
Other Schools – See Lincoln City, Toledo, Waldport

North Bend, Coos, Pop. 9,275
North Bend SD 13 3,900/K-12
1913 Meade St 97459 541-756-2521
Bill Yester, supt. Fax 756-1313
www.nbend.k12.or.us
Hillcrest ES 600/K-5
1100 Maine St 97459 541-756-8348
Jon Davison, prin. Fax 751-7991
North Bay ES 300/K-5
93670 Viking Ln 97459 541-756-8351
Bruce Martin, prin. Fax 751-0501
North Bend MS 300/6-8
1500 16th St 97459 541-756-8341
Darrell Johnston, prin. Fax 756-6460

Kingsview Christian S 100/PK-12
1850 Clark St 97459 541-756-1411

North Plains, Washington, Pop. 1,885
Hillsboro SD 1J
Supt. — See Hillsboro
North Plains ES 300/K-6
32030 NW North Ave 97133 503-844-1630
Becky Smith, prin Fax 844-1638

Nyssa, Malheur, Pop. 3,244
Nyssa SD 26 1,200/K-12
804 Adrian Blvd 97913 541-372-2275
Jana Iverson, supt. Fax 372-2204
www.nyssa.k12.or.us
Nyssa ES 500/K-5
809 Bower Ave 97913 541-372-3313
Matthew Murray, prin. Fax 372-5653
Nyssa MS 300/6-8
101 S 11th St 97913 541-372-3891
Luke Cleaver, prin. Fax 372-3260

Oakland, Douglas, Pop. 890
Oakland SD 1 500/K-12
PO Box 390 97462 541-459-4341
Patti Lovemark, supt. Fax 459-4120
www.oakland.k12.or.us
Lincoln MS 200/5-8
PO Box 420 97462 541-459-3407
Diana Sweeden, prin. Fax 459-9167
Oakland ES 200/K-4
PO Box 90 97462 541-459-2271
Anne Lamoreaux, prin. Fax 459-8998

Oakridge, Lane, Pop. 3,091
Oakridge SD 76 500/K-12
76499 Rose St 97463 541-782-2813
Dr. Donald Kordosky, supt. Fax 782-2982
www.oakridge.k12.or.us
Oakridge ES 300/K-6
48119 E 1st St 97463 541-782-3226
Tiffany O'Donnell, prin. Fax 782-3122

Odell, Hood River, Pop. 2,225
Hood River County SD
Supt. — See Hood River
Mid Valley ES 500/K-5
PO Box 188 97044 541-354-1691
Kim Yasui, prin. Fax 354-5109

Ontario, Malheur, Pop. 11,152
Ontario SD 8C 2,400/K-12
195 SW 3rd Ave 97914 541-889-5374
Nicole Albisu, supt. Fax 889-8553
www.ontario.k12.or.us
Aiken ES 300/K-5
1297 W Idaho Ave 97914 541-889-5584
Tobey Huddleston, prin. Fax 889-4762
Alameda ES 400/K-6
1252 Alameda Dr 97914 541-889-5497
Andrea Buchholz, prin. Fax 889-1993
Cairo ES 200/K-5
531 Highway 20 26 97914 541-889-5745
Jenny Dayton, prin. Fax 889-5745
Ontario MS 400/7-8
573 SW 2nd Ave 97914 541-889-5377
Lisa Longoria, prin. Fax 881-0060
Pioneer ES 100/K-5
4744 Pioneer Rd 97914 541-262-3902
Erin O'Hara-Rines, prin. Fax 262-3913
Roberts ES 400/K-6
590 NW 8th St 97914 541-889-5379
Marshell Hooker, prin. Fax 889-5370

St. Peter S 100/PK-6
98 SW 9th St 97914 541-889-7363
Armida Hernandez, lead tchr. Fax 889-2852
Treasure Valley Christian S 100/PK-12
386 N Verde Dr 97914 541-889-4662
Fran Renk, prin. Fax 889-9199

Oregon City, Clackamas, Pop. 30,976
Canby SD 86
Supt. — See Canby
Carus ES 400/K-6
14412 S Carus Rd 97045 503-263-7190
Sam Thompson, prin. Fax 632-3148

Oregon City SD 62 8,000/K-12
PO Box 2110 97045 503-785-8000
Larry Didway, supt. Fax 657-2492
www.orecity.k12.or.us
Gaffney Lane ES 500/K-5
13521 Gaffney Ln 97045 503-785-8600
Cyndi Borgmeier, prin. Fax 650-6688
Gardiner MS 800/6-8
180 Ethel St 97045 503-785-8200
Michael Sweeten, prin. Fax 650-5482
Holcomb ES 500/K-5
14625 Holcomb Blvd 97045 503-785-8100
Kelli Rhea, prin. Fax 657-4795
McLoughlin ES 600/K-5
19230 S End Rd 97045 503-785-8650
Candice Henkin, prin. Fax 657-2497
Ogden MS 900/6-8
14133 Donovan Rd 97045 503-785-8300
Lisa Normand, prin. Fax 657-2508
Redland ES 500/K-5
18131 S Redland Rd 97045 503-785-8500
Rebekah Beck, prin. Fax 631-7645
Other Schools – See Beavercreek, Milwaukie

North Clackamas Christian S 200/PK-12
19575 Sebastian Way 97045 503-655-5961
Tim Tutty, admin. Fax 655-4875
St. John the Apostle S 200/K-8
516 5th St 97045 503-742-8232
Erica Pyne, prin. Fax 742-8239

Paulina, Crook
Crook County SD
Supt. — See Prineville
Paulina S 50/K-8
70050 SE Paulina City Rd 97751 541-477-3182
Cheri Rasmussen, prin. Fax 477-3512

Pendleton, Umatilla, Pop. 16,180
Pendleton SD 16 2,900/PK-12
107 NW 10th St 97801 541-276-6711
Chris Fritsch, supt. Fax 278-3208
www.pendleton.k12.or.us
McKay Creek ES 300/K-5
1539 SW 44th St 97801 541-966-3000
Ronda Smith, prin. Fax 966-3046
Pendleton Early Learning Center 200/PK-K
455 SW 13th St 97801 541-966-3300
Lori Hale, prin. Fax 966-3339
Sherwood Heights ES 400/1-5
3235 SW Nye Ave 97801 541-276-1165
Theresa Owens, prin. Fax 966-3096
Sunridge MS 700/6-8
700 SW Runnion Ave 97801 541-276-4560
David Williams, prin. Fax 276-4724
Washington ES 300/1-5
1205 SE Byers Ave 97801 541-966-3550
Aimee VanNice, prin. Fax 966-3597

Harris Junior Academy 100/PK-10
3121 SW Hailey Ave 97801 541-276-0615

Philomath, Benton, Pop. 4,445
Philomath SD 17J 1,500/K-12
1620 Applegate St 97370 541-929-3169
Melissa Goff, supt. Fax 929-3991
www.philomath.k12.or.us
Clemens PS 100/K-1
535 S 19th St 97370 541-929-2082
Abby Couture, prin. Fax 929-3991
Philomath ES 400/2-5
239 S 16th St 97370 541-929-3253
Susan Halliday, prin. Fax 929-3281
Philomath MS 300/6-8
2021 Chapel Dr 97370 541-929-3167
Steve Bell, prin. Fax 929-3180
Other Schools – See Blodgett

Phoenix, Jackson, Pop. 4,376
Phoenix-Talent SD 4 2,700/K-12
PO Box 698 97535 541-535-1517
Brent Barry, supt. Fax 535-3928
www.phoenix.k12.or.us
Phoenix ES 400/K-5
PO Box 727 97535 541-535-3353
Jeff Carpenter, prin. Fax 535-7533
Other Schools – See Medford, Talent

Pilot Rock, Umatilla, Pop. 1,457
Pilot Rock SD 2 400/K-12
PO Box BB 97868 541-443-8291
Steve Staniak, supt. Fax 443-5000
www.pilotrock.k12.or.us
Pilot Rock ES 200/K-6
PO Box A 97868 541-443-2361
Steve Staniak, prin. Fax 443-3550

Pleasant Hill, Lane
Pleasant Hill SD 1 800/K-12
36386 Highway 58 97455 541-746-9646
Fax 746-2537
www.pleasanthill.k12.or.us
Pleasant Hill ES 400/K-5
36386 Highway 58 97455 541-736-0400
Devery Stoneberg, prin. Fax 736-0446

Emerald Christian Academy 100/K-10
35582 Zephyr Way 97455 541-746-1708

Plush, Lake, Pop. 56
Plush SD 18 50/K-8
18254 Morris Ln 97637 541-947-3933
Fax 947-4437
Plush ES 50/K-8
18254 Morris St 97637 541-947-3933
Lu Ann Anderson, prin. Fax 947-4437

Portland, Multnomah, Pop. 557,791

Beaverton SD 48J
Supt. — See Beaverton

Bonny Slope ES 600/K-5
11775 NW McDaniel Rd 97229 503-356-2040
Janet Maza, prin. Fax 356-2045

Cedar Mill ES 300/K-5
10265 NW Cornell Rd 97229 503-356-2050
Amy Chamberlain, prin. Fax 356-2055

Cedar Park MS 1,000/6-8
11100 SW Park Way 97225 503-356-2560
Shannon Anderson, prin. Fax 356-2565

Findley ES 800/K-5
4155 NW Saltzman Rd 97229 503-356-2100
Kathleen Skidmore-Dee, prin. Fax 356-2105

Hazeldale ES 500/K-5
650 NW 118th St 97229 503-356-2010
Angela Tran, prin. Fax 356-2015

Montclair ES 400/K-5
7250 SW Vermont St 97223 503-356-2190
Sean Leverty, prin. Fax 356-2195

Raleigh Hills S 500/K-8
5225 SW Scholls Ferry Rd 97225 503-356-2160
Peter McDougal, prin. Fax 356-2165

Raleigh Park ES 400/K-5
3670 SW 78th Ave 97225 503-356-2500
Brian Curl, prin. Fax 356-2505

Ridgewood ES 400/K-5
10100 SW Inglewood St 97225 503-356-2440
Carey Meier, prin. Fax 356-2445

Rock Creek ES 500/K-5
4125 NW 185th Ave 97229 503-356-2450
Tiffany Wiencken, prin. Fax 356-2455

Sato ES K-5
7775 NW Kaider Rd 97229 503-356-2530
Cheryl Hagseth, prin. Fax 356-2535

Springville S 800/K-8
6655 NW Joss Ave 97229 503-356-2480
Robin Kobrowski, prin. Fax 356-2485

Stoller MS 1,300/6-8
14141 NW Laidlaw Rd 97229 503-356-2680
Florence Richey, prin. Fax 356-2685

Terra Linda ES 400/K-5
1998 NW 143rd Ave 97229 503-356-2490
Christy Batsell, prin. Fax 356-2495

Walker ES 600/K-5
11940 SW Lynnfield Ln 97225 503-356-2520
Melissa Murray, prin. Fax 356-2525

West Tualatin View ES 300/K-5
8800 SW Leahy Rd 97225 503-356-2510
Kalay McNamee, prin. Fax 356-2515

Wismer ES 800/K-5
5477 NW Skycrest Pkwy 97229 503-356-2150
Joan McFadden, prin. Fax 356-2155

Centennial SD 28J 6,100/K-12
18135 SE Brooklyn St 97236 503-760-7990
Dr. Paul Coakley, supt. Fax 762-3689
csd28j.org

Centennial MS 1,000/7-8
17650 SE Brooklyn St 97236 503-762-3206
Rise' Hawley, prin. Fax 762-3236

Lynch Meadows ES 500/K-6
18009 SE Brooklyn St 97236 503-762-3208
Karen Weinert, prin. Fax 762-3238

Lynch View ES 400/K-6
1546 SE 169th Pl 97233 503-762-3203
Jim Mangan, prin. Fax 762-3243

Lynch Wood ES 500/K-6
3615 SE 174th Ave 97236 503-762-3204
Marin MIller, prin. Fax 762-3244

Oliver ES 400/K-6
15840 SE Taylor St 97233 503-762-3207
Jeb Hubbs, prin. Fax 762-3237

Parklane ES 400/K-6
15811 SE Main St 97233 503-762-3205
Jorge Meza, prin. Fax 762-3235

Other Schools – See Gresham

David Douglas SD 40 11,000/PK-12
11300 NE Halsey St 97220 503-252-2900
Ken Richardson, supt. Fax 261-8208
www.ddouglas.k12.or.us

Boyles ES 400/PK-5
10822 SE Bush St 97266 503-256-6554
Ericka Guynes, prin. Fax 261-8437

Cherry Park ES 500/PK-5
1930 SE 104th Ave 97216 503-256-6501
Kate Barker, prin. Fax 261-8428

Gilbert Heights ES 700/K-5
12839 SE Holgate Blvd 97236 503-256-6502
Dr. Shane Bassett, prin. Fax 261-8454

Gilbert Park ES 700/K-5
13132 SE Ramona St 97236 503-256-6531
Stacie Moncrief, prin. Fax 261-8413

Light MS 800/6-8
10800 SE Washington St 97216 503-256-6511
Doug Pease, prin. Fax 261-8423

Lincoln Park ES 600/K-5
13200 SE Lincoln St 97233 503-256-6504
Ceci DeValdenebro, prin. Fax 261-8444

Menlo Park ES 500/K-5
12900 NE Glisan St 97230 503-256-6506
Kellie Burkhardt, prin. Fax 261-8449

Mill Park ES 600/K-5
1900 SE 117th Ave 97216 503-256-6507
Bob Stelle, prin. Fax 261-8418

Ott MS 700/6-8
12500 SE Ramona St 97236 503-256-6510
Duane Larson, prin. Fax 261-8403

Russell MS 900/6-8
3955 SE 112th Ave 97266 503-256-6519
Thu Truong, prin. Fax 761-7246

Ventura Park ES 500/K-5
145 SE 117th Ave 97216 503-256-6508
Holly Schauer, prin. Fax 256-8439

West Powelhurst ES 500/K-5
2921 SE 116th Ave 97266 503-256-6509
Susan Olds, prin. Fax 261-8408

Hillsboro SD 1J
Supt. — See Hillsboro

Lenox ES 400/K-6
21200 NW Rock Creek Blvd 97229 503-844-1360
Gina McLain, prin. Fax 844-1369

North Clackamas SD 12
Supt. — See Milwaukie

View Acres ES 400/K-5
4828 SE View Acres Rd 97267 503-353-5640
Liz Manspeaker, prin. Fax 353-5655

Parkrose SD 3 3,300/PK-12
10636 NE Prescott St 97220 503-408-2100
Dr. Karen Fischer Gray, supt. Fax 408-2140
www.parkrose.k12.or.us

Parkrose MS 800/6-8
11800 NE Shaver St 97220 503-408-2700
Annette Sweeney, prin. Fax 408-2998

Prescott ES 400/PK-5
10410 NE Prescott St 97220 503-408-2150
Sam Maranto, prin. Fax 408-2190

Russell ES 400/K-5
2700 NE 127th Ave 97230 503-408-2750
Heather Bailey, prin. Fax 408-2790

Sacramento ES 400/K-5
11400 NE Sacramento St 97220 503-408-2800
Katie Barrett, prin. Fax 408-2840

Shaver ES 300/PK-5
3701 NE 131st Pl 97230 503-408-2850
Laura Goodman, prin. Fax 408-2890

Portland SD 1J 44,900/PK-12
PO Box 3107 97208 503-916-2000
Guadalupe Guerrero, supt. Fax 916-3107
www.pps.net

Abernethy ES 500/K-5
2421 SE Orange Ave 97214 503-916-6190
Heather Hull, prin. Fax 916-2600

Ainsworth ES 600/K-5
2425 SW Vista Ave 97201 503-916-6288
Kris Meyer, prin. Fax 916-2601

Alameda ES 800/K-5
2732 NE Fremont St 97212 503-916-6036
Raddy Lurie, prin. Fax 916-2602

Arleta ES 500/K-8
5109 SE 66th Ave 97206 503-916-6330
Seth Jones, prin. Fax 916-2604

Astor ES 500/K-8
5601 N Yale St 97203 503-916-6244
Sarah Zabel, prin. Fax 916-2605

Atkinson ES 400/K-5
5800 SE Division St 97206 503-916-6333
Ivonne Dibblee, prin. Fax 916-2606

Beach ES 600/PK-8
1710 N Humboldt St 97217 503-916-6236
Lisa Hawking, prin. Fax 916-2315

Beaumont MS 600/6-8
4043 NE Fremont St 97212 503-916-5610
Harriette Vimegnon, prin. Fax 916-2609

Boise-Eliot-Humboldt ES 500/PK-8
620 N Fremont St 97227 503-916-6171
Kevin Bacon, prin. Fax 916-2611

Bridger ES 400/K-8
7910 SE Market St 97215 503-916-6336
Melissa Schachner, prin. Fax 916-2612

Bridlemile ES 500/K-5
4300 SW 47th Dr 97221 503-916-6292
Brad Pearson, prin. Fax 916-2613

Buckman ES 500/K-5
320 SE 16th Ave 97214 503-916-6230
Susan Kosmala, prin. Fax 916-2615

Capitol Hill ES 400/K-5
8401 SW 17th Ave 97219 503-916-6303
Joy Williams, prin. Fax 916-2616

Chapman at the Ramona K-K
1545 NW 13th Ave 97209 503-916-5360
Pamela Van Der Wolf, prin. Fax 916-2717

Chapman ES 600/1-5
1445 NW 26th Ave 97210 503-916-6295
Pamela Van Der Wolf, prin. Fax 916-2617

Chavez ES 500/K-8
5103 N Willis Blvd 97203 503-916-5666
T.J. Fuller, prin. Fax 916-2663

Chief Joseph ES 400/K-5
2409 N Saratoga St 97217 503-916-6255
Amber Gerber, prin. Fax 916-2618

Clarendon Early Learning Academy PK-PK
9325 N Van Houten Ave 97213 503-916-6269
Eileen Isham, prin. Fax 916-2861

Cleary ES @ Fernwood Campus 4-8
1915 NE 33rd Ave 97212 503-916-6480
John Ferraro, prin. Fax 916-2626

Cleary ES @ Hollyrood Campus 100/K-K
3560 NE Hollyrood Ct 97212 503-916-6766
John Ferraro, prin. Fax 916-2635

Cleary ES @ Rose City Park 1-3
2334 NE 57th Ave 97213 503-916-6765
John Ferraro, prin.

Creative Science ES 400/K-8
1231 SE 92nd Ave 97216 503-916-6431
Meisha Plotske, admin. Fax 916-2620

Creston ES 400/K-8
4701 SE Bush St 97206 503-916-6340
Krista Blovad, prin. Fax 916-2621

Da Vinci Arts MS 500/6-8
2508 NE Everett St 97232 503-916-5356
Fred Locke, prin. Fax 916-2721

Duniway ES 400/K-5
7700 SE Reed College Pl 97202 503-916-6343
Matthew Goldstein, prin. Fax 916-2623

Faubion ES 500/PK-8
2930 NE Dekum St 97211 503-916-5686
Jennifer McCalley, prin. Fax 916-2625

Forest Park ES 500/K-5
9935 NW Durrett St 97229 503-916-5400
Lisa Newlyn, prin. Fax 916-2730

George MS 400/6-8
10000 N Burr Ave 97203 503-916-6262
Lavert Robertson, prin. Fax 916-2627

Glencoe ES 500/K-5
825 SE 51st Ave 97215 503-916-6207
Lori Clark, prin. Fax 916-2628

Gray MS 500/6-8
5505 SW 23rd Ave, 503-916-5676
Beth Madison, prin. Fax 916-2629

Grout ES 400/K-5
3119 SE Holgate Blvd 97202 503-916-6209
Annie Tabshy, prin. Fax 916-2632

Harrison Park ES 700/K-8
2225 SE 87th Ave 97216 503-916-5700
John Walden, prin. Fax 916-2610

Hayhurst ES 400/K-5
5037 SW Iowa St 97221 503-916-6300
Deanne Froehlich, prin. Fax 916-2633

Hosford International MS 600/6-8
2303 SE 28th Pl 97214 503-916-5640
Kristyn Westphal, prin. Fax 916-2637

Irvington ES 500/K-8
1320 NE Brazee St 97212 503-916-6185
Kathleen Ellwood, prin. Fax 916-2639

Jackson MS 500/6-8
10625 SW 35th Ave 97219 503-916-5680
Kevin Crotchett, prin. Fax 916-2640

John ES 500/K-5
7439 N Charleston Ave 97203 503-916-6266
Samantha Ragaisis, prin. Fax 916-2641

Kelly ES 600/K-5
9030 SE Cooper St 97266 503-916-6350
Amy Whitney, prin. Fax 916-2644

King ES 300/PK-8
4906 NE 6th Ave 97211 503-916-6456
Jill Sage, prin. Fax 916-2647

Lane MS 500/6-8
7200 SE 60th Ave 97206 503-916-6355
Jeandre Carbone, prin. Fax 916-2648

Laurelhurst ES 700/K-8
840 NE 41st Ave 97232 503-916-6210
Vanessa Martinez, prin. Fax 916-2649

Lee ES 500/K-8
2222 NE 92nd Ave 97220 503-916-6144
Isaac Cardona, prin. Fax 916-2650

Lent ES 600/K-8
5105 SE 97th Ave 97266 503-916-6322
Rene Canler, prin. Fax 916-2651

Lewis ES 400/K-5
4401 SE Evergreen St 97206 503-916-6360
Emily Glasgow, prin. Fax 916-2652

Llewellyn ES 600/K-5
6301 SE 14th Ave 97202 503-916-6216
Joe Galati, prin. Fax 916-2653

Maplewood ES 300/K-5
7452 SW 52nd Ave 97219 503-916-6308
Jill Bailey, prin. Fax 916-2654

Markham ES 400/K-5
10531 SW Capitol Hwy 97219 503-916-5681
Shawn Garnett, prin. Fax 916-2655

Marysville ES 400/K-8
7733 SE Raymond St 97206 503-916-6363
Lana Penley, prin. Fax 916-2656

Mt. Tabor MS 600/6-8
5800 SE Ash St 97215 503-916-5646
Sean Keating, prin. Fax 916-2659

Ockley Green MS 300/5-8
6031 N Montana Ave 97217 503-916-5660
Paula McCullough, prin. Fax 916-2661

Odyssey @ East Sylvan S 300/K-8
1849 SW 58th Ave 97221 503-916-6310
Deanne Froehlich, prin. Fax 916-2124

Parks ES 400/PK-5
8960 N Woolsey Ave 97203 503-916-6250
Tamala Newsome, prin. Fax 916-2607

Peninsula ES 400/K-8
8125 N Emerald Ave 97217 503-916-6275
Silvia Asson, prin. Fax 916-2662

Richmond ES 600/PK-5
2276 SE 41st Ave 97214 503-916-6220
David Allen, prin. Fax 916-2665

Rieke Immersion ES 400/K-5
1405 SW Vermont St 97219 503-916-5768
Sarah Lewins, prin. Fax 916-2666

Rigler ES 500/K-5
5401 NE Prescott St 97218 503-916-6451
Jennifer Fontana, prin. Fax 916-2667

Roseway Heights ES 600/K-8
7334 NE Siskiyou St 97213 503-916-5600
Jeremy Cohen, prin. Fax 916-2599

Sabin ES 500/PK-8
4013 NE 18th Ave 97212 503-916-6181
Reiko Williams, prin. Fax 916-2669

Scott ES 500/K-8
6700 NE Prescott St 97218 503-916-6369
G. Roletto, prin. Fax 916-2671

Sellwood MS 500/6-8
8300 SE 15th Ave 97202 503-916-5656
Karl Newsome, prin. Fax 916-2672

Sitton ES 400/K-5
9930 N Smith St 97203 503-916-6277
Dana Nerenberg, prin. Fax 916-2673

Skyline ES 300/K-8
11536 NW Skyline Blvd 97231 503-916-5212
B.G. Aguirre, prin. Fax 916-2765

Stephenson ES 300/K-5
2627 SW Stephenson St 97219 503-916-6318
Carlos Galindo, prin. Fax 916-2675

Vernon ES 400/PK-8
2044 NE Killingsworth St 97211 503-916-6415
Ben Keefer, prin. Fax 916-2678

Vestal ES 400/K-8
161 NE 82nd Ave 97220 503-916-6437
Sabrina Flamoe, prin. Fax 916-2679

West Sylvan MS 900/6-8
8111 SW West Slope Dr 97225 503-916-5690
Cherie Kinnersley, prin. Fax 916-2681
Whitman ES 300/K-5
7326 SE Flavel St 97206 503-916-6370
Ruth Tucker, prin. Fax 916-2684
Winterhaven ES 400/K-8
3830 SE 14th Ave 97202 503-916-6200
Mark Sandilands, prin. Fax 916-2614
Woodlawn ES 400/PK-5
7200 NE 11th Ave 97211 503-916-6282
Andrea Porter-Lopez, prin. Fax 916-2686
Woodmere ES 400/K-5
7900 SE Duke St 97206 503-916-6373
Katherine Polizos, prin. Fax 916-2687
Woodstock ES 500/K-5
5601 SE 50th Ave 97206 503-916-6300
Seth Johnson, prin. Fax 916-2688

Reynolds SD 7
Supt. — See Fairview
Alder ES 500/PK-5
17200 SE Alder St 97233 503-255-4673
Michael Clutter, prin. Fax 262-3786
Davis ES 500/K-5
19501 NE Davis St 97230 503-665-9193
Ashley Furlong, prin. Fax 667-6187
Four Corners ES K-5
14513 SE Stark St 97233 503-328-0420
Jessica Smrkovsky, prin. Fax 542-4796
Glenfair ES 500/K-5
15300 NE Glisan St 97230 503-252-3479
Lisa McDonald, prin. Fax 262-3788
Hartley ES 500/K-5
701 NE 185th Pl 97230 503-665-0134
Stephanie Murdock, prin. Fax 262-3789
Lee MS 800/6-8
1121 NE 172nd Ave 97230 503-255-5686
Danelle Heikkila, prin. Fax 328-0439
Scott ES 500/K-5
14700 NE Sacramento St 97230 503-255-2031
Debbie Nicolai, prin. Fax 262-3790
Wilkes ES 500/K-5
17020 NE Wilkes Rd 97230 503-255-6133
Candice Henkin, prin. Fax 262-3793

Riverdale SD 51J 600/K-12
11733 SW Breyman Ave 97219 503-262-4840
Terry Brandon, supt. Fax 262-4841
www.riverdaleschool.com
Riverdale Grade S 300/K-8
11733 SW Breyman Ave 97219 503-262-4842
Joanna Tobin, prin. Fax 262-4843

Tigard-Tualatin SD 23J
Supt. — See Tigard
Metzger ES 600/K-5
10350 SW Lincoln St 97223 503-431-4600
Todd Farris, prin. Fax 431-4610

All Saints S 400/PK-8
601 NE Cesar E Chavez Blvd 97232 503-236-6205
Rose Rosinski, prin. Fax 236-0781
Cathedral S 200/K-8
110 NW 17th Ave 97209 503-275-9370
Amy Biggs, prin. Fax 275-9378
Catlin Gabel S 700/PK-12
8825 SW Barnes Rd 97225 503-297-1894
Timothy Bazemore, head sch Fax 297-0139
Cedarwood S 300/PK-8
3030 SW 2nd Ave 97201 503-245-1477
Childpeace Montessori S 300/PK-8
1516 NW Thurman St 97209 503-222-1197
City Christian S 400/PK-12
9200 NE Fremont St 97220 503-252-5207
Columbia Christian S 200/PK-12
413 NE 91st Ave 97220 503-252-8577
Ami Vensel, prin. Fax 252-2108
Franciscan Montessori Earth S 300/PK-8
14750 SE Clinton St 97236 503-760-8220
Sr. Therese Gutting, head sch Fax 760-8333
Franciscan Montessori Earth S PK-6
14750 SE Clinton St 97236 503-760-8220
Sr. Therese Gutting, prin.
French American International S 500/PK-8
8500 NW Johnson St 97229 503-292-7776
Pam Dreisin, head sch Fax 292-7444
Grace Lutheran S 200/PK-8
2252 SE 92nd Ave 97216 503-777-8628
Mark Leitzke, prin. Fax 230-1354
Holy Cross S 200/1-8
5202 N Bowdoin St 97203 503-289-3010
Julie Johnson, prin. Fax 286-5006
Holy Family S 300/PK-8
7425 SE Cesar E Chavez Blvd 97202 503-774-8871
Loretta Wiltgen, prin. Fax 774-8872
Holy Redeemer S 200/K-8
127 N Rosa Parks Way 97217 503-283-5197
Anna Raineri, prin. Fax 283-9479
International S 500/PK-5
025 SW Sherman St 97201 503-226-2496
Robert Woods, hdmstr. Fax 525-0142
Islamic S of Portland 100/PK-8
10200 SW Capitol Hwy 97219 503-244-9606
ISMET/OIA PK-12
PO Box 283 97207 503-579-6621
Maayan Torah Day S 100/PK-8
PO Box 19452 97280 503-245-5568
Aviel Brodkin, prin.
Madeleine S 300/K-8
3240 NE 23rd Ave 97212 503-288-9197
Susan Steele, prin. Fax 280-1196
Maimonodies Jewish Day S 100/PK-6
6612 SW Capitol Hwy, 503-977-7850
Montessori S of Alameda 100/PK-3
4210 NE Going St 97218 503-335-3321
Montessori S of Beaverton 200/PK-6
11065 NW Crystal Creek Ln 97229 503-439-1597

Oregon Episcopal S 800/PK-12
6300 SW Nicol Rd 97223 503-246-7771
Mo Copeland, head sch Fax 293-1105
Portland Christian ES 300/PK-5
11845 SE Market St 97216 503-256-5455
Rhonda Rogers, prin. Fax 253-2666
Portland Jewish Academy 200/PK-8
6651 SW Capitol Hwy 97219 503-244-0126
Prince of Peace S 300/PK-K
14175 NW Cornell Rd 97229 503-645-1211
Carol Kluth, dir. Fax 531-2534
Renaissance S of Arts and Sciences K-8
0234 SW Bancroft St, 971-221-2311
St. Agatha S 200/PK-8
7960 SE 15th Ave 97202 503-234-5500
Chris Harris, prin. Fax 232-7240
St. Andrew Nativity S 100/6-8
4925 NE 9th Ave 97211 503-335-9600
Michael Chambers, prin. Fax 335-9494
St. Clare S 200/K-8
1807 SW Freeman St 97219 503-244-7600
Debbi Monahan, prin. Fax 293-2076
St. Ignatius S 200/K-8
3330 SE 43rd Ave 97206 503-774-5533
Kelli Clark, prin. Fax 788-1134
St. John Fisher S 200/K-8
7101 SW 46th Ave 97219 503-246-3234
Merrit Holub, prin. Fax 246-4117
St. Pius X S 300/K-8
1260 NW Saltzman Rd 97229 503-644-3244
Mary Thompson, prin. Fax 646-6568
St. Rose S 200/PK-8
5309 NE Alameda St 97213 503-281-5318
Karen Asbury, prin. Fax 281-0554
St. Therese S 200/K-8
1260 NE 132nd Ave 97230 503-253-9400
Joy Hunt, prin. Fax 253-9571
St. Thomas More S 200/K-8
3521 SW Patton Rd 97221 503-222-6105
Amy Jefferis, prin. Fax 227-5661
Shining Star Waldorf S 100/PK-8
2120 NE Tillamook St 97212 503-753-4459
Sunstone Montessori S 100/PK-6
6318 SW Corbett Ave, 503-768-3847
Trinity Lutheran S 100/PK-8
5520 NE Killingsworth St 97218 503-288-6403
Chris Herold, prin. Fax 288-1095
West Hills Christian S 400/K-8
7945 SW Capitol Hill Rd 97219 503-245-6688
Soo Chang, head sch Fax 245-4780

Port Orford, Curry, Pop. 1,095
Port Orford-Langlois SD 2CJ 200/K-12
PO Box 8 97465 541-366-2111
Steve Perkins, supt. Fax 332-0190
www.2cj.com
Driftwood S 100/K-8
PO Box 8 97465 541-332-2712
Christine Nichols, prin. Fax 332-0190

Powers, Coos, Pop. 625
Powers SD 31 100/K-12
PO Box 479 97466 541-439-2291
Matt Shorb, supt. Fax 439-2875
www.powersschools.com
Powers ES 100/K-6
PO Box 479 97466 541-439-2281
Matt Shorb, prin. Fax 439-2875

Prairie City, Grant, Pop. 882
Prairie City SD 4 100/K-12
PO Box 345 97869 541-820-3314
Julie Gurczynski, supt. Fax 820-4352
prairiecityschooldistrict.weebly.com
Prairie City S 100/K-12
PO Box 345 97869 541-820-3314
Julie Gurczynski, prin. Fax 820-4352

Prineville, Crook, Pop. 9,076
Crook County SD 2,700/K-12
471 NE Ochoco Plaza Dr 97754 541-447-5664
Dr. Duane Yecha, supt. Fax 447-3645
www.crookcounty.k12.or.us
Barnes Butte ES 600/K-5
1875 NE Iron Horse Dr 97754 541-416-4150
Jim Bates, prin. Fax 416-4151
Crook County MS 600/6-8
100 NE Knowledge St 97754 541-447-6283
Kurt Sloper, prin. Fax 447-3293
Crooked River ES 300/K-5
1400 SE 2nd St 97754 541-447-6488
Cheri Rasmussen, prin. Fax 447-8395
Other Schools – See Brothers, Paulina

High Desert Christian Academy 100/PK-12
839 S Main St 97754 541-416-0114
Maggie Hale, admin. Fax 416-0330

Rainier, Columbia, Pop. 1,842
Rainier SD 13 1,000/K-12
28168 Old Rainier Rd 97048 503-556-3777
R. Michael Carter, supt. Fax 556-3778
www.rainier.k12.or.us
Hudson Park ES 500/K-6
28176 Old Rainier Rd 97048 503-556-0196
Heidi Blakley, prin. Fax 556-8212

Redmond, Deschutes, Pop. 25,592
Redmond SD 2J 7,100/PK-12
145 SE Salmon Dr 97756 541-923-5437
Mike McIntosh, supt. Fax 923-5142
www.redmond.k12.or.us/
Gregory MS 600/6-8
1220 NW Upas Ave 97756 541-526-6440
Chad Lowe, prin. Fax 526-6441
Lynch ES 500/K-5
1314 SW Kalama Ave 97756 541-923-4876
Rayna Nordstrom, prin. Fax 923-4875

McCall ES 500/K-5
1200 NW Upas Ave 97756 541-526-6400
Drew Frank, prin. Fax 526-6401
Obsidian MS 600/6-8
1335 SW Obsidian Ave 97756 541-923-4900
Tami Nakamura, prin. Fax 923-6509
Patrick ES 400/K-5
3001 SW Obsidian Ave 97756 541-923-4830
Jennifer Hesse, prin. Fax 923-4833
Redmond Early Learning Center PK-PK
2105 W Antler Ave 97756 541-923-8900
Desiree Margo, prin.
Sage ES 600/K-5
2790 SW Wickiup Ave 97756 541-316-2830
Carolyn Espinosa, prin. Fax 316-2831
Tuck ES 400/K-5
209 NW 10th St 97756 541-923-4884
Dusty Porter, prin. Fax 923-4883
Other Schools – See Bend, Terrebonne

Central Christian S 300/PK-12
2731 SW Airport Way 97756 541-548-7803
Elisa Carlson, head sch Fax 548-2801
St. Thomas Academy 100/PK-5
1720 NW 19th St 97756 541-548-3785
Crystal Mooney, prin.

Reedsport, Douglas, Pop. 4,033
Reedsport SD 105 600/K-12
100 Ranch Rd 97467 541-271-3656
Dan Forbess, supt. Fax 271-3658
www.reedsport.k12.or.us
Highland ES 300/K-6
2605 Longwood Dr 97467 541-271-3616
Rebecca Lupton, prin. Fax 271-3618

Riddle, Douglas, Pop. 1,134
Riddle SD 70 300/K-12
PO Box 45 97469 541-874-3131
Dave Gianotti, supt. Fax 874-2345
www.riddle.k12.or.us
Riddle ES, PO Box 270 97469 200/K-6
Dave Gianotti, prin. 541-874-2226

Riley, Harney
Suntex SD 10
Supt. — See Hines
Suntex ES 50/K-8
68178 Silver Creek Rd 97758 541-493-2500
Janeen Starbuck, lead tchr. Fax 493-2245

Rockaway, Tillamook, Pop. 1,282
Neah-Kah-Nie SD 56 800/K-12
PO Box 28 97136 503-355-2222
Paul Erlebach, supt. Fax 355-3434
www.nknsd.org
Neah-Kah-Nie MS 200/6-8
25111 Highway 101 N 97136 503-355-2990
Leo Lawyer, prin. Fax 355-8514
Other Schools – See Garibaldi, Nehalem

Rogue River, Jackson, Pop. 2,091
Rogue River SD 35 800/K-12
PO Box 1045 97537 541-582-3235
Paul Young, supt. Fax 582-1600
www.rogueriver.k12.or.us
Rogue River ES 400/K-6
PO Box 1045 97537 541-582-3234
Janel Reed, prin. Fax 582-6007

Roseburg, Douglas, Pop. 20,494
Roseburg SD 6,000/PK-12
1419 NW Valley View Dr, 541-440-4015
Gerry Washburn, supt. Fax 440-4003
www.roseburg.k12.or.us
Eastwood ES 500/K-5
2550 SE Waldon Ave 97470 541-440-4180
Nicki Opp, prin. Fax 440-4182
Fir Grove ES 300/K-5
1360 W Harvard Ave, 541-440-4085
Lisa Dickover, prin. Fax 440-4086
Fremont MS 700/6-8
850 W Keady Ct, 541-440-4055
Ben Bentea, prin. Fax 440-4060
Fullerton IV ES 300/K-5
2560 W Bradford Ave, 541-440-4081
Katrina Hanson, prin. Fax 440-4082
Green ES 300/PK-5
4498 Carnes Rd, 541-440-4127
Amy Jo Rodriguez, prin. Fax 440-4017
Hucrest ES 400/K-5
1810 NW Kline St, 541-440-4189
Doug Freeman, prin. Fax 440-4191
Lane MS 700/6-8
2153 NE Vine St 97470 541-440-4104
Bill Bartlett, prin. Fax 440-4100
Melrose ES 300/K-5
2960 Melrose Rd, 541-440-4077
Tammy Rasmussen, prin. Fax 440-4078
Sunnyslope ES 300/K-5
2230 Cannon Ave, 541-440-4192
Don Schrader, prin. Fax 679-9485
Other Schools – See Winchester

Winston-Dillard SD 116
Supt. — See Winston
Lookingglass ES 200/K-6
7421 Lookingglass Rd, 541-679-3006
Oriole Inkster, prin. Fax 784-2639

Geneva Academy 100/K-12
PO Box 1154 97470 541-637-7500
Brian Turner, hdmstr.
Roseburg Junior Academy 50/K-8
1653 NW Troost St, 541-673-5278
St. Paul Lutheran S 100/PK-6
750 W Keady Ct, 541-673-7212
Kyle Crane, prin. Fax 677-9561

Umpqua Valley Christian S 100/PK-12
18585 Dixonville Rd 97470 541-679-4964
Adam Armstrong, head sch Fax 679-1881

Saint Helens, Columbia, Pop. 12,364
Saint Helens SD 502 3,200/K-12
474 N 16th St 97051 503-397-3085
Scot Stockwell, supt. Fax 397-1907
www.sthelens.k12.or.us
Lewis & Clark ES 700/K-6
111 S 9th St 97051 503-366-7603
Dustin Salisbury, prin. Fax 366-7656
McBride ES 700/K-6
2774 Columbia Blvd 97051 503-366-7700
Lisa Tyler, prin. Fax 366-7706
Saint Helens MS 500/7-8
354 N 15th St 97051 503-366-7300
Linda Hall, prin. Fax 366-7306
Other Schools – See Columbia City

Saint Paul, Marion, Pop. 420
St. Paul SD 45 300/PK-12
20449 Main St NE 97137 503-633-2541
Joseph Wehrli, supt. Fax 633-2540
www.stpaul.k12.or.us
Saint Paul ES 100/PK-6
20449 Main St NE 97137 503-633-2691
Joseph Wehrli, prin. Fax 633-2540

St. Paul S 100/PK-8
PO Box 188 97137 503-633-4622
Amanda Merrill, prin. Fax 633-4624

Salem, Marion, Pop. 148,676
Salem-Keizer SD 24J 40,300/PK-12
PO Box 12024 97309 503-399-3000
Christy Perry, supt. Fax 399-5579
www.salkeiz.k12.or.us
Auburn ES 700/K-5
4612 Auburn Rd NE 97301 503-399-3128
Katie Shumway, prin. Fax 391-4110
Battle Creek ES 500/K-5
1640 Waln Dr SE 97306 503-399-2062
Linda Dougherty, prin. Fax 399-2094
Brush College ES 300/K-5
2623 Doaks Ferry Rd NW 97304 503-399-3132
Artonya Gemmil, prin. Fax 391-4077
Bush ES 300/PK-5
410 14th St SE 97301 503-399-3134
Monica Takata, prin. Fax 391-4021
Candalaria ES 300/K-5
935 Hansen Ave S 97302 503-399-3136
Kerry Lohrman, prin. Fax 316-3525
Chapman Hill ES 400/K-5
1500 Doaks Ferry Rd NW 97304 503-399-3195
Rachael Harms, prin. Fax 375-7846
Chavez ES 700/K-5
2400 Walker Rd NE 97305 503-399-2571
Olga Cobb, prin. Fax 399-2576
Crossler MS 700/6-8
1155 Davis Rd S 97306 503-399-3444
Kristine Walton, prin. Fax 391-4005
Englewood ES 400/K-5
1132 19th St NE 97301 503-399-3143
Gary Etchemendy, prin. Fax 391-4085
Eyre ES 600/K-5
4868 Buffalo Dr SE, 503-399-3311
Corina Valencia-Cushman, prin. Fax 391-4078
Four Corners ES 500/K-5
500 Elma Ave SE, 503-399-3145
Phil Decker, prin. Fax 391-4148
Grant Community ES 400/PK-5
725 Market St NE 97301 503-399-3151
Marc Morris, prin. Fax 399-5557
Hallman ES 400/K-5
4000 Deerhaven Dr NE 97301 503-399-3451
Jessica Brenden, prin. Fax 391-4063
Hammond ES 500/K-5
4900 Bayne St NE 97305 503-399-3454
Lori Tan, prin. Fax 584-5174
Harritt ES 300/K-5
2112 Linwood St NW 97304 503-399-3457
Melinda Wilson, prin. Fax 361-2173
Hayesville ES 400/K-5
4545 Ward Dr NE 97305 503-399-3153
Michelle Halter, prin. Fax 391-4076
Highland ES 400/PK-5
530 Highland Ave NE 97301 503-399-3155
Christi Cheever, prin. Fax 391-4136
Hoover ES 500/K-5
1104 Savage Rd NE 97301 503-399-3157
Jen Vanslander, prin. Fax 375-7844
Houck MS 1,000/6-8
1155 Connecticut St SE, 503-399-3446
Suzanne Leonard, prin. Fax 391-4167
Judson MS 900/6-8
4512 Jones Rd SE 97302 503-399-3201
Alicia Kruska, prin. Fax 391-4041
Kalapuya ES 700/K-5
2085 Wilmington Ave NW 97304 503-399-2110
Jennifer Neitzel, prin. Fax 399-2112
Lamb ES 500/K-5
4930 Herrin Rd NE 97305 503-399-3477
Cherice Cochrane, prin. Fax 584-5079
Lee ES 300/K-5
5650 Venice St SE 97306 503-399-5570
Don Hakala, prin. Fax 399-3365
Leslie MS 800/6-8
3850 Pringle Rd SE 97302 503-399-3206
Denny McCarthy, prin. Fax 399-3479
Liberty ES 400/K-5
4871 Liberty Rd S 97306 503-399-3165
Lizi Aguilar-Nelson, prin. Fax 391-4185
McKinley ES 300/K-5
466 McGilchrist St SE 97302 503-399-3167
Michelle Nelson, prin. Fax 316-3527
Miller ES 400/K-5
1650 46th Pl SE, 503-399-3332
Laura Mata, prin. Fax 399-3318
Morningside ES 400/K-5
3513 12th St SE 97302 503-399-3173
Sarah Grimmer, prin. Fax 316-3528
Myers ES 400/K-5
2160 Jewel St NW 97304 503-399-3175
Stephanie Russell, prin. Fax 391-4094
Parrish MS 700/6-8
802 Capitol St NE 97301 503-399-3210
Dustin Purnell, prin. Fax 391-4004
Pringle ES 500/PK-5
5500 Reed Ln SE 97306 503-399-3178
Karl Paulson, prin. Fax 316-3529
Richmond ES 400/K-5
466 Richmond Ave SE 97301 503-399-3180
Bonney Dietrich, prin. Fax 316-3535
Salem Heights ES 300/K-5
3495 Liberty Rd S 97302 503-399-3187
Sarah Theis, prin. Fax 391-4036
Schirle ES 500/K-5
4875 Justice Way S 97302 503-399-3277
Clinton Gertenrich, prin. Fax 391-4087
Scott ES 500/K-5
4700 Arizona Ave NE 97305 503-399-3302
Tracy Moisan, prin. Fax 391-4030
Stephens MS 1,000/6-8
4962 Hayesville Dr NE 97305 503-399-3442
Jennie Madland, prin. Fax 391-4079
Straub MS 700/6-8
1920 Wilmington Ave NW 97304 503-399-2030
Laura Perez, prin. Fax 399-2032
Sumpter ES 500/K-5
525 Rockwood St SE 97306 503-399-3337
Janet Prats, prin. Fax 391-4080
Swegle ES 500/K-5
1751 Aguilas Ct NE 97301 503-399-3191
Suzanne West, prin. Fax 391-4138
Waldo MS 900/6-8
2805 Lansing Ave NE 97301 503-399-3215
Tricia Nelson, prin. Fax 391-4070
Walker MS 500/6-8
1075 8th St NW 97304 503-399-3220
Paul Myers, prin. Fax 399-5540
Washington ES 400/PK-5
3165 Lansing Ave NE 97301 503-399-3193
Scott Stenlund, prin. Fax 391-4086
Wright ES 500/K-5
4060 Lone Oak Rd SE 97302 503-399-3198
Sara Casebeer, prin. Fax 391-4090
Yoshikai ES 500/K-5
4900 Jade St NE 97305 503-399-3438
Zan Payne, prin. Fax 391-4071
Other Schools – See Keizer

Silver Falls SD 4J
Supt. — See Silverton
Pratum ES 100/K-8
8995 Sunnyview Rd NE 97305 503-362-8812
Lisa Freauff, lead tchr. Fax 585-6889

Abiqua Academy 200/PK-12
6974 Bates Rd S 97306 503-399-9020
Immanuel Lutheran S 100/PK-8
510 Idylwood Dr SE 97302 503-371-5473
Josh Roth, prin.
Livingstone Adventist Academy 200/PK-12
5771 Fruitland Rd NE, 503-363-9408
Our Savior's Christian ES 100/PK-5
1770 Baxter Road SE 97306 971-304-2013
Dawn Castronovo, prin.
Queen of Peace S 100/K-6
PO Box 3696 97302 503-362-3443
Carl Mucken, prin. Fax 589-9411
Riviera Christian S 200/PK-5
1650 Brush College Rd NW 97304 503-361-8779
Gordon Crowston, prin. Fax 362-9670
St. John Lutheran S 50/PK-K
1350 Court St NE 97301 503-588-0171
Kelly Crabtree, dir. Fax 585-2801
St. Joseph S 200/K-6
373 Winter St NE 97301 503-581-2147
Deborah Dewar, prin. Fax 399-7045
St. Vincent DePaul S 100/PK-6
1015 Columbia St NE 97301 503-363-8457
Maria Palacio, prin. Fax 363-1516
Salem Academy 700/PK-12
942 Lancaster Dr NE 97301 503-378-1219
John Tyler, supt. Fax 375-3522
Sonshine S 100/PK-7
395 Marion St NE 97301 503-375-5764
Donna Wiens, prin. Fax 391-9272

Sandy, Clackamas, Pop. 9,279
Oregon Trail SD 46 4,100/K-12
PO Box 547 97055 503-668-5541
Aaron Bayer, supt. Fax 668-7906
www.oregontrailschools.com
Cedar Ridge MS 400/6-8
17225 Smith Ave 97055 503-668-8067
Nicole Johnston, prin. Fax 668-3977
Firwood ES 500/K-5
42900 SE Trubel Rd 97055 503-668-8005
Tara Black, prin. Fax 668-3684
Sandy Grade S 300/K-5
38955 Pleasant St 97055 503-668-8065
Rachael George, prin. Fax 668-6246
Other Schools – See Boring, Welches

Scappoose, Columbia, Pop. 6,380
Scappoose SD 1J 2,300/K-12
33589 High School Way 97056 971-200-8000
Ron Alley, supt. Fax 543-7011
www.scappoose.k12.or.us
Petersen ES 400/4-6
52050 SE 3rd St 97056 971-200-8003
Matthew Wilding, prin. Fax 543-7120
Scappoose MS 400/7-8
52265 Columbia River Hwy 97056 503-543-7163
Troy Monson, prin. Fax 543-7917
Watts ES 400/K-3
52000 SE 3rd Pl 97056 971-200-8002
Jennifer Stearns, prin. Fax 543-6373
Other Schools – See Warren

Scappoose Adventist S 50/PK-8
54287 Columbia River Hwy 97056 503-543-6939

Scio, Linn, Pop. 809
Scio SD 95 4,200/K-12
38875 NW 1st Ave 97374 503-394-3261
Gary Tempel, supt. Fax 394-3920
www.scio.k12.or.us
Centennial ES 300/K-5
38875 NW 1st Ave 97374 503-394-3265
Luke Zedwick, prin. Fax 394-3247
Scio MS 200/6-8
38875 NW 1st Ave 97374 503-394-3271
Greg Nolan, prin. Fax 394-4042

Scotts Mills, Marion, Pop. 354
Silver Falls SD 4J
Supt. — See Silverton
Scotts Mills ES 100/K-8
PO Box 40 97375 503-873-4394
Kirstin Jorgenson, prin. Fax 873-3324

Seaside, Clatsop, Pop. 6,285
Jewell SD 8 100/PK-12
83874 Highway 103 97138 503-755-2451
Alice Hunsaker, supt. Fax 755-0616
www.jewell.k12.or.us
Jewell S 100/PK-12
83874 Highway 103 97138 503-755-2451
Terence Smyth, prin. Fax 755-0616

Seaside SD 10 1,500/K-12
1801 S Franklin St 97138 503-738-5591
Dr. Sheila Roley, supt. Fax 738-3471
www.seaside.k12.or.us
Broadway MS 400/6-8
1120 Broadway St 97138 503-738-5560
Robert Rusk, prin. Fax 738-3900
Seaside Heights ES 400/K-5
2000 Spruce Dr 97138 503-738-5161
John McAndrews, prin. Fax 738-7303
Other Schools – See Gearhart

Seneca, Grant, Pop. 198
Grant SD 3
Supt. — See Canyon City
Seneca ES 50/K-6
PO Box 69 97873 541-542-2542
Andrea Combs, lead tchr. Fax 542-2115

Shady Cove, Jackson, Pop. 2,835
Jackson County SD 9
Supt. — See Eagle Point
Shady Cove S 300/K-8
PO Box 138 97539 541-878-1400
Amy Isackson, prin. Fax 830-6226

Sheridan, Yamhill, Pop. 5,880
Sheridan SD 48J 1,000/K-12
435 S Bridge St 97378 971-261-6959
Dr. Steven Sugg, supt. Fax 843-3505
www.sheridan.k12.or.us
Faulconer-Chapman S 600/K-8
332 SW Cornwall St 97378 971-261-6960
Dave Kline, prin. Fax 843-3738

Delphian S 200/K-12
20950 SW Rock Creek Rd 97378 503-843-3521
Trevor Ott, hdmstr. Fax 843-4158

Sherwood, Washington, Pop. 17,504
Sherwood SD 88J 5,100/PK-12
23295 SW Main St 97140 503-825-5000
Dr. Heather Cordie, supt. Fax 825-5001
www.sherwood.k12.or.us
Archer Glen ES 500/K-5
16155 SW Sunset Blvd 97140 503-825-5100
Tim Smith, prin. Fax 825-5101
Edy Ridge ES 600/K-5
21472 SW Copper Ter 97140 503-825-5700
Amanda Hollenberg, prin. Fax 825-5701
Hopkins ES 500/PK-5
21920 SW Sherwood Blvd 97140 503-825-5200
Penny Salm, prin. Fax 825-5201
Laurel Ridge MS 500/6-8
21416 SW Copper Ter 97140 503-825-5800
Brian Bailey, prin. Fax 825-5801
Middleton ES 500/K-5
23505 SW Old Highway 99W 97140 503-825-5300
Jon Wollmuth, prin. Fax 825-5301
Sherwood MS 700/6-8
21970 SW Sherwood Blvd 97140 503-825-5400
Marianne Funderhide, prin. Fax 825-5401

St. Francis S 200/K-8
15643 SW Oregon St 97140 503-625-0497
William Summer, prin. Fax 625-5914

Silver Lake, Lake, Pop. 147
North Lake SD 14 200/PK-12
57566 Fort Rock Rd 97638 541-576-2121
Dave Kerr, supt. Fax 576-2705
www.nlake.k12.or.us/
North Lake S 200/PK-12
57566 Fort Rock Rd 97638 541-576-2121
Dave Kerr, admin. Fax 576-2705

Silverton, Marion, Pop. 9,064
Silver Falls SD 4J 3,300/K-12
612 Schlador St 97381 503-873-5303
Andy Bellando, supt. Fax 873-2936
silverfallsschools.org

Central Howell ES 200/K-8
8832 Silverton Rd NE 97381 503-873-4818
Dustin Hoehne, prin. Fax 873-5909
Evergreen ES 100/K-8
3727 Cascade Hwy NE 97381 503-873-4845
Jamie McCarty, prin. Fax 873-1495
Frost ES 400/3-6
201 Westfield St 97381 503-873-5301
Leslie Roache, prin. Fax 873-8910
Silver Crest ES 100/K-8
365 Loar Rd SE 97381 503-873-4428
Mark Hannan, prin. Fax 873-8457
Silverton MS 7-8
714 Schlador St 97381 503-873-5317
Brett Davisson, prin. Fax 873-7108
Twain ES 300/K-2
425 N Church St 97381 503-873-6341
Greg Kaatz, prin. Fax 873-8325
Victor Point S 200/K-8
1175 Victor Point Rd SE 97381 503-873-4987
Jamie McCarty, prin. Fax 873-8048
Other Schools – See Mount Angel, Salem, Scotts Mills

Silver Falls Christian S 50/PK-8
PO Box 828 97381 503-873-3991
Jamie Runion, head sch

Sisters, Deschutes, Pop. 2,007
Sisters SD 6 1,100/K-12
525 E Cascade Ave 97759 541-549-8521
Curtiss Scholl, supt. Fax 549-8951
www.sisters.k12.or.us
Sisters ES 300/K-4
611 E Cascade Ave 97759 541-549-8981
Becky Stoughton, prin. Fax 549-2093
Sisters MS 400/5-8
15200 McKenzie Hwy 97759 541-549-2099
Marshall Jackson, prin. Fax 549-2098

Sisters Christian Academy 100/PK-8
PO Box 1103 97759 541-549-4133
Cheryl Peterson, prin. Fax 549-1392

Spray, Wheeler, Pop. 157
Spray SD 1 50/PK-12
PO Box 230 97874 541-468-2226
Phil Starkey, supt. Fax 468-2630
www.spray.k12.or.us
Spray S 50/PK-12
PO Box 230 97874 541-468-2226
Phil Starkey, prin. Fax 468-2630

Springfield, Lane, Pop. 57,056
Springfield SD 19 10,500/K-12
525 Mill St 97477 541-747-3331
Susan Rieke-Smith Ed.D., supt. Fax 726-3312
www.springfield.k12.or.us
Briggs MS 500/6-8
2355 Yolanda Ave 97477 541-744-6350
Jeff Mather, prin. Fax 744-6354
Centennial ES 500/K-5
1315 Aspen St 97477 541-744-6383
Dan Sterling, prin. Fax 744-6489
Douglas Gardens ES 300/K-5
3680 Jasper Rd 97478 541-744-6387
Carla Smith, prin. Fax 744-6390
Hamlin MS 600/6-8
326 Centennial Blvd 97477 541-744-6356
Kevin Wright, prin. Fax 744-6360
Lee ES 300/K-5
755 Harlow Rd 97477 541-744-6391
Amber Mitchell, prin. Fax 744-6477
Maple ES 300/K-5
2109 J St 97477 541-744-6395
Sheila Minney, prin. Fax 744-6398
Mt. Vernon ES 500/K-5
935 Filbert Ln 97478 541-744-6403
Cindy Nees, prin. Fax 744-6405
Page ES 400/K-5
1300 Hayden Bridge Rd 97477 541-744-6407
Lacey MacDonald, prin. Fax 744-6410
Ridgeview ES 500/K-5
526 66th St 97478 541-744-6308
Jim Crist, prin. Fax 744-6311
Riverbend ES 500/K-5
320 51st St 97478 541-988-2511
Deborah Lange, prin. Fax 988-2519
Stewart MS 600/6-8
900 S 32nd St 97478 541-988-2520
Jeff Fuller, prin. Fax 988-2530
Thurston ES 500/K-5
7345 Thurston Rd 97478 541-744-6411
Nicki Gorham, prin. Fax 744-6414
Thurston MS 600/6-8
6300 Thurston Rd 97478 541-744-6368
Brandi Starck, prin. Fax 744-6372
Two Rivers-Dos Ros ES 400/K-5
1084 G St 97477 541-744-8865
Charlie Jett, prin. Fax 744-8876
Walterville ES 200/K-5
40589 Mckenzie Hwy 97478 541-744-6415
Dave Hulbert, prin. Fax 744-6417
Yolanda ES 400/K-5
2350 Yolanda Ave 97477 541-744-6418
Jeff Butler, prin. Fax 744-6421

Stanfield, Umatilla, Pop. 1,997
Stanfield SD 61 500/K-12
1120 N Main St 97875 541-449-8766
Shelley Liscom, supt. Fax 449-8768
www.stanfield.k12.or.us
Stanfield ES 200/K-5
1120 N Main St 97875 541-449-3305
Shelley Liscom, prin. Fax 449-8772

Stayton, Marion, Pop. 7,435
North Santiam SD 29J 2,400/K-12
1155 N 3rd Ave 97383 503-769-6924
Andrew Gardner, supt. Fax 769-3578
www.nsantiam.k12.or.us
Stayton ES 500/K-3
875 N 3rd Ave 97383 503-769-2336
Wendy Moore, prin. Fax 769-1709
Stayton MS 600/4-8
1021 Shaff Rd 97383 503-769-2198
Michael Proctor, prin. Fax 769-9524
Other Schools – See Lyons, Sublimity

Regis St. Mary S - St. Mary Campus 200/PK-8
1066 N 6th Ave 97383 503-769-2718
Richard Schindler, prin. Fax 769-0500

Sublimity, Marion, Pop. 2,632
North Santiam SD 29J
Supt. — See Stayton
Sublimity ES 400/K-8
PO Box 269 97385 503-769-2459
Missy Riesterer, prin. Fax 769-3383

Sunriver, Deschutes, Pop. 1,377
Bend-LaPine Administrative SD 1
Supt. — See Bend
Three Rivers S 300/K-8
56900 Enterprise Dr 97707 541-355-3000
Tim Broadbent, prin. Fax 355-3010

Sutherlin, Douglas, Pop. 7,596
Sutherlin SD 130 1,400/K-12
531 E Central Ave 97479 541-459-2228
Terry Prestianni, supt. Fax 459-2484
www.sutherlin.k12.or.us
Sutherlin East PS 400/K-3
323 E Third Ave 97479 541-459-2912
Debbie Foley, prin. Fax 459-0898
Sutherlin MS 200/7-8
649 E Fourth Ave 97479 541-459-2668
Jon Martz, prin. Fax 459-2047
Sutherlin West IS 300/4-6
531 N Comstock Rd 97479 541-459-3688
Trish McCracken, prin. Fax 459-5675

Sutherlin Adventist S 50/K-8
841 W Central Ave 97479 541-459-9940

Sweet Home, Linn, Pop. 8,693
Sweet Home SD 55 2,400/K-12
1920 Long St 97386 541-367-7126
Tom Yahraes, supt. Fax 367-7105
www.sweethome.k12.or.us
Hawthorne ES 300/K-6
3205 Long St 97386 541-367-7167
Terry Augustadt, prin. Fax 367-8903
Holley ES 100/K-6
40336 Crawfordsville Dr 97386 541-367-7162
Todd Barrett, prin. Fax 367-8904
Oak Heights ES 300/K-6
605 Elm St 97386 541-367-7165
Josh Dargis, prin. Fax 367-1128
Sweet Home JHS 300/7-8
880 22nd Ave 97386 541-367-7187
Colleen Henry, prin. Fax 367-7107
Other Schools – See Foster

Talent, Jackson, Pop. 5,873
Phoenix-Talent SD 4
Supt. — See Phoenix
Talent ES 500/K-5
PO Box 296 97540 541-535-1531
Curt Shenk, prin. Fax 535-1858
Talent MS 600/6-8
PO Box 359 97540 541-535-1552
Aaron Santi, prin. Fax 535-7532

Tangent, Linn, Pop. 1,128
Greater Albany SD 8J
Supt. — See Albany
Tangent ES 200/K-5
32100 Old Oak Dr 97389 541-967-4616
Gretchen Rayburn, prin. Fax 924-3716

Central Valley Christian S 100/PK-8
31630 Highway 34 97389 541-928-7820
Michael LaSage, prin. Fax 967-4410

Terrebonne, Deschutes, Pop. 1,235
Redmond SD 2J
Supt. — See Redmond
Terrebonne Community S 400/K-8
1199 B Ave 97760 541-923-4050
Trevor Flaherty, prin. Fax 923-4825

The Dalles, Wasco, Pop. 13,258
North Wasco County SD 21 3,000/K-12
3632 W 10th St 97058 541-506-3420
Candy Armstrong, supt. Fax 298-6018
www.nwasco.k12.or.us
Chenowith ES 500/K-5
922 Chenoweth Loop W 97058 541-506-3350
Anne Shull, prin. Fax 296-1316
Dry Hollow ES 500/K-5
1314 E 19th St 97058 541-506-3370
Theresa Peters, prin. Fax 298-6171
The Dalles MS 600/6-8
1100 E 12th St 97058 541-506-3380
Sandy Harris, prin. Fax 298-1942
Wright ES 300/K-5
610 W 14th St 97058 541-506-3360
Sharon Bonderud, prin. Fax 298-6145

St. Mary's Academy 200/PK-8
1112 Cherry Heights Rd 97058 541-296-6004
Kimberly Koch, prin. Fax 296-7858

Tigard, Washington, Pop. 46,005
Tigard-Tualatin SD 23J 12,600/K-12
6960 SW Sandburg St 97223 503-431-4000
Ernest Brown, supt. Fax 431-4047
www.ttsdschools.org
Deer Creek ES 600/K-5
16155 SW 131st Ave 97224 503-431-4450
Jarvis Gomes, prin. Fax 431-4460
Durham ES 600/K-5
7980 SW Durham Rd 97224 503-431-4500
Rhett Boudreau, prin. Fax 431-4510
Fowler MS 800/6-8
10865 SW Walnut St 97223 503-431-5000
Dan Busch, prin. Fax 431-5010
Rider ES 600/K-5
14850 SW 132nd Ter 97224 503-431-4900
Rory Moore, prin. Fax 431-4910
Templeton ES 600/K-5
9500 SW Murdock St 97224 503-431-4850
Carrie Ferguson, prin. Fax 431-4860
Tigard ES 600/K-5
12855 SW Grant Ave 97223 503-431-4400
Ryan Blasquez, prin. Fax 431-4410
Twality MS 1,000/6-8
14650 SW 97th Ave 97224 503-431-5200
Carol Kinch, prin. Fax 431-5210
Woodward ES 500/K-5
12325 SW Katherine St 97223 503-431-4700
Jerry Nihill, prin. Fax 431-4710
Other Schools – See Portland, Tualatin

Gaarde Christian S 200/PK-8
11265 SW Gaarde St 97224 503-639-5336
Kendra Jones, admin. Fax 684-6492
St. Anthony S 400/PK-8
12645 SW Pacific Hwy 97223 503-639-4179
Andy Nichols, prin. Fax 620-5117

Tillamook, Tillamook, Pop. 4,782
Tillamook SD 9 2,000/K-12
2510 1st St 97141 503-842-4414
Randy Schild, supt. Fax 842-6854
www.tillamook.k12.or.us
East ES 400/4-6
3905 Alder Ln 97141 503-842-7544
J.P. Richards, prin. Fax 842-1246
Liberty ES 300/K-1
1700 9th St 97141 503-842-7501
Jennifer Guarcello, prin. Fax 842-1314
South Prairie ES 300/2-3
6855 S Prairie Rd 97141 503-842-8401
Karen Therrell, prin. Fax 842-1452
Tillamook JHS 300/7-8
3906 Alder Ln 97141 503-842-7531
Melissa Radcliffe, prin. Fax 842-1349

Tillamook Adventist S 100/PK-8
4300 12th St 97141 503-842-6533
Fax 842-6236

Toledo, Lincoln, Pop. 3,349
Lincoln County SD
Supt. — See Newport
Toledo ES 400/K-6
600 SE Sturdevant Rd 97391 541-336-5121
Paul Tucker, prin. Fax 336-5407

Troutdale, Multnomah, Pop. 15,404
Reynolds SD 7
Supt. — See Fairview
Morey MS 600/6-8
2801 SW Lucas Ave 97060 503-491-1935
Tanya Pruett, prin. Fax 491-0245
Sweetbriar ES 400/K-5
501 SE Sweetbriar Ln 97060 503-666-9441
Marie Marianiello, prin. Fax 262-3791
Troutdale ES 400/K-5
648 SE Harlow Ave 97060 503-665-4182
Dr. Ed Krankowski, prin. Fax 262-3792

Tualatin, Washington, Pop. 25,026
Tigard-Tualatin SD 23J
Supt. — See Tigard
Bridgeport ES 500/K-5
5505 SW Borland Rd 97062 503-431-4200
Debbie Ebert, prin. Fax 431-4210
Byrom ES 500/K-5
21800 SW 91st Ave 97062 503-431-4300
Matt Coleman, prin. Fax 431-4310
Hazelbrook MS 1,000/6-8
11300 SW Hazelbrook Rd 97062 503-431-5100
Eric Nesse, prin. Fax 431-5110
Tualatin ES 600/K-5
20405 SW 95th Ave 97062 503-431-4800
Jamie Kingery, prin. Fax 431-4810

West Linn-Wilsonville SD 3J 9,100/PK-12
22210 SW Stafford Rd 97062 503-673-7000
Dr. Kathy Ludwig, supt. Fax 673-7001
www.wlwv.k12.or.us
Athey Creek MS 600/6-8
2900 SW Borland Rd 97062 503-673-7400
Joel Sebastian, prin. Fax 638-8302
Other Schools – See West Linn, Wilsonville

Horizon Christian Elementary and MS 400/PK-8
PO Box 2690 97062 503-692-9312
Judi Smith, prin. Fax 691-9677

Turner, Marion, Pop. 1,825
Cascade SD 5 2,200/K-12
10226 Marion Rd SE 97392 503-749-8010
Darin Drill, supt. Fax 749-8019
www.cascade.k12.or.us
Cascade JHS 500/6-8
10226 Marion Rd SE 97392 503-749-8030
Peter Rasmussen, prin. Fax 749-8039

Cloverdale ES 200/K-5
9666 Parrish Gap Rd SE 97392 503-749-8050
Bryan Dyer, prin. Fax 743-8059
Turner ES 200/K-5
PO Box 129 97392 503-749-8060
Dan Petersen, prin. Fax 749-8069
Other Schools – See Aumsville

Crosshill Christian S 200/PK-12
2707 Maranatha Ct SE 97392 503-391-9082
Adam Kronberger, supt. Fax 378-0507

Ukiah, Umatilla, Pop. 181
Ukiah SD 80R 50/K-12
PO Box 218 97880 541-427-3731
Norma Barber, supt. Fax 427-3730
www.ukiah.k12.or.us
Ukiah S 50/K-12
PO Box 218 97880 541-427-3740
Norma Barber, admin. Fax 427-3730

Umatilla, Umatilla, Pop. 6,845
Umatilla SD 6R 1,300/K-12
1001 6th St 97882 541-922-6500
Heidi Sipe, supt. Fax 922-6507
www.umatilla.k12.or.us
Brownell MS 300/6-8
1300 7th St 97882 541-922-6625
Liz Durant, prin. Fax 922-6507
McNary Heights ES 600/K-5
120 Columbia Ave 97882 541-922-6650
Rick Cotterell, prin. Fax 922-6699

Union, Union, Pop. 2,065
Union SD 5 300/K-12
PO Box K 97883 541-562-5166
Carter Wells, supt. Fax 562-8116
www.union.k12.or.us
Union ES 200/K-6
PO Box 868 97883 541-562-5278
Bill Johnson, prin. Fax 562-9028

Vale, Malheur, Pop. 1,833
Vale SD 84 900/K-12
403 E St W 97918 541-473-0201
Scott Linenberger, supt. Fax 473-3294
www.vale.k12.or.us
Vale ES 400/K-6
403 E St W 97918 541-473-3291
Alisha McBride, admin. Fax 473-3294
Vale MS 100/7-8
403 E St W 97918 541-473-0241
Jeri Schaffeld, prin. Fax 473-3293
Willowcreek ES 100/1-8
2300 9th Ave W 97918 541-473-2345
Alisha McBride, prin. Fax 473-3620

Veneta, Lane, Pop. 4,396
Fern Ridge SD 28J
Supt. — See Elmira
Veneta ES 400/K-5
PO Box 370 97487 541-935-8225
Lisa Leatham, prin. Fax 935-8228

Countryside Christian S 50/1-8
88401 Huston Rd 97487 541-935-6446

Vernonia, Columbia, Pop. 2,091
Vernonia SD 47J 600/K-12
1201 Texas Ave 97064 503-429-5891
Aaron Miller, supt. Fax 429-7742
www.vernonia.k12.or.us/
Vernonia ES 200/K-5
1000 Missouri Ave 97064 503-429-1333
Aaron Miller, prin. Fax 429-4539
Vernonia MS 100/6-8
1000 Missouri Ave 97064 503-429-1333
Nate Underwood, prin. Fax 429-4539
Other Schools – See Mist

Waldport, Lincoln, Pop. 1,936
Lincoln County SD
Supt. — See Newport
Crestview Heights ES 300/K-6
PO Box 830 97394 541-563-3237
Kelly Beaudry, prin. Fax 563-2467

Wallowa, Wallowa, Pop. 785
Wallowa SD 12 200/K-12
PO Box 425 97885 541-886-2061
Bret Uptmor, supt. Fax 886-7355
www.wallowa.k12.or.us/
Wallowa ES 100/K-6
PO Box 425 97885 541-886-2061
Bret Uptmor, admin. Fax 886-7355

Warm Springs, Jefferson, Pop. 2,866
Jefferson County SD 509J
Supt. — See Madras
Warm Springs K-8 Academy 500/K-8
50 Chukar Rd 97761 541-553-1128
Ken Parshall, prin. Fax 553-6321

Warren, Columbia, Pop. 1,740
Scappoose SD 1J
Supt. — See Scappoose
Warren ES 100/K-3
34555 Berg Rd 97053 503-397-2959
Laura LaMarsh, prin. Fax 397-7860

Columbia County Christian S 100/K-8
56523 Columbia River Hwy 97053 503-366-9209
Beth Winegar, admin. Fax 717-5568

Warrenton, Clatsop, Pop. 4,827
Warrenton-Hammond SD 30 900/K-12
820 SW Cedar Ave 97146 503-861-2281
Mark Jeffery, supt. Fax 861-2911
www.warrentonschools.com
Warrenton ES 600/K-8
820 SW Cedar Ave 97146 503-861-3376
Tom Rogozinski, prin. Fax 861-3378

Welches, Clackamas
Oregon Trail SD 46
Supt. — See Sandy
Welches S 200/K-8
24901 E Salmon River Rd 97067 503-622-3165
Kendra Payne, prin. Fax 622-4436

West Linn, Clackamas, Pop. 24,356
West Linn-Wilsonville SD 3J
Supt. — See Tualatin
Bolton PS 300/PK-5
5933 Holmes St 97068 503-673-7900
Holly Omlin-Ruback, prin. Fax 657-8711
Cedaroak Park PS 300/PK-5
4515 Cedaroak Dr 97068 503-673-7100
Carolyn Miller, prin. Fax 657-8722
Rosemont Ridge MS 700/6-8
20001 Salamo Rd 97068 503-673-7550
Debi Briggs-Crispin, prin. Fax 657-8720
Stafford PS 500/K-5
19875 SW Stafford Rd 97068 503-673-7150
Sara McCarney, prin. Fax 638-5313
Sunset PS 300/K-5
2351 Oxford St 97068 503-673-7200
Michelle Wilson, prin. Fax 657 6718
Trillium Creek PS 500/PK-5
1025 Rosemont Rd 97068 503-673-7950
Jim Mangan, prin.
Willamette ES 500/K-5
1403 12th St 97068 503-673-7250
Patrick Minor, prin. Fax 655-3706

Weston, Umatilla, Pop. 646
Athena-Weston SD 29RJ
Supt. — See Athena
Weston MS 200/4-8
PO Box 188 97886 541-566-3548
Ann Vescio, prin. Fax 566-2326

White City, Jackson, Pop. 7,814
Jackson County SD 9
Supt. — See Eagle Point
Academia Aguilitas Preschool 50/PK-PK
3275 Avenue G 97503 541-830-6240
Table Rock ES 400/K-5
2830 Maple Ct 97503 541-830-1350
Valerie Shehorn, prin. Fax 830-6307
White Mountain MS 400/6-8
550 Wilson Way 97503 541-830-6315
Karina Rizo, prin. Fax 830-6751

Willamina, Yamhill, Pop. 1,910
Willamina SD 30J 800/K-12
PO Box 1000 97396 503-876-4525
Carrie Zimbrick, supt. Fax 876-3610
www.willamina.k12.or.us
Willamina ES 400/K-6
PO Box 1000 97396 503-876-2374
Cera Norwood, prin. Fax 876-4321
Willamina MS 100/7-8
PO Box 1000 97396 503-876-2545
Tim France, prin. Fax 876-2511

Williams, Josephine, Pop. 1,050
Three Rivers SD
Supt. — See Grants Pass
Williams ES 100/K-5
20691 Williams Hwy 97544 541-846-7224
Steven Fuller, prin. Fax 846-7225

Wilsonville, Clackamas, Pop. 18,997
West Linn-Wilsonville SD 3J
Supt. — See Tualatin
Boeckman Creek ES 500/PK-5
6700 SW Wilsonville Rd 97070 503-673-7750
Lindy Sproul, prin. Fax 682-0738
Boones Ferry PS 500/PK-5
11495 SW Wilsonville Rd 97070 503-673-7300
Angela Freeman, prin. Fax 682-8761
Lowrie PS 500/PK-5
28995 SW Brown Rd 97070 503-673-7700
Patrick Meigs, prin. Fax 673-2221
Meridian Creek MS 6-8
6300 SW Hazel St 97070 503-673-7450
Annikke Olson, prin. Fax 570-0110
Wood MS 700/6-8
11055 SW Wilsonville Rd 97070 503-673-7500
Kelly Schmidt, prin. Fax 682-9109

Winchester, Douglas, Pop. 2,500
Roseburg SD
Supt. — See Roseburg
Winchester ES 400/PK-5
217 Pioneer Way 97495 541-440-4183
Melissa Locke-Warnicke, prin. Fax 440-4187

Winston, Douglas, Pop. 5,205
Winston-Dillard SD 116 1,500/K-12
620 NW Elwood Dr 97496 541-679-3000
Kevin Miller, supt. Fax 679-4819
www.wdsd.org
Brockway ES 400/K-3
2520 Brockway Rd 97496 541-679-3037
Kerry Dwight, prin. Fax 679-3051
McGovern ES 300/4-6
600 NW Elwood Dr 97496 541-679-3003
Jeremy Williams, prin. Fax 679-3027
Winston MS 200/7-8
330 SE Thompson Ave 97496 541-679-3002
David Welker, prin. Fax 679-3026
Other Schools – See Roseburg

Woodburn, Marion, Pop. 23,765
Woodburn SD 103 5,700/PK-12
1390 Meridian Dr 97071 503-981-9555
Chuck Ransom, supt. Fax 981-8018
www.woodburnsd.org
Creative Learning Center PK-PK
1274 N 5th St 97071 971-983-3043
French Prairie MS 600/6-8
1025 N Boones Ferry Rd 97071 971-983-3550
Ricardo Marquez, prin. Fax 981-2724
Heritage ES 900/K-5
440 Parr Rd 97071 503-981-2600
Greg Baisch, prin. Fax 981-2699
Lincoln ES 800/K-5
1041 N Boones Ferry Rd 97071 503-981-2825
Jennifer Caragol, prin. Fax 981-2831
Muir ES 500/K-5
1800 W Hayes St 97071 503-982-4300
Jeff Taylor, prin. Fax 982-4349
Valor MS 600/6-8
450 Parr Rd 97071 503-981-2750
Danny Nanez, prin. Fax 981-2790
Washington ES 600/K-5
777 E Lincoln St 97071 971-983-3050
Alfredo Belanger, prin. Fax 983-3063

St. Luke S 200/K-8
529 Harrison St 97071 503-981-7441
Angie Smith, prin. Fax 982-4697

Yamhill, Yamhill, Pop. 999
Yamhill-Carlton SD 1 1,200/K-12
120 N Larch 97148 503-852-6980
Charan Cline, supt. Fax 662-4931
www.ycsd.k12.or.us
Yamhill-Carlton IS 300/5-8
310 E Main St 97148 503-852-7680
Michael Fisher, prin. Fax 662-4079
Other Schools – See Carlton

Yoncalla, Douglas, Pop. 1,008
Yoncalla SD 32 200/K-12
PO Box 568 97499 541-849-2782
Jan Zarate, supt. Fax 849-2190
www.yoncalla.k12.or.us
Yoncalla ES 100/K-6
PO Box 568 97499 541-849-2158
Jan Zarate, prin. Fax 849-2121

PENNSYLVANIA

PENNSYLVANIA DEPARTMENT OF EDUCATION

333 Market St Fl 9, Harrisburg 17101-2215
Telephone 717-783-6788
Fax 717-787-7222
Website http://www.education.state.pa.us

Secretary of Education   Pedro Rivera

PENNSYLVANIA BOARD OF EDUCATION

333 Market St Fl 10, Harrisburg 17101-2210

Chairperson   Larry Wittig

INTERMEDIATE UNITS (IU)

Allegheny IU 3
Dr. Linda Hippert, dir. 412-394-5700
475 E Waterfront Dr Fax 394-5706
Homestead 15120
www.aiu3.net/

Appalachia IU 8
Dr. Thomas Butler, dir. 814-940-0223
4500 6th Ave, Altoona 16602 Fax 949-0984
www.iu08.org

ARIN IU 28
James Wagner, dir. 724-463-5300
2895 W Pike Rd, Indiana 15701 Fax 463-5315
www.iu28.org

Beaver Valley IU 27
Eric Rosendale, dir. 724-774-7800
147 Poplar Ave, Monaca 15061 Fax 774-4751
www.bviu.org/

Berks County IU 14
Dr. Jill Hackman, dir. 610-987-2248
PO Box 16050, Reading 19612 Fax 987-8400
www.berksiu.org

BLaST IU 17
Dr. Christina Reed, dir. 570-323-8561
PO Box 3609, Williamsport 17701 Fax 323-1738
www.iu17.org

Bucks County IU 22
Dr. Mark Hoffman, dir. 215-348-2940
705 N Shady Retreat Rd Fax 340-1964
Doylestown 18901
www.bucksiu.org

Capital Area IU 15
Dr. Andria Saia, dir. 717-732-8400
55 Miller St, Enola 17025 Fax 732-8421
www.caiu.org

Carbon-Lehigh IU 21
Elaine Eib Ed.D., dir. 610-769-4111
4210 Independence Dr Fax 769-1290
Schnecksville 18078
www.cliu.org

Central IU 10
Dr. Hugh Dwyer, dir. 814-342-0884
345 Link Rd, West Decatur 16878 Fax 342-5137
www.ciu10.com

Central Susquehanna IU 16
Dr. Kevin Singer, dir. 570-523-1155
90 Lawton Ln, Milton 17847 Fax 524-7104
www.csiu.org/

Chester County IU 24
Joseph Lubitsky, dir. 484-237-5000
455 Boot Rd, Downingtown 19335 Fax 237-5154
www.cciu.org/

IU 1
Charles Mahoney, dir. 724-938-3241
1 Intermediate Unit Dr Fax 938-6665
Coal Center 15423
www.iu1.org

Colonial IU 20
Dr. Charlene Brennan, dir. 610-252-5550
6 Danforth Dr, Easton 18045 Fax 252-5740
www.ciu20.org

Delaware County IU 25
Maria Edelberg Ed.D., dir. 610-938-9000
200 Yale Ave, Morton 19070 Fax 938-9887
www.dciu.org/

Lancaster-Lebanon IU 13
Dr. Brian Barnhart, dir. 717-606-1600
1020 New Holland Ave
Lancaster 17601
www.iu13.org

Lincoln IU 12
Dr. Jody Nace, dir. 717-624-4616
PO Box 70, New Oxford 17350 Fax 624-6519
www.iu12.org

Luzerne IU 18
Dr. Anthony Grieco, dir. 570-287-9681
368 Tioga Ave, Kingston 18704 Fax 287-5721
www.liu18.org/

Midwestern IU 4
Dr. Wayde Killmeyer, dir. 724-458-6700
453 Maple St, Grove City 16127 Fax 975-9519
www.miu4.k12.pa.us/

Montgomery County IU 23
Dr. John George, dir. 610-755-9400
2 W Lafayette St, Norristown 19401
www.mciu.org

Northeastern Educational IU 19
Bob McTiernan, dir. 570-876-9200
1200 Line St, Archbald 18403 Fax 876-8660
www.iu19.org

Northwest Tri-County IU 5
Dr. Dean Maynard, dir. 814-734-5610
252 Waterford St, Edinboro 16412 Fax 734-2303
www.iu5.org

Philadelphia IU 26
Dr. William Hite, dir. 215-400-4000
440 N Broad St, Philadelphia 19130
www.philasd.org

Pittsburgh/Mt. Oliver IU 2
Dr. Anthony Hamlet, dir. 412-224-4580
1305 Muriel St, Pittsburgh 15203 Fax 224-4583
www.pmoiu2.k12.pa.us

Riverview IU 6
Jeff Brown, dir. 814-226-7103
270 Mayfield Rd, Clarion 16214 Fax 226-4850
www.riu6.org/

Schuylkill IU 29
Dr. Gregory Koons, dir. 570-544-9131
PO Box 130, Mar Lin 17951 Fax 544-6412
www.iu29.org

Seneca Highlands IU 9
Don Wismar, dir. 814-887-5512
PO Box 1566, Smethport 16749 Fax 887-2157
www.iu9.org

Tuscarora IU 11
Dr. Kendra Trail, dir. 814-542-2501
2527 US Highway 522 S Fax 542-2569
Mc Veytown 17051
www.tiu11.org

Westmoreland IU 7
Dr. Jason Conway, dir. 724-836-2460
102 Equity Dr, Greensburg 15601 Fax 836-1747
wiu.k12.pa.us/

PUBLIC, PRIVATE AND CATHOLIC ELEMENTARY SCHOOLS

Abington, Montgomery, Pop. 56,600
Abington SD 7,600/K-12
970 Highland Ave 19001 215-884-4700
Amy Sichel Ph.D., supt. Fax 881-2545
www.abington.k12.pa.us
Highland ES 500/K-6
1301 Edge Hill Rd 19001 215-884-1048
Dr. James Etlen, prin. Fax 517-5039
Overlook ES 500/K-6
1750 Edge Hill Rd 19001 215-657-0857
Josha Perlman, prin. Fax 884-3237
Other Schools – See Elkins Park, Glenside, Huntingdon Valley, Roslyn, Rydal, Willow Grove

Adamstown, Lancaster, Pop. 1,761
Cocalico SD
Supt. — See Denver
Adamstown ES 400/K-5
256 W Main St 19501 717-484-1601
Denise Logue, prin. Fax 484-1613

Akron, Lancaster, Pop. 3,838
Ephrata Area SD
Supt. — See Ephrata
Akron ES 400/K-4
125 S 11th St 17501 717-859-0400
Sheri Horner, prin. Fax 859-4589

Albion, Erie, Pop. 1,497
Northwestern SD 1,500/K-12
100 Harthan Way 16401 814-756-9400
John Hansen, supt. Fax 756-9414
www.nwsd.org
Northwestern ES 400/K-5
10450 John Williams Ave 16401 814-756-9400
Terry Trimble, prin. Fax 756-9466
Northwestern MS 300/6-8
150 Harthan Way 16401 814-756-9400
Greg Lehman, prin. Fax 756-9415
Other Schools – See East Springfield

Albrightsville, Carbon, Pop. 201
Jim Thorpe Area SD
Supt. — See Jim Thorpe
Penn/Kidder S 700/K-8
2840 State Route 903 18210 570-722-1150
David McAndrew, prin. Fax 722-0317

Alburtis, Lehigh, Pop. 2,332
East Penn SD
Supt. — See Emmaus
Alburtis ES, 222 W 3rd St 18011 300/K-5
Dr. Ronald Renaldi, prin. 610-965-1633

Aldan, Delaware, Pop. 4,082
William Penn SD
Supt. — See Lansdowne
Aldan ES 200/K-6
1 N Woodlawn Ave 19018 610-626-3410
Janet Braker, prin. Fax 284-8059

Alexandria, Huntingdon, Pop. 344
Juniata Valley SD 800/K-12
PO Box 318 16611 814-669-9150
Michael Zinobile, supt. Fax 669-4492
www.jvhornets.com
Juniata Valley ES 400/K-6
PO Box 318 16611 814-669-4422
Jessica Quinter, prin. Fax 669-3413

Aliquippa, Beaver, Pop. 9,176
Aliquippa SD 1,200/K-12
800 21st St 15001 724-857-7500
Dr. Peter Carbone, supt. Fax 857-3404
www.quipsd.org
Aliquippa ES 700/K-6
800 21st St 15001 724-857-7500
A'Frica Sheppard, prin. Fax 857-7569

Central Valley SD
Supt. — See Monaca
Center Grange PS 500/K-2
225 Center Grange Rd 15001 724-775-5600
Carla Kosanovich, prin. Fax 775-4303

Hopewell Area SD 2,200/K-12
2354 Brodhead Rd 15001 724-375-6691
Dr. Michelle Miller, supt. Fax 375-0942
www.hopewell.k12.pa.us
Hopewell ES 300/K-4
3000 Kane Rd 15001 724-375-1111
Korri Kane, prin. Fax 375-4729
Hopewell JHS 700/5-8
2354 Brodhead Rd 15001 724-375-6691
Edward Katkich, prin. Fax 378-2594
Independence ES 300/K-4
103 School Rd 15001 724-375-3201
Korri Kane, prin. Fax 375-5141
Ross ES 200/K-4
1955 Maratta Rd 15001 724-375-2956
Korri Kane, prin. Fax 378-8555

Our Lady of Fatima S 200/PK-8
3005 Fatima Dr 15001 724-375-7565
Linda Liberatore, prin. Fax 375-0219
St. Francis Cabrini Preschool 100/PK-PK
115 Trinity Dr 15001 724-774-4888
Gayle Piroli, prin. Fax 775-3848

Allentown, Lehigh, Pop. 115,413
Allentown CSD 16,400/PK-12
31 S Penn St 18102 484-765-4000
Thomas Parker, supt. Fax 765-4239
www.allentownsd.org
Central ES 700/1-5
829 W Turner St 18102 484-765-4800
Rebecca Bodnar, prin. Fax 765-4810
Cleveland ES 300/K-5
424 N 9th St 18102 484-765-4820
Tonya Swavely, prin. Fax 765-4830
Dodd ES 700/K-5
1944 S Church St 18103 484-765-4500
Karen Boardman, prin. Fax 765-4510
Harrison-Morton MS 800/6-8
137 N 2nd St 18101 484-765-5700
Daria Custer, prin. Fax 765-5715
Jackson ECC 400/PK-K
517 N 15th St 18102 484-765-4701
Joshua Radcliffe, prin. Fax 765-5450
Jefferson ES 600/K-5
750 Saint John St 18103 484-765-4420
Christin Adams, prin. Fax 765-4430
Lehigh Parkway ES 300/1-5
1708 Coronado St 18103 484-765-4440
William Seng, prin. Fax 765-4450
McKinley ES 300/1-5
1124 W Turner St 18102 484-765-5460
Scott Cole, prin. Fax 765-5470
Mosser ES 700/K-5
129 S Dauphin St 18109 484-765-5880
Tiffany Polek, prin. Fax 765-5960
Muhlenberg ES 500/K-5
740 N 21st St 18104 484-765-4860
Jason Sizemore, prin. Fax 765-4878
Ramos ES 900/K-5
1430 W Allen St 18102 484-765-4840
Marybeth Kornfeind, prin. Fax 765-4850
Raub MS 900/6-8
102 S Saint Cloud St 18104 484-765-5300
Susan Elliott, prin. Fax 765-5310
Ritter ES 500/1-5
790 Plymouth St 18109 484-765-5660
Melissa Marcks, prin. Fax 765-5901
Roosevelt ES 700/K-5
210 W Susquehanna St 18103 484-765-4460
Erin Martin, prin. Fax 765-4470
Sheridan ES 700/1-5
521 N 2nd St 18102 484-765-4880
Lisa Lesko, prin. Fax 765-4890
South Mountain MS 1,100/6-8
709 W Emaus Ave 18103 484-765-4300
Frank Derrick, prin. Fax 765-4310
Trexler MS 900/6-8
851 N 15th St 18102 484-765-4600
Christine Piripavel, prin. Fax 765-4610
Union Terrace ES 800/K-5
1939 W Union St 18104 484-765-5480
David Hahn, prin. Fax 765-5489
Washington ES 500/1-5
837 N 9th St 18102 484-765-4940
Robert Wheeler, prin. Fax 765-4955

Parkland SD 9,200/K-12
1210 Springhouse Rd 18104 610-351-5503
Richard Sniscak, supt. Fax 351-5509
www.parklandsd.org
Cetronia ES 500/K-5
3635 Broadway 18104 610-351-5860
Jamie Giaquinto, prin. Fax 351-5869
Kratzer ES 400/K-5
2200 Huckleberry Rd 18104 610-351-5820
Karen Aulisio, prin. Fax 351-5829
Parkway Manor ES 500/K-5
768 Parkway Rd 18104 610-351-5850
Scott Bartman, prin. Fax 351-5859
Springhouse MS 1,200/6-8
1200 Springhouse Rd 18104 610-351-5700
Michelle Minotti, prin. Fax 351-5748
Other Schools – See Breinigsville, Coplay, Orefield, Schnecksville

Salisbury Township SD 1,600/K-12
1140 Salisbury Rd 18103 610-797-2062
Dr. Randy Ziegenfuss, supt. Fax 791-9983
www.salisburysd.org
Salisbury MS 400/6-8
3301 Devonshire Rd 18103 610-791-0830
Ken Parliman, prin. Fax 797-9648
Truman ES 400/K-5
1400 Gaskill St 18103 610-791-2800
Zachary Brem, prin. Fax 797-9640
Western Salisbury ES 200/K-5
3201 Devonshire Rd 18103 610-797-1688
Grace Hartman, prin. Fax 797-9641

Grace Montessori S 100/PK-5
814 W Linden St 18101 610-435-4060
Jewish Day S of the Lehigh Valley 100/PK-8
2313 W Pennsylvania St 18104 610-437-0721
Amy Golding, head sch Fax 437-1459
Lehigh Christian Academy 200/PK-8
1151 S Cedar Crest Blvd 18103 610-776-7301
Elizabeth Hauser, head sch Fax 776-1417
Our Lady Help of Christians S 200/K-8
934 Hanover Ave 18109 610-433-1592
Mary Vanya, prin. Fax 434-7123
Sacred Heart S 300/PK-8
325 N 4th St 18102 610-437-3031
James Krupka, prin. Fax 437-2724
St. John Vianney S 400/PK-8
210 N 18th St 18104 610-435-8981
Dr. Emily Kleintop, prin. Fax 437-7951
St. Thomas More S 600/K-8
1040 Flexer Ave 18103 610-432-0396
Dr. Carl Weber, prin. Fax 432-1395
Simplicity Christian Academy K-8
725 N 15th St Ste 17 18102 610-698-3074
Swain S 300/PK-8
1100 S 24th St 18103 610-433-4542
Dr. Shannan Boyle Schuster, head sch Fax 433-3844

Allison Park, Allegheny, Pop. 21,377
Hampton Township SD 3,000/K-12
4591 School Dr 15101 412-486-6000
Dr. Michael Loughead, supt.
www.ht-sd.org
Central ES 500/K-5
4100 Middle Rd 15101 412-492-6320
Dr. Amy Kern, prin. Fax 486-1144
Hampton MS 700/6-8
4589 School Dr 15101 412-492-6356
Marlynn Lux, prin. Fax 487-7544
Wyland ES 400/K-5
2284 Wyland Ave 15101 412-492-6345
Dr. Laurie Tocci, prin. Fax 486-6718
Other Schools – See Gibsonia

North Allegheny SD
Supt. — See Pittsburgh
Hosack ES 400/K-5
9275 Peebles Rd 15101 412-366-9664
Amanda Mathieson, prin. Fax 366-9019

Shaler Area SD
Supt. — See Glenshaw
Burchfield PS 400/K-3
1500 Burchfield Rd 15101 412-492-1200
Jeff Rojik, prin. Fax 486-7631
Rogers PS 200/K-3
1500 Burchfield Rd 15101 412-492-1200
Cynthia Foht, prin. Fax 487-0293

Providence Heights Alpha S 200/PK-8
9000 Babcock Blvd 15101 412-366-4455
Margaret Ruefle, prin. Fax 635-6317
St. Catherine of Sweden Preschool 50/PK-PK
2554 Wildwood Rd 15101 724-486-6001
Kathryn Sperdute, dir. Fax 486-6004
St. Ursula S 100/PK-8
3937 Kirk Ave 15101 412-486-5511
Judy Riegelnegg, prin. Fax 492-7295
Winchester Thurston S 100/PK-5
4225 Middle Rd 15101 412-486-8341
Gary Niels, head sch Fax 486-8378

Altoona, Blair, Pop. 45,425
Altoona Area SD 7,600/K-12
1415 6th Ave 16602 814-946-8211
Dr. Charles Prijatelj, supt. Fax 946-8226
www.aasdcat.com
Baker ES 400/K-6
108 W Ward Ave 16602 814-946-8388
Cathy Keefe, prin. Fax 946-8472
Ebner ES 600/K-6
308 Hillside Ave 16601 814-946-8400
Kelly Clouser, prin. Fax 946-8580
Juniata ES 600/K-6
418 N 8th Ave 16601 814-946-8394
Brandy Orner, prin. Fax 946-8582
Juniata Gap ES 600/K-6
3365 Juniata Gap Rd 16601 814-946-8401
Richard Adams, prin. Fax 946-8583
Logan ES 600/K-6
301 Sycamore St 16602 814-946-8370
Jill Daloisio, prin. Fax 946-8584
McAuliffe Heights S at Irving 300/K-6
110 Cherry Ave 16601 814-946-8392
Brandy Agnew, prin. Fax 946-8581
Penn-Lincoln ES 400/K-6
411 12th St 16602 814-946-8396
Eric Dambeck, prin. Fax 946-8585
Pleasant Valley ES 500/K-6
310 Cayuga Ave 16602 814-946-8397
Matthew Stinson, prin. Fax 946-8399

Great Commission S 100/PK-12
1100 6th Ave 16602 814-942-9710
Jennifer McConnell, supt. Fax 942-7147
Holy Trinity Catholic MS 300/5-8
5519 6th Ave 16602 814-942-7835
Elaine Spencer, prin. Fax 942-1095
Holy Trinity Catholic S PK-4
424 Wopsononock Ave 16601 814-381-7011
Elaine Spencer, prin. Fax 381-7015
Tender Love for Children S 100/PK-K
1401 12th Ave 16601 814-942-3816
Barbara Crago, dir.

Alverton, Westmoreland
Southmoreland SD
Supt. — See Scottdale
Southmoreland Primary Center 300/K-1
1431 Water St 15612 724-887-2026
Dan Clara, prin. Fax 887-2044

Ambler, Montgomery, Pop. 6,216
Wissahickon SD 4,400/K-12
601 Knight Rd 19002 215-619-8000
Dr. James Crisfield, supt. Fax 619-8002
wsdweb.org
Lower Gwynedd ES 600/K-5
571 Houston Rd 19002 215-619-8100
Nicole West, prin. Fax 619-8101
Shady Grove ES 600/K-5
351 W Skippack Pike 19002 215-619-8106
Toby Albanese, prin. Fax 619-8088
Wissahickon MS 1,000/6-8
500 Houston Rd 19002 215-619-8110
Elizabeth Bauer, prin. Fax 619-8111
Other Schools – See Blue Bell

Twin Spring Farm Day S 200/PK-6
1632 E Butler Pike 19002 215-646-2665

Ambridge, Beaver, Pop. 6,737
Ambridge Area SD 2,600/PK-12
901 Duss Ave 15003 724-266-2833
Dr. Laura Welter, supt. Fax 266-3981
www.ambridge.k12.pa.us
Highland ES 500/PK-6
1101 Highland Ave 15003 724-266-2833
Jo Ann Hoover, prin. Fax 524-1299
Other Schools – See Baden, Freedom

Anita, Jefferson
Punxsutawney Area SD
Supt. — See Punxsutawney
Parkview ES 100/K-3
PO Box 285 15711 814-938-5120
Dr. Sharon Weber, prin. Fax 938-3441

Annville, Lebanon, Pop. 4,714
Annville-Cleona SD 1,200/K-12
520 S White Oak St 17003 717-867-7600
Dr. Cheryl A. Potteiger, supt. Fax 867-7610
www.acschools.org
Annville ES 400/3-6
205 S White Oak St 17003 717-867-7620
Ross Hopple, prin. Fax 867-7624
Other Schools – See Cleona

Northern Lebanon SD
Supt. — See Jonestown
East Hanover ES 200/1-5
1098 School House Rd 17003 717-865-3595
Dr. Melissa McInerney, prin. Fax 865-0608

Apollo, Armstrong, Pop. 1,610
Apollo-Ridge SD 1,300/K-12
1825 State Route 56 15613 724-478-6000
Dr. Matthew E. Curci, supt. Fax 478-1149
www.apolloridge.com/
Other Schools – See Spring Church

Kiski Area SD
Supt. — See Leechburg
Kiski Area Upper ES 500/5-6
4350 State Route 66 15613 724-727-3421
Kenneth Pruitt, prin. Fax 727-2861

Archbald, Lackawanna, Pop. 6,931
Valley View SD 2,500/K-12
1 Columbus Dr 18403 570-876-5080
Dr. Rose Minniti, supt. Fax 876-6365
www.valleyviewsd.org
Valley View IS 600/3-5
3 Columbus Dr 18403 570-876-2263
Brian Durkin, prin. Fax 803-0355
Valley View MS 600/6-8
1 Columbus Dr 18403 570-876-6461
Craig Sweeney, prin. Fax 803-0276
Other Schools – See Peckville

Ardmore, Montgomery, Pop. 12,170
Haverford Township SD
Supt. — See Havertown
Chestnutwold ES 500/K-5
630 Loraine St 19003 610-853-5900
Joel DeBartolomeo, prin. Fax 853-5979

Lower Merion SD 7,800/K-12
301 E Montgomery Ave 19003 610-645-1800
Robert Copeland, supt. Fax 645-9772
www.lmsd.org
Other Schools – See Bala Cynwyd, Gladwyne, Merion Station, Narberth, Wynnewood

Ardsley, Montgomery

Good Shepherd Catholic Regional S 100/K-8
835 N Hills Ave 19038 215-886-4782
Sr. Patricia Healey, prin. Fax 517-6708

Arendtsville, Adams, Pop. 935
Upper Adams SD
Supt. — See Biglerville
Arendtsville IS 200/4-6
PO Box 340 17303 717-677-4300
Sonia Buckley, prin. Fax 677-6432

Armagh, Indiana, Pop. 121
United SD 1,100/PK-12
10780 Route 56 Hwy E 15920 814-446-5615
Dr. Barbara Parkins, supt. Fax 446-6615
www.unitedsd.net/
United ES 600/PK-6
10775 Route 56 Hwy E 15920 814-446-5615
Lewis Kindja, prin. Fax 446-4210

Arnold, Westmoreland, Pop. 4,917
New Kensington-Arnold SD
Supt. — See New Kensington
Berkey ES 300/1-2
1739 Victoria Ave 15068 724-337-7736
Thomas Rocchi, prin. Fax 594-1134
Hunt ES 500/3-6
1701 Alcoa Dr 15068 724-335-2511
Thomas Rocchi, prin. Fax 339-5532

Ashland, Schuylkill, Pop. 2,790
North Schuylkill SD 1,900/K-12
15 Academy Ln 17921 570-874-0466
Dr. Robert Ackell, supt. Fax 874-3334
www.northschuylkill.net
North Schuylkill ES 1,100/K-6
38 Line St 17921 570-874-3661
Missy Whitaker, prin. Fax 874-2857

Aspinwall, Allegheny, Pop. 2,766

Christ the Divine Teacher Academy 200/PK-8
205 Brilliant Ave 15215 412-781-7927
Mark Gurich, prin. Fax 781-0891

Aston, Delaware
Chichester SD 3,300/K-12
401 Cherry Tree Rd 19014 610-485-6881
Dr. Kathleen Sherman, supt. Fax 485-3086
www.chichestersd.org
Hilltop ES 400/K-4
401 Cherry Tree Rd 19014 610-485-6746
Christine Matijasich, prin. Fax 859-0606
Other Schools – See Boothwyn, Linwood, Marcus Hook

Penn-Delco SD 3,400/K-12
2821 Concord Rd 19014 610-497-6300
Dr. George Steinhoff, supt. Fax 497-1798
www.pdsd.org
Aston ES 500/K-5
900 Tryens Rd 19014 610-497-6300
Susan Phillips, prin. Fax 558-7881
Northley MS 800/6-8
2801 Concord Rd 19014 610-497-6300
Lanny Blair, prin. Fax 497-5737
Pennell ES 400/K-5
3300 Richard Rd 19014 610-497-6300
Eileen Martin, prin. Fax 485-5557
Other Schools – See Brookhaven, Parkside

Holy Family Regional Catholic S 200/PK-8
3265 Concord Rd 19014 610-494-0147
Nancy Franz, prin. Fax 494-4615

Atglen, Chester, Pop. 1,387
Octorara Area SD 2,500/K-12
228 Highland Rd Ste 1 19310 610-593-8238
Dr. Thomas Newcome, supt. Fax 593-6425
www.octorara.k12.pa.us
Octorara Area ES 400/3-4
104 Highland Rd 19310 610-593-8238
Brian Dikun, prin. Fax 593-8248
Octorara Area IS 400/5-6
221 Highland Rd 19310 610-593-8238
Christian Haller, prin. Fax 593-4611
Octorara Area JHS 400/7-8
228 Highland Rd 19310 610-593-8238
Dr. Scott Rohrer, prin. Fax 593-5185
Octorara Primary Learning Center 500/K-2
87 Highland Rd 19310 610-593-8350
Frank DiLeo, prin. Fax 593-8365

West Fallowfield Christian S 100/PK-8
PO Box 279 19310 610-593-5011
Robbie Martin, prin. Fax 593-6041

Athens, Bradford, Pop. 3,332
Athens Area SD 1,900/PK-12
401 W Frederick St 18810 570-888-7766
Craig Stage, supt. Fax 882-6250
www.athensasd.org
Lynch - Bustin ES 600/PK-5
253 Pennsylvania Ave 18810 570-888-7766
John Toscano, prin. Fax 888-8675
Rowe MS 200/6-8
116 W Pine St Ste 1 18810 570-888-7766
Stephen Boyce, prin. Fax 888-9536
Other Schools – See East Smithfield

Austin, Potter, Pop. 562
Austin Area SD 200/PK-12
138 Costello Ave 16720 814-647-8603
Dan Eskesen, supt. Fax 647-8869
www.austinsd.net
Austin Area ES 100/PK-6
138 Costello Ave 16720 814-647-8603
Dan Eskesen, prin. Fax 647-8869

Avella, Washington, Pop. 795
Avella Area SD 600/K-12
1000 Avella Rd 15312 724-356-2218
Cyril Walther, supt. Fax 356-2207
www.avella.k12.pa.us
Avella ES 300/K-6
1000 Avella Rd 15312 724-356-2294
Zachary Zebrasky, prin. Fax 356-7892

Avis, Clinton, Pop. 1,476

Walnut Street Christian S 200/PK-12
PO Box 616 17721 570-753-3400

Baden, Beaver, Pop. 4,097
Ambridge Area SD
Supt. — See Ambridge
State Street ES 300/K-6
600 Harmony Rd 15005 724-266-2833
Thomas McKelvey, prin. Fax 869-1030

Bala Cynwyd, Montgomery, Pop. 8,000
Lower Merion SD
Supt. — See Ardmore
Bala Cynwyd MS 900/6-8
510 Bryn Mawr Ave 19004 610-645-1480
Jason Potten, prin. Fax 664-2798
Belmont Hills ES 500/K-5
200 School St 19004 610-645-1420
Dr. Pamula Hart, prin. Fax 747-0645
Cynwyd ES 500/K-5
101 W Levering Mill Rd 19004 610-645-1430
Dr. Daniel Martino, prin. Fax 664-8127

French International S of Philadelphia 300/PK-8
150 N Highland Ave 19004 610-667-1284
Kathy Kotchick, head sch Fax 667-1286

Bally, Berks, Pop. 1,082

St. Francis Academy 200/PK-8
668 Pine St 19503 610-845-7364
Thomas Murphy, prin. Fax 845-2223

Bangor, Northampton, Pop. 5,192
Bangor Area SD 3,000/K-12
123 Five Points Richmond Rd 18013 610-588-2163
Dr. William Haws, supt. Fax 599-7040
www.bangor.k12.pa.us
Bangor Area MS 500/7-8
401 Five Points Richmond Rd 18013 610-599-7012
Allison Tucker, prin. Fax 599-7045
Defranco ES 500/5-6
267 Five Points Richmond Rd 18013 610-599-7013
Braden Hendershot, prin. Fax 599-7041
Five Points ES 600/K-4
363 Five Points Richmond Rd 18013 610-599-7015
Courtney Lepore, prin. Fax 599-7042
Washington ES 500/K-4
381 Washington Blvd 18013 610-599-7014
Scott Davis, prin. Fax 599-7046

Barto, Berks
Boyertown Area SD
Supt. — See Boyertown
Washington ES 600/K-6
1406 Route 100 19504 610-754-9589
Christopher Iacobelli, prin. Fax 754-8301

Bath, Northampton, Pop. 2,659
Northampton Area SD
Supt. — See Northampton
Moore ES 600/K-5
2835 Mountain View Dr 18014 610-837-1859
Curtis Dimmick, prin. Fax 837-7239
Wolf ES 600/K-5
300 Allen St 18014 610-837-1833
Stephen Serensits, prin. Fax 837-7308

Sacred Heart S 100/PK-8
115 Washington St 18014 610-837-6391
Karen Gabryluk, prin. Fax 837-2469

Beaver, Beaver, Pop. 4,471
Beaver Area SD 2,000/K-12
1300 5th St 15009 724-774-4021
Dr. Carrie Rowe, supt. Fax 774-8770
www.basd.k12.pa.us
Beaver Area MS 300/7-8
1 Gypsy Glen Rd 15009 724-774-0253
Jeff Beltz, prin. Fax 774-3926
College Square ES 400/K-2
375 College Ave 15009 724-774-9126
Jess Hiles, prin. Fax 774-1168
Dutch Ridge ES 600/3-6
2220 Dutch Ridge Rd 15009 724-774-1016
Justin Noel, prin. Fax 774-1033

SS. Peter & Paul S 100/K-8
370 E End Ave 15009 724-774-4450
Cynthia Baldrige, prin. Fax 774-5192

Beaver Falls, Beaver, Pop. 8,590
Big Beaver Falls Area SD 1,700/K-12
1503 8th Ave 15010 724-843-3420
Dr. Donna Nugent, supt. Fax 843-2360
www.tigerweb.org
Beaver Falls MS 400/6-8
1601 8th Ave 15010 724-846-5470
Thomas House, prin. Fax 846-2579
Central ES 500/K-5
805 15th St 15010 724-843-3420
Theresa Cherry, prin. Fax 843-5740
Other Schools – See Darlington

Blackhawk SD 2,000/K-12
500 Blackhawk Rd 15010 724-846-6600
Dr. Robert Postupac, supt. Fax 846-2021
www.bsd.k12.pa.us
Blackhawk IS 400/K-4
635 Shenango Rd 15010 724-843-5050
Jodi Boroni, prin. Fax 843-9175
Highland MS 600/5-8
402 Shenango Rd 15010 724-843-1700
Amy Anderson, prin. Fax 843-0934
Northwestern PS 300/K-2
635 Shenango Rd 15010 724-843-5050
Jodi Borroni, prin.
Patterson ES 200/K-2
701 Darlington Rd 15010 724-843-1268
Marianne LeDonne, prin. Fax 846-8082

Beaver County Christian ES 100/K-5
3601 Short St 15010 724-843-8331
Douglas Carson, prin. Fax 891-3315
Beaver County Christian MS 6-8
4001 6th Ave 15010 724-843-8331
Douglas Carson, prin.
St. Monica Catholic Academy 100/PK-8
609 10th St 15010 724-846-5955
Brad Diamond, prin. Fax 846-6868

Beaver Springs, Snyder, Pop. 668
Midd-West SD
Supt. — See Middleburg
West Snyder ES 400/K-5
645 Snyder Ave 17812 570-837-0046
Erin C. Sheedy, prin. Fax 658-7287

Bechtelsville, Berks, Pop. 934

Brookeside Montessori S 50/PK-6
1075 Route 100 19505 610-473-0408

Bedford, Bedford, Pop. 2,806
Bedford Area SD 1,900/K-12
330 E John St 15522 814-623-4290
Dr. Allen Sell, supt. Fax 623-4299
www.bedfordasd.org
Bedford ES 800/K-5
3639 Business 220 15522 814-623-4221
Leslie Turkovich, prin. Fax 623-3989
Bedford MS 500/6-8
440 E Watson St 15522 814-623-4200
Kevin Windows, prin. Fax 623-4214

St. Thomas the Apostle S 50/PK-4
129 W Penn St 15522 814-623-8873
Amy Higgins, prin. Fax 623-1208

Bellefonte, Centre, Pop. 6,107
Bellefonte Area SD 2,700/K-12
318 N Allegheny St 16823 814-355-4814
Dr. Michelle Saylor, supt. Fax 353-5342
www.basd.net
Bellefonte Area MS 600/6-8
100 N School St 16823 814-355-5466
Sommer Garman, prin. Fax 353-5350
Bellefonte ES 400/K-5
100 W Linn St 16823 814-355-5519
Jennifer Brown, prin. Fax 353-5338
Benner ES 300/K-5
490 Buffalo Run Rd 16823 814-355-2812
Kris Vancas, prin. Fax 353-5339
Marion-Walker ES 400/K-5
100 School Dr 16823 814-357-2425
Karen Krisch, prin. Fax 357-2426
Other Schools – See Pleasant Gap

Centre County Christian Academy 50/PK-12
100 Hertzler Dr 16823 814-355-7805
Kristy Smith, admin. Fax 355-9395
St. John the Evangelist S 100/PK-5
116 E Bishop St 16823 814-355-7859
Kristina Ticc, prin. Fax 355-2939

Belle Vernon, Fayette, Pop. 1,081
Belle Vernon Area SD 2,400/K-12
270 Crest Ave 15012 724-808-2500
Dr. John Wilkinson, supt. Fax 929-5598
www.bellevernonarea.net/bvasd/site/default.asp
Belle Vernon Area MS 200/7-8
500 Perry Ave 15012 724-808-2500
Greg Zborovancik, prin.
Marion ES, 500 Perry Ave 15012 700/K-6
Dr. Michele Dowell, prin. 724-808-2500
Rostraver ES, 300 Crest Ave 15012 700/K-6
Jennifer Godzak, prin. 724-808-2500

St. Sebastian Regional S 200/PK-8
815 Broad Ave 15012 724-929-5143
Giannina Zetty, prin. Fax 929-3038

Belleville, Mifflin, Pop. 1,819

Belleville Mennonite S 200/PK-12
4105 Front Mountain Rd 17004 717-935-2184
Starla Fogleman, supt. Fax 935-5641

Bellevue, Allegheny, Pop. 8,155
Northgate SD
Supt. — See Pittsburgh
Bellevue ES 300/K-6
435 Lincoln Ave 15202 412-732-3300
John Primrose, prin. Fax 734-8047

Bellwood, Blair, Pop. 1,814
Bellwood-Antis SD 1,300/K-12
300 Martin St 16617 814-742-2271
Dr. Thomas McInroy, supt. Fax 742-9049
moss.blwd.k12.pa.us
Bellwood-Antis MS 400/5-8
400 Martin St 16617 814-742-2273
Dr. Donald Wagner, prin. Fax 742-9817
Myers ES 500/K-4
220 Martin St 16617 814-742-2272
Terri Harpster, prin. Fax 742-9040

Bendersville, Adams, Pop. 631
Upper Adams SD
Supt. — See Biglerville
Bendersville IS 200/4-6
PO Box 447 17306 717-677-3300
Ann Wolfe, prin. Fax 677-9385

Bensalem, Bucks, Pop. 59,700
Bensalem Township SD 6,300/K-12
3000 Donallen Dr 19020 215-750-2800
Dr. Samuel Lee, supt. Fax 359-0181
www.bensalemsd.org/
Belmont Hills ES 500/K-6
5000 Neshaminy Blvd 19020 215-750-2800
Marla Zeisler, prin. Fax 750-2887
Cornwells ES 500/K-6
2215 Hulmeville Rd 19020 215-750-2800
Dr. Shawn Mark, prin. Fax 245-3559
Faust ES 600/K-6
2901 Bellview Dr 19020 215-750-2800
Jodie Sauers, prin. Fax 244-2973
Rush ES 400/K-6
3400 Hulmeville Rd 19020 215-750-2800
Joan D. Richey, prin. Fax 244-2976
Shafer MS 600/7-8
3333 Hulmeville Rd 19020 215-750-2800
Michael Stock, prin. Fax 244-2964
Snyder MS 400/7-8
3330 Hulmeville Rd 19020 215-750-2800
Dr. Thomas Evert, prin. Fax 244-2851
Struble ES 500/K-6
4300 Bensalem Blvd 19020 215-750-2800
Lana Judy, prin. Fax 244-2803

Valley ES 700/K-6
3100 Donallen Dr 19020 215-750-2800
Joan Toller, prin. Fax 750-2880

St. Charles Borromeo S 400/PK-8
1704 Bristol Pike 19020 215-639-3456
Sr. Kathleen Coffer, prin. Fax 639-0496
St. Ephrem S 500/K-8
5340 Hulmeville Rd 19020 215-639-9488
Sr. Shaun Thomas, prin. Fax 639-0206

Bentleyville, Washington, Pop. 2,539
Bentworth SD 1,200/K-12
150 Bearcat Dr 15314 724-239-2861
Scott Martin, supt. Fax 239-2865
bentworth.org
Bentworth ES 400/K-4
100 Bearcat Dr 15314 724-239-3606
Susanne Macik, prin. Fax 239-3205
Bentworth MS 400/5-8
563 Lincoln Ave 15314 724-239-4431
David Schreiber, prin. Fax 239-5889

Benton, Columbia, Pop. 821
Benton Area SD 700/K-12
600 Green Acres Rd 17814 570-925-6651
James M. Geffken, supt. Fax 925-6973
www.bentonsd.k12.pa.us/
Appleman ES 400/K-6
525 Park St 17814 570-925-6971
Robert Cashman, prin. Fax 925-5405

Berlin, Somerset, Pop. 2,084
Berlin Brothersvalley SD 800/K-12
1025 Main St 15530 814-267-4621
Dr. David Reeder, supt. Fax 267-6060
www.bbsd.com/
Berlin Brothersvalley ES 200/K-4
1025 Main St 15530 814-267-4623
Martin Mudry, prin. Fax 267-6060
Berlin Brothersvalley MS 300/5-8
1025 Main St 15530 814-267-6931
Martin Mudry, prin. Fax 267-6060

Bernville, Berks, Pop. 942
Tulpehocken Area SD
Supt. — See Bethel
Penn Bernville ES 400/K-6
24 Shartlesville Rd 19506 610-488-6248
Amanda Cipolla, prin. Fax 488-1188

Berwick, Columbia, Pop. 10,321
Berwick Area SD 2,900/K-12
500 Line St 18603 570-759-6400
Wayne Brookhart, supt. Fax 759-6439
www.berwicksd.org
Berwick Area MS 700/6-8
1100 Evergreen Dr 18603 570-759-6400
Greg Michael, prin. Fax 759-7978
Salem ES 500/K-5
810 E 10th St 18603 570-759-6400
Ralph Norce, prin. Fax 759-2784
West Berwick ES K-5
809 Sycamore St 18603 570-759-6400
Randy Peters, prin. Fax 759-2461
Other Schools – See Nescopeck

Holy Family Consolidated S 100/PK-5
728 Washington St 18603 570-752-2021
David Brown, prin. Fax 752-2914

Berwyn, Chester, Pop. 3,583
Tredyffrin-Easttown SD
Supt. — See Wayne
Hillside ES 500/K-4
507 Howellville Rd 19312 610-240-1500
Diane Cohle, prin. Fax 240-1510
Tredyffrin-Easttown MS 1,100/5-8
801 Conestoga Rd 19312 610-240-1200
Andrew Phillips, prin. Fax 240-1225

Bessemer, Lawrence, Pop. 1,097
Mohawk Area SD 1,500/K-12
PO Box 25 16112 724-667-7723
Michael Leitera, supt. Fax 667-0602
www.mohawk.k12.pa.us
Mohawk ES 800/K-6
PO Box 799 16112 724-667-7782
Bradlee Meehan, prin. Fax 667-7235

Bethel, Berks, Pop. 495
Tulpehocken Area SD 1,400/K-12
27 Rehrersburg Rd 19507 717-933-4611
Dr. Robert Schultz, supt. Fax 933-9724
www.tulpehocken.org
Bethel ES 400/K-6
8390 Lancaster Ave 19507 717-933-4131
Mark Brown, prin. Fax 933-8485
Other Schools – See Bernville

Bethel Dunkard Brethren Church S 1,300/K-12
5450 Four Point Rd 19507 717-933-5510

Bethel Park, Allegheny, Pop. 32,035
Bethel Park SD 4,500/K-12
301 Church Rd 15102 412-854-8402
Dr. Joseph W. Pasquerilla, supt. Fax 854-8430
www.bpsd.org
Armstrong MS 700/5-6
5800 Murray Ave 15102 412-854-8751
Ken Patterson, prin. Fax 833-5029
Bethel Memorial ES 300/K-4
3301 S Park Rd 15102 412-854-8506
Eric Chalus, prin. Fax 833-5014
Franklin ES 300/K-4
5400 Florida Ave 15102 412-854-8741
Teresa Doumont, prin. Fax 833-5016
Independence MS 700/7-8
2807 Bethel Church Rd 15102 412-854-8677
David Muench, prin. Fax 854-8732

Penn ES 200/K-4
110 Woodlet Ln 15102 412-854-8522
Brian Lenosky, prin. Fax 854-8411
Washington ES 300/K-4
515 Clifton Rd 15102 412-854-8546
Fred Pearson, prin. Fax 854-8435
Other Schools – See Pittsburgh

Hillcrest Christian Academy 200/PK-12
2500 Bethel Church Rd 15102 412-854-4040
Alan Ciechanowski, prin. Fax 854-4051
St. Valentine ECC 100/PK-PK
2709 Mesta St 15102 412-835-5539
Judy Mills, dir. Fax 835-4417

Bethlehem, Northampton, Pop. 73,573
Bethlehem Area SD 13,800/K-12
1516 Sycamore St 18017 610-861-0500
Dr. Joseph J. Roy, supt. Fax 807-5599
www.beth.k12.pa.us
Broughal MS 500/6-8
114 W Morton St 18015 610-866-5041
Ricky Amato, prin. Fax 807-5909
Buchanan ES 300/K-5
1621 Catasauqua Rd 18017 610-865-1766
Jill Moran, prin. Fax 807-5503
Calypso ES 200/K-5
1021 Calypso Ave 18018 610-691-0152
Kathleen Bast, prin. Fax 807-5565
Clearview ES 400/K-5
2121 Abington Rd 18018 610-868-5994
Heather Bennett-Knerr, prin. Fax 807-5525
Donegan ES 400/K-5
1210 E 4th St 18015 610-866-0031
Sonia Vazquez, prin. Fax 807-5524
East Hills MS 1,100/6-8
2005 Chester Rd 18017 610-867-0541
David Horvath, prin. Fax 807-5941
Fountain Hill ES 600/K-5
1330 Church St 18015 610-865-5881
Lisa Lynch, prin. Fax 807-5989
Hanover ES 200/K-5
3890 Jacksonville Rd 18017 610-691-3210
Timothy Lynch, prin. Fax 807-5560
Jefferson ES 200/K-5
404 E North St 18018 610-691-1776
Tracey Hirner, prin. Fax 807-5981
Lincoln ES 400/K-5
1260 Gresham St 18017 610-866-8727
Benita Draper, prin. Fax 807-5545
Marvine ES 300/K-5
1425 Livingston St 18017 610-865-0012
Karen Gomez, prin. Fax 849-6558
Miller Heights ES 400/K-5
3605 Allen St 18020 610-868-6441
Deborah Roeder, prin. Fax 807-5549
Nitschmann MS 800/6-8
1002 W Union Blvd 18018 610-866-5781
Peter Mayes, prin. Fax 866-1435
Northeast MS 800/6-8
1170 Fernwood St 18018 610-868-8581
Joseph Rahs, prin. Fax 807-5997
Packer ES 300/K-5
1650 Kenwood Dr 18017 610-865-0660
Jonathan Horvath, prin. Fax 807-5540
Penn ES 200/K-5
1002 Main St 18018 610-694-0116
Eric Fontanez, prin. Fax 807-5532
Spring Garden ES 500/K-5
901 North Blvd 18017 610-868-6071
Eric Smith, prin. Fax 807-5931
Wolf ES 400/K-5
1920 Butztown Rd 18017 610-867-8191
Theodoro Quinones, prin. Fax 867-6768
Other Schools – See Easton, Freemansburg

Southern Lehigh SD
Supt. — See Center Valley
Southern Lehigh IS 700/4-6
5438 Route 378 18015 610-861-4040
Mary Farris, prin. Fax 861-2881

Bethlehem Christian S Ebenezer Campus 50/K-4
3100 Hecktown Rd 18020 610-868-6020
Carol Aversa, head sch Fax 868-6939
Covenant Christian Academy 50/K-8
395 Bridle Path Rd 18017 610-868-7302
Philip Miller, prin. Fax 419-8008
Holy Infancy S 100/PK-8
127 E 4th St 18015 610-868-2621
Marjorie Manasse, prin. Fax 868-5402
Moravian Academy - Lower S 300/PK-5
422 Heckewelder Pl 18018 610-868-8571
Jeffrey Zemsky, hdmstr. Fax 868-9319
Moravian Academy MS 200/6-8
11 W Market St 18018 610-866-6677
Jeffrey Zemsky, hdmstr. Fax 866-6337
Notre Dame of Bethlehem S 400/PK-8
1835 Catasauqua Rd 18018 610-866-2231
Kathy Maziarz, prin. Fax 866-4374
Our Lady of Perpetual Help S 300/K-8
3221 Santee Rd 18020 610-868-6570
Daniel Moser, prin. Fax 868-7941
St. Anne S 400/PK-8
375 Hickory St 18017 610-868-4182
Karen Bentz, prin. Fax 868-8709
St. Michael the Archangel S 400/K-8
4121 Old Bethlehem Pike 18015 610-867-8422
Joanne LoFaso, prin. Fax 865-2098

Biglerville, Adams, Pop. 1,195
Upper Adams SD 1,600/K-12
161 N Main St 17307 717-677-7191
Dr. Wesley Doll, supt. Fax 677-9807
upperadams.org
Biglerville PS 500/K-3
3270 Biglerville Rd 17307 717-677-5200
James Kerstetter, prin. Fax 677-0101

Upper Adams MS 300/7-8
161 N Main St 17307 717-677-7191
Shane Brewer, prin. Fax 677-0219
Other Schools – See Arendtsville, Bendersville

Birdsboro, Berks, Pop. 5,083
Daniel Boone Area SD
Supt. — See Douglassville
Birdsboro Elementary Center 200/5-5
400 W 2nd St 19508 610-582-6190
Melanie Hefter, prin. Fax 582-6169
Monocacy ES 200/K-2
576 Monocacy Creek Rd 19508 610-385-6800
Melanie Hefter, prin. Fax 385-6810

Twin Valley SD
Supt. — See Elverson
Robeson ES 400/K-4
801 White Bear Rd 19508 610-582-9580
Dr. Christopher Stango, prin. Fax 582-9588

Berks Christian S 100/PK-12
926 Philadelphia Ter 19508 610-582-1000
Philip Warner, admin. Fax 404-0126
High Point Baptist Academy 200/K-12
200 Chapel Rd 19508 610-286-5942
Melissa Kauffman, admin. Fax 286-7525

Blain, Perry, Pop. 261
West Perry SD
Supt. — See Elliottsburg
Blain ES 300/PK-5
132 Blain Rd 17006 717-536-3219
Christopher Young, prin. Fax 536-3718

Blairsville, Indiana, Pop. 3,366
Blairsville-Saltsburg SD 1,700/PK-12
102 School Ln 15717 724-459-5500
Tammy Whitfield Ed.D., supt. Fax 459-9209
www.b-ssd.org
Blairsville ES 500/PK-5
106 School Ln 15717 724-459-8883
Fax 459-7985
Blairsville MS 200/6-8
104 School Ln 15717 724-459-8880
Allan Berkhimer, prin. Fax 459-0213
Other Schools – See Saltsburg

Blanchard, Centre, Pop. 735
Keystone Central SD
Supt. — See Mill Hall
Liberty Curtin ES 300/PK-5
PO Box 329 16826 570-962-2008
Michael Hall, prin. Fax 962-3124

Blandon, Berks, Pop. 7,039
Fleetwood Area SD
Supt. — See Fleetwood
Maier ES 300/K-4
355 Andrew Maier Blvd 19510 610-926-2502
Christopher Redding, prin. Fax 926-0923

Bloomsburg, Columbia, Pop. 14,675
Bloomsburg Area SD 1,600/K-12
728 E 5th St 17815 570-784-5000
Dr. Donald Wheeler, supt. Fax 387-8832
bloomsburgasd.schoolwires.com
Beaver-Main ES 100/K-5
245 Beaver Valley Rd 17815 570-784-0309
Joshua Tabor, prin. Fax 784-4308
Bloomsburg Area MS 400/6-8
1100 Railroad St 17815 570-784-9100
Marc Freeman, prin. Fax 387-3491
Evans Memorial ES 200/K-5
59 Perry Ave 17815 570-784-3167
Joshua Tabor, prin. Fax 784-4314
Memorial ES 500/K-5
500 Market St 17815 570-784-7885
Trevor Palmatier, prin. Fax 784-4341

Central Columbia SD 1,800/K-12
4777 Old Berwick Rd 17815 570-784-2850
Harry Mathias, supt. Fax 387-0192
www.ccsd.cc
Central Columbia ES 700/K-4
4777 Old Berwick Rd 17815 570-784-2850
Thomas Sharrow, prin. Fax 784-2582
Central Columbia MS 600/5-8
4777 Old Berwick Rd 17815 570-784-2850
Chad Heintzelman, prin. Fax 784-4935

Columbia County Christian S 200/K-12
123 Schoolhouse Rd 17815 570-784-2977
Daniel Thompson, head sch Fax 784-1755
St. Columba S 100/PK-8
40 E 3rd St 17815 570-784-5932
Dr. Robert Marande, admin. Fax 387-1257

Blossburg, Tioga, Pop. 1,532
Southern Tioga SD 1,600/K-12
241 Main St 16912 570-638-2183
Sam Rotella, supt. Fax 638-3512
www.southerntioga.org
Blossburg ES 300/K-6
133 Hannibal St 16912 570-638-2146
William Swingle, prin. Fax 638-2150
Other Schools – See Liberty, Mansfield

Blue Bell, Montgomery, Pop. 6,001
Wissahickon SD
Supt. — See Ambler
Blue Bell ES 400/K-5
801 Symphony Ln 19422 215-619-8102
Dr. Concetta Lupo, prin. Fax 619-8103
Stony Creek ES 400/K-5
1721 Yost Rd 19422 215-619-8108
Dr. Kevin McAneny, prin. Fax 619-8109

St. Helena S 500/K-8
1499 DeKalb Pike 19422 610-279-3345
Sr. Cathe Shoulberg, prin. Fax 279-3272

Bobtown, Greene, Pop. 741
Southeastern Greene SD
Supt. — See Greensboro
Bobtown ES 300/K-6
304 Grant St 15315 724-839-7241
Rick Menear, prin. Fax 839-7575

Boiling Springs, Cumberland, Pop. 3,185
Cumberland Valley SD
Supt. — See Mechanicsburg
Monroe ES 400/K-5
1240 Boiling Springs Rd 17007 717-258-6208
Megan Ward, prin. Fax 258-8819

South Middleton SD 2,100/K-12
4 Forge Rd 17007 717-258-6484
Bruce Deveney, supt. Fax 258-1214
www.smsd.us
Iron Forge ES 300/4-5
4 Academy St 17007 717-258-6484
Trisha Reed, prin. Fax 243-3009
Yellow Breeches MS 500/6-8
30 Academy St 17007 717-258-6484
Dr. Jesse White, prin. Fax 258-0301
Other Schools – See Mount Holly Springs

Boothwyn, Delaware, Pop. 4,830
Chichester SD
Supt. — See Aston
Boothwyn ES 300/K-4
2128 Blueball Ave 19061 610-485-4241
Joy Horstmyer, prin. Fax 494-1786
Chichester MS 1,000/5-8
925 Meetinghouse Rd 19061 610-485-6881
Stacie Hardy, prin. Fax 494-3064

Boswell, Somerset, Pop. 1,262
North Star SD 1,200/PK-12
1200 Morris Ave 15531 814-629-5631
Louis M. Lepley, supt. Fax 629-6181
www.nscougars.com
North Star Central ES 400/PK-4
1215 Morris Ave 15531 814-629-5627
Renee Lepley, prin. Fax 629-5295
Other Schools – See Stoystown

Boyertown, Berks, Pop. 4,017
Boyertown Area SD 7,100/K-12
911 Montgomery Ave 19512 610-367-6031
David Krem, supt. Fax 369-7620
www.boyertownasd.org
Boyertown ES 600/K-6
641 E 2nd St 19512 610-369-7462
Craig Kehl, prin. Fax 369-7687
Colebrookdale ES 300/K-6
1001 Montgomery Ave 19512 610-369-7427
Michael Stoudt, prin. Fax 369-7688
Earl ES 300/K-6
22 School House Rd 19512 610-369-7504
Stephan Pron, prin. Fax 369-7689
Pine Forge ES 300/K-6
8 Glendale Rd 19512 610-323-7609
Stephan Pron, prin. Fax 323-8651
Other Schools – See Barto, Frederick, Gilbertsville

Wagner SDA S 50/1-8
724 Douglass Dr 19512 610-323-0340
Shemika Campbell, prin. Fax 323-6750

Brackenridge, Allegheny, Pop. 3,200
Highlands SD
Supt. — See Natrona Heights
Fairmount PS 300/K-2
1060 Atlantic Ave 15014 724-224-5880
Ian Miller, prin. Fax 224-2413

Bradford, McKean, Pop. 8,658
Bradford Area SD 2,600/PK-12
PO Box 375 16701 814-362-3841
Katharine Pude, supt. Fax 362-2552
www.bradfordareaschools.org
Blaisdell ES 700/PK-2
265 Constitution Ave 16701 814-362-6834
Erin Waugaman, prin. Fax 362-5485
Fretz MS 600/6-8
140 Lorana Ave 16701 814-362-3508
Tina Slaven, prin. Fax 362-1812
School Street ES 500/3-5
76 School St 16701 814-368-3183
Sarah Tingley, prin. Fax 362-1741

Learning Center 100/PK-6
90 Jackson Ave 16701 814-368-6622
St. Bernard S 200/PK-8
450 W Washington St 16701 814-368-5302
Linda Cecchetti, prin. Fax 368-1404

Bradfordwoods, Allegheny, Pop. 1,160
North Allegheny SD
Supt. — See Pittsburgh
Bradford Woods ES 400/K-5
41 Forest Rd 15015 724-935-5081
Jaime Vernocy, prin. Fax 935-6076

Breezewood, Bedford
Everett Area SD
Supt. — See Everett
Breezewood ES 100/K-5
133 N Main St 15533 814-652-9114
Justin Hillegas, prin. Fax 735-2495

Breinigsville, Lehigh, Pop. 4,082
Parkland SD
Supt. — See Allentown
Fogelsville ES 500/K-5
312 S Route 100 18031 610-351-5800
Timothy A. Chorones, prin. Fax 351-5809
Jaindl ES 600/K-5
1051 Weilers Rd 18031 610-351-5880
Diana Schantz, prin. Fax 351-5889

Brentwood, Allegheny, Pop. 9,512
Brentwood Borough SD
Supt. — See Pittsburgh
Elroy Avenue ES 300/K-5
3129 Elroy Ave 15227 412-881-4484
Barbara Pagan, prin. Fax 881-9448

Bridgeport, Montgomery, Pop. 4,427
Upper Merion Area SD
Supt. — See King of Prussia
Bridgeport ES 400/K-4
900 Bush St 19405 610-205-3601
Dr. Carole Hoy, prin. Fax 205-3649

Bridgeville, Allegheny, Pop. 5,046
Chartiers Valley SD
Supt. — See Pittsburgh
Chartiers Valley MS 700/6-8
50 Thoms Run Rd 15017 412-429-2223
Adrienne Floro, prin. Fax 429-2226
Chartiers Valley PS 800/K-2
125 Thoms Run Rd 15017 412-429-3270
Anissa Rosenwald, prin. Fax 429-7030

Bristol, Bucks, Pop. 9,494
Bristol Borough SD 900/PK-12
1776 Farragut Ave 19007 215-781-1000
Dr. Thomas Shaffer, supt. Fax 781-1012
www.bbsd.org
Snyder-Girotti S, 450 Beaver St 19007 600/PK-8
Dr. Thomas Shaffer, prin. 215-781-1000

Bristol Township SD
Supt. — See Levittown
Roosevelt MS 500/6-8
1001 New Rodgers Rd 19007 267-599-2300
Kevin Boles, prin. Fax 599-2349

St. Mark S 200/K-8
1024 Radcliffe St 19007 215-785-0973
Maria Sanson, prin. Fax 781-0268

Brockway, Jefferson, Pop. 2,057
Brockway Area SD 1,000/K-12
40 North St 15824 814-265-8411
Daniel Hawkins, supt. Fax 265-8498
www.brockway.k12.pa.us/
Brockway Area ES 600/K-6
40 North St 15824 814-265-8417
Candace Patricelli, prin. Fax 265-8498

Brodheadsville, Monroe, Pop. 1,776
Pleasant Valley SD 4,900/K-12
2233 Route 115 Ste 100 18322 570-402-1000
David Piperato, supt. Fax 992-7275
www.pvbears.org
Pleasant Valley MS 900/7-8
2233 Route 115 18322 570-402-1000
Rocco Seiler, prin. Fax 992-6968
Other Schools – See Kunkletown

Brogue, York
Red Lion Area SD
Supt. — See Red Lion
Clearview ES 400/K-6
2650 Delta Rd 17309 717-927-6791
Sheila Hughes, prin. Fax 927-6545

Brookhaven, Delaware, Pop. 7,890
Chester-Upland SD
Supt. — See Chester
Toby Farms IS 500/4-8
201 Bridgewater Rd 19015 610-447-3815
Rene Garner, prin. Fax 499-3814

Penn-Delco SD
Supt. — See Aston
Coebourn ES 300/K-5
1 Coebourn Blvd 19015 610-497-6300
Teresa Ford, prin. Fax 876-4938

Christian Academy 400/K-12
4301 Chandler Dr 19015 610-872-5100
Dr. Timothy Sierer, hdmstr. Fax 876-2173

Brookville, Jefferson, Pop. 3,884
Brookville Area SD 1,600/K-12
PO Box 479 15825 814-849-1100
Dr. Robin Fillman, supt. Fax 849-6842
www.basd.us
Hickory Grove ES 500/3-6
PO Box 479 15825 814-849-1112
Brigette Matson, prin. Fax 849-1115
Northside ES 100/K-K
PO Box 479 15825 814-849-1118
Brigette Matson, prin. Fax 849-1130
Pinecreek ES 200/1-2
PO Box 479 15825 814-849-1119
Brigette Matson, prin. Fax 849-1131

Broomall, Delaware, Pop. 10,688
Marple Newtown SD
Supt. — See Newtown Square
Loomis ES 300/K-5
369 N Central Blvd 19008 610-359-4350
Thomas Grotchen, prin. Fax 359-4373
Paxon Hollow MS 800/6-8
815 Paxon Hollow Rd 19008 610-359-4320
Tina Kane Ed.D., prin. Fax 353-4061
Russell ES 400/K-5
2201 Sproul Rd 19008 610-359-4310
Dennis Reardon, prin. Fax 359-4371
Worrall ES 300/K-5
2979 Pennview Ave 19008 610-359-4300
John Beltrante, prin. Fax 359-1680

Grayson S, 35 N Malin Rd 19008 PK-8
Melissa Bilash, dir. 484-428-3241
St. Pius X S 500/PK-8
204 Lawrence Rd 19008 610-356-7222
Sr. Kathleen Touey, prin. Fax 356-5380

Brownstown, Lancaster, Pop. 741
Conestoga Valley SD
Supt. — See Lancaster
Brownstown ES 500/K-6
PO Box 250 17508 717-656-6021
Dr. Andrew Graybill, prin. Fax 656-9172

Brownsville, Fayette, Pop. 2,220
Brownsville Area SD 900/K-12
5 Falcon Dr 15417 724-785-2021
Dr. Keith Hartbauer, supt. Fax 785-6988
www.basd.org
Brownsville Area ES K-5
7 Falcon Dr 15417 724-785-9600
Frank Berdar, prin. Fax 785-5614
Brownsville Area MS 400/6-8
3 Falcon Dr 15417 724-785-2155
Shawn Clemmer, prin. Fax 785-2502

Bryn Athyn, Montgomery, Pop. 1,347

Bryn Athyn Church S 300/K-8
PO Box 277 19009 215-947-4086

Bryn Mawr, Montgomery, Pop. 3,647
Haverford Township SD
Supt. — See Havertown
Coopertown ES 400/K-5
800 Coopertown Rd 19010 610-853-5900
Elizabeth Mastrocola, prin. Fax 853-5976

Radnor Township SD
Supt. — See Wayne
Ithan ES 400/K-5
695 Clyde Rd 19010 610-527-1357
Tronya Boylan, prin. Fax 527-0459

Baldwin S 600/PK-12
701 Montgomery Ave 19010 610-525-2700
Marisa Porges Ph.D., head sch Fax 525-7534
Country Day S of the Sacred Heart 300/PK-12
480 S Bryn Mawr Ave 19010 610-527-3915
Deirdre Cryor, head sch Fax 527-0942
St. Aloysius Academy 200/K-8
401 S Bryn Mawr Ave 19010 610-525-1670
Sr. Stephen Anne Roderiguez, prin. Fax 525-5140
St. Thomas of Villanova PK-PK
1236 Montrose Ave 19010 610-525-7554
Mary Kurek, dir. Fax 525-6041
Shipley S 800/PK-12
814 Yarrow St 19010 610-525-4300
Dr. Steven Piltch, hdmstr. Fax 525-5082
SS. Colman & Neumann S 200/K-8
372 Highland Ln 19010 610-525-3266
Cathleen Lamberto, prin. Fax 525-6103

Buckingham, Bucks
Central Bucks SD
Supt. — See Doylestown
Buckingham ES 500/K-6
PO Box 158 18912 267-893-4200
Karl Funseth, prin. Fax 893-5802

Burgettstown, Washington, Pop. 1,365
Burgettstown Area SD 1,200/K-12
100 Bavington Rd 15021 724-947-8136
Dr. James Walsh, supt. Fax 947-8143
www.burgettstown.k12.pa.us
Burgettstown Area ES 500/K-5
100 Bavington Rd 15021 724-947-8150
Melissa Mankey, prin. Fax 947-8143

Tri State Christian Academy 100/PK-12
750 Steubenville Pike 15021 724-947-8722
John Massey, prin. Fax 947-0821

Butler, Butler, Pop. 13,451
Butler Area SD 5,500/K-12
110 Campus Ln 16001 724-287-8721
Dr. Brian White, supt. Fax 287-1802
www.basdk12.org
Brittain ES 400/K-6
338 N Washington St 16001 724-287-8721
Chad Broman, prin. Fax 282-1013
Butler Area MS 1,200/5-6
225 E North St 16001 724-214-3600
Jason Huffman, prin. Fax 287-7847
Center Avenue ES 200/K-6
102 Lincoln Ave 16001 724-287-8721
Keenan McGaughey, prin. Fax 287-0263
Center Township ES 600/K-6
950 Mercer Rd 16001 724-287-8721
Jeff Mathieson, prin. Fax 282-3503
McQuistion ES 400/K-6
210 Mechling Dr 16001 724-287-0721
Linda Peifer, prin. Fax 287-1119
Northwest ES 400/K-6
124 Staley Ave 16001 724-287-8721
Jack Ratica, prin. Fax 287-2516
Summit Township ES 200/K-6
351 Brinker Rd 16002 724-287-8721
William Chwalik, prin. Fax 287-2734
Other Schools – See Renfrew

Butler Catholic S 200/PK-8
515 E Locust St 16001 724-285-4276
Sr. John Ann Mulhern, prin. Fax 285-4896
First Baptist Christian S 100/PK-12
221 New Castle St 16001 724-287-1188
His Kids Christian S 50/PK-6
650 Saxonburg Rd 16002 724-352-8177
Debora Dawson, prin. Fax 352-8179
Holy Sepulcher S 200/PK-8
6515 Old Route 8 N 16002 724-586-5022
Sr. Anna Gaglia, prin. Fax 586-5073
Penn Christian Academy 300/PK-6
199 Airport Rd 16002 724-586-5200
Craig Carnahan, admin. Fax 586-2891

St. Mary of the Assmption Preschool 50/PK-PK
821 Herman Rd 16002 724-285-3285
Linda Green, dir. Fax 285-4715
St. Wendelin S 100/PK-8
211 Saint Wendelin Rd 16002 724-285-4986
JoLynn Clouse, prin. Fax 287-6253

Cabot, Butler

St. Joseph Preschool 50/PK-PK
315 Stoney Hollow Rd 16023 724-352-0333
Marcie Parks, lead tchr. Fax 352-7174
St. Luke Lutheran S 200/PK-8
330 Hannahstown Rd 16023 724-352-2221
Mark Wilt, prin. Fax 352-2355

Cairnbrook, Somerset, Pop. 520
Shade-Central CSD 500/K-12
203 McGregor Ave 15924 814-754-4648
John Krupper, supt. Fax 754-5848
www.shade.k12.pa.us
Cairnbrook ES 200/K-6
235 McGregor Ave 15924 814-754-5021
John Krupper, prin. Fax 754-5848

Cambridge Springs, Crawford, Pop. 2,577
PENNCREST SD
Supt. — See Saegertown
Cambridge Springs ES 500/K-6
130 Steele St 16403 814-398-4636
Jennifer Stevens, prin. Fax 398-4593

Camp Hill, Cumberland, Pop. 7,766
Camp Hill SD 1,300/K-12
2627 Chestnut St 17011 717-901-2401
Patricia Craig, supt. Fax 901-2421
www.camphillsd.k12.pa.us
Camp Hill MS 300/6-8
2401 Chestnut St 17011 717-901-2450
Leslee DeLong, prin. Fax 901-2573
Eisenhower ES 300/3-5
340 N 21st St 17011 717-901-2600
Dr. Sandra Fauser, prin. Fax 901-2461
Hoover ES 300/K-2
420 S 24th St 17011 717-901-2550
Eileen Czarnecki, prin. Fax 901-2594

East Pennsboro Area SD
Supt. — See Enola
West Creek Hills ES 500/K-4
400 Erford Rd 17011 717-732-0142
Melanie Shaver-Durham, prin. Fax 732-8943

West Shore SD
Supt. — See Lewisberry
Allen MS 500/6-8
4225 Gettysburg Rd 17011 717-901-9552
Brian Granger, prin. Fax 901-8201
Highland ES, 1325 Carlisle Rd 17011 500/K-5
Meghan Sheraw, prin. 717-901-9860
Lower Allen ES 200/K-2
4100 Gettysburg Rd 17011 717-761-8415
Amanda Lerew, prin.

Good Shepherd S 300/K-8
3400 Market St 17011 717-737-7261
Stephen Fry, admin. Fax 761-4673

Canonsburg, Washington, Pop. 8,707
Canon-McMillan SD 5,000/K-12
1 N Jefferson Ave 15317 724-746-2940
Michael Daniels, supt. Fax 746-9184
www.cmsd.k12.pa.us
Borland Manor ES 300/K-4
30 Giffin Dr 15317 724-745-2700
Marella McConnell, prin. Fax 873-5190
Canonsburg MS 800/7-8
25 E College St 15317 724-745-9030
Greg Taranto, prin. Fax 873-5230
Hills-Hendersonville ES 200/K-4
50 Mayview Rd 15317 724-745-8390
Shelley Brose, prin. Fax 873-5226
North Strabane IS 400/5-6
20 Giffin Dr 15317 724-873-5252
Mark Abbondanza, prin. Fax 873-5216
South Central ES 400/K-4
230 S Central Ave 15317 724-745-4475
Michelle Tomicek, prin. Fax 873-5228
Other Schools – See Eighty Four, Mc Donald, Muse

St. Patrick S 200/PK-8
200 Murdock St 15317 724-745-7977
Dr. Anthony Merante, prin. Fax 746-9778

Canton, Bradford, Pop. 1,948
Canton Area SD 1,000/K-12
509 E Main St 17724 570-673-3191
Eric Briggs, supt. Fax 673-3680
www.canton.k12.pa.us
Canton Area ES 600/K-6
545 E Main St 17724 570-673-5196
Michael Wells, prin. Fax 673-7929

Carbondale, Lackawanna, Pop. 8,778
Carbondale Area SD 1,600/PK-12
101 Brooklyn St 18407 570-282-2507
Robert Mehalick, supt. Fax 282-6988
www.carbondalearea.org
Carbondale ES 900/PK-6
103 Brooklyn St 18407 570-282-5656
William Vaverchak, prin. Fax 282-3203

Carlisle, Cumberland, Pop. 18,109
Carlisle Area SD 4,900/K-12
540 W North St 17013 717-240-6800
Christina M. Spielbauer, supt. Fax 240-6898
www.carlisleschools.org
Bellaire ES 400/K-5
540 W North St 17013 717-240-6800
Jeff Bell, prin. Fax 243-6074
Crestview ES 500/K-5
540 W North St 17013 717-240-6800
Carole Holly, prin. Fax 241-0302
Hamilton ES 300/K-5
540 W North St 17013 717-240-6800
Monique Pannebaker, prin. Fax 241-3263
Lamberton MS 600/6-8
540 W North St 17013 717-240-6800
Keith Colestock, prin. Fax 240-2066
Letort ES 300/K-5
540 W North St 17013 717-240-6800
Aaron Carmichael, prin. Fax 240-7002
Mooreland ES 300/K-5
540 W North St 17013 717-240-6800
Kim Truckenmiller, prin. Fax 241-0308
North Dickinson ES 200/K-5
540 W North St 17013 717-240-6800
Brian Gochenour, prin. Fax 241-3267
Wilson MS 600/6-8
540 W North St 17013 717-240-6800
Walt Bond, prin. Fax 240-2050
Other Schools – See Mount Holly Springs

Cumberland Valley SD
Supt. — See Mechanicsburg
Middlesex ES 400/K-5
250 N Middlesex Rd 17013 717-249-5586
Stephanie Eldridge, prin. Fax 249-0251

Carlisle Christian Academy 100/K-12
1412 Holly Pike, 717-249-3692
James Koser, admin. Fax 240-0644
Christian S of Grace Baptist 100/PK-8
777 W North St 17013 717-243-8820
Gene Drummond, hdmstr. Fax 249-0486
St. Patrick S 300/PK-8
87 Marsh Dr, 717-249-4826
Ricman Fly, prin. Fax 245-0522

Carmichaels, Greene, Pop. 473
Carmichaels Area SD 1,100/PK-12
225 N Vine St 15320 724-966-5045
John Menhart, supt. Fax 966-8793
www.carmarea.org
Carmichaels Area ES 500/PK-5
225 N Vine St 15320 724-966-5045
Fred Morecraft, prin. Fax 966-8789
Carmichaels Area MS 200/6-8
300 W Greene St 15320 724-966-5045
Ron Gallagher, prin. Fax 966-5556

Carnegie, Allegheny, Pop. 7,765
Carlynton SD 1,400/K-12
435 Kings Hwy 15106 412-429-8400
Dr. Gary D. Peiffer, supt. Fax 429-2502
www.carlynton.k12.pa.us
Carnegie ES 400/K-6
301 Franklin Ave 15106 412-429-2540
John McAdoo, prin. Fax 429-3253
Other Schools – See Crafton

Carrolltown, Cambria, Pop. 846
Cambria Heights SD
Supt. — See Patton
Cambria Heights ES 600/PK-5
PO Box 510 15722 814-344-8506
Hilary Yahner, prin. Fax 344-6274

St. Benedict S 100/PK-8
PO Box 596 15722 814-344-6512
Jeffrey Maucieri, prin. Fax 344-8530

Cashtown, Adams, Pop. 457
Gettysburg Area SD
Supt. — See Gettysburg
Franklin Township ES 400/K-5
PO Box 124 17310 717-334-6254
Dr. Shelly Lappi, prin. Fax 337-4432

Catasauqua, Lehigh, Pop. 6,277
Catasauqua Area SD 1,500/K-12
201 N 14th St 18032 610-264-5571
Robert Spengler, supt. Fax 264-5618
www.cattysd.org
Catasauqua MS 500/5-8
850 Pine St 18032 610-264-4341
Melissa Inselmann, prin. Fax 264-5458
Sheckler ES 600/K-4
251 N 14th St 18032 610-264-5601
Eric Dauberman, prin. Fax 403-1120

Catawissa, Columbia, Pop. 1,525
Southern Columbia Area SD 1,400/K-12
800 Southern Dr 17820 570-356-2331
Paul Caputo, supt. Fax 356-2892
www.scasd.us
Hartman ES 600/K-4
802 Southern Dr 17820 570-356-3250
John Fetterman, prin. Fax 356-7169
Southern Columbia Area MS 500/5-8
810 Southern Dr 17820 570-356-3400
William Callahan, prin. Fax 356-2835

Center Valley, Lehigh
Southern Lehigh SD 2,900/K-12
5775 Main St 18034 610-282-3121
Kathleen Evison, supt. Fax 282-0193
www.slsd.org
Hopewell ES 300/K-3
4625 W Hopewell Rd 18034 610-791-0200
Lori Limpar, prin. Fax 791-2444
Southern Lehigh MS 500/7-8
3715 Preston Ln 18034 610-282-3700
Dr. Edward Donahue, prin. Fax 282-2963
Other Schools – See Bethlehem, Coopersburg

Centre Hall, Centre, Pop. 1,260
Penns Valley Area SD
Supt. — See Spring Mills
Centre Hall-Potter ES 200/K-4
211 N Hoffer Ave 16828 814-364-1481
Kurt Nyquist, prin. Fax 364-9631

Chadds Ford, Chester
Unionville-Chadds Ford SD
Supt. — See Kennett Square
Chadds Ford ES 400/K-5
3 Baltimore Pike 19317 610-388-1112
Shawn Dutkiewicz, prin. Fax 388-8481
Hillendale ES 300/K-5
1850 Hillendale Rd 19317 610-388-1439
Michael Audevard, prin. Fax 388-2266

St. Cornelius S 100/K-5
160 Ridge Rd 19317 610-459-8663
Barbara Rosini, prin. Fax 459-7728

Chalfont, Bucks, Pop. 3,976
Central Bucks SD
Supt. — See Doylestown
Butler ES 800/K-6
200 Brittany Dr 18914 267-893-4250
Joseph Brereton, prin. Fax 893-5803

Plumstead Christian S - Lower Campus 100/PK-5
753 New Galena Rd 18914 215-822-0187
Patrick Fitzpatrick, hdmstr. Fax 822-5890
St. Jude S 400/PK-8
323 W Butler Ave 18914 215-822-9225
Sr. Elizabeth Marley, prin. Fax 822-0722

Chambersburg, Franklin, Pop. 19,639
Chambersburg Area SD 8,800/K-12
435 Stanley Ave 17201 717-263-9281
Dr. Joseph Padasak, supt. Fax 261-3321
casdonline.org
Buchanan ES 300/K-5
730 E Washington St 17201 717-261-3430
Dr. Angela Pollock, prin. Fax 261-3492
Chambersburg Area MS North 1,000/6-8
1957 Scotland Ave 17201 717-261-3366
Kurt Widmann, prin. Fax 261-3379
Chambersburg Area MS South 1,000/6-8
1151 E McKinley St 17201 717-261-3385
Melissa Cashdollar, prin. Fax 261-3401
Chambers ES 500/K-5
481 N Franklin St 17201 717-261-3442
Shawn Kimple, prin. Fax 262-6394
Falling Spring ES 300/K-5
1006 Falling Spring Rd, 717-261-3439
Sarah Herbert, prin. Fax 261-3493
Grandview ES 300/K-5
5538 Cumberland Hwy, 717-261-3445
Paul Swope, prin. Fax 261-3497
Guilford Hills ES 300/K-5
2105 Lincoln Way E, 717-352-2124
Dr. Sarah Herbert, prin. Fax 352-2733
Hamilton Heights ES 600/K-5
1589 Johnson Rd, 717-261-3448
Brian Hostetler, prin. Fax 261-1205
Marion ES 100/K-5
145 Colorado St, 717-375-2360
Dr. Angela Pollock, prin. Fax 375-4533
New Franklin ES 100/K-5
3584 Wayne Rd, 717-261-3454
Richard Snyder, prin. Fax 261-1429
Scotland ES 400/K-5
3832 Scotland Main St, 717-261-3460
Tom VanArsdale, prin. Fax 709-4099
South Hamilton ES 300/K-5
1019 Warm Spring Rd, 717-261-3466
Richard Snyder, prin. Fax 261-3498
Stevens ES 300/K-5
800 Hollywell Ave 17201 717-261-3469
Thomas Knepper, prin. Fax 261-3473
Other Schools – See Fayetteville, Lurgan

Corpus Christi S 300/PK-8
305 N 2nd St 17201 717-263-5036
Mary Geesaman, prin. Fax 263-6079
Cumberland Valley Christian S 400/PK-12
600 Miller St 17201 717-264-3266
Timothy Murr, prin. Fax 264-0416
Montessori Academy of Chambersburg 100/PK-12
875 Ragged Edge Rd, 717-261-1110
Shalom Christian Academy 400/PK-12
126 Social Island Rd, 717-375-2223
Angie Petersheim, admin. Fax 375-2224

Champion, Westmoreland

Champion Christian S 50/PK-4
2166 Indian Head Rd 15622 724-455-2122
Dr. D. Merle Skinner, dir. Fax 455-6651

Charleroi, Washington, Pop. 4,003
Charleroi Area SD 1,600/K-12
125 Fecsen Dr 15022 724-483-3509
Edward Zelich, supt. Fax 483-3776
www.charleroisd.org
Charleroi Area ES 700/K-5
75 Fecsen Dr 15022 724-483-5554
Steve Shields, prin. Fax 483-9367
Charleroi Area MS 400/6-8
100 Fecsen Dr 15022 724-483-3600
Adam Brewer, prin. Fax 489-9128

Cheltenham, Montgomery, Pop. 34,800
Cheltenham SD
Supt. — See Elkins Park
Cheltenham ES 400/K-4
7853 Front St 19012 215-635-7415
Nicolas Perez, prin. Fax 635-7548

Presentation BVM S 200/K-8
107 Old Soldiers Rd 19012 215-379-3798
Marianne Garnham, prin. Fax 379-4430

Chester, Delaware, Pop. 33,256
Chester-Upland SD 2,900/PK-12
232 W 9th St 19013 610-447-3600
Dr. Juan Baughn, supt. Fax 447-3616
www.chesteruplandsd.org
Chester Upland S of the Arts 300/PK-5
501 W 9th St 19013 610-447-3777
Sara Ferguson, prin. Fax 490-6139
Stetser ES 200/PK-5
808 E 17th St 19013 610-447-3795
Janet Baldwin, prin. Fax 447-3416
Other Schools – See Brookhaven, Upland

Douglass Christian S 100/PK-5
700 Central Ave 19013 610-499-9030
Janice Bowdre, prin. Fax 872-8479
Drexel Neumann Academy 200/PK-8
1901 Potter St 19013 610-872-7358
Sr. Cathy McGowan, prin. Fax 872-7833

Chester Springs, Chester
Downingtown Area SD
Supt. — See Downingtown
Pickering Valley ES 700/K-5
121 Byers Rd 19425 610-458-5324
Joseph Fernandes, prin. Fax 458-8356

Owen J. Roberts SD
Supt. — See Pottstown
West Vincent ES 600/K-6
2750 Conestoga Rd 19425 610-469-5108
Edward Smith, prin. Fax 469-1406

Montgomery S 300/PK-8
1141 Kimberton Rd 19425 610-827-7222
Sally Keidel, head sch Fax 827-7639

Cheswick, Allegheny, Pop. 1,738
Allegheny Valley SD 1,000/K-12
300 Pearl Ave 15024 724-274-5300
Patrick M. Graczyk, supt. Fax 274-8040
www.avsdweb.org
Acmetonia PS 300/K-3
300 Pearl Ave 15024 724-274-6500
Gregory Heavner, prin. Fax 274-2816
Other Schools – See Springdale

Deer Lakes SD 2,000/K-12
19 E Union Rd 15024 724-265-5300
Dr. Janell Logue-Belden, supt. Fax 265-5025
www.deerlakes.net
Deer Lakes MS 400/6-8
17 E Union Rd 15024 724-265-5310
David Campos, prin. Fax 265-3711
East Union Intermediate Center 500/3-5
57 E Union Rd 15024 724-265-5330
James Schweinberg, prin. Fax 265-1699
Other Schools – See Tarentum

Cheswick Christian Academy 200/K-12
1407 Pittsburgh St 15024 724-274-4846
Todd Rosio, prin. Fax 274-8300

Chicora, Butler, Pop. 1,038
Karns City Area SD
Supt. — See Karns City
Chicora ES 500/K-6
PO Box 241 16025 724-445-3680
Shane Spack, prin. Fax 445-2776

Chinchilla, Lackawanna, Pop. 2,076
Abington Heights SD
Supt. — See Clarks Summit
South Abington ES 300/K-4
640 Northern Blvd 18410 570-585-2100
Dr. Amy Williams, prin. Fax 585-2112

Christiana, Lancaster, Pop. 1,142
Solanco SD
Supt. — See Quarryville
Bart-Colerain ES 200/K-5
1336 Noble Rd 17509 717-529-2181
Sandra Haines, prin. Fax 529-6879

Churchville, Bucks, Pop. 4,092
Council Rock SD
Supt. — See Newtown
Churchville ES 600/K-6
100 New Rd 18966 215-944-1700
Jill Kingston, prin. Fax 944-1797
Welch ES 600/K-6
750 New Rd 18966 215-944-1800
Rebecca Grimm, prin. Fax 944-1896

Clairton, Allegheny, Pop. 6,590
Clairton CSD 800/K-12
502 Mitchell Ave 15025 412-233-7090
Dr. Ginny Hunt, supt. Fax 233-4755
www.ccsdbears.org
Clairton ES 400/K-5
501 Waddell Ave 15025 412-233-9200
Debra Maurizio, prin. Fax 233-4982

Clarion, Clarion, Pop. 5,178
Clarion Area SD 800/K-12
221 Liberty St 16214 814-226-6110
Dr. Michael Stahlman, supt. Fax 226-9292
www.clarion-schools.com
Clarion Area ES 400/K-6
800 Boundary St 16214 814-226-8118
Roger Walter, prin. Fax 226-4889

Immaculate Conception S 100/PK-6
729 Main St 16214 814-226-8433
Lori Cratty, prin. Fax 226-4998

Clarks Green, Lackawanna, Pop. 1,470

Our Lady of Peace S 400/K-8
410 N Abington Rd 18411 570-587-4152
Colleen Jumper, prin. Fax 586-5393

Clarks Summit, Lackawanna, Pop. 5,073
Abington Heights SD 3,300/K-12
200 E Grove St 18411 570-586-2511
Michael Mahon, supt. Fax 586-1756
www.ahsd.org
Abington Heights MS 1,000/5-8
1555 Newton Ransom Blvd 18411 570-586-1281
Dr. Michael Elia, prin. Fax 586-6361
Clarks Summit ES 400/K-4
401 W Grove St 18411 570-585-7300
Marc Wyandt, prin. Fax 585-7307
Newton-Ransom ES 300/K-4
1549 Newton Ransom Blvd 18411 570-585-8300
Dr. Amy Williams, prin.
Other Schools – See Chinchilla, Waverly

Claysburg, Blair, Pop. 1,606
Claysburg-Kimmel SD 900/K-12
531 Bedford St 16625 814-239-5141
Fax 239-5896
www.cksdbulldogs.com
Claysburg-Kimmel ES 500/K-6
240 C K Elementary Dr 16625 814-239-5144
Matt Hall, prin. Fax 239-8994

Claysville, Washington, Pop. 815
McGuffey SD 1,800/K-12
90 McGuffey Dr 15323 724-948-3731
Dr. Erica Kolat, supt. Fax 948-3769
www.mcguffey.k12.pa.us
Claysville ES 600/K-5
PO Box 421 15323 724-663-7772
Sheryl Fleck, prin. Fax 663-4298
McGuffey MS 400/6-8
86 McGuffey Dr 15323 724-948-3323
Michael Wilson, prin. Fax 948-2413
Other Schools – See Washington

Clearfield, Clearfield, Pop. 6,141
Clearfield Area SD 1,400/K-12
PO Box 710 16830 814-765-5511
Terry Struble, supt. Fax 765-5515
www.clearfield.org
Clearfield Area ES 600/K-6
700 High Level Rd 16830 814-762-8011
Mary Sayers, prin. Fax 762-8037

Clearfield Alliance Christian S 200/K-12
56 Alliance Rd 16830 814-765-0216
St. Francis S 200/PK-8
230 S 2nd St 16830 814-765-2618
Sheila Clancy, prin. Fax 765-6704

Cleona, Lebanon, Pop. 2,048
Annville-Cleona SD
Supt. — See Annville
Cleona ES 300/K-2
50 E Walnut St 17042 717-867-7640
Angela Love, prin. Fax 867-7644

Clifton Heights, Delaware, Pop. 6,525
Upper Darby SD
Supt. — See Drexel Hill
Westbrook Park ES 500/K-5
199 Westbrook Dr 19018 610-626-9363
Marc Comfort, prin.

St. Mark's Christian S 100/PK-K
436 N Oak Ave 19018 610-626-6837
Kathleen Cosentino, prin.

Clymer, Indiana, Pop. 1,351
Penns Manor Area SD 800/PK-12
6003 Route 553 Hwy 15728 724-254-2666
Daren Johnston, supt. Fax 254-3418
www.pennsmanor.org
Penns Manor Area ES 400/PK-5
6003 Route 553 Hwy 15728 724-254-2666
Kristen Zeglen, prin. Fax 254-3415

Coal Center, Washington, Pop. 134
California Area SD 800/K-12
11 Trojan Way Ste 100 15423 724-785-5800
Michael S. Sears, supt. Fax 785-4866
www.calsd.org/
California Area ES 300/K-4
40 Trojan Way 15423 724-785-5800
Rachel Nagy, prin. Fax 785-5458
California Area MS 200/5-8
40 Trojan Way 15423 724-785-5800
Raymond Huffman, prin. Fax 785-5458

Coal Township, Northumberland, Pop. 9,922
Shamokin Area SD 1,600/PK-12
2000 W State St 17866 570-648-5752
James Zack, supt. Fax 648-2592
www.indians.k12.pa.us/
Shamokin Area ES 900/PK-6
3000 W State St 17866 570-648-5721
Anthony Carnuccio, prin.

Our Lady of Lourdes Regional S 300/PK-12
2001 Clinton Ave 17866 570-644-0375
Martin McCarthy, admin. Fax 644-7655

Coatesville, Chester, Pop. 12,560
Coatesville Area SD
Supt. — See Thorndale
Friendship ES 400/K-5
296 Reeceville Rd 19320 610-383-3770
Brad Bentman, prin. Fax 383-3774
Kings Highway ES 600/K-5
841 W Kings Hwy 19320 610-383-3775
Stevan LeFever, prin. Fax 383-3779

North Brandywine MS 500/6-8
256 Reeceville Rd 19320 610-383-3745
Dr. Christopher Jahnke, prin. Fax 383-3749
Rainbow ES 800/K-5
1113 W Lincoln Hwy 19320 610-383-3780
Clifford Maloney, prin. Fax 383-3784
Reeceville ES 500/K-5
248 Reeceville Rd 19320 610-383-3785
Stephanie Sturdivant, prin. Fax 383-3789
Scott MS 500/6-8
800 Olive St 19320 610-383-6946
Chamise Taylor, prin. Fax 383-7110
South Brandywine MS 700/6-8
600 Doe Run Rd 19320 610-383-3750
Jeffrey Colf, prin. Fax 383-3754

Cochranton, Crawford, Pop. 1,120
Crawford Central SD
Supt. — See Meadville
Cochranton ES 400/K-6
225 S Franklin St 16314 814-425-2105
Shawn Ford, prin. Fax 425-3761

Cogan Station, Lycoming
Williamsport Area SD
Supt. — See Williamsport
Hepburn-Lycoming PS 400/K-3
355 State Route 973 E 17728 570-494-1112
Michelle Kunkle, prin. Fax 494-0534

Collegeville, Montgomery, Pop. 4,996
Methacton SD
Supt. — See Eagleville
Arrowhead ES 300/K-4
232 Level Rd 19426 610-489-5000
Aaron Roberts, prin. Fax 489-4350

Perkiomen Valley SD 5,800/K-12
3 Iron Bridge Dr 19426 610-489-8506
Dr. Barbara Russell, supt. Fax 489-2974
www.pvsd.org
Evergreen ES 600/K-5
98 Kagey Rd 19426 610-409-9751
Dr. Amy Sacks, prin. Fax 409-9756
Perkiomen Valley East MS 800/6-8
100 Kagey Rd 19426 610-409-8580
Dr. Seamus Clune, prin. Fax 489-8851
Perkiomen Valley South ES 600/K-5
200 E 3rd Ave 19426 610-489-2991
David D'Andrea, prin. Fax 409-8754
Skippack ES 800/K-5
4081 Heckler Rd 19426 610-409-6060
Ryan Stanson-Marsh, prin. Fax 409-6099
Other Schools – See Schwenksville, Zieglerville

Holy Cross Regional S 500/K-8
701 Locust St 19426 610-489-9434
Theresa Healy, prin. Fax 489-6137
Valley Forge Baptist Academy 200/K-12
616 S Trappe Rd 19426 610-792-1884
Lois Rall, admin. Fax 948-6423

Collingdale, Delaware, Pop. 8,482
Southeast Delco SD
Supt. — See Folcroft
Harris S 800/1-8
501 Sharon Ave 19023 610-522-4370
Shawn McDougal, prin. Fax 586-7161

Columbia, Lancaster, Pop. 10,150
Columbia Borough SD 1,000/K-12
200 N 5th St 17512 717-684-2283
Dr. Robert Hollister, supt. Fax 681-2220
www.columbiabsd.org
Columbia MS Hill Campus 7-8
901 Ironville Pike 17512 717-684-7500
Dr. Jodie Parkinson, prin. Fax 681-2219
Columbia MS Taylor Campus 300/5-6
45 N 9th St 17512 717-684-4010
Dr. Jodie Parkinson, prin. Fax 681-2748
Park ES 300/K-4
50 S 6th St 17512 717-684-9780
John Black, prin. Fax 681-2619

Our Lady of the Angels S 200/PK-8
404 Cherry St 17512 717-684-2433
Kimberly Winters, prin. Fax 684-5039

Colwyn, Delaware, Pop. 2,481
William Penn SD
Supt. — See Lansdowne
Colwyn ES 200/K-6
211 Pine St 19023 610-957-5470
Patricia Stewart, prin. Fax 957-5485

Commodore, Indiana, Pop. 325
Purchase Line SD 1,000/K-12
16559 Route 286 Hwy E 15729 724-254-4312
Joseph Bradley, supt. Fax 254-1621
www.plsd.k12.pa.us/
Purchase Line ES 500/K-6
16957 Route 286 Hwy E 15729 724-254-4312
Thomas Aurandt, prin. Fax 254-3113

Conestoga, Lancaster, Pop. 1,247
Penn Manor SD
Supt. — See Lancaster
Conestoga ES 300/K-6
100 Hill St 17516 717-872-9535
Tamara Baker, prin. Fax 872-9516

Confluence, Somerset, Pop. 758
Turkeyfoot Valley Area SD 400/PK-12
172 Turkeyfoot Rd 15424 814-395-3621
Jeffrey Malaspino, supt. Fax 395-3366
www.turkeyfoot.k12.pa.us
Turkeyfoot Valley Area ES 200/PK-6
172 Turkeyfoot Rd 15424 814-395-3623
Nicole Dice, prin. Fax 395-3366

Conneaut Lake, Crawford, Pop. 646
Conneaut SD
Supt. — See Linesville
Conneaut Lake ES 400/K-4
630 Line St 16316 814-382-8191
Douglas Parks, prin. Fax 382-4477
Conneaut Lake MS 100/5-8
10331 US Highway 6 16316 814-382-5315
Joel Wentling, prin. Fax 382-0165

Conneautville, Crawford, Pop. 765
Conneaut SD
Supt. — See Linesville
Conneaut Valley ES 400/K-4
22491 State Highway 18 16406 814-587-6326
Adam Jardina, prin. Fax 587-2930
Conneaut Valley MS 100/5-8
22154 State Highway 18 16406 814-587-2091
Kevin Burns, prin. Fax 587-2094

Connellsville, Fayette, Pop. 7,510
Connellsville Area SD 4,400/K-12
732 Rockridge Rd 15425 724-628-3300
Philip Martell, supt. Fax 628-9002
www.casdfalcons.org
Bullskin Township ES 400/K-5
125 Pleasant Valley Rd 15425 724-628-6540
Kristen Porter, prin. Fax 626-2838
Connellsville MS 800/6-8
710 Locust St 15425 724-628-8910
Jennifer Sanzone, prin. Fax 628-9293
Dunbar Township ES 600/K-5
711 Ridge Blvd 15425 724-628-6330
Geoffrey Snyder, prin. Fax 628-2180
West Crawford ES 300/K-5
215 Falls Ave 15425 724-628-4497
Traci Kuhns, prin. Fax 628-2666
Other Schools – See Normalville

Conn-Area Catholic S 100/PK-6
613 E Crawford Ave Fl 1 15425 724-628-5090
Cecilia Solan, prin. Fax 628-1745

Conshohocken, Montgomery, Pop. 7,703
Colonial SD
Supt. — See Plymouth Meeting
Conshohocken ES 200/K-3
301 Harry St 19428 610-828-0362
Dr. Terese Boegly, prin. Fax 828-4582
Ridge Park ES 400/K-3
200 Karrs Ln 19428 610-825-1083
Eileen Carr, prin. Fax 825-7983

Conshohocken Catholic ECC 100/PK-PK
210 Harry St 19428 610-828-0755
Michelle Borkowski, dir. Fax 828-0755
Miquon S 200/PK-6
2025 Harts Ln 19428 610-828-1231
Susannah Wolf, prin. Fax 828-6149

Coopersburg, Lehigh, Pop. 2,362
Southern Lehigh SD
Supt. — See Center Valley
Liberty Bell ES 300/K-3
960 W Oxford St 18036 610-282-1850
Samuel Hafner, prin. Fax 282-3676

Coplay, Lehigh, Pop. 3,161
Parkland SD
Supt. — See Allentown
Ironton ES 400/K-5
3135 Levans Rd 18037 610-351-5810
Robert Holmes, prin. Fax 351-5819

Coraopolis, Allegheny, Pop. 5,475
Cornell SD 600/K-12
1099 Maple Street Ext 15108 412-264-5010
Aaron Thomas, supt. Fax 264-1445
www.cornell.k12.pa.us
Cornell ES 400/K-6
1099 Maple Street Ext 15108 412-264-5010
Jeffrey Carter, prin. Fax 264-4142

Montour SD
Supt. — See Mc Kees Rocks
Williams MS 900/5-8
60 Gawaldo Dr 15108 412-771-8802
Dominic Salpeck, prin. Fax 771-3772

St. Malachy S 200/PK-8
343 Forest Grove Rd 15108 412-771-4545
Catherine Militzer, prin. Fax 771-0922

Corry, Erie, Pop. 6,515
Corry Area SD 1,400/PK-12
540 E Pleasant St 16407 814-664-4677
William Nichols, supt. Fax 664-9645
www.corrysd.net
Corry Area IS 100/3-5
100 W Main St 16407 814-665-9491
Gail Swank, prin. Fax 663-0411
Corry Area MS 300/6-8
534 E Pleasant St 16407 814-665-8297
L. Swartzfager, prin. Fax 664-3650
Corry Area PS 300/PK-2
423 Wayne St 16407 814-665-6341
Teresa Pearce, prin. Fax 663-4795

Corry Alliance Academy 50/K-6
721 Hatch St 16407 814-664-8658
Karen Brumagin, admin. Fax 665-8018

Coudersport, Potter, Pop. 2,519
Coudersport Area SD 800/K-12
698 Dwight St 16915 814-274-9480
Jacqueline A. Canter, supt. Fax 274-7551
www.coudyschools.net
Coudersport Area ES 400/K-6
802 Vine St 16915 814-274-8500
Sean Reams, prin. Fax 274-2235

Cowansville, Armstrong
Karns City Area SD
Supt. — See Karns City
Sugarcreek ES 300/K-6
1290 State Route 268 16218 724-545-2409
Michael Stimac, prin. Fax 543-5853

Crafton, Allegheny, Pop. 5,812
Carlynton SD
Supt. — See Carnegie
Crafton ES 300/K-6
1874 Crafton Blvd 15205 412-922-7196
Marsha Burleson, prin. Fax 922-7587

Cranberry Township, Butler
Seneca Valley SD
Supt. — See Harmony
Haine ES 800/K-4
1516 Haine School Rd 16066 724-776-1581
Fax 776-1481
Haine MS 700/5-6
1516 Haine School Rd 16066 724-776-1581
Cassandra Doggrell, admin. Fax 776-2213
Rowan ES 500/K-4
8051 Rowan Rd 16066 724-776-1518
Nannette Farmar, prin. Fax 776-9574

St. Killian S 500/PK-8
7076 Franklin Rd 16066 724-625-1665
Jane Pampena, prin. Fax 625-1922

Cresco, Monroe

Monsignor McHugh S 200/PK-8
212 Route 390 18326 570-595-7463
Virgilio Ogando, prin. Fax 595-9639

Cresson, Cambria, Pop. 1,702
Penn Cambria SD 1,700/PK-12
201 6th St 16630 814-886-8121
William Marshall, supt. Fax 886-4809
www.pcam.org
Penn Cambria Pre PS 100/PK-K
205 6th St 16630 814-886-8166
Cindy Pacifico, prin. Fax 886-4809
Other Schools – See Gallitzin, Lilly

All Saints Catholic S 200/PK-8
220 Powell Ave 16630 814-886-7942
Kathleen Maurer, prin. Fax 886-7942

Cressona, Schuylkill, Pop. 1,637
Blue Mountain SD
Supt. — See Orwigsburg
Blue Mountain El Cressona ES 200/4-5
45 Wilder St 17929 570-385-5580
Kristin Frederick, prin. Fax 385-7206

Croydon, Bucks, Pop. 9,779
Bristol Township SD
Supt. — See Levittown
Keystone ES K-5
1800 Keystone St 19021 267-599-2470
Margaret Deni, prin. Fax 781-1466

Curwensville, Clearfield, Pop. 2,529
Curwensville Area SD 1,100/K-12
650 Beech St 16833 814-236-1101
Ronald Matchock, supt. Fax 236-1103
www.curwensville.org
Curwensville Area ES 500/K-6
650 Beech St 16833 814-236-1411
Ken Veihdeffer, prin.

Dallas, Luzerne, Pop. 2,782
Dallas SD 2,700/K-12
PO Box 2000 18612 570-674-7221
Dr. Thomas Duffy, supt. Fax 674-7295
www.dallassd.com/
Dallas ES 600/K-5
PO Box 2000 18612 570-674-7271
Tom Traver, prin. Fax 674-7267
Dallas MS 700/6-8
PO Box 2000 18612 570-674-7245
Jeffrey Shaffer, prin. Fax 674-7219
Wycallis ES 500/K-5
PO Box 2000 18612 570-674-7283
Brian Bradshaw, prin. Fax 674-7288

Lake-Lehman SD 1,900/K-12
1237 Market St 18612 570-675-2165
James McGovern, supt. Fax 675-7657
www.llsd.org
Other Schools – See Harveys Lake, Lehman, Sweet Valley

Dallastown, York, Pop. 3,985
Dallastown Area SD 6,000/K-12
700 New School Ln 17313 717-244-4021
Dr. Ronald Dyer, supt. Fax 894-0583
www.dallastown.net
Dallastown Area MS 1,000/7-8
700 New School Ln 17313 717-244-4021
Chad Bumsted, prin. Fax 233-9796
Dallastown ES 200/K-3
105 S Charles St 17313 717-244-3785
Charles Patterson, prin. Fax 260-8470
Other Schools – See York

St. Joseph S 200/PK-6
271 E Main St 17313 717-244-9386
Margaret Snyder, prin. Fax 244-9478

Dalton, Lackawanna, Pop. 1,226
Tunkhannock Area SD
Supt. — See Tunkhannock
Mill City ES 200/K-4
1113 Buttermilk Rd 18414 570-219-4031
Katherine Felker, prin. Fax 219-4041

Damascus, Wayne
Wayne Highlands SD
Supt. — See Honesdale
Damascus Area S 300/K-8
174 High School Rd 18415 570-224-4114
David Jagger, prin. Fax 224-4997

Danville, Montour, Pop. 4,646
Danville Area SD 2,300/PK-12
733 Ironmen Ln 17821 570-271-3268
Fax 275-7712
www.danville.k12.pa.us
Danville Area MS 500/6-8
252 Northumberland St 17821 570-271-3268
Dr. Charles Smargiassi, prin. Fax 284-4943
Danville PS 500/PK-2
931 Ironmen Ln 17821 570-271-3268
John Bickhart, prin. Fax 274-6209
Liberty-Valley ES 500/3-5
327 Liberty Valley Rd 17821 570-271-3268
Lee Gump, prin. Fax 275-5047

St. Cyril K 50/PK-K
580 Railroad St 17821 570-275-1505
Sr. Donna Marie, prin. Fax 275-5997
St. Joseph S 100/1-8
511 Ferry St 17821 570-275-2435
Vincent Fayock, prin. Fax 275-3947

Darby, Delaware, Pop. 10,364
William Penn SD
Supt. — See Lansdowne
Park Lane ES 400/K-6
1300 Park Ln 19023 610-534-4880
Walter Rodriguez, prin. Fax 534-4495
Penn Wood MS 800/7-8
121 Summit St 19023 610-586-1804
Kyle Hill, prin. Fax 586-7372
Walnut Street ES 500/K-6
224 S 6th St 19023 610-534-5660
Joseph Williams, prin. Fax 534-4412

Blessed Virgin Mary S 200/K-8
47 N MacDade Blvd 19023 610-586-0638
Sr. Virginia Paschall, prin. Fax 586-1582

Darlington, Beaver, Pop. 254
Big Beaver Falls Area SD
Supt. — See Beaver Falls
Big Beaver ES 400/K-5
588 Friendship Rd 16115 724-827-2828
Theresa Cherry, prin. Fax 827-8453

Dauphin, Dauphin, Pop. 785
Central Dauphin SD
Supt. — See Harrisburg
Middle Paxton ES 300/K-5
931 Peters Mountain Rd 17018 717-265-7920
Daniel Iacavone, prin. Fax 921-3366

Davidsville, Somerset, Pop. 1,129
Conemaugh Township Area SD 1,000/K-12
300 W Campus Ave 15928 814-479-7575
Thomas Kakabar, supt. Fax 479-2620
www.ctasd.org
Other Schools – See Johnstown

Dayton, Armstrong, Pop. 542
Armstrong SD
Supt. — See Kittanning
Dayton ES 300/K-6
PO Box 418 16222 814-257-8816
Dr. John Giancola, prin. Fax 257-8459

Delta, York, Pop. 719
South Eastern SD
Supt. — See Fawn Grove
Delta-Peach Bottom ES 300/PK-4
1081 Atom Rd 17314 717-456-5313
Dr. Zane Fake, prin. Fax 456-6042

Denver, Lancaster, Pop. 3,812
Cocalico SD 3,100/PK-12
PO Box 800 17517 717-336-1413
Dr. Ella Musser, supt. Fax 336-1415
www.cocalico.org
Cocalico MS 700/6-8
650 S 6th St 17517 717-336-1471
Anthony DiMatteo, prin. Fax 336-1482
Denver ES 500/K-5
700 S 4th St 17517 717-336-1501
Angela Marley, prin. Fax 336-1503
Other Schools – See Adamstown, Reamstown

Eastern Lancaster County SD
Supt. — See New Holland
Brecknock ES 500/K-6
361 School Rd 17517 717-445-8600
Kimberly Andersen, prin. Fax 445-8604

Gehmans Mennonite S 100/K-12
650 Gehman School Rd 17517 717-484-4222

Derry, Westmoreland, Pop. 2,670
Derry Area SD 2,200/K-12
982 N Chestnut Street Ext 15627 724-694-1401
Cheryl Walters, supt. Fax 694-1429
derryasd.schoolwires.com/Page/1
Derry Area MS 500/6-8
994 N Chestnut Street Ext 15627 724-694-8231
Lisa Dubich, prin. Fax 694-0288
Grandview ES 1,000/K-5
188 Recreation Rd 15627 724-694-2400
Kristine Higgs, prin. Fax 694-1351

Devon, Chester, Pop. 1,486
Tredyffrin-Easttown SD
Supt. — See Wayne
Beaumont ES 400/K-4
575 Beaumont Rd 19333 610-240-1400
Dr. Stephanie Demming, prin. Fax 240-1410

Devon ES 500/K-4
400 S Fairfield Rd 19333 610-240-1450
Dr. Todd Parker, prin. Fax 240-1466

Delaware County Christian S - Lower Cmps 300/PK-5
905 S Waterloo Rd 19333 484-654-2400
Dr. Timothy Wiens, head sch Fax 654-2401

Dillsburg, York, Pop. 2,514
Northern York County SD 3,100/K-12
650 S Baltimore St 17019 717-432-8691
Dr. Eric Eshbach, supt. Fax 432-1421
www.northernpolarbears.com
Dillsburg ES 400/K-5
202 S Chestnut St 17019 717-432-8691
Dr. Patricia Franko, prin. Fax 432-7580
Northern ES 300/K-5
657 S Baltimore St 17019 717-432-8691
Joyce Cal, prin. Fax 502-8707
Northern MS 700/6-8
655 S Baltimore St 17019 717-432-8691
Sylvia Murray, prin. Fax 432-5889
South Mountain ES 500/K-5
711 S Mountain Rd 17019 717-432-8691
David Echelmeier, prin. Fax 502-1472
Other Schools – See Wellsville

Dingmans Ferry, Pike
Delaware Valley SD
Supt. — See Milford
Dingman-Delaware ES 600/3-5
1355 Route 739 18328 570-296-3120
Victoria McNeeley, prin. Fax 296-3171
Dingman-Delaware MS 700/6-8
1365 Route 739 18328 570-296-3140
James Mitchell, prin. Fax 296-3170
Dingman-Delaware PS 500/K-2
1375 Route 739 18328 570-296-3130
Kimberly Butaitis, prin. Fax 296-3173

East Stroudsburg Area SD
Supt. — See East Stroudsburg
Bushkill ES 400/K-5
131 N School Dr 18328 570-588-4400
Debra Padavano, prin. Fax 588-4406
Lehman IS 800/6-8
257 Timberwolf Dr 18328 570-588-4410
Dr. Robert Dilliplane, prin. Fax 588-4411

Douglassville, Berks, Pop. 444
Daniel Boone Area SD 2,900/K-12
2144 Weavertown Rd 19518 610-582-6140
James Harris, supt. Fax 689-6215
www.dboone.org
Amity ES 500/2-5
200 Boone Dr 19518 610-689-6240
Dane Miller, prin. Fax 689-6265
Boone Area MS 900/6-8
1845 Weavertown Rd 19518 610-689-6300
Jenny Rexrode, prin. Fax 689-6306
Other Schools – See Birdsboro

Immaculate Conception Academy 200/K-8
903 Chestnut St 19518 610-404-8645
Patricia Tarquinio, prin. Fax 404-4890

Dover, York, Pop. 1,967
Dover Area SD 3,500/K-12
101 Edgeway Rd 17315 717-292-3671
Tracy Krum, supt. Fax 292-9659
www.doversd.org
Dover Area ES 300/K-6
109 E Canal St 17315 717-292-8068
Galen Rupp, prin. Fax 292-4645
Dover Area IS 600/7-8
4500 Intermediate Ave 17315 717-292-8067
Victoria Gross, prin. Fax 292-9849
Leib ES 500/K-6
2925 Oakland Rd 17315 717-292-8070
Dr. Troy Wiestling, prin. Fax 292-4828
North Salem ES 500/K-6
5161 N Salem Church Rd 17315 717-292-8071
Christopher Cobb, prin. Fax 292-4388
Weigelstown ES 500/K-6
3205 Carlisle Rd 17315 717-292-8072
Tuesday Hufnagel, prin. Fax 292-6390

Downingtown, Chester, Pop. 7,678
Downingtown Area SD 11,100/K-12
540 Trestle Pl 19335 610-269-8460
Dr. Emilie Lonardi, supt. Fax 873-1404
www.dasd.org
Beaver Creek ES 500/K-5
601 W Pennsylvania Ave 19335 610-269-2790
Dr. Dawn Lawless, prin. Fax 269-4572
Bradford Heights ES 500/K-5
1330 Romig Rd 19335 610-269-6021
Andrew Hoffert, prin. Fax 518-0656
Brandywine-Wallace ES 400/K-5
435 Dilworth Rd 19335 610-269-2083
Linda Leib, prin. Fax 269-2829
Downingtown MS 900/7-8
115 Rock Raymond Rd 19335 610-518-0685
Dr. Nick Indeglio, prin. Fax 518-0685
East Ward ES 600/K-5
435 Washington Ave 19335 610-269-8282
Nick Argonish, prin. Fax 873-3440
Lionville ES 700/K-5
526 W Uwchlan Ave 19335 610-363-6580
Shelda Perry, prin. Fax 363-3065
Marsh Creek 6th Grade Center 6-6
489 Dorlan Mill Rd 19335 610-269-8460
Thomas Mulvey, prin.
Shamona Creek ES 400/K-5
501 Dorlan Mill Rd 19335 610-458-8703
Norma Jean Welsh, prin. Fax 458-9130
Uwchlan Hills ES 500/K-5
50 Peck Rd 19335 610-269-5656
Bob Giering, prin. Fax 269-6793

West Bradford ES 600/K-5
1475 Broadrun Rd 19335 610-384-9030
Dr. Dina Wert, prin. Fax 466-0914
Other Schools – See Chester Springs, Exton, Glenmoore

St. Joseph S 600/K-8
340 Manor Ave 19335 610-269-8999
Sr. Catherine Masino, prin. Fax 269-2252

Doylestown, Bucks, Pop. 8,255
Central Bucks SD 19,600/K-12
20 Weldon Dr 18901 267-893-2000
John Kopicki, supt. Fax 893-5800
www.cbsd.org
Cold Spring ES 600/K-6
4150 Durham Rd 267-893-3800
Brian Finger, prin. Fax 893-5804
Doyle ES 500/K-6
260 N West St 18901 267-893-4300
Susan Salvesen, prin. Fax 893-5806
Gayman ES 500/K-6
4440 Point Pleasant Pike, 267-893-4350
Kelly Carter, prin. Fax 348-4092
Groveland ES 900/K-6
1100 N Easton Rd, 267-893-4600
David Heineman, prin. Fax 893-5808
Kutz ES 600/K-6
1950 Turk Rd 18901 267-893-3900
Dr. Nadine Garvin, prin. Fax 340-9636
Linden ES 500/K-6
480 Linden Ave 18901 267-893-4400
Michael Testani, prin. Fax 348-4203
Other Schools – See Buckingham, Chalfont, Furlong, Jamison, New Britain, Warrington

Our Lady of Mt. Carmel S 400/K-8
225 E Ashland St 18901 215-348-5907
Dawn Parker, prin. Fax 348-5671

Dresher, Montgomery
Upper Dublin SD
Supt. — See Maple Glen
Jarrettown ES 500/K-5
1520 Limekiln Pike 19025 215-643-8951
Meg Place M.Ed., prin. Fax 641-9133
Sandy Run MS 1,000/6-8
520 Twining Rd 19025 215-576-3280
Dr. Jill Clark, prin. Fax 572-3886

Montessori S 100/PK-6
1701 Jarrettown Rd 19025 215-542-0740
Laura Stulb, head sch Fax 542-2381

Drexel Hill, Delaware, Pop. 27,609
Upper Darby SD 12,200/K-12
4611 Bond Ave 19026 610-789-7200
Daniel Nerelli, supt. Fax 789-8671
www.upperdarbysd.org
Aronimink ES, 4611 Bond Ave 19026 300/1-5
Brian Booher, prin. 610-853-4510
Drexel Hill MS, 3001 State Rd 19026 1,300/6-8
Frank Salerno, prin. 610-853-4580
Garrettford ES, 3830 Garrett Rd 19026 700/1-5
Thomas Christensen, prin. 610-626-9168
Hillcrest ES, 2601 Bond Ave 19026 700/K-5
Kristin O'Neill, prin. 610-853-4520
Kelly ES, 3400 Dennison Ave 19026 300/1-5
Dr. MelanieJo McCarthyFrick, prin. 610-638-1070
Upper Darby K, 3200 State Rd 19026 700/K-K
Dina Williams, prin. 610-284-7992
Other Schools – See Clifton Heights, Glenolden, Primos, Upper Darby

Holy Child Academy 200/PK-8
475 Shadeland Ave 19026 610-259-2712
Anne Wood, head sch Fax 259-1862
St. Andrew S 300/PK-8
535 Mason Ave 19026 610-259-5145
Helen McLean, prin. Fax 284-6956
St. Bernadette of Lourdes S 300/PK-8
1015 Turner Ave 19026 610-789-7676
Dr. Thomas Tobin, prin. Fax 789-9539
St. Dorothy S 400/K-8
1225 Burmont Rd 19026 610-789-4100
Louise Sheehan, prin. Fax 536-3101

Drums, Luzerne
Hazleton Area SD
Supt. — See Hazle Township
Drums S 800/K-8
85 S Old Turnpike Rd 18222 570-459-3221
Matthew Marnell, prin. Fax 788-3276

Du Bois, Clearfield, Pop. 7,711
Du Bois Area SD 3,800/K-12
500 Liberty Blvd 15801 814-371-2700
Dr. Luke Lansberry, supt. Fax 371-2544
www.dasd.k12.pa.us
Du Bois Area MS 900/6-8
404 Liberty Blvd 15801 814-375-8770
Darren Hack, prin. Fax 375-8775
Juniata ES 400/K-5
248 Juniata St 15801 814-371-1090
Barbara Jo Smith, prin. Fax 371-5235
Oklahoma ES 400/K-5
1032 Chestnut Ave 15801 814-371-3660
Tammy Cook, prin. Fax 371-5360
Wasson Avenue ES 400/K-5
300 Wasson Ave 15801 814-371-6171
Kathleen Ginther, prin. Fax 371-8635
Other Schools – See Reynoldsville

Du Bois Area Catholic ES 300/PK-5
PO Box 567 15801 814-371-2570
Fax 371-1551
Du Bois Area Catholic MS 100/6-8
PO Box 567 15801 814-371-3060
Dawn Bressler, prin. Fax 371-3215

DuBois Christian S 100/PK-12
197 Eastern Ave 15801 814-371-7395
Mark Montgomery M.Ed., admin. Fax 371-7399

Duke Center, McKean
Otto-Eldred SD 700/PK-12
143 Sweitzer Dr 16729 814-817-1380
Matthew D. Splain, supt. Fax 966-3911
www.ottoeldred.org
Other Schools – See Eldred

Duncannon, Perry, Pop. 1,503
Susquenita SD 1,700/K-12
1725 Schoolhouse Rd 17020 717-957-6000
Kent R. Smith, supt. Fax 957-2463
www.susq.k12.pa.us/
Susquenita ES 700/K-4
101 Susquenita Dr 17020 717-957-6000
Dr. Rebecca Lorfink, prin. Fax 957-3229
Susquenita MS 500/5-8
200 Susquenita Dr 17020 717-957-6000
William Quigley, prin. Fax 957-6022

Duncansville, Blair, Pop. 1,222
Hollidaysburg Area SD
Supt. — See Hollidaysburg
Foot of Ten ES 600/K-6
450 Foot of Ten Rd 16635 814-695-1941
Brian Keagy, prin. Fax 695-3753

Dunmore, Lackawanna, Pop. 13,930
Dunmore SD 1,600/K-12
300 W Warren St 18512 570-343-2110
John Marichak, supt. Fax 343-1458
www.dunmoreschooldistrict.net
Dunmore ES 800/K-6
300 W Warren St 18512 570-347-6794
Matthew Quinn, prin. Fax 207-6765
Dunmore MS 300/7-8
300 W Warren St 18512 570-207-9590
Timothy Hopkins, prin. Fax 346-5923

St. Mary of Mt. Carmel S 200/PK-8
325 Chestnut St 18512 570-346-4429
Kathleen Hubert, prin. Fax 346-3016

Duquesne, Allegheny, Pop. 5,349
Duquesne CSD 400/PK-6
300 Kennedy Ave 15110 412-466-9600
Nedene Gullen, supt.
www.dukecitysd.org
Duquesne ES 400/PK-6
300 Kennedy Ave 15110 412-466-9600
Jennifer Jennings, prin.

Duryea, Luzerne, Pop. 4,891

Holy Rosary S 300/PK-8
125 Stephenson St 18642 570-457-2553
Candice Lee, prin. Fax 457-3537

Eagleville, Montgomery, Pop. 4,719
Methacton SD 5,000/K-12
1001 Kriebel Mill Rd 19403 610-489-5000
Dr. David Zerbe, supt. Fax 489-5019
www.methacton.org
Arcola IS 800/7-8
4001 Eagleville Rd Ste A 19403 610-489-5000
Amy Mangano, prin. Fax 831-5317
Eagleville ES 400/K-4
125 Summit Ave 19403 610-489-5000
Dr. Zanthia Reddish, prin. Fax 831-5324
Skyview Upper ES 800/5-6
4001 Eagleville Rd Ste B 19403 610-489-5000
Melissa Gorla, prin. Fax 489-5046
Woodland ES 300/K-4
2700 Woodland Ave 19403 610-489-5000
Debra Euker, prin. Fax 831-5319
Other Schools – See Collegeville, Lansdale

East Earl, Lancaster, Pop. 1,139
Eastern Lancaster County SD
Supt. — See New Holland
Blue Ball ES 600/K-6
126 Ewell Rd 17519 717-354-1525
Curtis McCaskey, prin. Fax 354-1527

E Fallowfield, Chester
Coatesville Area SD
Supt. — See Thorndale
East Fallowfield ES 400/K-5
2254 Strasburg Rd 19320 610-383-3765
Wayne Wallace, prin. Fax 383-3769

East Greenville, Montgomery, Pop. 2,902
Upper Perkiomen SD
Supt. — See Pennsburg
Upper Perkiomen MS 700/6-8
510 Jefferson St 18041 215-679-6288
Jeffrey Fries, prin. Fax 679-3091

East Lansdowne, Delaware, Pop. 2,593
William Penn SD
Supt. — See Lansdowne
East Lansdowne ES 300/K-6
401 Emerson Ave 19050 610-626-2415
Phyllis Cubit, prin. Fax 284-8060

St. Cyril of Alexandria S 200/K-8
716 Emerson Ave 19050 610-623-1113
Sr. Barbara Montague, prin. Fax 623-2427

East Norriton, Montgomery, Pop. 13,324

Penn Christian Academy 200/PK-8
50 W Germantown Pike, 610-279-6628
Fax 279-1956

Easton, Northampton, Pop. 25,861
Bethlehem Area SD
Supt. — See Bethlehem

Farmersville ES 500/K-5
7036 William Penn Hwy 18045 610-868-0471
Jennifer Hilton, prin. Fax 807-5980

Easton Area SD 8,700/K-12
1801 Bushkill Dr 18040 610-250-2400
John Reinhart, supt. Fax 923-8954
www.eastonsd.org
Cheston ES 500/K-4
723 Coal St 18042 610-250-2542
Kyle Yanders, prin. Fax 923-6046
Easton Area MS 1,300/6-8
1010 Echo Trl 18040 610-250-2460
Dr. Charlene Symia, prin. Fax 250-2613
Forks ES 400/K-5
1709 Richmond Rd 18040 610-250-2536
Thomas Warren, prin. Fax 923-8933
March ES 400/K-4
429 Reeder St 18042 610-250-2531
Hector Bonilla, prin. Fax 250-2458
Palmer ES 600/K-5
3050 Green Pond Rd 18045 610-250-2521
Meredith Naumann, prin. Fax 923-6955
Paxinosa ES 700/K-4
1221 Northampton St 18042 610-250-2551
Anthony Viglianti, prin. Fax 923-8934
Shawnee ES 600/K-5
1315 Echo Trl 18040 610-250-2551
Josephine Galloway, prin. Fax 923-8934
Tracy ES 400/K-5
1243 Tatamy Rd 18045 610-250-2556
David Hightower, prin. Fax 250-2602

Wilson Area SD 2,200/K-12
2040 Washington Blvd 18042 484-373-6000
Douglas Wagner, supt. Fax 258-6421
www.wilsonareasd.org
Avona ES 200/K-4
2317 Front St 18042 484-373-6250
Michael Chromey, prin. Fax 258-9407
Williams Township ES 200/K-4
2660 Morgan Hill Rd 18042 484-373-6170
Kevin Steidle, prin. Fax 258-8717
Wilson Area IS 700/5-8
2400 Firmstone St 18042 484-373-6110
Anthony Tarsi, prin. Fax 258-4014
Wilson Borough ES 400/K-5
301 S 21st St 18042 484-373-6220
Amy Austin, prin. Fax 258-9436

Bethlehem Christian S Calvary Campus 50/5-8
5300 Green Pond Rd 18045 610-365-8176
Carol Aversa, head sch Fax 365-8407
St. Jane Frances deChantal S 500/PK-8
1900 Washington Blvd 18042 610-253-8442
Mary Beth Okula, prin. Fax 253-2427

East Petersburg, Lancaster, Pop. 4,408
Hempfield SD
Supt. — See Landisville
East Petersburg ES 500/K-6
5700 Lemon St 17520 717-569-1211
Kimberly Rauscher, prin. Fax 618-0998

East Prospect, York, Pop. 898
Eastern York SD
Supt. — See Wrightsville
Canadochly ES 500/K-5
PO Box 118 17317 717-252-3674
Mary Jo Moczulski, prin. Fax 252-5397

East Smithfield, Bradford
Athens Area SD
Supt. — See Athens
SRU ES 400/K-5
PO Box 38 18817 570-596-3171
Peter Henning, prin. Fax 596-4141

East Springfield, Erie
Northwestern SD
Supt. — See Albion
Springfield ES 200/K-5
PO Box 248 16411 814-756-9400
Richard Harvey, prin. Fax 922-3140

East Stroudsburg, Monroe, Pop. 9,606
East Stroudsburg Area SD 7,300/K-12
50 Vine St 18301 570-424-8500
Dr. William Riker, supt. Fax 424-5646
www.esasd.net
East Stroudsburg ES 700/K-5
93 Independence Rd 18301 570-421-1905
Irene Livingston, prin. Fax 420-8310
Hill ES 400/K-5
151 E Broad St 18301 570-424-8073
Michelle Arnold, prin. Fax 476-0720
Lambert IS 1,000/6-8
2000 Milford Rd 18301 570-424-8430
Craig Reichl, prin. Fax 476-0464
Middle Smithfield ES 600/K-5
5180 Milford Rd, 570-223-8082
David Baker, prin. Fax 223-2110
Resica ES 500/K-5
1 Gravel Ridge Rd, 570-223-6911
Gail Kulick, prin. Fax 223-2100
Smithfield ES 300/K-5
245 River Rd 18301 570-421-2841
Dr. William Vitulli, prin. Fax 476-0488
Other Schools – See Dingmans Ferry

Notre Dame ES 300/PK-6
60 Spangenburg Ave 18301 570-421-3651
Sr. Mary Alice Kane, prin. Fax 422-6935

Ebensburg, Cambria, Pop. 3,337
Central Cambria SD 1,700/K-12
208 Schoolhouse Rd 15931 814-472-8870
Vincent DiLeo Ed.D., supt. Fax 472-9695
www.cencam.org
Cambria ES 500/K-5
212 Schoolhouse Rd 15931 814-472-8432
Jennifer Mesoras, prin. Fax 472-8674
Central Cambria MS 400/6-8
206 Schoolhouse Rd 15931 814-472-6505
Christopher Santini, prin. Fax 472-4187
Other Schools – See Johnstown

Holy Name S 300/PK-8
215 W Horner St 15931 814-472-8817
Robin McMullen, prin. Fax 471-0500

Eddystone, Delaware, Pop. 2,345
Ridley SD
Supt. — See Folsom
Eddystone ES 200/K-5
1410 E 9th St 19022 610-534-1900
Jeffrey D'Orazio, prin. Fax 874-4321

Edinboro, Erie, Pop. 6,330
General McLane SD 2,200/K-12
11771 Edinboro Rd 16412 814-273-1033
Richard Scaletta, supt. Fax 273-1030
www.generalmclane.org
Edinboro ES 400/K-4
5390 Route 6N 16412 814-273-1033
Randy White, prin. Fax 273-1040
Parker MS 700/5-8
11781 Edinboro Rd 16412 814-273-1033
John Hansen, prin. Fax 273-1038
Other Schools – See Mc Kean

Eighty Four, Washington, Pop. 655
Canon-McMillan SD
Supt. — See Canonsburg
Wylandville ES 200/K-4
1254 Route 519 15330 724-222-2507
Christina Unitas, prin. Fax 225-5971

Elderton, Armstrong, Pop. 343
Armstrong SD
Supt. — See Kittanning
Elderton ES 300/K-6
239 S Lytle St 15736 724-354-2131
Paula Kijowski, prin. Fax 354-4619

Eldred, McKean, Pop. 808
Otto-Eldred SD
Supt. — See Duke Center
Otto-Eldred ES 400/PK-6
PO Box 309 16731 814-817-1380
Lindsay Burns, prin. Fax 225-4917

Elizabeth, Allegheny, Pop. 1,455
Elizabeth Forward SD 2,300/K-12
401 Rock Run Rd 15037 412-896-2312
Dr. Bart Hocco, supt. Fax 751-9483
www.efsd.net
Central ES 300/K-5
401 Rock Run Rd 15037 412-896-2318
Mary Perry, prin. Fax 751-0692
Elizabeth Forward MS 600/6-8
401 Rock Run Rd 15037 412-896-2335
Trisha Martell, prin. Fax 751-6669
Other Schools – See Mc Keesport, Monongahela

Elizabethtown, Lancaster, Pop. 11,397
Elizabethtown Area SD 3,900/K-12
600 E High St 17022 717-367-1521
Dr. Michele Balliet, supt. Fax 367-1920
www.etownschools.org
Bear Creek S 900/4-6
1459 Sheaffer Rd 17022 717-367-0210
Dr. Annette Spagnolo, prin. Fax 361-3788
East High Street ES 500/K-3
800 E High St 17022 717-361-0099
Amy Balsbaugh, prin. Fax 367-3826
Elizabethtown Area MS 600/7-8
600 E High St 17022 717-361-7525
Dr. Nathan Frank, prin. Fax 361-2597
Mill Road ES 200/K-3
35 Elm Ave 17022 717-361-7424
Amanda Baxter, prin. Fax 361-0184
Other Schools – See Rheems

Lower Dauphin SD
Supt. — See Hummelstown
Conewago ES 200/K-5
2809 Hershey Rd 17022 717-367-7233
Edward Gnall, prin. Fax 367-6893

Mt. Calvary Christian S 300/PK-12
629 Holly St 17022 717-367-1649
Dr. Daniel Sheard, hdmstr. Fax 367-5672

Elkins Park, Montgomery, Pop. 4,700
Abington SD
Supt. — See Abington
McKinley ES 700/K-6
370 Cedar Rd 19027 215-663-0430
Marie Kim, prin. Fax 663-0593

Cheltenham SD 4,600/K-12
2000 Ashbourne Rd 19027 215-886-9500
Dr. Wagner Marseille, supt. Fax 884-3029
www.cheltenham.org
Elkins Park S 700/5-6
8149 New Second St 19027 215-881-4941
Dr. Geraldine Doria, prin. Fax 635-7492
Myers ES 300/K-4
7609 Montgomery Ave 19027 215-517-4540
Dan Tahaney, prin. Fax 635-7437
Other Schools – See Cheltenham, Glenside, Wyncote

Perelman Jewish Day S 200/K-5
7601 Old York Rd 19027 215-635-3130

Elkland, Tioga, Pop. 1,798
Northern Tioga SD 2,100/K-12
110 Ellison Rd 16920 814-258-5642
Dr. Diane Barnes, supt. Fax 258-7083
www.ntiogasd.org
Wood ES 300/K-6
110A Ellison Rd 16920 814-258-5131
Jess Millard, prin. Fax 258-7484
Other Schools – See Tioga, Westfield

Elliottsburg, Perry
West Perry SD 2,500/PK-12
2606 Shermans Valley Rd 17024 717-789-3934
Dr. Michael O'Brien, supt. Fax 789-4997
www.westperry.org
West Perry MS 600/6-8
2620 Shermans Valley Rd 17024 717-789-3012
Renee LeDonne, prin. Fax 789-3393
Other Schools – See Blain, New Bloomfield, Shermans Dale

Ellwood City, Lawrence, Pop. 7,833
Ellwood City Area SD 1,800/K-12
501 Crescent Ave 16117 724-752-1591
Joseph Mancini, supt. Fax 752-8556
www.ellwood.k12.pa.us
Hartman ES 300/5-6
410 4th St 16117 724-752-1591
Frank Keally, prin. Fax 758-0534
North Side PS 400/K-2
501 Orchard Ave 16117 724-752-1591
Christine Gibson, prin. Fax 758-0329
Perry Lower IS 300/3-4
627 Portersville Rd 16117 724-752-1591
Frank Keally, prin. Fax 758-0534

Riverside Beaver County SD 1,500/PK-12
318 Country Club Dr 16117 724-758-7512
Dr. David Anney, supt. Fax 758-2070
www.riverside.k12.pa.us
Riverside ES 700/PK-5
302 Country Club Dr 16117 724-758-7512
Stephen Girting, prin. Fax 758-0919
Riverside MS 400/6-8
302 Country Club Dr 16117 724-758-7512
Alicia Dwyer, prin. Fax 758-0919

Holy Redeemer S 100/PK-6
311 Lawrence Ave 16117 724-758-5591
Sr. Joanne Kokosinski, prin. Fax 758-0705

Elverson, Chester, Pop. 1,218
Twin Valley SD 3,400/K-12
4851 N Twin Valley Rd 19520 610-286-8611
Dr. Robert Pleis, supt. Fax 286-8608
www.tvsd.org
Twin Valley ES 500/K-4
50 Mast Dr 19520 610-286-8670
Craig Sell, prin. Fax 286-8672
Twin Valley MS 1,100/5-8
770 Clymer Hill Rd 19520 610-286-8660
Dr. Gerald Catagnus, prin. Fax 286-8662
Other Schools – See Birdsboro, Honey Brook

Emmaus, Lehigh, Pop. 11,070
East Penn SD 8,100/K-12
800 Pine St 18049 610-966-8300
Michael Schilder Ed.D., supt. Fax 966-8339
new.eastpennsd.org
Jefferson ES 300/K-5
520 Elm St 18049 610-965-1645
Cheryl Scalzo, prin. Fax 966-8349
Lincoln ES, 233 Seem St 18049 400/K-5
Dr. Jacqueline Attinello, prin. 610-965-1636
Other Schools – See Alburtis, Macungie, Wescosville

St. Ann S 300/PK-8
435 S 6th St 18049 610-965-9220
Diana Kile, prin. Fax 967-4521

Emporium, Cameron, Pop. 2,061
Cameron County SD 600/K-12
601 Woodland Ave 15834 814-486-4000
Dr. Keith Wolfe, supt. Fax 486-4006
www.camcosd.org
Woodland ES 300/K-6
603 Woodland Ave 15834 814-486-4000
Amy Schwab, prin. Fax 486-4007

Enola, Cumberland, Pop. 5,946
Cumberland Valley SD
Supt. — See Mechanicsburg
Shaull ES 600/K-5
1 Shaull Dr 17025 717-732-2460
Deana Raymer, prin. Fax 732-8664

East Pennsboro Area SD 2,700/K-12
890 Valley St 17025 717-732-3601
Gregory Milbrand, supt. Fax 732-8927
www.epasd.k12.pa.us
East Pennsboro Area MS 900/5-8
529 N Enola Dr 17025 717-732-0771
Michael Sim, prin. Fax 732-8948
East Pennsboro ES 600/K-4
840 Panther Pkwy 17025 717-732-0441
Richard Tysarczyk, prin. Fax 732-8946
Other Schools – See Camp Hill

Ephrata, Lancaster, Pop. 13,209
Ephrata Area SD 4,200/K-12
803 Oak Blvd 17522 717-721-1400
Dr. Brian Troop, supt. Fax 721-1514
www.easdpa.org
Clay ES 500/K-4
250 Clay School Rd 17522 717-721-1100
Joy Darkes, prin. Fax 721-7082
Ephrata IS 600/5-6
957 Hammon Ave 17522 717-721-1405
Kevin Deemer, prin. Fax 721-1406

Ephrata MS 600/7-8
957 Hammon Ave 17522 717-721-1468
Kevin Deemer, prin. Fax 721-1469
Fulton ES 400/K-4
51 E Fulton St 17522 717-721-1130
Josh McCracken, prin. Fax 721-1133
Highland ES 400/K-4
99 Highland Ave 17522 717-721-1160
Brett Esbenshade, prin. Fax 721-1167
Other Schools – See Akron

Ephrata Mennonite S 200/K-10
598 Stevens Rd 17522 717-738-4266
Farmersville Mennonite S 100/1-9
05 E Farmersville Rd 17522 717-354-5070
Hinkletown Mennonite S 200/PK-12
272 Wanner Rd 17522 717-354-7100
Dawn Landes, admin. Fax 354-8438
Our Mother of Perpetual Help S 200/PK-8
330 Church Ave 17522 717-738-2414
Margaret Gardner, prin. Fax 738-3280
Pleasant Valley Mennonite S 100/K-12
144 Pleasant Valley Rd 17522 717-738-1833

Erdenheim, Montgomery

Philadelphia-Montgomery Christian Acad 300/K-12
35 Hillcrest Rd 19038 215-233-0782
Susan Liegel, head sch Fax 233-0829

Erie, Erie, Pop. 98,321
Erie CSD 11,700/PK-12
148 W 21st St 16502 814-874-6000
Brian Polito, supt. Fax 874-6010
www.eriesd.org
Cleveland ES 600/PK-5
1540 W 38th St 16508 814-874-6670
Michelle Fiorelli, prin. Fax 874-6675
Connell ES 600/PK-5
1820 E 38th St 16510 814-874-6785
Jesse Williams, prin. Fax 874-6789
Diehl S 500/PK-5
2327 Fairmont Pkwy 16510 814-874-6585
Tim Sabol, prin. Fax 874-6589
East MS 1,000/6-8
1001 Atkins St 16503 814-874-6400
Scherry Prater, prin. Fax 874-6407
Edison ES 500/PK-5
1921 E Lake Rd 16511 814-874-6470
Kevin Harper, prin. Fax 874-6475
Harding S 600/PK-5
820 Lincoln Ave 16505 814-874-6550
Kathleen Farnham, prin. Fax 874-6556
Jefferson ES 500/PK-5
230 E 38th St 16504 814-874-6650
Jeffrey Boam, prin. Fax 874-6656
Lincoln ES 400/PK-5
831 E 31st St 16504 814-874-6685
Carla Johnson, prin. Fax 874-6689
McKinley ES 600/PK-5
933 E 22nd St 16503 814-874-6870
Dana Suppa, prin. Fax 874-6875
Perry ES 500/PK-5
955 W 29th St 16508 814-874-6485
David Eubank, prin. Fax 874-6489
Pfeiffer-Burleigh S 800/K-8
235 E 11th St 16503 814-874-6750
Karin Ryan, prin. Fax 874-6756
Vincent MS 700/6-8
1330 W 8th St 16502 814-874-6500
Jeffrey Hutchinson, prin. Fax 874-6507
Wilson MS 800/6-8
718 E 28th St 16504 814-874-6600
Donald Orlando, prin. Fax 874-6607

Fort LeBoeuf SD
Supt. — See Waterford
Robison ES 400/K-5
1651 Robison Rd W 16509 814-796-3742
Jennifer Hopkins, prin. Fax 864-2017

Harbor Creek SD
Supt. — See Harborcreek
Clark ES 300/K-6
3650 Depot Rd 16510 814-897-2100
Donna Rose, prin. Fax 897-8723
Klein ES 300/K-6
5325 E Lake Rd 16511 814-897-2100
Tyler Cook, prin. Fax 898-0225
Rolling Ridge ES 500/K-6
3700 Ridge Pkwy 16510 814-897-2100
Cynthia Zajac, prin. Fax 898-1916

Iroquois SD, 800 Tyndall Ave 16511 1,200/PK-12
Shane Murray, supt. 814-899-7643
www.iroquoissd.org
Iroquois ES, 4231 Morse St 16511 600/PK-6
Brian Bronson, prin. 814-899-7643

Millcreek Township SD 7,200/PK-12
3740 W 26th St 16506 814-835-5300
William Hall, supt. Fax 835-5307
www.mtsd.org
Belle Valley ES 700/PK-5
5300 Henderson Rd 16509 814-835-5600
Stacy Camino, prin. Fax 835-5610
Chestnut Hill ES 400/K-5
1001 W 54th St 16509 814-835-5550
Dr. James Smith, prin. Fax 835-5590
Grandview ES 700/PK-5
4301 Lancaster Rd 16506 814-836-6300
Kristen Boyd, prin. Fax 836-5466
Tracy ES 600/K-5
2624 W 6th St 16505 814-835-5800
Jeremiah Bull, prin. Fax 835-5810
Westlake MS 700/PK-PK, 6-
4330 W Lake Rd 16505 814-835-5750
Marty Kaverman, prin. Fax 835-5770
Wilson MS 600/6-8
901 W 54th St 16509 814-835-5500
Terry Costello, prin. Fax 835-5542
Other Schools – See Fairview

Wattsburg Area SD 1,400/K-12
10782 Wattsburg Rd 16509 814-824-3400
Kenneth Berlin, supt. Fax 824-5200
www.wattsburg.org/
Wattsburg Area ES 500/K-4
10780 Wattsburg Rd 16509 814-824-3400
Hillary Barboni, prin. Fax 825-0302
Wattsburg Area MS 400/5-8
10774 Wattsburg Rd 16509 814-824-3400
Christopher Paris, prin. Fax 825-6337

Bethel Christian S of Erie 100/PK-12
1781 W 38th St 16508 814-868-2365
Kathe Gleason, admin. Fax 864-7674
Blessed Sacrament S 300/PK-8
2510 Greengarden Rd 16502 814-455-1387
Jane Wagner, prin. Fax 461-0247
Erie Day S 200/PK-8
1372 W 6th St 16505 814-452-4273
Dr. Karen Tyler, head sch Fax 455-5184
Erie First Christian Academy 300/PK-12
8150 Oliver Rd 16509 814-866-6979
John Richardson, supt. Fax 866-5829
Luther Memorial Academy 100/K-8
220 W 11th St 16501 814-454-0106
Susan Belott, prin. Fax 455-5832
Mother Teresa Academy 100/PK-8
1153 E 9th St 16503 814-452-4720
Jamie Brimm, prin. Fax 453-2275
Our Lady of Peace S 400/PK-8
2401 W 38th St Unit B 16506 814-838-3548
Lisa Panighetti, prin. Fax 838-9133
St. George S 500/PK-8
1612 Bryant St 16509 814-864-4821
Allison Reynolds, prin. Fax 866-8297
St. James S 200/PK-8
2602 Buffalo Rd 16510 814-899-3429
Lisa Ann Norton, prin. Fax 898-8285
St. Jude S 400/PK-8
606 Lowell Ave 16505 814-838-7676
Violet Kill, prin. Fax 838-6860
St. Luke S 400/PK-8
425 E 38th St 16504 814-825-7105
Julia Strzalka, prin. Fax 825-7169

Essington, Delaware
Interboro SD
Supt. — See Prospect Park
Tinicum S 300/K-8
91 Seneca St 19029 610-521-4450
Timothy Fanning, prin. Fax 521-5775

Etters, York, Pop. 937
West Shore SD
Supt. — See Lewisberry
Newberry ES 400/K-5
2055 Old Trail Rd 17319 717-938-2111
Travis Peck, prin.
Red Mill ES 600/K-5
700 Red Mill Rd 17319 717-938-3778
Kathleen Wagner, prin. Fax 932-5428

Evans City, Butler, Pop. 1,822
Seneca Valley SD
Supt. — See Harmony
Evans City ES 500/K-4
345 W Main St 16033 724-538-8800
Lauri Pendred, prin. Fax 538-3660
Evans City MS 500/5-6
345 W Main St 16033 724-538-8800
Mandy Toy, prin. Fax 538-3660

Everett, Bedford, Pop. 1,810
Everett Area SD 1,300/K-12
427 E South St 15537 814-652-9114
Dr. Danny Webb, supt. Fax 652-6191
www.everett.k12.pa.us
Everett Area ES 400/K-5
165 E 1st Ave 15537 814-652-9114
Justin Hillegas, prin. Fax 652-9640
Everett Area MS 300/6-8
1 Renaissance Cir 15537 814-652-9114
Laurie Criswell, prin. Fax 652-0107
Other Schools – See Breezewood

Foundations Christian Academy 50/PK-12
377 Upper Snake Spring Rd 15537 814-623-2840
Amy Will M.A., admin. Fax 623-4864

Exeter, Luzerne, Pop. 5,622
Wyoming Area SD 1,500/K-12
252 Memorial St 18643 570-655-2836
Janet Serino, supt. Fax 883-1280
www.wyomingarea.org
Wyoming Area Kindergarten Center 50/K-K
50 Penn Ave 18643 570-655-2146
Vito Quaglia, prin. Fax 602-0943
Other Schools – See West Pittston, Wyoming

Wyoming Area Catholic S 200/PK-8
1690 Wyoming Ave 18643 570-654-7982
Eileen Rishcoff, prin. Fax 654-0605

Export, Westmoreland, Pop. 912
Kiski Area SD
Supt. — See Leechburg
Kiski Area South PS 400/K-4
230 Mamont Dr 15632 724-327-4057
Brian Kutchak, prin. Fax 733-0689

Exton, Chester, Pop. 4,742
Downingtown Area SD
Supt. — See Downingtown
Lionville MS 1,100/7-8
550 W Uwchlan Ave 19341 610-524-6300
Jonathan Ross, prin. Fax 524-0152

West Chester Area SD 11,700/K-12
782 Springdale Dr 19341 484-266-1000
Dr. James R. Scanlon, supt. Fax 266-1175
www.wcasd.net
Exton ES 500/K-5
301 Hendricks Ave 19341 484-266-1400
Dr. Terri-Lynne Alston, prin. Fax 266-1499
Other Schools – See West Chester

SS. Philip & James S 500/PK-8
721 E Lincoln Hwy 19341 610-363-6530
Sr. Helen Thomas, prin. Fax 363-6495

Factoryville, Wyoming, Pop. 1,146
Lackawanna Trail SD 1,100/K-12
PO Box 85 18419 570-945-5184
Matthew Rakauskas, supt. Fax 945-3154
www.ltsd.org
Lackawanna Trail ES 600/K-6
PO Box 85 18419 570-945-5153
Brian Kearney, prin. Fax 945-3154

Fairchance, Fayette, Pop. 1,954
Albert Gallatin Area SD
Supt. — See Uniontown
Wilson ES 200/K-5
100 AL Wilson Dr 15436 724-564-7434
Krista Baker, prin. Fax 564-7423

Fairfield, Adams, Pop. 504
Fairfield Area SD 1,100/K-12
4840 Fairfield Rd 17320 717-642-8228
Karen Kugler, supt. Fax 642-2036
www.fairfieldpaschools.org/
Fairfield Area ES 400/K-4
4842 Fairfield Rd 17320 717-642-2016
Babara Richwine, prin. Fax 642-2018
Fairfield Area MS 400/5-8
4840 Fairfield Rd 17320 717-642-2005
Patricia Weber, prin. Fax 642-2030

Fairless Hills, Bucks, Pop. 8,316
Bristol Township SD
Supt. — See Levittown
Armstrong MS 500/6-8
475 Wistar Rd 19030 215-945-4940
Edward Dayton, prin. Fax 945-1664

Pennsbury SD
Supt. — See Fallsington
Oxford Valley ES 400/K-5
430 Trenton Rd 19030 215-949-6808
Donna Minnigh, prin. Fax 949-6810

Calvary Christian S 200/PK-8
676 Lincoln Hwy 19030 215-736-2391
Childrens House of Bucks County 100/PK-6
840 Trenton Rd 19030 215-943-3656
Lauren Fairfield, head sch Fax 946-3088
Pen Ryn S 200/PK-8
235 S Olds Blvd 19030 215-547-1800

Fairview, Erie, Pop. 2,337
Fairview SD 1,600/K-12
7466 McCray Rd 16415 814-474-2600
Erik Kincade, supt. Fax 474-5497
www.fairviewschools.org
Fairview ES 600/K-4
5145 Avonia Rd 16415 814-474-3123
Dr. Ben Horn, prin. Fax 474-2719
Fairview MS 500/5-8
4967 Avonia Rd 16415 814-474-2600
Steve Ferringer, prin. Fax 474-1640

Millcreek Township SD
Supt. — See Erie
Asbury ES 600/PK-5
5875 Sterrettania Rd 16415 814-836-6100
Donald Stark, prin. Fax 836-6110
Walnut Creek MS 500/PK-PK, 6-
5901 Sterrettania Rd 16415 814-835-5700
Marcie Morgan, prin. Fax 835-5720

Leadership Christian Academy 100/PK-8
5900 Sterrettania Rd 16415 814-833-0286
Rev. Diane Price, prin. Fax 314-0071

Fallsington, Bucks
Pennsbury SD 10,200/K-12
134 Yardley Ave 19054 215-428-4100
Dr. William Gretzula, supt. Fax 295-8912
www.pennsbury.k12.pa.us
Fallsington ES 200/K-5
134 Yardley Ave 19054 215-428-4170
Brian Shaffer, prin. Fax 428-5210
Other Schools – See Fairless Hills, Levittown, Morrisville, Yardley

Farmington, Fayette, Pop. 763
Uniontown Area SD
Supt. — See Uniontown
Wharton ES 200/K-5
136 Elliotsville Rd 15437 724-329-5510
Tracy Holesapple, prin. Fax 329-5349

Farrell, Mercer, Pop. 4,855
Farrell Area SD 800/K-12
1600 Roemer Blvd 16121 724-346-6585
Dr. Lora Adams-King, supt. Fax 346-0223
www.farrellareaschools.com
Farrell Area ES 400/K-6
1600 Roemer Blvd 16121 724-346-6585
Japraunika Wright, prin. Fax 509-1109

Fawn Grove, York, Pop. 449
South Eastern SD 2,800/PK-12
377 Main St 17321 717-382-4843
Jeffrey D. Hughes, supt. Fax 382-4769
www.sesdweb.net/
Fawn Area ES 300/K-4
504 Main St 17321 717-382-4220
Jennifer Herman, prin. Fax 382-1326
South Eastern IS 500/5-6
417 Main St 17321 717-382-4851
Jon Horton, prin. Fax 382-4786
South Eastern MS 400/7-8
375 Main St 17321 717-382-4851
Jon Horton, prin. Fax 382-9033
Other Schools – See Delta, Stewartstown

Fayetteville, Franklin, Pop. 3,069
Chambersburg Area SD
Supt. — See Chambersburg
Fayetteville ES 500/K-5
8 E Main St 17222 717-352-2774
Drew Nelson, prin. Fax 352-4109

Feasterville, Bucks, Pop. 3,026
Neshaminy SD
Supt. — See Langhorne
Ferderbar ES, 300 Heights Ln 19053 600/K-4
Judy Brown, prin. 215-809-6370
Poquessing MS 600/5-8
300 Heights Ln 19053 215-809-6210
Joann Holland, prin.

Finleyville, Washington, Pop. 453
Ringgold SD
Supt. — See New Eagle
Ringgold MS 700/6-8
6023 State Route 88 15332 724-348-7154
Mark Alberta, prin. Fax 348-8839
Ringold ES North 500/K-5
3685 Finleyville Elrama Rd 15332 724-348-7205
Ross Ference, prin. Fax 348-8839

Fishertown, Bedford
Chestnut Ridge SD 1,300/PK-12
3281 Valley Rd 15539 814-839-4195
Mark J. Kudlawiec, supt. Fax 839-2088
www.crsd.k12.pa.us
Chestnut Ridge MS 400/3-7
3281 Valley Rd 15539 814-839-4195
George Knisely, prin. Fax 839-9137
Other Schools – See New Paris

Fleetwood, Berks, Pop. 4,046
Fleetwood Area SD 2,600/K-12
801 N Richmond St 19522 610-944-9598
Dr. Greg Miller, supt. Fax 944-9408
www.fleetwoodasd.org
Fleetwood Area MS 800/5-8
407 N Richmond St 19522 610-944-7634
Gangi Cucciuffo, prin. Fax 944-5307
Richmond ES 200/K-4
14432 Kutztown Rd 19522 610-944-8279
Michelle Jackson, prin. Fax 944-8342
Willow Creek ES 500/K-4
605 Crisscross Rd 19522 610-944-8404
Courtney Stambaugh, prin. Fax 944-5341
Other Schools – See Blandon

Flinton, Cambria
Glendale SD 800/K-12
1466 Beaver Valley Rd 16640 814-687-3402
Edward DiSabato, supt. Fax 687-3341
www.gsd1.org
Glendale ES 400/K-6
1500 Beaver Valley Rd 16640 814-687-4263
Kate Bacher, prin. Fax 687-4083

Flourtown, Montgomery, Pop. 4,474
Springfield Township SD
Supt. — See Oreland
Springfield Twp ES - Erdenheim Campus 700/2-5
500 Haws Ln 19031 215-233-6085
Andre' McLaurin, prin. Fax 233-6094

St. Genevieve S 300/K-8
1237 Bethlehem Pike 19031 215-836-5644
Sr. Theresa Maugle, prin. Fax 836-0159

Folcroft, Delaware, Pop. 6,473
Southeast Delco SD 4,100/K-12
1560 Delmar Dr 19032 610-522-4300
Dr. Stephen D. Butz, supt. Fax 461-4874
www.sedelco.org
Delcroft S 600/1-8
799 School Ln 19032 610-522-4360
Stacey Ray, prin. Fax 534-3717
Other Schools – See Collingdale, Glenolden, Sharon Hill

Folsom, Delaware, Pop. 8,224
Ridley SD 5,500/K-12
901 Morton Ave 19033 610-534-1900
Lee Ann Wentzel, supt. Fax 534-2335
www.ridleysd.org/
Edgewood ES 300/K-5
525 8th Ave 19033 610-534-1900
Dr. Susan Kulp, prin. Fax 328-1840
Other Schools – See Eddystone, Morton, Ridley Park, Swarthmore, Woodlyn

Ford City, Armstrong, Pop. 2,961
Armstrong SD
Supt. — See Kittanning
Lenape ES 800/K-6
2300 Center Ave 16226 724-763-5299
Paula Kijowski, prin. Fax 763-2552

Divine Redeemer S 200/PK-6
726 4th Ave 16226 724-763-3761
Mark Talarico, prin. Fax 763-4112

Forest City, Susquehanna, Pop. 1,887
Forest City Regional SD 800/PK-12
100 Susquehanna St 18421 570-785-2400
Dr. Jessica Aquilina, supt. Fax 785-9557
www.fcrsd.org
Forest City Regional ES 400/PK-6
100 Susquehanna St 18421 570-785-2483
Brian Kelly, prin. Fax 785-2354

Fort Washington, Montgomery, Pop. 5,372
Upper Dublin SD
Supt. — See Maple Glen
Fort Washington ES 500/K-5
1010 Fort Washington Ave 19034 215-643-8961
Shawn McAleer, prin. Fax 643-8967

Germantown Academy 1,100/PK-12
340 Morris Rd 19034 215-646-3300
Rich Schellhas, head sch Fax 646-1216
Open Door Christian Academy 200/PK-8
1260 Fort Washington Ave 19034 215-542-9795
Tarah Ferrier, prin. Fax 646-6822

Forty Fort, Luzerne, Pop. 4,182
Wyoming Valley West SD
Supt. — See Kingston
Dana Street ES 600/K-5
50 Dana St 18704 570-283-0591
David Bond, prin. Fax 283-1802

Wyoming Seminary Lower S 400/PK-8
1560 Wyoming Ave 18704 570-718-6600
Kevin Rea, pres. Fax 718-6649

Foxburg, Clarion, Pop. 183
Allegheny-Clarion Valley SD 700/K-12
PO Box 100 16036 724-659-5820
David McDeavitt, supt. Fax 659-2963
www.acvsd.org/
Allegheny-Clarion Valley ES 300/K-6
PO Box 347 16036 724-659-3555
Lori Sherman, prin. Fax 659-2963

Franklin, Venango, Pop. 6,385
Franklin Area SD 1,900/K-12
702 Liberty St 16323 814-432-8917
Dr. Pamela Dye, supt. Fax 437-5754
www.fasd.k12.pa.us/
Central ES 400/K-6
1276 Otter St 16323 814-432-8419
Gary Canfora, prin. Fax 437-7819
Sandycreek ES 300/K-6
297 Pone Ln 16323 814-432-3819
George Forster, prin. Fax 437-7924
Other Schools – See Harrisville

Valley Grove SD 900/K-12
429 Wiley Ave 16323 814-432-4919
Kevin Briggs, supt. Fax 437-1243
www.vgsd.org
Valley Grove ES 500/K-6
389 Sugarcreek Dr 16323 814-432-3861
Jacob Saullo, prin. Fax 432-5223

St. Patrick S 100/PK-8
952 Buffalo St 16323 814-432-8689
Carol Long, prin. Fax 437-6538

Frederick, Montgomery, Pop. 397
Boyertown Area SD
Supt. — See Boyertown
New Hanover-Upper Frederick ES 800/K-6
2547 Big Rd 19435 610-754-9580
Brian Rohn, prin. Fax 754-8349

Fredericksburg, Lebanon, Pop. 1,345
Northern Lebanon SD
Supt. — See Jonestown
Fredericksburg ES 200/1-5
119 E Walnut St 17026 717-865-4107
Trevor Saylor, prin. Fax 865-0807
Northern Lebanon MS 400/6-8
PO Box 100 17026 717-865-2117
Bradly Reist, prin. Fax 865-5835

Fredericktown, Washington, Pop. 397
Bethlehem-Center SD 1,300/K-12
194 Crawford Rd 15333 724-267-4910
Thelma Szarell, supt. Fax 267-4904
www.bcasd.net
Bethlehem-Center ES 500/K-5
194 Crawford Rd 15333 724-267-4922
Joel Kirsch, prin. Fax 267-4905
Bethlehem-Center MS 300/6-8
136 Crawford Rd 15333 724-267-4935
Amanda Kinneer, prin. Fax 267-4937

Freedom, Beaver, Pop. 1,529
Ambridge Area SD
Supt. — See Ambridge
Ambridge Area JHS 400/7-8
401 1st St 15042 724-266-2833
Shaun Cooke, prin. Fax 869-5321
Economy ES 600/PK-6
1000 1st St 15042 724-266-2833
Aphrodite Galitsis, prin. Fax 869-3490

Freedom Area SD 1,200/K-12
1702 School St 15042 724-775-5464
Dr. Jeffrey Fuller, supt. Fax 775-7434
www.freedomareaschools.org
Freedom Area ES 500/K-4
1700 School St 15042 724-775-1122
Richard Edder, prin.
Freedom Area MS 200/5-8
1702 School St 15042 724-775-7641
Ryan Smith, prin. Fax 775-7748

Freeland, Luzerne, Pop. 3,500
Hazleton Area SD
Supt. — See Hazle Township
Freeland S 1,000/K-8
400 Alvin St 18224 570-459-3221
Joseph Barletta, prin. Fax 636-1043

Freemansburg, Northampton, Pop. 2,571
Bethlehem Area SD
Supt. — See Bethlehem
Freemansburg ES 400/K-5
501 Monroe St 18017 610-866-6681
Michael Alogna, prin. Fax 807-5988

Freeport, Armstrong, Pop. 1,775
Freeport Area SD
Supt. — See Sarver
South Buffalo ES 300/K-5
562 Freeport Rd 16229 724-295-9510
Jeffrey Lesko, prin. Fax 295-4860

Friedens, Somerset, Pop. 1,520
Shanksville-Stonycreek SD 300/PK-12
1325 Corner Stone Rd 15541 814-267-6499
Samuel Romesberg, supt. Fax 267-4372
www.sssd.com
Other Schools – See Shanksville

Friedensburg, Schuylkill, Pop. 852
Blue Mountain SD
Supt. — See Orwigsburg
Blue Mountain ES West 400/K-3
1383 Long Run Rd 17933 570-739-4461
Kristin Frederick, prin. Fax 739-4822

Friendsville, Susquehanna, Pop. 111
Montrose Area SD
Supt. — See Montrose
Choconut Valley ES 300/K-6
4458 Stanley Lake Rd 18818 570-278-7300
Christopher McComb, prin. Fax 553-2738

Furlong, Bucks
Central Bucks SD
Supt. — See Doylestown
Bridge Valley ES 900/K-6
2280 Sugar Bottom Rd 18925 267-893-3700
Kevin Cochran, prin. Fax 893-5825

Galeton, Potter, Pop. 1,134
Galeton Area SD 400/PK-12
27 Bridge St 16922 814-435-6571
Alanna Huck, supt. Fax 435-6981
gasd.net
Galeton Area S 400/PK-12
27 Bridge St 16922 814-435-6571
Alanna Huck, supt. Fax 435-6981

Gallitzin, Cambria, Pop. 1,656
Penn Cambria SD
Supt. — See Cresson
Penn Cambria MS 500/5-8
401 Division St 16641 814-886-4181
Jeff Baird, prin. Fax 886-9308

Gap, Lancaster, Pop. 1,905
Pequea Valley SD
Supt. — See Kinzers
Salisbury ES 300/K-6
422 School Lane Rd 17527 717-442-8268
Sheri McGowan, prin. Fax 442-9781

Garnet Valley, Delaware
Garnet Valley SD
Supt. — See Glen Mills
Bethel Springs ES 600/K-5
3280 Foulk Rd, 610-579-3000
Steven Piasecki, prin.

Gettysburg, Adams, Pop. 7,466
Gettysburg Area SD 3,000/K-12
900 Biglerville Rd 17325 717-334-6254
Dr. Jason Perrin, supt. Fax 334-5220
www.gettysburg.k12.pa.us
Gettysburg Area MS 700/6-8
37 Lefever St 17325 717-334-6254
Nancy Herb, prin. Fax 334-6999
Gettys ES 400/K-5
898 Biglerville Rd 17325 717-334-6254
Donna Harrison, prin. Fax 337-4434
Lincoln ES 400/K-5
98 Lefever St 17325 717-334-6254
Dr. Matthew McFarland, prin. Fax 337-4437
Other Schools – See Cashtown

Adams County Christian Academy 50/PK-12
1865 Biglerville Rd 17325 717-334-9177
Rhonda Fertich, prin. Fax 334-7691
Freedom Christian S 100/PK-12
3185 York Rd 17325 717-624-3884
Karen Trout, prin. Fax 624-1562
Gettysburg SDA S 50/1-8
1493 Biglerville Rd 17325 717-338-0131
St. Francis Xavier S 200/K-8
465 Table Rock Rd 17325 717-334-4221
Rebecca Sieg, prin. Fax 334-8883

Gibsonia, Allegheny, Pop. 2,710
Hampton Township SD
Supt. — See Allison Park
Poff ES 300/K-5
2990 Haberlein Rd 15044 412-492-6335
Colleen Hannagan, prin. Fax 443-4429

Pine-Richland SD 4,600/K-12
702 Warrendale Rd 15044 724-625-7773
Dr. Brian Miller, supt. Fax 625-1490
www.pinerichland.org
Eden Hall Upper ES 1,100/4-6
3900 Bakerstown Rd 15044 724-443-1450
Steven Smith, prin. Fax 443-1451
Hance ES 400/K-3
5518 Molnar Dr 15044 724-443-1541
Dr. John Mayberry, prin. Fax 443-1290

Pine-Richland MS 800/7-8
100 Logan Rd 15044 724-625-3111
Dr. David Kristofic, prin. Fax 625-3144
Richland ES 500/K-3
3811 Bakerstown Rd 15044 724-443-1558
Gene Nicastro, prin. Fax 443-2180
Other Schools – See Wexford

Aquinas Academy 300/K-12
2308 W Hardies Rd 15044 724-444-0722
Leslie Mitros, hdmstr. Fax 444-0750

Gilbertsville, Montgomery, Pop. 4,774
Boyertown Area SD
Supt. — See Boyertown
Gilbertsville ES 800/K-6
36 Congo Rd 19525 610-369-7485
Stephanie Landis, prin. Fax 369-7686

Girard, Erie, Pop. 3,073
Girard SD 1,800/PK-12
1203 Lake St 16417 814-774-5666
Donna Miller, supt. Fax 774-4220
www.girardsd.org
Rice Avenue MS 500/5-8
1100 Rice Ave 16417 814-774-5604
David Koma, prin. Fax 774-5259
Other Schools – See Lake City

Gladwyne, Montgomery, Pop. 4,000
Lower Merion SD
Supt. — See Ardmore
Gladwyne ES 700/K-5
230 Righters Mill Rd 19035 610-645-1440
Veronica Ellers, prin. Fax 649-3359

Gladwyne Montessori 300/PK-6
920 Youngs Ford Rd 19035 610-649-1761
Carrie Kries, head sch Fax 649-7978

Glen Mills, Delaware
Garnet Valley SD, 80 Station Rd 19342 4,800/K-12
Dr. Marc Bertrando, supt. 610-579-7300
www.garnetvalleyschools.com
Concord ES, 114 Station Rd 19342 700/K-2
Vanessa Stroup, prin. 610-579-6100
Garnet Valley ES 800/3-5
599 Smithbridge Rd 19342 610-579-4150
Dr. Jason Kotch, prin. Fax 579-4139
Garnet Valley MS 1,200/6-8
601 Smithbridge Rd 19342 610-579-5100
Lisa Stenz, prin.
Other Schools – See Garnet Valley

St. Thomas the Apostle S 400/K-8
430 Valleybrook Rd 19342 610-459-8134
John Keeley, prin. Fax 459-8120

Glenmoore, Chester
Downingtown Area SD
Supt. — See Downingtown
Springton Manor ES 400/K-5
400 Fairview Rd 19343 610-384-9030
Diane Boff, prin. Fax 466-0914

Glenolden, Delaware, Pop. 6,991
Interboro SD
Supt. — See Prospect Park
Glenolden S 600/K-8
198 S MacDade Blvd 19036 610-237-6430
Rachel Lambert, prin. Fax 586-1738

Southeast Delco SD
Supt. — See Folcroft
Darby Township S 600/1-8
801 W Ashland Ave 19036 610-522-4375
Dr. Ashwina Mosakowski, prin. Fax 522-9065
Kindergarten Center 400/K-K
1 School Ln 19036 610-522-4365
Colleen Burke, prin. Fax 522-1686

Upper Darby SD
Supt. — See Drexel Hill
Senkow ES, 15 Lamont Ave 19036 300/1-5
Dr. Tony Watson, prin. 610-957-5114

Glen Rock, York, Pop. 1,997
Southern York County SD 3,100/K-12
PO Box 128 17327 717-235-4811
Dr. Sandra Lemmon, supt. Fax 235-0863
www.syc.k12.pa.us
Friendship ES 500/K-6
PO Box 128 17327 717-235-4811
Beth Koontz, prin. Fax 235-0302
Shrewsbury ES 500/K-6
PO Box 128 17327 717-235-4811
Mary Dankosky, prin. Fax 227-2294
Southern ES 600/K-6
PO Box 128 17327 717-235-4811
James Hollinger, prin. Fax 235-8790
Southern MS 500/7-8
PO Box 128 17327 717-235-4811
Dr. Len Rappart, prin. Fax 227-9681

Glenshaw, Allegheny, Pop. 8,914
Shaler Area SD 4,600/K-12
1800 Mount Royal Blvd 15116 412-492-1200
Sean Aiken, supt. Fax 492-1293
www.sasd.k12.pa.us
Jeffery PS 200/K-3
201 Wetzel Rd 15116 412-492-1200
JoAnne Townsend, prin. Fax 492-1287
Shaler Area ES 1,000/4-6
700 Scott Ave 15116 412-492-1200
Ian Miller, prin. Fax 492-1317
Shaler Area MS 700/7-8
1810 Mount Royal Blvd 15116 412-492-1200
Martin Martynuska, prin. Fax 492-1237
Other Schools – See Allison Park, Pittsburgh

Montessori Centre Academy 100/PK-6
1014 William Flynn Hwy 15116 412-486-6239
St. Bonaventure S 300/PK-8
2001 Mount Royal Blvd Ste 2 15116 412-486-2608
Jacqueline Easley, prin. Fax 486-4583
St. Mary S 300/PK-8
2510 Middle Rd 15116 412-486-7611
Antoinette Pilarski, prin. Fax 487-9509

Glenside, Montgomery, Pop. 8,249
Abington SD
Supt. — See Abington
Copper Beech ES 1,100/K-6
825 N Easton Rd 19038 215-881-2000
Dr. Stephanie Viola, prin. Fax 884-9816

Cheltenham SD
Supt. — See Elkins Park
Glenside ES 500/K-4
400 Harrison Ave 19038 215-881-6440
Fax 886-6797

St. Joseph the Protector S 300/K-8
2336 Fairhill Ave 19038 215-884-0843
Dawn Perry, prin. Fax 884-4607

Glenville, York
South Western SD
Supt. — See Hanover
Manheim ES 300/K-5
5778 Blooming Grove Rd 17329 717-229-2930
Mary Kay Kelly, prin. Fax 227-9059

Grantville, Dauphin
Lower Dauphin SD
Supt. — See Hummelstown
East Hanover ES 400/K-5
2673 Sand Beach Rd 17028 717-469-2686
Gary Messinger, prin. Fax 469-0539

Greencastle, Franklin, Pop. 3,946
Greencastle-Antrim SD 3,000/K-12
500 Leitersburg St 17225 717-597-3226
Dr. Kendra Trail, supt. Fax 597-2180
www.gcasd.org
Greencastle-Antrim ES 700/3-5
500 Leitersburg St 17225 717-597-3226
Chad Stover, prin. Fax 597-3652
Greencastle-Antrim MS 700/6-8
370 S Ridge Ave 17225 717-597-3226
Mark Herman, prin. Fax 597-6468
Greencastle-Antrim PS 700/K-2
504 Leitersburg St 17225 717-597-3226
Angela Singer, prin. Fax 597-1306

Shady Grove Mennonite S 200/1-10
1442 Buchanan Trl E 17225 717-597-0843

Green Lane, Montgomery, Pop. 508
Upper Perkiomen SD
Supt. — See Pennsburg
Marlborough ES 700/K-5
1450 Gravel Pike 18054 215-541-7299
Lesley Motruk, prin. Fax 541-7286

Greensboro, Greene, Pop. 254
Southeastern Greene SD 600/K-12
1000 Mapletown Rd 15338 724-943-3630
Rich Pekar, supt. Fax 943-3052
www.segsd.org
Other Schools – See Bobtown

Greensburg, Westmoreland, Pop. 14,523
Greater Latrobe SD
Supt. — See Latrobe
Mountain View ES 700/K-6
1010 Mountain View Dr 15601 724-834-7399
Becki Pellis, prin. Fax 834-5338

Greensburg Salem SD 2,900/K-12
1 Academy Hill Pl 15601 724-832-2901
Dr. Eileen Amato, supt. Fax 832-2968
www.greensburgsalem.org
Greensburg Salem MS 600/6-8
301 N Main St 15601 724-832-2930
Adam Jones, prin. Fax 832-2937
Hutchinson ES 700/K-5
810 Welty St 15601 724-832-2885
Kevin Bringe, prin. Fax 832-2874
Nicely ES 400/K-5
55 McLaughlin Dr 15601 724-832-2865
Chris Thomas, prin. Fax 832-2860
Other Schools – See New Alexandria

Hempfield Area SD 5,900/K-12
4347 State Route 136 15601 724-834-2590
Dr. Tammy S. Wolicki, supt. Fax 850-2298
www.hasdpa.net
Ft. Allen ES 600/K-5
560 Baltzer Meyer Pike 15601 724-850-2501
Marty Rovedatti-Jackson, prin. Fax 850-2502
Harrold MS 400/6-8
1368 Middletown Rd 15601 724-850-2301
Jason Lochner, prin. Fax 850-2302
Maxwell ES 400/K-5
1101 Old Salem Rd 15601 724-850-3500
Alene Mancini, prin. Fax 850-3501
Wendover MS 500/6-8
425 Wendover Jr High Rd 15601 724-838-4070
Deanna Mikesic, prin. Fax 838-4071
West Point ES 400/K-5
533 Saint Andrews Dr 15601 724-850-2270
Audrey Dell, prin. Fax 850-2271
Other Schools – See Irwin, New Stanton

Aquinas Academy 200/PK-6
340 N Main St 15601 724-834-7940
Joseph Rice, prin. Fax 836-0497

Seton Montessori S 50/PK-K
294 Frye Farm Rd 15601 724-837-8500
Linda Fidazzo, prin. Fax 836-0772
Westmoreland Christian Academy 100/PK-12
538 Rugh St 15601 724-853-8308
Jordan Tomson, prin. Fax 836-7472

Greenville, Mercer, Pop. 5,850
Greenville Area SD 1,400/K-12
9 Donation Rd 16125 724-588-2500
Mark Ferrara, supt. Fax 588-5024
www.greenville.k12.pa.us
East ES 300/4-6
71 Columbia Ave 16125 724-588-1173
Matt Dieter, prin. Fax 588-1319
Hempfield ES 400/K-3
60 Fredonia Rd 16125 724-588-1018
Matt Dieter, prin. Fax 588-5036

Reynolds SD 1,100/PK-12
531 Reynolds Rd 16125 724-646-5501
John Sibeto, supt. Fax 646-5505
www.reynolds.k12.pa.us
Reynolds ES 600/PK-6
1609 Brentwood Dr 16125 724-646-5601
Amy Leczner, prin. Fax 646-5605

St. Michael S 100/PK-8
80 N High St 16125 724-588-7050
Nancy Kremm, prin. Fax 588-7056

Grove City, Mercer, Pop. 8,236
Grove City Area SD 2,100/K-12
511 Highland Ave 16127 724-458-6733
Jeffrey Finch, supt. Fax 458-5868
www.grovecity.k12.pa.us
Grove City Area MS 500/6-8
100 Middle School Dr 16127 724-458-8040
Larry Connelly, prin. Fax 450-0780
Highland PS 300/K-1
611 Highland Ave 16127 724-458-8101
Tammi Martin, prin. Fax 458-4399
Hillview IS 600/2-5
482 E Main Street Ext 16127 724-458-7570
Tammi Martin, prin. Fax 458-0444

Grove City Christian Academy 100/PK-8
301 N Madison Ave 16127 724-458-5253

Guys Mills, Crawford, Pop. 121

Faith Builders Christian S 100/1-12
28527 Guys Mills Rd 16327 814-789-2303
Gerald Miller, admin. Fax 789-3396

Hadley, Mercer
Commodore Perry SD 500/K-12
3002 Perry Hwy 16130 724-253-3255
Dr. Kimberly Zippie, supt. Fax 253-3467
www.cpanthers.org
Perry ES 300/K-6
3002 Perry Hwy 16130 724-253-2025
Michelle Young, prin. Fax 253-3467

Halifax, Dauphin, Pop. 814
Halifax Area SD 1,100/PK-12
3940 Peters Mountain Rd 17032 717-896-3416
Dr. Michele Orner, supt. Fax 896-3976
www.hasd.us
Enders-Fisherville ES 200/PK-1
791 Enders Rd 17032 717-896-3416
Carla Sauer, prin. Fax 362-6358
Halifax Area ES 300/2-5
3940 Peters Mountain Rd 17032 717-896-3416
Carla Sauer, prin. Fax 896-8337
Halifax Area MS 300/6-8
3940 Peters Mountain Rd 17032 717-896-3416
Rick Ansel, prin. Fax 896-3976

Hamburg, Berks, Pop. 4,259
Hamburg Area SD 2,300/K-12
Windsor St 19526 610-562-2241
Dr. Richard Mextorf, supt. Fax 562-2634
www.hasdhawks.org
Hamburg Area MS 600/6-8
Windsor St 19526 610-562-3990
Shawn Gravish, prin. Fax 562-1425
Tilden ES 600/K-5
524 W State St 19526 610-562-0291
Lacie Cacciuffo, prin. Fax 562-4451
Other Schools – See Shoemakersville

Blue Mountain SDA ES 50/PK-8
45 Woodland Ter 19526 610-562-5062
Mina Gravatt, prin. Fax 660-3386

Hanover, York, Pop. 15,077
Conewago Valley SD
Supt. — See New Oxford
Conewago Township ES 500/K-3
1189 W Elm Ave 17331 717-624-2157
Dr. Lawrence Sanders, prin. Fax 632-6553

Hanover Public SD 1,700/K-12
403 Moul Ave 17331 717-637-9000
Dr. John Scola, supt. Fax 630-4617
www.hanoverpublic.org
Clearview ES 300/K-4
801 Randolph St 17331 717-637-9000
Jay Czap, prin. Fax 630-4637
Hanover MS 500/5-8
300 Keagy Ave 17331 717-637-9000
Mark Hershner, prin. Fax 630-4632
Hanover Street ES 300/K-4
101 E Hanover St 17331 717-637-9000
Dr. Pamela Smith, prin. Fax 630-4636
Washington ES 200/K-4
301 Moul Ave 17331 717-637-9000
Dr. Thomas Krout, prin. Fax 630-4635

South Western SD 4,100/K-12
225 Bowman Rd 17331 717-632-2500
Dr. Jay Burkhart, supt. Fax 632-7993
www.swsd.k12.pa.us/
Baresville ES 500/K-5
135 Sanford Ave 17331 717-633-4870
Eric Klansek, prin. Fax 637-4241
Markle IS 1,000/6-8
225 Bowman Rd Ste 1 17331 717-633-4840
Jeffrey Smale, prin. Fax 633-7073
Park Hills ES 500/K-5
137 W Granger St 17331 717-633-4880
Eric Seibel, prin. Fax 633-1262
West Manheim ES 600/K-5
2000 Baltimore Pike 17331 717-633-4890
Brian Cromer, prin. Fax 637-2011
Other Schools – See Glenville

St. Joseph S 100/K-8
5125 Grandview Rd 17331 717-632-0118
Susan Mummert, prin. Fax 632-0030
St. Teresa of Calcutta S 300/K-8
55 Basilica Dr 17331 717-632-8715
Patricia Foltz, prin. Fax 632-6596

Hanover Twp, Lehigh
Hanover Area SD 2,000/K-12
1600 Sans Souci Pkwy 18706 570-831-2300
William Jones, supt. Fax 831-2322
www.hanoverarea.org
Hanover Area Memorial ES 500/4-6
80 W Saint Marys Rd 18706 570-822-5102
Ann Marie Mantione, prin. Fax 823-3096
Hanover Green ES 300/K-1
561 Main Rd 18706 570-824-3941
Dr. Terry Schnee, prin. Fax 408-1150
Lee Park ES 300/2-3
99 Lee Park Ave 18706 570-824-4741
Dr. Terry Schnee, prin. Fax 824-5714

Harborcreek, Erie
Harbor Creek SD 2,000/K-12
6375 Buffalo Rd 16421 814-897-2100
Kelly Hess, supt. Fax 897-2142
www.hcsd.iu5.org
Harbor Creek JHS 300/7-8
6375 Buffalo Rd 16421 814-897-2100
Andrew Krahe, prin. Fax 897-2121
Other Schools – See Erie

Harleysville, Montgomery, Pop. 9,178
North Penn SD
Supt. — See Lansdale
Nash ES 400/K-6
1560 Liberty Bell Dr 19438 215-368-2407
Jonathan Winkle, prin. Fax 368-7804

Souderton Area SD
Supt. — See Souderton
Indian Valley MS 800/6-8
130 Maple Ave 19438 215-256-8896
Dr. Dale Burkhard, prin. Fax 256-1288
Oak Ridge ES 500/K-5
465 Moyer Rd 19438 215-256-6633
Thomas Ferlick, prin. Fax 256-9258
Salford Hills ES 300/K-5
2721 Barndt Rd 19438 610-287-9197
David Purnell, prin. Fax 287-4030

Harmony, Butler, Pop. 882
Seneca Valley SD 7,200/K-12
124 Seneca School Rd 16037 724-452-6040
Dr. Tracy Vitale, supt. Fax 452-6105
www.svsd.net/
Seneca Valley MS 1,200/7-8
122 Seneca School Rd 16037 724-452-6040
Robert Ceh, prin. Fax 452-0331
Other Schools – See Cranberry Township, Evans City, Zelienople

Harrisburg, Dauphin, Pop. 47,794
Central Dauphin SD 10,800/K-12
600 Rutherford Rd 17109 717-545-4703
Dr. Carol Johnson, supt. Fax 657-4999
www.cdschools.org
Central Dauphin East MS 700/6-8
628 Rutherford Rd 17109 717-545-4703
Christine Miller, prin. Fax 657-4987
Central Dauphin MS 700/6-8
4600 Locust Ln 17109 717-540-4606
Jeffrey Matzner, prin. Fax 214-5055
Chambers Hill ES 200/K-5
6450 Chambers Hill Rd 17111 717-561-1655
Carol Lopez, prin. Fax 561-4977
Lawnton ES 200/K-5
4400 Franklin St 17111 717-558-9430
Stephanie Bruno, prin. Fax 558-7780
Linglestown ES 400/K-5
1044 N Mountain Rd 17112 717-657-3211
Scott Pavusek, prin. Fax 657-9698
Linglestown MS 700/6-8
1200 N Mountain Rd 17112 717-657-3060
Mickey Termin, prin. Fax 657-0537
Mountain View ES 400/K-5
400 Gibbel Rd 17112 717-657-8585
Stanley Roesch, prin. Fax 657-9733
North Side ES 500/K-5
4520 Devonshire Rd 17109 717-657-3201
Sarah Box, prin. Fax 657-9770
Paxtang ES 200/K-5
3530 Rutherford St 17111 717-265-7920
Robert Stewart, prin. Fax 561-4992
Paxtonia ES 600/K-5
6135 Jonestown Rd 17112 717-657-3202
Julia Batdorf, prin. Fax 657-9780
Phillips ES 400/K-5
100 Oakmont Rd 17109 717-657-3203
Erika Willis, prin. Fax 657-9790
Rutherford ES 400/K-5
6500 Clearfield St 17111 717-561-1990
Deron Doi, prin. Fax 561-5004
South Side ES 600/K-5
4525 Union Deposit Rd 17111 717-657-3204
Stacey Cherny, prin. Fax 657-9757
West Hanover ES 500/K-5
7740 Manor Dr 17112 717-657-3210
Lewis Correale, prin. Fax 657-9767
Other Schools – See Dauphin, Steelton

Harrisburg City SD 4,800/K-12
1601 State St 17103 717-703-4000
Dr. Sybil Knight-Burney, supt. Fax 703-4115
www.hbgsd.k12.pa.us
Camp Curtin Academy 400/5-8
2900 N 6th St 17110 717-703-4200
Portia Slaughter, prin. Fax 703-4225
Downey S 400/K-4
1313 Monroe St 17103 717-703-1240
Travis Peck, prin. Fax 703-1245
Foose S 500/K-4
1301 Sycamore St 17104 717-703-1280
Karen Wright, prin. Fax 703-1330
Franklin S 200/K-4
1205 N 6th St 17102 717-703-1200
Will Towson, prin. Fax 703-1215
Marshall Math Science Academy 200/5-8
301 Hale Ave 17104 717-703-1400
Marisol Craig, prin. Fax 703-1420
Melrose S 400/K-4
2041 Berryhill St 17104 717-703-1440
Lisa Crum, prin. Fax 703-1455
Rowland Academy 800/5-8
1842 Derry St 17104 717-703-4500
Roma Benjamin, prin. Fax 703-4520
Scott S 500/K-4
1900 Derry St 17104 717-703-4560
Donna Cheatham, prin. Fax 703-4580

Susquehanna Township SD 2,800/K-12
2579 Interstate Dr 17110 717-657-5100
Dr. Tamara Willis Ph.D., supt. Fax 724-1851
www.hannasd.org
Holtzman ES 600/3-5
1910 Linglestown Rd 17110 717-657-5158
Jacqueline Wapinsky, prin. Fax 657-9243
Lindemuth / Anna Carter PS 600/K-2
1201 N Progress Ave 17109 717-657-5122
Andrae Martin, prin. Fax 657-5148
Susquehanna Township MS 700/6-8
801 Wood St 17109 717-657-5125
Kenneth R. Edwards, prin. Fax 657-9841

Covenant Christian Academy 200/PK-12
1982 Locust Ln 17109 717-540-9885
Harrisburg Adventist S 50/PK-8
424 N Progress Ave 17109 717-545-7300
Harrisburg Catholic ES 100/K-8
555 S 25th St 17104 717-232-2551
David Rushinski, prin. Fax 232-9661
Harrisburg Christian S 300/K-12
2000 Blue Mountain Pkwy 17112 717-545-3728
Philip G. Puleo, supt. Fax 545-3729
Hillside Adventist S 50/K-8
1301 Cumberland St 17103 717-234-7388
Holy Name of Jesus S 600/K-8
6190 Allentown Blvd 17112 717-657-1704
Sr. Rita Smith, prin. Fax 657-9135
Londonderry S 200/PK-8
1800 Bamberger Rd 17110 717-540-0543
St. Catherine LaBoure S 400/PK-8
4020 Derry St 17111 717-564-1760
Sr. MaryAnne Sweeney, prin. Fax 564-3010
St. Margaret Mary S 400/PK-8
2826 Herr St 17103 717-232-3771
Jean Fennessy, prin. Fax 232-0776
St. Stephen's Episcopal S 100/PK-8
215 N Front St 17101 717-238-8590
Ruth Graffius, head sch Fax 238-0565
Silver Academy 100/PK-8
3301 N Front St 17110 717-238-8775
Debra Freeburn, prin. Fax 238-8773

Harrison City, Westmoreland, Pop. 134
Penn-Trafford SD 4,000/K-12
PO Box 530 15636 724-744-4496
Dr. Matthew Harris, supt. Fax 744-4016
www.penntrafford.org
Other Schools – See Irwin, Jeannette, Trafford

Harrisville, Butler, Pop. 888
Franklin Area SD
Supt. — See Franklin
Victory ES 200/K-6
1819 Georgetown Rd 16038 814-786-7311
George Forster, prin. Fax 786-7889

Harveys Lake, Luzerne, Pop. 2,754
Lake-Lehman SD
Supt. — See Dallas
Lake-Noxen ES 300/K-6
135 Westpoint Ave 18618 570-639-1129
Nancy Edkins, prin. Fax 639-3288

Hatboro, Montgomery, Pop. 7,268
Hatboro-Horsham SD
Supt. — See Horsham
Blair Mill ES 400/K-5
109 Bender Rd 19040 215-420-5200
Nancy Doherty, prin. Fax 420-5252
Crooked Billet ES 200/K-5
101 Meadowbrook Ave 19040 215-420-5300
Kelli Sendel, prin. Fax 420-5350
Pennypack ES 300/K-5
130 Spring Ave 19040 215-420-5400
Dr. Amy Roslevege, prin. Fax 420-5436

Upper Moreland Township SD
Supt. — See Willow Grove
Upper Moreland IS 700/3-5
3990 Orangemans Rd 19040 215-325-1700
Michael Bair Ed.D., prin. Fax 325-1701
Upper Moreland MS 700/6-8
4000 Orangemans Rd 19040 215-674-4185
Joseph Waters Ed.D., prin. Fax 956-1906
Upper Moreland PS 700/K-2
3980 Orangemans Rd 19040 215-325-1400
Susan Smith, prin. Fax 325-1401

Hatfield, Montgomery, Pop. 3,211
North Penn SD
Supt. — See Lansdale
Hatfield ES 500/K-6
726 Forty Foot Rd 19440 215-368-1585
Dr. D'Ana Waters, prin. Fax 368-6762
Kulp ES 500/K-6
801 Cowpath Rd 19440 215-368-3061
Neil Broxtermann, prin. Fax 368-7835

Haverford, Montgomery, Pop. 6,000

Friends S Haverford 100/PK-8
851 Buck Ln 19041 610-642-2334
Michael Zimmerman, head sch Fax 642-0870
Haverford S 1,000/PK-12
450 Lancaster Ave 19041 610-642-3020
Dr. John Nagl, hdmstr. Fax 649-4898

Havertown, Delaware, Pop. 30,000
Haverford Township SD 5,800/K-12
50 E Eagle Rd 19083 610-853-5900
Dr. Maureen Reusche Ed.D., supt. Fax 853-5942
www.haverford.k12.pa.us
Chatham Park ES 600/K-5
400 Allston Rd 19083 610-853-5900
Sara Christianson, prin. Fax 853-5974
Haverford MS 1,300/6-8
1701 Darby Rd 19083 610-853-5900
Daniel Horan, prin. Fax 853-5937
Lynnewood ES 600/K-5
1400 Lawrence Rd 19083 610-853-5900
Jillian McGilvery, prin. Fax 853-5977
Manoa ES 600/K-5
201 S Manoa Rd 19083 610-853-5900
George Ramoundos, prin. Fax 853-5978
Other Schools – See Ardmore, Bryn Mawr

Cardinal John Foley S 400/PK-8
300 E Eagle Rd 19083 610-446-4608
Mary Ann DeAngelo, prin. Fax 446-5707
Sacred Heart S 200/PK-8
109 N Manoa Rd 19083 610-446-9198
Celie Magee, prin. Fax 446-4861

Hawley, Pike, Pop. 1,191
Wallenpaupack Area SD 3,400/K-12
2552 Route 6 18428 570-226-4557
Michael Silsby, supt. Fax 226-0638
www.wallenpaupack.org/
Wallenpaupack Area MS 800/6-8
139 Atlantic Ave 18428 570-226-4557
Chris Caruso, prin. Fax 251-3165
Wallenpaupack North IS 500/3-5
187 Atlantic Ave 18428 570-226-4557
Amanda Cykosky, prin. Fax 226-1976
Wallenpaupack PS 500/K-2
158 Atlantic Ave 18428 570-226-4557
Anthony Cavallaro, prin. Fax 251-3151
Other Schools – See Newfoundland

Hawthorn, Clarion, Pop. 493
Redbank Valley SD
Supt. — See New Bethlehem
Redbank Valley IS 300/3-6
1306 Truittsburg Rd 16230 814-365-5141
Cheryl McCauley, prin. Fax 365-2427

Hazleton, Luzerne, Pop. 25,114
Hazleton Area SD
Supt. — See Hazle Township
Arthur Street ES 500/K-2
424 E 9th St 18201 570-459-3221
Phil Latella, prin. Fax 454-0357
Hazleton S 1,000/3-8
700 N Wyoming St 18201 570-459-3221
Maureen DeRose, prin. Fax 501-8433
Heights Terrace S 1,200/K-8
275 Mill St 18201 570-459-3221
Daniel Diehl, prin. Fax 459-1394

Hazleton Trinity K 100/PK-K
100 N Church St 18201 570-454-8123
Jeffrey Houston, dir. Fax 454-1014
Holy Family Academy 300/PK-8
601 N Laurel St 18201 570-455-9431
Donald Bayzick, prin. Fax 455-2847
Immanuel Christian S 100/K-12
725 N Locust St 18201 570-459-1111
Kelly Knowlden, head sch Fax 459-6920

Hazle Township, Luzerne
Hazleton Area SD 10,500/PK-12
1515 W 23rd St 18202 570-459-3111
Brian Uplinger, supt. Fax 459-3118
www.hasdk12.org
Hazle Township Early Learning Center PK-2
1400 W 23rd St, 570-459-3221
Phil Latella, prin.
Maple Manor ES 3-6
1700 W 22nd St, 570-459-3221
Jeanne Conahan, prin.
Other Schools – See Drums, Freeland, Hazleton, McAdoo, Sugarloaf, West Hazleton

Hellam, York, Pop. 2,635
Eastern York SD
Supt. — See Wrightsville

Kreutz Creek ES 300/K-5
50 N Lee St 17406 717-757-9682
Robert Walker, prin. Fax 757-2087

Hellertown, Northampton, Pop. 5,840
Saucon Valley SD 2,100/K-12
2097 Polk Valley Rd 18055 610-838-7026
Dr. Craig B. Butler, supt. Fax 838-6419
www.svpanthers.org
Saucon Valley ES 800/K-4
2085 Polk Valley Rd 18055 610-838-9331
Cynthia Motter, prin. Fax 838-7473
Saucon Valley MS 600/5-8
2095 Polk Valley Rd 18055 610-838-7071
Kenneth Napaver, prin. Fax 838-7473

St. Theresa S 200/PK-8
300 Leonard St 18055 610-838-8161
Colleen Weiss, prin. Fax 838-1915

Hereford, Berks, Pop. 906
Upper Perkiomen SD
Supt. — See Pennsburg
Hereford ES 900/K-5
1043 Gravel Pike 18056 215-679-4151
Maureen Zavadel, prin. Fax 679-6355

Herminie, Westmoreland, Pop. 785
Yough SD 2,200/K-12
915 Lowber Rd 15637 724-446-7272
Dr. Janet Sardon, supt. Fax 446-5017
www.youghsd.net
Good ES 300/K-4
1464 Herminie W Newton Rd 15637 724-446-5503
Amy Larcinese, prin. Fax 446-5509
Other Schools – See Ruffs Dale, West Newton

Hermitage, Mercer, Pop. 16,014
Hermitage SD 2,000/K-12
411 N Hermitage Rd 16148 724-981-8750
Dr. Daniel Bell, supt. Fax 981-5080
www.hermitage.k12.pa.us
Artman ES 600/K-3
343 N Hermitage Rd 16148 724-981-8750
Amy Wanchisn, prin. Fax 981-5080
Delahunty MS 300/6-7
419 N Hermitage Rd 16148 724-981-8750
Eric Trosch, prin. Fax 981-5080
Ionta ES 300/4-5
375 N Hermitage Rd 16148 724-981-8750
Eric Trosch, prin. Fax 981-5080

Kennedy Catholic MS 100/6-8
2120 Shenango Valley Fwy 16148 724-346-5531
William Lyon, hdmstr. Fax 346-3011
St. John Paul II ES 200/PK-5
2335 Highland Rd 16148 724-342-2205
Heidi Patterson, prin. Fax 704-7397

Herndon, Northumberland, Pop. 322
Line Mountain SD 1,200/K-12
185 Line Mountain Rd 17830 570-758-2640
David Campbell, supt. Fax 758-2842
www.linemountain.com
Line Mountain MS 400/5-8
187 Line Mountain Rd 17830 570-758-2011
Jeffrey Lagerman, prin.
Other Schools – See Trevorton

Hershey, Dauphin, Pop. 13,934
Derry Township SD 3,500/K-12
PO Box 898 17033 717-534-2501
Joseph McFarland, supt. Fax 533-4357
www.hershey.k12.pa.us
Hershey ECC 400/K-1
PO Box 898 17033 717-531-2211
Jackie Castleman, prin. Fax 531-2351
Hershey IS 600/4-5
PO Box 898 17033 717-531-2277
Jackie Castleman, prin. Fax 508-2266
Hershey MS 800/6-8
PO Box 898 17033 717-531-2222
Erick Valentin, prin. Fax 531-2245
Hershey PS 500/2-3
PO Box 898 17033 717-531-2277
Jackie Castleman, prin. Fax 508-2266

Lower Dauphin SD
Supt. — See Hummelstown
South Hanover ES 400/K-5
15 W 3rd St 17033 717-566-2564
Steven Schoessler, prin. Fax 566-1157

Hershey S 1,800/PK-12
PO Box 830 17033 717-520-2000
Peter Gurt, pres. Fax 520-2117
St. Joan of Arc S 300/PK-8
329 W Areba Ave 17033 717-533-2854
Sr. Eileen McGowan, prin. Fax 534-0755

Hilltown, Bucks

St. Agnes-Sacred Heart MS 100/4-8
PO Box 31 18927 215-822-9174
Margaret Graham, prin. Fax 822-7942

Holland, Bucks, Pop. 5,300
Council Rock SD
Supt. — See Newtown
Hillcrest ES 500/K-6
420 E Holland Rd 18966 215-944-1600
Nakia Jones-Tate, prin. Fax 944-1692
Holland ES 300/K-6
597 Beverly Rd 18966 215-944-1500
Joe MacClay, prin. Fax 944-1597
Holland MS 500/7-8
400 E Holland Rd 18966 215-944-2700
Richard Hollahan, prin. Fax 944-2789

Rolling Hills ES 400/K-6
340 Middle Holland Rd 18966 215-944-2000
Sam Smith, prin. Fax 944-2097

St. Katherine Drexel Regional S 300/K-8
1053 Holland Rd 18966 215-357-4720
Laura Clark, prin. Fax 355-9526

Hollidaysburg, Blair, Pop. 5,745
Hollidaysburg Area SD 3,400/K-12
405 Clark St 16648 814-696-4454
Dr. Robert Gildea, supt. Fax 695-2315
www.tigerwires.com
Frankstown ES 700/K-6
2459 Reservoir Rd 16648 814-695-4961
Frank Filkosky, prin. Fax 695-4833
Longer ES 500/K-6
1320 Union St 16648 814-695-4431
Timothy Gildea, prin. Fax 695-5091
Other Schools – See Duncansville

Holy Trinity Catholic S 200/PK-4
321 Spruce St 16648 814-695-6112
Elaine Spencer, prin. Fax 696-8960
Penn-Mont Academy 100/K-6
131 Holliday Hills Dr 16648 814-696-8801

Hollsopple, Somerset

Johnstown Christian S 200/PK-12
125 Christian School Rd 15935 814-288-2588
Cathy Sporu, prin. Fax 288-1447

Holtwood, Lancaster
Penn Manor SD
Supt. — See Lancaster
Martic ES 300/K-6
266 Martic Heights Dr 17532 717-284-4128
Dr. Jennifer Sugra, prin. Fax 284-5954

Home, Indiana, Pop. 1,345
Marion Center Area SD
Supt. — See Marion Center
Rayne ES 300/PK-6
2535 Route 119 Hwy N 15747 724-463-8615
Susan DeVaughn, prin.

Homer City, Indiana, Pop. 1,691
Homer-Center SD 900/K-12
65 Wildcat Ln 15748 724-479-8080
Dr. Charles Koren, supt. Fax 479-3967
homercenter.org/
Homer-Center ES 500/K-6
45 Wildcat Ln 15748 724-479-9077
Michael Stofa, prin. Fax 479-8768

Homestead, Allegheny, Pop. 3,024
Steel Valley SD
Supt. — See Munhall
Barrett ES 200/K-4
221 E 12th Ave 15120 412-464-3600
Kevin Walsh, prin. Fax 464-3632

Honesdale, Wayne, Pop. 4,431
Wayne Highlands SD 2,700/K-12
474 Grove St 18431 570-253-4661
Gregory Frigoletto, supt. Fax 253-9409
www.whsdk12.com
Lakeside ES 500/3-5
129 Lakeside Dr 18431 570-253-6820
Sandra Rickard, prin. Fax 253-6826
Stourbridge Primary Center 400/K-2
123 ABC Dr 18431 570-253-3010
Paula Brennan, prin. Fax 253-3236
Wayne Highlands MS 500/6-8
482 Grove St 18431 570-253-5900
Peter Jordan, prin. Fax 253-5259
Other Schools – See Damascus, Lakewood

Honey Brook, Lancaster, Pop. 1,675
Twin Valley SD
Supt. — See Elverson
Honey Brook ES 400/K-4
1530 Walnut Rd 19344 610-273-3615
Chasity Cooper M.Ed., prin. Fax 273-7053

Honey Grove, Juniata
Juniata County SD
Supt. — See Mifflintown
Lack-Tuscarora ES 100/K-5
3044 Middle Rd 17035 717-734-3172
Clint Mitchell, prin. Fax 734-3147

Hookstown, Beaver, Pop. 144
South Side Area SD 1,100/PK-12
4949 Route 151 15050 724-573-9581
Tamara Adams, supt. Fax 573-0414
www.sssd.k12.pa.us
South Side ES 200/PK-1
4949 Route 151 15050 724-573-9581
Andrea Welch, prin. Fax 573-2273
South Side ES 200/2-5
4949 Route 151 15050 724-573-9581
Timothy Strador, prin. Fax 573-2273
South Side MS 300/6-8
4949 Route 151 15050 724-573-9581
Samuel Adams, prin. Fax 573-0449

Horsham, Montgomery, Pop. 14,608
Hatboro-Horsham SD 4,700/K-12
229 Meetinghouse Rd 19044 215-420-5000
Dr. Curtis Griffin, supt. Fax 420-5262
www.hatboro-horsham.org
Hallowell ES 300/K-5
501 W Moreland Ave 19044 215-420-5900
Steven Glaize, prin. Fax 420-5951
Keith Valley MS 1,200/6-8
227 Meetinghouse Rd 19044 215-420-5050
Jonathan Kircher, prin. Fax 420-5291

Simmons ES 700/K-5
411 Babylon Rd 19044 215-420-5700
Karen Kanter, prin. Fax 420-5885
Other Schools – See Hatboro

Houston, Washington, Pop. 1,253
Chartiers-Houston SD 1,100/K-12
2020 W Pike St 15342 724-746-1400
John George, supt. Fax 746-3971
www.chbucs.k12.pa.us/
Allison Park ES 600/K-6
803 McGovern Rd 15342 724-745-4700
Annette Caruso, prin. Fax 745-1710

Central Christian Academy 200/PK-8
145 McGovern Rd 15342 724-746-4902
Kate Fisher M.Ed., admin. Fax 746-5053

Houtzdale, Clearfield, Pop. 791
Moshannon Valley SD 900/K-12
4934 Green Acre Rd 16651 814-378-7609
John Zesiger, supt. Fax 378-7100
www.movalley.org
Moshannon Valley ES 500/K-6
5026 Green Acre Rd 16651 814-378-7683
Sherri Campbell, prin. Fax 378-5988

Howard, Centre, Pop. 709
Bald Eagle Area SD
Supt. — See Wingate
Howard ES 100/K-5
PO Box 406 16841 814-625-2423
Nevin Pighetti, prin. Fax 625-2785

Hughesville, Lycoming, Pop. 2,101
East Lycoming SD 1,700/PK-12
349 Cemetery St 17737 570-584-2131
Michael Pawlik, supt. Fax 584-5701
www.eastlycoming.net
Ashkar ES 500/PK-6
350 S Broad St 17737 570-584-5121
Sherry Cowburn, prin. Fax 584-6301
Other Schools – See Lairdsville, Picture Rocks

Hummelstown, Dauphin, Pop. 4,481
Lower Dauphin SD 3,800/K-12
291 E Main St 17036 717-566-5300
Dr. Sherri L. Smith, supt. Fax 566-3670
www.ldsd.org
Lower Dauphin MS 900/6-8
251 Quarry Rd 17036 717-566-5310
Daniel Berra, prin. Fax 566-5383
Nye ES 300/K-5
200 S John St 17036 717-566-0300
Bryan MacLeod, prin. Fax 566-4814
Other Schools – See Elizabethtown, Grantville, Hershey, Middletown

---

Lancaster Mennonite S 300/K-12
1525 Sand Hill Rd 17036 717-533-4900

Hunker, Westmoreland, Pop. 283

Armbrust Christian Academy 100/PK-12
7786 State Route 819 15639 724-925-3830
Susan Stoner, head sch Fax 925-2523

Huntingdon, Huntingdon, Pop. 6,994
Huntingdon Area SD 2,000/K-12
2400 Cassady Ave Ste 2 16652 814-643-4140
Fred Foster, supt. Fax 643-6244
huntsd.org/
Huntingdon Area MS 500/6-8
2500 Cassady Ave 16652 814-643-2900
Travis Lee, prin. Fax 643-6513
Southside ES 400/K-5
10906 Station Rd 16652 814-627-1100
Dr. Kimberlie Rieffannacht, prin. Fax 627-0301
Standing Stone ES 500/K-5
10 W 29th St 16652 814-643-0771
Dr. Kimberlie Rieffannacht, prin. Fax 643-5947

Huntingdon Valley, Montgomery, Pop. 10,000
Abington SD
Supt. — See Abington
Rydal East ES 400/2-6
1160 Huntingdon Pike 19006 215-884-1308
Lyndsay Morgan, prin. Fax 884-8955

Lower Moreland Township SD 2,200/K-12
2551 Murray Ave 19006 215-938-0270
Dr. Marykay Feeley, supt. Fax 947-6933
www.lmtsd.org
Murray Avenue MS 500/6-8
2551 Murray Ave 19006 215-938-0230
Jennifer Dilks, prin. Fax 947-3697
Pine Road ES 900/K-5
3737 Pine Rd 19006 215-938-0290
Brian Swank, prin. Fax 502-4248

Huntingdon Valley Christian Academy 100/PK-10
1845 Byberry Rd 19006 215-947-6595
St. Albert the Great S 500/K-8
214 Welsh Rd 19006 215-947-2332
Cynthia Koons, prin. Fax 938-9360
Valley Christian S 100/PK-8
2364 Huntingdon Pike 19006 215-947-4581
Susan Caler, head sch Fax 947-4583

Huntington Mills, Luzerne
Northwest Area SD
Supt. — See Shickshinny
Northwest Area PS 200/PK-3
PO Box 28 18622 570-542-4126
Matthew Mills, prin. Fax 864-0836

Immaculata, Chester

Villa Maria Academy — 300/K-8
1140 King Rd 19345 — 610-644-4864
Sr. Susan Joseph, prin. — Fax 647-6403

Imperial, Allegheny, Pop. 2,507
West Allegheny SD — 3,300/K-12
PO Box 55 15126 — 724-695-3422
Dr. Jerri Lynn Lippert, supt. — Fax 695-3788
www.westasd.org
West Allegheny MS — 800/6-8
207 W Allegheny Rd 15126 — 724-695-8979
Frank Hernandez, prin. — Fax 695-8211
Wilson ES — 500/K-5
100 Bruno Ln 15126 — 724-695-3300
Rachael Gray, prin. — Fax 695-0610
Other Schools – See Oakdale

Indiana, Indiana, Pop. 13,787
Indiana Area SD — 2,200/PK-12
501 E Pike Rd 15701 — 724-463-8713
Dale Kirsch, supt. — Fax 463-0868
www.iasd.cc
East Pike ES — 200/PK-3
501 E Pike Rd 15701 — 724-463-8567
Donald Springer, prin. — Fax 463-0868
Eisenhower ES — 100/4-5
1460 School St 15701 — 724-463-8566
Marilyn Walther, prin. — Fax 465-8612
Franklin ES — 300/PK-3
95 Ben Franklin Rd S 15701 — 724-465-5637
Robert Rizzo, prin. — Fax 465-1070
Indiana Area JHS — 600/6-8
245 N 5th St 15701 — 724-463-8568
Dr. Michael Minnick, prin. — Fax 463-2133
Mann ES — 100/4-5
205 S 5th St 15701 — 724-463-8560
Lawra Stuart, prin. — Fax 463-9140

St. Bernard Regional S — 100/PK-8
300 Clairvaux Dr 15701 — 724-465-7139
Denise Swope, prin. — Fax 465-0803
Seeds of Faith Christian Academy — 100/PK-12
640 Church St 15701 — 724-463-7719
Erica Parks, admin. — Fax 463-8097

Irwin, Westmoreland, Pop. 3,935
Hempfield Area SD
Supt. — See Greensburg
West Hempfield ES — 500/K-5
469 Wendel Rd 15642 — 724-850-2780
Christopher Brasco, prin. — Fax 850-2781
West Hempfield MS — 500/6-8
156 Northumberland Dr 15642 — 724-850-2140
Aaron Steinly, prin. — Fax 850-2141

Penn-Trafford SD
Supt. — See Harrison City
Sunrise ES — 400/K-5
171 Sunrise Dr 15642 — 724-864-6700
Karin Coiner, prin. — Fax 864-0226

Jamestown, Mercer, Pop. 614
Jamestown Area SD — 500/K-12
PO Box 217 16134 — 724-932-5557
Tracy Reiser, supt. — Fax 932-5632
www.jamestown.k12.pa.us
Jamestown Area ES — 300/K-6
PO Box 217 16134 — 724-932-3181
Kristen Hope, dean

Jamison, Bucks
Central Bucks SD
Supt. — See Doylestown
Jamison ES — 600/K-6
2090 Land Rd 18929 — 267-893-3500
Matthew Croyle, prin. — Fax 343-9585
Warwick ES — 500/K-6
1340 Almshouse Rd 18929 — 267-893-4050
Chad Watters, prin. — Fax 343-9425

Jeannette, Westmoreland, Pop. 9,284
Jeannette CSD — 900/K-12
800 Florida Ave 15644 — 724-523-5497
Matthew Hutcheson, supt. — Fax 523-3289
www.jeannette.k12.pa.us
Jeannette McKee ES — 600/K-6
1000 Lowry Ave 15644 — 724-523-6522
Shelley Muto, prin. — Fax 523-9418

Penn-Trafford SD
Supt. — See Harrison City
Harrison Park ES — 500/K-5
18 Dell Ave 15644 — 724-744-2161
Jeff Swartz, prin. — Fax 744-1865
McCullough ES — 400/K-5
213 Watt Rd 15644 — 724-744-7441
Joseph Marasti, prin. — Fax 744-1076
Penn MS — 600/6-8
1007 Penn Middle Way 15644 — 724-744-4431
James Simpson, prin. — Fax 744-1215

Jefferson, Greene, Pop. 979
Jefferson-Morgan SD — 800/PK-12
PO Box 158 15344 — 724-883-2310
Joseph H. Orr, supt. — Fax 883-4942
www.jmsd.org/
Jefferson-Morgan ES — 400/PK-6
PO Box 158 15344 — 724-883-2310
Sam Silbaugh, prin. — Fax 883-2390

Jefferson Hills, Allegheny, Pop. 9,642
West Jefferson Hills SD — 2,800/K-12
835 Old Clairton Rd 15025 — 412-655-8450
Dr. Michael A. Panza, supt. — Fax 655-9544
www.wjhsd.net
Gill Hall ES — 300/K-5
829 Gill Hall Rd 15025 — 412-655-4732
Tina Mayer, prin. — Fax 655-3888
Jefferson ES — 500/K-5
875 Old Clairton Rd 15025 — 412-655-4163
Christopher Very, prin. — Fax 655-4973
Other Schools – See Pittsburgh

St. Thomas Becket Preschool — 100/PK-PK
139 Gill Hall Rd 15025 — 412-653-4322
Sr. Dolores Therasse, prin. — Fax 653-9979

Jenkintown, Montgomery, Pop. 4,346
Jenkintown SD — 600/K-12
325 Highland Ave 19046 — 215-885-3722
Dr. Jill Takacs, supt. — Fax 885-2090
www.jenkintown.org
Jenkintown ES — 400/K-6
325 Highland Ave 19046 — 215-884-2933
Keith Purcaro, prin.

Abington Friends S — 700/PK-12
575 Washington Ln 19046 — 215-576-3950
Richard Nourie, head sch — Fax 886-9143

Jersey Shore, Lycoming, Pop. 4,319
Jersey Shore Area SD — 2,600/K-12
175 A and P Dr 17740 — 570-398-1561
Dr. Jill Wenrich Ed.D., supt. — Fax 398-5089
www.jsasd.org
Avis ES — 300/K-5
1088 Third St 17740 — 570-753-5220
Jon Jean M.Ed., prin. — Fax 753-3460
Jersey Shore Area ES — 600/K-5
601 Locust St 17740 — 570-398-7120
Keith Veldhuis M.Ed., prin. — Fax 398-5624
Jersey Shore Area MS — 600/6-8
601 Thompson St 17740 — 570-398-7400
Laura Milarch M.Ed., prin. — Fax 398-5618
Salladasburg ES — 300/K-5
3490 Route 287 Hwy 17740 — 570-398-2931
Jon Jean M.Ed., prin. — Fax 398-5066

Jessup, Lackawanna, Pop. 4,627

LaSalle Academy — 200/PK-8
309 1st Ave 18434 — 570-489-2010
Ellen Murphy, prin. — Fax 489-3887

Jim Thorpe, Carbon, Pop. 4,724
Jim Thorpe Area SD — 2,100/K-12
410 Center Ave 18229 — 570-325-3691
Brian Gasper, supt. — Fax 325-3699
www.jimthorpesd.org/
Morris S — 800/K-8
150 W 10th St 18229 — 570-325-2703
Holly Mordaunt, prin. — Fax 325-8098
Other Schools – See Albrightsville

St. Joseph Regional Academy — 100/K-8
25 W 6th St 18229 — 570-325-3186
Amanda Salovay, prin. — Fax 325-2090

Johnsonburg, Elk, Pop. 2,464
Johnsonburg Area SD — 600/PK-12
315 High School Rd 15845 — 814-965-2536
Dennis Crotzer, supt. — Fax 965-5809
www.johnsonburgareaschooldistrict.net
Johnsonburg Area ES — 400/PK-6
1536 Wilcox Rd 15845 — 814-965-2577
Judy Allegretto, prin. — Fax 965-4101

Johnstown, Cambria, Pop. 20,140
Central Cambria SD
Supt. — See Ebensburg
Jackson ES — 200/K-5
3704 William Penn Ave 15909 — 814-749-8421
Joseph Strittmatter, prin. — Fax 749-0543

Conemaugh Township Area SD
Supt. — See Davidsville
Conemaugh Township Area ES — 400/K-5
1516 Tire Hill Rd 15905 — 814-479-4080
Nicole Dull, prin. — Fax 479-7497

Conemaugh Valley SD — 800/PK-12
1340 William Penn Ave 15906 — 814-535-5005
David Lehman, supt. — Fax 536-8902
www.cvk12.org/
Conemaugh Valley ES — 400/PK-6
1340 William Penn Ave 15906 — 814-535-6970
Rebecca Castiglione, prin. — Fax 536-8370

Ferndale Area SD — 700/PK-12
100 Dartmouth Ave 15905 — 814-535-1507
Carole Kakabar, supt. — Fax 535-8527
www.fasdk12.org
Ferndale ES — 400/PK-6
100 Dartmouth Ave 15905 — 814-535-6724
Rachelle Hrabosky, prin. — Fax 536-6506

Greater Johnstown SD — 3,100/PK-12
1091 Broad St 15906 — 814-533-5650
Michael Vuckovich, supt. — Fax 533-5662
www.gjsd.net
Greater Johnstown ES — 900/PK-4
196 Westgate Dr 15905 — 814-533-5540
Douglas Henry, prin. — Fax 533-5592
Greater Johnstown MS — 600/5-7
220 Messenger St 15902 — 814-533-5550
Dino Scarton, prin. — Fax 533-5548

Richland SD — 1,600/K-12
1 Academic Ave 15904 — 814-266-6063
Arnold Nadonley, supt. — Fax 266-7349
www.richlandsd.com/
Richland ES — 800/K-6
321 Schoolhouse Rd 15904 — 814-266-5757
Gregg Wilson, prin. — Fax 269-3499

Westmont Hilltop SD — 1,100/K-12
112 Lindberg Ave 15905 — 814-255-6751
Dr. Timothy Williams, supt. — Fax 255-7735
www.whsd.org
Westmont Hilltop ES — 600/K-6
827 Diamond Blvd 15905 — 814-255-8707
Nicole Kuzmiak, prin. — Fax 255-8793

Divine Mercy Catholic Academy East — 300/PK-6
2306 Bedford St 15904 — 814-266-3837
Thomas Smith, prin. — Fax 266-7718
Divine Mercy Catholic Academy MS — 7-8
25 Osborne St 15905 — 814-536-8991
Thomas Smith, prin. — Fax 535-4118
Divine Mercy Catholic Academy West — 300/PK-6
430 Tioga St 15905 — 814-539-5315
Thomas Smith, prin. — Fax 539-5315

Jones Mills, Westmoreland
Mt. Pleasant Area SD
Supt. — See Mount Pleasant
Donegal ES — 200/K-6
138 School House Ln 15646 — 724-547-4100
Scott Bryer, prin. — Fax 547-7713

Jonestown, Lebanon, Pop. 1,873
Northern Lebanon SD — 2,000/K-12
40 Fisher Ave 17038 — 717-865-2117
Dr. Erik Bentzel, supt. — Fax 865-0606
www.norleb.k12.pa.us
Jonestown ES — 400/K-5
135 S King St 17038 — 717-865-3193
John Rizzo, prin. — Fax 865-0805
Lickdale ES — 200/1-5
40 Fisher Ave 17038 — 717-865-4012
Trevor Saylor, prin. — Fax 865-5396
Other Schools – See Annville, Fredericksburg

Kane, McKean, Pop. 3,695
Kane Area SD — 1,200/K-12
400 W Hemlock Ave 16735 — 814-837-9570
Jeffrey Kepler, supt. — Fax 837-7450
www.kasd.net
Kane Area ES — 600/K-5
400 W Hemlock Ave 16735 — 814-837-7555
Linda Lorenzo, prin. — Fax 837-9207
Kane Area MS — 300/6-8
400 W Hemlock Ave 16735 — 814-837-6030
Todd Stanko, prin. — Fax 837-9133

Karns City, Butler, Pop. 209
Karns City Area SD — 1,500/K-12
1446 Kittanning Pike 16041 — 724-756-2030
Eric Ritzert, supt. — Fax 756-2121
www.kcasdk12.org
Other Schools – See Chicora, Cowansville

Kennett Square, Chester, Pop. 6,014
Kennett Consolidated SD — 4,200/K-12
300 E South St 19348 — 610-444-6600
Dr. Barry Tomasetti, supt. — Fax 444-6614
kcsd.org
Bancroft ES — 500/1-5
181 Bancroft Rd 19348 — 610-925-5711
Leah McComsey, prin. — Fax 925-5712
Greenwood ES — 600/K-5
420 Greenwood Rd 19348 — 610-388-5990
Tracey Marino, prin.
Lang Kindergarten — 300/K-K
409 Center St 19348 — 610-444-6260
April Reynolds, prin.
Other Schools – See Landenberg, Toughkenamon

Unionville-Chadds Ford SD — 4,100/K-12
740 Unionville Rd 19348 — 610-347-0970
Dr. John Sanville, supt. — Fax 347-0976
www.ucfsd.org
Patton MS — 1,000/6-8
760 Unionville Rd 19348 — 610-347-2000
Steve Dissinger, prin. — Fax 347-0421
Unionville ES — 400/K-5
1775 W Doe Run Rd 19348 — 610-347-1700
Dr. Michelle Lafferty, prin. — Fax 347-1443
Other Schools – See Chadds Ford, West Chester

London Grove Friends K — 50/K-K
500 W Street Rd 19348 — 610-268-8466
Deni-lyn Lane, prin.
Upland Country Day S — 200/PK-9
420 W Street Rd 19348 — 610-444-3035
Dr. Dan Hickey, head sch — Fax 444-2961

Kersey, Elk, Pop. 934
Saint Marys Area SD
Supt. — See Saint Marys
Fox Township ES — 200/K-5
376 Main St 15846 — 814-885-8076
Karen Lucanik, prin. — Fax 885-6331

St. Boniface S — 100/PK-5
359 Main St 15846 — 814-885-8093
Monica Schloder, prin. — Fax 885-8611

Kimberton, Chester

Kimberton Waldorf S — 300/PK-12
PO Box 350 19442 — 610-933-3635
Kevin Hughes, dean — Fax 935-6985

King of Prussia, Montgomery, Pop. 19,511
Upper Merion Area SD — 3,900/K-12
435 Crossfield Rd 19406 — 610-205-6401
Dr. John Toleno, supt. — Fax 205-6433
www.umasd.org
Caley ES — 400/K-4
725 Caley Rd 19406 — 610-205-3651
Steven Van Mater, prin. — Fax 205-3699
Candlebrook ES — 400/K-4
310 Prince Frederick St 19406 — 610-205-3701
Frank McCartney, prin. — Fax 205-3749

Upper Merion MS 1,200/5-8
450 Keebler Rd 19406 610-205-8801
Adam Slavin, prin. Fax 205-8999
Other Schools – See Bridgeport, Wayne

Mother Theresa Regional Catholic S 300/PK-8
405 Allendale Rd 19406 610-265-2323
Jack Bellantoni, prin. Fax 265-1816

Kingsley, Susquehanna
Mountain View SD 1,100/K-12
11748 State Route 106 18826 570-434-2180
Karen K. Voigt, supt. Fax 434-2404
www.mvsd.net
Mountain View ES 600/K-6
11748 State Route 106 18826 570-434-2181
Christine Kelly, prin. Fax 434-2755

Kingston, Luzerne, Pop. 12,983
Wyoming Valley West SD 4,200/K-12
450 N Maple Ave 18704 570-288-6551
Irvin T. DeRemer, supt. Fax 714-6948
www.wvwsd.org/
Chester Street ES 200/1-5
110 Chester St 18704 570-287-2438
Deborah Troy, admin. Fax 714-4140
Schuyler Avenue ES 300/K-5
715 Schuyler Ave 18704 570-287-6041
David Bond, prin. Fax 714-7329
State Street ES 600/K-5
355 E State St 18704 570-779-5381
Jake Sholtis, prin. Fax 779-2023
Third Avenue ES 200/K-5
111 3rd Ave 18704 570-288-2282
David Tosh, admin. Fax 714-3511
Wyoming Valley West MS 1,100/6-8
201 Chester St 18704 570-287-2131
Deborah Troy, prin. Fax 287-6343
Other Schools – See Forty Fort

Good Shepherd Academy 100/PK-8
316 N Maple Ave 18704 570-718-4724
James Jones, prin. Fax 718-4725
Wyoming Valley Montessori S 100/PK-6
851 W Market St 18704 570-288-3708

Kintnersville, Bucks
Palisades SD 1,800/K-12
39 Thomas Free Dr 18930 610-847-5131
Dr. Bridget O'Connell, supt. Fax 847-8116
www.palisadessd.org
Durham-Nockamixon ES 200/K-5
41 Thomas Free Dr 18930 610-847-5131
Marie Collie, prin. Fax 847-6960
Palisades MS 400/6-8
4710 Durham Rd 18930 610-847-5131
Zachary Fuller, prin. Fax 847-2691
Other Schools – See Pipersville, Quakertown

Kinzers, Lancaster
Pequea Valley SD 1,500/K-12
PO Box 130 17535 717-768-5530
Erik Orndorff, supt. Fax 768-7176
www.pequeavalley.org
Pequea Valley IS 300/7-8
PO Box 257 17535 717-768-5535
Arlen Mummau, prin. Fax 768-5656
Other Schools – See Gap, Paradise

Kittanning, Armstrong, Pop. 3,989
Armstrong SD 3,700/K-12
181 Heritage Park Dr Ste 2 16201 724-548-7200
Chris DeVivo, supt. Fax 548-7201
www.asd.k12.pa.us
West Hills IS 500/4-6
175 Heritage Park Dr 16201 724-543-1121
Chuck Kreinbucher, prin. Fax 548-8765
West Hills PS 700/K-3
181 Heritage Park Dr 16201 724-548-7651
Paula Berry, prin. Fax 548-8765
Other Schools – See Dayton, Elderton, Ford City, Rural Valley

---

Grace Christian S 100/PK-12
215 Arthur St 16201 724-543-4019
Darlene Edwards, head sch Fax 545-6738

Klingerstown, Schuylkill, Pop. 125
Tri-Valley SD
Supt. — See Valley View
Mahantongo Valley ES 100/K-6
1200 Ridge Rd 17941 570-648-6062
Robert Felty, prin. Fax 648-8739

Knox, Clarion, Pop. 1,139
Keystone SD 1,100/K-12
451 Huston Ave 16232 814-797-5921
Shawn Algoe, supt. Fax 797-2382
www.keyknox.com
Keystone ES 600/K-6
451 Huston Ave 16232 814-797-1251
Mike McCormick, prin. Fax 797-0205

Kunkletown, Monroe
Pleasant Valley SD
Supt. — See Brodheadsville
Pleasant Valley ES 1,000/K-3
476 Polk Township Rd 18058 610-681-3091
Erica Greer, prin. Fax 681-3018
Pleasant Valley IS 1,100/4-6
477 Polk Township Rd 18058 610-681-8591
Cassandra Herr, prin. Fax 681-8666

Kutztown, Berks, Pop. 4,969
Kutztown Area SD 1,400/K-12
251 Long Lane Rd 19530 610-683-7361
Dr. George Fiore, supt. Fax 683-7230
www.kasd.org
Kutztown Area MS 300/6-8
10 Deisher Ln 19530 610-683-3575
James Brown, prin. Fax 683-5460
Kutztown ES 300/K-5
40 Normal Ave 19530 610-683-3557
Deborah Barnes, prin. Fax 683-0254
Other Schools – See Lenhartsville

Northwestern Lehigh SD
Supt. — See New Tripoli
Weisenberg ES 500/K-5
2665 Golden Key Rd 19530 610-298-8661
Jill Berlet, prin. Fax 285-2677

Lafayette Hill, Montgomery, Pop. 6,700
Colonial SD
Supt. — See Plymouth Meeting
Whitemarsh ES 400/K-3
4120 Joshua Rd 19444 610-828-9092
Donna Drizin, prin. Fax 828-1516

St. Philip Neri S 500/PK-8
3015 Chestnut St 19444 610-828-3082
Elizabeth Veneziale, prin. Fax 828-2943

Lahaska, Bucks, Pop. 200

Buckingham Friends S 200/K-8
PO Box 159 18931 215-794-7491
Russell MacMullan, head sch Fax 794-7955

Lairdsville, Lycoming
East Lycoming SD
Supt. — See Hughesville
Renn ES 200/PK-6
183 School Ln 17742 570-584-3070
Jill Warg, prin. Fax 584-5393

Lake Ariel, Wayne
North Pocono SD
Supt. — See Moscow
Jefferson ES 300/K-3
825 Lions Rd 18436 570-689-2656
Judith Castrogiovanni, prin. Fax 689-3825

Western Wayne SD 2,100/PK-12
1970 Easton Tpke Bldg C 18436 800-321-9973
Dr. Matthew Barrett, supt. Fax 341-1221
www.westernwayne.org
EverGreen ES 600/PK-5
739 Easton Tpke 18436 800-321-9973
Justin Pidgeon, prin.
Western Wayne MS 500/6-8
1970 Easton Tpke Bldg B 18436 800-321-9973
Kristin Donohue, prin.
Other Schools – See Waymart

Canaan Christian Academy 200/PK-12
30 Hemlock Rd 18436 570-937-4848

Lake City, Erie, Pop. 2,990
Girard SD
Supt. — See Girard
Elk Valley ES 700/PK-4
2556 Maple Ave 16423 814-774-5602
Mike Trudnowski, prin. Fax 774-8885

Lakewood, Wayne
Wayne Highlands SD
Supt. — See Honesdale
Preston S 200/K-8
1493 Crosstown Hwy 18439 570-798-2516
David Jagger, prin. Fax 798-2677

Lancaster, Lancaster, Pop. 57,600
Conestoga Valley SD 4,300/K-12
2110 Horseshoe Rd 17601 717-397-2421
Dr. David Zuilkoski, supt. Fax 397-0442
www.conestogavalley.org
Fritz ES 700/K-6
845 Hornig Rd 17601 717-397-5246
Dr. Colleen Hovanec, prin. Fax 397-6481
Huesken MS 700/7-8
500 Mount Sidney Rd 17602 717-397-1294
Baron Jones, prin. Fax 397-4404
Smoketown ES 700/K-6
2426 Old Philadelphia Pike 17602 717-394-0555
Sally Bredeman, prin. Fax 394-2792
Other Schools – See Brownstown, Leola

Hempfield SD
Supt. — See Landisville
Centerville ES 500/K-6
901 Centerville Rd 17601 717-898-5575
Thomas Kramer, prin. Fax 618-1208
Centerville MS 600/7-8
865 Centerville Rd 17601 717-898-5580
Lisa Mumma, prin. Fax 618-0999
Rohrerstown ES 500/K-6
2200 Noll Dr 17603 717-299-7126
Dr. Kathleen Swantner, prin. Fax 618-0997

Lampeter-Strasburg SD 3,100/K-12
1600 Book Rd 17602 717-464-3311
Dr. Kevin Peart Ed.D., supt. Fax 464-4699
www.l-spioneers.org
Herr ES 700/3-5
1600 Book Rd 17602 717-464-3311
Dr. Jeffrey Smecker Ed.D., prin. Fax 509-0300
Lampeter ES 600/K-2
1600 Book Rd 17602 717-464-3311
Dr. William Bray Ed.D., prin. Fax 358-1880
Meylin MS 800/6-8
1600 Book Rd 17602 717-464-3311
Jamie Raum, prin. Fax 509-0289

Lancaster SD 10,700/K-12
251 S Prince St 17603 717-299-2700
Dr. Damaris Rau, supt. Fax 339-6844
www.lancaster.k12.pa.us
Buchanan ES 400/K-5
340 S West End Ave 17603 717-291-6151
Stacy Kain, prin. Fax 391-8608
Burrowes ES 400/K-5
1001 E Orange St 17602 717-291-6159
Gary Hess, prin. Fax 391-8607
Carter & MacRae ES 400/K-5
251 S Prince St 17603 717-396-6842
Rachel Esh, prin. Fax 295-7842
Fulton ES 400/K-5
225 W Orange St 17603 717-291-6110
Fax 396-6800
Hamilton ES 500/K-5
1300 Wabank Rd 17603 717-291-6166
Philip Ludwig, prin. Fax 390-2575
Hand MS 500/6-8
431 S Ann St 17602 717-291-6161
Mark Simms, prin. Fax 391-8600
King ES 500/K-5
466 Rockland St 17602 717-291-6178
Melinda Wells, prin. Fax 391-8616
Lafayette ES 400/K-5
1000 Fremont St 17603 717-291-6183
Wanda Suarez, prin. Fax 295-7847
Lincoln MS 500/6-8
1001 Lehigh Ave 17602 717-291-6187
Dr. Josh Keene, prin. Fax 399-6408
Martin ES 400/K-8
2000 Wabank Rd 17603 717-291-6193
Dr. Barbara Andrews, prin. Fax 390-2562
Price ES 400/K-5
615 Fairview Ave 17603 717-291-6252
Dr. Florence Krane, prin. Fax 291-6118
Reynolds MS 600/6-8
605 W Walnut St 17603 717-291-6257
Aaron Swinton, prin. Fax 396-6823
Ross ES 300/K-5
840 N Queen St 17603 717-291-6268
Camille Hopkins, prin. Fax 390-2576
Washington ES 600/K-5
545 S Ann St 17602 717-291-6275
Kathleen Wiercinski, prin. Fax 390-2563
Wharton ES 300/K-5
705 N Mary St 17603 717-291-6281
Melanie Martinez, prin. Fax 390-2561
Wheatland MS 600/6-8
919 Hamilton Park Dr 17603 717-291-6285
Donald Trost, prin. Fax 399-6411
Wickersham ES 500/K-5
401 N Reservoir St 17602 717-291-6291
Ashley Mercado, prin. Fax 390-2577

Manheim Township SD 5,700/K-12
PO Box 5134 17606 717-569-8231
Dr. Robin Felty, supt. Fax 569-3729
www.mtwp.net
Brecht ES 300/K-4
1250 Lititz Pike 17601 717-291-1733
Sharon Schaefer, prin. Fax 735-0939
Bucher ES 300/K-4
450 Candlewyck Rd 17601 717-569-4291
Andy Martin, prin. Fax 569-3060
Landis Run IS 900/5-6
PO Box 5134 17606 717-581-9124
William Gillis, prin. Fax 569-8226
Manheim Township MS 900/7-8
PO Box 5134 17606 717-560-3111
Karen Evans, prin. Fax 569-1670
Neff ES 300/K-4
PO Box 5134 17606 717-569-8502
Travis Bash, prin. Fax 569-8226
Nitrauer ES 500/K-4
811 Ashbourne Ave 17601 717-569-4239
Wendy Hancock, prin. Fax 569-7973
Schaeffer ES 300/K-4
875 Pleasure Rd 17601 717-392-6797
Christopher Zander, prin. Fax 392-0267
Other Schools – See Lititz

Penn Manor SD 4,700/K-12
2950 Charlestown Rd 17603 717-872-9500
Dr. Michael Leichliter, supt. Fax 872-9505
www.pennmanor.net
Hambright ES 400/K-6
3000 Charlestown Rd 17603 717-872-9503
Eric Howe, prin. Fax 842-2065
Manor MS 500/7-8
2950 Charlestown Rd 17603 717-872-9510
Dr. Dana Edwards, prin. Fax 872-9505
Other Schools – See Conestoga, Holtwood, Millersville, Pequea, Washington Boro, Willow Street

---

Lancaster Country Day S 600/PK-12
725 Hamilton Rd 17603 717-392-2916
Stephen Lisk, head sch Fax 392-0425
Lancaster Co. Christian S - Leola Campus 300/PK-12
2390 New Holland Pike 17601 717-556-0711
Beth Richardson, prin. Fax 656-4868
Lancaster Co. Christian S -West Lampeter 200/K-6
651 Lampeter Rd 17602 717-556-0711
Dr. Samuel Botta, head sch
Lancaster Mennonite S - Locust Grove 200/PK-7
2257 Old Philadelphia Pike 17602 717-394-7107
Lancaster Mennonite S - New Danville 100/PK-5
393 Long Ln 17603 717-872-2506
Eloy Rodriguez, prin. Fax 872-5201
Montessori Academy of Lancaster 200/PK-6
2750 Weaver Rd 17601 717-560-0815
New S of Lancaster 200/PK-8
935 Columbia Ave 17603 717-397-7655
Resurrection S 200/K-8
521 E Orange St 17602 717-392-3083
Brenda Weaver, prin. Fax 735-7793

Sacred Heart of Jesus S 200/PK-8
235 Nevin St 17603 717-393-8433
Sr. Mary Deering, prin. Fax 393-1028
St. Anne S 200/PK-8
108 E Liberty St 17602 717-394-6711
Suzanne Wood, prin. Fax 394-8628
St. Leo the Great S 300/PK-8
2427 Marietta Ave 17601 717-392-2441
Christine McLean, prin. Fax 392-4080
St. Philip the Apostle Preschool PK-PK
2111 Millersville Pike 17603 717-872-2166
Deborah Miehl, dir. Fax 872-2587
San Juan Baptista Preschool PK-PK
425 S Duke St 17602 717-283-0270

Landenberg, Chester
Kennett Consolidated SD
Supt. — See Kennett Square
Kennett MS, 195 Sunny Dell Rd 19350 1,000/6-8
Lorenzo DeAngelis, prin. 610-268-5800

Landenberg Christian Academy 50/PK-6
109 Gypsy Hill Rd 19350 610-255-5805
Julie Malone, admin. Fax 255-5515

Landisville, Lancaster, Pop. 1,881
Hempfield SD 6,800/K-12
200 Church St 17538 717-898-5564
Dr. Chris Adams, supt. Fax 898-5628
www.hempfieldsd.org
Landisville Intermediate Center 400/4-6
330 Mumma Dr 17538 717-898-5590
Ian Daecher, prin. Fax 618-0996
Landisville MS 500/7-8
340 Mumma Dr 17538 717-898-5607
Douglas Dandridge, prin. Fax 618-0871
Landisville Primary Center 600/K-3
320 Mumma Dr 17538 717-898-5519
Ronald Swantner, prin. Fax 618-1009
Other Schools – See East Petersburg, Lancaster, Mount Joy, Mountville

Langhorne, Bucks, Pop. 1,596
Neshaminy SD 7,700/K-12
2001 Old Lincoln Hwy 19047 215-809-6500
Joseph Jones, supt. Fax 809-6502
www.neshaminy.k12.pa.us
Hoover ES, 501 Trenton Rd 19047 700/K-4
Dr. David Glennon, prin. 215-809-6340
Maple Point MS 1,000/5-8
2250 Langhorne Yardley Rd 19047 215-809-6230
Matthew Sokol, prin.
Tawanka ES 700/K-4
2055 Brownsville Rd 19053 215-809-6310
Robin Klaiber, admin.
Other Schools – See Feasterville, Levittown

Lansdale, Montgomery, Pop. 15,885
Methacton SD
Supt. — See Eagleville
Worcester ES 400/K-4
3017 Skippack Pike 19446 610-489-5000
Jenifer Brucker, prin. Fax 831-5326

North Penn SD 12,700/K-12
401 E Hancock St 19446 215-368-0400
Dr. Curtis Dietrich, supt. Fax 368-3161
www.npenn.org
Bridle Path ES 600/K-6
200 Bridle Path Rd 19446 215-362-2200
Jeff Macosko, prin. Fax 362-7517
Gwynedd Square ES 600/K-6
1641 Supplee Rd 19446 215-855-4331
William Bowen, prin. Fax 412-7982
Inglewood ES 500/K-6
1313 Allentown Rd 19446 215-368-2992
Dr. Orlando Taylor, prin. Fax 368-7808
Knapp ES 600/K-6
698 Knapp Rd 19446 215-368-2054
Heather Mann, prin. Fax 368-6932
Oak Park ES 500/K-6
500 Squirrel Ln 19446 215-368-4017
Doug Povilaitis, prin. Fax 368-7862
Walton Farm ES 500/K-6
1610 Allentown Rd 19446 215-855-8800
Marc Gosselin, prin. Fax 412-8695
York Avenue ES 400/K-6
700 York Ave 19446 215-368-6002
Loretta Hoch, prin. Fax 368-7875
Other Schools – See Harleysville, Hatfield, North Wales

Calvary Baptist S 400/PK-12
1380 S Valley Forge Rd 19446 215-368-1100
Joshua Bacchus, prin. Fax 368-1003
Corpus Christi S 500/K-8
920 Sumneytown Pike 19446 215-368-0582
Maureen Lafferty, prin. Fax 361-5927
Mater Dei Regional S 400/K-8
493 E Main St 19446 215-368-0995
Diane McCaughan, prin. Fax 393-4869

Lansdowne, Delaware, Pop. 10,265
William Penn SD 5,200/K-12
100 Green Ave 19050 610-284-8000
Jane Harbert, supt. Fax 284-8054
www.williampennsd.org
Ardmore Avenue ES 500/K-6
161 Ardmore Ave 19050 610-623-7900
Joseph Denelsbeck, prin. Fax 284-2226
Other Schools – See Aldan, Colwyn, Darby, East Lansdowne, Yeadon

---

Lansdowne Friends S 100/PK-6
110 N Lansdowne Ave 19050 610-623-2548
John McKinstry, head sch Fax 623-3637

Lansford, Carbon, Pop. 3,876
Panther Valley SD 1,000/K-12
1 Panther Way 18232 570-645-4248
Dennis Kergick, supt. Fax 645-6232
www.panthervalley.org/
Panther Valley IS 100/4-6
678 Panther Pride Way 18232 570-645-2175
Lisa Mace, prin. Fax 645-9723
Other Schools – See Nesquehoning

Laporte, Sullivan, Pop. 316
Sullivan County SD 600/K-12
PO Box 240 18626 570-946-8200
Patricia A. Cross, supt. Fax 946-8210
www.sulcosd.k12.pa.us
Sullivan County ES 300/K-6
PO Box 115 18626 570-946-7471
Mary McClintock, prin. Fax 946-4272

Larksville, Luzerne, Pop. 4,445

Rock Solid Academy 50/K-12
1919 Mountain Rd 18651 570-338-1019
Lauren Dennis, head sch Fax 338-1021

Latrobe, Westmoreland, Pop. 8,261
Greater Latrobe SD 3,700/K-12
1816 Lincoln Ave 15650 724-539-4200
Judith Swigart, supt. Fax 539-4202
www.glsd.us
Baggaley ES 600/K-6
4080 State Route 982 15650 724-539-4531
Kim Stewart, prin. Fax 539-0448
Greater Latrobe JHS 700/7-8
130 High School Rd 15650 724-539-4265
Matt Shivetts, prin. Fax 539-4223
Latrobe ES 800/K-6
1501 Ligonier St 15650 724-539-9777
Sherri Holler, prin. Fax 539-4224
Other Schools – See Greensburg

Christ the Divine Teacher S 200/PK-7
323 Chestnut St 15650 724-539-1561
Kevin Frye, prin. Fax 532-3873

Laureldale, Berks, Pop. 3,857
Muhlenberg SD 3,500/K-12
801 E Bellevue Ave 19605 610-921-8000
Dr. Joseph Macharola, supt. Fax 921-8076
www.muhlsdk12.org
Other Schools – See Reading

Lebanon, Lebanon, Pop. 25,113
Cornwall-Lebanon SD 4,600/K-12
105 E Evergreen Rd 17042 717-272-2031
Dr. Philip Domencic, supt. Fax 274-2786
www.clsd.k12.pa.us
Cedar Crest MS 1,100/6-8
101 E Evergreen Rd 17042 717-272-2032
Dean Bozman, prin. Fax 389-1856
Cornwall ES 600/K-5
45 Burd Coleman Rd 17042 717-273-4571
Bernard McGinty, prin. Fax 389-1886
Ebenezer ES 600/K-5
1600 Colonial Cir 17046 717-272-1969
Cynthia Geesey, prin. Fax 389-1879
South Lebanon ES 500/K-5
1825 S 5th Ave 17042 717-273-4546
Barry Ferguson, prin. Fax 389-1865
Union Canal ES 400/K-5
400 Narrows Dr 17046 717-270-7227
Tracie Clemens, prin. Fax 389-1872

Lebanon SD 4,800/PK-12
1000 S 8th St 17042 717-270-6711
Dr. Arthur Abrom, supt. Fax 270-6778
www.lebanon.k12.pa.us
Harding ES, 622 Chestnut St 17042 600/PK-5
Michael Reager, prin. 717-273-9391
Houck ES, 315 E Lehman St 17046 400/PK-5
Pedro Cruz, prin. 717-273-9391
Lebanon MS 1,000/6-8
350 N 8th St 17046 717-273-9391
Dawn Connelly, prin. Fax 270-6859
Northwest ES, 900 Maple St 17046 600/PK-5
Neil Young, prin. 717-273-9391
Southeast ES 500/PK-5
499 E Pershing Ave 17042 717-273-9391
Michael Habecker, prin.
Southwest ES 500/PK-5
1500 Woodland St 17042 717-273-9391
Craig Coletti, prin.

Lebanon Catholic S 300/PK-12
1400 Chestnut St 17042 717-273-3731
Rose Kury, prin. Fax 274-5167
New Covenant Christian S 200/PK-12
452 Ebenezer Rd 17046 717-274-2423
James Hubbard, prin. Fax 274-9830

Leechburg, Armstrong, Pop. 2,128
Kiski Area SD 3,700/K-12
250 Hyde Park Rd 15656 724-845-2022
Dr. Timothy Scott, supt. Fax 842-0444
www.kiskiarea.com
Kiski Area IS 600/7-8
260 Hyde Park Rd 15656 724-845-2219
Michael Cardamone, prin. Fax 845-3208
Kiski Area North PS 500/K-4
1048 School Rd 15656 724-845-2032
Christine Ross, prin. Fax 845-0984
Other Schools – See Apollo, Export, Vandergrift

Leechburg Area SD 800/PK-12
210 Penn Ave 15656 724-842-9681
Tiffany Nix M.Ed., supt. Fax 845-2241
www.leechburg.k12.pa.us
Leech ES 400/PK-6
200 Siberian Ave 15656 724-845-6071
David Keibler B.S., prin. Fax 845-9723

Leesport, Berks, Pop. 1,904
Schuylkill Valley SD 2,000/K-12
929 Lakeshore Dr 19533 610-916-0957
Dr. Cindy Mierzejewski, supt. Fax 926-3960
www.schuylkillvalley.org/
Schuylkill Valley ES 800/K-4
62 Ashley Way 19533 610-926-4165
Melissa Kelchner, prin. Fax 916-5048
Schuylkill Valley MS 600/5-8
114 Ontelaunee Dr 19533 610-926-7111
Joshua Kuehner, prin. Fax 926-3321

Leetsdale, Allegheny, Pop. 1,172
Quaker Valley SD 1,900/K-12
100 Leetsdale Industrial Dr 15056 412-749-3600
Dr. Heidi Ondek, supt. Fax 749-3601
www.qvsd.org
Other Schools – See Sewickley

Lehighton, Carbon, Pop. 5,438
Lehighton Area SD 2,400/PK-12
1000 Union St 18235 610-377-4490
Jonathan J. Cleaver, supt. Fax 577-0035
www.lehighton.org/
East Penn ES 100/K-4
496 W Lizard Creek Rd 18235 610-377-6094
Suzanne Howland, prin. Fax 577-1008
Franklin ES 300/K-4
1122 Fairyland Rd 18235 610-377-6163
Suzanne Howland, prin. Fax 577-0067
Lehighton Area MS 700/5-8
301 Beaver Run Rd 18235 610-377-6535
Mark McGalla Ph.D., prin. Fax 377-6503
Mahoning ES 200/K-4
2466 Mahoning Dr E 18235 570-386-4678
Aaron Sebelin, prin. Fax 577-1009
Shull-David ES 300/PK-4
200 Beaver Run Rd 18235 610-377-7880
Aaron Sebelin, prin. Fax 377-0908

Palmerton Area SD
Supt. — See Palmerton
Towamensing ES 400/K-6
7920 Interchange Rd 18235 610-681-4024
Christine Steigerwalt, prin. Fax 681-6410

Lehman, Luzerne
Lake-Lehman SD
Supt. — See Dallas
Lehman-Jackson ES 500/K-6
PO Box 38 18627 570-675-2165
Donald James, prin. Fax 674-5907

Lemoyne, Cumberland, Pop. 4,428
West Shore SD
Supt. — See Lewisberry
Washington Heights ES 400/K-5
531 Walnut St 17043 717-761-8040
Michele Trevino, prin. Fax 901-9544

Lenhartsville, Berks, Pop. 164
Kutztown Area SD
Supt. — See Kutztown
Greenwich-Lenhartsville ES 300/K-5
1457 Krumsville Rd 19534 610-756-6948
Erin Anderson, prin. Fax 756-6858

Leola, Lancaster, Pop. 7,126
Conestoga Valley SD
Supt. — See Lancaster
Leola ES 500/K-6
11 School Dr 17540 717-656-2068
Dr. Colleen Pavlovec, prin. Fax 656-3247

Veritas Academy 200/PK-12
26 Hillcrest Ave 17540 717-556-0690
G. Tyler Fischer, hdmstr. Fax 556-0736

Levittown, Bucks, Pop. 52,008
Bristol Township SD 6,200/K-12
6401 Mill Creek Rd 19057 215-943-3200
Dr. Melanie Gehrens, supt. Fax 949-8889
www.btsd.us
Brookwood ES 500/K-5
2200 Haines Rd 19055 267-599-2400
Jacqueline Cubberly, prin. Fax 946-1390
Mill Creek ES 400/K-5
6501 Mill Creek Rd 19057 267-599-2440
Terrie Giardine, prin. Fax 547-8814
Other Schools – See Bristol, Croydon, Fairless Hills

Neshaminy SD
Supt. — See Langhorne
Buck ES 400/K-4
143 Top Rd 19056 215-809-6300
Brian Kern, prin. Fax 809-6303
Miller ES, 10 Cobalt Ridge Dr S 19057 400/K-4
Troy Bodolus, prin. 215-809-6360
Sandburg MS 500/5-8
30 Harmony Rd 19056 215-809-6220
Dawn Kelly, prin. Fax 809-6701
Schweitzer ES, 10 Harmony Rd 19056 300/K-4
Clarke Stoneback, prin. 215-809-6380

Pennsbury SD
Supt. — See Fallsington
Disney ES 400/K-5
200 Lakeside Dr 19054 215-949-6868
Laurie Ruffing, prin. Fax 949-6815
Manor ES 400/K-5
401 Penn Valley Rd 19054 215-949-6770
Terri Salvucci, prin. Fax 949-6772
Penn Valley ES 400/K-5
180 NorthTurn Ln 19054 215-949-6800
Barbara Hidalgo, prin. Fax 269-4827

Holy Family Regional S PK-8
2477 Trenton Rd 19056 215-269-9600
Linda Robinson, prin. Fax 269-9609

Hope Lutheran Christian S 200/PK-8
2600 Haines Rd 19055 215-946-3467
Elizabeth Mauro, prin. Fax 946-5926
St. Michael the Archangel S 300/PK-8
130 Levittown Pkwy 19054 215-943-0222
Stephen DiCicco, prin. Fax 943-9068

Lewisberry, York, Pop. 357
West Shore SD 7,600/K-12
507 Fishing Creek Rd 17339 717-938-9577
Dr. Todd Stoltz, supt. Fax 938-2779
www.wssd.k12.pa.us
Crossroads MS 700/6-8
535 Fishing Creek Rd 17339 717-932-1295
Christopher Konieczny, prin. Fax 938-3599
Fishing Creek ES 500/K-5
510 Fishing Creek Rd 17339 717-938-6565
Lisa Crum, prin.
Other Schools – See Camp Hill, Etters, Lemoyne, Mechanicsburg, New Cumberland

Lewisburg, Union, Pop. 5,667
Lewisburg Area SD 1,900/K-12
1951 Washington Ave 17837 570-523-3220
Dr. Steven Skalka, supt. Fax 522-3278
www.dragon.k12.pa.us
Eichhorn MS 400/6-8
2057 Washington Ave 17837 570-523-3220
George Drogin, prin. Fax 522-3331
Kelly ES 600/K-3
325 Hospital Dr 17837 570-523-3220
Christian Ruhl, prin. Fax 522-3296
Linntown ES 300/4-5
1951 Washington Ave 17837 570-523-3220
Jeremiah Bennett, prin. Fax 522-3259

Lewistown, Mifflin, Pop. 8,199
Mifflin County SD 5,100/K-12
201 8th St 17044 717-248-0148
James Estep, supt. Fax 248-5345
www.mcsdk12.org
East Derry ES 300/K-3
2316 Back Maitland Rd 17044 717-543-5615
Kevin O'Donnell, prin. Fax 543-6301
Lewistown ES 600/K-3
1 Manor Dr 17044 717-242-5823
Julie Lohr, prin. Fax 242-5810
Lewistown IS 600/4-5
212 Green Ave 17044 717-242-5801
Paul Maidens, prin. Fax 242-5804
Mifflin County MS 900/6-7
2 Manor Dr 17044 717-242-1401
Robert Reeder, prin. Fax 242-5805
Other Schools – See Mc Veytown, Reedsville

Sacred Heart of Jesus S 100/K-5
110 N Dorcas St 17044 717-248-5351
Dr. Joseph Maginnis, prin. Fax 248-1516

Liberty, Tioga, Pop. 247
Southern Tioga SD
Supt. — See Blossburg
Liberty ES 200/K-6
8622 Route 414 16930 570-324-2521
Joseph Eglesia, prin. Fax 324-2440

Ligonier, Westmoreland, Pop. 1,565
Ligonier Valley SD 1,600/K-12
339 W Main St 15658 724-238-5696
Dr. Christine Oldham Ed.D., supt. Fax 238-7877
lvsd.k12.pa.us
Ligonier Valley MS 400/6-8
536 Bell Street Ext 15658 724-238-6412
David Steimer, prin. Fax 238-2358
Mellon ES 400/K-5
559 Bell Street Ext 15658 724-238-5663
Edward Moran, prin. Fax 238-6335
Other Schools – See New Florence

Lilly, Cambria, Pop. 965
Penn Cambria SD
Supt. — See Cresson
Penn Cambria IS 300/3-4
376 Wood St 15938 814-886-8532
Dane Harrold, prin. Fax 886-5389
Penn Cambria PS 300/1-2
400 Main St 15938 814-886-2151
Cindy Pacifico, prin. Fax 886-5419

Limerick, Montgomery
Spring-Ford Area SD
Supt. — See Royersford
Evans ES 600/K-4
125 Sunset Rd 19468 610-705-6012
Jacqueline Havrilla, prin. Fax 705-6231

Linesville, Crawford, Pop. 1,024
Conneaut SD 1,300/K-12
219 W School Dr 16424 814-683-5900
Jarrin Sperry, supt. Fax 683-4127
www.conneautsd.org
Other Schools – See Conneaut Lake, Conneautville

Linwood, Delaware, Pop. 3,193
Chichester SD
Supt. — See Aston
Linwood ES 300/K-4
1403 Huddell Ave 19061 610-485-7351
Nicole Johnson, prin. Fax 485-7366

Lititz, Lancaster, Pop. 9,235
Manheim Township SD
Supt. — See Lancaster
Reidenbaugh ES 400/K-4
1001 Buckwalter Rd 17543 717-626-1000
Trudi Smith, prin. Fax 627-3887
Warwick SD 4,300/K-12
301 W Orange St 17543 717-626-3734
Dr. April Hershey, supt. Fax 626-3850
www.warwicksd.org/
Beck ES 500/K-6
418 E Lexington Rd 17543 717-626-3704
Lisa Bonfield, prin. Fax 627-6093
Bonfield ES 600/K-6
101 N Oak St 17543 717-626-3705
Stacie Bardell, prin. Fax 626-3890
Kissel Hill ES 600/K-6
215 Landis Valley Rd 17543 717-626-3703
Ryan Berardi, prin. Fax 627-6130
Lititz ES 500/K-6
20 S Cedar St 17543 717-626-3702
Jennifer Murphy, prin. Fax 627-6608
Warwick MS 700/7-8
401 Maple St 17543 717-626-3701
Steve Szobocsan, prin. Fax 627-6089

Lititz Area Mennonite S 300/PK-8
1050 E Newport Rd 17543 717-626-9551
Keith Garner, prin. Fax 626-0430
Lititz Christian S 300/PK-12
501 W Lincoln Ave 17543 717-626-9518
Rick Bernhardt, admin. Fax 626-9028
New Haven Mennonite S 100/1-12
225 Crest Rd 17543 717-626-1603

Littlestown, Adams, Pop. 4,373
Littlestown Area SD 1,700/K-12
162 Newark St 17340 717-359-4146
Christopher Bigger, supt. Fax 359-9617
www.lasd.k12.pa.us
Alloway Creek ES 300/K-5
162 Newark St 17340 717-359-4146
Chip Fissel, prin. Fax 359-5491
Maple Avenue MS 500/6-8
75 Maple Ave 17340 717-359-4146
Eric Naylor, prin. Fax 359-9617

Llewellyn, Schuylkill
Minersville Area SD
Supt. — See Minersville
Llewellyn ECC 200/PK-K
Llewellyn Rd 17944 570-544-1400
James Yacobacci, prin. Fax 544-5998

Lock Haven, Clinton, Pop. 9,648
Keystone Central SD
Supt. — See Mill Hall
Dickey ES 300/PK-5
102 S Fairview St 17745 570-748-2101
David Peters, prin. Fax 893-4949
Robb ES 400/PK-5
400 E Church St 17745 570-748-3501
Robin Taranto, prin. Fax 893-4951
Woodward ES 300/K-5
35 King St 17745 570-748-4025
Paula Lupold, prin. Fax 893-4952

Lock Haven Catholic S 200/K-8
311 W Water St 17745 570-748-7252
Michele Alexander, prin. Fax 748-1939

Loretto, Cambria, Pop. 1,282

St. Michael S 200/K-8
PO Box 67 15940 814-472-9117
Renee Phister, prin. Fax 472-9117

Lower Burrell, Westmoreland, Pop. 11,648
Burrell SD 1,800/K-12
1021 Puckety Church Rd 15068 724-334-1406
Dr. Shannon Wagner, supt. Fax 334-1429
www.burrell.k12.pa.us
Bon Air ES 500/K-3
3260 Leechburg Rd 15068 724-337-1463
Amy Lenart, prin. Fax 334-1479
Huston MS 400/6-8
1020 Puckety Church Rd 15068 724-334-1443
Brian Ferra, prin. Fax 334-1434
Stewart ES 300/4-5
2880 Leechburg Rd 15068 724-334-1483
James Croushore, prin. Fax 334-1490

Loysburg, Bedford
Northern Bedford County SD 1,000/PK-12
152 NBC Dr 16659 814-766-2221
Todd B. Beatty, supt. Fax 766-3772
www.nbcsd.org/
Northern Bedford County ES 500/PK-5
217 NBC Dr 16659 814-766-2221
Trevor Replogle, prin. Fax 766-2232
Northern Bedford County MS 200/6-8
152 NBC Dr 16659 814-766-2221
Wayne Sherlock, prin. Fax 766-3772

Loysville, Perry

Heritage Christian S 100/K-8
2401 Fort Robinson Rd 17047 717-789-0008
Alicia Miller, admin. Fax 789-0008

Lucinda, Clarion

St. Joseph S 100/PK-6
PO Box 9 16235 814-226-8018
Betsy Ochs, prin. Fax 223-9620

Lurgan, Franklin
Chambersburg Area SD
Supt. — See Chambersburg
Lurgan ES 200/K-5
8888 Roxbury Rd 17232 717-532-6125
Paul Swope, prin. Fax 532-7949

Lykens, Dauphin, Pop. 1,762
Upper Dauphin Area SD 1,300/K-12
5668 State Route 209 17048 717-362-8134
Evan Williams, supt. Fax 362-3050
www.udasd.org/
Upper Dauphin Area ES 500/K-4
5668 State Route 209 17048 717-362-4511
Jessica Megonnell, prin. Fax 362-0988
Upper Dauphin Area MS 400/5-8
5668 State Route 209 17048 717-362-8177
Jared Shade, prin. Fax 362-6567

McAdoo, Schuylkill, Pop. 2,280
Hazleton Area SD
Supt. — See Hazle Township
McAdoo-Kelayres S 900/K-8
15 Kelayres Rd 18237 570-459-3221
Frank Walton, prin. Fax 929-1581

Mc Alisterville, Juniata, Pop. 971
Juniata County SD
Supt. — See Mifflintown
Fayette Township ES 300/K-6
145 School St 17049 717-463-2236
Nancy Kramer, prin. Fax 463-2275

Juniata Mennonite S 200/K-12
289 Leonard Hill Rd 17049 717-463-2898
Tom Getz, admin. Fax 884-7876

Mc Clellandtown, Fayette
Albert Gallatin Area SD
Supt. — See Uniontown
Gallatin North MS 400/6-8
113 College Ave 15458 724-737-5423
Randy Wilson, prin. Fax 737-5312
Plava ES 300/K-5
120 Puritan Rd 15458 724-737-5424
Eric Witt, prin. Fax 737-5120

Mc Connellsburg, Fulton, Pop. 1,183
Central Fulton SD 1,000/PK-12
151 E Cherry St 17233 717-485-3183
Dr. Michelle Hall, supt. Fax 485-5984
www.cfsd.info
Mc Connellsburg ES 500/PK-5
151 E Cherry St 17233 717-485-4438
Alicia Mellott, prin. Fax 485-9002
Mc Connellsburg MS 200/6-8
151 E Cherry St 17233 717-485-3195
Christina Ramsey, prin. Fax 485-0175

Mc Donald, Washington, Pop. 2,125
Canon-McMillan SD
Supt. — See Canonsburg
Cecil IS 400/5-6
3676 Millers Run Rd 15057 724-745-2623
Robert Kleinhans, prin. Fax 873-5227

Fort Cherry SD 1,000/K-12
110 Fort Cherry Rd 15057 724-796-1551
Dr. Jill Jacoby, supt. Fax 796-0065
www.fortcherry.org
Fort Cherry ES 600/K-6
110 Fort Cherry Rd 15057 724-796-1551
Daniel S. Mayer, prin. Fax 356-2770

South Fayette Township SD 2,800/K-12
3680 Old Oakdale Rd 15057 412-221-4542
Dr. Bille Rondinelli, supt. Fax 693-2883
www.southfayette.org
South Fayette Township ES 700/K-2
3620 Old Oakdale Rd 15057 412-221-4542
Laurie Gray, prin. Fax 693-2762
South Fayette Township IS 700/3-5
1200 Lt Will Way 15057 412-221-4542
Thomas Kaminski, prin. Fax 693-8084
South Fayette Township MS 600/6-8
3700 Old Oakdale Rd 15057 412-221-4542
Kristin Deichler, prin. Fax 693-0860

Mc Kean, Erie, Pop. 382
General McLane SD
Supt. — See Edinboro
Mc Kean ES 300/K-4
5120 West Rd 16426 814-273-1033
Michael Getz, prin. Fax 273-1048

Mc Keesport, Allegheny, Pop. 18,886
Elizabeth Forward SD
Supt. — See Elizabeth
Greenock ES 200/K-2
1101 Greenock Buena Vista, 412-896-2324
Jennifer Meliton, prin. Fax 751-3818
Mt. Vernon ES 200/3-5
2400 Greenock Buena Vista, 412-896-2327
Jennifer Meliton, prin. Fax 751-1345

McKeesport Area SD 3,100/K-12
3590 Oneil Blvd, 412-664-3610
Dr. Mark Holtzman, supt. Fax 664-3638
www.mckasd.net
Founders Hall MS 500/6-8
3600 Oneil Blvd, 412-664-3690
Ashlee Boyle, prin. Fax 664-3768
Twin Rivers ES 500/K-2
1600 Cornell St, 412-664-3750
Paul Sweda, prin. Fax 664-3756
Other Schools – See White Oak

South Allegheny SD 1,600/PK-12
2743 Washington Blvd, 412-675-3070
Richard M. Fine, supt. Fax 672-2836
www.southallegheny.org
South Allegheny ECC 300/PK-1
1 Glendale St, 412-675-3070
Katelyn Vogel, prin. Fax 673-3991
South Allegheny ES 600/2-6
1707 Washington Blvd, 412-675-3070
Dave Hoffman, prin. Fax 672-8541

Mc Kees Rocks, Allegheny, Pop. 5,853
Montour SD 2,800/K-12
225 Clever Rd 15136 412-490-6500
Dr. Christopher Stone, supt. Fax 788-1196
www.montourschools.com
Montour ES, 221 Clever Rd 15136 1,100/K-4
Jason Burik, prin.
Other Schools – See Coraopolis

Sto-Rox SD 900/K-12
298 Ewing Rd 15136 412-771-3213
Frank Dalmas, supt. Fax 771-3848
www.srsd.k12.pa.us
Sto-Rox PS 500/K-3
300 Ewing Rd 15136 412-771-3213
Lori Sims, prin. Fax 771-8641
Sto-Rox Upper ES 100/4-6
298 Ewing Rd 15136 412-771-3213
Lori Sims, prin. Fax 771-3848

Holy Trinity S 400/PK-8
5720 Steubenville Pike 15136 412-787-2656
Kimberly Stevenson, prin. Fax 787-9487
Robinson Township Christian S 100/PK-12
77 Phillips Ln 15136 412-787-5919
Arthur Broadwick, prin. Fax 787-1558

Mc Murray, Washington, Pop. 4,622
Peters Township SD 4,300/K-12
631 E McMurray Rd 15317 724-941-6251
Dr. Jeannine French, supt. Fax 941-6565
www.ptsd.k12.pa.us
Mc Murray ES 1,000/4-6
626 E McMurray Rd 15317 724-941-5020
Blair Stoehr, prin. Fax 941-2769
Peters Township MS 700/7-8
625 E McMurray Rd 15317 724-941-2688
Adam Sikorski, prin. Fax 941-1426
Pleasant Valley ES 400/K-3
250 E McMurray Rd 15317 724-941-6260
Greg Marquis, prin. Fax 941-0708
Other Schools – See Venetia

St. Benedict the Abbot Preschool 100/PK-PK
120 Abington Dr 15317 724-941-9406
Beth Jurcic, dir.

Mc Sherrystown, Adams, Pop. 3,006

St. Joseph Academy 50/PK-PK
90 Main St 17344 717-630-9990
Sr. Anne Leonard, prin. Fax 637-2441
St. Teresa of Calcutta S 300/4-8
316 North St 17344 717-637-3135
Patricia Foltz, prin. Fax 637-1715

Macungie, Lehigh, Pop. 3,024
East Penn SD
Supt. — See Emmaus
Eyer MS, 5616 Buckeye Rd 18062 900/6-8
Michael Kelly, prin. 610-965-1600
Lower Macungie MS 1,100/6-8
6299 Lower Macungie Rd 18062 610-395-8593
Suzanne Vincent, prin. Fax 398-4385
Macungie ES 500/K-5
4062 Brookside Rd 18062 610-965-1617
James Best, prin. Fax 966-7583
Shoemaker ES 700/K-5
4068 N Fairview St 18062 610-965-1626
Lynn Brinckman, prin. Fax 965-2977
Willow Lane ES 700/K-5
6135 SauerKraut Ln 18062 484-519-3300
Dr. Anthony Moyer, prin.

Salem Christian S 200/PK-12
8031 Salem Bible Church Rd 18062 610-966-5823
Mark Stanton, head sch Fax 965-8368

Mc Veytown, Mifflin, Pop. 340
Mifflin County SD
Supt. — See Lewistown
Strodes Mills ES 200/K-3
185 Chestnut Ridge Rd 17051 717-248-7154
Frank Miller, prin. Fax 242-5839

Mahanoy City, Schuylkill, Pop. 4,109
Mahanoy Area SD 1,000/K-12
1 Golden Bear Dr 17948 570-773-3443
Dr. Joie Green, supt. Fax 773-2913
www.mabears.net
Mahanoy Area ES 400/K-6
1 Golden Bear Dr 17948 570-773-3443
Michael Heater, prin. Fax 773-4034

Malvern, Chester, Pop. 2,955
Great Valley SD 4,000/K-12
47 Church Rd 19355 610-889-2100
Dr. Regina Palubinsky, supt. Fax 889-2120
www.gvsd.org
Charlestown ES 300/K-5
2060 Charlestown Rd 19355 610-935-1555
Christopher Pickell, prin. Fax 935-4963
Great Valley MS 1,000/6-8
255 Phoenixville Pike 19355 610-644-6440
Dr. Edward Souders, prin. Fax 889-1166
Markley ES 600/K-5
354 Swedesford Rd 19355 610-644-1790
Victoria Morris, prin. Fax 407-0720
Sugartown ES 500/K-5
611 Sugartown Rd 19355 610-699-1500
Dr. Karen Schneck, prin. Fax 699-1512
Wayne ES 500/K-5
20 Devon Rd 19355 610-647-6651
Bonnie Citron, prin. Fax 889-2118

Christ Memorial Lutheran S 100/PK-K
89 Line Rd 19355 610-296-0650
Jodie Merow, admin. Fax 644-4677
St. Patrick S 300/K-8
115 Channing Ave 19355 610-644-5797
Patricia O'Donnell, prin. Fax 647-0535

Manchester, York, Pop. 2,703
Northeastern York SD 3,700/K-12
41 Harding St 17345 717-266-3667
Dr. Stacey Sidle, supt. Fax 266-5792
www.nesd.k12.pa.us
Orendorf ES 300/K-3
101 S Hartman St 17345 717-266-5621
Devin Moyer, prin. Fax 266-2058
Shallow Brook IS 400/4-6
213 S Hartman St 17345 717-266-7030
Scott D'Orazio, prin. Fax 266-7042
Spring Forge IS 500/4-6
100 S Hartman St 17345 717-266-9833
Beth Wolff, prin. Fax 266-1693
Other Schools – See Mount Wolf, York, York Haven

Manheim, Lancaster, Pop. 4,777
Manheim Central SD 2,400/K-12
281 White Oak Rd 17545 717-664-8540
Dr. Peter Aiken, supt. Fax 664-8539
www.manheimcentral.org
Burgard ES 400/K-6
111 S Penn St 17545 717-665-2209
Michael Pyle, prin. Fax 665-4600
Doe Run ES 400/K-6
281 Doe Run Rd 17545 717-665-8800
Arthur Paynter, prin. Fax 665-8860
Manheim Central MS 400/7-8
261 White Oak Rd 17545 717-664-1700
Dr. Seth Kensinger, prin. Fax 664-1859

Manheim Christian S 200/PK-8
686 Lebanon Rd 17545 717-665-4300
Jennifer Knecht, prin. Fax 664-4253

Mansfield, Tioga, Pop. 3,545
Southern Tioga SD
Supt. — See Blossburg
Miller ES 500/K-6
1 Dorsett Dr 16933 570-662-2192
Patricia White, prin. Fax 662-3180

New Covenant Academy 200/PK-12
310 Extension St 16933 570-662-2996
Bruce Reagan, admin. Fax 662-0272

Maple Glen, Montgomery, Pop. 6,682
Upper Dublin SD 4,300/K-12
1580 Fort Washington Ave 19002 215-643-8800
Dr. Deborah Wheeler, supt. Fax 643-8808
www.udsd.org
Maple Glen ES 400/K-5
1581 Fort Washington Ave 19002 215-643-3421
Timothy Bickhart M.Ed., prin. Fax 540-0988
Other Schools – See Dresher, Fort Washington, Willow Grove

Our Lady of Mercy Regional S 400/K-8
29 Conwell Dr 19002 215-646-0150
John McGrath, prin. Fax 646-7150

Mapleton Depot, Huntingdon, Pop. 435
Mt. Union Area SD
Supt. — See Mount Union
Mapleton-Union ES 200/K-6
13606 Smith Valley Rd 17052 814-542-4401
Kelly Hicks, lead tchr. Fax 542-8633

Marcus Hook, Delaware, Pop. 2,316
Chichester SD
Supt. — See Aston
Marcus Hook ES 300/K-4
711 Market St 19061 610-485-9780
Jim Adair, prin. Fax 485-7210

Marienville, Forest, Pop. 3,126
Forest Area SD
Supt. — See Tionesta
East Forest ES 100/PK-6
120 W Birch St 16239 814-927-6688
Debra Arner, prin. Fax 927-8452

Marietta, Lancaster, Pop. 2,552
Donegal SD
Supt. — See Mount Joy
Donegal IS 300/3-6
1177 River Rd 17547 717-426-1561
Dr. Clare Reich, prin. Fax 426-3105

Susquehanna Waldorf S 100/PK-8
15 W Walnut St 17547 717-426-4506

Marion Center, Indiana, Pop. 450
Marion Center Area SD 1,400/PK-12
PO Box 156 15759 724-397-5551
Clint Weimer, supt. Fax 397-9144
www.mcasd.net/
McCreery ES 500/PK-6
PO Box 199 15759 724-397-5551
Mark Magolis, prin. Fax 397-9093
Other Schools – See Home

Markleysburg, Fayette, Pop. 283
Uniontown Area SD
Supt. — See Uniontown
Marclay ES 100/K-5
111 Bruceton Rd 15459 724-329-4248
Tracy Holesapple, prin. Fax 329-5237
McMullen MS 200/6-8
4773 National Pike 15459 724-329-8811
Tracy Holesapple, prin. Fax 329-4696

Mars, Butler, Pop. 1,685
Mars Area SD 3,300/K-12
545 Route 228 16046 724-625-1518
Dr. Wesley Shipley, supt. Fax 625-1060
www.marsk12.org
Mars Area Centennial S 500/5-6
100 Winfield Manor Dr 16046 724-625-2601
Adam Kostewicz, prin. Fax 625-2660
Mars Area ES 700/2-4
549 Route 228 16046 724-625-3161
Robert Zaccari, prin. Fax 625-3499
Mars Area MS 500/7-8
1775 Three Degree Rd 16046 724-625-3145
Todd Kolson, prin. Fax 625-2147
Mars Area Primary Center 400/K-1
547 Route 228 16046 724-625-1588
Todd Lape, prin. Fax 625-2280

Martinsburg, Blair, Pop. 1,949
Spring Cove SD
Supt. — See Roaring Spring
Martinsburg ES 200/3-5
415 Spring St 16662 814-793-2014
Kendra Pritchett, prin. Fax 793-9447

Masontown, Fayette, Pop. 3,367
Albert Gallatin Area SD
Supt. — See Uniontown
Masontown ES 200/K-5
201 W Spring Ave 15461 724-583-1091
Lisa Haught, prin. Fax 583-1893

Matamoras, Pike, Pop. 2,433
Delaware Valley SD
Supt. — See Milford
Delaware Valley ES 500/PK-5
500 Avenue S 18336 570-296-1820
MaryAnn Olsommer, prin. Fax 296-3163

Mayfield, Lackawanna, Pop. 1,797
Lakeland SD
Supt. — See Scott Township
Lakeland ES - Mayfield Campus 300/K-6
501 Linden St 18433 570-254-9485
Kevin Sullivan, prin. Fax 876-3410

Meadowbrook, Montgomery

Meadowbrook S 100/PK-6
1641 Hampton Rd 19046 215-884-3238
Michael J Reardon, head sch Fax 884-9143

Meadville, Crawford, Pop. 13,058
Crawford Central SD 3,800/K-12
11280 Mercer Pike 16335 814-724-3960
Thomas Washington, supt. Fax 333-8731
www.craw.org
First District ES 400/K-6
725 N Main St 16335 814-724-1124
Jon Colinear, prin. Fax 337-5990
Meadville Area MS 500/7-8
974 North St 16335 814-333-1188
Scott Lynch, prin. Fax 333-2799
Neason Hill ES 400/K-6
11293 Williamson Rd 16335 814-724-7886
Carol Lilly, prin. Fax 337-2329
Second District ES 400/K-6
1216 S Main St 16335 814-724-7073
Kurt Meader, prin. Fax 337-5835
West End ES 500/K-6
12068 Brooks Rd 16335 814-724-1450
Tamara Clark, prin. Fax 337-5886
Other Schools – See Cochranton

Calvary Baptist Christian Academy 200/PK-12
543 Randolph St 16335 814-724-6606
Randy Thaxton, admin. Fax 337-4357
Seton S 200/PK-8
385 Pine St 16335 814-336-2320
Laura Blake, prin. Fax 336-2328

Mechanicsburg, Cumberland, Pop. 8,802
Cumberland Valley SD 8,300/K-12
6746 Carlisle Pike 17050 717-697-8261
Frederick Withum, supt. Fax 506-3302
www.cvschools.org
Eagle View MS 900/6-8
6746 Carlisle Pike 17050 717-766-0217
John Gallagher, prin. Fax 506-3806
Good Hope MS 1,000/6-8
451 Skyport Rd 17050 717-761-1865
Jeff Hosenfeld, prin. Fax 761-5910
Green Ridge ES 500/K-5
1 Green Ridge Rd 17050 717-766-4911
Amy Lena, prin. Fax 796-2482
Hampden ES 700/K-5
441 Skyport Rd 17050 717-737-4513
Connie Henry, prin. Fax 761-6780
Silver Spring ES 500/K-5
6746 Carlisle Pike 17050 717-506-3755
Dr. Anthony Parks, prin. Fax 506-3711
Sporting Hill ES 600/K-5
210 S Sporting Hill Rd 17050 717-761-5052
Dayl Shaddock, prin. Fax 761-6311
Other Schools – See Boiling Springs, Carlisle, Enola

Mechanicsburg Area SD 3,800/K-12
100 E Elmwood Ave 17055 717-691-4500
Mark K. Leidy Ed.D., supt. Fax 691-3438
www.mbgsd.org
Broad Street ES 200/1-5
200 S Broad St 17055 717-691-4574
Andrew B. Bitz, prin. Fax 697-7392
Elmwood ES 400/1-5
100 E Elmwood Ave 17055 717-691-4578
John P. McIntosh, prin. Fax 697-3655
Kindergarten Academy 300/K-K
505 S Filbert St 17055 717-506-0852
Kathleen M. Healey, prin. Fax 506-0853
Mechanicsburg MS 900/6-8
1750 S Market St 17055 717-691-4560
Joel A. Yohn, prin. Fax 791-7977
Northside ES 200/1-5
411 N Walnut St 17055 717-691-4581
Ashlyn Ecker, prin. Fax 697-8674

Shepherdstown ES 200/1-2
1849 S York St 17055 717-691-4589
Krista L. Archibald, prin. Fax 691-2474
Upper Allen ES 400/3-5
1790 S Market St 17055 717-691-4594
Stacy L. Alexander, prin. Fax 697-9107

West Shore SD
Supt. — See Lewisberry
Rossmoyne ES 200/3-5
1225 Rossmoyne Rd 17055 717-697-8578
Amanda Lerew, prin.

St. Joseph S 400/K-8
420 E Simpson St 17055 717-766-0561
John Cominsky, prin. Fax 766-1226

Media, Delaware, Pop. 5,231
Rose Tree Media SD 3,700/K-12
308 N Olive St 19063 610-627-6000
James Wigo, supt. Fax 891-0959
www.rtmsd.org
Glenwood ES 400/K-5
122 S Pennell Rd 19063 610-627-6900
Eric Bucci, prin. Fax 892-7193
Indian Lane ES 500/K-5
309 S Old Middletown Rd 19063 610-627-7100
John Reid, prin. Fax 566-6582
Media ES 500/K-5
100 E Front St 19063 610-627-6800
Dr. Paula Voshell, prin. Fax 566-3745
Rose Tree ES 300/K-5
1101 First Ave 19063 610-627-7200
Dr. Jenny Robinson, prin. Fax 566-5087
Springton Lake MS 800/6-8
1900 N Providence Rd 19063 610-627-6500
Dr. Robert Salladino, prin. Fax 566-8665

Benchmark S 100/1-8
2107 N Providence Rd 19063 610-565-3741
Dr. Robert Gaskins Ph.D., head sch Fax 565-3872
Media-Providence Friends S 200/PK-8
125 W Third St 19063 610-565-1960
Earl Sissell, head sch Fax 565-9866
St. Mary Magdalen S 400/K-8
2430 N Providence Rd 19063 610-565-1822
Denise Winterberger, prin. Fax 627-9670
Walden S 100/PK-8
901 N Providence Rd 19063 610-892-8000

Mehoopany, Wyoming
Tunkhannock Area SD
Supt. — See Tunkhannock
Mehoopany ES 200/K-4
400 Scottsville Rd 18629 570-712-2031
Michelle Knoebel, prin. Fax 219-4042

Mercer, Mercer, Pop. 1,978
Mercer Area SD 1,200/K-12
545 W Butler St 16137 724-662-5100
Dr. William Gathers, supt. Fax 662-5109
www.mercer.k12.pa.us
Mercer Area ES 600/K-6
301 Lamor Rd 16137 724-662-5102
Michelle Dietrich, prin. Fax 662-5103
Mercer Area MS 200/7-8
545 W Butler St 16137 724-662-5104
Michael Piddington, prin. Fax 662-2993

Mercersburg, Franklin, Pop. 1,540
Tuscarora SD 2,600/K-12
100 W Seminary St 17236 717-328-3127
Dr. Matthew Strine, supt. Fax 328-9316
www.tus.k12.pa.us
Buchanan MS 600/6-8
5191 Fort Loudon Rd 17236 717-328-5221
James Carbaugh, prin. Fax 328-9081
Mercersburg ES 300/K-5
30 S Park Ave 17236 717-328-5278
Ryan Kaczmark, prin. Fax 328-5628
Montgomery ES 300/K-5
9138 Fort Loudon Rd 17236 717-328-2023
Ryan Kaczmark, prin. Fax 328-9723
Mountain View ES 300/K-5
2311 Lemar Rd 17236 717-328-2191
Brett Kagarise, prin. Fax 328-9591
Other Schools – See Saint Thomas

Merion Station, Montgomery, Pop. 700
Lower Merion SD
Supt. — See Ardmore
Merion ES 500/K-5
540 S Bowman Ave 19066 610-645-1470
Anne Heffron, prin. Fax 664-8195

Kohelet Yeshiva 100/K-12
223 N Highland Ave 19066 610-667-2020
Rabbi Gil Perl, head sch Fax 667-2223
Waldron Mercy Academy 500/PK-8
513 Montgomery Ave 19066 610-664-9847
Nell Stetser, prin. Fax 664-6364

Meyersdale, Somerset, Pop. 2,169
Meyersdale Area SD 900/K-12
309 Industrial Park Rd 15552 814-634-5123
Dr. Tracey Karlie, supt. Fax 634-0832
www.masd.net
Meyersdale Area ES 400/K-5
1345 Shaw Mines Rd 15552 814-634-5123
Devin Pritts, prin. Fax 634-1812
Meyersdale Area MS 200/6-8
1353 Shaw Mines Rd 15552 814-634-5123
Wayne Miller, prin. Fax 634-0832

Middleburg, Snyder, Pop. 1,296
Midd-West SD 2,100/K-12
568 E Main St 17842 570-837-0046
Richard J. Musselman, supt. Fax 837-3018
www.mwsd.cc
Middleburg ES 700/K-5
600 Wagenseller St 17842 570-837-0046
Cynthia L. Hutchinson, prin. Fax 837-0579
Midd-West MS 300/6-7
10 Dock Hill Rd 17842 570-837-0551
Dane S. Aucker, prin. Fax 837-5061
Other Schools – See Beaver Springs

Middletown, Dauphin, Pop. 8,620
Lower Dauphin SD
Supt. — See Hummelstown
Londonderry ES 300/K-5
260 Schoolhouse Rd 17057 717-944-9462
Kathryn I. Ringso, prin. Fax 944-9529

Middletown Area SD 2,000/K-12
55 W Water St 17057 717-948-3300
Lori Suski Ed.D., supt. Fax 948-3329
www.raiderweb.org
Fink ES 200/K-5
150 N Race St 17057 717-948-3370
Thomas Shaffer, prin. Fax 948-3409
Kunkel ES 400/K-5
2401 Fulling Mill Rd 17057 717-939-6862
Daniel Borrelli, prin. Fax 939-3487
Middletown Area MS 600/6-8
215 Oberlin Rd 17057 717-930-0739
Kevin Cook, prin. Fax 944-0951
Reid ES 400/K-5
201 Oberlin Rd 17057 717-948-3360
Earl Bright, prin. Fax 702-1219

Seven Sorrows of BVM S 200/PK-8
360 E Water St 17057 717-944-5371
Angela Love, prin. Fax 944-5419

Midland, Beaver, Pop. 2,534
Midland Borough SD 300/PK-8
173 7th St 15059 724-643-8650
Sean Tanner, supt. Fax 643-4887
www.midlandpa.org
Midland ES 300/PK-8
173 7th St 15059 724-643-8650
Brenda S. Militello, prin. Fax 643-4887

Western Beaver County SD 700/PK-12
343 Ridgemont Dr 15059 724-643-9310
Dr. Robert Postupac, supt. Fax 643-8048
www.westernbeaver.org
Fairview ES 300/PK-5
343 Ridgemont Dr 15059 724-643-9680
Ron Busby, prin. Fax 643-5568

Mifflin, Juniata, Pop. 639
Juniata County SD
Supt. — See Mifflintown
Mountain View ES 200/K-5
23215 Route 35 S 17058 717-436-6816
Christie Holderman, prin. Fax 436-0011

Mifflinburg, Union, Pop. 3,516
Mifflinburg Area SD 2,100/K-12
178 Maple St 17844 570-966-8200
Daniel Lichtel, supt. Fax 966-8210
www.mifflinburg.org
Mifflinburg Area IS 500/3-5
250 Mabel St 17844 570-966-8270
Scott Zimmerman, prin. Fax 966-8273
Mifflinburg Area MS 500/6-8
100 Mabel St 17844 570-966-8290
Daryl Hunsberger, prin. Fax 966-8304
Mifflinburg ES 500/K-2
115 Shipton St 17844 570-966-8320
Karen Shaffer, prin. Fax 966-8339

Mifflintown, Juniata, Pop. 920
Juniata County SD 3,000/K-12
146 Weatherby Way 17059 717-436-2111
Keith Yarger, supt. Fax 436-0200
www.jcsdk12.org
Fermanagh-Mifflintown ES 300/K-5
75 S 7th St 17059 717-436-2111
Christie Holderman, prin. Fax 436-2777
Tuscarora JHS 400/6-8
3873 William Penn Hwy 17059 717-436-2165
Aaron Bennett, prin. Fax 436-5999
Walker Township ES 100/K-5
7864 William Penn Hwy 17059 717-436-6469
Christie Holderman, prin. Fax 436-2275
Other Schools – See Honey Grove, Mc Alisterville, Mifflin, Port Royal, Richfield, Thompsontown

Milford, Pike, Pop. 1,003
Delaware Valley SD 4,000/PK-12
236 Route 6 and 209 18337 570-296-1800
Dr. John Bell, supt. Fax 296-3172
www.dvsd.org
Delaware Valley MS 500/6-8
258 Route 6 and 209 18337 570-296-1830
Peter Ioppolo, prin. Fax 296-3162
Other Schools – See Dingmans Ferry, Matamoras, Shohola

Millersburg, Dauphin, Pop. 2,536
Millersburg Area SD 800/K-12
799 Center St 17061 717-692-2108
Thomas Haupt, supt. Fax 692-2895
www.mlbgsd.k12.pa.us/
Lenkerville ES 400/K-5
520 S Market St 17061 717-692-3072
Mike Lyter, prin. Fax 692-4255
Millersburg Area MS 200/6-8
799 Center St 17061 717-692-2108
David Shover, prin. Fax 692-2895

Northern Dauphin Christian S 100/PK-12
PO Box 233 17061 717-692-1940
JoAnn Kieffer, head sch Fax 692-1940

Millerstown, Perry, Pop. 664
Greenwood SD 800/K-12
405 E Sunbury St 17062 717-589-3117
Dr. Nicholas Guarente, supt. Fax 589-1017
www.greenwoodsd.org
Greenwood ES 400/K-5
405 E Sunbury St 17062 717-589-3115
Jeff Kuhns, prin. Fax 589-3013
Greenwood MS 200/6-8
405 E Sunbury St 17062 717-589-3116
Michele Dubaich, prin. Fax 589-1016

Millersville, Lancaster, Pop. 8,074
Penn Manor SD
Supt. — See Lancaster
Eshleman ES 600/K-6
545 Leaman Ave 17551 717-872-9540
Dr. Krista Cox, prin. Fax 872-9508

Mill Hall, Clinton, Pop. 1,602
Keystone Central SD 4,100/PK-12
86 Administration Dr 17751 570-893-4900
Kelly Hastings, supt. Fax 893-4923
www.kcsd.k12.pa.us
Central Mountain MS 900/6-8
200 Ben Ave 17751 570-726-3141
Justin Evey, prin. Fax 726-7227
Mill Hall ES 400/PK-5
210 Kyler Ave 17751 570-726-3105
Michael Hall, prin. Fax 726-7014
Other Schools – See Blanchard, Lock Haven, Renovo

Mill Village, Erie, Pop. 404
Fort LeBoeuf SD
Supt. — See Waterford
Mill Village ES 100/K-5
PO Box 56L 16427 814-796-2060
Jason Vaughn, prin. Fax 796-4850

Millville, Columbia, Pop. 940
Millville Area SD 700/K-12
PO Box 260 17846 570-458-5538
Cynthia Jenkins, supt. Fax 458-5584
www.millville.k12.pa.us
Millville Area ES 400/K-6
PO Box 300 17846 570-458-5538
Edward Sanders, prin. Fax 458-4715

Greenwood Friends S 100/PK-8
PO Box 438 17846 570-458-5532
Andrew Smith, head sch Fax 458-5533

Milton, Northumberland, Pop. 6,900
Milton Area SD 2,200/K-12
700 Mahoning St 17847 570-742-7614
Cathy Keegan M.Ed., supt. Fax 742-4523
www.miltonsd.org/
Baugher ES 600/K-5
60 Brenda Rovenolt Dr 17847 570-742-7631
Dave Slater, prin. Fax 742-6025
Milton Area MS 500/6-8
700 Mahoning St 17847 570-742-7685
Gregory Scoggins, prin. Fax 742-4857
Other Schools – See Montandon, New Columbia

Meadowbrook Christian S 400/PK-12
363 Stamm Rd 17847 570-742-2638
Rod Baughman M.Ed., admin. Fax 742-4710

Minersville, Schuylkill, Pop. 4,345
Minersville Area SD 1,300/PK-12
PO Box 787 17954 570-544-1400
Dr. Carl McBreen, supt. Fax 544-6162
www.battlinminers.com
Minersville Area ES 500/1-6
PO Box 787 17954 570-544-1400
James Yacobacci, prin. Fax 544-1404
Other Schools – See Llewellyn

St. Nicholas Ukranian Catholic S 200/PK-8
515 N Front St 17954 570-544-2800

Mohnton, Berks, Pop. 3,015
Governor Mifflin SD
Supt. — See Shillington
Brecknock ES 500/K-4
1332 Alleghenyville Rd 19540 610-775-5079
Dr. Maryellen Kueny, prin. Fax 685-3798

Mohrsville, Berks, Pop. 375

King's Academy 200/PK-12
1562 Main St 19541 610-926-9639
Michelle Goodman, head sch Fax 926-8089

Monaca, Beaver, Pop. 5,641
Central Valley SD 2,400/K-12
160 Baker Road Ext 15061 724-775-5600
Nicholas Perry, supt. Fax 775-4302
www.centralvalleysd.org
Central Valley MS 500/6-8
1500 Allen Ave 15061 724-775-5600
Brian Dolph, prin. Fax 775-4302
Todd Lane ES 600/3-5
113 Todd Ln 15061 724-775-5600
Dr. Kelly Sherbondy, prin. Fax 775-2799
Other Schools – See Aliquippa

Monessen, Westmoreland, Pop. 7,447
Monessen CSD 800/PK-12
1275 Rostraver St 15062 724-684-3600
Dr. Leanne Spazak, supt. Fax 684-6782
monessenschooldistrict.com
Monessen Elementary Center 400/PK-5
1275 Rostraver St 15062 724-684-4456
Bethanne Natali, prin. Fax 684-6782
Monessen MS 200/6-8
1245 State Rd 15062 724-684-6282
Eric Manko, prin. Fax 684-7931

Monongahela, Washington, Pop. 4,226
Elizabeth Forward SD
Supt. — See Elizabeth
Penn ES 300/K-5
392 William Penn Rd 15063 412-896-2330
Brad Simala, prin. Fax 384-4311

Ringgold SD
Supt. — See New Eagle
Ringgold ES South 800/K-5
120 Alexander St 15063 724-258-8454
Wendy Yonkers, prin. Fax 258-7050

Madonna Regional S 100/PK-8
731 Chess St 15063 724-258-3199
Donald Militzer, prin. Fax 258-6764

Monroeville, Allegheny, Pop. 28,591
Gateway SD 3,500/K-12
9000 Gateway Campus Blvd 15146 412-372-5300
William Short, supt. Fax 373-5731
www.gatewayk12.org
Evergreen ES 300/K-4
3831 Evergreen Dr 15146 412-373-5842
Michael Matteo, prin. Fax 373-5845
Gateway MS 600/7-8
4450 Old William Penn Hwy 15146 412-373-5780
Rocco Telli, prin. Fax 373-5794
Moss Side MS 500/5-6
9000 Gateway Campus Blvd 15146 412-373-5830
Eric Knorr, prin. Fax 373-5885
Ramsey ES 300/K-4
2200 Ramsey Rd 15146 412-373-5856
Joe DiLucente, prin. Fax 373-1058
Steward ES 300/K-4
5000 Gateway Campus Blvd 15146 412-373-5874
Dr. Celine Kandala, prin. Fax 858-1058
University Park ES 300/K-4
320 Noel Dr 15146 724-327-4113
Jennifer Hoffner, prin. Fax 733-9436

North American Martyrs S 100/PK-7
2526 Haymaker Rd 15146 412-373-0889
Nikole Laubham, prin. Fax 349-0175
St. Bernadette S 300/PK-8
245 Azalea Dr 15146 412-372-7255
Sr. Carol Arch, prin. Fax 372-7649

Montandon, Northumberland, Pop. 898
Milton Area SD
Supt. — See Milton
Montandon ES 200/K-5
PO Box 130 17850 570-523-3218
Philip Heggenstaller, prin. Fax 524-9665

Montgomery, Lycoming, Pop. 1,554
Montgomery Area SD 700/K-12
120 Penn St 17752 570-547-1608
Daphne Bowers, supt. Fax 547-6271
www.montasd.org
Montgomery ES 500/K-6
120 Penn St 17752 570-547-1608
Karen Snyder, prin. Fax 547-6055

Montoursville, Lycoming, Pop. 4,566
Loyalsock Township SD
Supt. — See Williamsport
Schick ES 700/K-5
2800 Four Mile Dr 17754 570-326-3554
Suzanne Foresman, prin. Fax 326-1498

Montoursville Area SD 2,000/K-12
50 N Arch St 17754 570-368-2491
Christina Bason, supt. Fax 368-3501
www.montoursville.k12.pa.us
Loyalsock Valley ES 300/K-4
3790 State Route 87 17754 570-435-0446
Darrin Feerrar, prin. Fax 435-3214
Lyter ES 500/K-4
900 Spruce St 17754 570-368-2614
Darrin Feerrar, prin. Fax 368-3535
McCall MS 600/5-8
600 Willow St 17754 570-368-2441
Daniel Taormina, prin. Fax 368-3521

Montrose, Susquehanna, Pop. 1,608
Montrose Area SD 1,400/K-12
273 Meteor Way 18801 570-278-6212
Carol Boyce, supt. Fax 278-4798
www.masd.info
Lathrop Street ES 400/K-6
130 Lathrop St 18801 570-278-0310
Gregory Adams, prin. Fax 278-4799
Other Schools – See Friendsville

Moon Township, Allegheny, Pop. 10,187
Moon Area SD 3,700/K-12
8353 University Blvd 15108 412-264-9440
Dr. Maureen Ungarean Ed.D., supt. Fax 264-3268
www.moonarea.net
Allard ES 200/K-4
170 Shafer Rd 15108 412-264-9440
Susan Kazmierczak, prin. Fax 262-2581
Bon Meade ES 500/K-4
1595 Brodhead Rd 15108 412-264-9440
Ashley Beeson, prin. Fax 457-0919
Brooks ES 300/K-4
1720 Hassam Rd 15108 412-264-9440
Lucas Furlow, prin. Fax 264-4743
Hyde ES, 110 Wallridge Dr 15108 200/K-4
Joseph Johnson, prin. 412-264-9440
McCormick ES 200/K-4
2801 Beaver Grade Rd 15108 412-264-9440
Dr. Julie Moore Ed.D., prin. Fax 893-0428
Moon Area Lower MS 600/5-6
904 Beaver Grade Rd 15108 412-264-9440
Melissa Heasley, prin.
Moon Area Upper MS 600/7-8
904 Beaver Grade Rd 15108 412-264-9440
Melissa Heasley, prin. Fax 264-3013

Rhema Christian S 100/PK-8
1301 Coraopolis Heights Rd 15108 412-269-9555
Christopher Berndt, prin. Fax 269-1914
St. Margaret Mary Child Care Center 100/PK-K
1 Parish Pl 15108 412-264-9716
Sandra Lubick, prin. Fax 262-3674

Moosic, Lackawanna, Pop. 5,672
Riverside SD
Supt. — See Taylor
Riverside ES East 300/3-6
900 School St 18507 570-562-2121
Nicole VanLuvender, prin. Fax 341-8298

Morgantown, Lancaster, Pop. 817

Conestoga Christian S 200/PK-12
2760 Main St 19543 610-286-0353
Kenneth Parris, admin. Fax 286-0350

Morrisdale, Clearfield, Pop. 747
West Branch Area SD 1,100/K-12
516 Allport Cutoff 16858 814-345-5615
Michelle Dutrow, supt. Fax 345-5220
www.westbranch.org
West Branch Area ES 600/K-6
356 Allport Cutoff 16858 814-345-5627
Mark Mitchell, prin. Fax 345-5220

Morrisville, Bucks, Pop. 8,532
Morrisville Borough SD 600/K-12
550 W Palmer St 19067 215-736-2681
Michael Kopakowski, supt. Fax 736-2413
mv.org
Grandview ES 200/K-2
80 Grandview Ave 19067 215-736-5280
Lynn Palumbo M.Ed., prin. Fax 736-5281
Morrisville IS, 550 W Palmer St 19067 100/3-5
Lynn Palumbo, prin. 215-736-5270

Pennsbury SD
Supt. — See Fallsington
Roosevelt ES 500/K-5
185 Walton Dr 19067 215-428-4256
Lisa Follman, prin. Fax 428-4263

Holy Trinity S 200/K-8
99 Osborne Ave 19067 215-295-6900
Elaine McDowell, prin. Fax 337-9079

Morton, Delaware, Pop. 2,597
Ridley SD
Supt. — See Folsom
Amosland ES 500/K-5
549 Amosland Rd 19070 610-534-1900
John Theodosiades, prin. Fax 237-8000

Our Lady of Angels Regional S 300/K-8
2130 Franklin Ave 19070 610-543-8350
Sr. Deborah Krist, prin. Fax 544-3203

Moscow, Lackawanna, Pop. 2,016
North Pocono SD 3,000/K-12
701 Church St 18444 570-842-7659
Bryan McGraw, supt. Fax 842-0886
www.npsd.org/
Moscow ES 600/K-3
851 Church St 18444 570-842-8464
Jeffery Hatala, prin. Fax 842-8905
North Pocono IS 500/4-5
701 Church St 18444 570-842-7676
Ian Farr, prin. Fax 842-4027
North Pocono MS 700/6-8
701 Church St 18444 570-842-4588
Matthew Montoro, prin. Fax 842-1783
Other Schools – See Lake Ariel

Mountain Top, Luzerne, Pop. 10,876
Crestwood SD 2,900/K-12
281 S Mountain Blvd 18707 570-474-6782
Joseph Gorham, supt. Fax 474-2254
www.csdcomets.org
Crestwood MS 500/7-8
281 S Mountain Blvd 18707 570-474-6782
Bonnie Gregory, prin. Fax 474-2254
Fairview ES 700/K-6
117 Spruce St 18707 570-474-5942
Peg Foster, prin. Fax 403-0496
Rice ES 800/K-6
3700 Church Rd 18707 570-868-3161
Kevin Seyer, prin. Fax 868-3147

St. Jude S 200/K-8
422 S Mountain Blvd 18707 570-474-5803
Sr. Ellen Fischer, prin. Fax 403-6159
Wyoming Valley SDA S 50/K-8
476 3rd St 18707 570-868-5958

Mount Carmel, Northumberland, Pop. 5,840
Mt. Carmel Area SD 1,300/PK-12
600 W 5th St 17851 570-339-1500
Bernard Stellar, supt. Fax 339-0487
www.mca.k12.pa.us
Mt. Carmel Area ES 900/PK-6
630 W 5th St 17851 570-339-1500
Susan Nestico, prin. Fax 339-5210

Mount Holly Springs, Cumberland, Pop. 1,983
Carlisle Area SD
Supt. — See Carlisle
Mt. Holly Springs ES 200/K-5
110 Mooreland Ave 17065 717-240-6800
Molli Davis, prin. Fax 486-3089

South Middleton SD
Supt. — See Boiling Springs
Rice ES 700/K-3
805 Holly Pike 17065 717-258-6484
David Boley, prin. Fax 486-3654

Mount Joy, Lancaster, Pop. 7,283
Donegal SD 2,300/K-12
1051 Koser Rd 17552 717-653-1447
Dr. J. Michael Lausch Ed.D., supt. Fax 492-1350
www.donegalsd.org
Donegal JHS 500/7-8
915 Anderson Ferry Rd 17552 717-928-2900
Judy Haugh, prin. Fax 928-2911
Donegal PS 700/K-2
1055 Koser Rd 17552 717-653-8812
Christopher Miller, prin. Fax 492-1341
Other Schools – See Marietta

Hempfield SD
Supt. — See Landisville
Farmdale ES 600/K-6
695 Prospect Rd 17552 717-684-2206
Trisha Pearson, prin. Fax 618-1007

Lancaster Mennonite S - Kraybill Campus 300/PK-8
598 Kraybill Church Rd 17552 717-653-5236

Mount Lebanon, Allegheny, Pop. 32,900

Mount Lebanon Montessori S 200/PK-6
550 Sleepy Hollow Rd 15228 412-563-2858

Mount Penn, Berks, Pop. 3,026
Antietam SD
Supt. — See Reading
Mount Penn ES 400/2-6
2310 Cumberland Ave 19606 610-779-3547
Shirley Feyers, prin. Fax 779-6937

Mount Pleasant, Westmoreland, Pop. 4,419
Mt. Pleasant Area SD 2,100/K-12
271 State St 15666 724-547-4100
Dr. Timothy Gabauer, supt. Fax 547-0629
www.mpasd.net
Mount Pleasant Area JHS 300/7-8
265 State St 15666 724-547-4100
Robert Gumbita, admin. Fax 547-0526
Norvelt ES 400/K-6
163 Lilac Ln 15666 724-547-4100
Scott Bryer, prin. Fax 423-2733
Ramsay ES 400/2-6
300 Eagle St 15666 724-547-4100
Lance Benteler, prin. Fax 547-0564
Rumbaugh ES 100/K-1
2414 School St 15666 724-547-4100
Lance Benteler, prin. Fax 547-1860
Other Schools – See Jones Mills

Verna Montessori S 100/PK-8
268 Prittstown Rd 15666 724-887-8810
Sr. Letizia Tribuzio, prin. Fax 887-2977

Mount Union, Huntingdon, Pop. 2,343
Mt. Union Area SD 1,500/K-12
603 N Industrial Dr 17066 814-542-8631
Dr. Brett Gilliland, supt. Fax 542-8633
www.muasd.org/
Mount Union JHS 300/7-8
706 N Shaver St 17066 814-542-9311
Amy Smith, prin.
Mount Union-Kistler ES 300/K-6
154 School St 17066 814-542-2595
Matthew Franks, prin. Fax 542-8633
Shirley Township ES 400/K-6
14188 2nd St 17066 814-542-9381
Dawn Holesa, prin. Fax 542-8633
Other Schools – See Mapleton Depot

Mountville, Lancaster, Pop. 2,760
Hempfield SD
Supt. — See Landisville
Mountville ES 600/K-6
200 College Ave 17554 717-285-5501
Maria Hoover, prin. Fax 618-1006

Dayspring Christian Academy 200/PK-12
120 College Ave 17554 717-285-2000
Dr. Michael Myers, hdmstr.

Mount Wolf, York, Pop. 1,367
Northeastern York SD
Supt. — See Manchester
Mt. Wolf ES 200/K-3
PO Box 1013 17347 717-266-6570
Jefferson Clifton, prin. Fax 266-6516
Northeastern MS 600/7-8
4855 Board Rd 17347 717-266-3676
Michael Alessandroni, prin. Fax 266-9735

Muncy, Lycoming, Pop. 2,457
Muncy SD 1,000/K-12
206 Sherman St 17756 570-546-3125
Dr. Craig Skaluba, supt. Fax 546-6676
www.muncysd.org
Myers ES 600/K-6
125 New St 17756 570-546-3129
Frank Jankowski, prin. Fax 546-7744

Munhall, Allegheny, Pop. 11,221
Steel Valley SD 1,400/K-12
220 E Oliver Rd 15120 412-464-3600
Edward Wehrer, supt. Fax 464-3626
steelvalleysd.org
Park ES 200/K-4
4102 Main St 15120 412-464-3600
Dr. Thomas Shaughnessy, prin. Fax 464-3661
Steel Valley MS 400/5-8
3114 Main St 15120 412-464-3600
Bryan Macuga, admin. Fax 326-0315
Other Schools – See Homestead

St. Therese S 300/PK-8
3 Saint Therese Ct 15120 412-462-8163
Sr. Eileen Johnston, prin. Fax 462-5865

Murrysville, Westmoreland, Pop. 19,098
Franklin Regional SD 3,600/K-12
3210 School Rd 15668 724-327-5456
Dr. Gennaro R. Piraino Ed.D., supt. Fax 327-6149
www.franklinregional.k12.pa.us
Franklin Regional MS 900/6-8
4660 Old William Penn Hwy 15668 724-327-5456
Andrew Leviski, prin. Fax 733-0949
Heritage ES 600/K-5
3240 School Rd 15668 724-327-5456
Dr. Robert Buffone, prin. Fax 327-8298
Newlonsburg ES 200/K-5
3170 School Rd 15668 724-327-5456
Tina Gillen, prin. Fax 327-4903
Sloan ES 600/K-5
4121 Sardis Rd 15668 724-327-5456
Jennifer DiFulvio, prin. Fax 733-5487

Mother of Sorrows S 300/PK-8
3264 Evergreen Dr 15668 724-733-8840
Theresa Szmed, prin. Fax 325-1144

Muse, Washington, Pop. 2,481
Canon-McMillan SD
Supt. — See Canonsburg
Muse ES 200/K-4
PO Box 430 15350 724-745-9014
Tom Theodore, prin. Fax 873-5233

Myerstown, Lebanon, Pop. 3,030
Eastern Lebanon County SD 2,400/K-12
180 Elco Dr 17067 717-866-7117
Julia R. Vicente M.A., supt. Fax 866-7084
www.elcosd.org/
Eastern Lebanon County IS 600/3-5
100 Evergreen Dr 17067 717-866-4521
Michael Gerhart, prin. Fax 866-6791
Eastern Lebanon County MS 600/6-8
60 Evergreen Dr 17067 717-866-6591
Christine Kassay, prin. Fax 866-5837
Jackson ES 200/K-2
558 W Main Ave 17067 717-866-2624
Tam Hower, prin. Fax 866-9690
Other Schools – See Richland

Lebanon Valley Christian S 100/1-12
7821 Lancaster Ave 17067 717-933-5171
Myerstown Mennonite S 100/1-12
739 E Lincoln Ave 17067 717-866-5667

Nanticoke, Luzerne, Pop. 10,349
Greater Nanticoke Area SD 2,200/K-12
427 Kosciuszko St 18634 570-735-1270
Dr. Ronald Grevera Ed.D., supt. Fax 735-1350
www.gnasd.com
GNA Elementary Center 500/3-5
601 Kosciuszko St 18634 570-735-1320
Sharon Baddick M.Ed., prin. Fax 733-1006
Greater Nanticoke Area Ed Center 400/6-7
600 E Union St 18634 570-735-2770
Sharon Baddick M.Ed., prin. Fax 740-2792
Kennedy S 200/2-2
513 Kosciuszko St 18634 570-735-6450
John Gorham, prin. Fax 740-2757
Smith ES 300/K-1
25 Robert St 18634 570-735-3740
John Gorham, prin. Fax 740-2704

Nanty Glo, Cambria, Pop. 2,702
Blacklick Valley SD 700/PK-12
555 Birch St 15943 814-749-9211
William Kanich, supt. Fax 749-8627
www.bvsd.k12.pa.us
Blacklick Valley ES 400/PK-6
1000 W Railroad St 15943 814-749-9211
Samuel Brunatti, prin. Fax 749-8710

Narberth, Montgomery, Pop. 4,161
Lower Merion SD
Supt. — See Ardmore
Penn Valley ES 600/K-5
301 Righters Mill Rd 19072 610-645-1460
Scott Mitchell, prin. Fax 664-7370
Welsh Valley MS 900/6-8
325 Tower Ln 19072 610-658-3920
Chris Hall, prin. Fax 667-4749

St. Margaret S 300/PK-8
227 N Narberth Ave 19072 610-664-2640
Micah Sumner, prin. Fax 664-4677

Natrona Heights, Allegheny, Pop. 11,400
Highlands SD 2,500/K-12
PO Box 288 15065 724-226-2400
Dr. Michael Bjalobok, supt. Fax 226-8437
www.goldenrams.com
Fawn PS 300/K-2
5591 Ridge Rd 15065 724-224-4844
Ian Miller, prin. Fax 224-9243
Highlands MS 600/6-8
1350 Broadview Blvd 15065 724-226-0600
Charles Mort, prin. Fax 226-3287
Other Schools – See Brackenridge, Tarentum

Our Lady of the Most Blessed Sacrament S 200/PK-8
800 Montana Ave 15065 724-226-2345
Sean Davis, prin. Fax 226-4934

Nazareth, Northampton, Pop. 5,699
Nazareth Area SD 4,600/K-12
1 Education Plz 18064 610-759-1170
Dr. Dennis L. Riker, supt. Fax 759-9637
www.nazarethasd.org
Butz ES 400/K-3
960 Bushkill Center Rd 18064 610-759-1118
Kelly Apruzzi, prin. Fax 759-0454
Lower Nazareth ES 400/K-3
4422 Newburg Rd 18064 610-759-7311
Michael Santos, prin. Fax 759-7922
Nazareth Area IS 1,100/4-6
355 Tatamy Rd 18064 484-292-1111
Joseph Yanek, prin. Fax 292-1120
Nazareth Area MS 700/7-8
94 Friedensthal Ave 18064 610-759-3350
Robert Bauder, prin. Fax 759-3725
Shafer ES 600/K-3
49 S Liberty St 18064 610-759-5228
William Mudlock, prin. Fax 759-2253

Pen Argyl Area SD
Supt. — See Pen Argyl
Plainfield ES 500/K-3
539 School Rd 18064 610-746-4436
Philip Giaquinto, prin. Fax 759-4227

Holy Family S 300/K-8
17 N Convent Ave 18064 610-759-5642
Christine Bruce, prin. Fax 759-0386

Nescopeck, Luzerne, Pop. 1,577
Berwick Area SD
Supt. — See Berwick
Nescopeck ES 300/K-5
315 Dewey St 18635 570-759-6400
Christopher Rivera, prin. Fax 759-4380

Nesquehoning, Carbon, Pop. 3,320
Panther Valley SD
Supt. — See Lansford
Panther Valley ES 600/K-3
1 N Mermon Ave 18240 570-669-9411
Robert Palazzo, prin. Fax 669-6043

New Alexandria, Westmoreland, Pop. 552
Greensburg Salem SD
Supt. — See Greensburg
Metzgar ES 300/K-5
140 CC Hall Dr 15670 724-668-2237
Tina Federico, prin. Fax 668-8297

New Bethlehem, Clarion, Pop. 986
Redbank Valley SD 1,100/K-12
920 Broad St 16242 814-275-2426
Michael Drzewiecki, supt. Fax 275-2428
www.redbankvalley.net/
Redbank Valley PS 300/K-2
600 Vine St 16242 814-275-2680
Cheryl McCauley, prin. Fax 275-4110
Other Schools – See Hawthorn

New Bloomfield, Perry, Pop. 1,237
West Perry SD
Supt. — See Elliottsburg
New Bloomfield ES 400/PK-5
300 W High St 17068 717-582-4318
Lucas Clouse, prin. Fax 582-7579

New Brighton, Beaver, Pop. 5,744
New Brighton Area SD 1,500/K-12
3225 43rd St 15066 724-843-1795
Dr. Joseph Guarino, supt. Fax 843-6144
www.nbasd.org
New Brighton Area ES 700/K-5
3200 43rd St 15066 724-843-1194
Jason Hall, prin. Fax 843-8769
New Brighton Area MS 300/6-8
901 Penn Ave 15066 724-846-8100
Julian Underwood, prin. Fax 846-2337

New Britain, Bucks, Pop. 3,100
Central Bucks SD
Supt. — See Doylestown
Pine Run ES 500/K-6
383 W Butler Ave 18901 267-893-4450
Amanda Mumford Ed.D., prin. Fax 893-5813

New Castle, Lawrence, Pop. 22,422
Laurel SD 1,300/K-12
2497 Harlansburg Rd 16101 724-658-8940
Leonard Rich, supt. Fax 658-2992
www.laurel.k12.pa.us
Laurel ES 600/K-6
223 McCaslin Rd 16101 724-658-2673
Daniel Svirbly M.Ed., prin. Fax 658-1167

Neshannock Township SD 1,300/K-12
3834 Mitchell Rd 16105 724-658-4793
Dr. Terence Meehan, supt. Fax 658-1828
www.neshannock.k12.pa.us
Neshannock JHS 200/7-8
3834 Mitchell Rd 16105 724-658-5513
Dr. Tracy McCalla, prin. Fax 657-8169
Neshannock Memorial ES 700/K-6
3832 Mitchell Rd 16105 724-652-8709
Matthew Heasley, prin. Fax 657-9721

New Castle Area SD 2,300/PK-12
420 Fern St 16101 724-656-4756
John Sarandrea, supt. Fax 656-4767
www.ncasd.com
Croton Pre K Center 100/PK-PK
420 Fern St 16101 724-656-4815
Debra DeBlasio, prin. Fax 656-4783
Lockley Early Learning Center 300/K-2
900 E Main St 16101 724-656-4735
Joseph Anderson, prin.
New Castle JHS 500/7-8
310 E Lincoln Ave 16101 724-656-4700
Carol Morrell, prin. Fax 658-6276
Washington IS 700/3-6
101 E Euclid Ave 16105 724-656-4729
Tabitha Marino, prin. Fax 658-7219

Shenango Area SD 1,200/K-12
2501 Old Pittsburgh Rd 16101 724-658-7287
Dr. Michael Schreck, supt. Fax 658-5370
www.shenango.k12.pa.us
Shenango ES 600/K-6
2501 Old Pittsburgh Rd 16101 724-658-5566
Adam Vincent, prin. Fax 658-7871
Union Area SD 600/K-12
2106 Camden Ave 16101 724-658-4775
Michael Ross, supt. Fax 658-5151
www.union.k12.pa.us/
Union Memorial ES 300/K-5
500 S Scotland Ln 16101 724-652-6683
Linda O'Neill, prin. Fax 658-5151

New Castle Christian Academy 100/PK-8
1701 Albert St 16105 724-658-5858
Greg Heotzler, admin. Fax 658-5861
St. Vitus S 100/PK-8
915 S Jefferson St 16101 724-654-9297
Cathy Ryan, prin. Fax 654-9364

New Columbia, Union, Pop. 998
Milton Area SD
Supt. — See Milton
White Deer ES 300/K-5
631 New Columbia Rd 17856 570-568-6201
Philip Heggenstaller, prin. Fax 568-0566

New Cumberland, Cumberland, Pop. 7,166
West Shore SD
Supt. — See Lewisberry
Fairview ES, 480 Lewisberry Rd 17070 300/K-5
Christopher Stine, prin. 717-774-2970
Hillside ES, 516 7th St 17070 600/K-5
Julie Dougherty, prin. 717-774-1321
New Cumberland MS 400/6-8
331 8th St 17070 717-774-0162
Melissa Herbert, prin. Fax 901-9474

St. Theresa S 400/PK-8
1200 Bridge St 17070 717-774-7464
Matthew Shore, prin. Fax 774-3154

New Eagle, Washington, Pop. 2,165
Ringgold SD 2,900/K-12
400 Main St 15067 724-258-9329
Dr. Karen Polkabla, supt. Fax 258-5363
www.ringgold.org
Other Schools – See Finleyville, Monongahela

New Florence, Westmoreland, Pop. 686
Ligonier Valley SD
Supt. — See Ligonier
Laurel Valley ES 200/K-5
137 Education Ln 15944 724-235-2723
Edward Moran, prin. Fax 235-9413

Newfoundland, Wayne
Wallenpaupack Area SD
Supt. — See Hawley
Wallenpaupack South ES 300/K-5
989 Main St 18445 570-676-3335
Mark Kirsten, prin. Fax 676-3389

New Freedom, York, Pop. 4,411

St. John the Baptist S 100/PK-5
315 N Constitution Ave 17349 717-235-3525
Susan Mareck, prin. Fax 235-8595
Shrewsbury Christian Academy 100/PK-8
701 Windy Hill Rd 17349 717-235-5763
Christine Huffman, prin. Fax 235-5357

New Holland, Lancaster, Pop. 5,286
Eastern Lancaster County SD 3,200/K-12
PO Box 609 17557 717-354-1500
Dr. Robert Hollister, supt. Fax 354-1512
www.elanco.org
Garden Spot MS 500/7-8
PO Box 609 17557 717-354-1560
Jeffrey Starr, prin. Fax 354-1129
New Holland ES 600/K-6
126 Eastern School Rd 17557 717-354-1520
Dr. Susan Sneath, prin. Fax 354-1541
Other Schools – See Denver, East Earl

New Hope, Bucks, Pop. 2,495
New Hope-Solebury SD 1,500/K-12
180 W Bridge St 18938 215-862-2552
Dr. Stephen M. Yanni, supt. Fax 744-6012
www.nhsd.org
New Hope-Solebury MS 400/6-8
184 W Bridge St 18938 215-862-0608
Dr. Christina Cortellessa, prin. Fax 862-2862
New Hope-Solebury Upper ES 400/3-5
186 W Bridge St 18938 215-862-8026
Dr. Michael McKenna, prin. Fax 862-8027
Other Schools – See Solebury

New Kensington, Westmoreland, Pop. 12,575
New Kensington-Arnold SD 1,400/PK-12
707 Stevenson Blvd 15068 724-335-4401
Dr. John Pallone J.D., supt. Fax 994-1212
www.nkasd.com
Martin ES 100/PK-K
1800 7th St 15068 724-335-4641
Thomas Rocchi, prin. Fax 334-7850
Other Schools – See Arnold

Mary Queen of Apostles S 300/PK-3
100 Freeport Rd 15068 724-335-5911
Catherine Collett, prin. Fax 335-3505
Mary Queen of Apostles S 100/4-8
110 Elmtree Rd 15068 724-339-4411
Catherine Collett, prin. Fax 337-6457

New Milford, Susquehanna, Pop. 860
Blue Ridge SD 1,000/PK-12
5150 School Rd 18834 570-465-3141
Matthew Button, supt. Fax 465-3148
www.brsd.org
Blue Ridge ES 500/PK-5
5150 School Rd 18834 570-465-3141
Danelle Decker, prin. Fax 465-3148

Blue Ridge MS 200/6-8
5150 School Rd 18834 570-465-3177
Peter Supko, prin. Fax 465-3148

New Oxford, Adams, Pop. 1,767
Conewago Valley SD 3,900/K-12
130 Berlin Rd 17350 717-624-2157
Dr. Russell Greenholt, supt. Fax 624-5020
www.conewago.k12.pa.us
Conewago Valley IS 900/4-6
175 700 Rd 17350 717-624-2157
Dr. Kenneth Armacost, prin. Fax 624-6667
New Oxford ES 600/K-3
116 N Berlin Ave 17350 717-624-2157
Misti Wildasin, prin. Fax 624-6570
New Oxford MS 600/7-8
130 Berlin Rd 17350 717-624-2157
Dr. Christopher Bowman, prin. Fax 624-6560
Other Schools – See Hanover

New Paris, Bedford, Pop. 183
Chestnut Ridge SD
Supt. — See Fishertown
Chestnut Ridge Central ES 400/PK-2
2534 Quaker Valley Rd 15554 814-839-4195
Dr. Amy Miller, prin. Fax 839-4418

Newport, Perry, Pop. 1,551
Newport SD 1,100/K-12
PO Box 9 17074 717-567-3806
Ryan Neuhard, supt. Fax 567-6468
www.newportsd.org
Newport ES 500/K-5
PO Box 9 17074 717-567-3806
Michael Smith, prin. Fax 567-9485
Newport MS 300/6-8
PO Box 9 17074 717-567-3806
Bryan Rehmeyer, prin. Fax 567-2619

New Providence, Lancaster
Solanco SD
Supt. — See Quarryville
Providence ES 400/K-5
137 Truce Rd 17560 717-786-3582
Christina McLaughlin, prin. Fax 786-1532

New Ringgold, Schuylkill, Pop. 272
Tamaqua Area SD
Supt. — See Tamaqua
West Penn Township ES 300/K-5
185 School Dr 17960 570-386-5051
Steven Behr, prin. Fax 386-3226

New Stanton, Westmoreland, Pop. 2,152
Hempfield Area SD
Supt. — See Greensburg
Stanwood ES 600/K-5
255 Arona Rd 15672 724-838-4000
John Behrendt, prin. Fax 838-4001

Newtown, Bucks, Pop. 2,215
Council Rock SD 11,200/K-12
30 N Chancellor St 18940 215-944-1000
Dr. Robert Fraser, supt. Fax 944-1031
www.crsd.org
Feinstone ES 700/K-6
1090 Eagle Rd 18940 215-944-2400
John Harlan, prin. Fax 944-2497
Goodnoe ES 800/K-6
298 Frost Ln 18940 215-944-2100
Nicole Crawford, prin. Fax 944-2197
Newtown ES 700/K-6
1 Wrights Rd 18940 215-944-2200
Kevin King, prin. Fax 944-2297
Newtown MS 900/7-8
116 Richboro Newtown Rd 18940 215-944-2600
Timothy Long, prin. Fax 944-2698
Other Schools – See Churchville, Holland, Richboro, Wrightstown

---

Newtown Friends S 300/PK-8
1450 Newtown Langhorne Rd 18940 215-968-2225
Dana Harrison, head sch Fax 968-9346
St. Andrew S 800/PK-8
51 Wrights Rd 18940 215-968-2685
Nancy Matteo, prin. Fax 968-4795

Newtown Square, Delaware, Pop. 11,300
Marple Newtown SD 3,300/K-12
40 Media Line Rd 19073 610-359-4256
Carol Cary Ed.D., supt. Fax 723-3340
www.mnsd.net
Culbertson ES 400/K-5
3530 Goshen Rd 19073 610-359-4340
James Wigo, prin. Fax 353-4183
Other Schools – See Broomall

Episcopal Academy 1,200/PK-12
1785 Bishop White Dr 19073 484-424-1400
Dr. Thomas Locke, hdmstr. Fax 424-1600
St. Anastasia S 600/PK-8
3309 West Chester Pike 19073 610-356-6225
Beth Doyle, prin. Fax 356-5748
Stratford Friends S 50/K-9
2 Bishop Hollow Rd 19073 610-355-9580
Jill Dougherty, head sch Fax 355-9585

New Tripoli, Lehigh, Pop. 887
Northwestern Lehigh SD 2,200/K-12
6493 Route 309 18066 610-298-8661
Dr. Mary Anne Wright Ph.D., supt. Fax 298-8002
www.nwlehighsd.org
Northwestern Lehigh ES 500/K-5
6493 Route 309 18066 610-298-8661
Maria Pulli, prin. Fax 298-8573
Northwestern Lehigh MS 500/6-8
6636 Northwest Rd 18066 610-298-8661
William Dovico, prin. Fax 298-8178
Other Schools – See Kutztown

Newville, Cumberland, Pop. 1,313
Big Spring SD 2,700/K-12
45 Mount Rock Rd 17241 717-776-2000
Dr. Richard Fry, supt. Fax 776-4428
www.bigspringsd.org
Big Spring MS 600/6-8
47 Mount Rock Rd 17241 717-776-2000
Dr. Linda Wilson, prin. Fax 776-2468
Mt. Rock ES 300/K-5
47 Mount Rock Rd 17241 717-776-2000
Karen Ward, prin. Fax 776-2025
Newville ES 300/K-5
100 Steelstown Rd 17241 717-776-2035
Clarissa Nace, prin. Fax 776-2038
Oak Flat ES 400/K-5
334 Centerville Rd 17241 717-776-2045
Stacey Kimble, prin. Fax 776-2495

New Wilmington, Lawrence, Pop. 2,444
Wilmington Area SD 1,200/K-12
300 Wood St 16142 724-656-8866
Jeffrey Matty, supt. Fax 946-8982
www.wilmington.k12.pa.us
Wilmington Area ES 300/K-4
450 Wood St 16142 724-656-8866
Robert Kwiat, prin.
Wilmington Area MS 400/5-8
400 Wood St 16142 724-656-8866
George Endrizzi, prin.

Nicktown, Cambria

Northern Cambria Catholic S 100/PK-8
PO Box 252 15762 814-948-8900
Theresa Burba, prin. Fax 948-8720

Normalville, Fayette
Connellsville Area SD
Supt. — See Connellsville
Springfield Township ES 300/K-5
PO Box 317 15469 724-455-3191
Stephanie Romanishan, prin. Fax 455-3114

Norristown, Montgomery, Pop. 33,250
Norristown Area SD 7,400/PK-12
401 N Whitehall Rd 19403 610-630-5000
Janet Samuels Ph.D., supt. Fax 630-5013
www.nasd.k12.pa.us
Cole Manor ES 500/K-4
2350 Springview Rd 19401 610-275-5525
Nicole Poncheri, prin. Fax 272-0529
East Norriton MS 900/5-8
330 Roland Dr 19401 610-275-6520
Dr. Christina Spink, prin. Fax 272-0531
Eisenhower MS 500/5-8
1601 Markley St 19401 610-277-8720
Christina Taylor, prin. Fax 270-2901
Fly ES 600/K-4
2920 Potshop Rd 19403 610-630-0380
Jason Smith, prin. Fax 630-1519
Gotwals ES 500/K-4
1 E Oak St 19401 610-275-1077
Jeanette Fernandez, prin. Fax 277-4622
Hancock ES 500/K-4
1520 Arch St 19401 610-275-5522
Sondra Stoczko, prin. Fax 272-0547
Marshall Street ES 600/PK-4
1525 W Marshall St 19403 610-630-8550
Mark Skoczynski, prin. Fax 630-1378
Musselman Learning Center 300/K-K
1020 Sandy Hill Rd 19401 484-270-2140
Stephanie Cole, prin.
Stewart MS 500/5-8
1315 W Marshall St 19401 610-275-6870
Martina Walls, prin. Fax 272-0560
Whitehall ES 500/K-4
399 N Whitehall Rd 19403 610-630-6000
Maryanne Hoskins, prin. Fax 630-1540

St. Francis of Assisi S 200/PK-8
601A Buttonwood St 19401 610-272-0501
Bridget Tigue, prin. Fax 272-8011
Visitation BVM S 600/PK-8
190 N Trooper Rd 19403 610-539-6080
Darlene Adams, prin. Fax 630-7946

Northampton, Northampton, Pop. 9,830
Northampton Area SD 5,100/K-12
2014 Laubach Ave 18067 610-262-7811
Joseph Kovalchik, supt. Fax 262-1150
www.nasdschools.org/
Borough ES 900/K-5
1677 Lincoln Ave 18067 610-262-6430
Renee Sallit, prin. Fax 262-6461
Northampton Area MS 900/6-8
1617 Laubach Ave 18067 610-262-7817
Patrice Turner, prin. Fax 262-6583
Other Schools – See Bath, Walnutport

Good Shepherd 300/PK-8
1300 Newport Ave 18067 610-262-9171
John Crescenzo, prin. Fax 262-2202

North Braddock, Allegheny, Pop. 4,701
Woodland Hills SD 2,300/K-12
531 Jones Ave, 412-731-1300
Alan Johnson, supt. Fax 273-3601
www.whsd.net
Other Schools – See Pittsburgh, Turtle Creek

North East, Erie, Pop. 4,255
North East SD 1,600/K-12
50 E Division St 16428 814-725-8671
Dr. Frank McClard, supt. Fax 725-9380
www.nesd1.org
Davis PS 400/K-2
50 E Division St 16428 814-725-8671
Dr. Jennifer Ritter, prin. Fax 725-0821
North East IS 400/3-5
50 E Division St 16428 814-725-8671
Brian Emick, prin. Fax 725-8643
North East MS 400/6-8
1903 Freeport Rd 16428 814-725-8671
Gregory Beardsley, prin. Fax 725-1086

St. Gregory S 100/PK-8
140 W Main St 16428 814-725-4571
Nancy Pierce, prin. Fax 725-4572

Northern Cambria, Cambria, Pop. 4,022
Northern Cambria SD 1,100/K-12
601 Joseph St 15714 814-948-5481
Robert Rocco, supt. Fax 948-6058
www.ncsd.k12.pa.us
Northern Cambria ES 400/K-5
601 Joseph St 15714 814-948-5880
Rebecca Roberts, prin. Fax 948-5561
Northern Cambria MS 200/6-8
601 Joseph St 15714 814-948-5880
Rebecca Roberts, prin. Fax 948-5561

North Huntingdon, Westmoreland, Pop. 28,158
Norwin SD 5,200/K-12
281 McMahon Dr 15642 724-861-3000
Dr. William Kerr, supt. Fax 863-9467
www.norwinsd.org
Hahntown ES 500/K-4
791 Entry Rd 15642 724-861-3020
Lisa Willig, prin. Fax 861-3020
Hillcrest IS 800/5-6
11091 Mockingbird Dr 15642 724-861-3015
Brian O'Neil, prin. Fax 864-7203
Norwin MS 800/7-8
10870 Mockingbird Dr 15642 724-863-5707
Robert Suman, prin. Fax 863-5408
Sheridan Terrace ES 500/K-4
1219 Morris St 15642 724-861-3025
Heather Newell, prin. Fax 863-4380
Stewartsville ES 500/K-4
101 Carpenter Ln 15642 724-861-3030
April Preisach, prin. Fax 863-9010
Sunset Valley ES 500/K-4
11605 Dickens Dr 15642 724-861-3035
Jason Cendroski, prin. Fax 863-4096

Queen of Angels S 300/PK-8
1 Main St 15642 724-978-0144
Sandra Stonebraker, prin. Fax 978-0171

Northumberland, Northumberland, Pop. 3,769
Shikellamy SD
Supt. — See Sunbury
Priestley ES 400/K-5
423 Cannery Rd 17857 570-473-3261
Roy Burns, prin. Fax 473-4495
Shikellamy MS 400/6-8
545 Permastone Dr 17857 570-286-3736
Dr. Mary Murphy Kahn, prin.

Northumberland Christian S 200/PK-12
351 5th St 17857 570-473-9786
Sunbury Christian Academy 100/PK-12
135 Spruce Hollow Rd 17857 570-473-7592
Richard Hennett, admin. Fax 473-7531

North Versailles, Allegheny, Pop. 12,302
East Allegheny SD 900/PK-12
1150 Jacks Run Rd 15137 412-824-8012
Donald MacFann, supt. Fax 824-1062
www.eawildcats.net
Logan ES 400/PK-6
1154 Jacks Run Rd 15137 412-824-6053
Sean Gildea, prin. Fax 824-6095

Praise Christian Academy 100/K-8
245 Foster Rd 15137 412-829-0400

North Wales, Montgomery, Pop. 3,136
North Penn SD
Supt. — See Lansdale
Gwyn-Nor ES 600/K-6
139 Hancock Rd 19454 215-368-7105
Sylvannya Dantzler, prin. Fax 368-7884
Montgomery ES 600/K-6
1221 Stump Rd 19454 215-368-6614
T.J. Seidenberger, prin. Fax 368-7882
North Wales ES 400/K-6
201 Summit St 19454 215-699-4471
Joe Covone, prin. Fax 616-0521

Gwynedd Friends K 50/PK-K
1101 DeKalb Pike 19454 215-699-5392
Daena Berdougo, dir.
Mary Mother of the Redeemer S 700/PK-8
1321 Upper State Rd 19454 215-412-7101
Denise Judge, prin. Fax 412-7197

Norwood, Delaware, Pop. 5,840
Interboro SD
Supt. — See Prospect Park
Norwood S 600/K-8
558 Seneca Ave 19074 610-237-6425
Daniel Mills, prin. Fax 237-1481

Oakdale, Allegheny, Pop. 1,442
West Allegheny SD
Supt. — See Imperial
Donaldson ES 500/K-5
600 Donaldson Rd 15071 724-213-1010
Patricia Nolan, prin. Fax 213-1002
McKee ES 500/K-5
1501 Oakdale Rd 15071 724-693-8451
Thomas Orr, prin. Fax 693-0924

Oakmont, Allegheny, Pop. 6,258
Riverview SD 1,000/K-12
701 10th St 15139 412-828-1800
Margaret DiNinno, supt. Fax 828-9346
www.rsd.k12.pa.us
Tenth Street ES 300/K-6
701 10th St 15139 412-828-1800
David Zolkowski, prin. Fax 828-7373
Other Schools – See Verona

St. Irenaeus S 100/PK-8
637 4th St 15139 412-828-8444
Sr. Carol Papp, prin. Fax 828-8749

Oaks, Montgomery
Spring-Ford Area SD
Supt. — See Royersford
Oaks ES 600/K-4
PO Box 396 19456 610-705-6008
Mark Moyer, prin. Fax 705-6247

Oil City, Venango, Pop. 10,397
Oil City Area SD 2,000/K-12
825 Grandview Rd 16301 814-676-1867
Patrick Gavin, supt. Fax 676-2211
www.ocasd.org
Hasson Heights ES 500/K-4
833 Grandview Rd 16301 814-677-8021
Matthew Siembida, prin. Fax 677-2225
Oil City Area MS 700/5-8
8 Lynch Blvd 16301 814-676-5702
Joy Zuck, prin. Fax 676-2306
Seventh Street ES 100/2-4
102 W 7th St 16301 814-677-3029
Tammie Newman, prin. Fax 677-3390
Smedley Street ES 100/K-1
310 Smedley St 16301 814-676-2294
Tammie Newman, prin. Fax 676-9314

St. Stephen S 200/PK-8
214 Reed St 16301 814-677-3035
Michael O'Brien, prin. Fax 677-2053

Old Forge, Lackawanna, Pop. 8,255
Old Forge SD 900/K-12
300 Marion St 18518 570-457-6721
John Rushefski, supt. Fax 457-8389
www.ofsd.cc
Old Forge ES 500/K-6
401 Melmore St 18518 570-457-8391
Nathan Barrett, prin. Fax 414-0516

Oley, Berks, Pop. 1,277
Oley Valley SD 1,700/K-12
17 Jefferson St 19547 610-987-4100
Dr. Tracy Shank Ed.D., supt. Fax 987-4138
www.oleyvalleysd.org
Oley Valley ES 700/K-5
3257 Friedensburg Rd 19547 610-987-4100
Dr. Matthew Broskey, prin. Fax 987-4173
Oley Valley MS 400/6-8
3247 Friedensburg Rd 19547 610-987-4100
Daniel Marks, prin. Fax 987-4240

Orefield, Lehigh
Parkland SD
Supt. — See Allentown
Kernsville ES 400/K-5
5051 Kernsville Rd 18069 610-351-5840
Michael Gehringer, prin. Fax 351-5849
Orefield MS 1,100/6-8
2675 PA Route 309 18069 610-351-5750
Todd Gombos, prin. Fax 351-5799

St. Joseph the Worker S 500/PK-8
1858 Applewood Dr 18069 610-395-7221
Jody Myers, prin. Fax 395-7904

Oreland, Montgomery, Pop. 5,575
Springfield Township SD 2,200/K-12
1901 Paper Mill Rd 19075 215-233-6000
Dr. Nancy Hacker, supt. Fax 233-5815
www.sdst.org
Springfield Township ES - Enfield Campus 400/K-1
1118 Church Rd 19075 215-233-6080
Catherine VanVooren, prin. Fax 233-4688
Springfield Township MS 500/6-8
1901 Paper Mill Rd 19075 215-233-6070
Zachary Fuller, prin. Fax 233-6091
Other Schools – See Flourtown

Orwigsburg, Schuylkill, Pop. 3,077
Blue Mountain SD 2,800/K-12
685 Red Dale Rd 17961 570-366-0515
Dr. David Helsel, supt. Fax 366-0838
www.bmsd.org
Blue Mountain ES East 700/K-5
675 Red Dale Rd 17961 570-366-1065
Mark Cesari, prin. Fax 366-1797
Blue Mountain MS 700/6-8
685 Red Dale Rd 17961 570-366-0546
James McGonigle, prin. Fax 366-2513
Other Schools – See Cressona, Friedensburg

Osceola Mills, Clearfield, Pop. 1,128
Philipsburg-Osceola Area SD
Supt. — See Philipsburg
Osceola Mills ES 300/K-4
400 Coal St 16666 814-339-6812
Brian Pelka, prin. Fax 339-7814

Ottsville, Bucks

St. John the Baptist S 200/PK-8
4040 Durham Rd 18942 610-847-5523
Michael Patterson, hdmstr. Fax 847-8357

Oxford, Chester, Pop. 4,949
Oxford Area SD 3,700/K-12
125 Bell Tower Ln 19363 610-932-6600
David Woods, supt. Fax 932-6614
www.oxfordasd.org
Elk Ridge S 400/1-2
200 Wickersham Rd 19363 610-932-6670
Herbert Hayes, prin. Fax 932-7836
Hopewell ES, 602 Garfield St 19363 600/5-6
Dr. Nicole Addis, prin. 484-365-6150
Jordan Bank ES 300/K-K
536 Hodgson St 19363 610-932-6625
Dr. David Hamburg, prin. Fax 932-6662
Nottingham S 600/3-4
736 Garfield St 19363 610-932-6632
Lisa Yingst, prin. Fax 932-4630
Penn's Grove S 600/7-8
301 S 5th St 19363 610-932-6615
Tami Motes, prin. Fax 932-6619

Bethany Christian S 300/PK-8
1137 Shadyside Rd 19363 610-998-0877
Stacey Cost, head sch Fax 998-0253
Sacred Heart S 200/PK-8
205 Church Rd 19363 610-932-3633
Steven Brunner, prin. Fax 932-6051

Palmerton, Carbon, Pop. 5,366
Palmerton Area SD 1,800/K-12
680 4th St 18071 610-826-7101
Scot Engler, supt. Fax 826-4958
www.palmerton.org/
Palmer ES 500/2-6
298 Lafayette Ave 18071 610-826-7101
Mary Brumbach, prin. Fax 826-7528
Palmerton Area JHS 300/7-8
3529 Fireline Rd 18071 610-826-2492
Richard DeSocio, prin. Fax 826-2366
Parkside Education Center 200/K-1
680 4th St 18071 610-826-4914
Mary Brumbach, prin. Fax 826-4915
Other Schools – See Lehighton

St. John Neuman S 100/K-8
259 Lafayette Ave 18071 610-826-2354
Sr. Virginia Bator, prin. Fax 826-6444

Palmyra, Lebanon, Pop. 7,238
Palmyra Area SD 3,300/K-12
1125 Park Dr 17078 717-838-3144
Lisa Brown, supt. Fax 838-5105
www.pasd.us
Forge Road ES 300/1-5
400 S Forge Rd 17078 717-838-1331
James Hale, prin. Fax 838-0481
Lingle Avenue ES 600/K-5
600 S Lingle Ave 17078 717-838-1331
Rebecca Hoover, prin. Fax 838-3759
Northside ES 200/1-5
301 E Spruce St 17078 717-838-1331
Nan Huffman, prin. Fax 838-0253
Palmyra Area MS 800/6-8
50 W Cherry St 17078 717-838-1331
Walter Popejoy, prin. Fax 838-4402
Pine Street ES 400/1-5
50 W Pine St 17078 717-838-1331
Robert Corcoran, prin. Fax 838-6792

Paoli, Chester, Pop. 5,479

International Montessori S at Paoli 100/PK-4
1510 Russell Rd 19301 610-640-3864
St. Norbert S 200/K-8
6 Greenlawn Rd 19301 610-644-1670
Mary Kay Hennessy, prin. Fax 644-0201

Paradise, Lancaster, Pop. 1,102
Pequea Valley SD
Supt. — See Kinzers
Paradise ES 400/K-6
20 N Belmont Rd 17562 717-768-5560
Beth Reinhart, prin. Fax 768-5654

Linville Hill Christian S 200/K-8
295 S Kinzer Rd 17562 717-442-4447
Matt Buckwalter, prin. Fax 442-9283

Parkside, Delaware, Pop. 2,277
Penn-Delco SD
Supt. — See Aston
Parkside ES 300/K-5
2 E Forestview Rd, 610-497-6300
Joshua Leight, prin. Fax 876-0043

Patton, Cambria, Pop. 1,764
Cambria Heights SD 1,400/PK-12
PO Box 66 16668 814-674-3626
Michael Strasser, supt. Fax 674-5411
www.chsd1.org/
Cambria Heights MS 300/6-8
PO Box 216 16668 814-674-6290
Jarrod Lewis, prin. Fax 674-5054
Other Schools – See Carrolltown

Peckville, See Blakely
Valley View SD
Supt. — See Archbald
Valley View ES 600/K-2
901 Main St 18452 570-489-7579
Maria Kishel, prin. Fax 489-7243

Pen Argyl, Northampton, Pop. 3,551
Pen Argyl Area SD 1,700/K-12
1620 Teels Rd 18072 610-863-3191
William Haberl Ed.D., supt. Fax 863-7040
www.penargylschooldistrict.org/penargyl/
Wind Gap MS 700/4-8
1620 Teels Rd 18072 610-863-9093
Sherri McNamara, prin. Fax 863-3817
Other Schools – See Nazareth

Penndel, Bucks, Pop. 2,269

Our Lady of Grace S 300/K-8
300 Hulmeville Ave 19047 215-757-5287
Denise Lewis, prin. Fax 757-6199

Pennsburg, Montgomery, Pop. 3,798
Upper Perkiomen SD 3,300/K-12
2229 E Buck Rd 18073 215-679-7961
Dr. Alexis McGloin, supt. Fax 679-6214
www.upsd.org
Other Schools – See East Greenville, Green Lane, Hereford

Penns Creek, Snyder, Pop. 711

Penn View Christian Academy 100/PK-12
PO Box 970 17862 570-837-1855
Brent Lenhart, prin. Fax 837-1865

Pequea, Lancaster
Penn Manor SD
Supt. — See Lancaster
Marticville MS 300/7-8
356 Frogtown Rd 17565 717-284-4135
Christine Smith, prin. Fax 284-5954

Perkasie, Bucks, Pop. 8,390
Pennridge SD 7,300/K-12
1200 N 5th St 18944 215-257-5011
Dr. Jacqueline Rattigan, supt. Fax 453-8699
www.pennridge.org
Bedminster ES 400/K-5
2914 Fretz Valley Rd 18944 215-795-2929
Mia DiPaolo, prin. Fax 795-2156
Deibler ES 500/K-5
1122 W Schwenkmill Rd 18944 215-257-1146
Deb Brady, prin. Fax 257-1173
Guth ES 500/K-5
601 N 7th St 18944 215-257-8057
Matthew Smith, prin. Fax 257-1389
Pennridge Central MS 600/6-8
144 N Walnut St 18944 215-258-0939
Christian Temchatin, prin. Fax 258-0938
Pennridge North MS 600/6-8
1500 N 5th St 18944 215-453-6932
Dr. Matthew Cole, prin. Fax 453-7867
Pennridge South MS 500/6-8
610 S 5th St 18944 215-257-0467
Dr. Felicia McAllister, prin. Fax 257-3094
Seylar ES 400/K-5
820 Callowhill Rd 18944 215-257-6272
Miles Roe, prin. Fax 257-2418
Other Schools – See Sellersville

Perryopolis, Fayette, Pop. 1,762
Frazier SD 1,200/PK-12
142 Constitution St 15473 724-736-4427
Dr. William Henderson, supt. Fax 736-0688
www.frazierschooldistrict.org
Frazier ES 500/PK-5
142 Constitution St 15473 724-736-9507
Kelly Muic, prin. Fax 736-0688
Frazier MS 300/6-8
142 Constitution St 15473 724-736-4428
Michael Turek, prin. Fax 736-0688

Philadelphia, Philadelphia, Pop. 1,493,502
Philadelphia CSD 177,900/PK-12
440 N Broad St 19130 267-758-2630
William Hite Ed.D., supt.
www.philasd.org/
Adaire S 400/K-8
1300 E Palmer St 19125 215-291-4712
Anna Jenkins, prin. Fax 291-6350
Allen ES 600/K-8
3200 W Lehigh Ave 19132 215-227-4404
Stefan Feaster-Eberhardt, prin. Fax 227-2971
Allen S 800/K-8
6329 Battersby St 19149 215-537-2530
Cassandra Houston, prin. Fax 537-2599
Anderson S 500/K-8
1034 S 60th St 19143 215-471-2903
Laurena Tolson, prin. Fax 471-6718
Arthur S 300/K-8
2000 Catharine St 19146 215-875-5774
Kimberly Newman, prin. Fax 875-8057
Bache-Martin S 400/K-8
2201 Brown St 19130 215-684-5074
Mark Vitvitsky, prin. Fax 684-5446
Baldi MS 1,200/6-8
8801 Verree Rd 19115 215-961-2003
Luke Hostetter, prin. Fax 961-2116
Barry S 800/K-8
5900 Race St 19139 215-471-2744
Derrick Hardy, prin. Fax 471-6320
Barton ES 800/K-2
4600 Rosehill St 19120 215-456-3007
Colleen Bowen, prin. Fax 456-5578
Bethune S 700/K-8
3301 Old York Rd 19140 215-227-4433
Jamina Dingle, prin. Fax 227-8658
Blaine S 400/K-8
3001 W Berks St 19121 215-684-5085
Gianeen Powell-Wali, prin. Fax 684-8858
Blankenburg S 500/K-8
4600 W Girard Ave 19131 215-581-5505
LeAndrea Baltimore-Hagan, prin. Fax 581-5922
Bregy S 500/K-8
1700 Bigler St 19145 215-952-6218
Shakeera Warthen, prin. Fax 952-0858
Bridesburg ES 500/K-8
2824 Jenks St 19137 215-537-2515
James Serpiello, prin. Fax 537-3145
Brown ES 600/K-8
1946 E Sergeant St 19125 215-291-4717
Connie Carnivale, prin. Fax 291-5836
Brown ES 500/K-6
3600 Stanwood St 19136 215-335-5650
Arthurea Smith, prin. Fax 335-5381

Bryant S 500/PK-8
6001 Cedar Ave 19143 215-471-2910
Paulette Gaddy, prin. Fax 471-8379

Carnell ES 1,000/K-5
1100 Devereaux Ave 19111 215-537-2527
Hilderbrand Pelzer, prin. Fax 537-6305

Cassidy Academics Plus 600/K-8
6523 Lansdowne Ave 19151 215-581-5506
Tangela McClam, prin. Fax 581-5581

Catharine ES 600/K-5
6600 Chester Ave 19142 215-727-2155
Lisa Wilmer, prin. Fax 727-5671

Cayuga ES 400/K-5
4344 N 5th St 19140 215-456-3167
Jason Carrion, prin. Fax 456-5622

Childs S 600/K-8
1599 Wharton St 19146 215-952-6213
Eileen Coutts, prin. Fax 952-6443

Clemente MS 500/6-8
122 W Erie Ave 19140 215-291-5400
Edward Penn, prin. Fax 291-5421

Comegys ES 500/PK-8
5100 Greenway Ave 19143 215-727-2162
Rauchaun DuPree, prin. Fax 727-2329

Comly ES 500/K-5
1001 Byberry Rd 19116 215-961-2008
Terri Salvucci, prin. Fax 961-2555

Conwell MS 600/5-8
1849 E Clearfield St 19134 215-291-4722
Erica Green, prin. Fax 291-5019

Cooke S 500/K-8
1300 W Louden St 19141 215-456-3002
Tara Brown, prin. Fax 456-3185

Cook-Wissahickon S 500/K-8
201 E Salaignac St 19128 215-487-4463
Michael Lowe, prin. Fax 487-4808

Cramp ES 600/K-5
3449 N Mascher St 19140 215-291-4704
Deanda Logan, prin. Fax 291-5694

Crossan ES 400/K-5
7350 Bingham St 19111 215-728-5014
Lynne Millard, prin. Fax 728-5955

Day S 500/K-8
6324 Crittenden St 19138 215-276-5250
Karen White, prin. Fax 276-5817

DeBurgos Bilingual Magnet S 800/K-8
401 W Lehigh Ave 19133 215-291-4065
Maritza Hernandez, prin. Fax 291-4084

Decatur S 1,000/K-8
3500 Academy Rd 19154 215-281-2606
Genevieve Endy-Okane, prin. Fax 281-5803

Dick S 500/K-8
2498 W Diamond St 19121 215-684-5081
Amy Agree-Williams, prin. Fax 684-8995

Disston S 800/K-8
6801 Cottage St 19135 215-335-5661
Kari Hill, prin. Fax 335-5030

Dobson S 300/K-8
4667 Umbria St 19127 215-487-4460
Patricia Cruice, prin. Fax 487-4804

Duckrey S 600/K-8
1501 W Diamond St 19121 215-684-5066
David Cohen, prin. Fax 684-8927

Dunbar S 200/K-8
1750 N 12th St 19122 215-684-5065
Dawn Moore, prin. Fax 684-8945

Edmonds ES 500/PK-7
8025 Thouron Ave 19150 215-276-5261
K. Lamia, prin. Fax 276-5811

Elkin ES 900/K-4
3199 D St 19134 215-291-4701
Evelyn Nunez, prin. Fax 291-4876

Ellwood ES 300/K-5
6701 N 13th St 19126 215-276-5286
Marilyn Quarterman, prin. Fax 276-5876

Emlen ES 500/K-5
6501 Chew Ave 19119 215-951-4010
Tammy Thomas, prin. Fax 951-4131

Farrell S 1,000/K-8
8300 Castor Ave 19152 215-728-5009
Nicholas Cirulli, prin. Fax 728-5225

Fell S 500/K-8
900 W Oregon Ave 19148 215-952-6237
Omahr Ashe, prin. Fax 952-6239

Feltonville Arts & Sciences MS 600/6-8
210 E Courtland St 19120 215-456-5603
John Piniat, prin. Fax 456-5614

Feltonville IS 700/3-5
238 E Wyoming Ave 19120 215-456-3012
Donald Anticoli, prin. Fax 456-0122

Finletter S 800/K-8
6100 N Front St 19120 215-276-5265
Tamara Edwards, prin. Fax 276-5285

Fitler Academics Plus 300/1-8
140 W Seymour St 19144 215-951-4009
Anthious Boone, prin. Fax 951-4502

Fitzpatrick S 900/K-8
11061 Knights Rd 19154 215-281-2602
Karen White, prin. Fax 281-3330

Forrest ES 1,100/K-6
7300 Cottage St 19136 215-335-5652
Paul Spina, prin. Fax 335-5983

Fox Chase ES 500/K-5
500 Rhawn St 19111 215-728-5016
Robert Caroselli, prin. Fax 728-5006

Frank ES 1,100/K-5
2000 Bowler St 19115 215-961-2005
Max Komins, prin. Fax 961-2551

Franklin S 1,000/K-8
5735 Rising Sun Ave 19120 215-728-5017
Roslynn Sample-Green, prin. Fax 728-5992

Gideon S 400/K-8
2817 W Glenwood Ave 19121 215-684-5072
Shauneille Taylor, prin. Fax 684-8917

Girard ES 600/K-4
1800 Snyder Ave 19145 215-952-8554
Thomas Koger, prin. Fax 952-6397

Gompers ES 300/K-8
5701 Wynnefield Ave 19131 215-581-5503
Phillip Deluca, prin. Fax 581-5686

Greenberg S 700/K-8
600 Sharon Ln 19115 215-961-2002
Gina Hubbard, prin. Fax 961-2560

Greenfield S 600/K-8
2200 Chestnut St 19103 215-299-3566
Daniel Lazar, prin. Fax 299-3567

Hackett ES 300/K-5
2161 E York St 19125 215-291-4706
Todd Kimmell, prin. Fax 291-4169

Hamilton S 600/K-8
5640 Spruce St 19139 215-471-2911
Leta Johnson, prin. Fax 471-2724

Hancock Demonstration S 500/K-5
3700 Morrell Ave 19114 215-281-2604
William Griffin, prin. Fax 281-5900

Harding MS 900/6-8
2000 Wakeling St 19124 215-537-2528
Mary Sanchez, prin. Fax 537-2850

Harrington ES 500/K-8
5300 Baltimore Ave 19143 215-471-2914
Mary Digiacomo, prin. Fax 471-5087

Hartranft S 500/K-8
720 W Cumberland St 19133 215-684-5088
Jason Lytle, prin. Fax 765-6515

Henry S 500/K-8
601 Carpenter Ln 19119 215-951-4006
Shavon Savage, prin. Fax 951-4505

Heston S 600/PK-8
1621 N 54th St 19131 215-581-5514
Angela Gaddie-Edwards, prin. Fax 581-5724

Holme ES 500/K-6
9120 Academy Rd 19114 215-335-5656
Crystle Roye-Gill, prin. Fax 335-5033

Hopkinson S 1,000/K-8
4001 L St 19124 215-537-2526
Margaret Shriver, prin. Fax 537-2900

Houston S 400/K-8
7300 Rural Ln 19119 215-248-6608
Leroy Hall, prin. Fax 248-6683

Howe ES 300/K-5
5800 N 13th St 19141 215-276-5270
Doaquin Jessup, prin. Fax 276-5380

Hunter S 500/K-8
2400 N Front St 19133 215-291-4710
Alberto Rivera, prin. Fax 291-5177

Jackson S 500/K-8
1213 S 12th St 19147 215-952-6223
Lisa Ciaranca-Kaplan, prin. Fax 952-6488

Jenks Academy 500/K-8
8301 Germantown Ave 19118 215-248-6604
Mary Lynskey, prin. Fax 248-6681

Jenks ES 300/K-5
2501 S 13th St 19148 215-952-6224
Siouda Chestnut, prin. Fax 952-6407

Juniata Park Academy 1,100/K-8
801 E Hunting Park Ave 19124 215-289-7930
Joan Richey, prin. Fax 289-7949

Kearny S 500/K-8
601 Fairmount Ave 19123 215-351-7343
Sabrina Scott-Feggins, prin. Fax 351-7129

Kelley S 400/K-8
1601 N 28th St 19121 215-684-5071
Amelia Coleman-Brown, prin. Fax 684-5179

Kelly ES 700/K-5
5116 Pulaski Ave 19144 215-951-4011
Christopher Byrd, prin. Fax 951-4182

Kenderton ES 300/K-8
1500 W Ontario St 19140 215-400-8340
Victoria Pressley, prin. Fax 400-8341

Key ES 500/K-6
2230 S 8th St 19148 215-952-6216
Stephanie Stover, prin. Fax 952-8505

Kirkbride S 500/K-8
1501 S 7th St 19147 215-952-6214
Rebecca Julien, prin. Fax 952-6253

Lamberton S 500/K-8
7501 Woodbine Ave 19151 215-581-5650
Yvette Duperon, prin. Fax 581-3403

Lawton ES 700/K-5
6101 Jackson St 19135 215-335-5659
Arnetta Imes, prin. Fax 335-5325

Lea S 600/K-8
4700 Locust St 19139 215-471-2915
Jennifer Duffy, prin. Fax 471-4355

Lingelbach S 400/K-8
6340 Wayne Ave 19144 215-951-4001
Lisa Matthews, prin. Fax 951-4514

Locke S 500/K-8
4550 Haverford Ave 19139 215-823-8202
Katherine Carter, prin. Fax 823-5721

Loesche ES 800/K-5
595 Tomlinson Rd 19116 215-961-2000
Sherin Philip Kurian, prin. Fax 961-2559

Logan ES 300/K-5
1700 Lindley Ave 19141 215-456-3006
Chuanica Sanders, prin. Fax 456-0271

Longstreth S 600/PK-8
5700 Willows Ave 19143 215-727-2158
Robin Cooper, prin. Fax 727-2260

Lowell ES 900/K-4
450 W Nedro Ave 19120 215-276-5272
David Lugo, prin. Fax 276-5278

Ludlow S 400/PK-8
550 W Master St 19122 215-684-5060
Carol Williams, prin. Fax 684-4387

Marshall ES 500/K-5
4500 Griscom St 19124 215-537-2521
Carla Glover, prin. Fax 537-2847

Marshall S 700/K-8
5120 N 6th St 19120 215-456-0170
Keith Arrington, prin. Fax 456-0187

Mayfair S 1,100/K-8
3001 Princeton Ave 19149 215-335-5651
Guy Lowery, prin. Fax 335-5035

McCall S 700/K-8
325 S 7th St 19106 215-351-7350
Rose Rock, prin. Fax 351-7349

McCloskey ES 400/K-8
8500 Pickering St 19150 215-248-6600
Del Jones, prin. Fax 248-6235

McClure ES 600/K-5
600 W Hunting Park Ave 19140 215-456-3001
Sharon Marino, prin. Fax 456-5587

McDaniel ES 800/K-8
1801 S 22nd St 19145 215-952-6380
Lachante Collier-Bacon, prin. Fax 952-6379

McKinley S 500/K-8
2101 N Orkney St 19122 215-291-4702
Marilyn Mejia, prin. Fax 291-5613

McMichael S 400/K-8
3543 Fairmount Ave 19104 215-823-8205
Brian Wallace, prin. Fax 386-3549

Meade S 400/K-8
1600 N 18th St 19121 215-684-5062
Donna Smith, prin. Fax 684-7006

Meehan MS 500/7-8
3001 Ryan Ave 19152 215-335-5654
Mary Jackson, prin. Fax 335-5992

Meredith S 500/K-8
725 S 5th St 19147 215-351-7360
Lauren Overton, prin. Fax 351-7190

Mifflin S 300/K-8
3624 Conrad St 19129 215-951-4007
Leslie Mason, prin. Fax 951-4510

Mitchell ES 700/K-8
5500 Kingsessing Ave 19143 215-727-2160
Stephanie Andrewlevich, prin. Fax 727-2218

Moffet ES 400/K-5
127 W Oxford St 19122 215-291-4721
Carmen Navarro, prin. Fax 291-5190

Moore ES 1,200/K-5
6900 Summerdale Ave 19111 215-728-5011
Timothy Glynn, prin. Fax 728-5692

Morrison S 700/K-8
5100 N 3rd St 19120 215-456-3004
Zaida Bultes, prin. Fax 456-5564

Morris S 500/K-8
2600 W Thompson St 19121 215-684-5087
Carolyn Williams, prin. Fax 684-8881

Morton ES 800/K-5
2501 S 63rd St 19142 215-727-2164
Carolyn Allen-Glass, prin. Fax 727-2341

Munoz-Marin S 700/K-8
3300 N 3rd St 19140 215-291-8825
Ariel Lajara, prin. Fax 291-8845

Nebinger S 300/K-8
601 Carpenter St 19147 215-952-6202
Anh Brown, prin. Fax 952-6392

Olney S 800/K-8
5301 N Water St 19120 215-456-3003
Michael Roth, prin. Fax 456-5566

Overbrook ES 300/PK-8
2032 N 62nd St 19151 215-581-5691
Michelle Hayes-Flores, prin. Fax 581-2175

Patterson ES 600/K-4
7000 Buist Ave 19142 215-492-6453
Kenneth Jessup, prin. Fax 492-6827

Penn Alexander S 500/K-8
4209 Spruce St 19104 215-823-5465
Michael Farrell, prin. Fax 382-2031

Pennell ES 400/K-5
1800 Nedro Ave 19141 215-276-5267
Jason Harris, prin. Fax 549-4562

Pennypacker ES 400/K-8
1858 E Washington Ln 19138 215-276-5271
Wendy Baldwin, prin. Fax 276-5886

Penrose S 700/K-8
2515 S 78th St 19153 215-492-6455
Huie Douglas, prin. Fax 492-6985

Pollock ES 800/K-6
2850 Welsh Rd 19152 215-961-2004
Dontae Wilson, prin. Fax 961-2597

Potter-Thomas S 600/K-8
3001 N 6th St 19133 215-227-4423
Dywonne Davis-Harris, prin. Fax 227-7196

Powel ES 300/K-4
301 N 36th St 19104 215-823-8201
Kimberly Ellerbee, prin. Fax 823-8215

Prince Hall ES 500/K-5
6101 N Gratz St 19141 215-276-5255
Donna Ragsdale, prin. Fax 276-5803

Rhawnhurst ES 600/K-5
7809 Castor Ave 19152 215-728-5013
Karen Howell-Toomer, prin. Fax 728-5931

Rhoads S 600/K-8
4901 Parrish St 19139 215-581-5504
Joe Dixon, prin. Fax 581-3405

Rhodes S 700/K-8
2900 W Clearfield St 19132 215-227-4402
Andrea Coleman-Hill, prin. Fax 227-4926

Richmond ES 700/K-5
2944 Belgrade St 19134 215-291-4718
Susan Rozanski, prin. Fax 291-4141

Roosevelt S 700/K-8
430 E Washington Ln 19144 215-951-4170
Matthew Hayes, prin. Fax 951-7762

Rowen ES 500/K-5
6841 N 19th St 19126 215-276-5251
James Murray, prin. Fax 276-5806

Sharswood S 500/K-8
2300 S 2nd St 19148 215-952-6212
Maureen Skalski, prin. Fax 952-6405

Shawmont S 600/K-8
535 Shawmont Ave 19128 215-487-4466
Eileen Hoffman, prin. Fax 487-4815

Sheppard ES 300/K-4
120 W Cambria St 19133 215-291-4711
Marisol Rodriguez, prin. Fax 291-4156

Sheridan ES 700/K-4
800 E Ontario St 19134 215-291-4724
Awilda Aguila, prin. Fax 291-5615

Solis-Cohen ES 1,300/K-6
7001 Horrocks St 19149 215-728-5012
Michelina Serianni, prin. Fax 728-5982

Southwark S 600/K-8
1835 S 9th St 19148 215-952-8606
Andrew Lukov, prin. Fax 952-8670

Spring Garden S 300/K-8
1146 Melon St 19123 215-684-5070
Laureal Robinson, prin. Fax 684-5059

Spruance S 1,300/K-8
6401 Horrocks St 19149 215-537-2514
Kwand Lang, prin. Fax 537-2933

Stanton S 300/K-8
1700 Christian St 19146 215-875-3185
Stacey Burnley, prin. Fax 875-3711

Stearne ES 500/PK-8
1655 Unity St 19124 215-537-2522
Jessica Ramos, prin. Fax 537-2918

Steel S 500/K-8
4301 Wayne Ave 19140 215-456-3008
Jamal Dennis, prin. Fax 457-1466

Sullivan ES 700/K-5
5300 Ditman St 19124 215-537-2524
Renee Morley, prin. Fax 537-2984

Taggart S 500/K-8
400 W Porter St 19148 215-952-6228
Nelson Reyes, prin. Fax 952-8502

Taylor ES 500/K-5
3698 N Randolph St 19140 215-227-4435
David Laver, prin. Fax 227-4900

Tilden MS 600/6-8
6601 Elmwood Ave 19142 215-492-6454
Brian Johnson, prin. Fax 492-6128

Vare-Washington S 400/K-8
1198 S 5th St 19147 215-952-8620
Zachary Duberstein, prin. Fax 952-8508

Wagner MS 600/6-8
1701 W Chelten Ave 19126 215-276-5252
Maya Johnstone, prin. Fax 276-5849

Waring S 300/K-8
1801 Green St 19130 215-684-5073
Brianna Dunn, prin. Fax 684-5479

Washington Jr. MS 600/5-8
201 E Olney Ave 19120 215-456-0422
Jovan Moore, prin. Fax 456-2181

Washington S 400/K-8
766 N 44th St 19104 215-823-8203
Allayna Ratliff, prin. Fax 823-8292

Webster ES 900/K-5
3400 Frankford Ave 19134 215-537-2525
Sherri Arabia, prin. Fax 537-2517

Welsh S 500/K-8
2331 N 4th St 19133 215-291-4708
Diana Garcia, prin. Fax 291-4153

Willard ES 000/K-4
1930 E Elkhart St 19134 215-291-4714
Ron Reilly, prin. Fax 291-4161

Wilson MS 1,200/6-8
1800 Cottman Ave 19111 215-728-5015
Stefanie Ressler, prin. Fax 728-5051

Wright S 400/K-5
2700 W Dauphin St 19132 215-684-5076
Jeannine Hendricks, prin. Fax 684-7018

Ziegler S 500/K-8
5935 Saul St 19149 215-537-2510
Robert Berretta, prin. Fax 537-2987

Al-Aqsa Islamic Academy 300/PK-12
1501 Germantown Ave 19122 215-765-6660

Beulah Baptist Christian Day S 100/K-8
5001 Spruce St Ste 21 19139 215-747-3347
Judith Barksdale, prin. Fax 747-7871

Blair Christian Academy 100/PK-8
220 W Upsal St 19119 215-438-6557
Dr. Karen Jenkins, admin. Fax 438-0661

Blessed Trinity Regional S 900/PK-8
3033 Levick St 19149 215-338-9797
Linda Milewski, prin. Fax 331-6457

Calvary Christian Academy 1,000/PK-12
13500 Philmont Ave 19116 215-969-1579

Calvary Temple Christian Academy 100/PK-8
3301 S 20th St 19145 215-462-2822
Eyvone Blunte, admin. Fax 551-7951

Cedar Grove Christian Academy 300/PK-8
6445 Bingham St 19111 215-725-3383
Jeffrey Howard, prin. Fax 725-7476

Christ the King S 400/K-8
3205 Chesterfield Rd 19114 215-632-1375
Sr. Trudy Helder, prin. Fax 632-0734

City S, 860 N 24th St 19130 200/PK-12
Jake Becker, head sch 215-765-5363

Community Partnership S 100/PK-5
1936 N Judson St 19121 215-235-0461
Eric Jones, head sch Fax 235-2875

Cornerstone Christian Academy 200/K-8
PO Box 5520 19143 215-724-6858
Deborah Lee, prin. Fax 724-2827

Depaul Catholic S 300/K-8
44 W Logan St 19144 215-842-1266
Katie Wardlow, prin. Fax 842-1400

Faith Tabernacle S 200/1-12
PO Box 46245 19160 215-221-0909

First Century Gospel S 200/1-10
6807 Rising Sun Ave 19111 215-742-6615

Frankford Friends S 100/PK-8
1500 Orthodox St 19124 215-533-5368
Kathryn Park Cook, head sch Fax 533-5523

Friends Select S 600/PK-12
1651 Benjamin Franklin Pkwy 19103 215-561-5900
Michael Gary, head sch Fax 864-2979

Germantown Friends S 900/PK-12
31 W Coulter St 19144 215-951-2300
Dana Weeks, head sch Fax 951-2312

Gesu S 500/PK-8
1700 W Thompson St 19121 215-763-3660
Sr. Ellen Convey, prin. Fax 763-9844

Girard College 500/1-12
2101 S College Ave 19121 215-787-2600
Clarence Armbrister, pres. Fax 787-2725

Greene Street Friends S 300/PK-8
5511 Greene St 19144 215-438-7000
Edward Marshall, head sch Fax 438-1121

Holmesburg Christian Academy 200/PK-8
7927 Frankford Ave 19136 215-335-4323

Holy Cross S 100/PK-8
144 E Mount Airy Ave 19119 215-242-0414
Emily Diefendorf, prin. Fax 242-0414

Holy Innocents Area S 300/K-8
1312 E Bristol St 19124 215-743-5909
Sr. Regina Mullen, prin. Fax 743-0199

Holy Redeemer S 300/K-8
915 Vine St 19107 215-922-0999
Mei-Hing Leung, prin. Fax 922-6674

Hope Church S 200/PK-12
6707 Old York Rd 19126 215-927-7770
Dr. Suzette Ajedho, prin. Fax 927-8070

Hunting Park Christian Academy 200/PK-8
4400 N 6th St 19140 267-331-8002
Kevin Deane, prin. Fax 535-2777

Immaculate Heart of Mary S 400/PK-8
815 E Cathedral Rd 19128 215-482-2029
Rochelle Grasso, prin. Fax 482-1075

Immanuel Lutheran S 200/PK-8
1015 Cottman Ave 19111 215-725-7265
Douglas Puls, prin. Fax 725-2145

Jubilee S 100/PK-6
4211 Chester Ave 19104 215-387-7592

LaSalle Academy 100/3-8
1434 N 2nd St 19122 215-739-5804
Teresa Diamond, prin. Fax 739-1664

Mary Mother of Peace Area Catholic S 200/K-8
6334 Buist Ave 19142 215-729-3603
Sr. Janet Walters, prin. Fax 729-2315

Maternity BVM S 500/PK-8
9222 Old Bustleton Ave 19115 215-673-0235
Mary Zawisza, prin. Fax 671-1347

Mother of Divine Grace S 200/K-8
2612 E Monmouth St 19134 215-426-7325
Jane Lockhart, prin. Fax 426-0753

Nazareth Academy 200/1-8
4701 Grant Ave 19114 215-637-7777
Sr. Linda Joseph, prin. Fax 637-5695

New Life Christian Academy 100/PK-6
1993 N 63rd St 19151 215-877-3440
Bonita Patterson, admin. Fax 877-3743

Norwood Fontbonne Academy 400/PK-8
8891 Germantown Ave 19118 215-247-3811
Sr. Mary Helen Beirne Ed.D., hdmstr. Fax 247-8405

Olney Christian S 100/K-6
425 E Roosevelt Blvd 19120 215-324-2323
Lisa Kuzma, head sch Fax 455-5430

Our Lady of Calvary S 900/PK-8
11023 Kipling Ln 19154 215-637-1648
Sr. Mildred Chesnavage, prin. Fax 637-3810

Our Lady of Hope Regional S 300/PK-8
1248 Jackson St 19148 215-467-5385
Patricia Cody, prin. Fax 336-5103

Our Lady of Port Richmond S PK-8
3233 E Thompson St 19134 215-739-1920
Sr. Mary Ripp, prin. Fax 739-0519

Our Mother of Consolation S 200/PK-8
17 E Chestnut Hill Ave 19118 215-247-1060
Theresa Ponte, prin. Fax 247-0590

Our Mother of Sorrows S 100/4-8
1008 N 48th St 19131 215-473-5828
Sr. Patricia Bonner, prin. Fax 473-3096

Penn Charter S 1,000/PK-12
3000 W School House Ln 19144 215-844-3460
Dr. Darryl Ford, head sch Fax 843-3939

Philadelphia Classical S 100/K-6
PO Box 2428 19147 267-443-8919
Katharine Savage, head sch

Philadelphia S 400/PK-8
2501 Lombard St 19146 215-545-5323
Carlye Nelson-Major, head sch Fax 546-1798

Politz Hebrew Academy 300/PK-8
9225 Old Bustleton Ave 19115 215-969-5960

Resurrection Regional Catholic S 500/PK-8
2020 Shelmire Ave 19152 215-742-1127
Joan Stulz, prin. Fax 742-0947

Roxborough Christian S 50/K-2
6301 Ridge Ave 19121 215-482-0293
Cindy Fleming-Powell, admin.

St. Anselm S 400/K-8
12650 Dunks Ferry Rd 19154 215-632-1133
Geraldine Murphy, prin. Fax 632-3264

St. Anthony of Padua Regional S 300/PK-8
913 Pierce St 19148 215-468-0353
Sr. Mary Esther Carsele, prin. Fax 334-4255

St. Athanasius S 300/K-8
7105 Limekiln Pike 19138 215-424-5045
Andrea Tomaino, prin. Fax 927-6615

St. Cecilia S 700/K-8
525 Rhawn St 19111 215-725-8588
Sr. Jane Carr, prin. Fax 725-0247

St. Christopher S 600/PK-8
13305 Proctor Rd 19116 215-673-5787
Mary Tremper, prin. Fax 673-8511

St. Dominic S 400/PK-8
8510 Frankford Ave 19136 215-333-6703
Kathleen Bruce, prin. Fax 333-9930

St. Francis Cabrini Regional S 200/PK-8
405 N 65th St 19151 215-748-2994
Stephani Finnin, prin. Fax 748-0288

St. Francis DeSales S 500/K-8
917 S 47th St 19143 215-387-1749
Sr. Mary McNulty, prin. Fax 387-6605

St. Francis Xavier S 200/PK-8
641 N 24th St 19130 215-763-6564
Dolores Butler, prin. Fax 236-2818

St. Gabriel S 200/PK-8
2917 Dickinson St 19146 215-468-7230
Sr. Noreen Friel, prin. Fax 468-2554

St. George S 200/PK-8
2700 E Venango St 19134 215-634-8803
Daniel Markowski, prin. Fax 634-3694

St. Helena/Incarnation Regional S 400/PK-8
6101 N 5th St 19120 215-549-2947
Claire Frosch, prin. Fax 549-5947

St. James S 5-8
3217 W Clearfield St 19132 215-226-1276
David Kasievich, head sch

St. Jerome S 500/PK-8
3031 Stamford St 19136 215-624-0637
Susan Gallagher, prin. Fax 624-5711

St. Katherine of Siena S 500/K-8
9738 Frankford Ave 19114 215-637-2181
Regina Tanghe, prin. Fax 637-4867

St. Laurentius S 200/K-8
1612 E Berks St 19125 215-423-8834
Elaine McKnight, prin. Fax 426-4675

St. Malachy S 200/K-8
1419 N 11th St 19122 215-232-0696
Steve Janczewski, prin. Fax 235-1434

St. Martha S 400/K-8
11321 Academy Rd 19154 215-632-0320
Karen Donofry, prin. Fax 632-5546

St. Martin De Porres S 400/K-8
2300 W Lehigh Ave 19132 215-223-6872
Sr. Nancy Fitzgerald, prin. Fax 233-4126

St. Martin of Tours S 500/PK-8
5450 Roosevelt Blvd 19124 215-535-2962
Sr. Ellen Giardino, prin. Fax 533-1579

St. Mary Interparochial S 300/K-8
247 S 5th St 19106 215-923-7522
Jeanne Meredith, prin. Fax 923-8502

St. Matthew S 800/K-8
3040 Cottman Ave 19149 215-333-3142
Sr. John Magdalen Eibell, prin. Fax 332-7242

St. Monica S - Junior Campus 200/K-3
1720 W Ritner St 19145 215-334-3777
Sr. Mary Matulka, prin. Fax 389-0355

St. Monica S - Senior Campus 200/4-8
2500 S 16th St 19145 215-467-5338
Sr. Mary Matulka, prin. Fax 467-4599

St. Peter's S 200/PK-8
319 Lombard St 19147 215-925-3963
Shawn Kelly, hdmstr. Fax 925-3351

St. Peter the Apostle S 200/PK-8
1009 N 5th St 19123 215-922-5958
Sr. Rosalia Federici, prin. Fax 922-1015

St. Pio Regional Catholic S 300/PK-8
1826 Pollock St 19145 215-467-5430
Marianne Garnham, prin. Fax 467-2391

St. Raymond of Penafort S 300/PK-8
7940 Williams Ave 19150 215-548-1919
Patricia Wright, prin. Fax 548-1925

St. Rose of Lima S 200/K-8
1522 N Wanamaker St 19131 215-473-6030
Sr. Rita Murphy, prin. Fax 473-2338

Saints Tabernacle Day S 50/PK-6
5800 N Marvine St 19141 215-548-6011
Cheryl Hurley, prin. Fax 548-4877

St. Thomas Aquinas S 200/PK-8
1719 Morris St 19145 215-334-0878
Nicole Unegbu, prin. Fax 334-2357

St. Veronica S 200/K-8
3521 N 6th St 19140 215-225-1575
Sr. Eileen Buichanan, prin. Fax 225-2595

Spring Garden Academy 100/PK-8
PO Box 15191 19130 215-226-1000
Candace Wegner, dir. Fax 563-8116

Springside Chestnut Hill Academy 500/PK-12
500 W Willow Grove Ave 19118 215-247-4700
Dr. Stephen Druggan, head sch Fax 247-8516

Timothy Academy 100/PK-8
303 W Lehigh Ave 19133 215-425-8886
Gwendolyn Hinton-Freeman, prin. Fax 425-4817

Trinity Christian S 50/PK-K
2300 S 18th St 19145 215-334-6657
David Oppold, prin.

Visitation BVM S 500/PK-8
300 E Lehigh Ave 19125 215-634-7280
Edward Coleman, prin. Fax 634-4062

Waldorf S of Philadelphia 200/PK-8
6000 Wayne Ave 19144 215-248-1662
Betsy Sweeney, admin.

Philipsburg, Centre, Pop. 2,742

Philipsburg-Osceola Area SD 1,800/K-12
200 Short St 16866 814-342-1050
Dr. Gregg Paladina, supt. Fax 342-7208
www.pomounties.org

Philipsburg ES 400/K-4
1810 Black Moshannon Rd 16866 814-342-2870
Jeffrey Baker, prin. Fax 342-7526

Philipsburg-Osceola Area MS 500/5-8
200 Short St 16866 814-342-4906
Susan Pritchard-Harris, prin. Fax 342-7532

Other Schools – See Osceola Mills

Phoenixville, Chester, Pop. 15,988

Phoenixville Area SD 3,600/K-12
386 City Line Ave 19460 484-927-5000
Dr. Alan Fegley, supt. Fax 983-3729
www.pasd.com

Barkley ES 500/2-5
320 2nd Ave 19460 484-927-5300
Dr. Keya Champagne-Lee, prin. Fax 933-6471

Manavon ES 2-5
2 Phantom Way 19460 484-927-5350
Robyn Spear, prin. Fax 927-5390

Phoenixville Area Early Learning Center K-1
1 Phantom Way 19460 484-927-5450
Mwenyewe Dawan, prin. Fax 927-5390

Phoenixville Area MS 800/6-8
1000 Purple Pride Pkwy 19460 484-927-5200
Dr. Frank Garritano, prin. Fax 933-6121

Schuylkill ES 700/2-5
290 S Whitehorse Rd 19460 484-927-5400
Dr. Kelley Harmer, prin. Fax 933-6237

Chesterbrook Academy 200/PK-5
711 Hollow Rd 19460 610-935-4400
Holy Family S 400/PK-8
221 3rd Ave 19460 610-933-7562
Ann Braca, prin. Fax 933-8823
Valley Forge Kinder House Montessori S 50/PK-6
865 Main St 19460 610-489-5757

Picture Rocks, Lycoming, Pop. 676
East Lycoming SD
Supt. — See Hughesville
Ferrell ES 200/K-6
34 Court St 17762 570-584-3341
Jill Warg, prin. Fax 584-5467

Pine Grove, Schuylkill, Pop. 2,160
Pine Grove Area SD 1,600/K-12
103 School St 17963 570-345-2731
Fax 345-2790
www.pgasd.com
Pine Grove Area MS 500/5-8
105 School St 17963 570-345-2731
Melissa Mekosh, prin. Fax 345-2791
Pine Grove ES 600/K-4
107 School St 17963 570-345-2731
Sandra Burns, prin. Fax 345-2792

Pine Grove Mills, Centre, Pop. 1,478
State College Area SD
Supt. — See State College
Ferguson Township ES 400/K-5
PO Box 237 16868 814-231-4119
Shelly Buckholtz, prin. Fax 231-4163

Pipersville, Bucks
Palisades SD
Supt. — See Kintnersville
Tinicum ES 200/K-5
162 E Dark Hollow Rd 18947 610-294-9311
Janet Link, prin. Fax 294-9182

Pittsburgh, Allegheny, Pop. 297,895
Avonworth SD 1,500/K-12
258 Josephs Ln 15237 412-369-8738
Dr. Thomas W. Ralston, supt. Fax 369-8746
www.avonworth.k12.pa.us
Avonworth ES 400/3-6
1320 Roosevelt Rd 15237 412-366-7170
William Battistone, prin. Fax 366-4146
Avonworth MS 300/7-8
256 Josephs Ln 15237 412-366-9650
Michael Hall, prin. Fax 358-9621
Avonworth Primary Center 400/K-2
1310 Roosevelt Rd 15237 412-366-7171
Dr. Scott Miller, prin.

Baldwin-Whitehall SD 4,100/K-12
4900 Curry Rd 15236 412-884-6300
Dr. Randal A. Lutz, supt. Fax 885-7802
www.bwschools.net/
Harrison MS 900/6-8
129 Windvale Dr 15236 412-885-7530
Jill Fleming-Salopek, prin. Fax 885-6766
McAnnulty ES 300/K-1
5151 McAnulty Rd 15236 412-714-2020
Daniel Emanuelson, prin. Fax 714-2024
Paynter ES 700/K-5
3454 Pleasantvue Dr 15227 412-885-7535
Patricia Fusco, prin. Fax 885-6641
Whitehall ES, 4900 Curry Rd 15236 700/2-5
Jennifer Marsteller, prin. 412-885-7525

Bethel Park SD
Supt. — See Bethel Park
Lincoln ES 300/K-4
1524 Hamilton Rd 15234 412-854-8618
Jay Johnson, prin. Fax 833-5010

Brentwood Borough SD 1,200/K-12
3601 Brownsville Rd 15227 412-881-2227
Dr. Amy Burch, supt. Fax 881-1640
www.bb-sd.com
Brentwood MS 300/6-8
3601 Brownsville Rd 15227 412-881-4940
David Radcliffe Ph.D., prin. Fax 881-4170
Moore ES 200/K-5
3809 Dalewood St 15227 412-881-7776
Bonnie Betler, prin. Fax 881-8994
Other Schools – See Brentwood

Chartiers Valley SD 3,400/K-12
2030 Swallow Hill Rd 15220 412-429-2201
Scott Seltzer, supt. Fax 429-2237
www.cvsd.net
Chartiers Valley IS 700/3-5
2030 Swallow Hill Rd 15220 412-429-2233
Patrick Myers, prin. Fax 429-2380
Other Schools – See Bridgeville

Fox Chapel Area SD 4,200/K-12
611 Field Club Rd 15238 412-963-9600
Dr. Gene Freeman Ed.D., supt. Fax 967-0697
www.fcasd.edu
Dorseyville MS 1,000/6-8
3732 Saxonburg Blvd 15238 412-767-5343
Jonathan Nauhaus, prin. Fax 767-4255
Fairview ES 300/K-5
738 Dorseyville Rd 15238 412-963-9315
Dr. Rebecca Stephan Ed.D., prin. Fax 967-2408
Hartwood ES 300/K-5
3730 Saxonburg Blvd 15238 412-767-5396
Dr. Rachel Fischbaugh Ed.D., prin. Fax 767-4565
Kerr ES 400/K-5
341 Kittanning Pike 15215 412-781-4105
Dr. Paul Noro Ed.D., prin. Fax 967-2497
O'Hara ES 700/K-5
115 Cabin Ln 15238 412-963-0333
Kristy Batis, prin. Fax 967-2510

Keystone Oaks SD 2,000/K-12
1000 Kelton Ave 15216 412-571-6000
Dr. William Stropkaj, supt. Fax 571-6006
www.kosd.org
Aiken ES 200/K-5
881 Greentree Rd 15220 412-921-9166
Dave Thomas, prin. Fax 571-6164
Dormont ES 300/K-5
3200 Annapolis Ave 15216 412-571-6152
Brian Werner, prin. Fax 571-6151
Keystone Oaks MS 400/6-8
1002 Kelton Ave 15216 412-571-6146
Jeffrey Kattan, prin. Fax 571-6092
Myrtle Ave ES 300/K-5
3724 Myrtle Ave 15234 412-571-6137
Scott Mizikar, prin. Fax 571-6051

Mt. Lebanon SD 5,200/K-12
7 Horsman Dr 15228 412-344-2077
Dr. Timothy Steinhauer, supt. Fax 344-2047
www.mtlsd.org
Foster ES 300/K-5
700 Vermont Ave 15234 412-344-2162
Jason Ramsey, prin. Fax 344-1121
Hoover ES 200/K-5
37 Robb Hollow Rd 15243 412-276-7411
Nicole Giehll, prin. Fax 276-5524
Howe ES 400/K-5
400 Broadmoor Ave 15228 412-344-2157
Dr. Michelle Murray, prin. Fax 344-2236
Jefferson ES 300/K-5
11 Moffett St 15243 412-344-2167
Dr. Sarah Shaw, prin. Fax 344-0870
Jefferson MS 600/6-8
21 Moffett St 15243 412-344-2123
Kelly Szesterniak, prin. Fax 344-1252
Lincoln ES 400/K-5
2 Ralston Pl 15216 412-344-2147
Ronald Kitsko, prin. Fax 344-0813
Markham ES 300/K-5
165 Crescent Dr 15228 412-344-2152
Dr. Robert Freil, prin. Fax 344-7088
Mellon MS 700/6-8
11 Castle Shannon Blvd 15228 412-344-2122
Christopher Wolfson, prin. Fax 344-0590
Washington ES 400/K-5
735 Washington Rd 15228 412-344-2142
Melissa Nelson, prin. Fax 344-3314

North Allegheny SD 8,200/K-12
200 Hillvue Ln 15237 412-366-2100
Dr. Robert Scherrer, supt. Fax 369-5513
www.northallegheny.org
Carson MS 600/6-8
300 Hillvue Ln 15237 412-369-5520
Katherine Jenkins, prin. Fax 630-5819
Ingomar ES 400/K-5
602 W Ingomar Rd 15237 412-366-9665
Kristen Silbaugh, prin. Fax 366-5679
Ingomar MS 700/6-8
1521 Ingomar Heights Rd 15237 412-358-1470
Heidi Stark, prin. Fax 366-4487
McKnight ES 800/K-5
500 Cumberland Rd 15237 412-635-4105
Christopher Shute, prin. Fax 635-4115
Peebles ES 400/K-5
8625 Peebles Rd 15237 412-366-9667
Susie Bjalobok, prin. Fax 635-2464
Other Schools – See Allison Park, Bradfordwoods, Sewickley, Wexford

North Hills SD 4,200/K-12
135 6th Ave 15229 412-318-1000
Dr. Patrick Mannarino, supt. Fax 318-1084
www.nhsd.net
Highcliff ES 500/K-6
156 Peony Ave 15229 412-318-1582
Kristy Bilderback, prin. Fax 318-1584
McIntyre ES 500/K-6
200 McIntyre Rd 15237 412-318-1622
Amy Mathieu, prin. Fax 318-1624
North Hills MS 700/7-8
55 Rochester Rd 15229 412-318-1450
Dave Lieberman, prin. Fax 318-1453
Ross ES 600/K-6
90 Houston Rd 15237 412-318-1542
Mary Grimm, prin. Fax 318-1544
West View ES 500/K-6
47 Chalfonte Ave 15229 412-318-1502
Jesse Simpson, prin. Fax 318-1504

Northgate SD 1,200/K-12
591 Union Ave 15202 412-732-3300
Dr. Caroline Johns, supt. Fax 734-8008
www.northgate.k12.pa.us
Avalon ES 300/K-6
721 California Ave 15202 412-732-3300
Joseph Peacock, prin. Fax 734-8054
Other Schools – See Bellevue

Penn Hills SD, 260 Aster St 15235 2,600/PK-12
Dr. Nancy Hines, supt. 412-793-7000
www.phsd.k12.pa.us
Linton MS, 250 Aster St 15235 1,200/5-8
Katie Friend, prin. 412-793-7000
Penn Hills ES PK-4
1079 Jefferson Rd 15235 412-793-7000
Kristin Brown, prin.

Pittsburgh SD 24,800/PK-12
341 S Bellefield Ave 15213 412-529-4357
Dr. Anthony Hamlet, supt. Fax 622-7920
www.pps.k12.pa.us
Chartiers ECC 100/PK-PK
3799 Chartiers Ave 15204 412-529-6792
Carol Martin, prin. Fax 928-6564
Pittsburgh Allegheny 6-8 300/6-8
810 Arch St 15212 412-529-4115
Yarra Howze, prin. Fax 323-4114
Pittsburgh Allegheny K-5 500/K-5
810 Arch St 15212 412-529-4100
Molly O'Malley-Argueta, prin. Fax 323-4109
Pittsburgh Arlington 3-8 400/PK-8
800 Rectenwald St 15210 412-488-3641
Holly Ballard, prin. Fax 488-3760
Pittsburgh Arsenal 6-8 200/6-8
220 40th St 15201 412-529-5740
Patti Camper, prin. Fax 622-5743
Pittsburgh Arsenal PreK-5 400/PK-5
215 39th St 15201 412-529-7307
Ruthie Rea, prin. Fax 622-7310
Pittsburgh Banksville K-5 300/K-5
1001 Carnahan Rd 15216 412-529-7400
David May, prin. Fax 571-7398
Pittsburgh Beechwood PreK-5 400/PK-5
810 Rockland Ave 15216 412-529-7390
Sally Rifugiato, prin. Fax 571-7393
Pittsburgh Brookline PreK-8 600/K-8
500 Woodbourne Ave 15226 412-529-7380
John Vater, prin. Fax 571-7386
Pittsburgh Carmalt PreK-8 600/PK-8
1550 Breining St 15226 412-529-7760
Dr. Sandra Och, prin. Fax 885-7764
Pittsburgh Classical 6-8 300/6-8
1463 Chartiers Ave 15220 412-529-3110
Valerie Merlo, prin. Fax 928-3106
Pittsburgh Colfax K-8 800/K-8
2332 Beechwood Blvd 15217 412-529-3525
Dr. Tamara Sanders-Woods, prin. Fax 422-4896
Pittsburgh Concord PreK-5 500/PK-5
2350 Brownsville Rd 15210 412-529-7755
Michael Perella, prin. Fax 885-7758
Pittsburgh Dilworth PreK-5 500/PK-5
6200 Stanton Ave 15206 412-529-5000
Dr. Monica Lamar, prin. Fax 665-5012
Pittsburgh Faison K-5 500/K-5
7430 Tioga St 15208 412-529-2305
Dr. Russell Patterson, prin. Fax 247-0105
Pittsburgh Fulton PreK-5 500/PK-5
5799 Hampton St 15206 412-529-4590
Karen Arnold, prin. Fax 665-4969
Pittsburgh Grandview K-5 300/K-5
845 McLain St 15210 412-529-6605
Sharon Fisher, prin. Fax 488-6846
Pittsburgh Greenfield PreK-8 400/PK-8
1 Alger St 15207 412-529-3535
Eric Rosenthall, prin. Fax 422-4879
Pittsburgh King PreK-8 600/PK-8
50 Montgomery Pl 15212 412-529-4160
Leah McCord, prin. Fax 323-4165
Pittsburgh Langley K-8 700/K-8
2940 Sheraden Blvd 15204 412-529-2100
Rodney Necciai, prin. Fax 778-2106
Pittsburgh Liberty K-5 400/K-5
601 Filbert St 15232 412-529-8450
Mark McClinchie, prin. Fax 622-8499
Pittsburgh Lincoln PreK-5 300/PK-5
328 Lincoln Ave 15206 412-529-3980
Virginia Hill, prin. Fax 665-4959
Pittsburgh Linden K-5 400/K-5
725 S Linden Ave 15208 412-529-3996
Victoria Burgess-Davis, prin. Fax 665-2035
Pittsburgh Manchester PreK-8 300/PK-8
1612 Manhattan St 15233 412-529-3100
Michilene Pegher, prin. Fax 323-3015
Pittsburgh Mifflin PreK-8 400/PK-8
1290 Mifflin Rd 15207 412-529-4350
Edward Littlehale, prin. Fax 464-4355
Pittsburgh Miller PreK-5 400/PK-5
2055 Bedford Ave 15219 412-529-3830
Dr. Margaret Starkes-Ross, prin. Fax 338-3834
Pittsburgh Minadeo PreK-5 500/PK-5
6502 Lilac St 15217 412-529-4035
Melissa Wagner, prin. Fax 422-4889
Pittsburgh Montessori PreK-5 300/PK-5
201 S Graham St 15206 412-529-2010
Kellie Meyer, prin. Fax 665-2038
Pittsburgh Morrow 5-8 5-8
3530 Fleming Ave 15212 412-529-6600
Darrel Prioleau, prin. Fax 734-6606
Pittsburgh Morrow PreK-4 500/PK-4
1611 Davis Ave 15212 412-529-6600
Darrel Prioleau, prin. Fax 734-6606
Pittsburgh Phillips K-5 300/K-5
1901 Sarah St 15203 412-529-5190
Michael Calvert, prin. Fax 488-4200
Pittsburgh Roosevelt 2-5 300/2-5
17 W Cherryhill St 15210 412-529-7780
Michael Perella, prin. Fax 885-7784
Pittsburgh Roosevelt PreK-1 100/PK-1
200 The Blvd 15210 412-529-7788
Michael Perella, prin. Fax 885-7789
Pittsburgh Schiller 6-8 200/6-8
1018 Peralta St 15212 412-529-4190
Paula Heinzman, prin. Fax 323-4192
Pittsburgh South Brook 6-8 500/6-8
779 Dunster St 15226 412-529-8170
Alexis Fadick, prin. Fax 572-8177
Pittsburgh South Hills 6-8 600/6-8
595 Crane Ave 15216 412-529-8130
Jacqueline Hale, prin. Fax 572-8148
Pittsburgh Spring Hill K-5 300/K-5
1351 Damas St 15212 412-529-3000
Erin McClay, prin. Fax 323-3008
Pittsburgh Sterrett 6-8 400/6-8
7100 Reynolds St 15208 412-529-7870
Dr. MiChele Holly, prin. Fax 247-7877
Pittsburgh Sunnyside PreK-8 400/PK-8
4801 Stanton Ave 15201 412-529-2040
Laura Dadey, prin. Fax 665-2042
Pittsburgh Weil PreK-5 200/PK-5
2250 Centre Ave 15219 412-529-3840
Anthony Pipkin, prin. Fax 338-3848
Pittsburgh West Liberty K-5 300/K-5
785 Dunster St 15226 412-571-7420
Deonne Arrington, prin. Fax 571-7424

Pittsburgh Westwood K-5 300/K-5
508 Shadyhill Rd 15205 412-529-6570
Dr. Nina Sacco, prin. Fax 928-6577
Pittsburgh Whittier K-5 300/K-5
150 Meridan St 15211 412-529-8211
Valerie Lucas, prin. Fax 488-4255
Pittsburgh Woolslair K-5 100/K-5
501 40th St 15224 412-529-8800
Lisa Gallagher, prin. Fax 623-8810
Spring Garden ECC 100/PK-PK
1502 Spring Garden Ave 15212 412-323-3000
Melissa Cujas, coord. Fax 323-3008

Plum Borough SD 3,600/K-12
900 Elicker Rd 15239 412-795-0100
Dr. Timothy Glasspool, supt. Fax 795-9115
www.pbsd.k12.pa.us
Center ES 400/K-6
201 Center New Texas Rd 15239 412-795-4420
D. Jason Knisely, prin. Fax 795-1650
Holiday Park ES 500/K-6
313 Holiday Park Dr 15239 412-795-4430
Fran Sciullo, prin. Fax 795-1723
O'Block JHS 600/7-8
440 Presque Isle Dr 15239 724-733-2400
Joseph Fishell, prin. Fax 798-6347
Pivik ES 600/K-6
151 School Rd 15239 412-795-4580
Kristen Gestrich, prin. Fax 795-2824
Regency Park ES 200/K-6
4795 Havana Dr 15239 412-795-0660
Dr. Jeff Hadley, prin. Fax 795-2923

Shaler Area SD
Supt. — See Glenshaw
Marzolf PS 300/K-3
101 Marzolf Road Ext 15209 412-492-1200
Rick Pelkofer, prin. Fax 486-8702
Reserve PS 200/K-3
2107 Lonsdale St 15212 412-492-1200
Eloise Groegler, prin. Fax 321-4507

Upper St. Clair SD
Supt. — See Upper Saint Clair
Baker ES 400/K-4
2300 Morton Rd 15241 412-833-1600
Pat McClintock-Comeaux, prin. Fax 221-5283
Boyce MS 700/5-6
1500 Boyce Rd 15241 412-833-1600
Karen Brown, prin. Fax 854-2161
Eisenhower ES 500/K-4
100 Warwick Dr 15241 412-833-1600
Mark Miller, prin. Fax 854-1295
Ft. Couch MS 700/7-8
515 Fort Couch Rd 15241 412-833-1600
Joseph DeMar, prin. Fax 854-3006
Streams ES 500/K-4
1560 Ashlawn Dr 15241 412-833-1600
Dr. Claire Miller, prin. Fax 854-4374

West Jefferson Hills SD
Supt. — See Jefferson Hills
McClellan ES 400/K-5
360 School Ln 15236 412-655-2700
Justin Liberatore, prin. Fax 655-3526
Pleasant Hills MS 700/6-8
404 Old Clairton Rd 15236 412-655-8680
Daniel Como, prin. Fax 655-5691

Woodland Hills SD
Supt. — See North Braddock
Edgewood PS 200/K-3
241 Maple Ave 15218 412-731-2238
Chad Burnheimer, prin. Fax 731-2256
Wilkins PS 200/K-3
362 Churchill Rd 15235 412-824-3231
Jean McAteer-Livingston, prin. Fax 824-3244
Woodland Hills Rankin Promise S 200/K-12
2550 Greensburg Pike 15221 412-731-1300
Licia Lentz, admin.

Assumption S 100/K-8
35 N Jackson Ave 15202 412-761-7887
Mary Ann Miller, prin. Fax 761-7620
Campus S of Carlow University 200/PK-8
3333 5th Ave 15213 412-578-6158
Tawana Purnell, head sch Fax 578-6676
Community Day S 300/PK-8
6424 Forward Ave 15217 412-521-1100
Avi Baran Munro, head sch Fax 521-4511
East Catholic S 300/K-8
2001 Ardmore Blvd 15221 412-351-5403
Sr. Judith Stojhovic, prin. Fax 273-9114
Eden Christian Academy - Berkeley Hills 400/PK-6
206 Siebert Rd 15237 412-364-8055
Kimberly A. Hyland, prin. Fax 364-8330
Ellis S 500/PK-12
6425 5th Ave 15206 412-661-5992
Macon Finley, head sch Fax 661-3979
Falk Laboratory S 400/K-8
4060 Allequippa St 15261 412-624-8020
Dr. Jeff Suzik Ph.D., dir. Fax 624-1303
Glen Montessori S 200/PK-6
950 Perry Hwy 15237 412-318-4885
Jackie Herrmann, head sch Fax 318-4423
Hillel Academy of Pittsburgh 200/K-12
5685 Beacon St 15217 412-521-8131
Imani Christian Academy 200/K-12
2150 E Hills Dr 15221 412-731-7982
Jubilee Christian S 100/K-5
255 Washington Rd 15216 412-561-5917
Robert Hart, prin. Fax 561-2857
Kentucky Avenue S 100/K-8
5701 Fifth Ave 15232 412-361-5332
Mt. Nazareth Learning Center 100/PK-PK
285 Bellevue Rd 15229 412-931-9761
Michelle Harrison, dir. Fax 931-4533
Northside Catholic S 200/PK-8
3854 Brighton Rd 15212 412-761-5043
Rosanne Kwiatkowski, prin. Fax 761-0840

Our Lady of Grace S 300/PK-8
1734 Bower Hill Rd 15243 412-279-6611
Sharon Brown, prin. Fax 279-6755
Pittsburgh Urban Christian S 100/K-8
809 Center St 15221 412-244-1779
Sacred Heart S 500/PK-8
325 Emerson St 15206 412-441-1582
Sr. Lynn Rettinger, prin. Fax 441-2798
St. Anne S 200/PK-8
4040 Willow Ave 15234 412-561-7720
Harmony Stewart, prin. Fax 561-7927
St. Bartholomew S 200/PK-8
111 Erhardt Dr 15235 412-242-2511
Harmony Shaw, prin. Fax 242-8317
St. Bede S 300/PK-8
6920 Edgerton Ave 15208 412-661-9425
Mary Drummond, prin. Fax 661-0447
St. Benedict the Moor S 200/PK-8
631 Watt St 15219 412-682-3755
Heather Hilterman, prin. Fax 682-4058
St. Bernard S 300/PK-8
401 Washington Rd 15216 412-341-5444
Sr. Daniela Bronka, prin. Fax 341-2044
St. Edmund's Academy 300/PK-8
5705 Darlington Rd 15217 412-521-1907
Chad Barnett, head sch Fax 521-2988
St. Elizabeth S 300/PK-8
1 Grove Pl Ste 5 15236 412-881-2958
Linda Bechtol, prin. Fax 882-0111
St. Gabriel Preschool PK-PK
5200 Greenridge Dr 15236 412-230-7572
Suzan Slezak, prin.
St. Gabriel S 400/K-8
5200 Greenridge Dr 15236 412-882-3353
Jessica Munscher, prin. Fax 882-2125
St. John Bosco S 100/PK-8
2690 Waddington Ave 15226 412-563-0858
Janet Salley-Rakoczy, prin. Fax 341-5610
St. John Fisher Preschool 50/PK-PK
33 Lewin Ln 15235 412-241-4722
Lynne Dominijanni, prin. Fax 241-4653
St. John the Baptist S 200/PK-8
418 Unity Center Rd 15239 412-793-0555
Beau Quattrone, prin. Fax 793-4001
St. Joseph Preschool 50/PK-PK
330 Dorseyville Rd 15215 412-963-8885
Nancy Whistler, dir.
St. Louise de Marillac S 500/K-8
310 McMurray Rd 15241 412-835-0600
Kenneth Klase, prin. Fax 835-2898
St. Margaret S 300/PK-8
915 Alice St 15220 412-922-4765
Celeste Cancilla, prin. Fax 922-4647
St. Maria Goretti S 200/PK-8
321 Edmond St 15224 412-621-5199
Sr. Mary Cook, prin. Fax 621-5601
St. Phillip S 400/PK-8
52 W Crafton Ave 15205 412-928-2742
Sr. Geraldine Marr, prin. Fax 920-7310
St. Raphael S 200/PK-8
1154 Chislett St 15206 412-661-0288
Robert Munz, prin. Fax 661-0420
St. Rosalia Academy 200/PK-8
411 Greenfield Ave 15207 412-521-3005
Sarah Tonski, prin. Fax 521-2763
St. Sebastian S 500/PK-8
307 Siebert Rd 15237 412-364-7171
Nancy Koslosky, prin. Fax 364-5891
St. Sylvester S 200/PK-8
30 W Willock Rd 15227 412-882-9900
Sr. Barbara Anne Quinn, prin. Fax 881-4142
St. Teresa of Avila S 300/PK-8
800 Avila Ct 15237 412-367-9001
Sr. Karen Brink, prin. Fax 364-1172
St. Thomas More S 500/PK-8
134 Fort Couch Rd 15241 412-833-1412
Setrak Haroutounian, prin. Fax 833-5597
Shady Side Academy Country Day S 100/PK-5
620 Squaw Run Rd E 15238 412-963-8644
Sharon Smith, head sch Fax 963-7123
Shady Side Academy Junior S 200/PK-5
400 S Braddock Ave 15221 412-473-4400
Ellen McConnell, head sch Fax 473-4420
Shady Side Academy MS 200/6-8
500 Squaw Run Rd E 15238 412-968-3100
Amy Nixon, head sch Fax 968-3008
SS. Simon & Jude ECC 100/PK-PK
1625 Greentree Rd 15220 412-563-1199
Maureen Torcasi, dir. Fax 563-8617
Trinity Christian S 300/K-12
299 Ridge Ave 15221 412-242-8886
Kennedy Henriquez, head sch Fax 242-8859
Waldorf S of Pittsburgh 100/PK-8
201 S Winebiddle St 15224 412-441-5792
K. Christopherson-Clark, head sch Fax 441-5179
Winchester Thurston S 700/PK-12
555 Morewood Ave 15213 412-578-7500
Gary Niels, hdmstr. Fax 578-7504
Yeshiva S of Pittsburgh 100/PK-12
2100 Wightman St 15217 412-422-7300

Pittston, Luzerne, Pop. 7,622
Pittston Area SD 3,300/K-12
5 Stout St 18640 570-654-2415
Kevin Booth, supt. Fax 654-5548
www.pittstonarea.com
Pittston Area IS 800/2-4
110 New St 18640 570-654-7176
Dr. Coreen Milazzo, prin. Fax 883-1385
Pittston Area MS 1,000/5-8
120 New St 18640 570-655-2928
Patrick Bilbow, prin. Fax 654-0862
Pittston Area PS 500/K-1
210 Rock St 18640 570-655-3785
Arthur Savokinas, prin. Fax 883-1381

Plains, Luzerne, Pop. 4,288
Wilkes-Barre Area SD
Supt. — See Wilkes Barre
Solomon/Plains ES 900/K-6
41 Abbott St 18705 570-826-7222
Sean Flynn, prin. Fax 820-3736
Solomon/Plains JHS 500/7-8
43 Abbott St 18705 570-826-7224
Sean Flynn, prin. Fax 820-3715

Pleasant Gap, Centre, Pop. 2,844
Bellefonte Area SD
Supt. — See Bellefonte
Pleasant Gap ES 200/K-5
230 S Main St 16823 814-359-2739
Daniel Besch, prin. Fax 359-4552

Pleasantville, Venango, Pop. 886
Titusville Area SD
Supt. — See Titusville
Pleasantville ES 200/1-5
374 N Main St 16341 814-827-2715
Shawn Fink, prin. Fax 827-0556

Plymouth Meeting, Montgomery, Pop. 6,092
Colonial SD 4,700/K-12
230 Flourtown Rd 19462 610-834-1670
Dr. Michael Christian, supt. Fax 834-7535
www.colonialsd.org
Colonial ES 700/4-5
230 Flourtown Rd 19462 610-941-0426
Rose Rock, prin. Fax 834-8701
Colonial MS 1,100/6-8
716 Belvoir Rd 19462 610-275-5100
Robert Fahler, prin. Fax 278-2447
Plymouth ES 500/K-3
542 Plymouth Rd 19462 610-825-8190
Rosemarie Gregitis, prin. Fax 825-7853
Other Schools – See Conshohocken, Lafayette Hill

Holy Rosary Regional Catholic S 200/PK-8
3040 Walton Rd 19462 610-825-0160
Lisa Hoban, prin. Fax 825-0460
Plymouth Meeting Friends S 100/PK-6
2150 Butler Pike 19462 610-828-2288
Sarah Sweeney-Denham, head sch Fax 828-2390

Pocono Pines, Monroe, Pop. 1,394
Pocono Mountain SD
Supt. — See Swiftwater
Tobyhanna Elementary Center 700/K-6
398 Old Route 940 18350 570-839-7121
Dr. Anastasia D'Angelo, prin. Fax 646-6147

Pocono Summit, Monroe
Pocono Mountain SD
Supt. — See Swiftwater
Pocono Mountain West JHS 800/7-8
180 Panther Ln 18346 570-839-7121
Dr. Eric Vogt, prin. Fax 839-7397

Point Marion, Fayette, Pop. 1,152
Albert Gallatin Area SD
Supt. — See Uniontown
Friendship Hill ES 200/K-5
218 New Geneva Rd 15474 724-725-9515
Amy Przybylinski, prin. Fax 725-9515
Gallatin South MS 400/6-8
224 New Geneva Rd 15474 724-725-5241
Joetta Britvich, prin. Fax 725-5424

Portage, Cambria, Pop. 2,610
Portage Area SD 900/PK-12
84 Mountain Ave 15946 814-736-9636
Eric Zelanko, supt. Fax 736-9634
www.portageareasd.org
Portage Area ES 500/PK-6
84 Mountain Ave 15946 814-736-9636
Christian Serenko, prin. Fax 736-4165

Port Allegany, McKean, Pop. 2,134
Port Allegany SD 900/PK-12
20 Oak St 16743 814-642-2596
Gary Buchsen, supt. Fax 642-9574
www.pahs.net
Port Allegany ES 500/PK-6
85 Clyde Lynch Dr 16743 814-642-9557
Tracy Kio, prin. Fax 642-7778

Portersville, Butler, Pop. 235

Portersville Christian S 200/PK-12
343 E Portersville Rd 16051 724-368-8787
Lee Saunders, head sch Fax 368-3100

Port Matilda, Centre, Pop. 601
Bald Eagle Area SD
Supt. — See Wingate
Port Matilda ES 100/K-5
PO Box 558 16870 814-692-7429
Terri Kenny, admin. Fax 692-8703

State College Area SD
Supt. — See State College
Gray's Woods ES 400/K-5
160 Brackenbourne Dr 16870 814-235-6100
Kristen Dewitt, prin. Fax 272-8152

Port Royal, Juniata, Pop. 916
Juniata County SD
Supt. — See Mifflintown
Tuscarora Valley ES 100/K-5
401 W 8th St 17082 717-527-4635
Clint Mitchell, prin. Fax 436-2777

Pottstown, Montgomery, Pop. 21,544
Owen J. Roberts SD 5,200/K-12
901 Ridge Rd 19465 610-469-5100
Dr. Michael Christian, supt. Fax 469-0403
www.ojrsd.com
East Coventry ES 600/K-6
932 Sanatoga Rd 19465 610-469-5103
Todd Oswald, prin. Fax 495-0346

French Creek ES 500/K-6
3590 Coventryville Rd 19465 610-469-5104
Dr. Malinda McKillip, prin. Fax 469-5738
North Coventry ES 600/K-6
475 Kemp Rd 19465 610-469-5105
Dr. Susan Lloyd, prin. Fax 469-5864
Roberts MS 800/7-8
881 Ridge Rd 19465 610-469-5102
Sean Burns, prin. Fax 469-5832
Other Schools – See Chester Springs, Spring City

Pottsgrove SD 3,200/K-12
1301 Kauffman Rd 19464 610-327-2277
William Shirk Ed.D., supt. Fax 327-2530
www.pgsd.org
Lower Pottsgrove ES 700/3-5
1329 Buchert Rd 19464 610-323-7510
Yolanda Williams, prin. Fax 323-1911
Pottsgrove MS 700/6-8
1351 N Hanover St 19464 610-326-8243
Matthew Boyer, prin. Fax 718-0581
Ringing Rocks ES 500/K-2
1401 Kauffman Rd 19464 610-323-0903
Lisa Jones, prin. Fax 970-6918
Other Schools – See Stowe

Pottstown SD 3,100/PK-12
230 Beech St 19464 610-323-8200
Stephen Rodriguez, supt. Fax 326-6540
www.pottstownschools.com
Barth ES 400/PK-4
467 W Walnut St 19464 610-970-6675
Ryan Oxenford, prin. Fax 970-4715
Franklin ES 400/PK-4
970 N Franklin St 19464 610-970-6640
Kevin Downes, prin. Fax 970-6742
Lincoln ES 300/PK-4
461 N York St 19464 610-970-6646
Calista Boyer, prin. Fax 970-6743
Pottstown MS 900/5-8
600 N Franklin St 19464 610-970-6665
Brian Hostetler, prin. Fax 970-8738
Rupert ES 400/PK-4
1230 South St 19464 610-970-6660
Matthew Moyer, prin. Fax 970-4188

Coventry Christian S 300/PK-12
699 N Pleasantview Rd 19464 610-326-3320
John Niehls, head sch Fax 948-1780
St. Aloysius S 300/K-8
220 N Hanover St 19464 610-326-6167
Sarah Kerins, prin. Fax 970-9960
West-Mont Christian Academy 300/K-12
873 S Hanover St 19465 610-326-7690
Dr. James Smock, admin. Fax 326-7126
Wyndcroft S 200/PK-8
1395 Wilson St 19464 610-326-0544
Gail Wolter, head sch Fax 326-9931

Pottsville, Schuylkill, Pop. 14,045
Pottsville Area SD 2,800/K-12
1501 Laurel Blvd 17901 570-621-2900
Dr. Jeffrey Zweibel, supt. Fax 621-2025
www.pottsville.k12.pa.us/
Clarke ES 1,000/K-4
601 N 16th St 17901 570-621-2945
Dr. Jared Gerace, prin. Fax 621-2038
Lengel MS 800/5-8
1541 Laurel Blvd 17901 570-621-2924
Michael Maley, prin. Fax 621-2999

Assumption BVM S 100/PK-8
112 S 7th St 17901 570-622-0106
Teresa Keating, prin. Fax 622-4737

Primos, Delaware
Upper Darby SD
Supt. — See Drexel Hill
Primos ES, 861 Bunting Ln 19018 500/K-5
Jonathan Wisneski, prin. 610-622-6755

St. Eugene S 200/K-8
110 S Oak Ave 19018 610-622-2909
Jane Magnatta, prin. Fax 622-6358

Prospect, Butler, Pop. 1,160
Slippery Rock Area SD
Supt. — See Slippery Rock
Moraine ES 400/K-5
350 Main St 16052 724-865-2010
Dr. Kristie Shulsky, prin. Fax 865-0023

Prospect Park, Delaware, Pop. 6,344
Interboro SD 3,400/K-12
900 Washington Ave 19076 610-461-6700
Bernadette Reiley, supt. Fax 583-1678
www.interborosd.org
Kindergarten Academy 300/K-K
900 Washington Ave 19076 610-957-5401
Nancy DeSanctis, prin. Fax 957-5403
Prospect Park S 500/K-8
901 Pennsylvania Ave 19076 610-237-6420
Robert Kelly, prin. Fax 586-7704
Other Schools – See Essington, Glenolden, Norwood

Punxsutawney, Jefferson, Pop. 5,912
Punxsutawney Area SD 2,200/K-12
475 Beyer Ave 15767 814-938-5151
Dr. Thomas Lesniewski, supt. Fax 938-6677
www.punxsy.k12.pa.us
Bell Township ES 100/K-3
662 Airport Rd 15767 814-938-5116
Dr. Sharon Weber, prin. Fax 938-6592
Jenks Hill ES 100/K-3
200 Jenks Ave 15767 814-938-5117
Dr. Sharon Weber, prin. Fax 938-2241
Longview ES 100/K-3
19466 Route 119 Hwy N 15767 814-938-5118
Dr. Sharon Weber, prin. Fax 938-8343
Mapleview ES 200/K-3
9329 Route 536 15767 814-938-5119
Dr. Sharon Weber, prin. Fax 938-9211
Punxsutawney Area MS 700/4-7
465 Beyer Ave 15767 814-938-5151
Travis Monroe, prin. Fax 938-2671
West End ES 100/K-3
300 Center St 15767 814-938-5122
Dr. Sharon Weber, prin. Fax 938-2241
Other Schools – See Anita

Punxsutawney Christian S 200/PK-12
216 N Jefferson St 15767 814-938-2295
Lori Galbraith, admin. Fax 938-2251
SS. Cosmas & Damian S 100/PK-6
205 Chestnut St 15767 814-938-4224
Jessica Dinger, prin. Fax 939-3759

Quakertown, Bucks, Pop. 8,835
Palisades SD
Supt. — See Kintnersville
Springfield ES 200/K-5
1950 Route 212 18951 610-346-7582
Scott Davis, prin. Fax 346-8124

Quakertown Community SD 5,200/K-12
100 Commerce Dr 18951 215-529-2000
William Harner Ph.D., supt. Fax 529-2042
www.qcsd.org
Neidig ES 400/K-5
201 N Penrose St 18951 215-529-2360
Scott Godshalk, prin. Fax 529-2361
Pfaff ES 400/K-5
1600 Sleepy Hollow Rd 18951 215-529-2850
K. Eric Thompson, prin. Fax 529-2851
Quakertown ES 300/K-5
123 S 7th St 18951 215-529-2410
Dr. Michael Zackon, prin. Fax 529-2411
Richland ES 400/K-5
500 Fairview Ave 18951 215-529-2450
Nicole Zuerblis, prin. Fax 529-2451
6th Grade Center 400/6-6
349 S 9th St 18951 267-371-1200
Derek Pieffer, prin. Fax 371-1201
Strayer MS 800/6-8
1200 Ronald Reagan Dr 18951 215-529-2290
Derek Peiffer, prin. Fax 529-2291
Trumbauersville ES 400/K-5
101 Woodview Dr 18951 215-529-2550
Adam Schmucker, prin. Fax 529-2551

Quakertown Christian S 200/PK-12
50 E Paletown Rd 18951 215-536-6970
Timothy Gray, admin. Fax 536-2115
St. Isidore S 300/PK-8
603 W Broad St 18951 215-536-6052
Robin Conboy, prin. Fax 536-8647
United Friends S 100/PK-8
1018 W Broad St 18951 215-538-1733
Nancy Donnelly, head sch Fax 538-3140

Quarryville, Lancaster, Pop. 2,535
Solanco SD 3,600/K-12
121 S Hess St 17566 717-786-8401
Dr. Brian A. Bliss, supt. Fax 786-8245
www.solanco.k12.pa.us
Clermont ES 600/K-5
1868 Robert Fulton Hwy 17566 717-548-2742
Kay Bandy, prin. Fax 548-6472
Quarryville ES 500/K-5
211 S Hess St 17566 717-786-2546
Rebecca Gajecki, prin. Fax 786-4997
Smith MS 400/6-8
645 Kirkwood Pike 17566 717-786-2244
Paul Gladfelter, prin. Fax 786-8796
Swift MS 400/6-8
1866 Robert Fulton Hwy 17566 717-548-2187
Paul Gladfelter, prin. Fax 548-3350
Other Schools – See Christiana, New Providence

Radnor, Delaware, Pop. 31,300
Radnor Township SD
Supt. — See Wayne
Radnor ES 600/K-5
20 Matsonford Rd 19087 610-788-9300
Therese Borden, prin. Fax 788-2378

Armenian Sisters Academy 100/PK-8
440 Upper Gulph Rd 19087 610-687-4100

Reading, Berks, Pop. 86,403
Antietam SD 1,000/K-12
100 Antietam Rd 19606 610-779-0554
Dr. Melissa G. Brewer, supt. Fax 779-4424
www.antietamsd.org
Mount Penn PS 200/K-1
201 N 25th St 19606 610-370-2898
Shirley Feyers, prin. Fax 370-2981
Other Schools – See Mount Penn

Exeter Township SD 3,700/K-12
200 Elm St 19606 610-779-0700
Dr. Robert Phillips, supt. Fax 779-7104
www.exeter.k12.pa.us
Exeter Township JHS 700/7-8
151 E 39th St 19606 610-779-3320
Eric Flamm, prin. Fax 370-0678
Jacksonwald ES 600/K-4
100 Church Lane Rd 19606 610-779-1820
Joseph Schlaffer Ed.D., prin. Fax 779-8844
Lorane ES 500/K-4
699 Rittenhouse Dr 19606 610-582-8608
Christy Haller, prin. Fax 582-4225
Owatin Creek ES K-4
5000 Boyertown Pike 19606 610-406-4580
Jeffrey Fries, prin. Fax 898-0910
Reiffton IS 600/5-6
4355 Dunham Dr 19606 610-779-7640
Gregory Fries Ed.D., prin. Fax 779-6995

Muhlenberg SD
Supt. — See Laureldale
Cole IS 500/5-6
3630 Kutztown Rd 19605 610-921-8212
Steven Baylor, prin. Fax 741-1198
Muhlenberg ES 1,200/K-4
610 Sharp Ave 19605 610-921-8028
Krista Venza, prin. Fax 921-7905

Reading SD 15,000/PK-12
800 Washington St 19601 610-371-5611
Dr. Khalid Mumin, supt. Fax 371-5971
www.readingsd.org
Glenside ES 400/PK-5
500 Lackawanna St 19601 610-371-5913
Melissa Fisher, prin. Fax 371-5916
Lauers Park ES 800/PK-5
251 N 2nd St 19601 610-371-5960
Gordon Hoodak, prin. Fax 371-5932
Millmont ES 700/PK-5
400 Summit Ave 19611 610-320-8947
Jennifer Murray, prin. Fax 371-5902
Northeast MS 800/6-7
1216 N 13th St 19604 610-371-5774
Robinette Armstrong, prin. Fax 371-5784
Northwest ES 800/PK-5
820 Clinton St 19601 610-371-5904
Maria Wengyn, prin. Fax 371-5614
Northwest MS 700/6-7
1000 N Front St 19601 610-371-5882
Joel Brigel, prin. Fax 371-5881
Riverside ES 900/K-5
1400 Centre Ave 19601 610-371-5896
JuliAnne Kline, prin. Fax 371-5899
Sixteenth and Haak ES 700/PK-5
1601 Haak St 19602 610-371-5760
Traci Webb, prin. Fax 371-5840
Southern MS 600/6-7
931 Chestnut St 19602 610-371-5802
Geina Beaver, prin. Fax 371-5814
Southwest MS 400/6-7
300 Chestnut St 19602 610-371-5934
Dennis Campbell, prin. Fax 371-5950
Stout ES 900/PK-5
321 S 10th St 19602 610-371-5815
Susan Higginson, prin. Fax 371-5822
Tenth and Green ES 800/PK-5
400 N 10th St 19604 610-371-5756
Susan Lozada, prin. Fax 371-5630
Tenth and Penn ES 500/K-5
955 Penn St 19601 610-320-6994
Rowbee'C Kasisky, prin. Fax 736-0491
Thirteenth and Green ES 700/K-5
501 N 13th St 19604 610-371-5766
Kevin Collins, prin. Fax 371-5878
Thirteenth and Union ES 900/PK-5
1600 N 13th St 19604 610-371-5795
Margaret Brown, prin. Fax 371-5801
Twelfth and Marion ES 600/K-5
1200 N 12th St 19604 610-371-5788
Fax 371-8776
Tyson-Schoener ES 700/PK-5
315 S 5th St 19602 610-371-5951
Salvador Sepulveda, prin. Fax 371-5877

Fairview Christian S 200/K-12
410 S 14th St 19602 610-372-8826
Holy Guardian Angels S 400/PK-8
3125 Kutztown Rd 19605 610-929-4124
Maureen Wallin, prin. Fax 929-1623
Reading Junior Academy 100/PK-10
309 N Kenhorst Blvd 19607 610-777-8424
St. Catherine of Siena S 300/PK-8
2330 Perkiomen Ave 19606 610-779-5810
Sr. Teresa Ballisty, prin. Fax 779-6888
St. Margaret S 200/K-8
233 Spring St 19601 610-375-1882
Sr. Marian Michele Smith, prin. Fax 376-2291
St. Peter S 200/K-8
225 S 5th St 19602 610-374-2447
Sr. Anna Musi, prin. Fax 374-3415

Reamstown, Lancaster, Pop. 3,340
Cocalico SD
Supt. — See Denver
Reamstown ES 500/PK-5
44 S Reamstown Rd 17567 717-336-1531
Dr. Beth Haldeman, prin. Fax 336-1533

Rebersburg, Centre, Pop. 489
Penns Valley Area SD
Supt. — See Spring Mills
Miles Township ES 100/K-4
80 Town Lane Rd 16872 814-349-8868
Kurt Nyquist, prin. Fax 349-8870

Rector, Westmoreland

Valley S of Ligonier 200/K-9
153 Lupine Ln 15677 724-238-6652
Dr. Jonathan Strecker, head sch Fax 238-6838

Red Hill, Montgomery, Pop. 2,355

Red Hill Christian S 100/PK-K
208 5th St 18076 215-679-6613

Red Lion, York, Pop. 6,289
Red Lion Area SD 5,500/K-12
696 Delta Rd 17356 717-244-4518
Dr. Scott Deisley, supt. Fax 244-2196
www.rlasd.net
Gable ES 500/K-6
100 E Prospect St 17356 717-244-5523
Brian Raab, prin. Fax 417-1204
Macaluso ES 700/K-6
1195 Windsor Rd 17356 717-246-8389
Kevin Peters, prin. Fax 246-8393

North Hopewell-Winterstown ES 300/K-6
12165 Winterstown Rd 17356 717-244-3164
Abby Gold, prin. Fax 417-1205
Pleasant View ES 400/K-6
700 Delta Rd 17356 717-244-5425
Elizabeth Stambaugh, prin. Fax 417-1202
Red Lion Area JHS 900/7-8
200 Country Club Rd 17356 717-244-1448
Shane Mack, prin. Fax 244-6160
Other Schools – See Brogue, Windsor, York

Red Lion Christian S 200/PK-12
105 Springvale Rd 17356 717-244-3905

Reedsville, Mifflin, Pop. 639
Mifflin County SD
Supt. — See Lewistown
Indian Valley ES 400/K-5
125 Kish Rd 17084 717-667-2123
Kevin O'Donnell, prin. Fax 667-6608

Renfrew, Butler, Pop. 350
Butler Area SD
Supt. — See Butler
Connoquenessing ES 300/K-6
102 Connoquenessing Schl Rd 16053 724-287-8721
Crystal Ross, prin. Fax 789-7478

Renovo, Clinton, Pop. 1,205
Keystone Central SD
Supt. — See Mill Hall
Renovo ES 200/PK-6
1301 Bucktail Ave 17764 570-923-2100
Betsy Dickey, prin. Fax 923-2857

Reynoldsville, Jefferson, Pop. 2,735
Du Bois Area SD
Supt. — See Du Bois
Johnson ES 300/K-5
923 Jackson St 15851 814-653-8254
Edward Dombroski, prin. Fax 653-2378

Rheems, Lancaster, Pop. 1,587
Elizabethtown Area SD
Supt. — See Elizabethtown
Rheems ES 300/K-3
130 Alida St 17570 717-367-9121
Jacques Viau, prin. Fax 361-2537

Richboro, Bucks, Pop. 6,518
Council Rock SD
Supt. — See Newtown
Richboro ES 500/K-6
125 Upper Holland Rd 18954 215-944-1900
Dr. Daneyelle Jordan, prin. Fax 944-1996
Richboro MS 500/7-8
98 Upper Holland Rd 18954 215-944-2500
Andrew Sanko, prin. Fax 944-2598

Richfield, Juniata, Pop. 545
Juniata County SD
Supt. — See Mifflintown
Monroe Township ES 200/K-6
54 Main St 17086 717-694-3961
Nancy Kramer, prin. Fax 694-3788

Richland, Lebanon, Pop. 1,507
Eastern Lebanon County SD
Supt. — See Myerstown
Ft. Zeller ES 300/K-2
243 N Sheridan Rd 17087 610-589-2575
Tam Hower, prin. Fax 589-5815

Ridgway, Elk, Pop. 4,043
Ridgway Area SD 900/K-12
PO Box 447 15853 814-773-3146
Heather McMahon-Vargas, supt. Fax 776-4299
www.rasd.us
Grandinetti ES 400/K-5
PO Box 447 15853 814-776-2176
Pamela Yeager, prin. Fax 776-4297
Ridgway Area MS 200/6-8
PO Box 447 15853 814-773-3156
Brice Benson, prin. Fax 776-4239

St. Leo S 200/PK-8
125 Depot St 15853 814-772-9775
Monica Schloder, prin. Fax 772-9295

Ridley Park, Delaware, Pop. 6,923
Ridley SD
Supt. — See Folsom
Lakeview ES 400/K-5
333 Constitution Ave 19078 610-534-1900
Gloria Goldoy, prin. Fax 237-8013
Leedom ES 200/K-5
620 E Chester Pike 19078 610-534-1900
Melissa Lodico O'Doherty, prin. Fax 237-8019
Ridley MS 1,300/6-8
400 Free St 19078 610-534-1900
Adam Staples, prin. Fax 237-8032

St. James Regional Catholic S 300/PK-8
500 Tome St 19078 610-583-3662
Barbara Burke, prin. Fax 583-3683

Rimersburg, Clarion, Pop. 942
Union SD 600/K-12
354 Baker St Ste 2 16248 814-473-6311
Jean McCleary, supt. Fax 473-8201
www.unionsd.net/
Rimersburg ES 100/4-6
88 School St 16248 814-473-3989
Thomas Minick, prin. Fax 473-8389
Other Schools – See Sligo

Roaring Spring, Blair, Pop. 2,566
Spring Cove SD 1,400/K-12
1100 E Main St 16673 814-224-5124
Betsy Baker, supt. Fax 224-5516
scsd.schoolwires.net
Spring Cove ES 200/K-2
137 Spring Cove Dr 16673 814-224-2311
Adam Macak, prin. Fax 224-5595
Spring Cove MS 400/6-8
185 Spring Cove Dr 16673 814-224-2106
Breanne Venios, prin. Fax 224-2842
Other Schools – See Martinsburg

Robesonia, Berks, Pop. 2,034
Conrad Weiser Area SD 2,700/PK-12
44 Big Spring Rd 19551 610-693-8545
Dr. Randall Grove, supt. Fax 693-8586
www.conradweiser.org
Weiser MS 900/5-8
347 E Penn Ave 19551 610-693-8514
R. Kenneth Buck, prin. Fax 693-8543
Other Schools – See Wernersville, Womelsdorf

Rochester, Beaver, Pop. 3,481
Rochester Area SD 800/K-12
540 Reno St 15074 724-775-7500
Dr. Jane W. Bovalino Ed.D., supt. Fax 775-4077
www.rasd.org
Rochester Area ES 400/K-5
540 Reno St 15074 724-775-7500
Michael Damon, prin. Fax 775-9266
Rochester Area MS 200/6-8
540 Reno St 15074 724-775-7500
Michael Damon, prin. Fax 775-9268

Rockhill Furnace, Huntingdon, Pop. 406
Southern Huntingdon County SD
Supt. — See Three Springs
Rockhill ES 200/K-5
PO Box 184 17249 814-447-5529
Brent Pistner, prin. Fax 447-3892

Rockwood, Somerset, Pop. 885
Rockwood Area SD 700/K-12
439 Somerset Ave 15557 814-926-4688
Mark Bower, supt. Fax 926-2880
www.rockwoodschools.org
Rockwood Area ES 400/K-6
435 Somerset Ave 15557 814-926-4677
Jonathon Hale, prin. Fax 926-4678

Rome, Bradford, Pop. 437
Northeast Bradford SD 900/K-12
526 Panther Ln 18837 570-744-2521
William J. Clark, supt. Fax 744-2933
www.nebpanthers.com
Northeast Bradford ES 500/K-6
210 Panther Ln 18837 570-744-2521
Fax 744-1614

North Rome Christian S 100/K-12
3376 N Rome Rd 18837 570-247-2800
Randy Reddinger, admin. Fax 247-7288

Rosemont, Montgomery

Holy Child S at Rosemont 300/PK-8
1344 Montgomery Ave 19010 610-922-1000
Thomas Lengel, head sch Fax 922-1030
Irwin S 700/PK-12
275 S Ithan Ave 19010 610-525-8400
Dr. Wendy Hill, head sch Fax 525-8908

Roseto, Northampton, Pop. 1,552

Faith Christian S 200/K-12
122 Dante St 18013 610-588-3414
Leeann Long, prin. Fax 588-8103

Rose Valley, Delaware, Pop. 895

School in Rose Valley 100/PK-6
20 School Ln 19063 610-566-1088
Rod Stanton, head sch Fax 566-4640

Roslyn, Montgomery, Pop. 10,000
Abington SD
Supt. — See Abington
Roslyn ES 400/K-6
2565 Susquehanna Rd 19001 215-884-3368
Dr. Kevin Osborne, prin. Fax 884-2386

Royersford, Montgomery, Pop. 4,653
Spring-Ford Area SD 7,800/K-12
857 S Lewis Rd 19468 610-705-6000
Dr. David Goodin, supt. Fax 705-6245
www.spring-ford.net
Brooke ES 400/K-4
339 N Lewis Rd 19468 610-705-6006
Mary Pat Long, prin. Fax 705-6248
Limerick ES 400/K-4
81 Limerick Center Rd 19468 610-705-6007
Mitchell Edmunds, prin. Fax 705-6246
Royersford ES 500/K-4
450 Spring St 19468 610-705-6005
Dr. Teresa Carboy, prin. Fax 705-6250
Spring-Ford IS 1,300/5-6
833 S Lewis Rd Bldg 2 19468 610-705-6003
Heather Nuneviller, prin. Fax 705-6254
Spring-Ford MS 7th Grade Center 600/7-7
833 S Lewis Rd Bldg 2 19468 610-705-6010
Heather Nuneviller, prin. Fax 705-6238
Spring-Ford MS 8th Grade Center 700/8-8
700 Washington St 19468 610-705-6002
Dr. Michael Siggins, prin. Fax 705-6255
Upper Providence ES 500/K-4
833 S Lewis Rd Bldg 3 19468 610-705-6009
Dr. Melissa Patschke, prin. Fax 705-6236
Other Schools – See Limerick, Oaks, Spring City

Ruffs Dale, Westmoreland
Yough SD
Supt. — See Herminie
Mendon ES 200/K-4
164 State Route 31 15679 724-872-6484
Jenifer Pappasergi, prin. Fax 872-6972
Yough MS 700/5-8
171 State Route 31 15679 724-872-5164
Kevin Smetak, prin. Fax 872-5319

Rural Valley, Armstrong, Pop. 873
Armstrong SD
Supt. — See Kittanning
Shannock Valley ES 300/K-6
PO Box 325 16249 724-783-6991
Dr. John Giancola, prin. Fax 783-7291

Russell, Warren, Pop. 1,393
Warren County SD 4,500/K-12
6820 Market St 16345 814-723-6900
Amy J. Stewart, supt.
www.wcsdpa.org
Eisenhower ES 400/K-5
3700 Route 957 16345 814-757-4507
Shannon Yeager, prin.
Other Schools – See Sheffield, Warren, Youngsville

Rydal, Montgomery
Abington SD
Supt. — See Abington
Rydal West ES 200/K-1
1231 Meetinghouse Rd 19046 215-884-0192
Lyndsay Morgan, prin. Fax 572-7963

St. Hilary of Poitiers S 200/1-8
920 Susquehanna Rd 19046 215-887-4520
Eileen Fagan, prin. Fax 887-6337
St. Marks Classical Academy 50/K-6
1162 Beverly Rd 19046 215-884-7660

Saegertown, Crawford, Pop. 988
PENNCREST SD 3,200/K-12
PO Box 808 16433 814-763-2323
Michael J. Healey, supt. Fax 763-5129
www.penncrest.org
Saegertown ES 500/K-6
18741 State Highway 198 16433 814-763-2314
Matthew Caro, prin. Fax 763-5125
Other Schools – See Cambridge Springs, Townville

Saint Clair, Schuylkill, Pop. 2,964
Saint Clair Area SD 600/K-8
227 S Mill St 17970 570-429-2716
Dr. Sarah Yoder, supt. Fax 429-2862
www.saintclairsd.org
Saint Clair Area S 600/K-8
227 S Mill St 17970 570-429-2716
Sarah Yoder, prin. Fax 429-2859

Saint Marys, Elk, Pop. 12,994
Saint Marys Area SD 2,200/K-12
977 S Saint Marys St 15857 814-834-7831
Dr. Brian Toth, supt. Fax 781-2190
smasd.org
Saint Marys Area MS 500/6-8
979 S Saint Marys St 15857 814-834-7831
Noel Petrosky, prin. Fax 781-2191
South St. Marys Street ES 600/K-5
370 S Saint Marys St 15857 814-834-3021
Christine Kuhar, prin. Fax 834-7814
Other Schools – See Kersey, Weedville

St. Mary's Catholic ES 300/PK-5
114 Queens Rd 15857 814-834-4169
Deborah Slay, prin. Fax 834-7830
St. Marys Catholic MS 100/6-8
600 Maurus St 15857 814-834-7800
John Schneider, prin. Fax 781-3441

Saint Thomas, Franklin
Tuscarora SD
Supt. — See Mercersburg
Saint Thomas ES 300/K-5
70 School House Rd 17252 717-369-3123
Andrew Kyle, prin. Fax 369-3183

Salisbury, Somerset, Pop. 724
Salisbury-Elk Lick SD 300/PK-12
PO Box 68 15558 814-662-2733
Joseph Renzi, supt. Fax 662-2544
selsd.com
Salisbury-Elk Lick ES 100/PK-6
PO Box 68 15558 814-662-2733
Joseph Renzi, supt. Fax 662-2544

Saltsburg, Indiana, Pop. 862
Blairsville-Saltsburg SD
Supt. — See Blairsville
Saltsburg ES 300/PK-5
199 Trojan Ln 15681 724-639-3556
Tracy Richards, prin. Fax 639-9322

Sarver, Butler
Freeport Area SD 1,600/K-12
621 S Pike Rd 16055 724-295-5141
Ian Magness, supt. Fax 295-3001
www.freeport.k12.pa.us
Buffalo ES 400/K-5
500 Sarver Rd 16055 724-353-9577
Steven Poleski, prin. Fax 353-1595
Freeport Area MS 300/6-8
629 S Pike Rd. 16055 724-295-9020
Donald Dell, prin. Fax 295-4630
Other Schools – See Freeport

Evangel Heights Christian Academy 200/PK-12
120 Beale Rd 16055 724-295-9199
Fax 295-9009

Saxonburg, Butler, Pop. 1,517
South Butler County SD 2,600/K-12
328 Knoch Rd 16056 724-352-1700
David Foley Ed.D., supt. Fax 352-3622
southbutler.org
Knoch MS 600/6-8
754 Dinnerbell Rd 16056 724-352-1700
Tyler Vargo, prin. Fax 352-0170

South Butler IS 400/4-5
340 Knoch Rd 16056 724-352-1700
Dr. Frank Moxie, prin. Fax 352-0380
South Butler PS 600/K-3
328 Knoch Rd 16056 724-352-1700
Gregory Mandalas, prin. Fax 352-8848

Saxton, Bedford, Pop. 730
Tussey Mountain SD 1,000/K-12
199 Front St 16678 814-635-3670
Dr. Gary Dawson, supt. Fax 635-3928
www.tmsd.net
Tussey Mountain ES 300/K-6
1110 Mifflin St 16678 814-635-2934
Wayland Heath, prin. Fax 635-3184

Sayre, Bradford, Pop. 5,530
Sayre Area SD 1,100/PK-12
333 W Lockhart St 18840 570-888-7615
Dr. Sherry Griggs Ph.D., supt. Fax 888-8248
www.sayresd.org
Snyder ES 600/PK-6
130 Cedar St 18840 570-888-7742
Michelle Murrelle, prin. Fax 888-6037

Epiphany S 100/K-8
627 Stevenson St 18840 570-888-5802
Sr. Kathleen Kelly, prin. Fax 888-2362

Schnecksville, Lehigh, Pop. 2,900
Parkland SD
Supt. — See Allentown
Schnecksville ES 400/K-5
4260 Sand Spring Rd 18078 610-351-5830
Karen Dopera, prin. Fax 351-5839

Schuylkill Haven, Schuylkill, Pop. 5,373
Schuylkill Haven Area SD 1,300/K-12
501 E Main St 17972 570-385-6705
Dr. Shawn Fitzpatrick, supt. Fax 385-6736
www.shasd.org
Schuylkill Haven ES 500/K-4
501 E Main St 17972 570-385-6731
Geno McGorry, prin. Fax 385-6742
Schuylkill Haven MS 300/5-7
120 Haven St 17972 570-385-6708
Matthew Buletza, prin. Fax 385-6743

St. Ambrose S 100/PK-8
302 Randel St 17972 570-385-2377
Jennifer Bowen, prin. Fax 385-2387

Schwenksville, Montgomery, Pop. 1,369
Perkiomen Valley SD
Supt. — See Collegeville
Schwenksville ES 600/K-5
55 2nd St 19473 484-961-7064
Dr. Barbara Powers, prin. Fax 961-7066

Blessed Teresa of Calcutta Education Ctr 300/PK-8
256 Swamp Pike 19473 610-287-2500
Anita Dixon, prin. Fax 287-2543
St. Mary S 300/PK-8
40 Spring Mount Rd 19473 610-287-7757
Kevin Conwell, prin. Fax 287-2562

Sciota, Monroe
Stroudsburg Area SD
Supt. — See Stroudsburg
Hamilton ES 200/K-4
5531 Hamilton S 18354 570-992-4960
Karen Houck, prin. Fax 992-9034

Immaculate Conception S 200/PK-8
290 W Babbit Ave 18354 610-863-4816
Sr. Maria Luz, prin. Fax 863-8158

Scotland, Franklin, Pop. 1,373

Providence Christian Academy 50/K-12
PO Box 369 17254 717-298-8090
Jeffrey Garner, head sch

Scottdale, Westmoreland, Pop. 4,332
Southmoreland SD 1,900/K-12
200 Scottie Way 15683 724-887-2005
Dr. John Molnar Ed.D., supt. Fax 887-2055
www.southmoreland.net
Southmoreland ES 600/2-5
100 Scottie Way 15683 724-887-2021
John L. Lee, prin. Fax 887-2024
Southmoreland MS 400/6-8
200 Scottie Way 15683 724-887-2029
Vince Mascia, prin. Fax 887-2032
Other Schools – See Alverton

Scott Township, Allegheny, Pop. 17,118
Lakeland SD 1,500/K-12
1355 Lakeland Dr 18433 570-254-9485
Andy Falonk, supt. Fax 254-6730
www.lakelandsd.org
Lakeland ES - Scott Campus 500/K-6
1333 Lakeland Dr, 570-254-9484
Alan King, prin. Fax 254-9224
Other Schools – See Mayfield

Scranton, Lackawanna, Pop. 74,482
Scranton SD 9,300/PK-12
425 N Washington Ave 18503 570-348-3465
Alexis Kirijan Ed.D., supt. Fax 348-3563
www.scrsd.org
Adams ES 300/K-5
927 Capouse Ave 18509 570-348-3655
Mario Emiliani, prin. Fax 348-3163
Armstrong ES 600/PK-5
1500 N Lincoln Ave 18508 570-348-3661
Chris Lazor, prin. Fax 348-3599
Bancroft ES 200/PK-5
1002 Albright Ave 18508 570-348-3667
Ann Grebeck, prin. Fax 348-3376
Kennedy ES 400/K-5
2300 Prospect Ave 18505 570-558-8970
Nathan Barrett, prin. Fax 558-8972
McNichols Plaza ES 400/PK-5
1111 S Irving Ave 18505 570-348-3685
Colleen Leonard, prin. Fax 348-3499
Morris ES, 1824 Boulevard Ave 18509 400/PK-5
Michael Coleman, prin. 570-348-3681
Northeast IS 800/6-8
721 Adams Ave 18510 570-348-3651
Robert Butka, prin. Fax 348-3608
Prescott ES 300/PK-5
838 Prescott Ave 18510 570-348-3683
Albert O'Donnell, prin. Fax 348-3167
South Scranton IS 500/6-8
355 Maple St 18505 570-348-3631
Dan Gilroy, prin. Fax 348-3609
Sumner ES 300/PK-5
372 N Sumner Ave 18504 570-348-3688
Rob DeLuca, prin. Fax 348-3370
Tripp ES 700/K-5
1000 N Everett Ave 18504 570-558-2700
Paul Stefani, prin. Fax 558-2707
West Scranton IS 700/6-8
1401 Fellows St 18504 570-348-3476
Paul Dougherty, prin. Fax 348-3670
Whittier ES 500/K-5
700 Orchard St 18505 570-348-3690
Tim Wolff, prin. Fax 348-3674
Willard ES 500/PK-5
1100 Eynon St 18504 570-348-3692
Meg Duffy, prin. Fax 348-1861

All Saints Academy 300/PK-8
1425 Jackson St 18504 570-343-8114
Doreen Dougherty, prin. Fax 343-0378
Lutheran Academy 100/1-8
1546 Monsey St 18509 570-507-9108
Heather Luklanchuk, prin.
St. Clare / St. Paul S - Main Campus 300/3-8
1527 Penn Ave 18509 570-343-7880
Douglas Workman, prin. Fax 343-0069
St. Clare / St. Paul S - Primary Campus 300/PK-2
2215 N Washington Ave 18509 570-343-2790
Douglas Workman, prin. Fax 343-4905
Scranton Hebrew Day S 100/K-8
520 Monroe Ave 18510 570-346-1576

Selinsgrove, Snyder, Pop. 5,582
Selinsgrove Area SD 2,700/K-12
401 18th St 17870 570-374-1144
Chad Cohrs, supt. Fax 372-2222
www.seal-pa.org/
Selinsgrove Area ES 600/K-2
600 N Broad St 17870 570-372-2285
Michelle L. Garman, prin. Fax 372-2287
Selinsgrove Area IS 700/3-5
301 18th St 17870 570-372-2270
Matthew Conrad, prin. Fax 372-2272
Selinsgrove Area MS 600/6-8
401 18th St 17870 570-372-2250
John Bohle, prin. Fax 372-2251

Sellersville, Bucks, Pop. 4,161
Pennridge SD
Supt. — See Perkasie
Grasse ES 500/K-5
600 Rickert Rd 18960 215-723-7501
Howard Vogel, prin. Fax 723-0541
Sellersville ES 500/K-5
122 W Ridge Ave 18960 215-257-6591
Sarah Baker, prin. Fax 257-2169
West Rockhill ES 500/K-5
1000 Washington Ave 18960 215-257-9200
Dr. Michelle Wiley, prin. Fax 257-2802

Faith Christian Academy 400/PK-12
700 N Main St 18960 215-257-4577
Ryan Clymer, hdmstr. Fax 534-0842
Upper Bucks Christian S 300/PK-12
754 E Rockhill Rd 18960 215-536-9200

Seneca, Venango, Pop. 1,053
Cranberry Area SD 1,100/K-12
3 Education Dr 16346 814-676-5628
William Vonada, supt. Fax 677-5728
www.edline.net/pages/cranberry_area_school_district
Cranberry ES 500/K-6
3 Education Dr 16346 814-676-1871
Robert Horner, prin. Fax 677-9957

Christian Life Academy 100/PK-12
3973 State Route 257 16346 814-676-9360
Lanny Williams, admin. Fax 676-2908

Sewickley, Allegheny, Pop. 3,749
North Allegheny SD
Supt. — See Pittsburgh
Franklin ES 500/K-5
2401 Rochester Rd 15143 412-366-9663
Jeff Anderchak, prin. Fax 366-5852

Quaker Valley SD
Supt. — See Leetsdale
Edgeworth ES 500/K-5
200 Meadow Ln 15143 412-749-3605
Carol Sprinker, prin. Fax 749-9867
Osborne ES 400/K-5
1414 Beaver St 15143 412-749-4003
Aaron Rea, prin. Fax 741-7369
Quaker Valley MS 500/6-8
618 Harbaugh St 15143 412-749-5079
Anthony Mooney, prin. Fax 749-9844

Montessori Children's Community 100/PK-8
474 Chadwick St 15143 412-741-8982
Terri Modic, hdmstr. Fax 741-7614
St. James S 200/PK-8
201 Broad St 15143 412-741-5540
Sr. Christine Hill, prin. Fax 741-9038
Sewickley Academy 700/PK-12
315 Academy Ave 15143 412-741-2230
Kolia John O'Connor, head sch Fax 741-1411

Shade Gap, Huntingdon, Pop. 104
Southern Huntingdon County SD
Supt. — See Three Springs
Shade Gap ES 100/K-5
22251 Shade Valley Rd 17255 814-447-5529
Brent Pistner, prin. Fax 259-3635

Shanksville, Somerset, Pop. 229
Shanksville-Stonycreek SD
Supt. — See Friedens
Shanksville-Stonycreek ES 200/PK-5
PO Box 128 15560 814-267-4649
Reno Barkman, prin. Fax 267-7229

Sharon, Mercer, Pop. 13,523
Sharon CSD 2,100/K-12
215 Forker Blvd 16146 724-983-4000
Michael Calla, supt. Fax 981-0844
sharoncitysd.schoolwires.com
Case Avenue ES 600/K-6
36 Case Ave 16146 724-983-4015
Traci Valentino, prin. Fax 983-4021
Musser ES 400/K-6
500 Cedar Ave 16146 724-981-4381
Jeff DeJulia, prin. Fax 981-4600
Sharon MS 300/7-8
1129 E State St 16146 724-983-4032
Matt Vannoy, prin. Fax 983-4050
West Hill ES 300/K-6
301 Ellsworth St 16146 724-981-4880
Michael Gay, prin. Fax 981-0482

Sharon Hill, Delaware, Pop. 5,504
Southeast Delco SD
Supt. — See Folcroft
Sharon Hill S 600/1-8
701 Coates St 19079 610-522-4355
Charles Baxter, prin. Fax 522-4364

Sharpsville, Mercer, Pop. 4,343
Sharpsville Area SD 1,300/K-12
701 Pierce Ave 16150 724-962-7874
John Vannoy, supt. Fax 962-7873
www.sharpsville.k12.pa.us/
Sharpsville Area ES 600/K-5
100 Hittle Ave 16150 724-962-8300
Jon Fry, prin. Fax 962-1003
Sharpsville Area MS 300/6-8
303 Blue Devil Way 16150 724-962-7863
Heidi AbiNader, prin. Fax 962-7891

Sheffield, Warren, Pop. 1,128
Warren County SD
Supt. — See Russell
Sheffield Area ES 200/K-5
6760 Route 6 16347 814-968-3720
Marcia Madigan, prin.

Shenandoah, Schuylkill, Pop. 5,009
Shenandoah Valley SD 1,100/PK-12
805 W Centre St 17976 570-462-1936
Brian Waite, supt. Fax 462-4611
www.svbluedevils.org
Shenandoah Valley ES 600/PK-6
805 W Centre St 17976 570-462-2796
Brooke Wowak, prin. Fax 462-1943

Trinity Academy 200/PK-8
233 W Cherry St 17976 570-462-3927
Sr. M. Judith Knowlton, prin. Fax 462-4603

Shermans Dale, Perry
West Perry SD
Supt. — See Elliottsburg
Carroll ES 400/PK-5
6670 Spring Rd 17090 717-582-4256
Kristi Wickard, prin. Fax 582-3547

Shickshinny, Luzerne, Pop. 832
Northwest Area SD 1,000/PK-12
243 Thorne Hill Rd 18655 570-542-4126
James McGovern, supt. Fax 542-0187
www.northwest.k12.pa.us
Northwest Area IS 300/4-6
20 Sunset Lake Rd 18655 570-542-4126
Matthew Mills, prin. Fax 256-3216
Other Schools – See Huntington Mills

Shillington, Berks, Pop. 5,201
Governor Mifflin SD 4,100/K-12
10 S Waverly St 19607 610-775-1461
Dr. Steven Gerhard, supt. Fax 775-6586
www.governormifflinsd.org
Cumru ES 500/K-4
10 S Waverly St 19607 610-775-5081
Dr. Richard Kaskey, prin. Fax 685-0404
Mifflin IS 600/5-6
10 S Waverly St 19607 610-775-5083
Lee Umberger, prin. Fax 685-3761
Mifflin MS 700/7-8
10 S Waverly St 19607 610-775-1465
Kevin Hohl, prin. Fax 685-3760
Mifflin Park ES 500/K-4
10 S Waverly St 19607 610-898-1489
Holly Garner, prin. Fax 898-0635
Other Schools – See Mohnton

LaSalle Academy 200/PK-8
440 Holland St 19607 610-777-7392
Stephen Mickulik, prin. Fax 777-1280

Shinglehouse, Potter, Pop. 1,122
Oswayo Valley SD 400/PK-12
277 S Oswayo St 16748 814-260-1700
Dr. Michele Hartzell, supt. Fax 697-7439
www.oswayovalley.com
Oswayo Valley ES 200/PK-5
277 S Oswayo St 16748 814-260-1702
Carolyn Fugate, prin. Fax 697-7799

Shippensburg, Cumberland, Pop. 5,366
Shippensburg Area SD 3,400/K-12
317 N Morris St 17257 717-530-2700
Dr. C. Gregory Hoover, supt. Fax 530-2724
www.shipk12.org
Burd ES 500/K-3
600 Brad St 17257 717-530-2780
Scott Shapiro, prin. Fax 530-2856
Grayson ES 500/K-3
301 Lurgan Ave 17257 717-530-2770
Susan Martin, prin. Fax 530-2542
Luhrs University ES 100/K-5
1871 Old Main Dr 17257 717-477-1612
Steven Smith, dir. Fax 477-4072
Shippensburg Area IS 500/4-5
601 Hollar Ave 17257 717-530-3189
Teri Mowery, prin. Fax 530-3627
Shippensburg Area MS 800/6-8
101 Park Pl W 17257 717-530-2750
David Rice, prin. Fax 530-2757

Shiremanstown, Cumberland, Pop. 1,540

Children's Garden of St. John's 200/PK-K
44 W Main St 17011 717-731-1095
Tracy Baxter, dir. Fax 731-1049
West Shore Christian Academy 400/PK-12
201 W Main St 17011 717-737-3550
Paul Beardmore, prin. Fax 761-3977

Shoemakersville, Berks, Pop. 1,376
Hamburg Area SD
Supt. — See Hamburg
Perry ES 300/K-5
201 4th St 19555 610-562-2241
Andrea Berger, prin. Fax 562-0469

Shohola, Pike
Delaware Valley SD
Supt. — See Milford
Shohola ES 500/K-5
940 Twin Lakes Rd 18458 570-296-3600
Diana Bixby, prin. Fax 296-3161

Sidman, Cambria, Pop. 430
Forest Hills SD 1,900/PK-12
PO Box 158 15955 814-487-7613
Edwin Bowser, supt. Fax 487-7775
www.fhrangers.org
Forest Hills ES 1,000/PK-6
PO Box 290 15955 814-487-7613
Lucas Jacobs, prin. Fax 487-2372

Sinking Spring, Berks, Pop. 3,938
Wilson SD
Supt. — See West Lawn
Cornwall Terrace ES 500/K-5
3100 Iroquois Ave 19608 610-670-0180
Beth Yeiser, prin. Fax 334-6447
Green Valley ES 400/K-5
270 Green Valley Rd 19608 610-670-0180
Laura Morgan, prin. Fax 334-6442
Shiloh Hills ES 400/K-5
301 Sage Dr 19608 610-670-0180
Dr. Matthew Flannery, prin. Fax 334-6443
Wilson Southern MS 700/6-8
3100 Iroquois Ave 19608 610-670-0180
Dr. Stephen Burnham, prin. Fax 334-6445
Wilson West MS 700/6-8
450 Faust Rd 19608 610-670-0180
Kyle Wetherhold, prin. Fax 334-6440

Slatington, Lehigh, Pop. 4,171
Northern Lehigh SD 1,700/K-12
1201 Shadow Oaks Ln 18080 610-767-9800
Fax 767-9809
www.nlsd.org
Northern Lehigh MS 300/7-8
600 Diamond St 18080 610-767-9812
Jill Chamberlain, prin. Fax 767-9850
Peters ES 400/K-2
4055 Friedens Rd 18080 610-767-9827
Paul Leonzi, prin. Fax 767-9857
Slatington ES 500/3-6
1201 Shadow Oaks Ln 18080 610-767-9821
Scott Pyne, prin. Fax 767-9808

Sligo, Clarion, Pop. 719
Union SD
Supt. — See Rimersburg
Sligo ES 200/K-3
2013 Madison Street Ext 16255 814-745-2152
Thomas Minick, prin. Fax 745-3017

Slippery Rock, Butler, Pop. 3,557
Slippery Rock Area SD 2,000/K-12
201 Kiester Rd 16057 724-794-2960
Dr. Alfonso Angelucci, supt. Fax 794-2001
www.slipperyrock.k12.pa.us
Slippery Rock Area ES 500/K-5
470 N Main St 16057 724-794-2960
W. Herbert Basham, prin. Fax 794-5461
Slippery Rock Area MS 500/6-8
201 Kiester Rd 16057 724-794-2960
Dr. Jacob Jefferis, prin. Fax 794-6265
Other Schools – See Prospect

Smethport, McKean, Pop. 1,646
Smethport Area SD 900/PK-12
414 S Mechanic St 16749 814-887-5543
David E. London, supt. Fax 887-5544
www.smethportschools.com/
Smethport Area ES 500/PK-6
414 S Mechanic St 16749 814-887-5012
Larry Rondinelli, prin. Fax 887-5540

Smithfield, Fayette, Pop. 871
Albert Gallatin Area SD
Supt. — See Uniontown
Smithfield ES 300/K-5
23 Liberty St 15478 724-569-9570
Renee Rosie, prin. Fax 569-1608

Mount Moriah Christian S 100/PK-8
PO Box 903 15478 724-569-4890

Snow Shoe, Centre, Pop. 763
Bald Eagle Area SD
Supt. — See Wingate
Mountaintop Area ES 200/K-5
100 School Dr 16874 814-387-6861
Mary Beth Crago, prin. Fax 387-4323

Solebury, Bucks
New Hope-Solebury SD
Supt. — See New Hope
New Hope-Solebury Lower ES 300/K-2
PO Box 569 18963 215-297-5438
Kenneth Silver, prin. Fax 297-0988

Somerset, Somerset, Pop. 6,210
Somerset Area SD 2,200/PK-12
645 S Columbia Ave Ste 110 15501 814-443-2831
Krista Mathias, supt. Fax 443-1964
sasd.us
Eagle View ES 500/3-5
191 Discovery Ln 15501 814-444-8455
Erick Fish, prin. Fax 445-3278
Maple Ridge ES 400/PK-2
105 New Centerville Rd 15501 814-445-6677
Joshua Spangler, prin. Fax 445-1821

St. Peter S 100/K-6
433 W Church St 15501 814-445-6662
Jill Harris, prin. Fax 445-7766

Souderton, Montgomery, Pop. 6,521
Souderton Area SD 6,300/K-12
760 Lower Rd 18964 215-723-6061
Frank Gallagher, supt. Fax 723-8897
www.soudertonsd.org
Crouthamel ES 300/K-5
143 S School Ln 18964 215-723-5949
Tamara Callahan, prin. Fax 723-1652
Franconia ES 500/K-5
366 Harleysville Pike 18964 215-723-2596
Gail Ryan, prin. Fax 723-4470
Indian Crest MS 800/6-8
139 Harleysville Pike 18964 215-723-9193
Jeff Pammer, prin. Fax 723-8897
West Broad Street ES 500/K-5
342 W Broad St 18964 215-723-1711
Marianne Boyd, prin. Fax 723-6909
Other Schools – See Harleysville, Telford

Dock Mennonite Academy 600/PK-8
420 Godshall Rd 18964 215-723-1196

South Abington, Lackawanna

Abington Christian Academy 100/PK-12
413 Layton Rd, 570-586-5270
Janet Wells M.Ed., admin. Fax 586-5270
Summit Christian Academy 100/PK-9
660 Griffin Pond Rd, 570-587-1545
Dr. Marianne Rivers, admin. Fax 309-0038

Southampton, Bucks, Pop. 11,500
Centennial SD
Supt. — See Warminster
Davis ES, 475 Maple Ave 18966 700/K-5
Shawanna James-Coles, prin. 215-364-5970
Klinger MS 600/6-8
1415 2nd Street Pike 18966 215-364-5950
Travis Bloom, prin. Fax 364-5955

Our Lady of Good Counsel S 400/PK-8
611 Knowles Ave 18966 215-357-1300
Frank Mokriski, prin. Fax 357-4452

South Park, Allegheny
South Park SD 1,900/K-12
2005 Eagle Ridge Dr 15129 412-655-3111
Wayne P. Gdovic, supt. Fax 655-2952
www.sparksd.org
South Park ES 700/K-4
2001 Eagle Pride Ln 15129 412-655-8510
Dr. L. Robert Furman, prin. Fax 655-6540
South Park MS 600/5-8
2500 Stewart Rd 15129 412-831-7200
Kevin Monaghan, prin. Fax 831-7204

South Williamsport, Lycoming, Pop. 6,306
South Williamsport Area SD 1,300/K-12
515 W Central Ave 17702 570-327-1581
Dr. Mark Stamm, supt. Fax 326-0641
www.mounties.k12.pa.us
Central ES 500/K-4
555 W Mountain Ave 17702 570-323-3694
Kathy Furman, prin. Fax 320-4492
Rommelt MS 200/5-6
515 W Central Ave 17702 570-320-4470
Matthew Fisher, prin. Fax 327-0641

Mountain View Christian S 50/PK-8
305 Fleming St 17702 570-327-9238

Spring Church, Armstrong
Apollo-Ridge SD
Supt. — See Apollo
Apollo-Ridge ES 600/K-5
PO Box 157 15686 724-478-6000
Courtney Anderson, prin. Fax 478-2967
Apollo-Ridge MS 300/6-8
1829 State Route 56 15686 724-478-6000
Travis Barta, prin. Fax 478-3730

Spring City, Chester, Pop. 3,247
Owen J. Roberts SD
Supt. — See Pottstown
East Vincent ES 500/K-6
340 Ridge Rd 19475 610-469-5185
Dr. Cheryl Bell, prin. Fax 469-5884

Spring-Ford Area SD
Supt. — See Royersford
Spring City ES 100/K-4
190 S Wall St 19475 610-705-6004
Mitchell Edmunds, prin. Fax 705-6253

Springdale, Allegheny, Pop. 3,373
Allegheny Valley SD
Supt. — See Cheswick
Colfax Upper ES 200/4-6
430 Colfax St 15144 724-274-7200
Jennifer Vecchio, prin. Fax 274-2187

Springfield, Delaware, Pop. 24,160
Springfield SD 3,900/K-12
111 W Leamy Ave 19064 610-938-6000
Dr. Anthony Barber, supt. Fax 938-6005
www.ssdcougars.org
Richardson MS 800/6-8
20 W Woodland Ave 19064 610-938-6300
Daniel Tracy, prin. Fax 938-6305
Sabold ES 600/2-5
468 E Thomson Ave 19064 610-938-6500
Peter Brigg, prin. Fax 938-6505
Scenic Hills ES 600/2-5
235 Hillview Dr 19064 610-938-6600
Dr. Madeleine O'Dowd, prin. Fax 938-6605
Springfield Literacy Center 600/K-1
210 W Woodland Ave 19064 610-690-3100
Susan Trella, prin.

Holy Cross S 300/PK-8
240 N Bishop Ave 19064 610-626-1709
Maureen Ward, prin. Fax 626-1859
St. Francis of Assisi S 300/K-8
112 Saxer Ave 19064 610-543-0546
Jill Carroll, prin. Fax 544-9431

Spring Grove, York, Pop. 2,145
Spring Grove Area SD 3,800/K-12
100 E College Ave 17362 717-225-4731
Dr. David J. Renaut, supt. Fax 225-6028
www.sgasd.org
Spring Grove Area IS 600/5-6
1480 Roth Church Rd 17362 717-225-4731
Craig Seelye, prin. Fax 225-7395
Spring Grove Area MS 600/7-8
244 Old Hanover Rd 17362 717-225-4731
Dr. Steve Guadagnino, prin. Fax 225-0146
Spring Grove ES 700/K-4
1450 Roth Church Rd 17362 717-225-4731
Jon Weaver, prin. Fax 225-9238
Other Schools – See Thomasville, York

Spring House, Montgomery, Pop. 3,766

Gwynedd Mercy Academy 500/K-8
PO Box 241 19477 215-646-4916
Sr. Anne Crampsie, prin. Fax 646-7250

Spring Mills, Centre, Pop. 267
Penns Valley Area SD 1,500/K-12
4528 Penns Valley Rd 16875 814-422-2000
Brian Griffith, supt. Fax 422-8020
www.pennsvalley.org
Penns Valley Area ES 400/K-6
4528 Penns Valley Rd 16875 814-422-8824
Danielle Yoder, prin. Fax 422-0374
Other Schools – See Centre Hall, Rebersburg

Springville, Susquehanna
Elk Lake SD 1,300/K-12
2380 Elk Lake School Rd 18844 570-278-1106
Dr. Kenneth Cuomo, supt. Fax 278-4838
www.elklakeschool.org
Elk Lake ES 700/K-6
2380 Elk Lake School Rd 18844 570-278-1106
Marc Weisgold, prin. Fax 278-4356

State College, Centre, Pop. 41,187
State College Area SD 6,700/K-12
240 Villa Crest Dr 16801 814-231-1011
Dr. Robert O'Donnell, supt. Fax 231-4130
www.scasd.org
Corl Street ES 200/K-5
235 Corl St 16801 814-231-1186
Charlotte Zmyslo, prin. Fax 235-4587
Easterly Parkway ES 300/K-5
234 Easterly Pkwy 16801 814-231-1170
Michael Maclay, prin. Fax 272-8861
Houserville/Lemont ES 300/K-5
675 Elmwood St 16801 814-231-5026
Todd Dishong, prin. Fax 231-5004
Mt. Nittany ES 400/K-5
700 Brandywine Dr 16801 814-272-5970
Mark Feldman, prin. Fax 272-5955
Mount Nittany MS 700/6-8
656 Brandywine Dr 16801 814-272-4050
Brian Ishler, prin. Fax 272-4055
Park Forest ES 500/K-5
2181 School Dr 16803 814-231-5010
Thomas Weed, prin. Fax 235-4558
Park Forest MS 800/6-8
2180 School Dr 16803 814-237-5301
Dr. Karen Wiser, prin. Fax 272-0196

Radio Park ES 400/K-5
800 W Cherry Ln 16803 814-231-4115
Zachary Wynkoop, prin. Fax 235-4592
Other Schools – See Pine Grove Mills, Port Matilda

Grace Lutheran Preschool & K 100/PK-K
205 S Garner St 16801 814-238-8110
Cathy Smarkusky, admin. Fax 238-4104
Nittany Christian S 100/K-8
1221 W Whitehall Rd 16801 814-234-5652
Anthony Wilson, hdmstr. Fax 234-5632
Our Lady of Victory S 300/PK-8
800 Westerly Pkwy 16801 814-238-1592
Samantha Weakland, prin. Fax 238-4553
State College Friends S 100/PK-8
1900 University Dr 16801 814-237-8386
Dan Hendey, head sch Fax 235-1446

Steelton, Dauphin, Pop. 5,688
Central Dauphin SD
Supt. — See Harrisburg
Swatara MS 600/6-8
1101 Highland St 17113 717-939-9363
Kelly Fowlkes, prin. Fax 939-2156
Tri Community ES 400/K-5
255 Cypress St 17113 717-939-9591
Jonathan Fried, prin. Fax 939-5591

Steelton-Highspire SD 1,300/K-12
250 Reynders St 17113 717-704-3800
Travis Waters, supt. Fax 704-3808
www.shsd.k12.pa.us
Steelton-Highspire ES 800/K-6
250 Reynders St 17113 717-704-3800
Scott Smith, prin. Fax 704-3808

Stewartstown, York, Pop. 2,058
South Eastern SD
Supt. — See Fawn Grove
Stewartstown ES 400/K-4
17945 Barrens Rd N 17363 717-993-2725
Barbara Lamond, prin. Fax 993-5256

Stoneboro, Mercer, Pop. 1,041
Lakeview SD 1,200/K-12
2482 Mercer St 16153 724-376-7911
Dr. Hedley Hoge, supt. Fax 376-7910
www.lakeview.k12.pa.us
Lakeview MS 400/6-8
2482 Mercer St 16153 724-376-7911
David Blakley, prin. Fax 376-7910
Oakview ES 400/K-5
1387 School Rd 16153 724-376-7911
Timothy Eiler, prin. Fax 376-7910

Stowe, Montgomery, Pop. 3,584
Pottsgrove SD
Supt. — See Pottstown
West Pottsgrove ES 300/K-2
25 Grosstown Rd 19464 610-323-6510
Terri Koehler, prin. Fax 340-2665

Stoystown, Somerset, Pop. 354
North Star SD
Supt. — See Boswell
North Star MS 300/5-8
3598 Whistler Rd 15563 814-893-5616
Cheryl Slade, prin. Fax 893-5922

Strafford, Chester, Pop. 4,500

Woodlynde S 200/K-12
445 Upper Gulph Rd 19087 610-687-9660
Dr. Christopher Fulco Ed.D., head sch Fax 687-4752

Strattanville, Clarion, Pop. 547
Clarion-Limestone Area SD 900/PK-12
4091 C L School Rd 16258 814-764-5111
Amy Glasl, supt. Fax 764-5729
www.clasd.net
Clarion-Limestone ES 400/PK-6
4091 C L School Rd 16258 814-764-6006
Kristie Taylor, prin. Fax 764-5806

Stroudsburg, Monroe, Pop. 5,412
Stroudsburg Area SD 4,700/K-12
123 Linden St 18360 570-421-1990
Dr. Cosmas Curry, supt. Fax 424-5986
www.sburg.org
Arlington Heights ES 300/K-4
853 Flagler St 18360 570-421-6952
Elise Hanna, prin. Fax 421-6065
Chipperfield ES 700/K-4
2015 Chipperfield Dr 18360 570-421-4834
Margaret Vitale M.Ed., prin. Fax 421-5370
Morey ES 200/K-4
1044 W Main St 18360 570-421-6371
Dr. Cynthia Miller, prin. Fax 421-4985
Stroudsburg MS 1,200/5-7
207 Mountaineer Dr 18360 570-213-0203
Jack Schalk, prin. Fax 213-0223
Other Schools – See Sciota

Pocono Adventist Christian S 50/PK-8
2001 W Main St 18360 570-421-5577

Sugarloaf, Luzerne
Hazleton Area SD
Supt. — See Hazle Township
Valley S 1,000/K-8
79 Rock Glen Rd 18249 570-459-3221
Kathy Brior, prin. Fax 788-4718

Sunbury, Northumberland, Pop. 9,716
Shikellamy SD 2,700/K-12
200 Island Blvd 17801 570-286-3720
Brett Misavage, supt. Fax 286-3776
www.shikbraves.org
Beck ES 300/K-5
600 Arch St 17801 570-286-3725
Susan Giberson, prin. Fax 286-3866
Chief Shikellamy ES 300/K-5
338 Memorial Dr 17801 570-286-3728
Todd VanKirk, prin. Fax 286-3730
Oaklyn ES 400/K-5
115 Oak St 17801 570-286-3731
Angela Farronato, prin. Fax 286-3762
Other Schools – See Northumberland

Susquehanna, Susquehanna, Pop. 1,631
Susquehanna Community SD 800/K-12
3192 Turnpike St 18847 570-853-4921
Bronson Stone, supt. Fax 853-3768
www.scschools.org/
Susquehanna Community ES 500/K-6
3192 Turnpike St 18847 570-853-4921
Bronson Stone, supt. Fax 853-3768

Swarthmore, Delaware, Pop. 5,977
Ridley SD
Supt. — See Folsom
Grace Park ES 300/K-5
1097 7th Ave 19081 610-534-1900
Dave DeYulis, prin. Fax 328-0110

Wallingford-Swarthmore SD
Supt. — See Wallingford
Swarthmore-Rutledge ES 600/K-5
100 College Ave 19081 610-892-3470
Dr. Angela Tuck, prin. Fax 338-0609

Notre Dame DeLourdes S 300/PK-8
990 Fairview Rd 19081 610-328-9330
Susan Lowe, prin. Fax 328-3955

Sweet Valley, Luzerne
Lake-Lehman SD
Supt. — See Dallas
Ross ES 300/K-6
5148 Main Rd 18656 570-477-5050
Lori Bednarek, prin. Fax 477-2461

Swiftwater, Monroe
Pocono Mountain SD 8,300/K-12
PO Box 200 18370 570-839-7121
Dr. Elizabeth Robison, supt. Fax 895-4768
www.pmsd.org
Pocono Mountain East JHS 700/7-8
PO Box 200 18370 570-839-7121
Dr. Kathy Fanelli, prin. Fax 839-3242
Swiftwater Elementary Center 1,100/K-3
PO Box 200 18370 570-839-7121
Tamala Toleno, prin. Fax 839-5935
Swiftwater IS 400/7-8
PO Box 200 18370 570-839-7121
Kristine Kunsman, prin. Fax 839-7820
Other Schools – See Pocono Pines, Pocono Summit, Tobyhanna

Tamaqua, Schuylkill, Pop. 7,032
Tamaqua Area SD 2,100/K-12
138 W Broad St 18252 570-668-2570
Raymond J. Kinder, supt. Fax 668-6850
www.tamaqua.k12.pa.us
Tamaqua Area MS 500/6-8
502 Penn St 18252 570-668-1210
Christopher Czapla, prin. Fax 668-5027
Tamaqua ES 500/K-5
Boyle Ave 18252 570-668-3306
Steven Behr, prin. Fax 668-3235
Other Schools – See New Ringgold

St. Jerome S 200/K-8
250 W Broad St 18252 570-668-2757
Amy Hannis-Miskar, prin. Fax 668-6101

Tarentum, Allegheny, Pop. 4,449
Deer Lakes SD
Supt. — See Cheswick
Curtisville Primary Center 500/K-2
1715 Saxonburg Blvd 15084 724-265-5340
Jennifer Cavalancia, prin. Fax 265-1488

Highlands SD
Supt. — See Natrona Heights
Grandview Upper ES 600/3-5
101 E 9th Ave 15084 724-224-0300
Heather Hauser, prin. Fax 224-3178

Taylor, Lackawanna, Pop. 6,195
Riverside SD 1,300/K-12
300 Davis St 18517 570-562-2121
Paul Brennan, supt. Fax 562-3205
www.riversidesd.com
Riverside ES West 200/K-2
300 Davis St 18517 570-562-2121
Scott Pentasuglio, prin. Fax 562-1790
Other Schools – See Moosic

Telford, Montgomery, Pop. 4,781
Souderton Area SD
Supt. — See Souderton
Vernfield ES 500/K-5
960 Long Mill Rd 18969 215-721-0606
Jonathan Graf, prin. Fax 721-6909

Terre Hill, Lancaster, Pop. 1,285

Shalom Mennonite S 100/K-8
1410 Union Grove Rd 17581 717-445-7020

Thomasville, York
Spring Grove Area SD
Supt. — See Spring Grove
Paradise ES 400/K-4
6923 Lincoln Hwy 17364 717-225-4731
Dr. Michael Holtzapple, prin. Fax 225-4861

St. Rose of Lima S 100/PK-6
115 N Biesecker Rd 17364 717-792-0889
Peggy Rizzuto, prin. Fax 792-3959

Thompsontown, Juniata, Pop. 692
Juniata County SD
Supt. — See Mifflintown
Thompsontown-Delaware ES 100/K-6
21 School St 17094 717-535-5520
Nancy Kramer, prin. Fax 535-5061

Thorndale, Chester, Pop. 3,357
Coatesville Area SD 7,300/K-12
3030 C G Zinn Rd 19372 610-466-2400
Dr. Cathy Taschner, supt. Fax 383-1426
casd.schoolwires.net
Caln ES 600/K-5
3609 Lincoln Hwy 19372 610-383-3760
Rebecca Richardson, prin. Fax 383-3764
Other Schools – See Coatesville, E Fallowfield

Three Springs, Huntingdon, Pop. 439
Southern Huntingdon County SD 1,300/K-12
10339 Pogue Rd 17264 814-447-5529
Dwayne Northcraft, supt. Fax 447-3967
shcsd.org
Spring Farms ES 200/K-5
12075 Old Plank Rd 17264 814-447-5529
Brent Pistner, prin. Fax 448-9170
Other Schools – See Rockhill Furnace, Shade Gap

Throop, Lackawanna, Pop. 4,041
Mid Valley SD 1,500/K-12
52 Underwood Rd 18512 570-307-1108
Patrick Sheehan, supt. Fax 307-1107
www.mvsd.us
Mid Valley Elementary Center 1,000/K-6
50 Underwood Rd 18512 570-307-3241
Carlos Lopez, prin. Fax 307-3239

Tioga, Tioga, Pop. 659
Northern Tioga SD
Supt. — See Elkland
Walter ES 500/K-6
65 Jct Cross Rd 16946 570-827-2171
Amy Wood, prin. Fax 827-3451

Tionesta, Forest, Pop. 478
Forest Area SD 500/PK-12
22318 Route 62 Unit 16 16353 814-755-4491
Amanda Hetrick, supt. Fax 755-2426
www.forestareaschools.org/
West Forest ES 200/PK-6
22318 Route 62 Unit 15 16353 814-755-3302
Elisha Pospisil, prin. Fax 755-2427
Other Schools – See Marienville

North Clarion County SD 600/PK-12
10439 Route 36 16353 814-744-8536
Steven Young, supt. Fax 744-9378
www.northclarion.org
North Clarion County ES 300/PK-6
10439 Route 36 16353 814-744-8541
Keith Hastings, prin. Fax 744-9229

Titusville, Crawford, Pop. 5,544
Titusville Area SD 2,100/PK-12
301 E Spruce St 16354 814-827-2715
Karen Jez, supt. Fax 827-7761
www.gorockets.org/
Early Childhood Learning Center 300/PK-K
330 E Spruce St 16354 814-827-2715
Diane Robbins, prin. Fax 827-0557
Hydetown ES 200/1-5
12294 Gresham Rd 16354 814-827-2715
Lisa Royek, prin. Fax 827-0554
Main Street ES 300/1-5
117 W Main St 16354 814-827-2715
Stephanie Keebler, prin. Fax 827-0555
Titusville MS 500/6-8
415 Water St 16354 814-827-2715
Jessica Stover, prin. Fax 827-0552
Other Schools – See Pleasantville

Tobyhanna, Monroe
Pocono Mountain SD
Supt. — See Swiftwater
Clear Run Elementary Center 700/K-2
780 Memorial Blvd 18466 570-839-7121
Heidi Donohue, prin. Fax 894-1286
Clear Run IS 400/3-6
800 Memorial Blvd 18466 570-839-7121
Regina Schank, prin. Fax 894-9329

Topton, Berks, Pop. 2,055
Brandywine Heights Area SD 1,400/K-12
200 W Weis St 19562 610-682-5100
Andrew Potteiger, supt. Fax 682-5136
www.bhasd.org
Brandywine Heights ES 400/K-3
200 W Weis St 19562 610-682-5171
Stephanie Kelly, prin. Fax 682-5176
Brandywine Heights Intermediate MS 400/4-8
200 W Weis St 19562 610-682-5131
Robert Farina, prin. Fax 682-5105

Toughkenamon, Chester, Pop. 1,486
Kennett Consolidated SD
Supt. — See Kennett Square
New Garden ES 500/K-5
265 New Garden Rd 19374 610-268-6900
Susan McArdle, prin.

Towanda, Bradford, Pop. 2,864
Towanda Area SD 1,600/K-12
410 State St 18848 570-265-9154
Dr. Amy Martell, supt. Fax 265-4881
www.tsd.k12.pa.us
Morrow PS 400/K-2
101 N 4th St 18848 570-265-4991
Karen Beirne-Getz, prin. Fax 265-6831
Towanda Area ES 400/3-6
420 State St 18848 570-265-6131
Susan Higley, prin. Fax 268-5070

St. Agnes S 100/PK-6
102 3rd St 18848 570-265-6803
Chad Shrawder, prin. Fax 265-3065

Tower City, Schuylkill, Pop. 1,337
Williams Valley SD 1,000/K-12
10330 Route 209 Rd 17980 717-647-2167
Dr. Diane Niederriter, supt. Fax 647-2055
www.wvschools.net
Williams Valley ES 600/K-6
10400 Route 209 Rd 17980 717-647-2167
Stephanie Carl, prin. Fax 647-7543

Townville, Crawford, Pop. 323
PENNCREST SD
Supt. — See Saegertown
Maplowood ES 500/K-6
32695 State Highway 408 16360 814-967-2675
Erin Fonzo, prin. Fax 967-2136

Trafford, Westmoreland, Pop. 3,138
Penn-Trafford SD
Supt. — See Harrison City
Level Green ES 200/K-5
650 Cypress Ct 15085 412-372-6603
Dan DiNapoli, prin. Fax 372-0114
Trafford ES 200/K-5
100 Brinton Ave 15085 412-372-6600
Dan DiNapoli, prin. Fax 372-1554
Trafford MS 400/6-8
100 Brinton Ave 15085 412-372-6600
Roger Sullivan, prin. Fax 372-1554

Trevorton, Northumberland, Pop. 1,820
Line Mountain SD
Supt. — See Herndon
Line Mountain ES 500/K-4
542 W Shamokin St 17881 570-797-3825
Jeanne Menko, prin. Fax 797-4001

Troy, Bradford, Pop. 1,340
Troy Area SD 1,500/K-12
68 Fenner Ave 16947 570-297-2750
Charles Young, supt. Fax 297-1600
www.troyareasd.org/
Croman PS 300/K-2
317 Canton St 16947 570-297-3145
Steven Brion, prin. Fax 297-3260
Troy Area IS 400/3-6
206 King St 16947 570-297-4565
Mary Abreu, prin. Fax 297-5186

Tunkhannock, Wyoming, Pop. 1,809
Tunkhannock Area SD 2,600/K-12
41 Philadelphia Ave 18657 570-836-3111
Heather McPherson, supt. Fax 836-2942
www.tasd.net
Evans Falls ES 200/K-4
2055 SR 29 S 18657 570-298-7011
Katherine Felker, prin. Fax 240-4811
Roslund ES 300/K-4
99 Digger Dr 18657 570-836-8270
Michelle Knoebel, prin. Fax 836-5622
Tunkhannock MS 800/5-8
200 Franklin Ave 18657 570-836-8242
Susan Bugno, prin. Fax 836-5796
Other Schools – See Dalton, Mehoopany

Turbotville, Northumberland, Pop. 705
Warrior Run SD 1,600/K-12
4800 Susquehanna Trl 17772 570-649-5138
Alan Hack Ed.D., supt. Fax 649-5475
www.wrsd.org
Turbotville ES 300/K-4
4800 Susquehanna Trl 17772 570-649-5164
Nathan Minium, prin. Fax 649-6160
Warrior Run MS 500/5-8
4800 Susquehanna Trl 17772 570-649-5135
Rebecca Perruquet, prin. Fax 649-6173

Turtle Creek, Allegheny, Pop. 5,197
Woodland Hills SD
Supt. — See North Braddock
Woodland Hills Academy 500/K-8
126 Monroeville Ave 15145 412-824-2450
Kelly Mann, prin. Fax 824-2597

Tyrone, Blair, Pop. 5,415
Tyrone Area SD 1,900/PK-12
701 Clay Ave 16686 814-684-0710
Cathy Harlow, supt. Fax 684-8408
www.tyrone.k12.pa.us
Tyrone Area ES 800/PK-4
601 Clay Ave 16686 814-684-1342
Lisa Hartsock, prin. Fax 684-2149
Tyrone Area MS 600/5-8
1001 Clay Ave 16686 814-684-4240
Kristen N. Pinter, prin. Fax 682-1013

St. Matthew S 100/PK-6
1105 Cameron Ave 16686 814-684-3510
Fax 684-7833

Ulysses, Potter, Pop. 619
Northern Potter SD 600/PK-12
745 Northern Potter Rd 16948 814-848-7506
Scott Graham, supt. Fax 848-7431
www.northernpottersd.org
Northern Potter Children's S 300/PK-6
745 Northern Potter Rd 16948 814-848-7563
Michael Morgan, prin. Fax 850-1208

Union City, Erie, Pop. 3,286
Union City Area SD 1,200/PK-12
107 Concord St 16438 814-438-3804
Dr. Sandra Myers, supt. Fax 438-2030
www.ucasd.org
Union City ES 600/PK-5
91 Miles St 16438 814-438-7611
Adam Shrout, prin. Fax 438-1085
Union City MS 300/6-8
105 Concord St 16438 814-438-7673
Melissa Tomcho, prin. Fax 438-8079

Uniontown, Fayette, Pop. 10,023
Albert Gallatin Area SD 3,300/K-12
2625 Morgantown Rd 15401 724-564-7190
Carl Bezjak, supt. Fax 564-7195
www.agasd.org
Other Schools – See Fairchance, Mc Clellandtown, Masontown, Point Marion, Smithfield

Laurel Highlands SD 3,300/K-12
304 Bailey Ave 15401 724-437-2821
Dr. Jesse Wallace Ed.D., supt. Fax 437-8929
www.lhsd.org
Clark ES 400/K-5
200 Water St 15401 724-437-9600
Emilie Kurek, prin. Fax 437-9688
Hatfield ES 400/K-5
370 Derrick Ave 15401 724-437-7371
Heidi Mears, prin. Fax 437-9229
Hutchinson ES 300/K-5
213 Mountain View Rd 15401 724-437-6208
Richard Hauger, prin. Fax 437-9774
Laurel Highlands MS 800/6-8
18 Hookton Ave 15401 724-437-2865
Mike Rozgony, prin. Fax 437-8518
Marshall ES 400/K-5
335 Park St 15401 724-438-5851
Jason Johns, prin. Fax 438-7858

Uniontown Area SD 2,800/K-12
205 Wilson Ave 15401 724-438-4501
Dr. Charles D. Machesky, supt. Fax 437-7007
uasdraiders.org
Franklin S 500/K-8
351 Morgantown St 15401 724-439-5020
Frank Aleman, prin. Fax 439-5018
Lafayette ES 300/K-5
303 Connellsville St 15401 724-438-3581
Tracey M. Kuchar, prin. Fax 439-5023
Lafayette MS 200/6-8
303 Connellsville St 15401 724-438-3581
Tracey M. Kuchar, prin. Fax 439-5023
Menallen ES 300/K-6
7527 National Pike 15401 724-438-4160
Joseph Galie, prin. Fax 430-7241
Other Schools – See Farmington, Markleysburg, Vanderbilt

Chestnut Ridge Christian Academy 100/PK-12
115 Downer Ave 15401 724-439-1090
Patricia D. Cowsert, prin. Fax 439-4540
St. John the Evangelist S 200/PK-8
52 Jefferson St 15401 724-438-8590
Christine Roskovensky, prin. Fax 438-8585

Upland, Delaware, Pop. 3,155
Chester-Upland SD
Supt. — See Chester
Main Street ES 300/PK-5
704 Main St 19015 610-447-3605
Nancy Butcher-Perez, prin. Fax 447-3684

Upper Black Eddy, Bucks

River Valley Waldorf S 100/PK-8
1395 Bridgeton Hill Rd, 610-982-5606

Upper Darby, See Darby
Upper Darby SD
Supt. — See Drexel Hill
Beverly Hills MS 1,500/6-8
1400 Garrett Rd 19082 610-626-9317
Kelley Simone, prin.
Bywood ES, 330 Avon Rd 19082 600/1-5
Timothy McEntee, prin. 610-352-6842
Highland Park ES 700/1-5
8301 W Chester Pike 19082 610-853-4530
Stephanie Sitek, prin.
Stonehurst Hills ES 600/1-5
7051 Ruskin Ln 19082 610-626-9111
Aaronda Beauford, prin.

St. Laurence S 400/PK-8
8245 W Chester Pike 19082 610-789-2670
Sr. Mary Anne Bolger, prin. Fax 789-1128

Upper Saint Clair, Allegheny, Pop. 19,692
Upper St. Clair SD 4,100/K-12
1820 McLaughlin Run Rd 15241 412-833-1600
Dr. Patrick O'Toole, supt. Fax 833-5535
www.uscsd.k12.pa.us
Other Schools – See Pittsburgh

Uwchland, Chester

St. Elizabeth S K-8
PO Box 780 19480 610-646-6540
Dr. Diane Greco, prin. Fax 646-6541
Windsor Christian Academy 100/K-8
PO Box 596 19480 610-458-7177
Susan Null, prin. Fax 458-2569

Valley View, Schuylkill, Pop. 1,675
Tri-Valley SD 900/K-12
110 W Main St 17983 570-682-9013
Dr. Mark Snyder, supt. Fax 682-9544
www.tri-valley.k12.pa.us
Hegins-Hubley ES 400/K-6
1801 W Main St 17983 570-682-9011
Robert Felty, prin. Fax 682-3124
Other Schools – See Klingerstown

Vanderbilt, Fayette, Pop. 465
Uniontown Area SD
Supt. — See Uniontown
Franklin ES 100/K-6
242 Buena Vista Rd 15486 724-628-6030
Joseph Galie, prin. Fax 529-7246

Vandergrift, Westmoreland, Pop. 5,061
Kiski Area SD
Supt. — See Leechburg
Kiski Area East PS 400/K-4
200 Poplar St 15690 724-567-6706
R. Patrick Marchand, prin. Fax 567-6261

Cardinal Maida Academy 100/PK-5
315 Franklin Ave 15690 724-568-3304
Patricia Visnick, prin. Fax 567-1900

Venetia, Washington
Peters Township SD
Supt. — See Mc Murray
Bower Hill ES 700/K-3
424 Bower Hill Rd 15367 724-941-0913
Robert Garvey, prin. Fax 941-0918

Verona, Allegheny, Pop. 2,433
Riverview SD
Supt. — See Oakmont
Verner ES 200/K-6
700 1st St 15147 412-828-1800
Mary Ann Plance, prin. Fax 828-8086

Redeemer Lutheran S 200/PK-12
700 Idaho Ave 15147 412-793-5884
Gail Holzer, admin.
St. Joseph S 200/K-8
825 2nd St 15147 412-828-7213
Sr. Jean Uzupis, prin. Fax 828-4008

Villanova, Delaware

Villanova Academy for Honor Studies 100/PK-6
1860 Montgomery Ave 19085 610-520-9624
Dr. Mustafa Ahmed, dir. Fax 520-1213

Wallingford, Delaware
Wallingford-Swarthmore SD 3,500/K-12
200 S Providence Rd 19086 610-892-3470
Dr. Lisa Palmer Ed.D., supt. Fax 892-3493
www.wssd.org
Nether Providence ES 500/K-5
410 Moore Rd 19086 610-892-3470
Al Heinle, prin. Fax 874-3561
Strath Haven MS 800/6-8
200 S Providence Rd 19086 610-892-3470
George King, prin. Fax 892-3492
Wallingford ES 500/K-5
20 S Providence Rd 19086 610-892-3470
Joshua Peterkin, prin. Fax 801-0486
Other Schools – See Swarthmore

Mother of Providence Regional S 200/PK-8
607 S Providence Rd 19086 610-876-7110
Therese Waters, prin. Fax 876-5923

Walnutport, Northampton, Pop. 2,045
Northampton Area SD
Supt. — See Northampton
Lehigh ES 500/K-5
800 Blue Mountain Dr 18088 610-767-1191
Dr. Lori Kuhns, prin. Fax 767-4731

Warfordsburg, Fulton
Southern Fulton SD 800/K-12
3072 Great Cove Rd Ste 100 17267 717-294-2203
Tara Will, supt. Fax 294-2207
sfsd.k12.pa.us
Southern Fulton ES 400/K-6
3072 Great Cove Rd 17267 717-294-3400
Kathy Cutchall, prin. Fax 294-6428

Warminster, Bucks, Pop. 32,400
Centennial SD 5,600/K-12
48 Swan Way 18974 215-441-6000
Dr. David Baugh, supt. Fax 441-5105
www.centennialsd.org
Log College MS 700/6-8
730 Norristown Rd 18974 215-441-6075
Andrew Doster, prin. Fax 441-6073
McDonald ES 900/K-5
666 Reeves Ln 18974 215-441-6157
Michael VanBuren, prin. Fax 441-6006
Willow Dale ES 800/K-5
720 Norristown Rd 18974 215-441-6093
Fax 441-6016
Other Schools – See Southampton

Nativity of Our Lord S 500/PK-8
585 W Street Rd 18974 215-675-2820
Roselee Maddaloni, prin. Fax 675-9413

Warren, Warren, Pop. 9,619
Warren County SD
Supt. — See Russell
Beaty-Warren MS 500/5-8
2 E 3rd Ave 16365 814-723-5200
Ann Ryan, prin. Fax 723-9503
Warren Area ES 900/K-5
343 E 5th Ave 16365 814-723-9061
Jennifer Hobbs, prin. Fax 723-2361

St. Joseph S 100/PK-5
608 Pennsylvania Ave W 16365 814-723-2030
Nancy Warner, prin. Fax 723-6042

Warrington, Bucks, Pop. 7,000
Central Bucks SD
Supt. — See Doylestown
Barclay ES 500/K-6
2015 Palomino Dr 18976 267-893-4100
Daniel Estep, prin. Fax 893-5801

Mill Creek ES 1,000/K-6
638 Bellflower Blvd 18976 267-893-3600
Shawn Ortman, prin. Fax 482-8214
Titus ES 600/K-6
2333 Lower Barness Rd 18976 267-893-4500
Stephen Cashman, prin. Fax 893-5814

St. Joseph St. Robert S 200/PK-8
850 Euclid Ave 18976 215-343-5100
Deborah Jaster, prin. Fax 343-7434

Washington, Washington, Pop. 13,036
McGuffey SD
Supt. — See Claysville
Walker ES 200/K-5
2510 Park Ave 15301 724-222-3061
Marie DeAngelis, prin. Fax 222-2630

Trinity Area SD 3,300/K-12
231 Park Ave 15301 724-223-2000
Michael Lucas, supt. Fax 228-2640
www.trinitypride.org
Trinity East ES 400/K-5
252 Cameron Rd 15301 724-225-8140
Saundra Deems, prin. Fax 225-4951
Trinity MS 800/6-8
50 Scenic Dr 15301 724-228-2112
Michelle Ostrosky, prin. Fax 228-1196
Trinity North ES 400/K-5
225 Midland Dr 15301 724-222-5064
Beth Tully, prin. Fax 229-1031
Trinity South ES 300/K-5
2500 S Main Street Ext 15301 724-225-7490
Peter Keruskin, prin. Fax 228-7658
Trinity West ES 400/K-5
1041 Gabby Ave 15301 724-222-4730
Carol Lee, prin. Fax 222-0180

Washington SD 1,500/K-12
311 Allison Ave 15301 724-223-5112
Dr. James R. Konrad, supt. Fax 223-5050
www.washington.k12.pa.us
Washington JHS 200/7-8
201 Allison Ave 15301 724-223-5060
Chet Henderson, prin. Fax 223-5123
Washington Park ES 800/K-6
801 E Wheeling St 15301 724-223-5150
Kelley Zebrasky, prin. Fax 223-5056

Faith Christian S 200/PK-12
524 E Beau St 15301 724-222-5440
Kennedy S 300/PK-8
111 W Spruce St 15301 724-225-1680
Dr. Kathleen Harrington, prin. Fax 225-4651

Washington Boro, Lancaster, Pop. 727
Penn Manor SD
Supt. — See Lancaster
Central Manor ES 600/K-6
3717 Blue Rock Rd 17582 717-872-1401
Brian Malek, prin. Fax 872-9515
Letort ES 300/K-6
561 Letort Rd 17582 717-872-9530
Carly McPherson, prin. Fax 872-9552

Waterfall, Fulton
Forbes Road SD 400/K-12
159 Red Bird Dr 16689 814-685-3866
Mark Loucks, supt. Fax 685-3159
www.frsd.k12.pa.us
Forbes Road ES 200/K-6
143 Red Bird Dr 16689 814-685-3865
Maria Scott-Bollman, prin. Fax 685-3217

Waterford, Erie, Pop. 1,509
Fort LeBoeuf SD 2,100/K-12
PO Box 810 16441 814-796-2638
Richard Emerick, supt. Fax 796-6459
www.fortleboeuf.net
Fort LeBoeuf MS 500/6-8
PO Box 516 16441 814-796-2681
Brent Holt, prin. Fax 796-4712
Waterford ES 400/K-5
PO Box 811 16441 814-796-4833
Yvonne Best-Proctor, prin. Fax 796-3306
Other Schools – See Erie, Mill Village

Waverly, Lackawanna, Pop. 603
Abington Heights SD
Supt. — See Clarks Summit
Waverly ES 300/K-4
103 Waverly Rd 18471 570-585-6300
Marc Wyandt, prin. Fax 586-4592

Waymart, Wayne, Pop. 1,323
Western Wayne SD
Supt. — See Lake Ariel
Wilson ES 300/PK-5
74 Belmont St 18472 800-321-9973
Maria Miller, prin. Fax 341-1224

Wayne, Delaware
Radnor Township SD 3,600/K-12
135 S Wayne Ave 19087 610-688-8100
Kenneth Batchelor, supt. Fax 687-3318
www.rtsd.org
Radnor MS 800/6-8
150 Louella Ave 19087 610-386-6300
Esther Purnell, prin. Fax 688-2491
Wayne ES 600/K-5
651 W Wayne Ave 19087 610-687-8480
Nancy Ferguson, prin. Fax 293-0490
Other Schools – See Bryn Mawr, Radnor

Tredyffrin-Easttown SD 6,500/K-12
940 W Valley Rd Ste 1700 19087 610-240-1900
Dr. Richard Gusick, supt. Fax 240-1965
www.tesd.net/
New Eagle ES 400/K-4
507 Pugh Rd 19087 610-240-1550
Karen Whyte, prin. Fax 240-1561
Valley Forge ES 500/K-4
99 Walker Rd 19087 610-240-1600
Rebecca Wills, prin. Fax 240-1615
Valley Forge MS 1,000/5-8
105 W Walker Rd 19087 610-240-1300
Matthew Gibson, prin. Fax 240-1325
Other Schools – See Berwyn, Devon

Upper Merion Area SD
Supt. — See King of Prussia
Roberts ES 400/K-4
889 Croton Rd 19087 610-205-3751
Dr. Anthony Grazel, prin. Fax 205-3799

Heritage S 200/PK-K
651 N Wayne Ave 19087 610-688-6342
Dr. Donald D. Dawes Ed.D., dir. Fax 989-0591
St. Katherine of Siena S 400/K-8
229 Windermere Ave 19087 610-688-5451
Bud Tosti, prin. Fax 688-6796

Waynesboro, Franklin, Pop. 10,360
Waynesboro Area SD 4,400/K-12
210 Clayton Ave 17268 717-762-1191
Dr. Tod Kline, supt. Fax 762-0028
www.wasd.k12.pa.us
Fairview Avenue ES 900/K-5
220 Fairview Ave 17268 717-762-1191
Dianne Eberhardt, prin. Fax 762-3939
Hooverville ES 400/K-5
10829 Buchanan Trl E 17268 717-762-1191
Barbara Martin, prin. Fax 762-4222
Mowrey ES 600/K-5
7891 Tomstown Rd 17268 717-762-1191
Emily Goodine, prin. Fax 749-5856
Summitview ES 600/K-5
840 E 2nd St 17268 717-762-1191
Diane McCallum, prin. Fax 762-3764
Waynesboro Area MS 700/6-8
702 E 2nd St 17268 717-762-1191
Aaron Taylor, prin. Fax 762-6566

St. Andrew S 100/K-6
213 E Main St 17268 717-762-3221
Patrick McDonald, prin. Fax 762-8474

Waynesburg, Greene, Pop. 4,116
Central Greene SD 1,900/K-12
PO Box 472 15370 724-627-8151
Brian Uplinger, supt. Fax 627-9591
www.cgsd.org
Bell MS 400/6-8
126 E Lincoln St 15370 724-852-2722
John Lipscomb, prin. Fax 627-0637
Waynesburg Central ES 900/K 5
90 Zimmerman Dr 15370 724-627-3081
Scott Headlee, prin. Fax 852-1160

West Greene SD 500/K-12
1367 Hargus Creek Rd 15370 724-499-5183
Brian Jackson, supt. Fax 499-5623
www.wgsd.org
West Greene ES 400/K-6
1350 Hargus Creek Rd 15370 724-499-5183
Donald Painter, prin.

St. Ann Preschool 50/PK-PK
232 E High St 15370 724-627-7568
Christine Bastaich, dir. Fax 627-7413

Weatherly, Carbon, Pop. 2,496
Weatherly Area SD 600/PK-12
602 6th St 18255 570-427-8681
Teresa Young, supt. Fax 427-8918
www.weatherlysd.org
Weatherly Area ES 300/PK-5
602 6th St 18255 570-427-8687
Sandra Slavick, prin. Fax 427-8918
Weatherly Area MS 200/6-8
602 6th St 18255 570-427-8689
Sandra Slavick, prin. Fax 427-8918

Weedville, Elk, Pop. 540
Saint Marys Area SD
Supt. — See Saint Marys
Bennetts Valley ES 100/K-5
19073 Bennetts Valley Hwy 15868 814-787-5481
Karen Lucanik, prin. Fax 787-8766

Wellsboro, Tioga, Pop. 3,220
Wellsboro Area SD 1,500/K-12
227 Nichols St 16901 570-724-4424
Dr. Brenda Freeman, supt. Fax 724-5103
www.wellsborosd.org
Butler MS 500/5-8
9 Nichols St 16901 570-724-2306
Michael Pietropola, prin. Fax 724-4143
Gill ES 300/2-4
10 Sherman St 16901 570-724-1811
Steven Adams, prin. Fax 724-1057
Lappla ES 200/K-1
32 Meade St 16901 570-724-1941
Steven Adams, prin. Fax 723-1916

Northern Tier Christian S 50/K-8
1292 Charleston Rd 16901 570-724-2321
Trinity Lutheran S 100/PK-6
53 West Ave 16901 570-724-7723
Janice Hughes, lead tchr. Fax 723-1053

Wellsville, York, Pop. 241
Northern York County SD
Supt. — See Dillsburg
Wellsville ES 200/K-5
1060 Zeigler Rd 17365 717-432-8691
Faithe Rotz, prin. Fax 502-0861

Wernersville, Berks, Pop. 2,469
Conrad Weiser Area SD
Supt. — See Robesonia
Weiser East ES 500/K-4
200 Lincoln Dr 19565 610-678-9901
Janet Heilman, prin. Fax 678-9279

Wescosville, Lehigh, Pop. 5,786
East Penn SD
Supt. — See Emmaus
Wescosville ES 600/K-5
1064 Liberty Ln 18106 610-395-5851
Tara Desiderio, prin.

West Brandywine, Chester

Pope John Paul II Regional S 600/K-8
2875 Manor Rd, 610-384-5961
Sr. Anne McGuire, prin. Fax 384-5730

West Chester, Chester, Pop. 18,141
Unionville-Chadds Ford SD
Supt. — See Kennett Square
Pocopson ES 600/K-5
1105 Pocopson Rd 19382 610-793-9241
Clifton Beaver, prin. Fax 793-7792

West Chester Area SD
Supt. — See Exton
East Bradford ES 300/K-5
820 Frank Rd 19380 484-266-2100
Dr. Christopher Alston, prin. Fax 266-2199
East Goshen ES 400/K-5
800 N Chester Rd 19380 484-266-1500
Dennis E. Brown, prin. Fax 266-1599
Fern Hill ES 500/K-5
915 Lincoln Ave 19380 484-266-1600
Rebecca L. Eberly, prin. Fax 266-1699
Fugett MS 900/6-8
500 Ellis Ln 19380 484-266-2900
Dr. Llewellyn Small, prin. Fax 266-2999
Glen Acres ES 500/K-5
1150 Delancey Pl 19382 484-266-1700
Donna Ryan, prin. Fax 266-1799
Hillsdale ES 600/K-5
725 W Market St 19380 484-266-2000
Julianne Pecorella, prin. Fax 266-2099
Howse ES 500/K-5
641 W Boot Rd 19380 484-266-1300
Dr. Stephen Catrambone, prin. Fax 266-1399
Peirce MS 800/6-8
1314 Burke Rd 19380 484-266-2500
Geoffrey Mills, prin. Fax 266-2599
Penn Wood ES 600/K-5
1470 Johnnys Way 19382 484-266-1900
Dr. Ellen M. Gacomis, prin. Fax 266-1999
Starkweather ES 600/K-5
1050 Wilmington Pike 19382 484-266-2200
John Meanix, prin. Fax 266-2299
Stetson MS 900/6-8
1060 Wilmington Pike 19382 484-266-2700
Dr. Charles A. Cognato, prin. Fax 266-2799
Westtown-Thornbury ES 400/K-5
750 Westbourne Rd 19382 484-266-1800
Nora O. Wheeler, prin. Fax 266-1899

Chesterbrook Academy PK-5
1190 McDermott Dr 19380 610-719-3061
Goshen Friends S 100/PK-5
814 N Chester Rd 19380 610-696-8869
Mimi Blackwell, head sch Fax 696-2578
Laurel Springs S 2,000/K-12
1615 W Chester Pike 19382 800-377-5890
Darby Carr, head sch
St. Agnes S 300/PK-8
211 W Gay St 19380 610-696-1260
Sr. Joan O'Reilly, prin. Fax 436-9631
St. Maximillian Kolbe S 300/PK-8
300 Daly Dr 19382 610-399-8400
Monica Malseed, prin. Fax 399-4684
SS. Peter & Paul S 300/PK-5
1327 E Boot Rd 19380 610-696-1000
Margaret Egan, prin. Fax 631-0181
SS. Simon & Jude S 400/K-8
6 Cavanaugh Ct 19382 610-696-5249
Sr. Janine Norton, prin. Fax 696-4682
West Chester Christian S 100/K-12
1237 Paoli Pike 19380 610-692-3700
West Chester Friends S 100/PK-5
415 N High St 19380 610-696-2962
Brian Fahey, head sch Fax 431-1457
Westtown S 700/PK-12
975 Westtown Rd 19382 610-399-0123
Victoria Jueds, head sch Fax 399-3760

Westfield, Tioga, Pop. 1,060
Northern Tioga SD
Supt. — See Elkland
Westfield Area ES 400/K-6
1355 Route 49 16950 814-367-2712
Cheryl Sottolano, prin. Fax 367-2776

West Grove, Chester, Pop. 2,811
Avon Grove SD 5,100/K-12
375 S Jennersville Rd 19390 610-869-2441
Dr. Michael Marchese, supt. Fax 869-8651
www.avongrove.org
Avon Grove IS 1,500/3-6
395 S Jennersville Rd 19390 610-869-2010
Jeffrey Detweiler, prin. Fax 667-4429
Engle MS 900/7-8
107 Schoolhouse Rd 19390 610-869-3022
Michael Berardi, prin. Fax 869-0827
Penn London ES 900/K-2
383 S Jennersville Rd 19390 610-869-9803
Dr. Cynthia Holland, prin. Fax 869-4512

Assumption BVM S 200/K-8
290 State Rd 19390 610-869-9576
Danielle White, prin. Fax 869-4049

West Hazleton, Luzerne, Pop. 4,544
Hazleton Area SD
Supt. — See Hazle Township
West Hazleton S 1,100/K-8
325 North St 18202 570-459-3221
Jocelyn Podlesney, prin. Fax 459-2584

West Lawn, Berks, Pop. 1,678
Wilson SD 5,500/K-12
2601 Grandview Blvd 19609 610-670-0180
Dr. Richard Faidley, supt. Fax 334-6430
www.wilsonsd.org
Whitfield ES 500/K-5
2700 Van Reed Rd 19609 610-670-0180
Dr. Krista Antonis, prin. Fax 334-6446
Other Schools – See Sinking Spring, Wyomissing

St. Ignatius Loyola S 400/PK-8
2700 Saint Albans Dr 19609 610-678-0111
Robert Birmingham, prin. Fax 670-5795

West Middlesex, Mercer, Pop. 850
West Middlesex Area SD 800/K-12
3591 Sharon Rd 16159 724-634-3030
Dr. David Foley, supt. Fax 528-0380
www.wmasd.k12.pa.us
Low ES 300/K-3
3591 Sharon Rd 16159 724-634-3030
Tammy Mild, prin. Fax 528-0380
Oakview ES 200/4-6
3591 Sharon Rd 16159 724-634-3030
Tammy Mild, prin. Fax 528-0380

West Mifflin, Allegheny, Pop. 19,950
West Mifflin Area SD 3,000/PK-12
1020 Lebanon Rd # 250 15122 412-466-9131
Dr. Daniel Castagna, supt. Fax 466-9260
www.wmasd.org
Barton ES 200/K-3
764 Beverly Dr 15122 412-466-9131
Noelle Haney, prin. Fax 469-3357
Homeville ES 400/PK-3
4315 Eliza St 15122 412-466-9131
Melissa Welsh, prin. Fax 461-5465
New Emerson ES 200/K-3
1922 Pennsylvania Ave 15122 412-466-9131
Christopher Hanna, prin. Fax 469-3373
West Mifflin Area MS 1,100/4-8
81 Commonwealth Ave 15122 412-466-9131
Brian Plichta, prin. Fax 466-0836

Cornerstone Christian Prep Academy 200/PK-12
1900 Clairton Rd 15122 412-466-1919
Cindi R. McCall, dir. Fax 466-0303
St. Agnes S 100/PK-8
653 Saint Agnes Ln 15122 412-466-6238
Sr. Cynthia Wessel, prin. Fax 466-2013

West Newton, Westmoreland, Pop. 2,599
Yough SD
Supt. — See Herminie
West Newton ES 200/K-4
1208 Vine St 15089 724-872-5877
Brian Sutherland, prin. Fax 872-5609

Westover, Clearfield, Pop. 390
Harmony Area SD 300/PK-12
5239 Ridge Rd 16692 814-845-2300
Darren McLaurin, supt. Fax 845-2305
www.harmonyowls.com
Harmony Area ES 200/PK-6
5239 Ridge Rd 16692 814-845-2300
Michelle Shirk, prin. Fax 845-7396

West Pittston, Luzerne, Pop. 4,815
Wyoming Area SD
Supt. — See Exeter
Wyoming Area Intermediate Center 200/4-6
100 Montgomery Ave 18643 570-654-1404
Joseph Long, prin. Fax 602-0555

West Reading, Berks, Pop. 4,092
Wyomissing Area SD
Supt. — See Wyomissing
West Reading ES 300/5-6
421 Chestnut St 19611 610-374-0739
Dr. Corbett Babb, prin. Fax 378-5739

Sacred Heart S 200/PK-8
701 Franklin St 19611 610-373-3316
Katherine Napolitano, prin. Fax 373-7299

West Sunbury, Butler, Pop. 190
Moniteau SD 1,300/K-12
1810 W Sunbury Rd 16061 724-637-2117
Sean Arney, supt. Fax 637-3862
www.moniteau.k12.pa.us
McKinney ES 700/K-6
391 Hooker Rd 16061 724-637-2321
Dustin Thompson, prin. Fax 637-3877

Wexford, Allegheny
North Allegheny SD
Supt. — See Pittsburgh
Marshall ES 700/K-5
5135 Wexford Run Rd 15090 724-935-4044
Marc Thornton, prin. Fax 935-1064
Marshall MS 600/6-8
5145 Wexford Run Rd 15090 724-934-6060
Daniel Swoger, prin. Fax 935-2474

Pine-Richland SD
Supt. — See Gibsonia
Wexford ES 400/K-3
250 Brown Rd 15090 724-935-4631
Dr. Rick Walsh, prin. Fax 935-3733

Eden Christian Academy - Wexford Campus 200/PK-6
12121 Perry Hwy 15090 724-935-9301
Carrie Powers, prin. Fax 935-9354
St. Alexis S 300/PK-8
10090 Old Perry Hwy 15090 724-935-3940
James Correll, prin. Fax 935-6070
St. Alphonsus S 400/PK-8
201 Church Rd 15090 724-935-1152
Robert Reese, prin. Fax 935-1110

Whitehall, Lehigh, Pop. 13,797
Whitehall-Coplay SD 4,200/K-12
2940 MacArthur Rd 18052 610-439-1431
Dr. Lorie Hackett, supt. Fax 435-0124
www.whitehallcoplay.org/districtsite/
Gockley ES 600/K-1
2932 Zephyr Blvd 18052 610-433-7551
Denise Saylor, prin. Fax 433-2241
Steckel ES 600/2-3
2928 Zephyr Blvd 18052 610-435-1521
Peter Bugbee, prin. Fax 435-4022
Whitehall-Coplay MS 1,000/6-8
2930 Zephyr Blvd 18052 610-439-1439
Glenn Noack, prin. Fax 740-9308
Zephyr ES 600/4-5
2934 Zephyr Blvd 18052 610-871-3671
Terri Miller, prin. Fax 871-3672

Lehigh Valley Adventist S 100/PK-8
3950 Mechanicsville Rd 18052 610-799-2341
St. Elizabeth S 200/K-8
433 Pershing Blvd 18052 610-264-0143
Linda Schiller, prin. Fax 264-1563
St. Stephen's Day S 200/PK-K
3900 Mechanicsville Rd 18052 610-435-4260

White Oak, Allegheny, Pop. 7,747
McKeesport Area SD
Supt. — See Mc Keesport
McClure ES 200/3-5
500 Longvue Dr 15131 412-664-3740
Tom Knight, prin. Fax 664-3747

Mary of Nazareth S 200/PK-8
1640 Fawcett Ave 15131 412-672-2360
Lynda McFarland, prin. Fax 672-0880

Wilkes Barre, Luzerne, Pop. 40,594
Wilkes-Barre Area SD 6,900/K-12
730 S Main St 18702 570-826-7111
Brian Costello, supt. Fax 829-5031
www.wbasd.k12.pa.us
Dodson ES 500/K-6
80 Jones St 18702 570-826-7185
James Geiger, prin. Fax 820-3717
Flood ES 500/K-6
565 N Washington St 18705 570-826-7245
Marlena Nockley, prin. Fax 820-3732
Heights/Murray ES 800/K-6
1 S Sherman St 18702 570-826-7256
Hal Gabriel, prin. Fax 820-3733
Kistler ES 1,000/K-6
301 Old River Rd 18702 570-826-7230
Margo Serafini, prin. Fax 820-3734
Other Schools – See Plains

St. Nicholas / St. Mary S 400/PK-8
242 S Washington St 18701 570-823-8089
Christopher Tigue, prin. Fax 823-1402
Wilkes-Barre Academy 200/PK-8
20 Stevens Rd 18702 570-823-7574
Janice Huntzinger, dir. Fax 823-9358

Wilkinsburg, Allegheny, Pop. 15,450
Wilkinsburg Borough SD 600/PK-6
718 Wallace Ave 15221 412-371-9667
Dr. Linda Iverson, supt. Fax 371-4058
www.wilkinsburgschools.org
Kelly ES 400/PK-6
400 Kelly Ave 15221 412-371-9504
Kerry Francis, prin. Fax 871-2217
Turner ES 200/PK-6
1833 Laketon Rd 15221 412-731-5883
Tanya Smith, prin. Fax 871-2157

Bowman Academy 200/PK-8
721 Rebecca Ave 15221 412-242-3515
April Perry, prin. Fax 241-3199

Williamsburg, Blair, Pop. 1,244
Williamsburg Community SD 500/K-12
515 W 3rd St 16693 814-832-2125
Lisa Murgas M.Ed., supt. Fax 832-3657
www.williamsburg.k12.pa.us/
Williamsburg Community ES 300/K-6
607 Sage Hill Dr 16693 814-832-2125
Jennifer Metzler, prin. Fax 832-3042

Williamsport, Lycoming, Pop. 28,270
Loyalsock Township SD 1,500/K-12
1605 Four Mile Dr 17701 570-326-6508
Gerald McLaughlin, supt. Fax 326-0770
www.loyalsocklancers.org
Loyalsock Township MS 400/6-8
2101 Loyalsock Dr 17701 570-323-9439
Dr. Charles Greevy, prin. Fax 323-5303
Other Schools – See Montoursville

Williamsport Area SD 5,100/K-12
2780 W 4th St 17701 570-327-5500
Dr. Tim Bowers, supt. Fax 327-8122
www.wasd.org
Cochran PS 500/K-3
1500 Cherry St 17701 570-322-9731
Cindy Schuyler, prin. Fax 322-9733
Curtin IS 600/4-6
85 Eldred St 17701 570-323-4785
David Michaels, prin. Fax 323-4974
Jackson PS 500/K-3
2500 Newberry St 17701 570-323-1992
Kirk Felix, prin. Fax 323-9006
Lycoming Valley IS 600/4-6
1825 Hays Ln 17701 570-494-1700
Timothy Fausnaught, prin. Fax 494-1706
Stevens PS 300/K-3
1150 Louisa St 17701 570-322-7853
James Ellis, prin. Fax 322-9949
Williamsport Area MS 800/7-8
2800 W 4th St 17701 570-323-6177
Reginald Fatherly, prin. Fax 326-6851
Other Schools – See Cogan Station

St. John Neumann Regional Academy ES 100/K-6
710 Franklin St 17701 570-326-3738
Susan Kaiser, prin. Fax 326-7385

Willow Grove, Montgomery, Pop. 15,410
Abington SD
Supt. — See Abington
Willow Hill ES 400/K-6
1700 Coolidge Ave 19090 215-657-3800
Damon Jordan, prin. Fax 884-0568

Upper Dublin SD
Supt. — See Maple Glen
Fitzwater ES 400/K-5
30 School Ln 19090 215-784-0381
Peter Alston M.Ed., prin. Fax 784-0797

Upper Moreland Township SD 3,100/K-12
2900 Terwood Rd 19090 215-830-1511
Robert Milrod Ph.D., supt. Fax 659-3421
www.umtsd.org
Other Schools – See Hatboro

Queen of Angels Regional S 200/PK-8
401 Easton Rd 19090 215-659-6393
Sr. Margaret Adams, prin. Fax 659-6377

Willow Hill, Franklin
Fannett-Metal SD 400/K-12
PO Box 91 17271 717-349-7172
David Burkett, supt. Fax 349-2748
fmtigers.org
Fannett-Metal ES 200/K-5
PO Box 91 17271 717-349-2513
Stephanie Shoemaker, prin. Fax 349-2748

Willow Street, Lancaster, Pop. 7,536
Penn Manor SD
Supt. — See Lancaster
Pequea ES 400/K-6
802 Millwood Rd 17584 717-464-3831
Shirley Murray, prin. Fax 464-3809

Windber, Somerset, Pop. 4,117
Windber Area SD 1,200/PK-12
2301 Graham Ave 15963 814-467-4567
Joseph Kimmel, supt.
www.windberschools.org
Windber Area ES 600/PK-5
421 Sugar Maple Dr 15963 814-467-4567
Jessica Shuster, prin. Fax 467-8594
Windber Area MS 300/6-8
2301 Graham Ave 15963 814-467-4567
Lance McGough, prin.

Windsor, York, Pop. 1,309
Red Lion Area SD
Supt. — See Red Lion
Windsor Manor ES 200/K-1
2110 Windsor Rd 17366 717-246-9312
Kitty Reinholt, prin. Fax 417-1201

Wingate, Centre
Bald Eagle Area SD 1,800/K-12
751 S Eagle Valley Rd 16823 814-355-4860
Jeffrey Miles, supt. Fax 355-1028
www.beasd.org
Wingate ES 400/K-5
751 S Eagle Valley Rd 16823 814-355-4872
James Orichosky, prin. Fax 355-5157
Other Schools – See Howard, Port Matilda, Snow Shoe

Womelsdorf, Berks, Pop. 2,779
Conrad Weiser Area SD
Supt. — See Robesonia
Weiser West ES 500/PK-4
102 S 3rd St 19567 610-589-2501
Nicole Moore, prin. Fax 589-9409

Woodlyn, Delaware, Pop. 9,319
Ridley SD
Supt. — See Folsom
Woodlyn ES 300/K-5
Colson Rd 19094 610-534-1900
Brenda Sweeney, prin. Fax 833-2487

Wormleysburg, Cumberland, Pop. 3,002

Harrisburg Academy 400/PK-12
10 Erford Rd 17043 717-763-7811
Dr. James Newman, head sch Fax 975-0894

Wrightstown, Bucks
Council Rock SD
Supt. — See Newtown
Wrightstown ES 300/K-4
729 Penns Park Rd 18940 215-944-2300
Beth Fox, prin. Fax 944-2397

Wrightsville, York, Pop. 2,269
Eastern York SD 2,500/K-12
PO Box 150 17368 717-252-1555
Dr. Darla Pianowski, supt. Fax 478-6000
www.easternyork.net
Eastern York MS 600/6-8
746 Cool Creek Rd 17368 717-252-3400
Dr. Keith Shoemaker, prin. Fax 252-4891
Wrightsville ES 400/K-5
320 Chestnut St 17368 717-252-3676
Doug Enders, prin. Fax 252-9844
Other Schools – See East Prospect, Hellam

Wyalusing, Bradford, Pop. 591
Wyalusing Area SD — 1,300/K-12
PO Box 157 18853 — 570-746-1600
Dr. Jason Bottiglieri, supt. — Fax 746-9156
www.wyalusingrams.com
Wyalusing Valley ES — 700/K-6
11450 Wyalusing New Albany 18853 — 570-746-1206
Deneen Lantz, prin. — Fax 746-1928

Wyncote, Montgomery, Pop. 2,980
Cheltenham SD
Supt. — See Elkins Park
Cedarbrook MS — 700/7-8
500 Rices Mill Rd 19095 — 215-881-6427
Marcia Hockfield, prin.
Wyncote ES — 400/K-4
333 Rices Mill Rd 19095 — 215-881-6410
Dr. Crystal Clark, prin. — Fax 881-6462

Ancillae-Assumpta Academy — 600/PK-8
2025 Church Rd 19095 — 215-885-1636
Sr. Maureen Gillespie, prin. — Fax 885-2740

Wynnewood, Montgomery, Pop. 7,800
Lower Merion SD
Supt. — See Ardmore
Penn Wynne ES — 600/K-5
250 Haverford Rd 19096 — 610-645-1450
Shawn Bernatowicz, prin. — Fax 642-2544

Friends' Central S - Lower Campus — 200/PK-5
228 Old Gulph Rd 19096 — 610-642-7575
Craig Sellers, hdmstr.
Perelman Jewish Day S — 200/K-5
49 Haverford Rd 19096 — 610-658-2518
Torah Academy of Greater Philadelphia — 300/PK-8
742 Argyle Rd 19096 — 610-642-7870

Wyoming, Luzerne, Pop. 3,048
Wyoming Area SD
Supt. — See Exeter
Wyoming Area Primary Center — 200/1-3
55 10th St 18644 — 570-693-1914
Vito Quaglia, prin. — Fax 613-0298

Wyomissing, Berks, Pop. 10,332
Wilson SD
Supt. — See West Lawn
Spring Ridge ES — 500/K-5
1211 Broadcasting Rd 19610 — 610-670-0180
Dawn Hart, prin. — Fax 334-6449

Wyomissing Area SD — 1,900/K-12
630 Evans Ave 19610 — 610-374-0739
Lynette Waller, admin. — Fax 374-0948
www.wyoarea.org/
Wyomissing Hills ES — 600/K-4
110 Woodland Rd 19610 — 610-374-0739
Kate Bobst, prin. — Fax 374-8487
Other Schools – See West Reading

Yardley, Bucks, Pop. 2,392
Pennsbury SD
Supt. — See Fallsington
Afton ES — 500/K-5
1673 Quarry Rd 19067 — 215-321-8540
Joseph Masgai, prin. — Fax 321-3620
Boehm MS — 700/6-8
866 Big Oak Rd 19067 — 215-428-4220
Theresa Ricci, prin. — Fax 428-9605
Edgewood ES — 500/K-5
899 Oxford Valley Rd 19067 — 215-321-2410
Stephanie Hultquist, prin. — Fax 321-2412
Makefield ES — 500/K-5
1939 Makefield Rd 19067 — 215-321-2420
Donna McCormick-Miller, prin. — Fax 321-2422
Penn MS — 1,000/6-8
1524 Derbyshire Rd 19067 — 215-428-4280
Christopher Becker, prin. — Fax 428-1549
Pennwood MS — 900/6-8
1523 Makefield Rd 19067 — 215-428-4237
Derek Majikas, prin. — Fax 428-4265
Quarry Hill ES — 500/K-5
1625 Quarry Rd 19067 — 215-321-2400
Dr. Peggy Schiavone, prin. — Fax 321-0804

Abrams Hebrew Academy — 200/PK-8
31 W College Ave 19067 — 215-493-1800
Grey Nun Academy — 200/PK-8
1750 Quarry Rd 19067 — 215-968-4151
Deborah Kost, head sch — Fax 860-7418
St. Ignatius of Antioch S — 200/PK-8
995 Reading Ave 19067 — 215-493-3867
Mary Ann DiTommaso, prin. — Fax 573-3550

Yeadon, Delaware, Pop. 11,214
William Penn SD
Supt. — See Lansdowne
Bell Avenue ES — 300/K-6
1000 Bell Ave 19050 — 610-284-6100
Mary Kramer, prin. — Fax 284-2257
Evans ES — 400/K-6
900 Baily Rd 19050 — 610-623-5975
Dr. Dawnee Watson-Bouie, prin. — Fax 284-2310

York, York, Pop. 41,931
Central York SD — 5,800/K-12
775 Marion Rd 17406 — 717-846-6789
Dr. Michael Snell, supt. — Fax 840-0451
www.cysd.k12.pa.us
Central York MS — 1,000/7-8
1950 N Hills Rd 17406 — 717-846-6789
Edmund McManama, prin.
Hayshire ES, 2801 Hayshire Dr 17406 — 600/K-3
Barbara Snare, prin. — 717-846-6789
North Hills ES, 1330 N Hills Rd 17406 — 700/4-6
Kevin Youcheff, prin. — 717-846-6789
Roundtown ES, 570 Church Rd 17404 — 500/K-3
Matthew Miller, prin. — 717-846-6789
Sinking Springs ES — 700/4-6
2850 N Susquehanna Trl 17406 — 717-846-6789
Joel Gugino, prin.
Stony Brook ES — 600/K-3
250 Silver Spur Dr 17402 — 717-846-6789
Diane Grondin, prin.

Dallastown Area SD
Supt. — See Dallastown
Dallastown Area IS — 1,400/4-6
94 Beck Rd 17403 — 717-244-4021
Dr. Erin Heffler, prin. — Fax 847-0968
Leaders Heights ES — 200/K-3
49 Indian Rock Dam Rd 17403 — 717-741-1826
Charles Patterson, prin. — Fax 601-2672
Loganville-Springfield ES — 400/K-3
169 N Main St 17403 — 717-428-2240
Kelly Kessler, prin. — Fax 227-6132
Ore Valley ES — 600/K-3
2620 Springwood Rd 17402 — 717-505-5051
Dr. Greg Anderson, prin. — Fax 828-9504
York Township ES — 500/K-3
2500 S Queen St 17402 — 717-741-2281
Marcus Bouchillon, prin. — Fax 601-2672

Northeastern York SD
Supt. — See Manchester
Conewago ES — 300/K-3
570 Copenhaffer Rd 17404 — 717-266-1644
Thomas Shaffer, prin. — Fax 266-6365

Red Lion Area SD
Supt. — See Red Lion
Locust Grove ES — 400/K-6
3620 E Prospect Rd 17402 — 717-757-2559
Amy Landis, prin. — Fax 755-9667

Spring Grove Area SD
Supt. — See Spring Grove
New Salem ES — 400/K-4
3745 Salem Rd, — 717-225-4731
Robert Shick, prin. — Fax 792-0329

West York Area SD — 2,300/K-12
2605 W Market St 17404 — 717-792-2796
Fax 792-5114
www.wyasd.k12.pa.us
Lincolnway ES — 300/2-3
2625 W Philadelphia St 17404 — 717-792-3902
Melissa Appnel, prin. — Fax 792-6646
Trimmer ES — 200/4-5
1900 Brenda Rd, — 717-764-6586
Jenna Sloan, prin. — Fax 764-5407
Wallace ES — 200/K-1
2065 High St, — 717-764-6869
Jonathan Hoffman, prin. — Fax 764-7056
West York Area MS — 700/6-8
1700 Bannister St 17404 — 717-845-1671
Dr. Brad Sterner, prin. — Fax 845-9083

York CSD — 3,500/K-12
PO Box 1927 17405 — 717-845-3571
Dr. Eric Holmes, supt. — Fax 849-1394
www.ycs.k12.pa.us
Davis S — 400/K-8
300 S Ogontz St 17403 — 717-849-1246
Mindy Sweitzer, prin. — Fax 849-1416
Devers S — 500/K-8
801 Chanceford Ave 17404 — 717-849-1210
Craig Linn, prin. — Fax 849-1416
Ferguson S — 600/K-8
525 N Newberry St 17404 — 717-849-1344
Melanie Still, prin. — Fax 846-3825
Goode S — 500/K-8
251 N Broad St 17403 — 717-849-1314
Deb Hummel, prin. — Fax 846-4612
Jackson S — 400/K-8
177 E Jackson St 17401 — 717-849-1223
Dr. Phillip Libvelsberger, prin. — Fax 846-4912
McKinley S — 300/K-8
600 Manor St 17401 — 717-849-1312
Keith Still, prin. — Fax 849-1240
STEAM Academy — 500/3-8
701 Texas Ave 17404 — 717-849-1240
Angela Ashley, prin. — Fax 849-1418

York Suburban SD — 2,800/K-12
1800 Hollywood Dr 17403 — 717-885-1210
Dr. Michele Merkle, supt. — Fax 885-1211
www.yssd.org/
East York ES — 400/3-5
701 Erlen Dr 17402 — 717-885-1240
Dr. Denise Fuhrman, prin. — Fax 885-1241
Indian Rock ES — 300/3-5
1500 Indian Rock Dam Rd 17403 — 717-885-1250
Dr. Gregory Gulley, prin. — Fax 885-1251
Valley View ES — 300/K-2
850 Southern Rd 17403 — 717-885-1220
Dr. Todd Monos, prin. — Fax 885-1221
Yorkshire ES — 300/K-2
295 Mills St 17402 — 717-885-1230
Dr. Kimberly Stoltz, prin. — Fax 885-1231
York Suburban MS — 700/6-8
455 Sundale Dr 17402 — 717-885-1260
Dr. Scott Krauser, prin. — Fax 885-1261

Bible Baptist Christian Academy — 100/PK-12
4190 N Susquehanna Trl 17404 — 717-266-2544
Christian S of York — 300/PK-12
907 Greenbriar Rd 17404 — 717-767-6842
Kevin Hofer, hdmstr. — Fax 767-4904
Keystone Christian Academy - York — PK-8
705 S Ogontz St 17403 — 717-850-0943
Patricia Eger M.Ed., head sch — Fax 850-0944
Logos Academy — 200/K-8
250 W King St 17401 — 717-848-9835
St. Joseph S — 300/PK-6
2945 Kingston Rd 17402 — 717-755-1797
Patricia Byrnes, prin. — Fax 751-0136
St. Patrick S — 200/PK-6
235 S Beaver St 17401 — 717-854-8263
Kathleen Smith, prin. — Fax 846-6049
T.L.C. Montessori S — 50/PK-3
6434 Susquehanna Trl 17407 — 717-428-9992
York Adventist Christian S — 50/PK-8
2220 Roosevelt Ave, — 717-764-5603
York Country Day S — 200/PK-12
1000 Indian Rock Dam Rd 17403 — 717-815-6700
Dr. Christine Heine, head sch — Fax 815-6769

York Haven, York, Pop. 686
Northeastern York SD
Supt. — See Manchester
York Haven ES — 300/K-3
PO Box 5 17370 — 717-266-5007
Raymond March, prin. — Fax 266-7089

York Springs, Adams, Pop. 827
Bermudian Springs SD — 2,000/K-12
7335 Carlisle Pike 17372 — 717-528-4113
Dr. Shane Hotchkiss, supt. — Fax 528-7981
www.bermudian.org
Bermudian Springs ES — 700/K-4
7335 Carlisle Pike 17372 — 717-528-5147
Shannon Myers, prin. — Fax 528-4007
Bermudian Springs MS — 600/5-8
7335 Carlisle Pike 17372 — 717-528-5137
Dr. Wade Hunt, prin. — Fax 528-0034

Youngsville, Warren, Pop. 1,716
Warren County SD
Supt. — See Russell
Youngsville Elementary MS — 600/K-8
232 2nd St 16371 — 814-563-7584
Elizabeth Kent, prin. — Fax 563-9032

Warren County Christian S — 50/K-12
165 Mead Run Rd 16371 — 814-563-4457
Konrad Kerr, admin. — Fax 563-7647

Zelienople, Butler, Pop. 3,781
Seneca Valley SD
Supt. — See Harmony
Connoquenessing Valley ES — 700/K-4
300 S Pittsburgh St 16063 — 724-452-8280
DeeAnn Graham, prin. — Fax 452-5640

St. Gregory S — 200/K-8
115 Pine St 16063 — 724-452-9731
Erin Harris, prin. — Fax 452-4064

Zieglerville, Montgomery
Perkiomen Valley SD
Supt. — See Collegeville
Perkiomen Valley West MS — 600/6-8
220 Big Rd 19492 — 484-977-7210
Dr. Kim Boyd, prin. — Fax 977-7212

RHODE ISLAND

RHODE ISLAND DEPARTMENT OF EDUCATION
255 Westminster St, Providence 02903-3414
Telephone 401-222-4600
Fax 401-277-6178
Website http://www.ride.ri.gov

Commissioner of Education Dr. Ken Wagner

RHODE ISLAND BOARD OF EDUCATION
255 Westminster St, Providence 02903-3414

Chairperson Barbara Cottam

PUBLIC, PRIVATE AND CATHOLIC ELEMENTARY SCHOOLS

Ashaway, Washington, Pop. 1,467
Chariho Regional SD
Supt. — See Wood River Junction
Ashaway ES 200/K-4
12 Hillside Ave Ste A 02804 401-377-2211
Jeffrey Scanapieco, prin. Fax 633-6208

Barrington, Bristol, Pop. 15,849
Barrington SD 3,300/PK-12
PO Box 95 02806 401-245-5000
Michael Messore, supt. Fax 245-5003
barringtonschools.org
Barrington MS 800/6-8
261 Middle Hwy 02806 401-247-3160
Dr. Andrew Anderson, prin. Fax 247-3164
Hampden Meadows S 500/4-5
297 New Meadow Rd 02806 401-247-3166
Tracey McGee, prin. Fax 245-5003
Nayatt S 300/K-3
400 Nayatt Rd 02806 401-247-3175
Tracey Whitehead, prin. Fax 245-5003
Primrose Hill S 300/PK-3
60 Middle Hwy 02806 401-247-3170
Patricia Tolento, prin. Fax 245-5003
Sowams S 300/K-3
364 Sowams Rd 02806 401-247-3180
James Callahan, prin. Fax 245-5003

Barrington Christian Academy 200/K-12
9 Old County Rd 02806 401-246-0113
Sean Hunley, head sch Fax 246-2540
St. Luke S 200/PK-8
10 Waldron Ave 02806 401-246-0990
Patricia Bartel, prin. Fax 246-2120

Block Island, Washington
New Shoreham SD 100/K-12
PO Box 1890 02807 401-466-7732
Dr. Judith Lundsten, supt. Fax 466-3249
blockislandschool.net/
Block Island S 100/K-12
PO Box 1890 02807 401-466-5600
Kristine Monje, prin. Fax 466-5610

Bristol, Bristol, Pop. 21,625
Bristol Warren Regional SD 3,400/PK-12
151 State St 02809 401-253-4000
Mario Andrade Ed.D., supt. Fax 253-1740
www.bwrsd.org
Colt Andrews ES 400/K-5
570 Hope St 02809 401-254-5987
Deborah Kearns, prin. Fax 254-3926
Guiteras ES 300/K-5
35 Washington St 02809 401-254-5932
Cynthia Sadler, prin. Fax 254-5942
Rockwell ES 300/K-5
1225 Hope St 02809 401-254-5930
Tara McAuliffe, prin. Fax 247-3746
Other Schools – See Warren

Our Lady of Mt. Carmel S 200/PK-8
127 State St 02809 401-253-8455
Janet Maloney, prin. Fax 254-8234

Central Falls, Providence, Pop. 18,222
Central Falls SD 2,700/PK-12
949 Dexter St 02863 401-727-7700
Victor Capellan, supt. Fax 727-7722
www.cfschools.net
Calcutt MS 600/5-8
112 Washington St 02863 401-727-7726
Jose Valerio, prin. Fax 724-0870
Hunt Early Learning 100/PK-PK
12 Kendall St 02863 401-727-7720
Beth Tanner, prin. Fax 724-0577
Risk ES 400/K-5
949 Dexter St 02863 401-727-7730
Buddy Comet, prin. Fax 725-5142
Robertson S 200/PK-K
135 Hunt St 02863 401-727-7733
Beth Tanner, prin. Fax 724-4164
Veterans Memorial ES 500/K-5
150 Fuller Ave 02863 401-727-7740
Jose Valerio, prin. Fax 725-0941

Charlestown, Washington
Chariho Regional SD
Supt. — See Wood River Junction
Charlestown ES 300/PK-4
363 Carolina Back Rd 02813 401-364-7716
Jennifer Poore, prin. Fax 633-7080

Chepachet, Providence, Pop. 1,658
Glocester SD 500/PK-5
PO Box B 02814 401-568-4160
Dr. Jenny Chan-Remka, supt. Fax 568-5850
www.glocesterri.org
West Glocester ES 200/PK-5
111 Reynolds Rd 02814 401-567-0350
Nancy Zambarano, prin. Fax 568-4104
Other Schools – See North Scituate

Clayville, Providence, Pop. 295
Scituate SD
Supt. — See North Scituate
Clayville ES 100/PK-5
3 George Washington Hwy 02815 401-647-4115
Courtney Francis, prin. Fax 647-4114

Coventry, Kent, Pop. 31,083
Coventry SD 5,000/PK-12
1675 Flat River Rd 02816 401-822-9400
Craig Levis, supt. Fax 822-9406
www.coventryschools.net
Blackrock ES 400/PK-5
12 La Casa Dr 02816 401-822-9450
Alicia Reniere, prin. Fax 822-9452
Feinstein MS of Coventry 1,200/6-8
15 Foster Dr 02816 401-822-9426
Joseph Lucian, prin. Fax 822-9469
Hopkins Hill ES 400/PK-5
95 Johnson Blvd 02816 401-822-9477
Katherine Tancrelle, prin. Fax 822-9454
Tiogue ES 400/PK-5
170 E Shore Dr 02816 401-822-9460
Domenic Giusti, prin. Fax 822-9453
Washington Oak ES 600/PK-5
801 Read School House Rd 02816 401-397-1976
Christine Mandese, prin. Fax 397-1094
Western Coventry ES 400/K-5
4588 Flat River Rd, Greene RI 02827 401-397-3355
Amy Anzalone, prin. Fax 397-4592

Father John Doyle S 400/PK-8
343 S Main St 02816 401-821-3756
Jae Smith, prin. Fax 828-8513

Cranston, Providence, Pop. 78,728
Cranston SD 10,500/PK-12
845 Park Ave 02910 401-270-8000
Jeannine Nota-Masse, supt. Fax 270-8703
www.cpsed.net
Arlington ES 300/PK-5
155 Princess Ave 02920 401-270-8179
Michelle David, prin. Fax 270-8139
Bain MS 400/6-8
135 Gansett Ave 02910 401-270-8010
Jeffrey Taylor, prin. Fax 270-8567
Barrows ES 200/PK-5
9 Beachmont Ave 02905 401-270-8160
Janet Antonelli, prin. Fax 270-8505
Dutemple ES 300/K-5
32 Garden St 02910 401-270-8104
Kim Magnelli, prin. Fax 270-8528
Eden Park ES 300/K-6
180 Oakland Ave 02910 401-270-8029
Courtney Sevigny, prin. Fax 270-8530
Edgewood Highland ES 300/PK-5
160 Pawtuxet Ave 02905 401-270-8065
Marlene Gamba, prin. Fax 270-8534
Garden City ES 300/PK-5
70 Plantation Dr 02920 401-270-8073
Dr. Tonianne Napolitano, prin. Fax 270-8536
Gladstone Street ES 600/K-5
50 Gladstone St 02920 401-270-8080
Susan Bounanno, prin. Fax 270-8540
Glen Hills ES 300/K-5
50 Glen Hills Dr 02920 401-270-8005
John DeCristofaro, prin. Fax 270-8544
Hope Highlands MS 400/6-8
300 Hope Rd 02921 401-270-8148
Alexander Kanelos, prin. Fax 270-8706
Oak Lawn ES 300/K-5
36 Stoneham St 02920 401-270-8004
James Zanfini, prin. Fax 270-8571
Orchard Farms ES 300/PK-6
1555 Scituate Ave 02921 401-270-8801
Beth Basile, prin. Fax 270-8805
Park View MS 500/6-8
25 Park View Blvd 02910 401-270-8090
Michael Crudale, prin. Fax 270-8527
Peters ES 400/K-5
15 Mayberry St 02920 401-270-8199
Patricia Caporelli, prin. Fax 270-8577
Stadium ES 300/PK-5
100 Crescent Ave 02910 401-270-8188
Cheri Sacco, prin. Fax 270-8597
Stone Hill ES 300/PK-5
21 Village Ave 02920 401-270-8022
Tricha Totolo, prin. Fax 270-8636
Waterman ES 200/PK-5
722 Pontiac Ave 02910 401-270-8013
Paul DePalma, prin. Fax 270-8614
Western Hills MS 700/6-8
400 Phenix Ave 02920 401-270-8030
Fax 270-8635
Woodridge ES 300/K-5
401 Budlong Rd 02920 401-270-8007
Charlotte Josephs, prin. Fax 270-8708
Other Schools – See Providence

Immaculate Conception S 300/PK-8
235 Garden Hills Dr 02920 401-942-7245
Andrea Spaziante, prin. Fax 943-5738
St. Mary S 200/PK-8
85 Chester Ave 02920 401-944-4107
Lisa Lepore, prin. Fax 944-2395
St. Paul S 200/PK-8
1789 Broad St 02905 401-941-2030
John Corry, prin. Fax 941-0644

Cumberland, Providence
Cumberland SD 4,500/PK-12
2602 Mendon Rd 02864 401-658-1600
Robert Mitchell, supt. Fax 658-4620
www.cumberlandschools.org/
Ashton ES 300/PK-5
130 Scott Rd 02864 401-333-0554
Nidia Karbonik, prin. Fax 334-1811
Community ES 600/K-5
15 Arnold Mills Rd 02864 401-333-5724
Cheryl Vaughn, prin. Fax 333-1412
Cumberland Preschool Center 100/PK-PK
130 Scott Rd 02864 401-658-1600
Kathleen Gibney, admin. Fax 334-1811
Garvin Memorial ES 400/K-5
1364 Diamond Hill Rd 02864 401-333-2557
Judith Bassignani, prin. Fax 333-2581
McCourt MS 400/6-8
45 Highland Ave 02864 401-725-2092
Jason Masterson Ed.D., prin. Fax 723-1188
McLaughlin Cumberland Hill ES 300/K-5
205 Manville Hill Rd 02864 401-658-1660
Debra Malcolm, prin. Fax 658-0046
North Cumberland MS 600/6-8
400 Nate Whipple Hwy 02864 401-333-6306
Bethany Coughlin, prin. Fax 333-1926
Norton ES 400/K-5
364 Broad St 02864 401-722-7610
Dina Cerra, prin. Fax 723-1084

Mercymount Country Day S 500/PK-8
35 Wrentham Rd 02864 401-333-5919
Sr. Martha Mulligan, prin. Fax 333-5150

East Greenwich, Kent, Pop. 11,865
East Greenwich SD 2,400/PK-12
111 Peirce St 02818 401-398-1201
Victor Mercurio, supt. Fax 886-3203
www.egsd.net
Cole MS 600/6-8
100 Cedar Ave 02818 401-398-1213
Alexis Meyer, prin. Fax 886-3283

Eldredge ES 300/3-5
101 1st Ave 02818 401-886-3246
Dan Seger, prin. Fax 886-3262
Frenchtown ES 200/K-2
1100 Frenchtown Rd 02818 401-398-1402
Cheryl Vaughn, prin. Fax 886-3204
Hanaford ES 300/3-5
200 Middle Rd 02818 401-398-1351
Beth Cauley, prin. Fax 886-3267
Meadowbrook Farms ES 300/PK-2
2 Chestnut Dr 02818 401-398-1602
Neil Marcaccio, prin. Fax 886-9657

Our Lady of Mercy Regional S 400/PK-8
55 4th Ave 02818 401-884-1618
Scott Fuller, prin. Fax 885-3138
Rocky Hill S 300/PK-12
530 Ives Rd 02818 401-884-9070
James Tracy Ph.D., head sch Fax 885-4985

East Providence, Providence, Pop. 44,064
East Providence SD 5,200/PK-12
145 Taunton Ave 02914 401-435-7500
Kathryn Crowley, supt. Fax 435-7507
www.epschoolsri.com
Hennessey ES 300/K-5
75 Fort St 02914 401-435-7831
Lindrey Reilly, prin. Fax 435-7835
Kent Heights ES 300/K-5
2680 Pawtucket Ave 02914 401-435-7824
Stephen Prew, prin. Fax 435-7839
Martin MS 600/6-8
111 Brown St 02914 401-435-7819
Fatima Avila, prin. Fax 435-7851
Martin Pre-K Annex PK-PK
111 Brown St 02914 401-270-2321
Karen Rebello, prin. Fax 919-5912
Orlo Avenue ES 300/K-5
25 Orlo Ave 02914 401-435-7836
Yanazia Gallant, prin. Fax 435-7825
Silver Spring ES 300/K-5
120 Silver Spring Ave 02915 401-435-7836
Fatima Avila, prin. Fax 435-7826
Whiteknact ES 300/K-5
261 Grosvenor Ave 02914 401-435-7828
Teresa Medeiros, prin. Fax 435-7862
Other Schools – See Riverside, Rumford

Gordon S 400/PK-8
45 Maxfield Ave 02914 401-434-3833
Ralph Wales, head sch Fax 431-0320
Ocean State Montessori S 100/PK-6
100 Grove Ave 02914 401-434-6913
Sacred Heart S 200/K-8
56 Purchase St 02914 401-434-1080
Rev. Peter DiTullio, prin. Fax 434-1080
St. Mary Academy-Bay View 700/PK-12
3070 Pawtucket Ave 02915 401-434-0113
Colleen Gribbin, prin. Fax 434-4756

Exeter, Washington
Exeter-West Greenwich Regional SD
Supt. — See West Greenwich
Metcalf ES 500/2-6
30 Nooseneck Hill Rd 02822 401-397-3375
Laurie Ratigan, prin. Fax 397-0011
Wawaloam ES 300/K-1
100 Victory Hwy 02822 401-295-8808
Melissa Marino, admin. Fax 295-5340

Montessori Pathways S 1-9
567 South County Trl # 307 02822 401-295-0677

Foster, Providence
Foster SD 300/PK-5
160 Foster Center Rd 02825 401-647-5100
Dr. Michael Barnes, supt. Fax 647-3750
www.paineschool.org
Paine ES 300/PK-5
160 Foster Center Rd 02825 401-647-5100
Kristen Danusis, prin. Fax 647-3750

Greenville, Providence, Pop. 8,588
Smithfield SD
Supt. — See Smithfield
Winsor ES 300/K-5
562 Putnam Pike 02828 401-949-2059
Brian Ackerman, prin. Fax 949-7385

Harrisville, Providence, Pop. 1,581
Burrillville SD 2,400/PK-12
2300 Broncos Hwy 02830 401-568-1301
Dr. Frank Pallotta, supt. Fax 568-4111
www.bsd-ri.net/
Burrillville MS 600/6-8
2220 Broncos Hwy 02830 401-568-1320
Kathryn Lord, prin. Fax 568-1317
Callahan ES 300/2-5
75 Callahan School St 02830 401-568-1330
David Brissette, prin. Fax 568-1328
Levy ES 400/PK-1
135 Harrisville Main St 02830 401-568-1340
Monica Tomson, prin. Fax 568-1318
Other Schools – See Pascoag

Hope, Providence
Scituate SD
Supt. — See North Scituate
Hope ES 200/K-5
391 North Rd 02831 401-821-3651
Dana Morel, prin. Fax 823-4976

Hope Valley, Washington, Pop. 1,583
Chariho Regional SD
Supt. — See Wood River Junction
Hope Valley ES 200/PK-4
15 Thelma Dr 02832 401-539-2321
Joe Gencarelli, prin. Fax 633-7099

Jamestown, Newport, Pop. 4,999
Jamestown SD 500/PK-8
76 Melrose Ave 02835 401-423-7020
Kenneth Duva, supt. Fax 423-7022
jsd-ri.schoolloop.com
Lawn S 200/5-8
55 Lawn Ave 02835 401-423-7010
Nathaniel Edmonds, prin. Fax 423-7012
Melrose S 300/PK-4
76 Melrose Ave 02835 401-423-7020
Carole Petersen, prin. Fax 423-7022

Johnston, Providence, Pop. 26,542
Johnston SD 3,100/PK-12
10 Memorial Ave 02919 401-233-1900
Dr. Bernard DiLullo, supt. Fax 233-1907
www.johnstonschools.org
Barnes ES 200/K-5
24 Barnes Ave 02919 401-231-8710
Jill Souza, prin. Fax 231-7470
Brown Avenue ES 200/1-5
14 Brown Ave 02919 401-934-0270
Helina Dlugon, prin. Fax 934-2115
ECC 200/K-K
10 Memorial Ave 02919 401-233-0054
Julie-Anne Zarrella, prin. Fax 233-0081
Ferri MS 700/6-8
10 Memorial Ave 02919 401-233-1930
Matthew Tsonos, admin. Fax 233-1943
Graniteville Preschool 50/PK-PK
6 Collins Ave 02919 401-231-8790
Maria Petronio-McAfee, prin. Fax 232-2060
Thornton ES 400/1-5
4 School St 02919 401-943-7369
Louise Denham, prin. Fax 943-6940
Winsor Hill ES 400/1-5
100 Theresa St 02919 401-831-4619
Michele Zarcaro, prin. Fax 421-5660

North Providence SD
Supt. — See North Providence
McGuire ES 300/K-5
7 Waveland Ave 02919 401-233-1135
Thomas Meagher, prin. Fax 232-5408

St. Rocco S 300/PK-8
931 Atwood Ave 02919 401-944-2993
Lorraine Moschella, prin. Fax 944-3019

Lincoln, Providence, Pop. 18,045
Lincoln SD 3,100/PK-12
1624 Lonsdale Ave 02865 401-721-3300
Georgia Fortunato, supt. Fax 728-5482
www.lincolnps.org/
Lincoln Central ES 300/K-5
1081 Great Rd 02865 401-334-2800
Patricia Gablinske, prin. Fax 334-4294
Lincoln MS 700/6-8
152 Jenckes Hill Rd 02865 401-721-3400
Heidi Godowski, prin. Fax 721-3428
Lonsdale ES 300/K-5
270 River Rd 02865 401-725-4200
Rosemary Stein, prin. Fax 722-0920
Saylesville ES 300/K-5
50 Woodland St 02865 401-723-5240
Reza Sarkarati, prin. Fax 722-1090
Other Schools – See Manville

Little Compton, Newport
Little Compton SD 300/PK-8
PO Box 178 02837 401-635-2351
Dr. Robert B. Power, supt. Fax 635-2191
www.lcsd.k12.ri.us
Wilbur & McMahon S 300/PK-8
PO Box 178 02837 401-635-2351
Sonya Whipp, prin. Fax 635-2191

Manville, Providence, Pop. 3,000
Lincoln SD
Supt. — See Lincoln
Northern Lincoln ES 500/PK-5
315 New River Rd 02838 401-769-0261
Alec Ciminello, prin. Fax 765-0530

Middletown, Newport, Pop. 3,400
Middletown SD 2,100/PK-12
26 Oliphant Ln 02842 401-849-2122
Rosemarie Kraeger, supt. Fax 849-0202
www.mpsri.net/
Aquidneck ES 400/PK-3
70 Reservoir Rd 02842 401-847-4921
Michelle Fonseca, prin. Fax 846-7010
Forest Ave ES 300/PK-3
315 Forest Ave 02842 401-849-9434
Stephen Ponte, prin. Fax 846-4709
Gaudet MS 700/4-8
1113 Aquidneck Ave 02842 401-846-6395
Beth Hayes, prin. Fax 847-7580

All Saints Academy 200/PK-8
915 W Main Rd 02842 401-848-4300
Anita Brouse, prin. Fax 848-5587

Narragansett, Washington, Pop. 3,721
Narragansett SD 1,400/PK-12
25 5th Ave 02882 401-792-9450
Peter Cummings Ed.D., supt. Fax 792-9439
www.narragansett.k12.ri.us
Narragansett ES 500/PK-4
55 Mumford Rd 02882 401-792-9420
Gail Dandurand, prin. Fax 792-9424
Narragansett Pier MS 400/5-8
235 S Pier Rd 02882 401-792-9430
Marianne Kirby, prin. Fax 792-9436

Quest Montessori S 100/PK-8
1150 Boston Neck Rd 02882 401-783-3222
Michael Barclay, head sch Fax 783-3229

Newport, Newport, Pop. 23,495
Newport SD 2,000/PK-12
109 Old Fort Rd 02840 401-847-2100
Colleen Jermain Ed.D., supt. Fax 849-0170
www.npsri.net
Pell ES 900/PK-4
35 Dexter St 02840 401-842-1900
Traci Westman, prin. Fax 847-0538
Thompson MS 600/5-8
55 Broadway 02840 401-847-1493
Robert Campion, prin. Fax 849-3426

St. Joseph of Cluny Sisters S 200/PK-8
75 Brenton Rd 02840 401-847-6043
William Lippe, prin. Fax 848-5678
St. Michael's Country Day S 200/PK-8
180 Rhode Island Ave 02840 401-849-5970
John Zurn, head sch Fax 849-7890

North Kingstown, Washington, Pop. 2,800
North Kingstown SD 4,200/PK-12
100 Romano Vineyard Way 02852 401-268-6400
Philip Auger, supt. Fax 268-6405
www.nksd.net
Davisville MS 500/6-8
200 School St 02852 401-541-6300
Ruthanne Logan, prin. Fax 541-6310
Fishing Cove ES 300/PK-5
110 Wickford Point Rd 02852 401-268-6580
Karen Seitler, prin. Fax 268-6590
Forest Park ES 300/K-5
50 Woodlawn Dr 02852 401-541-6380
Cynthia Scheller, prin. Fax 541-6390
Hamilton ES 400/K-5
25 Salisbury Ave 02852 401-268-6520
Kaitlin Donahue, prin. Fax 268-6530
Quidnessett ES 300/K-5
166 Mark Dr 02852 401-541-6360
Louise Denette, prin. Fax 541-6370
Stony Lane ES 400/K-5
825 Stony Ln 02852 401-268-6540
Nicole Hitchener, prin. Fax 268-6550
Wickford MS 400/6-8
250 Tower Hill Rd 02852 401-268-6470
Brian Lally, prin. Fax 268-6480

South County Montessori S 100/PK-3
1239 Tower Hill Rd 02852 401-294-3575
West Bay Christian Academy 100/PK-8
475 School St 02852 401-884-3600
Ken Amador, head sch Fax 886-1650

North Providence, Providence, Pop. 32,500
North Providence SD 3,400/PK-12
2240 Mineral Spring Ave 02911 401-233-1100
Brigette Morisseau, supt. Fax 233-1106
npsd.k12.ri.us
Birchwood MS 400/6-8
10 Birchwood Dr 02904 401-233-1120
Melissa Goho, prin. Fax 353-6903
Centredale ES 300/PK-5
41 Angell Ave 02911 401-233-1145
Joan Piccardi Ed.D., prin. Fax 232-5279
Greystone ES 300/PK-5
100 Morgan Ave 02911 401-233-1130
Lori DeSimone, prin. Fax 232-5403
Marieville ES 300/K-5
1135 Mineral Spring Ave 02904 401-725-0099
Bruce Butler, prin. Fax 727-3249
Olney ES 300/K-5
622 Woonasquatucket Ave 02911 401-233-1160
Janine Napolitano, prin. Fax 353-4356
Ricci MS 400/6-8
51 Intervale Ave 02911 401-233-1170
Thomas Mellen, prin. Fax 232-5421
Whelan ES 300/K-5
1440 Mineral Spring Ave 02904 401-233-1180
Dr. Andrea Pleau, prin. Fax 353-1465
Other Schools – See Johnston

North Scituate, Providence
Foster-Glocester Regional SD 1,200/6-12
91 Anan Wade Rd 02857 401-710-7500
Michael Barnes Ph.D., supt. Fax 710-9825
www.fg.k12.ri.us
Ponaganset MS 500/6-8
7 Rustic Hill Rd 02857 401-710-7500
Patricia Marcotte, prin. Fax 647-1792

Glocester SD
Supt. — See Chepachet
Fogarty Memorial ES 300/PK-5
736 Snake Hill Rd 02857 401-568-6211
Laurie Mokaba, prin. Fax 568-3776

Scituate SD 1,400/PK-12
PO Box 188 02857 401-647-4100
Dr. Lawrence P. Filippelli, supt. Fax 647-4102
www.scituateri.net
North Scituate ES 200/K-5
46 Institute Ln 02857 401-647-4110
Bryan Byerlee, prin. Fax 647-4112
Scituate MS 400/6-8
94 Trimtown Rd 02857 401-647-4123
Tonianne Napolitano, prin. Fax 647-4104
Other Schools – See Clayville, Hope

North Smithfield, Providence, Pop. 10,497
North Smithfield SD
Supt. — See Slatersville
North Smithfield ES 400/PK-3
2214 Providence Pike 02896 401-765-2260
Diane Jolin, prin. Fax 765-8665
North Smithfield MS 400/6-8
1850 Providence Pike 02896 401-597-6100
John Lahar, prin. Fax 597-6121

Pascoag, Providence, Pop. 4,517
Burrillville SD
Supt. — See Harrisville
Steere Farm ES 400/2-5
915 Steere Farm Rd 02859 401-568-1350
Dr. Janet Lyons, prin. Fax 568-1353

Pawtucket, Providence, Pop. 64,391
Pawtucket SD 8,500/PK-12
PO Box 388 02862 401-729-6300
Patti DiCenso, supt. Fax 727-1641
www.psdri.net
Baldwin ES 700/K-5
50 Whitman St 02860 401-729-6264
Dr. Edna Coia, prin. Fax 729-6269
Cunningham ES 600/K-5
40 Baldwin St 02860 401-729-6262
Kimberly McCaughey, prin. Fax 729-9201
Curtis Memorial ES 400/PK-5
582 Benefit St 02861 401-729-6252
Michael Lazzareschi, prin. Fax 721-2100
Curvin-McCabe ES 400/K-6
466 Cottage St 02861 401-729-6258
Gina Adams, prin. Fax 729-6538
Fallon Memorial ES 700/PK-5
62 Lincoln Ave 02861 401-729-6254
Paul Zona, prin. Fax 729-6306
Goff JHS 400/6-8
974 Newport Ave 02861 401-729-6500
Lisa Benedetti-Ramzi, prin. Fax 721-2105
Greene ES 600/K-5
285 Smithfield Ave 02860 401-729-6260
Dr. Monique Jacob, prin. Fax 729-9200
Jenks JHS 400/6-8
350 Division St 02860 401-729-6520
Matthew Bergeron, prin. Fax 729-6523
Little ES 500/K-6
60 S Bend St 02860 401-729-6256
Michael Gilmore, prin. Fax 729-6323
Potter-Burns ES 500/K-5
973 Newport Ave 02861 401-729-6250
Mark Andrade, prin. Fax 729-6337
Slater MS 500/6-8
281 Mineral Spring Ave 02860 401-729-6480
Mark DeCiccio, prin. Fax 729-6490
Varieur ES 400/PK-6
486 Pleasant St 02860 401-729-6266
Mary Murray, prin. Fax 729-6544
Winters ES 500/K-5
481 Broadway 02860 401-729-6272
Maria SanMartino, prin. Fax 729-6414

St. Cecilia S 300/PK-8
755 Central Ave 02861 401-723-9463
Mary Tetzner, prin. Fax 722-1444
St. Teresa S 200/PK-8
140 Woodhaven Rd 02861 401-726-1414
Allison Amodie, prin. Fax 722-6998
Woodlawn Catholic Regional S 300/PK-8
61 Hope St 02860 401-723-3759
Veronica Procopio, prin. Fax 722-4090

Peace Dale, See Wakefield
South Kingstown SD
Supt. — See Wakefield
Peace Dale ES 400/K-4
109 Kersey Rd 02879 401-360-1600
Lisa Wilson, prin. Fax 360-1601

Portsmouth, Newport, Pop. 3,600
Portsmouth SD 2,600/PK-12
29 Middle Rd 02871 401-683-1039
Ana C. Riley, supt. Fax 683-5204
www.portsmouthschoolsri.org
Hathaway ES 400/K-4
53 Tallman Ave 02871 401-683-0500
Lisa Little, prin. Fax 683-0525
Melville ES 300/PK-4
1351 W Main Rd 02871 401-683-1650
Elizabeth Viveiros, prin. Fax 683-3412
Portsmouth MS 1,000/5-8
125 Jepson Ln 02871 401-849-3700
Joao Arruda, prin. Fax 841-8420

Aquidneck Island Christian Academy 100/K-12
321 E Main Rd 02871 401-849-5550
Joshua White, hdmstr. Fax 849-6811
Pennfield S 200/PK-8
110 Sandy Point Ave 02871 401-849-4646
Rob Kelley, head sch Fax 847-6720
St. Philomena S 500/PK-8
324 Corys Ln 02871 401-683-0268
Brian Cordeiro, prin. Fax 683-6554

Providence, Providence, Pop. 170,517
Cranston SD
Supt. — See Cranston
Rhodes ES 300/K-6
160 Shaw Ave 02905 401-270-8110
Erica Stackhouse, prin. Fax 270-8579

Providence SD 23,400/PK-12
797 Westminster St 02903 401-456-9100
Christopher Maher, supt. Fax 456-9252
www.providenceschools.org
Bailey ES 500/K-5
65 Gordon Ave 02905 401-456-1735
Carolina Creel, prin. Fax 456-1786
Bishop MS 700/6-8
101 Sessions St 02906 401-456-9344
Kimberly Luca, prin. Fax 456-9110
Carnevale ES 600/PK-5
50 Springfield St 02909 401-278-0554
Mari-Ellen Boisclair, prin. Fax 278-0556
D'Abate ES 400/K-5
60 Kossuth St 02909 401-456-9416
Brent Kermen, prin. Fax 453-8647
DelSesto MS 1,000/6-8
152 Springfield St 02909 401-278-0557
Arzinia Gill, prin. Fax 278-0564
Feinstein ES 500/K-5
1450 Broad St 02905 401-456-9367
Michael Templeton, prin. Fax 456-9489
Feinstein ES 500/K-5
159 Sackett St 02907 401-456-9407
Carolyn Johnston, prin. Fax 453-8658
Fogarty ES 500/K-5
199 Oxford St 02905 401-456-9381
Courtney Monterecy, prin. Fax 453-8649
Fortes ES 400/PK-1
234 Daboll St 02907 401-278-0501
Tonya Costa, prin. Fax 278-0503
Greene MS 1,000/6-8
721 Chalkstone Ave 02908 401-456-9347
Michael Comella, prin. Fax 453-8630
Gregorian ES 400/PK-5
455 Wickenden St 02903 401-456-9377
Susan Stambler, prin. Fax 453-8650
Hopkins MS 600/6-8
480 Charles St 02904 401-456-9203
Gloria Jackson, prin. Fax 456-9226
Kennedy ES 500/K-5
195 Nelson St 02908 401-456-9403
Susan DeAthos, prin. Fax 453-8652
King ES 600/PK-5
35 Camp St 02906 401-456-9398
Kristen Lussier, prin. Fax 456-9497
Kizirian ES 600/K-5
60 Camden Ave 02908 401-456-9369
Daniel Smith, prin. Fax 456-9496
Lauro ES 900/K-5
99 Kenyon St 02903 401-456-9391
Suzanne Madden, prin. Fax 456-9246
Leviton Dual Language ES 100/K-1
65 Greenwich St 02907 401-278-2872
Dr. Javier Montanez, prin. Fax 278-2862
Lima ES 600/2-5
222 Daboll St 02907 401-278-0504
Kim Zona, prin. Fax 278-0506
Messer ES 600/K-5
1655 Westminster St 02909 401-456-9401
Denise Missry, prin. Fax 456-9486
Pleasant View ES 400/PK-5
50 Obediah Brown Rd 02909 401-456-9325
Colleen Loughlin, prin. Fax 453-8656
Reservoir Avenue ES 300/K-5
156 Reservoir Ave 02907 401-456-9406
Cheryl Merola, prin. Fax 453-8657
Spaziano Annex ES 200/K-1
240 Laban St 02909 401-456-1783
William Niemeyer, prin. Fax 456-1785
Spaziano ES 400/2-5
85 Laurel Hill Ave 02909 401-456-9389
William Niemeyer, prin. Fax 453-8653
Stuart MS 800/6-8
188 Princeton Ave 02907 401-456-9340
Scott Sutherland, prin. Fax 453-8659
Veazie Street ES 600/K-5
211 Veazie St 02904 401-453-8601
Colleen Caswell, prin. Fax 453-8660
Webster Avenue ES 400/K-5
191 Webster Ave 02909 401-456-9414
Alicia Jones, prin. Fax 453-8661
West Broadway MS 6-8
29 Bainbridge Ave 02909 401-456-1733
William Black, prin. Fax 278-0527
West ES 800/K-5
145 Beaufort St 02908 401-456-9337
Sandra Stuart, prin. Fax 456-9487
Williams MS 800/6-8
278 Thurbers Ave 02905 401-456-9355
Christina Gibbons, prin. Fax 453-8631
Young - Woods ES 700/PK-5
674 Prairie Ave 02905 401-278-0515
Edward Lee, prin. Fax 278-0541

Barnard Laboratory S 300/PK-5
600 Mount Pleasant Ave 02908 401-456-8127
Bishop McVinney Regional S 200/PK-8
155 Gordon Ave 02905 401-781-2370
Louis Hebert, prin. Fax 785-2618
Blessed Sacrament S 300/PK-8
240 Regent Ave 02908 401-831-3993
Christopher Weber, prin. Fax 223-0536
Brown S 800/PK-12
250 Lloyd Ave 02906 401-831-7350
Dr. Matt Glendinning, head sch Fax 455-0084
Community Preparatory S 100/4-8
135 Prairie Ave 02905 401-521-9696
French-American S of Rhode Island 200/PK-8
75 John St 02906 401-274-3325
Christophe Bonnet, head sch Fax 455-3437
Lincoln S 400/PK-12
301 Butler Ave 02906 401-331-9696
Suzanne Fogarty, head sch Fax 751-6670
Montessori Childrens House 100/PK-6
518 Lloyd Ave 02906 401-331-6120
Providence Hebrew Day S 200/PK-12
450 Elmgrove Ave 02906 401-331-5327
St. Augustine S 300/PK-8
635 Mount Pleasant Ave 02908 401-831-1213
Andrew Brassard, prin. Fax 831-4256
St. Pius V S 200/PK-8
49 Elmhurst Ave 02908 401-421-9750
Sr. Maria Wiley, prin. Fax 455-3928
St. Thomas Regional S 200/PK-8
15 Edendale Ave 02911 401-351-0403
Mary DiMuccio, prin. Fax 351-0403
San Miguel S 100/5-8
525 Branch Ave 02904 401-467-9777
John Wolf, dir. Fax 785-4976
Wheeler S 800/PK-12
216 Hope St 02906 401-421-8100
Allison Pell, head sch Fax 751-7674

Richmond, Washington

Meadowbrook Waldorf S 200/PK-8
300 Kingstown Rd 02892 401-491-9570

Riverside, See East Providence
East Providence SD
Supt. — See East Providence
Oldham ES 200/K-5
60 Bart Dr 02915 401-433-6209
Donna Peluso, prin. Fax 433-6247
Riverside MS 600/6-8
179 Forbes St 02915 401-433-6230
Dr. Cheri Guerra, prin. Fax 433-6261
Waddington ES 500/PK-5
101 Legion Way 02915 401-433-6235
Patricia Barlow, prin. Fax 433-6207

Rumford, See East Providence
East Providence SD
Supt. — See East Providence
Francis ES 400/K-5
64 Bourne Ave 02916 401-435-7829
Lloydanne Leddy, prin. Fax 435-7852

St. Margaret S 200/PK-8
42 Bishop Ave 02916 401-434-2338
Lee Nunes, prin. Fax 431-0266

Slatersville, Providence
North Smithfield SD 1,700/PK-12
PO Box 72 02876 401-769-5492
Michael St. Jean, supt. Fax 769-5493
www.northsmithfieldschools.com/
Halliwell Memorial ES 400/3-5
358 Victory Highway 02876 401-762-2793
Jennifer Daigneault, prin. Fax 765-8747
Other Schools – See North Smithfield

Smithfield, Providence, Pop. 19,163
Smithfield SD 2,400/PK-12
49 Farnum Pike 02917 401-231-6606
Judy Paolucci, supt. Fax 232-0870
www.smithfield-ps.org
Gallagher MS 600/6-8
10 Indian Run Trl 02917 401-949-2056
Laurie Beauvais, prin. Fax 949-5697
LaPerche ES 200/K-5
11 Limerock Rd 02917 401-231-6652
Julie Dorsey, prin. Fax 231-1141
McCabe ES 300/PK-5
100 Pleasant View Ave 02917 401-949-2058
Cathy Pleau, prin. Fax 949-5773
Old County Road ES 300/K-5
200 Old County Rd 02917 401-231-6613
Laurie Sullivan, prin. Fax 231-2292
Other Schools – See Greenville

St. Philip S 300/PK-8
618 Putnam Pike 02828 401-949-1130
Cynthia Senenko, prin. Fax 949-1141

Tiverton, Newport, Pop. 7,434
Tiverton SD 1,800/PK-12
100 N Brayton Rd 02878 401-624-8476
William Rearick, supt. Fax 624-4086
www.tivertonschools.org
Ft. Barton S 200/K-4
99 Lawton Ave 02878 401-624-6114
Suzette Wordell, prin. Fax 624-6115
Pocasset ES 200/PK-4
242 Main Rd 02878 401-624-6654
Deanne Reilly, prin. Fax 624-6655
Ranger ES 200/PK-4
278 N Brayton Rd 02878 401-624-8467
Manuel Cabral, prin. Fax 624-8468
Tiverton MS 600/5-8
10 Quintal Dr 02878 401-624-6668
Dr. Laurie Dias-Mitchell, prin. Fax 624-6669

Wakefield, Washington, Pop. 8,226
South Kingstown SD 3,400/PK-12
307 Curtis Corner Rd 02879 401-360-1300
Dr. Kristen Stringfellow Ed.D., supt. Fax 360-1330
www.skschools.net/
Broad Rock MS 500/5-6
351 Broad Rock Rd 02879 401-360-1800
Kathleen Egan, prin. Fax 360-1801
Curtis Corner MS 500/7-8
301 Curtis Corner Rd 02879 401-360-1333
Patricia Aull, prin. Fax 360-1334
Matunuck ES 200/K-4
380 Matunuck Beach Rd 02879 401-360-1234
Elizabeth McGuire, prin. Fax 360-1235
South Kingston Inclusionary Preschool 100/PK-PK
1157 South Rd 02879 401-360-1200
Coleen Smith, coord. Fax 360-1217
Wakefield ES 300/K-4
101 High St 02879 401-360-1400
Lynn Dougherty, prin. Fax 360-1401
Other Schools – See Peace Dale, West Kingston

Monsignor Matthew F. Clarke Regional S 400/PK-8
5074 Tower Hill Rd 02879 401-789-0860
Dr. John Finnegan, prin. Fax 789-3164

Warren, Bristol, Pop. 11,385
Bristol Warren Regional SD
Supt. — See Bristol
Cole ES 700/PK-5
50 Asylum Rd 02885 401-245-1460
Cindy Giroux, prin. Fax 245-8895
Kickemuit MS 700/6-8
525 Child St 02885 401-245-2010
Christine Homen, prin. Fax 254-5960

Warwick, Kent, Pop. 81,173
Warwick SD 8,400/PK-12
69 Draper Ave 02889 401-734-3000
Dr. Philip Thornton, supt. Fax 734-3003
www.warwickschools.org
Cedar Hill ES 400/K-6
35 Red Chimney Dr 02886 401-734-3535
Dr. Colleen Mercurio, prin. Fax 734-3538
Drum Rock ECC 200/PK-K
575 Centerville Rd Ste 3 02886 401-734-3490
Mindy Mertz, dir. Fax 734-3493
Francis ES 300/PK-6
325 Miantonomo Dr 02888 401-734-3340
Michelle Depot, prin. Fax 734-3343
Greenwood ES 300/K-6
93 Sharon St 02886 401-734-3290
Kenneth Rassler, prin. Fax 734-3293
Holden ES 200/K-6
61 Hoxsie Ave 02889 401-734-3455
Sabrina Antonelli, prin. Fax 734-3458
Holliman ES 300/PK-6
70 Deborah Rd 02888 401-734-3170
Joseph Coffey, prin. Fax 734-3173
Hoxsie ES 300/K-6
55 Glenwood Dr 02889 401-734-3555
Gary McCoombs, prin. Fax 734-3558
Lippitt ES 200/PK-6
30 Almy St 02886 401-734-3240
Martin Susla, prin. Fax 734-3243
Norwood ES 200/PK-6
266 Norwood Ave 02888 401-734-3525
John Gannon, prin. Fax 734-3528
Oakland Beach ES 400/PK-6
383 Oakland Beach Ave 02889 401-734-3420
Paul Heatherton, prin. Fax 734-3423
Park ES 300/PK-6
40 Asylum Rd 02886 401-734-3690
Marilyn Feeney, prin. Fax 734-3693
Robertson ES 300/PK-6
70 Nausauket Rd 02886 401-734-3470
Brian Dillon, prin. Fax 734-3473
Scott ES 300/PK-6
833 Centerville Rd 02886 401-734-3585
Virginia Bolano, prin. Fax 734-3588
Sherman ES 400/PK-6
120 Killey Ave 02889 401-734-3565
Dr. Michelle Paton, prin. Fax 734-3568
Veterans JHS 1,000/7-8
2401 W Shore Rd 02889 401-734-3200
David Tober, prin. Fax 734-3214
Warwick Neck ES 300/K-6
155 Rocky Point Ave 02889 401-734-3480
Patricia Cousineau, prin. Fax 734-3483
Wickes ES 300/K-6
50 Child Ln 02886 401-734-3575
Roy Costa, prin. Fax 734-3578
Winman JHS 500/7-8
575 Centerville Rd 02886 401-734-3375
Joanne Pelletier, prin. Fax 734-3385
Wyman ES 300/K-6
1 Columbia Ave 02888 401-734-3180
Ron Celio, prin. Fax 734-3183

St. Kevin S 200/PK-8
39 Cathedral Rd 02889 401-737-7172
Roger Parent, prin. Fax 738-1288
St. Peter S 200/PK-8
120 Mayfair Rd 02888 401-781-9242
Joan Sickinger, prin. Fax 467-5673
St. Rose of Lima S 300/PK-8
200 Brentwood Ave 02886 401-739-6937
Kimberly Izzi, prin. Fax 737-4632

Westerly, Washington, Pop. 17,600
Westerly SD 2,900/PK-12
23 Highland Ave 02891 401-315-1500
Dr. Mark Garceau, supt. Fax 348-2707
www.westerly.k12.ri.us
Dunns Corners ES 300/K-4
8 1/2 Plateau Rd 02891 401-348-2320
Steven Morrone, prin. Fax 348-2325
Springbrook ES 300/K-4
39 Springbrook Rd 02891 401-348-2296
Susan Martin, prin. Fax 348-2305
State Street ES 400/K-4
35 State St 02891 401-348-2340
Audrey Faubert, prin. Fax 348-2345
Westerly MS 900/5-8
10 Sandy Hill Rd 02891 401-348-2750
Paula Fusco, prin. Fax 348-2752

St. Pius X S 200/PK-8
32 Elm St 02891 401-596-5735
Janet Rufful, prin. Fax 596-5791

West Greenwich, Kent, Pop. 3,492
Exeter-West Greenwich Regional SD 1,600/PK-12
940 Nooseneck Hill Rd 02817 401-397-5125
James Erinakes M.Ed., supt. Fax 397-2407
www.ewg.k12.ri.us
Exeter-West Greenwich Regional JHS 300/7-8
930 Nooseneck Hill Rd 02817 401-397-6897
Mary Slattery, prin. Fax 392-0109
Lineham Preschool 50/PK-PK
859 Nooseneck Hill Rd 02817 401-397-3771
Robin Corsi, coord. Fax 392-0101
Other Schools – See Exeter

West Kingston, Washington
South Kingstown SD
Supt. — See Wakefield
West Kingston ES 300/K-4
3119 Ministerial Rd 02892 401-360-1130
Kim Leimer, prin. Fax 360-1131

West Warwick, Kent, Pop. 29,600
West Warwick SD 3,400/PK-12
10 Harris Ave 02893 401-821-1180
Karen A. Tarasevich M.Ed., supt. Fax 822-8463
www.westwarwickpublicschools.com/
Deering MS 1,000/5-8
2 Webster Knight Dr 02893 401-822-8445
Jeffrey Guiot, prin. Fax 822-8474
Greenbush ES 500/PK-4
127 Greenbush Rd 02893 401-822-8454
Derrick Ciesla, prin. Fax 822-8478
Horgan ES 500/PK-4
124 Providence St 02893 401-822-8449
Dr. Nicole L'Etoile, prin. Fax 822-8475
Wakefield Hills ES 400/PK-4
505 Wakefield St 02893 401-822-8452
Leah Bessette, prin. Fax 822-1509

Islamic School of Rhode Island 100/PK-9
840 Providence St 02893 401-821-8700
Abdelnasser Hussein M.Ed., head sch Fax 821-8701
St. Joseph S 300/PK-8
850 Wakefield St 02893 401-821-3450
James Woodmansee, prin. Fax 821-3516

Wood River Junction, Washington
Chariho Regional SD 3,400/PK-12
455A Switch Rd 02894 401-364-7575
Barry Ricci, supt. Fax 415-6076
www.chariho.k12.ri.us
Chariho Regional MS 1,000/5-8
455b Switch Rd 02894 401-364-0651
Gregory Zenion, prin. Fax 223-4925
Other Schools – See Ashaway, Charlestown, Hope Valley, Wyoming

Woonsocket, Providence, Pop. 39,726
Woonsocket SD 5,800/PK-12
108 High St 02895 401-767-4600
Dr. Patrick McGee, supt. Fax 767-4607
www.woonsocketschools.com
Bernon Heights ES 500/K-5
657 Logee St 02895 401-767-4864
Rob Desrosiers, prin. Fax 767-4865
Citizens Memorial ES 400/2-5
250 Winthrop St 02895 401-767-4850
Danielle Costa, prin. Fax 767-4851
Coleman ES 300/K-5
92 2nd Ave 02895 401-767-4859
Fax 767-4860
Globe Park ES 500/K-5
192 Avenue A 02895 401-767-4830
Tina Silva, prin. Fax 767-4831
Harris ES 400/K-5
60 High School St 02895 401-767-4855
Fax 767-4857
Pothier ES 500/PK-2
420 Robinson St 02895 401-767-4765
Danielle Costa, prin. Fax 767-4654
Savoie ES 400/K-5
990 Mendon Rd 02895 401-767-4820
Donna Coderre, prin. Fax 767-4821
Woonsocket MS at Hamlet 1,200/6-8
60 Florence Dr 02895 401-235-6110
Woonsocket MS at Villa Nova 6-8
240 Florence Dr 02895 401-235-6125

Good Shepherd Regional S 200/3-8
1210 Mendon Rd 02895 401-767-5906
Jennifer DeOliveira, prin. Fax 767-5905
Monsignor Gadoury Regional PS 200/PK-2
1371 Park Ave 02895 401-767-5902
Shawn Capron, prin. Fax 767-5902

Wyoming, Washington, Pop. 268
Chariho Regional SD
Supt. — See Wood River Junction
Richmond ES 500/PK-4
190 Kingstown Rd 02898 401-539-2441
Sharon Martin, prin. Fax 633-7139

SOUTH CAROLINA

SOUTH CAROLINA DEPARTMENT OF EDUCATION
1429 Senate St Ste 100, Columbia 29201-3730
Telephone 803-734-8500
Fax 803-734-3389
Website ed.sc.gov/

Superintendent of Education Molly Spearman

SOUTH CAROLINA BOARD OF EDUCATION
1429 Senate St Ste 100, Columbia 29201-3730

Chairperson Ivan Randolph

PUBLIC, PRIVATE AND CATHOLIC ELEMENTARY SCHOOLS

Abbeville, Abbeville, Pop. 5,157
Abbeville County SD 3,100/PK-12
400 Greenville St 29620 864-366-5427
Dr. Betty Jo Hall, supt. Fax 366-8531
www.acsdsc.org
Diamond Hill ES 300/K-7
104 Lake Secession Rd 29620 864-446-2600
Todd Ramey, prin. Fax 446-2602
Long Cane PS 400/K-2
815 E Greenwood St 29620 864-366-5924
Millie Ricketts, prin. Fax 366-4011
Westwood ES 400/3-5
124 Highway 28 Byp 29620 864-366-9604
Darren Gray, prin. Fax 366-5297
Wright MS 400/6-8
111 Highway 71 29620 864-366-5998
Skip Hopkins, prin. Fax 366-4282
Other Schools – See Calhoun Falls, Donalds

Aiken, Aiken, Pop. 29,094
Aiken County SD 23,900/PK-12
1000 Brookhaven Dr 29803 803-641-2428
Sean Alford Ph.D., supt. Fax 642-8903
www.acpsd.net
Aiken ES 800/K-5
2050 Pine Log Rd 29803 803-641-2740
Rebecca Koelker, prin. Fax 641-2526
Aiken MS 600/6-8
101 Gator Ln 29801 803-641-2570
Scott Floyd, prin. Fax 641-2578
Chukker Creek ES 800/K-5
1830 Chukker Creek Rd 29803 803-641-2474
Amy Gregory, prin. Fax 641-2537
East Aiken S of the Arts 600/K-5
223 Old Wagener Rd 29801 803-641-2450
Lisa Fallaw, prin. Fax 641-2527
Kennedy MS 1,000/6-8
274 E Pine Log Rd 29803 803-641-2470
Teresa Mitchem, prin. Fax 641-2405
Lever ES 500/K-5
2404 Columbia Hwy N 29805 803-641-2760
Michael Truitt, prin. Fax 641-2402
Millbrook ES 600/K-5
255 E Pine Log Rd 29803 803-641-2580
John Metts, prin. Fax 641-2449
North Aiken ES 400/K-5
100 Bears Rock Rd 29801 803-641-2690
Elisa Sandres-Pee, prin. Fax 641-2674
Oakwood-Windsor ES 400/K-5
3773 Charleston Hwy 29801 803-641-2560
Lynne Shrader, prin. Fax 641-2561
Redcliffe ES 700/K-5
22 Double Springs Rd 29803 803-827-3350
Julie Revelle, prin. Fax 827-3354
Schofield MS 700/6-8
224 Kershaw St NE 29801 803-641-2770
Denise McCray, prin. Fax 641-2529
Other Schools – See Belvedere, Burnettown, Clearwater, Gloverville, Graniteville, Jackson, New Ellenton, North Augusta, Ridge Spring, Wagener, Warrenville

---

Mead Hall S - St. Thaddeus Campus 100/PK-4
129 Pendleton St SW 29801 803-644-1122
St. Mary Help of Christians S 200/K-8
118 York St SE 29801 803-649-2071
Peggy Wertz, prin. Fax 643-0092
South Aiken Baptist Christian S 400/PK-12
980 Dougherty Rd 29803 803-648-7071

Anderson, Anderson, Pop. 26,180
Anderson SD 3
Supt. — See Iva
Flat Rock ES 400/PK-5
115 Thompson Rd 29624 864-296-9191
Christy Dodd, prin. Fax 296-5812

Anderson SD 5 12,800/PK-12
PO Box 439 29622 864-260-5000
Thomas Wilson, supt. Fax 260-5074
www.anderson5.net
Anderson MS 700/6-8
2302 Dobbins Bridge Rd 29626 864-716-3890
Leonard Galloway, prin. Fax 716-4070
Calhoun Academy of the Arts 600/K-5
1520 E Calhoun St 29621 864-260-5090
Ann Self, prin. Fax 231-2802
Centerville ES 700/K-5
1529 Whitehall Rd 29625 864-260-5100
Jenifer Seymour, prin. Fax 260-5051
Concord ES 700/K-5
2701 Calrossie Rd 29621 864-260-5105
Beryl Barclay, prin. Fax 964-0424
Glenview MS 700/6-8
2725 Old Williamston Rd 29621 864-716-4060
Walter Mayfield, prin. Fax 716-3883
Homeland Park PS 400/PK-2
3519 Wilmont St 29624 864-260-5125
Gary Bruhjell, prin. Fax 375-2042
McCants MS 700/6-8
2123 Marchbanks Ave 29621 864-260-5145
Kelly Elrod, prin. Fax 260-5846
McLees ES 700/K-5
4900 Dobbins Bridge Rd 29626 864-716-3600
Janet Mills, prin. Fax 716-3611
Midway ES 800/K-5
1221 Harriett Cir 29621 864-716-3800
Brandon Meares, prin. Fax 716-3811
Nevitt Forest ES 500/K-5
1401 Bolt Dr 29621 864-260-5190
Robin Gay, prin. Fax 375-2043
New Prospect ES 500/K-5
126 New Prospect Church Rd 29625 864-260-5195
Brian Williams, prin. Fax 964-2647
North Pointe ES 400/PK-5
3325 N Highway 81 29621 864-260-5040
Jill Gilreath, prin. Fax 260-5041
South Fant S of Early Education 200/PK-K
1700 S Fant St 29624 864-260-5225
Anthony Ware, prin. Fax 964-2694
Southwood Academy of the Arts 400/6-8
1110 Southwood St 29624 864-260-5205
Jamie Smith, prin. Fax 964-2607
Varennes ES 300/3-5
1820 Highway 29 S 29626 864-260-5215
Taria McIntosh, prin. Fax 964-2677
West Market S of Early Education 200/PK-K
1909 Dobbins Bridge Rd 29626 864-260-5200
Missy McKenzie, prin. Fax 716-3820
Whitehall ES 400/PK-5
702 Whitehall Rd 29625 864-260-5255
Jennifer Bufford, prin. Fax 375-2047

Anderson Christian S 200/PK-12
3902 Liberty Hwy 29621 864-224-7309
Dr. Michelle Cutler, admin. Fax 224-1085
Montessori S of Anderson 200/PK-12
280 Sam McGee Rd 29621 864-226-5344
New Covenant S 200/PK-12
303 Simpson Rd 29621 864-224-5675
Joseph Canney, hdmstr. Fax 224-5985
St. Joseph S 100/PK-8
1200 Cornelia Rd 29621 864-760-1619
Nadine DePape, prin. Fax 225-6432

Andrews, Georgetown, Pop. 2,842
Georgetown County SD
Supt. — See Georgetown
Andrews ES 800/PK-5
13072 County Line Rd 29510 843-264-3419
Adrienne Watford, prin. Fax 264-5511
Rosemary MS 500/6-8
12804 County Line Rd 29510 843-264-9780
LaTanya Goodson, prin. Fax 264-9787

Aynor, Horry, Pop. 554
Horry County SD
Supt. — See Conway
Aynor ES 700/PK-5
516 Jordanville Rd 29511 843-488-7070
Reggie Gasque, prin. Fax 488-7071

Bamberg, Bamberg, Pop. 3,560
Bamberg SD 1 900/PK-12
3830 Faust St 29003 803-245-3053
Phyllis Schwarting, supt. Fax 245-3056
www.bamberg1.com
Bamberg-Ehrhardt MS 200/7-8
897 North St 29003 803-245-3058
Denise L. Miller B.A., prin. Fax 245-6501
Carroll ES 200/PK-6
1980 Main Hwy 29003 803-245-3047
Stacey Walter, prin. Fax 245-3051

Barnwell, Barnwell, Pop. 4,670
Barnwell SD 45 2,500/PK-12
770 Hagood Ave 29812 803-541-1300
Crystal F. Stapleton, supt. Fax 541-1348
www.barnwell45.org
Barnwell ES 500/4-6
10524 Marlboro Ave 29812 803-541-1285
Dr. Carolyn Anderson, prin. Fax 541-1290
Barnwell PS 800/PK-3
734 Hagood Ave 29812 803-541-1321
Donna Selvey, prin. Fax 541-1313
Guinyard-Butler MS 400/7-8
779 Allen St 29812 803-541-1370
Dr. Jessica Brabham-James, prin. Fax 541-1306

Batesburg, Lexington, Pop. 5,296
Lexington County SD 3 2,000/PK-12
338 W Columbia Ave 29006 803-532-4423
Dr. Randall Gary, supt. Fax 532-8000
www.lex3.org
Batesburg-Leesville MS 400/6-8
425 Shealy Rd 29006 803-532-3831
Sharah Clark, prin. Fax 532-8021
Batesburg-Leesville PS 600/PK-2
800 Summerland Ave 29006 803-532-4452
Tonya Watson, prin. Fax 532-4453
Other Schools – See Leesville

King Academy 200/PK-12
1046 Sardis Rd 29006 803-532-6682

Beaufort, Beaufort, Pop. 12,089
Beaufort County SD 20,300/PK-12
PO Box 309 29901 843-322-2300
Dr. Jeffrey Moss, supt. Fax 322-2330
www.beaufort.k12.sc.us
Beaufort ES 600/PK-5
1800 Prince St 29902 843-322-2600
Melissa Holland, prin. Fax 322-2685
Beaufort MS 600/6-8
2501 Mossy Oaks Rd 29902 843-322-5700
Carole Ingram, prin. Fax 322-5723
Broad River ES 600/PK-5
474 Broad River Blvd 29906 843-322-8400
Constance Goodwine-Lewis, prin. Fax 322-8380
Coosa ES 400/PK-5
45 Middle Rd, 843-322-6100
Charles DelForge, prin. Fax 322-6170
Ladys Island ES 300/PK-5
73 Chowan Creek Blf, 843-322-2240
Marvelle Ulmer, prin. Fax 322-2281
Ladys Island MS 600/6-8
30 Cougar Dr, 843-322-3100
Gregory Hall, prin. Fax 322-3179
Mossy Oaks ES 400/PK-5
2510 Mossy Oaks Rd 29902 843-322-2900
Michelle Sackman, prin. Fax 322-2956
Shanklin ES 400/PK-5
121 Morrall Dr 29906 843-466-3400
Celestine LaVan, prin. Fax 466-3472
Smalls International Academy 600/PK-8
43 W K Alston Dr 29906 843-322-2500
Jennifer Morillo, prin. Fax 322-2564
Other Schools – See Bluffton, Hilton Head Island, Okatie, Port Royal, Saint Helena Island, Seabrook

---

Beaufort Academy 300/PK-12
240 Sams Point Rd, 843-524-3393
Dan Durbin Ed.D., head sch Fax 524-1171
Beaufort Christian S 100/PK-12
378 Parris Island Gtwy 29906 843-525-0635
Holy Trinity Classical Christian S 200/K-12
302 Burroughs Ave 29902 843-522-0660
St. Peter S 200/PK-8
70 Ladys Island Dr, 843-522-2163
Ann Feltner, prin. Fax 522-6513

Belton, Anderson, Pop. 4,063
Anderson SD 2
Supt. — See Honea Path
Belton ES 500/3-5
202 Watkins St 29627 864-338-7738
Tracy Hedrick, prin. Fax 338-3319
Belton MS 500/6-8
102 Cherokee Rd 29627 864-338-6595
Joshua Burton, prin. Fax 338-3301
Marshall PS 600/PK-2
218 Bannister St 29627 864-338-7611
Jenifer Fleming, prin. Fax 338-3309
Wright ES 200/K-5
1136 Wright School Rd 29627 864-296-1776
Laurie McCall, prin. Fax 296-9951

Belvedere, Aiken, Pop. 5,672
Aiken County SD
Supt. — See Aiken
Belvedere ES 600/K-5
201 Rhomboid Pl 29841 803-442-6330
Dr. Salvatore Minolfo, prin. Fax 442-6131

Bennettsville, Marlboro, Pop. 8,964
Marlboro County SD 4,100/PK-12
PO Box 947 29512 843-479-4016
Dr. Helena Tillar, supt. Fax 479-5944
www.marlboro.k12.sc.us
Bennettsville IS 400/3-5
701 Cheraw St 29512 843-479-5941
Rick Singletary, prin. Fax 479-5943
Bennettsville PS 500/PK-2
301 Jefferson St 29512 843-479-5936
Gail Redding, prin. Fax 479-5943
Other Schools – See Blenheim, Clio, Mc Coll, Wallace

Marlboro Academy 200/K-12
1035 Bennettsville Fire Twr 29512 843-479-6501

Bethune, Kershaw, Pop. 333
Kershaw County SD
Supt. — See Camden
Bethune ES 100/K-5
PO Box 477 29009 843-334-6278
Estelle Benson, prin. Fax 334-6275

Bishopville, Lee, Pop. 3,442
Lee County SD 2,300/PK-12
PO Box 507 29010 803-484-5327
Dr. Wanda Andrews, supt. Fax 484-9107
www.leeschooldistrictsc.org
Bishopville ES 600/PK-5
321 Roland St 29010 803-483-1005
Lamont Moore, prin. Fax 483-1007
Lee Central MS 500/6-8
41 Charlenes Ln 29010 803-428-2100
Gregory Jones, prin. Fax 428-2101
Other Schools – See Mayesville, Rembert

Lee Academy 400/K-12
630 Cousar St 29010 803-484-5532

Blacksburg, Cherokee, Pop. 1,800
Cherokee County SD
Supt. — See Gaffney
Blacksburg ES 300/3-5
402 Hardin St 29702 864-206-6518
Rita Martin, prin. Fax 839-5922
Blacksburg MS 400/6-8
101 London St 29702 864-206-6829
Virgil Hampton, prin. Fax 839-2390
Blacksburg PS 400/PK-2
1010 E Cherokee St 29702 864-206-6936
Deborah Hamrick, prin. Fax 839-1109

Blackville, Barnwell, Pop. 2,378
Barnwell SD 19 800/PK-12
297 Pascallas St 29817 803-284-5605
Dr. Shawn Johnson, supt. Fax 284-4417
www.barnwell19.k12.sc.us
Blackville-Hilda MS 100/6-8
PO Box 245 29817 803-284-5900
Eryl Smalls, prin. Fax 284-0961
Macedonia ES 400/PK-5
PO Box 246 29817 803-284-5800
Teresa Brown, prin. Fax 284-0959

Barnwell Christian S 100/1-12
5675 SC Highway 70 29817 803-259-2100
Patrick Heatwole, admin. Fax 259-2100
Davis Academy 200/K-12
5061 Hilda Rd 29817 803-284-2476

Blair, Fairfield
Fairfield County SD
Supt. — See Winnsboro
McCrorey-Liston ES 200/PK-6
1978 State Highway 215 S 29015 803-635-9490
Dr. Chandra Bell, prin. Fax 635-1557

Blenheim, Marlboro, Pop. 148
Marlboro County SD
Supt. — See Bennettsville
Blenheim S 500/PK-8
PO Box 250 29516 843-528-1492
James McCall, prin. Fax 528-1498

Bluffton, Beaufort, Pop. 12,248
Beaufort County SD
Supt. — See Beaufort
Bluffton ECC 100/PK-1
150 HE McCracken Cir 29910 843-707-0900
Christine Brown, prin. Fax 706-8542
Bluffton ES 400/2-5
160 HE McCracken Cir 29910 843-706-8500
Christine Brown, prin. Fax 706-8542
Bluffton MS 1,100/6-8
30 New Mustang Dr 29910 843-707-0700
Patricia Freda, prin. Fax 707-8117
Pritchardville ES 800/PK-5
9447 Evan Way 29910 843-707-0500
Brenda Blue, prin. Fax 707-8119
Red Cedar ES 800/PK-5
11 Box Elder St 29910 843-707-0600
Dr. Kathleen Corley, prin. Fax 707-0611
Riley ECC 200/PK-K
172 Burnt Church Rd 29910 843-707-0800
Adrienne Sutton, prin. Fax 706-8378
Riley ES 600/1-5
200 Burnt Church Rd 29910 843-706-8300
Adrienne Sutton, prin. Fax 706-8378
River Ridge Academy PK-8
3050 River Ridge Dr 29910 843-836-4600
Gary McCulloch, prin. Fax 836-4850

Cross Schools 300/PK-8
495 Buckwalter Pkwy 29910 843-706-2000
St. Gregory the Great S 200/PK-6
333 Fording Island Rd, 843-815-9988
Christopher Trott, prin. Fax 815-3150

Blythewood, Richland, Pop. 2,008
Richland SD 2
Supt. — See Columbia
Bethel/Hanberry ES 700/PK-5
125 Boney Rd 29016 803-691-6880
Tracy Footman, prin. Fax 691-6883
Blythewood MS 700/6-8
2351 Longtown Rd E 29016 803-691-6850
Karis Mazyck, prin. Fax 691-6860
Center for Knowledge ES K-5
1043 Muller Rd 29016 803-691-4895
Dr. Jo Lane Hall, prin.
Kelly Mill MS 900/6-8
1141 Kelly Mill Rd 29016 803-691-7210
Mark Sims, prin. Fax 691-7212
Lake Carolina ES - Lower 800/PK-2
1151 Kelly Mill Rd 29016 803-714-1300
Dr. Andrea Berry, prin. Fax 714-1301
Lake Carolina ES - Upper 400/3-5
1261 Kelly Mill Rd 29016 803-691-3360
Jeff Williams, prin.
Langford ES 500/PK-5
480 Langford Rd 29016 803-691-4091
Kaseena Jackson, prin. Fax 738-7535
Muller Road MS 700/6-8
1031 Muller Rd 29016 803-691-6851
Sean Bishton, prin. Fax 738-7531
Round Top ES 700/PK-5
449 Rimer Pond Rd 29016 803-691-8676
Jeaneen Tucker, prin. Fax 691-8677

Boiling Springs, Spartanburg, Pop. 8,098
Spartanburg SD 2
Supt. — See Chesnee
Boiling Springs ES 800/K-4
700 Double Bridge Rd 29316 864-578-1231
Michelle Kimbrell, prin. Fax 599-9163
Boiling Springs IS 600/5-5
2055 Hanging Rock Rd 29316 864-578-2884
Tammy Greer, prin. Fax 578-2426
Shoally Creek ES K-4
3777 Parris Bridge Rd 29316 864-594-3200
Laura Meyer, admin.

Branchville, Orangeburg, Pop. 1,014
Orangeburg County Consolidated SD 4
Supt. — See Cope
Lockett ES 300/PK-5
PO Box 218 29432 803-274-8588
Robert Eubanks, prin. Fax 274-8650

Brunson, Hampton, Pop. 550
Hampton SD 1
Supt. — See Varnville
Brunson ES 200/K-6
PO Box 130 29911 803-398-5584
Kristy Wood, prin. Fax 398-5585

Buffalo, Union, Pop. 1,254
Union County SD
Supt. — See Union
Buffalo ES 600/K-5
733 Main St 29321 864-429-1730
Stacy McAbee, prin. Fax 429-2100

Burnettown, Aiken, Pop. 2,629
Aiken County SD
Supt. — See Aiken
Jefferson ES 500/K-5
170 Flint Dr 29851 803-593-7180
Rebecca Wilson, prin. Fax 593-7112

Calhoun Falls, Abbeville, Pop. 1,964
Abbeville County SD
Supt. — See Abbeville
Calhoun ES 200/K-5
750 N Calhoun Shores Pkwy 29628 864-447-8016
Milton Scott, prin. Fax 447-8079

Camden, Kershaw, Pop. 6,772
Kershaw County SD 10,500/PK-12
2029 W Dekalb St 29020 803-432-8416
Dr. Frank Morgan, supt. Fax 425-8918
www.kcsdschools.com
Baron-DeKalb ES 200/PK-5
2684 Baron Dekalb Rd 29020 803-432-2483
Betty Turner, prin. Fax 425-8979
Camden ES of the Creative Arts 600/K-5
1304 Lyttleton St 29020 803-425-8960
Carol Przybyla, prin. Fax 425-7708
Camden MS 700/6-8
902 McRae Rd 29020 803-425-8975
Byron Johnson, prin. Fax 425-7867
Jackson S 500/PK-5
1730 Jefferson Davis Hwy 29020 803-425-8965
Matia Goodwin, prin. Fax 425-8967
Pine Tree Hill ES 500/K-5
938 Bishopville Hwy 29020 803-425-8970
Melissa Royalty, prin. Fax 425-7718
Other Schools – See Bethune, Cassatt, Elgin, Kershaw, Lugoff

Camden Adventist S 50/1-8
612 Boykin Rd 29020 803-432-0541

Campobello, Spartanburg, Pop. 498
Spartanburg SD 1 5,000/PK-12
PO Box 218 29322 864-472-2846
Dr. Ron Garner, supt. Fax 472-4118
www.spart1.org/do/
Campobello-Gramling S 800/PK-8
250 Fagan Ave 29322 864-472-9110
Jeremy Darby, prin. Fax 468-4210
Holly Springs-Motlow ES 400/PK-6
325 Motlow School Rd 29322 864-472-8120
Erika Center, prin. Fax 895-0620
Other Schools – See Inman, Landrum

Cassatt, Kershaw
Kershaw County SD
Supt. — See Camden
Midway ES 400/PK-5
1892 Highway 1 N 29032 803-432-6122
Dr. Charles King, prin. Fax 425-8929

Cayce, Lexington, Pop. 12,278
Lexington County SD 2
Supt. — See West Columbia
Busbee Creative Arts Academy 300/6-8
501 Bulldog Blvd 29033 803-739-4070
Dr. Dixon Brooks, prin. Fax 739-4133
Cayce ES 900/PK-5
515 Bulldog Blvd 29033 803-936-5500
Dr. Cecil McClary, admin. Fax 739-8396

Central, Pickens, Pop. 5,067
Pickens County SD
Supt. — See Easley
Central ES 300/K-5
608 Johnson Rd 29630 864-397-1400
Tish Goode, prin. Fax 639-5140
Edwards MS 800/6-8
1157 Madden Bridge Rd 29630 864-397-4200
Jeff Duncan, prin. Fax 624-4426

Chapin, Lexington, Pop. 1,420
SD Five of Lexington & Richland Counties
Supt. — See Irmo
Chapin ES 700/PK-4
940 Old Bush River Rd 29036 803-575-5900
Lauren Prochak, prin. Fax 575-5920
Chapin IS 5-6
1130 Old Lexington Hwy 29036 803-575-5700
Vann Holden, prin. Fax 575-5721
Chapin MS 1,100/6-8
11661 Broad River Rd 29036 803-726-6500
Anna Miller, prin. Fax 726-6521
Lake Murray ES 700/PK-4
1531 Three Dog Rd 29036 803-476-4600
Claire Thompson, prin. Fax 476-4620

Charleston, Charleston, Pop. 118,351
Berkeley County SD
Supt. — See Moncks Corner
Daniel Island S 1,400/K-8
2365 Daniel Island Dr 29492 843-471-2301
Kori Brown, prin. Fax 471-2304
Simmons ES K-4
2095 Seven Sticks Dr 29492 843-471-2580
Dr. Karen Whitley, prin. Fax 471-2566
Simmons MS 5-8
2065 Seven Sticks Dr 29492 843-471-2590
Anthony Dixon, prin. Fax 471-2599

Charleston County SD 45,100/PK-12
75 Calhoun St 29401 843-937-6300
Dr. Gerrita Postlewait, supt. Fax 937-6307
www.ccsdschools.com
Ashley River Creative Arts ES 600/K-5
1871 Wallace School Rd 29407 843-763-1555
Michelle Conner, prin. Fax 763-1567
Buist Academy for Advanced Studies 500/K-8
103 Calhoun St 29401 843-724-7750
Shawntay White, prin. Fax 724-1493
Burns ES 500/PK-5
3795 Spruill Ave 29405 843-745-7113
John Cobb, prin. Fax 529-3906
Camp Road MS 400/6-8
1484 Camp Rd 29412 843-762-2784
David Parler, prin. Fax 762-6209
Charleston Progressive Academy 400/PK-6
382 Meeting St 29403 843-720-2967
Wanda Wright-Sheats, prin. Fax 577-1680
Drayton Hall ES 700/PK-5
3183 Ashley River Rd 29414 843-852-0678
Brian Agnew, prin. Fax 852-2069
Harbor View ES 500/PK-5
1576 Harbor View Rd 29412 843-762-2749
Lara Latto, prin. Fax 762-6207
James Island ES 500/PK-5
1872 S Grimball Rd 29412 843-762-8240
Jonetta Gregory, prin. Fax 762-8250
Memminger S of Global Studies 300/PK-5
20 Beaufain St 29401 843-724-7778
Dr. Abigail Woods, prin. Fax 720-3142
Mitchell Math & Science ES 300/PK-5
2 Perry St 29403 843-724-7261
Deborah Smith, prin. Fax 720-3128
Montessori Community S 200/PK-8
2122 Wood Ave 29414 843-769-0346
Kim Hay, admin. Fax 852-4879
Murray-Lasaine ES 200/PK-6
691 Riverland Dr 29412 843-762-2765
Meredith Wallace, prin. Fax 762-6203

Oakland ES 500/PK-5
505 Arlington Dr Ste A 29414 843-763-1510
Elizabeth Nicodin, prin. Fax 769-2598
St. Andrew's S of Math-Science 700/PK-5
30 Chadwick Dr 29407 843-763-1503
Amy Cario, prin. Fax 769-2594
Sanders-Clyde S 600/K-5
805 Morrison Dr 29403 843-724-7783
Dr. Roshon Bradley, prin. Fax 720-3138
Simmons-Pinckney MS 6-8
244 President St 29403 843-724-7789
Nathan Nelson, prin. Fax 579-4363
Simons ES 200/PK-8
741 King St 29403 843-724-7763
Christine Ryan, prin. Fax 720-3129
Springfield ES 600/PK-5
2130 Pinehurst Ave 29414 843-763-1538
Megan Williams, prin. Fax 769-2236
Stiles Point ES 700/PK-5
883 Mikell Dr 29412 843-762-2767
Michael Ard, prin. Fax 762-2773
Stono Park ES 300/PK-5
721 Wappoo Rd 29407 843-763-1507
Michelle Simmons, prin. Fax 769-2248
West Ashley Advanced Studies Magnet MS 300/6-8
1776 William Kennerty Dr 29407 843-763-1546
Brant Glover, prin. Fax 852-6557
Williams MS 600/6-8
640 Butte St 29414 843-763-1529
Kevin Smith, prin. Fax 763-5955
Other Schools – See Edisto Island, Hollywood, Johns Island, Ladson, Mc Clellanville, Mount Pleasant, North Charleston, Ravenel, Sullivans Island, Wadmalaw Island

---

Addlestone Hebrew Academy 200/PK-8
1675 Raoul Wallenberg Blvd 29407 843-571-1105
Abby Levine, prin. Fax 571-6116
Ashley Hall 700/PK-12
172 Rutledge Ave 29403 843-722-4088
Jill Muti, head sch Fax 720-2868
Blessed Sacrament S 300/PK-8
7 Saint Teresa Dr 29407 843-766-2128
Katherine Murphy, prin. Fax 766-2154
Charleston Catholic S 200/PK-8
888 King St 29403 843-577-4495
Fred McKay, prin. Fax 577-6916
Charleston Christian S 100/PK-8
2234 Plainview Rd 29414 843-556-4480
Ashley Chandler, head sch Fax 766-4407
Charleston Day S 200/K-8
15 Archdale St 29401 843-377-0315
Brendan O'Shea, hdmstr. Fax 720-2143
Charleston SDA S 50/K-9
2518 Savannah Hwy 29414 843-571-7519
Charles Towne Montessori S 50/PK-6
56 Leinbach Dr 29407 843-571-1140
Cooper S 50/K-5
13 Oakdale Pl 29407 843-573-1033
Franci Bell, head sch Fax 225-7449
First Baptist S of Charleston 500/PK-12
48 Meeting St 29401 843-722-6646
Dr. Lee Cox, head sch Fax 720-2521
James Island Christian S 100/PK-8
15 Crosscreek Dr 29412 843-795-1762
Jeremy Schwartz, head sch Fax 762-1619
Mason Prep S 300/K-8
56 Halsey Blvd 29401 843-723-0664
Erik Kreutner, head sch Fax 723-1104
Meeting Street Academy 200/PK-5
642 Meeting St 29403 843-735-7102
Nativity S 100/PK-8
1125 Pittsford Cir 29412 843-795-3975
Patti Dukes, prin. Fax 795-7575
Porter-Gaud S 900/PK-12
300 Albemarle Rd 29407 843-556-3620
D. DuBose Egleston B.S., head sch Fax 556-7404
St. John S 100/PK-8
3921 Saint Johns Ave 29405 843-744-3901
Karen Durand, prin. Fax 744-3689
Trinity Montessori S 100/PK-6
1293 Orange Grove Rd 29407 843-556-6686

Cheraw, Chesterfield, Pop. 5,741
Chesterfield County SD
Supt. — See Chesterfield
Cheraw IS 500/3-5
421 Chesterfield Hwy 29520 843-921-1030
Scott Eddins, prin. Fax 921-1036
Cheraw PS 500/PK-2
321 High St 29520 843-921-1020
Molica Little, prin. Fax 921-1015
Long MS 500/6-8
1010 W Greene St 29520 843-921-1010
Karen Ellerbe, prin. Fax 921-1017

Faith Christian Academy 100/PK-8
220 Greene St 29520 843-537-0260

Chesnee, Spartanburg, Pop. 845
Spartanburg SD 2 9,400/K-12
3231 Old Furnace Rd 29323 864-578-0128
Scott Mercer, supt. Fax 578-8924
www.spartanburg2.k12.sc.us
Carlisle-Fosters Grove ES 500/K-4
625 Fosters Grove Rd 29323 864-578-2215
Cathy Garner, prin. Fax 599-7376
Chesnee ES 500/K-5
985 Fairfield Rd 29323 864-461-7322
Deana Watson, prin. Fax 431-7338
Chesnee MS 500/6-8
805 S Alabama Ave 29323 864-461-3900
Rob Hayes, prin. Fax 461-3950
Cooley Springs-Fingerville ES 300/K-5
140 Cooley Springs School 29323 864-592-1211
Amanda Ehlich, prin. Fax 592-3406

Rainbow Lake MS 700/6-8
1951 Riveroak Rd 29323 864-253-5700
Greg Lovelace, prin. Fax 253-5701
Other Schools – See Boiling Springs, Cowpens, Inman, Spartanburg

Chester, Chester, Pop. 5,520
Chester County SD 5,500/PK-12
509 District Office Dr 29706 803-385-6122
Angela H. Bain Ph.D., supt. Fax 581-6965
www.chester.k12.sc.us/
Chester MS 700/6-8
1014 McCandless Rd 29706 803-377-8192
Sheka Houston, prin. Fax 581-1875
Chester Park Ctr Literacy Through Tech 400/PK-5
835 Lancaster Hwy 29706 803-581-7275
Tammy Graham Ed.D., prin. Fax 581 7277
Chester Park ES of Inquiry 500/PK-5
835 Lancaster Hwy 29706 803-581-5184
Robin Taylor, prin. Fax 385-5435
Chester Park ES of the Arts 600/PK-5
835 Lancaster Hwy 29706 803-581-7279
Ruth Anne Pitt, prin. Fax 581-7281
Other Schools – See Great Falls, Richburg

Chesterfield, Chesterfield, Pop. 1,462
Chesterfield County SD 7,400/PK-12
401 West Blvd 29709 843-623-2175
Dr. Harrison Goodwin, supt. Fax 623-3434
www.chesterfieldschools.org
Chesterfield-Ruby MS 400/6-8
14445 Highway 9 29709 843-623-9401
Neil Adams, prin. Fax 623-9429
Edwards ES 500/PK-5
2411 West Blvd 29709 843-623-2351
Elizabeth Suggs, prin. Fax 623-9412
Other Schools – See Cheraw, Jefferson, Mc Bee, Pageland, Patrick, Ruby

Clearwater, Aiken, Pop. 4,288
Aiken County SD
Supt. — See Aiken
Clearwater ES 400/K-5
4552 Augusta Rd, 803-593-7240
Trey Laube, prin. Fax 593-7120

Clemson, Pickens, Pop. 13,699
Pickens County SD
Supt. — See Easley
Clemson ES 800/K-5
581 Berkeley Dr 29631 864-397-1500
Michelle Craddock, prin. Fax 624-4425

Clinton, Laurens, Pop. 8,368
Laurens County SD 56 3,100/PK-12
211 N Broad St Ste B 29325 864-833-0800
Dr. David O'Shields, supt. Fax 833-0804
www.laurens56.k12.sc.us
Bailey Child Development Center 200/PK-PK
625 Elizabeth St 29325 864-833-0836
Nancy Roland, dir. Fax 938-2320
Clinton ES 700/K-5
800 Chestnut St 29325 864-833-0812
Melodie Edwards, prin. Fax 833-0814
Clinton MS 700/6-8
800 N Adair St 29325 864-833-0807
Chris Winkler, prin. Fax 833-0810
Eastside ES 500/K-5
103 Old Colony Rd 29325 864-833-0827
Carol Anne Barnes, prin. Fax 833-0829
Other Schools – See Joanna

Clio, Marlboro, Pop. 720
Marlboro County SD
Supt. — See Bennettsville
Clio S 200/PK-8
2635 Highway 9 E 29525 843-586-9391
Julia Cain, prin. Fax 586-2234

Clover, York, Pop. 5,008
Clover SD 2 6,900/PK-12
604 Bethel St 29710 803-810-8000
Dr. Sheila Quinn, supt. Fax 222-8010
www.clover.k12.sc.us
Bethany ES 400/PK-5
337 Maynard Grayson Rd 29710 803-810-8800
Alison Churm, prin. Fax 222-8055
Bethel ES 400/PK-5
6000 Highway 55 E 29710 803-631-8100
Kimberly Ramsey, prin. Fax 631-2996
Clover MS 700/6-8
1233 Barrett Rd 29710 803-810-8300
Calub Courtwright, prin. Fax 222-8034
Crowders Creek ES 1,100/PK-5
5515 Charlotte Hwy 29710 803-810-8500
Kershena Dickey, prin. Fax 831-9471
Griggs Road ES 500/PK-5
100 Griggs Rd 29710 803-631-8200
Kenda Cook, prin. Fax 222-8066
Kinard ES 300/PK-5
201 Pressly St 29710 803-810-8700
Kathy Weathers, prin. Fax 222-8048
Larne ES 500/PK-5
3598 Filbert Hwy 29710 803-810-8600
Vickie Stine, prin. Fax 810-8670
Oakridge ES PK-5
5670 Oakridge Rd 29710 803-631-8400
Lori Maczko, prin. Fax 631-8475
Oakridge MS 900/6-8
5650 Highway 557 29710 803-631-8000
William Largen, prin. Fax 631-8102

Columbia, Richland, Pop. 126,841
Richland SD 1 24,300/PK-12
1616 Richland St 29201 803-231-7000
Dr. Craig Witherspoon, supt. Fax 231-7502
www.richlandone.org/
Alcorn MS 300/6-8
5125 Fairfield Rd 29203 803-735-3439
Dr. Carla Mathis, prin. Fax 735-3487

Arden ES 300/PK-5
1300 Ashley St 29203 803-735-3400
Dr. Peggie Grant, prin. Fax 691-4231
Bradley ES 400/PK-5
3032 Pine Belt Rd 29204 803-738-7200
Kezia Myers, prin. Fax 738-7346
Brennen ES 800/PK-5
4438 Devereaux Rd 29205 803-738-7204
Mark Shea, prin. Fax 738-7904
Brockman ES 300/PK-5
2245 Montclair Dr 29206 803-790-6743
Dr. Marian Crum-Mack, prin. Fax 790-6745
Burnside ES 300/PK-5
7300 Patterson Rd 29209 803-783-5530
Felicia Richardson, prin. Fax 783-5594
Burton-Pack ES 600/PK-5
111 Garden Dr 29204 803-691-5550
Sarah Smith, prin. Fax 691-5555
Carver-Lyon ES 400/PK-5
2100 Waverly St 29204 803-343-2900
Dr. Teresa Turner, prin. Fax 253-5721
Caughman Road ES 700/PK-5
7725 Caughman Rd 29209 803-783-5534
Shawn Hall, prin. Fax 783-5537
Crayton MS 1,100/6-8
5000 Clemson Ave 29206 803-738-7224
Angela Burns, prin. Fax 738-7901
Ford ES 700/K-5
5901 Satchel Ford Rd 29206 803-738-7209
Kevin Hasinger, prin. Fax 738-7218
Forest Heights ES 600/PK-5
2500 Blue Ridge Ter 29203 803-691-3780
Dr. Winnie Johnson, prin. Fax 691-3782
Gibbes MS 300/6-8
500 Summerlea Dr 29203 803-343-2942
Ericka Hursey, prin. Fax 733-3040
Hand MS 900/6-8
2600 Wheat St 29205 803-343-2947
Dr. Robin Hardy, prin. Fax 733-6173
Hyatt Park ES 500/PK-5
4200 N Main St 29203 803-735-3421
Lindell Brabham, prin. Fax 735-3391
Lewis Greenview ES 400/PK-5
726 Easter St 29203 803-735-3417
Delores Gilliard, prin. Fax 735-3495
Logan ES 300/PK-5
815 Elmwood Ave 29201 803-343-2915
Christopher Richards, prin. Fax 929 3896
Meadowfield ES 600/PK-5
525 Galway Ln 29209 803-783-5549
Lisa Davis, prin. Fax 695-3079
Mill Creek ES 400/PK-5
925 Universal Dr 29209 803-783-5553
Charles DeLaughter, prin. Fax 783-5572
Moore ES 400/PK-5
333 Etiwan Ave 29205 803-343-2910
Dr. Chantelle Baker, prin. Fax 929-3882
Perry MS 300/6-8
2600 Barhamville Rd 29204 803-256-6347
Dr. Robin Coletrain, prin. Fax 255-2262
Pine Grove ES 600/PK-5
111 Huffstetler Dr 29210 803-214-2380
Dr. Tracy Pickett, prin. Fax 214-2385
Rhame ES 500/PK-5
1300 Arrowwood Rd 29210 803-731-8900
Monica Owens-Carter, prin. Fax 750-4040
Rosewood ES 400/K-5
3300 Rosewood Dr 29205 803-343-2930
Elizabeth Williams, prin. Fax 929-3849
St. Andrews MS 700/6-8
1231 Bluefield Dr 29210 803-731-8910
Derrick Glover, prin. Fax 731-8913
Sandel ES 600/PK-5
2700 Seminole Rd 29210 803-731-8906
Claudia Brooks, prin. Fax 731-8977
Sanders MS 400/6-8
3455 Pine Belt Rd 29204 803-738-7575
Andrenna Smith, prin. Fax 738-7566
South Kilbourne ES 300/PK-5
1400 S Kilbourne Rd 29205 803-738-7215
Samantha Carlisle, prin. Fax 790-6734
Taylor ES 300/PK-5
200 McRae St 29203 803-343-2924
Debbie Hunter, prin. Fax 929-3851
Thomas ES 500/PK-5
6001 Weston Ave 29203 803-735-3430
Selina Latimore, prin. Fax 735-3369
Watkins-Nance ES 400/PK-5
2525 Barhamville Rd 29204 803-733-4321
Dr. Linda Norton, prin. Fax 733-4332
Other Schools – See Eastover, Gadsden, Hopkins

Richland SD 2 26,600/PK-12
124 Risdon Way 29223 803-787-1910
Dr. Baron Davis, supt. Fax 738-3334
www.richland2.org
Center for Achievement K-5
1000 Lake Carolina Dr 29229 803-691-7216
Kimberly Hutcherson, prin. Fax 691-7214
Center for Inquiry ES K-5
200 1/2 Summit Pkwy 29229 803-699-2969
Dr. Lyn Mueller, lead tchr. Fax 699-2963
Center for Knowledge ES K-5
3006 Appleby Ln 29223 803-699-2966
Jessica Agee, lead tchr. Fax 699-2967
Conder ES 800/PK-5
8040 Hunt Club Rd 29223 803-736-8720
Paula China, prin. Fax 699-3688
Dent MS 1,300/6-8
2721 Decker Blvd 29206 803-699-2750
Tamala Ashford, prin. Fax 699-2754
Forest Lake ES 600/PK-5
6801 Brookfield Rd 29206 803-782-0470
Dr. Kappy Steck, prin. Fax 738-7365
Jackson Creek ES K-5
1750 Trenholm Rd 29223 803-790-3800
Dr. Sabina Mosso-Taylor, prin.

Keels ES 700/PK-5
7500 Springcrest Dr 29223 803-736-8754
Alvera Butler, prin. Fax 736-8773
Killian ES 800/PK-5
2621 Clemson Rd 29229 803-699-2981
Stacey Franklin, prin. Fax 699-2971
Longleaf MS 700/6-8
1160 Longreen Pkwy 29229 803-691-4870
Robert Jackson, prin. Fax 691-4043
Nelson ES 500/PK-5
225 N Brickyard Rd 29223 803-736-8730
Karen Beaman, prin. Fax 699-3672
North Springs ES 800/PK-5
1300 Clemson Rd 29229 803-736-3183
Dr. David Holzendorf, prin. Fax 699-2732
Polo Road ES 600/K-5
1250 Polo Rd 29223 803-419-2226
Dr. Cassandra Bosier, prin. Fax 462-2173
Rice Creek ES 700/PK-5
4751 Hard Scrabble Rd 29229 803-699-2900
Stacey Gadson, prin. Fax 699-2907
Richland Two Child Development Center PK-PK
2621 Clemson Rd Ste A 29229 803-699-2536
Quinne Evans, prin. Fax 699-2695
Sandlapper ES 600/K-5
1001 Longtown Rd 29229 803-691-4045
Linda Hall, prin. Fax 691-2681
Summit Parkway MS 900/6-8
200 Summit Pkwy 29229 803-699-3580
April Shell, prin. Fax 699-3682
Windsor ES 700/PK-5
9800 Dunbarton Dr 29223 803-736-8723
Beth Elliott, prin. Fax 600-3648
Wright MS 1,100/6-8
2740 Alpine Rd 29223 803-736-8740
Malinda Taylor, prin. Fax 736-8798
Other Schools – See Blythewood, Elgin

SD Five of Lexington & Richland Counties
Supt. — See Irmo
CrossRoads IS 900/6-6
6949 Saint Andrews Rd 29212 803-476-8300
Jess Hutchinson, prin. Fax 476-8320
Harbison West ES 500/PK-5
257 Crossbow Dr 29212 803-476-3800
Edward Davis, prin. Fax 476-3820
Irmo MS 900/6-8
6051 Wescott Rd 29212 803-476-3600
Cassandra Paschal, prin. Fax 476-3620
Leaphart ES 500/PK-5
120 Piney Grove Rd 29210 803-476-4700
Courtney Long, prin. Fax 476-4720
Nursery Road ES 500/PK-5
6706 Nursery Rd 29212 803-476-4300
Love Ligons, prin. Fax 476-4320
Seven Oaks ES 500/PK-5
2800 Ashland Rd 29210 803-476-8500
Gina Mays, prin. Fax 476-8520

Center for Learning 100/PK-5
2729 Covenant Rd 29204 803-254-0068
Covenant Classical Christian S 100/K-12
3120 Covenant Rd 29204 803-787-0225
Kevin Bolen, admin. Fax 782-7309
Hammond S 900/PK-12
854 Galway Ln 29209 803-776-0295
Christopher Angel, prin. Fax 776-0122
Heathwood Hall Episcopal S 500/PK-12
3000 S Beltline Blvd 29201 803-765-2309
Chris Hinchey, head sch Fax 748-4755
Lippen ES 100/PK-5
500 Saint Andrews Rd 29210 803-807-4400
Tony Fajardo, hdmstr. Fax 807-4399
Lippen S 500/PK-12
7401 Monticello Rd 29203 803-807-4100
Tony Fajardo, hdmstr. Fax 744-1387
Montessori S of Columbia 100/PK-6
411 S Maple St 29205 803-783-8838
Karen Kuse, head sch
St. John Neumann S 400/PK-6
721 Polo Rd 29223 803-788-1367
Ron Poles, prin. Fax 788-7330
St. Joseph S 300/PK-6
3700 Devine St 29205 803-254-6736
Donavan Yarnall, prin. Fax 540-1913
St. Martin de Porres S 100/PK-6
2225 Hampton St 29204 803-254-5477
Sr. Roberta Fulton, prin. Fax 254-7335
St. Peter S 100/PK-6
1035 Hampton St 29201 803-252-8285
Kathy Preston, prin. Fax 254-4736
Timmerman S 300/K-8
2219 Atascadero Dr 29206 803-782-2748

Conway, Horry, Pop. 16,872
Horry County SD 41,200/PK-12
PO Box 260005 29528 843-488-6700
Dr. Rick Maxey, supt. Fax 488-6722
www.horrycountyschools.net
Black Water MS 800/6-8
900 E Cox Ferry Rd 29526 843-903-8440
Candace Lane, prin. Fax 903-8441
Conway ES 600/PK-5
1101 Snowhill Dr 29526 843-488-0696
Maquitta Davis, prin. Fax 488-0656
Conway MS 600/6-8
1104 Elm St 29526 843-488-6040
Regina Treadwell-Pertell, prin. Fax 488-0611
Homewood ES 600/PK-5
108 N Clemson Cir 29526 843-365-2512
Penny Foye, prin. Fax 365-7211
Kingston ES 600/PK-5
4580 Highway 472 29526 843-365-3777
Dr. Dawn Brooks, prin. Fax 365-2764
Pee Dee ES 800/PK-5
6555 Highway 134 29527 843-397-2579
Dr. Angela Huggins, prin. Fax 397-1426

South Conway ES 600/PK-5
3001 4th Ave 29527 843-488-0272
Leon Hayes, prin. Fax 488-0605
Waccamaw ES 800/PK-5
251 Claridy Rd 29526 843-347-4684
Fax 347-0398
Whittemore Park MS 700/6-8
1808 Rhue St 29527 843-488-0669
Quintina Livingston, prin. Fax 488-0665
Other Schools – See Aynor, Galivants Ferry, Garden City, Green Sea, Little River, Loris, Myrtle Beach, North Myrtle Beach

---

Conway Christian S 200/PK-12
PO Box 1245 29528 843-365-2005

Cope, Orangeburg, Pop. 75
Orangeburg County Consolidated SD 4 4,000/PK-12
6030 Slab Landing Rd 29038 803-534-8081
Dr. Tim Newman, supt. Fax 536-4638
www.ocsd4sc.net
Other Schools – See Branchville, Cordova, Neeses, Orangeburg

Cordova, Orangeburg, Pop. 167
Orangeburg County Consolidated SD 4
Supt. — See Cope
Carver-Edisto MS 600/6-8
2018 Carver School Rd, 803-534-3554
Dr. Jeannie Monson, prin. Fax 535-0937
Edisto PS 800/PK-2
3239 Cordova Rd 29039 803-536-4782
Susan Zeigler, prin. Fax 536-1458

Cottageville, Colleton, Pop. 752
Colleton County SD
Supt. — See Walterboro
Cottageville ES 500/PK-5
648 Peirce Rd 29435 843-782-4528
Janis Headden, prin. Fax 835-2095

Coward, Florence, Pop. 742
Florence County SD Three
Supt. — See Lake City
Lynch ES 500/PK-5
PO Box 140 29530 843-389-3323
Matthew Scandrol, prin. Fax 389-3322

Cowpens, Spartanburg, Pop. 2,133
Spartanburg SD 2
Supt. — See Chesnee
Mayo ES 300/K-5
1300 Springdale Rd 29330 864-461-2622
Cassandra Davis, prin. Fax 461-5102

Spartanburg SD 3
Supt. — See Glendale
Cowpens ES 400/PK-5
341 Foster St 29330 864-279-6300
Cindy Snead, prin. Fax 279-6310
Cowpens MS 500/6-8
150 Foster St 29330 864-279-6400
Mathew Davis, prin. Fax 279-6410

Cross, Berkeley
Berkeley County SD
Supt. — See Moncks Corner
Cross ES 400/K-6
1325 Ranger Dr 29436 843-899-8916
Dr. Carolyn Myers-Gillens, prin. Fax 899-8918

Dalzell, Sumter, Pop. 2,975
Sumter SD
Supt. — See Sumter
Hillcrest MS 400/6-8
4355 Peach Orchard Rd 29040 803-499-3341
Tarsha Staggers, prin. Fax 499-3353

Darlington, Darlington, Pop. 6,253
Darlington County SD 10,200/PK-12
PO Box 1117 29540 843-398-5100
Dr. Tim Newman, supt. Fax 398-5198
www.darlington.k12.sc.us
Brockington Magnet ES 400/3-5
413 Brockington Rd 29532 843-398-5095
Stephanie Bridges, prin. Fax 398-2495
Brunson-Dargan ES 200/3-5
400 Wells St 29532 843-398-2533
Ada Sindab, prin. Fax 398-2534
Cain ES 300/PK-2
607 1st St 29532 843-398-2450
Carla Watford, prin. Fax 398-2452
Darlington MS 1,000/6-8
150 Pinedale Dr 29532 843-398-5088
Eddie Shuler, prin. Fax 398-3390
Pate ES 400/PK-2
1010 Indian Branch Rd 29532 843-398-2400
Emily Lunn, prin. Fax 398-2397
St. John's ES 600/PK-5
140 Park St 29532 843-398-2350
Dr. Karen Kinloch, prin. Fax 398-5164
Other Schools – See Hartsville, Lamar, Society Hill

Denmark, Bamberg, Pop. 3,519
Denmark-Olar SD 2 700/PK-12
62 Holly Ave 29042 803-793-3346
Dr. Thelma Sojourner, supt. Fax 793-2006
www.bamberg2.org
Denmark-Olar ES 400/PK-5
1459 Sol Blatt Blvd 29042 803-793-3112
Dr. Lorraine Peeples, prin. Fax 793-2020
Denmark-Olar MS 100/6-8
64 Green St 29042 803-793-3383
Daryl Brockington, prin. Fax 793-2038

Dillon, Dillon, Pop. 6,694
Dillon SD Four 4,100/PK-12
1738 Highway 301 N 29536 843-774-1200
D. Ray Rogers, supt. Fax 774-1203
www.dillon.k12.sc.us

Dillon MS 500/6-8
1803 Joan Dr 29536 843-774-1212
Rodney Cook, prin. Fax 841-3616
East ES 600/PK-3
901 E Harrison St 29536 843-774-1222
Shannon Berry, prin. Fax 841-3881
Gordon ES 500/4-5
926 Perry Ave 29536 843-774-1227
Famon Whitfield, prin. Fax 841-3607
South ES 300/PK-3
900 Patriot St 29536 843-774-1210
Janet Powers-Penuel, prin. Fax 841-3685
Stewart Heights ES 400/PK-3
1001 W Calhoun St 29536 843-774-1219
Dr. Wendy Pace, prin. Fax 841-3689
Other Schools – See Lake View

Dillon Christian S 300/K-12
PO Box 151 29536 843-841-1000

Donalds, Abbeville, Pop. 341
Abbeville County SD
Supt. — See Abbeville
Cherokee Trail ES 400/PK-7
6219 Highway 184 E 29638 864-379-8500
Chester King, prin. Fax 379-8509

Dorchester, Dorchester
Dorchester SD 4
Supt. — See Saint George
Harleyville ES 300/PK-5
1650 E Main St 29437 843-462-7671
Chaquilla Green, prin. Fax 462-7647
Harleyville-Ridgeville MS 200/6-8
1650 E Main St 29437 843-462-2470
Jeffery Thompson, admin. Fax 462-2479

Duncan, Spartanburg, Pop. 3,086
Spartanburg SD 5 7,600/K-12
PO Box 307 29334 864-949-2350
Dr. Scott Turner, supt. Fax 439-0051
www.spart5.net
Abner Creek Academy 500/K-4
2050 Abner Creek Rd 29334 864-949-2334
Karen McMakin, prin. Fax 949-2307
Beech Springs IS 600/5-6
PO Box 411 29334 864-949-7600
Christoper McCants, prin. Fax 949-7604
Berry Shoals IS 600/5-6
300 Shoals Rd 29334 864-949-2300
Mike Powell, prin. Fax 949-2304
Duncan ES 600/K-4
100 S Danzler Rd 29334 864-949-2373
Susan Hill, prin. Fax 949-2374
Florence Chapel MS 600/7-8
290 Shoals Rd 29334 864-949-2310
Tammy White, prin. Fax 949-2315
Other Schools – See Lyman, Moore, Reidville, Wellford

Easley, Pickens, Pop. 19,670
Anderson SD 1
Supt. — See Williamston
Concrete PS 600/PK-2
535 Powdersville Main 29642 864-269-4571
Sherry Padgett, prin. Fax 269-6701
Hunt Meadows ES 400/PK-5
420 Hunt Rd 29642 864-850-3987
Carrie Pennington, prin. Fax 850-3810

Pickens County SD 15,800/K-12
1348 Griffin Mill Rd 29640 864-397-1000
Dr. Danny Merck, supt. Fax 850-5205
www.pickens.k12.sc.us
Crosswell ES 500/K-5
161 School Rd 29640 864-397-1600
Andy Holliday, prin. Fax 855-8161
Dacusville ES 600/K-5
200 Cherokee Trl 29640 864-397-2800
Wanda Tharpe, prin. Fax 850-2090
Dacusville MS 400/6-8
899 Thomas Mill Rd 29640 864-397-3525
Wanda Tharpe, prin. Fax 850-2094
East End ES 700/K-5
505 E 2nd Ave 29640 864-397-1700
Tammy Day, prin. Fax 855-7862
Forest Acres ES 700/K-5
401 McAlister Rd 29642 864-397-1800
Darian Byrd, prin. Fax 855-7867
Gettys MS 1,400/6-8
510 S Pendleton St 29640 864-397-3900
Michael Cory, prin. Fax 855-1268
McKissick ES 400/K-5
156 McKissick Rd 29640 864-397-2200
Gary Mohr, prin. Fax 855-7872
West End ES 700/K-5
314 Pelzer Hwy 29642 864-397-2500
Angie Rodgers, prin. Fax 850-2083
Other Schools – See Central, Clemson, Liberty, Pickens, Six Mile

Eastover, Richland, Pop. 803
Richland SD 1
Supt. — See Columbia
Webber ES 300/PK-5
140 Webber School Rd 29044 803-353-8771
Dr. Sommer Jones, prin. Fax 353-4032

Edgefield, Edgefield, Pop. 4,686
Edgefield County SD
Supt. — See Johnston
Parker ES 500/PK-5
41 Crest Rd 29824 803-637-4020
Gaye Holmes, prin. Fax 637-4058

Edisto Island, Charleston
Charleston County SD
Supt. — See Charleston
Edwards ES 100/PK-5
1960 Jane Edwards Rd 29438 843-559-4171
Susan Miles, prin. Fax 869-0627

Effingham, Florence
Florence County SD One
Supt. — See Florence
Carter ES 800/PK-6
4937 S Irby St 29541 843-664-8479
Wendy Frazier, prin. Fax 673-5771
Savannah Grove ES 700/K-6
2348 Savannah Grove Rd 29541 843-664-8463
David Copeland, prin. Fax 664-8185

Ehrhardt, Bamberg, Pop. 541

Jackson Academy 100/PK-12
7054 Broxton Bridge 29081 803-245-4810

Elgin, Kershaw, Pop. 1,286
Kershaw County SD
Supt. — See Camden
Blaney ES 800/K-5
1621 Smyrna Rd 29045 803-438-3241
Robert Yount, prin. Fax 408-0117
Stover MS 700/6-8
1649 Smyrna Rd 29045 803-438-7414
Mike Garity, prin. Fax 438-7014

Richland SD 2
Supt. — See Columbia
Bookman Road ES 500/PK-5
1245 Bookman Rd 29045 803-699-1724
Dr. Kendra Hill, prin. Fax 699-0892
Bridge Creek ES 600/K-5
121 Bombing Range Rd 29045 803-462-3900
Kristen Eubanks, prin. Fax 462-3901
Catawba Trail ES 500/K-5
1080 Old National Hwy 29045 803-699-3501
Denise Barth, prin. Fax 738-7530
Pontiac ES 700/PK-5
500 Spears Creek Church Rd 29045 803-699-2700
Dr. Katie Barber, prin. Fax 699-2704

Elloree, Orangeburg, Pop. 678
Orangeburg County Consolidated SD 3
Supt. — See Holly Hill
Elloree ES 500/PK-8
200 Warrior St 29047 803-897-2233
Dr. Debora Brunson, prin. Fax 897-2034

Estill, Hampton, Pop. 2,023
Hampton SD 2 900/PK-12
PO Box 1028 29918 803-625-5000
Martin Wright, supt. Fax 625-2573
www.hampton2.k12.sc.us
Estill ES 400/PK-5
PO Box 1028 29918 803-625-5030
Julia Lee, prin. Fax 625-2373
Estill MS 200/6-8
PO Box 817 29918 803-625-5200
Johnnie Miller, prin. Fax 625-3588

Henry Academy 300/PK-12
8766 Savannah Hwy 29918 803-625-2440

Eutawville, Orangeburg, Pop. 313
Orangeburg County Consolidated SD 3
Supt. — See Holly Hill
St. James/Gaillard ES 400/PK-5
1555 Gardensgate Rd 29048 803-854-9213
Loretta Gadson-Washington, prin. Fax 854-5202

Fairfax, Allendale, Pop. 2,023
Allendale County SD 900/PK-12
3249 Allendale Fairfax Hwy 29827 803-584-4603
Dr. Walter Tobin, supt. Fax 584-5303
www.acs.k12.sc.us
Allendale ES 200/3-6
3305 Allendale Fairfax Hwy 29827 803-584-3476
Sheila Leath, prin. Fax 584-5346
Allendale-Fairfax MS 200/7-8
3581 Allendale Fairfax Hwy 29827 803-584-3489
Darlene Hall, prin. Fax 584-5331
Fairfax ES 200/PK-2
734 14th St E 29827 803-632-2536
Fax 632-2822

Florence, Florence, Pop. 36,588
Florence County SD One 17,500/PK-12
319 S Dargan St 29506 843-673-1106
Randy Bridges, supt. Fax 292-1003
www.fsd1.org
Briggs ES 700/K-6
1012 Congaree Dr 29501 843-664-8169
Tara Newton, prin. Fax 664-8189
Carver ES 700/PK-4
515 N Cashua Dr 29501 843-664-8156
Chris Rogers, prin. Fax 664-8177
Child Development Center at Beck 100/PK-PK
1001 W Sumter St 29501 843-673-1129
Dr. Floyd Creech, coord.
Child Development Center at Woods Road PK-PK
1400 Woods Rd 29501 843-799-6006
Dr. Floyd Creech, prin.
Davis ES 600/K-4
200 Westfield Dr 29501 843-665-5977
Sonya Graves, admin. Fax 665-7017
Delmae Heights ES 600/PK-4
1211 S Cashua Dr 29501 843-664-8448
Roy Ann Jolley, prin. Fax 673-5777
Greenwood ES 800/K-6
2300 E Howe Springs Rd 29505 843-664-8451
Dr. Susan Hartwig-Collins, prin. Fax 664-8182
Lester ES 500/PK-6
3501 E Palmetto St 29506 843-664-8459
Janette Williams, prin. Fax 679-6753
McLaurin ES 900/PK-4
1400 McMillan Ln 29506 843-664-8457
Deborah Cribb, prin. Fax 664-8462
Moore MS 800/5-6
191 Westfield Dr 29501 843-664-8171
Carol Schweitz, prin. Fax 664-8188
North Vista ES 700/PK-6
1100 N Irby St 29501 843-664-8159
Sharon Dixon, prin. Fax 679-6752
Royall ES 700/K-6
1101 Cheraw Dr 29501 843-664-8167
Julie Smith, prin. Fax 292-1573
Sneed MS 1,000/7-8
1102 S Ebenezer Rd 29501 843-673-1199
Hayley Cagle, prin. Fax 679-6890
Southside MS 900/7-8
200 E Howe Springs Rd 29505 843-664-8467
Craig Washington, prin. Fax 673-5766
Timrod ES 400/PK-6
1901 E Old Marion Hwy 29506 843-664-8454
Michelle McBride, prin. Fax 664-8180
Wallace-Gregg ES 400/K-6
515 Francis Marion Rd 29506 843-664-8481
Debbie Donnelly, prin. Fax 664-8181
Williams MS 700/7-8
1119 N Irby St 29501 843-664-8162
Pam Johnson, prin. Fax 664-8178
Other Schools – See Effingham

All Saints' Episcopal Day S 300/PK-6
1425 Cherokee Rd 29501 843-662-8134
Florence Christian S 700/PK-12
2308 S Irby St 29505 843-662-0454
King's Academy 300/PK-12
1015 S Ebenezer Rd 29501 843-661-7464
David Wolff, head sch Fax 661-7647
Montessori S of Florence 100/PK-6
510 W Palmetto St 29501 843-629-2920
St. Anthony S 200/PK-8
2536 Hoffmeyer Rd 29501 843-662-1910
Tracy Hamner, prin. Fax 662-5335

Fort Mill, York, Pop. 10,605
Fort Mill SD 11,400/K-12
2233 Deerfield Dr 29715 803-548-2527
James Epps Ph.D., supt. Fax 547-4696
www.fortmillschools.org
Banks Trail MS 500/6-7
1640 Banks Rd 29715 803-578-2990
Mike Pratt, prin. Fax 578-2999
Dobys Bridge ES K-5
1000 Dragon Way 29715 803-835-5200
Jeanette Black, prin. Fax 547-5260
Fort Mill ES 800/K-5
192 Springfield Pkwy 29715 803-547-7546
Jocelyn Young, prin. Fax 547-7559
Fort Mill MS 600/6-8
200 Springfield Pkwy 29715 803-547-5553
Anthony Caricari, prin. Fax 548-2911
Orchard Park ES 900/K-5
474 Third Baxter St 29708 803-548-8170
Matthew Johnson, prin. Fax 548-8174
Pleasant Knoll ES 800/K-5
2346 Pleasant Rd 29708 803-835-0090
Travis Howard, prin. Fax 835-0099
Pleasant Knoll MS 800/6-8
2320 Pleasant Rd 29708 803-835-3721
Grey Young M.Ed., prin.
Riverview ES 600/K-5
1300 Spratt St 29715 803-548-4677
Annette Chinchilla, prin. Fax 548-4747
Springfield ES 700/K-5
1691 Springfield Pkwy 29715 803-548-8150
Peter Olinger, prin. Fax 548-8154
Springfield MS 700/6-8
1711 Springfield Pkwy 29715 803-548-8199
Keith Griffin, prin. Fax 547-1013
Sugar Creek ES 800/K-5
1599 Farmhouse Rd 29715 803-835-0150
Michelle Gritz, prin. Fax 835-0151
Other Schools – See Tega Cay

Fountain Inn, Greenville, Pop. 7,650
Greenville County SD
Supt. — See Greenville
Fountain Inn ES 700/K-5
608 Fairview St 29644 864-355-5100
Anthony Reabold, prin. Fax 355-5164

Gadsden, Richland, Pop. 1,618
Richland SD 1
Supt. — See Columbia
Gadsden ES 100/PK-5
1660 S Goodwin Cir 29052 803-353-2231
David Thorpe, prin. Fax 353-4035

Gaffney, Cherokee, Pop. 12,231
Cherokee County SD 9,100/PK-12
PO Box 460 29342 864-206-2201
Dr. Quincie Moore, supt. Fax 902-3541
www.cherokee1.k12.sc.us
Alma ES 300/PK-5
213 Alma St 29340 864-206-6482
Kim Camp, prin. Fax 902-3595
Bramlett ES 300/PK-5
301 Spruce St 29340 864-206-2520
Johnnette Nesbitt, prin. Fax 487-1236
Corinth ES 400/PK-5
128 Corinth Rd 29340 864-206-6600
Brenda Sharts, prin. Fax 487-7444
Draytonville ES 300/PK-5
2373 Wilkinsville Hwy 29340 864-206-6783
Isaac Wallace, prin. Fax 487-1218
Ewing MS 400/6-8
171 E Junior High Rd 29340 864-206-2449
Dr. Denise Wooten, prin. Fax 489-8534
Gaffney MS 700/6-8
805 E Frederick St 29340 864-206-6129
Dr. Eric Blanton, prin. Fax 902-3637
Goucher ES 300/PK-5
604 Goucher School Rd 29340 864-206-6890
Tanya Roberts, prin. Fax 902-3656
Granard MS 600/6-8
815 W Rutledge Ave 29341 864-206-2302
Dr. Gavin Fisher, prin. Fax 488-1553
Grassy Pond ES 500/PK-5
1146 Boiling Springs Hwy 29341 864-206-6671
Erik Gerstenacker, prin. Fax 487-1255
Lee ES 300/PK-5
401 Overbrook Dr 29341 864-206-6432
Sharon Jefferies, prin. Fax 902-3642
Limestone-Central ES 400/PK-5
727 Pacolet Hwy 29340 864-206-6620
Dr. Bryan Hullender, prin. Fax 487-1251
Northwest ES 500/PK-5
840 Green River Rd 29341 864-206-6727
Kathy Phillips, prin. Fax 487-1245
Vaughan ES 400/PK-5
192 Vaughn Rd 29341 864-206-6054
Janice Keller, prin. Fax 487-1253
Other Schools – See Blacksburg

Galivants Ferry, Horry
Horry County SD
Supt. — See Conway
Aynor MS 600/6-8
400 Frye Rd 29544 843-358-6000
Robbie Watkins, prin. Fax 358-5065
Midland ES 500/PK-5
3011 Nichols Hwy 29544 843-358-3036
Jennifer Parker, prin. Fax 358-0643

Garden City, Horry, Pop. 9,065
Horry County SD
Supt. — See Conway
Seaside ES 700/PK-5
1605 Woodland Drive Ext 29576 843-650-3490
Kristin Dowling, prin. Fax 650-3479

Gaston, Lexington, Pop. 1,599
Lexington County SD 4
Supt. — See Swansea
Mack IS 500/5-6
161 Gaston St 29053 803-490-7004
Sara Ankrapp, prin. Fax 399-7964
Sandhills MS 500/7-8
582 Meadowfield Rd 29053 803-490-7005
Patricia Carter, prin. Fax 399-7965

Georgetown, Georgetown, Pop. 9,055
Georgetown County SD 9,700/PK-12
2018 Church St 29440 843-436-7000
Dr. Randy Dozier, supt. Fax 436-7171
www.gcsd.k12.sc.us
Browns Ferry ES 200/PK-5
7292 Browns Ferry Rd 29440 843-527-1325
Kimberly Nesmith, prin. Fax 546-2138
Georgetown MS 900/6-8
2400 Anthuan Maybank St 29440 843-527-4495
Seth Hillman, prin. Fax 527-2290
Kensington ES 700/PK-5
86 Kensington Blvd 29440 843-546-8511
Maurice Cobb, prin. Fax 546-0605
Maryville ES 500/PK-5
2125 Poplar St 29440 843-546-8423
Stephanie Stuckey, prin. Fax 546-5038
McDonald ES 500/PK-5
532 McDonald Rd 29440 843-527-3485
Mack Burgess, prin. Fax 546-8674
Plantersville ES 100/PK-5
1668 Exodus Dr 29440 843-546-8453
Darryl Stanley, prin. Fax 527-2869
Sampit ES 400/PK-5
69 Woodland Ave 29440 843-527-4411
Sabrina Goff-Mack, prin. Fax 546-1226
Other Schools – See Andrews, Hemingway, Pawleys Island

Gilbert, Lexington, Pop. 564
Lexington County SD 1
Supt. — See Lexington
Gilbert ES 700/3-5
314 Main St 29054 803-821-1600
Preston Branham, prin. Fax 821-1603
Gilbert MS 700/6-8
120 Rikard Cir 29054 803-821-1700
Dr. Benji Ricard, prin. Fax 821-1703
Gilbert PS 700/K-2
520 Main St 29054 803-821-1400
Mylissa Apperson, prin. Fax 821-1403

Glendale, Spartanburg, Pop. 305
Spartanburg SD 3 2,900/PK-12
PO Box 267 29346 864-279-6000
Kenny Blackwood, supt. Fax 279-6010
www.spartanburg3.org
Other Schools – See Cowpens, Pacolet, Spartanburg

Gloverville, Aiken, Pop. 2,756
Aiken County SD
Supt. — See Aiken
Gloverville ES 300/K-5
114 Gloria Rush Cir 29828 803-593-7280
Dr. Mendi Tucker, prin. Fax 593-7281

Goose Creek, Berkeley, Pop. 34,642
Berkeley County SD
Supt. — See Moncks Corner
Boulder Bluff ES 800/PK-5
400 Judy Dr 29445 843-553-1223
Andrea Salters, prin. Fax 820-4086
Devon Forest ES 900/PK-5
1127 Dorothy St 29445 843-820-3880
Cristie Mitchum, prin. Fax 820-3883
Goose Creek PS 1,100/PK-2
200 Foster Creek Rd 29445 843-820-8008
Kathy Sullivan, prin. Fax 820-8016
Howe Hall Arts Infused Magnet S 400/K-5
115 Howe Hall Rd 29445 843-820-3899
Chris Swetckie, prin. Fax 820-5428

Marrington ES 500/PK-5
101 Gearing St 29445 843-572-3373
Jennifer Thielmann, prin. Fax 820-5429
Marrington MS of the Arts 400/6-8
109 Gearing St 29445 843-572-0313
Dara Harrop, prin. Fax 820-4063
Sedgefield IS 800/3-5
225 Garwood Dr 29445 843-820-4090
Dr. Creighton Eddings, prin. Fax 820-5433
Sedgefield MS 1,000/6-8
131 Charles B Gibson Blvd 29445 843-797-2620
Rebecca Davis, prin. Fax 820-5401
Westview ES 600/3-5
100 Westview Dr 29445 843-797-2992
Aimee Fulmer, prin. Fax 820-4012
Westview MS 900/6-8
101 Westview Dr 29445 843-572-1700
Sharon Perry M.Ed., prin. Fax 820-3728
Westview PS 600/PK-3
98 Westview Dr 29445 843-820-4082
Dr. Luci Carter, prin. Fax 820-4078

Graniteville, Aiken, Pop. 2,553
Aiken County SD
Supt. — See Aiken
Byrd ES 700/K-5
1225 Weldon Way 29829 803-663-4320
Ranae Enlow, prin. Fax 663-4321
Leavelle-McCampbell MS 500/6-8
1120 Weldon Way 29829 803-663-4300
Michelle Padgett, prin. Fax 663-4302

Gray Court, Laurens, Pop. 784
Laurens SD 55
Supt. — See Laurens
Gray Court - Owings S 600/PK-8
PO Box 128 29645 864-876-2131
Phillip Dean, prin. Fax 876-9597
Hickory Tavern S 400/PK-8
163 Neely Ferry Rd 29645 864-575-2126
Tina Faulkner, prin. Fax 575-3428

Great Falls, Chester, Pop. 1,942
Chester County SD
Supt. — See Chester
Great Falls ES 400/PK-5
301 Dearborn St 29055 803-482-2214
Tammy Taylor, prin. Fax 482-6800
Great Falls MS 200/6-8
409 Sunset Ave 29055 803-482-2220
Glenda Brunson, prin. Fax 482-6025

Greeleyville, Williamsburg, Pop. 428
Williamsburg County SD
Supt. — See Kingstree
Greeleyville ES 300/PK-5
7 Varner Ave 29056 843-426-2116
Berlinda Mack, prin. Fax 355-3213
Murray MS 100/6-8
222A C E Murray Blvd 29056 843-426-2121
Tamekia Morant, prin. Fax 355-3213

Green Sea, Horry
Horry County SD
Supt. — See Conway
Green Sea-Floyds ES 600/PK-5
5000 Tulip Grove Rd 29545 843-392-1078
Melissa Gause, prin. Fax 392-1090

Greenville, Greenville, Pop. 57,469
Anderson SD 1
Supt. — See Williamston
Powdersville ES 500/3-5
139 Hood Rd 29611 864-269-4431
Brad Moore, prin. Fax 269-4426
Powdersville MS 600/6-8
135 Hood Rd 29611 864-269-1821
Todd Binnicker, prin. Fax 269-0795

Greenville County SD 75,900/PK-12
PO Box 2848 29602 864-355-3100
W. Burke Royster, supt. Fax 241-4195
www.greenville.k12.sc.us
Alexander ES 400/K-5
1601 W Bramlett Rd 29611 864-355-1000
Dr. Sonya Campbell, prin. Fax 355-1044
Armstrong ES 400/K-5
8601 White Horse Rd 29617 864-355-1100
Tracy Atkins, prin. Fax 355-1158
Augusta Circle ES 500/K-5
100 Winyah St 29605 864-355-1200
Kerry Bannister, prin. Fax 355-1212
Beck Academy 1,100/6-8
901 Woodruff Rd 29607 864-355-1400
Jennifer Meisten, prin. Fax 355-1490
Berea ES 400/K-5
100 Berea Dr 29617 864-355-1500
Thomas Miller, prin. Fax 355-1558
Berea MS 700/6-8
151 Berea Middle School Rd 29617 864-355-1700
Robin Mill, prin. Fax 355-1777
Blythe Academy of Languages 800/K-5
100 Blythe Dr 29605 864-355-4400
Dr. Sandra Griffin, prin. Fax 355-4412
Cashion ES 700/K-5
1500 Fork Shoals Rd 29605 864-355-8000
Ryan Streetman, prin. Fax 355-8021
Cherrydale ES 500/K-5
302 Perry Rd 29609 864-355-3300
Debra Johnson, prin. Fax 355-3361
Collins ES 900/K-5
1200 Parkins Mill Rd 29607 864-355-3200
Dr. Melissa Burns, prin. Fax 355-3293
Duncan Chapel ES 600/K-5
210 Duncan Chapel Rd 29617 864-355-2700
Dr. Stephanie Lowry, prin. Fax 355-2769
East North Street Academy 600/K-5
1720 E North St 29607 864-355-2900
Dr. Dawn Hooker, prin. Fax 355-2980
Fisher MS 6-8
700 Millennium Blvd 29607 864-452-0800
Jane Garraux, prin. Fax 452-0890
Greenbrier ES 700/K-5
853 Log Shoals Rd 29607 864-355-5300
Lekeisha Brown, prin. Fax 355-5327
Greenview Child Development Center PK-K
625 Old Piedmont Hwy 29605 864-452-0400
Amanda Lecaroz, prin. Fax 452-0448
Greenville Middle Academy 800/6-8
339 Lowndes Ave 29607 864-355-5600
Nicky Andrews, prin. Fax 355-5682
Hollis Academy 600/K-5
200 Goodrich St 29611 864-355-4800
Miki Golden, prin. Fax 355-4826
Hughes Academy 900/6-8
122 Deoyley Ave 29605 864-355-6200
Jordan Finlay, prin. Fax 355-6275
Kerns ES 600/K-5
6650 Frontage Rd 29605 864-355-1300
Mark Adams, prin. Fax 355-1351
Lake Forest ES 800/K-5
16 Berkshire Ave 29615 864-355-4000
Julie Cooke, prin. Fax 355-4072
Lakeview MS 500/6-8
3801 Old Buncombe Rd 29617 864-355-6400
LaTonya Copeland, prin. Fax 355-6416
League Academy 800/6-8
125 Twin Lake Rd 29609 864-355-8100
Mary Leslie Anderson, prin. Fax 355-8160
Mitchell Road ES 500/K-5
4124 E North St 29615 864-355-6700
Amy Kern, prin. Fax 355-6719
Monaview ES 500/K-5
10 Monaview St 29617 864-355-4300
Damon Qualls, prin. Fax 355-4314
Northwest Crescent Child Development Ctr PK-K
925 N Franklin Rd 29617 864-355-4080
Amanda Lecaroz, prin. Fax 355-4097
Overbrook Child Development Center 800/K-K
111 Laurens Rd 29607 864-355-7350
Amanda Lecaroz, prin. Fax 355-7373
Pelham Road ES 700/K-5
100 All Star Way 29615 864-355-7600
Kristy Qualls, prin. Fax 355-7658
Sevier MS 700/6-8
1000 Piedmont Park Rd 29609 864-355-8200
Chad Maguire, prin. Fax 355-8255
Sterling S 800/K-8
99 John McCarroll Way 29607 864-355-4480
Dr. Josh Patterson, prin. Fax 355-4490
Stone Academy 600/K-5
115 Randall St 29609 864-355-8400
Brett Vaughn, prin. Fax 355-8455
Summit Drive ES 500/K-5
424 Summit Dr 29609 864-355-8800
Dr. Kelly Hellams, prin. Fax 355-8817
Tanglewood MS 600/6-8
44 Merriwoods Dr 29611 864-355-4500
Dr. Edward Anderson, prin. Fax 355-4512
Welcome ES 700/K-5
36 E Welcome Rd 29611 864-355-3900
Donna Ketron, prin. Fax 355-3961
Westcliffe ES 300/K-5
105 Eastbourne Rd 29611 864-355-0300
Carolyn Morgan, prin. Fax 355-0360
Whittenberg ES of Engineering 500/K-5
420 Westfield St 29601 864-452-0500
Dr. Susan Stevens, prin. Fax 452-0515
Other Schools – See Fountain Inn, Greer, Marietta, Pelzer, Piedmont, Simpsonville, Taylors, Travelers Rest

Bridgeway Christian Academy 200/PK-8
724 Garlington Rd 29615 864-297-6646
Kimberly Reeve, prin. Fax 627-1101
Christ Church Episcopal S 1,000/K-12
245 Cavalier Dr 29607 864-299-1522
Dr. Leonard Kupersmith, hdmstr. Fax 299-8861
Hampton Park Christian S 500/PK-12
875 State Park Rd 29609 864-233-0556
Jones Academy 1,300/PK-12
1700 Wade Hampton Blvd 29614 864-770-1395
Dr. Dan Nelson, admin. Fax 271-7278
Mitchell Road Christian Academy 400/PK-8
207 Mitchell Rd 29615 864-268-2210
Patrick Beaudine, head sch Fax 268-3184
Montessori S of Greenville 100/PK-3
305 Pelham Rd 29615 864-232-3447
Our Lady of the Rosary S 100/PK-8
2 James Dr 29605 864-277-5350
Thomas Curtin, prin. Fax 277-7745
St. Anthony of Padua S 100/PK-6
311 Gower St 29611 864-271-0167
Janie Harris, prin. Fax 271-2936
St. Mary S 300/PK-8
101 Hampton Ave 29601 864-271-3870
Steven Zimmerman, prin. Fax 271-0159
Shannon Forest Christian S 400/PK-12
829 Garlington Rd 29615 864-678-5107
Craig Bouvier, head sch Fax 281-9372

Greenwood, Greenwood, Pop. 22,959
Greenwood SD 50 9,200/PK-12
PO Box 248 29648 864-941-5400
Dr. Darrell Johnson, supt. Fax 941-5427
www.gwd50.org
Brewer MS 700/6-8
1000 Emerald Rd 29646 864-941-5500
Kathryn Benjamin, prin. Fax 941-5527
Greenwood ECC 400/PK-PK
1125 Cambridge Ave E 29646 864-941-5520
Ginny Metts, dir. Fax 941-3497
Lakeview ES 600/PK-5
660 Center St 29649 864-941-5760
Dr. Molly Smith, prin. Fax 941-3498
Mathews ES 600/K-5
725 Marshall Rd 29646 864-941-5680
Andrea Fulmer, prin. Fax 941-3496
Merrywood ES 500/K-5
329 Deadfall Rd W 29649 864-941-5700
Julian Gale, prin. Fax 388-2400
Northside MS 700/6-8
431 Deadfall Rd W 29649 864-941-5780
Cyndi Storer, prin. Fax 941-3434
Pinecrest ES 500/K-5
220 Northside Dr E 29649 864-941-5580
Susan Buchanan, prin. Fax 229-5284
Rice ES 500/PK-5
1802 Durst Ave E 29649 864-941-5660
Carlos Littlejohn, prin. Fax 388-2401
Springfield ES 600/K-5
1608 Florida Ave 29646 864-941-5535
Patrick Gardner, prin. Fax 388-2402
Westview MS 700/6-8
1410 W Alexander Rd 29646 864-229-4301
Dr. Steve Glenn, prin. Fax 229-4827
Woodfields ES 600/K-5
1032 Emerald Rd 29646 864-941-5540
Travis Blizzard, prin. Fax 388-7887
Other Schools – See Hodges

Cambridge Academy 100/PK-12
103 Eastman St 29649 864-229-2875
Greenwood Christian S 300/PK-12
2026 Woodlawn Rd 29649 864-229-2427
Palmetto Christian Academy of Greenwood 100/PK-12
308 Deadfall Rd W 29649 864-223-0391
David Douglas, head sch Fax 396-5316

Greer, Greenville, Pop. 25,060
Greenville County SD
Supt. — See Greenville
Blue Ridge MS 1,000/6-8
2423 E Tyger Bridge Rd 29651 864-355-1900
Rebecca Greene, prin. Fax 355-1966
Buena Vista ES 800/K-5
310 S Batesville Rd 29650 864-355-2200
David Burgess, prin. Fax 355-2214
Chandler Creek ES 900/K-5
301 Chandler Rd 29651 864-355-2400
Jane Mills, prin. Fax 355-2420
Crestview ES 600/K-5
509 American Legion Rd 29651 864-355-2600
David Langston, prin. Fax 355-2613
Dunbar Child Development Center PK-PK
200 Morgan St 29651 864-355-2270
Amanda Lecaroz, prin. Fax 355-2295
Greer MS 1,000/6-8
3032 E Gap Creek Rd 29651 864-355-5800
Daniel Bruce, prin. Fax 355-5880
Riverside MS 1,200/6-8
615 Hammett Bridge Rd 29650 864-355-7900
Kate Malone, prin. Fax 355-7918
Skyland ES 700/K-7
4221 N Highway 14 29651 864-355-7200
Dr. Carolyn Styles, prin. Fax 355-7215
Woodland ES 1,100/K-5
1730 Gibbs Shoals Rd 29650 864-355-0400
Katrina Miller, prin. Fax 355-0477

As-Sabeel Academy 100/PK-8
1601 Clement Rd 29650 864-674-7456

Gresham, Marion
Marion County SD
Supt. — See Marion
Brittons Neck ES 300/PK-5
223 Gresham Rd 29546 843-362-3510
Monica Kimbrough, prin. Fax 362-3519

Hampton, Hampton, Pop. 2,776
Hampton SD 1
Supt. — See Varnville
Hampton ES 400/4-6
505 Hoover St S 29924 803-943-3251
Cassandra Williams, prin. Fax 943-4128
Hazel PS 200/K-3
628 Railroad Ave W 29924 803-943-3659
Brandy Noll, prin. Fax 943-0532

Hanahan, Berkeley, Pop. 17,513
Berkeley County SD
Supt. — See Moncks Corner
Hanahan ES 1,100/PK-4
4000 Mabeline Rd 29410 843-553-3290
Tom Sparkman, prin. Fax 820-5421
Hanahan MS 900/5-8
5815 Murray Dr 29410 843-820-3800
Robin Rogers, prin. Fax 820-3804

Divine Redeemer S 100/PK-8
1104 Fort Dr 29410 843-553-1521
Paulette Walker, prin. Fax 553-7109

Hardeeville, Jasper, Pop. 2,902
Jasper County SD
Supt. — See Ridgeland
Hardeeville ES 600/PK-5
150 Hurricane Vly 29927 843-310-1888
Wanda McAllister, prin. Fax 784-2165
Hardeeville-Ridgeland MS 300/6-8
150 Hurricane Vly 29927 843-310-1898
Senaca Baines, prin. Fax 784-2167

Hartsville, Darlington, Pop. 7,682
Darlington County SD
Supt. — See Darlington
Carolina ES 300/1-5
719 W Carolina Ave 29550 843-383-3230
Donna Barrett, prin. Fax 857-3232
Hartsville MS 1,200/6-8
1427 14th St 29550 843-857-3000
Brian Hickman, prin. Fax 857-4510

North Hartsville ES 700/1-5
110 School Dr 29550 843-857-3200
Kristi Austin, prin. Fax 857-3190
Southside ECC 300/PK-K
1615 Blanding Dr 29550 843-383-3310
Patricia Toney, prin. Fax 857-3315
Thornwell ES for the Arts 400/1-5
437 W Carolina Ave 29550 843-383-3090
Dr. Lilkenya Jenkins, prin. Fax 383-6043
Washington Street ES 300/PK-3
325 W Washington St 29550 843-383-3141
Valerie Sawyer, prin. Fax 857-3351
West Hartsville ES 200/4-5
214 Clyde Rd 29550 843-383-3270
Julie Mahn, prin. Fax 857-3272

Hart Academy 200/PK-8
852 Flinns Rd 29550 843-332-4991

Heath Springs, Lancaster, Pop. 777
Lancaster County SD
Supt. — See Lancaster
Heath Springs ES 400/PK-5
158 Solar Rd 29058 803-273-3176
Sheri Watson, prin. Fax 273-3717

Hemingway, Williamsburg, Pop. 449
Georgetown County SD
Supt. — See Georgetown
Carvers Bay MS 300/6-8
13000 Choppee Rd 29554 843-545-0918
Comeletia Pyatt, prin. Fax 558-6937
Pleasant Hill ES 400/PK-5
127 Schoolhouse Dr 29554 843-558-9417
Teddy Graham, prin. Fax 558-7017

Williamsburg County SD
Supt. — See Kingstree
Hemingway ES 600/PK-5
160 Baxley Rd 29554 843-558-4444
Shaunta Mack, prin. Fax 355-3213
Hemingway M.B. Lee MS 200/6-8
400 S Main St 29554 843-558-2721
Bonita Glover, prin. Fax 355-3213

Hickory Grove, York, Pop. 429
York SD 1
Supt. — See York
Hickory Grove-Sharon ES 400/PK-6
4901 Hickory Grove Rd 29717 803-925-2116
Becky Dover, prin. Fax 925-2218

Hilton Head Island, Beaufort, Pop. 36,811
Beaufort County SD
Supt. — See Beaufort
Hilton Head Island ECC 500/PK-K
165 Pembroke Dr 29926 843-689-0400
Kim Bratt, prin. Fax 689-0552
Hilton Head Island ES 900/1-5
30 School Rd 29926 843-342-4100
Sarah Owens, prin. Fax 342-4299
Hilton Head Island MS 1,000/6-8
55 Wilborn Rd 29926 843-689-4500
Neodria Brown, prin. Fax 689-4600
Hilton Head Island S for Creative Arts 800/PK-5
10 Bus Dr 29926 843-342-4380
Gretchen Keefner, prin. Fax 689-7455

Hilton Head Christian Academy 400/PK-12
55 Gardner Dr 29926 843-681-2878
Hilton Head Preparatory S 400/PK-12
8 Fox Grape Rd 29928 843-671-2286
Jon Hopman, hdmstr. Fax 671-7624
St. Francis Catholic S 200/PK-8
45 Beach City Rd 29926 843-681-6501
Brian Pope, prin. Fax 689-3725
Sea Pines Montessori Academy 200/PK-8
9 Fox Grape Rd 29928 843-785-2534

Hodges, Greenwood, Pop. 152
Greenwood SD 50
Supt. — See Greenwood
Hodges ES 300/K-5
4717 Main St 29653 864-374-5000
Lori Corley, prin. Fax 374-5028

Holly Hill, Orangeburg, Pop. 1,261
Orangeburg County Consolidated SD 3 3,000/PK-12
1654 Camden Rd 29059 803-496-3288
Fax 496-5850
www.obg3.k12.sc.us
Holly Hill ES 500/PK-5
1490 Brant Ave 29059 803-496-3464
Sharon Wilson, prin. Fax 496-3526
Holly Hill-Roberts MS 500/6-8
530 Hesseman Ave 29059 803-496-3818
Robert Hemby, prin. Fax 496-9765
Other Schools – See Elloree, Eutawville, Vance

Holly Hill Academy 300/K-12
PO Box 757 29059 803-496-3243

Hollywood, Charleston, Pop. 4,680
Charleston County SD
Supt. — See Charleston
Hughes ES 200/PK-5
8548 Willtown Rd 29449 843-889-2976
Bridget Berry, prin. Fax 889-6758

Honea Path, Anderson, Pop. 3,518
Anderson SD 2 3,600/PK-12
10990 Belton Honea Path Hwy 29654 864-369-7364
Dr. Richard Rosenberger, supt. Fax 369-4006
www.anderson2.org
Honea Path ES 500/PK-5
806 E Greer St 29654 864-369-7612
Jeremy Sauceman, prin. Fax 369-4030
Honea Path MS 300/6-8
107 Brock Ave 29654 864-369-7641
Matthew Schult, prin. Fax 369-4034
Other Schools – See Belton

Hopkins, Richland, Pop. 2,838
Richland SD 1
Supt. — See Columbia
Hopkins ES 400/PK-5
6120 Cabin Creek Rd 29061 803-783-5541
Debora Varn, prin. Fax 783-5569
Hopkins MS 500/6-8
1601 Clarkson Rd 29061 803-695-3331
Bobbie Hartwell, prin. Fax 695-3320
Horrell Hill ES 600/PK-5
517 Horrell Hill Rd 29061 803-783-5545
Parthenia Satterwhite, prin. Fax 783-5593
Southeast MS 500/6-8
731 Horrell Hill Rd 29061 803-695-5700
Inger Ferguson, prin. Fax 695-5703

Huger, Berkeley
Berkeley County SD
Supt. — See Moncks Corner
Cainhoy S 300/K-8
2434 Cainhoy Rd 29450 843-899-8975
Aidra Shaw, prin. Fax 899-8970

Indian Land, Lancaster
Lancaster County SD
Supt. — See Lancaster
Harrisburg ES K-5
10251 Harrisburg Rd, 803-396-3737
Steven Puckett, prin. Fax 396-3761
Indian Land ES 1,500/K-5
4137 Dobys Bridge Rd, 803-548-2916
Elizabeth Blum, prin. Fax 548-3011
Indian Land MS 700/6-8
8361 Charlotte Hwy, 803-578-2500
Chris Thorpe, prin. Fax 578-2549

Inman, Spartanburg, Pop. 2,273
Spartanburg SD 1
Supt. — See Campobello
Inman ES 500/PK-3
25 Oakland Ave 29349 864-472-8403
John Hodge, prin. Fax 472-7839
Inman IS 300/4-6
10 W Miller St 29349 864-472-1510
Karen Bush, prin. Fax 472-1511
Mabry MS 400/7-8
35 Oakland Ave 29349 864-472-8402
Shelley Brown, prin. Fax 472-7438
New Prospect ES 400/PK-6
9251 Highway 9 29349 864-592-1970
Shameka Dawkins, prin. Fax 592-2010

Spartanburg SD 2
Supt. — See Chesnee
Boiling Springs MS 1,100/6-8
4801 Highway 9 29349 864-578-5954
Penny Atkinson, prin. Fax 599-5489
Oakland ES 600/K-4
151 Mudd Creek Rd 29349 864-814-3870
Lora McKillop, prin. Fax 814-3806

Irmo, Richland, Pop. 10,848
SD Five of Lexington & Richland Counties 16,300/PK-12
1020 Dutch Fork Rd 29063 803-476-8000
Dr. Stephen Hefner, supt. Fax 476-8217
www.lexrich5.org
Ballentine ES 700/PK-5
1040 Bickley Rd 29063 803-476-4500
Robin Bright, prin. Fax 475-4520
Corley ES 500/PK-5
1500 Chadford Rd 29063 803-476-4001
Dr. Jason Pollock, prin. Fax 476-4020
Dutch Fork ES 500/PK-5
7900 Broad River Rd 29063 803-476-3900
Julius Scott, prin. Fax 476-3920
Dutch Fork MS 1,100/6-8
1528 Old Tamah Rd 29063 803-476-4800
Vernon Sava, prin. Fax 476-4820
Irmo ES 500/K-5
7401 Gibbes St 29063 803-476-4200
Tina McCaskill, prin. Fax 476-4220
Oak Pointe ES 600/PK-5
1 River Bottom Rd 29063 803-476-4100
Kristie Smith, prin. Fax 476-4120
River Springs ES 600/PK-5
115 Connie Wright Rd 29063 803-476-4400
Melanie Cohen, prin. Fax 476-4420
Other Schools – See Chapin, Columbia

Iva, Anderson, Pop. 1,209
Anderson SD 3 2,600/PK-12
PO Box 118 29655 864-348-6196
Kathy Hipp, supt. Fax 348-6198
www.anderson3.k12.sc.us
Iva ES 400/PK-5
803 Antreville Hwy 29655 864-348-6400
Eric Hughes, prin. Fax 348-7071
Other Schools – See Anderson, Starr

Jackson, Aiken, Pop. 1,680
Aiken County SD
Supt. — See Aiken
Jackson STEM MS 300/6-8
18731 Atomic Rd 29831 803-279-3525
Perry Smith, prin. Fax 471-2202

Jefferson, Chesterfield, Pop. 722
Chesterfield County SD
Supt. — See Chesterfield
Jefferson ES 400/PK-5
809 W Elizabeth 29718 843-658-3295
Omoro King, prin. Fax 658-3309
New Heights MS 500/6-8
5738 Highway 151 29718 843-658-6830
Dr. Nikki Miller, prin. Fax 658-6812

Joanna, Laurens, Pop. 1,529
Laurens County SD 56
Supt. — See Clinton
Joanna-Woodson ES 300/K-5
510 S Ellis St 29351 864-697-6480
George Marshall, prin. Fax 697-4302

Johns Island, Charleston
Charleston County SD
Supt. — See Charleston
Angel Oak ES 400/PK-5
6134 Chisolm Rd 29455 843-559-6412
Judith Condon, prin. Fax 559-6415
Haut Gap MS 500/5-8
1861 Bohicket Rd 29455 843-559-6418
Travis Benintendo, prin. Fax 559-6439
Mt. Zion ES 300/PK-5
3464 River Rd 29455 843-559-3841
Deborah Fordham, prin. Fax 559-6440

Charleston Collegiate S 200/PK-12
2024 Academy Rd 29455 843-559-5506
Hacker Burr, head sch Fax 559-6172

Johnsonville, Florence, Pop. 1,455
Florence County SD Five 1,400/PK-12
PO Box 98 29555 843-386-2358
Randy Smiley, supt. Fax 386-3139
www.flo5.k12.sc.us
Johnsonville ES 600/PK-4
160 E Marion St 29555 843-386-2955
Dayne Coker, prin. Fax 386-3574
Johnsonville MS 400/5-8
PO Box 67 29555 843-386-2066
Randy Willis, prin. Fax 386-3786

Johnston, Edgefield, Pop. 2,346
Edgefield County SD 3,800/PK-12
3 Par Dr 29832 803-275-4601
Dr. Robert Maddox, supt. Fax 275-1795
www.edgefield.k12.sc.us
JET MS 500/6-8
1095 Columbia Rd 29832 803-275-1997
Debbie Courtney, prin. Fax 275-1783
Johnston ES 300/PK-5
514 Lee St 29832 803-275-1755
Tammy Martin, prin. Fax 275-1785
Other Schools – See Edgefield, North Augusta, Trenton

Wardlaw Academy 200/PK-12
1296 Columbia Rd 29832 803-275-4794

Jonesville, Union, Pop. 901
Union County SD
Supt. — See Union
Jonesville ES 300/K-8
350 New Hope Church Rd 29353 864-674-5518
Kathy Taylor, prin. Fax 674-1890

Kershaw, Lancaster, Pop. 1,779
Kershaw County SD
Supt. — See Camden
Mt. Pisgah ES 100/K-5
5160 Mount Pisgah Rd 29067 803-475-6791
Britt Gardner, prin. Fax 475-0602
North Central MS 400/6-8
805 Keys Ln 29067 803-424-2740
Dr. Burch Richardson Ed.D., prin. Fax 424-2742

Lancaster County SD
Supt. — See Lancaster
Jackson MS 500/6-8
6865 Kershaw Camden Hwy 29067 803-475-6021
Daryl Hinson, prin. Fax 475-8256
Kershaw ES 400/PK-5
108 N Rollins Dr 29067 803-475-6655
Kelli Farmer, prin. Fax 475-5784

Kingstree, Williamsburg, Pop. 3,310
Williamsburg County SD 3,900/PK-12
PO Box 1067 29556 843-355-5571
Carrie Brock, supt. Fax 355-3213
www.wcsd.k12.sc.us
Anderson PS 500/PK-2
500 Lexington Ave 29556 843-355-5493
Cynthia Brown, prin. Fax 355-3213
Gardner ES 400/3-5
1503 Woodland Dr 29556 843-355-7233
Myron Davis, prin. Fax 355-3213
Kingstree Middle Magnet S 500/6-8
710 3rd Ave 29556 843-355-1506
James Carraway, prin. Fax 355-3213
Other Schools – See Greeleyville, Hemingway

Williamsburg Academy 400/PK-12
1000 Sandy Bay Rd 29556 843-355-9400

Ladson, Berkeley, Pop. 13,352
Berkeley County SD
Supt. — See Moncks Corner
College Park ES 1,100/K-5
100 Davidson Dr 29456 843-797-2711
Amanda Prince, prin. Fax 820-4022
College Park MS 800/6-8
713 College Park Rd 29456 843-553-8300
Ingrid Dukes M.Ed., prin. Fax 820-4026
Sangaree MS 800/6-8
1050 Discovery Dr 29456 843-821-4028
Margaret Day, prin. Fax 871-8974

Charleston County SD
Supt. — See Charleston
Ladson ES 800/PK-5
3321 Ladson Rd 29456 843-764-2225
Celeste Spires, prin. Fax 569-5468

Dorchester SD 2
Supt. — See Summerville
Oakbrook ES 800/K-5
306 Old Fort Dr 29456 843-821-1165
Monica O'Dea, prin. Fax 821-3984
Oakbrook MS 1,000/6-8
286 Old Fort Dr 29456 843-873-9750
Brandon Pitcher, prin. Fax 821-3931
Pye ES 800/K-5
9701 Patriot Blvd 29456 843-695-2979
Wanda Carroll-Williams, prin. Fax 695-2983

William-Randolph Christian Prep S 50/PK-12
9659 Jamison Rd 29456 843-212-4289
Dr. Stephanie Wallace M.Ed., prin. Fax 771-0569

Lake City, Florence, Pop. 6,625
Florence County SD Three 2,600/PK-12
PO Box 1389 29560 843-374-8652
Laura Hickson, supt. Fax 374-2946
fsd3.org
Lake City ECC PK-2
906 N Matthews Rd 29560 843-374-2353
Mary Howard, prin. Fax 374-5480
Main Street ES 200/3-5
318 E Main St 29560 843-374-2221
Allana Prosser, prin. Fax 374-8697
McNair JHS 300/7-8
PO Box 1209 29560 843-374-8651
Kristi Anderson, prin. Fax 374-8504
Truluck IS 100/6-6
319 Carlisle St 29560 843-374-8685
Jeanette Altman, prin. Fax 374-7341
Other Schools – See Coward, Olanta, Scranton

Carolina Academy 200/PK-12
351 N Country Club Rd 29560 843-374-5485

Lake View, Dillon, Pop. 805
Dillon SD Four
Supt. — See Dillon
Lake View ES 400/PK-5
PO Box 685 29563 843-759-3003
Kim Walsh, prin. Fax 759-3013

Lamar, Darlington, Pop. 980
Darlington County SD
Supt. — See Darlington
Lamar ES 300/PK-2
214 N Darlington Ave 29069 843-326-7575
Garry Flowers, prin. Fax 326-7050
Spaulding ES 200/3-5
204 E Pearl St 29069 843-326-7666
Jacqueline Lynn, prin. Fax 326-1086
Spaulding MS 300/6-8
400 Cartersville Hwy 29069 843-326-7626
Chrissy Jones, prin. Fax 326-7656

Lancaster, Lancaster, Pop. 8,450
Lancaster County SD 12,000/PK-12
300 S Catawba St 29720 803-286-6972
Dr. Jonathan Phipps, supt. Fax 416-8860
www.lancastercsd.com
Brooklyn Springs ES 500/PK-5
1637 Billings Dr 29720 803-283-8471
Shirnetha Stinson, prin. Fax 285-8942
Buford ES 800/PK-5
1906 N Rocky River Rd 29720 803-286-0026
Andrea Ribelin, prin. Fax 286-9986
Buford MS 500/6-8
1890 N Rocky River Rd 29720 803-285-8473
Sheri Wells, prin. Fax 283-2023
Clinton ES 400/PK-5
110 Clinton School Rd 29720 803-285-5395
Michelle Crosby, prin. Fax 283-3998
Erwin ES 500/PK-5
1477 Locustwood Ave 29720 803-285-8484
Jane Gaston, prin. Fax 289-6332
McDonald Green ES 500/K-5
2763 Lynwood Dr 29720 803-285-7416
Tonya Hunter, prin. Fax 285-7417
North ES 700/PK-5
1100 Roddey Dr 29720 803-283-9918
Keishea McGriff-Mickles, prin. Fax 286-7769
Rucker MS 600/6-8
422 Old Dixie Rd 29720 803-416-8555
Anita Watts, prin. Fax 285-1534
South MS 600/6-8
1551 Billings Dr 29720 803-283-8416
Joyce Crimminger, prin. Fax 283-8417
Southside ECC 100/PK-PK
500 Hampton Rd 29720 803-283-3915
Dr. Linda Blackwell, admin. Fax 313-9587
Other Schools – See Heath Springs, Indian Land, Kershaw

Landrum, Spartanburg, Pop. 2,337
Spartanburg SD 1
Supt. — See Campobello
Earle ES 500/PK-5
100 Redland Rd 29356 864-457-3416
Brian Murray, prin. Fax 457-3913
Landrum MS 200/6-8
104 Redland Rd 29356 864-457-2629
Tucker Hamrick, prin. Fax 457-5372

Latta, Dillon, Pop. 1,366
Latta SD 1,200/PK-12
205 King St 29565 843-752-7101
Dr. John Kirby, supt. Fax 752-2081
www.dillon3.k12.sc.us
Latta ES 400/PK-4
300 Viking Dr 29565 843-752-5295
Dollie Morrell, prin. Fax 752-2713
Latta MS 400/5-8
612 N Richardson St 29565 843-752-7117
Debra Morris, prin. Fax 752-2722

Laurens, Laurens, Pop. 9,035
Laurens SD 55 5,500/PK-12
301 Hillcrest Dr 29360 864-984-3568
Dr. Stephen Peters, supt. Fax 984-8100
www.laurens55.org
Ford ES 500/PK-5
601 Lucas Ave 29360 864-984-3986
Zakaria Watson, prin. Fax 984-4724
Laurens ES 700/PK-5
301 Henry St 29360 864-984-3067
Randy Dendy, prin. Fax 984-5749
Laurens MS 400/6-8
1035 W Main St 29360 864-984-2400
Anna Brink, prin. Fax 984-6013
Morse ES 600/PK-5
200 Parkview Dr 29360 864-984-7777
Lynn Owings, prin. Fax 984-2926
Sanders MS 300/6-8
609 Green St 29360 864-984-0354
Dr. Lacresha Byrd, prin. Fax 984-2452
Other Schools – See Gray Court, Waterloo

Laurens Academy 200/PK-12
PO Box 425 29360 864-682-2324

Leesville, Lexington, Pop. 2,235
Lexington County SD 3
Supt. — See Batesburg
Batesburg-Leesville ES 400/3-5
403 S Lee St 29070 803-532-1155
Jamie Hembree, prin. Fax 532-8027

Lexington, Lexington, Pop. 17,606
Lexington County SD 1 23,600/K-12
PO Box 1869 29071 803-821-1000
Dr. Greg Little, supt. Fax 821-1010
www.lexington1.net
Carolina Springs ES 900/K-5
6340 Platt Springs Rd 29073 803-821-5100
Gregory Watchinski, prin. Fax 821-5103
Carolina Springs MS 800/6-8
6180 Platt Springs Rd 29073 803-821-4900
Dr. Brice Cockfield, prin. Fax 821-4903
Deerfield ES K-5
638 Longs Pond Rd 29073 803-821-5500
Janet Malone, prin. Fax 821-5503
Lake Murray ES 600/K-5
205 Wise Ferry Rd 29072 803-821-3100
Jennifer Stanley, prin. Fax 821-3103
Lexington ES 700/K-5
116 Azalea Dr 29072 803-821-4000
Jim Hamby, prin. Fax 821-4003
Lexington MS 800/6-8
702 N Lake Dr 29072 803-821-3700
Gloria Nester, prin. Fax 821-3703
Meadow Glen ES 900/K-5
510 Ginny Ln 29072 803-821-0400
Cheryl Fralick, prin. Fax 821-0403
Meadow Glen MS 900/6-8
440 Ginny Ln 29072 803-821-0600
Dr. Bill Coon, prin. Fax 821-0603
Midway ES 800/K-5
180 Midway Rd 29072 803-821-0300
Jan Fickling, prin. Fax 821-0303
New Providence ES 600/K-5
1118 Old Cherokee Rd 29072 803-821-3300
Debbie Poole, prin. Fax 821-3303
Oak Grove ES 600/K-5
479 Oak Dr 29073 803-821-0100
Sherry Cariens, prin. Fax 821-0103
Pleasant Hill ES 900/K-5
664 Rawl Rd 29072 803-821-2800
Margaret Mitchum, prin. Fax 821-2803
Pleasant Hill MS 1,000/6-8
660 Rawl Rd 29072 803-821-2700
Dr. Thomas Rivers, prin. Fax 821-2703
Red Bank ES 600/K-5
246 Community Dr 29073 803-821-4600
Marie Watson, prin. Fax 821-4603
Rocky Creek ES 600/K-5
430 Calks Ferry Rd 29072 803-821-4200
Brenda Nichols, prin. Fax 821-4203
Saxe Gotha ES 600/K-5
100 Bill Williamson Ct 29073 803-821-4800
Beth Houck, prin. Fax 821-4803
Other Schools – See Gilbert, Pelion, West Columbia

Columbia Adventist Academy 50/1-8
241 Riverchase Way 29072 803-796-0277
Denise Marshalleck-Smith, prin. Fax 796-2123
Northside Christian Academy PK-12
4347 Sunset Blvd 29072 803-520-5656
Rev. Scott Crede, head sch Fax 520-5661

Liberty, Pickens, Pop. 3,217
Pickens County SD
Supt. — See Easley
Chastain Road ES 500/K-5
940 Chastain Rd 29657 864-397-4800
Jessica Patterson, prin. Fax 843-4692
Liberty ES 500/K-5
251 N Hillcrest St 29657 864-397-2100
Dr. Lowell Haynes, prin. Fax 843-5822
Liberty MS 500/6-8
125 Falcon Ln 29657 864-397-3400
Lisa Cassidy, prin. Fax 843-5857

Little Mountain, Newberry, Pop. 289
Newberry County SD
Supt. — See Newberry
Little Mountain ES 400/K-5
692 Mill St 29075 803-945-7721
Kimberly Mack, prin. Fax 945-1058

Little River, Horry, Pop. 8,858
Horry County SD
Supt. — See Conway
North Myrtle Beach MS 1,100/6-8
11240 Highway 90 29566 843-399-6136
James LaPier, prin. Fax 399-2233
Riverside ES 700/PK-5
1283 Highway 57 S 29566 843-399-8800
Vicki Underwood, prin. Fax 399-8700
Waterway ES 700/K-5
700 Sandridge Rd 29566 843-399-2204
Melissa Graham, prin. Fax 399-2250

Lockhart, Union, Pop. 478
Union County SD
Supt. — See Union
Lockhart S 200/K-8
212 Lockhart Dr 29364 864-545-6501
Gerard Wood, prin. Fax 545-2175

Longs, Horry

Holy Trinity S 50/PK-8
1760 Living Stones Ln 29568 843-390-4108
Karen Luzzo, prin. Fax 390-4097
North Myrtle Beach Christian S 100/PK-12
9535 Highway 90 29568 843-399-7181

Loris, Horry, Pop. 2,350
Horry County SD
Supt. — See Conway
Daisy ES 600/PK-5
2801 Red Bluff Rd 29569 843-756-5136
Michelle Dunsford, prin. Fax 756-3965
Loris ES 700/PK-5
901 Highway 9 Business E 29569 843-390-6860
Angela Gore, prin. Fax 390-6861
Loris MS 700/6-8
5209 Highway 66 29569 843-756-2181
Shelley Todd, prin. Fax 756-0522

Lugoff, Kershaw, Pop. 7,335
Kershaw County SD
Supt. — See Camden
Doby's Mill ES 500/PK-5
1964 Fort Jackson Rd 29078 803-438-4055
Ginger Catoe, prin. Fax 438-7925
Lugoff ES 600/K-5
994 Ridgeway Rd 29078 803-438-8000
Dr. Melissa Lloyd, prin. Fax 438-8024
Lugoff-Elgin MS 700/6-8
1244 Highway 1 S 29078 803-438-3591
Karen Bullard, prin. Fax 438-8027
Wateree ES 600/PK-5
424 Wildwood Ln 29078 803-438-8018
Gail Stehle, prin. Fax 438-8020

Lyman, Spartanburg, Pop. 3,187
Spartanburg SD 5
Supt. — See Duncan
Hill MS 600/7-8
PO Box 1329 29365 864-949-2370
Terry Glasgow, prin. Fax 949-2369
Lyman ES 600/K-4
PO Box 1119 29365 864-949-2330
Tim Henson, prin. Fax 949-2339

Mc Bee, Chesterfield, Pop. 855
Chesterfield County SD
Supt. — See Chesterfield
Mc Bee ES 400/PK-6
PO Box 368 29101 843-335-8347
Dr. David Nutt, prin. Fax 335-5671

Mc Clellanville, Charleston, Pop. 499
Charleston County SD
Supt. — See Charleston
St. James-Santee ES 200/PK-5
8900 N Highway 17 29458 843-723-0863
LaCarma Brown-McMillan, prin. Fax 887-3357

Mc Coll, Marlboro, Pop. 2,113
Marlboro County SD
Supt. — See Bennettsville
Mc Coll S 800/PK-8
700 N Main St 29570 843-523-5371
Mark Phillips, prin. Fax 523-9147

Mc Cormick, McCormick, Pop. 2,752
McCormick County SD 800/PK-12
821 N Mine St 29835 864-852-2435
Don Doggett, supt. Fax 852-2883
www.mccormick.k12.sc.us
McCormick ES 400/PK-5
6977 SC Highway 28 S 29835 864-443-2292
Nynita Paul, prin. Fax 443-2755
McCormick MS 200/6-8
6979 SC Highway 28 S 29835 864-443-2243
Gena Wideman, prin. Fax 443-3298

Manning, Clarendon, Pop. 4,077
Clarendon SD 2 3,000/PK-12
PO Box 1252 29102 803-435-4435
John Tindal, supt. Fax 435-8172
www.clarendon2.k12.sc.us
Manning ECC 600/PK-1
2759 Raccoon Rd 29102 803-473-4744
Otis Reed, prin. Fax 473-4777
Manning ES 600/4-6
311 W Boyce St 29102 803-435-5066
Allyson Goff, prin. Fax 435-0340
Manning JHS 400/7-8
1101 WL Hamilton Rd 29102 803-435-8195
Terrie Ard, prin. Fax 435-6848
Manning PS 500/2-3
125 N Boundary St 29102 803-435-2268
Brenda Clark, prin. Fax 435-8737

Laurence Manning Academy 1,000/PK-12
PO Box 278 29102 803-435-2114

Marietta, Greenville, Pop. 2,245
Greenville County SD
Supt. — See Greenville

Slater-Marietta ES 400/K-5
100 Baker Cir 29661 864-355-2000
George Champlin, prin. Fax 355-2016

Marion, Marion, Pop. 6,862
Marion County SD 5,200/PK-12
719 N Main St 29571 843-423-1811
Dr. Kandace Bethea, supt. Fax 423-8328
www.marion.k12.sc.us
Easterling PS 800/PK-2
600 E Northside Ave 29571 843-423-8335
Shalah Sweeney, prin. Fax 423-8314
Johnakin MS 600/6-8
601 Gurley St 29571 843-423-8360
Rebecca Ford, prin. Fax 423-8383
Marion IS 600/3-5
2320 N Highway 41A 29571 843-423-8345
Melonie Dozier, prin. Fax 423-8378
Other Schools – See Gresham, Mullins

Mauldin, Greenville, Pop. 22,445

Montessori S of Mauldin 100/PK-6
205 E Butler Rd Ste B 29662 864-288-8613

Mayesville, Sumter, Pop. 731
Lee County SD
Supt. — See Bishopville
Lower Lee ES 200/PK-5
5142 St Charles Rd 29104 803-428-3637
Shelia Stukes Ed.D., prin. Fax 428-3658

Moncks Corner, Berkeley, Pop. 7,746
Berkeley County SD 31,600/PK-12
PO Box 608 29461 843-899-8600
Dr. Eddie Ingram, supt. Fax 899-8791
www.bcsdschools.net
Berkeley ES 600/K-2
715 Highway 6 29461 843-899-8860
Kelly Gabriel, prin. Fax 899-8865
Berkeley IS 600/3-5
777 Stony Landing Rd 29461 843-899-8870
Mike Shaw, prin. Fax 899-8873
Berkeley MS 1,100/6-8
320 N Live Oak Dr 29461 843-899-8840
Mike Wilkerson, prin. Fax 899-8846
Bonner ES 800/PK-5
171 Macedonia Foxes Cir 29461 843-899-8950
Melissa Willis, prin. Fax 899-8928
Macedonia MS 400/6-8
200 Macedonia Foxes Cir 29461 843-899-8940
Don Walton, prin. Fax 899-8929
Whitesville ES 900/PK-5
324 Gaillard Rd 29461 843-899-8880
Katie Taie, prin. Fax 899-8883
Other Schools – See Charleston, Cross, Goose Creek, Hanahan, Huger, Ladson, Pineville, Saint Stephen, Summerville

St. John's Christian Academy 300/PK-12
204 W Main St 29461 843-761-8539

Moore, Spartanburg
Spartanburg County SD 6
Supt. — See Roebuck
Anderson Mill ES 700/PK-5
1845 Old Anderson Mill Rd 29369 864-576-6539
Beth Haun, prin. Fax 595-2452
Dawkins MS 900/6-8
1300 E Blackstock Rd 29369 864-576-8088
Jay Seegars, prin. Fax 595-2418

Spartanburg SD 5
Supt. — See Duncan
River Ridge ES 600/K-4
5960 Reidville Rd 29369 864-949-7620
Dr. Glenda Bigby, prin. Fax 949-7627

Mount Pleasant, Charleston, Pop. 67,140
Charleston County SD
Supt. — See Charleston
Belle Hall ES 700/PK-5
385 Egypt Rd 29464 843-849-2841
Kevin Conklin, prin. Fax 849-2893
Cario MS 1,300/6-8
3500 Thomas Cario Blvd 29466 843-856-4595
Sharon Randall, prin. Fax 856-4599
Carolina Park ES PK-5
3650 Park Ave 29466 843-856-8060
Michael Antonelli, prin. Fax 881-4247
Edwards S of Global Leadership 600/PK-5
855 Von Kolnitz Rd 29464 843-849-2805
Robin Fountain, prin. Fax 849-2892
Laing MS of Science & Technology 700/6-8
2705 Bulrush Basket Ln 29466 843-849-2809
James Whitehair, prin. Fax 849-2895
Laurel Hill PS 1,100/PK-2
3100 Thomas Cario Blvd 29466 843-849-2200
Ashley Dorsey, prin. Fax 849-3377
Moore ES for the Creative Arts 800/PK-5
2725 Bulrush Basket Ln 29466 843-849-2815
Karen Felder, prin. Fax 849-2891
Moultrie MS 800/6-8
645 Coleman Blvd 29464 843-849-2819
Ryan Cumback, prin. Fax 849-2899
Mount Pleasant Academy 600/PK-5
605 Center St 29464 843-849-2826
Kim Jackson, prin. Fax 849-2097
Pinckney ES 1,200/3-5
3300 Thomas Cario Blvd 29466 843-856-4585
Leanne Sheppard, prin. Fax 856-4594
Whitesides ES 700/PK-5
1565 Rifle Range Rd 29464 843-849-2838
Cynthia Perez, prin. Fax 849-2884

Christ Our King / Stella Maris S 600/PK-8
1183 Russell Dr 29464 843-884-4721
Susan Splendido, prin. Fax 971-7850

Coastal Christian Preparatory S 300/PK-12
681 McCants Dr 29464 843-884-3663
Dr. David Piccolo, head sch Fax 884-9608
Palmetto Christian Academy 500/PK-12
361 Egypt Rd 29464 843-881-9967
J.D. Zubia, hdmstr. Fax 881-4662
Sundrops Montessori S 200/PK-9
955 Houston Northcutt Blvd 29464 843-849-3652

Mullins, Marion, Pop. 4,600
Marion County SD
Supt. — See Marion
McCormick ES 400/3-5
1123 Sandy Bluff Rd 29574 843-464-3760
Patricia Burch, prin. Fax 464-3763
Mullins ECC PK-PK
111 Academy St 29574 843-464-3725
Stacy Wilbanks, prin. Fax 464-3728
North Mullins PS 500/PK-2
105 Charles St 29574 843-464-3750
Sharron Crowner Ed.D., prin. Fax 464-3756
Palmetto MS 400/6-8
305 ONeal St 29574 843-464-3730
Kelvin Edwards, prin. Fax 464-3736

Pee Dee Academy 400/PK-12
PO Box 449 29574 843-423-1771

Murrells Inlet, Horry, Pop. 7,501

St. Michael S 100/PK-8
542 Cypress Ave 29576 843-651-6795
Pamela Walters, prin. Fax 651-6803

Myrtle Beach, Horry, Pop. 26,336
Horry County SD
Supt. — See Conway
Burgess ES 700/PK-5
9645 Scipio Ln 29588 843-650-4600
Samantha Coy, prin. Fax 650-4602
Carolina Forest ES 900/PK-5
285 Carolina Forest Blvd 29579 843-236-0001
Dennis Devorick, prin. Fax 236-0152
Forestbrook ES 1,000/PK-5
4000 Panthers Pkwy 29588 843-236-8100
Janet Brown, prin. Fax 236-8103
Forestbrook MS 1,100/6-8
4430 Gator Ln 29588 843-236-7300
Beverly Holt-Pilkey, prin. Fax 236-8065
Lakewood ES 900/PK-5
1675 Highway 396 29575 843-650-6768
Katherine Roberts, prin. Fax 650-6748
Myrtle Beach ES 700/2-3
620 29th Ave N 29577 843-448-1774
Michelle Green-Graham, prin. Fax 448-1115
Myrtle Beach IS 700/4-5
3301 N Oak St 29577 843-626-5831
Deb Colliver, prin. Fax 626-8528
Myrtle Beach MS 1,000/6-8
3101 N Oak St 29577 843-448-3932
Dr. Janice Christy, prin. Fax 448-1182
Myrtle Beach PS 900/PK-1
612 29th Ave N 29577 843-448-1658
Christel Arnette, prin. Fax 448-0139
Ocean Bay ES 700/PK-5
950 International Dr 29579 843-903-8400
Rebecca Schroyer, prin. Fax 903-8401
Ocean Bay MS 1,200/6-8
905 International Dr 29579 843-903-8420
Barbara McGinnis, prin. Fax 903-8421
Palmetto Bays ES 600/PK-5
8900 Highway 544 29588 843-236-6200
Dawn McKinney, prin. Fax 236-7900
River Oaks ES 700/PK-5
700 Augusta Plantation Dr 29579 843-903-6300
Robert Homer, prin. Fax 903-6301
St. James ES 900/PK-5
9711 Saint James Rd 29588 843-650-8220
Felisa McDavid, prin. Fax 650-7909
St. James IS 5-6
9641 Scipio Ln 29588 843-903-6005
David Cupolo, prin. Fax 650-9794
St. James MS 1,200/6-8
9775 Saint James Rd 29588 843-650-5543
Dr. Olga Toggas, prin. Fax 650-5610
Socastee ES 800/PK-5
4223 Socastee Blvd 29588 843-650-2606
Krista Finklea, prin. Fax 650-2629
Socastee MS 6-8
151 Esso Rd 29588 843-903-6051
Lisa Melchione, prin. Fax 293-3244
Ten Oaks MS 6-8
150 Revolutionary War Way 29579 843-488-8896
Ben Prince, prin. Fax 236-0014

Calvary Christian S 200/PK-12
4511 Dick Pond Rd 29588 843-650-2829
Chabad Jewish Academy 100/PK-8
2803 N Oak St 29577 843-448-0035
Leah Aizenman, prin. Fax 626-6403
Christian Academy of Myrtle Beach 400/K-12
291 Ronald McNair Blvd 29579 843-236-6222
Katherine Cannon, head sch Fax 236-2262
Myrtle Beach SDA S 50/1-8
2351 Carolina Forest Blvd 29579 843-236-1452
Risen Christ Lutheran S 100/PK-12
10595 Highway 17 N 29572 843-272-8163
Sean O'Connor, prin. Fax 272-4039
St. Andrew S 200/K-8
3601 N Kings Hwy 29577 843-448-6062
Debbie Wilfong, prin. Fax 626-8644

Neeses, Orangeburg, Pop. 371
Orangeburg County Consolidated SD 4
Supt. — See Cope
Hunter-Kinard-Tyler ES 300/PK-5
7066 Norway Rd 29107 803-263-4441
Gloria Jenkins, prin. Fax 263-4404

Newberry, Newberry, Pop. 10,123
Newberry County SD 5,800/PK-12
PO Box 718 29108 803-321-2600
Jim Suber, supt. Fax 321-2604
www.newberry.k12.sc.us
Boundary Street ES 500/PK-5
1406 Boundary St 29108 803-321-2616
Allison Stribble, prin. Fax 321-2605
Gallman ES 500/PK-5
255 Hawkins Rd 29108 803-321-2655
Nikki Hunter, prin. Fax 321-2657
Newberry ES 500/PK-5
1829 Nance St 29108 803-321-2670
Reggie Wicker, prin. Fax 321-2671
Newberry MS 700/6-8
125 ONeal St 29108 803-321-2640
Kimberly Hamilton, prin. Fax 321-2647
Reuben ES 200/PK-5
3605 Spearman Rd 29108 803-321-2664
Mike Stroud, prin. Fax 321-2665
Other Schools – See Little Mountain, Pomaria, Prosperity, Whitmire

Newberry Academy 200/PK-12
2055 Smith Rd 29108 803-276-2760

New Ellenton, Aiken, Pop. 1,998
Aiken County SD
Supt. — See Aiken
Greendale ES 400/K-5
505 S Boundary Ave 29809 803-652-8170
Robin Hill-Davidson, prin. Fax 652-8173
New Ellenton Middle STEAM Magnet S 200/6-8
814 Main St S 29809 803-652-8200
Shunte Dugar, prin. Fax 652-8203

New Zion, Clarendon
Clarendon SD 3
Supt. — See Turbeville
Walker Gamble ES 600/PK-5
PO Box 7 29111 843-659-2102
Allen Kirby, prin. Fax 659-2129

Ninety Six, Greenwood, Pop. 1,979
Greenwood SD 52 1,700/PK-12
605 Johnston Rd 29666 864-543-3100
Fax 543-3704
www.greenwood52.org
Edgewood MS 400/6-8
644 S Cambridge St 29666 864-543-3511
David Schoolfield, prin. Fax 543-4994
Ninety Six ES 400/3-5
810 Johnston Rd 29666 864-543-4995
Charlene Louden, prin. Fax 543-4962
Ninety Six PS 500/PK-2
121 S Cambridge St 29666 864-543-3112
Becky Corbin, prin. Fax 543-4427

North, Orangeburg, Pop. 730
Orangeburg Consolidated SD 5
Supt. — See Orangeburg
Dover ES 300/PK-5
PO Box 218 29112 803-247-2184
Sylvia Williams, prin. Fax 247-5010

North Augusta, Aiken, Pop. 20,954
Aiken County SD
Supt. — See Aiken
Hammond Hill ES 800/K-5
901 W Woodlawn Ave 29841 803-442-6170
Eric Jeffcoat, prin. Fax 442-6112
Knox MS 700/6-8
1804 Wells Rd 29841 803-442-6300
Jason Holt, prin. Fax 442-6302
Mossy Creek ES 700/K-5
421 W Five Notch Rd 29841 803-442-6090
Stephanie Hammond, prin. Fax 442-6092
North Augusta ES 600/K-5
400 E Spring Grove Ave 29841 803-442-6280
Patricia Wilson, prin. Fax 442-6282
North Augusta MS 700/6-8
725 Old Edgefield Rd 29841 803-442-6200
Phyllis Gamble, prin. Fax 442-6202

Edgefield County SD
Supt. — See Johnston
Merriwether ES 700/PK-5
565 Springhaven Dr 29860 803-279-9993
Bruce Lee, prin. Fax 279-8898
Merriwether MS 400/6-8
430 Murrah Rd 29860 803-279-2511
Derrick Forrest, prin. Fax 279-1710

Our Lady of Peace S 100/PK-8
856 Old Edgefield Rd 29841 803-279-8396
Stephen Hickey, prin. Fax 301-6770

North Charleston, Charleston, Pop. 95,273
Charleston County SD
Supt. — See Charleston
Chicora S of Communication 400/PK-5
3100 Carner Ave 29405 843-746-2211
Mary Reynolds, prin. Fax 566-7792
Corcoran ES 700/PK-5
8585 Vistavia Rd 29406 843-764-2218
Quenetta White, prin. Fax 764-2234
Deer Park MS 5-8
2263 Otranto Rd 29406 843-990-5200
Paul Padron, prin. Fax 863-5383
Dunston PS 300/PK-3
1825 Remount Rd 29406 843-745-7109
Janice Malone, prin. Fax 529-3905
Ford ES 400/PK-5
3180 Thomasina McPherson 29405 843-745-7131
LaDene Conroy, prin. Fax 529-3927
Goodwin ES 600/PK-5
5501 Dorchester Rd 29418 843-767-5911
Diane Ross, prin. Fax 767-5929

Hunley Park ES 500/PK-5
1000 Michigan Ave 29404 843-767-5914
Dr. Michael Griggs, prin. Fax 767-5932
Hursey ES 400/PK-8
4542 Simms Ave 29405 843-745-7105
Dr. Timothy Schavel, prin. Fax 529-3903
Lambs ES 400/PK-5
6800 Dorchester Rd 29418 843-767-5900
Jarmalar Logan, prin. Fax 767-5928
Meeting Street ES at Brentwood PK-5
2865 Leeds Ave 29405 843-529-3130
Sarah Campbell, prin.
Midland Park PS 400/PK-1
2415 Midland Park Rd 29406 843-574-2183
Beth McCraw, prin. Fax 569-5476
Morningside MS 6-8
1999 Singley St 29405 843-745-2000
Stephanie Flock, prin. Fax 745-7191
North Charleston Creative Arts ES 200/PK-5
5200 Lackawanna Blvd 29405 843-529-2831
Eric Hansen, dir. Fax 529-2848
North Charleston ES 600/PK-5
4921 Durant Ave 29405 843-745-7107
Jeffrey Beckwith, prin. Fax 554-5716
Northwoods MS 900/6-8
7763 Northside Dr 29420 843-764-2212
Colleen Knauer, prin. Fax 569-5466
Pepperhill ES 600/PK-5
3300 Creola Rd 29420 843-767-5905
Tanya Underwood, prin. Fax 767-5927
Pinehurst ES 500/1-5
7753 Northside Dr 29420 843-824-8728
Dianne Benton, prin. Fax 824-8729
Zucker Science MS 500/6-8
6401 Dorchester Rd 29418 843-767-8383
Jacob Perlmutter, prin. Fax 207-3073

Dorchester SD 2
Supt. — See Summerville
Eagle Nest ES 900/K-5
8640 River Oaks Dr 29420 843-695-2460
Dr. Tamara Diebold, prin. Fax 695-2465
River Oaks MS 1,000/6-8
8642 River Oaks Dr 29420 843-695-2470
Scott Matthews, prin. Fax 695-2475
Windsor Hill ES 700/K-5
8600 William Moultrie Dr 29420 843-760-9820
Robert Neuner, prin. Fax 760-4469

Cathedral Academy 300/K-12
PO Box 41129, 843-760-1192
Patrick Stuart, head sch Fax 760-1197

North Myrtle Beach, Horry, Pop. 13,575
Horry County SD
Supt. — See Conway
Ocean Drive ES 900/PK-5
901 11th Ave N 29582 843-390-6900
Renea Fowler, prin. Fax 390-6901

Okatie, Beaufort
Beaufort County SD
Supt. — See Beaufort
Okatie ES 600/PK-5
53 Cherry Point Rd, 843-322-7700
Jamie Pinckney, prin. Fax 322-7710

Olanta, Florence, Pop. 553
Florence County SD Three
Supt. — See Lake City
Olanta ES 300/PK-5
PO Box 628 29114 843-396-4457
Dr. Cutina Barrineau, prin. Fax 396-9512

Orangeburg, Orangeburg, Pop. 13,823
Orangeburg Consolidated SD 5 6,500/PK-12
578 Ellis Ave 29115 803-534-5454
Dr. Jesse Washington, supt. Fax 533-7953
www.ocsd5schools.org
Brookdale ES 300/K-5
394 Brookdale Dr 29115 803-534-5982
Dr. Sharon Hampton, prin. Fax 533-6472
Clark MS 700/6-8
919 Bennett St 29115 803-531-2200
Donyale Mosely, prin. Fax 533-6503
Howard MS 400/6-8
1255 Belleville Rd 29115 803-534-5470
Dr. Charlene Stokes, prin. Fax 535-1606
Marshall ES 800/K-5
1441 Marshall St 29118 803-534-7865
Dyisha Taylor, prin. Fax 535-1645
Mellichamp ES 400/3-5
350 Murray Rd 29115 803-534-8044
Hayward Jean, prin. Fax 533-6492
Rivelon ES 200/PK-2
350 Thomas Eklund Cir 29115 803-534-2949
Dr. Rena Bowman, prin. Fax 533-6540
Sheridan ES 500/K-5
1139 Hillsboro Rd 29115 803-534-7504
Sammie Gordon, prin. Fax 535-1650
Whittaker ES 600/K-5
790 Whittaker Pkwy 29115 803-534-6559
Dr. Teresa Jennings, prin. Fax 533-6466
Other Schools – See North, Rowesville

Orangeburg County Consolidated SD 4
Supt. — See Cope
Edisto ES 600/3-5
136 Woodolive St 29115 803-531-7646
Ronda Simmons, prin. Fax 531-7614

Mendinghall SDA Jr. Academy 50/K-8
1204 Decatur St 29118 803-535-3730
Orangeburg Preparatory S 800/PK-12
2651 North Rd 29118 803-534-7970
Evan Powell, head sch Fax 535-2190

Pacolet, Spartanburg, Pop. 2,212
Spartanburg SD 3
Supt. — See Glendale
Middle School of Pacolet 200/6-8
850 Sunny Acres Rd 29372 864-279-6600
Max Deaton, prin. Fax 279-6610
Pacolet ES 400/PK-5
150 McDowell St 29372 864-279-6500
Allison Berry, prin. Fax 279-6510

Pageland, Chesterfield, Pop. 2,713
Chesterfield County SD
Supt. — See Chesterfield
Pageland ES 400/3-5
715 W McGregor St 29728 843-672-2400
Ellen Middleton, prin. Fax 672-5585
Petersburg PS 400/PK-2
326 N Arnold St 29728 843-672-6241
Janice Kiser, prin. Fax 672-5866

Richards Adventist S K-8
1463 S Pearl St 29728 843-672-6634
South Pointe Christian S 200/PK-12
PO Box 188 29728 843-672-2760
Susan Waller, head sch Fax 672-3913

Pamplico, Florence, Pop. 1,212
Florence County SD 2 1,200/PK-12
2121 S Pamplico Hwy 29583 843-493-2502
Neal Vincent, supt. Fax 493-1912
www.fsd2.org
Hannah-Pamplico S 900/PK-8
2131 S Pamplico Hwy 29583 843-493-5588
Legrande Richardson, prin. Fax 493-5461

Patrick, Chesterfield, Pop. 347
Chesterfield County SD
Supt. — See Chesterfield
Plainview ES 200/PK-6
16002 Highway 102 29584 843-498-6633
Beth Melton, prin. Fax 498-6024

Pauline, Spartanburg
Spartanburg County SD 6
Supt. — See Roebuck
Pauline-Glenn Springs ES 500/PK-5
PO Box 95 29374 864-583-1868
Jennifer Million, prin. Fax 573-8534

Pawleys Island, Georgetown, Pop. 101
Georgetown County SD
Supt. — See Georgetown
Waccamaw ES 700/PK-3
1364 Waverly Rd 29585 843-237-4233
Ashley Cameron, prin. Fax 237-2015
Waccamaw IS 600/4-6
320 Wildcat Way 29585 843-237-7071
Dr. Timothy Carnahan, prin. Fax 237-7031
Waccamaw MS 500/7-8
247 Wildcat Way 29585 843-237-0106
Jamie Curry, prin. Fax 237-0237

Lowcountry Preparatory S 100/K-12
300 Blue Stem Dr 29585 843-237-4147
Scott Gibson, head sch Fax 237-4543

Pelion, Lexington, Pop. 671
Lexington County SD 1
Supt. — See Lexington
Forts Pond ES 500/K-5
7350 Fish Hatchery Rd 29123 803-821-2500
Michelle Smith, prin. Fax 821-2503
Pelion ES 500/K-5
1202 Pine St 29123 803-821-2000
Wendy West, prin. Fax 821-2003
Pelion MS 600/6-8
758 Magnolia St 29123 803-821-2300
Jeffrey Matthews, prin. Fax 821-2303

Pelzer, Anderson, Pop. 87
Greenville County SD
Supt. — See Greenville
Fork Shoals ES 700/K-5
916 McKelvey Rd 29669 864-355-5000
Kim Reid, prin. Fax 355-5012
Riley Child Development Center PK-K
9130 Augusta Rd 29669 864-355-3400
Amanda Lecaroz, prin. Fax 355-3440
Woodside ES 600/K-5
9122 Augusta Rd 29669 864-355-4900
Mimi Melehes, prin. Fax 355-4965

Pendleton, Anderson, Pop. 2,884
Anderson SD 4 2,800/K-12
315 E Queen St 29670 864-403-2000
Dr. Joanne Avery Ph.D., supt. Fax 403-2029
www.anderson4.org
La France ES 400/K-6
550 Williams St 29670 864-403-2300
Hope Bass, prin. Fax 646-8011
Mt. Lebanon ES 500/K-6
2850 Lebanon Rd 29670 864-403-2400
Elliott Southard, prin. Fax 716-3654
Pendleton ES 400/K-6
902 E Queen St 29670 864-403-2500
Jeffrey Simpson, prin. Fax 646-8016
Riverside MS 500/7-8
458 Riverside St 29670 864-403-2200
Jeff Boozer, prin. Fax 646-8025
Other Schools – See Townville

Pickens, Pickens, Pop. 3,062
Pickens County SD
Supt. — See Easley
Ambler ES 200/K-5
838 Ambler School Rd 29671 864-397-1200
Dr. Carlton Lewis, prin. Fax 898-5589
Hagood ES 300/K-5
435 Sparks Ln 29671 864-397-1900
Paula Alexander, prin. Fax 878-8719
Pickens ES 400/K-5
567 Hampton Ave 29671 864-397-2300
Donna Harden, prin. Fax 898-5627
Pickens MS 800/6-8
140 Torch Dr 29671 864-397-4100
Reggia Stapleton, prin. Fax 878-9224

Lakeview Christian S 200/PK-12
107 Mauldin Lake Rd 29671 864-878-6959

Piedmont, Greenville, Pop. 5,025
Anderson SD 1
Supt. — See Williamston
Spearman ES 500/PK-5
2001 Easley Hwy 29673 864-947-9787
Jason Lesley, prin. Fax 947-1162
Wren ES 500/PK-5
226 Roper Rd 29673 864-850-5950
Tommy Bolger, prin. Fax 850-5951
Wren MS 800/6-8
1010 Wren School Rd 29673 864-850-5930
Dr. Andy Hooker, prin. Fax 850-5941

Greenville County SD
Supt. — See Greenville
Cleveland ES 600/K-5
375 Woodmont School Rd Ext 29673 864-355-4200
Christie Payne, prin. Fax 355-4215
Grove ES 700/K-5
1220 Old Grove Rd 29673 864-355-5900
Deborah Bauer, prin. Fax 355-5965
Woodmont MS 700/6-8
325 N Flat Rock Rd 29673 864-355-8500
Greg Scott, prin. Fax 355-8587

Pineville, Berkeley
Berkeley County SD
Supt. — See Moncks Corner
Gourdin ES 200/PK-5
1649 Highway 45 29468 843-567-3637
Lorene Bradley, prin. Fax 567-3069

Pinewood, Sumter, Pop. 537
Sumter SD
Supt. — See Sumter
Manchester ES 500/PK-5
200 E Clark St 29125 803-452-5454
Dr. Joan Tye, prin. Fax 452-5423

Pomaria, Newberry, Pop. 178
Newberry County SD
Supt. — See Newberry
Pomaria-Garmany ES 300/PK-5
7288 US Highway 176 29126 803-321-2651
Lindsey Folk, prin. Fax 321-2652

Port Royal, Beaufort, Pop. 10,354
Beaufort County SD
Supt. — See Beaufort
Port Royal ES 200/PK-5
1214 Paris Ave 29935 843-322-0820
Chavon Browne, prin. Fax 322-0841

Prosperity, Newberry, Pop. 1,173
Newberry County SD
Supt. — See Newberry
Mid-Carolina MS 600/6-8
6794 US Highway 76 29127 803-364-3634
Deedee Westwood, prin. Fax 364-4877
Prosperity-Rikard ES 400/PK-5
381 S Wheeler Ave 29127 803-364-2321
Tim Lyden, prin. Fax 364-4484

Ravenel, Charleston, Pop. 2,438
Charleston County SD
Supt. — See Charleston
Ellington ES 300/PK-6
5400 Old Jacksonboro Rd 29470 843-889-9411
Wanda Hughes, prin. Fax 889-2205

Reidville, Spartanburg, Pop. 590
Spartanburg SD 5
Supt. — See Duncan
Reidville ES 300/K-4
PO Box 189 29375 864-949-2388
Kim Deering, prin. Fax 949-2390

Rembert, Sumter, Pop. 296
Lee County SD
Supt. — See Bishopville
West Lee ES 200/K-5
55 W Lee School Rd 29128 803-428-3147
Damon Officer, prin. Fax 428-3184

Sumter SD
Supt. — See Sumter
Rafting Creek ES 200/PK-5
4100 Highway 261 N 29128 803-432-2994
Jennifer Howard, prin. Fax 425-7386

Sumter Academy 400/PK-12
5265 Camden Hwy 29128 803-499-3378
Dr. Frank Martin Ed.D., head sch Fax 499-3391

Richburg, Chester, Pop. 273
Chester County SD
Supt. — See Chester
Lewisville ES 600/PK-5
4006 Lewisville High School 29729 803-789-5164
Anne Stone, prin. Fax 789-3954
Lewisville MS 300/6-8
PO Box 280 29729 803-789-5858
Brian Edmond, prin. Fax 789-6159

Ridgeland, Jasper, Pop. 4,009
Jasper County SD 2,500/PK-12
10942 N Jacob Smart Blvd 29936 843-489-8892
Donald Andrews, supt. Fax 717-1199
www.jcsd.net

Ridgeland ES 900/PK-5
250 Jaguar Trl 29936 843-489-8845
Renata Johnson-Green, prin. Fax 717-3274
Other Schools – See Hardeeville

Heyward Academy 300/PK-12
1727 Malphrus Rd 29936 843-726-3673

Ridge Spring, Saluda, Pop. 720
Aiken County SD
Supt. — See Aiken
Ridge Spring-Monetta S 600/K-8
422 Hazzard Cir 29129 803-685-2000
Callie Herlong, prin. Fax 685-2008

Ridgeville, Dorchester, Pop. 1,972
Dorchester SD 4
Supt. — See Saint George
Clay Hill ES 200/PK-5
387 S Railroad Ave 29472 843-851-7386
Tracy Elmore Jackson, prin. Fax 873-0571

Ridgeway, Fairfield, Pop. 317
Fairfield County SD
Supt. — See Winnsboro
Geiger ES 300/PK-6
150 Cook Rd 29130 803-337-8288
Myra Bramlett, prin. Fax 337-8185

Rock Hill, York, Pop. 64,898
Rock Hill SD 3 17,600/PK-12
1234 Flint Street Ext 29730 803-981-1000
Dr. Kelly Pew, supt. Fax 981-1094
www.rock-hill.k12.sc.us
Belleview ES 400/K-5
501 Belleview Rd 29730 803-981-1181
Kevin Hood, prin. Fax 981-1193
Castle Heights MS 800/6-8
2382 Fire Tower Rd 29730 803-981-1400
John Kirell, prin. Fax 981-1430
Central Child Development Center 400/PK-PK
414 E Black St 29730 803-980-2060
Damon Ward, dir. Fax 980-2070
Children's ES at Sylvia Circle 300/K-5
929 Sylvia Cir 29730 803-981-1380
Jaqueline Jones, prin. Fax 981-1494
Dutchman Creek MS 900/6-8
4757 Mount Gallant Rd 29732 803-985-1700
Dr. Norris Williams, prin. Fax 985-1740
Ebenezer Avenue ES Montessori 300/PK-6
242 Ebenezer Ave 29730 803-981-1380
Chris Beard, prin. Fax 981-1925
Ebinport ES 600/K-5
2142 India Hook Rd 29732 803-981-1550
Rhonda Kelsey, prin. Fax 981-1492
Finley Road ES 400/K-5
1089 Finley Rd 29730 803-981-1280
Christopher Roorda, prin. Fax 981-1294
Independence ES 500/K-5
132 W Springdale Rd 29730 803-981-1135
Kimberly Odom, prin. Fax 981-2010
India Hook ES 600/K-5
2068 Yukon Dr 29732 803-985-1600
Crystal Guyton, prin. Fax 985-1620
Lesslie ES 400/K-5
250 Neely Store Rd 29730 803-981-1910
Seberina Myles, prin. Fax 981-1916
Mount Gallant ES 500/K-5
4664 Mount Gallant Rd 29732 803-981-1360
Jacob Moree, prin. Fax 981-1366
Mount Holly ES 500/K-5
1800 Porter Rd 29730 803-985-1650
Dr. Nakia Barnes, prin. Fax 985-1660
Northside ES 500/K-5
840 Annafrel St 29730 803-981-1570
Lesley King, prin. Fax 981-1926
Oakdale ES 400/K-5
1129 Oakdale Rd 29730 803-981-1585
Denise Khaalid, prin. Fax 981-1593
Old Pointe ES 600/K-5
380 Old Pointe School Rd 29732 803-980-2040
Brian Hammond, prin. Fax 980-2045
Rawlinson Road MS 600/6-8
2631 W Main St 29732 803-981-1500
Dr. Jean Dickson, prin. Fax 981-1532
Richmond Drive ES 600/K-5
1162 Richmond Dr 29732 803-981-1930
Pat Maness, prin. Fax 981-1929
Rosewood ES 600/PK-5
2240 Rosewood Dr 29732 803-981-1540
Deborah Greenwood, prin. Fax 981-1568
Saluda Trail MS 800/6-8
2300 Saluda Rd 29730 803-981-1800
Elissa Cox, prin. Fax 981-1888
Sullivan MS 800/6-8
1825 Eden Ter 29730 803-981-1450
Shane Goodwin, prin. Fax 981-1456
Sunset Park ES 500/K-5
1036 Ogden Rd 29730 803-981-1260
Dr. Tammy White, prin. Fax 981-1269
York Road ES 400/K-5
2254 W Main St 29732 803-981-1950
Patrick Robinson, prin. Fax 981-1961

St. Anne S 300/PK-12
1698 Bird St 29730 803-324-4814
Shaileen Riginos, prin. Fax 324-0189
Westminster Catawba Christian S 500/PK-12
2650 India Hook Rd 29732 803-366-4119
Scott Dillon, head sch Fax 328-5465

Roebuck, Spartanburg, Pop. 2,173
Spartanburg County SD 6 12,000/PK-12
1390 Cavalier Way 29376 864-576-4212
Dr. Darryl Owings, supt. Fax 574-6265
www.spart6.org
Gable MS 800/6-8
198 Otts Shoals Rd 29376 864-576-3500
Matt Talley, prin. Fax 595-2428
Roebuck ES 700/PK-5
2401 E Blackstock Rd 29376 864-576-6151
Jennifer Faulkner, prin. Fax 595-2429
Other Schools – See Moore, Pauline, Spartanburg

Rowesville, Orangeburg, Pop. 302
Orangeburg Consolidated SD 5
Supt. — See Orangeburg
Bethune-Bowman ES 300/K-5
4857 Charleston Hwy 29133 803-533-6371
Lakekia Lewis, prin. Fax 533-6373

Ruby, Chesterfield, Pop. 357
Chesterfield County SD
Supt. — See Chesterfield
Ruby ES 300/PK-5
249 Thurman Ave 29741 843-634-6310
Caroline Miles, prin. Fax 634-5013

Ruffin, Colleton
Colleton County SD
Supt. — See Walterboro
Bells ES 300/PK-5
12088 Bells Hwy 29475 843-782-0012
Lauren Behie, prin. Fax 866-7361

Saint George, Dorchester, Pop. 2,077
Dorchester SD 4 2,300/PK-12
500 Ridge St 29477 843-563-4535
Dr. Morris Ravenell Ed.D., supt. Fax 563-9269
www.dorchester4.k12.sc.us
Saint George MS 300/6-8
600 Minus St 29477 843-563-3171
Benjamin Kennedy, prin. Fax 563-5936
Williams Memorial ES 700/PK-5
290 S Metts St 29477 843-563-3231
Shannon Stephens, prin. Fax 563-5929
Other Schools – See Dorchester, Ridgeville

Dorchester Academy 300/PK-12
234 Academy Rd 29477 843-563-9511

Saint Helena Island, Beaufort
Beaufort County SD
Supt. — See Beaufort
St. Helena ES 400/PK-5
1025 Sea Island Pkwy 29920 843-838-0300
Dr. Tara Mack, prin. Fax 838-0373

Saint Matthews, Calhoun, Pop. 2,002
Calhoun County SD 1,800/PK-12
PO Box 215 29135 803-655-7310
Dr. Steve Wilson, supt. Fax 655-7393
www.ccpsonline.net
St. Matthews ES 700/PK-8
135 Saints Ave 29135 803-665-2750
Treda Keith, prin. Fax 874-3273
Other Schools – See Swansea

Calhoun Academy 400/PK-12
PO Box 526 29135 803-874-2734

Saint Stephen, Berkeley, Pop. 1,670
Berkeley County SD
Supt. — See Moncks Corner
Saint Stephen ES 400/PK-5
PO Box 338 29479 843-567-2813
Dr. Elaine Norton, prin. Fax 567-3064
Saint Stephen MS 300/6-8
225 Carolina Dr 29479 843-567-3128
Brenda Fleming, prin. Fax 567-8162

Saluda, Saluda, Pop. 3,519
Saluda SD 2,200/PK-12
404 N Wise Rd 29138 864-445-8441
David M. Mathis Ed.D., supt. Fax 445-9598
www.saludaschools.org
Hollywood ES 400/PK-5
1261 Hollywood Rd 29138 864-445-8333
Tammie Shore, prin. Fax 445-3518
Saluda ES 300/3-5
400 W Butler Ave 29138 864-445-2564
Marcie Enlow, prin. Fax 445-8833
Saluda MS 500/6-8
140 Ivory Key Rd 29138 864-445-3767
Don Hardie, prin. Fax 445-3980
Saluda PS 400/PK-2
200 Matthews Dr 29138 864-445-2469
Peggy Trivelas, prin. Fax 445-4374

Scranton, Florence, Pop. 927
Florence County SD Three
Supt. — See Lake City
Scranton ES 400/PK-5
PO Box 129 29591 843-389-2531
Allana Prosser, prin. Fax 389-2548

Seabrook, Beaufort
Beaufort County SD
Supt. — See Beaufort
Whale Branch ES 400/PK-4
15 Stuart Point Rd 29940 843-466-1000
Anita Singleton, prin. Fax 466-1073
Whale Branch MS 400/5-8
2009 Trask Pkwy 29940 843-466-3000
Freddie Lawton, prin. Fax 466-3087

Seneca, Oconee, Pop. 7,931
Oconee County SD
Supt. — See Walhalla
Blue Ridge ES 600/PK-5
995 S Oak St 29678 864-886-4550
Lisa Simmons, prin. Fax 886-4551
Keowee ES 400/PK-5
7051 Keowee School Rd 29672 864-886-4475
Josh Holliday, prin. Fax 886-4474
Northside ES 600/PK-5
710 N Townville St 29678 864-886-4445
Geoff Smith, prin. Fax 886-4446
Ravenel ES 500/PK-5
150 Ravenel School Rd 29678 864-885-5026
Angie Henderson, prin. Fax 885-5063
Seneca MS 800/6-8
810 W South 4th St 29678 864-886-4455
Al LeRoy, prin. Fax 886-4452

Oconee Christian Academy 100/PK-12
150 His Way Cir 29672 864-882-6925
Dean Bare, dir. Fax 882-7217

Shaw AFB, Sumter
Sumter SD
Supt. — See Sumter
High Hills ES 500/4-5
4971 Frierson Rd 29152 803-499-3327
Dr. Mary Kay Norton, prin. Fax 499-9553
Shaw Heights ES 500/2-3
5121 Frierson Rd 29152 803-666-2335
Dr. Melissa Morris, prin. Fax 666-3719

Simpsonville, Greenville, Pop. 17,848
Greenville County SD
Supt. — See Greenville
Bells Crossing ES 1,000/K-5
804 Scuffletown Rd 29681 864-355-3800
Chris Ross, prin. Fax 355-3885
Bethel ES 900/K-5
111 Bethel School Rd 29681 864-355-4100
Nerissa Lewis, prin. Fax 355-4180
Bryson ES 900/K-5
703 Bryson Dr 29681 864-355-3600
Andreya Boggs, prin. Fax 355-3696
Bryson MS 1,100/6-8
3657 S Industrial Dr 29681 864-355-2100
Dr. Adrienne Davenport, prin. Fax 355-2194
Chandler MS 700/6-8
4231 Fork Shoals Rd 29680 864-452-0300
Jeffrey Jenkins, prin. Fax 452-0365
Golden Strip Child Development Center PK-K
1200 Howard Dr 29681 864-355-5070
Amanda Lecaroz, prin. Fax 355-5090
Gordon ES 700/K-5
1507 Scuffletown Rd 29681 864-452-0200
Jackie Parker, prin. Fax 452-0242
Hillcrest MS 1,000/6-8
510 Garrison Rd 29681 864-355-6100
William Price, prin. Fax 355-6120
Mauldin ES 900/K-5
1194 Holland Rd 29681 864-355-3700
Dr. Jamie Spinks, prin. Fax 355-3783
Mauldin MS 1,200/6-8
1190 Holland Rd 29681 864-355-6770
Chris Killan, prin. Fax 355-6988
Monarch ES 800/K-5
224 Five Forks Rd 29681 864-452-0600
Vaughan Overman, prin. Fax 452-0690
Oakview ES 1,000/K-5
515 Godfrey Rd 29681 864-355-7100
Dr. Phillip Reavis, prin. Fax 355-7115
Plain ES 900/K-5
506 Neely Ferry Rd 29680 864-355-7700
Deborah Mihalic, prin. Fax 355-7774
Simpsonville ES 800/K-5
200 Morton Ave 29681 864-355-8300
Jackie Earle, prin. Fax 355-8360

Abiding Peace Academy PK-5
401 Batesville Rd 29681 864-509-6408
Zach Seeger, prin.
Five Oaks Academy 200/PK-8
1101 Jonesville Rd 29681 864-228-1881
Kathleen Trewhella-Grant, dir. Fax 228-9888
Greenville Classical Academy 100/PK-12
2519 Woodruff Rd 29681 864-329-9884
Eric Woernle, prin.
Southside Christian S 1,100/PK-12
2211 Woodruff Rd 29681 864-234-7595
Dr. Sam Barfell, supt. Fax 234-7048

Six Mile, Pickens, Pop. 670
Pickens County SD
Supt. — See Easley
Six Mile ES 400/K-5
777 N Main St 29682 864-397-2400
Melissa Terry, prin. Fax 868-4011

Society Hill, Darlington, Pop. 552
Darlington County SD
Supt. — See Darlington
Rosenwald S 100/PK-8
508 Church St 29593 843-378-4011
Kimberly Mason, prin. Fax 398-2694

Spartanburg, Spartanburg, Pop. 36,415
Spartanburg County SD 6
Supt. — See Roebuck
Arcadia ES 400/PK-5
375 Spring St 29301 864-576-1371
Bobby Rollins, prin. Fax 595-2408
Bobo ES 500/K-5
495 Powell Mill Rd 29301 864-576-2085
Catherine Pogue, prin. Fax 576-3180
District 6 Child Development Center PK-PK
3050 N Blackstock Rd 29301 864-576-4886
Krishenda Alexander, prin. Fax 576-0402
Fairforest ES 800/K-5
1005 Mount Zion Rd 29303 864-439-5000
Dr. Stephen Krawczyk, prin. Fax 661-1476
Fairforest MS 800/6-8
4120 N Blackstock Rd 29301 864-576-1270
Dean Ledford, prin. Fax 576-2600
Lone Oak ES 400/K-5
7314 Lone Oak Rd 29303 864-503-9088
Keith Burton, prin. Fax 503-9090

West View ES 800/PK-5
400 Oak Grove Rd 29301 864-576-1833
Dr. Lindi Metcalf, prin. Fax 595-2436
Woodland Heights ES 500/PK-5
1216 John B White Sr Blvd 29306 864-576-0506
Dr. Cindy Pridgen, prin. Fax 595-2439

Spartanburg SD 2
Supt. — See Chesnee
Hendrix ES 700/K-4
1084 Springfield Rd 29316 864-578-1288
Tina Humphries, prin. Fax 578-6162

Spartanburg SD 3
Supt. — See Glendale
Cannons ES 200/PK-5
1315 Old Converse Rd 29307 864-279-6100
Karen Grimm, prin. Fax 279-6110
Clifdale ES 300/PK-5
451 Heritage Hills Dr 29307 864-279-6200
Windy Hodge, prin. Fax 279-6210

Spartanburg SD 7 7,300/PK-12
PO Box 970 29304 864-594-4400
Dr. Russell W. Booker, supt. Fax 594-4406
spartanburg7.org
Boyd ES 400/K-5
1505 Fernwood Glendale Rd 29307 864-594-4430
Meredith Rose, prin. Fax 594-6143
Carver MS 500/6-8
467 S Church St 29306 864-594-4435
Nicole Thompson, prin. Fax 594-6144
Chapman ES 400/K-5
230 Bryant Rd 29303 864-594-4440
Eric Mathison, prin. Fax 594-6145
Cleveland Academy of Leadership 500/K-6
151 Franklin St 29303 864-594-4444
Fred Logan, prin. Fax 594-6146
Early Learning Center Park Hills 300/PK-PK
301 Crescent Ave 29306 864-594-4465
Charlene Doctor, prin. Fax 594-6149
Houston ES 400/K-5
1475 Skylyn Dr 29307 864-594-4448
Mark Hendry, prin. Fax 594-6147
McCracken MS 700/6-8
300 Webber Rd 29307 864-594-4457
Margaret Peach, prin. Fax 596-8418
Meeting Street Academy - Spartanburg PK-3
201 E Broad St Ste 110 29306 864-253-1800
Raine Hackler, prin. Fax 253-1802
Pine Street S 700/K-5
500 S Pine St 29302 864-594-4470
Anne Chapman-Jeter, prin. Fax 594-6150
Todd S 900/PK-8
150 Old Canaan Rd 29306 864-594-4475
Katrina Robinson, prin. Fax 594-6152
Wright ES 500/PK-5
457 S Church St 29306 864-594-4477
Dr. Marc Zachary, prin. Fax 594-6153

Eddlemon Adventist S 50/K-8
1217 John B White Sr Blvd 29306 864-576-2234
Oakbrook Preparatory S 500/K-12
190 Lincoln School Rd 29301 864-587-2060
St. Paul the Apostle S 100/PK-8
152 Alabama St 29302 864-582-6645
Patricia Lanthier, prin. Fax 582-1225
Spartanburg Christian Academy 500/PK-12
8740 Asheville Hwy 29316 864-578-4238
Robert McDonald, hdmstr. Fax 542-1846
Spartanburg Day S 400/PK-12
1701 Skylyn Dr 29307 864-582-7539
Rachel Deems, head sch Fax 582-7530

Starr, Anderson, Pop. 170
Anderson SD 3
Supt. — See Iva
Starr ES 400/PK-5
400 Professor Brown Ln 29684 864-352-6154
Melissa Davis, prin. Fax 352-6158
Starr-Iva MS 600/6-8
1034 Rainey Rd 29684 864-352-6146
Daniel Crawford, prin. Fax 352-2095

Sullivans Island, Charleston, Pop. 1,780
Charleston County SD
Supt. — See Charleston
Sullivans Island ES 500/PK-5
2014 Mike Perkis Pl 29482 843-883-3118
Susan King, prin. Fax 883-3134

Summerton, Clarendon, Pop. 994
Clarendon SD 1 800/PK-12
PO Box 38 29148 803-485-2325
Barbara Champagne, supt. Fax 485-2822
www.clarendon1.k12.sc.us
St. Paul ES 200/3-6
9297 Alex Harvin Hwy 29148 803-574-2150
Joaquin Brown, prin. Fax 478-2780
Scott's Branch MS 100/7-8
9253 Alex Harvin Hwy 29148 803-574-2100
Corey Burgess, prin. Fax 478-7659
Summerton ECC 300/PK-2
8 S Church St 29148 803-485-2102
Patricia Middleton, prin. Fax 485-8708

Clarendon Hall S 200/PK-12
PO Box 609 29148 803-485-3550
Phillip Rizzo, hdmstr. Fax 485-3205

Summerville, Dorchester, Pop. 42,232
Berkeley County SD
Supt. — See Moncks Corner
Cane Bay ES 900/PK-4
1247 Cane Bay Blvd, 843-899-5100
Melissa LaBerge, prin. Fax 899-5104
Cane Bay MS 700/5-8
1175 Cane Bay Blvd, 843-899-1857
Carol Beckmann-Bartlett, prin. Fax 899-1861
Nexton ES K-5
200 Scholar Way, 843-900-3222
Nancy Leigh, prin. Fax 900-3255
Sangaree ES 900/PK-2
1460 Royle Rd, 843-820-3865
Barbara Webber, prin. Fax 820-3874
Sangaree IS 700/3-5
201 School House Ln, 843-820-3850
Angela Siegling, prin. Fax 820-3854

Dorchester SD 2 23,800/K-12
115 Devon Rd 29483 843-873-2901
Joseph Pye, supt. Fax 821-4053
www.edlinesites.net/pages/Dorchester_County_SD
Alston-Bailey ES K-5
820 W 5th North St 29483 843-695-5210
Vernisa Bodison, prin. Fax 695-5211
Alston MS 900/6-8
500 Bryan St 29483 843-873-3890
Thad Schmenk, prin. Fax 821-3978
Beech Hill ES 1,200/K-5
1001 Beech Hill Rd 29485 843-821-3970
Rene Harris, prin. Fax 821-3979
DuBose MS 1,100/6-8
1005 DuBose School Rd 29483 843-875-7012
Ted Brinkley, prin. Fax 821-3995
Flowertown ES 1,000/K-5
20 King Charles Cir 29485 843-871-7400
Teresa Kelly, prin. Fax 821-3980
Fort Dorchester ES 1,100/K-5
5201 Old Glory Ln 29485 843-832-5550
Harolyn Hess, prin. Fax 832-5553
Gregg MS 1,100/6-8
500 Greenwave Blvd 29483 843-871-3150
Will Wilson, prin. Fax 821-3992
Knightsville ES 1,300/K-5
847 Orangeburg Rd 29483 843-873-4851
Clair Sieber, prin. Fax 821-3983
Newington ES 800/K-5
10 King Charles Cir 29485 843-871-3230
Camilla Groome, prin. Fax 821-3981
Reeves ES 1,100/K-5
1003 DuBose School Rd 29483 843-695-2450
Natalie Hayes, prin. Fax 695-2455
Rollings MS of the Arts 700/6-8
815 S Main St 29483 843-873-3610
Dr. Kathy Sobolewski, prin. Fax 821-3985
Sand Hill ES K-5
324 Gnarly Oak Ln 29485 843-695-5201
Dr. Wally Baird, prin. Fax 695-5202
Sires ES K-5
301 Chandler Creek Rd 29485 843-695-5205
Laura Blanchard, prin. Fax 695-5206
Spann ES 800/K-5
901 John Mckissick Way 29483 843-873-3050
Shane Sanford, prin. Fax 821-3987
Summerville ES 700/K-5
835 S Main St 29483 843-873-2372
Katie Barker, prin. Fax 821-3988
Other Schools – See Ladson, North Charleston

Faith Christian S 300/PK-12
337 Farmington Rd, 843-873-8464
Northwood Academy 400/K-5
102 Charger Dr, 843-572-0940
Melanie Van Deusen, prin. Fax 764-2274
Oaks Christian S 200/PK-8
505 Gahagan Rd 29485 843-875-7667
Robin Boehler, head sch
Pinewood Preparatory S 800/PK-12
1114 Orangeburg Rd 29483 843-873-1643
Stephen Mandell, hdmstr. Fax 821-4257
Ridge Christian Academy 200/PK-12
2168 Ridge Church Rd 29483 843-873-9856
Summerville Catholic S 200/PK-8
226 Black Oak Blvd 29485 843-873-9310
Charlie Tisdale, prin. Fax 873-5709

Sumter, Sumter, Pop. 39,747
Sumter SD 16,800/PK-12
1345 Wilson Hall Rd 29150 803-469-6900
Dr. Debra Hamm, supt. Fax 469-3769
sumterschools.net
Alice Drive ES 700/PK-5
251 Alice Dr 29150 803-775-0857
Suzanna Foley, prin. Fax 775-7580
Alice Drive MS 800/6-8
40 Miller Rd 29150 803-775-0821
Jeannie Pressley, prin. Fax 778-2929
Bates MS 700/6-8
715 Estate St 29150 803-775-0711
Dr. Ayesha Hunter, prin. Fax 775-0715
Cherryvale ES 400/PK-5
1420 Furman Dr 29154 803-494-8200
Dr. Henrietta Green, prin. Fax 494-8233
Chestnut Oaks MS 500/6-8
1200 Oswego Hwy 29153 803-775-7272
Dr. Maggie Wright, prin. Fax 775-7601
Crosswell Drive ES 600/PK-5
301 Crosswell Dr 29150 803-775-0679
Dr. Shawn Hagerty, prin. Fax 778-2857
Crosswell Park ECC PK-PK
475 Crosswell Dr 29150 803-774-5900
Dr. Cynthia Graham, dir. Fax 774-5901
Davis ES 300/PK-5
345 Eastern School Rd 29153 803-495-3247
Michelle McBride, prin. Fax 495-3211
Ebenezer MS 400/6-8
3440 Ebenezer Rd 29153 803-469-8571
Marlene DeWit, prin. Fax 469-8575
Furman MS 900/6-8
3400 Bethel Church Rd 29154 803-481-8519
Michael Riggins, prin. Fax 481-8923
Kingsbury ES 700/PK-5
825 Kingsbury Dr 29154 803-775-6244
Phillip Jackson, prin. Fax 775-7021
Lemira ES 600/PK-5
952 Fulton St 29153 803-775-0658
Dr. Vanessa Canty, prin. Fax 778-2730
Mayewood MS 200/6-8
4300 E Brewington Rd 29153 803-495-8014
Anita Hunter, prin. Fax 495-8016
Millwood ES 700/PK-5
24 Pinewood Rd 29150 803-775-0648
Dr. Cornelius Leach, prin. Fax 436-2987
Oakland PS 600/PK-1
5415 Oakland Dr 29154 803-499-3366
Josh Campbell, prin. Fax 499-3361
Pocalla Springs ES 900/PK-5
2060 Bethel Church Rd 29154 803-481-5800
Dr. Laura Brown, prin. Fax 481-5813
Wilder ES 400/PK-5
975 S Main St 29150 803-773-5723
David Wright, prin. Fax 778-2918
Willow Drive ES 600/PK-5
26 Willow Dr 29150 803-773-5796
Trevor Ivey, prin. Fax 778-2847
Other Schools – See Dalzell, Pinewood, Rembert, Shaw AFB, Wedgefield

---

Berea Academy 50/K-8
675 S Lafayette Dr 29150 803-773-6875
St. Anne & St. Jude Catholic S 100/PK-8
11 S Magnolia St 29150 803-775-3632
Kristi Doyle, prin. Fax 938-9074
St. James Lutheran S PK-5
1137-A Alice Dr 29150 803-934-8727
Kristin Ross, admin. Fax 934-8728
Sumter Christian S 200/PK-12
420 S Pike W 29150 803-773-1902
Wilson Hall 800/PK-12
520 Wilson Hall Rd 29150 803-469-3475

Swansea, Lexington, Pop. 808
Calhoun County SD
Supt. — See Saint Matthews
Sandy Run S 600/PK-8
450 Old Swamp Rd 29160 803-791-8866
Brenda Goodwin, prin. Fax 791-8975

Lexington County SD 4 3,300/PK-12
607 E 5th St 29160 803-490-7000
Dr. Linda Lavender, supt. Fax 399-7960
www.lexington4.net
ECC 600/PK-K
135 Lewis Rast Rd 29160 803-490-7001
Lisa Evans, prin. Fax 399-7961
Sandhills ES 500/3-4
130 Lewis Rast Rd 29160 803-490-7003
Bryan Evans, prin. Fax 399-7963
Sandhills PS 500/1-2
140 Lewis Rast Rd 29160 803-490-7002
Bryan Evans, prin.
Other Schools – See Gaston

Tamassee, Oconee
Oconee County SD
Supt. — See Walhalla
Tamassee-Salem ES 300/PK-5
9950 N Highway 11 29686 864-886-4540
Bobby Norizsan, prin. Fax 886-4539

Taylors, Greenville, Pop. 21,240
Greenville County SD
Supt. — See Greenville
Brook Glenn ES 400/K-5
2003 E Lee Rd 29687 864-355-4700
Bernice Jackson, prin. Fax 355-4755
Brushy Creek ES 900/K-5
1344 Brushy Creek Rd 29687 864-355-5400
Charles Davis, prin. Fax 355-5413
Mountain View ES 800/K-5
6350 Mountain View Rd 29687 864-355-6800
Jennifer Gibson, prin. Fax 355-6856
Northwood MS 900/6-8
710 Ikes Rd 29687 864-355-7000
Treva Lee, prin. Fax 355-7077
Paris ES 600/K-5
32 E Belvue Rd 29687 864-355-4260
David Wise, prin. Fax 355-4391
Taylors ES 800/K-5
809 Reid School Rd 29687 864-355-7450
Rhonda Rhodes, prin. Fax 355-7477
Tigerville ES 200/K-5
25 Tigerville Elem School 29687 864-355-4600
Diane Jackson, prin. Fax 355-4646

Prince of Peace S 300/PK-8
1209 Brushy Creek Rd 29687 864-322-2233
Marianne Tully, prin. Fax 331-2153

Tega Cay, York, Pop. 7,516
Fort Mill SD
Supt. — See Fort Mill
Gold Hill ES 900/K-5
1000 Dave Gibson Blvd 29708 803-548-8250
Terry Brewer, prin. Fax 548-8373
Gold Hill MS 700/6-8
1025 Dave Gibson Blvd 29708 803-548-8300
Matthew Wallace, prin. Fax 548-8322
Tega Cay ES K-5
2185 Gold Hill Rd 29708 803-548-8282
Chris Gardner, prin. Fax 548-8619

Timmonsville, Florence, Pop. 2,312
Florence County SD Four 700/PK-12
304 Kemper St 29161 843-346-3956
Dr. Zona W. Jefferson, supt. Fax 346-5159
www.florence4.k12.sc.us
Brockington ES 400/PK-5
304 Kemper St 29161 843-346-4953
Teresa Gamble, prin. Fax 346-5159
Johnson MS 200/6-8
304 Kemper St 29161 843-346-4586
Tonya Addison, prin. Fax 346-5159

Townville, Anderson
Anderson SD 4
Supt. — See Pendleton
Townville ES 300/K-6
PO Box 10 29689 864-403-2600
Denise Fredericks, prin. Fax 287-5716

Travelers Rest, Greenville, Pop. 4,504
Greenville County SD
Supt. — See Greenville
Gateway ES 600/K-5
200 Hawkins Rd 29690 864-355-5200
Susan Stubley, prin. Fax 355-5259
Heritage ES 600/K-5
1592 Geer Hwy 29690 864-355-6000
Heather Hester, prin. Fax 355-6046
Northwest MS 800/6-8
1606 Geer Hwy 29690 864-355-6900
Patrick Jarrett, prin. Fax 355-6920

Trenton, Edgefield, Pop. 196
Edgefield County SD
Supt. — See Johnston
Douglas ES 300/PK-5
215 Samuel E Diggs Rd 29847 803-275-1752
Bobby Turner, prin. Fax 275-1751

Turbeville, Clarendon, Pop. 765
Clarendon SD 3 1,200/PK-12
PO Box 270 29162 843-659-2188
Fax 659-3204
www.clarendon3.org
Other Schools – See New Zion

Union, Union, Pop. 8,281
Union County SD 3,800/K-12
PO Box 907 29379 864-429-1740
William F. Roach Ph.D., supt. Fax 429-1745
www.union.k12.sc.us
Foster Park ES 500/K-5
901 Arthur Blvd 29379 864-429-1737
Ott Sizemore, prin. Fax 429-1799
Monarch ES 400/K-5
218 Monarch School Dr 29379 864-429-1733
Mickey Connolly, prin. Fax 429-1789
Sims MS 700/6-8
2200 Whitmire Hwy 29379 864-429-1755
Eric Childers, prin. Fax 429-2811
Other Schools – See Buffalo, Jonesville, Lockhart

Vance, Orangeburg, Pop. 169
Orangeburg County Consolidated SD 3
Supt. — See Holly Hill
Vance/Providence ES 300/PK-5
633 Camden Rd 29163 803-492-7766
Latonya Durant, prin. Fax 492-3901

Varnville, Hampton, Pop. 2,133
Hampton SD 1 2,400/PK-12
372 Pine St E 29944 803-943-4576
Dr. Ronald Wilcox, supt. Fax 943-5943
www.hampton1.org
North District MS 400/7-8
PO Box 368 29944 803-943-3507
Patricia Brantley, prin. Fax 943-4074
Varnville ES 400/PK-6
PO Box 367 29944 803-943-2376
Donna Kinard, prin. Fax 943-5715
Other Schools – See Brunson, Hampton, Yemassee

Wadmalaw Island, Charleston
Charleston County SD
Supt. — See Charleston
Frierson ES 100/PK-5
6133 Maybank Hwy 29487 843-559-4500
Dr. Deborah Fickling, prin. Fax 559-6438

Wagener, Aiken, Pop. 778
Aiken County SD
Supt. — See Aiken
Busbee ES 500/K-5
20 Corbett Cir 29164 803-564-1000
Sonya Colvin, prin. Fax 564-1010
Corbett MS 200/6-8
10 A L Corbett Cir 29164 803-564-1050
Sonya Colvin, prin. Fax 564-1058

Walhalla, Oconee, Pop. 4,200
Oconee County SD 10,900/PK-12
414 S Pine St 29691 864-886-4400
Dr. Michael Thorsland, supt. Fax 886-4408
www.oconee.k12.sc.us
Brown ES 700/PK-5
225 Coffee Rd 29691 864-886-4470
Ashley Robertson, prin. Fax 886-4471
Walhalla ES 600/PK-5
508 Fowler Rd 29691 864-886-4480
Shanon Lusk, prin. Fax 886-4481
Walhalla MS 800/6-8
151 Razorback Ln 29691 864-886-4485
Scott Dixon, prin. Fax 886-4483
Other Schools – See Seneca, Tamassee, Westminster

Wallace, Marlboro, Pop. 872
Marlboro County SD
Supt. — See Bennettsville
Wallace S 400/PK-8
3643 Highway 9 W 29596 843-537-7493
Mahilda Douglas, prin. Fax 537-4435

Walterboro, Colleton, Pop. 5,325
Colleton County SD 6,100/PK-12
213 N Jefferies Blvd 29488 843-782-4510
Dr. Franklin Foster, supt. Fax 549-2606
www.colletonsd.org
Black Street ECC 400/PK-K
256 Smith St 29488 843-782-4516
Barbara Kulisek, coord. Fax 549-6220
Colleton MS 1,500/6-8
1379 Tuskegee Airmen Dr 29488 843-782-0040
Matthew Brantley, prin. Fax 782-0041
Forest Hills ES 700/1-5
633 Hiers Corner Rd 29488 843-782-4512
Amy Libenrood, prin. Fax 782-3853
Hendersonville ES 400/PK-5
6089 Hendersonville Hwy 29488 843-782-0027
Marcella Owens, prin. Fax 844-7361
Northside ES 600/1-5
1929 Industrial Rd 29488 843-782-0015
Wilsey Hamilton, prin. Fax 538-3478
Other Schools – See Cottageville, Ruffin

Colleton Prep Academy 200/PK-12
PO Box 1426 29488 843-538-8959
Jill Burttram, head sch Fax 538-8260

Ware Shoals, Greenwood, Pop. 2,149
Greenwood SD 51 800/PK-12
56 S Greenwood Ave 29692 864-456-7496
Dr. Fay Sprouse, supt. Fax 626-4565
www.gwd51.org
Ware Shoals MS 100/5-8
45 W Main St 29692 864-456-2711
Nancy Brown, prin. Fax 456-2153
Ware Shoals PS 300/PK-4
15269 Indian Mound Rd 29692 864-861-2261
Debbie Bishop, prin. Fax 861-4338

Warrenville, Aiken, Pop. 1,205
Aiken County SD
Supt. — See Aiken
Langley-Bath-Clearwater MS 600/6-8
29 Lions Trl 29851 803-593-7260
Paul Spadaro, prin. Fax 593-7119
Warrenville ES 400/K-5
569 Howlandville Rd 29851 803-663-4270
Charlene Heard, prin. Fax 663-4271

Waterloo, Laurens, Pop. 163
Laurens SD 55
Supt. — See Laurens
Waterloo ES 300/PK-5
10457 Highway 221 S 29384 864-677-4670
Jennifer Abercrombie, prin. Fax 677-4674

Wedgefield, Sumter, Pop. 1,581
Sumter SD
Supt. — See Sumter
DeLaine ES 200/K-5
5355 Cane Savannah Rd 29168 803-494-2661
Maria Newton-Ta'Bon, prin. Fax 494-2675

Wellford, Spartanburg, Pop. 2,329
Spartanburg SD 5
Supt. — See Duncan
Wellford Academy of Science & Technology 400/K-4
684 Syphrit Rd 29385 864-949-2385
Angie Showalter, prin. Fax 949-2386

West Columbia, Lexington, Pop. 14,742
Lexington County SD 1
Supt. — See Lexington
White Knoll ES 700/K-5
132 White Knoll Way 29170 803-821-4500
Nicole Mitchell, prin. Fax 821-4503
White Knoll MS 800/6-8
116 White Knoll Way 29170 803-821-4300
Guy Smith, prin. Fax 821-4303

Lexington County SD 2 8,800/PK-12
715 9th St 29169 803-796-4708
Dr. William B. James Ph.D., supt. Fax 739-4063
www.lex2.org/
Brookland-Cayce Grammar S #1 400/K-5
114 Hook Ave 29169 803-739-4075
Christopher Dickey, prin. Fax 739-8384
Congaree ES 400/2-5
1221 Ramblin Rd 29172 803-755-7430
Jeff Becker, prin. Fax 755-7405
Congaree-Wood ECC 700/PK-1
739 Pine Ridge Dr 29172 803-755-7474
Leonard Frierson, prin. Fax 755-7482
Fulmer MS 700/6-8
1614 Walterboro St 29170 803-822-5660
Megan Carrero, prin. Fax 822-5664
Northside MS 600/6-8
157 Cougar Dr 29169 803-739-4190
Mary Paige Damm, prin. Fax 739-3188
Pine Ridge MS 500/6-8
735 Pine Ridge Dr 29172 803-755-7400
Dr. David Basile, prin. Fax 755-7449
Pineview ES 700/K-5
3035 Leaphart Rd 29169 803-739-4090
David Sims, prin. Fax 739-3190
Saluda River Academy for the Arts 400/K-5
1520 Duke St 29169 803-739-4095
Tonya Fryer, prin. Fax 739-3198
Springdale ES 500/K-5
361 Wattling Rd 29170 803-739-4175
Hope Vrana, prin. Fax 739-3198
Wood ES 500/2-5
737 Pine Ridge Dr 29172 803-755-7420
Leonard Frierson, prin. Fax 755-7447
Other Schools – See Cayce

Westminster, Oconee, Pop. 2,380
Oconee County SD
Supt. — See Walhalla
Fair-Oak ES 400/PK-5
1964 Oakway Rd 29693 864-886-4505
David Thompson, prin. Fax 886-4506
Orchard Park ES 400/PK-5
600 Toccoa Hwy 29693 864-886-4515
Josh Wittrock, prin. Fax 886-4516
Westminster ES 500/PK-5
206 Hamilton Dr 29693 864-886-4520
Sherrie McAllister, prin. Fax 886-4521
West Oak MS 700/6-8
501 Westminster Hwy 29693 864-886-4525
Brandon Blackwell, prin. Fax 886-4524

Poplar Springs SDA S 50/K-8
4279A S Highway 11 29693 864-638-2347

West Pelzer, Anderson, Pop. 867
Anderson SD 1
Supt. — See Williamston
West Pelzer ES 500/PK-5
10 W Stewart St, 864-947-6424
Dr. Stacy Hashe, prin. Fax 947-2014

Whitmire, Newberry, Pop. 1,424
Newberry County SD
Supt. — See Newberry
Whitmire Community S 300/PK-12
2597 Hwy 66 29178 803-694-2320
Daniel McGlohorn, prin. Fax 694-3835

Williamston, Anderson, Pop. 3,887
Anderson SD 1 9,400/PK-12
PO Box 99 29697 864-847-7344
David Havird, supt. Fax 847-3543
www.anderson1.k12.sc.us
Cedar Grove ES 600/PK-5
107 Melvin Ln 29697 864-847-3500
Kristie Finley, prin. Fax 847-3502
Palmetto ES 600/PK-5
1 Roberts Blvd 29697 864-847-5442
Amy Cothran, prin. Fax 847-3504
Palmetto MS 800/6-8
803 N Hamilton St 29697 864-847-4333
Jason McCauley, prin. Fax 847-3529
Other Schools – See Easley, Greenville, Piedmont, West Pelzer

Williston, Barnwell, Pop. 3,095
Williston SD 29 1,000/PK-12
12255 Main St 29853 803-266-7878
Dr. Missoura G. Ashe, supt. Fax 266-3879
www.williston.k12.sc.us
Edwards ES 500/PK-5
1071 Elko St 29853 803-266-3737
Nakeisha Baxley, prin. Fax 266-7061
Williston-Elko MS 200/6-8
12333 Main St 29853 803-266-3430
Greg Sweet, prin. Fax 266-7623

Winnsboro, Fairfield, Pop. 3,508
Fairfield County SD 3,100/PK-12
PO Box 622 29180 803-635-4607
Dr. J.R. Green, supt. Fax 635-6578
www.fairfield.k12.sc.us
Fairfield ES 600/PK-6
175 Medley Rd 29180 803-635-5594
Dr. Tammy Martin, prin. Fax 635-1721
Fairfield Magnet S for Math and Science 400/PK-6
1647 US Highway 321 Byp N 29180 803-635-4810
Gale Whitfield, prin. Fax 635-1803
Fairfield MS 400/7-8
728 US Highway 321 Byp S 29180 803-635-4270
Terrence Harris, prin. Fax 635-9108
Miller ES 300/PK-6
255 Kelly Miller Rd 29180 803-635-2961
Kathy Woodard, prin. Fax 635-4564
Other Schools – See Blair, Ridgeway

Winn Academy 300/PK-12
PO Box 390 29180 803-635-5494

Woodruff, Spartanburg, Pop. 3,990
Spartanburg SD 4 2,800/PK-12
118 McEdco Rd 29388 864-476-3186
Dr. W. Rallie Liston, supt. Fax 476-8616
www.spartanburg4.org
Woodruff ES 600/3-5
915 Cross Anchor Rd 29388 864-476-3123
Jennifer Turner, prin. Fax 476-6193
Woodruff MS 600/6-8
205 SJ Workman Hwy 29388 864-476-3150
Denise Brown, prin. Fax 476-6036
Woodruff PS 700/PK-2
200 Lucy P Edwards Rd 29388 864-476-3174
Ann Hodge, prin. Fax 476-7067

Yemassee, Hampton, Pop. 1,011
Hampton SD 1
Supt. — See Varnville
Fennell ES 200/K-6
131 Yemassee Rd 29945 843-398-5591
Willie Coker, prin. Fax 589-8043

York, York, Pop. 7,594
York SD 1 5,100/PK-12
PO Box 770 29745 803-684-9916
Dr. Vernon Prosser, supt. Fax 684-1903
www.york.k12.sc.us
Cotton Belt ES 400/PK-4
1176 Black Hwy 29745 803-684-1947
Jennifer Bolin, prin. Fax 684-1949
Hunter Street ES 400/PK-4
1100 Hunter St 29745 803-684-1926
Jane Wallace, prin. Fax 684-1931
Jefferson ES 500/PK-4
1543 Chester Hwy 29745 803-684-1942
Mattie Hughes, prin. Fax 684-1944
Johnson ES 500/PK-4
400 E Jefferson St 29745 803-818-6040
Crystal Sandifer, prin. Fax 818-6042
York IS 600/5-6
1280 Johnson Rd 29745 803-684-2311
Keith McSwain, prin. Fax 684-1918
York MS 800/7-8
1010 Devinney Rd 29745 803-684-5008
Richard Ball, prin. Fax 684-1916
Other Schools – See Hickory Grove

Blessed Hope Christian Academy 200/PK-8
PO Box 609 29745 803-684-9819

SOUTH DAKOTA

SOUTH DAKOTA DEPARTMENT OF EDUCATION
800 Governors Dr, Pierre 57501
Telephone 605-773-3134
Fax 605-773-6139
Website doe.sd.gov/
Secretary of Education Donald Kirkegaard

SOUTH DAKOTA BOARD OF EDUCATION
700 Governors Dr, Pierre 57501-2291
President Donald Kirkegaard

EDUCATIONAL COOPERATIVES

NE Educational Services Cooperatives
Gerald Aberle, dir. 605-783-3607
310 5th St, Hayti 57241
nesc.k12.sd.us/

Northwest Area Schools
Quinn Lenk, dir. 605-466-2206
PO Box 35, Isabel 57633 Fax 466-2207
www.nwascoop.org

South Central Cooperative
Carol Rempp, dir. 605-589-3134
PO Box 430, Tyndall 57066 Fax 589-3661
www.southcentralcoop.k12.sd.us

Southeast Area Cooperative
Tricia West, dir. 605-763-5096
1109 W Cedar St, Beresford 57004 Fax 763-2206
southeastareacoop.org

Teachwell Solutions
Joan Frevik, dir. 605-367-7680
715 E 14th St, Sioux Falls 57104 Fax 367-6036
teachwell.org/

PUBLIC, PRIVATE AND CATHOLIC ELEMENTARY SCHOOLS

Aberdeen, Brown, Pop. 25,591
Aberdeen SD 6-1 4,200/K-12
1224 S 3rd St 57401 605-725-7100
Dr. Becky Guffin, supt. Fax 725-7199
www.aberdeen.k12.sd.us
Holgate MS 500/6-8
2200 N Dakota St 57401 605-725-7700
Dr. Greg Aas, prin. Fax 725-7799
Lee ES 400/K-5
1900 N State St 57401 605-725-7500
Christopher Osborn, prin. Fax 725-7599
Lincoln ES 400/K-5
414 S 10th St 57401 605-725-7200
Lisa McNeely, prin. Fax 725-7299
Miller ES K-5
3010 Milwaukee Ave NE 57401 605-725-7800
Nicole Schutter, prin.
Overby ES 400/K-5
612 14th Ave SE 57401 605-725-7300
Mike Neubert, prin. Fax 725-7399
Simmons ES 400/K-5
1500 S 3rd St 57401 605-725-7600
Kim Aman, prin. Fax 725-7699
Simmons MS 500/6-8
1300 S 3rd St 57401 605-725-7900
Dr. Colleen Murley, prin. Fax 725-7999
Tiffany ES 400/K-5
819 8th Ave NE 57401 605-725-7400
Jared Ahlberg, prin. Fax 725-7499

Aberdeen Christian S 200/PK-12
1500 N Highway 281 57401 605-225-2053
Eric Kline, supt. Fax 226-2106
Roncalli ES 200/3-6
501 3rd Ave SE 57401 605-229-4100
Paula Florey, prin. Fax 229-4101
Roncalli PS 200/PK-2
419 1st Ave NE 57401 605-225-3460
Kelsie Sather, prin. Fax 229-4101
Trinity Lutheran S 50/PK-8
923 S Dakota St 57401 605-229-4697
Aaron Kjenstad, prin. Fax 229-4697

Alcester, Union, Pop. 801
Alcester-Hudson SD 61-1 300/PK-12
PO Box 198 57001 605-934-1890
Tim Rhead, supt. Fax 934-1936
www.alcester-hudson.k12.sd.us
Alcester-Hudson ES 200/PK-6
409 E 6th St 57001 605-934-2171
Tim Rhead, prin. Fax 934-1765
Alcester-Hudson JHS 100/7-8
PO Box 198 57001 605-934-1890
LeeAnn Haisch, prin. Fax 934-1936

Alexandria, Hanson, Pop. 613
Hanson SD 30-1 400/PK-12
PO Box 490 57311 605-239-4387
James Bridge, supt. Fax 239-4293
www.hanson.k12.sd.us/
Hanson ES 200/PK-5
PO Box 490 57311 605-239-4387
Josh Oltmanns, prin. Fax 239-4293
Hanson MS 100/6-8
PO Box 490 57311 605-239-4387
Ray Slaba, prin. Fax 239-4293
Oaklane Colony S 50/PK-8
PO Box 490 57311 605-239-4387
Josh Oltmanns, prin. Fax 239-4293
Other Schools – See Mitchell

Mitchell SD 17-2
Supt. — See Mitchell
Rockport Colony S 50/K-8
25209 Rockport Rd 57311 605-239-4214
Lisa Heckenlaible, prin. Fax 239-4372

Arlington, Kingsbury, Pop. 909
Arlington SD 38-1 300/PK-12
PO Box 359 57212 605-983-5597
Justin Downes, supt. Fax 983-2820
www.arlington.k12.sd.us
Arlington ES 200/PK-6
PO Box 359 57212 605-983-5741
Rhonda Gross, prin. Fax 983-4652
Arlington JHS 50/7-8
PO Box 359 57212 605-983-5598
Rhonda Gross, prin. Fax 983-4652

Oldham-Ramona SD 39-5
Supt. — See Ramona
Spring Lake Colony S 50/K-8
21727 452nd Ave 57212 605-482-8244
Andrew Johnson, prin. Fax 482-8282

Armour, Douglas, Pop. 693
Armour SD 21-1 200/K-12
PO Box 640 57313 605-724-2153
Andrea Powell, supt. Fax 724-2977
www.armour.k12.sd.us/
Armour ES 100/K-5
PO Box 640 57313 605-724-2698
Andrea Powell, prin. Fax 724-2977
Armour MS 50/6-8
PO Box 640 57313 605-724-2698
Andrea Powell, prin. Fax 724-2799

Artesian, Sanborn, Pop. 130
Sanborn Central SD 55-5
Supt. — See Forestburg
Upland Colony S 50/K-8
24221 412th Ave 57314 605-495-4183
Connie Vermeulen, prin. Fax 495-4185

Avon, Bon Homme, Pop. 586
Avon SD 4-1 300/PK-12
PO Box 407 57315 605-286-3291
Tom Culver, supt. Fax 286-3712
www.avon.k12.sd.us
Avon ES 100/PK-6
PO Box 407 57315 605-286-3291
Kathryn Blaha, prin. Fax 286-3712
Avon JHS 50/7-8
PO Box 407 57315 605-286-3291
Kathryn Blaha, prin. Fax 286-3510

Baltic, Minnehaha, Pop. 1,070
Baltic SD 49-1 500/PK-12
PO Box 309 57003 605-529-5464
Robert Sittig, supt. Fax 529-5443
www.balticschool.org
Baltic ES 200/PK-5
PO Box 309 57003 605-529-5464
Robert Sittig, prin. Fax 529-5443
Baltic MS 100/6-8
PO Box 309 57003 605-529-5461
James Aisenbrey, prin. Fax 529-5467

Batesland, Shannon, Pop. 108
Oglala Lakota County SD 65-1 1,500/PK-8
PO Box 109 57716 605-288-1921
Dr. Julie Ertz, supt. Fax 288-1814
www.olcsd.com
Batesland S 200/PK-8
PO Box 49 57716 605-288-1948
Dr. Wendy Castaneda, prin. Fax 288-1986
Other Schools – See Hermosa, Pine Ridge, Porcupine

Belle Fourche, Butte, Pop. 5,472
Belle Fourche SD 9-1 1,400/K-12
2305 13th Ave 57717 605-723-3355
Dr. Steve Willard, supt. Fax 723-3366
www.bellefourcheschools.org
Belle Fourche MS 400/5-8
2305 13th Ave 57717 605-723-3367
Kevin Smidt, prin. Fax 723-3374
North Park ES 100/K-K
2305 13th Ave 57717 605-723-3379
Ryan Young, prin. Fax 723-3381
South Park ES 500/1-4
2305 13th Ave 57717 605-723-3382
Ryan Young, prin. Fax 723-3384

Beresford, Union, Pop. 1,991
Beresford SD 61-2 600/PK-12
301 W Maple St 57004 605-763-4293
Brian Field, supt. Fax 763-5305
www.beresford.k12.sd.us/
Beresford ES 300/PK-5
209 S 4th St 57004 605-763-5012
Kevin Nelson, prin. Fax 763-2205
Beresford MS 200/6-8
205 W Maple St 57004 605-763-2139
Dustin Degen, prin. Fax 763-5305

Big Stone City, Grant, Pop. 465
Big Stone CSD 25-1 100/PK-8
655 Walnut St 57216 605-862-8108
Christopher Folk, supt. Fax 862-8640
bigstonecitylions.weebly.com
Big Stone City ES 100/PK-5
655 Walnut St 57216 605-862-8108
Shelley Haggerty, prin. Fax 862-8640
Big Stone City JHS 50/6-8
655 Walnut St 57216 605-862-8108
Shelley Haggerty, prin. Fax 862-8640

Bison, Perkins, Pop. 326
Bison SD 52-1 100/K-12
PO Box 9 57620 605-244-5961
Marilyn Azevedo, supt. Fax 244-5276
www.bison.k12.sd.us/
Bison ES 100/K-6
PO Box 9 57620 605-244-5271
Marilyn Azevedo, supt. Fax 244-5276
Bison JHS 50/7-8
PO Box 9 57620 605-244-5271
Marilyn Azevedo, supt. Fax 244-5276

Black Hawk, Meade, Pop. 2,803
Rapid City Area SD 51-4
Supt. — See Rapid City
Black Hawk ES 400/K-5
7108 Seeaire St 57718 605-787-6701
Holly Yamada, prin. Fax 787-6654

Blunt, Hughes, Pop. 349
Agar-Blunt-Onida SD 58-3
Supt. — See Onida
Blunt ES, PO Box 207 57522 50/K-6
Shana Davis, prin. 605-258-2617

Bonesteel, Gregory, Pop. 272
South Central SD 26-5 100/PK-12
401 Birdsell St 57317 605-654-2314
Brad Peters, supt.
southcentral.k12.sd.us
South Central ES 100/PK-5
401 Birdsell St 57317 605-654-2314
Jeremy Wollman, prin.
South Central MS 50/6-8
401 Birdsell St 57317 605-654-2314
Jeremy Wollman, prin.

Bowdle, Edmunds, Pop. 501
Bowdle SD 22-1 100/K-12
PO Box 563 57428 605-285-6272
Hector Serna, supt. Fax 285-6830
www.bowdle.k12.sd.us
Bowdle ES 100/K-6
PO Box 563 57428 605-285-6590
Hector Serna, prin. Fax 285-6830
Bowdle JHS 50/7-8
PO Box 563 57428 605-285-6590
Hector Serna, prin. Fax 285-6830

Box Elder, Pennington, Pop. 7,381
Douglas SD 51-1 2,700/PK-12
400 Patriot Dr 57719 605-923-0000
Alan Kerr, supt. Fax 923-0018
www.dsdk12.net
Badger Clark ES 500/K-1
401 Don Williams Dr 57719 605-923-0080
Troy Volesky, prin. Fax 923-0081
Carrousel Preschool 100/PK-PK
421 Don Williams Dr 57719 605-923-0090
Joan Dunmire, dir. Fax 923-0091
Case ES 500/2-3
441 Don Williams Dr 57719 605-923-0070
Jeannie Clark, prin. Fax 923-0071
Douglas MS 600/6-8
401 Tower Rd 57719 605-923-0050
Dan Baldwin, prin. Fax 923-0051
Vandenberg ES 400/4-5
561 Briggs St 57719 605-923-0060
Lezlie Larsen, prin. Fax 923-0061

Brandon, Minnehaha, Pop. 8,690
Brandon Valley SD 49-2 3,200/PK-12
300 S Splitrock Blvd 57005 605-582-2049
Dr. Jarod Larson, supt. Fax 582-7456
brandonvalley.k12.sd.us/district/home.htm
Bennis ES 500/K-4
2001 S Sioux Blvd 57005 605-582-8010
Kristin Hofkamp, prin. Fax 582-8012
Brandon ES 600/PK-4
501 E Holly Blvd 57005 605-582-6315
Merle Horst, prin. Fax 582-2709
Brandon Valley IS 5-6
201 W Park St 57005 605-582-6035
Nick Skibsted, prin. Fax 582-6036
Brandon Valley MS 500/7-8
700 E Holly Blvd 57005 605-582-3214
Brad Thorson, prin. Fax 582-7206
Other Schools – See Sioux Falls, Valley Springs

Risen Saviour Preschool PK-PK
301 N Splitrock Blvd 57005 605-582-6902
Val Minihan, admin. Fax 582-3993

Bridgewater, McCook, Pop. 491
Bridgewater-Emery SD 30-3 300/PK-12
PO Box 350 57319 605-729-2541
Jason Bailey, supt. Fax 449-4270
www.bridgewater-emery.k12.sd.us/
Bridgewater ES 100/PK-5
PO Box 350 57319 605-729-2541
Kim Aman, prin. Fax 729-2580
Other Schools – See Emery

Britton, Marshall, Pop. 1,232
Britton-Hecla SD 45-4 500/PK-12
PO Box 190 57430 605-448-2234
Steve Benson, supt. Fax 448-5994
www.britton.k12.sd.us
Britton-Hecla ES 200/PK-6
PO Box 190 57430 605-448-2234
Kyla Richter, prin. Fax 448-5994
Britton-Hecla JHS 50/7-8
PO Box 190 57430 605-448-2234
Carrie James, prin. Fax 448-5994
Sunset Colony S 50/K-8
PO Box 190 57430 605-448-2234
Steve Benson, admin. Fax 448-5994
Westwood Rural S 50/K-8
PO Box 190 57430 605-448-2234
Steve Benson, admin. Fax 448-5994

Brookings, Brookings, Pop. 21,716
Brookings SD 5-1 3,200/K-12
2130 8th St S 57006 605-696-4700
Dr. Klint Willert, supt. Fax 696-4704
www.brookings.k12.sd.us
Camelot IS 500/4-5
1401 15th St S 57006 605-696-4400
Tim Lease, prin. Fax 696-4424
Dakota Prairie ES K-3
111 26th St S 57006 605-696-4900
Kirstin Girard, prin. Fax 696-4905
Hillcrest ES 600/K-3
304 15th Ave 57006 605-696-4600
Brad Olinger, prin. Fax 696-4642
Medary ES 600/K-3
718 5th St S 57006 605-696-4300
Jessica Enderson, prin. Fax 696-4362
Mickelson MS 700/6-8
1801 12th St S 57006 605-696-4500
Tim Steffensen, prin. Fax 696-4506

St. Thomas More S PK-K
1700 8th St S 57006 605-692-4361
Cate Luvaas, prin.

Buffalo, Harding, Pop. 328
Harding County SD 31-1 200/K-12
PO Box 367 57720 605-375-3241
Josh Page, supt. Fax 375-3246
hardingcounty.k12.sd.us
Buffalo ES 100/K-5
PO Box 367 57720 605-375-3241
Kelly Messmer, prin. Fax 375-3246
Harding County MS 50/6-8
PO Box 367 57720 605-375-3241
Kelly Messmer, prin. Fax 375-3246
Other Schools – See Camp Crook, Ludlow

Burke, Gregory, Pop. 594
Burke SD 26-2 200/PK-12
PO Box 382 57523 605-775-2644
Erik Person, supt. Fax 775-2468
www.burke.k12.sd.us
Burke ES 100/PK-6
PO Box 382 57523 605-775-2246
Mark Otten, prin. Fax 775-2468
Burke MS 50/7-8
PO Box 382 57523 605-775-2645
Mark Otten, prin. Fax 775-2468

Camp Crook, Harding, Pop. 63
Harding County SD 31-1
Supt. — See Buffalo
Camp Crook S 50/K-8
Box 58 / 3rd N 57724 605-375-3241
Kelly Messmer, prin. Fax 375-3246

Canistota, McCook, Pop. 646
Canistota SD 43-1 200/K-12
PO Box 8 57012 605-296-3458
Larry Nebelsick, supt. Fax 296-3158
www.canistota.k12.sd.us
Canistota ES 100/K-5
PO Box 8 57012 605-296-3458
Lenny Schroeder, prin. Fax 296-3158
Canistota MS 50/6-8
PO Box 8 57012 605-296-3458
Lenny Schroeder, prin. Fax 296-3158

Canton, Lincoln, Pop. 3,010
Canton SD 41-1 900/PK-12
800 N Main St 57013 605-764-2706
Terry Gerber, supt. Fax 764-2700
www.canton.k12.sd.us
Canton MS 200/6-8
800 N Main St 57013 605-764-2706
Russell Townsend, prin. Fax 764-2700
Lawrence ES 400/PK-5
724 N Sanborn St 57013 605-764-2579
Gabe Devitt, prin. Fax 764-5003

Carpenter, Clark
Clark SD 12-2
Supt. — See Clark
Fordham Colony S 50/K-8
533 Fordham Dr 57322 605-532-3606
Jerry Hartley, prin. Fax 532-3608

Willow Lake SD 12-3
Supt. — See Willow Lake
Shamrock Colony ES 50/K-8
19087 413th Ave 57322 605-625-5945
Chris Lee, prin. Fax 625-3103

Castlewood, Hamlin, Pop. 623
Castlewood SD 28-1 300/PK-12
310 E Harry St 57223 605-793-2497
Keith Fodness, supt. Fax 793-2679
www.castlewood.k12.sd.us/
Castlewood ES 200/PK-6
310 E Harry St 57223 605-793-2497
Brandon Girard, prin. Fax 793-2679
Castlewood JHS 50/7-8
310 E Harry St 57223 605-793-2497
Keith Fodness, prin. Fax 793-2679
Claremont Colony S 50/K-8
46271 184th St 57223 605-793-2497
Brandon Girard, prin. Fax 793-2679

Centerville, Turner, Pop. 877
Centerville SD 60-1 200/PK-12
PO Box 100 57014 605-563-2291
Eric Knight, supt. Fax 563-2615
www.centerville.k12.sd.us
Centerville ES 100/PK-4
PO Box 100 57014 605-563-2291
Eric Knight, prin. Fax 563-2615
Centerville JHS 100/5-8
PO Box 100 57014 605-563-2291
Doug Edberg, prin. Fax 563-2615

Chamberlain, Brule, Pop. 2,326
Chamberlain SD 7-1 900/PK-12
PO Box 119 57325 605-234-4477
Debra Johnson, supt. Fax 234-4479
www.chamberlain.k12.sd.us
Chamberlain ES 500/PK-6
PO Box 119 57325 605-234-4460
Rocky Almond, prin. Fax 234-4479
Chamberlain JHS 100/7-8
PO Box 119 57325 605-234-4467
Rick Pearson, prin. Fax 234-4479

St. Joseph Indian S 200/1-8
PO Box 300 57325 800-341-2235
Fax 734-3483

Chester, Lake, Pop. 257
Chester Area SD 39-1 600/PK-12
PO Box 159 57016 605-489-2411
Heath Larson, supt. Fax 489-2413
www.chester.k12.sd.us
Chester ES 200/PK-5
PO Box 159 57016 605-489-2411
Amy Johnson, prin. Fax 489-2413
Chester MS 100/6-8
PO Box 159 57016 605-489-2411
Julie Eppard, prin. Fax 489-2413
Other Schools – See Madison

Claremont, Brown, Pop. 126
Langford SD 45-5
Supt. — See Langford
Newport Colony S 50/K-8
11796 414th Ave 57432 605-493-6454
Monte Nipp, prin. Fax 493-6447

Clark, Clark, Pop. 1,130
Clark SD 12-2 400/PK-12
220 N Clinton St 57225 605-532-3605
Luanne Warren, supt. Fax 532-3600
clark.k12.sd.us/
Clark ES 100/PK-4
200 2nd Ave NW 57225 605-532-3606
Brian Heupel, prin. Fax 532-3608
Clark MS 100/5-8
220 N Clinton St 57225 605-532-3604
Jerry Hartley, prin. Fax 532-3600
Silver Creek Colony S 50/K-8
17354 430th Ave 57225 605-532-3606
Luanne Warren, prin. Fax 532-3608
Other Schools – See Carpenter, Garden City

Clear Lake, Deuel, Pop. 1,256
Deuel SD 19-4 500/PK-12
PO Box 770 57226 605-874-2161
Chad Schiernbeck, supt. Fax 874-8585
www.deuel.k12.sd.us
Deuel ES 300/PK-3
PO Box 770 57226 605-874-2162
Todd Rahlf, prin. Fax 874-8585
Deuel MS 100/6-8
PO Box 770 57226 605-874-2162
Todd Rahlf, prin. Fax 874-8585
Deuel Midway MS 4-5
PO Box 770 57226 605-874-2162
Todd Rahlf, prin. Fax 874-8585

Colman, Moody, Pop. 586
Colman-Egan SD 50-5 200/K-12
200 S Loban Ave 57017 605-534-3534
Tracey Olson, supt. Fax 534-3670
www.colman-egan.k12.sd.us
Colman-Egan JHS 50/7-8
200 S Loban Ave 57017 605-534-3534
Scott Hemmer, prin. Fax 534-3670
Colman ES 100/K-6
200 S Loban Ave 57017 605-534-3534
Scott Hemmer, prin. Fax 534-3670

Colome, Tripp, Pop. 291
Colome SD 59-3 200/PK-12
PO Box 367 57528 605-842-1624
Ryan Orrock, supt. Fax 842-0783
www.colome.k12.sd.us
Colome ES 100/PK-5
PO Box 367 57528 605-842-1992
Anna LaDeaux, prin. Fax 842-0783
Colome JHS 50/6-8
PO Box 367 57528 605-842-1624
Anna LaDeaux, prin. Fax 842-0783
Other Schools – See Wood

Colton, Minnehaha, Pop. 682
Tri-Valley SD 49-6 800/PK-12
46450 252nd St 57018 605-446-3538
Mike Lodmel, supt. Fax 446-3520
www.tri-valley.k12.sd.us/
Tri-Valley ES 400/PK-6
46450 252nd St 57018 605-446-3538
Nancy Johnson, prin. Fax 446-3520
Tri-Valley JHS 100/7-8
46450 252nd St 57018 605-446-3538
Tim Pflanz, prin. Fax 446-3520

Corsica, Douglas, Pop. 584
Corsica Stickney SD 21-3 100/PK-12
120 S Napoleon Ave 57328 605-946-5475
Scott Muckey, supt. Fax 946-5607
corsica-stickney.k12.sd.us
Other Schools – See Stickney

Dakota Christian S 100/PK-12
37614 SD Highway 44 57328 605-243-2211
Donald Mitchell, admin. Fax 243-2379

Custer, Custer, Pop. 2,043
Custer SD 16-1 800/PK-12
527 Montgomery St 57730 605-673-3154
Mark Naugle, supt. Fax 673-5607
www.csd.k12.sd.us
Custer ES 300/PK-6
1415 Wild Cat Ln 57730 605-673-4483
Barb Paulson, prin. Fax 673-4515
Other Schools – See Hermosa

Deadwood, Lawrence, Pop. 1,248
Lead-Deadwood SD 40-1
Supt. — See Lead
Lead-Deadwood ES 400/PK-5
716 Main St 57732 605-717-3884
Tim Kosters, prin. Fax 717-2823

Dell Rapids, Minnehaha, Pop. 3,605
Dell Rapids SD 49-3 900/K-12
1216 N Garfield Ave 57022 605-428-5473
Summer Schultz, supt. Fax 428-5609
dr-k12.org
Dell Rapids ES 300/K-4
1216 N Garfield Ave 57022 605-428-5473
Jay Nelson, prin. Fax 428-5609
Dell Rapids MS 300/5-8
1216 N Garfield Ave 57022 605-428-5473
Fran Ruesink, prin. Fax 428-5609

St. Mary S 100/PK-6
812 N State Ave 57022 605-428-3459
Deb Kallhoff, prin. Fax 428-5377

Delmont, Douglas, Pop. 230
Tripp-Delmont SD 33-5
Supt. — See Tripp
Clearfield Colony S 50/K-8
40248 293rd St 57330 605-935-6766
Mark Sampson, prin. Fax 935-6507
Greenwood Colony S 50/K-8
28781 402nd Ave 57330 605-935-6766
Hiddy Heinz, prin. Fax 935-6507

De Smet, Kingsbury, Pop. 1,084
De Smet SD 38-2 300/K-12
PO Box 157 57231 605-854-3423
Abi Van Regenmorter, supt. Fax 854-9138
www.desmet.k12.sd.us

De Smet MS 100/6-8
PO Box 157 57231 605-854-3423
Mike Warne, prin. Fax 854-9138
Wilder ES 100/K-5
PO Box 157 57231 605-854-3963
Abi Van Regenmorter, prin. Fax 854-9138

Dewey, Custer
Elk Mountain SD 16-2 50/K-12
10222 Valley Rd 57735 605-749-2258
Lisa Richardson, admin. Fax 749-2258
Elk Mountain S 50/K-12
10222 Valley Rd 57735 605-749-2258
Lisa Richardson, admin. Fax 749-2258

Doland, Spink, Pop. 180
Doland SD 56-2 200/K-12
PO Box 385 57436 605-635-6302
Jim Hulscher, supt. Fax 635-6504
www.doland.k12.sd.us/
Doland ES 50/K-6
PO Box 385 57436 605-635-6241
Jeremy Wieseler, prin. Fax 635-6504
Doland JHS 50/7-8
PO Box 385 57436 605-635-6241
Jim Hulscher, prin. Fax 635-6504
Hillside Colony S 50/K-8
18248 Hillside Ln 57436 605-635-6302
Jim Hulscher, prin. Fax 635-6504
Other Schools – See Frankfort, Raymond

Dupree, Ziebach, Pop. 511
Dupree SD 64-2 400/PK-12
PO Box 10 57623 605-365-5140
Brian Shanks, supt. Fax 365-5514
www.dupree.k12.sd.us
Dupree ES 300/PK-6
PO Box 10 57623 605-365-5140
Cindy Lindskov, prin. Fax 365-5514
Dupree JHS 100/7-8
PO Box 10 57623 605-365-5140
Pandi Pittman, prin. Fax 365-5514

Eagle Butte, Dewey, Pop. 1,279
Eagle Butte SD 20-1 300/K-12
PO Box 260 57625 605-964-4911
Carol Veit, supt. Fax 964-4912
ceb.k12.sd.us
Eagle Butte JHS 50/7-8
PO Box 672 57625 605-964-7841
Dr. Kathie Bowker, prin. Fax 964-1224
Eagle Butte PS 100/K-2
PO Box 672 57625 605-964-7920
Jennifer Bowman, prin. Fax 964-7923
Eagle Butte Upper ES 200/3-6
PO Box 260 57625 605-964-2702
Cora Petersen, prin. Fax 964-4912

Windswept Academy 100/K-10
PO Box 1576 57625 605-200-0757
Clint Holley, hdmstr. Fax 964-7600

Edgemont, Fall River, Pop. 746
Edgemont SD 23-1 200/K-12
PO Box 29 57735 605-662-7294
Dave Cortney, supt. Fax 662-7721
edgemont.k12.sd.us
Edgemont S 100/K-8
PO Box 29 57735 605-662-7254
Dave Cortney, admin. Fax 662-7721

Elk Point, Union, Pop. 1,939
Elk Point-Jefferson SD 61-7 700/PK-12
PO Box 578 57025 605-356-5950
Al Leber, supt. Fax 356-5953
www.epj.k12.sd.us
Elk Point-Jefferson ES 300/PK-5
PO Box 578 57025 605-356-5800
Janet Ries, prin. Fax 356-5802
Elk Point-Jefferson MS 100/6-8
PO Box 578 57025 605-356-5900
Travis Aslesen, prin. Fax 356-5999

Elkton, Brookings, Pop. 721
Elkton SD 5-3 300/PK-12
PO Box 190 57026 605-542-2541
Brian Jandahl, supt. Fax 542-4441
elkton.k12.sd.us
Elkton ES 200/PK-6
PO Box 190 57026 605-542-2541
Kelly Neill, prin. Fax 542-4441
Elkton JHS 100/7-8
PO Box 190 57026 605-542-2541
Kelly Neill, prin. Fax 542-4441
Newdale Colony S 50/K-8
21336 484th Ave 57026 605-542-2541
Kelly Neill, prin. Fax 542-4441
Other Schools – See White

Emery, Hanson, Pop. 443
Bridgewater-Emery SD 30-3
Supt. — See Bridgewater
Bridgewater-Emery MS 100/6-8
130 N 6th St 57332 605-449-4271
Christena Schultz, prin. Fax 449-4270
Emery ES 50/PK-5
130 N 6th St 57332 605-449-4271
Kim Aman, prin. Fax 449-4270

Enning, Meade
Meade SD 46-1
Supt. — See Sturgis
Enning ES 50/K-5
1745 Highway 34 57737 605-269-2264
Bev Rosenboom, prin. Fax 269-2099

Estelline, Hamlin, Pop. 763
Estelline SD 28-2 300/K-12
PO Box 306 57234 605-873-2201
Jim Lentz, supt. Fax 873-2102
www.estelline.k12.sd.us
Estelline JHS 50/7-8
PO Box 306 57234 605-873-2203
Jim Lentz, prin. Fax 873-2102
Estelline S 200/K-6
PO Box 306 57234 605-873-2203
Justin Pitts, prin. Fax 873-2102

Ethan, Davison, Pop. 328
Ethan SD 17-1 300/PK-12
PO Box 169 57334 605-227-4211
Terry Eckstaine, supt. Fax 227-4236
www.ethan.k12.sd.us/
Ethan ES 200/PK-6
PO Box 169 57334 605-227-4211
Terry Eckstaine, prin. Fax 227-4236
Ethan JHS 50/7-8
PO Box 169 57334 605-227-4211
Tim Hawkins, prin. Fax 227-4236

Parkston SD 33-3
Supt. — See Parkston
New Elm Spring Colony S 50/PK-8
41844 269th St 57334 605-928-3040
Matt Yost, prin. Fax 928-7284

Eureka, McPherson, Pop. 856
Eureka SD 44-1 200/PK-12
PO Box 10 57437 605-284-2875
Bo Beck, supt. Fax 284-2810
www.eureka.k12.sd.us/
Eureka ES 100/PK-5
PO Box 10 57437 605-284-2875
Bo Beck, prin. Fax 284-2810
Eureka MS 50/6-8
PO Box 10 57437 605-284-2875
Bo Beck, prin. Fax 284-2810

Faith, Meade, Pop. 405
Faith SD 46-2 200/PK-12
PO Box 619 57626 605-967-2152
Kelly Daughters, supt. Fax 967-2153
www.faith.k12.sd.us/
Faith ES 100/PK-6
PO Box 619 57626 605-967-2152
Don Kraemer, supt. Fax 967-2153
Faith JHS 50/7-8
PO Box 619 57626 605-967-2152
Don Kraemer, supt. Fax 967-2153
Maurine S 50/K-8
PO Box 619 57626 605-967-2152
Don Kraemer, supt. Fax 967-2153

Faulkton, Faulk, Pop. 724
Faulkton Area SD 24-4 300/K-12
PO Box 308 57438 605-598-6266
Derek Barrios, supt. Fax 598-6666
www.faulkton.k12.sd.us
Brentwood S 50/K-8
15442 343rd Ave 57438 605-598-4333
Derek Barrios, prin. Fax 598-6576
Faulkton ES 100/K-6
PO Box 308 57438 605-598-6266
Derek Barrios, prin. Fax 598-6666
Faulkton JHS 50/7-8
PO Box 308 57438 605-598-6266
Craig Cassens, prin. Fax 598-6666
Other Schools – See Wecota

Flandreau, Moody, Pop. 2,264
Flandreau SD 50-3 600/K-12
600 W Community Dr 57028 605-997-3263
Rick Weber, supt. Fax 997-2457
www.flandreau.k12.sd.us
Flandreau ES 300/K-5
500 W Community Dr 57028 605-997-2780
Jay Swatek, prin. Fax 997-2457
Flandreau MS 100/6-8
700 W Community Dr 57028 605-997-2705
Brian Relf, prin. Fax 997-2457
Pleasant Valley Colony S 50/K-8
22941 487th Ave 57028 605-997-2780
Jay Swatek, prin. Fax 997-2559

Florence, Codington, Pop. 370
Florence SD 14-1 200/PK-12
PO Box 66 57235 605-758-2412
Gary Leighton, supt. Fax 758-2433
www.florence.k12.sd.us/
Florence ES 100/PK-6
PO Box 66 57235 605-758-2412
Jean Case, lead tchr. Fax 758-2433
Florence JHS 50/7-8
PO Box 66 57235 605-758-2412
Matthew Bastian, prin. Fax 758-2433

Forestburg, Sanborn, Pop. 70
Sanborn Central SD 55-5 200/PK-12
40405 SD Highway 34 57314 605-495-4183
Justin Siemsen, supt. Fax 495-4185
www.sanborncentral.com
Sanborn Central ES 100/PK-5
40405 SD Highway 34 57314 605-495-4183
Connie Vermeulen, prin. Fax 495-4185
Sanborn Central MS 50/6-8
40405 SD Highway 34 57314 605-495-4183
Connie Vermeulen, prin. Fax 495-4185
Other Schools – See Artesian

Fort Pierre, Stanley, Pop. 2,009
Stanley County SD 57-1 300/K-12
PO Box 370 57532 605-223-7741
Joel Price, supt. Fax 223-7750
www.stanleycounty.k12.sd.us
Stanley County ES 200/K-5
PO Box 370 57532 605-223-7745
Terri Mehlhaff, prin. Fax 223-7760
Other Schools – See Hayes

Frankfort, Spink, Pop. 149
Doland SD 56-2
Supt. — See Doland
Camrose Colony S 50/K-8
16950 400th Ave 57440 605-635-6302
Jim Hulscher, admin. Fax 635-6504

Hitchcock-Tulare SD 56-6
Supt. — See Tulare
Hitchcock-Tulare Glendale Colony S 50/K-8
17866 Glendale Dr 57440 605-266-2151
Jeff Clark, prin. Fax 266-2160
Hitchcock-Tulare Spink Colony S 50/K-8
18206 Spink Ln 57440 605-266-2151
Jeff Clark, prin. Fax 266-2160

Frederick, Brown, Pop. 197
Frederick Area SD 6-2 200/PK-12
PO Box 486 57441 605-329-2145
Jeff Kosters, supt. Fax 329-2722
www.frederickarea.k12.sd.us
Frederick Area ES 100/PK-6
PO Box 486 57441 605-329-2145
Jessica Ringgenberg, prin. Fax 329-2722
Frederick Area JHS 50/7-8
PO Box 486 57441 605-329-2145
Jessica Ringgenberg, prin. Fax 329-2722

Freeman, Hutchinson, Pop. 1,290
Freeman SD 33-1 300/PK-12
PO Box 220 57029 605-925-4214
Kevin Kunz, supt. Fax 925-4814
www.freeman.k12.sd.us
Freeman ES 100/PK-6
PO Box 220 57029 605-925-4216
Shane Voss, prin. Fax 925-4814
Freeman JHS 50/7-8
PO Box 220 57029 605-925-4214
Kevin Kunz, prin. Fax 925-4814
Other Schools – See Olivet

Freeman Academy 100/1-12
PO Box 1000 57029 605-925-4237
Nathan Epp, prin. Fax 925-4271

Garden City, Clark, Pop. 53
Clark SD 12-2
Supt. — See Clark
Hillcrest Colony S 50/K-8
1004 Hillcrest Dr 57236 605-532-3606
Jerry Hartley, prin. Fax 532-3608

Garretson, Minnehaha, Pop. 1,155
Garretson SD 49-4 500/PK-12
PO Box C 57030 605-594-3451
Guy Johnson, supt. Fax 594-3443
www.garretson.k12.sd.us/
Garretson ES 300/PK-5
PO Box C 57030 605-594-3453
Teresa Johnson, prin. Fax 594-3443
Garretson MS 100/6-8
PO Box C 57030 605-594-3452
Chris Long, prin. Fax 594-3443

Gayville, Yankton, Pop. 403
Gayville-Volin SD 63-1 300/K-12
PO Box 158 57031 605-267-4476
Jason Selchert, supt. Fax 267-4294
www.gayvillevolin.k12.sd.us/
Gayville-Volin ES 100/K-6
PO Box 158 57031 605-267-4476
Patrick Beeman, prin. Fax 267-4294
Gayville-Volin MS 50/7-8
PO Box 158 57031 605-267-4476
Tom Rice, prin. Fax 267-4294

Gettysburg, Potter, Pop. 1,150
Gettysburg SD 53-1 300/K-12
100 E King Ave 57442 605-765-2436
Chip Sundberg, supt. Fax 765-2249
www.gettysburg.k12.sd.us
Gettysburg ES 100/K-6
100 E King Ave 57442 605-765-2436
Chip Sundberg, prin. Fax 765-2249
Gettysburg JHS 50/7-8
100 E King Ave 57442 605-765-2436
Wendy Smith, prin. Fax 765-2249

Gregory, Gregory, Pop. 1,270
Gregory SD 26-4 400/K-12
PO Box 438 57533 605-835-9651
Sara Klein, supt. Fax 835-8146
www.gregory.k12.sd.us/
Gregory ES 200/K-6
PO Box 438 57533 605-835-8771
Jeff Determan, prin. Fax 835-8744
Gregory JHS 50/7-8
PO Box 438 57533 605-835-8771
Jeff Determan, prin. Fax 835-8744

Groton, Brown, Pop. 1,444
Groton Area SD 6-6 600/PK-12
PO Box 410 57445 605-397-2351
Joe Schwan, supt. Fax 397-8453
www.grotonarea.com/
Groton ES 300/PK-5
PO Box 410 57445 605-397-2317
Brett Schwan, prin. Fax 397-2344
Groton MS 100/6-8
PO Box 410 57445 605-397-8381
Kiersten Sombke, prin. Fax 397-8453

Harrisburg, Lincoln, Pop. 4,018
Harrisburg SD 41-2 3,300/PK-12
PO Box 187 57032 605-743-2567
James Holbeck, supt. Fax 743-2569
harrisburgdistrict41-2.org
Harrisburg Freedom ES 300/K-5
1101 Tom Sawyer Trl 57032 605-743-2567
Tanja Pederson, prin. Fax 213-2010
Harrisburg Liberty ES 400/PK-5
PO Box 306 57032 605-743-2567
Aaron Weaver, prin. Fax 213-0111
Harrisburg South MS 300/6-8
600 S Cliff Ave 57032 605-743-2567
Darren Ellwein, prin. Fax 743-5630
Other Schools – See Sioux Falls

Hartford, Minnehaha, Pop. 2,498
West Central SD 49-7 1,300/PK-12
PO Box 730 57033 605-528-3217
Brad Berens, supt. Fax 528-3219
www.westcentral49-7.com
Hartford ES 300/PK-2
PO Box 730 57033 605-528-3215
Matt Alley, prin. Fax 528-3399
West Central MS 300/6-8
PO Box 730 57033 605-528-3799
Mark Rockafellow, prin. Fax 528-3702
Other Schools – See Humboldt

Hayes, Stanley
Stanley County SD 57-1
Supt. — See Fort Pierre
Cheyenne S 50/K-8
24882 196th St 57537 605-223-7745
Terri Mehlhaff, prin. Fax 223-7760

Hayti, Hamlin, Pop. 381
Hamlin SD 28-3 800/PK-12
44577 188th St 57241 605-783-3631
Patrick Kraning, supt. Fax 783-3632
www.hamlin.k12.sd.us
Hamlin ES 400/PK-5
44577 188th St 57241 605-783-3631
Gail Krause, prin. Fax 783-3632
Hamlin MS 200/6-8
44577 188th St 57241 605-783-3644
Jeff Sheehan, prin. Fax 783-3632

Henry, Codington, Pop. 264
Henry SD 14-2 200/K-12
PO Box 8 57243 605-532-5364
Philip Schonebaum, supt. Fax 532-3795
www.henry.k12.sd.us
Henry ES 100/K-4
PO Box 8 57243 605-532-5364
Jon Redmond, prin. Fax 532-3795
Henry MS 50/5-8
PO Box 8 57243 605-532-5364
Jon Redmond, prin. Fax 532-3795

Hereford, Meade
Meade SD 46-1
Supt. — See Sturgis
Hereford S 50/K-8
15998 Cross S Rd 57785 605-269-2264
Bev Rosenboom, prin. Fax 269-2099

Hermosa, Custer, Pop. 379
Custer SD 16-1
Supt. — See Custer
Hermosa S 200/K-8
PO Box 27 57744 605-255-4345
Jeremy Hurd, prin. Fax 255-4190

Oglala Lakota County SD 65-1
Supt. — See Batesland
Red Shirt Table S 100/PK-8
Red Shirt Village 57744 605-255-4224
Marilyn Erickson, prin. Fax 255-5396

Herreid, Campbell, Pop. 436
Herreid SD 10-1 100/K-12
PO Box 276 57632 605-437-2263
Daniel Hoey, supt. Fax 437-2264
herreid.k12.sd.us
Herreid ES 50/K-5
PO Box 276 57632 605-437-2263
Daniel Hoey, admin. Fax 437-2264
Herreid MS 50/6-8
PO Box 276 57632 605-437-2263
Daniel Hoey, admin. Fax 437-2264

Highmore, Hyde, Pop. 788
Highmore-Harrold SD 34-2 300/PK-12
PO Box 416 57345 605-852-2275
Quinton Cermak, supt. Fax 852-2295
www.highmore.k12.sd.us
Highmore ES 100/PK-6
PO Box 416 57345 605-852-2276
Grant VanderVorst M.Ed., prin. Fax 852-2295
Highmore JHS 50/7-8
PO Box 416 57345 605-852-2275
Quinton Cermak M.Ed., prin. Fax 852-2295

Hill City, Pennington, Pop. 926
Hill City SD 51-2 500/PK-12
PO Box 659 57745 605-574-3030
Mike Hanson, supt. Fax 574-3031
hillcity.sd.schoolwebpages.com
Hill City ES 200/PK-5
PO Box 659 57745 605-574-3013
Chip Franke, prin. Fax 574-3028
Hill City MS 100/6-8
PO Box 659 57745 605-574-3032
Blake Gardner, prin. Fax 574-3044

Hitchcock, Beadle, Pop. 88
Hitchcock-Tulare SD 56-6
Supt. — See Tulare
Hitchcock-Tulare ES 100/PK-6
235 Palm St 57348 605-266-2151
Jeff Clark, prin. Fax 266-2160

Hosmer, Edmunds, Pop. 205
Edmunds Central SD 22-5
Supt. — See Roscoe
Boulder Colony S K-8
301 E Main St 57448
Angie Preszler, prin.

Hot Springs, Fall River, Pop. 3,587
Hot Springs SD 23-2 800/PK-12
1609 University Ave 57747 605-745-4145
Kevin Coles, supt. Fax 745-4178
www.hssd.k12.sd.us
Hot Springs ES 400/PK-5
1609 University Ave 57747 605-745-4149
John Fitzgerald, prin. Fax 745-4165
Hot Springs MS 200/6-8
1609 University Ave 57747 605-745-4146
Liz Baker, prin. Fax 745-6389

Bethesda Lutheran S 50/PK-2
1537 Baltimore Ave 57747 605-745-6676
Marianne Allen, lead tchr. Fax 745-6676

Hoven, Potter, Pop. 401
Hoven SD 53-2 100/PK-12
PO Box 128 57450 605-948-2252
Bob Graham, supt. Fax 948-2477
www.hoven.k12.sd.us
Hoven ES 100/PK-6
PO Box 188 57450 605-948-2252
Dr. Pat Jones, prin. Fax 948-2477
Hoven JHS 50/7-8
PO Box 128 57450 605-948-2252
Dr. Pat Jones, prin. Fax 948-2477

Howard, Miner, Pop. 846
Howard SD 48-3 400/PK-12
500 N Section Line St 57349 605-772-5515
Todd Lee, supt. Fax 772-5516
www.howard.k12.sd.us
Howard ES 200/PK-6
201 N Minnie St 57349 605-772-4443
Dr. Christopher Noid, prin. Fax 772-4445
Howard JHS 50/7-8
500 N Section Line St 57349 605-772-5515
Todd Lee, prin. Fax 772-5516
Other Schools – See Winfred

Humboldt, Minnehaha, Pop. 578
West Central SD 49-7
Supt. — See Hartford
Humboldt ES 400/K-5
PO Box 136 57035 605-363-3131
Matt Alley, prin. Fax 363-3818

Hurley, Turner, Pop. 413
Viborg-Hurley SD 60-6
Supt. — See Viborg
Viborg-Hurley MS 50/5-8
PO Box 278 57036 605-238-5221
Brett Mellem, prin. Fax 238-5223

Huron, Beadle, Pop. 12,413
Huron SD 2-2 1,600/K-12
PO Box 949 57350 605-353-6990
Terry Nebelsick Ed.D., supt. Fax 353-6994
www.huron.k12.sd.us
4th/5th Grade Center at Washington 100/4-5
PO Box 949 57350 605-353-7805
Beth Foss, prin. Fax 353-7898
Huron Colony S 50/K-8
40068 399th Ave 57350 605-353-6978
Kari Hinker, prin. Fax 353-7888
Huron MS 500/6-8
PO Box 949 57350 605-353-6900
Michael Taplett, prin. Fax 353-6913
Kindergarten/1st Grade Center Buchanan 200/K-1
PO Box 949 57350 605-353-7875
Peggy Heinz, prin. Fax 353-7877
Riverside Colony S 50/K-8
RR 1 57350 605-353-6980
Kari Hinker, prin. Fax 353-7888
2nd/3rd Grade Center at Madison 100/2-3
1680 Idaho Ave SE 57350 605-353-7885
Heather Rozell, prin. Fax 353-7888

Holy Trinity S 200/PK-6
425 21st St SW 57350 605-352-9344
Michelle Schoenfelder, prin. Fax 353-0889
James Valley Christian S 300/PK-12
1550 Dakota Ave N 57350 605-352-7737
Brian Held, admin. Fax 352-9893

Interior, Jackson, Pop. 84
Kadoka Area SD 35-2
Supt. — See Kadoka
Interior S 50/K-8
301 A St 57750 605-837-2173
Karen Byrd, prin. Fax 837-2176

Ipswich, Edmunds, Pop. 945
Ipswich SD 22-6 400/PK-12
PO Box 306 57451 605-426-6571
Trent Osborne, supt. Fax 426-6029
www.ipswich.k12.sd.us
Deerfield Colony S 50/PK-8
PO Box 306 57451 605-426-6832
Matt Pollock, prin. Fax 426-6029
Ipswich ES 200/PK-5
PO Box 306 57451 605-426-6832
Mathew Pollock, prin. Fax 426-6029
Ipswich MS 100/6-8
PO Box 306 57451 605-426-6571
Dan Knuth, prin. Fax 426-6029
Pembrook Colony S 50/PK-8
PO Box 306 57451 605-426-6832
Matt Pollock, prin. Fax 426-6029
Other Schools – See Leola

Irene, Yankton, Pop. 419
Irene-Wakonda SD 13-3 300/PK-12
PO Box 5 57037 605-263-3311
David Hutchison, supt. Fax 263-3316
www.irene-wakonda.k12.sd.us/
Other Schools – See Wakonda

Iroquois, Kingsbury, Pop. 263
Iroquois SD 2-3 300/PK-12
111 E Washita St 57353 605-546-2210
Mike Ruth, supt. Fax 546-8540
www.iroquois.k12.sd.us/
Iroquois ES 100/PK-5
111 E Washita St 57353 605-546-2262
Mike Ruth, prin. Fax 546-8540
Iroquois MS 50/6-8
111 E Washita St 57353 605-546-2426
Rick Soma, prin. Fax 546-8540
Pearl Creek Colony S 50/K-8
21085 415th Ave 57353 605-546-2210
Mike Ruth, prin. Fax 546-8540

Willow Lake SD 12-3
Supt. — See Willow Lake
Collins Colony ES 50/K-8
19606 Collins Ave 57353 605-625-5945
Chris Lee, prin. Fax 625-3103

Jefferson, Union, Pop. 542

St. Peter S 50/PK-PK
PO Box 98 57038 605-966-5529
Erin Hammitt, prin. Fax 966-5746

Kadoka, Jackson, Pop. 622
Kadoka Area SD 35-2 400/PK-12
PO Box 99 57543 605-837-2175
Jamie Hermann, supt. Fax 837-2176
www.kadoka.k12.sd.us
Kadoka S 200/PK-8
PO Box 99 57543 605-837-2173
Karen Byrd, prin. Fax 837-2176
Other Schools – See Interior, Long Valley, Midland

Kennebec, Lyman, Pop. 232
Lyman SD
Supt. — See Presho
Kennebec ES 100/PK-5
PO Box 188 57544 605-869-2213
Rene Lillebo, prin. Fax 869-2283
Lyman MS 100/6-8
PO Box 188 57544 605-869-2213
Rene Lillebo, prin. Fax 895-2283

Kimball, Brule, Pop. 698
Kimball SD 7-2 300/PK-12
PO Box 479 57355 605-778-6232
Tim Mayclin, supt. Fax 778-6393
www.kimball.k12.sd.us
Grass Ranch S 50/K-8
PO Box 479 57355 605-778-6231
Tim Mayclin, prin. Fax 778-6393
Kimball ES 100/PK-4
PO Box 479 57355 605-778-6231
Tim Mayclin, prin. Fax 778-6393
Kimball MS 100/5-8
PO Box 479 57355 605-778-6231
Matt Dykstra, prin. Fax 778-6393

Kyle, Shannon, Pop. 840

Lakota Waldorf S K-6
PO Box 527 57752 605-455-2487

Lake Andes, Charles Mix, Pop. 832
Andes Central SD 11-1 400/PK-12
PO Box 40 57356 605-487-7671
Debera Lucas, supt. Fax 487-7051
www.andescentral.k12.sd.us/
Andes Central ES 200/PK-6
PO Box 40 57356 605-487-5243
William Kitchenmaster, prin. Fax 487-7656
Andes Central JHS 50/7-8
PO Box 40 57356 605-487-7671
Rocky Brinkman, prin. Fax 487-7051
Lakeview Colony S 50/PK-8
28748 386th Ave 57356 605-487-7797
William Kitchenmaster, prin. Fax 487-7051

Lake Preston, Kingsbury, Pop. 595
Lake Preston SD 38-3 200/K-12
300 1st St NE 57249 605-847-4455
Tim Casper, supt. Fax 847-4311
www.lakepreston.k12.sd.us
Lake Preston ES 100/K-6
300 1st St NE 57249 605-847-4464
Dana Felderman, prin. Fax 847-4311
Lake Preston JHS 50/7-8
300 1st St NE 57249 605-847-4455
Tim Casper, prin. Fax 847-4311

Langford, Marshall, Pop. 312
Langford SD 45-5 200/PK-12
PO Box 127 57454 605-493-6454
Monte Nipp, supt. Fax 493-6447
www.langford.k12.sd.us/
Langford ES 100/PK-5
PO Box 127 57454 605-493-6454
Monte Nipp, prin. Fax 493-6447
Langford MS 50/6-8
PO Box 127 57454 605-493-6454
Toni Brown, prin. Fax 493-6447
Other Schools – See Claremont

Lead, Lawrence, Pop. 3,058
Lead-Deadwood SD 40-1 800/PK-12
320 S Main St 57754 605-717-3890
Dr. Dan Leikvold, supt. Fax 717-2813
www.lead-deadwood.k12.sd.us/
Lead-Deadwood MS 200/6-8
234 S Main St 57754 605-717-3898
Jay Beagle, prin. Fax 717-2821
Other Schools – See Deadwood

Lemmon, Perkins, Pop. 1,211
Lemmon SD 52-4 200/PK-12
209 3rd St W 57638 605-374-3762
Craig Johnson, supt. Fax 374-3562
www.lemmon.k12.sd.us
Lemmon ES 100/PK-6
905 5th Ave W 57638 605-374-3784
Steve Bucks, prin. Fax 374-5424
Lemmon JHS 50/7-8
209 3rd St W 57638 605-374-3784
Craig Johnson, prin. Fax 374-3562

Lennox, Lincoln, Pop. 2,100
Lennox SD 41-4 900/PK-12
PO Box 38 57039 605-647-2203
Chad Conaway, supt. Fax 647-2201
www.lennox.k12.sd.us
Lennox ES 400/PK-6
PO Box 38 57039 605-647-2203
Darin Elch, prin. Fax 647-6043
Lennox JHS 100/7-8
PO Box 38 57039 605-647-2203
Chad Allison, prin. Fax 647-2502

Other Schools – See Worthing

Leola, McPherson, Pop. 451
Ipswich SD 22-6
Supt. — See Ipswich
Rosette Colony S 50/PK-8
12465 359th Ave 57456 605-426-6832
Matt Pollock, prin. Fax 426-6029

Leola SD 44-2 200/K-12
PO Box 350 57456 605-439-3477
Brian Heupel, supt. Fax 439-3206
www.leola.k12.sd.us/
Leola ES 100/K-5
PO Box 350 57456 605-439-3477
Beverly Myer, prin. Fax 439-3206
Leola JHS 50/6-8
PO Box 350 57456 605-439-3477
Beverly Myer, prin. Fax 439-3206
Other Schools – See Westport, Wetonka

Long Valley, Jackson
Kadoka Area SD 35-2
Supt. — See Kadoka
Long Valley S 50/K-8
26840 Sd Hwy 73 57547 605-837-2173
Karen Byrd, prin. Fax 837-2176

Ludlow, Harding
Harding County SD 31-1
Supt. — See Buffalo
Ludlow S 50/K-8
HC 63 57755 605-375-3241
Kelly Messmer, prin. Fax 375-3246

Mc Intosh, Corson, Pop. 167
Mc Intosh SD 15-1 200/PK-12
PO Box 80 57641 605-273-4298
Rod Broadnax, supt. Fax 273-4531
www.mcintosh.k12.sd.us
Mc Intosh ES 100/PK-6
PO Box 80 57641 605-273-4298
Rod Broadnax, prin. Fax 273-4531
Mc Intosh JHS 50/7-8
PO Box 80 57641 605-273-4298
Rod Broadnax, prin. Fax 273-4531

Mc Laughlin, Corson, Pop. 634
Mc Laughlin SD 15-2 500/PK-12
PO Box 880 57642 605-823-4484
Scott Lepke, supt. Fax 823-4886
www.mclaughlin.k12.sd.us
McLaughlin ES 300/PK-5
PO Box 880 57642 605-823-4484
Peggy Freidel, prin. Fax 823-4880
McLaughlin MS 100/6-8
PO Box 880 57642 605-823-4484
Jeremy Hurd, prin. Fax 823-4481

Madison, Lake, Pop. 6,389
Chester Area SD 39-1
Supt. — See Chester
Rustic Acres S 50/K-8
24243 40056th Ave 57042 605-489-2411
Amy Johnson, prin. Fax 489-2413

Madison Central SD 39-2 1,100/K-12
800 NE 9th St 57042 605-256-7700
Joel Jorgenson, supt. Fax 256-7711
www.madison.k12.sd.us
Madison ES 500/K-5
700 NW 9th St 57042 605-256-7721
Janel Guse, prin. Fax 256-7729
Madison MS 300/6-8
830 NE 9th St 57042 605-256-7717
Cotton Koch, prin. Fax 256-7728

St. Thomas S 100/PK-5
401 N Van Eps Ave 57042 605-256-4419
Cate Luvaas, prin. Fax 256-3953

Marion, Turner, Pop. 780
Marion SD 60-3 200/PK-12
PO Box 207 57043 605-648-3615
E. David Colberg, supt. Fax 648-3652
marion.k12.sd.us
Marion ES 100/PK-5
PO Box 207 57043 605-648-3615
E. David Colberg, prin. Fax 648-3652
Marion MS 50/6-8
PO Box 207 57043 605-648-3615
Katie Minster, prin. Fax 648-3617

Martin, Bennett, Pop. 986
Bennett County SD 3-1 500/PK-12
PO Box 580 57551 605-685-6697
Stacy Halverson, supt. Fax 685-6694
www.bennettco.k12.sd.us/
Bennett County JHS 100/7-8
PO Box 580 57551 605-685-6343
Belinda Ready, prin. Fax 685-6935
Martin ES 300/PK-6
PO Box 580 57551 605-685-6717
Amie Kuxhaus, prin. Fax 685-6147

Mellette, Spink, Pop. 205
Northwestern Area SD 56-7 300/PK-12
221 3rd St 57461 605-887-3467
Ryan Bruns, supt. Fax 887-3101
www.northwestern.k12.sd.us
Northwestern ES 100/PK-5
221 3rd St 57461 605-887-3467
Ryan Bruns, prin. Fax 887-3101
Northwestern MS 100/6-8
221 3rd St 57461 605-887-3467
Richard Osborn, prin. Fax 887-3101

Menno, Hutchinson, Pop. 603
Menno SD 33-2 300/PK-12
PO Box 346 57045 605-387-5161
Dr. Charlene Crosswait, supt. Fax 387-5171
www.menno.k12.sd.us/
Menno ES 100/PK-5
PO Box 346 57045 605-387-5161
Dr. Charlene Crosswait, prin. Fax 387-5171
Menno MS 50/6-8
PO Box 346 57045 605-387-5161
Cameron Kerkhove, prin. Fax 387-5171
Other Schools – See Scotland, Utica

Midland, Haakon, Pop. 128
Kadoka Area SD 35-2
Supt. — See Kadoka
Midland ES 50/K-8
104 Main St 57552 605-837-2173
Karen Byrd, prin. Fax 837-2176

Milbank, Grant, Pop. 3,335
Milbank SD 25-4 900/K-12
1001 E Park Ave 57252 605-432-5579
Tim Graf, supt. Fax 432-4137
www.milbankschooldistrict.com
Koch ES 400/K-5
410 E 10th Ave 57252 605-432-6615
Amy Brandriet, prin. Fax 432-4137
Milbank MS 200/6-8
1001 E Park Ave 57252 605-432-5519
Kristopher Evje, dean Fax 432-4137

St. Lawrence S 100/PK-6
113 S 6th St 57252 605-432-5673
Brenda Anderson, prin. Fax 432-5846

Milesville, Haakon
Haakon SD 27-1
Supt. — See Philip
Milesville S 50/K-8
22061 200th St 57553 605-544-3231
Jeff Rieckman, prin. Fax 859-3005

Miller, Hand, Pop. 1,475
Miller SD 29-4 400/PK-12
PO Box 257 57362 605-853-2614
Dan Trefz, supt. Fax 853-3041
www.miller.k12.sd.us/
Millerdale Colony S 50/K-8
PO Box 257 57362 605-853-2711
Knute Reierson, prin. Fax 853-3041
Miller ES 200/PK-6
PO Box 257 57362 605-853-2711
Knute Reierson, prin. Fax 853-3041
Miller JHS 100/7-8
PO Box 257 57362 605-853-2455
Steve Schumacher, prin. Fax 853-3041

Sunshine Bible Academy 100/K-12
400 Sunshine Dr 57362 605-853-3071
Jason Watson, supt. Fax 853-3072

Mission, Todd, Pop. 1,157
Todd County SD 66-1 2,200/K-12
PO Box 87 57555 605-856-3501
Dr. Karen Whitney, supt. Fax 856-2449
www.tcsdk12.org/
Todd County Achievement MS 6-8
PO Box 87 57555 605-856-8701
Aries Yumul, prin.
Todd County ES 800/K-5
PO Box 87 57555 605-856-3506
Bobbie Cox, prin. Fax 856-2432
Todd County MS 400/6-8
PO Box 248 57555 605-856-3504
Linda Bordeaux, prin. Fax 856-2032
Other Schools – See O Kreek, Parmelee, Rosebud, Saint Francis

Mitchell, Davison, Pop. 15,009
Hanson SD 30-1
Supt. — See Alexandria
Millbrook Colony S 50/K-8
41659 256th St 57301 605-239-4387
Josh Oltmanns, prin. Fax 239-4293

Mitchell SD 17-2 2,800/K-12
821 N Capital St 57301 605-995-3010
Dr. Joseph Graves, supt. Fax 995-3089
mitchell.k12.sd.us
Longfellow ES 400/K-5
110 N Mentzer St 57301 605-995-3092
Lisa Heckenlaible, prin. Fax 995-3084
Mitchell MS 600/6-8
800 W 10th Ave 57301 605-995-3051
Justin Zajic, prin. Fax 995-3037
Rogers ES 400/K-5
1301 N Kimball St 57301 605-995-3091
Vicki Harmdierks, prin. Fax 996-6610
Rosedale Colony S 50/K-8
25986 Rosedale Rd 57301 605-239-4215
Lisa Heckenlaible, prin. Fax 239-4346
Williams ES 500/K-5
1420 W University Ave 57301 605-995-3090
Becky Roth, prin. Fax 996-5286
Other Schools – See Alexandria

John Paul II S 200/PK-6
1510 W Elm Ave 57301 605-996-2365
Robin Cahoy, prin. Fax 995-0378
Mitchell Christian S 200/PK-12
805 W 18th Ave 57301 605-996-8861
Dr. Gary Cookson, prin. Fax 996-3642

Mobridge, Walworth, Pop. 3,357
Mobridge-Pollock SD 62-6 700/PK-12
1107 1st Ave E 57601 605-845-9200
Tim Frederick, supt. Fax 845-3455
www.mobridge-pollock.k12.sd.us/
Davis ES 200/PK-2
1107 1st Ave E 57601 605-845-9200
Jill Olson, prin. Fax 845-3455
Mobridge-Pollock MS 200/6-8
1107 1st Ave E 57601 605-845-9200
Erin Dale, prin. Fax 845-3455
Mobridge-Pollock Upper ES 100/3-5
1107 1st Ave E 57601 605-845-9200
Erin Dale, prin. Fax 845-3455

Montrose, McCook, Pop. 466
Montrose SD 43-2 200/K-12
309 S Church Ave 57048 605-363-5025
Lonny Johnson, supt. Fax 363-3513
www.montroseschool.k12.sd.us
Montrose ES 100/K-5
309 S Church Ave 57048 605-363-5025
Sam Jacobs, prin. Fax 363-3513
Montrose JHS 50/6-8
309 S Church Ave 57048 605-363-5025
Sam Jacobs, prin. Fax 363-3513
Orland Colony S 50/K-8
309 S Church Ave 57048 605-363-5025
Sam Jacobs, prin. Fax 363-3513

Mount Vernon, Davison, Pop. 457
Mount Vernon SD 17-3 200/PK-12
PO Box 46 57363 605-236-5237
Patrick Mikkonen, supt. Fax 236-5604
www.mtvernon.k12.sd.us
Mount Vernon ES 100/PK-5
PO Box 46 57363 605-236-5237
Fax 236-5604
Mount Vernon MS 50/6-8
PO Box 46 57363 605-236-5237
Fax 236-5604

Murdo, Jones, Pop. 476
Jones County SD 37-3 200/PK-12
PO Box 109 57559 605-669-2297
Lorrie Esmay, supt. Fax 669-3248
jonesco.k12.sd.us
Jones County ES 100/PK-6
PO Box 109 57559 605-669-2297
Lorrie Esmay, prin. Fax 669-3248
Jones County MS 50/7-8
PO Box 109 57559 605-669-2258
Missy Valburg, dean Fax 669-2904

Newell, Butte, Pop. 575
Newell SD 9-2 300/PK-12
PO Box 99 57760 605-456-2393
Robin Dutt, supt. Fax 456-2395
www.newell.k12.sd.us
Newell ES 200/PK-5
PO Box 99 57760 605-456-0102
Jennifer Nehl, prin. Fax 456-2395
Newell MS 100/6-8
PO Box 99 57760 605-456-0102
Jennifer Nehl, prin. Fax 456-2395

New Underwood, Pennington, Pop. 640
New Underwood SD 51-3 300/K-12
PO Box 128 57761 605-754-6485
George Seiler, supt. Fax 754-6492
www.newunderwood.k12.sd.us
New Underwood ES 100/K-6
PO Box 128 57761 605-754-6485
Katie Albers, prin. Fax 754-6492
New Underwood JHS 50/7-8
PO Box 128 57761 605-754-6485
Katie Albers, prin. Fax 754-6492

Norris, Mellette
White River SD 47-1
Supt. — See White River
Norris ES 100/K-5
501 E 3rd St 57560 605-462-6455
Gayle Cady-Leboeuf, prin. Fax 259-3133

North Sioux City, Union, Pop. 2,476
Dakota Valley SD 61-8 1,000/K-12
1150 Northshore Dr 57049 605-422-3800
Dr. Jerry Rasmussen, supt. Fax 422-3807
www.dakotavalley.k12.sd.us
Dakota Valley ES 400/K-3
1150 Northshore Dr 57049 605-422-3840
Dr. Tami Hummel, prin. Fax 422-3847
Dakota Valley MS 200/6-8
1150 Northshore Dr 57049 605-422-3830
Harlan Halverson, prin. Fax 422-3837
Dakota Valley Upper ES 100/4-5
1150 Northshore Dr 57049 605-422-3800
Harlan Halverson, prin. Fax 422-3800

Oelrichs, Fall River, Pop. 123
Oelrichs SD 23-3 100/PK-12
PO Box 65 57763 605-535-2631
Dr. Mitch Stone, supt. Fax 535-2046
www.oelrichs.k12.sd.us
Oelrichs ES 50/PK-5
PO Box 65 57763 605-535-2631
Deana Castro, prin. Fax 535-2046
Oelrichs JHS 50/6-8
PO Box 65 57763 605-535-2631
Deana Castro, prin. Fax 535-2046

O Kreek, Todd, Pop. 260
Todd County SD 66-1
Supt. — See Mission
O'Kreek ES 50/K-8
PO Box 180 57563 605-856-3507
Christine Rhodes, prin. Fax 856-2081

Olivet, Hutchinson, Pop. 71
Freeman SD 33-1
Supt. — See Freeman
Tschetter Colony S 50/K-8
27709 Tschetter Ave 57052 605-925-4216
Fax 925-4814
Wolf Creek Colony S 50/PK-8
42906 Colony Rd 57052 605-925-4216
Fax 925-4814

Onida, Sully, Pop. 643
Agar-Blunt-Onida SD 58-3 300/K-12
PO Box 205 57564 605-258-2618
Kevin Pickner, supt. Fax 258-2361
www.abo.k12.sd.us
Onida ES 100/K-6
PO Box 205 57564 605-258-2617
Shana Davis, prin. Fax 258-2361
Sully Buttes JHS 50/7-8
PO Box 205 57564 605-258-2618
Jeremy Chicoine, prin. Fax 258-2361

Other Schools – See Blunt

Opal, Meade
Meade SD 46-1
Supt. — See Sturgis
Opal S 50/K-8
18010 Opal Rd 57758 605-269-2264
Bev Rosenboom, prin. Fax 269-2099

Parker, Turner, Pop. 1,005
Parker SD 60-4 400/K-12
PO Box 517 57053 605-297-3456
Dr. Donavan DeBoer, supt. Fax 297-4381
parker.k12.sd.us
Parker ES 200/K-6
PO Box 517 57053 605-297-3237
Donavan DeBoer, prin. Fax 297-4381
Parker JHS 100/7-8
PO Box 517 57053 605-297-3456
Bill Leberman, prin. Fax 297-4381

Parkston, Hutchinson, Pop. 1,496
Parkston SD 33-3 600/PK-12
102C S Chapman Dr 57366 605-928-3368
Shayne McIntosh, supt. Fax 928-7284
www.parkston.k12.sd.us
Old Elm Spring Colony S 50/PK-8
42021 268th St 57366 605-928-3368
Matt Yost, prin. Fax 928-7284
Parkston ES 300/PK-6
102C S Chapman Dr 57366 605-928-3368
Matt Yost, prin. Fax 928-7284
Parkston JHS 100/7-8
102A S Chapman Dr 57366 605-928-3368
Eric Norden, prin. Fax 928-4032
Other Schools – See Ethan

Parmelee, Todd, Pop. 562
Todd County SD 66-1
Supt. — See Mission
He Dog ES 100/K-5
PO Box 260 57566 605-747-2438
Deb Boyd, prin. Fax 747-5168

Philip, Haakon, Pop. 760
Haakon SD 27-1 300/PK-12
PO Box 730 57567 605-859-2679
Jeff Rieckman, supt. Fax 859-3005
www.philip.k12.sd.us
Philip ES 100/PK-6
PO Box 730 57567 605 859 2001
Jeff Rieckman, prin. Fax 859-3005
Philip MS 100/7-8
PO Box 730 57567 605-859-2680
Mandie Menzel, prin. Fax 859-3550
Other Schools – See Milesville

Piedmont, Meade, Pop. 221
Meade SD 46-1
Supt. — See Sturgis
Piedmont Valley ES 600/K-6
PO Box 90 57769 605-787-5295
Ethan Dschaak, prin. Fax 787-5954

Pierre, Hughes, Pop. 13,369
Pierre SD 32-2 2,600/PK-12
211 S Poplar Ave 57501 605-773-7300
Dr. Kelly Glodt, supt. Fax 773-7304
www.pierre.k12.sd.us
Buchanan ES 400/PK-5
100 N Buchanan Ave 57501 605-773-7310
Ryan Noyes, prin. Fax 773-7314
Jefferson ES 400/PK-5
900 N Poplar Ave 57501 605-773-7320
Bill Kaiser, prin. Fax 773-7318
Kennedy ES 400/PK-5
2306 Brookstone Loop 57501 605-773-7370
Kelly Hansen, prin. Fax 773-7374
Morse MS 600/6-8
309 E Capitol Ave 57501 605-773-7330
Dr. Kyley Cumbow, prin. Fax 773-7338

St. Joseph S 200/K-5
210 E Broadway Ave 57501 605-224-7185
Darlene Braun, prin. Fax 224-1014

Pine Ridge, Shannon, Pop. 3,284
Oglala Lakota County SD 65-1
Supt. — See Batesland
Wolf Creek Lower ES 500/PK-4
PO Box 469 57770 605-867-5174
Jeannine Metzger, prin. Fax 867-5067
Wolf Creek Upper ES 200/5-8
PO Box 469 57770 605-867-5174
Darrell Eagle Bull, prin. Fax 867-5067

Red Cloud Indian S 200/PK-12
100 Mission Dr 57770 605-867-5888

Plankinton, Aurora, Pop. 706
Plankinton SD 1-1 300/PK-12
PO Box 190 57368 605-942-7743
Steve Randall, supt. Fax 942-7453
www.plankinton.k12.sd.us
Plankinton ES 200/PK-6
PO Box 190 57368 605-942-7743
LeeAnn Nussbaum, prin. Fax 942-7453
Plankinton JHS 50/7-8
PO Box 190 57368 605-942-7743
Steve Randall, admin. Fax 942-7453

Platte, Charles Mix, Pop. 1,219
Platte-Geddes SD 11-5 500/PK-12
PO Box 140 57369 605-337-3391
Joel Bailey, supt. Fax 337-2549
www.platte-geddes.k12.sd.us/
Cedar Grove Colony S 50/K-8
PO Box 140 57369 605-337-2468
Joel Bailey, prin. Fax 337-2549
Platte Colony S 50/K-8
PO Box 140 57369 605-337-2468
Joel Bailey, prin. Fax 337-2549
Platte-Geddes ES 200/PK-6
PO Box 140 57369 605-337-2468
Joel Bailey, prin. Fax 337-2549
Platte JHS 100/7-8
PO Box 140 57369 605-337-3391
Steve Randall, prin. Fax 337-2549

Porcupine, Shannon, Pop. 1,058
Oglala Lakota County SD 65-1
Supt. — See Batesland
Rockyford ES 300/PK-4
HC 49 Box 175 57772 605-455-2438
Dr. Jennifer Sierra, prin. Fax 455-2091
Rockyford Upper ES 200/5-8
HC 49 Box 175 57772 605-455-6300
Dr. Jennifer Sierra, prin. Fax 455-2091

Presho, Lyman, Pop. 489
Lyman SD 400/PK-12
201 S Birch Ave 57568 605-895-2579
Rob Davis, supt. Fax 895-2216
www.lyman.k12.sd.us
Presho ES 100/PK-5
PO Box 1000 57568 605-895-2579
Jon Boer, prin. Fax 895-2216
Other Schools – See Kennebec

Ramona, Lake, Pop. 174
Oldham-Ramona SD 39-5 100/PK-12
PO Box 8 57054 605-482-8244
Michael Fischer, supt. Fax 482-8282
www.oldhamramona.k12.sd.us
Oldham-Ramona ES 100/PK-6
PO Box 8 57054 605-482-8244
Andrew Johnson, prin. Fax 482-8282
Oldham-Ramona JHS 50/7-8
PO Box 8 57054 605-482-8244
Andrew Johnson, prin. Fax 482-8282
Other Schools – See Arlington

Rapid City, Pennington, Pop. 65,557
Rapid City Area SD 51-4 13,400/PK-12
300 6th St 57701 605-394-4031
Dr. Lori Simon, supt. Fax 394-2514
www.rcas.org
Beadle ES 500/PK-5
10 Van Buren St 57701 605-394-1841
Cary Davis, prin. Fax 394-1739
Canyon Lake ES 400/PK-5
1500 Evergreen Dr 57702 605-394-1817
Dave Swank, prin. Fax 355-3013
Corral Drive ES 500/K-5
4503 Park Dr 57702 605-394-6789
Kyle Yamada, prin. Fax 394-3341
East MS 600/6-8
4860 Homestead St 57703 605-394-4092
Scott Phares, prin. Fax 394-6935
Grandview ES 500/K-5
3301 Grandview Dr 57701 605-394-1829
Rick Owen, prin. Fax 394-5831
Knollwood Heights ES 500/K-5
1701 Downing St 57701 605-394-1851
Shannon Schaefers, prin. Fax 394-5391
Mann ES 300/K-5
902 Anamosa St 57701 605-394-1847
Kelly Gorman, prin. Fax 394-4194
Meadowbrook ES 500/K-5
3125 W Flormann St 57702 605-394-1821
Danny Janklow, prin. Fax 394-1780
North MS 500/6-8
1501 N Maple Ave 57701 605-394-4042
Jackie Talley, prin. Fax 394-6120
Pinedale ES 400/K-5
4901 W Chicago St 57702 605-394-1805
Dr. Lisa Hafer, prin. Fax 394-5830
Rapid Valley ES 600/PK-5
2601 Covington St 57703 605-393-2221
Cher Daniel, prin. Fax 393-1973
Robbinsdale ES 500/PK-5
424 E Indiana St 57701 605-394-1825
Michele Seaholm, prin. Fax 394-1827
South Canyon ES 300/K-5
218 Nordby Ln 57702 605-394-1801
Dr. Erin Lehmann, prin. Fax 394-1803
South MS 700/6-8
2 Indiana St 57701 605-394-4024
Larry Stevens, prin. Fax 394-5834
South Park ES 400/K-5
207 Flormann St 57701 605-394-1833
Brad Jungwirth, prin. Fax 394-1853
Southwest MS 700/6-8
4501 Park Dr 57702 605-394-6792
Lindsey Ruml, prin. Fax 355-3095
Valley View ES 600/K-5
4840 Homestead St 57703 605-393-2812
Gregg McNabb, prin. Fax 393-2861
West MS 700/6-8
1003 Soo San Dr 57702 605-394-4033
Dan Conrad, prin. Fax 394-1889
Wilson ES 400/K-5
827 Franklin St 57701 605-394-1837
Brad Chaney, prin. Fax 394-1832
Other Schools – See Black Hawk

Calvary Christian S 200/PK-5
PO Box 2434 57709 605-348-5175
Chris Causey, admin. Fax 342-0773
Creekside Christian S 100/K-5
2225 E Saint Patrick St 57703 605-343-2980
Rev. Christi Hendrickson, prin.
Rapid City SDA S 50/K-8
305 N 39th St 57702 605-343-2785
Kelli Vigil, lead tchr. Fax 343-2785
St. Elizabeth Seton S 400/PK-5
2101 City Springs Rd #100 57702 605-716-5213
Colleen Lecy, prin. Fax 716-5216
St. Paul's Lutheran S 100/PK-8
835 E Fairmont Blvd 57701 605-341-5385
Stephen Gurgel M.A., prin. Fax 342-8717
St. Thomas More MS 200/6-8
424 Fairmont Blvd 57701 605-348-1477
Mary Helen Olsen, prin. Fax 342-4367
Zion Lutheran S 200/PK-5
4550 Mount Rushmore Rd 57701 605-342-5749
Ann Solinsky, prin. Fax 342-4469

Raymond, Spink, Pop. 50
Doland SD 56-2
Supt. — See Doland
Clark Colony S 50/K-8
41181 179th St 57258 605-635-6302
Jim Hulscher, prin. Fax 635-6504

Redfield, Spink, Pop. 2,312
Redfield SD 56-4 700/PK-12
PO Box 560 57469 605-472-4520
Shad Storley, supt. Fax 472-4525
www.redfield.k12.sd.us
Redfield ES 400/PK-6
PO Box 560 57469 605 472 4520
Samantha Walder, prin. Fax 472-4525
Redfield JHS 100/7-8
PO Box 560 57469 605-472-4520
Rob Lewis, prin. Fax 472-4525

Renner, Minnehaha
Sioux Falls SD 49-5
Supt. — See Sioux Falls
Renberg ES 200/K-5
47260 258th St 57055 605-543-5273
Anne Williams, prin. Fax 543-5076

Roscoe, Edmunds, Pop. 323
Edmunds Central SD 22-5 100/PK-12
PO Box 317 57471 605-287-4251
Karen Fox, supt. Fax 287-4813
www.echs.k12.sd.us
Edmunds Central ES 100/PK-5
PO Box 317 57471 605-287-4251
Karen Fox, prin. Fax 287-4813
Edmunds Central MS 50/6-8
PO Box 317 57471 605-287-4251
Karen Fox, prin. Fax 287-4813
Other Schools – See Hosmer

Rosebud, Todd, Pop. 1,575
Todd County SD 66-1
Supt. — See Mission
Rosebud ES 300/K-5
PO Box 310 57570 605-747-2411
George Shipley, prin. Fax 747-4334

Rosholt, Roberts, Pop. 406
Rosholt SD 54-4 200/PK-12
PO Box 106 57260 605-537-4283
Teresa Appel, supt. Fax 537-4285
www.rosholt.k12.sd.us/
Rosholt ES 100/PK-6
PO Box 106 57260 605-537-4283
Teresa Appel, prin. Fax 537-4285
Rosholt JHS 50/7-8
PO Box 106 57260 605-537-4278
Spencer Oland, prin. Fax 537-4285
White Rock Colony S 50/K-8
PO Box 106 57260 605-537-4790
Kay Brandenburger, prin. Fax 537-4285

Rutland, Lake
Rutland SD 39-4 100/PK-12
102 School St 57057 605-586-4352
Peter Books, supt. Fax 586-4343
www.rutland.k12.sd.us
Camridge Colony S K-8
102 School St 57057 605-586-4352
Teri Jaspers, lead tchr. Fax 586-4343
Rutland ES 100/PK-5
102 School St 57057 605-586-4352
Brian Brosnahan, prin. Fax 586-4343
Rutland JHS 50/6-8
102 School St 57057 605-586-4352
Brian Brosnahan, prin. Fax 586-4343

Saint Francis, Todd, Pop. 708
Todd County SD 66-1
Supt. — See Mission
Spring Creek ES 100/K-8
233 Yellow Cloud Dr 57572 605-747-2541
Erin Grant, prin. Fax 747-4369

Salem, McCook, Pop. 1,343
McCook Central SD 43-7 400/PK-12
PO Box 310 57058 605-425-2264
Dr. Cheryl Thaler, supt. Fax 425-2079
www.mccookcentral.k12.sd.us/
Goldenview Colony S 50/PK-8
PO Box 310 57058 605-425-2264
Dr. Deb Eichacker, prin. Fax 425-2079
McCook Central ES 200/PK-4
PO Box 310 57058 605-425-2264
Dr. Deb Eichacker, prin. Fax 425-2079
McCook Central MS 100/5-8
PO Box 310 57058 605-425-2264
Masey Pechholt, prin. Fax 425-2079

St. Mary S 100/K-8
PO Box 40 57058 605-425-2607
Linda Merkwan, prin. Fax 425-3310

Scotland, Bon Homme, Pop. 830
Menno SD 33-2
Supt. — See Menno
Maxwell Colony S 100/K-8
42805 Maxwell Rd 57059 605-387-5161
Dr. Charlene Crosswait, prin. Fax 387-5171

Scotland SD 4-3 300/PK-12
711 4th St 57059 605-583-2237
Tim Hagedorn, supt. Fax 583-2239
www.scotland.k12.sd.us
Scotland ES 100/PK-5
711 4th St 57059 605-583-2717
Tim Hagedorn, prin. Fax 583-2718
Scotland MS 50/6-8
711 4th St 57059 605-583-2237
Chris McGregor, prin. Fax 583-2239

Selby, Walworth, Pop. 634
Selby Area SD 62-5 — 200/PK-12
PO Box 324 57472 — 605-649-7818
Darrel McFarland, supt. — Fax 649-7282
www.selby.k12.sd.us/
Selby Area ES — 100/PK-6
PO Box 324 57472 — 605-649-7818
Darrel McFarland, prin. — Fax 649-7282
Selby Area JHS — 50/7-8
PO Box 324 57472 — 605-649-7818
Yvette Houck, prin. — Fax 649-7282

Sioux Falls, Minnehaha, Pop. 150,371
Brandon Valley SD 49-2
Supt. — See Brandon
Assam ES — 500/PK-4
7700 E Willowwood St 57110 — 605-582-1500
Susan Foster, prin. — Fax 332-0947

Harrisburg SD 41-2
Supt. — See Harrisburg
Harrisburg Endeavor ES — 400/K-5
2401 W 95th St 57108 — 605-743-2567
Mike Munzke, prin. — Fax 271-0410
Harrisburg Explorer ES — 300/PK-5
4010 W 82nd St 57108 — 605-743-2567
Doug Eppard, prin. — Fax 367-4695
Harrisburg Horizon ES — K-5
5800 S Bahnson Ave 57108 — 605-743-2567
Lisa Garrett, prin. — Fax 271-4694
Harrisburg Journey ES — 500/PK-5
6801 S Grange Ave 57108 — 605-743-2567
Rob Sylliaasen, prin. — Fax 367-0017
Harrisburg North MS — 400/6-8
2201 W 95th St 57108 — 605-743-2567
Micah Fesler, prin. — Fax 275-9140

Sioux Falls SD 49-5 — 22,300/PK-12
201 E 38th St 57105 — 605-367-7900
Dr. Brian Maher, supt. — Fax 367-4637
www.sf.k12.sd.us
All City ES — 100/K-5
2511 W Brookings St 57104 — 605-367-6120
Jane Hannemann, prin. — Fax 367-6063
Anderson ES — 300/PK-5
1600 N Wayland Ave 57103 — 605-367-6130
Jayne Zielenski, prin. — Fax 367-6064
Anthony ES — K-5
2000 S Dakota Ave 57105 — 605-367-4560
Marie Rickert, prin. — Fax 367-6082
Challenge Center S — 200/K-5
3101 S 4th Ave 57105 — 605-367-6170
Colleen Werner, prin. — Fax 367-6171
Cleveland ES — 500/PK-5
1000 S Edward Dr 57103 — 605-367-6150
Mitch Sheaffer, prin. — Fax 367-6066
Discovery ES — 700/PK-5
1506 S Discovery Ave 57106 — 605-362-3530
Lois Running, prin. — Fax 362-3535
Dunn ES — 600/PK-5
2400 S Bahnson Ave 57103 — 605-371-4120
Patti Pannell, prin. — Fax 371-4122
Edison MS — 900/6-8
2101 S West Ave 57105 — 605-367-7643
Shane Hieronimus, prin. — Fax 367-8457
Field A+ ES — 300/K-5
501 S Highland Ave 57103 — 605-367-6160
Linda McDaniel, prin. — Fax 367-6069
Frost ES — 500/PK-5
3101 S 4th Ave 57105 — 605-367-6170
Colleen Werner, prin. — Fax 367-6071
Garfield ES — 400/PK-5
705 S Roberts Dr 57104 — 605-367-6180
Kristin Skogstad, prin. — Fax 367-6072
Harris ES — 600/K-5
3501 E 49th St 57103 — 605-371-4111
Nancy Hagen, prin. — Fax 371-4110
Hawthorne ES — 500/PK-5
601 N Spring Ave 57104 — 605-367-4580
Stephanie Jones, prin. — Fax 367-6074
Hayward ES — 800/PK-5
400 N Valley View Rd 57107 — 605-367-4590
Jeff Sheets, prin. — Fax 367-6075
Henry MS — 1,100/6-8
2200 S 5th Ave 57105 — 605-367-7639
Kim Sharping, prin. — Fax 367-7693
Howe ES — 600/K-5
2801 S Valley View Rd 57106 — 605-362-2752
Larry Larsen, prin. — Fax 362-2724
Kennedy ES — 600/K-5
4501 S Holbrook Ave 57106 — 605-362-2784
Patty Vincent, prin. — Fax 362-2776
Lowell MST ES — 500/PK-5
710 W 18th St 57104 — 605-367-8378
Diane Kennedy, prin. — Fax 367-6079
Mann ES — 200/K-5
1401 E 26th St 57105 — 605-367-6190
Tara Eckstaine, prin. — Fax 367-6080
McGovern MS — 700/6-8
6221 W Maple St 57107 — 605-367-4440
Lynn Gillette, prin. — Fax 367-4434
Memorial MS — 1,100/6-8
1401 S Sertoma Ave 57106 — 605-362-2785
Carrie Aaron, prin. — Fax 362-2790
Parks Global Studies ES — 600/K-5
5701 E Red Oak Dr 57110 — 605-371-4170
Kiersta Machacek, prin. — Fax 371-4174
Pettigrew ES — 700/PK-5
7900 W 53rd St 57106 — 605-362-3560
Kevin Dick, prin. — Fax 362-3564
Redlin ES — 500/PK-5
1721 E Austin St 57103 — 605-367-6140
Ryan DeGraff, prin. — Fax 367-6065
Sullivan ES — 700/PK-5
3701 E 3rd St 57103 — 605-367-6084
Dr. Kirk Zeeck, prin. — Fax 367-6088
Whittier MS — 1,000/6-8
930 E 6th St 57103 — 605-367-7620
Twaine Fink, prin. — Fax 367-8357
Wilder ES — 400/K-5
2300 S Lyndale Ave 57105 — 605-367-4570
Nancy Krueger, prin. — Fax 367-8487
Other Schools – See Renner

Tea Area SD 41-5
Supt. — See Tea
Tea Area Frontier ES — 100/K-5
2700 S Lancaster Dr 57106 — 605-271-7331
Barbara Hansen, prin. — Fax 271-7394

Baan Dek Montessori S — PK-K
1836 W Grand Arbor Cir 57108 — 605-271-9945
Bethel Lutheran S — 50/K-8
1801 S Valley View Rd 57106 — 605-362-8231
Dyllan Jensen, prin. — Fax 362-8231
Christ the King S — 100/PK-6
1801 S Lake Ave 57105 — 605-338-5103
Julie Kolbeck, prin. — Fax 335-1231
Good Shepherd Lutheran S — 100/PK-8
4800 S Southeastern Ave 57103 — 605-371-0047
Timothy Schubkegel, admin.
Holy Spirit S — 500/PK-6
4309 S Bahnson Ave 57103 — 605-371-1481
Regan Manning, prin. — Fax 371-1483
O'Gorman JHS — 400/7-8
3100 W 41st St 57105 — 605-988-0546
Wade Charron, prin. — Fax 336-9839
Providence Classical Christian Academy — PK-4
3800 W 15th St 57103 — 605-610-8697
St. Katharine Drexel S — PK-6
1800 S Katie Ave 57106 — 605-275-6994
Stacy Charron, prin. — Fax 275-6996
St. Lambert S — 200/K-6
1000 S Bahnson Ave 57103 — 605-338-7042
Colleen Davis, prin. — Fax 336-8727
St. Mary S — 300/PK-6
2001 S 5th Ave 57105 — 605-334-9881
Michelle Shields, prin. — Fax 334-9224
St. Michael S — 300/PK-6
1600 S Marion Rd 57106 — 605-361-0021
Lisa Huemoeller, prin. — Fax 361-0094
Sioux Falls Christian S — 400/PK-12
6120 S Charger Cir 57108 — 605-334-1422
Jay Woudstra, supt. — Fax 334-6928
Sioux Falls Lutheran S — 300/PK-8
308 W 37th St 57105 — 605-335-1923
Tia Esser, admin. — Fax 335-1930
Sioux Falls SDA S — 50/K-8
7100 E 26th St 57110 — 605-333-0197

Sisseton, Roberts, Pop. 2,369
Sisseton SD 54-2 — 900/K-12
516 8th Ave W 57262 — 605-698-7613
Tammy Meyer, supt. — Fax 698-3032
www.sisseton.k12.sd.us
Sisseton MS — 200/6-8
516 8th Ave W 57262 — 605-698-7613
Eric Heath, prin. — Fax 698-7487
Westside ES — 400/K-5
516 8th Ave W 57262 — 605-698-7613
Dr. April Moen, prin. — Fax 698-7404

Spearfish, Lawrence, Pop. 10,283
Spearfish SD 40-2 — 2,200/PK-12
525 E Illinois St 57783 — 605-717-1201
Kirk Easton, supt. — Fax 717-1200
www.spearfish.k12.sd.us
Creekside ES — 500/3-5
525 E Illinois St 57783 — 605-717-1210
Dan Olson, prin. — Fax 717-1231
Mountain View ES — 200/PK-K
525 E Illinois St 57783 — 605-717-1209
Nick Gottlob, prin. — Fax 717-0426
Spearfish MS — 500/6-8
525 E Illinois St 57783 — 605-717-1215
Don Lyon, prin. — Fax 717-1252
West ES — 400/1-2
525 E Illinois St 57783 — 605-717-1205
Nick Gottlob, prin. — Fax 717-1232

Black Hills Christian Academy — 100/PK-8
630 S 32nd St 57783 — 605-722-1276
Jullie Totino, admin. — Fax 722-1217
Spearfish Classical Christian S — 100/PK-12
PO Box 723 57783 — 605-717-4019

Springfield, Bon Homme, Pop. 1,945
Bon Homme SD 4-2
Supt. — See Tyndall
Springfield ES — 50/K-5
1008 Walnut St 57062 — 605-369-2282
Michael Duffek, prin. — Fax 369-2438

Stickney, Aurora, Pop. 284
Corsica-Stickney SD 21-3
Supt. — See Corsica
Corsica-Stickney ES — 100/PK-6
PO Box 67 57375 — 605-732-4221
Ferra Kemp, prin. — Fax 732-4281

Sturgis, Meade, Pop. 6,462
Meade SD 46-1 — 2,600/K-12
1230 Douglas St 57785 — 605-347-2523
John Pedersen, supt. — Fax 347-0005
meade.k12.sd.us
Sturgis ES — 700/K-5
1121 Ballpark Rd 57785 — 605-347-2386
Chantal Ligtenberg, prin. — Fax 347-0005
Sturgis IS, 1230 Douglas St 57785 — 5-6
Chantal Ligtenberg, prin. — 605-347-2523
Sturgis Williams MS — 500/6-8
1425 Cedar St 57785 — 605-347-5232
Ann Monnast, prin. — Fax 720-0190
Other Schools – See Enning, Hereford, Opal, Piedmont, Union Center, Wasta, Whitewood

Summit, Roberts, Pop. 270
Summit SD 54-6 — 200/PK-12
PO Box 791 57266 — 605-398-6211
Kurt Jensen, supt. — Fax 398-6311
www.summit.k12.sd.us
Summit ES — 100/PK-8
PO Box 791 57266 — 605-398-6211
Kurt Jensen, prin. — Fax 398-6311

Tabor, Bon Homme, Pop. 415
Bon Homme SD 4-2
Supt. — See Tyndall
Hutterische Colony S — 50/K-8
31232 Colony Rd 57063 — 605-589-3388
Dr. Mike Elsberry, prin. — Fax 589-3468
Tabor ES — 50/K-5
227 N Lidice Ave 57063 — 605-463-2271
Michael Duffek, prin. — Fax 463-9511

Tea, Lincoln, Pop. 3,745
Tea Area SD 41-5 — 1,600/K-12
PO Box 488 57064 — 605-498-2700
Jennifer Lowery, supt. — Fax 498-2702
www.teaschools.k12.sd.us
Tea Area Legacy ES — 400/K-2
PO Box 488 57064 — 605-498-2700
Betsy Drew, prin. — Fax 498-4134
Tea Area MS — 300/6-8
PO Box 488 57064 — 605-498-2700
Chris Fechner, prin. — Fax 498-0280
Other Schools – See Sioux Falls

Timber Lake, Dewey, Pop. 419
Timber Lake SD 20-3 — 400/PK-12
PO Box 1000 57656 — 605-865-3654
Dan Martin, supt. — Fax 865-3294
www.tls.new.rschooltoday.com
Timber Lake ES — 200/PK-5
PO Box 1000 57656 — 605-865-3654
Danae Paxton, prin. — Fax 865-3294
Timber Lake MS — 100/6-8
PO Box 1000 57656 — 605-865-3654
Julie Marshall, prin. — Fax 865-3294

Toronto, Deuel, Pop. 212
Deubrook Area SD 5-6
Supt. — See White
Deubrook ES — 200/K-6
PO Box 399 57268 — 605-794-1151
Mitch Reed, prin. — Fax 794-2492
Red Willow Colony S — 50/K-8
47360 197th St 57268 — 605-629-1152
Mitch Reed, prin. — Fax 794-2492

Tripp, Hutchinson, Pop. 645
Tripp-Delmont SD 33-5 — 200/PK-12
PO Box 430 57376 — 605-935-6766
Gail Swenson, supt. — Fax 935-6507
www.tridel.k12.sd.us/
Tripp-Delmont S — 100/PK-8
PO Box 430 57376 — 605-935-6766
Gail Swenson, prin. — Fax 935-6507
Other Schools – See Delmont

Tulare, Spink, Pop. 205
Hitchcock-Tulare SD 56-6 — 200/PK-12
PO Box 108 57476 — 605-266-2151
Jeff Clark, supt. — Fax 266-2160
www.hitchcock-tulare.k12.sd.us/
Hitchcock-Tulare JHS — 50/7-8
PO Box 108 57476 — 605-596-4171
Bill Barrie, prin. — Fax 596-4150
Other Schools – See Frankfort, Hitchcock

Tyndall, Bon Homme, Pop. 1,060
Bon Homme SD 4-2 — 500/PK-12
PO Box 28 57066 — 605-589-3388
Dr. Mike Elsberry, supt. — Fax 589-3468
www.bonhomme.k12.sd.us/
Bon Homme MS — 100/6-8
PO Box 28 57066 — 605-589-3387
Cory Lambley, prin. — Fax 589-3468
Tyndall ES — 100/PK-5
PO Box 28 57066 — 605-589-3389
Michael Duffek, prin. — Fax 589-3468
Other Schools – See Springfield, Tabor

Union Center, Meade
Meade SD 46-1
Supt. — See Sturgis
Atall S — 50/K-8
16375 Atall Rd 57787 — 605-269-2264
Bev Rosenboom, prin. — Fax 269-2099
Union Center S — 50/6-8
1700 SD Highway 34 57787 — 605-269-2264
Bev Rosenboom, prin. — Fax 269-2099

Utica, Yankton, Pop. 63
Menno SD 33-2
Supt. — See Menno
Jamesville Colony S — 50/K-8
43582 NE Jim River Rd 57067 — 605-387-5161
Dr. Charlene Crosswait, prin. — Fax 387-5171

Valley Springs, Minnehaha, Pop. 744
Brandon Valley SD 49-2
Supt. — See Brandon
Valley Springs ES — 100/K-5
PO Box 130 57068 — 605-757-6285
Tanya Palmer, prin. — Fax 582-6795

Vermillion, Clay, Pop. 10,331
Vermillion SD 13-1 — 1,200/PK-12
17 Prospect St 57069 — 605-677-7000
Damon Alvey, supt. — Fax 677-7002
www.vermillion.k12.sd.us
Austin ES — 200/PK-1
300 High St 57069 — 605-677-7010
Kim Johnson, prin. — Fax 677-7022
Jolley ES — 300/2-5
224 S University St 57069 — 605-677-7015
Sue Galvin, prin. — Fax 677-7022
Vermillion MS — 300/6-8
422 Princeton St 57069 — 605-677-7025
Tim Koehler, prin. — Fax 677-7028

St. Agnes S — 100/PK-5
909 Lewis St 57069 — 605-624-4144
Darla Hamm, prin. — Fax 624-6239

Viborg, Turner, Pop. 777
Viborg-Hurley SD 60-6 — 300/PK-12
PO Box 397 57070 — 605-766-5418
Peggy Petersen, supt. — Fax 766-5635
www.viborg-hurleyk12.com

Cameron Colony ES 50/K-6
28971 447th Ave 57070 605-766-5418
Brett Mellem, prin. Fax 766-5635
Viborg-Hurley ES 200/PK-4
PO Box 397 57070 605-766-5418
Peggy Petersen, prin. Fax 766-5635
Other Schools – See Hurley

Volga, Brookings, Pop. 1,762
Sioux Valley SD 5-5 600/PK-12
PO Box 278 57071 605-627-5657
Laura Schuster, supt. Fax 627-5291
www.svs.k12.sd.us/
Sioux Valley ES 300/PK-5
PO Box 278 57071 605-627-5657
Heather Hiltunen, prin. Fax 627-5291
Sioux Valley MS 100/6-8
PO Box 278 57071 605-627-5657
Belinda Miller, prin. Fax 627-5291

Volga Christian S 100/PK-8
223 E 6th St 57071 605-627-9286
Richard Brubakken, admin. Fax 627-9286

Wagner, Charles Mix, Pop. 1,520
Wagner Community SD 11-4 900/PK-12
101 Walnut Ave SW 57380 605-384-3677
Linda Foos, supt. Fax 384-3678
www.wagner.k12.sd.us/
Wagner ES 200/1-4
101 Walnut Ave SW 57380 605-384-3393
Carol Ersland, prin. Fax 384-3002
Wagner MS 200/5-8
101 Walnut Ave SW 57380 605-384-3913
Steve Petry, prin. Fax 384-3678
Wagner PS 200/PK-K
101 Walnut Ave SW 57380 605-384-4354
Lori Bouza, prin. Fax 384-3888

Wakonda, Clay, Pop. 321
Irene-Wakonda SD 13-3
Supt. — See Irene
Irene-Wakonda ES 200/PK-6
PO Box 268 57073 605-267-2644
Debra Lyle, prin. Fax 267-2645

Wakpala, Corson
Smee SD 15-3 200/PK-12
PO Box B 57658 605-845-3040
Jay Shillingstad, supt. Fax 845-7244
www.smee.k12.sd.us
Wakpala ES 100/PK-5
PO Box B 57658 605-845-3040
Karyl Knudson, prin. Fax 845-7244
Wakpala MS 50/6-8
PO Box B 57658 605-845-3040
Barry Mann, prin. Fax 845-7244

Wall, Pennington, Pop. 739
Wall SD 51-5 200/K-12
PO Box 414 57790 605-279-2156
Cooper Garnos, supt. Fax 279-2613
www.wall.k12.sd.us
Big White ES 50/K-6
PO Box 414 57790 605-279-2156
Charles Sykora, prin. Fax 279-2613
Wall ES 100/K-6
PO Box 414 57790 605-279-2156
Charles Sykora, prin. Fax 279-2613
Wall MS 50/7-8
PO Box 414 57790 605-279-2156
Cooper Garnos, prin. Fax 279-2613

Warner, Brown, Pop. 453
Warner SD 6-5 300/K-12
PO Box 20 57479 605-225-6397
Michael Kroll, supt. Fax 225-0007
www.warner.k12.sd.us/
Warner ES 200/K-5
PO Box 20 57479 605-225-6194
Roby Johnson, prin. Fax 225-0007
Warner MS 100/6-8
PO Box 20 57479 605-225-6194
Michael Kroll, prin. Fax 225-0007

Wasta, Pennington, Pop. 80
Meade SD 46-1
Supt. — See Sturgis
Elm Springs S 50/K-8
21309 Elm Springs Rd 57791 605-269-2264
Bev Rosenboom, prin. Fax 269-2099

Watertown, Codington, Pop. 21,216
Watertown SD 14-4 3,900/PK-12
PO Box 730 57201 605-882-6312
Jeff Danielsen, supt. Fax 882-6327
www.watertown.k12.sd.us
Jefferson ES 400/K-4
1701 N Maple 57201 605-882-6390
Laura Morrow, prin. Fax 882-6391
Lincoln ES 400/K-4
1100 13th St NE 57201 605-882-6340
Dr. Susan Patrick, prin. Fax 882-6343
McKinley ES 300/PK-4
5 12th St SW 57201 605-882-6350
Shannon Knopf, prin. Fax 882-6351
Mellette ES 300/K-4
619 2nd St NW 57201 605-882-6385
John Decker, prin. Fax 882-6382
Roosevelt ES 200/K-4
412 2nd St SE 57201 605-882-6360
Gregg DeSpiegler, prin. Fax 882-6361
Watertown IS 600/5-6
601 11th St NE 57201 605-882-6355
Jennifer Bollinger, admin. Fax 882-6395
Watertown MS 600/7-8
1700 11th St NE 57201 605-882-6370
Dr. Todd Brist, prin. Fax 886-6372

Immaculate Conception S 200/PK-6
109 3rd St SE 57201 605-886-3883
Carol Dagel, prin. Fax 886-0199
St. Martin Lutheran S 100/PK-8
1200 2nd St NE 57201 605-886-4976
Mark Renner, prin. Fax 886-6362
Watertown Christian S 100/PK-8
15 12th Ave NE 57201 605-882-0949
Nancy Weber, admin. Fax 882-5935

Waubay, Day, Pop. 561
Waubay SD 18-3 200/PK-12
202 W School Rd 57273 605-947-4529
Dean Jones M.A., supt. Fax 947-4243
www.waubay.k12.sd.us/
Waubay ES 100/PK-5
202 W School Rd 57273 605-947-4529
Dean Jones M.A., prin. Fax 947-4243
Waubay MS 50/6-8
202 W School Rd 57273 605-947-4529
Dean Jones M.A., prin. Fax 947-4243

Waverly, Codington, Pop. 37
Waverly SD 14-5 200/PK-12
319 Mary Pl, 605-886-9174
Jon Meyer, supt. Fax 886-6630
www.waverly.k12.sd.us
Waverly/South Shore ES 100/PK-5
319 Mary Pl, 605-886-9174
Joe Dalton, prin. Fax 886-6630
Waverly/South Shore MS 50/6-8
319 Mary Pl, 605-886-9174
Joe Dalton, prin. Fax 886-6630

Webster, Day, Pop. 1,853
Webster Area SD 18-4 500/PK-12
102 E 9th Ave 57274 605-345-3548
Dr. James Block, supt. Fax 345-4421
www.webster.k12.sd.us/
Webster Area ES 300/PK-5
102 E 9th Ave 57274 605-345-4651
Craig Case, prin. Fax 345-4421
Webster Area MS 100/6-8
102 E 9th Ave 57274 605-345-4651
Craig Case, prin. Fax 345-4421

Wecota, Faulk
Faulkton Area SD 24-4
Supt. — See Faulkton
Blumengard Colony S 50/K-8
35075 148th St 57438 605-324-3243
Derek Barrios, prin.
Thunderbird Colony S 50/K-8
15185 346th Ave 57438 605-324-3241
Derek Barrios, prin.

Wessington Springs, Jerauld, Pop. 954
Wessington Springs SD 36-2 300/PK-12
PO Box 449 57382 605-539-9391
Lance Witte, supt. Fax 539-1029
www.wessingtonsprings.k12.sd.us
Spring Valley Colony ES 50/K-8
PO Box 449 57382 605-539-1754
Jason Kolousek, prin. Fax 539-1583
Wessington Springs ES 200/PK-6
PO Box 449 57382 605-539-9500
Carrie Azure, prin. Fax 539-1583
Wessington Springs JHS 50/7-8
PO Box 449 57382 605-539-9311
Jason Kolousek, prin. Fax 539-1029

Westport, Brown, Pop. 133
Leola SD 44-2
Supt. — See Leola
Grassland Colony S 50/K-8
11865 370th Ave 57481 605-439-3477
Beverly Myer, prin. Fax 439-3206

Wetonka, McPherson, Pop. 8
Leola SD 44-2
Supt. — See Leola
Longlake Colony S 50/K-8
36848 123rd St 57481 605-439-3477
Beverly Myer, prin. Fax 439-3206

White, Brookings, Pop. 482
Deubrook Area SD 5-6 300/K-12
PO Box 346 57276 605-629-1100
Dr. Kimberly Kludt, supt. Fax 629-3701
www.deubrook.com
Norfeld Colony S 50/K-8
PO Box 346 57276 605-794-1152
Mitch Reed, prin. Fax 794-2492
Other Schools – See Toronto

Elkton SD 5-3
Supt. — See Elkton
Rolland Colony S 50/K-8
48088 210th St 57276 605-542-2541
Kelly Neill, prin. Fax 542-4441

White Lake, Aurora, Pop. 368
White Lake SD 1-3 100/PK-12
PO Box 246 57383 605-249-2251
Robert Schroeder, supt. Fax 249-2725
www.whitelake.k12.sd.us/
White Lake ES 100/PK-6
PO Box 246 57383 605-249-2251
Robert Schroeder, prin. Fax 249-2725
White Lake JHS 50/7-8
PO Box 246 57383 605-249-2251
Robert Schroeder, prin. Fax 249-2725

White River, Mellette, Pop. 529
White River SD 47-1 400/PK-12
PO Box 273 57579 605-259-3311
Thomas Cameron, supt. Fax 259-3133
www.whiteriver.k12.sd.us/
White River ES 200/PK-5
PO Box 273 57579 605-259-3137
Celia Hermsen, prin. Fax 259-3133
White River MS 100/6-8
PO Box 273 57579 605-259-3135
Kendra Becker, prin. Fax 259-3133
Other Schools – See Norris

Whitewood, Lawrence, Pop. 897
Meade SD 46-1
Supt. — See Sturgis
Whitewood ES 100/K-6
603 Garfield St 57793 605-269-2264
Bev Rosenboom, prin. Fax 269-2099

Willow Lake, Clark, Pop. 262
Willow Lake SD 12-3 200/PK-12
PO Box 170 57278 605-625-5945
Scott Klaudt, supt. Fax 625-3103
www.willowlake.k12.sd.us
Mayfield Colony ES 50/K-8
PO Box 170 57278 605-625-5945
Chris Lee, prin. Fax 625-3103
Willow Lake ES 100/PK-5
PO Box 170 57278 605-625-5945
Chris Lee, prin. Fax 625-3103
Willow Lake MS 50/6-8
PO Box 170 57278 605-625-5945
Chris Lee, prin. Fax 625-3103
Other Schools – See Carpenter, Iroquois

Wilmot, Roberts, Pop. 481
Wilmot SD 54-7 200/PK-12
PO Box 100 57279 605-938-4647
Larry Hulscher, supt. Fax 938-4185
www.wilmot.k12.sd.us
Wilmot ES 100/PK-5
PO Box 100 57279 605-938-4647
Mike Schmidt, prin. Fax 938-4185
Wilmot MS 50/6-8
PO Box 100 57279 605-938-4647
Mike Schmidt, prin. Fax 938-4185

Winfred, Lake, Pop. 52
Howard SD 48-3
Supt. — See Howard
Shannon Colony S 50/K-8
43952 235th St 57076 605-772-4443
Dr. Christopher Noid, prin. Fax 772-4445

Winner, Tripp, Pop. 2,819
Winner SD 59-2 500/K-12
PO Box 231 57580 605-842-8101
Keven Morehart, supt. Fax 842-8120
www.winner.k12.sd.us
Winner ES 300/K-5
PO Box 231 57580 605-842-8170
Brian Naasz, prin. Fax 842-8123

Wolsey, Beadle, Pop. 376
Wolsey-Wessington SD 2-6 300/K-12
375 Ash St SE 57384 605-883-4221
James Cutshaw, supt. Fax 883-4720
www.wolsey-wessington.k12.sd.us
Wolsey-Wessington ES 200/K-5
375 Ash St SE 57384 605-883-4221
Carol Rowen, prin. Fax 883-4720
Wolsey-Wessington MS 100/6-8
375 Ash St SE 57384 605-883-4221
Carol Rowen, prin. Fax 883-4720

Wood, Mellette, Pop. 52
Colome SD 59-3
Supt. — See Colome
Wood S 50/K-8
PO Box 458 57585 605-452-3251
Anna LaDeaux, prin. Fax 452-3252

Woonsocket, Sanborn, Pop. 652
Woonsocket SD 55-4 200/PK-12
PO Box 428 57385 605-796-4431
Dr. Rodrick Weber, supt. Fax 796-4352
www.woonsocket.k12.sd.us/
Woonsocket ES 200/PK-8
PO Box 428 57385 605-796-4431
Paula Lynch, prin. Fax 796-4432

Worthing, Lincoln, Pop. 866
Lennox SD 41-4
Supt. — See Lennox
Worthing ES 100/K-4
230 Cedar St 57077 605-372-4114
Kym Johnston, prin. Fax 372-6046

Yankton, Yankton, Pop. 14,259
Yankton SD 63-3 2,800/PK-12
PO Box 738 57078 605-665-3998
Dr. Wayne Kindle, supt. Fax 665-1422
www.ysd.k12.sd.us
Beadle ES 400/K-5
PO Box 738 57078 605-665-2282
Carey Mitzel, prin. Fax 655-5961
Lincoln ES 400/K-5
PO Box 738 57078 605-665-7392
Paul Struck, prin. Fax 665-0301
Stewart ES 300/K-5
PO Box 738 57078 605-665-5765
Jerome Klimisch, prin. Fax 668-0762
Webster ES 300/PK-5
PO Box 738 57078 605-665-2484
Melanie Ryken, prin. Fax 655-0006
Yankton MS 600/6-8
PO Box 738 57078 605-665-2419
Todd Dvoracek, prin. Fax 665-6239

Missouri Valley Christian Academy 50/K-8
PO Box 902 57078 605-665-4470
Fax 665-4470
Sacred Heart ES 200/PK-4
1500 Saint Benedict Dr 57078 605-665-5841
Laura Haberman, prin. Fax 260-3400
Sacred Heart MS 5-8
504 Capitol St 57078 605-665-1808
Dr. Tim Mulhair, prin. Fax 260-9787

TENNESSEE

TENNESSEE DEPARTMENT OF EDUCATION
710 James Robertson Pkwy, Nashville 37243-1219
Telephone 615-741-2731
Fax 615-532-4791
Website tn.gov/education

Commissioner of Education Candice McQueen

TENNESSEE BOARD OF EDUCATION
710 James Robertson Pkwy, Nashville 37243

Executive Director B. Fielding Rolston

PUBLIC, PRIVATE AND CATHOLIC ELEMENTARY SCHOOLS

Adamsville, McNairy, Pop. 2,170
Hardin County SD
Supt. — See Savannah
West Hardin ES 200/PK-5
25105 Highway 69 38310 731-632-0413
Carmen Blankenship, prin. Fax 632-0253

McNairy County SD
Supt. — See Selmer
Adamsville ES 600/K-6
220 S Elm St 38310 731-439-4137
Danny Combs, prin. Fax 632-5007

Afton, Greene
Greene County SD
Supt. — See Greeneville
Chuckey Doak MS 500/6-8
120 Chuckey Doak Rd 37616 423-787-2038
Steve Broyles, prin. Fax 787-2096

Alamo, Crockett, Pop. 2,420
Alamo CSD 700/PK-6
265 E Park St 38001 731-696-5515
Jake Nichols, supt. Fax 696-2541
www.alamoschool.org
Alamo ES 700/PK-6
265 E Park St 38001 731-696-5515
Jake Nichols, admin. Fax 696-2541

Crockett County SD 2,000/PK-12
102 N Cavalier Dr 38001 731-696-2604
Bobby Mullins, supt. Fax 696-4734
www.ccschools.net
Crockett County MS 600/6-8
497 N Cavalier Dr 38001 731-696-5583
Bobby McLaughlin, prin. Fax 696-2034
Maury City ES 200/PK-5
3916 Highway 88 38001 731-656-2244
Ashley Dodd, prin. Fax 656-2936
Other Schools – See Friendship, Gadsden

Alcoa, Blount, Pop. 8,239
Alcoa CSD 1,900/PK-12
524 Faraday St 37701 865-984-0531
Dr. Brian Bell, supt. Fax 984-5832
www.alcoaschools.net/
Alcoa ES 500/PK-2
1200 Springbrook Rd 37701 865-982-3120
Monique Maples, prin. Fax 984-4458
Alcoa IS, 1325 Springbrook Rd 37701 400/3-5
Michelle Knight, admin. 865-984-0531
Alcoa MS 500/6-8
532 Faraday St 37701 865-982-5211
Dr. Scott Porter, prin. Fax 380-2533

Algood, Putnam, Pop. 3,428
Putnam County SD
Supt. — See Cookeville
Algood ES 600/K-4
2525 Old Walton Rd, Cookeville TN 38506
931-303-0362
Patience Cannon, prin. Fax 537-2079
Algood MS 800/PK-PK, 5-
540 Dry Valley Rd, Cookeville TN 38506
931-537-6141
Tim Martin, prin. Fax 537-3700

Allardt, Fentress, Pop. 632
Fentress County SD
Supt. — See Jamestown
Allardt ES 400/PK-8
220 Portland Ave 38504 931-879-9515
Ernest Campbell, prin. Fax 879-2702

Allons, Overton
Overton County SD
Supt. — See Livingston
Allons S 300/PK-8
321 Old Celina Rd 38541 931-823-5921
Jenny Smith, prin. Fax 823-7496

Altamont, Grundy, Pop. 1,042
Grundy County SD 2,300/PK-12
PO Box 97 37301 931-692-3467
Dr. William Childers Ed.D., dir. Fax 692-2188
www.grundycoschools.com
North ES 300/PK-8
PO Box 7 37301 931-692-3710
Kathy Hill, prin. Fax 692-2664
Other Schools – See Coalmont, Gruetli Laager, Palmer, Pelham, Tracy City

Andersonville, Anderson, Pop. 469
Anderson County SD
Supt. — See Clinton
Andersonville ES 300/PK-5
1951 Mountain Rd 37705 865-494-7695
Beth Roeder, prin. Fax 494-5484

Antioch, Davidson
Metropolitan Nashville SD
Supt. — See Nashville
Antioch MS 700/5-8
5050 Blue Hole Rd 37013 615-333-5642
Celia Conley, prin. Fax 333-5053
Apollo MS 800/5-8
631 Richards Rd 37013 615-333-5025
Shawn Lawrence, prin. Fax 333-5029
Cambridge Early Learning Center PK-PK
2325 Hickory Highlands Dr 37013 615-687-4560
DeeAnne Miree, prin.
Cane Ridge ES 900/K-4
3884 Asheford Trce 37013 615-641-7824
Donna Wilburn, prin.
Cole ES 800/PK-4
5060 Colemont Dr 37013 615-333-5043
Dr. Darwin Mason, prin. Fax 298-8052
Edison ES 700/PK-4
6130 Mount View Rd 37013 615-501-8800
Dr. Kesha Walrond, prin. Fax 262-6656
Kelley ES, 5834 Pettus Rd 37013 700/PK-4
Heather Bethurum, prin. 615-941-7535
Kennedy MS Prep 800/5-8
2087 Hobson Pike 37013 615-501-7900
Dr. Sam Braden, prin.
Marshall MS, 5832 Pettus Rd 37013 800/5-8
Roderick Webb, prin. 615-941-7515
Maxwell ES 600/PK-4
5535 Blue Hole Rd 37013 615-333-7180
Dr. Darwin Mason, prin. Fax 333-7183
Moss ES 900/PK-4
4701 Bowfield Dr 37013 615-333-5200
Carl Febles, prin. Fax 333-5208
Mount View ES 700/PK-4
3820 Murfreesboro Pike 37013 615-641-9393
Julia Lamb, prin. Fax 641-9395
Smith Springs ES PK-4
3132 Smith Springs Rd 37013 615-645-6465
Lance High, prin.

Ezell-Harding Christian S 600/PK-12
574 Bell Rd 37013 615-367-0532
Lighthouse Christian S 600/PK-12
5100 Blue Hole Rd 37013 615-331-6286

Apison, Hamilton, Pop. 2,442
Hamilton County SD
Supt. — See Chattanooga
Apison ES 600/PK-5
10433 E Brainerd Rd 37302 423-236-4322
Ronald Hughes, prin. Fax 236-4000

Coon Adventist S 50/K-8
11429 Bates Rd 37302 423-236-4926

Arlington, Shelby, Pop. 11,290
Arlington Community SD 5,000/K-12
12060 Arlington Trl 38002 901-389-2497
Tamara Mason, supt. Fax 389-2498
www.acsk-12.org
Arlington ES 900/K-5
11825 Douglass St 38002 901-867-6000
Anna Jones, prin. Fax 867-6006
Arlington MS 1,100/6-8
5470 Lamb Rd 38002 901-867-6015
Dr. Allison Clark, prin. Fax 867-7080
Donelson ES 600/K-5
12140 Donelson Farms Pkwy 38002 901-389-6973
Cherry Davidson, prin. Fax 389-6982
Shelby County SD
Supt. — See Memphis
Barrets Chapel S 300/K-8
10280 Godwin Rd 38002 901-416-0325
Jenae Scott-Robinson, prin. Fax 416-0321

Macon Road Baptist S - East 400/K-12
11015 Highway 64 38002 901-867-8161

Ashland City, Cheatham, Pop. 4,449
Cheatham County SD 6,600/PK-12
102 Elizabeth St 37015 615-792-5664
Dr. Cathy Beck, supt. Fax 792-2551
www.cheathamcountyschools.net
Ashland City ES 500/PK-4
108 Elizabeth St 37015 615-792-4296
Chip Roney, prin. Fax 792-2030
Cheatham MS 700/5-8
700 Scoutview Rd 37015 615-792-2334
Linda Owen, prin. Fax 792-2337
East Cheatham ES 500/PK 4
3201 Bearwallow Rd 37015 615-746-5251
Wendy Cox, prin. Fax 746-4594
Other Schools – See Chapmansboro, Kingston Springs, Pegram, Pleasant View

Athens, McMinn, Pop. 13,106
Athens CSD 1,700/PK-8
943 Crestway Dr 37303 423-745-2863
Dr. Melanie Miller, dir. Fax 745-9041
www.athenscityschools.net
Athens City MS 500/6-8
200 Keith Ln 37303 423-745-1177
Michael Simmons, prin. Fax 745-9679
City Park ES 400/PK-2
203 Keith Ln 37303 423-745-3862
Kristine Walden, prin. Fax 745-9577
Ingelside ES 400/PK-2
200 Guille St 37303 423-745-3671
Jill Swafford, prin. Fax 745-9665
North City ES 300/3-5
1601 Palos St 37303 423-745-4210
Holly Owens, prin. Fax 745-9306
Westside ES 200/3-5
700 Westside St 37303 423-745-4721
Tracy Lee, prin. Fax 745-0621

McMinn County SD 5,900/PK-12
3 S Hill St 37303 423-745-1612
Mickey Blevins Ed.D., dir. Fax 744-1641
www.mcminn.k12.tn.us
Baker S 300/PK-8
1044 County Road 172 37303 423-745-2760
. Amy Bohannon, prin. Fax 745-5986
Rogers Creek S 400/PK-8
137 County Road 82 37303 423-745-2123
Glen Puryear, prin. Fax 745-4286
Other Schools – See Calhoun, Englewood, Etowah, Niota, Riceville

---

Christ's Legacy Academy 100/K-12
964 County Road 180 37303 423-649-0040
Dr. Shane Arnold Ph.D., head sch
Fairview Christian Academy 100/PK-12
261 County Road 439 37303 423-745-6781
Liberty Christian S 100/K-12
PO Box 1555 37371 423-745-9248

Atoka, Tipton, Pop. 8,222
Tipton County SD
Supt. — See Covington
Atoka ES 900/PK-5
870 Rosemark Rd 38004 901-840-9525
Lisa Rose, prin. Fax 840-9541

Atwood, Carroll, Pop. 925
West Carroll Special SD 1,000/PK-12
1415 State Route 77 38220 731-662-4200
Dexter Williams, dir. Fax 662-4250
www.wcssd.org
Other Schools – See Mc Lemoresville, Trezevant

Auburntown, Cannon, Pop. 265
Cannon County SD
Supt. — See Woodbury

Auburn S 100/K-8
150 Vantrease Ave 37016 615-464-4342
Melinda Crook, prin. Fax 464-4344

Bartlett, Shelby, Pop. 53,815
Bartlett CSD 7,900/K-12
5650 Woodlawn St 38134 901-202-0855
David Stephens, supt. Fax 202-0854
www.bartlettschools.org
Altruria ES 700/K-5
6641 Deermont Dr 38134 901-373-2600
Marva Johnson, prin. Fax 373-1418
Appling MS 700/6-8
3700 Appling Rd 38133 901-373-1410
Dr. Keshia McMickens, prin. Fax 373-1360
Bartlett ES 800/K-5
3932 Billy Maher Rd 38135 901-373-2610
Page Watson, prin. Fax 373-1394
Bon Lin ES 800/K-5
3940 N Germantown Rd 38133 901-937-2344
Kasandra Berry, prin. Fax 937-3387
Bon Lin MS 600/6-8
3862 N Germantown Rd 38133 901-347-1520
Cody Duncan, prin. Fax 347-1491
Ellendale ES 600/K-5
6950 Dawnhill Rd 38135 901-373-2636
Dr. Bess Anne Mcknight, prin. Fax 373-1395
Elmore Park MS 600/6-8
6330 Althorne Rd 38134 901-373-2642
Ethan Randle, prin. Fax 373-1361
Oak ES 600/K-5
3573 Oak Rd 38135 901-373-2646
Marie DeLockery, prin. Fax 373-1415
Rivercrest ES 700/K-5
4825 Rivercrest Ln 38135 901-373-1373
Portia Tate, prin. Fax 373-1380

Bartlett Baptist K & Preschool 100/PK-K
3465 Kirby Whitten Pkwy 38135 901-333-3352
Susan Myatt, prin. Fax 386-7480

Baxter, Putnam, Pop. 1,354
Putnam County SD
Supt. — See Cookeville
Baxter PS 200/PK-1
125 Elmore Town Rd 38544 931-858-3110
Marsha Wyatt, admin. Fax 858-4644
Cornerstone ES 2-4
371 1st Ave S 38544 931-858-9190
Tammy Hoover, admin. Fax 858-9189
Upperman MS 5-8
6700 Nashville Hwy 38544 931-858-6601
Shannon Pirtle, admin. Fax 858-6637

Bean Station, Grainger, Pop. 2,804
Grainger County SD
Supt. — See Rutledge
Bean Station S 600/PK-6
200 Bean Station School Rd 37708 865-767-2131
Dwayne Brabson, prin. Fax 767-2248

Bells, Crockett, Pop. 2,394
Bells CSD 400/PK-5
4547 Highway 88 S 38006 731-663-2041
Mark Wallace, dir. Fax 663-2161
www.bellscityschool.org
Bells ES 400/PK-5
4547 Highway 88 S 38006 731-663-2041
Brooks Rawson, prin. Fax 663-2161

Benton, Polk, Pop. 1,374
Polk County SD 2,600/PK-12
PO Box 665 37307 423-299-0471
Dr. James Jones, dir. Fax 338-2691
www.polk-schools.com
Benton ES 500/PK-5
PO Box 190 37307 423-338-4510
Dr. Tracy McAbee, prin. Fax 338-7977
Chilhowee MS 400/6-8
PO Box 977 37307 423-299-0086
Connie Dunn, prin. Fax 338-3158
Other Schools – See Copperhill, Oldfort

Bethel Springs, McNairy, Pop. 715
McNairy County SD
Supt. — See Selmer
Bethel Springs S 500/K-8
4733 Main St 38315 731-934-7288
Terry Moore, prin. Fax 934-0046

Bethpage, Sumner, Pop. 280
Sumner County SD
Supt. — See Gallatin
Bethpage ES 300/K-5
420 Old Highway 31 E 37022 615-841-3212
David Woodard, prin. Fax 841-3998
North Sumner ES 200/K-5
1485 N Sumner Rd 37022 615-888-2281
Terry Herndon, prin. Fax 888-3560

Big Rock, Stewart
Stewart County SD
Supt. — See Dover
North Stewart ES 400/PK-5
2201 Highway 79 37023 931-232-5505
Debbie Grasty, prin. Fax 232-8139

Big Sandy, Benton, Pop. 553
Benton County SD
Supt. — See Camden
Big Sandy S 300/K-12
13305 Highway 69A 38221 731-593-3221
Marty Caruthers, prin. Fax 593-3245

Blountville, Sullivan, Pop. 3,052
Sullivan County SD 10,500/PK-12
PO Box 306 37617 423-354-1000
Evelyn Rafalowski, supt. Fax 354-1004
www.sullivank12.net
Blountville ES 500/PK-5
155 School Ave 37617 423-354-1650
Dr. Becky Olinger, prin. Fax 354-1656
Blountville MS 300/6-8
1651 Blountville Blvd 37617 423-354-1600
Becky Olinger, prin. Fax 354-1606
Central Heights ES 200/PK-5
158 Central Heights Rd 37617 423-354-1575
Angie Baker, prin. Fax 354-1581
Holston ES 300/PK-5
2348 Highway 75 37617 423-354-1550
Lesley Fleenor, prin. Fax 354-1555
Holston MS 400/6-8
2348 Highway 75 37617 423-354-1500
Bill Miller, prin. Fax 354-1505
Innovation Academy 200/6-7
2348 Highway 75 37617 423-354-1730
Billy Miller, admin. Fax 354-1736
Other Schools – See Bluff City, Bristol, Kingsport, Piney Flats

---

Tri-Cities Christian S 400/PK-12
1500 Highway 75 37617 423-323-7128

Bluff City, Sullivan, Pop. 1,717
Sullivan County SD
Supt. — See Blountville
Bluff City ES 500/K-4
282 J Forrest Thomas St 37618 423-354-1825
Cathy Nester, prin. Fax 354-1831
Bluff City MS 400/5-8
337 Carter St 37618 423-354-1801
Greg Stallcup, prin. Fax 354-1818

Bolivar, Hardeman, Pop. 5,360
Hardeman County SD 4,000/PK-12
10815 Old Highway 64 38008 731-658-2510
Warner Ross, dir. Fax 658-2061
www.hardemancountyschools.org
Bolivar ES 900/PK-5
445 Nuckolls Rd 38008 731-658-3981
James Rutherford, prin. Fax 658-2641
Bolivar MS 400/6-8
915 Pruitt St 38008 731-658-3050
Mary Ann Polk, prin. Fax 658-6625
Other Schools – See Grand Junction, Hornsby, Middleton, Toone, Whiteville

Bradford, Gibson, Pop. 1,036
Bradford Special SD 500/PK-12
PO Box 220 38316 731-742-3180
Dan Black, supt. Fax 742-3994
www.bradfordssd.schoolinsites.com
Bradford ES 300/PK-6
PO Box 99 38316 731-742-2118
Kelly Knott, prin. Fax 742-3062

Bradyville, Cannon
Cannon County SD
Supt. — See Woodbury
Woodland S 400/PK-8
8383 Jim Cummings Hwy 37026 615-765-5498
Angela Cossey, prin. Fax 765-7496

Brentwood, Williamson, Pop. 36,506
Metropolitan Nashville SD
Supt. — See Nashville
Granbery ES 700/K-4
5501 Hill Rd 37027 615-333-5112
Chad High, prin. Fax 262-6901

Williamson County SD
Supt. — See Franklin
Brentwood MS 1,300/6-8
5324 Murray Ln 37027 615-472-4250
Dr. Brandon Barkley, prin. Fax 472-4263
Crockett ES 700/K-5
9019 Crockett Rd 37027 615-472-4340
Bronwyn Rector, prin. Fax 472-4351
Edmondson ES 700/K-5
851 Edmondson Pike 37027 615-472-4360
Trent Satterfield, prin. Fax 472-4371
Grassland ES 500/K-5
6803 Manley Ln 37027 615-472-4480
Dr. Ann Gordon, prin. Fax 472-4492
Kenrose ES 800/K-5
1702 Raintree Pkwy 37027 615-472-4630
Rebekah Loffi, prin. Fax 472-4646
Lipscomb ES 900/PK-5
8011 Concord Rd 37027 615-472-4650
Michelle Contich, prin. Fax 472-4661
Scales ES 700/K-5
6430 Murray Ln 37027 615-472-4830
Dr. Melonye Lowe, prin. Fax 472-4841
Sunset ES 800/K-5
100 Sunset Trl 37027 615-472-5020
Karen Caldwell, prin. Fax 472-5030
Sunset MS 800/6-8
200 Sunset Trl 37027 615-472-5040
Dr. Tim Brown, prin. Fax 472-5050
Woodland MS 800/6-8
1500 Volunteer Pkwy 37027 615-472-4930
Priscilla Fizer, prin. Fax 472-4941

Currey Ingram Academy 300/K-12
6544 Murray Ln 37027 615-507-3242
Dr. Jeffrey Mitchell, head sch Fax 507-3170
Montessori Academy 100/PK-8
6021 Cloverland Dr 37027 615-833-3610

Briceville, Anderson
Anderson County SD
Supt. — See Clinton
Briceville ES 100/K-5
103 Slatestone Rd 37710 865-426-2289
Travis Hutcheson, prin. Fax 426-6451

Brighton, Tipton, Pop. 2,690
Tipton County SD
Supt. — See Covington
Brighton ES 800/PK-5
1201 Old Highway 51 S 38011 901-837-5860
Brooke Shipley, prin. Fax 837-5879
Brighton MS 1,000/6-8
7785 Highway 51 S 38011 901-837-5600
Sabrina Sneed-Mathews, prin. Fax 837-5625

Bristol, Sullivan, Pop. 26,322
Bristol CSD 4,000/PK-12
615 Martin Luther King Blvd 37620 423-652-9451
Dr. Gary Lilly, dir. Fax 652-9238
www.btcs.org
Anderson ES 400/PK-6
901 9th St 37620 423-652-9444
Dr. Ginger Christian, prin. Fax 652-9497
Avoca ES 500/PK-6
2440 Volunteer Pkwy 37620 423-652-9445
Dr. Vonda Beavers, prin. Fax 652-4616
Fairmount ES 500/PK-6
821 Virginia Ave 37620 423-652-9311
Dr. Kyle Evans, prin. Fax 652-9436
Haynesfield ES 400/PK-6
201 Bluff City Hwy 37620 423-652-9292
Dr. Rachel Walk, prin. Fax 652-9214
Holston View ES 400/PK-6
1840 King College Rd 37620 423-652-9470
Dr. Kristie Coleman, prin. Fax 652-9472
Vance MS 600/7-8
815 Edgemont Ave 37620 423-652-9449
Dr. Amy Scott, prin. Fax 652-9297

Sullivan County SD
Supt. — See Blountville
Emmett ES 400/K-5
753 Emmett Rd 37620 423-354-1865
Deborah Stevenson, prin. Fax 354-1871
Holston Valley MS 200/6-8
1717 Bristol Caverns Hwy 37620 423-354-1880
Jess Lockhart, prin. Fax 354-1891

Brownsville, Haywood, Pop. 10,196
Haywood County SD 3,300/PK-12
900 E Main St 38012 731-772-9613
Joey Hassell, dir. Fax 772-3275
www.haywoodschools.com
Anderson ECC 400/PK-K
620 W Main St 38012 731-772-9053
Charles Byrum, prin. Fax 772-7621
East Side IS 500/4-5
1315 E Jefferson St 38012 731-772-1233
Sandra Humphreys, prin. Fax 772-0991
Haywood ES 800/1-3
313 N Grand Ave 38012 731-772-0732
Anna Roberts, prin. Fax 779-1995
Haywood JHS 800/6-8
1201 Haralson St 38012 731-772-3265
Morris Long, prin. Fax 772-3352

Bruceton, Carroll, Pop. 1,455
Hollow Rock-Bruceton Special SD 700/PK-12
29590 Broad St 38317 731-418-4180
David Duncan, supt. Fax 418-4188
www.hrbedu.org
Central ES, 29590 Broad St 38317 300/PK-5
Deborah Martin, prin. 731-418-4168
Central MS 100/6-8
29590 Broad St 38317 731-418-4167
Joe Norval, prin. Fax 418-4188

Buchanan, Henry
Henry County SD
Supt. — See Paris
Lakewood ES 600/PK-5
6745 Highway 79 N Ste A 38222 731-644-1600
Amy Veazey, prin. Fax 644-0680
Lakewood MS 300/6-8
6745 Highway 79 N Ste B 38222 731-644-1600
Mike Bell, prin. Fax 644-0680

Bulls Gap, Hawkins, Pop. 730
Hawkins County SD
Supt. — See Rogersville
Bulls Gap S 400/PK-8
315 Allen Dr 37711 423-235-5201
Sharon Southern, prin. Fax 235-7687
St. Clair ES 200/K-5
1350 Melinda Ferry Rd 37711 423-235-2721
Mary Ann Davis, prin. Fax 235-2033

Burns, Dickson, Pop. 1,449
Dickson County SD
Supt. — See Dickson
Stuart-Burns ES 600/PK-5
3201 Highway 96 37029 615-446-2791
Amanda Nicks, prin. Fax 441-4140

Greater Things Christian Academy 100/PK-8
2612 White Bluff Rd 37029 615-441-4822
Chris Harris, supt.

Butler, Carter
Carter County SD
Supt. — See Elizabethton
Little Milligan ES 100/PK-8
4226 Highway 321 37640 423-768-4400
Howard Campbell, prin. Fax 768-4403

Byrdstown, Pickett, Pop. 803
Pickett County SD 800/PK-12
141 Skyline Dr 38549 931-864-3123
Diane Elder, supt. Fax 864-7185
pickett.k12tn.net/
Pickett County S 500/PK-8
1016 Woodlawn Dr 38549 931-864-3496
Kenny Tompkins, prin. Fax 864-3268

Calhoun, McMinn, Pop. 483
McMinn County SD
Supt. — See Athens
Calhoun S 400/PK-8
PO Box 129 37309 423-336-2974
Larson Frerichs, prin. Fax 336-3878

Camden, Benton, Pop. 3,542
Benton County SD 2,300/PK-12
197 Briarwood St 38320 731-584-6111
Mark Florence, supt. Fax 584-8142
www.bcos.org
Briarwood MS 400/3-5
169 Briarwood St 38320 731-584-4257
Lisa Bell, prin. Fax 584-2985
Camden ES 400/PK-2
208 Washington Ave 38320 731-584-4918
Sherri Crutchfield, prin. Fax 584-4147
Camden JHS 400/6-8
75 Schools Dr 38320 731-584-4518
Michelle Leonard, prin. Fax 584-5958
Other Schools – See Big Sandy, Holladay

Carthage, Smith, Pop. 2,267
Smith County SD 3,200/PK-12
126 Smith Co Middle Schl Ln 37030 615-735-9625
Barry Smith, dir. Fax 735-8271
www.smithcoedu.com
Carthage ES 400/PK-4
149 Skyline Dr 37030 615-735-0433
Tracy Brooks, prin. Fax 735-8256
Defeated S 200/PK-8
451 Defeated Creek Hwy 37030 615-774-3150
Meranda Cook, prin. Fax 774-3900
Smith County MS 400/5-8
134 Smith Co Mid School Ln 37030 615-735-8277
Mike Lytle, prin. Fax 735-8255
Union Heights S 300/PK-8
663 Lebanon Hwy 37030 615-735-1975
Wendolyn Kittrell, prin. Fax 736-0667
Other Schools – See Elmwood, Gordonsville

Caryville, Campbell, Pop. 2,278
Campbell County SD
Supt. — See Jacksboro
Caryville ES 600/PK-5
120 Cardinal Ln 37714 423-562-2687
Lori Adkins, prin. Fax 566-8918

Cedar Hill, Robertson, Pop. 308
Robertson County SD
Supt. — See Springfield
Byrns ES 500/PK-5
6399 Highway 41 N 37032 615-696-0533
Sarah Jane Moore, prin. Fax 696-0795

Celina, Clay, Pop. 1,478
Clay County SD 1,100/PK-12
PO Box 469 38551 931-243-3310
Matt Eldridge, dir. Fax 243-3706
www.clayedu.com
Celina K-8 S 600/PK-8
1324 Mitchell St 38551 931-243-2391
Alicia Dailey, prin. Fax 243-4428
Other Schools – See Red Boiling Springs

Centerville, Hickman, Pop. 3,602
Hickman County SD 3,600/PK-12
115 Murphree Ave 37033 931-729-3391
Michelle Gilbert, dir. Fax 729-3834
www.hickmank12.org
Centerville ES 400/PK-2
104 Maryfield Ave 37033 931-729-2212
Jill Hunt, prin. Fax 729-6094
Centerville IS 400/3-5
110 Maryfield Ave 37033 931-729-2748
Alicia Spears, prin. Fax 729-5497
Hickman County MS 400/6-8
1639 Bulldog Blvd 37033 931-729-4234
Tina Thigpen, prin. Fax 729-5688
Other Schools – See Lyles

Chapel Hill, Marshall, Pop. 1,427
Marshall County SD
Supt. — See Lewisburg
Chapel Hill ES 500/K-3
415 S Horton Pkwy 37034 931-246-4255
Dawn Kirby, prin. Fax 246-4252
Delk-Henson IS 4-6
425 S Horton Pkwy 37034 931-536-0491
Robert Reasonover, admin. Fax 536-0494

Chapmansboro, Cheatham
Cheatham County SD
Supt. — See Ashland City
West Cheatham ES 400/K-4
3120 Highway 12 N 37035 615-792-5167
Amber Raymer, prin. Fax 792-1230

Charleston, Bradley, Pop. 646
Bradley County SD
Supt. — See Cleveland
Charleston ES 300/K-5
PO Box 435 37310 423-336-2232
Candice Belt, prin. Fax 336-3692

Candies Creek Academy 100/K-12
294 Old Eureka Rd NW 37310 423-790-5660

Charlotte, Dickson, Pop. 1,221
Dickson County SD
Supt. — See Dickson
Charlotte ES 600/PK-5
200 Humphries St 37036 615-740-5803
Dr. Malissa Johnson, prin. Fax 789-6388
Charlotte MS 500/6-8
250 Humphries St 37036 615-740-6060
Dr. Justin Barden, prin. Fax 789-7033

Chattanooga, Hamilton, Pop. 164,861
Hamilton County SD 42,200/PK-12
3074 Hickory Valley Rd 37421 423-498-7020
Dr. Bryan Johnson, supt. Fax 209-8601
www.hcde.org
Alpine Crest ES 300/K-5
4700 Stagg Rd 37415 423-874-1921
Norma Faerber, prin. Fax 874-1939
Barger Academy of Fine Arts 400/K-5
4808 Brainerd Rd 37411 423-493-0348
Gregory Bagby, prin. Fax 493-0354
Battle Academy for Teaching and Learning 400/PK-5
1601 S Market St 37408 423-209-5747
Jesse Goins, prin. Fax 209-5748
Brown International Academy 400/PK-5
718 E 8th St 37403 423-209-5760
Emily Baker, prin. Fax 209-5761
Chattanooga S for Arts & Sciences 400/K-5
865 E 3rd St 37403 423-498-6845
Kelly Coffelt, prin. Fax 209-5817
Chattanooga S for Liberal Arts 400/K-8
6579 E Brainerd Rd 37421 423-855-2614
Krystal Scarbrough, prin. Fax 855-9429
Clifton Hills ES 600/PK-5
1815 E 32nd St 37407 423-493-0357
Lindsay Starnes, prin. Fax 493-0362
Dalewood MS 300/6-8
1300 Shallowford Rd 37411 423-493-0323
Arielle Hayes, prin. Fax 493-0327
Donaldson Environmental Science Academy 400/PK-5
927 W 37th St 37410 423-825-7337
Megan Bray, prin. Fax 825-7335
DuPont ES 300/K-5
4134 Hixson Pike 37415 423-870-0615
Ruthie Panni, prin. Fax 870-0631
East Brainerd ES 700/K-5
7453 E Brainerd Rd 37421 423-855-2600
Dr. Martha Young, prin. Fax 855-2610
East Lake Academy of Fine Arts 500/6-8
2700 E 34th St 37407 423-493-0334
Lakesha Carson, prin. Fax 493-0343
East Lake ES 500/PK-5
3600 13th Ave 37407 423-493-0366
Joyce Lancaster, prin. Fax 493-0370
East Ridge ES 1,000/PK-5
1014 John Ross Rd 37412 423-493-9296
Gail Huffstutler, prin. Fax 493-9298
East Ridge MS 700/6-8
4400 Bennett Rd 37412 423-867-6214
Angela Cass, prin. Fax 867-6226
East Side ES 600/K-5
1603 S Lyerly St 37404 423-493-7780
Stephanie Hinton, prin. Fax 493-7784
Hardy ES 500/PK-5
2100 Glass St 37406 423-493-0300
Shannon Braziel, prin. Fax 493-0302
Hillcrest ES 400/PK-5
4302 Bonny Oaks Dr 37416 423-855-2602
Vonetta Maston, prin. Fax 855-2604
Lakeside Academy 500/PK-5
4850 Jersey Pike 37416 423-855-2605
Andrea Johnson, prin. Fax 855-2607
Lookout Valley ES 300/PK-5
701 Browns Ferry Rd 37419 423-825-7370
Alisan Taylor, prin. Fax 825-7371
Normal Park Museum Magnet Lower S 500/K-5
1009 Mississippi Ave 37405 423-209-5900
Blake Freeman, prin. Fax 209-5901
Normal Park Museum Magnet S 200/6-8
1219 W Mississippi Ave 37405 423-498-6880
Carrie Willmore, prin. Fax 498-1499
Orchard Knob ES 600/PK-5
400 N Orchard Knob Ave 37404 423-493-0385
Lafrederick Thirkill, prin. Fax 493-0388
Orchard Knob MS 400/6-8
500 N Highland Park Ave 37404 423-493-7793
Tiffany Earvin, prin. Fax 493-7795
Red Bank ES 600/PK-5
1100 Mountain Creek Rd 37405 423-874-1917
Haley Brown, prin. Fax 874-1918
Red Bank MS 600/6-8
3701 Tom Weathers Dr 37415 423-874-1908
Andrea Edmondson, prin. Fax 874-1938
Rivermont ES 400/PK-5
3330 Hixson Pike 37415 423-870-0610
Nikki Bailey, prin. Fax 870-0611
Shepherd ES 600/K-5
7126 Tyner Rd 37421 423-855-2611
Valerie Brown, prin. Fax 855-2668
Spring Creek ES 700/PK-5
1100 Spring Creek Rd 37412 423-855-6138
Phil Iannarone, prin. Fax 855-6150
Tyner Middle Academy 500/6-8
6837 Tyner Rd 37421 423-855-2648
Crystal Sorrells, prin. Fax 855-2699
Westview ES 700/K-5
9629 E Brainerd Rd 37421 423-855-6141
Margo Williams, prin. Fax 892-2199
Woodmore ES 400/PK-5
800 Woodmore Ln 37411 423-493-0394
Dionne Upton, prin. Fax 493-0396
Other Schools – See Apison, Harrison, Hixson, Lookout Mountain, Ooltewah, Sale Creek, Signal Mountain, Soddy Daisy

---

Avondale SDA S 50/PK-8
1201 N Orchard Knob Ave 37406 423-698-5028
Belvoir Christian Academy 200/PK-8
800 Belvoir Ave 37412 423-622-3755
Linda Dahnke, head sch Fax 622-0177
Boyd-Buchanan S 900/PK-12
4650 Buccaneer Trl 37411 423-622-6177
Brainerd Baptist S 300/PK-5
PO Box 8099 37414 423-622-3873
Sean Corcoran, hdmstr. Fax 624-5164
Bright S 300/PK-5
1950 McDade Ln 37405 423-267-8546
O.J. Morgan, hdmstr. Fax 265-0025
Calvary Christian S 200/PK-12
4601 North Ter 37411 423-622-2181
Dan Davis, admin. Fax 622-0150
Chattanooga Christian S 1,200/PK-12
3354 Charger Dr 37409 423-265-6411
Chad Dirkse, pres. Fax 756-4044
Grace Baptist Academy 600/PK-12
7815 Shallowford Rd 37421 423-892-8224
Matt Pollock, hdmstr. Fax 892-1194
Hickory Valley Christian S 100/PK-5
6605 Shallowford Rd 37421 423-894-3200
Montessori S 300/PK-8
300 Montessori Way 37404 423-622-6366
Allison Driver, head sch Fax 622-6027
Our Lady of Perpetual Help S 300/PK-8
505 S Moore Rd 37412 423-622-1481
Leslie Fox, prin. Fax 622-2016
St. Jude S 400/PK-8
930 Ashland Ter 37415 423-877-6022
Jamie Goodhard, prin. Fax 875-8920
St. Nicholas S 200/PK-5
7525 Min Tom Dr 37421 423-899-1999
Mark Fallo, head sch Fax 899-0109
St. Peter's Episcopal S 200/PK-5
848 Ashland Ter 37415 423-870-1794
Meredith Ruffner, head sch Fax 877-2604
Silverdale Baptist Academy 1,000/PK-12
7236 Bonny Oaks Dr 37421 423-892-2319
Rebecca Hansard, hdmstr. Fax 648-7600
Standifer Gap SDA S 100/K-8
8255 Standifer Gap Rd 37421 423-892-6013
Joel Mcquistan, prin. Fax 664-4891

Christiana, Rutherford
Rutherford County SD
Supt. — See Murfreesboro
Christiana ES 700/K-5
4701 Shelbyville Pike 37037 615-896-0614
Angie Baker-Templeton, prin. Fax 896-3715
Christiana MS 900/6-8
4675 Shelbyville Pike 37037 615-904-3885
Dr. Crystal Hastings, prin. Fax 904-3886

Chuckey, Greene
Greene County SD
Supt. — See Greeneville
Chuckey ES 400/PK-5
1605 Chuckey Hwy 37641 423-257-2108
Leann Myers, prin. Fax 257-3938

Washington County SD
Supt. — See Jonesborough
South Central S 300/K-8
2955 Highway 107 37641 423-753-1135
Cheryl McHone, prin. Fax 753-1135

Church Hill, Hawkins, Pop. 6,688
Hawkins County SD
Supt. — See Rogersville
Carters Valley ES 300/K-4
1006 N Central Ave 37642 423-357-7450
Denise McKee, prin. Fax 357-5169
Church Hill ES 400/K-4
400 Old Stage Rd 37642 423-357-5621
Hope Malone, prin. Fax 357-4422
Church Hill IS 400/5-6
301 Park Ave 37642 423-357-0252
Sherry Price, prin. Fax 357-0267
Church Hill MS 400/7-8
211 Oak St 37642 423-357-3051
Scott Jones, prin. Fax 357-9873
McPheeters Bend ES 100/K-5
1115 Goshen Valley Rd 37642 423-357-6822
Renee Bernard, prin. Fax 357-5437

Clairfield, Claiborne
Claiborne County SD
Supt. — See Tazewell
Clairfield S 100/K-8
6360 Highway 90 37715 423-784-6052
Tom Zachary, prin. Fax 784-6052

Clarksville, Montgomery, Pop. 126,966
Clarksville-Montgomery County SD 30,700/PK-12
621 Gracey Ave 37040 931-648-5600
Dr. Millard House, dir. Fax 648-5612
www.cmcss.net
Barkers Mill ES 900/K-5
1230 Little Bobcat Ln 37042 931-906-7235
Rhonda Kennedy, prin. Fax 503-2643
Barksdale ES 600/K-5
1920 Madison St 37043 931-648-5685
Melinda Harris, prin. Fax 533-2087
Burt ES 200/3-5
110 Bailey St 37040 931-648-5630
Melody Nix, prin. Fax 553-2088
Carmel ES 500/K-5
4925 Sango Rd 37043 931-802-5025
Rosanne Sanford, prin. Fax 802-5026
Cumberland Heights ES 700/PK-5
2093 Ussery Rd S 37040 931-648-5695
Dr. Tonya Cunningham, prin. Fax 503-3400
Darden ES 600/K-5
609 E St 37042 931-648-5615
Jessica Harris, prin. Fax 553-2089
East Montgomery ES 600/K-5
230 McAdoo Creek Rd 37043 931-358-2868
Janet Staggs, prin. Fax 358-4092
Glenellen ES 900/K-5
825 Needmore Rd 37040 931-920-6158
Patti Koloski, prin. Fax 920-6163
Hazelwood ES 800/PK-5
2623 Tiny Town Rd 37042 931-553-2075
Cynthia Kerr, prin. Fax 503-3403
Kenwood ES 700/K-5
1101 Peachers Mill Rd 37042 931-553-2059
Kim Masters, prin. Fax 503-3401
Kenwood MS 900/6-8
241 E Pine Mountain Rd 37042 931-553-2080
Dr. Marlon Heaston, prin. Fax 552-3080
Liberty ES 800/K-5
849 S Liberty Church Rd 37042 931-905-5729
Sherry Baker, prin. Fax 905-5734
Minglewood ES 800/K-5
215 Cunningham Ln 37042 931-648-5646
Michelle Brock-Demps, prin. Fax 503-3402
Moore Magnet ES 500/K-5
1350 Madison St 37040 931-648-5635
Kim Smith, prin. Fax 503-3404

New Providence MS 1,100/6-8
146 Cunningham Ln 37042 931-648-5655
Scott Wainwright, prin. Fax 503-3409
Northeast ES 800/K-5
3705 Trenton Rd 37040 931-648-5662
Dr. Regina Lyle, prin. Fax 553-6986
Northeast MS 1,100/6-8
3703 Trenton Rd 37040 931-648-5665
Laura Boss, prin. Fax 503-3410
Oakland ES K-5
1050 Cherry Blossom Ln 37040 931-920-7422
Cindy Adams, prin. Fax 920-7421
Pisgah ES 700/K-5
1770 Hazelwood Rd 37042 931-802-6790
Sallie Oden, prin. Fax 802-6791
Richview MS 1,000/6-8
2350 Memorial Drive Ext 37043 931-648-5620
Lisa Clark, prin. Fax 551-8111
Ringgold ES 700/K-5
240 Ringgold Rd 37042 931-648-5625
Angela Lovelace, prin. Fax 503-3406
Rossview ES 1,100/K-5
2235 Cardinal Ln 37043 931-645-1403
Madeline Haller, prin. Fax 920-9949
Rossview MS 1,200/6-8
2265 Cardinal Ln 37043 931-920-6150
Laura Barnett Ed.D., prin. Fax 920-6147
St. Bethlehem ES 500/PK-2
2450 Old Russellville Pike 37040 931-648-5670
Melisse Williams, prin. Fax 503-3408
Sango ES 600/K-5
3585 Sango Rd 37043 931-358-4093
Erin Hedrick, prin. Fax 358-4098
Smith ES 600/K-5
740 Greenwood Ave 37040 931-648-5660
Emily Clark, prin. Fax 503-3405
West Creek ES 600/K-5
1201 W Creek Coyote Trl 37042 931-802-8637
Lynne Rains, prin. Fax 920-9977
West Creek MS 1,000/6-8
1200 W Creek Coyote Trl 37042 931-503-3288
Damaris Last, prin. Fax 503-3296
Other Schools – See Cunningham, Woodlawn

Clarksville Academy 600/PK-12
710 N 2nd St 37040 931-647-6311
Clarksville Christian S 100/PK-12
505 Highway 76 37043 931-647-8180
Amanda Binkley, prin. Fax 741-0953
Immaculate Conception S 100/PK-8
1901 Madison St 37043 931-645-1865
Stephanie Stafford, prin. Fax 645-1160
Little Country Schoolhouse 50/PK-1
840 Highway 76 37043 931-358-5775
Power and Grace Prep Academy PK-5
219 B Dunbar Cave Rd 37043 931-320-9862
Katobwa Stallworth, prin.
Tabernacle Christian S 50/PK-5
301 Market St 37042 931-552-9431
Donna Shanks, prin. Fax 552-9148

Cleveland, Bradley, Pop. 40,418
Bradley County SD 10,200/PK-12
800 S Lee Hwy 37311 423-476-0620
Dr. Linda Cash, dir. Fax 476-0485
www.bradleyschools.org
Black Fox ES 500/K-5
3119 Varnell Rd SW 37311 423-478-8800
Dr. Kim Fisher, prin. Fax 478-8850
Hopewell ES 500/K-5
5350 Freewill Rd NW 37312 423-478-8802
Tim Riggs, prin. Fax 478-8804
Lake Forest MS 1,100/6-8
610 Kile Lake Rd SE 37323 423-478-8821
Ritchie Stevenson, prin. Fax 478-8832
Michigan Avenue ES 400/K-5
188 Michigan Avenue School 37323 423-478-8807
Angela Lawson, prin. Fax 478-8856
North Lee ES 500/K-5
205 Sequoia Rd NW 37312 423-478-8809
Dana Yost, prin. Fax 478-8811
Oak Grove ES 500/PK-5
400 Durkee Rd SE 37323 423-478-8812
Buck Watson, prin. Fax 478-8866
Ocoee MS 1,300/6-8
2250 N Ocoee St 37311 423-476-0630
Ron Spangler, prin. Fax 476-0588
Park View ES 500/K-5
300 Minnis Rd NE 37323 423-476-6620
Jodie Grannan, prin. Fax 476-2292
Prospect ES 400/K-5
2450 Prospect School Rd NW 37312 423-478-8814
Steve Montgomery, prin. Fax 478-8815
Taylor ES 200/K-5
5265 Bates Pike SE 37323 423-478-8817
Elizabeth Kaylor, prin. Fax 478-8853
Valley View ES 300/K-5
5607 Spring Place Rd SE 37323 423-478-8825
Corey Limburg, prin. Fax 478-8826
Waterville Community ES 600/K-5
4081 Dalton Pike SE 37323 423-478-8827
Jennifer Huskins, prin. Fax 478-8873
Other Schools – See Charleston

Cleveland CSD 5,200/K-12
4300 Mouse Creek Rd NW 37312 423-472-9571
Dr. Russell Dyer, dir. Fax 472-3390
www.clevelandschools.org
Arnold Memorial ES 400/K-5
473 8th St NW 37311 423-472-2241
Michael Chai, prin. Fax 472-9877
Blythe-Bower ES 500/K-5
604 20th St SE 37311 423-479-5121
Joel Barnes, prin. Fax 472-2459
Cleveland MS 1,200/6-8
3635 Georgetown Rd NW 37312 423-479-9641
Dr. Leneda Laing, prin. Fax 479-9553
Mayfield ES 500/K-5
501 20th St NE 37311 423-472-4541
Randall Stephens, prin. Fax 472-2539
Ross ES 300/3-5
4340 Mouse Creek Rd NW 37312 423-479-7274
Lisa Earby, prin. Fax 472-9763
Stuart ES 500/K-5
802 20th St NW 37311 423-476-8246
Richelle Shelton, prin. Fax 479-5016
Yates PS 300/K-2
750 Mouse Creek Rd NW 37312 423-479-1723
Michael Collier, prin. Fax 472-2388

Bowman Hills SDA S 100/PK-8
300 Westview Dr NE 37312 423-476-6014
Cleveland Christian S 100/K-12
695 S Ocoee St 37311 423-476-2642
Tennessee Christian Preparatory S 200/PK-12
4995 N Lee Hwy 37312 423-559-8939
Brad Benton, pres. Fax 476-4971
United Christian Academy 100/PK-8
2200 Peerless Rd NW 37311 423-478-2500

Clifton, Wayne, Pop. 2,664
Wayne County SD
Supt. — See Waynesboro
Hughes S 400/PK-12
PO Box A 38425 931-676-3325
Brian Jones, prin. Fax 676-3903

Clinton, Anderson, Pop. 9,667
Anderson County SD 6,800/PK-12
101 S Main St 37716 865-463-2800
Dr. Tim Parrott, supt. Fax 457-9157
www2.acs.ac
Clinton MS 700/6-8
110 N Hicks St 37716 865-457-3451
RaeAnn Owens, prin. Fax 457-9486
Dutch Valley ES 200/PK-5
1044 Old Dutch Valley Rd 37716 865-457-2599
Stephanie Sherwood, prin. Fax 457-0152
Grand Oaks ES 300/PK-5
1033 Oliver Springs Hwy 37716 865-435-7506
Jessica Conatser, prin. Fax 435-5346
Other Schools – See Andersonville, Briceville, Heiskell, Lake City, Norris, Oliver Springs, Powell

Clinton CSD 900/PK-6
212 N Hicks St 37716 865-457-0225
Kelly Johnson, dir. Fax 463-0668
www.clintonschools.org
Clinton ES 500/K-6
210 N Hicks St 37716 865-457-0616
Jenna Sharp, prin. Fax 457-1024
North Clinton ES 200/PK-6
305 Beets St 37716 865-457-2784
Monica Rael, prin. Fax 457-1193
South Clinton ES 200/K-6
242 Hiway Dr 37716 865-457-2684
LeighAnn Bonesteel, prin. Fax 457-1089

Coalfield, Morgan, Pop. 2,425
Morgan County SD
Supt. — See Wartburg
Coalfield S 500/K-12
PO Box 98 37719 865-435-7332
Matthew Murphy, prin. Fax 435-2646

Coalmont, Grundy, Pop. 825
Grundy County SD
Supt. — See Altamont
Coalmont ES 300/PK-8
PO Box 148 37313 931-592-9453
Dr. Russell Ladd, prin. Fax 592-9455

Collegedale, Hamilton, Pop. 8,113

Collegedale Adventist MS 50/6-8
PO Box 598 37315 423-396-3020
Spalding ES 300/PK-5
PO Box 568 37315 423-396-2122
Tom Fogg, prin. Fax 396-2218

College Grove, Williamson
Williamson County SD
Supt. — See Franklin
College Grove ES 300/PK-5
6668 Arno College Grove Rd 37046 615-472-4320
Katherine Lillard, prin. Fax 472-4331

Collierville, Shelby, Pop. 43,413
Collierville SD, 146 College St 38017 7,800/PK-12
John Aitken, supt. 901-861-7000
www.colliervilleschools.org
Bailey Station ES 900/K-5
3435 Bailey Station Rd 38017 901-853-6380
Cynthia Tesreau, prin. Fax 853-7380
Collierville ES 800/PK-5
590 Peterson Lake Rd 38017 901-853-3300
Tyler Salyer, prin. Fax 853-3326
Collierville MS 900/6-8
580 Quinn Rd 38017 901-853-3320
Roger Jones, prin. Fax 853-3327
Crosswind ES 700/K-5
831 Shelton Rd 38017 901-853-3330
Andre Crafford, prin. Fax 854-2343
Schilling Farms MS 1,000/6-8
935 Colbert St S 38017 901-854-2345
Beth Robbins, prin. Fax 854-8200
Sycamore ES 800/K-5
1155 Sycamore Rd 38017 901-854-8202
Julie Reagan, prin. Fax 854-8207
Tara Oaks ES 700/K-5
600 E Harpers Ferry Rd 38017 901-853-3337
Tricia Marshall, prin. Fax 854-2349

Incarnation ES 200/PK-8
360 Bray Station Rd 38017 901-853-7804
Michael Zientek M.Ed., prin. Fax 854-0536

Collinwood, Wayne, Pop. 979
Wayne County SD
Supt. — See Waynesboro
Collinwood ES 400/PK-4
450 N Trojan Blvd 38450 931-724-9118
Greg Pigg, prin. Fax 724-6447
Collinwood MS 300/5-8
300 4th Ave N 38450 931-724-9510
Rob Vandiver, prin. Fax 924-2519

Columbia, Maury, Pop. 33,976
Maury County SD 12,000/PK-12
501 W 8th St 38401 931-388-8403
Dr. Chris Marczak, dir. Fax 840-4410
www.mauryk12.org
Baker ES 300/PK-4
1301 Hampshire Pike 38401 931-388-3319
Jon-Micah Clanton, prin. Fax 840-4414
Brown ES 400/PK-4
301 Cord Dr 38401 931-388-3601
Robert Busch, prin. Fax 380-1670
Cox MS 800/5-8
633 Bear Creek Pike 38401 931-840-3902
Kevin Eady, prin. Fax 840-3903
Highland Park ES 300/PK-4
1606 Highland Ave 38401 931-388-7325
Kelly Meyers, prin. Fax 380-4862
Howell ES 500/K-4
653 Bear Creek Pike 38401 931-540-1032
Michael Ford, prin. Fax 540-1034
McDowell ES 400/PK-4
714 W 7th St 38401 931-840-4418
Breckon Pennell, prin. Fax 381-2320
Riverside ES 400/PK-4
203 Carter St 38401 931-840-4422
Reggie Holmes, prin. Fax 380-4696
Whitthorne MS 900/5-8
915 Lion Pkwy 38401 931-388-2558
Lance Evans, prin. Fax 380-4684
Woodard ES 500/PK-4
207 Rutherford Ln 38401 931-380-2872
Dr. Stan Curtis, prin. Fax 380-4667
Other Schools – See Culleoka, Hampshire, Mount Pleasant, Santa Fe, Spring Hill

---

Agathos Classical S 100/PK-12
1201 Mapleash Ave 38401 931-388-0556
Ted Trainor, hdmstr. Fax 388-0538
Columbia Academy 600/PK-12
1101 W 7th St 38401 931-388-5363
Dr. James Thomas, pres. Fax 398-5344
Zion Christian Academy 500/PK-12
6901 Old Zion Rd 38401 931-388-5731
Paul Brenner, hdmstr. Fax 388-5842

Cookeville, Putnam, Pop. 29,908
Jackson County SD
Supt. — See Gainesboro
Dodson Branch S 200/PK-8
16221 Dodson Branch Hwy 38501 931-268-0761
Tammy Woolbright, prin. Fax 268-1891

Putnam County SD 10,000/PK-12
1400 E Spring St 38506 931-526-9777
Jerry S. Boyd, dir. Fax 528-6942
www.pcsstn.com
Cane Creek ES 500/PK-4
1500 W Jackson St 38501 931-520-1173
Emily Pierce, prin. Fax 520-1426
Capshaw ES 500/PK-4
1 Cougar Ln 38501 931-526-2414
Dr. Kim Wright, prin. Fax 372-0383
Northeast ES 500/PK-4
575 N Old Kentucky Rd 38501 931-526-2978
Dr. Melissa Palk, prin. Fax 372-0385
Park View ES 400/PK-4
545 Scott Ave 38501 931-526-2516
Bobby Winningham, prin. Fax 520-0209
Prescott South ES 500/PK-4
115 W Cemetery Rd 38506 931-526-2275
Catherine Jones, prin. Fax 525-4807
Prescott South MS 700/5-8
1859 S Jefferson Ave 38506 931-528-3647
Trey Upchurch, prin. Fax 520-2019
Sycamore ES 400/PK-4
452 Ellis Ave 38501 931-526-9322
Tracy Nabors, prin. Fax 372-0387
Trace MS 700/5-8
230 Raider Dr 38501 931-520-2200
Michael Miehls, prin. Fax 520-2204
Whitson ES 300/PK-4
178 E Jere Whitson Rd 38501 931-526-6575
Thomas Fuhrman, prin. Fax 372-0384
Other Schools – See Algood, Baxter, Monterey

Algood Christian ES 100/K-8
2600 Highway 111 N 38506 931-854-0259
Heavenly Host Lutheran S 100/PK-8
777 S Willow Ave 38501 931-520-3766
Reid Otto, admin. Fax 372-2016
Highland Rim Academy 100/K-12
PO Box 3022 38502 931-526-4472

Copperhill, Polk, Pop. 348
Polk County SD
Supt. — See Benton
Copper Basin ES 400/PK-6
206 Cougar Dr 37317 423-496-3271
Jill Franklin, prin. Fax 496-3272

Cordova, Shelby
Shelby County SD
Supt. — See Memphis
Chimneyrock ES 900/K-5
8601 Chimneyrock Blvd 38016 901-416-2067
Crystal Andrews, prin. Fax 416-3791
Cordova ES 800/K-5
750 N Sanga Rd 38018 901-416-1700
Kimbrelle Lewis, prin. Fax 416-1701
Cordova MS 900/6-8
900 N Sanga Rd 38018 901-416-2189
Stephanie Beach, prin. Fax 416-2191

Dexter ES 600/PK-5
7105 Dexter Rd 38016 901-416-0355
Dr. Timothy Gough, prin. Fax 373-8561
Dexter MS 500/6-8
6998 Raleigh LaGrange Rd 38018 901-416-0360
Dr. Phyllis Jones, prin. Fax 373-3378
Macon-Hall ES 1,100/K-5
9800 Macon Rd 38016 901-416-2625
Mary Anne Spencer, prin. Fax 759-4536
Mt. Pisgah MS 600/6-8
1444 Pisgah Rd 38016 901-416-2620
LaVonda Jones, prin. Fax 756-2306
Riverwood ES 1,000/K-5
1330 Stern Ln 38016 901-416-2310
Toya Riddick, prin. Fax 416-2325

First Assembly Christian S 800/PK-12
8650 Walnut Grove Rd 38018 901-458-5543
Harding Academy of Memphis - Cordova 300/PK-6
8350 Macon Rd 38018 901-624-0522
Lamplighter Montessori S 100/PK-8
8563 Fay Rd 38018 901-751-2000
St. Francis of Assisi S 1,000/PK-8
2100 N Germantown Pkwy 38016 901-388-7321
Kathy Scherer, prin. Fax 388-8201

Cornersville, Marshall, Pop. 1,184
Marshall County SD
Supt. — See Lewisburg
Cornersville ES 400/K-6
485 N Main St 37047 931-246-4230
Cheryl Ewing, prin. Fax 246-4184

Corryton, Knox, Pop. 100
Knox County SD
Supt. — See Knoxville
Corryton ES 200/K-5
7200 Corryton Rd 37721 865-687-4573
Aaron Maddox, prin. Fax 689-0867
Gibbs ES 800/K-5
7715 Tazewell Pike 37721 865-689-1497
Joe Cameron, prin. Fax 688-0712

New Hope Christian S 100/PK-8
7602 Bud Hawkins Rd 37721 865-688-5330
Emily Pursiful, prin. Fax 688-3052

Cosby, Cocke
Cocke County SD
Supt. — See Newport
Cosby S 600/K-8
3320 Cosby Hwy 37722 423-487-3850
Christy Edmonds, prin. Fax 487-2845
Smoky Mountain S 200/PK-8
135 S Highway 32 37722 423-487-2255
Joe Burchette, prin. Fax 487-5382

Sevier County SD
Supt. — See Sevierville
Jones Cove S 200/PK-8
4554 Jones Cove Rd 37722 865-453-9325
Rodney Helton, prin. Fax 453-2779

Cottage Grove, Henry, Pop. 88

Cottage Grove Christian S 50/K-10
6800 Church St 38224 731-782-3711
Mark Atkins, dir.

Cottontown, Sumner, Pop. 364
Sumner County SD
Supt. — See Gallatin
Oakmont ES 100/K-5
3323 Highway 76 37048 615-325-5313
Bryant Brewer, prin. Fax 325-5316

Counce, Hardin
Hardin County SD
Supt. — See Savannah
Pickwick Southside S 200/PK-8
1970 Highway 57 38326 731-689-5185
Jennifer Burks, prin. Fax 689-5214

Covington, Tipton, Pop. 8,910
Tipton County SD 11,600/PK-12
1580 Highway 51 S 38019 901-476-7148
Dr. William Bibb, dir. Fax 476-4870
www.tipton-county.com
Covington Integrated Arts Academy 600/PK-8
760 Bert Johnston Ave 38019 901-476-1444
Autrell Williams, prin. Fax 475-2786
Crestview ES 1,000/PK-5
151 Mark Walker Dr 38019 901-475-5925
Anne Adams, prin. Fax 475-2632
Crestview MS 600/6-8
201 Mark Walker Dr 38019 901-475-5900
Steve Maclin, prin. Fax 475-2607
Peay ES 700/PK-5
474 Academic Dr 38019 901-475-5121
Jill McIntyre, prin. Fax 475-2793
Other Schools – See Atoka, Brighton, Drummonds, Munford

Tipton Christian Academy 300/PK-12
2105 Highway 59 S 38019 901-475-4990
Lisa Blalack, head sch Fax 475-4930

Cowan, Franklin, Pop. 1,690
Franklin County SD
Supt. — See Winchester
Cowan ES 300/PK-5
501 Cumberland St E 37318 931-967-7353
Cynthia Young, prin. Fax 967-7915
South MS 400/6-8
601 Cumberland St W 37318 931-967-7355
Derrick Crutchfield, prin. Fax 967-1413

Crab Orchard, Cumberland, Pop. 747
Cumberland County SD
Supt. — See Crossville
Crab Orchard S 400/PK-8
240 School Rd 37723 931-484-7400
Dr. Michelle England, prin. Fax 456-5655

Crawford, Overton
Overton County SD
Supt. — See Livingston
Wilson S 200/PK-8
2210 Hanging Limb Hwy 38554 931-445-3335
Ashley Fisher, prin. Fax 445-3005

Cross Plains, Robertson, Pop. 1,691
Robertson County SD
Supt. — See Springfield
East Robertson ES 600/PK-5
5177 E Robertson Rd 37049 615-654-3874
Renae Fehrman, prin. Fax 654-4029

Crossville, Cumberland, Pop. 10,670
Cumberland County SD 7,400/PK-12
368 Fourth St 38555 931-484-6135
Janet Graham, supt. Fax 484-6491
ccschools.k12tn.net/
Brown S 500/PK-8
3766 Dunbar Rd 38572 931-788-2248
Stephanie Speich, prin. Fax 788-2554
Homestead S 700/PK-8
3889 Highway 127 S 38572 931-456-8344
Robin Perry, prin. Fax 456-8342
Martin S 700/PK-8
1362 Miller Ave 38555 931-484-7547
Christie Thompson, prin. Fax 484-8785
North Cumberland S 700/PK-8
7657 Highway 127 N 38571 931-484-5174
Jennifer Magnusson, prin. Fax 707-5556
South Cumberland S 700/PK-8
3536 Lantana Rd 38572 931-788-6713
Darrell Threet, prin. Fax 788-1116
Stone ES 700/PK-8
1219 Cook Rd 38555 931-456-5636
Justin Whittenbarger, prin. Fax 456-5369
Other Schools – See Crab Orchard, Pleasant Hill, Rockwood

Christian Academy of the Cumberlands 100/PK-12
325 Braun St 38555 931-707-9540
Darci Bernabei, prin. Fax 707-9545
Wrenn SDA S 50/K-10
PO Box 2659 38557 931-484-3150

Culleoka, Maury
Maury County SD
Supt. — See Columbia
Culleoka S 1,000/PK-12
1921 Warrior Way 38451 931-987-2511
Penny Love, prin. Fax 987-2594

Hopewell Church Covenant Family S 50/1-12
3886 Hopewell Rd 38451 931-505-1624
Thomas Vierra, prin. Fax 523-3217

Cunningham, Montgomery
Clarksville-Montgomery County SD
Supt. — See Clarksville
Montgomery Central ES 400/K-5
4011 Highway 48 37052 931-387-3208
Loralee BeCraft, prin. Fax 387-2565
Montgomery Central MS 800/6-8
3941 Highway 48 37052 931-387-2575
Vicki Winner, prin. Fax 387-3391

Dandridge, Jefferson, Pop. 2,785
Jefferson County SD 8,100/PK-12
PO Box 190 37725 865-397-3194
Dr. Charles Edmonds, dir. Fax 397-3301
jc-schools.net/
Dandridge ES 500/PK-5
780 Highway 92 S 37725 865-397-3127
Tommy Arnold, prin. Fax 397-1465
Maury MS 600/6-8
965 Maury Cir 37725 865-397-3424
Michelle Walker, prin. Fax 397-4253
Piedmont ES 400/PK-5
1100 W Dumplin Valley Rd 37725 865-397-2939
Melanie Simpson, prin. Fax 397-1865
Other Schools – See Jefferson City, New Market, Strawberry Plains, Talbott, White Pine

Dayton, Rhea, Pop. 7,052
Dayton CSD 900/PK-8
520 Cherry St 37321 423-775-8414
Robert Greene, dir. Fax 775-4002
www.daytoncity.net
Dayton City S 900/PK-8
520 Cherry St 37321 423-775-8414
Fax 775-4002

Rhea County SD 4,500/PK-12
305 California Ave 37321 423-775-7812
Jerry Levengood, dir. Fax 775-7831
www.rheacounty.org
Frazier ES 400/K-5
3900 Double S Rd 37321 423-775-7854
Dwayne Price, prin. Fax 775-6754
Graysville ES 300/PK-5
606 Long St 37321 423-775-7850
Dedra Sims, prin. Fax 570-2096
Rhea Central ES 700/K-5
1005 Delaware Ave 37321 423-775-7842
Rhonda Freeman, prin. Fax 775-7843
Other Schools – See Evensville, Spring City

Decatur, Meigs, Pop. 1,593
Meigs County SD 1,800/PK-12
345 N Main St 37322 423-334-5793
Don Roberts, supt. Fax 334-1462
www.meigscounty.net
Meigs MS 400/6-8
564 N Main St 37322 423-334-9187
Ronnie Woods, prin. Fax 334-1353
Meigs North ES 400/PK-5
22015 State Highway 58 N 37322 423-334-5454
James Boshears, prin. Fax 334-1366
Meigs South ES 400/PK-5
9638 State Highway 58 S 37322 423-334-5444
Rachel Moore, prin. Fax 334-1801

Decaturville, Decatur, Pop. 853
Decatur County SD 1,600/PK-12
PO Box 369 38329 731-852-2391
Rhonda Mitchell, dir. Fax 852-2960
www.decaturcountyschools.org
Decaturville ES 300/PK-4
820 S West St 38329 731-852-4616
Melinda Thompson, prin. Fax 852-2009
Other Schools – See Parsons

Decherd, Franklin, Pop. 2,304
Franklin County SD
Supt. — See Winchester
Decherd ES 400/PK-5
401 N Bratton St 37324 931-967-5483
Chris Hawkersmith, prin. Fax 967-2525

Deer Lodge, Morgan, Pop. 300

Meister Memorial SDA S 50/1-8
1145 Meister Hills Rd 37726 931-863-4944

Del Rio, Cocke
Cocke County SD
Supt. — See Newport
Del Rio S 200/K-8
500 Highway 107 S 37727 423-487-5570
Kaye Ramsey, prin. Fax 487-5411

Denmark, Madison
Jackson-Madison County SD
Supt. — See Jackson
Denmark ES 400/PK-5
535 Denmark Jackson Rd 38391 731-427-5986
Kimberly Quinn, prin. Fax 427-3083

Dickson, Dickson, Pop. 14,179
Dickson County SD 8,800/PK-12
817 N Charlotte St 37055 615-446-7571
Dr. Danny Weeks, dir. Fax 441-1375
www.dicksoncountyschools.org
Centennial ES 700/PK-5
198 Upper Lake Dr 37055 615-446-0355
Crysti Sheley, prin. Fax 446-8186
Dickson ES 300/PK-5
120 W Broad St 37055 615-740-5837
Amanda Roche, prin. Fax 441-4136
Dickson IS 400/6-6
507 Henslee Dr 37055 615-740-5829
Corey Duke, prin. Fax 441-4137
Dickson MS 1,200/6-8
401 E College St 37055 615-446-2273
Dr. William Burton, prin. Fax 441-4139
Discovery S 200/K-5
101 Henslee Dr 37055 615-441-4163
Debbie Bogdan, prin. Fax 740-6679
Oakmont ES 600/K-5
630 Highway 46 S 37055 615-446-2435
Misty Hodge, prin. Fax 441-4138
Other Schools – See Burns, Charlotte, Vanleer, White Bluff

Dickson Adventist S 50/K-8
PO Box 706 37055 615-446-4131
Raquel Soler, lead tchr. Fax 446-9646

Dover, Stewart, Pop. 1,392
Stewart County SD 2,100/PK-12
PO Box 433 37058 931-232-5176
Leta Joiner, dir. Fax 232-5390
stewartcountyschools.net
Dover ES 500/K-5
115 Dr Robert Lee Rd 37058 931-232-5442
Bryan Saunders, prin. Fax 232-3106
Stewart County MS 500/6-8
PO Box 1001 37058 931-232-9112
Andy Luton, prin. Fax 232-4608
Other Schools – See Big Rock

Doyle, White, Pop. 532
White County SD
Supt. — See Sparta
Doyle ES 200/PK-5
174 W Gooseneck Rd 38559 931-657-2287
Brenda Knox, prin. Fax 657-5041

Dresden, Weakley, Pop. 2,945
Weakley County SD 4,500/PK-12
8319 Highway 22 Ste A 38225 731-364-2247
Randy Frazier, supt. Fax 364-2662
www.weakleycountyschools.com
Dresden ES 500/PK-4
759 Linden St Ste B 38225 731-364-3401
Mike Laughrey, prin. Fax 364-5537
Dresden MS 400/5-8
759 Linden St Ste A 38225 731-364-2407
David Lewellen, prin. Fax 364-5840
Other Schools – See Gleason, Greenfield, Martin, Sharon

Drummonds, Tipton
Tipton County SD
Supt. — See Covington
Drummonds ES 700/PK-5
5068 Drummonds Rd 38023 901-835-3571
Patricia Mills, prin. Fax 837-5799

Duff, Campbell
Campbell County SD
Supt. — See Jacksboro
White Oak S 100/K-8
5634 White Oak Rd 37729 423-784-6051
Mike Miller, prin. Fax 784-9386
Wynn Habersham ES 200/PK-8
174 Habersham Rd 37729 423-784-9482
Bob Walden, prin. Fax 784-9380

Dunlap, Sequatchie, Pop. 4,760
Sequatchie County SD 2,300/PK-12
PO Box 488 37327 423-949-3617
Michael Swafford, dir. Fax 949-5257
sequatchieschools.net
Griffith ES 1,000/PK-4
PO Box 819 37327 423-949-2105
William Childers, prin. Fax 949-6872
Sequatchie County MS 700/5-8
PO Box 789 37327 423-949-4149
Devona Smith, prin. Fax 949-4140

Dunlap Adventist Christian S 50/K-8
105 Apache Ln 37327 423-949-2920
Sequatchie Valley Preparatory Academy 50/K-12
1050 Ray Hixson Rd 37327 423-554-4677
Robert Young, admin. Fax 554-4398

Dyer, Gibson, Pop. 2,288
Gibson County Special SD 4,000/PK-12
PO Box 60 38330 731-692-3803
Eddie Pruett, dir. Fax 692-4375
www.gcssd.org
Dyer S 500/PK-8
PO Box 220 38330 731-692-2444
Brad Garner, prin. Fax 692-2751
Other Schools – See Kenton, Medina, Newbern, Rutherford, Trenton

Dyersburg, Dyer, Pop. 16,802
Dyer County SD 3,800/PK-12
159 Everett Ave 38024 731-285-6712
Dr. Larry Lusk, dir. Fax 286-6721
www.dyercs.net
Fifth Consolidated ES 400/K-5
2150 Millsfield Hwy 38024 731-285-2840
Greg Cherry, prin. Fax 285-2915
Powell ES 300/PK-5
988 Highway 210 S 38024 731-285-1994
Alice Seratt, prin. Fax 285-9108
Three Oaks MS 500/6-8
3200 Upper Finley Rd 38024 731-285-3100
Matt Stafford, prin. Fax 285-3360
Other Schools – See Finley, Newbern, Trimble

Dyersburg CSD 2,800/PK-12
509 Lake Rd 38024 731-286-3600
Neel Durbin, dir. Fax 286-2754
www.dyersburgcityschools.org/
Dyersburg IS 600/3-5
725 Tibbs St 38024 731-286-3620
Lenita Click, prin. Fax 286-3622
Dyersburg MS 600/6-8
400 Frank Maynard Dr 38024 731-286-3625
Cal Johnson, prin. Fax 286-3624
Dyersburg PS 800/PK-2
1425 Frank Maynard Dr 38024 731-286-3615
Linda DeBerry, prin. Fax 286-3617

Christ Classical Academy 100/PK-8
1005 US Highway 51 Byp W 38024 731-285-3727
Kim Mullins, admin. Fax 285-3726

Eads, Shelby

Briarcrest Christian S 300/PK-12
76 S Houston Levee Rd 38028 901-765-4600
Caron Swatley, hdmstr. Fax 765-4667

Eagleville, Rutherford, Pop. 600
Rutherford County SD
Supt. — See Murfreesboro
Eagleville S 900/PK-12
500 Old Highway 99 37060 615-904-6710
Bill Tollett, prin. Fax 274-6859

Elizabethton, Carter, Pop. 13,969
Carter County SD 5,600/PK-12
305 Academy St 37643 423-547-4000
Dr. Kevin Ward, dir. Fax 542-7560
carter.k12.tn.us
Happy Valley MS 500/5-8
163 Warpath Ln 37643 423-547-4070
Katherine Hyder, prin. Fax 547-8352
Hunter ES 500/PK-8
145 Hope St 37643 423-547-4074
Mark Revis, prin. Fax 547-4075
Keenburg ES 300/PK-8
139 Keenburg Rd 37643 423-547-4047
Jason Hartley, prin. Fax 547-4048
Unaka ES 300/PK-8
120 Unaka Dr 37643 423-474-4110
Diana Bowers, prin. Fax 474-4111
Valley Forge ES 300/PK-5
1485 Riverview Dr 37643 423-547-4085
LeeAnn Carr, prin. Fax 547-4081
Other Schools – See Butler, Hampton, Johnson City, Roan Mountain

Elizabethton CSD 2,500/PK-12
804 S Watauga Ave 37643 423-547-8000
Dr. Corey R. Gardenhour, supt. Fax 547-8929
www.ecschools.net
Dugger JHS 600/6-8
306 W E St 37643 423-547-8025
Randy Little, prin. Fax 547-8021
East Side ES 300/K-5
800 Siam Rd 37643 423-547-8010
Travis Hurley, prin. Fax 547-8038
McCormick ES 400/K-5
226 S Cedar Ave 37643 423-547-8020
Eric Wampler, prin. Fax 547-8120
Wandell Early Learning Center 100/PK-PK
800 Siam Rd 37643 423-547-8035
Travis Thompson, dir. Fax 542-2882
West Side ES 300/K-5
1310 Burgie St 37643 423-547-8030
John Wright, prin. Fax 547-8031

Elkton, Giles, Pop. 557
Giles County SD
Supt. — See Pulaski
Elkton ES 300/PK-8
176 College St 38455 931-468-2285
Lanny Rich, prin. Fax 468-2350

Elmwood, Smith
Smith County SD
Supt. — See Carthage
Forks River S 200/PK-8
611 Cookeville Hwy 38560 615-897-2676
Leslie Pope, prin. Fax 897-2222

Englewood, McMinn, Pop. 1,491
McMinn County SD
Supt. — See Athens
Englewood S 700/PK-8
PO Box 47 37329 423-887-5260
Kristie Darnell, prin. Fax 887-7327

Erin, Houston, Pop. 1,288
Houston County SD 1,400/PK-12
PO Box 209 37061 931-289-4148
Kris McAskill, dir. Fax 289-5543
www.houston.k12.tn.us
Erin ES, 6500 Highway 13 37061 400/PK-5
Cynthia Ryan, prin. 931-289-3127
Houston County MS 300/6-8
3460 W Main St 37061 931-289-5591
Anita Gray, prin. Fax 289-5599
Other Schools – See Tennessee Ridge

Erwin, Unicoi, Pop. 6,036
Unicoi County SD 2,600/PK-12
100 Nolichucky Ave 37650 423-743-1600
John English, dir. Fax 743-1615
www.unicoischools.com/
Love Chapel ES 200/K-5
650 S Mohawk Dr 37650 423-743-1657
Ben Evely, prin. Fax 743-1662
Rock Creek ES 200/K-5
1121 E Erwin Rd 37650 423-743-1648
Larry Howell, prin. Fax 743-1664
Temple Hill ES 100/PK-5
797 Old Highway Rd 37650 423-743-1661
Angie Vaughn, prin. Fax 743-1663
Unicoi County MS 600/6-8
599 S Mohawk Dr 37650 423-735-0236
Jordan Simmons, prin. Fax 735-0728
Other Schools – See Unicoi

Estill Springs, Franklin, Pop. 2,017
Franklin County SD
Supt. — See Winchester
Rock Creek ES 400/PK-5
901 Rock Creek Rd 37330 931-649-5135
Celina Benere, prin. Fax 649-2040

Ethridge, Lawrence, Pop. 461
Lawrence County SD
Supt. — See Lawrenceburg
Ethridge S 500/K-8
33 Main St 38456 931-201-5880
Christy Crews, prin. Fax 201-5882

Etowah, McMinn, Pop. 3,410
Etowah CSD 400/PK-8
858 8th St 37331 423-263-5483
Dr. Mike Frazier, dir. Fax 263-3401
www.etowahcityschool.com
Etowah City S 400/PK-8
858 8th St 37331 423-263-5483
Brian Trammell, prin. Fax 263-3401

McMinn County SD
Supt. — See Athens
Mountain View S 700/PK-8
145 County Road 627 37331 423-263-2498
Angie Piercy, prin. Fax 263-5671

Evensville, Rhea
Rhea County SD
Supt. — See Dayton
Rhea County MS 700/6-8
405 Pierce Rd 37332 423-775-7821
Doug Keylon, prin. Fax 775-7823

Fairview, Williamson, Pop. 7,635
Williamson County SD
Supt. — See Franklin
Fairview ES 500/PK-5
2640 Fairview Blvd 37062 615-472-4380
Brent Oakley, prin. Fax 472-4391
Fairview MS 600/6-8
7200 Cumberland Dr 37062 615-472-4430
Heather Hayes, prin. Fax 472-4441
Westwood ES 600/PK-5
7200 Tiger Trl 37062 615-472-4890
Valerie Garcia, prin. Fax 472-4901

Fall Branch, Washington, Pop. 1,282
Washington County SD
Supt. — See Jonesborough
Fall Branch S 300/K-8
1061 Highway 93 37656 423-348-1200
Mark Merriman, prin. Fax 348-1207

Fayetteville, Lincoln, Pop. 6,705
Fayetteville CSD 1,500/PK-12
110 Elk Ave S Ste 200 37334 931-433-5542
Dr. Janine M. Wilson Ed.D., supt. Fax 433-7499
www.fcsboe.org
Askins ES 800/PK-4
901 Shady Ln 37334 931-433-4319
Dr. Bridgette Jones Ed.D., prin. Fax 433-0513
Fayetteville MS 400/5-8
1800 Wilson Pkwy Ste A 37334 931-438-2533
Steve Giffin, prin. Fax 438-2539

Lincoln County SD 4,100/PK-12
206 Davidson St E 37334 931-433-3565
Bill Heath, dir. Fax 433-7397
www.lcdoe.org
Highland Rim S 700/PK-8
111 Highland Rim Rd 37334 931-433-4197
Billy Owes, prin. Fax 438-1472
South Lincoln S 700/PK-8
362 Smith Mill Rd 37334 931-937-7385
Jennifer Turpen, prin. Fax 937-7886
Stone Bridge Academic Learning Center 100/PK-PK
1107 Hedgemont Ave 37334 931-433-3939
Kathy Morris, prin. Fax 438-1707
Other Schools – See Flintville, Petersburg, Taft

Riverside Christian Academy 400/PK-12
PO Box 617 37334 931-438-4722
James Bryant, head sch Fax 438-4727

Finger, McNairy, Pop. 296

Pioneer Christian S 50/K-8
802 Sweet Lips Rd 38334 731-934-7327
Salome Kinniburgh, admin. Fax 934-7327

Finley, Dyer
Dyer County SD
Supt. — See Dyersburg
Finley ES 300/PK-5
72 Poplar St 38030 731-285-7050
Carolyn Tyler, prin. Fax 287-8931

Flintville, Lincoln, Pop. 613
Lincoln County SD
Supt. — See Fayetteville
Flintville S 600/PK-8
37 Flintville School Rd 37335 931-937-8271
David Golden, prin. Fax 937-6739

Franklin, Williamson, Pop. 61,495
Franklin Special SD 3,800/PK-8
507 New Highway 96 W 37064 615-794-6624
Dr. David Snowden Ph.D., supt. Fax 790-4716
www.fssd.org
Franklin ES 300/PK-4
1501 Figuers Dr 37064 615-794-1187
David Esslinger Ed.D., prin. Fax 591-2800
Freedom IS 600/5-6
840 Glass Ln 37064 615-790-4718
Dr. Joel Hoag, prin. Fax 790-4717
Freedom MS 600/7-8
750 New Highway 96 W 37064 615-794-0987
Dr. Kristi Jefferson Ed.D., prin. Fax 790-4742
Johnson ES 400/PK-4
815 Glass Ln 37064 615-794-4837
Tocha Robinson Baugh, prin. Fax 790-4749
Liberty ES 500/PK-4
600 Liberty Pike 37064 615-790-0892
Dr. Cheryl Robey, prin. Fax 790-4714
Moore ES 500/PK-4
1061 Lewisburg Pike 37064 615-790-4700
Lisa Burgin, prin. Fax 790-4748
Poplar Grove ES 500/PK-4
2959 Del Rio Pike 37069 615-790-4720
Alisha Erickson, prin. Fax 790-4729
Poplar Grove MS 400/5-8
2959 Del Rio Pike 37069 615-790-4721
Chris Treadway, prin. Fax 790-4730

Williamson County SD 34,000/PK-12
1320 W Main St Ste 202 37064 615-472-4000
Dr. Michael Looney, supt. Fax 472-4190
www.wcs.edu
Clovercroft ES 800/K-5
9336 Clovercroft Rd 37067 615-472-5170
Dr. Elizabeth Vest, prin. Fax 472-5181
Grassland MS 900/6-8
2390 Hillsboro Rd 37069 615-472-4500
Darren Kennedy, prin. Fax 472-4511
Hillsboro S 500/PK-8
5412 Pinewood Rd 37064 615-472-4560
Alicia Justice, prin. Fax 472-4572
Hunters Bend ES 600/K-5
2121 Fieldstone Pkwy 37069 615-472-4580
Yolanda Blackburn, prin. Fax 472-4591
Oak View ES 600/K-5
2390 Henpeck Ln 37064 615-472-4710
Dr. Tom Morris, prin. Fax 472-4725
Page MS 1,000/6-8
6262 Arno Rd 37064 615-472-4760
Dr. Eric Lifsey, prin. Fax 472-4771
Pearre Creek ES 600/K-5
1811 Townsend Blvd 37064 615-472-5150
Dr. Stephanie Goff, prin. Fax 472-5161
Trinity ES 600/PK-5
4410 Murfreesboro Rd 37067 615-472-4850
Chris Schwartz, prin. Fax 472-4861
Walnut Grove ES 600/K-5
326 Stable Rd 37069 615-472-4870
Dr. Kate Donnelly, prin. Fax 472-4881
Winstead ES 500/PK-5
4080 Columbia Pike 37064 615-472-4910
Kathy Wells, prin. Fax 472-4921
Other Schools – See Brentwood, College Grove, Fairview, Nolensville, Spring Hill, Thompsons Station

---

Battle Ground Academy 900/K-12
336 Ernest Rice Ln 37069 615-794-3501
William F. Kesler, head sch Fax 567-8360
Classical Academy of Franklin 200/PK-12
810 Del Rio Pike 37064 615-790-8556
Eric Van Gorden, head sch Fax 790-8617
Franklin Classical S 100/K-12
PO Box 1601 37065 615-528-3777
Jeff Dokkestul, prin. Fax 528-9432
Grace Christian Academy 200/PK-12
3279 Southall Rd 37064 615-591-3017
Robbie Mason, hdmstr.
Montessori S of Franklin 100/PK-6
244 Noah Dr 37064 615-794-0567

New Hope Academy 200/PK-6
1820 Downs Blvd 37064 615-595-0324
St. Matthew S 400/K-8
533 Sneed Rd W 37069 615-662-4044
Tim Forbes, prin. Fax 662-6822

Friendship, Crockett, Pop. 665
Crockett County SD
Supt. — See Alamo
Friendship ES 200/PK-5
6229 State Highway 189 38034 731-677-2718
Cindy Nolen, prin. Fax 677-2331

Friendsville, Blount, Pop. 902
Blount County SD
Supt. — See Maryville
Friendsville ES 200/K-5
210 E 4th Ave 37737 865-980-1252
Stan Painter, prin. Fax 980-1253
Union Grove ES 400/PK-5
330 S Old Grey Ridge Rd 37737 865-980-1515
Kristy Brewer, prin. Fax 980-1520
Union Grove MS 800/6-8
334 S Old Grey Ridge Rd 37737 865-980-1320
John Webb, prin. Fax 980-1323

Gadsden, Crockett, Pop. 463
Crockett County SD
Supt. — See Alamo
Gadsden ES 200/PK-5
19040 Highway 79 38337 731-663-2453
Marsha Foust, prin. Fax 663-3938

Gainesboro, Jackson, Pop. 959
Jackson County SD 1,600/PK-12
711 School Dr 38562 931-268-0268
Joe Barlow, dir. Fax 268-3647
jacksoncoschools.com
Gainesboro ES 400/PK-3
611 S Main St 38562 931-268-9775
Tina Cassetty, prin. Fax 268-3674
Jackson County MS 500/PK-PK, 4-
170 Blue Devil Ln 38562 931-268-9779
Gail Myers, prin. Fax 268-9413
Other Schools – See Cookeville

Gallatin, Sumner, Pop. 29,705
Sumner County SD 28,200/PK-12
695 E Main St 37066 615-451-5200
Dr. Del Phillips, dir. Fax 451-5216
www.sumnerschools.org
Bills ES 700/K-5
1030 Union School Rd 37066 615-451-6577
Ken Henderson, prin. Fax 451-6575
Guild ES 700/PK-5
1018 S Water Ave 37066 615-452-5583
Mel Sawyers, prin. Fax 451-6582
Howard ES 400/K-5
805 Long Hollow Pike 37066 615-452-3025
Cindy Swafford, prin. Fax 451-6567
Rucker-Stewart MS 700/6-8
350 Hancock St 37066 615-452-1734
Dr. Jodi Green, prin. Fax 451-5297
Shafer MS 600/6-8
240 Albert Gallatin Ave 37066 615-452-9100
David Hallman, prin. Fax 451-6545
Station Camp ES 1,000/PK-5
1020 Bison Trl 37066 615-230-0387
Dr. Phillip Holt, prin. Fax 230-8518
Station Camp MS 700/6-8
281 Big Station Camp Blvd 37066 615-206-0116
Brian Smith, prin. Fax 206-0165
Stuart ES 700/K-5
780 Hart St 37066 615-452-1486
Jessica Thurman, prin. Fax 451-5281
Union Elementary STEM S 500/K-5
516 Carson St 37066 615-452-0737
Lance Taylor, prin. Fax 451-6543
Other Schools – See Bethpage, Cottontown, Goodlettsville, Hendersonville, Portland, Westmoreland, White House

---

St. John Vianney S 100/PK-8
501 N Water Ave 37066 615-230-7048
Jennifer McCormick, prin. Fax 206-9839
Sumner Academy 200/PK-8
464 Nichols Ln 37066 615-452-1914

Gatlinburg, Sevier, Pop. 3,902
Sevier County SD
Supt. — See Sevierville
Pi Beta Phi S 500/PK-8
125 Cherokee Orchard Rd 37738 865-436-5076
Carey Woods, prin. Fax 436-9494
Pittman Center S 300/PK-8
2455 E Parkway 37738 865-436-4515
Wendy Patterson, prin. Fax 430-3068

Germantown, Shelby, Pop. 38,412
Germantown Municipal SD 5,100/K-12
6685 Poplar Ave Ste 202 38138 901-752-7900
Jason Manuel, supt. Fax 757-6479
www.gmsdk12.org
Dogwood ES 600/K-5
8945 Dogwood Rd 38139 901-756-2310
Teresa Price, prin. Fax 751-7852
Farmington ES 700/K-5
2085 Cordes Rd 38139 901-756-2320
Zachary Percoski, prin. Fax 756-2308
Houston MS 900/6-8
9400 Wolf River Blvd 38139 901-756-2366
Liz Dias, prin. Fax 756-2346
Riverdale S 1,200/K-8
7391 Neshoba Rd 38138 901-756-2300
Joseph Bond, prin. Fax 759-4520

Shelby County SD
Supt. — See Memphis
Germantown ES 800/K-5
2730 Cross Country Dr 38138 901-416-0904
Kimberly Sanders, prin. Fax 756-2302
Germantown MS 700/6-8
7925 CD Smith Rd 38138 901-416-0950
Amie Marsh, prin. Fax 416-0952

Evangelical Christian ES 200/PK-5
1920 Forest Hill Irene Rd 38139 901-754-4420
Dr. Dan Peterson, head sch Fax 751-6782
Our Lady of Perpetual Help S 300/PK-8
8151 Poplar Ave 38138 901-753-1181
Cristy Sneed, prin. Fax 754-1475
St. George's Independent S 400/PK-5
8250 Poplar Ave 38138 901-261-2300
J. Ross Peters, head sch Fax 261-2311

Gladeville, Wilson
Wilson County SD
Supt. — See Lebanon
Gladeville ES 500/PK-5
8840 Stewarts Ferry Pike 37071 615-444-5694
Monica Fox, prin. Fax 449-3435

Gleason, Weakley, Pop. 1,427
Weakley County SD
Supt. — See Dresden
Gleason S 500/PK-12
9299 State Championship Dr 38229 731-648-5351
Trish Price, prin. Fax 648-9199

Goodlettsville, Davidson, Pop. 15,590
Metropolitan Nashville SD
Supt. — See Nashville
Goodlettsville ES 400/PK-4
514 Donald St 37072 615-859-8950
Tracy Gibson, prin. Fax 783-2820
Goodlettsville MS 500/5-8
300 S Main St 37072 615-859-8956
Beatriz Salgado, prin. Fax 859-8961
Old Center ES 400/PK-4
1245 S Dickerson Rd 37072 615-859-8968
Brenda Steele, prin. Fax 859-8970

Sumner County SD
Supt. — See Gallatin
Madison Creek ES 800/K-5
1040 Madison Creek Rd 37072 615-859-4991
Jon Duncan, prin. Fax 859-3963
Millersville ES 300/K-5
1248 Louisville Hwy 37072 615-859-1439
Tracey Carson, prin. Fax 859-5224

Gordonsville, Smith, Pop. 1,200
Smith County SD
Supt. — See Carthage
Gordonsville ES 400/3-6
100 Main St E 38563 615-683-8245
Scott Clemons, prin. Fax 683-8253
New Middleton S 200/PK-2
402 New Middleton Hwy 38563 615-683-8411
Shawn Frye, prin. Fax 683-8422

Grand Junction, Hardeman, Pop. 319
Hardeman County SD
Supt. — See Bolivar
Grand Junction ES 200/PK-6
750 Pledge St 38039 731-764-2841
Linda Buggs, prin. Fax 764-6913

Gray, Washington, Pop. 1,206
Washington County SD
Supt. — See Jonesborough
Boones Creek ES 500/K-4
348 Christian Church Rd 37615 423-283-3500
J.W. McKinney, prin. Fax 283-3510
Gray S 600/K-8
755 Gray Station Rd 37615 423-477-1640
Erika Patterson, prin. Fax 477-1644
Ridgeview S 700/K-8
252 Sam Jenkins Rd 37615 423-788-7340
Kelly Harrell, prin. Fax 788-7348

Living Springs Christian Academy 50/K-8
PO Box 9215 37615 423-494-3328

Greenback, Loudon, Pop. 1,059
Loudon County SD
Supt. — See Loudon
Greenback S 600/PK-12
6945 Morganton Rd 37742 865-856-3028
Michael Casteel, prin. Fax 856-7348

Greenbrier, Robertson, Pop. 6,354
Robertson County SD
Supt. — See Springfield
Greenbrier ES 800/PK-5
2658 Highway 41 S 37073 615-643-4529
Kim Cassetty, prin. Fax 643-0238
Greenbrier MS 600/6-8
2450 Highway 41 S 37073 615-643-7823
Kathy Carroll, prin. Fax 643-4580

Dayspring Academy 100/PK-12
2838 Heights Circle Dr 37073 615-672-9650
Monecca Brewer M.Ed., head sch Fax 672-5175

Greeneville, Greene, Pop. 14,821
Greene County SD 7,300/PK-12
910 W Summer St 37743 423-639-4194
David McLain, dir. Fax 639-1615
www.greenek12.org
Baileyton S 300/PK-8
6535 Horton Hwy 37745 423-234-6411
Randy Richards, prin. Fax 234-3100
Camp Creek S 300/PK-8
2941 Camp Creek Rd 37743 423-798-2644
Dennis Wilds, prin. Fax 798-0446
DeBusk S 400/PK-8
740 Debusk Rd 37743 423-638-7233
Diann Musgrove, prin. Fax 638-8364
Doak ES 600/PK-5
70 West St 37745 423-638-3197
Sunshine Broyles, prin. Fax 638-5276
Glenwood S 200/K-8
3860 Warrensburg Rd 37743 423-638-7120
Jennifer Whitson, prin. Fax 638-8688
Nolachuckey S 400/PK-8
565 Nolichuckey Rd 37743 423-639-7731
Amy Brooks, prin. Fax 798-2659
Ottway S 300/PK-8
2705 Ottway Rd 37745 423-234-8511
Dr. Kevin Ridley, prin. Fax 234-3281
West Pines S 200/PK-8
3500 W Pines Rd 37745 423-234-8022
Alan Cobble, prin. Fax 234-3109
Other Schools – See Afton, Chuckey, Mohawk, Mosheim

Greeneville CSD 2,800/PK-12
PO Box 1420 37744 423-787-8000
Dr. Jeff Moorhouse, dir. Fax 638-2540
www.gcschools.net
Eastview ES 400/PK-5
454 E Bernard Ave 37745 423-638-6351
Dale Landers, prin. Fax 638-2651
Greeneville MS 600/6-8
433 E Vann Rd 37743 423-639-7841
Jack Evans, prin. Fax 639-4112
Henard ES 400/PK-5
425 E Vann Rd 37743 423-638-3511
Janet Ricker, prin. Fax 638-2900
Highland ES 200/PK-5
208 N Highland Ave 37745 423-638-3341
Sheila Newland, prin. Fax 638-1780
Tusculum View ES 400/PK-5
1725 Lafayette St 37745 423-639-2751
DeAnna Martin, prin. Fax 639-2198

Greeneville Adventist Academy 100/K-10
305 Takoma Ave 37743 423-639-2011
Towering Oaks Christian S 200/PK-8
1985 Buckingham Rd 37745 423-639-0791
Jimmy Webb, admin. Fax 638-6026

Greenfield, Weakley, Pop. 2,162
Weakley County SD
Supt. — See Dresden
Greenfield S 600/PK-12
319 W Main St 38230 731-235-3424
Don McCurley, prin. Fax 235-3480

Grimsley, Fentress, Pop. 1,149
Fentress County SD
Supt. — See Jamestown
South Fentress ES 600/PK-8
5018 Wilder Rd 38565 931-863-3131
Linda Hodgen, prin. Fax 863-3980

Gruetli Laager, Grundy, Pop. 1,795
Grundy County SD
Supt. — See Altamont
Swiss Memorial ES 200/PK-8
PO Box 129 37339 931-779-3129
Jamie Ruehling, prin. Fax 779-3179

Faith Missionary Academy 100/K-12
495 Red Barn Rd 37339 931-779-3338

Halls, Lauderdale, Pop. 2,218
Lauderdale County SD
Supt. — See Ripley
Halls ES 900/PK-6
601 Carmen St 38040 731-836-9651
Andy Campbell, prin. Fax 836-5573
Halls JHS 200/7-8
800 W Tigrett St 38040 731-836-5579
Michael Blackwood, prin. Fax 836-5555

Hampshire, Maury
Maury County SD
Supt. — See Columbia
Hampshire S 300/K-12
4235 Old State Rd 38461 931-285-2300
Sonya Booker Cathey, prin. Fax 285-2612

Hampton, Carter
Carter County SD
Supt. — See Elizabethton
Hampton ES 700/PK-8
408 Highway 321 37658 423-725-5220
Brandon Carpenter, prin. Fax 725-5221

Harriman, Roane, Pop. 6,223
Roane County SD
Supt. — See Kingston
Bowers ES 600/PK-5
120 Breazeale St 37748 865-882-1185
Brenda Arwood, prin. Fax 882-3203
Harriman MS 300/6-8
1025 Cumberland St 37748 865-882-1727
Leslie Smith, prin. Fax 882-6285
Midtown ES 300/K-5
2830 Roane State Hwy 37748 865-882-1228
Kendra Inman, prin. Fax 882-8165

Harrison, Hamilton, Pop. 7,602
Hamilton County SD
Supt. — See Chattanooga
Brown MS 500/6-8
5716 Highway 58 37341 423-344-1439
David Carpenter, prin. Fax 344-1471
Harrison ES 400/K-5
5637 Highway 58 37341 423-344-1428
Wendy Jung, prin. Fax 344-1430

Harrogate, Claiborne, Pop. 4,333
Claiborne County SD
Supt. — See Tazewell
Forge Ridge S 300/PK-8
160 Hill Rd 37752 423-869-2768
Travis Bailey, prin. Fax 869-4977
Livesay MS 300/5-8
PO Box 460 37752 423-869-4663
Karyn Clark, prin. Fax 869-8389

Myers ES 300/PK-4
275 Nettleton Rd 37752 423-869-2172
Karen Fultz, prin. Fax 869-0353

Hartford, Cocke
Cocke County SD
Supt. — See Newport
Grassy Fork S 100/K-8
4120 Big Creek Rd 37753 423-487-5835
Dr. Judy Webb, prin. Fax 487-5387

Hartsville, Trousdale, Pop. 2,373
Trousdale County SD 1,200/K-12
103 Lock Six Rd 37074 615-374-2193
Dr. Clint Satterfield, dir. Fax 374-1108
www.tcschools.org
Satterfield MS 300/6-8
210 Damascus St 37074 615-374-2748
James McCall, prin. Fax 374-2602
Trousdale County ES 600/K-5
115 Lock Six Rd 37074 615-374-3752
Demetrice Badru, prin. Fax 374-1121

Heiskell, Anderson
Anderson County SD
Supt. — See Clinton
Fairview ES 300/PK-5
6715 Hickory Valley Rd 37754 865-494-7959
Karen Cupples, prin. Fax 494-6880

Henderson, Chester, Pop. 6,177
Chester County SD 2,800/PK-12
PO Box 327 38340 731-989-5134
Troy Kilzer, supt. Fax 989-4755
www.chestercountyschools.org
Chester County JHS 700/6-8
930 E Main St 38340 731-989-8135
Dr. Belinda Anderson, prin. Fax 989-8137
Chester County MS 400/4-5
634 E Main St 38340 731-989-8110
Tommie Kirk, prin. Fax 989-8117
East Chester ES 500/PK-3
708 E Main St 38340 731-989-8145
Kim Scott, prin. Fax 989-8147
West Chester ES 300/K-3
1243 W Main St 38340 731-989-8150
Amy Wooley, prin. Fax 989-8151
Other Schools – See Jacks Creek

Hendersonville, Sumner, Pop. 50,488
Sumner County SD
Supt. — See Gallatin
Anderson ES 600/K-5
250 Shute Ln 37075 615-264-5830
Tressa Sanders, prin. Fax 824-0470
Beech ES 600/PK-5
3120 Long Hollow Pike 37075 615-824-2700
Bobby Elrod, prin. Fax 264-6089
Berry ES 600/K-5
138 Indian Lake Rd 37075 615-822-3123
Justin Thomas, prin. Fax 264-6009
Brown ES 500/K-5
174 Imperial Blvd 37075 615-824-8633
Keith Parrack, prin. Fax 264-5819
Burrus ES K-5
1336 Drakes Creek Rd 37075
Mary Reynolds, prin.
Ellis MS 600/6-8
100 Indian Lake Rd 37075 615-264-6093
Adam Cripps, prin. Fax 264-5800
Hawkins MS 500/6-8
487A Walton Ferry Rd 37075 615-824-3456
Mitch Flood, prin. Fax 264-6003
Hunter MS 700/6-8
2101 New Hope Rd 37075 615-822-4720
Eric Bowman, prin. Fax 264-6036
Hyde Magnet S 700/K-12
128 Township Dr 37075 615-264-6543
Darren Frank, prin. Fax 264-6546
Indian Lake ES 600/K-5
505 Indian Lake Rd 37075 615-824-6810
Ondie Mitchell, prin. Fax 264-6064
Knox Doss MS 600/6-8
1338 Drakes Creek Rd 37075 615-824-8383
Mike Hayes, prin. Fax 824-8448
Lakeside Park ES 300/K-5
204 Dolphus Dr 37075 615-824-5151
Racheal Mason, prin. Fax 264-6550
Walton Ferry ES 400/K-5
732 Walton Ferry Rd 37075 615-824-3217
Bertie Alligood, prin. Fax 264-5809
Whitten ES 400/K-5
140 Scotch St 37075 615-824-3258
Rhonda Roach, prin. Fax 264-6556

Hendersonville Christian Academy 300/PK-12
355 Old Shackle Island Rd 37075 615-824-1550

Henry, Henry, Pop. 455
Henry County SD
Supt. — See Paris
Henry S 400/PK-8
937 Pioneer Rd 38231 731-243-7114
Marshall Kibbler, prin. Fax 243-2951

Hermitage, See Nashville
Metropolitan Nashville SD
Supt. — See Nashville
Dodson ES 500/PK-4
4401 Chandler Rd 37076 615-885-8806
Tiffany Curtis, prin. Fax 262-6962
DuPont Tyler MS 700/5-8
431 Tyler Dr 37076 615-885-8827
Dr. Bianca Jefferson, prin. Fax 847-7322
Hermitage ES 300/PK-4
3800 Plantation Dr 37076 615-885-8838
Dr. Matthew Owensby, prin. Fax 321-8389
Major ES 600/K-4
5141 John Hager Rd 37076 615-232-2203
Michael Westveer, prin. Fax 232-7108

Tulip Grove ES 600/PK-4
441 Tyler Dr 37076 615-885-8944
Allyson Johnson, prin. Fax 292-5154

Hilham, Overton
Overton County SD
Supt. — See Livingston
Hilham S 300/PK-8
2305 Hilham Highway 38568 931-823-6816
Kim Dillon, prin. Fax 823-5203

Hillsboro, Coffee, Pop. 448
Coffee County SD
Supt. — See Manchester
Hillsboro ES 500/PK-5
284 Winchester Hwy 37342 931-596-2775
Angela Harris, prin. Fax 596-2107

Hixson, See Chattanooga
Hamilton County SD
Supt. — See Chattanooga
Big Ridge ES 500/K-5
5210 Cassandra Smith Rd 37343 423-843-4793
Jeana Johnson, prin. Fax 843-4794
Ganns Middle Valley ES 600/K-5
1609 Thrasher Pike 37343 423-843-4700
Allyson DeYoung, prin. Fax 843-4731
Hixson ES 500/K-5
5950 Winding Ln 37343 423-870-0621
Julie Fine, prin. Fax 870-0628
Hixson MS 700/6-8
5681 Old Hixson Pike 37343 423-847-4810
LeAngela Rogers, prin. Fax 847-4811
Loftis MS 600/6-8
8611 Columbus Rd 37343 423-843-4749
Brentley Eller, prin. Fax 843-4758
McConnell ES 500/K-5
8629 Columbus Rd 37343 423-843-4704
Ruth Pohlman, prin. Fax 843-4706

Berean Academy 300/PK-12
441 Berean Ln 37343 423-877-1288

Hohenwald, Lewis, Pop. 3,706
Lewis County SD 1,900/PK-12
206 S Court St 38462 931-796-3264
Benny Pace, supt. Fax 796-5127
www.lewis.k12.tn.us
Lewis County ES 500/PK-2
305 S Oak St 38462 931-796-5621
Dr. Mike Taylor, prin. Fax 796-5762
Lewis County IS 400/3-5
310 S Park St 38462 931-796-1029
Mary McDonald, prin. Fax 796-7651
Lewis County MS 400/6-8
207 S Court St 38462 931-796-4586
Steve Edwards, prin. Fax 796-7601

Holladay, Benton
Benton County SD
Supt. — See Camden
Holladay S 200/K-8
148 Stokes Rd 38341 731-584-6874
Marty Arnold, prin. Fax 584-0984

Hornbeak, Obion, Pop. 419
Obion County SD
Supt. — See Union City
Black Oak ES 300/PK-8
365 N Shawtown Rd 38232 731-538-2271
Travis Johnson, prin. Fax 538-3001

Hornsby, Hardeman, Pop. 301
Hardeman County SD
Supt. — See Bolivar
Hornsby S 200/PK-8
105 Church St 38044 731-658-5707
Ted Kessler, prin. Fax 658-9999

Humboldt, Gibson, Pop. 8,376
Humboldt CSD 900/PK-12
2602 Viking Dr 38343 731-784-2652
Dr. Versie Hamlett, supt. Fax 784-2480
www.hcsvikings.org
East ES 300/2-6
1560 N 30th Ave 38343 731-784-4171
Charlotte Shivley, prin. Fax 784-1900
Stigall PS 300/PK-1
301 Westside Dr 38343 731-784-2825
Richard Willis, prin. Fax 784-9410

Huntingdon, Carroll, Pop. 3,896
Huntingdon Special SD 1,200/PK-12
PO Box 648 38344 731-986-2222
Pat Dillahunty, supt. Fax 986-4365
www.huntingdonschools.net
Huntingdon MS 400/4-8
199 Browning Ave 38344 731-986-4544
Scott Carter, prin. Fax 986-8609
Huntingdon PS 400/PK-3
191 Cox St E 38344 731-986-3091
Alan Eubanks, prin. Fax 986-0525

South Carroll County Special SD 400/PK-12
145 Clarksburg Rd 38344 731-986-4534
Dr. Tony Tucker, supt. Fax 986-4562
www.rocketsonline.org
Clarksburg S 400/PK-12
145 Clarksburg Rd 38344 731-986-3165
Porsche McClerking, prin. Fax 986-4562

Huntland, Franklin, Pop. 866
Franklin County SD
Supt. — See Winchester
Huntland S 700/PK-12
400 Gore St 37345 931-469-7506
Ken Bishop, prin. Fax 469-0590

Huntsville, Scott, Pop. 1,235
Scott County SD 3,100/PK-12
PO Box 37 37756 423-663-2159
Bill Hall, supt. Fax 663-9682
www.scottcounty.net

Fairview S 500/PK-8
8702 Baker Hwy 37756 423-663-3700
Scott Cash, prin. Fax 663-4447
Huntsville ES 500/PK-4
3221 Baker Hwy 37756 423-663-2520
Lisa Hamilton, prin. Fax 663-2971
Huntsville MS 300/5-8
3101 Baker Hwy 37756 423-663-2192
Donna Goodman, prin. Fax 663-2967
Other Schools – See Oneida, Robbins, Winfield

Huron, Henderson
Henderson County SD
Supt. — See Lexington
Westover ES 600/K-8
300 Crucifer Rd 38345 731-968-9846
Stacey Valle, prin. Fax 968-9699

Jacksboro, Campbell, Pop. 2,000
Campbell County SD 5,900/PK-12
172 Valley St 37757 423-562-8377
Larry Nidiffer, dir. Fax 566-7562
www.campbell.k12.tn.us
Jacksboro ES 600/PK-5
PO Box 437 37757 423-562-7433
Pam Walden, prin. Fax 566-8957
Jacksboro MS 500/6-8
150 Eagle Cir 37757 423-562-3773
Jennifer Fields, prin. Fax 562-8994
Other Schools – See Caryville, Duff, Jellico, La Follette, Pioneer

Jacks Creek, Chester
Chester County SD
Supt. — See Henderson
Jacks Creek ES 100/K-3
65 State Route 22A S 38347 731-989-8155
Tangie Sweatman, prin. Fax 989-8156

Jackson, Madison, Pop. 64,311
Jackson-Madison County SD 11,300/PK-12
310 N Parkway 38305 731-664-2592
Dr. Eric Jones, supt. Fax 664-2502
www.jmcss.org
Alexander ES 300/PK-5
900 N Highland Ave 38301 731-422-1841
Carolyn Caldwell, prin. Fax 424-4801
Arlington International Leadership S 700/PK-5
701 Arlington Ave 38301 731-265-9784
Kippi Jordan, prin. Fax 265-9803
Barker ES 700/K-5
1470 Ashport Rd 38305 731-668-8831
Timothy Gilmer, prin. Fax 668-8126
Community Montessori S 200/K-5
716 Westwood Ave 38301 731-422-3116
Dr. Melinda Harris, prin. Fax 427-3290
East ES 400/PK-5
2480 Ashport Rd 38305 731-988-3860
Judy Record, prin. Fax 988-3866
Jackson Careers and Technology ES 400/4-8
668 Lexington Ave 38301 731-427-4581
James Shaw, prin. Fax 427-2334
Jackson ES 500/K-5
211 Old Hickory Blvd 38305 731-668-8023
Ramonica Dorsey, prin. Fax 668-5933
Lane Technology Magnet ES 500/PK-3
746 Lexington Ave 38301 731-423-4720
Janet Gore, prin. Fax 423-4797
Lincoln ES 400/PK-5
425 Berry St 38301 731-988-3800
LaDonna Braswell, prin. Fax 988-3801
Northeast MS 500/6-8
2665 Christmasville Rd 38305 731-422-6687
Dr. Teresa Tritt, prin. Fax 423-1805
North Parkway MS 500/6-8
1341 N Parkway 38305 731-427-3384
Tiffany Taylor, prin. Fax 427-2591
Pope ES 500/K-6
1071 Old Humboldt Rd 38305 731-668-0350
Tracey Vowell, prin. Fax 668-5348
Rose Hill ES 500/PK-8
2233 Beech Bluff Rd 38301 731-423-6170
Pam Betler, prin. Fax 423-6171
West Bemis MS 400/6-8
230 D St 38301 731-988-3810
David Wicker, prin. Fax 988-3814
Whitehall Pre K Center 200/PK-PK
248 Bedford White Rd 38305 731-427-6396
Tisa Day, prin. Fax 423-6168
Other Schools – See Denmark, Pinson

Augustine S 100/PK-12
1171 Old Humboldt Rd 38305 731-660-6822
Donna Nelson, admin. Fax 660-6833
Jackson Christian S 800/PK-12
832 Country Club Ln 38305 731-668-8055
Montessori Center of Jackson 50/PK-6
PO Box 10516 38308 731-668-9197
Teri Canaday Freeman, dir. Fax 688-8644
St. Mary's S 400/K-8
1665 Highway 45 Byp 38305 731-668-2525
Jo-Ann Wormer, prin. Fax 668-1164
Trinity Christian Academy 700/PK-12
10 Windy City Rd 38305 731-668-8500
Jon Holley, head sch Fax 668-3232
University S of Jackson 1,100/PK-12
232 McClellan Rd 38305 731-664-0812
Stuart Hirstein, hdmstr. Fax 664-5046

Jamestown, Fentress, Pop. 1,935
Fentress County SD 2,400/PK-12
1011 Old Highway 127 S 38556 931-879-9218
Mike Jones, dir. Fax 879-4050
www.fentressboe.com
Pine Haven S 500/PK-8
800 N York Hwy 38556 931-879-9525
Sheri York, prin. Fax 879-2773
York ES 500/PK-8
218 School Ave 38556 931-879-5832
John Cargile, prin. Fax 879-2739
Other Schools – See Allardt, Grimsley

Jasper, Marion, Pop. 3,248
Marion County SD 4,300/PK-12
204 Betsy Pack Dr 37347 423-942-3434
Dr. Mark Griffith, supt. Fax 942-4210
www.marionschools.org/
Jasper ES 700/PK-4
495 Warrior Dr 37347 423-942-2110
Kimberly Shurett, prin. Fax 942-8817
Jasper MS 500/5-8
601 Elm Ave 37347 423-942-6251
Ramona McEntyre, prin. Fax 942-0141
Other Schools – See Monteagle, South Pittsburg, Whitwell

Jasper Adventist Christian S 50/K-8
PO Box 787 37347 423-942-1819

Jefferson City, Jefferson, Pop. 7,885
Jefferson County SD
Supt. — See Dandridge
Jefferson ES 600/PK-5
321 W Broadway Blvd 37760 865-475-4712
Craig Day, prin. Fax 475-8719
Jefferson MS 600/6-8
361 W Broadway Blvd 37760 865-475-6133
Joel Sanford, prin. Fax 471-6878
Mt. Horeb ES 600/PK-5
500 Dumplin Valley Rd E 37760 865-397-9472
Sandra Austin, prin.

Jellico, Campbell, Pop. 2,326
Campbell County SD
Supt. — See Jacksboro
Jellico ES 300/PK-8
551 Sunset Trl 37762 423-784-6565
Debra Loveday, prin. Fax 784-8196

Jellico SDA S 50/K-8
170 Adventist Ln 37762 423-784-9355

Joelton, See Nashville
Metropolitan Nashville SD
Supt. — See Nashville
Joelton ES 300/PK-4
7141 Whites Creek Pike 37080 615-876-5110
Dr. Rebecca Welch, prin. Fax 847-7336
Joelton MS Prep 300/5-8
3500 Old Clarksville Pike 37080 615-876-5100
Todd Irving, prin.

Johnson City, Washington, Pop. 61,881
Carter County SD
Supt. — See Elizabethton
Central ES 300/PK-8
252 Taylortown Rd 37601 423-547-4045
Terry Morley, prin. Fax 547-4056
Happy Valley ES 600/PK-4
1840 Milligan Hwy 37601 423-547-4028
Stephan Garland, prin. Fax 547-8323

Johnson City SD 7,800/PK-12
PO Box 1517 37605 423-434-5200
Dr. Steve Barnett, supt. Fax 218-4968
www.jcschools.org
Cherokee ES 400/K-4
2100 Cherokee Rd 37604 423-434-5281
Mary Nell McIntyre, prin. Fax 434-5591
Fairmont ES 600/PK-4
1405 Lester Harris Rd 37601 423-434-5275
Carol McGill, prin. Fax 434-5278
Indian Trail IS 1,100/5-6
307 Car Mol Dr 37601 423-610-6000
James Jacobs, prin. Fax 610-6010
Lake Ridge ES 500/K-4
1001 Lake Ridge Sq 37601 423-610-6030
John Phillips, prin. Fax 610-6033
Liberty Bell MS 1,200/7-8
806 Morningside Dr 37604 423-232-2192
Tammy Pearce, prin.
Mountain View ES 500/K-4
907 King Springs Rd 37601 423-434-5260
Melissa Stukes, prin. Fax 434-5596
North Side ES 300/PK-4
1000 N Roan St 37601 423-434-5249
Dr. Sharon Pickering, prin. Fax 434-5295
South Side ES 300/PK-4
1011 Southwest Ave 37604 423-434-5290
Dr. Anne Littleford, prin. Fax 434-5291
Towne Acres ES 300/K-4
2310 Larkspur Dr 37604 423-854-4800
Dr. Steven Barnett, prin. Fax 854-4810
Woodland ES 400/PK-4
2303 Indian Ridge Rd 37604 423-434-5267
Dr. Karen Reach, prin. Fax 434-5298

Washington County SD
Supt. — See Jonesborough
Boones Creek MS 300/5-8
4352 N Roan St 37615 423-283-3520
Mike Edmonds, prin. Fax 283-3524

Ashley Academy 100/PK-8
1502 Knob Creek Rd 37604 423-929-7888
Providence Academy 500/K-12
2788 Carroll Creek Rd 37615 423-854-9819
Jerry Williams, admin. Fax 854-8958
St. Mary S 200/PK-8
2211 E Lakeview Dr 37601 423-282-3397
Randi Wright-McKee, prin. Fax 282-0224

Jonesborough, Washington, Pop. 4,977
Washington County SD 8,900/PK-12
405 W College St 37659 423-753-1100
Kimber Halliburton, dir. Fax 753-1114
www.wcde.org
Jonesborough ES 500/PK-4
306 Forrest Dr 37659 423-753-1180
Matthew Combs, prin. Fax 753-1181
Jonesborough MS 400/5-8
308 Forrest Dr 37659 423-753-1190
Brandon McKee, prin. Fax 753-1570
Lamar S 600/K-8
3261 Highway 81 S 37659 423-753-1130
Leslie Lyons, prin. Fax 753-1134
Sulphur Springs S 500/K-8
1518 Gray Sulphur Springs 37659 423-753-1140
Cathy Humphries, prin. Fax 753-1146
Other Schools – See Chuckey, Fall Branch, Gray, Johnson City, Limestone, Telford

Kenton, Gibson, Pop. 1,268
Gibson County Special SD
Supt. — See Dyer
Kenton ES 100/PK-4
101 Tommy Wade Dr 38233 731-749-0007
Kevin Turner, prin. Fax 749-8023

Kingsport, Sullivan, Pop. 47,353
Kingsport CSD 7,200/PK-12
400 Clinchfield St Ste 200 37660 423-378-2100
Dwain Arnold, supt. Fax 378-2120
www.k12k.com/
Adams ES 400/K-5
2727 Edinburgh Channel Rd 37664 423-378-1400
Christy Free, prin. Fax 378-1424
Jackson ES 600/K-5
600 Jackson St 37660 423-378-2250
Dr. Krissy Turner, prin. Fax 378-2242
Jefferson ES 500/K-5
2216 Westmoreland Ave 37664 423-378-2270
Mike Fulkerson, prin. Fax 378-2277
Johnson ES 500/PK-5
1001 Ormond Dr 37664 423-378-2300
Stacy Edwards, prin. Fax 378-2310
Kennedy ES 300/K-5
1500 Woodland Ave 37665 423-857-2700
Dr. Janice Irvin, prin. Fax 378-2340
Lincoln ES 500/PK-5
1000 Summer St 37664 423-378-2360
Suzanne Zahner, prin. Fax 378-2375
Robinson MS 900/6-8
1517 Jessee St 37664 423-378-2200
Dr. Jim Wernke, prin. Fax 378-2220
Roosevelt ES 300/PK-5
1051 Lake St 37660 423-856-2600
Dr. Kelli Seymour, prin. Fax 378-2395
Sevier MS 800/6-8
1200 Wateree St 37660 423-378-2450
Dr. Holly Flora, prin. Fax 378-2430
Washington ES 500/K-5
1100 Bellingham Dr 37660 423-378-2480
Heather Wolf, prin. Fax 378-2470

Sullivan County SD
Supt. — See Blountville
Colonial Heights MS 500/6-8
415 Lebanon Rd 37663 423-354-1360
Bill Dunham, prin. Fax 354-1365
Indian Springs ES 400/PK-5
333 Hill Rd 37664 423-354-1685
Jeff Hickam, prin. Fax 354-1691
Ketron ES 700/K-5
3301 Bloomingdale Rd 37660 423-354-1710
Sherri DeVault, prin. Fax 354-1716
Miller Perry ES 400/K-5
904 Fordtown Rd 37663 423-354-1760
Mike Wilson, prin. Fax 354-1766
Rock Springs ES 500/PK-5
1238 Moreland Dr 37664 423-354-1380
Alesia Dinsmore, prin. Fax 354-1389
Sullivan Gardens ES 300/PK-5
209 Rosemont St 37660 423-354-1770
Dr. Darrell Moore, prin. Fax 354-1775
Sullivan North MS 300/6-8
2533 N John B Dennis Hwy 37660 423-354-1750
Josh Davis, admin. Fax 354-1459

Appalachian Christian S 50/K-12
1044 New Beason Well Rd 37660 423-288-3352
Br. Newl Dotson, admin. Fax 288-3354
Cedar View Christian School 200/PK-12
PO Box 143 37662 423-245-6341
St. Dominic S 100/PK-5
1474 E Center St 37664 423-245-8491
Tucker Davis, prin. Fax 245-2907

Kingston, Roane, Pop. 5,854
Roane County SD 6,700/PK-12
105 Bluff Rd 37763 865-376-5592
Dr. Leah Watkins Ed.D., dir. Fax 376-1284
www.roaneschools.com
Cherokee MS 500/6-8
200 Paint Rock Ferry Rd 37763 865-376-9281
Elizabeth Rose, prin. Fax 376-8525
Kingston ES 700/PK-5
2000 Kingston Hwy 37763 865-376-5252
Tim Thompson, prin. Fax 376-8535
Midway ES 400/PK-5
130 Laurel Bluff Rd 37763 865-376-2341
Travis Langley, prin. Fax 376-8512
Other Schools – See Harriman, Oliver Springs, Rockwood, Ten Mile

Kingston Springs, Cheatham, Pop. 2,732
Cheatham County SD
Supt. — See Ashland City
Harpeth MS 600/5-8
170 Harpeth View Trl 37082 615-952-2293
Ryan Phillipe, prin. Fax 952-4527
Kingston Springs ES 400/K-4
166 W Kingston Springs Rd 37082 615-952-9060
Dawn Wenning, prin. Fax 952-3650

Knoxville, Knox, Pop. 174,475
Knox County SD 58,000/PK-12
PO Box 2188 37901 865-594-1800
Bob Thomas, dir. Fax 594-1627
www.knoxschools.org
Amherst ES 800/K-5
5101 Schaad Rd 37931 865-560-7001
Sharon Yarbrough, prin. Fax 560-7005
Ball Camp ES 600/K-5
9801 Middlebrook Pike 37931 865-539-7888
Sarah Brengle, prin. Fax 539-3042
Bearden ES 400/K-5
5717 Kingston Pike 37919 865-909-9000
Susan Dunlap, prin. Fax 909-9007
Bearden MS 1,200/6-8
1000 Francis Rd 37909 865-539-7839
Michael Toth, prin. Fax 539-7851
Beaumont Magnet ES 500/K-5
1211 Beaumont Ave 37921 865-594-1272
Windy Clayton, prin. Fax 594-1375
Belle Morris ES 500/K-5
2308 Washington Pike 37917 865-594-1277
Terry Hursey, prin. Fax 594-1125
Blue Grass ES 700/K-5
8901 Bluegrass Rd 37922 865-539-7864
Jamie Cantrill, prin. Fax 531-2164
Bonny Kate ES 300/K-5
7608 Martin Mill Pike 37920 865-579-2108
Linda Norris, prin. Fax 579-8256
Brickey - McCloud ES 900/K-5
1810 Dry Gap Pike 37918 865-689-1499
Robbie Norman, prin. Fax 689-0814
Burnett ES 600/K-5
4521 Brown Gap Rd 37918 865-689-1474
Michelle Wolfenbarger, prin. Fax 689-1476
Carter ES 600/K-5
8455 Strawberry Plains Pike 37924 865-933-4172
Jessica Birdsong, prin. Fax 932-8190
Cedar Bluff ES 1,100/K-5
705 N Cedar Bluff Rd 37923 865-539-7721
Keith Cottrell, prin. Fax 539-8667
Cedar Bluff MS 600/6-8
707 N Cedar Bluff Rd 37923 865-539-7891
Terry Nieporte, prin. Fax 539-7792
Chilhowee IS 300/3-5
5005 Asheville Hwy 37914 865-594-1285
Sherry Hensley, prin. Fax 594-1286
Christenberry ES 500/PK-5
927 Oglewood Ave 37917 865-594-8500
Melissa Johnson, prin. Fax 594-8508
Dogwood ES 700/K-5
705 Tipton Ave 37920 865-579-5677
Lana Shelton-Lowe, prin. Fax 579-6051
Farragut IS 1,100/3-5
208 W End Ave, 865-966-6703
Dr. Chris Henderson, prin. Fax 671-7074
Farragut MS 1,400/6-8
200 W End Ave, 865-966-9756
Wes Edmonds, prin. Fax 671-7048
Farragut PS 1,000/PK-2
509 N Campbell Station Rd, 865-966-5848
Gina Byrd, prin. Fax 671-1787
Fountain City ES 400/K-5
2910 Montbelle Dr 37918 865-689-1445
Ina Langston, prin. Fax 689-1491
Gap Creek ES 100/K-5
1920 Kimberlin Heights Rd 37920 865-577-4860
Lisa Light, prin. Fax 579-2112
Greene Magnet Technology Academy 700/K-5
3001 Brooks Ave 37914 865-594-1328
Amy Brace, prin. Fax 594-1169
Green Math Science Academy 300/K-5
801 Townview Dr 37915 865-594-1324
Jessica Holman, prin. Fax 594-1938
Gresham MS 800/6-8
500 Gresham Rd 37918 865-689-1430
Donna Parker, prin. Fax 689-7437
Halls ES 800/K-5
7502 Andersonville Pike 37938 865-922-7445
Mitchell Cox, prin. Fax 925-7409
Halls MS 1,200/6-8
4317 E Emory Rd 37938 865-922-7494
Jessica Strickland, prin. Fax 925-7439
Hardin Valley ES 1,000/K-5
11445 Hardin Valley Rd 37932 865-470-2088
Sunny Poe, prin. Fax 560-1480
Hill Family Community Center 200/K-K
1725 Delaware Ave 37921 865-594-3632
Wendy Jo Laman, prin. Fax 594-3847
Holston MS 900/6-8
600 N Chilhowee Dr 37924 865-594-1300
Kathryn Lutton, prin. Fax 594-4429
Inskip ES 500/K-5
4701 High School Rd 37912 865-689-1450
Lynn Jacomen, prin. Fax 689-0806
Karns ES 1,200/K-5
8108 Beaver Ridge Rd 37931 865-539-7767
Shay Siler, prin. Fax 539-7774
Karns MS 1,400/6-8
2925 Gray Hendrix Rd 37931 865-539-7732
Sherry Smith, prin. Fax 539-7745
Lonsdale ES 400/K-5
1317 Louisiana Ave 37921 865-594-1330
Wendy Hansard, prin. Fax 594-1208
Lotts ES 800/K-5
9320 Westland Dr 37922 865-539-8611
Cindy Bosse, prin. Fax 539-8632
Maynard ES 200/K-5
737 College St 37921 865-594-1333
Kim Wilburn-Cullom, prin. Fax 594-1120
Mooreland Heights ES 400/K-5
5315 Magazine Rd 37920 865-579-2105
Brandi Self, prin. Fax 579-2189
Mt. Olive ES 300/K-5
2507 Maryville Pike 37920 865-579-2170
Casey Cutter, prin. Fax 579-2175
New Hopewell ES 200/K-5
757 Kimberlin Heights Rd 37920 865-579-2194
Patricia Moore, prin. Fax 579-2113
Northshore ES 900/K-5
1889 Thunderhead Rd 37922 865-670-4104
Brandon Pratt, prin. Fax 670-7614

Northwest MS 800/6-8
5301 Pleasant Ridge Rd 37912 865-594-1345
Bill Baldwin, prin. Fax 594-1339
Norwood ES 600/K-5
1909 Merchant Dr 37912 865-689-1460
Robyn Ellis, prin. Fax 689-9140
Pleasant Ridge ES 400/K-5
3013 Walnoaks Rd 37921 865-594-1354
Sandy Roach, prin. Fax 594-1355
Pond Gap ES 300/K-5
4530 Papermill Dr 37909 865-909-9040
Shelly McGill, prin. Fax 909-9012
Ritta ES 600/K-5
6228 Washington Pike 37918 865-689-1496
Shawnda Ernst, prin. Fax 689-0501
Rocky Hill ES 700/K-5
1200 Morrell Rd 37919 865-539-7844
Tina Holt, prin. Fax 539-7845
Sequoyah ES 400/K-5
942 Southgate Rd 37919 865-594-1360
Alisha Hinton, prin. Fax 594-1137
Shannondale ES 400/K-5
5316 Shannondale Rd 37918 865-689-1465
Megan O'Dell, prin. Fax 689-9158
South-Doyle MS 1,100/6-8
3900 Decatur Dr 37920 865-579-2133
Andrew Brown, prin. Fax 579-2128
South Knoxville ES 100/K-5
801 Sevier Ave 37920 865-579-2100
Tanna Nicely, prin. Fax 579-2199
Spring Hill ES 400/K-5
4711 Mildred Dr 37914 865-594-1365
Beth Lackey, prin. Fax 594-1370
Sterchi ES 400/PK-5
900 Oaklett Dr 37912 865-689-1470
Lynn White, prin. Fax 689-1471
Sunnyview PS 300/PK-2
412 Bagwell Rd 37924 865-594-1173
Sydney Upton, prin. Fax 594-1174
Vine MS 300/6-8
1807 Martin Luther King Jr 37915 865-594-4461
Desiree Jones, prin. Fax 594-1702
West Haven ES 300/K-5
3620 Sisk Rd 37921 865-594-4467
Paula Brown, prin. Fax 594-3743
West Hills ES 800/K-5
409 Vanosdale Rd 37909 865-539-7850
Kimberle Harrison, prin. Fax 539-7876
West Valley MS 1,200/6-8
9118 George Williams Rd 37922 865-539-5145
David Claxton, prin. Fax 539-5155
West View ES 200/K-5
1714 Mingle Ave 37921 865-594-4471
Beth Blevins, prin. Fax 594-1669
Whittle Springs MS 500/6-8
2700 White Oak Ln 37917 865-594-4474
Joann Bost, prin. Fax 594-1132
Other Schools – See Corryton, Mascot, Powell, Strawberry Plains

---

Annoor Academy of Knoxville 100/PK-8
724 Foxvue Rd 37922 865-525-3399
Apostolic Christian S 100/K-12
5020 Pleasant Ridge Rd 37912 865-523-5261
Berean Christian S 400/PK-12
2329 Prosser Rd 37914 865-521-6054
George Waller M.A., hdmstr. Fax 788-1465
Cedar Springs Weekday S 200/PK-K
9132 Kingston Pike 37923 865-291-5252
Christian Academy of Knoxville 1,000/PK-12
529 Academy Way 37923 865-690-4721
Robert Neu, head sch Fax 690-4752
Concord Christian S 400/K-12
11704 Kingston Pike, 865-966-8858
Mark Kelly, head sch Fax 288-1617
Episcopal S of Knoxville 300/PK-8
950 Episcopal School Way 37932 865-777-9032
Dr. Jack Talmadge, head sch Fax 777-9034
First Lutheran S 100/PK-8
1207 N Broadway St 37917 865-524-0308
Lindsey Hofman, prin. Fax 524-5636
Freedom Christian Academy 200/PK-12
PO Box 6010 37914 865-525-7807
Melanie Stipes, prin. Fax 246-3423
Garden Montessori S 100/PK-8
3225 Garden Dr 37918 865-688-6776
Grace Christian Academy 900/K-12
5914 Beaver Ridge Rd 37931 865-691-3427
Rob Hammond, head sch Fax 342-3827
Grace Covenant Baptist Academy 50/PK-6
9956 Dutchtown Rd 37923 865-690-3681
Dr. Alan Smith, head sch Fax 690-3681
Knoxville Adventist S 100/K-10
3615 Kingston Pike 37919 865-522-9929
Knoxville Christian S 200/PK-12
11549 Snyder Rd 37932 865-966-7060
Jarra Snyder, pres. Fax 671-2148
Mead Montessori S 100/PK-8
2647 Bafford Pl 37920 865-577-0760
Nature's Way Montessori S 200/PK-8
4710 Murphy Rd 37918 865-689-8976
Paideia Academy 200/PK-12
10825 Yarnell Rd 37932 865-670-0440
Mark Hamilton, hdmstr. Fax 474-1476
River's Edge Christian Academy 300/PK-12
PO Box 31733 37930 865-212-5575
Brian Beemer, admin. Fax 317-2443
Sacred Heart Cathedral S 700/PK-8
711 S Northshore Dr 37919 865-588-0415
Daniel Breen, prin. Fax 558-4139
St. John Neumann S 300/PK-8
625 Saint John Ct, 865-777-0077
Bill Derbyshire, prin. Fax 777-0087
St. Joseph S 200/PK-8
1810 Howard Dr 37918 865-689-3424
Andy Zengel, prin. Fax 687-7885
Tate's S 200/PK-8
9215 Bob Gray Rd 37923 865-693-3021
Kaye Simmons, prin. Fax 693-8532

University SDA S 50/K-8
1837 Brandau St 37921 865-524-1424
Jamie Mitchell, prin. Fax 524-5066
Webb S of Knoxville 1,100/PK-12
9800 Webb School Dr 37923 865-693-0011
Michael McBrien, pres. Fax 691-8057
West End Academy 100/PK-12
5311 McKamey Rd 37921 865-690-1720

Kodak, Sevier
Sevier County SD
Supt. — See Sevierville
Northview MS 400/4-6
3295 Douglas Dam Rd 37764 865-933-7985
Rene Walker, prin. Fax 933-7387
Northview PS 500/PK-3
3293 Douglas Dam Rd 37764 865-933-2415
Missy Wade, prin. Fax 932-4322

Lafayette, Macon, Pop. 4,440
Macon County SD 3,800/PK-12
501 College St 37083 615-666-2125
Tony Boles, dir. Fax 666-7878
www.maconcountyschools.com
Central ES 400/2-3
905 Sycamore St 37083 615-666-3265
Daniel Cook, prin. Fax 666-4028
Fairlane ES 400/PK-1
305 Fairlane Dr 37083 615-666-2970
Carroll Gunter, prin. Fax 666-7477
Lafayette ES 300/4-5
401 Meador Dr 37083 615-666-8868
Terry Marsh, prin. Fax 666-9489
Macon County JHS 700/6-8
1003 Highway 52 Byp E 37083 615-666-7545
Jamie Kelley, prin. Fax 666-9264
Other Schools – See Red Boiling Springs, Westmoreland

La Follette, Campbell, Pop. 7,339
Campbell County SD
Supt. — See Jacksboro
La Follette ES 800/PK-5
195 Myers Ln 37766 423-562-3439
Meredith Arnold, prin. Fax 566-3432
La Follette MS 500/6-8
1309 E Central Ave 37766 423-562-8448
Howard St. John, prin. Fax 562-2107
Valley View ES 400/PK-5
1187 Old Middlesboro Hwy 37766 423-562-5278
Jason Dotson, prin. Fax 562-8098

Christian Academy of Campbell County 100/PK-8
2709 Gnrl Carl W Stiner Hwy 37766 423-566-5294

Lake City, Anderson, Pop. 1,756
Anderson County SD
Supt. — See Clinton
Lake City ES 500/PK-5
402 Lindsay Ave 37769 865-426-2108
Henry Baggett, prin. Fax 426-2110
Lake City MS 300/6-8
1132 S Main St 37769 865-426-2609
Kelvin McCullom, prin. Fax 426-9319

Lakeland, Shelby, Pop. 12,270
Lakeland SD 800/K-8
10001 Highway 70 38002 901-867-5412
Dr. Ted Horrell, supt. Fax 867-2063
lakelandk12.org
Lakeland ES 800/K-4
10050 Oakseed Ln 38002 901-867-7071
Joretha Lockhart, prin. Fax 867-2801
Lakeland Middle Prep S 5-8
5020 Lions Crest Dr 38002 901-290-0505
Matt Adler, prin. Fax 290-1226

Lascassas, Rutherford
Rutherford County SD
Supt. — See Murfreesboro
Lascassas ES 500/K-5
6300 Lascassas Pike 37085 615-893-0758
Tamera Blair, prin. Fax 893-1275

Laurel Bloomery, Johnson
Johnson County SD
Supt. — See Mountain City
Laurel ES 100/K-6
300 Gentry Creek Rd 37680 423-727-2685
Leon Henley, prin. Fax 727-2631

La Vergne, Rutherford, Pop. 31,758
Rutherford County SD
Supt. — See Murfreesboro
La Vergne Lake ES 1,000/K-5
201 Davids Way 37086 615-904-6730
Paige Johnson, prin. Fax 904-6731
La Vergne MS 1,000/6-8
382 Stones River Rd 37086 615-904-3877
Cary Holman, prin. Fax 904-3878
La Vergne PS 500/PK-1
220 Stones River Rd 37086 615-904-6735
Angela Thomas-Maupin, prin. Fax 793-5952
Rock Springs ES 900/PK-5
1000 Waldron Rd 37086 615-904-3820
Stephen Lewis, prin. Fax 904-3821
Waldron S 800/2-5
125 Floyd Mayfield Dr 37086 615-904-3785
Tiffany Dukes, prin. Fax 904-3786

Lawrenceburg, Lawrence, Pop. 10,194
Lawrence County SD 6,800/PK-12
700 Mahr Ave 38464 931-762-3581
Dr. Johnny McDaniel, supt. Fax 762-7299
www.lcss.us
Coffman MS 400/6-8
111 Lafayette Ave 38464 931-762-6395
Sarah Cope, prin. Fax 762-7176
Crockett ES 500/PK-6
2301 W Gaines St 38464 931-762-2288
Renee Jackson, prin. Fax 766-0683

Lawrenceburg ES 500/PK-6
600 Prosser Rd 38464 931-762-3282
Nick Davis, prin. Fax 766-5605
New Prospect S 400/PK-8
4520 Pulaski Hwy 38464 931-762-2934
Dr. Anisha Jones, prin. Fax 762-3820
Sowell ES 500/PK-5
510 7th St 38464 931-762-4438
Jeff Riddle, prin. Fax 762-4487
Other Schools – See Ethridge, Leoma, Loretto, Summertown

Egly SDA S 50/1-8
11 Valley Rd 38464 931-762-6297
Sacred Heart S 100/PK-8
220 Berger St 38464 931-762-6125
Rosemary Harris, prin. Fax 762-6125

Lebanon, Wilson, Pop. 25,677
Lebanon Special SD 3,800/PK-8
397 N Castle Heights Ave 37087 615-449-6060
Scott Benson, dir. Fax 449-5673
www.lssd.org
Baird MS 600/6-8
131 WJB Pride Ln 37087 615-444-2190
Pam Sampson, prin. Fax 453-2690
Byars Dowdy ES 700/PK-5
904 Hickory Ridge Rd 37087 615-444-6651
Becky Siever, prin. Fax 443-0212
Castle Heights ES 600/PK-5
1007 N Castle Heights Ave 37087 615-444-2483
Michael Pigg, prin. Fax 443-6314
Coles Ferry ES 700/PK-5
511 Coles Ferry Pike 37087 615-443-1946
Brian Hutto, prin. Fax 443-0215
Houston ES 600/PK-5
207 Oakdale Dr 37087 615-444-7494
Julie Beasley, prin. Fax 443-0243
Winfree Bryant MS 600/6-8
1213 Leeville Pike 37090 615-449-4560
Becky Kegley, prin. Fax 449-4590

Wilson County SD 16,900/PK-12
351 Stumpy Ln 37090 615-444-3282
Dr. Donna Wright, dir. Fax 449-3858
www.wcschools.com
Carroll-Oakland S 700/PK-8
4664 Hunters Point Pike 37087 615-444-5208
Jason Dunn, prin. Fax 449-3914
Southside S 900/PK-8
1224 Murfreesboro Rd 37090 615-444-6330
Dr. Frank Tittle, prin. Fax 443-2668
Tuckers Crossroads S 400/K-8
5905 Trousdale Ferry Pike 37087 615-444-3956
Anna Raines, prin. Fax 444-3958
Other Schools – See Gladeville, Mount Juliet, Watertown

Cedars Preparatory Academy 100/PK-5
410 W Main St 37087 615-547-4612
Friendship Christian S 500/PK-12
5400 Coles Ferry Pike 37087 615-449-1573

Lenoir City, Loudon, Pop. 8,520
Lenoir CSD 2,400/PK-12
200 E Broadway St 37771 865-986-8058
Dr. Jeanne Barker, dir. Fax 988-6732
www.lenoircityschools.com/
Lenoir City ES 500/PK-3
203 Kelly Ln 37771 865-986-2009
Don Maloney, prin. Fax 988-7250
Lenoir City Intermediate MS 600/4-8
2141 Harrison Ave 37771 865-986-2038
Brandee Hoglund, prin. Fax 988-1964

Loudon County SD
Supt. — See Loudon
Eaton ES 800/PK-4
423 Hickory Creek Rd 37771 865-986-2420
Ashley Talley, prin. Fax 988-5550
Highland Park ES 400/PK-4
4404 Highway 11 E 37772 865-986-2241
Kathy Winsor, prin. Fax 988-7495
North MS 800/5-8
421 Hickory Creek Rd 37771 865-986-9944
Matthew Tinker, prin. Fax 988-9089

Crossroads Christian Academy 100/PK-12
1963 Martel Rd 37772 865-986-9823
Lenoir City Christian Academy 100/PK-7
2085 Simpson Rd E 37772 865-986-6716
Melinda McGill, prin. Fax 988-3903

Leoma, Lawrence
Lawrence County SD
Supt. — See Lawrenceburg
Leoma S 500/PK-8
2612 Highway 43 S 38468 931-231-8199
Kathy Burns, prin. Fax 852-2829

Lewisburg, Marshall, Pop. 10,852
Marshall County SD 5,000/PK-12
700 Jones Cir 37091 931-359-1581
Jacob Sorrells, dir. Fax 270-8816
www.k12marshall.net
Lewisburg MS 500/7-8
500 Tiger Blvd 37091 931-359-1265
Randy Hubbell, prin. Fax 359-4030
Marshall ES 400/2-3
401 Tiger Blvd 37091 931-359-7149
Bonnie Reese, prin. Fax 359-8669
Oak Grove ES 500/PK-1
1645 Franklin Pike 37091 931-270-1855
Dr. Tracy Kilpatrick, prin. Fax 270-8052
Westhills ES 700/4-6
1351 W Ellington Pkwy 37091 931-359-3909
Rachel Perryman, prin. Fax 359-3999
Other Schools – See Chapel Hill, Cornersville

Lexington, Henderson, Pop. 7,427
Henderson County SD 4,000/PK-12
35 E Wilson St 38351 731-968-3661
Steve Wilkinson, dir. Fax 968-9457
hcschoolstn.org
Bargerton ES 300/PK-8
6141 Poplar Spgs Bargerton 38351 731-968-7484
Danny Leasure, prin. Fax 968-9498
Pin Oak ES 400/PK-8
19925 Highway 412 E 38351 731-968-7341
Steve Meyer, prin. Fax 968-9490
South Haven ES 300/PK-8
5455 Highway 22A 38351 731-968-6890
Stephanie Coffman, prin. Fax 968-9705
Other Schools – See Huron, Reagan, Scotts Hill, Wildersville

Lexington CSD 1,000/PK-8
99 Monroe Ave 38351 731-967-5591
Gail Walker, dir. Fax 967-0794
www.caywood.org
Caywood ES 700/PK-5
162 Monroe Ave 38351 731-968-8457
Angela Blankenship, prin. Fax 968-2938
Lexington MS 300/6-8
112 Airways Dr 38351 731-968-8457
Beth Deere, prin. Fax 967-7130

Liberty, DeKalb, Pop. 308
DeKalb County SD
Supt. — See Smithville
Dekalb West S 400/PK-8
101 Bull Dog Ln 37095 615-536-5332
Sabrina Farler, prin.

Limestone, Washington
Washington County SD
Supt. — See Jonesborough
West View S 500/K-8
2847 Old State Route 34 37681 423-753-1175
Dr. Patton Gamble, prin. Fax 753-1583

Linden, Perry, Pop. 889
Perry County SD 1,200/PK-12
857 Squirrel Hollow Dr 37096 931-589-2102
Eric Lomax, dir. Fax 589-5110
www.perrycountyschools.us
Linden ES 400/PK-4
331 Brooklyn Ave 37096 931-589-2531
Kathy Whitt, prin. Fax 589-2158
Linden MS 200/5-8
130 College Ave 37096 931-589-5000
Brent Cunningham, prin. Fax 589-3685
Other Schools – See Lobelville

Livingston, Overton, Pop. 4,018
Overton County SD 3,300/PK-12
302 Zachary St 38570 931-823-1287
Mark Winningham, dir. Fax 823-4673
www.overtoncountyschools.net
Livingston MS 300/5-8
216 Bilbrey St 38570 931-823-5917
Doug Smith, prin. Fax 823-7549
Roberts ES 400/PK-4
301 Zachary St 38570 931-823-5551
Richard Melton, prin. Fax 823-5965
Other Schools – See Allons, Crawford, Hilham, Rickman

Lobelville, Perry, Pop. 883
Perry County SD
Supt. — See Linden
Lobelville S 200/PK-8
196 E Fourth Ave 37097 931-593-2354
J.B. Trull, prin. Fax 593-2613

Lookout Mountain, Hamilton, Pop. 1,813
Hamilton County SD
Supt. — See Chattanooga
Lookout Mountain ES 200/K-5
321 N Bragg Ave 37350 423-821-6116
Ruth White, prin. Fax 825-7384

Loretto, Lawrence, Pop. 1,696
Lawrence County SD
Supt. — See Lawrenceburg
South Lawrence S 700/PK-8
PO Box 310 38469 931-281-5884
Brian Tucker, prin. Fax 853-4945

Sacred Heart S 100/PK-8
PO Box 277 38469 931-853-4388
Tina Neese, prin. Fax 853-4388

Loudon, Loudon, Pop. 5,315
Loudon County SD 4,900/PK-12
100 River Rd 37774 865-458-5411
Jason Vance, dir. Fax 458-6138
www.loudoncounty.org/
Ft. Loudoun MS 300/6-8
1083 Mulberry St 37774 865-458-2026
Christie Amburn, prin. Fax 458-6611
Loudon ES 500/PK-5
2175 Roberts Rd 37774 865-458-2001
Kim Greenway, prin. Fax 458-1405
Steekee ES 200/PK-5
4500 Steekee School Rd 37774 865-458-3322
Donna Stapleton, prin. Fax 458-9921
Other Schools – See Greenback, Lenoir City, Philadelphia

Louisville, Blount, Pop. 2,408
Blount County SD
Supt. — See Maryville
Middlesettlements ES 400/PK-5
3105 Miser Station Rd 37777 865-983-6644
April Herron, prin. Fax 982-6137

Luttrell, Union, Pop. 1,050
Union County SD
Supt. — See Maynardville
Luttrell ES 400/PK-5
241 Tazewell Pike 37779 865-992-3441
Sonja Saylor, prin. Fax 992-9154

Lyles, Hickman, Pop. 722
Hickman County SD
Supt. — See Centerville
East Hickman ES 500/PK-2
5191 Highway 100 37098 931-670-3044
Leigha Coble, prin. Fax 670-5433
East Hickman IS 400/3-5
5198 E Eagle Dr 37098 931-670-0227
Becky Malugin, prin. Fax 670-4360
East Hickman MS 400/6-8
9414 E Eagle Dr 37098 931-670-4237
Eric Cannon, prin. Fax 670-4239

Lynchburg, Moore, Pop. 5,241
Moore County SD 900/K-12
PO Box 219 37352 931-759-7303
Chad Moorehead, dir. Fax 759-6386
www.moorecountyschools.net
Lynchburg ES 500/K-6
276 Mechanic St N 37352 931-759-7388
Melissa Eslick, prin.

Lynnville, Giles, Pop. 286
Giles County SD
Supt. — See Pulaski
Richland ES 400/PK-5
10333 Columbia Hwy 38472 931-527-0663
Velena Newton, prin. Fax 527-3279

Mc Ewen, Humphreys, Pop. 1,735
Humphreys County SD
Supt. — See Waverly
McEwen ES 400/K-5
220 Swift St E 37101 931-582-6913
Sherry McClurkan, prin. Fax 582-3267
McEwen JHS 200/6-8
365 Melrose St 37101 931-582-8417
T. Coleman, prin. Fax 582-8418

St. Patrick S 100/PK-8
175 Saint Patrick St 37101 931-582-3493
Sr. Mary Grace Watson, prin. Fax 582-6386

Mc Kenzie, Carroll, Pop. 5,208
Mc Kenzie Special SD 1,400/PK-12
114 Bell Ave 38201 731-352-2246
Lynn Watkins, dir. Fax 352-7550
www.mckenzieschools.org
Mc Kenzie ES 600/PK-4
165 Brooks Ave 38201 731-352-5272
Tim Barker, prin. Fax 352-6076
Mc Kenzie MS 400/5-8
80 Woodrow Ave 38201 731-352-2792
Dorethea Royle, prin. Fax 352-4709

Mc Lemoresville, Carroll, Pop. 347
West Carroll Special SD
Supt. — See Atwood
West Carroll PS 200/PK-2
PO Box 219 38235 731-986-8359
Jackie Wester, prin. Fax 986-4509

Mc Minnville, Warren, Pop. 13,384
Warren County SD 6,600/PK-12
2548 Morrison St 37110 931-668-4022
John R. Cox, dir. Fax 815-2685
www.warrenschools.com
Centertown S 500/PK-8
376 Warrior Blvd 37110 931-939-2261
Pam Cowan, prin. Fax 939-2050
Dibrell S 500/PK-8
1759 Mike Muncey Rd 37110 931-934-2301
Sheila Gann, prin. Fax 934-2092
Hickory Creek ES 700/PK-5
270 Pioneer Ln 37110 931-668-5100
Mike Mansfield, prin. Fax 668-7260
Irving College S 200/PK-8
115 Dry Creek Rd 37110 931-668-8693
Rachel Graves, prin. Fax 668-9351
Ray Memorial ES 600/PK-5
504 N Chancery St 37110 931-473-9006
Monti Hillis, prin. Fax 506-5245
Warren County MS 900/6-8
200 Caldwell St 37110 931-473-6557
Gerald Tidwell, prin. Fax 473-2432
West ES 500/PK-5
400 Clark Blvd 37110 931-473-3801
Michelle Lewis, prin. Fax 473-0863
Other Schools – See Morrison, Rock Island

Boyd Christian S 100/PK-12
806 Morrison St 37110 931-473-9631
Covenant Academy 100/PK-12
1079 Country Club Dr 37110 931-668-6185
Faulkner Springs Christian S 50/1-8
201 Bluff Springs Rd 37110 931-668-4092

Madison, See Nashville
Metropolitan Nashville SD
Supt. — See Nashville
Amqui ES 600/PK-4
319 Anderson Ln 37115 615-612-3678
Latoya Cobb, prin. Fax 612-3684
Chadwell ES, 321 Port Dr 37115 300/PK-4
Elnora Mitchell, prin. 615-860-1459
Gateway ES 200/K-4
1524 Monticello Ave 37115 615-860-1465
John Garland, prin.
Madison MS Prep 800/5-8
300 W Old Hickory Blvd 37115 615-684-4018
Brian Mells, prin. Fax 612-3664
Stratton ES 700/PK-4
310 W Old Hickory Blvd 37115 615-860-1486
Renita Perkins, prin. Fax 262-6957

Goodpasture Christian S 900/PK-12
619 W Due West Ave 37115 615-868-2600
Ricky Perry, pres. Fax 865-1766
Madison Campus ES 200/PK-8
1515 Sutherland Dr 37115 615-865-4575
Susan Mulraine, prin. Fax 612-4409
St. Joseph S 400/PK-8
1225 Gallatin Pike S 37115 615-865-1491
C.J. Martin, prin. Fax 612-0228

Madisonville, Monroe, Pop. 4,500
Monroe County SD 5,400/PK-12
205 Oak Grove Rd 37354 423-442-2373
Tim Blankenship, dir. Fax 442-1389
www.monroe.k12.tn.us/
Madisonville IS 500/3-5
1000 Green Rd 37354 423-442-2454
Terry Moser, prin. Fax 442-1534
Madisonville MS 600/6-8
175 Oak Grove Rd 37354 423-442-4137
Sheryl Debity, prin. Fax 442-9338
Madisonville PS 600/PK-2
268 Warren St 37354 423-442-2236
Angie Kyle, prin. Fax 442-2215
Other Schools – See Tellico Plains, Vonore

Manchester, Coffee, Pop. 9,924
Coffee County SD 4,100/PK-12
1343 McArthur St 37355 931-723-5150
Dr. LaDonna McFall, dir. Fax 723-5153
www.coffeecountyschools.com/
Coffee County MS 1,000/6-8
3063 Woodbury Hwy 37355 931-723-5177
Kimberly Aaron, prin. Fax 723-5180
Deerfield ES 300/PK-5
9123 Woodbury Hwy 37355 931-570-2652
Traci McCoy, prin. Fax 723-7298
East Coffee ES 300/PK-5
6264 McMinnville Hwy 37355 931-723-5185
Kelvin Shores, prin. Fax 723-3231
New Union ES 300/PK-5
3320 Woodbury Hwy 37355 931-723-5187
Jill Potts, prin. Fax 723-5197
North Coffee ES 300/PK-5
6790 Murfreesboro Hwy 37355 931-723-5183
Adam Clark, prin. Fax 723-3230
Other Schools – See Hillsboro, Tullahoma

Manchester CSD 1,300/PK-8
215 E Fort St 37355 931-728-2316
Sandra Morris, supt. Fax 728-7075
www.manchestercitysch.org
College Street ES 400/PK-5
405 College St 37355 931-728-2805
Tom Jacobs, prin. Fax 728-5100
Westwood ES 500/PK-5
912 Oakdale St 37355 931-728-3412
Melissa Glenn, prin. Fax 723-0221
Westwood MS 400/6-8
505 E Taylor St 37355 931-728-2071
Julie Green, prin. Fax 728-0962

Martin, Weakley, Pop. 11,280
Weakley County SD
Supt. — See Dresden
Martin ES 400/3-5
300 S College St 38237 731-587-2290
Terri Stephenson, prin. Fax 587-2877
Martin MS 400/6-8
700 Fowler Rd 38237 731-587-2346
Nate Holmes, prin. Fax 588-0529
Martin PS 500/PK-2
215 S College St 38237 731-587-9033
Tracey Bell, prin. Fax 587-6699

Maryville, Blount, Pop. 26,990
Blount County SD 11,300/PK-12
831 Grandview Dr 37803 865-984-1212
Rob Britt, dir. Fax 980-1002
www.blountk12.org
Blount ES 600/PK-5
131 S Old Glory Rd 37801 865-980-1430
Dr. Jesse Robinette, prin. Fax 980-1428
Carpenters ES 600/PK-5
915 Huffstetler Rd 37803 865-980-1490
Katrina Gravitte, prin. Fax 980-1495
Carpenters MS 700/6-8
920 Huffstetler Rd 37803 865-980-1414
Jon Young, prin. Fax 980-1404
Eagleton ES 500/PK-5
708 Sam Houston School Rd 37804 865-980-1455
Buffy Wyrosdick, prin. Fax 980-1451
Eagleton MS 400/6-8
2610 Cinema Dr 37804 865-982-3211
Tony Shultz, prin. Fax 982-4203
Fairview ES 300/PK-5
2130 Old Niles Ferry Rd 37803 865-982-0630
Greg England, prin. Fax 977-0712
Heritage MS 800/6-8
3737 E Lamar Alexander Pkwy 37804 865-980-1300
Dr. Steve Moser, prin. Fax 980-1281
Lanier ES 400/PK-5
6006 Lanier Rd 37801 865-980-1075
Teresa Robinson, prin. Fax 980-1053
Montvale ES 400/K-5
3128 Montvale Rd 37803 865-983-2666
Donna Russell, prin. Fax 977-0240
Porter ES 300/K-5
4520 Wildwood Springs Rd 37804 865-983-4071
Jared Smith, prin. Fax 981-4928
Other Schools – See Friendsville, Louisville, Rockford, Seymour, Townsend, Walland

Maryville CSD 5,100/PK-12
833 Lawrence Ave 37803 865-982-7121
Dr. Mike Winstead, supt. Fax 977-5055
www.maryville-schools.org
Coulter Grove IS 800/4-7
2025 Sevierville Rd 37804 865-982-6345
Dr. Ramona Best, prin. Fax 982-6312

Foothills ES 500/K-3
520 Sandy Springs Rd 37803 865-681-0364
Karen Schito, prin. Fax 681-0366
Houston ES 500/PK-3
330 Melrose St 37803 865-983-3241
Heather Hilton, prin. Fax 977-0756
Montgomery Ridge IS 800/4-7
835 Montgomery Ln 37803 865-980-0590
Kevin Myers, prin. Fax 980-0589
Sevier ES 600/PK-3
2001 Sequoyah Ave 37804 865-983-8551
Ginny Boles, prin. Fax 977-0725

Adventist Christian S of Maryville 50/K-8
2921 Sevierville Rd 37804 865-982-7504
Apostolic Christian Academy 100/PK-12
1331 William Blount Dr 37801 865-982-4901
Maryville Christian S 400/PK-12
2525 Morganton Rd 37801 865-681-3205
Kris Schottleutner, admin. Fax 681-4086

Mascot, Knox, Pop. 2,357
Knox County SD
Supt. — See Knoxville
East Knox County ES 500/K-5
9315 Rutledge Pike 37806 865-933-3493
Kristina Woods, prin. Fax 933-8178

Maynardville, Union, Pop. 2,385
Union County SD 5,600/PK-12
PO Box 10 37807 865-992-5466
Dr. James Carter, dir. Fax 992-0126
www.ucps.org
Big Ridge ES 200/PK-5
3420 Hickory Valley Rd 37807 865-992-8687
Kim Turner, prin. Fax 992-8647
Maynard MS 700/6-8
PO Box 669 37807 865-992-1030
Greg Clay, prin. Fax 992-1060
Maynardville ES 400/PK-5
PO Box 339 37807 865-992-8391
Lisa Carter, prin. Fax 992-8392
Paulette ES 400/PK-5
PO Box 999 37807 865-745-0517
Dr. Jason Bailey, prin. Fax 745-0518
Other Schools – See Luttrell, Sharps Chapel

Medina, Gibson, Pop. 3,452
Gibson County Special SD
Supt. — See Dyer
Medina ES 600/PK-2
PO Box 99 38355 731-783-3660
Billy Carey, prin. Fax 783-3778
Medina MS 1,100/3-8
PO Box 369 38355 731-783-1962
Steve Maloan, prin. Fax 783-1964

Memphis, Shelby, Pop. 639,057
Achievement SD 7,400/PK-12
1350 Concourse Ave Ste 434 38104 901-260-9649
Kathleen Airhart, dir.
achievementschooldistrict.org
Corning Achievement ES 300/PK-5
1662 Dabbs Ave 38127 901-416-3926
Danielle Harris, prin. Fax 416-3928
Frayser Achievement ES 400/PK-5
1602 Dellwood Ave 38127 901-416-3840
Jessica Tang, prin. Fax 416-4836
Georgian Hills Achievement ES 300/PK-5
3930 Leweir St 38127 901-416-3750
Yolanda Dandridge, prin. Fax 416-3903
Westside Achievement MS 500/6-8
3389 Dawn Dr 38127 901-416-3700
Rasheedah Jemison, prin. Fax 416-3701

Shelby County SD 106,700/PK-12
160 S Hollywood St 38112 901-321-2500
Dorsey Hopson, supt. Fax 321-2501
www.scsk12.org/
Airways Achievement Academy K-8
2601 Ketchum Rd 38114 901-416-5006
Dr. Billy Walker, prin. Fax 416-8458
Alcy ES 300/PK-5
1750 E Alcy Rd 38114 901-416-7800
Pamela Cleaves, prin. Fax 416-7862
Alton ES 400/PK-5
2020 Alton Ave 38106 901-416-7430
Latisha Brown, prin. Fax 416-7414
American Way MS 800/6-8
3805 American Way 38118 901-416-1250
Anne Webb, prin. Fax 416-1251
Balmoral/Ridgeway ES 400/K-5
5905 Grosvenor Ave 38119 901-416-2128
Sharonda Beard, prin. Fax 416-2130
Belle Forest Community S PK-5
3135 Ridgeway Rd 38115 901-416-7200
Dinah Taylor, prin. Fax 416-7198
Bellevue MS 500/6-8
575 S Bellevue Blvd 38104 901-416-4488
Frederick Malone, prin. Fax 416-4490
Berclair ES 600/PK-5
810 N Perkins Rd 38122 901-416-8800
Dr. Sam Shaw, prin. Fax 416-8802
Bethel Grove ES 300/PK-5
2459 Arlington Ave 38114 901-416-5012
Audrean Bond-Jones, prin. Fax 416-5005
Bond ES 1,100/K-5
2727 Kate Bond Rd 38133 901-416-0020
Dr. Yvette Williams-Renfroe, prin. Fax 416-0021
Bond MS 1,100/6-8
2737 Kate Bond Rd 38133 901-416-0640
Christopher Murrah, prin. Fax 416-7962
Brewster ES 600/PK-5
2605 Sam Cooper Blvd 38112 901-416-7150
Dr. Angela Askew, prin. Fax 416-7151
Brownsville Road ES 700/K-5
5292 Banbury Ave 38135 901-416-4300
Charles Newborn, prin. Fax 416-4302

Bruce ES 500/PK-5
581 S Bellevue Blvd 38104 901-416-4495
Archie Moss, prin. Fax 416-4494
Campbell ES 400/PK-5
3232 Birchfield Dr 38127 901-416-1000
Jaron Carson, prin. Fax 416-1001
Campus ES 300/1-5
535 Zach Curlin Rd 38152 901-678-2285
Dr. Susan Copeland, dir. Fax 678-4235
Charjean ES 400/PK-5
2140 Charjean Rd 38114 901-416-5016
Tameka Allen, prin. Fax 416-5018
Cherokee ES 500/PK-5
3061 Kimball Ave 38114 901-416-5028
Sunya Payne, prin. Fax 416-5010
Chickasaw MS 400/6-8
4060 Westmont Rd 38109 901-416-8134
Veda Turner, prin. Fax 416-8139
Church ES 600/PK-5
4100 Millbranch Rd 38116 901-416-0198
Christye Lowe, prin. Fax 416-2248
Colonial MS 1,200/6-8
1370 Colonial Rd 38117 901-416-8980
Marqui Fifer, prin. Fax 416-8996
Craigmont MS 800/6-8
3455 Covington Pike 38128 901-416-7780
LaTrenda Hicks, prin. Fax 416-1454
Cromwell ES 500/K-5
4989 Cromwell Ave 38118 901-416-2500
Dr. Stephanie Waller, prin. Fax 416-2517
Crump ES 1,000/K-5
4405 Crump Rd 38141 901-416-1970
Lyne Ssebikindu, prin. Fax 416-1973
Cummings S 600/K-8
1037 Cummings St 38106 901-416-7810
Keyundah Coleman, prin. Fax 416-7812
Delano ES 300/K-5
1716 Delano Ave 38127 901-416-3932
Patrice Shipp, prin. Fax 416-3934
Double Tree ES 500/PK-5
4560 Double Tree Rd 38109 901-416-8144
Tonya Miller, prin. Fax 416-8149
Douglass S 400/K-8
1650 Ash St 38108 901-416-5946
Kamiah Turner, prin. Fax 416-8085
Downtown ES 600/PK-5
10 N 4th St 38103 901-416-8400
Debra Martin, prin. Fax 416-8406
Dunbar ES 300/PK-5
2606 Select Ave 38114 901-416-5000
Dr. Anniece Gentry, prin. Fax 416-5002
Egypt ES 600/K-5
4160 Karen Cv 38128 901-416-4150
Dionna Pruitt, prin. Fax 416-4163
Evans ES 600/K-5
4949 Cottonwood Rd 38118 901-416-2504
Charlette McCants, prin. Fax 416-8475
Ford Road ES 600/PK-5
3336 Ford Rd 38109 901-416-8150
LaQuita Tate, prin. Fax 416-8156
Fox Meadows ES 700/K-5
2960 Emerald St 38115 901-416-2530
Rhonda Bowles Howard, prin. Fax 416-2550
Freeman Optional S 500/K-8
5250 Tulane Rd 38109 901-416-3156
Randi Howard, prin. Fax 416-3127
Gardenview ES 400/K-5
4075 Hartz Dr 38116 901-416-3068
Faye Anderson, prin. Fax 416-6773
Geeter MS 400/6-8
4649 Horn Lake Rd 38109 901-416-8157
Pamela Yancy-Taylor, prin. Fax 416-8160
Georgian Hills MS 300/6-8
3925 Denver St 38127 901-416-3740
Ticada Guyton, prin. Fax 416-6500
Germanshire ES 800/PK-5
3965 S Germantown Rd 38125 901-416-3733
Antuan Knapp, prin. Fax 416-3723
Getwell ES 400/K-5
2795 Getwell Rd 38118 901-416-0267
Dr. Trina Holly, prin. Fax 416-6774
Goodlett ES 400/K-5
3001 S Goodlett St 38118 901-416-2510
Nadiyah McMurray, prin. Fax 416-2512
Gordon Achievement Academy 300/K-8
815 Breedlove St 38107 901-416-3212
Leviticus Pointer, prin. Fax 416-3214
Grahamwood ES 1,000/K-5
3950 Summer Ave 38122 901-416-5952
John Johnson, prin. Fax 416-5954
Grandview Heights MS 400/6-8
2342 Clifton Ave 38127 901-416-3940
DeArtis Barbor, prin. Fax 416-3923
Hamilton ES 400/PK-5
1378 Ethlyn Ave 38106 901-416-7826
Brian Ingram, prin. Fax 416-7827
Hamilton MS 400/6-8
1478 Wilson St 38106 901-416-7832
Audrey Johnson, prin. Fax 416-3314
Havenview MS 900/6-8
1481 Hester Rd 38116 901-416-3092
Darla Young, prin. Fax 416-3093
Hawkins Mill ES 400/PK-5
4295 Mountain Terrace St 38127 901-416-3944
Antonio Harvey, prin. Fax 416-3948
Hickory Ridge ES 900/K-5
3890 Hickory Hill Rd 38115 901-416-1195
Regina Nichols, prin. Fax 416-1474
Hickory Ridge MS 900/6-8
3920 Ridgeway Rd 38115 901-416-9337
Cedric Smith, prin. Fax 416-9210
Highland Oaks ES 1,000/K-5
5252 Annandale Dr 38125 901-416-0330
Marchera James, prin. Fax 756-2304
Highland Oaks MS 900/6-8
5600 Meadowbriar Trl 38125 901-416-0340
Monica Bates, prin. Fax 416-0345

Hill ES 300/K-5
345 E Olive Ave 38106 901-416-7844
Melody Smith, prin. Fax 416-7890
Holmes Road ES 600/K-5
1083 E Holmes Rd 38116 901-416-6469
Debra Fox, prin. Fax 416-2469
Idlewild ES 500/K-5
1950 Linden Ave 38104 901-416-4566
Randy Thompson, prin. Fax 416-4492
Jackson ES 300/PK-5
3925 Wales Ave 38108 901-416-4222
Yolanda Heidelberg, prin. Fax 416-4277
Keystone ES 400/PK-5
4301 Old Allen Rd 38128 901-416-3924
Dr. Deelene Weedon, prin. Fax 416-3947
Kingsbury ES 500/K-5
4055 Bayliss Ave 38108 901-416-6020
Wynn Earle, prin. Fax 416-6041
Kingsbury MS 400/6-8
1276 N Graham St 38122 901-416-6040
Tarcia Gilliam, prin. Fax 416-6058
Knight Road ES 500/K-5
3237 Knight Rd 38118 901-416-2514
Femetres Gray, prin. Fax 416-2516
LaRose ES 300/PK-5
864 S Wellington St 38126 901-416-7848
Robert Davis, prin. Fax 416-7850
Levi ES 400/K-5
135 W Levi Rd 38109 901-416-8166
Dr. Janice Tankson, prin. Fax 416-8167
Lowrance S 900/PK-8
7740 Lowrance Rd 38125 901-416-2330
Kelvin Bates, prin. Fax 759-3011
Magnolia ES 400/PK-5
2061 Livewell Cir 38114 901-416-4578
Netarsha McDaniel-Rone, prin. Fax 416-4580
Manor Lake ES 300/K-5
4900 Horn Lake Rd 38109 901-416-8170
Tiffany Curry, prin. Fax 416-8172
Newberry ES 500/K-5
5540 Newberry Ave 38115 901-416-2510
James Gordon, prin. Fax 416-8184
Northaven ES 300/PK-5
5157 N Circle Rd 38127 901-416-2800
Louis Padgett, prin. Fax 353-8586
Oak Forest ES 900/PK-5
7440 Nonconnah View Cv 38119 901-416-2257
LaShinda Hughes, prin. Fax 416-2264
Oakhaven ES 600/K-5
3795 Bishops Bridge Rd 38118 901-416-2320
Perry Horner, prin. Fax 416-2335
Oakhaven MS 200/6-8
3125 Ladbrook Rd 38118 901-416-2380
Rod Peterson, prin. Fax 416-9780
Oakshire ES 500/K-5
1765 E Holmes Rd 38116 901-416-3140
Gloria Golden, prin. Fax 416-3142
Peabody ES 400/PK-5
2086 Young Ave 38104 901-416-4606
Melanie Nelson, prin. Fax 416-4611
Raleigh-Bartlett Meadows ES 500/K-5
5195 Twin Woods Ave 38134 901-416-4336
Divalyn Gordon, prin. Fax 416-4339
Richland ES 800/K-5
5440 Rich Rd 38120 901-416-2148
Sharon McNary, prin. Fax 416-2150
Ridgeway MS 800/6-8
6333 Quince Rd 38119 901-416-1588
Corey Williams, prin. Fax 416-1477
Riverview S 300/PK-8
241 Majuba Ave 38109 901-416-7340
Latasha Harris, prin. Fax 416-7343
Ross ES 900/K-5
4890 Ross Rd 38141 901-416-1990
Evette Smith, prin. Fax 416-1964
Rozelle ES 300/K-5
993 Roland St 38114 901-416-4612
Carl Johnson, prin. Fax 416-4619
Scenic Hills ES 400/K-5
3450 Scenic Hwy 38128 901-416-4342
Todd Shaffer, prin. Fax 416-4303
Sea Isle ES 500/K-5
5250 Sea Isle Rd 38117 901-416-2104
Renee Meeks, prin. Fax 416-2109
Shady Grove ES 400/K-5
5360 Shady Grove Rd 38120 901-416-2166
Kiersten Schnacke, prin. Fax 416-2168
Sharpe ES 400/K-5
3431 Sharpe Ave 38111 901-416-5020
Gary Zimmerman, prin. Fax 416-5022
Sheffield ES 400/K-5
4290 Chuck Ave 38118 901-416-2360
Patricia Merriweather, prin. Fax 416-2371
Shelby Oaks ES 900/K-5
6053 Summer Ave 38134 901-416-4305
Dr. Catherine Diezi, prin. Fax 416-4311
Sherwood ES 700/PK-5
1156 Robin Hood Ln 38111 901-416-4864
Tonya Miller, prin. Fax 416-4869
Sherwood MS 600/6-8
3480 Rhodes Ave 38111 901-416-4870
Michael Henry, prin. Fax 416-4881
Smith STEAM Academy 300/6-8
750 E Parkway S 38104 901-416-4536
Michael Demster, prin. Fax 416-4539
Snowden S 1,600/K-8
1870 N Parkway 38112 901-416-4621
Jamie Stallsmith, prin. Fax 416-4620
South Park ES 500/K-5
1720 Getwell Rd 38111 901-416-5024
Felicia Strickland, prin. Fax 416-5025
Southwind ES 800/K-5
8155 Meadow Vale Dr 38125 901-416-2805
Dennis Kimbrough, prin. Fax 416-2807
Springdale ES 300/K-5
880 N Hollywood St 38108 901-416-4883
Carmen Gregory, prin. Fax 416-9280

Treadwell ES 700/PK-5
3538 Given Ave 38122 901-416-6130
Dr. Tanisha Heaston, prin. Fax 416-6132
Treadwell MS 400/6-8
920 N Highland St 38122 901-416-6100
Roger Faulkner, prin. Fax 416-6133
Vollentine ES 300/K-5
1682 Vollintine Ave 38107 901-416-4632
Tamika Jackson, prin. Fax 416-3603
Walker MS 600/6-8
1900 E Raines Rd 38116 901-416-1030
Dr. Terrence Brittenum, prin. Fax 416-1075
Wells Academy 100/K-8
995 S Lauderdale St 38126 901-416-3210
Robert Davis, prin. Fax 416-3205
Wells Station ES 700/PK-5
1610 Wells Station Rd 38108 901-416-2172
Kesia Jackson, prin. Fax 416-2175
Westhaven ES 500/PK-5
4585 Hodge Rd 38109 901-416-8740
Rodney Rowan, prin. Fax 416-8741
Westside ES 400/K-5
3347 Dawn Dr 38127 901-416-3725
Kimberly Adams, prin. Fax 416-3729
Whitehaven ES 400/K-5
4783 Elvis Presley Blvd 38116 901-416-7431
Tommy Elliott, prin. Fax 416-9358
White Station ES 600/K-5
4840 Chickasaw Rd 38117 901-416-8900
Tracie Thomas, prin. Fax 416-8911
White Station MS 900/6-8
5465 Mason Rd 38120 901-416-2184
Dr. Charlotte Danley, prin. Fax 416-2187
Willow Oaks ES 700/PK-5
4417 Willow Rd 38117 901-416-2196
Dr. Angela Nichols, prin. Fax 416-2198
Winchester ES 600/PK-5
3587 Boeingshire Dr 38116 901-416-3152
Flora Childres, prin. Fax 416-3154
Winridge ES 700/K-5
3500 Ridgeway Rd 38115 901-416-6618
Dr. Linda Campbell, prin. Fax 416-4467
Other Schools – See Arlington, Cordova, Germantown, Millington

---

Binghampton Christian Academy 100/PK-8
PO Box 11109 38111 901-323-4092
Tari Harris, head sch Fax 888-7952
Bornblum Jewish Community S 100/K-8
6641 Humphreys Blvd 38120 901-747-2665
Briarcrest Christian ES - East Memphis 200/PK-5
6000 Briarcrest Ave 38120 901-765-4662
Karen Fienup, prin. Fax 765-4675
Brinkley Heights Urban Academy 100/PK-12
3260 Macon Rd 38122 901-324-3022
Central Baptist S 200/PK-12
5470 Raleigh LaGrange Rd 38134 901-386-8161
Christ Methodist Day S 200/PK-4
411 S Grove Park Rd 38117 901-683-6873
Christ the King Lutheran S 300/PK-8
5296 Park Ave 38119 901-682-8405
Felicia Calhoun, admin. Fax 682-7687
Creative Life Preparatory S 50/PK-12
1222 Riverside Blvd 38106 901-775-0304
Dr. Carolyn Bibbs, pres. Fax 946-5433
De La Salle S at Blessed Sacrament 100/K-8
2540 Hale Ave 38112 901-866-9084
Chris Reid, prin. Fax 866-9086
Grace-St. Luke's Episcopal S 500/PK-8
246 S Belvedere Blvd 38104 901-278-0200
Thor Kvande, head sch Fax 272-7119
Greater Memphis Adventist Academy 50/K-8
3333 Old Brownsville Rd 38134 256-679-6819
Harding Acad of Memphis - White Station 200/PK-6
1106 Colonial Rd 38117 901-767-2093
Holy Rosary S 500/PK-8
4841 Park Ave 38117 901-685-1231
Darren Mullis, prin. Fax 818-0335
Hutchison S 900/PK-12
1740 Ridgeway Rd 38119 901-761-2220
Dr. Kristen Ring, head sch Fax 683-3510
Immaculate Conception Cathedral S 200/PK-12
1695 Central Ave 38104 901-725-2705
Tracey Ford, prin. Fax 725-2701
Immanuel Lutheran S 200/PK-8
6319 Raleigh Lagrange Rd 38134 901-388-0205
Todd Baringer, prin. Fax 377-7371
Lausanne Collegiate S 800/PK-12
1381 W Massey Rd 38120 901-474-1000
Little Flower PS 100/PK-2
1666 Jackson Ave 38107 901-725-9900
Tunia Sangster, prin. Fax 725-5779
Lord's Tabernacle Christian Academy 100/PK-6
PO Box 11067 38111 901-454-7060
Stephane Cole, head sch Fax 323-3040
Margolin Hebrew Academy 200/PK-12
390 S White Station Rd 38117 901-682-2400
Maria Montessori S 100/PK-8
740 Harbor Bend Rd 38103 901-527-3444
Memphis Junior Academy 100/PK-10
50 N Mendenhall Rd 38117 901-683-1061
Tracy Fry, prin. Fax 683-1012
New Hope Christian Academy 400/PK-6
3000 University St 38127 901-358-3183
Our Lady of Sorrows S 100/PK-8
3690 Thomas St 38127 901-358-7431
Connie Hegwood, prin. Fax 353-1153
Pleasant View S 200/PK-12
1888 Bartlett Rd 38134 901-380-0122
Presbyterian Day S 600/PK-6
4025 Poplar Ave 38111 901-842-4600
Steven Hancock, hdmstr. Fax 842-4620
Resurrection S PK-6
5475 Newberry Ave 38115 901-546-9926
James Shelton, prin. Fax 546-9929
St. Agnes Academy/St. Dominic S 400/PK-12
4830 Walnut Grove Rd 38117 901-767-1356
Tom Hood, pres. Fax 435-5866
St. Ann S 400/PK-8
6529 Stage Rd 38134 901-386-3328
Marie Borkowski, prin. Fax 386-1030
St. Augustine S 100/PK-6
1169 Kerr Ave 38106 901-942-8002
Kelsey Bourquin, prin. Fax 942-4564
St. George's Independent S 200/PK-5
3749 Kimball Ave 38111 901-261-3920
J. Ross Peters, head sch Fax 261-3999
St. John S 100/PK-6
2718 Lamar Ave 38114 901-743-6700
Rhiannon Thomas, prin. Fax 743-6720
St. Joseph S 100/PK-6
3851 Neely Rd 38109 901-344-0021
Leslie Harden, prin. Fax 348-0787
St. Louis S 500/K-8
5192 Shady Grove Rd 38117 901-255-1900
Teddi Niedzwiedz, prin. Fax 328-9798
St. Mary's Episcopal S 800/PK-12
60 Perkins Ext 38117 901-537-1472
Albert L. Throckmorton, head sch Fax 682-0119
St. Michael S 100/PK-8
3880 Forrest Ave 38122 901-323-2162
Mary Anne Chiozza, prin. Fax 323-0481
St. Patrick ES 100/PK-6
277 S 4th St 38126 901-521-3252
Susan Pittman, prin. Fax 521-8265
St. Paul Catholic S 300/PK-6
1425 E Shelby Dr 38116 901-346-0862
Sr. Mary Lawrence, prin. Fax 396-2677
Westminster Academy 300/PK-12
2500 Ridgeway Rd 38119 901-380-9192
Ralph Janikowsky, hdmstr. Fax 405-2019
Woodland Presbyterian S 400/PK-8
5217 Park Ave 38119 901-685-0976
Adam Moore M.Ed., head sch Fax 761-2406
Word of Faith Christian Academy 100/PK-12
3528 Sharpe Ave 38111 901-744-4061

Michie, McNairy, Pop. 589
McNairy County SD
Supt. — See Selmer
Michie S 400/K-8
6418 Highway 57 E 38357 731-439-4135
Dr. Matt Alred, prin. Fax 632-4945

Middleton, Hardeman, Pop. 695
Hardeman County SD
Supt. — See Bolivar
Middleton ES 400/PK-6
PO Box 537 38052 731-376-0160
Doris Keller, prin. Fax 376-9111

Milan, Gibson, Pop. 7,701
Milan Special SD 2,100/PK-12
1165 S Main St 38358 731-686-0844
Jonathan Criswell, dir. Fax 686-8781
www.milanssd.org
Milan ES 800/PK-4
1100 Middle Rd 38358 731-686-0840
Tammy Rushing, prin. Fax 686-3282
Milan MS 700/5-8
4040 Middle Rd 38358 731-686-7232
Chris Jones, prin. Fax 723-8872

Millington, Shelby, Pop. 9,878
Millington Municipal SD 2,800/PK-12
5020 2nd Ave 38053 901-873-5680
Dr. David Roper, dir. Fax 873-5699
www.millingtonschools.org
Harrold ES 400/PK-5
4943 W Union Rd 38053 901-873-8165
Dr. Amanda Compton, prin. Fax 873-8121
Millington ES 600/PK-5
6445 William L Osteen Dr 38053 901-873-8433
Kathy Wilson, prin. Fax 873-8439
Millington MS 500/6-8
4964 Cuba Millington Rd 38053 901-873-8130
Selina Sparkman, prin. Fax 873-8136

Shelby County SD
Supt. — See Memphis
Jeter S 200/K-8
7662 Benjestown Rd 38053 901-416-2955
Paulette Bond, prin. Fax 416-2957
Lucy ES 600/K-5
6269 Amherst Rd 38053 901-416-2610
Jonathan Humphrey, prin. Fax 416-2068
Woodstock MS 500/6-8
5885 Woodstock Cuba Rd 38053 901-416-4180
Eric Linsy, prin. Fax 416-4182

Faith Heritage Christian Academy 100/PK-12
PO Box 157 38083 901-872-0828
Lighthouse Christian Academy 200/PK-12
3660 Shelby Rd 38053 901-873-3353
Tipton-Rosemark Academy 600/PK-12
8696 Rosemark Rd 38053 901-829-6500

Minor Hill, Giles, Pop. 536
Giles County SD
Supt. — See Pulaski
Minor Hill S 400/PK-8
13099 Minor Hill Hwy 38473 931-565-3117
Vickie Beard, prin. Fax 565-4504

Mohawk, Greene
Greene County SD
Supt. — See Greeneville
McDonald S 400/PK-8
8120 McDonald Rd 37810 423-235-5406
Chris Sharp, prin. Fax 235-7778

Monteagle, Marion, Pop. 1,178
Marion County SD
Supt. — See Jasper
Monteagle S 300/PK-8
120 E Main St 37356 931-924-2136
Janet Layne, prin. Fax 924-2104

Monterey, Putnam, Pop. 2,832
Putnam County SD
Supt. — See Cookeville
Burks ES 500/PK-6
300 Crossville St 38574 931-839-7641
Kevin Maynard, prin. Fax 839-6683

Mooresburg, Hawkins, Pop. 937
Hawkins County SD
Supt. — See Rogersville
Mooresburg ES 200/PK-5
305 Highway 31 37811 423-272-9597
Jason Roach, prin. Fax 921-8970

Morrison, Warren, Pop. 681
Warren County SD
Supt. — See Mc Minnville
Morrison S 400/PK-8
500 S Fair St 37357 931-635-2512
Kim Cantrell, prin. Fax 635-3233

Morristown, Hamblen, Pop. 28,494
Hamblen County SD 10,000/K-12
210 E Morris Blvd 37813 423-586-7700
Dr. Jeff Perry, dir. Fax 586-7747
www.hcboe.net
Alpha ES 600/K-5
5620 Old Highway 11E 37814 423-586-3332
Kim Dyke, prin. Fax 585-3737
Fairview-Marguerite ES 500/K-5
2125 Fairview Rd 37814 423-586-4098
Suzanne Wampler, prin. Fax 585-3746
Hay ES 300/K-5
501 Britton Ct 37814 423-586-1080
Matthew Drinnon, prin. Fax 585-3753
Hillcrest ES 500/K-5
407 S Liberty Hill Rd 37813 423-586-7472
Paula Davis, prin. Fax 585-3750
Lincoln Heights ES 500/K-5
215 Lincoln Ave 37813 423-586-2062
Janet Dalton, prin. Fax 585-3757
Lincoln Heights MS 500/6-8
219 Lincoln Ave 37813 423-581-3200
Joseph Ely, prin. Fax 585-3763
Manley ES 500/K-5
551 W Economy Rd 37814 423-586-7400
Debra Dickenson, prin. Fax 585-3875
Meadowview MS 500/6-8
1623 Meadowview Ln 37814 423-581-6360
Karen Holweg, prin. Fax 585-3771
Union Heights ES 300/K-5
3366 Tornado Trl 37813 423-586-1502
James Patrick, prin. Fax 585-3822
West ES 500/K-5
235 W Converse St 37814 423-586-1263
Krista Crum, prin. Fax 585-3810
West View MS 600/6-8
1 Indian Path 37813 423-581-2407
Rebekah Patrick, prin. Fax 585-3807
Witt ES 200/K-5
4650 S Davy Crockett Pkwy 37813 423-586-2862
Lisa Templin, prin. Fax 585-3754
Other Schools – See Russellville, Whitesburg

All Saints' Episcopal S 100/PK-8
3275 Maple Valley Rd 37813 423-586-3280
Mark Workman, head sch Fax 586-9355
Cornerstone Academy 200/PK-12
260 Jacobs Rd 37813 423-307-1189
Ben Holland, hdmstr.
Lighthouse Christian Academy 50/K-8
360 W Economy Rd 37814 423-586-4198

Moscow, Fayette, Pop. 552
Fayette County SD
Supt. — See Somerville
LaGrange-Moscow ES 300/PK-5
15655 Highway 57 38057 901-877-6854
Dr. Kerri Anne Breeden, prin. Fax 877-3165

Mosheim, Greene, Pop. 2,337
Greene County SD
Supt. — See Greeneville
Mosheim S 1,100/PK-8
297 W School St 37818 423-422-4123
Tim Shelton, prin. Fax 422-6490

Mountain City, Johnson, Pop. 2,508
Johnson County SD 2,300/PK-12
211 N Church St 37683 423-727-2640
Dr. Mischelle Simcox, dir. Fax 727-2663
jocoed.net
Doe ES 200/PK-6
7164 Highway 67 W 37683 423-727-2682
Teresa Stansberry, prin. Fax 727-2698
Johnson County MS 300/7-8
278 Fairground Hill 37683 423-727-2600
Edna Miller, prin. Fax 727-4141
Mountain City ES 500/PK-6
301 Donnelly St 37683 423-727-2621
Gay Triplett, prin. Fax 727-2631
Roan Creek ES 500/PK-6
2410 Roan Creek Rd 37683 423-727-4964
Dr. Cheri Long, prin. Fax 727-2164
Other Schools – See Laurel Bloomery, Shady Valley

Mount Carmel, Hawkins, Pop. 5,390
Hawkins County SD
Supt. — See Rogersville
Mt. Carmel ES 300/PK-4
127 Cherry St 37645 423-357-7221
Kelli Campbell, prin. Fax 357-9863

Mount Juliet, Wilson, Pop. 23,208
Wilson County SD
Supt. — See Lebanon
Lakeview ES 700/K-5
6211 Saundersville Rd 37122 615-758-5619
Tracey Burge, prin. Fax 758-5600
Mount Juliet ES 700/K-5
2521 W Division St 37122 615-758-5654
Ginger Ash, prin. Fax 758-5602

Mount Juliet MS 1,500/6-8
3565 N Mount Juliet Rd 37122 615-754-6688
Leigh Ann Rainey, prin. Fax 754-7566
Patton ES 600/PK-5
1003 Woodridge Pl 37122 615-444-3282
Wilma Hawkins, prin. Fax 773-5394
Rutland ES 900/PK-5
1995 S Rutland Rd 37122 615-754-1800
Cathy York, prin. Fax 754-1801
Springdale ES 600/PK-5
5675 Central Pike 37122 615-773-9640
Christine Miller, prin. Fax 754-7580
Stoner Creek ES 700/K-5
1035 N Mount Juliet Rd 37122 615-754-6300
Michael Hickman, prin. Fax 754-5784
West ES 600/K-5
9315 Lebanon Rd 37122 615-758-5846
Chris Plummer, prin. Fax 754-5798
West Wilson MS 1,100/6-8
935 N Mount Juliet Rd 37122 615-758-5152
Wendell Marlowe, prin. Fax 758-5283
Wright ES 700/PK-5
5017 Market Pl 37122 615-754-6200
Bryan Adams, prin. Fax 754-5282

Heritage Christian Academy - Mt. Juliet 300/K-12
PO Box 1135 37121 615-604-0564
Katrina Hagerty, prin.
Mt. Juliet Christian Academy 500/PK-12
735 N Mount Juliet Rd 37122 615-758-2427
Dr. Mike Lee, head sch Fax 758-3662

Mount Pleasant, Maury, Pop. 4,471
Maury County SD
Supt. — See Columbia
Mount Pleasant ES 600/PK-4
600 Locust St 38474 931-379-5040
Julie Tidwell, prin. Fax 379-2095
Mt. Pleasant MS of Visual/Performing Art 400/5-8
410 Gray Ln 38474 931-379-1100
Marrkus Marshall, prin. Fax 379-1108

Munford, Tipton, Pop. 5,823
Tipton County SD
Supt. — See Covington
Munford ES 800/PK-5
1200 McLaughlin Dr 38058 901-837-0152
Varissa Richardson, prin. Fax 837-5778
Munford MS 900/6-8
100 Education Ave 38058 901-837-1700
Vicki Shipley, prin. Fax 837-5749

Murfreesboro, Rutherford, Pop. 106,177
Murfreesboro CSD 7,600/PK-6
2552 S Church St 37127 615-893-2313
Dr. Linda Gilbert, dir. Fax 893-2352
www.cityschools.net
Black Fox ES 800/PK-6
1753 S Rutherford Blvd 37130 615-893-6395
Joe Thompson, prin. Fax 893-0121
Bradley Academy 400/K-6
511 Mercury Blvd 37130 615-895-2672
Jenny Ortiz, prin. Fax 898-7131
Cason Lane Academy ES 900/PK-6
1330 Cason Ln 37128 615-898-7145
Shavon Davis-Louis, prin. Fax 898-7156
Discovery S at Bellwood 400/K-6
1165 Middle Tennessee Blvd 37130 615-895-2123
Kristina Maddux, prin. Fax 898-7155
Hobgood ES 500/PK-6
307 S Baird Ln 37130 615-895-2744
Dr. Tammy Garrett, prin. Fax 896-3627
Mitchell-Neilson ES 300/2-6
711 W Clark Blvd 37129 615-890-7841
Robin Newell, prin. Fax 904-2416
Mitchell-Neilson PS 200/PK-1
1303 Jones Blvd 37129 615-895-2904
Robin Newell, prin. Fax 848-5300
Northfield ES 700/PK-6
550 W Northfield Blvd 37129 615-895-7324
Dr. Gene Loyd, prin. Fax 898-7158
Overall Creek ES 600/K-6
429 Otter Trl 37128 615-624-5500
Don Bartch, admin. Fax 624-5501
Pittard ES K-6
745 DeJarnette Ln 37130 615-396-0240
Adam Bryson, prin. Fax 396-0249
Reeves-Rogers ES 1,100/PK-6
1807 Greenland Dr 37130 615-895-4973
Dr. Kimberly Osborne, prin. Fax 898-7110
Scales ES 1,100/PK-6
2340 Saint Andrews Dr 37128 615-895-5279
Maria Johnson, prin. Fax 217-2482
Siegel ES 700/PK-6
135 W Thompson Ln 37129 615-904-1002
Emily Spencer, prin. Fax 904-1007

Rutherford County SD 41,400/PK-12
2240 Southpark Dr 37128 615-893-5812
Don Odom, dir. Fax 898-7940
www.rcschools.net
Barfield ES 900/PK-5
350 Barfield Crescent Rd 37128 615-904-3810
Judy Goodwin, prin. Fax 904-3811
Blackman ES 1,100/K-5
586 Fortress Blvd 37128 615-904-3795
Cynthia Ford, prin. Fax 904-3796
Blackman MS 1,200/6-8
3945 Blaze Dr 37128 615-904-3860
Will Shelton, prin. Fax 904-3861
Brown's Chapel ES 700/PK-5
6128 Baker Rd 37129 615-904-6755
Kellye Goostree, prin. Fax 904-6756
Buchanan ES 500/K-5
6050 Manchester Pike 37127 615-893-3651
Ashley Witt, prin. Fax 893-6222
Hill ES 300/PK-5
6309 Lebanon Rd 37129 615-893-8046
Helen Campbell, prin. Fax 848-5272
McFadden S of Excellence 400/K-5
221 Bridge Ave 37129 615-893-7251
Dr. Clark Blair, prin. Fax 898-7724
Oakland MS 1,100/6-8
853 Dejarnette Ln 37130 615-904-6760
Tori Ruis, prin. Fax 904-6761
Pittard Campus S 300/K-6
923 E Lytle St 37130 615-895-1030
Dr. Sherry King, prin. Fax 904-7502
Siegel MS 1,100/6-8
355 W Thompson Ln 37129 615-904-3830
Kimberly Stoecker, prin. Fax 904-3831
Whitworth-Buchanan MS 700/6-8
5555 Manchester Pike 37127 615-904-6765
Avy Seymore, prin. Fax 904-6766
Wilson ES 800/K-5
1545 Cutoff Rd 37129 615-904-3840
Jon Dinkins, prin. Fax 904-3841
Other Schools – See Christiana, Eagleville, Lascassas, La Vergne, Readyville, Rockvale, Smyrna

---

Franklin Road Christian S 300/PK-12
3124 Franklin Rd 37128 615-890-0894
Kenton Kramer, admin. Fax 893-2837
Middle Tennessee Christian S 700/PK-12
100 E MTCS Rd 37129 615-893-0601
Providence Christian Academy 300/PK-12
410 Dejarnette Ln 37130 615-904-0902
Dr. Bill Mott, hdmstr. Fax 904-0859
Redeemer Classical Academy 100/K-12
PO Box 12169 37129 615-904-0350
Rice Christian Academy 100/K-9
627 Bill Rice Ranch Rd 37128 615-893-2767
St. Rose of Lima S 300/PK-8
1601 N Tennessee Blvd 37130 615-898-0555
Sr. Marie Hannah, prin. Fax 890-0977

Nashville, Davidson, Pop. 588,359
Metropolitan Nashville SD 79,600/PK-12
2601 Bransford Ave 37204 615-259-4636
Shawn Joseph, dir. Fax 214-8897
www.mnps.org
Allen MS Prep 500/5-8
500 Spence Ln 37210 615-291-6385
Kisha Stinson-Cox, prin. Fax 291-6066
Baxter MS 400/5-8
350 Hart Ln 37207 615-262-6710
Miriam Harrington, prin. Fax 262-6743
Bellevue MS 700/5-8
655 Colice Jeanne Rd 37221 615-662-3000
Mark Pittman, prin. Fax 662-5728
Bellshire Design Center ES 500/PK-4
1128 Bell Grimes Ln 37207 615-860-1452
Robbin Masters, prin. Fax 860-9810
Binkley ES 500/PK-4
4700 W Longdale Dr 37211 615-333-5037
James Urquhart, prin. Fax 333-5041
Buena Vista Enhanced Option ES 400/PK-4
1531 9th Ave N 37208 615-291-6762
Myra Taylor, prin. Fax 291-6768
Caldwell Enhanced Option ES 200/K-4
244 Foster St 37207 615-291-6361
Dr. Ronald Wooding, prin. Fax 291-6363
Carter-Lawrence Magnet ES 400/PK-4
1118 12th Ave S 37203 615-291-7333
Inta Sanford, prin. Fax 291-7323
Casa Azafran ECC PK-PK
2195 Nolensville Pike 37211 615-291-4672
Dr. Dalia Duarte, prin.
Charlotte Park ES 500/PK-4
480 Annex Ave 37209 615-353-2006
Dr. Amy Downey, prin. Fax 353-2008
Churchwell Magnet ES 500/PK-4
1625 Dr DB Todd Jr Blvd 37208 615-687-4024
Marcia Northern, prin.
Cockrill ES 500/PK-4
4701 Indiana Ave 37209 615-298-8075
Keri Hanes, prin. Fax 783-2806
Cotton STEM ES 500/PK-4
1033 W Greenwood Ave 37206 615-262-6981
Jocelyn Adams, prin. Fax 333-5659
Creswell MS of the Arts 500/5-8
3500 John Mallette Dr 37218 615-291-6515
Trellaney Lane, prin. Fax 291-5326
Crieve Hall ES 400/K-4
498 Hogan Rd 37220 615-333-5059
Nate Miley, prin. Fax 329-8183
Croft Design Center MS 700/5-8
482 Elysian Fields Rd 37211 615-332-0217
Dr. Jeremy Lewis, prin. Fax 333-5650
Cumberland ES 300/K-4
4247 Cato Rd 37218 615-291-6370
Carolyn Cobbs, prin. Fax 332-0645
Davis Early Learning Center 50/PK-PK
1910 S Hamilton Rd 37218 615-291-6355
Jessica Hardin, prin. Fax 291-6313
Donelson MS 700/5-8
110 Stewarts Ferry Pike 37214 615-884-4080
Jennifer Rheinecker, prin. Fax 885-8970
Eakin ES 600/K-4
2500 Fairfax Ave 37212 615-298-8076
Dr. Matthew Nelson, prin. Fax 298-8497
Early Museum Magnet MS Prep 500/5-8
1000 Cass St 37208 615-291-6369
Rise Pope, prin. Fax 298-8497
East Nashville Magnet MS Prep 5-8
2000 Greenwood Ave 37206 615-262-6670
Paul Brunette, prin.
Explore Community S K-3
217 S 10th St 37206 615-784-8222
Jon Driscoll, prin.
Fall-Hamilton Enhanced Option ES 300/PK-4
510 Wedgewood Ave 37203 615-291-6380
Matthew Portell, prin. Fax 291-6317
Glencliff ES 500/PK-4
120 Antioch Pike 37211 615-333-5105
Julie Hopkins, prin. Fax 333-5003
Glendale ES 400/PK-4
800 Thompson Ave 37204 615-279-7970
Jeanna Collins, prin. Fax 279-7978
Glengarry ES 500/PK-4
200 Finley Dr 37217 615-360-2900
Ricki Gibbs, prin. Fax 279-7978
Glenn Enhanced Option ES 100/K-4
322 Cleveland St 37207 615-262-6682
Dexter Adams, prin. Fax 360-2932
Glenview ES 800/PK-4
1020 Patricia Dr 37217 615-360-2906
Dr. Marsha McGill, prin. Fax 262-6667
Gower ES 700/PK-4
650 Old Hickory Blvd 37209 615-353-2012
Barbara Frazier, prin. Fax 859-8961
Gra-Mar MS Prep 400/5-8
575 Joyce Ln 37216 615-262-6685
Sonya Brooks, prin. Fax 262-6901
Green ES 600/K-4
3500 Hobbs Rd 37215 615-298-8082
Dr. Andy Davis, prin. Fax 783-2814
Harpeth Valley ES 800/PK-4
7840 Learning Ln 37221 615-662-3015
Dr. Ann-Marie Gleason, prin. Fax 662-3011
Haynes Health/Medical Science Design Ctr 200/5-8
510 W Trinity Ln 37207 615-262-6688
Dr. Iris Olige, prin. Fax 298-8084
Haywood ES 900/PK-4
3790 Turley Dr 37211 615-333-5118
Megan Galloway, prin. Fax 333-5646
Head MS Magnet Prep 600/5-8
1830 Jo Johnston Ave 37203 615-329-8160
Dr. Tonja Williams, prin. Fax 321-8389
Hickman ES 600/PK-4
112 Stewarts Ferry Pike 37214 615-884-4020
Dr. Kimberly Fowler, prin. Fax 884-4028
Hill MS 600/5-8
150 Davidson Rd 37205 615-353-2020
Dr. Carrie Jones, prin. Fax 884-4028
Hull-Jackson Montessori S 500/PK-4
1015 Kellow St 37208 615-291-6601
Martha Phillips, prin. Fax 262-6763
Inglewood ES 300/PK-4
1700 Riverside Dr 37216 615-262-6697
Tracy McPherson, prin. Fax 860-7541
Jones Paideia Magnet ES 400/K-4
1800 9th Ave N 37208 615-291-6382
Dr. Debra Smith, prin.
Joy ES 600/PK-4
2201 Jones Ave 37207 615-262-6724
Sandra Moorman, prin. Fax 258-1079
Kirkpatrick Enhanced Option ES 200/PK-PK, 3-
1000 Sevier St 37206 615-262-6708
LaToya Cobb, prin. Fax 262-6615
Lakeview Design Center ES 900/PK-4
455 Rural Hill Rd 37217 615-360-2912
Dr. Claire Jasper, prin. Fax 360-2915
Lillard ES 300/K-4
3200 Kings Ln 37218 615-876-5126
Derek Sanborn, prin. Fax 876-5104
Litton MS 300/5-8
4601 Hedgewood Dr 37216 615-262-6700
Chara Rand, prin. Fax 262-6995
Lockeland Design Center ES 300/K-4
105 S 17th St 37206 615-258-1330
Christie Conyers-Lewis, prin. Fax 258-1336
McGavock ES 300/PK-4
275 Mcgavock Pike 37214 615-885-8912
Hildateri Smith, prin. Fax 316-7752
McKissack MS Prep 400/5-8
915 38th Ave N 37209 615-329-8170
Thomas Chappelle, prin. Fax 329-8183
McMurray MS 700/5-8
520 McMurray Dr 37211 615-333-5126
T-Shaka Coverson, prin. Fax 333-5125
Meigs Magnet MS 700/5-8
713 Ramsey St 37206 615-271-3222
Dr. Samuel Underwood, prin. Fax 271-3223
Mills ES 600/PK-4
4106 Kennedy Ave 37216 615-262-6677
Fax 226-4796
Moore MS 600/5-8
4425 Granny White Pike 37204 615-298-8095
Dr. Gary Hughes, prin. Fax 298-8452
Napier Enhanced Option ES 500/PK-4
60 Fairfield Ave 37210 615-291-6400
Dr. Watechia Lawless, prin. Fax 291-6003
Oliver MS Prep 800/5-8
6211 Nolensville Pike 37211 615-332-3011
Jeanna Collins, prin. Fax 332-3019
Paragon Mills ES 900/PK-4
260 Paragon Mills Rd 37211 615-333-5170
Dr. Joie Austria, prin. Fax 333-5615
Park Avenue Enhanced Option ES 500/PK-4
3703 Park Ave 37209 615-298-8412
Deltina Short, prin. Fax 298-6751
Pennington ES 400/PK-4
2817 Donna Hill Dr 37214 615-885-8918
Jacqueline Kinzer, prin. Fax 885-8920
Priest ES 600/K-4
1700 Otter Creek Rd 37215 615-298-8416
Melinda Williams, prin. Fax 665-8283
Rosebank ES 300/PK-4
1012 Preston Dr 37206 615-262-6720
Kellee Akers, prin. Fax 333-5178
Rose Park Math/Science MS 400/5-8
1025 9th Ave S 37203 615-291-6405
Rommie Vasser, prin. Fax 262-6717
Ross Early Learning Center 50/PK-PK
601 McFerrin Ave 37206 615-262-6721
Miatta Alexander, prin. Fax 262-6638
Shayne ES 800/PK-4
6217 Nolensville Pike 37211 615-332-3020
Elayna Wilson, prin. Fax 262-6638
Shwab ES 400/PK-4
1500 Dickerson Pike 37207 615-262-6725
Dr. Natalyn Gibbs, prin. Fax 332-3028

Stanford Montesori Design Center ES 400/PK-4
2417 Maplecrest Dr 37214 615-885-8822
Angela Bailey, prin. Fax 885-8928

Stratford STEM MS 5-8
1800 Stratford Ave 37216 615-262-6730
Dr. Janet Wallace, prin.

Sylvan Park Paideia Design Center 500/K-4
4801 Utah Ave 37209 615-298-8423
Robin Elder, prin. Fax 292-5154

Tusculum ES 600/PK-4
440 McMurray Dr 37211 615-333-5179
Dr. Alison McMahan, prin. Fax 885-8965

Two Rivers MS Prep 600/5-8
2991 Mcgavock Pike 37214 615-885-8931
Dr. Shelly Dunaway, prin. Fax 333-5641

Una ES 900/PK-4
2018 Murfreesboro Pike 37217 615-360-2921
Amelia Dukes, prin. Fax 885-8954

Warner Enhanced Option ES 300/PK-4
626 Russell St 37206 615-291-6395
Denise Jacono, prin. Fax 353-2090

Waverly - Belmont ES K-4
2301 10th Ave S 37204 615-800-7690
Susan Blankenship, prin.

West End MS Prep 500/5-8
3529 W End Ave 37205 615-298-8425
Dr. Russell Young, prin.

Westmeade ES 500/K-4
6641 Clearbrook Dr 37205 615-353-2066
Stephen Breese, prin. Fax 298-8450

Whitsitt ES 500/PK-4
110 Whitsett Rd 37210 615-333-5600
Justin Uppinghouse, prin. Fax 876-5134

Wright MS 900/5-8
180 McCall St 37211 615-333-5189
Dr. Sharada Deaton, prin. Fax 333-5635

Other Schools – See Antioch, Brentwood, Goodlettsville, Hermitage, Joelton, Madison, Old Hickory, Whites Creek

---

Abintra Montessori S 100/PK-8
914 Davidson Dr 37205 615-352-4317

Akiva S 100/K-6
809 Percy Warner Blvd 37205 615-356-1880
Daniella Pressner, prin. Fax 356-1850

Bambini Montessori S 100/PK-4
2501 Lakeland Dr 37214 615-885-2739

Born Again Christian Academy 200/PK-4
858 W Trinity Ln 37207 615-228-1430
Fax 228-9598

Christ Presbyterian Academy 1,000/PK-12
2323A Old Hickory Blvd 37215 615-373-9550
Nathaniel Morrow, hdmstr. Fax 370-0884

Christ the King S 300/PK-8
3105 Belmont Blvd 37212 615-292-9465
Sherry Woodman, prin. Fax 292-2477

Covenant S 100/PK-6
33 Burton Hills Blvd 37215 615-467-2313

Davidson Academy 700/PK-12
1414 Old Hickory Blvd 37207 615-860-5300

Donelson Christian Academy 800/PK-12
300 Danyacrest Dr 37214 615-883-2926
Keith Singer, hdmstr. Fax 883-2998

Ensworth S 1,100/K-12
211 Ensworth Ave 37205 615-383-0661
David Braemer, head sch Fax 269-4840

Episcopal S of Nashville PK-3
413 Woodland St 37206 615-928-8611
Harrison Stuart, head sch

Franklin Road Academy 800/PK-12
4700 Franklin Pike 37220 615-832-8845
Sean Casey, head sch Fax 834-4137

Harding Academy 500/PK-8
170 Windsor Dr 37205 615-356-5510
Dave Skeen, head sch Fax 356-0441

Holy Rosary Academy 400/PK-8
190 Graylynn Dr 37214 615-883-1108
Peter Rodgers, prin. Fax 885-5100

Jenkins Preparatory S 100/K-8
814 Youngs Ln 37207 615-227-8992

Linden Waldorf S 200/PK-8
3201 Hillsboro Pike 37215 615-354-0270
Tricia Drake, admin. Fax 354-0247

Lipscomb Academy 1,300/PK-12
3901 Granny White Pike 37204 615-966-1600

Montessori Centre 100/PK-K
4608 Granny White Pike 37220 615-373-0897

Montessori East 100/PK-6
801 Porter Rd 37206 615-226-4588
Faye E. Hunt, dir. Fax 659-1665

Nashville Christian S 600/PK-12
7555 Sawyer Brown Rd 37221 615-356-5600
Connie Jo Shelton, pres. Fax 352-1324

Nashville International Academy 100/PK-8
7335 Charlotte Pike 37209 615-352-5903

Oak Hill S 500/PK-6
4815 Franklin Rd 37220 615-297-6544
Brenda Boon, head sch Fax 298-9555

Overbrook S 300/PK-8
4210 Harding Pike 37205 615-292-5134
Sr. Julia Marie, prin. Fax 783-0560

St. Ann S 200/K-8
5105 Charlotte Pike 37209 615-269-0568
Dr. Adelaide Nicholson, prin. Fax 297-1383

St. Bernard Academy 300/PK-8
2304 Bernard Ave 37212 615-385-0440
Carl Sabo, prin. Fax 783-0241

St. Edward S 400/PK-8
190 Thompson Ln 37211 615-833-5770
Dr. Lisa Redmon, prin. Fax 833-9739

St. Henry S 600/PK-8
6401 Harding Pike 37205 615-352-1328
Sr. Maria Greve, prin. Fax 356-9293

St. Paul Christian Academy 400/PK-6
5033 Hillsboro Pike 37215 615-269-4751
Dr. Jason Powell, head sch Fax 269-4713

St. Pius X Classical Academy 100/PK-8
2750 Tucker Rd 37218 615-255-2049
Lori Patton, prin. Fax 255-2049

University S of Nashville 1,000/K-12
2000 Edgehill Ave 37212 615-321-8000
Dr. Vincent Durnan, dir. Fax 321-0889

Newbern, Dyer, Pop. 3,269

Dyer County SD
Supt. — See Dyersburg

Newbern ES 600/PK-5
401 N York St 38059 731-627-2139
Betty Jackson, prin. Fax 627-9610

Northview MS 400/6-8
820 Williams St 38059 731-627-3713
Lynn Garner, prin. Fax 627-4823

Gibson County Special SD
Supt. — See Dyer

Yorkville S 200/PK-8
56 Nebo Yorkville Rd 38059 731-483-4138
Sharon Lee, prin. Fax 643-6635

New Johnsonville, Humphreys, Pop. 1,923

Humphreys County SD
Supt. — See Waverly

Lakeview S 300/K-8
802 Long St 37134 931-535-2513
John Tidwell, prin. Fax 535-3593

New Market, Jefferson, Pop. 1,317

Jefferson County SD
Supt. — See Dandridge

New Market ES 400/PK-5
1559 W Old A J Hwy 37820 865-475-3551
Vickie Forgety, prin. Fax 475-7122

Newport, Cocke, Pop. 6,817

Cocke County SD 4,800/PK-12
305 Hedrick Dr 37821 423-623-7821
Manney Moore, dir. Fax 625-3947
www.cocke.k12.tn.us

Bridgeport S 300/K-8
1935 Edwina Bridgeport Rd 37821 423-623-5780
April Cody, prin. Fax 623-5722

Centerview S 300/PK-8
2400 Highway 160 37821 423-623-4947
Pam Messer, prin. Fax 623-2038

Edgemont S 600/PK-8
375 Carson Springs Rd 37821 423-623-2288
Nathan Chambers, prin. Fax 623-0345

Northwest S 400/K-8
344 Woodson Rd 37821 423-623-4697
Dr. Shannon Grooms, prin. Fax 623-3432

Other Schools – See Cosby, Del Rio, Hartford, Parrottsville

Newport CSD 800/PK-8
301 College St 37821 423-623-3811
Sandra W. Burchette, dir. Fax 613-8029
newportcityschools.org

Newport Grammar S 800/PK-8
301 College St 37821 423-623-3811
Michael Short, prin. Fax 623-4599

New Tazewell, Claiborne, Pop. 2,986

Claiborne County SD
Supt. — See Tazewell

Alpha Preschool 100/PK-PK
910 Alpha Dr 37825 423-626-3323
JoAnn Wells, prin. Fax 626-3634

Midway S 400/PK-8
4411 Clouds Rd 37825 423-626-3067
Sharon Tolliver, prin. Fax 626-1864

Tazewell New Tazewell ES 500/K-4
501 Davis Dr 37825 423-626-9502
Suzanne Anders, prin. Fax 626-0484

Niota, McMinn, Pop. 706

McMinn County SD
Supt. — See Athens

Niota S 600/PK-8
418 S Burn Rd 37826 423-568-2247
Jon Franks, prin. Fax 568-2687

Nolensville, Williamson, Pop. 5,749

Williamson County SD
Supt. — See Franklin

Mill Creek ES, 100 York Trl 37135 K-5
Julie Sparrow, admin. 615-472-5230

Mill Creek MS, 200 York Trl 37135 6-8
Kari Miller, admin. 615-472-5250

Nolensville ES 900/K-5
2338 Rocky Fork Rd 37135 615-472-4690
Amanda Fuller, prin. Fax 472-4701

Norris, Anderson, Pop. 1,472

Anderson County SD
Supt. — See Clinton

Norris ES 300/K-5
PO Box 949 37828 865-494-7422
Renee Branham, prin. Fax 494-9764

Norris MS 500/6-8
PO Box 980 37828 865-494-7171
Jeff Harshbarger, prin. Fax 494-6693

Oakdale, Morgan, Pop. 205

Morgan County SD
Supt. — See Wartburg

Oakdale S 600/K-12
225 Clifty Creek Rd 37829 423-369-3885
Heath Snow, prin. Fax 369-2821

Oakland, Fayette, Pop. 6,569

Fayette County SD
Supt. — See Somerville

Oakland ES 600/PK-5
PO Box 388 38060 901-465-3804
Josie Currie, prin. Fax 465-1284

West JHS 400/6-8
13100 Highway 194 38060 901-465-9213
Courtney Breeden, prin. Fax 465-1599

Oak Ridge, Anderson, Pop. 28,500

Oak Ridge CSD 4,700/PK-12
PO Box 6588 37831 865-425-9001
Dr. Bruce Borchers, dir. Fax 425-9070
www.ortn.edu

Glenwood ES 400/K-4
125 Audubon Rd 37830 865-425-9401
Pearl Goins, prin. Fax 425-9360

Jefferson MS 700/5-8
200 Fairbanks Rd 37830 865-425-9301
Phil Cox, prin. Fax 425-9339

Linden ES 500/K-4
700 Robertsville Rd 37830 865-425-5701
Roger Ward, prin. Fax 425-5713

Oak Ridge Preschool 200/PK-PK
PO Box 6588 37831 865-425-9101
Lisa Downard, prin. Fax 425-9120

Robertsville MS 700/5-8
245 Robertsville Rd 37830 865-425-9201
Garfield Adams, prin. Fax 425-9236

Willow Brook ES 400/K-4
298 Robertsville Rd 37830 865-425-3201
Sherrie Fairchild-Keyes, prin. Fax 425-3268

Woodland ES 400/K-4
168 Manhattan Ave 37830 865-425-9501
D.T. Hobby, prin. Fax 425-9432

St. Mary S 200/PK-8
323 Vermont Ave 37830 865-483-9700
Sr. Marie Blanchette Cumming, prin. Fax 483-8305

Oldfort, Polk

Polk County SD
Supt. — See Benton

South Polk ES 400/PK-5
964 Old Federal Rd 37362 423-338-4512
Frances Bramblett, prin. Fax 338-5683

Old Hickory, See Nashville

Metropolitan Nashville SD
Supt. — See Nashville

Dupont ES 500/PK-4
1311 9th St 37138 615-847-7305
Stephanie Hoskins, prin. Fax 847-7311

DuPont Hadley MS 600/5-8
1901 Old Hickory Blvd 37138 615-847-7300
Dr. Kevin Armstrong, prin. Fax 847-7311

Jackson ES 500/PK-4
110 Shute Ln 37138 615-847-7317
Tara Loba, prin. Fax 847-7336

Academy for G.O.D. K-12
401 Center St 37138 615-722-7107
Alison Sherrod, admin. Fax 246-2719

Oliver Springs, Morgan, Pop. 3,166

Anderson County SD
Supt. — See Clinton

Norwood ES 300/PK-5
809 E Tri County Blvd 37840 865-435-2519
Karri Hobby, prin. Fax 435-2758

Norwood MS 200/6-8
803 E Tri County Blvd 37840 865-435-7749
Dan Jenkins, prin. Fax 435-5426

Morgan County SD
Supt. — See Wartburg

Petros-Joyner S 200/K-8
125 Petros Joyner School Rd 37840 423-324-8600
Laura Bunch, prin. Fax 324-2558

Roane County SD
Supt. — See Kingston

Dyllis Springs ES 200/PK-5
120 Ollis Rd 37840 865-435-6357
Jennifer Spakes, prin. Fax 435-3402

Oliver Springs MS 300/6-8
317 Roane St 37840 865-435-0011
Nancy Wilson, prin. Fax 435-1621

Oneida, Scott, Pop. 3,699

Oneida Special SD 1,300/PK-12
PO Box 4819 37841 423-569-8912
Dr. Jeanny Hatfield Ph.D., dir. Fax 569-2201
www.oneidaschools.org/

Oneida ES 600/PK-5
330 Claude Terry Dr 37841 423-569-8340
Rick Harper, prin. Fax 569-2406

Oneida MS 300/6-8
376 N Main St 37841 423-569-2468
Kelly Posey, prin. Fax 569-5977

Scott County SD
Supt. — See Huntsville

Burchfield S 600/PK-8
1112 W 3rd Ave 37841 423-569-4935
Tonja Crabtree, prin. Fax 569-1756

Ooltewah, Hamilton, Pop. 676

Hamilton County SD
Supt. — See Chattanooga

Hunter MS 700/6-8
6810 Teal Ln 37363 423-344-1474
Robert Alford, prin. Fax 344-1485

Ooltewah ES 800/K-5
8890 Snowy Owl Rd 37363 423-238-4204
Thomas Arnold, prin. Fax 238-4250

Ooltewah MS 900/6-8
5100 Ooltewah Ringgold Rd 37363 423-238-5732
Chrissy Easterly, prin. Fax 238-5735

Smith ES 700/K-5
6930 Teal Ln 37363 423-344-1425
Sharon Dodds, prin. Fax 344-1462

Snow Hill ES 500/PK-5
9042 Career Ln 37363 423-344-1456
Lea Ann Burk, prin. Fax 344-1472

Wolftever Creek ES 500/PK-5
5080 Ooltewah Ringgold Rd 37363 423-238-7300
Penny Leffew, prin. Fax 238-6502

Ooltewah Adventist S 100/K-8
9209 Amos Rd 37363 423-238-4449

Palmer, Grundy, Pop. 667
Grundy County SD
Supt. — See Altamont
Palmer ES 200/PK-8
PO Box 9 37365 931-779-3383
Donald Partin, prin. Fax 779-3445

Paris, Henry, Pop. 9,926
Henry County SD 3,100/PK-12
217 Grove Blvd 38242 731-642-9733
Dr. Brian Norton, dir. Fax 642-8073
www.henryk12.net/
Other Schools – See Buchanan, Henry, Puryear

Paris Special SD 1,800/PK-8
1219 Highway 641 S 38242 731-642-9322
Norma Gerrell, supt. Fax 642-9327
www.parisssd.org/
Inman MS 500/6-8
400 Harrison St 38242 731-642-8131
Jason Scarbrough, prin. Fax 642-8209
Paris ES 600/3-5
650 Volunteer Dr Ste B 38242 731-642-3675
Chip Gray, prin. Fax 644-0734
Rhea ES 700/PK-2
115 S Wilson St 38242 731-642-0961
Sandra Paschall, prin. Fax 642-5171

Holy Cross Preschool PK-PK
1210 E Wood St 38242 731-642-4681
Angie Taylor, dir. Fax 644-9668

Parrottsville, Cocke, Pop. 249
Cocke County SD
Supt. — See Newport
Parrottsville S 500/K-8
1901 Old Parrottsville Hwy 37843 423-623-1612
Dr. Robert Vick, prin. Fax 623-3332

Parsons, Decatur, Pop. 2,355
Decatur County SD
Supt. — See Decaturville
Decatur County MS 500/5-8
2740 Highway 641 S 38363 731-847-6510
Chris Villaflor, prin. Fax 847-6572
Parsons ES 400/K-4
182 W 4th St 38363 731-847-7317
Renae Lomax, prin. Fax 847-6669

Pegram, Cheatham, Pop. 2,071
Cheatham County SD
Supt. — See Ashland City
Pegram ES 300/PK-4
4552 Dogwood Ln 37143 615-646-6637
Detra Emery, prin. Fax 662-4736

Pelham, Grundy, Pop. 397
Grundy County SD
Supt. — See Altamont
Pelham ES 100/PK-8
PO Box 37 37366 931-467-3276
Jamie Hill, prin. Fax 467-2262

Petersburg, Lincoln, Pop. 535
Lincoln County SD
Supt. — See Fayetteville
Unity S 400/PK-8
259 Boonshill Petersburg Rd 37144 931-433-9018
Emily Pierce, prin. Fax 732-4374

Philadelphia, Loudon, Pop. 649
Loudon County SD
Supt. — See Loudon
Philadelphia ES 600/PK-8
300 Spring St 37846 865-458-6801
Marvin Feezell, prin. Fax 458-6805

Pigeon Forge, Sevier, Pop. 5,787
Sevier County SD
Supt. — See Sevierville
Pigeon Forge MS 600/5-8
300 Wears Valley Rd 37863 865-453-2401
Scott Hensley, prin. Fax 453-0799

Pikeville, Bledsoe, Pop. 1,590
Bledsoe County SD 2,000/PK-12
478 Spring St 37367 423-447-2914
Jennifer Terry, dir. Fax 447-7135
www.bledsoecountyschools.org
Bledsoe County MS 400/6-8
PO Box 147 37367 423-447-3212
Chris Cagle, prin. Fax 447-3085
Pikeville ES 400/PK-5
41068 SR 30 37367 423-447-2457
James Ellis, prin. Fax 447-6230
Rigsby ES 200/K-5
8231 New Harmony Rd 37367 423-447-2891
Carl Brown, prin. Fax 447-7369
Wheeler ES 300/PK-5
33073 SR 30 37367 423-881-3394
Candi Kempton, prin. Fax 881-3867

Piney Flats, Sullivan
Sullivan County SD
Supt. — See Blountville
Hughes S 500/K-8
240 N Austin Springs Rd 37686 423-354-1835
Randy Gentry, prin. Fax 354-1841

Pinson, Madison
Jackson-Madison County SD
Supt. — See Jackson
South ES 300/PK-5
570 Stone Rd 38366 731-988-5413
Scott Nelson, prin. Fax 988-5463

Pioneer, Campbell
Campbell County SD
Supt. — See Jacksboro

Elk Valley ES 100/K-8
6691 Highway 297 37847 423-784-6866
Nancy Lay, prin. Fax 784-5826

Pleasant Hill, Cumberland, Pop. 559
Cumberland County SD
Supt. — See Crossville
Pleasant Hill S 600/PK-8
PO Box 10 38578 931-277-3677
Missy Carter, prin. Fax 277-3880

Pleasant View, Cheatham, Pop. 4,108
Cheatham County SD
Supt. — See Ashland City
Pleasant View ES 500/K-4
2625 Church St 37146 615-746-5035
Keith Miller, prin. Fax 746-8215
Sycamore MS 800/5-8
1025 Old Clarksville Pike 37146 615-746-8852
Robyn Miller, prin. Fax 746-5770

Pleasant View Christian S 300/PK-12
160 Hicks Edgen Rd 37146 615-746-8555

Portland, Sumner, Pop. 11,308
Sumner County SD
Supt. — See Gallatin
Portland East MS 400/6-8
604 S Broadway St 37148 615-325-4146
Jackson Howell, prin. Fax 325-5320
Portland Gateview ES 600/K-5
1098 Gateview Dr 37148 615-323-7638
Timberly Denning, prin. Fax 323-0273
Portland West MS 500/6-8
110 Nolan Private Dr 37148 615-325-8066
Cam MacLean, prin. Fax 325-4073
Riggs ES 200/K-5
211 Fountain Head Rd 37148 615-325-2391
Terry Darnell, prin. Fax 325-5315
Watt Hardison ES 500/K-5
300 Gibson St 37148 615-325-3233
Phyllis Gilman, prin. Fax 325-5305
Wiseman ES 500/K-5
922 S Broadway St 37148 615-325-8580
Sabrina McClard, prin. Fax 325-8581

Highland ES 100/PK-8
234 Highland Circle Dr 37148 615-325-3184
Portland Montessori Academy 50/PK-8
613 College St 37148 615-323-1065

Powell, Knox, Pop. 7,534
Anderson County SD
Supt. — See Clinton
Claxton ES 600/PK-5
2218 Clinton Hwy 37849 865-945-2222
Jennifer Coleman, prin. Fax 945-3797

Knox County SD
Supt. — See Knoxville
Copper Ridge ES 500/K-5
2502 E Brushy Valley Rd 37849 865-938-7002
Dr. Jennifer Atkins, prin. Fax 947-4336
Powell ES 900/K-5
1711 Spring St 37849 865-938-2048
Denise Blefko, prin. Fax 947-1805
Powell MS 1,000/6-8
3329 W Emory Rd 37849 865-938-9008
Christine Oehler, prin. Fax 947-4357

First Baptist Academy 300/PK-12
7706 Ewing Rd 37849 865-947-8503
Matt Mercer, hdmstr. Fax 961-6525
Temple Baptist Academy 200/PK-12
1700 W Beaver Creek Dr 37849 865-938-8181
Dr. Jeff Jones, prin. Fax 938-8147

Pulaski, Giles, Pop. 7,654
Giles County SD 4,000/PK-12
270 Richland Dr 38478 931-363-4558
Phillip Wright, dir. Fax 363-8975
www.giles-lea.giles.k12.tn.us
Bridgeforth MS 400/6-8
1051 Bridgeforth Cir 38478 931-363-7526
Cathie White, prin. Fax 424-7021
Pulaski ES 500/PK-2
606 S Cedar Ln 38478 931-363-5233
Mary Britton, prin. Fax 424-7027
Southside ES 400/3-5
707 S Cedar Ln 38478 931-424-7005
Carmen Hayes, prin. Fax 424-1644
Other Schools – See Elkton, Lynnville, Minor Hill

Puryear, Henry, Pop. 660
Henry County SD
Supt. — See Paris
Harrelson S 600/PK-8
143 Puryear Country Club Rd 38251 731-247-3152
Maria Cox, prin. Fax 247-3154

Ramer, McNairy, Pop. 316
McNairy County SD
Supt. — See Selmer
Ramer S 400/K-8
PO Box 8 38367 731-645-3996
Dr. Sondra Kiser, prin. Fax 645-3990

Readyville, Cannon
Cannon County SD
Supt. — See Woodbury
West Side S 200/PK-8
3714 Murfreesboro Rd 37149 615-563-4482
Karen King, prin. Fax 563-1911

Rutherford County SD
Supt. — See Murfreesboro
Kittrell ES 300/PK-5
7001 Old Woodbury Pike 37149 615-893-7604
Ynetia Avant, prin. Fax 849-2187

Reagan, Henderson
Henderson County SD
Supt. — See Lexington
South Side ES 300/PK-8
29855 Highway 104 S 38368 731-549-3718
Marty Johnson, prin. Fax 549-2431

Red Boiling Springs, Macon, Pop. 1,106
Clay County SD
Supt. — See Celina
Hermitage Springs S 200/PK-8
17580 Clay County Hwy 37150 615-699-2414
John Denton, prin. Fax 699-2410

Macon County SD
Supt. — See Lafayette
Red Boiling Springs ES 300/PK-5
415 Hillcrest Dr 37150 615-699-2222
Michael Owens, prin. Fax 699-3445

Riceville, McMinn, Pop. 659
McMinn County SD
Supt. — See Athens
Riceville S 700/PK-8
3592 Highway 11 S 37370 423-462-2294
David McDonald, prin. Fax 462-2534

Rickman, Overton, Pop. 750
Overton County SD
Supt. — See Livingston
Rickman S 700/PK-8
631 Rickman Monterey Hwy 38580 931-498-2825
Donnie Holman, prin. Fax 498-2095

Ridgely, Lake, Pop. 1,772
Lake County SD
Supt. — See Tiptonville
Kendall S 400/PK-8
200 N College St 38080 731-264-5586
Kathy Todd, prin. Fax 264-5587

Ridgetop, Robertson, Pop. 1,852
Robertson County SD
Supt. — See Springfield
Watauga ES 400/K-5
PO Box 190 37152 615-859-5252
Kelley Armstrong, prin. Fax 859-5933

Ridgetop Adventist S 50/PK-8
PO Box 829 37152 615-859-0259
Aaron Raines, prin.

Ripley, Lauderdale, Pop. 8,322
Lauderdale County SD 4,600/PK-12
321 Armory St 38063 731-635-2941
Shawn Kimble, supt. Fax 635-7985
www.lced.net
Ripley ES 700/3-5
100 Highway 19 E 38063 731-221-3066
Teresa White, prin. Fax 221-3055
Ripley MS 700/6-8
309 Charles Griggs St 38063 731-635-1391
Cindy Anderson, prin. Fax 635-0028
Ripley PS 900/PK-2
225 Volz Ave 38063 731-635-0691
Lillie Treadway, prin. Fax 635-0312
Other Schools – See Halls

Roan Mountain, Carter, Pop. 1,355
Carter County SD
Supt. — See Elizabethton
Cloudland ES 400/PK-6
8540 Highway 19 E 37687 423-772-5310
Becky Raulston, prin. Fax 772-5311

Robbins, Scott, Pop. 287
Scott County SD
Supt. — See Huntsville
Robbins S 300/PK-8
355 School House Rd 37852 423-627-4354
Robbin Newman, prin. Fax 627-2200

Rockford, Blount, Pop. 840
Blount County SD
Supt. — See Maryville
Rockford ES 400/PK-5
3728 Williams Mill Rd 37853 865-982-1415
Chad Tipton, prin. Fax 681-1788

Rock Island, Warren
Warren County SD
Supt. — See Mc Minnville
Eastside S 500/PK-8
2121 Old Rock Island Rd 38581 931-686-2392
Dr. Carol Prater, prin. Fax 686-2118

Rockvale, Rutherford
Rutherford County SD
Supt. — See Murfreesboro
Rockvale ES 900/PK-5
6550 Highway 99 37153 615-904-3881
Dayna Nichols, prin. Fax 274-2761
Rockvale MS 1,000/6-8
6543 Highway 99 37153 615-904-6745
Fred Barlow, prin. Fax 904-6746

Rockwood, Roane, Pop. 5,395
Cumberland County SD
Supt. — See Crossville
Pine View S 200/PK-8
349 Daysville Rd 37854 865-354-1986
Dr. Sharon Daniels, prin. Fax 354-1922

Roane County SD
Supt. — See Kingston
Ridge View ES 700/PK-5
625 Pumphouse Rd 37854 865-354-2111
Angela Spurgeon, prin. Fax 354-5150
Rockwood MS 400/6-8
434 W Rockwood St 37854 865-354-0931
Amanda Evans, prin. Fax 354-5160

Rogersville, Hawkins, Pop. 4,364
Hawkins County SD 7,300/PK-12
200 N Depot St 37857 423-272-7629
Steve Starnes, dir. Fax 272-2207
www.hck12.net
Hawkins ES 300/3-5
1121 E Main St 37857 423-272-2632
Barry Bellamy, prin. Fax 272-9066
Keplar ES 100/K-5
1914 Burem Rd 37857 423-272-9390
Sandy Williams, prin. Fax 921-9929
Rogers PS 400/PK-2
2001 E Main St 37857 423-272-9110
Lori Allen, prin. Fax 272-7211
Rogersville MS 500/6-8
958 E Mckinney Ave 37857 423-272-7603
Greg Simpson, prin. Fax 272-0185
Other Schools – See Bulls Gap, Church Hill, Mooresburg, Mount Carmel, Sneedville, Surgoinsville

Rogersville CSD 700/PK-8
116 W Broadway St 37857 423-272-7651
Rebecca Isaacs, dir. Fax 272-7790
www.rcschool.net
Rogersville S 700/PK-8
116 W Broadway St 37857 423-272-7651
Rhonda Winstead, prin. Fax 272-7790

Rossville, Fayette, Pop. 656

Rossville Christian Academy 300/K-12
PO Box 369 38066 901-853-0200

Russellville, Hamblen
Hamblen County SD
Supt. — See Morristown
Russellville ES 600/K-5
5655 Old Russellville Pike 37860 423-586-6560
Samuel Taylor, prin. Fax 585-3796

Rutherford, Gibson, Pop. 1,144
Gibson County Special SD
Supt. — See Dyer
Rutherford S 300/K-8
PO Box 70 38369 731-483-4006
Jody Hinson, prin. Fax 665-6638

Rutledge, Grainger, Pop. 1,113
Grainger County SD 3,700/PK-12
PO Box 38 37861 865-828-3611
Edwin Jarnagin, dir. Fax 828-4357
www.grainger.k12.tn.us/
Joppa ES 500/PK-6
4745 Rutledge Pike 37861 865-828-5721
Pam Roach, prin. Fax 828-5603
Rutledge ES 400/2-6
7480 Rutledge Pike 37861 865-828-5530
Tim Collins, prin. Fax 828-5797
Rutledge MS 500/7-8
140 Pioneer Dr 37861 865-828-3366
Lynn Jones, prin. Fax 828-3364
Rutledge PS 200/PK-1
470 Water St 37861 865-828-5614
Dr. April Sell, prin. Fax 828-5849
Other Schools – See Bean Station, Washburn

Sale Creek, Hamilton, Pop. 2,811
Hamilton County SD
Supt. — See Chattanooga
North Hamilton County ES 400/K-5
601 Industrial Blvd 37373 423-332-8848
Jacqueline Hauth, prin. Fax 332-8850

Santa Fe, Maury
Maury County SD
Supt. — See Columbia
Santa Fe S 700/PK-12
2629 Santa Fe Pike 38482 931-682-2172
Leigh Ann Willey, prin. Fax 682-2606

Savannah, Hardin, Pop. 6,820
Hardin County SD 3,700/PK-12
155 Guinn St 38372 731-925-3943
Michael Davis, dir. Fax 925-7313
www.hardincountyschools.net
East Hardin ES 400/PK-5
100 Freewill Ln 38372 731-926-4620
Todd Buczynski, prin. Fax 926-4621
Hardin County MS 700/6-8
299 Lacefield Dr 38372 731-925-9037
Dr. Duane Eliff, prin. Fax 925-0253
Northside ES 500/PK-5
1450 Main St E 38372 731-926-4520
Gary Gober, prin. Fax 926-4521
Parris South ES 500/PK-5
169 Lacefield Dr 38372 731-925-2480
Todd Harrison, prin. Fax 925-4022
Other Schools – See Adamsville, Counce

Harbert Hills Academy 100/1-12
3575 Lonesome Pine Rd 38372 731-925-3098
Savannah Christian Academy 100/PK-8
3514 Cravens Rd 38372 731-926-1504
Brian Reid, prin. Fax 925-2605

Scotts Hill, Decatur, Pop. 979
Henderson County SD
Supt. — See Lexington
Scotts Hill ES 300/PK-8
1 Highway 114 S 38374 731-549-3145
Brian Lane, prin. Fax 549-2430

Selmer, McNairy, Pop. 4,308
McNairy County SD 4,200/K-12
530 Mulberry Ave 38375 731-645-3267
Wayne Henry, dir. Fax 645-8085
www.mcnairy.org
Selmer ES 500/K-4
533 E Poplar Ave 38375 731-645-3131
Pamela Simon, prin. Fax 645-9756
Selmer MS 400/5-8
635 E Poplar Ave 38375 731-645-7977
Dr. Brenda Armstrong, prin. Fax 645-6377
Other Schools – See Adamsville, Bethel Springs, Michie, Ramer

Sevierville, Sevier, Pop. 14,595
Sevier County SD 14,900/PK-12
226 Cedar St 37862 865-453-4671
Dr. Jack Parton, supt. Fax 522-1497
www.sevier.org
Boyds Creek S 600/K-8
1729 Indian Warpath Rd 37876 865-774-8285
Kim Grosser, prin. Fax 429-2083
Catlettsburg S 600/K-6
1409 Catlettsburg Rd 37876 865-428-2171
Kim Conrad, prin. Fax 428-2464
Catons Chapel S 500/PK-8
3135 Catons Chapel Rd 37876 865-453-2132
Bill Hatcher, prin. Fax 453-2693
New Center S 700/K-8
2701 Old Newport Hwy 37876 865-453-2123
Dustin Huffaker, prin. Fax 453-7321
Pigeon Forge PS 700/PK-4
1766 Waldens Creek Rd 37862 865-428-3016
Dr. Connie Cottongim, prin. Fax 428-3053
Sevierville IS 700/3-5
416 High St 37862 865-428-8925
Terri Dodge, prin. Fax 428-7846
Sevierville MS 600/6-8
520 High St 37862 865-453-0311
Donna Rolen, prin. Fax 428-2316
Sevierville PS 800/K-2
1146 Blanton Dr 37862 865-453-2824
Tammy Valentine, prin. Fax 428-5443
Wearwood S 200/K-8
3150 Wearwood Dr 37862 865-453-2252
Jon Manning, prin. Fax 453-8943
Other Schools – See Cosby, Gatlinburg, Kodak, Pigeon Forge, Seymour

Sewanee, Franklin, Pop. 2,295
Franklin County SD
Supt. — See Winchester
Sewanee ES 200/PK-5
PO Box 696 37375 931-598-5951
Kim Tucker, prin. Fax 598-0943

Seymour, Sevier, Pop. 10,811
Blount County SD
Supt. — See Maryville
Prospect ES 400/K-5
1535 Burnett Station Rd 37865 865-980-1565
John Parham, prin. Fax 980-1570

Sevier County SD
Supt. — See Sevierville
Seymour IS 600/3-5
212 N Pitner Rd 37865 865-609-0030
Peggy Oakes, prin. Fax 609-2258
Seymour MS 700/6-8
737 Boyds Creek Hwy 37865 865-579-0730
David Loy, prin. Fax 579-0905
Seymour PS 500/K-2
717 Boyds Creek Hwy 37865 865-577-5970
Jannese Moore, prin. Fax 573-9236

King's Academy 500/PK-12
202 Smothers Rd 37865 865-573-8321
Dr. Walter Grubb, hdmstr. Fax 573-8323
Seymour Community Christian S 100/PK-12
PO Box 849 37865 865-577-5500

Shady Valley, Johnson
Johnson County SD
Supt. — See Mountain City
Shady Valley ES 100/PK-6
423 Highway 133 37688 423-739-2422
Dana Smith, prin. Fax 739-9278

Sharon, Weakley, Pop. 934
Weakley County SD
Supt. — See Dresden
Sharon S 200/PK-8
254 N Woodlawn Ave 38255 731-456-2672
Dr. Michelle Clements, prin. Fax 456-2750

Sharps Chapel, Union
Union County SD
Supt. — See Maynardville
Sharps Chapel ES 200/PK-5
1550 Sharps Chapel Rd 37866 865-278-3294
Roger Flatford, prin. Fax 278-3993

Shelbyville, Bedford, Pop. 19,855
Bedford County SD 8,300/PK-12
500 Madison St 37160 931-684-3284
Don Embry, supt. Fax 684-1133
www.bedfordk12tn.com/
Eakin ES 600/PK-5
1100 Glenoaks Rd 37160 931-684-7852
Dulcie Davis, prin. Fax 684-0553
East Side ES 400/PK-5
421 Elliott St 37160 931-684-7112
Xavier Hamler, prin. Fax 684-7108
Harris MS 1,000/6-8
570 Eagle Blvd 37160 931-684-5195
Neil Watson, prin. Fax 685-9455
Learning Way ES 600/K-5
200 Learning Way Dr 37160 931-685-1425
Kathy Reed, prin. Fax 684-6165
Liberty ES 700/K-8
500 Snell Rd 37160 931-684-7809
Cort Huffman, prin. Fax 685-0627
Southside ES 400/PK-5
903 S Cannon Blvd 37160 931-684-7545
Reita Vaughn, prin. Fax 685-0912
Thomas Magnet S 400/K-5
515 Tate Ave 37160 931-684-6818
LeEllen Carter, prin. Fax 684-7174
Other Schools – See Unionville, Wartrace

Signal Mountain, Hamilton, Pop. 7,474
Hamilton County SD
Supt. — See Chattanooga
Nolan ES 700/K-5
4435 Shackleford Ridge Rd 37377 423-886-0898
Shane Harwood, prin. Fax 886-0897
Thrasher ES 600/K-5
1301 James Blvd 37377 423-886-0882
Jeff Paulson, prin. Fax 886-0888

Signal Mountain Christian S 100/K-5
808 Key Hulse Rd 37377 423-886-1115
Danette Kelley, prin. Fax 424-4144

Smithville, DeKalb, Pop. 4,481
DeKalb County SD 3,000/PK-12
110 S Public Sq 37166 615-597-4084
Patrick Cripps, supt. Fax 597-6326
www.dekalbschools.net
DeKalb MS 600/6-8
1132 W Broad St 37166 615-597-7987
Amanda Dakas, prin. Fax 597-2640
Northside ES 600/2-5
400 N Congress Blvd 37166 615-597-1575
Karen Knowles, prin. Fax 597-1585
Smithville ES 600/PK-2
221 E Bryant St 37166 615-597-4415
Dr. Julie Vincent, prin. Fax 597-7547
Other Schools – See Liberty

Smyrna, Rutherford, Pop. 39,070
Rutherford County SD
Supt. — See Murfreesboro
Cedar Grove ES 900/PK-5
354 Chaney Rd 37167 615-904-3777
Paige Jorge, prin. Fax 904-3760
Colemon ES 500/PK-5
1098 Espey Dr 37167 615-904-6740
Ann Haley, prin. Fax 459-0936
Francis Arts Academy 800/K-8
221 Todd Ln 37167 615-904-6715
Jeff McCann, prin. Fax 459-7710
Rock Springs MS 1,000/6-8
3301 Rock Springs Rd 37167 615-904-3825
Steven Wayne, prin. Fax 904-3826
Rocky Fork MS 6-8
100 Thunderstorm Ln 37167 615-904-6780
Dr. Jimmy Sullivan, prin. Fax 904-6781
Smyrna ES 800/PK-5
1001 Sam Davis Rd 37167 615-904-6725
Amy Patton, prin. Fax 904-6726
Smyrna MS 1,000/6-8
712 Hazelwood Dr 37167 615-904-3845
Steve Luker, prin. Fax 904-3846
Smyrna PS 600/PK 5
200 Walnut St 37167 615-904-6720
Felicia James, prin. Fax 355-5609
Stewartsboro ES 900/PK-5
10479 Old Nashville Hwy 37167 615-904-6705
Gary Seymore, prin. Fax 904-6706
Stewarts Creek ES 800/K-5
200 Red Hawk Blvd 37167 615-904-6750
Ginger Tucker, prin. Fax 904-6751
Stewarts Creek MS 900/6-8
400 Red Hawk Blvd 37167 615-904-6700
Letoni Murry, prin. Fax 904-6701
Youree ES 800/K-5
250 Todd Ln 37167 615-904-6775
Scott Bolden, prin. Fax 904-6776

Lancaster Christian Academy 500/PK-12
150 Soccer Way 37167 615-223-0451

Sneedville, Hancock, Pop. 1,364
Hancock County SD 1,000/K-12
PO Box 629 37869 423-733-2591
Anthony Seal, dir. Fax 733-8757
www.hancockcountyschools.com
Hancock County ES 500/K-5
373 Newmans Ridge Rd 37869 423-733-2534
Angela Kinsler, prin. Fax 733-9820

Hawkins County SD
Supt. — See Rogersville
Clinch S 100/K-12
1540 Clinch Valley Rd 37869 423-272-3202
George Barton, prin. Fax 272-3207

Soddy Daisy, Hamilton, Pop. 12,577
Hamilton County SD
Supt. — See Chattanooga
Allen ES 600/PK-5
9811 Dallas Hollow Rd 37379 423-843-4713
Earlene Weeks, prin. Fax 843-4714
Daisy ES 500/PK-5
620 Sequoyah Rd 37379 423-332-8815
Samantha Walter, prin. Fax 332-8816
Soddy Daisy MS 500/6-8
200 Turner Rd 37379 423-332-8800
Jane Reynolds, prin. Fax 332-8810
Soddy ES 400/PK-5
260 School St 37379 423-332-8823
Kimberly Roden, prin. Fax 332-8843

Somerville, Fayette, Pop. 3,069
Fayette County SD 3,100/PK-12
PO Box 9 38068 901-465-5260
Dr. Marlon King, dir. Fax 466-0078
www.fcsk12.net
Buckley Carpenter ES 200/PK-5
12580 S Main St 38068 901-235-4242
Constance Wright, prin. Fax 235-4244
East JHS 400/6-8
400 Leach Dr 38068 901-465-3151
Shalonda Franklin, prin. Fax 465-5084
Other Schools – See Moscow, Oakland, Williston

Fayette Academy 700/PK-12
PO Box 130 38068 901-465-3241
Courtney Burnette, head sch Fax 465-2141

South Fulton, Obion, Pop. 2,320
Obion County SD
Supt. — See Union City
South Fulton ES 300/PK-5
209 John C Jones Pkwy 38257 731-479-2304
Don Capps, prin. Fax 479-1447

South Pittsburg, Marion, Pop. 2,934
Marion County SD
Supt. — See Jasper
South Pittsburg ES 500/PK-6
310 Elm Ave 37380 423-837-6117
Candace Powers, prin. Fax 837-6168

Richard CSD 300/PK-12
1620 Hamilton Ave 37380 423-837-7282
Cindy Blevins, dir. Fax 837-0641
www.richardhardy.org
Hardy Memorial S 300/PK-12
1620 Hamilton Ave 37380 423-837-7282
Beth Webb, prin. Fax 837-0641

Sparta, White, Pop. 4,841
White County SD 4,100/PK-12
136 Baker St 38583 931-836-2229
Kurt Dronebarger, dir. Fax 836-8128
www.whitecoschools.net
Bon De Croft ES 200/PK-5
8095 Crossville Hwy 38583 931-935-2359
Sara Cope, prin. Fax 935-2399
Cassville ES 200/PK-5
261 Will Thompson Rd 38583 931-761-2277
Juli Johnson, prin. Fax 761-5102
Findlay ES 500/PK-5
576 Hale St 38583 931-738-2412
Rebecca Ryan, prin. Fax 738-3007
Northfield ES 300/PK-5
570 S Bunker Hill Rd 38583 931-761-7979
Stacy Hinds, prin. Fax 761-7969
White County MS 900/6-8
300 Turn Table Rd 38583 931-738-9238
Farrah Griffith, prin. Fax 738-9271
Woodland Park ES 500/PK-5
88 Panther Dr 38583 931-738-3505
Dr. Larry Thompson, prin. Fax 738-5071
Other Schools – See Doyle, Walling

Speedwell, Claiborne
Claiborne County SD
Supt. — See Tazewell
Powell Valley S 400/K-8
255 Powell Valley School Ln 37870 423-869-4659
Melissa Edwards, prin. Fax 869-8343

Spencer, Van Buren, Pop. 1,580
Van Buren County SD 800/PK-12
PO Box 98 38585 931-946-2242
Cheryl Cole, dir. Fax 946-2858
www.vanburenschools.org
Spencer ES 400/PK-5
311 Sparta St 38585 931-946-2171
Laura Duncan, prin. Fax 946-7113

Spring City, Rhea, Pop. 1,936
Rhea County SD
Supt. — See Dayton
Spring City ES 700/PK-5
270 E Jackson Ave 37381 423-365-6451
Tamaria Boles, prin. Fax 365-7075
Spring City MS 300/6-8
751 Wassom Memorial Hwy 37381 423-365-9105
Lesia Garrison, prin. Fax 365-9102

Springfield, Robertson, Pop. 16,188
Robertson County SD 11,500/PK-12
800 MS Couts Blvd Ste 2 37172 615-384-5588
Fax 384-9749
www.rcstn.net
Bransford ES 100/PK-PK
700 Bransford Dr 37172 615-384-4313
Harold Barbee, prin. Fax 384-3213
Cheatham Park ES 200/3-5
301 Locust St 37172 615-384-0232
Amy West, prin. Fax 382-2305
Coopertown ES 400/K-3
3746 Highway 49 W 37172 615-384-7642
Tiffany Hyde, prin. Fax 384-1176
Coopertown MS 500/4-8
3820 Highway 49 W 37172 615-382-4166
Stacie Batson, prin. Fax 382-4171
Crestview ES 800/PK-5
1160 Jaden Gavin Dr 37172 615-382-2222
Lori Smith, admin.
Krisle ES 600/PK-5
6712 Highway 49 E 37172 615-384-2596
Angel Wiliams, prin. Fax 384-9022
Springfield MS 600/6-8
715 5th Ave W 37172 615-384-4821
Dr. Grant Bell, prin. Fax 382-7890
Westside ES 200/K-2
309 Alsup Dr 37172 615-384-8495
Michelle Darnell, prin. Fax 384-0230
Other Schools – See Cedar Hill, Cross Plains, Greenbrier, Ridgetop, White House

South Haven Christian S 400/PK-12
112 Academy Dr 37172 615-384-5073
Dr. Steve Blaser, admin. Fax 425-2403

Spring Hill, Maury, Pop. 28,520
Maury County SD
Supt. — See Columbia
Spring Hill ES 600/PK-4
5359 Main St 37174 931-486-2291
Renata Powell, prin. Fax 486-2294
Spring Hill MS 800/5-8
3501 Cleburne Rd 37174 931-451-1531
Shanda Sparrow, prin. Fax 486-3954
Wright ES 600/K-4
4714 Derryberry Ln 37174 931-486-3586
Marisa Massey, prin. Fax 486-3588

Williamson County SD
Supt. — See Franklin
Allendale ES 800/K-5
2100 Prescott Way 37174 615-472-5130
Dr. Cindy Davis, prin. Fax 472-5141
Chapman's Retreat ES 800/PK-5
1000 Secluded Ln 37174 615-472-4300
Carol Garrett, prin. Fax 472-4312
Longview ES 700/K-5
2929 Commonwealth Dr 37174 615-472-5060
Kathy Ball, prin. Fax 472-5071
Spring Station MS 1,100/6-8
1000 Spring Station Dr 37174 615-472-5080
Paula Pulliam, prin. Fax 472-5091

Columbia Academy Spring Hill PK-6
756 Beechcroft Rd 37174 615-486-1002
Nathan Hixson, prin.
Spring Hill Christian Academy 100/PK-7
PO Box 2055 37174 615-435-9476

Strawberry Plains, Jefferson
Jefferson County SD
Supt. — See Dandridge
Rush Strong S 600/PK-8
3081 W Old Andrew Johnson 37871 865-933-5313
Ron Overton, prin. Fax 933-3331

Knox County SD
Supt. — See Knoxville
Carter MS 800/6-8
204 N Carter School Rd 37871 865-933-3426
Thomas Watson, prin. Fax 932-8170

Blue Springs Christian Academy 50/PK-12
3265 Blue Springs Rd 37871 865-932-7603
Don Ingram, admin.

Summertown, Lawrence, Pop. 852
Lawrence County SD
Supt. — See Lawrenceburg
Summertown ES 600/PK-6
319 Corbin St 38483 931-964-3614
Ricky Mabry, prin. Fax 964-4164

Sunbright, Morgan, Pop. 550
Morgan County SD
Supt. — See Wartburg
Sunbright S 600/K-12
PO Box 129 37872 423-628-2244
Ron Treadway, prin. Fax 628-2120

Surgoinsville, Hawkins, Pop. 1,786
Hawkins County SD
Supt. — See Rogersville
Surgoinsville ES 400/K-4
1010 Main St 37873 423-345-2153
Amanda Smith, prin. Fax 345-2154
Surgoinsville MS 300/5-8
1044 Main St 37873 423-345-2252
Dr. Rodney Roberson, prin. Fax 345-3598

Sweetwater, Monroe, Pop. 5,664
Sweetwater CSD 1,600/PK-8
PO Box 231 37874 423-337-7051
Rodney Boruff, supt. Fax 337-7051
www.compurdy.com/scs2/
Brown IS 300/5-6
135 Starrett St 37874 423-337-5905
Heather Henry, prin. Fax 337-0791
Sweetwater ES 300/3-4
301 Broad St 37874 423-337-7062
Brandi Smith, prin. Fax 337-7609
Sweetwater JHS 300/7-8
1013 Cannon Ave 37874 423-337-7336
Jaime Downs, prin. Fax 337-7360
Sweetwater PS 600/PK-2
500 Highway 322 E 37874 423-351-7004
Darrin Nichols, prin. Fax 351-7089

Cross Creek Christian S 200/PK-12
501 Sweetwater-Vonore Rd 37874 423-337-9330
Melissa Whitfield, admin. Fax 337-9335

Taft, Lincoln
Lincoln County SD
Supt. — See Fayetteville
Blanche S 300/PK-8
1649 Ardmore Hwy 38488 931-425-6141
Christy Wright, prin. Fax 425-9160

Talbott, Jefferson
Jefferson County SD
Supt. — See Dandridge
Talbott ES 200/PK-5
848 Talbott Kansas Rd 37877 865-475-2988
Sandi Ramey, prin. Fax 475-8808

Tazewell, Claiborne, Pop. 2,172
Claiborne County SD 4,700/PK-12
PO Box 179 37879 423-626-3543
Dr. Joseph Miller, dir. Fax 626-5945
www.clabornecountyschools.com
Soldiers Memorial MS 500/5-8
1510 Legion St 37879 423-626-3531
Lisa Jessie, prin. Fax 626-2151
Springdale ES 500/PK-6
1915 Highway 25E S 37879 423-626-9142
Jim Shipley, prin. Fax 626-3936
Other Schools – See Clairfield, Harrogate, New Tazewell, Speedwell

Telford, Washington, Pop. 913
Washington County SD
Supt. — See Jonesborough
Grandview S 600/K-8
2891 Highway 11 E 37690 423-257-7400
Rachel Price, prin. Fax 257-7401

Tellico Plains, Monroe, Pop. 866
Monroe County SD
Supt. — See Madisonville

Coker Creek S 100/K-8
130 Ruritan Rd 37385 423-261-2241
Joey Debity, prin. Fax 261-2394
Rural Vale S 300/K-8
395 Daugherty Spring Rd 37385 423-253-3551
Dennis Hicks, prin. Fax 253-2009
Tellico Plains ES 300/K-4
121 Old High School Rd 37385 423-253-2626
Robert Hooper, prin. Fax 253-7962
Tellico Plains JHS 300/5-8
120 Old High School Rd 37385 423-253-2250
Ruthie Hunt, prin. Fax 253-7824

Ten Mile, Roane
Roane County SD
Supt. — See Kingston
Midway MS 200/6-8
104 Dogtown Rd 37880 865-717-5464
Amy Cawood, prin. Fax 376-0948

Tennessee Ridge, Houston, Pop. 1,358
Houston County SD
Supt. — See Erin
Tennessee Ridge ES 300/PK-5
135 School St 37178 931-721-3780
Rob Randolph, prin.

Thompsons Station, Williamson, Pop. 2,172
Williamson County SD
Supt. — See Franklin
Bethesda ES 600/PK-5
4907 Bethesda Rd 37179 615-472-4200
Jill Justus, prin. Fax 472-4211
Heritage ES 700/PK-5
4801 Columbia Pike 37179 615-472-4520
Shannon Robertson, prin. Fax 472-4531
Heritage MS 900/6-8
4803 Columbia Pike 37179 615-472-4540
Dr. Dana Finch, prin. Fax 472-4553

Tiptonville, Lake, Pop. 4,409
Lake County SD 900/PK-12
819 McBride St 38079 731-253-6601
Sherry Darnell, supt. Fax 253-7111
www.lcfalcons.net
Newton ES 300/PK-5
819 Church St 38079 731-253-7253
Gamble Snyder, prin. Fax 253-7178
Other Schools – See Ridgely

Toone, Hardeman, Pop. 360
Hardeman County SD
Supt. — See Bolivar
Toone S 300/PK-8
160 Neely St 38381 731-658-5606
Chris Cranford, prin. Fax 658-9880

Townsend, Blount, Pop. 436
Blount County SD
Supt. — See Maryville
Townsend ES 100/K-5
140 Tiger Dr 37882 865-980-1202
Steve Stout, prin. Fax 980-1205

Tracy City, Grundy, Pop. 1,468
Grundy County SD
Supt. — See Altamont
Tracy City ES 400/PK-8
276 3rd St 37387 931-592-5741
Glenda Dykes, prin. Fax 592-5750

Trenton, Gibson, Pop. 4,197
Gibson County Special SD
Supt. — See Dyer
Spring Hill S 100/K-8
84 State Route 188 38382 731-483-4489
Jenifer Clark, prin. Fax 559-4337

Trenton Special SD 1,400/PK-12
201 W 10th St 38382 731-855-1191
Sandra Harper, supt. Fax 855-1414
www.trentonssd.org
Trenton ES 600/PK-4
811 S College St 38382 731-855-0971
Cortnee Wilkes, prin. Fax 855-2732
Trenton Rosenwald MS 400/5-8
2065 US Highway 45 Byp S 38382 731-855-2422
Paul Pillow, prin. Fax 855-1826

Trezevant, Carroll, Pop. 849
West Carroll Special SD
Supt. — See Atwood
West Carroll ES 300/3-6
PO Box 278 38258 731-669-3831
Molly Ashley, prin. Fax 669-3173

Trimble, Dyer, Pop. 623
Dyer County SD
Supt. — See Dyersburg
Trimble ES 200/PK-5
256 College St 38259 731-297-5512
Cindy Hutching, prin. Fax 297-5514

Troy, Obion, Pop. 1,363
Obion County SD
Supt. — See Union City
Hillcrest ES 600/PK-8
605 S Main St 38260 731-536-4222
Patresa Rogers, prin. Fax 536-4609

Tullahoma, Coffee, Pop. 18,247
Coffee County SD
Supt. — See Manchester
Hickerson ES 200/PK-5
5017 Old Manchester Hwy 37388 931-455-9576
Jimmy Anderson, prin. Fax 455-3758

Franklin County SD
Supt. — See Winchester
North Lake ES 300/PK-5
10626 Old Tullahoma Rd 37388 931-455-6239
George Butler, prin. Fax 455-6273

Tullahoma CSD 3,500/PK-12
510 S Jackson St 37388 931-454-2600
Dr. Dan Lawson, supt. Fax 454-2642
www.tcsedu.net
Bel Aire ES 400/K-5
500 Stone Blvd 37388 931-454-2610
April Norris, prin. Fax 454-2656
East Lincoln ES 600/PK-5
700 E Lincoln St 37388 931-454-2612
Scott Hargrove, prin. Fax 454-2609
East MS 400/6-8
908 Country Club Dr 37388 931-454-2632
Dr. Charles Lawson, prin. Fax 454-2660
Farrar ES 300/K-5
215 Westside Dr 37388 931-454-2608
Debbie Edens, prin. Fax 454-2658
Lee ES 400/K-5
313 Layne St 37388 931-454-2637
Dr. Woody Dillehay, prin. Fax 454-2649
West MS 400/6-8
90 Hermitage Dr 37388 931-454-2605
Dr. Mickey Shuran, prin. Fax 454-2661

Tullahoma SDA Christian S 50/1-8
231 Turkey Creek Dr 37388 931-455-1924

Unicoi, Unicoi, Pop. 3,607
Unicoi County SD
Supt. — See Erwin
Unicoi ES 300/PK-5
404 Massachusetts Ave 37692 423-743-1665
Michael Riddell, prin. Fax 743-1667

Union City, Obion, Pop. 10,735
Obion County SD 3,900/PK-12
1700 N 5th St 38261 731-885-9743
Russell J. Davis, dir. Fax 885-4902
www.obioncountyschools.com
Lake Road S 600/PK-8
1130 E Highway 22 38261 731-885-5304
Linda Crigger, prin. Fax 885-5784
Ridgemont ES 500/PK-8
1285 N Highway 45 W 38261 731-536-5171
Jon Kerr, prin. Fax 536-0664
Other Schools – See Hornbeak, South Fulton, Troy

Union CSD 1,500/PK-12
PO Box 749 38281 731-885-3922
Wesley Kennedy, dir. Fax 885-6033
tornadotouch.net
Union City ES 800/PK-5
1100 S Miles Ave 38261 731-885-1632
Rene Flood, prin. Fax 885-9699
Union City MS 400/6-8
1111 High School Dr 38261 731-885-2901
Lance Morgan, prin. Fax 885-3677

Unionville, Bedford, Pop. 1,363
Bedford County SD
Supt. — See Shelbyville
Community ES 700/PK-5
3480 Highway 41A N 37180 931-685-1417
Whitney Yoes, prin. Fax 294-2444
Community MS 400/6-8
3470 Highway 41A N 37180 931-685-1426
Tony Garrette, prin. Fax 294-5126

Vanleer, Dickson, Pop. 393
Dickson County SD
Supt. — See Dickson
Vanleer ES 300/PK-5
4456 Highway 49 W 37181 615-740-5760
Sue Stringfield, prin. Fax 763-3100

Vonore, Monroe, Pop. 1,458
Monroe County SD
Supt. — See Madisonville
Vonore ES 400/K-4
PO Box 159 37885 423-884-6392
Melissa Moree, prin. Fax 884-6981
Vonore MS 200/5-8
414 Hall St 37885 423-884-2730
Matt Conley, prin. Fax 884-2731

Walland, Blount, Pop. 259
Blount County SD
Supt. — See Maryville
Walland ES 300/K-5
247 E Millers Cove Rd 37886 865-983-2801
Kim Sullivan, prin. Fax 681-6219

Walling, White
White County SD
Supt. — See Sparta
Central View ES 100/K-5
14484 Old Kentucky Rd 38587 931-761-2907
Melea Johnson, prin. Fax 761-2906

Wartburg, Morgan, Pop. 898
Morgan County SD 3,100/K-12
136 Flat Fork Rd 37887 423-346-6214
Dr. Ronald Wilson, supt. Fax 346-6043
mcsed.net/
Central ES 600/K-5
1315 Knoxville Hwy 37887 423-346-6683
Julie Smith, prin. Fax 346-5556
Central MS 300/6-8
146 Liberty Rd 37887 423-346-2800
Dr. Larry Davis, prin. Fax 346-2805
Other Schools – See Coalfield, Oakdale, Oliver Springs, Sunbright

Wartrace, Bedford, Pop. 637
Bedford County SD
Supt. — See Shelbyville
Cascade ES 600/K-5
2998 Fairfield Pike 37183 931-389-0031
Sherry Crawford, prin. Fax 389-0032
Cascade MS 300/6-8
1165 Bell Buckle Wartrace 37183 931-389-9389
David Parker, prin. Fax 389-6223

Washburn, Grainger
Grainger County SD
Supt. — See Rutledge
Washburn S 600/PK-12
7925 Highway 131 37888 865-497-2557
Ginny McElhaney, prin. Fax 497-2934

Watertown, Wilson, Pop. 1,450
Wilson County SD
Supt. — See Lebanon
Watertown ES 700/PK-5
PO Box 127 37184 615-237-3821
Anita Christian, prin. Fax 237-9544
Watertown MS 300/6-8
515 W Main St 37184 615-237-4000
Kayla Price, prin. Fax 237-3643

Waverly, Humphreys, Pop. 4,056
Humphreys County SD 3,000/PK-12
2443 Highway 70 E 37185 931-296-2568
Richard Rawlings, supt. Fax 296-6501
www.hcss.org
Waverly ES 600/PK-3
612 E Main St 37185 931-296-2371
Vivian Spencer, prin. Fax 296-6515
Waverly JHS 500/4-8
520 E Main St 37185 931-296-4514
Andy Daniels, prin. Fax 296-6507
Other Schools – See Mc Ewen, New Johnsonville

Waynesboro, Wayne, Pop. 2,423
Wayne County SD 2,500/PK-12
PO Box 658 38485 931-722-3548
Marlon Davis, supt. Fax 722-7579
www.waynetn.net/
Waynesboro ES 500/PK-4
115 Helton St 38485 931-722-5580
Brad Stooksberry, prin. Fax 722-3006
Waynesboro MS 300/5-8
PO Box 657 38485 931-722-5545
Jason Morris, prin. Fax 722-3953
Other Schools – See Clifton, Collinwood

Westmoreland, Sumner, Pop. 2,182
Macon County SD
Supt. — See Lafayette
Westside ES 300/PK-5
8025 Old Highway 52 37186 615-666-3128
Angela Marshall, prin. Fax 666-6873

Sumner County SD
Supt. — See Gallatin
Westmoreland ES 500/K-5
4178 Hawkins Dr 37186 615-644-2340
Dr. David Stafford, prin. Fax 644-3924
Westmoreland MS 400/6-8
4128 Hawkins Dr 37186 615-644-3003
Danny Robinson, prin. Fax 644-5584

White Bluff, Dickson, Pop. 3,171
Dickson County SD
Supt. — See Dickson
James MS 300/6-8
3030 Trace Creek Rd 37187 615-740-5770
Jan Ford, prin. Fax 797-6401
White Bluff ES 600/PK-5
377 School Rd 37187 615-740-5775
Gail Mosley, prin. Fax 797-6400

White House, Sumner, Pop. 10,123
Robertson County SD
Supt. — See Springfield
White House-Heritage ES 600/3-6
220 West Dr 37188 615-672-4595
Angie Freye, prin. Fax 672-4583
Woodall ES 400/K-2
300 Edenway Dr 37188 615-672-7772
Dinah Maupin, prin. Fax 672-7276

Sumner County SD
Supt. — See Gallatin
White House MS 700/6-8
2020 Highway 31 W 37188 615-672-4379
Mark Mills, prin. Fax 672-6409
Williams ES 700/K-5
115 S Palmers Chapel Rd 37188 615-672-6432
Jeff Wiit, prin. Fax 672-0996

Christian Community Schools 300/PK-12
506 Hester Dr 37188 615-672-6949
Bob Cook, dir. Fax 616-1330

White Pine, Jefferson, Pop. 2,154
Jefferson County SD
Supt. — See Dandridge
White Pine S 900/PK-8
3060 Roy Messer Hwy 37890 865-674-2596
Bill Walker, prin. Fax 674-8383

Whitesburg, Hamblen
Hamblen County SD
Supt. — See Morristown
East Ridge MS 600/6-8
6595 Saint Clair Rd 37891 423-581-3041
James Templin, prin. Fax 585-3765
Whitesburg ES 300/K-5
7859 E Andrew Johnson Hwy 37891 423-235-2547
William Southern, prin. Fax 235-6315

Whites Creek, See Nashville
Metropolitan Nashville SD
Supt. — See Nashville
Green ES 400/PK-4
3921 Lloyd Rd 37189 615-876-5105
Robyn Beard, prin. Fax 333-5667

Edwards Classical Academy K-12
4479 Jackson Rd 37189 615-876-7291
Ryan Boomershine, hdmstr.

Whiteville, Hardeman, Pop. 4,622
Hardeman County SD
Supt. — See Bolivar
Whiteville S 300/PK-8
2510 US Highway 64 38075 731-254-8013
Cedric Crisp, prin. Fax 254-9528

Whitwell, Marion, Pop. 1,684
Marion County SD
Supt. — See Jasper
Whitwell ES 600/PK-4
150 Tiger Trl 37397 423-658-5313
David Smith, prin. Fax 658-0306
Whitwell MS 400/5-8
1 Butterfly Ln 37397 423-658-5635
Kim Headrick, prin. Fax 658-6949

Wildersville, Henderson
Henderson County SD
Supt. — See Lexington
Beaver ES 300/PK-8
19830 Highway 22 N 38388 731-968-2109
Denny McDaniel, prin. Fax 968-9706

Williston, Fayette, Pop. 394
Fayette County SD
Supt. — See Somerville
Southwest ES 300/PK-5
8095 Highway 194 38076 901-465-8317
Dr. Fabre Ford, prin. Fax 466-1981

Winchester, Franklin, Pop. 8,370
Franklin County SD 5,800/PK-12
215 S College St 37398 931-967-0626
Stanley K. Bean, supt. Fax 967-7832
www.fcstn.net
Broadview ES 300/PK-5
4980 Lynchburg Rd 37398 931-967-0132
Sandy Schultz, prin. Fax 967-0292
Clark Memorial ES 600/PK-5
500 N Jefferson St 37398 931-967-2407
David Carson, prin. Fax 967-9655
North MS 700/6-8
2990 Decherd Blvd 37398 931-967-5323
Leah Harrell, prin. Fax 967-1413
Other Schools – See Cowan, Decherd, Estill Springs, Huntland, Sewanee, Tullahoma

Winchester Christian Academy 200/PK-5
PO Box 715 37398 931-967-5466

Winfield, Scott, Pop. 954
Scott County SD
Supt. — See Huntsville
Winfield S 300/PK-8
23366 Scott Hwy 37892 423-569-8288
Sharon Stanley, prin. Fax 569-9835

Woodbury, Cannon, Pop. 2,647
Cannon County SD 2,100/PK-12
301 W Main St Ste 100 37190 615-563-5752
Barbara Parker, supt. Fax 563-2716
www.ccstn.com/
East Side S 100/K-8
5658 McMinnville Hwy 37190 615-563-4196
Connie Foster, prin. Fax 563-6252
Short Mountain S 100/PK-8
5988 Short Mountain Rd 37190 615-563-4418
Robert Pitts, prin. Fax 563-4596
Woodbury Grammar S 500/PK-8
530 W Adams St 37190 615-563-2220
Rick Meacham, prin. Fax 563-6153
Other Schools – See Auburntown, Bradyville, Readyville

Woodbury SDA S 50/1-8
PO Box 290 37190 615-765-5330

Woodlawn, Montgomery
Clarksville-Montgomery County SD
Supt. — See Clarksville
Woodlawn ES 600/K-5
2250 Woodlawn Rd 37191 931-648-5680
Jennifer Silvers, prin. Fax 503-3407

TEXAS

TEXAS EDUCATION AGENCY
1701 Congress Ave, Austin 78701-1494
Telephone 512-463-9734
Fax 512-463-9838
Website tea.texas.gov/

Commissioner of Education Mike Morath

TEXAS BOARD OF EDUCATION
1701 Congress Ave, Austin 78701-1402

Chairperson Donna Bahorich

REGIONAL EDUCATION SERVICE CENTERS (RESC)

Region 1 ESC
Dr. Cornelia Gonzalez, dir. 956-984-6000
1900 W Schunior St, Edinburg Fax 984-7655
www.esc1.net

Region 2 ESC
Dr. Rick Alvarado Ph.D., dir. 361-561-8400
209 N Water St Fax 883-3442
Corpus Christi 78401
www.esc2.net

Region 3 ESC
Charlotte Baker, dir. 361-573-0731
1905 Leary Ln, Victoria 77901 Fax 576-4804
www.esc3.net

Region 4 ESC
Dr. Pam Wells, dir. 713-462-7708
7145 W Tidwell Rd, Houston 77092 Fax 744-6514
www.esc4.net

Region 5 ESC
Dr. Danny Lovett, dir. 409-951-1700
350 Pine St Ste 500 Fax 951-1800
Beaumont 77701
www.esc5.net

Region 6 ESC
Michael Holland, dir. 936-435-8400
3332 Montgomery Rd Fax 435-8484
Huntsville 77340
www.esc6.net

Region 7 ESC
Elizabeth Abernethy, dir. 903-988-6700
1909 N Longview St, Kilgore 75662 Fax 988-6708
www.esc7.net/

Region 8 ESC
Dr. David Fitts, dir. 903-572-8551
4845 US Highway 271 N Fax 575-2611
Pittsburg 75686
www.reg8.net

Region 9 ESC
Wes Pierce, dir. 940-322-6928
301 Loop 11, Wichita Falls 76306 Fax 767-3836
www.esc9.net

Region 10 ESC
Dr. Gordon Taylor, dir. 972-348-1700
400 E Spring Valley Rd Fax 231-3642
Richardson 75081
www.region10.org

Region 11 ESC
Dr. Clyde Steelman, dir. 817-740-3600
1451 S Cherry Ln Fax 740-7600
Fort Worth 76108
www.esc11.net

Region 12 ESC
Dr. Jerry Maze, dir. 254-297-1212
2101 W Loop 340, Waco 76712 Fax 666-0823
www.esc12.net

Region 13 ESC
Rich Elsasser, dir. 512-919-5313
5701 Springdale Rd, Austin 78723 Fax 919-5374
www4.esc13.net

Region 14 ESC
Ronnie Kincaid, dir. 325-675-8600
1850 State Highway 351 Fax 675-8659
Abilene 79601
www.esc14.net/

Region 15 ESC
Casey Callahan, dir. 325-658-6571
PO Box 5199, San Angelo 76902 Fax 655-4823
www.netxv.net

Region 16 ESC
Ray Cogburn, dir. 806-677-5000
5800 Bell St, Amarillo 79109 Fax 677-5001
www.esc16.net

Region 17 ESC
Dr. Kyle Wargo, dir. 806-792-4000
1111 W Loop 289, Lubbock 79416 Fax 792-1523
www.esc17.net/

Region 18 ESC
Dr. Dewitt Smith, dir. 432-563-2380
PO Box 60580, Midland 79711 Fax 567-3290
www.esc18.net

Region 19 ESC
Dr. Armando Aguirre, dir. 915-780-1919
PO Box 971127, El Paso 79997 Fax 780-6537
www.esc19.net/

Region 20 ESC
Dr. Jeff Goldhorn, dir. 210-370-5200
1314 Hines, San Antonio 78208 Fax 370-5750
www.esc20.net

PUBLIC, PRIVATE AND CATHOLIC ELEMENTARY SCHOOLS

Abbott, Hill, Pop. 355

Abbott ISD 300/PK-12
PO Box 226 76621 254-582-3011
Eric Pustejovsky, supt. Fax 582-5430
www.abbottisd.org

Abbott S 300/PK-12
PO Box 226 76621 254-582-3011
Jon Coker, prin. Fax 582-5430

Abernathy, Hale, Pop. 2,787

Abernathy ISD 800/PK-12
505 7th St 79311 806-298-4940
Glen Teal Ed.D., supt. Fax 298-2400
www.abernathyisd.com

Abernathy ES 400/PK-5
505 7th St 79311 806-298-4930
Lela Taubert, prin. Fax 298-2400

Abernathy JHS 200/6-8
505 7th St 79311 806-298-4921
Kelly Carlisle, prin. Fax 298-4775

Abilene, Taylor, Pop. 114,633

Abilene ISD 16,600/PK-12
PO Box 981 79604 325-677-1444
Dr. David Young, supt. Fax 794-1325
www.abileneisd.org

Austin ES 600/K-5
2341 Greenbriar Dr 79605 325-690-3920
Allson Camp, prin. Fax 794-1350

Bassetti ES 600/K-5
5749 US Highway 277 S 79606 325-690-3720
Keri Thornburg, prin. Fax 794-1351

Bonham ES 600/K-5
717 Buccaneer Dr 79605 325-690-3745
Stevanie Jackson, prin. Fax 794-1352

Bowie ES 600/K-5
2034 Jeanette St 79602 325-671-4770
Tina Jones, prin. Fax 794-1353

Clack MS 800/6-8
1610 Corsicana Ave 79605 325-692-1961
Todd Bramwell, prin. Fax 794-1371

Craig MS 1,000/6 8
702 S Judge Ely Blvd 79602 325-794-4100
Joey Gonzales, prin. Fax 794-1385

Dyess ES 600/K-5
402 Delaware Rd 79605 325-690-3795
Mike Newton, prin. Fax 794-1355

Jackson ES 500/K-5
2650 S 32nd St 79605 325-690-3602
Deb Hollingsworth, prin. Fax 794-1357

Johnston ES 600/K-5
3633 N 14th St 79603 325-671-4845
Roger Thomas, prin. Fax 794-1358

Lee ES 400/K-5
1026 N Pioneer Dr 79603 325-671-4895
Andy Blessing, prin. Fax 794-1359

Long Early Learning Center PK-PK
3600 Sherry Ln 79603 325-671-4594
Jennifer Putnam, dir.

Madison MS 900/6-8
3145 Barrow St 79605 325-692-5661
Tina Wyatt, prin. Fax 794-1313

Mann MS 900/6-8
2545 Mimosa Dr 79603 325-672-8493
Kathy Walker, prin. Fax 794-1374

Martinez ES 800/K-5
1200 Merchant St 79603 325-794-4160
Mildred Petty, prin. Fax 794-1356

Ortiz ES 600/K-5
2550 Vogel St 79603 325-671-4945
Debra Stewart, prin. Fax 794-1361

Reagan ES 500/PK-5
5340 Hartford St 79605 325-690-3627
Chris Halifax, prin. Fax 794-1362

Taylor ES 600/K-5
916 E North 13th St 79601 325-671-4970
Lavon Burton, prin. Fax 794-1364

Thomas ES 600/K-5
1240 Lakeside Dr 79602 325-671-4995
Cindy Hay, prin. Fax 794-1365

Ward ES 500/K-5
3750 Paint Brush Dr 79606 325-690-3666
Alison Sims, prin. Fax 794-1366

Wylie ISD 3,800/PK-12
6251 Buffalo Gap Rd 79606 325-692-4353
Joey Light, supt. Fax 695-3438
www.wyliebulldogs.org

Wylie ECC 400/PK-K
6249 Buffalo Gap Rd 79606 325-437-2350
Lisa Salmon, prin. Fax 437-2351

Wylie ES 600/1-2
7650 Hardwick Rd 79606 325-692-6554
Robin McPherson, prin. Fax 695-4645

Wylie IS 600/3-4
3158 Beltway S 79606 325-692-7961
Terry Hagler, prin. Fax 695-4647

Wylie JHS 600/6-8
4010 Beltway S 79606 325-695-1910
Rob Goodenough, prin. Fax 692-5786

Wylie MS, 4134 Beltway S 79606 600/5-6
Phil Boone, prin. 325-695-6870

Abilene Christian S 300/PK-12
2550 N Judge Ely Blvd 79601 325-672-9200
Kirk Wade, pres. Fax 672-1262

Abilene Jr. Academy 50/1-6
2542 E Overland Trl 79605 325-428-8004

St. John's Episcopal S 200/PK-5
1600 Sherman Dr 79605 325-695-8870

Ackerly, Dawson, Pop. 220

Sands Consolidated ISD 200/PK-12
PO Box 218 79713 432-353-4888
Wayne Henderson, supt. Fax 353-4650
sands.esc17.net

Sands S 200/PK-12
PO Box 218 79713 432-353-4888
Lenny Morrow, prin. Fax 353-4650

Addison, Dallas, Pop. 12,782

Dallas ISD
Supt. — See Dallas

Bush ES 700/PK 5
3939 Spring Valley Rd 75001 972-925-1700
Carol Crowling, prin.

Greenhill S 1,300/PK-12
4141 Spring Valley Rd 75001 972-628-5400
Scott Griggs, head sch Fax 404-8217
Trinity Christian Academy 1,500/PK-12
17001 Addison Rd 75001 972-931-8325
David Delph, hdmstr. Fax 931-8923

Adrian, Oldham, Pop. 165
Adrian ISD 100/PK-12
PO Box 189 79001 806-538-6203
Steve Reynolds, supt. Fax 538-6291
www.adrianisd.net
Adrian S 100/PK-12
PO Box 189 79001 806-538-6203
Maritssa Flores, prin. Fax 538-6291

Afton, Dickens
Patton Springs ISD 100/PK-12
PO Box 32 79220 806-689-2220
Bryan White, supt. Fax 249-9600
pattonsprings.net
Patton Springs S 100/PK-12
PO Box 32 79220 806-689-2220
Bryan White, admin. Fax 249-9600

Agua Dulce, Nueces, Pop. 795
Agua Dulce ISD 400/PK-12
PO Box 250 78330 361-998-2542
Wayne Kelly, supt. Fax 998-2816
www.adisd.net
Agua Dulce ES 200/PK-5
PO Box 250 78330 361-998-2335
Nora Lopez, prin. Fax 998-2333

Alamo, Hidalgo, Pop. 18,315
Donna ISD
Supt. — See Donna
Salinas II ES 600/PK-5
333 E Business Highway 83 78516 956-783-1332
San Juanita Franco, prin. Fax 782-9175

Pharr-San Juan-Alamo ISD
Supt. — See Pharr
Alamo MS 700/6-8
1819 W US Highway 83 78516 956-354-2550
Yolanda Gomez, prin. Fax 354-3188
Farias ES 500/PK-5
1100 W Acacia Ave 78516 956-354-2760
Criselda Trevino, prin. Fax 354-3254
Garza ES 600/PK-5
810 El Gato Rd 78516 956-354-2780
Claudia Gonzalez, prin. Fax 354-3262
Guerra ES 600/PK-5
807 State Highway 495 78516 956-354-2810
Graciela Gonzalez, prin. Fax 354-3264
McKeever ES 600/PK-5
1310 Ridge Rd 78516 956-354-2680
Irma Gomez, prin. Fax 354-3240
Murphy MS 1,000/6-8
924 Sioux Rd 78516 956-354-2530
Lizette Longoria, prin. Fax 354-3224
Santos Livas ES 700/PK-5
733 N Alamo Rd 78516 956-354-2840
Sylvia Hernandez, prin. Fax 354-3272

Valley Christian Heritage S 100/PK-12
932 N Alamo Rd 78516 956-787-9743

Alba, Wood, Pop. 497
Alba-Golden ISD 800/PK-12
1373 County Road 2377 75410 903-768-2472
Dwayne Ellis, supt. Fax 768-2593
www.agisd.com
Alba-Golden ES 400/PK-5
1373 County Road 2377 75410 903-768-2472
Kevin Wright, prin. Fax 768-2593

Albany, Shackelford, Pop. 1,992
Albany ISD 500/PK-12
PO Box 2050 76430 325-762-2823
Shane Fields, supt. Fax 762-3876
www.albanyisd.net
Smith ES 300/PK-6
PO Box 2499 76430 325-762-3384
Jonathan Scott, prin. Fax 762-3070

Aledo, Parker, Pop. 2,690
Aledo ISD 4,500/PK-12
1008 Bailey Ranch Rd 76008 817-441-8327
Dr. Derek Citty, supt. Fax 441-5144
aledo.schoolfusion.us
Aledo MS 700/7-8
416 S FM 1187 76008 817-441-5198
Mandy Musselwhite, prin. Fax 441-5133
Coder ES 400/PK-5
12 Vernon Rd 76008 817-441-6095
Amy Sadler, prin. Fax 441-5135
McAnally IS 400/6-6
151 S FM 5 76008 817-441-8347
Zachary Tarrant, prin. Fax 441-5177
Stuard ES 500/K-5
200 Thunder Head Ln 76008 817-441-5103
Ron Shelton, prin. Fax 441-5116
Vandagriff ES 400/K-5
408 S FM 1187 76008 817-441-8771
Stephanie Covington, prin. Fax 441-5150
Other Schools – See Fort Worth, Willow Park

Alice, Jim Wells, Pop. 19,053
Alice ISD 5,400/PK-12
2 Coyote Trl 78332 361-664-0981
Dr. Alma Charles, supt. Fax 660-2113
www.aliceisd.net
Adams MS 800/7-8
901 E 3rd St 78332 361-660-2055
Dr. Judy Holmgreen, prin. Fax 660-2094
Dubose IS 400/5-6
1000 N Cameron St 78332 361-664-7512
Dina Hinojosa, prin. Fax 660-2074
Garcia ES 200/PK-4
3051 Old Kingsville Rd 78332 361-660-2050
Vanessa Snyder, prin. Fax 660-2051
Hillcrest ES 300/PK-4
1400 Morningside Dr 78332 361-660-2095
Monica Morales, prin. Fax 660-2163
Memorial IS 300/5-6
900 W 3rd St 78332 361-660-2080
Kimberly Rodriguez, prin. Fax 660-2081
Noonan ES 500/PK-4
701 W 3rd St 78332 361-664-7591
Melissa Barrington, prin. Fax 660-2024
Saenz ES 500/PK-4
400 Palo Blanco St 78332 361-664-4981
Marina Garza, prin. Fax 660-2167
Salazar ES 300/PK-4
1028 Pierce St 78332 361-664-6263
Lorie Ann Orta, prin. Fax 660-2026
Schallert ES 600/PK-4
1001 Jim Wells Dr 78332 361-664-6361
Dr. Stephanie Ashworth, prin. Fax 660-2169

Alice Christian S 50/K-12
1200 N Stadium Rd 78332 361-668-6636
Sammy Garcia, prin. Fax 668-0840
St. Elizabeth S 200/PK-6
615 E 5th St 78332 361-664-6271
Macaria Gonzalez, prin. Fax 668-4250
St. Joseph S 200/PK-8
311 Dewey Ave 78332 361-664-4642
Mary Sandoval, prin. Fax 664-5511

Allen, Collin, Pop. 82,168
Allen ISD 20,300/PK-12
PO Box 13 75013 972-727-0511
Dr. Scott Niven, supt. Fax 727-0500
www.allenisd.org
Anderson ES 600/K-6
305 N Alder Dr 75002 972-396-6924
Alani Chisum, prin. Fax 396-6929
Boon ES 800/K-6
1050 Comanche Dr 75013 972-747-3331
Tammie James, prin. Fax 727-3335
Boyd ES 700/K-6
800 S Jupiter Rd 75002 972-727-0560
Judith Coffman, prin. Fax 727-0566
Chandler ES 700/K-6
1000 Water Oak Dr 75002 469-467-1400
Cindy Blair, prin. Fax 467-1410
Cheatam ES 600/K-6
1501 Hopewell Dr 75013 972-396-3016
Stephanie Logan, prin. Fax 396-3035
Curtis MS 1,100/7-8
1530 Rivercrest Blvd 75002 972-727-0340
Sonya Pitcock, prin. Fax 727-0345
Ereckson MS 1,100/7-8
450 Tatum Dr 75013 972-747-3308
Leslie Norris, prin. Fax 747-3311
Evans ES 600/K-6
1225 Walnut Springs Dr 75013 972-747-3373
Pam Hale, prin. Fax 747-3374
Ford MS 900/7-8
630 Park Place Dr 75002 972-727-0590
Matt Russell, prin. Fax 727-0596
Green ES 700/K-6
1315 Comanche Dr 75013 972-727-0370
Stacia Butler, prin. Fax 727-0373
Kerr ES 700/K-6
1325 Glendover Dr 75013 214-495-6765
Ardath Streitmatter, prin. Fax 495-6771
Marion ES 800/K-6
1595 Stablerun Dr 75002 214-495-6784
Brooke Cherry, prin. Fax 495-6787
Norton ES 600/PK-6
1120 Newport Dr 75013 972-396-6918
Julie DeLeon, prin. Fax 396-6923
Olson ES 800/PK-6
1751 E Exchange Pkwy 75002 972-562-1800
Amanda Reyes, prin. Fax 562-1835
Preston ES, 2455 Hilliard Dr 75013 K-6
Johnna Walker, prin. 972-908-8780
Reed ES 600/K-6
1200 Rivercrest Blvd 75002 972-727-0580
Susanne Miller, prin. Fax 727-0588
Rountree ES 500/PK-6
800 E Main St 75002 972-727-0550
Lara Utecht, prin. Fax 727-0555
Story ES 600/PK-6
1550 Edelweiss Dr 75002 972-727-0570
Amanda Tabor, prin. Fax 727-0573
Vaughan ES 500/K-6
820 Cottonwood Dr 75002 972-727-0470
Debbie Burt, prin. Fax 727-0579
Other Schools – See Mc Kinney, Parker

Lovejoy ISD 3,700/K-12
259 Country Club Rd 75002 469-742-8000
Ted Moore, supt. Fax 742-8001
www.lovejoyisd.net/
Lovejoy ES 400/K-5
256 Country Club Rd 75002 469-742-8100
Wendy Craft, prin. Fax 742-8101
Other Schools – See Fairview, Lucas

Plano ISD
Supt. — See Plano
Beverly ES 500/K-5
715 Duchess Dr 75013 469-752-0400
Cindy Savant, prin. Fax 752-0401

Montessori School at Starcreek 100/K-6
915 Ridgeview Dr 75013 972-727-2800
Watters Montessori Academy 50/PK-3
1292 Bossy Boots Dr 75013 214-383-9000

Alpine, Brewster, Pop. 5,819
Alpine ISD 1,000/PK-12
704 W Sul Ross Ave 79830 432-837-7700
Becky Watley, supt. Fax 837-7740
www.alpine.esc18.net
Alpine ES 500/PK-4
200 W Avenue A 79830 432-837-7730
Judith Pardo-Alferez, prin. Fax 837-7744
Alpine MS 300/5-8
801 Middle School Dr 79830 432-837-7720
Justin Gonzales, prin. Fax 837-9814

Altair, Colorado
Rice Consolidated ISD 1,200/PK-12
PO Box 338 77412 979-234-3531
Bill Hefner, supt. Fax 234-3409
www.ricecisd.org
Rice JHS 200/6-8
PO Box 338 77412 979-234-3531
John Post, prin. Fax 234-3191
Other Schools – See Eagle Lake, Garwood, Sheridan

Alto, Cherokee, Pop. 1,204
Alto ISD 600/PK-12
244 County Road 2429 75925 936-858-7101
Kerry Birdwell, supt. Fax 858-2101
www.alto.esc7.net/
Alto ES 300/PK-4
236 County Road 2429 75925 936-858-7170
Martha Gresham, prin. Fax 858-4382
Alto MS 200/5-8
240 County Road 2429 75925 936-858-7140
Kelly West, prin. Fax 858-4579

Alton, Hidalgo, Pop. 12,339
La Joya ISD
Supt. — See La Joya
Trevino MS 900/6-8
301 S Inspiration Blvd, 956-323-2810
Jose T. Garcia, prin. Fax 323-2811

Mission Consolidated ISD
Supt. — See Mission
Alton ES 500/PK-5
205 N Chicago St, 956-323-7600
Araceli Escalona, prin. Fax 323-7617
Alton Memorial JHS 900/6-8
521 S Los Ebanos Blvd, 956-323-5000
Sylvia Garcia, prin. Fax 323-5045
Cantu ES 500/PK-5
920 W Main Ave, 956-323-7400
Enrique Alvarez, prin. Fax 323-7415
Cavazos ES 500/PK-5
803 S Los Ebanos Blvd, 956-323-7200
Nelly Flores, prin. Fax 323-7225
Salinas ES 500/PK-5
10820 N Conway Ave, 956-323-6200
Martina Garcia, prin. Fax 323-6219
Waitz ES 700/PK-5
842 W Saint Francis Ave, 956-323-6600
Rubicela Rodriguez, prin. Fax 323-6618

Alvarado, Johnson, Pop. 3,699
Alvarado ISD 3,400/PK-12
PO Box 387 76009 817-783-6800
Dr. Kenneth Estes, supt. Fax 783-3844
www.alvaradoisd.net/
Alvarado ES North 400/PK-3
PO Box 387 76009 817-783-6863
Lou Ann Stephens, prin. Fax 783-6871
Alvarado ES South 400/PK-3
PO Box 387 76009 817-783-6880
Karla Moore, prin. Fax 783-6889
Alvarado IS 800/4-6
PO Box 387 76009 817-783-6825
Tamara Morris, prin. Fax 783-6837
Alvarado JHS 500/7-8
PO Box 387 76009 817-783-6840
Melodye Brooks, prin. Fax 783-6844
Lillian ES 400/PK-3
PO Box 387 76009 817-783-6815
Ricky Lewis, prin. Fax 783-6823

Rooted Life Montessori S 50/PK-3
PO Box 658 76009 817-578-6556

Alvin, Brazoria, Pop. 23,976
Alvin ISD 20,000/PK-12
301 E House St 77511 281-388-1130
Dr. Buck Gilcrease, supt. Fax 388-2719
www.alvinisd.net
Alvin ES 500/3-5
1910 Rosharon Rd 77511 281-585-2511
Tracy Olvera, prin. Fax 331-2217
Alvin JHS 800/6-8
2300 W South St 77511 281-245-2770
Leroy Castro, prin. Fax 331-5926
Alvin PS 600/PK-2
2200 W Park Dr 77511 281-585-2531
Karla Kyling, prin. Fax 331-9888
Disney ES 600/3-5
5000 Mustang Rd 77511 281-585-6234
Dale Tribble, prin. Fax 585-6503
Fairview JHS 900/6-8
2600 County Road 190 77511 281-245-3100
Greg Bingham, prin. Fax 245-3213
Harby JHS 700/6-8
1500 Heights Rd 77511 281-585-6626
Juan Gonzales, prin. Fax 388-2247
Hasse ES K-5
1200 House St 77511 281-585-3397
DeeDee Baker, prin. Fax 331-1190
Hood-Case ES 700/PK-5
1450 Heights Rd 77511 281-585-5786
Donna Reynolds, prin. Fax 388-0692
Passmore ES 700/PK-5
600 Kost Rd 77511 281-585-6696
Rosemary Reed, prin. Fax 331-6697

Stevenson PS 700/PK-2
4715 Mustang Rd 77511 281-585-3349
Dale Tribble, prin. Fax 245-2904
Twain ES 800/PK-5
345 Kendall Crest Dr 77511 281-585-5318
Brenda Vincent, prin. Fax 331-2584
Other Schools – See Manvel, Pearland, Rosharon

Living Stones Christian S 200/PK-12
1407 Victory Ln 77511 281-331-0086
Jessica Sanders, admin. Fax 331-6747

Alvord, Wise, Pop. 1,324
Alvord ISD 700/PK-12
PO Box 70 76225 940-427-5975
Dr. Randy Brown, supt. Fax 427-2313
www.alvordisd.net
Alvord ES 300/PK-5
PO Box 70 76225 940-427-2881
Bridget Williams, prin. Fax 427-2377
Alvord MS 200/6-8
PO Box 70 76225 940-427-5511
Jessica Bull, prin. Fax 427-2461

Amarillo, Potter, Pop. 187,598
Amarillo ISD 32,500/PK-12
7200 W Interstate 40 79106 806-326-1000
Dr. Dana West, supt. Fax 354-4378
www.amaisd.org
Allen 6th Grade Campus 200/6-6
700 N Lincoln St 79107 806-326-3770
Dalea Tatum, prin. Fax 371-5829
Austin MS 800/6-8
1808 Wimberly Rd 79109 806-326-3000
David Manchee, prin. Fax 356-4802
Avondale ES 600/PK-5
1500 S Avondale St 79106 806-326-4000
Randalyn Huyck, prin. Fax 354-4498
Belmar ES 400/PK-5
6342 Adirondack Trl 79106 806-326-4050
Nicki Roush, prin. Fax 354-5081
Bivins ES 500/PK-5
1500 S Fannin St 79102 806-326-4100
Benny Barraza, prin. Fax 371-6133
Bonham MS 800/6-8
5600 SW 49th Ave 79109 806-326-3100
Andrea Pfeifer, prin. Fax 356-4865
Bowie 6th Grade Campus 6-6
2905 Tee Anchor Blvd 79104 806-326-3270
Kim Lackey, prin.
Bowie MS 700/7-8
2901 Tee Anchor Blvd 79104 806-326-3200
JoAnn Ramirez, prin. Fax 371-6016
Carver Academy 400/2-5
1905 NW 12th Ave 79107 806-326-4150
Melody Fox, prin. Fax 371-6081
Carver Early Childhood Academy 400/PK-1
1800 N Travis St 79107 806-326-4200
Mitzi Malcolm, prin. Fax 371-6178
Coronado ES 500/PK-5
3210 Wimberly Rd 79109 806-326-4250
Bria Galt, prin. Fax 356-4821
Crockett MS 900/6-8
4720 Floyd Ave 79106 806-326-3300
Lisa Loan, prin. Fax 356-4873
de Zavala MS 400/5-8
2801 N Coulter St 79124 806-326-3400
Mike Manchee, prin. Fax 354-4286
Eastridge ES 800/PK-5
1314 Evergreen St 79107 806-326-4300
Genie Baca, prin. Fax 381-7333
Emerson ES 600/PK-5
600 N Cleveland St 79107 806-326-4350
Jessica Cardenas, prin. Fax 371-6055
Fannin MS 600/6-8
4627 S Rusk St 79110 806-326-3500
Nathan Culwell, prin. Fax 354-4588
Forest Hill ES 600/PK-5
3515 E Amarillo Blvd 79107 806-326-4400
Bethany Rose, prin. Fax 381-7221
Glenwood ES 400/PK-5
2407 S Houston St 79103 806-326-4450
Holly Holder, prin. Fax 371-5848
Hamlet ES 400/PK-5
705 Sycamore St 79107 806-326-4500
Kym Daniel, prin. Fax 381-7366
Houston MS 800/6-8
815 S Independence St 79106 806-326-3600
Melody Stephenson, prin. Fax 371-5577
Humphrey's Highland ES 700/PK-5
3901 SE 15th Ave 79104 806-326-4550
Lisa Morgan, prin. Fax 371-5822
Lamar ES 300/PK-5
3800 S Lipscomb St 79110 806-326-4600
Ginny Smith, prin. Fax 356-4871
Landergin ES 300/PK-5
3209 S Taylor St 79110 806-326-4650
Ramon Garcia, prin. Fax 371-6034
Lawndale ES 400/PK-5
2215 S Bivins St 79103 806-326-4700
Bama Coward, prin. Fax 371-5687
Lee ES 400/PK-5
119 NE 15th Ave 79107 806-326-4750
Maggie Ogden, prin. Fax 371-6046
Mann MS 400/7-8
610 N Buchanan St 79107 806-326-3700
Tammie Villarreal, prin. Fax 371-5617
Mesa Verde ES 500/PK-5
4011 Beaver Dr 79107 806-326-4800
Charla Cobb, prin. Fax 381-7323
Oak Dale ES 400/PK-5
2711 S Hill St 79103 806-326-4850
Justin Ruiz, prin. Fax 371-6106
Olsen Park ES 500/PK-5
2409 Anna St 79106 806-326-4900
Kris Schellhamer, prin. Fax 356-4944
Paramount Terrace ES 400/PK-5
3906 Cougar Dr 79109 806-326-4950
Pam Camarata, prin. Fax 354-4623
Pleasant Valley ES 300/PK-5
4413 River Rd 79108 806-326-5000
Dr. Curtis Crump, prin. Fax 381-7372
Puckett ES 400/K-5
6700 Oakhurst Dr 79109 806-326-5050
Casey Newman, prin. Fax 356-4833
Ridgecrest ES 500/PK-5
5306 SW 37th Ave 79109 806-326-5100
Lesley McCoy, prin. Fax 356-4835
Rogers ES 600/PK-5
920 N Mirror St 79107 806-326-5150
Terri Huseman, prin. Fax 371-5718
Sanborn ES 700/PK-5
700 S Roberts St 79102 806-326-5250
Melissa Schooler, prin. Fax 371-6171
San Jacinto ES 700/PK-5
3400 W 4th Ave 79106 806-326-5200
Mary Scobey, prin. Fax 371-5843
Sleepy Hollow ES 600/K-5
3435 Reeder Dr 79121 806-326-5300
Amy Krieger, prin. Fax 354-5079
South Georgia ES 500/PK-5
5018 Susan Dr 79110 806-326-5350
Leslie Callahan, prin. Fax 356-4959
South Lawn ES 500/PK-5
4719 Bowie St 79110 806-326-5400
Donna Harris, prin. Fax 356-4879
Sunrise ES 300/PK-5
5123 E 14th Ave 79104 806-326-5450
Shelley Baloglou, prin. Fax 371-5841
Tradewind ES 500/K-5
4300 S Williams St 79118 806-326-5500
Kim Bentley, prin. Fax 371-6535
Travis 6th Grade Campus 6-6
2801 NE 24th Ave 79107 806-326-3870
Brandy Self, prin.
Travis MS 700/7-8
2815 Martin Rd 79107 806-326-3800
Jennifer Wilkerson, prin. Fax 381-7207
Western Plateau ES 300/K-5
4927 Shawnee Trl 79109 806-326-5550
Lori Berryman, prin. Fax 356-4872
Whittier ES 600/PK-5
2004 N Marrs St 79107 806-326-5600
Bea Enevoldsen, prin. Fax 381-7322
Wills ES 500/PK-5
3500 SW 11th Ave 79106 806-326-5650
Chris Altman, prin. Fax 371-5842
Windsor ES 400/K-5
6700 Hyde Pkwy 79109 806-326-5700
Bobby Payne, prin. Fax 356-4090
Wolflin ES 400/PK-5
2026 S Hughes St 79109 806-326-5750
Steffanie Chew, prin. Fax 371-6101
Woodlands ES 400/K-4
2501 N Coulter St 79124 806-326-5800
Traci Gabel, prin. Fax 356-4926

Canyon ISD
Supt. — See Canyon
Arden Road ES 500/K-4
6801 Learning Tree Ln 79119 806-677-2360
John Forbis, prin. Fax 677-2379
City View ES 500/K-4
3400 Knoll Dr 79118 806-677-2500
Andrew Burgoon, prin. Fax 677-2519
Greenways IS 900/5-6
8100 Pineridge Dr 79119 806-677-2460
Toby King, prin. Fax 677-2499
Hillside ES 300/K-4
9600 Perry Ave 79119 806-677-2520
Amy Duggan, prin. Fax 677-2539
Howe ES 400/K-4
5108 Pico Blvd 79110 806-677-2380
Nicole Johnston, prin. Fax 677-2399
Lakeview ES 500/PK-4
6407 Lair Rd 79118 806-677-2830
Dana Stokes, prin. Fax 677-2849
Sundown Lane ES 300/PK-4
4715 W Sundown Ln 79118 806-677-2400
Noe Renteria, prin. Fax 677-2419
Westover Park JHS 900/7-8
7200 Pinnacle Dr 79119 806-677-2420
Doug Voran, prin. Fax 677-2439

Highland Park ISD 900/PK-12
PO Box 30430 79120 806-335-2823
Jimmy Hannon, supt. Fax 335-3547
www.hpisd.net
Highland Park ES 400/PK-5
PO Box 30430 79120 806-335-1334
Vanette Barnett, prin. Fax 335-3184
Highland Park MS 200/6-8
PO Box 30430 79120 806-335-2821
Tim Landon, prin. Fax 335-3215

River Road ISD 1,400/PK-12
9500 N US Highway 287 79108 806-381-7800
Richard Kelley, supt. Fax 381-1357
www.rrisd.net
River Road MS 200/7-8
9500 N US Highway 287 79108 806-383-8721
Penny Rosson, prin. Fax 381-7815
Rolling Hills ES 600/PK-4
2800 W Cherry Ave 79108 806-383-8621
Erin Brandstatt, prin. Fax 381-7814
Willow Vista IS 200/5-6
7600 Pavillard Dr 79108 806-383-8820
Mike Cheverier, prin. Fax 381-7821

St. Andrews Episcopal S 200/PK-8
1515 S Georgia St 79102 806-376-9501
Joe Bicknell, hdmstr. Fax 376-8421
St. Joseph S 100/PK-5
4118 S Bonham St 79110 806-359-1604
David Hernandez, prin. Fax 359-1604
St. Mary's Cathedral S 200/PK-5
1200 S Washington St 79102 806-376-9112
Linda Aranda, prin. Fax 376-4314
San Jacinto Christian Academy 400/PK-12
PO Box 3428 79116 806-372-2285
Ed Thomas, supt. Fax 376-6712
Trinity Lutheran Christian S 100/PK-5
5005 W Interstate 40 79106 806-352-5620
Rick Ryan, prin. Fax 353-7785

Amherst, Lamb, Pop. 712
Amherst ISD 200/PK-12
PO Box 248 79312 806-246-3221
Joel Rodgers, supt. Fax 246-3494
www.amherstisd.com
Amherst S 200/PK-12
PO Box 248 79312 806-246-3221
Joel Rodgers, prin. Fax 246-3649

Anahuac, Chambers, Pop. 2,205
Anahuac ISD 1,200/PK-12
PO Box 369 77514 409-267-3600
James Hopper, supt. Fax 267-3855
www.anahuacisd.net
Anahuac ES 600/PK-5
PO Box 399 77514 409-267-3600
Mitzi Higginbotham, prin. Fax 267-2068
Anahuac MS 300/6-8
PO Box 849 77514 409-267-2040
Tammy Duhon, prin. Fax 267-2046

Anderson, Grimes, Pop. 220
Anderson - Shiro Consolidated ISD 800/PK-12
458 FM 149 Rd W 77830 936-873-4500
Scott Beene, supt. Fax 873-4515
www.ascisd.net
Anderson - Shiro ES 400/PK-5
458 FM 149 Rd W 77830 936-873-4525
Marcy Pavlock, prin. Fax 873-4530

Andrews, Andrews, Pop. 10,989
Andrews ISD 3,800/PK-12
405 NW 3rd St 79714 432-523-3640
Bobby Azam, supt. Fax 523-3343
www.andrews.esc18.net
Andrews MS 800/6-8
405 NW 3rd St 79714 432-523-3640
Dewayne Wilkins, prin. Fax 524-1904
Clearfork ES 800/PK-1
405 NW 3rd St 79714 432-523-3640
Suzanne Mata, prin. Fax 523-1903
Devonian ES 600/2-3
405 NW 3rd St 79714 432-523-3640
Arturo Roman, prin. Fax 524-1905
Underwood ES 600/4-5
405 NW 3rd St 79714 432-523-3640
Terry Justice, prin. Fax 524-1906

Angleton, Brazoria, Pop. 18,559
Angleton ISD 6,500/PK-12
1900 N Downing Rd 77515 979-864-8000
Patricia Montgomery Ed.D., supt. Fax 864-8070
www.angletonisd.net/
Angleton JHS 1,500/6-8
1201 W Henderson Rd 77515 979-849-8206
Alice Clayton, prin. Fax 864-8675
Central ES 600/PK-5
429 E Locust St 77515 979-849-1226
Annette Jones, prin. Fax 864-8704
Frontier ES 400/K-5
5200 Airline Rd 77515 979-849-8241
Vicki Harmon, prin. Fax 864-8715
Northside ES 500/K-5
1000 Ridgecrest St 77515 979-849-6189
Lori Gonzalez, prin. Fax 864-8696
Rancho Isabella ES 400/K-5
100 Corral Loop 77515 979-849-2418
Christopher Kocurek, prin. Fax 864-8725
Southside ES 400/K-5
1200 Park Ln 77515 979-849-5245
Jerri McNeill, prin. Fax 864-8730
Westside ES 1,000/K-5
1001 W Mulberry St 77515 979-848-8990
Robin Braun, prin. Fax 864-8686

Angleton Christian S 100/PK-12
3133 N Valderas St 77515 979-864-3842
Gordon Smith, head sch Fax 864-3843

Anna, Collin, Pop. 8,055
Anna ISD 2,600/PK-12
501 S Sherley Ave 75409 972-924-1000
Pete Slaughter, supt. Fax 924-1001
www.annaisd.org
Anna MS 600/6-8
501 S Sherley Ave 75409 972-924-1200
Tressi Brown, prin. Fax 924-1201
Bryant ES 500/1-5
501 S Sherley Ave 75409 972-924-1300
Cinda Owen, prin. Fax 924-1301
Harlow ES PK-5
501 S Sherley Ave 75409 972-924-1500
Karen Reddelll, prin. Fax 924-1501
Rattan ES 600/1-5
501 S Sherley Ave 75409 972-924-1400
Todd Frazier, prin. Fax 924-1401

Anson, Jones, Pop. 2,396
Anson ISD 700/PK-12
1431 Commercial Ave 79501 325-823-3671
Jay Baccus, supt. Fax 823-4444
www.ansontigers.com
Anson ES 400/PK-5
922 Avenue M 79501 325-823-3361
Amy McIntire, prin. Fax 823-3127

Anson MS 200/6-8
1120 Avenue M 79501 325-823-2771
David Hagler, prin. Fax 823-3667

Anthony, El Paso, Pop. 4,964
Anthony ISD 800/PK-12
840 6th St 79821 915-886-6500
Dr. Steven Saldivar, supt. Fax 886-2420
www.anthonyisd.net
Anthony ES 400/PK-5
610 6th St 79821 915-886-6510
Oralia Moseley, prin. Fax 886-3205
Anthony MS 200/6-8
813 6th St 79821 915-886-6530
Oscar Troncoso, prin. Fax 886-3875

Anton, Hockley, Pop. 1,117
Anton ISD 300/PK-12
PO Box 309 79313 806-997-2301
Dwight Rice, supt. Fax 997-2062
www.antonisd.org
Anton S 300/PK-12
PO Box 309 79313 806-997-2301
Dwight Rice, admin. Fax 997-2062

Apple Springs, Trinity
Apple Springs ISD 200/PK-12
PO Box 125 75926 936-831-3344
Cody Moree, supt. Fax 831-2824
www.asisd.com/
Apple Springs ES 100/PK-6
PO Box 125 75926 936-831-2241
Kevin Plotts, prin. Fax 831-2824

Aquilla, Hill, Pop. 108
Aquilla ISD 300/PK-12
404 N Richards 76622 254-694-3770
David Edison, supt. Fax 694-6237
www.aquillaisd.net
Aquilla S 300/PK-12
404 N Richards 76622 254-694-3770
Andrew Christian, prin. Fax 694-6237

Aransas Pass, San Patricio, Pop. 8,090
Aransas Pass ISD 1,900/PK-12
2300 McMullen Ln Ste 600 78336 361-758-3466
Mark Kemp, supt. Fax 758-2962
www.apisd.org
Blunt MS 400/6-8
2103 Demory Ln 78336 361-758-2711
Martha Rose, prin. Fax 758-4690
Faulk ECC 400/PK-1
430 S 8th St 78336 361-758-3141
Thomas Grajek, prin. Fax 758-5493
Kieberger ES 300/2-3
748 W Goodnight Ave 78336 361-758-3113
Josh Rombs, prin. Fax 758-3605
Marshall ES 300/4-5
2300 McMullen Ln 78336 361-758-3455
Thomas Grajek, prin. Fax 758-3046

Archer City, Archer, Pop. 1,806
Archer City ISD 500/PK-12
PO Box 926 76351 940-574-4536
C.D. Knobloch, supt. Fax 574-4051
www.archercityisd.net
Archer City ES 200/PK-6
PO Box 926 76351 940-574-4506
Ay Huseman, prin. Fax 574-4051

Argyle, Denton, Pop. 3,241
Argyle ISD 1,700/PK-12
800 Eagle Dr 76226 940-464-7241
Dr. Telena Wright, supt. Fax 464-7297
www.argyleisd.com
Argyle IS 100/4-5
800 Eagle Dr 76226 940-464-5100
Renee Funderburg, prin. Fax 464-7245
Argyle MS 300/6-8
800 Eagle Dr 76226 940-246-2126
Scott Gibson, prin. Fax 246-2128
Hilltop ES 500/PK-3
800 Eagle Dr 76226 940-464-0564
Mandi Murphy, prin. Fax 464-4017

Denton ISD
Supt. — See Denton
Blanton ES 800/K-5
9501 Stacee St 76226 940-369-0700
Linda Bozeman, prin. Fax 241-1423
Harpool MS 1,000/6-8
9601 Stacee Ln 76226 940-369-1700
Jeff Smith, prin. Fax 241-1342
Rayzor ES 700/K-5
377 Rayzor Rd 76226 940-369-4100
Mary Dunlevy, prin. Fax 455-2658

Liberty Christian S 1,300/PK-12
1301 S US Highway 377 76226 940-294-2000
Dr. Rodney Haire, pres. Fax 294-2045
Selwyn S 200/K-12
2270 Copper Canyon Rd 76226 940-382-6771
Deb Hof M.S., head sch Fax 382-6773

Arlington, Tarrant, Pop. 357,280
Arlington ISD 61,600/PK-12
1203 W Pioneer Pkwy 76013 682-867-4611
Dr. Marcelo Cavazos, supt. Fax 459-7299
www.aisd.net
Adams ES 800/PK-6
2220 Sherry St 76010 682-867-2130
Lesley Rhodes, prin. Fax 867-2135
Amos ES 600/PK-6
3100 Daniel Dr 76014 682-867-4700
Susan Laird, prin. Fax 419-4708
Anderson ES 900/PK-6
1101 Timberlake Dr 76010 682-867-7750
Dr. Donna Trevino-Jones, prin. Fax 867-7773
Ashworth ES 500/PK-6
6700 Silo Rd 76002 682-867-4800
Patrick Guy, prin. Fax 867-4808
Atherton ES 700/PK-6
2101 Overbrook Dr 76014 682-867-4900
Nidia Zaravar, prin. Fax 867-4916
Bailey JHS 800/7-8
2411 Winewood Ln 76013 682-867-0700
Tiffany Benavides, prin. Fax 867-0708
Barnett JHS 900/7-8
2101 E Sublett Rd 76018 682-867-5000
Stephanie Hawthorne, prin. Fax 419-5005
Bebensee ES 700/PK-6
5900 Inks Lake Dr 76018 682-867-5100
Charlotte Carter, prin. Fax 867-5108
Beckham ES 600/PK-6
1700 Southeast Pkwy 76018 682-867-6600
Susi Mitchell, prin. Fax 867-6617
Berry ES 800/PK-6
1800 Joyce St 76010 682-867-0850
Tammy Rogers, prin. Fax 867-0857
Blanton ES 700/PK-6
1900 S Collins St 76010 682-867-1000
Joshua Leonard, prin. Fax 867-0987
Boles JHS 700/7-8
3900 SW Green Oaks Blvd 76017 682-867-8000
Jeff Provence, prin. Fax 561-8005
Bryant ES 600/PK-6
2201 Havenwood Dr 76018 682-867-5200
Randi Smith, prin. Fax 867-5211
Burgin ES 800/PK-6
401 E Mayfield Rd 76014 682-867-1300
Christi Wilks, prin. Fax 867-1369
Butler ES 700/K-6
2121 Margaret Dr 76012 682-867-1010
Stacie Humbles, prin. Fax 867-1071
Carter JHS 1,100/7-8
701 Tharp St 76010 682-867-1700
Reny Lizardo, prin. Fax 867-1721
Corey Acad of Fine Arts & Dual Language 600/PK-6
5200 Kelly Elliott Rd 76017 682-867-3900
Dr. Matt Varnell, prin. Fax 867-3904
Crow ES 600/PK-6
1201 Coke Dr 76010 682-867-1850
Jamie MacDougall, prin. Fax 867-1847
Ditto ES 700/PK-6
3001 Quail Ln 76016 682-867-3100
Karie Kuster, prin. Fax 867-3176
Duff ES 700/K-6
3100 Lynnwood Dr 76013 682-867-2000
Cynthia Harbison, prin. Fax 867-2003
Dunn ES 500/K-6
2201 Woodside Dr 76013 682-867-3200
Mary Burnett, prin. Fax 867 3203
Ellis ES 1,000/PK-6
2601 Shadow Ridge Dr 76006 682-867-7900
Keith Boyd, prin. Fax 867-7903
Fitzgerald ES 600/PK-6
5201 Creek Valley Dr 76018 682-867-5300
Grayson Toperzer, prin. Fax 867-5347
Foster ES 800/PK-6
1025 High Point Rd 76015 682-867-5350
Jacquelyn Burden, prin. Fax 867-5806
Goodman ES 600/PK-6
1400 Rebecca Ln 76014 682-867-2200
Selina Elizondo, prin. Fax 867-2275
Gunn JHS 500/7-8
3000 S Fielder Rd 76015 682-867-5400
Juan Villarreal, prin. Fax 867-5405
Hale ES 600/K-6
2400 E Mayfield Rd 76014 682-867-1530
Claudia Morales, prin. Fax 867-1956
Hill ES 700/K-6
2020 W Tucker Blvd 76013 682-867-2300
Melinda Schweig, prin. Fax 867-2375
Johns ES 800/PK-6
1900 Sherry St 76010 682-867-2500
Vanessa Colon, prin. Fax 867-2505
Jones Acad of Fine Arts & Dual Language PK-6
2001 Van Buren Dr 76011 682-867-3580
Katiuska Herrador, prin. Fax 867-3505
Key ES 500/K-6
3621 Roosevelt Dr 76016 682-867-5500
Hallema Jackson, prin. Fax 867-5502
Knox ES 600/PK-6
2315 Stonegate St 76010 682-867-2051
Rose Ravin, prin. Fax 867-2104
Kooken Education Center 300/PK-PK
423 N Center St 76011 682-867-7152
Dr. Connie Spence, prin. Fax 867-7154
Little ES 700/K-6
3721 Little Rd 76016 682-867-3300
Beth Anne Woodard, prin. Fax 867-3305
McNutt ES PK-6
3609 S Center St 76014 682-867-9100
Ginger Cole-Leffel, prin. Fax 867-9105
Miller ES 800/PK-6
6401 W Pleasant Ridge Rd 76016 682-867-8400
Shelly Osten, prin. Fax 867-8405
Moore ES 600/K-6
5500 Park Springs Blvd 76017 682-867-8900
Tyson Jones, prin. Fax 867-8970
Morton ES 1,000/PK-6
2900 Barrington Pl 76014 682-867-5600
Tashalon McDonald, prin. Fax 867-5679
Nichols JHS 800/7-8
2201 Ascension Blvd 76006 682-867-2600
Marcus Brannon, prin. Fax 867-2649
Ousley JHS 600/7-8
950 Southeast Pkwy 76018 682-867-5700
Lora Thurston, prin. Fax 419-5705
Peach ES PK-6
2020 Baird Farm Rd 76006 682-867-6100
Stephanie Lee, prin. Fax 867-6105
Pearcy ES 500/PK-6
601 E Harris Rd 76002 682-867-5555
Codi Van Duzee, prin. Fax 867-5561
Pope ES 700/PK-6
901 Chestnut Dr 76012 682-867-2750
Celina Kilgore, prin. Fax 867-2795
Rankin ES 700/PK-6
1900 Oleander St 76010 682-867-2800
Raul Espinosa, prin. Fax 867-2805
Roark ES 800/PK-6
2401 Roberts Cir 76010 682-867-2900
Anna Anderson, prin. Fax 867-2904
Shackelford JHS 700/7-8
2000 N Fielder Rd 76012 682-867-3600
Jerod Zahn, prin. Fax 801-3605
Sherrod ES 800/PK-6
2626 Lincoln Dr 76006 682-867-3700
Shundra Brown, prin. Fax 867-3705
Short ES 500/PK-6
2000 California Ln 76015 682-867-5850
Tracey Cross, prin. Fax 867-5895
South Davis ES 700/PK-6
2001 S Davis Dr 76013 682-867-3800
David Gutierrez, prin. Fax 867-3817
Speer ES 800/PK-6
811 Fuller St 76012 682-867-4000
Rosa Orosco, prin. Fax 867-4005
Swift ES 600/PK-6
1101 S Fielder Rd 76013 682-867-4100
Bailey Morris, prin. Fax 867-4109
Thornton ES 900/PK-6
2301 E Park Row Dr 76010 682-867-4200
Alicia Rodriguez, prin. Fax 867-4295
Webb ES 900/PK-6
1200 N Cooper St 76011 682-867-4300
Elena Lopez, prin. Fax 867-4349
Williams ES 800/PK-6
4915 Red Birch Dr 76018 682-867-5900
Mark Kammlah, prin. Fax 867-5904
Wimbish ES 600/PK-6
1601 Wright St 76012 682-867-6000
Kari Pride, prin. Fax 867-6019
Wood ES 700/PK-6
3300 Pimlico Dr 76017 682-867-1100
David Dillard, prin. Fax 867-1105
Workman JHS 600/7-8
701 E Arbrook Blvd 76014 682-867-1200
Inelda Acosta, prin. Fax 419-1205
Young JHS 800/7-8
3200 Woodside Dr 76016 682-867-3400
Kelly Hastings, prin. Fax 492-3405
Other Schools – See Grand Prairie

Hurst-Euless-Bedford ISD
Supt. — See Bedford
Viridian ES PK-6
4001 Cascade Sky Dr 76005 817-864-0550
Dr. Angelique Brading, prin. Fax 354-3280

Kennedale ISD
Supt. — See Kennedale
Patterson ES 400/K-4
6621 Kelly Elliott Rd 76001 817-563-8600
Cari Blackstone, prin. Fax 483-3638

Mansfield ISD
Supt. — See Mansfield
Anderson ES 500/PK-4
2122 W Nathan Lowe Rd 76017 817-299-7760
Sheira Petty, prin. Fax 472-3216
Brockett ES 700/PK-4
810 Dove Meadows Dr 76002 817-299-6620
Tamara Liddell, prin. Fax 453-6835
Coble MS 700/7-8
1200 Ballweg Rd 76002 682-314-4900
Winston Gipson, prin. Fax 453-7331
Cross Timber IS 800/5-6
2934 Russell Rd 76001 817-299-3560
Gina Rietfors, prin. Fax 561-3814
Davis ES 600/PK-4
900 Eden Rd 76001 817-299-7840
Lacye Redmond, prin. Fax 472-3267
Gideon ES 500/PK-4
1201 Mansfield Webb Rd 76002 817-299-7800
Shanee Charles, prin. Fax 472-3292
Harmon ES 600/PK-4
5700 Petra Dr 76017 817-299-7780
Robyn Rinearson, prin. Fax 472-3228
Holt ES 500/PK-4
7321 Ledbetter Rd 76001 817-299-6460
Thelma Foster, prin. Fax 561-3888
Howard MS 900/7-8
7501 Calendar Rd 76001 682-314-1050
Alma Martinez, prin. Fax 561-3840
Icenhower IS 600/5-6
8100 Webb Ferrell Rd 76002 817-299-2700
Mendy Gregory, prin. Fax 453-6890
Jones ES 600/PK-4
7650 S Watson Rd 76002 817-299-6940
Dameon Gray, prin. Fax 472-3247
Morris ES 500/PK-4
7900 Tin Cup Dr 76001 817-299-7860
Tara Sublette, prin. Fax 473-5362
Reid ES 700/PK-4
500 Country Club Dr 76002 817-299-6960
Rebecca Stephens, prin. Fax 453-7360

Arlington Faith Academy 50/PK-12
PO Box 170718 76003 817-483-0119
Evelyn Kazsuk, prin. Fax 483-4292
Burton Adventist Academy 300/PK-12
4611 Kelly Elliott Rd 76017 817-572-0081
Darlene White, prin. Fax 561-4237
Children's University 300/PK-6
4621 Park Springs Blvd 76017 817-784-6655
Regina Wright, head sch Fax 784-1650
Goines STEM Academy 50/5-7
2455 SE Green Oaks Blvd 76018 817-466-8967
Terri Alford, admin.
Grace Preparatory Academy 400/K-12
PO Box 170958 76003 817-557-3399

Merryhill S Arlington PK-6
711 W Arbrook Blvd 76015 817-472-9494
Montessori Academy 200/PK-6
3428 W Arkansas Ln 76016 817-274-1548
Oakridge S 900/PK-12
5900 W Pioneer Pkwy 76013 817-451-4994
Jon Kellam, head sch Fax 457-6681
Pantego Christian Academy 800/PK-12
2201 W Park Row Dr 76013 817-460-3315
Dr. Jeffrey Potts, pres. Fax 459-4687
Park Row Christian Academy 100/PK-6
915 W Park Row Dr 76013 817-277-1021
St. Joseph Catholic S 400/PK-8
2015 SW Green Oaks Blvd 76017 817-419-6800
Diane Price, prin. Fax 419-7080
St. Maria Goretti Catholic S 500/PK-8
1200 S Davis Dr 76013 817-275-5081
Kimberly Pierce, prin. Fax 277-4193
St. Paul's Preparatory Academy 200/PK-12
6900 US 287 Hwy 76001 817-561-3500
Gayla Rockwell, prin. Fax 561-3408
Tate Springs Christian S 200/PK-6
4001 Little Rd 76016 817-478-7091

Arp, Smith, Pop. 957
Arp ISD 900/PK-12
PO Box 70 75750 903-859-8482
Dwight Thomas, supt. Fax 859-2621
home.arpisd.org
Arp ES 400/PK-5
PO Box 70 75750 903-859-4650
Stephanie Schminkey, prin. Fax 859-3683
Arp JHS 200/6-8
PO Box 70 75750 903-859-4936
Bryan Hurst, prin. Fax 859-3186

Aspermont, Stonewall, Pop. 909
Aspermont ISD 200/PK-12
PO Box 549 79502 940-989-3355
Tim Bartram, supt. Fax 989-3353
www.aspermontisd.com
Aspermont ES 100/PK-5
PO Box 549 79502 940-989-3323
L'Rae Watson, prin. Fax 989-2954

Atascosa, Bexar
Southwest ISD
Supt. — See San Antonio
Elm Creek ES 700/PK-5
11535 Pearsall Rd 78002 210-622-4430
J. Luis Rojas, prin. Fax 622-4431
McNair MS 1,100/6-8
11553 Old Pearsall Rd 78002 210-622-4480
Anitra Crisp, prin. Fax 622-4481

Athens, Henderson, Pop. 12,562
Athens ISD 3,400/PK-12
104 Hawn St 75751 903-677-6900
Blake Stiles, supt. Fax 677-6908
www.athensisd.net
Athens MS 700/6-8
6800 State Highway 19 S 75751 903-677-3030
Jennifer Risinger, prin. Fax 677-2111
Bel Air ES 600/PK-5
215 Willowbrook Dr 75751 903-677-6980
Lisa Howell, prin. Fax 677-6986
Central Athens ES 500/PK-5
307 Madole St 75751 903-677-6960
Shannon Pursley, prin. Fax 677-6987
South Athens ES 600/PK-5
718 Robbins Rd 75751 903-677-6970
Claudia Stiles, prin. Fax 677-3470

Athens Christian Academy 100/K-6
105 S Carroll St 75751 903-675-5135
Brent Williams, admin. Fax 675-4708

Atlanta, Cass, Pop. 5,585
Atlanta ISD 1,800/PK-12
106 W Main St 75551 903-796-4194
Sidney Harrist, supt. Fax 799-1004
www.atlisd.net
Atlanta ES 400/2-4
902 Abc Ln 75551 903-796-7164
Todd Marshall, prin. Fax 799-1018
Atlanta MS 500/5-8
600 High School Ln 75551 903-796-7928
Jay Wylie, prin. Fax 799-1021
Atlanta PS 400/PK-1
505 Rabbit Blvd 75551 903-796-8115
Donna Rice, prin. Fax 799-1014

Aubrey, Denton, Pop. 2,543
Aubrey ISD 1,900/PK-12
415 Tisdell Ln 76227 940-668-0060
Dr. David Belding, supt. Fax 365-2627
www.aubreyisd.net
Aubrey MS 500/5-8
815 W Sherman Dr 76227 940-668-0200
Karen Wright, prin. Fax 365-3135
Brockett ES 400/K-4
900 Chestnut St 76227 940-668-0036
Kari Abrams, prin. Fax 668-0037
Monaco ES 500/PK-4
9350 Cape Cod Blvd 76227 940-668-0000
Derek Leary, prin. Fax 668-0001

Denton ISD
Supt. — See Denton
Cross Oaks ES 500/K-5
600 Liberty Rd 76227 972-347-7100
Matthew Preston, prin. Fax 440-9770
Navo MS 1,000/6-8
1701 Navo Rd 76227 972-347-7500
Dr. Beth Kelly, prin. Fax 346-2562
Paloma Creek ES 600/K-5
1600 Navo Rd 76227 972-347-7300
Natalie Mead, prin. Fax 346-9501

Providence ES 600/K-5
1000 FM 2931 76227 940-369-1900
Jairia Diggs, prin. Fax 369-2985
Savannah ES 700/PK-5
1101 Cotton Exchange Dr 76227 972-347-7400
Michael McWilliams, prin. Fax 346-3352

Austin, Travis, Pop. 774,864
Austin ISD 83,600/PK-12
1111 W 6th St 78703 512-414-1700
Dr. Paul Cruz, supt. Fax 414-1707
www.austinisd.org
Allison ES 500/PK-5
515 Vargas Rd 78741 512-414-2004
Guadalupe Velasquez, prin. Fax 385-0905
Andrews ES 700/PK-5
6801 Northeast Dr 78723 512-414-1770
Saleem Blevins, prin. Fax 926-6635
Bailey MS 900/6-8
4020 Lost Oasis Holw 78739 512-414-4990
John Rocha, prin. Fax 292-0898
Baldwin ES 700/PK-5
12200 Meridian Park Blvd 78739 512-841-8900
Jennifer Murray, prin. Fax 841-8901
Baranoff ES 1,000/K-5
12009 Buckingham Gate Rd 78748 512-841-7100
Megan Counihan, prin. Fax 841-7104
Barrington ES 500/K-5
400 Cooper Dr 78753 512-414-2008
Gilma Sanchez, prin. Fax 836-4077
Barton Hills ES 400/K-6
2108 Barton Hills Dr 78704 512-414-2013
Katie Achtermann, prin. Fax 841-3849
Becker ES 300/PK-5
906 W Milton St 78704 512-414-2019
Valerie Borchers, prin. Fax 442-1759
Bedichek MS 1,000/6-8
6800 Bill Hughes Rd 78745 512-414-3265
Michael Herbin, prin. Fax 444-4382
Blackshear ES 200/PK-5
1712 E 11th St 78702 512-414-2021
Richard Garner, prin. Fax 477-7640
Blanton ES 600/PK-5
5408 Westminster Dr 78723 512-414-2026
Dora Molina, prin. Fax 926-8553
Blazier ES 1,000/PK-5
8601 Vertex Blvd 78744 512-841-8800
Leti Pena-Wilk M.Ed., prin. Fax 841-8801
Boone ES 500/PK-5
8101 Croftwood Dr 78749 512-414-2537
Alan Stevens, prin. Fax 280-3307
Brentwood ES 600/PK-5
6700 Arroyo Seco 78757 512-414-2039
Amber Laroche, prin. Fax 453-8928
Brooke ES 400/PK-5
3100 E 4th St 78702 512-414-2043
Elia Diaz-Ortiz, prin. Fax 385-3862
Brown ES 500/PK-6
505 W Anderson Ln 78752 512-414-2047
Veronica Sharp, prin. Fax 452-6097
Bryker Woods ES 400/K-6
3309 Kerbey Ln 78703 512-414-2054
Jane Kronke, prin. Fax 459-9047
Burnet MS 1,100/6-8
8401 Hathaway Dr 78757 512-414-3225
Gavino Barrera, prin. Fax 452-0695
Campbell ES 300/PK-5
2613 Rogers Ave 78722 512-414-2056
Keith Moore, prin. Fax 841-1246
Casey ES 700/PK-5
9400 Texas Oaks Dr 78748 512-841-6900
Lina Villarreal, prin. Fax 841-6925
Casis ES 800/PK-5
2710 Exposition Blvd 78703 512-414-2062
Samuel Tinnon, prin. Fax 477-1776
Clayton ES 900/K-5
7525 La Crosse Ave 78739 512-841-9200
Amy Gonzales, prin. Fax 841-9201
Cook ES 900/K-5
1511 Cripple Creek Dr 78758 512-414-2510
Framy Diaz, prin. Fax 837-5983
Covington MS 700/6-8
3700 Convict Hill Rd 78749 512-414-3276
Shannon Sellstrom, prin. Fax 892-4547
Cowan ES 800/PK-5
2817 Kentish Dr 78748 512-841-2700
Debbie Warnken, prin. Fax 841-2755
Cunningham ES 400/PK-5
2200 Berkeley Ave 78745 512-414-2067
Amy Lloyd, prin. Fax 441-6006
Davis ES 700/PK-5
5214 Duval Rd 78727 512-414-2580
Jennifer Daniel, prin. Fax 346-7384
Dawson ES 300/PK-5
3001 S 1st St 78704 512-414-2070
Tania Jedele, prin. Fax 442-5765
Dobie MS 700/6-8
1200 E Rundberg Ln 78753 512-414-3270
Jesse De La Huerta, prin. Fax 836-8411
Doss ES 800/PK-5
7005 Northledge Dr 78731 512-414-2365
Janna Griffin, prin. Fax 345-0013
Fulmore MS 1,000/6-8
201 E Mary St 78704 512-414-3207
Lisa Bush, prin. Fax 441-3129
Galindo ES 600/PK-5
3800 S 2nd St 78704 512-414-1756
Natascha Barreto-Romero, prin. Fax 414-0448
Garcia Young Men's Leadership Academy 500/6-8
7414 Johnny Morris Rd 78724 512-841-9400
Sterlin McGruder, prin. Fax 841-9401
Gorzycki MS 1,300/6-8
7412 W Slaughter Ln 78749 512-841-8600
Cathryn Mitchell, prin. Fax 841-8601
Govalle ES 600/PK-5
3601 Govalle Ave 78702 512-414-2078
Paula Reyes, prin. Fax 926-4820

Graham ES 700/PK-5
11211 Tom Adams Dr 78753 512-414-2395
Yolanda Wilkins, prin. Fax 835-4562
Gullett ES 500/K-5
6310 Treadwell Blvd 78757 512-414-2082
Janie Ruiz, prin. Fax 451-2036
Harris ES 700/PK-5
1711 Wheless Ln 78723 512-414-2085
Monica Martinez, prin. Fax 929-7347
Hart ES 700/PK-5
8301 Furness Dr 78753 512-841-2100
Sonia Tosh, prin. Fax 841-2190
Henry MS 1,000/6-8
2610 W 10th St 78703 512-414-3229
Karen Aidman, prin. Fax 477-7428
Highland Park ES 700/K-5
4900 Fairview Dr 78731 512-414-2090
Katherine Pena, prin. Fax 414-2626
Hill ES 800/PK-5
8601 Tallwood Dr 78759 512-414-2369
Beth Newton, prin. Fax 841-8105
Houston ES 800/PK-5
5409 Ponciana Dr 78744 512-414-2517
Elia Diaz-Camarillo, prin. Fax 448-4869
Jordan Early College Prep S 800/PK-5
6711 Johnny Morris Rd 78724 512-414-2578
Adrienne Williams, prin. Fax 926-8299
Joslin ES 300/PK-5
4500 Manchaca Rd 78745 512-414-2094
Jennifer Pace, prin. Fax 443-3011
Kealing MS 1,100/6-8
1607 Pennsylvania Ave 78702 512-414-3214
Kenisha Coburn, prin. Fax 478-9133
Kiker ES 1,000/PK-5
5913 La Crosse Ave 78739 512-414-2584
Lori Schneider, prin. Fax 288-5779
Kocurek ES 500/PK-5
9800 Curlew Dr 78748 512-414-2547
Heather Scholl, prin. Fax 282-7824
Lamar MS 700/6-8
6201 Wynona Ave 78757 512-414-3217
George Llewellyn, prin. Fax 467-6862
Langford ES 800/PK-5
2206 Blue Meadow Dr 78744 512-414-1765
Dounna Poth, prin. Fax 447-4808
Lee ES 400/K-6
3308 Hampton Rd 78705 512-414-2098
John Hewlett, prin. Fax 478-4463
Linder ES 500/PK-5
2800 Metcalfe Rd 78741 512-414-2398
Beverly Odom, prin. Fax 447-3222
Maplewood ES 500/PK-6
3808 Maplewood Ave 78722 512-414-4402
Vickie Jacobson, prin. Fax 472-8559
Martin MS 600/6-8
1601 Haskell St 78702 512-414-3243
Monica DeLaGarza-Conness, prin. Fax 320-0125
Mathews ES 400/PK-6
906 Westlynn St 78703 512-414-4406
Grace Martino-Brewster, prin. Fax 476-2108
McBee ES 600/K-5
1001 W Braker Ln 78758 512-841-2500
Maggie Delarosa, prin. Fax 841-2333
Menchaca ES 700/PK-5
12120 Manchaca Rd 78748 512-414-2333
Eliza Loyola, prin. Fax 282-4043
Mendez MS 900/6-8
5106 Village Square Dr 78744 512-414-3284
Kathy Ryan, prin. Fax 442-5738
Metz ES 400/PK-5
84 Robert T Martinez Jr St 78702 512-414-4408
Martha Castillo, prin. Fax 472-3412
Mills ES 800/PK-5
6201 Davis Ln 78749 512-841-2400
Lalla Beachum, prin. Fax 841-2490
Murchison MS 1,400/6-8
3700 N Hills Dr 78731 512-414-3254
Rebekah Van Ryn, prin. Fax 343-1710
Norman ES 300/PK-5
4001 Tannehill Ln 78721 512-414-2347
Cynthia Gonzales, prin. Fax 926-6321
Oak Hill ES 800/PK-5
6101 Patton Ranch Rd 78735 512-414-2336
Lori Komassa, prin. Fax 892-2279
Oak Springs ES 300/PK-5
3601 Webberville Rd 78702 512-414-4413
Monica Woods, prin. Fax 472-5005
Odom ES 500/PK-5
1010 Turtle Creek Blvd 78745 512-414-2388
Sondra McWilliams, prin. Fax 443-6170
Ortega ES 400/PK-5
1135 Garland Ave 78721 512-414-4417
Jennifer Stephens, prin. Fax 929-7906
Overton ES 700/PK-5
7201 Colony Loop Dr 78724 512-841-9300
Courtney Colvin, prin. Fax 841-9301
Padron ES PK-5
2011 W Rundberg Ln 78758 512-841-9600
Rafael Soriano, prin. Fax 841-9601
Palm ES 500/PK-5
7601 Dixie Dr 78744 512-414-2545
Rhoda Coleman, prin. Fax 280-2769
Paredes MS 1,100/6-8
10100 S Mary Moore Searight 78748 512-841-6800
Valeria Torres-Solis, prin. Fax 841-7036
Patton ES 1,000/PK-5
6001 Westcreek Dr 78749 512-414-1780
Dr. Amanda Brantley, prin. Fax 892-6541
Pease ES 300/K-6
1106 Rio Grande St 78701 512-414-4428
Cynthia Jackson, prin. Fax 477-3009
Pecan Springs ES 500/PK-6
3100 Rogge Ln 78723 512-414-4445
Elaine McKinney, prin. Fax 926-0001
Perez ES 900/PK-5
7500 S Pleasant Valley Rd 78744 512-841-9100
Kara Mitchell-Santibanez, prin. Fax 841-9101

Pickle ES 800/PK-5
1101 Wheatley Ave 78752 512-841-8400
Lauro Devalos, prin. Fax 841-8444
Pillow ES 600/PK-5
3025 Crosscreek Dr 78757 512-414-2350
Brian Hill, prin. Fax 467-2513
Pleasant Hill ES 500/PK-5
6405 Circle S Rd 78745 512-414-4453
Kristi Cisneros, prin. Fax 442-4741
Read Pre K S 500/PK-PK
2608 Richcreek Rd 78757 512-414-9400
Ami Cortes, prin. Fax 414-9401
Reilly ES 300/PK-5
405 Denson Dr 78752 512-414-4464
Corrine Saenz, prin. Fax 453-1193
Ridgetop ES 300/PK-5
5005 Caswell Ave 78751 512-414-4469
Joaquin Gloria, prin. Fax 459-9187
Rodriguez ES 900/PK-5
4400 Franklin Park Dr 78744 512-841-7200
Monica Villasenor, prin. Fax 841-7205
Sadler Means Young Womens Leadership Acd 6-8
6401 N Hampton Dr 78723 512-414-3234
Christina Almaraz-Ortiz, prin. Fax 926-6146
St. Elmo ES 300/PK-5
600 W Saint Elmo Rd 78745 512-414-4477
Adriana Gonzales, prin. Fax 442-6871
Sanchez ES 500/PK-5
73 San Marcos St 78702 512-414-4423
Azucena Garcia, prin. Fax 472-9493
Sims ES 300/PK-5
1203 Springdale Rd 78721 512-414-4488
Freda Mills, prin. Fax 841-1282
Small MS 1,000/6-8
4801 Monterey Oaks Blvd 78749 512-841-6700
Matthew Nelson, prin. Fax 841-6703
Summitt ES 800/PK-5
12207 Brigadoon Ln 78727 512-414-4484
Dedra Standish, prin. Fax 832-1458
Sunset Valley ES 500/PK-5
3000 Jones Rd 78745 512-414-2392
Emily Bush, prin. Fax 892-7206
Thompson ES PK-5
102 E Rundberg Ln 78753 512-414-8400
Lakesha Drinks, prin. Fax 414-8401
Travis Heights ES 500/PK-5
2010 Alameda Dr 78704 512-414-4495
Lisa Robertson, prin. Fax 442-9537
Uphaus ECC 300/PK-K
5200 Freidrich Ln 78744 512-414-5520
Leticia Botello, prin. Fax 414-5521
Walnut Creek ES 700/PK-5
401 W Braker Ln 78753 512-414-4499
Dinorah Bores, prin. Fax 837-6789
Webb MS 700/6-8
601 E Saint Johns Ave 78752 512-414-3258
Raul Sanchez, prin. Fax 452-9683
Webb PS 200/PK-2
601 E Saint Johns Ave 78752 512-414-8830
Raul Sanchez, prin. Fax 414-8834
Widen ES 700/PK-5
5605 Nuckols Crossing Rd 78744 512-414-2556
Kimberly Royal, prin. Fax 441-8971
Williams ES 600/PK-5
500 Mairo St 78748 512-414-2525
Mary Cisneros, prin. Fax 292-3041
Winn ES 300/PK-5
3500 Susquehanna Ln 78723 512-414-2390
Anayansi Blessum, prin. Fax 926-9211
Wooldridge ES 800/K-5
1412 Norseman Ter 78758 512-414-2353
Sheri Mull, prin. Fax 339-6583
Wooten ES 700/PK-5
1406 Dale Dr 78757 512-414-2315
Angelo San Segundo, prin. Fax 459-9227
Zavala ES 300/PK-6
310 Robert T Martinez Jr St 78702 512-414-2318
Nicole Anderson, prin. Fax 477-2361
Zilker ES 500/PK-5
1900 Bluebonnet Ln 78704 512-414-2327
Randall Thomson, prin. Fax 442-3992

Del Valle ISD
Supt. — See Del Valle
Baty ES 800/PK-5
2101 Faro Dr 78741 512-386-3450
Jennifer Garcia, prin. Fax 386-3455
Dailey MS 800/6-8
14000 Westall 78725 512-386-3600
Mario Palacios, prin. Fax 386-3630
Gilbert ES 800/PK-5
5412 Gilbert Rd 78724 512-386-3800
Laurie Jurado, prin. Fax 386-3805
Hillcrest ES 700/PK-5
6910 E William Cannon Dr 78744 512-386-3550
Jeni Bristol, prin. Fax 386-3555
Hornsby-Dunlap ES 700/PK-5
13901 FM 969 78724 512-386-3650
Marisol Rocha, prin. Fax 386-3655
Ojeda MS 1,000/6-8
4900 McKinney Falls Pkwy 78744 512-386-3500
Sarah Reuwsaat, prin. Fax 386-3505
Smith ES 700/PK-5
4209 Smith School Rd 78744 512-386-3850
Frances Maldonado, prin. Fax 386-3855

Dripping Springs ISD
Supt. — See Dripping Springs
Rooster Springs ES 800/PK-5
1001 Belterra Dr 78737 512-465-6200
Mandy Sargent, prin. Fax 465-6299
Sycamore Springs ES PK-5
14451 Sawyer Ranch Rd 78737 512-858-3900
Kristen Ray, prin. Fax 858-3999
Sycamore Springs MS 6-8
14451 Sawyer Ranch Rd 78737 512-858-3600
Dan Diehl, prin. Fax 858-3699

Eanes ISD 8,000/PK-12
601 Camp Craft Rd 78746 512-732-9000
Dr. Tom Leonard, supt. Fax 732-9005
www.eanesisd.net
Barton Creek ES 500/PK-5
1370 Patterson Rd 78733 512-732-9180
Tiffany Phelps, prin. Fax 732-9189
Bridge Point ES 800/PK-5
6401 Cedar St 78746 512-732-9200
Heather Meek, prin. Fax 732-9209
Cedar Creek ES 500/PK-5
3301 Pinnacle Rd 78746 512-732-9120
Jessica Brown, prin. Fax 732-9129
Eanes ES 700/PK-5
4101 Bee Cave Rd 78746 512-732-9100
Lesley Ryan, prin. Fax 732-9109
Hill Country MS 1,000/6-8
1300 Walsh Tarlton Ln 78746 512-732-9220
Kathleen Sullivan, prin. Fax 732-9229
West Ridge MS 900/6-8
9201 Scenic Bluff Dr 78733 512-732-9240
Robin Lowe, prin. Fax 732-9249
Other Schools – See West Lake Hills

Lake Travis ISD 8,300/PK-12
3322 Ranch Road 620 S 78738 512-533-6000
Brad Lancaster, supt. Fax 533-6001
www.ltisdschools.org/
Hudson Bend MS 900/6-8
15600 Lariat Trl 78734 512-533-6400
Thomas Payne, prin. Fax 533-6401
Lake Pointe ES 600/PK-5
11801 Sonoma Dr 78738 512-533-6500
Kelly Freed, prin. Fax 533-6501
Lake Travis ES 1,000/PK-5
15303 Kollmeyer Dr 78734 512-533-6300
Angela Frankhouser, prin. Fax 533-6301
Lakeway ES 700/PK-5
1701 Lohmans Crossing Rd 78734 512-533-6350
Samuel Hicks, prin. Fax 533-6351
Serene Hills ES 700/PK-5
3301 Serene Hills Dr 78738 512-533-7400
Julie Nederveld, prin. Fax 533-7401
Other Schools – See Bee Cave, Spicewood

Leander ISD
Supt. — See Leander
Bush ES 800/PK-5
12600 Country Trl 78732 512-570-6100
Kristine Kline, prin. Fax 570-6105
Canyon Ridge MS 1,200/6-8
12601 Country Trl 78732 512-570-3500
Susan Sullivan, prin. Fax 570-3505
Four Points MS 600/6-8
9700 McNeil Dr 78750 512-570-3700
Dr. Joe Ciccarelli, prin. Fax 570-3705
Grandview Hills ES 500/K-5
12024 Vista Parke Dr 78726 512-570-6800
Kathy Goecke, prin. Fax 570-6805
River Place ES 800/K-5
6500 Sitio Del Rio Blvd 78730 512-570-6900
Tina Pasak, prin. Fax 570-6905
River Ridge ES 1,000/K-5
12900 Tierra Grande Trl 78732 512-570-7300
Shelley Roberts, prin. Fax 570-7305
Rutledge ES 800/PK-5
11501 Staked Plains Dr 78717 512-570-6500
Elizabeth Mohler, prin. Fax 570-6505
Steiner Ranch ES 600/K-5
4001 N Quinlan Park Rd 78732 512-570-5700
Catherine Robinson, prin. Fax 570-5705

Manor ISD
Supt. — See Manor
Bluebonnet Trail ES 500/PK-5
11316 Farmhaven Rd 78754 512-278-4125
Brandon Powell, prin. Fax 278-4140
Decker ES 800/PK-5
8500 Decker Ln 78724 512-278-4150
Angel DeLuna, prin. Fax 278-4174
Decker MS 900/6-8
8104 Decker Ln 78724 512-278-4630
Dayna Anthony-Swain, prin. Fax 278-4654
Oak Meadows ES 600/PK-5
5600 Decker Ln 78724 512-278-4175
Salvador Vega, prin. Fax 278-4199
Pioneer Crossing ES 600/PK-5
11300 Samsung Blvd 78754 512-278-4250
Ryan Marcum, prin. Fax 278-4259

Pflugerville ISD
Supt. — See Pflugerville
Copperfield ES 500/PK-5
12135 Thompkins Dr 78753 512-594-5800
Georgie Arenaz, prin. Fax 594-5805
Delco PS 500/PK-2
12900 Dessau Rd Ste A 78754 512-594-6200
Sonya Collins, prin. Fax 594-6205
Dessau ES 400/3-5
1501 Dessau Ridge Ln 78754 512-594-4600
Jesusita Avalos, prin. Fax 594-4605
Dessau MS 800/6-8
12900 Dessau Rd 78754 512-594-2600
Jeremy LeJeune, prin. Fax 594-2605
Northwest ES 500/PK-5
14014 Thermal Dr 78728 512-594-4400
Nathan Steenport, prin. Fax 594-4405
Parmer Lane ES 400/K-5
1806 W Parmer Ln 78727 512-594-4000
Barry Miller, prin. Fax 594-4005
River Oaks ES 500/PK-5
12401 Scofield Farms Dr 78758 512-594-5000
Aracely Suarez, prin. Fax 594-5005
Westview MS 900/6-8
1805 Scofield Ln 78727 512-594-2200
Amanda Johnson, prin. Fax 594-2205

Round Rock ISD
Supt. — See Round Rock
Anderson Mill ES 500/PK-5
10610 Salt Mill Holw 78750 512-428-3700
Trana Allen, prin. Fax 428-3790
Canyon Creek ES 500/K-5
10210 Ember Glen Dr 78726 512-428-2800
April Crawford, prin. Fax 428-2890
Canyon Vista MS 1,300/6-8
8455 Spicewood Springs Rd 78759 512-464-8100
Nicole Hagerty, prin. Fax 464-8210
Caraway ES 700/PK-5
11104 Oak View Dr 78759 512-464-5500
Katrina Bailey, prin. Fax 464-5590
Cedar Valley MS 1,300/6-8
8139 Racine Trl 78717 512-428-2300
Matt Groff, prin. Fax 428-2420
Deerpark MS 900/6-8
8849 Anderson Mill Rd 78729 512-464-6600
Jonathan Smith, prin. Fax 464-6740
England ES 600/K-5
8801 Pearson Ranch Rd 78717 512-704-1200
Jana Stowe, prin. Fax 704-1290
Forest North ES 400/K-5
13414 Broadmeade Ave 78729 512-464-6750
Amy Jacobs, prin. Fax 464-6794
Grisham MS 700/6-8
10805 School House Ln 78750 512-428-2650
Kim Winters, prin. Fax 428-2790
Johnson ES K-5
2800 Sauls Dr 78728 512-704-1400
Gabi Nino, prin. Fax 704-1490
Jollyville ES 500/PK-5
6720 Corpus Christi Dr 78729 512-428-2200
Scott Morgan, prin. Fax 428-2299
Laurel Mountain ES 800/PK-5
10111 D K Ranch Rd 78759 512-464-4300
Jan Richards, prin. Fax 464-4390
Live Oak ES 600/PK-5
8607 Anderson Mill Rd 78729 512-428-3800
Katie Holding, prin. Fax 428-3890
Pearson Ranch MS 6-8
8901 Pearson Ranch Rd 78717 512-464-5000
Kim Winters, prin. Fax 464-5090
Pond Springs ES 600/PK-5
7825 Elkhorn Mountain Trl 78729 512-464-4200
Brooke Bailey, prin. Fax 464-4290
Purple Sage ES 300/PK-5
11801 Tanglebriar Trl 78750 512-428-3500
Sara Nelson, prin. Fax 428-3590
Sommer ES 900/K-5
16200 Avery Ranch Blvd 78717 512-704-0600
Nancy Varljen, prin. Fax 704-0690
Spicewood ES 800/PK-5
11601 Olson Dr 78750 512-428-3600
Jiae Kim, prin. Fax 428-3690
Wells Branch ES 1,000/PK-5
14650 Merriltown Rd 78728 512-428-3400
Belinda Cini, prin. Fax 428-3490

ACE Academy 200/PK-12
3901 Shoal Creek Blvd 78756 512-206-4070
AESA Prep Academy 100/2-12
14101 Canonade 78737 512-774-4822
All Saints' Episcopal S 100/PK-K
209 W 27th St 78705 512-472-8866
Cindy LaPorte, head sch Fax 477-5215
Austin Jewish Academy 100/K-8
7300 Hart Ln 78731 512-735-8350
Austin Montessori S - Great Northern Cmp PK-6
5006 Sunset Trl 78745 512-323-2313
Austin Montessori S - Sunset Valley Cmps 300/PK-6
5006 Sunset Trl 78745 512-892-0253
Austin Peace Academy 200/PK-12
5110 Manor Rd 78723 512-926-1737
Austin Waldorf S 400/K-12
8700 South View Rd 78737 512-288-5942
Bannockburn Christian Academy 200/PK-5
7100 Brodie Ln 78745 512-892-2706
Bobbi Flowers, prin. Fax 899-1161
Boys S of Austin K-4
PO Box 300547 78703 512-553-2690
Brentwood Christian S 700/PK-12
11908 N Lamar Blvd 78753 512-835-5983
Cathedral S of St. Mary 100/PK-8
910 San Jacinto Blvd 78701 512-476-1480
Robert LeGros, prin. Fax 476-9922
Emergent Academy 1-8
1044 Liberty Park Dr 78746 512-358-1672
Girls' School of Austin 100/K-8
2007 McCall Rd 78703 512-478-7827
Lisa Schmitt, head sch Fax 478-5456
Good Shepherd Episcopal S 200/PK-K
PO Box 5250 78763 512-476-4393
Headwaters S 200/PK-12
801 Rio Grande St 78701 512-480-8142
Ted Graf, head sch Fax 480-0278
Hebrew Prep S PK-5
2127 W Parmer Ln 78727 512-977-0770
Hill Country Christian S of Austin 500/PK-12
12124 Ranch Road 620 N 78750 512-331-7036
Tim Hillen, head sch Fax 257-4190
Holy Family Catholic S 500/PK-8
9400 Neenah Ave 78717 512-246-4455
Kelly Laster, prin. Fax 246-4454
Holy Word Christian Academy 50/K-8
10601 Bluff Bend Dr 78753 512-836-4264
Hyde Park Baptist S - Central Campus 300/K-8
PO Box 4486 78765 512-465-8338
Kirby Hall S 200/PK-12
306 W 29th St 78705 512-474-1770
Magellan International S 100/PK-8
7938 Great Northern Blvd 78757 512-782-2327
Mariposa Montessori S 50/PK-8
3338 Paisano Tr 78745 512-891-0093

Paragon Preparatory S 200/PK-8
2001 Koenig Ln 78756 512-459-5040
David McGrath, hdmstr. Fax 459-1875
Rawson Saunders School 100/1-12
2614 Exposition Blvd Bldg A 78703 512-476-8382
Laura Steinbach M.Ed., head sch Fax 476-1132
Reedemer Lutheran S 500/PK-8
1500 W Anderson Ln 78757 512-451-6478
Carol Mueller, prin. Fax 610-8809
Regents S of Austin 900/K-12
3230 Travis Country Cir 78735 512-899-8095
Ronnie Long, head sch Fax 899-8623
Renaissance Academy 200/PK-12
14401 Owen-Tech Blvd 78728 512-252-2277
St. Andrew's Episcopal S 500/K-8
1112 W 31st St 78705 512-299-9800
Sean Murphy, head sch Fax 299-9822
St. Austin Catholic S 200/PK-8
1911 San Antonio St 78705 512-477-3751
Tara Cevallos, prin. Fax 477-3079
St. Francis S 400/PK-8
300 E Huntland Dr 78752 512-454-0848
Barbara Porter, head sch Fax 453-2982
St. Gabriel's Catholic S 400/PK-8
2500 Wimberly Ln 78735 512-327-7755
Dan McKenna, head sch Fax 327-4334
St. Ignatius Martyr Catholic S 300/PK-8
120 W Oltorf St 78704 512-442-8547
Jennifer Malone, prin. Fax 442-8685
St. Louis Catholic S 200/PK-8
2114 Saint Joseph Blvd 78757 512-614-6622
Cindy Gee, prin.
St. Matthew's Episcopal S 100/PK-K
8134 Mesa Dr 78759 512-345-3040
Page Race, head sch Fax 345-5866
St. Theresa's Catholic S 400/PK-8
4311 Small Dr 78731 512-451-7105
Ann Walters, pres. Fax 451-8808
School in the Hills PK-3
10819 Ranch Road 2222 78730 512-266-8180
Trinity Episcopal S of Austin 400/K-8
3901 Bee Cave Rd 78746 512-472-9525
Marie Kidd, head sch Fax 472-2337
Veritas Academy 500/PK-12
PO Box 90517 78709 512-891-1673

Avalon, Ellis
Avalon ISD 300/PK-12
PO Box 455 76623 972-627-3251
Dr. David Del Bosque, supt. Fax 627-3220
www.avalonisd.net
Avalon S 300/PK-12
PO Box 455 76623 972-627-3251
Khristopher Marshall, prin. Fax 627-3220

Avery, Red River, Pop. 482
Avery ISD 300/PK-12
150 San Antonio St 75554 903-684-3460
Debbie Drew, supt. Fax 684-3294
www.averyisd.net/
Avery ES 100/PK-5
150 San Antonio St 75554 903-684-3116
Karen Downs, prin. Fax 684-3294
Avery MS 100/6-8
150 San Antonio St 75554 903-684-3079
Jill Mahan, prin. Fax 684-3294

Avinger, Cass, Pop. 437
Avinger ISD 200/PK-12
245 Conner 75630 903-562-1355
Jacquelyn Smith, supt. Fax 562-1271
www.avingerisd.net/
Avinger S 200/PK-12
245 Conner 75630 903-562-1355
Terry Giddens, prin. Fax 562-1271

Axtell, McLennan
Axtell ISD 700/PK-12
308 Ottawa 76624 254-863-5301
Dr. J.R. Proctor, supt. Fax 863-5651
www.axtellisd.net
Axtell ES 300/PK-5
1178 Longhorn Pkwy 76624 254-863-5419
Danette Stranacher, prin. Fax 863-5944
Axtell MS 200/6-8
308 Ottawa 76624 254-863-5301
Penny Kocian, prin. Fax 863-5651

Azle, Tarrant, Pop. 10,777
Azle ISD 5,900/PK-12
300 Roe St 76020 817-444-3235
Tanya Anderson, supt. Fax 444-6866
www.azleisd.net
Azle ES 500/5-6
301 Church St 76020 817-444-1312
Gina Lee, prin. Fax 444-6934
Azle JHS 500/7-8
201 School St 76020 817-444-2564
Brian Roberts, prin. Fax 270-0880
Cross Timbers ES 500/K-4
831 Jackson Trl 76020 817-444-3802
Doo Gilloy, prin. Fax 444-0730
Forte JHS 400/7-8
479 Sandy Beach Rd 76020 817-270-1133
Dianne Boone, prin. Fax 270-1157
Hoover ES 500/5-6
484 Sandy Beach Rd 76020 817-444-7766
Joni Bettis, prin. Fax 270-1425
Liberty ES 400/PK-4
11450 Liberty School Rd 76020 817-444-1317
Kella Rogers, prin. Fax 444-1937
Silver Creek ES 500/PK-4
10300 S FM 730 76020 817-444-0257
Heidi Nelson, prin. Fax 270-2383
Walnut Creek ES 500/PK-4
1010 Boyd Rd 76020 817-444-4045
Jessica Hanson, prin. Fax 270-2576
Other Schools – See Fort Worth

Springtown ISD
Supt. — See Springtown
Reno ES 400/PK-4
172 W Reno Rd 76020 817-221-5001
Traunsa Reeves, prin. Fax 677-1214

Azle Christian S 100/PK-12
1801 S Stewart St 76020 817-444-9964
April Geeslin, admin. Fax 444-9914

Bacliff, Galveston, Pop. 8,503
Dickinson ISD
Supt. — See Dickinson
Little ES 700/PK-4
622 Oklahoma Ave 77518 281-229-7000
Brooke Newell, prin. Fax 229-7001

Baird, Callahan, Pop. 1,483
Baird ISD 300/PK-12
PO Box 1147 79504 325-854-1400
Jarod Bellar, supt. Fax 854-2058
www.bairdisd.net
Baird ES 200/PK-5
PO Box 1147 79504 325-854-1400
Cynthia Bessent, prin. Fax 854-2327
Baird JHS 100/6-8
PO Box 1147 79504 325-854-1400
Cynthia Bessent, prin. Fax 854-2808

Balch Springs, Dallas, Pop. 23,383
Dallas ISD
Supt. — See Dallas
Young Womens STEAM Academy 1,400/6-8
710 Cheyenne Rd 75180 972-892-5800
Gabriell Dickson, prin.

Mesquite ISD
Supt. — See Mesquite
Floyd ES 900/PK-5
3025 Hickory Tree Rd 75180 972-882-7100
Dr. Tonya Mamantov, prin. Fax 882-7110
Gray ES 900/PK-6
3500 Pioneer Rd 75180 972-882-7280
Dr. Jennifer LaPlante, prin. Fax 882-7288
Hodges ES 900/PK-6
14401 Spring Oaks Dr 75180 972-290-4040
Dr. Kim Broadway, prin. Fax 290-4046
Mackey ES 900/K-6
14900 N Spring Ridge Cir 75180 972-290-4160
Lynne Noe, prin. Fax 290-4179

Ballinger, Runnels, Pop. 3,731
Ballinger ISD 1,000/PK-12
PO Box 231 76821 325-365-3588
Jeff Butts, admin. Fax 365-5920
www.ballingerisd.net
Ballinger ES 500/PK-5
PO Box 231 76821 325-365-3527
Jamie Dudley, prin. Fax 365-2943
Ballinger JHS 200/6-8
PO Box 231 76821 325-365-3537
Stacy Tucker, prin. Fax 365-5420

Balmorhea, Reeves, Pop. 479
Balmorhea ISD 200/PK-12
PO Box 368 79718 432-375-2223
Manuel Espino, supt. Fax 375-2511
www.bisdbears.esc18.net
Balmorhea S 200/PK-12
PO Box 368 79718 432-375-2223
Teri Barragan, prin. Fax 375-2511

Bandera, Bandera, Pop. 852
Bandera ISD 2,400/PK-12
PO Box 727 78003 830-796-3313
Regina Howell, supt. Fax 796-6238
www.banderaisd.net
Alkek ES 600/PK-5
PO Box 727 78003 830-796-6223
Chip Jackson, prin. Fax 796-6232
Bandera MS 500/6-8
PO Box 727 78003 830-796-6270
Donald Tosh, prin. Fax 796-6277
Other Schools – See Pipe Creek

Bangs, Brown, Pop. 1,570
Bangs ISD 1,100/PK-12
PO Box 969 76823 325-752-6612
Tony Truelove, supt. Fax 752-6253
www.bangsisd.net
Bangs MS 300/5-8
PO Box 969 76823 325-752-6088
Scott Patrick, prin. Fax 752-6253
Stephens ES 400/PK-4
PO Box 969 76823 325-752-7236
Candace Wilson, prin. Fax 752-6974

Banquete, Nueces, Pop. 721
Banquete ISD 900/PK-12
PO Box 369 78339 361-387-2551
Dr. Max Thompson, supt. Fax 387-7188
www.banqueteisd.esc2.net/
Banquete ES 400/PK-5
PO Box 369 78339 361-387-1329
Adriana Tagle, prin. Fax 767-8105
Banquete JHS 200/6-8
PO Box 369 78339 361-387-6504
Ramiro Pena, prin. Fax 387-7051

Barksdale, Edwards
Nueces Canyon Consolidated ISD 300/K-12
PO Box 118 78828 830-234-3514
Kristi Powers, supt. Fax 234-3435
www.nccisd.net/
Other Schools – See Camp Wood

Bartlett, Bell, Pop. 1,605
Bartlett ISD 400/PK-12
PO Box 170 76511 254-527-4247
Travis Edwards, supt. Fax 527-3340
www.bartlett.txed.net
Bartlett S 400/PK-12
PO Box 170 76511 254-527-4247
Angie Peace, prin. Fax 527-3340

Bastrop, Bastrop, Pop. 7,084
Bastrop ISD 9,600/PK-12
906 Farm St 78602 512-772-7100
Steve Murray, supt. Fax 321-7469
www.bisdtx.org/
Bastrop IS 700/5-6
509 Old Austin Hwy 78602 512-772-7450
Daniel Brown, prin. Fax 321-4348
Bastrop MS 700/7-8
725 Old Austin Hwy 78602 512-772-7400
Dr. Christopher Julian, prin. Fax 321-1557
Bluebonnet ES 800/PK-4
416 FM 1209 78602 512-772-7680
Alison Hall, prin. Fax 308-1306
Emile ES 600/PK-4
601 Martin Luther King Dr 78602 512-772-7620
Windy Burnett, prin. Fax 321-3564
Lost Pines ES 700/PK-4
151 Tiger Woods Dr 78602 512-772-7700
Melinda Gardner, prin. Fax 321-2385
Mina ES 500/K-4
1203 Hill St 78602 512-772-7640
Reba King, prin. Fax 321-4354
Other Schools – See Cedar Creek, Red Rock

Calvary Episcopal S 100/PK-6
PO Box 626 78602 512-321-1610
Glennie Burgess, prin.

Batesville, Zavala, Pop. 1,066
Uvalde Consolidated ISD
Supt. — See Uvalde
Batesville ES 100/1-6
496 Garden St 78829 830-376-4221
Dr. Hector Lopez, prin. Fax 376-4223

Bay City, Matagorda, Pop. 17,441
Bay City ISD 3,600/PK-12
PO Box 2510 77404 979-401-1000
Marshall Scott, supt. Fax 245-3175
www.bcblackcats.net
Bay City JHS 800/6-8
1507 Sycamore Ave 77414 979-401-1600
Dr. Keely Coufal, prin. Fax 245-1419
Cherry ES 700/PK-5
2509 8th St 77414 979-401-1300
Meredith Dodd, prin. Fax 245-1702
Holmes ES 700/PK-5
3200 5th St 77414 979-401-1400
Estella Reyes, prin. Fax 245-1645
Roberts ES 500/PK-5
1212 Whitson St 77414 979-401-1500
Melissa Carroll, prin. Fax 245-1573

Holy Cross S 100/PK-6
2001 Katy Ave 77414 979-245-5632
Inez Kucera, prin. Fax 245-6120

Baytown, Harris, Pop. 70,920
Barbers Hill ISD
Supt. — See Mont Belvieu
Barbers Hill MS South 6-8
9600 Eagle Dr, 281-576-2221
Dennis Wagner, prin. Fax 576-3350

Goose Creek Consolidated ISD 22,200/PK-12
PO Box 30 77522 281-420-4800
Randal O'Brien, supt. Fax 420-4815
www.gccisd.net
Alamo ES 600/K-5
6100 N Main St 77521 281-420-4595
Andrea Zepeda, prin. Fax 420-4905
Austin ES 900/K-5
3022 Massey Tompkins Rd 77521 281-420-4620
Michelle Duhon, prin. Fax 420-4899
Banuelos ES K-5
7770 Eastpoint Blvd 77521 281-420-1230
Renee Meyer, prin.
Baytown JHS 800/6-8
7707 Bayway Dr 77520 281-420-4560
Matthew Bolinger, prin. Fax 420-4908
Bowie ES 800/PK-5
2200 Clayton Dr 77520 281-420-4605
Blanca Capetillo, prin. Fax 420-4609
Carver ES 800/PK-5
610 S Pruett St 77520 281-420-4600
Barrett Cobb, prin. Fax 420-4983
Cedar Bayou JHS 1,000/6-8
2610 Elvinta St 77520 281-420-4570
Michael Curl, prin. Fax 420-4569
Clark ES, 6033 N Highway 146, K-5
Katherine Cruz, prin. 281-420-7450
Crockett ES 700/PK-5
4500 Barkaloo Rd 77521 281-420-4645
Michelle James, prin. Fax 420-4649
De Zavala ES 800/PK-5
305 Tri City Beach Rd 77520 281-420-4920
Theresa Keel, prin. Fax 420-4342
Gentry JHS 1,000/6-8
1919 E Archer Rd 77521 281-420-4590
Kathryn Holland, prin. Fax 420-4909
Harlem ES 1,000/PK-5
3333 Interstate 10 77521 281-420-4910
Beatrice Baca, prin. Fax 426-5358
Lamar ES 900/PK-5
816 N Pruett St 77520 281-420-4625
Kami Hale, prin. Fax 420-4626
Mann JHS 1,000/6-8
310 S Highway 146 77520 281-420-4585
Erica Tran, prin. Fax 420-4664
San Jacinto ES 600/PK-5
2615 Virginia St 77520 281-420-4670
Rachel McAdam, prin. Fax 420-4599

Smith ES 800/PK-5
403 E James St 77520 281-420-4615
Martessa Humphries, prin. Fax 420-4940
Travis ES 900/PK-5
100 Robin Rd 77520 281-420-4660
Mary Beebe, prin. Fax 420-4986
Walker ES 1,000/PK-5
4711 Seabird St 77521 281-420-1800
Monica Juarez, prin. Fax 421-3204
Other Schools – See Highlands

Baytown Christian Academy 200/PK-12
5555 N Main St 77521 281-421-4150
Jim Twardowski, hdmstr. Fax 421-4038
St. Joseph S 200/PK-8
1811 Carolina St 77520 281-422-9749
Deborah Francis, prin. Fax 422-7001

Beasley, Fort Bend, Pop. 638
Lamar Consolidated ISD
Supt. — See Rosenberg
Beasley ES 400/PK-5
7511 Avenue J 77417 832-223-1100
Laura Haugvoll, prin. Fax 223-1101

Beaumont, Jefferson, Pop. 116,638
Beaumont ISD 19,400/PK-12
3395 Harrison Ave 77706 409-617-5000
Dr. John Frossard, supt. Fax 617-5184
www.bmtisd.com
Amelia ES 800/PK-5
565 S Major Dr 77707 409-617-6000
Dimitrise Haynes, prin. Fax 617-6024
Bingman Head Start 500/PK-PK
5265 Kenneth Ave 77705 409-617-6200
Carolyn Little, prin. Fax 617-6203
Blanchette ES 500/K-5
2550 Sarah St 77705 409-617-6300
April Johnston, prin. Fax 617-6296
Caldwood ES 700/PK-5
565 S Major Dr 77707 409-617-6025
Julie Corona, prin. Fax 617-6048
Charlton-Pollard ES 600/PK-5
1695 Irving St 77701 409-617-6075
Charisma Popillion, prin. Fax 617-6098
Curtis ES 600/K-5
6225 N Circuit Dr 77706 409-617-6050
Glenetta Henley, prin. Fax 617-6073
Dishman ES 600/PK-5
3475 Champions Dr 77707 409-617-6250
Mellow Tatmon, prin. Fax 617-6274
Fehl-Price ES 600/K-5
3350 Blanchette St 77701 409-617-6400
Chandra Walters, prin. Fax 617-6423
Fletcher ES 600/K-5
1055 Avenue F 77701 409-617-6100
Gloria Guillory, prin. Fax 617-6123
Guess ES 600/PK-5
8055 Voth Rd 77708 409-617-6125
Debbie Oge, prin. Fax 617-6148
Homer Drive ES 700/PK-5
8950 Homer Dr 77708 409-617-6225
Paul Shipman, prin. Fax 617-6248
Jones-Clark ES 800/K-5
3525 Cleveland St 77703 409-617-6350
Fax 617-6346
King MS 300/6-8
1400 Avenue A 77701 409-617-5850
Dion Varnado, prin. Fax 617-5873
Lucas Pre K Center 300/PK-PK
1750 E Lucas Dr 77703 409-617-6450
Valencia Greenwood, prin. Fax 617-6448
Marshall MS 800/6-8
6455 Gladys Ave 77706 409-617-5900
Paul Breaux, prin. Fax 617-5924
Martin ES 700/PK-5
3500 Pine St 77703 409-617-6425
Tamara Long, prin. Fax 617-6446
Odom Academy 800/6-8
2550 W Virginia St 77705 409-617-5925
Jeffrey Farley, prin. Fax 617-5949
Pietzsch-MacArthur ES 900/PK-5
4301 Highland Ave 77705 409-617-6475
Audrey Collins, prin. Fax 617-6498
Regina-Howell ES 800/PK-5
5850 Regina Ln 77706 409-617-6190
Kimberly Screen, prin. Fax 617-6199
Smith MS 600/6-8
4415 Concord Rd 77703 409-617-5825
Anetra Cheatham, prin. Fax 617-5848
South Park MS 400/6-8
4500 Highland Ave 77705 409-617-5875
Calvin Rice, prin. Fax 617-5899
Vincent MS 700/6-8
350 Eldridge Dr 77707 409-617-5950
Melanie Gimble, prin. Fax 617-5974

Hamshire-Fannett ISD
Supt. — See Hamshire
Hamshire-Fannett ES 500/PK-3
23395 Burrell Wingate Rd 77705 409-794-1412
Karen Reneau, prin. Fax 794-1049
Hamshire-Fannett IS 400/4-6
11407 Dugat Rd 77705 409-794-1558
Amanda Jenkins M.Ed., prin. Fax 794-1787
Hamshire-Fannett MS 300/7-8
11375 Dugat Rd 77705 409-794-2361
Shawn Clubb, prin. Fax 794-3042

All Saints Episcopal S 400/PK-8
4108 Delaware St 77706 409-892-1755
Scootie Clark, head sch Fax 892-0166
Legacy Christian Academy 300/PK-12
8200 Highway 105 77713 409-924-0500
St. Anne Catholic S 600/PK-8
375 N 11th St 77702 409-832-5939
Alison Kiker, prin. Fax 832-4655

St. Anthony Cathedral Basilica S 200/PK-8
850 Forsythe St 77701 409-832-3486
Fax 838-9051
Veritas Classical Academy 100/PK-10
PO Box 5344 77726 409-225-9107

Beckville, Panola, Pop. 830
Beckville ISD 700/PK-12
PO Box 37 75631 903-678-3311
Devin Tate, supt. Fax 678-2157
www.beckvilleisd.net/
Beckville JHS 200/6-8
PO Box 37 75631 903-678-3851
Loretta Blair, prin. Fax 678-3827
Beckville Sunset ES 300/PK-5
PO Box 37 75631 903-678-3601
Jason Bridges, prin. Fax 678-2257

Bedford, Tarrant, Pop. 45,838
Hurst-Euless-Bedford ISD 22,100/PK-12
1849 Central Dr Ste A 76022 817-283-4461
Steven Chapman, supt. Fax 354-3311
www.hebisd.edu
Bedford Heights ES 800/K-6
1000 Cummings Dr 76021 817-788-3150
Brad Mengwasser, prin. Fax 788-3112
Bell Manor ES 800/PK-6
1300 Winchester Way 76022 817-354-3370
Patti Bearden, prin. Fax 354-3374
Meadow Creek ES 800/PK-6
3001 Harwood Rd 76021 817-354-3500
Doreen Mengwasser, prin. Fax 354-3329
Shady Brook ES 600/K-6
2601 Shady Brook Dr 76021 817-354-3513
Shannon Gauntt, prin. Fax 354-3336
Spring Garden ES 700/PK-6
2400 Cummings Dr 76021 817-354-3395
Sheila Walker, prin. Fax 354-3337
Stonegate ES 500/K-6
900 Bedford Rd 76022 817-285-3250
Gena Jackson, prin. Fax 285-3210
Other Schools – See Arlington, Euless, Fort Worth, Hurst

Bee Cave, Travis, Pop. 3,811
Lake Travis ISD
Supt. — See Austin
Bee Cave ES 900/PK-5
14300 Hamilton Pool Rd 78738 512-533-6250
Jennifer Andjelic, prin. Fax 533-6251

Beeville, Bee, Pop. 12,739
Beeville ISD 3,400/PK-12
201 N Saint Marys St 78102 361-358-7111
Dr. Marc Puig, supt. Fax 362-6046
www.beevilleisd.net
Barnhart Academy 7-8
301 N Minnesota St 78102 361-358-7111
Jaime Rodriguez, prin.
FMC ES 500/1-2
100 Pfeil Ln 78102 361-362-6050
Martina Villarreal, prin. Fax 362-6054
Hall ES 500/3-4
1100 W Huntington St 78102 361-362-6060
Belinda Aguirre, prin. Fax 362-6059
Hampton-Moreno-Dugat ECC 400/PK-K
2000 S Mussett 78102 361-362-6040
Annette Sanchez, prin. Fax 362-6049
Jefferson ES 500/5-6
701 E Hayes St 78102 361-362-6070
Elinor Straecner, prin. Fax 362-6069
Moreno MS 600/7-8
301 N Minnesota St 78102 361-358-6262
Jaime Rodriguez, prin. Fax 362-6092

St. Philip's Episcopal S 100/PK-6
105 N Adams St 78102 361-358-6242
Carol Reagan, head sch Fax 358-8232

Bellaire, Harris, Pop. 16,508
Houston ISD
Supt. — See Houston
Condit ES 700/PK-5
7000 S 3rd St 77401 713-295-5255
Daniel Greenberg, prin. Fax 668-5738
Horn ES 800/K-5
4530 Holly St 77401 713-295-5264
Vanessa Flores, prin. Fax 295-5286
Pin Oak MS 1,200/6-8
4601 Glenmont St 77401 713-295-6500
Rita Graves, prin. Fax 295-6511

Post Oak S 400/PK-12
4600 Bissonnet St 77401 713-661-6688
Maura Joyce, head sch Fax 661-4959
Veritas Christian Academy of Houston 200/PK-8
7000 Ferris St 77401 713-773-9605
Brad Sewell, head sch Fax 773-9753

Bellevue, Clay, Pop. 360
Bellevue ISD 100/K-12
PO Box 38 76228 940-928-2104
Dean Gilstrap, supt. Fax 928-2583
www.bellevueisd.org/
Bellevue S 100/K-12
PO Box 38 76228 940-928-2104
Michael Qualls, prin. Fax 928-2583

Bells, Grayson, Pop. 1,356
Bells ISD 800/PK-12
1550 Ole Ambrose Rd 75414 903-965-7721
Joe Moore, supt. Fax 965-7036
bellsisd.net/
Bells ES 400/PK-5
110 Scott Rd 75414 903-965-7725
Yalonda Ivers, prin. Fax 965-0140
Prichard JHS 200/6-8
1510 Ole Ambrose Rd 75414 903-965-4835
Will Steger, prin. Fax 965-7428

Bellville, Austin, Pop. 4,068
Bellville ISD 2,100/PK-12
518 S Mathews St 77418 979-865-3133
Mike Coker, supt. Fax 865-8591
www.bellvilleisd.org
Bellville JHS 500/6-8
518 S Mathews St 77418 979-865-5966
Daniel Symm, prin. Fax 865-7060
O'Bryant IS 300/4-5
518 S Mathews St 77418 979-865-3671
Natalie Jones, prin. Fax 865-7049
O'Bryant PS 600/PK-3
518 S Mathews St 77418 979-865-5907
Natalie Jones, prin. Fax 865-7039
Other Schools – See Industry

Faith Academy 200/PK-12
12177 Highway 36 77418 979-865-1811
Merlene Byler, head sch Fax 865-2454

Belton, Bell, Pop. 17,870
Belton ISD 8,700/PK-12
PO Box 269 76513 254-215-2000
Dr. Susan Kincannon, supt. Fax 215-2001
www.bisd.net
Belton ECC PK-PK
501 E 4th Ave 76513 254-215-3700
Sue Banfield, prin. Fax 215-3701
Chisholm Trail ES K-5
1082 S Wheat Rd 76513 254-316-5100
Elizabeth McMurtry, prin. Fax 316-5102
Leon Heights ES 300/K-5
1501 N Main St 76513 254-215-3200
Tiffany Weiss, prin. Fax 215-3201
Miller Heights ES 400/K-5
1110 Fairway Dr 76513 254-215-3300
Jennifer Conner, prin. Fax 215-3301
South Belton MS 800/6-8
805 Sage Brush 76513 254-215-3000
Kevin Taylor, prin. Fax 215-3001
Southwest ES 400/K-5
611 Saunders St 76513 254-215-3500
Stacy Cox, prin. Fax 215-3501
Sparta ES 700/K-5
1800 Sparta Rd 76513 254-215-3600
Julee Manley, prin. Fax 215-3601
Other Schools – See Temple

Providence Preparatory S 200/PK-12
506 N Main St 76513 254-307-1165

Benavides, Duval, Pop. 1,353
Benavides ISD 400/PK-12
PO Box P 78341 361-256-3003
Adell Cueva, supt. Fax 256-3002
www.benavidesisd.net
Benavides ES 200/PK-6
PO Box P 78341 361-256-3030
Sandra Perez, prin. Fax 256-3032

Ben Bolt, Jim Wells
Ben Bolt-Palito Blanco ISD 600/PK-12
PO Box 547 78342 361-664-9904
Dr. Timothy Little, supt. Fax 668-0446
www.bbpbschools.net
Palito Blanco ES 200/PK-6
PO Box 547 78342 361-664-3201
Gloria Hamill, prin. Fax 668-0549

Benbrook, Tarrant, Pop. 20,889
Fort Worth ISD
Supt. — See Fort Worth
Benbrook ES 600/K-5
800 Mercedes St 76126 817-815-6400
Shelly Mayer, prin. Fax 815-6450
Leonard MS 800/6-8
8900 Chapin Rd 76116 817-815-6200
Cathy Williams-Ridley, prin. Fax 815-6250
Waverly Park ES 800/PK-5
3604 Cimmaron Trl 76116 817-815-6700
Valorie Bedford, prin. Fax 815-6750
Westpark ES 500/PK-5
10202 Jerry Dunn Pkwy 76126 817-815-7000
Susan Hill, prin. Fax 815-7050

Benjamin, Knox, Pop. 256
Benjamin ISD 100/K-12
PO Box 166 79505 940-459-2231
Olivia Gloria, supt. Fax 459-2007
www.benjaminisd.net/
Benjamin S 100/K-12
PO Box 166 79505 940-459-2231
Olivia Gloria, prin. Fax 459-2007

Ben Wheeler, Van Zandt
Martins Mill ISD 500/PK-12
301 FM 1861 75754 903-479-3872
James Oliver, supt. Fax 479-3711
www.martinsmillisd.net
Martins Mill ES 300/PK-6
301 FM 1861 75754 903-479-3706
Suzzette Stringer, prin. Fax 479-3754

Bertram, Burnet, Pop. 1,339
Burnet Consolidated ISD
Supt. — See Burnet
Bertram ES 400/PK-5
315 Main St 78605 512-355-2111
Jennifer Simpson, prin. Fax 355-2261

Big Bend National Park, Brewster, Pop. 250
San Vicente ISD 50/K-8
PO Box 195 79834 432-477-2220
Eric Stoddard, supt. Fax 477-2221
San Vicente ES 50/K-8
PO Box 195 79834 432-477-2220
Eric Stoddard, prin. Fax 477-2221

Big Lake, Reagan, Pop. 2,917
Reagan County ISD 900/PK-12
1111 E 12th St 76932 325-884-3705
Steve Long, supt. Fax 884-3021
www.rcisd.net
Reagan County ES 500/PK-5
501 N Texas Ave 76932 325-884-3741
Mandy Traylor, prin. Fax 884-2194
Reagan County MS 200/6-8
500 N Pennsylvania Ave 76932 325-884-3728
David Kohutek, prin. Fax 884-2327

Big Sandy, Upshur, Pop. 1,325
Big Sandy ISD 700/PK-12
PO Box 598 75755 903 636 5287
Jay Ratcliff, supt. Fax 636-5111
www.bigsandyisd.org
Big Sandy ES 300/PK-5
PO Box 598 75755 903-636-5287
Donna Varnado, prin. Fax 636-5111
Big Sandy JHS 200/6-8
PO Box 598 75755 903-636-5287
Kim Stradley, prin. Fax 636-5111

Harmony ISD 1,000/PK-12
9788 State Highway 154 W 75755 903-725-5492
Dennis Glenn, supt. Fax 725-6737
www.harmonyisd.net
Harmony JHS 200/6-8
9788 State Highway 154 W 75755 903-725-5485
Lonnie Henry, prin. Fax 725-7270
Irons-Smith IS 100/4-5
9788 State Highway 154 W 75755 903-725-7077
Ginger Cargal, prin. Fax 725-7370
Poole ES 300/PK-3
9788 State Highway 154 W 75755 903-725-5496
Cara Rendon, prin. Fax 725-7078

Big Spring, Howard, Pop. 26,933
Big Spring ISD 3,500/PK-12
708 E 11th Pl 79720 432-264-3600
Chris Wigington, supt. Fax 264-3646
www.bsisd.esc18.net
Big Spring IS 5-6
708 E 11th Pl 79720 432-264-4121
Patsy Sanchez, prin. Fax 264-3646
Big Spring JHS 600/7-8
708 E 11th Pl 79720 432-264-4135
Rebecca Otto, prin. Fax 264-4196
Goliad ES 500/4-4
708 E 11th Pl 79720 432-264-4111
Rosie Lain, prin. Fax 264-3610
Kentwood ECC 100/PK-K
708 E 11th Pl 79720 432-264-4130
Kelli Wigington, prin. Fax 264-3612
Marcy ES 500/K-2
708 E 11th Pl 79720 432-264-4144
Alecia Hancock, prin. Fax 264-3627
Moss ES 400/K-2
708 E 11th Pl 79720 432-264-4148
Kaitlin Jeffrey, prin. Fax 264-3619
Washington ES 500/3-3
708 E 11th Pl 79720 432-264-4126
Kari Eggleston, prin. Fax 264-3611

Bishop, Nueces, Pop. 3,126
Bishop Consolidated ISD 1,300/PK-12
719 E 6th St 78343 361-584-3591
Christina Gutierrez, supt. Fax 584-3147
www.bishopcisd.net
Bishop ES 300/3-5
200 S Fir Ave 78343 361-584-3571
Rosalinda Trevino, prin. Fax 584-3147
Bishop PS 300/PK-2
705 W Main St 78343 361-584-2434
Amy Leos, prin. Fax 584-7600
Luehrs JHS 200/6-8
717 E 6th St 78343 361-584-3576
Ray Garza, prin. Fax 584-3577
Other Schools – See Robstown

St. Paul Lutheran S 50/PK-4
801 E Main St 78343 361-584-2778
Tawnya Denkeler, prin. Fax 584-2691

Blackwell, Nolan, Pop. 309
Blackwell Consolidated ISD 100/PK-12
PO Box 505 79506 325-282-2311
Abe Gott, supt. Fax 282-2027
www.blackwellhornets.org
Blackwell S 100/PK-12
PO Box 505 79506 325-282-2311
Bryan Shipman, prin. Fax 282-2027

Blanco, Blanco, Pop. 1,722
Blanco ISD 1,000/PK-12
814 11th St 78606 830-833-4414
Clay Rosenbaum, supt. Fax 833-2019
www.blancoisd.com
Blanco ES 500/PK-5
814 11th St 78606 830-833-4338
Jowie Walker, prin. Fax 833-4389
Blanco MS 200/6-8
814 11th St 78606 830-833-5570
Dr. Kathryn Korelich, prin. Fax 833-2507

Blanket, Brown, Pop. 382
Blanket ISD 200/K-12
901 Avenue H 76432 325-748-5311
David Whisenhunt, supt. Fax 748-3391
www.blanketisd.net
Blanket ES 200/K-8
901 Avenue H 76432 325-748-5311
Kay Ribble, prin. Fax 748-2110

Blessing, Matagorda, Pop. 923
Tidehaven ISD
Supt. — See Elmaton
Blessing ES, PO Box 170 77419 200/PK-5
Selina Garcia, prin. 979-843-4330

Bloomburg, Cass, Pop. 398
Bloomburg ISD 300/PK-12
307 W Cypress St 75556 903-728-5216
Brian Stroman, supt. Fax 728-5399
www.bloomburgisd.net
Bloomburg ES 100/PK-5
307 W Cypress St 75556 903-728-5216
Silvia Stroman, prin. Fax 728-5399

Blooming Grove, Navarro, Pop. 812
Blooming Grove ISD 900/PK-12
PO Box 258 76626 903-695-2541
Jack Lee, supt. Fax 695-2594
www.bgisd.org
Blooming Grove ES 400/PK-5
PO Box 258 76626 903-695-2541
Tiffany Munoz, prin. Fax 695-2009
Blooming Grove JHS 200/6-8
PO Box 258 76626 903-695-4201
Doyle Bell, prin. Fax 695-4601

Bloomington, Victoria, Pop. 2,445
Bloomington ISD
Supt. — See Victoria
Bloomington ES 300/2-5
PO Box 668 77951 361-333-8003
Louise Torres, prin. Fax 333-8007
Bloomington MS 200/6-8
PO Box 158 77951 361-333-8008
Abbie Barnett, prin. Fax 333-8010

Blossom, Lamar, Pop. 1,476
Prairiland ISD
Supt. — See Pattonville
Blossom ES 400/PK-5
310 High St 75416 903-982-5230
Brad Bassano, prin. Fax 982-5260

Blue Ridge, Collin, Pop. 807
Blue Ridge ISD 700/PK-12
318 School St 75424 972-752-5554
John Wink, supt. Fax 752-9084
brisd.net
Blue Ridge ES 300/PK-5
425 N Church St 75424 972-752-5554
Matthew Todd, prin. Fax 752-9950
Blue Ridge MS 200/6-8
710 Tiger Pride Cir 75424 972-752-5554
Phillip Lentz, prin. Fax 752-5363

Bluff Dale, Erath
Bluff Dale ISD 100/K-12
PO Box 101 76433 254-728-3277
Bill Morgan, supt. Fax 728-3298
www.bdisd.net
Bluff Dale S 100/K-12
PO Box 101 76433 254-728-3277
Scott Wells, prin. Fax 728-3298

Blum, Hill, Pop. 439
Blum ISD 400/PK-12
PO Box 520 76627 254-874-5231
Jeff Sanders, supt. Fax 874-5233
www.blumisd.net
Blum S 200/PK 12
PO Box 520 76627 254-874-5231
Traci Bellomy, prin. Fax 874-5233

Boerne, Kendall, Pop. 10,349
Boerne ISD 6,700/PK-12
235 Johns Rd 78006 830-357-2000
Thomas Price, supt. Fax 357-2009
www.boerne-isd.net
Boerne MS - North 500/6-8
240 Johns Rd 78006 830-357-3100
Tommy Hungate, prin. Fax 357-3199
Boerne MS - South 700/6-8
10 Cascade Caverns Rd 78015 830-357-3300
Georgia Franks, prin. Fax 357-3399
Cibolo Creek ES 600/PK-5
300 Herff Ranch Blvd 78006 830-357-4400
Eleanor Maxwell, prin. Fax 357-4499
Curington ES 600/PK-5
601 Adler St 78006 830-357-4000
Tanya Tate, prin. Fax 357-4099
Fabra ES 500/PK-5
723 Johns Rd 78006 830-357-4200
Heberto Hinojosa, prin. Fax 357-4299
Kendall ES 600/K-5
141 Old San Antonio Rd 78006 830-357-4600
Marshay Wolff, prin. Fax 357-4699
Other Schools – See Fair Oaks Ranch

Northside ISD
Supt. — See San Antonio
McAndrew ES 200/K-5
26615 Toutant Beauregard Rd 78006
DeAnn Upright, prin. 210-398-1750

Geneva S of Boerne 500/K-12
113 Cascade Caverns Rd 78015 830-775-6101
Hill Country Montessori S 100/PK-8
50 Stone Wall Dr 78006 830-229-5377
Steve Whewell, head sch Fax 229-5378
Summit Christian Academy 50/K-12
631 S School St 78006 210-254-4534
Beth Miller, prin. Fax 247-9607

Bogata, Red River, Pop. 1,141
Rivercrest ISD 700/PK-12
4100 US Highway 271 S 75417 903-632-5205
Stanley Jessee, supt. Fax 632-4691
www.rivercrestisd.net
Rivercrest ES 300/PK-5
4220 US Highway 271 S 75417 903-632-5214
Carrie Gray, prin. Fax 632-2424
Rivercrest JHS 200/6-8
4100 US Highway 271 S 75417 903-632-0878
Lee Wilson, prin. Fax 632-4691

Boling, Wharton, Pop. 1,118
Boling ISD 1,100/PK-12
PO Box 160 77420 979-657-2770
Wade Stidevent, supt. Fax 657-3265
www.bolingisd.net
Iago JHS 300/6-8
PO Box 89 77420 979-657-2826
Brett Pohler, prin. Fax 657-2828
Newgulf ES 500/PK-5
PO Box 9 77420 979-657-2837
Gerald Floyd, prin. Fax 657-3604

Bonham, Fannin, Pop. 9,979
Bonham ISD 1,800/PK-12
1005 Chestnut St 75418 903-583-5526
Dr. Marvin Beaty, supt. Fax 583-8463
www.bonhamisd.org/
Bailey Inglish ECC PK-PK
201 E 10th St 75418 903-583-8141
Rodolfo Rodriguez, prin. Fax 583-0025
Evans MS 400/4-6
1300 N Main St 75418 903-583-2914
Karli Fowler, prin. Fax 583-7133
Finley-Oates ES 600/K-3
1901 Albert Broadfoot St 75418 903-640-4090
Mary Lou Fox, prin. Fax 640-8140
Rather JHS 300/7-8
1201 N Main St 75418 903-583-7474
Traci Daniel, prin. Fax 583-3713

Morning Star Academy 100/PK-8
PO Box 236 75418 903-583-5974
Brandy Burns, head sch Fax 583-6035

Booker, Lipscomb, Pop. 1,488
Booker ISD 400/PK-12
PO Box 288 79005 806-658-4501
Dr. Brian Holt, supt. Fax 658-4503
www.bookerisd.net
Kirksey ES 200/PK-5
PO Box 288 79005 806-658-4559
Kelli Cates, prin. Fax 658-9279

Borger, Hutchinson, Pop. 13,012
Borger ISD 2,800/PK-12
200 E 9th St 79007 806-273-1000
Chance Welch, supt. Fax 273-1066
www.borgerisd.net
Belton ES 400/PK-K
800 N McGee St 79007 806-273-1059
Daniel Kotara, prin. Fax 273-1070
Borger IS 200/5-6
1321 S Florida St 79007 806-273-4342
Brandon Harris, prin. Fax 273-4343
Borger MS 600/7-8
1321 S Florida St 79007 806-273-1037
Michael Cano, prin. Fax 273-1069
Crockett ES 400/3-4
400 Kaye St 79007 806-273-1054
Randal Hatfield, prin. Fax 273-1067
Gateway ES 400/1-2
401 Tristram St 79007 806-273-1044
Teresa Bodey, prin. Fax 273-1071

Bovina, Parmer, Pop. 1,863
Bovina ISD 500/PK-12
PO Box 70 79009 806-251-1336
Denise Anderson, supt. Fax 251-1578
www.bovinaisd.org
Bovina ES 300/PK-5
PO Box 70 79009 806-251-1336
Dawn Waston, prin. Fax 251-1578
Bovina MS 100/6-8
PO Box 70 79009 806-251-1336
Mark Barnes, prin. Fax 251-1578

Bowie, Montague, Pop. 5,161
Bowie ISD 1,700/PK-12
PO Box 1168 76230 940-872-1151
Steven Monkres, supt. Fax 872-5979
www.bowieisd.net/
Bowie ES 500/PK-2
405 Lovers Ln 76230 940-872-3696
Steven Valkenaar, prin. Fax 872-3041
Bowie IS 400/3-5
800 N Mill St 76230 940-872-1153
Russell Black, prin. Fax 872-8978
Bowie JHS 400/6-8
501 E Tarrant St 76230 940-872-1152
Hector Madrigal, prin. Fax 872-8921

Gold-Burg ISD 100/PK-12
468 Prater Rd 76230 940-872-3562
Roger Ellis, supt. Fax 872-5933
www.goldburgisd.net
Gold-Burg S 100/PK-12
468 Prater Rd 76230 940-872-3562
Kim Williams, prin. Fax 872-5933

Boyd, Wise, Pop. 1,184
Boyd ISD 1,200/PK-12
PO Box 92308 76023 940-433-2327
Ted West, supt. Fax 433-9569
www.boydisd.net
Boyd ES 400/PK-3
PO Box 92308 76023 940-433-2327
Anke Bracey, prin. Fax 433-9536
Boyd IS 200/4-6
PO Box 92308 76023 940-433-2327
Daniel Bourgeois, prin. Fax 433-9568
Boyd MS 200/7-8
PO Box 92308 76023 940-433-2327
Barbara Stice, prin. Fax 433-9568

Boys Ranch, Oldham, Pop. 281
Boys Ranch ISD 300/K-12
PO Box 219 79010 806-534-2221
Kenneth Brown, supt. Fax 534-2384
www.boysranchisd.org/

Blakemore MS 100/6-8
PO Box 219 79010 806-534-2361
Brandon Sanders, prin. Fax 534-0041
Farley ES 50/K-5
PO Box 219 79010 806-534-2248
Debbie Byrd, prin. Fax 534-0111

Brackettville, Kinney, Pop. 1,675
Brackett ISD 600/PK-12
PO Box 586 78832 830-563-2491
Guillermo Mancha Ph.D., supt. Fax 563-9264
www.brackettisd.net
Brackett IS 100/4-5
PO Box 586 78832 830-563-2492
Tonya Senne Ph.D., prin. Fax 563-9355
Brackett JHS 100/6-8
PO Box 586 78832 830-563-2480
Christy Price, prin. Fax 563-9559
Jones ES 200/PK-3
PO Box 586 78832 830-563-2492
Tonya Senne Ph.D., prin. Fax 563-9355

Brady, McCulloch, Pop. 5,490
Brady ISD 1,300/PK-12
1003 W 11th St 76825 325-597-2301
Duane Limbaugh, supt. Fax 597-3984
www.bradyisd.org
Brady ES 600/PK-5
1003 W 11th St 76825 325-597-2590
Angela Bierman, prin. Fax 597-0490
Brady MS 300/6-8
1003 W 11th St 76825 325-597-8110
Shona Moore, prin. Fax 597-4166

Brazoria, Brazoria, Pop. 2,978
Columbia-Brazoria ISD
Supt. — See West Columbia
Barrow ES 600/PK-6
112 Gaines St 77422 979-799-1740
Tara Belote, prin. Fax 798-6784
West Brazos JHS 500/7-8
111 Roustabout Dr 77422 979-799-1730
Robert McReynolds, prin. Fax 798-8000
Wild Peach ES 400/PK-6
3311 County Road 353 77422 979-799-1750
Mary McCarthy, prin. Fax 798-9198

Breckenridge, Stephens, Pop. 5,738
Breckenridge ISD 1,500/PK-12
PO Box 1738 76424 254-522-9600
Timothy Seymore, supt. Fax 522-9600
www.breckenridgeisd.org
Breckenridge JHS 200/7-8
502 W Lindsey St 76424 254-212-4311
Michelene Etzel, prin. Fax 212-4311
East ES 300/PK-1
1310 E Elm St 76424 254-212-4311
Barbara Collinsworth, prin. Fax 212-4311
North ES 200/2-3
300 W 7th St 76424 254-212-4661
Jennifer Gillard, prin. Fax 212-4661
South ES 300/4-6
1001 W Elliott St 76424 254-212-4691
Kenna Rainey, prin. Fax 212-4691

Bremond, Robertson, Pop. 926
Bremond ISD 400/PK-12
601 W Collins St 76629 254-746-7145
Daryl Stuard, supt. Fax 746-7726
www.bremondisd.net
Bremond ES 200/PK-5
601 W Collins St 76629 254-746-7145
Ronnie Groholski, prin. Fax 746-7726
Bremond MS 100/6-8
601 W Collins St 76629 254-746-7145
John Burnett, prin. Fax 746-7726

Brenham, Washington, Pop. 15,543
Brenham ISD 4,900/PK-12
PO Box 1147 77834 979-277-3700
Walter Jackson Ed.D., supt. Fax 277-3701
www.brenhamisd.net
Alton ES 500/K-4
1210 S Market St 77833 979-277-3870
Michael Ogg, prin. Fax 277-3871
Brenham Early Childhood Learning Center 200/PK-PK
PO Box 1147 77834 979-277-3770
Toni Schwartz, prin. Fax 277-3771
Brenham ES 800/K-4
1000 W Blue Bell Rd 77833 979-277-3880
Jennifer Vest, prin. Fax 277-3881
Brenham JHS 800/7-8
1200 Carlee Dr 77833 979-277-3830
Bryan Bryant, prin. Fax 277-3831
Brenham MS 700/5-6
1600 S Blue Bell Rd 77833 979-277-3845
Peggy Still, prin. Fax 277-3846
Krause ES 700/K-4
2201 E Stone St 77833 979-277-3860
Courtney Mason, prin. Fax 277-3861

Brenham Christian Academy 50/PK-12
2111 S Blue Bell Rd 77833 979-830-8480
Sheila Suders, prin. Fax 830-1687
First Baptist Church S 200/PK-6
302 Pahl St 77833 979-836-6411
Nancy Jahns, admin. Fax 836-3269
Grace Lutheran S 100/PK-8
1212 W Jefferson St 77833 979-836-2030
Rev. Thomas Obersat, prin. Fax 836-0510
St. Paul's Christian Day S 300/PK-6
305 W Third St 77833 979-836-1145
Sherrie Winkelmann, prin. Fax 836-5795

Bridge City, Orange, Pop. 7,734
Bridge City ISD 2,800/PK-12
1031 W Round Bunch Rd 77611 409-735-1500
Todd Lintzen, supt. Fax 735-1512
www.bridgecityisd.net
Bridge City ES 800/PK-2
1035 W Round Bunch Rd 77611 409-735-0900
Melanie Toups, prin. Fax 735-0906
Bridge City IS 600/3-5
1029 W Round Bunch Rd 77611 409-792-8800
Dr. Tara Fountain, prin. Fax 792-8827
Bridge City MS 600/6-8
300 Bower Dr 77611 409-735-1513
Dr. Lydia Gonzales-Burton, prin. Fax 735-1517

Bridgeport, Wise, Pop. 5,936
Bridgeport ISD 2,100/PK-12
2107 15th St 76426 940-683-5124
Brandon Peavey, supt. Fax 683-4268
www.bridgeportisd.net
Bridgeport ES 600/PK-2
1408 Elementary Dr 76426 940-683-5955
Martha Bock, prin. Fax 683-5079
Bridgeport IS 400/3-5
1400 US Highway 380 76426 940-683-5784
Rita Lemoine, prin. Fax 683-4086
Bridgeport MS 500/6-8
702 17th St 76426 940-683-2273
Travis Whisenant, prin. Fax 683-5812

Briscoe, Wheeler
Fort Elliott Consolidated ISD 100/PK-12
PO Box 138 79011 806-375-2454
Frank Belcher, supt. Fax 375-2327
www.fecisd.net
Ft. Elliott S 100/PK-12
PO Box 138 79011 806-375-2454
Maria Gomez, prin. Fax 375-2327

Broaddus, San Augustine, Pop. 202
Broaddus ISD 400/PK-12
PO Box 58 75929 936-872-3041
Mark Anglin, supt. Fax 872-3699
www.broaddusisd.net
Broaddus ES 200/PK-5
PO Box 58 75929 936-872-3315
Lucas Holloway, prin. Fax 872-3439

Brock, Parker
Brock ISD 1,000/K-12
410 Eagle Spirit Ln 76087 817-594-7642
Scott Drillette, supt. Fax 599-3246
www.brockisd.net
Brock ES 500/K-4
100 Grindstone Rd 76087 817-594-8017
Erin Griffith, prin. Fax 599-5117
Brock MS 200/5-8
300 Grindstone Rd 76087 817-594-3195
Ingia Saxton, prin. Fax 594-3191

Bronte, Coke, Pop. 986
Bronte ISD 300/PK-12
PO Box 670 76933 325-473-2511
Tim Siler, supt. Fax 473-2313
www.bronteisd.net
Bronte ES 100/PK-6
PO Box 670 76933 325-473-2251
John Phillips, prin. Fax 473-2313

Brookeland, Sabine
Brookeland ISD 400/PK-12
187 Wildcat Walk 75931 409-698-2677
Kevin McCugh, supt. Fax 698-2533
www.brookelandisd.net
Brookeland ES 200/PK-5
187 Wildcat Walk 75931 409-698-2152
Charlotte Odom, prin. Fax 698-9874

Brookesmith, Brown
Brookesmith ISD 200/PK-12
PO Box 706 76827 325-643-3023
Steve Mickelson, supt. Fax 643-3378
www.brookesmithisd.net/
Brookesmith S 200/PK-12
PO Box 706 76827 325-643-3023
Sandy Lehman, supt. Fax 643-3378

Brookshire, Waller, Pop. 4,653
Royal ISD
Supt. — See Pattison
Royal ECC 400/PK-1
2300 Durkin Rd 77423 281-934-3147
Susan Hopkins, prin. Fax 934-4122
Royal ES 800/2-5
2222 Durkin Rd 77423 281-934-3166
Kerry Kernwein, prin. Fax 934-3358
Royal JHS 400/6-8
2520 Durkin Rd 77423 281-934-2241
Justin Johnston, prin. Fax 934-2329
Royal STEM Academy 200/2-8
2500 Durkin Rd 77423 281-934-3181
K.T. Trimbur-Glenn, admin. Fax 934-3186

Brownfield, Terry, Pop. 9,594
Brownfield ISD 1,800/PK-12
601 E Tahoka Rd 79316 806-637-2591
Tanya Monroe, supt. Fax 637-9208
www.brownfieldisd.net
Bright Beginnings Academic Center 200/PK-PK
1202 Seagraves Rd 79316 806-637-0757
Kathleen Crooks, prin.
Brownfield MS 400/6-8
1001 E Broadway St 79316 806-637-7521
Artemio Ontiveros, prin. Fax 637-2919
Colonial Heights ES 300/K-1
1100 E Reppto St 79316 806-637-4282
Vicki Hathaway, prin. Fax 637-1815
Oak Grove ES 500/2-5
1000 E Cactus Ln 79316 806-637-6455
Susan Brisendine, prin. Fax 637-3636

Brownsboro, Henderson, Pop. 1,031
Brownsboro ISD 2,800/PK-12
PO Box 465 75756 903-852-3701
Tommy Hunter, supt. Fax 852-3957
www.gobearsgo.net
Brownsboro ES 500/PK-3
PO Box 465 75756 903-852-6461
Robbi McCarter, prin. Fax 852-2718
Brownsboro IS 300/4-6
PO Box 465 75756 903-852-7325
Laura Ballard, prin. Fax 852-6745
Brownsboro JHS 400/7-8
PO Box 465 75756 903-852-6931
Bradley Robertson, prin. Fax 852-5238
Other Schools – See Chandler

Brownsville, Cameron, Pop. 174,679
Brownsville ISD 49,100/PK-12
1900 Price Rd 78521 956-548-8000
Dr. Esperanza Zendejas, supt. Fax 548-8010
www.bisd.us
Aiken ES 800/PK-5
6290 Southmost Rd 78521 956-986-5200
Dora Fasci-Marquez, prin. Fax 986-5208
Benavides ES 600/PK-5
3101 McAllen Rd 78520 956-350-3250
Sherry Stout, prin. Fax 350-3273
Besteiro MS 900/6-8
6280 Southmost Rd 78521 956-544-3900
Teresa Nunez, prin. Fax 544-3946
Breeden ES 700/PK-5
3955 Dana Ave 78526 956-554-4730
Mandy Delgado, prin. Fax 547-4305
Brite ES 700/PK-5
450 S Browne Ave 78521 956-698-3000
Nicole Clint, prin. Fax 831-5146
Burns ES 900/PK-5
1974 E Alton Gloor Blvd 78526 956-548-8490
Alma Garza, prin. Fax 548-8489
Canales ES 700/PK-5
1811 International Blvd 78521 956-548-8900
Dr. Edward Ude, prin. Fax 548-8912
Castaneda ES 600/PK-5
3201 Lima St 78521 956-548-8800
Nora Camargo, prin. Fax 548-8811
Champion ES 900/PK-5
4750 Bowie Rd 78521 956-832-6200
Ricardo Torres, prin. Fax 832-6225
Cromack ES 700/PK-5
3200 E 30th St 78521 956-548-8820
Frank Ortiz, prin. Fax 548-8824
Cummings MS 700/6-8
1800 Cummings Pl 78520 956-548-8630
Teresa Nunez, prin. Fax 548-8218
Del Castillo ES 500/PK-5
105 Morningside Rd 78521 956-982-2600
Petra Torres, prin. Fax 982-2622
Egly ES 1,000/PK-5
445 Land O Lakes Dr 78521 956-548-8850
Pedro Vidal, prin. Fax 982-3074
El Jardin ES 800/PK-5
6911 Boca Chica Blvd 78521 956-831-6000
Marina Flores, prin. Fax 831-6024
Faulk MS 900/6-8
2000 Roosevelt St 78521 956-548-8500
Benita Villarreal, prin. Fax 548-8507
Gallegos ES 700/PK-5
2700 Rancho Viejo Ave 78526 956-547-4230
Theresa Villafuerte, prin. Fax 547-4232
Garcia MS 1,100/6-8
5701 FM 802 78526 956-832-6300
Kathleen Jimenez, prin. Fax 832-6304
Garden Park ES 700/PK-5
855 Military Rd 78520 956-982-2630
Victor Caballero, prin. Fax 982-2644
Garza ES 700/PK-5
200 Esperanza Rd 78521 956-982-2660
Maria Lara, prin. Fax 982-2682
Gonzalez ES 900/PK-5
4350 Jaime J Zapata Ave 78521 956-831-6030
Dr. Timothy Cuff, prin. Fax 831-6040
Hudson ES 900/PK-5
2980 FM 802 78526 956-574-6400
Rachel Ayala, prin. Fax 574-6403
Keller ES 600/K-5
2540 W Alton Gloor Blvd 78520 956-547-4400
Javier Garza, prin. Fax 554-7150
Longoria ES 400/PK-5
2400 E Van Buren St 78520 956-982-2700
Myrta Garza, prin. Fax 982-2723
Lucio MS 1,100/6-8
300 N Vermillion Ave 78521 956-831-4550
Chester Arizmendi, prin. Fax 838-2298
Manzano MS 900/6-8
2580 W Alton Gloor Blvd 78520 956-548-9800
Marisol Trevino, prin. Fax 548-6772
Martin ES 700/PK-5
1701 Stanford Ave 78520 956-982-2730
Gilda Pena, prin. Fax 982-3032
Morningside ES 700/PK-5
1025 Morningside Rd 78521 956-982-2760
Jose Martinez, prin. Fax 982-2787
Oliveira MS 1,200/6-8
444 Land O Lakes Dr 78521 956-548-8530
Cynthia Castro, prin. Fax 544-3968
Ortiz ES 600/PK-5
2500 W Alton Gloor Blvd 78520 956-698-1100
Patricia Garza, prin. Fax 546-6611
Palm Grove ES 600/PK-5
7942 Southmost Rd 78521 956-982-3850
Patricia Chacon, prin. Fax 986-5070
Paredes ES 900/PK-5
3700 Heritage Trl 78526 956-574-5582
Melissa Werbiski, prin. Fax 574-5584
Pena ES 600/K-5
4975 Salida De Luna 78526 956-547-7100
Yolanda Turbeville, prin. Fax 838-6545
Perez ES 600/PK-5
2514 Shidler Dr 78521 956-982-2800
Michael Moreno, prin. Fax 982-2806
Perkins MS 1,100/6-8
4750 Austin Rd 78521 956-831-8770
Beatriz Hernandez, prin. Fax 831-8789

Pullam ES 500/K-5
3200 Madrid Ave 78520 956-547-3700
Celia de los Santos, prin. Fax 350-2880
Putegnat ES 500/PK-5
730 E 8th St 78520 956-548-8930
Dr. Aidee Vasquez, prin. Fax 548-8947
Resaca ES 300/PK-5
901 E Filmore St 78520 956-982-2900
Lucy Hernandez, prin. Fax 982-2916
Russell ES 900/PK-5
800 Lakeside Blvd 78520 956-548-8960
Oscar Cantu, prin. Fax 548-8889
Sharp ES 500/PK-5
1439 Palm Blvd 78520 956-982-2930
Irma Segura, prin. Fax 982-2948
Skinner ES 600/PK-5
411 W Saint Charles St 78520 956-982-2830
Kim Moore, prin. Fax 982-2849
Southmost ES 500/PK-5
5245 Southmost Rd 78521 956-548-8870
Anabela Almanza, prin. Fax 554-4245
Stell MS 1,100/6-8
1105 E Los Ebanos Blvd 78520 956-548-8560
Obed Leal, prin. Fax 546-2579
Stillman MS 900/6-8
2977 W Tandy Rd 78520 956-698-1000
Eduardo Martinez, prin. Fax 350-3231
Vela MS 1,000/6-8
4905 Paredes Line Rd 78526 956-548-7770
Joel Wood, prin. Fax 548-7780
Vermillion Road ES 900/PK-5
6895 FM 802 78526 956-831-6060
Socorro Houghtaling, prin. Fax 831-1093
Victoria Heights ES 400/PK-5
2801 E 13th St 78521 956-982-2960
Ruben Martinez, prin. Fax 982-2988
Villa Nueva ES 500/PK-5
7455 Old Military Rd 78520 956-542-3957
Melissa Gutierrez, prin. Fax 544-0720
Yturria ES 500/PK-5
2955 W Tandy Rd 78520 956-350-3200
Sandra Cortez, prin. Fax 350-3207

Los Fresnos Consolidated ISD
Supt. — See Los Fresnos
Olmito ES 600/PK-5
2500 Arroyo Blvd 78526 956-233-3950
Linda Rodriguez, prin. Fax 350-8835
Rancho Verde ES 600/PK-5
101 Rancho Alegre 78521 956-254-5232
Maria E. Pineda, prin. Fax 350-8843
Romero ES 400/PK-5
9705 Cajun Blvd 78521 956-254-5210
Veronica Grimaldo, prin. Fax 350-2645

Brownsville Montessori Academy 100/PK-8
36 S Coria St 78520 956-548-1952
Coram Deo Classical Academy 50/1-11
1175 W Price Rd Ste 3 78520 956-459-7162
Episcopal Day S 300/PK-6
34 N Coria St 78520 956-542-5231
Lynda McCrocklin, head sch Fax 504-9486
First Baptist S 300/PK-12
1600 Boca Chica Blvd 78520 956-542-4854
Terry Roberts, supt. Fax 542-6188
Guadalupe Regional MS 100/6-8
1214 Lincoln St 78521 956-504-5568
Maria Alvarado, prin. Fax 504-9393
Incarnate Word Academy 300/PK-8
244 Resaca Blvd 78520 956-546-4486
Sr. Marilyn Springs, prin. Fax 504-3960
Kenmont S 500/PK-8
2734 N Coria St 78520 956-542-0500
St. Luke S 200/PK-8
2850 E Price Rd 78521 956-544-7982
Anne Serrato, prin. Fax 544-4874
St. Mary's S 500/PK-6
1300 E Los Ebanos Blvd 78520 956-546-1805
Ana Gomez M.Ed., prin. Fax 546-0787

Brownwood, Brown, Pop. 19,003
Brownwood ISD 3,500/PK-12
PO Box 730 76804 325-643-5644
Dr. Joe Young, supt. Fax 643-5640
www.brownwoodisd.org
Brownwood MS 500/7-8
1600 Calvert Rd 76801 325-646-9545
Richard Sweaney, prin. Fax 646-3785
Coggin IS 300/4-6
800 Rogan St 76801 325-646-0462
Todd Lewis, prin. Fax 646-9317
East ES 400/PK-3
2700 Vincent St 76801 325-646-2937
Nanda Wilbourn, prin. Fax 646-5900
Northwest ES 500/PK-3
311 Bluffview Dr 76801 325-646-0707
Christine Young, prin. Fax 646-2449
Woodland Heights ES 500/PK-3
3900 4th St 76801 325-646-8633
Jenny Swanzy, prin. Fax 641-0109

Victory Life Academy 100/PK-12
PO Box 940 76804 325-641-2223
Debbie Hagood, head sch Fax 641-8063

Bruni, Webb, Pop. 377
Webb Consolidated ISD 300/PK-12
PO Box 206 78344 361-747-5415
Heriberto Gonzalez, supt. Fax 747-5202
www.webbcisd.org
Bruni MS 100/6-8
PO Box 206 78344 361-747-5415
Sandra Castillo, prin. Fax 747-5298
Other Schools – See Oilton

Bryan, Brazos, Pop. 75,248
Bryan ISD 15,400/PK-12
101 N Texas Ave 77803 979-209-1000
Dr. Christie Whitbeck, supt. Fax 209-1004
www.bryanisd.org
Austin MS 800/7-8
800 S Coulter Dr 77803 979-209-6700
Rachel Layton, prin. Fax 209-6741
Bonham ES 800/PK-5
3100 Wilkes St 77803 979-209-1200
Gloria Garcia-Rhodes, prin. Fax 209-1218
Bowen ES 400/K-4
3870 Copperfield Dr 77802 979-209-1300
Bridget Cooper, prin. Fax 209-1306
Branch ES 600/K-4
2040 W Villa Maria Rd 77807 979-209-2900
Karen Kaspar, prin. Fax 209-2910
Crockett ES 500/PK-4
401 Elm Ave 77801 979-209-2960
Debi Ehrhardt, prin. Fax 209-2965
Davila MS 600/7-8
2751 N Earl Rudder Fwy 77803 979-209-7150
Shannon McGehee, prin. Fax 209-7151
Fannin ES 500/PK-4
1200 Baker Ave 77803 979-209-3800
Rebecca Ryberg, prin. Fax 209-3826
Henderson ES 500/K-4
801 Matous Dr 77802 979-209-1560
Danielle Legg, prin. Fax 209-1566
Houston ES 500/K-4
4501 Canterbury Dr 77802 979-209-1360
Susan Finch, prin. Fax 209-1364
Johnson ES 500/K-4
3800 Oak Hill Dr 77802 979-209-1460
Amy Newbold, prin. Fax 209-1462
Jones ES 700/PK-4
1400 Pecan St 77803 979-209-3900
Linda Montoya, prin. Fax 209-3912
Kemp-Carver ES 600/PK-4
750 Bruin Trce 77803 979-209-3760
Alison Boggan, prin. Fax 209-3764
Long IS 1,100/5-6
1106 N Harvey Mitchell Pkwy 77803 979-209-6500
Cody Satterfield, prin. Fax 209-6566
Mitchell ES 500/K-4
2500 Austins Colony Pkwy 77808 979-209-1400
Donna Wallace, prin Fax 209-1420
Navarro ES 600/K-4
4619 Northwood Dr 77803 979-209-1260
Sara Rueda, prin. Fax 209-1270
Neal ES 500/K-4
801 W Martin Luther King Jr 77803 979-209-3860
Juantia Collins, prin. Fax 209-3863
Rayburn IS 800/5-6
1048 N Earl Rudder Fwy 77802 979-209-6600
Justin Smith, prin. Fax 209-6611
Sul Ross ES 400/K-4
3300 Parkway Ter 77802 979-209-1500
Kristina Brunson, prin. Fax 209-1513

Allen Academy 300/PK-12
3201 Boonville Rd 77802 979-776-0731
Dr. Matthew Rush, head sch Fax 774-7769
Brazos Christian S 400/PK-12
3000 W Villa Maria Rd 77807 979-823-1000
Dr. Jeff McMaster, hdmstr. Fax 823-1774
Brazos Valley Cornerstone Christian Acad 100/K-12
3200 Cavitt Ave 77801 979-694-8200
St. Joseph Catholic ES 200/PK-5
901 E Wm J Bryan Pkwy 77803 979-822-6643
Jim Rike, prin. Fax 779-2810
St. Michael's Episcopal S 100/PK-12
2500 S College Ave 77801 979-822-2715
Still Creek Christian Academy 100/K-12
6055 Hearne Rd 77808 979-589-1816
James Inmon, prin. Fax 589-2152

Bryson, Jack, Pop. 518
Bryson ISD 200/PK-12
300 N McCloud St 76427 940-392-3281
David Stout, supt. Fax 392-2086
www.brysonisd.net
Bryson S 200/PK-12
300 N McCloud St 76427 940-392-3281
Eric Wilson, prin. Fax 392-2086

Buckholts, Milam, Pop. 513
Buckholts ISD 200/PK-12
PO Box 248 76518 254-593-2744
Nancy Sandlin, supt. Fax 593-2270
www.buckholtsisd.net
Buckholts S 200/PK-12
PO Box 248 76518 254-593-2744
Kris Shaver, prin. Fax 593-2270

Buda, Hays, Pop. 7,167
Hays Consolidated ISD
Supt. — See Kyle
Barton MS 900/6-8
4950 Jack C Hays Trl 78610 512-268-1472
Teri Eubank, prin. Fax 268-1610
Buda ES 500/PK-5
300 N San Marcos St 78610 512-268-8439
Tim Robinson, prin. Fax 295-2946
Carpenter Hill ES 600/PK-5
4410 Route 967 78610 512-268-8509
Debbie Brown, prin. Fax 295-4049
Dahlstrom MS 900/6-8
3600 FM 967 78610 512-268-8441
Dr. Michael Watson, prin. Fax 295-5346
Elm Grove ES 600/K-5
801 S FM 1626 78610 512-268-8440
Kathy Faulks, prin. Fax 295-6809
Green ES 600/PK-5
1301 Old Goforth Rd 78610 512-268-8438
Dr. Tracie Robinson, prin. Fax 295-4107
McCormick MS 6-8
5700 Dacy Ln 78610 512-268-8508
James Cruz, prin. Fax 295-4696
Pfluger ES 600/K-5
4951 Marsh Ln 78610 512-268-8510
Kathy Noack, prin. Fax 295-6826

Santa Cruz Catholic S 200/PK-8
PO Box 160 78610 512-312-2137
Susan Flanagan, prin. Fax 312-2143

Buffalo, Leon, Pop. 1,845
Buffalo ISD 900/PK-12
708 Cedar Creek Rd 75831 903-322-3765
Lacy Freeman, supt. Fax 322-3091
www.buffaloisd.net
Buffalo ES 300/PK-2
1700 E Commerce St 75831 903-322-3562
Lisa Boudiette, prin. Fax 322-4077
Buffalo JHS 300/3-8
335 Bison Trl 75831 903-322-4340
Greg Kennedy, prin. Fax 322-4803

Buffalo Gap, Taylor, Pop. 460
Jim Ned Consolidated ISD
Supt. — See Tuscola
Buffalo Gap ES 200/PK-5
PO Box 608 79508 325-572-3533
Cristi Doty, prin. Fax 572-3850

Bullard, Smith, Pop. 2,447
Bullard ISD 2,300/PK-12
PO Box 250 75757 903-894-6639
Todd Schneider, supt. Fax 894-9291
www.bullardisd.net
Bullard ECC, PO Box 250 75757 PK-K
Michelle Hurst, prin. 903-894-6389
Bullard ES 500/3-4
PO Box 250 75757 903-894-2930
Jenny Kasson, prin. Fax 894-2931
Bullard IS 300/5-6
PO Box 250 75757 903-894-6793
Jodie Albritton, prin. Fax 894-3982
Bullard MS 400/7-8
PO Box 250 75757 903-894-6533
Kenley Dover, prin. Fax 894-7592
Bullard PS 400/1-2
PO Box 250 75757 903-894-2890
Michelle Hurst, prin. Fax 894-2893

Brook Hill S 500/PK-12
1051 N Houston St 75757 903-894-5000
Rod Fletcher, head sch Fax 894-6332

Bulverde, Comal, Pop. 4,570
Comal ISD
Supt. — See New Braunfels
Johnson Ranch ES 200/PK-5
30501 Johnson Way 78163 830-885-8600
Suzanne Seabolt, prin. Fax 885-8601
Rahe Bulverde ES 400/PK-5
1715 E Ammann Rd 78163 830-885-1600
Amy Malone, prin. Fax 885-1601

Bracken Christian S 300/PK-12
670 Old Boerne Rd 78163 830-438-3211
Ed Thomas, supt. Fax 980-2327
Gloria Deo Academy 100/PK-12
1100 Bulverde Rd 78163 830-980-8511
Jamie King, head sch Fax 438-2179
Living Rock Academy 100/K-12
2500 Bulverde Rd 78163 830-387-2929
James Johnson, head sch

Buna, Jasper, Pop. 2,103
Buna ISD 1,500/PK-12
PO Box 1087 77612 409-994-5101
Dr. Steve Hyden, supt. Fax 994-4808
www.bunaisd.net
Buna ES 800/PK-5
PO Box 1087 77612 409-994-4840
Julie Motomura, prin. Fax 994-4808
Buna JHS 400/6-8
PO Box 1087 77612 409-994-4860
Amber Flowers, prin. Fax 994-4808

Burkburnett, Wichita, Pop. 10,638
Burkburnett ISD 3,500/PK-12
416 Glendale St 76354 940-569-3326
Tylor Chaplin, supt. Fax 569-4776
www.burkburnettisd.org
Burkburnett MS 700/6-8
108 S Avenue D 76354 940-569-3381
Michael Baughman, prin. Fax 569-7116
Evans ES 600/PK-5
1015 S Berry St 76354 940-569-3311
Michelle Wiese, prin. Fax 569-2719
Hardin ES 500/PK-5
100 N Avenue D 76354 940-569-5253
Kendy Johnston, prin. Fax 569-1509
Other Schools – See Wichita Falls

Burke, Angelina, Pop. 734

Crimson Christian Academy 50/K-12
7020 S Highway 59, 936-639-1222
Crimson Christian Academy K-12
7020 S US Highway 59, 936-639-1222

Burkeville, Newton
Burkeville ISD 200/PK-12
PO Box 218 75932 409-565-2201
Dr. Brant Graham, supt. Fax 565-2012
www.burkevilleisd.org
Burkeville ES 100/PK-6
PO Box 218 75932 409-565-4284
Kimberly Urie, prin. Fax 565-2461

Burleson, Johnson, Pop. 36,116
Burleson ISD 11,400/PK-12
1160 SW Wilshire Blvd 76028 817-245-1000
Dr. Bret Jimerson, supt. Fax 447-5737
www.burlesonisd.net
Academy at Nola Dunn 700/K-5
201 S Dobson St 76028 817-245-3300
Lindsey Byrd, prin. Fax 447-0523
Academy of Arts at Bransom 500/PK-5
820 S Hurst Rd 76028 817-245-3600
Joy Burchfield, prin. Fax 447-5888
Acad of Leadership & Technology @ Mound 400/K-5
205 SW Thomas St 76028 817-245-3100
Marla Bennett, prin. Fax 447-5845
Brock ES 600/PK-5
12000 Oak Grove Rd S 76028 817-245-3800
Kim Kimberling, prin. Fax 293-0488
Clinkscale ES 600/K-5
600 Blayke St 76028 817-245-3900
Lauri Allen, prin. Fax 295-4651
Frazier ES 600/PK-5
1125 NW Summercrest Blvd 76028 817-245-3000
Dena Schimming, prin. Fax 447-4916
Hajek ES 600/K-5
555 NE McAlister Rd 76028 817-245-3700
Jeanie French, prin. Fax 447-4921
Hughes MS 1,200/6-8
316 SW Thomas St 76028 817-245-0600
Ben Renner, prin. Fax 447-5748
Kerr MS 1,200/6-8
517 SW Johnson Ave 76028 817-245-0750
Dr. Miller Beaird, prin. Fax 447-5742
Norwood ES 400/PK-5
619 Evelyn Ln 76028 817-245-3400
Tracy Besgrove, prin. Fax 447-5831
STEAM Academy at Stribling 400/K-5
1881 E Renfro St 76028 817-245-3500
Dr. Jim Calvin, prin. Fax 447-5835
STEAM MS, 201 S Hurst Rd 76028 600/6-8
Brandon Johnson, prin. 817-245-1000
Taylor ES 500/PK-5
400 NE Alsbury Blvd 76028 817-245-3200
Ryan Timm, prin. Fax 447-5841

Joshua ISD
Supt. — See Joshua
Nichols MS 600/6-8
2845 FM 731 76028 817-202-2500
Brian Rosatelli, prin. Fax 202-2649
North Joshua ES 600/PK-5
100 Ranchway Dr 76028 817-202-2500
Dr. Somer Yocom, prin. Fax 295-9836

Mansfield ISD
Supt. — See Mansfield
Tarver-Rendon ES 600/PK-4
6065 Retta Mansfield Rd 76028 817-299-7880
Jamie Norwood, prin. Fax 453-6599

Burleson Adventist S 100/PK-8
1635 Fox Ln 76028 817-295-6812
Holy Cross Christian Academy 200/PK-8
PO Box 3113 76097 817-295-7232
Karen Matejka, admin. Fax 295-6307

Burnet, Burnet, Pop. 5,927
Burnet Consolidated ISD 3,200/PK-12
208 E Brier Ln 78611 512-756-2124
Keith McBurnett, supt. Fax 756-7498
www.burnetcisd.net
Burnet MS 700/6-8
1401 N Main St 78611 512-756-6182
Steve Grant, prin. Fax 756-7955
Richey ES 500/3-5
500 E Graves St 78611 512-756-2609
B. J. Gates, prin. Fax 756-2624
Shady Grove ES 700/PK-2
111 Shady Grove Rd 78611 512-756-2126
Bonnie Sullivan, prin. Fax 756-6993
Other Schools – See Bertram

Burton, Washington, Pop. 298
Burton ISD 400/PK-12
PO Box 37 77835 979-289-3131
Dr. Edna Kennedy, supt. Fax 289-3076
www.burtonisd.net
Burton ES 200/PK-6
PO Box 129 77835 979-289-2175
Melinda Fuchs, prin. Fax 289-0170

Bushland, Potter
Bushland ISD 1,500/PK-12
PO Box 60 79012 806-359-6683
Don Wood, supt. Fax 359-6769
www.bushlandisd.net
Bushland ES 500/PK-4
PO Box 60 79012 806-359-5410
Bobbye Morgan, prin. Fax 322-1166
Bushland MS 400/5-8
PO Box 60 79012 806-359-5418
Jessica Garrett, prin. Fax 355-2841

Bynum, Hill, Pop. 197
Bynum ISD 200/PK-12
PO Box 68 76631 254-531-2341
Larry Mynarcik, supt. Fax 531-2342
www.bynumisd.net
Bynum S 200/PK-12
PO Box 68 76631 254-531-2341
Lyndsey Pederson, prin. Fax 531-2342

Cactus, Moore, Pop. 3,093
Dumas ISD
Supt. — See Dumas
Cactus ES 400/PK-4
PO Box 368 79013 806-966-5102
T.J. Funderburg, prin. Fax 966-5561

Caddo Mills, Hunt, Pop. 1,323
Caddo Mills ISD 1,500/PK-12
PO Box 160 75135 903-527-6056
Vicki Payne, supt. Fax 527-4883
www.caddomillsisd.org/caddomillsisd/site/default.asp
Caddo Mills MS 400/6-8
PO Box 160 75135 903-527-3161
Anne Payne, prin. Fax 527-2379
Griffis ES 400/PK-5
PO Box 160 75135 903-527-3525
Kendra Mosher, prin. Fax 527-3597
Lee ES 300/PK-5
PO Box 160 75135 903-527-3162
Vonda Farmer, prin. Fax 527-0166

Caldwell, Burleson, Pop. 4,063
Caldwell ISD 1,800/PK-12
203 N Gray St 77836 979-567-2400
Andrew Peters, supt. Fax 567-9876
caldwellisd.net
Caldwell ES 500/PK-2
203 N Gray St 77836 979-567-2404
Erin Supak, prin. Fax 567-9422
Caldwell IS 400/3-5
203 N Gray St 77836 979-567-2403
Shaunna Savage, prin. Fax 567-7131
Caldwell MS 400/6-8
203 N Gray St 77836 979-567-2402
Nathan Goodlett, prin. Fax 567-7433

First Baptist S 100/PK-8
PO Box 687 77836 979-567-3771
Tabbatha Pipes, admin. Fax 567-9267

Callisburg, Cooke, Pop. 352
Callisburg ISD 1,200/PK-12
148 Dozier St, 940-665-0540
Steve Clugston, supt. Fax 668-2706
www.cisdtx.net
Callisburg MS 300/6-8
148 Dozier St, 940-665-0961
Bronwyn Werts, prin. Fax 665-2849
Other Schools – See Gainesville

Calvert, Robertson, Pop. 1,179
Calvert ISD 200/PK-12
PO Box 7 77837 979-364-2824
Lynn Ponder, supt. Fax 364-2468
www.calvertisd.com/
Calvert S 200/PK-12
PO Box 7 77837 979-364-2824
Ronnell Trotter, prin. Fax 364-2468

Cameron, Milam, Pop. 5,512
Cameron ISD 1,700/PK-12
PO Box 712 76520 254-697-3512
Allan Sapp, supt. Fax 697-2448
www.cameronisd.net
Cameron ES 400/3-5
PO Box 712 76520 254-697-2381
Wendy Mahan, prin. Fax 605-0356
Cameron JHS 400/6-8
PO Box 712 76520 254-697-2131
Wendy Mahan, prin. Fax 605-0379
Milam ES 500/PK-2
PO Box 712 76520 254-697-3641
Rod Allen, prin. Fax 605-0354

Campbell, Hunt, Pop. 622
Campbell ISD 400/PK-12
480 N Patterson St 75422 903-862-3259
Dr. Denise Morgan, supt. Fax 862-2222
www.campbellisd.org
Campbell ES 200/PK-5
480 N Patterson St 75422 903-862-3253
Stephenia Erwin, prin. Fax 862-3546

Camp Wood, Real, Pop. 689
Nueces Canyon Consolidated ISD
Supt. — See Barksdale
Nueces Canyon ES 100/K-6
Highway 337 78833 830-597-3218
Luci Harmon, prin. Fax 597-6197

Canadian, Hemphill, Pop. 2,631
Canadian ISD 1,000/PK-12
800 Hillside Ave 79014 806-323-5393
Kyle Lynch, supt. Fax 323-8143
www.canadianisd.net
Baker ES 200/3-5
800 Hillside Ave 79014 806-323-5386
Jamie Copley, prin. Fax 323-9916
Canadian ES 300/PK-2
800 Hillside Ave 79014 806-323-9331
Reagan Oles, prin. Fax 323-6852
Canadian MS 200/6-8
800 Hillside Ave 79014 806-323-5351
Bruce Bryant, prin. Fax 323-8791

Canton, Van Zandt, Pop. 3,519
Canton ISD 2,100/PK-12
1045 S Buffalo St 75103 903-567-4179
Jay Tullos, supt. Fax 567-2370
www.cantonisd.net
Canton ES 500/PK-2
1163 S Buffalo St 75103 903-567-6521
Kelly Lamar, prin. Fax 567-5373
Canton IS 400/3-5
1190 W Highway 243 75103 903-567-6418
Marsha Robison, prin. Fax 567-2956
Canton JHS 500/6-8
1115 S Buffalo St 75103 903-567-4329
Henry Tracy, prin. Fax 567-1298

Canutillo, El Paso, Pop. 6,297
Canutillo ISD
Supt. — See El Paso
Alderete MS 700/6-8
PO Box 100 79835 915-877-6600
Dr. Oscar Rico, prin. Fax 877-6607
Canutillo ES 700/PK-5
PO Box 100 79835 915-877-7600
Julieta Melendez, prin. Fax 877-7607
Canutillo MS 700/6-8
PO Box 100 79835 915-877-7900
Mark Paz, prin. Fax 877-7907
Childress ES 500/PK-5
PO Box 100 79835 915-877-7700
Maria Reyna Salcedo, prin. Fax 877-7707
Damian ES 600/PK-5
PO Box 100 79835 915-877-6800
Jesus Barba, prin. Fax 877-6819
Davenport ES 400/PK-5
PO Box 100 79835 915-886-6400
Marta Strobach, prin. Fax 886-6407

Canyon, Randall, Pop. 13,164
Canyon ISD 9,400/PK-12
PO Box 899 79015 806-677-2600
Darryl Flusche, supt. Fax 677-2659
www.canyonisd.net
Canyon IS 600/5-6
506 8th St 79015 806-677-2800
Tricia Cook, prin. Fax 677-2829
Canyon JHS 600/7-8
910 9th Ave 79015 806-677-2700
Kirk Kear, prin. Fax 677-2739
Crestview ES 500/K-4
80 Hunsley Rd 79015 806-677-2780
Shelly Willeford, prin. Fax 677-2799
Reeves-Hinger ES 700/PK-4
1005 21st St 79015 806-677-2870
Brandi Parker, prin. Fax 677-2889
Other Schools – See Amarillo

Canyon Lake, Comal, Pop. 20,951
Comal ISD
Supt. — See New Braunfels
Mountain Valley ES 400/PK-5
310 Cannan Rd 78133 830-885-9500
Jennifer Smith, prin. Fax 885-9501
Startzville ES 500/PK-5
42111 FM 3159 78133 830-885-8000
Jan Bettersworth, prin. Fax 885-8001

Carmine, Fayette, Pop. 250
Round Top - Carmine ISD 300/PK-12
PO Box 385 78932 979-249-3200
Brandon Schovajsa, supt. Fax 249-4084
www.rtcisd.net
Other Schools – See Round Top

Carrizo Springs, Dimmit, Pop. 5,350
Carrizo Springs Consolidated ISD 2,200/PK-12
300 N 7th St 78834 830-876-2473
Dr. Jesse Salazar, supt. Fax 876-9700
www.cscisd.net
Carrizo Springs ES 800/PK-3
300 N 7th St 78834 830-876-3513
Elisa Martinez, prin. Fax 876-4183
Carrizo Springs IS 400/4-6
300 N 7th St 78834 830-876-3561
Jose Talamantez, prin. Fax 876-5132
Carrizo Springs JHS 400/7-8
300 N 7th St 78834 830-876-2496
Maria Villarreal, prin. Fax 876-3655

Carrollton, Denton, Pop. 116,719
Carrollton-Farmers Branch ISD 26,200/PK-12
PO Box 115186 75011 972-968-6100
Dr. Bobby Burns, supt. Fax 968-6210
www.cfbisd.edu
Blalack MS 1,000/6-8
1706 E Peters Colony Rd 75007 972-968-3500
Dr. Lance Hamlin, prin. Fax 968-3510
Blanton ES 600/K-5
2525 Scott Mill Rd 75006 972-968-1100
Eva Medina-Walker, prin. Fax 968-1110
Carrollton ES 700/PK-5
1805 Pearl St 75006 972-968-1200
Monica Koen, prin. Fax 968-1210
Central ES 700/PK-5
1600 S Perry Rd 75006 972-968-1300
Robert Atchison, prin. Fax 968-1310
Country Place ES 300/PK-5
2115 Raintree Dr 75006 972-968-1400
Brianna Neumann, prin. Fax 968-1410
Davis ES 600/K-5
3205 Dorchester Dr 75007 972-968-1500
Lisa Williams, prin. Fax 968-1510
Furneaux ES 400/PK-5
3210 Furneaux Ln 75007 972-968-1800
Lori Parker, prin. Fax 968-1810
Good ES 600/PK-5
1012 Study Ln 75006 972-968-1900
Shahnaj Ahmad, prin. Fax 968-1910
Kent ES 400/K-5
1800 W Rosemeade Pkwy 75007 972-968-2000
Debbie Williams, prin. Fax 968-2010
McCoy ES 400/K-5
2425 McCoy Rd 75006 972-968-2300
Dawn Rink, prin. Fax 968-2310
McLaughlin/Strickland ES 400/K-5
1500 Webb Chapel Rd 75006 972-968-2500
DeDe Lacy, prin. Fax 968-2510
Perry MS 1,000/6-8
1709 E Belt Line Rd 75006 972-968-4400
Adam Toy, prin. Fax 968-4410
Polk MS 1,100/6-8
2001 Kelly Blvd 75006 972-968-4600
Kelly O'Sullivan, prin. Fax 968-4610
Rainwater ES 400/PK-5
1408 E Frankford Rd 75007 972-968-2800
Charlotte Thomas, prin. Fax 968-2810
Rosemeade ES 400/PK-5
3550 Kimberly Dr 75007 972-968-3000
M. Amy Miller, prin. Fax 968-3010

Thompson ES 500/K-5
2915 Scott Mill Rd 75007 972-968-3400
Shashawn Campbell, prin. Fax 968-3410
Other Schools – See Coppell, Dallas, Farmers Branch, Irving

Dallas ISD
Supt. — See Dallas
Junkins ES 800/PK-5
2808 Running Duke Dr 75006 972-502-2400
Jennifer Hernandez, prin. Fax 502-2401

Lewisville ISD
Supt. — See Flower Mound
Arbor Creek MS 900/6-8
2109 Arbor Creek Dr 75010 469-713-5971
Joanie Finch, prin. Fax 350-9163
Coyote Ridge ES 600/PK-5
4520 Maumee Dr 75010 469-713-5994
Padgett Cervantes M.Ed., prin. Fax 350-9026
Creek Valley MS 700/6-8
4109 Creek Valley Blvd 75010 469-713-5184
Steffanie Webb, prin. Fax 350-9172
Hebron Valley ES 600/PK-5
4108 Creek Valley Blvd 75010 469-713-5182
Tina Krol, prin. Fax 350-9068
Homestead ES 600/PK-5
1830 E Branch Hollow Dr 75007 469-713-5181
Sean Perry, prin. Fax 350-9083
Indian Creek ES 600/PK-5
2050 Arbor Creek Dr 75010 469-713-5180
Amy Teddy, prin. Fax 350-9085
Polser ES 500/PK-5
1520 Polser Rd 75010 469-713-5978
Adam Gray, prin. Fax 350-9134

Carrollton Christian Academy 300/K-12
1529 E Hebron Pkwy 75010 972-395-5104
Elaine Marchant, prin.
Prince of Peace Christian S 900/PK-12
4004 Midway Rd 75007 972-447-0532
Chris Hahn, hdmstr. Fax 267-4202

Carthage, Panola, Pop. 6,679
Carthage ISD 2,700/PK-12
1 Bulldog Dr 75633 903-693-3806
Dr. J. Glenn Hambrick Ed.D., supt. Fax 693-3650
www.carthageisd.org
Baker-Koonce ES 600/4-6
1 Bulldog Dr 75633 903-693-8611
Clarinda Collins, prin. Fax 693-5948
Carthage JHS 400/7-8
1 Bulldog Dr 75633 903-693-2751
Wade Watson, prin. Fax 693-9582
Carthage PS 600/PK-1
1 Bulldog Dr 75633 903-693-2254
Kiley Schumacher, prin. Fax 693-3287
Libby ES 400/2-3
1 Bulldog Dr 75633 903-693-8862
Staci Davis, prin. Fax 693-4696

Castroville, Medina, Pop. 2,662
Medina Valley ISD 3,900/PK-12
8449 FM 471 S 78009 830-931-2243
Dr. Kenneth Rohrbach, supt. Fax 931-4050
www.mvisd.com
Castroville ES 600/PK-5
1000 Madrid St 78009 830-931-2243
Ken Center, prin. Fax 931-3973
Medina Valley MS 900/6-8
8395 FM 471 S 78009 830-931-2243
Justin Russell, prin. Fax 931-3258
Medina Valley MS 6-8
8395 FM 471 S 78009 830-931-2243
Justin Russell, prin. Fax 931-3258
Other Schools – See La Coste, San Antonio

St. Louis S 100/PK-5
607 Madrid St 78009 830-931-3544
Karen Rothe, prin. Fax 931-0155

Cayuga, Anderson
Cayuga ISD 600/PK-12
PO Box 427 75832 903-928-2102
Dr. Rick Webb, supt. Fax 928-2646
www.cayugaisd.com
Cayuga ES 200/PK-5
PO Box 427 75832 903-928-2295
Tracie Campbell, prin. Fax 928-2646
Cayuga MS 100/6-8
PO Box 427 75832 903-928-2699
Sherri McInnis, prin. Fax 928-2646

Cedar Creek, Bastrop
Bastrop ISD
Supt. — See Bastrop
Cedar Creek ES 800/PK-4
5582 FM 535 78612 512-772-7600
Dr. Dolores Godinez, prin. Fax 321-6905
Cedar Creek IS 800/5-6
151 Voss Pkwy 78612 512-772-7475
Krystal Gabriel, prin. Fax 321-3484
Cedar Creek MS 800/7-8
125 Voss Pkwy 78612 512-772-7425
Edgar Rincon, prin. Fax 332-2631

Cedar Hill, Dallas, Pop. 44,182
Cedar Hill ISD 6,600/PK-12
285 Uptown Blvd Ste 300 75104 972-291-1581
Dr. Larry Watson, supt. Fax 291-5231
www.chisd.net
Bray ES 200/PK-5
218 N Broad St 75104 972-291-4231
Marchelle Sterling, prin. Fax 291-6098
Cedar Hill Collegiate Academy MS 6-8
1533 High Pointe Ln 75104 469-272-2021
Niki Edwards, prin.
Cedar Hill Collegiate Preparatory ES PK-5
975 Pickard Dr 75104 972-293-4502
Heath Koenig, prin. Fax 291-5213
Coleman MS 600/6-8
1208 E Pleasant Run Rd 75104 972-293-4505
Avesgus Tetterton, prin. Fax 272-9445
Highlands ES 600/PK-5
131 Sims Dr 75104 972-291-0496
Damian Patton, prin. Fax 291-5764
High Pointe ES 500/K-5
1351 High Pointe Ln 75104 972-291-7874
Charmon Barksdale, prin. Fax 291-5695
Lake Ridge ES 300/K-5
1020 Lake Ridge Pkwy 75104 972-293-4501
Marquita Anderson, prin. Fax 291-5210
Permenter MS 600/6-8
431 W Parkerville Rd 75104 972-291-5270
Tonya Haddox, prin. Fax 291-5296
Plummer ES 500/PK-5
1203 S Clark Rd 75104 972-291-4058
Sherese Nix, prin. Fax 291-4980
Waterford Oaks ES 600/PK-5
401 N Waterford Oaks Dr 75104 972-291-5290
Dr. Trevena Taylor, prin. Fax 293-2381

Ashleys Private S 200/PK-5
310 W Belt Line Rd 75104 972-291-1313
Fax 293-8056
Trinity Christian S 600/PK-12
1231 E Pleasant Run Rd 75104 972-291-2505

Cedar Park, Williamson, Pop. 47,764
Leander ISD
Supt. — See Leander
Cedar Park MS 1,400/6-8
2100 Sunchase Blvd 78613 512-570-3100
Sandra Stewart, prin. Fax 570-3105
Cox ES 800/PK-5
1001 Brushy Creek Rd 78613 512-570-6000
Sheri Hawthorn, prin. Fax 570-6005
Cypress ES 800/PK-5
2900 El Salido Pkwy 78613 512-570-5400
Vicky Draper, prin. Fax 570-5405
Deer Creek ES 800/PK-5
2420 Zeppelin Dr 78613 512-570-6300
Tol Wilhite, prin. Fax 570-6305
Faubion ES 600/PK-5
1209 Cypress Creek Rd 78613 512-570-7500
Bobbie Steiner, prin. Fax 570-7505
Giddens ES 500/PK-5
1500 Timberwood Dr 78613 512-570-5600
Sally Hill, prin. Fax 570-5605
Henry MS 1,300/6-8
100 N Vista Ridge Pkwy 78613 512-570-3400
Dr. David Ellis, prin. Fax 570-3405
Knowles ES 700/PK-5
2101 Cougar Country 78613 512-570-6200
Lara Labbe-Maginel, prin. Fax 570-6205
Mason ES 700/PK-5
1501 N Lakeline Blvd 78613 512-570-5500
Abby Kennell, prin. Fax 570-5505
Naumann ES 800/PK-5
1201 Brighton Bend Ln 78613 512-570-5800
Keith Morgan, prin. Fax 570-5805
Reagan ES 1,000/PK-5
1700 E Park St 78613 512-570-7200
Steve Crawford, prin. Fax 570-7205
Reed ES PK-5
1515 Little Elm Trl 78613 512-570-7700
Paige Collier, prin. Fax 570-7705
Running Brushy MS 1,300/6-8
2303 N Lakeline Blvd 78613 512-570-3300
Jim Rose, prin. Fax 570-3305
Westside ES 800/PK-5
300 Ryan Jordan Ln 78613 512-570-7000
Tracie Montanio, prin. Fax 570-7005

Cedar Park Montessori S 100/PK-6
400 E Whitestone Blvd 78613 512-259-8495
Kalika Sarathkumara M.Ed., head sch Fax 259-3989
Sapientia Montessori S 100/PK-6
1220 Cottonwood Creek Trl 78613 512-260-2261
Kalika Sarathkumara, head sch Fax 259-4410
Summit Christian Academy of Cedar Park 300/PK-12
2121 Cypress Creek Rd 78613 512-250-1369
Shannon Dare, hdmstr. Fax 257-1851

Celeste, Hunt, Pop. 800
Celeste ISD 500/PK-12
207 S 5th St 75423 903-568-4825
Brad Connelly, supt. Fax 568-4495
www.celesteisd.org/
Celeste ES 200/PK-5
207 S 5th St 75423 903-568-4721
Dr. Beth Ray, prin. Fax 568-4651
Celeste JHS 100/6-8
207 S 5th St 75423 903-568-4721
Staci Beadles, prin. Fax 568-4277

Celina, Collin, Pop. 5,948
Celina ISD 2,100/PK-12
205 S Colorado St 75009 469-742-9100
Rick DeMasters M.Ed., supt. Fax 382-3607
www.celinaisd.com
Celina ES 500/1-5
550 S Utah St 75009 469-742-9103
Starla Martin M.Ed., prin. Fax 382-3789
Celina JHS 300/7-8
710 E Pecan St 75009 469-742-9101
Russell McDaniel, prin. Fax 382-4258
Celina MS 400/6-6
706 E Pecan St 75009 469-742-9105
Kim Kincaid M.Ed., prin. Fax 382-8543
Celina PS 300/PK-K
507 E Malone St 75009 469-742-9104
Nancy Alvarez M.Ed., prin. Fax 382-4792
O'Dell ES 400/1-5
750 Punk Carter Pkwy 75009 469-742-9100
Stacy Ceci M.Ed., prin.

Prosper ISD
Supt. — See Prosper
Light Farms ES PK-5
1100 Cypress Creek Way 75009 469-219-2140
Daphne Morris, admin. Fax 346-9630

Center, Shelby, Pop. 5,149
Center ISD 2,800/PK-12
PO Box 1689 75935 936-598-5642
James Hockenberry, supt. Fax 598-1515
www.centerisd.org/
Center ES 600/1-3
621 Rough Rider Dr 75935 936-598-3625
Shelly Norvell, prin. Fax 598-1507
Center IS 400/4-5
624 Malone Dr 75935 936-598-6148
Heath Hagler, prin. Fax 598-1555
Center MS 600/6-8
302 Kennedy St 75935 936-598-5619
Jake Henson, prin. Fax 598-1534
Moffett PS 500/PK-K
294 Stadium Dr 75935 936-598-6266
Inez Hughes, prin. Fax 598-1545

Excelsior ISD 100/PK-8
11270 State Highway 7 W 75935 936-598-5866
Wayne Mason, supt. Fax 598-2076
excelsiorisd.weebly.com
Excelsior S 100/PK-8
11270 State Highway 7 W 75935 936-598-5866
Johnny Lewis, prin. Fax 598-2076

Center Point, Kerr
Center Point ISD 600/PK-12
PO Box 377 78010 830-634-2171
Cody Newcomb, supt. Fax 634-2254
www.cpisd.net
Center Point ES 300/PK-5
PO Box 377 78010 830-634-2257
Jennifer George, prin. Fax 634-2119
Center Point MS 100/6-8
PO Box 377 78010 830-634-2533
Keith Mills, prin. Fax 634-7825

Centerville, Leon, Pop. 862
Centerville ISD 700/PK-12
813 S Commerce St 75833 903-536-7812
Jason Jeitz, supt. Fax 536-7148
www.centerville.k12.tx.us
Centerville ES 400/PK-6
813 S Commerce St 75833 903-536-2235
Dottio Sullivan, prin. Fax 536-3525

Chandler, Henderson, Pop. 2,689
Brownsboro ISD
Supt. — See Brownsboro
Chandler ES 500/PK-3
PO Box 99 75758 903-849-3400
Ricky Daily, prin. Fax 849-3628
Chandler IS 300/4-6
22250 Barron Rd 75758 903-849-6436
Lisa Brown, prin. Fax 849-3019

Channelview, Harris, Pop. 37,941
Channelview ISD 9,000/PK-12
828 Sheldon Rd 77530 281-452-8002
Greg Ollis, supt. Fax 452-8001
www.cvisd.org
Channelview Pre K 500/PK-PK
911 Sheldon Rd 77530 281-860-3827
Emily Laird, prin. Fax 860-3801
Cobb ES 400/K-5
915 Dell Dale St 77530 281-452-7788
Chad Nuetzmann, prin. Fax 452-7413
Crenshaw ES 600/K-5
16204 Wood Dr 77530 281-457-3080
Audry Lane, prin. Fax 457-5434
De Zavala ES 600/K-5
16150 2nd St 77530 281-452-6008
Ruben Rodriguez, prin. Fax 452-3562
Hamblen ES 700/K-5
1019 Dell Dale St 77530 281-457-8720
Jose Lopez, prin. Fax 457-8724
Johnson JHS 1,000/6-8
15500 Proctor St 77530 281-452-8030
Jules Pichon, prin. Fax 452-1022
McMullan ES 600/K-5
1290 Dell Dale St 77530 281-452-1154
Gina Ervin, prin. Fax 452-1367
Schochler ES 500/K-5
910 Deerpass Dr 77530 281-452-2880
Ann Garza, prin. Fax 452-3709
Other Schools – See Houston

Channing, Hartley, Pop. 363
Channing ISD 100/PK-12
PO Box A 79018 806-235-3719
Robert McLain, supt. Fax 235-2609
www.channingisd.net/
Channing S 100/PK-12
PO Box A 79018 806-235-3719
Forrest Herbert, prin. Fax 235-2609

Charlotte, Atascosa, Pop. 1,708
Charlotte ISD 500/PK-12
PO Box 489 78011 830-277-1431
Mario Sotelo, supt. Fax 277-1551
www.charlotteisd.net
Charlotte ES 200/PK-4
PO Box 489 78011 830-277-1710
Laura Mikolajczyk, prin. Fax 277-1675
Charlotte MS 200/5-8
PO Box 489 78011 830-277-1646
Roger Solis, prin. Fax 277-1654

Cherokee, San Saba
Cherokee ISD 100/K-12
PO Box 100 76832 325-622-4298
Eldon Franco, supt. Fax 622-4430
www.cherokeeisd.net
Cherokee S 100/K-12
PO Box 100 76832 325-622-4298
Randy Gartman, prin. Fax 622-4430

Chester, Tyler, Pop. 312
Chester ISD 200/PK-12
273 Yellow Jacket Dr 75936 936-969-2371
Cory Hines, supt. Fax 969-2080
www.chesterisd.com
Chester ES 100/PK-5
273 Yellow Jacket Dr 75936 936-969-2211
Cory Hines, supt. Fax 969-2080

Chico, Wise, Pop. 994
Chico ISD 600/PK-12
PO Box 95 76431 940-644-2228
Don Elsom, supt. Fax 644-5642
www.chicoisdtx.net
Chico ES 300/PK-5
PO Box 95 76431 940-644-2220
Karen Decker, prin. Fax 644-5642
Chico MS 100/6-8
PO Box 95 76431 940-644-5550
Monte Sewell, prin. Fax 644-5642

Childress, Childress, Pop. 6,037
Childress ISD 1,100/PK-12
PO Box 179 79201 940-937-2501
Rick Teran, supt. Fax 937-2938
www.childressisd.net/
Childress ES 600/PK-5
300 3rd St SE 79201 940-937-6313
Janet Word, prin. Fax 937-2165
Childress JHS 200/6-8
700 Commerce St 79201 940-937-3641
Marsha Meacham, prin. Fax 937-8427

Chillicothe, Hardeman, Pop. 698
Chillicothe ISD 200/PK-12
PO Box 418 79225 940-852-5391
Todd Wilson, supt. Fax 852-5269
www.cisd-tx.net
Chillicothe ES 100/PK-6
PO Box 538 79225 940-852-5391
Brenda Dunlap, prin. Fax 852-5012

Chilton, Falls, Pop. 896
Chilton ISD 500/PK-12
PO Box 488 76632 254-546-1200
Brandon Hubbard, supt. Fax 546-1201
www.chiltonisd.org
Chilton ES 300/PK-5
PO Box 488 76632 254-122-1225
Leo Darden, prin. Fax 546-1202

China, Jefferson, Pop. 1,140
Hardin-Jefferson ISD
Supt. — See Sour Lake
China ES 400/PK-5
PO Box 398 77613 409-981-6410
Dianne Timberlake, prin. Fax 752-3623

China Spring, McLennan, Pop. 1,276
China Spring ISD 2,400/PK-12
PO Box 250 76633 254-836-1115
Marc Faulkner, supt. Fax 836-0559
www.chinaspringisd.net
China Spring ES 800/PK-3
200 Bob Johnson Rd 76633 254-836-4635
Kim Coe, prin. Fax 836-4637
China Spring MS 400/7-8
7201 N River Xing 76633 254-836-4611
Mike Kelly, prin. Fax 836-4777
Other Schools – See Waco

Chireno, Nacogdoches, Pop. 378
Chireno ISD 300/PK-12
PO Box 85 75937 936-362-2132
Tim Norman, supt. Fax 362-2490
www.chirenoisd.org/
Chireno ES 200/PK-6
PO Box 85 75937 936-362-2132
Brandy Gray, prin. Fax 362-2490

Christoval, Tom Green, Pop. 503
Christoval ISD 500/K-12
PO Box 162 76935 325-896-2520
Dr. David Walker, supt. Fax 896-7405
www.christovalisd.org
Christoval ES 200/K-5
PO Box 162 76935 325-896-2446
Tracy Knighton, prin. Fax 896-1145

Cibolo, Guadalupe, Pop. 14,799
Schertz-Cibolo-Universal City ISD
Supt. — See Schertz
Cibolo Valley ES K-4
4093 Green Valley Rd 78108 210-619-4700
LaCreasha Stille, admin.
Dobie JHS 1,100/7-8
395 W Borgfeld Rd 78108 210-619-4100
Vernon Simmons, prin. Fax 619-4142
Jordan IS 600/5-6
515 Thistle Creek Dr 78108 210-619-4250
Tina Curtis, prin. Fax 619-4277
Schlather IS 800/5-6
230 Elaine S Schlather Pkwy 78108 210-619-4300
Yvette Ross, prin. Fax 619-4340
Watts ES 700/PK-4
100 Deer Meadow Blvd 78108 210-619-4400
Deanna Jackson, prin. Fax 619-4419
Wiederstein ES 800/PK-4
171 W Borgfeld Rd 78108 210-619-4550
Luis Chavez, prin. Fax 619-4590

Cisco, Eastland, Pop. 3,863
Cisco ISD 900/PK-12
PO Box 1645 76437 254-442-3056
Kelly West, supt. Fax 442-1412
www.ciscoisd.net/
Cisco ES 400/PK-5
PO Box 1645 76437 254-442-1219
Sharon Wilcoxen, prin. Fax 442-4836
Cisco JHS 200/6-8
PO Box 1645 76437 254-442-3004
Mark Lewis, prin. Fax 442-1832

Clarendon, Donley, Pop. 1,994
Clarendon ISD 500/PK-12
PO Box 610 79226 806-874-2062
Michael Norrell, supt. Fax 874-2579
www.clarendonisd.net
Clarendon ES 200/PK-5
PO Box 610 79226 806-874-3855
Mike Word, prin. Fax 874-2082
Clarendon JHS 100/6-8
PO Box 610 79226 806-874-3232
John Taylor, prin. Fax 874-9748

Clarksville, Red River, Pop. 3,231
Clarksville ISD 500/PK-12
1500 W Main St 75426 903-427-3891
Dr. Pamela Bryant Ed.D., supt. Fax 427-5071
www.clarksvilleisd.net
Cheatham ES 300/PK-5
1500 W Main St 75426 903-427-3891
Marianne Whitehouse, prin. Fax 427-1747

Claude, Armstrong, Pop. 1,174
Claude ISD 400/PK-12
PO Box 209 79019 806-226-7331
Brock Cartwright, supt. Fax 226-2244
www.claudeisd.net/
Claude ES 200/PK-6
PO Box 209 79019 806-226-3522
Doug Rawlins, prin. Fax 226-2244

Cleburne, Johnson, Pop. 28,861
Cleburne ISD 6,500/PK-12
505 N Ridgeway Dr Ste 100 76033 817-202-1100
Dr. Kyle Heath, supt. Fax 202-1460
www.cleburne.k12.tx.us/
Adams ES 500/PK-5
1492 Island Grove Rd 76031 817-202-2000
Dawn Hitt, prin. Fax 202-1482
Coleman ES 500/PK-5
920 W Westhill Dr 76033 817-202-2030
Marla Roth, prin. Fax 202-1484
Cooke ES 500/K-5
902 Phillips St 76033 817-202-2060
Jacob Walker, prin. Fax 202-1483
Gerard ES 500/K-5
1212 Hyde Park Blvd 76033 817-202-2130
Tracy White, prin. Fax 202-1485
Irving ES 500/PK-5
345 Hix Rd 76031 817-202-2100
Joel Blalock, prin. Fax 202-1486
Marti ES 400/K-5
2020 W Kilpatrick St 76033 817-202-1650
Mary Boedeker, prin. Fax 202-1487
Santa Fe ES 500/PK-5
1601 E Henderson St 76031 817-202-2300
Sabina Landeros, prin. Fax 202-1497
Smith MS 700/6-8
1710 Country Club Rd 76033 817-202-1500
Amber White, prin. Fax 202-1475
Wheat MS 700/6-8
810 N Colonial Dr 76033 817-202-1300
Suzanne Keesee, prin. Fax 202-1479

Cleburne Adventist Christian S 50/PK-8
111 Meadow View Dr 76033 817-645-4300
Cleburne Christian Academy 100/K-12
PO Box 2017 76033 817-641-2857

Cleveland, Liberty, Pop. 7,571
Cleveland ISD 3,800/PK-12
316 E Dallas St 77327 281-592-8717
Dr. Darrell Myers, supt. Fax 592-8283
www.clevelandisd.org
Cleveland MS 600/7-8
2000 E Houston St 77327 281-593-1148
Sheila Stephens, prin. Fax 593-3400
Eastside ES 600/PK-PK, 5-
1602 Shell Ave 77327 281-592-0125
Rebecca Smith, prin. Fax 592-0277
Northside ES 600/3-4
1522 N Blair Ave 77327 281-592-4628
Edward Husk, prin. Fax 592-9679
Southside PS 1,100/K-2
303 E Fort Worth St 77327 281-592-0594
Janie Snyder, prin. Fax 592-2185

Tarkington ISD 1,900/PK-12
2770 FM 163 Rd 77327 281-592-8781
Kevin Weldon, supt. Fax 592-3969
www.tarkingtonisd.net/
Tarkington IS 300/4-5
2770 FM 163 Rd 77327 281-592-6134
Calesta House, prin. Fax 592-2453
Tarkington MS 500/6-8
2770 FM 163 Rd 77327 281-592-7737
Michael Kelley, prin. Fax 592-5241
Tarkington PS 600/PK-3
2770 FM 163 Rd 77327 281-592-7736
Angie Thomas, prin. Fax 592-2361

Clifton, Bosque, Pop. 3,399
Clifton ISD 1,000/PK-12
1102 Key St 76634 254-675-2827
Rhoda White, supt. Fax 675-4351
www.cliftonisd.org
Clifton ES 500/PK-5
706 W 11th St 76634 254-675-1875
Ronda Kroll, prin. Fax 675-8725
Clifton MS 200/6-8
1102 Key St 76634 254-675-1855
Andy Ball, prin. Fax 675-2005

Clint, El Paso, Pop. 926
Clint ISD
Supt. — See El Paso
Clint JHS 500/6-8
12625 Alameda Ave 79836 915-926-8000
Noemi Hernandez, prin. Fax 851-3895
Surratt ES 1,000/PK-5
12675 Alameda Ave 79836 915-926-8200
Melissa Williams, prin. Fax 851-3489

Clute, Brazoria, Pop. 11,087
Brazosport ISD 11,900/PK-12
301 W Brazoswood Dr 77531 979-730-7000
Danny Massey, supt. Fax 266-2409
www.brazosportisd.net
Clute IS 900/5-8
421 E Main St 77531 979-730-7230
Chris Loftin, prin. Fax 730-7363
Griffith ES 500/PK-4
101 Lexington Ave 77531 979-730-7180
Karen Matt, prin. Fax 266-2469
Ogg ES 400/PK-4
208 N Lazy Ln 77531 979-730-7195
Kristi Traylor, prin. Fax 266-2488
Other Schools – See Freeport, Jones Creek, Lake Jackson, Richwood

Clyde, Callahan, Pop. 3,655
Clyde Consolidated ISD 1,500/PK-12
PO Box 479 79510 325-893-4222
Kenny Berry, supt. Fax 893-4024
www.clyde.esc14.net
Clyde ES 400/PK-2
318 Forrest Rd 79510 325-893-4788
Kim Jones, prin. Fax 893-5642
Clyde IS 300/3-5
505 N Hays Rd 79510 325-893-2815
Jill Morphis, prin. Fax 893-3067
Clyde JHS 400/6-8
211 S 3rd St W 79510 325-893-5788
Jared Duncum, prin. Fax 893-2134

Eula ISD 300/PK-12
6040 FM 603 79510 325-529-3186
Tim Kelley, supt. Fax 529-4461
www.eulaisd.us
Eula ES 200/PK-6
6040 FM 603 79510 325-529-3212
Cody Bob Williams, prin. Fax 529-2001

Coahoma, Howard, Pop. 815
Coahoma ISD 900/PK-12
PO Box 110 79511 432-394-5000
Dr. Amy Jacobs, supt. Fax 394-4302
www.coahomaisd.com
Coahoma ES 400/PK-5
PO Box 110 79511 432-394-5000
Alison Alvarez, prin. Fax 394-4419
Coahoma JHS 200/6-8
PO Box 110 79511 432-394-5000
Ashley Roberts, prin. Fax 394-4419

Coldspring, San Jacinto, Pop. 837
Coldspring-Oakhurst Consolidated ISD 1,500/PK-12
PO Box 39 77331 936-653-1115
Dr. Leland Moore, supt. Fax 653-2197
www.cocisd.org
Coldspring IS 300/3-5
PO Box 39 77331 936-653-1152
Stephanie Mizelle, prin. Fax 653-3689
Lincoln JHS 300/6-8
PO Box 39 77331 936-653-1166
Todd White, prin. Fax 653-3688
Street ES 400/PK-2
PO Box 39 77331 936-653-1187
Stephanie Mizelle, prin. Fax 653-3690

Coleman, Coleman, Pop. 4,660
Coleman ISD 800/PK-12
PO Box 900 76834 325-625-3575
Skip McCambridge, supt. Fax 625-4751
www.colemanisd.org
Coleman ES 400/PK-4
303 15th St 76834 325-625-3546
Joy Thompson, prin. Fax 625-4064
Coleman JHS 200/5-8
301 15th St 76834 325-625-3593
Amy Flippin, prin. Fax 625-3358

College Station, Brazos, Pop. 92,151
College Station ISD 11,700/PK-12
1812 Welsh Ave 77840 979-764-5400
Dr. Clark Ealy Ph.D., supt. Fax 764-5535
www.csisd.org
A & M Consolidated MS 900/7-8
105 Holik St 77840 979-764-5575
Jeff Mann, prin. Fax 764-5577
College Hills ES 700/PK-4
1101 Williams St 77840 979-764-5565
Josh Hatfield, prin. Fax 764-5497
College Station MS 900/7-8
900 Rock Prairie Rd 77845 979-764-5545
Oliver Hadnot, prin. Fax 764-5557
Creek View ES 700/PK-4
1001 Eagle Ave 77845 979-694-5890
Jeff Durand, prin. Fax 694-5893
Cypress Grove IS 800/5-6
900 Graham Rd 77845 979-694-5600
Holly Scott, prin. Fax 694-5604
Forest Ridge ES 600/PK-4
1950 Greens Prairie Rd W 77845 979-694-5801
Terresa Katt, prin. Fax 694-5805
Greens Prairie ES 700/PK-4
4315 Greens Prairie Trl 77845 979-694-5870
Donna Bairrington, prin. Fax 694-5871

Oakwood IS 900/5-6
106 Holik St 77840 979-764-5530
Josh Symank, prin. Fax 764-5533
Pebble Creek ES 600/PK-4
200 Parkview Dr 77845 979-764-5595
Annette Roraback, prin. Fax 764-5478
Pecan Trail IS 800/5-6
4319 Greens Prairie Tr 77845 979-694-5874
Kellie Deegear, prin.
Rock Prairie ES 700/PK-4
3400 Welsh Ave 77845 979-764-5570
Robyn Jones, prin. Fax 764-5486
South Knoll ES 600/PK-4
1220 Boswell St 77840 979-764-5580
Laura Richter, prin. Fax 764-5485
Southwood Valley ES 600/PK-4
2700 Brothers Blvd 77845 979-764-5590
Kristiana Hamilton, prin. Fax 764-5488
Spring Creek ES PK-PK, 4-
2450 Brewster Dr 77845 979-694-5838
Stormy Hickman, prin.

St. Thomas Early Learning Center 100/PK-K
906 George Bush Dr 77840 979-696-1728

Colleyville, Tarrant, Pop. 22,415
Grapevine-Colleyville ISD
Supt. — See Grapevine
Bransford ES 400/K-5
601 Glade Rd 76034 817-305-4920
Jamie Halliburton, prin. Fax 428-1203
Colleyville ES 500/K-5
5911 Pleasant Run Rd 76034 817-305-4940
Sheila Shimmick, prin. Fax 498-2062
Colleyville MS 700/6-8
1100 Bogart Dr 76034 817-305-4900
David Arencibia, prin. Fax 498-9764
Glenhope ES 500/PK-5
6600 Glenhope Cir N 76034 817-251-5720
Wynette Griffin, prin. Fax 329-5618
Heritage MS 900/6-8
5300 Heritage Ave 76034 817-305-4790
Scott Saettel, prin. Fax 267-9929
Taylor ES 400/PK-5
5300 Pool Rd 76034 817-305-4870
Lisa Young, prin. Fax 540-3940

Keller ISD
Supt. — See Keller
Liberty ES 400/K-4
1101 W McDonwell School Rd 76034 817-744-6000
Janet Travis, prin. Fax 743-0314

Covenant Christian Academy 600/PK-12
901 Cheek Sparger Rd 76034 817-281-4333
Crown of Life Lutheran S 200/PK-8
6605 Pleasant Run Rd 76034 817-251-1881
Laura Cleland, prin. Fax 421-9263
Waypoint Montessori S 200/PK-6
1513 Hall Johnson Rd 76034 817-354-6670

Collinsville, Grayson, Pop. 1,601
Collinsville ISD 400/PK-12
PO Box 49 76233 903-429-6272
Mark Dykes, supt. Fax 429-6665
www.collinsvilleisd.org
Collinsville ES 200/PK-6
PO Box 49 76233 903-429-3077
Ken Kemp, prin. Fax 429-1004

Colmesnell, Tyler, Pop. 588
Colmesneil ISD 400/PK-12
PO Box 37 75938 409-837-5757
Angela Matterson, supt. Fax 837-9107
www.colmesneilisd.net
Colmesneil ES 200/PK-6
PO Box 37 75938 409-837-2229
Yvette Carlton, prin. Fax 837-9119

Colorado City, Mitchell, Pop. 4,115
Colorado ISD 1,000/PK-12
PO Box 1268 79512 325-728-5312
Reggy Spencer, supt. Fax 728-1015
www.ccity.esc14.net
Colorado ES PK-5
PO Box 1268 79512 325-728-5312
Colorado MS 200/6-8
312 E 12th St 79512 325-728-2673
Robby Russell, prin. Fax 728-1051

Columbus, Colorado, Pop. 3,623
Columbus ISD 1,600/PK-12
105 Cardinal Ln 78934 979-732-5704
Dr. Brian Morris, supt. Fax 732-5960
www.columbusisd.org
Columbus ES 800/PK-5
1324 Bowie St 78934 979-732-2078
Shana Neisner, prin. Fax 732-8627
Columbus JHS 400/6-8
702 Rampart St 78934 979-732-2891
Gary leopold, prin. Fax 732-9081

St. Anthony S 100/PK-8
635 Bonham St 78934 979-732-5505
John O'Leary, prin. Fax 732-9758

Comanche, Comanche, Pop. 4,301
Comanche ISD 1,000/PK-12
200 E Highland Ave 76442 325-356-2727
Gary Speegle, supt. Fax 356-2312
www.comancheisd.net
Comanche ECC 300/PK-PK
200 E Highland Ave 76442 325-356-2440
Melinda Megna, dir. Fax 356-1454
Comanche ES 200/PK-5
310 FM 3381 76442 325-356-3900
Curtis Stahnke, prin. Fax 356-3990
Jeffries JHS 200/6-8
1 Valley Forge St 76442 325-356-5220
Joseph Simmons, prin. Fax 356-1949

Combes, Cameron, Pop. 2,890
Harlingen Consolidated ISD
Supt. — See Harlingen
Dishman ES 500/PK-5
309 Madeley 78535 956-427-3100
Irma Davis, prin. Fax 427-3103

Comfort, Kendall, Pop. 2,348
Comfort ISD 1,100/PK-12
PO Box 398 78013 830-995-6400
Dennis Hill, supt. Fax 995-2236
www.comfort.txed.net
Comfort ES 500/PK-5
PO Box 157 78013 830-995-6410
Don Love, prin. Fax 995-4153
Comfort MS 300/6-8
PO Box 187 78013 830-995-6420
Josh Limmer, prin. Fax 995-2248

Commerce, Hunt, Pop. 7,851
Commerce ISD 1,500/PK-12
3315 Washington St 75428 903-886-3755
Charles Alderman, supt. Fax 886-6025
www.commerceisd.org
Commerce ES 400/PK-2
3315 Washington St 75428 903-886-3757
Diane Stegall, prin. Fax 886-6112
Commerce MS 300/6-8
3315 Washington St 75428 903-886-3795
Dr. Shenequa Miller, prin. Fax 886-6102
Williams ES 300/3-5
3315 Washington St 75428 903-886-3758
Lisa Palazzetti, admin. Fax 468-8030

Como, Hopkins, Pop. 696
Como-Pickton Consolidated ISD 700/PK-12
PO Box 18 75431 903-488-3671
Greg Bower, supt. Fax 488-3133
www.cpcisd.net
Como-Pickton S 700/PK-12
PO Box 18 75431 903-488-3671
Kelly Baird, prin. Fax 488-3133

Comstock, Val Verde
Comstock ISD 200/K-12
PO Box 905 78837 432-292-4444
Orlie Wolfenbarger, supt. Fax 292-4436
www.comstockisd.net/
Comstock S 200/K-12
PO Box 905 78837 432-292-4444
Travis Grubbs, prin. Fax 292-4436

Conroe, Montgomery, Pop. 55,526
Conroe ISD 54,600/PK-12
3205 W Davis St 77304 936-709-7751
Dr. Don Stockton, supt. Fax 709-9701
www.conroeisd.net
Anderson ES 900/PK-4
1414 E Dallas St 77301 936-709-5300
Laura Quinones, prin. Fax 709-5312
Armstrong ES 800/PK-4
110 Gladstell St 77301 936-709-3400
Patricia Thacker, prin. Fax 709-3415
Austin ES 900/PK-4
14796 Highway 105 E 77306 936-709-8400
Dr. Serena Pierson, prin. Fax 709-8403
Bozman IS 700/5-6
800 Beach Airport Rd 77301 936-709-1800
Amber Debeaumont, prin. Fax 709-1899
Creighton ES 800/PK-4
12089 FM 1485 Rd 77306 936-709-2900
Jennifer Watson, prin. Fax 709-2999
Cryar IS 700/5-6
2375 Montgomery Park Blvd 77304 936-709-7300
Bethany Medford, prin. Fax 709-7313
Giesinger ES 600/PK-4
2323 White Oak Blvd 77304 936-709-2600
Melissa Hammond, prin. Fax 709-2699
Grangerland IS 1,000/5-6
16283 FM 3083 Rd 77302 936-709-3500
Karen Jones, prin. Fax 709-3565
Houser ES 800/PK-4
27370 Oak Ridge School Rd 77385 832-663-4000
Angela Lozano, prin. Fax 663-4076
Houston ES 900/PK-4
1000 N Thompson St 77301 936-709-5100
Viviana Harris, prin. Fax 709-5103
Irons JHS 1,000/7-8
16780 Needham Rd 77385 936-709-8500
Jeff Fuller, prin. Fax 709-8599
Milam ES 900/PK-4
16415 FM 3083 Rd 77302 936-709-5200
Gilberto Lozano, prin. Fax 709-5203
Moorhead JHS 1,100/7-8
13475 FM 1485 Rd 77306 936-709-2400
Robert Garcia, prin. Fax 709-2499
Oak Ridge ES 500/PK-4
19675 Interstate 45 S 77385 832-592-5900
Tami Eldridge, prin. Fax 592-5968
Patterson ES PK-4
670 Beach Airport Rd 77301 936-709-4300
Julie Miller, prin. Fax 709-4399
Peet JHS 1,200/7-8
1895 Longmire Rd 77304 936-709-3700
Tasha Smith, prin. Fax 709-3828
Reaves ES 700/K-4
1717 N Loop 336 W 77304 936-709-5400
Nicole Walker, prin. Fax 709-5407
Rice ES 700/PK-4
904 Gladstell Rd 77304 936-709-2700
Malinda Stewart, prin. Fax 709-2799
Runyan ES 600/PK-4
1101 Foster Dr 77301 936-709-2800
Tracy Voelker, prin. Fax 709-2899
San Jacinto ES 600/PK-4
17601 FM 1314 Rd 77302 281-465-7700
Krista McWilliams, prin. Fax 465-7799
Travis IS 500/5-6
1100 N Thompson St 77301 936-709-7000
Charita Smith, prin. Fax 709-7019
Washington JHS 600/7-8
507 Dr Martin Luther King 77301 936-709-7400
Hartwell Brown, prin. Fax 709-7492
Wilkinson ES 600/PK-4
2575 Ed Kharbat Dr 77301 936-709-1500
Victor Uher, prin. Fax 709-1599
Other Schools – See Montgomery, Spring, The Woodlands

Adventist Christian Academy of Texas 100/PK-12
3601 S Loop 336 E 77301 936-756-5078
Calvary Baptist S 200/PK-12
3401 N Frazier St 77303 936-756-0743
Rev. Mark Parker, admin. Fax 756-0764
Covenant Christian S 300/PK-12
4503 Interstate 45 N 77304 936-890-8080
Dr. Glenn Slater, head sch Fax 890-5343
Lifestyle Christian S 100/K-12
3993 Interstate 45 N 77304 936-756-9383
Montie Mansur, prin. Fax 760-3003
PCAL Christian S 100/PK-12
9268 Highway 242 77385 936-273-6464
Sacred Heart S 300/PK-8
615 McDade St 77301 936-756-3848
Deborah Brown, prin. Fax 756-4097

Converse, Bexar, Pop. 17,584
Judson ISD
Supt. — See Live Oak
Converse ES 800/PK-5
6720 FM 1516 N 78109 210-945-1210
MaryKay Tyson, prin. Fax 658-8162
Copperfield ES 600/PK-5
7595 E Loop 1604 N 78109 210-619-0460
Sherri Wrather, prin.
Elolf ES 700/PK-5
6335 Beech Trail Dr 78109 210-661-1130
Scott Wilson, prin. Fax 666-0536
Judson MS 1,000/6-8
9695 Schaefer Rd 78109 210-357-0801
Liza Guerrero, prin. Fax 659-8769
Judson STEM Academy 100/6-8
9695 Schaefer Rd 78109 210-945-1159
Dawn Worley, dir.
Masters ES 700/K-5
2650 Woodlake Pkwy 78109 210-945-1150
Theodore Haynes, prin. Fax 310-0650
Miller's Point ES 600/K-5
7027 Misty Ridge Dr 78109 210-945-5114
Barbara Smejkal, prin. Fax 590-4254

St. Monica S 300/K-8
PO Box 429 78109 210-658-6701
Kristy Geyer, prin. Fax 658-6945

Coolidge, Limestone, Pop. 937
Coolidge ISD 300/PK-12
PO Box 70 76635 254-786-4612
Dr. Robert Lowry, supt. Fax 786-4835
www.coolidge.k12.tx.us
Coolidge ES 200/PK-5
PO Box 70 76635 254-786-2206
Laci Lowry, prin. Fax 786-4835

Cooper, Delta, Pop. 1,923
Cooper ISD 800/PK-12
PO Box 478 75432 903-395-2111
Denicia Hohenberger, supt. Fax 395-2117
www.cooperisd.net/
Cooper ES 400/PK-5
PO Box 478 75432 903-395-2111
Lynn Byrd, prin. Fax 395-2019
Cooper JHS 200/6-8
PO Box 429 75432 903-395-2111
Julie Silman, prin. Fax 395-2382

Coppell, Dallas, Pop. 37,827
Carrollton-Farmers Branch ISD
Supt. — See Carrollton
Riverchase ES 400/PK-5
272 S MacArthur Blvd 75019 972-968-2900
Pam Henderson, prin. Fax 968-2910

Coppell ISD 11,400/PK-12
200 S Denton Tap Rd 75019 214-496-6000
Dr. Brad Hunt, supt. Fax 496-6036
www.coppellisd.com
Austin ES 600/PK-5
161 S Moore Rd 75019 214-496-7300
Lorie Squalls, prin. Fax 496-7306
Coppell MS East 800/6-8
400 Mockingbird Ln 75019 214-496-6600
Laura Springer, prin. Fax 496-6603
Coppell MS North 900/6-8
120 Natches Trce 75019 214-496-7100
Gregory Axelson, prin. Fax 496-7103
Coppell MS West 1,000/6-8
1301 Wrangler Cir 75019 214-496-8600
Emily Froese, prin. Fax 496-8606
Cottonwood Creek ES 500/PK-5
615 Minyard Dr 75019 214-496-8300
Dr. Andra Penny, prin. Fax 496-8306
Denton Creek ES 600/PK-5
250 Natches Trce 75019 214-496-8100
Shannon Edwards, prin. Fax 496-8106
Lakeside ES 600/PK-5
1100 Village Pkwy 75019 214-496-7600
Gema Hall, prin. Fax 496-7606
Lee ES K-5
8808 Chaparral Waters Way 75019 214-496-7900
Chantel Kastrounis, prin. Fax 496-7906

Mockingbird ES 700/PK-5
300 Mockingbird Ln 75019 214-496-8200
Laura Flynn, prin. Fax 496-8206
Pinkerton ES 400/PK-5
260 Southwestern Blvd 75019 214-496-6800
Kristi Mikkelsen, prin. Fax 496-6806
Town Center ES 500/PK-5
185 N Heartz Rd 75019 214-496-7800
Angie Applegate, prin. Fax 496-7806
Wilson ES 600/PK-5
200 S Coppell Rd 75019 214-496-7500
Cooper Hilton, prin. Fax 496-7506
Other Schools – See Irving

Copperas Cove, Coryell, Pop. 30,055
Copperas Cove ISD 7,500/PK-12
703 W Avenue D 76522 254-547-1227
Dr. Joe Burns, supt. Fax 547-7060
www.ccisd.com
Clements\Hollie Parsons ES 700/K-5
1115 Northern Dancer Dr 76522 254-547-2235
Jimmy Shuck, prin. Fax 547-0845
Copperas Cove JHS 800/6-8
702 Sunny Ave 76522 254-547-6959
Amanda Crawley, prin. Fax 518-2620
Fairview\Miss Jewell ES 500/K-5
710 S 5th St 76522 254-547-4530
Leah Miller, prin. Fax 547-6378
Halstead ES 300/K-5
910 N Main St 76522 254-547-3440
Brian Jost, prin. Fax 547-6896
House Creek ES 700/K-5
351 Lutheran Church Rd 76522 254-518-3000
Larea Gamble, prin. Fax 518-7400
Lee JHS 800/6-8
1205 Courtney Ln 76522 254-542-7877
Kayleen Love, prin. Fax 542-8103
Stevens Early Learning Academy 400/PK-PK
302 Manning Dr 76522 254-547-8289
Mary Derrick, prin. Fax 547-8325
Walker ES 400/K-5
100 FM 3046 76522 254-547-2283
Earl Parcell, prin. Fax 547-5984
Williams\Lovett Ledger ES 600/K-5
909 Courtney Ln 76522 254-542-3070
Marla Sullivan, prin. Fax 542-3348

Lampasas ISD
Supt. — See Lampasas
Taylor Creek ES 500/PK-5
2096 Big Divide Rd 76522 512-564-2585
Renee Cummings, prin. Fax 564-2606

Corinth, Denton, Pop. 19,502
Denton ISD
Supt. — See Denton
Crownover MS 900/6-8
1901 Creekside Dr 76210 940-369-4700
Charlene Parham, prin. Fax 321-0502

Lake Dallas ISD
Supt. — See Lake Dallas
Corinth ES 500/K-5
3501 Cliff Oaks Dr 76210 940-497-4010
Randall Caldwell, prin. Fax 497-8479

Corpus Christi, Nueces, Pop. 301,876
Calallen ISD 4,100/PK-12
4205 Wildcat Dr 78410 361-242-5600
Dr. Arturo Almendarez, supt. Fax 242-5620
www.calallen.org
Calallen East ES 600/PK-3
3709 Lott Ave 78410 361-242-5938
Kimberly Rodriguez, prin. Fax 242-5944
Calallen MS 900/6-8
4602 Cornett Dr 78410 361-242-5672
Marcos Flores, prin. Fax 242-0628
Magee ES 600/4-5
4201 Calallen Dr 78410 361-242-5900
Dr. Dalia Torres, prin. Fax 242-5913
Wood River ES 600/PK-3
15118 Dry Creek Dr 78410 361-242-7560
Dr. Debbie Litton, prin. Fax 387-3114

Corpus Christi ISD 39,100/PK-12
PO Box 110 78403 361-695-7200
Dr. Roland Hernandez, supt. Fax 886-9109
www.ccisd.us
Adkins MS 6-8
2402 Ennis Joslin Rd 78414 361-878-3800
Norma Cullum, prin. Fax 878-3828
Allen ES 400/PK-5
1414 18th St 78404 361-878-2140
Elodia Gutierrez, prin. Fax 886-9874
Baker MS 1,000/6-8
3445 Pecan St 78411 361-878-4600
John Dobbins, prin. Fax 878-1834
Barnes ES 600/PK-5
2829 Oso Pkwy 78414 361-994-5051
Delma Yzaguirre, prin. Fax 994-0860
Berlanga ES 700/PK-5
4120 Carroll Ln 78411 361-878-2160
Aurelia Barrera, prin. Fax 878-2303
Browne MS 800/6-8
4301 Schanen Blvd 78413 361-878-4270
John Trevino, prin. Fax 878-1836
Calk-Wilson ES 600/PK-5
3925 Fort Worth St 78411 361-878-2860
Sheila Thomas, prin. Fax 878-1831
Club Estates ES 500/K-5
5222 Merganser Dr 78413 361-994-3642
Kay Bircher, prin. Fax 994-3615
Crockett ES 500/PK-5
2625 Belton St 78416 361-878-2220
Dr. Olivia Ballesteros, prin. Fax 878-2366
Cullen Place MS 500/6-8
5225 Greely Dr 78412 361-878-2960
George Lerma, prin. Fax 994-3624
Cunningham MS 600/6-8
4321 Prescott St 78416 361-878-4630
Sandy Salinas-Deleon, prin. Fax 878-1838
Dawson ES 600/K-5
6821 Sanders Dr 78413 361-878-4800
Dr. Jamie Copeland, prin. Fax 878-4805
Driscoll MS 800/6-8
3501 Kenwood Dr 78408 361-878-4660
Bruce Wilson, prin. Fax 886-9890
Early Childhood Development Center 200/PK-5
6300 Ocean Dr 78412 361-825-3366
Dr. Criselda Castillo, prin. Fax 825-3301
Evans Special Emphasis S 400/PK-5
1315 Comanche St 78401 361-878-2240
Amanda Cameron, prin. Fax 886-9877
Fannin ES 600/PK-5
2730 Gollihar Rd 78415 361-878-2260
Analisa Farrah, prin. Fax 878-1820
Galvan ES 700/PK-5
3126 Masterson Dr 78415 361-878-2800
Hope Ramos-Uribe, prin. Fax 878-1821
Garcia ES 700/PK-5
1945 Gollihar Rd 78416 361-878-2280
Norma DeLeon, prin. Fax 878-2367
Gibson ES 500/PK-5
5723 Hampshire Rd 78408 361-878-2500
Julissa Segovia, prin. Fax 289-7406
Grant MS 1,200/6-8
4350 Aaron Dr 78413 361-878-3740
Carla Rosa-Villarreal, prin. Fax 878-1871
Haas MS 600/6-8
6630 McArdle Rd 78412 361-878-4240
Dr. Lynda DeLeon, prin. Fax 994-3626
Hamlin MS 700/6-8
3900 Hamlin Dr 78411 361-878-4210
Tommy Whitehead, prin. Fax 878-1839
Hicks ES 700/K-5
3602 McArdle Rd 78415 361-878-2200
Norma Reyna, prin. Fax 806-0578
Houston ES 500/PK-5
363 Norton St 78415 361-878-2520
Prudence Farrell, prin. Fax 878-1823
Jones ES 600/PK-5
7533 Lipes Blvd 78413 361-994-3674
Lisa Bowers, prin. Fax 994-3616
Kaffie MS 1,200/6-8
5922 Brockhampton St 78414 361-878-3700
Patti Heiland, prin. Fax 994-3604
Kolda ES 400/K-5
3730 Rodd Field Rd 78414 361-878-2980
Kostoryz ES 600/PK-5
3602 Panama Dr 78415 361-878-2540
Debra Aguilar, prin. Fax 878-2329
Los Encinos Special Emphasis S 400/PK-5
1826 Frio St 78417 361-878-2600
Christine Sierra, prin. Fax 878-1826
Martin Special Emphasis S 700/6-8
3502 Greenwood Dr 78416 361-878-4690
Javier Granados, prin. Fax 878-2455
Meadowbrook ES 600/PK-5
901 Meadowbrook Dr 78412 361-878-2620
LaTricia Johnson, prin. Fax 994-3650
Menger ES 400/PK-5
2401 S Alameda St 78404 361-878-2640
Christina Barrera, prin. Fax 886-9880
Metropolitan S of Design 600/K-6
1707 Ayers St 78404 361-878-2780
Robin Conde, prin. Fax 886-9892
Mireles ES 600/PK-5
7658 Cimarron Blvd 78414 361-994-6960
Alexis Soulas, prin. Fax 994-6970
Montclair ES 400/PK-5
5241 Kentner St 78412 361-994-3651
Steve Barrera, prin. Fax 994-6940
Moore ES 600/PK-5
6121 Durant Dr 78414 361-878-2660
Christine Marroquin, prin. Fax 994-3619
Oak Park Special Emphasis S 700/PK-5
3801 Leopard St 78408 361-878-2120
Kellye Loving, prin. Fax 878-2139
Sanders ES 400/PK-5
4102 Republic Dr 78413 361-878-2820
Dr. John Prezas, prin. Fax 878-1829
Schanen Estates ES 400/PK-5
5717 Killarmet Dr 78413 361-878-2940
Pamela Wright, prin. Fax 878-1830
Shaw Special Emphasis S 600/PK-5
2920 Soledad St 78405 361-878-2100
Rebecca Casas, prin. Fax 878-2109
Smith ES 500/PK-5
6902 Williams Dr 78412 361-878-2760
Rebecca Raesz, prin. Fax 994-3681
South Park MS 500/6-8
3001 McArdle Rd 78415 361-878-4720
Anna Marie Fuentes, prin. Fax 878-1844
Travis ES 500/PK-5
3210 Churchill Dr 78415 361-878-2700
Laura Quiroz-Colunga, prin. Fax 844-0341
Webb ES 600/K-5
6953 Boardwalk Ave 78414 361-878-2740
Jennifer Hammond, prin. Fax 878-2759
Windsor Park ES 700/1-5
4525 S Alameda St 78412 361-994-3664
Kimberly Bissell, prin. Fax 994-3621
Woodlawn ES 400/PK-5
1110 Woodlawn Dr 78412 361-878-2900
Kathryn Ortiz, prin. Fax 994-3622
Yeager ES 400/PK-5
5414 Tripoli Dr 78411 361-878-2920
Tammy Gathright, prin. Fax 878-1832
Zavala ES 800/PK-5
3125 Ruth St 78405 361-878-2720
Rolando Gonzalez, prin. Fax 886-9884
Flour Bluff ISD 5,800/PK-12
2505 Waldron Rd 78418 361-694-9000
Brian Schuss, supt. Fax 694-9800
flourbluffschools.us
Flour Bluff ECC 500/PK-K
2505 Waldron Rd 78418 361-694-9036
Amy Seeds, prin. Fax 694-9810
Flour Bluff ES 800/3-4
2505 Waldron Rd 78418 361-694-9500
Dr. Nikol Youngberg, prin. Fax 694-9805
Flour Bluff IS 800/5-6
2505 Waldron Rd 78418 361-694-9400
Salvador Alvarado, prin. Fax 694-9804
Flour Bluff JHS 1,000/7-8
2505 Waldron Rd 78418 361-694-9300
Cindy Holder, prin. Fax 694-9803
Flour Bluff PS 800/1-2
2505 Waldron Rd 78418 361-694-9600
Shea Hernandez, prin. Fax 694-9806

London ISD 800/PK-12
1306 FM 43 78415 361-855-0092
David Freeman Ed.D., supt. Fax 855-0198
www.londonisd.net
London ES 400/PK-4
1306 FM 43 78415 361-855-0092
Jessica Gutierrez, prin. Fax 255-0198
London MS 300/5-8
1306 FM 43 78415 361-855-0092
Amanda Barmore, prin. Fax 855-0098

Tuloso-Midway ISD 3,500/PK-12
PO Box 10900 78460 361-903-6400
Dr. Sue Nelson, supt. Fax 241-5836
www.tmisd.us
Tuloso-Midway IS 600/3-5
PO Box 10900 78460 361-903-6550
David Calk, prin. Fax 903-6572
Tuloso-Midway MS 900/6-8
PO Box 10900 78460 361-903-6600
Fax 242-9829
Tuloso-Midway PS 800/PK-2
PO Box 10900 78460 361-903-6500
Margaret Canales, prin. Fax 241-5617

West Oso ISD 1,900/PK-12
5050 Rockford Dr 78416 361-806-5900
Conrado Garcia, supt. Fax 225-8308
www.westosoisd.net
Kennedy PS 500/PK-2
1102 Villarreal Dr 78416 361-806-5920
Marcy Davis, prin. Fax 806-5969
West Oso ES 400/3-5
1526 Cliff Maus Dr 78416 361-806-5930
Fernando Gonzalez, prin. Fax 225-8956
West Oso JHS 500/6-8
5202 Bear Ln 78405 361-806-5950
Margaret Evans, prin. Fax 299-3111

Annapolis Christian Academy 200/PK-12
3875 S Staples St 78411 361-991-6004
Peter Hansen, hdmstr. Fax 232-5629
Arlington Heights Christian S 200/PK-12
9550 Leopard St 78410 361-241-0090
Leanne Isom, admin. Fax 242-9284
Bishop Garriga MS 200/6-8
3114 Saratoga Blvd 78415 361-851-0853
Rene Gonzalez, prin. Fax 853-5145
Central Catholic ES 100/PK-5
1218 Comanche St 78401 361-883-3873
Larry Manschot, prin. Fax 883-5879
Coggin Memorial S 50/PK-10
6645 Downing St 78414 361-991-6968
First Baptist S 200/PK-5
3115 Ocean Dr 78404 361-884-8931
Melinda Lyles, prin. Fax 888-5905
Holy Family S 200/PK-5
2526 Soledad St 78416 361-884-9142
Sr. Marilyn Springs, prin. Fax 884-1750
Incarnate Word Academy 300/PK-5
450 Chamberlain St 78404 361-883-0857
Pamela Carrillo, prin. Fax 881-9519
Incarnate Word Academy 200/6-8
2917 Austin St 78404 361-883-0857
Adolfo Garza, prin. Fax 882-9193
Most Precious Blood S 200/PK-5
3502 Saratoga Blvd 78415 361-852-4800
Nelda Bazan, prin. Fax 855-8707
Our Lady of Perpetual Help Academy 200/PK-8
5814 Williams Dr 78412 361-991-3305
Raul Ramon, prin. Fax 994-1806
Our Lady of the Rosary S 50/PK-K
2237 Waldron Rd 78418 361-939-9847
Josephine Taban-ud, prin. Fax 937-0890
St. James Episcopal S 200/PK-8
602 S Carancahua St 78401 361-883-0835
Galen Hoffstadt, hdmstr. Fax 883-0837
St. Patrick S 300/PK-6
3340 S Alameda St 78411 361-852-1211
Evelyn Burton, prin. Fax 852-4855
St. Pius X S 200/PK-6
737 Saint Pius Dr 78412 361-992-1343
Brian Krnavek, prin. Fax 992-0329
SS. Cyril & Methodius S 100/PK-5
5002 Kostoryz Rd 78415 361-853-9392
Lilly Samaniego, prin. Fax 853-0280
Yorktown Christian Academy 200/PK-8
5025 Yorktown Blvd Ste A 78413 361-985-9960
John Gilbert, admin. Fax 985-9821

Corrigan, Polk, Pop. 1,578
Corrigan-Camden ISD 900/PK-12
504 S Home St 75939 936-398-4040
Sherry Hughes, supt. Fax 398-4616
www.ccisdtx.com
Corrigan-Camden ES 100/PK-5
504 S Home St 75939 936-398-2341
Barbara Roden, prin. Fax 398-2986

Corrigan-Camden JHS 100/6-8
504 S Home St 75939 936-398-2341
Robert Elliott, prin. Fax 398-4928

Corsicana, Navarro, Pop. 23,195
Corsicana ISD 6,000/PK-12
2200 W 4th Ave 75110 903-874-7441
Dr. Diane Frost Ph.D., supt. Fax 602-8515
www.cisd.org
Bowie ES 700/K-4
1800 Bowie Dr 75110 903-872-6541
Amy Gibbs, prin. Fax 872-6298
Carroll ES 800/K-4
1101 E 13th Ave 75110 903-872-3074
Cheryl Murdock, prin. Fax 641-4153
Collins IS 900/5-6
1500 Dobbins Rd 75110 903-872-3979
Stephanie Howell, prin. Fax 874-1423
Corsicana MS, 4101 FM 744 75110 7-8
Darla Nolan, prin. 430-775-6167
Drane Learning Center PK-PK
100 S 18th St 75110 903-874-8281
Lisa West, dir. Fax 641-4130
Fannin ES 600/K-5
3201 N Beaton St 75110 903-874-3728
Karen Miller-Kopp, prin. Fax 874-0758
Houston ES 400/K-4
1213 W 4th Ave 75110 903-874-6971
Tracey Jordan, prin. Fax 641-4114
Navarro ES 600/K-4
601 S 45th St 75110 903-874-1011
Lauren Hodge, prin. Fax 874-3874

Mildred ISD 700/K-12
5475 S US Highway 287 75109 903-872-6505
Shannon Baker, supt. Fax 872-1341
www.mildredisd.org
Mildred ES 300/K-5
5475 S US Highway 287 75109 903-872-0381
Jana Schwarz, prin. Fax 872-3584

Collins Catholic S 200/PK-8
3000 W State Highway 22 75110 903-872-1751
Vicky Morrison, prin. Fax 872-1186

Cotton Center, Hale
Cotton Center ISD 100/PK-12
PO Box 350 79021 806-879-2160
Jeff Kirby M.Ed., supt. Fax 879-2175
www.cottoncenterisd.org
Cotton Center S 100/PK-12
PO Box 350 79021 806-879-2176
Jeff Kirby, admin. Fax 879-2175

Cotulla, LaSalle, Pop. 3,594
Cotulla ISD 1,400/PK-12
310 N Main St 78014 830-879-3073
Dr. Jack Seals, supt. Fax 879-3609
www.cotullaisd.org
Newman MS 300/6-8
310 N Main St 78014 830-879-2224
Dr. Brenda Jirasek, prin. Fax 879-4357
Ramirez-Burks ES 600/PK-5
310 N Main St 78014 830-879-2511
Cynthia Flores-Perkins, prin. Fax 879-4361
Other Schools – See Encinal

Coupland, Williamson
Coupland ISD 100/K-8
620 S Commerce St 78615 512-856-2422
Tammy Brinkman, supt. Fax 856-2222
www.couplandisd.org
Coupland ES 100/K-8
620 S Commerce St 78615 512-856-2422
Tammy Brinkman, prin. Fax 856-2222

Covington, Hill, Pop. 269
Covington ISD 300/PK-12
501 N Main 76636 254-854-2215
Dr. Christopher Heskett, supt. Fax 854-2272
www.covingtonisd.org/
Covington S 300/PK-12
501 N Main 76636 254-854-2215
Sherry Abbott, prin. Fax 854-2272

Crandall, Kaufman, Pop. 2,834
Crandall ISD 3,200/PK-12
PO Box 128 75114 972-427-6000
Dr. Robert Jolly, supt. Fax 427-6036
www.crandall-isd.net
Crandall MS 700/7-8
PO Box 490 75114 972-427-6080
Amy McAfee, prin. Fax 427-8031
Martin ES 400/PK-6
PO Box 460 75114 972-427-6020
David Christensen, prin. Fax 427-6039
Wilson ES 500/K-6
PO Box 430 75114 972-427-6040
Ginger Sikes, prin. Fax 427-8111
Other Schools – See Heartland

Crane, Crane, Pop. 3,329
Crane ISD 1,100/PK-12
511 W 8th St 79731 432-558-1022
Jim Rumage, supt. Fax 558-1025
www.craneisd.com/css/home.htm
Crane ES 600/PK-5
511 W 8th St 79731 432-558-1050
Nicole Jeffery, prin. Fax 558-1077
Crane MS 300/6-8
511 W 8th St 79731 432-558-1040
Lori Schulze, prin. Fax 558-1046

Cranfills Gap, Bosque, Pop. 280
Cranfills Gap ISD 100/PK-12
PO Box 67 76637 254-597-2505
Monti Parchman, supt. Fax 597-0001
www.cranfillsgapisd.net
Cranfills Gap S 100/PK-12
PO Box 67 76637 254-597-2505
Shana Campbell, prin. Fax 597-0001

Crawford, McLennan, Pop. 703
Crawford ISD 600/K-12
200 Pirate Dr 76638 254-486-2381
Kenneth Hall, supt. Fax 486-2198
www.crawford-isd.net
Crawford ES 300/K-6
100 Leonard Love Dr 76638 254-486-9083
Linda Stout, prin. Fax 486-9085

Creedmoor, Travis, Pop. 201
Del Valle ISD
Supt. — See Del Valle
Creedmoor ES 800/PK-5
5604 FM 1327, 512-386-3950
T.J. Moreno, prin. Fax 386-3955

Crockett, Houston, Pop. 6,873
Crockett ISD 1,300/PK-12
1400 W Austin St 75835 936-544-2125
Terry Myers, supt. Fax 544-5727
www.crockettisd.net
Crockett ECC 200/PK-K
1400 W Austin St 75835 936-544-2125
Dylis Bobbitt, dir. Fax 544-9678
Crockett ES 500/1-5
1400 W Austin St 75835 936-544-2125
Robin Stowe, prin. Fax 544-2088
Crockett JHS 300/6-8
1400 W Austin St 75835 936-544-2125
Michael Woodard, prin. Fax 544-4164

Jordan S 100/PK-6
1303 E Houston Ave 75835 936-544-4049

Crosby, Harris, Pop. 2,268
Crosby ISD 5,200/PK-12
706 Runneburg Rd 77532 281-328-9200
Keith Moore Ed.D., supt. Fax 328-9208
www.crosbyisd.org
Barrett PS 700/1-2
815 FM 1942 Rd 77532 281-328-9320
Karen Walthall, prin. Fax 328-9374
Crosby ES 200/1-5
5910 Pecan St 77532 281-328-9360
Christy Erb, prin. Fax 328-9213
Crosby K 600/PK-K
805 Runneburg Rd 77532 281-328-9370
Jennifer Roach, prin. Fax 328-9379
Crosby MS 800/7-8
14705 FM 2100 Rd 77532 281-328-9264
Dustin Bromley, prin. Fax 328-9356
Drew IS 800/5-6
223 Red Oak Ave 77532 281-328-9306
Christy Tisdom, prin. Fax 328-9376
Newport ES 700/3-4
430 N Diamondhead Blvd 77532 281-328-9330
Christy Covan, prin. Fax 328-9378

Sacred Heart S 100/PK-8
907 Runneburg Rd 77532 281-328-6561
Susan Harris, prin. Fax 462-0072

Crosbyton, Crosby, Pop. 1,731
Crosbyton Consolidated ISD 300/PK-12
204 S Harrison St 79322 806-675-7331
Shawn Mason, supt. Fax 675-2409
www.crosbyton.k12.tx.us
Crosbyton ES 200/PK-5
204 S Harrison St 79322 806-675-7331
Sharon West, prin. Fax 675-2409

Cross Plains, Callahan, Pop. 974
Cross Plains ISD 300/PK-12
700 N Main St 76443 254-725-6121
Phil Mitchell, supt. Fax 725-6559
www.crossplains.esc14.net/
Cross Plains ES 200/PK-6
700 N Main St 76443 254-725-6123
Leslie Lawrence, prin. Fax 725-6559

Crowell, Foard, Pop. 945
Crowell ISD 200/PK-12
PO Box 239 79227 940-684-1403
Pam Norwood, supt. Fax 684-1616
www.crowellisd.net
Crowell ES 100/PK-8
PO Box 239 79227 940-684-1403
Pam Norwood, admin. Fax 684-1616

Crowley, Tarrant, Pop. 12,575
Crowley ISD 15,000/PK-12
PO Box 688 76036 817-297-5800
Dr. Michael McFarland, supt. Fax 297-5005
www.crowleyisdtx.org
Crowley IS 400/5-6
10525 McCart Ave 76036 817-297-5960
Deidra Castro, prin. Fax 297-5964
Deer Creek ES 500/PK-4
805 S Crowley Rd 76036 817-297-5880
MaLisa Horton, prin. Fax 297-5884
Race ES 700/PK-6
537 S Heights Dr 76036 817-297-5080
Holly Anderson, prin. Fax 297-5084
Stevens MS 900/7-8
940 N Crowley Rd 76036 817-297-5840
Kimberly Buckhalton, prin. Fax 297-5850
Summer Creek MS 800/7-8
10236 Summercreek Dr 76036 817-297-5090
Cayla Grossman, prin. Fax 297-5094
Other Schools – See Fort Worth

Nazarene Christian Academy 400/K-12
2001 E Main St 76036 817-297-7003
Angelica Adams, prin. Fax 297-1509

Crystal City, Zavala, Pop. 7,131
Crystal City ISD 2,100/PK-12
805 E Crockett St 78839 830-374-2367
Imelda Salinas, supt. Fax 374-8004
www.crystalcityisd.org
Fly JHS 300/7-8
805 E Crockett St 78839 830-374-2371
Sarah Garcia, prin. Fax 374-9124
Juarez MS 300/5-6
805 E Crockett St 78839 830-374-8105
Carmel Diaz, prin. Fax 374-0043
Rivera ES 500/PK-1
805 E Crockett St 78839 830-374-8078
Andrea Guerrero, prin. Fax 374-8024
Zavala ES 500/2-4
805 E Crockett St 78839 830-374-8080
Yolanda Luna, prin. Fax 374-8092

Cuero, DeWitt, Pop. 6,679
Cuero ISD 2,000/PK-12
960 E Broadway St 77954 361-275-1914
Micah Dyer, supt. Fax 275-2981
www.cueroisd.org
Cuero JHS 400/6-8
608 Jr High Dr 77954 361-275-1900
Kim Fleener, prin. Fax 275-6912
French K 300/PK-1
611 E Prairie 77954 361-275-1900
Jennifer Bauer, prin. Fax 275-5313
Hunt ES 400/2-5
550 Industrial Blvd 77954 361-275-1900
Bridgette Cerny, prin. Fax 275-3474

St. Michael S 100/PK-6
208 N McLeod St 77954 361-277-3854
Jennifer Saenz, prin. Fax 275-3618

Cumby, Hopkins, Pop. 769
Cumby ISD 400/PK-12
303 Sayle St 75433 903-994-2260
Shelly Slaughter, supt. Fax 994-2399
www.cumbyisd.net
Cumby ES 200/PK-6
303 Sayle St 75433 903-994-2260
Doug Wicks, prin. Fax 994-2847

Miller Grove ISD 300/PK-12
7819 Farm Road 275 S 75433 903-459-3288
Steve Johnson, supt. Fax 459-3744
www.mgisd.net
Miller Grove S 300/PK-12
7819 Farm Road 275 S 75433 903-459-3288
Gary Billingsley, prin. Fax 459-3744

Cushing, Nacogdoches, Pop. 594
Cushing ISD 500/PK-12
PO Box 337 75760 936-326-4890
Michael Davis, supt. Fax 326-4115
www.cushingisd.org
Cushing ES 200/PK-5
PO Box 337 75760 936-326-4234
Stefani Jackson, prin. Fax 326-4265

Cypress, Harris
Cypress-Fairbanks ISD
Supt. — See Houston
Andre ES 1,200/K-5
8111 Fry Rd 77433 281-463-5500
Laura Novacinski, prin. Fax 463-5507
Anthony MS 6-8
10215 Greenhouse Rd 77433 281-373-5660
Vivian Bennett, prin. Fax 373-5661
Arnold MS 1,600/6-8
11111 Telge Rd 77429 281-897-4700
Jodi Matteson, prin. Fax 807-8610
Ault ES 1,000/PK-5
21010 Maple Village Dr 77433 281-373-2800
Jeff LaCoke, prin. Fax 373-2823
Black ES 1,000/K-5
14155 Grant Rd 77429 281-320-7145
Melissa LeDoux, prin. Fax 320-7144
Farney ES 1,100/K-5
14425 Barker Cypress Rd 77429 281-373-2850
Patricia Reilly, prin. Fax 373-2855
Goodson MS 1,200/6-8
17333 Huffmeister Rd 77429 281-373-2350
Sheri McCaig, prin. Fax 373-2355
Hamilton ES 1,000/PK-5
12050 Old Kluge Rd 77429 281-370-0990
Joni Conn, prin. Fax 320-7067
Hamilton MS 1,500/6-8
12330 Kluge Rd 77429 281-320-7000
Kim Sempe, prin. Fax 320-7021
Hopper MS 1,400/6-8
7811 Fry Rd 77433 281-463-5353
Wendi Whitthaus, prin. Fax 463-5354
Keith ES 900/PK-5
20550 Fairfield Green Blvd 77433 281-213-1744
Dawn Tryon, prin. Fax 213-1749
Lamkin ES 1,000/PK-5
11521 Telge Rd 77429 281-897-4775
Gale Parker, prin. Fax 807-8163
Millsap ES 700/K-5
12424 Huffmeister Rd 77429 281-897-4470
Joy Dauphin, prin. Fax 807-8635
Pope ES 1,000/K-5
19019 N Bridgeland Lake Pky 77433 281-373-2340
Becky Koop, prin. Fax 373-2341
Postma ES 900/K-5
18425 West Rd 77433 281-345-3660
Kim Freed, prin. Fax 345-3545
Rennell ES 1,100/PK-5
10600 Tuckorton Rd 77433 281-213-1550
Leslie Thomas, prin. Fax 213-1551
Robison ES 900/PK-5
17100 Robison Woods Rd 77429 281-213-1700
Kelly Gerletti, prin. Fax 213-1705

Salyards MS 1,500/6-8
21757 Fairfield Place Dr 77433 281-373-2400
Liz Wood, prin. Fax 373-2425
Sampson ES 1,100/K-5
16002 Coles Crossing Dr 77429 281-213-1600
Heather Motzny, prin. Fax 213-1605
Smith MS 1,900/6-8
10300 Warner Smith Blvd 77433 281-213-1010
Susan Higgins, prin. Fax 213-1020
Spillane MS 1,300/6-8
13403 Woods Spillane Blvd 77429 281-213-1645
Michael Maness, prin. Fax 213-1799
Swenke ES 1,200/K-5
22400 Fairfield Place Dr 77433 281-213-1200
Elizabeth Miller, prin. Fax 213-1210
Warner ES 900/K-5
10400 Warner Smith Blvd 77433 281-213-1650
Schonda Kidd, prin. Fax 213-1651
Wells ES PK-5
10607 Mason Rd 77433 832-349-7400
Cheryl Fisher, prin. Fax 349-7410
Woodard ES PK-5
17501 Cypress North Houston 77433 281-373-2303
Susan Brenz, prin. Fax 373-2304

Tomball ISD
Supt. — See Tomball
Oakcrest IS 5-6
18202 Shaw Rd 77429 281-357-3033
Lee Wright, prin. Fax 357-3034

Connection S of Houston 100/K-12
15815 House and Hahl Rd 77433 832-544-6031
Kathleen Wrobleske, head sch Fax 286-3088
Covenant Academy 200/K-12
11711 Telge Rd 77429 281-373-2233
Leslie Collins, head sch Fax 588-8227
Longwood Montessori S 100/PK-K
12839 Louetta Rd 77429 281-655-5900
Victoria Turner, prin. Fax 349-7990
Oaks Adventist Christian S 100/PK-12
11735 Grant Rd 77429 713-896-0071

Daingerfield, Morris, Pop. 2,512
Daingerfield-Lone Star ISD 1,100/PK-12
200 Tiger Dr 75638 903-645-2239
Sandra Quarles, supt. Fax 645-2137
www.dlsisd.org
Daingerfield JHS 200/6-8
200 Texas St 75638 903-645-2261
Amy Billingslea, prin. Fax 645-4010
South ES 200/3-5
701 Linda Dr 75638 903-645-3501
Daniel Pritchett, prin. Fax 645-2295
West ES 300/PK-2
1305 W W M Watson Blvd 75638 903-645-2901
Lesia Lewis, prin. Fax 645-7178

Daisetta, Liberty, Pop. 957
Hull-Daisetta ISD 500/PK-12
PO Box 477 77533 936-536-6321
Mary Huckabay, supt. Fax 536-6251
www.hdisd.net/
Hull-Daisetta JHS 100/7-8
PO Box 477 77533 936-536-6321
Quinn Godwin, prin. Fax 536-3839
Other Schools – See Hull

Dale, Caldwell
Lockhart ISD
Supt. — See Lockhart
Strawn ES K-5
9000 FM 1854 78616 512-398-0630
Patricia Rocha, prin. Fax 398-0631

Dalhart, Dallam, Pop. 7,836
Dalhart ISD 1,800/PK-12
701 E 10th St 79022 806-244-7810
John Massey, supt. Fax 244-7822
www.dalhartisd.org
Dalhart ES 600/PK-2
701 E 10th St 79022 806-244-7350
Claudia Montoya, prin. Fax 244-7352
Dalhart IS 200/3-5
701 E 10th St 79022 806-244-7380
Misty Heiskell, prin. Fax 244-7387
Dalhart JHS 400/6-8
701 E 10th St 79022 806-244-7825
Shannon Marshall, prin. Fax 244-7835

Dalhart Christian Academy 100/PK-7
PO Box 987 79022 806-244-6482
Melissa Ritchey, admin. Fax 244-3542
St. Anthony of Padua Catholic S 100/PK-6
PO Box 1329 79022 806-244-4811
Shay Batenhorst, prin. Fax 244-0462

Dallardsville, Polk
Big Sandy ISD 500/PK-12
PO Box 188 77332 936-563-1000
Eric Carpenter, supt. Fax 563-1010
www.bigsandyisd.net
Big Sandy S 500/PK-12
PO Box 188 77332 936-563-1000
Eric Carpenter, admin. Fax 563-1010

Dallas, Dallas, Pop. 1,183,449
Carrollton-Farmers Branch ISD
Supt. — See Carrollton
Long MS 800/6-8
2525 Frankford Rd 75287 972-968-4100
Charde Dockery, prin. Fax 968-4110
McKamy ES 500/PK-5
3443 Briargrove Ln 75287 972-968-2400
Matt Pruitt, prin. Fax 968-2410
McWhorter ES 800/PK-5
3678 Timberglen Rd 75287 972-968-2800
Yanet Cardoza, prin. Fax 968-2810
Sheffield ES 500/K-5
18111 Kelly Blvd 75287 972-968-3100
Amy Miller, prin. Fax 968-3110

Dallas ISD 156,100/PK-12
9400 N Central Expy 75231 972-925-3700
Michael Hinojosa Ed.D., supt. Fax 925-3201
www.dallasisd.org
Adams ES 700/PK-5
8239 Lake June Rd 75217 972-794-1200
Maria Totsuka-Reyes, prin. Fax 794-1201
Adams ES 600/PK-5
12600 Welch Rd 75244 972-794-2600
Dora Renaud, prin. Fax 794-2601
Alexander ES 400/PK-5
1830 Goldwood Dr 75232 972-749-3100
Valarie Kendrick, prin. Fax 749-3101
Anderson ES 800/PK-5
620 N Saint Augustine Dr 75217 972-749-6200
Silvia Garcia, prin. Fax 749-6201
Arcadia Park ES 700/PK-5
1300 N Justin Ave 75211 972-502-5300
Kelly O'Hara, prin. Fax 502-5301
Atwell Law Academy 1,000/6-8
1303 Reynoldston Ln 75232 972-794-6400
Selena Deboskie, prin. Fax 794-6401
Bayles ES 600/PK-5
2444 Telegraph Ave 75228 972-749-8900
Robby Wilson, prin. Fax 749-8901
Bethune ES 700/PK-5
1665 Duncanville Rd 75211 972-502-1300
Teresa Hernandez, prin. Fax 502-1301
Blair ES 800/PK-5
7720 Gayglen Dr 75217 972-794-1600
Umoja Turner, prin. Fax 794-1601
Blanton ES 700/PK-5
8915 Greenmound Ave 75227 972-794-1700
Laura Garza, prin. Fax 794-1701
Botello ES 500/PK-5
225 S Marsalis Ave 75203 214-502-4600
Maria Puentemejia, prin. Fax 932-5094
Bowie ES 500/PK-5
330 N Marsalis Ave 75203 972-925-6600
Carolina Wilson, prin. Fax 925-6601
Brashear ES 700/PK-5
2959 S Hampton Rd 75224 972-502-2600
Sonja Barnes, prin. Fax 502-2601
Browne MS 700/7-8
3333 Sprague Dr 75233 972-502-2500
Lakisha Thomas, prin. Fax 502-2501
Bryan ES 600/PK-5
2001 Deer Path Dr 75216 972-502-8500
Tonya Anderson, prin. Fax 502-8501
Budd ES 600/PK-5
2121 S Marsalis Ave 75216 972-502-8400
Anita Barnes, prin. Fax 502-8401
Burleson ES 700/PK-5
6300 Elam Rd 75217 972-749-4500
LaJoyce Johnson, prin. Fax 749-4501
Burnet ES 1,100/PK-5
3200 Kinkaid Dr 75220 972-794-3000
Sonia Loskot, prin. Fax 794-3001
Bushman ES 600/PK-5
4200 Bonnie View Rd 75216 972-749-1800
Yolanda Knight, prin. Fax 749-1801
Cabell ES 600/PK-5
12701 Templeton Trl 75234 972-794-2400
Fabian Hypolite, prin. Fax 794-2401
Caillet ES 700/PK-5
3033 Merrell Rd 75229 972-794-3200
Janeen Pantoja, prin. Fax 794-3201
Callejo ES, 7817 Military Pkwy 75227 700/PK-5
Sandra Fernandez, prin. 972-892-5700
Carpenter ES 400/PK-5
2121 Tosca Ln 75224 972-794-6000
Charmain Curtis, prin. Fax 794-6001
Carr ES 400/PK-5
1952 Bayside St 75212 972-794-4300
Carlotta Hooks, prin. Fax 794-4301
Cary MS 600/6-8
3978 Killion Dr 75229 972-502-7600
Ben Dickerson, prin. Fax 502-7601
Casa View ES 700/PK-5
2100 N Farola Dr 75228 972-749-7700
Thania Garibay, prin. Fax 749-7701
Chavez Learning Center 600/PK-5
1710 N Carroll Ave 75204 972-925-1000
Vincent Garcia, prin. Fax 925-1001
Cigarroa ES 700/PK-5
9990 Webb Chapel Rd 75220 972-502-2900
Douglas Burak, prin. Fax 502-2901
Cochran ES 600/PK-5
6000 Keeneland Pkwy 75211 972-794-4600
Melissa Gonzalez, prin. Fax 794-4601
Comstock MS 600/7-8
7044 Hodde St 75217 972-794-1300
Willie Johnson, prin. Fax 794-1301
Conner ES 700/PK-5
3037 Green Meadow Dr 75228 972-749-8200
Kiashan King-Corbett, prin. Fax 749-8201
Cowart ES 600/PK-5
1515 S Ravinia Dr 75211 972-794-5500
Lucia Salinas, prin. Fax 794-5501
Cuellar ES 800/PK-5
337 Pleasant Vista Dr 75217 972-749-6400
Lonnie Russell, prin. Fax 749-6401
Dade Learning Center 800/6-8
2727 Al Lipscomb Way 75215 972-749-3800
Al Way, prin. Fax 749-3801
Dallas Environmental Science Academy 400/6-8
3531 N Westmoreland Rd 75212 972-794-3950
Arnold Zuniga, prin. Fax 794-3951
Dealey Montessori 400/PK-8
6501 Royal Ln 75230 972-794-8400
Beverly Lusk, prin. Fax 794-8401
DeGolyer ES 400/PK-5
3453 Flair Dr 75229 972-794-2800
Tara Mays, prin. Fax 794-2801
De Zavala ES 400/PK-5
3214 N Winnetka Ave 75212 972-892-6400
Lisa Miramontes, prin. Fax 892-6401
Donald ES 500/PK-5
1218 Phinney Ave 75211 972-794-5300
Katherine Carter, prin. Fax 794-5301
Dorsey ES 500/PK-5
133 N Saint Augustine Dr 75217 972-749-6300
Rubinna Sanchez, prin. Fax 749-6301
Douglass ES 600/PK-5
226 N Jim Miller Rd 75217 972-794-1400
Marquetaa Masters, prin. Fax 794-1401
Dunbar Learning Center 600/PK-5
4200 Metropolitan Ave 75210 972-794-6600
Verna Farmer, prin. Fax 794-6601
Edison MS 600/6-8
2940 Singleton Blvd 75212 972-794-4100
Luis Valdez, prin. Fax 794-4101
Ervin ES 700/PK-5
3722 Black Oak Dr 75241 972-749-3700
Dr. James Wallace, prin. Fax 749-3701
Field ES 500/PK-5
2151 Royal Ln 75229 972-794-2700
Shondula Whitfield, prin. Fax 794-2701
Foster ES 900/PK-5
3700 Clover Ln 75220 972-794-8100
Irma De La Guardia, prin. Fax 794-8101
Frank ES 1,200/PK-5
5201 Celestial Rd 75254 972-502-5900
Beverly Mullins Ford, prin. Fax 502-5901
Franklin MS 1,000/6-8
6920 Meadow Rd 75230 972-502-7100
Joseph Sotelo, prin. Fax 502-7101
Garcia MS, 700 E 8th St 75203 900/6-8
Gary Auld, prin. 972-502-5500
Gaston MS 1,100/6-8
9565 Mercer Dr 75228 972-502-5400
Sharon Stauss, prin. Fax 502-5401
Gill ES 800/PK-5
10910 Ferguson Rd 75228 972-749-8400
Shawki Freelon, prin. Fax 749-8401
Gonzalez ES 700/PK-5
6610 Lake June Rd 75217 972-502-3300
Reymundo Guajardo, prin. Fax 502-3301
Gooch ES 300/PK-5
4030 Calculus Dr 75244 972-794-2500
Kim Ashmore, prin. Fax 794-2501
Greiner Exploratory Arts Academy 1,500/6-8
501 S Edgefield Ave 75208 972-925-7100
Yvonne Rojas, prin. Fax 925-7101
Guzick ES 800/PK-5
5000 Berridge Ln 75227 972-502-3900
Adreana Davis, prin. Fax 502-3901
Hall ES 600/PK 5
2120 Keats Dr 75211 972-794-5400
Adriana Gonzalez, prin. Fax 794-5401
Halliday ES 600/PK-5
10210 Teagarden Rd 75217 972-925-1800
Tangela Carter, prin.
Harllee ECC, 1216 E 8th St 75203 PK-PK
Onjaleke Brown, prin. 972-925-6500
Hawthorne ES 500/PK-5
7800 Umphress Rd 75217 972-749-4700
Ana Fernandez, prin. Fax 749-4701
Henderson ES 500/PK-5
2200 S Edgefield Ave 75224 972-749-2900
Ida Escobedo, prin. Fax 749-2901
Hernandez ES 400/PK-5
5555 Maple Ave 75235 972-925-2700
Oscar Aponte, prin. Fax 925-2701
Hexter ES 600/PK-5
9720 Waterview Rd 75218 972-502-5800
Jennifer Jackson, prin. Fax 502-5801
Highland Meadows ES 900/PK-5
8939 Whitewing Ln 75238 972-502-5200
Julian Davis, prin. Fax 502-5201
Hill MS 900/6-8
505 Easton Rd 75218 972-502-5700
Candice Ruiz, prin. Fax 502-5701
Hogg ES 300/PK-5
1144 N Madison Ave 75208 972-502-8600
Jairo Casco, prin. Fax 502-8601
Holland ES 300/PK-5
4203 S Lancaster Rd 75216 972-749-1900
Kieshla Wiley, prin. Fax 749-1901
Holmes Classical Academy 800/6-8
2001 E Kiest Blvd 75216 972-925-8500
Sharron Jackson, prin. Fax 925-8501
Holmes MS 1,200/6-8
2939 Saint Rita Dr 75233 214-932-7800
Barbara Moham, prin. Fax 932-7801
Hooe ES 500/PK-5
2419 Gladstone Dr 75211 972-794-6700
Fernando Rodriguez, prin. Fax 794-6701
Hotchkiss ES 1,000/PK-5
6929 Town North Dr 75231 972-749-7000
Cecilia Criner, prin. Fax 749-7001
Houston ES 200/PK-5
2827 Throckmorton St 75219 972-749-5800
Oscar Nandayapa, prin. Fax 749-5801
Ireland ES 600/PK-5
1515 N Jim Miller Rd 75217 972-749-4900
Stephanie Amaya, prin. Fax 749-4901
Jackson ES 600/K-5
5828 E Mockingbird Ln 75206 972-749-7200
Melanie Schiff, prin. Fax 749-7201
Johnston ES 500/PK-5
2020 Mouser Ln 75203 972-925-7400
Michele Martin, prin. Fax 925-7401
Jones ES 700/PK-5
3901 Meredith Ave 75211 972-794-4700
Alberto Herrera, prin. Fax 794-4701
Jordan ES 600/PK-5
1111 W Kiest Blvd 75224 972-925-8100
Lucy Hopkins, prin. Fax 925-8101
Kahn ES 700/PK-5
610 N Franklin St 75211 972-502-1400
Monica Marquez, prin. Fax 502-1401

Kennedy-Curry MS 700/6-8
6605 Sebring Dr 75241 972-925-1600
David Welch, prin.
Kennedy Learning Center 700/PK-5
1802 Moser Ave 75206 972-794-7100
Linda Olivarez, prin. Fax 794-7101
Kiest ES 700/PK-5
2611 Healey Dr 75228 972-502-5600
Yasmine Cruz, prin. Fax 502-5601
King Learning Center 500/PK-5
1817 Warren Ave 75215 972-502-8100
Gloria Kennedy, prin. Fax 502-8101
Kleberg ES 600/PK-5
1450 Edd Rd 75253 972-749-6500
Amy Zbylut, prin. Fax 749-6501
Knight ES 600/PK-5
2615 Anson Rd 75235 972-749-5300
Enrique Escobedo, prin. Fax 749-5301
Kramer ES 600/PK-5
7131 Midbury Dr 75230 972-794-8300
Kate Walker, prin. Fax 794-8301
Lagow ES 500/PK-5
637 Edgeworth Dr 75217 972-749-6600
Joseph Luedecke, prin. Fax 749-6601
Lakewood ES 900/PK-5
3000 Hillbrook St 75214 972-749-7300
Kate Wilke, prin. Fax 749-7301
Lang MS, 1678 Chenault St 75228 1,000/6-8
Kimberly Robinson, prin. 972-925-2400
Lanier Center for Arts 600/PK-5
1400 Walmsley Ave 75208 972-794-4400
Alyssa Peraza, prin. Fax 794-4401
Lee ES 400/PK-5
2911 Delmar Ave 75206 972-749-7400
Bernard Hart, prin. Fax 749-7401
Lee ES 600/PK-5
7808 Racine Dr 75232 972-749-3900
Roshonda Clayton-Brown, prin. Fax 749-3901
Lipscomb ES 500/PK-5
5801 Worth St 75214 972-794-7300
Daisy Briones, prin. Fax 794-7301
Longfellow Career Academy 400/6-8
5314 Boaz St 75209 972-749-5400
Lorena Hernandez, prin. Fax 749-5401
Long MS 1,300/6-8
6116 Reiger Ave 75214 972-502-4700
Chandra Hooper-Barnett, prin. Fax 502-4701
Lowe ES 600/PK-5
7000 Holly Hill Dr 75231 972-502-1700
Yesenia Cardoza, prin. Fax 502-1701
Macon ES 500/PK-5
650 Holcomb Rd 75217 972-794-1500
Gerald Bennett, prin. Fax 794-1501
Maple Lawn ES 600/PK-5
3120 Inwood Rd 75235 972-925-2500
Carmen Derrick, prin. Fax 925-2501
Marcus ES 1,000/PK-5
2911 Northaven Rd 75229 972-794-2900
Holly Wallace, prin. Fax 794-2901
Marsalis ES 500/PK-5
5640 S Marsalis Ave 75241 972-749-3500
Kimberly Richardson, prin. Fax 749-3501
Marsh Preparatory Academy 1,200/6-8
3838 Crown Shore Dr 75244 972-502-6600
Martha Bujanda, prin. Fax 502-6601
Martinez Learning Center 500/PK-5
4500 Bernal Dr 75212 972-794-6900
Josefina Murillo, prin. Fax 794-6901
Mata IS 200/PK-5
7420 La Vista Dr 75214 972-749-7500
Tomeka Williams, prin. Fax 749-7501
May ES, 9818 Brockbank Dr 75220 PK-5
Israel Rivera, prin. 972-925-3700
McNair ES 800/PK-5
3150 Bainbridge Ave 75237 972-794-6200
Ariss Rider, prin. Fax 794-6201
McShan ES 700/PK-5
8307 Meadow Rd 75231 972-502-3800
Dayanna Carson, prin. Fax 502-3801
Medrano ES 600/PK-5
2221 Lucas Dr 75219 972-794-3300
Mariela Magro Malo, prin. Fax 794-3301
Medrano MS 900/6-8
9815 Brockbank Dr 75220 972-925-1300
Theresa Sigurdson, prin. Fax 925-1301
Milam ES 300/PK-5
4200 Mckinney Ave 75205 972-749-5600
Anna Gamez, prin. Fax 749-5601
Miller ES 400/PK-5
3111 Bonnie View Rd 75216 972-502-8700
Nikkie Hudson, prin. Fax 502-8701
Mills ES 500/PK-5
1515 Lynn Haven Ave 75216 972-925-7500
LaTonya Clark, prin. Fax 925-7501
Moreno ES 500/PK-5
2115 S Hampton Rd 75224 972-502-3100
Tammie Brooks, prin. Fax 502-3101
Moseley ES 800/PK-5
10400 Rylie Rd 75217 972-749-6700
Rocio Bernal, prin. Fax 749-6701
Mt. Auburn ES 600/PK-5
6012 E Grand Ave 75223 972-749-8500
Michele Hill, prin. Fax 749-8501
Oliver ES 400/PK-5
4010 Idaho Ave 75216 972-749-3400
Cheryl Freeman, prin. Fax 749-3401
Peabody ES 600/PK-5
3101 Raydell Pl 75211 972-794-5200
Sherry Rogers Hall, prin. Fax 794-5201
Pease ES 600/PK-5
2914 Cummings St 75216 214-932-3800
Shavannia Dash, prin. Fax 932-3801
Peeler ES 400/PK-5
810 S Llewellyn Ave 75208 972-502-8300
Sofia Villareal, prin. Fax 502-8301
Pershing ES 500/PK-5
5715 Meaders Ln 75229 972-794-8600
Margarita Hernandez, prin. Fax 794-8601

Piedmont Global Academy 6-8
7625 Hume Dr 75227 972-749-4100
LaTonya Lockhart, prin. Fax 749-4101
Pleasant Grove ES 600/PK-5
1614 N Saint Augustine Dr 75217 972-892-5000
Anabel Ruiz, prin. Fax 892-5001
Polk Center for Talented & Gifted 600/PK-5
6911 Victoria Ave 75209 972-794-8900
Misty Rothermund, prin. Fax 794-8901
Preston Hollow ES 400/PK-5
6423 Walnut Hill Ln 75230 972-794-8500
Tom Brandt, prin. Fax 794-8501
Quintanilla MS 800/7-8
2700 Remond Dr 75211 972-502-3200
Salem Hussain, prin. Fax 502-3201
Ray Learning Center 400/PK-5
2211 Caddo St 75204 972-794-7700
Sheryl Wilson, prin. Fax 794-7701
Reagan ES 600/PK-5
201 N Adams Ave 75208 972-502-8200
Ruby Garza Ramirez, prin. Fax 502-8201
Reilly ES 500/PK-5
11230 Lippitt Ave 75218 972-749-7800
Marion Jackson, prin. Fax 749-7801
Reinhardt ES 600/PK-5
10122 Losa Dr 75218 972-749-7900
Phoebe Montgomery, prin. Fax 749-7901
Rhoads Learning Center 700/PK-5
4401 S 2nd Ave 75210 972-749-1000
Bridget Ransom, prin. Fax 749-1001
Rice Learning Center 600/PK-5
2425 Pine St 75215 972-749-1100
Alpher Garrett-Jones, prin. Fax 749-1101
Richards MS 1,200/6-8
3831 N Prairie Creek Rd 75227 972-892-5400
Francine Taylor, prin.
Richardson ES, 7203 Bruton Rd 75217 600/PK-5
Courtney Thomas Loy, prin. 972-892-8100
Roberts ES 600/PK-5
4919 E Grand Ave 75223 972-749-8700
Eneida Padro-Colon, prin. Fax 749-8701
Rogers ES 500/PK-5
5314 Abrams Rd 75214 972-794-8800
Lisa Lovato, prin. Fax 794-8801
Rosemont ES 400/3-5
719 N Montclair Ave 75208 972-749-5000
Rachel Moon, prin. Fax 749-5001
Rosemont PS - Semos Campus 700/PK-2
1919 Stevens Forest Dr 75208 972-502-3850
Rachel Moon, prin. Fax 502-3851
Rowe ES 500/PK-5
4918 Hovenkamp Dr 75227 972-749-8800
Cynthia McFarland, prin. Fax 749-8801
Runyon ES 700/PK-5
10750 Cradlerock Dr 75217 972-749-6100
Sherry Williams, prin. Fax 749-6101
Rusk MS 700/6-8
2929 Inwood Rd 75235 972-925-2000
Juan Cordoba, prin. Fax 925-2001
Russell ES 800/PK-5
3031 S Beckley Ave 75224 972-925-8300
Marco Baker, prin. Fax 925-8301
Salazar ES 700/PK-5
1120 S Ravinia Dr 75211 972-502-1800
Nicole Bixby, prin. Fax 502-1801
Saldivar ES 1,000/PK-5
9510 Brockbank Dr 75220 972-794-2000
Chaundra Macklin, prin. Fax 794-2001
Sanger ES 600/PK-5
8410 San Leandro Dr 75218 972-749-7600
Hector Martinez, prin. Fax 749-7601
San Jacinto ES 500/PK-5
7900 Hume Dr 75227 972-749-4200
Celia Sanchez, prin. Fax 749-4201
Seagoville MS 1,100/6-8
950 N Woody Rd 75253 972-892-7100
Javier Chaparro, prin. Fax 892-7101
Silberstein ES 800/PK-5
5940 Hollis Ave 75227 972-794-1900
Richie Heffernan, prin. Fax 794-1901
Solar Preparatory S for Girls 300/K-2
2617 N Henderson Ave 75206 972-749-4300
Nancy Bernardino, prin.
Soto ES 700/PK-5
4510 W Jefferson Blvd 75211 972-502-5100
Perla Kwiatkowski, prin. Fax 502-5101
Spence Talented/Gifted Academy 1,000/6-8
4001 Capitol Ave 75204 972-925-2300
Deardra Hayes-Whigham, prin. Fax 925-2301
Starks ES 300/PK-5
3033 Tips Blvd 75216 972-502-8800
Lynette Howard, prin. Fax 502-8801
STEAM MS at Hulcy 6-8
9339 S Polk St 75232 214-932-7400
Jonica Crowder-Lockwood, prin.
Stemmons ES 800/PK-5
2727 Knoxville St 75211 972-794-4900
Arnoldo Zuniga, prin. Fax 794-4901
Stevens Park ES 700/PK-5
2615 W Colorado Blvd 75211 972-794-4200
Cameron Ramirez, prin. Fax 794-4201
Stockard MS 900/7-8
2300 S Ravinia Dr 75211 972-794-5700
Adam Varrassi, prin. Fax 794-5701
Stone ES at Vickery Meadows 300/PK-5
6606 Ridgecrest Rd 75231 972-502-7900
Rosalinda Pratt, prin. Fax 502-7901
Stone Montessori S 200/PK-8
4747 Veterans Dr 75216 972-794-3400
Niki Jones, prin. Fax 794-3401
Storey MS 700/6-8
3000 Maryland Ave 75216 972-925-8700
JoAnn Jackson, prin. Fax 925-8701
Tasby MS 900/6-8
7001 Fair Oaks Ave 75231 972-502-1900
Audrey Delacruz, prin. Fax 502-1901

Tatum ES 700/PK-5
3002 N Saint Augustine Dr 75227 972-502-2000
Juan Pecina, prin. Fax 502-2001
Terry ES 400/PK-5
6661 Greenspan Ave 75232 972-749-3200
Alicia Bradley, prin. Fax 749-3201
Thornton ES 500/PK-5
6011 Old Ox Rd 75241 972-794-8000
Christofor Stephens, prin. Fax 794-8001
Titche ES 1,000/PK-5
9560 Highfield Dr 75227 972-794-2100
Damien Stovall, prin. Fax 794-2101
Tolbert ES 500/PK-5
4000 Blue Ridge Blvd 75233 972-794-5900
LaKeisha Smith, prin. Fax 794-5901
Travis Academy 100/4-8
3001 McKinney Ave 75204 972-794-7500
Mari Smith, prin. Fax 794-7501
Truett ES 1,000/PK-5
1811 Gross Rd 75228 972-749-8000
Terre Evans, prin. Fax 749-8001
Turner ES 400/PK-5
5505 S Polk St 75232 972-749-6300
Michael Nickson, prin. Fax 794-6301
Twain Leadership Vanguard ES 400/PK-5
724 Green Cove Ln 75232 972-749-3000
Derrick Ross, prin. Fax 749-3001
Urban Park ES 600/PK-5
6901 Military Pkwy 75227 972-794-1100
Lisa Falcon, prin. Fax 794-1101
Walker MS 800/6-8
12532 Nuestra Dr 75230 972-502-6100
Dr. Laura Stout, prin. Fax 502-6101
Walnut Hill ES 400/PK-5
10115 Midway Rd 75229 972-502-7800
Robert McLaurin, prin. Fax 502-7801
Webster ES 700/PK-5
3815 S Franklin St 75233 972-794-6100
Clement Alexander, prin. Fax 794-6101
Weiss ES 500/PK-5
8601 Willoughby Blvd 75232 972-749-4000
Lakiesha Merritt, prin. Fax 749-4001
Williams ES 300/PK-5
4518 Pomona Rd 75209 972-794-8700
Michael Jackson, prin. Fax 794-8701
Wilmer-Hutchins ES 900/PK-5
7475 J J Lemmon Rd 75241 972-925-2600
Michael Gipson, prin.
Winnetka ES 900/PK-5
1151 S Edgefield Ave 75208 972-749-5100
Lourdes Garduno, prin. Fax 749-5101
Withers ES 400/PK-5
3959 Northaven Rd 75229 972-794-5000
Wendy Miller, prin. Fax 794-5001
Young ES 600/PK-5
4601 Veterans Dr 75216 972-749-2000
Christie Samuell, prin. Fax 749-2001
Young Mens Leadership Academy Florence 800/6-8
1625 N Masters Dr 75217 972-749-6000
Christopher Barksdale, prin. Fax 749-6001
Zaragosa ES 500/PK-5
4550 Worth St 75246 972-749-8600
Angela Bell, prin. Fax 749-8601
Zumwalt MS 500/6-8
2445 E Ledbetter Dr 75216 972-749-3600
Troy Tyson, prin. Fax 749-3601
Other Schools – See Addison, Balch Springs, Carrollton, Mesquite, Seagoville, Wilmer

Duncanville ISD
Supt. — See Duncanville
Acton ES 500/PK-4
9240 County View Rd 75249 972-708-2400
Kyalla Bowens, prin. Fax 708-2424
Bilhartz ES 700/PK-4
6700 Wandt Dr 75236 972-708-6600
Valerie Nelms-Harris, prin. Fax 708-6666
Hyman ES 600/PK-4
8441 Fox Creek Trl 75249 972-708-6700
Brandee King, prin. Fax 708-6767
Kennemer MS 700/7-8
7101 W Wheatland Rd 75249 972-708-3600
Monica Smith, prin. Fax 708-3636

Highland Park ISD 7,000/PK-12
7015 Westchester Dr 75205 214-780-3000
Dr. Tom Trigg, supt. Fax 780-3099
www.hpisd.org
Armstrong ES 600/PK-4
3600 Cornell Ave 75205 214-780-3100
Dr. Skip Moran, prin. Fax 780-3199
Bradfield ES 700/K-4
4300 Southern Ave 75205 214-780-3200
Regina Dumar, prin. Fax 780-3299
Highland Park MS 1,100/7-8
3555 Granada Ave 75205 214-780-3600
Dr. Laurie Hitzelberger, prin. Fax 780-3699
Hyer ES 700/K-4
3920 Caruth Blvd 75225 214-780-3300
Jeremy Gilbert, prin. Fax 780-3399
McCulloch IS 1,100/5-6
3555 Granada Ave 75205 214-780-3500
Dr. Laurie Hitzelberger, prin. Fax 780-3599
University Park ES 700/K-4
3505 Amherst Ave 75225 214-780-3400
Candace Judd, prin. Fax 780-3402

Mesquite ISD
Supt. — See Mesquite
Henrie ES, 253 W Lawson Rd 75253 K-6
Lisa Millsaps, prin. 972-290-4200

Plano ISD
Supt. — See Plano
Frankford MS 1,100/6-8
7706 Osage Plaza Pkwy 75252 469-752-5200
Kristopher Vernon, prin. Fax 752-5201

Haggar ES 600/PK-5
17820 Campbell Rd 75252 469-752-1400
Katie Brittain, prin. Fax 752-1401
Mitchell ES 700/K-5
4223 Briargrove Ln 75287 469-752-2800
Bob Farris, prin. Fax 752-2801

Richardson ISD
Supt. — See Richardson
Aikin ES 800/PK-6
12300 Pleasant Valley Dr 75243 469-593-1820
Fax 593-1763
Audelia Creek ES 700/PK-6
12600 Audelia Rd 75243 469-593-1820
Raymie Venable, prin. Fax 593-1763
Bowie ES 600/K-6
7643 La Manga Dr 75248 469-593-6000
Staci Low, prin. Fax 593-6066
Brentfield ES 600/K-6
6768 Brentfield Dr 75248 469-593-5740
Steve Lemons, prin. Fax 593-5723
Bukhair ES 800/1-6
13900 Maham Rd 75240 469-593-4900
Lanette Massey-Stinnett, prin. Fax 593-4901
RISD Academy 900/1-6
13630 Coit Rd 75240 469-593-3300
Rebecca Henriquez, prin. Fax 593-3307
Dobie PS 700/PK-1
14040 Rolling Hills Ln 75240 469-593-4100
Kirstyn Hart, prin. Fax 593-4011
Forest Lane Academy 800/PK-6
9663 Forest Ln 75243 469-593-1850
Lariza Liner, prin. Fax 593-1919
Forest Meadow JHS 700/7-8
9373 Whitehurst Dr 75243 469-593-1500
Kerri Jones, prin. Fax 593-1461
Forestridge ES 700/PK-6
10330 Bunchberry Dr 75243 469-593-8500
Misty Wilson, prin. Fax 593-8502
Hamilton Park Pacesetter Magnet ES 700/PK-6
8301 Towns St 75243 469-593-3900
Michael Thomas, prin. Fax 593-3950
Lake Highlands ES 700/PK-6
9501 Ferndale Rd 75238 469-593-2100
Becky Stevens, prin. Fax 593-2088
Lake Highlands JHS 800/7-8
10301 Walnut Hill Ln 75238 469-593-1600
Carrie Breedlove, prin. Fax 593-1606
Marshall ES 700/PK-6
9666 W Ferris Branch Blvd 75243 469-593-6800
Sharon Newman, prin. Fax 593-6801
Merriman Park ES 400/K-6
7101 Winedale Dr 75231 469-593-2800
Susan Burt, prin. Fax 593-2741
Moss Haven ES 400/K-6
9202 Moss Farm Ln 75243 469-593-2200
Philip Henderson, prin. Fax 593-2158
Northlake ES 600/PK-6
10059 Ravensway Dr 75238 469-593-2300
Mary Kellagher, prin. Fax 593-2309
Northwood Hills ES 400/K-6
14532 Meandering Way 75254 469-593-4300
Roxxy Griffin, prin. Fax 593-4301
Prestonwood ES 400/K-6
6525 La Cosa Dr 75248 469-593-6700
Pam Aitken, prin. Fax 593-6712
Skyview ES 700/K-6
9229 Meadowknoll Dr 75243 469-593-2400
Ingrid Dodd, prin. Fax 593-2423
Spring Creek ES 300/PK-6
7667 Roundrock Rd 75248 469-593-4500
Sharon Erickson, prin. Fax 593-4501
Spring Valley ES 400/PK-6
13535 Spring Grove Ave 75240 469-593-4600
Kelly Colburn, prin. Fax 593-4609
Stults Road ES 700/PK-6
8700 Stults Rd 75243 469-593-2500
Jennifer Balch, prin. Fax 593-2521
Wallace ES 700/K-6
9921 Kirkhaven Dr 75238 469-593-2600
Frank Patranella, prin. Fax 593-2610
White Rock ES 700/K-6
9229 Chiswell Rd 75238 469-593-2700
Lee Walker, prin. Fax 593-2706

Akiba Academy 300/PK-8
12324 Merit Dr 75251 214-295-3400
Alcuin S 500/PK-12
6144 Churchill Way 75230 972-239-1745
Walter Sorensen, head sch Fax 934-8727
All Saints Catholic S 400/PK-8
7777 Osage Plaza Pkwy 75252 214-217-3300
Dr. Laura McCorkle, prin. Fax 217-3339
Calvary Lutheran S 100/PK-8
9807 Church Rd 75238 214-343-7457
James Henrickson, prin. Fax 348-1424
Choices Leadership Academy 50/5-8
18106 Marsh Ln 75287 972-662-0665
Christ the King Catholic S 400/K-8
4100 Colgate Ave 75225 214-365-1234
Patrick O'Sullivan, prin. Fax 365-1236
Coram Deo Academy 100/PK-8
7777 Lyndon B Johnson Fwy 75251 972-385-6410
Beverly McMullin, dir. Fax 385-6410
Covenant S 500/K-12
7300 Valley View Ln 75240 214-358-5818
Dallas Christian Academy 100/PK-12
4025 N Central Expy 75204 214-528-6327
Maeli Dang M.Ed., prin. Fax 528-6450
Episcopal S of Dallas 400/PK-4
4344 Colgate Ave 75225 214-353-5818
Meredyth Cole, head sch Fax 353-5861
Fellowship Christian Academy 400/PK-8
1821 W Camp Wisdom Rd 75232 214-672-9206
Karen Gosby M.Ed., head sch Fax 672-9201
First Baptist Academy 300/PK-12
1606 Patterson St 75201 214-969-7861

Good Shepherd Episcopal S 600/PK-8
11110 Midway Rd 75229 214-357-1610
Dr. Julie McLeod, head sch Fax 357-4105
Grace Academy of Dallas 100/PK-6
11306 Inwood Rd Ste A 75229 214-696-5648
Jim Clarke, hdmstr. Fax 696-8713
Highland Park Presbyterian Day S 200/PK-K
3821 University Blvd 75205 214-525-6500
Sarah Good M.Ed., dir.
Hockaday S 1,100/PK-12
11600 Welch Rd 75229 214-363-6311
Dr. Karen Coleman, head sch Fax 360-6563
Holy Trinity Catholic S 200/PK-8
3815 Oak Lawn Ave 75219 214-526-5113
Marian Davis, prin. Fax 526-4524
Kessler S PK-6
1215 Turner Ave 75208 214-942-2220
Vanessa Ullmann, head sch Fax 942-1223
Lakehill Prep S 400/K-12
2720 Hillside Dr 75214 214-826-2931
Roger Perry, hdmstr. Fax 826-4623
Lakewood Montessori S 100/PK-6
6210 E Mockingbird Ln 75214 214-821-9466
Lamplighter S 400/PK-4
11611 Inwood Rd 75229 214-369-9201
Dr. Joan Hill, head sch
Levine Academy 300/PK-8
18011 Hillcrest Rd 75252 972-248-3032
Montessori S of North Dallas 100/PK-6
18303 Davenport Rd 75252 972-985-8844
Mount St. Michael S 200/PK-8
PO Box 225159 75222 214-337-0244
Gretchen Montgomery, prin. Fax 339-1702
Our Lady of Perpetual Help Catholic S 200/PK-8
7625 Cortland Ave 75235 214-351-3396
Maleli Paniagua, prin. Fax 351-9889
Our Redeemer Lutheran S 200/PK-6
7611 Park Ln 75225 214-368-1371
Lois Frischmann, prin. Fax 368-1473
Parish Episcopal S 1,100/PK-12
4101 Sigma Rd 75244 972-239-8011
David Monaco, head sch Fax 991-1237
St. Bernard of Clairvaux Catholic S 200/PK-8
1420 Old Gate Ln 75218 214-321-2897
Michael Davies, prin. Fax 321-4060
St. Cecilia Catholic S 200/PK-8
635 Mary Cliff Rd 75208 214-948-8628
Candice Barbosa, prin. Fax 948-4956
St. Elizabeth of Hungary Catholic S 300/PK-8
4019 S Hampton Rd 75224 214-331-5139
Rachel Dzurilla, prin. Fax 467-4346
St. James Episcopal S 50/PK-K
9845 McCree Rd 75238 214-348-1349
Loree Birkenback, head sch Fax 348-1368
St. John's Episcopal S 500/PK-8
848 Harter Rd 75218 214-328-9131
Mark Crotty, head sch Fax 320-0205
St. Marks S of Texas 900/1-12
10600 Preston Rd 75230 214-346-8000
David Dini, hdmstr. Fax 346-8002
St. Mary of Carmel Catholic S 200/PK-8
1716 Singleton Blvd 75212 214-748-2934
Kaitlyn Aguilar, prin. Fax 760-9052
St. Monica Catholic S 900/PK-8
4140 Walnut Hill Ln 75229 214-351-5688
Phil Riley, prin. Fax 352-2608
St. Patrick Catholic S 500/PK-8
9635 Ferndale Rd 75238 214-348-8070
Julie Hendry, prin. Fax 503-7230
St. Philip & St. Augustine Catholic Acad 200/PK-8
8151 Military Pkwy 75227 214-381-4973
Erica Romero, prin. Fax 381-0466
St. Philip's S & Community Center 200/PK-6
1600 Pennsylvania Ave 75215 214-421-5221
St. Pius X Catholic S 300/K-8
3030 Gus Thomasson Rd 75228 972-279-2339
Tana Scott, prin. Fax 613-2059
St. Rita Catholic S 700/K-8
12525 Inwood Rd 75244 972-239-3203
Dr. Carol Everling-Walsh, prin. Fax 934-0657
St. Thomas Aquinas Catholic S 900/PK-8
3741 Abrams Rd 75214 214-826-0566
Patrick Magee, pres. Fax 826-0251
St. Timothy School 50/PK-12
4333 Cole Ave 75205 214-521-6062
Rev. Tony Melton, hdmstr. Fax 521-5200
Santa Clara Catholic Academy 200/PK-8
321 Calumet Ave 75211 214-333-9423
Stephanie Matous, prin. Fax 333-2556
Scofield Christian S 100/PK-6
7730 Abrams Rd 75231 214-349-6843
Dr. Shailendra Thomas, head sch Fax 342-2061
Southwest Adventist Jr. Academy 50/PK-8
1600 Bonnie View Rd 75203 214-948-1666
Torah Day S of Dallas 300/PK-8
6921 Frankford Rd 75252 972-964-0090
Tyler Street Christian Academy 200/PK-12
915 W 9th St 75208 214-941-9717
Dr. Karen Egger, supt. Fax 941-0324
Wesley Prep S 400/PK-6
9200 Inwood Rd 75220 214-706-9568
West Dallas Community S 300/PK-8
2300 Canada Dr 75212 214-634-1927
Stan Newton, head sch Fax 688-1928
Westwood S 300/PK-12
14340 Proton Rd 75244 972-239-8598
White Rock Montessori 200/PK-8
1601 Oates Dr 75228 214-324-5580
White Rock North S 300/PK-6
9727 White Rock Trl 75238 214-348-7410
Winston S 200/K-12
5707 Royal Ln 75229 214-691-6950
Rebbie Evans, head sch Fax 691-1509
Zion Lutheran S 300/PK-8
6121 E Lovers Ln 75214 214-363-1630
Jeff Thorman, prin. Fax 361-2049

Damon, Brazoria, Pop. 543
Damon ISD 200/PK-8
PO Box 429 77430 979-742-3457
Dr. Donald Rhodes, supt. Fax 742-3275
www.damonisd.net/
Damon S 200/PK-8
PO Box 429 77430 979-742-3457
Dave Demiglio, supt. Fax 742-3275

Danbury, Brazoria, Pop. 1,690
Danbury ISD 700/PK-12
PO Box 378 77534 979-922-1218
Greg Anderson, supt. Fax 922-8246
www.danburyisd.org
Danbury ES 300/PK-5
PO Box 716 77534 979-922-8787
Jennifer Williams, prin. Fax 922-1589
Danbury MS 100/6-8
PO Box 586 77534 979-922-1226
Jon Hill, prin. Fax 922-1051

Darrouzett, Lipscomb, Pop. 347
Darrouzett ISD 100/PK-12
PO Box 98 79024 806-624-2221
Troy Humphrey, supt. Fax 624-4361
www.darrouzettisd.net
Darrouzett S 100/PK-12
PO Box 98 79024 806-624-2221
Donavan Ferguson, prin. Fax 624-4361

Dawson, Navarro, Pop. 793
Dawson ISD 500/PK-12
199 N School Ave 76639 254-578-1031
Stacy Henderson, supt. Fax 578-1721
www.dawsonisd.net/
Dawson ES 300/PK-6
199 N School Ave 76639 254-578-1416
Andrea Farrish, prin. Fax 578-1721

Dayton, Liberty, Pop. 7,114
Dayton ISD 4,700/PK-12
PO Box 248 77535 936-258-2667
Dr. Jessica Johnson, supt. Fax 258-5616
www.daytonisd.net
Austin ES 700/K-5
PO Box 248 77535 936-258-2535
Nelly Tinkle, prin. Fax 257-4138
Brown ES 700/K-5
PO Box 248 77535 936-257-2796
Jessica Ott, prin. Fax 257-4154
Colbert ES 200/PK-PK
PO Box 248 77535 936-258-2727
Jennifer Narvaez, admin. Fax 257-4151
Richter ES 700/K-5
PO Box 248 77535 936-258-7126
Lecia Eubanks, prin. Fax 257-4179
Wilson JHS 800/6-8
PO Box 248 77535 936-258-2309
Matt Barnett, prin. Fax 257-4109

Veritas Christian S 50/K-5
202 E Houston St 77535 936-258-8231

Decatur, Wise, Pop. 6,000
Decatur ISD 2,700/PK-12
307 S Cates St 76234 940-393-7100
Judi Whitis, supt. Fax 627-3141
www.decaturisd.us/
Carson ES 500/PK-5
2100 S Business 287 76234 940-393-7500
LeeAnn Farris, prin. Fax 627-4792
McCarroll MS 500/6-8
1201 W Thompson St 76234 940-393-7300
Dewayne Tamplen, prin. Fax 627-2497
Rann ES 500/PK-5
1300 Deer Park Rd 76234 940-393-7600
Kaci Cook, prin. Fax 627-6198
Young ES 400/PK-5
379 Buchanan Rd 76234 940-393-7400
Lana Coffman, prin. Fax 627-0082

Victory Christian Academy 200/PK-12
PO Box 32 76234 940-626-4730

Deer Park, Harris, Pop. 31,669
Deer Park ISD 15,700/PK-12
2800 Texas Ave 77536 832-668-7000
Victor White, supt. Fax 930-4638
www.dpisd.org
Bonnette JHS 800/6-8
5010 W Pasadena Blvd 77536 832-668-7700
John Wegman, prin. Fax 930-4756
Carpenter ES 800/PK-5
5002 W Pasadena Blvd 77536 832-668-8400
Suzanne Holcomb, prin. Fax 930-4970
Dabbs ES 700/K-5
302 E Lambuth Ln 77536 832-668-8100
Mandy Davis, prin. Fax 930-4910
Deer Park ES 800/PK-5
2920 Luella Ave 77536 832-668-8000
Lisa McLaughlin, prin. Fax 930-4930
Deer Park JHS 800/6-8
410 E 9th St 77536 832-668-7500
Dr. Tiffany Regan, prin. Fax 930-4726
San Jacinto ES 900/K-5
1302 E 13th St 77536 832-668-7900
Dr. Robin Evans, prin. Fax 930-4950
Other Schools – See Pasadena

La Porte ISD
Supt. — See La Porte
College Park ES 500/PK-5
4315 Luella Ave 77536 281-604-4400
Camilla Whitlock, prin. Fax 604-4460
Heritage ES 600/K-5
4301 East Blvd 77536 281-604-2600
Grisel Wallace, prin. Fax 604-2605

De Kalb, Bowie, Pop. 1,672
De Kalb ISD — 800/PK-12
101 Maple St 75559 — 903-667-2566
Dr. John Booth, supt. — Fax 667-3791
www.dekalbisd.net
De Kalb ES — 400/PK-4
101 W Fannin St 75559 — 903-667-2328
Emily Lee, prin. — Fax 667-5151
De Kalb MS — 200/5-8
929 W Grizzley St 75559 — 903-667-2834
Clayton Little, prin. — Fax 667-5509

Hubbard ISD — 100/PK-8
3347 US Highway 259 S 75559 — 903-667-2645
Traci Drake, supt. — Fax 667-5835
hubbardisd.net
Hubbard S — 100/PK-8
3347 US Highway 259 S 75559 — 903-667-2645
Traci Drake, prin. — Fax 667-5835

De Leon, Comanche, Pop. 2,226
De Leon ISD — 600/PK-12
425 S Texas St 76444 — 254-893-8210
Dr. Dana Marable Ph.D., supt. — Fax 893-8214
www.deleonisd.net
De Leon ES — 300/PK-5
425 S Texas St 76444 — 254-893-8220
Lori Womack, prin. — Fax 893-8224
Perkins MS — 200/6-8
425 S Texas St 76444 — 254-893-8230
Liesa Nowlin, prin. — Fax 893-8234

Dell City, Hudspeth, Pop. 357
Dell City ISD — 100/K-12
PO Box 37 79837 — 915-964-2663
Jody Kotys, supt. — Fax 964-2473
dellcity.schoolwires.com
Dell City S — 100/K-12
PO Box 37 79837 — 915-964-2663
Jody Kotys, admin. — Fax 964-2473

Del Rio, Val Verde, Pop. 35,427
San Felipe-Del Rio Consolidated ISD — 10,700/PK-12
PO Box 428002 78842 — 830-778-4000
Carlos Rios Ed.D., supt. — Fax 774-9892
www.sfdr-cisd.org
Buena Vista ES — 900/K-5
PO Box 428002 78842 — 830-778-4600
Jennifer Sutton, prin. — Fax 774-9875
Calderon ES — 600/K-5
PO Box 428002 78842 — 830-778-4620
Jane Villarreal, prin. — Fax 774-9975
Cardwell Preschool — 600/PK-PK
PO Box 428002 78842 — 830-778-4650
Rufina Adams, prin. — Fax 774-9855
Chavira ES — 600/PK-5
PO Box 428002 78842 — 830-778-4668
Maria Correa, prin. — Fax 778-4921
Del Rio MS — 1,500/7-8
PO Box 428002 78842 — 830-778-4530
Sergio Jimenez, prin. — Fax 778-4912
Garfield ES — 900/K-6
PO Box 428002 78842 — 830-778-4700
Genella Rubio, prin. — Fax 774-9928
Green ES — 700/K-5
PO Box 428002 78842 — 830-778-4750
Cheryl Pond, prin. — Fax 774-9532
Lamar ES — 600/K-5
PO Box 428002 78842 — 830-778-4730
Maryvel Flores, prin. — Fax 774-9493
North Heights ES — 700/PK-8
PO Box 428002 78842 — 830-778-4770
Mattye Soliz, prin. — Fax 778-4922
San Felipe Memorial MS — 700/6-6
PO Box 428002 78842 — 830-778-4560
Celia Zuniga-Barrera, prin. — Fax 778-4920

Sacred Heart S — 200/PK-8
209 E Greenwood St 78840 — 830-775-3274
Araceli Faz, prin. — Fax 774-2800
St. James Episcopal S — 200/PK-5
PO Box 4000 78841 — 830-775-9911

Del Valle, Travis
Del Valle ISD — 11,600/PK-12
5301 Ross Rd 78617 — 512-386-3000
Kelly Crook Ph.D., supt. — Fax 386-3015
dvisd.net
Del Valle ES — 900/PK-5
5400 Ross Rd 78617 — 512-386-3350
Bertha Hernandez, prin. — Fax 386-3355
Del Valle MS — 900/6-8
5500 Ross Rd 78617 — 512-386-3400
Natasha Staten, prin. — Fax 386-3440
Popham ES — 700/PK-5
7014 Elroy Rd 78617 — 512-386-3750
Suzi Gonzales, prin. — Fax 386-3755
Other Schools – See Austin, Creedmoor

Denison, Grayson, Pop. 22,067
Denison ISD — 3,500/PK-12
1201 S Rusk Ave 75020 — 903-462-7000
Dr. Henry Scott, supt. — Fax 462-7002
www.denisonisd.net
Houston ES — 300/PK-5
1100 W Morgan St 75020 — 903-462-7300
Kyle Uber, prin. — Fax 462-7419
Hyde Park ES — 300/K-5
1701 S Hyde Park Ave 75020 — 903-462-7350
Kerry Kaai, prin. — Fax 462-7455
Lamar ES — 400/PK-5
1000 S 5th Ave 75021 — 903-462-7400
Janet Mobley, prin. — Fax 462-7495
Mayes ES — 600/PK-5
201 Jennie Ln 75020 — 903-462-7500
Natalie Hicks, prin. — Fax 462-7563
McDaniel IS — 300/5-6
400 S Lillis Ln 75020 — 903-462-7200
Alvis Dunlap, prin. — Fax 462-7328
Scott MS — 7-8
1901 S Mirick Ave 75020 — 903-462-7180
John Parker, prin. — Fax 462-7342
Terrell ES — 400/PK-5
230 Martin Luther King St 75020 — 903-462-7550
Amy Dunn, prin. — Fax 462-7609

Denton, Denton, Pop. 110,797
Denton ISD — 26,100/PK-12
1307 N Locust St 76201 — 940-369-0000
Dr. Jamie Wilson, supt. — Fax 369-4982
www.dentonisd.org
Borman ES — 500/PK-5
1201 Parvin St 76205 — 940-369-2500
Michele Sandefur, prin. — Fax 369-4903
Calhoun MS — 700/6-8
709 W Congress St 76201 — 940-369-2400
Paul Martinez, prin. — Fax 369-4939
Evers Park ES — 600/K-5
3300 Evers Pkwy 76207 — 940-369-2600
Linda Tucker, prin. — Fax 369-4906
Ginnings ES — 600/K-5
2525 Yellowstone Pl 76209 — 940-369-2700
Marcy Auchter, prin. — Fax 369-4909
Gonzalez Pre K Ctr — 300/PK-PK
1212 Long Rd 76207 — 940-369-4360
Felicia Sprayberry, prin. — Fax 382-4285
Hawk ES — 700/K-5
2300 Oakmont Dr 76210 — 940-369-1800
Robin Brownell, prin. — Fax 321-1872
Hodge ES — 700/PK-5
3900 Grant Pkwy 76208 — 940-369-2800
Patty Jensen, prin. — Fax 369-4912
Houston ES — 600/PK-5
3100 Teasley Ln 76205 — 940-369-2900
Teresa Andress, prin. — Fax 369-4915
Lee ES — 600/K-5
800 Mack Dr 76209 — 940-369-3500
Lorena Salas, prin. — Fax 369-4918
McMath MS — 700/6-8
1900 Jason Dr 76205 — 940-369-3300
Dr. Debra Nobles, prin. — Fax 369-4946
McNair ES — 500/PK-5
1212 Hickory Creek Rd 76210 — 940-369-3600
Lacey Hailey, prin. — Fax 369-4921
Nelson ES — 600/K-5
3909 Teasley Ln 76210 — 940-369-1400
Erika Timmons, prin. — Fax 383-3534
Pecan Creek ES — 700/K-5
4400 Lakeview Blvd 76208 — 940-369-4400
Lacey Rainey, prin. — Fax 369-4904
Rayzor ES — 600/PK-5
1400 Malone St 76201 — 940-369-3700
Cecilia Holt, prin. — Fax 369-4924
Rivera ES — 600/PK-5
701 Newton St 76205 — 940-369-3800
Roshaunda Thomas, prin. — Fax 369-4927
Ryan ES — 600/K-5
201 W Ryan Rd 76210 — 940-369-4600
Nicole Poole, prin. — Fax 369-4936
Strickland MS — 900/6-8
324 E Windsor Dr 76209 — 940-369-4200
Kathleen Carmona, prin. — Fax 369-4950
Wilson ES — 600/K-5
1306 E Windsor Dr 76209 — 940-369-4500
Caleb Leath, prin. — Fax 369-4933
Windle S for Young Children — 300/PK-PK
901 Audra Ln 76209 — 940-369-3900
Angela Hellman, prin. — Fax 369-4930
Other Schools – See Argyle, Aubrey, Corinth, Lantana, Little Elm, Oak Point, Shady Shores

---

Denton Calvary Academy — 200/K-12
PO Box 2414 76202 — 940-320-1944
Immaculate Conception S — 300/PK-8
2301 N Bonnie Brae St 76207 — 940-381-1155
Elaine Schad, prin. — Fax 381-1837

Denver City, Yoakum, Pop. 4,445
Denver City ISD — 1,200/PK-12
501 Mustang Dr 79323 — 806-592-5900
Gary Davis, supt. — Fax 592-5909
www.dcisd.org
Dodson PS — PK-2
600 N Soland Ave 79323 — 806-592-5930
Angie Sutton, prin. — Fax 592-5939
Gravitt JHS — 400/6-8
419 Mustang Dr 79323 — 806-592-5940
Billy Moore, prin. — Fax 592-5949
Kelley ES — 400/3-5
500 N Soland Ave 79323 — 806-592-5920
Lori Alexander, prin. — Fax 592-5929

Deport, Lamar, Pop. 566
Prairiland ISD
Supt. — See Pattonville
Deport ES — 200/PK-5
PO Box 218 75435 — 903-652-3325
Lanny Mathews, prin. — Fax 652-2212

DeSoto, Dallas, Pop. 48,350
De Soto ISD — 7,600/PK-12
200 E Belt Line Rd 75115 — 972-223-6666
Dr. David Harris, supt. — Fax 274-8209
www.desotoisd.org
Amber Terrace Early Childhood Academy — 100/PK-PK
224 Amber Ln 75115 — 972-223-8757
Keishla Coleman, prin. — Fax 274-8247
Cockrell Hill ES — 500/K-5
425 S Cockrell Hill Rd 75115 — 972-230-1692
Leetha Harper, prin. — Fax 274-8081
De Soto East MS — 600/6-8
601 E Belt Line Rd 75115 — 972-223-0690
Brandon Ward, prin. — Fax 274-8156
De Soto West MS — 700/6-8
800 N Westmoreland Rd 75115 — 972-230-1820
James McBride, prin. — Fax 274-8183
Meadows ES — 400/K-5
1016 The Meadows Pkwy 75115 — 972-224-0960
Shana Hawthorne, prin. — Fax 228-7908
Northside ES — 500/K-5
525 Ray Ave 75115 — 972-224-6709
Dr. Lori Mathis, prin. — Fax 228-7925
Woodridge ES — 600/K-5
1001 Woodridge Dr 75115 — 972-223-3800
Deidre Hannible, prin. — Fax 274-8204
Young ES — 600/K-5
707 N Young Blvd 75115 — 972-223-6505
Shanta Duren, prin. — Fax 274-8221
Other Schools – See Glenn Heights

Canterbury Episcopal S — 300/PK-12
1708 N Westmoreland Rd 75115 — 972-572-7200
DeSoto Private S — 100/PK-6
301 E Beltline Rd 75115 — 972-223-6450

Detroit, Red River, Pop. 712
Detroit ISD — 500/PK-12
110 E Garner St 75436 — 903-674-6131
Brian Howie, supt. — Fax 674-2478
www.detroiteagles.net
Detroit ES — 300/PK-5
110 E Garner St 75436 — 903-674-3137
Paul Allen, prin. — Fax 674-2407
Detroit JHS — 100/6-8
110 E Garner St 75436 — 903-674-2646
Amanda Tidwell, prin. — Fax 674-2206

Devers, Liberty, Pop. 439
Devers ISD — 200/PK-8
PO Box 488 77538 — 936-549-7591
Elizabeth A. Harris, supt. — Fax 549-7595
www.deversisd.net
Devers ES — 100/PK-5
PO Box 488 77538 — 936-549-7591
Elizabeth A. Harris, admin. — Fax 549-7595
Devers JHS — 50/6-8
PO Box 488 77538 — 936-549-7591
Elizabeth A. Harris, admin. — Fax 549-7595

Devine, Medina, Pop. 4,321
Devine ISD — 2,000/PK-12
605 W Hondo Ave 78016 — 830-851-0795
Scott Sostarich, supt. — Fax 663-6706
www.devineisd.org
Ciavarra ES — 500/PK-2
112 Bentson Dr 78016 — 830-851-0395
Brenda Gardner, prin. — Fax 663-6730
Devine IS — 400/3-5
900 Atkins Ave 78016 — 830-851-0495
Blain Martin, prin. — Fax 663-6746
Devine MS — 400/6-8
400 Cardinal Dr 78016 — 830-851-0695
Kandi Darnell, prin. — Fax 663-6769

Deweyville, Newton, Pop. 997
Deweyville ISD
Supt. — See Orange
Deweyville ES — 300/PK-6
683 County Road 4156 77614 — 409-746-2681
LaJuan Addison, prin.

D Hanis, Medina, Pop. 845
D'Hanis ISD — 300/PK-12
PO Box 307 78850 — 830-363-7216
Scott Higgins, supt. — Fax 363-7390
www.dhanisisd.net/
D'Hanis MSHS — 300/PK-12
PO Box 307 78850 — 830-363-7217
Kurt Schumacher, prin. — Fax 363-7390

Diana, Upshur
New Diana ISD — 1,000/PK-12
1373 US Highway 259 S 75640 — 903-663-8000
Carl Key, supt. — Fax 241-7393
www.ndisd.org
Hunt ES East — 100/4-5
1379 US Highway 259 S 75640 — 903-663-8003
Teresa Beckham, prin. — Fax 663-9588
Hunt ES West — 300/PK-3
11150 State Highway 154 E 75640 — 903-663-8004
Teresa Beckham, prin. — Fax 663-7575
New Diana MS — 200/6-8
11854 State Highway 154 E 75640 — 903-663-8002
Joaquin Guerero, prin. — Fax 663-1812

Diboll, Angelina, Pop. 4,716
Diboll ISD — 2,000/PK-12
PO Box 550 75941 — 936-829-4718
Vicki Thomas, supt. — Fax 829-5558
www.dibollisd.com
Diboll JHS — 300/7-8
403 Dennis St 75941 — 936-829-5225
Mark Kettering, prin. — Fax 829-5848
Diboll PS — 200/PK-PK
113 Hendrick St 75941 — 936-829-4671
Diana Moore, prin. — Fax 829-4977
Temple ES — 600/K-3
PO Box 550 75941 — 936-829-6950
Nikki Miller, prin. — Fax 829-6960
Temple IS — 400/4-6
PO Box 550 75941 — 936-829-6900
Nikki Miller, prin. — Fax 829-6910

Dickinson, Galveston, Pop. 18,370
Dickinson ISD — 10,000/PK-12
PO Box Z 77539 — 281-229-6000
Vicki Mims, supt. — Fax 229-6011
www.dickinsonisd.org
Barber MS — 700/5-6
5651 FM 517 Rd E 77539 — 281-229-6900
Kimberly Kelley, prin. — Fax 229-6901
Bay Colony ES — 800/PK-4
101 Bay Colony Elmentary Dr 77539 — 281-229-6200
Amy Smith, prin. — Fax 229-6201

Dunbar MS 800/5-6
2901 23rd St 77539 281-229-6600
Nancy Flores, prin. Fax 229-6601
Hughes Road ES 700/PK-4
11901 Hughes Rd 77539 281-229-6700
Kelly Colburn Jackson, prin. Fax 229-6701
McAdams JHS 1,400/7-8
11415 Hughes Rd 77539 281-229-7100
Rachelle Joseph, prin. Fax 229-7101
Silbernagel ES 700/PK-4
4201 25th St 77539 281-229-6800
Leslie Burke, prin. Fax 229-6801
Other Schools – See Bacliff, League City, San Leon

Pine Drive Christian S 200/PK-12
705 FM 517 Rd E 77539 281-534-4881
Frances Templeton, admin. Fax 534-4318
True Cross S 100/PK-8
400 FM 517 Rd E 77539 281-337-5212
Yolanda Agrella, prin. Fax 337-5779

Dilley, Frio, Pop. 3,879
Dilley ISD 1,000/PK-12
245 W FM 117 78017 830-965-1912
Clint McLain, supt. Fax 965-4069
dilleyisd.net
Dilley ES 500/PK-5
245 W FM 117 78017 830-965-1313
Delma Carrion, prin. Fax 965-1178
Harper MS 200/6-8
245 W FM 117 78017 830-965-2195
Jennifer Torres, prin. Fax 965-2171

Dime Box, Lee
Dime Box ISD 100/PK-12
PO Box 157 77853 979-884-2324
Nicholas West, supt. Fax 884-0106
www.dimeboxisd.net
Dime Box ES PK-6
PO Box 157 77853 979-884-2324
James Smith, prin. Fax 884-0106

Dimmitt, Castro, Pop. 4,377
Dimmitt ISD 1,200/PK-12
608 W Halsell St 79027 806-647-3101
Bryan Davis, supt. Fax 647-5433
www.dimmittisd.net
Dimmitt MS 400/5-8
1505 Western Cir 79027 806-647-3108
Tiffany Seaton, prin. Fax 647-2996
Richardson ES 600/PK-4
708 W Stinson St 79027 806-647-4131
Angelica Okamoto, prin. Fax 647-4438

Dodd City, Fannin, Pop. 356
Dodd City ISD 400/PK-12
602 N Main St 75438 903-583-7585
Craig Reed, supt. Fax 583-9545
www.doddcityisd.org
Dodd City S 400/PK-12
602 N Main St 75438 903-583-7585
Jason Crow, prin. Fax 583-9545

Donna, Hidalgo, Pop. 15,775
Donna ISD 15,400/PK-12
116 N 10th St 78537 956-464-1600
Fernando Castillo, supt. Fax 464-1752
www.donnaisd.net
Adame ES 900/PK-5
116 N 10th St 78537 956-461-4010
Maria Partida, prin. Fax 461-4017
Caceres ES 500/PK-5
116 N 10th St 78537 956-464-1995
Celia Martinez, prin. Fax 464-1743
Garza ES 800/PK-5
116 N 10th St 78537 956-464-1886
Maria M. Gomez, prin. Fax 464-1891
Guzman ES 500/PK-5
116 N 10th St 78537 956-464-1920
Emmy De La Garza, prin. Fax 464-1926
Lenoir ES 600/PK-5
116 N 10th St 78537 956-464-1685
Karen Nieto, prin. Fax 464-1877
Munoz ES 900/PK-5
116 N 10th St 78537 956-464-1310
Nelda Calderon, prin. Fax 464-1316
Ochoa ES 500/PK-5
116 N 10th St 78537 956-464-1900
Melisa Smith, prin. Fax 464-1918
Price ES 500/PK-5
116 N 10th St 78537 956-464-1303
Crystal S. Garza, prin. Fax 464-1676
Rivas ES 500/PK-5
116 N 10th St 78537 956-464-1990
Rosalinda Navarro, prin. Fax 464-1869
Runn ES 300/PK-5
116 N 10th St 78537 956-464-1864
Alicia Sarmiento, prin. Fax 464-1934
Salazar ES 600/PK-5
116 N 10th St 78537 956-464-1977
Leticia Chavez, prin. Fax 464-1983
Sauceda MS 800/6-8
116 N 10th St 78537 956-464-1360
Adela Troncoso, prin. Fax 464-1349
Singleterry ES 500/PK-5
116 N 10th St 78537 956-454-1845
Christopher Park, prin. Fax 454-1849
Solis MS 700/6-8
116 N 10th St 78537 956-464-1650
Mary Lou Rodriguez, prin. Fax 464-1649
Stainke ES 600/PK-5
116 N 10th St 78537 956-464-1940
Griselda Alvarez, prin. Fax 464-1790
Todd MS 900/6-8
116 N 10th St 78537 956-464-1800
Labrado DeHoyos, prin. Fax 464-1824
Veterans MS 900/6-8
116 N 10th St 78537 956-464-1350
Claudia Guerrero, prin. Fax 464-1356

Other Schools – See Alamo

Doss, Gillespie
Doss Consolidated Common SD 50/PK-8
PO Box 50 78618 830-669-2411
Fax 669-2303
www.dossccsd.org
Doss ES 50/PK-8
PO Box 50 78618 830-669-2411
Fax 669-2303

Douglass, Nacogdoches
Douglass ISD 400/K-12
PO Box 38 75943 936-569-9804
Walter Peddy, supt. Fax 569-9446
www.douglassisd.com
Douglass S 400/K-12
PO Box 38 75943 936-569-9804
Jeffrey Roquemore, prin. Fax 569-9446

Dripping Springs, Hays, Pop. 1,763
Dripping Springs ISD 5,100/PK-12
PO Box 479 78620 512-858-3002
Bruce Gearing Ed.D., supt. Fax 858-3099
www.dsisdtx.us
Dripping Springs ES 900/PK-5
PO Box 479 78620 512-858-3700
Kellie Raymond, prin. Fax 858-3799
Dripping Springs MS 1,200/6-8
PO Box 479 78620 512-858-3400
Jason Certain, prin. Fax 858-3499
Walnut Springs ES 800/PK-5
PO Box 479 78620 512-858-3800
Julie Pryor, prin. Fax 858-3899
Other Schools – See Austin

Dripping Springs Christian Academy 50/PK-12
800 W Hwy 290 Bldg C # 100 78620 512-858-9738
Becky Welborn, head sch
King's Academy 50/K-8
PO Box 39 78620 512-858-4700
Shelby Hubbard, prin. Fax 686-3305

Driscoll, Nueces, Pop. 733
Driscoll ISD, PO Box 238 78351 100/PK-8
Dr. Cynthia Garcia, supt. 361-387-7349
www.driscollisd.us
Driscoll Elementary MS 100/PK-8
PO Box 238 78351 361-387-7349
Lynn Landenberger, prin.

Dublin, Erath, Pop. 3,617
Dublin ISD 1,200/PK-12
PO Box 169 76446 254-445-3341
Rodney Schneider, supt. Fax 445-3345
www.dublinisd.us
Dublin ES 400/PK-3
PO Box 169 76446 254-445-2577
Lisa Weaver, prin. Fax 445-2570
Dublin IS 300/4-6
PO Box 169 76446 254-445-2618
Chesta Schneider, prin. Fax 445-3383

Dumas, Moore, Pop. 14,542
Dumas ISD 4,600/PK-12
PO Box 615 79029 806-935-6461
Monty Hysinger, supt. Fax 935-6275
www.dumasisd.org
Dumas IS 700/5-6
PO Box 978 79029 806-935-6474
Philip Rhodes, prin. Fax 935-6484
Dumas JHS 600/7-8
PO Box 697 79029 806-935-4155
Kurt Baxter, prin. Fax 934-1434
Green Acres ES 500/PK-4
PO Box 736 79029 806-935-4157
Andrea Cox, prin. Fax 934-1444
Hillcrest ES 300/PK-4
PO Box 715 79029 806-935-5629
Stephanie Schilling, prin. Fax 934-1439
Morningside ES 400/PK-4
PO Box 698 79029 806-935-4153
Stan Stroebel, prin. Fax 934-1438
Sunset ES 400/PK-4
PO Box 716 79029 806-935-2127
Kelly Carrell, prin. Fax 934-1441
Other Schools – See Cactus

Duncanville, Dallas, Pop. 38,022
Duncanville ISD 13,100/PK-12
710 S Cedar Ridge Dr 75137 972-708-2000
Dr. Marc Smith, supt. Fax 708-2020
www.duncanvilleisd.org
Alexander ES 500/PK-4
510 Softwood Dr 75137 972-708-2500
Eduardo Gonzalez, prin. Fax 708-2525
Brandenburg IS 500/5-6
1903 Blueridge Dr 75137 972-708-3100
Tamra Thompson, prin. Fax 708-3131
Byrd MS 700/7-8
1040 W Wheatland Rd 75116 972-708-3400
Kendria Davis-Martin, prin. Fax 708-3434
Central ES 600/PK-4
302 E Freeman St 75116 972-708-2600
Sherri Smith, prin. Fax 708-2626
Daniel IS 700/5-6
1007 Springwood Ln 75137 972-708-3200
Kim Edmondson, prin. Fax 708-3232
Fairmeadows ES 600/PK-4
101 E Fairmeadows Dr 75116 972-708-2700
Patonia Bell, prin. Fax 708-2727
Hardin IS 700/5-6
426 E Freeman St 75116 972-708-3300
Pamela Brown, prin. Fax 708-3333
Hastings ES 500/PK-4
602 W Center St 75116 972-708-2800
Keith Agnes, prin. Fax 708-2828
Merrifield ES 500/PK-4
102 E Vinyard Rd 75137 972-708-2900
Tanji Towels, prin. Fax 708-2929

Reed MS 500/7-8
530 E Freeman St 75116 972-708-3500
Pam Wilson, prin. Fax 708-3535
Smith ES 500/PK-4
1010 Big Stone Gap Rd 75137 972-708-3000
Brandi Lee, prin. Fax 708-3030
Other Schools – See Dallas

Eagle Lake, Colorado, Pop. 3,613
Rice Consolidated ISD
Supt. — See Altair
Eagle Lake IS 100/3-5
701 Tate Ave 77434 979-234-3531
Gene Glover, prin. Fax 234-5027
Eagle Lake PS 300/PK-2
600 Johnnie D Hutchins 77434 979-234-3531
Kimberly Etheridge, prin. Fax 234-6337

Eagle Pass, Maverick, Pop. 26,203
Eagle Pass ISD 15,000/PK-12
1420 Eidson Rd 78852 830-773-5181
Gilberto Gonzalez, supt. Fax 773-7252
www.eaglepassisd.net
Benavides Heights ES 300/1-6
1750 Mesa Dr 78852 830-758-7006
Veronica Soto-Gonzalez, prin. Fax 758-0216
Cerna ES 400/1-6
2268 Mondragon Blvd 78852 830-757-7004
Sandra Lopez, prin. Fax 757-2731
Darr ES 500/1-6
841 Memo Robinson Rd 78852 830-758-7060
Veronica Chacon, prin. Fax 758-0090
Eagle Pass JHS 1,200/7-8
1750 N Bibb Ave 78852 830-758-7037
Mario Escobar, prin. Fax 757-1278
ECC 500/PK-K
636 Kelso Dr 78852 830-758-7027
Letty Sandoval, prin. Fax 757-1153
Gallego ES 400/1-6
300 Azucena St 78852 830-758-7130
Jose Villalobos, prin. Fax 757-5795
Glass ES 500/1-6
1501 Boehmer Ave 78852 830-758-7042
Rosanna Rios, prin. Fax 773-5989
Gonzalez ES 500/1-6
400 Balcones Blvd 78852 830-758-7099
Carmen Garcia, prin. Fax 757-3274
Graves ES 500/1-6
720 Kelso Dr 78852 830-758-7043
Sandra Koenig, prin. Fax 758-0342
Houston ES 500/1-6
2789 FM 1021 78852 830-758-7069
Amalia Riojas, prin. Fax 757-6639
Kennedy Hall S 400/PK-K
1610 Del Rio Blvd 78852 830-758-7189
Lisa Ruiz, prin. Fax 758-7192
Language Development Center 500/PK-K
724 FM 3443 78852 830-758-7047
Rosella Even, prin. Fax 757-1528
Lee ES 400/1-6
300 S Monroe St 78852 830-758-7062
Blanca Muzquiz, prin. Fax 773-3471
Liberty ES 600/1-6
1850 Flowers 78852 830-758-7156
Rosa Barcena, prin. Fax 757-3237
Memorial JHS 1,100/7-8
1800 Lewis St 78852 830-758-7053
Maria Sumpter, prin. Fax 773-8900
Perfecto Mancha ES 500/1-6
3269 Fletcher Rd 78852 830-758-7216
Jose Jimenez, prin. Fax 758-7201
Rosita Valley ES 500/1-6
735 Rosita Valley Rd 78852 830-758-7065
Luz Lazarski, prin. Fax 757-2098
Rosita Valley Literacy Academy 300/PK-K
811 Rosita Valley Rd 78852 830-758-7067
Aida Pang-Villa, prin. Fax 773-8859
San Luis ES 500/1-6
2090 Williams St 78852 830-758-7071
Sylvia Saucedo, prin. Fax 773-1632
Seco Mines ES 400/1-6
2900 Diaz St 78852 830-758-7073
Maribel Martinez, prin. Fax 773-8725
Other Schools – See Quemado

Our Lady of Refuge S 300/PK-8
577 Washington St 78852 830-773-3531
Katrina Harper, prin. Fax 773-7310

Early, Brown, Pop. 2,720
Early ISD 1,200/PK-12
PO Box 3315, Brownwood TX 76803 325-646-7934
Wes Beck, supt. Fax 646-9238
www.earlyisd.net
Early ES 300/3-5
PO Box 3315, Brownwood TX 76803 325-646-5511
Sharon Watson, prin. Fax 646-5469
Early MS 300/6-8
PO Box 3315, Brownwood TX 76803 325-643-5665
Chad Burleson, prin. Fax 646-9972
Early PS 200/PK-2
PO Box 3315, Brownwood TX 76803 325-643-9622
Brian Callaway, prin. Fax 646-5336

Earth, Lamb, Pop. 1,057
Springlake-Earth ISD 400/PK-12
PO Box 130 79031 806-257-3310
Denver Crum, supt. Fax 257-3927
www.springlake-earth.org
Springlake-Earth S 300/PK-7
PO Box 130 79031 806-257-3863
Cindy Furr, prin. Fax 257-3927

East Bernard, Wharton, Pop. 2,255
East Bernard ISD 1,000/PK-12
723 College St 77435 979-335-7519
Courtney Hudgins, supt. Fax 335-6561
www.ebisd.org

East Bernard ES 300/PK-4
723 College St 77435 979-335-7519
Philip Gaudette M.Ed., prin. Fax 335-6561
East Bernard JHS 300/5-8
723 College St 77435 979-335-7519
Emmett Tugwell M.Ed., prin. Fax 335-6561

Eastland, Eastland, Pop. 3,922
Eastland ISD 1,100/PK-12
PO Box 31 76448 254-631-5120
Jason Cochran, supt. Fax 631-5126
www.eastlandisd.net/
Eastland MS 300/6-8
PO Box 31 76448 254-631-5040
Jason Henry, prin. Fax 631-5049
Siebert ES 500/PK-5
PO Box 31 76448 254-631-5080
Scott Allen, prin. Fax 631-5085

Ector, Fannin, Pop. 677
Ector ISD 300/PK-12
PO Box 128 75439 903-961-2355
Gary Bohannon, supt. Fax 961-2110
www.ectorisd.net
Ector ES 200/PK-6
PO Box 128 75439 903-961-2355
Brad Evans, prin. Fax 961-2110

Edcouch, Hidalgo, Pop. 3,161
Edcouch-Elsa ISD 4,800/PK-12
PO Box 127 78538 956-262-6000
Ronaldo Cavazos, supt. Fax 262-6032
www.eeisd.org
Garcia ES 400/1-6
PO Box 127 78538 956-262-6002
Jesus Ramos, prin. Fax 262-6004
Gutierrez ECC 700/PK-K
PO Box 127 78538 956-262-0040
Norma Hernandez, prin. Fax 262-0043
Rodriguez ES 400/1-6
PO Box 127 78538 956-262-6062
Maricela Olivarez, prin. Fax 262-6061
Other Schools – See Elsa

Eddy, McLennan, Pop. 1,113
Bruceville-Eddy ISD 800/PK-12
1 Eagle Dr 76524 254-859-5525
Richard Kilgore, supt. Fax 859-4023
www.beisd.net
Bruceville-Eddy ES 200/PK-3
1 Eagle Dr 76524 254-859-5465
Sharon Johnson, prin. Fax 859-4023
Bruceville-Eddy IS 200/4-6
1 Eagle Dr 76524 254-859-5525
Sharon Johnson, prin. Fax 859-5638
Bruceville-Eddy MS 100/7-8
1 Eagle Dr 76524 254-859-5525
Mike Hawkins, prin. Fax 859-3207

Eden, Concho, Pop. 2,753
Eden Consolidated ISD 200/K-12
PO Box 988 76837 325-869-4121
Kent Coker, supt. Fax 869-5210
www.edencisd.net
Eden ES 100/K-5
PO Box 988 76837 325-869-4121
Rebecca Bunger, prin. Fax 869-5672

Edgewood, Van Zandt, Pop. 1,419
Edgewood ISD 900/PK-12
804 E Pine St 75117 903-896-4332
Emmett Baker, supt. Fax 896-7056
www.edgewood-isd.net
Edgewood ES 200/PK-2
804 E Pine St 75117 903-896-4773
Kristy Jones, prin. Fax 896-7056
Edgewood IS 200/3-5
804 E Pine St 75117 903-896-2134
Becky Goodwin, prin. Fax 896-7056
Edgewood MS 200/6-8
804 E Pine St 75117 903-896-1530
Lyndsay Hayes, prin. Fax 896-7056

Edinburg, Hidalgo, Pop. 76,876
Edinburg Consolidated ISD 34,000/PK-12
PO Box 990 78540 956-289-2300
Dr. Rene Gutierrez, supt. Fax 383-3576
www.ecisd.us/
Austin ES 400/PK-5
PO Box 990 78540 956-289-2331
Homero Cano, prin. Fax 316-7560
Avila ES 700/PK-5
PO Box 990 78540 956-289-2307
Susana Aguilar, prin. Fax 385-3330
Barrientes MS 1,300/6-8
PO Box 990 78540 956-289-2430
Robert Lopez, prin. Fax 316-7749
Betts ES 500/PK-5
PO Box 990 78540 956-289-2560
Jesus Cantu, prin. Fax 384-5312
Brewster S 400/PK-8
PO Box 990 78540 956-289-2334
Cipriano Pena, prin. Fax 316-7510
Cano-Gonzales ES 600/PK-5
PO Box 990 78540 956-289-2380
Nelda Gaytan, prin. Fax 316-7457
Canterbury ES 600/PK-5
PO Box 990 78540 956-289-2374
Ricardo Perez, prin. Fax 316-7606
Crawford ES 700/PK-5
PO Box 990 78540 956-289-2410
Alondo Navarro, prin. Fax 287-0700
De Escandon ES 600/PK-5
PO Box 990 78540 956-289-2545
Ruth Torres, prin. Fax 316-7647
De La Vina ES 600/PK-5
PO Box 990 78540 956-289-2366
Erika Playle, prin. Fax 316-7782
De Zavala ES 700/PK-5
PO Box 990 78540 956-289-2350
Dr. Graciela Perez, prin. Fax 316-7605
Edinburg South MS 1,500/6-8
PO Box 990 78540 956-289-2415
Dr. Mary Garza, prin. Fax 316-8817
Eisenhower ES 700/PK-5
PO Box 990 78540 956-289-2540
Sylvia Faz, prin. Fax 316-7554
Esparza ES 500/PK-5
PO Box 990 78540 956-289-2308
Arnoldo Pesina, prin. Fax 385-3310
Flores-Zapata ES 600/PK-5
PO Box 990 78540 956-289-2445
Victoria Martinez, prin. Fax 383-0957
Garza MS 1,100/6-8
PO Box 990 78540 956-289-2480
Anibal Gorena, prin. Fax 316-3109
Gonzalez ES 500/PK-5
PO Box 990 78540 956-289-2520
Nadia Torres, prin. Fax 316-7420
Gorena ES, PO Box 990 78540 600/PK-5
Diane Willis, prin. 956-289-2460
Guerra ES 700/PK-5
PO Box 990 78540 956-289-2530
Lisa Valdez, prin. Fax 384-5352
Harwell MS 1,400/6-8
PO Box 990 78540 956-289-2440
Dr. Marissa Garza, prin. Fax 316-7303
Jefferson ES 400/PK-5
PO Box 990 78540 956-289-2385
Ana Villalobos Salinas, prin. Fax 316-7427
Johnson ES 500/PK-5
PO Box 990 78540 956-289-2358
Enrique DeLaCruz, prin. Fax 316-7630
Kennedy ES 600/PK-5
PO Box 990 78540 956-289-2390
Gloria Alonzo, prin. Fax 384-5131
Lee ES 500/PK-5
PO Box 990 78540 956-289-2342
Leticia Duarte, prin. Fax 316-7596
Lincoln ES 600/PK-5
PO Box 990 78540 956-289-2525
Eva Sandoval, prin. Fax 384-5208
Longoria MS 1,000/6-8
PO Box 990 78540 956-289-2486
Antonio Ballesteros, prin. Fax 381-6442
Magee ES 500/PK-5
PO Box 990 78540 956-289-2306
Marla Cavazos, prin. Fax 385-3320
Memorial MS 1,200/6-8
PO Box 990 78540 956-289-2470
Fermin Gonzalez, prin. Fax 316-7581
Monte Cristo ES 600/PK-5
PO Box 990 78540 956-289-2362
Diana Cervantes-Smith, prin. Fax 316-7471
Ramirez ES 500/PK-5
PO Box 990 78540 956-289-2425
Clarissa Ramirez, prin. Fax 316-2355
San Carlos ES 500/PK-5
PO Box 990 78540 956-289-2370
Belinda De La Rosa, prin. Fax 316-7364
Travis ES 400/PK-5
PO Box 990 78540 956-289-2354
E. Flores, prin. Fax 316-7637
Trevino ES 600/PK-5
PO Box 990 78540 956-289-2550
Rosalinda Munoz, prin. Fax 384-5372
Truman ES 600/PK-5
PO Box 990 78540 956-289-2555
Jose Garza, prin. Fax 316-7527
Villarreal ES 600/PK-5
PO Box 990 78540 956-289-2377
Odilia Villarreal, prin. Fax 381-4782
Other Schools – See Hargill, Mc Allen

South Texas ISD
Supt. — See Mercedes
South Texas Preparatory Academy 600/7-8
724 S Sugar Rd 78539 956-381-5522
Ana Castro, prin. Fax 381-1177

Discovery S 200/PK-6
1711 W Alberta Rd 78539 956-381-1117
St. Joseph S 300/PK-8
119 W Fay St 78539 956-383-3957
Elida Paris, prin. Fax 318-0681

Edna, Jackson, Pop. 5,438
Edna ISD 1,600/PK-12
601 N Wells 77957 361-782-3573
Robert O'Connor, supt. Fax 781-1002
www.ednaisd.org
Edna ES 800/PK-5
400 Apollo Dr 77957 361-782-2953
Katie Kucera, prin. Fax 781-1028
Edna JHS 300/6-8
505 W Gayle St 77957 361-782-2351
Brandie Roe, prin. Fax 781-1025

Edna Christian Academy 50/PK-12
PO Box 885 77957 361-782-2052
Rev. Darrell Clark, prin.

El Campo, Wharton, Pop. 11,547
El Campo ISD 3,600/PK-12
700 W Norris St 77437 979-543-6771
Kelly Waters M.Ed., supt. Fax 543-1670
www.ecisd.org
El Campo MS 800/6-8
4010 FM 2765 Rd 77437 979-543-6362
Mark Freeman, prin. Fax 541-5210
Hutchins ES 600/2-3
1006 Roberts St 77437 979-543-5481
Alicia Stary, prin. Fax 543-2418
Myatt ES 700/PK-1
501 W Webb St 77437 979-543-7514
Maurie Couey, prin. Fax 543-5188
Northside ES 600/4-5
2610 Meadow Ln 77437 979-543-5812
Rebecca Crowell, prin. Fax 578-0682

St. Philip S 300/PK-8
302 W Church St 77437 979-543-2901
Gwen Edwards, prin. Fax 578-8835

Eldorado, Schleicher, Pop. 1,941
Schleicher ISD 600/PK-12
PO Box W 76936 325-853-2514
Robert Gibson, supt. Fax 853-2695
www.scisd.net
Eldorado ES 300/PK-4
PO Box W 76936 325-853-2514
Michael Rudewick, prin. Fax 853-2177
Eldorado MS 200/5-8
PO Box W 76936 325-853-2514
Ezra Walling, prin. Fax 853-2895

Electra, Wichita, Pop. 2,739
Electra ISD 300/PK-12
PO Box 231 76360 940-495-3683
Scott Hogue, supt. Fax 495-3945
www.electraisd.net
Electra ES 100/PK-6
621 S Bailey St 76360 940-495-2533
Steven Wallace, prin. Fax 495-3627

Elgin, Bastrop, Pop. 7,996
Elgin ISD 4,200/PK-12
PO Box 351 78621 512-281-3434
Dr. Jodi Duron, supt. Fax 285-5388
www.elginisd.net
Elgin ES 800/PK-5
1005 W 2nd St 78621 512-281-3457
Sarah Juarez-Farias, prin. Fax 281-9772
Elgin MS 900/6-8
1351 N Avenue C 78621 512-281-3382
Riza Cooper, prin. Fax 281-9781
Neidig ES 600/PK-5
13700 County Line Rd 78621 512-281-9702
April Wallace, prin. Fax 281-9703
Washington ES 600/PK-5
510 M L K Dr 78621 512-281-3411
Glenell Bankhead, prin. Fax 281-9749

Elkhart, Anderson, Pop. 1,338
Elkhart ISD 1,200/PK-12
301 E Parker St 75839 903-764-2952
Dr. Ray DeSpain, supt. Fax 764-2466
www.elkhartisd.org/
Elkhart ES 300/PK-2
301 E Parker St 75839 903-764-2979
Tana Horring, prin. Fax 764-8286
Elkhart IS 300/3-5
301 E Parker St 75839 903-764-8535
Greg Herring, prin. Fax 764-2466
Elkhart MS 300/6-8
301 E Parker St 75839 903-764-2459
Ron Mays, prin. Fax 764-8287

Slocum ISD 300/PK-12
5765 E State Highway 294 75839 903-478-3624
Cliff Lasiter, supt. Fax 478-3030
www.slocumisd.org
Slocum PK-8 S 200/PK-8
5765 E State Highway 294 75839 903-478-3624
Mark Leuschner, prin. Fax 478-3030

El Lago, Harris, Pop. 2,653
Clear Creek ISD
Supt. — See League City
White ES 500/K-5
1708 Les Talley Dr 77586 281-284-4300
Matthew Paulson, prin. Fax 284-4305

Elmaton, Matagorda
Tidehaven ISD, PO Box 129 77440 800/PK-12
Dr. Andrew Seigrist, supt. 979-843-4302
www.tidehavenisd.com
Tidehaven IS, PO Box 130 77440 200/6-8
Patrick Talbert, prin. 979-843-4320
Other Schools – See Blessing, Markham

Elm Mott, McLennan
Connally ISD
Supt. — See Waco
Connally JHS 500/6-8
100 Hancock Dr 76640 254-296-7700
Thurman Brown, prin. Fax 829-2354
Connally PS 400/1-3
100 Little Cadet Ln 76640 254-296-7600
Marlo Moore, prin. Fax 829-1273

El Paso, El Paso, Pop. 643,027
Canutillo ISD 6,000/PK-12
7965 Artcraft Rd 79932 915-877-7400
Dr. Pedro Galaviz, supt. Fax 877-7414
www.canutillo-isd.org
Garcia ES 600/PK-5
6550 Westside Dr 79932 915-877-1200
Jesica Arellano, prin. Fax 877-1219
Reyes S PK-5
7440 Northern Pass 79911 915-872-2300
Dr. Debra Kerney, prin. Fax 872-2319
Other Schools – See Canutillo

Clint ISD 11,800/PK-12
14521 Horizon Blvd 79928 915-926-4000
Juan Martinez, supt. Fax 926-4009
www.clintweb.net
East Montana MS 700/6-8
3490 Ascension Rd 79938 915-926-5200
Dr. Juanita Guerra, prin. Fax 855-0821
Montana Vista ES 800/PK-5
3550 Mark Jason Dr 79938 915-926-5300
Cain Castillo, prin. Fax 857-0631
Red Sands ES 900/PK-5
4250 OShea St 79938 915-926-5400
Jaime Hernandez, prin. Fax 855-8294

Other Schools – See Clint, Horizon City

El Paso ISD 60,900/PK-12
PO Box 20100 79998 915-230-2000
Juan Cabrera, supt. Fax 887-5484
www.episd.org

Alta Vista ES 400/PK-5
1000 N Grama St 79903 915-236-8000
Angelica Negrete, prin. Fax 566-0971

Aoy ES 700/PK-5
901 S Campbell St 79901 915-774-4020
Anabel Tanabe, prin. Fax 313-0163

Armendariz MS 800/6-8
2231 Arizona Ave 79930 915-546-9012
Lorenzo Munoz, prin. Fax 577-0848

Barron ES 500/PK-5
11155 Whitey Ford St 79934 915-849-4220
Lidia Anguiano, prin. Fax 822-1460

Bassett MS 700/6-8
4400 Elm St 79930 915-231-2260
Michael Mendoza, prin. Fax 565-1562

Beall ES 500/PK-5
320 S Piedras St 79905 915-236-8075
Maria Guerra, prin. Fax 533-7044

Bliss ES 600/PK-5
4401 Sheridan Rd 79906 915-236-5150
Narichica Handy, prin. Fax 566-2806

Bond ES 500/PK-5
250 Lindbergh Ave 79932 915-832-6930
Rachel Villalobos, prin. Fax 581-1220

Bonham ES 300/K-5
7024 Cielo Vista Dr 79925 915-881-6950
Sandra Sanchez, prin. Fax 778-0525

Bradley ES 400/PK-5
5330 Sweetwater Dr 79924 915-849-2840
Kathleen Ese, prin. Fax 821-0628

Brown MS 900/6-8
7820 Helen Of Troy Dr 79912 915-774-4080
Laurie Enloe, prin. Fax 581-6424

Burleson ES 500/PK-5
4400 Blanco Ave 79905 915-236-8300
Jesus Medina, prin. Fax 533-0967

Burnet ES 300/PK-5
3700 Thomason Ave 79904 915-231-2580
Francis Ezenwa, prin. Fax 566-3951

Canyon Hills MS 800/6-8
8930 Eclipse St 79904 915-231-2240
Ronald Haugen, prin. Fax 757-8067

Charles MS 700/6-8
4909 Trojan Dr 79924 915-236-6550
David Zamora, prin. Fax 821-0505

Cielo Vista ES 300/PK-5
9000 Basil Ct 79925 915-236-8375
Kathryn Mcmillan, prin. Fax 599-2965

Clardy ES 600/PK-5
5508 Delta Dr 79905 915-887-4040
Leticia Foster, prin. Fax 778-1580

Clendenin ES 500/PK-5
2701 Harrison Ave 79930 915-231-2640
Martha Martinez, prin. Fax 566-4459

Coldwell ES 500/PK-5
4101 Altura Ave 79903 915-236-8525
Jose Gijon, prin. Fax 566-4634

Collins ES 500/PK-5
4860 Tropicana Ave 79924 915-231-2600
Leticia Ewing, prin. Fax 759-7315

Cooley ES 600/PK-5
107 N Collingsworth St 79905 915-780-1020
Suzanne Hansen-Gibson, prin. Fax 775-1272

Crockett ES 600/PK-5
3200 Wheeling Ave 79930 915-587-2640
Elco Ramos, prin. Fax 566-4950

Crosby ES 600/PK-5
5411 Wren Ave 79924 915-236-5450
Yvette Hernandez, prin. Fax 759-7409

Douglass ES 500/PK-5
101 S Eucalyptus St 79905 915-496-8070
Alonzo Barraza, prin. Fax 533-3716

Dowell ES 300/PK-5
5249 Bastille Ave 79924 915-231-2560
Yeni Ontiveros, prin. Fax 759-7713

Fannin ES 600/PK-5
5425 Salem Dr 79924 915-849-3910
Peggy Gustafson, prin. Fax 821-0680

Green ES 400/PK-5
5430 Buckley Dr 79912 915-231-2700
Charlotte Quintana, prin. Fax 833-8794

Guerrero ES 600/PK-5
7530 Lakehurst Rd 79912 915-231-2680
Jill Crossley, prin. Fax 581-4418

Guillen MS 900/6-8
900 S Cotton St 79901 915-496-4620
Teresa Zamarripa, prin. Fax 532-1143

Hart ES 400/PK-5
1110 Park St 79901 915-236-8825
Elizabeth Prangner, prin. Fax 533-3726

Hawkins ES 400/PK-5
5816 Stephenson Ave 79905 915-587-2660
Adriana Ruiz, prin. Fax 775-2699

Henderson MS 800/6-8
5505 Robert Alva Ave 79905 915-887-3080
Elizabeth Maldonado, prin. Fax 772-3425

Herrera ES 500/PK-5
350 Coates Dr 79932 915-774-7700
Alberto Reyes, prin. Fax 581-2377

Hillside ES 600/PK-5
4500 Clifton Ave 79903 915-587-2560
Cynthia Anderson, prin. Fax 566-5210

Hornedo MS 1,200/6-8
6101 High Ridge Dr 79912 915-881-2900
Micaela Varela, prin. Fax 581-7371

Hughey ES 700/PK-5
6201 Hughey Cir 79925 915-832-6670
Lilia Aguilera, prin. Fax 779-6911

Johnson ES 600/PK-5
499 Cabaret Dr 79912 915-832-3940
Karla Montemayor, prin. Fax 581-0917

Kohlberg ES 700/PK-5
1445 Nardo Goodman Dr 79912 915-832-4880
Michelle Pringle, prin. Fax 833-4628

Lamar ES 600/PK-5
1440 E Cliff Dr 79902 915-351-3200
Bertha Martinez, prin. Fax 534-0083

Lea ES 800/PK-5
4851 Marcus Uribe Dr 79934 915-774-7725
Michelle Casillas, prin. Fax 821-3665

Lee ES 700/PK-5
7710 Pandora St 79904 915-587-3560
Terry Montes, prin. Fax 759-8115

Lincoln MS 1,000/6-8
500 Mulberry Ave 79932 915-231-2180
Heidi Appel, prin. Fax 581-1371

Logan ES 500/PK-5
3200 Ellerthorpe Ave 79904 915-231-2720
Sharon Aziz, prin. Fax 566-8550

Lundy ES 700/PK-5
6201 High Ridge Dr 79912 915-774-7750
Lourdes Lugo, prin. Fax 584-1972

MacArthur S 700/K-8
8101 Whitus Dr 79925 915-236-0625
Rose Ann Martinez, prin. Fax 779-2281

Magoffin MS 800/6-8
4931 Hercules Ave 79904 915-774-4040
Rogelio Segovia, prin. Fax 757-7675

Mesita ES 800/PK-5
3307 N Stanton St 79902 915-774-4100
Laila Ferris, prin. Fax 532-2068

Milam ES 500/PK-5
5000 Luke St 79908 915-587-2520
Wanda Johnson, prin. Fax 562-6448

Morehead MS 800/6-8
5625 Confetti Dr 79912 915-231-2140
Armando Gallegos, prin. Fax 587-5355

Moreno ES 500/PK-5
2300 San Diego Ave 79930 915-832-6650
Fernando Vasquez, prin. Fax 566-5163

Moye ES 600/PK-5
4500 Alps Dr 79904 915-774-4000
Mary Broderick-Vargas, admin. Fax 751-7810

Newman ES 500/PK-5
10275 Alcan St 79924 915-587-3580
Pauletta Howard, prin. Fax 759-8306

Nixon ES 600/PK-5
11141 Loma Roja Dr 79934 915-849-5700
Christine Miles, prin. Fax 821-6582

Park ES 600/PK-5
3601 Edgar Park Ave 79904 915-587-3540
Carmen Dwyer, prin. Fax 759-8315

Polk ES 600/K-5
940 Belvidere St 79912 915-236-2775
Sandra Spivey, prin. Fax 236-2049

Powell ES 600/PK-5
4750 Ellerthorpe Ave 79904 915-774-7775
Andrew Veilleux, prin. Fax 564-5086

Putnam ES 500/PK-5
6508 Fiesta Dr 79912 915-832-6700
Cynthia Sanchez, prin. Fax 585-2304

Richardson MS 700/6-8
11350 Loma Franklin Dr 79934 915-822-8829
Ragen Chappell, prin. Fax 822-8812

Rivera ES 500/PK-5
6445 Escondido Dr 79912 915-231-2780
Cindy Contreras, prin. Fax 585-2337

Roberts ES 500/PK-5
341 Thorn Ave 79932 915-231-2660
Rafael Guardado, prin. Fax 585-2729

Ross MS 1,000/6-8
6101 Hughey Cir 79925 915-887-3060
Jason Yturralde, prin. Fax 771-6792

Rusk ES 400/PK-5
3601 N Copia St 79930 915-587-2580
Monica Brinkley, prin. Fax 565-1666

Schuster ES 300/PK-5
5515 Will Ruth Ave 79924 915-231-2760
Nancy Hanson, prin. Fax 759-9315

Stanton ES 600/PK-5
5414 Hondo Pass Dr 79924 915-587-3520
Dr. Sarah Chavez-Gibson, prin. Fax 759-9415

Terrace Hills MS 700/6-8
4835 Blossom Ave 79924 915-231-2120
Darren Cole, prin. Fax 759-0615

Tippin ES 600/PK-5
6541 Bear Ridge Dr 79912 915-585-4750
Gina Nunez, prin. Fax 833-2140

Travis ES 400/PK-5
5000 N Stevens St 79930 915-236-6200
Armando Llanos, prin. Fax 565-2013

Western Hills ES 500/K-5
530 Thunderbird Dr 79912 915-774-4060
Sandra Sanchez, prin. Fax 875-0183

Whitaker ES 600/PK-5
4700 Rutherford Dr 79924 915-231-2820
Antoinette Carpenter, prin. Fax 751-9436

White ES 500/PK-5
4256 Roxbury Dr 79922 915-236-2700
Jocelyn Scott, prin. Fax 585-3619

Wiggs MS 900/6-8
1300 Circle Dr 79902 915-231-2100
Timothy Luther, prin. Fax 533-2902

Zavala ES 300/PK-5
51 N Hammett St 79905 915-496-8160
Alma Brockhoff, prin. Fax 542-1760

Socorro ISD 45,900/PK-12
12440 Rojas Dr 79928 915-937-0000
Jose Espinoza Ed.D., supt. Fax 851-7572
www.sisd.net

Antwine S 1,100/K-5
3830 Rich Beem 79938 915-937-6400
Michelle Romero, prin. Fax 851-7830

Ball ES 900/PK-5
1950 Firehouse Dr 79936 915-937-8200
Ana Soto, prin. Fax 856-1478

Butler ES 800/PK-5
14251 Ralph Seitsinger 79938 915-937-8900
Rosa Chavez-Avedician, prin. Fax 937-5098

Campestre ES 600/PK-5
11399 Socorro Rd 79927 915-937-7300
Alma Rosa Vasquez, prin. Fax 851-1715

Chavez ES 800/K-5
11720 Pebble Hills Blvd 79936 915-937-8300
Rosemary Yates, prin. Fax 856-9993

Clarke MS 1,000/6-8
1515 Bob Hope Dr 79936 915-937-5600
Ivan Ramirez, prin. Fax 857-3765

Cooper ES 700/PK-5
1515 Rebecca Ann Dr 79936 915-937-7700
Leticia Terrazas, prin. Fax 855-7645

Desert Wind S 800/PK-8
1100 Colina de Paz 79928 915-937-7800
Patricia Franco, prin. Fax 851-7840

Drugan S 1,100/PK-8
12451 Pellicano Dr 79928 915-937-6800
Adalberto Garcia, prin. Fax 937-6815

Ensor MS 1,000/6-8
13600 Ryderwood Dr 79928 915-937-6000
Lisa Estrada-Batson, prin. Fax 851-7590

Escontrias ECC 400/PK-1
10400 Alameda Ave 79927 915-937-4200
Jesse Aguirre, prin. Fax 937-4292

Escontrias ES 600/2-5
205 Buford Rd 79927 915-937-4100
Jesse Aguirre, prin. Fax 937-4196

Hambric S 1,400/PK-8
3535 Nolan Richardson Dr 79936 915-937-4600
Carolyn Thomas, prin. Fax 851-7560

Hernando MS 900/6-8
3451 Rich Beem 79938 915-937-9800
Venessa Betancourt, prin. Fax 937-9898

Hilley ES 700/PK-5
693 N Rio Vista Rd 79927 915-937-8400
Fernando Miranda, prin. Fax 860-3778

Horizon Heights ES 1,100/PK-5
13601 Ryderwood Dr 79928 915-937-7400
Jenifer Hansen, prin. Fax 937-7497

Hueco ES 600/PK-5
300 Old Hueco Tanks Rd 79927 915-937-7600
Anjelica Herrera, prin. Fax 860-1125

Ituarte ES 800/K-5
12860 Tierra Sonora 79938 915-937-7000
Elizabeth Castro, prin. Fax 937-7095

Jordan ES 800/K-5
13995 Jason Crandall Dr 79938 915-937-8800
Maribel Pidone, prin. Fax 937-8889

KEYS ES 50/1-5
205 Buford Rd 79927 915-937-4104
Jesse Aguirre, prin. Fax 937-9212

Loma Verde ES 800/PK-5
12150 Ted Houghton 79936 915-937-8600
Leslie Chavez, prin. Fax 851-7780

Lujan-Chavez ES 1,200/PK-5
2200 Sun Country Dr 79938 915-937-8700
Lilia Campoya, prin. Fax 937-8790

Martinez ES 700/PK-5
2640 Robert Wynn St 79936 915-937-8000
Greg Hatch, prin. Fax 937-8090

Mission Ridge ES K-5
150 Nonap Rd 79928 915-938-2200
Jesus Mendez, prin. Fax 852-8559

Montwood MS 800/6-8
11710 Pebble Hills Blvd 79936 915-937-5800
Sylvia Esparza, prin. Fax 856-9909

O'Shea-Keleher ES 800/PK-5
1800 Leroy Bonse Dr 79936 915-937-7200
Josefina Perez, prin. Fax 921-1506

Paso del Norte S 1,200/K-8
12300 Tierra Este Rd 79938 915-937-6200
Nathan Ballard, prin. Fax 851-7800

Puentes MS 600/6-8
3216 Tim Foster 79938 915-937-9200
Monica Castro, prin. Fax 851-7855

Purple Heart ES K-4
14400 G R Campuzano Dr 79938 915-938-2200
Jennifer Parker, prin. Fax 851-7134

Rojas ES 600/PK-5
500 Bauman Rd 79927 915-937-8500
Jessica Macias, prin. Fax 937-8589

Sanchez MS 700/6-8
321 N Rio Vista Rd 79927 915-937-5200
Rosa Barrio, prin. Fax 859-6636

Serna S 700/PK-8
11471 Alameda Ave 79927 915-937-4800
Alejandro Olvera, prin. Fax 851-7580

Shook ES 900/PK-5
13777 Paseo Del Este Dr 79928 915-937-7100
Donna Smith, prin. Fax 937-7197

Sierra Vista ES 900/PK-5
1501 Bob Hope Dr 79936 915-937-8100
Christine De La Cruz, prin. Fax 849-1263

Slider MS 800/6-8
11700 School Ln 79936 915-937-5400
Enrique Herrera, prin. Fax 857-5804

Socorro MS 600/6-8
321 Bovee Rd 79927 915-937-5000
Mauro Guerrero, prin. Fax 859-6955

Sun Ridge MS 900/6-8
2210 Sun Country Dr 79938 915-937-6600
Ignacio Estorga, prin. Fax 851-7730

Sybert S 1,200/PK-8
11530 Edgemere Blvd 79936 915-937-4400
Gabriela Elliott, prin. Fax 851-7777

Vista Del Sol ES 700/PK-5
11851 Vista Del Sol Dr 79936 915-937-7500
Cynthia Velasquez, prin. Fax 855-7523

Ysleta ISD 42,200/PK-12
9600 Sims Dr 79925 915-434-0000
Dr. Xavier De La Torre, supt. Fax 591-4144
www.yisd.net
Ascarate ES 400/K-6
7090 Alameda Ave 79915 915-434-7400
Claudia Ureno-Olivas, prin. Fax 772-8051
Bel Air MS 500/7-8
8040 Yermoland Dr 79907 915-434-2200
Dana DeRouen, prin. Fax 591-9439
Camino Real MS 700/6-8
9393 Alameda Ave 79907 915-434-8300
Ida Resendez-Perales, prin. Fax 858-3743
Capistrano ES 600/K-5
240 Mecca Dr 79907 915-434-8600
Lynn Musel, prin. Fax 860-2750
Cedar Grove ES 600/PK-6
218 Barker Rd 79915 915-434-7600
Dolores Acosta, prin. Fax 772-8092
Chacon International S 800/K-8
221 S Prado Rd 79907 915-434-9200
Ruben Cadena, prin. Fax 859-2131
Del Norte Heights ES 400/K-6
1800 Winslow Rd 79915 915-434-2400
Claudia Poblano, prin. Fax 591-8862
Del Valle ES 400/K-5
9251 Escobar Dr 79907 915-434-9300
Lisa Lopez, prin. Fax 434-9306
Desertaire ES 800/K-5
6301 Tiger Eye Dr 79924 915-434-6400
Beth Harbison, prin. Fax 821-0634
Desert View MS 500/6-8
1641 Billie Marie Dr 79936 915-434-5300
Maryann Olivas, prin. Fax 591-9327
Dolphin Terrace ES 600/K-5
9790 Pickerel Dr 79924 915-434-6500
Lorraine Martinez, prin. Fax 757-8073
East Point ES 900/PK-6
2400 Zanzibar Rd 79925 915-434-4500
Dana Boyd, prin. Fax 591-8958
Eastwood Heights ES 700/PK-6
10530 Janway Dr 79925 915-434-4600
Raul Mendoza, prin. Fax 591-8960
Eastwood Knolls S 800/K-8
10000 Buckwood Ave 79925 915-434-4400
Robert Martinez, prin. Fax 592-0339
Eastwood MS 1,000/7-8
2612 Chaswood St 79935 915-434-4300
Sarah Venegas, prin. Fax 591-9426
Edgemere ES 600/PK-6
10300 Edgemere Blvd 79925 915-434-4700
Jose Perez, prin. Fax 590-8335
Glen Cove ES 900/PK-5
10955 Sam Snead Dr 79936 915-434-5500
Margarita Mendoza, prin. Fax 591-9024
Hacienda Heights ES 500/K-6
7530 Acapulco Ave 79915 915-434-2500
Maria Aguilar, prin. Fax 591-9044
Hulbert ES 400/K-6
7755 Franklin Dr 79915 915-434-6900
James McIntyre, prin. Fax 772-8166
Indian Ridge MS 800/6-8
11201 Pebble Hills Blvd 79936 915-434-5400
Pauline Muela, prin. Fax 591-9447
Lancaster ES 500/K-5
9230 Elgin Dr 79907 915-434-3400
Veronica Frias, prin. Fax 860-2315
Le Barron Park ES 400/K-5
920 Burgundy Dr 79907 915-434-3500
Norma Sierra, prin. Fax 860-2817
Loma Terrace ES 600/PK-6
8200 Ryland Ct 79907 915-434-2600
Lourdes Hinojosa, prin. Fax 591-9111
Marian Manor ES 400/K-5
8300 Forrest Haven Ct 79907 915-434-3600
Natalie Alvarez, prin. Fax 591-9131
Mesa Vista ES 500/PK-6
8032 Alamo Ave 79907 915-434-2700
Heather Karnes, prin. Fax 591-9171
Mission Valley ES 600/PK-5
8674 N Loop Dr 79907 915-434-3700
Veronica Alvidrez, prin. Fax 860-0049
North Loop ES 500/K-6
412 Emerson St 79915 915-434-2800
Denise Jones, prin. Fax 591-9202
North Star ES 500/K-5
5950 Sean Haggerty Dr 79924 915-434-6700
Maritza Balderrama, prin. Fax 822-9386
Parkland ES 900/PK-5
6330 Deer Ave 79924 915-434-6600
Roxanne Morfa, prin. Fax 757-9458
Parkland MS 1,200/6-8
6045 Nova Way 79924 915-434-6300
Javier Salgado, prin. Fax 757-6608
Parkland Pre-K Center PK-PK
10080 Chick-a-Dee 79924 915-435-7800
Rita Lopez, prin. Fax 435-7896
Pasodale ES 700/PK-5
8253 McElroy Ave 79907 915-434-8500
David Medina, prin. Fax 858-1269
Pebble Hills ES 700/PK-5
11145 Edgemere Blvd 79936 915-434-5600
Stacy Vasquez, prin. Fax 591-9222
Presa ES 400/K-5
128 Presa Pl 79907 915-434-8700
Wendy Banegas, prin. Fax 860-2810
Ramona ES 300/PK-6
351 Nichols Rd 79915 915-434-7700
Irene Medlin, prin. Fax 772-8153
Rio Bravo MS 500/6-8
525 Greggerson Dr 79907 915-434-8400
Dr. Sandra Calzada, prin. Fax 872-0269
Riverside MS 600/7-8
7615 Mimosa Ave 79915 915-434-7300
Jonathan Valdez, prin. Fax 772-7549
Sageland ES 500/K-6
7901 Santa Monica Ct 79915 915-434-2900
Carmen Crawford, prin. Fax 591-9228
Scotsdale ES 900/PK-6
2901 Mcrae Blvd 79925 915-434-4800
Sheri Pellicotte, prin. Fax 591-9270
South Loop ES 400/K-5
520 Southside Rd 79907 915-434-8800
Rosa Lujan, prin. Fax 860-9075
Thomas Manor ES 500/K-6
7988 Alameda Ave 79915 915-434-7800
Sandra Valdez, prin. Fax 858-0873
Tierra Del Sol ES 700/PK-6
1832 Tommy Aaron Dr 79936 915-434-5800
Juan Guzman, prin. Fax 591-9271
Valley View MS 700/6-8
8660 N Loop Dr 79907 915-434-3300
Alejandro Armendariz, prin. Fax 858-3615
Vista Hills ES 700/K-6
10801 La Subida Dr 79935 915-434-5700
Laura Calderon, prin. Fax 591-9305
Washington ES 500/K-6
3505 N Lee Trevino Dr 79936 915-434-5900
Mauricio Cano, prin. Fax 590-6535
Young Women's Leadership Academy 400/6-7
7615 Yuma Dr 79915 915-434-2300
Malinda Villalobos, prin. Fax 592-0036
Ysleta ES 500/K-5
8624 Dorbandt Cir 79907 915-434-8900
Norma Corral, prin. Fax 859-9311
Ysleta MS 600/6-8
8691 Independence Dr 79907 915-434-8200
David Gonzalez, prin. Fax 858-0261
Ysleta Pre K Center 700/PK-PK
7940 Craddock Ave 79915 915-434-9500
Sandra Perez, prin. Fax 591-9325

Community of Faith Christian S 100/PK-8
4539 Emory Rd 79922 915-584-2561
Blanca Mixer, prin. Fax 584-8263
El Paso Adventist Junior Academy 100/PK-9
3510 George Dieter Dr 79936 915-855-7312
El Paso Country Day S 100/PK-8
220 E Cliff Dr 79902 915-533-4492
El Paso Jewish Academy 100/K-8
805 Cherry Hill Ln 79912 915-833-0808
Faith Christian Academy 500/PK-12
8960 Escobar Dr 79907 915-594-3305
Shannon Nieman, supt. Fax 593-5474
Father Yermo ES 200/PK-8
237 Tobin Pl 79905 915-533-4693
Sr. Martha Santamaria, prin. Fax 532-6807
Immanuel Christian S 600/PK-12
1201 Hawkins Blvd 79925 915-778-6160
John Davis, head sch Fax 772-8207
Jesus Chapel S 200/PK-12
10200 Album Ave 79925 915-591-9330
Alba Wilcox, prin. Fax 593-1113
Loretto Academy 700/PK-12
1300 Hardaway St 79903 915-566-8400
Abe Ramirez, prin. Fax 564-0563
Most Holy Trinity S 100/PK-8
10000 Pheasant Rd 79924 915-751-2566
James Horan, prin. Fax 751-2596
Our Lady of Assumption S 100/PK-8
4805 Byron St 79930 915-565-3411
Jim Horan, prin. Fax 564-5724
Our Lady of the Valley S 300/PK-8
8600 Winchester Rd 79907 915-859-6448
Cynthia Vargas, prin. Fax 859-3908
Palm Tree Academy 50/PK-5
143 Paragon Ln 79912 915-581-7729
Radford S 100/PK-12
2001 Radford St 79903 915-565-2737
St. Clement's Parish S 400/PK-8
600 Montana Ave 79902 915-533-4248
Dr. John Roskosky, head sch Fax 544-1778
St. Joseph S 500/PK-8
1300 Lamar St 79903 915-566-1661
Marcela Hernandez, prin. Fax 566-1664
St. Mark's S 500/PK-8
5005 Love Rd 79922 915-581-2032
Linda Smith, prin. Fax 581-4701
St. Matthew S 200/PK-8
400 W Sunset Rd 79922 915-581-8801
Olga Macias, prin. Fax 581-8816
St. Patrick S 300/PK-8
1111 N Stanton St 79902 915-532-4142
Liliana Esparza M.Ed., prin. Fax 532-8297
St. Pius X S 500/PK-8
1007 Geronimo Dr 79905 915-772-6598
Ana Silva, prin. Fax 225-0010
St. Raphael S 500/PK-8
2310 Woodside Dr 79925 915-598-2241
O. Yapor, prin. Fax 598-3002

Elsa, Hidalgo, Pop. 5,655
Edcouch-Elsa ISD
Supt. — See Edcouch
Johnson ES 400/1-6
200 S Fannin St 78543 956-262-6010
Aminta Limas, prin. Fax 262-6012
Kennedy ES 400/1-6
500 W 9th St 78543 956-262-6027
Criselda Martinez, prin. Fax 262-6029
Truan JHS 800/7-8
E 9th St 78543 956-262-6082
Jose Rios, prin. Fax 262-6079

Elysian Fields, Harrison
Elysian Fields ISD 1,000/PK-12
PO Box 120 75642 903-633-2420
Maynard Chapman, supt. Fax 633-2498
www.efisd.net
Elysian Fields ES 500/PK-5
PO Box 119 75642 903-633-2420
Martha Lovaasen, prin. Fax 633-2187
Elysian Fields MS 200/6-8
PO Box 120 75642 903-633-2420
Brandon Goswick, prin. Fax 633-2326

Emory, Rains, Pop. 1,215
Rains ISD 1,600/PK-12
PO Box 247 75440 903-473-2222
John Rouse, supt. Fax 473-3053
www.rainsisd.org
Rains ES 400/PK-2
PO Box 247 75440 903-473-2222
Angie Trull, prin. Fax 473-7259
Rains IS 400/3-5
PO Box 247 75440 903-473-2222
Rachel Traylor, prin. Fax 473-5162
Rains JHS 400/6-8
PO Box 247 75440 903-473-2222
Gina Hildebrandt, prin. Fax 473-5162

Encinal, LaSalle, Pop. 553
Cotulla ISD
Supt. — See Cotulla
Encinal ES 200/PK-5
503 Encinal Blvd 78019 956-948-5324
Louisa Franklin, prin. Fax 948-5534

Ennis, Ellis, Pop. 18,329
Ennis ISD 5,700/PK-12
PO Box 1420 75120 972-872-7000
Dr. John Chapman, supt. Fax 875-8667
www.ennis.k12.tx.us
Austin ES 300/1-3
1500 Austin Dr 75119 972-872-7190
Bobby White, prin. Fax 875-7216
Bowie ES 400/1-3
501 Jeter Dr 75119 972-872-7234
John Peterson, prin. Fax 875-3407
Carver ECC 300/PK-K
600 E Martin Luther King Dr 75119 972-872-3730
Susan Jones, prin. Fax 872-3731
Crockett ECC 400/PK-K
1701 W Lampasas St 75119 972-872-7131
Deanna Gryder, prin. Fax 872-9829
Ennis JHS 800/7-8
3101 Ensign Rd 75119 972-872-3850
Wade Bishop, prin. Fax 875-9044
Houston ES 300/1-3
1701 S Hall St 75119 972-872-7285
Lori Redning, prin. Fax 875-4816
Lummus IS 700/4-6
501 N Clay St 75119 972-872-7060
Rodney McNeill, prin. Fax 875-8030
Miller IS 600/4-6
2200 W Lampasas St 75119 972-872-3775
Lindsey Wood, prin. Fax 872-9370
Travis ES 300/1-3
200 N Shawnee St 75119 972-872-7455
Philip Black, prin. Fax 875-4205

Era, Cooke
Era ISD 400/K-12
108 Hargrove St 76238 940-665-5961
Dr. Jeremy Thompson, supt. Fax 665-5311
www.eraisd.net
Era ES 200/K-6
108 Hargrove St 76238 940-665-5961
Courtney Stevens, prin. Fax 665-5311

Etoile, Nacogdoches
Etoile ISD 200/PK-8
PO Box 98 75944 936-465-9404
Sarah Hottman, supt. Fax 854-2241
www.etoile.esc7.net
Etoile ES 200/PK-8
PO Box 98 75944 936-465-9404
Adam Craft, prin. Fax 854-2241

Euless, Tarrant, Pop. 48,852
Grapevine-Colleyville ISD
Supt. — See Grapevine
Bear Creek ES 700/K-5
401 Bear Creek Dr 76039 817-305-4860
Bryan Calvert, prin. Fax 267-3863

Hurst-Euless-Bedford ISD
Supt. — See Bedford
Lakewood ES 700/K-6
1600 Donley Dr 76039 817-354-3375
Julie McAvoy, prin. Fax 354-3525
Midway Park ES 700/PK-6
409 N Ector Dr 76039 817-354-3380
Sarah Williams, prin. Fax 354-3332
North Euless ES 700/PK-6
1101 Denton Dr 76039 817-354-3505
Melissa Meadows, prin. Fax 354-3334
Oakwood Terrace ES 700/PK-6
700 Ranger St 76040 817-354-3386
Anmarie Garcia, prin. Fax 354-3335
South Euless ES 800/PK-6
605 S Main St 76040 817-354-3521
Maureen Sterling, prin. Fax 354-3523
Wilshire ES 800/PK-6
420 Wilshire Dr 76040 817-354-3529
Jodie Ramos, prin. Fax 354-3338

New Life Academy 100/PK-6
601 E Airport Fwy 76039 817-267-1000
Renee DeLorge, head sch Fax 267-5000

Eustace, Henderson, Pop. 976
Eustace ISD 1,500/PK-12
PO Box 188 75124 903-425-5151
Dr. Coy Holcombe, supt. Fax 425-5147
www.eustaceisd.net
Eustace IS 300/3-5
PO Box 188 75124 903-425-5181
Robert Reeve, prin. Fax 425-5294
Eustace MS 300/6-8
PO Box 188 75124 903-425-5171
Truman Oakley, prin. Fax 425-5146
Eustace PS 400/PK-2
PO Box 188 75124 903-425-5191
Shelby Adams, prin. Fax 425-5148

Evadale, Jasper, Pop. 1,471
Evadale ISD 500/PK-12
PO Box 497 77615 409-276-1337
Gary Fairchild, supt. Fax 276-1908
www.evadalek12.net
Evadale ES 200/PK-5
PO Box 497 77615 409-276-1337
Cheryl Jones, prin. Fax 276-1588
Evadale JHS 100/6-8
PO Box 497 77615 409-276-1337
Cheryl Jones, prin. Fax 276-1588

Evant, Coryell, Pop. 421
Evant ISD 200/PK-12
PO Box 339 76525 254-471-5536
Ken Wimberley, supt. Fax 471-5629
www.evantisd.org/
Evant ES 100/PK-6
PO Box 339 76525 254-471-5536
Craig Taylor, prin. Fax 471-5629

Everman, Tarrant, Pop. 6,051
Everman ISD 5,500/PK-12
608 Townley Dr 76140 817-568-3500
Curtis Amos, supt. Fax 568-3508
www.eisd.org
Baxter JHS 800/7-8
3038 Shelby Rd 76140 817-568-3530
Kentrel Phillips, prin. Fax 568-3594
Bishop ES 500/PK-4
501 Vaughn Ave 76140 817-568-3575
Ollie Clark, prin. Fax 568-3572
Hommel ES 400/PK-4
308 W Enon Ave 76140 817-568-3540
Martin DeHoyos, prin. Fax 568-3543
Souder ES 500/PK-4
201 N Forest Hill Dr 76140 817-568-3580
Hyacinth Hall, prin. Fax 568-3589
Townley ES 500/PK-4
2200 McPherson Rd 76140 817-568-3560
Wendy Simpson, prin. Fax 568-5177
Other Schools – See Fort Worth

Fabens, El Paso, Pop. 8,249
Fabens ISD 2,400/PK-12
PO Box 697 79838 915-765-2600
Poncho Garcia, supt. Fax 764-2968
www.fabensisd.net/
Fabens ES 800/PK-3
PO Box 697 79838 915-765-2650
Richard Lopez, prin. Fax 765-2655
Fabens MS 500/6-8
PO Box 697 79838 915-765-2630
Dr. Joe Keith, prin. Fax 764-7263
O'Donnell IS 300/4-5
PO Box 697 79838 915-765-2640
Michele Gonzalez, prin. Fax 764-4358

Fairfield, Freestone, Pop. 2,920
Fairfield ISD 1,800/PK-12
615 Post Oak Rd 75840 903-389-2532
Tony Price, supt. Fax 389-7050
www.fairfieldisd.net
Fairfield ES 500/PK-2
615 Post Oak Rd 75840 903-389-2148
Carroll Cain M.Ed., prin. Fax 389-5314
Fairfield JHS 400/6-8
615 Post Oak Rd 75840 903-389-4210
Bryan Gawryszewski M.Ed., prin. Fax 389-5454
Fairview IS 400/3-5
615 Post Oak Rd 75840 903-389-7095
Beth Henrichs M.Ed., prin. Fax 389-7101

Fair Oaks Ranch, Bexar, Pop. 5,916
Boerne ISD
Supt. — See Boerne
Fair Oaks Ranch ES 700/K-5
29085 Ralph Fair Rd 78015 830-357-4800
Jamie Robinson, prin. Fax 357-4899

Fairview, Collin, Pop. 7,141
Lovejoy ISD
Supt. — See Allen
Puster ES 400/K-5
856 Stoddard Rd 75069 469-742-8300
Kevin Parker, prin. Fax 742-8301
Sloan Creek IS 600/5-6
440 Country Club Rd 75069 469-742-8400
Wendy Craft, prin. Fax 742-8401

Falfurrias, Brooks, Pop. 4,970
Brooks County ISD 1,500/PK-12
PO Box 589 78355 361-325-8000
Dr. Maria Casas, supt. Fax 325-1913
www.bcisdistrict.net
Falfurrias ES 400/2-5
PO Box 589 78355 361-325-8040
Marie Vidaurri, prin. Fax 325-1010
Falfurrias JHS 300/6-8
PO Box 589 78355 361-325-8071
Cynthia Perez, prin. Fax 325-8156
Lasater ES 400/PK-1
PO Box 589 78355 361-325-8060
Elda Ramos, prin. Fax 325-2673

La Gloria ISD 100/PK-6
182 E County Road 401 78355 361-325-2330
David Braswell, supt. Fax 325-2533
www.lagloriaisd.esc2.net/
La Gloria ES 100/PK-6
182 E County Road 401 78355 361-325-2330
David Braswell, prin. Fax 325-2533

Falls City, Karnes, Pop. 604
Falls City ISD 400/K-12
PO Box 399 78113 830-254-3551
Todd Pawelek, supt. Fax 254-3354
www.fcisd.net
Falls City ES 200/K-6
PO Box 399 78113 830-254-3551
Christy Blocker, prin. Fax 254-3354

Farmers Branch, Dallas, Pop. 28,241
Carrollton-Farmers Branch ISD
Supt. — See Carrollton
Blair ES 700/K-5
14055 Heartside Pl 75234 972-968-1000
Kim Chow-Jackson, prin. Fax 968-1010
Farmers Branch ES 500/PK-5
13521 Tom Field Rd 75234 972-968-6100
Susan Machayo, prin. Fax 968-6110
Field MS 900/6-8
13551 Dennis Ln 75234 972-968-3900
Stephanie Jimenez, prin. Fax 968-3910
Stark ES 700/PK-5
12400 Josey Ln 75234 972-968-3200
Shanah Brown, prin. Fax 968-3210

Mary Immaculate Catholic S 500/K-8
14032 Dennis Ln 75234 972-243-7105
Matthew Krause, prin. Fax 241-7678

Farmersville, Collin, Pop. 3,235
Farmersville ISD 1,500/PK-12
501A State Highway 78 N 75442 972-782-6601
Jeff Adams, supt. Fax 784-7293
www.farmersvilleisd.net
Farmersville IS 500/2-5
807 N Main St 75442 972-782-8108
Tad Myers, prin. Fax 782-7527
Farmersville JHS 400/6-8
501 State Highway 78 N 75442 972-782-6202
Dr. Josh Martin, prin. Fax 782-7029
Tatum ES 300/PK-1
405 N Washington St 75442 972-782-7251
Ginger Ketcher, prin. Fax 782-8109

Farwell, Parmer, Pop. 1,360
Farwell ISD 500/PK-12
PO Box F 79325 806-481-3371
Colby Waldrop, supt. Fax 481-9275
www.farwellschools.org
Farwell ES 300/PK-5
PO Box F 79325 806-481-9131
Michael Johnson, prin. Fax 481-3255
Farwell JHS 100/6-8
PO Box F 79325 806-481-9260
Kristy White, prin. Fax 481-9258

Fate, Rockwall, Pop. 6,255
Rockwall ISD
Supt. — See Rockwall
Stevenson ES 400/PK-6
636 Stevenson Dr, 469-698-7474
Mike Pitcher, prin. Fax 698-7495

Royse City ISD
Supt. — See Royse City
Vernon ES 600/PK-4
100 Miss May Ave 75132 972-635-5006
Shannon Hayes, prin. Fax 722-8577

Fayetteville, Fayette, Pop. 257
Fayetteville ISD 200/PK-12
PO Box 129 78940 979-378-4242
Jeff Harvey, supt. Fax 378-4246
www.fayettevilleisd.net
Fayetteville S 200/PK-12
PO Box 129 78940 979-378-4242
Brynn Lopez, prin. Fax 378-4246

Ferris, Ellis, Pop. 2,412
Ferris ISD 2,300/PK-12
303 E 5th St 75125 972-544-3858
James Hartman, supt. Fax 544-2784
www.ferrisisd.org
Ferris IS 400/4-5
601 FM 664 75125 972-544-8662
Lance Keating, prin. Fax 544-3085
Ferris JHS 400/6-8
1002 E 8th St 75125 972-544-2279
Ivan Reyes, prin. Fax 544-2281
Ingram ES 400/PK-K
600 S Central St 75125 972-544-3212
Richard McClesky, prin. Fax 544-3405
McDonald ES 500/1-3
500 FM 983 75125 972-544-2574
Rhonda Renner, prin. Fax 544-2116

Flatonia, Fayette, Pop. 1,376
Flatonia ISD 600/PK-12
PO Box 189 78941 361-865-2941
Beverly Mikulenka, supt. Fax 865-2940
www.flatoniaisd.net
Flatonia ES 400/PK-6
PO Box 189 78941 361-865-2947
Nicole Ramirez, prin. Fax 865-2945

Florence, Williamson, Pop. 1,128
Florence ISD 1,000/PK-12
306 College Ave 76527 254-793-2850
Paul Michalewicz, supt. Fax 793-3055
florenceisd.net
Florence ES 500/PK-5
304 College Ave 76527 254-793-2497
Kay Bradford, prin. Fax 793-3158
Florence MS 200/6-8
718 S Patterson 76527 254-793-2504
Catherine Beckerley, prin. Fax 793-3054

Floresville, Wilson, Pop. 6,407
Floresville ISD 3,800/PK-12
1200 5th St 78114 830-393-5300
Dr. Sherri Bays Ed.D., supt. Fax 393-5399
www.fisd.us
Floresville MS 900/6-8
2601 B St 78114 830-393-5350
Marcia Gonzales, prin. Fax 393-5339
Floresville North ES 900/PK-5
14905 FM 775 78114 830-393-5310
Griselda Raley, prin. Fax 393-5315
Floresville South ES 900/PK-5
2000 Tiger Ln 78114 830-393-5325
Shelley Keck, prin. Fax 393-5320

Sacred Heart S 100/PK-5
1007 Trail St 78114 830-393-2117
Hilary Reile, prin. Fax 393-6968

Flower Mound, Denton, Pop. 63,499
Lewisville ISD 49,700/PK-12
1800 Timber Creek Rd 75028 469-713-5200
Kevin Rogers Ed.D., supt. Fax 350-9500
www.lisd.net
Bluebonnet ES 500/K-5
2000 Spinks Rd 75028 469-713-5195
Lana Fisher, prin. Fax 350-9005
Bridlewood ES 500/K-5
4901 Remington Park Dr 75028 469-713-5193
Robin Block, prin. Fax 350-9007
Donald ES 500/PK-5
2400 Forest Vista Dr 75028 469-713-5198
Michelle Wooten, prin. Fax 350-9033
Downing MS 700/6-8
5555 Bridlewood Blvd 75028 469-713-5962
Lisa Lingren, prin. Fax 350-9176
Flower Mound ES 500/PK-5
4101 Churchill Dr 75028 469-713-5955
Gayle Nurre, prin. Fax 350-9046
Forest Vista ES 500/PK-5
900 Forest Vista Dr 75028 469-713-5194
Dr. Patrick Schott, prin. Fax 350-9047
Forestwood MS 700/6-8
2810 Morriss Rd 75028 469-713-5972
Dave Tickner, prin. Fax 350-9184
Garden Ridge ES 500/PK-5
2220 S Garden Ridge Blvd 75028 469-713-5956
Kelly Roden, prin. Fax 350-9052
Lamar MS 800/6-8
4000 Timber Creek Rd 75028 469-713-5966
Chad Russell, prin. Fax 350-9204
Liberty ES 700/PK-5
4600 Quail Run 75022 469-713-5958
Tim Greenwell, prin. Fax 350-9098
McKamy MS 1,100/6-8
2401 Old Settlers Rd 75022 469-713-5991
Kelly Knight, prin. Fax 350-9477
Old Settlers ES 700/PK-5
2525 Old Settlers Rd 75022 469-713-5993
Kelly Hayunga, prin. Fax 350-9126
Prairie Trail ES 500/K-5
5555 Timber Creek Rd 75028 469-713-5980
Wendi Vaughn, prin. Fax 350-9135
Shadow Ridge MS 800/6-8
2050 Aberdeen Dr 75028 469-713-5984
Gary Gibson, prin. Fax 350-9215
Timbercreek ES 400/K-5
1900 Timber Creek Rd 75028 469-713-5961
Amy Acosta, prin. Fax 350-9146
Vickery ES 600/PK-5
3301 Wager Dr 75028 469-713-5969
Patricia Cheatham, prin. Fax 350-9157
Wellington ES 900/PK-5
3900 Kenwood Dr 75022 469-713-5989
Dr. Tami Braun, prin. Fax 350-9160
Other Schools – See Carrollton, Frisco, Highland Village, Lewisville, The Colony

---

Alden Montessori S 100/PK-3
4010 Justin Rd, 972-584-0400
Coram Deo Academy 1,100/PK-12
4900 Wichita Trl 75022 682-237-0232
Paula Dwyer, admin. Fax 237-0232
Explorations Preparatory S 100/PK-8
1501 Flower Mound Rd 75028 972-539-0601
Lamb of God Lutheran Preschool 400/PK-K
1401 Cross Timbers Rd 75028 972-539-0055
Brandy Simmons, dir. Fax 539-8194
Temple Christian Academy 200/K-12
2501 Northshore Blvd 75028 972-874-8700
Wonderland Montessori Academy 100/PK-5
3701 Auburn Dr 75022 972-225-5962

Floydada, Floyd, Pop. 3,029
Floydada ISD 700/PK-12
226 W California St 79235 806-983-3498
Dr. Gilbert Trevino, supt. Fax 983-5739
www.floydadaisd.esc17.net
Duncan ES 400/PK-6
1011 S 8th St 79235 806-983-5332
Carlos Munoz, prin. Fax 983-4976
Floydada JHS 100/7-8
618 Whirlwind Aly 79235 806-983-4961
Wayne Morren, prin. Fax 983-5739

Follett, Lipscomb, Pop. 459
Follett ISD 200/PK-12
PO Box 28 79034 806-653-2301
George Auld, supt. Fax 653-2036
www.follettisd.net
Follett S 200/PK-12
PO Box 28 79034 806-653-2301
Brianna Ethridge, prin. Fax 653-2036

Forestburg, Montague
Forestburg ISD 200/PK-12
PO Box 415 76239 940-964-2323
John Metzler, supt. Fax 964-2531
www.forestburgisd.net
Forestburg S 200/PK-12
PO Box 415 76239 940-964-2323
Karen Wiley, prin. Fax 964-2531

Forest Hill, Tarrant, Pop. 12,191
Fort Worth ISD
Supt. — See Fort Worth
Beal ES 500/PK-5
5615 Forest Hill Dr 76119 817-815-8500
Alfreida Colvin, prin. Fax 815-8550

Sellars ES 700/PK-5
4200 Dorsey St 76119 817-815-9200
Steven Mattic, prin. Fax 815-9250

Forney, Kaufman, Pop. 14,459
Forney ISD 8,600/PK-12
600 S Bois d Arc St 75126 972-564-4055
Suzanne McWilliams, supt. Fax 552-3038
www.forneyisd.net
Blackburn ES 600/PK-6
2401 Concord St 75126 972-564-7008
Courtney Parker, prin. Fax 355-0491
Brown MS 700/7-8
1050 Windmill Farms Blvd 75126 972-564-3967
Dr. Pamelia Luttrull, prin. Fax 355-1099
Claybon ES 500/K-6
1011 FM 741 75126 972-564-7023
Kristie Crabtree, prin. Fax 552-3274
Criswell ES 600/K-6
401 FM 740 N 75126 972-564-1609
Rachel Bonner, prin. Fax 552-3304
Crosby ES 400/K-6
495 Diamond Creek Dr 75126 972-564-7002
Leslie Rader, prin. Fax 355-0531
Henderson ES 600/PK-6
12755 FM 1641 75126 972-564-7100
Laurie Branch, prin. Fax 552-3335
Johnson ES 500/K-6
701 S Bois d Arc St 75126 972-564-3397
Nancy McElroy, prin. Fax 552-3336
Lewis ES 400/K-6
1309 Luckenbach Dr 75126 972-564-7102
Jenny Harstrom, prin. Fax 355-2128
Rhea ES 700/PK-6
250 Monitor Dr 75126 469-762-4157
Barbi Donehoo, prin. Fax 355-0191
Smith ES 500/PK-6
1750 Iron Gate Blvd 75126 469-762-4158
Jeff Hutcheson, prin. Fax 355-0154
Warren MS 700/7-8
811 S Bois D Arc St 75126 469-762-4156
Sondra Floyd, prin. Fax 552-1693

Forsan, Howard, Pop. 209
Forsan ISD 700/PK-12
PO Box 689 79733 432-457-2223
Randy Johnson, supt. Fax 457-2225
forsan.esc18.net
Forsan ES 300/PK-5
PO Box 689 79733 432-457-0091
Hanna Carter, prin. Fax 457-0040

Fort Davis, Jeff Davis, Pop. 1,186
Fort Davis ISD 200/PK-12
PO Box 1339 79734 432-426-4440
Graydon Hicks, supt. Fax 426-3841
www.fdisd.com
Dirks-Anderson ES 100/PK-5
PO Box 1339 79734 432-426-4440
Allison Scott, prin. Fax 426-4456

Fort Hancock, Hudspeth, Pop. 1,741
Fort Hancock ISD 500/PK-12
PO Box 98 79839 915-769-3811
Jose Franco, supt. Fax 769-3940
www.forthancockisd.net
Fort Hancock MS 100/6-8
PO Box 98 79839 915-769-3811
Daniel Medina, prin. Fax 769-0045
Martinez ES 200/PK-5
PO Box 98 79839 915-769-3811
Yadira Munoz, prin. Fax 769-0043

Fort Hood, Bell, Pop. 27,754
Killeen ISD
Supt. — See Killeen
Clarke ES 600/PK-3
51612 Comanche Ave 76544 254-336-1510
Laura Dart, prin. Fax 336-1528
Clear Creek ES 700/PK-5
4800 Washington St 76544 254-336-1550
Maryann Ramos, prin. Fax 336-1567
Duncan ES 600/PK-5
52425 Muskogee Dr 76544 254-336-1620
Pamela Disher, prin. Fax 336-1643
Meadows ES 700/PK-5
423 27th St 76544 254-336-1870
Peter Hartley, prin. Fax 336-1893
Montague Village ES 600/PK-5
84001 Clements Dr 76544 254-336-2230
Renee Cook, prin. Fax 336-2238
Murphy MS 500/6-8
53393 Sun Dance Dr 76544 254-336-6530
Mike Quinn, prin. Fax 336-6579
Oveta Culp Hobby ES 600/PK-5
53210 Lost Moccasin 76544 254-336-6500
Jennifer Warren, prin. Fax 336-6505
Venable Village ES 500/PK-5
60160 Venable Dr 76544 254-336-1980
Vickie Wasson, prin. Fax 336-2015

Fort Stockton, Pecos, Pop. 8,231
Fort Stockton ISD 2,400/PK-12
101 W Division St 79735 432-336-4000
Ralph Traynham, supt. Fax 336-4008
www.fsisd.net/
Alamo ES 500/K-3
101 W Division St 79735 432-336-4016
Adrienne Horton, prin. Fax 336-4028
Apache ES 400/PK-3
101 W Division St 79735 432-336-4161
Betty McCallister, prin. Fax 336-4167
Fort Stockton IS 400/4-5
101 W Division St 79735 432-336-4141
Matthew Calkins, prin. Fax 336-4147
Fort Stockton MS 500/6-8
101 W Division St 79735 432-336-4131
Roy Alvarado, prin. Fax 336-4136

Fort Worth, Tarrant, Pop. 728,297
Aledo ISD
Supt. — See Aledo
Walsh ES, 14113 Walsh Ave, 400/K-5
Sheri Coll, prin. 817-441-8327

Azle ISD
Supt. — See Azle
Eagle Heights ES 500/PK-4
6505 Lucerne Dr 76135 817-237-4161
Amy Rollmann, prin. Fax 237-0656

Castleberry ISD 3,900/PK-12
5228 Ohio Garden Rd 76114 817-252-2000
John Ramos, supt. Fax 252-2097
www.castleberryisd.net
Castleberry ES 800/PK-5
1100 Roberts Cut Off Rd 76114 817-252-2300
Michelle Stapp, prin. Fax 252-2399
James ES 500/PK-5
5300 Buchanan St 76114 817-252-2500
Leigh Ann Turner, prin. Fax 252-2599
Marsh MS 900/6-8
415 Hagg Dr 76114 817-252-2200
Kalyn Perkins, prin. Fax 738-3454
Other Schools – See River Oaks

Crowley ISD
Supt. — See Crowley
Carden ES 500/PK-4
3701 Garden Springs Dr 76123 817-370-5600
Paula Brooks, prin. Fax 370-5604
Crouch IS 500/5-6
8036 Cedar Lake Ln 76123 817-370-5670
Camcea Stapinski, prin. Fax 370-5676
Crowley MS 700/7-8
3800 W Risinger Rd 76123 817-370-5650
Omarian Brown, prin. Fax 370-5656
Dallas Park ES 700/PK-4
8700 Viridian Ln 76123 817-370-5620
Kevin Hunt, prin. Fax 370-5624
Hargrave ES 600/PK-4
9200 Poynter St 76123 817-370-5630
Paula Brooks, prin. Fax 370-5635
Harris IS 600/5-6
8400 W Cleburne Rd 76123 817-370-7571
Clarence Williams, prin. Fax 294-1594
Meadowcreek ES 700/PK-4
2801 Country Creek Ln 76123 817-370-5690
Dr. Arthurlyn Morgan, prin. Fax 370-5694
Oakmont ES 600/PK-4
6651 Oakmont Trl 76132 817-370-5610
Dr. Kim Scoggins, prin. Fax 370-5615
Parkway ES 700/PK-4
1320 W Everman Pkwy 76134 817-568-5710
Roslyn Bell, prin. Fax 568-5714
Poynter ES 500/PK-4
521 Ashdale Dr 76140 817-568-5730
Shaketa Traylor, prin. Fax 568-5734
Sycamore ES 600/PK-4
1601 Country Manor Rd 76134 817-568-5700
Rebekah Hunt, prin. Fax 568-5704
Walker IS 600/5-6
9901 Hemphill St 76134 817-568-2745
Jose Lara, prin. Fax 568-2209

Eagle Mountain.-Saginaw ISD 18,000/PK-12
1200 Old Decatur Rd 76179 817-232-0880
Jim Chadwell Ed.D., supt. Fax 847-6124
www.emsisd.com
Bryson ES 500/K-5
8601 Old Decatur Rd 76179 817-237-8306
Whitney Wheeler, prin. Fax 238-8991
Chisholm Ridge ES 600/K-5
8301 Running River Ln 76131 817-232-0715
Susan Cook, prin. Fax 306-4391
Comanche Springs ES 600/K-5
8100 Comanche Springs Dr 76131 817-847-8700
Melissa Davis, prin. Fax 847-0941
Creekview MS 700/6-8
6716 Bob Hanger St 76179 817-237-4261
Anthe Anagnostis, prin. Fax 237-2387
Dozier ES, 6201 Redeagle Dr 76179 K-5
Beth Epps, prin. 817-847-6340
Eagle Mountain ES 600/K-5
9700 Morris Dido Newark Rd 76179 817-236-7191
Terri Floyd, prin. Fax 236-1461
Elkins ES 600/K-5
7250 Elkins School Rd 76179 817-237-0805
Kori Werth, prin. Fax 237-0948
Gililland ES 500/K-5
701 Waggoman Rd 76131 817-232-0331
Christy Fehler, prin. Fax 232-8822
Greenfield ES 700/K-5
6020 Ten Mile Bridge Rd 76135 817-237-0357
Cathe Bragg, prin. Fax 237-5809
Highland MS 900/6-8
1001 E Bailey Boswell Rd 76131 817-847-5143
Karen Pressley, prin. Fax 847-1922
Lake Pointe ES 600/K-5
5501 Park Dr 76179 817-236-8801
Dr. Audrey Arnold, prin. Fax 236-8805
Northbrook ES 600/K-5
2500 Cantrell Sansom Rd 76131 817-232-0086
Gina Mayfield, prin. Fax 232-9861
Parkview ES 700/K-5
6225 Crystal Lake Dr 76179 817-237-5121
Mindy Miller, prin. Fax 237-5187
Prairie Vista MS 900/6-8
8000 Comanche Springs Dr 76131 817-847-9210
Anna King, prin. Fax 847-4255
Remington Point ES 600/K-5
6000 Old Decatur Rd 76179 817-232-1342
Chaney Curran, prin. Fax 232-2594
Wayside MS 900/6-8
1300 Old Decatur Rd 76179 817-232-0541
Jason Sneed, prin. Fax 232-2391

Willkie MS 900/6-8
6129 Texas Shiner Dr 76179 817-237-9631
Daniel Knowles, prin. Fax 237-9643
Other Schools – See Saginaw

Everman ISD
Supt. — See Everman
Johnson 6th Grade Campus 400/6-6
8901 Oak Grove Rd 76140 817-615-3670
Mary Preston, prin. Fax 615-3675
Powell IS 400/5-5
8875 Oak Grove Rd 76140 817-568-3523
Tanisha Boone, prin. Fax 568-3533
Ray ES 500/PK-4
7309 Sheridan Rd 76134 817-568-3545
Eva Quinonez, prin. Fax 568-3544

Fort Worth ISD 83,000/PK-12
100 N University Dr 76107 817-814-2000
Dr. Kent Scribner, supt. Fax 871-2112
www.fwisd.org
Bonnie Brea ES 400/K-5
3504 Kimbo Rd 76111 817-814-3700
Samantha Gonzalez, prin. Fax 814-3750
Briscoe ES 400/PK-5
2751 Yuma Ave 76104 817-814-0300
Octavia Johnson, prin. Fax 814-0350
Burton Hill ES 500/PK-5
519 Burton Hill Rd 76114 817-815-1400
Terrance Bigley, prin. Fax 815-1450
Carter Park ES 700/PK-5
1204 E Broadus Ave 76115 817-815-8600
Howard Robinson, prin. Fax 815-8650
Chavez ES 600/PK-5
3710 Deen Rd 76106 817-815-0300
Monica Ordaz, prin. Fax 815-0350
Clarke ES 400/PK-5
3300 S Henderson St 76110 817-814-6100
Kimberly Benavides, prin. Fax 814-6150
Clayton ES 500/PK-5
2000 Park Place Ave 76110 817-814-5400
Stephanie Hughes, prin. Fax 814-5450
Como ES 500/PK-5
4000 Horne St 76107 817-815-6500
Valencia Rhines, prin. Fax 815-6550
Como Montessori ES 300/PK-8
4001 Littlepage St 76107 817-815-7200
Janna Bennett, prin. Fax 815-7250
Contreras ES 700/PK-5
4100 Lubbock Ave 76115 817-814-7800
Diana Puente-Vargas, prin. Fax 814-7850
Daggett ES 800/PK-5
958 Page Ave 76110 817-814-5500
Patty Cole, prin. Fax 814-5550
Daggett MS 400/6-8
1108 Carlock St 76110 817-814-5200
Monica Garrett, prin. Fax 814-5250
Daggett Montessori S 500/K-8
801 W Jessamine St 76110 817-814-6300
Veronica Delgado, prin. Fax 814-6350
Davis ES 700/PK-5
4300 Campus Dr 76119 817-815-8700
Pamela Henderson, prin. Fax 815-8750
De Zavala ES 400/PK-5
1419 College Ave 76104 817-814-5600
Victorius Eugenio, prin. Fax 814-5650
Diamond Hill ES 600/PK-5
2000 Dewey St 76106 817-815-0400
Marlyn Martinez, prin. Fax 815-0450
Dillow ES 700/PK-5
4000 Avenue N 76105 817-814-0400
Erika Moody, prin. Fax 814-0450
Eastern Hills ES 600/PK-5
5917 Shelton St 76112 817-815-4500
Whitney Scott, prin. Fax 815-4550
East Handley ES 400/PK-5
2617 Mims St 76112 817-815-4400
Alleia Hobbs, prin. Fax 815-4450
Elder MS 1,200/6-8
709 NW 21st St 76164 817-814-4100
Ronald Schultze, prin. Fax 814-4150
Elliott ES 600/PK-5
2501 Cooks Ln 76120 817-815-4600
Steven Moore, prin. Fax 815-4650
Ellis PS 500/PK-K
215 NE 14th St 76164 817-814-3800
Leticia Sparks, prin. Fax 814-3850
Forest Oak MS 800/6-8
3221 Pecos St 76119 817-815-8200
Seretha Lofton, prin. Fax 815-8250
Glencrest 6th Grade S 400/6-6
4801 Eastline Dr 76119 817-815-8400
Keith Christmas, prin. Fax 815-8450
Glen Park ES 800/PK-5
3601 Pecos St 76119 817-815-8800
Ellen Verreault, prin. Fax 815-8850
Greenbriar ES 600/PK-5
1605 Grady Lee St 76134 817-814-7400
Nicole Montalvo, prin. Fax 814-7450
Green ES 700/PK-5
4612 David Strickland Rd 76119 817-815-8900
Edra Bailey, prin. Fax 815-8950
Handley MS 500/6-8
2801 Patino Rd 76112 817-815-4200
Cheryl Johnson, prin. Fax 815-4250
Helbing ES 600/PK-5
3524 N Crump St 76106 817-815-0500
Ana Morales, prin. Fax 815-0550
Hubbard Heights ES 700/PK-5
1333 W Spurgeon St 76115 817-814-7500
Amparo Martinez, prin. Fax 814-7550
Huerta ES 600/PK-5
3309 W Long Ave 76106 817-814-4400
Carla Coscia, prin. Fax 814-4450
Jacquet MS 500/7-8
2501 Stalcup Rd 76119 817-815-3500
Latanya Sadler, prin. Fax 815-3550

James MS 1,100/6-8
1101 Nashville Ave 76105 817-814-0200
Joycelyn Barnett, prin. Fax 814-0250
Jara ES 700/PK-5
2100 Lincoln Ave 76164 817-814-4500
Marta Plata, prin. Fax 814-4550
Kirkpatrick ES 500/PK-5
3229 Lincoln Ave 76106 817-814-4600
Christine Renteria, prin. Fax 814-4650
Kirkpatrick MS 500/6-8
3201 Refugio Ave 76106 817-814-4200
Jeffrey Bartolotta, prin. Fax 814-4250
Logan ES 400/PK-5
2300 Dillard St 76105 817-815-3700
Robert Ray, prin. Fax 815-3750
Lowery Road ES 700/PK-5
7600 Lowery Rd 76120 817-815-4700
Debra Williamson, prin. Fax 815-4750
McClung MS 800/6-8
3000 Forest Ave 76112 817-815-5300
Norbert Whitaker, prin. Fax 815-5350
McDonald ES 700/PK-5
1850 Barron Ln 76112 817-815-4800
Nkosi Geary-Smith, prin. Fax 815-4850
McLean MS 1,000/7-8
3816 Stadium Dr 76109 817-814-5300
Barbara Ozuna, prin. Fax 814-8350
McLean Sixth Grade S 500/6-6
3201 S Hills Ave 76109 817-814-5700
Karen Brown, prin. Fax 814-5750
McRae ES 700/PK-5
3316 Avenue N 76105 817-814-0500
Kendall Miller, prin. Fax 814-0550
Meacham MS 700/6-8
3600 Weber St 76106 817-815-0200
Oscar Martinez, prin. Fax 815-0250
Meadowbrook ES 700/PK-5
4330 Meadowbrook Dr 76103 817-815-4900
Terri McGuire, prin. Fax 815-4950
Meadowbrook MS 500/6-8
2001 Ederville Rd S 76103 817-815-4300
Marron McWilliams, prin. Fax 815-4350
Mendoza ES 500/PK-5
1412 Denver Ave 76164 817-814-4700
Jennifer Sanchez, prin. Fax 814-4750
Merrett ES 600/PK-5
7325 Kermit Ave 76116 817-815-6600
Anitra Perry, prin. Fax 815-6650
Mitchell Blvd ES 500/PK-5
3601 Mitchell Blvd 76105 817-815-9000
Aileen Martina-Quinones, prin. Fax 815-9050
Monnig MS 500/6-8
3136 Bigham Blvd 76116 817-815-1200
Kellye Kirkpatrick, prin. Fax 815-1250
Moore ES 500/PK-5
1809 NE 36th St 76106 817-815-0600
Elizabeth Yoder, prin. Fax 815-0650
Morningside ES 700/PK-5
2601 Evans Ave 76104 817-814-0600
Ronnita Carridine, prin. Fax 814-0650
Morningside MS 700/6-8
2751 Mississippi Ave 76104 817-815-8300
Justin Edwards, prin. Fax 815-8350
Moss ES 400/PK-5
4108 Eastland St 76119 817-815-3600
Charla Staten, prin. Fax 815-3650
Nash ES 300/PK-5
401 Samuels Ave 76102 817-814-9400
Blanca Galindo, prin. Fax 814-9450
North Hi Mount ES 300/PK-5
3801 W 7th St 76107 817-815-1500
Myrna Blanchard, prin. Fax 815-1550
Oakhurst ES 700/PK-5
2700 Yucca Ave 76111 817-814-9500
Guadalupe Cortez, prin. Fax 814-9550
Oaklawn ES 600/PK-5
3220 Hardeman St 76119 817-815-9100
Maria Anguiano, prin. Fax 815-9150
Pate ES 500/PK-5
3800 Anglin Dr 76119 817-815-3800
Rochelle Horton, prin. Fax 815-3850
Peace ES K-5
7555 Trail Lake Dr 76133 817-814-8800
Cassandra McCalister, prin. Fax 814-8850
Peak ES 500/PK-5
1201 E Jefferson Ave 76104 817-814-0700
Kimberley Blackwell, prin. Fax 814-0750
Phillips ES 500/PK-5
3020 Bigham Blvd 76116 817-815-1600
Whitney Clark, prin. Fax 815-1650
Ridglea Hills ES 600/PK-5
6817 Cumberland Rd 76116 817-815-1700
Crenesha Cotton, prin. Fax 815-1750
Riverside MS 1,100/6-8
1600 Bolton St 76111 817-814-9200
Victor Alfaro, prin. Fax 814-9250
Rosemont 6th Grade S 500/6-6
3908 Mccart Ave 76110 817-814-7300
Kathrina Andersen, prin. Fax 814-7350
Rosemont ES 600/K-5
1401 W Seminary Dr 76115 817-815-5200
Rodolfo Valdez, prin. Fax 815-5250
Rosemont MS 900/7-8
1501 W Seminary Dr 76115 817-814-7200
Oscar Adams, prin. Fax 814-7250
Rosen ES 500/K-5
2613 Roosevelt Ave 76164 817-814-4800
Julia Yost, prin. Fax 814-4850
Sagamore Hill ES 800/PK-5
701 S Hughes Ave 76103 817-815-5000
Dirrick Butler, prin. Fax 815-5050
Seminary Hills Park ES 400/PK-5
5037 Townsend Dr 76115 817-814-7600
Lorena Delgado, prin. Fax 814-7650
Shulkey ES 500/PK-5
5533 Whitman Ave 76133 817-814-8400
Vanessa Tritten, prin. Fax 814-8450

Sims ES 700/PK-5
3500 Crenshaw Ave 76105 817-814-0800
Andrea Harper, prin. Fax 814-0850
South Hills ES 800/PK-5
3009 Bilglade Rd 76133 817-814-5800
Melissa Russell, prin. Fax 814-5850
South Hi Mount ES 500/K-5
4101 Birchman Ave 76107 817-815-1800
Melissa Bryan, prin. Fax 815-1850
Springdale ES 500/PK-5
3207 Hollis St 76111 817-814-9600
LeAnn Moreno, prin. Fax 814-9650
Stevens ES 300/PK-5
6161 Wrigley Way 76133 817-814-8500
Jessica Johnson-McNeal, prin. Fax 814-8550
Stripling MS 700/6-8
2100 Clover Ln 76107 817-815-1300
Amy Bishop, prin. Fax 815-1350
Sunrise-McMillian ES 400/PK-5
3409 Stalcup Rd 76119 817-815-3900
LaTres Cole, prin. Fax 815-3950
Tanglewood ES 700/PK-5
3060 Overton Park Dr W 76109 817-814-5900
Connie Smith, prin. Fax 814-5950
Turner ES 600/PK-5
3000 NW 26th St 76106 817-814-4900
Elida Gonzalez, prin. Fax 814-4950
Van Zandt-Guinn ES 300/PK-5
600 S Kentucky Ave 76104 817-815-2000
Keith Besses, prin. Fax 815-2050
Walton ES 400/PK-5
5816 Rickenbacker Pl 76112 817-815-3300
Christina Turner Hanson, prin. Fax 815-3350
Washington Heights ES 400/PK-5
3214 Clinton Ave 76106 817-815-0700
Mary Cantu, prin. Fax 815-0750
Wedgwood 6th Grade S 500/6-6
4212 Belden Ave 76132 817-814-8300
Tremanya Thomas, prin. Fax 814-8350
Wedgwood MS 900/7-8
3909 Wilkie Way 76133 817-814-8200
Robert Burrell, prin. Fax 814-8250
Westcliff ES 500/PK-5
4300 Clay Ave 76109 817-814-6000
Sara Gillaspie, prin. Fax 814-6050
Westcreek ES 700/PK-5
3401 Walton Ave 76133 817-814-8600
Julia Cortina, prin. Fax 814-8650
Western Hills ES 800/2-5
2805 Laredo Dr 76116 817-815-6800
Alexandra Montes, prin. Fax 815-6850
Western Hills PS 600/PK-1
8300 Mojave Trl 76116 817-815-6900
Sonya Kelly, prin. Fax 815-6950
West Handley ES 500/K-5
2749 Putnam St 76112 817-815-5100
Julie Moynihan, prin. Fax 815-5150
White ES 700/K-5
7300 John T White Rd 76120 817-814-7900
Tamera Dugan, prin. Fax 814-7950
Williams ES 500/PK-5
901 Baurline St 76111 817-814-9700
Angela Wright, prin. Fax 814-9750
Wilson ES 600/PK-5
900 W Fogg St 76110 817-814-7700
Angeles Gonzalez, prin. Fax 814-7750
Woodway ES 600/PK-5
6701 Woodway Dr 76133 817-814-8700
Bryan Johnson, prin. Fax 814-8750
Worth Heights ES 700/PK-5
519 E Butler St 76110 817-814-6200
Andrea Lange, prin. Fax 814-6250
Other Schools – See Benbrook, Forest Hill, Haltom City

Hurst-Euless-Bedford ISD
Supt. — See Bedford
River Trails ES 600/K-6
8850 Elbe Trl 76118 817-285-3235
Tammy Daggs, prin. Fax 285-3238

Keller ISD
Supt. — See Keller
Basswood ES 500/K-4
3100 Clay Mountain Trl 76137 817-744-6500
Tony Johnson, prin. Fax 750-5168
Bluebonnet ES 600/K-4
7000 Teal Dr 76137 817-744-4500
Rhonda McGee, prin. Fax 581-3441
Caprock ES 700/K-4
12301 Grey Twig Dr, 817-744-6400
Amy Erb, prin. Fax 744-6438
Chisholm Trail IS 900/5-6
3901 Summerfields Blvd 76137 817-744-3800
Trish McKeel, prin. Fax 306-5393
Eagle Ridge ES 800/K-4
4600 Alta Vista Rd, 817-744-6300
Stacy Blevins, prin. Fax 741-1856
Fossil Hill MS 1,000/7-8
3821 Staghorn Cir S 76137 817-744-3050
Jennifer Gonzales, prin. Fax 847-6990
Freedom ES 500/PK-4
5401 Wall Price Keller Rd, 817-744-4800
Gary Mantz, prin. Fax 741-9913
Friendship ES 600/K-4
5400 Shiver Rd, 817-744-6200
Casey Riles, prin. Fax 741-5853
Heritage ES 600/K-4
4001 Thompson Rd, 817-744-4900
Dawn Bailey M.Ed., prin. Fax 337-3656
Hillwood MS 1,200/7-8
8250 Parkwood Hill Blvd 76137 817-744-3350
Kathleen Eckert, prin. Fax 581-1810
Independence ES 500/K-4
11773 Bray Birch Ln, 817-744-6100
Mark Basham, prin. Fax 744-6138
Keller Early Learning Center 600/PK-PK
10310 Old Denton Rd, 817-744-6700
David Riche, dir. Fax 744-6738

Keller Early Learning South PK-PK
3975 Summerfields Blvd 76137 817-743-8300
Christy Johnson, prin.
Lone Star ES 700/K-4
4647 Shiver Rd, 817-744-5200
Steve Hurst, prin. Fax 379-6231
North Riverside ES 500/K-4
7900 N Riverside Dr 76137 817-744-5300
Dr. Jackie Green-August, prin. Fax 306-1474
Park Glen ES 600/K-4
5100 Glen Canyon Rd 76137 817-744-5400
Leslee Shepherd, prin. Fax 485-2067
Parkview ES 700/K-4
6900 Bayberry Dr 76137 817-744-5500
Doreen Krebs, prin. Fax 232-8693
Parkwood Hill IS 1,100/5-6
8201 Parkwood Hill Blvd 76137 817-744-4000
Brad Tyler, prin. Fax 581-0085
Perot ES 700/K-4
9345 General Worth Dr, 817-744-4600
Lisa Young, prin. Fax 741-3659
Sunset Valley ES K-5
2032 Canchim St 76131 817-743-8200
Kristen Eriksen, prin.
Timberview MS 1,100/5-8
10300 Old Denton Rd, 817-744-2600
Carrie Jackson, prin. Fax 744-2638
Trinity Meadows IS 1,000/5-6
3500 Keller Hicks Rd, 817-744-4300
Susan Mackey, prin. Fax 741-6923
Trinity Springs MS 1,000/7-8
3550 Keller Hicks Rd, 817-744-3500
Justin Barrett, prin. Fax 744-3538
Vista Ridge MS 6-8
3201 Thompson Rd 76177 817-743-8400
Chelsea Allison, prin.
Woodland Springs ES 500/K-4
12120 Woodland Springs Dr, 817-744-5900
Cindy Daniel, prin. Fax 741-0354

Lake Worth ISD
Supt. — See Lake Worth
Collins MS 500/7-8
3651 Santos Dr 76106 817-306-4250
Kathy Harmon, prin. Fax 624-7058
Marine Creek ES 600/PK-4
4801 Huffines Blvd 76135 817-306-4270
Craig Beasley, prin. Fax 238-6726
Miller ES 600/PK-4
5250 Estrella St 76106 817-306-4280
Brent McClain, prin. Fax 624-9007

Northwest ISD
Supt. — See Justin
Granger ES 900/K-5
12771 Saratoga Springs Cir, 817-698-1100
Michelle McAdams, prin. Fax 698-1170
Nance ES 500/K-5
701 Tierra Vista Way 76131 817-698-1950
Penny Bowles, prin. Fax 698-1960
Peterson ES 700/PK-5
2000 Winter Hawk Dr 76177 817-698-5000
Justin Vercher, prin. Fax 698-5070

White Settlement ISD 6,600/PK-12
401 S Cherry Ln 76108 817-367-1300
Frank Molinar, supt. Fax 367-1351
www.wsisd.com/
Blue Haze ES 800/PK-4
601 Blue Haze Dr 76108 817-367-2583
Sarah Deslatte, prin. Fax 367-1344
Fine Arts Academy 400/K-6
8301 Downe Dr 76108 817-367-5396
Heather Crow, prin. Fax 367-1396
North ES 900/PK-4
9850 Legacy Dr 76108 817-367-1323
Connie Bitters, prin. Fax 367-1308
Tannahill IS 800/5-6
701 American Flyer Blvd 76108 817-367-1370
Randy Summerhill, prin. Fax 367-1371
Other Schools – See White Settlement

Alliance Christian Academy PK-10
13105 Harmon Rd 76177 817-439-8425
Dr. Christy Wilson, head sch Fax 840-7657
All Saints Catholic S 100/PK-8
2006 N Houston St 76164 817-624-2670
Arica Prado, prin. Fax 624-1221
All Saints' Episcopal S 900/PK-12
9700 Saints Cir 76108 817-560-5700
Dr. Thaddeus Bird, head sch Fax 560-9805
Anderson Private S 50/PK-12
14900 White Settlement Rd 76108 817-448-8484
Bethesda Christian S 400/K-12
4700 N Beach St 76137 817-281-6446
Vicki Vaughn, admin. Fax 581-5123
Calvary Christian Academy 400/PK-12
1401 Oakhurst Scenic Dr 76111 817-332-3351
Sue Tidwell, admin. Fax 332-4621
Christian Life Preparatory S 200/K-12
5253 Altamesa Blvd 76123 817-293-1500
Covenant Classical S 200/K-12
1701 Wind Star Way 76108 817-820-0884
Ekklesia Christian S 50/PK-6
1200 Bessie St 76104 817-332-1202
Fort Worth Academy 200/K-8
7301 Dutch Branch Rd 76132 817-370-1191
Shannon Elders, head sch Fax 294-1323
Ft. Worth Adventist Jr Academy 100/PK-8
3040 Sycamore School Rd 76133 817-370-7177
Fort Worth Country Day S 1,100/K-12
4200 Country Day Ln 76109 817-302-3209
Eric Lombardi, head sch Fax 377-3425
Fort Worth Save Our Children S 100/PK-7
4217 Avenue M 76105 817-536-3033
Vernon James, prin. Fax 536-3033

Harvest Christian Academy 300/PK-12
7200 Denton Hwy 76148 817-485-1660
Terry Caywood, hdmstr. Fax 514-6279
Holy Family Catholic S 200/PK-8
6146 Pershing Ave 76107 817-737-4201
Dr. John Shreve, prin. Fax 738-1542
ITOP Christian Academy K-12
2010 E Lancaster Ave 76103 817-885-8875
Lake Country Christian S 400/PK-12
7050 Lake Country Dr 76179 817-236-8703
Mark Earwood, head sch Fax 904-2022
Miss Endy's Christian Academy 50/PK-6
5837 Humbert Ave 76107 817-737-9031
Wilbernita Crosby, prin. Fax 377-1719
Montessori S of Fort Worth 100/PK-8
3420 Clayton Rd E 76116 817-732-0252
Our Lady of Victory Catholic S 100/PK-8
3320 Hemphill St 76110 817-924-5123
Linda Kuntz, prin. Fax 923-9621
Pathway Christian Academy 50/K-12
7460 McCart Ave 76133 817-370-7000
Steve Allen, hdmstr.
Rivertree Academy 100/PK-5
PO Box 101268 76185 817-420-9310
Emily Ryan, prin.
St. Andrew Catholic S 700/PK-8
3304 Dryden Rd 76109 817-924-8917
Veronica Tucker, prin. Fax 927-8507
St. George Catholic S 200/PK-8
824 Hudgins Ave 76111 817-222-1221
Mary Longoria, prin. Fax 838-0424
St. Paul Lutheran S 200/PK-8
1800 West Fwy 76102 817-332-2281
Scott Browning, prin. Fax 332-2640
St. Peter's Classical S 100/PK-12
7601 Bellaire Dr S 76132 817-294-0124
St. Peter the Apostle Catholic S 100/PK-8
1201 S Cherry Ln 76108 817-246-2032
Lisa Giardino, prin. Fax 246-3686
St. Rita S 200/PK-8
712 Weiler Blvd 76112 817-451-9383
Mary Burns, prin. Fax 446-4465
Southwest Christian ES 400/PK-6
6801 Dan Danciger Rd 76133 817-294-0350
Justin Kirk, prin. Fax 294-0752
Temple Christian S 800/PK-12
6824 Randol Mill Rd 76120 817-457-0770
Neil Childs, hdmstr. Fax 457-0777
Trinity Baptist Temple Academy 100/PK-12
6045 WJ Boaz Rd 76179 817-237-4255
Kelley McDowell, prin. Fax 237-5233
Trinity Valley S 1,000/K-12
7500 Dutch Branch Rd 76132 817-321-0100
Ian Craig, head sch Fax 321-0105

Franklin, Robertson, Pop. 1,547
Franklin ISD 1,000/PK-12
PO Box 909 77856 979-828-7000
Timothy Bret Lowry, supt. Fax 828-1910
www.franklinisd.net/
Franklin MS 200/5-8
PO Box 909 77856 979-828-7200
Susan Nelson, prin. Fax 828-7207
Reynolds ES 500/PK-4
PO Box 909 77856 979-828-7300
Christie Smitherman, prin. Fax 828-5048

Frankston, Anderson, Pop. 1,210
Frankston ISD 800/PK-12
PO Box 428 75763 903-876-2556
John Allen, supt. Fax 876-4558
www.frankstonisd.net
Frankston ES 400/PK-5
PO Box 428 75763 903-876-2214
Melissa McIntire, prin. Fax 876-4558
Frankston MS 200/6-8
PO Box 428 75763 903-876-2215
Melanie Blackwell, prin. Fax 876-4558

Fred, Tyler
Warren ISD
Supt. — See Warren
Fred ES 200/PK-5
PO Box 10 77616 409-429-3240
Chris Carter, prin. Fax 429-3488

Fredericksburg, Gillespie, Pop. 10,449
Fredericksburg ISD 2,900/PK-12
234 Friendship Ln 78624 830-997-9551
Dr. Eric Wright, supt. Fax 997-6164
www.fisd.org/
Fredericksburg ES 1,000/2-5
1608 N Adams St 78624 830-997-9595
Monica Ward, prin. Fax 997-7209
Fredericksburg MS 600/6-8
110 W Travis St 78624 830-997-7657
Missy Wright, prin. Fax 997-1927
Fredericksburg PS 300/PK-1
1110 S Adams St 78624 830-997-7421
Dr. Delesa Styles, prin. Fax 990-0002
Other Schools – See Stonewall

Ambleside S of Fredericksburg PK-12
106 S Edison St 78624 830-990-9059
Heritage S 200/K-12
310 Smokehouse Rd 78624 830-997-6597
Christopher Acton, head sch Fax 997-4900
St. Mary Catholic S 300/PK-8
202 S Orange St 78624 830-997-3914
John Mein, prin. Fax 997-2382

Freeport, Brazoria, Pop. 11,851
Brazosport ISD
Supt. — See Clute
Fleming ES 200/PK-1
PO Box Z 77542 979-730-7175
Maria Espinoza, prin. Fax 237-6332
Freeport IS 600/7-8
PO Box Z 77542 979-730-7240
Brooke Merritt, prin. Fax 237-6329
O'Hara Lanier MS 500/5-6
PO Box Z 77542 979-730-7220
Bridgette Percle, prin. Fax 237-6348
Velasco ES 600/PK-4
PO Box Z 77542 979-730-7210
Margaret Meadows, prin. Fax 237-6318

Freer, Duval, Pop. 2,808
Freer ISD 800/PK-12
PO Box 240 78357 361-394-6025
Conrad Cantu, supt. Fax 394-5005
www.freerisd.org/
Freer JHS 200/6-8
PO Box 240 78357 361-394-7102
Rosalva Campos, prin. Fax 394-5016
Thomas ES 400/PK-5
PO Box 240 78357 361-394-6800
Dr. Ray Garza, prin. Fax 394-5014

Fresno, Fort Bend, Pop. 18,750
Fort Bend ISD
Supt. — See Sugar Land
Burton ES 800/K-5
1625 Hunter Green Ln 77545 281-634-5080
Keli Mullins, prin. Fax 634-5094
Goodman ES 600/K-5
1100 W Sycamore St 77545 281-634-5985
Dr. Felicia Bolden, prin. Fax 634-6000
Parks ES 600/PK-5
19101 Chimney Rock Rd 77545 281-634-6390
Linda Espericueta, prin. Fax 327-6390

Friendswood, Galveston, Pop. 35,202
Clear Creek ISD
Supt. — See League City
Brookside IS 800/6-8
3535 E FM 528 Rd 77546 281-284-3600
Lauren Ambeau, prin. Fax 284-3605
Landolt ES 900/PK-5
2104 Pilgrims Point Dr 77546 281-284-5200
Deb Reno, prin. Fax 284-5205
Wedgewood ES 800/PK-5
4000 Friendswood Link Rd 77546 281-284-5700
Buffie Johnson, prin. Fax 284-5705
Westbrook IS 1,100/6-8
302 W El Dorado Blvd 77546 281-284-3800
Stephanie Cooper, prin. Fax 284-3805

Friendswood ISD 5,900/PK-12
302 Laurel Dr 77546 281-482-1267
Thad Roher, supt. Fax 996-2513
www.myfisd.com
Bales IS 400/3-5
211 Stadium Ln 77546 281-482-8255
J.T. Patton, admin. Fax 996-2551
Cline ES 900/K-3
505 Briarmeadow Ave 77546 281-482-1201
Barry Clifford, prin. Fax 996-2557
Friendswood JHS 1,500/6-8
1000 Manison Pkwy 77546 281-996-6200
Dana Drew, prin. Fax 996-6262
Westwood ES 500/PK-2
506 W Edgewood Dr 77546 281-482-3341
Kristin Moffitt, prin. Fax 996-2542
Windsong IS 500/3-5
2100 W Parkwood Ave 77546 281-482-0111
Nelda Guerra, prin. Fax 996-2594

Galloway S PK-5
3200 W Bay Area Blvd 77546 281-338-9510
Lord of Life Lutheran S 50/PK-8
4425 FM 2351 Rd 77546 281-482-0481
Andrew Van Weele, prin. Fax 648-4189

Friona, Parmer, Pop. 4,104
Friona ISD 1,200/PK-12
909 E 11th St 79035 806-250-2747
Dr. Pamela Nelson-Ray, supt. Fax 250-3805
www.frionaisd.com
Friona ES 300/2-5
909 E 11th St 79035 806-250-3340
Travis Victory, prin. Fax 250-5078
Friona JHS 300/6-8
909 E 11th St 79035 806-250-2788
Jesus Galdean, prin. Fax 250-8155
Friona PS 300/PK-1
909 E 11th St 79035 806-250-2240
Ashley Smith, prin. Fax 250-3937

Frisco, Collin, Pop. 113,923
Frisco ISD 46,000/PK-12
5515 Ohio Dr 75035 469-633-6000
Dr. Mike Waldrip, supt. Fax 633-6050
www.friscoisd.org
Allen ES 600/K-5
5800 Legacy Dr 75034 469-633-3800
Chastity Johnson, prin. Fax 633-3810
Ashley ES 900/K-5
15601 Christopher Ln 75035 469-633-3700
Kimberly Frankson, prin. Fax 633-3710
Bledsoe ES 800/K-5
1900 Timber Ridge Dr 75034 469-633-3600
Jamie Peden, prin. Fax 633-3610
Boals ES 700/K-5
2035 Jaguar Dr, 469-633-3300
Christina Beran, prin. Fax 633-3350
Bright ES 600/K-5
7600 Woodstream Dr 75034 469-633-2700
Serita Dodson, prin. Fax 633-2750
Carroll ES 700/K-5
4380 Throne Hall Dr, 469-633-3725
Lauren Cypert, prin. Fax 633-3735
Christie ES 700/K-5
10300 Huntington Rd 75035 469-633-2400
Katie Babb, prin. Fax 633-2450
Clark MS 900/6-8
4600 Colby Dr 75035 469-633-4600
Charese Duffey, prin. Fax 633-4650
Cobb MS 900/6-8
9400 Teel Pkwy, 469-633-4300
Kecia Theodore, prin. Fax 633-4310
Corbell ES 700/K-5
11095 Monarch Dr, 469-633-3550
Brenda Youngblood, prin. Fax 633-3560
Curtsinger ES 800/K-5
12450 Jereme Trl 75035 469-633-2100
Angela Borgarello, prin. Fax 633-2150
Early Childhood S 600/PK-PK
10330 Red Cedar Dr 75035 469-633-3825
Melissa Ellis, prin. Fax 633-3835
Fisher ES 700/K-5
2500 Old Orchard Rd, 469-633-2600
Nancy Fatheree, prin. Fax 633-2650
Griffin MS 700/6-8
3703 Eldorado Pkwy, 469-633-4900
Elizabeth Holcomb, prin. Fax 633-4950
Gunstream ES 700/K-5
7600 Rockyridge Dr 75035 469-633-3100
David Smolka, prin. Fax 633-3150
Hosp ES K-5
5050 Lone Star Ranch Pkwy 75034 469-633-4050
Aaron Else, prin. Fax 633-4060
Hunt MS 700/6-8
4900 Legendary Dr 75034 469-633-5200
Amanda Ziaer, prin. Fax 633-5210
Isbell ES 700/K-5
6000 Maltby Dr 75035 469-633-3400
Kandra Wooten, prin. Fax 633-3450
Maus MS 800/6-8
12175 Coit Rd 75035 469-633-5250
Chakosha Powell, prin. Fax 633-5260
McSpedden ES K-5
14140 Countrybrook Dr 75035 469-633-4025
Kranti Singh, prin. Fax 633-4035
Nelson MS K-5
10100 Independence Pkwy 75035 469-633-4100
Mitzi Garner, prin. Fax 633-4110
Newman ES K-5
12333 Briar Ridge Rd, 469-633-3975
Rachael Gilbert, prin. Fax 633-3985
Nichols ES 700/K-5
7411 Nichols Trl 75034 469-633-3950
Zach Wiley, prin. Fax 633-3960
Norris ES K-5
10101 Shepton Ln 75035 469-633-4075
Loryn Tobey, prin. Fax 633-4085
Pearson MS 6-8
2323 Stonebrook Pkwy 75034 469-633-4450
Jamie Wisneski, prin. Fax 633-4460
Phillips ES 800/K-5
2285 Little River Rd, 469-633-3925
Dana Solomon, prin. Fax 633-3935
Pink ES 700/K-5
3650 Overhill Dr, 469-633-3500
Danielle Record, prin. Fax 633-3510
Pioneer Heritage MS 900/6-8
1649 High Shoals Dr 75034 469-633-4700
Rocky Agan, prin. Fax 633-4750
Purefoy ES 700/K-5
11880 Teel Pkwy, 469-633-3875
Kena Robertson, prin. Fax 633-3885
Roach MS 900/6-8
12499 Independence Pkwy 75035 469-633-5000
Terri Gladden, prin. Fax 633-5010
Rogers ES 600/K-5
10500 Rogers Rd, 469-633-2000
Jennifer McGowan, prin. Fax 633-2050
Sem ES 600/K-5
12721 Honeygrove Dr 75035 469-633-3575
Alex Mira, prin. Fax 633-3585
Shawnee Trail ES 600/K-5
10701 Preston Vineyard Dr 75035 469-633-2500
Pam Schaeffer, prin. Fax 633-2550
Smith ES 600/K-5
9800 Sean Dr 75035 469-633-2200
Catherine Young, prin. Fax 633-2250
Sparks ES 700/K-5
8200 Otis Dr 75034 469-633-3000
Amy Baker, prin. Fax 633-3050
Spears ES 700/K-5
8500 Wade Blvd 75034 469-633-2900
Becca Bustillos, prin. Fax 633-2950
Stafford MS 1,000/6-8
2288 Little River Rd, 469-633-5100
Robin Scott, prin. Fax 633-5110
Staley MS 700/6-8
6927 Stadium Ln, 469-633-4500
Anita Lightfoot, prin. Fax 633-4550
Tadlock ES 800/K-5
12515 Godfrey Dr 75035 469-633-3775
Kellie Rapp, prin. Fax 633-3785
Trent MS 6-8
13131 Coleto Creek Dr, 469-633-4400
Shawn Perry, prin. Fax 633-4410
Vandeventer MS 900/6-8
6075 Independence Pkwy 75035 469-633-4350
Paige Hoes, prin. Fax 633-4360
Vaughn ES K-5
3535 Guinn Gate Dr 75034 469-633-2575
Susie Graham, prin. Fax 633-2585
Wester MS 900/6-8
12293 Shepherds Hill Ln 75035 469-633-4800
Richard Manuel, prin. Fax 633-4850
Other Schools – See Little Elm, Mc Kinney, Plano

Lewisville ISD
Supt. — See Flower Mound
Hicks ES 600/PK-5
3651 Compass Dr 75034 469-713-5981
Curtis Martin, prin. Fax 350-9075

Little Elm ISD
Supt. — See Little Elm
Hackberry ES 700/PK-5
7200 Snug Harbor Cir 75034 972-947-9453
Stephen Richardson, prin. Fax 947-9327

Frisco Montessori Academy 100/PK-8
8890 Meadow Hill Dr, 972-712-7400
Frisco Trails Montessori S 200/PK-K
8600 Teel Pkwy 75034 469-365-9100
Legacy Christian Academy 900/PK-12
5000 Academy Dr 75034 469-633-1330
Bill McGee, hdmstr. Fax 633-1348
St. Martin de Porres S 50/PK-6
303 King Rd 75034 469-362-2400
Nancy Kirkpatrick, prin. Fax 370-5524
St. Philip's Episcopal S - Frisco PK-5
6400 Stonebrook Pkwy 75034 972-335-8171
Beverly Woodson, prin. Fax 387-9531
Starwood Montessori S 200/PK-6
6600 Lebanon Rd 75034 972-712-8080

Fritch, Hutchinson, Pop. 2,086
Sanford-Fritch ISD 800/PK-12
PO Box 1290 79036 806-397-0159
Jim McClellan, supt. Fax 397-0629
www.sfisd.net
Sanford-Fritch ES 400/PK-5
PO Box 1290 79036 806-397-0159
Edie Allen, prin. Fax 397-0627
Sanford-Fritch JHS 200/6-8
PO Box 1290 79036 806-397-0159
Dixie Watson, prin. Fax 397-0626

Frost, Navarro, Pop. 641
Frost ISD 400/PK-12
PO Box K 76641 903-682-2711
Mickie Jackson, supt. Fax 682-2107
www.frostisd.org
Frost ES 200/PK-5
PO Box K 76641 903-682-2541
Mickie Jackson, prin. Fax 682-2107

Fruitvale, Van Zandt, Pop. 408
Fruitvale ISD 400/PK-12
PO Box 77 75127 903-896-1191
Rebecca Bain, supt. Fax 896-1011
www.fruitvaleisd.com
Fruitvale MS 100/6-8
PO Box 77 75127 903-896-4363
Charles Harford, prin. Fax 896-1011
Randall ES 200/PK-5
PO Box 77 75127 903-896-4466
Zach Masterson, prin. Fax 896-1011

Fulshear, Fort Bend, Pop. 1,120
Katy ISD
Supt. — See Katy
Randolph ES K-6
5303 Flewellen Oaks Ln 77441 281-234-3800
Kristin Harper, prin. Fax 644-1930

Lamar Consolidated ISD
Supt. — See Rosenberg
Huggins ES 600/PK-5
1 Huggins Dr 77441 832-223-1600
Janice Harvey, prin. Fax 223-1601
Leaman JHS 1,000/6-8
9320 Charger Way 77441 832-223-5200
Mike Semmler, prin. Fax 223-5201

Fulton, Aransas, Pop. 1,332
Aransas County ISD
Supt. — See Rockport
Fulton 4-5 Learning Center 500/4-5
314 6th St 78358 361-790-2240
Rose Tran, prin. Fax 790-2274

Gail, Borden, Pop. 230
Borden County ISD 300/K-12
PO Box 95 79738 806-756-4313
Billy Collins, supt. Fax 756-4310
www.bcisd.net/
Borden S 300/K-12
PO Box 95 79738 806-756-4313
Bart McMeans, prin. Fax 756-4310

Gainesville, Cooke, Pop. 15,668
Callisburg ISD
Supt. — See Callisburg
Callisburg ES 500/PK-5
648 FM 3164 76240 940-612-4196
Derrick Conley, prin. Fax 612-4804

Gainesville ISD 2,400/PK-12
800 S Morris St 76240 940-665-4362
Jeffrey L. Brasher, supt. Fax 665-4473
www.gainesvilleisd.org
Chalmers ES 500/2-4
600 Radio Hill Rd 76240 940-665-4147
Brittenie Polk, prin. Fax 665-9290
Edison ES 600/PK-1
1 Edison Dr 76240 940-665-6091
Pablo De Santiago, prin. Fax 665-5728
Gainesville JHS 400/7-8
1201 S Lindsay St 76240 940-665-4062
David Glancy, prin. Fax 665-1432
Lee IS 200/5-6
2100 N Grand Ave 76240 940-668-6662
Dee Dosher, prin. Fax 668-0353

Sivells Bend ISD 100/PK-8
1053 County Road 403 76240 940-665-6411
Lisa Slaughter, supt. Fax 665-2527
www.sivellsbendisd.net
Sivells Bend S 100/PK-8
1053 County Road 403 76240 940-665-6411
Lisa Slaughter, admin. Fax 665-2527

Walnut Bend ISD 100/PK-8
47 County Road 198 76240 940-665-5990
Debra Sikes, supt. Fax 665-9660
www.walnutbendisd.net
Walnut Bend ES 100/PK-8
47 County Road 198 76240 940-665-5990
Debra Sikes, admin. Fax 665-9660

St. Mary Catholic S 200/PK-8
931 N Weaver St 76240 940-665-5395
Karen Lee, prin. Fax 665-9538

Galena Park, Harris, Pop. 10,842
Galena Park ISD
Supt. — See Houston
Galena Park ES 700/PK-5
401 N Main St 77547 832-386-1670
Jaime Rocha, prin. Fax 386-1692
Galena Park MS 1,000/6-8
400 Keene St 77547 832-386-1700
L. Ramirez, prin. Fax 386-1738
MacArthur ES 700/PK-5
1801 N Main St 77547 832-386-4630
Maria Munoz, prin. Fax 386-4631

Our Lady of Fatima S 100/PK-8
1702 9th St 77547 713-674-5832
Khanh Pham, prin. Fax 674-3877

Galveston, Galveston, Pop. 47,004
Galveston ISD 6,400/PK-12
PO Box 660 77553 409-766-5100
Dr. Kelli Moulton, supt. Fax 762-8391
www.gisd.org
Austin Magnet MS 500/5-8
1514 Avenue N 1/2 77550 409-761-3500
Cathy Vanness, prin. Fax 765-5946
Burnet ES PK-4
5501 Avenue S 77551 409-761-6470
Beatriz Rodriguez, prin. Fax 740-5106
Central MS 300/5-8
3014 Sealy St 77550 409-761-6200
Monique Lewis, dir. Fax 770-0649
Collegiate Academy 500/5-8
7100 Stewart Rd 77551
Debra Owens, prin.
Moody ECC, 1110 21st St 77550 PK-PK
Mary Patrick, admin. 409-766-5172
Morgan ES 600/PK-4
1410 37th St 77550 409-761-6700
Divya Nagpal, prin. Fax 763-0122
Oppe ES 700/PK-4
2915 81st St 77554 409-761-6500
Alice Prets, prin. Fax 744-1905
Parker ES 600/PK-4
6802 Jones Dr 77551 409-761-6600
Liz Murphy, prin. Fax 744-8312
Other Schools – See Port Bolivar

Holy Family Catholic S 100/PK-8
2601 Ursuline St 77550 409-765-6607
Rita Hesse, prin. Fax 765-5154
Trinity Episcopal S 200/PK-8
720 Tremont St 77550 409-765-9391
Mark Ravelli, head sch Fax 762-7000

Ganado, Jackson, Pop. 1,997
Ganado ISD 700/PK-12
PO Box 1200 77962 361-771-4200
Dr. John Hardwick Ed.D., supt. Fax 771-2280
www.ganadoisd.org
Ganado ES 400/PK-5
PO Box 1200 77962 361-771-4250
Virgil Knowlton, prin. Fax 771-2280
Ganado JHS 200/6-8
PO Box 1200 77962 361-771-4309
Joey Rosalez, prin. Fax 771-4310

Garden City, Glasscock, Pop. 334
Glasscock County ISD 300/PK-12
PO Box 9 79739 432-354-2230
Tom Weeaks, supt. Fax 354-2503
www.gckats.net
Glasscock County ES 200/PK-5
PO Box 9 79739 432-354-2243
Scott Bicknell, prin. Fax 354-2503

Garden Ridge, Comal, Pop. 3,224
Comal ISD
Supt. — See New Braunfels
Garden Ridge ES 600/K-5
9401 Municipal Pkwy 78266 830-837-7000
Julie Cronkhite, prin. Fax 837-7001

Garland, Dallas, Pop. 223,158
Garland ISD 57,200/PK-12
PO Box 469026 75046 972-494-8201
Dr. Deborah Cron, supt. Fax 485-4928
www.garlandisd.net
Abbett ES 700/K-5
730 W Muirfield Rd 75044 972-675-3000
Betsy Cummins, prin. Fax 675-3005
Austin Academy for Excellence MS 900/6-8
1125 Beverly Dr 75040 972-926-2620
John Fishpaw, prin. Fax 926-2633
Beaver Technology ES 600/K-5
3232 March Ln 75042 972-494-8301
Shannon Trimble, prin. Fax 494-8702
Bradfield ES 500/K-5
3817 Bucknell Dr 75042 972-494-8303
Karla Massey, prin. Fax 494-8729
Bullock ES 600/PK-5
3909 Edgewood Dr 75042 972-494-8308
Brian Trichell, prin. Fax 494-8704
Bussey MS 900/6-8
1204 Travis St 75040 972-494-8391
Carol Goff, prin. Fax 494-8971
Caldwell ES 500/K-5
3400 Saturn Rd 75041 972-926-2500
Raelyn Scroggin, prin. Fax 926-2505
Carver ES 700/PK-5
2200 Wynn Joyce Rd 75043 972-487-4415
Wendy Williams, prin. Fax 240-8042
Centerville ES 400/K-5
600 Keen Dr 75041 972-926-2510
Amie Pennington, prin. Fax 926-2515
Cisneros Preschool 600/PK-PK
2826 S 5th St 75041 972-271-7160
Andy Kiser, prin. Fax 271-7165
Classical Center at Brandenburg MS 1,200/6-8
626 Nickens Rd 75043 972-926-2630
Elise Mosty, prin. Fax 926-2633
Classical Center at Vial ES 600/K-5
126 Creekview Dr 75043 972-240-3710
Beatris Martinez, prin. Fax 240-3711
Club Hill ES 500/K-5
1330 Colonel Dr 75043 972-926-2520
Dr. Spencer Hughes, prin. Fax 926-2526
Cooper ES 600/K-5
1200 Kingsbridge Dr 75040 972-675-3010
Bobbie Carter, prin. Fax 675-3015
Couch ES 600/PK-5
4349 Waterhouse Blvd 75043 972-240-1801
Angelee Shipp-Morales, prin. Fax 240-9276
Daugherty ES 700/K-5
500 W Miller Rd 75041 972-926-2530
Dr. Bonnie Barrett, prin. Fax 926-2535
Davis ES 700/K-5
1621 McCallum Dr 75042 972-494-8205
Patricia Tatum, prin. Fax 494-8707
Ethridge ES 700/K-5
2301 Sam Houston Dr 75044 972-675-3020
Jill Vincent, prin. Fax 675-3025
Freeman ES 400/K-5
1220 W Walnut St 75040 972-494-8371
Kelly Garcia, prin. Fax 494-8835
Golden Meadows ES 500/K-5
1726 Travis St 75042 972-494-8373
Jacqueline Rhymes, prin. Fax 494-8709
Handley ES 600/K-5
3725 Broadway Blvd 75043 972-926-2540
Aishley Cohns, prin. Fax 926-2545
Heather Glen ES 600/K-5
5119 Heather Glen Dr 75043 972-270-2881
Melissa True, prin. Fax 681-0078
Hickman ES 600/PK-5
3114 Pinewood Dr 75044 972-675-3150
Kara Onken, prin. Fax 675-3155
Hillside Academy for Excellence 500/K-5
2014 Dairy Rd 75041 972-926-2550
Sonya Palmer, prin. Fax 926-2555
Houston MS 1,100/6-8
2232 Sussex Dr 75041 972-926-2640
Don Hernandez, prin. Fax 926-2647
Jackson Tech Center for Math & Science 1,200/6-8
1310 Bobbie Ln 75042 972-494-8362
David Dunphy, prin. Fax 494-8802
Kimberlin Academy for Excellence 500/K-5
1520 Cumberland Dr 75040 972-926-2560
Tobi Schmidt, prin. Fax 926-2565
Lister ES 500/K-5
3131 Mars Dr 75040 972-675-3030
Cheryl Alexander, prin. Fax 675-3036
Luna ES 500/PK-5
1050 Lochness Ln 75044 972-675-3040
Deborah Wilkerson, prin. Fax 675-3045
Lyles MS 900/6-8
4655 S Country Club Rd 75043 972-240-3720
Adam Varrassi, prin. Fax 240-3723
Montclair ES 500/PK-5
5200 Broadmoor Dr 75043 972-279-4041
James Iorio, prin. Fax 681-0565
Northlake ES 700/PK-5
1626 Bosque Dr 75040 972-494-8359
Dr. Kathy Metzinger, prin. Fax 494-8717
O'Banion MS 1,100/6-8
700 Birchwood Dr 75043 972-279-6103
John Tucci, prin. Fax 613-9532
Park Crest ES 500/K-5
2232 Parkcrest Dr 75041 972-926-2571
Andrea Kleckner, prin. Fax 926-2575
Parsons Preschool 600/PK-PK
2202 Richoak Dr 75044 972-675-8065
Disa McEwen, prin. Fax 675-8061
Roach ES 400/K-5
1811 Mayfield Ave 75041 972-926-2580
Aurora Trichell, prin. Fax 926-2585
Sellers MS 800/6-8
1009 Mars Dr 75040 972-494-8337
Vikki Mahagan, prin. Fax 494-8607
Shorehaven ES 500/K-5
600 Shorehaven Dr 75040 972-494-8346
Deborah Henson, prin. Fax 494-8720
Shugart ES 600/PK-5
4726 Rosehill Rd 75043 972-240-3700
Kelly Williams, prin. Fax 240-3701
Southgate ES 400/K-5
1115 Mayfield Ave 75041 972-926-2590
Quinton Darden, prin. Fax 926-2595
Spring Creek ES 600/K-5
1510 Spring Creek Dr 75040 972-675-3060
Sue Sheridan, prin. Fax 675-3065
Toler ES 700/PK-5
3520 Guthrie Rd 75043 972-226-3922
Valerie Nobles, prin. Fax 226-0262
Walnut Glen Academy For Excellence 500/PK-5
3101 Edgewood Dr 75042 972-494-8330
Lisa Alexander, prin. Fax 494-8725
Watson Technology Ctr for Math & Science 600/PK-5
2601 Dairy Rd 75041 972-926-2600
Chris Grey, prin. Fax 926-2606
Weaver ES 500/PK-5
805 Pleasant Valley Rd 75040 972-494-8311
Ernest Espino, prin. Fax 494-8721

Webb MS 1,100/6-8
1610 Spring Creek Dr 75040 972-675-3080
Kenneth Washington, prin. Fax 675-3089
Williams ES 300/K-5
1821 Oldgate Ln 75042 972-926-2610
Chucky Viernes, prin. Fax 926-2615
Other Schools – See Rowlett, Sachse

Mesquite ISD
Supt. — See Mesquite
Price ES 500/K-6
630 Stroud Ln 75043 972-290-4100
Tomika Johnson, prin. Fax 290-4110

Richardson ISD
Supt. — See Richardson
Big Springs ES 400/K-6
3301 W Campbell Rd 75044 469-593-8100
Denise May, prin. Fax 593-8114
Henry ES 500/PK-6
4100 Tynes Dr 75042 469-593-8200
Jennifer Wills, prin. Fax 593-8221

Brighter Horizons Academy 700/PK-12
3145 Medical Plaza Dr 75044 972-675-2062
Firewheel Christian Academy 200/PK-9
5500 Lavon Dr 75040 972-495-0851
Rev. Adam Herod, hdmstr. Fax 495-3927
Garland Christian Academy 300/PK-12
1516 Lavon Dr 75040 972-487-0043
Cathey Ondrusek, admin. Fax 276-4079
Garland Christian Adventist S 1-4
1702 E Centerville Rd 75041 972-271-1154
Good Shepherd Catholic S 200/PK-8
214 S Garland Ave 75040 972-272-6533
Gail Richardson-Bassett, prin. Fax 272-0512
Mount Hebron Christian Academy 50/PK-2
901 Dairy Rd 75040 972-272-8095
Carolyn Primm, dir. Fax 276-8203
New Century Montessori Academy 200/PK-8
1625 Ferris Rd 75044 214-802-7770

Garrison, Nacogdoches, Pop. 884
Garrison ISD 700/PK-12
459 N US Highway 59 75946 936-347-7000
Richard Cooper, supt. Fax 347-2529
www.garrisonisd.com
Garrison ES 300/PK-5
459 N US Highway 59 75946 936-347-7010
Colleen Hill, prin. Fax 347-7004
Garrison MS 200/6-8
459 N US Highway 59 75946 936-347-7020
Clark Bynum, prin. Fax 347-7004

Garwood, Colorado
Rice Consolidated ISD
Supt. — See Altair
Garwood ES 100/K-5
7827 Highway 71 77442 979-234-3531
Leroy Stavinoha, prin. Fax 758-9032

Gary, Panola
Gary ISD 500/PK-12
132 Bobcat Trl 75643 903-685-2291
Todd Greer, supt. Fax 685-2639
www.garyisd.org
Gary S 500/PK-12
132 Bobcat Trl 75643 903-685-2291
Tony Wood, prin. Fax 685-2639

Gatesville, Coryell, Pop. 15,526
Gatesville ISD 2,600/PK-12
311 S Lovers Ln 76528 254-865-7251
Eric Penrod, supt. Fax 865-2279
www.gatesvilleisd.org
Gatesville ES 500/1-3
311 S Lovers Ln 76528 254-865-7262
Pamela Bone, prin. Fax 248-0077
Gatesville IS 700/4-6
311 S Lovers Ln 76528 254-865-2526
Nickolas Smith, prin. Fax 865-2932
Gatesville JHS 500/7-8
311 S Lovers Ln 76528 254-865-8271
Cindy Venable, prin. Fax 865-2252
Gatesville PS 200/PK-K
311 S Lovers Ln 76528 254-865-7264
Bridget Register, prin. Fax 865-2160

Gause, Milam
Gause ISD 200/PK-8
PO Box 38 77857 979-279-5891
Brad Jones, supt. Fax 279-5142
www.gauseisd.net
Gause ES 200/PK-8
PO Box 38 77857 979-279-5891
Brad Jones, prin. Fax 279-5142

Georgetown, Williamson, Pop. 46,741
Georgetown ISD 10,500/PK-12
603 Lakeway Dr 78628 512-943-5000
Dr. Fred Brent, supt. Fax 943-5004
www.georgetownisd.org
Benold MS 900/6-8
3407 Northwest Blvd 78628 512-943-5090
Joseph Ferguson, prin. Fax 943-5099
Carver ES 400/PK-5
4901 Scenic Lake Dr 78626 512-943-5070
Nancy Bottlinger, prin. Fax 943-5079
Cooper ES 600/K-5
1921 NE Inner Loop 78626 512-943-5060
Susan Peacock, prin. Fax 943-5069
Forbes MS 700/6-8
1911 NE Inner Loop 78626 512-943-5150
Brian Booker, prin. Fax 943-5159
Ford ES 500/K-5
210 Woodlake Dr, 512-943-5180
Jessica McMullen, prin. Fax 943-5189
Frost ES 400/PK-5
711 Lakeway Dr 78628 512-943-5020
Janet Mormon, prin. Fax 943-5028

McCoy ES 600/K-5
401 Bellaire Dr 78628 512-943-5030
Tyra Storie, prin. Fax 943-5039
Mitchell ES 600/K-5
1601 Rockride Ln 78626 512-943-1820
Meredith Gandy, prin. Fax 943-1829
Pickett ES 300/PK-5
1100 Thousand Oaks Blvd 78628 512-943-5050
Natalia Ramback, prin. Fax 943-5059
Purl ES 600/PK-2
1953 Maple St 78626 512-943-5080
Denisse Baldwin, prin. Fax 943-5089
Rancho Sienna ES PK-4
751 Bonnet Blvd 78628 512-260-4450
Melanie Bowman, prin. Fax 260-4460
Tippit MS 800/6-8
1601 Leander Rd 78628 512-943-5040
Brian Dawson, prin. Fax 943-5049
Village ES 400/PK-5
400 Village Commons Blvd, 512-943-5140
Debra Barker, prin. Fax 943-5149
Wagner MS 6-8
1621 Rockride Ln 78626 512-943-1830
Lindsay Harris, prin. Fax 943-1839

Leander ISD
Supt. — See Leander
Parkside ES 800/PK-5
301 Garner Park Dr 78628 512-570-7100
Kimberly Waltmon, prin. Fax 570-7105

Community Montessori S 100/PK-6
500 Pleasant Valley Dr 78626 512-863-7920
Stephanie Sayre, dir. Fax 819-9617
Grace Academy 200/K-12
225 Grace Blvd, 512-864-9500
St. Helen Catholic S 200/PK-8
2700 E University Ave 78626 512-868-0744
Mary Kay Sims, prin. Fax 869-3244
Zion Lutheran S, 6101 FM 1105 78626 200/PK-8
Thomas W. Wrege, prin. 512-863-5345

George West, Live Oak, Pop. 2,431
George West ISD 1,100/PK-12
913 Houston St 78022 361-449-1914
Ty Sparks, supt. Fax 449-1426
www.gwisd.esc2.net/
George West ES 300/4-6
910 Houston St 78022 361-449-1914
Pat James, prin. Fax 449-1426
George West JHS 200/7-8
900 Houston St 78022 361-449-1914
Ashley Lowe, prin. Fax 449-3909
George West PS 300/PK-3
405 Travis St 78022 361-449-1914
Pat James, prin. Fax 449-8921

Giddings, Lee, Pop. 4,822
Giddings ISD 1,900/PK-12
PO Box 389 78942 979-542-2854
Roger Dees, supt. Fax 542-9264
www.giddings.txed.net
Giddings ES 600/PK-3
PO Box 389 78942 979-542-2886
Alisa Niemeyer, prin. Fax 542-1153
Giddings IS 300/4-5
PO Box 389 78942 979-542-4403
Sarah Borowicz, prin. Fax 542-4327
Giddings MS 400/6-8
PO Box 389 78942 979-542-2057
Charlotte Penn, prin. Fax 542-3941

Immanual Lutheran S 100/PK-8
382 N Grimes St 78942 979-542-3319
Daniel Schaefer, prin. Fax 542-9084
St. Paul Lutheran S 100/PK-8
1578 County Road 211 78942 979-366-2218
Rev. John Schmidt, prin. Fax 366-2200

Gilmer, Upshur, Pop. 4,805
Gilmer ISD 2,500/PK-12
500 S Trinity St 75644 903-841-7400
Rick Albritton, supt. Fax 843-5279
www.gilmerisd.org
Bruce JHS 300/7-8
111 Bruce St 75645 903-841-7600
Bill Bradshaw, prin. Fax 843-6108
Gilmer ES 1,000/PK-4
1625 US Highway 271 N 75644 903-841-7700
Kimberly Kemp, prin. Fax 797-3773
Gilmer IS 400/5-6
1623 US Highway 271 N 75644 903-841-7800
Gina Treadway, prin. Fax 797-6346

Union Hill ISD 300/PK-12
2197 FM 2088 75644 903-762-2140
Dr. Troy Batts, supt. Fax 762-6845
www.uhisd.com
Richardson ES 200/PK-6
2197 FM 2088 75644 903-762-2139
Sara Batts, prin. Fax 762-6845

Gladewater, Gregg, Pop. 6,285
Gladewater ISD 1,600/PK-12
500 W Quitman Ave 75647 903-845-6991
Sedric Clark, supt. Fax 845-6994
www.gladewaterisd.com
Gladewater MS 400/6-8
414 S Loop 485 75647 903-845-2243
Chris Langford, prin. Fax 844-1738
Gladewater PS 400/PK-3
100 W Gay Ave 75647 903-845-2254
Amanda Langford, prin. Fax 845-2555
Weldon IS 300/4-5
314 E Saunders St 75647 903-845-6921
Cathy Bedair, prin. Fax 845-6923

Sabine ISD 1,400/PK-12
5424 FM 1252 W 75647 903-984-8564
Stacey Bryce, supt. Fax 984-6108
www.sabineisd.org
Sabine MS 300/6-8
5424 FM 1252 W 75647 903-984-4767
Stanton Reaves, prin. Fax 984-8823
Other Schools – See Kilgore

Union Grove ISD 600/PK-12
PO Box 1447 75647 903-845-5509
Brian Gray, supt. Fax 845-6178
www.ugisd.org
Union Grove ES 400/PK-6
PO Box 1447 75647 903-845-3481
Lynn Whitaker, prin. Fax 845-6270

Glenn Heights, Dallas, Pop. 11,061
De Soto ISD
Supt. — See DeSoto
McCowan MS 900/6-8
1500 Majestic Meadows Dr 75154 972-274-8090
Emory Price, prin. Fax 274-8099
Moates ES 600/K-5
1500 Heritage Blvd 75154 972-230-2881
Wesley Pittman, prin. Fax 274-8073

Red Oak ISD
Supt. — See Red Oak
Schupmann ES 400/PK-5
401 E Ovilla Rd 75154 972-617-2685
Rob Waller, prin. Fax 617-4388
Shields ES 500/PK-5
223 W Ovilla Rd 75154 972-617-4799
Shondra Jones, prin. Fax 617-4798

Glen Rose, Somervell, Pop. 2,402
Glen Rose ISD 1,700/PK-12
PO Box 2129 76043 254-898-3900
Wayne Rotan, supt. Fax 897-3651
www.grisd.net
Glen Rose ES 400/PK-2
PO Box 2129 76043 254-898-3500
Debbie Morris, prin. Fax 897-3086
Glen Rose IS 400/3-5
PO Box 2129 76043 254-898-3600
Lauri Mapes, prin. Fax 897-9707
Glen Rose JHS 400/6-8
PO Box 2129 76043 254-898-3700
Vicki Goebel, prin. Fax 897-4059

Godley, Johnson, Pop. 999
Godley ISD 1,700/PK-12
313 N Pearson St 76044 817-389-2536
Dr. Rich Dear, supt. Fax 389-2543
www.godleyisd.net/
Godley ES 600/PK-3
604 N Pearson St 76044 817-389-3838
Keri Grimsley, prin. Fax 389-4404
Godley IS 400/4-6
309 N Pearson St 76044 817-389-2383
Airemy Caudle, prin. Fax 389-2394
Godley MS 300/7-8
409 N Pearson St 76044 817-389-2121
Leigh Brown, prin. Fax 389-4357

Goldthwaite, Mills, Pop. 1,857
Goldthwaite ISD 600/PK-12
PO Box 608 76844 325-648-3531
Ronny Wright, supt. Fax 648-2456
www.goldisd.net/
Goldthwaite ES 300/PK-5
PO Box 608 76844 325-648-3055
DeeDee Wright, prin. Fax 648-3528
Goldthwaite MS 100/6-8
PO Box 608 76844 325-648-3630
Landon Sanderson, prin. Fax 648-3571

Goliad, Goliad, Pop. 1,901
Goliad ISD 900/PK-12
PO Box 830 77963 361-645-3259
Dave Plymale, supt. Fax 645-3614
www.goliadisd.org
Goliad ES 300/PK-6
PO Box 830 77963 361-645-3206
Patricia Huber, prin. Fax 645-2578
Goliad MS 200/7-8
PO Box 830 77963 361-645-3146
Mary Tippin, prin. Fax 645-8040

Gonzales, Gonzales, Pop. 7,175
Gonzales ISD 2,500/PK-12
PO Box 157 78629 830-672-9551
Dr. Kimberly Strozier Ed.D., supt. Fax 672-7159
www.gonzalesisd.net
East Avenue PS 200/1-2
1615 Saint Louis St 78629 830-672-2826
Dr. Damaris Womack, prin. Fax 672-6161
Gonzales ES 400/3-4
1600 Saint Andrew St 78629 830-672-1467
Jim Workman, prin. Fax 672-5758
Gonzales JHS 400/7-8
426 N College St 78629 830-672-8641
Rogue Thompson, prin. Fax 672-6466
Gonzalez Primary Academy 400/PK-K
222 Saint Joseph 78629 830-519-4110
Christi Leonhardt, prin. Fax 519-4112
North Avenue IS 400/5-6
1032 N Saint Joseph St 78629 830-672-9557
Hector Dominguez, prin. Fax 672-4350

Goodrich, Polk, Pop. 267
Goodrich ISD 200/PK-12
PO Box 789 77335 936-365-1100
Dr. Gary Bates, supt. Fax 365-3518
www.goodrichisd.net
Goodrich ES 100/PK-5
PO Box 789 77335 936-365-1100
Dr. Kathryn Washington, prin. Fax 365-2375

Goodrich MS 50/6-8
PO Box 789 77335 936-365-1100
Lara Devillier, prin. Fax 365-2371

Gordon, Palo Pinto, Pop. 475
Gordon ISD 200/PK-12
PO Box 47 76453 254-693-5582
Michael Steck, supt. Fax 693-5503
www.gordonisd.net
Gordon S 200/PK-12
PO Box 47 76453 254-693-5342
Fax 693-5503

Gorman, Eastland, Pop. 1,079
Gorman ISD 300/PK-12
PO Box 8 76454 254-734-3171
Mike Winter, supt. Fax 734-3393
www.gormanisd.net
Gorman MS 100/6-8
PO Box 8 76454 254-734-3171
Vanessa Oakley, prin. Fax 734-3425
Maxfield ES 200/PK-5
PO Box 8 76454 254-734-3171
Susan Walker, prin. Fax 734-3445

Graford, Palo Pinto, Pop. 570
Graford ISD 300/PK-12
400 W Division Ave 76449 940-664-3101
Dennis Holt, supt. Fax 664-2123
www.grafordisd.net
Graford ES 200/PK-5
400 W Division Ave 76449 940-664-3101
Wes Corzine, prin. Fax 664-2123

Graham, Young, Pop. 8,817
Graham ISD 2,600/PK-12
400 3rd St 76450 940-549-0595
Sonny Cruse, supt. Fax 549-8656
www.grahamisd.com
Crestview ES 600/1-3
1317 Old Jacksboro Rd 76450 940-549-6023
Amanda Townley, prin. Fax 549-6025
Graham JHS 600/6-8
1000 2nd St 76450 940-549-2002
Ginger Robbins, prin. Fax 549-6991
Pioneer K 300/PK-K
1425 1st St 76450 940-549-2442
Lisa Budarf, prin. Fax 549-2460
Woodland ES 400/4-5
1219 Cliff Dr 76450 940-549-4090
Donna Gatlin, prin. Fax 549-4093

Open Door Christian S 100/PK-5
735 Oak St 76450 940-549-2339
Tim Guice, prin. Fax 549-2331

Granbury, Hood, Pop. 7,903
Granbury ISD 6,100/PK-12
600 W Pearl St 76048 817-408-4000
James Largent Ed.D., supt. Fax 408-4014
www.granburyisd.org
Acton ES 700/PK-5
3200 Acton School Rd 76049 817-408-4200
Anna Roe, prin. Fax 408-4299
Acton MS 800/6-8
1300 James Rd 76049 817-408-4800
Jimmy Dawson, prin. Fax 408-4849
Baccus ES 500/PK-5
901 Loop 567 76048 817-408-4300
Robert Herrera, prin. Fax 408-4399
Brawner IS 400/3-5
1520 S Meadows Dr 76048 817-408-4950
Jincy Ross, prin. Fax 408-4999
Granbury MS 700/6-8
2000 Crossland Rd 76048 817-408-4850
Pat Yelverton, prin. Fax 408-4899
Mambrino ES 500/PK-5
3835 Mambrino Hwy 76048 817-408-4900
Stacie Brown, prin. Fax 408-4949
Oak Woods ES 400/PK-PK, 1-
311 Davis Rd 76049 817-408-4750
Donnie Cody, prin. Fax 408-4799
Roberson ES 500/PK-2
1500 Misty Meadow Dr 76048 817-408-4500
Kellie Lambert, prin. Fax 408-4599

Cornerstone Christian Academy 100/PK-12
5150 N Gate Rd 76049 817-573-6485
Marci Martinez, admin. Fax 573-7604
Grace Classical Christian Academy 50/PK-6
PO Box 41 76048 682-936-4566
North Central Texas Academy 200/PK-12
3846 N Highway 144 76048 254-897-4822
Todd Shipman, pres. Fax 897-7650

Grandfalls, Ward, Pop. 353
Grandfalls-Royalty ISD 100/PK-12
PO Box 10 79742 432-547-2266
Joe Helms, supt. Fax 547-2960
www.grisd.com
Grandfalls-Royalty S 100/PK-12
PO Box 10 79742 432-547-2266
Steven Parker, prin. Fax 547-2960

Grand Prairie, Dallas, Pop. 172,425
Arlington ISD
Supt. — See Arlington
Crouch ES 1,100/PK-6
2810 Prairie Hill Dr 75051 682-867-0200
Delisse Hardy, prin. Fax 867-0217
Farrell ES 800/PK-6
3410 Paladium Dr 75052 682-867-0300
Glen Brunk, prin. Fax 867-0370
Larson ES 800/PK-6
2620 E Avenue K 75050 682-867-0000
Teri Conley, prin. Fax 867-0079
Patrick ES PK-6
755 Timber Oaks Ln 75051 682-867-0600
Ena Meyers, prin. Fax 867-0605
Remynse ES 600/PK-6
2720 Fall Dr 75052 682-867-0500
Selena Ozuna, prin. Fax 867-0507
Starrett ES 700/PK-6
2675 Fairmont Dr 75052 682-867-0400
John Wofford, prin. Fax 867-0405
West ES 700/K-6
2911 Kingswood Blvd 75052 682-867-0100
Wendy Brittton, prin. Fax 867-0190

Grand Prairie ISD 27,600/PK-12
PO Box 531170 75053 972-264-6141
Dr. Susan Simpson Hull, supt. Fax 237-5440
www.gpisd.org
Adams MS 600/6-8
833 W Tarrant Rd 75050 972-262-1934
Darwert Johnson, prin. Fax 522-3099
Austin ES 500/PK-5
815 NW 7th St 75050 972-343-4600
Tanya Gilliam, prin. Fax 343-4699
Bonham Early Education S 400/PK-PK
1301 E Coral Way 75051 972-262-4255
Julio Toro, prin. Fax 522-3199
Bowie ES 400/PK-5
425 Alice Dr 75051 972-262-7348
Ana Holland, prin. Fax 264-6219
Crockett Early Education S 500/PK-PK
1340 Skyline Rd 75051 972-262-5353
Alisha Crumley, prin. Fax 343-6299
Daniels Elementary Academy Science Math 700/PK-5
801 SW 19th St 75051 972-264-7803
Norman Jones, prin. Fax 343-4574
De Zavala Environmental Science Academy 800/PK-5
3410 Kirby Creek Dr 75052 972-642-0448
Mary Smith, prin. Fax 264-9495
Dickinson ES 500/PK-5
1902 Palmer Trl 75052 972-641-1664
Whitney Carlisle, prin. Fax 641-8601
Eisenhower ES 700/PK-5
2102 N Carrier Pkwy 75050 972-262-3717
Dr. Shelley Handcock, prin. Fax 264-9473
Fannin MS 800/6-8
301 NE 28th St 75050 972-262-8668
Larry Jones, prin. Fax 343-4799
Garcia ES 600/PK-5
2444 Graham St 75050 972-237-0001
Rachel Mendoza, prin. Fax 237-9660
Garner Fine Arts Academy 600/PK-5
145 W Polo Rd 75052 972-262-5000
Vikki Vogel, prin. Fax 522-3399
Global Leadership Academy at Bush ES 600/PK-5
511 E Springdale Ln 75052 972-237-1628
Dina Jammer, prin. Fax 237-1059
Hill ES 500/PK-5
4213 S Robinson Rd 75052 972-264-0802
Dr. Catherine Bridges, prin. Fax 264-9475
Jackson MS 1,000/6-8
3504 Corn Valley Rd 75052 972-343-7500
Robert Wallace, prin. Fax 343-7599
Lee ES 800/K-5
401 E Grand Prairie Rd 75051 972-262-6785
Tony Vessakosal, prin. Fax 343-6099
Marshall Leadership Academy 600/PK-5
1160 W Warrior Trl 75052 972-522-7200
Gordon Carlisle, prin. Fax 522-7299
Moore College & Career Preparatory 600/PK-5
3150 Waterwood Dr 75052 972-660-2261
Nichole Holland, prin. Fax 343-4899
Moseley ES 600/PK-5
1851 W Camp Wisdom Rd 75052 972-522-2800
Tuyet Huynh, prin. Fax 522-2899
Ochoa STEM Academy at Milam ES 800/PK-5
2030 Proctor Dr 75051 972-262-7131
Dinnah Escanilla, prin. Fax 264-9492
Powell ES 500/K-5
5009 S Carrier Pkwy 75052 972-642-3961
Maura Ayers, prin. Fax 642-4049
Rayburn STEAM Academy 500/K-5
2800 Reforma Dr 75052 972-264-8900
Jennifer Oliver, prin. Fax 522-3899
Reagan MS 700/6-8
4616 Bardin Rd 75052 972-522-7300
Dr. Wendy Mathis, prin. Fax 522-7399
Seguin ES 500/K-5
1450 SE 4th St 75051 972-522-7100
Deedie Jones, prin. Fax 522-7199
Truman MS 600/6-8
1501 Coffeyville Trl 75052 972-641-7676
Letycia Fowler, prin. Fax 522-3999
Whitt Fine Arts Academy 600/PK-5
3320 S Edelweiss Dr 75052 972-264-5024
April Shaw, prin. Fax 343-4999
Williams ES 600/K-5
1635 SE 14th St 75051 972-522-2700
Ami Potts, prin. Fax 522-2799
World Language Academy at Travis ES 600/PK-6
525 NE 15th St 75050 972-262-2990
Joetta Wesley, prin. Fax 343-6198
Young Mens Leadership Academy 1,000/6-8
2205 SE 4th St 75051 972-264-8651
Joseph Melms, prin. Fax 522-3699

Mansfield ISD
Supt. — See Mansfield
Cabaniss ES 600/PK-4
6080 Mirabella Blvd 75052 972-299-6480
Dr. Kisha McDonald, prin. Fax 472-3030
Daulton ES 700/PK-4
2607 N Grand Peninsula Dr 75054 817-299-6640
Dr. Susan Gerlach, prin. Fax 453-6570
Spencer ES 600/K-4
3140 S Camino Lagos 75054 817-299-6680
Georgie Swize, prin. Fax 453-6580

Immaculate Conception Catholic S 100/PK-8
400 NE 17th St 75050 972-264-8777
Linda Santos, prin. Fax 264-7742

Grand Saline, Van Zandt, Pop. 3,102
Grand Saline ISD 1,100/PK-12
400 Stadium Dr 75140 903-962-7546
Micah Lewis, supt. Fax 962-7464
www.grandsalineisd.net
Grand Saline ES 300/PK-2
405 Stadium Dr 75140 903-962-7526
Lori Hooton, prin. Fax 962-7438
Grand Saline IS 200/3-5
200 Stadium Dr 75140 903-962-5515
Tina Core, prin. Fax 962-3783
Grand Saline MS 200/6-8
400 Stadium Dr 75140 903-962-7537
Duane Petty, prin. Fax 962-7474

Grandview, Johnson, Pop. 1,542
Grandview ISD 900/PK-12
PO Box 310 76050 817-866-4500
Joe Perrin, supt. Fax 866-3351
www.gvisd.org
Grandview ES 200/PK-5
PO Box 310 76050 817-866-4600
Kathrine Stewart, prin. Fax 866-2452
Grandview JHS 200/6-8
PO Box 310 76050 817-866-4660
Jeff Hudson, prin. Fax 866-3912

Granger, Williamson, Pop. 1,404
Granger ISD 400/PK-12
PO Box 578 76530 512-859-2173
Randy Willis, supt. Fax 859-2446
www.grangerisd.net
Granger S 400/PK-12
PO Box 578 76530 512-859-2173
Mike Abbott, prin. Fax 859-2446

Granite Shoals, Burnet, Pop. 4,859
Marble Falls ISD
Supt. — See Marble Falls
Highland Lakes ES 600/PK-5
8200 W FM 1431 78654 830-798-3650
Bethany Birdwell, prin. Fax 598-9349

Grapeland, Houston, Pop. 1,478
Grapeland ISD 500/PK-12
PO Box 249 75844 936-687-4619
Don Jackson, supt. Fax 687-4624
www.grapelandisd.net
Grapeland ES 200/PK-5
PO Box 249 75844 936-687-2317
Cassie Satterwhite, prin. Fax 687-2341
Grapeland JHS 100/6-8
PO Box 249 75844 936-687-2351
Rick Frauenberger, admin. Fax 687-5285

Grapevine, Tarrant, Pop. 45,499
Grapevine-Colleyville ISD 13,600/PK-12
3051 Ira E Woods Ave 76051 817-251-5200
Dr. Robin Ryan, supt. Fax 251-5375
www.gcisd-k12.org
Cannon ES 500/PK-5
1300 W College St 76051 817-251-5680
Tona Blizzard, prin. Fax 421-0982
Cross Timbers MS 800/6-8
2301 Pool Rd 76051 817-251-5320
Alex Fingers, prin. Fax 424-4296
Dove ES 600/K-5
1932 Dove Rd 76051 817-251-5700
Heather Landrum, prin. Fax 481-6730
Grapevine ES 500/K-5
1801 Hall Johnson Rd 76051 817-251-5735
Laura Hilcher, prin. Fax 481-6451
Grapevine MS 700/6-8
301 Pony Pkwy 76051 817-251-5660
Laura Koehler, prin. Fax 424-1626
Heritage ES 500/PK-5
4500 Heritage Ave 76051 817-305-4820
Jill Hemme, prin. Fax 540-2892
Silver Lake ES 600/PK-5
1301 N Dooley St 76051 817-251-5750
Shannon Cole, prin. Fax 329-4536
Timberline ES 700/PK-5
3220 Timberline Dr 76051 817-251-5770
Shelley Ingram, prin. Fax 329-5666
Other Schools – See Colleyville, Euless

Grapevine Faith Christian S 800/PK-12
730 E Worth St 76051 817-442-9144
Dr. Ed Smith Ed.D., pres. Fax 442-9904
Holy Trinity Catholic S 400/PK-8
3750 William D Tate Ave 76051 817-421-8000
Jeff Heiple, prin. Fax 421-4468
Novus Academy 100/K-12
204 N Dooley St 76051 817-488-4555
Kathleen Edwards M.Ed., head sch Fax 488-4533

Greenville, Hunt, Pop. 25,073
Bland ISD
Supt. — See Merit
Bland ES 300/PK-5
5123 FM 2194 75401 903-776-2239
Jason Hammack, prin. Fax 527-5481

Greenville ISD 4,700/PK-12
4004 Moulton St 75401 903-457-2500
Demetrus Liggins, supt. Fax 457-2504
www.greenvilleisd.com
Bowie ES 500/K-5
6005 Stonewall St 75402 903-457-2676
Dale Mason, prin. Fax 457-0725
Carver ES 500/K-5
2110 College St 75401 903-457-0777
Michelle Baird, prin. Fax 457-0786
Crockett ES 400/K-5
1316 Wolfe City Dr 75401 903-457-2684
Shannon Orsborn, prin. Fax 457-0722
Greenville 6th Grade Center 400/6-6
3201 Stanford St 75401 903-457-2660
James Evans, prin. Fax 457-2533

Greenville MS 600/7-8
3611 Texas St 75401 903-457-2620
David Gish, prin. Fax 457-2628
Johnson STEM Academy K-5
9315 Jack Finney Blvd 75402 903-454-5050
Stacey Kluttz, prin. Fax 454-5070
Lamar ES 600/K-5
6321 Jack Finney Blvd 75402 903-457-0765
Jason Tharp, prin. Fax 457-0774
Travis ES 400/K-5
3201 Stanford St 75401 903-457-2696
Matthew Spivy, prin. Fax 457-2533
Waters ECC 300/PK-PK
2504 Carver St 75401 903-457-2680
Judy Evans, prin. Fax 457-0745

Greenville Christian S 200/PK-12
8420 Jack Finney Blvd 75402 903-454-1111
Steven Bowers, hdmstr. Fax 455-8470

Gregory, San Patricio, Pop. 1,900
Gregory-Portland ISD
Supt. — See Portland
Austin ES 400/PK-5
308 N Gregory Ave 78359 361-777-4252
Gloria Dornak, prin. Fax 777-4261

Groesbeck, Limestone, Pop. 4,255
Groesbeck ISD 1,300/PK-12
PO Box 559 76642 254-729-4100
Dr. Harold Ramm, supt. Fax 729-5167
www.groesbeckisd.net
Enge-Washington IS 500/3-6
PO Box 559 76642 254-729-4103
Beth Westhoff, prin. Fax 729-5309
Groesbeck MS 300/7-8
410 Elwood Enge Dr 76642 254-729-4102
Dayne Duncan, prin. Fax 729-8763
Whitehurst ES 50/PK-2
801 S Ellis St 76642 254-729-4104
Ladena King, prin. Fax 729-2798

Groom, Carson, Pop. 567
Grandview-Hopkins ISD 50/PK-6
11676 FM 293 79039 806-669-3831
John Wilson, supt. Fax 669-3044
www.gvhisd.net
Grandview-Hopkins ES 50/PK-6
11676 FM 293 79039 806-669-3831
John Wilson, prin. Fax 669-3044

Groom ISD 100/PK-12
PO Box 598 79039 806-248-7557
Jay Lamb, supt. Fax 248-7949
www.groomisd.net
Groom S 100/PK-12
PO Box 598 79039 806-248-7474
Jay Lamb, admin. Fax 248-7949

Groves, Jefferson, Pop. 15,978
Port Neches-Groves ISD
Supt. — See Port Neches
Groves ES 300/4-5
3901 Cleveland Ave 77619 409-962-1531
Mandie Champagne, prin. Fax 963-2484
Groves MS 600/6-8
5201 Wilson St 77619 409-962-0225
James Arnett, prin. Fax 963-1898
Van Buren ES 300/K-3
6400 Van Buren St 77619 409-962-6511
Joe Cegielski, prin. Fax 962-2043
West Groves Early Learning Center PK-PK
5840 W Jefferson St 77619 409-963-1215
Tanya Davis, prin.

Triangle Adventist Christian S 50/PK-8
PO Box H 77619 409-963-3806

Groveton, Trinity, Pop. 1,043
Centerville ISD 100/PK-12
10327 N State Highway 94 75845 936-642-1597
Mark Brown, supt. Fax 642-2810
www.centervilleisd.net
Centerville ES 100/PK-6
10327 N State Highway 94 75845 936-642-1597
Andja Sailer, prin. Fax 642-2810

Groveton ISD 700/PK-12
PO Box 728 75845 936-642-1473
Don Hamilton, supt. Fax 642-1628
www.grovetonisd.net
Groveton ES 300/PK-5
PO Box 580 75845 936-642-1182
Phil Gersbach, prin. Fax 642-3254

Grulla, Starr, Pop. 1,621
Rio Grande City ISD
Supt. — See Rio Grande City
Grulla MS 800/6-8
PO Box 338 78548 956-487-5558
Rene Pena, prin. Fax 487-5633

Gruver, Hansford, Pop. 1,190
Gruver ISD 400/PK-12
PO Box 650 79040 806-733-2001
Troy Seagler, supt. Fax 733-5416
www.gruverisd.net
Gruver ES 200/PK-4
PO Box 1139 79040 806-733-2031
Amber Holland, prin. Fax 733-5412
Gruver JHS 100/5-8
PO Box 709 79040 806-733-2081
Wade Callaway, prin. Fax 733-5523

Gun Barrel City, Henderson, Pop. 5,589
Mabank ISD
Supt. — See Mabank
Lakeview ES 400/K-4
306 Harbor Point Rd, 903-880-1360
Kevyn Pate, prin. Fax 880-1363

Gunter, Grayson, Pop. 1,485
Gunter ISD 800/PK-12
PO Box 109 75058 903-433-4750
Dr. Jill Siler, supt. Fax 433-1053
www.gunterisd.org
Gunter ES 300/PK-4
PO Box 109 75058 903-433-5315
Dara Arrington, prin. Fax 433-1184
Gunter MS 200/5-8
PO Box 109 75058 903-433-1545
Kim Patterson, prin. Fax 433-9306

Gustine, Comanche, Pop. 473
Gustine ISD 200/PK-12
503 W Main St 76455 325-667-7303
Patti Blue, supt. Fax 667-7281
www.gustine.esc14.net/
Gustine S 200/PK-12
503 W Main St 76455 325-667-7303
Patti Blue, prin. Fax 667-0203

Guthrie, King, Pop. 160
Guthrie Common SD 100/PK-12
PO Box 70 79236 806-596-4466
Kevin Chisum, supt. Fax 596-4519
www.guthriejags.com
Guthrie S 100/PK-12
PO Box 70 79236 806-596-4466
Jodie Reel, prin. Fax 596-4519

Hale Center, Hale, Pop. 2,231
Hale Center ISD 700/PK-12
PO Box 1210 79041 806-839-2451
Steven Pyburn, supt. Fax 839-2195
www.hcisdowls.net
Akin ES 300/PK-4
PO Box 1210 79041 806-839-2121
Jackie King, prin. Fax 839-4404
Carr MS 200/5-8
PO Box 1210 79041 806-839-2141
Jimmi Johnson, prin. Fax 839-4417

Hallettsville, Lavaca, Pop. 2,529
Ezzell ISD 100/PK-8
20500 FM 531 77964 361-798-4448
Lisa Berckenhoff, supt. Fax 798-9331
www.ezzellisd.org
Ezzell ES 100/PK-8
20500 FM 531 77964 361-798-4448
Lisa Berckenhoff, supt. Fax 798-9331

Hallettsville ISD 1,000/PK-12
PO Box 368 77964 361-798-2242
Dr. JoAnn Bludau, supt. Fax 798-5902
www.hisdbrahmas.org
Hallettsville ES 400/PK-4
PO Box 368 77964 361-798-2242
Jason Harris, prin. Fax 798-4349
Hallettsville JHS 300/5-8
PO Box 368 77964 361-798-2242
Sophie Teltschik, prin. Fax 798-3573

Vysehrad ISD 100/PK-8
595 County Road 182 77964 361-798-4118
Jason Appelt, supt. Fax 798-3131
www.vysehrad.k12.tx.us
Vysehrad S 100/PK-8
595 County Road 182 77964 361-798-4118
Jason Appelt, supt. Fax 798-3131

Sacred Heart S 300/PK-12
313 S Texana St 77964 361-798-4251
Kevin Haas, prin. Fax 798-4970

Hallsville, Harrison, Pop. 3,526
Hallsville ISD 4,800/PK-12
PO Box 810 75650 903-668-5990
Jeff Collum, supt. Fax 668-5990
www.hisd.com
East ES 700/K-3
PO Box 810 75650 903-668-5990
Melissa Goulden, prin. Fax 668-5990
Hallsville IS 700/4-5
PO Box 810 75650 903-668-5990
Tracy Conway, prin. Fax 668-5990
Hallsville JHS 1,100/6-8
PO Box 810 75650 903-668-5990
Amy Whittle, prin. Fax 668-5990
Little Cats Learning Center 100/PK-PK
PO Box 810 75650 903-668-5990
Barbara Stevens, coord. Fax 668-5990
North ES 700/K-3
PO Box 810 75650 903-668-5990
Danieli Parker, prin. Fax 668-5990

Haltom City, Tarrant, Pop. 41,719
Birdville ISD 24,300/PK-12
6125 E Belknap St 76117 817-847-5700
Dr. Darrell Brown, supt. Fax 547-5530
www.birdvilleschools.net
Birdville ES 400/PK-5
3111 Carson St 76117 817-547-1500
Cherie Wagoner, prin. Fax 831-5736
Cheney at South Birdville ES 500/PK-5
2600 Solona St 76117 817-547-2300
Darrell Brown, prin. Fax 831-5798
Francisco ES 400/PK-5
3701 Layton Ave 76117 817-547-1700
Angela Limon, prin. Fax 831-5724
Haltom MS 900/6-8
5000 Hires Ln 76117 817-547-4000
Dr. Jill Balzer, prin. Fax 831-5778
North Oaks MS 600/6-8
4800 Jordan Park Dr 76117 817-547-4600
Dr. Jennifer Klaerner, prin. Fax 581-5352
Smith ES 400/PK-5
3701 Haltom Rd 76117 817-547-1600
Jennifer Martin, prin. Fax 831-5817

Spicer ES 700/PK-5
4300 Estes Park Rd 76137 817-547-3300
Dr. Cheryl Waddell, prin. Fax 581-5497
Stowe ES 800/PK-5
4201 Rita Ln 76117 817-547-2400
Mike Moon, prin. Fax 581-5328
West Birdville ES 700/PK-5
3001 Layton Ave 76117 817-547-2500
Tim Drysdale, prin. Fax 831-5795
Other Schools – See Hurst, North Richland Hills, Richland Hills, Watauga

Fort Worth ISD
Supt. — See Fort Worth
Howell ES 500/PK-5
1324 Kings Hwy 76117 817-814-9300
Monica Granados, prin. Fax 814-9350

Hamilton, Hamilton, Pop. 3,076
Hamilton ISD 700/PK-12
400 S College St 76531 254-386-3149
Clay Tarpley, supt. Fax 386-8885
hamiltonisd.org
Hamilton JHS 200/6-8
400 S College St 76531 254-386-8168
Mona Gloff, prin. Fax 386-8885
Whitney ES 400/PK-5
400 S College St 76531 254-386-8166
Jennifer Zschiesche, prin. Fax 386-3316

Hamlin, Jones, Pop. 2,109
Hamlin ISD 400/PK-12
PO Box 338 79520 325-576-2722
Randy Burks, supt. Fax 576-2152
www.hamlin.esc14.net
Hamlin ES 200/PK-6
405 NW 5th St 79520 325-576-3191
Kenda Cox, prin. Fax 576-2358

Hamshire, Jefferson
Hamshire-Fannett ISD 1,700/PK-12
PO Box 223 77622 409-243-2133
Dwaine Augustine Ed.D., supt. Fax 243-3437
www.hfisd.net
Other Schools – See Beaumont

Happy, Swisher, Pop. 670
Happy ISD 200/PK-12
PO Box 458 79042 806-558-5331
Ray Keith, supt. Fax 558-2070
www.happyisd.net
Happy ES 100/PK-6
PO Box 458 79042 806-558-2561
Toni Waldo, prin. Fax 558-2484

Hardin, Liberty, Pop. 804
Hardin ISD 1,300/PK-12
PO Box 330 77561 936-298-2112
Bob Parker, supt. Fax 298-9161
www.hardinisd.net/
Hardin ES 600/PK-5
PO Box 330 77561 936-298-2114
Jennifer Stein, prin. Fax 298-9153
Hardin IS 200/6-6
PO Box 330 77561 936-298-2054
Julia Hall, prin. Fax 298-3264
Hardin JHS 200/7-8
PO Box 330 77561 936-298-2054
Cami Jones, prin. Fax 298-3264

Hargill, Hidalgo, Pop. 877
Edinburg Consolidated ISD
Supt. — See Edinburg
Hargill ES 400/PK-5
13394 4th St 78549 956-289-2338
Modesta Segundo, prin. Fax 845-6337

Harker Heights, Bell, Pop. 25,289
Killeen ISD
Supt. — See Killeen
Eastern Hills MS 800/6-8
300 Indian Trl 76548 254-336-1100
Jeremy Key, prin. Fax 336-1115
Harker Heights ES 800/PK-5
726 S Ann Blvd 76548 254-336-2050
Carolyn Dugger, prin. Fax 336-2073
Mountain View ES 700/PK-5
500 Mountain Lion Rd 76548 254-336-1900
Randy Podhaski, prin. Fax 336-1919
Skipcha ES 1,000/PK-5
515 Prospector Trl 76548 254-336-6690
Carrie Parker, prin. Fax 336-6711
Union Grove MS 900/6-8
101 E Iowa Dr 76548 254-336-6580
Dagmar Harris, prin. Fax 336-6593

Harleton, Harrison
Harleton ISD 700/PK-12
PO Box 510 75651 903-777-2372
Dr. Craig Coleman, supt. Fax 777-2406
www.harletonisd.net/
Harleton ES 400/PK-5
PO Box 400 75651 903-777-4092
Traci Jones, prin. Fax 777-3009
Harleton JHS 200/6-8
PO Box 610 75651 903-777-3010
Paul Davis, prin. Fax 777-3009

Harlingen, Cameron, Pop. 64,588
Harlingen Consolidated ISD 18,300/PK-12
407 N 77 Sunshine Strip 78550 956-430-9500
Dr. Arturo Cavazos, supt. Fax 430-9514
www.hcisd.org
Austin ES 400/PK-5
700 E Austin Ave 78550 956-427-3060
Magda Gonzalez, prin. Fax 427-3063
Bonham ES 700/PK-5
2400 E Jefferson Ave 78550 956-427-3070
Minnie Ramirez, prin. Fax 427-3073

Bowie ES 400/PK-5
309 W Lincoln Ave 78550 956-427-3080
Adriana Arellano, prin. Fax 427-3083
Coakley MS 800/6-8
1402 S 6th St 78550 956-427-3000
Pedro Sanchez, prin. Fax 427-3006
Crockett ES 400/PK-5
1406 W Jefferson Ave 78550 956-427-3090
Juan Garcia, prin. Fax 427-3093
Gutierrez MS 800/6-8
3205 Wilson Rd 78552 956-430-4400
Mike Reyes, prin. Fax 430-4480
Houston ES 500/PK-5
301 E Taft Ave 78550 956-427-3110
Virginia Armstrong, prin. Fax 427-3114
Jefferson ES 300/PK-5
601 S J St 78550 956-427-3120
Alejandra Lara, prin. Fax 427-3127
Lamar ES 700/PK-5
1100 S M St 78550 956-427-3130
Alma Atkinson, prin. Fax 427-3133
Long ES 700/PK-5
2601 N 7th St 78550 956-427-3140
Bobbie Jo Hushen, prin. Fax 427-3144
Means ES 600/PK-5
1201 E Loop 499 78550 956-427-3377
Mindy Sanchez, prin. Fax 427-3376
Memorial MS 800/6-8
1901 Rio Hondo Rd 78550 956-427-3020
Alex Gonzalez, prin. Fax 427-3024
Milam ES 500/PK-5
1215 S Rangerville Rd 78552 956-427-3150
Dr. Rosalinda Cobarrubias, prin. Fax 427-3153
Rodriguez ES 700/K-5
8402 Wilson Rd 78552 956-430-4060
Traci Gonzalez, prin. Fax 430-4065
Stuart Place ES 700/PK-5
6701 W Business 83 78552 956-427-3160
William Snavely, prin. Fax 427-3159
Travis ES 400/PK-5
600 E Polk St 78550 956-427-3170
Beulah Rangel, prin. Fax 427-3173
Treasure Hills ES 700/K-5
2525 Haine Dr 78550 956-427-3180
Roland Ingram, prin. Fax 427-3187
Vela MS 800/6-8
801 S Palm Blvd 78552 956-427-3479
Tony Gonzales, prin. Fax 427-3549
Vernon MS 700/6-8
125 S 13th St 78550 956-427-3040
Gracie Gutierrez, prin. Fax 427-3046
Wilson ES 500/PK-5
16495 Primera Rd 78552 956-427-3190
Kristi David, prin. Fax 427-3197
Zavala ES 400/PK-5
1111 N B St 78550 956-427-3200
Tanya Garza, prin. Fax 427-3203
Other Schools – See Combes

Calvary Christian S 300/PK-8
1815 N 7th St 78550 956-425-1882
St. Alban's Episcopal S 200/PK-6
1417 E Austin Ave 78550 956-428-2326
Mary Katherine Duffy, head sch Fax 428-8457
St. Anthony S 200/PK-8
1015 E Harrison Ave 78550 956-423-2486
Kathy Stapleton, prin. Fax 412-0084
St. Paul Academy 100/PK-8
1920 E Washington Ave 78550 956-423-3926
Jim House M.Ed., prin. Fax 423-0926

Harper, Gillespie, Pop. 1,183
Harper ISD 500/PK-12
PO Box 68 78631 830-864-4044
Chris Stevenson M.Ed., supt. Fax 864-4060
www.harper.txed.net/
Harper ES 200/PK-4
PO Box 68 78631 830-864-4044
Jay Harper M.Ed., prin. Fax 864-5240
Harper MS 100/5-8
PO Box 68 78631 830-864-4044
Julie Fiedler M.Ed., prin. Fax 864-4748

Harrold, Wilbarger
Harrold ISD 100/K-12
18106 Stewart St 76364 940-886-2213
David Thweatt, supt. Fax 886-2215
www.harroldisd.net/
Harrold S 100/K-12
18106 Stewart St 76364 940-886-2213
Craig Templeton, prin. Fax 886-2215

Hart, Castro, Pop. 1,112
Hart ISD 200/PK-12
PO Box 490 79043 806-938-2143
David Cox, supt. Fax 938-2610
www.hartisd.net
Hart ES 100/PK-5
PO Box 490 79043 806-938-2142
Ramona Neudorf, prin. Fax 938-2188

Hartley, Hartley, Pop. 536
Hartley ISD 200/PK-12
PO Box 408 79044 806-365-4458
Scott Vincent, supt. Fax 365-4459
www.hartleyisd.net
Hartley S 200/PK-12
PO Box 408 79044 806-365-4458
Scott Vincent, supt. Fax 365-4459

Haskell, Haskell, Pop. 3,278
Haskell Consolidated ISD 600/PK-12
PO Box 937 79521 940-864-2602
Bill Alcorn, supt. Fax 864-8096
www.haskell.esc14.net/
Haskell ES 300/PK-5
PO Box 937 79521 940-864-2654
James Lisle, prin. Fax 864-2369
Haskell JHS 100/6-8
PO Box 937 79521 940-864-5981
Kent Colley, prin. Fax 864-5982

Paint Creek ISD 100/PK-12
4485 FM 600 79521 940-864-2868
Dr. Cheryl Floyd, supt. Fax 863-4488
www.paintcreek.esc14.net
Paint Creek S 100/PK-12
4485 FM 600 79521 940-864-2868
Roy Gardner, prin. Fax 863-4488

Haslet, Tarrant, Pop. 1,481
Northwest ISD
Supt. — See Justin
Adams MS, 1069 Eagle Blvd 76052 6-8
Cynthia Webber, prin. 817-215-0000
Haslet ES 500/K-5
501 Schoolhouse Rd 76052 817-215-0850
Melissa Webber, prin. Fax 215-0870
Schluter ES 500/K-5
1220 Mesa Crest Dr 76052 817-698-3900
Amy Howell, prin. Fax 698-3970
Sendera Ranch ES 600/K-5
1216 Diamond Back Ln 76052 817-698-3500
John Booles, prin. Fax 698-3515
Thompson ES 500/K-5
440 E Wishbone Ln 76052 817-698-3800
Dr. Leigh Anne Romer, prin. Fax 698-3870
Wilson MS 800/6-8
14250 Sendera Ranch Blvd 76052 817-698-7900
Mike Blankenship, prin. Fax 698-7970

Legacy Classical Christian Academy 50/PK-12
12501 US Highway 287 76052 817-363-3652

Hawkins, Wood, Pop. 1,237
Hawkins ISD 700/PK-12
PO Box 1430 75765 903-769-2181
Morris Lyon, supt. Fax 769-0505
www.hawkinsisd.org
Hawkins ES 300/PK-5
PO Box 1430 75765 903-769-0536
Stephanie McConnell, prin. Fax 769-0531
Hawkins MS 200/6-8
PO Box 1430 75765 903-769-0552
Jason Boyd, prin. Fax 769-0583

Hawley, Jones, Pop. 626
Hawley ISD 700/PK-12
PO Box 440 79525 325-537-2214
Jimmy J. Burns, supt. Fax 537-2265
www.hawley.esc14.net
Hawley ES 300/PK-5
PO Box 440 79525 325-537-2721
Laurie Florence, prin. Fax 537-2265
Hawley MS 200/6-8
PO Box 440 79525 325-537-2070
Chad Hoffman, prin. Fax 537-2265

Hearne, Robertson, Pop. 4,418
Hearne ISD 900/PK-12
900 Wheelock St 77859 979-279-3200
Dr. Adrain Johnson, supt. Fax 279-3631
www.hearneisd.com
Hearne ES 600/PK-6
1210 Hackberry St 77859 979-279-3341
Latisha Crockett, prin. Fax 279-8011
Hearne JHS 100/7-8
1201B W Brown St 77859 979-279-2449
Jannie Mitchell, prin. Fax 279-8033

Heartland, Kaufman
Crandall ISD
Supt. — See Crandall
Dietz ES, 2080 Sunnybrook Dr, K-6
Melissa Smith, prin. 972-427-6050
Walker ES 500/K-6
4060 Abbey Rd, 972-427-6030
Abby Baker, prin. Fax 427-6031

Heath, Rockwall, Pop. 6,837
Rockwall ISD
Supt. — See Rockwall
Lyon ES, 2186 Trophy Dr, PK-6
Megan Gist, prin.
Parks-Heath ES 700/K-6
330 Laurence Dr 75032 972-772-4300
Megan Smith, prin. Fax 772-2098

Fulton S 200/PK-8
1626 Smirl Dr 75032 972-772-4445
Johnathan Bryant, head sch Fax 772-9558

Hebbronville, Jim Hogg, Pop. 4,553
Jim Hogg County ISD 1,100/PK-12
PO Box 880 78361 361-527-3203
Susana Garza, supt. Fax 527-4928
www.jhcisdpk12.org
Hebbronville ES 600/PK-5
200 W Lucille St 78361 361-527-3203
Leonor Hernandez, prin. Fax 527-2133
Hebbronville JHS 200/6-8
PO Box 880 78361 361-527-3203
Anna Canales, prin. Fax 527-5986

Hedley, Donley, Pop. 328
Hedley ISD 100/PK-12
PO Box 69 79237 806-856-5323
Terry Stevens, supt. Fax 856-5372
www.hedleyisd.net
Hedley S 100/PK-12
PO Box 69 79237 806-856-5323
Garrett Bains, prin. Fax 856-5372

Helotes, Bexar, Pop. 7,218
Northside ISD
Supt. — See San Antonio
Beard ES 800/K-5
8725 Sonoma Pkwy 78023 210-397-6600
Blanca Hemann, prin. Fax 695-3849
Helotes ES 400/K-5
13878 Riggs Rd 78023 210-397-3800
Rhonda Johnson, prin. Fax 695-3827
Kuentz ES 800/K-5
12303 Leslie Rd 78023 210-397-8050
Lori Gallegos, prin. Fax 695-4810
Los Reyes ES 400/K-5
10785 Triana Pkwy 78023 210-398-1200
Erika Pruneda, prin. Fax 695-5394

Hemphill, Sabine, Pop. 1,176
Hemphill ISD 900/PK-12
PO Box 1950 75948 409-787-3371
Reese Briggs, supt. Fax 787-4005
www.hemphill.esc7.net
Hemphill ES 400/PK-4
PO Box 1950 75948 409-787-3371
Susan Smith, prin. Fax 787-4005
Hemphill MS 300/5-8
PO Box 1950 75948 409-787-3371
Jeremy McDaniel, prin. Fax 787-4005

Hempstead, Waller, Pop. 5,718
Hempstead ISD 1,100/PK-12
PO Box 1007 77445 979-826-3304
Dr. Angela Gutsch, supt. Fax 826-5510
www.hempsteadisd.org
Hempstead ES 300/PK-5
PO Box 1007 77445 979-826-2452
Stacey Baughn-Hunt, prin. Fax 826-5524
Hempstead MS 400/6-8
PO Box 1007 77445 979-826-2530
Erin Meadows, prin. Fax 826-5583

Henderson, Rusk, Pop. 13,557
Carlisle ISD 700/PK-12
8960 FM 13 W 75654 903-861-3801
Michael Payne, supt. Fax 861-3932
www.carlisleisd.org
Carlisle ES 300/PK-5
8960 FM 13 W 75654 903-861-3612
Stephanie Rowan, prin. Fax 861-0063
Carlisle JHS 100/6-8
8960 FM 13 W 75654 903-861-0040
Fax 861-0014

Henderson ISD 3,500/PK-12
PO Box 728 75653 903-655-5000
Keith Boles, supt. Fax 657-9271
www.hendersonisd.org/
Henderson MS 800/6-8
PO Box 728 75653 903-655-5400
Hardy Dotson, prin. Fax 657-6499
Northside ES 500/4-5
PO Box 728 75653 903-655-5300
Dea Henry, prin. Fax 657-5238
Wylie ES 900/1-3
PO Box 728 75653 903-655-5200
Deidra Sutton, prin. Fax 655-5299
Wylie PS 500/PK-K
PO Box 728 75653 903-655-5100
Deana Griffith, prin. Fax 655-5199

Full Armor Christian Academy 100/K-12
PO Box 2035 75653 903-655-8489
Tricia Hall, head sch Fax 657-8267

Henrietta, Clay, Pop. 3,103
Henrietta ISD 900/PK-12
1801 E Crafton St 76365 940-720-7900
Jeff McClure, supt. Fax 538-7505
www.henrietta-isd.net
Henrietta ES 500/PK-5
1600 E Crafton St 76365 940-720-7910
Kendra Bennett, prin. Fax 538-7515
Henrietta JHS 200/6-8
308 E Gilbert St 76365 940-720-7920
Fax 538-7525

Midway ISD 100/PK-12
12142 State Highway 148 S 76365 940-476-2215
Randal Beaver, supt. Fax 476-2226
www.midwayisd.net
Midway S 100/PK-12
12142 State Highway 148 S 76365 940-476-2222
Shane Coker, prin. Fax 476-2226

Hereford, Deaf Smith, Pop. 15,284
Hereford ISD 4,300/PK-12
601 N 25 Mile Ave 79045 806-363-7600
Sheri Blankenship, supt. Fax 363-7647
www.herefordisd.net
Aikman ES 400/K-5
900 Avenue K 79045 806-363-7640
Sandy Maldonado, prin. Fax 363-7699
Bluebonnet ES 300/K-5
221 16th St 79045 806-363-7650
Linda Gonzalez, prin. Fax 363-7699
Hereford JHS 600/6-7
704 La Plata St 79045 806-363-7630
Cuca Salinas, prin. Fax 363-7697
Hereford Preparatory Academy 300/8-8
704 La Plata St 79045 806-363-7740
Amy Clifton, prin. Fax 363-7699
Northwest ES 500/K-5
400 Moreman St 79045 806-363-7660
Nancy Neusch, prin. Fax 363-7699
Stanton Learning Center 300/PK-PK
711 E Park Ave 79045 806-363-7610
Brenda Bice, prin. Fax 363-7699
Tierra Blanca ES 300/K-5
615 Columbia Dr 79045 806-363-7680
Ortencia Mendez, prin. Fax 363-7699
West Central ES 300/K-5
120 Campbell St 79045 806-363-7690
Suzanne Gaitan, prin. Fax 363-7699

Walcott ISD 100/PK-6
4275 Highway 214 79045 806-289-5222
Bill McLaughlin, supt. Fax 289-5224
Walcott ES 100/PK-6
4275 Highway 214 79045 806-289-5222
Billy McLaughlin, prin. Fax 289-5224

St. Anthony S 100/PK-6
120 W Park Ave 79045 806-364-1952
Ana Copeland, prin. Fax 364-7179

Hermleigh, Scurry, Pop. 343
Hermleigh ISD 200/PK-12
8010 Business 84 H 79526 325-863-2772
Brent Dawson, supt. Fax 863-2713
www.hermleigh.esc14.net
Hermleigh S 200/PK-12
8010 Business 84 H 79526 325-863-2482
Amber Palmer, prin. Fax 863-2713

Hewitt, McLennan, Pop. 13,309
Midway ISD
Supt. — See Woodway
Castleman Creek ES 500/PK-4
755 S Hewitt Dr 76643 254-761-5755
Mandy Johnson, prin. Fax 761-5759
Hewitt ES 500/PK-4
900 W Panther Way 76643 254-761-5750
Christy Watley, prin. Fax 666-7540
Midway MS 1,200/7-8
800 N Hewitt Dr 76643 254-761-5680
Dr. Herbert Cox, prin. Fax 761-5775
Spring Valley ES 500/PK-4
610 W Spring Valley Rd 76643 254-761-5710
Jay Fischer, prin. Fax 666-4654

Hico, Hamilton, Pop. 1,369
Hico ISD 500/PK-12
PO Box 218 76457 254-796-2181
Jon Hartgraves, supt. Fax 796-2446
www.hico-isd.net
Hico ES 300/PK-5
PO Box 218 76457 254-796-2183
Ben Eubanks, prin. Fax 796-2446

Hidalgo, Hidalgo, Pop. 11,192
Hidalgo ISD 3,200/PK-12
PO Box 8220 78557 956-843-4401
Xavier Salinas, supt. Fax 843-3343
www.hidalgo-isd.com
Diaz JHS 700/6-8
PO Box 8220 78557 956-843-4350
Dr. George Guzman, prin. Fax 843-3198
Hidalgo ES 400/PK-5
PO Box 8220 78557 956-843-4225
Raquel Reyes-Alvarez, prin. Fax 843-3158
Hidalgo Park ES 400/PK-5
PO Box 8220 78557 956-843-4275
Gregorio Solano, prin. Fax 781-4631
Salinas ES 400/PK-5
PO Box 8220 78557 956-843-4251
Jose Esquivel, prin. Fax 843-3357
Other Schools – See Pharr

Valley View ISD
Supt. — See Pharr
Lucas ES 400/PK-4
1300 N McColl St 78557 956-340-1700
Dr. Rosemarie Gomez, prin. Fax 843-3039
Valley View South ES 400/PK-4
900 S McColl St 78557 956-340-1650
Elizabeth Reyes, prin. Fax 843-7787

Higgins, Lipscomb, Pop. 392
Higgins ISD 100/PK-12
PO Box 218 79046 806-852-2631
Michael Lee, supt. Fax 852-3502
www.higginsisd.net
Higgins S 100/PK-12
PO Box 218 79046 806-852-2631
Steve James, supt. Fax 852-3502

High Island, Galveston
High Island ISD 100/PK-12
PO Box 246 77623 409-286-5317
Travis Grubbs, supt. Fax 286-5351
www.highislandisd.com
High Island S 100/PK-12
PO Box 246 77623 409-286-5314
Travis Grubbs, prin. Fax 286-2120

Highlands, Harris, Pop. 7,443
Goose Creek Consolidated ISD
Supt. — See Baytown
Highlands ES 900/2-5
200 E Wallisville Rd 77562 281-420-4900
Edward Villanueva, prin. Fax 426-5099
Highlands JHS 1,100/6-8
1212 E Wallisville Rd 77562 281-420-4695
Gary Guy, prin. Fax 426-4301
Hopper PS 600/PK-1
405 E Houston St 77562 281-420-4685
Maria Rosas, prin. Fax 426-5179

Highland Village, Denton, Pop. 14,764
Lewisville ISD
Supt. — See Flower Mound
Briarhill MS 1,000/6-8
2100 Briarhill Blvd 75077 469-713-5975
Chris Mattingly, prin. Fax 350-9167
Heritage ES 700/PK-5
100 Barnett Dr 75077 469-713-5985
Toby Maxson, prin. Fax 350-9072
Highland Village ES 400/PK-5
301 Brazos Blvd 75077 469-713-5957
Leslye Mitchell, prin. Fax 350-9079
McAuliffe ES 500/PK-5
2300 Briarhill Blvd 75077 469-713-5959
Jennifer Mattingly, prin. Fax 350-9116

Hillsboro, Hill, Pop. 8,341
Hillsboro ISD 1,900/PK-12
121 E Franklin St 76645 254-582-8585
Vicki Adams, supt. Fax 582-4165
www.hillsboroisd.org
Franklin ES 200/PK-PK
103 Country Club Rd 76645 254-582-4130
Tiffanye Oliver, coord. Fax 582-4133
Hillsboro ES 500/K-2
115 Jane Ln 76645 254-582-4140
Robin Ralston, prin. Fax 582-4145
Hillsboro IS 400/3-5
1000 Old Bynum Rd 76645 254-582-4170
Stephanie Tucker, prin. Fax 582-4175
Hillsboro JHS 300/6-8
210 E Walnut St 76645 254-582-4120
Cathryn Patterson, prin. Fax 582-4122

Hitchcock, Galveston, Pop. 6,879
Hitchcock ISD 1,100/PK-12
7801 Neville Ave 77563 409-316-6545
Carla Vickroy, supt. Fax 986-5141
www.hitchcockisd.org
Crosby MS 200/6-8
6625 FM 2004 Rd 77563 409-316-6542
Kellie Edmundson, prin. Fax 986-9254
Hitchcock PS 400/PK-2
5901 FM 2004 Rd 77563 409-316-6467
Angela Mancini, prin. Fax 986-3168
Stewart ES 200/3-5
7013 Stewart St 77563 409-316-6543
Donette Line, prin. Fax 986-5563

Our Lady of Lourdes S 100/PK-6
10114 Highway 6 77563 409-925-3224
Mark Priest, prin. Fax 925-9900

Hockley, Harris
Waller ISD
Supt. — See Waller
Roberts Road ES 500/PK-5
24920 Zube Rd 77447 936-931-0300
Angie Davis, prin. Fax 373-3164
Turlington ES 700/PK-5
23400 Hegar Rd 77447 936-372-0100
Mindy Peper, prin. Fax 372-3868

Holland, Bell, Pop. 1,111
Holland ISD 600/PK-12
PO Box 217 76534 254-657-0175
Cindy Gunn, supt. Fax 657-0172
www.hollandisd.org
Holland ES 300/PK-5
PO Box 217 76534 254-657-2525
Shane Downing, prin. Fax 657-2250
Holland MS 200/6-8
PO Box 217 76534 254-657-2224
Leah Smith, prin. Fax 657-2872

Holliday, Archer, Pop. 1,747
Holliday ISD 900/PK-12
PO Box 689 76366 940-586-1281
Dr. Kevin Dyes, supt. Fax 586-1492
www.hollidayisd.net
Holliday ES 400/PK-5
PO Box 978 76366 940-586-1986
Tara Kirkland, prin. Fax 586-0538
Holliday MS 200/6-8
PO Box 977 76366 940-586-1314
Kelly Carver, prin. Fax 586-4480

Hondo, Medina, Pop. 8,749
Hondo ISD 2,200/PK-12
PO Box 308 78861 830-426-3027
Dr. A'Lann Truelock, supt. Fax 426-7683
www.hondoisd.net
McDowell MS 500/6-8
1602 27th St S 78861 830-426-2261
Scott Backus, prin. Fax 426-7624
Meyer ES 600/PK-2
2502 Avenue Q 78861 830-426-3161
Misty Ptasnik, prin. Fax 426-7679
Woolls IS 500/3-5
2802 Avenue Q 78861 830-426-7666
Steve Ayers, prin. Fax 426-7669

Honey Grove, Fannin, Pop. 1,640
Honey Grove ISD 600/PK-12
1206 17th St 75446 903-378-2264
Todd Morrison, supt. Fax 378-2991
www.honeygroveisd.net/
Honey Grove ES 300/PK-5
1206 17th St 75446 903-378-2264
Catherine Sherwood, prin. Fax 900-4725
Honey Grove MS 100/6-8
1206 17th St 75446 903-378-2264
Lee Frost, prin. Fax 900-4725

Hooks, Bowie, Pop. 2,693
Hooks ISD 900/PK-12
100 E 5th St 75561 903-547-6077
Shane Krueger, supt. Fax 547-2943
www.hooksisd.net
Hooks ES 300/PK-4
401 Precinct Rd 75561 903-547-2291
Kenny Turner, prin. Fax 547-3172
Hooks JHS 300/5-8
3921 FM 560 75561 903-547-2568
Craig Mahar, prin. Fax 547-2595

Leary ISD 100/PK-8
PO Box 519 75561 903-838-8960
Jim Tankersley, supt. Fax 838-6036
www.learyisd.net/
Leary ES 100/PK-8
PO Box 519 75561 903-838-8960
Jennifer Dear, prin. Fax 838-6036

Horizon City, El Paso, Pop. 16,659
Clint ISD
Supt. — See El Paso
Desert Hills ES 1,100/PK-5
300 N Kenazo Ave 79928 915-926-4500
Michael Mackeben, prin. Fax 852-3570
Horizon MS 1,000/6-7
400 N Kenazo Ave 79928 915-926-4700
Veronica Candelaria, prin. Fax 852-9274
Macias ES 1,200/PK-5
14400 Golden Eagle Dr 79928 915-926-4600
Dawn Davis, prin. Fax 852-7547
Welch ES 900/PK-5
14510 McMahon Ave 79928 915-926-4400
Margarita Flores, prin. Fax 852-7230

Houston, Harris, Pop. 2,071,912
Aldine ISD 66,300/PK-12
2520 WW Thorne Blvd 77073 281-449-1011
Dr. Wanda Bamberg, supt. Fax 449-4911
www.aldineisd.org
Aldine MS 900/7-8
14908 Aldine Westfield Rd 77032 281-985-6580
Marcus Pruitt, prin. Fax 985-6480
Anderson Academy 700/1-3
7401 Wheatley St 77088 281-878-0370
Kimberly Martin, prin. Fax 591-8549
Bethune Academy 400/3-4
2500 S Victory Dr 77088 281-878-0380
Dr. Eunetra Simpson, prin. Fax 878-0383
Black ES 800/K-4
160 Mill Stream Ln 77060 281-878-0350
Ash Kirk, prin. Fax 878-0389
Bussey ES 1,100/K-4
11555 Airline Dr 77037 281-878-1501
Kathy Sandoval, prin. Fax 878-1506
Calvert ES 900/K-4
1925 Marvell Dr 77032 281-985-6360
Cheryl LaFleur, prin. Fax 985-6364
Caraway IS 800/5-6
3031 Ellington St 77088 281-878-0320
Todd Roede, prin. Fax 878-0326
Carmichael ES 1,100/K-4
6902 Silver Star Dr 77086 281-878-0345
Monica Stogsdill, prin. Fax 878-0379
Carroll Academy 1,100/K-4
423 W Gulf Bank Rd 77037 281-878-0340
Jennifer Price, prin. Fax 591-8527
Carter Academy 1,000/K-4
3111 Fallbrook Dr 77038 281-878-7760
Lee Wold, prin. Fax 878-7767
Conley ES 900/K-4
3345 W Greens Rd 77066 281-537-5418
LaDon Ward, prin. Fax 895-5005
Cypresswood ES K-4
6901 Cypresswood Point Ave, 281-227-3370
Innetta Carter, prin.
deSantiago ECC 700/PK-PK
1420 Aldine Meadows Rd 77032 281-985-7500
Maria Galindo, prin. Fax 985-7509
Drew Academy 600/7-8
1910 W Little York Rd 77091 281-878-0360
Earnest Washington, prin. Fax 447-4694
Dunn ES 1,000/K-4
2003 WW Thorne Blvd 77073 281-233-4320
Cheryl Davis, prin. Fax 233-4328
Eckert IS 800/5-6
1430 Aldine Meadows Rd 77032 281-985-6380
Mark Herndon, prin. Fax 985-6117
Ermel ES 700/K-4
7103 Woodsman Trl 77040 713-466-5220
Martha Escalante, prin. Fax 856-4256
Escamilla IS 1,000/5-6
5241 Mount Houston Rd 77093 281-985-6390
Susan Rehan, prin. Fax 985-6137
Francis ES 800/K-4
14815 Lee Rd 77032 281-985-6500
Dana Stelly, prin. Fax 985-6504
Garcia-Leza ECC 700/PK-PK
5311 Mount Houston Rd 77093 281-985-6037
Orfelinda Todd, prin. Fax 985-6044
Goodman ES 800/K-4
9325 Deer Trail Dr 77088 281-878-0355
Angeles Perez, prin. Fax 878-0330
Grantham Academy 1,100/7-8
13300 Chrisman Rd 77039 281-985-6590
Jessica Scott, prin. Fax 985-6595
Gray ES 1,000/K-4
700 West Rd 77038 281-878-0660
Scott Dubberke, prin. Fax 878-0664
Greenspoint ES 1-4
18028 Chisholm Tr 77060 281-985-7800
Tami Schuler, prin.
Hambrick MS 1,000/7-8
4600 Aldine Mail Rd 77039 281-985-6570
Rebecca Sanford, prin. Fax 442-9036
Harris Academy 700/K-4
3130 Holder Forest Dr 77088 281-878-7900
Cicely Bailey, prin. Fax 878-7913
Hill IS 800/5-6
2625 W Mount Houston Rd 77038 281-878-7775
Ivan Hepworth, prin. Fax 878-7779
Hinojosa Pre K Center 600/PK-PK
1620 Lauder Rd 77039 281-985-4750
Denise Meister, prin. Fax 985-4754
Hoffman MS 700/7-8
6101 W Little York Rd 77091 713-613-7670
Rosalyn Sweat, prin. Fax 613-7675
Houston Academy 700/5-6
8103 Carver Rd 77088 281-878-7745
Rhonda Shelby, prin. Fax 878-7755
Johnson ES 900/K-4
5801 Hamill Rd 77039 281-985-6510
Pamela Riggans-Johnson, prin. Fax 985-6494
Keeble ECC 900/PK-PK
203 W Gulf Bank Rd 77037 281-878-6860
Andrenetta Marshall, prin. Fax 878-6869

Kujawa ECC 700/PK-PK
7111 Fallbrook Dr 77086 281-878-1514
Andrea Davis, prin. Fax 878-1545
Kujawa ES 900/K-4
7007 Fallbrook Dr 77086 281-878-1530
Debera Thomas, prin. Fax 878-1536
Lewis MS 1,000/7-8
21255 W Hardy Rd 77073 281-209-8257
Cassandra Bell, prin. Fax 209-8267
Marcella IS 800/5-6
16250 Cotillion Dr 77060 281-878-0860
Demedia Edwards, prin. Fax 878-0805
Mendel ES 300/K-4
3735 Topping St 77093 713-694-8002
Karen Wilkerson, prin. Fax 696-4155
Odom ES 800/K-4
14701 Henry Rd 77060 281-878-0390
Delilah St. Julian, prin. Fax 878-0397
Oleson ES 1,000/K-4
12345 Vickery St 77039 281-985-6530
Guadalupe Munoz, prin. Fax 985-6143
Orange Grove ES 900/K-4
4514 Mount Houston Rd 77093 281-985-6540
Kelly James, prin. Fax 985-6544
Parker IS 900/5-6
19850 E Hardy Rd 77073 281-233-8930
Candace Hardin, prin. Fax 233-8935
Plummer MS 900/7-8
11429 Spears Rd 77067 281-539-4000
Andrea Cain, prin. Fax 539-4017
Raymond Academy 1,100/K-4
1605 Connorvale Rd 77039 281-985-6550
Constance White, prin. Fax 985-6555
Reece Academy 700/PK-K
2223 Esther Dr 77088 281-878-0800
Theresa Craft, prin. Fax 878-0808
Reed Academy 900/5-6
1616 Lauder Rd 77039 281-985-6670
Jeana Morrison-Adams, prin. Fax 985-6679
Sammons ES 800/K-4
2301 Frick Rd 77038 281-878-0955
Jose Almendarez, prin. Fax 591-8546
Shotwell MS 1,100/7-8
6515 Trail Valley Way 77086 281-878-0960
Denise Winchester, prin. Fax 591-8564
Smith Academy 600/K-4
5815 W Little York Rd 77091 713-613-7650
Raymond Stubblefield, prin. Fax 613-7653
Spence ES 1,100/K-4
1300 Gears Rd 77067 281-539-4050
Susana Bazan, prin. Fax 539-4054
Stehlik IS 1,000/5-6
400 West Rd 77038 281-878-0300
Christi Van Wassenhove, prin. Fax 878-0305
Stephens ES 1,000/K-4
2402 Aldine Mail Rd 77039 281-985-6560
Shauna Showers, prin. Fax 985-6564
Stovall Academy 600/K-4
3025 Ellington St 77088 281-591-8500
Everette Taylor, prin. Fax 591-8507
Stovall MS 1,000/7-8
11201 Airline Dr 77037 281-878-0670
Elsa Wright, prin. Fax 448-0636
Thompson ES 900/K-4
220 Casa Grande Dr 77060 281-878-0333
Sandra Doria, prin. Fax 878-0339
Vines Pre K Center 600/PK-PK
7220 Inwood Park Dr 77088 281-878-7950
Linda Reed, prin. Fax 878-7959
Wilson IS 1,000/5-6
3131 Fallbrook Dr 77038 281-878-0990
Dana Baker, prin. Fax 878-0995
Worsham ES 900/K-4
3007 Hartwick Rd 77093 281-985-6520
Lidia Calderon, prin. Fax 985-6524
Other Schools – See Humble

Alief ISD 45,800/PK-12
4250 Cook Rd 77072 281-498-8110
H.D. Chambers, supt. Fax 498-8730
www.aliefisd.net
Albright MS 1,300/7-8
6315 Winkleman Rd 77083 281-983-8411
Lori Wyatt, prin. Fax 983-8443
Alexander ES 900/PK-4
8500 Brookwulf Dr 77072 281-983-8300
Kathleen DiFelice, prin. Fax 983-8454
Alief MS 700/7-8
4415 Cook Rd 77072 281-983-8422
David Lopez, prin. Fax 983-8053
Best ES 900/PK-4
10000 Centre Pkwy 77036 713-988-6445
Yvonne Canales, prin. Fax 272-3211
Boone ES 900/PK-4
11400 Bissonnet St 77099 281-983-8308
Angela Chapman, prin. Fax 983-8035
Budewig IS 1,200/5-6
12570 Richmond Ave 77082 281-988-3200
Rosalind Burroughs, prin. Fax 497-7293
Bush ES 1,000/PK-4
9730 Stroud Dr 77036 713-272-3220
Gloria Price, prin. Fax 272-3230
Chambers ES 800/PK-4
10700 Carvel Ln 77072 281-983-8313
Jannae Jernberg, prin. Fax 983-8493
Chancellor ES 700/PK-4
4350 Boone Rd 77072 281-983-8318
Lisa Saarie, prin. Fax 983-8033
Collins ES 1,000/PK-4
9829 Town Park Dr 77036 713-272-3250
Courtney Marshall, prin. Fax 272-3260
Cummings ES 600/PK-4
10455 S Kirkwood Rd 77099 281-983-8328
Jeanette Byrd, prin. Fax 983-8096
Hearne ES 1,200/PK-4
13939 Rio Bonito Rd 77083 281-983-8333
Johanna Sanchez, prin. Fax 983-8060
Heflin ES 700/PK-4
3303 Synott Rd 77082 281-531-1144
Robin Human, prin. Fax 531-3418
Hicks ES 700/PK-4
8520 Hemlock Hill Dr 77083 281-983-8040
Mary Kesler, prin. Fax 983-8064
Holmquist ES 1,200/PK-4
15040 Westpark Dr 77082 281-988-3024
Kimberly Toney, prin. Fax 556-1050
Holub MS 900/7-8
9515 S Dairy Ashford Rd 77099 281-983-8433
Pauline Beckley, prin. Fax 983-8398
Horn ES 1,100/PK-4
10734 Bissonnet St 77099 281-988-3223
Mary Starling, prin. Fax 530-5262
Kennedy ES 800/PK-4
10200 Huntington Place Dr 77099 281-983-8338
Sara Caldwell, prin. Fax 983-8390
Killough MS 1,000/7-8
7600 Synott Rd 77083 281-983-8444
Bert Bilton, prin. Fax 983-8067
Klentzman IS 1,000/5-6
11100 Stancliff Rd 77099 281-983-8477
Courtney Holman, prin. Fax 983-8373
Landis ES 900/PK-4
10255 Spice Ln 77072 281-983-8343
Kelli Upshaw, prin. Fax 983-8072
Liestman ES 900/PK-4
7610 Synott Rd 77083 281-983-8348
Noe Galindo, prin. Fax 983-8086
Mahanay ES 700/PK-4
13215 High Star Dr 77083 281-983-8355
Carmilla Nandlal, prin. Fax 983-8083
Martin ES 900/PK-4
11718 Hendon Ln 77072 281-983-8363
Ting-Ling Sha, prin. Fax 983-7705
Mata IS 800/5-6
9225 S Dairy Ashford Rd 77099 281-983-7800
Amy Coleman, prin. Fax 983-7810
Miller IS 900/5-6
15025 Westpark Dr 77082 281-531-3430
Stacy Frenchwood, prin. Fax 531-3446
O'Donnell MS 1,300/6-8
14041 Alief Clodine Rd 77082 281-495-6000
Andy Velasquez, prin. Fax 568-5029
Olle MS 1,100/7-8
9200 Boone Rd 77099 281-983-8455
Nelda Billescas, prin. Fax 983-8077
Outley ES 1,100/PK-6
12355 Richmond Ave 77082 281-584-0655
Sharonda Newby, prin. Fax 531-3421
Owens IS 1,000/5-6
6900 Turtlewood Dr 77072 281-983-8466
Lorena Augustus, prin. Fax 983-8098
Petrosky ES 700/PK-4
6703 Winkleman Rd 77083 281-983-8366
Bernadette Bentley, prin. Fax 983-7708
Rees ES 700/PK-4
16305 Kensley Dr 77082 281-531-1444
Paul Baez, prin. Fax 531-3429
Smith ES 800/PK-4
11300 Stancliff Rd 77099 281-983-8380
Jennifer Silva, prin. Fax 983-7710
Sneed ES 1,200/PK-4
9855 Pagewood Ln 77042 713-789-6979
Elizabeth Maldonado, prin. Fax 260-7307
Youens ES 1,000/PK-4
12141 High Star Dr 77072 281-983-8383
Tangela Hughes-Beston, prin. Fax 983-8055
Youngblood IS 1,100/5-6
8410 Dairy View Ln 77072 281-983-8020
Gwen Sandles, prin. Fax 983-8051

Channelview ISD
Supt. — See Channelview
Aguirre JHS 900/6-8
15726 Wallisville Rd 77049 281-860-3300
Eric Lathan, prin. Fax 860-3320
Brown ES 800/K-5
16550 Wallisville Rd 77049 281-860-1400
LaKeisha LeBlanc, prin. Fax 860-9916

Clear Creek ISD
Supt. — See League City
Bayou ES 500/PK-5
16000 Hickory Knoll Dr 77059 281-284-5100
Jenny Thomas, prin. Fax 284-5105
Brookwood ES 700/K-5
16850 Middlebrook Dr 77059 281-284-5600
Kathryn Gouger, prin. Fax 284-5605
Clear Lake City ES 600/PK-5
1707 Fairwind Rd 77062 281-284-4200
Jepsey Kimble, prin. Fax 284-4205
Clear Lake IS 1,000/6-8
15545 El Camino Real 77062 281-284-3200
Lonnie Leal, prin. Fax 284-3205
Falcon Pass ES 600/PK-5
2465 Falcon Pass Dr 77062 281-284-6200
Monica Giuffre, prin. Fax 284-6205
North Pointe ES 800/PK-5
3200 Almond Creek Dr 77059 281-284-5900
Jennifer Buckels, prin. Fax 284-5905
Space Center IS 1,100/6-8
17400 Saturn Ln 77058 281-284-3300
Ann Thornton, prin. Fax 284-3305
Ward ES 600/K-5
1440 Bouldercrest Dr 77062 281-284-5400
Sara Konesheck, prin. Fax 284-5405
Weber ES 900/PK-5
11955 Blackhawk Blvd 77089 281-284-6300
Cheryl Chaney, prin. Fax 284-6305
Whitcomb ES 700/PK-5
900 Reseda Dr 77062 281-284-4900
Diana Kattner, prin. Fax 284-4905

Cypress-Fairbanks ISD 110,100/PK-12
PO Box 692003 77269 281-897-4000
Dr. Mark Henry, supt. Fax 897-4125
www.cfisd.net
Adam ES 900/PK-5
11303 Honey Grove Ln 77065 281-897-4485
Beth May, prin. Fax 517-2089
Aragon MS 1,600/6-8
16823 West Rd 77095 281-856-5100
Maria Mamaux, prin. Fax 856-5105
Bane ES 900/PK-5
5805 Kaiser St 77040 713-460-6140
Carrie Marz, prin. Fax 460-7847
Bang ES 1,000/PK-5
8900 Rio Grande Dr 77064 281-897-4760
Erwann Wilson, prin. Fax 517-2095
Birkes ES 1,300/K-5
8500 Queenston Blvd 77095 281-345-3300
Stacie Everson, prin. Fax 345-3305
Bleyl MS 1,600/6-8
10800 Mills Rd 77070 281-897-4340
Stacia Carew, prin. Fax 897-4353
Campbell MS 1,200/6-8
11415 Bobcat Rd 77064 281-897-4300
Laura Perry, prin. Fax 807-8634
Cook MS 1,600/6-8
9111 Wheatland Dr 77064 281-897-4400
Sherma Duck, prin. Fax 897-3850
Copeland ES 1,100/PK-5
18018 Forest Heights Dr 77095 281-856-1400
Ann Melancon, prin. Fax 463-5510
Danish ES 1,000/K-5
11850 Fallbrook Dr 77065 281-955-4981
Kelly Dalton, prin. Fax 955-4994
Dean MS 1,500/6-8
14104 Reo St 77040 713-460-6153
Heather Bergman, prin. Fax 460-6197
Emmott ES 800/PK-5
11750 Steeple Way Blvd 77065 281-897-4500
Jessica Hernandez, prin. Fax 897-3888
Fiest ES 1,100/PK-5
8425 Pine Falls Dr 77095 281-463-5838
Dr. Jeanette Gerault, prin. Fax 856-1174
Francone ES 1,000/PK-5
11250 Perry Rd 77064 281-897-4512
Tonya Goree, prin. Fax 897-4518
Frazier ES 1,100/PK-5
8300 Little River Rd 77064 713-896-3475
Gloria Vasquez, prin. Fax 896-5013
Gleason ES 900/PK-5
9203 Willowbridge Park Blvd 77064 281-517-6800
Christine Melancon, prin. Fax 517-6805
Hairgrove ES 900/PK-5
7120 N Eldridge Pkwy 77041 713-896-5015
Darynda Klein, prin. Fax 896-5020
Hancock ES 1,100/PK-5
13801 Schroeder Rd 77070 281-897-4523
Lissa Archuletta, prin. Fax 807-8166
Holbrook ES 1,100/PK-5
6402 Langfield Rd 77092 713-460-6165
Yvette Garcia, prin. Fax 460-7866
Holmsley ES 900/PK-5
7315 Hudson Oaks Dr 77095 281-463-5885
Ana Diaz, prin. Fax 463-5529
Horne ES 1,100/PK-5
14950 W Little York Rd 77084 281-463-5954
Stephanie Thomas, prin. Fax 856-1451
Kahla MS 1,500/6-8
16212 W Little York Rd 77084 281-345-3260
Virgil Maddox, prin. Fax 345-5275
Kirk ES 1,000/PK-5
12421 Tanner Rd 77041 713-849-8250
Onica Mayers, prin. Fax 849-8255
Labay MS 1,500/6-8
15435 Willow River Dr 77095 281-463-5800
Lanette Bellamy, prin. Fax 463-5804
Lee ES 800/K-5
12900 W Little York Rd 77041 713-849-8281
Susan Epperson, prin. Fax 849-8249
Lieder ES 1,000/PK-5
17003 Kieth Harrow Blvd 77084 281-463-5928
Dr. Karen Stockton, prin. Fax 463-5531
Lowery ES 900/PK-5
15950 Ridge Park Dr 77095 281-463-5900
April Wright, prin. Fax 463-5516
Matzke ES 900/PK-5
13102 Jones Rd 77070 281-897-4450
Cathy Jacobs, prin. Fax 897-4454
Metcalf ES 1,000/PK-5
6100 Queenston Blvd 77084 281-856-1152
John Steward, prin. Fax 856-1154
Moore ES 900/K-5
13734 Lakewood Forest Dr 77070 281-370-4040
Patricia Myers, prin. Fax 320-7978
Owens ES 1,000/PK-5
7939 Jackrabbit Rd 77095 281-463-5915
Amy Frank, prin. Fax 463-5526
Post ES 1,100/PK-5
7600 Equador St 77040 713-896-3488
Tomicka Williams, prin. Fax 896-3497
Reed ES 1,000/PK-5
8700 Tami Renee Ln 77040 713-896-5035
Kandy Bond, prin. Fax 896-5051
Tipps ES 1,100/K-5
5611 Queenston Blvd 77084 281-345-3350
Kari Hough, prin. Fax 345-3355
Truitt MS 1,400/6-8
6600 Addicks Satsuma Rd 77084 281-856-1100
Teresa Baranowski, prin. Fax 856-1104
Watkins MS 1,300/6-8
4800 Cairnvillage St 77084 281-463-5850
Dr. Jose Martinez, prin. Fax 856-1565
Willbern ES 1,000/PK-5
10811 Goodspring Dr 77064 281-897-3820
Connie Roberson, prin. Fax 517-2162
Wilson ES 1,000/K-5
18015 Kieth Harrow Blvd 77084 281-463-5941
Tamara Felder, prin. Fax 463-5944

Yeager ES 1,000/PK-5
13615 Champion Forest Dr 77069 281-440-4914
Laura Barrett, prin. Fax 587-7516
Other Schools – See Cypress, Katy

Fort Bend ISD
Supt. — See Sugar Land
Blue Ridge ES 600/PK-5
6241 McHard Rd 77053 281-634-4520
Heather Welker, prin. Fax 634-4533
Fleming ES 700/PK-5
14850 Bissonnet St 77083 281-634-4600
Jason Soileau, prin. Fax 634-4615
Hodges Bend MS 1,200/6-8
16510 Bissonnet St 77083 281-634-3000
Dr. Ashley Causey, prin. Fax 634-3028
Holley ES 800/PK-5
16655 Bissonnet St 77083 281-634-3850
Laureen Sanford, prin. Fax 634-3856
McAuliffe MS 800/6-8
16650 S Post Oak Rd 77053 281-634-3360
Andre Roberson, prin. Fax 634-3393
Mission Bend ES 800/PK-5
16200 Beechnut St 77083 281-634-4240
Anna Hinojosa, prin. Fax 634-4250
Mission Glen ES 500/PK-5
16053 Mission Glen Dr 77083 281-634-4280
Dr. Yvette Blake, prin. Fax 634-4296
Mission West ES 800/PK-5
7325 Clodine Reddick Rd 77083 281-634-4320
Rhonda Mason, prin. Fax 634-4334
Ridgegate ES 700/PK-5
6015 W Ridgecreek Dr 77053 281-634-4840
Felicia Holmes, prin. Fax 634-4855
Ridgemont ES 900/PK-5
4910 Raven Ridge Dr 77053 281-634-4880
Stephanie Houston, prin. Fax 634-4896

Galena Park ISD 22,500/PK-12
14705 Woodforest Blvd 77015 832-386-1000
Dr. Angi Williams, supt. Fax 386-1298
tx02217083.schoolwires.net
Cimarron ES 800/PK-5
816 Cimarron St 77015 832-386-3240
Cynthia Galaviz, prin. Fax 386-3241
Cloverleaf ES 900/PK-5
1035 Frankie St 77015 832-386-3200
Lee Brown, prin. Fax 386-3201
Cobb Sixth Grade Campus 1,200/6-6
6722 Uvalde Rd 77049 832-386-2100
Fax 386-2101
Cunningham MS 900/7-8
14110 Wallisville Rd 77049 832-386-4470
Shaunte Morris, prin. Fax 386-4471
Green Valley ES 800/PK-5
13350 Woodforest Blvd 77015 832-386-4390
Grace Devost, prin. Fax 386-4391
Havard ES 700/PK-5
15150 Wallisville Rd 77049 832-386-3710
Toshia Gouard, prin. Fax 386-3711
Houston ES 800/PK-5
4101 E Sam Houston Pkwy N 77015 832-386-4430
Michelle Cavazos, prin. Fax 386-4431
Jacinto City ES 900/PK-5
10910 Wiggins St 77029 832-386-4600
Rebecca Gardea, prin. Fax 386-4601
Normandy Crossing ES 600/PK-5
12500 Normandy Crossing Dr 77015 832-386-1600
Irene Benzor, prin. Fax 386-1642
North Shore ES 900/PK-5
14310 Duncannon Dr 77015 832-386-4660
Esmeralda Perez, prin. Fax 386-4661
North Shore MS 1,300/7-8
120 Castlegory Rd 77015 832-386-2600
James Cline, prin. Fax 386-2643
Purple Sage ES 500/PK-5
6500 Purple Sage Rd 77049 832-386-3100
W. Magee, prin. Fax 386-3106
Pyburn ES 700/PK-5
12302 Coulson St 77015 832-386-3150
Conrad Rivera, prin. Fax 386-3168
Tice ES 700/PK-5
14120 Wallisville Rd 77049 832-386-4050
Aronda Green, prin. Fax 386-4053
Williamson ES 700/PK-5
6720 New Forest Pkwy 77049 832-386-4000
J. Sutton, prin. Fax 386-4025
Woodland Acres ES 400/PK-5
12936 Sarahs Ln 77015 832-386-2220
Sandra Rodriguez, prin. Fax 386-2221
Woodland Acres MS 500/6-8
12947 Myrtle Ln 77015 832-386-4700
A. Gonzalez, prin. Fax 386-4701
Other Schools – See Galena Park

Houston ISD 211,000/PK-12
4400 W 18th St 77092 713-556-6000
Richard Carranza, supt. Fax 556-6323
www.houstonisd.org
Alcott ES 400/PK-5
5859 Bellfort St 77033 713-732-3540
Dimitrie Rainey, prin. Fax 732-3542
Almeda ES 800/PK-5
14226 Almeda School Rd 77047 713-434-5620
Gerardo Medina, prin. Fax 434-5622
Anderson ES 600/PK-5
5727 Ludington Dr 77035 713-726-3600
Roslyn Vaughn, prin. Fax 726-3603
Arabic Immersion Magnet S PK-2
812 W 28th St 77008 713-556-8940
Mahassen Ballouli, prin. Fax 556-8944
Ashford ES 500/PK-3
1815 Shannon Valley Dr 77077 281-368-2120
Valarie Sikes, prin. Fax 368-2123
Askew ES 900/PK-5
11200 Wood Lodge Dr 77077 281-368-2100
Ebony Cumby, prin. Fax 368-2103
Atherton ES 500/PK-6
2011 Solo St 77020 713-671-4100
Albert Lemons, prin. Fax 671-4104
Attucks MS 500/6-8
4330 Bellfort St 77051 713-732-3670
Renita Perry, prin. Fax 732-3677
Barrick ES 700/PK-5
12001 Winfrey Ln 77076 281-405-2500
Yolanda Garrido, prin. Fax 405-2502
Bastian ES 700/PK-5
5051 Bellfort St 77033 713-732-5830
Everett Hare, prin. Fax 732-3552
Baylor College of Medicine Academy 200/6-8
2610 Elgin St 77004 713-942-1932
Jyoti Malhan, prin. Fax 942-1943
Baylor Coll of Medicine Biotech Academy 500/PK-8
2805 Garrow St 77003 713-226-4543
Jesus Herrera, prin. Fax 226-4546
Bell ES 800/PK-5
12323 Shaftsbury Dr 77031 281-983-2800
Brishaun Sutton, prin. Fax 983-2802
Bellfort ECC 400/PK-K
7647 Bellfort St 77061 713-640-0950
Cheryl Lewis, prin. Fax 640-0957
Benavidez ES 900/PK-5
6262 Gulfton St 77081 713-778-3350
Zabeth Parra-Malek, prin. Fax 778-3358
Benbrook ES 600/PK-5
4026 Bolin Rd 77092 713-613-2502
Dana Darden, prin. Fax 613-2281
Berry ES 700/PK-5
2310 Berry Rd 77093 713-696-2700
Armando Lujan, prin. Fax 696-2701
Black MS 800/6-8
1575 Chantilly Ln 77018 713-613-2505
Paolo Castagnoli, prin. Fax 613-2233
Blackshear ES 300/PK-6
2900 Holman St 77004 713-942-1481
Alicia Lewis, prin. Fax 942-1486
Bonham ES 1,100/PK-5
8302 Braes River Dr 77074 713-778-3480
Anna White, prin. Fax 778-3482
Bonner ES 1,000/PK-5
8100 Elrod St 77017 713-943-5740
Franklin Cahuasqui, prin. Fax 943-5741
Braeburn ES 900/PK-5
7707 Rampart St 77081 713-295-5210
Santos Reyes, prin. Fax 295-5289
Briargrove ES 900/PK-5
6145 San Felipe St 77057 713-917-3600
Thayer Hutcheson, prin. Fax 917-3601
Briarmeadow Charter S 600/PK-8
3601 Dunvale Rd 77063 713-458-5500
Peter Heinze, prin. Fax 458-5506
Briscoe ES 400/PK-6
321 Forest Hill Blvd 77011 713-924-1740
Daniel Hernandez, prin. Fax 924-1742
Brookline ES 1,000/PK-5
6301 South Loop E 77087 713-845-7400
Rick Nagir, prin. Fax 847-4717
Browning ES 600/PK-5
607 Northwood St 77009 713-867-5140
Julia Elizondo, prin. Fax 867-5148
Bruce ES 600/PK-6
510 Jensen Dr 77020 713-226-4560
Raquel Sosa-Gonzalez, prin. Fax 226-4562
Burbank ES 900/PK-5
216 Tidwell Rd 77022 713-696-2690
Diego Calderon-Duran, prin. Fax 696-2691
Burbank MS 1,400/6-8
315 Berry Rd 77022 713-696-2720
David Knittle, prin. Fax 696-2723
Burnet ES 500/PK-6
5403 Canal St 77011 713-924-1780
Cynthia Galaviz, prin. Fax 924-1783
Burrus ES 400/PK-5
701 E 33rd St 77022 713-867-5180
Jessie Woods, prin. Fax 867-5182
Bush ES 800/PK-5
13800 Westerloch Dr 77077 281-368-2150
Theresa Rose, prin. Fax 368-2153
Cage ES 600/PK-5
4528 Leeland St 77023 713-924-1700
Jose Covarrubia, prin. Fax 924-1704
Carrillo ES 600/PK-5
960 S Wayside Dr 77023 713-924-1870
Mary Hallinan, prin. Fax 924-1873
Clifton MS 900/6-8
6001 Golden Forest Dr 77092 713-613-2516
Georgina Castilleja, prin. Fax 613-2523
Codwell ES 600/PK-5
5225 Tavenor Ln 77048 713-732-3580
Kristy Love, prin. Fax 732-3582
Cook ES 800/PK-5
7115 Lockwood Dr 77016 713-636-6040
Lysette Cooper, prin. Fax 636-6088
Coop ES 800/PK-5
10130 Aldine Westfield Rd 77093 713-696-2630
Tudon Martinez, prin. Fax 696-2633
Cornelius ES 900/PK-5
7475 Westover St 77087 713-845-7405
Angel Wilson, prin. Fax 845-7448
Crespo ES 1,000/PK-5
7500 Office City Dr 77012 713-845-7492
Mayra Ramon, prin. Fax 847-4716
Crockett ES 500/PK-5
2112 Crockett St 77007 713-802-4780
Priscilla Rivas, prin. Fax 802-4783
Cullen MS 700/6-8
6900 Scott St 77021 713-746-8180
Clayton Crook, prin. Fax 746-8181
Cunningham ES 800/PK-5
5100 Gulfton St 77081 713-295-5223
Enrique Cruz, prin. Fax 668-6217
Daily ES 700/PK-5
12909 Briar Forest Dr 77077 281-368-2111
Stephanie Rhodes, prin. Fax 368-7463
Davila ES 500/PK-5
7610 Dahlia St 77012 713-924-1851
Berzayda Ochoa, prin. Fax 924-1853
Deady MS 900/6-8
2500 Broadway St 77012 713-845-7411
Edward Cuevas, prin. Fax 649-5816
DeAnda ES 800/PK-5
7980 Almeda Genoa Rd 77075 713-556-9550
Lauren Mailhiot, prin. Fax 556-9552
DeChaumes ES 800/PK-5
155 Cooper Rd 77076 713-696-2676
Elizabeth Garcia, prin. Fax 696-2680
De Zavala ES 600/PK-5
7521 Avenue H 77012 713-924-1888
Victoria Orozco-Martinez, prin. Fax 924-1891
Dogan ES 600/PK-6
4202 Liberty Rd 77026 713-671-4110
Sandra Menxueiro, prin. Fax 671-4142
Durham ES 500/PK-5
4803 Brinkman St 77018 713-613-2527
Amy Poerschke, prin. Fax 613-2515
Durkee ES 700/PK-5
7301 Nordling Rd 77076 713-696-2835
Irma Sandate, prin. Fax 696-2837
Edison MS 700/6-8
6901 Avenue I 77011 713-924-1800
Richard Smith, prin. Fax 924-1316
Eliot ES 600/PK-5
6411 Laredo St 77020 713-671-3670
Zandra Aguilar, prin. Fax 671-3676
Elmore ES 800/K-5
8200 Tate St 77028 713-672-7466
Joyce Fugit, prin. Fax 671-3565
Elrod ES 700/PK-5
6230 Dumfries Dr 77096 713-778-3330
Leigh Curry, prin. Fax 778-3333
Emerson ES 900/PK-5
9533 Skyline Dr 77063 713-917-3630
Alexander Rodriguez, prin. Fax 917-3634
Farias ECC 400/PK-PK
515 E Rittenhouse St 77076 713-691-8730
Maria Solis, prin. Fax 691-8746
Field ES 500/PK-5
703 E 17th St 77008 713-867-5190
John Hendrickson, prin. Fax 867-5194
Fleming MS 500/6-8
4910 Collingsworth St 77026 713-671-4170
Sabrina Cuby-King, prin. Fax 671-4176
Foerster ES 700/PK-5
14200 Fonmeadow Dr 77035 713-726-3604
Alicia Craig, prin. Fax 726-3629
Fondren ES 500/PK-6
12405 Carlsbad St 77085 713-726-3611
Tabitha Dudley, prin. Fax 726-3646
Fondren MS 800/6-8
6333 S Braeswood Blvd 77096 713-778-3360
Latonya Hodge, prin. Fax 778-3362
Fonville MS 1,100/6-8
725 E Little York Rd 77076 713-696-2825
Paula Pierre, prin. Fax 696-2829
Fonwood ECC 500/PK-PK
9709 Mesa Dr 77078 713-633-0781
Kimberly Agnew, prin. Fax 636-7940
Forest Brook MS 1,000/6-8
7525 Tidwell Rd 77016 713-631-7720
Tannisha Gentry, prin. Fax 636-4114
Foster ES 400/PK-5
3919 Ward St 77021 713-746-8260
Traci Lightfoot, prin. Fax 746-8263
Franklin ES 500/PK-6
7101 Canal St 77011 713-924-1820
Wilfredo Montanez, prin. Fax 924-1823
Frost ES 600/PK-5
5002 Almeda Genoa Rd 77048 713-732-3490
David Terrell, prin. Fax 732-3498
Gallegos ES 500/PK-5
7415 Harrisburg Blvd 77011 713-924-1830
Jessica Tejada, prin. Fax 924-1833
Garcia ES 700/PK-5
9550 Aldine Westfield Rd 77093 713-696-2900
Linda Bellard, prin. Fax 696-2904
Garden Oaks ES 700/PK-8
901 Sue Barnett Dr 77018 713-696-2930
Lindsey Pollock, prin. Fax 696-2932
Garden Villas ES 800/PK-5
7185 Santa Fe Dr 77061 713-845-7484
Kimberly Thompson, prin. Fax 847-4714
Golfcrest ES 800/PK-5
7414 Fairway Dr 77087 713-845-7425
Bertha Espinosa-Garza, prin. Fax 847-4705
Gregg ES 500/PK-5
6701 Roxbury Rd 77087 713-845-7432
David Jackson, prin. Fax 847-4708
Gregory-Lincoln Education Center 700/PK-8
1101 Taft St 77019 713-942-1400
Alecia Bell, prin. Fax 942-1406
Grissom ES 600/PK-5
4900 Simsbrook Dr 77045 713-434-5660
Diana Fernandez-Chavez, prin. Fax 434-5664
Gross ES 700/PK-5
12583 S Gessner Rd 77071 713-778-8450
Traci Hart-Jackson, prin. Fax 778-8454
Halpin ECC 500/PK-K
10901 Sandpiper Dr 77096 713-778-6720
Constance Lathan, prin. Fax 778-6724
Hamilton MS 1,300/6-8
139 E 20th St 77008 713-802-4725
Wendy Hampton, prin. Fax 802-4731
Harris ES 600/PK-5
801 Broadway St 77012 713-924-1860
Judith Garcia, prin. Fax 924-1863
Harris ES 600/PK-5
1262 Mae Dr 77015 713-450-7100
Adelina Alcala, prin. Fax 450-7103
Hartman MS 1,400/6-8
7111 Westover St 77087 713-845-7435
Gerrol Johnson, prin. Fax 847-4706

Hartsfield ES 400/PK-5
5001 Perry St 77021 713-746-8280
Travis Johnson, prin. Fax 746-8283
Harvard ES 700/PK-5
810 Harvard St 77007 713-867-5210
Laura Alaniz, prin. Fax 867-5215
Helms ES 500/PK-5
503 W 21st St 77008 713-867-5130
Dolores Lasheras, prin. Fax 867-5133
Henderson ES 800/PK-5
1800 Dismuke St 77023 713-924-1730
Maria Barrientos, prin. Fax 924-1735
Henderson North ES 400/PK-6
701 Solo St 77020 713-671-4195
Erika Kimble, prin. Fax 671-4197
Henry MS 900/6-8
10702 E Hardy Rd 77093 713-696-2650
Kenneth Brantley, prin. Fax 696-2657
Herod ES 800/PK-5
5627 Jason St 77096 713-778-3315
Michelle Turek, prin. Fax 778-3317
Herrera ES 900/PK-5
525 Bennington St 77022 713-696-2800
Christopher Carnes, prin. Fax 696-2804
Highland Heights ES 600/PK-5
865 Paul Quinn St 77091 713-696-2920
Geraldine Cox, prin. Fax 696-2922
High School Ahead Academy 300/6-8
5320 Yale St 77091 713-696-2643
Yolanda Jones, prin. Fax 696-2999
Hilliard ES 900/K-5
8115 E Houston Rd 77028 713-635-3085
Edrick Moultry, prin. Fax 636-7905
Hines-Caldwell ES 800/PK-5
5515 W Orem Dr 77085 713-726-3700
Torrye Hooper, prin.
Hobby ES 800/PK-5
4021 Woodmont Dr 77045 713-434-5650
Isaac Daniels, prin. Fax 434-5652
Hogg MS 700/6-8
1100 Merrill St 77009 713-802-4700
Angela Sugarek, prin. Fax 802-4708
Holland MS 700/6-8
1600 Gellhorn Dr 77029 713-671-3860
Lashonda Bilbo-Ervin, prin. Fax 671-3874
Isaacs ES 400/PK-6
3830 Pickfair St 77026 713-671-4120
Rosemarie Cumings, prin. Fax 671-4122
Janowski ES 600/PK-5
7500 Bauman Rd 77022 713-696-2844
Myrna Bazan, prin. Fax 696-2847
Jefferson ES 500/PK-5
5000 Sharman St 77009 713-696-2778
Lilly Rincon, prin. Fax 696-2784
Kashmere Gardens ES 400/PK-6
4901 Lockwood Dr 77026 713-671-4160
Regnald Bush, prin. Fax 671-4163
Kelso ES 400/PK-5
5800 Southmund St 77033 713-845-7451
Myra Castle, prin. Fax 847-4710
Kennedy ES 800/PK-6
400 Victoria Dr 77022 713-696-2686
Diana Lum, prin. Fax 696-2689
Ketelsen ES 500/K-5
600 Quitman St 77009 713-220-5050
Cynthia Banda, prin. Fax 220-5074
Key MS 700/6-8
4000 Kelley St 77026 713-636-6000
Joseph Williams, prin. Fax 636-6008
King ECC 400/PK-PK
3930 W Fuqua St 77045 713-797-7900
Tremeka Collins, prin. Fax 797-7904
Kolter ES 600/PK-5
9710 Runnymeade Dr 77096 713-726-3630
Julianne Dickinson, prin. Fax 726-3663
Lanier MS 1,400/6-8
2600 Woodhead St 77098 713-942-1900
Katherine Bradarich, prin. Fax 942-1907
Lantrip ES 800/PK-6
100 Telephone Rd 77023 713-924-1670
Magdalena Strickland, prin. Fax 924-1672
Las Americas MS 200/4-8
6501 Bellaire Blvd 77074 713-773-5300
Maria Moreno, prin. Fax 773-5303
Laurenzo ECC 300/PK-K
205 N Delmar St 77011 713-924-0350
Carmen Lopez-Rogina, prin. Fax 924-0390
Law ES 800/PK-5
12401 S Coast Dr 77047 713-732-3630
Hannah Harvey, prin. Fax 732-3633
Lawson MS 1,100/6-8
14000 Stancliff St 77045 713-434-5600
Kasey Bailey, prin. Fax 434-5608
Lewis ES 1,000/PK-5
6745 Tipperary Ln 77061 713-845-7453
Marlen Martinez, prin. Fax 847-4711
Lockhart ES 700/PK-5
3200 Rosedale St 77004 713-942-1950
Monica Cooper, prin. Fax 942-1953
Longfellow ES 700/K-5
3617 Norris Dr 77025 713-295-5268
Katherine Keafer, prin. Fax 295-5257
Looscan ES 500/PK-5
3800 Robertson St 77009 713-696-2760
Erin Chavez, prin. Fax 696-2765
Love ES 500/PK-5
1120 W 13th St 77008 713-867-0840
Robert Chavarria, prin. Fax 867-0841
Lovett ES 700/K-5
8814 S Rice Ave 77096 713-295-5258
Dawn Thompson, prin. Fax 295-5291
Lyons ES 1,000/PK-5
800 Roxella St 77076 713-696-2870
Cecilia Gonzales, prin. Fax 696-2877
MacGregor ES 500/PK-5
4801 La Branch St 77004 713-942-1990
Tara Garrett, prin. Fax 942-1993

Mading ES 600/PK-5
8511 Crestmont St 77033 713-732-3560
Nicole Haskins, prin. Fax 732-3563
Mandarin Immersion Magnet S 300/PK-7
5445 W Alabama St 77056 713-295-5276
Chaolin Chang, prin. Fax 662-3527
Marshall ES 800/K-5
6200 Winfield Rd 77050 713-636-4606
Jane Ocanas, prin. Fax 986-6475
Marshall MS 1,000/6-8
1115 Noble St 77009 713-226-2600
Benjamin Hernandez, prin. Fax 226-2605
Martinez ES 600/PK-5
901 Hays St 77009 713-224-1424
Rita Sotelo, prin. Fax 224-1304
Martinez ES 500/PK-5
7211 Market St 77020 713-671-3680
Philip Steuernagel, prin. Fax 671-3684
McGowen ES 400/PK-6
6820 Homestead Rd 77028 713-636-6982
Jeffrey Whitaker, prin. Fax 636-6983
McNamara ES 800/PK-5
8714 McAvoy Dr 77074 713-778-3460
Tiffany Chenier, prin. Fax 778-3431
McReynolds MS 600/6-8
5910 Market St 77020 713-671-3650
Steven Stapleton, prin. Fax 671-3657
Memorial ES 400/PK-5
6401 Arnot St 77007 713-867-5150
Maria Garcia, prin. Fax 867-5151
Meyerland MS 1,700/6-8
10410 Manhattan Dr 77096 713-726-3616
Jose Sarabia, prin. Fax 726-3622
Milne ES 700/PK-5
7800 Portal Dr 77071 713-778-3420
Terese Pollard, prin. Fax 778-3424
Mistral ECC 400/PK-K
6203 Jessamine St 77081 713-773-6253
Kristina Troutman, prin. Fax 773-6257
Mitchell ES 500/PK-5
10900 Gulfdale Dr 77075 713-991-8190
Elizabeth Castillo, prin. Fax 991-8193
Montgomery ES 600/PK-5
4000 Simsbrook Dr 77045 713-434-5640
Faye McNeil, prin. Fax 434-5643
Moreno ES 800/PK-5
620 E Canino Rd 77037 281-405-2150
Adriana Abarca-Castro, prin. Fax 405-2176
Navarro MS 900/6-8
5100 Polk St 77023 713-924-1760
Kelly Pichon, prin. Fax 924-1768
Neff ECC 600/PK-1
8200 Carvel Ln 77036 713-778-3470
Gerardo Leal, prin. Fax 778-3473
Neff ES 700/2-5
8301 Neff St 77036 713-556-9566
Amanda Wingard, prin. Fax 556-9567
Northline ES 600/PK-5
821 E Witcher Ln 77076 713-696-2890
Diana DeLaRosa, prin. Fax 696-2894
Oak Forest ES 800/K-5
1401 W 43rd St 77018 713-613-2536
April Williams, prin. Fax 613-2244
Oates ES 400/PK-6
10044 Wallisville Rd 77013 713-671-3800
Maria Palacios, prin. Fax 671-3803
Ortiz MS 1,000/6-8
6767 Telephone Rd 77061 713-845-5650
Noelia Longoria, prin. Fax 845-5646
Osborne ES 400/PK-5
800 Ringold St 77088 281-405-2525
Jacqueline Parnell, prin. Fax 405-2528
Paige ES 400/PK-5
7501 Curry Rd 77093 713-696-2855
Iliana Salinas, prin. Fax 696-2858
Parker ES 800/PK-5
10626 Atwell Dr 77096 713-726-3634
Lori Frodine, prin. Fax 726-3660
Park Place ES 1,000/PK-5
8235 Park Place Blvd 77017 713-845-7458
Nirmol Lim, prin. Fax 845-7460
Patterson ES 1,000/PK-5
5302 Allendale Rd 77017 713-943-5750
Juan Gonzalez, prin. Fax 943-5755
Peck ES 600/PK-5
5001 Martin Luther King Jr 77021 713-845-7463
Carlotta Brown, prin. Fax 847-4701
Pershing MS 1,700/6-8
3838 Blue Bonnet Blvd 77025 713-295-5240
Steven Shetzer, prin. Fax 295-5252
Petersen ES 600/PK-6
14404 Waterloo Dr 77045 713-434-5630
Danitra Arredondo, prin. Fax 434-5634
Pilgrim Academy 1,100/PK-8
6302 Skyline Dr 77057 713-458-4672
Diana Castillo, prin. Fax 458-4693
Piney Point ES 1,200/PK-5
8921 Pagewood Ln 77063 713-917-3610
Bobbie Swaby, prin. Fax 917-3613
Pleasantville ES 300/PK-5
1431 Gellhorn Dr 77029 713-671-3840
Gwendolyn Hunter, prin. Fax 671-3844
Poe ES 800/PK-5
5100 Hazard St 77098 713-535-3780
Jeffrey Amerson, prin. Fax 535-3784
Port Houston ES 300/PK-6
1800 Mccarty St 77029 713-671-3890
Victor Garcia, prin. Fax 671-3893
Project Chrysalis MS 200/6-8
4528 Leeland St 77023 713-924-1700
Jose Covarrubia, prin. Fax 924-1704
Pugh ES 400/PK-5
1147 Kress St 77020 713-671-3820
Jason Davila, prin. Fax 671-3825
Reagan S 1,200/PK-8
4842 Anderson Rd 77053 713-556-9575
Tabitha Davis, prin. Fax 556-9576

Red ES 600/PK-5
4520 Tonawanda Dr 77035 713-726-3638
Melissa Alvarez, prin. Fax 726-3698
Revere MS 1,200/6-8
10502 Briar Forest Dr 77042 713-917-3500
Christian Delariva, prin. Fax 917-3505
Reynolds ES 500/PK-5
9601 Rosehaven Dr 77051 713-731-5590
Rhonda Honore, prin. Fax 731-5598
Rice S 1,200/K-8
7550 Seuss Dr 77025 713-349-1800
Kimberly Hobbs, prin. Fax 349-1828
River Oaks ES 700/PK-5
2008 Kirby Dr 77019 713-942-1460
Keri Fovargue, prin. Fax 942-1463
Roberts ES 800/PK-5
6000 Greenbriar St 77030 713-295-5272
Trealla Epps, prin. Fax 295-5282
Robinson ES 700/PK-5
12425 Wood Forest Dr 77013 713-450-7108
Paige Fernandez, prin. Fax 450-7129
Rodriguez ES 1,000/PK-5
5858 Chimney Rock Rd 77081 713-295-3870
Elena Martinez Buley, prin. Fax 295-3875
Rogers S 800/K-12
5840 San Felipe St 77057 713-917-3565
David Muzyka, prin. Fax 917-3555
Roosevelt ES 700/PK-5
6700 Fulton St 77022 713-696-2820
Mar Azcarraga, prin. Fax 696-2821
Ross ES 400/PK-5
2819 Bay St 77026 713-226-4550
Erica Carter, prin. Fax 226-4554
Rucker ES 600/PK-5
5201 Vinett St 77017 713-845-7467
Bernadette Blanco, prin. Fax 845-5083
Sanchez ES 600/PK-5
2700 Berkley St 77012 713-845-7472
Emeterio Cruz, prin. Fax 847-4755
Scarborough ES 800/PK-5
3021 Little York Rd 77093 713-696-2710
Miriam Medina, prin. Fax 696-2712
School at St. George Place 800/PK-5
5430 Hidalgo St 77056 713-625-1499
Dave Wheat, prin. Fax 985-7455
Scroggins ES 600/PK-5
400 Boyles St 77020 713-671-4130
Brenda Garcia-Salazar, prin. Fax 671-4133
Seguin ES 700/PK-5
5905 Waltrip St 77087 713-845-5600
Nora Sada, prin. Fax 845-5615
Shadowbriar ES 400/PK-5
2650 Shadowbriar Dr 77077 281-368-2160
Mark Samuel, prin. Fax 368-2170
Shadydale ES 800/PK-5
5905 Tidwell Rd 77016 713-633-5150
Tammie Daily, prin. Fax 636-7925
Shearn ES 600/PK-5
9802 Stella Link Rd 77025 713-295-5236
Mayra Romero, prin. Fax 295-5253
Sherman ES 600/PK-5
1909 McKee St 77009 713-226-2627
Melba Johnson, prin. Fax 236-8417
Sinclair ES 500/K-5
6410 Grovewood Ln 77008 713-867-5161
Lee Mashburn, prin. Fax 867-5162
Smith ES 800/PK-5
4802 Chrystell Ln 77092 713-613-2542
Dr. Queinnise Miller, prin. Fax 613-2578
Southmayd ES 700/PK-5
1800 Coral St 77012 713-924-1720
Siomara Saenz-Phillips, prin. Fax 924-1722
Stevens ES 700/PK-5
1910 Lamonte Ln 77018 713-613-2546
Lucy Anderson, prin. Fax 613-2541
Stevenson MS 1,400/6-8
9595 Winkler Dr 77017 713-943-5700
Ruth Ruiz, prin. Fax 943-5711
Sugar Grove MS 700/6-8
8405 Bonhomme Rd 77074 713-271-0214
Eric Tingle, prin. Fax 771-9342
Sutton ES 1,100/PK-5
7402 Albacore Dr 77074 713-778-3400
Luis Landa, prin. Fax 778-3407
Tanglewood MS 600/6-8
5215 San Felipe St 77056 713-625-1411
Gretchen Kasper-Hoffman, prin. Fax 625-1415
Thomas MS 500/6-8
5655 Selinsky Rd 77048 713-732-3500
Connie Smith, prin. Fax 732-3511
Thompson ES 600/PK-5
6121 Tierwester St 77021 713-746-8250
Tanya Edwards, prin. Fax 746-8253
Tijerina ES 500/PK-6
6501 Sherman St 77011 713-924-1790
Richard Pena, prin. Fax 924-1792
Tinsley ES 800/1-5
11035 Bob White Dr 77096 713-778-8400
Christopher Walker, prin. Fax 778-8405
Travis ES 800/PK-5
3311 Beauchamp St 77009 713-802-4790
Thomas Day, prin. Fax 802-4795
Twain ES 900/PK-5
7500 Braes Blvd 77025 713-295-5230
Melissa Patin, prin. Fax 295-5283
Valley West ES 800/PK-5
10707 S Gessner Rd 77071 713-773-6151
Brian Vannest, prin. Fax 773-6156
Wainwright ES 800/PK-5
5330 Milwee St 77092 713-613-2550
Christina Aguirre, prin. Fax 613-2549
Walnut Bend ES 700/PK-5
10620 Briar Forest Dr 77042 713-917-3540
Susan Shenker, prin. Fax 917-3656
Welch MS 900/6-8
11544 S Gessner Rd 77071 713-778-3300
Inge Garibaldi, prin. Fax 995-6067

Wesley ES 400/PK-5
800 Dillard St 77091 713-696-2860
Cornelius Anderson, prin. Fax 696-2866
West Briar MS 1,200/6-8
13733 Brimhurst Dr 77077 281-368-2140
Gabriel Lopez, prin. Fax 368-2194
West University ES 1,300/PK-5
3756 University Blvd 77005 713-295-5215
John Threet, prin. Fax 667-8514
Wharton Dual Language Academy 400/K-8
1101 Taft St 77019 713-535-3771
Jennifer Day, prin. Fax 535-3772
Whidby ES 500/PK-5
7625 Springhill St 77021 713-746-8170
Roshanda Griffin, prin. Fax 746-8173
White ES 900/PK-5
9001 Triola Ln 77036 713-778-3490
Paulette Caston, prin. Fax 778-3493
White ES, 2515 Old Farm Rd 77063 K-5
Lisa Hernandez, prin. 713-556-6571
Whittier ES 600/PK-6
10511 La Crosse St 77029 713-671-3810
Lori Lueptow, prin. Fax 671-3812
Williams Charter MS 500/6-8
6100 Knox St 77091 713-696-2600
Christina Lovette, prin. Fax 696-2604
Wilson Montessori S 500/PK-8
2100 Yupon St 77006 713-942-1470
Merrie Bonnette, prin. Fax 942-1472
Windsor Village ES 800/PK-5
14440 Polo St 77085 713-726-3642
Shantelle Louis, prin. Fax 726-3647
Woodson S 900/PK-8
10720 Southview St 77047 713-732-3600
Stephan Gittens, prin. Fax 732-3606
Young ES 400/PK-5
3555 Bellfort St 77051 713-732-3590
Novelyn Robinson, prin. Fax 732-3592
Other Schools – See Bellaire

Humble ISD
Supt. — See Humble
Lakeshore ES 900/K-5
13333 Breakwater Path Dr 77044 281-641-3501
Annette Nevermann, prin. Fax 641-3517
Summerwood ES 600/K-5
14000 Summerwood Lakes Dr 77044 281-641-3000
Shannon Lalmansingh, prin. Fax 641-3017
Woodcreek MS 1,200/6-8
14600 Woodson Park Dr 77044 281-641-5200
Bryan Applegate, prin. Fax 641-5217

Katy ISD
Supt. — See Katy
Bear Creek ES 700/K-5
4815 Hickory Downs Dr 77084 281-237-5600
Dr. Lorena Zertuche, prin. Fax 644-1500
Mayde Creek ES 800/PK-5
2698 Greenhouse Rd 77084 281-237-3950
Felicia Sheedy, prin. Fax 644-1555
Mayde Creek JHS 1,100/6-8
2700 Greenhouse Rd 77084 281-237-3900
Dr. David Paz, prin. Fax 644-1650
Schmalz ES 1,100/K-5
18605 Green Land Way 77084 281-237-4500
Jaime Shipley, prin. Fax 644-1615
Wolfe ES 400/K-5
502 Addicks Howell Rd 77079 281-237-2250
Teresa Garcia, prin. Fax 644-1620

Klein ISD
Supt. — See Klein
Eiland ES 600/PK-5
6700 N Klein Circle Dr 77088 832-484-6900
Sheldon Barr, prin. Fax 484-7854
England ECC 500/PK-PK
7535 Prairie Oak Dr 77086 832-375-7900
Ann Dristas, prin. Fax 375-7925
Epps Island ES 800/PK-5
7403 Smiling Wood Ln 77086 832-484-5800
Maribel Scarbrough, prin. Fax 484-7856
Greenwood Forest ES 700/PK-5
12100 Misty Valley Dr 77066 832-484-5700
Alisha Elrod, prin. Fax 484-7858
Kaiser ES 800/PK-5
13430 Bammel N Houston Rd 77066 832-484-6100
Betty Zavala, prin. Fax 484-7864
Klein IS 1,200/6-8
4710 W Mount Houston Rd 77088 832-249-4900
Charles Woods, prin. Fax 249-4046
Klenk ES 800/PK-5
6111 Bourgeois Rd 77066 832-484-6800
Allie Martin, prin. Fax 484-7866
McDougle ES 700/PK-5
10410 Kansack Ln 77086 832-484-7550
Kathy Rachal, prin. Fax 484-7699
Nitsch ES 800/PK-5
4702 W Mount Houston Rd 77088 832-484-6400
Amber Kent, prin. Fax 484-7878
Ulrich IS 1,100/6-8
10103 Spring Cypress Rd 77070 832-375-7500
Leslie Kompelien, prin. Fax 375-7599
Wunderlich IS 1,500/6-8
11800 Misty Valley Dr 77066 832-249-5200
Chris Ruggerio, prin. Fax 249-4050

Pasadena ISD
Supt. — See Pasadena
Atkinson ES 600/K-5
9602 Kingspoint Rd 77075 713-740-0520
Lena Rohne-Ortiz, prin. Fax 740-4128
Beverly Hills IS 1,000/6-8
11111 Beamer Rd 77089 713-740-0420
Stacy Barber, prin. Fax 740-4051
Burnett ES 600/K-5
11825 Teaneck Dr 77089 713-740-0536
Jae Lee, prin. Fax 740-4130

Bush ES 1,000/K-4
9100 Blackhawk Blvd 77075 713-740-0928
Stephanie Miller, prin. Fax 740-4126
Frazier ES 500/K-5
10503 Hughes Rd 77089 713-740-0560
Wendy Wiseburn, prin. Fax 740-4132
Freeman ES 400/K-5
2323 Theta St 77034 713-740-0568
Michael Van Loenen, prin. Fax 740-4107
Garfield ES 900/PK-5
10301 Hartsook St 77034 713-740-0584
Courtney Merilatt, prin. Fax 740-4134
Genoa ES 700/K-5
12900 Almeda Genoa Rd 77034 713-740-0592
Tiffany Bennett, prin. Fax 740-4135
Hancock ES K-5
9604 Minnesota 77034 713-740-5430
Veronica Sandoval, prin. Fax 740-5977
Jessup ES 900/PK-5
9301 Almeda Genoa Rd 77075 713-740-0616
Ryan Pavone, prin. Fax 740-4112
Meador ES 600/PK-5
10701 Seaford Dr 77089 713-740-0648
Beverly Bolton, prin. Fax 740-4105
Melillo MS 1,000/5-6
9220 Hughes Rd 77089 713-740-5260
Diane Wheeler, prin. Fax 740-5908
Milstead MS 900/5-6
338 Gilpin St 77034 713-740-5238
Scott Pollack, prin. Fax 740-4176
Moore ES 500/K-5
8880 Southbluff Blvd 77089 713-740-0656
Jill Lacamu, prin. Fax 740-4140
Morris MS 900/5-6
10415 Fuqua St 77089 713-740-0672
Daniel Hoppie, prin. Fax 740-4047
Queens IS 700/6-8
1452 Queens St 77017 713-740-0470
Troy Jones, prin. Fax 740-4102
Roberts MS, 13402 Conklin Ln 77034 6-8
Jorly Thomas, prin. 713-740-5390
Schneider MS 900/5-6
8420 Easthaven Blvd 77075 713-740-0920
Kristin Still, prin. Fax 740-4125
South Belt ES 500/PK-5
1801 Riverstone Ranch Rd 77089 713-740-5276
Candy Howard, prin. Fax 740-5924
Stuchbery ES 700/PK-5
11210 Hughes Rd 77089 713-740-0752
Joey Hernandez, prin. Fax 740-4147
Thompson IS 1,000/6-8
11309 Sagedowne Ln 77089 713-740-0510
Melissa Allen, prin. Fax 740-4083

Sheldon ISD 8,000/PK-12
11411 C E King Pkwy 77044 281-727-2000
King Davis, supt. Fax 727-2085
www.sheldonisd.com
Carroll ES 700/1-5
10210 C E King Pkwy 77044 281-727-4100
Alina Young, prin. Fax 727-4175
Cravens Early Childhood Acad 600/PK-K
13210 Tidwell Rd 77044 281-727-2100
Denise Mustin, prin. Fax 727-2160
Garrett ES 500/1-5
12017 Garrett Rd 77044 281-727-4200
Stephanie Chavez, prin. Fax 727-4275
King MS 900/6-8
8530 C E King Pkwy 77044 281-727-4300
Raff Saeed, prin. Fax 459-7452
Monahan ES 500/1-5
8901 Deep Valley Dr 77044 281-454-2900
Cheri Dixon, prin. Fax 454-2975
Null MS 900/6-8
12117 Garrett Rd 77044 281-436-2800
Leroy Bradley, prin. Fax 436-2875
Royalwood ES 600/1-5
7715 Royalwood Dr 77049 281-454-2700
Lorena Carrasco, prin. Fax 454-2775
Sheldon Early Childhood Academy 500/PK-K
17010 Beaumont Hwy 77049 281-456-6800
Christopher Dickson, prin. Fax 456-6875
Sheldon ES 700/1-5
17203 Hall Shepperd Rd 77049 281-456-6700
Rachelle Ysquierdo, prin. Fax 456-6775

Spring Branch ISD 35,100/PK-12
955 Campbell Rd 77024 713-464-1511
Scott Muri Ed.D., supt. Fax 365-4664
www.springbranchisd.com
Bear Blvd S 300/PK-PK
8860 Westview Dr 77055 713-251-7900
Kim Hammer, dir. Fax 251-7915
Buffalo Creek ES 700/PK-5
2801 Blalock Rd 77080 713-251-5300
David Rodriguez, prin. Fax 329-6605
Bunker Hill ES 700/K-5
11950 Taylorcrest Rd 77024 713-251-5400
Dana Johnson, prin. Fax 251-5415
Cedar Brook ES 900/PK-5
2121 Ojeman Rd 77080 713-251-5500
Alejandra Perez, prin. Fax 365-5027
Edgewood ES 800/PK-5
8757 Kempwood Dr 77080 713-251-5600
Jessica Tejada, prin. Fax 365-5615
Frostwood ES 700/PK-5
12214 Memorial Dr 77024 713-251-5700
Pamela Pennington, prin. Fax 251-5715
Hollibrook ES 800/PK-5
3602 Hollister St 77080 713-251-5800
Karen Liska, prin. Fax 251-5815
Housman ES 600/K-5
6705 Housman St 77055 713-251-5900
Lindy Robertson, prin. Fax 251-5915
Hunters Creek ES 600/K-5
10650 Beinhorn Rd 77024 713-251-6000
Robalyn Snyder, prin. Fax 251-6015

Landrum MS 800/6-8
2200 Ridgecrest Dr 77055 713-251-3700
Steven Speyrer, prin. Fax 251-3715
Lion Lane S 300/PK-PK
2210 Ridgecrest Dr 77055 713-251-6100
Sharee Cantrell, dir. Fax 251-6115
Meadow Wood ES 500/PK-5
14230 Memorial Dr 77079 713-251-6200
Hailey Haynes, prin. Fax 251-6215
Memorial Drive ES 500/PK-5
11202 Smithdale Rd 77024 713-251-6300
Jennifer Jordan, prin. Fax 251-6315
Memorial MS 1,400/6-8
12550 Vindon Dr 77024 713-251-3900
Daniel Bauer, prin. Fax 251-3915
Northbrook MS 900/6-8
3030 Rosefield Dr 77080 713-251-4100
Sarah Guerrero, prin. Fax 251-4102
Nottingham ES 500/K-5
570 Nottingham Oaks Trl 77079 713-251-6400
Roy Moore, prin. Fax 251-6415
Panda Path S 200/PK-PK
8575 Pitner Rd 77080 713-251-8000
Sara Hannes, dir. Fax 251-8015
Pine Shadows ES 800/K-5
9900 Neuens Rd 77080 713-251-6500
Christina Winstead, prin. Fax 251-6515
Ridgecrest ES 900/K-5
2015 Ridgecrest Dr 77055 713-251-6600
Michelle Garcia, prin. Fax 251-6615
Rummel Creek ES 600/K-5
625 Brittmoore Rd 77079 713-251-6700
Nancy Harn, prin. Fax 251-6715
Shadow Oaks ES 700/PK-5
1335 Shadowdale Dr 77043 713-251-6800
Julie Baggerly, prin. Fax 251-6815
Sherwood ES 500/PK-5
1700 Sherwood Forest St 77043 713-251-6900
Stefanie Spencer, prin. Fax 251-6903
Spring Branch Academic Institute K-8
8390 Westview Dr 77055 713-251-2219
Lynda Maxwell, dir.
Spring Branch ES 600/PK-5
1700 Campbell Rd 77080 713-251-7000
Lynn Austin, prin. Fax 365-4159
Spring Branch MS 1,200/6-8
1000 Piney Point Rd 77024 713-251-4400
Bryan Williams, prin. Fax 251-4415
Spring Forest MS 800/6-8
14240 Memorial Dr 77079 713-251-4600
Dr. Raymorris Barnes, prin. Fax 251-4615
Spring Oaks MS 800/6-8
2150 Shadowdale Dr 77043 713-251-4800
Mary Lou Davalos, prin. Fax 251-4815
Spring Shadows ES 800/K-5
9725 Kempwood Dr 77080 713-251-7100
Rachel Martinez, prin. Fax 329-6480
Spring Woods MS 900/6-8
9810 Neuens Rd 77080 713-251-5000
Deborah Silber, prin. Fax 251-5015
Terrace ES 500/K-5
10400 Rothbury St 77043 713-251-7200
April Blanco, prin. Fax 251-7215
Thornwood ES 500/K-5
14400 Fern Dr 77079 713-251-7300
Chyla Weaver, prin. Fax 251-7315
Tiger Trail S 300/PK-PK
10406 Tiger Trl 77043 713-251-8100
Vidal Garza, dir. Fax 251-8115
Treasure Forest ES 600/K-5
7635 Amelia Rd 77055 713-251-7400
Celeste Barretto, prin. Fax 251-7415
Valley Oaks ES 600/PK-5
8390 Westview Dr 77055 713-251-7500
Kimberly Reynolds, prin. Fax 251-7515
Westwood ES 700/K-5
10595 Hammerly Blvd 77043 713-251-2100
Kay Kennard, prin. Fax 251-2134
Wilchester ES 700/PK-5
13618 Saint Marys Ln 77079 713-251-7700
Rian Evans, prin. Fax 251-7715
Wildcat Way S 300/PK-PK
12754 Kimberley Ln 77024 713-251-8200
Morella Tapia, dir. Fax 365-4745
Woodview ES 600/PK-5
9749 Cedardale Dr 77055 713-251-7800
Becky Hagan, prin. Fax 251-7815

Spring ISD 36,500/PK-12
16717 Ella Blvd 77090 281-891-6000
Dr. Rodney Watson, supt. Fax 891-6006
www.springisd.org
Bammel ES 900/PK-5
17309 Red Oak Dr 77090 281-891-8150
Dr. Berkey Hernandez-Owolabi, prin. Fax 891-8151
Bammel MS 1,300/6-8
16711 Ella Blvd 77090 281-891-7900
La'Quesha Grigsby, prin. Fax 891-7901
Beneke ES 800/PK-5
3840 Briarchase Dr 77014 281-891-8450
LaTracey Harris, prin. Fax 891-8451
Booker ES 1,000/PK-5
22352 Imperial Valley Dr 77073 281-891-8750
Keisha Womack, prin. Fax 891-8751
Clark IS 800/2-5
1825 Rushworth Dr 77014 281-891-8540
Torrance Brooks, prin. Fax 891-8541
Clark PS 800/PK-1
12625 River Laurel Dr 77014 281-891-8600
Micah Bachemin, prin. Fax 891-8601
Claughton MS 1,200/6-8
3000 Spears Rd 77067 281-891-7950
Domonica Amerson, prin. Fax 891-7951
Cooper ES 800/PK-5
18655 Imperial Valley Dr 77073 281-891-8660
Leticia Gonzalez, prin. Fax 209-0035

Eickenroht ES 600/PK-5
15252 Grand Point Rd 77090 281-891-8840
Robbie Green, prin. Fax 891-8841
Heritage ES 500/PK-5
12255 T C Jester Blvd 77067 281-891-8510
H.P. Hyder Ph.D., prin. Fax 891-8511
Hoyland ES 900/PK-5
2200 Wittershaw Dr 77090 281-891-8810
Cynthia Gomez, prin. Fax 891-8811
Lewis ES 700/PK-5
3230 Spears Rd 77067 281-891-8720
Grace Leal, prin. Fax 891-8676
Link ES 700/PK-5
2815 Ridge Hollow Dr 77067 281-891-8390
Justin Jones, prin. Fax 891-8391
Major ES 700/PK-5
16855 Sugar Pine Dr 77090 281-891-8870
Shamethia Dillard, prin. Fax 891-8871
Meyer ES 700/PK-5
16330 Forest Way Dr 77090 281-891-8270
C'ne Dawkins, prin. Fax 895-0807
Ponderosa ES 700/PK-5
17202 Butte Creek Rd 77090 281-891-8180
Shanna Swearingen, prin. Fax 891-8181
Reynolds ES 700/PK-5
3975 Gladeridge Dr 77068 281-891-8240
Rodney Louis, prin. Fax 891-8241
Roberson MS 1,100/6-8
1500 Southridge 77090 281-891-7700
Tracey Walker, prin. Fax 891-7701
Thompson ES 700/PK-5
12470 Walters Rd 77014 281-891-8480
Robert Long Ed.D., prin. Fax 891-8481
Wells MS 1,300/6-8
4033 Gladeridge Dr 77068 281-891-7750
Henri Lewi, prin. Fax 891-7751
Other Schools – See Spring

Abiding Word Lutheran S 100/PK-8
17123 Red Oak Dr 77090 281-895-7048
Ben Carlovsky, prin. Fax 895-7048
Al-Hadi S of Accelerative Learning 300/PK-12
2313 S Voss Rd 77057 713-787-5000
Dr. Humaira Bokhari, prin. Fax 513-5315
Annunciation Orthodox S 700/PK-8
3600 Yoakum Blvd 77006 713-470-5600
Mark Kelly, hdmstr. Fax 470-5605
Ascension Episcopal S 100/PK-5
2525 Seagler Rd 77042 713-783-0260
Nancy Clausey, head sch Fax 787-9162
Assumption Catholic S 200/PK-8
801 Roselane St 77037 281-447-2132
John Bates, prin. Fax 447-1825
Awty International S 1,300/PK-12
7455 Awty School Ln 77055 713-686-4850
Lisa Darling, head sch Fax 686-4956
Banff S 100/PK-12
13726 Cutten Rd 77069 281-444-9326
Bay Area Montessori S 50/PK-8
17222 Mercury Dr 77058 281-480-7022
Bayou Montessori S 50/PK-5
16204 Hickory Knoll Dr 77059 281-480-1648
Beren Academy 300/PK-12
11333 Cliffwood Dr 77035 713-723-7170
Dr. Paul Oberman, head sch Fax 723-8343
Beth Yeshurun Day S 300/PK-5
4525 Beechnut St 77096 713-666-1884
Dr. Dan Ahlstrom, head sch Fax 666-2924
Branch S 100/PK-8
1424 Sherwood Forest St 77043 713-465-0288
Christian S of Northwest Houston 100/PK-5
6720 W Tidwell Rd 77092 713-462-7125
Lucila Villarreal, dir. Fax 462-0855
Christ Memorial Lutheran S 100/PK-K
14200 Memorial Dr 77079 281-497-2055
Barb Tanz, dir. Fax 293-7734
Christ the Redeemer Catholic S PK-6
11511 Huffmeister Rd 77065 281-469-8440
Dan Courtney, prin. Fax 894-9669
Clay Road Baptist S 100/PK-8
9151 Clay Rd 77080 713-939-1023
Clear Lake Christian S 300/K-12
14325 Crescent Landing Dr 77062 281-488-4883
Dr. Bruce Guillot M.S., prin. Fax 480-3287
Corpus Christi S 200/PK-8
4005 Cheena Dr 77025 713-664-3351
Dr. Mazie McCoy, prin. Fax 664-6095
Cypress Christian S 600/K-12
11123 Cypress N Houston Rd 77065 281-469-8829
Stephen Novotny J.D., dir. Fax 469-6040
Darul Arqam North PK-12
11815 Adel Rd 77067 281-583-1984
Darul Arqam Southeast 100/PK-6
8830 Old Galveston Rd 77034 713-948-0094
Duchesne Academy of the Sacred Heart 500/PK-12
10202 Memorial Dr 77024 713-468-8211
Patricia Swenson, head sch Fax 465-9809
Elim Christian S 50/K-12
5151 Addicks Satsuma Rd 77084 281-855-3546
Dianne Hornor M.A., prin.
Epiphany Lutheran S 200/PK-8
14423 West Rd 77041 713-896-1843
Tim Miesner, prin. Fax 896-7568
Eternity Christian S 100/PK-12
1122 West Rd 77038 281-999-5107
Beth Bashinski, admin. Fax 999-0107
Family Christian Academy 300/PK-12
14718 Woodford Dr 77015 713-455-4483
John Bohacek, admin. Fax 450-3730
Fay S 300/PK-5
105 N Post Oak Ln 77024 713-681-8300
Bob Meyer, head sch Fax 681-6826
First Baptist Academy 500/PK-8
7450 Memorial Woods Dr 77024 713-290-2500
Teresa Chambers, head sch Fax 290-2508

Goudeau Accelerated Preparatory Academy 50/K-5
11410 Hall Rd 77089 281-481-3630
Linda Goudeau, prin. Fax 481-3665
Grace S 500/PK-8
10219 Ella Lee Ln 77042 713-782-4421
Dr. Liz Walgamuth Ed.D., head sch Fax 267-5056
Holy Ghost S 100/PK-8
6920 Chimney Rock Rd 77081 713-668-5327
Christina Mendez, prin. Fax 667-4410
Holy Spirit Episcopal S 300/PK-8
12535 Perthshire Rd 77024 713-468-5138
Holy Trinity Episcopal S 100/PK-12
11810 Lockwood Rd 77044 281-459-4323
Jeff Matthews, head sch Fax 459-4302
Houston Quran Academy 200/PK-12
1902 Baker Rd 77094 281-717-4622
Dr. Hamed Ghazali, prin.
ILM Academy 100/PK-3
1209 Conrad Sauer Dr 77043 713-464-4720
Iman Academy Southwest 400/1-12
6240 Highway 6 S 77083 281-498-1345
Imani S 400/PK-8
12401 S Post Oak Rd 77045 713-723-0616
Patricia Hogan-Williams, head sch Fax 723-6143
Kardia Christian Academy 400/PK-6
10555 Spring Cypress Rd 77070 281-378-4050
Kim Watson, head sch Fax 378-4081
Kinkaid S 1,400/PK-12
201 Kinkaid School Dr 77024 713-782-1640
Andrew Martire Ed.D., hdmstr. Fax 782-3543
Kipling S 200/PK-5
600 Shepherd Dr 77007 713-880-3318
Lutheran South Academy 800/PK-12
12555 Ryewater Dr 77089 281-464-8299
Sheila Psencik, head sch Fax 464-6119
Memorial Lutheran S 200/PK-8
5800 Westheimer Rd 77057 713-782-4022
Rev. Robert Paul, hdmstr. Fax 782-1749
Montessori Country Day S 300/PK-K
5117 La Branch St 77004 713-520-0738
Montessori Learning Institute 50/PK-7
5701 Beechnut St 77074 713-771-5600
Northland Christian S 600/PK-12
4363 Sylvanfield Dr 77014 281-440-1060
Our Lady of Guadalupe S 200/PK-8
2405 Navigation Blvd 77003 713-224-6904
Irazema Ortiz, prin. Fax 225-2122
Our Lady of Mt. Carmel S 100/PK-8
6703 Whitefriars Dr 77087 713-643-0676
Maribel Mendoza, prin. Fax 649-1835
Our Savior Lutheran S 200/PK-8
5000 W Tidwell Rd 77091 713-290-8277
Lance Gerard, prin. Fax 290-0850
Paratus Classical Academy 100/PK-9
1415 S Voss Rd #110-436 77057 281-547-0060
Pilgrim Lutheran S 200/PK-8
8601 Chimney Rock Rd 77096 713-432-7082
David Topp, prin. Fax 666-6585
Presbyterian S 500/PK-8
5300 Main St 77004 713-520-0284
Dr. Mark Carleton, hdmstr. Fax 620-6390
Queen of Peace S 200/PK-8
2320 Oakcliff St 77023 713-921-1558
Jan Krametbauer, prin. Fax 921-0855
Rainard S for Gifted Students 100/PK-12
11059 Timberline Rd 77043 713-647-7246
Redd S 200/PK-8
4820 Strack Rd 77069 281-440-1106
Regis S 300/PK-8
7330 Westview Dr 77055 713-682-8383
Dennis Phillips, head sch Fax 682-8388
Resurrection S 100/PK-8
916 Majestic St 77020 713-674-5545
Felicia Nichols, prin. Fax 674-2151
River Oaks Baptist S 900/PK-8
2300 Willowick Rd 77027 713-623-6938
Leanne Reynolds, head sch Fax 621-8216
St. Ambrose S 400/PK-8
4213 Mangum Rd 77092 713-686-6990
Judy Fritsch, prin. Fax 686-6902
St. Anne S 500/PK-8
2120 Westheimer Rd 77098 713-526-3279
Kathy Barnosky, prin. Fax 526-8025
St. Augustine S 200/PK-8
5500 Laurel Creek Way 77017 713-946-9050
Denise Rios, prin. Fax 943-3444
St. Catherine's Montessori S 200/PK-9
9821 Timberside Dr 77025 713-665-2195
Susan Tracy, head sch Fax 665-1478
St. Cecilia S 600/PK-8
11740 Joan of Arc Dr 77024 713-468-9515
Jeff Matthews, prin. Fax 468-4698
St. Christopher S 200/PK-8
8134 Park Place Blvd 77017 713-649-0009
Claudia Cavazos, prin. Fax 649-1104
St. Clare of Assisi S 200/PK-8
3131 El Dorado Blvd 77059 281-286-3395
Dr. Alfred Varisco, prin. Fax 461-6585
St. Constantine S PK-12
6000 Dale Carnegie Ln 77036 832-975-7075
Dr. John Reynolds, pres.
St. Elizabeth Ann Seton S 600/PK-8
6646 Addicks Satsuma Rd 77084 281-463-1444
Ignacio Aguilera, prin. Fax 463-8707
St. Francis De Sales S 500/PK-8
8100 Roos Rd 77036 713-774-4447
Diane Wooten, prin. Fax 271-6744
St. Francis Episcopal S 800/PK-8
335 Piney Point Rd 77024 713-458-6100
Dr. Susan Lair, head sch Fax 782-4720
St. Francis of Assisi S 200/PK-8
5100 Dabney St 77026 713-674-1966
Tawana Fulmer, prin. Fax 674-9901
St. Jerome S 300/PK-8
8825 Kempwood Dr 77080 713-468-7946
Patricia Jackson, prin. Fax 464-0325

St. John Paul II S 700/PK-8
1400 Parkway Plaza Dr 77077 281-496-1500
Rebecca Bogard, prin. Fax 496-2943
St. John's S 1,300/K-12
2401 Claremont Ln 77019 713-850-0222
Mark Desjardins, hdmstr. Fax 622-2309
St. Mark Lutheran S 300/PK-8
1515 Hillendahl Blvd 77055 713-468-2623
Dallas Lusk M.Ed., prin. Fax 468-6735
St. Mark's Episcopal S 400/PK-8
3816 Bellaire Blvd 77025 713-667-7030
Garhett Wagers, hdmstr. Fax 349-0419
St. Mary of the Purification S 100/PK-5
3002 Rosedale St 77004 713-522-9276
Natalie Garrett, prin. Fax 522-1879
St. Michael S 500/PK-8
1833 Sage Rd 77056 713-621-6847
Kathleen Cox, prin. Fax 877-8812
St. Peter the Apostle S 100/PK-8
6220 La Salette St 77021 713-747-9484
Toni Marshall, prin. Fax 842-7055
St. Rose of Lima S 200/PK-8
3600 Brinkman St 77018 713-691-0104
Bernadette Drabek, prin. Fax 692-8073
St. Stephen's Episcopal School - Houston 200/PK-8
1800 Sul Ross St 77098 713-821-9100
David Coe M.S., head sch Fax 821-9156
St. Theresa S 200/PK-8
6623 Rodrigo St 77007 713-864-4536
Melissa Ilski, prin. Fax 869-5184
St. Thomas' Episcopal S 600/PK-12
4900 Jackwood St 77096 713-666-3111
Michael Cusack, hdmstr. Fax 668-3887
St. Thomas More S 500/PK-8
5927 Wigton Dr 77096 713-729-3434
Kristen Thome, prin. Fax 721-5644
St. Thomas the Apostle Episcopal S 100/PK-5
18300 Upper Bay Rd 77058 281-333-1340
Teresa McMillan, dir. Fax 333-1340
St. Vincent De Paul S 500/PK-8
6802 Buffalo Speedway 77025 713-666-2345
Carolyn Sears, prin. Fax 663-3562
School of the Woods 400/PK-12
1321 Wirt Rd 77055 713-686-8811
Second Baptist S 1,100/PK-12
6410 Woodway Dr 77057 713-365-2310
Sherwood Forest Montessori S 100/PK-6
1331 Sherwood Forest St 77043 713-464-5791
Shlenker S 400/PK-5
5600 N Braeswood Blvd 77096 713-270-6127
Ricki Komiss, hdmstr. Fax 270-6114
Smaller Scholars Montessori S 300/PK-6
1685 S Dairy Ashford Rd 77077 281-558-3515
Noreen Martin, head sch Fax 559-0917
Southhampton Montessori S 300/PK-8
5012 Morningside Dr 77005 713-526-7458
Southwest Christian Academy 200/K-12
7400 Eldridge Pkwy 77083 281-561-7400
Paula Thurmond, prin. Fax 561-9823
Texas Christian S 200/PK-12
17810 Kieth Harrow Blvd 77084 281-550-6060
Beckie Soliz, head sch Fax 550-2400
Torah Day S 100/PK-8
10900 Fondren Rd 77096 713-777-2000
Trafton Academy 200/PK-8
4711 McDermed St 77035 713-723-3732
Trinity Classical School of Houston 400/PK-10
7941 Katy Freeway #110 77024 281-656-1880
Trinity Lutheran S - Downtown 300/PK-8
1316 Washington Ave 77002 832-301-3100
Matthew Meier, prin. Fax 224-0685
Village S 900/PK-12
2005 Gentryside Dr 77077 281-496-7900
Gabriella Rowe, head sch Fax 496-7799
Wesley Academy 100/PK-8
10570 Westpark Dr 77042 281-266-3341
Westbury Christian S 500/PK-12
10420 Hillcroft St 77096 713-551-8100
Western Academy 100/3-8
1511 Butlercrest St 77080 713-461-7000
Westside Montessori S 100/PK-8
13555 Briar Forest Dr 77077 281-556-5970
Bonita Lea, head sch Fax 556-5961
Yellowstone Academy 400/PK-8
3000 Trulley St 77004 713-741-8000
Yeshiva Torat Emet 200/PK-8
11330 Braesridge Dr 77071 713-721-3900
Yorkshire Academy 200/PK-5
14120 Memorial Dr 77079 281-531-6088

Howe, Grayson, Pop. 2,551

Howe ISD 1,100/PK-12
105 W Tutt St 75459 903-532-3228
Kevin Wilson, supt. Fax 532-3205
www.howeisd.net
Howe ES 400/PK-4
315 Roberts St 75459 903-532-3320
Clarissia Doty, prin. Fax 532-3321
Howe MS 300/5-8
300 Beatrice St 75459 903-532-3286
Clay Wilson, prin. Fax 532-3287

Hubbard, Hill, Pop. 1,406

Hubbard ISD 400/PK-12
PO Box 218 76648 254-576-2564
Dr. Wayne Guidry, supt. Fax 576-5019
www.hubbardisd.com
Hubbard ES 200/PK-5
PO Box 218 76648 254-576-2359
Donna Vardeman, prin. Fax 576-5018
Hubbard MS 100/6-8
PO Box 218 76648 254-576-2758
James Wright, prin. Fax 576-5017

Huffman, Harris

Huffman ISD 2,800/PK-12
PO Box 2390 77336 281-324-1871
Dr. Benny Soileau Ed.D., supt. Fax 324-4319
www.huffmanisd.net

Bowen ECC 600/PK-1
PO Box 2390 77336 281-324-1399
Melissa Hutchinson, prin. Fax 324-1646
Copeland ES 500/2-5
PO Box 2390 77336 281-324-7100
Amy Turner, prin. Fax 324-2076
Huffman MS 800/6-8
PO Box 2390 77336 281-324-2598
Adam Skinner, prin. Fax 324-2710

Hughes Springs, Cass, Pop. 1,726
Hughes Springs ISD 1,200/PK-12
871 Taylor St 75656 903-639-3800
Sarah Dildine, supt. Fax 639-2624
www.hsisd.net
Hughes Springs ES 600/PK-5
809 Russell 75656 903-639-3881
Scott Hanes, prin. Fax 639-3930
Hughes Springs JHS 300/6-8
609 Russell 75656 903-639-3812
Stephen Barnes, prin. Fax 639-3929

Hull, Liberty, Pop. 664
Hull-Daisetta ISD
Supt. — See Daisetta
Hull-Daisetta ES 200/PK-6
7243 FM 834E 77564 936-536-6667
Kevin Frauenberger, prin. Fax 536-3800

Humble, Harris, Pop. 14,835
Aldine ISD
Supt. — See Houston
Jones ECC 700/PK-K
8003 Forest Point Dr 77338 281-446-1576
Gladys Moton, prin. Fax 985-6010
Jones ES 1,100/1-4
7903 Forest Point Dr 77338 281-446-6168
Cheryl Fontenot, prin. Fax 985-6022
Magrill ES 1,100/K-4
21701 Rayford Rd 77338 281-233-4300
Mark Malo, prin. Fax 233-4303
Rayford IS 700/5-6
21919 Rayford Rd 77338 281-233-8901
Margraet Doran, prin. Fax 233-8907
Teague MS 900/7-8
21700 Rayford Rd 77338 281-233-4310
Sonya Hicks, prin. Fax 233-4318

Humble ISD 38,100/PK-12
PO Box 2000 77347 281-641-1000
Dr. Elizabeth Fagen, supt. Fax 641-1050
www.humble.k12.tx.us
Atascocita MS 1,100/6-8
18810 W Lake Houston Pkwy 77346 281-641-4600
Karl Koehler, prin. Fax 641-4617
Atascocita Springs ES 900/K-5
13515 Valley Lodge Pkwy 77346 281-641-3600
Kathy Shealy, prin. Fax 641-3617
Eagle Springs ES 700/PK-5
12500 Will Clayton Pkwy 77346 281-641-3100
April Maldonado, prin. Fax 641-3117
Fall Creek ES 700/K-5
14435 Mesa Dr 77396 281-641-3400
Yvonne Stroud, prin. Fax 641-3417
Fields ES 500/PK-5
2505 S Houston Ave 77396 281-641-2700
Karen Weeks, prin. Fax 641-2717
Groves ES PK-5
11902 Madera Run Pkwy 77346 281-641-5000
Dr. Brian Peters, prin. Fax 641-5017
Humble ES 500/PK-5
20252 Fieldtree Dr 77338 281-641-1100
Stacy Trost, prin. Fax 641-1117
Humble MS 1,200/6-8
11207 Will Clayton Pkwy 77346 281-641-4000
Sarahdia Johnson, prin. Fax 641-4117
Lakeland ES 800/PK-5
1500 Montgomery Ln 77338 281-641-1200
Lucy Anderson, prin. Fax 641-1217
Maplebrook ES 700/PK-5
7935 Farmingham Rd 77346 281-641-2900
Tiffany Caseltine, prin. Fax 641-2917
North Belt ES 600/PK-5
8105 E North Belt 77396 281-641-1300
Christina Morris, prin. Fax 641-1317
Oak Forest ES 700/K-5
6400 Kingwood Glen Dr 77346 281-641-2800
Linda Schmidt, prin. Fax 641-2817
Oaks ES 600/PK-5
5858 Upper Lake Dr 77346 281-641-1890
Cheryl Fennell, prin. Fax 641-1817
Park Lakes ES 700/PK-5
4400 Wilson Rd 77396 281-641-3200
Sarah Ballard, prin. Fax 641-3217
Pine Forest ES 700/K-5
19702 W Lake Houston Pkwy 77346 281-641-2100
T.J. Hall, prin. Fax 641-2117
Ridge Creek ES 500/K-5
15201 Woodland Hills Dr 77396 281-641-3700
Stephanie Davis, prin. Fax 641-3717
River Pines ES 800/PK-5
2400 Cold River Dr 77396 281-641-3300
Sharon Lee, prin. Fax 641-3317
Sterling MS 900/6-8
1131 Wilson Rd 77338 281-641-6000
Damico Bartley, prin. Fax 641-6017
Timbers ES 700/PK-5
6910 Lonesome Woods Trl 77346 281-641-2000
Alison Pierce, prin. Fax 641-2017
Timberwood MS 1,300/6-8
18450 Timber Forest Dr 77346 281-641-3800
Kenneth Buck, prin. Fax 641-3817
Whispering Pines ES 700/K-5
17321 Woodland Hills Dr 77346 281-641-2500
Patricia Gnatzig, prin. Fax 641-2517
Other Schools – See Houston, Kingwood

Humble Christian S 300/PK-12
16202 Old Humble Rd 77396 281-441-1313
Ted Howell, admin. Fax 441-1329
St. Mary Magdalene S 300/PK-8
530 Ferguson St 77338 281-446-8535
Joshua Raab, prin. Fax 446-8527

Hunt, Kerr
Hunt ISD 200/PK-8
PO Box 259 78024 830-238-4893
Dr. Crystal Dockery, supt. Fax 238-4691
www.huntisd.com
Hunt S 200/PK-8
PO Box 259 78024 830-238-4893
Dr. Crystal Dockery, supt. Fax 238-4691

Huntington, Angelina, Pop. 2,087
Huntington ISD 1,800/PK-12
PO Box 328 75949 936-876-4287
David Flowers, supt. Fax 876-3212
www.huntingtonisd.com/
Huntington ES 500/PK-3
PO Box 328 75949 936-876-5194
Geoff Gregory, prin. Fax 422-4450
Huntington IS 200/4-5
PO Box 328 75949 936-876-3432
Sandy Flowers, prin. Fax 422-4419
Huntington MS 400/6-8
PO Box 328 75949 936-876-4722
Matt Clifton, prin. Fax 876-4009

Huntsville, Walker, Pop. 38,042
Huntsville ISD 6,500/PK-12
441 FM 2821 Rd E 77320 936-435-6300
Dr. Howell Wright Ed.D., supt. Fax 435-6648
www.huntsville-isd.org
Gibbs Prekindergarten Center 400/PK-PK
441 FM 2821 Rd E 77320 936-435-6550
Sharonda Johnson, prin. Fax 435-6600
Houston ES 600/K-4
441 FM 2821 Rd E 77320 936-435-6750
Renee Royal, prin. Fax 435-6605
Huntsville ES 500/K-4
441 FM 2821 Rd E 77320 936-435-6500
Christy Cross, prin. Fax 435-6611
Huntsville IS 900/5-6
441 FM 2821 Rd E 77320 936-435-6500
Tim Maresch, prin. Fax 435-6614
Johnson ES 700/K-4
441 FM 2821 Rd E 77320 936-435-6250
Shannon Williams, prin. Fax 435-6608
Mance Park MS 900/7-8
441 FM 2821 Rd E 77320 936-435-6400
Samantha Mullens, prin. Fax 435-6617
Stewart ES 700/K-4
441 FM 2821 Rd E 77320 936-435-6700
Sara Williams, prin. Fax 435-6602

Alpha Omega Academy 400/PK-12
PO Box 8419 77340 936-438-8833
Paul Davidhizar, hdmstr. Fax 438-8844
Faith Lutheran S 100/PK-4
111 Sumac Rd 77340 936-291-1706
Kristie Pacher, prin. Fax 291-0128
Summit Christian Academy 100/PK-12
PO Box 1590 77342 936-295-9601
Krystal Nunez, head sch Fax 295-9236

Hurst, Tarrant, Pop. 36,447
Birdville ISD
Supt. — See Haltom City
Porter ES 500/PK-5
2750 Prestondale Dr 76054 817-547-2900
Greg Bicknell, prin. Fax 581-5381

Hurst-Euless-Bedford ISD
Supt. — See Bedford
Bellaire ES 800/PK-6
501 Bellaire Dr 76053 817-285-3230
Katrina Rhodes, prin. Fax 285-3203
Donna Park ES 500/PK-6
1125 Scott Dr 76053 817-285-3285
Sharon Wynn, prin. Fax 285-3289
Harrison Lane ES 600/PK-6
1000 Harrison Ln 76053 817-285-3270
Kathleen Harrell, prin. Fax 285-3207
Hurst Hills ES 500/PK-6
525 Billie Ruth Ln 76053 817-285-3295
Misty Donaho, prin. Fax 285-3208
Shady Oaks ES 500/PK-6
1400 Cavender Dr 76053 817-285-3240
Darla Clark, prin. Fax 285-3209
West Hurst ES 500/PK-6
501 Precinct Line Rd 76053 817-285-3290
Debra Day, prin. Fax 285-3212

Hutto, Williamson, Pop. 14,315
Hutto ISD 5,900/PK-12
200 College St 78634 512-759-3771
Eduardo Ramos, admin. Fax 759-4797
www.hipponation.org
Cottonwood Creek ES 700/PK-5
3160 Limmer Loop 78634 512-759-5430
Kyle Ruggirello, prin. Fax 759-5431
Farley MS 700/6-8
303 County Road 137 78634 512-759-2050
Jorge Franco, prin. Fax 759-2033
Hutto ES 600/PK-5
100 Mager Ln 78634 512-759-2094
Gaye Rosser, prin. Fax 759-4778
Hutto MS 700/6-8
1005 Exchange Blvd 78634 512-759-4541
Jason McAuliffe, prin. Fax 759-4753
Johnson ES 700/PK-5
480 Carl Stern Dr 78634 512-759-5400
Jacqueline Tealer, prin. Fax 759-5401

Norman ES K-5
101 Llano River Tr 78634 512-749-5480
Greg Nestle, prin. Fax 759-4757
Ray ES 600/PK-5
225 Swindoll Ln 78634 512-759-5450
Adrienne King, prin. Fax 759-5451
Other Schools – See Round Rock

Idalou, Lubbock, Pop. 2,236
Idalou ISD 1,000/PK-12
PO Box 1338 79329 806-892-1900
Jim Waller, supt. Fax 892-3204
www.idalouisd.net/
Idalou ES 400/PK-4
PO Box 1399 79329 806-892-1900
Steve Gunter, prin. Fax 892-2666
Idalou MS 300/5-8
PO Box 1343 79329 806-892-1900
Josh Damron, prin. Fax 892-3204

Imperial, Pecos, Pop. 277
Buena Vista ISD 200/PK-12
PO Box 310 79743 432-536-2225
Mark Dominguez, supt. Fax 536-2469
www.bvisd.net
Buena Vista S 200/PK-12
PO Box 310 79743 432-536-2225
Julian Castillo, prin. Fax 536-2469

Industry, Austin, Pop. 294
Bellville ISD
Supt. — See Bellville
West End ES 200/K-5
7453 Ernst Pkwy 78944 979-357-2595
Dr. Tony Hancock, prin. Fax 357-4799

Inez, Victoria, Pop. 2,080
Industrial ISD
Supt. — See Vanderbilt
Industrial ES West 200/PK-5
599 FM 444 S 77968 361-284-3226
Cynthia Adams, prin. Fax 782-0010

Ingleside, San Patricio, Pop. 9,243
Ingleside ISD 2,300/PK-12
PO Box 1320 78362 361-776-7631
Troy Mircovich, supt. Fax 776-0267
www.inglesideisd.org
Blaschke/Sheldon ES 400/5-6
2624 Mustang Dr 78362 361-776-3050
Jill Blankenship, prin. Fax 776-7912
Ingleside PS 500/PK-1
2100 Achievement Blvd 78362 361-776-3060
Stephanie Gibson, prin. Fax 775-2070
Mircovich ES 500/2-4
2720 Big Oak Ln 78362 361-776-1683
Heather Cohea, prin. Fax 776-0509
Taylor JHS 400/7-8
2739 Mustang Dr 78362 361-776-2232
Heather Waugh, prin. Fax 776-2192

Ingram, Kerr, Pop. 1,786
Ingram ISD 1,000/PK-12
510 College St 78025 830-367-5517
Dr. Robert Templeton, supt. Fax 367-4869
www.ingramisd.net
Ingram ES 500/PK-5
510 College St 78025 830-367-5751
Donna Jenschke, prin. Fax 367-7333
Ingram MS 200/6-8
510 College St 78025 830-367-4111
Joey McRorey, prin. Fax 367-7335

Iola, Grimes, Pop. 393
Iola ISD 500/PK-12
PO Box 159 77861 936-394-2361
Dr. Chad Jones, supt. Fax 394-2132
www.iolaisd.net
Iola ES 200/PK-6
PO Box 159 77861 936-394-2361
Scott Martindale, prin. Fax 394-2051

Iowa Park, Wichita, Pop. 6,289
Iowa Park Consolidated ISD 1,800/PK-12
PO Box 898 76367 940-592-4193
Steve Moody, supt. Fax 592-2136
www.ipcisd.net/
Bradford ES 400/3-5
809 Texowa Rd 76367 940-592-5841
Brandi Swenson, prin. Fax 592-2059
George MS 400/6-8
412 E Cash St 76367 940-592-2196
Darla Biddy, prin. Fax 592-2801
Kidwell ES 500/PK-2
1200 N 3rd St 76367 940-592-4322
James Kennedy, prin. Fax 592-2487

Ira, Scurry
Ira ISD 300/K-12
6143 W FM 1606 79527 325-573-2629
Brian Patterson, supt. Fax 573-5825
www.ira.esc14.net/
Ira S 300/K-12
6123 W FM 1606 79527 325-573-2628
Dale Jones, prin. Fax 573-5825

Iraan, Pecos, Pop. 1,225
Iraan-Sheffield ISD 600/PK-12
PO Box 486 79744 432-639-2512
Kevin Allen, supt. Fax 639-2501
isisd.net
Iraan ES 200/PK-5
PO Box 486 79744 432-639-2512
Dr. Candra Cade, prin. Fax 639-2501
Iraan JHS 100/6-8
PO Box 486 79744 432-639-2512
Amy Frazier, prin. Fax 639-2501

Iredell, Bosque, Pop. 338
Iredell ISD 100/PK-12
PO Box 39 76649 254-364-2411
Patrick Murphy, supt. Fax 364-2206
www.iredell-isd.com
Iredell S 100/PK-12
PO Box 39 76649 254-364-2411
Patrick Murphy, prin. Fax 364-2206

Irving, Dallas, Pop. 212,044
Carrollton-Farmers Branch ISD
Supt. — See Carrollton
Bush MS 700/6-8
515 Cowboys Pkwy 75063 972-968-3700
Matt Warnock, prin. Fax 968-3710
Freeman ES 600/PK-5
8757 Valley Ranch Pkwy W 75063 972-968-1700
Robyn Campbell, prin. Fax 968-1710
Landry ES 400/K-5
265 Red River Trl 75063 972-968-2100
Stephanie Lopez, prin. Fax 968-2110
Las Colinas ES 500/K-5
2200 Kinwest Pkwy 75063 972-968-2200
Ahveance Jones, prin. Fax 968-2210
La Villita ES 500/K-5
1601 Camino Lago 75039 972-968-6900
Deama Mayfield, prin. Fax 968-6910

Coppell ISD
Supt. — See Coppell
Valley Ranch ES 700/PK-5
9800 Rodeo Dr 75063 214-496-8500
Cynthia Arterbery, prin. Fax 496-8506

Irving ISD 35,300/PK-12
PO Box 152637 75015 972-600-5000
Dr. Jose L. Parra, supt. Fax 215-5201
www.irvingisd.net
Austin MS 1,000/6-8
825 E Union Bower Rd 75061 972-600-3100
Toscha Reeves, prin. Fax 721-3105
Barton ES 800/K-5
2931 Conflans Rd 75061 972-600-4100
Kelly Giddens, prin. Fax 313-4110
Bowie MS 1,000/6-8
600 E 6th St 75060 972-600-3000
Jennifer Anderson, prin. Fax 721-3044
Brandenburg ES 900/K-5
2800 Hillcrest Dr 75062 972-600-7100
Julie Miller, prin. Fax 258-7199
Britain ES 700/K-5
631 Edmondson Dr 75060 972-600-3800
Adriana Rico, prin. Fax 554-3899
Brown ES 800/K-5
2501 10th St 75060 972-600-4000
Jason Barnett, prin. Fax 513-4099
Clifton ECC 800/PK-PK
3950 Pleasant Run Rd 75038 972-600-4200
Leigh Ann McNeese, prin. Fax 261-2849
Crockett MS 800/6-8
2431 Hancock St 75061 972-600-4700
Francisco Miranda, prin. Fax 313-4770
Davis ES 900/K-5
310 Davis Dr 75061 972-600-4900
Angela Long, prin. Fax 313-4949
de Zavala MS 800/6-8
707 W Pioneer Dr 75061 972-600-6000
Anika Horgan, prin. Fax 273-8924
Elliott ES 700/K-5
1900 S Story Rd 75060 972-600-4300
Sheila Peragine, prin. Fax 313-4316
Farine ES 800/K-5
615 Metker St 75062 972-600-7900
Joe Estrada, prin. Fax 261-2799
Gilbert ES 800/K-5
1501 E Pioneer Dr 75061 972-600-0400
Jorge Acosta, prin. Fax 721-8480
Good ES 900/K-5
1200 E Union Bower Rd 75061 972-600-3300
Dr. Jill Tokumoto, prin. Fax 721-3379
Haley ES 800/K-5
1100 Schulze Dr 75060 972-600-6600
Lindsey Sanders, prin. Fax 273-6608
Haley ES 800/K-5
3601 Cheyenne St 75062 972-600-7000
Alberto Zavala, prin. Fax 261-2599
Hanes ES 700/K-5
2730 Cheyenne St 75062 972-600-3600
Ed Henderson, prin. Fax 261-2950
Houston MS 900/6-8
3033 Country Club Dr W 75038 972-600-7500
Jeffrey Dorman, prin. Fax 261-2399
Johnson MS 1,000/6-8
3601 W Pioneer Dr 75061 972-600-0500
James Clark, prin. Fax 986-6830
Johnston ES 800/K-5
2801 Rutgers Dr 75062 972-600-7700
Stephen Pollard, prin. Fax 659-7799
Keyes ES 800/K-5
1501 N Britain Rd 75061 972-600-3400
Blanca De La Sierra, prin. Fax 721-3405
Kinkeade ECC 700/PK-PK
2333 Cameron Pl 75060 972-600-6500
Jennifer McKee, prin. Fax 273-6549
Lamar MS 800/6-8
219 Crandall Rd 75060 972-600-4400
Eric Ogle, prin. Fax 313-4499
Lee ES 800/K-5
1600 Carlisle St 75062 972-600-7800
Angel Rico, prin. Fax 261-2629
Lively ES 900/K-5
1800 Plymouth Dr W 75061 972-600-6700
Sean Flynn, prin. Fax 273-6710
Pierce ECC 600/PK-PK
901 N Britain Rd 75061 972-600-3700
Jennifer Dickson, prin. Fax 554-3749
Schulze ES 800/K-5
1200 S Irving Heights Dr 75060 972-600-3500
Robin Latiolais, prin. Fax 785-3599
Stipes ES 800/K-5
3100 Cross Timbers Dr 75060 972-600-4500
Bonnie Richardson, prin. Fax 986-4598
Townley ES 700/K-5
1030 W Vilbig St 75060 972-600-6800
Shirley Sturges, prin. Fax 273-6877
Townsell ES 900/K-5
3700 Pleasant Run Rd 75038 972-600-5500
Frances Adams, prin. Fax 255-6008
Travis MS 1,000/6-8
1600 Finley Rd 75062 972-600-0100
Denise Anderson, prin. Fax 261-2450

Highlands S 400/PK-12
1451 E Northgate Dr 75062 972-554-1980
Daniel Ray, prin. Fax 721-1691
Holy Family of Nazareth Catholic Academy 200/PK-8
2323 Cheyenne St 75062 972-255-0205
Kathy Carruth, prin. Fax 252-0448
Islamic S of Irving 500/PK-12
2555 Esters Rd 75062 972-812-2230
Redeemer Montessori S 100/PK-6
2700 Warren Cir 75062 972-257-3517
Shanon Flowers, head sch Fax 258-9882
StoneGate Christian Academy 100/PK-12
1705 Esters Rd 75061 972-790-0070
Rhonda Tuttle, head sch Fax 790-6560
Wonderland Montessori Academy 200/PK-6
2090 Market Pl Blvd 75063 972-506-9500

Italy, Ellis, Pop. 1,835
Italy ISD 500/PK-12
300 College 76651 972-483-1815
Lee Joffre, supt. Fax 483-6152
www.italyisd.info/
Stafford ES 200/PK-6
300 College 76651 972-483-6342
Pamela Thomas, prin. Fax 483-6892

Itasca, Hill, Pop. 1,623
Itasca ISD 600/PK-12
123 N College St 76055 254-687-2922
Mark Parsons, supt. Fax 687-2637
www.itascaisd.org
Itasca ES 300/PK-4
300 N Files St 76055 254-687-2922
Amy Reyna, prin. Fax 687-2637
Itasca MS 200/5-8
208 N Files St 76055 254-687-2922
Kristi Sargent, prin. Fax 687-2637

Ivanhoe, Fannin, Pop. 869
Sam Rayburn ISD 500/PK-12
9363 E FM 273 75447 903-664-2255
Cole McClendon, supt. Fax 664-2406
www.srisd.org
Rayburn ES 300/PK-6
9363 E FM 273 75447 903-664-2005
Jim Shaw, prin. Fax 664-2307

Jacksboro, Jack, Pop. 4,489
Jacksboro ISD 1,000/PK-12
750 W Belknap St 76458 940-567-7203
Dwain Milam, supt. Fax 567-2214
www.jacksboroisd.net/
Jacksboro ES 500/PK-5
1677 N Main St 76458 940-567-7206
Dr. Tina Alvarado, prin. Fax 567-2603
Jacksboro MS 200/6-8
812 W Belknap St 76458 940-567-7205
Sara Mathis, prin. Fax 567-2681

Jacksonville, Cherokee, Pop. 14,356
Jacksonville ISD 4,900/PK-12
PO Box 631 75766 903-586-6511
Dr. Chad Kelly, supt. Fax 586-3133
www.jisd.org
Douglass ES 600/PK-4
PO Box 631 75766 903-586-6519
Rachel Sherman, prin. Fax 589-4341
East Side ES 600/PK-4
PO Box 631 75766 903-586-5146
Jodi Alderete, prin. Fax 589-4977
Jacksonville MS 700/7-8
PO Box 631 75766 903-586-3686
Holly Searcy, prin. Fax 586-8071
Nichols IS 700/5-6
PO Box 631 75766 903-541-0213
Holly Searcy, prin. Fax 541-0199
West Side ES 500/PK-4
PO Box 631 75766 903-586-5165
Geoffrey Sherman, prin. Fax 586-6196
Wright ES 500/PK-4
PO Box 631 75766 903-586-5286
Cindy Slovacek, prin. Fax 589-8108

Jarrell, Williamson, Pop. 971
Jarrell ISD 900/PK-12
PO Box 9 76537 512-746-2124
Dr. Bill Chapman, supt. Fax 746-2518
www.jarrellisd.org
Jarrell ES 300/PK-2
PO Box 9 76537 512-746-2170
Jack Wilson, prin. Fax 746-2575
Jarrell IS, PO Box 9 76537 3-5
Dr. Becky Snow, prin. 512-746-4805
Jarrell MS 300/6-8
PO Box 9 76537 512-746-4180
Abbe Lester, prin. Fax 746-4280

Jasper, Jasper, Pop. 7,490
Jasper ISD 2,000/PK-12
128 Park Ln 75951 409-384-2401
Dr. Gerald Hudson, supt. Fax 382-1084
www.jasperisd.net
Few PS 800/PK-3
225 Bulldog Ave 75951 409-489-9808
Ron Vickers, prin. Fax 382-1399
Jasper JHS 400/6-8
211 2nd St 75951 409-384-3585
John Seybold, prin. Fax 382-1160
Parnell ES 200/4-5
151 Park Ln 75951 409-384-2212
William Davis, prin. Fax 382-1114

Jayton, Kent, Pop. 530
Jayton-Girard ISD 100/PK-12
PO Box 168 79528 806-237-2991
Trig Overbo, supt. Fax 237-2670
www.jaytonjaybirds.com
Jayton S 100/PK-12
PO Box 168 79528 806-237-2991
Lyle Lackey, prin. Fax 237-2670

Jefferson, Marion, Pop. 2,067
Jefferson ISD 1,200/PK-12
1600 Martin Luther King Dr 75657 903-665-2461
Rob Barnwell, supt. Fax 665-7367
jeffersonisd.org/
Jefferson ES 400/1-4
301 W Harrison St 75657 903-665-2461
Anthony Keith McGill, prin. Fax 665-6401
Jefferson JHS 300/5-8
804 N Alley St 75657 903-665-2461
Clint Coyne, prin. Fax 665-7149
Jefferson PS 200/PK-K
304 W Broadway St 75657 903-665-2461
Lindsey Whitaker, prin. Fax 665-7092

Cypress Bend Adventist ES 50/PK-8
2997 FM 728 75657 903-665-7402

Jewett, Leon, Pop. 1,158
Leon ISD 700/PK-12
12168 US Highway 79 75846 903-626-1400
William Rains, supt. Fax 626-1420
www.leonisd.net/
Leon ES 400/PK-5
12168 US Highway 79 75846 903-626-1425
Geoffery Bowdoin, prin. Fax 626-1440
Leon JHS 200/6-8
12168 US Highway 79 75846 903-626-1450
J.D. Foley, prin. Fax 626-1455

Joaquin, Shelby, Pop. 818
Joaquin ISD 800/PK-12
11109 US Highway 84 E 75954 936-269-3128
Phil Worsham, supt. Fax 269-3615
www.joaquinisd.net/
Joaquin ES 400/PK-5
11109 US Highway 84 E 75954 936-269-3258
Sherry Scruggs, prin. Fax 269-3324
Joaquin JHS 200/6-8
11109 US Highway 84 E 75954 936-269-3128
Terri Gray, prin. Fax 269-9123

Johnson City, Blanco, Pop. 1,640
Johnson City ISD 700/K-12
PO Box 498 78636 830-868-7410
Richard Kolek, supt. Fax 868-7375
www.jc.txed.net
Johnson ES 300/K-4
PO Box 498 78636 830-868-4028
Amanda Haley, prin. Fax 868-7375
Johnson MS 200/5-8
PO Box 498 78636 830-868-9025
Russell Maedgen, prin. Fax 868-7375

Jonesboro, Coryell
Jonesboro ISD 200/PK-12
PO Box 125 76538 254-463-2111
Matt Dossey, supt. Fax 463-2275
www.jonesboroisd.net
Jonesboro S 200/PK-12
PO Box 125 76538 254-463-2111
Kendra Gustin, admin. Fax 463-2275

Jones Creek, Brazoria, Pop. 1,982
Brazosport ISD
Supt. — See Clute
Austin ES 300/PK-6
7351 Stephen F Austin Rd 77541 979-730-7160
Melania Gutierrez, prin. Fax 237-6341

Joshua, Johnson, Pop. 5,826
Joshua ISD 5,000/PK-12
PO Box 40 76058 817-202-2500
Fran Marek, supt. Fax 641-2738
www.joshuaisd.org
Caddo Grove ES 600/PK-5
7301 FM 1902 76058 817-202-2500
Julie Rohleder, prin. Fax 645-6420
Elder ES 600/PK-5
513 Henderson St 76058 817-202-2500
Lance Cathey, prin. Fax 641-2951
Loflin MS 800/6-8
6801 FM 1902 76058 817-202-2500
Damon Patterson, prin. Fax 202-9140
Plum Creek ES 500/PK-5
500 Plum St 76058 817-202-2500
Shelly Green, prin. Fax 202-9133
Staples ES 500/PK-5
505 S Main St 76058 817-202-2500
Toby Cox, prin. Fax 556-0450
Other Schools – See Burleson

Joshua Adventist Multigrade S 100/PK-8
1912 Conveyor Dr 76058 817-556-2109
Joshua Christian Academy 100/PK-12
PO Box 1379 76058 817-295-7377
Brian Archer, admin.

Jourdanton, Atascosa, Pop. 3,848
Jourdanton ISD 1,500/PK-12
200 Zanderson Ave 78026 830-769-3548
Theresa McAllister, supt. Fax 769-3272
www.jourdantonisd.net

Jourdanton ES 700/PK-5
200 Zanderson Ave 78026 830-769-2121
Chandra Camp, prin. Fax 769-2208
Jourdanton JHS 400/6-8
200 Zanderson Ave 78026 830-769-2234
Robert Rutkowski, prin. Fax 769-2998

Junction, Kimble, Pop. 2,554
Junction ISD 700/PK-12
1700 College St 76849 325-446-3510
Mike Carter, supt. Fax 446-4413
www.junctionisd.net
Junction ES 300/PK-5
1700 College St 76849 325-446-2055
Jurahee Silvers, prin. Fax 446-4569
Junction MS 100/6-8
1700 College St 76849 325-446-2464
Joe Jones, prin. Fax 446-2255

Justin, Denton, Pop. 3,207
Northwest ISD 18,800/PK-12
2001 Texan Dr 76247 817-215-0000
Ryder Warren Ed.D., supt. Fax 215-0170
www.nisdtx.org
Hatfield ES 500/K-5
2051 Texan Dr 76247 817-215-0350
Carrie Pierce, prin. Fax 215-0369
Justin ES 500/PK-5
425 Boss Range Rd 76247 817-215-0800
Dr. Lisa Ransleben, prin. Fax 215-0840
Love ES 600/K-5
16301 Elementary Dr 76247 817-698-6600
Jaimie McAllister, prin. Fax 698-6670
Pike MS 800/6-8
2200 Texan Dr 76247 817-215-0400
Christopher Jones, prin. Fax 215-0425
Other Schools – See Fort Worth, Haslet, Newark, Rhome, Roanoke, Trophy Club

Karnack, Harrison
Karnack ISD 100/PK-8
PO Box 259 75661 903-679-3117
Amy Dickson, supt. Fax 679-4252
karnackisd.org
Carver ES 100/PK-8
PO Box 259 75661 903-679-3111
Amy Dickson, prin. Fax 679-3163

Karnes City, Karnes, Pop. 3,027
Karnes City ISD 800/PK-12
314 N Highway 123 78118 830-780-2321
Jeanette Winn, supt. Fax 780-3823
www.kcisd.net
Karnes City JHS 200/6-8
410 N Highway 123 78118 830-780-2321
Theresa Molina, prin. Fax 780-4382
Karnes City PS PK-1
203 E Mayfield 78118 830-780-2321
Jennifer Foster, prin. Fax 780-5376
Sides ES 300/2-5
221 N Esplanade St 78118 830-780-2321
Phyllis Campbell, prin. Fax 780-4427

Katy, Harris, Pop. 13,902
Cypress-Fairbanks ISD
Supt. — See Houston
Duryea ES 1,000/PK-5
20150 Arbor Creek Dr 77449 281-856-5174
Kenneth Henry, prin. Fax 856-5179
Emery ES 800/K-5
19636 Plantation Myrtle 77449 281-855-9080
Michelle Merricks, prin.
Hemmenway ES 800/K-5
20400 W Little York Rd 77449 281-856-9870
Dr. Jae Simpson-Butler, prin. Fax 856-9850
Hoover ES PK-2
6425 Greenhouse Rd 77449 832-667-7301
Michelle Rice, prin. Fax 667-7310
Jowell ES 1,000/PK-5
6355 Greenhouse Rd 77449 281-463-5966
Kimberley Criswell, prin. Fax 345-3628
McFee ES 1,100/K-5
19315 Plantation Cove Ln 77449 281-463-5380
Donna Harden, prin. Fax 463-5680
Robinson ES 900/K-5
4321 Westfield Village Dr 77449 281-855-1240
Irene Ruiz, prin. Fax 855-0740
Sheridan ES 900/PK-5
19790 Kieth Harrow Blvd 77449 281-856-1420
Gina Guidry, prin. Fax 856-1461
Thornton MS 1,300/6-8
19802 Kieth Harrow Blvd 77449 281-856-1500
Reginald Mitchell, prin. Fax 856-1548
Walker ES 1,100/PK-5
6424 Settlers Village Dr 77449 281-345-3200
Kimberly Dameron, prin. Fax 345-3205

Katy ISD 65,800/PK-12
PO Box 159 77492 281-396-6000
Dr. Lance Hindt, supt. Fax 644-1800
www.katyisd.org
Alexander ES 1,000/K-5
6161 S Fry Rd 77494 281-237-7100
Dr. Charmaine Hobin, prin. Fax 644-1585
Beckendorff JHS 1,700/6-8
8200 S Fry Rd 77494 281-237-8800
Dr. Ethan Crowell, prin Fax 644-1635
Beck JHS 1,100/6-8
5200 S Fry Rd 77450 281-237-3300
Carra Daniels, prin. Fax 644-1630
Bethke ES K-5
4535 E Ventana Pkwy 77493 281-234-4200
Carrie Lowery, prin. Fax 644-1935
Bryant ES K-5
29801 Kingsland Blvd 77494 281-234-4300
Dr. William Rhodes, prin. Fax 644-1965
Cardiff JHS 1,000/6-8
3900 Dayflower Dr 77449 281-234-0600
Bryan Rounds, prin. Fax 644-1855
Cimarron ES 600/K-5
1100 S Peek Rd 77450 281-237-6900
Youshawna Hunt, prin. Fax 644-1505
Cinco Ranch JHS 1,200/6-8
23420 Cinco Ranch Blvd 77494 281-237-7300
Elizabeth Nicklas, prin. Fax 644-1640
Creech ES 800/K-5
4242 S Mason Rd 77450 281-237-8850
Euberta Lucas, prin. Fax 644-1605
Davidson ES K-6
26906 Pine Mill Ranch Dr 77494 281-234-2500
Jessie Miller, prin. Fax 644-1925
Exley ES 1,000/PK-5
21800 Westheimer Pkwy 77450 281-237-8400
Juli Noeldner, prin. Fax 644-1535
Fielder ES 1,000/K-5
2100 Greenway Village Dr 77494 281-237-6450
Ramona Cardin, prin. Fax 644-1515
Franz ES 1,000/PK-5
2751 N Westgreen Blvd 77449 281-237-8600
Yvette Sylvan, prin. Fax 644-1520
Golbow ES 800/PK-5
3535 Lakes of Bridgewater 77449 281-237-5350
Dr. Ann LaLime, prin. Fax 644-1525
Griffin ES 800/K-5
7800 S Fry Rd 77494 281-237-8700
Jackie Keithan, prin. Fax 644-1850
Hayes ES 600/K-5
21203 Park Timbers Ln 77450 281-237-3200
Heather Mulcahy, prin. Fax 644-1541
Holland ES 900/K-5
23720 Seven Meadows Pkwy 77494 281-234-0500
Linnea Griffith, prin. Fax 644-1695
Hutsell ES 800/PK-5
5360 Franz Rd 77493 281-237-6500
Dr. Margie Blount, prin. Fax 644-1530
Jenks ES K-5
27602 Westridge Creek Ln 77494 281-234-4100
Troy Kemp, prin Fax 644-1940
Katy ES 500/PK-5
5726 George Bush Dr 77493 281-237-6550
Elizabeth Grimet, prin. Fax 644-1550
Katy JHS 1,400/6-8
5350 Franz Rd 77493 281-237-6800
Dr. Jake Leblanc, prin. Fax 644-1645
Kilpatrick ES 1,000/K-5
26100 Cinco Ranch Blvd 77494 281-237-7600
Malynn Rodriguez, prin. Fax 644-1570
King ES 1,100/K-5
1901 Charlton House Ln 77493 281-237-6850
Tammi Wilhelm, prin. Fax 644-1595
Lindsey ES 500/PK-5
2431 Joan Collier Tr 77494 832-223-5400
Heather Williams, prin. Fax 223-5401
McDonald JHS 1,000/6-8
3635 Lakes of Bridgewater 77449 281-237-5300
Dr. Kenneth Cummings, prin. Fax 644-1655
McMeans JHS 1,100/6-8
21000 Westheimer Pkwy 77450 281-237-8000
Dr. Susan Rice, prin Fax 644-1660
McRoberts ES 800/PK-5
3535 N Fry Rd 77449 281-237-2000
Rahsan Smith, prin. Fax 644-1580
Memorial Parkway ES 900/PK-5
21603 Park Tree Ln 77450 281-237-5850
Dr. Doreen Martinez, prin. Fax 644-1560
Memorial Parkway JHS 900/6-8
21203 Highland Knolls Dr 77450 281-237-5800
Dr. Emily Craig, prin. Fax 644-1665
Morton Ranch ES 700/K-5
2502 N Mason Rd 77449 281-234-0300
Deb Hubble, prin. Fax 644-1685
Morton Ranch JHS 1,300/6-8
2498 N Mason Rd 77449 281-237-7400
Dr. Sanee Bell, prin. Fax 644-1670
Nottingham Country ES 600/K-5
20500 Kingsland Blvd 77450 281-237-5500
Tracy Stroud, prin. Fax 644-1566
Pattison ES 800/PK-5
19910 Stonelodge Dr 77450 281-237-5450
Debra Barker, prin. Fax 644-1575
Rhoads ES 1,100/PK-5
19711 Clay Rd 77449 281-237-8500
Amanda Weaver, prin. Fax 644-1590
Rylander ES 1,300/K-5
24831 Westheimer Pkwy 77494 281-237-8300
Gwendolyn Coffey, prin. Fax 644-1600
Seven Lake JHS 1,600/6-8
6026 Katy Gaston Rd 77494 281-234-2100
Dr. Imelda Medrano, prin. Fax 644-1885
Shafer ES 1,300/K-5
5150 Ranch Point Dr 77494 281-234-1900
Melissa Salyer, prin. Fax 644-1880
Stanley ES 1,300/K-5
26633 Cinco Terrace Dr 77494 281-234-1400
Rebecca Wingfield, prin. Fax 644-1865
Stephens ES 700/K-5
2715 N Fry Rd 77449 281-234-0200
Stephanie Vaughan, prin. Fax 644-1680
Stockdick JHS, 4777 Peek Rd 77449 6-8
Mark McCord, prin. 281-234-2700
Sundown ES 900/PK-5
20100 Saums Rd 77449 281-237-5400
Martha Pulido, prin. Fax 644-1610
Tays JHS 6-8
26721 Hawks Prairie Blvd 77494 281-234-2400
Dr. Kris Mitzner, prin. Fax 644-1945
West Memorial ES 800/PK-5
22605 Provincial Blvd 77450 281-237-6600
Paul Moussavi, prin. Fax 644-1625
West Memorial JHS 700/6-8
22311 Provincial Blvd 77450 281-237-6400
Gina Cobb, prin. Fax 644-1675
Williams ES 700/K-5
3900 S Peek Rd 77450 281-237-7200
Angel Bateman, prin. Fax 644-1545
Wilson ES 900/K-5
5200 Falcon Landing Blvd 77494 281-234-1600
Rhonda Henderson, prin. Fax 644-1870
Winborn ES 700/PK-5
22555 Prince George St 77449 281-237-6650
Leah Lowry, prin. Fax 644-1510
Wolman ES 1,000/K-5
28727 N Firethorne Rd 77494 281-234-1700
Kelly Ricks, prin. Fax 644-1875
WoodCreek ES 1,400/K-5
1155 WoodCreek Bend Ln 77494 281-234-0100
Ronnie Mosher, prin. Fax 644-1690
WoodCreek JHS 1,600/6-8
1801 WoodCreek Bend Ln 77494 281-234-0800
Dr. Melinda Stone, prin. Fax 644-1860
Other Schools – See Fulshear, Houston

CrossPoint Christian S 400/PK-K
700 Westgreen Blvd 77450 281-945-5133
Amy Sanders, dir. Fax 599-9446
Faith West Academy 600/PK-12
2225 Porter Rd 77493 281-391-5683
Mary Strickland, prin. Fax 391-2606
Katy Adventist Christian S 50/PK-8
1913 East Ave 77493 281-392-5603

Kaufman, Kaufman, Pop. 6,619
Kaufman ISD 3,900/PK-12
1000 S Houston St 75142 972-932-2622
Dr. Lori Blaylock, supt. Fax 932-3325
www.kaufmanisd.net
Edwards ECC 500/PK-K
1605 Rand Rd 75142 972-932-0800
Melanie Bowers, prin. Fax 932-6850
Monday PS 600/1-2
905 S Madison St 75142 972-932-3513
Kathy Allen, prin. Fax 932-2758
Nash IS 600/5-6
1002 S Houston St 75142 972-932-6415
Alicia Thurston, prin. Fax 932-4028
Norman JHS 600/7-8
3701 S Houston St 75142 972-932-2410
Jeremy Melton, prin. Fax 932-7771
Phillips ES 600/3-4
1501 Royal Dr 75142 972-932-4500
Kara Holley, prin. Fax 932-7633

Kaufman Christian S 100/PK-12
401 N Shannon St 75142 972-932-6111
Christy Butler, admin. Fax 962-6111

Keene, Johnson, Pop. 5,659
Keene ISD 900/PK-12
PO Box 656 76059 817-774-5200
Ricky Stephens, supt. Fax 774-5400
www.keeneisd.org/
Keene ES 400/PK-5
PO Box 656 76059 817-774-5320
Jamie Ingram, prin. Fax 774-5303
Keene JHS 200/6-8
PO Box 656 76059 817-774-5270
Heather Archer, prin. Fax 774-5402

Keene Adventist ES 200/PK-8
302 Pecan St 76059 817-645-9125

Keller, Tarrant, Pop. 38,916
Keller ISD 33,800/PK-12
350 Keller Pkwy 76248 817-744-1000
Dr. Rick Westfall, supt. Fax 744-1263
www.kellerisd.net
Bear Creek IS 800/5-6
801 Bear Creek Pkwy 76248 817-744-3650
Amanda Burruel, prin. Fax 377-5200
Hidden Lakes ES 500/K-4
900 Preston Ln 76248 817-744-5000
Melanie Graham, prin. Fax 741-1260
Indian Springs MS 900/7-8
305 Bursey Rd 76248 817-744-3200
Sandy Troudt, prin. Fax 431-4432
Keller-Harvel ES 500/K-4
635 Norma Ln 76248 817-744-5100
Leslie Tewell, prin. Fax 337-3551
Keller MS 900/7-8
300 College Ave 76248 817-744-2900
Sandra Chapa, prin. Fax 377-3512
Ridgeview ES 600/K-4
1601 Marshall Ridge Pkwy 76248 817-744-6600
Becky Wilder, prin. Fax 744-6438
Shady Grove ES 500/K-4
1400 Sarah Brooks Dr 76248 817-744-5600
Anna Renfro, prin. Fax 428-2895
Willis Lane ES 500/K-4
1620 Willis Ln 76248 817-744-5700
Cheryl Hudson, prin. Fax 337-3830
Other Schools – See Colleyville, Fort Worth, Southlake, Watauga

---

Messiah Lutheran Classical Academy 100/PK-10
1308 Whitley Rd 76248 817-431-5486
Betsy Kirk, hdmstr. Fax 431-8536
St. Elizabeth Ann Seton Catholic S 600/PK-8
2016 Willis Ln 76248 817-431-4845
William Perales, prin. Fax 431-4165

Kemah, Galveston, Pop. 1,747
Clear Creek ISD
Supt. — See League City
Stewart ES 700/PK-5
330 FM 2094 Rd 77565 281-284-4700
Dr. Britani Moses, prin. Fax 284-4705

Kemp, Kaufman, Pop. 1,139
Kemp ISD 1,400/PK-12
905 S Main St 75143 903-498-1314
Phil Edwards, supt. Fax 498-1315
www.kempisd.org

Kemp IS 300/3-5
101 Old State Highway 40 Rd 75143 903-498-1362
Kim McDowell, prin. Fax 498-1379
Kemp JHS 400/6-8
1000 Tolosa Rd 75143 903-498-1343
Clay Tracy, prin. Fax 498-1359
Kemp PS 400/PK-2
601 E 8th St 75143 903-498-1404
Angela Barton, prin. Fax 498-2136

Kenedy, Karnes, Pop. 3,282
Kenedy ISD 700/PK-12
401 FM 719 78119 830-583-4100
Travis McClellan, supt. Fax 583-9950
www.kenedy.isd.tenet.edu
Kenedy ES 400/PK-5
401 FM 719 78119 830-583-4100
Melanie Witte, prin. Fax 583-3973
Kenedy MS 200/6-8
401 FM 719 78119 830-583-4100
Dr. Richard Cardin, prin. Fax 583-9519

Kennard, Houston, Pop. 331
Kennard ISD 300/PK-12
304 State Highway 7 E 75847 936-655-2161
Malinda Lindsey, supt. Fax 655-2327
www.kennardisd.net
Kennard ES 200/PK-6
304 State Highway 7 E 75847 936-655-2724
Oscar Encarnacion, prin. Fax 655-2327

Kennedale, Tarrant, Pop. 6,631
Kennedale ISD 3,200/PK-12
PO Box 467 76060 817-563-8000
Gary Dugger, supt. Fax 483-3610
www.kennedaleisd.net
Arthur IS 500/5-6
PO Box 448 76060 817-563-8300
Frankie Bryson, prin. Fax 483-3628
Delaney ES 800/PK-4
PO Box 1287 76060 817-563-8400
Katina Martinez, prin. Fax 483-3653
Kennedale JHS 500/7-8
PO Box 489 76060 817-563-8200
Bel Williams, prin. Fax 483-3655
Other Schools – See Arlington

Fellowship Academy 200/PK-12
PO Box 738 76060 817-483-2400
Monica Collier, admin. Fax 483-2404

Kerens, Navarro, Pop. 1,548
Kerens ISD 600/PK-12
200 Bobcat Ln 75144 903-396-2924
Jason Adams, supt. Fax 396-2334
www.kerensisd.org
Kerens S 600/PK-12
200 Bobcat Ln 75144 903-396-2931
Greg Priddy, prin. Fax 396-2334

Kermit, Winkler, Pop. 5,630
Kermit ISD 1,300/PK-12
601 S Poplar St 79745 432-586-1000
Denise Shetter, supt. Fax 586-1016
www.kisd.esc18.net
Kermit ES 700/PK-4
601 S Poplar St 79745 432-586-1020
Sonia Gonzales, prin. Fax 586-1023
Kermit JHS 300/5-8
601 S Poplar St 79745 432-586-1040
Laura Miller, prin. Fax 586-1045

Kerrville, Kerr, Pop. 22,087
Kerrville ISD 5,000/PK-12
1009 Barnett St 78028 830-257-2200
Dr. Mark Foust, supt. Fax 257-2249
www.kerrvilleisd.net
Daniels ES 600/K-5
2002 Singing Wind Dr 78028 830-257-2208
Amy Billeiter, prin. Fax 257-1310
ECC 300/PK-PK
1011 3rd St 78028 830-257-1335
Susana Alejandro, prin. Fax 257-7885
Nimitz ES 500/K-5
100 Valley View Dr 78028 830-257-2209
Julie Johnson, prin. Fax 895-7905
Peterson MS 700/7-8
1607 Sidney Baker St 78028 830-257-2204
Tamela Crawford, prin. Fax 257-1300
Starkey ES 500/PK-5
1030 W Main St 78028 830-257-2210
Amy Ahrens, prin. Fax 792-3727
Tally ES 600/K-5
1840 Goat Creek Pkwy 78028 830-257-2222
Holly Jones, prin. Fax 257-2288
Wilson Sixth Grade S 400/6-6
605 Tivy St 78028 830-257-2207
James Harmon, prin. Fax 257-1316

Hill Country Adventist S 50/1-8
611 Harper Rd 78028 830-257-3903
Notre Dame Catholic S 100/PK-8
907 Main St 78028 830-257-6707
Sandi Killo, prin. Fax 792-4370

Kilgore, Gregg, Pop. 12,762
Kilgore ISD 4,000/PK-12
301 N Kilgore St 75662 903-988-3900
Cara Cooke, supt. Fax 983-3212
www.kisd.org
Chandler ES 600/2-3
301 N Kilgore St 75662 903-988-3904
Dr. Cindy Lindley, prin. Fax 986-8026
Kilgore IS 600/4-5
301 N Kilgore St 75662 903-988-3903
Kim Slayter, prin. Fax 984-7879
Kilgore MS 900/6-8
301 N Kilgore St 75662 903-988-3902
April Cox, prin. Fax 984-6225
Kilgore PS 900/PK-1
301 N Kilgore St 75662 903-988-3905
Tamara Dean, prin. Fax 984-2176

Sabine ISD
Supt. — See Gladewater
Sabine ES 700/PK-5
645 Access Rd 75662 903-984-5320
Teri Bass, prin. Fax 984-4101

Killeen, Bell, Pop. 120,349
Killeen ISD 40,700/PK-12
PO Box 967 76540 254-336-0000
Dr. John Craft, supt. Fax 526-0010
www.killeenisd.org
Bellaire ES 600/PK-5
108 W Jasper Dr 76542 254-336-1410
Lavonda Loney, prin. Fax 336-1437
Brookhaven ES 700/PK-5
3221 Hilliard Ave 76543 254-336-1440
Iris Felder, prin. Fax 336-1463
Cedar Valley ES 700/PK-5
4801 Chantz Dr 76542 254-336-1480
Connie Morris, prin. Fax 336-1496
Clifton Park ES 500/PK-5
2200 Trimmier Rd 76541 254-336-1580
Catherine Snyder, prin. Fax 336-1598
Cross ES 800/PK-5
1910 Herndon Dr 76543 254-336-2550
Tomas Sias, prin. Fax 336-2560
Douse ES PK-5
700 Rebecca Lynn Ln 76542 254-336-7480
Pamela Disher, prin. Fax 336-7490
East Ward ES 500/PK-5
1608 E Rancier Ave 76541 254-336-1650
Norma Baker, prin. Fax 336-1669
Fowler ES 400/PK-5
4910 Katy Creek Ln 76549 254-336-1760
Joyce Lauer, prin. Fax 336-1789
Hay Branch ES 700/PK-5
6101 Westcliff Rd 76543 254-336-2080
Cassandra Spearman, prin. Fax 336-2097
Haynes ES 1,100/PK-5
3309 Canadian River Loop 76549 254-336-6750
Angela Donovan, prin. Fax 336-2798
Iduma ES 1,000/PK-5
4400 Foster Ln 76549 254-336-2590
Katy Bohannon, prin. Fax 336-2598
Liberty Hill MS 900/6-8
4500 Kit Carson Trl 76542 254-336-1370
Jorge Soldevila, prin. Fax 336-1403
Live Oak Ridge MS 800/6-8
2600 Robinett Rd 76549 254-336-2490
Wanda Stidom, prin. Fax 336-2498
Manor MS 700/6-8
1700 S W S Young Dr 76543 254-336-1310
Jennifer Washington, prin. Fax 336-1317
Maxdale ES 800/PK-5
2600 Westwood Dr 76549 254-336-2460
Bobbie Evans, prin. Fax 336-2469
Nolan MS 700/6-8
505 E Jasper Dr 76541 254-336-1150
Lolly Garcia, prin. Fax 336-1162
Palo Alto MS 900/6-8
2301 W Elms Rd 76549 254-336-1200
Matt Widacki, prin. Fax 336-1217
Patterson MS 1,100/6-8
8383 W Trimmier Rd 76542 254-336-7100
Jill Balzer, prin. Fax 336-7136
Peebles ES 700/PK-5
1800 N W S Young Dr 76543 254-336-2120
Gayle Dudley, prin. Fax 336-2131
Pershing Park ES 800/PK-5
1500 W Central Texas Expy 76549 254-336-1790
Linda Butler, prin. Fax 336-1804
Rancier MS 700/6-8
3301 Hilliard Ave 76543 254-336-1250
Micah Wells, prin. Fax 336-1254
Reeces Creek ES 900/PK-5
400 W Stan Schlueter Loop 76542 254-336-2150
Michelle Taylor, prin. Fax 336-2165
Saegert ES 1,200/PK-5
5600 Schorn Dr 76542 254-336-6660
Eli Lopez, prin. Fax 336-6684
Smith MS 6-8
6000 Brushy Creek Dr 76549 254-336-1050
Chad Wolf, prin. Fax 336-1056
Sugar Loaf ES 500/PK-5
1517 Barbara Ln 76549 254-336-1940
Violet Simmons, prin. Fax 336-1945
Timber Ridge ES 1,000/PK-5
5402 White Rock Dr 76542 254-336-6630
Tanya Dockery, prin. Fax 336-6653
Trimmier ES 900/PK-5
4400 Success Dr 76542 254-336-2270
Penny Batts, prin. Fax 336-2284
West Ward ES 500/PK-5
709 W Dean Ave 76541 254-336-1830
Maureen Adams, prin. Fax 336-1861
Willow Springs ES 1,000/PK-5
2501 W Stan Schlueter Loop 76549 254-336-2020
Denise Pennington, prin. Fax 336-2047
Other Schools – See Fort Hood, Harker Heights, Nolanville

Grace Lutheran S 50/PK-K
1007 Bacon Ranch Rd 76542 254-634-4424
Naomi Matthys, admin. Fax 634-5475
Killeen Adventist Junior Academy 100/PK-8
3412 Lake Rd 76543 254-699-9466
Memorial Christian Academy 300/PK-12
PO Box 11269 76547 254-526-5403
Dr. Barbara Carpenter, admin. Fax 634-2030
St. Joseph Catholic S 100/PK-6
2901 E Rancier Ave 76543 254-634-7272
Katie Grooms, prin. Fax 634-1224

Kingsland, Llano, Pop. 5,947
Llano ISD
Supt. — See Llano
Packsaddle ES 500/PK-5
150 Pioneer Ln 78639 325-388-8129
Maela Edmonson, prin. Fax 388-7000

Kingsville, Kleberg, Pop. 25,996
Kingsville ISD 3,400/PK-12
PO Box 871 78364 361-592-3387
Carol G. Perez Ed.D., supt. Fax 595-7805
www.kingsvilleisd.com
Gillett IS 400/5-6
PO Box 871 78364 361-595-8200
Guadalupe Martinez, prin. Fax 595-9008
Harrel ES 300/PK-4
PO Box 871 78364 361-592-9305
Leo Ramos, prin. Fax 516-1313
Harvey ES 500/PK-4
PO Box 871 78364 361-592-4327
Dawn Mireles, prin. Fax 595-9130
Kleberg ES 400/PK-4
PO Box 871 78364 361-592-2615
Connie Herrera, prin. Fax 595-9145
Memorial MS 500/7-8
PO Box 871 78364 361-595-8675
Dr. Alys Williams, prin. Fax 592-4198
Perez ES 400/PK-4
PO Box 871 78364 361-592-8511
Emily Salazar, prin. Fax 516-1468

Ricardo ISD 700/PK-8
138 W County Road 2160 78363 361-592-6465
Dr. Maria Canales, supt. Fax 592-3101
www.ricardoisd.us
Ricardo ES 400/PK-4
138 W County Road 2160 78363 361-592-6465
Marci Braswell, prin. Fax 593-0704
Ricardo MS 300/5-8
138 W County Road 2160 78363 361-592-6465
Dr. Cynthia Flores, prin. Fax 593-0707

Santa Gertrudis ISD 600/PK-12
PO Box 592 78364 361-384-5087
Dr. Corey Seymour, supt. Fax 592-7736
www.sgisd.net
Santa Gertrudis ES 300/PK-8
PO Box 592 78364 361-384-5046
Dr. Veronica Alfaro, prin. Fax 592-3128

St. Gertrude S 100/PK-6
400 E Caesar Ave 78363 361-592-6522
Griselda Gonzalez White, prin. Fax 592-0100

Kingwood, Harris, Pop. 37,397
Humble ISD
Supt. — See Humble
Bear Branch ES 600/PK-5
3500 Garden Lake Dr 77339 281-641-1600
Kakie Palmer, prin. Fax 641-1617
Creekwood MS 1,100/6-8
3603 W Lake Houston Pkwy 77339 281-641-4400
Walt Winicki, prin. Fax 641-4417
Deerwood ES 600/PK-5
2920 Forest Garden Dr 77345 281-641-2200
Macaire McDonough-Davies, prin. Fax 641-2217
Elm Grove ES 500/K-5
2815 Clear Ridge Dr 77339 281-641-1700
Donna Fife, prin. Fax 641-1717
Foster ES 600/PK-5
1800 Trailwood Village Dr 77339 281-641-1400
Diane Zelezinski, prin. Fax 641-1417
Greentree ES 700/K-5
3502 Brook Shadow Dr 77345 281-641-1900
Linda Pearce, prin. Fax 641-1917
Hidden Hollow ES 500/PK-5
4104 Appalachian Trl 77345 281-641-2400
Janice Wiederhold, prin. Fax 641-2417
Kingwood MS 1,000/6-8
2407 Pine Terrace Dr 77339 281-641-4200
Bob Atteberry, prin. Fax 641-4217
Riverwood MS 1,100/6-8
2910 High Valley Dr 77345 281-641-4800
Donnie Bodron, prin. Fax 641-4817
Shadow Forest ES 600/K-5
2300 Mills Branch Dr 77345 281-641-2600
Lisa Lackey, prin. Fax 641-2617
Willow Creek ES 600/K-5
2002 Willow Terrace Dr 77345 281-641-2300
Scott Duncan, prin. Fax 641-2317
Woodland Hills ES 500/K-5
2222 Tree Ln 77339 281-641-1500
Debi Beard, prin. Fax 641-1517

New Caney ISD
Supt. — See New Caney
Kings Manor ES 600/PK-5
21111 Royal Crossing Dr 77339 281-577-2940
Stacey Paine, prin. Fax 359-6391

Christian Life Center Academy 200/PK-12
806 Russell Palmer Rd 77339 281-319-0077
Covenant Preparatory S 200/PK-6
1711 Hamblen Rd 77339 281-359-1090
Brad Baggett, head sch Fax 359-5560
Good Shepherd Episcopal S 200/PK-K
2929 Woodland Hills Dr 77339 281-359-1895
Kingwood Montessori S 50/PK-6
2510 Mills Branch Dr Ste 10 77345 281-548-1452
Pines Montessori S 100/PK-8
3535 Cedar Knolls Dr 77339 281-358-8933
Patricia Sobelman, head sch Fax 358-3162
St. Martha S 400/PK-8
2411 Oak Shores Dr 77339 281-358-5523
Jessica Munscher, prin. Fax 358-5526

Kirbyville, Jasper, Pop. 2,112
Kirbyville Consolidated ISD 1,300/PK-12
206 E Main St 75956 409-423-2284
Dr. Thomas Wallis, supt. Fax 423-2367
www.kirbyvillecisd.org
Kirbyville ES 700/PK-5
2100 S Margaret Ave 75956 409-423-8526
Kristi Gore, prin. Fax 423-3753
Kirbyville JHS 200/6-8
2200 S Margaret Ave 75956 409-420-0692
Rodney Anderson, prin. Fax 423-6654

Klein, Harris, Pop. 12,000
Klein ISD 48,600/PK-12
7200 Spring Cypress Rd 77379 832-249-4000
Dr. Bret Champion, supt. Fax 249-4015
www.kleinisd.net
Benfer ES 700/PK-5
18027 Kuykendahl Rd Ste B 77379 832-484-6000
Shannon Strole, prin. Fax 484-7850
Benignus ES 900/PK-5
7225 Alvin A Klein Dr 77379 832-484-7750
Dawn Proctor, prin. Fax 484-7796
Bernshausen ES 700/PK-5
11116 Mahaffey Rd, 832-375-8000
Cassandra Christian, prin. Fax 375-8050
Blackshear ES 900/PK-5
11211 Lacey Rd, 832-375-7600
Meagan White, prin. Fax 375-7725
Brill ES 700/PK-5
9102 Herts Rd 77379 832-484-6150
Samantha Hinson, prin. Fax 484-7851
Doerre IS 1,200/6-8
18218 Theiss Mail Route Rd 77379 832-249-5700
Amana Land, prin. Fax 249-4054
Ehrhardt ES 700/PK-5
6603 Rosebrook Ln 77379 832-484-6200
Darrel Luedeker, prin. Fax 484-7853
Frank ES 600/PK-5
9225 Crescent Clover Dr 77379 832-375-7000
Eve Messina, prin. Fax 375-7100
Hassler ES 700/PK-5
9325 Lochlea Ridge Dr 77379 832-484-7100
Sarah Brown, prin. Fax 484-7860
Kleb IS 1,400/6-8
7425 Louetta Rd 77379 832-249-5500
Clay Huggins, prin. Fax 249-4053
Krahn ES 800/PK-5
9502 Eday Dr 77379 832-484-6500
Frank Ward, prin. Fax 484-7868
Krimmel IS 1,100/6-8
7070 FM 2920 Rd 77379 832-375-7200
Prentiss Harper, prin. Fax 375-7150
Kuehnle ES 700/PK-5
5510 Winding Ridge Dr 77379 832-484-6650
Julia Funk, prin. Fax 484-7870
Mahaffey ES PK-5
10255 Mahaffey Rd, 832-375-8300
Christy Petross, prin.
Mittelstadt ES 900/PK-5
7525 Kleingreen Ln 77379 832-484-6700
Cynthia Levy, prin. Fax 484-7876
Mueller ES 800/PK-5
7074 FM 2920 Rd 77379 832-375-7300
Pattie Holecek, prin. Fax 375-7425
Strack IS 1,200/6-8
18027 Kuykendahl Rd Ste S 77379 832-249-5400
Andrea Comer, prin. Fax 249-4051
Theiss ES 600/PK-5
17510 Theiss Mail Route Rd 77379 832-484-5900
JoAnn Keenan, prin. Fax 484-7886
Other Schools – See Houston, Spring, Tomball

Trinity Lutheran S 700/PK-8
18926 Klein Church Rd 77379 281-376-5810
Keith Goedecke, prin. Fax 290-4950

Knippa, Uvalde, Pop. 688
Knippa ISD 400/PK-12
PO Box 99 78870 830-934-2176
Elda Alejandro, supt. Fax 934-2490
www.knippaisd.net
Knippa S 400/PK-12
PO Box 99 78870 830-934-2177
Jeff Cottrill, prin. Fax 934-2490

Knox City, Knox, Pop. 1,121
Knox City-O'Brien Consolidated ISD 300/PK-12
606 E Main St 79529 940-657-3521
Louis Baty, supt. Fax 657-3379
www.knoxcityschools.net
Knox City ES 100/PK-4
606 E Main St 79529 940-657-3147
Marsha Quade, prin. Fax 657-3379
Other Schools – See O Brien

Kopperl, Bosque
Kopperl ISD 200/PK-12
PO Box 67 76652 254-889-3502
Kenneth Bateman, supt. Fax 889-3443
www.kopperlisd.org
Kopperl S 200/PK-12
PO Box 67 76652 254-889-3502
Katrina Adcock, prin. Fax 889-3443

Kountze, Hardin, Pop. 2,103
Kountze ISD 1,200/PK-12
PO Box 460 77625 409-246-3352
John Ferguson, supt. Fax 246-3217
kountzeisd.org
Kountze ES 400/PK-3
PO Box 460 77625 409-246-3877
Dr. Shane Reyenga, prin. Fax 246-4138
Kountze IS 300/4-6
PO Box 460 77625 409-246-8230
Connie Joubert, prin. Fax 246-3857
Kountze MS 200/7-8
PO Box 460 77625 409-246-3551
Thomas Cooley, prin. Fax 246-8907

Kress, Swisher, Pop. 707
Kress ISD 200/PK-12
200 E 5th St 79052 806-684-2652
Leah Zeigler, supt. Fax 684-2687
www.kressonline.net
Kress ES 100/PK-6
401 Ripley Ave 79052 806-684-2326
Shawn Langston, prin. Fax 684-2778

Krum, Denton, Pop. 4,096
Krum ISD 2,000/PK-12
1200 Bobcat Blvd 76249 940-482-6000
Cody Carroll, supt. Fax 482-3929
www.krumisd.net
Dodd IS 300/4-5
1200 Bobcat Blvd 76249 940-482-2603
Patricia Bolz, prin. Fax 482-3368
Dyer ES 300/2-3
1200 Bobcat Blvd 76249 940-482-2604
Lindsey Boone, prin. Fax 482-8203
Krum Early Education Center 400/PK-1
1200 Bobcat Blvd 76249 940-482-2605
Tammy Morris, prin. Fax 482-6232
Krum MS 400/6-8
1200 Bobcat Blvd 76249 940-482-2602
Robert Butler, prin. Fax 482-6299

Kyle, Hays, Pop. 27,512
Hays Consolidated ISD 17,200/PK-12
21003 Interstate 35 78640 512-268-2141
Dr. Ann Dixon, supt. Fax 268-2147
www.hayscisd.net
Chapa MS 700/6-8
3311 Dacy Ln 78640 512-268-8500
Lisa Walls, prin. Fax 295-7824
Fuentes ES 600/PK-5
901 Goforth Rd 78640 512-268-7827
Regina Butcher, prin. Fax 268-5968
Hemphill ES 800/PK-5
3995 E FM 150 78640 512-268-4688
Cynthia Vasquez, prin. Fax 268-6208
Kyle ES 700/PK-5
500 W Blanco St 78640 512-268-3311
Karen Lucita, prin. Fax 268-1417
Negley ES 800/K-5
5940 McNaughton 78640 512-268-8501
Melody Crowther, prin. Fax 268-8582
Science Hall ES 700/K-5
1510 Bebee Rd 78640 512-268-8502
Soor-El Puga, prin. Fax 268-8784
Simon MS 600/6-8
3839 E FM 150 78640 512-268-8507
Dr. Jose Puga, prin. Fax 268-4146
Tobias ES 700/PK-5
1005 E FM 150 78640 512-268-8437
Paige Collier, prin. Fax 268-8447
Wallace MS 800/6-8
1500 W Center St 78640 512-268-2891
Sarah Hodges, prin. Fax 268-1853
Other Schools – See Buda, Niederwald, San Marcos

La Coste, Medina, Pop. 1,105
Medina Valley ISD
Supt. — See Castroville
LaCoste ES 600/PK-5
PO Box 280 78039 830-931-2243
Natalie Benke, prin. Fax 985-3732

Ladonia, Fannin, Pop. 606
Fannindel ISD 200/PK-12
601 W Main St 75449 903-367-7251
Drew Thomas, supt. Fax 367-7252
www.fannindel.net
Other Schools – See Pecan Gap

La Feria, Cameron, Pop. 7,287
La Feria ISD 3,600/PK-12
PO Box 1159 78559 956-797-8300
Cathy Lee Hernandez, supt. Fax 797-3737
www.laferiaisd.org/
Dominguez ES 600/5-6
PO Box 1159 78559 956-797-8430
Yvette Cantu, prin. Fax 797-2600
Green JHS 500/7-8
PO Box 1159 78559 956-797-8400
Michael Torres, prin. Fax 797-2157
Houston ES 600/PK-4
PO Box 1159 78559 956-797-8490
Maria Rodriguez, prin. Fax 797-5169
Sanchez ES 500/PK-4
PO Box 1159 78559 956-797-8550
Umberto Flores, prin. Fax 797-8530
Vail ES 500/PK-4
PO Box 1159 78559 956-797-8460
Rosalinda Garza, prin. Fax 797-3429

Lago Vista, Travis, Pop. 5,961
Lago Vista ISD 1,300/PK-12
PO Box 4929 78645 512-267-8300
Darren Webb, supt. Fax 267-8304
www.lagovistaisd.net
Lago Vista ES 400/PK-3
PO Box 4929 78645 512-267-8300
Michelle Jackson, prin. Fax 267-8362
Lago Vista IS 100/4-5
PO Box 4929 78645 512-267-8300
Stacie Davis, prin. Fax 267-8304
Lago Vista MS 300/6-8
PO Box 4929 78645 512-267-8300
Davin Vogler, prin. Fax 267-8329

La Grange, Fayette, Pop. 4,573
La Grange ISD 1,500/PK-12
PO Box 100 78945 979-968-7000
William D. Wagner, supt. Fax 968-8155
www.lgisd.net/
Hermes ES 600/PK-6
PO Box 100 78945 979-968-4700
Fax 968-5694
La Grange MS 300/7-8
PO Box 100 78945 979-968-4747
Cliff Kinder, prin. Fax 968-6419

Sacred Heart Catholic S 200/PK-6
545 E Pearl St 78945 979-968-3223
LaDonna Voelkel, prin. Fax 968-6382

La Joya, Hidalgo, Pop. 3,984
La Joya ISD 29,900/PK-12
201 W Expressway 83 78560 956-323-2000
Dr. Alda T. Benavides, supt. Fax 323-2001
www.lajoyaisd.com
De Zavala MS 700/6-8
603 Tabasco Rd 78560 956-323-2770
Dr. Antonio Uresti, prin. Fax 323-2771
Tabasco ES 800/PK-5
223 S Leo Ave 78560 956-323-2440
Marena Contreras, prin. Fax 323-2441
Other Schools – See Alton, Mission, Palmview, Penitas, Sullivan City

Lake Dallas, Denton, Pop. 6,973
Lake Dallas ISD 4,000/PK-12
PO Box 548 75065 940-497-4039
Gayle Stinson, supt. Fax 497-3737
www.ldisd.net
Lake Dallas ES 700/PK-5
PO Box 548 75065 940-497-2222
Jennifer Perry, prin. Fax 497-2807
Lake Dallas MS 900/6-8
PO Box 548 75065 940-497-4037
Jim Parker, prin. Fax 497-4028
Other Schools – See Corinth, Shady Shores

Lake Jackson, Brazoria, Pop. 26,471
Brazosport ISD
Supt. — See Clute
Beutel ES 500/PK-4
300 Ligustrum St 77566 979-730-7165
Laura Morris, prin. Fax 292-2821
Brannen ES 500/PK-4
802 That Way St 77566 979-730-7170
Julie Evans, prin. Fax 292-2834
Lake Jackson IS 900/7-8
100 Oyster Creek Dr 77566 979-730-7250
Susan Wood, prin. Fax 292-2804
Ney ES 500/PK-4
308 Winding Way St 77566 979-730-7190
Vicky Parr, prin. Fax 292-2829
Rasco MS 800/5-6
92 Lake Rd 77566 979-730-7225
J. Gonzalez, prin. Fax 292-2817
Roberts ES 500/PK-4
110 Cedar St 77566 979-730-7205
Jennifer Nabors, prin. Fax 292-2825

Brazosport Christian S 200/PK-12
200 Willow Dr Ste B 77566 979-297-0563
Todd Landers, head sch Fax 297-8455

Lake Worth, Tarrant, Pop. 4,497
Lake Worth ISD 3,200/PK-12
6805 Telephone Rd 76135 817-306-4200
John Hebert, supt. Fax 237-2583
www.lwisd.org
Howry IS 500/5-6
4000 Dakota Trl 76135 817-306-4240
Karen Miller, prin. Fax 237-3687
Morris ES 400/PK-4
3801 Merrett Dr 76135 817-306-4260
Eric Moore, prin. Fax 237-3625
Tadpole Learning Center 50/PK-PK
6817 Telephone Rd 76135 817-306-4200
Ami Edwards, dir. Fax 237-5131
Other Schools – See Fort Worth

La Marque, Galveston, Pop. 14,302
Texas City ISD
Supt. — See Texas City
La Marque ES, 1217 Vauthier 77568 300/2-4
Sharon Williams, prin. 409-908-5100
La Marque MS, 1431 Bayou Rd 77568 5-8
Dr. Florence Adkins, prin. 409-938-4286
La Marque PS, 100 Lake Rd 77568 400/PK-1
Patti Martin, prin. 409-935-3020

Abundant Life Christian S PK-12
5130 Hallam Rd 77568 409-935-8773
Cynthia Hallam, admin.

Lamesa, Dawson, Pop. 9,364
Klondike ISD 300/PK-12
2911 County Road H 79331 806-462-7334
Steve McLaren, supt. Fax 462-7333
klondike.esc17.net
Klondike S 300/PK-12
2911 County Road H 79331 806-462-7332
Tony Bushong, prin. Fax 462-7333

Lamesa ISD 2,100/PK-12
PO Box 261 79331 806-872-5461
Jim Knight, supt. Fax 872-6220
www.lamesa.esc17.net
Lamesa MS 500/6-8
PO Box 261 79331 806-872-8301
Leroy Mitchell, prin. Fax 872-2949
North ES 400/3-5
PO Box 261 79331 806-872-5428
Dalia Benavides, prin. Fax 872-8324
South ES 700/PK-2
PO Box 261 79331 806-872-5401
Shelley Mann, prin. Fax 872-9161

Lampasas, Lampasas, Pop. 6,551
Lampasas ISD 3,400/PK-12
207 W 8th St 76550 512-556-6224
Chane Rascoe Ed.D., supt. Fax 556-8711
www.lampasas.k12.tx.us

Hanna Springs ES 600/K-5
207 W 8th St 76550 512-556-2152
Leslie Talamantes, prin. Fax 556-0225
Kline Whitis ES 400/PK-5
207 W 8th St 76550 512-556-8291
Wes Graham, prin. Fax 556-8285
Lampasas MS 800/6-8
207 W 8th St 76550 512-556-3101
Dana Holcomb, prin. Fax 556-0245
Other Schools – See Copperas Cove

Lancaster, Dallas, Pop. 35,843
Lancaster ISD 6,800/PK-12
422 S Centre Ave 75146 972-218-1400
Dr. Elijah Granger, supt. Fax 218-1401
www.lancasterisd.org
Beltline ES 600/PK-5
1355 W Belt Line Rd 75146 972-218-1608
Wendy Hawthorne, prin. Fax 218-1620
Carver STEM 6th Grade Learning Ctr 500/6-6
1005 Westridge Ave 75146 972-218-1577
Cosheda Hurd, prin. Fax 218-1589
Houston ES 700/PK-5
2929 Marquis Ln 75134 972-218-1512
Tatanisha Sparks, prin. Fax 218-1524
Lancaster ES 600/PK-5
1109 W Main St 75146 972-218-1590
Nakesha Reddick, prin. Fax 218-1607
Lancaster MS 1,000/7-8
822 W Pleasant Run Rd 75146 972-218-1660
Shon Joseph, prin. Fax 218-3080
Parks/Millbrook ES 500/PK-5
630 Millbrook Dr 75146 972-218-1564
Marlon Waites, prin. Fax 218-1576
Pleasant Run ES 400/PK-5
427 W Pleasant Run Rd 75146 972-218-1538
Kelli Watson, prin. Fax 218-1550
Rolling Hills ES 600/PK-5
450 Rolling Hills Pl 75146 972-218-1525
Rolanda McKenzie, prin. Fax 218-1537
West Main ES 300/PK-5
531 W Main St 75146 972-218-1551
Nakesha Reddick, prin. Fax 218-1563

Berne Academy 100/PK-8
1311 Johns Ave 75134 972-218-7373

Laneville, Rusk
Laneville ISD 200/PK-12
7415 FM 1798 W 75667 903-863-5353
Teresa Shelton, supt. Fax 863-2736
www.lanevilleisd.org
Laneville S 200/PK-12
7415 FM 1798 W 75667 903-863-5353
Joshua Tremont, prin. Fax 863-2376

Lantana, Denton
Denton ISD
Supt. — See Denton
Adkins ES, 1701 Monahan Dr 76226 K-5
Emily McLarty, prin. 940-369-1300

La Porte, Harris, Pop. 33,263
La Porte ISD 7,600/PK-12
1002 San Jacinto St 77571 281-604-7000
Lloyd Graham, supt. Fax 604-7010
www.lpisd.org
Baker Sixth Grade Campus 500/6-6
1002 San Jacinto St 77571 281-604-6800
Alcia Upchurch, prin. Fax 604-6885
Bayshore ES 500/PK-5
1002 San Jacinto St 77571 281-604-4600
Donna Spaugh, prin. Fax 604-4680
La Porte ES 500/PK-5
1002 San Jacinto St 77571 281-604-4700
Carol Williams, prin. Fax 604-4787
La Porte JHS 600/7-8
1002 San Jacinto St 77571 281-604-6600
Candace Pohl, prin. Fax 604-6605
Lomax ES 500/PK-5
1002 San Jacinto St 77571 281-604-4300
Patricia Herrera-Johnson, prin. Fax 604-4355
Lomax JHS 600/7-8
1002 San Jacinto St 77571 281-604-6700
Dr. Larry Gerhart, prin. Fax 604-6730
Reid ES 500/PK-5
1002 San Jacinto St 77571 281-604-4500
Diane Weeden, prin. Fax 604-4555
Rizzuto ES 600/PK-5
1002 San Jacinto St 77571 281-604-6500
Deanna Narcisse, prin. Fax 604-6555
Other Schools – See Deer Park

La Pryor, Zavala, Pop. 1,634
La Pryor ISD 500/PK-12
PO Box 519 78872 830-365-4000
Matthew McHazlett, supt. Fax 365-4006
www.lapryor.net
La Pryor ES 300/PK-6
PO Box 519 78872 830-365-4009
Esequiel de la Fuente, prin. Fax 365-4021

Laredo, Webb, Pop. 235,714
Laredo ISD 24,900/PK-12
1702 Houston St 78040 956-273-1000
Dr. Sylvia Rios, supt. Fax 273-1403
www.laredoisd.org/
Bruni ES 700/PK-5
1508 San Eduardo Ave 78040 956-273-3000
Miguel Castillo, prin. Fax 795-3913
Christen MS 1,400/6-8
2001 Santa Maria Ave 78040 956-273-6400
Lizzy Newsome, prin. Fax 795-3732
Cigarroa MS 1,400/6-8
2600 Palo Blanco St 78046 956-273-6100
Jose Cerda, prin. Fax 718-2208
Daiches ES 600/PK-5
1401 Green St 78040 956-273-3200
Lisa Soto, prin. Fax 795-3933
Dovalina ES 600/PK-5
1700 Anna Ave 78040 956-273-3320
Alma Gonzalez, prin. Fax 795-3943
Farias ES 800/PK-5
1510 Chicago St 78041 956-273-3400
San Juana Garza, prin. Fax 795-3954
Gallego ES 700/PK-5
520 Clark Blvd 78040 956-273-3100
Imelda Martinez, prin. Fax 795-3923
Hachar ES 600/PK-5
3000 Guadalupe St 78043 956-273-3500
Cynthia Villarreal, prin. Fax 795-3963
Heights ES 600/PK-5
1208 Market St 78040 956-273-3600
Adriana Padilla, prin. Fax 795-3973
Kawas ES 600/PK-5
2100 S Milmo Ave 78046 956-273-3700
Vanessa Ortegon, prin. Fax 795-3982
Lamar MS 1,400/6-8
1818 N Arkansas Ave 78043 956-273-6200
Margarita Taboada, prin. Fax 795-3766
Leyendecker ES 600/PK-5
1311 Garden St 78040 956-273-3800
Maria Oviedo, prin. Fax 795-3992
Ligarde ES 800/PK-5
2800 S Canada Ave 78046 956-273-3900
Rosalba Martinez, prin. Fax 795-4002
MacDonell ES 800/PK-5
1606 Benavides St 78040 956-273-4000
Cathy DeLeon, prin. Fax 795-4012
Martin ES 700/PK-5
1600 Monterrey Ave 78040 956-273-4100
Manuel Gerardo Escalante, prin. Fax 795-4025
Memorial MS 800/6-8
2002 Marcella Ave 78040 956-273-6600
Sandra Garcia, prin. Fax 795-3780
Milton ES 900/PK-5
2500 E Ash St 78043 956-273-4200
Flor Diaz, prin. Fax 795-4033
Pierce ES 900/PK-5
800 E Eistetter St 78041 956-273-4300
Noralva Johnson, prin. Fax 795-4053
Ryan ES 1,000/PK-5
2401 Clark Blvd 78043 956-273-4400
Elsa Flores, prin. Fax 795-4061
Sanchez/Ochoa ES 700/PK-5
211 E Ash St 78040 956-273-4500
Elba Contreras, prin. Fax 795-4042
Santa Maria ES 700/PK-5
3817 Santa Maria Ave 78041 956-273-4600
Jose DeLeon, prin. Fax 795-4082
Santo Nino ES 800/PK-5
2701 Bismark St 78043 956-273-4700
Jose Perez, prin. Fax 795-4093
Tarver ES 600/PK-5
3200 Tilden Ave 78040 956-273-4800
Sara Montemayor, prin. Fax 795-4103
Zachry ES 700/PK-5
3200 Chacota St 78046 956-273-4900
Diana Martinez, prin. Fax 795-4122

United ISD 42,500/PK-12
201 Lindenwood Dr 78045 956-473-6201
Roberto J. Santos, supt. Fax 728-8691
www.uisd.net
Arndt ES 900/PK-5
610 Santa Martha Blvd 78046 956-473-2800
Juanita Zepeda, prin. Fax 473-2899
Benavides ES 1,000/PK-5
10702 Kirby Dr 78045 956-473-4900
Dr. Myrtha Villarreal, prin. Fax 473-4999
Borchers ES 900/PK-5
9551 Backwoods Trl 78045 956-473-7200
Mucia R. Flores, prin. Fax 473-7299
Bruni-Vergar MS 900/6-8
5910 Saint Luke 78046 956-473-6600
Clare G. Flores, prin. Fax 473-6699
Centeno ES 900/PK-5
2710 La Pita Mangana Rd 78046 956-473-8800
Amabilia Gonzalez, prin. Fax 473-8899
Clark ES 500/PK-5
500 W Hillside Rd 78041 956-473-4600
Gabriela N. Perez, prin. Fax 473-4699
Clark MS 800/6-8
500 W Hillside Rd 78041 956-473-7500
Melissa Chapa Ramirez, prin. Fax 473-7599
Cuellar ES 700/PK-5
6431 Casa Del Sol Blvd 78043 956-473-2700
Melissa Shinn, prin. Fax 473-2799
De Llano ES 600/PK-5
1415 Shiloh Dr 78045 956-473-4000
Diana Korrodi, prin. Fax 473-4099
Fasken ES 1,000/PK-5
11111 Atlanta Dr 78045 956-473-4700
Melba Gutierrez, prin. Fax 473-4799
Finley ES 500/PK-5
2001 Lowry Rd 78045 956-473-4500
Joe Garza, prin. Fax 473-4599
Freedom ES PK-5
415 EG Ranch Rd 78046 956-473-1600
Laura De Los Santos, prin. Fax 473-1699
Garcia ES 1,000/PK-5
1453 Concord Hills Blvd 78046 956-473-8900
Patricia Lanas, prin. Fax 473-8999
Garcia MS 500/6-8
499 Pena Dr 78046 956-473-5000
Alfredo Palapa, prin. Fax 473-5099
Gonzalez MS 1,200/6-8
5208 Santa Claudia 78043 956-473-7000
Clotilde Gamez, prin. Fax 473-7099
Gutierrez ES 700/PK-5
505 Calle Del Norte 78041 956-473-4400
Laura Gonzalez-Vasquez, prin. Fax 473-4499
Juarez-Lincoln at D.D. Hachar ES 800/PK-5
1003 Espejo Molina Rd 78046 956-473-3000
Roberto Ortiz, prin. Fax 473-3099
Kazen ES 600/PK-5
9620 Albany Dr 78045 956-473-4200
Maria Arambula-Ruiz, prin. Fax 473-4299
Kennedy-Zapata ES 500/PK-5
3809 Espejo Molina Rd 78046 956-473-4100
Thelma J. Martinez, prin. Fax 473-4199
Killam ES 800/PK-5
5315 Fairfield Dr 78043 956-473-2600
Agapito Palizo, prin. Fax 473-2699
Los Obispos MS 1,000/6-8
4801 S Ejido Ave 78046 956-473-7800
Jessica C. Salazar, prin. Fax 473-1899
Malakoff ES 900/PK-5
2810 Havana 78045 956-473-4800
Anna R. Martinez, prin. Fax 473-4899
Muller ES 900/PK-5
4430 Muller Memorial Blvd 78045 956-473-3900
Mayra N. Ramirez, prin. Fax 473-3999
Newman ES 600/PK-5
1300 Alta Vista Dr 78041 956-473-3800
Leticia R. Garcia, prin. Fax 473-3899
Nye ES 800/PK-5
101 E Del Mar Blvd 78041 956-473-3700
Cynthia Caballero, prin. Fax 473-3799
Perez ES 1,100/PK-5
500 Sierra Vista Blvd 78046 956-473-3600
Salud Hernandez, prin. Fax 473-3699
Prada ES 800/PK-5
510 Soria Dr 78046 956-473-3500
Raquel Alvarado, prin. Fax 473-3599
Roosevelt ES 700/PK-5
3301 Sierra Vista Blvd 78046 956-473-3400
Sylvia A. Ruiz, prin. Fax 473-3499
Ruiz ES 1,000/PK-5
1717 Los Presidentes Ave 78046 956-473-3300
Caryn Fox, prin. Fax 473-3399
Salinas ES 800/PK-5
1000 Century Dr W 78046 956-473-3200
Abraham Rodriguez, prin. Fax 473-3299
Trautmann ES 800/PK-5
810 Lindenwood Dr 78045 956-473-3100
Zaida Gonzalez, prin. Fax 473-3199
Trautmann MS 6th Grade 6-6
909 E Del Mar Blvd 78041 956-473-1700
Martha Valdez, prin. Fax 473-1799
Trautmann MS 1,800/6-8
8501 Curly Ln 78045 956-473-7400
Leticia Menchaca, prin. Fax 473-7499
United MS 1,100/6-8
700 E Del Mar Blvd 78041 956-473-7300
Rebecca Morales, prin. Fax 473-7399
United South MS 1,400/6-8
3707 Los Presidentes Ave 78046 956-473-7700
Martha Alvarez, prin. Fax 473-7799
Veterans Memorial ES PK-5
5909 Saint Luke 78046 956-473-1200
Luz Edith Serna Ramirez, prin. Fax 473-1299
Washington MS 1,300/6-8
10306 Riverbank Dr 78045 956-473-7600
Beth Porter, prin. Fax 473-7699
Zaffirini ES 1,100/PK-5
5210 Santa Claudia 78043 956-473-2900
Claudia Y. Benavides, prin. Fax 473-2999

Blessed Sacrament S 200/PK-8
1501 N Bartlett Ave 78043 956-722-1222
Selma Santos, prin. Fax 722-5635
Mary Help of Christians S 500/PK-8
10 E Del Mar Blvd 78041 956-722-3966
Sr. Vuong Do, prin. Fax 722-1413
Our Lady of Guadalupe S 100/PK-6
400 Callaghan St 78040 956-722-3915
Herlinda Martinez, prin. Fax 727-2840
St. Augustine ES 400/PK-8
1300 Galveston St 78040 956-724-1176
Barbra Zurita, prin. Fax 724-9891
St. Peters Memorial S 100/PK-8
PO Box 520 78042 956-723-6302
Dr. Linda Mitchell, prin. Fax 725-2671
United Day S 500/PK-8
1701 San Isidro Pkwy 78045 956-723-7261

LaRue, Henderson
La Poynor ISD 500/PK-12
13155 US Highway 175 E 75770 903-876-4057
James Young, supt. Fax 876-4541
www.lapoynorisd.net/
La Poynor ES 300/PK-5
13155 US Highway 175 E 75770 903-876-5293
Marsha Mills, prin. Fax 876-4543
La Poynor JHS 100/6-8
13155 US Highway 175 E 75770 903-876-2373
Garland Willis, prin. Fax 876-2374

Lasara, Willacy, Pop. 1,039
Lasara ISD 500/PK-12
PO Box 57 78561 956-642-3598
Sara Alvarado, supt. Fax 642-3546
www.lasaraisd.net/
Lasara S 400/PK-8
PO Box 57 78561 956-642-3271
Melissa Garza, prin. Fax 642-3546

Latexo, Houston, Pop. 319
Latexo ISD 500/PK-12
PO Box 975 75849 936-544-5664
Dr. Stacy Easterly, supt. Fax 544-5332
www.latexoisd.net
Latexo ES 300/PK-6
PO Box 975 75849 936-544-5664
Sandy Simpson, prin. Fax 546-2220

La Vernia, Wilson, Pop. 1,011
La Vernia ISD 3,100/PK-12
13600 US Highway 87 W 78121 830-779-6600
Dr. Jose Moreno, supt. Fax 779-2304
lvisd.org

La Vernia IS 700/3-5
369 S FM 1346 78121 830-779-6640
Scott Cales, prin. Fax 779-6642
La Vernia JHS 800/6-8
195 Bluebonnet Rd 78121 830-779-6650
Anthony Kosub, prin. Fax 779-6651
La Vernia PS 700/PK-2
249 S FM 1346 78121 830-779-6660
Tiffany Wehe, prin. Fax 779-7031

La Villa, Hidalgo, Pop. 1,955
La Villa ISD 600/PK-12
PO Box 9 78562 956-262-4755
Dr. Jose A. Cervantes, supt. Fax 262-7323
www.lavillaisd.org
La Villa MS 100/6-8
PO Box 9 78562 956-262-4760
Paul Abundez, prin. Fax 262-5243
Munoz ES 300/PK-5
PO Box 9 78562 956-262-9357
Edward Rivera, prin. Fax 262-9452

Lavon, Collin, Pop. 2,184
Community ISD
Supt. — See Nevada
NeSmith ES 400/PK-5
801 President Blvd 75166 972-843-8620
Julie Meek, prin. Fax 843-8621

Lawn, Taylor, Pop. 308
Jim Ned Consolidated ISD
Supt. — See Tuscola
Lawn ES 200/PK-5
PO Box 118 79530 325-583-2256
David Hogan, prin. Fax 583-2511

Lazbuddie, Parmer
Lazbuddie ISD 200/PK-12
PO Box 9 79053 806-965-2156
Steve Wolf, supt. Fax 965-2892
www.lazbuddieisd.org
Lazbuddie S 200/PK-12
PO Box 9 79053 806-965-2152
Ken Hoskins, prin. Fax 965-2892

League City, Galveston, Pop. 81,913
Clear Creek ISD 39,900/PK-12
PO Box 799 77574 281-284-0000
Dr. Greg Smith, supt. Fax 284-0005
www.ccisd.net
Bauerschlag ES 900/PK-5
2051 W League City Pkwy 77573 281-284-6100
Kelly Chapman, prin. Fax 284-6105
Bayside IS 700/6-8
4430 Village Way 77573 281-284-3000
James Thomas, prin. Fax 284-3005
Clear Creek IS 800/6-8
2451 E Main St 77573 281-284-2300
Marshall Ponce, prin. Fax 284-2305
Creekside IS 800/6-8
4320 W Main St 77573 281-284-3500
Peter Caterina, prin. Fax 284-3505
Ferguson ES 800/K-5
1910 S Compass Rose Blvd 77573 281-284-5500
Jennifer Serrano, prin. Fax 284-5505
Gilmore ES 900/K-5
3552 W League City Pkwy 77573 281-284-6400
Suzanne Jones, prin. Fax 284-6405
Goforth ES 600/K-5
2610 Webster St 77573 281-284-6000
Mark Smith, prin. Fax 284-6005
Hall ES 700/PK-5
5931 Meadowside St 77573 281-284-5300
Stephanie King, prin. Fax 284-5305
Hyde ES 600/PK-5
3700 FM 518 Rd E 77573 281-284-5800
Tony Nastasi, prin. Fax 284-5805
League City ES 600/PK-5
709 E Wilkins St 77573 281-284-4400
Xan Wood, prin. Fax 284-4405
League City IS 900/6-8
2588 Webster St 77573 281-284-3400
Kimberly Brouillard, prin. Fax 284-3405
Mossman ES 800/PK-5
4050 Village Way 77573 281-284-4000
Deborah Johnson, prin. Fax 284-4006
Parr ES 800/K-5
1315 Highway 3 S 77573 281-284-4100
Jane Kelling, prin. Fax 284-4106
Ross ES 700/PK-5
2401 W Main St 77573 281-284-4500
Kellly Mooney, prin. Fax 284-4505
Victory Lakes IS 900/6-8
2880 W Walker St 77573 281-284-3700
Adam Douglas, prin. Fax 284-3705
Other Schools – See El Lago, Friendswood, Houston, Kemah, Seabrook, Webster

Dickinson ISD
Supt. — See Dickinson
Calder Road ES 800/PK-4
6511 Calder Dr 77573 281-229-7500
Sophia Acevedo, prin. Fax 229-7501
Lobit ES PK-4
1251 W FM 517 77573 281-229-7600
Stephanie Williams, prin. Fax 229-7601
Lobit MS 5-6
1251 W FM 517 77573 281-229-7700
Theresa Bruce, prin. Fax 229-7701

Bay Area Christian S 700/PK-12
4800 W Main St 77573 281-332-4814
Jason Nave, head sch Fax 554-5495
St. Mary S 200/PK-8
1612 E Walker St 77573 281-332-4014
Laura Noonan, prin. Fax 332-5148
South Shore Montessori S 100/PK-6
201 S Shore Blvd 77573 281-334-7345

Leakey, Real, Pop. 417
Leakey ISD 300/PK-12
PO Box 1129 78873 830-232-5595
Dr. Barbara Skipper, supt. Fax 232-5535
www.leakeyisd.org
Leakey S 300/PK-12
PO Box 1129 78873 830-232-5595
DeeAnn Blanton, prin. Fax 232-5535

Leander, Williamson, Pop. 25,831
Leander ISD 35,400/PK-12
PO Box 218 78646 512-570-0000
Dr. Dan Troxell, supt. Fax 570-0054
www.leanderisd.org
Akin ES K-5
3261 Barley Rd 78641 512-570-8000
Beckie Webster, prin. Fax 570-8005
Bagdad ES 600/PK-5
800 Deercreek Ln 78641 512-570-5900
Christy Hilbun, prin. Fax 570-5905
Block House Creek ES 700/PK-5
401 Creek Run Dr 78641 512-570-7600
Dr. Deana Cady, prin. Fax 570-7605
Camacho ES PK-5
501 Municipal Dr 78641 512-570-7800
Gena Fleming, prin. Fax 570-7805
Leander MS 800/6-8
410 S West Dr 78641 512-570-3200
Mark Koller, prin. Fax 570-3205
Plain ES 800/PK-5
501 S Brook Dr 78641 512-570-6600
Evelyn Crisp, prin. Fax 570-6605
Pleasant Hill ES 700/PK-5
1800 Horizon Park Blvd 78641 512-570-6400
Heather Robbins, prin. Fax 570-6405
Stiles MS 800/6-8
3250 Barley Rd 78641 512-570-3800
Melody Maples, prin. Fax 570-3805
Whitestone ES 800/PK-5
2000 Crystal Falls Pkwy 78641 512-570-7400
Niki Prindle, prin. Fax 570-7405
Wiley MS 1,000/6-8
1526 Raider Way 78641 512-570-3600
Brandon Evans, prin. Fax 570-3605
Winkley ES 800/PK-5
2100 Pow Wow 78641 512-570-6700
Donna Brady, prin. Fax 570-6705
Other Schools – See Austin, Cedar Park, Georgetown

Sterling Classical S 200/PK-12
11880 Old 2243 W Ste 700 78641 512-259-2722

Lefors, Gray, Pop. 490
Lefors ISD 200/PK-12
PO Box 390 79054 806-835-2533
Joe Waldron, supt. Fax 835-2238
www.leforsisd.net
Lefors S 200/PK-12
PO Box 390 79054 806-835-2533
Kelley Porter, prin. Fax 835-2238

Leggett, Polk
Leggett ISD 200/PK-12
PO Box 68 77350 936-398-2804
Jana Lowe, supt. Fax 398-2078
www.leggettisd.net
Leggett ES 100/PK-6
PO Box 68 77350 936-398-2412
Jana Lowe, prin. Fax 398-0889

Lenorah, Martin
Grady ISD 200/PK-12
3500 FM 829 79749 432-459-2444
Leandro Gonzales, supt. Fax 459-2729
grady.tx.schoolwebpages.com
Grady S 200/PK-12
3500 FM 829 79749 432-459-2445
Gary Jones, prin. Fax 459-2729

Leonard, Fannin, Pop. 1,933
Leonard ISD 900/PK-12
1 Tiger Aly 75452 903-587-2318
Brad Maxwell, supt. Fax 587-2845
www.leonardisd.net
Leonard ES 300/PK-3
1 Tiger Aly 75452 903-587-2316
Julie Burnett, prin. Fax 587-2392
Leonard IS 100/4-5
1 Tiger Aly 75452 903-587-8303
Sarah Day, prin. Fax 587-4414
Leonard JHS 200/6-8
1 Tiger Aly 75452 903-587-2315
Tammy Hutchings, prin. Fax 587-2228

Levelland, Hockley, Pop. 13,427
Levelland ISD 3,100/PK-12
704 11th St 79336 806-894-9628
Jeff Northern, supt. Fax 894-2583
www.levellandisd.net
Capitol ES 300/1-3
704 11th St 79336 806-894-4715
Joanna Runkles, prin. Fax 894-9860
Levelland Academic Beginnings Center 500/PK-K
704 11th St 79336 806-894-6959
Sky Tucker, prin. Fax 894-5512
Levelland IS 400/4-5
704 11th St 79336 806-894-3060
Terri White, prin. Fax 894-0957
Levelland MS 600/6-8
704 11th St 79336 806-894-6355
John Clanton, prin. Fax 894-8935
South ES 400/1-3
704 11th St 79336 806-894-6255
Ben Prowell, prin. Fax 894-1283

Levelland Christian S 50/PK-7
1905 Cactus Dr 79336 806-894-6019
Heather Scoggins, head sch Fax 897-0522

Lewisville, Denton, Pop. 93,105
Lewisville ISD
Supt. — See Flower Mound
Castle Hills ES 800/PK-5
1025 Holy Grail Dr 75056 469-713-5952
Donna Taylor, prin. Fax 350-9018
Central ES 1,000/PK-5
400 High School Dr 75057 469-713-5976
Lea Devers, prin. Fax 350-9019
College Street ES 300/K-5
350 W College St 75057 469-713-5965
Susan Heintzman, prin. Fax 350-9024
Creekside ES 400/PK-5
901 Valley View Dr 75067 469-713-5953
Rod McGinnis, prin. Fax 350-9027
Degan ES 600/PK-5
1680 College Pkwy 75077 469-713-5967
Vanessa Stuart, prin. Fax 350-9028
Delay MS 900/6-8
2103 Savage Ln 75057 469-713-5191
Jim Baker, prin. Fax 350-9174
Durham MS 800/6-8
2075 S Edmonds Ln 75067 469-713-5963
Gary Holt, prin. Fax 350-9182
Hedrick ES 600/PK-5
1532 Bellaire Blvd 75067 469-713-5189
Trish Cuckler, prin. Fax 350-9071
Hedrick MS 700/6-8
1526 Bellaire Blvd 75067 469-713-5188
Barbara Hamric, prin. Fax 350-9196
Huffines MS 900/6-8
1440 N Valley Pkwy 75077 469-713-5990
Estella Rupard, prin. Fax 350-9199
Independence ES 700/PK-5
2511 Windhaven Pkwy 75056 469-713-5212
Teddie Winslow, prin. Fax 350-9479
Jackson ECC 700/PK-PK
1651 S Valley Pkwy 75067 469-713-5986
Dulia Longoria, prin. Fax 350-9103
Killian MS 900/6-8
2561 FM 544 75056 469-713-5977
Deanne Angonia, prin. Fax 350-9200
Lakeland ES 800/PK-5
800 Fox Ave 75067 469-713-5992
James Crockett, prin. Fax 350-9092
Lewisville ES 800/PK-5
285 Country Rdg 75067 469-713-5995
Lakshmi Valdes-Natividad, prin. Fax 626-1620
Parkway ES 600/PK-5
2100 S Valley Pkwy 75067 469-713-5979
Valerie Parsons, prin. Fax 350-9132
Rockbrook ES 700/K-5
2751 Rockbrook Dr 75067 469-713-5968
Dawn Jordan, prin. Fax 350-9139
Southridge ES 700/PK-5
495 W Corporate Dr 75067 469-713-5187
Wyvona Ulman, prin. Fax 350-9140
Valley Ridge ES 600/K-5
1604 N Garden Ridge Blvd 75077 469-713-5982
Rachel Garrett, prin. Fax 350-9155

Knowledge Seekers Christian S 50/PK-8
1471 W Corporate Dr 75067 972-353-3981
Lakeland Christian Academy 600/PK-12
397 S Stemmons Fwy 75067 972-219-3939
Thom Wilder, head sch Fax 219-9601

Lexington, Lee, Pop. 1,158
Lexington ISD 900/PK-12
8731 N Highway 77 78947 979-773-2254
Dr. Frances McArthur, supt. Fax 773-4455
www.lexingtonisd.net
Lexington ES 500/PK-5
8731 N Highway 77 78947 979-773-2525
Lynette Brown, prin. Fax 773-4455
Lexington MS 200/6-8
8731 N Highway 77 78947 979-773-2255
William Paul, prin. Fax 773-4455

Liberty, Liberty, Pop. 8,274
Liberty ISD, 1600 Grand Ave 77575 2,100/PK-12
Dr. Cody Abshier, supt. 936-336-7213
www.libertyisd.net
Liberty ES 600/2-5
1002 Bowie St 77575 936-336-3603
Stephanie Cox, prin. Fax 336-6077
Liberty MS 400/6-8
2515 Jefferson Dr 77575 936-336-3582
Rhonda Smith, prin. Fax 336-1021
San Jacinto ES 400/PK-1
1629 Grand Ave 77575 936-336-3161
Tom Connelly, prin. Fax 336-5751

Liberty Hill, Williamson, Pop. 951
Liberty Hill ISD 3,000/PK-12
301 Forrest St 78642 512-260-5580
Dr. Rob Hart, supt. Fax 260-5581
www.libertyhill.txed.net
Liberty Hill Bill Burden ES 600/PK-4
315 Stonewall Pkwy 78642 512-260-4400
Terrie Chambers M.Ed., prin. Fax 260-4410
Liberty Hill ES 500/PK-4
1400 Loop 332 78642 512-515-6514
Heather Collison, prin. Fax 778-5942
Liberty Hill IS 400/5-6
101 Loop 332 78642 512-379-3200
Josh Curtis, prin. Fax 379-3210
Liberty Hill JHS 500/7-8
13125 W State Highway 29 78642 512-379-3300
Annette Coe, prin. Fax 379-3310

Fortis Academy 200/PK-12
PO Box 580 78642 512-432-5152

Lindale, Smith, Pop. 4,737
Lindale ISD 3,800/PK-12
PO Box 370 75771 903-881-4000
Stan Surratt, supt. Fax 881-4004
www.lindaleeagles.org
College Street ES 400/1-3
PO Box 370 75771 903-881-4350
Dana Sustaire, prin. Fax 881-4351
Lindale ECC 400/PK-K
PO Box 370 75771 903-881-4400
Kaela Deslatte, prin. Fax 881-4401
Lindale JHS 600/7-8
PO Box 370 75771 903-881-4150
Jeremy Chilek, prin. Fax 881-4049
Moss IS 800/4-6
PO Box 370 75771 903-881-4200
Kyle Wright, prin. Fax 881-4201
Penny ES 400/1-3
PO Box 370 75771 903-881-4250
Monica Moore, prin. Fax 881-4251

Mercy Ships Academy 50/PK-12
15862 Highway 110 N 75771 903-939-7183
Nikki Aldum, dir. Fax 939-7114

Linden, Cass, Pop. 1,960
Linden-Kildare Consolidated ISD 800/PK-12
205 Kildare Rd 75563 903-756-5027
Keri Winters, supt. Fax 756-7242
www.lkcisd.net
Linden ES 400/PK-5
205 Kildare Rd 75563 903-756-5471
Shekita Martin, prin. Fax 756-5022
Stephens JHS 200/6-8
205 Kildare Rd 75563 903-756-5381
Randall Wright, prin. Fax 756-8832

Lindsay, Cooke, Pop. 1,000
Lindsay ISD 500/K-12
PO Box 145 76250 940-668-8923
Trevor Rogers, supt. Fax 668-2662
www.lindsayisd.org
Lindsay ES 300/K-6
PO Box 145 76250 940-668-8923
Pat Autry, prin. Fax 668-2662

Lingleville, Erath
Lingleville ISD 200/PK-12
PO Box 134 76461 254-968-2596
Curt Haley, supt. Fax 965-5821
www.lingleville.us
Lingleville S 200/PK-12
PO Box 134 76461 254-968-2596
Cheryl Hudson, prin. Fax 965-5821

Lipan, Hood, Pop. 426
Lipan ISD 300/PK-8
211 N Kickapoo St 76462 254-646-2266
Cindy Edwards, supt. Fax 646-3499
www.lipanindians.net/
Lipan ES 200/PK-6
211 N Kickapoo St 76462 254-646-2266
Kelly Kunkel, prin. Fax 646-3498
Lipan JHS 50/7-8
211 N Kickapoo St 76462 254-646-2266
Steve Bryant, prin. Fax 646-3499

Little Elm, Denton, Pop. 25,208
Denton ISD
Supt. — See Denton
Bell ES, 601 Villa Paloma Blvd 75068 K-5
Dr. Lauren Shapiaro, prin. 972-347-7200

Frisco ISD
Supt. — See Frisco
Miller ES K-5
300 Cypress Hill Dr 75068 469-633-2075
Ashley Miller, prin. Fax 633-2085
Robertson ES 800/K-5
2501 Woodlake Pkwy 75068 469-633-3675
James Iorio, prin. Fax 633-3685

Little Elm ISD 6,600/PK-12
PO Box 6000 75068 972-947-9340
Daniel Gallagher, supt. Fax 294-1107
www.leisd.ws
Brent ES 600/PK-5
500 Witt Rd 75068 972-647-9451
Virginia Gwyn, prin. Fax 947-9330
Chavez ES 600/PK-5
2600 Hart Rd 75068 972-947-9452
Doug Sevier, prin. Fax 947-9331
Lakeside MS 1,000/7-8
400 Lobo Ln 75068 972-947-9445
Clint Miller, prin. Fax 947-9332
Lakeview ES 600/PK-5
1800 Waterside Dr 75068 972-947-9454
Kelly Carr, prin. Fax 947-9328
Powell 6th Grade Center 6-6
500 Lobo Ln 75068 972-947-9446
Elizabeth Miller, prin. Fax 947-9325
Other Schools – See Frisco, Oak Point, The Colony

Littlefield, Lamb, Pop. 6,333
Littlefield ISD 1,400/PK-12
1207 E 14th St 79339 806-385-4150
Robert Dillard, supt. Fax 385-4195
www.littlefield.k12.tx.us
Littlefield ES 300/3-5
1207 E 14th St 79339 806-385-4150
Tom Whistler, prin. Fax 385-4193
Littlefield JHS 300/6-8
1207 E 14th St 79339 806-385-4150
Mitchell McNeese, prin. Fax 385-4192
Littlefield PS 400/PK-2
1207 E 14th St 79339 806-385-4150
Jan Richards, prin. Fax 385-4194

Little River, Bell, Pop. 1,936
Academy ISD 1,000/PK-12
704 E Main St 76554 254-982-4304
Kevin Sprinkles, supt. Fax 982-0023
www.academyisd.net
Academy ES 300/PK-2
311 N Bumblebee Dr 76554 254-982-4621
Emily Nichols, prin. Fax 982-4584
Academy IS, 107 S Pondalily 76554 3-5
Dana Coleman, prin. 254-982-0150
Academy MS 300/6-8
501 E Main St 76554 254-982-4620
Stephen Ash, prin. Fax 982-4776

Live Oak, Bexar, Pop. 12,703
Judson ISD 23,500/PK-12
8012 Shin Oak Dr 78233 210-945-5100
Dr. Carl Montoya, supt. Fax 945-6900
www.judsonisd.org
Crestview ES 600/PK-5
7710 Narrow Pass St 78233 210-945-5111
Yvonne Munoz, prin. Fax 590-4300
Other Schools – See Converse, San Antonio, Universal City

Livingston, Polk, Pop. 5,275
Livingston ISD 4,000/PK-12
PO Box 1297 77351 936-328-2100
Dr. Brent Hawkins, supt. Fax 328-2109
www.livingstonisd.com
Cedar Grove ES PK-3
819 W Church St 77351 936-328-2240
Erin Barnes, prin. Fax 328-2259
Livingston IS 600/4-5
1 Lions Ave 77351 936-328-2150
Sheri Murphy, prin. Fax 328-2159
Livingston JHS 900/6-8
1801 Highway 59 Loop N 77351 936-328-2120
Jared Nettles, prin. Fax 328-2139
Pine Ridge ES 700/PK-3
1200 Mill Rdg 77351 936-328-2160
Mary Hill, prin. Fax 328-2179
Timber Creek ES 700/PK-3
701 N Willis Ave 77351 936-328-2180
Ryan Young, prin. Fax 328-2199

Llano, Llano, Pop. 3,210
Llano ISD 1,800/PK-12
1400 Oatman St 78643 325-247-4747
Mac Edwards, supt. Fax 247-5623
www.llanoisd.org
Llano ES 400/PK-5
1600 Oatman St 78643 325-247-5718
Doug DeBord, prin. Fax 247-5731
Llano JHS 400/6-8
400 E State Highway 71 78643 325-247-4659
Todd Keele, prin. Fax 247-5821
Other Schools – See Kingsland

Llano Christian Academy 100/PK-12
PO Box 728 78643 325-247-4942
Dr. Alice Smith, hdmstr.

Lockhart, Caldwell, Pop. 12,574
Lockhart ISD 5,100/PK-12
PO Box 120 78644 512-398-0000
Tina Knudsen, supt. Fax 398-0025
www.lockhartisd.org
Bluebonnet ES 600/PK-5
211 Mockingbird Ln 78644 512-398-0900
Belinda Vasquez, prin. Fax 398-0901
Carver K 500/PK-K
371 Carver St 78644 512-398-0060
Karen Nixon, prin. Fax 398-0110
Clear Fork ES 500/1-5
1102 Clearfork St 78644 512-398-0450
Heidi Gudelman, prin. Fax 398-0536
Lockhart JHS 1,100/6-8
500 City Line Rd 78644 512-398-0770
Lori Davis, prin. Fax 398-0772
Navarro ES 400/1-5
715 S Medina St 78644 512-398-0690
Deanna Juarez, prin. Fax 398-0692
Plum Creek ES 600/1-5
710 Flores St 78644 512-398-0570
Jamee Griebel, prin. Fax 398-0572
Other Schools – See Dale

Lockney, Floyd, Pop. 1,837
Lockney ISD 500/PK-12
PO Box 428 79241 806-652-2115
Jim Baum, supt. Fax 652-4920
www.lockneyisd.net
Lockney ES 300/PK-5
PO Box 127 79241 806-652-3321
Jean Anne Williams, prin. Fax 652-2956
Lockney JHS 100/6-8
PO Box 550 79241 806-652-2236
Craig Setliff, prin. Fax 652-4920

Lohn, McCulloch
Lohn ISD 100/PK-12
PO Box 277 76852 325-344-5749
Leon Freeman, supt. Fax 344-5790
www.lohnisd.net
Lohn S 100/PK-12
PO Box 277 76852 325-344-5749
Dr. Stacy Rush, prin. Fax 344-5790

Lometa, Lampasas, Pop. 834
Lometa ISD 300/PK-12
PO Box 250 76853 512-752-3384
David Fisher, supt. Fax 752-3424
www.lometaisd.net
Lometa S 300/PK-12
PO Box 250 76853 512-752-3384
Jamie Smart, prin. Fax 752-3424

Lone Oak, Hunt, Pop. 584
Lone Oak ISD 1,000/PK-12
8162 US Highway 69 S 75453 903-662-5427
Lance Campbell, supt. Fax 662-5290
www.loisd.net
Lone Oak ES 400/PK-5
8080 US Highway 69 S 75453 903-662-5022
Beth Luhn, prin. Fax 662-0973
Lone Oak MS 200/6-8
8160 US Highway 69 S 75453 903-662-5121
Dr. Shannon Wilhite, prin. Fax 662-5017

Longview, Gregg, Pop. 79,235
Longview ISD 8,600/PK-12
PO Box 3268 75606 903-381-2200
Dr. James Wilcox, supt. Fax 753-5389
w3.lisd.org
Bramlette ES 700/1-5
PO Box 3268 75606 903-803-5600
Nikita Mumphrey, prin. Fax 758-6964
East Texas Montessori Prep Academy PK-K
PO Box 3268 75606 903-803-5000
Dr. Jacqueline Burnett, prin. Fax 753-5389
Everhart ES 700/1-5
PO Box 3268 75606 903-803-5400
Arthur Brown, prin. Fax 803-5401
Forest Park MS 500/6-8
PO Box 3268 75606 903-446-2510
Cynthia Wise, prin. Fax 446-2501
Foster MS 800/6-8
PO Box 3268 75606 903-446-2710
John York, prin. Fax 758-2052
Hudson ES 600/1-5
PO Box 3268 75606 903-803-5100
Sue Wilson, prin. Fax 803-5101
Johnston-McQueen ES 700/PK-5
PO Box 3268 75606 903-803-5300
Donald Fisher, prin. Fax 663-2135
Judson MS 500/6-8
PO Box 3268 75606 903-446-2610
William Houff, prin. Fax 663-0275
South Ward ES 700/1-5
PO Box 3268 75606 903-803-5200
Dr. Rebeca Cooper, prin. Fax 753-2961
Ware ES 800/1-5
PO Box 3268 75606 903-803-5700
Sarah Sheppard, prin. Fax 803-5701
Williams ES 500/1-5
PO Box 3268 75606 903-803-5500
Cynthia Wise, prin. Fax 803-5501

Pine Tree ISD 5,000/PK-12
PO Box 5878 75608 903-295-5000
Dr. T.J. Farler, supt. Fax 295-5004
www.ptisd.org
Pine Tree Birch ES 800/1-4
PO Box 5878 75608 903-295-5120
Jill Clay, prin. Fax 295-5126
Pine Tree JHS 700/7-8
PO Box 5878 75608 903-295-5081
Vanessa Robinson, prin. Fax 295-5082
Pine Tree MS 700/5-6
PO Box 5878 75608 903-295-5160
Mickey White, prin. Fax 295-5162
Pine Tree Parkway ES 700/1-4
PO Box 5878 75608 903-295-5151
Melanie Keoun, prin. Fax 295-5155
Pine Tree PS 500/PK-K
PO Box 5878 75608 903-295-5095
Cristi Parsons, prin. Fax 295-5098

Spring Hill ISD 1,900/PK-12
3101 Spring Hill Rd 75605 903-759-4404
Steven Snell, supt. Fax 297-0141
www.shisd.net
Spring Hill IS 400/3-5
3101 Spring Hill Rd 75605 903-323-7701
Dana Robertson, prin. Fax 323-7762
Spring Hill JHS 400/6-8
3101 Spring Hill Rd 75605 903-323-7718
David Lynch, prin. Fax 323-7765
Spring Hill PS 500/PK-2
3101 Spring Hill Rd 75605 903-323-7848
Deanna Turner, prin. Fax 323-7847

Christian Heritage S 200/PK-12
2715 FM 1844 75605 903-663-4151
East Texas Christian S 200/PK-12
PO Box 8053 75607 903-757-7891
Dr. Renee Sawyer, admin. Fax 619-0349
Longview Christian S 200/K-12
1236 Pegues Pl 75601 903-297-3501
Ben Cammack, admin. Fax 212-2541
Oak Forest Montessori S 200/PK-6
2000 Greenleaf St 75605 903-297-0634
St. Mary's Catholic S 200/PK-12
405 Hollybrook Dr 75605 903-753-1657
Amy Blalock, prin. Fax 758-7347
Trinity S of Texas 300/PK-12
215 N Teague St 75601 903-753-0612
Gary Whitwell, head sch Fax 753-4812

Loop, Gaines, Pop. 223
Loop ISD 100/PK-12
PO Box 917 79342 806-487-6411
Darrell Ericson, supt. Fax 487-6416
www.loopisd.net
Loop S 100/PK-12
PO Box 917 79342 806-487-6411
Darrell Ericson, supt. Fax 487-6416

Loraine, Mitchell, Pop. 595
Loraine ISD 200/PK-12
PO Box 457 79532 325-737-2225
Brandon McDowell, supt. Fax 737-2701
loraine.esc14.net
Loraine S 200/PK-12
PO Box 457 79532 325-737-2225
James Womack, prin. Fax 737-2701

Lorena, McLennan, Pop. 1,682
Lorena ISD 1,400/PK-12
PO Box 97 76655 254-857-3239
Dr. Sandra Talbert, supt. Fax 857-4533
www.lorenaisd.net
Lorena ES 200/3-5
PO Box 97 76655 254-857-4613
Lowell Anderson, prin. Fax 857-9019
Lorena MS 400/6-8
PO Box 97 76655 254-857-4621
Dr. Jennifer Allison, prin. Fax 857-3419
Lorena PS 300/PK-2
PO Box 97 76655 254-857-8909
Liza Cunningham, prin. Fax 857-8815

Lorenzo, Crosby, Pop. 1,134
Lorenzo ISD 300/PK-12
PO Box 520 79343 806-634-5591
Oran Hamilton, supt. Fax 634-5928
www.lorenzoisd.net
Lorenzo ES 200/PK-6
PO Box 520 79343 806-634-5593
Jose Molina, prin. Fax 634-8419

Los Fresnos, Cameron, Pop. 5,528
Los Fresnos Consolidated ISD 10,400/PK-12
PO Box 309 78566 956-254-5010
Gonzalo Salazar, supt. Fax 233-4031
www.lfcisd.net
Lopez-Riggins ES 600/PK-5
PO Box 309 78566 956-233-6916
Claudia Larrasquitu, prin. Fax 233-3696
Los Cuates MS 900/6-8
PO Box 309 78566 956-254-5182
Antonio Padilla, prin. Fax 233-6265
Los Fresnos ES 600/PK-5
PO Box 309 78566 956-233-6900
Rosemary Leal, prin. Fax 233-6235
Reseca MS 900/6-8
PO Box 309 78566 956-254-5159
Elizabeth Swantner, prin. Fax 233-6209
Other Schools – See Brownsville, Olmito, San Benito

Lott, Falls, Pop. 750
Rosebud-Lott ISD 500/PK-12
1789 US Highway 77 76656 254-583-4510
Dr. Steve Brownlee, supt. Fax 583-4469
www.rlisd.org
Lott ES 50/4-6
513 S 5th St 76656 254-584-4251
Natalie Parcus, prin. Fax 584-4050
Rosebud-Lott MS 100/7-8
1789 US Highway 77 76656 254-583-7962
Todd Williams, prin. Fax 583-2904
Other Schools – See Rosebud

Westphalia ISD 200/K-8
124 County Road 3000 76656 254-584-4988
Robert Hudson, supt. Fax 584-2963
www.westphaliaisd.org/
Westphalia S 200/K-8
124 County Road 3000 76656 254-584-4988
Robert Hudson, supt. Fax 584-2963

Louise, Wharton, Pop. 991
Louise ISD 500/PK-12
PO Box 97 77455 979-648-2982
Dr. Garth Oliver, supt. Fax 648-2520
louiseisd.net
Louise ES 200/PK-5
PO Box 97 77455 979-648-2262
Pamela Lechlar, prin. Fax 648-2520
Louise JHS 100/6-8
PO Box 97 77455 979-648-2262
Brady Peterson, prin. Fax 648-2520

Lovelady, Houston, Pop. 635
Lovelady ISD 500/PK-12
PO Box 99 75851 936-636-7616
Wendy Tullos, supt. Fax 636-2212
www.loveladyisd.net
Lovelady ES 300/PK-6
PO Box 250 75851 936-636-7832
Rhonda Lowery, prin. Fax 636-2529

Lubbock, Lubbock, Pop. 226,600
Frenship ISD
Supt. — See Wolfforth
Crestview ES 600/K-5
6020 81st St 79424 806-794-3661
Stacy Davis, prin. Fax 798-2373
Heritage MS 800/6-8
6110 73rd St 79424 806-794-9400
Gina Laughlin, prin. Fax 793-8956
Legacy ES PK-3
6424 Kemper St 79416 806-792-3800
Cheryl Booher, prin. Fax 792-3801
North Ridge ES 800/K-5
6302 11th Pl 79416 806-793-6686
Shannon Morrison, prin. Fax 792-3798
Oak Ridge ES 700/K-5
6514 68th St 79424 806-794-5200
Shane Langen, prin. Fax 698-0440
Terra Vista MS 600/6-8
1111 Upland Ave 79416 806-796-0076
Brent Lowrey, prin. Fax 796-1540
Upland Heights ES K-5
10020 Upland Ave 79424 806-698-6611
Denise Stewart, prin.
Westwind ES 700/PK-5
6401 43rd St 79407 806-799-3731
Todd Newberry, prin. Fax 799-1087
Willow Bend ES 600/PK-5
8816 13th St 79416 806-796-0090
Dr. LeAnn Fisher, prin. Fax 796-1517

Lubbock ISD 27,500/PK-12
1628 19th St 79401 806-219-0000
Dr. Berhl Robertson, supt. Fax 766-1210
www.lubbockisd.org
Alderson ES 600/K-5
219 Walnut Ave 79403 806-219-8000
Cicely Alexander, prin. Fax 766-1490
Atkins MS 600/6-8
5401 Avenue U 79412 806-766-1522
Chris Huber, prin. Fax 766-2226
Bayless ES 600/K-5
2115 58th St 79412 806-219-5000
Amy Stephens, prin. Fax 766-1651
Bean ES 500/K-5
3001 Avenue N 79411 806-219-5100
Thomas Thomas, prin. Fax 766-1671
Bowie ES 200/K-5
2902 Chicago Ave 79407 806-219-5200
Kimberly Callison, prin. Fax 766-0551
Brown ES 400/K-5
2315 36th St 79412 806-219-5300
Staci Sumners, prin. Fax 766-0832
Cavazos MS 600/6-8
210 N University Ave 79415 806-219-3200
Marti Makuta, prin. Fax 766-6627
Centennial ES 700/K-5
1301 N Utica Ave 79416 806-219-7800
Davida Burks, prin. Fax 766-1982
Dunbar College Preparatory Academy 600/6-8
2010 E 26th St 79404 806-766-1300
Lori Alexander, prin. Fax 766-1320
Dupre ES 200/K-5
2008 Avenue T 79411 806-219-5400
Robin Conkwright, prin. Fax 766-1691
Ervin ES 700/PK-5
1802 E 28th St 79404 806-219-8200
Joshlyn Cotton, prin. Fax 766-1875
Evans MS 900/6-8
4211 58th St 79413 806-219-3600
Flo Touchstone, prin. Fax 766-0570
Guadulupe ES 200/K-5
101 N Avenue P 79401 806-219-5500
Ofelia Mendez, prin. Fax 766-1702
Hardwick ES 400/K-5
1420 Chicago Ave 79416 806-219-5600
Melissa Portwood, prin. Fax 766-0842
Harwell ES 400/K-5
4101 Avenue D 79404 806-219-5700
Jorge Sanchez, prin. Fax 766-1713
Hodges ES 400/K-5
5001 Avenue P 79412 806-219-5800
Elsa Montes, prin. Fax 766-1730
Honey ES 400/K-5
3615 86th St 79423 806-219-5900
Phillip Neeb, prin. Fax 766-0864
Hutchinson MS 800/6-8
3102 Canton Ave 79410 806-219-3800
Heidi Dye, prin. Fax 766-0538
Irons MS 700/6-8
5214 79th St 79424 806-219-4000
Philip Riewe, prin. Fax 766-2070
Jackson ES 200/K-5
201 Vernon Ave 79415 806-219-6000
Edwina Medrano, prin. Fax 766-1765
MacKenzie MS 700/6-8
5402 12th St 79416 806-219-4200
John Martinez, prin. Fax 766-0510
Maedgen ES 400/K-5
4401 Nashville Ave 79413 806-219-6200
Drue Coleman, prin. Fax 766-0990
McWhorter ES 500/K-5
2711 1st St 79415 806-219-6100
Karla Mann, prin. Fax 766-1797
Miller ES 600/K-5
6705 Joliet Dr 79413 806-219-8100
Kevin Booe, prin. Fax 766-0852
Overton ES 300/K-5
2902 Louisville Ave 79410 806-219-6300
Ann Archer, prin. Fax 766-0895
Parsons ES 400/K-5
2811 58th St 79413 806-219-6400
Bonnie Bowman, prin. Fax 766-0902
Roberts ES 700/K-5
7901 Ave P 79423 806-766-7900
Shirley Hutchins, prin. Fax 766-6222
Rush ES 400/K-5
4702 15th St 79416 806-219-6700
Mary McGann, prin. Fax 766-0929
Slaton MS 600/6-8
1602 32nd St 79411 806-219-4400
Damon McCall, prin. Fax 766-1571
Smith ES 600/K-5
8707 Dover Ave 79424 806-219-6800
Gale Latimer, prin. Fax 798-0173
Stewart ES 400/K-5
4815 46th St 79414 806-219-6900
Jaci Underwood, prin. Fax 766-0943
Waters ES 700/K-5
3006 78th St 79423 806-219-7000
Karen Thornton, prin. Fax 766-6209
Wester ES 400/K-5
4602 Chicago Ave 79414 806-219-7100
Amy Kimbley, prin. Fax 766-0962
Wheelock ES 400/K-5
3008 42nd St 79413 806-219-7200
Stacy Carter, prin. Fax 766-0976
Whiteside ES 500/K-5
7508 Albany Ave 79424 806-219-7300
Brandi Lay, prin. Fax 766-2081
Williams ES 400/PK-5
4812 58th St 79414 806-219-7400
Denise Neeb, prin. Fax 766-0989
Wilson ES 500/K-5
2807 25th St 79410 806-219-7500
Paula January, prin. Fax 766-0525
Wilson MS 500/6-8
4402 31st St 79410 806-219-4600
Kelly Brownfield, prin. Fax 766-0814

Wolffarth ES 400/K-5
3202 Erskine St 79415 806-219-7600
Christy Gillespie, prin. Fax 766-1893
Wright ES 200/K-5
1302 Adrian St 79403 806-219-7700
Stacy Hurst, prin. Fax 766-1906

Lubbock-Cooper ISD 5,000/PK-12
16302 Loop 493 79423 806-863-7100
Keith Bryant, supt. Fax 863-3130
www.lcisd.net
Lubbock-Cooper Bush MS 600/6-8
3425 118th St 79423 806-776-0750
Edna Parr, prin. Fax 776-0751
Lubbock-Cooper Central ES 600/PK-5
16302 Loop 493 79423 806-776-2150
Candice Cross, prin. Fax 776-2151
Lubbock-Cooper MS 500/6-8
16302 Loop 493 79423 806-863-7104
Tami Gunset, prin. Fax 863-7163
Lubbock-Cooper North ES 800/PK-5
3202 108th St 79423 806-776-2100
Annie Crawford, prin. Fax 687-2714
Lubbock-Cooper South ES 700/PK-5
16302 Loop 493 79423 806-863-7102
Frances Alonzo, prin. Fax 863-3830
Lubbock-Cooper West ES 600/PK-5
10101 Fulton Ave 79424 806-776-0700
Sasha Bennett, prin. Fax 771-9970

Roosevelt ISD 1,100/PK-12
1406 County Road 3300 79403 806-842-3282
Dallas Grimes, supt. Fax 842-3266
www.roosevelt.k12.tx.us/
Roosevelt ES 500/PK-5
1406 County Road 3300 79403 806-842-3284
Delynn Wheeler, prin. Fax 842-3930
Roosevelt JHS 200/6-8
1406 County Road 3300 79403 806-842-3218
Tim Crane, prin. Fax 842-3337

All Saints Episcopal S 300/PK-11
3222 103rd St 79423 806-745-7701
Christ the King Cathedral S 300/PK-12
4011 54th St 79413 806-795-8283
Christine Wanjura, prin. Fax 795-9715
Kingdom Preparatory Academy 200/PK-12
PO Box 64028 79464 806-767-9334
Lubbock Christian S 300/PK-12
2604 Dover Ave 79407 806-796-8700
Lubbock Junior Academy 50/K-10
PO Box 6277 79493 806-795-4481
Southcrest Christian S 300/PK-12
3801 S Loop 289 79423 806-797-7400
Linda Merriott M.Ed., supt. Fax 776-0540
Trinity Christian ES 300/PK-3
7002 Canton Ave 79413 806-791-6581
Jill Roberts, prin. Fax 791-6596

Lucas, Collin, Pop. 5,074
Lovejoy ISD
Supt. — See Allen
Hart ES 400/K-5
450 Country Club Rd, 469-742-8200
Lacey Moser, prin. Fax 742-8201
Willow Springs MS 700/7-8
1101 W Lucas Rd, 469-702-8500
Kent Messer, prin. Fax 702-8501

Lueders, Jones, Pop. 342
Lueders-Avoca ISD 100/PK-12
334 Vandeventer St 79533 325-228-4211
Bob Spikes, supt. Fax 228-4513
www.laisd.esc14.net
Lueders-Avoca S 100/PK-8
334 Vandeventer St 79533 325-228-4211
Bob Spikes, supt. Fax 228-4513

Lufkin, Angelina, Pop. 34,621
Hudson ISD 2,800/PK-12
6735 Ted Trout Dr 75904 936-875-3351
Donald Webb, supt. Fax 875-9209
www.hudsonisd.org
Bonner ES 600/3-5
536 FM 3258 75904 936-875-9212
Scott Mackey, prin. Fax 875-9314
Hudson MS 600/6-8
6735 Ted Trout Dr 75904 936-875-9292
Richard Crenshaw, prin. Fax 875-9317
Peavy PS 700/PK-2
6920 State Highway 94 75904 936-875-9344
Laura Mikeal, prin. Fax 875-9378

Lufkin ISD 8,300/PK-12
PO Box 1407 75902 936-634-6696
Dr. LaTonya Goffney, supt. Fax 634-8864
www.lufkinisd.org
Anderson ES 300/3-5
381 Champions Dr 75901 936-632-5527
Cindy Tierney, prin. Fax 632-5487
Brandon ES 400/3-5
1612 Sayers St 75904 936-632-5513
Dr. Brandon Boyd, prin. Fax 632-5617
Brookhollow ES 300/3-5
1009 Live Oak Ln 75904 936-634-8415
April Sebesta, prin. Fax 634-8543
Burley PS 500/K-2
502 Joyce Ln 75901 936-633-6211
Betsy Mijares, prin. Fax 633-6222
Coston ES 300/3-5
707 Trenton St 75901 936-639-3118
Kathy Jost, prin. Fax 639-3289
Dunbar PS 300/1-2
1806 Mrtn Lthr King Jr Blvd 75904 936-630-4500
Dorinda Wade, prin. Fax 630-4511
Garrett PS 400/PK-K
507 Kurth Dr 75904 936-634-8418
LaMona Coleman, prin. Fax 634-8406

Hackney PS 300/PK-PK
708 Lubbock St 75901 936-634-3324
Kelly Proutt, prin. Fax 634-0463
Herty PS 400/PK-2
2804 Paul Ave 75901 936-639-2241
Jill Riggs, prin. Fax 639-2480
Kurth PS 400/PK-2
521 York Dr 75901 936-639-3279
Karen Vinson, prin. Fax 639-3415
Lufkin MS 1,700/6-8
900 E Denman Ave 75901 936-630-4444
Jesus Gomez, prin. Fax 632-4444
Slack ES 400/3-5
1305 Fuller Springs Dr 75901 936-639-2279
Danny Whisenant, prin. Fax 639-3693
Trout PS 400/PK-2
1014 Allendale Dr 75904 936-639-3274
Cindy Nerren, prin. Fax 639-3873

St. Cyprian's Episcopal S 200/PK-8
1115 S John Reddit Dr 75904 936-632-1720
St. Patrick Catholic S 100/PK-8
2116 Lowry St 75901 936-634-6719
Martha Lopez Coleman, prin. Fax 639-2776

Luling, Caldwell, Pop. 5,365

Luling ISD 1,500/PK-12
212 E Bowie St 78648 830-875-3191
Tim Glover, supt. Fax 875-3193
www.luling.txed.net
Gerdes JHS 300/6-8
214 E Bowie St 78648 830-875-2121
Kelly Meshell, prin. Fax 875-5482
Luling PS 400/PK-2
118 W Bowie St 78648 830-875-2223
Laura Eubank, prin. Fax 875-6712
Shanklin ES 300/3-5
122 E Houston St 78648 830-875-2515
Stephanie Heinchon, prin. Fax 875-6708

Lumberton, Hardin, Pop. 11,830

Lumberton ISD 3,800/PK-12
121 S Main St 77657 409-923-7580
John Valastro, supt. Fax 755-7848
www.lumberton.k12.tx.us
Lumberton Early Childhood S 400/PK-K
1020 S Main St 77657 409-923-7695
Kevin Wing, prin. Fax 755-6607
Lumberton IS 800/4-6
107 S LHS Dr 77657 409-923-7790
Paige Wing, prin. Fax 755-6716
Lumberton MS 600/7-8
123 S Main St 77657 409-923-7581
Leanna Stringer, prin. Fax 751-0641
Lumberton PS 900/1-3
128 E Candlestick Dr 77657 409-923-7490
Kathrine Waldrop, prin. Fax 923-7444

Lyford, Willacy, Pop. 2,606

Lyford Consolidated ISD 1,600/PK-12
PO Box 220 78569 956-347-3900
Eduardo Infante, supt. Fax 347-5588
www.lyfordcisd.net
Lyford ES 800/PK-5
PO Box 220 78569 956-347-3911
Veronica Lerma, prin. Fax 347-3577
Lyford MS 300/6-8
PO Box 220 78569 956-347-3910
Jose Escamilla, prin. Fax 347-2351

Lytle, Atascosa, Pop. 2,470

Lytle ISD 1,800/PK-12
PO Box 745 78052 830-709-5100
Michelle Carroll Smith, supt. Fax 709-5104
lytleisd.com
Lytle ES 500/2-5
PO Box 1060 78052 830-709-5130
Wendy Conover, prin. Fax 709-5136
Lytle JHS 400/6-8
PO Box 825 78052 830-709-5115
Kenneth Dykes, prin. Fax 709-5119
Lytle PS 300/PK-1
PO Box 460 78052 830-709-5140
Wendy Carroll-Conover, prin. Fax 709-5142

Mabank, Kaufman, Pop. 2,981

Mabank ISD 3,400/PK-12
310 E Market St 75147 903-880-1300
Dr. Russell Marshall, supt. Fax 880-1303
www.mabankisd.net
Central ES 600/PK-4
310 E Market St 75147 903-880-1380
Chelsea Capehart, prin. Fax 880-1383
Mabank IS 500/5-6
310 E Market St 75147 903-880-1640
Debbie DeRosa, prin. Fax 880-1643
Mabank JHS 500/7-8
310 E Market St 75147 903-880-1670
Barbie Conrad, prin. Fax 880-1673
Southside ES 400/K-4
310 E Market St 75147 903-880-1340
Brandi Dyer, prin. Fax 880-1343
Other Schools – See Gun Barrel City

Mc Allen, Hidalgo, Pop. 129,344

Edinburg Consolidated ISD
Supt. — See Edinburg
Cavazos ES 600/PK-5
1501 Freddy Gonzales Rd 78504 956-289-2535
Christine Gordon, prin. Fax 384-5147

McAllen ISD 25,200/PK-12
2000 N 23rd St 78501 956-618-6000
Jose Gonzalez, supt. Fax 686-8362
www.mcallenisd.org
Alvarez ES 500/PK-5
2606 Gumwood Ave 78501 956-971-4471
Juan Montes, prin. Fax 972-5668
Bonham ES 400/PK-5
2400 Jordan Ave 78503 956-971-4440
Clarissa Partida, prin. Fax 971-4284
Brown MS 900/6-8
2700 S Ware Rd 78503 956-632-8700
Alfredo Gutierrez, prin. Fax 632-8709
Castaneda ES 600/PK-5
4100 N 34th St 78504 956-632-8882
Jessica Estringel, prin. Fax 632-3627
Cathey MS 1,000/6-8
1800 N Cynthia St 78501 956-971-4300
Melvin L. Benford, prin. Fax 632-2811
De Leon MS 700/6-8
4201 N 29th Ln 78504 956-632-8800
Philip Grossweiler, prin. Fax 632-8805
Escandon ES 500/PK-5
2901 Colbath Ave 78503 956-971-4511
Carlos Mora, prin. Fax 971-4508
Fields ES 600/PK-5
500 Dallas Ave 78501 956-971-4344
Rosey Solis-Guerra, prin. Fax 971-4351
Fossum MS 800/6-8
7800 N Ware Rd 78504 956-971-1105
Monica Kaufmann, prin. Fax 618-9718
Garza ES 700/PK-5
6300 N 29th St 78504 956-971-4554
Rachel Villanueva, prin. Fax 971-4235
Gonzalez ES 900/PK-5
201 E Martin Ave 78504 956-971-4577
Christina Hernandez, prin. Fax 971-4575
Hendricks ES 500/PK-5
3900 Goldcrest Ave 78504 956-971-1145
Sandra Salinas, prin. Fax 618-9726
Houston ES 600/PK-5
3221 Olga Ave 78503 956-971-4484
Debra Loya-Thomas, prin. Fax 971-4295
Jackson ES 800/PK-5
501 W Harvey St 78501 956-971-4277
Pedro Garcia, prin. Fax 632-5179
Lincoln MS 700/6-8
1601 N 27th St 78501 956-971-4200
Maribelle Elizondo, prin. Fax 971-4273
McAuliffe ES 700/PK-5
3000 Daffodil Ave 78501 956-971-4400
Sandra Pitchford, prin. Fax 971-4482
Milam ES 1,000/PK-5
3800 N Main St 78501 956-971-4333
Linda McGurk, prin. Fax 972-5649
Morris MS 900/6-8
1400 Trenton Rd 78504 956-618-7300
Brian McClenny, prin. Fax 632-3666
Navarro ES 500/PK-5
2100 W Hackberry Ave 78501 956-971-4455
Leticia Infante, prin. Fax 972-5692
Perez ES 600/PK-5
7801 N Main St 78504 956-971-1125
Albert Irlas, prin. Fax 632-2880
Rayburn ES 600/PK-5
7000 N Main St 78504 956-971-4363
Nancy Dillard, prin. Fax 632-8453
Roosevelt ES 600/PK-5
4801 S 26th St 78503 956-971-4424
Gerardo Gonzalez, prin. Fax 618-7362
Sanchez ES 500/PK-5
2901 Incarnate Word Ave 78504 956-971-1100
Cynthia Rodriguez, prin. Fax 618-9705
Seguin ES 500/PK-5
2200 N 29th St 78501 956-971-4565
Juan Nevarez, prin. Fax 971-4589
Thigpen/Zavala ES 600/PK-5
2500 Galveston Ave 78501 956-971-4377
Sonia Casas, prin. Fax 972-5660
Travis MS 700/6-8
600 W Houston Ave 78501 956-971-4242
Efrain Amaya, prin. Fax 632-8454
Wilson ES 600/PK-5
1200 E Hackberry Ave 78501 956-971-4525
Kristina Garza, prin. Fax 971-4597

Sharyland ISD
Supt. — See Mission
Bentsen ES 600/PK-6
2101 S Taylor Rd 78503 956-668-0426
Cecilia Boyd, prin. Fax 668-0430
Sharyland North JHS 800/7-8
5100 W Dove Ave 78504 956-686-1415
Lorene Bazan, prin. Fax 668-0425
Wernecke ES 800/PK-6
4500 W Dove Ave 78504 956-928-1063
Lela Culberson, prin. Fax 928-0221

Covenant Christian Academy 500/PK-12
4201 N Ware Rd 78504 956-686-7886
Milton Gonzalez, prin. Fax 686-9470
Our Lady of Sorrows S 600/PK-8
1100 Gumwood Ave 78501 956-686-3651
Luisa DeLeon, prin. Fax 686-1996
St. Paul Lutheran S 200/PK-8
300 Pecan Blvd 78501 956-682-2345
Dr. Jeanne Kretzmann, prin. Fax 682-7148
South Texas Christian Academy 300/PK-12
7001 N Ware Rd 78504 956-682-1117
Eric Enright, prin. Fax 682-7398
Taylor Christian S 50/PK-8
2021 W Jackson Ave 78501 956-686-7574
Christina McBride B.A., dir. Fax 682-4945

Mc Camey, Upton, Pop. 1,870

Mc Camey ISD 500/PK-12
PO Box 1069 79752 432-652-3666
Ronnie Golson, supt. Fax 652-4219
www.mcisd.esc18.net
Mc Camey MS 100/5-8
PO Box 1069 79752 432-652-3666
Blanca Smith, prin. Fax 652-4246
Mc Camey PS 200/PK-4
PO Box 1069 79752 432-652-3666
Gina Schreiner, prin. Fax 652-4247

Mc Dade, Bastrop, Pop. 682

Mc Dade ISD 200/PK-12
PO Box 400 78650 512-273-2522
Barbara Marchbanks, supt. Fax 273-2101
www.mcdadeisd.com/
Mc Dade ES 200/PK-6
PO Box 400 78650 512-273-2522
Frances Williams, prin. Fax 273-2101

Mc Gregor, McLennan, Pop. 4,934

Mc Gregor ISD 1,000/PK-12
PO Box 356 76657 254-840-2828
James Lenamon, supt. Fax 840-4077
www.mcgregor-isd.org
Isbill JHS 300/6-8
PO Box 356 76657 254-840-3251
Kelly Tharpe, prin. Fax 840-3572
Mc Gregor ES 300/2-5
PO Box 356 76657 254-840-3204
Tonya Burgess, prin. Fax 840-3540
Mc Gregor PS PK-1
923 Bluebonnet Pkwy 76657 254-840-2973
Cheri Zacharias, prin. Fax 840-3345

Midway ISD
Supt. — See Woodway
River Valley IS 600/5-6
4750 Speegleville Rd 76657 254-761-5699
Sarah Holland, prin. Fax 761-5698

Mc Kinney, Collin, Pop. 128,217

Allen ISD
Supt. — See Allen
Lindsey ES 700/K-6
5730 Wilford Dr 75070 972-908-4000
Melissa Pursifull, prin. Fax 319-6999

Frisco ISD
Supt. — See Frisco
Comstock ES 500/K-5
7152 Silverado Trl 75070 469-633-3900
Pam Orr, prin. Fax 633-3910
Elliott ES 600/K-5
3721 Hudson Xing 75070 469-633-3750
Dr. Natalie Miller, prin. Fax 633-3760
Mooneyham ES 800/K-5
2301 Eden Dr 75070 469-633-3650
Michele Lott, prin. Fax 633-3660
Ogle ES 700/K-5
4200 Big Fork Trl 75070 469-633-3525
Phyllis Pope, prin. Fax 633-3535
Scoggins MS 700/6-8
7070 Stacy Rd 75070 469-633-5150
Barbara Warner, prin. Fax 633-5160
Scott ES K-5
10550 Millbend Dr 75070 469-633-4000
Paige Brewer, prin. Fax 633-4010
Sonntag ES 800/K-5
2001 Reagan Dr 75070 469-633-3850
Shannon Acosta, prin. Fax 633-3860

Mc Kinney ISD 24,500/PK-12
1 Duvall St 75069 469-302-4000
Dr. Rick McDaniel, supt. Fax 302-4071
www.mckinneyisd.net
Bennett ES 500/K-5
7760 Coronado Dr 75070 469-302-5400
Amy Holderman, prin. Fax 302-5401
Burks ES 500/PK-5
1801 Hill St 75069 469-302-6200
Pam Bendorf, prin. Fax 302-6201
Caldwell ES 500/K-5
601 W Louisiana St 75069 469-302-5500
Kelly Flowers, prin. Fax 302-5501
Cockrill MS 1,400/6-8
1351 Hardin Rd 75071 469-302-7900
Dr. Amber Epperson, prin. Fax 302-7901
Dowell MS 1,200/6-8
301 Ridge Rd 75070 469-302-6700
Holly Rogers, prin. Fax 302-6701
Eddins ES 500/K-5
311 Peregrine Dr 75070 469-302-6600
Sharon Havard, prin. Fax 302-6601
Evans MS 1,500/6-8
6998 Eldorado Pkwy 75070 469-302-7100
Darla Jackson, prin. Fax 302-7101
Faubion MS 900/6-8
2000 Rollins St 75069 469-302-6900
Jimmy Bowser, prin. Fax 302-6901
Finch ES 400/K-5
1205 S Tennessee St 75069 469-302-5600
Erika Echegaray, prin. Fax 302-5601
Glen Oaks ES 500/K-5
6100 Glen Oaks Dr 75070 469-302-6400
Mollky Hovan, prin. Fax 302-6401
Johnson ES 600/K-5
3400 Ash Ln 75070 469-302-6500
Michelle Baumann, prin. Fax 302-6501
Johnson MS 900/6-8
3400 Community Ave 75071 469-302-4900
Mitch Curry, prin. Fax 302-4901
Lawson ECC 700/PK-PK
500 Dowell St 75071 469-302-2400
Susie Towber, prin. Fax 302-2401
Malvern ES 500/K-5
1100 Eldorado Pkwy 75069 469-302-5300
Dr. Rhonda Gilliam, prin. Fax 302-5301
McClure ES 600/K-5
1753 N Ridge Rd 75071 469-302-9450
Melanie Raleeh, prin. Fax 302-9451
McGowen ES 700/K-5
4300 Columbus Dr 75070 469-302-7500
Jennifer Little, prin. Fax 302-7501
McNeil ES 500/K-5
3650 S Hardin Blvd 75070 469-302-5200
Tracy Meador, prin. Fax 302-5201
Minshew ES 600/PK-5
300 Joplin Dr 75071 469-302-7300
Al Conley, prin. Fax 302-7301

Naomi Press ES 500/K-5
4101 Shawnee Rd 75071 469-302-7600
Chris Clark, prin. Fax 302-7601
Slaughter ES 700/K-5
2706 Wolford St 75071 469-302-6100
Nick DeFelice, prin. Fax 302-6101
Valley Creek ES 500/K-5
2800 Valley Creek Trl 75070 469-302-4800
Megan Richards, prin. Fax 302-4801
Vega ES 600/K-5
2511 Cattleman Dr 75071 469-302-5100
Michael Forsyth, prin. Fax 302-5101
Walker ES 500/K-5
4000 Cockrill Dr 75070 469-302-4600
Deborah Sanchez, prin. Fax 302-4601
Webb ES 400/K-5
810 E Louisiana St 75069 469-302-6000
Kyle Luthi, prin. Fax 302-6001
Wilmeth ES 600/K-5
901 La Cima Dr 75071 469-302-7400
Judy Bragg, prin. Fax 302-7401
Wolford ES 600/K-5
6951 Berkshire Rd 75070 469-302-4700
Francine Gratt, prin. Fax 302-4701

Prosper ISD
Supt. — See Prosper
Baker ES 600/K-5
3125 Bluewood Dr 75071 469-219-2120
Garry Gorman, prin. Fax 529-1142
Hughes ES K-5
1551 Prestwick Hollow Dr 75071 469-219-2230
Tiffany Johns, prin. Fax 346-9620

Cornerstone Christian Academy 300/K-12
PO Box 3143 75070 214-491-5700
McKinney Christian Academy 500/PK-12
3601 Bois D Arc Rd 75071 214-544-2658
Bob Lovelady, head sch Fax 542-5056
Montessori S of Excellence 50/PK-6
7701 W Virginia Pkwy Ste B 75071 214-491-6090
Asma Ismail, prin. Fax 859-9620
Wonderland Montessori Acad of McKinney 200/PK-6
3132 Hudson Xing 75070 972-325-5962

Mc Lean, Gray, Pop. 771
McLean ISD 200/PK-12
PO Box 90 79057 806-779-2571
Oscar Muniz, supt. Fax 779-2248
www.mcleanisd.com
McLean S 200/PK-12
PO Box 90 79057 806-779-2671
Raymond Glass, prin. Fax 779-2248

Mc Leod, Cass
Mc Leod ISD 400/PK-12
PO Box 350 75565 903-796-7181
Cathy May, supt. Fax 796-8443
www.mcleodisd.net
Mc Leod ES 200/PK-5
PO Box 350 75565 903-796-7181
Jim Spurlin, prin. Fax 796-8443
Mc Leod MS 100/6-8
PO Box 350 75565 903-796-7181
Jim Spurlin, prin. Fax 796-8443

Mc Queeney, Guadalupe, Pop. 2,512
Seguin ISD
Supt. — See Seguin
Mc Queeney ES 400/K-5
8860 FM 725 78123 830-401-8738
Yomeida Guerra, prin. Fax 557-6981

Madisonville, Madison, Pop. 4,327
Madisonville Consolidated ISD 2,300/PK-12
PO Box 879 77864 936-348-2797
Keith Smith, supt. Fax 348-2751
www.madisonvillecisd.org
Madisonville ES 700/PK-2
PO Box 849 77864 936-348-2261
Rhodena Brooks, prin. Fax 349-8028
Madisonville IS 500/3-5
PO Box 635 77864 936-348-2921
Tawnya Nail, prin. Fax 348-2249
Madisonville JHS 500/6-8
PO Box 819 77864 936-348-3587
Dr. Rhonda Morgan, prin. Fax 348-5603

Magnolia, Montgomery, Pop. 1,381
Magnolia ISD 12,100/PK-12
PO Box 88 77353 281-356-3571
Dr. Todd Stephens Ph.D., supt. Fax 356-1328
www.magnoliaisd.org
Bear Branch 6th Grade Campus 500/6-6
PO Box 1559 77353 281-252-2031
Tommy Burns, prin. Fax 252-2032
Bear Branch ES 600/K-5
PO Box 999 77353 281-356-4771
Holly Ray, prin. Fax 252-2074
Bear Branch JHS 900/7-8
PO Box 606 77353 281-356-0000
Ben King Ed.D., prin. Fax 252-2060
Ellisor ES 700/K-5
PO Box 909 77353 281-252-7400
Coni Felinski, prin. Fax 252-7401
Lyon ES 800/PK-5
PO Box 907 77353 281-356-8115
Tammy Haley, prin. Fax 252-2170
Magnolia 6th Grade Campus 500/6-6
PO Box 1540 77353 281-252-2033
Lisa Bertrand, prin. Fax 252-2024
Magnolia ES 700/K-5
PO Box 638 77353 281-356-6434
Letty Roman, prin. Fax 252-2150
Magnolia JHS 1,000/7-8
PO Box 476 77353 281-356-1327
David Slater, prin. Fax 252-2125
Magnolia Parkway ES 700/PK-5
PO Box 460 77353 281-252-7440
Megan Baker, prin. Fax 252-7446
Nichols Sawmill ES 700/PK-5
PO Box 450 77353 281-252-2133
Carrie Quinn, prin. Fax 252-2138
Smith ES 700/PK-5
PO Box 1166 77353 281-252-2300
Dion Rivera, prin. Fax 252-2304
Williams ES 700/PK-5
PO Box 320 77353 281-356-6866
Kelly Jones, prin. Fax 252-2504

Tomball ISD
Supt. — See Tomball
Decker Prairie ES 600/PK-4
27427 Decker Prairie Rosehl 77355 281-357-3134
JoAnn Colson, prin. Fax 357-3293

Malakoff, Henderson, Pop. 2,275
Cross Roads ISD 600/PK-12
14434 FM 59 75148 903-489-2001
Richard Tedder, supt. Fax 489-2527
www.crossroadsisd.org
Cross Roads ES 300/PK-5
14434 FM 59 75148 903-489-1774
Kari Cahil, prin. Fax 489-1843
Cross Roads JHS 200/6-8
14434 FM 59 75148 903-489-2667
Julie Koepp, prin. Fax 489-3840

Malakoff ISD 1,300/PK-12
1308 FM 3062 75148 903-489-1152
Randy Perry, supt. Fax 489-2566
www.malakoffisd.org/
Malakoff ES 400/PK-5
310 N Terry St 75148 903-489-1964
Ronny Snow, prin. Fax 489-1536
Malakoff MS 300/6-8
106 N Cedar St 75148 903-489-0264
Quintin Watkins, prin. Fax 489-1812
Other Schools – See Tool

Malone, Hill, Pop. 265
Malone ISD 100/PK-8
PO Box 38 76660 254-533-2321
Linda Buffe, supt. Fax 533-5660
www.maloneisd.org
Malone ES 100/PK-8
PO Box 38 76660 254-533-2321
Linda Buffe, admin. Fax 533-5660

Manor, Travis, Pop. 4,931
Manor ISD 8,600/PK-12
10335 US Highway 290 E 78653 512-278-4000
Royce Avery, supt. Fax 278-4017
www.manorisd.net
Blake Manor ES 700/PK-5
18010 Blake Manor Rd 78653 512-278-4200
Jamie Haywood, prin. Fax 278-4209
Lagos ES, 11817 Murchison St 78653 K-5
Malaki Hawkins, admin. 512-278-4363
Manor ES 800/PK-5
12904 Gregg Manor Rd 78653 512-278-4100
Niccole Delestre, prin. Fax 278-4104
Manor MS 900/6-8
12900 Gregg Manor Rd 78653 512-278-4600
Donald Wise, prin. Fax 278-4285
Manor New Tech MS 6-8
12116 Joyce Turner Dr 78653 512-278-4463
Christopher Smith, admin.
Presidential Meadows ES 800/PK-5
13252 George Bush St 78653 512-278-4225
Lanica Failey, prin. Fax 278-4231
Shadowglen ES PK-5
12000 Shadowglen Trace 78653 512-278-4700
Andrea Easley, prin. Fax 278-4701
Other Schools – See Austin

Mansfield, Tarrant, Pop. 55,102
Mansfield ISD 30,800/PK-12
605 E Broad St 76063 817-299-6300
Dr. Jim Vaszauskas, supt. Fax 473-5465
www.mansfieldisd.org
Boren ES 500/K-4
1401 Country Club Dr 76063 817-299-7740
Tracy Johnson, prin. Fax 473-5727
Brown ES 600/PK-4
1860 Cannon Dr 76063 817-299-5860
Kyna Eastlick, prin. Fax 473-5392
Jobe MS 800/7-8
2491 Gertie Barrett Rd 76063 682-314-4400
Trent Dowd, prin. Fax 561-3899
Jones MS 1,000/7-8
4500 E Broad St 76063 682-314-4600
Travis Moore, prin. Fax 453-7380
Lillard IS 1,000/5-6
1301 N Day Miar Rd 76063 817-276-6260
Dr. Matthew Herzberg, prin. Fax 548-2285
Low IS 900/5-6
1526 N Walnut Creek Dr 76063 817-299-3640
Jason Short, prin. Fax 453-6577
Miller ES PK-4
403 N Holland Rd 76063 817-299-7550
Jenny Roberson, prin. Fax 473-5706
Nash ES 600/PK-4
1050 Magnolia St 76063 817-299-6900
Tiffanie King, prin. Fax 453-7300
Neal ES 400/PK-4
280 Nelson Wyatt Rd 76063 817-299-1270
Tameka Patton, prin. Fax 561-3820
Orr IS 900/5-6
2900 E Broad St 76063 817-299-2600
Duane Thurston, prin. Fax 473-5747
Perry ES 300/PK-4
1261 S Main St 76063 817-804-2800
Willie Wimbrey, prin. Fax 453-6760
Ponder ES 500/PK-4
101 Pleasant Ridge Dr 76063 817-299-7700
David Thayer, prin. Fax 473-5658
Shepard IS 800/5-6
1280 Highway 1187 76063 817-299-5940
Matthew Brown, prin. Fax 453-6812
Sheppard ES 600/PK-4
1701 Highway 1187 76063 817-299-6600
Dr. Lylia King, prin. Fax 453-6870
Smith ES 700/PK-4
701 S Holland Rd 76063 817-299-6980
Lea Boiles, prin. Fax 453-7340
Tipps ES 700/PK-4
3001 N Walnut Creek Dr 76063 817-299-6920
Cristina Hernandez, prin. Fax 453-7320
Wester MS 900/7-8
1520 N Walnut Creek Dr 76063 817-314-1800
Jennifer Powers, prin. Fax 453-7213
Worley MS 900/7-8
500 Pleasant Ridge Dr 76063 682-314-5100
Dr. Julia McMains, prin. Fax 473-5623
Other Schools – See Arlington, Burleson, Grand Prairie

Pantego Christian Academy - Mansfield 100/PK-6
2351 Country Club Dr 76063 817-522-5900
Jamye Autrey, prin. Fax 453-6342

Manvel, Brazoria, Pop. 5,107
Alvin ISD
Supt. — See Alvin
Duke ES 800/K-5
2900 County Road 59 77578 281-245-3400
Fulvia Shaw, prin. Fax 489-2160
Jeter ES 900/PK-5
2455 County Road 58 77578 281-245-3055
Craig Rhodes, prin. Fax 489-4630
Manvel JHS 6-8
7302 McCoy Rd 77578 281-245-3700
Raymond Root, prin. Fax 692-9078
Mason ES 700/PK-5
7400 Lewis Ln 77578 281-245-2832
Dixie Jones, prin. Fax 489-9181
Pomona ES K-5
4480 Kirby Dr 77578 281-245-3670
Renae Rives, prin. Fax 245-2412
Rodeo Palms JHS 900/6-8
101 Palm Desert Dr 77578 281-245-2078
Aeniqua Flowers, prin. Fax 489-8169

Marathon, Brewster, Pop. 427
Marathon ISD 50/PK-12
PO Box 416 79842 432-386-4431
Dr. Guadalupe Singh, supt. Fax 386-4395
www.marathonisd.net
Marathon S 50/PK-12
PO Box 416 79842 432-386-4431
Dr. Guadalupe Singh, admin. Fax 386-4395

Marble Falls, Burnet, Pop. 5,987
Marble Falls ISD 4,000/PK-12
1800 Colt Cir 78654 830-693-4357
Dr. Chris Allen, supt. Fax 693-5685
www.marblefallsisd.org
Colt ES 600/PK-5
2200 Manzano Mile 78654 830-693-3474
Keith Powell, prin. Fax 693-7092
Marble Falls ES 500/PK-5
901 Avenue U 78654 830-693-2385
Michael Haley, prin. Fax 693-5421
Marble Falls MS 900/6-8
1511 Pony Dr 78654 830-693-4439
Roger Barr, prin. Fax 693-7788
Other Schools – See Granite Shoals, Spicewood

Faith Academy of Marble Falls 200/K-12
PO Box 1240 78654 830-798-1333
Joseph Rispoli, admin. Fax 798-1332
First Baptist Christian S 200/PK-8
901 La Ventana 78654 830-693-3930
Living Word Academy 50/1-12
918 2nd St 78654 – Robert Hill, prin. 830-693-3339
St. Peters S 50/PK-K
1803 FM 1431 78654 830-798-2253
Tracy Knight, dir. Fax 693-6772

Marfa, Presidio, Pop. 1,967
Marfa ISD 300/PK-12
PO Box T 79843 432-729-5500
Oscar Aguero, supt. Fax 729-4310
www.marfaisd.com
Marfa ES 200/PK-6
PO Box I 79843 432-729-5500
Amy White, prin. Fax 729-4310

Marion, Guadalupe, Pop. 1,060
Marion ISD 1,300/PK-12
PO Box 189 78124 830-914-2803
Kelly Walters, supt. Fax 420-3268
www.marionisd.net
Krueger ES Karrer Campus 300/3-5
PO Box 189 78124 830-914-2803
Paul Goetzke, prin. Fax 420-3268
Krueger PS 300/PK-2
PO Box 189 78124 830-914-2803
Julie Brown, prin. Fax 420-3238
Marion MS 300/6-8
PO Box 189 78124 830-914-2803
Susan Thetford, prin. Fax 420-3206

Markham, Matagorda, Pop. 1,058
Tidehaven ISD
Supt. — See Elmaton
Markham ES, PO Box 317 77456 200/PK-5
Stacie Murry, prin. 979-843-4340

Marlin, Falls, Pop. 5,913
Marlin ISD 1,000/PK-12
130 Coleman St 76661 254-883-3585
Michael Seabolt, supt. Fax 883-6612
www.marlinisd.org
Marlin MS 200/6-8
678 Success Dr 76661 254-883-9241
Patti Ward, prin. Fax 883-2839
Marlin Primary Academy 500/PK-5
602 Donohoo St 76661 254-883-3232
Kimberly McKnight, prin. Fax 883-5237

Marshall, Harrison, Pop. 23,237
Marshall ISD 5,500/PK-12
1305 E Pinecrest Dr 75670 903-927-8700
Dr. Jerry Gibson, supt. Fax 935-0203
www.marshallisd.com
Crockett ES 600/K-5
700 Jasper Dr 75672 903-927-8880
Angela Fitzpatrick, prin. Fax 927-8885
Houston ES 400/K-5
2905 E Travis St 75672 903-927-8860
Jerry Hancock, prin. Fax 927-8863
Marshall JHS 800/6-8
2710 E Travis St 75672 903-927-8830
Yolonda Martin, prin. Fax 927-8837
Travis ES 400/K-5
300 W Carolanne Blvd 75672 903-927-8780
Loyed Jones, prin. Fax 927-8782
Washington ECC 300/PK-PK
1202 Evans St 75670 903-927-8790
Detrice Fisher, prin. Fax 927-8794
Young ES 400/K-5
1501 Sanford St 75670 903-927-8850
Nakeisha Pegues, prin. Fax 927-8888

Trinity Episcopal S 200/PK-8
2905 Rosborough Springs Rd 75672 903-938-3513

Mart, McLennan, Pop. 2,183
Mart ISD 500/PK-12
700 E Navarro Ave 76664 254-876-2523
Leonard Williams, supt. Fax 876-3028
www.martisd.org
Mart ES 200/PK-6
700 E Navarro Ave 76664 254-876-2762
Amy Stone, prin. Fax 876-2613

Mason, Mason, Pop. 2,094
Mason ISD 700/PK-12
PO Box 410 76856 325-347-1144
John Schumacher, supt. Fax 294-4412
www.masonisd.net
Mason ES 300/PK-4
PO Box 410 76856 325-347-1122
Shanda Schmidt, prin. Fax 347-5461
Mason JHS 200/5-8
PO Box 410 76856 325-347-1122
Lauren Walch, prin. Fax 347-5461

Matador, Motley, Pop. 605
Motley County ISD 200/PK-12
PO Box 310 79244 806-347-2676
William Cochran, supt. Fax 347-2871
www.motleyco.org
Motley County S 200/PK-12
PO Box 310 79244 806-347-2676
James Richards, prin. Fax 347-2871

Matagorda, Matagorda, Pop. 498
Matagorda ISD 200/PK-8
PO Box 657 77457 979-863-7693
Susan Phillips, supt. Fax 863-2230
www.matagordaisd.org/
Matagorda S 200/PK-8
PO Box 657 77457 979-863-7693
Laura Shay, prin. Fax 863-2230

Mathis, San Patricio, Pop. 4,929
Mathis ISD 1,700/PK-12
PO Box 1179 78368 361-547-3378
Benny Hernandez, supt. Fax 547-4198
www.mathisisd.org
Mathis ES 500/PK-2
PO Box 1179 78368 361-547-4106
Jesse Dolin, prin. Fax 547-4162
Mathis IS 400/3-5
PO Box 1179 78368 361-547-2472
Cynthia Westbrook, prin. Fax 547-4119
Mathis MS 400/6-8
PO Box 1179 78368 361-547-2381
Randy Tiemman, prin. Fax 547-4156

Maud, Bowie, Pop. 1,042
Maud ISD 500/PK-12
PO Box 1028 75567 903-585-2219
Chris Bradshaw, supt. Fax 585-5451
www.maudisd.net
Maud S 500/PK-12
PO Box 1028 75567 903-585-2219
Scott Sanders, prin. Fax 585-5451

May, Brown
May ISD 300/PK-12
3400 E County Road 411 76857 254-259-2091
Steve Howard, supt. Fax 259-3514
www.mayisd.com
May ES 100/PK-6
3400 E County Road 411 76857 254-259-3711
Allison Williams, prin. Fax 259-2135

Maypearl, Ellis, Pop. 920
Maypearl ISD 1,100/PK-12
PO Box 40 76064 972-435-1000
Ritchie Bowling M.Ed., supt. Fax 435-1001
www.maypearlisd.org
Kirkpatrick ES 400/PK-4
PO Box 40 76064 972-435-1010
Cristin Votaw, prin. Fax 435-1011
Maypearl IS 200/5-6
PO Box 40 76064 972-435-1099
Jessica Lee, admin. Fax 435-1098
Maypearl JHS 200/7-8
PO Box 40 76064 972-435-1015
Jessica Lee, prin. Fax 435-1016

Meadow, Terry, Pop. 593
Meadow ISD 300/PK-12
604 4th St 79345 806-539-2246
Darrian Dover, supt. Fax 539-2529
www.meadowisd.net
Meadow ES 200/PK-5
604 4th St 79345 806-539-2527
Dennis Berger, prin. Fax 539-2334

Meadows Place, Fort Bend, Pop. 4,547
Fort Bend ISD
Supt. — See Sugar Land
Meadows ES 400/K-5
12037 Pender Ln, 281-634-4720
Michele Labus, prin. Fax 634-4734

Medina, Bandera, Pop. 3,931
Medina ISD 100/PK-12
PO Box 1470 78055 830-589-2855
Kevin Newsom, supt. Fax 589-7150
www.medinaisd.org
Medina S 100/PK-12
PO Box 1470 78055 830-589-2851
Dr. Sarah McCrae, prin. Fax 589-7150

Melissa, Collin, Pop. 4,615
Melissa ISD 1,800/PK-12
1904 Cooper St 75454 972-837-2411
Keith Murphy, supt. Fax 837-4233
www.melissaisd.org
McKillop ES 700/PK-3
3509 Liberty Way 75454 972-837-2632
Walter Perez, prin. Fax 837-2836
Melissa MS 300/6-8
2950 Cardinal Dr 75454 972-837-4355
Jim Miller, prin. Fax 837-4497
Melissa Ridge IS 300/4-5
3233 Fannin Rd 75454 972-837-4530
Michele Austin, prin. Fax 837-4333

Memphis, Hall, Pop. 2,281
Memphis ISD 500/PK-12
PO Box 460 79245 806-259-5900
William Alexander, supt. Fax 259-2515
www.memphisisd.net
Austin ES 100/3-5
PO Box 460 79245 806-259-5930
Leigh Ann Hawthorne, prin. Fax 259-2786
Memphis MS 100/6-8
PO Box 460 79245 806-259-5920
Kennith Hardin, prin. Fax 259-2051
Travis ES 100/PK-2
PO Box 460 79245 806-259-5940
Victoria Davis, prin. Fax 259-3119

Menard, Menard, Pop. 1,468
Menard ISD 300/PK-12
PO Box 729 76859 325-396-2404
Amy Bannowsky, supt. Fax 396-2143
www.menardisd.net
Menard ES 200/PK-5
PO Box 729 76859 325-396-2348
Cordelia Kothmann, admin. Fax 396-2761
Menard JHS 100/6-8
PO Box 729 76859 325-396-2348
Cordelia Kothmann, admin. Fax 396-2761

Mercedes, Hidalgo, Pop. 15,537
Mercedes ISD 5,300/PK-12
PO Box 419 78570 956-514-2000
Dr. Daniel Trevino, supt. Fax 514-2033
www.misdtx.net
Chacon MS 900/6-8
PO Box 419 78570 956-514-2200
Orlando Rodriguez, prin. Fax 514-2212
Harrell MS 6-8
PO Box 419 78570 956-825-5140
Elva Rivera, prin. Fax 514-2323
Hinojosa ES 600/PK-5
PO Box 419 78570 956-514-2277
Michelle Guajardo, prin. Fax 514-2292
Kennedy ES 400/PK-5
PO Box 419 78570 956-514-2300
Elva Rivera, prin. Fax 514-2311
Taylor ES 500/PK-5
PO Box 419 78570 956-514-2388
David Aguirre, prin. Fax 514-2377
Travis ES 600/PK-5
PO Box 419 78570 956-514-2366
Miguel Chacon, prin. Fax 514-2373

South Texas ISD 3,400/7-12
100 Med High Dr 78570 956-565-2454
Marla Guerra Ed.D., supt. Fax 565-9129
www.stisd.net
Other Schools – See Edinburg, San Benito

Immanuel Lutheran S 50/PK-5
703 W 3rd St 78570 956-565-1518
Virginia Guzman, prin.

Meridian, Bosque, Pop. 1,479
Meridian ISD 500/PK-12
PO Box 349 76665 254-435-2081
Dr. Kim Edwards, supt. Fax 435-2025
www.meridianisd.org
Meridian ES 300/PK-5
PO Box 349 76665 254-435-2731
Jaime Leinhauser, prin. Fax 435-6099

Merit, Hunt
Bland ISD 600/PK-12
PO Box 216 75458 903-776-2239
Rick Tidwell, supt. Fax 776-2240
www.blandisd.net
Bland MS 100/6-8
PO Box 216 75458 903-776-2239
Jason Hammack, prin. Fax 527-5491
Other Schools – See Greenville

Merkel, Taylor, Pop. 2,564
Merkel ISD 800/PK-12
PO Box 430 79536 325-928-5813
Bryan Allen, supt. Fax 928-3910
www.merkel.esc14.net
Merkel ES 300/PK-5
PO Box 430 79536 325-928-4795
Tammy Nall, prin. Fax 928-3174
Merkel MS 200/6-8
PO Box 430 79536 325-928-5511
Larry Bills, prin. Fax 928-3138

Mertzon, Irion, Pop. 768
Irion County ISD 300/K-12
PO Box 469 76941 325-835-6111
Billy Barnett, supt. Fax 835-2017
www.irion-isd.org
Irion County ES 200/K-6
PO Box 469 76941 325-835-3991
Jessica Parker, prin. Fax 835-2281

Mesquite, Dallas, Pop. 137,317
Dallas ISD
Supt. — See Dallas
Smith ES 800/PK-5
5299 Gus Thomasson Rd 75150 972-502-4800
Lora Morris, prin. Fax 502-4801

Mesquite ISD 39,500/PK-12
3819 Towne Crossing Blvd 75150 972-288-6411
Dr. David Vroonland, supt. Fax 882-7787
www.mesquiteisd.org
Achziger ES 900/PK-5
3300 Ridge Ranch Rd 75181 972-290-4180
Kristi Gregory, prin. Fax 290-4190
Agnew MS 800/7-8
729 Wilkinson Dr 75149 972-882-5750
Kelly Long, prin. Fax 882-5760
Austin ES 500/PK-6
3020 Poteet Dr 75150 972-882-7220
Jonathan Royle, prin. Fax 882-7225
Beasley ES 400/K-6
919 Green Canyon Dr 75150 972 882 5160
Kelly McCollom, prin. Fax 882-5161
Berry MS 900/6-8
2675 Bear Dr 75181 972-882-5850
Gerald Sarpy, prin. Fax 882-5888
Black ES 600/K-6
328 Newsome Rd 75149 972-882-7240
Darla Franklin, prin. Fax 882-7250
Cannaday ES 500/K-6
2701 Chisolm Trl 75150 972-882-5060
Lauren Chism, prin. Fax 882-5070
Florence ES 600/PK-6
4600 Ashwood Dr 75150 972-290-4080
LaDonna Gulley, prin. Fax 290-4088
Galloway ES 800/PK-6
200 Clary Dr 75149 972-882-5101
Wanda Mingle, prin. Fax 882-5110
Gentry ES 800/PK-6
1901 Twin Oaks Dr 75181 972-290-4140
Rashunda Price, prin. Fax 290-4150
Hanby ES 1,000/PK-5
912 Cascade St 75149 972-882-5040
Tammy Zeller, prin. Fax 882-5050
Kimball ES 300/K-6
4010 Coryell Way 75150 972-290-4120
Stacy Sheffield, prin. Fax 290-4130
Kimbrough MS 900/7-8
3900 N Galloway Ave 75150 972-882-5900
Chris Brott, prin. Fax 882-5942
Lawrence ES 500/PK-6
3811 Richman Dr 75150 972-882-7000
Cathy Swann, prin. Fax 882-7010
McDonald MS 1,000/7-8
2930 N Town East Blvd 75150 972-882-5700
Debra Bassinger, prin. Fax 882-5710
McKenzie ES 600/K-6
3535 Stephens Green Dr 75150 972-882-5140
Aimee Lewis, prin. Fax 882-5151
McWhorter ES 900/PK-6
1700 Hickory Tree Rd 75149 972-882-7020
Tammi Froning, prin. Fax 882-7030
Moss ES 500/PK-6
1208 New Market Rd 75149 972-882-7130
Michael Pierotti, prin. Fax 882-7146
Motley ES 400/K-6
3719 Moon Dr 75150 972-882-5080
Shawna DeLamar, prin. Fax 882-5090
New MS 800/7-8
3700 S Belt Line Rd 75181 972-882-5600
Stacy Carpenter, prin. Fax 882-5620
Pirrung ES 500/PK-5
1500 Creek Valley Rd 75181 972-882-7170
Paige Brison, prin. Fax 882-7189
Porter ES 600/PK-6
517 Via Avenida 75150 972-290-4000
Becky Rasco, prin. Fax 290-4004
Range ES 600/K-6
2600 Bamboo St 75150 972-882-5180
Sherrie Beard, prin. Fax 882-5190
Rugel ES 500/PK-6
2701 Sybil Dr 75149 972-882-7260
Renee Duckworth, prin. Fax 882-7270
Rutherford ES 500/PK-5
1607 Sierra Dr 75149 972-290-4060
Holly Grubbs, prin. Fax 290-4068

Seabourn ES 600/PK-6
2249 Picadilly Blvd 75149 972-882-7040
Renae Kern, prin. Fax 882-7050
Shands ES 900/K-6
4836 Shands Dr 75150 972-290-4020
Brandi Lewis, prin. Fax 290-4030
Shaw ES 800/PK-6
707 Purple Sage Trl 75149 972-882-7060
Kim Dumaine-Banuelos, prin. Fax 882-7070
Smith ES 500/PK-5
2300 Mesquite Valley Rd 75149 972-882-7080
Charlene Goss, prin. Fax 882-7090
Terry MS 900/6-8
2351 Edwards Church Rd 75181 972-882-5650
Danny Taylor, prin. Fax 882-5660
Thompson ES 600/PK-5
2525 Helen Ln 75181 972-882-7190
Kristy Morse, prin. Fax 882-7197
Tisinger ES 800/PK-5
1701 Hillcrest St 75149 972-882-5120
Valerie Nelson, prin. Fax 882-5130
Tosch ES 800/K-6
2424 Larchmont Dr 75150 972-882-5000
Amy Childress, prin. Fax 882-5010
Vanston MS 800/7-8
3230 Karla Dr 75150 972-882-5801
Karen Morris, prin. Fax 882-5848
Wilkinson MS 900/6-8
2100 Crest Park Dr 75149 972-882-5950
Molly Purl, prin. Fax 882-5988
Other Schools – See Balch Springs, Dallas, Garland

Dallas Christian S 600/PK-12
1515 Republic Pkwy 75150 972-270-5495

Mexia, Limestone, Pop. 7,378
Mexia ISD 1,700/PK-12
PO Box 2000 76667 254-562-4000
Dr. Lyle DuBus, supt. Fax 562-4007
www.mexiaisd.net
McBay ES 500/PK-2
PO Box 2000 76667 254-562-4030
Joe Tyus, prin. Fax 562-0074
Mexia JHS 400/6-8
PO Box 2000 76667 254-562-4020
Kurt Hulett Ph.D., prin. Fax 562-5053
Sims IS 200/3-5
PO Box 2000 76667 254-562-4025
Lisa Lauderdale, prin. Fax 562-4028

Meyersville, DeWitt
Meyersville ISD 100/PK-8
PO Box 1 77974 361-277-5817
Kelly Dunn, supt. Fax 275-5034
www.meyersvilleisd.org
Meyersville S 100/PK-8
PO Box 1 77974 361-275-3639
Kelly Dunn, supt. Fax 275-5034

Miami, Roberts, Pop. 592
Miami ISD 200/PK-12
PO Box 368 79059 806-868-3971
Donna Hale, supt. Fax 868-3171
www.miamiisd.net
Miami S 200/PK-12
PO Box 368 79059 806-868-3971
Charles Driskell, prin. Fax 868-3171

Midland, Midland, Pop. 109,776
Greenwood ISD 1,800/PK-12
2700 FM 1379 79706 432-683-6461
Ariel Elliott, supt. Fax 685-7804
www.greenwood.esc18.net
Brooks MS 500/5-8
2700 FM 1379 79706 432-253-6696
John-Paul Huber, prin. Fax 253-6731
Greenwood ES 800/PK-4
2700 FM 1379 79706 432-253-6703
Crysten Hopkins, prin. Fax 685-7822

Midland ISD 23,400/PK-12
615 W Missouri Ave 79701 432-240-1000
Orlando Riddick, supt. Fax 689-1976
www.midlandisd.net
Abell JHS 900/7-8
3201 Heritage Blvd 79707 432-689-6200
Jennifer Seybert, prin. Fax 689-6217
Alamo JHS 800/7-8
3800 Storey Ave 79703 432-689-1700
Leann Dumas, prin. Fax 689-1712
Bonham ES 800/PK-6
909 Bonham St 79703 432-240-6000
Juan Dominguez, prin. Fax 240-6001
Bowie Fine Arts Academy 500/PK-6
805 Elk Ave 79701 432-240-6100
Melissa Horner, prin. Fax 240-6101
Bunche ES, 702 S Jackson St 79701 PK-6
Sha Burdsal, prin. 432-240-8605
Burnet ES 600/PK-6
900 Raymond Rd 79703 432-240-6200
Angie Aron, prin. Fax 240-6201
Bush ES 600/PK-6
5001 Preston Dr 79707 432-240-6300
Stephanie Ramos, prin. Fax 240-6301
Carver Center 400/2-6
1300 E Wall St 79701 432-240-6400
Stephanie Carnett, prin. Fax 240-6401
DeZavala ES 500/PK-6
705 N Lee St 79701 432-240-6600
Ray Portillo, prin. Fax 240-6601
Emerson ES 600/PK-6
2800 Moss Ave 79705 432-240-6700
Edgar Tibayan, prin. Fax 240-6701
Fannin ES 600/K-6
2400 Fannin Ave 79705 432-240-6800
Tara Crockett, prin. Fax 240-6801
Fasken ES, 5806 Val Verde Dr 79707 PK-6
Lina Baiza, prin. 432-240-8405

Franks ES PK-6
401 E Parker Ave 79701 432-240-6500
Leslie Goodrum, prin. Fax 240-6501
Goddard JHS 1,000/7-8
2500 Haynes Dr 79705 432-689-1300
Shelly King, prin. Fax 689-1321
Greathouse ES 700/PK-6
5107 Greathouse Ave 79707 432-240-6900
Brandy Copeland, prin. Fax 240-6901
Henderson ES 500/PK-6
4800 Graceland Dr 79703 432-240-7000
Tanya Bell, prin. Fax 240-7001
Houston ES 600/PK-6
2000 W Louisiana Ave 79701 432-240-7100
Dolores Cano, prin. Fax 240-7101
Jones ES 500/PK-6
4919 Shadylane Dr 79703 432-240-7200
Lisa LeClear, prin. Fax 240-7201
Lamar ES 600/PK-6
3200 Kessler Ave 79701 432-240-7300
Amy Clark, prin. Fax 240-7301
Long ES 600/PK-6
4200 Cedar Spring Dr 79703 432-240-7400
Terri Rimer, prin. Fax 689-1836
Milam ES 600/K-6
301 E Dormard Ave 79705 432-240-7500
Iliana Bermea, prin. Fax 240-7501
Parker ES 500/PK-6
3800 Norwood St 79707 432-240-7600
Tracie Burrow, prin. Fax 240-7601
Pease Technology & Communication S 500/PK-6
1700 Magnolia Ave 79705 432-240-7700
Holly Roberts, prin. Fax 240-7701
Rusk ES 600/PK-6
2601 Wedgwood St 79707 432-240-7800
Dora Flores, prin. Fax 240-7801
San Jacinto JHS 700/7-8
1400 N N St 79701 432-689-1350
Deborah Kendricks, prin. Fax 689-1385
Santa Rita ES 600/PK-6
5306 Whitman Dr 79705 432-240-7900
Debra Alba, prin. Fax 240-7901
Scharbauer ES 800/K-6
2115 Hereford Blvd 79707 432-240-8000
Sharla Butler, prin. Fax 240-8001
South ES 500/PK-6
201 W Dakota Ave 79701 432-240-8100
Lety Amalla, prin. Fax 240-8101
Travis ES 800/PK-6
900 E Gist Ave 79701 432-240-8200
Terri Matthews, prin. Fax 240-8201
Washington STEM Academy 500/PK-6
1800 E Wall St 79701 432-240-8300
Banay Newton, prin. Fax 240-8301
Yarbrough ES PK-6
6000 Riverfront Dr 79706 432-240-8500
Jill Arthur, prin.

Midland Christian S 1,200/PK-12
2001 Culver Dr 79705 432-694-1661
St. Anns Catholic S 300/PK-8
2000 W Texas Ave 79701 432-684-4563
Joan Wilmoe, prin. Fax 687-2468
Trinity S of Midland 500/PK-12
3500 W Wadley Ave 79707 432-697-3281
Don North, head sch Fax 697-7403

Midlothian, Ellis, Pop. 17,760
Midlothian ISD 7,700/PK-12
100 Walter Stephenson Rd 76065 972-775-8296
Dr. Lane Ledbetter, supt. Fax 775-1757
www.misd.gs
Baxter ES 600/PK-5
1050 Park Place Blvd 76065 972-775-8281
Harper Stewart, prin. Fax 775-3154
Irvin ES 400/K-5
700 W Avenue H 76065 972-775-8239
Josh Roberts, prin. Fax 775-3179
Longbranch ES 700/PK-5
6631 FM 1387 76065 972-775-2830
Karena Blackwell, prin. Fax 775-2024
McClatchey ES, 6631 Shiloh Rd 76065 K-5
Stacy Germany, prin. 972-775-8296
Miller ES 500/K-5
2800 Sudith Ln 76065 972-775-4497
Shannon West, prin. Fax 775-4316
Mt. Peak ES 600/PK-5
5201 FM 663 76065 972-775-2881
Shannon Thompson, prin. Fax 775-2054
Seale MS 900/6-8
700 George Hopper Rd 76065 972-775-6145
Coy Tipton, prin. Fax 775-1502
Vitovsky ES 600/PK-5
333 Church St 76065 972-775-5536
Hollye Walker, prin. Fax 775-5532
Walnut Grove MS 1,000/6-8
990 N Walnut Grove Rd 76065 972-775-5355
Brian Blackwell, prin. Fax 775-8127

Milano, Milam, Pop. 425
Milano ISD 400/PK-12
PO Box 145 76556 512-455-2533
Robert Westbrook, supt. Fax 455-9311
www.milanoisd.net
Milano ES 200/PK-5
PO Box 145 76556 512-455-2062
Courtney Todd, prin. Fax 455-2267
Milano JHS 100/6-8
PO Box 145 76556 512-455-6701
Frederick Kutcher, prin. Fax 455-9186

Miles, Runnels, Pop. 823
Miles ISD 400/PK-12
PO Box 308 76861 325-468-2861
Robert Gibson, supt. Fax 468-2179
www.milesisd.net

Miles ES 200/PK-6
PO Box 308 76861 325-468-2861
Sharla Arp, prin. Fax 468-2179

Milford, Ellis, Pop. 717
Milford ISD 200/PK-12
PO Box 545 76670 972-493-2911
Don Clingenpeel, supt. Fax 493-2429
www.milfordisd.org
Milford S 200/PK-12
PO Box 545 76670 972-493-2921
Don Clingenpeel, prin. Fax 493-4600

Millsap, Parker, Pop. 400
Millsap ISD 800/PK-12
201 E Brazos St 76066 940-682-3100
Deann Lee, supt. Fax 682-4476
www.millsapisd.net
Millsap ES 400/PK-5
101 Wilson Bend Rd 76066 940-682-4489
Cathy Bradshaw, prin. Fax 682-4158
Millsap MS 200/6-8
301 E Brazos St 76066 940-682-4994
Jeff Clark, prin. Fax 682-4476

Mineola, Wood, Pop. 4,457
Mineola ISD 1,600/PK-12
1695 W Loop 564 75773 903-569-2448
Kim Tunnell, supt. Fax 569-5155
www.mineolaisd.net
Mineola ES 400/3-5
1695 W Loop 564 75773 903-569-2466
Stacy Morris, prin. Fax 569-3061
Mineola MS 400/6-8
1695 W Loop 564 75773 903-569-5338
Kendall Gould, prin. Fax 569-5339
Mineola PS 400/PK-2
1695 W Loop 564 75773 903-569-5488
Jole Ray, prin. Fax 569-5489

Mineral Wells, Palo Pinto, Pop. 16,580
Mineral Wells ISD 3,300/PK-12
906 SW 5th Ave 76067 940-325-6404
John Kuhn, supt. Fax 325-6378
www.mwisd.net/
Houston ES 500/2-3
300 SW 13th St 76067 940-325-3427
Dianna Leggett, prin. Fax 325-7683
Lamar ES 700/PK-1
2012 SE 12th St 76067 940-325-5303
Kendra Fowler, prin. Fax 328-0152
Mineral Wells JHS 500/7-8
1301 SE 14th Ave 76067 940-325-0711
Shanna Coker, prin. Fax 328-0450
Travis ES 700/4-6
1001 SE Martin Luther King 76067 940-325-7001
David Wells, prin. Fax 328-0972

Community Christian S 100/PK-12
2501 Garrett Morris Pkwy 76067 940-328-1333
Doug Jefferson, admin. Fax 328-1277

Mission, Hidalgo, Pop. 76,804
La Joya ISD
Supt. — See La Joya
Bentsen ES 800/PK-5
3301 W Mile 3 Rd, 956-323-2480
Magda Palacios, prin. Fax 323-2481
Camarena ES 700/PK-5
2612 N Moorefield Rd, 956-323-2720
Maria Lily Garza, prin. Fax 323-2721
Cavazos ES 600/PK-5
4563 N Minnesota Rd, 956-323-2430
Marisa Garza, prin. Fax 323-2431
Chapa ES 600/PK-5
5670 N Doffing Rd, 956-323-2400
Linda Lopez, prin. Fax 323-2401
Chavez MS 900/6-8
78 Showers Rd 78572 956-323-2800
Rolando Rios, prin. Fax 323-2801
De Escandon ES 700/PK-5
700 N Schuerbach Rd 78572 956-323-2410
Mary Sepulveda, prin. Fax 323-2411
De La Garza ES 500/PK-5
5441 N La Homa Rd, 956-323-2380
Irene Fernandez, prin. Fax 323-2381
Diaz-Villarreal ES 800/PK-5
5543 N La Homa Rd, 956-580-6170
Yolanda Salazar, prin. Fax 580-6016
Flores ES 600/PK-5
1913 Roque Salinas Rd 78572 956-323-2760
Maria Flores, prin. Fax 323-2761
Garcia MS 800/6-8
933 Paula St, 956-323-2840
Santana Galven, prin. Fax 323-2841
Garza ES 800/PK-5
8731 N Doffing Rd, 956-323-2350
Maria Flores-Guerra, prin. Fax 323-2351
Gonzalez ES 700/PK-5
3912 N FM 492, 956-323-2460
Dianabel Villarrea, prin. Fax 323-2461
Leo ES 600/PK-5
1625 Roque Salinas Rd 78572 956-323-2370
Maria Jazinski, prin. Fax 323-2371
Memorial MS 700/6-8
2610 N Moorefield Rd, 956-323-2820
Daniel Villarreal, prin. Fax 323-2821
Mendiola ES 600/PK-5
6401 N Abram Rd, 956-323-2420
Alicia Gutierrez, prin. Fax 323-2421
Paredes ES 600/PK-5
5301 N Bentsen Palm Dr, 956-323-2730
Erika Covarrubia, prin. Fax 323-2731
Perez ES 700/PK-5
4431 N Minnesota Rd, 956-323-2450
Myra Trigo Ramos, prin. Fax 323-2451
Richards MS 900/6-8
7005 Ann Richards Rd 78572 956-323-2860
Thomas Ocana, prin. Fax 323-2861

Salinas MS 800/6-8
6101 N Bentsen Palm Dr, 956-323-2850
Nidia Ortiz, prin. Fax 323-2851
Seguin ES 900/PK-5
8500 Western Rd, 956-323-2710
Jacqueline Escobedo, prin. Fax 323-2711
Zapata ES 800/PK-5
9100 N La Homa Rd, 956-323-2700
Rosa Gonzalez, prin. Fax 323-2701

Mission Consolidated ISD 15,200/PK-12
1201 Bryce Dr 78572 956-323-5505
Dr. Ricardo Lopez, supt. Fax 323-5634
www.mcisd.net
Bryan ES 700/PK-5
1201 Bryce Dr 78572 956-323-4800
Linda Sanchez, prin. Fax 323-4819
Castro ES 600/PK-5
1201 Bryce Dr 78572 956-323-6800
Myra Garza, prin. Fax 323-6818
Escobar/Rios ES 600/PK-5
1201 Bryce Dr 78572 956-323-8400
Blanca Lopez, prin. Fax 323-8480
Leal ES 600/PK-5
1201 Bryce Dr 78572 956-323-4600
Trinidad Pena, prin. Fax 323-4615
Marcell ES 500/PK-5
1201 Bryce Dr 78572 956-323-6400
Marissa Saenz, prin. Fax 323-6419
Mims ES 600/PK-5
1201 Bryce Dr 78572 956-323-4400
Yvonne Zamora, prin. Fax 323-4418
Mission JHS 900/6-8
1201 Bryce Dr 78572 956-323-3300
Adan Ramirez, prin. Fax 323-3338
O'Grady ES 500/PK-5
1201 Bryce Dr 78572 956-323-4200
Angelina Garcia, prin. Fax 323-4220
Pearson ES 500/PK-5
1201 Bryce Dr 78572 956-323-4000
Melissa Davis, prin. Fax 323-4015
White JHS 900/6-8
1201 Bryce Dr 78572 956-323-3600
Brenda Betancourt, prin. Fax 323-3632
Other Schools – See Alton, Palmhurst

Sharyland ISD 10,300/PK-12
1106 N Shary Rd 78572 956-580-5200
Dr. Robert O'Connor, supt. Fax 580-5229
www.sharylandisd.org
Garza ES 600/PK-6
1106 N Shary Rd 78572 956-580-5353
Veronica Rodriguez, prin. Fax 580-5363
Gray JHS 800/7-8
1106 N Shary Rd 78572 956-580-5333
Ericka Carranza, prin. Fax 580-5346
Hinojosa ES 500/PK-6
1106 N Shary Rd 78572 956-584-4990
Lou Ann Sarachene, prin. Fax 584-4998
Jensen ES 700/PK-6
1106 N Shary Rd 78572 956-580-5252
Niranda Flores, prin. Fax 580-5266
Martinez ES 700/PK-6
1106 N Shary Rd 78572 956-584-4900
Nayeli Perez, prin. Fax 584-4908
Shary ES 800/PK-6
1106 N Shary Rd 78572 956-580-5282
Rebekah Gerlach, prin. Fax 580-5294
Shimotsu ES 600/PK-6
1106 N Shary Rd 78572 956-583-5643
Anthony Limon, prin. Fax 519-1079
Other Schools – See Mc Allen

Agape Christian S 200/PK-6
1401 E 24th St, 956-585-9773
Criselda Zambrano, dir. Fax 585-9775

Missouri City, Fort Bend, Pop. 65,862
Fort Bend ISD
Supt. — See Sugar Land
Armstrong ES 700/PK-5
3440 Independence Blvd 77459 281-634-9410
Millie Alvarez, prin. Fax 327-9409
Baines MS 1,500/6-8
9000 Sienna Ranch Rd 77459 281-634-6870
Jennifer Roberts, prin. Fax 634-6880
Briargate ES 500/PK-5
15817 Blueridge Rd 77489 281-634-4560
Deanna Olson, prin. Fax 634-4576
Glover ES 500/PK-5
1510 Columbia Blue Dr 77489 281-634-4920
Nikki Roberts, prin. Fax 634-4934
Hunters Glen ES 500/PK-5
695 Independence Blvd 77489 281-634-4640
Crystal Gardner, prin. Fax 634-4656
Jones ES 700/PK-5
302 Martin Ln 77489 281-634-4960
Tim Clark, prin. Fax 634-4974
Lake Olympia MS 1,200/6-8
3100 Lake Olympia Pkwy 77459 281-634-3520
Janis Longmire, prin. Fax 634-3549
Lantern Lane ES 500/K-5
3323 Mission Valley Dr 77459 281-634-4680
Dr. Trenae Hill, prin. Fax 634-4694
Leonetti ES K-5
1757 Waters Lake Blvd 77459 281-327-3190
Joy Schwinger, prin. Fax 327-3191
Lexington Creek ES 500/K-5
2335 Dulles Ave 77459 281-634-5000
Christina Hopkins, prin. Fax 634-5014
Missouri City MS 1,200/6-8
202 Martin Ln 77489 281-634-3440
Jerrie Kammerman, prin. Fax 634-3473
Palmer ES 600/K-5
4208 Crow Valley Dr 77459 281-634-4760
Kellie Clay, prin. Fax 634-4773
Quail Valley ES 600/PK-5
3500 Quail Village Dr 77459 281-634-5040
Carla Patton, prin. Fax 634-5054
Quail Valley MS 1,300/6-8
3019 FM 1092 Rd 77459 281-634-3600
Jeff Post, prin. Fax 634-3632
Scanlan Oaks ES 1,000/K-5
9000 Camp Sienna Trl 77459 281-634-3950
Jaimie Geis, prin. Fax 634-3915
Schiff ES 900/K-5
7400 Discovery Ln 77459 281-634-9450
Lucretia DeFlora, prin. Fax 327-9449
Sienna Crossing ES 1,000/K-5
10011 Steep Bank Trce 77459 281-634-3680
Kandy Bond, prin. Fax 634-3799

Casa Dei Bambini Montessori S 200/PK-5
20211 S University Blvd 77459 281-261-2272
Excel Adventist Academy 50/PK-8
PO Box 2240 77459 281-835-0770
Hesketh Henry, prin. Fax 835-1275
Sienna Lutheran Academy 100/K-8
770 Waters Lake Blvd 77459 281-778-3003
Patrick Cortright, prin. Fax 778-3074
Southminster S 100/PK-5
4200 Cartwright Rd 77459 281-261-8872
Tiera Pennix M.Ed., head sch Fax 499-4430

Monahans, Ward, Pop. 6,896
Monahans-Wickett-Pyote ISD 2,200/PK-12
606 S Betty Ave 79756 432-943-6711
Kellye Riley, supt. Fax 943-2307
www.mwpisd.esc18.net
Cullender K 300/PK-K
1100 S Leon Ave 79756 432-943-5252
Marielena Saenz, prin. Fax 943-4768
Sudderth ES 500/4-6
701 N Carol Ave 79756 432-943-2414
Adam Alaniz, prin. Fax 943-2685
Tatom ES 500/1-3
1600 S Calvin Ave 79756 432-943-2769
Jill Steen, prin. Fax 943-3952
Walker JHS 300/7-8
800 S Faye Ave 79756 432-943-4622
Mayna Benavides, prin. Fax 943-3723

Montague, Montague, Pop. 304
Montague ISD 100/PK-8
PO Box 78 76251 940-894-2811
Carla Hennessey, supt. Fax 894-6605
www.montagueisd.org
Montague ES 100/PK-8
PO Box 78 76251 940-894-2811
Angela Kleinhans, prin. Fax 894-6605

Mont Belvieu, Chambers, Pop. 3,784
Barbers Hill ISD 4,000/PK-12
PO Box 1108 77580 281-576-2221
Greg Poole, supt. Fax 576-3410
www.bhisd.net/
Barbers Hill ES North 300/2-5
PO Box 1108 77580 281-576-2221
Stephanie Martin, prin. Fax 576-3434
Barbers Hill ES South 700/2-5
PO Box 1108 77580 281-576-2221
Elizabeth Filer, prin. Fax 576-3420
Barbers Hill K 400/PK-K
PO Box 1108 77580 281-576-2221
Lisa Watkins, prin. Fax 576-3412
Barbers Hill MS North 800/6-8
PO Box 1108 77580 281-576-2221
Lance Murphy, prin. Fax 576-3353
Barbers Hill PS 400/1-1
PO Box 1108 77580 281-576-2221
Mandy Malone, prin. Fax 576-3415
Other Schools – See Baytown

Monte Alto, Hidalgo, Pop. 1,914
Monte Alto ISD 1,000/PK-12
25149 1st St 78538 956-262-1381
Dr. Richard Rivera, supt. Fax 262-5535
www.montealtoisd.org
Monte Alto ES 500/PK-5
25149 1st St 78538 956-262-6101
Alma Cerda, prin. Fax 262-6112
Monte Alto MS 200/6-8
25149 1st St 78538 956-262-1374
Perla Benavidez, prin. Fax 262-1377

Montgomery, Montgomery, Pop. 621
Conroe ISD
Supt. — See Conroe
Stewart ES K-6
680 Fish Creek Thoroughfare 77316 936-709-4200
Dr. Julie English, prin. Fax 709-4299

Montgomery ISD 7,500/PK-12
PO Box 1475 77356 936-276-2000
Dr. Beau Rees, supt. Fax 276-2101
www.misd.org
Keenan ES 700/PK-PK, 5-
19180 Keenan Cut Off Rd 77316 936-276-5500
Mallory Kirby, prin. Fax 276-5501
Lone Star ES 800/PK-5
16600 FM 2854 Rd 77316 936-276-4500
Catherine Bartlett, prin. Fax 276-4501
Madeley Ranch ES 600/K-5
3500 Madeley Ranch Rd 77356 936-276-4600
Andrea Smith, prin. Fax 276-4601
Montgomery ES 700/PK-5
13755 Liberty St 77316 936-276-3600
Carrie Fitzpatrick, prin. Fax 276-3601
Montgomery JHS 1,300/6-8
19000 Stewart Creek Rd 77356 936-276-3300
Angie Chapman, prin. Fax 276-3301
Oak Hills JHS 6-8
19190 Keenan Cut Off Rd 77316 936-276-4300
Tim Williams, prin. Fax 276-4301
Stewart Creek ES 800/PK-5
18990 Stewart Creek Rd 77356 936-276-3500
Michele Salter, prin. Fax 276-3501

Moody, McLennan, Pop. 1,359
Moody ISD 700/PK-12
12084A S Lone Star Pkwy 76557 254-853-2172
Gary Martel, supt. Fax 853-2886
www.moodyisd.org
Moody ES 200/PK-4
200 Ave D 76557 254-853-2155
Tina Eaton, prin. Fax 853-3009
Moody MS 200/5-8
107 Coralee Ln 76557 254-853-2182
Eric Cox, prin. Fax 853-2886

Moran, Shackelford, Pop. 270
Moran ISD 100/PK-12
PO Box 98 76464 325-945-3101
Danny Freeman, supt. Fax 945-2741
www.moran.esc14.net
Moran S 100/PK-12
PO Box 98 76464 325-945-3101
Danny Freeman, prin. Fax 945-2741

Morgan, Bosque, Pop. 480
Morgan ISD 100/PK-12
PO Box 300 76671 254-635-2311
John Bryant, supt. Fax 635-2224
www.morganisd.org
Morgan S 100/PK-12
PO Box 300 76671 254-635-2311
Juan Ramirez, prin. Fax 635-2224

Morgan Mill, Erath
Morgan Mill ISD 100/K-8
PO Box 8 76465 254-968-4921
Wendy Sanders, supt. Fax 968-4814
www.mmisd.us
Morgan Mill S 100/K-8
PO Box 8 76465 254-968-4921
Barrett Hutchison, prin. Fax 968-4921

Morse, Hansford, Pop. 147
Pringle-Morse Consolidated ISD 100/PK-8
PO Box 109 79062 806-733-2507
Scott Burrow, supt. Fax 733-2351
www.pringlemorsecisd.net
Pringle-Morse S 100/PK-8
PO Box 109 79062 806-733-2507
Scott Burrow, supt. Fax 733-2351

Morton, Cochran, Pop. 1,996
Morton ISD 400/PK-12
500 Champion Dr 79346 806-266-5505
Karen Saunders, supt. Fax 266-5449
www.mortonisd.net/
Morton ES 200/PK-5
500 Champion Dr 79346 806-266-5505
Kellye Kuehler, prin. Fax 266-5793
Morton JHS 100/6-8
500 Champion Dr 79346 806-266-5505
David Van Wettering, prin. Fax 266-5739

Moulton, Lavaca, Pop. 877
Moulton ISD 300/K-12
PO Box C 77975 361-596-4609
Todd Grandjean, supt. Fax 596-7578
www.moultonisd.net
Moulton ES 200/K-6
PO Box C 77975 361-596-4605
David Hayward, prin. Fax 596-4894

Mountain Home, Kerr
Divide ISD 50/PK-6
120 Divide School Rd 78058 830-640-3322
Bill Bacon, supt. Fax 640-3323
Divide ES 50/PK-6
120 Divide School Rd 78058 830-640-3322
Bill Bacon, prin. Fax 640-3323

Mount Calm, Hill, Pop. 312
Mount Calm ISD 100/PK-12
PO Box 105 76673 254-993-2611
James Wright, supt. Fax 993-1022
www.mcisd1.org
Mount Calm S 100/PK-12
PO Box 105 76673 254-993-2611
Pamela Taylor, prin. Fax 993-1022

Mount Enterprise, Rusk, Pop. 445
Mount Enterprise ISD 400/PK-12
301 NW 3rd St 75681 903-822-3721
Byron Jordan, supt. Fax 822-3633
www.meisd.esc7.net
Mount Enterprise ES 200/PK-5
301 NW 3rd St 75681 903-822-3545
Andy Lee, prin. Fax 822-3633

Mount Pleasant, Titus, Pop. 15,466
Chapel Hill ISD 1,000/PK-12
1069 County Road 4660 75455 903-572-8096
Marc Levesque, supt. Fax 572-1086
www.chisddevils.com
Chapel Hill ES 500/PK-5
1069 County Road 4660 75455 903-572-1086
Jamie Martinez, prin. Fax 577-9176
Chapel Hill JHS 200/6-8
1069 County Road 4660 75455 903-572-1086
Mike Clifton, prin. Fax 572-9747

Harts Bluff ISD 500/K-8
3506 Farm Road 1402 75455 903-577-1146
Dr. Bobby Rice, supt. Fax 572-4699
www.hbisd.net
Harts Bluff S 500/K-8
3506 Farm Road 1402 75455 903-577-1146
Tracie Rose, prin. Fax 577-8710

Mount Pleasant ISD 5,400/PK-12
PO Box 1117 75456 903-575-2000
Judd Marshall, supt. Fax 575-2014
www.mpisd.net
Brice ES 500/K-4
PO Box 1117 75456 903-575-2057
Craig Toney, prin. Fax 575-2061
Child Development Center 600/PK-PK
PO Box 1117 75456 903-575-2092
Jamie Cook, prin. Fax 575-2077
Corprew ES 500/K-4
PO Box 1117 75456 903-575-2050
Amanda Jones, prin. Fax 575-2052
Fowler ES 500/K-4
PO Box 1117 75456 903-575-2070
Cindy Davis, prin. Fax 575-2075
Mount Pleasant JHS 700/7-8
PO Box 1117 75456 903-575-2110
Kelli Glenn, prin. Fax 575-2117
Sims ES 500/K-4
PO Box 1117 75456 903-575-2062
Tonya Murray, prin. Fax 575-2064
Wallace MS 700/5-6
PO Box 1117 75456 903-575-2040
James Gibson, prin. Fax 575-2047

Mount Vernon, Franklin, Pop. 2,608
Mount Vernon ISD 1,600/PK-12
501 Texas Highway 37 75457 903-537-2546
Gregg Weiss, supt. Fax 537-4784
www.mtvernonisd.net
Mount Vernon ES 700/PK-4
501 Texas Highway 37 75457 903-537-2266
Jennifer Driver, prin. Fax 537-2057
Mount Vernon MS 200/5-8
501 Texas Highway 37 75457 903-537-2267
Craig Watson, prin. Fax 537-3601

Muenster, Cooke, Pop. 1,534
Muenster ISD 500/PK-12
PO Box 608 76252 940-759-2281
Steven Self, supt. Fax 759-5200
www.muensterisd.net
Muenster ES 300/PK-6
PO Box 608 76252 940-759-2281
Lou Heers, prin. Fax 759-4614

Sacred Heart S 200/PK-12
153 E 6th St 76252 940-759-2511
Elizabeth Bartush, prin. Fax 759-4422

Muleshoe, Bailey, Pop. 5,137
Muleshoe ISD 1,500/PK-12
514 W Avenue G 79347 806-272-7400
Dr. R.L. Richards, supt. Fax 272-4120
www.muleshoeisd.net
DeShazo ES 300/3-5
514 W Avenue G 79347 806-272-7364
Erin Boatmun, prin. Fax 272-7370
Dillman ES 500/PK-2
514 W Avenue G 79347 806-272-7383
Letti Tovar, prin. Fax 272-7388
Watson JHS 300/6-8
514 W Avenue G 79347 806-272-7349
Melvin Nusser, prin. Fax 272-4983

Mullin, Mills, Pop. 179
Mullin ISD 100/PK-12
PO Box 128 76864 325-985-3374
Kristi Mickelson, supt. Fax 985-3372
www.mullinisd.net
Mullin ES 50/PK-6
PO Box 128 76864 325-985-3374
Sarah McDowell, admin. Fax 985-3372

Mumford, Robertson
Mumford ISD 600/PK-12
9755 FM 50, 979-279-3678
Pete Bienski, supt. Fax 279-5044
www.mumford.k12.tx.us
Mumford ES 400/PK-6
9755 FM 50, 979-279-3678
Pete Bienski, prin. Fax 279-5044

Munday, Knox, Pop. 1,285
Munday Consolidated ISD 400/PK-12
PO Box 300 76371 940-422-4241
Kristi Bufkin, supt. Fax 422-5331
www.esc9.net
Munday ES 200/PK-6
PO Box 300 76371 940-422-4322
Kristi Bufkin, prin. Fax 422-5331

Murchison, Henderson, Pop. 593
Murchison ISD 200/PK-8
PO Box 538 75778 903-469-3636
Kimberly Followwell, supt. Fax 469-3887
murchisonisd.com
Murchison S 200/PK-8
PO Box 538 75778 903-469-3636
Kimberly Followell, admin. Fax 469-3887

Murphy, Collin, Pop. 17,219
Plano ISD
Supt. — See Plano
Boggess ES 800/K-5
225 Glen Ridge Dr 75094 469-752-4000
Shurandia Holden, prin. Fax 752-4001
Hunt ES 700/K-5
415 Oriole Dr 75094 469-752-4400
Arron Moeller, prin. Fax 752-4401
Murphy MS 1,200/6-8
620 N Murphy Rd 75094 469-752-7000
Matthew Conrad, prin. Fax 752-7001

Wylie ISD
Supt. — See Wylie
Tibbals ES 700/K-4
621 Waters Edge Way 75094 972-429-2520
Melinda Sarles, prin. Fax 429-2260

Nacogdoches, Nacogdoches, Pop. 32,466
Central Heights ISD 1,100/PK-12
10317 US Highway 259 75965 936-564-2681
Bryan Lee, supt. Fax 569-6889
www.centralhts.org
Central Heights ES 500/PK-5
10317 US Highway 259 75965 936-552-3424
Jana Muckleroy, prin. Fax 569-6889
Central Heights MS 300/6-8
10317 US Highway 259 75965 936-552-3441
Andrew Binford, prin. Fax 564-0177

Martinsville ISD 400/PK-12
12952 E State Highway 7 75961 936-564-3455
David Simmons, supt. Fax 569-0498
www.martinsvilleisd.com
Martinsville S 400/PK-12
12952 E State Highway 7 75961 936-564-3455
Zach Crawford, prin. Fax 569-0498

Nacogdoches ISD 6,600/PK-12
PO Box 631521 75963 936-569-5000
Sandra Dowdy, supt. Fax 569-5797
www.nacisd.org
Brooks-Quinn-Jones ES 800/PK-5
PO Box 631521 75963 936-569-5040
Tom Miller, prin. Fax 569-5796
Carpenter ES 400/PK-5
PO Box 631521 75963 936-569-5070
Dr. Jackie Briggs-Vaughn, prin. Fax 569-3165
Fredonia ES 600/PK-5
PO Box 631521 75963 936-569-5080
Melinda Wiebold, prin. Fax 569-3168
Marshall Academy of Dual Language 400/PK-5
PO Box 631521 75963 936-569-5062
Bradley Durham, prin. Fax 569-5038
McMichael MS 800/6-8
PO Box 631521 75963 936-552-0519
Tim Mullican, prin. Fax 552-0523
Moses MS 600/6-8
PO Box 631521 75963 936-569-5001
Stephen Autrey, prin. Fax 569-5031
Raguet ES 500/K-5
PO Box 631521 75963 936-569-5052
Julia Wells, prin. Fax 569-5060
Rusk Academy of Fine Arts 700/K-5
PO Box 631521 75963 936-569-3100
Paula Harshbarger, prin. Fax 569-5759

Christ Episcopal S 100/PK-6
1428 N Mound St 75961 936-564-0621
Catherine Oliver, head sch Fax 552-7120
Regents Academy 100/PK-12
200 NE Stallings Dr 75961 936-560-7343
David Bryant, hdmstr.

Nash, Bowie, Pop. 2,894
Texarkana ISD
Supt. — See Texarkana
Nash ES 700/PK-5
100 E Burton St 75569 903-838-4321
Patti O'Bannon, prin. Fax 831-7158

Natalia, Medina, Pop. 1,422
Natalia ISD 1,100/PK-12
PO Box 548 78059 830-663-4416
Dr. Hensley Cone, supt. Fax 663-4186
www.nataliaisd.net
Natalia ECC 200/PK-1
PO Box 548 78059 830-663-9739
Carmen Maglievaz, prin. Fax 663-4186
Natalia ES 300/2-5
PO Box 548 78059 830-663-2837
Carmen Maglievaz, prin. Fax 663-9693
Natalia JHS 200/6-8
PO Box 548 78059 830-663-4027
Edgar Camacho, prin. Fax 663-2347

Navasota, Grimes, Pop. 6,996
Navasota ISD 3,100/PK-12
PO Box 511 77868 936-825-4200
Dr. Stu Musick, supt. Fax 825-4297
www.navasotaisd.org
Brule ES 300/PK-5
PO Box 511 77868 936-825-4275
Amy Bay-Wetherwax, prin. Fax 825-8523
High Point ES 400/PK-5
PO Box 511 77868 936-825-1130
Melissa Boenker, prin. Fax 894-3195
Navasota JHS 700/6-8
PO Box 511 77868 936-825-4225
Melody Hudspeth, prin. Fax 825-4260
Webb ES 900/PK-5
PO Box 511 77868 936-825-1120
Todd Nesloney, prin. Fax 825-2802

Nazareth, Castro, Pop. 311
Nazareth ISD 200/PK-12
PO Box 189 79063 806-945-2231
Glen Waldo, supt. Fax 945-2431
www.nazarethisd.net/
Nazareth S 200/PK-12
PO Box 189 79063 806-945-2231
Jeanie Birkenfeld, prin. Fax 945-2431

Neches, Anderson
Neches ISD 400/PK-12
PO Box 310 75779 903-584-3311
Randy Snider, supt. Fax 584-3686
www.nechesisd.com
Other Schools – See Palestine

Nederland, Jefferson, Pop. 17,344
Nederland ISD 5,000/PK-12
220 N 17th St 77627 409-724-2391
Dr. Robin Perez, supt. Fax 724-4280
www.nederland.k12.tx.us
Central MS 700/5-8
220 N 17th St 77627 409-727-5765
Charles Jehlen, prin. Fax 724-4275
Helena Park ES 500/K-4
220 N 17th St 77627 409-722-0462
Tina Oliver, prin. Fax 726-2698
Highland Park ES 400/K-4
220 N 17th St 77627 409-722-0236
Sissy Yeaman, prin. Fax 726-2694
Hillcrest ES 600/PK-4
220 N 17th St 77627 409-722-3484
Dr. Kevin Morrison, prin. Fax 726-2690
Langham ES 400/PK-4
220 N 17th St 77627 409-722-4324
Rosetta Morgan, prin. Fax 724-4286
Wilson MS 800/5-8
220 N 17th St 77627 409-727-6224
Scott Clemmons, prin. Fax 726-2699

Needville, Fort Bend, Pop. 2,792
Needville ISD 2,800/PK-12
PO Box 412 77461 979-793-4308
Curtis Rhodes, supt. Fax 793-3823
www.needvilleisd.com
Needville ES 1,100/PK-4
PO Box 412 77461 979-793-4241
Stacey Stavinoha, prin. Fax 793-2299
Needville JHS 500/7-8
PO Box 412 77461 979-793-4250
Karen Smart, prin. Fax 793-4575
Needville MS 400/5-6
PO Box 412 77461 979-793-3027
Marla Sebesta, prin. Fax 793-7665

Nevada, Collin, Pop. 815
Community ISD 1,700/PK-12
PO Box 400 75173 972-843-8400
Roosevelt Nivens, supt. Fax 843-8401
www.communityisd.org
Edge MS 400/6-8
PO Box 400 75173 972-843-8411
David Girardi, prin. Fax 843-8412
McClendon ES 400/PK-5
PO Box 400 75173 972-843-8409
Patricia Sandy, prin. Fax 843-8410
Other Schools – See Lavon

Newark, Wise, Pop. 987
Northwest ISD
Supt. — See Justin
Seven Hills ES 600/PK-5
654 FM 3433 76071 817-215-0700
Kim Blackburn, prin. Fax 215-0740

Victory in Christ Classical Luth Academy 50/PK-12
508 Main St 76071 817-489-5400
Ruth Rohloff, prin.

New Boston, Bowie, Pop. 4,450
Malta ISD 100/PK-6
6178 W US Highway 82 75570 903-667-2950
Brian Bobbitt, supt. Fax 667-2984
www.maltaisd.net/
Malta S 100/PK-6
6178 W US Highway 82 75570 903-667-2950
Stacy Starrett, prin. Fax 667-2984

New Boston ISD 1,400/PK-12
201 Rice St 75570 903-628-2521
Dr. Rose Mary Neshyba, supt. Fax 628-8990
www.nbschools.net
Crestview ES 300/3-5
604 N McCoy Blvd 75570 903-628-6521
Melissa Reid, prin. Fax 628-4205
New Boston MS 300/6-8
1215 N State Highway 8 75570 903-628-6588
Denise Davis, prin. Fax 628-5132
Oakview PS 400/PK-2
530 Hospital Dr 75570 903-628-8900
Patty Green, prin. Fax 628-2235

New Braunfels, Comal, Pop. 57,097
Comal ISD 19,200/PK-12
1404 N Interstate 35 78130 830-221-2000
Andrew Kim, supt. Fax 221-2001
www.comalisd.org
Canyon MS 1,000/6-8
2014 FM 1101 78130 830-221-2300
Matthew Deloach, prin. Fax 221-2301
Church Hill MS 900/6-8
1275 N Business IH 35 78130 830-221-2800
Scott Hammond, prin. Fax 221-2801
Clear Spring ES 600/PK-5
550 Avery Pkwy 78130 830-837-7300
Julie Hardy, prin. Fax 837-7301
Frazier ES 400/K-5
1441 N Business IH 35 78130 830-221-2200
Carolyn Gump, prin. Fax 221-2201
Freiheit ES 500/K-5
2002 FM 1101 78130 830-221-2700
Shelly Crofford, prin. Fax 221-2701
Hoffmann Lane ES 600/K-5
4600 FM 306 78132 830-221-2500
Krista Moffatt, prin. Fax 221-2501
Morningside ES 600/PK-5
3855 Morningside Dr 78132 830-837-7100
Ashley Fredo, prin. Fax 837-7101
Mountain Valley MS 700/6-8
1165 Sattler Rd 78132 830-885-1300
Kristy Castilleja, prin. Fax 885-1301
Oak Creek ES 500/K-5
3060 Goodwin Ln 78130 830-837-7200
Stacy Wilkie, prin. Fax 837-7201
Other Schools – See Bulverde, Canyon Lake, Garden Ridge, San Antonio, Spring Branch

New Braunfels ISD 8,000/PK-12
PO Box 311688 78131 830-643-5700
Randy Moczygemba, supt. Fax 643-5701
www.nbisd.org/
County Line ES 600/K-5
1200 W County Line Rd 78130 830-627-6610
Deanna Callahan, prin. Fax 627-6611

Klein Road ES 700/K-5
2620 Klein Way 78130 830-221-1700
Chris Russell, prin. Fax 221-1701
Lamar ES 500/K-5
240 N Central Ave 78130 830-627-6890
Danielle Taylor, prin. Fax 627-6891
Lone Star ECC 300/PK-PK
2343 W San Antonio St 78130 830-627-6820
Heather Salas, prin. Fax 627-6821
Memorial ES 400/K-5
1911 S Walnut Ave 78130 830-627-6470
Nicole Haecker, prin. Fax 627-6471
New Braunfels MS 700/7-8
656 S Guenther Ave 78130 830-627-6270
Greg Hughes, prin. Fax 627-6271
Oakrun MS 1,000/6-8
415 Oak Run Pt 78132 830-627-6400
Shana Behling, prin. Fax 627-6401
Schurz ES 500/K-5
633 W Coll St 78130 830-627-6680
Duane Trujillo, prin. Fax 627-6681
Seele ES 500/PK-5
540 Howard St 78130 830-627-6750
Leah Droddy, prin. Fax 627-6751
Veramendi ES K-5
2290 Oak Run Pkwy 78132 830-608-5900
David MacRoberts, prin. Fax 608-5901
Voss Farms ES K-5
2510 Pahmeyer Rd 78130 830-608-5800
Deborah Cary, prin. Fax 608-5801
Walnut Springs ES 500/K-5
1900 S Walnut Ave 78130 830-627-6540
David Lewis, prin. Fax 627-6541

Cross Lutheran S 100/PK-8
2171 Common St 78130 830-625-3969
Corey Brandenburger, prin. Fax 625-5019
New Braunfels Christian Academy 400/PK-12
220 FM 1863 78132 830-629-1821
Jill R. White M.Ed., head sch Fax 639-1880
SS. Peter & Paul Catholic S 300/PK-8
198 W Bridge St 78130 830-625-4531
Janet Buras, prin. Fax 606-6916

New Caney, Montgomery, Pop. 3,000
New Caney ISD 11,700/PK-12
21580 Loop 494 77357 281-577-8600
Kenn Franklin, supt. Fax 354-2639
www.newcaneyisd.org
Dogwood ES, 600 Dogwood Ln 77357 PK-5
Kerry Hamilton, prin. 281-577-2960
Keefer Crossing MS 1,000/7-8
20350 FM 1485 Rd 77357 281-577-8840
Andy Pearson, prin. Fax 399-9859
New Caney ES 700/PK-5
20501 FM 1485 Rd 77357 281-577-8720
Gail London, prin. Fax 399-2174
Oakley ES 900/PK-5
22320 Loop 494 77357 281-577-5970
Shay Thompson, prin. Fax 354-3384
Tavola ES K-5
18885 Winding Summit Dr 77357 281-577-2900
Sheri Lowe, prin. Fax 399-9946
Other Schools – See Kingwood, Porter

Newcastle, Young, Pop. 582
Newcastle ISD 200/PK-12
PO Box 129 76372 940-846-3551
Ty Spitzer, supt. Fax 846-3452
www.newcastle-isd.net
Newcastle S 200/PK-12
PO Box 129 76372 940-846-3531
Ty Spitzer, admin. Fax 846-3452

New Deal, Lubbock, Pop. 782
New Deal ISD 700/PK-12
PO Box 280 79350 806-746-5833
Jimmy Noland, supt. Fax 746-5707
www.ndisd.net
New Deal ES 300/PK-4
PO Box 240 79350 806-746-5849
Rebecca Cooper, prin. Fax 746-5142
New Deal MS 200/5-8
PO Box 308 79350 806-746-6633
Jesus Arenas, prin. Fax 746-5244

New Home, Lynn, Pop. 334
New Home ISD 300/PK-12
225 N Main St, 806-924-7543
Shane Fiedler, supt. Fax 924-7520
www.newhomeisd.org
New Home S 300/PK-12
225 N Main St, 806-924-7543
Koby Abney, prin. Fax 924-7520

New London, Rusk, Pop. 978
West Rusk ISD 1,000/PK-12
PO Box 168 75682 903-392-7850
Lawrence Coleman, supt. Fax 392-7866
www.westrusk.esc7.net
West Rusk ES 300/PK-2
PO Box 168 75682 903-392-7857
Carlette Mills, prin. Fax 392-7866
West Rusk IS 200/3-5
PO Box 168 75682 903-392-7856
Connie Lawrence, prin. Fax 392-7866
West Rusk JHS 300/6-8
PO Box 168 75682 903-392-7855
Brian Keith, prin. Fax 392-7866

New Summerfield, Cherokee, Pop. 1,102
New Summerfield ISD 500/PK-12
PO Box 6 75780 903-726-3306
Dr. Brian Nichols, supt. Fax 726-3405
www.nsisd.sprnet.org
New Summerfield S 500/PK-12
PO Box 6 75780 903-726-3306
Josh Faucett, supt. Fax 726-3405

Newton, Newton, Pop. 2,458
Newton ISD 1,100/PK-12
720 Rusk St 75966 409-420-6600
Michelle Barrow, supt. Fax 379-5130
www.newtonisd.net
Newton ES 500/PK-5
720 Rusk St 75966 409-420-6600
Sarah Richardson, prin. Fax 379-2801
Newton MS 300/6-8
720 Rusk St 75966 409-420-6600
Judy Holleman, prin. Fax 379-5082

New Waverly, Walker, Pop. 1,019
New Waverly ISD 900/PK-12
355 Front St 77358 936-344-6751
Dr. Darol Hail, supt. Fax 344-2438
www.new-waverly.k12.tx.us
New Waverly ES 300/PK-3
355 Front St 77358 936-344-2900
Tiffany Forester, prin. Fax 344-2905
New Waverly IS 100/4-5
355 Front St 77358 936-344-6601
Kathy Lepley, prin. Fax 344-2331
New Waverly JHS 200/6-8
355 Front St 77358 936-344-2246
Dudley Hawkes, prin. Fax 344-8313

Niederwald, Hays, Pop. 562
Hays Consolidated ISD
Supt. — See Kyle
Camino Real ES 700/PK-5
170 Las Brisas Blvd 78640 512-268-8505
Yvette Soliz, prin. Fax 398-5599

Nixon, Gonzales, Pop. 2,375
Nixon-Smiley Consolidated ISD 1,100/PK-12
PO Box 400 78140 830-582-1536
Cathy L. Lauer Ph.D., supt. Fax 582-1920
www.nixonsmiley.net
Nixon-Smiley MS 300/5-8
PO Box 400 78140 830-582-1536
Anita Van Auken, prin. Fax 582-2258
Other Schools – See Smiley

Nocona, Montague, Pop. 3,004
Nocona ISD 800/PK-12
220 Clay St 76255 940-825-3267
Dr. Vickie Gearheart, supt. Fax 825-4945
www.noconaisd.net/
Nocona ES 400/PK-5
220 Clay St 76255 940-825-3151
Rod Bailey, prin. Fax 825-4253
Nocona MS 200/6-8
220 Clay St 76255 940-825-3121
Amy Murphey, prin. Fax 825-6151

Prairie Valley ISD 100/PK-12
12920 FM 103 76255 940-825-4425
W. Tucker, supt. Fax 825-4650
www.prairievalleyisd.net/
Prairie Valley ES 100/PK-5
12920 FM 103 76255 940-825-4425
Lisa Sadler, prin. Fax 825-4650

Nolanville, Bell, Pop. 4,095
Killeen ISD
Supt. — See Killeen
Cavazos ES 600/PK-5
1200 N 10th St 76559 254-336-7000
Joe Gullekson, prin. Fax 336-3159
Nolanville ES 700/PK-5
901 Old Nolanville Rd 76559 254-336-2180
Wendy Haider, prin. Fax 336-2202

Nordheim, DeWitt, Pop. 305
Nordheim ISD 200/PK-12
500 Broadway 78141 361-938-5211
Kevin Wilson, supt. Fax 938-5266
www.nordheimisd.org
Nordheim S 200/PK-12
500 Broadway 78141 361-938-5211
Lisa Karnei, prin. Fax 938-5266

Normangee, Leon, Pop. 671
Normangee ISD 500/PK-12
PO Box 219 77871 936-396-3111
Luke Allison, supt. Fax 396-3112
www.normangeeisd.org
Normangee ES 200/PK-5
PO Box 219 77871 936-396-9999
Tera Phillips, prin. Fax 396-2609
Normangee MS 100/6-8
PO Box 219 77871 936-396-6111
Teddy Clevenger, prin. Fax 396-6879

North Richland Hills, Tarrant, Pop. 62,179
Birdville ISD
Supt. — See Haltom City
Academy at Carrie F. Thomas ES 700/PK-5
8200 O Brian Way 76180 817-547-3000
Dr. Sabrina Lindsey, prin. Fax 581-5490
Foster Village ES 600/PK-5
6800 Springdale Ln 76182 817-547-3100
Jody Fadely, prin. Fax 581-5382
Green Valley ES 500/PK-5
7900 Smithfield Rd 76182 817-547-3400
Dawn Demas, prin. Fax 581-5477
Holiday Heights ES 700/PK-5
5221 Susan Lee Ln 76180 817-547-2600
Mike Dukes, prin. Fax 581-5396
Mullendore ES 400/PK-5
4100 Flory St 76180 817-547-1900
Billy Pope, prin. Fax 581-5326
North Richland MS 900/6-8
4801 Redondo St 76180 817-547-4200
Steve Ellis, prin. Fax 581-5372
North Ridge ES 600/PK-5
7331 Holiday Ln 76182 817-547-3200
Deborah Coulson, prin. Fax 581-5440
North Ridge MS 800/6-8
7332 Douglas Ln 76182 817-547-5200
John Davis, prin. Fax 581-5460
Smithfield ES 400/PK-5
6724 Smithfield Rd 76182 817-547-2100
Melissa Minix, prin. Fax 581-5377
Smithfield MS 800/6-8
8400 Main St 76182 817-547-5000
Kyle Pekurney, prin. Fax 581-5480
Snow Heights ES 400/PK-5
4801 Vance Rd 76180 817-547-2200
Susan Nall, prin. Fax 581-5323
Walker Creek ES 600/PK-5
8780 Bridge St 76180 817-547-3500
Marsha Perry, prin. Fax 581-2932

Fort Worth Christian S 900/PK-12
6200 Holiday Ln 76180 817-520-6200
North Park Christian Academy 50/PK-4
7025 Mid Cities Blvd 76182 817-498-8456
Jane Edwards, admin. Fax 428-2060
North Richland Hills Montessori 100/PK-3
8725 N Tarrant Pkwy 76182 817-281-9992
Young Academy K-12
8521 Davis Blvd 76182 817-427-4888
Kathy Lyda, head sch

North Zulch, Madison
North Zulch ISD 400/PK-12
PO Box 158 77872 936-241-7100
Alan Andrus, supt. Fax 241-7093
www.nzisd.org
North Zulch ES 200/PK-6
PO Box 158 77872 936-241-7100
Rick Panter, prin. Fax 241-7093

Oak Point, Denton, Pop. 2,748
Denton ISD
Supt. — See Denton
Rodriguez MS, 8650 Martop Rd, 6-8
Renee Koontz, prin. 972-347-7050

Little Elm ISD
Supt. — See Little Elm
Oak Point ES 600/PK-5
401 Shahan Prairie Rd 75068 972-947-9455
Debbie Clark, prin. Fax 947-9329

Oak Ridge North, Montgomery, Pop. 3,010

Sojourn Academy 100/PK-12
27420 Robinson Rd, 281-298-5800
Becky Staggs, prin. Fax 292-2818

Oakwood, Leon, Pop. 506
Oakwood ISD 200/PK-12
631 N Holly St 75855 903-545-2600
Donny Lee, supt. Fax 545-2310
www.oakwoodisd.net
Oakwood ES 100/PK-6
631 N Holly St 75855 903-545-2106
Tina Rayborn, prin. Fax 545-1130

O Brien, Haskell, Pop. 105
Knox City-O'Brien Consolidated ISD
Supt. — See Knox City
O'Brien MS 100/5-8
711 9th St 79539 940-657-3731
Mark Tucker, prin. Fax 657-3379

Odem, San Patricio, Pop. 2,386
Odem-Edroy ISD 1,000/PK-12
1 Owl Sq 78370 361-368-8121
Dr. Lisa Gonzales, supt. Fax 368-2879
www.oeisd.org/
Odem ES 500/PK-2
1 Owl Sq 78370 361-368-8121
Esmerelda Martinez, prin. Fax 368-2317
Odem IS, 1 Owl Sq 78370 3-5
Jana Kieschnick, prin. 361-368-8121
Odem JHS 200/6-8
1 Owl Sq 78370 361-368-8121
Traci Pogue, prin. Fax 368-2033

Odessa, Ector, Pop. 98,924
Ector County ISD 26,600/PK-12
PO Box 3912 79760 432-456-0000
Tom Crowe, supt. Fax 456-9878
www.ectorcountyisd.org
Austin Montessori Magnet S 500/PK-5
PO Box 3912 79760 432-456-1029
Crystal Marquez, prin. Fax 456-1028
Blackshear Magnet ES 800/K-5
PO Box 3912 79760 432-456-1279
Marissa King, prin. Fax 456-1278
Blanton ES 500/K-5
PO Box 3912 79760 432-456-1259
Stacey Molyneaux, prin. Fax 456-1258
Bonham MS 900/6-8
PO Box 3912 79760 432-456-0429
James Ramage, prin. Fax 456-0428
Bowie JHS 700/6-8
PO Box 3912 79760 432-456-0439
Mark Ferrer, prin. Fax 456-0438
Buice ES, PO Box 3912 79760 K-5
Alicia Press, prin. 432-456-1339
Burleson ES 700/K-5
PO Box 3912 79760 432-456-1039
Tristan Specter, prin. Fax 456-1038
Burnet ES 700/K-5
PO Box 3912 79760 432-456-1049
Tristan Specter, prin. Fax 456-1048
Cameron Dual Language Magnet ES 600/PK-5
PO Box 3912 79760 432-456-1059
David Bargas, prin. Fax 456-1058
Carver Early Education Center 600/PK-PK
PO Box 3912 79760 432-456-1069
Sherry Palmer, prin. Fax 456-1068

Cavazos ES 800/K-6
PO Box 3912 79760 432-456-1309
Brandon Chesser, prin. Fax 456-1308
Crockett MS 600/6-8
PO Box 3912 79760 432-456-0449
Maribel Aranda, prin. Fax 456-0448
Dowling ES 700/K-5
PO Box 3912 79760 432-456-1079
Valerie Rivera, prin. Fax 456-1078
Downing ES, PO Box 3912 79760 K-5
Marcos Lopez, prin. 432-456-1319
Ector MS 1,100/6-8
PO Box 3912 79760 432-456-0479
Kendra Herrera, prin. Fax 456-0478
Fly ES 700/PK-5
PO Box 3912 79760 432-456-1269
Sammy Martinez, prin. Fax 456-1268
Goliad ES 500/K-5
PO Box 3912 79760 432-456-1109
Lauren Tavarez, prin. Fax 456-1108
Gonzales ES 600/K-6
PO Box 3912 79760 432-456-1119
Sunny Rodriguez, prin. Fax 456-1118
Hays Magnet ES 400/PK-5
PO Box 3912 79760 432-456-1129
Amy Anderson, prin. Fax 456-1128
Houston ES 600/K-5
PO Box 3912 79760 432-456-1139
Sandra Banda, prin. Fax 456-1138
Ireland Magnet ES 500/K-5
PO Box 3912 79760 432-456-1149
Jaime Miller, prin. Fax 456-1148
Johnson ES 700/K-5
PO Box 3912 79760 432-456-1289
Alisha Holguin, prin. Fax 456-1288
Jordan ES 800/K-5
PO Box 3912 79760 432-456-1299
Linda Voss, prin. Fax 456-1298
Lamar Early Education Center 600/PK-PK
PO Box 3912 79760 432-456-1159
Martha Mitchell, prin. Fax 456-1158
Milam Magnet ES 600/PK-5
PO Box 3912 79760 432-456-1169
Natalie Fitzgerald, prin. Fax 456-1168
Nimitz MS 800/6-8
PO Box 3912 79760 432-456-0469
Teresa Willison, prin. Fax 456-0468
Noel ES 800/K-6
PO Box 3912 79760 432-456-1249
Stacy Johnson, prin. Fax 456-1248
Pease ES 700/K-5
PO Box 3912 79760 432-456-1179
Autumn Sloan, prin. Fax 456-1178
Pond-Alamo ES 500/PK-5
PO Box 3912 79760 432-456-1019
Regina Lee, prin. Fax 456-1018
Reagan Magnet ES 600/K-5
PO Box 3912 79760 432-456-1189
Wayne Squiers, prin. Fax 456-1188
Ross ES 700/K-5
PO Box 3912 79760 432-456-1199
Becky Phillips, prin. Fax 456-1198
San Jacinto ES 600/K-5
PO Box 3912 79760 432-456-1219
Pam Walker, prin. Fax 456-1218
Travis Magnet ES 600/K-5
PO Box 3912 79760 432-456-1229
Tanya Galindo, prin. Fax 456-1228
West ES, PO Box 3912 79760 K-5
Gisela Davila, prin. 432-456-1329
Wilson & Young Medal of Honor MS 500/6-8
PO Box 3912 79760 432-456-0459
Yolanda Hernandez, prin. Fax 456-0458
Zavala Magnet ES 500/K-5
PO Box 3912 79760 432-456-1239
Amanda Warber, prin. Fax 456-1238

UTPB STEM Academy K-12
4901 E University Blvd 79762 432-552-2020
Fax 552-2581
utpbstemacademy.org
UTPB STEM Academy K-12
4901 E University Blvd 79762 432-552-2580
Oscar Rendon, prin. Fax 552-2581

Odessa Christian S 100/PK-8
2000 Doran Dr 79761 432-362-6311
St. Johns Episcopal S 200/PK-7
401 N County Rd W 79763 432-337-6431
Emily McDoniel, head sch Fax 335-0815
St. Marys S 200/K-8
1703 Adams Ave 79761 432-337-6052
Benjamin Villarreal, prin. Fax 332-2942

O Donnell, Lynn, Pop. 817
O'Donnell ISD 100/PK-12
PO Box 487 79351 806-428-3241
Dr. Cathy York-Palmer, supt. Fax 428-3395
odonnell.esc17.net
O'Donnell S 100/PK-12
PO Box 487 79351 806-428-3241
Cody White, prin. Fax 428-3395

Oglesby, Coryell, Pop. 480
Oglesby ISD 200/PK-12
125 College Ave 76561 254-456-2271
David Maass, supt. Fax 456-2522
www.oglesbyisd.net
Oglesby S 200/PK-12
125 College Ave 76561 254-456-2271
Brianna Ethridge, supt. Fax 456-2916

Oilton, Webb, Pop. 353
Webb Consolidated ISD
Supt. — See Bruni
Oilton ES 200/PK-5
301 Despain St 78371 361-747-5415
Josie Castillo, prin. Fax 747-4939

Olmito, Cameron
Los Fresnos Consolidated ISD
Supt. — See Los Fresnos
Villareal ES 400/PK-5
7700 E Lakeside Blvd 78575 956-233-3975
Pablo Leal, prin. Fax 350-2087

Olney, Young, Pop. 3,242
Olney ISD 700/PK-12
809 W Hamilton St 76374 940-564-3519
Dr. Greg Roach, supt. Fax 564-5205
www.olneyisd.net
Olney ES 400/PK-5
801 W Hamilton St 76374 940-564-5608
Gunter Rodriguez, prin. Fax 564-3518
Olney JHS 100/6-8
300 S Avenue H 76374 940-564-3517
Amanda Barrientes, prin. Fax 564-8824

Olton, Lamb, Pop. 2,197
Olton ISD 600/PK-12
PO Box 388 79064 806-285-2641
Dr. G. Steve Mills, supt. Fax 285-2724
www.oltonisd.net
Olton JHS 200/6-8
PO Box 509 79064 806-285-2681
Brian Hunt, prin. Fax 285-3348
Webb ES 300/PK-5
PO Box 1007 79064 806-285-2657
Stacie Ramage, admin. Fax 285-2438

Omaha, Morris, Pop. 1,001
Pewitt Consolidated ISD 1,000/PK-12
PO Box 1106 75571 903-884-2804
Dr. Andy Reddock, supt. Fax 884-2866
www.pewittcisd.net
Pewitt ES 500/PK-5
PO Box 1106 75571 903-884-2404
Amy Barron, prin. Fax 884-3076
Pewitt JHS 200/6-8
PO Box 1106 75571 903-884-2505
Floyd Giles, prin. Fax 884-2142

Onalaska, Polk, Pop. 1,736
Onalaska ISD 900/PK-12
PO Box 2289 77360 936-646-1000
Lynn Redden, supt. Fax 646-2605
www.onalaskaisd.net
Onalaska ES 600/PK-6
PO Box 2289 77360 936-646-1010
David Murphy, prin. Fax 646-1019

Orange, Orange, Pop. 18,289
Deweyville ISD 700/PK-12
43200 State Highway 87 S 77632 409-746-2731
Keith Jones, supt. Fax 349-9338
www.deweyvilleisd.com
Other Schools – See Deweyville

Little Cypress-Mauriceville Cons ISD 3,300/PK-12
6586 FM 1130 77632 409-883-2232
Dr. Pauline Hargrove, supt. Fax 883-3509
www.lcmcisd.org/
Little Cypress ES 600/PK-3
5723 Meeks Dr 77632 409-886-2838
Kayla Casey, prin. Fax 886-8172
Little Cypress IS 300/4-5
2300 Allie Payne Rd 77632 409-886-4245
Michael Ridout, prin. Fax 886-1828
Little Cypress JHS 500/6-8
6765 FM 1130 77632 409-883-2317
Ryan DuBose, prin. Fax 883-5044
Mauriceville ES 600/PK-5
20040 FM 1130 77632 409-745-1615
Carie Broussard, prin. Fax 745-5187
Mauriceville MS 300/6-8
19952 FM 1130 77632 409-745-3970
Kim Cox, prin. Fax 745-3383

West Orange-Cove Consolidated ISD 2,400/PK-12
PO Box 1107 77631 409-882-5500
Rickie R. Harris, supt. Fax 882-5452
www.woccisd.net
North Early Learning Center 300/PK-PK
PO Box 1107 77631 409-882-5434
Sherry Hardin, prin. Fax 882-5449
West Orange-Stark ES 1,100/K-5
PO Box 1107 77631 409-882-5630
Glenetta Henley, prin. Fax 882-5644
West Orange-Stark MS 500/6-8
PO Box 1107 77631 409-882-5520
Anthony Moten, prin. Fax 882-5545

Community Christian S 200/PK-12
3400 Martin Luther King Jr 77632 409-883-4531
Laurie Beard M.Ed., head sch Fax 883-8855
St. Mary Catholic S 200/PK-8
2600 Bob Hall Rd 77630 409-883-8913
Donna Darby, prin. Fax 883-0827

Orangefield, Orange
Orangefield ISD 1,800/PK-12
PO Box 228 77639 409-735-5337
Dr. Stephen D. Patterson, supt. Fax 735-2080
www.orangefieldisd.net
Orangefield ES 700/PK-4
PO Box 228 77639 409-735-5346
Amanda Jenkins, prin. Fax 735-3940
Orangefield JHS 500/5-8
PO Box 228 77639 409-735-6737
Deena VanPelt, prin. Fax 792-9605

Orange Grove, Jim Wells, Pop. 1,306
Orange Grove ISD 1,900/PK-12
PO Box 534 78372 361-384-2495
Randy Hoyer, supt. Fax 384-2148
www.ogisd.net
Orange Grove ES 300/2-3
PO Box 534 78372 361-384-9358
Arnold Diaz, prin. Fax 384-2186
Orange Grove IS 300/4-5
PO Box 534 78372 361-384-9358
Arnold Diaz, prin. Fax 384-2118
Orange Grove JHS 400/6-8
PO Box 534 78372 361-384-2323
Carlos Flores, prin. Fax 384-9579
Orange Grove PS 400/PK-1
PO Box 534 78372 361-384-2316
Herlinda Perez, prin. Fax 384-9171

Orchard, Fort Bend, Pop. 350
Brazos ISD
Supt. — See Wallis
Brazos ES 400/PK-5
PO Box 30 77464 979-478-6610
Lauren Almanza, prin. Fax 478-6031

Ore City, Upshur, Pop. 1,130
Ore City ISD 800/PK-12
100 Rebel Rd N 75683 903-968-3300
Lynn Heflin, supt. Fax 968-3797
www.ocisd.net
Ore City ES 400/PK-5
1000 US Highway 259 S 75683 903-968-3300
Louann Orms, prin. Fax 968-6903
Ore City JHS 200/6-8
100 Rebel Rd N 75683 903-968-3300
Beau Vincent, prin. Fax 968-4913

Overton, Rusk, Pop. 2,503
Leveretts Chapel ISD 300/PK-12
8956 State Highway 42/135 N 75684 903-834-6675
Donna Johnson, supt. Fax 834-6602
www.leverettschapelisd.net
Leveretts Chapel ES 200/PK-5
8956 State Highway 42/135 N 75684 903-834-3181
Nikki Saxton, prin. Fax 834-6602
Leveretts Chapel JHS 100/6-8
8956 State Highway 42/135 N 75684 903-834-3181
Matt Everett, prin. Fax 834-6602

Overton ISD 500/PK-12
PO Box 130 75684 903-834-6145
Stephen DuBose, supt. Fax 834-6755
www.overtonisd.net
Overton ES 300/PK-5
PO Box 130 75684 903-834-6144
Nichole Fenter, prin. Fax 834-3913
Overton MS 100/6-8
PO Box 130 75684 903-834-6146
Cindy Bundrick, prin. Fax 834-3256

Ovilla, Ellis, Pop. 3,449

Ovilla Christian S 400/PK-12
3251 Ovilla Rd 75154 972-617-1177
Penny Hayes, dean Fax 218-0135

Ozona, Crockett, Pop. 3,206
Crockett County Consolidated SD 800/PK-12
PO Box 400 76943 325-392-5501
Raul Chavarria, supt. Fax 392-5177
www.ozonaschools.net
Ozona ES 400/PK-5
PO Box 400 76943 325-392-5501
Tamara McWilliams, prin. Fax 392-5177
Ozona MS 200/6-8
PO Box 400 76943 325-392-5501
Rick Bachman, prin. Fax 392-5177

Paducah, Cottle, Pop. 1,174
Paducah ISD 200/PK-12
PO Box P 79248 806-492-3524
Gary Waitman, supt. Fax 492-2432
www.paducahisd.org
Paducah S 200/PK-12
810 Goodwin Ave 79248 806-492-2009
Will Flemons, prin. Fax 492-2193

Paint Rock, Concho, Pop. 270
Paint Rock ISD 200/PK-12
PO Box 277 76866 325-732-4314
Ron Cline, supt. Fax 732-4384
www.paintrockisd.net
Paint Rock S 200/PK-12
PO Box 277 76866 325-732-4314
Ron Cline, prin. Fax 732-4384

Palacios, Matagorda, Pop. 4,670
Palacios ISD 1,500/PK-12
1209 12th St 77465 361-972-5491
Alexandro Flores, supt. Fax 972-3567
www.palaciosisd.org
Central ES 500/PK-3
1001 5th St 77465 361-972-2911
Nancy Flores, prin. Fax 972-5539
East Side IS 300/4-6
901 2nd St 77465 361-972-2544
Amy Marroquin, prin. Fax 972-2695
Palacios JHS 200/7-8
200 Shark Dr 77465 361-972-2417
Buddy Kelley, prin. Fax 972-6372

Palestine, Anderson, Pop. 18,404
Neches ISD
Supt. — See Neches
Neches ES 300/PK-8
3055 FM 2574 75803 903-584-3401
Kim Snider M.Ed., prin. Fax 584-3278

Palestine ISD 3,300/PK-12
1007 E Park Ave 75801 903-731-8000
Jason Marshall, supt. Fax 766-4983
www.palestineschools.org/
Northside PS 600/K-1
2509 N State Highway 155 75803 903-731-8020
Barbara Dutton, prin. Fax 655-0742
Palestine JHS 400/7-8
233 Ben Milam Dr 75801 903-731-8008
Stephen Cooksey, prin. Fax 655-0731

Southside ES 500/2-3
201 E Gillespie St 75801 903-731-8023
Grace Mancilla, prin. Fax 655-0734
Story IS 700/4-6
5300 N Loop 256 75801 903-731-8015
Jaime Clark, prin. Fax 655-0732
Washington ECC 200/PK-PK
1020 W Hamlett St 75803 903-731-8030
Sheila Bradley, prin. Fax 645-9497

Westwood ISD 1,600/PK-12
PO Box 260 75802 903-729-1776
Wade Stanford, supt. Fax 729-3696
www.westwoodisd.net
Westwood ES 500/3-6
PO Box 260 75802 903-729-1771
Michelle Carroll, prin. Fax 723-0169
Westwood JHS 200/7-8
PO Box 260 75802 903-723-0423
Sonya Brown, prin. Fax 723-6765
Westwood PS 400/PK-2
PO Box 260 75802 903-729-1787
Sonya Brown, prin. Fax 729-8839

Christian Heritage Academy 100/K-8
1500 Crockett Rd 75801 903-723-4685
Tammy Patton, admin. Fax 729-1175

Palmer, Ellis, Pop. 1,973
Palmer ISD 1,100/PK-12
PO Box 790 75152 972-449-3389
Kevin Noack, supt. Fax 845-2112
www.palmer-isd.org
Palmer ES 400/PK-4
PO Box 790 75152 972-449-3132
Allyson Spurgeon, prin. Fax 449-3472
Palmer MS 400/5-8
PO Box 790 75152 972-449-3319
Kristin Middlebrooks, prin. Fax 845-3380

Palmhurst, Hidalgo, Pop. 2,600
Mission Consolidated ISD
Supt. — See Mission
Cantu JHS 800/6-8
5101 N Stewart Rd 78572 956-323-7800
Ana Lisa Flores, prin. Fax 323-7880
Midkiff ES 600/PK-5
4201 N Mayberry St, 956-323-7000
Dora Villalobos, prin. Fax 323-7025

Faith Christian Academy 100/PK-12
4301 N Shary Rd, 956-581-7777
Rev. Robert Munne, prin. Fax 581-7786

Palmview, Hidalgo, Pop. 5,455
La Joya ISD
Supt. — See La Joya
Reyna ES 700/PK-5
707 E Veterans Blvd 78572 956-323-2390
Idalia Perez, prin. Fax 323-2391

Palo Pinto, Palo Pinto, Pop. 329
Palo Pinto ISD 100/PK-6
PO Box 280 76484 940-659-2745
Eric Cederstrom, supt. Fax 659-2936
www.palopintoisd.net/
Palo Pinto ES 100/PK-6
PO Box 280 76484 940-659-2745
Wendell Barker, prin. Fax 659-2936

Pampa, Gray, Pop. 17,739
Pampa ISD 3,700/PK-12
1233 N Hobart St 79065 806-669-4700
Tanya Larkin, supt. Fax 665-0506
www.pampaisd.net
Austin ES 500/K-5
1900 Duncan St 79065 806-669-4760
Susan Baker, prin. Fax 669-4731
Lamar ES 700/PK-5
1234 S Nelson St 79065 806-669-4880
Jamie Winborne, prin. Fax 669-4735
Pampa JHS 800/6-8
4000 Bad Cattle Company Rd 79065 806-669-4901
Jennifer Studebaker, prin. Fax 669-4742
Travis ES 400/K-5
2300 Primrose Ln 79065 806-669-4901
April Cross, prin. Fax 669-4737
Wilson ES 500/K-5
801 E Browning Ave 79065 806-669-4970
Keana Daughtry, prin. Fax 669-4736

Panhandle, Carson, Pop. 2,431
Panhandle ISD 700/PK-12
PO Box 1030 79068 806-537-3568
Blair Brown, supt. Fax 537-5553
www.panhandleisd.net
Panhandle ES 300/PK-5
PO Box 1030 79068 806-537-3579
Taylor Norvell, prin. Fax 537-4230
Panhandle JHS 100/6-8
PO Box 1030 79068 806-537-3541
Blair Brown, prin. Fax 537-5725

Paradise, Wise, Pop. 438
Paradise ISD 1,100/PK-12
338 School House Rd 76073 940-969-5000
Robert Criswell, supt. Fax 969-5008
www.pisd.net
Paradise ES 400/PK-3
338 School House Rd 76073 940-969-5046
Robyn Gibson, prin. Fax 969-5043
Paradise IS 100/4-5
338 School House Rd 76073 940-969-5032
Kristin Gage, prin. Fax 969-5031
Paradise MS 300/6-8
338 School House Rd 76073 940-969-5034
Greg Fletcher, prin. Fax 969-5025

Paris, Lamar, Pop. 24,458
Chisum ISD 900/PK-12
3250 S Church St 75462 903-737-2830
Tommy Chalaire, supt. Fax 737-2831
www.chisumisd.org
Chisum ES 400/PK-5
3250 S Church St 75462 903-737-2820
Wendy Ruthart, prin. Fax 737-2831
Chisum MS 200/6-8
3250 S Church St 75462 903-737-2806
Aaron Bridges, prin. Fax 737-2831

North Lamar ISD 2,900/PK-12
3201 Lewis Ln 75460 903-737-2000
John McCullough, supt. Fax 669-0129
www.northlamar.net
Bailey IS 400/4-5
3201 Lewis Ln 75460 903-737-7971
Angela Compton, prin. Fax 669-0179
Everett ES 300/2-3
3201 Lewis Ln 75460 903-737-2061
Lora Sanders, prin. Fax 669-0169
Higgins ES 400/PK-1
3201 Lewis Ln 75460 903-737-2081
Lori Malone, prin. Fax 669-0189
Stone MS 700/6-8
3201 Lewis Ln 75460 903-737-2041
Kelli Stewart, prin. Fax 669-0149
Other Schools – See Powderly

Paris ISD 3,400/PK-12
1920 Clarksville St 75460 903-737-7473
Paul Jones, supt. Fax 737-7484
www.parisisd.net
Aikin ES 900/K-4
3100 Pine Mill Rd 75460 903-737-7443
Kimberly Donnan, prin. Fax 737-7517
Crockett IS 500/5-6
655 S Collegiate Dr 75460 903-737-7450
Brock Blassingame, prin. Fax 737-7526
Givens Pre-Kindergarten 100/PK-PK
655 Martin Luther King Jr 75460 903-737-7466
Sheila Ensey, prin. Fax 737-7531
Justiss ES 500/K-4
401 18th St NW 75460 903-737-7458
Renee Elmore, prin. Fax 737-7530
Paris JHS 500/7-8
2400 Jefferson Rd 75460 903-737-7434
Stephen Long, prin. Fax 737-7534

Trinity Christian Academy 100/PK-12
2190 Farm Road 79 75460 903-785-9557

Parker, Collin, Pop. 3,708
Allen ISD
Supt. — See Allen
Bolin ES 700/K-6
5705 Cheyenne Dr, Allen TX 75002 214-495-6750
Reena Varughese, prin. Fax 495-6756

Pasadena, Harris, Pop. 147,777
Deer Park ISD
Supt. — See Deer Park
Deepwater ES 700/3-5
309 Glenmore Dr 77503 832-668-8300
Dr. Belinda Box, prin. Fax 475-6150
Deepwater JHS 600/6-8
501 Glenmore Dr 77503 832-668-7600
Scott Davis, prin. Fax 475-6138
ECC 400/PK-PK
401 Glenmore Dr 77503 832-668-8390
Jenny Martinez, prin. Fax 668-8395
Fairmont ES 800/K-5
4315 Heathfield Dr 77505 832-668-8500
Lea Ann Boswell, prin. Fax 998-4411
Fairmont JHS 800/6-8
4911 Holly Bay Ct 77505 832-668-7800
Neil Munro, prin. Fax 998-4456
Parkwood ES 700/K-2
404 Parkwood Dr 77503 832-668-8200
Debbie Yampey, prin. Fax 475-6180

Pasadena ISD 53,900/PK-12
1515 Cherrybrook Ln 77502 713-740-0000
Deeann Powell, supt. Fax 740-4042
www.pasadenaisd.org
Bailey ES 800/K-5
2707 Lafferty Rd 77502 713-740-0528
Karyn Johnson, prin. Fax 740-4129
Bondy IS 1,000/6-8
5101 Keith Rd 77505 713-740-0430
Roneka Lee, prin. Fax 740-4152
DeZavala MS 800/5-6
101 Jackson Ave 77506 713-740-0544
Melissa Garza, prin. Fax 740-4159
Fisher ES 800/PK-5
2920 Watters Rd 77502 713-740-0552
Norma Gomez-Valenzuela, prin. Fax 740-4131
Gardens ES 600/PK-5
1105 Harris Ave 77506 713-740-0576
Lindsey Lesniewski, prin. Fax 740-4133
Golden Acres ES 500/PK-5
5232 Sycamore Ave 77503 713-740-0600
Lisa Davis, prin. Fax 740-4136
Jackson IS 800/6-8
1020 Thomas Ave 77506 713-740-0440
Paula Sword, prin. Fax 740-4109
Jensen ES 700/PK-5
3514 Tulip St 77504 713-740-0608
Judy Diaz, prin. Fax 740-4137
Keller MS 600/5-6
3102 San Augustine Ave 77503 713-740-5284
Diane Phelan, prin. Fax 740-5915
Kendrick MS 6-8
3000 Watters 77504 713-740-5380
Melissa Messenger, prin. Fax 740-5980
Kruse ES 700/PK-5
400 Main St 77506 713-740-0624
Sandra Buckner, prin. Fax 740-4138
Lomax MS 1,000/5-6
1519 Genoa Red Bluff Rd 77504 713-740-5230
Norma Penny, prin. Fax 740-4175
McMasters ES 400/K-5
1011 Bennett Dr 77503 713-740-0640
Andrea Gilger, prin. Fax 740-4079
Miller IS 900/6-8
1002 Fairmont Pkwy 77504 713-740-0450
Vanessa Reyes, prin. Fax 740-4106
Morales ES 500/PK-5
305 W Harris Ave 77506 713-740-0664
Lisa Haws, prin. Fax 740-4104
Parks ES 500/PK-5
3302 San Augustine Ave 77503 713-740-0680
Frances Burley, prin. Fax 740-4141
Park View IS 1,000/6-8
3003 Dabney Dr 77502 713-740-0460
Rob Hasson, prin. Fax 740-4115
Pomeroy ES 1,000/PK-5
920 Burke Rd 77506 713-740-0696
Stephen Harding, prin. Fax 740-4103
Red Bluff ES 600/PK-5
416 Bearle St 77506 713-740-0704
Tammie Hinton, prin. Fax 740-4143
Richey ES 900/PK-5
610 Richey St 77506 713-740-0712
Andrea Zapata, prin. Fax 740-4098
San Jacinto IS 600/6-8
3600 Red Bluff Rd 77503 713-740-0480
Dianna Walker, prin. Fax 740-4153
Shaw MS 800/5-6
1200 Houston Ave 77502 713-740-5268
Darby Hickman, prin. Fax 740-5909
Smythe ES 600/K-5
2202 Pasadena Blvd 77502 713-740-0728
Denise Moody, prin. Fax 740-4114
Southmore IS 900/6-8
2000 Patricia Ln 77502 713-740-0500
Derek Moody, prin. Fax 740-4154
South Shaver ES 600/PK-5
2020 Shaver St 77502 713-740-0842
Erica Ordogne, prin. Fax 740-4145
Sparks ES 500/PK-5
2503 Southmore Ave 77502 713-740-0744
Sherri Means, prin. Fax 740-4146
Sullivan MS, 1112 Queens Rd 77502 6-8
Kelly Cook, prin. 713-740-5420
Teague ES 700/K-5
4200 Crenshaw Rd 77504 713-740-0760
Valorie Morris, prin. Fax 740-4148
Turner ES 500/PK-5
4333 Lily St 77505 713-740-0768
Donna Duke, prin. Fax 740-4149
Williams ES 800/PK-5
1522 Scarborough Ln 77502 713-740-0776
Michael Hanson, prin. Fax 740-4150
Young ES 700/K-5
4221 Fox Meadow Ln 77504 713-740-0784
Shirlyn Ross, prin. Fax 740-4151
Other Schools – See Houston, South Houston

Faith Christian Academy K-12
3519 Burke Rd 77504 713-943-9978
First Baptist Christian Academy 400/PK-12
7500 Fairmont Pkwy 77505 281-991-9191
Freddie Cullins, head sch Fax 946-8632
St. Pius V S 200/PK-8
812 Main St 77506 713-472-5172
Sheryl Calton, prin. Fax 534-6270

Pattison, Waller, Pop. 462
Royal ISD 2,400/PK-12
PO Box 489 77466 281-934-2248
Dr. Stacy Ackley, supt. Fax 934-2846
www.royal-isd.net
Other Schools – See Brookshire

Pattonville, Lamar
Prairiland ISD 1,100/PK-12
466 Farm Road 196 75468 903-652-6476
Jeff Ballard, supt. Fax 652-3738
www.prairiland.net
Prairiland JHS 200/6-8
466 Farm Road 196 75468 903-652-5681
Leslie Watson, prin. Fax 652-3232
Other Schools – See Blossom, Deport

Pawnee, Bee, Pop. 164
Pawnee ISD 200/PK-8
PO Box 569 78145 361-456-7256
Michelle Hartmann, supt. Fax 456-7388
www.pawneeisd.net
Pawnee Elementary JHS 200/PK-8
PO Box 569 78145 361-456-7256
Kendra Wuest, prin. Fax 456-7388

Pearland, Brazoria, Pop. 89,386
Alvin ISD
Supt. — See Alvin
Brothers ES PK-5
2910 Half Moon Bay Dr 77584 281-245-3660
Krystal Hawks, prin. Fax 245-2411
Marek ES 900/PK-5
1947 Kirby St 77584 281-245-3232
Roman Nieto, prin. Fax 436-3796
Ryan JHS 1,200/6-8
11500 Shadow Creek Pkwy 77584 281-245-3210
Christina Lovette, prin. Fax 245-3221
Wilder ES 900/PK-5
2225 Kingsley Dr 77584 281-245-3090
Stacie Van Loenen, prin. Fax 340-0694
York ES 800/PK-5
2720 Kingsley Dr 77584 281-245-2100
Lisa Hicks, prin. Fax 340-1797

Pearland ISD, PO Box 7 77588 — 20,000/PK-12
John Kelly Ph.D., supt. — 281-485-3203
www.pearlandisd.org
Alexander MS — 700/5-6
3001 Old Alvin Rd 77581 — 832-736-6700
Dr. Brad Hayes, prin.
Carleston ES, 3010 Harkey Rd 77584 — 800/PK-4
Amy Beverly, prin. — 281-412-1412
Challenger ES — 700/PK-4
9434 Hughes Ranch Rd 77584 — 281-485-7912
Lisa Nelson, prin.
Cockrell ES, 3500 McHard Rd 77581 — 800/PK-4
Kathy Behrendsen, prin. — 832-736-6600
Harris ES, 2314 Schleider Dr 77581 — 700/PK-4
Brenda Keimig, prin. — 281-485-4024
Jamison MS, 2506 Woody Rd 77581 — 800/5-6
Sharon Bradley, prin. — 281-412-1440
Lawhon ES, 5810 Brookside Rd 77581 — 700/PK-4
Jennifer Walker, prin. — 281-412-1445
Magnolia ES, 5350 Magnolia Dr 77584 — 800/PK-4
Sharon Gifford, prin. — 281-727-1750
Massey Ranch ES — 700/PK-4
3900 Manvel Rd 77584 — 281-727-1700
Heather Block, prin.
Miller JHS, 3301 Manvel Rd 77584 — 900/7-8
Kim Brooks, prin. — 281-997-3900
Pearland JHS East — 700/7-8
2315 Old Alvin Rd 77581 — 281-485-2481
Charles Allen, prin.
Pearland JHS South — 800/7-8
4719 Bailey Rd 77584 — 281-727-1500
Jason Frerking, prin.
Pearland JHS West — 800/7-8
2337 N Galveston Ave 77581 — 281-412-1222
Dana Miles, prin.
Rogers MS, 3121 Manvel Rd 77584 — 900/5-6
Lakesha Vaughn, prin. — 832-736-6400
Rustic Oak ES, 1302 Rustic Ln 77581 — 600/PK-4
Beth West, prin. — 281-482-5400
Sablatura MS — 800/5-6
2201 N Galveston Ave 77581 — 281-412-1500
Verna Tipton, prin.
Shadycrest ES — 600/PK-4
2405 Shadybend Dr 77581 — 281-412-1404
Michelle Kiefer, prin.
Silvercrest ES — 800/PK-4
3003 Southwyck Pkwy 77584 — 832-736-6000
Lori Campbell, prin.
Silverlake ES — 700/PK-4
2550 County Road 90 77584 — 713-436-8000
Shayla McGrew, prin.

Eagle Heights Christian Academy — 300/PK-12
3005 Pearland Pkwy 77581 — 281-485-6330
John Stahl, head sch — Fax 485-8682
Heritage Christian Academy — 200/PK-5
12006 Shadow Creek Pkwy 77584 — 713-436-8422
Kara A. Marsh, admin. — Fax 893-6104
Montessori S of Downtown Silverlake — 300/PK-3
2525 County Road 90 77584 — 281-412-5763
St. Helen S — 200/K-8
2213 Old Alvin Rd 77581 — 281-485-2845
Dr. Phyliss Coleman, prin. — Fax 485-7607
Silverline Montessori S — 200/PK-5
2505 Old Chocolate Bayou Rd 77584 — 281-997-3700
Silverline Montessori S — 300/PK-4
2080 Reflection Bay Dr 77584 — 713-436-5070

Pearsall, Frio, Pop. 9,098
Pearsall ISD — 2,100/PK-12
318 Berry Ranch Rd 78061 — 830-334-8001
Dr. Nobert Rodriguez, supt. — Fax 334-8007
www.pearsallisd.org
Flores ES — 500/PK-2
321 W Pena St 78061 — 830-334-4108
Silvia Martinez, prin. — Fax 334-5047
Pearsall IS — 500/3-5
415 E Florida St 78061 — 830-334-3316
Juliana Lingo, prin. — Fax 334-5007
Pearsall JHS — 600/6-8
607 E Alabama St 78061 — 830-334-8021
Devon Zamzow, prin. — Fax 334-8025

Pecan Gap, Delta, Pop. 199
Fannindel ISD
Supt. — See Ladonia
Fannindel ES — 100/PK-5
409 W Main St 75469 — 903-359-6314
Drew Thomas B.S., prin. — Fax 359-6315

Pecos, Reeves, Pop. 8,754
Pecos-Barstow-Toyah ISD — 2,300/PK-12
PO Box 869 79772 — 432-447-7201
Jim Haley, supt. — Fax 447-7262
www.pbtisd.esc18.net
Austin ES — 600/1-3
PO Box 869 79772 — 432-447-7541
Alicia Mitchell, prin. — Fax 447-4248
Crockett MS — 500/6-8
PO Box 869 79772 — 432-447-7461
Jennifer Guillory, prin. — Fax 447-4853
Haynes ES — 400/4-5
PO Box 869 79772 — 432-447-7497
Omar Salgado, prin. — Fax 445-1612
Pecos K — 300/PK-K
PO Box 869 79772 — 432-447-7596
LeeAnn McGraw, prin. — Fax 445-4203

Penelope, Hill, Pop. 198
Penelope ISD — 200/PK-12
PO Box 68 76676 — 254-533-2215
Scot Kelley, supt. — Fax 533-2262
www.penelopeisd.org/
Penelope S — 200/PK-12
PO Box 68 76676 — 254-533-2215
Scot Kelley, supt. — Fax 533-2262

Penitas, Hidalgo, Pop. 4,401
La Joya ISD
Supt. — See La Joya
Clinton ES — 700/PK-5
39202 Mile 7 Rd 78576 — 956-323-2740
Martin Munoz, prin. — Fax 323-2471
Corina-Sanchez Pena ES — 800/PK-5
4800 Liberty Blvd 78576 — 956-323-2750
Raul G. Luna, prin. — Fax 323-2751
Kennedy ES — 800/PK-5
1801 Diamond Ave 78576 — 956-323-2330
Maria Guerra, prin. — Fax 323-2339
Saenz MS — 700/6-8
39200 Mile 7 Rd 78576 — 956-323-2830
Belen Martinez, prin. — Fax 323-2831

Perrin, Jack, Pop. 396
Perrin-Whitt Consolidated ISD — 300/PK-12
216 N Benson St 76486 — 940-798-3718
Cliff Gilmore, supt. — Fax 798-3071
www.pwcisd.net
Perrin ES — 200/PK-6
216 N Benson St 76486 — 940-798-2395
Amy Salazar, prin. — Fax 798-3071

Perryton, Ochiltree, Pop. 8,746
Perryton ISD — 2,400/PK-12
PO Box 1048 79070 — 806-435-5478
Robert Hall, supt. — Fax 435-4689
www.perrytonisd.com
Perryton JHS — 500/6-8
PO Box 1048 79070 — 806-435-3601
Dimitri Garcia, prin. — Fax 435-3624
Perryton K — 300/PK-K
PO Box 1048 79070 — 806-435-2463
Dent Felix, prin. — Fax 435-6093
Williams IS — 400/4-5
PO Box 1048 79070 — 806-435-3436
Read Cates, prin. — Fax 435-9231
Wright ES — 600/1-3
PO Box 1048 79070 — 806-435-2371
Tiffany Bietz, prin. — Fax 434-8844

Petersburg, Hale, Pop. 1,201
Petersburg ISD — 300/PK-12
PO Box 160 79250 — 806-667-3585
Dr. Drew Howard, supt. — Fax 667-3463
www.petersburgisd.net
Petersburg ES — 200/PK-6
PO Box 160 79250 — 806-667-3585
Donna Carnagey, prin. — Fax 667-3463

Petrolia, Clay, Pop. 676
Petrolia ISD — 500/PK-12
PO Box 176 76377 — 940-524-3555
David Hedges, supt. — Fax 524-3370
www.petroliaisd.org
Petrolia ES — 300/PK-6
PO Box 176 76377 — 940-524-3343
Travis Barnes, prin. — Fax 524-3302

Pettus, Bee, Pop. 551
Pettus ISD — 400/PK-12
PO Box D 78146 — 361-375-2296
Jaime Velasco, supt. — Fax 375-2295
www.pettusisd.com
Pettus ES — 200/PK-5
PO Box D 78146 — 361-375-2296
Klaire DeLeon, prin. — Fax 375-2930

Pflugerville, Travis, Pop. 45,841
Pflugerville ISD — 23,600/PK-12
1401 Pecan St W 78660 — 512-594-0000
Douglas Killian Ph.D., supt. — Fax 594-0005
www.pfisd.net
Barron ES — 700/K-5
14850 Harris Ridge Blvd 78660 — 512-594-4300
Virginia Caudle, prin. — Fax 594-4305
Brookhollow ES — 500/K-5
1200 N Railroad Ave 78660 — 512-594-5200
Lisa Harris, prin. — Fax 594-5205
Cele MS — 700/6-8
6000 Cele Rd 78660 — 512-594-3000
Brian Ernest, prin. — Fax 594-3005
Highland Park ES — 800/PK-5
428 Kingston Lacy Blvd 78660 — 512-594-6800
Tana Ruckel, prin. — Fax 594-6805
Kelly Lane MS — 1,000/6-8
18900 Falcon Pointe Blvd 78660 — 512-594-2800
Dina Schaefer, prin. — Fax 594-2805
Mott ES, 20101 Hodde Ln 78660 — PK-5
Tammy Rebecek, prin. — 512-594-4700
Murchison ES — 900/PK-5
2215 Kelly Ln 78660 — 512-594-6000
Reese Weirich, prin. — Fax 594-6005
Park Crest MS — 900/6-8
1500 N Railroad Ave 78660 — 512-594-2400
Zachary Kleypas, prin. — Fax 594-2405
Pflugerville ES — 500/K-5
701 Immanuel Rd 78660 — 512-594-3800
Genia Antoine, prin. — Fax 594-3805
Pflugerville MS — 1,100/6-8
1600 Settlers Valley Dr 78660 — 512-594-2000
Robert Stell, prin. — Fax 594-2005
Riojas ES — 600/K-5
3400 Crispin Hall Ln 78660 — 512-594-4100
Christi Siegel, prin. — Fax 594-4105
Rowe Lane ES — 900/K-5
3112 Speidel Dr 78660 — 512-594-6600
Ben O'Conner, prin. — Fax 594-6605
Spring Hill ES — 700/PK-5
600 S Heatherwilde Blvd 78660 — 512-594-5400
Camille Ramirez-Longoria, prin. — Fax 594-5405
Timmerman ES — 500/PK-5
700 Pecan St W 78660 — 512-594-4200
Sara Watson, prin. — Fax 594-4205
Wieland ES — 500/PK-5
900 Tudor House Rd 78660 — 512-594-3900
Jared Stevenson, prin. — Fax 594-3905
Windermere ES — 500/3-5
1101 Picadilly Dr 78660 — 512-594-4800
Kate Shaum, prin. — Fax 594-4805
Windermere PS — 500/PK-2
429 Grand Avenue Pkwy 78660 — 512-594-5600
Christi Siegel, prin. — Fax 594-5605
Other Schools – See Austin, Round Rock

Stonehill Christian Academy — 50/PK-8
900 Pecan St E Ste 300 78660 — 512-763-2776

Pharr, Hidalgo, Pop. 70,290
Hidalgo ISD
Supt. — See Hidalgo
Kelly ES — 400/PK-5
PO Box 8220 78577 — 956-843-4200
Beatriz Solano, prin. — Fax 781-5972

Pharr-San Juan-Alamo ISD — 31,400/PK-12
PO Box 1150 78577 — 956-354-2000
Dr. Daniel King, supt. — Fax 702-5648
www.psjaisd.us/
Anaya ES — 700/PK-5
1000 W Dicker Dr 78577 — 956-784-8500
Joe Garza, prin. — Fax 354-3284
Arnold ES — 600/PK-5
615 W El Dora Rd 78577 — 956-354-2710
Rafaela Romero, prin. — Fax 354-3238
Chavez ES — 700/PK-5
401 E Thomas Rd 78577 — 956-354-2720
Roel Faz, prin. — Fax 354-3248
Escalante MS — 600/6-8
6123 S Cage Blvd 78577 — 956-354-2670
Rafael Gonzalez, prin. — Fax 354-3200
Escobar ES — 800/PK-5
901 W Kelly Ave 78577 — 956-354-2920
Eleticia Nava, prin. — Fax 354-3288
Ford ES — 500/PK-5
1110 E Polk Ave 78577 — 956-354-2770
Priscilla Salinas, prin. — Fax 354-3256
Garcia ES — 700/PK-5
1002 W Juan Balli Rd 78577 — 956-354-2790
Sandra Garcia, prin. — Fax 354-3258
Johnson MS — 900/6-8
500 E Sioux Rd 78577 — 956-354-2590
Linda Soto, prin. — Fax 354-3212
Kelly-Pharr ES — 800/PK-5
500 E Sam Houston Blvd 78577 — 956-354-2870
Lydia Trevino, prin. — Fax 354-3276
Kennedy MS — 800/6-8
600 W Hall Acres Rd 78577 — 956-354-2650
Luis Villarreal, prin. — Fax 354-3206
Liberty MS — 1,000/6-8
1212 S Fir St 78577 — 956-354-2610
Alfredo Carrillo, prin. — Fax 354-3218
Long ES — 900/PK-5
700 N Raiders Dr 78577 — 956-354-2750
Concepcion Ipina, prin. — Fax 354-3266
Longoria ES — 500/PK-5
2500 N Cypress 78577 — 956-354-2820
Rosalina Dorrego, prin. — Fax 354-3268
Palacios ES — PK-5
801 E Thomas Rd 78577 — 956-354-2930
Michelle Cardoza, prin. — Fax 354-3290
Palmer ES — 500/PK-5
1200 W Hall Acres Rd 78577 — 956-354-2860
Brisa Gonzalez, prin. — Fax 354-3274
PSJA Early Start Pre K — 700/PK-PK
903 N Flag St 78577 — 956-354-2270
Consuelo Casas, prin. — Fax 354-3236
Ramirez ES — 600/PK-5
1920 N Hibiscus St 78577 — 956-354-2880
Leonel Avila, prin. — Fax 354-3278
Other Schools – See Alamo, San Juan

Valley View ISD — 4,600/PK-12
9701 S Jackson Rd 78577 — 956-340-1000
Rolando Ramirez, supt. — Fax 843-8688
www.vviewisd.net
Valley View 5th Grade Campus — 300/5-5
9701 S Jackson Rd 78577 — 956-340-1400
Tomas Villagomez , prin. — Fax 843-3756
Valley View ES — 500/PK-4
9701 S Jackson Rd 78577 — 956-340-1450
Jesus Cerda, prin. — Fax 843-8526
Valley View JHS — 700/6-7
9701 S Jackson Rd 78577 — 956-340-1300
Antonio De La Cerda, prin. — Fax 843-3031
Valley View North ES — 500/PK-4
9701 S Jackson Rd 78577 — 956-340-1600
Marina Leal, prin. — Fax 783-1163
Other Schools – See Hidalgo

Oratory Academy — 700/PK-12
1407 W Moore Rd 78577 — 956-781-3056
Fr. Leo Daniels, head sch — Fax 787-1516

Pilot Point, Denton, Pop. 3,793
Pilot Point ISD — 1,400/PK-12
829 S Harrison St 76258 — 940-686-8700
Dan Gist, supt. — Fax 686-8705
www.pilotpointisd.com
Pilot Point ES — 400/PK-2
829 S Jefferson St 76258 — 940-686-8710
Rae Ann Strittmatter, prin. — Fax 686-8715
Pilot Point IS — 400/3-6
501 Carroll St 76258 — 940-686-8720
Dustin Toth, prin. — Fax 686-8725
Pilot Point MS - J. Earl Selz Campus — 200/7-8
828 S Harrison St 76258 — 940-686-8730
Zane Stapp, prin. — Fax 686-8735

Pineland, Sabine, Pop. 835
West Sabine ISD — 700/PK-12
PO Box 869 75968 — 409-584-2655
Mike Pate, supt. — Fax 584-2139
www.westsabineisd.net

West Sabine ES 300/PK-5
PO Box 869 75968 409-584-2205
Debbie Lane, prin. Fax 584-3096

Pipe Creek, Bandera
Bandera ISD
Supt. — See Bandera
Hill Country ES 500/PK-5
6346 FM 1283 78063 830-535-6151
Laura Klein, prin. Fax 535-5111

Pipe Creek Christian S 50/PK-6
PO Box 63778 78063 830-510-6131
Don Myers, head sch Fax 510-6136

Pittsburg, Camp, Pop. 4,399
Pittsburg ISD 2,500/PK-12
PO Box 1189 75686 903-856-3628
Judy Pollan, supt. Fax 856-0269
pittsburgisd.net
Pittsburg ES 500/2-4
110 Fulton St 75686 903-856-6472
Terri Brown, prin. Fax 855-3370
Pittsburg IS 400/5-6
209 Lafayette St 75686 903-855-3395
Sarah Richmond, prin. Fax 855-3398
Pittsburg JHS 300/7-8
313 Broach St 75686 903-856-6432
Kristane Moore, prin. Fax 855-3357
Pittsburg PS 500/PK-1
405 Broach St 75686 903-856-6482
Vicki Rockett, prin. Fax 855-3385

Placedo, Victoria, Pop. 685
Bloomington ISD
Supt. — See Victoria
Placedo ES 200/PK-1
PO Box 156 77977 361-333-8000
Edna Salinas, prin. Fax 333-8002

Plains, Yoakum, Pop. 1,468
Plains ISD 400/PK-12
PO Box 479 79355 806-456-7401
Dr. Stephanie Howard, supt. Fax 456-4325
plainsisd.net/
Plains ES 200/PK-5
PO Box 479 79355 806-456-7438
Tracy Heflin, prin. Fax 456-4325
Plains MS 100/6-8
PO Box 479 79355 806-456-7490
Jorge Mendez, prin. Fax 456-4325

Plainview, Hale, Pop. 21,983
Plainview ISD 5,200/PK-12
PO Box 1540 79073 806-293-6000
Dr. Rocky Kirk, supt. Fax 296-4014
www.plainviewisd.org
College Hill ES 400/PK-5
707 Canyon St 79072 806-293-6035
Lori Glenn, prin. Fax 296-4102
Coronado MS 400/6-8
2501 Joliet St 79072 806-293-6020
Andrew Hannon, prin. Fax 296-4169
Edgemere ES 500/PK-5
2600 W 20th St 79072 806-293-6040
Angie Valdez, prin. Fax 296-4103
Estacado MS 400/6-8
2200 W 20th St 79072 806-293-6015
Ritchie Thornton, prin. Fax 290-4109
Highland ES 500/PK-5
1707 W 11th St 79072 806-293-6045
Becky Buxton, prin. Fax 296-4139
Hillcrest ES 400/PK-5
315 SW Alpine Dr 79072 806-293-6050
Yesenia Pardo, prin. Fax 296-4106
La Mesa ES 600/PK-5
600 S Ennis St 79072 806-293-6055
Vickie Young, prin. Fax 296-9425
Thunderbird ES 500/PK-5
1200 W 32nd St 79072 806-293-6060
Amy Meek, prin. Fax 296-4125

Plainview Christian Academy 200/PK-12
310 S Ennis St 79072 806-296-6034
Karen Earhart, admin. Fax 686-0988

Plano, Collin, Pop. 253,492
Frisco ISD
Supt. — See Frisco
Anderson ES 600/K-5
2800 Oakland Hills Dr 75025 469-633-2300
Laura Del Hierro, prin. Fax 633-2350
Borchardt ES 700/K-5
4300 Waskom Dr 75024 469-633-2800
Jodi Davis, prin. Fax 633-2850
Fowler MS 900/6-8
3801 McDermott Rd 75025 469-633-5050
Donnie Wiseman, prin. Fax 633-5060
Riddle ES 800/K-5
8201 Robinson Rd 75024 469-633-3200
Heather Cox, prin. Fax 633-3250
Taylor ES 700/K-5
9865 Gillespie Dr 75025 469-633-3625
Christy Garza, prin. Fax 633-3635

Plano ISD 54,100/PK-12
2700 W 15th St 75075 469-752-8100
Dr. Brian Binggeli, supt. Fax 752-8096
www.pisd.edu
Andrews ES 700/K-5
2520 Scenic Dr 75025 469-752-3900
Joy Lovell, prin. Fax 752-3901
Armstrong MS 700/6-8
3805 Timberline Dr 75074 469-752-4600
Melissa Blank, prin. Fax 752-4601
Barksdale ES 600/K-5
2424 Midway Rd 75093 469-752-0100
Jennifer Caplinger, prin. Fax 752-0101
Barron ES 500/K-5
3300 P Ave 75074 469-752-0200
Tricia Lancaster, prin. Fax 752-0201
Beaty Early Childhood S 600/PK-PK
1717 Nevada Dr 75093 469-752-4200
Dr. Dina Rowe, prin. Fax 752-4201
Bethany ES 400/K-5
2418 Micarta Dr 75025 469-752-0300
Bryan Bird, prin. Fax 752-0301
Bowman MS 800/6-8
2501 Jupiter Rd 75074 469-752-4800
Brooks Baca, prin. Fax 752-4801
Brinker ES 700/K-5
3800 Clark Pkwy 75093 469-752-0500
Barbara Lange, prin. Fax 752-0501
Carlisle ES 500/K-5
6525 Old Orchard Dr 75023 469-752-0600
Linda Patrick, prin. Fax 752-0601
Carpenter MS 800/6-8
3905 Rainier Rd 75023 469-752-5000
Courtney Washington, prin. Fax 752-5001
Centennial ES 500/K-5
2609 Ventura Dr 75093 469-752-0700
Sara Stewart, prin. Fax 752-0701
Christie ES 700/PK-5
3801 Rainier Rd 75023 469-752-0800
Ryan Steele, prin. Fax 752-0801
Daffron ES 600/K-5
3900 Preston Meadow Dr 75093 469-752-0900
Stefanie Ramos, prin. Fax 752-0901
Davis ES 500/K-5
2701 Parkhaven Dr 75075 469-752-1000
Karma Cunningham, prin. Fax 752-1001
Dooley ES 400/K-5
2425 San Gabriel Dr 75074 469-752-1100
Tramy Tran, prin. Fax 752-1101
Forman ES 600/K-5
3600 Timberline Dr 75074 469-752-1200
Talle Gomez, prin. Fax 752-1201
Gulledge ES 600/K-5
6801 Preston Meadow Dr 75024 469-752-1300
Deni Bleggi, prin. Fax 752-1301
Haggard MS 900/6-8
2832 Parkhaven Dr 75075 469-752-5400
Julie-Anne Dean, prin. Fax 752-5401
Harrington ES 400/K-5
1540 Baffin Bay Dr 75075 469-752-1500
Ann Irvine, prin. Fax 752-1501
Haun ES 500/K-5
4500 Quincy Ln 75024 469-752-1600
Jayne Smith, prin. Fax 752-1601
Hedgcoxe ES 400/K-5
7701 Prescott Dr 75025 469-752-1700
Kristi Graham, prin. Fax 752-1701
Hendrick MS 800/6-8
7400 Red River Dr 75025 469-752-5600
Lisa Long, prin. Fax 752-5601
Hickey ES 600/K-5
4100 Coldwater Creek Ln 75074 469-752-4100
Jane Oestreich, prin. Fax 752-4101
Hightower ES 500/K-5
2601 Decator Dr 75093 469-752-1800
Mariea Sprott, prin. Fax 752-1801
Huffman ES 500/PK-5
5510 Channel Isle Dr 75093 469-752-1900
Jamey Allen, prin. Fax 752-1901
Hughston ES 400/K-5
2601 Cross Bend Rd 75023 469-752-2000
Carrie D'Argo, prin. Fax 752-2001
Isaacs Early Childhood S 500/PK-PK
3400 E Parker Rd 75074 469-752-3480
Kris Benson, prin. Fax 752-3481
Jackson ES 700/PK-5
1101 Jackson Dr 75075 469-752-2100
Andrea Cockrell, prin. Fax 752-2101
Mathews ES 600/K-5
7500 Marchman Way 75025 469-752-2300
Jill Stoker, prin. Fax 752-2301
McCall ES 600/K-5
6601 Cloverhaven Way 75074 469-752-4500
Stacy Kimbriel, prin. Fax 752-4501
Meadows ES 600/K-5
2800 18th St 75074 469-752-2400
Katherine Foster, prin. Fax 752-2401
Memorial ES 500/PK-5
2200 Laurel Ln 75074 469-752-2500
Mary Hardin, prin. Fax 752-2501
Mendenhall ES 600/PK-5
1330 19th St 75074 469-752-2600
Jana Prince, prin. Fax 752-2601
Otto MS 1,000/6-8
504 N Star Rd 75074 469-752-8500
Antoine Spencer, prin. Fax 752-8501
Pearson Early Childhood S 400/PK-PK
4000 Eagle Pass 75023 469-752-4300
Dr. Cheri Izbicki, prin. Fax 752-4301
Rasor ES 500/K-5
945 Hedgcoxe Rd 75025 469-752-2900
Zack Pruett, prin. Fax 752-2901
Renner MS 1,300/6-8
5701 W Parker Rd 75093 469-752-5800
Jill Engelking, prin. Fax 752-5801
Rice MS 1,200/6-8
8500 Gifford Dr 75025 469-752-6000
Chris Glasscock, prin. Fax 752-6001
Robinson MS 1,000/6-8
6701 Preston Meadow Dr 75024 469-752-6200
Billie Jean Lee, prin. Fax 752-6201
Saigling ES 400/K-5
3600 Matterhorn Dr 75075 469-752-3000
Chris Dunkle, prin. Fax 752-3001
Schimelpfenig MS 1,000/6-8
2400 Maumelle Dr 75023 469-752-6400
Dr. Brant Perry, prin. Fax 752-6401
Shepard ES 400/K-5
1000 Wilson Dr 75075 469-752-3100
Kristin Bishop, prin. Fax 752-3101
Sigler ES 500/K-5
1400 Janwood Dr 75075 469-752-3200
Matthew Arend, prin. Fax 752-3201
Skaggs ES 500/K-5
3201 Russell Creek Dr 75025 469-752-3300
Karen Lee, prin. Fax 752-3301
Thomas ES 600/K-5
1800 Montana Trl 75023 469-752-3500
Lynn Swanson, prin. Fax 752-3501
Weatherford ES 500/PK-5
2941 Mollimar Dr 75075 469-752-3600
Ben Benavides, prin. Fax 752-3601
Wells ES 600/K-5
3427 Mission Ridge Rd 75023 469-752-3700
Sara Meyer, prin. Fax 752-3701
Wilson MS 900/6-8
1001 Custer Rd 75075 469-752-6700
Selenda Sager, prin. Fax 752-6701
Wyatt ES 500/K-5
8900 Coit Rd 75025 469-752-3800
Cynthia Hentges, prin. Fax 752-3801
Other Schools – See Allen, Dallas, Murphy, Richardson

Alpha Montessori S 100/PK-3
4815 Rasor Blvd 75024 972-872-2825
Rupali Abdulpurkar, dir. Fax 872-2829
Bethany Christian S 100/PK-12
3300 W Parker Rd 75075 972-596-5811
Dr. Marvin Effa, prin. Fax 596-5814
Coram Deo Academy 300/PK-12
9645 Independence Pkwy 75025 469-854-1300
Toby Oaks, admin. Fax 854-1300
Faith Lutheran S 100/PK-12
1701 E Park Blvd 75074 972-423-7448
Rev. Stephen Kieser, hdmstr. Fax 423-9618
Good Tree Academy 100/PK-9
3600 K Ave 75074 972-836-6322
Messiah Lutheran Lambs S 50/PK-K
1801 W Plano Pkwy 75075 972-398-7560
Amy Myers, dir. Fax 398-7598
Montessori: New Beginnings Academy 200/PK-6
4660 Legacy Dr 75024 972-491-1230
New Hope Christian Academy PK-6
1501 H Ave 75074 972-656-9951
DeeDee Mims, head sch
Prestonwood Christian Academy 1,400/PK-12
6801 W Park Blvd 75093 972-820-5300
Dr. Larry Taylor, head sch Fax 930-4008
Prince of Peace Catholic S 800/PK-8
5100 W Plano Pkwy 75093 972-380-5505
Chad Evans, pres. Fax 380-2570
St. Mark the Evangelist Catholic S 600/K-8
1201 Alma Dr 75075 972-578-0610
Patricia Opon, prin. Fax 423-3299
Spring Creek Academy 200/K-12
6000 Custer Rd 75023 972-517-6730
Erin Thomas, dir. Fax 517-8750
Yorktown Education 100/K-12
5170 Village Creek Dr 75093 972-521-8610

Pleasanton, Atascosa, Pop. 8,878
Pleasanton ISD 3,200/PK-12
831 Stadium Dr 78064 830-569-1200
Matthew Mann, supt. Fax 569-2171
www.pisd.us
Pleasanton ES 500/2-5
831 Stadium Dr 78064 830-569-1340
Erica Bernal, prin. Fax 569-1360
Pleasanton JHS 500/6-8
831 Stadium Dr 78064 830-569-1280
Jennifer Garcia, prin. Fax 569-1290
Pleasanton PS 700/PK-1
831 Stadium Dr 78064 830-569-1325
Kari Vickers, prin. Fax 569-5208

Our Lady of Grace Catholic S PK-5
626 Market St 78064 830-569-8073
Jeannette Geyer, prin. Fax 569-8065

Pollok, Angelina
Central ISD 1,600/PK-12
7622 N US Highway 69 75969 936-853-2216
Dr. Allen Garner, supt. Fax 853-2215
www.centralisd.com
Central ES 600/PK-4
7622 N US Highway 69 75969 936-853-9390
Anita Byrd, prin. Fax 853-9329
Central JHS 500/5-8
7622 N US Highway 69 75969 936-853-2115
Ty Cauthen, prin. Fax 853-2348

Ponder, Denton, Pop. 1,372
Ponder ISD 1,300/PK-12
400 W Bailey St 76259 940-479-8200
Bruce Yeager, supt. Fax 479-8209
www.ponderisd.net
Ponder ES 600/PK-5
400 W Bailey St 76259 940-479-8230
Janell Wilbanks, prin. Fax 479-8239
Ponder JHS 300/6-8
400 W Bailey St 76259 940-479-8220
Ted Heers, prin. Fax 479-8229

Poolville, Parker
Poolville ISD 500/PK-12
PO Box 96 76487 817-594-4452
Jimmie Dobbs, supt. Fax 594-2651
www.poolville.net
Poolville ES 200/PK-5
PO Box 96 76487 817-599-3308
Kathy Pierce, prin. Fax 599-6593
Poolville JHS 100/6-8
PO Box 96 76487 817-594-4539
Matt Scott, prin. Fax 594-0081

Port Aransas, Nueces, Pop. 3,435
Port Aransas ISD 500/PK-12
100 S Station St 78373 361-749-1205
Sharon McKinney, supt. Fax 749-1215
www.paisd.net
Brundrett MS 100/6-8
100 S Station St 78373 361-749-1209
James Garrett, prin. Fax 749-1218
Olsen ES 200/PK-5
100 S Station St 78373 361-749-1212
Gina McKeever, prin. Fax 749-1219

Port Arthur, Jefferson, Pop. 53,210
Port Arthur ISD 8,700/PK-12
PO Box 1388 77641 409-989-6100
Dr. Mark Porterie Ed.D., supt. Fax 989-6229
www.paisd.org
Adams ES 700/PK-5
5701 9th Ave 77642 409-984-4100
Cheryl Tripplett, prin. Fax 983-2528
DeQueen ES 300/3-5
740 DeQueen Blvd 77640 409-984-8900
Jerry Gloston, prin. Fax 982-1843
Dowling ES 300/PK-5
6301 Pat Ave 77640 409-984-4960
Amy Newcomb-Jordan, prin. Fax 736-2406
Houston ES 700/PK-5
3245 36th St 77642 409-984-4800
Marcia Sharp, prin. Fax 985-8701
Jefferson MS 1,100/6-8
2200 Jefferson Dr 77642 409-984-4860
Randy Lupton, prin. Fax 960-6057
Lee ES 800/PK-5
3900 10th St 77642 409-984-8300
Reuben Sampson, prin. Fax 983-1649
Lincoln MS 800/6-8
1023 Abe Lincoln Ave 77640 409-984-8700
LaSonya Baptiste, prin. Fax 982-2847
Travis ES 700/PK-5
1115 Lakeview Ave 77642 409-984-4700
Israel Taylor, prin. Fax 982-8966
Tyrrell ES 700/PK-5
4401 Ferndale Dr 77642 409-984-4660
Dr. Lisa Chambers, prin. Fax 963-2765
Washington ES 200/PK-2
1300 Freeman Ave 77640 409-984-8600
Erica Seastrunk, prin. Fax 982-3569
Wheatley S of Early Childhood Programs 400/PK-PK
1100 Jefferson Dr 77642 409-984-8750
Fredia Reynolds, prin. Fax 985-5487

Port Neches-Groves ISD
Supt. — See Port Neches
Taft ES 500/PK-3
2500 Taft Ave 77642 409-962-2262
Staci Gary, prin. Fax 963-1923

St. Catherine of Siena Catholic S 200/PK-8
3840 Woodrow Dr 77642 409-962-3011
Haldee Todora, prin. Fax 962-5019

Port Bolivar, Galveston
Galveston ISD
Supt. — See Galveston
Crenshaw S 200/PK-8
416 Highway 87 77650 409-684-8526
Tracie Camp, prin. Fax 684-7916

Porter, Montgomery, Pop. 7,000
New Caney ISD
Supt. — See New Caney
Bens Branch ES 800/PK-5
24160 Briar Berry Ln 77365 281-577-8700
Catherine Olano, prin. Fax 354-4296
Crippen ES 800/PK-5
18690 Cumberland Blvd 77365 281-577-8740
Crystal Mayes, prin. Fax 354-6823
New Caney MS 1,000/6-8
22784 Highway 59 77365 281-577-8860
Eric Holton, prin. Fax 354-8725
Porter ES 700/PK-5
22256 Ford Rd 77365 281-577-2920
Sheri Bonsal, prin. Fax 354-7583
Sorters Mill ES 700/PK-5
23300 Sorters Rd 77365 281-577-8780
Hollie Hanks, prin. Fax 354-0164
Valley Ranch ES 600/PK-5
21700 Valley Ranch Crossing 77365 281-577-8760
Nicole Jones, prin. Fax 577-9209
White Oak MS 900/7-8
24161 Briar Berry Ln 77365 281-577-8800
Everett Simons, prin. Fax 354-5186
Woodridge Forest MS 6-8
4540 Woodridge Pkwy 77365 281-577-8800
Bridgette Heine, admin.

Port Isabel, Cameron, Pop. 4,982
Point Isabel ISD 2,600/PK-12
101 Port Rd 78578 956-943-0000
Dr. Lisa Garcia, supt. Fax 943-0014
www.pi-isd.net/
Derry ES 600/2-5
101 Port Rd 78578 956-943-0070
Maribel Valdez, prin. Fax 943-0074
Garriga ES 800/PK-3
101 Port Rd 78578 956-943-0080
Reina Salinas, prin. Fax 943-0640
Port Isabel JHS 600/6-8
101 Port Rd 78578 956-943-0060
Nancy Gonzalez, prin. Fax 943-0055

Portland, San Patricio, Pop. 14,859
Gregory-Portland ISD 4,200/PK-12
608 College St 78374 361-777-1091
Dr. Paul Clore, supt. Fax 777-1093
www.g-pisd.org
Andrews ES 300/PK-5
1100 Lang Rd 78374 361-777-4048
Jana Tarkington, prin. Fax 643-0775
Clark ES 600/PK-5
2250 Memorial Pkwy 78374 361-777-4045
Bobby Rister, prin. Fax 777-4046
East Cliff ES 400/PK-5
1140 E Broadway Blvd 78374 361-777-4255
Alma Munoz, prin. Fax 777-3207
Gregory-Portland IS 300/6-6
4200 Wildcat Dr 78374 361-777-4258
Leticia Villa, prin. Fax 777-4259
Gregory-Portland JHS 700/7-8
4600 Wildcat Dr 78374 361-777-4042
Gabe Alvarado, prin. Fax 643-3187
Other Schools – See Gregory

Port Lavaca, Calhoun, Pop. 12,146
Calhoun County ISD 4,300/PK-12
525 N Commerce St 77979 361-552-9728
Dr. James B. Cowley, supt. Fax 551-2648
www.calcoisd.org
Harrison/Jefferson/Madison ES 800/PK-5
605 N Commerce St 77979 361-552-5253
Tiffany O'Donnell, prin. Fax 551-2628
Jackson/Roosevelt ES 1,000/PK-5
1512 Jackson St 77979 361-552-3317
Sherry Phillips, prin. Fax 551-2691
Travis MS 900/6-8
705 N Nueces St 77979 361-552-3784
Jimmy Sides, prin. Fax 551-2692
Other Schools – See Port O Connor, Seadrift

Our Lady of the Gulf S 100/PK-8
301 S San Antonio St 77979 361-552-6140
Theresa Dent M.Ed., prin. Fax 552-7485

Port Neches, Jefferson, Pop. 12,912
Port Neches-Groves ISD 4,800/PK-12
620 Avenue C 77651 409-722-4244
Dr. Jimmy Creel, supt. Fax 724-7864
www.pngisd.org
Port Neches ES 400/4-5
2101 Llano St 77651 409-722-2262
Amy Gil, prin. Fax 729-7003
Port Neches MS 600/6-8
749 Central Dr 77651 409-722-8115
Kyle Hooper, prin. Fax 727-8342
Ridgewood ES 400/K-3
2820 Merriman St 77651 409-722-7641
Julie Gauthier, prin. Fax 721-9721
Woodcrest ES 400/PK-3
1522 Heisler St 77651 409-724-2309
Fae Sandifer, prin. Fax 729-9480
Other Schools – See Groves, Port Arthur

Port O Connor, Calhoun, Pop. 1,242
Calhoun County ISD
Supt. — See Port Lavaca
Port O Connor ES 100/PK-5
PO Box 687 77982 361-983-2341
Melissa Hoggett, prin. Fax 551-2605

Post, Garza, Pop. 5,351
Post ISD 900/PK-12
501 S Avenue K 79356 806-495-3343
Mike Comeaux, supt. Fax 495-2945
www.postisd.net
Post ES 500/PK-5
211 W 8th St 79356 806-495-3414
Cassie Petty, prin. Fax 495-2381
Post MS 200/6-8
200 W 6th St 79356 806-495-2874
Robert Wilson, prin. Fax 495-2426

Poteet, Atascosa, Pop. 3,241
Poteet ISD 1,800/PK-12
PO Box 138 78065 830-742-3567
Andres Castillo, supt. Fax 742-3332
www.poteet.k12.tx.us
Poteet ES 600/PK-3
PO Box 138 78065 830-742-3503
Donisha Miller, prin. Fax 742-8487
Poteet IS 200/4-5
PO Box 138 78065 830-742-3697
Tina Gillespie, prin. Fax 742-3194
Poteet JHS 400/6-8
PO Box 138 78065 830-742-3571
Shelly Ortiz, prin. Fax 742-8495

Poth, Wilson, Pop. 1,900
Poth ISD 800/PK-12
PO Box 250 78147 830-484-3330
Paula Renken, supt. Fax 484-2961
www.pothisd.us
Poth ES 400/PK-5
PO Box 250 78147 830-484-3321
Laura Kroll, prin. Fax 484-1271
Poth JHS 200/6-8
PO Box 250 78147 830-484-3323
Todd Deaver, prin. Fax 484-3682

Pottsboro, Grayson, Pop. 2,115
Pottsboro ISD 1,200/PK-12
PO Box 555 75076 903-771-0083
Dr. Kevin Matthews, supt. Fax 786-9085
www.pottsboroisd.org
Pottsboro ES 400/PK-4
PO Box 555 75076 903-771-2981
Danielle Curry, prin. Fax 786-4903
Pottsboro MS 300/5-8
PO Box 555 75076 903-771-2982
John Reves, prin. Fax 786-4902

Powderly, Lamar, Pop. 1,159
North Lamar ISD
Supt. — See Paris
Parker ES 200/PK-5
98 County Road 44112 75473 903-732-3066
Kristin Hughes, prin. Fax 669-0139

Prairie Lea, Caldwell
Prairie Lea ISD 200/PK-12
PO Box 9 78661 512-488-2370
Larry Markert, supt. Fax 488-9006
www.plisd.net
Prairie Lea S 200/PK-12
PO Box 9 78661 512-488-2328
Larry Markert, prin. Fax 488-2425

Prairie View, Waller, Pop. 5,483
Waller ISD
Supt. — See Waller
Jones ES 300/PK-5
PO Box 248 77446 936-931-0395
Carol Bates, prin. Fax 857-5050

Premont, Jim Wells, Pop. 2,649
Premont ISD 600/PK-12
PO Box 530 78375 361-348-3915
Steve Vamatre, supt. Fax 348-2882
www.premontisd.net
Premont Early College Academy 300/PK-5
PO Box 1165 78375 361-348-3915
Misty Benavides, prin. Fax 348-5010

Presidio, Presidio, Pop. 4,416
Presidio ISD 1,200/PK-12
PO Box 1401 79845 432-229-3275
Dennis McEntire, supt. Fax 229-4228
www.presidio-isd.net
Franco MS 200/6-8
PO Box 1401 79845 432-229-3113
Yvette DeAnda, prin. Fax 229-4087
Presidio ES 700/PK-5
PO Box 1401 79845 432-229-3200
Glenn Omar, prin. Fax 229-4267

Priddy, Mills
Priddy ISD 100/K-12
PO Box 40 76870 325-966-3323
Adrianne Burden, supt. Fax 966-3380
www.priddyisd.net
Priddy S 100/K-12
PO Box 40 76870 325-966-3323
Adrianne Burden, prin. Fax 966-3380

Princeton, Collin, Pop. 6,693
Princeton ISD 4,100/PK-12
321 Panther Pkwy 75407 469-952-5400
Philip Anthony, supt. Fax 736-3505
www.princetonisd.net
Clark JHS 500/7-8
301 Panther Pkwy 75407 469-952-5400
Casey Gunnels, prin. Fax 736-5903
Godwin ES 700/PK-5
1019 N 6th St 75407 469-952-5400
Marlena Brown, prin. Fax 736-3533
Harper ES 500/PK-5
8080 County Road 398 75407 469-952-5400
Nichole Powell, prin. Fax 736-2621
Huddleston IS 300/6-6
301 N 5th St 75407 469-952-5400
Richard Boring, prin. Fax 736-6162
Lacy ES 600/PK-5
224 E College St 75407 469-952-5400
Elizabeth Goen, prin. Fax 736-6795
Smith ES 400/PK-5
2101 Forest Meadow Dr 75407 469-952-5400
Rachel Nicks, admin. Fax 952-5421

Progreso, Hidalgo, Pop. 5,505
Progreso ISD 2,000/PK-12
PO Box 610 78579 956-565-3002
Martin Cuellar, supt. Fax 565-2128
progreso.schooldesk.net
Progreso East ES, PO Box 610 78579 300/5-6
Yulia Molina, prin. 956-825-7294
Progreso North ES 500/PK-4
PO Box 610 78579 956-514-9502
Idalia Flores, prin. Fax 514-9503
Progreso West ES 600/PK-4
PO Box 610 78579 956-565-1103
Edith Zuniga, prin. Fax 565-6473
Thompson MS 300/7-8
PO Box 610 78579 956-565-6539
Yulia Molina, prin. Fax 565-5412

Prosper, Collin, Pop. 9,238
Prosper ISD 5,600/PK-12
605 E 7th St 75078 469-219-2000
Drew Watkins Ed.D., supt. Fax 346-9247
www.prosper-isd.net
Cockrell ES 800/K-5
1075 Escalante Trl 75078 469-219-2130
Glenda Dophied, prin. Fax 346-2456
Folsom ES 600/K-5
800 Somerville Dr 75078 469-219-2110
Laine Jones, prin. Fax 346-9245
Reynolds MS 900/6-8
700 N Coleman St 75078 469-219-2165
Greg Bradley, prin. Fax 346-2455
Rogers MS 500/6-8
1001 S Coit Rd 75078 469-219-2150
Todd Shirley, prin. Fax 346-9248
Rucker ES 600/K-5
402 S Craig Rd 75078 469-219-2100
Machelle Scogin, prin. Fax 346-9249
Windsong Ranch ES PK-5
800 Copper Canyon Dr 75078 469-219-2220
Kardel Miller, prin. Fax 346-9615
Other Schools – See Celina, Mc Kinney

Quanah, Hardeman, Pop. 2,586
Quanah ISD 500/PK-12
PO Box 150 79252 940-663-2281
Ryan Turner, supt. Fax 663-2875
www.qisd.net
Reagan ES 300/PK-5
PO Box 150 79252 940-663-2171
Lillie Cary, prin. Fax 663-2209

Travis MS 100/6-8
PO Box 150 79252 940-663-2226
Gayle McKinley, prin. Fax 663-6361

Queen City, Cass, Pop. 1,456
Queen City ISD 1,000/PK-12
PO Box 128 75572 903-796-8256
Charlotte Williams, supt. Fax 796-0248
www.qcisd.net
Hileman ES 400/PK-4
PO Box 128 75572 903-796-6304
David Estes, prin. Fax 799-5275
Upchurch MS 300/5-8
PO Box 128 75572 903-796-6412
Steve Holmes, prin. Fax 796-0834

Quemado, Maverick, Pop. 230
Eagle Pass ISD
Supt. — See Eagle Pass
Kirchner ES 100/PK-6
1st and Crockett St 78877 830-758-7045
Veronica Chacon, prin. Fax 758-0328

Quinlan, Hunt, Pop. 1,373
Boles ISD 500/PK-12
9777 FM 2101 75474 903-883-4464
Dr. Graham Sweeney, supt. Fax 883-4531
www.bolesisd.com
Boles ES 200/PK-4
9777 FM 2101 75474 903-883-2161
Shirley Duran, prin. Fax 883-9094
Boles MS 200/5-8
9777 FM 2101 75474 903-883-4464
Gordon Jordan, prin. Fax 883-3097

Quinlan ISD 2,600/PK-12
401 E Richmond 75474 903-356-1200
Dr. Debra Crosby, supt. Fax 356-1201
www.quinlanisd.net
Butler IS 600/3-5
410 Clardy Dr 75474 903-356-1400
Jo Lynn Hughes, prin. Fax 356-0034
Cannon ES 700/PK-2
315 Business Highway 34 75474 903-356-1300
Angela House, prin. Fax 356-3952
Thompson MS 600/6-8
423 Panther Path 75474 903-356-1500
Brian Kinsworthy, prin. Fax 356-2414

Quitman, Wood, Pop. 1,780
Quitman ISD 1,100/PK-12
1201 E Goode St 75783 903-763-5000
Rhonda Turner, supt. Fax 763-2710
www.quitmanisd.net/
Quitman ES 600/PK-5
902 E Goode St 75783 903-763-5000
Mary Nichols, prin. Fax 763-4151
Quitman JHS 200/6-8
1101 E Goode St 75783 903-763-5000
Lance Morrow, prin. Fax 763-5526

Ralls, Crosby, Pop. 1,930
Ralls ISD 500/PK-12
1082 4th St 79357 806-253-2500
Chris Wade, supt. Fax 253-2508
rallsisd.org
Ralls ES 300/PK-5
1082 4th St 79357 806-253-2546
Chelsey Campbell, prin. Fax 253-3112
Ralls MS 100/6-8
1082 4th St 79357 806-253-2549
Jeremy Griffith, prin. Fax 253-4031

Randolph AFB, Bexar, Pop. 1,177
Randolph Field ISD 1,200/PK-12
Building 1225 78148 210-357-2300
Lance Johnson, supt. Fax 357-2469
www.rfisd.net
Randolph ES 600/PK-5
Building 146 78148 210-357-2345
Allana Hemenway, prin. Fax 357-2346
Randolph MS 300/6-8
Building 1225 78148 210-357-2400
Merrie Fox, prin. Fax 357-2475

Ranger, Eastland, Pop. 2,441
Ranger ISD 400/PK-12
1842 E Loop 254 76470 254-647-1187
Mike Thompson, supt. Fax 647-5215
www.ranger.esc14.net
Ranger ES 300/PK-5
1842 E Loop 254 76470 254-647-1138
Michelle Arnold, prin. Fax 647-1895
Ranger MS 6-8
1842 E Loop 254 76470 254-647-3216
Jessie Ellerbe, prin. Fax 647-1895

Rankin, Upton, Pop. 776
Rankin ISD 200/PK-12
PO Box 90 79778 432-693-2461
Sammy Wyatt, supt. Fax 693-2353
www.rankinisd.net
Gossett ES 100/PK-5
PO Box 90 79778 432-693-2455
Brad Riker, prin. Fax 693-2552

Raymondville, Willacy, Pop. 11,257
Raymondville ISD 2,200/PK-12
419 FM 3168 78580 956-689-8176
Stetson Roane, supt. Fax 689-0201
www.raymondvilleisd.org/
Green MS 500/6-8
419 FM 3168 78580 956-689-8171
Raul Valdez, prin. Fax 689-5330
Pittman ES 600/PK-5
419 FM 3168 78580 956-689-8173
Sulema Davila, prin. Fax 689-1141
Smith ES 500/PK-5
419 FM 3168 78580 956-689-8172
Antonio Guerra, prin. Fax 689-5871

Realitos, Duval, Pop. 183
Ramirez Common SD 50/PK-6
10492 School St 78376 361-539-4343
Angela Gonzalez Ed.D., supt. Fax 539-4482
www.ramirezcsd.esc2.net
Ramirez ES 50/PK-6
10492 School St 78376 361-539-4343
Angela Gonzalez, prin. Fax 539-4482

Red Oak, Ellis, Pop. 10,592
Red Oak ISD 5,200/PK-12
PO Box 9000 75154 972-617-2941
Michael Goddard, supt. Fax 617-4333
www.redoakisd.org
Eastridge ES 400/PK-5
PO Box 9000 75154 972-617-2266
Michelle Owen, prin. Fax 617-4417
Red Oak ES 600/PK-5
PO Box 9000 75154 972-617-3523
Megan Corns, prin. Fax 576-3423
Red Oak MS 900/6-8
PO Box 9000 75154 972-617-0066
Cristi Watts, prin. Fax 617-4786
Wooden ES 500/PK-5
PO Box 9000 75154 972-617-2977
Rebecca Vega, prin. Fax 576-8927
Other Schools – See Glenn Heights

Red Rock, Bastrop
Bastrop ISD
Supt. — See Bastrop
Red Rock ES 700/PK-4
2401 FM 20 78662 512-772-7660
Laura Krcmar, prin. Fax 321-2038

Redwater, Bowie, Pop. 1,037
Redwater ISD 1,100/PK-12
PO Box 347 75573 903-671-3481
Kelly Burns, supt. Fax 671-2019
www.redwaterisd.org
Redwater ES 300/PK-3
PO Box 347 75573 903-671-3425
Kasey Coggin, prin. Fax 671-3196
Redwater JHS 200/7-8
PO Box 347 75573 903-671-3227
Kim Cody, prin. Fax 671-9921
Redwater MS 300/4-6
PO Box 347 75573 903-671-3412
Audrey Shumate, prin. Fax 671-2444

Refugio, Refugio, Pop. 2,860
Refugio ISD 700/PK-12
212 W Vance St 78377 361-526-2325
Melissa Gonzales, supt. Fax 526-2326
www.refugioisd.net
Refugio ES 400/PK-6
212 W Vance St 78377 361-526-4844
Twyla Thomas, prin. Fax 526-1053
Refugio JHS, 212 W Vance St 78377 100/7-8
Brandon Duncan, prin. 361-526-2434

Rhome, Wise, Pop. 1,498
Northwest ISD
Supt. — See Justin
Chisholm Trail MS 900/6-8
583 FM 3433 76078 817-215-0600
Matrice Raven, prin. Fax 215-0648
Prairie View ES 400/PK-5
609 FM 3433 76078 817-215-0550
Yolanda Wallace, prin. Fax 215-0598

Rice, Ellis, Pop. 908
Rice ISD 900/PK-12
1302 SW McKinney St 75155 903-326-4287
Lynn Jantzen, supt. Fax 326-4164
www.rice-isd.org
Rice ES 200/PK-2
PO Box 450 75155 903-326-4151
Kelly Walters, prin. Fax 326-4900
Rice IS 400/3-8
1402 SW McKinney St 75155 903-326-4190
Robert Allen, prin. Fax 326-4620

Richards, Grimes
Richards ISD 100/PK-12
9477 Panther Dr 77873 936-851-2364
William Boyce, supt. Fax 851-2210
www.richardsisd.net
Richards ES 100/PK-6
9477 Panther Dr 77873 936-851-2364
William Boyce, prin. Fax 851-2210

Richardson, Dallas, Pop. 96,979
Plano ISD
Supt. — See Plano
Aldridge ES 500/K-5
720 Pleasant Valley Ln 75080 469-752-0000
AntreShawn Buhl, prin. Fax 752-0001
Miller ES 500/K-5
5651 Coventry Dr 75082 469-752-2700
Jennifer Bero, prin. Fax 752-2701
Schell ES 700/K-5
5301 E Renner Rd 75082 469-752-6600
Jeanne Beall, prin. Fax 752-6601
Stinson ES 700/K-5
4201 Greenfield Dr 75082 469-752-3400
Michele Taylor, prin. Fax 752-3401

Richardson ISD 36,100/PK-12
400 S Greenville Ave 75081 469-593-0000
Jeannie Stone Ed.D., supt. Fax 593-0402
www.risd.org
Arapaho Classical Magnet S 500/K-6
1300 Cypress Dr 75080 469-593-6400
Kristin Strickland, prin. Fax 593-6448
Canyon Creek ES 300/K-6
2100 Copper Ridge Dr 75080 469-593-8100
Carol Mixon, prin. Fax 593-8114
Dartmouth ES 300/K-6
417 Dartmouth Ln 75081 469-593-8400
Stacey Marx, prin. Fax 593-8408
Dover ES 600/PK-6
700 Dover Dr 75080 469-593-4200
Brona Hudson, prin. Fax 593-4201
Greenwood Hills ES 400/PK-6
1313 W Shore Dr 75080 469-593-6100
Misti Lehman, prin. Fax 593-6111
Harben ES 400/PK-6
600 S Glenville Dr 75081 469-593-8800
Emily Good, prin. Fax 593-8801
Math/Science/Technology Magnet ES 600/K-6
450 Abrams Rd 75081 469-593-7300
Helena Lopez, prin. Fax 593-7301
Mohawk ES 400/K-6
1500 Mimosa Dr 75080 469-593-6600
Megan Cox, prin. Fax 593-6610
Northrich ES 500/PK-6
1301 Custer Rd 75080 469-593-6200
La'Shon Easter, prin. Fax 593-6201
Prairie Creek ES 300/K-6
2120 E Prairie Creek Dr 75080 469-593-6300
Kyle Stuard, prin. Fax 593-6308
Richardson Heights ES 500/PK-6
101 N Floyd Rd 75080 469-593-4400
Jenny Lanier, prin. Fax 593-4401
Richardson Terrace ES 500/PK-6
300 N Dorothy Dr 75081 469-593-8700
Michelle Zupa, prin. Fax 593-8781
Richland ES 600/PK-6
550 Park Bend Dr 75081 469-593-4650
Jason Tharp, prin. Fax 593-4654
Springridge ES 400/PK-6
1801 E Spring Valley Rd 75081 469-593-8600
Katie Barrett, prin. Fax 593-8603
Twain ES 500/PK-6
1200 Larkspur Dr 75081 469-593-4800
Catherine Kelly, prin. Fax 593-4799
Yale ES 400/K-6
1900 E Collins Blvd 75081 469-593-8300
Suzanne Davis, prin. Fax 593-8362
Other Schools – See Dallas, Garland

Breckinridge Montessori S 200/PK-5
3900 Breckinridge Blvd 75082 972-664-1177
IANT Quranic Academy 200/K-12
840 Abrams Rd 75081 972-231-8451
Br. Matthew Moes, prin.
North Dallas Adventist Academy 200/PK-12
2800 Custer Parkway 75080 972-234-6322
Orton Varona, head sch Fax 234-6325
St. Joseph Catholic S 400/K-8
600 S Jupiter Rd 75081 972-234-4679
Camille Antes, prin. Fax 692-4594
St. Paul the Apostle Catholic S 300/PK-8
720 S Floyd Rd 75080 972-235-3263
Darbie Safford, prin. Fax 690-1542
Salam Academy PK-12
1515 Blake Dr 75081 972-704-4373

Richland Hills, Tarrant, Pop. 7,627
Birdville ISD
Supt. — See Haltom City
Binion ES 800/PK-5
7400 Glenview Dr 76180 817-547-1800
Hilda Hager, prin. Fax 595-5111
Richland ES 300/PK-5
3250 Scruggs Park Dr 76118 817-547-2000
Kerri Sands, prin. Fax 595-5110
Richland MS 600/6-8
7400 Hovenkamp Ave 76118 817-547-4400
Mark McCanlies, prin. Fax 595-5139

St. John the Apostle Catholic S 300/PK-8
7421 Glenview Dr 76180 817-284-2228
Amy Felton, prin. Fax 284-1800

Richland Springs, San Saba, Pop. 332
Richland Springs ISD 100/PK-12
700 W Coyote Trl 76871 325-452-3524
Don Fowler, supt. Fax 452-3230
www.rscoyotes.net
Richland Springs S 100/PK-12
700 W Coyote Trl 76871 325-452-3427
Don Fowler, prin. Fax 452-3580

Richmond, Fort Bend, Pop. 11,601
Fort Bend ISD
Supt. — See Sugar Land
Bowie MS 900/6-8
700 Plantation Dr 77406 281-327-6200
Brian Shillingburg, prin. Fax 327-6201
Crockett MS 800/6-8
19001 Beechnut St, 281-634-6380
Tonya Curtis, prin. Fax 327-6380
Jordan ES 900/K-5
17800 W Oaks Village Dr, 281-634-2800
Lakisha Anthony, prin. Fax 634-2801
Madden ES K-5
17727 Abermore Ln, 281-327-2740
Pamela Brown, prin. Fax 327-2742
Neill ES K-5
3830 Harvest Corner Dr 77406 281-327-3760
Lori Hoeffken, prin. Fax 327-3761
Oakland ES 1,100/K-5
4455 Waterside Estates Dr 77406 281-634-3730
Nancy Hummel, prin. Fax 634-3738
Patterson ES K-5
18702 Beechnut St, 281-327-4260
Kari Bruhn, prin. Fax 327-4261
Pecan Grove ES 600/PK-5
3330 Old South Dr 77406 281-634-4800
Ruth Riha, prin. Fax 634-4814
Seguin ES 700/PK-5
7817 Grand Mission Blvd, 281-634-9850
Fidel Maffuz, prin. Fax 327-7029

Lamar Consolidated ISD
Supt. — See Rosenberg
Adolphus ES 500/K-5
7910 Winston Ranch Pkwy 77406 832-223-4700
Stacy Boarman, prin. Fax 223-4701
Arredondo ES PK-5
6110 August Green Dr 77469 832-223-4800
Amber Barbarow, prin.
Austin ES 600/PK-5
1630 Pitts Rd 77406 832-223-1000
Bud Whileyman, prin. Fax 223-1001
Bentley ES 600/PK-5
9910 FM 359 77406 832-223-4900
Thomas Thompson, prin. Fax 223-4901
Briscoe JHS 1,100/7-8
4300 FM 723 Rd 77406 832-223-4000
Juan Pineda, prin. Fax 223-4001
Frost ES 400/PK-5
3306 Skinner Ln 77406 832-223-1500
Dr. Shannon Hood, prin. Fax 223-1501
Hubenak ES 900/PK-5
11344 Rancho Bella Pkwy 77406 832-223-2900
Diane Parks, prin. Fax 223-2901
Hutchison ES 800/PK-5
3602 Ransom Rd 77469 832-223-1700
Mark Melendez, prin. Fax 223-1701
Long ES 600/PK-5
907 Main St 77469 832-223-1900
Jill Nehls, prin. Fax 223-1901
McNeill ES 800/PK-5
7300 S Mason Rd, 832-223-2800
Toni Scott, prin. Fax 223-2801
Meyer ES 600/PK-5
1930 J Meyer Rd 77469 832-223-2000
Lisa McKey, prin. Fax 223-2001
Pink ES 600/PK-5
1001 Collins Rd 77469 832-223-2100
Chandra Woods, prin. Fax 223-2101
Reading JHS 1,100/7-8
8101 FM 762 Rd 77469 832-223-4400
Juan Nava, prin. Fax 223-4401
Ryon MS 500/6-6
7901 FM 762 Rd 77469 832-223-4500
Heather Patterson, prin. Fax 223-4501
Seguin ECC 400/PK-PK
605 Mabel St 77469 832-223-2200
Mary Ellen Rocha, dir. Fax 223-2201
Smith ES 500/PK-5
2014 Lamar Dr 77469 832-223-2300
Carla Thomas, prin. Fax 223-2301
Thomas ES 900/PK-5
6822 Irby Cobb Blvd 77469 832-223-4600
Vicki Stevenson, prin. Fax 223-4601
Velasquez ES 700/PK-5
402 Macek Rd 77469 832-223-2600
Brian Gibson, prin. Fax 223-2601
Williams ES 700/PK-5
5111 FM 762 Rd 77469 832-223-2700
Henva Bhola, prin. Fax 223-2701

Calvary Episcopal Preparatory 200/PK-12
1201 Austin St 77469 281-342-3161
Malcolm Smith, hdmstr. Fax 232-9449
Montessori House for Children 100/PK-3
20625 Lakemont Bend Ln, 281-239-3400
Westlake Preparatory Lutheran Academy 200/PK-8
23300 Bellaire Blvd 77406 281-341-9910
Judy Gerber, head sch Fax 341-9915

Richwood, Brazoria, Pop. 3,442
Brazosport ISD
Supt. — See Clute
Polk ES 500/PK-4
600 Audubon Woods Dr, Clute TX 77531
979-730-7200
Tara Fulton, prin. Fax 266-2478

Foundation Prep S 50/3-12
2400 Brazosport Blvd N, Clute TX 77531
979-265-1111
Our Lady Queen of Peace S 200/PK-8
1600 Highway 2004, Clute TX 77531 979-265-3909
Marianne Mechura, prin. Fax 265-9780

Riesel, McLennan, Pop. 994
Riesel ISD 600/PK-12
600 E Frederick St 76682 254-896-5000
Brian Garner, supt. Fax 896-2981
www.rieselisd.org
Foster ES 300/PK-6
200 Williams 76682 254-896-5000
Brittni Summers, prin. Fax 896-2981

Rio Grande City, Starr, Pop. 13,814
Rio Grande City ISD 10,900/PK-12
1 S Fort Ringgold St 78582 956-716-6700
Alfredo Garcia, supt. Fax 487-8506
www.rgccisd.org
Alto Bonito ES 600/PK-5
753 N FM 2360 78582 956-487-6295
Yvette Pena, prin. Fax 487-5755
Grulla ES 600/PK-5
443 Old Military Rd 78582 956-487-3306
Liliana Olivarez, prin. Fax 716-8615
Guerra ES 800/PK-5
1600 W Main St 78582 956-716-6982
Laura Barrera, prin. Fax 487-1046
Hinojosa ES 500/PK-5
2448 Embassy St 78582 956-487-3710
Marissa Saldivar, prin. Fax 487-4942
La Union ES 500/PK-5
6300 NE Highway 83 78582 956-487-3404
Garcia Teresa, prin. Fax 487-4076
North Grammar ES 600/PK-5
1400 N Lopez St 78582 956-716-6618
Nora Rivera, prin. Fax 716-8634

Ramirez ES 600/PK-5
8001 Trophy Rd 78582 956-487-4457
Dr. Daniel Ramirez, prin. Fax 487-4415
Ringgold ES 500/PK-5
1 S Fort Ringgold St 78582 956-716-6928
Dr. Idani Salinas, prin. Fax 716-6930
Ringgold MS 800/6-8
1 S Fort Ringgold St 78582 956-716-6849
Jorge Pena, prin. Fax 716-6807
Sanchez ES 800/PK-5
2801 W Eisenhower St 78582 956-487-7095
Adela Rivera, prin. Fax 487-7133
Veterans MS 900/6-8
2700 W Eisenhower St 78582 956-488-0252
Enrique Cantu, prin. Fax 488-0261
Other Schools – See Grulla

Roma ISD
Supt. — See Roma
Barrera MS 700/6-8
258 N FM 649 78582 956-486-2670
Rodrigo Bazan, prin. Fax 486-2607

Immaculate Conception S 200/PK-8
305 N Britton Ave 78582 956-487-2558
Maria Olivarez, prin. Fax 487-6478

Rio Hondo, Cameron, Pop. 2,354
Rio Hondo ISD 2,200/PK-12
215 W Colorado St 78583 956-748-1000
Ismael Garcia, supt. Fax 748-1038
www.riohondoisd.net
Rio Hondo ES 600/PK-2
215 W Colorado St 78583 956-748-1050
Adriana Lippa, prin. Fax 748-1054
Rio Hondo IS 400/3-5
215 W Colorado St 78583 956-748-1100
Mary Leal, prin. Fax 748-1104
Rio Hondo JHS 500/6-8
215 W Colorado St 78583 956-748-1150
Asael Ruvalcaba, prin. Fax 748-1154

Rio Vista, Johnson, Pop. 866
Rio Vista ISD 700/PK-12
PO Box 369 76093 817-373-2009
Tim Wright, supt. Fax 373-2076
www.rvisd.net
Rio Vista ES 300/PK-5
PO Box 369 76093 817-373-2151
Jaylynn Cauthen, prin. Fax 373-3042
Rio Vista MS 200/6-8
PO Box 369 76093 817-373-2009
Brent Batch, prin. Fax 373-3046

Rising Star, Eastland, Pop. 829
Rising Star ISD 200/PK-12
PO Box 37 76471 254-643-1986
Joe Branham, supt. Fax 643-1922
www.risingstarisd.org
Rising Star ES 100/PK-6
PO Box 37 76471 254-643-2431
Barbara Long, prin. Fax 643-1002

River Oaks, Tarrant, Pop. 7,362
Castleberry ISD
Supt. — See Fort Worth
Cato ES 800/PK-5
4501 Barbara Rd 76114 817-252-2400
Charles Rodriguez, prin. Fax 252-2499

Riviera, Kleberg, Pop. 688
Riviera ISD 400/PK-12
203 Seahawk Dr 78379 361-296-3101
Karen Unterbrink, supt. Fax 296-3108
www.rivieraisd.us
Nanny ES 200/PK-6
203 Seahawk Dr 78379 361-296-2446
Tarrah Dobson, prin. Fax 296-3461

Roanoke, Denton, Pop. 5,845
Northwest ISD
Supt. — See Justin
Cox ES 300/K-5
1100 Litsey Rd 76262 817-698-7200
Kim Becan, prin. Fax 698-7270
Hughes ES 500/PK-5
13824 Lost Spurs Rd 76262 817-698-1900
Jessica McDonald, prin. Fax 698-1918
Roanoke ES 600/K-5
1401 Lancelot Dr 76262 817-215-0650
Kristi King, prin. Fax 215-0670
Tidwell MS 1,000/6-8
3937 Haslet Roanoke Rd 76262 817-698-5900
Rhett King, prin. Fax 698-5870

Robert Lee, Coke, Pop. 1,034
Robert Lee ISD 200/PK-12
1323 W Hamilton St 76945 325-453-4555
Dr. Aaron Hood, supt. Fax 453-2326
www.rlisd.net
Robert Lee ES 100/PK-6
1323 W Hamilton St 76945 325-453-4557
Lee McCown, prin. Fax 453-2326

Robinson, McLennan, Pop. 10,380
Robinson ISD 2,300/PK-12
500 W Lyndale Ave 76706 254-662-0194
Dr. Michael Hope, supt. Fax 662-0215
www.risdweb.org
Robinson ES 300/2-3
500 W Lyndale Ave 76706 254-662-5000
Kati Fuqua, prin. Fax 662-3140
Robinson IS 300/4-5
500 W Lyndale Ave 76706 254-662-6113
Sara Laughlin, prin. Fax 662-6183
Robinson JHS 500/6-8
500 W Lyndale Ave 76706 254-662-3843
Shelly Chudej, prin. Fax 662-1845

Robinson PS 400/PK-1
500 W Lyndale Ave 76706 254-662-0251
Missy Zacharias, prin. Fax 662-3361

Robstown, Nueces, Pop. 11,474
Bishop Consolidated ISD
Supt. — See Bishop
Petronila ES 100/PK-5
2391 County Road 67 78380 361-387-2834
Rick Gutierrez, prin. Fax 767-0429

Robstown ISD 2,600/PK-12
801 N 1st St 78380 361-767-6600
Dr. Maria Vidaurri, supt. Fax 387-6311
www.robstownisd.org/
Driscoll ES, 122 E Avenue H 78380 600/PK-3
Manuel Lunoff, prin. 361-767-6641
Lotspeich ES 300/PK-3
1000 Ruben Chavez Rd 78380 361-767-6655
Angelita Lopez, prin. Fax 387-6374
Ortiz IS 200/4-5
208 E Avenue H 78380 361-767-6662
Lorena Ceballos, prin. Fax 767-2651
San Pedro ES 300/PK-3
800 W Avenue D 78380 361-767-6648
Laura Cueva, prin. Fax 767-3043
Seale JHS 500/6-8
401 E Avenue G 78380 361-767-6631
Maribel Trevino, prin. Fax 387-6202

River Hills Christian Academy 50/PK-4
16318 FM 624 78380 361-933-1114
Shayla Floyd, prin. Fax 387-7584
St. Anthony S 100/PK-8
203 Dunne Ave 78380 361-387-3814
Sr. Fe Gamotin, prin. Fax 387-3814

Roby, Fisher, Pop. 640
Roby Consolidated ISD 200/PK-12
PO Box 519 79543 325-776-2222
Heath Dickson, supt. Fax 776-2823
www.robycisd.org
Roby S 200/PK-8
PO Box 519 79543 325-776-2224
Misty McWilliams, prin. Fax 776-3215

Rochelle, McCulloch
Rochelle ISD 200/PK-12
PO Box 167 76872 325-243-5224
Dave Lewis, supt. Fax 243-5283
www.rochelleisd.net
Rochelle S 200/PK-12
PO Box 167 76872 325-243-5224
Matthew Fields, prin. Fax 243-5283

Rockdale, Milam, Pop. 5,537
Rockdale ISD 1,600/PK-12
PO Box 632 76567 512-430-6000
Denise Monzingo, supt. Fax 446-3460
www.rockdaleisd.net
Rockdale ES 400/PK-2
PO Box 632 76567 512-430-6030
Alesha Eoff, prin. Fax 446-5229
Rockdale IS 400/3-5
PO Box 632 76567 512-430-6200
Kathy Pelzel, prin. Fax 446-3682
Rockdale JHS 300/6-8
PO Box 632 76567 512-430-6100
Kelly Blair, prin. Fax 446-2597

Rockport, Aransas, Pop. 8,668
Aransas County ISD 3,200/PK-12
PO Box 907 78381 361-790-2212
Joseph Patek, supt. Fax 790-2299
www.acisd.org
Little Bay PS 300/PK-K
PO Box 907 78381 361-790-2000
Kathy Stephenson, prin. Fax 790-2245
Live Oak 1-3 Learning Center 700/1-3
PO Box 907 78381 361-790-2260
Robin Rice, prin. Fax 790-2207
Rockport-Fulton MS 800/6-8
PO Box 907 78381 361-790-2230
Michael Hannum, prin. Fax 790-2030
Other Schools – See Fulton

Sacred Heart S 100/PK-5
111 N Church St 78382 361-729-2672
Katherine Barnes, prin. Fax 729-9382

Rocksprings, Edwards, Pop. 1,182
Rocksprings ISD 300/PK-12
PO Box 157 78880 830-683-4137
Christopher Yeschke, supt. Fax 683-4141
www.rockspringsisd.net
Rocksprings ES 200/PK-8
PO Box 157 78880 830-683-2140
Callie Hough, prin. Fax 683-4141

Rockwall, Rockwall, Pop. 36,881
Rockwall ISD 14,400/PK-12
1050 Williams St 75087 972-771-0605
Dr. John Villarreal, supt. Fax 771-2637
www.rockwallisd.com
Cain MS 900/7-8
6620 FM 3097 75032 972-772-1170
Derrice Randle, prin. Fax 772-2414
Dobbs ES 500/K-6
101 S Clark St 75087 972-771-5232
Dr. Ruth Johnson, prin. Fax 772-1145
Hartman ES 700/PK-6
1325 Petaluma Dr 75087 972-772-2080
Rebecca Reidling, prin. Fax 772-5794
Hays ES 400/PK-6
1880 Tannerson Dr 75087 469-698-2800
Tammi Schmitt, prin. Fax 698-2809
Jones ES 600/PK-6
2051 Trail Gln 75032 972-772-1070
Teresa Twedell, prin. Fax 772-5789

Pullen ES 600/K-6
6492 FM 3097 75032 972-772-1177
Michael Stuart, prin. Fax 772-2424
Reinhardt ES 500/K-6
615 Highland Dr 75087 972-771-5247
Amanda Payne, prin. Fax 772-2097
Rochell ES 600/PK-6
899 Rochell Ct 75032 972-771-3317
Kelli Crossland, prin. Fax 771-0829
Shannon ES 600/PK-6
3130 Fontana Blvd 75032 469-698-2900
Steven Pesek, prin. Fax 698-2909
Springer ES 600/PK-6
3025 Limestone Hill Ln 75032 972-772-7160
Sara Reeves, prin. Fax 772-2464
Utley MS 700/7-8
1201 T L Townsend Dr 75087 972-771-5281
Dane Steinberger, prin. Fax 772-1164
Williams ES 600/K-6
350 Dalton Rd 75087 972-772-0502
Lisa Gielow, prin. Fax 772-2046
Williams MS 800/7-8
625 E FM 552 75087 972-771-8313
David Blake, prin. Fax 772-2033
Other Schools – See Fate, Heath, Rowlett

Heritage Christian Academy 300/PK-12
1408 S Goliad St 75087 972-772-3003
Dr. Brad Helmer, hdmstr. Fax 772-3770
Providence Academy 100/PK-8
3021 Ridge Rd A22 75032 469-500-3150
Rebecca Hunt, head sch Fax 550-4988

Rogers, Bell, Pop. 1,192
Rogers ISD 900/PK-12
1 Eagle Dr 76569 254-642-3802
Joe Craig, supt. Fax 642-3851
www.rogersisd.org
Rogers ES 400/PK-5
1 Eagle Dr 76569 254-642-3250
Garrett Layne, prin. Fax 642-3145
Rogers MS 200/6-8
1 Eagle Dr 76569 254-642-3011
Lucinda Smith, prin. Fax 642-0033

Roma, Starr, Pop. 9,764
Roma ISD 6,500/PK-12
PO Box 187 78584 956-849-1377
Carlos Guzman, supt. Fax 849-3118
www.romaisd.com/
Barrera ES 700/PK-5
PO Box 187 78584 956-486-2475
Olga Gonzalez, prin. Fax 486-2474
Escobar ES 600/PK-5
PO Box 187 78584 956-849-4800
Edgar Garza, prin. Fax 849-4566
Roma MS 700/6-8
PO Box 187 78584 956-849-1434
Nicolasa Sarabia, prin. Fax 849-1895
Saenz ES 500/PK-5
PO Box 187 78584 956-849-7230
Odette Garcia, prin. Fax 849-7503
Scott ES 500/PK-5
PO Box 187 78584 956-849-1175
Diana Salinas, prin. Fax 849-7274
Vera ES 600/PK-5
PO Box 187 78584 956-849-4552
Yvonne Guerrero, prin. Fax 849-1118
Veterans Memorial ES 500/PK-5
PO Box 187 78584 956-849-1717
Leida Reyes, prin. Fax 849-3854
Other Schools – See Rio Grande City

Ropesville, Hockley, Pop. 433
Ropes ISD 300/PK-12
304 Ranch Rd 79358 806-562-4031
Joel Willmon, supt. Fax 562-4059
www.ropesisd.us
Ropes ES 200/PK-5
304 Ranch Rd 79358 806-562-4031
Dr. Danny McNabb, prin. Fax 562-4059

Roscoe, Nolan, Pop. 1,308
Highland ISD 200/PK-12
6625 FM 608 79545 325-766-3652
Duane Hyde, supt. Fax 766-2281
www.highland.esc14.net/
Highland S 200/PK-12
6625 FM 608 79545 325-766-3652
Karry Owens, supt. Fax 766-3869

Roscoe Collegiate ISD 500/PK-12
PO Box 579 79545 325-766-3629
Dr. Kim Alexander, supt. Fax 766-3138
www.roscoe.esc14.net
Roscoe Collegiate ES 300/PK-5
PO Box 129 79545 325-766-3323
Crystal Althof, prin. Fax 766-3605

Rosebud, Falls, Pop. 1,384
Rosebud-Lott ISD
Supt. — See Lott
Rosebud PS 200/PK-3
512 S 5th St 76570 254-583-7965
Alushka Driska, prin. Fax 583-2642

Rosenberg, Fort Bend, Pop. 30,297
Lamar Consolidated ISD 27,600/PK-12
3911 Avenue I 77471 832-223-0000
Dr. Thomas Randle, supt. Fax 223-0002
www.lcisd.org
Bowie ES 700/PK-5
2304 Bamore Rd 77471 832-223-1200
Belynda Billings, prin. Fax 223-1201
George JHS 1,000/7-8
4601 Airport Ave 77471 832-223-3600
Stephen Judice, prin. Fax 223-3601
Jackson ES 400/PK-5
301 3rd St 77471 832-223-1800
Deana Gonzalez, prin. Fax 223-1801
Lamar JHS 800/7-8
4814 Mustang Ave 77471 832-223-3200
Creighton Jaster, prin. Fax 223-3201
Navarro MS 500/6-6
4700 Avenue N 77471 832-223-3700
Stephanie McElroy, prin. Fax 223-3701
Ray ES 600/PK-5
2611 Avenue N 77471 832-223-2400
Ben Perez, prin. Fax 223-2401
Travis ES 700/PK-5
2700 Avenue K 77471 832-223-2500
Jearine Jordan, prin. Fax 223-2501
Wertheimer MS 500/6-6
4240 FM 723 Rd 77471 832-223-4100
Jennifer Zebold, prin. Fax 223-4101
Wessendorff MS 500/6-6
5201 Mustang Ave 77471 832-223-3300
Sonya Sanzo, prin. Fax 223-3301
Other Schools – See Beasley, Fulshear, Richmond, Sugar Land

Holy Rosary S 200/PK-8
1426 George St 77471 281-342-5813
Linda Bradford, prin. Fax 344-1107
Living Water Christian S 100/PK-12
4808 Airport Ave 77471 281-238-8946
Gamila Frank, admin. Fax 342-9951

Rosharon, Brazoria, Pop. 1,128
Alvin ISD
Supt. — See Alvin
Meridiana ES PK-5
9815 Meridiana Pkwy 77583 281-245-3636
Julie Weiss, prin. Fax 245-3665
Savannah Lakes ES 700/K-5
5151 Savannah Pkwy 77583 281-245-3214
Charles Bagley, prin. Fax 245-3161

Fort Bend ISD
Supt. — See Sugar Land
Heritage Rose ES 500/PK-5
636 Glendale Lakes Dr 77583 281-327-5400
Lavanta Williams, prin. Fax 327-5401

Rotan, Fisher, Pop. 1,488
Rotan ISD 200/PK-12
102 N McKinley Ave 79546 325-735-2332
Greg Decker, supt. Fax 735-2686
www.rotan.org
Rotan ES 200/PK-5
102 N McKinley Ave 79546 325-735-3182
Jody Helms, prin. Fax 735-2686

Round Rock, Williamson, Pop. 97,480
Hutto ISD
Supt. — See Hutto
Veterans Hill ES 400/PK-5
555 Limmer Loop, 512-759-3030
Misty Patureau, prin. Fax 759-5485

Pflugerville ISD
Supt. — See Pflugerville
Caldwell ES 700/PK-5
1718 Picadilly Dr 78664 512-594-6400
Colby Self, prin. Fax 594-6405
Dearing ES PK-5
4301 Gattis School Rd 78664 512-594-4500
Christy Chandler, prin. Fax 594-4505

Round Rock ISD 46,100/PK-12
1311 Round Rock Ave 78681 512-464-5000
Steve Flores Ph.D., supt. Fax 464-5090
www.roundrockisd.org
Berkman ES 500/PK-5
400 W Anderson Ave 78664 512-464-8250
Kathy Cawthron, prin. Fax 464-8315
Blackland Prairie ES 900/PK-5
2005 Via Sonoma Dr, 512-424-8600
Sue Hildebrand, prin. Fax 424-8690
Bluebonnet ES 600/PK-5
1010 Chisholm Valley Dr 78681 512-428-7700
Sharon Wilkes, prin. Fax 428-7790
Brushy Creek ES 800/PK-5
3800 Stonebridge Dr 78681 512-428-3000
Valerie Tidwell, prin. Fax 428-3080
Cactus Ranch ES 1,000/K-5
2901 Goldenoak Cir 78681 512-424-8000
Vicki Crain, prin. Fax 424-8090
Caldwell Heights ES 600/K-5
4010 Eagles Nest St, 512-428-7300
Barbara Bergman, prin. Fax 428-7390
Callison ES 800/K-5
1750 Thompson Trl 78664 512-704-0700
Krista Kuwamura, prin. Fax 704-0790
Chandler Oaks ES 600/K-5
3800 Stone Oak Dr 78681 512-704-0400
Kelley Hirt, prin. Fax 704-0490
Chisholm Trail MS 1,100/6-8
500 Oakridge Dr 78681 512-428-2500
Steven Swain, prin. Fax 428-2629
Deep Wood ES 400/K-5
705 Saint Williams Ave 78681 512-464-4400
Reba Mussey, prin. Fax 464-4494
Double File Trail ES 700/PK-5
2400 Chandler Creek Blvd, 512-428-7400
Abigail Duffy, prin. Fax 428-7490
Fern Bluff ES 700/PK-5
17815 Park Valley Dr 78681 512-428-2100
Dr. Elizabeth Wilson, prin. Fax 428-2160
Forest Creek ES 800/K-5
3505 Forest Creek Dr 78664 512-464-5350
Denise Sharp, prin. Fax 464-5430
Fulkes MS 800/6-8
300 W Anderson Ave 78664 512-428-3100
Laura Ihonvbere, prin. Fax 428-3240
Gattis ES 800/PK-5
2920 Round Rock Ranch Blvd, 512-428-2000
Jennifer Lucas, prin. Fax 428-2065
Great Oaks ES 700/PK-5
16455 S Great Oaks Dr 78681 512-464-6850
Heath Frazer, prin. Fax 464-6930
Hernandez MS 900/6-8
1901 Sunrise Rd 78664 512-424-8800
Nachelle Scott, prin. Fax 424-8940
Herrington ES 700/K-5
2850 Paloma Lake Blvd, 512-704-1900
Julie Nelson, prin. Fax 704-1990
Hopewell MS 900/6-8
1535 Gulf Way, 512-464-5200
Lynda Garinger, prin. Fax 464-5349
Old Town ES 800/PK-5
2200 Chaparral Dr 78681 512-428-7600
Leah Ionnotti, prin. Fax 428-7690
Ridgeview MS 1,400/6-8
2000 Via Sonoma Dr, 512-424-8400
Travis Mutscher, prin. Fax 424-8540
Robertson ES 500/PK-5
1415 Bayland St 78664 512-428-3300
Patricia Ephlin, prin. Fax 428-3370
Teravista ES 800/K-5
4419 Teravista Club Dr, 512-704-0500
Michael Wakefield, prin. Fax 704-0590
Union Hill ES 800/K-5
1511 Gulf Way, 512-424-8700
Kimberly Connelly, prin. Fax 424-8790
Voigt ES 600/PK-5
1201 Cushing Dr 78664 512-428-7500
Cheryl Hester, prin. Fax 428-7590
Walsh MS 1,400/6-8
3850 Walsh Ranch Blvd 78681 512-704-0800
Brenda Agnew, prin. Fax 704-0940
Other Schools – See Austin

Applegate Adventist Academy 50/PK-9
PO Box 729 78680 512-388-7870
Round Rock Christian Academy 500/PK-12
301 N Lake Creek Dr Ste A 78681 512-255-4491
Rebecca Blauser, head sch Fax 255-6043
Round Rock Montessori S 100/PK-3
1818 Sam Bass Rd 78681 512-733-1818

Round Top, Fayette, Pop. 90
Round Top - Carmine ISD
Supt. — See Carmine
Round Top - Carmine ES 200/PK-6
608 N Washington St 78954 979-249-3200
Kate Schoen, prin. Fax 249-4084

Rowena, Runnels
Olfen ISD 100/PK-8
1122 Private Road 2562 76875 325-442-4301
Gabriel Zamora, supt. Fax 442-2133
www.olfenisd.net
Olfen S 100/PK-8
1122 Private Road 2562 76875 325-442-4301
Lizette Paceley, admin. Fax 442-2133

Rowlett, Dallas, Pop. 55,115
Garland ISD
Supt. — See Garland
Back ES 500/PK-5
7300 Bluebonnet Dr 75089 972-475-1884
Teresa McCutcheon, prin. Fax 412-5245
Coyle MS 1,200/6-8
4500 Skyline Dr 75088 972-475-3711
Nikketta Wilson, prin. Fax 412-7222
Dorsey ES 600/PK-5
6200 Dexham Rd 75089 972-463-5595
Leslie Russell, prin. Fax 463-1805
Giddens-Steadham ES 500/K-5
6200 Danridge Rd 75089 972-463-5887
Lakisha Culpepper, prin. Fax 463-7147
Herfurth ES 400/K-5
7500 Miller Rd 75088 972-475-7994
Jessica Hicks, prin. Fax 475-7391
Keeley ES 600/K-5
8700 Liberty Grove Rd 75089 972-412-2140
Sheri Taylor, prin. Fax 412-7061
Liberty Grove ES 600/PK-5
10201 Liberty Grove Rd 75089 972-487-4416
Elisa Wittrock, prin. Fax 227-5348
Pearson ES 700/PK-5
5201 Nita Pearson Dr 75088 972-463-7568
James Howard, prin. Fax 463-7623
Rowlett ES 600/K-5
3315 Carla Dr 75088 972-475-3380
Keith Ellis, prin. Fax 412-4485
Schrade MS 1,200/6-8
6201 Danridge Rd 75089 972-463-8790
Rachael Brown, prin. Fax 463-8793
Stephens ES 500/K-5
3700 Cheyenne Dr 75088 972-463-5790
Jeffrey Waller, prin. Fax 463-5794

Rockwall ISD
Supt. — See Rockwall
Cullins Lake Point ES 800/K-6
5701 Scenic Dr 75088 972-412-3070
Jill Baird, prin. Fax 412-7920

Roxton, Lamar, Pop. 632
Roxton ISD 200/PK-12
PO Box 307 75477 903-346-3213
Kelly R. Pickle, supt. Fax 346-3356
www.roxtonisd.org
Roxton S 200/PK-12
PO Box 307 75477 903-346-3213
Katie Exum, prin. Fax 346-3356

Royse City, Rockwall, Pop. 9,169
Royse City ISD 5,000/PK-12
PO Box 479 75189 972-636-2413
Kevin Worthy, supt. Fax 635-7037
www.rcisd.org
Cherry IS 400/5-6
PO Box 479 75189 972-636-3301
Richard Pense, prin. Fax 635-5008

Davis ES 500/PK-4
PO Box 479 75189 972-636-9549
Cynthia Pense, prin. Fax 635-2535
Fort ES 500/PK-4
PO Box 479 75189 972-636-3304
Danette Dodson, prin. Fax 874-4050
Herndon IS 400/5-6
PO Box 479 75189 469-721-8101
Shanna Brown, prin. Fax 874-2186
Royse City MS 800/7-8
PO Box 479 75189 972-636-9544
Jere Craighead, prin. Fax 635-5093
Scott ES 500/PK-4
PO Box 479 75189 972-636-3300
Don Jacobs, prin. Fax 635-6503
Other Schools – See Fate

Rule, Haskell, Pop. 627
Rule ISD 100/PK-12
1100 Union Ave 79547 940-997-2521
Rick Moeller, supt. Fax 997-2446
www.rule.esc14.net
Rule S 100/PK-12
1100 Union Ave 79547 940-997-2246
Tim Holt, prin. Fax 997-2446

Runge, Karnes, Pop. 1,025
Runge ISD 300/PK-12
PO Box 158 78151 830-239-4315
Dr. Ronny Beard, supt. Fax 239-4816
www.rungeisd.org
Runge ES 200/PK-5
PO Box 158 78151 830-239-4315
Kyle Spivey, prin. Fax 239-4816

Rusk, Cherokee, Pop. 5,468
Rusk ISD 2,200/PK-12
203 E 7th St 75785 903-683-5592
Scott Davis, supt. Fax 683-2104
www.ruskisd.net
Rusk ES 300/2-3
203 E 7th St 75785 903-683-2595
Debbie Welch, prin. Fax 683-6104
Rusk IS 300/4-5
203 E 7th St 75785 903-683-1726
Carlene Clayton, prin. Fax 683-5167
Rusk JHS 500/6-8
203 E 7th St 75785 903-683-2502
John Burkhalter, prin. Fax 683-4363
Rusk PS 500/PK-1
203 E 7th St 75785 903-683-6106
Tammy Hancock, prin. Fax 683-6299

Sabinal, Uvalde, Pop. 1,672
Sabinal ISD 500/PK-12
PO Box 338 78881 830-988-2472
Richard Grill, supt. Fax 988-7151
www.sabinalisd.net
Sabinal ES 200/PK-5
PO Box 667 78881 830-988-2436
Dr. Patrick Peabody, prin. Fax 988-7142
Sabinal JHS 200/6-8
PO Box 338 78881 830-988-2475
Steve Alvarado, prin. Fax 988-7170

Sabine Pass, Jefferson
Sabine Pass ISD 400/PK-12
PO Box 1148 77655 409-971-2321
Kristi Heid, supt. Fax 971-2120
www.sabinepass.net
Sabine Pass S 400/PK-12
PO Box 1148 77655 409-971-2321
Kristi Heid, admin. Fax 971-2120

Sachse, Dallas, Pop. 19,902
Garland ISD
Supt. — See Garland
Armstrong ES 800/PK-5
4750 Ben Davis Rd 75048 972-414-7480
Brandy Schneider, prin. Fax 414-7488
Hudson MS 1,200/6-8
4405 Hudson Park 75048 972-675-3070
Carmen Blakeyh, prin. Fax 675-3077
Sewell ES 500/K-5
4400 Hudson Park 75048 972-675-3050
Kimberly Marsh, prin. Fax 675-3053

Wylie ISD
Supt. — See Wylie
Cox ES 600/K-4
7009 Woodbridge Pkwy 75048 972-429-2500
Krista Wilson, prin. Fax 429-4435
Whitt ES 600/K-4
7520 Woodcreek Way 75048 972-429-2560
Amber Teamann, prin. Fax 941-8564

Sadler, Grayson, Pop. 336
S&S Consolidated ISD 900/PK-12
PO Box 837 76264 903-564-6051
Roger Reed, supt. Fax 564-3492
www.sscisd.net
S&S Consolidated MS 200/6-8
PO Box 837 76264 903-564-7626
Lance Johnson, prin. Fax 564-7857
Other Schools – See Southmayd

Saginaw, Tarrant, Pop. 19,433
Eagle Mountain-Saginaw ISD
Supt. — See Fort Worth
Hafley Development Center 300/PK-PK
616 W McLeroy Blvd 76179 817-232-2071
Carol Renfro, prin. Fax 232-5126
High Country ES 600/K-5
1301 High Country Trl 76131 817-306-8007
Karen Sutton, prin. Fax 306-5852
Saginaw ES 400/K-5
301 W McLeroy Blvd 76179 817-232-0631
Amber Beene, prin. Fax 232-3357
Willow Creek ES 700/K-5
1100 E McLeroy Blvd 76179 817-232-2845
Christal Hollinger, prin. Fax 847-1859

Saint Jo, Montague, Pop. 1,027
Saint Jo ISD 300/PK-12
PO Box L 76265 940-995-2668
Curtis Eldridge, supt. Fax 995-2024
www.saintjoisd.net
Saint Jo ES 200/PK-6
PO Box L 76265 940-995-2668
Denise Thurman, prin. Fax 995-2024

Salado, Bell, Pop. 2,113
Salado ISD 1,500/PK-12
PO Box 98 76571 254-947-5479
Dr. Michael Novotny, supt. Fax 947-5605
www.saladoisd.org
Arnold ES 300/PK-2
PO Box 98 76571 254-947-5191
Katie Mullins, prin. Fax 947-6924
Salado IS 400/3-6
PO Box 98 76571 254-947-1700
Beth Aycock, prin. Fax 947-6954
Salado JHS 200/7-8
PO Box 98 76571 254-947-6935
Marvin Rainwater, prin. Fax 947-6934

Saltillo, Hopkins
Saltillo ISD 300/PK-12
PO Box 269 75478 903-537-2386
David Stickels, supt. Fax 537-2191
www.saltilloisd.net
Saltillo S 300/PK-12
PO Box 269 75478 903-537-2386
David Stickels, admin. Fax 537-2191

San Angelo, Tom Green, Pop. 91,751
Grape Creek ISD 1,100/PK-12
8207 US Highway 87 N 76901 325-658-7823
Angie Smetana, supt. Fax 658-8719
www.grapecreekisd.net/
Grape Creek IS 200/3-5
8207 US Highway 87 N 76901 325-655-1735
Denver Bilyeu, prin. Fax 658-2623
Grape Creek MS 200/6-8
8207 US Highway 87 N 76901 325-655-1735
Tim Jetton, prin. Fax 657-2997
Grape Creek PS 300/PK-2
8207 US Highway 87 N 76901 325-655-1735
Dana Felts, prin. Fax 658-2623

San Angelo ISD 14,600/PK-12
1621 University Ave 76904 325-947-3700
Dr. Carl Dethloff, supt. Fax 947-3771
www.saisd.org
Alta Loma ES 400/PK-5
1700 N Garfield St 76901 325-947-3914
Karen Clark, prin. Fax 947-3952
Austin ES 500/PK-5
700 N Van Buren St 76901 325-659-3636
Blanca Casillas, prin. Fax 657-4089
Belaire ES 400/PK-5
700 Stephen St 76905 325-659-3639
Lindsay Carr, prin. Fax 657-4093
Bonham ES 500/K-5
4630 Southland Blvd 76904 325-947-3917
Heidi Wierzowiecki, prin. Fax 947-3945
Bowie ES 400/K-5
3700 Forest Trl 76904 325-947-3921
Cindy Lee, prin. Fax 947-3947
Bradford ES 500/PK-5
2302 Bradford St 76903 325-659-3645
Berta Carrasco, prin. Fax 659-3692
Crockett ES 300/K-5
2104 Johnson Ave 76904 325-947-3925
Clayton Hubbard, prin. Fax 947-3951
Fannin ES 400/PK-5
1702 Wilson St 76901 325-947-3930
David Danner, prin. Fax 947-3944
Fort Concho ES 500/K-5
310 E Washington Dr 76903 325-659-3654
Lori Barton, prin. Fax 657-4083
Glenmore ES 400/PK-5
323 Penrose St 76903 325-659-3657
Misty Zesch, prin. Fax 657-4086
Glenn MS 1,200/6-8
2201 University Ave 76904 325-947-3841
Michael Kalnbach, prin. Fax 947-3847
Goliad ES 600/K-5
120 E 39th St 76903 325-659-3660
Zachary Ramirez, prin. Fax 657-4097
Holiman ES 400/K-5
1900 Ricks Dr 76905 325-659-3663
Ginger Luther, prin. Fax 659-3696
Lamar ES 500/K-5
3444 School House Dr 76904 325-947-3900
Sharon Lane, prin. Fax 947-3901
Lee MS 1,000/6-8
2500 Sherwood Way 76901 325-947-3871
Rikke Black, prin. Fax 947-3890
Lincoln MS 1,000/6-8
255 Lake View Heroes Dr 76903 325-659-3550
Christy Diego, prin. Fax 659-3559
McGill ES 300/PK-5
201 Millspaugh St 76901 325-947-3934
Dr. John Rueter, prin. Fax 947-3946
Reagan ES 400/PK-5
1600 Volney St 76903 325-659-3666
Brandy Tyner, prin. Fax 657-4096
San Jacinto ES 400/PK-5
800 Spaulding St 76903 325-659-3675
Kimberly Spurgers, prin. Fax 657-4092
Santa Rita ES 300/K-5
615 S Madison St 76901 325-659-3672
Kay Scott, prin. Fax 657-4094

Ambleside S of San Angelo 100/PK-12
511 W Harris Ave 76903 325-659-1654
Angelo Catholic S 100/PK-8
2315 A and M Ave 76904 325-949-1747
Becky Trojcak, prin. Fax 942-1547
Cornerstone Christian S 200/PK-12
1502 N Jefferson St 76901 325-655-3439
Cheryl Mathes, dir. Fax 658-8998
San Angelo Christian Academy 100/PK-12
518 Country Club Rd 76904 325-651-8363
Trinity Lutheran S 200/PK-8
3516 Lutheran Way 76904 325-947-1275
Ron Fritsche, prin. Fax 947-1377

San Antonio, Bexar, Pop. 1,308,790
Alamo Heights ISD 4,800/PK-12
7101 Broadway St 78209 210-824-2483
Dr. Kevin Brown, supt. Fax 822-2221
www.ahisd.net
Alamo Heights JHS 1,100/6-8
7607 N New Braunfels Ave 78209 210-824-3231
Laura Ancira, prin. Fax 832-5825
Cambridge ES 800/1-5
1001 Townsend Ave 78209 210-822-3611
Jana Needham, prin. Fax 832-5840
Howard ECC 400/PK-K
7800 Broadway St 78209 210-832-5900
Susan Peery, prin. Fax 832-5898
Woodridge ES 900/1-5
100 Woodridge Dr 78209 210-826-8021
Gerrie Spellmann, prin. Fax 832-5871

Comal ISD
Supt. — See New Braunfels
Indian Springs ES 700/K-5
25751 Wilderness Oak 78261 830-609-6298
Marisa Wulfsberg, prin. Fax 885-9301
Kinder Ranch ES 600/PK-5
2035 Kinder Pkwy 78260 830-885-8900
Dr. Judy Murray, prin. Fax 885-8901
Specht ES 600/K-5
25815 Overlook Pkwy 78260 830-885-1500
Jackie Sundt, prin. Fax 885-1501
Timberwood Park ES 500/K-5
26715 S Glenrose Rd 78260 830-885-8500
Kim Lyssy, prin. Fax 885-8501

East Central ISD 9,700/PK-12
6634 New Sulphur Springs Rd 78263 210-648-7861
Roland Toscano, supt. Fax 648-0931
www.ecisd.net
East Central Development Center 300/PK-PK
12271 Donop Rd 78223 210-633-3020
Damon Trainer, prin. Fax 633-0323
East Central Heritage MS 1,100/6-8
8004 New Sulphur Springs Rd 78263 210-648-4546
Mary Alice Gomez, prin. Fax 648-3501
Glenn ES 500/K-3
7284 FM 1628 78263 210-649-2021
Darlene Gorhum, prin. Fax 649-1226
Harmony ES 600/K-3
10625 Green Lake St 78223 210-633-0231
Stephanie Orsak, prin. Fax 633-2176
Highland Forest ES 500/K-3
3736 SE Military Dr 78223 210-333-7385
Irma Jean Williams, prin. Fax 333-4069
Legacy MS 1,200/6-8
5903 SE Loop 410 78222 210-648-3118
Nicole Lewis, prin. Fax 648-1068
Oak Crest IS 700/4-5
7806 New Sulphur Springs Rd 78263 210-648-9484
Brenda Law, prin. Fax 648-6967
Pecan Valley ES 500/PK-3
3966 E Southcross Blvd 78222 210-333-1230
Kristin Wurzbach, prin. Fax 359-1352
Salado IS 700/4-5
3602 S WW White Rd 78222 210-648-3310
Teresa Triana, prin. Fax 359-1245
Sinclair ES 600/K-3
6126 Sinclair Rd 78222 210-648-4620
Janice Williams, prin. Fax 648-0422

Edgewood ISD 12,200/PK-12
5358 W Commerce St 78237 210-444-4500
Dr. Emilio Castro, supt. Fax 444-4602
www.eisd.net
Brentwood MS 800/6-8
1626 Thompson Pl 78226 210-444-7675
Eva Reyna, prin. Fax 444-7698
Burleson ECC 200/PK-K
4415 Monterey St 78237 210-444-7725
Fax 444-7748
Cardenas Center 300/PK-PK
3300 Ruiz St 78228 210-444-7826
Claudia Barrios, prin. Fax 444-7848
Cisneros ES 600/K-5
3011 Ruiz St 78228 210-444-7850
Graciela Martinez, prin. Fax 444-7873
Garcia MS 800/6-8
3306 Ruiz St 78228 210-444-8075
Pam Reece, prin. Fax 444-8098
Gardendale ES 500/K-5
1731 Dahlgreen Ave 78237 210-444-8150
Kristin Willman, prin. Fax 444-8173
Gonzalez ES 500/K-5
2803 Castroville Rd 78237 210-444-7800
Mario Goff, prin. Fax 444-7823
Johnson ES 500/K-5
6515 W Commerce St 78227 210-444-8175
Walter Allen, prin. Fax 444-8198
Las Palmas ES 600/K-5
115 Las Palmas Dr 78237 210-444-8050
Monica Munoz, prin. Fax 444-8073
Loma Park ES 800/PK-5
400 Aurora Ave 78228 210-444-8250
Wendy Salazar, prin. Fax 444-8273
Perales ES 600/K-5
1507 Ceralvo St 78237 210-444-8350
Teresa Silva, prin. Fax 444-8373
Roosevelt ES 700/K-5
3823 Fortuna Ct 78237 210-444-8375
Tina Garcia, prin. Fax 444-7798

Stafford ECC 400/PK-K
611 SW 36th St 78237 210-444-7900
Kerry Smith, prin. Fax 444-7923
Stafford ES 600/K-5
415 SW 36th St 78237 210-444-8400
Roger Gonzales, prin. Fax 444-8423
Winston ES 600/K-5
2500 S General McMullen Dr 78226 210-444-8450
Lilly Benavidez, prin. Fax 444-8473
Wrenn MS 800/6-8
627 S Acme Rd 78237 210-444-8475
Nicole Cannon, prin. Fax 444-8498

Fort Sam Houston ISD 1,500/PK-12
4005 Winans Rd 78234 210-368-8701
Dr. Gail Siller, supt. Fax 368-8741
www.fshisd.net
Ft. Sam Houston ES 800/PK-5
4351 Nursery Rd 78234 210-368-8800
Joseph Cerna, prin. Fax 368-8801

Harlandale ISD 15,200/PK-12
102 Genevieve Dr 78214 210-989-4300
Reynaldo Madrigal, supt. Fax 921-4481
www.harlandale.net
Adams ES 800/PK-5
135 E Southcross Blvd 78214 210-989-2800
Leticia Cerda-Rodriguez, prin. Fax 977-1407
Bellaire ES 700/PK-5
142 E Amber St 78221 210-989-2850
Elizabeth Lozano, prin. Fax 977-1421
Bell ES 600/PK-5
906 March Ave 78214 210-989-2900
Taleen Bloom, prin. Fax 977-1438
Collier ES 600/PK-5
834 W Southcross Blvd 78211 210-989-2950
Patricia Garcia, prin. Fax 977-1452
Columbia Heights ES 500/PK-5
1610 Fitch St 78211 210-989-3000
Santos Flores, prin. Fax 977-1466
Fenley Center PK-PK
934 Flanders Ave 78211 210-921-7000
Elizabeth Libby, prin. Fax 977-1481
Gilbert ES 600/PK-5
931 E Southcross Blvd 78214 210-989-3050
H. Martinez-Longoria, prin. Fax 977-1496
Gillette ES 700/PK-5
625 Gillette Blvd 78221 210-989-3100
Lorena Jasso, prin. Fax 921-8356
Harlandale MS 900/6-8
300 W Huff Ave 78214 210-989-2000
Ricardo Marroquin, prin. Fax 977-8764
Kingsborough MS 600/6-8
422 E Ashley Rd 78221 210-989-2200
Sylvia Tovar, prin. Fax 977-9463
Leal MS 800/6-8
743 W Southcross Blvd 78211 210-989-2400
Geraldine Balleza, prin. Fax 977-1459
Morrill ES 500/PK-5
5200 S Flores St 78214 210-989-3150
Tina Mireles, prin. Fax 977-1527
Rayburn ES 500/PK-5
635 Rayburn Dr 78221 210-989-3200
Faith Molina, prin. Fax 977-1541
Schulze ES 800/PK-5
9131 Yett Ave 78221 210-989-3250
Vanessa Trevino, prin. Fax 977-1571
Stonewall Flanders ES 900/PK-5
804 Stonewall St 78211 210-989-3300
Dr. Traci Smith, prin. Fax 977-1481
Vestal ES 500/PK-5
1111 W Vestal Pl 78221 210-989-3350
Marianela Gonzalez, prin. Fax 977-1587
Wells MS 700/6-8
422 W Hutchins Pl 78221 210-989-2600
Jessica Gipprich, prin. Fax 923-5126
Wright ES 500/PK-5
115 E Huff Ave 78214 210-989-3400
Martha Gonzales, prin. Fax 977-1596

Judson ISD
Supt. — See Live Oak
Candlewood ES 600/PK-5
3635 Candleglenn 78244 210-662-1060
Christopher Galloway, prin. Fax 662-9327
Franz ES 400/PK-5
12301 Welcome Dr 78233 210-655-6241
Kelle Lofton, prin. Fax 590-4649
Hartman ES 800/PK-5
7203 Woodlake Pkwy 78218 210-564-1520
Yliana Gonzalez, prin. Fax 590-3096
Hopkins ES 900/PK-5
2440 Ackerman Rd 78219 210-661-1120
Terry Combs, prin. Fax 662-9585
Kirby MS 900/6-8
5441 Seguin Rd 78219 210-661-1140
Jerome Johnson, prin. Fax 662-9275
Metzger MS 900/6-8
7475 Binz Engleman Rd 78244 210-662-2210
Tracey Valree, prin. Fax 662-8390
Park Village ES 600/PK-5
5855 Midcrown Dr 78218 210-653-1822
Gregory Mihleder, prin. Fax 590-4302
Paschall ES 800/PK-5
6351 Lakeview Dr 78244 210-662-2240
Tricia Davila, prin. Fax 666-4129
Rolling Meadows ES 700/PK-5
17222 FM 2252 78266 210-945-5700
Michelle La Rue, prin. Fax 945-6914
Spring Meadows ES 600/K-5
7135 Elm Trail Dr 78244 210-662-1050
Destiny Barrera, prin. Fax 662-9082
Woodlake ES 700/K-5
5501 Lakebend East Dr 78244 210-662-2220
Kristin Saunders, prin. Fax 662-9338
Woodlake Hills MS 900/6-8
6625 Woodlake Pkwy 78244 210-661-1110
Daniel Brooks, prin. Fax 666-0169

Lackland ISD 900/PK-12
2460 Kenly Ave Bldg 8265 78236 210-357-5000
Dr. Burnie L. Roper, supt. Fax 357-5050
www.lacklandisd.net/
Lackland ES 700/K-5
2460 Kenly Ave Bldg 8265 78236 210-357-5053
Teresa Leija, prin. Fax 357-5060

Medina Valley ISD
Supt. — See Castroville
Luckey Ranch ES K-5
12045 Luckey River 78252 830-931-2243
Georgia Neuman, prin.
Potranco ES 700/PK-5
190 County Road 381 S 78253 830-931-2243
Thomas Grajek, prin. Fax 931-9575

North East ISD 67,500/PK-12
8961 Tesoro Dr 78217 210-407-0000
Dr. Brian Gottardy, supt. Fax 804-7017
www.neisd.net
Bradley MS 1,200/6-8
14819 Heimer Rd 78232 210-356-2600
Todd Bloomer, prin. Fax 491-8314
Bulverde Creek ES 900/K-5
3839 Canyon Pkwy 78259 210-407-1000
Michelle McCoy, prin. Fax 491-8333
Bush MS 1,600/6-8
1500 Evans Rd 78258 210-356-2900
Gary Comalander, prin. Fax 491-8471
Camelot ES 500/K-5
7410 Ray Bon Dr 78218 210-407-1400
Wilma Payne, prin. Fax 564-1782
Canyon Ridge ES 600/K-5
20522 Stone Oak Pkwy 78258 210-407-1600
Laura Huggins, prin. Fax 482-2293
Castle Hills ES 500/K-5
200 Lemonwood Dr 78213 210-407-1800
Betsy Asheim, prin. Fax 442-0607
Cibolo Green ES 1,000/PK-5
24315 Bulverde Grn 78261 210-407-1200
Adam Schwab, prin. Fax 438-3540
Clear Spring ES 400/K-5
4311 Clear Spring Dr 78217 210-407-2000
Carlos Hoffman, prin. Fax 407-2009
Coker ES 900/K-5
302 Heimer Rd 78232 210-407-2200
Andrea Hall, prin. Fax 491-8408
Colonial Hills ES 800/K-5
2627 Kerrybrook Ct 78230 210-407-2400
Jenae Mai, prin. Fax 442-0730
Dellview ES 600/PK-5
7235 Dewhurst Rd 78213 210-407-2600
Kelli Nungesser, prin. Fax 442-0781
Driscoll MS 900/6-8
17150 Jones Maltsberger Rd 78247 210-356-3200
John Hill, prin. Fax 491-6467
East Terrell Hills ES 700/PK-5
4415 Bloomdale 78218 210-407-2800
Jennifer Gutierrez, prin. Fax 564-1604
Eisenhower MS 1,200/6-8
8231 Blanco Rd 78216 210-356-3500
John Smith, prin. Fax 442-0537
El Dorado ES 700/K-5
12634 El Sendero St 78233 210-407-3000
Christopher Specia, prin. Fax 650-1458
Encino Park ES 700/PK-5
2550 Encino Rio 78259 210-407-3200
James Miller, prin. Fax 497-6238
Fox Run ES 800/K-5
6111 Fox Creek St 78247 210-407-3400
Kimberly Orihuela, prin. Fax 564-1732
Garner MS 1,000/6-8
4302 Harry Wurzbach Rd 78209 210-805-5100
John Bojescul, prin. Fax 805-5138
Hardy Oak ES 800/PK-5
22900 Hardy Oak Blvd 78258 210-407-3600
Lola Folkes, prin. Fax 481-4004
Harmony Hills ES 700/PK-5
10727 Memory Ln 78216 210-407-3800
Dr. Phillip Bennett, prin. Fax 442-0631
Harris MS 1,400/6-8
5300 Knollcreek 78247 210-356-4100
Jeremi Niehoff, prin. Fax 657-8892
Hidden Forest ES 600/K-5
802 Silver Spruce St 78232 210-407-4000
Cody Miller, prin. Fax 491-8432
Hill MS 6-8
21314 Bulverde Rd 78259 210-356-8000
Charles Reininger, prin. Fax 494-2380
Huebner ES 800/PK-5
16311 Huebner Rd 78248 210-407-4200
Carol Pierce, prin. Fax 408-5529
Jackson-Keller ES 900/K-5
1601 Jackson Keller Rd 78213 210-407-4400
Anna Nicolai, prin. Fax 442-0706
Jackson MS 1,000/6-8
4538 Vance Jackson Rd 78230 210-356-4400
Erin Deason, prin. Fax 442-0580
Krueger MS, 438 Lanark Dr 78218 1,200/6-8
Cynthia Rubio, prin. 210-356-4700
Larkspur ES 900/PK-5
1802 Larkspur 78213 210-407-4600
Edward Balderas, prin. Fax 407-4609
Las Lomas ES 600/PK-5
20303 Hardy Oak Blvd 78258 210-356-7000
Jennifer Lomas, prin. Fax 481-4012
Long's Creek ES 700/K-5
15806 OConnor Rd 78247 210-407-4800
Glenn Forde, prin. Fax 657-8754
Lopez MS 1,500/6-8
23103 Hardy Oak Blvd 78258 210-356-5000
Eric Wernli, prin. Fax 481-4072
Montgomery ES 500/K-5
7047 Montgomery 78239 210-407-5000
Elizabeth Fischer, prin. Fax 564-1758

Nimitz MS 1,000/6-8
5426 Blanco Rd 78216 210-442-0450
Dana Stolhandske, prin. Fax 442-0489
Northern Hills ES 600/PK-5
13901 Higgins Rd 78217 210-407-5200
Randy Barr, prin. Fax 650-1482
Northwood ES 500/K-5
519 Pike Rd 78209 210-407-5400
Catherine Harper, prin. Fax 805-5157
Oak Grove ES 500/PK-5
3250 Nacogdoches Rd 78217 210-407-5600
Harold Massey, prin. Fax 650-1558
Oak Meadow ES 500/PK-5
2800 Hunters Green St 78231 210-407-5800
Lynn Dockery, prin. Fax 408-5512
Olmos ES 700/PK-5
1103 Allena Dr 78213 210-407-6000
Gaila Booth, prin. Fax 442-0654
Redland Oaks ES 500/PK-5
16650 Redland Rd 78247 210-407-6200
Shawn Hayden, prin. Fax 491-8383
Regency Place ES 600/K-5
2635 MacArthur Vw 78217 210-407-6400
Estelia Wallace, prin. Fax 650-1532
Ridgeview ES 700/PK-5
8223 Mccullough Ave 78216 210-407-6600
Veronica Garza, prin. Fax 805-5208
Roan Forest ES 700/PK-5
22710 Roan Park 78259 210-407-6800
Martha Staufert, prin. Fax 481-4053
Royal Ridge ES 700/K-5
5933 Royal Rdg 78239 210-407-7000
Jana Carter, prin. Fax 564-1620
Serna ES 600/PK-5
2569 NE Loop 410 78217 210-407-7200
Joel Luther, prin. Fax 650-1508
Stahl ES 900/PK-5
5222 Stahl Rd 78247 210-407-7400
Emma Yates, prin. Fax 564-1682
STEM Academy Nimitz 6-8
5426 Blanco Rd 78216 210-356-5501
Jennifer Jensen, dir. Fax 442-0476
Steubing Ranch ES 900/K-5
5100 Knollcreek 78247 210-407-7600
Mario Guillen, prin. Fax 650-1248
Stone Oak ES 600/PK-5
21045 Crescent Oaks 78258 210-407-7800
Jana Smith, prin. Fax 497-6204
Tejeda MS 1,500/6-8
2909 E Evans Rd 78259 210-356-5600
David Crowe, prin. Fax 482-2277
Thousand Oaks ES 800/K-5
16080 Henderson Pass 78232 210-407-8000
Jennifer Barton, prin. Fax 491-8358
Tuscany Heights ES 900/PK-5
25001 Wilderness Oak 78260 210-407-8200
Tara Bailey, prin. Fax 438-6330
Vineyard Ranch ES 700/PK-5
16818 Huebner Rd 78258 210-356-7200
Diadra Williams, prin. Fax 408-5515
Walzem ES 600/K-5
4618 Walzem Rd 78218 210-407-8400
John Hinds, prin. Fax 564-1630
West Avenue ES 400/K-5
3915 West Ave 78213 210-407-8600
Victor Saldana, prin. Fax 442-0756
Wetmore ES 700/K-5
3250 Thousand Oaks Dr 78247 210-407-8800
America Gonzalez-Rosas, prin. Fax 481-4037
White MS 900/6-8
7800 Midcrown Dr 78218 210-650-1400
Brent Brummet, prin. Fax 650-1443
Wilderness Oak ES 800/K-5
21019 Wilderness Oak 78258 210-407-9200
Ross McGlothlin, prin. Fax 491-8371
Wilshire ES 400/PK-5
6523 Cascade Pl 78218 210-407-9400
Stacy Deming-Garcia, prin. Fax 805-5181
Windcrest ES 700/K-5
465 Faircrest Dr 78239 210-407-9600
Todd Voges, prin. Fax 564-1657
Wood MS 1,100/6-8
14800 Judson Rd 78233 210-650-1300
Marcus Alvarez, prin. Fax 650-1309
Woodstone ES 900/PK-5
5602 Fountainwood St 78233 210-407-9800
Kelli Halliburton, prin. Fax 564-1708

Northside ISD 100,700/PK-12
5900 Evers Rd 78238 210-397-8500
Dr. Brian Woods, supt. Fax 706-8772
www.nisd.net
Adams Hill ES 500/PK-5
9627 Adams Hill Dr 78245 210-397-1400
Annette Robinson, prin. Fax 678-2937
Allen ES 600/PK-5
101 Dumont Dr 78227 210-397-0800
Erika Zagala, prin. Fax 678-2946
Aue ES 700/K-5
24750 Baywater Stage 78255 210-397-6750
Kathryn Hayes, prin. Fax 698-4422
Behlau ES 700/K-5
2355 Camp Light Way 78245 210-398-1000
Jody Fries, prin. Fax 645-2100
Bernal MS 6-8
14045 Bella Vista Pl 78253 210-398-1900
Glenda Munson, prin. Fax 679-8216
Boldt ES PK-5
310 Hollimon Pkwy 78253 210-398-2000
Debra Pinon, prin. Fax 398-2048
Boone ES 700/PK-5
6614 Spring Time St 78249 210-397-1450
Manuela Haberer, prin. Fax 561-5143
Brauchle ES 600/PK-5
8555 Bowens Crossing St 78250 210-397-1500
Adriana Garza, prin. Fax 706-7463

Braun Station ES 600/PK-5
8631 Tezel Rd 78254 210-397-1550
Jack Funkhouser, prin. Fax 706-7463

Briscoe MS 1,300/6-8
4265 Lone Star Pkwy 78253 210-398-1100
Christina Rather, prin. Fax 674-0220

Burke ES 500/PK-5
10111 Terra Oak 78250 210-397-1300
Misty Knapp, prin. Fax 257-1305

Cable ES 800/PK-5
1706 Pinn Rd 78227 210-397-2850
Rosie Siller, prin. Fax 678-2878

Carnahan ES 600/K-5
6839 Babcock Rd 78249 210-397-5850
Andi Sosa, prin. Fax 561-2050

Carson ES 700/PK-5
8151 Old Tezel Rd 78250 210-397-1100
Lori Shaw, prin. Fax 257-1103

Cody ES 800/PK-5
10403 Dugas Dr 78245 210-397-1650
Kittiya Johnson, prin. Fax 678-2797

Cole ES, 13185 Tillman Ridge 78253 PK-5
Tod Kuenning, prin. 210-398-2100

Colonies North ES 700/PK-5
9915 Northampton Dr 78230 210-397-1700
Kris Cotton, prin. Fax 561-5240

Connally MS 1,100/6-8
8661 Silent Sunrise 78250 210-397-1000
Jaime Liendo, prin. Fax 257-1004

Coon ES 900/PK-5
3110 Timber View Dr 78251 210-397-7250
Mary Lou Mendoza, prin. Fax 706-7288

Driggers ES 600/PK-5
6901 Shadow Mist 78238 210-397-5900
Paul Brusewitz, prin. Fax 257-4993

Ellison ES K-5
7132 Oak Dr 78256 210-398-1850
Carin Adermann, prin. Fax 687-1093

Elrod ES 600/PK-5
8885 Heath Circle Dr 78250 210-397-1800
Mark Garcia, prin. Fax 706-7493

Esparza ES 700/PK-5
5700 Hemphill Dr 78228 210-397-1850
Gabriela Garcia, prin. Fax 431-5843

Evers ES 900/PK-5
1715 Richland Hills Dr 78251 210-397-2550
Talia Hernandez, prin. Fax 706-7564

Fernandez ES 600/PK-5
6845 Ridgebrook St 78250 210-397-1900
Chaisleigh Southworth, prin. Fax 706-7376

Fields ES, 9570 FM 1560 N 78254 PK-5
Daeon Harris, prin. 210-398-2150

Fisher ES 800/K-5
3430 Barrel Pass 78245 210-397-4450
Jeffrey Davenport, prin. Fax 645-3911

Folks MS 600/6-8
9855 Swayback Rnch 78254 210-398-1600
Shawn McKenzie, prin. Fax 257-3060

Forester ES 900/K-5
10726 Rousseau St 78245 210-397-0200
Kelly Mantle, prin. Fax 257-1030

Franklin ES 500/PK-5
9180 Silver Spot 78254 210-398-1700
Brenda Gallardo, prin. Fax 257-3013

Galm ES 700/PK-5
1454 Saxonhill Dr 78253 210-397-1150
Jill Holmes, prin. Fax 678-2863

Garcia MS 1,500/6-8
14900 Kyle Seale Pkwy 78255 210-397-8400
Tracy Wernli, prin. Fax 695-3830

Glass ES 600/PK-5
519 Clearview Dr 78228 210-397-1950
Amber Gonzales, prin. Fax 431-5817

Glenn ES 700/PK-5
2385 Horal St 78227 210-397-2250
Kristine Bolstad, prin. Fax 678-2891

Glenoaks ES 600/PK-5
5103 Newcome Dr 78229 210-397-2300
Maria Elena Meza, prin. Fax 617-5452

Hatchett ES 800/PK-5
10700 Ingram Rd 78245 210-397-6850
Adam Bock, prin. Fax 645-5222

Henderson ES 600/PK-5
14605 Kallison Bnd 78254 210-398-1050
Thomas Mackey, prin. Fax 256-0985

Hobby MS 1,000/6-8
11843 Vance Jackson Rd 78230 210-397-6300
Lawrence Carranco, prin. Fax 690-6332

Hoffman ES 700/K-5
12118 Voluntoor Pkwy 78253 210-397-8350
Carrie Squyres, prin. Fax 645-3305

Howsman ES 700/PK-5
11431 Vance Jackson Rd 78230 210-397-2350
Thomas Buente, prin. Fax 561-5047

Hull ES 700/PK-5
7320 Remuda Dr 78227 210-397-0950
Patricia Noriega, prin. Fax 678-2917

Jefferson MS 1,500/6-8
10900 Shaenfield Rd 78254 210-397-3700
Kevin Kearns, prin. Fax 257 4988

Jones MS 1,200/6-8
1256 Pinn Rd 78227 210-397-2100
Michella Wheat, prin. Fax 678-2113

Jordan MS 1,400/6-8
1725 Richland Hills Dr 78251 210-397-6150
Anabel Romero, prin. Fax 523-4876

Kallison ES K-5
8610 Ranch View E 78254 210-398-2350
William Navin, prin.

Knowlton ES 700/PK-5
9500 Timber Path 78250 210-397-2600
Dr. Maricela Alarcon, prin. Fax 706-7534

Krueger ES 1,000/K-5
9900 Wildhorse Pkwy 78254 210-397-3850
LaNeil Belko, prin. Fax 257-1130

Langley ES 600/K-5
14185 Bella Vista Pl 78253 210-397-0150
Leticia Ramirez, prin. Fax 645-3325

Leon Springs ES 600/K-5
23881 W Interstate 10 78257 210-397-4400
Griselda Espinoza, prin. Fax 698-4407

Leon Valley ES 700/PK-5
7111 Huebner Rd 78240 210-397-4650
Rebecca Barron-Flores, prin. Fax 706-7391

Lewis ES 700/K-5
1000 Seascape 78251 210-397-2650
Angela Fry, prin. Fax 257-3004

Lieck ES 600/K-5
12600 Reid Ranch Rd 78245 210-398-1450
Rachel Delgado, prin. Fax 678-2108

Linton ES 600/PK-5
2103 Oakhill Rd 78238 210-397-0750
Juan Perez, prin. Fax 706-7186

Locke Hill ES 600/K-5
5050 De Zavala Rd 78249 210-397-1600
Danielle Frei, prin. Fax 561-5062

Luna MS 1,200/6-8
200 Grosenbacher Rd N 78253 210-397-5300
Lisa Richard, prin. Fax 645-5246

Martin ES 800/PK-5
730 Canterbury 78228 210-398-1400
Evelyn Cobarruvias, prin. Fax 431-5810

May ES 700/PK-5
15707 Chase Hill Blvd 78256 210-397-2000
Geraldina Benitez, prin. Fax 561-2024

McDermott ES 700/PK-5
5111 Usaa Blvd 78240 210-397-5100
Belinda Trevino, prin. Fax 561-5118

Mead ES 800/K-5
3803 Midhorizon Dr 78229 210-397-1750
Annette Lopez, prin. Fax 366-0770

Meadow Village ES 700/PK-5
1406 Meadow Way Dr 78227 210-397-0650
Jennifer Escamilla, prin. Fax 678-2846

Michael ES 800/PK-5
3155 Quiet Plain Dr 78245 210-397-3900
Melissa Lopez-Brouse, prin. Fax 645-3905

Mireles ES 800/K-5
12260 Rockwall Ml 78253 210-398-1500
Norma Farrell, prin. Fax 257-3044

Murnin ES 800/K-5
9019 Dugas Dr 78251 210-397-4550
Amber Freeman, prin. Fax 257-4335

Myers ES 700/PK-5
3031 Village Pkwy 78251 210-397-6650
Tesilia Garza, prin. Fax 706-6674

Neff MS 1,200/6-8
5227 Evers Rd 78238 210-397-4100
Yvonne Correa, prin. Fax 523-4566

Nichols ES 500/K-5
9560 Braun Rd 78254 210-397-4050
Sonya Kirkham, prin. Fax 767-5951

Northwest Crossing ES 600/PK-5
10255 Dover Rdg 78250 210-397-0600
Paul Moreno, prin. Fax 706-7546

Oak Hills Terrace ES 600/K-5
5710 Cary Grant Dr 78240 210-397-0550
Kendra Merrell, prin. Fax 706-7348

Ott ES 800/PK-5
100 Grosenbacher Rd N 78253 210-397-5550
Madeline Bueno, prin. Fax 645-5235

Passmore ES 600/PK-5
570 Pinn Rd 78227 210-397-0500
Dr. Veronica Arteaga, prin. Fax 678-2808

Pease MS 1,200/6-8
201 Hunt Ln 78245 210-397-2950
Katherine Lyssy, prin. Fax 678-2974

Powell ES 500/PK-5
6003 Thunder Dr 78238 210-397-0450
Priscilla Paul, prin. Fax 706-7361

Raba ES 800/PK-5
9740 Raba Dr 78251 210-397-1350
Victor Raga, prin. Fax 257-1335

Rawlinson MS 1,200/6-8
14100 Vance Jackson Rd 78249 210-397-4900
Mark Rustan, prin. Fax 767-4055

Rayburn MS 1,000/6-8
1400 Cedarhurst Dr 78227 210-397-2150
Dr. Scott McKenzie, prin. Fax 678-2181

Rhodes ES 600/K-5
5714 N Knoll 78240 210-397-4000
Vicki Kilpatrick, prin. Fax 697-4020

Ross MS 1,100/6-8
3630 Callaghan Rd 78228 210-397-6350
Faustino Ortega, prin. Fax 431-6383

Rudder MS 1,000/6-8
6558 Horn Blvd 78240 210-397-5000
Dr. Mary Jewell, prin. Fax 561-5022

Scarborough ES 700/PK-5
12280 Silver Pointe 78254 210-397-8000
Mirella Campbell, prin. Fax 257-1019

Scobee ES 600/PK-5
11223 Cedar Park 78249 210-397-0700
Ron Tatsch, prin. Fax 561-5076

Steubing ES 500/PK-5
11655 Braefield 78249 210-397-4350
Dr. Mary Usrey, prin. Fax 706-4374

Stevenson MS 1,400/6-8
8403 Tezel Rd 78254 210-397-7300
Chuck Baldridge, prin. Fax 706-7336

Stinson MS 1,200/6-8
13200 Skyhawk Dr 78249 210-397-3600
Lourdes Medina, prin. Fax 561-3609

Thornton ES 700/PK-5
6450 Pembroke Rd 78240 210-397-3950
Justin Bledsoe, prin. Fax 561-5128

Timberwilde ES 800/PK-5
8838 Timberwilde St 78250 210-397-0400
Wendy Tiemann, prin. Fax 706-7478

Valo MS 1,400/6-8
2120 N Ellison Dr 78251 210-397-5700
Dana Gilbert-Perry, prin. Fax 257 1000

Valley Hi ES 400/PK-5
8503 Ray Ellison Blvd 78227 210-397-0350
Andrew Morris, prin. Fax 678-2928

Villarreal ES 800/PK-5
2902 White Tail Dr 78228 210-397-5800
April Mata-Tausch, prin. Fax 431-5809

Wanke ES 800/K-5
10419 Old Prue Rd 78249 210-397-6700
Claudia Lizcano, prin. Fax 257-4340

Ward ES 900/K-5
8400 Cavern Hl 78254 210-397-6800
Sunday Nelson, prin. Fax 257-1195

Westwood Terrace ES 700/PK-5
2315 Hackamore Ln 78227 210-397-0300
Tom Knapp, prin. Fax 678-2786

Zachry MS 1,000/6-8
9410 Timber Path 78250 210-397-7400
Susan Allain, prin. Fax 706-7432

Other Schools – See Boerne, Helotes, Shavano Park

San Antonio ISD 49,900/PK-12
141 Lavaca St 78210 210-554-2200
Pedro Martinez, supt.
www.saisd.net

Advanced Learning Academy PK-3
621 W Euclid Ave 78212 210-738-9760
Kathy Bieser, prin. Fax 224-8792

Arnold ES 600/PK-5
467 Freiling 78213 210-438-6530
Belinda Hernandez, prin. Fax 732-5192

Ball ES 500/PK-5
343 Koehler Ct 78223 210-438-6845
Gregory Rivers, prin. Fax 533-1215

Baskin ES 500/PK-6
630 Crestview Dr 78201 210-438-6535
Valarie Garcia, prin. Fax 735-5962

Beacon Hill ES 500/PK-5
1411 W Ashby Pl 78201 210-738-9765
Laryn Nelson, prin. Fax 735-6683

Bowden ES 500/PK-5
515 Willow 78202 210-738-9770
Anita O'Neal, prin. Fax 226-8150

Brackenridge ES 700/PK-8
1214 Guadalupe St 78207 210-978-7950
Marco Morales, prin. Fax 224-4933

Cameron ES 400/PK-5
3635 Belgium Ln 78219 210-978-7960
Monica Guillory, prin. Fax 224-2954

Carroll ECC 300/PK-PK
463 Holmgreen Rd 78220 210-978-7965
Dr. Alejandra Barraza, dir. Fax 333-1133

Carvajal ECC 400/PK-PK
225 Arizona 78207 210-978-7970
Sonya Cardenas, dir. Fax 432-7828

Collins Garden ES 600/PK-5
167 Harriman Pl 78204 210-228-3310
Cynthia De La Garza, prin. Fax 226-9958

Cotton ES 200/PK-5
1616 Blanco Rd 78212 210-738-9780
Sonia Morales, prin. Fax 733-0830

Crockett ES 1,000/PK-5
2215 Morales St 78207 210-738-9785
Anna Garcia, prin. Fax 434-6476

Davis MS 600/6-8
4702 E Houston St 78220 210-978-7920
Rashad Ray, prin. Fax 662-8189

De Zavala ES 600/PK-5
2311 San Luis St 78207 210-978-7975
Donna Venable Finch, prin. Fax 226-8627

Douglass ES 400/PK-6
318 Martin Luther King Dr 78203 210-228-3315
Dr. Stephanie Ratliff, prin. Fax 532-1618

Fenwick ES 400/PK-5
1930 Waverly Ave 78228 210-438-6540
Dr. Tambrey Ozuna, prin. Fax 732-4693

Forbes ES 400/PK-5
2630 Sally Gay Dr 78223 210-438-6850
Erica Lopez, prin. Fax 534-2695

Foster ES 600/PK-5
6718 Pecan Valley Dr 78223 210-438-6855
Sandra Sandoval, prin. Fax 333-1873

Franklin ES 500/PK-5
1915 W Olmos Dr 78201 210-738-9790
Graciela Luna-Buster, prin. Fax 733-8479

Gates ES 300/PK-5
510 Morningview Dr 78220 210-978-7980
Sonya Mora, prin. Fax 333-3644

Gonzales ECC PK-PK
518 E Magnolia Ave 78212 210-438-6830
Lisa Garcia, prin. Fax 228-3138

Graebner ES 800/PK-5
530 Hoover Ave 78225 210-228-3320
Noemi Saldivar, prin. Fax 923-0626

Green ES 200/PK-5
122 W Whittier St 78210 210-228-3325
Jeanette Vasquez, prin. Fax 534-6865

Herff ES 300/PK-2
996 S Hackberry 78210 210-228-3330
Elida Navarro, prin. Fax 533-9500

Highland Hills ES 700/PK-5
734 Glamis Ave 78223 210-438-6860
Deborah Esparza, prin. Fax 534-6484

Hillcrest ES 600/PK-5
211 W Malone Ave 78214 210-228-3340
Jennifer Sanchez, prin. Fax 534-0691

Hirsch ES 500/PK-5
4826 Seabreeze Dr 78220 210-978-7985
Mary Rodriguez, prin. Fax 648-1925

Huppertz ES 400/PK-5
247 Bangor Dr 78228 210-438-6580
Ronnie Cantu, prin. Fax 433-4984

Japhet ES 500/PK-5
314 Astor St 78210 210-228-3345
Natasha Gould, prin. Fax 534-1665

Kelly ES 300/PK-5
1026 Thompson Pl 78226 210-228-3350
Cynthia Rocha, prin. Fax 223-9065

King ES 400/PK-5
1001 Ceralvo St 78207 210-978-7990
Dr. Gloria Martinez, prin. Fax 433-6477

Knox ECC 400/PK-PK
302 Tipton Ave 78204 210-228-3365
David Chavarria, dir. Fax 533-5539
Lamar ES 200/PK-5
201 Parland Pl 78209 210-738-9800
Brian Sparks, prin. Fax 822-7874
Longfellow MS 1,000/6-8
1130 E Sunshine Dr 78228 210-438-6520
Dr. Aurora Terry, prin. Fax 433-0375
Madison ES 600/PK-5
2900 W Woodlawn Ave 78228 210-438-6545
Lianna Cano, prin. Fax 736-3356
Margil ES 500/PK-5
1000 Perez St 78207 210-738-9805
Cynthia Perez-Gomez, prin. Fax 223-4984
Maverick ES 700/PK-5
107 Raleigh Pl 78201 210-438-6550
Leila Garza, prin. Fax 735-2444
Miller ES 400/PK-5
207 Lincolnshire Dr 78220 210-978-7995
Dr. Christine Weiland, prin. Fax 333-0563
Mission Academy 700/PK-8
9210 S Presa St 78223 210-438-6880
Noemi Davilla, prin. Fax 633-9427
Neal ES 700/PK-5
3407 Capitol Ave 78201 210-738-9810
Valerie Henry, prin. Fax 735-0839
Nelson ECC PK-PK
1014 Waverly Ave 78201 210-438-6555
Marisa Mendez, prin. Fax 228-3057
Ogden ES 300/PK-5
2215 Leal St 78207 210-738-9815
Ixchell Gonzalez, prin. Fax 432-0755
Page MS 400/6-8
401 Berkshire Ave 78210 210-228-1230
Stephanie Mihleder, prin. Fax 533-7369
Pershing ES 400/PK-5
600 Sandmeyer St 78208 210-738-9820
Casey Calland, prin. Fax 226-4656
Poe MS 700/6-8
814 Aransas Ave 78210 210-228-1235
Krista Hays, prin. Fax 534-7299
Rodriguez ES 400/PK-5
3626 W Cesar E Chavez Blvd 78207 210-978-8000
Beth Brady, prin. Fax 433-6846
Rogers ES 700/PK-5
620 McIlvaine 78212 210-738-9825
Cynthia Carielo, prin. Fax 734-4026
Rogers MS 600/6-8
314 Galway St 78223 210-438-6840
Julie May, prin. Fax 333-7954
Schenck ES 700/PK-5
101 Kate Schenck Ave 78223 210-438-6865
Michelle Hickman, prin. Fax 333-0680
Smith ES 500/PK-5
823 S Gevers St 78203 210-228-3360
Vanessa Fox Norton, prin. Fax 533-1066
Stewart ES 500/PK-5
1950 Rigsby Ave 78210 210-438-6875
Kathleen St. Clair, prin. Fax 333-2597
Tafolla MS 800/6-8
1303 W Cesar E Chavez Blvd 78207 210-978-7930
Jeff Price, prin. Fax 227-7044
Twain Dual Language Academy 400/PK-2
2411 San Pedro Ave 78212 210-738-9745
David Garcia, prin. Fax 738-0518
Tynan ECC 300/PK-PK
925 Gulf 78202 210-738-9835
Gregorio Velazquez, dir. Fax 226-5799
Washington ES 500/PK-5
1823 Nolan 78202 210-738-9840
Phyllis Foley-Davis, prin. Fax 226-6589
Wilson ES 500/PK-5
1421 Clower 78201 210-738-9845
Yvonne Martinez, prin. Fax 733-8756
Woodlawn Academy 500/K-8
1717 W Magnolia Ave 78201 210-438-6560
Dorene Benavides, prin. Fax 732-2037
Woodlawn Hills ES 600/PK-5
110 W Quill Dr 78228 210-438-6565
Francisca Whitaker, prin. Fax 432-5341
Young Mens Leadership Academy 4-8
415 Gabriel St 78202 210-354-9652
Derrick Brown, prin. Fax 228-3070

South San Antonio ISD 9,900/PK-12
5622 Ray Ellison Blvd 78242 210-977-7000
Dr. Abelardo Saavedra, supt. Fax 977-7021
www.southsanisd.net
Armstrong ES 500/PK-5
7111 Apple Valley Dr 78242 210-623-8787
Nichole Speer, prin. Fax 623-8792
Athens ES 400/PK-5
2707 W Gerald Ave 78211 210-977-7475
Sandra Sandoval, prin. Fax 921-1194
Benavidez ES 600/PK-5
8340 Interstate 35 S 78224 210-977-7175
Johnny Diaz, prin. Fax 977-7184
Carrillo ES 500/PK-5
500 Price Ave 78211 210-977-7550
Valerie Garcia, prin. Fax 977-7558
Dwight MS 500/6-8
2454 W Southcross Blvd 78211 210-977-7300
Yvonne Hernandez, prin. Fax 977-7316
Five Palms ES 400/PK-5
7138 Five Palms Dr 78242 210-645-3850
Greg Martinez, prin. Fax 645-3853
Hutchins ES 600/PK-5
1919 W Hutchins Pl 78224 210-977-7200
Elizabeth Martinez, prin. Fax 977-7211
Kazen MS 500/6-8
1520 Gillette Blvd 78224 210-977-7150
Joseph Carranza, prin. Fax 977-7155
Kindred ES 500/PK-5
7811 Kindred St 78224 210-977-7575
Marisa Mendez, prin. Fax 977-7586

Madla ES 700/PK-5
6100 Royalgate Dr 78242 210-645-3800
Jo Ann Buchanan, prin. Fax 645-3807
Palo Alto ES 600/PK-5
1725 Palo Alto Rd 78211 210-977-7125
Judith Benavidez, prin. Fax 977-7132
Price ES 400/PK-5
245 Price Ave 78211 210-977-7225
Florinda Castillo, prin. Fax 977-7236
Shepard MS 600/6-8
5558 Ray Ellison Blvd 78242 210-623-1875
Chriselda Bazaldua, prin. Fax 623-1894
Zamora MS 600/6-8
8638 Larkia St 78224 210-977-7278
Rosanna Carmona-Mercado, prin. Fax 977-7285

Southside ISD 5,100/PK-12
1460 Martinez Losoya Rd 78221 210-882-1600
Mark E. Eads, supt. Fax 626-0101
www.southsideisd.org/
Freedom ES 600/PK-4
1460 Martinez Losoya Rd 78221 210-882-1603
Thomasina Montana, prin. Fax 626-9866
Gallardo ES 600/PK-4
1460 Martinez Losoya Rd 78221 210-882-1609
Karen Feldman, prin. Fax 626-2161
Heritage ES 600/PK-4
1460 Martinez Losoya Rd 78221 210-882-1607
Elise Puente, prin. Fax 626-9788
Losoya IS 800/5-6
1460 Martinez Losoya Rd 78221 210-882-1602
Manuel Ornelas, prin. Fax 626-0116
Matthey MS 800/7-8
1460 Martinez Losoya Rd 78221 210-882-1601
Miguel Martell, prin. Fax 626-0113
Pearce PS 500/PK-4
1460 Martinez Losoya Rd 78221 210-882-1605
Brenda Gonzales, prin. Fax 626-0117

Southwest ISD 13,000/PK-12
11914 Dragon Ln 78252 210-622-4300
Dr. Lloyd Verstuyft, supt. Fax 622-4301
www.swisd.net/
Big Country ES 700/K-5
11914 Dragon Ln 78252 210-645-7560
Wendy Quillin, prin. Fax 645-7561
Hidden Cove ES 600/PK-5
11914 Dragon Ln 78252 210-623-6220
Roxie Freeman, prin. Fax 623-6219
Hope ES 400/K-5
11914 Dragon Ln 78252 210-927-8180
Brian Pennartz, prin. Fax 927-8181
Indian Creek ES 600/K-5
11914 Dragon Ln 78252 210-623-6520
Julie Verstuyft, prin. Fax 623-6521
Kriewald Road ES 600/PK-5
11914 Dragon Ln 78252 210-645-7550
Rosie Hidalgo, prin. Fax 645-7551
McAuliffe MS 1,000/6-8
11914 Dragon Ln 78252 210-623-6260
Joseph Guidry, prin. Fax 623-6261
Medio Creek ES 500/K-5
11914 Dragon Ln 78252 210-622-4950
Gasper DeLeon, prin. Fax 622-4951
Scobee MS 1,000/6-8
11914 Dragon Ln 78252 210-645-7500
Darin Kasper, prin. Fax 645-7501
Sky Harbour ES 600/K-5
11914 Dragon Ln 78252 210-623-6580
Sylvia Acuna, prin. Fax 623-6584
Southwest ES 700/PK-5
11914 Dragon Ln 78252 210-622-4420
Judy Foster, prin. Fax 622-4421
Spicewood Park ES 500/K-5
11914 Dragon Ln 78252 210-622-4999
Krista Nail, prin. Fax 622-4131
Sun Valley ES 600/K-5
11914 Dragon Ln 78252 210-645-7570
Veronica Cuenca-Wilson, prin. Fax 645-7571
Other Schools – See Atascosa, Von Ormy

Atonement Academy 600/PK-12
15415 Red Robin Rd 78255 210-695-2240
John Markovetz, hdmstr. Fax 695-9679
Blessed Sacrament Catholic S 300/PK-8
600 Oblate Dr 78216 210-824-3381
Michael Fierro, prin. Fax 826-6146
Buckner Fanning Christian S 200/PK-9
975 Mission Spgs 78258 210-721-4700
Child Montessori S 100/PK-5
2829 Hunters Green St 78231 210-493-6550
Jean Stein, head sch Fax 493-6550
Christian S at Castle Hills 400/PK-12
2216 NW Military Hwy 78213 210-878-1000
Michael Pinkston, supt. Fax 878-1099
Concordia Lutheran S 500/PK-8
16801 Huebner Rd 78258 210-479-1477
Sally McBee, prin. Fax 479-9416
Cornerstone Christian S 700/PK-12
17702 NW Military Hwy 78257 210-979-6161
Dr. Jerry Eshleman, supt.
Holy Name Catholic S 200/PK-8
3814 Nash Blvd 78223 210-333-7356
Jennifer Tiller, prin. Fax 333-7642
Holy Spirit Catholic S 400/PK-8
770 W Ramsey Rd 78216 210-349-1169
Margaret Webb, prin. Fax 349-1247
Islamic Academy of San Antonio 100/PK-5
8638 Fairhaven St 78229 210-614-0202
Br. Musa Sadek, prin.
Keystone S 400/PK-12
119 E Craig Pl 78212 210-735-4022
James Lindsey, head sch Fax 732-4905
Legacy Christian Academy 200/PK-12
2255 Horal St 78227 210-674-0490
Pedro Garza, prin. Fax 674-3615

Little Flower Catholic S 300/PK-8
905 Kentucky Ave 78201 210-732-9207
Nora Mozingo, prin. Fax 732-3214
Maranatha Adventist S 50/K-8
2526 Goliad Rd 78223 210-333-8861
Montessori School of San Antonio 300/PK-8
17722 Rogers Ranch Pkwy 78258 210-492-3553
Mt. Sacred Heart Catholic S 400/PK-8
619 Mount Sacred Heart Rd 78216 210-342-6711
Veronica Beck, prin. Fax 342-4032
Northwest Hills Christian S 400/PK-8
8511 Heath Circle Dr 78250 210-522-1102
Gilpatrick Peyton, prin. Fax 522-1103
Oak Island Academy 50/PK-4
2627 Oak Island Dr 78264 210-624-3237
Janie Rodriguez, prin.
River City Believers Academy 100/PK-12
16765 Lookout Rd 78233 210-656-2999
Dr. Victor Fordyce, prin. Fax 496-2888
Rolling Hills Catholic S 200/PK-8
21140 Gathering Oak 78260 210-497-0323
Jonathan Kiesler, prin. Fax 497-5192
St. Anthony Catholic S 400/PK-8
205 W Huisache Ave 78212 210-732-8801
Patricia Ramirez, prin. Fax 732-5968
St. David's Episcopal S 200/PK-K
1300 Wiltshire Ave 78209 210-824-2481
Ashley Miles, head sch Fax 824-7870
St. George Episcopal S 500/PK-8
6900 West Ave 78213 210-342-4263
Robert Devlin, head sch Fax 342-4681
St. Gregory the Great Catholic S 600/PK-8
700 Dewhurst Rd 78213 210-342-0281
Daniel Martinez, prin. Fax 308-7177
St. James the Apostle Catholic S 200/PK-8
907 W Theo Ave 78225 210-924-1201
Sr. Debbie Walker, prin. Fax 924-0201
St. John Berchmans Catholic S 400/PK-8
PO Box 28187 78226 210-433-0411
Nora Garcia, prin. Fax 433-2335
St. John Bosco Catholic S 300/PK-8
5630 W Commerce St 78237 210-432-8011
Roxanne LeBlanc, prin. Fax 214-8083
St. Leo the Great Catholic S 200/PK-8
119 Octavia Pl 78214 210-532-3166
Carol Johnson, prin. Fax 532-5997
St. Luke Catholic S 500/PK-8
4603 Manitou 78228 210-434-2011
Mary Helen Cover, prin. Fax 433-2778
St. Luke's Episcopal S 300/PK-8
15 Saint Lukes Ln 78209 210-826-0664
Thomas McLaughlin, head sch Fax 826-8520
St. Mary Magdalen Catholic S 200/PK-8
1700 Clower 78201 210-735-1381
William Daily, prin. Fax 735-2406
St. Mary's Hall 500/PK-12
9401 Starcrest Dr 78217 210-483-9100
Jonathan Eades, head sch Fax 483-9299
St. Matthew Catholic S 700/PK-8
10703 Wurzbach Rd 78230 210-478-5099
Alvin Caro, prin. Fax 696-7624
St. Paul Catholic S 200/K-8
307 John Adams Dr 78228 210-732-2741
Mary Crow, prin. Fax 732-7702
St. Peter Prince of the Apostles S 300/PK-8
112 Marcia Pl 78209 210-824-3171
Gabriel Duarte, prin. Fax 822-4504
St. Pius X Catholic S 300/PK-8
7734 Robin Rest Dr 78209 210-824-6431
Jane Zarate, prin. Fax 824-7454
St. Thomas Episcopal S 200/PK-5
1416 N Loop 1604 E 78232 210-494-3509
Dr. Debra Root, head sch Fax 494-0678
St. Thomas More Catholic S 100/PK-8
4427 Moana Dr 78218 210-655-2882
Kimberly Gutierrez, prin. Fax 655-9603
San Antonio Academy 300/PK-8
117 E French Pl 78212 210-733-7331
Clint DuBose, head sch Fax 734-0711
San Antonio Christian S 500/PK-12
19202 Redland Rd 78259 210-340-1864
Fax 340-0461
San Antonio Country Day Montessori S 100/PK-6
4194 Jung Rd 78247 210-816-5916
Scenic Hills Christian Academy 50/PK-12
11223 Bandera Rd 78250 210-523-2312
Jon Dickerson, prin.
Shepherd of the Hills Lutheran S 300/PK-8
6914 Wurzbach Rd 78240 210-614-3741
Susan Gary, prin. Fax 692-1639
Torah Academy of San Antonio 50/K-8
3003 Sholom Dr #200 78230 210-607-7261
Rabbi Dov Nimchinsky, head sch
Trinity Christian Academy 200/K-12
5401 N Loop 1604 E 78247 210-653-2800
Sharon Ausbury, prin. Fax 653-0303
Trinity United Methodist S 100/PK-5
5319 Newcome Dr 78229 210-684-5214
Village Parkway Christian S 100/PK-5
3002 Village Pkwy 78251 210-680-8187
Winston S San Antonio 100/K-12
8565 Ewing Halsell Dr 78229 210-615-6544
Dr. Charles J. Karulak, hdmstr. Fax 615-6627

San Augustine, San Augustine, Pop. 2,090
San Augustine ISD 800/PK-12
1002 Barrett St 75972 936-275-2306
Dr. Virginia Liepman, supt. Fax 275-9776
www.saisd.us
San Augustine ES 400/PK-5
1002 Barrett St 75972 936-275-3424
Anna Sharp, prin. Fax 275-9719

San Benito, Cameron, Pop. 24,199
Los Fresnos Consolidated ISD
Supt. — See Los Fresnos

Las Yescas ES 500/PK-5
23413 FM 803 78586 956-233-6955
Oscar De La Rosa, prin. Fax 748-2540
Laureles ES 700/PK-5
31383 FM 2893 78586 956-254-5141
Celia Ontiveros, prin. Fax 233-3690
Liberty Memorial MS 800/6-8
31579 FM 2893 78586 956-233-3900
Annice Garza, prin. Fax 233-1074
Palmer-Laakso ES 600/PK-5
30515 Farm Road 1847 78586 956-254-5121
Jerri Gomez, prin. Fax 233-3659

San Benito Consolidated ISD 10,900/PK-12
240 N Crockett St 78586 956-361-6100
Dr. Nate Carman, supt. Fax 361-6115
www.sbcisd.net
Booth ES 600/PK-5
705 Zaragosa St 78586 956-361-6860
Nedia Espinoza, prin. Fax 361-6868
Cabaza MS 900/6-8
2901 Shafer Rd 78586 956-361-6600
Saul Ibarra, prin. Fax 361-6608
Cash ES 600/PK-5
400 Poinciana St 78586 956-361-6700
Dilia Cornett, prin. Fax 361-6708
De La Fuente ES 400/PK-5
2700 S Sam Houston St 78586 956-361-6820
Rolando Diaz, prin. Fax 361-6828
Downs ES 500/PK-5
1302 N Dick Dowling St 78586 956-361-6720
Manuela Lopez, prin. Fax 361-6728
Garza ES 400/PK-5
845 8th St 78586 956-361-6900
Elsa Lambert, prin. Fax 361-6908
Jordan MS 900/6-8
700 N McCullough St 78586 956-361-6650
Alfredo Perez, prin. Fax 361-6658
La Encantada ES 600/PK-5
35001 FM 1577 78586 956-361-6760
Gracie Martinez, prin. Fax 361-6768
Landrum ES 300/PK-5
450 S Dick Dowling St 78586 956-361-6800
Dr. Lupita Monsevalles, prin. Fax 361-6808
La Paloma ES 400/PK-5
35076 Padilla St 78586 956-361-6780
Libby Flores, prin. Fax 361-6788
Leal ES 500/PK-5
33356 FM 732 78586 956-276-5055
Virginia Romero, prin. Fax 361-6193
Rangerville ES 400/PK-5
17558 Landrum Park Rd 78586 956-361-6840
Diana Atkinson, prin. Fax 361-6848
Roberts ES 400/PK-5
451 Biddle St 78586 956-361-6740
Linda Molina, prin. Fax 361-6748
San Benito Riverside MS 700/6-8
35428 Padilla St 78586 956-361-6940
Amy Rodriguez, prin. Fax 361-6948
Sullivan ES 500/PK-5
900 Elizabeth St 78586 956-361-6880
Stephanie Ramirez, prin. Fax 361-6888

South Texas ISD
Supt. — See Mercedes
Rising Scholars Academy of South Texas 7-8
151 S Helen Moore Rd 78586 956-399-4358
Carrie Saucedo, prin. Fax 399-3570

Sanderson, Terrell, Pop. 834
Terrell County ISD 100/PK-12
PO Box 747 79848 432-345-2515
Amanda Magallan, supt. Fax 345-2404
www.terrell.esc18.net
Sanderson S 100/PK-12
PO Box 747 79848 432-345-2515
Amanda Magallan, prin. Fax 345-2670

San Diego, Duval, Pop. 4,473
San Diego ISD 1,300/PK-12
609 W Labbe Ave 78384 361-279-3382
Dr. Samuel Bueno, supt. Fax 279-1830
www.sdisd.us
Collins-Parr ES 700/PK-5
609 W Labbe Ave 78384 361-279-3382
Monica Perez, prin. Fax 279-1822
Jaime JHS 300/6-8
609 W Labbe Ave 78384 361-279-3382
Debbie Guerra, prin. Fax 279-3139

San Elizario, El Paso, Pop. 13,596
San Elizario ISD 4,100/PK-12
PO Box 920 79849 915-872-3900
Jeannie Meza-Chavez, supt. Fax 872-3903
www.seisd.net
Alarcon ES 700/1-6
PO Box 920 79849 915-872-3930
Julissa Esquivel, prin. Fax 872-3931
Borrego ES 600/1-6
PO Box 920 79849 915-872-3910
Norma Casillas, prin. Fax 872-3911
Garcia-Enriquez MS 600/7-8
PO Box 920 79849 915-872-3960
April Marioni, prin. Fax 872-3961
Loya PS 700/PK-K
PO Box 920 79849 915-872-3940
George Augustain, prin. Fax 872-3941
Sambrano ES 500/1-6
PO Box 920 79849 915-872-3950
Teresa Wilks, prin. Fax 872-3951

Sanger, Denton, Pop. 6,799
Sanger ISD 2,700/PK-12
601 Elm St 76266 940-458-7438
Dr. Sandra McCoy-Jackson, supt. Fax 458-5140
www.sangerisd.net/
Butterfield ES 500/PK-5
291 Indian Ln 76266 940-458-4377
Larry Beam, prin. Fax 458-5591
Chisholm Trail ES 400/K-2
812 Keaton Rd N 76266 940-458-5297
Alice Ford, prin. Fax 458-2537
Clear Creek IS 300/3-5
1901 S Stemmons St 76266 940-458-7476
Stephanie Lance, prin. Fax 458-2539
Sanger 6th Grade Campus 200/6-6
508 N 7th St 76266 940-458-3699
Larry Shuman, prin. Fax 458-3795
Sanger MS 500/7-8
105 Berry St 76266 940-458-7916
Sally Herrell, prin. Fax 458-5111

San Isidro, Starr, Pop. 240
San Isidro ISD 300/PK-12
PO Box 10 78588 956-481-3110
Mario Alvarado, supt. Fax 481-3930
www.sanisidroisd.org
San Isidro ES, PO Box 10 78588 200/PK-8
Anna Garcia, prin. 956-481-3107

San Juan, Hidalgo, Pop. 33,835
Pharr-San Juan-Alamo ISD
Supt. — See Pharr
Austin MS 700/6-8
804 S Stewart Rd 78589 956-354-2570
Liza Navarro, prin. Fax 354-3194
Cantu ES 800/PK-5
2900 N Raul Longoria Rd 78589 956-354-2850
Yvette Mancillas, prin. Fax 354-3244
Carman ES 700/PK-5
100 Ridge Rd 78589 956-354-2700
Adrian Karr, prin. Fax 354-3246
Clover ES 600/PK-5
800 Carroll Ln 78589 956-354-2730
Rosalinda Diaz, prin. Fax 354-3250
Doedyns ES 800/PK-5
1401 N Raul Longoria Rd 78589 956-354-2740
Maria Guerrero, prin. Fax 354-3252
Garza-Pena ES 500/PK-5
501 E FM 495 78589 956-354-2800
Karla Montemayor, prin. Fax 354-3260
Reed & Mock ES 600/PK-5
400 E Eldora Rd 78589 956-354-2890
Jose Montelongo, prin. Fax 354-3280
Sorensen ES 700/PK-5
701 E Sam Houston Blvd 78589 956-354-2910
Maricela Cortez, prin. Fax 354-3282
Trevino ES 700/PK-5
901 E Eldora Rd 78589 956-354-2900
Jill Wright, prin. Fax 354-3286
Yzaguirre MS 900/6-8
605 E FM 495 78589 956-354-2630
Rebecca Luna, prin. Fax 354-3230

San Leon, Galveston, Pop. 4,915
Dickinson ISD
Supt. — See Dickinson
San Leon ES 800/PK-4
2655 Broadway St 77539 281-229-7400
Sherri Blackburn, prin. Fax 229-7401

San Marcos, Hays, Pop. 44,109
Hays Consolidated ISD
Supt. — See Kyle
Blanco Vista ES 800/PK-5
2951 Blanco Vista Blvd 78666 512-268-8506
Sean Fox, prin. Fax 393-2082

San Marcos Consolidated ISD 7,600/PK-12
PO Box 1087 78667 512-393-6700
Michael Cardona, supt. Fax 393-6709
www.smcisd.net
Bonham Pre K 500/PK-PK
PO Box 1087 78667 512-393-6031
Rosemary Garza, prin. Fax 353-0671
Bowie ES 700/K-5
PO Box 1087 78667 512-393-6200
Pam Thomas, prin. Fax 393-6210
Crockett ES 500/K-5
PO Box 1087 78667 512-393-6400
Keith Cunningham, prin. Fax 393-3557
De Zavala ES 500/K-5
PO Box 1087 78667 512-393-6250
Elena Villanueva, prin. Fax 393-7115
Goodnight MS 1,000/6-8
PO Box 1087 78667 512-393-6550
Rose Pearson, prin. Fax 393-6560
Hernandez ES 400/K-5
PO Box 1087 78667 512-393-6100
Amber Owens, prin. Fax 393-6109
Mendez ES 500/K-5
PO Box 1087 78667 512-393-6060
Karen McGowan, prin. Fax 393-6839
Miller MS 700/6-8
PO Box 1087 78667 512-393-6660
Richard Duvall, prin. Fax 393-6602
Travis ES 700/K-5
PO Box 1087 78667 512-393-6450
Niki Konecki, prin. Fax 393-6476

Master's S 100/K-7
1664 Center Point Rd 78666 512-392-4322
Tucker Blythe, head sch Fax 754-6017
San Marcos Academy 300/K-12
2801 Ranch Road 12 78666 512-753-8000
Jimmie Scott, pres. Fax 753-8031
San Marcos Adventist Academy 100/PK-10
1523 Old Ranch Road 12 78666 512-392-9475

San Perlita, Willacy, Pop. 573
San Perlita ISD 300/PK-12
PO Box 37 78590 956-248-5563
Albert Pena, supt. Fax 248-5561
www.spisd.org
San Perlita ES 100/PK-5
PO Box 37 78590 956-248-5250
Laurie Kilbourn, prin. Fax 248-5103
San Perlita MS 100/6-8
PO Box 37 78590 956-248-5250
Adrian Montemayor, prin. Fax 248-5103

San Saba, San Saba, Pop. 3,082
San Saba ISD 700/PK-12
808 W Wallace St 76877 325-372-3771
Michael Bohensky, supt. Fax 372-5977
www.san-saba.net
San Saba ES 300/PK-4
808 W Wallace St 76877 325-372-3019
Kay Shackelford, prin. Fax 372-6187
San Saba MS 200/5-8
808 W Wallace St 76877 325-372-3200
Dustin Anders, prin. Fax 372-5228

Santa Anna, Coleman, Pop. 1,086
Santa Anna ISD 200/PK-12
701 Bowie St 76878 325-348-3136
David Robinett, supt. Fax 348-3141
www.santaannaisd.net
Santa Anna ES 100/PK-6
701 Bowie St 76878 325-348-3138
Aletha Patterson, prin. Fax 348-3142

Santa Fe, Galveston, Pop. 12,112
Santa Fe ISD 4,600/PK-12
PO Box 370 77510 409-925-9001
Dr. Leigh Wall, supt. Fax 925-4002
www.sfisd.org/
Kubacak ES 1,000/3-5
PO Box 370 77510 409-925-9600
Destini Martin, prin. Fax 927-8262
Santa Fe JHS 1,100/6-8
PO Box 370 77510 409-925-9300
Ryan Kopp, prin. Fax 927-4106
Wollam ES 1,100/PK-2
PO Box 370 77510 409-925-2770
Michelle Pourchot, prin. Fax 925-4276

Santa Maria, Cameron, Pop. 732
Santa Maria ISD 700/PK-12
PO Box 448 78592 956-565-6308
Maria Chavez, supt. Fax 565-0598
www.smisd.net
Gonzalez ES 400/PK-5
PO Box 448 78592 956-565-5348
Cindy Taylor, prin. Fax 565-2698
Santa Maria MS 200/6-8
PO Box 448 78592 956-565-6309
Rogelio Campa, prin. Fax 565-6720

Santa Rosa, Cameron, Pop. 2,866
Santa Rosa ISD 1,200/PK-12
PO Box 368 78593 956-636-9800
Heriberto Villarreal, supt. Fax 636-1439
www.srtx.org
Barrera ES 600/PK-5
PO Box 368 78593 956-636-9870
Sylvia Ramos, prin. Fax 636-2746
Nelson MS 200/6-8
PO Box 368 78593 956-636-9850
John Gray, prin. Fax 636-1519

Santo, Palo Pinto
Santo ISD 500/PK-12
PO Box 67 76472 940-769-2835
Greg Gilbert, supt. Fax 769-3116
www.santoisd.net/
Santo ES 200/PK-5
PO Box 67 76472 940-769-3215
Cathy Longley, prin. Fax 769-3116

San Ygnacio, Zapata, Pop. 666
Zapata County ISD
Supt. — See Zapata
Benavides ES 100/PK-5
307 Lincoln St 78067 956-765-5611
Diana Brandon, prin. Fax 765-3942

Saratoga, Hardin
West Hardin County Consolidated ISD 400/PK-12
39227 Highway 105 77585 936-274-5061
James Armstrong, supt. Fax 274-4321
westhardin.org
West Hardin ES 300/PK-6
39227 Highway 105 77585 936-274-5061
Tiffany Merriwether, prin. Fax 274-4039

Sarita, Kenedy, Pop. 235
Kenedy County Wide Common SD 100/PK-6
PO Box 100 78385 361-294-5381
Johnny Johnson, supt. Fax 294-5718
www.saritaschool.net
Sarita ES 100/PK-6
PO Box 100 78385 361-294-5381
Kristen Tinsley, prin. Fax 294-5718

Savoy, Fannin, Pop. 820
Savoy ISD 300/PK-12
302 W Hayes St 75479 903-965-5262
Brian Neal, supt. Fax 965-7282
www.savoyisd.org
Savoy ES 100/PK-6
302 W Hayes St 75479 903-965-7738
Korey Kennedy, prin. Fax 965-4389

Schertz, Guadalupe, Pop. 30,563
Schertz Cibolo Universal City ISD 14,100/PK-12
1060 Elbel Rd 78154 210-945-6200
Greg Gibson Ed.D., supt. Fax 945-6292
www.scuc.txed.net
Corbett JHS 1,100/7-8
12000 Ray Corbett Dr 78154 210-619-4150
Tracey Bandy, prin. Fax 619-4190
Green Valley ES 700/PK-4
1694 Green Valley Rd 78154 210-619-4450
Shannon Mills, prin. Fax 619-4478
Paschal ES 700/PK-4
590 Savannah Dr 78154 210-619-4500
Allison Miller, prin. Fax 619-4518

Schertz ES 900/PK-4
701 Curtiss St 78154 210-619-4650
Geri Pope, prin. Fax 619-4690
Sippel ES 1,000/PK-4
420 Fairlawn Ave, 210-619-4600
Lisa Newman, prin. Fax 619-4630
Wilder IS 700/5-6
806 Savannah Dr 78154 210-619-4200
Sarah Dauphinais, prin. Fax 619-4220
Other Schools – See Cibolo, Universal City

Schulenburg, Fayette, Pop. 2,828
Schulenburg ISD 700/PK-12
521 North St 78956 979-743-3448
Lisa Meysembourg, supt. Fax 743-4721
schulenburgisd.net
Schulenburg ES 300/PK-5
300 Bucek St 78956 979-743-4221
Brooke de la Garza, prin. Fax 743-4864
Schulenburg JHS 200/6-8
512 North St 78956 979-743-4295
Britina Pesak, admin. Fax 743-3540

St. Rose of Lima S 200/PK-8
405 Black St 78956 979-743-3080
Rosanne Gallia, prin. Fax 743-4228

Scurry, Kaufman, Pop. 668
Scurry-Rosser ISD 1,000/PK-12
10705 S State Highway 34 75158 972-452-8823
James Sanders, supt. Fax 452-8586
www.scurry-rosser.com
Scurry-Rosser ES 300/PK-3
9511 Silver Creek Dr 75158 972-452-8823
Kandy Shirey, prin. Fax 452-3434
Scurry-Rosser MS 400/4-8
10729 S State Highway 34 75158 972-452-8823
Grant Miller, prin. Fax 452-8902

Seabrook, Harris, Pop. 11,727
Clear Creek ISD
Supt. — See League City
Bay ES 800/PK-5
1502 Bayport Blvd 77586 281-284-4600
Erin Tite, prin. Fax 284-4605
Robinson ES 500/K-5
451 Kirby Rd 77586 281-284-6500
Yolanda Jones, prin. Fax 284-6505
Seabrook IS 1,000/6-8
2401 N Meyer Ave 77586 281-284-3100
Sharon Lopez, prin. Fax 284-3105

Seadrift, Calhoun, Pop. 1,355
Calhoun County ISD
Supt. — See Port Lavaca
Seadrift S 300/PK-8
PO Box 979 77983 361-785-3451
Melissa Hoggett, prin. Fax 785-4006

Seagoville, Dallas, Pop. 14,610
Dallas ISD
Supt. — See Dallas
Central ES 500/PK-5
902 Shady Ln 75159 972-749-6800
Julie Singleton, prin. Fax 749-6801
Seagoville ES 600/PK-5
304 N Kaufman St 75159 972-892-7900
Katrina Allen-Gibson, prin. Fax 892-7901
Seagoville North ES 700/PK-5
1906 Seagoville Rd 75159 972-892-5300
Norma Martinez, prin.

Seagraves, Gaines, Pop. 2,405
Seagraves ISD 600/PK-12
PO Box 577 79359 806-387-2035
Dr. Josh Goen, supt. Fax 387-2944
www.seagravesisd.net/
Seagraves ES 400/PK-5
1300 Avenue J 79359 806-387-2015
Ovidio Martinez, prin. Fax 387-3339
Seagraves JHS 100/6-8
PO Box 938 79359 806-387-2646
Glenn Thompson, prin. Fax 387-2451

Sealy, Austin, Pop. 5,953
Sealy ISD 2,800/PK-12
939 Tiger Ln 77474 979-885-3516
Sheryl Moore, supt. Fax 885-6457
www.sealyisd.com
Sealy JHS 600/6-8
939 Tiger Ln 77474 979-885-3292
Lisa Svoboda, prin. Fax 877-0743
Selman ES 900/PK-3
1741 Highway 90 W 77474 979-885-6659
Mary Gajewski, prin. Fax 885-1338
Selman IS 400/4-5
939 Tiger Ln 77474 979-885-3852
David Janecek, prin. Fax 885-0162

Seguin, Guadalupe, Pop. 24,967
Navarro ISD 1,700/PK-12
6450 N State Highway 123 78155 830-372-1930
Dee Carter, supt. Fax 372-1853
www.nisd.us
Navarro ES 500/PK-3
380 Link Rd 78155 830-372-1933
Kim Schlichting, prin. Fax 379-3145
Navarro IS 400/4-6
300 Link Rd 78155 830-372-1943
Bobbi Supak, prin. Fax 379-3170
Navarro JHS 300/7-8
6450 N State Highway 123 78155 830-401-5550
Luke Morales, prin. Fax 379-3135

Seguin ISD 6,900/PK-12
1221 E Kingsbury St 78155 830-401-8600
Matthew Gutierrez, supt. Fax 379-0392
www.seguin.k12.tx.us
Ball ECC 500/PK-PK
812 Shannon Ave 78155 830-401-1281
Dr. Laura Flack, prin. Fax 379-5590
Barnes MS 500/6-8
1539 Joe Carrillo Blvd 78155 830-379-4717
Michael Garza, prin. Fax 379-4239
Briesemeister MS 500/6-8
1616 W Court St 78155 830-379-0600
Elisa Carter, prin. Fax 379-0615
Jefferson Avenue ES 400/K-5
215 Short Ave 78155 830-401-8727
Merry White, prin. Fax 379-0950
Koennecke ES 500/K-5
1441 Joe Carrillo Blvd 78155 830-372-5430
Cindy Moreno, prin. Fax 372-3317
Patlan ES 500/K-5
2501 Breustedt St 78155 830-401-1221
Linda Guzman, prin. Fax 372-4565
Rodriguez ES 500/K-5
1567 W Kingsbury St 78155 830-401-8770
Allison Seidenberger, prin. Fax 386-0001
Vogel ES 400/K-5
16121 FM 725 78155 830-401-8745
Chanda Bloch, prin. Fax 372-2174
Weinert ES 500/K-5
1111 Bruns St 78155 830-401-1241
Brandi Bell-Wiatrek, prin. Fax 372-2720
Other Schools – See Mc Queeney

Lifegate Christian S 200/K-12
395 Lifegate Ln 78155 830-372-0850
Mark Peters, prin. Fax 372-0895
St. James Catholic S 200/PK-8
507 S Camp St 78155 830-379-2878
Dr. Cindy Cummins, prin. Fax 379-0047

Selma, Bexar, Pop. 5,403

Our Lady of Perpetual Help S 500/PK-8
16075 N Evans Rd 78154 210-651-6811
Frank Burns, prin. Fax 651-5516

Seminole, Gaines, Pop. 6,373
Seminole ISD 2,700/PK-12
207 SW 6th St 79360 432-758-3662
Gary Laramore, supt. Fax 758-9833
www.seminoleisd.net
Seminole ES 400/4-5
401 SW Avenue B 79360 432-758-3615
Kevin McCasland, prin. Fax 758-9064
Seminole JHS 600/6-8
600 NW Avenue J 79360 432-758-9431
Bryan Ritchey, prin. Fax 758-5795
Seminole PS 400/2-3
508 SW Avenue D 79360 432-758-5841
Kathy Moore, prin. Fax 758-5299
Young ES 600/PK-1
2100 SW Avenue B 79360 432-758-3637
Sherrie Warren, prin. Fax 758-2066

Seymour, Baylor, Pop. 2,715
Seymour ISD 600/PK-12
409 W Idaho St 76380 940-889-3525
Dr. John Baker, supt. Fax 889-5340
www.seymour-isd.net
Seymour ES 200/PK-4
409 W Idaho St 76380 940-889-2533
John Anderson, prin. Fax 889-8890
Seymour MS 200/5-8
409 W Idaho St 76380 940-889-4548
Morris Davis, prin. Fax 889-4962

Shady Shores, Denton, Pop. 2,560
Denton ISD
Supt. — See Denton
Myers MS 700/6-8
131 N Garza Rd 76208 940-369-1500
Angela Ricks, prin. Fax 498-0050
Stephens ES 500/K-5
133 N Garza Rd 76208 940-369-0800
Chris Rangel, prin. Fax 321-1318

Lake Dallas ISD
Supt. — See Lake Dallas
Shady Shores ES 500/PK-5
300 Dobbs Rd 76208 940-497-4035
Vangee Duessen, prin. Fax 497-4036

Shallowater, Lubbock, Pop. 2,469
Shallowater ISD 1,600/PK-12
1100 Avenue K 79363 806-832-4531
Dr. Kenny Border, supt. Fax 832-4350
www.shallowaterisd.net
Shallowater ES 300/PK-1
1100 Avenue K 79363 806-832-4531
Tori Mitchell, prin. Fax 832-4534
Shallowater IS 400/2-4
1100 Avenue K 79363 806-832-4531
Donna Bowles, prin. Fax 832-1884
Shallowater MS 500/5-8
1100 Avenue K 79363 806-832-4531
Dr. Aron Strickland, prin. Fax 832-5543

Shamrock, Wheeler, Pop. 1,874
Shamrock ISD 400/PK-12
100 S Illinois St 79079 806-256-3492
Kenneth Shields, supt. Fax 256-3628
www.shamrockisd.net
Shamrock ES 300/PK-5
100 S Illinois St 79079 806-256-3227
Ed Berngen, prin. Fax 256-3628
Shamrock JHS 50/6-8
100 S Illinois St 79079 806-256-3492
Ed Berngen, admin. Fax 256-3628

Shavano Park, Bexar, Pop. 2,986
Northside ISD
Supt. — See San Antonio
Blattman ES 600/K-5
3300 N Loop 1604 W 78231 210-397-4600
Donna Gavegan, prin. Fax 408-6219

Shelbyville, Shelby
Shelbyville ISD 800/PK-12
PO Box 325 75973 936-598-2641
Dr. Ray West, supt. Fax 598-6842
www.shelbyville.k12.tx.us
Shelbyville S 800/PK-12
PO Box 325 75973 936-598-7323
Mario Osby, prin. Fax 598-6842

Shepherd, San Jacinto, Pop. 2,281
Shepherd ISD 1,900/PK-12
1401 S Byrd Ave 77371 936-628-3396
Rick Hartley, supt. Fax 628-3841
www.shepherdisd.net/
Shepherd IS 400/3-5
1401 S Byrd Ave 77371 936-628-6764
Mary Williams, prin. Fax 628-6507
Shepherd MS 500/6-8
1401 S Byrd Ave 77371 936-628-3377
Denise Weatherford, prin. Fax 628-6749
Shepherd PS 600/PK-2
1401 S Byrd Ave 77371 936-628-3302
Sandra Meekins, prin. Fax 628-6459

Sheridan, Colorado
Rice Consolidated ISD
Supt. — See Altair
Sheridan ES 100/K-5
5526 Main St 77475 979-234-3531
Mike Keenon, prin. Fax 234-6322

Sherman, Grayson, Pop. 37,575
Sherman ISD 7,100/PK-12
2701 N Loy Lake Rd 75090 903-891-6400
Dr. David Hicks, supt. Fax 891-6407
www.shermanisd.net
Crutchfield ES 400/K-4
521 S Dewey Ave 75090 903-891-6565
Rhonda Johnson, prin. Fax 891-6570
Dillingham IS 1,000/5-6
1701 Gallagher Dr 75090 903-891-6495
Brett Counce, prin. Fax 891-6499
Douglass ECC 300/PK-PK
505 E College St 75090 903-891-6545
Deloris Dowell, prin. Fax 891-6549
Fairview ES 400/K-4
501 W Taylor St 75092 903-891-6580
Michelle Eackles, prin. Fax 891-6585
Jefferson ES 300/K-4
608 N Lee Ave 75090 903-891-6610
Tammy MacDonald, prin. Fax 891-6615
Neblett ES 400/K-4
1505 Gallagher Dr 75090 903-891-6670
Susan Taraba, prin. Fax 893-0263
Piner MS 1,000/7-8
402 W Pecan St 75090 903-891-6470
Amy Porter, prin. Fax 891-6475
Sory ES 600/K-4
120 Binkley Park Dr 75092 903-891-6650
Steven Traw, prin. Fax 892-6307
Wakefield ES 400/K-4
400 Sunset Blvd 75092 903-891-6595
Eartha Linson, prin. Fax 891-6600
Washington ES 400/K-4
815 S Travis St 75090 903-891-6700
Amy Pesina, prin. Fax 893-0141

Grayson Institute K-8
475 Old Dorchester Rd 75092 903-436-0102
Michelle Chapman, head sch
Montessori Academy of North Texas 100/PK-6
906 Cottonwood St 75090 903-893-3500
Angela Magers, prin. Fax 767-0999
St. Mary's Catholic S 200/PK-8
713 S Travis St 75090 903-893-2127
Phillip Scheibmeir, prin. Fax 893-3233
Texoma Christian S 300/PK-12
3500 W Houston St 75092 903-893-7076
Jeff Burley, head sch Fax 891-8486

Shiner, Lavaca, Pop. 2,046
Shiner ISD 600/PK-12
PO Box 804 77984 361-594-3121
Trey Lawrence, supt. Fax 594-3925
www.shinerisd.net
Shiner ES 300/PK-6
PO Box 804 77984 361-594-3251
Greg Murrile, prin. Fax 594-8106

Shiner Catholic S 300/PK-12
PO Box 725 77984 361-594-2313
Neely Yackel, prin. Fax 594-8599

Sidney, Comanche
Sidney ISD 100/PK-12
PO Box 190 76474 254-842-5500
Doug Bowden, supt. Fax 842-5731
www.sidney.esc14.net/
Sidney S 100/PK-12
PO Box 190 76474 254-842-5500
James Rucker, prin. Fax 842-5731

Sierra Blanca, Hudspeth, Pop. 550
Sierra Blanca ISD 100/PK-12
PO Box 308 79851 915-369-3741
Evelyn Loeffler, supt. Fax 369-2605
Sierra Blanca S 100/PK-12
PO Box 308 79851 915-369-2781
Fax 369-2605

Silsbee, Hardin, Pop. 6,524
Silsbee ISD 2,200/PK-12
415 Highway 327 W 77656 409-980-7800
Richard Bain, supt. Fax 980-7897
www.silsbeeisd.org
Edwards-Johnson Memorial Silsbee MS 600/6-8
1140 Highway 327 E 77656 409-980-7800
Sunee Stephens, prin. Fax 980-7875
Reeves PS 400/PK-K
695 Woodrow St 77656 409-980-7800
Terry Deaver, prin. Fax 980-7868
Silsbee ES 400/1-5
770 S 7th St 77656 409-980-7856
Terry Deaver, prin. Fax 980-7861

Silverton, Briscoe, Pop. 724
Silverton ISD 200/PK-12
PO Box 608 79257 806-823-2476
Michelle Francis, supt. Fax 823-2276
www.silvertonisd.net
Silverton S 200/PK-12
PO Box 608 79257 806-823-2476
Michelle Francis, supt. Fax 823-2276

Simms, Bowie
Simms ISD 500/PK-12
PO Box 9 75574 903-543-2219
Rex Burks, supt. Fax 543-2512
www.simmsisd.net/
Bowie ES 200/PK-5
PO Box 9 75574 903-543-2245
Justin Tyndell, prin. Fax 543-2512
Bowie MS 100/6-8
PO Box 9 75574 903-543-2219
Lisa Hudgeons, prin. Fax 543-2512

Simonton, Fort Bend, Pop. 799

Simonton Christian Academy 100/PK-4
PO Box 490 77476 281-346-2303
Amy Oglesby, admin. Fax 346-2393

Sinton, San Patricio, Pop. 5,646
Sinton ISD 2,200/PK-12
PO Box 1337 78387 361-364-6800
Pari Whitten, supt. Fax 364-6905
www.sintonisd.net/
Sinton ES 500/3-5
200 S Bowie St 78387 361-364-6900
Lori Trevino, prin. Fax 364-6914
Smith MS 500/6-8
1000 S San Patricio St 78387 361-364-6840
Jennifer Davis, prin. Fax 364-6856
Welder ES 600/PK-2
901 Hamilton St 78387 361-364-6600
Luci Rodriguez, prin. Fax 364-6608

Skellytown, Carson, Pop. 468
Spring Creek ISD 100/K-8
9849 FM 2171 79080 806-273-6791
Mandy Poer, supt. Fax 273-7479
www.springcreekisd.net
Spring Creek ES 100/K-8
9849 FM 2171 79080 806-273-6791
Shawna Lamb, prin. Fax 273-7479

Skidmore, Bee, Pop. 917
Skidmore-Tynan ISD 800/K-12
224 W Main St 78389 361-287-3426
Dr. Dustin Barton, supt. Fax 287-3442
www.stbobcats.net
Skidmore-Tynan ES 300/K-5
224 W Main St 78389 361-287-3426
Corina Garcia, prin. Fax 287-0104
Skidmore-Tynan JHS 200/6-8
224 W Main St 78389 361-287-3426
Stella Resio, prin. Fax 287-0714

Slaton, Lubbock, Pop. 6,048
Slaton ISD 1,300/PK-12
140 E Panhandle St 79364 806-828-6591
Julee Becker, supt. Fax 828-5506
www.slatonisd.net/
Austin ES 200/PK-K
740 S 7th St 79364 806-828-5813
David Martinez, prin. Fax 828-2079
Slaton JHS 300/6-8
300 W Jean St 79364 806-828-6583
Jim Andrus, prin. Fax 828-2080
Thomas ES 500/1-5
615 W Lubbock St 79364 806-828-5805
Lori Andrus, prin. Fax 828-2046

St. Joseph S 100/PK-5
1305 W Division St 79364 806-828-6761
Sr. Brenda Haynes, prin. Fax 828-5396

Slidell, Wise
Slidell ISD 200/PK-12
PO Box 69 76267 940-466-3118
Greg Enis, supt. Fax 466-3062
www.slidellisd.net
Slidell ES 100/PK-5
PO Box 69 76267 940-466-3118
Theresa Stevens, prin. Fax 466-3016

Smiley, Gonzales, Pop. 546
Nixon-Smiley Consolidated ISD
Supt. — See Nixon
Nixon-Smiley ES 500/PK-4
500 Anglin St 78159 830-582-1536
Lundy Atkins, prin. Fax 582-1920

Smithville, Bastrop, Pop. 3,753
Smithville ISD 1,800/PK-12
PO Box 479 78957 512-237-2487
Dr. Rock McNulty, supt. Fax 237-2775
www.smithvilleisd.org
Brown PS 500/PK-2
PO Box 479 78957 512-237-2519
Dr. Michael Caudill, prin. Fax 237-5635
Smithville ES 400/3-5
PO Box 479 78957 512-237-2406
Tammie Hewitt, prin. Fax 237-5614
Smithville JHS 400/6-8
PO Box 479 78957 512-237-2407
Dr. Bethany Logan, prin. Fax 237-5624

Smyer, Hockley, Pop. 469
Smyer ISD 400/PK-12
PO Box 206 79367 806-234-2935
Dane Kerns, supt. Fax 234-2411
www.smyer-isd.org
Smyer ES 200/PK-6
PO Box 206 79367 806-234-2935
Tony Igo, prin. Fax 234-2411

Snook, Burleson, Pop. 502
Snook ISD 400/PK-12
PO Box 87 77878 979-272-8307
Brenda Krchnak, supt. Fax 272-5041
www.snookisd.org
Snook ES 200/PK-5
PO Box 87 77878 979-272-8307
Shari Hedstrom, prin. Fax 272-5041

Snyder, Scurry, Pop. 11,101
Snyder ISD 2,100/PK-12
2901 37th St 79549 325-574-8900
Dr. Eddie Bland, supt. Fax 573-9025
www.snyderisd.net
Snyder IS 400/4-5
2901 37th St 79549 325-574-8650
Jerry Russell, prin. Fax 574-6034
Snyder JHS 600/6-8
2901 37th St 79549 325-574-8700
Rebecca Mebane, prin. Fax 574-6024
Snyder PS 500/PK-3
2901 37th St 79549 325-574-8600
Canita Rhodes, prin. Fax 573-0342

Somerset, Bexar, Pop. 1,624
Somerset ISD 4,000/PK-12
PO Box 279 78069 866-852-9858
Dr. Saul Hinojosa, supt. Fax 852-9860
www.sisdk12.net
Somerset ECC 400/PK-K
PO Box 279 78069 866-852-9865
Sara Gonzalez, prin. Fax 667-2599
Somerset ES 700/1-4
PO Box 279 78069 866-852-9864
Deborah Van Brunt, prin. Fax 667-2602
Other Schools – See Von Ormy

Somerville, Burleson, Pop. 1,362
Somerville ISD 500/PK-12
PO Box 997 77879 979-596-2153
Charles Camarillo, supt. Fax 596-1778
www.somervilleisd.org
Somerville ES 300/PK-6
PO Box 997 77879 979-596-1502
Stephanie Longoria, prin. Fax 596-1778

Sonora, Sutton, Pop. 3,018
Sonora ISD 900/PK-12
807 S Concho Ave 76950 325-387-6940
Ross Aschenbeck, supt. Fax 387-5090
www.sonoraisd.net
Sonora ES 200/PK-5
807 S Concho Ave 76950 325-387-6940
Michael Kissire, prin. Fax 387-9604
Sonora JHS 200/6-8
807 S Concho Ave 76950 325-387-6940
Daron Worrell, prin. Fax 387-2007

Sour Lake, Hardin, Pop. 1,788
Hardin-Jefferson ISD 2,100/PK-12
PO Box 490 77659 409-981-6400
Shannon Holmes Ed.D., supt. Fax 287-2283
www.hjisd.net/
Henderson MS, PO Box 649 77659 500/6-8
Darrell Westfall, prin. 409-981-6420
Sour Lake ES 600/PK-5
PO Box 340 77659 409-981-6440
Danny McFarland, prin. Fax 287-3987
Other Schools – See China

South Houston, Harris, Pop. 16,918
Pasadena ISD
Supt. — See Pasadena
Matthys ES 700/PK-5
1500 Main St 77587 713-740-0632
Becky Vargas, prin. Fax 740-4139
Pearl Hall ES 800/PK-5
1504 9th St 77587 713-740-0688
Allison Tamez, prin. Fax 740-4142
Smith ES 800/PK-5
1401 Avenue A 77587 713-740-0720
Cathy Danna, prin. Fax 740-4113
South Houston ES 600/PK-5
900 Main St 77587 713-740-0736
Karina Zarzosa, prin. Fax 740-4144
South Houston IS 900/6-8
900 College Ave 77587 713-740-0490
Laura Gomez, prin. Fax 740-4097

Southlake, Tarrant, Pop. 26,042
Carroll ISD 7,800/PK-12
2400 N Carroll Ave 76092 817-949-8282
Dr. David J. Faltys, supt. Fax 949-8228
www.southlakecarroll.edu
Carroll ES 500/PK-4
1705 W Continental Blvd 76092 817-949-4300
Stacy Wagnon, prin. Fax 949-4343
Carroll MS 700/7-8
1800 Kirkwood Blvd 76092 817-949-5400
Stephanie Mangels, prin. Fax 949-5454
Dawson MS 700/7-8
400 S Kimball Ave 76092 817-949-5500
Ryan Wilson, prin. Fax 949-5555
Durham IS 600/5-6
801 Shady Oaks Dr 76092 817-949-5300
Michael Wyrick, prin. Fax 949-5353
Eubanks IS 600/5-6
500 S Kimball Ave 76092 817-949-5200
Mary Stockton, prin. Fax 949-5252
Johnson ES 500/K-4
1301 N Carroll Ave 76092 817-949-4500
Lori Allison, prin. Fax 949-4545
Old Union ES 400/PK-4
1050 S Carroll Ave 76092 817-949-4600
Jon Fike, prin. Fax 949-4646
Rockenbaugh ES 500/PK-4
301 Byron Nelson Pkwy 76092 817-949-4700
Janet Blackwell, prin. Fax 949-4747
Walnut Grove ES 600/K-4
2520 N White Chapel Blvd 76092 817-949-4400
Mike Landers, prin. Fax 949-4444

Keller ISD
Supt. — See Keller
Florence ES 500/K-4
3095 Johnson Rd 76092 817-744-4700
Jacque Hughes, prin. Fax 377-3607

Clariden S 100/PK-12
100 Clariden Ranch Rd 76092 682-237-0400

Southland, Garza
Southland ISD 200/K-12
190 Eighth St 79364 806-996-5599
Wynn Robinson, supt. Fax 996-5342
www.southlandisd.net
Southland S 200/K-12
190 Eighth St 79364 806-996-5339
Wynn Robinson, admin. Fax 996-5595

Southmayd, Grayson, Pop. 984
S&S Consolidated ISD
Supt. — See Sadler
S&S Consolidated ES 400/PK-5
4217 Elementary Dr 76268 903-893-0767
Jenna Frye, prin. Fax 891-9338

Spearman, Hansford, Pop. 3,341
Spearman ISD 900/PK-12
403 E 11th Ave 79081 806-659-3233
Wm. Clay Montgomery, supt. Fax 659-2079
www.spearmanisd.net
Birdwell ES 400/PK-5
511 Townsend St 79081 806-659-2565
Dr. Randy Lamb, prin. Fax 659-2257
Spearman JHS 200/6-8
313 W 5th Ave 79081 806-659-2563
Shane Whiteley, prin. Fax 659-2243

Spicewood, Burnet
Lake Travis ISD
Supt. — See Austin
Lake Travis MS 1,000/6-8
4932 Bee Creek Rd 78669 512-533-6200
Jodie Villemaire, prin. Fax 533-6201
West Cypress Hills ES K-5
6112 Cypress Ranch Blvd 78669 830-533-7500
Amanda Prehn, prin. Fax 533-7399

Marble Falls ISD
Supt. — See Marble Falls
Spicewood ES 200/PK-5
1005 Spur 191 78669 830-798-3675
Susan Cox, prin. Fax 798-3676

Splendora, Montgomery, Pop. 1,597
Splendora ISD 3,200/PK-12
23419 FM 2090 Rd 77372 281-689-3128
Dr. Jeffrey Burke, supt. Fax 689-7509
www.splendoraisd.org/
Greenleaf ES 600/K-5
26275 FM 2090 Rd 77372 281-689-8020
Dr. Carolyn King, prin. Fax 689-3213
Peach Creek ES 500/K-5
14455 Cox St 77372 281-689-3114
Julie Gillespie, prin. Fax 689-7128
Piney Woods ES 500/PK-5
23395 FM 2090 Rd 77372 281-689-3073
Heath Lucas, prin. Fax 689-7975
Splendora JHS 500/6-8
23411 FM 2090 Rd 77372 281-689-6343
Kent Broussard, prin. Fax 689-8702

Spring, Harris, Pop. 53,043
Conroe ISD
Supt. — See Conroe
Birnham Woods ES 800/PK-4
31150 Birnham Woods Dr 77386 832-663-4200
Natalie Buckley, prin. Fax 663-4299
Bradley ES K-5
4200 Falls Lake Dr 77386 832-482-6800
Dr. Christine Butler, prin. Fax 482-6899
Broadway ES 800/K-4
2855 Spring Trails Bnd 77386 281-465-2900
Nikki Conley, prin. Fax 465-2903
Cox IS 1,000/5-6
3333 Waterbend Cv 77386 281-465-3200
Deborah Spoon, prin. Fax 465-3299
Ford ES 1,000/PK-4
25460 Richards Rd 77386 832-592-5700
Paola Gorman, prin. Fax 592-5709
Kaufman ES 900/K-4
2760 Northridge Forest Dr 77386 832-592-5600
Tina Oliver, prin. Fax 592-5617
Snyder ES 800/K-6
28601 Birnham Woods Dr 77386 832-663-4400
Lindsay Ardoin, prin. Fax 663-4499
Vogel IS 1,100/5-6
27125 Geffert Wright Rd 77386 832-663-4300
Tara Vandermark, prin. Fax 663-4399

York JHS 900/7-8
3515 Waterbend Cv 77386 832-592-8600
Dr. Christopher Povich, prin. Fax 592-8684

Klein ISD
Supt. — See Klein
French ES 500/PK-5
5802 W Rayford Rd 77389 832-375-8100
Carole Mason, prin. Fax 375-8175
Haude ES 700/PK-5
3111 Louetta Rd 77388 832-484-5600
Rachel Wall, prin. Fax 484-7862
Hildebrandt IS 1,100/6-8
22800 Hildebrandt Rd 77389 832-249-5100
Lauren Marti, prin. Fax 249-4068
Kreinhop ES 900/PK-5
20820 Ella Blvd 77388 832-484-7400
Sherri Trammell, prin. Fax 484-7404
Lemm ES 600/PK-5
19034 Joanleigh Dr 77388 832-484-6300
Kathy Brown, prin. Fax 484-7872
Metzler ES 800/K-5
8500 W Rayford Rd 77389 832-484-7900
Lakita Combs, prin. Fax 484-7999
Northampton ES 800/PK-5
6404 Root Rd 77389 832-484-5550
Evelyn Castillo, prin. Fax 484-7880
Roth ES 700/PK-5
21623 Castlemont Ln 77388 832-484-6600
Gail McGuire, prin. Fax 484-7882
Schindewolf IS 1,300/6-8
20903 Ella Blvd 77388 832-249-5900
Dr. Curtis Simmons, prin. Fax 249-4072
Zwink ES 900/PK-5
22200 Frassati Way 77389 832-375-7800
Cathryn Turner, prin. Fax 375-7850

Spring ISD
Supt. — See Houston
Anderson ES 700/PK-5
6218 Lynngate Dr 77373 281-891-8360
Kristin Falcon, prin. Fax 891-8361
Bailey MS 1,200/6-8
3377 James Leo Dr 77373 281-891-8000
Dr. George Flores, prin. Fax 891-8001
Burchett ES 700/PK-5
3366 James Leo Dr 77373 281-891-8630
Michael Walker, prin. Fax 528-6351
Dueitt MS 1,000/6-8
1 Eagle Xing 77373 281-891-7800
Dr. Benjamin Bostick, prin. Fax 528-6611
Hirsch ES 700/PK-5
2633 Trailing Vine Rd 77373 281-891-8330
John Baker, prin. Fax 891-8331
Jenkins ES 800/PK-5
4615 Reynaldo Dr 77373 281-891-8300
Tiffany Weston, prin. Fax 891-8301
Marshall ES 700/PK-5
24505 Birnamwood Dr 77373 281-891-4900
Debra Broughton, prin. Fax 891-4901
McNabb ES 700/PK-5
743 E Cypresswood Dr 77373 281-891-8690
Melissa Warford, prin. Fax 528-5980
Northgate Crossing ES 700/PK-5
23437 Northgate Crossing Bl 77373 281-891-8780
Kristi Brown, prin. Fax 891-8781
Salyers ES 700/PK-5
25705 W Hardy Rd 77373 281-891-8570
Sharon Carpenter, prin. Fax 891-8571
Smith ES 600/PK-5
26000 Cypresswood Dr 77373 281-891-8420
Kimberly Culley, prin. Fax 891-8421
Twin Creeks MS 1,000/6-8
27100 Old Cypresswood Dr 77373 281-891-7850
Kenisha Williams, prin. Fax 891-7851
Winship ES 500/PK-5
2175 Spring Creek Dr 77373 281-891-8210
Todd Armelin, prin. Fax 528-9158

Abercrombie Academy 100/PK-5
17102 Theiss Mail Route Rd 77379 281-374-1730
Cunae International S 100/PK-12
5655 Creekside Forest Dr 77389 281-516-3770
Founders Christian S 100/K-12
24724 Aldine Westfield Rd 77373 281-602-8006
Joe Jones, head sch Fax 403-2420
Houston Peace Academy PK-4
16700 Old Louetta Rd 77379 281-257-8988
Providence Classical S 400/PK-12
18100 Stuebner Airline Rd 77379 281-320-0500
Richard Halloran, head sch Fax 379-2039
St. Edward S 300/PK-8
2601 Spring Stuebner Rd 77389 281-353-4570
Tina Lewis, prin. Fax 353-8255
Spell Well Montessori S 100/PK-6
17512 Strack Dr 77379 281-376-0811
Spring Baptist Academy 100/PK-8
633 E Louetta Rd 77373 281-353-5448

Spring Branch, Comal
Comal ISD
Supt. — See New Braunfels
Brown ES 600/PK-5
20410 State Highway 46 W 78070 830-885-1400
Sarah Permenter, prin. Fax 885-1401
Rebecca Creek ES 500/PK-5
125 Quest Ave 78070 830-885-1800
Jodie Wymore, prin. Fax 885-1801
Seay ES 400/K-5
20911 State Highway 46 W 78070 830-885-8700
Shay Strain, prin. Fax 885-8701
Smithson Valley MS 1,000/6-8
6101 FM 311 78070 830-885-1200
Michael Keranen, prin. Fax 885-1201
Spring Branch MS 1,000/6-8
21053 State Highway 46 W 78070 830-885-8800
Chris Smith, prin. Fax 885-8801

Springtown, Parker, Pop. 2,624
Springtown ISD 3,400/PK-12
301 E 5th St 76082 817-220-1700
Mike Kelley, supt. Fax 523-5766
www.springtownisd.net
Goshen Creek ES 600/PK-4
401 S Po Jo Dr 76082 817-220-0272
Wesley Thomas, prin. Fax 220-0471
Springtown ES 500/PK-4
416 E 3rd St 76082 817-220-2498
Pearl Russell, prin. Fax 523-4094
Springtown IS 500/5-6
300 Po Jo Dr 76082 817-220-1219
Joe Brown, prin. Fax 220-0889
Springtown MS 500/7-8
500 Pojo Dr 76082 817-220-7455
Mark Wilson, prin. Fax 220-2395
Other Schools – See Azle

Spur, Dickens, Pop. 1,312
Spur ISD 300/PK-12
PO Box 250 79370 806-271-3272
Craig Hamilton, supt. Fax 271-4575
www.spurbulldogs.com
Spur ES 200/PK-5
PO Box 250 79370 806-271-4531
Michael Norman, prin. Fax 271-4575

Spurger, Tyler
Spurger ISD 400/PK-12
PO Box 38 77660 409-429-3464
Kendall Smith, supt. Fax 429-3770
www.spurgerisd.org
Spurger ES 200/PK-6
PO Box 38 77660 409-429-3464
Kimberley Parker, prin. Fax 429-3770

Stafford, Fort Bend, Pop. 17,344
Stafford Municipal SD 3,500/PK-12
1625 Staffordshire Rd 77477 281-261-9200
Dr. Robert Bostic, supt. Fax 261-9249
www.staffordmsd.org
Stafford ES 700/2-4
1625 Staffordshire Rd 77477 281-261-9229
Valerie Orum Ed.D., prin. Fax 261-9262
Stafford IS 500/5-6
1625 Staffordshire Rd 77477 281-208-6100
Cornelius Anderson, prin. Fax 208-6111
Stafford MS 500/7-8
1625 Staffordshire Rd 77477 281-261-9215
Andre Roberson, prin. Fax 261-9349
Stafford PS 700/PK-1
1625 Staffordshire Rd 77477 281-261-9203
Karen Hattor, prin. Fax 261-9348

Everest Academy 300/PK-8
610 Brand Ln 77477 281-261-3030

Stamford, Jones, Pop. 3,075
Stamford ISD 700/PK-12
507 S Orient St 79553 325-773-2705
Shaun Barnett, supt. Fax 773-5684
www.stamford.esc14.net
Oliver ES 400/PK-5
507 S Orient St 79553 325-773-5713
Kyle Chambers, prin. Fax 773-4077
Stamford MS 100/6-8
507 S Orient St 79553 325-773-2651
Kevin White, prin. Fax 773-4052

Stanton, Martin, Pop. 2,466
Stanton ISD 900/PK-12
PO Box 730 79782 432-607-3700
Merl Brandon, supt. Fax 756-2052
www.stanton.esc18.net/
Stanton ES 400/PK-5
PO Box 730 79782 432-607-3700
Leah Mitchell, prin. Fax 756-2151
Stanton MS 200/6-8
PO Box 730 79782 432-607-3700
Albert Chavez, prin. Fax 756-2702

Stephenville, Erath, Pop. 16,950
Huckabay ISD 200/K-12
200 County Road 421 76401 254-968-8476
Troy Roberts, supt. Fax 965-3740
www.hisd.us
Huckabay S 200/K-12
200 County Road 421 76401 254-968-5274
Nick Heupel, prin. Fax 965-3740

Stephenville ISD 3,700/PK-12
2655 W Overhill Dr 76401 254-968-7990
Matt Underwood, supt. Fax 968-5942
www.sville.us
Central ES 400/PK-K
780 W Washington St 76401 254-965-3716
Kelly Magin, prin. Fax 965-5319
Chamberlin ES 600/1-2
1601 W Frey St 76401 254-968-2311
Jennifer Salyards, prin. Fax 968-5399
Gilbert IS 600/5-6
950 N Dale Ave 76401 254-968-4664
Mary Laigle, prin. Fax 968-8696
Henderson JHS 600/7-8
2798 W Frey St 76401 254-968-6967
Donna Ward, prin. Fax 965-7018
Hook ES 600/3-4
1067 W Jones St 76401 254-968-3213
Daresa Rhine, prin. Fax 968-6758

Three Way ISD 100/PK-9
247 County Road 207 76401 254-965-6496
Paul Ryan, supt. Fax 965-3357
www.twisd.us
Three Way ES 100/PK-9
247 County Road 207 76401 254-965-6496
Paul Ryan, prin. Fax 965-3357

Stephenville Christian S 100/PK-6
1120 County Road 351 76401 254-965-4821
Michelle Castillo, admin. Fax 965-6853

Sterling City, Sterling, Pop. 875
Sterling City ISD 300/K-12
PO Box 786 76951 325-378-4781
Bob Rauch, supt. Fax 378-2283
www.sterlingcityisd.net
Sterling City S 100/K-12
PO Box 786 76951 325-378-5821
Ty Stevens, prin. Fax 378-2087

Stinnett, Hutchinson, Pop. 1,860
Plemons-Stinnett-Phillips Cons ISD 600/PK-12
PO Box 3440 79083 806-878-2858
Bill Wiggins, supt. Fax 878-3585
www.pspcisd.net
West Texas ES 300/PK-5
PO Box 3440 79083 806-878-2103
Jeff Quisenberry, prin. Fax 878-3585
West Texas MS 200/6-8
PO Box 3440 79083 806-878-2247
Kevin Freriks, prin. Fax 878-3585

Stockdale, Wilson, Pop. 1,428
Stockdale ISD 800/K-12
PO Box 7 78160 830-996-3551
Daniel Fuller, supt. Fax 996-1071
www.stockdaleisd.org
Stockdale ES 300/K-5
PO Box 7 78160 830-996-3557
Lee Dockery, prin. Fax 996-3236
Stockdale JHS 200/6-8
PO Box 7 78160 830-996-3153
Sharon Dunn, prin. Fax 996-3055

Stonewall, Gillespie, Pop. 505
Fredericksburg ISD
Supt. — See Fredericksburg
Stonewall ES 100/K-5
220 Peach St 78671 830-990-4599
Lori Maxcey, prin. Fax 990-4549

Stratford, Sherman, Pop. 2,009
Stratford ISD 600/PK-12
PO Box 108 79084 806-366-3300
Mike Dominguez, supt. Fax 366-3304
www.stratfordisd.net
Allen ES 300/PK-4
PO Box 108 79084 806-366-3340
Jennifer Deanda, prin. Fax 366-3343
Stratford JHS 200/5-8
PO Box 108 79084 806-366-3320
Clint Seward, prin. Fax 366-3307

Strawn, Palo Pinto, Pop. 647
Strawn ISD 200/PK-12
PO Box 428 76475 254-672-5313
Richard Mitchell, supt. Fax 672-5662
www.strawnschool.net
Strawn S 200/PK-12
PO Box 428 76475 254-672-5776
Melanie Cormack, prin. Fax 672-5389

Sudan, Lamb, Pop. 949
Sudan ISD 400/PK-12
PO Box 249 79371 806-227-2431
Scott Harrell, supt. Fax 227-2146
www.sudanisd.net
Sudan ES 300/PK-7
PO Box 659 79371 806-227-2431
DeAnn Wilson, prin. Fax 227-2146

Sugar Land, Fort Bend, Pop. 76,889
Fort Bend ISD 70,700/PK-12
16431 Lexington Blvd 77479 281-634-1000
Charles Dupre Ed.D., supt. Fax 634-1700
www.fortbendisd.com
Austin Parkway ES 800/PK-5
4400 Austin Pkwy 77479 281-634-4001
Sue Sierra, prin. Fax 634-4014
Barrington Place ES 800/PK-5
2100 Squire Dobbins Dr 77478 281-634-4040
Ellie Garza, prin. Fax 634-4057
Brazos Bend ES 600/K-5
621 Cunningham Creek Blvd 77479 281-634-5180
Ida Ford, prin. Fax 634-5200
Colony Bend ES 600/K-5
2720 Planters St 77479 281-634-4080
Elizabeth Williams, prin. Fax 634-4092
Colony Meadows ES 800/PK-5
4510 Sweetwater Blvd 77479 281-634-4120
Melissa Bolding, prin. Fax 634-4136
Commonwealth ES 1,000/K-5
4909 Commonwealth Blvd 77479 281-634-5120
Dr. Latecha Bogle, prin. Fax 634-5140
Cornerstone ES 900/K-5
1800 Chatham Ave 77479 281-634-6400
Sonya Smith-Watson, prin. Fax 327-6400
Drabek ES 900/PK-5
11325 Lake Woodbridge Dr, 281-634-6570
Wendy Nunez, prin. Fax 634-6572
Dulles ES 700/K-5
630 Dulles Ave 77478 281-634-5830
Kyella Griffin, prin. Fax 634-5843
Dulles MS 1,200/6-8
500 Dulles Ave 77478 281-634-5750
Dee Knox, prin. Fax 634-5781
First Colony MS 1,200/6-8
3225 Austin Pkwy 77479 281-634-3240
Sarah Laberge, prin. Fax 634-3267
Fort Settlement MS 1,200/6-8
5440 Elkins Rd 77479 281-634-6440
Michael Hejducek, prin. Fax 634-6456
Garcia MS 1,200/6-8
18550 Old Richmond Rd, 281-634-3160
Dr. Cory Collins, prin. Fax 634-3166

Highlands ES 600/PK-5
2022 Colonist Park Dr 77478 281-634-4160
Angela Dow, prin. Fax 634-4176
Lakeview ES 600/K-5
314 Lakeview Dr, 281-634-4200
Alena McClanahan, prin. Fax 634-4214
Oyster Creek ES 800/K-5
16425 Mellow Oaks Ln, 281-634-5910
Lisa Langston, prin. Fax 634-5925
Sartartia MS 1,300/6-8
8125 Homeward Way 77479 281-634-6310
Melissa King-Knowles, prin. Fax 634-6373
Settlers Way ES 800/PK-5
3015 Settlers Way Blvd 77479 281-634-4360
Rachel Rosier, prin. Fax 634-4376
Sugar Land MS 1,300/6-8
321 7th St, 281-634-3080
Keith Fickel, prin. Fax 634-3108
Sugar Mill ES 700/K-5
13707 Jess Pirtle Blvd, 281-634-4440
Lori Craig, prin. Fax 634-4459
Sullivan ES K-5
17828 Winding Waters Ln 77479 281-327-2860
Donna Whisonant, prin. Fax 327-2861
Townewest ES 800/PK-5
13927 Old Richmond Rd, 281-634-4480
Erika Edmond, prin. Fax 634-4494
Walker Station ES 800/K-5
6200 Homeward Way 77479 281-634-4400
Kathryn Kargbo, prin. Fax 634-4413
Other Schools – See Fresno, Houston, Meadows Place, Missouri City, Richmond, Rosharon

Lamar Consolidated ISD
Supt. — See Rosenberg
Campbell ES 700/K-5
1000 Shadow Bend Dr 77479 832-223-1300
Michelle Koerth, prin. Fax 223-1301
Dickinson ES 600/K-5
7110 Greatwood Pkwy 77479 832-223-1400
Dr. Karen Mumphord, prin. Fax 223-1401

Casa Dei Bambini Montessori S 100/PK-6
108 Telfair Central Blvd 77479 281-207-9700
Cornerstone Christian Academy 400/PK-8
2140 First Colony Blvd 77479 281-980-0842
Darul Arqam S Southwest 200/PK-8
10415 Synott Rd, 281-495-4015
Ft. Bend Christian Academy 800/PK-12
1250 7th St 77478 281-263-9175
David Pitre Ph.D., head sch Fax 263-9147
Honor Roll S 800/PK-8
4111 Sweetwater Blvd 77479 281-265-7888
Tom Heinly, head sch Fax 265-7880
Logos Preparatory S K-12
13303 Southwest Fwy, 281-565-6467
Riverbend Montessori S 100/PK-6
4225 Elkins Rd 77479 281-980-4123
St. Laurence S 700/PK-8
2630 Austin Pkwy 77479 281-980-0500
Suzanne Barto, prin. Fax 980-0026
St. Theresa S 100/PK-6
705 St Theresa Blvd, 281-494-1157
Dr. Mark Newcomb, prin. Fax 240-4870
Trent Internationale S 200/PK-12
2553 Cordes Dr 77479 281-980-5800
Sr. Huda Ahmed, prin. Fax 980-6106

Sullivan City, Hidalgo, Pop. 4,002
La Joya ISD
Supt. — See La Joya
Benavides ES 500/PK-5
1882 El Pinto Rd 78595 956-323-2360
Donna Martinez, prin. Fax 323-2361
Fordyce ES 500/PK-5
801 FM 886 78595 956-323-2490
Roxana Pena, prin. Fax 323-2491

Sulphur Bluff, Hopkins
Sulphur Bluff ISD 200/PK-12
PO Box 30 75481 903-945-2460
Dustin Carr, supt. Fax 945-2459
www.sulphurbluffisd.net/
Sulphur Bluff S 200/PK-12
PO Box 30 75481 903-945-2460
Amy Northcutt, prin. Fax 945-2459

Sulphur Springs, Hopkins, Pop. 15,115
North Hopkins ISD 500/PK-12
1994 Farm Road 71 W 75482 903-945-2192
Dr. Darin Jolly, supt. Fax 945-2531
www.northhopkins.net
North Hopkins ES 300/PK-5
1994 Farm Road 71 W 75482 903-945-2192
Kodi Wright, prin. Fax 945-9003

Sulphur Springs ISD 4,200/PK-12
631 Connally St 75482 903-885-2153
Michael Lamb, supt. Fax 439-6162
www.ssisd.net/
Bowie PS 200/1-2
1400 Mockingbird Ln 75482 903-885-3772
Angela Edwards, prin. Fax 885-5754
Douglas IS 300/5-5
600 Calvert St 75482 903-885-4516
Holly Folmar, prin. Fax 439-1181
Early Childhood Learning Center 600/PK-K
390 N Hillcrest Dr 75482 903-439-6170
Amanda Fenton, prin. Fax 439-6177
Lamar PS 200/1-2
825 Church St 75482 903-885-4550
Rowena Johnson, prin. Fax 439-6144
Sulphur Springs ES 600/3-4
829 Bell St 75482 903-885-8466
Ashanta Alexander, prin. Fax 885-5451
Sulphur Springs MS 1,000/6-8
832 Wildcat Way 75482 903-885-7741
Jena Williams, prin. Fax 439-6126

Travis PS 200/1-2
130 Garrison St 75482 903-885-5246
Michelle Wallace, prin. Fax 438-2251

Sundown, Hockley, Pop. 1,386
Sundown ISD 700/PK-12
PO Box 1110 79372 806-229-3021
Scott Marshall, supt. Fax 229-2004
www.sundownisd.com
Sundown ES 400/PK-5
PO Box 1110 79372 806-229-3021
Jason Powell, prin. Fax 229-2004
Sundown MS 200/6-8
PO Box 1110 79372 806-229-4691
Eddie Carter, prin. Fax 229-2004

Sunnyvale, Dallas, Pop. 5,012
Sunnyvale ISD 1,400/PK-12
417 E Tripp Rd 75182 972-226-5974
Doug Williams, supt. Fax 226-6882
www.sunnyvaleisd.com
Sunnyvale ES 500/PK-4
416 Hounsel Ln 75182 972-226-7601
Sara Staley, prin. Fax 226-4812
Sunnyvale MS 400/5-8
216 N Collins Rd 75182 972-226-2922
Brandon Tunnell, prin. Fax 226-0982

Sunray, Moore, Pop. 1,899
Sunray ISD 500/PK-12
PO Box 240 79086 806-948-4411
Marshall Harrison, supt. Fax 948-5274
www.sunrayisd.net
Sunray ES 200/PK-4
PO Box 240 79086 806-948-4222
Stacie Jones, prin. Fax 948-4180
Sunray MS 200/5-8
PO Box 240 79086 806-948-4444
Pam Keisling, prin. Fax 948-4208

Sweeny, Brazoria, Pop. 3,645
Sweeny ISD 1,900/PK-12
1310 N Elm St 77480 979-491-8000
Toy Hill, supt. Fax 491-8030
www.sweenyisd.org
Sweeny ES 900/PK-5
1310 N Elm St 77480 979-491-8300
Michael Heinroth, prin. Fax 491-8373
Sweeny JHS 500/6-8
1310 N Elm St 77480 979-491-8200
Michael Saul, prin. Fax 491-8274

Sweeny Christian S 100/PK-7
PO Box 156 77480 979-548-6001

Sweet Home, Lavaca
Sweet Home ISD 100/PK-8
PO Box 326 77987 361-293-3221
Shane Wagner, supt. Fax 741-2499
www.sweethomeisd.org/
Sweet Home ES 100/PK-8
PO Box 326 77987 361-293-3221
Shane Wagner, prin. Fax 741-2499

Sweetwater, Nolan, Pop. 10,784
Sweetwater ISD 2,200/PK-12
207 Musgrove St 79556 325-235-8601
Dr. George McFarland, supt. Fax 235-5561
www.sweetwaterisd.net/
Cowen ECC 200/PK-PK
1200 Corral St 79556 325-235-3482
Crystal Meneses, prin. Fax 235-2771
East Ridge ES 400/2-3
1700 E 12th St 79556 325-235-5282
Vicki Mayberry, prin. Fax 235-3740
Southeast ES 400/PK-1
1201 Mustang Dr 79556 325-235-9222
Peggy Elliott, prin. Fax 235-0260
Sweetwater IS 300/4-5
705 E 3rd St 79556 325-235-3491
Doug Young, prin. Fax 235-8016
Sweetwater MS 500/6-8
305 Lamar St 79556 325-236-6303
Jeff Withrow, prin. Fax 236-6941

Taft, San Patricio, Pop. 3,018
Taft ISD 1,100/PK-12
400 College St 78390 361-528-2636
Jose Lopez, supt. Fax 528-2223
www.taftisd.net
Petty ES 500/PK-5
401 Peach St 78390 361-528-2636
Joshua Rombs, prin. Fax 528-2717
Taft JHS 200/6-8
727 McIntyre Ave 78390 361-528-2636
Christine Acosta, prin. Fax 528-5477

Tahoka, Lynn, Pop. 2,660
Tahoka ISD 600/PK-12
PO Box 1230 79373 806-561-4105
Alan Umholtz, supt. Fax 561-4160
www.tahokaisd.us
Tahoka ES 300/PK-5
PO Box 1560 79373 806-561-4350
Christa Ritchey, prin. Fax 561-5334
Tahoka MS 100/6-8
PO Box 1500 79373 806-561-4538
Kelly Kieth, prin. Fax 561-6082

Tatum, Rusk, Pop. 1,369
Tatum ISD 1,600/PK-12
PO Box 808 75691 903-947-6482
Dr. Jerry Richardson Ed.D., supt. Fax 947-3295
www.tatumisd.org
Tatum ES 300/3-5
PO Box 808 75691 903-947-6482
Kelly Sorenson, prin. Fax 765-7659
Tatum MS 400/6-8
PO Box 808 75691 903-947-6482
Kin Bryan, prin. Fax 765-7782

Tatum PS 400/PK-2
PO Box 808 75691 903-947-6482
Kathy Baumgardner, prin. Fax 765-7376

Taylor, Williamson, Pop. 14,982
Taylor ISD 3,100/PK-12
3101 N Main St Ste 104 76574 512-365-1391
Keith Brown, supt. Fax 365-3800
www.taylorisd.org
Johnson ES 300/PK-K
3100 Duck Ln 76574 512-365-7114
Jenni Cork, prin. Fax 365-7112
Main Street IS 500/4-5
3101 N Main St 76574 512-365-1999
Keith Thompson, prin. Fax 309-4471
Pasemann ES 700/1-3
2809 North Dr 76574 512-365-2278
Jennifer Patschke, prin. Fax 365-2280
Taylor MS 700/6-8
304 Carlos Parker Blvd NW 76574 512-365-8591
Travis Motal, prin. Fax 365-8589

St. Marys Catholic S 200/PK-8
520 Washburn St 76574 512-352-2313
Heidi Altman, prin. Fax 365-5313
St. Paul Lutheran S 100/PK-5
610 Fowzer St 76574 512-365-6161
Sherrie Halpain M.Ed., prin. Fax 365-1509

Teague, Freestone, Pop. 3,527
Dew ISD 100/PK-8
606 County Road 481 75860 903-389-2828
Darrell Evans, supt. Fax 389-5104
www.dewisd.net
Dew S 100/PK-8
606 County Road 481 75860 903-389-2828
Darrell Evans, admin. Fax 389-5104

Teague ISD 1,300/PK-12
420 N 10th Ave 75860 254-739-1300
Dr. Nate Carman, supt. Fax 739-5223
www.teagueisd.org
Teague ES 400/PK-3
420 N 10th Ave 75860 254-739-1350
Christina Fuller, prin. Fax 739-3605
Teague IS 200/4-5
420 N 10th Ave 75860 254-739-1400
Vickey Little, prin. Fax 739-3561
Teague JHS 300/6-8
420 N 10th Ave 75860 254-739-1450
Drake Paris, prin. Fax 739-5896

Temple, Bell, Pop. 64,746
Belton ISD
Supt. — See Belton
High Point ES 600/K-5
1635 Starlight Dr 76502 254-215-5000
Amy Armstrong, prin. Fax 215-5003
Lake Belton MS 800/6-8
8818 Tarver Dr 76502 254-215-2900
Kris Hobson, prin. Fax 215-2901
Lakewood ES 600/K-5
11200 W Adams Ave 76502 254-215-3100
Judy Schiller, prin. Fax 215-3101
North Belton MS 6-8
7907 Prairie View Rd 76502 254-316-5200
Joe Brown, prin. Fax 316-5201
Pirtle ES 700/K-5
714 S Pea Ridge Rd 76502 254-215-3400
Rebecca Vaughn, prin. Fax 215-3401
Tarver ES 400/K-5
7949 Stonehollow Dr 76502 254-215-3800
Michelle Tish, prin. Fax 774-9684

Temple ISD 8,000/PK-12
PO Box 788 76503 254-215-8473
Dr. Robin Battershell, supt. Fax 215-6783
www.tisd.org
Bonham MS 500/6-8
4600 Midway Dr 76502 254-215-6600
Sandra Atmar, prin. Fax 215-6634
Cater ES 400/K-5
4111 Lark Trl 76502 254-215-7444
Adrian Lopez, prin. Fax 215-7479
Garcia ES 500/K-5
2525 Lavendusky Dr 76501 254-215-6100
Sandra Reyes, prin. Fax 215-6122
Jefferson ES 800/K-5
2616 N 3rd St 76501 254-215-5500
Dr. Beth Giniewicz, prin. Fax 215-5545
Kennedy-Powell ES 500/K-5
3707 W Nugent Ave 76504 254-215-6000
Dr. Kelly Madden, prin. Fax 215-6032
Lamar MS 600/6-8
2120 N 1st St 76501 254-215-6444
Billy Madden, prin. Fax 215-6483
Meridith-Dunbar ECC 50/PK-PK
1717 E Avenue J 76501 254-215-6700
Lynne Brock, prin.
Raye-Allen ES 500/K-5
5015 S 5th St 76502 254-215-5800
Fran Smetana, prin. Fax 215-5843
Scott ES 500/K-5
2301 W Avenue P 76504 254-215-6222
Chrystal Thomas, prin. Fax 215-6251
Thornton ES 500/K-5
2900 Pin Oak Dr 76502 254-215-5700
Craig Wilson, prin. Fax 215-5746
Travis Science Academy 700/6-8
1551 S 25th St 76504 254-215-6300
Kristina Carter, prin. Fax 215-6352
Western Hills ES 500/K-5
600 Arapaho Dr 76504 254-215-5600
Angie Peace, prin. Fax 215-5624

Central Texas Christian S 600/PK-12
4141 W FM 93 76502 254-939-5700
Brian Littlefield, head sch Fax 939-5769

St. Marys Catholic S 200/PK-8
1019 S 7th St 76504 254-778-8141
Theresa Wyles, prin. Fax 778-1396

Tenaha, Shelby, Pop. 1,146
Tenaha ISD 600/PK-12
PO Box 318 75974 936-248-5000
Scott Tyner, supt. Fax 248-3902
www.tenahaisd.com/
Tenaha ES 300/PK-5
PO Box 318 75974 936-248-5000
Linda Jacobs, prin. Fax 248-4216

Terlingua, Brewster, Pop. 54
Terlingua Common SD 50/K-12
PO Box 256 79852 432-371-2281
Bobbie Jones, supt. Fax 371-2245
www.terlinguacsd.com
Big Bend S 50/K-12
PO Box 256 79852 432-371-2281
Bobbie Jones, admin. Fax 371-2245

Terrell, Kaufman, Pop. 15,583
Terrell ISD 4,200/PK-12
700 N Catherine St 75160 972-563-7504
Micheal French, supt. Fax 563-1406
www.terrellisd.org
Burnett S 600/PK-PK
921 S Rockwall Ave 75160 972-563-1452
Raquel Villarreal, prin. Fax 563-4782
Furlough MS 600/6-8
1351 Colquitt Rd 75160 972-563-7501
Jay Thompson, prin. Fax 563-5721
Long ES 600/K-5
300 Creekside Dr 75160 972-563-1448
Melissa Nichols, prin. Fax 563-4780
Willie ES 700/K-5
1400 S Rockwall Ave 75160 972-563-1443
Suzanne Fields, prin. Fax 563-4783
Wood ES 600/K-5
121 Poetry Rd 75160 972-563-3750
Tracie Pritchett, prin. Fax 563-4774

Poetry Community Christian S 200/K-12
18688 FM 986 75160 972-563-7227
Dr. Anne Horan, admin. Fax 563-0025

Texarkana, Bowie, Pop. 35,750
Liberty-Eylau ISD 2,300/PK-12
2901 Leopard Dr 75501 903-832-1535
Ronnie Thompson, supt. Fax 838-9444
www.leisd.net
Liberty-Eylau C.K. Bender ES 600/1-4
2300 Buchanan Rd 75501 903-831-5347
Joanna Taylor, prin. Fax 831-5393
Liberty-Eylau MS 400/5-8
5555 Leopard Dr 75501 903-838-5555
Jakeb Goff, prin. Fax 832-6700
Liberty-Eylau Pre - K Center 300/PK-K
3105 Norris Cooley Dr 75501 903-831-5352
Amy Norwood, prin. Fax 831-5354

Pleasant Grove ISD 2,000/PK-12
8500 N Kings Hwy 75503 903-831-4086
Dr. Jason Smith, supt. Fax 831-4435
www.pgisd.net
Pleasant Grove ES 500/PK-2
6500 Pleasant Grove Rd 75503 903-838-0528
Chad Blain, prin. Fax 831-3799
Pleasant Grove IS 400/3-5
8480 N Kings Hwy 75503 903-832-0001
Pam Bradford, prin. Fax 832-0147
Pleasant Grove MS 500/6-8
5605 Cooks Ln 75503 903-831-4295
Linda Erie, prin. Fax 831-5501

Red Lick ISD 500/K-8
3511 N FM 2148 75503 903-838-8230
Nick Blain, supt. Fax 831-6134
www.redlickisd.com
Red Lick ES 300/K-4
3511 N FM 2148 75503 903-838-8230
Debbie Cooper, prin. Fax 831-6134
Red Lick MS 200/5-8
3511 N FM 2148 75503 903-838-6006
Jason Dempsey, prin. Fax 831-6134

Texarkana ISD 7,100/PK-12
4241 Summerhill Rd 75503 903-794-3651
Paul Norton, supt. Fax 792-2632
www.txkisd.net
Dunbar ECC 300/PK-PK
2315 W 10th St 75501 903-794-8112
Lakesha Taylor, prin. Fax 794-5841
Highland Park ES 400/PK-5
401 W 25th St 75503 903-794-8001
Jennifer Cross, prin. Fax 793-1702
Jones Early Literacy Center 400/K-2
2600 W 15th St 75501 903-793-4871
Melodie White, prin. Fax 793-7596
Morriss Math & Engineering ES 400/K-5
4826 University Park 75503 903-791-2262
Brandy Debenport, prin. Fax 798-6875
Spring Lake Park ES 400/PK-5
4324 Ghio Fish Blvd 75503 903-794-7525
Anne Slade, prin. Fax 794-0633
Texas MS 1,500/6-8
2100 College Dr 75503 903-793-5631
Tim Lambert, prin. Fax 792-2935
Waggoner Creek ES K-5
6335 Gibson Ln 75503 903-255-3301
Angie Griffin, prin. Fax 223-7945
Westlawn ES 400/3-5
410 Westlawn Dr 75501 903-223-4252
Taryn Wells, prin. Fax 223-4262
Other Schools – See Nash, Wake Village

Bethel SDA S 50/K-8
PO Box 660 75504 903-832-6036

St. James Day S 200/PK-6
5501 N State Line Ave 75503 903-793-5554
Cheryl Brown, head sch Fax 793-1775

Texas City, Galveston, Pop. 44,454
Texas City ISD 7,200/PK-12
PO Box 1150 77592 409-916-0100
Dr. Rodney Cavness, supt. Fax 942-2655
www.tcisd.org
Blocker MS 900/7-8
1800 9th Ave N 77590 409-916-0700
Tony Furman, prin. Fax 942-2755
Fry IS 900/5-6
300 25th Ave N 77590 409-916-0600
Felicia Garrett, prin. Fax 916-0696
Guajardo ES 600/K-4
2300 21st St N 77590 409-916-0300
Debbie Fuller, prin. Fax 942-2839
Heights ES 500/PK-4
300 N Logan St 77590 409-916-0500
Erica Allen, prin. Fax 942-2450
Kohfeldt ES 500/K-4
1705 13th Ave N 77590 409-916-0400
Matthew Salley, prin. Fax 916-0496
Roosevelt-Wilson ES 600/K-4
301 16th Ave N 77590 409-916-0200
Wendy Patterson, prin. Fax 942-2871
Vincent ECC PK-PK
1805 13th Ave N 77590 409-916-0512
Susan Wilson, prin. Fax 916-0596
Other Schools – See La Marque

Our Lady of Fatima S 100/PK-8
1600 9th Ave N 77590 409-945-3326
Gail Rodgers, prin. Fax 945-3389

Texhoma, Sherman, Pop. 342
Texhoma ISD 200/PK-4
PO Box 10080, 806-827-7400
James Mireles, supt. Fax 827-7657
www.texhomaisd.net
Texhoma ES 200/PK-4
PO Box 10080, 806-827-7400
James Mireles, admin. Fax 827-7657

Texline, Dallam, Pop. 485
Texline ISD 100/PK-12
PO Box 60 79087 806-362-4667
Jody Johnson, supt. Fax 362-4538
www.texlineisd.net
Texline S 100/PK-12
PO Box 60 79087 806-362-4284
Terrell Jones, prin. Fax 362-4938

The Colony, Denton, Pop. 35,324
Lewisville ISD
Supt. — See Flower Mound
Camey ES 500/PK-5
4949 Arbor Glen Rd 75056 469-713-5951
Angela Cortez, prin. Fax 350-9015
Ethridge ES 500/PK-5
6001 Ethridge Dr 75056 469-713-5954
Tasia Thompson, prin. Fax 350-9036
Griffin MS 700/6-8
5105 N Colony Blvd 75056 469-713-5973
Amy Boughten, prin. Fax 350-9187
Lakeview MS 800/6-8
4300 Keys Dr 75056 469-713-5974
Jeremy Turner, prin. Fax 350-9202
Morningside ES 400/PK-5
6350 Paige Rd 75056 469-713-5970
Rita Bacque, prin. Fax 350-9117
Owen ES 400/K-5
5640 Squires Dr 75056 469-713-5950
Jennifer Spitzer, prin. Fax 350-9000
Peters Colony ES 700/K-5
5101 Nash Dr 75056 469-713-5179
Toni Hall, prin. Fax 350-9133
Stewarts Creek ES 500/PK-5
4431 Augusta St 75056 469-713-5960
Eric Cockerham, prin. Fax 350-9145

Little Elm ISD
Supt. — See Little Elm
Prestwick STEM Academy 700/K-8
3101 Stonefield 75056 972-947-9446
Christine Gibson, prin. Fax 947-9325

The Woodlands, Montgomery, Pop. 92,202
Conroe ISD
Supt. — See Conroe
Buckalew ES 700/K-4
4909 Alden Bridge Dr 77382 281-465-3400
Jill Price, prin. Fax 465-3499
Bush ES 700/K-4
7420 Crownridge Dr 77382 936-709-1600
Judy Mills, prin. Fax 709-1699
Collins IS 600/5-6
6020 Shadow Bend Pl 77381 281-298-3800
Shellie LeBlanc, prin. Fax 298-3803
David ES 600/K-4
5301 Shadow Bend Pl 77381 281-298-4700
Lee Allen, prin. Fax 298-4703
Deretchin ES 1,200/K-6
11000 Merit Oaks Dr 77382 832-592-8700
Alicia Reeves, prin. Fax 592-8780
Galatas ES 700/K-4
9001 Cochrans Crossing Dr 77381 936-709-5000
Denae Wilker, prin. Fax 709-5003
Glen Loch ES 600/PK-4
27505 Glen Loch Dr 77381 281-298-4900
Cassie Hertzenberg, prin. Fax 298-4903
Hailey ES 700/K-4
12051 Sawmill Rd 77380 832-663-4100
Tracy Horne, prin. Fax 663-4199
Knox JHS 1,300/7-8
12104 Sawmill Rd 77380 832-592-8400
Joe Daw, prin. Fax 592-8410
Lamar ES 700/K-4
1300 Many Pines Rd 77380 832-592-5800
Mary Kirbo, prin. Fax 592-5810
McCullough JHS 2,300/7-8
3800 S Panther Creek Dr 77381 832-592-5100
Chris McCord, prin. Fax 592-5116
Mitchell IS 1,200/5-6
6800 Alden Bridge Dr 77382 832-592-8500
Paula Klapesky, prin. Fax 592-8518
Powell ES 800/K-4
7332 Cochrans Crossing Dr 77381 936-709-1700
Lisa Garrison, prin. Fax 709-1799
Ride ES 500/K-4
4920 W Panther Creek Dr 77381 281-465-2800
Megan Burnham, prin. Fax 465-2803
Tough ES 1,100/K-6
11660 Cranebrook Dr 77382 281-465-5900
Shawn Creswell, prin. Fax 465-5959
Wilkerson IS 700/5-6
12312 Sawmill Rd 77380 832-592-8900
Jennifer Daw, prin. Fax 592-8910

Tomball ISD
Supt. — See Tomball
Creekside Forest ES 800/K-5
5949 Creekside Forest Dr, 281-357-4526
Jeanine Deyoe, prin. Fax 357-4535
Creekside Park JHS 6-8
8711 Creekside Green Dr, 281-357-3282
Mindy Munoz, prin. Fax 516-9606
Creekview ES 900/K-5
8877 W New Harmony Trl, 281-357-3070
Niesa Glenewinkel, prin. Fax 357-3071
Timber Creek ES 500/K-5
8455 Creekside Green Dr, 281-357-3060
Lauren Thompson, prin. Fax 357-3061

Center for Teaching and Learning 100/PK-8
PO Box 131541 77393 832-474-8214
Christ Community S 200/PK-6
1488 Wellman Rd 77384 936-321-6300
Gerald Evans, head sch Fax 447-9324
Cooper S 1,000/PK-12
1 John Cooper Dr 77381 281-367-0900
Michael Maher, head sch Fax 292-9201
Esprit International S 100/PK-12
4890 W Panther Creek Dr 77381 281-298-9200
Legacy Preparatory Christian Academy 200/PK-12
9768 Research Forest Dr, 936-337-2000
Audra May, admin. Fax 755-1797
Rubicon Academy 50/PK-9
14211 Horseshoe Bend 77384 936-273-9111
Dr. Franci Roberts, prin.
St. Anthony of Padua S 500/PK-8
7901 Bay Branch Dr 77382 281-296-0300
Renee Nunez, prin. Fax 296-7236
The Woodlands Methodist S 200/PK-8
1915 Lake Front Cir 77380 281-882-8220
Tim Patton, prin. Fax 297-5912
Woodlands Christian Academy 400/PK-12
5800 Academy Way 77384 936-273-2555
Julie Ambler, head sch Fax 271-3115

Thorndale, Milam, Pop. 1,329
Thorndale ISD 600/PK-12
PO Box 870 76577 512-898-2538
Adam Ivy, supt. Fax 898-5356
www.thorndale.txed.net
Thorndale ES 300/PK-5
PO Box 870 76577 512-898-2912
Meghan Esau, prin. Fax 898-5541
Thorndale MS 200/6-8
PO Box 870 76577 512-898-2670
Lee Hafley, prin. Fax 898-5505

St. Paul Lutheran S 100/PK-8
PO Box 369 76577 512-898-2711
Corey Moss, prin. Fax 898-5298

Thrall, Williamson, Pop. 832
Thrall ISD 500/PK-12
201 S Bounds St 76578 512-898-0062
Tommy Hooker, supt. Fax 898-5349
www.thrallisd.com
Thrall ES 300/PK-4
201 S Bounds St 76578 512-898-5293
Sherri Maruska, prin. Fax 898-2879

Three Rivers, Live Oak, Pop. 1,845
Three Rivers ISD 600/PK-12
351 S School Rd 78071 361-786-3626
Dr. Mary Springs, supt. Fax 786-2555
www.trisd.org
Three Rivers ES 400/PK-6
351 S School Rd 78071 361-786-3592
Les Dragon, prin. Fax 786-2555

Throckmorton, Throckmorton, Pop. 823
Throckmorton ISD 100/PK-12
210 College St 76483 940-849-2411
Nelson Coulter, supt. Fax 849-3345
www.throck.org
Throckmorton S 100/PK-12
210 College St 76483 940-849-2421
David Farquhar, prin. Fax 849-3345

Tilden, McMullen, Pop. 261
McMullen County ISD 200/PK-12
PO Box 359 78072 361-274-2000
Jason Jones, supt. Fax 274-3665
www.mcisd.us
McMullen County S 200/PK-12
PO Box 359 78072 361-274-2000
Joe Timms, prin. Fax 274-3580

Timpson, Shelby, Pop. 1,144
Timpson ISD 600/PK-12
PO Box 370 75975 936-254-2463
Mid Johnson, supt. Fax 254-3878
www.timpsonisd.com
Timpson ES 300/PK-5
PO Box 370 75975 936-254-2462
Dewayne Carrington, prin. Fax 254-3261
Timpson MS 200/6-8
PO Box 370 75975 936-254-2078
Calvin Smith, prin. Fax 254-2355

Tioga, Grayson, Pop. 788
Tioga ISD 300/PK-12
PO Box 159 76271 940-437-2366
Dr. Charles Holloway, supt. Fax 437-9986
www.tiogaisd.net/
Tioga S 300/PK-12
PO Box 159 76271 940-437-2366
Jana Smith, prin. Fax 437-9986

Tivoli, Refugio, Pop. 475
Austwell-Tivoli ISD 200/K-12
207 Redfish St 77990 361-286-3212
Dr. Antonio Aguirre, supt. Fax 286-3637
www.atisd.net
Austwell-Tivoli ES 100/K-6
207 Redfish St 77990 361-286-3151
Stephen Maldonado, prin. Fax 286-3637

Tolar, Hood, Pop. 677
Tolar ISD 700/PK-12
PO Box 368 76476 254-835-4718
Travis Stilwell, supt. Fax 835-4704
www.tolarisd.org
Tolar ES 300/PK-5
PO Box 368 76476 254-835-4028
Kristen Carey, prin. Fax 835-4319
Tolar JHS 200/6-8
PO Box 368 76476 254-835-5207
Dr. Lindsay Morgan, prin. Fax 835-5208

Tomball, Harris, Pop. 10,569
Klein ISD
Supt. — See Klein
Kohrville ES 700/K-5
11600 Woodland Shore Dr 77375 832-484-7200
Vicki Bland, prin. Fax 484-7890
Schultz ES 900/PK-5
7920 Willow Forest Dr 77375 832-484-7000
Sherri Davenport, prin. Fax 484-7884

Tomball ISD 13,400/PK-12
310 S Cherry St 77375 281-357-3100
Dr. Martha Salazar-Zamora, supt. Fax 357-3128
www.tomballisd.net
Canyon Pointe ES 800/PK-4
13002 Northpointe Blvd 77377 281-357-3122
Barbara Coleman, prin. Fax 357-3147
Lakewood ES 800/PK-4
15614 Gettysburg Dr 77377 281-357-3260
Deanna Porter, prin. Fax 357-3271
Northpointe IS 900/5-6
11855 Northpointe Blvd 77377 281-357-3020
Darrell McReynolds, prin. Fax 357-3026
Rosehill ES 600/PK-4
17950 Tomball Waller Rd 77377 281-357-3075
Gregory Chappell, prin. Fax 357-3099
Tomball ES 700/PK-4
1110 Inwood St 77375 281-357-3280
Chad Schmidt, prin. Fax 357-3288
Tomball IS 700/5-6
723 W Main St 77375 281-357-3150
Beatriz Shaughnessy, prin. Fax 357-3148
Tomball JHS 800/7-8
30403 Quinn Rd 77375 281-357-3000
Chad Allman, prin. Fax 357-3027
Wildwood ES PK-4
13802 Northpointe Blvd 77377 281-357-3040
Sherry Baker, prin. Fax 357-3041
Willow Creek ES 900/K-4
18302 N Eldridge Pkwy 77377 281-357-3080
Teresa Sullivan, prin. Fax 357-3092
Willow Wood JHS 1,000/7-8
11770 Gregson Rd 77377 281-357-3030
Robert Frost, prin. Fax 357-3045
Other Schools – See Cypress, Magnolia, The Woodlands

Rosehill Christian S 400/PK-12
19830 FM 2920 Rd 77377 281-351-8114
Dean Unsicker, head sch Fax 516-3418
St. Anne S 400/PK-8
1111 S Cherry St 77375 281-351-0093
Joseph Noonan, prin. Fax 357-1905
Salem Lutheran S 500/PK-8
22601 Lutheran Church Rd 77377 281-351-8223
Dr. Mary Beth Gaertner, dir. Fax 520-4287
Step by Step Christian S 100/PK-8
1119 S Cherry St 77375 281-351-2888
Jerianne Green, head sch Fax 378-4412
Woodlands Preparatory S 300/PK-12
27440 Kuykendahl Rd 77375 281-516-0600
Daniel Fernandez, head sch Fax 516-1155

Tom Bean, Grayson, Pop. 1,019
Tom Bean ISD 700/K-12
PO Box 128 75489 903-546-6076
Kelly Lusk, supt. Fax 546-6104
www.tbisd.org
Tom Bean ES 300/K-5
PO Box 128 75489 903-546-6333
Patrice Counts, prin. Fax 546-6572
Tom Bean MS 200/6-8
PO Box 128 75489 903-546-6161
Sara McCarty, prin. Fax 546-6798

Tool, Henderson, Pop. 2,205
Malakoff ISD
Supt. — See Malakoff
Tool ES 200/PK-5
1201 S Tool Dr, 903-432-2637
Christal Calhoun, prin. Fax 432-3666

Tornillo, El Paso, Pop. 1,568
Tornillo ISD 1,100/PK-12
PO Box 170 79853 915-765-3000
Dr. Rosa Vega-Barrio, supt. Fax 765-3099
www.tisd.us/
Tornillo ES 300/PK-2
PO Box 170 79853 915-765-3100
Thomas Cervantes, prin. Fax 765-3199
Tornillo IS 200/3-5
PO Box 170 79853 915-765-3300
Roberto Guerrero, prin. Fax 765-3399
Tornillo JHS 200/6-8
PO Box 170 79853 915-765-3400
Marco Tristan, prin. Fax 765-3499

Trent, Taylor, Pop. 330
Trent ISD 200/PK-12
PO Box 105 79561 325-862-6125
Leanna West, supt. Fax 862-6448
www.trentisd.org
Trent S 200/PK-12
PO Box 105 79561 325-862-6125
Leanna West, admin. Fax 862-6448

Trenton, Fannin, Pop. 627
Trenton ISD 500/PK-12
PO Box 5 75490 903-989-2245
Rick Foreman, supt. Fax 989-2767
sites.google.com/trentonisd.com/tisd/
Trenton ES 200/PK-4
PO Box 5 75490 903-989-2244
Mandi Alexander, prin. Fax 989-2415
Trenton MS 100/5-8
PO Box 5 75490 903-989-2243
Trent Hamilton, prin. Fax 989-2668

Trinidad, Henderson, Pop. 863
Trinidad ISD 200/PK-12
105 W Eaton St 75163 903-778-2673
Corey Jenkins, supt. Fax 778-4120
www.trinidadisd.com
Trinidad S 200/PK-12
105 W Eaton St 75163 903-778-2673
Corey Jenkins, admin. Fax 778-4120

Trinity, Trinity, Pop. 2,644
Trinity ISD 1,200/PK-12
PO Box 752 75862 936-594-3569
John Kaufman, supt. Fax 594-8425
www.trinityisd.net
Lansberry ES 600/PK-5
PO Box 752 75862 936-594-3567
Kelli Robinson, prin. Fax 594-2646
Trinity MS 300/6-8
PO Box 752 75862 936-594-2321
Brittaney Cassidy, prin. Fax 594-3041

Trophy Club, Denton, Pop. 7,926
Northwest ISD
Supt. — See Justin
Beck ES 700/K-5
401 Parkview Dr 76262 817-215-0450
Sandy Conklin, prin. Fax 215-0498
Lakeview ES 600/PK-5
100 Village Trl 76262 817-215-0750
Mary Seltzer, prin. Fax 215-0770
Medlin MS 1,000/6-8
601 Parkview Dr 76262 817-215-0500
Dr. Paige Cantrell, prin. Fax 215-0548

Troup, Smith, Pop. 1,837
Troup ISD 1,100/PK-12
PO Box 578 75789 903-842-3067
Stuart Bird, supt. Fax 842-4563
www.troupisd.org
Troup ES 500/PK-5
PO Box 578 75789 903-842-3071
Melanie Johnson, prin. Fax 842-4563
Troup MS 300/6-8
PO Box 578 75789 903-842-3081
Ava Johnson, prin. Fax 842-4563

Troy, Bell, Pop. 1,625
Troy ISD 1,400/PK-12
PO Box 409 76579 254-938-2595
Neil Jeter, supt. Fax 938-7323
www.troyisd.org
Mays ES 300/PK-1
PO Box 409 76579 254-938-0304
Kelli Frisch, prin. Fax 938-0233
Mays MS 300/6-8
PO Box 409 76579 254-938-2543
Michelle Jolliff, prin. Fax 938-2880
Troy ES 400/2-5
PO Box 409 76579 254-938-2503
Andrea Durbin, prin. Fax 938-2080

Tulia, Swisher, Pop. 4,912
Tulia ISD 1,100/PK-12
702 NW 8th St 79088 806-995-4591
Steve Post, supt. Fax 995-3169
www.tuliaisd.net
Swinburn ES 300/3-5
300 N Dallas Ave 79088 806-995-4309
Johnny Lara, prin. Fax 995-4448
Tulia Highland ES 300/PK-2
800 NW 9th St 79088 806-995-4141
Pam White Miner, prin. Fax 995-2265
Tulia JHS 200/6-8
421 NE 3rd St 79088 806-995-4842
Casey McBroom, prin. Fax 995-4498

Turkey, Hall, Pop. 416
Turkey-Quitaque ISD 200/PK-12
11826 Highway 86 79261 806-455-1411
Jackie Jenkins, supt. Fax 455-1718
www.valleypatriots.com
Valley S 200/PK-12
11826 Highway 86 79261 806-455-1411
Jerry Smith, prin. Fax 455-1718

Tuscola, Taylor, Pop. 734
Jim Ned Consolidated ISD 1,100/PK-12
PO Box 9 79562 325-554-7500
Bobby Easterling, supt. Fax 554-7740
www.jimned.esc14.net
Jim Ned MS 300/6-8
PO Box 9 79562 325-554-7870
Jay Wise, prin. Fax 554-7750
Other Schools – See Buffalo Gap, Lawn

Tyler, Smith, Pop. 95,596
Chapel Hill ISD 3,500/PK-12
11134 County Road 2249 75707 903-566-2441
Donni Cook Ed.D., supt. Fax 566-8469
www.chapelhillisd.org
Chapel Hill MS 800/6-8
13174 State Highway 64 E 75707 903-566-1491
Debbie Black, prin. Fax 565-5125
Jackson ES 400/PK-5
16406 FM 2767 75705 903-566-3530
Dr. Jennifer Bailey, prin. Fax 566-5158
Kissam ES 700/PK-5
12800 State Highway 64 E 75707 903-566-8334
Charla McClure, prin. Fax 565-5195
Wise Fine Arts Magnet S 500/PK-5
10659 State Highway 64 E 75707 903-566-2271
Patricia Duck, prin. Fax 566-5135

Tyler ISD 17,500/PK-12
PO Box 2035 75710 903-262-1000
Dr. Marty Crawford, supt. Fax 262-1178
www.tylerisd.org
Austin ES 500/PK-5
1105 W Franklin St 75702 903-262-1765
Brandy Holland, prin. Fax 262-1767
Bell ES 500/PK-5
1409 E Hankerson St 75701 903-262-1820
Sheri Barberee, prin. Fax 262-1821
Birdwell ES 500/PK-5
2010 S Talley Ave 75701 903-262-1870
Bethany Moody, prin. Fax 262-1871
Bonner ES 400/PK-5
235 S Saunders Ave 75702 903-262-1920
Zaqueo Cazares, prin. Fax 262-1921
Boulter Creative Arts Magnet S 600/6-8
2926 Garden Valley Rd 75702 903-262-1390
Tara Hinton, prin. Fax 262-1392
Caldwell Elementary Arts Academy 700/PK-5
331 S College Ave 75702 903-262-2250
Bobby Markle, prin. Fax 262-2252
Clarkston ES 400/PK-5
2915 Williamsburg Dr 75701 903-262-1980
Gretchen Nabi, prin. Fax 262-1981
Dixie ES 600/PK-5
213 Patton Ln 75704 903-262-2040
Joanne Saul, prin. Fax 262-2041
Dogan MS 500/6-8
2621 N Border Ave 75702 903-262-1450
Vanessa Holmes, prin. Fax 262-1451
Douglas ES 700/PK-5
1525 N Carlyle Ave 75702 903-262-2100
Christina Roach, prin. Fax 262-2101
Griffin ES 600/PK-5
2650 N Broadway Ave 75702 903-262-2310
Brandon Chandler, prin. Fax 262-2311
Hogg MS 600/6-8
920 S Broadway Ave 75701 903-262-1500
Eddie Dunn, prin. Fax 262-1501
Hubbard MS 800/6-8
1300 Hubbard Dr 75703 903-262-1560
Kevin Blain, prin. Fax 262-1566
Jack ES 700/K-5
1900 Balsam Gap 75703 903-262-3260
Patti Henderson, prin. Fax 262-3329
Jones ES 300/PK-5
3450 Chandler Hwy 75702 903-262-2360
Natasha Crain, prin. Fax 262-2362
Moore MST Magnet MS 900/6-8
2101 Devine St 75701 903-262-1640
Claude Lane, prin. Fax 262-1648
Orr ES 700/PK-5
3350 Pine Haven Rd 75702 903-262-2400
Steven Young, prin. Fax 262-2401
Owens ES 600/K-5
11780 County Road 168 75703 903-262-2175
Laurie Greathouse, prin. Fax 262-2176
Peete ES 400/PK-5
1511 Bellwood Rd 75701 903-262-2460
Jonathon Kegler, prin. Fax 262-2461
Ramey ES 500/PK-5
2000 N Forest Ave 75702 903-262-2505
Cassandra Chapa, prin. Fax 262-2506
Rice ES 600/PK-5
5215 Old Bullard Rd 75703 903-262-2555
Shelly Bosley, prin. Fax 262-2556
St. Louis ECC, 2800 Walton Rd 75701 100/PK-PK
Stacy Miles, prin. 903-262-1180
Three Lakes MS 6-8
2445 Three Lakes Pkwy 75703 903-952-4400
Christopher Blake, prin.
Woods ES 600/K-5
3131 Fry Ave 75701 903-262-1280
Georgeanna Jones, prin. Fax 262-1281

All Saints Episcopal S 700/PK-12
2695 S Southwest Loop 323 75701 903-579-6000
Mike Cobb, head sch Fax 579-6002
Christian Heritage S 100/K-12
961 County Road 1143 75704 903-593-2702
Calvin Todd, admin. Fax 531-2226
East Texas Christian Academy 300/PK-12
2448 Roy Rd 75707 903-561-8642
Dr. Mike Weimer, pres. Fax 561-9620

Good Shepherd S 100/PK-12
2525 Old Jacksonville Rd 75701 903-592-4045
Walter Banek, head sch Fax 596-7149
Grace Community S Lower Campus 500/PK-5
3215 Old Jacksonville Rd 75701 903-593-1977
Jay Ferguson, hdmstr. Fax 593-2897
King's Academy Christian S 100/K-12
7330 S Broadway Ave 75703 903-534-9992
Erin Baggs, admin. Fax 526-7929
Oak Hill Montessori S 200/PK-4
6720 Oak Hill Blvd 75703 903-561-1002
Promise Academy 50/K-1
PO Box 7353 75711 903-630-7369
Sarah Cumming, head sch
St. Gregory Cathedral S 300/PK-5
500 S College Ave 75702 903-595-4109
Patty Brittain, prin. Fax 592-8626
Tyler SDA S 50/K-8
2931 S Southeast Loop 323 75701 903-595-6706

Universal City, Bexar, Pop. 18,038
Judson ISD
Supt. — See Live Oak
Coronado Village ES 500/PK-5
213 Amistad Blvd 78148 210-945-5110
Cynthia Davis, prin. Fax 659-0579
Kitty Hawk MS 1,300/6-8
840 Old Cimarron Trl 78148 210-945-1220
Beverly Broom, prin. Fax 659-0687
Olympia ES 500/PK-5
8439 Athenian Dr 78148 210-945-5113
Karli Sitton, prin. Fax 659-6172
Salinas ES 900/K-5
10560 Old Cimarron Trl 78148 210-659-5045
Martin Silverman, prin. Fax 659-2367

Schertz-Cibolo-Universal City ISD
Supt. — See Schertz
Rose Garden ES 500/PK-4
506 North Blvd 78148 210-619-4350
Sherri Schlather, prin. Fax 619-4369

First Baptist Academy 500/PK-12
1401 Pat Booker Rd 78148 210-658-5331
Christine Povolish, hdmstr. Fax 658-7024

Utopia, Uvalde, Pop. 224
Utopia ISD 200/PK-12
PO Box 880 78884 830-966-1928
John Walts, supt. Fax 966-6162
www.utopiaisd.net
Utopia S 200/PK-12
PO Box 880 78884 830-966-3339
Jessica Milam, prin. Fax 966-6162

Uvalde, Uvalde, Pop. 15,676
Uvalde Consolidated ISD 4,800/PK-12
PO Box 1909 78802 830-278-6655
Jeanette Ball, supt. Fax 591-4909
www.ucisd.net
Anthon ES 700/1-2
PO Box 1909 78802 830-591-2988
Bryan Perez, prin. Fax 591-2993
Dalton ECC 700/PK-K
PO Box 1909 78802 830-591-4933
Abraham Contreras, prin. Fax 591-4936
Flores ES 700/5-6
PO Box 1909 78802 830-591-2976
Michelle Rodriguez, prin. Fax 591-2987
Morales JHS 400/7-8
PO Box 1909 78802 830-591-2980
Isidro Esamilla, prin. Fax 591-2975
Robb ES 700/3-4
PO Box 1909 78802 830-591-4947
Becky Reinhardt, prin. Fax 591-4937
Other Schools – See Batesville

Sacred Heart S 100/PK-6
401 W Leona St 78801 830-278-2661
Janice Estrada, prin. Fax 279-0634
St. Philip's Episcopal Day S 100/PK-4
343 N Getty St 78801 830-278-1350
Jean Ann Chisum, head sch Fax 278-2093
Uvalde Classical Academy 100/PK-12
PO Box 2004 78802 830-591-2242

Valentine, Jeff Davis, Pop. 134
Valentine ISD 50/PK-12
PO Box 188 79854 432-467-2671
Debbie Engle, supt. Fax 467-2004
www.valentineisd.com
Valentine S 50/PK-12
PO Box 188 79854 432-467-2671
Debbie Engle, supt. Fax 467-2004

Valera, Coleman
Panther Creek Consolidated ISD 100/PK-12
129 Private Road 3421 76884 325-357-4506
Dwin Nanny, supt. Fax 357-4470
www.pcreek.net
Panther Creek S 100/PK-12
129 Private Road 3421 76884 325-357-4449
Dwin Nanny, admin. Fax 357-4470

Valley Mills, Bosque, Pop. 1,193
Valley Mills ISD 600/PK-12
PO Box 518 76689 254-932-5210
Dr. Alan Oakley, supt. Fax 932-6601
www.vmisd.net
Valley Mills ES 400/PK-6
PO Box 518 76689 254-932-5526
Chris Dowdy, prin. Fax 932-6601
Valley Mills JHS 100/7-8
PO Box 518 76689 254-932-5251
Jason Sansom, prin. Fax 932-6601

Valley View, Cooke, Pop. 748
Valley View ISD 700/PK-12
106 Newton St 76272 940-726-3659
William Stokes, supt. Fax 726-3614
www.vvisd.net
Valley View ES 300/PK-4
106 Newton St 76272 940-726-3681
Susan Smith, prin. Fax 726-3647
Valley View MS 200/5-8
106 Newton St 76272 940-726-3244
Jesse Newton, prin. Fax 726-3786

Van, Van Zandt, Pop. 2,615
Van ISD 2,300/PK-12
PO Box 697 75790 903-963-8328
Don Dunn, supt. Fax 963-8799
www.vanschools.org
Rhodes ES 400/PK-1
PO Box 697 75790 903-963-8386
Jonnie Smith, prin. Fax 963-8794
Van IS 300/2-3
PO Box 697 75790 903-963-8331
Marty Moore, prin. Fax 963-5582
Van JHS 400/7-8
PO Box 697 75790 903-963-8321
Richard Pride, prin. Fax 963-3277
Van MS 500/4-6
PO Box 697 75790 903-963-1461
Shelby Davidson, prin. Fax 963-1472

Van Alstyne, Grayson, Pop. 2,993
Van Alstyne ISD 1,300/PK-12
549 Miller Ln 75495 903-482-8802
Dr. David Brown, supt. Fax 482-6086
www.vanalstyneisd.org
Van Alstyne ES 500/PK-4
201 Newport Dr 75495 903-482-8805
Sherry Stillman, prin. Fax 482-8820
Van Alstyne MS 400/5-8
1314 N Waco St 75495 903-482-8804
Ryan Coleman, prin. Fax 482-8890

Kingdom Country Academy K-12
PO Box 1423 75495 903-225-9064
Karen Love, prin.

Vanderbilt, Jackson, Pop. 392
Industrial ISD 1,200/PK-12
PO Box 369 77991 361-284-3226
Paul Darilek, supt. Fax 284-3349
www.industrialisd.org
Industrial ES East 300/PK-5
PO Box 368 77991 361-284-3226
Kim Schaefer, prin. Fax 284-3377
Industrial JHS 300/6-8
PO Box 367 77991 361-284-3226
Caleb McCain, prin. Fax 284-3049
Other Schools – See Inez

Van Horn, Culberson, Pop. 2,041
Culberson County-Allamore ISD 300/PK-12
PO Box 899 79855 432-283-2245
Ken Baugh, supt. Fax 283-9062
www.ccaisd.net/
Van Horn S 300/PK-12
PO Box 899 79855 432-283-2245
Kittie Gibson, prin. Fax 283-9062

Van Vleck, Matagorda, Pop. 1,828
Van Vleck ISD 900/PK-12
142 S 4th St 77482 979-245-8518
John O'Brien, supt. Fax 245-1214
www.vvisd.org
Herman MS 200/6-8
719 1st St 77482 979-245-6401
Shannon Jedlicka, prin. Fax 245-8538
Rudd IS 100/4-5
128 5th St 77482 979-245-6561
Shannon Jedlicka, prin. Fax 245-1214
Van Vleck ES 200/PK-3
178 S 4th St 77482 979-245-8681
Sarah Roper, prin. Fax 323-0479

Vega, Oldham, Pop. 874
Vega ISD 300/PK-12
PO Box 190 79092 806-267-2123
Dr. Paul Uttley, supt. Fax 267-2146
www.vegalonghorn.com
Vega ES 200/PK-4
PO Box 190 79092 806-267-2126
Johnette Stribling, prin. Fax 267-2146
Vega JHS 5-8
PO Box 190 79092 806-267-2123
Tracey Bell, prin. Fax 267-2146

Venus, Johnson, Pop. 2,914
Venus ISD 1,900/PK-12
100 Student Dr 76084 972-366-3448
Dr. Melissa Sulak, supt. Fax 366-2141
www.venusisd.net
Venus ES 600/2-5
20 Bulldog Dr 76084 972-366-3748
Tammy Witten, prin. Fax 366-8808
Venus MS 400/6-8
1 Bulldog Dr 76084 972-366-3358
Kimberly Buck, prin. Fax 366-1740
Venus PS 400/PK-1
102 Student Dr 76084 972-366-3268
Steven Nazworth, prin. Fax 366-1826

Veribest, Tom Green
Veribest ISD 300/PK-12
PO Box 490 76886 325-655-4912
Bobby Fryar, supt. Fax 655-3355
www.veribestisd.net
Veribest ES 100/PK-6
PO Box 490 76886 325-655-2851
Kalum McKay, prin. Fax 653-0551

Vernon, Wilbarger, Pop. 10,848
Northside ISD 200/K-12
18040 US Highway 283 76384 940-552-2551
Mark Haught, supt. Fax 553-4919
www.northsideisd.us
Northside S 200/K-12
18040 US Highway 283 76384 940-552-2551
Molly Lemon, prin. Fax 553-4913

Vernon ISD 2,100/PK-12
1713 Wilbarger St 76384 940-553-1900
Jeff Byrd, supt. Fax 553-3802
www.vernonisd.org
Central ES 400/2-3
1300 Paradise St 76384 940-553-1859
Kacy Hunter, prin. Fax 553-1138
McCord ES 400/PK-1
2915 Sand Rd 76384 940-553-4381
Scott Mills, prin. Fax 552-0056
Shive ES 300/4-5
3130 Bacon St 76384 940-553-4309
Stefanie Merrell, prin. Fax 552-5597
Vernon MS 500/6-8
2200 Yamparika St 76384 940-552-6231
Michael Campos, prin. Fax 552-0504

Victoria, Victoria, Pop. 61,923
Bloomington ISD 900/PK-12
2875 FM 616 77905 361-333-8016
Abbie Barnett, supt. Fax 333-8026
www.bisd-tx.org/
Other Schools – See Bloomington, Placedo

Nursery ISD 100/K-5
13254 Nursery Dr 77904 361-575-6882
Chris Ulcak, supt. Fax 576-9212
www.nurseryisd.org
Nursery ES 100/K-5
13254 Nursery Dr 77904 361-575-6882
Chris Ulcak, admin. Fax 576-9212

Victoria ISD 14,900/PK-12
PO Box 1759 77902 361-576-3131
Dr. Robert Jaklich Ed.D., supt. Fax 788-9643
www.visd.net/
Aloe ES 500/PK-5
PO Box 1759 77902 361-788-9509
Kristina Hurley, prin. Fax 788-9662
Cade MS 800/6-8
PO Box 1759 77902 361-788-2840
Jill Lau, prin. Fax 788-2886
Chandler ES 600/PK-5
PO Box 1759 77902 361-788-9587
Melanie Reed, prin. Fax 788-9590
Crain ES 900/PK-5
PO Box 1759 77902 361-573-7453
Melissa Correll, prin. Fax 574-3411
De Leon ES 500/PK-5
PO Box 1759 77902 361-788-9553
Selina Reyna, prin. Fax 788-9634
Dudley GT Magnet ES 600/PK-5
PO Box 1759 77902 361-788-9517
Diane Billo, prin. Fax 788-9523
Gross ES 400/PK-5
PO Box 1759 77902 361-788-9500
Mary Noble, prin. Fax 788-9504
Guadalupe ES 100/K-5
PO Box 1759 77902 361-788-9906
Laura Longoria, prin. Fax 788-9357
Hopkins ES 500/PK-5
PO Box 1759 77902 361-788-9527
Leandra Hill, prin. Fax 788-9635
Howell MS 800/6-8
PO Box 1759 77902 361-578-1561
Jo Beth Jones, prin. Fax 788-9547
Mission Valley ES 200/PK-5
PO Box 1759 77902 361-788-9514
Eric Amsler, prin. Fax 788-9689
O'Connor ES 500/PK-5
PO Box 1759 77902 361-788-9572
Vickie Dunseth, prin. Fax 788-9575
Rowland ES 500/PK-5
PO Box 1759 77902 361-788-9549
Tammy Garza, prin. Fax 788-9902
Schorlemmer ES 400/PK-5
PO Box 1759 77902 361-788-2860
Lynn Guerra, prin. Fax 788-9283
Shields ES 500/PK-5
PO Box 1759 77902 361-788-9593
Heather Mascorro, prin. Fax 788-9691
Smith ES 600/PK-5
PO Box 1759 77902 361-788-9605
Michelle Graves, prin. Fax 788-9688
Stroman MS 800/6-8
PO Box 1759 77902 361-578-2711
Dawn Maroney, prin. Fax 788-9800
Torres ES 600/PK-5
PO Box 1759 77902 361-788-2850
Crystal Rice, prin. Fax 788-9278
Vickers ES 500/PK-5
PO Box 1759 77902 361-788-9579
Steve Carroll, prin. Fax 788-9663
Welder MS 700/6-8
PO Box 1759 77902 361-575-4553
Denise Canchola, prin. Fax 788-9629
Wood ES 100/K-5
PO Box 1759 77902 361-788-9533
Katherine Schuelke, prin. Fax 788-9912

Faith Academy 400/PK-12
PO Box 4824 77903 361-572-4568
Rev. Larry Long M.A., supt. Fax 573-5058
Nazareth Academy 300/PK-8
206 W Convent St 77901 361-573-6651
Sr. Evelyn Korenek, prin. Fax 573-1829
Our Lady of Victory S 500/PK-8
1311 E Mesquite Ln 77901 361-575-5391
Sr. Laura Toman, prin. Fax 575-3473

Trinity Episcopal S 200/PK-8
1504 N Moody St 77901 361-573-3220
Kristy Nelson, head sch Fax 573-2964
Victoria Adventist Academy PK-8
3103 E Mockingbird Ln 77904 361-572-3887
Victoria Christian S 100/PK-6
3310 N Ben Jordan St 77901 361-573-5345

Vidor, Orange, Pop. 10,443
Vidor ISD 5,000/PK-12
120 E Bolivar St 77662 409-951-8700
Dr. Jay Killgo, supt. Fax 769-0093
www.vidorisd.org/
Oak Forest ES 800/PK-4
2400 Highway 12 77662 409-951-8860
Carolyn Wedgeworth, prin. Fax 769-2678
Pine Forest ES 700/PK-4
4150 N Main St 77662 409-951-8800
Preston Clark, prin. Fax 786-1728
Vidor ES 600/PK-4
400 E Railroad St 77662 409-951-8830
Jeff Leger, prin. Fax 769-0211
Vidor JHS 800/7-8
945 N Tram Rd 77662 409-951-8970
Dr. James McDowell, prin. Fax 769-6754
Vidor MS 700/5-6
2500 Highway 12 77662 409-951-8880
Jason Yeaman, prin. Fax 783-0309

Von Ormy, Bexar, Pop. 1,084
Somerset ISD
Supt. — See Somerset
Barrera Veterans ES 600/PK-4
4135 Smith Rd 78073 866-465-8808
Geneva Salinas, prin. Fax 465-8818
Savannah Heights IS 600/5-6
5040 Smith Rd 78073 866-852-9863
Julie Riedel, prin. Fax 488-4341
Somerset JHS 600/7-8
4730 W Loop 1604 78073 866-852-9862
Ellida Guerra, prin. Fax 448-2738

Southwest ISD
Supt. — See San Antonio
Resnik MS 6-8
4495 SW Verano Pkwy 78073 210-623-6589
Odilia Martinez, prin. Fax 623-2700

Waco, McLennan, Pop. 122,806
Bosqueville ISD 600/PK-12
7636 Rock Creek Rd 76708 254-757-3113
James Skeeler, supt. Fax 752-4909
www.bosquevilleisd.org
Bosqueville ES 300/PK-5
7636 Rock Creek Rd 76708 254-752-6006
Kelly Bray, prin. Fax 759-7065
Bosqueville MS 100/6-8
7636 Rock Creek Rd 76708 254-759-7077
Sara Mynarcik, prin. Fax 752-5459

China Spring ISD
Supt. — See China Spring
China Spring IS 600/4-6
4001 Flat Rock Rd 76708 254-759-1200
Heather Jenkins, prin. Fax 759-1208

Connally ISD 1,900/PK-12
200 Cadet Way 76705 254-296-6460
Wesley Holt, supt. Fax 412-5530
www.connally.org
Connally ECC PK-K
200 Cadet Way 76705 254-296-6771
Melissa Sulak, prin. Fax 412-5530
Connally ES 400/4-5
300 Cadet Way 76705 254-750-7100
Gina Pasisis, prin. Fax 412-5525
Other Schools – See Elm Mott

Gholson ISD 200/PK-12
137 Hamilton Dr 76705 254-829-1528
Pamela Brown, supt. Fax 829-0054
www.gholsonisd.org
Gholson S 200/PK-12
137 Hamilton Dr 76705 254-829-1528
Heather McCartney, prin. Fax 829-0054

Hallsburg ISD 100/PK-6
2313 Hallsburg Rd 76705 254-875-2331
Dr. Kent Reynolds, supt. Fax 875-2436
hallsburgisd.com
Hallsburg ES 100/PK-6
2313 Hallsburg Rd 76705 254-875-2331
Dr. Kent Reynolds, prin. Fax 875-2436

La Vega ISD 2,900/PK-12
400 E Loop 340 76705 254-799-4963
Dr. Sharon Shields, supt. Fax 799-8642
www.lavegaisd.org
La Vega ES 700/1-3
3100 Wheeler St 76705 254-799-1721
Shaunte Stewart, prin. Fax 799-4453
La Vega IS H.P Miles Campus 600/4-6
4201 Williams Rd 76705 254-799-5553
Kristi Rizo, prin. Fax 799-9738
La Vega JHS George Dixon Campus 400/7-8
4401 Orchard Ln 76705 254-799-2428
Chris Borland, prin. Fax 799-8943
La Vega PS 400/PK-K
4400 Harrison St 76705 254-799-6229
Lisa Seawright, prin. Fax 799-1369

Midway ISD
Supt. — See Woodway
South Bosque ES 600/PK-4
1 Wickson Rd 76712 254-761-5720
Stacy Voigt, prin. Fax 776-2493
Speegleville ES 200/PK-4
101 Maywood Dr 76712 254-761-5730
Christopher Eberlein, prin. Fax 848-9751

Woodgate IS 600/5-6
9400 Chapel Rd 76712 254-761-5690
Aaron Pena Ed.D., prin. Fax 666-0928
Woodway ES 600/PK-4
325 Estates Dr 76712 254-761-5740
Beth Olson, prin. Fax 761-5765

Waco ISD 14,300/PK-12
PO Box 27 76703 254-755-9473
Marcus Nelson Ed.D., supt. Fax 755-9690
www.wacoisd.org
Alta Vista ES 500/PK-5
3637 Alta Vista Dr 76706 254-662-3050
Karmen Logan, prin. Fax 662-7353
ATLAS Academy 6-8
6100 Tennyson Dr 76710 254-754-5491
Sandra Gibson, dean Fax 750-3576
Bells Hill ES 800/PK-5
2100 Ross Ave 76706 254-754-4171
Rebekah Mechell, prin. Fax 750-3559
Brook Avenue ES 400/PK-5
720 Brook Ave 76708 254-750-3562
Sarah Pedrotti, prin. Fax 750-3545
Carver MS 500/6-8
1601 J J Flewellen Rd 76704 254-757-0787
Alonza McAdoo, prin. Fax 750-3442
Cedar Ridge ES 700/PK-5
2115 Meridian Ave 76708 254-756-1241
Helen Smith, prin. Fax 750-3531
Chavez MS 900/6-8
700 S 15th St 76706 254-750-3736
Suzanne Hamilton, prin. Fax 750-3739
Crestview ES 700/PK-5
1120 N New Rd 76710 254-776-1704
Jacob Donnell, prin. Fax 741-4910
Dean Highland ES 800/PK-5
3300 Maple Ave 76707 254-752-3751
Thia Allen, prin. Fax 750-3458
Hillcrest ES 400/PK-5
4225 Pine Ave 76710 254-772-4286
Amy Mathews-Perez, prin. Fax 741-4938
Hines ES 500/PK-5
301 Garrison St 76704 254-753-1362
Julie Sapaugh, prin. Fax 750-3799
Kendrick ES 500/PK-5
1801 Kendrick Ln 76711 254-752-3316
Tonya Coleman, prin. Fax 750-3472
Lake Air Montessori S 700/PK-8
4601 Cobbs Dr 76710 254-772-1910
Stephanie Tankersley, prin. Fax 741-4945
Mountainview ES 400/PK-4
5901 Bishop Dr 76710 254-772-2520
Melissa Pritchard, prin. Fax 741-4961
Parkdale ES 500/PK-4
6400 Edmond Ave 76710 254-772-2170
Marsha Henry, prin. Fax 741-4979
Provident Heights ES 400/PK-5
2415 Bosque Blvd 76707 254-750-3930
Debbie Sims, prin. Fax 750-3934
South Waco ES 600/PK-5
2104 Gurley Ln 76706 254-753-6802
Twana Lee, prin. Fax 750-3527
Tennyson MS 800/6-8
6100 Tennyson Dr 76710 254-772-1440
Lisa Hall, prin. Fax 741-4970
West Avenue ES 400/PK-5
1101 N 15th St 76707 254-750-3900
Joseph Alexander, prin. Fax 750-3904

Live Oak Classical S 200/PK-12
PO Box 647 76703 254-714-1007
New Creation Adventist S 50/K-10
800 W State Highway 6 76712 254-772-8775
St. Louis Catholic S 300/PK-8
2208 N 23rd St 76708 254-754-2041
Nisa Lagle, prin. Fax 754-2091
St. Paul's Episcopal S 200/PK-6
517 Columbus Ave 76701 254-753-0246
M'Lissa Howen, head sch Fax 755-7488
Waco Montessori S 300/PK-6
1920 Columbus Ave 76701 254-754-3966
Woodway Christian S 200/PK-8
13000 Woodway Dr 76712 254-772-1298
Nancy Purdy, admin.

Waelder, Gonzales, Pop. 1,062
Waelder ISD 300/PK-12
PO Box 247 78959 830-788-7161
Jon Orozco, supt. Fax 788-7429
www.waelderisd.org
Waelder S 300/PK-12
PO Box 247 78959 830-788-7151
Dr. Ron Lilie, prin. Fax 788-7323

Wake Village, Bowie, Pop. 5,381
Texarkana ISD
Supt. — See Texarkana
Wake Village ES 700/PK-5
400 Wildcat Dr 75501 903-838-4261
Kassie Watson, prin. Fax 832-6809

Wall, Tom Green
Wall ISD, PO Box 259 76957 1,100/K-12
Russell Dacy, supt. 325-651-7790
www.wallisd.net
Wall ES, PO Box 259 76957 500/K-5
Matt Fore, prin. 325-651-7790
Wall MS, PO Box 259 76957 300/6-8
Matt Rivers, prin. 325-651-7790

Waller, Waller, Pop. 2,288
Waller ISD 5,900/PK-12
2214 Waller St 77484 936-931-3685
Danny Twardowski, supt. Fax 372-5576
www.wallerisd.net
Fields Store ES 700/PK-5
31670 Giboney Rd 77484 936-931-4050
Melissa Crosby, prin. Fax 372-4100

Holleman ES 700/PK-5
2200 Brazeal St 77484 936-372-9196
Michael Skinner, prin. Fax 372-2468
Schultz JHS 700/6-8
19010 Stokes Rd 77484 936-931-9103
Stephanie Fletcher, prin. Fax 372-9302
Waller JHS 700/6-8
2402 Waller St 77484 936-931-1353
Eric Meldahl, prin. Fax 931-4044
Other Schools – See Hockley, Prairie View

Waller Christian Academy 50/PK-9
PO Box 1717 77484 936-372-0901
Richard Keithley M.Ed., head sch Fax 202-2322

Wallis, Austin, Pop. 1,240
Brazos ISD 800/PK-12
PO Box 819 77485 979-478-6551
Brian Thompson, supt. Fax 478-6413
www.brazosisd.net/
Brazos MS 200/6-8
PO Box 879 77485 979-478-6814
Clay Hudgins, prin. Fax 478-2574
Other Schools – See Orchard

Walnut Springs, Bosque, Pop. 805
Walnut Springs ISD 200/PK-12
PO Box 63 76690 254-797-2133
Pat Garrett, supt. Fax 797-2191
www.walnutspringsisd.net
Walnut Springs S 200/PK-12
PO Box 63 76690 254-797-2133
Michele Garza, prin. Fax 797-2191

Warren, Tyler, Pop. 751
Warren ISD 1,300/PK-12
PO Box 69 77664 409-547-2241
Brad McEachern, supt. Fax 547-3405
www.warrenisd.net
Warren ES 400/PK-5
PO Box 550 77664 409-547-2247
Dr. Steven Cox, prin. Fax 547-0146
Warren JHS 300/6-8
PO Box 205 77664 409-547-2241
Kristina Wiedman, prin. Fax 547-2740
Other Schools – See Fred

Waskom, Harrison, Pop. 2,131
Waskom ISD 900/PK-12
PO Box 748 75692 903-687-3361
Jimmy Cox, supt. Fax 687-3253
www.waskomisd.net
Waskom ES 300/PK-5
PO Box 748 75692 903-687-3361
Wade Youngblood, prin. Fax 687-3377
Waskom MS 300/6-8
PO Box 748 75692 903-687-3361
Bonita Cherry, prin. Fax 687-3372

Watauga, Tarrant, Pop. 22,948
Birdville ISD
Supt. — See Haltom City
Hardeman ES 800/PK-5
6100 Whispering Ln 76148 817-547-2800
Lindi Talbott, prin. Fax 581-5496
Watauga ES 900/PK-5
5937 Whitley Rd 76148 817-547-2700
Sarah Upchurch, prin. Fax 581-5425
Watauga MS 700/6-8
6300 Maurie Dr 76148 817-547-4800
Shannon Houston, prin. Fax 581-5369

Keller ISD
Supt. — See Keller
Whitley Road ES 500/K-4
7600 Whitley Rd 76148 817-744-5800
Rodrigo Cano, prin. Fax 281-4023

Water Valley, Tom Green
Water Valley ISD 300/PK-12
PO Box 250 76958 325-484-2478
Fabian Gomez, supt. Fax 484-3359
www.wvisd.net/
Water Valley ES 100/PK-6
PO Box 250 76958 325-484-2478
Wayland Cooksey LL.D., prin. Fax 484-3359

Waxahachie, Ellis, Pop. 29,212
Waxahachie ISD 7,800/PK-12
411 N Gibson St 75165 972-923-4631
Jeremy Glenn Ed.D., supt. Fax 923-4759
www.wisd.org
Clift ES 500/K-5
650 Parks School House Rd 75165 972-923-4720
Christi Kubin, prin. Fax 937-5367
Dunaway ES 600/K-5
600 S Highway 77 75165 972-923-4646
Emily Camarena, prin. Fax 923-4752
Felty ES 600/K-5
231 Park Place Blvd 75165 972-923-4616
Carrie Kazda, prin. Fax 923-9394
Finley JHS 800/6-8
2401 Brown St 75165 972-923-4680
Adan Casas, prin. Fax 923-4687
Howard JHS 900/6-8
265 Broadhead Rd 75165 972-923-4771
Jacob Perry, prin. Fax 923-3817
Marvin ES 200/K-5
110 Brown St 75165 972-923-4670
Christi Bailey, prin. Fax 923-4677
Northside ES 600/K-5
801 Brown St 75165 972-923-4610
Jennifer Burns, prin. Fax 923-4750
Shackelford ES 600/K-5
1001 Butcher Rd 75165 972-923-4666
Theresa Burkhalter, prin. Fax 923-4753
Turner Prekindergarten Academy PK-PK
614 N Getzendaner St 75165 972-923-4690
Fax 923-4699

Wedgeworth ES 600/K-5
405 Solon Rd 75165 972-923-4640
Lynda Solis, prin. Fax 923-4751

St. Joseph Catholic S 200/PK-8
506 E Marvin Ave 75165 972-937-0956
Deborah Timmerman, prin. Fax 937-1742
Waxahachie Preparatory Academy 100/K-12
PO Box P 75168 972-937-0440
Scott Marks, admin. Fax 937-5033

Weatherford, Parker, Pop. 24,879
Garner ISD 200/PK-8
2222 Garner School Rd 76088 940-682-4251
Rebecca Hallmark, supt. Fax 682-4141
www.garnerisd.net
Garner S 200/PK-8
2222 Garner School Rd 76088 940-682-4251
Diane Shaw, prin. Fax 682-4141

Peaster ISD 900/PK-12
3602 Harwell Lake Rd 76088 817-341-5000
Matt Adams, supt. Fax 341-5003
www.peaster.net
Peaster ES 500/PK-6
3400 Harwell Lake Rd 76088 817-341-5000
Michelle Madison, prin. Fax 594-1890
Peaster MS 200/7-8
8512 FM Road 920 76088 817-341-5000
Darren Grudt, prin. Fax 341-5052

Weatherford ISD 7,700/PK-12
1100 Longhorn Dr 76086 817-598-2800
Dr. Jeffrey Hanks, supt. Fax 598-0216
www.weatherfordisd.com
Austin ES 600/K-5
1776 Texas Dr 76086 817-598-2848
Jenny Morris, prin. Fax 598-2978
Crockett ES 500/PK-5
1015 Jameson St 76086 817-598-2811
Marie Hernandez, prin. Fax 598-2813
Curtis ES 700/K-5
501 W Russell St 76086 817-598-2838
Lorie Bratcher, prin. Fax 598-2840
Hall MS 600/6-8
823 S Bowie Dr 76086 817-598-2822
Jeanette McNeely, prin. Fax 598-2854
Ikard ES 700/PK-5
100 Ikard Ln 76086 817-598-2818
Christy Burton, prin. Fax 598-2805
Martin ES 600/K-5
719 N Oakridge Dr 76087 817-598-2910
Amy Crippen, prin. Fax 598-2912
Seguin ES 600/PK-5
499 E 8th St 76086 817-598-2814
Jessica Shugart, prin. Fax 598-2826
Tison MS 600/6-8
102 Meadowview Rd 76087 817-598-2960
Eric Sams, prin. Fax 598-2963
Wright ES 600/PK-5
1309 Charles St 76086 817-598-2828
Tra Hall, prin. Fax 598-2830

Couts Christian Academy 200/PK-8
802 N Elm St 76086 817-599-8601
Amy Nesler, admin. Fax 594-5516
Weatherford Christian S 200/PK-12
111 E Columbia St 76086 817-596-7807
Dr. Beth Riley, head sch Fax 596-0529

Webster, Harris, Pop. 10,170
Clear Creek ISD
Supt. — See League City
Greene ES 800/PK-5
2903 Friendswood Link Rd 77598 281-284-5000
Lesa Gaffey, prin. Fax 284-5005
McWhirter ES 800/PK-5
300 Pennsylvania St 77598 281-284-4800
Dr. Michael Marquez, prin. Fax 284-4805

Iman Academy Southeast 300/PK-10
825 Jetstream 77598 281-204-8710
Br. Hisham Youssef, pres. Fax 204-8717
Westminster Christian Academy 200/PK-8
670 E Medical Center Blvd 77598 281-280-9829

Weimar, Colorado, Pop. 2,127
Weimar ISD 600/PK-12
506 W Main St 78962 979-725-9504
Jon Wunderlich, supt. Fax 725-8737
www.weimarisd.org/
Weimar ES 300/PK-4
515 W Main St 78962 979-725-6009
Karen Bellue, prin. Fax 725-9527
Weimar JHS 200/5-8
101 N West St 78962 979-725-9515
Stacey Heger, prin. Fax 725-8383

St. Michael S 100/PK-8
103 E North St 78962 979-725-8461
Carolanne McAfee, prin. Fax 725-8344

Welch, Dawson, Pop. 221
Dawson ISD 200/PK-12
PO Box 180 79377 806-489-7568
Jeff Fleenor, supt. Fax 489-7463
www.dawsonisd.us
Dawson S 200/PK-12
PO Box 180 79377 806-489-7461
Jeff Fleenor, prin. Fax 489-7463

Wellington, Collingsworth, Pop. 2,160
Wellington ISD 600/PK-12
609 15th St 79095 806-447-3102
Kurt Ashmore, supt. Fax 447-5124
www.wellingtonisd.net
Wellington ES 300/PK-5
606 16th St 79095 806-447-3112
Dane Richardson, prin. Fax 447-5097
Wellington JHS 100/6-8
1504 Amarillo St 79095 806-447-3152
Tim Webb, prin. Fax 447-5089

Wellman, Terry, Pop. 202
Wellman-Union Consolidated ISD 200/PK-12
PO Box 69 79378 806-637-4910
Aaron Waldrip, supt. Fax 637-2585
wellman.esc17.net
Wellman-Union ES 100/PK-5
PO Box 129 79378 806-637-4619
Bridget Brown, prin. Fax 637-2585

Wells, Cherokee, Pop. 772
Wells ISD 300/PK-12
PO Box 469 75976 936-867-4466
James Moore, supt. Fax 867-4497
www.wells.esc7.net
Wells ES 200/PK-6
PO Box 469 75976 936-867-4400
Charles Caughlin, prin. Fax 867-4466

Weslaco, Hidalgo, Pop. 35,580
Weslaco ISD 17,200/PK-12
PO Box 266 78599 956-969-6500
Priscilla Canales, supt. Fax 969-2664
www.wisd.us
Airport ES 700/PK-5
410 N Airport Dr 78596 956-969-6770
Ida Cuadra, prin. Fax 968-4062
Central MS 1,000/6-8
503 E 6th St 78596 956-969-6710
Patricia Munoz, prin. Fax 969-0779
Cleckler/Heald ES 900/PK-5
1601 W Sugar Cane Dr 78599 956-969-6888
Monica Vanderveer, prin. Fax 968-6808
Cuellar MS 800/6-8
1201 S Bridge Ave 78596 956-969-6720
Desi Rodriguez, prin. Fax 973-9797
Garza MS 1,100/6-8
1111 W Sugar Cane Dr 78599 956-969-6774
John Garlic, prin. Fax 447-0484
Gonzalez ES 800/PK-5
3801 N Mile 5 1/2 W 78599 956-969-6760
Rosa Garcia, prin. Fax 969-9828
Hoge MS 1,000/6-8
2302 N International Blvd 78596 956-969-6730
Pablo Vallejo, prin. Fax 514-0903
Houston ES 100/PK-5
608 N Cantu St 78596 956-969-6740
Selma Guiterrez, prin. Fax 973-9404
Margo ES 1,100/PK-5
1701 S Bridge Ave 78596 956-969-6800
Rubelina Martinez, prin. Fax 969-8868
Memorial ES 900/PK-5
1700 S Border Ave 78596 956-969-6780
Rhonda Sellman, prin. Fax 968-5506
North Bridge ES 800/PK-5
2001 N Bridge Ave 78599 956-969-6810
Daniel Budimir, prin. Fax 968-1521
Rico ES 900/PK-5
2202 N International Blvd 78596 956-969-6815
Jaqueline Padilla, prin. Fax 565-4676
Roosevelt ES 700/PK-5
814 E Plaza St 78596 956-969-6750
Jennifer Luna, prin. Fax 968-6154
Silva ES 800/PK-5
1001 W Mile 10 N 78599 956-969-6790
Sonia Gonzalez, prin. Fax 968-6937
21st Century Early Learning Foundations 600/PK-PK
400 S Oklahoma Ave 78596 956-969-6620
Janie Pena, prin.
Ybarra ES 700/PK-5
1800 E Mile 10 N 78599 956-969-6587
Selma Gutierrez, prin. Fax 969-6518

San Martin de Porres S 100/PK-5
905 N Texas Blvd 78596 956-973-8642
Reyna Ortega, prin. Fax 973-0522

West, McLennan, Pop. 2,777
West ISD 1,300/PK-12
801 N Reagan St 76691 254-951-2000
David Truitt, supt. Fax 826-7503
www.westisd.net/
West ES 600/PK-5
801 N Reagan St 76691 254-981-2200
Cari Detlefsen, prin. Fax 826-7543
West MS 300/6-8
801 N Reagan St 76691 254-981-2120
Michele Scott, prin. Fax 826-7524

St. Marys Catholic S 100/PK-8
PO Box 277 76691 254-826-5991
Ericka Sammon, prin. Fax 826-7047

Westbrook, Mitchell, Pop. 253
Westbrook ISD 300/PK-12
PO Box 99 79565 325-644-2311
Todd Burleson, supt. Fax 644-5101
www.westbrookisd.com
Westbrook S 300/PK-12
PO Box 99 79565 325-644-2311
Sherry Rowden, prin. Fax 644-5101

West Columbia, Brazoria, Pop. 3,841
Columbia-Brazoria ISD 3,000/PK-12
PO Box 158 77486 979-345-5147
Steven Galloway, supt. Fax 345-4890
www.cbisd.com
West Columbia ES 800/PK-6
PO Box 158 77486 979-799-1760
Roxana Bolton, prin. Fax 345-3170
Other Schools – See Brazoria

Westhoff, DeWitt
Westhoff ISD 100/PK-8
244 Lynch Ave 77994 830-236-5519
David Kennedy Ed.D., supt. Fax 236-5583
www.westhoffisd.org
Westhoff S 100/PK-8
244 Lynch Ave 77994 830-236-5519
Fax 236-5583

West Lake Hills, Travis, Pop. 3,003
Eanes ISD
Supt. — See Austin
Forest Trail ES 600/K-5
1203 S Capital Of Texas Hwy 78746 512-732-9160
Cody Spraberry, prin. Fax 732-9169
Valley View ES 500/K-5
1201 S Capital Of Texas Hwy 78746 512-732-9140
Jennifer Dusek, prin. Fax 732-9149

Wharton, Wharton, Pop. 8,727
Wharton ISD 1,800/PK-12
2100 N Fulton St 77488 979-532-6201
Tina Herrington, supt. Fax 532-6228
www.whartonisd.net
Sivells ES 500/PK-2
1605 N Alabama Rd 77488 979-532-6866
Trisha Terrell, prin. Fax 532-6873
Wharton ES 500/3-6
2030 E Boling Hwy 77488 979-532-6882
Jennifer Mann, prin. Fax 532-6884
Wharton JHS 300/7-8
1120 N Rusk St 77488 979-532-6840
Dr. Jerrell Barron, prin. Fax 532-6849

Wheeler, Wheeler, Pop. 1,576
Kelton ISD 100/PK-12
16703 FM 2697 79096 806-826-5795
Doug Rice, supt. Fax 826-3601
keltonisd.com
Kelton S 100/PK-12
16703 FM 2697 79096 806-826-5795
Johnny James, prin. Fax 826-3601

Wheeler ISD 500/PK-12
PO Box 1010 79096 806-826-5241
Bryan Markham, supt. Fax 826-3118
www.wheelerschools.net
Wheeler S 500/PK-12
PO Box 1010 79096 806-826-5241
Mike Bailey, prin. Fax 826-3118

White Deer, Carson, Pop. 983
White Deer ISD 300/PK-12
PO Box 517 79097 806-883-2311
Karl Vaughn, supt. Fax 883-2321
www.whitedeerisd.net/
White Deer ES 200/PK-6
PO Box 37 79097 806-883-2311
Rob Groves, prin. Fax 883-5008

Whiteface, Cochran, Pop. 442
Whiteface Consolidated ISD 400/PK-12
PO Box 7 79379 806-287-1154
Dr. Cassidy McBrayer, supt. Fax 287-1131
www.whitefaceschool.net
Whiteface S 200/PK-12
PO Box 7 79379 806-287-1104
Chris Mendez, prin. Fax 287-1131

Whitehouse, Smith, Pop. 7,533
Whitehouse ISD 4,600/PK-12
106 Wildcat Dr 75791 903-839-5500
Dr. Christopher Moran, supt. Fax 839-5515
www.whitehouseisd.org
Brown ES 300/PK-5
104 State Highway 110 N 75791 903-839-5610
Lisa Schwartz, prin. Fax 839-5607
Cain ES 600/PK-5
801 State Highway 110 S 75791 903-839-5600
Sandi Jones, prin. Fax 839-5604
Higgins ES 700/PK-5
306 Bascom Rd 75791 903-839-5580
Forrest Kaiser, prin. Fax 839-5584
Holloway 6th Grade S 300/6-6
701 E Main St 75791 903-839-5656
Susan Limmer, prin. Fax 839-1568
Stanton - Smith ES 600/PK-5
500 Zavala Trl 75791 903-839-5730
Sterling Haskell, prin. Fax 839-5744
Whitehouse JHS 700/7-8
108 Wildcat Dr 75791 903-839-5590
Josh Garred, prin. Fax 839-5518

White Oak, Gregg, Pop. 6,394
White Oak ISD 1,400/PK-12
200 S White Oak Rd 75693 903-291-2000
Michael Gilbert, supt. Fax 291-2222
www.woisd.net
White Oak IS 400/3-5
200 S White Oak Rd 75693 903-291-2100
Jenifer Rock, prin. Fax 291-2196
White Oak MS 300/6-8
200 S White Oak Rd 75693 903-291-2050
Rebecca Balboa, prin. Fax 291-2035
White Oak PS 300/PK-2
200 S White Oak Rd 75693 903-291-2150
Claire Koonce, prin. Fax 291-2132

Whitesboro, Grayson, Pop. 3,755
Whitesboro ISD 1,600/PK-12
115 4th St 76273 903-564-4200
Ryan Harper, supt. Fax 564-9303
www.whitesboroisd.org
Hayes PS 400/PK-2
117 4th St 76273 903-564-4200
Patti Achimon, prin. Fax 564-4123
Whitesboro IS 400/3-5
211 N College St 76273 903-564-4180
Gina Henley, prin. Fax 564-6808

Whitesboro MS 400/6-8
600 4th St 76273 903-564-4240
Ted Beal, prin. Fax 564-5939

White Settlement, Tarrant, Pop. 15,816
White Settlement ISD
Supt. — See Fort Worth
Brewer MS 1,000/7-8
1000 S Cherry Ln 76108 817-367-1267
Sherri Kottwitz, prin. Fax 367-1268
Liberty ES 500/PK-4
7976 Whitney Dr 76108 817-367-1312
Michael Dickinson, prin. Fax 367-1313
West ES 500/PK-4
8901 White Settlement Rd 76108 817-367-1334
Lisa Edmunds, prin. Fax 367-1333

Whitewright, Grayson, Pop. 1,571
Whitewright ISD 800/PK-12
PO Box 888 75491 903-364-2155
Steve Arthur, supt. Fax 364-2839
whitewrightisd.com
Whitewright ES 400/PK-5
PO Box 888 75491 903-364-2155
Brandon Whiten, prin. Fax 364-5799
Whitewright MS 200/6-8
PO Box 888 75491 903-364-2155
Charles Nash, prin. Fax 364-5263

Whitharral, Hockley
Whitharral ISD 200/K-12
PO Box 225 79380 806-299-1184
Ed Sharp, supt. Fax 299-1257
www.whitharralisd.org/
Whitharral S 200/K-12
PO Box 225 79380 806-299-1135
Nick McCollister, prin. Fax 299-1257

Whitney, Hill, Pop. 2,048
Whitney ISD 1,500/PK-12
PO Box 518 76692 254-694-2254
Gene Solis, supt. Fax 694-4001
www.whitney.k12.tx.us
Whitney ES 400/PK-2
PO Box 518 76692 254-694-3456
Amber Seely, prin. Fax 694-2059
Whitney IS 300/3-5
PO Box 518 76692 254-694-7303
Russell Gauer, prin. Fax 694-7029
Whitney MS 300/6-8
PO Box 518 76692 254-694-3446
Wayne Redding, prin. Fax 694-2064

Wichita Falls, Wichita, Pop. 102,278
Burkburnett ISD
Supt. — See Burkburnett
Tower ES 600/PK-5
5200 Hooper Dr 76306 940-855-3221
Jason Nolan, prin. Fax 851-9812

City View ISD 1,000/PK-12
1025 City View Dr 76306 940-855-4042
Dr. Brad Lewis, supt. Fax 851-8889
www.cityview-isd.net/
City View ES 600/PK-6
1023 City View Dr 76306 940-855-2351
Stephanie Spear, prin. Fax 855-7943

Wichita Falls ISD 12,500/PK-12
PO Box 97533 76307 940-235-1000
Michael Kuhrt, supt. Fax 720-3228
www.wfisd.net
Barwise MS 400/6-8
3807 Kemp Blvd 76308 940-235-1108
Cody Blair, prin. Fax 235-1109
Brook Village ECC 300/PK-PK
2222 Brook Ave 76301 940-235-1132
Letitia Willis, prin. Fax 235-1133
Burgess ES 500/PK-5
3106 Maurine St 76306 940-235-1136
Jeff Hill, prin. Fax 235-1137
Crockett ES 500/K-5
3015 Avenue I 76309 940-235-1140
Kory Dorman, prin. Fax 235-1141
Cunningham ES 400/PK-5
4107 Phillips Dr 76308 940-235-1144
Ashley Davis, prin. Fax 235-1145
Fain ES 600/PK-5
1562 Norman St 76302 940-235-1148
Clarisa Richie, prin. Fax 235-1149
Fowler ES 600/K-5
5100 Ridgecrest Dr 76310 940-235-1152
Alex Martin, prin. Fax 235-1153
Franklin ES 400/K-5
2112 Speedway Ave 76308 940-235-1156
Angie Betts, prin. Fax 235-1157
Haynes Northwest Academy 300/PK-5
1705 Katherine Dr 76306 940-235-1160
Cindy Underwood, prin. Fax 235-1161
Jefferson ES 500/PK-5
4628 Mistletoe Dr 76310 940-235-1168
Peter Braveboy, prin. Fax 235-1169
Kirby MS 400/6-8
1715 Loop 11 76306 940-235-1113
Troy Farris, prin. Fax 235-1114
Lamar ES 400/PK-5
2206 Lucas Ave 76301 940-235-1172
Amanda Garcia, prin. Fax 235-1173
McNiel MS 700/6-8
4712 Barnett Rd 76310 940-235-1118
Tania Rushing, prin. Fax 235-1119
Milam ES 500/PK-5
2901 Boren Ave 76308 940-235-1176
Ana Griffiths, prin. Fax 235-1305
Scotland Park ES 500/PK-5
1415 N 5th St 76306 940-235-1180
Laura Scott, prin. Fax 235-1303
Sheppard A F B ES 300/PK-5
301 Anderson Dr 76311 940-235-1184
Cindy Waddell, prin. Fax 235-1185

Southern Hills ES 600/PK-5
3920 Armory Rd 76302 940-235-1188
Noami Alejandro, prin. Fax 235-1304
Washington ES 400/PK-5
1300 Harding St 76301 940-235-1196
Mark Davis, prin. Fax 235-1197
West Foundation ES 500/K-5
5220 Lake Wellington Pkwy 76310 940-235-1192
Kim Smith, prin. Fax 235-1193
Zundy ES K-5
1706 Polk St 76309 940-235-1123
Stacey Darnall, admin. Fax 235-1124

Christ Academy 200/PK-12
5105 Stone Lake Dr 76310 940-692-2853
Dr. Jerry Meadows, hdmstr. Fax 692-2657
Notre Dame S 200/PK-12
2821 Lansing Blvd 76309 940-692-6041
Michael Edghill, prin. Fax 692-2811
Wichita Christian S 300/K-12
1615 Midwestern Pkwy 76302 940-763-1347
Thomas Snell, supt. Fax 687-0744

Wildorado, Oldham
Wildorado ISD 100/PK-9
PO Box 120 79098 806-426-3317
Troy Duck, supt. Fax 426-3523
www.wildoradoisd.org
Wildorado S 100/PK-9
PO Box 120 79098 806-426-3317
Trish Giacomazzi, prin. Fax 426-3523

Willis, Montgomery, Pop. 5,574
Willis ISD 6,800/PK-12
204 W Rogers St 77378 936-856-1200
Dr. Tim Harkrider, supt. Fax 856-5182
www.willisisd.org/
Brabham MS 800/6-8
10000 FM 830 Rd 77318 936-890-2312
Tiffany Mathews, prin. Fax 856-2910
Cannan ES 600/PK-5
7639 County Line Rd 77378 936-890-8660
Tamara Good, prin. Fax 890-2616
Hardy ES 700/PK-5
701 Gerald St 77378 936-856-1241
Lorie Oram, prin. Fax 856-1242
Lucas MS 800/6-8
1304 N Campbell St 77378 936-856-1274
Kim Sprayberry, prin. Fax 856-1065
Meador ES 800/PK-5
10020 FM 830 Rd 77318 936-890-7550
Nan Seith, prin. Fax 890-7540
Parmley ES 700/PK-5
600 N Campbell St 77378 936-856-1231
Calandra Lewis, prin. Fax 856-1239
Turner ES 600/PK-5
10101 N Highway 75 77378 936-856-1289
Kameron Wilder, prin. Fax 856-1677

Willow Park, Parker, Pop. 3,938
Aledo ISD
Supt. — See Aledo
McCall ES 400/K-5
400 Scenic Trl 76087 817-441-4500
Julie Choate, prin. Fax 441-4535

Trinity Christian Academy 400/PK-12
4954 E IH-20 Service Rd S 76087 817-441-5897
Michael Skaggs, head sch Fax 441-9063

Wills Point, Van Zandt, Pop. 3,473
Wills Point ISD 2,500/PK-12
338 W North Commerce St 75169 903-873-5100
Scott Caloss, supt. Fax 873-2462
www.wpisd.com
Wills Point JHS 400/7-8
200 Tiger Dr 75169 903-873-4924
Casey Cochran, prin. Fax 873-4873
Wills Point MS 400/5-6
101 School St 75169 903-873-3617
Kim Calvery, prin. Fax 873-2465
Wills Point PS 500/PK-1
447 Terrace Dr 75169 903-873-2491
Kim White, prin. Fax 873-3051
Woods IS 500/2-4
307 Wingo Way 75169 903-873-2841
Melanie Mullin, prin. Fax 873-3134

New Frontiers Christian Academy 50/K-12
24385 Interstate 20 75169 903-873-2440
Julann Goldsmith, admin. Fax 873-2440

Wilmer, Dallas, Pop. 3,621
Dallas ISD
Supt. — See Dallas
Wilmer ECC, 211 Walnut St 75172 PK-PK
Dr. Sharonda Pruitt, prin. 469-660-7296

Wilson, Lynn, Pop. 487
Wilson ISD 100/PK-12
PO Box 9 79381 806-628-6271
Jerry Burger, supt. Fax 628-6441
www.wilson.esc17.net
Wilson S 100/PK-12
PO Box 9 79381 806-628-6271
Richard Soliz, prin. Fax 628-6441

Wimberley, Hays, Pop. 2,602
Wimberley ISD 2,100/PK-12
951 FM 2325 78676 512-847-2414
Dwain York, supt. Fax 847-2142
www.wimberleyisd.net
Danforth JHS 500/6-8
200 Texan Blvd 78676 512-847-2181
Greg Howard, prin. Fax 847-7897
Jacob's Well ES 600/2-5
3470 FM 2325 78676 512-847-5558
Andrea Pope, prin. Fax 847-6176

Scudder PS 300/PK-1
400 Green Acres Dr 78676 512-847-3407
Dara Richardson, prin. Fax 847-2738

Windthorst, Archer, Pop. 398
Windthorst ISD 500/PK-12
PO Box 190 76389 940-423-6688
Lonnie Hise, supt. Fax 423-6505
www.windthorstisd.net
Windhorst JHS 100/7-8
PO Box 190 76389 940-423-6680
Roy Longcrier, prin. Fax 423-6505
Windthorst ES 200/PK-6
PO Box 190 76389 940-423-6679
Ann Armendarez, prin. Fax 423-6505

Winfield, Titus, Pop. 518
Winfield ISD 200/PK-8
PO Box 298 75493 903-524-2221
Rhonda Burchinal, supt. Fax 524-2410
www.winfieldisd.net
Winfield S 200/PK-8
PO Box 298 75493 903-524-2221
Marshall Moore, prin. Fax 524-2410

Wink, Winkler, Pop. 931
Wink-Loving ISD 400/PK-12
PO Box 637 79789 432-527-3880
Scotty Carman, supt. Fax 527-3505
www.wlisd.net
Wink ES 300/PK-6
PO Box 637 79789 432-527-3880
Lance Wineinger, prin. Fax 527-3505

Winnie, Chambers, Pop. 3,222
East Chambers ISD 1,400/PK-12
1955 State Highway 124 77665 409-296-6100
Scott Campbell, supt. Fax 296-3528
www.eastchambers.net
East Chambers ES 600/PK-4
316 E Fear Rd 77665 409-296-6100
Becky Dale, prin. Fax 296-3259
East Chambers IS 200/5-6
213 School Rd 77665 409-296-6100
Lou Ann Rainey, prin. Fax 296-2724
East Chambers JHS 200/7-8
1931 State Highway 124 77665 409-296-6100
Lou Ann Rainey, prin. Fax 296-2724

Winnsboro, Wood, Pop. 3,395
Winnsboro ISD 1,500/PK-12
207 E Pine St 75494 903-342-3737
Susan Morton, supt. Fax 342-3380
www.winnsboroisd.org
Memorial MS 400/5-8
505 S Chestnut St 75494 903-342-5711
Jeff Akin, prin. Fax 342-6689
Winnsboro ES 700/PK-4
310 W Coke Rd 75494 903-342-3548
Kristie Amason, prin. Fax 342-6858

Winona, Smith, Pop. 574
Winona ISD 1,000/PK-12
611 Wildcat Dr 75792 903-939-4001
Cody Mize, supt. Fax 877-9387
www.winonaisd.org
Winona ES 400/PK-3
611 Wildcat Dr 75792 903-939-4800
Joshua Snook, prin. Fax 877-2457
Winona IS 200/4-5
611 Wildcat Dr 75792 903-939-4800
Joshua Snook, prin. Fax 877-2457
Winona MS 200/6-8
611 Wildcat Dr 75792 903-939-4040
Mark McDonald, prin. Fax 877-9150

Winters, Runnels, Pop. 2,547
Winters ISD 600/PK-12
603 N Heights St 79567 325-754-5574
Bruce Davis, supt. Fax 754-5374
www.wintersisd.org
Winters ES 300/PK-5
603 N Heights St 79567 325-754-5577
Kari Calcote, prin. Fax 754-4686
Winters JHS 100/6-8
603 N Heights St 79567 325-754-5518
Kathy Horner, prin. Fax 754-5085

Woden, Nacogdoches
Woden ISD 800/PK-12
PO Box 100 75978 936-564-2073
Brady Taylor, supt. Fax 564-1250
www.wodenisd.org/
Woden ES 400/PK-5
PO Box 100 75978 936-564-2386
Jesse Stroud, prin. Fax 564-3322
Woden JHS 200/6-8
PO Box 100 75978 936-564-2481
Dr. Jerry Meador, prin. Fax 462-4982

Wolfe City, Hunt, Pop. 1,375
Wolfe City ISD 600/PK-12
505 W Dallas St 75496 903-496-7333
Vernon Richardson, supt. Fax 496-7905
www.wcisd.net
Wolfe City ES 300/PK-5
PO Box L 75496 903-496-7333
Brent Fitzgerald, prin. Fax 496-2233
Wolfe City MS 200/6-8
PO Box L 75496 903-496-7333
Melanie Williams, prin. Fax 496-2112

Wolfforth, Lubbock, Pop. 3,636
Frenship ISD 8,300/PK-12
PO Box 100 79382 806-866-9541
Dr. Michelle McCord, supt. Fax 866-4135
www.frenship.net
Bennett ES 800/PK-5
PO Box 100 79382 806-866-4443
Michelle Elliott, prin. Fax 866-4715

Frenship MS 600/6-8
PO Box 100 79382 806-866-4464
Jerry Jerabek, prin. Fax 866-2181
Other Schools – See Lubbock

Woodsboro, Refugio, Pop. 1,498
Woodsboro ISD 500/PK-12
PO Box 770 78393 361-543-4518
Janice Sykora, supt. Fax 543-4856
www.wisd.net
Woodsboro ES 200/PK-6
PO Box 770 78393 361-543-4380
Leslie Garza, prin. Fax 543-5478

Woodson, Throckmorton, Pop. 262
Woodson ISD 100/PK-12
PO Box 287 76491 940-345-6528
Gordon Thomas, supt. Fax 345-6549
www.woodsonisd.net
Woodson S 100/PK-12
PO Box 287 76491 940-345-6521
Casey Adams, prin. Fax 345-6549

Woodville, Tyler, Pop. 2,545
Woodville ISD 1,300/PK-12
505 N Charlton St 75979 409-283-3752
Glen Conner, supt. Fax 283-7962
www.woodvilleeagles.org
Wheat ES 400/PK-2
505 N Charlton St 75979 409-283-2452
Carrie Garsee, prin. Fax 331-3409
Woodville IS 300/3-5
505 N Charlton St 75979 409-283-2549
Ashley Weatherford, prin. Fax 331-3412
Woodville MS 300/6-8
505 N Charlton St 75979 409-283-7109
Dwayne Hollingsworth, prin. Fax 331-3418

Woodway, McLennan, Pop. 8,360
Midway ISD 7,500/PK-12
13885 Woodway Dr 76712 254-761-5600
George Kazanas Ed.D., supt. Fax 761-5789
www.midwayisd.org
Other Schools – See Hewitt, Mc Gregor, Waco

Wortham, Freestone, Pop. 1,060
Wortham ISD 500/PK-12
PO Box 247 76693 254-765-3095
David R. Allen, supt. Fax 765-3473
www.worthamisd.org
Wortham ES 200/PK-5
PO Box 247 76693 254-765-3080
Dee Ann Allen, prin. Fax 765-3540
Wortham MS 100/6-8
PO Box 247 76693 254-765-3523
David Hayes, prin. Fax 765-3512

Wylie, Dallas, Pop. 40,460
Wylie ISD 14,300/PK-12
PO Box 490 75098 972-429-3000
Dr. David Vinson, supt. Fax 442-5368
www.wylieisd.net
Akin ES 500/K-4
PO Box 490 75098 972-429-3400
Valerie Mann, prin. Fax 442-5744
Birmingham ES 500/K-4
PO Box 490 75098 972-429-3420
Tiffany Doolan, prin. Fax 442-1215
Burnett JHS 700/7-8
PO Box 490 75098 972-429-3200
Ryan Bickley, prin. Fax 442-1447
Bush ES, PO Box 490 75098 600/K-4
Maricela Helm, admin. 972-429-3000
Cooper JHS 700/7-8
PO Box 490 75098 972-429-3250
Shawn Miller, prin. Fax 941-9175
Davis IS 600/5-6
PO Box 490 75098 972-429-3325
Barbara Rudolph, prin. Fax 429-9729
Dodd ES 600/K-4
PO Box 490 75098 972-429-3440
Nicole Duvall, prin. Fax 442-9856
Draper IS 900/5-6
PO Box 490 75098 972-429-3350
Beth Craighead, prin. Fax 442-9317
Groves ES 600/K-4
PO Box 490 75098 972-429-3460
Jill Vasquez, prin. Fax 429-7906
Harrison IS 600/5-6
PO Box 490 75098 972-429-3300
Christa Smyder, prin. Fax 442-3971
Hartman ES 500/PK-4
PO Box 490 75098 972-429-3480
Shawna Ballast, prin. Fax 442-7072
McMillan JHS 700/7-8
PO Box 490 75098 972-429-3225
Jon Peters, prin. Fax 941-6372
Smith ES 600/K-4
PO Box 490 75098 972-429-2540
Kellye Morton, prin. Fax 442-5493
Watkins ES 500/K-4
PO Box 490 75098 972-429-2580
Jennifer Speicher, prin. Fax 429-9345
Other Schools – See Murphy, Sachse

Wylie Preparatory Academy 300/K-12
4110 Skyview Ct 75098 972-442-1388

Yantis, Wood, Pop. 386
Yantis ISD 400/PK-12
105 W Oak St 75497 903-383-2463
Jerry Brem, supt. Fax 383-7620
www.yantisisd.net
Yantis ES 200/PK-5
105 W Oak St 75497 903-383-2463
Tracey Helfferich, prin. Fax 383-7620

Yoakum, Lavaca, Pop. 5,752
Yoakum ISD 1,600/PK-12
315 E Gonzales St 77995 361-293-3162
Tom Kelley, supt. Fax 293-6678
www.yoakumisd.net/
Yoakum IS 300/3-5
208 Aubrey St 77995 361-293-2741
Gabe Adamek, prin. Fax 293-6562
Yoakum JHS 300/6-8
103 McKinnon St 77995 361-293-3111
Patrick Frank, prin. Fax 293-5787
Yoakum PS 200/1-2
800 W Grand Ave 77995 361-293-2011
Darrin Stansberry, prin. Fax 293-2688
Yoakum PS Annex 200/PK-K
412 Simpson St 77995 361-293-3312
Pat Brewer, prin. Fax 293-6937

St. Joseph S 100/PK-8
310 Orth St 77995 361-293-9000
Sean Mooney, prin. Fax 293-3004

Yorktown, DeWitt, Pop. 2,079
Yorktown ISD 500/PK-12
PO Box 487 78164 361-564-2252
Chad Gee, supt. Fax 564-2254
www.yisd.org
Yorktown ES 200/PK-5
PO Box 487 78164 361-564-2252
Pamela Edwards Flores, prin. Fax 564-2270
Yorktown JHS 100/6-8
PO Box 487 78164 361-564-2252
Dr. Ashley Chandler, prin. Fax 564-2289

Zapata, Zapata, Pop. 5,080
Zapata County ISD 3,600/PK-12
1302 Glenn St 78076 956-765-6546
Carlos Gonzalez, supt. Fax 765-8350
www.zcisd.org
Villarreal ES 600/PK-5
805 Mira Flores Ave 78076 956-765-4321
Marlen Guerra, prin. Fax 765-5124
Zapata MS 700/6-8
702 E 17th Ave 78076 956-765-6542
Elsa Martinez, prin. Fax 765-9204
Zapata North ES 600/PK-5
502 E 17th Ave 78076 956-765-6921
Elma Almaraz, prin. Fax 765-8512
Zapata South ES 600/PK-5
500 Delmar St 78076 956-765-4332
Dahlia Garcia, prin. Fax 765-3320
Other Schools – See San Ygnacio

Faith Academy Christian S 50/K-4
1302 Lincoln St 78076 956-765-6549
Victoria Rodriguez, lead tchr. Fax 765-5626

Zavalla, Angelina, Pop. 708
Zavalla ISD 400/PK-12
431 E Main St 75980 936-897-2271
Ricky Oliver, supt. Fax 897-2674
www.zavallaisd.org
Zavalla ES 200/PK-5
431 E Main St 75980 936-897-2611
Shana McCugh, prin. Fax 897-2674

Zephyr, Brown
Zephyr ISD 200/PK-12
11625 County Road 281 76890 325-739-5331
Stanton Marwitz, supt. Fax 739-5906
zephyrisd.net
Zephyr S 200/PK-12
11625 County Road 281 76890 325-739-5331
Kelsa Blair, prin. Fax 739-2126

UTAH

UTAH OFFICE OF EDUCATION
PO Box 144200, Salt Lake City 84114-4200
Telephone 801-538-7500
Fax 801-538-7768
Website http://www.schools.utah.gov/main/

Superintendent of Public Instruction Dr. Sydnee Dickson

UTAH BOARD OF EDUCATION
250 E 500 S, Salt Lake City 84111-3204

Chairperson

REGIONAL SERVICE CENTERS (RSC)

Central Utah Educational Services
Jason Strate, dir. 435-896-4469
820 N Main St, Richfield 84701 Fax 896-4767
www.mycues.org

Northeastern Utah Educational Services
Duke Mossman, dir. 435-654-1921
35 S Main St, Heber City 84032 Fax 654-2403
www.nucenter.org

Southeast Educational Service Center
J.J. Grant, dir. 435-637-1173
685 E 200 S, Price 84501 Fax 637-1178
seschools.org

Southwest Educational Development Ctr
Edna LaMarca, dir. 435-586-2865
520 W 800 S, Cedar City 84720 Fax 586-2868
www.sedck12.org

PUBLIC, PRIVATE AND CATHOLIC ELEMENTARY SCHOOLS

Alpine, Utah, Pop. 9,390
Alpine SD
Supt. — See American Fork
Alpine ES 700/K-6
400 E 300 N 84004 801-610-8700
Dave Perdue, prin. Fax 756-8527
Westfield ES 800/K-6
380 S Long Dr 84004 801-610-8720
Salonna Thomas, prin. Fax 763-7044

Altamont, Duchesne, Pop. 222
Duchesne SD
Supt. — See Roosevelt
Altamont ES 400/K-6
PO Box 40 84001 435-738-1375
Lori Oman, prin. Fax 738-1396

American Fork, Utah, Pop. 25,678
Alpine SD 72,000/K-12
575 N 100 E 84003 801-610-8400
Sam Jarman, supt. Fax 610-8516
alpineschools.org
Barratt ES 600/K-6
168 N 900 E 84003 801-610-8701
Dan Griffy, prin. Fax 756-8530
Forbes ES 600/K-6
281 N 200 E 84003 801-610-8705
Kim Jones, prin. Fax 756-8571
Greenwood ES 600/K-6
50 E 200 S 84003 801-610-8708
Matt Killpack, prin. Fax 756-8536
Legacy ES 800/K-6
28 E 1340 N 84003 801-610-8711
Tom Tillman, prin. Fax 756-8568
Shelley ES 1,000/K-6
602 N 200 W 84003 801-610-8718
Mike Ericksen, prin. Fax 763-7020
Other Schools – See Alpine, Cedar Fort, Cedar Hills, Eagle Mountain, Highland, Lehi, Lindon, Orem, Pleasant Grove, Saratoga Sprngs, Vineyard

---

American Heritage S 500/K-12
736 N 1100 E 84003 801-642-0055
Grant Beckwith, prin. Fax 642-0060

Antimony, Garfield, Pop. 120
Garfield SD
Supt. — See Panguitch
Antimony ES 50/K-6
PO Box 120026 84712 435-624-3221
Julie Allen, lead tchr. Fax 624-3286

Bear River City, Box Elder, Pop. 850
Box Elder SD
Supt. — See Brigham City
Century ES 400/K-5
5820 N 4800 W 84301 435-279-2651
Jason Sparks, prin. Fax 279-2654

Beaver, Beaver, Pop. 3,076
Beaver SD 1,500/K-12
PO Box 31 84713 435-438-2291
Dr. Ray Terry, supt. Fax 438-5898
www.beaver.k12.ut.us
Belknap ES 500/K-6
PO Box 686 84713 435-438-2281
Monte Hawkins, prin. Fax 438-5385
Other Schools – See Milford, Minersville

Beryl, Iron
Iron SD
Supt. — See Cedar City
Escalante Valley ES 100/K-6
202 N Beryl Hwy 84714 435-439-5550
Trevor Heaton, prin. Fax 439-5552

Bicknell, Wayne, Pop. 324
Wayne SD 500/PK-12
PO Box 127 84715 435-425-3813
Dr. John M. Fahey Ed.D., supt. Fax 425-3806
www.waynesd.org
Wayne MS 100/6-8
PO Box 128 84715 435-425-3421
Lance Peterson, prin. Fax 425-3130
Other Schools – See Hanksville, Loa

Big Water, Kane, Pop. 468
Kane SD
Supt. — See Kanab
Big Water ES 50/K-6
PO Box 410126 84741 435-675-5821
Andrew Roundy, prin. Fax 675-5821

Blanding, San Juan, Pop. 3,283
San Juan SD 3,000/K-12
200 N Main St 84511 435-678-1200
Edward Lyman, supt. Fax 678-1272
www.sjsd.org
Blanding ES 600/K-5
302 S 100 W 84511 435-678-1872
Mark Burge, prin. Fax 678-1877
Lyman MS 300/6-8
535 N 100 E 84511 435-678-1398
Aaron Brewer, prin. Fax 678-1399
Other Schools – See Bluff, La Sal, Mexican Hat, Montezuma Creek, Monticello

Bluff, San Juan, Pop. 251
San Juan SD
Supt. — See Blanding
Bluff ES 100/K-6
PO Box 130 84512 435-678-1296
Barbara Silversmith, prin. Fax 678-1297

Bluffdale, Salt Lake, Pop. 7,468
Jordan SD
Supt. — See West Jordan
Bluffdale ES 900/K-6
14323 S 2700 W 84065 801-254-8090
Karen Eagan, prin. Fax 302-4909

Boulder, Garfield, Pop. 226
Garfield SD
Supt. — See Panguitch
Boulder ES 50/K-6
PO Box 1447 84716 435-335-7322
Elizabeth Julian, lead tchr. Fax 335-7354

Bountiful, Davis, Pop. 41,539
Davis SD
Supt. — See Farmington
Adelaide ES 600/K-6
731 W 3600 S 84010 801-402-1250
Jeri Thomas, prin. Fax 402-1251
Boulton ES 500/PK-6
2611 Orchard Dr 84010 801-402-1300
Brooke Murdock, prin. Fax 402-1301
Bountiful ES 400/K-6
1620 S 50 W 84010 801-402-1350
Bryan Skelton, prin. Fax 402-1351
Holbrook ES 500/K-6
1018 E 250 N 84010 801-402-1450
Neesha Killpack, prin. Fax 402-1451
Meadowbrook ES 400/PK-6
700 N 325 W 84010 801-402-1600
James Campbell, prin. Fax 402-1601
Muir ES 700/K-6
2275 S Davis Blvd 84010 801-402-1550
Marilyn Merkley, prin. Fax 402-1551
Oak Hills ES 400/PK-6
1235 E 600 S 84010 801-402-1650
Ruthanne Keller, prin. Fax 402-1651
Tolman ES 400/PK-6
300 E 1200 N 84010 801-402-1900
Steve Hammer, prin. Fax 402-1901
Valley View ES 500/PK-6
1305 S 600 E 84010 801-402-2050
Kimberly Johnston, prin. Fax 402-2051
Washington ES 300/PK-6
340 W 650 S 84010 801-402-1950
Sandra Carmony, prin. Fax 402-1951

St. Olaf S 100/PK-8
1793 Orchard Dr 84010 801-295-5341
Laurie Jacobs, prin. Fax 295-5915

Brigham City, Box Elder, Pop. 17,553
Box Elder SD 11,300/PK-12
960 S Main St 84302 435-734-4800
Steven E. Carlsen, supt. Fax 734-4833
www.besd.net
Discovery ES 500/K-5
820 N 500 W 84302 435-734-4910
Jeff Morris, prin. Fax 734-4912
Foothill ES 400/K-5
820 N 100 E 84302 435-734-4916
David Lee, admin. Fax 734-4918
Lake View ES 600/K-5
851 S 200 W 84302 435-734-4922
Mark Johnson, admin. Fax 734-4924
Mountain View ES 400/K-5
650 E 700 S 84302 435-734-4926
Bryce Day, prin. Fax 734-4928
Young IS 900/6-7
830 S Law Dr 84302 435-734-4940
Corey Thompson, prin. Fax 734-4950
Other Schools – See Bear River City, Corinne, Fielding, Garland, Grouse Creek, Park Valley, Perry, Snowville, Tremonton, Willard

Castle Dale, Emery, Pop. 1,623
Emery County SD
Supt. — See Huntington
Castle Dale ES 200/K-6
PO Box 539 84513 435-381-5221
Melinda Durrant, prin. Fax 381-5220

Cedar City, Iron, Pop. 28,202
Iron SD 6,300/K-12
2077 W Royal Hunte Dr 84720 435-586-2804
Dr. Shannon Dulaney, supt. Fax 586-2815
irondistrict.org
Canyon View MS 900/6-8
1865 N Main St 84721 435-586-2830
Robert Wagner, prin. Fax 586-2837
Cedar MS 900/6-8
2215 W Royal Hunte Dr 84720 435-586-2810
Bylynda Murray, prin. Fax 586-2829
Cedar North ES 400/K-5
550 W 200 N 84720 435-586-2845
Ray Whittier, prin. Fax 586-2846
Cedar South ES 500/K-5
499 W 400 S 84720 435-586-2850
Jerry Oldroyd, prin. Fax 586-2852
Fiddlers Canyon ES 500/K-5
475 E 1935 N 84721 435-586-2860
Michelle Jones, prin. Fax 586-2861
Other Schools – See Beryl, Parowan

Cedar Fort, Utah, Pop. 357
Alpine SD
Supt. — See American Fork

Cedar Valley ES 100/K-6
40 E Center St 84013 801-610-8702
Jory Schmidt, prin. Fax 766-1370

Cedar Hills, Utah, Pop. 9,597
Alpine SD
Supt. — See American Fork
Cedar Ridge ES 1,000/K-6
4501 W Cedar Hills Dr 84062 801-610-8103
Jeremy Brunner, prin. Fax 763-9537
Deerfield ES 900/K-6
4353 W Harvey Blvd 84062 801-610-8106
Caroline Knadler, prin. Fax 796-3145

Centerville, Davis, Pop. 15,086
Davis SD
Supt. — See Farmington
Centerville ES 500/PK-6
350 N 100 E 84014 801-402-1400
Dan Hansen, prin. Fax 402-1401
Reading ES 600/K-6
360 W 2025 N 84014 801-402-1750
Scott Hughes, prin. Fax 402-1751
Stewart ES 700/K-6
1155 N Main St 84014 801-402-1850
Amanda Keller, prin. Fax 402-1851
Taylor ES 400/K-6
293 E Pages Ln 84014 801-402-1500
Chris Laypath, prin. Fax 402-1501

Circleville, Piute, Pop. 540
Piute County SD
Supt. — See Junction
Circleville ES 100/PK-6
PO Box 228 84723 435-577-2912
Eugene King, lead tchr. Fax 577-2927

Clearfield, Davis, Pop. 28,950
Davis SD
Supt. — See Farmington
Antelope ES 800/PK-6
1810 S Main St 84015 801-402-2100
Jennie DeFriez, prin. Fax 402-2101
Hill Field ES 500/K-6
389 S 1000 E 84015 801-402-2350
Doug Forsgren, prin. Fax 402-2351
Holt ES 600/PK-6
448 N 1000 W 84015 801-402-2400
Bryan Tesch, prin. Fax 402-2401
South Clearfield ES 700/PK-6
990 E 700 S 84015 801-402-2500
Buck Ekstrom, prin. Fax 402-2501
Wasatch ES 500/PK-6
210 Center St 84015 801-402-2650
Robert Kinghorn, prin. Fax 402-2651

Cleveland, Emery, Pop. 464
Emery County SD
Supt. — See Huntington
Cleveland ES 200/PK-6
PO Box 220 84518 435-653-2235
Jerel Lofley, prin. Fax 653-2370

Clinton, Davis, Pop. 19,830
Davis SD
Supt. — See Farmington
Clinton ES 600/PK-6
1101 W 1800 N 84015 801-402-2150
Jake Heidrich, prin. Fax 402-2151
Parkside ES 600/K-6
2262 N 1500 W 84015 801-402-1150
Chris Bertoldi, prin. Fax 402-1151
West Clinton ES 800/PK-6
2826 W 1800 N 84015 801-402-2700
Ryan Van Natter, prin. Fax 402-2701

Coalville, Summit, Pop. 1,348
North Summit SD 1,000/PK-12
PO Box 497 84017 435-336-5654
Jerre Holmes, supt. Fax 336-2401
www.nsummit.org
North Summit ES 400/PK-4
PO Box 497 84017 435-336-2101
Wade Murdock, prin. Fax 336-2064
North Summit MS 300/5-8
PO Box 497 84017 435-336-5678
Brett Richins, prin. Fax 336-4474

Corinne, Box Elder, Pop. 668
Box Elder SD
Supt. — See Brigham City
Early Learning Center 200/PK-PK
2275 N 3900 W 84307 435-774-2468
Corynn Arehart, admin. Fax 744-2628

Cottonwood Heights, Salt Lake, Pop. 32,636
Canyons SD
Supt. — See Sandy
Bella Vista ES 300/K-5
2131 E 7000 S, 801-826-7825
Cory Anderson, prin. Fax 826-7826
Butler MS 900/6-8
7530 S 2700 E, 801-826-6800
Paula Logan, prin. Fax 826-6809
Ridgecrest ES 600/K-5
1800 E 7200 S, 801-826-9250
Julie Winfrey, prin. Fax 826-9251

Delta, Millard, Pop. 3,399
Millard SD 2,600/PK-12
285 E 450 N 84624 435-864-1000
David Styler, supt. Fax 864-5684
www.millardk12.org
Delta MS 400/6-8
251 E 300 N 84624 435-864-5660
Rebecca Callister, prin. Fax 864-5669
Delta North ES 300/3-5
50 N 100 E 84624 435-864-5680
Delna Bliss, prin. Fax 864-5689
Delta South ES 200/PK-2
450 S Center St 84624 435-864-5670
Rhonda Harrison, prin. Fax 864-5679
Other Schools – See Fillmore, Garrison

Draper, Salt Lake, Pop. 41,208
Canyons SD
Supt. — See Sandy
Draper ES 700/K-5
1080 E 12660 S 84020 801-826-8275
Piper Riddle, prin. Fax 826-8276
Draper Park MS 1,400/6-8
13133 S 1300 E 84020 801-826-6900
Mary Anderson, prin. Fax 826-6909
Oak Hollow ES 700/K-5
884 E 14400 S 84020 801-826-8875
Julie Mootz, prin. Fax 826-8876
Willow Springs ES 800/K-5
13288 S Lone Peak Dr 84020 801-826-9700
Marianne Yule, prin. Fax 826-9701

St. John the Baptist ES 600/PK-5
300 E 11800 S 84020 801-984-7123
Nikki Ward, prin. Fax 984-7649
St. John the Baptist MS 400/6-8
300 E 11800 S 84020 801-984-7613
Patrick Reeder, prin. Fax 984-7649

Duchesne, Duchesne, Pop. 1,664
Duchesne SD
Supt. — See Roosevelt
Duchesne ES 400/K-6
PO Box 370 84021 435-738-1290
David Taylor, prin. Fax 738-1313

Dugway, Tooele, Pop. 749
Tooele County SD
Supt. — See Tooele
Dugway S 100/K-12
Bldg 5010 School St 84022 435-831-4090
Jeff Wyatt, prin. Fax 831-4091

Dutch John, Daggett, Pop. 144
Daggett SD
Supt. — See Manila
Flaming Gorge ES 50/PK-5
PO Box 289 84023 435-885-3112
Bruce Northcott, prin. Fax 885-3218

Eagle Mountain, Utah, Pop. 20,745
Alpine SD
Supt. — See American Fork
Black Ridge ES K-6
9358 N Sunset Dr, 801-610-8729
Cami Larsen, prin. Fax 789-5370
Eagle Valley ES 800/K-6
4475 Heritage Dr, 801-610-8704
Paula Tucker, prin. Fax 789-8304
Hidden Hollow ES 1,300/K-6
7447 N Hidden Valley Pkwy, 801-610-8721
Brad Davies, prin. Fax 789-7806
Mountain Trails ES 600/K-6
3951 N Wood Rd, 801-610-8724
David Turner, prin. Fax 789-6080
Pony Express ES 1,200/K-6
3985 E Smith Ranch Rd, 801-610-8714
Vicki Smith, prin. Fax 789-2604

Eden, Weber, Pop. 593
Weber SD
Supt. — See Ogden
Valley ES 600/K-6
5821 E 1900 N 84310 801-452-4180
Jon England, prin. Fax 452-4199

Enterprise, Washington, Pop. 1,701
Washington County SD
Supt. — See Saint George
Enterprise ES 400/PK-6
PO Box 459 84725 435-878-2236
Luke Rowley, prin. Fax 878-2510

Ephraim, Sanpete, Pop. 5,963
South Sanpete SD
Supt. — See Manti
Ephraim ES 600/PK-5
570 S 300 E 84627 435-283-4171
Gannon Jones, prin. Fax 283-6892
Ephraim MS 500/6-8
555 S 100 E 84627 435-283-4037
Timothy Miller, prin. Fax 283-4885

Escalante, Garfield, Pop. 794
Garfield SD
Supt. — See Panguitch
Escalante ES 100/K-6
PO Box 248 84726 435-826-4247
Chip Sharpe, prin. Fax 826-4789

Eureka, Juab, Pop. 666
Tintic SD 300/PK-12
PO Box 210 84628 435-433-6363
Kodey Hughes, supt. Fax 433-6643
www.tintic.k12.ut.us
Eureka ES 100/PK-6
PO Box 170 84628 435-433-6927
Brian Ward, prin. Fax 433-6622
Other Schools – See Trout Creek

Fairview, Sanpete, Pop. 1,236
North Sanpete SD
Supt. — See Mount Pleasant
Fairview ES 300/K-6
651 E 150 N 84629 435-427-9204
Allynne Mower, prin. Fax 427-9201

Farmington, Davis, Pop. 17,985
Davis SD 68,800/PK-12
PO Box 588 84025 801-402-5261
Reid Newey, supt. Fax 402-5249
www.davis.k12.ut.us
Canyon Creek ES K-6
755 S 1100 W 84025 801-402-0300
Vonzaa Hewitt, prin. Fax 402-0301
Eagle Bay ES 1,000/K-6
1933 Clark Ln 84025 801-402-3800
Janeal Magalei, prin. Fax 402-3801
Farmington ES 500/K-6
50 W 200 S 84025 801-402-2950
Cameron Forbush, prin. Fax 402-2951

Knowlton ES 800/PK-6
801 Shepard Ln 84025 801-402-3000
Daryl Fluckiger, prin. Fax 402-3001
Other Schools – See Bountiful, Centerville, Clearfield, Clinton, Kaysville, Layton, North Salt Lake, South Weber, Sunset, Syracuse, West Bountiful, West Point, Woods Cross

Ferron, Emery, Pop. 1,614
Emery County SD
Supt. — See Huntington
Ferron ES 300/PK-6
PO Box 910 84523 435-384-2383
Brian Dawes, prin. Fax 384-2550

Fielding, Box Elder, Pop. 451
Box Elder SD
Supt. — See Brigham City
Fielding ES 400/K-5
PO Box 98 84311 435-458-2700
Colleen Shaffer, prin. Fax 458-2702

Fillmore, Millard, Pop. 2,397
Millard SD
Supt. — See Delta
Fillmore ES 500/PK-4
555 W 400 S 84631 435-743-5670
Harold Robison, prin. Fax 743-5679
Fillmore MS 300/5-8
435 S 500 W 84631 435-743-5660
Dennis Alldredge, prin. Fax 743-5669

Fountain Green, Sanpete, Pop. 1,059
North Sanpete SD
Supt. — See Mount Pleasant
Fountain Green ES 100/K-6
PO Box 38 84632 435-445-3316
Robyn Cox, prin. Fax 445-3305

Garland, Box Elder, Pop. 2,370
Box Elder SD
Supt. — See Brigham City
Garland ES 700/K-5
450 S 100 W 84312 435-257-2600
Shaylyn Ekins, admin. Fax 257-2602

Garrison, Millard
Millard SD
Supt. — See Delta
Garrison 7th & 8th S 50/7-8
1000 Circle Dr 84728 435-855-2148
Nomi Sheppard, lead tchr. Fax 855-2148
Garrison ES 50/K-2
PO Box 10 84728 435-855-2321
Cecelia Phillips, lead tchr. Fax 855-2195

Goshen, Utah, Pop. 917
Nebo SD
Supt. — See Spanish Fork
Goshen ES 400/K-6
60 N Center 84633 801-667-3361
Lynette DeGraffenried, prin. Fax 667-3374

Grantsville, Tooele, Pop. 8,741
Tooele County SD
Supt. — See Tooele
Grantsville ES 800/K-6
50 Park St 84029 435-884-9991
Jeff Zaleski, prin. Fax 884-9992
Grantsville JHS 400/7-8
318 S Hale St 84029 435-884-4510
Charles Mohler, prin. Fax 884-4513
Willow ES 700/K-6
439 Willow St 84029 435-884-4527
Angie Gillette, prin. Fax 884-4531

Green River, Emery, Pop. 946
Emery County SD
Supt. — See Huntington
Book Cliff ES 100/K-6
PO Box 448 84525 435-564-8102
Jerry R. Jones, prin. Fax 564-8327

Grouse Creek, Box Elder
Box Elder SD
Supt. — See Brigham City
Grouse Creek S 50/K-10
PO Box 16 84313 435-747-7321
Viola Foy, lead tchr. Fax 747-7182

Gunnison, Sanpete, Pop. 3,235
South Sanpete SD
Supt. — See Manti
Gunnison Valley ES 500/PK-5
PO Box 369 84634 435-528-7880
Arleen Jensen, prin. Fax 528-7474
Gunnison Valley MS 300/6-8
PO Box 1090 84634 435-528-5337
Alan Peterson, prin. Fax 528-5397

Hanksville, Wayne, Pop. 216
Wayne SD
Supt. — See Bicknell
Hanksville ES 50/K-6
PO Box 69 84734 435-542-3291
Cindy Wilkins, lead tchr. Fax 542-2025

Heber City, Wasatch, Pop. 11,241
Wasatch SD 5,800/K-12
101 E 200 N 84032 435-654-0280
Paul Sweat, supt. Fax 654-4714
www.wasatch.edu/
Heber Valley ES 700/K-4
730 S 600 W 84032 435-654-0112
DeAnna Lloyd, prin. Fax 654-7540
Old Mill ES 500/K-4
1600 E 980 S 84032 435-657-3130
Stephanie Discher, prin. Fax 654-9055
Rocky Mountain MS 900/7-8
800 School House Way 84032 435-654-9350
Justin Kelly, prin. Fax 654-9343
Smith ES 500/K-4
235 E 500 N 84032 435-654-2201
Ryan Brown, prin. Fax 654-0167

Timpanogos IS 900/5-6
200 E 800 S 84032 435-654-0550
David McNaughtan, prin. Fax 654-0622
Other Schools – See Midway

Helper, Carbon, Pop. 2,166
Carbon SD
Supt. — See Price
Helper MS 100/6-8
151 Uintah St 84526 435-472-5441
Mika Salas, prin. Fax 472-3502
Mauro ES 400/K-5
20 S 2nd Ave 84526 435-472-5311
Jarad Hardy, prin. Fax 472-3687

Herriman, Salt Lake, Pop. 21,297
Jordan SD
Supt. — See West Jordan
Bastian ES K-6
5692 W American Park Dr, 801-567-8920
Doree Strauss, prin. Fax 256-5955
Blackridge ES K-6
14131 S Rosecrest Rd, 801-254-0326
Steve Giles, prin. Fax 302-4927
Butterfield Canyon ES 1,300/K-6
6860 W Mary Leizan Ln, 801-254-0737
Amanda Bollinger, prin. Fax 302-4977
Herriman ES 1,100/K-6
13170 S 6000 W, 801-446-3215
Kim Gibson, prin. Fax 302-4936
Silver Crest ES 1,100/K-6
12937 S Elementary Dr, 801-253-1034
Amanda Edwards, prin. Fax 302-4917

Highland, Utah, Pop. 15,197
Alpine SD
Supt. — See American Fork
Freedom ES 1,200/K-6
10326 N 6800 W 84003 801-610-8707
Michelle Stephenson, prin. Fax 766-5272
Highland ES 900/K-6
10865 N 6000 W 84003 801-610-8710
Reed Hodson, prin. Fax 763-7001
Ridgeline ES 900/K-6
6250 W 11800 N 84003 801-610-8715
Dr. Ken Higgins, prin. Fax 492-0263

Hildale, Washington, Pop. 2,719
Washington County SD
Supt. — See Saint George
Water Canyon S PK-12
250 W Newel Ave 84784 435-668-2847
Darin Thomas, prin.

Holladay, Salt Lake
Granite SD
Supt. — See Salt Lake City
Cottonwood ES 500/K-6
5205 S Holladay Blvd 84117 385-646-4798
Paulette McMillan, prin. Fax 646-4799
Oakwood ES 500/K-6
5815 S Highland Dr 84121 385-646-4942
Dianne Phillips, prin. Fax 646-4943

Hooper, Weber, Pop. 7,107
Weber SD
Supt. — See Ogden
Freedom ES 800/K-6
4555 W 5500 S 84315 801-452-4100
Diane Rockwood, prin. Fax 452-4119
Hooper ES 600/K-6
5500 S 5900 W 84315 801-452-4320
Dave Gerstheimer, prin. Fax 452-4339

Huntington, Emery, Pop. 2,105
Emery County SD 2,300/PK-12
PO Box 120 84528 435-687-9846
Larry Davis, supt. Fax 687-9849
www.emeryschools.org
Huntington ES 300/K-6
PO Box 190 84528 435-687-9954
Garth Johnson, prin. Fax 687-2796
Other Schools – See Castle Dale, Cleveland, Ferron, Green River, Orangeville

Hurricane, Washington, Pop. 13,404
Washington County SD
Supt. — See Saint George
Hurricane ES 600/PK-5
948 W 325 N 84737 435-635-4668
Matthew Lowe, prin. Fax 635-4670
Hurricane IS 600/6-7
1325 S 700 W 84737 435-635-8931
Brad Christensen, prin. Fax 635-8937
Three Falls ES 600/K-5
789 S 700 W 84737 435-635-7229
Brad Jolley, prin. Fax 635-7273

Hyde Park, Cache, Pop. 3,797
Cache County SD
Supt. — See North Logan
Cedar Ridge MS 700/6-7
65 N 200 W 84318 435-563-6229
Mike Thompson, prin. Fax 563-3915

Hyrum, Cache, Pop. 7,476
Cache County SD
Supt. — See North Logan
Canyon ES 500/K-6
270 S 1300 E 84319 435-792-7684
Stacie Williamson, prin. Fax 792-7685
Lincoln ES 400/K-6
90 S Center St 84319 435-245-6442
Jeni Buist, prin. Fax 245-4411

Ibapah, Tooele
Tooele County SD
Supt. — See Tooele
Ibapah ES 50/K-6
PO Box 6087 84034 435-234-1113
Heather Castagno, prin. Fax 234-1175

Ivins, Washington, Pop. 6,591
Washington County SD
Supt. — See Saint George

Red Mountain ES 500/PK-5
263 E 200 S 84738 435-656-3802
Amy Mitchell, prin. Fax 656-3812

Junction, Piute, Pop. 190
Piute County SD 300/PK-12
PO Box 69 84740 435-577-2912
Shane Erickson, supt. Fax 577-2561
www.piutek12.org
Other Schools – See Circleville, Marysvale

Kamas, Summit, Pop. 1,803
South Summit SD 1,500/PK-12
285 E 400 S 84036 435-783-4301
Dr. Shad Sorenson, supt. Fax 783-4501
www.ssummit.org
South Summit ES 600/PK-4
535 E 300 S 84036 435-783-4318
Lisa Flinders, prin. Fax 783-2805
South Summit MS 500/5-8
355 E 300 S 84036 435-783-4341
Steve Camp, prin. Fax 783-2787

Kanab, Kane, Pop. 4,263
Kane SD 1,200/K-12
746 S 175 E 84741 435-644-2555
Ben Dalton, supt. Fax 644-2509
www.kane.k12.ut.us
Kanab ES 500/K-6
41 W 100 N 84741 435-644-2329
Braxton Bateman, prin. Fax 644-5041
Kanab MS 100/7-8
690 Cowboy Way 84741 435-644-5800
Mandie Luce, prin. Fax 644-5121
Other Schools – See Big Water, Lake Powell, Orderville

Kaysville, Davis, Pop. 26,897
Davis SD
Supt. — See Farmington
Burton ES 700/K-6
827 E 200 S 84037 801-402-3150
Denece Johnson, prin. Fax 402-3151
Columbia ES 700/PK-6
378 S 50 W 84037 801-402-3350
Darryl Denhalter, prin. Fax 402-3351
Creekside ES 700/K-6
275 W Mutton Hollow Rd 84037 801-402-3650
David Birch, prin. Fax 402-3651
Endeavour ES 1,000/K-6
1870 S 25 W 84037 801-402-0400
Traci Robbins, prin. Fax 402-0401
Kay's Creek ES K-6
2260 W Island Dr 84037 801-402-0050
Julie Larsen, prin. Fax 402-0051
Kaysville ES 700/PK-6
50 N 100 E 84037 801-402-3400
Meggan Nichols, prin. Fax 402-3401
Morgan ES 800/K-6
1065 Thornfield Rd 84037 801-402-3450
Alisha Johnson, prin. Fax 402-3451
Snow Horse ES 800/K-6
1095 W Smith Ln 84037 801-402-7350
Rachel Alberts, prin. Fax 402-7351
Windridge ES 700/PK-6
1300 S 700 E 84037 801-402-3550
Tiffany Midgley, prin. Fax 402-3551

Kearns, Salt Lake, Pop. 34,126
Granite SD
Supt. — See Salt Lake City
Bacchus ES 500/K-6
5925 S Copper City Dr 84118 385-646-4762
Becki Monson, prin. Fax 646-4763
Beehive ES 700/K-6
5655 S 5220 W 84118 385-646-4768
Nichole Higgins, prin. Fax 646-4769
Gourley ES 700/K-6
4905 S 4300 W 84118 385-646-4846
Allesen Peck, prin. Fax 646-4847
Oquirrh Hills ES 400/PK-6
5241 S 4280 W 84118 385-646-4948
Karen Marberger, prin. Fax 646-4949
Silver Hills ES 500/PK-6
5770 W 5100 S 84118 385-646-5014
Nykola Patton, prin. Fax 646-5015
South Kearns ES 500/PK-6
4430 W 5570 S 84118 385-646-5026
Debbie Koji, prin. Fax 646-5027
Western Hills ES 500/PK-6
5190 S Heath Ave 84118 385-646-5091
Dr. Mardel Higginson, prin. Fax 646-5092
West Kearns ES 900/PK-6
4900 S 4620 W 84118 385-646-5073
Brent Nelson, prin. Fax 646-5074

Koosharem, Sevier, Pop. 311
Sevier SD
Supt. — See Richfield
Koosharem ES 50/K-6
75 E Center 84744 435-638-7303
Alcea Bagley, prin. Fax 638-7516

Lake Powell, San Juan, Pop. 15
Kane SD
Supt. — See Kanab
Lake Powell ES 50/K-6
1000 Ferry Rd 84533 435-684-2268
Gordon Miller, prin. Fax 684-3821

Laketown, Rich, Pop. 240
Rich SD
Supt. — See Randolph
North Rich ES 100/K-5
PO Box 129 84038 435-946-3359
Kip Motta, prin. Fax 946-3366
Rich MS 100/6-8
PO Box 129 84038 435-946-3359
Kip Motta, prin. Fax 946-3366

Lapoint, Uintah
Uintah SD
Supt. — See Vernal
Lapoint ES 300/K-6
HC 67 Box 151 84039 435-247-2637
Dennis Atkin, prin. Fax 247-2639

La Sal, San Juan, Pop. 395
San Juan SD
Supt. — See Blanding
La Sal ES 50/K-4
PO Box 367 84530 435-678-1292
Shelly Thayn, lead tchr. Fax 678-1293

La Verkin, Washington, Pop. 3,978
Washington County SD
Supt. — See Saint George
La Verkin ES 500/PK-5
51 W Center St 84745 435-635-4619
Steve Leavenworth, prin. Fax 635-7953

Layton, Davis, Pop. 65,397
Davis SD
Supt. — See Farmington
Adams ES 600/K-6
2200 E Sunset Dr 84040 801-402-3100
Jackie Corbridge, prin. Fax 402-3101
Crestview ES 400/PK-6
185 W Golden Ave 84041 801-402-3200
Lori Hawthorne, prin. Fax 402-3201
East Layton ES 600/PK-6
2470 E Cherry Ln 84040 801-402-3250
Lisa Brown, prin. Fax 402-3251
Ellison Park ES 900/K-6
800 Cold Creek Way 84041 801-402-7300
Debbie Marshall, prin. Fax 402-7301
Heritage ES 1,000/PK-6
1354 Weaver Ln 84041 801-402-1200
Chris Whitaker, prin. Fax 402-1201
King ES 600/K-6
601 E Gordon Ave 84041 801-402-3300
Roy Warren, prin. Fax 402-3301
Layton ES 700/PK-6
369 W Gentile St 84041 801-402-3500
Diane Hammer, prin. Fax 402-3501
Legacy JHS 800/7-8
411 N 3200 W 84041 801-402-4700
Chadli Bodily, prin. Fax 402-4701
Lincoln ES 700/PK-6
591 W Antelope Dr 84041 801-402-2450
Sue Caldwell, prin. Fax 402-2451
Mountain View ES 800/PK-6
2025 E 3100 N 84040 801-402-3700
Chris Mudrow, prin. Fax 402-3701
Sand Springs ES 1,000/K-6
242 N 3200 W 84041 801-402-3850
Jody Schaap, prin. Fax 402-3851
Vae View ES 500/PK-6
1750 W 1600 N 84041 801-402-2800
David Pendergast, prin. Fax 402-2801
Whitesides ES 500/PK-6
233 Colonial Ave 84041 801-402-3600
Diane Ramsey, prin. Fax 402-3601

Layton Christian Academy 500/PK-12
2352 E Highway 193 84040 801-771-7141
Greg Miller, admin. Fax 771-0921

Lehi, Utah, Pop. 46,111
Alpine SD
Supt. — See American Fork
Dry Creek ES K-6
1301 W 1450 S 84043 801-610-8730
Sam Rencher, prin. Fax 766-8818
Eaglecrest ES 1,000/K-6
2760 N 300 W 84043 801-610-8703
Rex Becker, prin. Fax 768-7039
Fox Hollow ES 1,100/K-6
1450 W 3200 N 84043 801-610-8706
Darrin Johnson, prin. Fax 768-2742
Lehi ES 600/K-6
765 N Center St 84043 801-610-8712
Joel Miller, prin. Fax 768-7022
Meadow ES 1,200/K-6
176 S 500 W 84043 801-610-8713
Carolyn Johnson, prin. Fax 768-7018
North Point ES 1,200/K-6
1901 N 2300 W 84043 801-610-8722
Kim Roper, prin. Fax 768-0337
River Rock ES K-6
520 N 1700 W 84043 801-610-8731
Jason Benson, prin. Fax 768-7060
Sego Lily ES 1,000/K-6
550 E 900 N 84043 801-610-8717
Courtney Johnson, prin. Fax 768-7034
Snow Springs ES 1,200/K-6
850 S 1700 W 84043 801-610-8719
Shelley Schroeder, prin. Fax 768-7049
Traverse Mountain ES 900/K-6
2500 W Chapel Ridge Rd 84043 801-610-8725
Ilene Strong, prin. Fax 701-6280

Challenger S 300/PK-8
3920 Traverse Mountain Blvd 84043 801-407-8777
Benjamin Celver, hdmstr. Fax 407-6944

Lewiston, Cache, Pop. 1,738
Cache County SD
Supt. — See North Logan
Lewiston ES 500/K-6
181 S 200 E 84320 435-258-2923
Leslie Burt, prin. Fax 258-2707

Lindon, Utah, Pop. 9,825
Alpine SD
Supt. — See American Fork
Lindon ES 700/K-6
30 N Main St 84042 801-610-8111
Kate Ross, prin. Fax 785-8749
Rocky Mountain ES 600/K-6
55 S 500 E 84042 801-610-8117
Katie Bowman, prin. Fax 796-3133

Loa, Wayne, Pop. 562
Wayne SD
Supt. — See Bicknell
Loa ES 200/PK-5
PO Box 130 84747 435-836-2851
Cherie Blackburn, prin. Fax 836-2335

Logan, Cache, Pop. 47,175
Cache County SD
Supt. — See North Logan
Greenville ES 600/K-6
2450 N 400 E 84341 435-750-7888
Dee Ashcroft, prin. Fax 755-0112
Nibley ES 300/K-6
2545 S 660 W 84321 435-752-8303
Kelly Rindlisbacher, prin. Fax 752-8401
North Park ES 500/K-6
2800 N 800 E 84341 435-752-5121
Sharyle Shaffer, prin. Fax 752-5019
River Heights ES 500/K-6
780 E 600 S 84321 435-753-4948
Glen Harris, prin. Fax 753-4973

Logan CSD 6,100/PK-12
101 W Center St 84321 435-755-2300
Frank Schofield, supt. Fax 755-2311
www.loganschools.org
Adams ES 400/K-5
415 E 500 N 84321 435-755-2320
Sundee Ware, prin. Fax 755-2322
Bridger ES 600/K-5
1261 N 400 W 84341 435-755-2345
John Taggart, prin. Fax 755-2348
Ellis ES 400/K-5
348 W 300 N 84321 435-755-2330
Jed Grunig, prin. Fax 755-2332
Hillcrest ES 500/K-5
960 N 1400 E 84321 435-755-2360
Spencer Holmgren, prin. Fax 755-2362
Mt. Logan MS 1,300/6-8
875 N 200 E 84321 435-755-2370
Daryl Guymon, prin. Fax 755-2370
Riverside Preschool 100/PK-K
1075 Sumac Dr 84321 435-755-2337
Marci Elliott, prin. Fax 755-2342
Wilson ES 400/1-5
89 S 500 E 84321 435-755-2340
Sue Sorenson, prin. Fax 755-2342
Woodruff ES 700/K-5
950 W 600 S 84321 435-755-2350
Eric Markworth, prin. Fax 755-2352

Magna, Salt Lake, Pop. 25,413
Granite SD
Supt. — See Salt Lake City
Copper Hills ES 500/K-6
7635 W 3715 S 84044 385-646-4792
Tracy Rose, prin. Fax 646-4793
Elk Run ES 700/K-6
3550 S Helen Dr 84044 385-646-4786
Dona Harris, prin. Fax 646-4787
Lake Ridge ES 500/K-6
7400 W 3400 S 84044 385-646-4888
Karly Chavez, prin. Fax 646-4889
Magna ES 600/PK-6
8500 W 3100 S 84044 385-646-4900
Brett Bawden, prin. Fax 646-4901
Pleasant Green ES 700/K-6
8201 W 2700 S 84044 385-646-4972
Dr. Sharon Prescott, prin. Fax 646-4973

Manila, Daggett, Pop. 308
Daggett SD 200/PK-12
PO Box 249 84046 435-784-3174
Bruce Northcott, supt. Fax 784-3920
www.dsdf.org
Manila ES 100/PK-6
PO Box 249 84046 435-784-3174
Alan Staggs, prin. Fax 784-3209
Other Schools – See Dutch John

Manti, Sanpete, Pop. 3,220
South Sanpete SD 3,300/PK-12
39 S Main St 84642 435-835-2261
Kent Larsen, supt. Fax 835-2265
www.ssanpete.org/
Manti ES 500/PK-5
150 W 100 S 84642 435-835-2271
Karen Soper, prin. Fax 835-2278
Other Schools – See Ephraim, Gunnison

Mapleton, Utah, Pop. 7,784
Nebo SD
Supt. — See Spanish Fork
Hobble Creek ES 600/K-6
1145 E 1200 N 84664 801-489-2863
Michael Johnson, prin. Fax 489-2868
Maple Ridge ES PK-6
2340 W Harvest Pkwy 84664 801-489-1800
Sara Matis, prin. Fax 489-1819
Mapleton ES 700/K-6
120 W Maple St 84664 801-489-2850
Julie Peery, prin. Fax 489-2887

Marysvale, Piute, Pop. 405
Piute County SD
Supt. — See Junction
Oscarson ES 50/PK-6
PO Box 39 84750 435-326-4341
Jodi Johnson, lead tchr. Fax 326-4247

Mendon, Cache, Pop. 1,262
Cache County SD
Supt. — See North Logan
Mountainside ES 500/K-6
PO Box 518 84325 435-792-7688
Lynette Riggs, prin. Fax 792-7690

Mexican Hat, San Juan, Pop. 31
San Juan SD
Supt. — See Blanding
Tsebii'nidzisgai ES 300/K-6
101 W Medical Dr 84531 435-678-1286
Kristine Fitzgerald, prin. Fax 678-1244

Midvale, Salt Lake, Pop. 27,166
Canyons SD
Supt. — See Sandy
Copperview ES 500/K-5
8449 S 150 W 84047 801-826-8125
Christie Webb, prin. Fax 826-8126
East Midvale ES 500/K-5
6990 S 300 E 84047 801-826-8350
Justin Pitcher, prin. Fax 826-8351
Midvale ES 700/K-5
7830 S Chapel St 84047 801-826-8725
Chip Watts, prin. Fax 826-8726
Midvale MS 900/6-8
7852 S Pioneer St 84047 801-826-7300
Wendy Dau, prin. Fax 826-7309
Midvalley ES 500/K-5
217 E 7800 S 84047 801-826-8800
Jeff Nalwalker, prin. Fax 826-8801

Midway, Wasatch, Pop. 3,812
Wasatch SD
Supt. — See Heber City
Midway ES 600/K-4
225 S 100 E 84049 435-654-0472
Brian Thorne, prin. Fax 654-7426

Milford, Beaver, Pop. 1,385
Beaver SD
Supt. — See Beaver
Milford ES 200/K-6
PO Box 309 84751 435-387-2841
Fax 387-5050

Millville, Cache, Pop. 1,804
Cache County SD
Supt. — See North Logan
Millville ES 400/K-6
PO Box 230 84326 435-752-7162
Gary Thomas, prin. Fax 755-5758

Minersville, Beaver, Pop. 902
Beaver SD
Supt. — See Beaver
Minersville S 100/K-8
PO Box 189 84752 435-386-2382
Jody Heaps, prin. Fax 386-2484

Moab, Grand, Pop. 4,967
Grand SD 1,500/PK-12
264 S 400 E 84532 435-259-5317
Dr. Scott Crane, supt. Fax 259-6212
www.grandschools.org
Grand County MS 200/7-8
439 S 100 E 84532 435-259-7158
Melinda Snow, prin. Fax 259-6221
Knight ES 800/K-6
505 Mivida Dr 84532 435-259-7350
Taryn Kay, prin. Fax 259-8094
Sundwall Preschool 50/PK-PK
190 E 100 N 84532 435-259-3068
Sherie Buckingham, dir. Fax 259-6276

Mona, Juab, Pop. 1,524
Juab SD
Supt. — See Nephi
Mona ES 400/K-6
260 E 200 S, 435-623-2082
Mary Wohlforth, prin. Fax 623-2661

Monroe, Sevier, Pop. 2,221
Sevier SD
Supt. — See Richfield
Monroe ES 600/K-5
40 W Center St 84754 435-527-4691
Ted Chappell, prin. Fax 527-4660
Monroe Preschool, 25 N 100 W 84754 PK-PK
Dawnanna Topham, prin. 435-527-3014
South Sevier MS 300/6-8
300 E Center St 84754 435-527-4607
Michelle Nielson, prin. Fax 527-4636

Montezuma Creek, San Juan, Pop. 332
San Juan SD
Supt. — See Blanding
Montezuma Creek ES 200/K-6
PO Box 630 84534 435-678-1261
Boyd Silversmith, prin. Fax 678-1850

Monticello, San Juan, Pop. 1,935
San Juan SD
Supt. — See Blanding
Monticello ES 300/K-6
PO Box 189 84535 435-678-1180
Julie Holt, prin. Fax 678-1179

Monument Valley, San Juan

Monument Valley SDA Mission S 50/K-8
PO Box 360013 84536 435-727-3270

Morgan, Morgan, Pop. 3,652
Morgan SD 2,600/PK-12
PO Box 530 84050 801-829-3411
Dr. Doug Jacobs, supt. Fax 829-3531
www.morgansd.org
Morgan ES 700/PK-5
344 E Young St 84050 801-829-3438
Andrew Jensen, prin. Fax 829-0589
Morgan MS 600/6-8
PO Box 470 84050 801-829-3467
Reynold Hoopes, prin. Fax 829-0645
Mountain Green ES 500/K-5
6064 Silver Leaf Dr 84050 801-876-3041
Dr. Heidi Andreasen, prin. Fax 876-3518

Moroni, Sanpete, Pop. 1,398
North Sanpete SD
Supt. — See Mount Pleasant
Moroni ES 400/K-6
PO Box 279 84646 435-436-8291
Stacey Peterson, prin. Fax 436-8401
North Sanpete MS 400/7-8
PO Box 307 84646 435-436-8206
ODee Hansen, prin. Fax 436-8208

Mount Pleasant, Sanpete, Pop. 3,193
North Sanpete SD 2,300/PK-12
220 E 700 S 84647 435-462-2485
Dr. Sam Ray, supt. Fax 462-2480
www.nsanpete.org
Mount Pleasant ES 500/PK-6
579 S 400 E 84647 435-462-2077
Rena Orton, prin. Fax 462-3608
Other Schools – See Fairview, Fountain Green, Moroni, Spring City

Murray, Salt Lake, Pop. 45,548
Granite SD
Supt. — See Salt Lake City
Twin Peaks ES 500/K-6
5325 S 1045 E 84117 385-646-5049
Dr. Julie Lorentzon, prin. Fax 646-5051
Woodstock ES 400/K-6
6015 S 1300 E 84121 385-646-5108
Brenda Zimmerman, prin. Fax 646-5109

Murray CSD
Supt. — See Salt Lake City
Grant ES 400/K-6
662 W Bulldog Cir 84123 801-264-7416
Matthew Nelson, prin. Fax 264-7437
Horizon ES 700/K-6
5180 S Glendon St 84123 801-264-7420
Heather Nicholas, prin. Fax 264-7444
Liberty ES 400/K-6
140 W 6100 S 84107 801-264-7424
Natalie Stouffer, prin. Fax 264-7449
Longview ES 400/K-6
6240 S Longview Dr 84107 801-264-7428
Chad Sanders, prin. Fax 264-7452
McMillan ES 500/K-6
315 E 5900 S 84107 801-264-7430
Joy Sanford, prin. Fax 264-7451
Parkside ES 600/K-6
495 E 5175 S 84107 801-264-7434
Colleen Smith, prin. Fax 264-7453
Viewmont ES 500/K-6
745 W Anderson Ave 84123 801-264-7438
Melissa Bueno-Hamilton, prin. Fax 264-7454

Mt. Vernon Academy 100/K-12
184 E Vine St 84107 801-266-5521

Myton, Duchesne, Pop. 554
Duchesne SD
Supt. — See Roosevelt
Myton ES 200/K-5
PO Box 186 84052 435-725-4735
Jennifer Tuckett, prin. Fax 725-4746

Neola, Duchesne, Pop. 450
Duchesne SD
Supt. — See Roosevelt
Neola ES 200/K-5
PO Box 220 84053 435-725-4715
Kendra Embleton, prin. Fax 725-4730

Nephi, Juab, Pop. 5,328
Juab SD 2,300/K-12
346 E 600 N 84648 435-623-1940
Rick Robins, supt. Fax 623-1941
www.juabsd.org
Juab JHS 300/7-8
555 E 800 N 84648 435-623-1541
Ken Rowley, prin. Fax 623-4995
Nebo View ES 300/K-6
380 E 200 N 84648 435-623-1812
John Samuelson, prin. Fax 623-5039
Red Cliff ES 500/K-6
1199 S Main St 84648 435-623-0328
Richard Pay, prin. Fax 623-4212
Other Schools – See Mona

Nibley, Cache, Pop. 5,368
Cache County SD
Supt. — See North Logan
Heritage ES 500/K-6
925 W 3200 S 84321 435-792-7696
Alden Jack, prin. Fax 792-7698

North Logan, Cache, Pop. 8,096
Cache County SD 16,700/K-12
2063 N 1200 E 84341 435-752-3925
Dr. Steven Norton, supt. Fax 753-2168
www.ccsdut.org
Other Schools – See Hyde Park, Hyrum, Lewiston, Logan, Mendon, Millville, Nibley, Providence, Richmond, Smithfield, Wellsville

North Ogden, Weber, Pop. 17,100
Weber SD
Supt. — See Ogden
Bates ES 700/K-6
850 E 3100 N 84414 801-452-4580
Laura Wright, prin. Fax 452-4599
Green Acres ES 500/K-6
640 E 1900 N 84414 801-452-4420
Lisa Gilstrap, prin. Fax 452-4439
North Ogden ES 600/K-6
530 E 2650 N 84414 801-452-4300
Phil Nestoryak, prin. Fax 452-4319

North Salt Lake, Davis, Pop. 15,698
Davis SD
Supt. — See Farmington
Foxboro ES 1,100/K-6
587 N Foxboro Dr 84054 801-402-5050
Kevin Prusse, prin. Fax 402-5051
Orchard ES 700/K-6
205 E Center St 84054 801-402-1700
Michael Volmar, prin. Fax 402-1701

Ogden, Weber, Pop. 80,717
Ogden CSD 12,400/K-12
1950 Monroe Blvd 84401 801-737-7300
Sandy Coroles, supt. Fax 627-7654
www.ogdensd.org
Bonneville ES 500/K-6
490 Gramercy Ave 84404 801-737-8900
Janice Bukey, prin. Fax 627-7681
Gramercy ES 500/K-6
1270 Gramercy Ave 84404 801-737-7500
Jim Mieure, prin. Fax 625-8795

Heritage ES 800/K-6
373 S 150 W 84404 801-737-8000
Don Mendenhall, prin. Fax 737-8047
Hillcrest ES 500/K-6
130 N Eccles Ave 84404 801-737-7550
Jenny Decorso, prin. Fax 334-4411
Lincoln ES 500/K-6
1235 Canfield Dr 84404 801-737-7650
Ross Lunceford, prin. Fax 625-8816
Madison ES 600/K-6
2563 Monroe Blvd 84401 801-737-8200
Shannon Wilcox, prin. Fax 627-7606
Mann ES 500/K-6
1300 9th St 84404 801-737-7600
Jileen Xochimitl, prin. Fax 627-7694
New Bridge ES K-6
2150 Jefferson Ave 84401 801-737-8100
Vincent Ardizzone, prin. Fax 737-8854
Odyssey ES 600/K-6
375 Goddard St 84401 801-737-8400
LeeAnne Rich, prin. Fax 737-8511
Polk ES 400/K-6
2615 Polk Ave 84401 801-737-8300
Maridee Harrison, prin. Fax 625-8829
Shadow Valley ES 600/K-6
4911 S 1500 E 84403 801-737-8150
Suzanne Bolar, prin. Fax 737-8157
Smith ES 500/K-6
3295 Gramercy Ave 84403 801-737-8350
Terry Humphreys, prin. Fax 627-7660
Taylor Canyon ES 500/K-6
2130 Taylor Ave 84401 801-737-8950
Bev Jenson, prin. Fax 737-8957
Wasatch ES 400/K-6
3370 Polk Ave 84403 801-737-8450
Dr. Donna Corby, prin. Fax 627-7685

Weber SD 30,300/K-12
5320 Adams Avenue Pkwy 84405 801-476-7800
Dr. Jeff Stephens, supt. Fax 476-7800
www.wsd.net
Burch Creek ES K-6
4300 Madison Ave 84405 801-476-5300
Rick Proffer, prin. Fax 476-5319
Child ES 500/K-6
655 E 5500 S 84405 801-452-4140
Karen Neiswender, prin. Fax 452-4159
Farr West ES 900/K-6
2190 W 2700 N 84404 801-452-4360
Dave Hales, prin. Fax 452-4379
Majestic ES 900/K-6
425 W 2550 N 84414 801-452-4260
Dave Wallace, prin. Fax 452-4279
Pioneer ES 500/K-6
250 N 1600 W 84404 801-452-4560
Brian Anderson, prin. Fax 452-4579
Plain City ES 700/K-6
2335 N 3600 W 84404 801-452-4220
Quinn Karlinsey, prin. Fax 452-4239
Riverdale ES 600/K-6
1160 W 4400 S 84405 801-452-4540
Melanie Johnson, prin. Fax 452-4559
Roosevelt ES 500/K-6
190 W 5100 S 84405 801-452-4520
Kitty Barney, prin. Fax 452-4539
Uintah ES 700/K-6
6115 S 2250 E 84403 801-452-4980
Joanne Hobbs, prin. Fax 452-4999
Washington Terrace ES 500/K-6
20 E 4600 S 84405 801-452-4200
Katie Amsden, prin. Fax 452-4219
West Weber ES 500/K-6
4178 W 900 S 84404 801-452-4280
Mike Fazzio, prin. Fax 452-4299
Other Schools – See Eden, Hooper, North Ogden, Pleasant View, Roy, West Haven

---

Deamude Adventist Christian S 50/K-8
1765 W 2100 S 84401 801-731-3140
Del Jean Butler, prin. Fax 752-0620
St. Joseph S 400/PK-8
2980 Quincy Ave 84403 801-393-6051
Nancy Essary, prin. Fax 393-6086

Orangeville, Emery, Pop. 1,463
Emery County SD
Supt. — See Huntington
Cottonwood ES 200/PK-6
PO Box 679 84537 435-748-2481
John Hughes, prin. Fax 748-2130

Orderville, Kane, Pop. 575
Kane SD
Supt. — See Kanab
Valley ES 200/K-6
PO Box 129 84758 435-648-2277
Tracy Stevens, prin. Fax 648-2131

Orem, Utah, Pop. 85,397
Alpine SD
Supt. — See American Fork
Aspen ES 400/K-6
945 W 2000 N 84057 801-610-8100
T. Freeman, prin. Fax 227-8786
Bonneville ES 700/K-6
1245 N 800 W 84057 801-610-8101
Shawn Brooks, prin. Fax 227-8705
Cascade ES 700/K-6
160 N 800 E 84097 801-610-8102
Boyce Campbell, prin. Fax 227-8709
Cherry Hill ES 600/K-6
250 E 1650 S 84058 801-610-8105
Alisa Hart, prin. Fax 227-8712
Foothill ES 600/K-6
921 N 1240 E 84097 801-610-8107
Dr. Joseph Backman, prin. Fax 227-2466
Geneva ES 500/K-6
665 W 400 N 84057 801-610-8108
Keith Conley, prin. Fax 227-8716
Hillcrest ES 400/K-6
651 E 1400 S 84097 801-610-8110
Zach Eager, prin. Fax 227-8719
Northridge ES 700/K-6
1660 N 50 E 84057 801-610-8114
Eric Woodhouse, prin. Fax 227-8726
Orchard ES 700/K-6
1035 N 800 E 84097 801-610-8115
Aaron Stevenson, prin. Fax 227-2433
Orem ES 700/K-6
450 W 400 S 84058 801-610-8116
Andrea Park, prin. Fax 227-8729
Scera Park ES 500/K-6
450 S 400 E 84097 801-610-8118
Lori Bellitti, prin. Fax 227-8732
Sharon ES 400/K-6
525 N 400 E 84097 801-610-8119
Mike Larson, prin. Fax 227-8735
Suncrest ES 500/K-6
668 W 150 N 84057 801-610-8120
Linda Anderson, prin. Fax 227-8738
Westmore ES 400/K-6
1150 S Main St 84058 801-610-8123
John Shelton, prin. Fax 227-8744
Windsor ES 500/K-6
1315 N Main St 84057 801-610-8124
Lani Sitake, prin. Fax 227-8747

Arches Academy, 280 S 400 E 84097 100/PK-9
Annette Warnick, head sch 801-374-5480

Panguitch, Garfield, Pop. 1,509
Garfield SD 900/K-12
PO Box 398 84759 435-676-8821
Tracy Davis, supt. Fax 676-8266
www.garfk12.org
Panguitch ES 300/K-6
PO Box 386 84759 435-676-8847
Nick Reynolds, prin. Fax 676-1346
Panguitch MS 100/7-8
PO Box 393 84759 435-676-8225
Russ Torgersen, prin. Fax 676-2518
Other Schools – See Antimony, Boulder, Escalante, Tropic

Park City, Summit, Pop. 7,439
Park City SD 4,700/K-12
2700 Kearns Blvd 84060 435-645-5600
Ember Conley, supt. Fax 645-5609
www.pcschools.us
Ecker Hill International MS 700/6-7
2465 Kilby Rd 84098 435-645-5610
Traci Evans, prin. Fax 645-5619
Jeremy Ranch ES 500/K-5
3050 Rasmussen Rd 84098 435-645-5670
Shawn Kuennen, prin. Fax 645-5679
McPolin ES 400/K-5
2270 Kearns Blvd 84060 435-645-5630
Bob Edmiston, prin. Fax 645-5639
Parley's Park ES 600/K-5
4600 Silver Springs Dr 84098 435-645-5620
David Gomez, prin. Fax 645-5629
Trailside ES 500/K-5
5700 Trailside Dr 84098 435-645-5680
Carolyn Sinan, prin. Fax 645-5689

Park City Day S 200/PK-8
3120 Pinebrook Rd 84098 435-649-2791
Ian Crossland, head sch Fax 649-6759
Soaring Wings International Montessori S 100/PK-9
2083 Equestrian Ct 84060 435-649-3626
Bruce W. King, admin.

Park Valley, Box Elder
Box Elder SD
Supt. — See Brigham City
Park Valley S 50/K-10
788 Education Dr 84329 435-871-4411
Melissa Morris, lead tchr. Fax 871-4444

Parowan, Iron, Pop. 2,772
Iron SD
Supt. — See Cedar City
Parowan ES 400/K-6
PO Box 458 84761 435-477-3368
Kevin Porter, prin. Fax 477-1108

Payson, Utah, Pop. 18,014
Nebo SD
Supt. — See Spanish Fork
Barnett ES 500/K-6
456 N 300 E 84651 801-465-6000
Angela Stoddard, prin. Fax 465-6001
Park View ES 600/PK-6
360 S 100 E 84651 801-465-6010
Shanna Stirland, prin. Fax 465-6011
Taylor ES 500/K-6
92 S 500 W 84651 801-465-6050
Billi Robbins, prin Fax 465-6039
Wilson ES 500/PK-6
590 W 500 S 84651 801-465-6060
Shawn Rawlings, prin. Fax 465-6068

Perry, Box Elder, Pop. 4,433
Box Elder SD
Supt. — See Brigham City
Three Mile Creek S 600/2-5
2625 S 1050 W 84302 435-734-4930
AshLee Nelson, prin. Fax 734-4932

Pleasant Grove, Utah, Pop. 32,692
Alpine SD
Supt. — See American Fork
Central ES 500/K-6
95 N 400 E 84062 801-610-8104
Ryan Wells, prin. Fax 785-8741
Grovecrest ES 800/K-6
1037 N 300 E 84062 801-610-8109
Kyle Hoopes, prin. Fax 785-8715
Manila ES 800/K-6
1726 N 600 W 84062 801-610-8112
Dr. Nancy Sorensen, prin. Fax 785-8784
Mt. Mahogany ES 1,000/K-6
618 N 1300 W 84062 801-610-8113
Megan Miller, prin. Fax 785-8798
Valley View ES 500/K-6
941 Orchard Dr 84062 801-610-8121
Carl Stubbs, prin. Fax 785-8725

Liahona Preparatory Academy 200/PK-12
2464 W 450 S 84062 801-785-7850
Breanne Dedrickson, admin. Fax 785-4723

Pleasant View, Weber, Pop. 7,835
Weber SD
Supt. — See Ogden
Lomond View ES 600/K-6
3644 N 900 W 84414 801-452-4780
Justin Skeen, prin. Fax 452-4799

Price, Carbon, Pop. 8,585
Carbon SD 2,900/K-12
251 W 400 N 84501 435-637-1732
Dr. Lance Hatch, supt. Fax 637-9417
www.carbonschools.org
Castle Heights ES 500/K-5
750 Homestead Blvd 84501 435-637-7177
Christopher Winfree, prin. Fax 637-4645
Creekview ES 400/K-5
590 W 500 S 84501 435-637-0828
John Thomas, prin. Fax 637-4902
Mont Harmon MS 400/6-8
60 W 400 N 84501 435-637-0510
Seth Allred, prin. Fax 637-6074
Other Schools – See Helper, Sunnyside, Wellington

Providence, Cache, Pop. 6,963
Cache County SD
Supt. — See North Logan
Providence ES 500/K-6
91 E Center St 84332 435-752-6010
Trudy Wilson, prin. Fax 753-1937
Spring Creek MS 700/6-7
350 W 100 N 84332 435-753-6200
Blake Pickett, prin. Fax 753-1979

Provo, Utah, Pop. 108,411
Provo CSD 14,300/PK-12
280 W 940 N 84604 801-374-4800
Keith C. Rittel, supt. Fax 374-4808
www.provo.edu
Canyon Crest ES 500/K-6
4664 N Canyon Rd 84604 801-221-9873
Darren Johnson, prin. Fax 221-9989
Centennial MS 1,000/7-8
305 E 2320 N 84604 801-374-4621
Kyle Bates, prin. Fax 374-4626
Dixon MS 800/7-8
750 W 200 N 84601 801-374-4980
John Anderson, prin. Fax 374-4884
Earhart ES 600/K-6
2585 W 200 S 84601 801-370-4630
Ryan McCarty, prin. Fax 370-4633
Edgemont ES 600/K-6
566 E 3650 N 84604 801-221-9984
Gaye Gibbs, prin. Fax 221-9987
Franklin ES 500/K-6
350 S 600 W 84601 801-374-4925
Kimberli Hawkins, prin. Fax 374-4886
Lakeview ES 700/K-6
2899 W 1390 N 84601 801-374-4990
Drew Daniels, prin. Fax 374-4991
Provo Peaks ES 500/K-6
665 E Center St 84606 801-374-4940
Geovanni Guzman, prin. Fax 374-4982
Provost ES 400/K-6
629 S 1000 E 84606 801-374-4960
Dr. Steve Oliverson, prin. Fax 374-4962
Rock Canyon ES 600/K-6
435 E 2320 N 84604 801-374-4935
Dean Nielson, prin. Fax 374-5081
Spring Creek ES 600/K-6
1740 Nevada Ave 84606 801-370-4650
Jill Franklin, prin. Fax 370-4653
Sunrise Preschool 300/PK-PK
87 N 700 E 84606 801-374-4915
Jeremy Barker, prin. Fax 374-4917
Sunset View ES 500/K-6
1520 W 600 S 84601 801-374-4950
Chris Chilcoat, prin. Fax 374-4951
Timpanogos ES 700/K-6
449 N 500 W 84601 801-374-4955
Carrie Rawlins, prin. Fax 374-4958
Wasatch ES 900/K-6
1080 N 900 E 84604 801-374-4910
Rene' Cunningham, prin. Fax 374-4912
Westridge ES 900/K-6
1720 W 1460 N 84604 801-374-4870
Rebekah Thomas, prin. Fax 374-4873

Ivy Hall Academy 100/PK-8
1598 W 820 N 84601 801-356-1000
Fax 356-0484

Randolph, Rich, Pop. 458
Rich SD 500/K-12
PO Box 67 84064 435-793-2135
Dale Lamborn, supt. Fax 793-2136
www.richschool.org
South Rich ES 100/K-5
PO Box 67 84064 435-793-2135
Dale Lamborn, prin. Fax 793-2136
Other Schools – See Laketown

Richfield, Sevier, Pop. 7,458
Sevier SD 4,800/PK-12
180 E 600 N 84701 435-896-8214
Cade Douglas, supt. Fax 896-8804
www.seviersd.org
Ashman ES 500/K-2
70 N 200 W 84701 435-896-8415
Jill Porter, prin. Fax 896-6958
Pahvant ES 500/3-5
520 N 300 W 84701 435-896-4403
Chad Johnson, prin. Fax 896-9479
Red Hills MS 500/6-8
400 S 600 W 84701 435-896-6421
Selena Terry, prin. Fax 896-6423

Richfield Preschool 100/PK-PK
80 W Center St 84701 435-896-8776
Dawnanna Topham, dir.
Other Schools – See Koosharem, Monroe, Salina

Richmond, Cache, Pop. 2,447
Cache County SD
Supt. — See North Logan
Park ES 300/K-6
90 S 100 W 84333 435-258-2344
Shellie Healy, prin. Fax 258-5202
White Pine MS 500/6-7
184 W 100 N 84333 435-258-2111
Randy Bennion, prin. Fax 258-5523

Riverton, Salt Lake, Pop. 37,974
Jordan SD
Supt. — See West Jordan
Foothills ES 1,100/K-6
13717 S Shaggy Peak Dr, 801-302-8599
Cherie Wilson, prin. Fax 302-4976
Midas Creek ES 1,200/K-6
11901 S Park Haven Ln, 801-254-7407
Carolyn Bona, prin. Fax 302-4919
Riverton ES 800/K-6
13150 S 1830 W 84065 801-254-8050
Cynthia Tingey, prin. Fax 302-4952
Rosamond ES 700/K-6
12195 S 1975 W 84065 801-254-8043
Colleen Wheeler, prin. Fax 302-4957
Rose Creek ES 900/K-6
12812 S 3600 W 84065 801-254-8082
Tami Bird, prin. Fax 302-4963
Southland ES 800/K-6
12675 S 2700 W 84065 801-254-8047
Lisa Jackson, prin. Fax 302-4961

Montessori at Riverton 100/PK-8
1646 W 13200 S 84065 801-253-4000
Emily Aune, head sch
St. Andrew S 300/PK-8
11835 S 3600 W 84065 801-253-6000
Dr. Patrick Jefferies, prin. Fax 254-1142

Roosevelt, Duchesne, Pop. 5,853
Duchesne SD 5,100/K-12
1010 E 200 N 84066 435-725-4500
Dr. David Brotherson, supt. Fax 725-4511
www.dcsd.org
Centennial ES, 490 S 500 E 84066 K-5
Bruce Guymon, admin. 435-725-4450
East ES 700/K-2
700 E 400 N Ste 107-10 84066 435-725-4665
Russ Nielsen, prin. Fax 725-4709
Kings Peak ES 600/3-5
437 N 300 W Ste 425-2 84066 435-725-4630
Michlel Bostick, prin. Fax 725-4661
Roosevelt JHS 700/6-8
350 W 200 S 84066 435-725-4585
Mike Ross, prin. Fax 725-4622
Other Schools – See Altamont, Duchesne, Myton, Neola, Tabiona

Uintah SD
Supt. — See Vernal
Eagle View S 500/K-8
301 N 5750 E 84066 435-722-2247
Robert Stearmer, prin. Fax 722-2240

Roy, Weber, Pop. 35,969
Weber SD
Supt. — See Ogden
Lakeview ES 500/K-6
2025 W 5000 S 84067 801-452-4380
Shirley Passey, prin. Fax 452-4399
Midland ES 600/K-6
3100 W 4800 S 84067 801-476-5400
Mary Jo Williams, prin. Fax 476-5459
Municipal ES 400/K-6
5775 S 2200 W 84067 801-452-4120
Kevin Chase, prin. Fax 452-4139
North Park ES 400/K-6
4046 S 2175 W 84067 801-452-4340
Riko Reese, prin. Fax 452-4359
Roy ES 500/K-6
2888 W 5600 S 84067 801-452-4160
Brent Hogan, prin. Fax 452-4179
Valley View ES 500/K-6
2465 W 4500 S 84067 801-476-5200
Ann Holdaway, prin. Fax 476-5219

Saint George, Washington, Pop. 70,848
Washington County SD 26,500/PK-12
121 W Tabernacle St 84770 435-673-3553
Larry Bergeson, supt. Fax 673-3216
www.washk12.org
Bloomington ES 500/K-5
425 Man O War Rd 84790 435-673-6266
Melissa Lane, prin. Fax 674-6497
Bloomington Hills ES 600/K-5
919 E Brigham Rd 84790 435-674-6495
Michelle North, prin. Fax 652-4703
Coral Cliffs ES 600/PK-5
2040 W 2000 N 84770 435-652-4712
Amy Wilcox, prin. Fax 652-4716
Crimson View ES 600/K-5
2835 E 2000 S 84790 435-634-7000
Nathan Esplin, prin. Fax 652-4713
Diamond Valley ES 300/K-5
1411 W Diamond Valley Dr 84770 435-574-2009
Brandon Yost, prin. Fax 574-2013
Dixie Sun ES 600/PK-5
1795 W 1230 N 84770 435-673-8978
Kim Heki, prin. Fax 673-6303
Fossil Ridge IS 800/6-7
383 S Mall Dr 84790 435-652-4706
Jonathan Howell, prin. Fax 652-4758
Heritage ES 600/PK-5
747 E Riverside Dr 84790 435-628-4427
Adam Baker, prin. Fax 628-5771
Legacy ES 600/PK-5
280 E 100 S 84770 435-673-6191
Teria Mortensen, prin. Fax 673-6248
Little Valley ES 500/K-5
2330 E Horsemans Park Dr 84790 435-652-4771
Rob Stevenson, prin. Fax 652-4770
Panorama ES 500/K-5
301 N 2200 E 84790 435-628-6881
Steve Gregoire, prin. Fax 634-1476
Sandstone ES 600/PK-5
850 N 2450 E 84790 435-674-6460
Rod Broadhead, prin. Fax 674-6463
Sunrise Ridge IS 800/6-7
3167 S 2350 E 84790 435-652-4772
Sandy Ferrell, prin. Fax 652-4777
Sunset ES 600/PK-5
495 N Westridge Dr 84770 435-673-5669
Anthony Horrocks, prin. Fax 673-3544
Tonaquint IS 700/6-7
1210 W Curly Hollow Dr 84770 435-688-2238
Barbara Garrett, prin. Fax 688-2504
Other Schools – See Enterprise, Hildale, Hurricane, Ivins, La Verkin, Santa Clara, Springdale, Washington

---

Trinity Lutheran S 50/PK-7
2260 Red Cliffs Dr 84790 435-628-6115
Duane Nyen, prin. Fax 628-1850

Salem, Utah, Pop. 6,343
Nebo SD
Supt. — See Spanish Fork
Foothills ES 800/K-6
412 S 810 E 84653 801-423-9172
Keri Huntsman, prin. Fax 423-6538
Mt. Loafer ES 500/K-6
1025 S 250 W 84653 801-423-2705
Sarah Blackhurst, prin. Fax 423-3593
Salem ES 500/K-6
140 W 100 S 84653 801-423-1182
Jim Wellburn, prin. Fax 423-2746

Salina, Sevier, Pop. 2,467
Sevier SD
Supt. — See Richfield
North Sevier MS 300/6-8
135 N 100 W 84654 435-529-3841
Rod Hinck, prin. Fax 529-7377
Salina ES 500/K-5
210 W 300 N 84654 435-529-7462
Nolan Andersen, prin. Fax 529-7463
Salina Preschool, 210 W 300 N 84654 PK-PK
Dawnanna Topham, dir. 435-529-3872

Salt Lake City, Salt Lake, Pop. 178,350
Canyons SD
Supt. — See Sandy
Butler ES 500/K-5
7000 S 2700 E 84121 801-826-7975
Christine Waddell, prin. Fax 826-7976
Canyon View ES 400/K-5
3050 E 7800 S 84121 801-826-8050
B.J. Weller, prin. Fax 826-8051

Granite SD 67,200/PK-12
2500 S State St 84115 385-646-5000
Dr. Martin Bates, supt. Fax 646-4207
www.graniteschools.org
Crestview ES 700/K-6
2100 E Lincoln Ln 84124 385-646-4804
Teri Cooper, prin. Fax 646-4805
Driggs ES 600/K-6
4340 S 2700 E 84124 385-646-4810
Ben Peters, prin. Fax 646-4811
Eastwood ES 500/K-6
3305 S Wasatch Blvd 84109 385-646-4816
Naomi Hopf, prin. Fax 646-4817
Lincoln ES 600/PK-6
450 E 3700 S 84115 385-646-4894
Milton Collins, prin. Fax 646-4895
Mill Creek ES 500/PK-6
3761 S 1100 E 84106 385-646-4912
Ann Kane, prin. Fax 646-4913
Morningside ES 700/K-6
4170 S 3000 E 84124 385-646-4924
Tod Cracroft, prin. Fax 646-4925
Moss ES 500/K-6
4399 S 500 E 84107 385-646-4930
Judith Simmons-Kissell, prin. Fax 646-4931
Oakridge ES 600/K-6
4325 S Jupiter Dr 84124 385-646-4936
Christine Drummond, prin. Fax 646-4937
Penn ES 700/K-6
1670 E Siggard Dr 84106 385-646-4960
Kent Nixon, prin. Fax 646-4961
Roosevelt ES 500/K-6
3225 S 800 E 84106 385-646-4996
Malynda Cloward, prin. Fax 646-4997
Rosecrest ES 500/K-6
2420 E Fisher Ln 84109 385-646-5002
Kyle Anderson, prin. Fax 646-5003
Spring Lane ES 600/K-6
5315 S 1700 E 84117 385-646-4906
Afton Lambson, prin. Fax 646-4907
Upland Terrace ES 600/K-6
3700 S Sunnydale Dr 84109 385-646-5055
Jennifer Reed, prin. Fax 646-5056
Wilson ES 900/PK-6
2567 S Main St 84115 385-646-5102
Christine Golze, prin. Fax 646-5106
Wright ES 800/K-6
6760 W 3100 S 84128 385-646-5480
Kristie Reather, prin. Fax 646-5481
Other Schools – See Holladay, Kearns, Magna, Murray, Taylorsville, West Jordan, West Valley

Murray CSD 6,400/K-12
5102 S Commerce Dr 84107 801-264-7400
Dr. Steven Hirase, supt. Fax 264-7456
www.murrayschools.org
Other Schools – See Murray

Salt Lake City SD 24,900/PK-12
440 E 100 S 84111 801-578-8599
Dr. Alexa Cunningham, supt. Fax 578-8248
www.slcschools.org
Backman ES 600/K-6
601 N 1500 W 84116 801-578-8100
Heather Newell, prin. Fax 578-8155
Beacon Heights ES 400/K-6
1850 S 2500 E 84108 801-481-4814
Rae Louie, prin. Fax 481-4900
Bennion ES 300/K-6
429 S 800 E 84102 801-578-8108
Dahlia Cordova, prin. Fax 578-8111
Bonneville ES 600/K-6
1145 S 1900 E 84108 801-584-2913
Donna Reid, prin. Fax 584-2919
Bryant MS 400/7-8
40 S 800 E 84102 801-578-8118
Larry Madden, prin. Fax 578-8125
Clayton MS 700/7-8
1470 S 1900 E 84108 801-481-4810
Jared Wright, prin. Fax 481-4884
Dilworth ES 600/K-6
1953 S 2100 E 84108 801-481-4806
Jeremy Chatterton, prin. Fax 481-4924
Edison ES 600/K-5
466 S Cheyenne St 84104 801-974-8300
Sue Damm, prin. Fax 974-8352
Emerson ES 600/K-6
1017 E Harrison Ave 84105 801-481-4819
April Reynolds, prin. Fax 481-4914
Ensign ES 300/K-6
775 E 12th Ave 84103 801-578-8150
Bobbie Kirby, prin. Fax 578-8107
Escalante ES 500/K-6
1810 W 900 N 84116 801-578-8496
Liz Gonzalez, prin. Fax 578-8499
Franklin ES 500/K-6
1115 W 300 S 84104 801-578-8158
Randy Miller, prin. Fax 578-8163
Glendale MS 800/6-8
1430 W Andrew Ave 84104 801-974-8319
Jill Baillie, prin. Fax 974-8356
Hawthorne ES 500/K-6
1675 S 600 E 84105 801-481-4824
Marian Broadhead, prin. Fax 481-4927
Highland Park ES 700/K-6
1738 E 2700 S 84106 801-481-4833
Debora Cluff, prin. Fax 481-4920
Hillside MS 500/7-8
1825 S Nevada St 84108 801-481-4828
Jane Bernston, prin. Fax 481-4831
Indian Hills ES 500/K-6
2496 E Saint Marys Dr 84108 801-584-2908
Earl Arnoldson, prin. Fax 584-2932
Jackson ES 500/K-6
750 W 200 N 84116 801-578-8165
Jana Edward, prin. Fax 578-8172
Liberty ES 500/K-6
1090 S Roberta St 84111 801-578-8180
JaNeal Rodriguez, prin. Fax 578-8188
Meadowlark ES 500/K-6
497 N Morton Dr 84116 801-578-8529
Heidi Greene, prin. Fax 578-8534
Mountain View ES 600/K-5
1380 S Navajo St 84104 801-974-8315
Kenneth Limb, prin. Fax 974-8332
Newman ES 500/K-6
1269 N Colorado St 84116 801-578-8537
Debra Andrews, prin. Fax 578-8544
Nibley Park S 500/K-8
2785 S 800 E 84106 801-481-4842
Frances Battle, prin. Fax 481-4899
North Star ES 700/K-6
1545 N Morton Dr 84116 801-578-8448
Dr. Nathan Elkins, prin. Fax 578-8445
Northwest MS 800/7-8
1730 W 1700 N 84116 801-578-8547
Marissa Zuchetto, prin. Fax 578-8558
Parkview ES 500/K-5
970 S Emery St 84104 801-974-8304
Valerie Bergera, prin. Fax 974-8329
Riley ES 400/K-5
1410 S 800 W 84104 801-974-8310
James Martin, prin. Fax 974-8354
Rose Park ES 500/K-6
1105 W 1000 N 84116 801-578-8554
Nicole O'Brien, prin. Fax 578-8373
Uintah ES 600/K-6
1571 E 1300 S 84105 801-584-2940
Ken Obrien, prin. Fax 584-2944
Wasatch ES 500/K-6
30 R St 84103 801-578-8564
Deborah Candler, prin. Fax 578-8117
Washington ES 400/K-6
420 N 200 W 84103 801-578-8140
John Kelly, prin. Fax 578-8147
Whittier ES 700/K-6
1600 S 300 E 84115 801-481-4846
Greg Proffitt, prin. Fax 481-4849

Challenger S 200/PK-K
4555 S 2300 E 84117 801-278-4797
Max Kleber, dir. Fax 278-4798
Challenger S 500/PK-8
1325 S Main St 84115 801-487-9984
Cindee Winter, head sch Fax 487-9986
Cosgriff Memorial S 400/PK-8
2335 E Redondo Ave 84108 801-486-3197
Betsy Hunt, prin. Fax 484-8270
Elizabeth Academy 200/PK-9
2870 S Connor St 84109 801-281-4848
Jennifer Spikner, head sch Fax 485-1093
Intermountain Christian S 300/PK-12
6515 S Lion Ln 84121 801-365-0370
Mitch Menning, head sch Fax 942-8813
Kearns-St. Ann S 300/PK-8
430 E 2100 S 84115 801-486-0741
Shirley Redle, prin. Fax 486-0742

Madeleine Choir S 300/PK-8
205 E 1st Ave 84103 801-323-9850
Jill Baillie, prin. Fax 323-0581
McGillis S 300/K-8
668 S 1300 E 84102 801-583-0094
Jim Brewer, head sch Fax 583-0720
Our Lady of Lourdes Catholic S 200/K-8
1065 E 700 S 84102 801-364-5624
Christine Bergquist, prin. Fax 364-0925
Redeemer Lutheran S 100/K-6
1955 E Stratford Ave 84106 801-487-6283
Melody Barenbrugge, lead tchr. Fax 463-7904
Reid S 100/PK-12
2965 E 3435 S 84109 801-466-4214
Dr. Ethna R. Reid, prin. Fax 466-4214
Rowland Hall ES 500/PK-5
720 S Guardsman Way 84108 801-355-7485
Alan Sparrow, head sch Fax 363-5521
Rowland Hall MS 200/6-8
970 E 800 S 84102 801-355-0272
Alan Sparrow, head sch Fax 355-0474
St. Francis Xavier S 200/PK-8
4501 W 5215 S 84118 801-966-1571
Marianne Rozsahegyi, prin. Fax 966-1639
St. Vincent de Paul S 300/PK-8
1385 E Spring Ln 84117 801-277-6702
Gary Green, prin. Fax 424-0450
Summit Christian Academy 100/PK-8
4020 S 900 E 84124 801-613-1722

Sandy, Salt Lake, Pop. 85,199
Canyons SD 33,900/K-12
9361 S 300 E 84070 801-826-5000
Dr. James Briscoe, supt. Fax 826-5053
www.canyonsdistrict.org
Albion MS 900/6-8
2755 E Newcastle Dr 84093 801-826-6700
Molly Hart, prin. Fax 826-6709
Altara ES 600/K-5
800 E 11000 S 84094 801-826-7675
Nicole Svee-Magann, prin. Fax 826-7676
Alta View ES 600/K-5
10333 S Crocus St 84094 801-826-7600
Karen Medlin, prin. Fax 826-7601
Bell View ES 400/K-5
9800 S 800 E 84094 801-826-7750
Chanci Loran, prin. Fax 826-7751
Brookwood ES 500/K-5
8640 S Snowbird Dr 84093 801-826-7900
Corrie Barrett, prin. Fax 826-7901
Crescent ES 700/K-5
11100 S 230 E 84070 801-826-8200
Mindy Robison, prin. Fax 826-8201
Eastmont MS 900/6-8
10100 S 1300 E 84094 801-826-7000
Stacy Kurtzhals, prin. Fax 826-7009
East Sandy ES 500/K-5
8295 S 870 E 84094 801-826-8425
Kenna Sorenson, prin. Fax 826-8426
Edgemont ES 400/K-5
1085 E Galena Dr 84094 801-826-8500
Cathleen Schino, prin. Fax 826-8501
Granite ES 400/K-5
9760 S 3100 E 84092 801-826-8575
Ronnie Mulqueen, prin. Fax 826-8576
Indian Hills MS 1,100/6-8
1180 E Sanders Rd 84094 801-826-7100
Doug Graham, prin. Fax 826-7109
Lone Peak ES 700/K-5
11515 S High Mesa Dr 84092 801-826-8650
Tracy Stacy, prin. Fax 826-8651
Mt. Jordan MS 700/6-8
9351 S Mountaineer Ln 84070 801-826-7400
Cindy Hanson, prin. Fax 826-7409
Oakdale ES 400/K-5
1900 E Creek Rd 84093 801-826-8950
Kierstin Draper, prin. Fax 826-8951
Park Lane ES 400/K-5
9955 S Eastdell Dr 84092 801-826-9025
Justin Jeffrey, prin. Fax 826-9026
Peruvian Park ES 500/K-5
1545 E 8425 S 84093 801-826-9100
Leslie Jewkes, prin. Fax 826-9101
Quail Hollow ES 500/K-5
2625 E Newcastle Dr 84093 801-826-9175
Shad DeMill, prin. Fax 826-9176
Sandy ES 500/K-5
8725 S 280 E 84070 801-826-9325
McKay Robinson, prin. Fax 826-9326
Silver Mesa ES 600/K-5
8920 S 1700 E 84093 801-826-9400
Julie Fielding, prin. Fax 826-9401
Sprucewood ES 500/K-5
12025 S 1000 E 84094 801-826-9475
Lori Jones, prin. Fax 826-9476
Sunrise ES 600/K-5
1520 E 11265 S 84092 801-826-9550
Margaret Swanicke, prin. Fax 826-9551
Union MS 900/6-8
615 E 8000 S 84070 801-826-7500
Kelly Tauteoli, prin. Fax 826-7509
Willow Canyon ES 400/K-5
9650 S 1700 E 84092 801-826-9625
Marilyn Williams, prin. Fax 826-9626
Other Schools – See Cottonwood Heights, Draper, Midvale, Salt Lake City

---

Blessed Sacrament S 300/PK-8
1745 E 9800 S 84092 801-572-5311
Bryan Penn, prin. Fax 572-0251
Challenger S 400/PK-8
10685 S 1000 E 84094 801-572-6686
Mary Gourgeon, hdmstr. Fax 572-6687
Grace Lutheran S 200/PK-8
1815 E 9800 S 84092 801-572-3793
Shelly Davis, prin. Fax 553-2403
Waterford S 900/PK-12
1480 E 9400 S 84093 801-816-2201
Andrew Menke, head sch Fax 523-6229

Santa Clara, Washington, Pop. 5,889
Washington County SD
Supt. — See Saint George
Arrowhead ES 700/K-5
545 Arrowhead Trl 84765 435-674-2027
Susan Harrah, prin. Fax 674-2038
Lava Ridge IS 800/6-7
2425 Rachel 84765 435-652-4742
Kalyn Gubler, prin. Fax 652-4747
Santa Clara ES 400/K-5
2950 Crestview Dr 84765 435-628-2624
Nadine Hancey, prin. Fax 628-3785

Santaquin, Utah, Pop. 9,030
Nebo SD
Supt. — See Spanish Fork
Orchard Hills ES 700/K-6
168 E 610 S 84655 801-754-3237
Ryan Murray, prin. Fax 754-5106
Santaquin ES 700/K-6
25 S 400 W 84655 801-754-3611
Chad Argyle, prin. Fax 754-3612

Saratoga Sprngs, Utah, Pop. 17,223
Alpine SD
Supt. — See American Fork
Harvest ES 900/K-6
2105 N Providence Dr, 801-610-8709
Charles Stewart, prin. Fax 768-1947
Riverview ES 700/K-6
273 W Aspen Hills Blvd, 801-610-8726
Matt Dias, prin. Fax 766-2252
Sage Hills ES 1,100/K-6
3033 Swainson Ave, 801-610-8723
Brady Rowley, prin. Fax 341-5915
Saratoga Shores ES 1,000/K-6
1415 S Parkside Dr, 801-610-8716
Dr. Vallen Thomas, prin. Fax 766-6443
Springside ES K-6
694 S Highpoint Dr, 801-610-8732
Gary Gibb, prin. Fax 854-5505
Thunder Ridge ES 1,000/K-6
264 N 750 W, 801-610-8727
Jason Theler, prin. Fax 766-2311

Smithfield, Cache, Pop. 9,375
Cache County SD
Supt. — See North Logan
Birch Creek ES 600/K-6
675 W 220 N 84335 435-792-7692
John Anderson, prin. Fax 792-7694
Summit ES 500/K-6
80 W Center St 84335 435-563-6269
Troy Pugmire, prin. Fax 563-6422
Sunrise ES 500/K-6
225 S 455 E 84335 435-563-3866
Kathy Toolson, prin. Fax 563-5738

Snowville, Box Elder, Pop. 165
Box Elder SD
Supt. — See Brigham City
Snowville ES 50/K-5
PO Box 669 84336 435-872-2771
Joylene Ritchie, lead tchr. Fax 872-2772

South Jordan, Salt Lake, Pop. 49,075
Jordan SD
Supt. — See West Jordan
Daybreak ES 1,100/K-6
4544 W Harvest Moon Dr, 801-302-0553
Kristy Whiteside, prin. Fax 302-4915
Eastlake ES 1,300/K-6
4389 W Isla Daybreak Rd, 801-446-0778
Suzanne Williams, prin. Fax 302-4918
Elk Meadows ES 800/K-6
3448 W 9800 S 84095 801-446-3200
Aaron Ichimura, prin. Fax 302-4926
Jordan Ridge ES 1,000/K-6
2636 W 9800 S 84095 801-254-8025
Melissa Beck, prin. Fax 302-4933
Monte Vista ES 1,000/K-6
11121 S 2700 W 84095 801-254-8040
Meredith Doleac, prin. Fax 302-4946
South Jordan ES 1,100/K-6
11205 S Black Cherry Way 84095 801-254-8000
Ken Westwood, prin. Fax 302-4960
Welby ES 1,000/K-6
4130 W 9580 S, 801-280-1456
Jennifer Fisher, prin. Fax 302-4967

American Heritage of South Jordan 300/K-12
11100 S Redwood Rd 84095 801-254-3882

South Weber, Davis, Pop. 5,945
Davis SD
Supt. — See Farmington
South Weber ES 500/3-6
1285 E Lester Dr 84405 801-402-3750
Marjorie Conrad, prin. Fax 402-3751
South Weber K-2 Center 300/K-2
7450 S 1160 E 84405 801-402-3770
Fax 402-7363

Spanish Fork, Utah, Pop. 33,849
Nebo SD 31,200/PK-12
350 S Main St 84660 801-354-7400
Rick Nielsen, supt. Fax 798-4010
www.nebo.edu
Brockbank ES 600/PK-6
340 W 500 N 84660 801-798-4025
Larraine Nelson, prin. Fax 798-4026
Canyon ES 600/K-6
1492 E 1240 S 84660 801-798-4610
Dave Harlan, prin. Fax 798-3493
East Meadows ES 800/K-6
1287 S 2130 E 84660 801-798-4015
Celeste Glodhill, prin. Fax 798-4022
Larsen ES 500/K-6
1175 E Flonette Ave 84660 801-798-4035
Camille Thomas, prin. Fax 798-4036
Park ES 500/K-6
90 N 600 E 84660 801-798-4045
Ryan Kay, prin. Fax 798-4046

Rees ES 700/PK-6
574 N Rees Ave 84660 801-798-4055
Adam Gull, prin. Fax 798-4056
Riverview ES 800/K-6
628 Westpark Dr 84660 801-798-4050
Angela Killian, prin. Fax 798-4051
Sierra Bonita ES 900/K-6
53 S 1800 E 84660 801-798-4480
Garrett Andersen, prin. Fax 798-4481
Spanish Oaks ES 600/K-6
2701 E Canyon Crest Dr 84660 801-798-7411
Kali Brown, prin. Fax 794-2845
Other Schools – See Goshen, Mapleton, Payson, Salem, Santaquin, Spring Lake, Springville

Spring City, Sanpete, Pop. 978
North Sanpete SD
Supt. — See Mount Pleasant
Spring City ES 100/K-6
PO Box 159 84662 435-462-2169
John Thomas, prin. Fax 462-3445

Springdale, Washington, Pop. 524
Washington County SD
Supt. — See Saint George
Springdale ES 50/K-6
PO Box 509 84767 435-772-3279
Chris Snodgress, prin. Fax 772-3124

Spring Lake, Utah
Nebo SD
Supt. — See Spanish Fork
Spring Lake ES 800/K-6
1750 S 500 W 84651 801-465-6070
Teresa Jordan, prin. Fax 465-6075

Springville, Utah, Pop. 28,786
Nebo SD
Supt. — See Spanish Fork
Art City ES 600/K-6
121 N 900 E 84663 801-489-2820
Lisa Muirbrook, prin. Fax 489-6042
Brookside ES 800/K-6
750 E 400 S 84663 801-489-2830
Dana Beckert, prin. Fax 489-2834
Cherry Creek ES 800/K-6
484 S 200 E 84663 801-489-2810
Mike Duncan, prin. Fax 489-2814
Meadow Brook ES K-6
748 S 950 W 84663 801-489-2897
Heather Balli, prin. Fax 489-2898
Sage Creek ES 700/K-6
1050 S 700 E 84663 801-489-2860
Alison Hansen, prin. Fax 489-2865
Westside ES 800/K-6
740 W Center St 84663 801-489-2800
Lori Pruitt, prin. Fax 489-2825

Stansbury Park, Tooele, Pop. 5,041
Tooele County SD
Supt. — See Tooele
Rose Springs ES 800/K-6
5349 Innsbrook Pl 84074 435-833-9015
Lori Buhr, prin. Fax 833-9207
Stansbury Park ES 900/K-6
485 Country Clb 84074 435-833-1968
Gina Ruiz, prin. Fax 833-1972

Sunnyside, Carbon, Pop. 367
Carbon SD
Supt. — See Price
Bruin Point ES 100/K-5
PO Box 399 84539 435-888-4474
Dina Wise, prin. Fax 888-9938

Sunset, Davis, Pop. 4,981
Davis SD
Supt. — See Farmington
Doxey ES 400/PK-6
944 N 250 W 84015 801-402-2250
Midori Clough, prin. Fax 402-2263
Fremont ES 300/K-6
2525 N 160 W 84015 801-402-2300
Don Beatty, prin. Fax 402-2301
Sunset ES 400/PK-6
2014 N 250 W 84015 801-402-2550
Laura Bond, prin. Fax 402-2551

Syracuse, Davis, Pop. 23,777
Davis SD
Supt. — See Farmington
Bluff Ridge ES 1,000/K-6
2680 S Bluff Ridge Dr 84075 801-402-2850
Vanessa Mori, prin. Fax 402-2851
Buffalo Point ES 1,000/K-6
1924 Doral Dr 84075 801-402-8400
Kristy Nelson, prin. Fax 402-8401
Cook ES 800/PK-6
1175 W 1350 S 84075 801-402-2200
Roger King, prin. Fax 402-2201
Syracuse ES 1,000/K-6
1503 S 2000 W 84075 801-402-2600
Michelle Fredericks, prin. Fax 402-2601

Tabiona, Duchesne, Pop. 166
Duchesne SD
Supt. — See Roosevelt
Tabiona ES 100/K-6
PO Box 470 84072 435-738-1320
Darin Jenkins, prin. Fax 738-1332

Taylorsville, Salt Lake, Pop. 56,089
Granite SD
Supt. — See Salt Lake City
Arcadia ES 500/K-6
3461 W 4850 S, 385-646-4756
Dr. Cecilia Jabakumar, prin. Fax 646-4757
Bennion ES 600/K-6
5775 S Sierra Grande Dr, 385-646-4774
Lynne Rada, prin. Fax 646-4775
Fox Hills ES 800/K-6
3775 W 6020 S, 385-646-4828
Teri Daynes, prin. Fax 646-4829

Fremont ES 500/K-6
4249 S 1425 W 84123 385-646-4834
Dr. Paul McCarty, prin. Fax 646-4835
Plymouth ES 700/K-6
5220 S 1470 W 84123 385-646-4978
Matthew Graham, prin. Fax 646-4979
Smith ES 700/K-6
2150 W 6200 S, 385-646-5020
Cindy Dunn, prin. Fax 646-5021
Taylorsville ES 600/K-6
2010 W Mantle Ave, 385-646-5038
Andrea McMillan, prin. Fax 646-5039
Vista ES 800/PK-6
4925 S 2200 W, 385-646-5067
Jolene Randall, prin. Fax 646-5068
Westbrook ES 700/K-6
3451 W 6200 S, 385-646-5085
Crista Holt, prin. Fax 646-5086

Prince of Peace Lutheran S 100/PK-8
1441 W Tamarack Rd 84123 801-261-3808
Justin Vilski, prin. Fax 747-0108

Tooele, Tooele, Pop. 30,935
Tooele County SD 14,300/K-12
92 Lodestone Way 84074 435-833-1900
Scott Rogers, supt. Fax 833-1912
www.tooeleschools.org
Copper Canyon ES 600/K-6
1600 N Broadway Ave 84074 435-843-3820
Linda Clegg, prin. Fax 843-3824
East ES 500/K-6
135 S 7th St 84074 435-833-1951
Shanz Leonelli, prin. Fax 833-1952
Johnsen JHS 900/7-8
2152 N 400 W 84074 435-833-1939
Jared Small, prin. Fax 843-3816
Middle Canyon ES 500/K-6
751 E 1000 N 84074 435-833-1906
Jerri Sagers, prin. Fax 843-3802
Northlake ES 500/K-6
268 N Coleman St 84074 435-833-1940
Renee Milne, prin. Fax 833-1943
Overlake ES 600/K-6
2052 N 170 W 84074 435-843-3805
Jonathan Marble, prin. Fax 843-3809
Settlement Canyon ES 700/K-6
935 Timpie Rd 84074 435-882-4597
Betsy Swynenburg, prin. Fax 882-0760
Sterling ES 400/K-6
251 N 1st St 84074 435-833-1961
Andy Peterson, prin. Fax 833-1965
Tooele JHS 800/7-8
411 W Vine St 84074 435-833-1921
Bill Gochis, prin. Fax 833-1923
West ES 400/K-6
451 W 300 S 84074 435-833-1931
Clint Poole, prin. Fax 833-1933
Other Schools – See Dugway, Grantsville, Ibapah, Stansbury Park, Vernon, Wendover

---

St. Marguerite S 100/PK-8
15 S 7th St 84074 435-882-0081
Lorena Needham, prin. Fax 882-3866

Tremonton, Box Elder, Pop. 7,535
Box Elder SD
Supt. — See Brigham City
Harris IS 700/6-7
515 N 800 W 84337 435-257-2560
Alison Williams, prin. Fax 257-4133
McKinley ES 600/K-5
120 W 500 S 84337 435-257-2590
Clay Chournos, prin. Fax 257-2593
North Park ES 600/K-5
50 E 700 N 84337 435-257-2580
Jeremy Young, admin. Fax 257-2583

Tropic, Garfield, Pop. 524
Garfield SD
Supt. — See Panguitch
Bryce Valley ES 200/K-6
PO Box 286 84776 435-679-8619
Layne LeFevre, prin. Fax 679-8936

Trout Creek, Tooele
Tintic SD
Supt. — See Eureka
West Desert ES 50/K-6
440 Pony Express Rd 84083 435-693-3193
Mario Johnson, head sch Fax 693-3193

Vernal, Uintah, Pop. 8,901
Uintah SD 7,600/PK-12
635 W 200 S 84078 435-781-3100
Mark Dockins Ed.D., supt. Fax 781-3107
www.uintah.net/
Ashley ES 700/K-5
350 N 1150 W 84078 435-781-3170
Carrie Weldon, prin. Fax 781-3178
Central Cove Specialized Preschool PK-PK
250 S Vernal Ave 84078 435-781-3125
Tami Chew, coord. Fax 781-3127
Davis ES 600/K-5
4101 S 2500 E 84078 435-781-3155
Rick Johnson, prin. Fax 781-3193
Discovery ES 700/K-5
650 W 1200 S 84078 435-781-3146
Tammy Christensen, prin. Fax 781-3147
Maeser ES 700/K-5
2670 W 1000 N 84078 435-781-3160
Denise Williams, prin. Fax 781-3162
Naples ES 700/K-5
635 W 200 S 84078 435-781-3150
Deborah Chatham, prin. Fax 781-3152
Uintah MS 1,000/6-8
161 N 1000 W 84078 435-781-3130
Kathleen Hawkins, prin. Fax 781-3134
Vernal MS 1,000/6-8
721 W 100 S 84078 435-781-3140
Mistalyn Leis, prin. Fax 781-3143
Other Schools – See Lapoint, Roosevelt

Uintah Basin Christian Academy 100/PK-8
PO Box 1548 84078 435-789-9332
Torrey Pitchford, admin.

Vernon, Tooele, Pop. 238
Tooele County SD
Supt. — See Tooele
Vernon ES 50/K-6
70 N Main St 84080 435-839-3433
Jeff Wyatt, prin. Fax 839-3433

Vineyard, Utah, Pop. 137
Alpine SD
Supt. — See American Fork
Vineyard ES 800/K-6
620 E Holdaway Rd 84058 801-610-8122
Vic Larsen, prin. Fax 227-2454

Washington, Washington, Pop. 18,376
Washington County SD
Supt. — See Saint George
Coral Canyon ES 700/PK-5
3435 E Canyon Crest Ave 84780 435-652-4787
Jennifer Eggleston, prin. Fax 652-4792
Horizon ES 600/K-5
1970 S Arabian Way 84780 435-652-4781
Mona Haslem, prin. Fax 652-4784
Riverside ES 700/K-5
2500 S Harvest Ln 84780 435-652-4760
Burke Staheli, prin. Fax 652-4765
Washington ES 500/PK-5
300 N 300 E 84780 435-673-3012
Kelly Mitchell, prin. Fax 634-5748

Wellington, Carbon, Pop. 1,637
Carbon SD
Supt. — See Price
Wellington ES 300/K-5
250 W 200 N 84542 435-637-2570
Stacy Basinger, prin. Fax 637-5043

Wellsville, Cache, Pop. 3,383
Cache County SD
Supt. — See North Logan
Wellsville ES 400/K-6
525 N 200 W 84339 435-245-3764
Cody Dobson, prin. Fax 245-4586

Wendover, Tooele, Pop. 1,381
Tooele County SD
Supt. — See Tooele
Smith ES 300/K-6
PO Box 879 84083 435-665-0470
Heather Castagno, prin. Fax 665-7562

West Bountiful, Davis, Pop. 5,130
Davis SD
Supt. — See Farmington
West Bountiful ES 600/PK-6
750 W 400 N 84087 801-402-2000
Regina Oechsle, prin. Fax 402-2001

West Haven, Weber, Pop. 10,042
Weber SD
Supt. — See Ogden
Country View ES 500/K-6
4650 W 4800 S 84401 801-452-4400
Melissa Copeland, prin. Fax 452-4419
Kanesville ES 700/K-6
3112 S 3500 W 84401 801-452-4680
Justin Willie, prin. Fax 452-4699
West Haven ES 800/K-6
4385 S 3900 W 84401 801-452-4960
Heather Neilson, prin. Fax 452-4979

West Jordan, Salt Lake, Pop. 99,828
Granite SD
Supt. — See Salt Lake City
Bridger ES 600/K-6
5368 W Cyclamen Way, 385-646-4780
Milicent Larsen-Fogarty, prin. Fax 646-4781

Jordan SD 52,900/K-12
7387 S Campus View Dr 84084 801-567-8100
Dr. Patrice Johnson, supt. Fax 567-8064
www.jordandistrict.org
Columbia ES 700/K-6
3505 W 7800 S 84088 801-280-3279
Kathe Riding, prin. Fax 302-4911
Copper Canyon ES 800/K-6
8917 S Copperwood Dr, 801-260-0222
Patty Bowen, prin. Fax 302-4975
Falcon Ridge ES 900/K-6
6111 W 7000 S, 801-282-2437
Michelle Peterson, prin. Fax 302-4928
Fox Hollow ES 900/K-6
6020 W 8200 S, 801-282-1818
Kevin Pullan, prin. Fax 302-4921
Hayden Peak ES 1,000/K-6
5120 W Hayden Peak Dr, 801-280-0722
David Butler, prin. Fax 302-4931
Heartland ES 700/K-6
1451 W 7000 S 84084 801-565-7533
Shelly Davis, prin. Fax 302-4932
Jordan Hills ES 700/K-6
8892 S 4800 W 84088 801-280-0238
Michelle Lovell, prin. Fax 302-4934
Majestic ES 400/K-6
7430 S Redwood Rd 84084 801-565-7458
Todd Theobald, prin. Fax 302-4938
Mountain Shadows ES 800/K-6
5255 W 7000 S, 801-963-0291
Annette Huff, prin. Fax 302-4945
Oakcrest ES 1,000/K-6
8462 S Hilltop Oak Dr, 801-280-7243
Joel Pullan, prin. Fax 302-4914
Oquirrh ES 700/K-6
7165 S Paddington Rd 84084 801-565-7474
Mandy Thurman, prin. Fax 302-4947
Riverside ES 800/K-6
8737 S 1220 W 84088 801-565-7484
Ronna Hoffman, prin. Fax 302-4953
Terra Linda ES 600/K-6
8400 S 3400 W 84088 801-282-8036
Karen Gorringe, prin. Fax 302-4962
West Jordan ES 500/K-6
7220 S 2370 W 84084 801-565-7506
Jennifer Ludlow, prin. Fax 302-4968
Westland ES 700/K-6
2925 W 7180 S 84084 801-565-7508
Lauren Goodsell, prin. Fax 302-4970
Westvale ES 700/K-6
2300 W Gardner Ln 84088 801-565-7510
Brenda Anderson, prin. Fax 302-4969
Other Schools – See Bluffdale, Herriman, Riverton, South Jordan

---

Challenger S 500/PK-1
2247 W 8660 S 84088 801-565-1058
Annette Matthews, head sch Fax 565-1059

West Point, Davis, Pop. 9,305
Davis SD
Supt. — See Farmington
Lakeside ES 800/K-6
2941 W 800 N 84015 801-402-2900
Kurt Farnsworth, prin. Fax 402-2901
West Point ES 800/K-6
3788 W 300 N 84015 801-402-2750
Loren Clark, prin. Fax 402-2751

West Valley, Salt Lake, Pop. 122,084
Granite SD
Supt. — See Salt Lake City
Academy Park ES 600/K-6
4580 Westpoint Dr 84120 385-646-4750
Dr. Pauline Longberg, prin. Fax 646-4751
Armstrong Academy 700/PK-6
5194 W Highbury Pkwy 84120 385-646-5284
Matt Goebel, prin. Fax 646-5286
Diamond Ridge ES 800/PK-6
6034 W Mill Valley Ln, 385-646-4858
Monica Thayer, prin. Fax 646-4859
Farnsworth ES 600/K-6
3751 S Sunnyvale Dr 84120 385-646-4822
Joan Bramble, prin. Fax 646-4823
Frost ES 500/K-6
3444 W 4400 S 84119 385-646-4840
Andrew Carbaugh, prin. Fax 646-4841
Granger ES 1,000/K-6
3700 S 1950 W 84119 385-646-4852
Amber Clayton, prin. Fax 646-4853
Hillsdale ES 900/PK-6
3275 W 3100 S 84119 385-646-4864
Deb Woolley, prin. Fax 646-4865
Hillside ES 700/PK-6
4283 S 6000 W 84128 385-646-4870
Dr. Sharon Sonnenreich, prin. Fax 646-4871
Hunter ES 600/K-6
4351 S 5400 W 84120 385-646-4876
Kayla Mackay, prin. Fax 646-4877
Jackling ES 500/K-6
3760 S Atlas Way 84120 385-646-4882
Robyn Roper, prin. Fax 646-4883
Monroe ES 700/PK-6
4450 W 3100 S 84120 385-646-4918
Dave Holt, prin. Fax 646-4919
Orchard ES 700/PK-6
6744 W 3800 S 84128 385-646-4954
Leona Chandler, prin. Fax 646-4955
Pioneer ES 600/K-6
3860 S 3380 W 84119 385-646-4966
Doug Johnson, prin. Fax 646-4967
Redwood ES 800/PK-6
2650 S Redwood Rd 84119 385-646-4984
Jolynn Koehler, prin. Fax 646-4985
Rolling Meadows ES 600/PK-6
2950 W Whitehall Dr 84119 385-646-4990
Connie McCann, prin. Fax 646-4995
Sandburg ES 400/PK-6
3900 S Rancho Vista Ln 84120 385-646-5008
Julie Wilson, prin. Fax 646-5009
Stansbury ES 1,000/PK-6
3050 S Constitution Blvd 84119 385-646-5032
Ernie Broderick, prin. Fax 646-5033
Truman ES 600/K-6
4639 S 3200 W 84119 385-646-5044
Jared Broderick, prin. Fax 646-5045
Valley Crest ES 600/K-6
5240 W 3100 S 84120 385-646-5061
Jane McClure, prin. Fax 646-5062
West Valley ES 600/K-6
6049 W Brud Dr 84128 385-646-5079
Shauna Jensen, prin. Fax 646-5080
Whittier ES 700/K-6
3585 S 6000 W 84128 385-646-5096
Lynette Golze, prin. Fax 646-5097

Willard, Box Elder, Pop. 1,738
Box Elder SD
Supt. — See Brigham City
Willard ES 300/K-1
40 W 50 S 84340 435-734-4934
Corynn Arehart, prin. Fax 734-4936

Woods Cross, Davis, Pop. 9,426
Davis SD
Supt. — See Farmington
Odyssey ES K-6
2050 S 1955 W 84087 801-402-0200
Julie Peters, prin. Fax 402-0201
Woods Cross ES 800/PK-6
745 W 1100 S 84087 801-402-1800
Eric Holmes, prin. Fax 402-1801

VERMONT

VERMONT DEPARTMENT OF EDUCATION
120 State St, Montpelier 05620-0002
Telephone 802-828-3135
Fax 802-828-3140
Website education.vermont.gov/

Secretary of Education Rebecca Holcombe

VERMONT BOARD OF EDUCATION
120 State St, Montpelier 05620-0002

Chairperson Krista Huling

PUBLIC, PRIVATE AND CATHOLIC ELEMENTARY SCHOOLS

Addison, Addison
Addison Northwest SD
Supt. — See Vergennes
Addison Central S 100/K-6
121 VT Route 17 W 05491 802-759-2131
Travis Park, prin. Fax 759-2631

Albany, Orleans, Pop. 191
Orleans Central Supervisory Union
Supt. — See Barton
Albany Community S 100/K-8
351 Main St 05820 802-755-6168
Stephen Owens, prin. Fax 755-6263

Alburg, Grand Isle, Pop. 457
Grand Isle Supervisory Union
Supt. — See North Hero
Alburg Community Education Center 200/PK-8
14 N Main St 05440 802-796-3573
James Ross, prin. Fax 796-3068

Arlington, Bennington, Pop. 1,195
Battenkill Valley Supervisory Union 400/K-12
530A E Arlington Rd 05250 802-375-9744
Judith Pullinen, supt. Fax 375-2368
www.bvsu.org
Fisher ES 200/K-5
504 E Arlington Rd 05250 802-375-6409
Deanne LaCoste, prin. Fax 375-1544

Ascutney, Windsor, Pop. 532
Windsor Southeast Supervisory Union
Supt. — See Windsor
Weathersfield S 200/K-8
PO Box 279 05030 802-674-5400
JeanMarie Oakman, prin. Fax 674-9963

Bakersfield, Franklin
Franklin Northeast Supervisory Union
Supt. — See Richford
Bakersfield S 200/PK-8
PO Box 17 05441 802-827-6611
Anissa Seguin, prin. Fax 827-3170

Barnard, Windsor
Windsor Central Supervisory Union
Supt. — See Woodstock
Barnard Academy 100/PK-6
PO Box 157 05031 802-234-9763
Anne Koop, prin. Fax 234-9641

Barnet, Caledonia, Pop. 127
Caledonia Central Supervisory Union
Supt. — See Danville
Barnet S 200/PK-8
163 Kid Row 05821 802-633-4978
Shawn Gonyaw, prin. Fax 633-4497

Barre, Washington, Pop. 8,882
Barre Supervisory Union 2,500/PK-12
120 Ayers St 05641 802-476-5011
John Pandolfo, supt. Fax 476-4944
www.bsuvt.org
Barre City S 900/PK-8
50 Parkside Ter 05641 802-476-6541
James Taffe, prin. Fax 476-1492
Barre Town S 900/PK-8
70 Websterville Rd 05641 802-476-6617
Scott Griggs, prin. Fax 479-5723

Montessori S of Central Vermont 100/PK-6
84 Pine Hill Rd 05641 802-479-0912
St. Monica - St. Michael S 100/PK-8
79 Summer St 05641 802-476-5015
Brenda Buzzell, prin. Fax 476-0861

Barton, Orleans, Pop. 727
Orleans Central Supervisory Union 1,100/PK-12
130 Kinsey Rd 05822 802-525-1204
Bev Davis, supt. Fax 525-1276
www.ocsu.org
Barton Academy & Graded S 200/K-8
PO Box 588 05822 802-525-6244
Kimberly Wheelock, prin. Fax 525-1170
Orleans Central ECC PK-PK
130 Kinsey Rd 05822 802-525-6253
Julie Lavine, dir. Fax 525-1276
Other Schools – See Albany, Brownington, Glover, Irasburg, Orleans

---

St. Paul S 100/PK-8
54 Eastern Ave 05822 802-525-6578
Joanne Beloin, prin. Fax 525-3869

Bellows Falls, Windham, Pop. 3,056
Windham Northeast Supervisory Union 1,200/K-12
25 Cherry St 05101 802-463-9958
Christopher Kibbe, supt. Fax 463-9705
www.wnesu.org
Bellows Falls MS 200/5-8
15 School St 05101 802-463-4366
Karen Bukowski, prin. Fax 463-9738
Central ES 200/K-4
50 School Street Ext 05101 802-463-4346
Keith Nemlich, prin. Fax 463-0131
Other Schools – See Grafton, Putney, Saxtons River, Westminster

Bennington, Bennington, Pop. 8,960
Southwest Vermont Supervisory Union 2,800/K-12
246 S Stream Rd 05201 802-447-7501
James Culkeen, supt. Fax 447-0475
www.svsu.org
Bennington ES 300/K-5
128 Park St 05201 802-442-5256
Jim Law, prin. Fax 442-1272
Monument ES 100/K-5
66 Main St 05201 802-447-7979
Donna Cauley, prin. Fax 442-2822
Mt. Anthony Union MS 600/6-8
747 East Rd 05201 802-447-7541
Tim Payne, prin. Fax 442-1262
Stark ES 400/K-5
181 Orchard Rd 05201 802-442-2692
Dr. Michael Mugits, prin. Fax 442-1736
Woodford Hollow ES 50/K-6
955 VT Route 9 05201 802-442-4071
Sandy Foster, prin. Fax 442-2996
Other Schools – See Pownal, Shaftsbury

Grace Christian S 200/PK-12
104 Kocher Dr 05201 802-447-2233
Shawn Smith, head sch Fax 442-8403
Sacred Heart/St Francis de Sales S 100/PK-8
307 School St 05201 802-442-2446
David Estes, prin. Fax 442-2344
Ward Memorial S 50/1-8
404 Houghton Ln 05201 802-681-7029
Heidi Ewing, prin. Fax 442-4579

Benson, Rutland, Pop. 304
Addison-Rutland Supervisory Union
Supt. — See Fair Haven
Benson Village S 100/PK-8
32 School St 05743 802-537-2491
Kim Prehoda, prin. Fax 537-2494

Berlin, See Montpelier
Washington Central Supervisory Union
Supt. — See Montpelier
Berlin ES 200/PK-6
372 Paine Tpke N 05602 802-223-2796
Carol Amos, prin. Fax 229-0222

Bethel, Windsor, Pop. 558
White River Valley Supervisory Union
Supt. — See South Royalton
Bethel ES 200/PK-6
273 Pleasant St 05032 802-234-6607
Owen Bradley, prin. Fax 234-5779

Bolton, Chittenden
Chittenden East Supervisory Union
Supt. — See Richmond
Smilie Memorial ES 100/PK-4
2712 Theodore Roosevelt Hwy 05676 802-434-2757
Barbara Tomasi-Gay, prin. Fax 434-2098

Bondville, Bennington

Mountain S at Winhall 100/PK-8
9 School St 05340 802-297-2662
Peter Ahlfeld, head sch Fax 297-2590

Bradford, Orange, Pop. 774
Orange East Supervisory Union 1,300/K-12
530 Waits River Rd 05033 802-222-5216
Dr. Sandra Stanley, supt. Fax 222-4451
www.oesu.org
Bradford ES 200/K-6
143 Fairground Rd 05033 802-222-4077
Adam Norwood, prin. Fax 222-5196
Other Schools – See East Corinth, Newbury, Thetford

Braintree, Orange
Orange Southwest Supervisory Union
Supt. — See Randolph
Braintree ES 100/K-6
66 Bent Hill Rd 05060 802-728-9373
Pat Miller, prin. Fax 728-5044

Brandon, Rutland, Pop. 1,631
Rutland Northeast Supervisory Union 1,500/PK-12
49 Court Dr 05733 802-247-5757
Jeanne Collins, supt. Fax 247-5548
www.rnesu.org
Neshobe ES 400/PK-6
17 Neshobe Cir 05733 802-247-3721
Judi Pulsifer, prin. Fax 247-5699
Other Schools – See Chittenden, Leicester, Pittsford, Sudbury, Whiting

Brattleboro, Windham, Pop. 7,206
Windham Southeast Supervisory Union 2,400/K-12
53 Green St 05301 802-254-3730
Lyle Holiday, supt. Fax 254-3733
www.wsesu.org
Academy S 400/K-6
860 Western Ave 05301 802-254-3743
Andrew Paciulli, prin. Fax 254-3756
Brattleboro Area MS 300/7-8
109 Sunny Acres Rd 05301 802-451-3500
Keith Lyman, prin. Fax 451-3502
Green Street ES 200/K-6
164 Green St 05301 802-254-3737
Mark Speno, prin. Fax 254-3753
Oak Grove ES 100/K-6
15 Moreland Ave 05301 802-254-3740
Jeri Curry, prin. Fax 254-3633
Other Schools – See East Dummerston, Guilford, Putney, Vernon

---

Hilltop Montessori S 100/PK-8
99 Stafford Farm Rd 05301 802-257-0500
Tamara Mount, head sch Fax 254-2671
St. Michael S 100/PK-11
48 Walnut St 05301 802-254-6320
Elaine Beam, prin. Fax 254-5229

Bridport, Addison
Addison Central Supervisory Union
Supt. — See Middlebury
Bridport Central ES 100/PK-6
3442 VT Route 22A 05734 802-758-2331
Jennefer Eaton, prin. Fax 758-2866

Bristol, Addison, Pop. 1,992
Addison Northeast Supervisory Union 1,600/PK-12
72 Munsill Ave Ste 601 05443 802-453-3657
Patrick Reen, supt. Fax 453-2029
www.anesu.org
Bristol ES 300/PK-6
57 Mountain St 05443 802-453-3227
W. Kevin Robinson, prin. Fax 453-4666
Other Schools – See Lincoln, Monkton, New Haven, Starksboro

Brookfield, Orange
Orange Southwest Supervisory Union
Supt. — See Randolph
Brookfield ES 100/K-6
1728 Ridge Rd 05036 802-276-3153
Susan McKelvie, prin. Fax 276-3189

Brownington, Orleans
Orleans Central Supervisory Union
Supt. — See Barton
Brownington Central S 100/K-8
103 Chase Rd 05860 802-754-8467
Larry Fliegelman, prin. Fax 754-6177

Brownsville, Windsor
Windsor Southeast Supervisory Union
Supt. — See Windsor
Albert Bridge ES 100/K-6
PO Box 88 05037 802-484-3344
Jenifer Aldrich, prin. Fax 484-5105

Burlington, Chittenden, Pop. 41,355
Burlington SD 3,700/PK-12
150 Colchester Ave 05401 802-865-5332
Yaw Obeng, supt. Fax 864-8501
www.bsdvt.org
Champlain ES 300/K-5
800 Pine St 05401 802-864-8477
Dorinne Dorfman, prin. Fax 864-2157
Edmunds ES 400/K-5
299 Main St 05401 802-864-1791
Shelley Mathias, prin. Fax 864-2166
Edmunds MS 400/6-8
275 Main St 05401 802-864-8486
Megan McDonough, prin. Fax 864-2218
Flynn ES 400/K-5
1645 North Ave, 802-864-8478
Graham Clarke, prin. Fax 864-2145
Hunt MS 400/6-8
1364 North Ave, 802-864-8469
Len Phelan, prin. Fax 864-8467
Integrated Arts Academy at H.O. Wheeler 300/PK-5
6 Archibald St 05401 802-864-8475
Bobby Riley, prin. Fax 864-2162
Smith ES 300/K-5
332 Ethan Allen Pkwy, 802-864-8479
Amy Mellencamp, prin. Fax 864-4923
Sustainability Academy at Barnes S 200/PK-5
123 North St 05401 802-864-8480
Lashawn Whitmore-Sells, prin. Fax 864-2161

Christ the King S 300/PK-8
136 Locust St 05401 802-862-6696
Angela Pohlen, prin. Fax 658-6553
Mater Christi S 200/PK-8
50 Mansfield Ave 05401 802-658-3992
Tim Loescher, head sch Fax 863-1196

Cabot, Washington, Pop. 226
Washington NE Supervisory Union
Supt. — See Plainfield
Cabot S 200/PK-12
25 Common Rd 05647 802-563-2289
David Schilling, prin. Fax 563-6089

,
Essex-Caledonia Supervisory Union
Supt. — See Concord
Waterford S 200/PK-8
276 Duck Pond Rd 05819 802-748-9393
Kelley Brooks, prin. Fax 748-2806

Cambridge, Chittenden, Pop. 227
Franklin West Supervisory Union
Supt. — See Fairfax
Fletcher ES 100/PK-6
340 School Rd 05444 802-849-6251
Christopher Dodge, prin. Fax 849-6509

Canaan, Essex, Pop. 390
Essex North Supervisory Union 200/PK-12
PO Box 100 05903 802-266-3330
Christopher Masson, supt. Fax 266-7085
www.essexnorth.org
Canaan S 200/PK-12
99 School St 05903 802-266-8910
Deborah Lynch, prin. Fax 266-7068

Castleton, Rutland, Pop. 1,470
Addison-Rutland Supervisory Union
Supt. — See Fair Haven
Castleton ES 300/PK-5
PO Box 68 05735 802-468-5624
Kathleen Kilbourne, prin. Fax 468-5625
Castleton Village S 100/6-8
PO Box 68 05735 802-468-2203
Linda Peltier, prin. Fax 468-5131

Charlotte, Chittenden
Champlain Valley SD
Supt. — See Shelburne
Charlotte Central S 500/PK-8
408 Hinesburg Rd 05445 802-425-2771
Barbara Komons-Montroll, prin. Fax 425-2122

Chelsea, Orange
White River Valley Supervisory Union
Supt. — See South Royalton
Chelsea S 200/K-12
6 School St 05038 802-685-4551
Mark Blount, prin. Fax 685-3310

Chester, Windsor, Pop. 997
Two Rivers Supervisory Union
Supt. — See Ludlow
Chester-Andover ES 200/K-6
72 Main St 05143 802-875-2108
Katherine Fogg, prin. Fax 875-3998

Chittenden, Rutland
Rutland Northeast Supervisory Union
Supt. — See Brandon
Barstow Memorial S 200/PK-8
223 Chittenden Rd 05737 802-773-3763
Renee Castillo, prin. Fax 747-4814

Colchester, Chittenden
Colchester SD 2,200/PK-12
PO Box 27 05446 802-264-5999
Amy Minor, supt. Fax 863-4774
www.csdvt.org
Colchester MS 400/6-8
PO Box 30 05446 802-264-5800
Michele Cote, prin. Fax 264-5858
Malletts Bay ES 500/PK-PK, 3-
PO Box 28 05446 802-264-5900
Julie Benay, prin. Fax 264-5901
Porters Point ES 300/K-2
PO Box 32 05446 802-264-5920
Carolyn Millham, prin. Fax 862-6835
Union Memorial ES 200/K-2
PO Box 48 05446 802-264-5959
Chris Antonicci, prin. Fax 879-5350

Concord, Essex, Pop. 268
Essex-Caledonia Supervisory Union 400/PK-8
PO Box 255 05824 802-695-3373
Michael Clark, supt. Fax 695-1334
www.ecsuvt.org
Concord S, 173 School St 05824 100/PK-8
Julia Donahue, prin. 802-695-2550
Other Schools – See , Gilman, Lunenburg

Cornwall, Addison
Addison Central Supervisory Union
Supt. — See Middlebury
Cornwall ES 100/K-6
112 School Rd 05753 802-462-2463
Jennifer Kravitz, prin. Fax 462-2462

Coventry, Orleans, Pop. 95
North Country Supervisory Union
Supt. — See Newport
Coventry Village S 100/PK-8
PO Box 92 05825 802-754-6464
Matthew Baughman, prin. Fax 754-8508

Craftsbury Common, Orleans
Orleans Southwest Supervisory Union
Supt. — See Hardwick
Craftsbury S 200/PK-12
PO Box 73 05827 802-586-2541
Merri Greenia, prin. Fax 586-7524

Danby, Rutland
Bennington-Rutland Supervisory Union
Supt. — See Sunderland
Currier Memorial ES 100/PK-6
234 N Main St 05739 802-293-5191
Carolyn Parillo, prin. Fax 293-5518

Danville, Caledonia, Pop. 378
Caledonia Central Supervisory Union 700/PK-12
PO Box 216 05828 802-684-3801
Dr. Mathew Forest, supt. Fax 684-1190
www.ccsuonline.org
Danville S 400/PK-12
148 Peacham Rd 05828 802-684-3651
Kerin Hoffman, prin. Fax 684-1192
Other Schools – See Barnet, Peacham, West Danville

Derby, Orleans, Pop. 595
North Country Supervisory Union
Supt. — See Newport
North Country Union JHS 300/7-8
57 Jr High Dr 05829 802-766-2276
Nicole Corbett, prin. Fax 766-2287

Derby Line, Orleans, Pop. 670
North Country Supervisory Union
Supt. — See Newport
Derby ES 400/PK-6
907 Elm St 05830 802-873-3162
Stacey Urbin, prin. Fax 873-9106

Dorset, Bennington, Pop. 249
Bennington-Rutland Supervisory Union
Supt. — See Sunderland
Dorset S 200/K-8
130 School Dr 05251 802-362-2606
Rosanna Moran, prin. Fax 362-0894

Duxbury, See Waterbury
Harwood Unified UNSD
Supt. — See Waitsfield
Crossett Brook MS 300/5-8
5672 VT Route 100 05676 802-244-6100
Tom Drake, prin. Fax 244-6899

East Barre, Washington, Pop. 822
Orange North Supervisory Union
Supt. — See Williamstown
Orange Center S 100/K-8
357 US Route 302 05649 802-476-3278
Timothy Francke, prin. Fax 476-1389

East Corinth, Orange
Orange East Supervisory Union
Supt. — See Bradford
Waits River Valley S 200/K-8
6 Waits River Vly School Rd 05040 802-439-5534
Carlotta Perantoni, prin. Fax 439-6444

East Dover, Windham
Windham Central Supervisory Union
Supt. — See Townshend
Dover ES 100/PK-6
9 Schoolhouse Rd 05341 802-464-5386
Matt Martyn, prin. Fax 464-0562

East Dummerston, Windham
Windham Southeast Supervisory Union
Supt. — See Brattleboro
Dummerston S 200/K-8
52 School House Rd, 802-254-2733
Jo Carol Ratti, prin. Fax 257-5751

East Montpelier, Washington, Pop. 77
Washington Central Supervisory Union
Supt. — See Montpelier
East Montpelier ES 200/PK-6
665 Vincent Flats Rd 05651 802-223-7936
Alicia Lyford, prin. Fax 223-3736

Orchard Valley Waldorf S 200/PK-8
2290 VT Route 14 N 05651 802-456-7400

Eden, Lamoille
Lamoille North Supervisory Union
Supt. — See Hyde Park
Eden Central S 100/PK-6
PO Box 29 05652 802-635-6630
Melinda Mascolino, prin. Fax 635-3670

Enosburg Falls, Franklin, Pop. 1,309
Franklin Northeast Supervisory Union
Supt. — See Richford
Enosburg Falls ES 300/PK-5
PO Box 510 05450 802-933-2171
Michelle Lussier, prin. Fax 933-5013
Enosburg Falls MS 100/6-8
PO Box 417 05450 802-933-7777
Rachel Reynolds, prin. Fax 933-5013

Essex Junction, Chittenden, Pop. 9,092
Chittenden Central Supervisory Union 2,600/PK-12
51 Park St 05452 802-879-5579
Judith DeNova, supt. Fax 878-1370
www.ccsuvt.org
Fleming ES 200/4-5
21 Prospect St 05452 802-878-1381
Daniel Ryan, prin. Fax 879-5598
Hiawatha ES 300/PK-3
30 Hiawatha Ave 05452 802-878-1384
Thomas Bochanski, prin. Fax 879-8190
Lawton MS 400/6-8
104 Maple St 05452 802-878-1388
Jennifer Wood, prin. Fax 879-8175
Summit Street ES 300/PK-3
17 Summit St 05452 802-878-1377
Suzanne Gruendling, prin. Fax 878-1380
Other Schools – See Westford

Essex Town SD 1,300/PK-8
58 Founders Rd 05452 802-878-8168
Mark Andrews, supt. Fax 878-5190
www.etsdvt.org
Essex ES 500/PK-2
1 Bixby Hill Rd 05452 802-878-2584
Peter Farrell, prin. Fax 879-0602
Essex MS 400/6-8
60 Founders Rd 05452 802-879-7173
Kevin Briggs, prin. Fax 879-1363
Founders Memorial ES 400/3-5
33 Founders Rd 05452 802-879-6326
Wendy Cobb, prin. Fax 879-6139

Fairfax, Franklin
Franklin West Supervisory Union 1,300/PK-12
4497 Highbridge Rd 05454 802-370-3113
Ned Kirsch, supt. Fax 370-3115
www.fwsu.org
Bellows Free Academy Fairfax 600/PK-12
75 Hunt St 05454 802-849-6711
Thomas Walsh, prin. Fax 849-2611
Other Schools – See Cambridge, Georgia

Fairfield, Franklin
Maple Run USD
Supt. — See Saint Albans
Fairfield Center S 200/PK-8
57 Park St 05455 802-827-6639
Dr. Sean O'Dell, prin. Fax 827-3604

Fair Haven, Rutland, Pop. 2,236
Addison-Rutland Supervisory Union 1,400/PK-12
49 Main St 05743 802-265-4905
Brooke Olsen-Farrell, supt. Fax 265-2158
www.arsu.org
Fair Haven ES 300/PK-8
115 N Main St 05743 802-265-3883
Wayne Cooke, prin. Fax 265-2343
Other Schools – See Benson, Castleton, Orwell

Fairlee, Orange, Pop. 186
Rivendell Interstate SD
Supt. — See Orford, NH
Morey ES 200/PK-6
214 School St 05045 802-333-9755
Gail Keiling, prin. Fax 333-9601

Fayston, Washington
Harwood Unified UNSD
Supt. — See Waitsfield
Fayston ES 100/PK-6
782 German Flats Rd 05673 802-496-3636
Jean Berthiaume, prin. Fax 496-5297

Ferrisburgh, Addison
Addison Northwest SD
Supt. — See Vergennes
Ferrisburgh Central S 200/K-6
56 Little Chicago Rd, 802-877-3463
Beth Brodie, prin. Fax 877-6377

Franklin, Franklin
Franklin Northwest Supervisory Union
Supt. — See Swanton
Franklin Central ES 100/PK-6
PO Box 146 05457 802-285-2100
Joyce Hakey, prin. Fax 285-2111

Georgia, Chittenden
Franklin West Supervisory Union
Supt. — See Fairfax
Georgia ES 600/PK-8
4416 Ethan Allen Hwy, 802-524-6358
Steve Emery, prin. Fax 524-1781

Gilman, Essex
Essex-Caledonia Supervisory Union
Supt. — See Concord
Gilman MS 50/5-8
PO Box 97 05904 802-892-5969
Cheryl McVetty, prin. Fax 892-9045

Glover, Orleans, Pop. 294
Orleans Central Supervisory Union
Supt. — See Barton
Glover Community S 100/K-8
100 School St 05839 802-525-6958
Angelique Brown, prin. Fax 525-4955

Grafton, Windham
Windham Northeast Supervisory Union
Supt. — See Bellows Falls
Athens/Grafton ES 100/K-6
PO Box 226 05146 802-843-2495
Cela Dorr, prin. Fax 843-2496

Grand Isle, Grand Isle
Grand Isle Supervisory Union
Supt. — See North Hero
Grand Isle S 200/K-8
224 US Route 2 05458 802-372-6913
Eric Arnzen, prin. Fax 372-5292

Greensboro, Orleans, Pop. 109
Orleans Southwest Supervisory Union
Supt. — See Hardwick
Lakeview Union ES 100/K-6
189 Lauredon Ave 05841 802-533-7066
Eric Erwin, prin. Fax 533-2962

Guilford, Windham
Windham Southeast Supervisory Union
Supt. — See Brattleboro
Guilford Central S 100/K-8
374 School Rd 05301 802-254-2271
John Gagnon, prin. Fax 258-2848

Hardwick, Caledonia, Pop. 1,309
Orleans Southwest Supervisory Union 1,000/PK-12
PO Box 338 05843 802-472-6531
Joanne LeBlanc, supt. Fax 472-6250
www.ossu.org
Hardwick ES 200/PK-6
PO Box 515 05843 802-472-5411
Patrick Pennock, prin. Fax 472-3325
Other Schools – See Craftsbury Common, Greensboro, Wolcott, Woodbury

Hartland, Windsor, Pop. 372
Windsor Southeast Supervisory Union
Supt. — See Windsor
Hartland S 300/K-8
97 Martinsville Rd 05048 802-436-2255
Christine Bourne, prin. Fax 436-2091

Highgate Center, Franklin
Franklin Northwest Supervisory Union
Supt. — See Swanton
Highgate ES 300/K-6
PO Box 163 05459 802-868-4170
Patrick Hartnett, prin. Fax 868-4572

Hinesburg, Chittenden, Pop. 642
Champlain Valley SD
Supt. — See Shelburne
Hinesburg Community S 600/PK-8
10888 Route 116 05461 802-482-2106
Jeff O'Hara, prin. Fax 482-2003

Holland, Orleans
North Country Supervisory Union
Supt. — See Newport
Holland ES 100/PK-6
26 School Rd 05830 802-895-4455
Kelli Dean, prin. Fax 895-4161

Huntington, Chittenden
Chittenden East Supervisory Union
Supt. — See Richmond
Brewster-Pierce ES 200/PK-4
120 School St 05462 802-434-2074
Sally Hayes, prin. Fax 434-5575

Hyde Park, Lamoille, Pop. 449
Lamoille North Supervisory Union 1,900/PK-12
96 Cricket Hill Rd 05655 802-888-3142
Catherine Gallagher, supt. Fax 888-7908
lnsu.org
Hyde Park ES 300/PK-6
50 E Main St 05655 802-888-2237
Diane Reilly, prin. Fax 888-8591
Lamoille Union MS 200/7-8
736 VT 15 W 05655 802-851-1300
Wendy Savery, prin. Fax 851-1397
Other Schools – See Eden, Jeffersonville, Johnson, Waterville

Irasburg, Orleans, Pop. 159
Orleans Central Supervisory Union
Supt. — See Barton
Irasburg Village S 100/K-8
292 Route 58 E 05845 802-754-8810
Paul Simmons, prin. Fax 754-2855

Island Pond, Essex, Pop. 809
North Country Supervisory Union
Supt. — See Newport
Brighton ES 100/PK-8
PO Box 419 05846 802-723-4373
Denise Russell, prin. Fax 723-4114

Isle La Motte, Grand Isle
Grand Isle Supervisory Union
Supt. — See North Hero
Isle La Motte ES 50/K-6
42 School St Ext 05463 802-928-3231
Thomas Tregan, prin. Fax 928-3702

Jamaica, Windham
Windham Central Supervisory Union
Supt. — See Townshend
Jamaica Village ES 100/PK-6
PO Box 488 05343 802-874-4822
Laura Hazard, prin. Fax 874-7170

Jay, Orleans
North Country Supervisory Union
Supt. — See Newport
Jay/Westfield Joint ES 100/PK-6
257 Revoir Flat Rd 05859 802-988-4042
Kristy Ellis, prin. Fax 988-9813

Jeffersonville, Lamoille, Pop. 714
Lamoille North Supervisory Union
Supt. — See Hyde Park
Cambridge ES 400/PK-6
PO Box 160 05464 802-644-8821
Mary Anderson, prin. Fax 644-6531

Jericho, Chittenden, Pop. 1,303
Chittenden East Supervisory Union
Supt. — See Richmond
Browns River MS 400/5-8
20 River Rd 05465 802-899-3711
Kevin Hamilton, prin. Fax 899-4281
Jericho ES 300/K-4
90 VT Route 15 05465 802-899-2272
Victoria Graf, prin. Fax 899-1059
Underhill I.D. ES 100/K-4
10 River Rd 05465 802-899-4680
David Wells, prin. Fax 899-4001

Johnson, Lamoille, Pop. 1,395
Lamoille North Supervisory Union
Supt. — See Hyde Park
Johnson ES 300/PK-6
57 College Hill 05656 802-635-2211
David Manning, prin. Fax 635-7663

Killington, Rutland
Windsor Central Supervisory Union
Supt. — See Woodstock
Killington ES 100/PK-6
686 Schoolhouse Rd 05751 802-422-3366
Mary Guggenberger, prin. Fax 422-3367

Lake Elmore, Lamoille
Lamoille South Supervisory Union
Supt. — See Morrisville
Lake Elmore ES 50/1-3
PO Box 122 05657 802-888-2966
Tracy Wrend, prin. Fax 888-2966

Leicester, Addison
Rutland Northeast Supervisory Union
Supt. — See Brandon
Leicester Central ES 100/PK-6
68 Schoolhouse Rd 05733 802-247-8825
Thomas Fleury, prin. Fax 247-5619

Lincoln, Addison
Addison Northeast Supervisory Union
Supt. — See Bristol
Lincoln Community S 100/K-6
795 E River Rd 05443 802-453-2119
Tory Riley, prin. Fax 453-3370

Londonderry, Windham
Bennington-Rutland Supervisory Union
Supt. — See Sunderland
Flood Brook S 300/K-8
PO Box 547 05148 802-824-6811
Neal McIntyre, prin. Fax 824-4105

Lowell, Orleans, Pop. 227
North Country Supervisory Union
Supt. — See Newport
Lowell Graded S 100/PK-8
52 Gelo Park Rd 05847 802-744-6641
Anita Gagner, prin. Fax 744-9989

Ludlow, Windsor, Pop. 795
Two Rivers Supervisory Union 1,100/PK-12
609 VT Route 103 S 05149 802-875-3365
Meg Powden, supt. Fax 875-6439
su.trsu.org/
Ludlow ES 100/PK-6
45 Main St 05149 802-228-5151
Karen Trimboli, prin. Fax 228-5026
Other Schools – See Chester, Mount Holly, Proctorsville

Lunenburg, Essex
Essex-Caledonia Supervisory Union
Supt. — See Concord
Lunenburg ES 100/PK-4
PO Box 39 05906 802-895-5955
Cheryl McVetty, prin. Fax 892-7734

Lyndon Center, Caledonia

Stevens S 100/K-8
PO Box 274 05850 802-626-0370

Lyndonville, Caledonia, Pop. 1,188
Caledonia North Supervisory Union 1,000/PK-8
PO Box 107 05851 802-626-6100
Jennifer Botzojorns, supt. Fax 626-3423
www.cnsuschools.org
Lyndon Town S 500/PK-8
2591 Lily Pond Rd 05851 802-626-3209
Amy Gale, prin. Fax 626-5872
Other Schools – See Sheffield, Sutton, West Burke

Riverside S 100/PK-8
30 Lily Pond Rd 05851 802-626-8552

Manchester Center, Bennington, Pop. 2,105
Bennington-Rutland Supervisory Union
Supt. — See Sunderland
Manchester S 400/PK-8
PO Box 1526 05255 802-362-1597
Marty Nadler, prin. Fax 362-3883

Maple Street S 100/K-8
322 Maple St 05255 802-362-7137
Fanning Hearon, head sch Fax 362-3492

Marlboro, Windham
Windham Central Supervisory Union
Supt. — See Townshend
Marlboro S 100/PK-8
PO Box D 05344 802-254-2668
Wayne Kermenski, prin. Fax 254-8768

Middlebury, Addison, Pop. 6,363
Addison Central Supervisory Union 1,700/PK-12
49 Charles Ave 05753 802-382-1274
Dr. Peter Burrows, supt. Fax 388-0024
www.acsdvt.org
Hogan ES 400/K-6
201 Mary Hogan Dr 05753 802-382-1400
Thomas Buzzell, prin. Fax 382-1405
Middlebury Union MS 300/7-8
48 Deerfield Ln 05753 802-382-1600
K. Holsman-Francoeur, prin. Fax 382-1215
Other Schools – See Bridport, Cornwall, Ripton, Salisbury, Shoreham, Weybridge

Middlesex, See Montpelier
Washington Central Supervisory Union
Supt. — See Montpelier
Rumney Memorial ES 200/PK-6
433 Shady Rill Rd 05602 802-223-5429
Adam Rosen, prin. Fax 223-0750

Middletown Springs, Rutland
Rutland Southwest Supervisory Union
Supt. — See Poultney
Middletown Springs ES 100/PK-6
PO Box 1267 05757 802-235-2365
Rick Beal, prin. Fax 235-9226

Milton, Chittenden, Pop. 1,843
Milton Town SD 1,700/PK-12
42 Herrick Ave 05468 802-893-5400
Ann Bradshaw, supt. Fax 893-3213
www.mtsd-vt.org
Milton ES 800/PK-5
42 Herrick Ave 05468 802-893-5400
Bridget Gagne, prin. Fax 893-3224
Milton MS 400/6-8
42 Herrick Ave 05468 802-893-5400
Brandy Brown, prin. Fax 893-3213

Monkton, Addison
Addison Northeast Supervisory Union
Supt. — See Bristol
Monkton Central ES 100/K-6
1036 Monkton Rd 05469 802-453-2314
Betsy Knox, prin. Fax 453-6123

Montgomery Center, Franklin
Franklin Northeast Supervisory Union
Supt. — See Richford
Montgomery S 100/PK-8
249 School Dr 05471 802-326-4632
Sandra Alexander, prin. Fax 326-4618

Montpelier, Washington, Pop. 7,675
Montpelier SD 900/PK-12
5 High School Dr Unit 1 05602 802-223-9796
Dr. Brian Ricca, supt. Fax 223-9795
www.mpsvt.org/
Main Street MS 200/5-8
170 Main St 05602 802-223-3404
Pamela Arnold, prin. Fax 223-9225
Union ES 500/PK-4
1 Park Ave 05602 802-223-6343
Chris Hennessey, prin. Fax 223-9219

Washington Central Supervisory Union 1,600/PK-12
1130 Gallison Hill Rd 05602 802-229-0553
William Kimball, supt. Fax 229-2761
www.wcsu32.org
Other Schools – See Berlin, East Montpelier, Middlesex, Plainfield, Worcester

Moretown, Washington
Harwood Unified UNSD
Supt. — See Waitsfield
Moretown ES 100/PK-6
940 Route 100 B 05660 802-496-3742
Duane Pierson, prin. Fax 496-3749

Morrisville, Lamoille, Pop. 1,933
Lamoille South Supervisory Union 1,600/K-12
46 Copley Ave 05661 802-888-4541
Tracy Wrend, supt. Fax 888-6710
www.lamoillesouthsu.org
Morristown ES 300/K-4
548 Park St 05661 802-888-3101
Kate Torrey, prin. Fax 888-7550
Peoples Academy MS 300/5-8
202 Copley Ave 05661 802-888-1402
Karen Weeks, prin. Fax 888-6488
Other Schools – See Lake Elmore, Stowe

Marshall S 100/PK-8
680 Laporte Rd 05661 802-888-4758
Carrie Wilson, hdmstr. Fax 888-3137

Mount Holly, Rutland
Two Rivers Supervisory Union
Supt. — See Ludlow
Mt. Holly ES 100/PK-6
150 School Dr 05758 802-259-2392
Craig Hutt-Vater, prin. Fax 259-2692

Newbury, Orange, Pop. 360
Orange East Supervisory Union
Supt. — See Bradford
Newbury ES 100/K-6
PO Box 68 05051 802-866-5621
Chance Lindsley, prin. Fax 866-3345

Newfane, Windham, Pop. 118
Windham Central Supervisory Union
Supt. — See Townshend
Newbrook ES 100/K-6
14 School St 05345 802-365-7536
Scotty Tabachnick, prin. Fax 365-7177

New Haven, Addison
Addison Northeast Supervisory Union
Supt. — See Bristol
Beeman ES 100/K-6
50 North St 05472 802-453-2331
Kristine Evarts, prin. Fax 453-4637

Newport, Orleans, Pop. 4,495
North Country Supervisory Union 2,700/PK-12
121 Duchess Ave Ste A 05855 802-334-5847
John A. Castle, supt. Fax 334-6528
www.ncsuvt.org
Newport City ES 300/PK-6
166 Sias Ave 05855 802-334-2455
Elaine Collins, prin. Fax 334-0161
Other Schools – See Coventry, Derby, Derby Line, Holland, Island Pond, Jay, Lowell, Newport Center, North Troy, West Charleston

---

United Christian Academy 100/K-12
65 School St 05855 802-334-3112
Dr. Vincent Montoro, head sch Fax 334-2305

Newport Center, Orleans, Pop. 273
North Country Supervisory Union
Supt. — See Newport
Newport Town S 100/PK-8
PO Box 48 05857 802-334-5201
Wendy Wood, prin. Fax 334-7541

North Bennington, Bennington, Pop. 1,606

Village S of North Bennington 100/PK-6
PO Box 847 05257 802-442-5955
Timothy Newbold, head sch Fax 447-2397

North Clarendon, Rutland
Mill River USD 900/PK-12
64 Grange Hall Rd 05759 802-775-3264
Dave Younce, supt. Fax 775-8063
millriverschools.org
Clarendon ES 200/PK-6
84 Grange Hall Rd 05759 802-775-5379
Fred Valastro, prin. Fax 747-7584
Other Schools – See Shrewsbury, Tinmouth, Wallingford

Northfield, Washington, Pop. 2,049
Washington South Supervisory Union 600/PK-12
37 Cross St Ste 1 05663 802-485-7755
Laurie Gossens, supt. Fax 485-3348
www.wssu.org
Northfield ES 300/PK-5
10 Cross St 05663 802-485-6161
Wayne Howe, prin. Fax 485-3471
Other Schools – See Roxbury

North Hero, Grand Isle
Grand Isle Supervisory Union 600/PK-8
5038 US Route 2 05474 802-372-6921
Fax 372-4898
www.gisu.org
North Hero ES 100/PK-6
6441 US Route 2 05474 802-372-8866
Joe Restighini, prin. Fax 372-4867
Other Schools – See Alburg, Grand Isle, Isle La Motte, South Hero

North Troy, Orleans, Pop. 614
North Country Supervisory Union
Supt. — See Newport
Troy S 200/PK-8
PO Box 110 05859 802-988-2565
Christopher Young, prin. Fax 988-2635

Norwich, Windsor, Pop. 834
Hanover SD
Supt. — See Hanover, NH
Cross ES 300/K-6
PO Box 900 05055 802-649-1703
Bill Hammond, prin. Fax 649-3640

Orleans, Orleans, Pop. 796
Orleans Central Supervisory Union
Supt. — See Barton
Orleans ES 100/K-8
53 School St 05860 802-754-6650
Kim Hastings, prin. Fax 754-2636

Orwell, Addison
Addison-Rutland Supervisory Union
Supt. — See Fair Haven
Orwell Village S 100/K-8
494 Main St 05760 802-948-2871
Patrick Walters, prin. Fax 948-2754

Peacham, Caledonia
Caledonia Central Supervisory Union
Supt. — See Danville
Peacham ES 50/PK-6
PO Box 271 05862 802-592-3513
Ashley Gray, prin. Fax 592-3517

Pittsford, Rutland, Pop. 731
Rutland Northeast Supervisory Union
Supt. — See Brandon
Lothrop ES 200/PK-6
3447 US Route 7 05763 802-483-6361
Debbie Alexander, prin. Fax 483-2146

Plainfield, Washington, Pop. 393
Washington Central Supervisory Union
Supt. — See Montpelier
Calais ES 100/PK-6
321 Lightening Ridge Rd 05667 802-454-7777
Catherine Fair, prin. Fax 454-1580

Washington NE Supervisory Union 600/PK-12
PO Box 470 05667 802-454-9924
Mark Tucker, supt. Fax 454-9934
washnesu.org
Twinfield Union S 400/PK-12
106 Nasmith Brook Rd 05667 802-426-3213
Mark Mooney, prin. Fax 426-4085
Other Schools – See Cabot

Poultney, Rutland, Pop. 1,589
Rutland Southwest Supervisory Union 600/PK-12
168 York St 05764 802-287-5286
Joan Paustian Ed.D., supt. Fax 287-2284
www.rswsu.org
Poultney ES 200/K-6
96 School Cir 05764 802-287-5212
Kristen Caligiuri, prin. Fax 287-2470
Other Schools – See Middletown Springs, Wells

Pownal, Bennington
Southwest Vermont Supervisory Union
Supt. — See Bennington
Pownal ES 200/K-6
94 Schoolhouse Rd 05261 802-823-7333
Todd Phillips, prin. Fax 823-4031

Proctor, Rutland
Rutland Central Supervisory Union
Supt. — See Rutland
Proctor ES 200/PK-6
14 School St 05765 802-459-2225
Christy Colouitti, prin. Fax 459-2103

Proctorsville, Windsor, Pop. 450
Two Rivers Supervisory Union
Supt. — See Ludlow
Cavendish Town ES 100/K-6
PO Box 236 05153 802-226-7758
George Thomson, prin. Fax 226-7312

Putney, Windham, Pop. 508
Windham Northeast Supervisory Union
Supt. — See Bellows Falls
Westminster West ES 50/1-4
3724 Westminster West Rd 05346 802-387-5756
Doug Kussius, prin. Fax 387-4309

Windham Southeast Supervisory Union
Supt. — See Brattleboro
Putney Central S 200/K-8
182 Westminster Rd 05346 802-387-5521
Herve Pelletier, prin. Fax 387-2776

Grammar S 100/PK-8
69 Hickory Ridge Rd S 05346 802-387-5364
Nick Perry, head sch Fax 387-4744

Quechee, Windsor, Pop. 648
Hartford SD
Supt. — See White River Junction
Ottauquechee S 300/PK-5
PO Box 353 05059 802-295-8654
Cathy Newton, prin. Fax 295-8656

Mid Vermont Christian S 100/PK-12
399 W Gilson Ave 05059 802-295-6800
Robert Bracy M.Ed., hdmstr. Fax 295-3748
Upper Valley Waldorf S 200/PK-8
PO Box 709 05059 802-296-2496

Randolph, Orange, Pop. 1,947
Orange Southwest Supervisory Union 1,100/PK-12
24 Central St 05060 802-728-5052
Dr. Brent Kay, supt. Fax 728-4844
www.orangesouthwest.org
Randolph ES 300/PK-6
40 Ayers Brook Rd 05060 802-728-9555
Erica McLaughlin, prin. Fax 728-6709
Other Schools – See Braintree, Brookfield

Reading, Windsor
Windsor Central Supervisory Union
Supt. — See Woodstock
Reading ES 100/PK-6
PO Box 176 05062 802-484-7230
Cathy Knight, prin. Fax 484-3818

Readsboro, Bennington, Pop. 319
Windham Southwest Supervisory Union
Supt. — See Wilmington
Readsboro S 100/PK-8
301 Phelps Ln 05350 802-423-7786
Barbara Barrett, prin. Fax 423-9914

Richford, Franklin, Pop. 1,314
Franklin Northeast Supervisory Union 1,600/PK-12
PO Box 130 05476 802-848-7661
Lynn Cota, supt. Fax 848-3531
fnesu.net
Berkshire S 200/PK-8
4850 Water Tower Rd 05476 802-933-2290
Lynn Cota, prin. Fax 933-2812
Richford ES 200/PK-5
1 Elementary School Rd 05476 802-848-7453
Beth O'Brien, prin. Fax 848-7720
Other Schools – See Bakersfield, Enosburg Falls, Montgomery Center

Richmond, Chittenden, Pop. 707
Chittenden East Supervisory Union 2,700/PK-12
PO Box 282 05477 802-434-2128
John Alberghini, supt. Fax 434-2196
www.cesuvt.org
Camels Hump MS 400/5-8
173 School St 05477 802-434-2188
Mark Carbone, prin. Fax 434-2192
Richmond ES 300/PK-4
125 School St 05477 802-434-2461
Ben White, prin. Fax 434-7241
Other Schools – See Bolton, Huntington, Jericho, Underhill Center

Ripton, Addison
Addison Central Supervisory Union
Supt. — See Middlebury
Ripton ES 50/PK-6
PO Box 155 05766 802-388-2208
Tracey Harrington, prin. Fax 388-2208

Rochester, Windsor, Pop. 297
White River Valley Supervisory Union
Supt. — See South Royalton
Rochester S 100/PK-4
222 S Main St 05767 802-767-3161
Daniella Stamm, prin. Fax 767-1130

Roxbury, Washington
Washington South Supervisory Union
Supt. — See Northfield
Roxbury Village ES 50/PK-6
1559 Roxbury Rd 05669 802-485-7768
Ben Brownell, prin. Fax 485-9304

Rutland, Rutland, Pop. 16,220
Rutland Central Supervisory Union 1,000/PK-12
16 Evelyn St 05701 802-775-4342
Dr. Debra Taylor, supt. Fax 775-7319
www.rcsu.org
Rutland Town S 300/K-8
1612 Post Rd 05701 802-775-0566
Aaron Boynton, prin. Fax 775-8951
Other Schools – See Proctor, West Rutland

Rutland City SD 2,200/K-12
6 Church St 05701 802-773-1900
Mary Moran, supt. Fax 773-1927
www.rutlandcitypublicschools.org
Rutland IS 600/3-6
65 Library Ave 05701 802-773-1932
Jay Slenker, prin. Fax 773-1913
Rutland MS 300/7-8
67 Library Ave 05701 802-773-1960
Robert Johnson, prin. Fax 773-1914
Rutland Northeast PS 200/K-2
117 Temple St 05701 802-773-1940
Suzanne Engels, prin. Fax 773-1941
Rutland Northwest PS 200/K-2
80 Pierpoint Ave 05701 802-773-1946
Kristin Hubert, prin. Fax 773-1912

Christ the King S 200/PK-8
60 S Main St 05701 802-773-0500
Sarah Fortier, prin. Fax 773-0554
Rutland Area Christian S 100/PK-12
112 Lincoln Ave 05701 802-775-0709
Dia Lind, prin. Fax 786-0111

Saint Albans, Franklin, Pop. 6,736
Maple Run USD 2,800/PK-12
28 Catherine St 05478 802-524-2600
Dr. Kevin Dirth, supt. Fax 524-1540
www.maplerun.org
St. Albans City S 800/PK-8
29 Bellows St 05478 802-527-0565
Joan Cavallo, prin. Fax 527-0153
St. Albans Town Educational Center 700/PK-8
169 S Main St 05478 802-527-7191
Angela Stebbins, prin. Fax 527-7043
Other Schools – See Fairfield

Saint Johnsbury, Caledonia, Pop. 6,424
Saint Johnsbury SD 700/PK-8
161 Western Ave 05819 802-748-8912
Dr. Margaret Bledsoe, supt. Fax 748-2542
district.stjsd.org
Saint Johnsbury S 700/PK-8
257 Western Ave 05819 802-748-8912
Michael Redmon, prin. Fax 748-1095

Caledonia Christian S 50/K-8
54 Southard St 05819 802-748-9528
Good Shepherd S 200/PK-8
121 Maple St 05819 802-751-8223
Lynn Cartularo, prin. Fax 751-8111

Salisbury, Addison
Addison Central Supervisory Union
Supt. — See Middlebury
Salisbury Community ES 100/PK-6
286 Kelly Cross Rd 05769 802-352-4291
Fernanda Canales, prin. Fax 352-1067

Saxtons River, Windham, Pop. 550
Windham Northeast Supervisory Union
Supt. — See Bellows Falls
Saxtons River ES 100/K-5
PO Box 308 05154 802-869-2637
Nancy Erickson, prin. Fax 869-2631

Shaftsbury, Bennington
Southwest Vermont Supervisory Union
Supt. — See Bennington
Shaftsbury ES 200/K-6
150 Buck Hill Rd 05262 802-442-4373
Jeffrey Johnson, prin. Fax 442-3588

Sharon, Windsor
White River Valley Supervisory Union
Supt. — See South Royalton
Sharon ES 100/PK-6
75 Vermont Route 132 05065 802-763-7425
Barrett Williams, prin. Fax 763-2056

Sheffield, Caledonia
Caledonia North Supervisory Union
Supt. — See Lyndonville
Millers Run S 100/PK-8
3249 VT Route 122 05866 802-626-9755
Patrick Ham, prin. Fax 626-4316

Shelburne, Chittenden, Pop. 581
Champlain Valley SD 3,100/PK-12
5420 Shelburne Rd Ste 300 05482 802-383-1234
Elaine Pinckney, supt. Fax 383-1242
www.cvsdvt.org
Shelburne Community S 800/PK-8
345 Harbor Rd 05482 802-985-3331
Allan Miller, prin. Fax 985-8951
Other Schools – See Charlotte, Hinesburg, Williston

Lake Champlain Waldorf S 200/PK-8
359 Turtle Ln 05482 802-985-2827
Renaissance S 100/K-5
PO Box 339 05482 802-985-8209

Sheldon, Franklin
Franklin Northwest Supervisory Union
Supt. — See Swanton
Sheldon S 300/K-8
78 Poor Farm Rd 05483 802-933-4909
Christie Martin, prin. Fax 933-6405

Shoreham, Addison
Addison Central Supervisory Union
Supt. — See Middlebury
Shoreham ES 100/K-6
130 School Rd 05770 802-897-7181
Michael Lenox, prin. Fax 897-2463

Shrewsbury, Rutland
Mill River USD
Supt. — See North Clarendon
Shrewsbury ES 100/PK-6
300 Mountain School Rd 05738 802-492-3435
Deb Fishwick, prin. Fax 492-6107

South Burlington, Chittenden, Pop. 17,544
South Burlington SD 2,400/K-12
550 Dorset St 05403 802-652-7250
David Young, supt. Fax 652-7257
www.sbschools.net
Chamberlin ES 200/K-5
262 White St 05403 802-652-7400
Holly Rouelle, prin. Fax 658-9048
Marcotte Central ES 400/K-5
10 Market St 05403 802-652-7200
Brent Coon, prin. Fax 658-9047
Orchard ES 400/K-5
2 Baldwin Ave 05403 802-652-7300
Mark Trifilio, prin. Fax 658-9037
Tuttle MS 600/6-8
500 Dorset St 05403 802-652-7100
Karsten Schlenter, prin. Fax 652-7152

South Hero, Grand Isle
Grand Isle Supervisory Union
Supt. — See North Hero
Folsom Education & Community Center 100/K-8
75 South St 05486 802-372-6600
Leonard Badeau, prin. Fax 372-5188

South Royalton, Windsor, Pop. 674
White River Valley Supervisory Union 1,300/PK-12
461 Waterman Rd 05068 802-763-8840
Bruce Labs, supt. Fax 763-3235
wrvsu.org
South Royalton S 400/PK-12
223 S Windsor St 05068 802-763-8844
Dean Stearns, prin. Fax 763-3233
Other Schools – See Bethel, Chelsea, Rochester, Sharon, South Strafford, Stockbridge, Tunbridge

South Strafford, Orange
White River Valley Supervisory Union
Supt. — See South Royalton
Newton S 100/K-8
PO Box 239 05070 802-765-4351
Gregory Bagnato, prin. Fax 765-4785

Springfield, Windsor, Pop. 3,895
Springfield SD 1,300/K-12
60 Park St 05156 802-885-5141
Zachary McLaughlin, supt. Fax 885-8169
www.ssdvt.org
Elm Hill PS 300/K-2
10 Hoover St 05156 802-885-5154
Dana Jacobson-Goodhue, prin. Fax 885-5159
Riverside MS 300/6-8
13 Fairground Rd 05156 802-885-8490
Steve Cone, prin. Fax 885-8442
Union Street ES 300/3-5
43 Union St 05156 802-885-5155
Nancy Wiese, prin. Fax 885-8481

Stamford, Bennington
Windham Southwest Supervisory Union
Supt. — See Wilmington
Stamford S 100/K-8
986 Main Rd 05352 802-694-1379
Micah Hayre, prin. Fax 694-8512

Starksboro, Addison
Addison Northeast Supervisory Union
Supt. — See Bristol
Robinson ES 200/K-6
PO Box 10 05487 802-453-2949
Edorah Frazer, prin. Fax 453-6062

Stockbridge, Windsor
White River Valley Supervisory Union
Supt. — See South Royalton
Stockbridge Central ES 100/PK-6
2933 VT Route 107 05772 802-234-9248
Barbara Woods, prin. Fax 767-9248

Stowe, Lamoille, Pop. 492
Lamoille South Supervisory Union
Supt. — See Morrisville
Stowe ES 300/K-5
PO Box 760 05672 802-253-4154
Martha Sorrell-Lacasse, prin. Fax 253-6915
Stowe MS 200/6-8
413 Barrows Rd 05672 802-253-6913
Dan Morrison, prin. Fax 253-5314

Sudbury, Rutland
Rutland Northeast Supervisory Union
Supt. — See Brandon
Sudbury Country S 50/PK-6
31 Schoolhouse Ln 05733 802-623-7771
Roderick Driscoll, prin. Fax 623-7772

Sunderland, Bennington
Bennington-Rutland Supervisory Union 1,200/PK-8
6378 VT Route 7A 05250 802-362-2452
Jacquelyne Wilson, supt. Fax 362-2455
www.brsu.org
Sunderland ES 100/K-6
98 Bear Ridge Rd 05250 802-375-6100
Skyler LaBombard, prin. Fax 375-6555
Other Schools – See Danby, Dorset, Londonderry, Manchester Center, West Pawlet

Sutton, Caledonia
Caledonia North Supervisory Union
Supt. — See Lyndonville
Sutton Village S 100/K-8
95 Underpass Rd 05867 802-467-3492
Kenneth Hayes, prin. Fax 467-3023

Swanton, Franklin, Pop. 2,303
Franklin Northwest Supervisory Union 2,100/PK-12
100 Robin Hood Dr 05488 802-868-4967
Winton Goodrich, supt. Fax 868-4265
www.fnwsu.org
Babcock ES 300/PK-2
24 4th St 05488 802-868-4920
Dena St. Amour, prin. Fax 868-3389
Swanton Central ES 300/K-6
24 4th St 05488 802-868-5346
Dena St. Amour, prin. Fax 868-4861
Other Schools – See Franklin, Highgate Center, Sheldon

Thetford, Orange
Orange East Supervisory Union
Supt. — See Bradford
Thetford ES 200/K-6
PO Box 182 05074 802-785-2426
Kevin Petrone, prin. Fax 785-2645

Tinmouth, Rutland
Mill River USD
Supt. — See North Clarendon
Tinmouth ES 100/PK-6
573 Route 140 05773 802-446-2458
Maureen Fitzgerald-Riker, prin. Fax 446-2466

Townshend, Windham
Windham Central Supervisory Union 900/PK-12
1219 VT Route 30 05353 802-365-9510
William Anton, supt. Fax 365-7934
www.windhamcentral.org
Townshend ES 100/PK-6
PO Box 236 05353 802-365-7506
Craig Roach, prin. Fax 365-7955
Other Schools – See East Dover, Jamaica, Marlboro, Newfane, Wardsboro, Windham

Tunbridge, Orange
White River Valley Supervisory Union
Supt. — See South Royalton
Tunbridge Central S 100/PK-8
PO Box 8 05077 802-889-3310
Scott Farnsworth, prin. Fax 889-3214

Underhill Center, Chittenden
Chittenden East Supervisory Union
Supt. — See Richmond
Underhill Central ES 200/PK-4
6 Irish Settlement Rd 05490 802-899-4676
Barbara Nason, prin. Fax 899-5173

Vergennes, Addison, Pop. 2,536
Addison Northwest SD 1,000/K-12
11 Main St Ste B100 05491 802-877-3332
JoAn Canning, supt. Fax 877-3628
www.anwsd.org
Vergennes Union ES 300/K-6
43 East St 05491 802-877-3761
Matt DeBlois, prin. Fax 877-1115
Other Schools – See Addison, Ferrisburgh

Champlain Valley Christian S 50/PK-8
2 Church St 05491 802-877-3640
Linda Larocque, admin. Fax 877-1103

Vernon, Windham
Windham Southeast Supervisory Union
Supt. — See Brattleboro
Vernon ES 200/K-6
381 Governor Hunt Rd 05354 802-254-5373
Dana Gordon-Macey, prin. Fax 257-0988

Waitsfield, Washington, Pop. 162
Harwood Unified UNSD 1,800/PK-12
340 Mad River Park Ste 7 05673 802-496-2272
Brigid Nease, supt. Fax 496-6515
www.wwsu.org/
Waitsfield ES 200/PK-6
3951 Main St 05673 802-496-3643
Kaiya Korb, prin. Fax 496-3226
Other Schools – See Duxbury, Fayston, Moretown, Warren, Waterbury

Wallingford, Rutland, Pop. 822
Mill River USD
Supt. — See North Clarendon
Wallingford ES 100/K-6
126 School St 05773 802-446-2141
Helen Richards-Peelle, prin. Fax 446-2996

Wardsboro, Windham
Windham Central Supervisory Union
Supt. — See Townshend
Wardsboro ES 100/PK-6
PO Box 107 05355 802-896-6210
Tammy Bates, prin. Fax 896-6687

Warren, Washington
Harwood Unified UNSD
Supt. — See Waitsfield
Warren ES 200/PK-6
293 School Rd 05674 802-496-2487
Beth Peterson, prin. Fax 496-2570

Washington, Orange
Orange North Supervisory Union
Supt. — See Williamstown
Washington Village S 100/PK-8
72 School Ln 05675 802-883-2312
Amy Harlow, prin. Fax 883-5411

Waterbury, Washington, Pop. 1,738
Harwood Unified UNSD
Supt. — See Waitsfield
Thatcher Brook PS 400/PK-4
47 Stowe St 05676 802-244-7195
Denise Goodnow, prin. Fax 244-1158

Waterville, Lamoille
Lamoille North Supervisory Union
Supt. — See Hyde Park
Waterville ES 100/PK-6
3414 VT Route 109 05492 802-644-2224
Jan Epstein, prin. Fax 644-2726

Wells, Rutland, Pop. 392
Rutland Southwest Supervisory Union
Supt. — See Poultney
Wells Village S 100/K-6
135 VT Route 30 05774 802-645-0386
Lisa Yates, prin. Fax 645-1906

Wells River, Orange, Pop. 387
Blue Mountain SD 400/PK-12
2420 Route 302 05081 802-757-2766
Emilie Knisley, supt. Fax 757-2790
www.bmuschool.org
Blue Mountain Union S 21 400/PK-12
2420 Route 302 05081 802-757-2711
Scott Blood, prin. Fax 757-3894

West Burke, Caledonia, Pop. 338
Caledonia North Supervisory Union
Supt. — See Lyndonville
Burke Town S 200/PK-8
3293 Burke Hollow Rd 05871 802-467-3385
Stacy Rice, prin. Fax 467-3323
Newark Street S 100/K-8
1448 Newark St 05871 802-467-3401
Timothy Mulligan, prin. Fax 467-1001

West Charleston, Orleans
North Country Supervisory Union
Supt. — See Newport
Charleston ES 100/PK-8
255 Center School Rd 05872 802-895-2915
Jessica Applegate, prin. Fax 895-2611

West Danville, Caledonia
Caledonia Central Supervisory Union
Supt. — See Danville
Walden S 100/PK-8
135 Cahoon Farm Rd 05873 802-563-3000
Liz Benoit, prin. Fax 563-3030

West Fairlee, Orange
Rivendell Interstate SD
Supt. — See Orford, NH
Westshire ES 100/PK-4
744 VT Route 113 05083 802-333-4668
Tammy MacQueen, prin. Fax 333-4744

Westford, Chittenden
Chittenden Central Supervisory Union
Supt. — See Essex Junction
Westford S 200/PK-8
146 Brookside Rd 05494 802-878-5932
Marcie Lewis, prin. Fax 879-0874

West Halifax, Windham
Windham Southwest Supervisory Union
Supt. — See Wilmington
Halifax S 100/K-8
246 Branch Rd 05358 802-368-2888
Sandra Pentak, prin. Fax 368-7847

Westminster, Windham, Pop. 291
Windham Northeast Supervisory Union
Supt. — See Bellows Falls
Westminster Center ES 200/K-6
301 School St 05158 802-722-3241
Doug Kussius, prin. Fax 722-9536

West Pawlet, Rutland
Bennington-Rutland Supervisory Union
Supt. — See Sunderland
Mettawee Community S 200/PK-6
5788 VT Route 153 05775 802-645-9009
Brooke DeBonis, prin. Fax 645-0907

West Rutland, Rutland, Pop. 2,007
Rutland Central Supervisory Union
Supt. — See Rutland
West Rutland S 300/PK-12
713 Main St 05777 802-438-2288
Sarah Merrill, prin. Fax 438-5708

Weybridge, Addison
Addison Central Supervisory Union
Supt. — See Middlebury
Weybridge ES 50/K-6
210 Quaker Village Rd 05753 802-545-2113
Christina Johnson, prin. Fax 545-2439

White River Junction, Windsor, Pop. 2,238
Hartford SD 1,600/PK-12
73 Highland Ave 05001 802-295-8600
Tom DeBalsi, supt. Fax 295-8602
www.hsdvt.com
Dothan Brook S 300/PK-5
2300 Christian St 05001 802-295-8647
Rick Dustin-Eichler, prin. Fax 295-8649
Hartford Memorial MS 300/6-8
245 Highland Ave 05001 802-295-8640
Tristan Upson, prin. Fax 295-8641
White River S 200/PK-5
102 Pine St 05001 802-295-8650
Sheila Powers, prin. Fax 295-8652
Other Schools – See Quechee

Whiting, Addison
Rutland Northeast Supervisory Union
Supt. — See Brandon
Whiting ES 50/PK-6
87 S Main St 05778 802-623-7991
Roderick Driscoll, prin. Fax 623-7992

Williamstown, Orange
Orange North Supervisory Union 800/PK-12
111B Brush Hill Rd 05679 802-433-5818
Susette Bollard, supt. Fax 433-5825
www.onsu.org/
Williamstown ES 200/PK-5
100 Brush Hill Rd 05679 802-433-6653
Jamie Kinnarney, prin. Fax 433-6266
Other Schools – See East Barre, Washington

Williston, Chittenden
Champlain Valley SD
Supt. — See Shelburne
Williston Central S 700/3-8
195 Central School Dr 05495 802-878-2762
Greg Marino, prin. Fax 871-6101

Brownell Mountain SDA S 50/1-8
5330 St George Rd 05495 802-878-3830

Wilmington, Windham, Pop. 457
Windham Southwest Supervisory Union 500/PK-12
1 School St 05363 802-464-1300
Dr. Christopher A. Pratt Ed.D., supt. Fax 464-1303
www.windhamsw.k12.vt.us/
Twin Valley ES 100/PK-5
360 VT Route 100 N 05363 802-464-5177
Rebecca Fillion, prin. Fax 464-1246
Other Schools – See Readsboro, Stamford, West Halifax

Windham, Windham
Windham Central Supervisory Union
Supt. — See Townshend
Windham ES 50/K-6
5940 Windham Hill Rd 05359 802-874-4159
Mickey Parker-Jennings, prin. Fax 874-4929

Windsor, Windsor, Pop. 2,011
Windsor Southeast Supervisory Union 1,100/K-12
105 Main St Ste 200 05089 802-674-2144
David Baker, supt. Fax 674-6357
www.wsesu.net
Windsor State Street ES 300/K-6
127 State St 05089 802-674-2310
Tiffany Cassano, prin. Fax 674-9803
Other Schools – See Ascutney, Brownsville, Hartland

Winooski, Chittenden, Pop. 7,032
Winooski SD 800/PK-12
60 Normand St 05404 802-655-0485
Sean McMannon, supt. Fax 655-7602
www.wsdschools.org
Kennedy ES 400/PK-5
60 Normand St 05404 802-655-0411
Sara Raabe, prin. Fax 654-1032
Winooski MS 200/6-8
60 Normand St 05404 802-655-3530
Kate Grodin, prin. Fax 655-6538

St. Francis Xavier S 200/PK-8
5 Saint Peter St 05404 802-655-2600
Eric Becker, prin. Fax 655-3096

Wolcott, Lamoille
Orleans Southwest Supervisory Union
Supt. — See Hardwick
Wolcott ES 100/PK-6
PO Box 179 05680 802-472-6551
Matthew Foster, prin. Fax 472-6295

Woodbury, Washington
Orleans Southwest Supervisory Union
Supt. — See Hardwick
Woodbury ES 50/K-6
PO Box 328 05681 802-472-5715
Amy Masse, prin. Fax 472-6923

Woodstock, Windsor, Pop. 897
Windsor Central Supervisory Union 900/PK-12
70 Amsden Way 05091 802-457-1213
Mary Beth Banios, supt. Fax 457-2989
www.wcsu.net
Woodstock ES 200/K-6
15 South St 05091 802-457-2522
Maggie Mills, prin. Fax 457-3732
Woodstock Union MS 100/7-8
100 Amsden Way 05091 802-457-1330
Dana Peterson, prin. Fax 457-5048
Other Schools – See Barnard, Killington, Reading

Worcester, Washington, Pop. 112
Washington Central Supervisory Union
Supt. — See Montpelier
Doty Memorial ES 100/PK-6
24 Calais Rd 05682 802-223-5656
Matt Young, prin. Fax 223-0216

VIRGINIA

VIRGINIA DEPARTMENT OF EDUCATION
PO Box 2120, Richmond 23218-2120
Telephone 804-225-2020
Fax 804-371-2099
Website http://www.pen.k12.va.us

Superintendent of Public Instruction Steven Constantine

VIRGINIA BOARD OF EDUCATION
PO Box 2120, Richmond 23218-2120

President Billy Cannaday

PUBLIC, PRIVATE AND CATHOLIC ELEMENTARY SCHOOLS

Abingdon, Washington, Pop. 8,107
Washington County SD 7,400/PK-12
812 Thompson Dr 24210 276-739-3000
Dr. Brian Ratliff, supt. Fax 628-1874
www.wcs.k12.va.us
Abingdon ES 500/PK-5
19431 Woodland Hills Rd 24210 276-739-3400
Megan de Nobriga, prin. Fax 623-4121
Greendale ES 300/PK-5
13092 McGuffie Rd 24210 276-739-3500
Allyson Willis, prin. Fax 623-4102
Stanley MS 700/6-8
297 Stanley St 24210 276-739-3300
Scott Allen, prin. Fax 676-1945
Watauga ES 600/PK-5
23181 Watauga Rd 24211 276-739-3600
Dr. Marie Stanley, prin. Fax 628-1847
Other Schools – See Bristol, Damascus, Glade Spring, Meadowview

Cornerstone Christian Academy 200/PK-12
PO Box 2228 24212 276-623-7164
Dr. Clay Brinson, head sch Fax 628-2481

Accomac, Accomack, Pop. 513
Accomack County SD 5,200/PK-12
PO Box 330 23301 757-787-5754
Warren Holland, supt. Fax 787-2951
www.accomack.k12.va.us
Accawmacke ES 600/PK-5
PO Box 389 23301 757-787-8013
Javan Thompson, prin. Fax 787-8032
Other Schools – See Chincoteague, Mappsville, Melfa, Oak Hall, Onley, Parksley, Tangier

Afton, Nelson
Nelson County SD
Supt. — See Lovingston
Rockfish River ES 400/PK-5
200 Chapel Hollow Rd 22920 434-361-1791
Kim Candler, prin. Fax 361-1795

Afton Christian S 50/PK-12
9357 Critzers Shop Rd 22920 540-456-6853
Lori Knight, head sch Fax 456-6236

Alberta, Brunswick, Pop. 294
Brunswick County SD
Supt. — See Lawrenceville
Red Oak-Sturgeon ES 200/PK-5
4081 Flat Rock Rd 23821 434-949-7820
Dr. Mark Harrison, prin. Fax 949-7519

Aldie, Loudoun
Loudoun County SD
Supt. — See Ashburn
Aldie ES 100/PK-5
PO Box 25 20105 703-957-4380
Tracy Stephens, prin. Fax 327-9898
Arcola ES 800/PK-5
41740 Tall Cedar Pkwy 20105 703-957-4390
Andrew Stevens, prin. Fax 327-7801
Buffalo Trail ES 800/K-5
42190 Seven Hills Dr 20105 703-722-2780
Alisa Rogaliner, prin. Fax 542-2340
Mercer MS 1,000/6-8
42149 Greenstone Dr 20105 703-957-4340
Robert Phillips, prin. Fax 444-8068
Pinebrook ES 1,200/K-5
25480 Mindful Ct 20105 703-957-4325
Paul Thiessen, prin. Fax 542-7178

Leport S - Aldie 100/PK-K
24328 Marrwood Dr 20105 703-542-5522

Alexandria, Alexandria, Pop. 135,858
Alexandria CSD 12,000/PK-12
1340 Braddock Pl 22314 703-619-8000
Dr. Lois Berlin, supt. Fax 619-8090
www.acps.k12.va.us
Adams ES 900/PK-5
5651 Rayburn Ave 22311 703-824-6970
Ginja Canton, prin. Fax 379-4853
Barrett ES 400/PK-5
1115 Martha Custis Dr 22302 703-824-6960
Seth Kennard, prin. Fax 379-3782
Hammond MS 500/6-8
4646 Seminary Rd 22304 703-461-4100
Meilin Jao, prin. Fax 461-4111
Henry ES 600/PK-8
4643 Taney Ave 22304 703-461-4170
Ingrid Bynum, prin. Fax 823-3350
Jefferson-Houston S for Arts & Academics 400/PK-8
1501 Cameron St 22314 703-706-4400
Christopher Phillips Ed.D., prin. Fax 836-7923
Kelly S for Math Science & Technology 400/PK-5
3600 Commonwealth Ave 22305 703-706-4420
Jasibi Crews-West, prin. Fax 706-4425
Lyles-Crouch Traditional Academy 400/K-5
530 S Saint Asaph St 22314 703-706-4430
Dr. Patricia Zissios, prin. Fax 684-0252
MacArthur ES 700/K-5
1101 Janneys Ln 22302 703-461-4190
Rae Covey, prin. Fax 370-2719
Mason ES 500/K-5
2601 Cameron Mills Rd 22302 703 706-4470
Brian Orrenmaa, prin. Fax 683-9011
Maury ES 400/K-5
600 Russell Rd 22301 703-706-4440
Victor Powell, prin. Fax 683-5146
Mt. Vernon Community S 800/PK-5
2601 Commonwealth Ave 22305 703-706-4460
Liza Burrell-Aldana, prin. Fax 706-4466
Polk ES 700/K-5
5000 Polk Ave 22304 703-461-4180
PreeAnn Johnson, prin. Fax 751-8614
Ramsay ES 800/PK-5
5700 Sanger Ave 22311 703-824-6950
Michael Routhouska, prin. Fax 379-7824
Tucker ES 700/K-5
435 Ferdinand Day Dr 22304 703-933-6300
Rene Paschal, prin. Fax 212-8465
Washington MS 600/6-8
1005 Mount Vernon Ave 22301 703-706-4500
Jesse Mazur, prin. Fax 299-7597

Fairfax County SD
Supt. — See Falls Church
Belle View ES 500/K-6
6701 Fort Hunt Rd 22307 703-660-8300
Tom Kuntz, prin. Fax 660-8397
Bren Mar Park ES 500/K-5
6344 Beryl Rd 22312 703-914-7200
Jason Pannutti, prin. Fax 914-7297
Bucknell ES 300/PK-6
6925 University Dr 22307 703-660-2900
LaRonda Peterson, prin. Fax 660-2997
Bush Hill ES 500/K-6
5927 Westchester St 22310 703-924-5600
Mary Duffy, prin. Fax 924-5697
Cameron ES 500/K-6
3434 Campbell Dr 22303 703-329-2100
Timothy Slayter, prin. Fax 329-2197
Clermont ES 500/K-6
5720 Clermont Dr 22310 703-921-2400
Anne Stokowski, prin. Fax 921-2497
Fort Hunt ES 600/K-6
8832 Linton Ln 22308 703-619-2600
Thomas Fitzpatrick, prin. Fax 619-2697
Franconia ES 600/K-6
6301 Beulah St 22310 703-822-2200
Terri Edmunds-Heard, prin. Fax 822-2297
Glasgow MS 1,500/6-8
4101 Fairfax Pkwy 22312 703-813-8700
Shawn DeRose, prin. Fax 813-8797
Groveton ES 800/K-6
6900 Harrison Ln 22306 703-718-8000
James Swoger, prin. Fax 718-8097
Hayfield ES 700/K-6
7633 Telegraph Rd 22315 703-924-4500
Jessica Lewis, prin. Fax 924-4597
Hollin Meadows ES 600/K-6
2310 Nordok Pl 22306 703-718-8300
Jon Gates, prin. Fax 718-8397
Holmes MS 1,000/6-8
6525 Montrose St 22312 703-658-5900
Margaret Barnes, prin. Fax 658-5997
Hybla Valley ES 900/K-6
3415 Lockheed Blvd 22306 703-718-7000
Lauren Sheehy Ed.D., prin. Fax 718-7097
Island Creek ES 700/PK-6
7855 Morning View Ln 22315 571-642-6300
Michael Macrina, prin. Fax 642-6397
Lane ES 800/K-6
7137 Beulah St 22315 703-924-7700
Eleanor Contreras, prin. Fax 924-7797
Mt. Eagle ES 400/K-6
6116 N Kings Hwy 22303 703-721-2100
Jean Consolla, prin. Fax 721-2197
Mt. Vernon Woods ES 700/PK-6
4015 Fielding St 22309 703-619-2800
Clint Mitchell, prin. Fax 619-2897
Parklawn ES 700/K-5
4116 Braddock Rd 22312 703-914-6900
Rebecca Forgy, prin. Fax 914-6997
Riverside ES 700/K-6
8410 Old Mount Vernon Rd 22309 703-799-6000
Paul Basdekis, prin. Fax 799-6097
Rose Hill ES 700/PK-6
6301 Rose Hill Dr 22310 703-313-4200
Elizabeth Obester, prin. Fax 313-4297
Sandburg MS 1,300/7-8
8428 Fort Hunt Rd 22308 703-799-6100
Darwin Barker, prin. Fax 799-6197
Stratford Landing ES 900/PK-6
8484 Riverside Rd 22308 703-619-3600
Maureen Marshall, prin. Fax 619-3697
Twain MS 900/7-8
4700 Franconia Rd 22310 703-313-3700
Charles Miller, prin. Fax 313-3797
Washington Mill ES 600/K-6
9100 Cherrytree Dr 22309 703-619-2500
Brad Bennink, prin. Fax 619-2597
Waynewood ES 700/K-6
1205 Waynewood Blvd 22308 703-704-7100
Katie Reynolds, prin. Fax 704-7197
Weyanoke ES 600/K-5
6520 Braddock Rd 22312 703-813-5400
Felicia Usher, prin. Fax 813-5497
Whitman MS 1,000/7-8
2500 Parkers Ln 22306 703-660-2400
Craig Herring, prin. Fax 660-2497
Woodlawn ES 800/K-6
8505 Highland Ln 22309 703-619-4800
Dawn Hendrick, prin. Fax 619-4897
Woodley Hills ES 700/K-6
8718 Old Mount Vernon Rd 22309 703-799-2000
Sharon Aldredge, prin. Fax 799-2097

Alexandria Country Day S 200/K-8
2400 Russell Rd 22301 703-548-4804
Scott Baytosh, hdmstr. Fax 549-9022
Aquinas Montessori S 100/PK-6
8334 Mount Vernon Hwy 22309 703-780-8484
Blessed Sacrament S 300/PK-8
1417 W Braddock Rd 22302 703-998-4170
Valerie Garcia, prin. Fax 998-5033
Browne Academy 300/PK-8
5917 Telegraph Rd 22310 703-960-3000
Peggy Otey, head sch Fax 777-5867
Burgundy Farm Country Day S 300/PK-8
3700 Burgundy Rd 22303 703-960-3431
Jeff Sindler, hdmstr. Fax 960-5056
Calvary Road Christian S 200/PK-6
6811 Beulah St 22310 703-971-8004
Kevin Lewis, admin. Fax 971-0130
Commonwealth Academy 100/3-12
1321 Leslie Ave 22301 703-548-6912
Peri-Anne Chobot Ed.D., head sch Fax 548-6914
Grace Episcopal S 100/PK-5
3601 Russell Rd 22305 703-549-5067
Patti Culbreth, head sch Fax 549-9545
Immanuel Lutheran S 100/PK-8
109 Bellaire Rd 22301 703-549-0155
Julia Habrecht, hdmstr.
Montessori S of Alexandria 100/PK-6
6300 Florence Ln 22310 703-960-3498
Potomac Crescent Waldorf S 100/PK-5
3846 King St 22302 703-486-1309

Queen of Apostles S 200/K-8
4409 Sano St 22312 703-354-0714
Kathryn Littlefield, prin. Fax 354-1820
St. Louis S 400/PK-8
2901 Popkins Ln 22306 703-768-7732
Kathleen McNutt, prin. Fax 768-3836
St. Mary S 700/PK-8
400 Green St 22314 703-549-1646
Janet Cantwell, prin. Fax 519-0840
St. Rita S 200/PK-8
3801 Russell Rd 22305 703-548-1888
Mary Schlickenmaier, prin. Fax 519-9389
St. Stephen's and St. Agnes S 1,100/PK-12
1000 Saint Stephens Rd 22304 703-751-2700
Kirsten Adams, head sch Fax 751-7142
Washington International Academy 200/PK-8
6408 Edsall Rd 22312 703-941-6977

Altavista, Campbell, Pop. 3,366
Campbell County SD
Supt. — See Rustburg
Altavista ES 600/K-5
2190 Lynch Mill Rd 24517 434-369-5665
Wendy Thomas, prin. Fax 369-2859

Alton, Halifax
Halifax County SD
Supt. — See Halifax
Cluster Springs ES 600/K-5
7091 Huell Matthews Hwy 24520 434-517-2600
Catherine Glass, prin. Fax 517-2610

Amelia Court House, Amelia, Pop. 1,087
Amelia County SD 1,800/PK-12
8701 Otterburn Rd Ste 101 23002 804-561-2621
Dr. Jack McKinley, supt. Fax 561-3057
www.amelia.k12.va.us
Amelia County ES 700/PK-4
8533 N Five Forks Rd 23002 804-561-2433
Cynthia Reasoner, prin. Fax 561-6524
Amelia County MS 500/5-8
8740 Otterburn Rd 23002 804-561-4422
Dr. Jan Medley, prin. Fax 561-6525

Amelia Academy 200/PK-12
PO Box 106 23002 804-561-2270

Amherst, Amherst, Pop. 2,173
Amherst County SD 4,300/PK-12
PO Box 1257 24521 434-946-9387
Dr. Steven Nichols, supt. Fax 946-9346
www.amherst.k12.va.us
Amherst ES 300/PK-5
156 Davis St 24521 434-946-9704
Julie Steele, prin. Fax 946-9706
Amherst MS 400/6-8
165 Gordons Fairgrounds Rd 24521 434-946-0691
Amy Snead, prin. Fax 946-0258
Central ES 300/PK-5
575 Union Hill Rd 24521 434-946-9700
Wanda Smith, prin. Fax 946-9702
Temperance ES 100/PK-5
1981 Lowesville Rd 24521 434-946-2811
Michael O'Brien, prin. Fax 277-5594
Other Schools – See Madison Heights

Annandale, Fairfax, Pop. 39,850
Fairfax County SD
Supt. — See Falls Church
Annandale Terrace ES 700/K-5
7604 Herald St 22003 703-658-5600
Lisa Pilson, prin. Fax 658-5697
Braddock ES 800/PK-5
7825 Heritage Dr 22003 703-914-7300
Keesha Jackson-Muir, prin. Fax 914-1185
Camelot ES 600/PK-6
8100 Guinevere Dr 22003 703-645-7000
Aileen Flaherty, prin. Fax 645-7097
Canterbury Woods ES 700/PK-6
4910 Willet Dr 22003 703-764-5600
Barbara Messinger, prin. Fax 764-5697
Columbia ES 500/K-5
6720 Alpine Dr 22003 703-916-2500
Michael Cunningham, prin. Fax 916-2597
Mason Crest ES 500/K-5
3705 Crest Dr 22003 571-226-2600
Tim Stanley, prin. Fax 226-2697
Poe MS 900/6-8
7000 Cindy Ln 22003 703-813-3800
Maria Eck, prin. Fax 813-3897

Holy Spirit S 400/PK-8
8800 Braddock Rd 22003 703-978-7117
Maureen Ashby, prin. Fax 978-7438
Montessori S of Northern Virginia 200/PK-6
6820 Pacific Ln 22003 703-256-9577
Betsy Mitchell, head sch Fax 256-9851
Pinecrest S 100/PK-6
7209 Quiet Cv 22003 703-354-3446
St. Ambrose S 200/PK-8
3827 Woodburn Rd 22003 703-698-7171
Angela Rowley, prin. Fax 698-7170
St. Michael S 200/PK-8
7401 Saint Michaels Ln 22003 703-256-1222
Daniel Cinalli, prin. Fax 256-3490
Westminster S 300/PK-8
3819 Gallows Rd 22003 703-256-3620
Ellis Glover, head sch

Appomattox, Appomattox, Pop. 1,694
Appomattox County SD 2,300/PK-12
PO Box 548 24522 434-352-8251
Dorinda Grasty Ed.D., supt. Fax 352-0883
va02205093.schoolwires.net
Appomattox ES 500/3-5
176 Kids Pl 24522 434-352-7463
Karen Cyrus, prin. Fax 352-8134
Appomattox MS 500/6-8
2020 Church St 24522 434-352-8257
Cheryl Servis, prin. Fax 352-5621
Appomattox PS 600/PK-2
185 Learning Ln 24522 434-352-5766
Allison Maxwell, prin. Fax 352-7476

Appomattox Christian Academy 50/PK-12
PO Box 517 24522 434-352-7373
Cornerstone Christian Academy 100/PK-12
PO Box 897 24522 434-352-2345
Dr. Geoffrey Hubler Ph.D., head sch Fax 352-2345

Ararat, Patrick
Patrick County SD
Supt. — See Stuart
Blue Ridge ES 300/PK-7
PO Box 30 24053 276-251-5271
Rozina Turner, prin. Fax 251-1354

Arlington, Arlington, Pop. 201,587
Arlington County SD 24,300/PK-12
1426 N Quincy St 22207 703-228-6000
Dr. Patrick Murphy, supt. Fax 228-6188
www.apsva.us
Abingdon ES 600/PK-5
3035 S Abingdon St 22206 703-228-6650
Joanne Uyeda, prin. Fax 931-1804
Arlington Science Focus ES 600/PK-5
1501 N Lincoln St 22201 703-228-7670
Mary Begley, prin. Fax 525-2452
Arlington Traditional ES 500/PK-5
855 N Edison St 22205 703-228-6290
Holly Hawthorne, prin. Fax 522-1482
Ashlawn ES 600/PK-5
5950 8th Rd N 22205 703-228-5270
Judy Apostolico-Buck, prin. Fax 534-3685
Barcroft ES 500/PK-5
625 S Wakefield St 22204 703-228-5838
Judy Apostolico-Buck, prin. Fax 271-0948
Barrett ES 500/PK-5
4401 N Henderson Rd 22203 703-228-6288
Dan Redding, prin. Fax 228-8544
Campbell ES 400/PK-5
737 S Carlin Springs Rd 22204 703-228-6770
Maureen Nesselrode, prin. Fax 671-0062
Carlin Springs ES 600/PK-5
5995 5th Rd S 22204 703-228-6645
Eileen Delaney, prin. Fax 998-5341
Claremont Immersion ES 700/PK-5
4700 S Chesterfield Rd 22206 703-228-2500
Jessica Panfil, prin. Fax 820-4264
Discovery ES, 5241 36th St N 22207 PK-5
Dr. Erin Russo, prin. 703-228-2685
Drew Model ES 600/PK-5
3500 23rd St S 22206 703-228-5825
Catharina Genove, prin. Fax 979-0892
Glebe ES 600/PK-5
1770 N Glebe Rd 22207 703-228-6280
Jamie Borg, prin. Fax 527-2040
Gunston MS 800/6-8
2700 S Lang St 22206 703-228-6900
Dr. Lori Wiggins, prin. Fax 519-9183
Henry ES 500/PK-5
701 S Highland St 22204 703-228-5820
Andrea Turner, prin. Fax 486-8971
Hoffman-Boston ES 400/PK-5
1415 S Queen St 22204 703-228-5845
Kimberley Graves, prin. Fax 892-4526
Jamestown ES 600/PK-5
3700 N Delaware St 22207 703-228-5275
Kenwyn Schaffner, prin. Fax 538-2612
Jefferson MS 900/6-8
125 S Old Glebe Rd 22204 703-228-5900
Keisha Boggan, prin. Fax 979-3744
Kenmore MS 900/6-8
200 S Carlin Springs Rd 22204 703-228-6800
David McBride, prin. Fax 998-3069
Key ES 700/PK-5
2300 Key Blvd 22201 703-228-4210
Dr. Marjorie Myers, prin. Fax 524-2236
Long Branch ES 500/PK-5
33 N Fillmore St 22201 703-228-4220
Felicia Russo, prin. Fax 875-2868
McKinley ES 500/PK-5
1030 N Mckinley Rd 22205 703-228-5280
Colin Brown, prin. Fax 538-4982
Nottingham ES 700/PK-5
5900 Little Falls Rd 22207 703-228-5290
Mary Beth Pelosky, prin. Fax 228-2300
Oakridge ES 700/PK-5
1414 24th St S 22202 703-228-5840
Dr. Lynne Wright, prin. Fax 271-0529
Randolph ES 400/PK-5
1306 S Quincy St 22204 703-228-5830
Dr. Donna Snyder, prin. Fax 521-2516
Swanson MS 1,100/6-8
5800 Washington Blvd 22205 703-228-5500
Bridget Loft, prin. Fax 536-2775
Taylor ES 700/PK-5
2600 N Stuart St 22207 703-228-6275
Harold Pellegreen, prin. Fax 228-2352
Tuckahoe ES 700/PK-5
6550 26th St N 22213 703-228-5288
Mitch Pascal, prin. Fax 237-1548
Williamsburg MS 1,100/6-8
3600 N Harrison St 22207 703-228-5450
Bryan Boykin, prin. Fax 536-2870

Our Savior Lutheran S 100/PK-8
825 S Taylor St 22204 703-892-4846
Joshua Klug, prin.
St. Agnes S 400/PK-8
2024 N Randolph St 22207 703-527-5423
Kristine Carr, prin. Fax 525-4689
St. Ann S 200/PK-8
980 N Frederick St 22205 703-525-7599
Mary Therrell, prin. Fax 525-2687
St. Charles ECC 200/PK-PK
3299 Fairfax Dr 22201 703-527-0608
Amy Fry, dir.
St. Thomas More S 400/PK-8
105 N Thomas St 22203 703-528-6781
Eleanor McCormack, prin. Fax 528-5048

Arrington, Nelson, Pop. 700
Nelson County SD
Supt. — See Lovingston
Tye River ES 500/PK-5
5198 Thomas Nelson Hwy 22922 434-263-8960
Marti Bradt, prin. Fax 263-8964

Ashburn, Loudoun, Pop. 41,992
Loudoun County SD 70,400/PK-12
21000 Education Ct 20148 571-252-1000
Dr. Eric Williams, supt. Fax 252-1003
www.lcps.org/
Ashburn ES 700/PK-5
44062 Fincastle Dr 20147 571-252-2350
Michelle Walthour, prin. Fax 223-2656
Belmont Station ES 800/PK-5
20235 Nightwatch St 20147 571-252-2240
Lori Mercer, prin. Fax 223-3805
Brambelton MS 6-8
23070 Learning Cir 20148 703-957-4450
Renee Dawson, prin. Fax 349-3260
Carter ES 900/K-5
43330 Loudoun Reserve Dr 20148 703-957-4490
Ann Hines, prin. Fax 661-8313
Cedar Lane ES 700/PK-5
43700 Tolamac Dr 20147 571-252-2120
Robert Marple, prin. Fax 771-6521
Creighton's Corner ES 800/K-5
23171 Minerva Dr 20148 703-957-4480
Christopher Knott, prin. Fax 327-4164
Discovery ES 700/PK-5
44020 Grace Bridge Dr 20147 571-252-2370
Christopher Painter, prin. Fax 858-7032
Dominion Trail ES 700/PK-5
44045 Bruceton Mills Cir 20147 571-252-2340
Jeff Joseph, prin. Fax 858-0978
Eagle Ridge MS 1,200/6-8
42901 Waxpool Rd 20148 571-252-2140
Scott Phillips, prin. Fax 779-8977
Farmwell Station MS 1,300/6-8
44281 Gloucester Pkwy 20147 571-252-2320
Sherryl Loya, prin. Fax 771-6495
Hillside ES 700/K-5
43000 Ellzey Dr 20148 571-252-2170
Chris Mills, prin. Fax 858-0504
Legacy ES 1,100/PK-5
22995 Minerva Dr 20148 703-957-4425
Matthew Dickersheid, prin. Fax 542-7193
Madison's Trust ES K-5
42380 Creighton Rd 20148 703-957-4470
David Stewart, prin. Fax 327-9196
Mill Run ES 900/K-5
42940 Ridgeway Dr 20148 571-252-2160
John Cornely, prin. Fax 779-8932
Moorefield Station ES 900/PK-5
22325 Mooreview Pkwy 20148 571-252-2380
Karen Roche, prin. Fax 729-6404
Newton-Lee ES 900/K-5
43335 Gloucester Pkwy 20147 571-252-1535
Shawn Lyons, prin. Fax 223-0793
Sanders Corner ES 600/PK-5
43100 Ashburn Farm Pkwy 20147 571-252-2250
Michael Jacques, prin. Fax 771-6614
Stone Hill MS 1,600/6-8
23415 Evergreen Ridge Dr 20148 703-957-4420
Kathryn Clark, prin. Fax 223-0585
Trailside MS 6-8
20325 Claiborne Pkwy 20147 571-252-2280
Bridget Beichler, prin. Fax 724-1086
Weller ES 800/K-5
20700 Marblehead Dr 20147 571-252-2360
Julia Burton, prin. Fax 223-2282
Other Schools – See Aldie, Centreville, Chantilly, Hamilton, Leesburg, Lovettsville, Middleburg, Purcellville, Round Hill, South Riding, Sterling, Waterford

---

Arris Montessori Academy 50/PK-3
44675 Cape Ct 20147 703-858-2800
Kathleen Opiola, dir. Fax 291-2598
County Christian S 400/PK-8
21673 Beaumeade Cir Ste 600 20147 703-729-5968
Marie Barker, prin. Fax 729-6635
Ha'penny Montessori S 100/PK-K
20854 Stubble Rd 20147 703-729-5755
Leport S - Broadlands 200/PK-6
42945 Waxpool Rd 20148 703-723-3364
Montessori Academy at Belmont Greene 100/PK-3
20300 Bowfonds St 20147 703-729-7200
St. Theresa S 500/K-8
21370 St Theresa Ln 20147 703-729-3577
Carol Krichbaum, prin. Fax 729-8068
Virginia Academy 600/PK-12
19790 Ashburn Rd 20147 571-209-5500
Michael Taylor, supt. Fax 209-5845

Ashland, Hanover, Pop. 7,029
Hanover County SD 17,800/K-12
200 Berkley St 23005 804-365-4500
Dr. Michael Gill, supt. Fax 365-4680
www.hcps.us
Clay ES 300/K-2
310 S James St 23005 804-365-8120
Teresa Keck, prin. Fax 365-8139
Elmont ES 400/K-5
12007 Cedar Ln 23005 804-365-8100
Pamela Harvey, prin. Fax 365-8111

Gandy ES 300/3-5
201 Archie Cannon Dr 23005 804-365-4640
Leigh Finch, prin. Fax 365-4659
Liberty MS 1,100/6-8
13496 Liberty School Rd 23005 804-365-8060
Donald Latham, prin. Fax 365-8061
Other Schools – See Beaverdam, Mechanicsville, Montpelier

Atkins, Smyth, Pop. 1,134
Smyth County SD
Supt. — See Marion
Atkins ES 200/PK-5
5903 Lee Hwy 24311 276-783-3366
Gary Roberts, prin. Fax 783-0901

Austinville, Wythe
Carroll County SD
Supt. — See Hillsville
Laurel ES 300/PK-5
26 Pleasantview Rd 24312 276-728-9247
Angela Beamer, prin. Fax 728-5742

Wythe County SD
Supt. — See Wytheville
Jackson Memorial ES 200/PK-5
4424 Fort Chiswell Rd 24312 276-699-0160
Tammy Watson, prin. Fax 699-9650

Axton, Henry
Henry County SD
Supt. — See Collinsville
Axton ES 400/PK-5
1500 Axton School Rd 24054 276-650-1193
Ben Boone, prin. Fax 650-1462

Carlisle S 500/PK-12
300 Carlisle Rd 24054 276-632-7288

Bassett, Henry, Pop. 1,078
Henry County SD
Supt. — See Collinsville
Campbell Court ES 400/PK-5
220 Campbell Ct 24055 276-629-5344
Shonna Pilson, prin. Fax 629-3849
Sanville ES 300/PK-5
19 Sanville School Rd 24055 276-629-5301
Elizabeth Motley, prin. Fax 629-4648

Bastian, Bland
Bland County SD 400/PK-12
361 Bears Trl 24314 276-688-3361
Scott Meade, supt. Fax 688-4659
www.bland.k12.va.us
Other Schools – See Bland

Bealeton, Fauquier, Pop. 4,295
Fauquier County SD
Supt. — See Warrenton
Cedar-Lee MS 600/6-8
11138 Marsh Rd 22712 540-422-7430
David Lee, prin. Fax 422-7449
Miller ES 500/PK-5
6248 Catlett Rd 22712 540-422-7590
Bruce McDaniel, prin. Fax 422-7609
Walter ES 400/PK-5
4529 Morrisville Rd 22712 540-422-7710
Alex O'Dell, prin. Fax 422-7729

Beaverdam, Hanover
Hanover County SD
Supt. — See Ashland
Beaverdam ES 400/K-5
15485 Beaverdam School Rd 23015 804-449-6373
Charles Joseph, prin. Fax 449-6510

Bedford, Bedford, Pop. 6,098
Bedford County SD 9,700/K-12
PO Box 748 24523 540-586-1045
Dr. Douglas Schuch, supt. Fax 586-7703
bedford.sharpschool.net
Bedford ES 400/2-5
806 Tiger Trl 24523 540-586-0275
Scott Graham, prin. Fax 586-7619
Bedford MS 600/6-8
503 Longwood Ave 24523 540-586-7735
Rhetta Watkins, prin. Fax 586-4957
Bedford PS 200/K-1
807 College St 24523 540-586-8339
Lisa Dellis, prin. Fax 586-7654
Other Schools – See Big Island, Forest, Goode, Goodview, Huddleston, Lynchburg, Moneta, Montvale

Bent Mountain, Roanoke

Bent Mountain Christian Academy 50/K-12
PO Box 66 24059 540-494-8356
Karen Scott, admin. Fax 929-9028

Berryville, Clarke, Pop. 4,082
Clarke County SD 2,300/PK-12
309 W Main St 22611 540-955-6100
Chuck Bishop, supt. Fax 955-6109
www.clarke.k12.va.us
Cooley ES 400/1-5
240 Westwood Rd 22611 540-955-6110
Molly Tinsman, prin. Fax 955-6111
Cooley PS 400/PK-K
34 Westwood Rd 22611 540-955-6120
Molly Tinsman, prin. Fax 955-6124
Johnson-Williams MS 400/6-8
200 Swan Ave 22611 540-955-6160
Evan Robb, prin. Fax 955-6169
Other Schools – See Boyce

Big Island, Bedford, Pop. 302
Bedford County SD
Supt. — See Bedford
Big Island ES 100/K-5
1114 Schooldays Rd 24526 434-299-5863
Andy Bliss, prin. Fax 299-6037

Big Stone Gap, Wise, Pop. 5,523
Wise County SD
Supt. — See Wise
Powell Valley MS 500/5-8
3137 2nd Ave E 24219 276-523-0195
Paul Clendenon, prin. Fax 523-4762
Powell Valley PS 700/PK-4
2945 2nd Ave E 24219 276-523-4900
Heather Sykes, prin. Fax 523-4901

King's Christian Academy 50/PK-5
PO Box 339 24219 276-523-0004
Allison Giles, head sch Fax 523-0294

Birchleaf, Dickenson
Dickenson County SD
Supt. — See Clintwood
Sandlick ES 400/PK-5
PO Box 188 24220 276-865-5361
Dennis Deel, prin. Fax 865-4448

Blacksburg, Montgomery, Pop. 41,455
Montgomery County SD
Supt. — See Christiansburg
Beeks ES 400/PK-5
709 Airport Rd 24060 540-951-5700
Micah Mefford, prin. Fax 951-5703
Blacksburg MS 800/6-8
3109 Prices Fork Rd 24060 540-951-5800
Amanda Weidner, prin. Fax 951-5808
Harding Avenue ES 300/K-5
429 Harding Ave 24060 540-951-5732
Stephanie Sedor, prin. Fax 951-5729
Kipps ES 400/K-5
2801 Prices Fork Rd 24060 540-951-5760
Carey Stewart, prin. Fax 951-5764
Linkous ES 400/PK-5
813 Toms Creek Rd 24060 540-951-5726
Carol Slonka, prin. Fax 951-5725
Prices Fork ES 400/PK-5
4021 Prices Fork Rd 24060 540-951-5834
Kelly Roark, prin. Fax 951-5840

Dayspring Christian Academy 300/K-12
PO Box 909 24063 540-552-7777
William Hampton, admin. Fax 552-7778
St. John Neumann Academy 100/PK-8
2470 Research Center Dr 24060 540-552-7562
Julia Wharton, dir. Fax 951-5540

Blackstone, Nottoway, Pop. 3,575
Nottoway County SD
Supt. — See Nottoway
Blackstone PS 500/PK-4
615 East St 23824 434-292-5300
Dr. Carrie Gravely, prin. Fax 292-4802

Kenston Forest S 300/PK-12
75 Ridge Rd 23824 434-292-7218

Blairs, Pittsylvania, Pop. 903
Pittsylvania County SD
Supt. — See Chatham
Southside ES 500/K-5
440 E Witt Rd 24527 434-836-0006
Leslie Hackworth, prin. Fax 836-3615

Bland, Bland, Pop. 406
Bland County SD
Supt. — See Bastian
Bland County ES 200/PK-6
31 Rocket Dr 24315 276-688-3621
Laura Radford, prin. Fax 688-3403

Bluefield, Tazewell, Pop. 5,359
Tazewell County SD
Supt. — See Tazewell
Abbs Valley-Boissevain ES 200/PK-5
7030 Abbs Valley Rd 24605 276-945-5969
Chad Brown, prin. Fax 945-2395
Dudley PS 300/PK-2
1840 Tazewell Ave 24605 276-326-1507
Susan Maupin, prin. Fax 322-1197
Graham IS 300/3-5
808 Greever Ave 24605 276-326-3737
Todd Baker, prin. Fax 326-1440
Graham MS 400/6-8
1 Academic Cir 24605 276-326-1101
Lee Salyers, prin. Fax 322-1409

Blue Ridge, Botetourt, Pop. 3,056
Botetourt County SD
Supt. — See Fincastle
Colonial ES 400/PK-5
2941 Webster Rd 24064 540-977-6773
Tammy Riggs, prin. Fax 977-4219

Bon Air, Chesterfield, Pop. 16,027
Chesterfield County SD
Supt. — See Chesterfield
Bon Air ES 600/PK-5
8701 Polk St 23235 804-560-2700
Elizabeth Lowe, prin. Fax 560-0309

Boones Mill, Franklin, Pop. 235
Franklin County SD
Supt. — See Rocky Mount
Boones Mill ES 300/PK-5
265 Taylors Rd 24065 540-334-4000
Amy Shaver, prin. Fax 334-4001

Bowling Green, Caroline, Pop. 1,090
Caroline County SD 4,400/PK-12
16261 Richmond Tpke 22427 804-633-5088
Dr. George Parker, supt. Fax 633-5563
www.ccps.us
Other Schools – See Milford, Ruther Glen

Boyce, Clarke, Pop. 566
Clarke County SD
Supt. — See Berryville
Boyce ES 300/K-5
119 W Main St 22620 540-955-6115
Pam Egbert, prin. Fax 955-6119

Powhatan S 200/PK-8
49 Powhatan Ln 22620 540-837-1009
Susan Scarborough, head sch Fax 837-5061

Boydton, Mecklenburg, Pop. 430
Mecklenburg County SD 4,600/PK-12
PO Box 190 23917 434-738-6111
Paul Nichols, supt. Fax 738-6679
mcpsweb.org
Other Schools – See Chase City, Clarksville, La Crosse, Skipwith, South Hill

Bridgewater, Rockingham, Pop. 5,553
Rockingham County SD
Supt. — See Harrisonburg
Wayland ES 600/PK-5
801 N Main St 22812 540-828-6081
Karen Ridder, prin. Fax 828-4439

Blue Ridge Christian S 200/PK-12
PO Box 207 22812 540-828-2233
Karen Shomo, head sch Fax 828-4372

Bristol, Bristol, Pop. 17,490
Bristol CSD 2,300/PK-12
220 Lee St 24201 276-821-5600
Dr. Keith Perrigan, supt. Fax 821-5601
www.bvps.org
Highland View ES 200/PK-5
1405 Eads Ave 24201 276-821-5710
Pam Smith, prin. Fax 821-5711
Jackson ES 300/PK-5
2045 Euclid Ave 24201 276-821-5740
Dr. Linda Brittle, prin. Fax 821-5741
Van Pelt ES 400/PK-5
200 Spring Hill Ter 24201 276-821-5770
Jared Rader, prin. Fax 821-5771
Virginia MS 500/6-8
501 Piedmont Ave 24201 276-821-5660
Jason Mallock, prin. Fax 821-5661
Washington Lee ES 200/PK-5
900 Washington Lee Dr 24201 276-821-5800
Faith Mabe, prin. Fax 821-5801

Washington County SD
Supt. — See Abingdon
High Point ES 600/PK-5
14091 Sinking Creek Rd 24202 276-642-5600
Dr. Sherry King, prin. Fax 645-2360
Valley Institute ES 300/PK-5
4350 Gate City Hwy 24202 276-642-5500
Cynthia Jackson, prin. Fax 645-2394
Wallace MS 500/6-8
13077 Wallace Pike 24202 276-642-5400
David Lambert, prin. Fax 645-2365

St. Anne Catholic S 200/PK-8
300 Euclid Ave 24201 276-669-0048
Billie Schneider, prin. Fax 669-3523
Sullins Academy 200/PK-8
22218 Sullins Academy Dr 24202 276-669-4101

Bristow, Prince William
Prince William County SD
Supt. — See Manassas
Bristow Run ES 700/K-5
8990 Worthington Dr 20136 703-753-7741
Rhonda Jeck, prin. Fax 753-7604
Cedar Point ES 700/K-5
12601 Braemar Pkwy 20136 703-365-0963
Mark Marinoble, prin. Fax 365-0954
Marsteller MS 1,500/6-8
14000 Sudley Manor Dr 20136 703-393-7608
Roberta Knetter, prin. Fax 530-6327
Piney Branch ES 700/K-5
8301 Linton Hall Rd 20136 571-261-5300
Damon Cerrone, prin. Fax 261-5305
Victory ES 900/K-5
12001 Tygart Lake Dr 20136 703-257-0356
Christopher Wray, prin. Fax 257-1682
Yung ES K-5
12612 Fog Light Way 20136 571-598-3500
Kathy Notyce, prin. Fax 367-9064

Bristow Montessori S 100/PK-K
9050 Devlin Rd 20136 703-468-1191
Linton Hall S 200/PK-8
9535 Linton Hall Rd 20136 703-368-3157
Elizabeth Poole, prin. Fax 368-3036

Broadway, Rockingham, Pop. 3,640
Rockingham County SD
Supt. — See Harrisonburg
Hillyard MS 800/6-8
226 Hawks Hill Dr 22815 540-896-8961
Dave Baker, prin. Fax 896-6641
Myers ES 500/PK-5
290 Raider Rd 22815 540-896-2297
Rebecca Roadcap, prin. Fax 896-1576

Brookneal, Campbell, Pop. 1,102
Campbell County SD
Supt. — See Rustburg
Brookneal ES 400/PK-5
PO Box 900 24528 434-376-2042
Keith Bennett, prin. Fax 376-2371

Buchanan, Botetourt, Pop. 1,142
Botetourt County SD
Supt. — See Fincastle

Buchanan ES 300/PK-5
255 Schoolhouse Rd 24066 540-254-2084
Debbie Garrett, prin. Fax 254-1473

Buckingham, Buckingham, Pop. 370
Buckingham County SD 2,200/PK-12
15595 W James Anderson Hwy 23921 434-969-6100
Dr. Cecil Snead, supt. Fax 969-1176
www.bcpschools.org
Buckingham County MS 400/6-8
1184 High School Rd 23921 434-969-1044
Zane Harshman, prin. Fax 969-4290
Buckingham Preschool 100/PK-PK
77 Buckingham Preschool Rd 23921 434-969-4490
Fax 969-1004

Other Schools – See Dillwyn

Buena Vista, Buena Vista, Pop. 6,530
Buena Vista CSD 1,000/K-12
2329 Chestnut Ave Ste A 24416 540-261-2129
Dr. John Keeler, supt. Fax 261-2967
www.bvcps.net
Enderly Heights ES 200/3-5
101 Woodland Ave 24416 540-261-6151
Troy Clark, prin. Fax 261-7009
Kling ES 200/K-2
3400 Lombardy Ave 24416 540-261-6717
Lisa Clark, prin. Fax 261-1389
McCluer MS 200/6-7
2329 Chestnut Ave 24416 540-261-7340
Debbie Gilbert, prin. Fax 261-3292

Rockbridge County SD
Supt. — See Lexington
Mountain View ES 100/PK-5
20 Burger Cir 24416 540-261-2418
Lori Teague, prin. Fax 261-8082

Bumpass, Louisa

Piedmont Christian S 100/PK-12
2382 Bethany Church Rd 23024 540-872-3543
Andy Fahey, admin. Fax 872-3873

Burke, Fairfax, Pop. 39,726
Fairfax County SD
Supt. — See Falls Church
Cherry Run ES 500/PK-6
9732 Ironmaster Dr 22015 703-923-2800
Mark Bibbee, prin. Fax 923-2897
Terra Centre ES 600/PK-6
6000 Burke Centre Pkwy 22015 703-249-1400
Rebecca Gidoni, prin. Fax 249-1497
White Oaks ES 800/K-6
6130 Shiplett Blvd 22015 703-923-1400
Ryan Richardson, prin. Fax 923-1497

Nativity S 300/PK-8
6398 Nativity Ln 22015 703-455-2300
Maria Kelly, prin. Fax 569-8109

Callaway, Franklin
Franklin County SD
Supt. — See Rocky Mount
Callaway ES 200/PK-5
8451 Callaway Rd 24067 540-483-0364
Pam Brown, prin. Fax 483-0523

Cana, Carroll, Pop. 1,240
Carroll County SD
Supt. — See Hillsville
St. Paul S 300/PK-7
231 Flower Gap Rd 24317 276-755-3512
Leonard Davidson, prin. Fax 755-3211

Cape Charles, Northampton, Pop. 1,004
Northampton County SD
Supt. — See Machipongo
Kiptopeke ES 500/PK-6
24023 Fairview Rd 23310 757-678-5151
Subrina Parker, prin. Fax 331-3219

Capron, Southampton, Pop. 165
Southhampton County SD
Supt. — See Courtland
Capron ES 200/PK-5
18414 Southampton Pkwy 23829 434-658-4348
Allison Francis, prin. Fax 658-4118

Carrollton, Isle of Wight, Pop. 4,460
Isle of Wight County SD
Supt. — See Smithfield
Carrollton ES 600/PK-3
14440 New Town Haven Ln 23314 757-357-8850
Robert Brennan, prin. Fax 238-2536

Carrsville, Isle of Wight, Pop. 358
Isle of Wight County SD
Supt. — See Smithfield
Carrsville ES 200/K-5
5355 Carrsville Hwy 23315 757-357-8844
Clint Walters, prin. Fax 562-2607

Castlewood, Russell, Pop. 2,028
Russell County SD
Supt. — See Lebanon
Castlewood ES 500/1-7
242 Blue Devil Cir 24224 276-762-2315
Paula Banner, prin. Fax 762-9261
Copper Creek S 100/PK-K
23894 US Highway 58 24224 276-794-9306
Paula Banner, prin. Fax 794-7934

Learning Center 100/PK-11
PO Box 133 24224 276-762-5700
James Nunley, admin. Fax 762-7116

Catlett, Fauquier, Pop. 294
Fauquier County SD
Supt. — See Warrenton

Pearson ES 400/PK-5
9347 Bastable Mill Rd 20119 540-422-7610
Wendy Wilcox, prin. Fax 422-7629

Cedar Bluff, Tazewell, Pop. 1,127
Tazewell County SD
Supt. — See Tazewell
Cedar Bluff ES 400/K-5
1089 Cedar Valley Dr 24609 276-963-5765
Charity McDaniel, prin. Fax 963-4253

Centreville, Fairfax, Pop. 68,513
Fairfax County SD
Supt. — See Falls Church
Bull Run ES 900/K-6
15301 Lee Hwy 20121 703-227-1400
Jason Pensler, prin. Fax 227-1497
Centre Ridge ES 800/K-6
14400 New Braddock Rd 20121 703-227-2600
Margo Dias-Pareja, prin. Fax 227-2697
Centreville ES 900/K-6
14330 Green Trails Blvd 20121 703-502-3500
Joshua Douds, prin. Fax 502-3597
Cub Run ES 600/PK-6
5301 Sully Station Dr 20120 703-633-7500
Jennifer Coakley, prin. Fax 633-7597
Deer Park ES 700/PK-6
15109 Carlbern Dr 20120 703-802-5000
Carol Larsen, prin. Fax 802-5097
London Towne ES 900/K-6
6100 Stone Rd 20120 703-227-5400
Wiatta Padmore, prin. Fax 227-5497
Powell ES 1,000/K-6
13340 Leland Rd 20120 571-522-6000
Jamie Luerssen, prin. Fax 522-6097
Stone MS 800/7-8
5500 Sully Park Dr 20120 703-631-5500
Amielia Mitchell, prin. Fax 631-5598
Virginia Run ES 800/K-6
15450 Martins Hundred Dr 20120 703-988-8900
Laraine Edwards, prin. Fax 988-8997

Loudoun County SD
Supt. — See Ashburn
Cardinal Ridge ES PK-5
26155 Bull Run Post Office 20120 571-367-4020
Dr. Ricardy Anderson, prin. Fax 327-6302

Ad Fontes Academy 200/K-12
PO Box 916 20122 703-673-1145

Chantilly, Fairfax, Pop. 22,194
Fairfax County SD
Supt. — See Falls Church
Brookfield ES 800/K-6
4200 Lees Corner Rd 20151 703-814-8700
Mary Miller, prin. Fax 803-7695
Franklin MS 900/7-8
3300 Lees Corner Rd 20151 703-904-5100
Sharon Eisenberg, prin. Fax 904-5197
Poplar Tree ES 600/K-6
13440 Melville Ln 20151 703-633-7400
Susan Andujar, prin. Fax 633-7497
Rocky Run MS 1,100/7-8
4400 Stringfellow Rd 20151 703-802-7700
Amy Goodloe, prin. Fax 802-7797

Loudoun County SD
Supt. — See Ashburn
Lunsford MS 1,400/6-8
26020 Ticonderoga Rd 20152 703-722-2660
Carrie Simms, prin. Fax 327-2420

Auburn S 50/K-12
3800 Concorde Pkwy Ste 500 20151 703-793-9353
Joshua Metz, head sch Fax 793-9355
Chesterbrook Academy Kids Campus 100/PK-K
3753 Centerview Dr 20151 703-397-0555
Chelsie Magone, prin.
Leport S - Chantilly 200/PK-6
4550 Walney Rd 20151 571-321-0364
Montessori S of Fairfax 100/PK-6
3411 Lees Corner Rd 20151 703-323-0222
St. Timothy S 600/PK-8
13809 Poplar Tree Rd 20151 703-378-9408
Joseph McLaughlin, prin. Fax 378-1273
St. Veronica S 300/PK-8
3460 Centreville Rd 20151 703-773-2020
Elizabeth Goldman, prin. Fax 991-9103

Charles City, Charles City, Pop. 131
Charles City County SD 600/PK-12
10910 Courthouse Rd 23030 804-652-4612
Dr. David Gaston, supt. Fax 829-6723
www.ccps.net
Charles City ES 300/PK-6
10049 Courthouse Rd 23030 804-829-2512
Edward Van Dyke, prin. Fax 829-9256

Charlotte Court House, Charlotte, Pop. 538
Charlotte County SD 1,900/PK-12
PO Box 790 23923 434-542-5151
Dr. Nancy Leonard, supt. Fax 542-4261
www.ccpsk12.org
Central MS 400/6-8
PO Box 748 23923 434-542-4536
Michael Haskins, prin. Fax 542-4630
Other Schools – See Keysville, Phenix, Saxe

Charlottesville, Charlottesville, Pop. 42,217
Albemarle County SD 13,500/PK-12
401 McIntire Rd 22902 434-296-5826
Dr. Pamela Moran, supt. Fax 296-5869
www.k12albemarle.org/
Agnor-Hurt ES 500/PK-5
3201 Berkmar Dr 22901 434-973-5211
Doug Granger, prin. Fax 974-7046

Baker-Butler ES 600/PK-5
2740 Proffit Rd 22911 434-974-7777
Dr. Stephen Saunders, prin. Fax 964-4684
Burley MS 600/6-8
901 Rose Hill Dr 22903 434-295-5101
James Asher, prin. Fax 984-4975
Cale ES 600/PK-5
1757 Avon Street Ext 22902 434-293-7455
Lisa Jones, prin. Fax 293-2067
Greer ES 600/PK-5
190 Lambs Ln 22901 434-973-8371
Robyn Bolling, prin. Fax 973-0629
Hollymead ES 500/PK-5
2775 Powell Creek Dr 22911 434-973-8301
Nancy Teel, prin. Fax 978-3687
Jouett MS 600/6-8
210 Lambs Ln 22901 434-975-9320
Kathryn Baylor, prin. Fax 975-9325
Lewis ES 400/PK-5
1610 Owensville Rd 22901 434-293-9304
Dr. Michael Irani, prin. Fax 979-3850
Murray ES 300/PK-5
3251 Morgantown Rd 22903 434-977-4599
Mark Green, prin. Fax 979-5416
Stone-Robinson ES 400/PK-5
958 N Milton Rd 22911 434-296-3754
Kristen Williams, prin. Fax 296-7645
Sutherland MS 600/6-8
2801 Powell Creek Dr 22911 434-975-0599
Brandi Robertson, prin. Fax 975-0852
Walton MS 400/6-8
4217 Red Hill Rd 22903 434-977-5615
Josh Walton, prin. Fax 296-6648
Woodbrook ES 400/PK-5
100 Woodbrook Dr 22901 434-973-6600
Lisa Molinaro, prin. Fax 973-0317
Other Schools – See Crozet, Earlysville, Keswick, North Garden, Scottsville

Charlottesville CSD 4,300/PK-12
1562 Dairy Rd 22903 434-245-2400
Dr. Rosa Atkins, supt. Fax 245-2603
charlottesvilleschools.org
Buford MS 500/7-8
1000 Cherry Ave 22903 434-245-2411
Eric Johnson, prin. Fax 245-2611
Burnley-Moran ES 400/PK-4
1300 Long St 22901 434-245-2413
Dr. Dawn LoCasale, prin. Fax 245-2613
Clark ES 300/PK-4
1000 Belmont Ave 22902 434-245-2414
Deanna Isley, prin. Fax 245-2614
Greenbrier ES 400/PK-4
2228 Greenbrier Dr 22901 434-245-2415
Pat Cuomo, prin. Fax 245-2615
Jackson-Via ES 300/PK-4
508 Harris Rd 22903 434-245-2416
Dr. Justin Malone, prin. Fax 245-2616
Johnson ES 300/PK-4
1645 Cherry Ave 22903 434-245-2417
Summerlyn Thompson, prin. Fax 245-2617
Venable ES 300/PK-4
406 14th St NW 22903 434-245-2418
Erin Kershner, prin. Fax 245-2618
Walker Upper ES 500/5-6
1564 Dairy Rd 22903 434-245-2412
Linda Humphries, prin. Fax 245-2612

Charlottesville Catholic S 300/PK-8
1205 Pen Park Rd 22901 434-964-0400
Michael Riley, prin. Fax 964-1373
Charlottesville Waldorf S 200/PK-8
120 Waldorf School Rd 22901 434-973-4946
Covenant S 500/K-12
175 Hickory St 22902 434-220-7329
Mountaintop Montessori S 200/PK-8
440 Pinnacle Pl 22911 434-979-8886
Peabody S 100/PK-8
1232 Stoney Ridge Rd 22902 434-296-6901
Robert Orlando, head sch Fax 296-5751
Regents S of Charlottesville 100/K-10
200 Bob Finley Way 22903 434-293-0633
St. Anne's-Belfield S 900/PK-12
2132 Ivy Rd 22903 434-296-5106
David Lourie, hdmstr. Fax 979-1486

Chase City, Mecklenburg, Pop. 2,295
Mecklenburg County SD
Supt. — See Boydton
Chase City ES 400/PK-5
5450 Highway Forty Seven 23924 434-372-4770
Fred Taylor, prin. Fax 372-5294

Chatham, Pittsylvania, Pop. 1,254
Pittsylvania County SD 9,200/PK-12
PO Box 232 24531 434-432-2761
Dr. Mark R. Jones, supt. Fax 432-9560
www.pcs.k12.va.us
Chatham ES 300/K-5
245 Chatham Elementary Ln 24531 434-432-5441
Wanda Carter, prin. Fax 432-2227
Chatham MS 500/6-8
11650 US Highway 29 24531 434-432-2169
Julia Woodward, prin. Fax 432-2842
Union Hall ES 300/PK-5
100 Union Hall Elem Cir 24531 434-724-7010
Amy Emond, prin. Fax 724-1850
Other Schools – See Blairs, Danville, Dry Fork, Gretna, Hurt, Ringgold

Check, Floyd
Floyd County SD
Supt. — See Floyd
Check ES 300/PK-7
6810 Floyd Hwy N 24072 540-745-9410
Steven Lin, prin. Fax 745-9491

Chesapeake, Chesapeake, Pop. 216,170
Chesapeake CSD 39,000/PK-12
PO Box 16496 23328 757-547-0153
Dr. James Roberts, supt. Fax 547-0196
cpschools.com
Butts Road IS 800/3-5
1571 Mount Pleasant Rd 23322 757-482-4566
Nancy Cruz, prin. Fax 482-4066
Butts Road PS 500/PK-2
1000 Mount Pleasant Rd 23322 757-482-5820
Brenda Hobbs, prin. Fax 482-5095
Camelot ES 600/K-5
2901 Guenevere Dr 23323 757-558-5347
Robert Sander, prin. Fax 558-5351
Carver IS 500/3-5
2601 Broad St 23324 757-494-7505
Michelle Ferebee, prin. Fax 494-7685
Cedar Road ES 800/K-5
1605 Cedar Rd 23322 757-547-0166
Tracy Cioppa, prin. Fax 547-0538
Chittum ES 700/K-5
2008 Dock Landing Rd 23321 757-465-6300
Sharon Miles, prin. Fax 465-6304
Crestwood IS 800/3-5
1240 Great Bridge Blvd 23320 757-494-7565
Renee Davis, prin. Fax 494-7598
Crestwood MS 600/6-8
1420 Great Bridge Blvd 23320 757-494-7560
Michael Ward, prin. Fax 494-7599
Deep Creek Central ES 600/K-5
2448 Shipyard Rd 23323 757-558-5356
Barbara Fortner, prin. Fax 558-5358
Deep Creek ES 700/K-5
2809 Forehand Dr 23323 757-558-5333
Dr. Barry Brown, prin. Fax 558-5337
Deep Creek MS 500/6-8
1955 Deal Dr 23323 757-558-5321
Brian Haughinberry, prin. Fax 558-5320
Georgetown PS 700/K-3
436 Providence Rd 23325 757-578-7060
Terry Reitz, prin. Fax 578-7064
Grassfield ES 900/K-5
2248 Averill Dr 23323 757-558-8923
Kimberly Pinello, prin. Fax 558-4486
Great Bridge IS 600/3-5
253 Hanbury Rd W 23322 757-482-4405
Heather Martin, prin. Fax 482-4027
Great Bridge MS 1,300/6-8
441 Battlefield Blvd S 23322 757-482-5128
Craig Mills, prin. Fax 482-0210
Great Bridge PS 500/K-2
408 Cedar Rd 23322 757-547-1135
Theresa Myers, prin. Fax 547-1820
Greenbrier IS 600/3-5
1701 River Birch Run N 23320 757-578-7080
Keith Hyater, prin. Fax 578-7084
Greenbrier MS 900/6-8
1016 Greenbrier Pkwy 23320 757-548-5309
Dr. Michael Mustain, prin. Fax 548-8921
Greenbrier PS 700/K-2
1551 Eden Way S 23320 757-436-3428
Joan Raybourn, prin. Fax 436-0208
Hickory ES 400/K-5
109 Benefit Rd 23322 757-421-7080
James Lewter, prin. Fax 421-7096
Hickory MS 1,500/6-8
1997 Hawk Blvd 23322 757-421-0468
Dr. Deborah Hutchens, prin. Fax 421-0475
Indian River MS 800/6-8
2300 Old Greenbrier Rd 23325 757-578-7030
Terre Werts, prin. Fax 578-7036
Jolliff MS 800/6-8
1021 Jolliff Rd 23321 757-465-5246
Quentin Hicks, prin. Fax 465-1646
Marshall ES 500/K-5
2706 Border Rd 23324 757-494-7515
Karen Lopez, prin. Fax 494-7651
Norfolk Highlands PS 400/K-3
1115 Myrtle Ave 23325 757-578-7092
Shawnia Smiley, prin. Fax 578-7096
Owens MS 1,100/6-8
1997 Horseback Run 23323 757-558-5382
Alaina Britt, prin. Fax 558-5386
Portlock PS 600/K-2
1857 Varsity Dr 23324 757-494-7555
Regina Ratcliff, prin. Fax 494-7650
Smith MS 1,000/6-8
2500 Rodgers St 23324 757-494-7590
Kinyatta Garrett, prin. Fax 494-7680
Southeastern ES 700/K-5
1853 Battlefield Blvd S 23322 757-421-7676
Donna Weingand, prin. Fax 421-7053
Southwestern ES 500/K-5
4410 Airline Blvd 23321 757-465-6310
Sonya Beasley, prin. Fax 465-6314
Sparrow Road IS 500/4-5
1605 Sparrow Rd 23325 757-578-7050
Sharon Popson, prin. Fax 578-7054
Treakle ES 500/K-5
2500 Gilmerton Rd 23323 757-558-5361
Sheila Johnson, prin. Fax 558-5365
Truitt IS 300/3-5
1100 Holly Ave 23324 757-494-8014
Kimberly Lowden, prin. Fax 494-8083
Western Branch IS 700/3-5
4013 Terry Dr 23321 757-638-7941
Jataune Jones, prin. Fax 638-7945
Western Branch MS 900/6-8
4201 Hawksley Dr 23321 757-638-7920
Kambar Khoshaba, prin. Fax 638-7926
Western Branch PS 600/K-2
4122 Terry Dr 23321 757-638-7951
Gayle Bartlett, prin. Fax 638-7954
Williams PS 800/K-2
1100 Battlefield Blvd N 23320 757-547-0238
Thomas Moyer, prin. Fax 547-3475
Wright PS 300/K-2
600 Park Ave 23324 757-494-7585
Micheal Ottley, prin. Fax 494-7681

Cathedral of Faith Christian S 50/PK-2
2020 Portlock Rd 23324 757-545-8050
Andre Small, prin. Fax 545-0953
Cedar Road Christian Academy 100/PK-4
916 Cedar Rd 23322 757-547-9553
Chesapeake Montessori S 200/PK-6
2013 Scenic Pkwy 23323 757-547-7673
Faith Diamond Christian Academy 100/PK-5
1023 Deep Creek Blvd 23323 757-487-1800
Debra Cromwell, dir. Fax 487-6311
Greenbrier Christian Academy 600/PK-12
311 Kempsville Rd 23320 757-547-9595
Dr. Ron White, supt. Fax 547-9569
Hickory Ridge Academy 50/PK-8
3320 Battlefield Blvd S 23322 757-421-7500
Sherry Corbitt M.Ed., head sch Fax 204-4375
Mt. Pleasant Christian S 100/PK-8
1613 Mount Pleasant Rd 23322 757-482-9557
Wendy Walker, prin. Fax 482-3447
StoneBridge S 300/PK-12
PO Box 9247 23321 757-488-2214
Kathy Rader, head sch Fax 465-7637
Tidewater Adventist Academy 50/PK-8
1136 Centerville Tpke N 23320 757-479-0002
Veritas Christian Academy 100/PK-12
1208 Centerville Tpke N 23320 757-410-5095

Chester, Chesterfield, Pop. 20,491
Chesterfield County SD
Supt. — See Chesterfield
Carver MS 1,100/6-8
3800 Cougar Trl 23831 804-524-3620
Jason Trueblood, prin. Fax 520-0189
Curtis ES 700/PK-5
3600 W Hundred Rd 23831 804-768-6175
Susan Pereira, prin. Fax 768-9008
Davis MS 1,200/6-8
601 Corvus Ct 23836 804-541-4700
Edward Maynes, prin. Fax 530-2717
Ecoff ES 700/PK-5
5200 Ecoff Ave 23831 804-768-6185
Dr. Joshua Cole, prin. Fax 778-7247
Harrowgate ES 500/PK-5
15501 Harrowgate Rd 23831 804-520-6015
Christina Serola, prin. Fax 520-6021
Scott ES 900/PK-5
813 Beginners Trail Loop 23836 804-541-4660
Julie Buntich, prin. Fax 541-4679
Wells ES 700/PK-5
13101 S Chester Rd 23831 804-768-6265
Fredrick Geissler, prin. Fax 768-0356

Life Christian Academy 100/PK-12
16801 Harrowgate Rd 23831 804-526-5941

Chesterfield, Chesterfield
Chesterfield County SD 59,200/PK-12
PO Box 10 23832 804-748-1405
Dr. James Lane, supt. Fax 796-7178
mychesterfieldschools.com
Chalkley ES 900/K-5
3301 Turner Rd 23832 804-674-1300
Nicole Boone, prin. Fax 675-1478
Gates ES 700/PK-5
10001 Courthouse Rd 23832 804-768-6195
Nina Brink, prin. Fax 768-0697
Jacobs Road ES 700/PK-5
8800 Jacobs Rd 23832 804-674-1320
Eileen Traveline, prin. Fax 276-9045
Winterpock ES 800/K-5
9000 Elementary Way Loop 23832 804-763-5051
Karen Dubiel, prin. Fax 763-5056
Other Schools – See Bon Air, Chester, Ettrick, Matoaca, Midlothian, Moseley, N Chesterfield, Richmond, S Chesterfield

---

Guardian Christian Academy 300/PK-12
6851 Courthouse Rd 23832 804-715-3210
Glenda Paul, dir. Fax 715-3237
Richmond Christian S 300/K-12
6511 Belmont Rd 23832 804-276-3193
Cliff Williams, head sch Fax 276-9106

Chilhowie, Smyth, Pop. 1,774
Smyth County SD
Supt. — See Marion
Chilhowie ES 600/PK-5
PO Box 348 24319 276-646-8220
Jason Kilbourne, prin. Fax 646-2848
Chilhowie MS 300/6-8
PO Box 5018 24319 276-646-3942
Sam Blevins, prin. Fax 646-0210

Chincoteague, Accomack, Pop. 2,859
Accomack County SD
Supt. — See Accomac
Chincoteague ES 200/PK-5
6078 Hallie Whealton Smith 23336 757-336-5545
Jessie Duncil, prin. Fax 336-5586

Christiansburg, Montgomery, Pop. 20,645
Montgomery County SD 9,700/PK-12
750 Imperial St 24073 540-382-5100
Mark Miear Ed.D., supt. Fax 381-6127
www.mcps.org
Christiansburg ES 400/3-5
160 Wades Ln 24073 540-382-5172
Malinda Morgan, prin. Fax 381-6143
Christiansburg MS 800/6-8
1205 Buffalo Dr 24073 540-394-2180
Jason Garretson, prin. Fax 394-2197
Christiansburg PS 500/PK-2
240 Betty Dr 24073 540-382-5175
Oliver Lewis, prin. Fax 381-6162
Falling Branch ES 500/PK-5
735 Falling Branch Rd 24073 540-381-6145
Julie Vanidestine, prin. Fax 381-6148
Other Schools – See Blacksburg, Elliston, Radford, Riner, Shawsville

Church Road, Dinwiddie
Dinwiddie County SD
Supt. — See Dinwiddie
Midway ES 400/K-5
5511 Midway Rd 23833 804-265-4205
Penny Brooks, prin. Fax 265-4209

Churchville, Augusta, Pop. 190
Augusta County SD
Supt. — See Verona
Churchville ES 300/K-5
3710 Churchville Ave 24421 540-337-6036
Laura Hodges, prin. Fax 337-8803

Clarksville, Mecklenburg, Pop. 1,125
Mecklenburg County SD
Supt. — See Boydton
Clarksville ES 500/PK-5
1696 Noblin Farm Rd 23927 434-374-8668
Ann Dalton, prin. Fax 374-8157

Clear Brook, Frederick
Frederick County SD
Supt. — See Winchester
Stonewall ES 500/K-5
3165 Martinsburg Pike 22624 540-662-2289
Darren Thomas, prin. Fax 723-8903

Clifton, Fairfax, Pop. 280
Fairfax County SD
Supt. — See Falls Church
Liberty MS 1,100/7-8
6801 Union Mill Rd 20124 703-988-8100
Catherine Cipperly, prin. Fax 988-8197
Union Mill ES 1,000/K-6
13611 Springstone Dr 20124 703-322-8500
Kathleen Case, prin. Fax 322-8597

St. Andrew the Apostle S 200/PK-8
6720 Union Mill Rd 20124 703-817-1774
Mary Baldwin, prin. Fax 817-1721

Clifton Forge, Alleghany, Pop. 3,785
Alleghany County SD
Supt. — See Low Moor
Sharon ES 200/K-5
100 Sharon School Cir 24422 540-863-1712
Sherman Callahan, prin. Fax 863-1717

Clintwood, Dickenson, Pop. 1,403
Dickenson County SD 2,200/PK-12
PO Box 1127 24228 276-926-4643
Haydee Robinson, supt. Fax 926-6374
www.dickenson.k12.va.us
Clintwood ES 500/PK-5
PO Box 585 24228 276-926-6088
Betty Newton, prin. Fax 926-6505
Ridgeview MS 500/6-8
320 Wolf Pack Way 24228 276-835-1601
John Whitner, prin.
Other Schools – See Birchleaf, Nora

Cloverdale, Botetourt, Pop. 3,095
Botetourt County SD
Supt. — See Fincastle
Cloverdale ES 300/K-5
833 Cougar Dr 24077 540-992-1086
Jessica Martin, prin. Fax 992-8378
Read Mountain MS 700/6-8
182 Orchard Hill Dr 24077 540-966-8655
Beth Mast, prin. Fax 966-8656

Coeburn, Wise, Pop. 2,115
Wise County SD
Supt. — See Wise
Coeburn MS 400/5-8
PO Box 670 24230 276-395-2135
Diedre Church, prin. Fax 395-5453
Coeburn PS 500/PK-4
PO Box 1337 24230 276-395-6100
Marsha Christian, prin. Fax 395-3242

Collinsville, Henry, Pop. 7,233
Henry County SD 7,400/PK-12
PO Box 8958 24078 276-634-4700
Dr. Jared Cotton, supt. Fax 638-2925
www.henry.k12.va.us
Collinsville PS 400/PK-2
15 Primary School Rd 24078 276-647-8932
Judy Edmonds, prin. Fax 647-9585
Fieldale-Collinsville MS 900/6-8
645 Miles Rd 24078 276-647-3841
Laryssa Hairston-Penn, prin. Fax 647-4090
Smith ES 300/PK-PK, 3-
40 School Dr 24078 276-647-7676
Judy Edmonds, prin. Fax 647-9434
Other Schools – See Axton, Bassett, Martinsville, Ridgeway, Stanleytown

Colonial Beach, Westmoreland, Pop. 3,440
Colonial Beach SD 600/PK-12
16 Irving Ave N 22443 804-224-0906
Dr. Kevin Newman, supt. Fax 224-8357
www.cbschools.net
Colonial Beach ES 400/PK-7
102 1st St 22443 804-224-9897
Michele Coates, prin. Fax 224-0304

Westmoreland County SD
Supt. — See Montross
Washington District ES 500/PK-5
454 Oak Grove Rd 22443 804-224-9100
Sandy Herdle, prin. Fax 224-1644

Colonial Heights, Colonial Heights, Pop. 17,059
Colonial Heights CSD 2,800/K-12
512 Boulevard, 804-524-3400
Dr. Joseph Cox, supt. Fax 526-4524
www.colonialhts.net
Colonial Heights MS 700/6-8
500 Conduit Rd, 804-524-3420
William Hortz, prin. Fax 526-9288
Lakeview ES 300/K-5
401 Taswell Ave, 804-524-3435
Patrick Neuman, prin. Fax 520-4158
North ES 300/K-5
3201 Dale Ave, 804-524-3430
Travis Ridley, prin. Fax 526-8800
Tussing ES 600/K-5
5501 Conduit Rd, 804-524-3440
Remus James, prin. Fax 526-7938

Concord, Campbell, Pop. 1,439
Campbell County SD
Supt. — See Rustburg
Concord ES 400/K-5
9339 Village Hwy 24538 434-477-5595
Whitney Rinella, prin. Fax 993-3509

Courtland, Southampton, Pop. 1,266
Southhampton County SD 2,900/PK-12
PO Box 96 23837 757-653-2692
Dr. Gwendolyn Shannon, supt. Fax 653-9422
www.southampton.k12.va.us
Riverdale ES 600/PK-5
31023 Camp Pkwy 23837 757-562-3007
Will Melbye, prin. Fax 562-6424
Southampton MS 600/6-8
23450 Southampton Pkwy 23837 757-653-9250
Darian Bell, prin. Fax 653-7251
Other Schools – See Capron, Newsoms, Sedley

Southampton Academy 300/PK-12
26495 Old Plank Rd 23837 757-653-2512

Covington, Covington, Pop. 5,839
Alleghany County SD
Supt. — See Low Moor
Callaghan ES 200/K-5
4018 Midland Trl 24426 540-965-1810
Nancy Moga, prin. Fax 965-1814
Clifton MS 600/6-8
1000 Riverview Farm Rd 24426 540-863-1726
Sarah Rowe, prin. Fax 863-1731
Mountain View ES 500/K-5
100 Gleason Dr 24426 540-863-1737
April Easton, prin. Fax 863-1740

Covington CSD 1,000/PK-12
340 E Walnut St 24426 540-965-1400
Melinda Snead-Johnson, supt. Fax 965-1404
www.covington.k12.va.us
Edgemont PS 400/PK-3
574 W Indian Valley Rd 24426 540-965-1420
Cynthia Morgan, prin.
Jeter-Watson IS 300/4-7
560 W Indian Valley Rd 24426 540-965-1430
Robert Bennett, prin.

Craigsville, Augusta, Pop. 920
Augusta County SD
Supt. — See Verona
Craigsville ES 100/K-5
100 E 1st St 24430 540-997-9184
Crystal Coffman, prin. Fax 997-0432

Crewe, Nottoway, Pop. 2,296
Nottoway County SD
Supt. — See Nottoway
Crewe PS 300/1-4
1953 Sunnyside Rd 23930 434-645-8149
Dr. Sherry Saunders, prin. Fax 645-1604
Nottoway IS 300/5-6
5285 Old Nottoway Rd 23930 434-292-5353
Marcia Martin, prin. Fax 298-0612
Nottoway MS 300/7-8
5279 Old Nottoway Rd 23930 434-292-5375
Jane Geyer, prin. Fax 292-7479

Critz, Patrick
Patrick County SD
Supt. — See Stuart
Hardin-Reynolds Memorial MS 200/4-7
3597 Dogwood Rd 24082 276-694-3631
Kirk Renegar, prin. Fax 694-5805

Crozet, Albemarle, Pop. 5,475
Albemarle County SD
Supt. — See Charlottesville
Brownsville ES 700/PK-5
5870 Rockfish Gap Tpke 22932 434-823-4658
Jason Crutchfield, prin. Fax 823-5120
Crozet ES 300/PK-5
1407 Crozet Ave 22932 434-823-4800
Gwedette Crummie, prin. Fax 823-6470
Henley MS 800/6-8
5880 Rockfish Gap Tpke 22932 434-823-4393
Dr. Beth Costa, prin. Fax 823-2711

Crozier, Goochland
Goochland County SD
Supt. — See Goochland
Randolph ES 400/K-5
1552 Sheppard Town Rd 23039 804-556-5385
Dan Gardner, prin. Fax 784-2674

Culpeper, Culpeper, Pop. 15,837
Culpeper County SD 7,900/K-12
450 Radio Ln 22701 540-825-3677
Dr. Anthony S. Brads, supt. Fax 829-2111
www.culpeperschools.org
Binns MS 800/6-8
205 E Grandview Ave 22701 540-825-6894
Nathan Bopp, prin. Fax 829-9926
Culpeper County MS 1,100/6-8
14300 Achievement Dr 22701 540-825-4140
Cathy Timmons, prin. Fax 825-7543
Emerald Hill ES 800/K-5
11245 Rixeyville Rd 22701 540-937-7361
Pamela Gatewood, prin. Fax 937-7365
Farmington ES 600/K-5
500 Sunset Ln 22701 540-825-0713
Gail Brewer, prin. Fax 829-0865
Richardson ES 600/K-5
18370 Simms Dr 22701 540-825-0616
Susan Bridges, prin. Fax 825-5807
Sample ES 600/K-5
18480 Simms Dr 22701 540-825-5448
Kristin Williams, prin. Fax 829-2118
Sycamore Park ES 600/K-5
451 Radio Ln 22701 540-825-8847
Derek McWilliams, prin. Fax 825-6384
Yowell ES 600/K-5
701 Yowell Dr 22701 540-825-9484
Susan Campbell, prin. Fax 825-7509

Culpeper Christian S 100/PK-8
810 Old Rixeyville Rd 22701 540-825-4208
Michael Owings, admin. Fax 829-0910
Epiphany S 100/PK-8
1211 E Grandview Ave 22701 540-825-9017
James Oliver, prin. Fax 825-8987

Cumberland, Cumberland, Pop. 383
Cumberland County SD 1,400/PK-12
PO Box 170 23040 804-492-4212
Dr. Amy Griffin Ed.D., supt. Fax 492-9869
www.cucps.k12.va.us
Cumberland ES 600/PK-4
PO Box 190 23040 804-492-4212
Virginia Gills, prin. Fax 492-9867
Cumberland MS 400/5-8
PO Box 184 23040 804-492-4212
Michael Camden, prin. Fax 492-9868

Dahlgren, King George, Pop. 2,565
King George County SD
Supt. — See King George
Potomac ES 700/K-6
PO Box 314 22448 540-663-3322
Angela Harris, prin. Fax 663-2947

Dale City, Prince William, Pop. 63,241
Prince William County SD
Supt. — See Manassas
Neabsco ES 600/PK-5
3800 Cordell Ave 22193 703-670-2147
Griff Carmichael, prin. Fax 670-0892

Holy Family S 200/PK-8
14160 Ferndale Rd 22193 703-670-3138
Sarah Chevlin, prin. Fax 563-9118

Damascus, Washington, Pop. 807
Washington County SD
Supt. — See Abingdon
Damascus MS 200/6-8
32101 Government Rd 24236 276-739-4100
Scott Keith, prin. Fax 475-4032

Danville, Danville, Pop. 42,537
Danville CSD 6,300/PK-12
PO Box 9600 24543 434-799-6400
Stanley Jones, supt. Fax 799-5008
www.danvillepublicschools.org
Bonner MS 800/6-8
300 Apollo Ave 24540 434-799-6446
Kim Agnor, prin. Fax 797-8867
Forest Hills ES 400/K-5
155 Mountain View Ave 24541 434-799-6430
Jo Beth Clark, prin. Fax 799-8922
Gibson ES 600/K-5
1215 Industrial Ave 24541 434-799-6426
Jay Jones, prin. Fax 797-8857
Grove Park Preschool 100/PK-PK
1070 S Main St 24541 434-799-6437
Lou Ann Long, prin. Fax 797-8921
Johnson ES 600/PK-5
680 Arnett Blvd 24540 434-799-6433
Thomas Takacs, prin. Fax 797-8926
Northside Preschool 200/PK-PK
121 Gloucester St 24540 434-773-8301
Rhonda Wright, prin. Fax 773-8304
Park Avenue ES 500/K-5
661 Park Ave 24541 434-799-6452
Melissa Newton, prin. Fax 797-8891
Schoolfield Academy 600/K-5
1400 W Main St 24541 434-799-6455
Everette Johnson, prin. Fax 797-8923
Westwood MS 600/6-8
500 Apollo Ave 24540 434-797-8860
Debra Kinsey, prin. Fax 797-8874
Woodberry Hills ES 400/K-5
614 Audubon Dr 24540 434-799-6466
Wayne Mayo, prin. Fax 797-8927

Pittsylvania County SD
Supt. — See Chatham
Brosville ES 200/K-5
195 Bulldog Ln 24541 434-685-7787
Felita Atkins, prin. Fax 685-3362
Stony Mill ES 500/PK-5
100 Stony Mill Elem Cir 24541 434-685-7545
Kimberly Haymore, prin. Fax 685-4328
Twin Springs ES 800/K-5
100 Twin Springs Elementary 24540 434-724-2666
Patricia Hawkins, prin. Fax 724-2851

Epiphany Episcopal S 100/PK-8
115 Jefferson Ave 24541 434-792-4334
Suzanne Miller, dean Fax 792-0786
Sacred Heart S 200/PK-9
540 Central Blvd 24541 434-793-2656
Kira Kania, prin. Fax 793-2658
Westover Christian Academy 400/PK-12
5665 Riverside Dr 24541 434-822-0800
John Cline, admin. Fax 822-0441

Dayton, Rockingham, Pop. 1,520
Rockingham County SD
Supt. — See Harrisonburg
Ottobine ES 200/PK-5
8646 Waggys Creek Rd 22821 540-879-2091
Dr. Todd Johnson, prin. Fax 879-2556
Pence MS 800/6-8
375 Bowman Rd 22821 540-879-2535
Camala Kite, prin. Fax 879-2179

Dendron, Surry, Pop. 267
Surry County SD
Supt. — See Surry
Jackson MS 300/5-8
4255 New Design Rd 23839 757-267-2810
Trina Craddox, prin. Fax 267-0809
Surry ES 400/PK-4
1600 Hollybush Rd 23839 757-267-2558
Ann Marie Nelin, prin. Fax 267-0107

Dillwyn, Buckingham, Pop. 440
Buckingham County SD
Supt. — See Buckingham
Buckingham ES 500/3-5
40 Frank Harris Rd 23936 434-505-0000
Bryan Jackson, prin. Fax 983-1366
Buckingham PS 500/K-2
128 Frank Harris Rd 23936 434-505-0001
Angela Jones, prin. Fax 983-1386

Central Virginia Christian S 100/PK-8
164 Industrial Park Rd 23936 434-983-4810
Dr. Cherie Brickhill, admin. Fax 983-4811

Dinwiddie, Dinwiddie
Dinwiddie County SD 4,400/K-12
PO Box 7 23841 804-469-4190
Dr. Kari Weston, supt. Fax 469-4197
www.dinwiddie.k12.va.us
Dinwiddie County MS 1,000/6-8
PO Box 340 23841 804-469-5430
Jason Chandler, prin. Fax 469-3389
Dinwiddie ES 400/K-5
13811 Boydton Plank Rd 23841 804-469-4580
Davis Roberts, prin. Fax 469-4585
Southside ES 400/K-5
10305 Boydton Plank Rd 23841 804-469-4480
Charles E. Moss, prin. Fax 469-4484
Other Schools – See Church Road, Mc Kenney, Sutherland

Disputanta, Prince George
Prince George County SD
Supt. — See Prince George
Harrison ES 600/PK-5
12900 E Quaker Rd 23842 804-991-2242
Christopher Scruggs, prin. Fax 991-2123
Moore MS 1,000/6-7
11455 Prince George Dr 23842 804-733-2740
Stephanie Bishop, prin. Fax 733-2697
South ES 500/PK-5
13400 Prince George Dr 23842 804-733-2755
Susan Braswell, prin. Fax 732-5844

Dryden, Lee, Pop. 1,195
Lee County SD
Supt. — See Jonesville
Dryden ES 400/PK-5
176 School House Ridge Rd 24243 276-546-4443
Mona Baker, prin. Fax 546-5185

Powell Valley Christian S 50/PK-8
187 Stairway Dr 24243 276-523-0464

Dry Fork, Pittsylvania
Pittsylvania County SD
Supt. — See Chatham
Tunstall MS 700/6-8
1160 Tunstall High Rd 24549 434-724-7086
Deborah Stowe, prin. Fax 724-7907

Heritage Academy 100/PK-8
1461 Dry Fork Rd 24549 434-432-8380
Ann Haymes, head sch Fax 432-8381

Dublin, Pulaski, Pop. 2,500
Pulaski County SD
Supt. — See Pulaski
Dublin ES 500/PK-5
600 Dunlap Rd 24084 540-643-0337
Elizabeth Webb, prin. Fax 674-1351
Dublin MS 600/6-8
650 Giles Ave 24084 540-643-0367
Adam Joyce, prin. Fax 674-0813

Duffield, Scott, Pop. 90
Scott County SD
Supt. — See Gate City
Duffield PS 300/PK-4
663 Duff Patt Hwy 24244 276-431-2244
Greg Ervin, prin. Fax 431-2131
Rye Cove IS 200/5-7
158 Memorial School Ln 24244 276-940-2322
Chris Stapleton, prin. Fax 940-4161

Dumfries, Prince William, Pop. 4,762
Prince William County SD
Supt. — See Manassas
Covington-Harper ES K-5
2500 River Heritage Blvd 22026 703-466-4500
Ronald Whitten, prin. Fax 221-0917

Dumfries ES 600/PK-5
3990 Cameron St 22026 703-221-3101
Marlene Coleman, prin. Fax 221-0047
Montclair ES 600/K-5
4920 Tallowwood Dr, 703-730-1072
Amanda Parks, prin. Fax 878-0356
Pattie ES 700/K-5
16125 Dumfries Rd, 703-670-3173
Robert Lucciotti, prin. Fax 583-7233
Potomac MS 1,200/6-8
3130 Panther Pride Dr 22026 703-221-4996
Kevin Smith, prin. Fax 221-4998
Swans Creek ES 600/K-5
17700 Wayside Dr 22026 703-445-0930
Amanda Broy, prin. Fax 445-0546
Williams ES 900/K-5
3100 Panther Pride Dr 22026 703-445-8376
Lynmara Colon, prin. Fax 445-8378

Dungannon, Scott, Pop. 331
Scott County SD
Supt. — See Gate City
Dungannon IS 100/4-7
113 Fifth Ave 24245 276-467-2281
Jennifer Meade, prin. Fax 467-2654

Eagle Rock, Botetourt
Botetourt County SD
Supt. — See Fincastle
Eagle Rock ES 100/PK-5
145 Eagles Nest Dr 24085 540-884-2421
Sandy Gould, prin. Fax 473-8377

Earlysville, Albemarle
Albemarle County SD
Supt. — See Charlottesville
Broadus Wood ES 300/PK-5
185 Buck Mountain Rd 22936 434-973-3865
Amy Morris, prin. Fax 973-3833

Eastville, Northampton, Pop. 300
Northampton County SD
Supt. — See Machipongo
Northampton MS 300/7-8
16041 Courthouse Rd 23347 757-678-5151
Laurel Crenshaw, prin. Fax 678-5244

Elkton, Rockingham, Pop. 2,698
Rockingham County SD
Supt. — See Harrisonburg
Elkton ES 400/PK-5
302 W B St 22827 540-298-1511
Chris Bryant, prin. Fax 298-1471
Elkton MS 500/6-8
21063 Blue and Gold Dr 22827 540-298-1228
Dr. Ramona Pence, prin. Fax 298-0029
River Bend ES 300/PK-5
14556 Rockingham Pike 22827 540-298-5301
Sharon Martz, prin. Fax 298-5305

Elliston, Montgomery, Pop. 900
Montgomery County SD
Supt. — See Christiansburg
Eastern Montgomery ES 500/PK-5
4580 Eastern Montgomery Ln 24087 540-268-1147
Denise Boyle, prin. Fax 268-1244

Emporia, Emporia, Pop. 5,846
Greensville County SD 2,600/PK-12
105 Ruffin St 23847 434-634-3748
Dr. Angela Wilson, supt. Fax 634-3495
www.gcps1.com
Belfield ES 200/5-5
515 Belfield Rd 23847 434-634-5566
Mary Person, prin. Fax 634-5395
Greensville ES, 1101 Sussex Dr 23847 1,100/PK-4
Nicole Coker, prin. 434-336-0907
Wyatt MS 600/6-8
206 Slagles Lake Rd 23847 434-634-5159
Jami Clements, prin. Fax 634-0442

Ettrick, Chesterfield, Pop. 6,505
Chesterfield County SD
Supt. — See Chesterfield
Ettrick ES 500/PK-5
20910 Chesterfield Ave 23803 804-520-6005
Dr. Randi Smith, prin. Fax 520-0430

Ewing, Lee, Pop. 438
Lee County SD
Supt. — See Jonesville
Elydale ES 200/K-7
128 Elydale Rd 24248 276-445-4439
Kelli Mooney, prin. Fax 445-5207

Exmore, Northampton, Pop. 1,433
Northampton County SD
Supt. — See Machipongo
Occohannock ES 500/PK-6
4208 Seaside Rd 23350 757-678-5151
Ron Yorko, prin. Fax 442-6349

Broadwater Academy 300/PK-12
PO Box 546 23350 757-442-9041
Joseph Spagnolo, head sch Fax 442-9615
Shore Christian Academy 100/PK-8
11624 Occohannock Rd 23350 757-442-9791
Shannon Drummond, prin. Fax 442-3998

Fairfax, Fairfax, Pop. 21,900
Fairfax County SD
Supt. — See Falls Church
Bonnie Brae ES 700/K-6
5420 Sideburn Rd 22032 703-321-3900
April Cage, prin. Fax 321-3997
Daniels Run ES 800/K-6
3705 Old Lee Hwy 22030 703-279-8400
Adam Erbrecht, prin. Fax 279-8497
Eagle View ES 700/PK-6
4500 Dixie Hill Rd 22030 703-322-3100
Kanchana Lyer, prin. Fax 322-3197
Fairfax Villa ES 600/PK-6
10900 Santa Clara Dr 22030 703-267-2800
Elizabeth Bumbrey, prin. Fax 267-2897
Fairhill ES 600/K-6
3001 Chichester Ln 22031 703-208-8100
Candace Hunstad, prin. Fax 208-8197
Frost MS 1,100/7-8
4101 Pickett Rd 22032 703-426-5700
Eric McCann, prin. Fax 426-5797
Greenbriar East ES 1,000/PK-6
13006 Point Pleasant Dr 22033 703-633-6400
Linda Cohen, prin. Fax 378-7790
Greenbriar West ES 1,100/K-6
13300 Poplar Tree Rd 22033 703-633-6700
Patty Granada, prin. Fax 633-6797
Lanier MS 1,200/7-8
3801 Jermantown Rd 22030 703-934-2400
Erin Lenart, prin. Fax 934-2497
Laurel Ridge ES 800/K-6
10110 Commonwealth Blvd 22032 703-426-3700
Tonya Wassenberg, prin. Fax 426-3797
Lees Corner ES 700/K-6
13500 Hollinger Ave 22033 703-227-3500
Robert D'Amato, prin. Fax 227-3597
Little Run ES 400/PK-6
4511 Olley Ln 22032 703-503-3500
Monica Mohr, prin. Fax 503-3597
Mantua ES 1,000/K-6
9107 Horner Ct 22031 703-645-6300
Jan-Marie Fernandez, prin. Fax 645-6397
Mosby Woods ES 1,000/K-6
9819 Five Oaks Rd 22031 703-937-1600
Mahri Aste, prin. Fax 937-1697
Navy ES 900/K-6
3500 W Ox Rd 22033 703-262-7100
Jon Coch, prin. Fax 262-7197
Oak View ES 800/K-6
5004 Sideburn Rd 22032 703-764-7100
Sarah Brooker, prin. Fax 764-7197
Olde Creek ES 400/K-6
9524 Old Creek Dr 22032 703-426-3100
Dustin Wright, prin. Fax 426-3197
Providence ES 900/K-6
3616 Jermantown Rd 22030 703-460-4400
Dan Phillips, prin. Fax 460-4497
Wakefield Forest ES 500/K-6
4011 Iva Ln 22032 703-503-2300
Sharyn Prindle, prin. Fax 503-2397
Willow Springs ES 1,000/K-6
5400 Willow Springs School 22030 703-679-6000
Dylan Taylor, prin. Fax 687-6097

Gesher Jewish Day S 200/K-8
4800 Mattie Moore Ct 22030 703-978-9789
Leport S - Fairfax 100/PK-K
3909 Oak St 22030 703-934-0920
Merritt Academy 300/PK-8
9211 Arlington Blvd 22031 703-273-8000
Palm Tree S 50/K-12
8900 Lee Hwy 22031 703-665-9915
St. Leo the Great S 500/PK-8
3704 Old Lee Hwy 22030 703-273-1211
Dave DiPippa, prin. Fax 273-6913
St. Mary of Sorrows Preschool PK-PK
5222 Sideburn Rd 22032 703-978-4557
Elena Quartuccio, prin.
Trinity Christian S 700/K-12
11204 Braddock Rd 22030 703-273-8787
Dr. David Vanderpoel, hdmstr. Fax 226-0512

Fairfax Station, Fairfax, Pop. 11,680
Fairfax County SD
Supt. — See Falls Church
Fairview ES 700/K-6
5815 Ox Rd 22039 703-503-3700
Lynn Mayer, prin. Fax 978-5492
Halley ES 700/PK-6
8850 Cross Chase Cir 22039 703-551-5700
Jamey Chianetta, prin. Fax 551-5797
Silverbrook ES 800/K-6
9350 Crosspointe Dr 22039 703-690-5100
Melaney Mackin, prin. Fax 690-5197

Fairfax Baptist Temple Academy 300/PK-12
6401 Missionary Ln 22039 703-323-8100

Fairfield, Rockbridge
Rockbridge County SD
Supt. — See Lexington
Fairfield ES 400/PK-5
20 Fairfield School Rd 24435 540-340-5202
Kelly Holmes, prin. Fax 377-2601

Fairlawn, Pulaski, Pop. 2,345
Pulaski County SD
Supt. — See Pulaski
Riverlawn ES 400/PK-5
8100 Beth Nelson Dr 24141 540-643-0748
Kimberly Sink, prin. Fax 639-0882

Falls Church, Falls Church, Pop. 11,898
Fairfax County SD 181,400/PK-12
8115 Gatehouse Rd 22042 703-423-1000
Dr. Steven Lockard, supt. Fax 423-1007
www.fcps.edu
Baileys ES for the Arts & Sciences 1,300/PK-2
6111 Knollwood Dr 22041 703-575-6800
Dr. Julie Easa, prin. Fax 575-6897
Bailey's Upper ES 600/3-5
6245 Leesburg Pike 22044 703-503-2700
Marie Lemmon, prin.
Beech Tree ES 400/K-5
3401 Beechtree Ln 22042 703-531-2600
Karim Daugherty, prin. Fax 237-7785
Belvedere ES 700/PK-5
6540 Columbia Pike 22041 703-916-6800
Cecilia Vanderhye, prin. Fax 916-6897
Glen Forest ES 1,000/K-5
5829 Glen Forest Dr 22041 703-578-8000
Cindi Choate, prin. Fax 578-8097
Graham Road ES 500/K-6
2831 Graham Rd 22042 703-226-2700
Lindsay Elliott, prin. Fax 226-2797
Haycock ES 900/K-6
6616 Haycock Rd 22043 703-531-4000
Jereme Donnelly, prin. Fax 531-4097
Jackson MS 1,300/7-8
3020 Gallows Rd 22042 703-204-8100
Chad Lehman, prin. Fax 204-8197
Lemon Road ES 500/K-6
7230 Idylwood Rd 22043 703-714-6400
Andrew Camarda, prin. Fax 714-6497
Longfellow MS 1,300/7-8
2000 Westmoreland St 22043 703-533-2600
Carole Kihm, prin. Fax 533-2697
Pine Spring ES 600/PK-6
7607 Willow Ln 22042 571-226-4400
Armando Peri, prin. Fax 226-4497
Shrevewood ES 700/K-6
7525 Shreve Rd 22043 703-645-6600
Michelle Eugene, prin. Fax 645-6697
Sleepy Hollow ES 500/K-5
3333 Sleepy Hollow Rd 22044 703-237-7000
Eric Johnson, prin. Fax 237-7097
Timber Lane ES 600/PK-6
2737 West St 22046 703-206-5300
Kimberly Cook, prin. Fax 206-5397
Westgate ES 600/K-6
7500 Magarity Rd 22043 703-610-5700
Hallie Demetriades, prin. Fax 610-5797
Westlawn ES 700/K-6
3200 Westley Rd 22042 703-241-5100
Linda Ferguson, prin. Fax 241-5197
Woodburn ES 500/K-6
3401 Hemlock Dr 22042 703-641-8200
Bridget Chapin, prin. Fax 641-8297
Other Schools – See Alexandria, Annandale, Burke, Centreville, Chantilly, Clifton, Fairfax, Fairfax Station, Fort Belvoir, Great Falls, Herndon, Lorton, Mc Lean, Oakton, Reston, Springfield, Vienna

Falls Church CSD 2,400/K-12
800 W Broad St Ste 203 22046 703-248-5600
Dr. Peter Noonan, supt. Fax 248-5613
www.fccps.org
Henderson MS 500/6-8
7130 Leesburg Pike 22043 703-720-5700
Valerie Hardy, prin. Fax 720-5710
Jefferson ES 700/2-5
601 S Oak St 22046 703-248-5660
Paul Swanson, prin. Fax 248-5666
Mount Daniel ES 400/K-1
2328 N Oak St 22046 703-248-5640
Erin Kelly, prin. Fax 248-5642

Congressional S 300/PK-8
3229 Sleepy Hollow Rd 22042 703-533-9711
Janet Marsh, head sch Fax 532-5467
Corpus Christi ECC 200/PK-PK
7506 Saint Philips Ct 22042 703-573-4570
Ann Stich, dir. Fax 573-6832
Corpus Christi S 200/K-8
3301 Glen Carlyn Rd 22041 703-820-7450
Marie Bonard, prin. Fax 820-9635
Grace Christian Academy 100/PK-8
3233 Annandale Rd 22042 703-534-5517
Patrick Hurley, prin. Fax 534-1394
Montessori S of Holmes Run 50/PK-8
3527 Gallows Rd 22042 703-573-4652
Christy Clarke Choi, head sch Fax 573-2807
Nur Montessori S PK-6
6329 Arlington Blvd Ste L 22044 703-237-5400
St. James S 500/K-8
830 W Broad St 22046 703-533-1182
Sr. Mary Sue Carwile, prin. Fax 532-8316

Falmouth, Stafford, Pop. 4,116
Stafford County SD
Supt. — See Stafford
Drew MS 500/6-8
501 Cambridge St 22405 540-371-1415
Tammara Hanna, prin. Fax 371-1447
Falmouth ES 500/K-5
1000 Forbes St 22405 540-373-7458
Sallie Johnakin-Putnam, prin. Fax 371-1757

Fancy Gap, Carroll, Pop. 236
Carroll County SD
Supt. — See Hillsville
Fancy Gap ES 200/PK-5
63 Winding Ridge Rd 24328 276-728-7504
Dr. Jeanne Edwards, prin. Fax 728-4619

Farmville, Prince Edward, Pop. 8,093
Prince Edward County SD 2,200/K-12
35 Eagle Dr 23901 434-315-2100
Dr. Barbara Johnson, supt. Fax 392-1911
www.pecps.k12.va.us
Prince Edward ES 800/K-4
35 Eagle Dr 23901 434-315-2110
Carolyn Jones, prin. Fax 392-1583
Prince Edward MS 700/5-8
35 Eagle Dr 23901 434-315-2120
Dr. Julie Gilliam, prin. Fax 392-4286

Fuqua S, PO Box 328 23901 400/PK-12
John Melton, head sch 434-392-4131

Ferrum, Franklin, Pop. 1,932
Franklin County SD
Supt. — See Rocky Mount
Ferrum ES 200/PK-5
660 Ferrum School Rd 24088 540-365-7194
Jennifer Talley, prin. Fax 365-7307

Fincastle, Botetourt, Pop. 352
Botetourt County SD 5,400/PK-12
143 Poor Farm Rd 24090 540-473-8263
John S. Busher, supt. Fax 473-8298
www.bcps.k12.va.us
Breckinridge ES 200/PK-5
331 Springwood Rd 24090 540-473-8386
Debra Deitrich, prin. Fax 473-8361
Central Academy MS 500/6-8
367 Poor Farm Rd 24090 540-473-8333
Tim McClung, prin. Fax 473-8398
Other Schools – See Blue Ridge, Buchanan, Cloverdale, Eagle Rock, Troutville

Fishersville, Augusta, Pop. 7,346
Augusta County SD
Supt. — See Verona
Wilson ES 700/K-5
127 Woodrow Wilson Ave 22939 540-245-5040
Dawn Young, prin. Fax 245-5042
Wilson MS 600/6-8
232 Hornet Rd 22939 540-245-5185
Steven Eckstrom, prin. Fax 245-5189

Flint Hill, Rappahannock, Pop. 207

Wakefield Country Day S 200/PK-12
PO Box 739 22627 540-635-8555

Floyd, Floyd, Pop. 419
Floyd County SD 2,100/PK-12
140 Harris Hart Rd NE 24091 540-745-9400
John Wheeler, supt. Fax 745-9496
www.floyd.k12.va.us
Floyd ES 600/PK-7
531 Oak Hill Dr SE 24091 540-745-9440
Amber Burnett, prin. Fax 745-9494
Other Schools – See Check, Radford, Willis

Forest, Bedford, Pop. 9,010
Bedford County SD
Supt. — See Bedford
Forest ES 400/K-5
1 Scholar Ln 24551 434-525-2681
Lorri Manley, prin. Fax 525-7186
Forest MS 1,000/6-8
100 Ashwood Dr 24551 434-525-6630
Scott Simmons, prin. Fax 525-1284
Jefferson ES 600/K-5
1255 Patriot Pl 24551 434-534-6159
Andy Greenough, prin. Fax 534-6240
New London Academy 300/K-5
1133 Academy Ln 24551 434-525-2177
Dr. Tammy Parlier, prin. Fax 525-0935

Timberlake Christian S 400/PK-12
202 Horizon Dr 24551 434-237-5943
Jeff Abbett, admin. Fax 239-3319

Fork Union, Fluvanna
Fluvanna County SD
Supt. — See Palmyra
Carysbrook ES 600/3-4
9172 James Madison Hwy 23055 434-842-1241
Scott Lucas, prin. Fax 842-1186

Fort Belvoir, Fairfax, Pop. 6,658
Fairfax County SD
Supt. — See Falls Church
Fort Belvoir PS 1,100/PK-3
5970 Meeres Rd 22060 703-781-2700
Kate Graham, prin. Fax 781-2712
Fort Belvoir Upper ES 4-6
5980 Meeres Rd 22060 703-982-1300
Carol Padgett, prin. Fax 982-1397

Fort Blackmore, Scott
Scott County SD
Supt. — See Gate City
Fort Blackmore ES 100/K-3
214 Big Stoney Creek Rd 24250 276-995-2471
Jennifer Meade, prin. Fax 995-2654

Fort Defiance, Augusta
Augusta County SD
Supt. — See Verona
Clymore ES 600/K-5
184 Fort Defiance Rd 24437 540-245-5043
Fonda Morris, prin. Fax 245-5095
Stewart MS 600/6-8
118 Fort Defiance Rd 24437 540-245-5046
Michael Conner, prin. Fax 245-5049

Fort Eustis, See Newport News
Newport News CSD
Supt. — See Newport News
Stanford ES 500/K-5
929 Madison Ave 23604 757-888-3200
Diane Willis, prin. Fax 888-3354

Franklin, Southampton, Pop. 8,431
Franklin CSD 1,300/PK-12
207 W 2nd Ave 23851 757-569-8111
Tamara Sterling, supt. Fax 516-1015
www.fcpsva.org
King MS 300/6-8
501 Charles St 23851 757-562-4631
Lisa B. Francis, prin. Fax 562-0231
Morton ES 700/PK-5
300 Morton St 23851 757-562-5458
Dr. Sherie Davis, prin. Fax 562-6178

Fredericksburg, Fredericksburg, Pop. 23,462
Fredericksburg CSD 3,500/PK-12
210 Ferdinand St 22401 540-372-1130
Dr. David Melton, supt. Fax 372-1111
www.cityschools.com
Lafayette Upper ES 700/3-5
3 Learning Ln 22401 540-310-0029
Matthew Terry, prin. Fax 310-0671
Mercer ES 900/K-2
2100 Cowan Blvd 22401 540-372-1115
Marjorie Tankersley, prin. Fax 372-6753
Original Walker-Grant S 200/PK-PK
210 Ferdinand St 22401 540-372-1065
Walker-Grant MS 700/6-8
1 Learning Ln 22401 540-372-1145
Melanie Kay-Wyatt, prin. Fax 891-5449

Spotsylvania County SD 23,500/PK-12
8020 River Stone Dr 22407 540-834-2500
Scott Baker Ed.D., supt. Fax 834-2550
www.spotsylvania.k12.va.us
Battlefield ES 600/K-5
11108 Leavells Rd 22407 540-786-4532
Susan Fines, prin. Fax 786-3149
Battlefield MS 800/6-8
11120 Leavells Rd 22407 540-786-4400
Sheila Smith, prin. Fax 786-7109
Cedar Forest ES 700/K-5
3412 Massaponax Church Rd 22408 540-834-4569
Amy Williams, prin. Fax 834-4577
Chancellor ES 400/K-5
5995 Plank Rd 22407 540-786-6123
Shawn Hudson, prin. Fax 786-5487
Chancellor MS 900/6-8
6320 Harrison Rd 22407 540-786-8099
Deborah Frazier, prin. Fax 785-9392
Freedom MS 900/6-8
7315 Smith Station Rd 22407 540-548-1030
Dr. Eric Wright, prin. Fax 786-0782
Harrison Road ES 800/K-5
6230 Harrison Rd 22407 540-548-4864
Deborah Frazier, prin. Fax 548-4863
Lee Hill ES 700/K-5
3600 Lee Hill School Dr 22408 540-898-1433
Carroll Lewter, prin. Fax 898-9223
Parkside ES 700/K-5
5620 Smith Station Rd 22407 540-710-5190
Thomas Eichenberg, prin. Fax 710-7451
Salem ES 700/PK-5
4501 Jackson Rd 22407 540-786-8218
Harold Morton, prin. Fax 786-5006
Smith Station ES 800/K-5
7320 Smith Station Rd 22407 540-786-5443
Terrie Cagle, prin. Fax 785-2880
Spotswood ES 500/K-5
400 Lorraine Ave 22408 540-898-1514
Chad Armstrong, prin. Fax 898-8571
Other Schools – See Spotsylvania

Stafford County SD
Supt. — See Stafford
Conway ES 900/PK-5
105 Primmer House Rd 22405 540-361-1455
William Raybold, prin. Fax 361-4493
Dixon-Smith MS 800/6-8
503 Deacon Rd 22405 540-899-0860
Lisa Besceglia, prin. Fax 899-0881
Ferry Farm ES 600/K-5
20 Pendleton Rd 22405 540-373-7366
Robert Freeman, prin. Fax 371-3788
Gayle MS 900/6-8
100 Panther Dr 22406 540-373-0383
Robin Lloyd, prin. Fax 373-8856
Grafton Village ES 500/PK-5
501 Deacon Rd 22405 540-373-5454
Michael Sidebotham, prin. Fax 373-1498
Hartwood ES 500/K-5
14 Shackelford Well Rd 22406 540-752-4441
Scott Elchenko, prin. Fax 752-4320
Rocky Run ES 800/K-5
95 Reservoir Rd 22406 540-286-1956
Nicholas Roman, prin. Fax 286-1955

Cornerstone Life Academy 50/PK-5
56 McWhirt Loop 22406 540-374-1876
Laura Howell, prin.
Faith Baptist S 300/PK-12
4105 Plank Rd 22407 540-786-4953
Fredericksburg Academy 400/PK-12
10800 Academy Dr 22408 540-898-0020
Karen Moschetto, head sch Fax 898-0440
Fredericksburg Christian Lower S 300/PK-5
2231 Jefferson Davis Hwy 22401 540-373-5357
Susan Cheatham, prin. Fax 899-6211
Holy Cross Academy 600/PK-8
250 Stafford Lakes Pkwy 22406 540-286-1600
Sr. Susan Eder, prin. Fax 286-1625
St. Patrick S 200/PK-8
9151 Elys Ford Rd 22407 540-786-2277
George Elliott, prin. Fax 785-2213
Tree of Life Christian Prep 50/1-8
6050 Plank Rd 22407 540-786-2019

Fries, Grayson, Pop. 478
Grayson County SD
Supt. — See Independence
Fries S 200/PK-7
PO Box 446 24330 276-744-7201
John Alexander, prin. Fax 744-3384

Front Royal, Warren, Pop. 14,067
Warren County SD 5,400/K-12
210 N Commerce Ave 22630 540-635-2171
L. Gregory Drescher, supt. Fax 636-4195
www.wcps.k12.va.us
Barbour ES 500/K-5
290 Westminster Dr 22630 540-622-8090
Amanda Roller, prin. Fax 636-1053
Jeffries ES 600/K-5
320 E Criser Rd 22630 540-636-6824
Doris Dean, prin. Fax 635-3803
Keyser ES 600/K-5
1015 E Stonewall Dr 22630 540-635-3125
Danelle Sperling, prin. Fax 635-6978
Morrison ES 500/K-5
40 Crescent St 22630 540-635-4188
Nicole Jensen, prin. Fax 635-5640
Rhodes ES 300/K-5
224 W Strasburg Rd 22630 540-635-4556
Lori Layman, prin. Fax 635-2821
Skyline MS 6-8
240 Luray Ave 22630 540-636-0909
Robert Johnston, prin. Fax 635-6981
Warren County MS 800/6-8
522 Heritage Dr 22630 540-635-2194
Amy Gubler, prin. Fax 631-3200

Front Royal Christian S 100/PK-12
80 N Lake Ave 22630 540-635-6799
Lorraine Hewitt M.Ed., head sch Fax 635-6152

Fulks Run, Rockingham
Rockingham County SD
Supt. — See Harrisonburg
Fulks Run ES 200/PK-5
11089 Brocks Gap Rd 22830 540-896-7635
Alisa Sims, prin. Fax 896-1606

Gainesville, Prince William, Pop. 11,049
Prince William County SD
Supt. — See Manassas
Buckland Mills ES 1,100/PK-5
10511 Wharfdale Pl 20155 703-530-1560
Connie Balkcom, prin. Fax 530-1563
Bull Run MS 1,100/6-8
6308 Catharpin Rd 20155 703-753-9969
Matthew Phythian, prin. Fax 753-9610
Gainesville MS 1,300/6-8
8001 Limestone Dr 20155 703-753-2997
Catherine Porter-Lucas, prin. Fax 753-4331
Glenkirk ES 900/PK-5
8584 Sedge Wren Dr 20155 703-753-1702
Marisa Miranda, prin. Fax 753-4981
Tyler ES 700/K-5
14500 John Marshall Hwy 20155 703-754-7181
Jennifer Perilla, prin. Fax 754-4869

Montessori S of Gainesville 50/PK-K
14130 Glenkirk Rd 20155 703-754-0946
Deepa Simlot, admin. Fax 754-9961

Galax, Galax, Pop. 6,941
Carroll County SD
Supt. — See Hillsville
Gladeville ES 300/PK-5
3117 Glendale Rd 24333 276-236-5449
Marlin Campbell, prin. Fax 238-1625
Oakland ES 200/PK-5
4930 Pipers Gap Rd 24333 276-236-3049
Larry Williams, prin. Fax 236-5367

Galax CSD 1,300/K-12
223 Long St 24333 276-236-2911
Bill Sturgill, supt. Fax 236-5776
www.gcps.k12.va.us
Galax ES 500/K-4
225 Academy Dr 24333 276-236-6159
Dr. Kristie Legg, prin. Fax 236-5839
Galax MS 300/5-7
202 Maroon Tide Dr 24333 276-236-6124
Derrick Spence, prin. Fax 236-4162

Grayson County SD
Supt. — See Independence
Baywood ES 100/PK-5
247 Grammer Ln 24333 276-236-4868
Michael Reavis, prin. Fax 236-3791
Fairview ES 100/K-5
2323 Fairview Rd 24333 276-236-2365
Michael Reavis, prin. Fax 236-6807

Gate City, Scott, Pop. 2,016
Scott County SD 3,800/PK-12
340 East Jackson St 24251 276-386-6118
John Ferguson, supt. Fax 386-2684
scott.k12.va.us
Shoemaker ES 600/PK-6
218 Shoemaker Dr 24251 276-386-7002
Renee Dishner, prin. Fax 386-7932
Yuma ES 200/K-6
130 Grover Cleveland Ln 24251 276-386-3109
Valerie Babb, prin. Fax 386-6183
Other Schools – See Duffield, Dungannon, Fort Blackmore, Hiltons, Nickelsville, Weber City

Glade Hill, Franklin
Franklin County SD
Supt. — See Rocky Mount
Glade Hill ES 300/PK-5
8081 Old Franklin Tpke 24092 540-576-3010
Kimberly Poindexter, prin. Fax 576-3404

Glade Spring, Washington, Pop. 1,443
Washington County SD
Supt. — See Abingdon
Glade Spring MS 300/6-8
33474 Stagecoach Rd 24340 276-739-3800
Andrew Hockett, prin. Fax 429-4211

Glen Allen, Henrico, Pop. 14,427
Henrico County SD
Supt. — See Richmond
Colonial Trail ES 500/K-5
12101 Liesfeld Farm Dr 23059 804-364-0055
Kirk Eggleston, prin. Fax 364-0877
Echo Lake ES 600/K-5
5200 Francistown Rd 23060 804-527-4672
Cynthia Foust, prin. Fax 527-4674
Glen Allen ES 600/K-5
11101 Mill Rd 23060 804-756-3040
Melissa Halquist-Pruden, prin. Fax 756-0486
Greenwood ES 600/K-5
10960 Greenwood Rd 23059 804-261-2970
Ryan Stein, prin.

Holman MS 900/6-8
600 Concourse Blvd 23059 804-346-1300
Brian Fellows Ph.D., prin. Fax 346-1309
Hungary Creek MS 1,000/6-8
4909 Francistown Rd 23060 804-527-2640
Robert Moose, prin. Fax 527-2642
Kaechele ES 400/K-5
5680 Pouncey Tract Rd 23059 804-364-8080
Cindy Patterson, prin. Fax 364-8085
Longdale ES 500/K-5
9500 Norfolk St 23060 804-261-5095
Lara Brooks, prin. Fax 515-1198
Rivers Edge ES 600/K-5
11600 Holman Ridge Rd 23059 804-935-6760
Pamela James, prin. Fax 935-6668
Shady Grove ES 700/K-5
12200 Wyndham Lake Dr 23059 804-360-0825
Dr. Stacey Austin, prin. Fax 364-0844
Short Pump MS 800/6-8
4701 Pouncey Tract Rd 23059 804-360-0800
Thomas McAuley, prin. Fax 360-0808
Springfield Park ES 700/K-5
4301 Fort McHenry Pkwy 23060 804-527-4630
Amanda Mulholland, prin. Fax 527-4631
Twin Hickory ES 700/K-5
4900 Twin Hickory Lake Dr 23059 804-360-4700
Michael Dussault, prin. Fax 360-4419

Gloucester, Gloucester
Gloucester County SD 5,600/PK-12
6099 T C Walker Rd 23061 804-693-5300
Dr. Walter Clemons, supt. Fax 693-7886
gets.gc.k12.va.us
Bethel ES 500/PK-5
2991 Hickory Fork Rd 23061 804-693-2360
Eileen Kersmarki, prin. Fax 693-0403
Botetourt ES 600/PK-5
6361 Main St 23061 804-693-2151
Felicia Hudgins, prin. Fax 693-3954
Page MS 500/6-8
5198 T C Walker Rd 23061 804-693-2540
Patricia McMahon, prin. Fax 693-2111
Peasley MS 800/6-8
2885 Hickory Fork Rd 23061 804-693-1499
Katharine Litton, prin. Fax 693-1497
Petsworth ES 300/PK-5
10658 George Washington Mem 23061
804-693-6161
Cathy Balderson, prin. Fax 693-1238
Other Schools – See Hayes

Gloucester Montessori S 50/PK-3
PO Box 1510 23061 804-693-6455
Ware Academy 100/PK-8
7936 John Clayton Mem Hwy 23061 804-693-3825

Goochland, Goochland, Pop. 840
Goochland County SD 2,400/PK-12
PO Box 169 23063 804-556-5630
Jeremy Raley, supt. Fax 556-3847
goochlandschools.org
Byrd ES 300/PK-5
2704 Hadensville Fife Rd 23063 804-556-5380
James Hopkins, prin. Fax 457-9303
Goochland ES 300/K-5
3150 River Rd W 23063 804-556-5321
Tina McCay, prin. Fax 556-6054
Goochland MS 600/6-8
3250-B River Rd W 23063 804-556-5320
Jennifer Rucker, prin. Fax 556-6223
Other Schools – See Crozier

Goode, Bedford
Bedford County SD
Supt. — See Bedford
Otter River ES 200/K-5
1044 Otter River Dr 24556 540-586-9210
Georgia Hairston, prin. Fax 586-7635

Goodview, Bedford
Bedford County SD
Supt. — See Bedford
Goodview ES 500/K-5
1374 Rivermont Academy Rd 24095 540-892-5674
Kim Morris, prin. Fax 892-5677
Stewartsville ES 400/K-5
1138 Wildcat Rd 24095 540-890-2174
Denise Gerstler, prin. Fax 890-0955

Gordonsville, Orange, Pop. 1,460
Orange County SD
Supt. — See Orange
Gordon-Barbour ES 300/K-5
500 W Baker St 22942 540-661-4500
Nick Sodano, prin. Fax 661-4499

Grafton, York
York County SD
Supt. — See Yorktown
Grafton Bethel ES 600/K-5
410 Lakeside Dr 23692 757-898-0350
Lisa Ruffieux, prin. Fax 898-0359

Great Falls, Fairfax, Pop. 14,902
Fairfax County SD
Supt. — See Falls Church
Forrestville ES 600/K-6
1085 Utterback Store Rd 22066 703-404-6000
Todd Franklin, prin. Fax 404-6097
Great Falls ES 600/K-6
701 Walker Rd 22066 703-757-2100
Sara Harper, prin. Fax 757-2197

Siena Academy 100/PK-5
1020 Springvale Rd 22066 703-759-4129
Ruth Barwick, prin. Fax 759-3753

Gretna, Pittsylvania, Pop. 1,254
Pittsylvania County SD
Supt. — See Chatham
Gretna ES 600/PK-5
PO Box 595 24557 434-656-2231
Paula Cocke, prin. Fax 656-2661
Gretna MS 500/6-8
201 Coffey St 24557 434-656-2217
Carter Lowry, prin. Fax 656-6122
Mt. Airy ES 200/PK-5
100 Mount Airy Elem Cir 24557 434-335-5291
Pamela Fields, prin. Fax 335-5585

Grottoes, Rockingham, Pop. 2,633
Rockingham County SD
Supt. — See Harrisonburg
South River ES 400/PK-5
2101 Elm Ave 24441 540-249-4001
Ashley Houff, prin. Fax 249-3110

Grundy, Buchanan, Pop. 1,011
Buchanan County SD 3,100/PK-12
1176 Booth Branch Rd 24614 276-935-4551
Melanie Hibbitts, supt. Fax 935-7150
www.buc.k12.va.us
Bevins ES 100/PK-5
8668 Slate Creek Rd 24614 276-244-3200
Karen Brown, prin. Fax 244-3201
Riverview S 800/PK-8
27382 Riverside Dr 24614 276-935-1613
Kimberly Hess, prin. Fax 935-0782
Other Schools – See Honaker, Hurley, Oakwood

Hague, Westmoreland
Westmoreland County SD
Supt. — See Montross
Cople ES 400/PK-5
7114 Cople Hwy 22469 804-472-2081
Leslie Steele, prin. Fax 472-2759

Halifax, Halifax, Pop. 1,298
Halifax County SD 5,500/PK-12
PO Box 1849 24558 434-476-2171
Dr. Mark Lineburg, supt. Fax 476-1858
www.halifax.k12.va.us
Sinai ES 300/K-5
1011 Sinai Elementary Dr 24558 434-476-6193
Dawn Miller, prin. Fax 830-3053
Other Schools – See Alton, Nathalie, Scottsburg, South Boston

Hamilton, Loudoun, Pop. 498
Loudoun County SD
Supt. — See Ashburn
Culbert ES 500/K-5
38180 W Colonial Hwy 20158 540-751-2540
Monica Kissel, prin. Fax 338-3108
Hamilton ES 200/PK-5
54 S Kerr St 20158 540-751-2570
Kelly Meisenzahl, prin. Fax 338-6882
Harmony MS 1,100/6-8
38174 W Colonial Hwy 20158 540-751-2500
Eric Stewart, prin. Fax 751-2501

Hampton, Hampton, Pop. 132,850
Hampton CSD 21,100/PK-12
1 Franklin St 23669 757-727-2000
Dr. Jeffrey Smith, supt. Fax 727-2002
www.hampton.k12.va.us
Aberdeen ES 500/K-5
1424 Aberdeen Rd 23666 757-825-4624
Karla Young, prin. Fax 825-4538
Andrews S 1,300/PK-8
3120 Victoria Blvd 23661 757-268-3333
Jeffrey Blowe, prin. Fax 727-2308
Armstrong ES for the Arts 300/K-5
3401 Matoaka Rd 23661 757-727-1067
Millicent Rogers, prin. Fax 727-1436
Asbury ES 400/K-5
140 Beach Rd 23664 757-850-5075
Marye Werling, prin. Fax 848-2332
Barron Fundamental ES 400/K-5
45 Fox Hill Rd 23669 757-850-5100
Karen Johnson, prin. Fax 850-5126
Bassette ES 400/K-5
671 Bell St 23661 757-727-1071
Dr. Bryce Johnson, prin. Fax 727-1275
Booker ES 400/K-5
160 Apollo Dr 23669 757-850-5096
Brynne Cere, prin. Fax 850-5283
Bryan ES 400/K-5
1021 N Mallory St 23663 757-727-1056
Lynette Nelms, prin. Fax 727-1467
Burbank ES 400/PK-5
40 Tide Mill Ln 23666 757-825-4642
Ashley Ide, prin. Fax 896-7806
Cary ES 400/K-5
2009 Andrews Blvd 23663 757-850-5092
Dr. Heidi Brezinski, prin. Fax 850-5068
Cooper ES 400/K-5
200 Marcella Rd 23666 757-825-4645
Tracie Albea, prin. Fax 825-4631
Davis MS 700/6-8
1435 Todds Ln 23666 757-825-4520
Violet Whiteman, prin. Fax 825-4533
Eaton MS 700/6-8
2108 Cunningham Dr 23666 757-825-4540
Sharon Slater, prin. Fax 825-4551
Forrest ES 500/K-5
1406 Todds Ln 23666 757-825-4627
Elizabeth Cromartie, prin. Fax 896-6731
Jones Magnet MS 600/6-8
1819 Nickerson Blvd 23663 757-850-7900
Dr. Daniel Bowling, prin. Fax 850-5395
Kraft ES 400/K-5
600 Concord Dr 23666 757-825-4634
Kara McCord, prin. Fax 825-4507

Langley ES 500/K-5
16 Rockwell Rd 23669 757-850-5105
Elizabeth Franks, prin. Fax 850-5409
Lindsay MS 700/6-8
1636 Briarfield Rd 23661 757-825-4560
Dr. Chevese Thomas, prin. Fax 825-4839
Machen ES 500/K-5
20 Sacramento Dr 23666 757-727-2900
Jennifer Humble, prin. Fax 766-5297
Moton ECC 300/PK-PK
339 Old Buckroe Rd 23663 757-727-1061
Joanne Drew, prin. Fax 727-8615
Phenix S 1,500/PK-8
1061 Big Bethel Rd 23666 757-268-3500
Robin Hunt-Crenshaw, prin. Fax 825-4741
Phillips ES 400/K-5
703 Lemaster Ave 23669 757-850-5079
Shelley Lawrence, prin. Fax 850-5622
Smith ES 400/K-5
379 Woodland Rd 23669 757-850-5088
Patrina Jenkins, prin. Fax 850-5455
Spratley Gifted Center 600/3-8
339 Woodland Rd 23669 757-850-5032
Dr. Kenneth Crum, prin. Fax 850-5186
Syms MS 1,000/6-8
170 Fox Hill Rd 23669 757-850-5050
Michael Blount, prin. Fax 850-5413
Tucker-Capps ES 400/K-5
113 Wellington Dr 23666 757-825-4641
Dr. Tiffany Geddie-Suggs, prin. Fax 825-4698
Tyler ES 400/K-5
57 Salina St 23669 757-727-1075
Shelly Spain, prin. Fax 727-1439

Calvary Christian Academy 100/PK-4
2311 Tower Pl 23666 757-325-4222
Calvary Classical S 100/PK-8
403 Whealton Rd 23666 757-262-0062
Ryan Noppen, head sch Fax 826-4017
Faith Outreach Education Center 100/PK-12
3105 W Mercury Blvd 23666 757-838-8927
Rev. Bobby Hartman, admin. Fax 838-4434
First Friends Christian Academy 100/PK-6
1062 Big Bethel Rd 23666 757-265-6966
Gloria Dei Lutheran S 400/PK-8
250 Fox Hill Rd 23669 757-851-6292
Linda Robinson, prin. Fax 850-3935
Hampton Christian Academy 200/PK-12
2419 N Armistead Ave 23666 757-838-7427
Meredith Cowley M.Ed., head sch Fax 827-8067
St. Mary Star of the Sea S 200/PK-8
14 N Willard Ave 23663 757-723-6358
Sr. Mary John, prin Fax 723-6544

Hardy, Bedford
Franklin County SD
Supt. — See Rocky Mount
Windy Gap ES 300/PK-5
465 Truman Hill Rd 24101 540-719-2809
Matthew Brain, prin. Fax 719-2816

Harrisonburg, Harrisonburg, Pop. 47,739
Harrisonburg CSD 5,200/PK-12
1 Court Sq 22802 540-434-9916
Scott Kizner, supt. Fax 434-5196
www.harrisonburg.k12.va.us
Bluestone ES K-5
750 Garbers Church Rd 22801
Anne Lintner, admin.
Harrison MS 800/6-8
1311 W Market St 22801 540-434-1949
Don Vale, prin. Fax 434-4052
Keister ES 500/K-5
100 Maryland Ave 22801 540-434-6585
Julie Zook, prin. Fax 434-4452
Rhodes Early Learning Center PK-PK
474 Linda Ln 22802
Sharon Shuttle, dir.
Skyline MS 700/6-8
470 Linda Ln 22802 540-434-6862
Daniel Kirwan, prin. Fax 434-6453
Smithland ES 500/K-5
474 Linda Ln 22802 540-434-6075
Janis Churchill, prin. Fax 434-6059
Spotswood ES 400/K-5
400 Mountain View Dr 22801 540-434-3429
Joy Blosser, prin. Fax 434-4453
Stone Spring ES 300/K-5
1575 Peach Grove Ave 22801 540-574-1199
Kathleen Taylor, prin. Fax 432-0053
Waterman ES 500/K-5
451 Chicago Ave 22802 540-434-8352
Jill Hart, prin. Fax 434-9996

Rockingham County SD 11,900/PK-12
100 Mount Clinton Pike 22802 540-564-3200
Dr. Oskar Scheikl, supt. Fax 564-3241
www.rockingham.k12.va.us
Lacey Spring ES 200/PK-5
8621 N Valley Pike 22802 540-433-7819
Donna Robinson, prin. Fax 433-0383
Mountain View ES 500/PK-5
2800 Rawley Pike 22801 540-438-1965
Karen Thomsen, prin. Fax 438-0455
Pleasant Valley ES 200/PK-5
215 Pleasant Valley Rd 22801 540-434-4557
Sara Hammill, prin. Fax 433-3528
Other Schools – See Bridgewater, Broadway, Dayton, Elkton, Fulks Run, Grottoes, Linville, Mc Gaheysville, Penn Laird, Timberville

---

Cornerstone Christian S 100/PK-8
197 Cornerstone Dr 22802 540-432-9816
Ben Frenchak, prin. Fax 438-0116
Eastern Mennonite S 400/K-12
801 Parkwood Dr 22802 540-236-6000

Hayes, Gloucester
Gloucester County SD
Supt. — See Gloucester
Abingdon ES 600/PK-5
7087 Powhatan Dr 23072 804-642-9885
Anna Harwood, prin. Fax 642-9692
Achilles ES 500/PK-5
9306 Guinea Rd 23072 804-642-9140
Katina Keener, prin. Fax 642-9406

Haymarket, Prince William, Pop. 1,713
Prince William County SD
Supt. — See Manassas
Alvey ES 800/K-5
5300 Waverly Farm Dr 20169 571-261-2556
Amber Macerelli, prin. Fax 261-2557
Gravely ES 800/K-5
4670 Waverly Farm Dr 20169 571-248-4930
Michael Kelchlin, prin. Fax 248-4932
Haymarket ES PK-5
15500 Learning Ln 20169 571-468-2800
Norma Moore, prin. Fax 285-0092
Mountain View ES 700/K-5
5600 Mcleod Way 20169 703-754-4161
Adriane Harrison, prin. Fax 754-8416
Reagan MS 1,300/6-8
15801 Tanning House Pl 20169 571-402-3500
Alfie Turner, prin. Fax 782-1638

St. Michael's Academy 200/PK-5
6735 Fayette St 20169 703-754-1948
Lorrie Crockett, prin. Fax 743-9150

Heathsville, Northumberland, Pop. 142
Northumberland County SD
Supt. — See Lottsburg
Northumberland ES 700/PK-5
757 Academic Ln 22473 804-580-8032
Stephanie Baker, prin.
Northumberland MS 300/6-8
175 Academic Ln 22473 804-580-5753
Javornda Ashton, prin.

Henry, Franklin
Franklin County SD
Supt. — See Rocky Mount
Henry ES 200/PK-5
200 Henry School Rd 24102 540-483-5676
Robin Whitmer, prin. Fax 483-0399

Herndon, Fairfax, Pop. 22,605
Fairfax County SD
Supt. — See Falls Church
Carson MS 1,300/7-8
13618 McLearen Rd 20171 703-925-3600
Gordon Stokes, prin. Fax 925-3697
Clearview ES 700/PK-6
12635 Builders Rd 20170 703-708-6000
Kimberly Willison, prin. Fax 708-6097
Coates ES 800/K-6
2480 River Birch Rd 20171 703-713-3000
Jesse Kraft, prin. Fax 713-3097
Crossfield ES 700/K-6
2791 Fox Mill Rd 20171 703-295-1100
Mark Granieri, prin. Fax 295-1197
Dranesville ES 700/K-6
1515 Powells Tavern Pl 20170 703-326-5200
Rae Mitchell, prin. Fax 326-5297
Floris ES 700/K-6
2708 Centreville Rd 20171 703-561-2900
Gail Porter, prin. Fax 561-2997
Fox Mill ES 600/K-6
2611 Viking Dr 20171 703-262-2700
Brian Moose, prin. Fax 262-2797
Herndon ES 900/K-6
630 Dranesville Rd 20170 703-326-3100
Teresa Fennessy, prin. Fax 326-3197
Herndon MS 1,000/7-8
901 Locust St 20170 703-904-4800
Justine Klena, prin. Fax 904-4897
Hutchison ES 900/K-6
13209 Parcher Ave 20170 703-925-8300
Ray Lonnett, prin. Fax 925-8397
McNair ES 1,100/PK-6
2499 Thomas Jefferson Dr 20171 703-793-4800
Melissa Goddin, prin. Fax 793-4897
Oak Hill ES 900/K-6
3210 Kinross Cir 20171 703-467-3500
Holly DeVore, prin. Fax 467-3597

Leport S - Herndon 100/PK-K
13251 Woodland Park Rd 20171 571-203-8686
Leport S - Reston 100/PK-K
11579 Cedar Chase Rd 20170 703-404-9733
Montessori S of Herndon 100/PK-6
840 Dranesville Rd 20170 703-437-8229
Mt. Pleasant Christian Academy 50/PK-3
2516 Squirrel Hill Rd 20171 703-793-1196
Margaret Aghayere, dir. Fax 793-1197
Nysmith S for the Gifted 600/PK-8
13625 EDS Dr 20171 703-713-3332
Oak Hill Christian S 100/PK-12
13525 Dulles Technology Dr 20171 703-796-6887
St. Joseph S 600/K-8
750 Peachtree St 20170 703-880-4350
Cindi Conroy, prin. Fax 880-4320
Temple Baptist S 200/PK-12
1545 Dranesville Rd 20170 703-437-7400

Highland Springs, Henrico, Pop. 15,359
Henrico County SD
Supt. — See Richmond
Fair Oaks ES 300/K-5
201 Jennings Rd 23075 804-328-4085
Candace Wilkerson, prin. Fax 328-4028
Highland Springs ES 500/K-5
600 Pleasant St 23075 804-328-4045
Dr. Shawnya Tolliver, prin. Fax 328-4038

Hillsville, Carroll, Pop. 2,663
Carroll County SD 4,000/PK-12
605 Pine St Ste 9 24343 276-730-3200
Dr. Shirley Perry, supt. Fax 730-3210
www.ccpsd.k12.va.us
Carroll County MS 900/6-8
1036 N Main St 24343 276-728-2382
Marc Quesenberry, prin. Fax 728-4089
Gladesboro ES 100/PK-5
7845 Snake Creek Rd 24343 276-398-2493
Franklin Hawks, prin. Fax 398-3384
Hillsville ES 500/PK-5
90 Patriot Ln 24343 276-728-7312
Samantha Reed, prin. Fax 728-3943
Other Schools – See Austinville, Cana, Fancy Gap, Galax

Hiltons, Scott
Scott County SD
Supt. — See Gate City
Hilton ES 200/PK-6
303 Academy Rd 24258 276-386-7430
Kelsey Taylor, prin. Fax 386-3192

Hiwassee, Pulaski, Pop. 260
Pulaski County SD
Supt. — See Pulaski
Snowville ES 200/PK-5
4858 Lead Mine Rd 24347 540-643-0766
Amy Shrewsbury, prin. Fax 639-0842

Honaker, Russell, Pop. 1,440
Buchanan County SD
Supt. — See Grundy
Council S 200/PK-7
7608 Helen Henderson Hwy 24260 276-859-9329
Joan Hart, prin. Fax 859-0631

Russell County SD
Supt. — See Lebanon
Honaker ES 700/PK-7
PO Box 744 24260 276-873-6301
Greg Mullins, prin. Fax 873-7263

Hopewell, Hopewell, Pop. 21,953
Hopewell CSD 4,300/PK-12
103 N 12th Ave 23860 804-541-6400
Dr. Melody Hackney, supt. Fax 541-6401
www.hopewell.k12.va.us
Copeland ES 700/K-5
400 Westhill Rd 23860 804-541-6410
Byron Davis, prin. Fax 541-6411
Dupont ES 700/K-5
300 S 18th Ave 23860 804-541-6406
Carla Fizer, prin. Fax 541-6407
James ES 700/K-5
1807 Arlington Rd 23860 804-541-6408
Judy Barnes, prin. Fax 541-6409
Woodlawn Learning Center 300/PK-PK
1100 Dinwiddie Ave 23860 804-541-6414
Joyce Jones, prin. Fax 458-2064
Woodson MS 900/6-8
1000 Winston Churchill Dr 23860 804-541-6404
Shannon Royster, prin. Fax 541-6405

West End Christian S 200/PK-12
1600 Atlantic St 23860 804-458-6142
Amy Griggs, prin. Fax 458-7183

Hot Springs, Bath, Pop. 727
Bath County SD
Supt. — See Warm Springs
Valley ES 300/PK-7
98 Panther Dr 24445 540-839-5395
Steve Sizemore, prin. Fax 839-5392

Huddleston, Bedford
Bedford County SD
Supt. — See Bedford
Huddleston ES 200/K-5
1027 Huddleston Dr 24104 540-297-5144
Traci Oakes, prin. Fax 297-8230

Hurley, Buchanan
Buchanan County SD
Supt. — See Grundy
Hurley S 400/PK-7
6911 Hurley Rd 24620 276-566-8523
Ruth Tester, prin. Fax 566-7751

Hurt, Pittsylvania, Pop. 1,295
Pittsylvania County SD
Supt. — See Chatham
Hurt ES 300/PK-5
315 Prospect Rd 24563 434-324-7231
Kathryn Lowry, prin. Fax 324-7233

Faith Christian Academy 200/PK-12
PO Box 670 24563 434-324-8276
Bruce Devers, admin. Fax 324-8279

Independence, Grayson, Pop. 933
Grayson County SD 1,700/PK-12
PO Box 888 24348 276-773-2832
Kelly Wilmore, supt. Fax 773-2939
www.grayson.k12.va.us
Independence ES 300/K-5
PO Box 429 24348 276-773-2722
Susan Mitchell, prin. Fax 773-9566
Independence MS 200/6-8
PO Box 155 24348 276-773-3020
Jamey Hale, prin. Fax 773-0479
Other Schools – See Fries, Galax, Trout Dale

Irvington, Lancaster, Pop. 430

Chesapeake Academy 100/PK-8
PO Box 8 22480 804-438-5575

Isle of Wight, Isle of Wight

Isle of Wight Academy 600/PK-12
PO Box 105 23397 757-357-3866

Jonesville, Lee, Pop. 1,025
Lee County SD 3,400/PK-12
153 School Board Pl 24263 276-346-2107
Dr. Brian Austin, supt. Fax 346-0307
sites.google.com/leecoschools.com/lcps
Flatwoods ES 400/PK-5
205 Flatwoods School Rd 24263 276-346-2799
Michelle Warner, prin. Fax 346-4162
Jonesville MS 200/6-8
160 Bulldog Cir 24263 276-346-1011
Stacey Belcher, prin. Fax 346-1411
Other Schools – See Dryden, Ewing, Pennington Gap, Rose Hill, Saint Charles

Keezletown, Rockingham

Redeemer Classical S 100/PK-8
1688 Indian Trail Rd 22832 540-437-0880
Teresa Patton, prin.

Kenbridge, Lunenburg, Pop. 1,244
Lunenburg County SD 1,600/PK-12
PO Box 710 23944 434-676-2467
Charles Berkley, supt. Fax 676-1000
www.lun.k12.va.us
Kenbridge ES 400/PK-5
215 Nottoway Falls Rd 23944 434-676-2491
Lucy Hall, prin. Fax 676-8636
Other Schools – See Victoria

Keswick, Albemarle
Albemarle County SD
Supt. — See Charlottesville
Stony Point ES 300/PK-5
3893 Stony Point Rd 22947 434-973-6405
Andy Johnson, prin. Fax 973-9751

Keysville, Charlotte, Pop. 820
Charlotte County SD
Supt. — See Charlotte Court House
Eureka ES 400/PK-5
315 Eureka School Rd 23947 434-736-8458
Brian Hamilton, prin. Fax 736-9830

Kilmarnock, Lancaster, Pop. 1,466
Lancaster County SD
Supt. — See Weems
Lancaster MS 500/4-8
191 School St 22482 804-462-5100
Jessica Davis, prin. Fax 435-0589

King and Queen Court House, King and Queen, Pop. 84
King & Queen County SD 800/PK-12
PO Box 97 23085 804-785-5981
Dr. Carol Carter, supt. Fax 785-5686
www.kqps.net
Other Schools – See Mattaponi, Saint Stephens Church

King George, King George, Pop. 4,296
King George County SD 4,200/K-12
PO Box 1239 22485 540-775-5833
Dr. Robert B. Benson, supt. Fax 775-2165
www.kgcs.k12.va.us
King George ES 900/K-6
10381 Ridge Rd 22485 540-775-5411
Ronald Monroe, prin. Fax 775-2715
King George MS 600/7-8
8246 Dahlgren Rd 22485 540-775-2331
Jennifer Collins, prin. Fax 775-0263
Sealston ES 800/K-6
11048 Fletchers Chapel Rd 22485 540-775-3400
Cynthia Malyevac, prin. Fax 775-9953
Other Schools – See Dahlgren

King William, King William, Pop. 228
King William County SD 2,200/K-12
PO Box 185 23086 804-769-3434
Dr. David O. White, supt. Fax 769-3312
www.kwcps.k12.va.us
Acquinton ES 500/3-5
18550 King William Rd 23086 804-769-3434
Shelley Nester, prin.
Cool Spring PS 500/K-2
7301 Acquinton Church Rd 23086 804-769-3434
Rachel Ball, prin.
Hamilton-Holmes MS 500/6-8
18444 King William Rd 23086 804-769-3434
Tina Rudd, prin.

La Crosse, Mecklenburg, Pop. 596
Mecklenburg County SD
Supt. — See Boydton
La Crosse ES 400/PK-5
1000 School Cir 23950 434-757-7374
Connie Puckett, prin. Fax 757-1378

Lake Ridge, Prince William, Pop. 39,354

Prince William Academy 200/PK-6
3480 Commission Ct 22192 703-491-1444

Lancaster, Lancaster
Lancaster County SD
Supt. — See Weems
Lancaster PS 400/PK-3
36 Primary School Cir 22503 804-462-5100
Michael Daddario, prin. Fax 435-0989

Langley AFB, See Hampton
York County SD
Supt. — See Yorktown
Bethel Manor ES 500/K-5
1797 1st St 23665 757-867-7439
Dr. David Reitz, prin. Fax 867-7435

Lawrenceville, Brunswick, Pop. 1,414
Brunswick County SD 1,900/PK-12
1718 Farmers Field Rd 23868 434-848-3138
Dora Wynn M.Ed., supt. Fax 848-4001
www.brunswickcps.org
Meherrin-Powellton ES 300/PK-5
11555 Dry Bread Rd 23868 434-577-5000
Sandra King, prin. Fax 577-5001
Russell MS 400/6-8
19400 Christanna Hwy 23868 434-848-2132
Dr. Virginia Berry, prin. Fax 848-6201
Totaro ES 400/PK-5
19350 Christanna Hwy 23868 434-848-3209
Carolyn Meredith, prin.
Other Schools – See Alberta

Brunswick Academy 300/PK-12
2100 Planters Rd 23868 434-848-2220

Lebanon, Russell, Pop. 3,395
Russell County SD 4,200/PK-12
PO Box 8 24266 276-889-6500
Dr. Greg Brown, supt. Fax 889-6508
www.russell.k12.va.us
Lebanon ES 300/2-4
PO Box 668 24266 276-889-6531
Tabitha Long, prin. Fax 889-2008
Lebanon MS 400/5-7
PO Box 577 24266 276-889-6548
Nathan Breeding, prin. Fax 889-4262
Lebanon PS 300/PK-1
919 E Main St 24266 276-889-4507
Rebecca Sykes, prin. Fax 889-4509
Other Schools – See Castlewood, Honaker, Rosedale, Swords Creek

Leesburg, Loudoun, Pop. 41,241
Loudoun County SD
Supt. — See Ashburn
Ball's Bluff ES 600/PK-5
821 Battlefield Pkwy NE 20176 571-252-2880
Dr. Melinda Carper, prin. Fax 779-8804
Belmont Ridge MS 1,500/6-8
19045 Upper Belmont Pl 20176 571-252-2220
Dr. Ryan Hitchman, prin. Fax 669-1455
Catoctin ES 600/PK-5
311 Catoctin Cir SW 20175 571-252-2940
Janet Platenberg, prin. Fax 771-6773
Cool Spring ES 700/PK-5
501 Tavistock Dr SE 20175 571-252-2890
Chris Cadwell, prin. Fax 771-6764
Douglass ES 700/PK-5
510 Principal Drummond SE 20175 571-252-1920
Melissa Logan, prin. Fax 258-0595
Evergreen Mill ES 700/PK-5
491 Evergreen Mill Rd SE 20175 571-252-2900
Michael Pellegrino, prin. Fax 779-8837
Harper Park MS 1,000/6-8
701 Potomac Station Dr NE 20176 571-252-2820
Elizabeth Robinson, prin. Fax 779-8867
Leesburg ES 600/K-5
323 Plaza St NE 20176 571-252-2860
Angela Robinson, prin. Fax 771-6725
Lucketts ES 300/K-5
14550 James Monroe Hwy 20176 571-252-2070
Carolyn Clement, prin. Fax 771-6692
Reid ES 700/PK-5
800 N King St 20176 571-252-2050
Brenda Jochems, prin. Fax 669-1469
Seldens Landing ES 900/K-5
43345 Coton Commons Dr 20176 571-252-2260
Garett Brazina, prin. Fax 779-8953
Simpson MS 1,000/6-8
490 Evergreen Mill Rd SE 20175 571-252-2840
Lenny Compton, prin. Fax 771-6643
Smart's Mill MS 1,100/6-8
850 N King St 20176 571-252-2030
William Waldman, prin. Fax 669-1485
Sycolin Creek ES 700/PK-5
21100 Evergreen Mills Rd 20175 571-252-2910
Derek Racino, prin. Fax 771-9616
Tolbert ES 800/K-5
691 Potomac Station Dr NE 20176 571-252-2870
Susan Ward, prin. Fax 779-8989

Loudoun Country Day S 300/PK-8
20600 Red Cedar Dr 20175 703-777-3841
Dr. Randall Hollister Ph.D., hdmstr. Fax 771-1346
Montessori S of Leesburg 100/PK-K
166 Fort Evans Rd NE 20176 703-779-7791
Providence Academy 200/K-8
835 Lee Ave SW Ste 604 20175 571-252-9259
Kevin Lockerbie, head sch Fax 779-3561
St. John the Apostle Preschool PK-PK
101 Oakcrest Manor Dr NE 20176 703-777-7873
Dr. Jane Taylor, dir. Fax 771-9016

Lexington, Lexington, Pop. 6,907
Lexington CSD 500/K-8
300 Diamond St 24450 540-463-7146
Dr. Scott Jefferies, supt. Fax 464-5230
www.lexedu.org
Harrington-Waddell ES 300/K-5
100 Pendleton Pl 24450 540-463-5353
Rebecca Walters, prin. Fax 464-3250
Lylburn-Downing MS 200/6-8
302 Diamond St 24450 540-463-3532
Jason White, prin.

Rockbridge County SD 2,800/PK-12
2893 Collierstown Rd 24450 540-463-7386
Dr. Phillip Thompson, supt. Fax 463-7823
www.rockbridge.k12.va.us
Central ES 500/PK-5
85 Central Rd 24450 540-463-4500
Robin Parker, prin. Fax 463-2225
Maury River MS 500/6-8
600 Waddell St 24450 540-463-3129
Billy Thomas, prin. Fax 464-4838
Other Schools – See Buena Vista, Fairfield, Natural Bridge Station

---

Rockbridge Christian Academy 100/PK-12
PO Box 570 24450 540-463-5456
Mary Phillips, admin. Fax 463-3485

Linville, Rockingham
Rockingham County SD
Supt. — See Harrisonburg
Linville-Edom ES 200/PK-5
3653 Linville Edom Rd 22834 540-833-6916
Dr. Amy Painter, prin. Fax 833-2267

Locust Grove, Orange
Orange County SD
Supt. — See Orange
Locust Grove ES 400/3-5
31208 Constitution Hwy 22508 540-661-4440
Evan Straub, prin. Fax 661-4483
Locust Grove MS 600/6-8
6368 Flat Run Rd 22508 540-661-4480
Todd Satterwhite, prin. Fax 854-6430
Locust Grove PS 400/K-2
31230 Constitution Hwy 22508 540-661-4420
Lee Erik Finger, prin. Fax 661-4419

Locust Hill, Middlesex
Middlesex County SD
Supt. — See Saluda
Middlesex ES 600/PK-5
PO Box 375 23092 804-758-2496
Danielle Allen, prin. Fax 758-2369
St. Clare Walker MS 300/6-8
PO Box 9 23092 804-758-2561
Elizabeth Sanders, prin. Fax 758-0834

Lorton, Fairfax, Pop. 17,779
Fairfax County SD
Supt. — See Falls Church
Gunston ES 600/K-6
10100 Gunston Rd 22079 703-541-3600
JoVon Rogers, prin. Fax 541-3697
Laurel Hill ES 900/K-6
8390 Laurel Crest Dr 22079 703-551-5300
Janice Dalton, prin. Fax 551-5397
Lorton Station ES 1,000/K-6
9298 Lewis Chapel Rd 22079 571-642-6000
Joanne Jackson, prin. Fax 642-6097
South County MS 1,100/7-8
8700 Laurel Crest Dr 22079 703-690-5500
Marsha Manning, prin. Fax 690-5597

Lottsburg, Northumberland
Northumberland County SD 1,400/PK-12
2172 Northumberland Hwy 22511 804-529-6134
Dr. Holly Wargo, supt. Fax 529-6449
www.nucps.net
Other Schools – See Heathsville

Louisa, Louisa, Pop. 1,520
Louisa County SD
Supt. — See Mineral
Jefferson ES 500/PK-5
1782 Jefferson Hwy 23093 540-967-0492
Dr. William F. Caten Ed.D., prin. Fax 967-0337
Moss-Nuckols ES 700/PK-5
2055 Courthouse Rd 23093 540-967-1347
Anita Roane, prin. Fax 967-3173
Trevilians ES 400/PK-5
2035 South Spotswood Trl 23093 540-967-1108
Gary Black, prin. Fax 967-3695

Lovettsville, Loudoun, Pop. 1,565
Loudoun County SD
Supt. — See Ashburn
Lovettsville ES 500/K-5
49 S Loudoun St 20180 540-751-2470
Dennis Racke, prin. Fax 771-6703

Lovingston, Nelson, Pop. 495
Nelson County SD 2,000/PK-12
PO Box 276 22949 434-260-7646
Dr. Jeff Comer, supt. Fax 263-7115
www.nelson.k12.va.us
Nelson MS 400/6-8
6925 Thomas Nelson Hwy 22949 434-263-4801
Dr. Roger Dunnick, prin. Fax 263-4483
Other Schools – See Afton, Arrington

Low Moor, Alleghany, Pop. 252
Alleghany County SD 2,400/K-12
PO Box 140 24457 540-863-1800
Eugene Kotulka, supt. Fax 863-1804
www.alleghany.k12.va.us/
Other Schools – See Clifton Forge, Covington

Luray, Page, Pop. 4,837
Page County SD 3,500/PK-12
735 W Main St 22835 540-743-6533
Donna Whitley-Smith, supt. Fax 743-7784
www.pagecounty.k12.va.us
Luray ES 500/PK-5
555 1st St 22835 540-743-4078
Dr. Teresa Wiita, prin. Fax 743-1014
Luray MS 400/6-8
14 Luray Ave 22835 540-843-2660
Kelly Lawton, prin. Fax 743-1709
Other Schools – See Rileyville, Shenandoah, Stanley

Lynchburg, Lynchburg, Pop. 73,910
Bedford County SD
Supt. — See Bedford
Boonsboro ES 300/K-5
1234 Eagle Cir 24503 434-384-2881
Beth Williams, prin. Fax 384-4661

Campbell County SD
Supt. — See Rustburg
Brookville MS 700/6-8
320 Bee Dr 24502 434-239-9267
Edwin Martin, prin. Fax 237-8974
Leesville Road ES 600/PK-5
25 Lewis Way 24502 434-239-0303
Amy Hunley, prin. Fax 239-0355
Tomahawk ES 700/PK-5
155 Bee Dr 24502 434-237-4090
Toby Ackerman, prin. Fax 239-2162

Lynchburg CSD 8,600/PK-12
PO Box 2497 24505 434-515-5000
Dr. Larry A. Massie, supt. Fax 846-1500
www.lcsedu.net
Bass ES 300/PK-5
1730 Seabury Ave 24501 434-515-5200
Monica H. Hendricks, prin. Fax 522-2374
Bedford Hills ES 600/PK-5
4330 Morningside Dr 24503 434-515-5210
Sherri L. Steele, prin. Fax 384-1703
Dearington ES for Innovation 200/PK-5
210 Smyth St 24501 434-515-5220
Daniel J. Rule, prin. Fax 522-2351
Dunbar MS for Innovation 600/6-8
1200 Polk St 24504 434-515-5310
Derrick R. Brown, prin. Fax 522-3727
Heritage ES 400/PK-5
501 Leesville Rd 24502 434-515-5230
Sharon J. Anderson, prin. Fax 582-1175
Linkhorne ES 500/PK-5
2501 Linkhorne Dr 24503 434-515-5240
Karen K. Dearden, prin. Fax 384-9620
Linkhorne MS 600/6-8
2525 Linkhorne Dr 24503 434-515-5330
Karin H. Blay, prin. Fax 384-2810
Miller ES for Innovation 300/PK-5
600 Mansfield Ave 24501 434-515-5300
Dr. Amy D. Huskin, prin. Fax 522-2301
Munro ES 300/PK-5
4641 Locksview Rd 24503 434-515-5260
Donna D. Bear, prin. Fax 386-3067
Payne ES 500/PK-5
1201 Floyd St 24501 434-515-5270
Kellie S. Baldwin, prin. Fax 522-3791
Perrymont ES 500/PK-5
409 Perrymont Ave 24502 434-515-5250
Karen S. Nelson, prin. Fax 582-1108
Sandusky ES 400/PK-5
5828 Apache Ln 24502 434-515-5280
Derrick E. Womack, prin. Fax 582-1184
Sandusky MS 600/6-8
805 Chinook Pl 24502 434-515-5350
Matthew A. Mason, prin. Fax 582-1183
Sheffield ES 500/PK-5
115 Kenwood Pl 24502 434-515-5290
Lisa P. Lee, prin. Fax 582-1174

Doss Junior Academy 100/K-12
19 George St 24502 434-237-1899
Holy Cross Regional S 200/PK-12
2125 Langhorne Rd 24501 434-847-5436
Mary Sherry, prin. Fax 847-4156
James River Day S 300/K-8
5039 Boonsboro Rd 24503 434-384-7385
Peter Twadell, head sch Fax 384-5937
Liberty Christian Academy 2,000/PK-12
100 Mountain View Rd 24502 434-832-2000
John Patterson, supt. Fax 832-2027
New Covenant S 400/K-12
122 Fleetwood Dr 24501 434-847-8313
Tree of Life Academy 100/PK-5
2812 Greenview Dr 24502 434-455-0294
Dr. Fay Andrist, admin. Fax 455-5952

Mc Gaheysville, Rockingham
Rockingham County SD
Supt. — See Harrisonburg
Mc Gaheysville ES 300/PK-5
9508 Spotswood Trl 22840 540-289-3004
Pam Dowrey, prin. Fax 289-6832

Machipongo, Northampton
Northampton County SD 1,700/PK-12
7207 Young St 23405 757-678-5151
Charles E. Lawrence, supt. Fax 678-7267
www.ncpsk12.com
Other Schools – See Cape Charles, Eastville, Exmore

Mc Kenney, Dinwiddie, Pop. 469
Dinwiddie County SD
Supt. — See Dinwiddie
Sunnyside ES 200/K-5
PO Box 250 23872 804-478-2313
Wanda Snodgrass, prin. Fax 478-2315

Mc Lean, Fairfax, Pop. 46,663
Fairfax County SD
Supt. — See Falls Church
Chesterbrook ES 700/K-6
1753 Kirby Rd 22101 703-714-8200
Robert Fuqua, prin. Fax 448-0971
Churchill Road ES 900/K-6
7100 Churchill Rd 22101 703-288-8400
Donald Hutzel, prin. Fax 288-8497
Cooper MS 800/7-8
977 Balls Hill Rd 22101 703-442-5800
Arlene Randall, prin. Fax 442-5897
Kent Gardens ES 900/K-6
1717 Melbourne Dr 22101 703-394-5600
Holly McGuigan, prin. Fax 394-5697
Sherman ES 400/PK-6
6633 Brawner St 22101 703-506-7900
Kathleen Quigley, prin. Fax 506-7997
Spring Hill ES 1,000/K-6
8201 Lewinsville Rd 22102 703-506-3400
William Olk, prin. Fax 506-3497

BASIS Independent McLean PK-12
8000 Jones Branch Dr 22102 703-854-1253
Ron Kim, head sch
Brooksfield S 100/PK-4
1830 Kirby Rd 22101 703-356-5437
Langley S 500/PK-8
1411 Balls Hill Rd 22101 703-356-1920
Dr. Elinor Scully, head sch Fax 790-9712
Montessori S of McLean 200/PK-6
1711 Kirby Rd 22101 703-790-1049
Potomac S 1,000/K-12
1301 Potomac School Rd 22101 703-356-4100
John Kowalik, head sch Fax 883-9031
St. John Academy 300/PK-8
6422 Linway Ter 22101 703-356-7554
Michael Busekrus, prin. Fax 448-3811
St. Luke S 200/PK-8
7005 Georgetown Pike 22101 703-356-1508
Louis Silvano, prin. Fax 356-1141

Madison, Madison, Pop. 214
Madison County SD 1,900/PK-12
60 School Board Ct 22727 540-948-3780
Dr. Matthew Eberhardt, supt. Fax 948-6988
www2.madisonschools.k12.va.us
Madison PS 500/PK-2
158 Primary School Dr 22727 540-948-3781
Mike Coiner, prin. Fax 948-3365
Wetsel MS 400/6-8
186 Mountaineer Ln 22727 540-948-3783
Donald Dodson, prin. Fax 948-4809
Yowell ES 400/3-5
1809 N Main St 22727 540-948-4511
Joe Kubricki, prin. Fax 948-3969

Madison Heights, Amherst, Pop. 11,015
Amherst County SD
Supt. — See Amherst
Amelon ES 500/PK-5
132 Amer Cir 24572 434-528-6498
Jay Sales, prin. Fax 929-1547
Elon ES 300/PK-5
147 Younger Dr 24572 434-528-6496
Kimberly Scott, prin. Fax 386-9300
Madison Heights ES 500/PK-5
287 Learning Ln 24572 434-846-2151
Marvin McGinnis, prin. Fax 845-5109
Monelison MS 600/6-8
257 Trojan Rd 24572 434-846-1307
Regina Phillips, prin. Fax 846-5318

Temple Christian S 300/PK-12
PO Box 970 24572 434-846-0024

Manakin Sabot, Goochland

Hunter Classical Christian S 50/K-6
635 Manakin Rd 23103 804-708-0048
Dr. Ann McLean, head sch

Manassas, Manassas, Pop. 36,735
Manassas CSD 7,100/PK-12
8700 Centreville Rd Ste 400 20110 571-377-6000
Dr. Catherine Magouyrk, supt. Fax 257-8801
www.mcpsva.org
Baldwin ES 600/PK-4
9000 Tudor Ln 20110 571-377-6100
Laura Goldzung, prin. Fax 257-8654
Baldwin IS, 1978 Eagle Way 20110 5-6
Amanda Wagner, prin. 571-921-8000
Dean ES 600/K-4
9601 Prince William St 20110 571-377-6300
Dr. Zella Jones, prin. Fax 257-8688
Haydon ES 600/PK-4
9075 Park Ave 20110 571-377-6200
Amanda Wilder, prin. Fax 257-8708
Mayfield IS 1,000/5-6
9400 Mayfield Ct 20110 571-377-6600
Kara Mills, prin. Fax 257-1562
Metz JHS 1,000/7-8
9700 Fairview Ave 20110 571-377-6800
Kimberly Buckheit, prin. Fax 257-8615
Round ES 500/K-4
10100 Hastings Dr 20110 571-377-6400
Scott Baldwin, prin. Fax 257-8759
Weems ES 600/K-4
8750 Weems Rd 20110 571-377-6500
Dave Rupert, prin. Fax 257-8786

Prince William County SD 85,100/PK-12
PO Box 389 20108 703-791-7200
Steven Walts Ed.D., supt. Fax 791-8033
www.pwcs.edu
Ashland ES 900/K-5
15300 Bowmans Folly Dr 20112 703-583-8774
Andrew Jacks, prin. Fax 583-9542
Bennett ES 800/K-5
8800 Old Dominion Dr 20110 703-361-8261
Matthew Ritter, prin. Fax 361-1147
Benton MS 1,300/6-8
7411 Hoadly Rd 20112 703-791-0727
Joseph Graczyk, prin. Fax 791-0977
Coles ES 500/K-5
7405 Hoadly Rd 20112 703-791-3141
Kathryn Forgas, prin. Fax 791-4761
Ellis ES 600/PK-5
10400 Kim Graham Ln 20109 703-365-0287
Salvador Rivera, prin. Fax 365-0257
Loch Lomond ES 500/K-5
7900 Augusta Rd 20111 703-368-4128
Kimberly Werle, prin. Fax 257-8438
Marshall ES 600/K-5
12505 Kahns Rd 20112 703-791-2099
Dr. Kris Waldrop, prin. Fax 791-0032
Mullen ES 700/K-5
8000 Rodes Dr 20109 703-330-0427
Rhonda Ellington, prin. Fax 330-7415
Parkside MS 1,200/6-8
8602 Mathis Ave 20110 703-361-3106
Dr. Mary Jane Boynton, prin. Fax 361-8993
Pennington S 600/1-8
9305 Stonewall Rd 20110 703-369-6644
Amanda McCulla, prin. Fax 369-4206
Saunders MS 1,100/6-8
13557 Spriggs Rd 20112 703-670-9188
Sheila Huckestein, prin. Fax 670-3078
Signal Hill ES 600/PK-5
9553 Birmingham Dr 20111 703-530-7541
Carrie Webb, prin. Fax 530-7542
Sinclair ES 800/PK-5
7801 Garner Dr 20109 703-361-4811
Dr. Sharon Woodson, prin. Fax 361-7787
Stonewall MS 1,200/6-8
10100 Lomond Dr 20109 703-361-3185
John Miller, prin. Fax 368-1266
Sudley ES 800/K-5
9744 Copeland Dr 20109 703-361-3444
Kendra Chapman, prin. Fax 361-8795
West Gate ES 700/PK-5
8031 Urbanna Rd 20109 703-368-4404
Julie Svendsen, prin. Fax 361-0503
Woodbine Preschool Center 200/PK-PK
13225 Canova Dr 20112 703-791-3151
Fax 791-2669
Yorkshire ES 900/PK-5
7610 Old Centreville Rd 20111 703-361-3124
Lyn Marsilio, prin. Fax 361-6184
Other Schools – See Bristow, Dale City, Dumfries, Gainesville, Haymarket, Montclair, Nokesville, Triangle, Woodbridge

---

All Saints S 600/PK-8
9294 Stonewall Rd 20110 703-368-4400
David Conroy, prin. Fax 393-2157
Emmanuel Christian S 200/PK-5
8302 Spruce St 20111 703-369-3950
Dave Melander, head sch Fax 330-9285
Manassas Adventist Preparatory S 50/K-8
8225 Barrett Dr 20109 703-361-5593
Manassas Christian S 200/PK-8
9296 West Carondelet Dr 20111 703-393-6555

Manassas Park, Manassas Park, Pop. 13,791
Manassas Park CSD 3,200/PK-12
1 Park Center Ct Ste A 20111 703-335-8850
Dr. C. Bruce McDade, supt. Fax 361-4583
www.mpark.net
Cougar ES 900/PK-2
9330 Brandon St 20111 703-392-1317
Ann Gwynn, prin. Fax 392-7204
Manassas Park ES 700/3-5
9298 Cougar Ct 20111 703-368-2032
Stacey Mamon, prin. Fax 396-7172
Manassas Park MS 800/6-8
8202 Euclid Ave 20111 703-361-1510
Pam Kalso, prin. Fax 331-3538

Mappsville, Accomack, Pop. 419
Accomack County SD
Supt. — See Accomac
Kegotank ES 700/PK-5
PO Box 28 23407 757-824-4756
Jennifer Annis, prin. Fax 824-4601

Marion, Smyth, Pop. 5,878
Smyth County SD 4,800/PK-12
121 Bagley Cir Ste 300 24354 276-783-3791
Dr. Dennis Carter, supt. Fax 783-3291
www.scsb.org
Marion ES 400/PK-5
188 Star Mountain Dr 24354 276-783-3021
Dr. Kimberly Williams, prin. Fax 781-2053
Marion MS 500/6-8
134 Wilden St 24354 276-783-4466
Damon Mazoff, prin. Fax 783-4952
Oak Point ES 500/PK-5
138 Oak Point Dr 24354 276-783-2609
Dr. Gary Foulke, prin. Fax 783-9463
Other Schools – See Atkins, Chilhowie, Saltville, Sugar Grove

Marshall, Fauquier, Pop. 1,447
Fauquier County SD
Supt. — See Warrenton
Thompson ES 300/PK-5
3284 Rectortown Rd 20115 540-422-7690
Marypat Warter, prin. Fax 422-7709

Martinsville, Martinsville, Pop. 13,595
Henry County SD
Supt. — See Collinsville
Carver ES 500/PK-5
220 Trott Cir 24112 276-957-2226
Marcie Seay, prin. Fax 957-4234
Laurel Park MS 800/6-8
280 Laurel Park Ave 24112 276-632-7216
Jo Ellen Hylton, prin. Fax 632-4865
Mt. Olivet ES 300/PK-5
255 Lancer Ln 24112 276-638-1022
Elizabeth Minter, prin. Fax 638-2281
Rich Acres ES 300/PK-5
400 Rich Acres School Rd 24112 276-638-3366
Renee Scott, prin. Fax 638-2462

Martinsville CSD 2,100/PK-12
PO Box 5548 24115 276-403-5820
Dr. Zebedee Talley, supt. Fax 403-5825
www.martinsville.k12.va.us
Clearview Early Learning Center 100/PK-PK
800 Ainsley St 24112 276-403-5800
Sheliah Williams, dir. Fax 638-3031
Harris ES 500/K-4
710 Smith St 24112 276-403-5838
Renee Brown, prin. Fax 632-3069
Henry ES 400/K-4
1810 E Church Street Ext 24112 276-403-5812
Cameron Cooper, prin. Fax 656-1928
Martinsville MS 500/5-8
201 Brown St 24112 276-403-5886
Cynthia Tarpley, prin. Fax 638-4140

Mathews, Mathews, Pop. 530
Mathews County SD 1,100/K-12
PO Box 369 23109 804-725-3909
Nancy Welch, supt. Fax 725-3951
www.mathews.k12.va.us
Hunter MS 300/5-8
PO Box 339 23109 804-725-2434
Laurel Byrd, prin. Fax 725-2337
Lee-Jackson ES 400/K-4
PO Box 219 23109 804-725-2580
Andrew Greve, prin. Fax 725-3428

Matoaca, Chesterfield, Pop. 2,359
Chesterfield County SD
Supt. — See Chesterfield
Matoaca ES 500/PK-5
6627 River Rd 23803 804-590-3100
Mary Thrift, prin. Fax 590-1323
Matoaca MS 1,100/6-8
6001 Hickory Rd 23803 804-590-3110
Dr. Gayle Hines, prin. Fax 590-9378

Mattaponi, King and Queen
King & Queen County SD
Supt. — See King and Queen Court House
King & Queen ES 300/PK-7
24667 The Trail 23110 804-785-5830
Allison Jordan, prin. Fax 785-3611

Max Meadows, Wythe, Pop. 559
Wythe County SD
Supt. — See Wytheville
Ft. Chiswell MS 400/6-8
101 Pioneer Trl 24360 276-637-4400
Brett Booher, prin. Fax 637-4452
Max Meadows ES 300/PK-5
PO Box 326 24360 276-637-3211
Kimley Frye, prin. Fax 637-6568

Meadows of Dan, Patrick
Patrick County SD
Supt. — See Stuart
Meadows of Dan ES 400/PK-7
3003 Jeb Stuart Hwy 24120 276-952-2424
Jason Wood, prin. Fax 952-1160

Meadowview, See Emory
Washington County SD
Supt. — See Abingdon
Meadowview ES 600/PK-5
14050 Glenbrook Ave 24361 276-739-3900
Tammy Williams, prin. Fax 944-2113
Rhea Valley ES 400/PK-5
31305 Rhea Valley Rd 24361 276-739-4200
Michael Colston, prin. Fax 475-4055

Mechanicsville, Hanover, Pop. 35,793
Hanover County SD
Supt. — See Ashland
Battlefield Park ES 500/K-5
5501 Mechanicsville Tpke 23111 804-723-3600
Judy Bradley, prin. Fax 723-3605
Chickahominy MS 1,200/6-8
9450 Atlee Station Rd 23116 804-723-2160
Mark Beckett, prin. Fax 723-2191
Cold Harbor ES 500/K-4
6740 Cold Harbor Rd 23111 804-723-3620
Dr. Cheri Fisher, prin. Fax 723-3630
Cool Spring ES 700/K-5
9964 Honey Meadows Rd 23116 804-723-3560
Dr. Paula Brown, prin. Fax 723-3564
Jackson MS 1,100/6-8
8021 Lee Davis Rd 23111 804-723-2260
Dr. Quentin Ballard, prin. Fax 723-2261
Kersey Creek ES 600/K-5
10004 Learning Ln 23116 804-723-3440
Lisa Thompson, prin. Fax 723-3450
Laurel Meadow ES 700/K-5
8248 Lee Davis Rd 23111 804-723-2040
Sandra Crowder, prin. Fax 723-2058
Mechanicsville ES 600/K-5
7425 Mechanicsville Elem Dr 23111 804-723-3640
Dr. Amy Robinson, prin. Fax 723-3643
Oak Knoll MS 900/6-8
10295 Chamberlayne Rd 23116 804-365-4740
Caroline Harris, prin. Fax 365-4741
Pearsons Corner ES 500/K-5
8290 New Ashcake Rd 23116 804-723-3660
Dawn Armstrong, prin. Fax 723-3663
Pole Green ES 600/K-5
8993 Pole Green Park Ln 23116 804-365-4700
Rhonda Voorhees, prin. Fax 365-4717
Rural Point ES 400/K-5
7161 Studley Rd 23116 804-723-3580
Nicolle Currie, prin. Fax 723-3594
Washington-Henry ES 500/K-5
9025 Washington Henry Dr 23116 804-723-2300
Dr. Dana Jackson, prin. Fax 723-2301

Liberty Christian S 100/PK-5
8094 Liberty Cir 23111 804-746-3062

Melfa, Accomack, Pop. 396
Accomack County SD
Supt. — See Accomac
Pungoteague ES 500/PK-5
28480 Bobtown Rd 23410 757-787-4032
Brian Patterson, prin. Fax 787-1838

Middleburg, Loudoun, Pop. 655
Loudoun County SD
Supt. — See Ashburn

Banneker ES 200/PK-5
35231 Snake Hill Rd 20117 540-751-2480
Robert Carter, prin. Fax 771-6782

Hill S 200/K-8
PO Box 65 20118 540-687-5897

Middletown, Frederick, Pop. 1,237
Frederick County SD
Supt. — See Winchester
Middletown ES 500/K-5
190 Mustang Ln 22645 540-869-4615
Dr. Amy Larrick, prin. Fax 869-5150

Midland, Fauquier, Pop. 218

Midland Christian Academy 100/PK-8
10456 Old Carolina Rd 22728 540-439-2606
Peter Mannix, admin. Fax 439-7082

Midlothian, Chesterfield
Chesterfield County SD
Supt. — See Chesterfield
Bailey Bridge MS 1,400/6-8
12501 Bailey Bridge Rd 23112 804-739-6200
Melanie Knowles, prin. Fax 739-6211
Clover Hill ES 800/PK-5
5700 Woodlake Village Pkwy 23112 804-739-6220
Allie Strollo, prin. Fax 739-6227
Crenshaw ES 700/PK-5
11901 Bailey Bridge Rd 23112 804-739-6250
Brian Campos, prin. Fax 763-4479
Evergreen ES 1,000/PK-5
1701 E Evergreen Pkwy 23114 804-378-2400
Matt Maher, prin. Fax 378-2403
Midlothian MS 1,200/6-8
13501 Midlothian Tpke 23113 804-378-2460
Dr. Patrick Stanfield, prin. Fax 378-7556
Robious ES 700/PK-5
2801 Robious Crossing Dr 23113 804-378-2500
Casta Childress, prin. Fax 378-2507
Robious MS 1,300/6-8
2701 Robious Crossing Dr 23113 804-378-2510
Dr. Derek Wasnock, prin. Fax 378-2519
Smith ES 700/PK-5
13200 Bailey Bridge Rd 23112 804-739-6295
Jana Kline, prin. Fax 739-0583
Spring Run ES 800/PK-5
13901 Spring Run Rd 23112 804-639-6352
Christopher Hart, prin. Fax 639-9015
Swift Creek ES 800/PK-5
13800 Genito Rd 23112 804-739-6305
Peggy Innes, prin. Fax 739-6309
Swift Creek MS 1,000/6-8
3700 Old Hundred Rd S 23112 804-739-6315
Dr. James Frye, prin. Fax 739-6330
Tomahawk Creek MS 1,300/6-8
1600 Learning Place Loop 23114 804-378-7120
Dr. David Ellena, prin. Fax 794-2672
Watkins ES 1,000/PK-5
501 Coalfield Rd 23114 804-378-2530
Deborah Weatherford, prin. Fax 378-5182
Weaver ES 700/PK-5
3600 James River Rd 23113 804-378-2540
Lindsay Mottley, prin. Fax 379-4555
Woolridge ES 700/PK-5
5401 Timber Bluff Pkwy 23112 804-739-6330
Kathleen Matheny, prin. Fax 639-5422

Al Madina S of Richmond PK-12
10700 Academy Dr 23112 804-330-4888
Millwood S 200/PK-12
15100 Millwood School Ln 23112 804-639-3200

Milford, Caroline
Caroline County SD
Supt. — See Bowling Green
Bowling Green ES 800/PK-5
17502 New Baltimore Rd 22514 804-596-2391
Michelle Jones, prin. Fax 633-2151
Caroline MS 1,000/6-8
13325 Devils Three Jump Rd 22514 804-633-6561
Karen Foster, prin. Fax 633-9014

Millboro, Bath
Bath County SD
Supt. — See Warm Springs
Millboro ES 100/PK-7
411 Church St 24460 540-997-5452
Allison Hicklin, prin. Fax 997-0123

Millers Tavern, Essex

Aylett Country Day S 200/PK-8
PO Box 70 23115 804-443-3214

Mineral, Louisa, Pop. 464
Louisa County SD 4,800/PK-12
953 Davis Hwy 23117 540-894-5115
J. Douglas Straley, supt. Fax 894-0252
www.lcps.k12.va.us
Jouett ES 600/PK-5
315 Jouett School Rd 23117 540-872-3931
Justin Grigg, prin. Fax 872-4323
Louisa MS 1,100/6-8
1009 Davis Hwy 23117 540-894-5457
Todd Weidow, prin. Fax 894-5096
Other Schools – See Louisa

Moneta, Bedford
Bedford County SD
Supt. — See Bedford
Moneta ES 200/K-5
12718 N Old Moneta Rd 24121 540-297-4411
Dr. Shawn Trosper, prin. Fax 297-3280
Staunton River MS 700/6-8
1293 Golden Eagle Dr 24121 540-297-4152
Dr. Karen Woodford, prin. Fax 297-4076

Montclair, Prince William, Pop. 18,769
Prince William County SD
Supt. — See Manassas
Henderson ES 600/K-5
3799 Waterway Dr, 703-670-2885
Suzanne Bevans, prin. Fax 670-5521

Monterey, Highland, Pop. 147
Highland County SD 200/PK-12
PO Box 250 24465 540-468-6300
Dr. Thomas Schott Ed.D., supt. Fax 468-6306
www.highland.k12.va.us
Highland ES 100/PK-5
PO Box 310 24465 540-468-6360
Teresa Kay Blum, prin. Fax 468-6333

Montpelier, Hanover
Hanover County SD
Supt. — See Ashland
South Anna ES 600/K-5
13122 Waltons Tavern Rd 23192 804-883-6089
Alicia Todd, prin. Fax 730-2576

Montross, Westmoreland, Pop. 382
Westmoreland County SD 1,700/PK-12
141 Opal Ln 22520 804-493-8018
Rebecca Lowry, supt. Fax 493-9323
division.wmlcps.org
Montross MS 400/6-8
8884 Menokin Rd 22520 804-493-9818
William Bowen, prin. Fax 493-0918
Other Schools – See Colonial Beach, Hague

Montvale, Bedford, Pop. 691
Bedford County SD
Supt. — See Bedford
Montvale ES 200/K-5
1 Little Patriot Dr 24122 540-947-2241
Krista Moore, prin. Fax 947-5300

Moseley, Chesterfield
Chesterfield County SD
Supt. — See Chesterfield
Grange Hall ES 800/PK-5
19301 Hull Street Rd 23120 804-739-6265
Courtney Jones, prin.

Mount Solon, Augusta
Augusta County SD
Supt. — See Verona
North River ES 300/K-5
3395 Scenic Hwy 22843 540-350-2463
Lori Cox, prin. Fax 886-8550

Narrows, Giles, Pop. 2,019
Giles County SD
Supt. — See Pearisburg
Narrows S 500/PK-7
401 Wolf St 24124 540-726-2391
Chris Gautier, prin. Fax 726-7345

Nathalie, Halifax, Pop. 183
Halifax County SD
Supt. — See Halifax
Jennings ES 200/K-5
1011 Sydnor Jennings Rd 24577 434-349-1013
Linda Owen, prin. Fax 349-1076
Meadville ES 200/K-5
1011 Meadville School Loop 24577 434-349-1012
Kevin Neal, prin. Fax 349-5619

Natural Bridge Station, Rockbridge
Rockbridge County SD
Supt. — See Lexington
Natural Bridge ES 300/PK-5
PO Box 280 24579 540-291-2292
Vicki Stevens, prin. Fax 291-2966

New Baltimore, Fauquier, Pop. 7,965
Fauquier County SD
Supt. — See Warrenton
Ritchie ES 400/PK-5
4416 Broad Run Church Rd 20187 540-422-7650
Cristy Thorpe, prin. Fax 422-7669

New Castle, Craig, Pop. 151
Craig County SD 700/PK-12
PO Box 245 24127 540-864-5191
Jeanette Warwick, supt. Fax 864-6885
www.craig.k12.va.us
McCleary ES 300/PK-5
25345 Craigs Creek Rd 24127 540-864-5173
Gerri VanDyke, prin. Fax 864-8349

New Kent, New Kent, Pop. 227
New Kent County SD 3,000/PK-12
PO Box 110 23124 804-966-9650
Dr. David Myers, supt. Fax 966-8556
www.newkentschools.org
New Kent County ES 700/PK-5
11705 New Kent Hwy 23124 804-966-9663
John Moncrief, prin. Fax 966-2506
New Kent County MS 700/6-8
7501 Egypt Rd 23124 804-966-9655
Kelley Gray, prin. Fax 966-2703
Other Schools – See Quinton

New Market, Shenandoah, Pop. 2,116

Shenandoah Valley Adventist ES 100/PK-8
115 Bindery Rd 22844 540-740-8237
Tim LaPierre, prin. Fax 740-4562

Newport News, Newport News, Pop. 174,010
Newport News CSD 29,600/PK-12
12465 Warwick Blvd 23606 757-591-4500
Dr. Ashby Kilgore, supt.
www.sbo.nn.k12.va.us
Achievable Dream Academy 700/K-5
726 16th St 23607 757-928-6827
Terra Harris, prin. Fax 247-1720
Carver ES 700/K-5
6160 Jefferson Ave 23605 757-591-4950
Izzie Brown, prin. Fax 827-7936
Charles ES 600/K-5
701 Menchville Rd 23602 757-886-7750
Anthony Perry, prin. Fax 988-1673
Crittenden MS 800/6-8
6158 Jefferson Ave 23605 757-591-4900
Felicia Barnett, prin. Fax 838-8261
Deer Park ES 500/K-5
11541 Jefferson Ave 23601 757-591-7470
Mary Jo Anastasio, prin. Fax 591-7448
Denbigh ECC 500/PK-PK
15638 Warwick Blvrd 23608 757-886-7789
Amelia Hunt, prin. Fax 988-1676
Discovery STEM Academy 600/K-4
1712 Chestnut Ave 23607 757-928-6838
Christine Pilger, prin. Fax 247-0422
Dozier MS 1,100/6-8
432 Industrial Park Dr 23608 757-888-3300
Crystal Haskins, prin. Fax 887-3662
Dutrow ES 500/K-5
60 Curtis Tignor Rd 23608 757-886-7760
Kelly Stewart, prin. Fax 989-0932
Epes ES 500/K-5
855 Lucas Creek Rd 23608 757-886-7755
Dr. Reggie Alston, prin. Fax 989-0015
Gildersleeve MS 1,100/6-8
1 Minton Dr 23606 757-591-4862
Dr. Windy Nichols, prin. Fax 596-2059
Greenwood ES 700/K-5
13460 Woodside Ln 23608 757-886-7744
Camisha Davis, prin. Fax 989-0231
Hall ECC 200/PK-PK
17346 Warwick Blvd 23603 757-888-3329
Lauren Gray, prin. Fax 888-3352
Hall ES 600/K-5
17346 Warwick Blvd 23603 757-888-3320
Darra White, prin. Fax 888-0212
Hidenwood ES 600/K-5
501 Blount Point Rd 23606 757-591-4766
Annette Walls, prin. Fax 599-4451
Hilton ES 400/K-5
225 River Rd 23601 757-591-4772
Barbara Nagel, prin. Fax 599-4382
Hines MS 900/6-8
561 McLawhorne Dr 23601 757-591-4878
Lisa Gatz, prin. Fax 591-0119
Huntington MS 600/6-8
3401 Orcutt Ave 23607 757-928-6846
Courtney Mompoint, prin. Fax 245-8451
Jenkins ES 400/K-5
80 Menchville Rd 23602 757-881-5400
Terri McCaughan, prin. Fax 881-9211
Kiln Creek ES 700/K-5
1501 Kiln Creek Pkwy 23602 757-886-7961
Kathryn Hermann, prin. Fax 989-0153
Marshall ECC 300/PK-PK
743 24th St 23607 757-928-6832
Vanessa Keller, prin. Fax 247-0530
McIntosh ES 400/K-5
185 Richneck Rd 23608 757-886-7767
Ethel Francis, prin. Fax 989-0326
Nelson ES 500/K-5
826 Moyer Rd 23608 757-886-7783
Dr. Melody Camm, prin. Fax 989-0381
Newsome Park ES 500/1-5
4200 Marshall Ave 23607 757-928-6810
Kimberly Judge, prin. Fax 247-3218
Palmer ES 500/K-5
100 Palmer Ln 23602 757-881-5000
Karen Lynch, prin. Fax 249-4261
Passage MS 1,000/6-8
400 Atkinson Way 23608 757-886-7600
Janelle Spitz, prin. Fax 886-7661
PEEP 100/PK-PK
1241 Gatewood Rd 23601 757-591-4963
Dr. Heather Jankovich, admin. Fax 591-4695
Richneck ES 700/K-5
205 Tyner Dr 23608 757-886-7772
Troy Latuch, prin. Fax 874-6315
Riverside ES 600/PK-5
1100 Country Club Rd 23606 757-591-4740
Jacky Barber, prin. Fax 599-4518
Sanford ES 700/K-5
480 Colony Rd 23602 757-886-7778
Brian Lieberman, prin. Fax 989-0385
Saunders ES 600/K-5
853 Harpersville Rd 23601 757-591-4781
Shannon Pipkin, prin. Fax 599-4571
Sedgefield ES 600/K-5
804 Main St 23605 757-591-4792
Raquel Cox, prin. Fax 599-5064
Washington MS 400/6-8
3700 Chestnut Ave 23607 757-928-6860
Dr. Sean Callender, prin. Fax 247-1119
Watkins ECC 500/PK-PK
21 Burns Dr 23601 757-591-4815
Sue Waxman, admin. Fax 591-7690
Yates ES 500/K-5
73 Maxwell Ln 23606 757-881-5450
Timothy Edwards, prin. Fax 930-1417
Other Schools – See Fort Eustis

Calvary Seventh-Day Adventist S 50/K-8
1200 17th St 23607 757-244-5438
Denbigh Baptist Christian S 300/PK-12
13010 Mitchell Point Rd 23602 757-249-2654
Robert Law, admin. Fax 249-9480
Denbigh Christian Academy 100/PK-K
1233 Shields Rd 23608 757-874-8661
Linda Amiss, dir. Fax 234-4377
First Baptist Church Denbigh CDCA 100/PK-5
3628 Campbell Rd 23602 757-833-7261
Rev. Sylvia Harris M.S., admin. Fax 833-7450

Hampton Roads Academy 600/PK-12
739 Academy Ln 23602 757-884-9100
Peter Mertz, hdmstr. Fax 884-9137
Our Lady of Mt. Carmel S 400/PK-8
52 Harpersville Rd 23601 757-596-2754
Sr. Maria Frassati, prin. Fax 596-1570
St. Andrew's Episcopal S 100/PK-5
45 Main St 23601 757-596-6261
Janna Outlaw, head sch Fax 596-7218
Summit Christian Academy 100/PK-6
69 Saunders Rd 23601 757-599-9424
Tim Grimes, hdmstr. Fax 599-1898
Trinity Lutheran S 200/PK-8
6812 River Rd 23607 757-245-2576
Kevin Goetz, head sch Fax 245-4111
Warwick River Christian S 200/PK-8
252 Lucas Creek Rd 23602 757-877-2941
Jenny Mahone, head sch Fax 877-6510

Newsoms, Southampton, Pop. 321
Southhampton County SD
Supt. — See Courtland
Meherrin ES 300/PK-5
28600 Grays Shop Rd 23874 757-654-6461
Tasha Ricks, prin. Fax 654-6028

Nickelsville, Scott, Pop. 382
Scott County SD
Supt. — See Gate City
Nickelsville ES 200/K-7
11415 Nickelsville Hwy 24271 276-479-2676
Tracy Stallard, prin. Fax 479-2121

Nokesville, Prince William, Pop. 1,327
Fauquier County SD
Supt. — See Warrenton
Greenville ES 500/PK-5
7389 Academic Ave 20181 540-422-7570
Tim Gardner, prin. Fax 422-7589

Prince William County SD
Supt. — See Manassas
Nokesville S 500/K-8
12375 Aden Rd 20181 703-781-3040
Eric Worcester, prin. Fax 594-2068
Wood ES 1,000/K-5
10600 Kettle Run Rd 20181 703-594-3990
Andrew Buchheit, prin. Fax 594-2653

Nora, Dickenson
Dickenson County SD
Supt. — See Clintwood
Ervinton ES 200/PK-5
PO Box 519 24272 276-835-8423
Brian Baker, prin. Fax 835-8796

Norfolk, Norfolk, Pop. 234,855
Norfolk CSD 31,300/PK-12
PO Box 1357 23501 757-670-3945
Dr. Melinda Boone, supt. Fax 628-3820
www.npsk12.com
Academy of Discovery at Lakewood 3-8
1701 Alsace Ave 23509 757-628-2477
Thomas Smigiel, prin. Fax 628-2486
Academy of Intl Studies at Rosemont 100/6-8
1330 Branch Rd 23513 757-852-4610
Dorie Banks, prin. Fax 852-4615
Azalea Gardens MS 900/6-8
7721 Azalea Garden Rd 23518 757-531-3000
James Kirk, prin. Fax 531-3013
Bay View ES 700/PK-5
1434 E Bayview Blvd 23503 757-531-3030
Dr. Valerie Walton, prin. Fax 531-3025
Berkley/Compostella ECC 200/PK-PK
1530 Cypress St 23523 757-494-3870
Dr. Doreatha White, prin. Fax 494-3290
Blair MS 1,200/6-8
730 Spotswood Ave 23517 757-628-2400
Dr. Mark Makovec, prin. Fax 628-2422
Bowling ES 500/PK-5
2700 E Princess Anne Rd 23504 757-628-2515
Eric Goodman, prin. Fax 628-2512
Calcott ES 500/PK-5
137 E Westmont Ave 23503 757-531-3039
Danielle McIntyre, prin. Fax 531-3041
Camp Allen ES 500/PK-5
501 C St 23505 757-451-4170
Deena Copeland, prin. Fax 451-4172
Chesterfield Academy 500/PK-5
2915 Westminster Ave 23504 757-628-2544
Dr. Lawrence Taylor, prin. Fax 628-2541
Coleman Place ES 700/PK-5
2445 Palmyra St 23513 757-852-4641
Dr. Pamela Tatem, prin. Fax 852-4648
Crossroads S 900/PK-8
8021 Old Ocean View Rd 23518 757-531-3050
Dr. Kristen Nichols, prin. Fax 531-3046
Easton Preschool 200/PK-PK
6045 Curlew Dr 23502 757-892-3290
Dr. Tami White, coord. Fax 892-3285
Fairlawn ES 200/3-5
1132 Wade St 23502 757-892-3260
Michele Logan, prin. Fax 892-3255
Ghent S 500/K-8
200 Shirley Ave 23517 757-628-2565
Dr. Thomas McAnulty, prin. Fax 628-2564
Granby ES 600/PK-5
7101 Newport Ave 23505 757-451-4150
Kathryn Verhappen, prin. Fax 451-4157
Ingleside ES 400/K-5
976 Ingleside Rd 23502 757-892-3270
Dr. Alana Balthazar, prin. Fax 892-3265
Jacox ES 700/PK-5
1300 Marshall Ave 23504 757-628-2433
Dr. Lucy Litchmore, prin. Fax 628-2435
Lake Taylor MS 900/6-8
1380 Kempsville Rd 23502 757-892-3230
Melanie Patterson, prin. Fax 892-3240
Larchmont ES 600/K-5
1145 Bolling Ave 23508 757-451-4180
Dennis Fifer, prin. Fax 451-4188
Larrymore ES 500/K-5
7600 Halprin Dr 23518 757-531-3070
David Faircloth, prin. Fax 531-3071
Lindenwood ES 400/PK-5
2700 Ludlow St 23504 757-628-2577
Dr. Lisa Corbin, prin. Fax 628-2576
Little Creek ES 800/PK-5
7900 Tarpon Pl 23518 757-531-3080
Cheryl Coghlan, prin. Fax 531-3083
Monroe ES 500/PK-5
520 W 29th St 23508 757-628-3500
Leigh Kovalcik, prin. Fax 628-3563
Northside MS 800/6-8
8720 Granby St 23503 757-531-3150
Richard Fraley, prin. Fax 531-3144
Norview ES 500/PK-5
6401 Chesapeake Blvd 23513 757-852-4660
Kathryn Caple, prin. Fax 852-4658
Norview MS 1,100/6-8
6325 Sewells Point Rd 23513 757-852-4600
Patrick Doyle, prin. Fax 852-4590
Oceanair ES 500/PK-5
600 Dudley Ave 23503 757-531-3095
Lenthia Willie-Clark, prin. Fax 531-3099
Ocean View ES 600/PK-5
350 W Government Ave 23503 757-531-3105
Dr. James Peterson, prin. Fax 531-3111
Poplar Halls ES 200/PK-2
5523 Pebble Ln 23502 757-892-3280
Cassandra Washington, prin. Fax 892-3275
Ruffner Academy 800/6-8
610 May Ave 23504 757-628-2466
Jeryl Scott, prin. Fax 628-2465
St. Helena ES 400/PK-5
903 S Main St 23523 757-494-3884
Vandelyn Hodges, prin. Fax 494-3888
Sewells Point ES 600/K-5
7928 Hampton Blvd 23505 757-451-4160
Mary Wrushen, prin. Fax 451-4165
Sherwood Forest ES 600/PK-5
3035 Sherwood Forest Ln 23513 757-852-4550
Cheryl Jordan, prin. Fax 852-4532
Southside STEM Academy at Campostella 700/PK-6
1106 Campostella Rd 23523 757-494-3850
Katrina Rountree, prin. Fax 494-3860
Suburban Park ES 500/PK-5
310 Thole St 23505 757-531-3118
Brenda Shepherd, prin. Fax 531-3120
Tanners Creek ES 700/PK-5
1335 Longdale Dr 23513 757-852-4555
Maritsa Alger, prin. Fax 852-4553
Tarrallton ES 400/PK-5
2080 Tarrallton Dr 23518 757-531-1800
Daniel White, prin. Fax 531-1802
Taylor ES 400/PK-5
1122 W Princess Anne Rd 23507 757-628-2525
Charlene Feliton, prin. Fax 628-2531
Tidewater Park ES 100/3-5
1045 E Brambleton Ave 23504 757-628-2500
Dr. Sharon Phillips, prin. Fax 628-2501
Willard Model ES 600/K-5
1511 Willow Wood Dr 23509 757-628-2721
Julie Honeycutt, prin. Fax 628-3997
Willoughby ES 200/PK-5
9500 4th View St 23503 757-531-3127
June Lightfoot, prin. Fax 531-3125
Young ES 500/PK-5
543 E Olney Rd 23510 757-628-2588
Dwana White, prin. Fax 628-2582

Christ the King S 300/PK-8
3401 Tidewater Dr 23509 757-625-4951
Dr. Francine Gagne, prin. Fax 623-5212
Norfolk Academy 1,200/1-12
1585 Wesleyan Dr 23502 757-461-6236
Dennis Manning, hdmstr. Fax 455-3181
Norfolk Christian Lower S 400/PK-5
7000 Granby St 23505 757-423-5812
Norfolk Collegiate Lower S 200/PK-5
5429 Tidewater Dr 23509 757-625-0471
Cleteus Smith, head sch Fax 623-9246
Ocean View Christian Academy 50/PK-12
9504 Selby Pl 23503 757-583-1808
Amy Dunnavant, prin. Fax 583-5706
READY Academy Christian S 100/PK-5
418 E Bute St 23510 757-622-5650
Amanda Murray M.Ed., admin. Fax 622-5653
St. John Lutheran S 100/PK-2
8918 Tidewater Dr 23503 757-588-8227
St. Patrick S 400/PK-8
1000 Bolling Ave 23508 757-440-5500
Stephen Hammond, prin. Fax 440-5200
St. Pius X S 300/PK-8
7800 Halprin Dr 23518 757-588-6171
Sr. Linda Taber, prin. Fax 587-6580
Williams S 200/K-8
419 Colonial Ave 23507 757-627-1383
Michael Spencer, head sch Fax 333-9707

N Chesterfield, Chesterfield
Chesterfield County SD
Supt. — See Chesterfield
Bellwood ES 500/PK-5
9536 Dawnshire Rd, 804-743-3600
Jennifer Rudd, prin. Fax 275-3227
Bensley ES 600/PK-5
6600 Strathmore Rd, 804-743-3610
Dr. Patrice Wilson, prin. Fax 271-2670
Beulah ES 600/PK-5
4216 Beulah Rd, 804-743-3620
Christina Allen-Roach, prin. Fax 271-3894
Falling Creek ES 700/PK-5
4800 Hopkins Rd, 804-743-3630
Pamela Johnson, prin. Fax 275-9269
Falling Creek MS 1,200/6-8
4724 Hopkins Rd, 804-743-3640
Aurelia Ortiz, prin. Fax 743-3735
Gordon ES 700/PK-5
11701 Gordon School Rd, 804-378-2410
Rosemary Harris, prin. Fax 379-2983
Greenfield ES 600/PK-5
10751 Savoy Rd, 804-560-2720
Melissa Reams, prin. Fax 272-6739
Hening ES 900/PK-5
5230 Chicora Dr, 804-743-3655
Bruce Fillman, prin. Fax 743-3658
Hopkins Road ES 600/PK-5
6000 Hopkins Rd, 804-743-3665
Dr. Lisa Hill, prin. Fax 743-3671
Salem Church MS 900/6-8
9700 Salem Church Rd, 804-768-6225
Lashante Knight, prin. Fax 768-6230

Southside Baptist Christian S 100/K-12
411 Branchway, 804-745-8699

North Garden, Albemarle
Albemarle County SD
Supt. — See Charlottesville
Red Hill ES 200/PK-5
3901 Red Hill School Rd 22959 434-293-5332
Arthur Stow, prin. Fax 293-7300

North Tazewell, See Tazewell
Tazewell County SD
Supt. — See Tazewell
North Tazewell ES 300/PK-5
300 W Riverside Dr 24630 276-988-4510
Suzanne Grindstaff, prin. Fax 988-0183
Springville ES 200/PK-5
144 Schoolhouse Rd 24630 276-322-5900
Chad Brown, prin. Fax 322-0254

Norton, Norton, Pop. 3,857
Norton CSD 800/PK-12
PO Box 498 24273 276-679-2330
Dr. Gina Wohlford, supt. Fax 679-4315
www.nortoncityschools.org/
Norton ES 500/PK-7
205 E Park Ave 24273 276-679-0971
Dr. Scott Addison, prin. Fax 679-5914

Nottoway, Nottoway
Nottoway County SD 2,300/PK-12
10321 E Colonial Trail Hwy 23955 434-645-9596
Dr. Rodney Berry, supt. Fax 645-1266
www.nottowayschools.org
Other Schools – See Blackstone, Crewe

Oak Hall, Accomack, Pop. 245
Accomack County SD
Supt. — See Accomac
Arcadia MS 500/6-8
PO Box 220 23416 757-824-4862
Brian Tupper, prin. Fax 824-6618

Oakton, Fairfax, Pop. 32,914
Fairfax County SD
Supt. — See Falls Church
Oakton ES 800/K-6
3000 Chain Bridge Rd 22124 703-937-6100
Christine Kelley, prin. Fax 937-6197
Waples Mill ES 900/PK-6
11509 Waples Mill Rd 22124 703-390-7700
Gregory Brotemarkle, prin. Fax 390-7797

Dominion Christian S 200/K-12
10922 Vale Rd 22124 703-758-1055
Matthew Michell, head sch
Flint Hill S 1,100/PK-12
3320 Jermantown Rd 22124 703-584-2300
John Thomas, hdmstr. Fax 584-2369
Montessori S of Oakton 100/PK-6
12113 Vale Rd 22124 703-715-0611
Carolyn Linke, head sch
Pinnacle Academy 200/PK-12
2854 Hunter Mill Rd 22124 703-537-0355
Fatih Kandil M.Ed., prin. Fax 782-9449

Oakwood, Buchanan
Buchanan County SD
Supt. — See Grundy
Twin Valley S 400/PK-7
9017 Riverside Dr 24631 276-498-4537
Kevin Yates, prin. Fax 498-7046

Onley, Accomack, Pop. 509
Accomack County SD
Supt. — See Accomac
Nandua MS 500/6-8
20330 Warrior Dr 23418 757-787-7037
John Killmon, prin. Fax 787-8807

Orange, Orange, Pop. 4,610
Orange County SD 5,000/K-12
200 Dailey Dr 22960 540-661-4550
Dr. Brenda Tanner, supt. Fax 661-4599
www.ocss-va.org
Orange ES 500/K-5
230 Montevista Ave 22960 540-661-4450
Sherri McGhee, prin. Fax 661-4449
Prospect Heights MS 500/6-8
202 Dailey Dr 22960 540-661-4400
Renee Bourke, prin. Fax 661-4399
Other Schools – See Gordonsville, Locust Grove, Unionville

Grymes Memorial S 200/PK-8
PO Box 1160 22960 540-672-1010
Dr. Elisabeth Work, head sch Fax 672-9167

Palmyra, Fluvanna, Pop. 102
Fluvanna County SD 3,700/PK-12
14455 James Madison Hwy 22963 434-589-8208
Chuck Winkler, supt. Fax 589-5393
www.fluco.org
Central ES 500/1-2
3340 Central Plains Rd 22963 434-589-8318
Sue Davies, prin. Fax 589-4275
Fluvanna MS 800/5-7
3717 Central Plains Rd 22963 434-510-1000
Bradley Stang, prin. Fax 510-1019
West Central PS 300/PK-K
3188 Central Plains Rd 22963 434-510-1016
Clint Estes, prin. Fax 510-1014
Other Schools – See Fork Union

Parksley, Accomack, Pop. 829
Accomack County SD
Supt. — See Accomac
Metompkin ES 600/PK-5
24501 Parksley Rd 23421 757-665-1299
Belinda Rippon, prin. Fax 665-5283

Patrick Springs, Patrick, Pop. 1,824
Patrick County SD
Supt. — See Stuart
Patrick Springs ES 200/PK-3
75 Elementary Ln 24133 276-694-3396
Marcie Murphy, prin. Fax 694-5806

Pearisburg, Giles, Pop. 2,771
Giles County SD 2,500/PK-12
151 School Rd 24134 540-921-1421
Dr. Terry Arbogast, supt. Fax 921-1424
sbo.gilesk12.org
McClaugherty S 500/PK-7
1001 Henson Ave 24134 540-921-1363
Kevin White, prin. Fax 921-3130
Other Schools – See Narrows, Pembroke

Pembroke, Giles, Pop. 1,105
Giles County SD
Supt. — See Pearisburg
Eastern ES 500/PK-7
6899 Virginia Ave 24136 540-626-7281
Jason Mills, prin. Fax 626-7175

Penhook, Franklin, Pop. 792
Franklin County SD
Supt. — See Rocky Mount
Snow Creek ES 200/PK-5
5393 Snow Creek Rd 24137 540-483-5599
Ken Grindstaff, prin. Fax 483-5604

Pennington Gap, Lee, Pop. 1,760
Lee County SD
Supt. — See Jonesville
Elk Knob ES 400/PK-5
159 School Rd 24277 276-546-1837
Brian Huff, prin. Fax 546-4161
Pennington MS 400/6-8
201 Middle School Dr 24277 276-546-1453
Sherry Collier, prin. Fax 546-3515

Penn Laird, Rockingham
Rockingham County SD
Supt. — See Harrisonburg
Cub Run ES 600/PK-5
1451 S Montevideo Cir 22846 540-289-5854
Kenny Boyers, prin. Fax 289-5901
Montevideo MS 700/6-8
7648 McGaheysville Rd 22846 540-289-3401
Drew Miller, prin. Fax 289-3601
Peak View ES 400/PK-5
641 Lawyer Rd 22846 540-289-7510
Marcy Williams, prin. Fax 289-7439

Petersburg, Petersburg, Pop. 31,887
Petersburg CSD 4,800/PK-12
255 E South Blvd 23805 804-732-0510
Marcus Newsome Ed.D., supt. Fax 732-0514
www.petersburg.k12.va.us
Cool Spring ES 500/K-5
1450 Talley Ave 23803 804-862-7002
Jennifer Kelley, prin. Fax 862-7182
Johns MS, 3101 Homestead Dr 23805 600/6-8
Danielle Davis, prin. 804-862-7018
Lakemont ES 500/K-5
51 Gibbons Ave 23803 804-862-7007
Sheryl Doswell, prin. Fax 861-5041
Pleasants Lane ES 500/K-5
100 Pleasants Ln 23803 804-862-7013
Tracy Stith-Johnson, prin. Fax 861-2197
Walnut Hill ES 600/K-5
300 W South Blvd 23805 804-862-7005
Belinda Urquhart, prin. Fax 861-4032
Westview Early Childhood Ed Center 300/PK-PK
1100 Patterson St 23803 804-861-1274
Stacie Parham, admin. Fax 861-3920

Grace and Hope Academy PK-7
PO Box 3264 23805 804-431-5717
Letetia Mullenix, head sch Fax 431-5718
St. Joseph S 200/PK-9
123 Franklin St 23803 804-732-3931
Joseph Whitmore, prin. Fax 732-6479

Phenix, Charlotte, Pop. 222
Charlotte County SD
Supt. — See Charlotte Court House
Phenix ES 200/PK-5
400 Red House Rd 23959 434-542-5570
Jamie Brown, prin. Fax 542-5572

Poquoson, Poquoson, Pop. 11,990
Poquoson CSD 2,100/PK-12
500 City Hall Ave 23662 757-868-3055
Dr. Jennifer Parish, supt. Fax 868-3107
www.poquoson.k12.va.us
Poquoson ES 500/3-5
1033 Poquoson Ave 23662 757-868-6921
Dr. Barbara Wood, prin. Fax 868-8058
Poquoson MS 500/6-8
985 Poquoson Ave 23662 757-868-6031
Melissa Bunting, prin. Fax 868-4220
Poquoson PS 400/PK-2
19 Odd Rd 23662 757-868-4403
Janet Harper, prin. Fax 868-6846

Portsmouth, Portsmouth, Pop. 93,145
Portsmouth CSD 15,000/PK-12
PO Box 998 23705 757-393-8751
Dr. Elie Bracy, supt. Fax 393-5236
ppsk12.us
Brighton ES 500/K-6
1100 Portsmouth Blvd 23704 757-393-8870
Kathy Mangum-Parker, prin. Fax 393-5133
Churchland Academy 700/K-6
4061 River Shore Rd 23703 757-686-2527
Karen Clark, prin. Fax 686-2529
Churchland ES 800/K-6
5601 Michael Ln 23703 757-686-2523
Dr. Jamill Jones, prin. Fax 686-2526
Churchland MS 900/7-8
4051 River Shore Rd 23703 757-686-2512
Barbara Kimzey, prin. Fax 686-2515
Churchland Preschool 200/PK-PK
4061 River Shore Rd 23703 757-686-2533
Robyn McIntyre, prin. Fax 686-2534
Churchland Primary & IS 600/K-6
5700 Hedgerow Ln 23703 757-686-2519
Rosalyn Exum, prin. Fax 686-2521
Cradock MS 600/7-8
21 Alden Ave 23702 757-393-8788
Sonya Harrell, prin. Fax 393-5020
Douglass Park ES 700/K-6
34 Grand St 23701 757-393-8646
Dusti Johnson, prin. Fax 393-8286
Hodges Manor ES 500/K-6
1201 Cherokee Rd 23701 757-465-2921
Dr. Faye Felton, prin. Fax 465-2922
Hurst ES 700/K-6
18 Dahlgren Ave 23702 757-558-2811
Morris Barco, prin. Fax 558-2812
Lakeview ES 500/K-6
1300 Horne Ave 23701 757-465-2901
Dr. Camilla Ferebee, prin. Fax 465-1895
Mt. Hermon Preschool 200/PK-PK
3000 North St 23707 757-393-8825
Patricia Williams, prin. Fax 393-1349
Olive Branch Preschool 200/PK-PK
415 Mimosa Rd 23701 757-465-2926
Lois Reickhoff, prin. Fax 465-2927
Park View ES 600/K-6
260 Elm Ave 23704 757-393-8647
Angela Flowers, prin. Fax 393-8126
Simonsdale ES 700/K-6
4841 Clifford St 23701 757-465-2917
Darlene Bright, prin. Fax 465-2918
Spong Preschool 100/PK-PK
2200 Piedmont Ave 23704 757-393-5247
Venessa Whichard-Harris, prin. Fax 397-4514
Tyler ES 700/K-6
3649 Hartford St 23707 757-393-8879
Heidi Lewis, prin. Fax 393-5876
Victory ES 500/K-6
2828 Greenwood Dr 23701 757-393-8806
Dr. J. Wayne Williams, prin. Fax 393-5139
Waters MS 600/7-8
600 Roosevelt Blvd 23701 757-558-2813
Ricardo Randall, prin. Fax 485-2829
Westhaven ES 500/K-6
3701 Clifford St 23707 757-393-8855
Venessa Whichard-Harris, prin. Fax 393-8410

Alliance Christian Academy 200/PK-12
5809 Portsmouth Blvd 23701 757-488-5552
Central Christian Academy 100/PK-6
1200 Hodges Ferry Rd 23701 757-488-4477
Dawn Stephens, admin. Fax 488-4836
Christopher Academy 200/PK-5
3300 Cedar Ln 23703 757-484-6776
Miriam Terry, head sch Fax 484-6774
Portsmouth Catholic S 200/PK-8
2301 Oregon Ave 23701 757-488-6744
Mary Ellen Paul, prin. Fax 465-8833
Portsmouth Christian S 700/PK-12
3214 Elliott Ave 23702 757-393-0725
Nancy Stafford, admin. Fax 397-7487
St. Mark Christian Academy 100/PK-4
2714 Frederick Blvd 23704 757-399-7176
Mya Braxton, prin. Fax 399-7023
Toras Chaim S 100/PK-8
3110 Sterling Point Dr 23703 757-686-2480

Potomac Falls, Loudoun

Our Lady of Hope S 200/K-8
46633 Algonkian Pkwy 20165 703-433-6760
Mary Pittman, prin. Fax 433-6761

Pound, Wise, Pop. 1,022
Wise County SD
Supt. — See Wise
Adams Combined S 600/PK-8
10824 Orby Cantrell Hwy 24279 276-796-5419
Rick Bolling, prin. Fax 796-4698

Powhatan, Powhatan
Powhatan County SD 3,200/PK-12
2320 Skaggs Rd 23139 804-598-5700
Dr. Eric Jones, supt. Fax 598-5705
www.powhatan.k12.va.us
Flat Rock ES 600/PK-5
2210 Batterson Rd 23139 804-598-5743
Tanja Atkins-Nelson, prin. Fax 598-8235
Pocahontas ES 500/PK-5
4294 Anderson Hwy 23139 804-598-5717
Thomas Sulzer, prin. Fax 598-6320
Pocahontas MS 300/6-8
4290 Anderson Hwy 23139 804-598-5720
Dr. Samantha Martin, prin. Fax 598-1485
Powhatan ES 400/K-5
4111 Old Buckingham Rd 23139 804-598-5730
Constance Deal, prin. Fax 598-1484

Blessed Sacrament S 300/PK-12
2501 Academy Rd 23139 804-598-4211
Paula Ledbetter, prin. Fax 598-1053

Prince George, Prince George, Pop. 2,019
Prince George County SD 6,400/PK-12
PO Box 400 23875 804-733-2700
Renee P. Williams, supt. Fax 733-2737
pgs.k12.va.us
Beazley ES 700/PK-5
6700 Courthouse Rd 23875 804-733-2745
Robin Germanos, prin. Fax 732-1627
North ES 700/PK-5
11106 Old Stage Rd 23875 804-458-8922
Christina Romig, prin. Fax 452-3917
Walton ES 600/PK-5
4101 Courthouse Rd 23875 804-733-2750
Sharon Kushma, prin. Fax 732-1592
Other Schools – See Disputanta

Pulaski, Pulaski, Pop. 8,916
Pulaski County SD 4,500/PK-12
202 N Washington Ave 24301 540-994-2550
Dr. Kevin Siers, supt. Fax 994-2552
www.pcva.us
Critzer ES 400/PK-5
100 Critzer Dr 24301 540-643-0274
Amy Williams, prin. Fax 980-8627
Pulaski ES 500/PK-5
2004 Morehead Ln 24301 540-643-0737
Rebecah Smith, prin. Fax 643-0990
Pulaski MS 400/6-8
500 Pico Ter 24301 540-643-0767
William Atwood, prin. Fax 980-8571
Other Schools – See Dublin, Fairlawn, Hiwassee

Purcellville, Loudoun, Pop. 7,498
Loudoun County SD
Supt. — See Ashburn
Blue Ridge MS 900/6-8
551 E A St 20132 540-751-2520
Brion Bell, prin. Fax 338-6823
Emerick ES 500/PK-5
440 S Nursery Ave 20132 540-751-2440
Dawn Haddock, prin. Fax 338-6876
Lincoln ES 100/K-5
18048 Lincoln Rd 20132 540-751-2430
David Michener, prin. Fax 338-6862
Mountain View ES 500/PK-5
36803 Allder School Rd 20132 540-751-2550
Jill Broaddus, prin. Fax 338-0821

Montessori S of Purcellville 50/PK-6
280 N Hatcher Ave 20132 540-751-1065

Quicksburg, Shenandoah
Shenandoah County SD
Supt. — See Woodstock
Ashby Lee ES 600/PK-5
480 Stonewall Ln 22847 540-477-2927
Steve Povlish, prin. Fax 477-2844
North Fork MS 300/6-8
1018 Caverns Rd 22847 540-477-2953
Todd Lynn, prin. Fax 477-2562

Quinton, New Kent
New Kent County SD
Supt. — See New Kent
Watkins ES 700/PK-5
6501 New Kent Hwy 23141 804-966-9660
Russell Macomber, prin. Fax 932-8459

Radford, Radford, Pop. 16,003
Floyd County SD
Supt. — See Floyd
Indian Valley ES 200/K-7
4130 Indian Valley Rd NW 24141 540-745-9420
Robert Ratcliffe, prin. Fax 745-9490

Montgomery County SD
Supt. — See Christiansburg
Belview ES 300/PK-5
3187 Peppers Ferry Rd 24141 540-633-3200
Timothy Moeller, prin. Fax 639-5235

Radford CSD 1,600/PK-12
1612 Wadsworth St 24141 540-731-3647
Robert Graham, supt. Fax 731-4419
www.rcps.org/
Belle Heth ES 500/3-6
151 George St 24141 540-731-3653
Tara Grant, prin. Fax 731-3697
Dalton IS 300/7-8
60 Dalton Dr 24141 540-731-3651
Jerry King, prin. Fax 731-5033
McHarg ES 400/PK-2
700 12th St 24141 540-731-3652
Dr. Michael Brown, prin. Fax 731-3696

Raven, Tazewell, Pop. 2,239
Tazewell County SD
Supt. — See Tazewell
Raven ES 200/K-5
22 School St 24639 276-964-9437
Blendia Walls, prin. Fax 963-5179

Remington, Fauquier, Pop. 581
Fauquier County SD
Supt. — See Warrenton

Pierce ES 500/PK-5
12074 James Madison St 22734 540-422-7630
Laura Hoover, prin. Fax 422-7649

Reston, Fairfax, Pop. 56,325
Fairfax County SD
Supt. — See Falls Church
Aldrin ES 700/PK-6
11375 Center Harbor Rd 20194 703-904-3800
Shane Wolfe, prin. Fax 904-3897
Armstrong ES 500/K-6
11900 Lake Newport Rd 20194 703-375-4800
James Quinn, prin. Fax 375-4897
Dogwood ES 800/K-6
12300 Glade Dr 20191 703-262-3100
Mie Devers, prin. Fax 262-3197
Forest Edge ES 800/PK-6
1501 Becontree Ln 20190 703-925-8000
Leona Smith-Vance, prin. Fax 925-8097
Hughes MS 1,000/7-8
11401 Ridge Heights Rd 20191 703-715-3600
Aimee Monticchio, prin. Fax 715-3697
Hunters Woods ES for the Arts & Sciences 1,100/K-6
2401 Colts Neck Rd 20191 703-262-7400
Emily Cope, prin. Fax 262-7497
Lake Anne ES 600/K-6
11510 North Shore Dr 20190 703-326-3500
Jill Stewart, prin. Fax 326-3597
Sunrise Valley ES 600/K-6
10824 Cross School Rd 20191 703-715-3800
Kevin West, prin. Fax 715-3897
Terraset ES 500/K-6
11411 Ridge Heights Rd 20191 703-390-5600
Lindsay Trout, prin. Fax 390-5697

Academy of Christian Education 200/PK-5
10800 Parkridge Blvd # 150 20191 703-471-2132
Kristen Rogers, head sch Fax 471-5790
Al Fatih Academy 200/PK-8
12300 Pinecrest Rd 20191 703-437-9382
Farah Imam, prin. Fax 437-9383
Reston Montessori S 200/PK-6
1928 Isaac Newton Sq W 20190 703-481-2922
Sunset Hills Montessori S 200/PK-8
11180 Ridge Heights Rd 20191 703-476-7477

Richlands, Tazewell, Pop. 5,766
Tazewell County SD
Supt. — See Tazewell
Richlands ES 600/PK-5
309 Front St 24641 276-964-4112
Melanie Lashinsky, prin. Fax 964-4278
Richlands MS 600/6-8
185 Learning Ln 24641 276-963-5370
Glayde Brown, prin. Fax 963-0210

Richmond, Richmond, Pop. 200,073
Chesterfield County SD
Supt. — See Chesterfield
Crestwood ES 500/PK-5
7600 Whittington Dr 23225 804-560-2710
Lindsay Porzio, prin. Fax 320-8520
Davis ES 700/PK-5
415 S Providence Rd 23236 804-674-1310
Kenya Batts, prin. Fax 675-0243
Manchester MS 1,400/6-8
7401 Hull Street Rd 23235 804-674-1385
Sarah Fraher, prin. Fax 674-1394
Providence ES 700/PK-5
11001 W Providence Rd 23236 804-674-1345
Dr. Sharon Rucker, prin. Fax 745-2339
Providence MS 800/6-8
900 Starlight Ln 23235 804-674-1355
Amanda Voelker, prin. Fax 674-1361
Reams Road ES 500/PK-5
10141 Reams Rd 23236 804-674-1370
Jodi Seitz, prin. Fax 745-3391
Salem Church ES 600/K-5
9600 Salem Church Rd 23237 804-768-6215
Monique Booth, prin. Fax 796-9499

Henrico County SD 49,800/PK-12
PO Box 23120 23223 804-652-3600
Dr. Patrick Kinlaw, supt. Fax 652-3856
henricoschools.us
Adams ES 400/K-5
600 S Laburnum Ave 23223 804-226-8745
Tijuana Lowery, prin. Fax 226-8768
Ashe ES 400/K-5
1001 Cedar Fork Rd 23223 804-343-6550
Dr. Kecia Lipscomb, prin. Fax 343-6514
Baker ES 500/K-5
6651 Willson Rd 23231 804-226-8755
Dr. Beverly Allen-Hardy, prin. Fax 226-8769
Brookland MS 1,100/6-8
9200 Lydell Dr 23228 804-261-5000
Dr. Nicholas Barlett, prin. Fax 261-5003
Carver ES 500/K-5
1801 Lauderdale Dr 23238 804-750-2640
Dr. Eric Armbruster, prin. Fax 750-2648
Chamberlayne ES 400/K-5
8200 St Charles Rd 23227 804-261-5030
Dwight VanRossum, prin. Fax 261-1734
Crestview ES 300/K-5
1901 Charles St 23226 804-673-3775
Jennifer Drake, prin. Fax 673-3742
Davis ES 500/K-5
8801 Nesslewood Dr 23229 804-527-4620
Christine Bonner, prin. Fax 527-4658
Dumbarton ES 600/K-5
9000 Hungary Spring Rd 23228 804-756-3030
Deia Champ, prin. Fax 756-3014
Fairfield MS 1,000/6-8
5121 Nine Mile Rd 23223 804-328-4020
Dr. Angela Thompson, prin. Fax 328-4031
Gayton ES 500/K-5
12481 Church Rd 23233 804-360-0820
Kim Sower, prin. Fax 360-0811

Glen Lea ES 500/K-5
3909 Austin Ave 23222 804-228-2725
Kimberly Lee, prin. Fax 228-2732
Harvie ES 600/PK-5
3401 Harvie Rd 23223 804-343-7010
Tonya Holmes, prin. Fax 343-7013
Holladay ES 600/K-5
7300 Galaxie Rd 23228 804-261-5040
Kimberly Olsen, prin. Fax 261-5054
Johnson ES 500/K-5
5600 Bethlehem Rd 23230 804-673-3735
Dr. Tracie Daniels, prin. Fax 673-3753
Laburnum ES 500/K-5
500 Meriwether Ave 23222 804-228-2720
Nicole Henderson, prin. Fax 228-2733
Lakeside ES 500/K-5
6700 Cedar Croft St 23228 804-261-5050
Debbie Samuel, prin. Fax 261-5069
Longan ES 500/K-5
9200 Mapleview Ave 23294 804-527-4640
Melanie Peugh, prin. Fax 527-4639
Maybeury ES 600/K-5
901 Maybeury Dr 23229 804-750-2650
Bradley Fernald, prin. Fax 750-2649
Mehfoud ES 300/K-2
8320 Buffin Rd 23231 804-795-7020
Stacie Carlisle, prin. Fax 795-7023
Montrose ES 400/K-5
2820 Williamsburg Rd 23231 804-226-8765
Ted Durniak, prin. Fax 226-8771
Moody MS 1,000/6-8
7800 Woodman Rd 23228 804-261-5015
Denise Doss, prin. Fax 261-5024
Nuckols Farm ES 600/K-5
12351 Graham Meadows Dr 23233 804-364-0840
Lisa Merriam, prin. Fax 364-0843
Pemberton ES 300/K-5
1400 Pemberton Rd 23238 804-750-2660
Dr. Joseph Koontz, prin. Fax 750-2663
Pinchbeck ES 500/K-5
1275 Gaskins Rd 23238 804-750-2670
Sarah Modrak, prin. Fax 750-2664
Pocahontas MS 900/6-8
12000 Three Chopt Rd 23233 804-364-0830
Kimberly Sigler, prin. Fax 364-0847
Quioccasin MS 1,000/6-8
9400 Quioccasin Rd 23238 804-750-2630
Cheri Guempel, prin. Fax 750-2629
Ratcliffe ES 400/K-5
2901 Thalen St 23223 804-343-6535
Joy Reed, prin. Fax 343-6516
Ridge ES 500/K-5
8910 Three Chopt Rd 23229 804-673-3745
Anna Hatfield, prin. Fax 673-3754
Rolfe MS 1,000/6-8
6901 Messer Rd 23231 804-226-8730
Dr. Michael Jackson, prin. Fax 226-8739
Short Pump ES 600/K-5
3425 Pump Rd 23233 804-360-0812
Dr. Sarah Slaughter, prin. Fax 364-0845
Skipwith ES 500/K-5
2401 Skipwith Rd 23294 804-527-4650
Todd Smith, prin. Fax 527-4664
Three Chopt ES 200/K-5
1600 Skipwith Rd 23229 804-673-3755
Dana Baldacci, prin. Fax 673-3748
Trevvett ES 500/K-5
2300 Trevvett Dr 23228 804-261-5060
Erica Broudy, prin. Fax 515-1199
Tuckahoe ES 700/K-5
701 Forest Ave 23229 804-673-3765
Sonia Ford, prin. Fax 673-3749
Tuckahoe MS 1,100/6-8
9000 Three Chopt Rd 23229 804-673-3720
Ann Greene, prin. Fax 673-3731
Varina ES 300/3-5
2551 New Market Rd 23231 804-795-7010
Mark Tyler, prin. Fax 795-7028
Ward ES 500/K-5
3400 Darbytown Rd 23231 804-795-7030
Tiffany Chatman, prin. Fax 795-7017
Wilder MS 900/6-8
6900 Wilkinson Rd 23227 804-515-1100
Solomon Jefferson, prin. Fax 515-1110
Other Schools – See Glen Allen, Highland Springs, Sandston

Richmond CSD 22,700/PK-12
301 N 9th St 23219 804-780-7700
Thomas Kranz, supt. Fax 780-4122
www.rvaschools.net
Bellevue Model ES 400/PK-5
2301 E Grace St 23223 804-780-4417
Regina Farr, prin. Fax 780-4436
Binford MS 200/6-8
1701 Floyd Ave 23220 804-780-6231
Melissa Rickey, prin. Fax 780-6057
Blackwell ES 700/PK-5
300 E 15th St 23224 804-780-5078
Kate Outten, prin. Fax 319-3012
Boushall MS 600/6-8
3400 Hopkins Rd 23234 804-780-5016
LaTonya Waller, prin. Fax 780-5396
Broad Rock ES 700/PK-5
4615 Ferguson Ln 23234 804-780-5048
Teya Green, prin. Fax 319-3133
Brown MS 800/6-8
6300 Jahnke Rd 23225 804-319-3015
Stacy Gaines, prin. Fax 319-3009
Carver ES 600/PK-5
1110 W Leigh St 23220 804-780-6247
Kiwana Yates, prin. Fax 780-8046
Cary ES 300/PK-5
3021 Maplewood Ave 23221 804-780-6252
Michael Powell, prin. Fax 780-8407
Chimborazo ES 500/PK-5
3000 E Marshall St 23223 804-780-8392
David Peck, prin. Fax 780-8154

Elkhardt-Thompson MS 500/6-8
7825 Forest Hill Ave 23225 804-272-7554
Jacquelyn Murphy, prin. Fax 560-5115
Fairfield Court ES 600/K-5
2510 Phaup St 23223 804-780-4639
Ellena Ebanks, prin. Fax 780-4087
Fisher ES 400/PK-5
3701 Garden Rd 23235 804-327-5612
Cleveland Walton, prin. Fax 327-5611
Fox ES 600/PK-5
2300 Hanover Ave 23220 804-780-6259
Daniela Jacobs, prin. Fax 780-8409
Francis ES 500/PK-5
5146 Snead Rd 23224 804-745-3702
Kecia Ryan, prin. Fax 319-3030
Ginter Park ES 600/PK-5
3817 Chamberlayne Ave 23227 804-780-8193
Indira Williams, prin. Fax 780-4313
Greene ES 500/PK-5
1745 Catalina Dr 23224 804-780-5082
Linda Sims, prin. Fax 319-3022
Henderson MS 600/6-8
4319 Old Brook Rd 23227 804-780-8288
Cynthia Heckstall, prin. Fax 228-5357
Hill MS 500/6-8
3400 Patterson Ave 23221 804-780-6107
Cherita Sears, prin. Fax 780-8754
Holton ES 600/PK-5
1600 W Laburnum Ave 23227 804-228-5310
Charlene Brooks, prin. Fax 262-1501
Jones ES 600/PK-5
200 Beaufont Hills Dr 23225 804-319-3185
Sonya Shaw, prin. Fax 319-3187
King MS 600/6-8
1000 Mosby St 23223 804-780-8011
Inett Dabney, prin. Fax 780-5590
King Preschool Learning Center PK-PK
900 Mosby St 23223 804-648-5959
Dr. Johnnye Johnson, prin. Fax 648-5966
Mason ES 500/PK-5
813 N 28th St 23223 804-780-4401
Rose Ferguson, prin. Fax 780-8155
MathScience Innovation Center K-12
2401 Hartman St 23223 804-343-6525
Fax 343-6529
Maymount Preschool Learning Center PK-PK
1211 S Allen Ave 23220 804-780-6263
Debra Hall, prin. Fax 780-8411
Munford ES 500/K-5
211 Westmoreland St 23226 804-780-6267
Gregory Muzik, prin. Fax 780-6051
Oak Grove-Bellemeade ES PK-5
2409 Webber Ave 23224 804-780-5008
Mary Townes, prin. Fax 319-3117
Overby-Sheppard ES 400/PK-5
1101 Dance St 23220 804-329-2515
Kara Lancaster-Gay, prin. Fax 780-4321
Redd ES 500/PK-5
5601 Jahnke Rd 23225 804-780-5061
Sherry Wharton-Carey, prin. Fax 780-5013
Regional Preschool Lrng Ctr at Blackwell PK-PK
238 E 14th St 23224 804-780-5064
Dr. Johnnye Johnson, prin. Fax 319-3098
Reid ES 700/PK-5
1301 Whitehead Rd 23225 804-745-3550
Angela Delaney, prin. Fax 319-3029
Scott Regional Preschool Learning Center PK-PK
4011 Moss Side Ave 23222 804-780-8463
Dr. Johnnye Johnson, prin.
Southampton ES 500/PK-5
3333 Cheverly Rd 23225 804-320-2434
Sheleta Crews, prin. Fax 560-2853
Stuart ES 400/PK-5
3101 Fendall Ave 23222 804-780-4879
Jennifer Moore, prin. Fax 780-4320
Summer Hill Preschool Learning Center PK-PK
2717 Alexander Ave 23234 804-780-5041
Dr. Johnnye Johnson, prin.
Swansboro ES 300/PK-5
3160 Midlothian Tpke 23224 804-780-5030
Wayne Scott, prin. Fax 319-3027
Westover Hills ES 400/PK-5
1211 Jahnke Rd 23225 804-780-5002
Virginia Loving, prin. Fax 319-3028
Woodville ES 500/PK-5
2000 N 28th St 23223 804-780-4821
Shannon Washington, prin. Fax 780-8156

Academy of Academic Excellence 50/PK-5
12345 Gayton Rd 23238 804-740-6500
All Saints Catholic S 100/PK-8
3418 Noble Ave 23222 804-329-7524
Wanda Wallin, prin. Fax 329-4201
Banner Christian S 200/K-12
1501 S Providence Rd 23236 804-276-5200
Dr. Thomas Burkett, hdmstr. Fax 276-7620
Central Montessori S of Virginia 100/PK-6
323 N 20th St 23223 804-447-7493
Collegiate S 1,600/PK-12
103 N Mooreland Rd 23229 804-741-7077
Stephen Hickman, hdmstr. Fax 741-9797
Cooper Episcopal S 100/4-8
2124 N 29th St 23223 804-822-6610
Mike Maruca, head sch Fax 447-5784
East End Christian Academy 50/PK-12
3294 Britton Rd 23231 804-795-9266
Suzanne Helland, dir. Fax 795-2222
Elijah House Academy 200/PK-8
6627 Jahnke Rd Ste B 23225 804-755-7051
Jesse Kell, head sch Fax 377-6800
Ephesus Adventist Jr. Academy 100/PK-8
3700 Midlothian Tpke 23224 804-233-4582
Jasmine Johnson, prin. Fax 291-9180
Good Shepherd Episcopal S 100/K-8
4207 Forest Hill Ave 23225 804-231-1452
Ken Seward, hdmstr. Fax 231-9925

Grove Christian S 200/PK-12
8701 Ridge Rd 23229 804-741-2860
Julia Lloyd, admin. Fax 754-8534
Orchard House S 100/5-8
500 N Allen Ave 23220 804-228-2436
Laura Haskins, dir. Fax 228-1069
Our Lady of Lourdes S 400/PK-8
8250 Woodman Rd 23228 804-262-1770
Kelly Taylor, prin. Fax 200-6295
Precious Blessing Academy 50/PK-12
4823 Bryce Ln 23224 804-232-7180
Lois Bias, dean Fax 232-2490
Richmond Academy 100/PK-12
12285 Patterson Ave 23238 804-784-0036
Nancy Melashenko, prin. Fax 784-1558
Richmond Montessori S 300/PK-8
499 N Parham Rd 23229 804-741-0040
Grainne Murray, head sch Fax 741-5341
Richmond Waldorf S 100/PK-8
1000 Westover Hills Blvd 23225 804-377-8024
Rudlin Torah Academy 100/K-8
3809 Patterson Ave 23221 804-353-1110
Sabot at Stony Point 200/PK-8
3400 Stony Point Rd 23235 804-272-1341
Dr. Irene Carney Ph.D., head sch Fax 560-9255
St. Andrew's S 100/K-5
227 S Cherry St 23220 804-648-4545
Cyndy Weldon-Lassiter Ed.D., head sch Fax 612-4175
St. Benedict S 200/PK-8
3100 Grove Ave 23221 804-254-8850
Sean Cruess, prin. Fax 254-9163
St. Bridget S 500/K-8
6011 York Rd 23226 804-288-1994
George Sadler, prin. Fax 288-5730
St. Catherine's S 900/PK-12
6001 Grove Ave 23226 804-288-2804
Dr. Terrie Scheckelhoff Ph.D., head sch Fax 285-8169
St. Christopher's S 1,000/PK-12
711 Saint Christophers Rd 23226 804-282-3185
Mason Lecky, head sch Fax 285-3914
St. Edward-Epiphany S 400/PK-8
10701 W Huguenot Rd 23235 804-272-2881
Emily Elliott, prin. Fax 327-0788
St. Mary S 500/PK-8
9501 Gayton Rd 23229 804-740-1048
Dr. Thomas Dertinger, prin. Fax 740-1310
St. Michael's Episcopal S 400/K-8
8706 Quaker Ln 23235 804-272-3514
Michael Turner, hdmstr. Fax 323-3280
Seven Hills S 100/5-8
1311 Overbrook Rd 23220 804-329-6300
Dagan Rowe, head sch Fax 329-2408
Steward S 600/PK-12
11600 Gayton Rd 23238 804-740-3394
Dan Frank, head sch Fax 740-1464
Veritas S 300/PK-12
3400 Brook Rd 23227 804-272-9517
Keith Nix, head sch Fax 272-9518
Victory Christian Academy 200/PK-5
8491 Chamberlayne Rd 23227 804-262-8256
Kimberly Perez B.S., prin. Fax 553-1905
West End Montessori S 100/PK-6
9307 Quioccasin Rd 23229 804-523-7536

Ridgeway, Henry, Pop. 734
Henry County SD
Supt. — See Collinsville
Drewry Mason ES 400/PK-5
45 Drewry Mason School Rd 24148 276-956-3154
Dr. Sherri Lewis, prin. Fax 956-3156

Rileyville, Page
Page County SD
Supt. — See Luray
Springfield ES 200/PK-5
158 Big Spring Ln 22650 540-743-3750
Sue Davies, prin. Fax 743-4699

Riner, Montgomery, Pop. 845
Montgomery County SD
Supt. — See Christiansburg
Auburn ES 500/PK-5
1760 Auburn School Dr 24149 540-381-6521
Marcia Settle, prin. Fax 381-6530
Auburn MS 300/6-8
4163 Riner Rd 24149 540-382-5165
Meggan Marshall, prin. Fax 381-6562

Ringgold, Pittsylvania
Pittsylvania County SD
Supt. — See Chatham
Dan River MS 500/6-8
5875 Kentuck Rd 24586 434-822-6027
Emily Reynolds, prin. Fax 822-6548
Kentuck ES 600/PK-5
100 Kentuck Elementary Cir 24586 434-822-5944
Bobby Shields, prin. Fax 822-5923

Roanoke, Roanoke, Pop. 94,517
Roanoke CSD 13,500/PK-12
PO Box 13145 24031 540-853-2502
Dr. Rita Bishop, supt. Fax 853-2951
www.rcps.info
Addison MS 600/6-8
1220 5th St NW 24016 540-853-2681
Robert Johnson, prin. Fax 853-1424
Breckinridge MS 500/6-8
3901 Williamson Rd NW 24012 540-853-2251
Tracey Anderson, prin. Fax 853-6505
Crystal Spring ES 300/PK-5
2620 Carolina Ave SW 24014 540-853-2976
Kathleen Tate, prin. Fax 853-1914
Fairview ES 500/PK-5
648 Westwood Blvd NW 24017 540-853-2978
April Plympton, prin. Fax 853-1038
Fallon Park ES 700/PK-5
502 19th St SE 24013 540-853-2535
Nikki Mitchem, prin. Fax 853-2094
Fishburn Park ES 300/PK-5
3057 Colonial Ave SW 24015 540-853-2931
Tammy Brown, prin. Fax 853-2330
Garden City ES 300/PK-5
3718 Garden City Blvd SE 24014 540-853-2971
Jill Lane, prin. Fax 853-1237
Grandin Court ES 300/PK-5
2815 Spessard Ave SW 24015 540-853-2867
Theresa Pritchard, prin. Fax 853-1399
Highland Park Magnet ES 400/PK-5
1212 5th St SW 24016 540-853-2963
Dr. Mark Crummey, prin. Fax 853-1692
Hurt Park ES 400/PK-5
1525 Salem Ave SW 24016 540-853-2986
Regina Gregory, prin. Fax 853-2397
Jackson MS 600/6-8
1004 Montrose Ave SE 24013 540-853-6040
Cindy Delp, prin. Fax 853-6027
Lincoln Terrace ES 300/PK-5
1802 Liberty Rd NW 24012 540-853-2994
Stacie Wright, prin. Fax 853-2729
Madison MS 600/6-8
1160 Overland Rd SW 24015 540-853-2351
Whitney Johnson, prin. Fax 853-1050
Monterey ES 600/PK-5
4501 Oliver Rd NE 24012 540-853-2933
Morgan Johnson-Strother, prin. Fax 853-1126
Morningside ES 300/PK-5
1716 Wilson St SE 24013 540-853-2991
Ann Kreft, prin. Fax 853-1552
Preston Park ES 400/PK-5
3142 Preston Ave NW 24012 540-853-2996
Eric Fisher, prin. Fax 853-1168
Roanoke Academy/Math & Science 500/PK-5
1616 19th St NW 24017 540-853-2751
Toni Belton, prin. Fax 853-1192
Round Hill ES 600/PK-5
2020 Oakland Blvd NW 24012 540-853-2756
Dr. Cory Hawks, prin. Fax 853-1118
Virginia Heights ES 400/K-5
1210 Amherst St SW 24015 540-853-2937
Theresa Schmitt, prin. Fax 853-2496
Wasena ES 300/PK-5
1125 Sherwood Ave SW 24015 540-853-2914
Josh Burton, prin. Fax 853-1189
Westside ES 800/PK-5
1441 Westside Blvd NW 24017 540-853-2967
Dr. Beth Poff, prin. Fax 853-1429
Wilson MS 500/6-8
1813 Carter Rd SW 24015 540-853-2358
Rosalind Henderson, prin. Fax 853-2004

Roanoke County SD 14,000/K-12
5937 Cove Rd 24019 540-562-3700
Dr. Gregory Killough, supt. Fax 562-3994
www.rcs.k12.va.us
Back Creek ES 300/K-5
7130 Bent Mountain Rd 24018 540-772-7565
Virginia Sharp, prin. Fax 776-7144
Bonsack ES 400/K-5
5437 Crumpacker Dr 24019 540-977-5870
Melissa Jones, prin. Fax 977-5879
Burlington ES 400/K-5
6533 Peters Creek Rd 24019 540-561-8165
Susan Brown, prin. Fax 561-8162
Cave Spring ES 500/K-5
5404 Springlawn Ave 24018 540-772-7558
Jodi Poff, prin. Fax 776-7145
Cave Spring MS 700/6-8
4880 Brambleton Ave 24018 540-772-7560
Fiona Hill, prin. Fax 772-2195
Clearbrook ES 300/K-5
5205 Franklin Rd SW 24014 540-772-7555
Beth Grim, prin. Fax 776-7148
Glen Cove ES 400/K-5
5901 Cove Rd 24019 540-561-8135
Stephanie Hogan, prin. Fax 561-8164
Green Valley ES 400/K-5
3838 Overdale Rd 24018 540-772-7556
Kimberly Bradshaw, prin. Fax 776-7149
Hidden Valley MS 600/6-8
4902 Hidden Valley School 24018 540-772-7570
Mike Riley, prin. Fax 772-7519
Mountain View ES 400/K-5
5901 Plantation Cir 24019 540-561-8175
Leigh Smith, prin. Fax 561-8167
Mt. Pleasant ES 300/K-5
3216 Mount Pleasant Blvd 24014 540-427-1879
Ellen Walton, prin. Fax 427-5779
Northside MS 700/6-8
6810 Northside High School 24019 540-561-8145
Dr. Paul Lineburg, prin. Fax 561-8152
Oak Grove ES 400/K-5
5005 Grandin Road Ext 24018 540-772-7580
Cindy Klimaitis, prin. Fax 776-7150
Penn Forest ES 500/K-5
6328 Merriman Rd 24018 540-772-7590
Karen Pendleton, prin. Fax 776-7151
Other Schools – See Salem, Vinton

Faith Christian S 300/PK-12
3585 Buck Mountain Rd 24018 540-769-5200
New Vista Montessori S 50/PK-K
541 Luck Ave SW Ste 110 24016 540-342-1173
North Cross S 500/PK-12
4254 Colonial Ave 24018 540-989-6641
Dr. Christian Proctor, head sch Fax 989-7299
Parkway Christian Academy 300/PK-12
3230 King St NE 24012 540-982-2400
Erica Dixon, admin. Fax 982-2005
Roanoke Adventist Prep S 50/K-8
4120 Challenger Ave 24012 540-977-0346
Roanoke Catholic S 500/PK-12
621 N Jefferson St 24016 540-982-3532
Patrick Patterson, prin. Fax 345-0785
Roanoke Valley Christian S 300/PK-12
PO Box 7010 24019 540-366-2432
Rick Brown, admin. Fax 366-9719

Rocky Mount, Franklin, Pop. 4,700
Franklin County SD 7,400/PK-12
25 Bernard Rd 24151 540-483-5138
W. Mark Church Ph.D., supt. Fax 483-5806
www.frco.k12.va.us
Franklin MS East 500/6-6
375 Middle School Rd 24151 540-483-5105
Dr. Bernice Cobbs, prin. Fax 483-5501
Franklin MS West 900/7-8
225 Middle School Rd 24151 540-483-5105
Dr. Bernice Cobbs, prin. Fax 483-5585
Rocky Mount ES 400/PK-5
555 School Board Rd 24151 540-483-5040
Dr. Lisa Newell, prin. Fax 483-5454
Sontag ES 300/PK-5
3101 Sontag Rd 24151 540-483-5667
Gail Brendle, prin. Fax 483-5652
Waid ES 400/PK-5
540 E Court St 24151 540-483-5736
Gregg Cuddy, prin. Fax 483-9674
Other Schools – See Boones Mill, Callaway, Ferrum, Glade Hill, Hardy, Henry, Penhook, Wirtz

---

Christian Heritage Academy 100/PK-12
625 Glennwood Dr 24151 540-483-5855
Tony Quist, head sch Fax 483-9355

Rosedale, Russell
Russell County SD
Supt. — See Lebanon
Belfast ES 100/K-5
PO Box G 24280 276-880-2283
Georgia McCoy, prin. Fax 880-1330

Rose Hill, Lee, Pop. 791
Lee County SD
Supt. — See Jonesville
Rose Hill ES 300/PK-7
150 Rose Hill Dr 24281 276-445-4094
Lora Lawson, prin. Fax 445-5315

Round Hill, Loudoun, Pop. 534
Loudoun County SD
Supt. — See Ashburn
Round Hill ES 600/PK-5
17115 Evening Star Dr 20141 540-751-2450
Andrew Davis, prin. Fax 338-6834

Ruckersville, Greene, Pop. 1,105
Greene County SD
Supt. — See Stanardsville
Ruckersville ES 600/K-5
105 Progress Pl 22968 434-939-9006
Erika Liddle, prin. Fax 990-9432

Rural Retreat, Wythe, Pop. 1,472
Wythe County SD
Supt. — See Wytheville
Rural Retreat ES 400/PK-5
100 Martha DeBord Way 24368 276-686-4125
Alan Rouse, prin. Fax 686-4467
Rural Retreat MS 300/6-8
325 E Buck Ave 24368 276-686-5200
Shannon Vaught, prin. Fax 686-4944

Rustburg, Campbell, Pop. 1,389
Campbell County SD 8,300/PK-12
PO Box 99 24588 434-332-3458
Dr. Robert Johnson, supt. Fax 528-1655
www.campbell.k12.va.us
Rustburg ES 500/PK-5
25 Webbs Way 24588 434-332-5215
Mary Lynne Arnold, prin. Fax 332-1151
Rustburg MS 700/6-8
PO Box 130 24588 434-332-5141
Christie Cundiff, prin. Fax 332-2058
Yellow Branch ES 600/PK-5
377 Dennis Riddle Dr 24588 434-821-1021
Betsy Brown, prin. Fax 821-5871
Other Schools – See Altavista, Brookneal, Concord, Lynchburg

Ruther Glen, Caroline
Caroline County SD
Supt. — See Bowling Green
Lewis & Clark ES 900/PK-5
18101 Clark And York Blvd 22546 804-448-0175
Cynthia Aref, prin. Fax 448-0293
Madison ES 500/PK-5
9075 Chance Pl 22546 804-448-2171
Fax 448-4395

Carmel S 100/PK-12
PO Box 605 22546 804-448-3288

Saint Charles, Lee, Pop. 128
Lee County SD
Supt. — See Jonesville
Saint Charles ES 200/PK-7
2434 Saint Charles Rd 24282 276-383-4531
Kellie Leonard, prin. Fax 383-4422

Saint Paul, Wise, Pop. 957
Wise County SD
Supt. — See Wise
Saint Paul ES 200/PK-7
PO Box 1067 24283 276-762-5941
Karen Dickenson, prin. Fax 762-0481

Saint Stephens Church, King and Queen
King & Queen County SD
Supt. — See King and Queen Court House
Lawson-Marriott ES 300/PK-7
1599 Newtown Rd 23148 804-769-3116
David Copsmith, prin. Fax 769-8846

Salem, Salem, Pop. 24,439
Roanoke County SD
Supt. — See Roanoke
Ft. Lewis ES 200/K-5
3115 W Main St 24153 540-387-6594
Julie Sandzimier, prin. Fax 387-6348
Glenvar ES 400/K-5
4507 Malus Dr 24153 540-387-6540
Lisa Coleman, prin. Fax 387-6351
Glenvar MS 400/6-8
4555 Malus Dr 24153 540-387-6322
Josh Whitlow, prin. Fax 387-6283
Masons Cove ES 200/K-5
3370 Bradshaw Rd 24153 540-387-6530
Matt Johnson, prin. Fax 384-6087

Salem CSD 3,800/PK-12
510 S College Ave 24153 540-389-0130
Dr. H. Alan Seibert, supt. Fax 389-4135
www.salem.k12.va.us
Carver ES 400/K-5
6 E 4th St 24153 540-387-2492
Kristyn Schmidt, prin. Fax 375-4105
East Salem ES 500/PK-5
1765 Roanoke Blvd 24153 540-375-7001
Diane Rose, prin. Fax 343-6623
Lewis MS 900/6-8
616 S College Ave 24153 540-387-2513
James Garst, prin. Fax 389-8914
South Salem ES 400/K-5
1600 Carolyn Rd 24153 540-387-2478
Margaret Humphrey, prin. Fax 389-4810
West Salem ES 400/K-5
520 N Bruffey St 24153 540-387-2503
Debbie Carroll, prin. Fax 389-4923

Salem Montessori S 100/PK-6
101 Corporate Cir 24153 540-387-1523

Saltville, Smyth, Pop. 2,062
Smyth County SD
Supt. — See Marion
Northwood MS 200/6-8
156 Long Hollow Rd 24370 276-624-3341
Mariann Blevins, prin. Fax 624-3535
Rich Valley ES 200/PK-5
196 Long Hollow Rd 24370 276-624-3314
Tamela Hahn, prin. Fax 624-3426
Saltville ES 300/PK-5
PO Box C 24370 276-496-4751
Mitzi Frye, prin. Fax 496-3958

Saluda, Middlesex, Pop. 753
Middlesex County SD 1,200/PK-12
PO Box 205 23149 804-758-2277
Dr. Peter Gretz, supt. Fax 758-3727
www.mcps.k12.va.us/
Other Schools – See Locust Hill

Sandston, Henrico, Pop. 7,426
Henrico County SD
Supt. — See Richmond
Donahoe ES 500/K-5
1801 Graves Rd 23150 804-328-4035
Rebecca Roper, prin. Fax 328-4022
Elko MS 900/6-8
5901 Elko Rd 23150 804-328-4110
Dominique Friend, prin. Fax 328-4115
Sandston ES 200/K-5
7 Naglee Ave 23150 804-328-4055
Kim Powell, prin. Fax 328-4017
Seven Pines ES 500/K-5
301 Beulah Rd 23150 804-328-4065
Terri Mothershead, prin. Fax 328-4043

New Bridge Academy 100/K-12
5701 Elko Rd 23150 804-737-7833
Rev. J.D. Sluss, admin. Fax 737-1181

Saxe, Charlotte
Charlotte County SD
Supt. — See Charlotte Court House
Bacon District ES 200/PK-5
840 Bacon School Rd 23967 434-735-8612
Sylvia Lockett, prin. Fax 735-8505

Scottsburg, Halifax, Pop. 119
Halifax County SD
Supt. — See Halifax
Clays Mill ES 200/K-5
1011 Clays Mill School Rd 24589 434-476-3022
David Duffer, prin. Fax 476-1891
Scottsburg ES 300/K-5
1010 Scottsburg School Trl 24589 434-454-6454
Sherry Cowan, prin. Fax 454-1210

Scottsville, Albemarle, Pop. 557
Albemarle County SD
Supt. — See Charlottesville
Scottsville ES 200/PK-5
7868 Scottsville School Rd 24590 434-974-8040
Sharon Amato-Wilcox, prin. Fax 286-2442

Seaford, York
York County SD
Supt. — See Yorktown
Seaford ES 500/K-5
1105 Seaford Rd 23696 757-898-0352
Christina Head Ed.D., prin. Fax 898-0413

Sedley, Southampton, Pop. 465
Southhampton County SD
Supt. — See Courtland
Nottoway ES 300/PK-5
13093 Ivor Rd 23878 757-859-6539
Susan Melbye, prin. Fax 859-9392

Shawsville, Montgomery, Pop. 1,291
Montgomery County SD
Supt. — See Christiansburg
Shawsville MS 200/6-8
4179 Oldtown Rd 24162 540-268-2262
Andrew Hipple, prin. Fax 268-1868

Shenandoah, Page, Pop. 2,351
Page County SD
Supt. — See Luray
Grove Hill Preschool 100/PK-PK
7979 US Highway 340 22849 540-652-5844
Eric Benson, coord.
Page County MS 400/6-8
198 Panther Dr 22849 540-652-3400
Lance Moran, prin. Fax 652-8308
Shenandoah ES 400/K-5
529 4th St 22849 540-652-8621
Denise Atkins, prin. Fax 652-1711

Skipwith, Mecklenburg
Mecklenburg County SD
Supt. — See Boydton
Bluestone MS 400/6-8
250 Middle School Rd 23968 434-372-3266
Paige Lacks, prin. Fax 372-3362

Smithfield, Isle of Wight, Pop. 7,922
Isle of Wight County SD 5,500/PK-12
820 W Main St 23430 757-357-4393
Dr. James Thornton M.Ed., supt. Fax 357-0849
www.iwcs.k12.va.us
Hardy ES 500/PK-3
9311 Hardy Cir 23430 757-357-3204
Shante Denson, prin. Fax 365-0236
Smithfield MS 600/7-8
14175 Turner Dr 23430 757-365-4100
Fred Eng, prin. Fax 365-4222
Westside ES 800/4-6
800 W Main St 23430 757-357-3021
Marsha Cale, prin. Fax 365-4222
Other Schools – See Carrollton, Carrsville, Windsor

South Boston, Halifax, Pop. 8,032
Halifax County SD
Supt. — See Halifax
Cluster Springs Early Learning Center 100/PK-PK
1011 Cluster Springs Elem R 24592 434-572-4121
Priscilla Price, prin. Fax 572-4682
Halifax MS 1,200/6-8
1011 Middle School Cir 24592 434-572-4100
Magie Wilkerson, prin. Fax 572-4106
South Boston Early Learning Center 100/PK-PK
1927 Jeffress Blvd 24592 434-572-4273
Priscilla Price, prin. Fax 572-4275
South Boston ES 800/K-5
2320 Parker Ave 24592 434-517-2620
Dennis Seamster, prin. Fax 517-2630

S Chesterfield, Chesterfield
Chesterfield County SD
Supt. — See Chesterfield
Christian ES 700/PK-5
14801 Woods Edge Rd, 804-530-5730
Jennifer Lenz, prin. Fax 530-0217
Enon ES 500/PK-5
14801 Woods Edge Rd, 804-530-5720
Jennifer Hinson, prin. Fax 530-5739

South Hill, Mecklenburg, Pop. 4,561
Mecklenburg County SD
Supt. — See Boydton
Park View MS 600/6-8
365 Dockery Rd 23970 434-447-3761
Dr. Brian Matney, prin. Fax 447-4920
South Hill ES 800/PK-5
1290 Plank Rd 23970 434-447-8134
Michele Icenhour, prin. Fax 447-6511

South Riding, Loudoun, Pop. 23,365
Loudoun County SD
Supt. — See Ashburn
Hutchison Farm ES 800/PK-5
42819 Center St 20152 703-957-4350
Heidi Smith, prin. Fax 444-8020
Liberty ES 1,100/K-5
25491 Riding Center Dr 20152 703-957-4370
Paul Pack, prin. Fax 327-5118
Little River ES 800/PK-5
43464 Hyland Hills St 20152 703-957-4360
Kevin Murphy, prin. Fax 327-4855

Speedwell, Wythe
Wythe County SD
Supt. — See Wytheville
Speedwell ES 100/PK-5
6820 Cedar Springs Rd 24374 276-621-4622
Kim Ingo, prin. Fax 621-4687

Spotsylvania, Spotsylvania
Spotsylvania County SD
Supt. — See Fredericksburg
Berkeley ES 300/K-5
5979 Partlow Rd, 540-582-5141
Robin Monroe, prin. Fax 582-8110
Brock Road ES 800/PK-5
10207 Brock Rd 22553 540-972-3870
Shonda Collins-Richey, prin. Fax 972-3170
Courthouse Road ES 800/K-5
9911 Courthouse Rd 22553 540-891-0400
Marcie Fields, prin. Fax 891-0405
Courtland ES 500/K-5
6601 Smith Station Rd 22553 540-898-5422
Katie Simitoski, prin. Fax 891-4658
Lee ES 500/K-5
7415 Brock Rd 22553 540-582-5445
Robert MacDonald, prin. Fax 582-3462
Livingston ES 400/K-5
6057 Courthouse Rd, 540-895-5101
Cynthia Franzen, prin. Fax 895-9338
Ni River MS 700/6-8
11632 Catharpin Rd 22553 540-785-3990
Brian Bartoszek, prin. Fax 785-0658
Post Oak MS 800/6-8
6959 Courthouse Rd, 540-582-7517
Scott Belako, prin. Fax 582-7510
Riverview ES 700/K-5
7001 N Roxbury Mill Rd, 540-582-7617
Darnella Cunningham, prin. Fax 582-7622
Spotsylvania MS 800/6-8
8801 Courthouse Rd 22553 540-582-6341
Lane Byrd, prin. Fax 582-3207
Thornburg MS 700/6-8
6929 N Roxbury Mill Rd, 540-582-7600
Daryl Lann, prin. Fax 582-7606
Wilderness ES 700/K-5
11600 Catharpin Rd 22553 540-786-9817
Dianne Holmes, prin. Fax 785-2652

Springfield, Fairfax, Pop. 29,504
Fairfax County SD
Supt. — See Falls Church
Cardinal Forest ES 600/K-6
8600 Forrester Blvd 22152 703-923-5200
Karen Kenna, prin. Fax 923-5297
Crestwood ES 600/K-6
6010 Hanover Ave 22150 703-923-5400
Tim Kasik, prin. Fax 923-5497
Forestdale ES 600/PK-6
6530 Elder Ave 22150 703-313-4300
Merrell Dade, prin. Fax 313-4397
Garfield ES 400/K-6
7101 Old Keene Mill Rd 22150 703-923-2900
Christine Slattery, prin. Fax 923-2997
Hunt Valley ES 600/K-6
7107 Sydenstricker Rd 22152 703-913-8800
David Fee, prin. Fax 913-8897
Irving MS 1,000/7-8
8100 Old Keene Mill Rd 22152 703-912-4500
Cindy Conley, prin. Fax 912-4597
Keene Mill ES 700/K-6
6310 Bardu Ave 22152 703-644-4700
Renee Miller, prin. Fax 644-4797
Key MS 800/7-8
6402 Franconia Rd 22150 703-313-3900
Aimee Holleb, prin. Fax 313-3997
Kings Glen ES 500/4-6
5401 Danbury Forest Dr 22151 703-239-4000
Samuel Elson, prin. Fax 239-4097
Kings Park ES 700/K-3
5400 Harrow Way 22151 703-426-7000
Dotty Lin, prin. Fax 426-7097
Lynbrook ES 600/K-6
5801 Backlick Rd 22150 703-866-2940
Jay Nocco, prin. Fax 866-2997
Newington Forest ES 600/K-6
8001 Newington Forest Ave 22153 703-923-2600
Angela Thompson, prin. Fax 923-2697
North Springfield ES 500/PK-5
7602 Heming Ct 22151 703-658-5500
Chad McRae, prin. Fax 658-5597
Orange Hunt ES 800/K-6
6820 Sydenstricker Rd 22152 703-913-6800
Karen Tuttle, prin. Fax 913-6897
Ravensworth ES 500/PK-6
5411 Nutting Dr 22151 703-426-3600
Roxanne Salata, prin. Fax 426-3697
Rolling Valley ES 600/K-6
6703 Barnack Dr 22152 703-923-2700
Maureen Boland, prin. Fax 923-2797
Sangster ES 900/K-6
7420 Reservation Dr 22153 703-644-8200
Lisa Reddel, prin. Fax 644-8297
Saratoga ES 700/K-6
8111 Northumberland Rd 22153 703-440-2600
Amy Miller, prin. Fax 440-2697
Springfield Estates ES 700/K-6
6200 Charles Goff Dr 22150 703-921-2300
Mary Randolph, prin. Fax 921-2397
West Springfield ES 400/K-6
6802 Deland Dr 22152 703-912-4400
Kelly Sheers, prin. Fax 912-4457

Angelus Academy PK-8
7644 Dynatech Ct 22153 703-924-3996
Vivian Zini, prin. Fax 924-9683
Immanuel Christian S 700/K-8
6915 Braddock Rd 22151 703-941-1220
Stephen Danish, head sch Fax 563-3772
Prince of Peace Lutheran S 200/PK-K
8306 Old Keene Mill Rd 22152 703-451-6177
Cindy Deatherage, prin. Fax 451-9728
St. Bernadette S 500/PK-8
7602 Old Keene Mill Rd 22152 703-451-8696
Beth Monroe, prin. Fax 269-1121
Springs Montessori S 200/PK-3
7719 Fullerton Rd 22153 703-455-1000
Word of Life Christian Academy 200/PK-8
5225 Backlick Rd 22151 703-354-4222
Bonnie Johnson, admin. Fax 750-1306

Stafford, Stafford
Stafford County SD 27,100/PK-12
31 Stafford Ave 22554 540-658-6000
Dr. W. Bruce Benson, supt. Fax 658-5963
www.staffordschools.net
Barrett ES 800/K-5
150 Duffey Dr, 540-658-6464
Kim Austin, prin. Fax 658-6465
Brent ES 900/K-5
2125 Mountain View Rd, 540-658-6790
Brian Fitzgerald, prin. Fax 658-6799
Burns ES 700/K-5
60 Gallery Rd 22554 540-658-6800
Caroline Goddard, prin. Fax 658-6807
Garrisonville ES 500/PK-5
100 Wood Dr, 540-658-6260
Alexis White, prin. Fax 658-6255
Hampton Oaks ES 800/K-5
107 Northampton Blvd 22554 540-658-6280
Allen Hicks, prin. Fax 658-6276

Heim MS 900/6-8
320 Telegraph Rd 22554 540-658-5910
Mary McGraw, prin. Fax 658-0329
Moncure ES 700/K-5
75 Moncure Ln, 540-658-6300
Gregory Machi, prin. Fax 658-6292
Park Ridge ES 600/PK-5
2000 Parkway Blvd 22554 540-658-6320
Keana Sirmans-Butler, prin. Fax 658-6314
Poole MS 800/6-8
800 Eustace Rd 22554 540-658-6190
Robert Bingham, prin. Fax 658-6176
Rockhill ES 600/K-5
50 Wood Dr, 540-658-6360
Terri Rivero, prin. Fax 658-6355
Stafford ES 700/K-5
1349 Courthouse Rd 22554 540-658-6340
Mary Foreman, prin. Fax 658-6332
Stafford MS 500/6-8
101 Spartan Dr 22554 540-658-6210
Mark Smith, prin. Fax 658-6204
Thompson MS 1,100/6-8
75 Walpole St 22554 540-658-6420
Andrew Grider, prin. Fax 658-6430
Widewater ES 900/PK-5
101 Den Rich Rd 22554 540-658-6380
Kristen McKinney-Nash, prin. Fax 658-6378
Winding Creek ES 700/PK-5
475 Winding Creek Rd 22554 540-658-6400
Rebecca Wardlow, prin. Fax 658-6401
Wright MS 800/6-8
100 Wood Dr, 540-658-6240
William Boatwright, prin. Fax 658-6238
Other Schools – See Falmouth, Fredericksburg

Grace Preparatory S 100/PK-12
2202 Jefferson Davis Hwy 22554 540-657-4500
Ted Smith, head sch Fax 628-0323
St. William of York S 200/PK-8
3130 Jefferson Davis Hwy 22554 540-659-5207
Frank Nicely, prin. Fax 659-9863

Stanardsville, Greene, Pop. 363
Greene County SD 3,100/PK-12
PO Box 1140 22973 434-939-9000
Dr. Andrea Whitmarsh, supt. Fax 985-4686
www.greenecountyschools.com
Greene ES 400/3-5
8094 Spotswood Trl 22973 434-939-9001
Adam Midock, prin. Fax 985-5287
Greene PS 500/PK-2
64 Monroe Dr 22973 434-939-9002
Danielle Alicea, prin. Fax 985-1321
Monroe MS 700/6-8
148 Monroe Dr 22973 434-939-9003
Eileen Oliver-Eggert, prin. Fax 985-1359
Other Schools – See Ruckersville

Stanley, Page, Pop. 1,681
Page County SD
Supt. — See Luray
Stanley ES 500/K-5
306 Aylor Grubbs Ave 22851 540-778-2612
Chris Hopkins, prin. Fax 778-1913

Stanley SDA S 50/PK-8
118 Church Ave 22851 540-778-3377

Stanleytown, Henry, Pop. 1,409
Henry County SD
Supt. — See Collinsville
Stanleytown ES 400/PK-5
74 Edgewood Dr 24168 276-629-5084
Turonne Hunt, prin. Fax 629-2925

Staunton, Staunton, Pop. 23,179
Augusta County SD
Supt. — See Verona
Beverley Manor MS 700/6-8
58 Cedar Green Rd 24401 540-886-5806
Dr. Sarah Melton, prin. Fax 886-4019
Riverheads ES 500/K-5
239 Don Hanger Circle 24401 540-337-2535
John Matherly, prin. Fax 337-1454

Staunton CSD 2,600/K-12
116 W Beverley St 24401 540-332-3920
Dr. Garett Smith, supt. Fax 332-3924
www.staunton.k12.va.us
McSwain ES 500/K-5
1101 N Coalter St 24401 540-332-3936
Kim Crocker, prin. Fax 332-3955
Shelburne MS 600/6-8
300 Grubert Ave 24401 540-332-3930
Jennifer Morris, prin. Fax 332-3933
Ware ES 400/K-5
330 Grubert Ave 24401 540-332-3938
Dr. Sharon Barker, prin. Fax 332-3957
Weller ES 400/K-5
600 Greenville Ave 24401 540-332-3940
Donald Rhodes, prin. Fax 332-3959

Grace Christian Elementary & MS 200/PK-8
511 Thornrose Ave 24401 540-886-0937
Joanne Kinder, prin. Fax 886-2761
Richards Christian Academy 50/K-8
414 Sterling St 24401 540-886-4984

Stephens City, Frederick, Pop. 1,772
Frederick County SD
Supt. — See Winchester
Aylor MS 700/6-8
901 Aylor Rd 22655 540-869-3736
David Rudy, prin. Fax 867-2756
Bass-Hoover ES 600/K-5
471 Aylor Rd 22655 540-869-4700
Amy Williams, prin. Fax 869-0668

Eukarya Christian Academy 50/PK-12
PO Box 664 22655 540-868-0081
Legacy Christian Academy 100/PK-12
5933 Valley Pike 22655 540-877-7336
Shenandoah Valley Christian Academy 200/PK-12
PO Box 1360 22655 540-869-4600

Sterling, Loudoun, Pop. 26,953
Loudoun County SD
Supt. — See Ashburn
Algonkian ES 500/PK-5
20196 Carter Ct 20165 571-434-3240
Brian Blubaugh, prin. Fax 444-1917
Countryside ES 700/K-5
20624 Countryside Blvd 20165 571-434-3250
Richard Rudnick, prin. Fax 444-8055
Forest Grove ES 600/PK-5
46245 Forest Ridge Dr 20164 571-434-4560
Shontel Simon, prin. Fax 444-7598
Guilford ES 500/K-5
600 W Poplar Rd 20164 571-434-4550
Lauren Sprowls, prin. Fax 444-7424
Horizon ES 700/PK-5
46665 Broadmore Dr 20165 571-434-3260
Jennifer Ewing, prin. Fax 444-7418
Lowes Island ES 700/PK-5
20755 Whitewater Dr 20165 571-434-4450
Bruce Shafferman, prin. Fax 430-6355
Meadowland ES 400/K-5
729 Sugarland Run Dr 20164 571-434-4440
Herman Mizell, prin. Fax 444-7435
Potowmack ES 600/PK-5
46465 Esterbrook Cir 20165 571-434-3270
Jennifer Rule, prin. Fax 444-7526
River Bend MS 1,200/6-8
46240 Algonkian Pkwy 20165 571-434-3220
David Shaffer, prin. Fax 444-7578
Rolling Ridge ES 500/K-5
500 E Frederick Dr 20164 571-434-4540
Lottie Spurlock, prin. Fax 444-7442
Seneca Ridge MS 1,000/6-8
98 Seneca Ridge Dr 20164 571-434-4420
Nicholas Cottone, prin. Fax 444-7567
Sterling ES 500/PK-5
200 W Church Rd 20164 571-434-4580
Jennifer Meres, prin. Fax 450-1583
Sterling MS 1,000/6-8
201 W Holly Ave 20164 571-434-4520
Gus Martinez, prin. Fax 444-7492
Sugarland ES 600/PK-5
65 Sugarland Run Dr 20164 571-434-4460
Gail Brady, prin. Fax 444-7463
Sully ES 500/PK-5
300 Circle Dr 20164 571-434-4570
Colleen O'Neill, prin. Fax 444-7473

Chesterbrook Academy 100/PK-8
46100 Woodshire Dr 20166 703-404-0202
Lydia Soto, prin.

Stony Creek, Sussex, Pop. 195
Sussex County SD 1,100/K-12
21302 Sussex Dr 23882 434-246-1099
Arthur Jarrett Ed.D., supt. Fax 246-8214
www.sussex.k12.va.us
Sussex Central ES 500/K-5
21392 Sussex Dr 23882 434-246-8960
Morris Taylor, prin. Fax 246-2027
Sussex Central MS 300/6-8
21356 Sussex Dr 23882 434-246-2251
Dr. Jennifer Tindle, prin. Fax 246-8912

Strasburg, Shenandoah, Pop. 6,272
Shenandoah County SD
Supt. — See Woodstock
Sandy Hook ES 1,000/PK-5
162 Stickley Loop 22657 540-465-8281
Robin Shrum, prin. Fax 465-5443
Signal Knob MS 500/6-8
687 Sandy Hook Rd 22657 540-465-3422
Dr. Holly Rusher, prin. Fax 465-5412

Stuart, Patrick, Pop. 1,391
Patrick County SD 2,800/PK-12
PO Box 346 24171 276-694-3163
William Sroufe Ed.D., supt. Fax 694-3170
www.patrick.k12.va.us
Stuart ES 500/PK-7
314 Staples Ave 24171 276-694-7139
Sandra Clement, prin. Fax 694-5807
Other Schools – See Ararat, Critz, Meadows of Dan, Patrick Springs, Woolwine

Stuarts Draft, Augusta, Pop. 9,108
Augusta County SD
Supt. — See Verona
Stuarts Draft ES 700/K-5
63 School Blvd 24477 540-337-2951
Tina Bowersox, prin. Fax 946-7620
Stuarts Draft MS 500/6-8
1088 Augusta Farms Rd 24477 540-946-7611
Scott Musick, prin. Fax 946-7613
Stump ES 400/K-5
115 Draft Ave 24477 540-337-1549
Shawn Baska, prin. Fax 337-1761

Ridgeview Christian S 100/PK-12
PO Box 477 24477 540-337-1025
Jeremy Woody, prin. Fax 337-3718

Suffolk, Suffolk, Pop. 82,776
Suffolk CSD 14,200/PK-12
100 N Main St 23434 757-925-6750
Dr. Deran Whitney, supt. Fax 925-6751
www.spsk12.net/
Benn ES 700/PK-5
1253 Nansemond Pkwy 23434 757-934-6224
David LeFevre, prin. Fax 925-5644
Creekside ES 1,000/PK-5
1000 Bennetts Creek Park Rd 23435 757-923-4251
Tara Moore, prin. Fax 686-2640
Driver ES 300/PK-5
4270 Driver Ln 23435 757-923-4106
Melodie Griffin, prin. Fax 538-5407
Elephants Fork ES 700/PK-5
2316 William Reid Dr 23434 757-923-5250
Jessica Avery, prin. Fax 925-5596
Forest Glen MS 400/6-8
200 Forest Glen Dr 23434 757-925-5780
Melvin Bradshaw, prin. Fax 925-5557
Hillpoint ES 800/K-5
1101 Hillpoint Rd 23434 757-923-5252
Catherine Pichon, prin. Fax 538-5442
Kennedy MS 600/6-8
2325 E Washington St 23434 757-934-6212
Bryan Thrift, prin. Fax 925-5594
Kilby Shores ES 600/PK-5
111 Kilby Shores Dr 23434 757-934-6214
Lorri Banks, prin. Fax 925-5569
King's Fork MS 1,000/6-8
350 Kings Fork Rd 23434 757-923-5246
Jennifer Presson, prin. Fax 925-5754
Nansemond Parkway ES 600/PK-5
3012 Nansemond Pkwy 23434 757-923-4167
Chanel Woods, prin. Fax 538-5415
Northern Shores ES 800/PK-5
6701 Respass Beach Rd 23435 757-923-4169
Lori White, prin. Fax 925-5602
Oakland ES 500/PK-5
5505 Godwin Blvd 23434 757-923-5248
Temesha Dabney, prin. Fax 925-5562
Pioneer ES 500/PK-5
150 Pioneer Rd 23437 757-934-6213
Danielle Belton, prin. Fax 925-5592
Washington ES 500/PK-5
204 Walnut St 23434 757-934-6226
Lori Mounie, prin. Fax 925-5558
Yeates MS 1,100/6-8
4901 Bennetts Pasture Rd 23435 757-923-4105
Shawn Green, prin. Fax 538-5416

Nansemond-Suffolk Academy 800/PK-12
3373 Pruden Blvd 23434 757-539-8789
Deborah Russell, head sch Fax 934-8363
Suffolk Christian Academy 200/K-12
917 Carolina Rd 23434 757-809-6606
Tamra VanDorn, hdmstr. Fax 924-1194

Sugar Grove, Smyth, Pop. 744
Smyth County SD
Supt. — See Marion
Sugar Grove ES 200/PK-8
242 Teas Rd 24375 276-677-3311
Amy Wheeler, prin. Fax 677-3846

Surry, Surry, Pop. 239
Surry County SD 900/PK-12
PO Box 317 23883 757-294-5229
Dr. Michael Thornton, supt. Fax 294-5263
www.surryschools.net
Other Schools – See Dendron

Sutherland, Dinwiddie
Dinwiddie County SD
Supt. — See Dinwiddie
Sutherland ES 600/K-5
6000 R B Pamplin Dr 23885 804-732-4168
C. Michelle Powell, prin. Fax 732-4620

Swords Creek, Russell
Russell County SD
Supt. — See Lebanon
Swords Creek ES 100/PK-7
3867 Swords Creek Rd 24649 276-991-0016
Georgia McCoy, prin. Fax 991-0102

Tangier, Accomack, Pop. 722
Accomack County SD
Supt. — See Accomac
Tangier S 100/K-12
PO Box 245 23440 757-891-2234
Dr. Nina Pruitt, prin. Fax 891-2572

Tappahannock, Essex, Pop. 2,335
Essex County SD 1,600/PK-12
PO Box 756 22560 804-443-4366
Dr. Scott Burckbuchler, supt. Fax 443-4498
www.essex.k12.va.us
Essex IS 500/4-7
PO Box 609 22560 804-443-3040
Heather Gentry, prin. Fax 445-1079
Tappahannock ES 600/PK-3
PO Box 399 22560 804-443-5301
Angela Gross, prin. Fax 443-1176

Tappahannock Junior Academy 100/PK-8
PO Box 790 22560 804-443-5076

Tazewell, Tazewell, Pop. 4,565
Tazewell County SD 6,300/PK-12
506 Jeffersonville St 24651 276-988-5511
George Brown, supt. Fax 988-6765
www.tazewell.k12.va.us
Tazewell ES 500/PK-5
175 Parkview Dr 24651 276-988-4441
Chandra Ashby, prin. Fax 988-0445
Tazewell MS 500/6-8
367 Hope St 24651 276-988-6513
Charity Hurst, prin. Fax 988-2363
Other Schools – See Bluefield, Cedar Bluff, North Tazewell, Raven, Richlands

The Plains, Fauquier, Pop. 213
Fauquier County SD
Supt. — See Warrenton

Coleman ES 300/K-5
4096 Zulla Rd 20198 540-422-7550
Joy Seward, prin. Fax 422-7569
Marshall MS 500/6-8
4048 Zulla Rd 20198 540-422-7450
David Graham, prin. Fax 422-7469

Wakefield S 400/PK-12
PO Box 107 20198 540-253-7500
David Colon, head sch Fax 253-5492

Timberville, Rockingham, Pop. 2,485
Rockingham County SD
Supt. — See Harrisonburg
Plains ES 400/PK-5
225 American Legion Dr 22853 540-896-8956
Joseph Kapuchuck, prin. Fax 896-8908

Toano, James City
Williamsburg-James City County SD
Supt. — See Williamsburg
Toano MS 700/6-8
7817 Richmond Rd 23168 757-566-4251
Tracey Jones, prin. Fax 566-3006

Triangle, Prince William, Pop. 7,762
Prince William County SD
Supt. — See Manassas
Graham Park MS 900/6-8
3613 Graham Park Rd 22172 703-221-2118
Maria Ramadane, prin. Fax 221-1079
Triangle ES 800/PK-5
3615 Lions Field Rd 22172 703-221-4114
Laura Elliott, prin. Fax 221-3956

St. Francis of Assisi S 400/PK-8
18825 Fuller Heights Rd 22172 703-221-3868
Dr. Tricia Barber, prin. Fax 221-0700

Trout Dale, Grayson, Pop. 176
Grayson County SD
Supt. — See Independence
Grayson Highlands S 200/PK-7
6459 Troutdale Hwy 24378 276-773-2832
Bobby Cheeks, prin.

Troutville, Botetourt, Pop. 422
Botetourt County SD
Supt. — See Fincastle
Greenfield ES 400/PK-5
288 Etzler Rd 24175 540-992-4416
Laura Camp, prin. Fax 992-3174
Troutville ES 300/PK-5
12 Barron Dr 24175 540-992-1871
Steven Anderson, prin. Fax 992-8382

Unionville, Orange
Orange County SD
Supt. — See Orange
Lightfoot ES 300/3-5
11360 Zachary Taylor Hwy 22567 540-661-4520
Jewel Williams, prin. Fax 661-4519
Unionville ES 300/K-2
10285 Zachary Taylor Hwy 22567 540-661-4540
Peggy Kinser, prin. Fax 661-4539

Verona, Augusta, Pop. 4,194
Augusta County SD 10,400/K-12
PO Box 960 24482 540-245-5100
Dr. Eric Bond, supt. Fax 245-5115
www.augusta.k12.va.us
Other Schools – See Churchville, Craigsville, Fishersville, Fort Defiance, Mount Solon, Staunton, Stuarts Draft, Waynesboro

---

Stuart Hall S K-5
74 Quicks Mill Rd 24482 540-248-2404
Mark Eastham, head sch Fax 248-5323

Victoria, Lunenburg, Pop. 1,693
Lunenburg County SD
Supt. — See Kenbridge
Lunenburg MS 400/6-8
583 Tomlinson Rd 23974 434-696-2161
Dr. Sharon Stanislause, prin. Fax 696-2162
Victoria ES 400/K-5
1521 8th St 23974 434-696-2163
Casey Jackson, prin. Fax 696-2096

Vienna, Fairfax, Pop. 15,197
Fairfax County SD
Supt. — See Falls Church
Archer ES 800/K-6
324 Nutley St NW 22180 703-937-6200
Michelle Makrigiorgos, prin. Fax 937-6297
Colvin Run ES 900/K-6
1400 Trap Rd 22182 703-757-3000
Kenneth Junge, prin. Fax 757-3097
Cunningham Park ES 500/PK-6
1001 Park St SE 22180 703-255-5600
Katharine Le, prin. Fax 255-5697
Flint Hill ES 700/K-6
2444 Flint Hill Rd 22181 703-242-6100
Jennifer Hertzberg, prin. Fax 242-6197
Freedom Hill ES 600/PK-6
1945 Lord Fairfax Rd 22182 703-506-7800
Scott Bloom, prin. Fax 506-7897
Kilmer MS 1,300/7-8
8100 Wolftrap Rd 22182 703-846-8800
Ronald James, prin. Fax 846-8897
Marshall Road ES 700/K-6
730 Marshall Rd SW 22180 703-937-1500
Jennifer Heiges, prin. Fax 937-1597
Stenwood ES 500/PK-6
2620 Gallows Rd 22180 703-208-7600
Peggy Dammeyer, prin. Fax 208-7697
Thoreau MS 800/7-8
2505 Cedar Ln 22180 703-846-8000
Yusef Azimi, prin. Fax 846-8097
Vienna ES 400/PK-6
128 Center St S 22180 703-937-6000
John Carmichael, prin. Fax 937-6000
Westbriar ES 600/K-6
1741 Pine Valley Dr 22182 703-937-1700
Mary Tam, prin. Fax 937-1700
Wolftrap ES 600/K-6
1903 Beulah Rd 22182 703-319-7300
Teresa Khuluki, prin. Fax 319-7397

Fairfax Christian S 200/K-12
1624 Hunter Mill Rd 22182 703-759-5100
Jo Thoburn, pres. Fax 759-2143
Green Hedges S 200/PK-8
415 Windover Ave NW 22180 703-938-8323
Robert Gregg, head sch Fax 938-1485
Our Lady of Good Counsel S 500/K-8
8601 Wolftrap Rd 22182 703-938-3600
Austin Poole, prin. Fax 938-2933
St. Mark S 400/PK-8
9972 Vale Rd 22181 703-281-9103
Darcie Girmus, prin. Fax 766-3430
Vienna Adventist Academy 100/PK-12
340 Courthouse Rd SW 22180 703-938-6200

Vinton, Roanoke, Pop. 7,942
Roanoke County SD
Supt. — See Roanoke
Byrd MS 800/6-8
2910 E Washington Ave 24179 540-890-1035
Todd Kageals, prin. Fax 890-0703
Cundiff ES 500/K-5
1200 Hardy Rd 24179 540-857-5009
Ashley McCallum, prin. Fax 857-5065
Horn ES 400/K-5
1002 Ruddell Rd 24179 540-857-5007
Peggy Stovall, prin. Fax 857-5062

Mineral Springs Christian S 100/PK-12
1030 Bible Ln 24179 540-890-4465
Dr. Kim Morris, admin. Fax 890-3185

Virginia Beach, Virginia Beach, Pop. 422,328
Virginia Beach CSD 69,500/PK-12
PO Box 6038 23456 757-263-1000
Dr. Aaron Spence, supt. Fax 263-1397
www.vbschools.com/
Alanton ES 700/PK-5
1441 Stephens Rd 23454 757-648-2000
Charlene Garran, prin. Fax 496-6841
Arrowhead ES 500/K-5
5549 Susquehanna Dr 23462 757-648-2040
Benjamin Gillikin, prin. Fax 473-5101
Bayside 6th Grade Campus 6-6
4722 Jericho Rd 23462 757-648-4440
Camille Harmon, prin. Fax 333-4167
Bayside ES 500/PK-5
5649 Bayside Rd 23455 757-648-2080
Catherine Brumm, prin. Fax 460-7513
Bayside MS 700/7-8
965 Newtown Rd 23462 757-648-4400
Dr. Paula Johnson, prin. Fax 473-5185
Birdneck ES 800/PK-5
957 S Birdneck Rd 23451 757-648-2120
Robert Yoshida, prin. Fax 437-4792
Brandon MS 1,200/6-8
1700 Pope St 23464 757-648-4450
Dr. Christy McQueeney, prin. Fax 366-4550
Brookwood ES 700/PK-5
601 S Lynnhaven Rd 23452 757-648-2160
Christine Alarcon, prin. Fax 431-4631
Centerville ES 700/PK-5
2201 Centerville Tpke 23464 757-648-2200
Teresa Ritzel, prin. Fax 502-0324
Christopher Farms ES 700/K-5
2828 Pleasant Acres Dr, 757-648-2240
Teri Breaus, prin. Fax 427-3656
College Park ES 400/K-5
1110 Bennington Rd 23464 757-648-2280
Dr. Sterling White, prin. Fax 366-4532
Cooke ES 600/PK-5
1501 Mediterranean Ave 23451 757-648-2320
Pamela Bennis, prin. Fax 437-4711
Corporate Landing ES 500/PK-5
1590 Corporate Landing Pkwy 23454 757-648-2360
Kelly Coon, prin. Fax 437-4760
Corporate Landing MS 1,300/6-8
1597 Corporate Landing Pkwy 23454 757-648-4500
Dr. Freddie Alarcon, prin. Fax 437-6487
Creeds ES 300/K-5
920 Princess Anne Rd 23457 757-648-2400
Casey Conger, prin. Fax 426-7837
Dey ES 900/PK-5
1900 N Great Neck Rd 23454 757-648-2440
Elizabeth Bianchi, prin. Fax 496-6784
Diamond Springs ES 700/PK-1
5225 Learning Cir 23462 757-648-4240
Gloria Coston, prin. Fax 493-5458
Fairfield ES 500/K-5
5428 Providence Rd 23464 757-648-2480
Douglas Knapp, prin. Fax 366-4530
Glenwood ES 900/PK-5
2213 Round Hill Dr 23464 757-648-2520
David French, prin. Fax 471-5817
Great Neck MS 1,100/6-8
1848 N Great Neck Rd 23454 757-648-4550
Dr. Eugene Soltner, prin. Fax 496-6774
Green Run ES 500/PK-5
1200 Green Garden Cir, 757-648-2560
Sheila Wynn, prin. Fax 427-6558
Hermitage ES 700/PK-5
1701 Pleasure House Rd 23455 757-648-2600
Angela Munari, prin. Fax 460-7138
Holland ES 600/PK-5
3340 Holland Rd 23452 757-648-2640
Dr. Callie Richardson, prin. Fax 427-0028
Independence MS 1,300/6-8
1370 Dunstan Ln 23455 757-648-4600
Carey Manugo, prin. Fax 460-0508
Indian Lakes ES 600/PK-5
1240 Homestead Dr 23464 757-648-2680
Jennifer Born, prin. Fax 474-8454
Kempsville ES 500/PK-5
570 Kempsville Rd 23464 757-648-2720
Lori Hasher, prin. Fax 474-8513
Kempsville Meadows ES 500/K-5
736 Edwin Dr 23462 757-648-2760
Mikelle Williams, prin. Fax 474-8489
Kempsville MS 800/6-8
860 Churchill Dr 23464 757-648-4700
Dr. Patti Jenkins, prin. Fax 474-8449
Kings Grant ES 600/K-5
612 N Lynnhaven Rd 23452 757-648-2800
Dr. Lorena Kelly, prin. Fax 431-4092
Kingston ES 600/K-5
3532 Kings Grant Rd 23452 757-648-2840
Dr. Sharon Shewbridge, prin. Fax 431-4017
Landstown ES 800/PK-5
2212 Recreation Dr 23456 757-648-2880
Jeffrey Hofmann, prin. Fax 430-2775
Landstown MS 1,500/6-8
2204 Recreation Dr 23456 757-648-4750
John Parkman, prin. Fax 430-3247
Larkspur MS 1,700/6-8
4696 Princess Anne Rd 23462 757-648-4800
Dr. Melanie Hamblin, prin. Fax 474-8598
Linkhorn Park ES 800/K-5
977 First Colonial Rd 23454 757-648-2920
Barbara Sessoms, prin. Fax 496-6750
Luxford ES 600/PK-5
4808 Haygood Rd 23455 757-648-2960
Danielle Colucci, prin. Fax 473-5103
Lynnhaven ES 500/PK-5
210 Dillon Dr 23452 757-648-3000
Katherine Everett, prin. Fax 431-4634
Lynnhaven MS 1,000/6-8
1250 Bayne Dr 23454 757-648-4850
Dr. Kellie Mason, prin. Fax 496-6793
Malibu ES 400/PK-5
3632 Edinburgh Dr 23452 757-648-3040
Micah Harris, prin. Fax 431-4099
New Castle ES 800/PK-5
4136 Dam Neck Rd 23456 757-648-3080
Heather Quinn, prin. Fax 430-8977
Newtown ES 500/2-3
5277 Learning Cir 23462 757-648-3120
H. Rinehart-Richardson, prin. Fax 493-5461
North Landing ES 500/PK-5
2929 North Landing Rd 23456 757-648-3160
Jill Barger, prin. Fax 427-6086
Ocean Lakes ES 600/PK-5
1616 Upton Dr 23454 757-648-3200
Dr. Linda Reese, prin. Fax 721-4009
Old Donation S 600/2-8
4633 Honeygrove Rd 23455 757-648-3240
Dr. Kelly Hedrick, prin. Fax 648-3265
Parkway ES 600/K-5
4180 Ohare Dr, 757-648-3280
Krista Barton-Arnold, prin. Fax 471-5818
Pembroke ES 500/PK-5
4622 Jericho Rd 23462 757-648-3320
Dr. Linda Hayes, prin. Fax 473-5624
Pembroke Meadows ES 500/K-5
820 Cathedral Dr 23455 757-648-3360
Dr. Charles Spivey, prin. Fax 473-5261
Plaza MS 1,100/6-8
3080 S Lynnhaven Rd 23452 757-648-4900
Deborah Price, prin. Fax 431-5331
Point O'View ES 600/K-5
5400 Parliament Dr 23462 757-648-3440
John Chowns, prin. Fax 473-5262
Princess Anne ES 500/PK-5
2444 Seaboard Rd 23456 757-648-3480
Patrick Wroton, prin. Fax 427-1447
Princess Anne MS 1,500/6-8
2323 Holland Rd, 757-648-4950
Dr. Alex Bergren, prin. Fax 430-0972
Providence ES 600/K-5
4968 Providence Rd 23464 757-648-3520
Michael Taylor, prin. Fax 474-8522
Red Mill ES 700/PK-5
1860 Sandbridge Rd 23456 757-648-3560
Michelle Miller, prin. Fax 426-9600
Rosemont ES 400/K-5
1257 Rosemont Rd, 757-648-3600
Cari Hall, prin. Fax 427-6411
Rosemont Forest ES 500/K-5
1716 Grey Friars Chase 23456 757-648-3640
Gregory Furlich, prin. Fax 471-5816
Salem ES 500/K-5
3961 Salem Lakes Blvd 23456 757-648-3680
Dr. Ann Shufflebarger, prin. Fax 471-5813
Salem MS 1,000/6-8
2380 Lynnhaven Pkwy 23464 757-648-5000
Dr. James Smith, prin. Fax 474-8467
Seatack ES 400/K-5
912 S Birdneck Rd 23451 757-648-3720
Vincent Darby, prin. Fax 437-7747
Shelton Park ES 500/PK-5
1700 Shelton Rd 23455 757-648-3760
Tara Brewer, prin. Fax 460-7515
Strawbridge ES 700/PK-5
2553 Strawbridge Rd 23456 757-648-3800
Jacqueline Sargent, prin. Fax 427-5031
Tallwood ES 600/PK-5
2025 Kempsville Rd 23464 757-648-3840
Dr. T. Singletary-Johnson, prin. Fax 502-0308
Thalia ES 600/PK-5
421 Thalia Rd 23452 757-648-3880
Crystal Wilkerson, prin. Fax 431-4641
Thoroughgood ES 700/PK-5
1444 Dunstan Ln 23455 757-648-3920
Dr. Cheryl Zigrang, prin. Fax 460-7516

Three Oaks ES 800/PK-5
2201 Elson Green Ave 23456 757-648-3960
Linda Sidone, prin. Fax 430-3758
Trantwood ES 500/K-5
2344 Inlynnview Rd 23454 757-648-4000
Lou Anne Metzger, prin. Fax 496-6785
Virginia Beach MS 900/6-8
600 25th St 23451 757-648-5050
Dr. Sandra Brown, prin. Fax 437-4708
White Oaks ES 800/PK-5
960 Windsor Oaks Blvd 23462 757-648-4040
Stephanie Haus, prin. Fax 474-8515
Williams ES 400/PK-5
892 Newtown Rd 23462 757-648-4080
Timothy Sullivan, prin. Fax 473-5263
Windsor Oaks ES 600/PK-5
3800 Van Buren Dr 23452 757-648-4120
Sherri Archer, prin. Fax 431-4637
Windsor Woods ES 400/K-5
233 Presidential Blvd 23452 757-648-4160
Matthew Orebaugh, prin. Fax 431-4638
Woodstock ES 700/K-5
6016 Providence Rd 23464 757-648-4200
Amy Hedrick, prin. Fax 366-4578

Atlantic Shores Christian ES 400/PK-6
1861 Kempsville Rd 23464 757-479-1125
Gale Hall, prin. Fax 479-8742
Cape Henry Collegiate 900/PK-12
1320 Mill Dam Rd 23454 757-481-2446
Dr. Christopher S. Garran, head sch Fax 481-9194
Friends S of Virginia Beach PK-12
1537 Laskin Rd 23451 757-428-7534
Jack Lewis, head sch Fax 428-7511
Galilee Montessori S 200/PK-2
3928 Pacific Ave 23451 757-428-1034
Gateway Christian Academy 200/PK-12
5473 Virginia Beach Blvd 23462 757-499-6551
Hebrew Academy of Tidewater 200/PK-5
5000 Corporate Woods Dr 180 23462 757-424-4327
Heather Moore, head sch Fax 420-0915
Holy Family Day S PK-K
1279 N Great Neck Rd 23454 757-481-1180
Cynthia Girard, dir. Fax 481-3989
Ivy League Academy 100/PK-12
4413 Wishart Rd 23455 757-656-5725
Ruby De Castro-Brown, prin.
Norfolk Christian S 300/PK-5
1265 Laskin Rd 23451 757-428-1284
OakTree Academy 200/PK-12
817 Kempsville Rd 23464 757-248-9560
Terri Turley, dir. Fax 248-9594
St. Gregory the Great S 700/PK-8
5343 Virginia Beach Blvd 23462 757-497-1811
Gina Coss, prin. Fax 497-7005
St. John the Apostle S 300/PK-8
1968 Sandbridge Rd 23456 757-821-1100
Miriam Cotton, prin. Fax 821-1047
St. Matthew S 500/PK-8
3316 Sandra Ln 23464 757-420-2455
Louis Goldberg, prin. Fax 420-4880
Star of the Sea Regional S 200/PK-8
309 15th St 23451 757-428-8400
Kelly Lazzara, prin. Fax 428-2794
Tidewater Classical Academy 100/PK-8
1201 Rosemont Rd, 757-427-5683
Alyson Crews, prin. Fax 430-1040
Virginia Beach Friends S 100/PK-12
1537 Laskin Rd 23451 757-428-7534

Wakefield, Sussex, Pop. 921

Tidewater Academy 200/PK-12
217 W Church St 23888 757-899-5401

Warm Springs, Bath, Pop. 122
Bath County SD 600/PK-12
PO Box 67 24484 540-839-2722
Sue Hirsh, supt. Fax 839-3040
www.bath.k12.va.us
Other Schools – See Hot Springs, Millboro

Warrenton, Fauquier, Pop. 9,361
Fauquier County SD 11,100/PK-12
320 Hospital Dr Ste 40 20186 540-422-7000
Dr. David Jeck, supt. Fax 422-7057
www.fcps1.org
Auburn MS 600/6-8
7270 Riley Rd 20187 540-422-7410
Steve Kadilak, prin. Fax 422-7429
Bradley ES 500/PK-5
674 Hastings Ln 20186 540-422-7510
Beth Banks, prin. Fax 422-7529
Brumfield ES 600/PK-5
550 Alwington Blvd 20186 540-422-7530
Julie Gagnon, prin. Fax 422-7549
Smith ES 400/K-5
6176 Dumfries Rd 20187 540-422-7670
Linda Smith, prin. Fax 422-7689
Taylor MS 400/6-8
350 E Shirley Ave 20186 540-422-7470
Nick Napolitano, prin. Fax 422-7489
Warrenton MS 500/6-8
244 Waterloo St 20186 540-422-7490
Barbara Bannister, prin. Fax 422-7509
Other Schools – See Bealeton, Catlett, Marshall, New Baltimore, Nokesville, Remington, The Plains

---

Covenant Christian Academy 100/K-12
4177 Bludau Dr 20187 540-680-4111
Amber Sabia, head sch
Highland S 500/PK-12
597 Broadview Ave 20186 540-878-2700
Providence Christian Academy 100/PK-12
4258 Burrough Dr 20187 540-349-4989
Rev. Young Shin, hdmstr. Fax 349-3915

St. James' Episcopal S 100/PK-5
73 Culpeper St 20186 540-347-3855
Stacey Irvin, head sch Fax 202-9328
St. John the Evangelist S 200/PK-8
111 John E Mann St 20186 540-347-2458
Temple MacDonald, prin. Fax 349-8007

Warsaw, Richmond, Pop. 1,495
Richmond County SD 900/K-12
PO Box 1507 22572 804-333-3681
James Smith Ed.D., supt. Fax 333-5586
www.richmond-county.k12.va.us
Richmond County ES 600/K-7
361 Walnut St 22572 804-333-3510
Jason Strong, prin. Fax 333-5484

Washington, Rappahannock, Pop. 133
Rappahannock County SD 900/K-12
6 School House Rd 22747 540-227-0023
Shannon Grimsley, supt. Fax 987-8896
www.rappahannockschools.us
Rappahannock ES 600/K-7
34 School House Rd 22747 540-227-0200
Benjamin Temple, prin. Fax 987-1130

Waterford, Loudoun
Loudoun County SD
Supt. — See Ashburn
Waterford ES 200/PK-5
15513 Loyalty Rd 20197 540-751-2460
Andrew Heironimus, prin. Fax 771-6662

Waynesboro, Waynesboro, Pop. 20,421
Augusta County SD
Supt. — See Verona
Cassell ES 500/K-5
1301 Rockfish Rd 22980 540-946-7635
Dr. Mindy Garber, prin. Fax 946-7637

Waynesboro CSD 3,200/PK-12
301 Pine Ave 22980 540-946-4600
Dr. Jeffrey Cassell, supt. Fax 946-4608
www.waynesboro.k12.va.us
Berkeley Glenn ES 300/K-5
1020 Jefferson Ave 22980 540-946-4680
Leola Burks, prin. Fax 946-4684
Collins MS 600/6-8
1625 Ivy St 22980 540-946-4635
Janet Buchheit, prin. Fax 946-4642
Perry ES 500/K-5
840 King Ave 22980 540-946-4650
Tammy Hipes, prin. Fax 946-4656
Wayne Hills Preschool Center 200/PK-PK
937 Fir St 22980 540-946-4626
Dr. Diane Behrens, prin.
Wenonah ES 300/K-5
125 N Bayard Ave 22980 540-946-4660
Tonya Carter, prin. Fax 946-4663
Westwood Hills ES 400/K-5
548 Rosser Ave 22980 540-946-4670
Renae Deffenbaugh, prin. Fax 946-4673

Weber City, Scott, Pop. 1,321
Scott County SD
Supt. — See Gate City
Weber City ES 300/PK-6
322 Jennings St 24290 276-386-7981
Cindy Dorton, prin. Fax 386-9289

Weems, Lancaster
Lancaster County SD 1,300/PK-12
2330 Irvington Rd 22576 804-462-5100
Steve Parker, supt. Fax 435-3309
www.lcs.k12.va.us
Other Schools – See Kilmarnock, Lancaster

West Point, King William, Pop. 3,232
West Point SD 800/PK-12
PO Box T 23181 804-843-4368
Laura Abel, supt. Fax 843-4421
www.wpschools.net
West Point ES 300/PK-5
1060 Thompson Ave 23181 804-843-2030
Kim Haskins, prin. Fax 843-3557
West Point MS 200/6-8
1040 Thompson Ave 23181 804-843-9810
Nathan Leach, prin. Fax 843-9812

Williamsburg, Williamsburg, Pop. 13,648
Williamsburg-James City County SD 11,000/K-12
PO Box 8783 23187 757-603-6400
Dr. Olwen Herron Ed.D., supt.
wjccschools.org
Baker ES 500/K-5
3131 Ironbound Rd 23185 757-221-0949
Mike Hurley, prin. Fax 229-1591
Berkeley MS 900/6-8
1118 Ironbound Rd 23188 757-229-8051
Panagiotis Tsigaridas, prin. Fax 229-6133
Blayton ES 400/K-5
800 Jolly Pond Rd 23188 757-565-9300
Amy Stamm, prin. Fax 565-9301
Hornsby MS 900/6-8
850 Jolly Pond Rd 23188 757-565-9400
Dr. Jessica Ellison, prin. Fax 565-9401
James River ES 500/K-5
8901 Pocahontas Trl 23185 757-887-1768
Dr. Michael Stutt, prin. Fax 887-2162
Laurel Lane ES 400/K-5
112 Laurel Ln 23185 757-229-7597
Karen Swann, prin. Fax 229-0237
Matoaka ES 700/K-5
4001 Brick Bat Rd 23188 757-564-4001
Andy Jacobs, prin. Fax 564-4000
Montague ES 400/K-5
5380 Centerville Rd 23188 757-258-3022
Cathy Vazquez, prin. Fax 258-3910
Norge ES 600/K-5
7311 Richmond Rd 23188 757-564-3372
Veronda Matthews, prin. Fax 220-1763

Stonehouse ES 700/K-5
3651 Rochambeau Dr 23188 757-566-4300
Melissa White, prin. Fax 566-2323
Whaley ES 500/K-5
301 Scotland St 23185 757-229-1931
Robin Ford, prin. Fax 221-0286
Other Schools – See Toano

York County SD
Supt. — See Yorktown
Magruder ES 600/K-5
700 Penniman Rd 23185 757-220-4067
Mark Kirk, prin. Fax 220-4081
Queens Lake MS 400/6-8
124 W Queens Dr 23185 757-220-4080
Scott Meadows, prin. Fax 220-4074
Waller Mill Fine Arts Magnet S 300/K-5
314 Waller Mill Rd 23185 757-220-4060
Jennifer Goodwin, prin. Fax 220-4063

Greenwood Christian Academy 100/PK-6
5251 John Tyler Hwy Ste 37 23185 757-345-0905
Marilyn Dayton, prin. Fax 645-4587
Providence Classical S 200/K-12
6000 Easter Cir 23188 757-565-2900
Susan Oweis, head sch Fax 565-3720
Walsingham Academy 500/PK-12
1100 Jamestown Rd 23185 757-229-6026
Sr. Mary Oesterle, pres. Fax 259-1401
Walsingham Academy Lower S 200/PK-7
PO Box 8702 23187 757-229-2642
Sr. Mary Jeanne Osterle, prin. Fax 259-1404
Williamsburg Christian Academy 200/PK-12
101 School House Ln 23188 757-220-1978
Dr. David Breslin, head sch Fax 345-5597
Williamsburg Montessori S 50/PK-8
4200 Longhill Rd 23188 757-565-0977
Sandra Andrews, head sch Fax 220-6655

Willis, Floyd
Floyd County SD
Supt. — See Floyd
Willis ES 300/PK-7
PO Box 10 24380 540-745-9430
Sandra Montgomery, prin. Fax 745-9493

Winchester, Winchester, Pop. 25,545
Frederick County SD 13,100/K-12
PO Box 3508 22604 540-662-3888
Dr. David Sovine, supt. Fax 722-2788
www.frederick.k12.va.us
Apple Pie Ridge ES 600/K-5
349 Apple Pie Ridge Rd 22603 540-662-4781
Justin Raymond, prin. Fax 722-3918
Armel ES 600/K-5
2239 Front Royal Pike 22602 540-869-1657
Heather Miller, prin. Fax 869-5342
Byrd MS 900/6-8
134 Rosa Ln 22602 540-662-0500
Jessica Nail, prin. Fax 662-7790
Evendale ES 500/K-5
220 Rosa Ln 22602 540-662-0531
Elizabeth Mistretta, prin. Fax 662-6530
Frederick County MS 700/6-8
4661 N Frederick Pike 22603 540-888-4296
Jerry Putt, prin. Fax 888-3101
Gainesboro ES 500/K-5
4651 N Frederick Pike 22603 540-888-4550
Patricia Black, prin. Fax 888-4579
Greenwood Mill ES 800/K-5
281 Channing Dr 22602 540-667-7863
Jennifer Muldowney, prin.
Indian Hollow ES 400/K-5
1548 N Hayfield Rd 22603 540-877-2283
Sharon Cooley, prin. Fax 877-2353
Orchard View ES 400/K-5
4275 Middle Rd 22602 540-869-8642
Crystal Nicola, prin. Fax 868-2035
Redbud Run ES 700/K-5
250 First Woods Dr 22603 540-678-1868
Joseph Strong, prin. Fax 678-0703
Wood MS 900/6-8
1313 Amherst St 22601 540-667-7500
Grant Javersak, prin. Fax 667-7500
Other Schools – See Clear Brook, Middletown, Stephens City

Winchester CSD 4,200/PK-12
PO Box 551 22604 540-667-4253
Dr. Jason Van Heukelum, supt. Fax 667-4253
www.wps.k12.va.us
Douglass ES 500/PK-4
100 W Cedarmeade Ave 22601 540-662-7656
Stephanie Downey, prin. Fax 665-1081
Kerr ES 300/PK-4
427 Meadowbranch Ave 22601 540-662-3945
Laura Evy, prin. Fax 662-4728
Morgan IS 5-6
48 S Purcell Ave 22601 540-667-7171
Matthew Wygal Ed.D., admin. Fax 662-6398
Morgan MS 1,300/7-8
48 S Purcell Ave 22601 540-667-7171
Jennifer Buckley, prin. Fax 723-8897
Quarles ES 500/PK-4
1310 S Loudoun St 22601 540-662-3575
Joanie Hovatter, prin. Fax 662-8449
Virginia Avenue / DeHart ES 500/PK-4
550 Virginia Ave 22601 540-665-6330
Nikea Hurt, prin. Fax 665-6334

Mountain View Christian Academy 100/K-12
153 Narrow Ln 22602 540-868-1231
Dr. Minta Hardman, admin. Fax 869-8976
Sacred Heart Academy 200/PK-8
110 Keating Dr 22601 540-662-7177
Susan Parks, prin. Fax 722-2894

Sharon's Centre 100/PK-1
1855 Senseny Rd 22602 540-667-7002
Abby Sours, admin. Fax 667-6224

Windsor, Isle of Wight, Pop. 2,598
Isle of Wight County SD
Supt. — See Smithfield
Tyler MS 400/6-8
23320 N Court St 23487 757-242-3229
Jessica Harding, prin. Fax 242-8105
Windsor ES 600/PK-5
20008 Courthouse Hwy 23487 757-242-4193
Ellen Couch, prin. Fax 242-3842

Wirtz, Franklin
Franklin County SD
Supt. — See Rocky Mount
Burnt Chimney ES 300/PK-5
80 Burnt Chimney Rd 24184 540-721-2936
Jason Guilliams, prin. Fax 721-2003
Dudley ES 300/PK-5
7250 Brooks Mill Rd 24184 540-721-2621
Dana Kelley, prin. Fax 721-3741

Wise, Wise, Pop. 3,248
Wise County SD 6,200/PK-12
PO Box 1217 24293 276-328-8017
Dr. Greg Mullins, supt. Fax 328-3350
www.wisek12.org
Addington MS 500/5-8
PO Box 977 24293 276-328-8821
Greg Jessee, prin. Fax 328-2044
Wise PS 700/PK-4
323 Railroad Ave SE 24293 276-328-8019
Susan Mullins, prin. Fax 328-6809
Other Schools – See Big Stone Gap, Coeburn, Pound, Saint Paul

---

Wise County Christian S 100/PK-12
PO Box 3297 24293 276-328-3297
Eddie Mullins, admin. Fax 328-3248

Woodbridge, Prince William, Pop. 3,887
Prince William County SD
Supt. — See Manassas
Antietam ES 600/PK-5
12000 Antietam Rd 22192 703-497-7619
Marica Wieduwilt, prin. Fax 491-7603
Bel Air ES 600/PK-5
14151 Ferndale Rd 22193 703-670-4050
Antoinette McDonald, prin. Fax 670-5593
Belmont ES 500/K-5
751 Norwood Ln 22191 703-494-4945
Karen Giacometti, prin. Fax 491-2650
Beville MS 1,100/6-8
4901 Dale Blvd 22193 703-878-2593
Timothy Keenan, prin. Fax 730-1274
Dale City ES 500/K-5
14450 Brook Dr 22193 703-670-2208
Cindy Crow-Miller, prin. Fax 670-8425
Enterprise ES 500/K-5
13900 Lindendale Rd 22193 703-590-1558
Kelly Nickerson, prin. Fax 878-0404
Featherstone ES 500/K-5
14805 Blackburn Rd 22191 703-491-1156
Daria Groover, prin. Fax 491-2052
Fitzgerald ES 900/K-5
15500 Benita Fitzgerald Dr 22193 703-583-4195
Bridget Outlaw, prin. Fax 583-4097
Hampton MS 1,100/6-8
14800 Darbydale Ave 22193 703-670-6166
Jehovanni Mitchell, prin. Fax 670-9888
Kerrydale ES 500/K-5
13199 Kerrydale Rd 22193 703-590-1262
Kimberly Gudinas, prin. Fax 670-6259
Kilby ES 500/PK-5
1800 Horner Rd 22191 703-494-6677
Amy Jordan, prin. Fax 497-7371
King ES 500/K-5
13224 Nickleson Dr 22193 703-590-1616
Amy Larsen, prin. Fax 590-0304
Lake Ridge ES 600/K-5
11970 Hedges Run Dr 22192 703-494-9153
Stefanie Sanders, prin. Fax 494-2272
Lake Ridge MS 1,200/6-8
12350 Mohican Rd 22192 703-494-5154
Skyles Calhoun, prin. Fax 494-8246
Leesylvania ES 800/PK-5
15800 Neabsco Rd 22191 703-670-8268
Margaret MacGregor, prin. Fax 670-9235
Lynn MS 1,000/6-8
1650 Prince William Pkwy 22191 703-494-5157
Hamish Brewer, prin. Fax 491-5141
Marumsco Hills ES 700/K-5
14100 Page St 22191 703-494-3252
Meisram Hernandez, prin. Fax 494-9789
McAuliffe ES 500/K-5
13540 Princedale Dr 22193 703-680-7270
Janice Herritt, prin. Fax 897-1960
Minnieville ES 600/K-5
13639 Greenwood Dr 22193 703-670-6106
Nathaniel Provencio, prin. Fax 878-0695
Occoquan ES 600/K-5
12915 Occoquan Rd 22192 703-494-2195
Michael Lint, prin. Fax 494-2158
Old Bridge ES 700/K-5
3051 Old Bridge Rd 22192 703-491-5614
Anita Flemons, prin. Fax 491-0561
Parks ES 800/K-5
13446 Princedale Dr 22193 703-580-9665
Susan Danielson, prin. Fax 580-9667
Penn ES 700/K-5
12980 Queen Chapel Rd 22193 703-590-0344
Dr. Elliott Bolles, prin. Fax 590-1528
Porter S 700/1-8
15311 Forest Grove Dr 22191 703-580-6501
Darci Whitehead, prin. Fax 580-6646
Potomac View ES 800/PK-5
14601 Lamar Rd 22191 703-491-1126
Latiesa Green, prin. Fax 491-1292
Rippon MS 1,200/6-8
15101 Blackburn Rd 22191 703-491-2171
Scott Bergquist, prin. Fax 491-2487
River Oaks ES 700/PK-5
16950 McGuffeys Trl 22191 703-441-0050
Aerica Williams, prin. Fax 441-1012
Rockledge ES 600/K-5
2300 Mariner Ln 22192 703-491-2108
Amy Schott, prin. Fax 491-0240
Springwoods ES 700/K-5
3815 Marquis Pl 22192 703-590-9874
Janeen Mainor, prin. Fax 590-1457
Vaughan ES 800/K-5
2200 York Dr 22191 703-494-3220
Mark Boyd, prin. Fax 497-4774
Westridge ES 700/K-5
12400 Knightsbridge Dr 22192 703-590-3711
Laurence Khan, prin. Fax 590-0074
Wilson ES PK-5
5710 Liberty Hill Ct 22193 571-589-4327
Felicia Norwood, prin. Fax 782-0209
Woodbridge MS 1,200/6-8
2201 York Dr 22191 703-494-3181
Angela Owens, prin. Fax 491-1441

Cardinal Montessori S 100/PK-4
1424 G St 22191 703-491-3810
Christ Chapel Academy 600/PK-12
13909 Smoketown Rd 22192 703-670-3822
Rev. Paul Miklich, admin. Fax 897-7905
Heritage Christian S 400/PK-12
14510 Spriggs Rd 22193 703-680-6629
St. Thomas Aquinas Regional S 500/PK-8
13750 Marys Way 22191 703-491-4447
Sr. Kateri Masters, prin. Fax 492-8828
Victory Christian Preschool & Academy 100/PK-K
14747 Arizona Ave 22191 703-491-7100
Beverly Ellis, admin. Fax 490-8489

Woodstock, Shenandoah, Pop. 5,017
Shenandoah County SD 6,200/PK-12
600 N Main St Ste 200 22664 540-459-6222
Dr. Mark Johnston, supt. Fax 459-6707
www.shenandoah.k12.va.us
Muhlenberg MS 600/6-8
1251 Susan Ave 22664 540-459-2941
Morgan Saeler, prin. Fax 459-5965
Robinson ES 1,200/PK-5
1231 Susan Ave 22664 540-459-5155
Jennifer Proctor, prin. Fax 459-5992
Other Schools – See Quicksburg, Strasburg

Woolwine, Patrick
Patrick County SD
Supt. — See Stuart
Woolwine ES 200/PK-7
9993 Woolwine Hwy 24185 276-930-2811
Jeannie King, prin. Fax 694-1238

Wytheville, Wythe, Pop. 8,065
Wythe County SD 4,300/PK-12
1570 W Reservoir St 24382 276-228-5411
Dr. Jeff Perry, supt. Fax 228-9192
wythe.k12.va.us/
Scott Memorial MS 300/6-8
950 S 7th St 24382 276-228-2851
Brad Haga, prin. Fax 228-8261
Sheffey ES 300/PK-5
621 Piney Mountain Rd 24382 276-699-1771
Chad Newman, prin. Fax 699-1031
Spiller ES 700/PK-5
330 Tazewell St 24382 276-228-3561
Russell Street, prin. Fax 228-7277
Other Schools – See Austinville, Max Meadows, Rural Retreat, Speedwell

Yorktown, York, Pop. 195
York County SD 12,300/PK-12
302 Dare Rd 23692 757-898-0300
Dr. Victor Shandor, supt. Fax 890-0771
www.yorkcountyschools.org
Coventry ES 600/K-5
200 Owen Davis Blvd 23693 757-898-0403
Paula Sasin, prin. Fax 867-7446
Dare ES 400/K-5
300 Dare Rd 23692 757-898-0324
Lindsey Caccavale, prin. Fax 898-0371
Grafton MS 900/6-8
405 Grafton Dr 23692 757-898-0525
Paul Rice, prin. Fax 898-0534
Mt. Vernon ES 500/PK-5
310 Mount Vernon Dr 23693 757-898-0497
Kristin Bolam, prin. Fax 867-7444
Tabb ES 600/K-5
3711 Big Bethel Rd 23693 757-898-0372
Mary Lugo, prin. Fax 867-7433
Tabb MS 900/6-8
300 Yorktown Rd 23693 757-898-0320
Heather Young, prin. Fax 867-7425
Yorktown Math/Science/Tech Magnet S 700/K-5
131 Siege Ln 23692 757-898-0358
Kelly Denny, prin. Fax 898-0415
Yorktown MS 800/6-8
11201 George Washington Mem 23690 757-898-0360
Susan Hutton, prin. Fax 898-0412
Other Schools – See Grafton, Langley AFB, Seaford, Williamsburg

WASHINGTON

WASHINGTON DEPARTMENT OF EDUCATION
PO Box 47200, Olympia 98504-7200
Telephone 360-725-6000
Fax 360-753-6712
Website http://www.k12.wa.us

Superintendent of Public Instruction Chris Reykdal

WASHINGTON BOARD OF EDUCATION
PO Box 47206, Olympia 98504-7206

Executive Director

EDUCATIONAL SERVICE DISTRICTS (ESD)

North Central ESD 171
Dr. Richard McBride, supt. 509-665-2610
PO Box 1847, Wenatchee 98807 Fax 662-9027
www.ncesd.org
Northeast Washington ESD 101
Dr. Michael Dunn, supt. 509-789-3800
4202 S Regal St, Spokane 99223 Fax 789-3780
www.esd101.net
Northwest ESD 189
Larry Francois, supt. 360-299-4000
1601 R Ave, Anacortes 98221 Fax 299-4070
www.nwesd.org

Olympic ESD 114
Greg Lynch, supt. 360-479-0993
105 National Ave N Fax 405-5813
Bremerton 98312
www.oesd114.org
ESD 123
Darcy Weisner, supt. 509-547-8441
3924 W Court St, Pasco 99301 Fax 544-5795
www.esd123.org
Puget Sound ESD
John Welch, supt. 800-917-7600
800 Oakesdale Ave SW Fax 917-7777
Renton 98057
www.psesd.org

ESD 113
Dana Anderson, supt. 360-464-6700
6005 Tyee Dr SW, Tumwater 98512 Fax 464-6900
www.esd113.org
ESD 112
Dr. Tim Merlino, supt. 360-750-7500
2500 NE 65th Ave Fax 750-9706
Vancouver 98661
www.esd112.org
ESD 105
Kevin Chase, supt. 509-575-2885
33 S 2nd Ave, Yakima 98902 Fax 575-2918
www.esd105.org

PUBLIC, PRIVATE AND CATHOLIC ELEMENTARY SCHOOLS

Aberdeen, Grays Harbor, Pop. 16,223
Aberdeen SD 5 3,300/PK-12
216 N G St 98520 360-538-2000
Dr. Alicia Henderson Ph.D., supt. Fax 538-2014
www.asd5.org
Central Park ES 200/K-6
601 School Rd 98520 360-538-2170
Barbara Page, prin. Fax 538-2172
Gray ES 300/PK-6
1516 N B St 98520 360-538-2140
Dr. Rick Bates, prin. Fax 538-2142
Hopkins Preschool Center 50/PK-PK
1313 Pacific Ave 98520 360-538-2190
Cindy Mitby, coord. Fax 538-2192
McDermoth ES 400/K-6
409 N K St 98520 360-538-2120
Brandon Winkelman, prin. Fax 538-2122
Miller JHS 500/7-8
100 E Lindstrom St 98520 360-538-2100
Lisa Griebel, prin. Fax 538-2106
Stevens ES 500/PK-6
301 S Farragut St 98520 360-538-2150
Arnie Lewis, prin. Fax 538-2156
West ES 400/PK-6
1801 Bay Ave 98520 360-538-2130
John Meers, prin. Fax 538-2132

Wishkah Valley SD 117 100/K-12
4640 Wishkah Rd 98520 360-532-3128
Dennis Johnson, supt. Fax 533-4638
www.wishkah.org
Wishkah Valley S 100/K-12
4640 Wishkah Rd 98520 360-532-3128
Dennis Johnson, supt. Fax 533-4638

St. Mary S 200/PK-8
518 N H St 98520 360-532-1230
Nicole Franson, prin. Fax 532-1209

Acme, Whatcom, Pop. 234
Mt. Baker SD 507
Supt. — See Deming
Acme ES 200/K-6
PO Box 9 98220 360-383-2045
Carly Takata, prin. Fax 383-2049

Addy, Stevens, Pop. 244
Summit Valley SD 202 100/PK-8
2360 Addy Gifford Rd 99101 509-935-6362
Bill Glidewell, supt. Fax 935-6364
www.svalley.k12.wa.us
Summit Valley S 100/PK-8
2360 Addy Gifford Rd 99101 509-935-6362
Bill Glidewell, supt. Fax 935-6364

Airway Heights, Spokane, Pop. 5,820
Cheney SD 360
Supt. — See Cheney
Sunset ES 400/PK-5
12824 W 12th Ave 99001 509-559-4600
Ty McGregor, prin. Fax 244-0906

Almira, Lincoln, Pop. 276
Almira SD 17 100/K-8
PO Box 217 99103 509-639-2414
Shauna Schmerer, supt. Fax 639-2620
www.almirasd.org
Almira ES 100/K-8
PO Box 217 99103 509-639-2414
Shauna Schmerer, prin. Fax 639-2620

Amanda Park, Grays Harbor, Pop. 240
Lake Quinault SD 97 200/K-12
PO Box 38 98526 360-288-2260
Rich DuBois, supt. Fax 288-2732
www.lakequinaultschools.org
Lake Quinault ES 100/K-5
PO Box 38 98526 360-288-2414
Keith Samplawski, prin. Fax 288-2209

Amboy, Clark, Pop. 1,593
Battle Ground SD 119
Supt. — See Brush Prairie
Amboy MS 600/5-8
22115 NE Chelatchie Rd 98601 360-885-6050
Michael Maloney, prin. Fax 885-6055

Anacortes, Skagit, Pop. 15,315
Anacortes SD 103 2,700/PK-12
2200 M Ave 98221 360-293-1200
Dr. Mark Wenzel, supt. Fax 293-1222
www.asd103.org
Anacortes MS 400/7-8
2202 M Ave 98221 360-293-1230
Patrick Harrington, prin. Fax 293-1231
Fidalgo ES 400/K-6
13590 Gibralter Rd 98221 360-293-9545
Dr. Tara Dowd, prin. Fax 299-1852
Island View ES 500/K-6
2501 J Ave 98221 360-293-3149
Brian Hanrahan, prin. Fax 299-1853
Mount Erie ES 500/K-6
1313 41st St 98221 360-293-9541
Peter Donaldson, prin. Fax 299-1854
Whitney ECC 100/PK-K
1200 M Ave 98221 360-293-9536
Kevin Schwartz, prin Fax 503-1288

Lopez Island SD 144
Supt. — See Lopez Island
Decatur Island S 50/K-8
0 Decatur Is 98221 360-375-6004
Joanne Wester, lead tchr. Fax 375-6005

Anderson Island, Pierce, Pop. 1,014
Steilacoom Historical SD 1
Supt. — See Steilacoom
Anderson Island ES 50/K-5
13005 Camus Rd 98303 253-884-4901
Susan Greer, prin. Fax 884-7835

Ariel, Cowlitz
Woodland SD 404
Supt. — See Woodland
Yale ES 50/K-5
11842 Lewis River Rd 98603 360-231-4246
Asha Riley, prin. Fax 231-4446

Arlington, Snohomish, Pop. 17,235
Arlington SD 16 6,200/PK-12
315 N French Ave 98223 360-618-6200
Dr. Chrys Sweeting Ed.D., supt. Fax 618-6221
www.asd.wednet.edu
APPLE Preschool 700/PK-PK
1216 E 5th St 98223 360-618-6434
Carrie Saunders, dir.
Eagle Creek ES 500/K-5
1216 E 5th St 98223 360-618-6270
Bethany Belisle, prin. Fax 618-6275
Haller MS 700/6-8
600 E 1st St 98223 360-618-6400
Trever Summers, prin. Fax 618-6411
Kent Prairie ES 600/K-5
8110 207th St NE 98223 360-618-6260
Karl Olson, prin. Fax 618-6265
Pioneer ES 600/K-5
8213 Eaglefield Dr 98223 360-618-6230
Kerri Helgeson, prin. Fax 618-6234
Post MS 600/6-8
1220 E 5th St 98223 360-618-6450
Voni Walker, prin. Fax 618-6455
Presidents ES 600/PK-5
505 E 3rd St 98223 360-618-6240
Derek Larsen, prin. Fax 618-6245

Lakewood SD 306
Supt. — See Marysville
Cougar Creek ES 400/K-5
16216 11th Ave NE 98223 360-652-4517
Bill Landry, prin. Fax 652-4519

Arlington Christian S 50/PK-12
PO Box 3337 98223 360-652-2988
Wendy Tavenner, admin.

Ashford, Pierce, Pop. 212
Eatonville SD 404
Supt. — See Eatonville
Columbia Crest STEM S 100/K-8
24503 State Route 706 E 98304 360-569-2567
Angie Ellenbecker, prin. Fax 569-2917

Asotin, Asotin, Pop. 1,220
Asotin-Anatone SD 420 600/PK-12
PO Box 489 99402 509-243-1100
Dale Bonfield, supt. Fax 243-4251
www.aasd.wednet.edu
Asotin ES 300/PK-5
PO Box 489 99402 509-243-4147
Wes Nicholas, prin. Fax 243-7720

Auburn, King, Pop. 65,915
Auburn SD 408 14,800/K-12
915 4th St NE 98002 253-931-4900
Dr. Alan Spicciati, supt. Fax 931-8006
www.auburn.wednet.edu
Cascade MS 700/6-8
1015 24th St NE 98002 253-931-4995
Isaiah Johnson, prin. Fax 833-7580
Chinook ES 400/K-5
3502 Auburn Way S 98092 253-931-4980
Jennifer Davidson, prin. Fax 931-4728
Evergreen Heights ES 500/K-5
5602 S 316th St 98001 253-931-4974
Anne Gayman, prin. Fax 931-4860
Gildo Rey ES 500/K-5
1005 37th St SE 98002 253-931-4952
Lenny Holloman, prin. Fax 931-4731
Hazelwood ES 600/K-5
11815 SE 304th St 98092 253-931-4740
Sally Colburn, prin. Fax 804-4520

Ilalko ES 600/K-5
301 Oravetz Pl SE 98092 253-931-4748
Tim Carstens, prin. Fax 804-4522
Jacobsen ES 500/K-5
29205 132nd Ave SE 98092 253-630-2441
Eric Daniel, prin. Fax 630-1323
Lakeland Hills ES 700/K-5
1020 Evergreen Way SE 98092 253-876-7711
Colleen Barlow, prin. Fax 876-7714
Lake View ES 300/K-5
16401 SE 318th St 98092 253-931-4830
John Aiken, prin. Fax 931-4832
Lea Hill ES 400/K-5
30908 124th Ave SE 98092 253-931-4982
Ed Herda, prin. Fax 931-4733
Mt. Baker MS 900/6-8
620 37th St SE 98002 253-804-4555
Greg Brown, prin. Fax 931-0661
Olympic MS 700/6-8
1825 K St SE 98002 253-931-4966
Jason Hill, prin. Fax 939-2753
Pioneer ES 500/K-5
2301 M St SE 98002 253-931-4986
Debra Gary, prin. Fax 931-4734
Rainier MS 900/6-8
30620 116th Ave SE 98092 253-931-4843
Justin Maier, prin. Fax 939-4318
Scobee ES 500/K-5
1031 14th St NE 98002 253-931-4984
Adam Couch, prin. Fax 804-4514
Terminal Park ES 400/K-5
1101 D St SE 98002 253-931-4978
Tom Dudley, prin. Fax 804-4532
Washington ES 400/K-5
20 E St NE 98002 253-931-4988
Pauline Thomas, prin. Fax 931-4736
Other Schools – See Pacific

Federal Way SD 210
Supt. — See Federal Way
Camelot ES 300/PK-5
4041 S 298th St 98001 253-945-2500
Joe Kosty, prin. Fax 945-2525
Kilo MS 500/6-8
4400 S 308th St 98001 253-945-4700
Margaret Peterson, prin. Fax 945-4747
Lake Dolloff ES 400/PK-5
4200 S 308th St 98001 253-945-2800
Sara Gill, prin. Fax 945-2828
Lakeland ES 400/K-5
35827 32nd Ave S 98001 253-945-3000
Ra'Jeanna Conerly, prin. Fax 945-3030
Sequoyah MS 500/6-8
3425 S 360th St 98001 253-945-3670
Mike McCarthy, prin. Fax 945-3699
Valhalla ES 600/K-5
27847 42nd Ave S 98001 253-945-4300
Kristen Schroeder, prin. Fax 945-4343

Buena Vista SDA S 200/PK-8
3320 Academy Dr SE 98092 253-833-0718
Gregg Wahlstrom, prin. Fax 833-0385
Holy Family S 200/PK-8
505 17th St SE 98002 253-833-8688
Michele Corey, prin. Fax 833-9311
Overcomer Academy 100/PK-7
33415 Military Rd S 98001 253-886-5710
Medgar Wells, prin. Fax 886-5759
RCS Kent View Christian S 300/PK-6
20 49th St NE 98002 253-852-5145
Valley Christian S 200/PK-8
1312 2nd St SE 98002 253-833-3541
Joshua Snyder, admin. Fax 833-4239

Bainbridge Island, Kitsap, Pop. 22,174
Bainbridge Island SD 303 3,800/PK-12
8489 Madison Ave NE 98110 206-842-4714
Dr. Peter Bang-Knudsen, supt. Fax 842-2928
www.bisd303.org
Blakely ES 400/PK-4
4704 Blakely Ave NE 98110 206-842-4752
Reese Ande, prin. Fax 780-2040
Ordway ES 400/PK-4
8555 Madison Ave NE 98110 206-842-7637
Melinda Reynvaan, prin. Fax 780-1560
Sakai IS 600/5-6
9343 Sportsman Club Rd NE 98110 206-780-6500
Jim Corsetti, prin. Fax 780-6565
Wilkes ES 400/K-4
12781 Madison Ave NE 98110 206-842-4411
Amii Pratt, prin. Fax 780-3000
Woodward MS 500/7-8
9125 Sportsman Club Rd NE 98110 206-842-4787
Mike Florian, prin. Fax 780-4525

Island S 100/K-5
8553 NE Day Rd E 98110 206-842-0400
Madrona S, PO Box 11371 98110 100/PK-8
Missi Goss, hdmstr. 206-855-8041
St. Cecilia S 100/PK-8
1310 Madison Ave N 98110 206-842-2017
Susan Kilbane, prin. Fax 842-6988

Battle Ground, Clark, Pop. 16,976
Battle Ground SD 119
Supt. — See Brush Prairie
Chief Umtuch MS 600/5-8
PO Box 200 98604 360-885-6350
Elizabeth Beattie, prin. Fax 885-6355
Daybreak MS 500/5-8
PO Box 200 98604 360-885-6900
Kevin Palena, prin. Fax 885-6948
Daybreak PS 600/K-4
PO Box 200 98604 360-885-6950
Matt Kauffman, prin. Fax 885-6998
Maple Grove K-8 500/K-8
PO Box 200 98604 360-885-6700
Michelle Reinhardt, admin. Fax 885-6747
Strong PS 600/K-4
PO Box 200 98604 360-885-6400
Angela Knight, prin. Fax 885-6432
Tukes Valley MS 500/5-8
PO Box 200 98604 360-885-6250
Brian Amundson, prin. Fax 885-6297
Tukes Valley PS 600/K-4
PO Box 200 98604 360-885-6200
Jennifer Paulsen, prin. Fax 885-6247

Firm Foundation Christian S 400/PK-12
1919 SW 25th Ave 98604 360-687-8382
Julie Olson, prin. Fax 687-8799
Meadow Glade Adventist ES 200/K-8
18717 NE 109th Ave 98604 360-687-5121

Belfair, Mason, Pop. 3,769
North Mason SD 403 2,100/PK-12
250 E Campus Dr 98528 360-277-2300
Dana Rosenbach, supt. Fax 277-2320
www.nmsd.wednet.edu
Belfair ES 500/PK-5
22900 NE State Route 3 98528 360-277-2233
Dan King, prin. Fax 275-8842
Hawkins MS 400/6-8
200 E Campus Dr 98528 360-277-2302
Joanne Warren, prin. Fax 277-2324
Sand Hill ES 400/K-5
791 NE Sand Hill Rd 98528 360-277-2330
Jason Swaser, prin. Fax 277-2307

Bellevue, King, Pop. 117,650
Bellevue SD 405 18,700/PK-12
PO Box 90010 98009 425-456-4000
Dr. Ivan Duran Ed.D., supt. Fax 456-4176
www.bsd405.org
Ardmore ES 400/K-5
16616 NE 32nd St 98008 425-456-4700
Chas Miller, prin. Fax 456-4706
Bennett ES 400/K-5
301 151st Pl NE 98007 425-456-4800
David Staight, prin. Fax 456-4824
Cherry Crest ES 700/K-5
12400 NE 32nd St 98005 425-456-4900
Dusty Steere, prin. Fax 456-4911
Chinook MS 900/6-8
2001 98th Ave NE 98004 425-456-6300
Dr. Russell White, prin. Fax 456-6304
Clyde Hill ES 600/K-5
9601 NE 24th St 98004 425-456-5000
Mary Olin, prin. Fax 456-5036
Eastgate ES 500/K-5
4255 153rd Ave SE 98006 425-456-5100
Steven Lesco, prin. Fax 456-5119
Enatai ES 500/K-5
301 151st Pl NE 98007 425-456-5200
Amy MacDonald, prin. Fax 456-5213
Highland MS 500/6-8
15027 Bel Red Rd 98007 425-456-6400
Katie Klug, prin. Fax 456-6499
Jing Mei ES 100/K-4
12635 SE 56th St 98006 425-456-6900
Tina Bogucharova, prin. Fax 456-6939
Lake Hills ES 500/K-5
14310 SE 12th St 98007 425-456-5300
Chris Jones, prin. Fax 456-5302
Newport Heights ES 600/K-5
5225 119th Ave SE 98006 425-456-5500
Cathy Leaver, prin. Fax 456-5506
Odle MS 800/6-8
11650 SE 60th St 98006 425-456-6600
Aaron Miller, prin. Fax 456-6616
Phantom Lake ES 300/K-5
1050 160th Ave SE 98008 425-456-5600
Erin King, prin. Fax 456-5606
Puesta del Sol S 600/K-5
3810 132nd Ave SE 98006 425-456-6100
Jonathan Shearer, prin. Fax 456-6104
Sherwood Forest ES 400/K-5
16411 NE 24th St 98008 425-456-5700
Danelle Edwards, prin. Fax 456-5702
Somerset ES 600/K-5
14100 SE Somerset Blvd 98006 425-456-5800
Judy Bowllby, prin. Fax 456-5804
Spiritridge ES 700/K-5
16401 SE 24th St 98008 425-456-5900
Scott Hetherington, prin. Fax 456-5967
Stevenson ES 500/K-5
14220 NE 8th St 98007 425-456-6000
Anissa Bereano, prin. Fax 456-6015
Tillicum MS 700/6-8
11650 SE 60th St 98006 425-456-6700
James Peterson, prin. Fax 456-6770
Tyee MS 900/6-8
13630 SE Allen Rd 98006 425-456-6800
Susan Thomas, prin. Fax 456-6801
Woodridge ES 600/PK-5
12619 SE 20th Pl 98005 425-456-6200
Nicole Hepworth, prin. Fax 456-6204
Other Schools – See Medina

Issaquah SD 411
Supt. — See Issaquah
Cougar Ridge ES 600/K-5
4630 167th Ave SE 98006 425-837-7300
Drew Terry, prin. Fax 837-7230
Sunset ES 600/PK-5
4229 W Lake Sammamish Pkwy 98008 425-837-5600
Amanda Dorey, prin. Fax 837-5660

Bellevue Childrens Academy 500/PK-5
14640 NE 24th St 98007 425-556-0791
Bellevue Montessori S 200/PK-6
2411 112th Ave NE 98004 425-454-7439
Bel-Red BiLingual Academy 100/PK-3
15061 Bel Red Rd 98007 425-283-0717
Cedar Park Christian S - Bellevue 100/PK-6
625 140th Ave NE 98005 425-746-3258
Dana Johnson, admin. Fax 274-0469
Chestnut Hill Academy 200/K-5
13633 SE 26th St 98005 425-372-2800
Holly Senaga M.Ed., admin. Fax 372-2850
Chestnut Montessori S 100/PK-3
10723 NE 38th Pl 98004 425-822-6001
Dartmoor S 100/1-12
2340 130th Ave NE 98005 425-885-6296
Kimm Conroy M.Ed., head sch Fax 885-1137
Eastside Christian S 300/PK-8
14615 SE 22nd St 98007 425-641-5570
Mark Migliore, prin. Fax 746-3155
Eton S 300/PK-8
2701 Bellevue Redmond Rd 98008 425-881-4230
Dr. Russell Smith, head sch Fax 861-8011
French Immersion S of Washington 200/PK-5
4211 W Lake Sammamish SE 98008 425-653-3970
Jewish Day S of Metro Seattle 200/PK-8
15749 NE 4th St 98008 425-460-0200
Hamutal Gavish, head sch Fax 460-0201
Little S 50/PK-6
2812 116th Ave NE 98004 425-827-8708
Peter Berner-Hays, head sch Fax 827-3814
Living Montessori Academy 100/PK-6
2445 140th Ave NE Ste B-200 98005 425-373-5437
Afrose Amlani-Duncan, head sch Fax 746-2434
Medina Academy 200/PK-8
16242 Northup Way 98008 425-643-2678
Robert Mond, admin.
Open Window S 300/K-8
6128 168th Pl SE 98006 425-747-2911
Jeff Stroebel, head sch Fax 562-4035
Sacred Heart S 400/PK-8
9450 NE 14th St 98004 425-451-1773
David Burroughs, prin. Fax 450-3918
St. Louise S 500/PK-8
133 156th Ave SE 98007 425-746-4220
Dan Fitzpatrick, prin. Fax 644-3294
St. Madeleine Sophie S 200/PK-8
4400 130th Pl SE 98006 425-747-6770
Dan Sherman, prin. Fax 747-1825
Seattle Waldorf S - Three Cedars Campus 100/PK-8
556 124th Ave NE 98005 425-401-9874
Janine Cleland, dir. Fax 865-9093

Bellingham, Whatcom, Pop. 77,637
Bellingham SD 501 11,200/PK-12
1306 Dupont St 98225 360-676-6400
Dr. Greg Baker, supt. Fax 676-2793
bellinghamschools.org
Alderwood ES 300/K-5
3400 Hollywood Ave 98225 360-676-6404
Micah Smith, prin. Fax 647-6896
Birchwood ES 300/PK-5
3200 Pinewood Ave 98225 360-676-6466
Matt Whitten, prin. Fax 647-6875
Columbia ES 300/K-5
2508 Utter St 98225 360-676-6413
Aaron Darragh, prin. Fax 647-6880
Cordata ES 500/K-5
4420 Aldrich Rd 98226 360-676-6461
Analisa Ficklin, prin. Fax 676-6462
Cozier ES 300/K-5
1330 Lincoln St, 360-676-6410
Eric Paige, prin. Fax 676-6578
Fairhaven MS 600/6-8
110 Parkridge Rd 98225 360-676-6450
Robert Kalahan, prin. Fax 647-6887
Geneva ES 400/K-5
1401 Geneva St, 360-676-6416
Steven Ruthford, prin. Fax 647-6893
Happy Valley ES 300/K-5
1041 24th St 98225 360-676-6420
Karen Tolliver, prin. Fax 676-4989
King ES 500/K-5
2155 Yew Street Rd, 360-647-6840
Stephanie Johnson, prin. Fax 647-6841
Kulshan MS 600/6-8
1250 Kenoyer Dr, 360-676-4886
Meagan Dawson, prin. Fax 647-6892
Lowell ES 300/K-5
935 14th St 98225 360-676-6430
Mary Sepler, prin. Fax 647-6894
Northern Heights ES 500/K-5
4000 Magrath Rd 98226 360-647-6820
Pam Pottle, prin. Fax 647-6824
Parkview ES 300/K-5
3033 Coolidge Dr 98225 360-676-6433
Mylo Allen, prin. Fax 647-6882
Roosevelt ES 400/K-5
2900 Yew St 98226 360-676-6440
Tom Gresham, prin. Fax 647-6895
Shuksan MS 600/6-8
2717 Alderwood Ave 98225 360-676-6454
Amy Carder, prin. Fax 647-6879
Silver Beach ES 400/K-5
4101 Academy St 98226 360-676-6443
Nicole Talley, prin. Fax 647-6884
Sunnyland ES 300/K-5
2800 James St 98225 360-676-6446
Lynn Heimsoth, prin. Fax 647-6891
Whatcom MS 600/6-8
810 Halleck St 98225 360-676-6460
Jeffrey Coulter, prin. Fax 647-6881

Meridian SD 505 1,800/PK-12
214 W Laurel Rd 98226 360-398-7111
Tom Churchill, supt. Fax 398-8966
www.meridian.wednet.edu
Other Schools – See Everson, Lynden

Mt. Baker SD 507
Supt. — See Deming
Harmony ES 400/K-6
5060 Sand Rd 98226 360-383-2050
Dr. Todd Mathews, prin. Fax 383-2054

Assumption S 200/PK-8
2116 Cornwall Ave 98225 360-733-6133
Daniel Anderson, prin. Fax 647-4372
Baker View Christian S 100/1-8
5353 Waschke Rd 98226 360-384-8155
Bellingham Christian S 200/PK-8
1600 E Sunset Dr 98226 360-733-7303
Shawn Cunningham, prin. Fax 647-0683

Lynden Christian S-Evergreen Campus 100/PK-8
567 E Kellogg Rd 98226 360-738-8248
Glen Hendricks, admin. Fax 738-1020
St. Paul's Academy PK-8
1509 E Victor St 98225 360-733-1750
Trinity Classical S 50/PK-6
2826 Birchwood Ave 98225 360-733-2695
Diana Lim, dir.
Whatcom Hills Waldorf S 200/PK-8
941 Austin St, 360-733-3164

Benge, Adams
Benge SD 122 50/K-6
2978 E Benge Winona Rd 99105 509-887-2370
Robert Moore, supt. Fax 887-2360
Benge ES 50/K-6
2978 E Benge Winona Rd 99105 509-887-2370
Robert Moore, admin. Fax 887-2360

Benton City, Benton, Pop. 2,971
Kiona-Benton City SD 52 1,400/PK-12
1105 Dale Ave 99320 509-588-2000
Wade Haun, supt. Fax 588-5580
www.kibesd.org
Kiona-Benton City IS 200/3-5
1105 Dale Ave 99320 509-588-2009
Corey Williams, prin. Fax 588-5580
Kiona-Benton City MS 300/6-8
1105 Dale Ave 99320 509-588-2040
Chuck Feth, prin. Fax 588-2905
Kiona-Benton City PS 400/PK-2
1105 Dale Ave 99320 509-588-2090
Linda Hardy, prin. Fax 588-2729

Bickleton, Klickitat, Pop. 87
Bickleton SD 203 100/K-12
PO Box 10 99322 509-896-5473
Tom Whitmore, supt. Fax 896-2071
www.bickletonschools.org
Bickleton S 100/K-12
PO Box 10 99322 509-896-5473
Tom Whitmore, prin. Fax 896-2071

Black Diamond, King, Pop. 4,019
Kent SD 415
Supt. — See Kent
Sawyer Woods ES 400/K-6
31135 228th Ave SE 98010 253-373-7750
Tim Helgeson, prin. Fax 373-7757

Blaine, Whatcom, Pop. 4,469
Blaine SD 503 2,100/PK-12
765 H St 98230 360-332-5881
Ron Spanjer Ed.D., supt. Fax 332-7568
www.blaine.k12.wa.us
Blaine ES 400/3-5
836 Mitchell Ave 98230 360-332-5213
Dr. Craig Baldwin, prin. Fax 332-0555
Blaine MS 500/6-8
975 H St 98230 360-332-8226
Darren Benson, prin. Fax 332-0444
Blaine PS 500/PK-2
820 Boblett St 98230 360-332-1300
Nancy Bakarich, prin. Fax 332-0666
Other Schools – See Point Roberts

Bonney Lake, Pierce, Pop. 16,669
Sumner SD 320
Supt. — See Sumner
Bonney Lake ES 500/K-5
18715 80th St E, 253-891-4450
Sandy Miller, prin. Fax 891-4472
Crestwood ES 400/K-5
3914 W Tapps Dr E, 253-891-4550
Kay Gallo, prin. Fax 891-4572
Eismann ES 500/K-5
13802 Canyon View Blvd E, 253-891-4500
Susie Black, prin. Fax 891-4522
Emerald Hills ES 400/K-5
19515 S Tapps Dr E, 253-891-4750
Andrea Landes, prin. Fax 891-4772
Lakeridge MS 600/6-8
5909 Myers Rd E, 253-891-5100
Toby Udager, prin. Fax 891-5145
Liberty Ridge ES 400/K-5
12202 209th Avenue Ct E, 253-891-4800
Julana Hardtke, prin. Fax 891-4822
Mountain View MS 700/6-8
10921 199th Avenue Ct E, 253-891-5200
Curtis Hurst, prin. Fax 891-5245
Victor Falls ES 600/K-5
11401 188th Avenue Ct E, 253-891-4700
Martina Scheerer, prin. Fax 891-4722

Bonney Lake Christian Academy 50/PK-8
8201 Locust Ave E, 253-507-0235
Dr. Susan Kobes, supt.

Bothell, King, Pop. 32,149
Everett SD 2
Supt. — See Everett
Cedar Wood ES 600/PK-5
3414 168th St SE 98012 425-385-7700
David Jones, prin. Fax 385-7702
Woodside ES 700/K-5
17000 23rd Ave SE 98012 425-385-7800
Dr. Betty Cobbs, prin. Fax 385-7802

Northshore SD 417 20,000/PK-12
3330 Monte Villa Pkwy 98021 425-408-7701
Dr. Michelle Reid Ed.D., supt. Fax 408-7702
www.nsd.org
Canyon Creek ES 700/K-5
21400 35th Ave SE 98021 425-408-5700
Bruce Denton, prin. Fax 408-5702
Canyon Park MS 800/6-8
23723 23rd Ave SE 98021 425-408-6300
Sebastian Ziz, prin. Fax 408-6302
Crystal Springs ES 600/K-5
21615 9th Ave SE 98021 425-408-4300
May Pelto, prin. Fax 408-4302
Fernwood ES 700/K-5
3933 Jewell Rd 98012 425-408-4500
Kate Bradshaw, prin. Fax 408-4502
Lockwood ES 500/K-5
24118 Lockwood Rd 98021 425-408-5800
Gary Keeler, prin. Fax 408-5802
Love ES 600/K-5
303 224th St SW 98021 425-408-4600
Katy French, prin. Fax 408-4602
Maywood Hills ES 600/K-5
19510 104th Ave NE 98011 425-408-5000
Sonja Hoeft, prin. Fax 408-5002
Northshore MS 700/6-8
12101 NE 160th St 98011 425-408-6700
Tiffany Rodriguez, prin. Fax 408-6702
Shelton View ES 400/K-5
23400 5th Ave W 98021 425-408-5200
Bethel Santos, prin. Fax 408-5202
Skyview MS 900/6-8
21404 35th Ave SE 98021 425-408-6800
Dawn Mark, prin. Fax 408-6802
Sorenson ECC 100/PK-PK
19705 88th Ave NE 98011 425-408-5570
Doreen Milburn, prin. Fax 408-5572
Westhill ES 500/PK-5
19515 88th Ave NE 98011 425-408-5500
Dana Whitehurst, prin. Fax 408-5502
Woodin ES 600/K-5
12950 NE 195th St 98011 425-408-5400
Dawn Bowers, prin. Fax 408-5402
Woodmoor ES 900/K-5
12225 NE 160th St 98011 425-408-5600
Angela Kerr, prin. Fax 408-5602
Other Schools – See Kenmore, Redmond, Woodinville

Cedar Park Christian S - Bothell 1,100/PK-12
16300 112th Ave NE 98011 425-488-9778
Adam Lynch, admin. Fax 483-5765
Evergreen Academy 200/K-5
16017 118th Pl NE 98011 425-488-8000
Heritage Christian Academy 300/PK-8
19527 104th Ave NE 98011 425-485-2585
Brenda Chadwick, prin. Fax 486-2895
Providence Classical Christian S 200/PK-12
18943 120th Ave NE 98011 425-774-6622
St. Brendan S 200/PK-8
10049 NE 195th St 98011 425-483-8300
Catherine Shumate, prin. Fax 483-2839
UCIC Learning Center 300/PK-6
3727 240th St SE 98021 425-770-6606
Dr. Seungho Pi, dir.
Whole Earth Montessori S 100/PK-8
2930 228th St SE 98021 425-486-3037
Woodinville Montessori S - North Creek 300/PK-12
19102 N Creek Pkwy 98011 425-482-3184

Bow, Skagit
Burlington-Edison SD 100
Supt. — See Burlington
Allen ES 500/K-8
17145 Cook Rd 98232 360-757-3352
Dr. Steven Finch, prin. Fax 757-2503
Edison ES 500/K-8
5801 Main St 98232 360-757-3375
Amy Staudenraus, prin. Fax 766-6272

Bremerton, Kitsap, Pop. 34,864
Bremerton SD 100-C 5,000/PK-12
134 Marion Ave N 98312 360-473-1000
Dr. Aaron Leavell, supt. Fax 473-1040
www.bremertonschools.org
Crownhill ES 400/K-5
1500 Rocky Point Rd NW 98312 360-473-4200
Teneka Morley, prin. Fax 473-4220
Jahr ES 400/K-5
800 Dibb St 98310 360-473-4100
Mike Sellers, prin. Fax 473-4120
Kitsap Lake ES 400/K-5
1111 Carr Blvd 98312 360-473-4300
Susan Stone, prin. Fax 473-4320
Mountain View MS 800/6-8
2400 Perry Ave 98310 360-473-0600
Michaeleen Gelhaus, prin. Fax 473-0620
Naval Avenue Early Learning Center 400/PK-3
900 Olympic Ave 98312 360-473-4400
John Welsh, prin. Fax 473-4420
View Ridge ES 500/PK-5
3250 Spruce Ave 98310 360-473-4500
Korene Calderwood, prin. Fax 473-4520
West Hills STEM Academy 600/PK-8
520 S National Ave 98312 360-473-4600
Lisa Heaman, prin. Fax 473-4620

Central Kitsap SD 401
Supt. — See Silverdale
Brownsville ES 300/K-5
8795 Illahee Rd NE 98311 360-662-8000
Stacey Krumsick, prin. Fax 662-8001
Cottonwood ES 300/K-5
330 NE Foster Rd 98311 360-662-8300
Bethany LaHaie, prin. Fax 662-8301
Esquire Hills ES 400/K-5
2650 NE John Carlson Rd 98311 360-662-8600
Susan Zetty, prin. Fax 662-8601
Fairview MS 400/6-8
8107 Central Valley Rd NE 98311 360-662-2600
Adrienne Nestor, prin. Fax 662-2601
Green Mountain ES 400/K-5
3860 Boundary Trl NW 98312 360-662-8700
Thomasina Rogers, prin. Fax 662-8701
Hawk ES at Jackson Park 400/K-5
2900 Austin Dr 98312 360-662-9000
Chris Visserman, prin. Fax 662-9001
PineCrest ES 400/K-5
5530 Pine Rd NE 98311 360-662-9200
Shaun Takenouchi, prin. Fax 662-9201
Woodlands ES 400/K-5
7420 Central Valley Rd NE 98311 360-662-9700
Amy Archuleta, prin. Fax 662-9701

Christ the King Lutheran S 100/PK-8
8065 Chico Way NW 98312 360-692-8799
Chris Hintz, prin. Fax 307-9179
Crosspoint 200/K-12
4012 Chico Way NW 98312 360-377-7700
Nick Sweeney, admin. Fax 351-0030
Kitsap Adventist Christian S 50/K-8
5088 NW Taylor Rd 98312 360-377-4542
Our Lady Star of the Sea S 200/PK-8
1516 5th St 98337 360-373-5162
Jeannette Wolfe, prin. Fax 616-4727
Peace Lutheran S 200/PK-8
1234 NE Riddell Rd 98310 360-373-2116
Sheri Juszczak B.A., prin. Fax 377-0686

Brewster, Okanogan, Pop. 2,353
Brewster SD 111 700/PK-12
PO Box 97 98812 509-689-3418
Eric Driessen, supt. Fax 689-0749
brewsterbears.org
Brewster ES 500/PK-5
PO Box 97 98812 509-689-2581
Lynnette Blackburn, prin. Fax 689-0965
Brewster MS 6-8
PO Box 97 98812 509-689-3449
Greg Austin, admin. Fax 689-0675

Brewster Adventist S 50/PK-9
115 Valley Rd 98812 509-689-3213
John McCombs, prin.

Bridgeport, Douglas, Pop. 2,379
Bridgeport SD 75 800/PK-12
PO Box 1060 98813 509-686-5656
Scott Sattler, supt. Fax 686-2221
www.bridgeport.wednet.edu
Bridgeport ES 300/PK-4
PO Box 1060 98813 509-686-2201
Jesse Macy, prin. Fax 686-0773
Bridgeport MS 200/5-8
PO Box 1060 98813 509-686-9501
Hanna Coffman, prin. Fax 686-4052

Brier, Snohomish, Pop. 5,840
Edmonds SD 15
Supt. — See Lynnwood
Brier ES 400/K-6
3625 232nd St SW 98036 425-431-7854
Johnna Stewart, prin. Fax 431-7853
Brier Terrace MS 600/7-8
22200 Brier Rd 98036 425-431-7834
Alex Alexander, prin. Fax 431-7836

Brinnon, Jefferson, Pop. 767
Brinnon SD 46 50/PK-8
46 Schoolhouse Rd 98320 360-796-4646
Patricia Beathard, supt. Fax 796-4113
www.bsd46.org
Brinnon ES 50/PK-8
46 Schoolhouse Rd 98320 360-796-4646
Patricia Beathard, prin. Fax 796-4113

Brush Prairie, Clark, Pop. 2,603
Battle Ground SD 119 13,200/K-12
11104 NE 149th St 98606 360-885-5300
Mark Ross, supt. Fax 885-5310
www.battlegroundps.org
Other Schools – See Amboy, Battle Ground, Vancouver, Yacolt

Hockinson SD 98 1,500/K-12
17912 NE 159th St 98606 360-448-6400
Sandra Yager, supt. Fax 448-6409
www.hocksd.org
Hockinson Heights ES 300/K-5
20000 NE 164th St 98606 360-448-6430
Joshua Robertson, prin. Fax 448-6439
Hockinson MS 500/6-8
15916 NE 182nd Ave 98606 360-448-6440
Brian Lehner, prin. Fax 448-6449

Buckley, Pierce, Pop. 4,221
White River SD 416 3,600/PK-12
PO Box 2050 98321 360-829-0600
Janel Keating Hambly, supt. Fax 829-3358
www.whiteriver.wednet.edu
Elk Ridge ES 300/PK-5
PO Box 1685 98321 360-829-3354
Christine Ellenwood, prin. Fax 829-3392
Foothills ES 500/PK-5
PO Box 2210 98321 360-829-3355
Mark Cushman, prin. Fax 829-3381
Glacier MS 800/6-8
PO Box 1976 98321 360-829-3395
Nick Hedman, prin. Fax 829-3391
Mountain Meadow ES 500/PK-5
PO Box 2390 98321 360-829-3356
Jeff Byrnes, prin. Fax 829-3388
Other Schools – See Wilkeson

Burbank, Walla Walla, Pop. 3,235
Columbia SD 400 900/PK-12
755 Maple St 99323 509-547-2136
Dr. Lou Gates, supt. Fax 546-0603
www.csd400.org/
Columbia ES 400/PK-5
977 Maple St 99323 509-547-9393
Ian Yale, prin. Fax 545-6382
Columbia MS 200/6-8
835 Maple St 99323 509-545-8571
Mike Taylor, prin. Fax 547-4277

Burien, King, Pop. 31,292
Highline SD 401 18,600/PK-12
15675 Ambaum Blvd SW 98166 206-631-3000
Dr. Susan Enfield, supt. Fax 631-3393
www.highlineschools.org
Cedarhurst ES 700/K-6
611 S 132nd St 98168 206-631-3600
Bobbi Giammona, prin. Fax 631-3604

Gregory Heights ES 700/PK-6
16201 16th Ave SW 98166 206-631-3800
Robin Totten, prin. Fax 631-3862
Hazel Valley ES 600/K-6
402 SW 132nd St 98146 206-631-8900
Casey Jeannot, prin. Fax 631-3962
Seahurst ES 600/K-6
14603 14th Ave SW 98166 206-631-4800
Terry Holtgraves, prin. Fax 631-4854
Shorewood ES 500/K-6
2725 SW 116th St 98146 206-631-4900
Colin Ryan, prin. Fax 631-4999
Sylvester MS 600/7-8
16222 Sylvester Rd SW 98166 206-631-6000
Gil Parsons, prin. Fax 631-6064
Other Schools – See Des Moines, Normandy Park, SeaTac, Seattle

---

Glendale Lutheran S 50/PK-8
13455 2nd Ave SW 98146 206-244-6085
Diane Schukar, dir. Fax 244-0601
St. Bernadette S 200/PK-8
1028 SW 128th St 98146 206-244-4934
Carol Mendoza, prin. Fax 244-4943
St. Francis of Assisi S 500/K-8
15216 21st Ave SW 98166 206-243-5690
Rosemary Leifer, prin. Fax 433-8593
Three Tree Montessori S 100/PK-6
220 SW 160th St 98166 206-242-5100

Burlington, Skagit, Pop. 8,211
Burlington-Edison SD 100 3,800/K-12
927 E Fairhaven Ave 98233 360-757-3311
Laurel Browning, supt. Fax 755-9198
www.be.wednet.edu/
Bay View ES 600/K-8
15241 Josh Wilson Rd 98233 360-757-3322
Amy Reisner, prin. Fax 757-1582
Umbarger ES 700/K-8
820 S Skagit St 98233 360-757-3366
Nicholas Hayes, prin. Fax 755-0047
West View ES 400/K-6
515 W Victoria Ave 98233 360-757-3391
Tamara Skeen, prin. Fax 757-3306
Other Schools – See Bow

Skagit Adventist Academy 100/PK-12
530 N Section St 98233 360-755-9261
Aubrey Fautheree, prin.

Camano Island, See Stanwood
Stanwood-Camano SD 401
Supt. — See Stanwood
Elger Bay ES 300/K-5
1810 Elger Bay Rd 98282 360-629-1290
Victor Hanzeli, prin. Fax 629-1291
Utsalady ES 300/K-5
608 Arrowhead Rd 98282 360-629-1260
Colleen Keller, prin. Fax 629-1261

Camas, Clark, Pop. 18,670
Camas SD 117 6,400/K-12
841 NE 22nd Ave 98607 360-335-3000
Jeff Snell, supt. Fax 335-3001
www.camas.wednet.edu/
Baller ES 500/K-5
1954 NE Garfield St 98607 360-833-5720
Aaron Parman, prin. Fax 833-5721
Fox ES 500/K-5
2623 NW Sierra St 98607 360-833-5700
Dr. Cathy Sork, prin. Fax 833-5701
Grass Valley ES 500/K-5
3000 NW Grass Valley Dr 98607 360-833-5710
Sean McMillan, prin. Fax 833-5711
Lacamas Heights ES 300/K-5
4600 NE Garfield St 98607 360-833-5740
Julie Mueller, prin. Fax 833-5741
Liberty MS 700/6-8
1612 NE Garfield St 98607 360-833-5850
Gary Moller, prin. Fax 833-5851
Prune Hill ES 500/K-5
1601 NW Tidland St 98607 360-833-5730
Julie Swan, prin. Fax 833-5731
Skyridge MS 900/6-8
5220 NW Parker St 98607 360-833-5800
Clint Williams, prin. Fax 833-5801
Woodburn ES 500/K-5
2400 NE Woodburn Dr 98607 360-833-5860
Brian Graham, prin. Fax 833-5861

Evergreen SD 114
Supt. — See Vancouver
Illahee ES 700/K-5
19401 SE 1st St 98607 360-604-3350
Erin Lucich, prin. Fax 604-3352

Camas Christian Academy 100/PK-8
717 SE Everett Rd 98607 360-833-0558
Cindie Boyles, prin. Fax 834-7654

Carbonado, Pierce, Pop. 597
Carbonado Historical SD 19 200/PK-8
PO Box 131 98323 360-829-0121
Scott Hubbard, supt. Fax 829-0471
www.carbonado.k12.wa.us/
Carbonado S 200/PK-8
PO Box 131 98323 360-829-0121
Scott Hubbard, supt. Fax 829-0471

Carnation, King, Pop. 1,754
Riverview SD 407
Supt. — See Duvall
Carnation ES 400/PK-5
4950 Tolt Ave 98014 425-844-4550
Chris Lupo, prin. Fax 844-4552
Stillwater ES 500/K-5
11530 320th Ave NE 98014 425-844-4680
Jack Madigan, prin. Fax 844-4682
Tolt MS 700/6-8
3740 Tolt Ave 98014 425-844-4600
Amy Karkainen, prin. Fax 844-4602

Carson, Skamania, Pop. 2,177
Stevenson-Carson SD 303
Supt. — See Stevenson
Carson ES 200/3-6
351 Hot Springs Ave 98610 509-427-5939
Brian Howe, prin. Fax 427-5874

Cashmere, Chelan, Pop. 3,023
Cashmere SD 222 1,500/PK-12
210 S Division St 98815 509-782-3355
Glenn Johnson, supt. Fax 782-4747
www.cashmere.wednet.edu
Cashmere MS 500/5-8
300 Tigner Rd 98815 509-782-2001
Sara Graves, prin. Fax 782-2547
Vale ES 600/PK-4
101 Pioneer Ave 98815 509-782-2211
Sean McKenna, prin. Fax 782-1214

Castle Rock, Cowlitz, Pop. 1,912
Castle Rock SD 401 1,300/PK-12
600 Huntington Ave S 98611 360-501-2940
Jim Mabbott, supt. Fax 501-3140
www.crschools.org
Castle Rock IS 600/3-5
700 Huntington Ave S 98611 360-501-2910
David Starkey, prin. Fax 501-3121
Castle Rock MS 300/6-8
615 Front Ave SW 98611 360-501-2920
Tiffany Golden, prin. Fax 501-3125
Castle Rock PS 300/PK-2
700 Huntington Ave S 98611 360-501-2910
Veronica Heller, prin. Fax 501-2910

Cathlamet, Wahkiakum, Pop. 521
Wahkiakum SD 200 400/K-12
PO Box 398 98612 360-795-3971
Bob Garrett, supt. Fax 795-0545
www.wahksd.k12.wa.us
Thomas MS 100/6-8
PO Box 398 98612 360-795-3261
Theresa Libby, prin. Fax 795-3205
Wendt ES 200/K-5
PO Box 398 98612 360-795-3261
Theresa Libby, prin. Fax 795-3205

Centerville, Klickitat, Pop. 108
Centerville SD 215 100/K-8
2315 Centerville Hwy 98613 509-773-4893
Dr. Mark Mansell, supt. Fax 773-4902
www.centervilleschool.org
Centerville S 100/K-8
2315 Centerville Hwy 98613 509-773-4893
Dr. Mark Mansell, admin. Fax 773-4902

Centralia, Lewis, Pop. 15,816
Centralia SD 401 3,500/K-12
PO Box 610 98531 360-330-7600
Mark Davalos, supt. Fax 330-7604
www.centralia.k12.wa.us
Centralia MS 600/7-8
901 Johnson Rd 98531 360-330-7619
Heidi Bunker, prin. Fax 330-7622
Edison ES 300/K-3
607 H St 98531 360-330-7631
Andy Justice, prin. Fax 807-6223
Fords Prairie ES 400/K-3
1620 Harrison Ave 98531 360-330-7633
David Roberts, prin. Fax 330-7698
Jefferson-Lincoln ES 400/K-3
400 W Summa St 98531 360-330-7636
David Eacker, prin. Fax 330-7803
Oakview ES 400/4-6
201 E Oakview Ave 98531 360-330-7638
Heidi Jenkins, prin. Fax 330-7812
Washington ES 300/4-6
800 Field Ave 98531 360-330-7641
Danielle Vekich, prin. Fax 330-7815

Centralia Christian S 200/PK-10
PO Box 1209 98531 360-736-7657
Dr. Ann Stout, prin. Fax 807-9161

Chattaroy, Spokane
Riverside SD 416 1,400/PK-12
34515 N Newport Hwy 99003 509-464-8201
Dr. Ken Russell, supt. Fax 464-8206
www.riversidesd.org
Chattaroy ES 200/PK-4
25717 N Yale Rd 99003 509-464-8250
Juanita Murray, prin. Fax 464-8294
Riverside ES 400/PK-5
3802 E Deer Park Milan Rd 99003 509-464-8350
Samantha Griggs, prin. Fax 464-8365
Riverside MS 400/6-8
3814 E Deer Park Milan Rd 99003 509-464-8450
Michael Syron, prin. Fax 464-8447

Chehalis, Lewis, Pop. 7,074
Adna SD 226 600/K-12
179 Dieckman Rd 98532 360-748-0362
Jim Forrest, supt. Fax 748-9217
www.adnaschools.org
Adna ES 200/K-5
220 Dieckman Rd 98532 360-748-7029
Lisa Dallas, prin. Fax 740-9419

Chehalis SD 302 2,800/PK-12
310 SW 16th St 98532 360-807-7200
Ed Rothlin, supt. Fax 748-8899
chehalisschools.org
Bennett ES 400/2-3
233 S Market Blvd 98532 360-807-7220
Trisha Smith, prin. Fax 748-7256
Cascade ES 400/PK-1
89 SW 3rd St 98532 360-807-7215
Bob Hunt, prin. Fax 748-6167
Chehalis MS 600/6-8
1060 SW 20th St 98532 360-807-7230
Chris Simpson, prin. Fax 740-1849

Olympic ES 400/4-5
2057 SW Salsbury Ave 98532 360-807-7225
Brett Ellingson, prin. Fax 740-1952

Lewis County Adventist S 100/K-10
PO Box 1203 98532 360-748-3213
St. Joseph S 100/PK-8
123 SW 6th St 98532 360-748-0961
Carissa Talley, prin. Fax 748-8502

Chelan, Chelan, Pop. 3,828
Lake Chelan SD 129 1,300/K-12
PO Box 369 98816 509-682-3515
Barry DePaoli, supt. Fax 682-5842
www.chelanschools.org
Chelan MS 300/6-8
PO Box 369 98816 509-682-4073
Brian Wood, prin. Fax 682-5001
Holden Village Community S 50/K-12
PO Box 369 98816 509-682-3515
Fax 682-5842
Morgen Owings ES 600/K-5
PO Box 369 98816 509-682-4031
Heidi Busk, prin. Fax 682-3373

Cheney, Spokane, Pop. 10,120
Cheney SD 360 4,200/PK-12
12414 S Andrus Rd 99004 509-559-4599
Robert Roettger, supt. Fax 559-4508
www.cheneysd.org
Betz ES 400/K-5
317 N 7th St 99004 509-559-4800
Carla Hudson, prin. Fax 559-4837
Cheney MS 500/6-8
740 W Betz Rd 99004 509-559-4400
Mike Stark, prin. Fax 559-4479
Salnave ES 400/K-5
1015 Salnave Rd 99004 509-559-4700
Celina Brennan, prin. Fax 559-4740
Snowdon ES 400/K-5
6323 S Holly Rd 99004 509-559-4300
Shawna Fraser, prin. Fax 559-4310
Other Schools – See Airway Heights, Spokane

Chewelah, Stevens, Pop. 2,514
Chewelah SD 36 800/PK-12
PO Box 47 99109 509-685-6800
Richard Linehan, supt. Fax 935-8605
www.chewelah.k12.wa.us
Gess ES 300/PK-6
PO Box 7 99109 509-685-6800
Julie Price, prin. Fax 935-4860

Chimacum, Jefferson
Chimacum SD 49 1,000/K-12
PO Box 278 98325 360-302-5890
Rick Thompson, supt. Fax 732-4336
www.csd49.org
Chimacum ES 200/3-5
PO Box 278 98325 360-302-5855
Jason Lynch, prin. Fax 732-0274
Chimacum MS 200/6-8
PO Box 278 98325 360-302-5944
David Carthum, prin. Fax 732-6859
Other Schools – See Port Hadlock

Clallam Bay, Clallam, Pop. 345
Cape Flattery SD 401
Supt. — See Sekiu
Clallam Bay S 100/K-12
PO Box 337 98326 360-963-2324
Kirs Hanson, prin. Fax 963-2228

Clarkston, Asotin, Pop. 7,028
Clarkston SD J 250-185 2,700/K-12
PO Box 70 99403 509-758-2531
Tim Winter, supt. Fax 758-3326
www.csdk12.org
Grantham ES 200/K-6
1253 Poplar St 99403 509-758-2503
Don Lee, prin. Fax 758-1639
Heights ES 400/K-6
1917 4th Ave 99403 509-758-8180
Samantha Ogden, prin. Fax 758-8212
Highland ES 300/K-6
1432 Highland Ave 99403 509-758-5531
Angela Baldus, prin. Fax 758-5532
Lincoln MS 400/7-8
1945 4th Ave 99403 509-758-5506
Mike Sperry, prin. Fax 758-7838
Parkway ES 400/K-6
1103 4th St 99403 509-758-2553
Eric Price, prin. Fax 758-5020

Holy Family S 100/PK-6
1002 Chestnut St 99403 509-758-6621
Sharon Shelley-Ray, prin. Fax 758-4997

Clearlake, Skagit
Sedro-Woolley SD 101
Supt. — See Sedro Woolley
Clearlake ES 200/K-6
PO Box 128 98235 360-855-3530
Dina Fox, prin. Fax 855-3531

Cle Elum, Kittitas, Pop. 1,804
Cle Elum-Roslyn SD 404 900/PK-12
2690 State Route 903 98922 509-649-4850
Gary Wargo, supt. Fax 649-2404
www.cersd.org
Cle Elum-Roslyn ES 400/PK-5
2696 State Route 903 98922 509-649-4700
Matt Chase, prin. Fax 649-3634
Strom MS 200/6-8
2694 State Route 903 98922 509-649-4800
Lara Gregorich-Bennett, prin. Fax 649-3634

Clinton, Island, Pop. 906

Whidbey Island Waldorf S 100/PK-8
PO Box 469 98236 360-341-5686
Lori Barian, admin.

Colbert, Spokane
Mead SD 354
Supt. — See Mead
Colbert ES 500/K-6
4625 E Greenbluff Rd 99005 509-465-6300
Rob Haugen, prin. Fax 465-6320
Midway ES 500/K-6
821 E Midway Rd 99005 509-465-6700
Josh Westermann, prin. Fax 465-6720
Mountainside MS 700/7-8
4717 E Day Mount Spokane Rd 99005 509-465-7400
Craig Busch, prin. Fax 465-7420

Northwest Christian Lower Campus 400/PK-8
5028 E Bernhill Rd 99005 509-292-6700
Dr. Jack Hancock, hdmstr. Fax 230-2342

Colfax, Whitman, Pop. 2,773
Colfax SD 300 600/K-12
1207 N Morton St 99111 509-397-3042
Jerry Pugh, supt. Fax 397-5835
www.colfax.k12.wa.us
Jennings ES 300/K-6
1207 N Morton St 99111 509-397-2181
Travis Howell, prin. Fax 397-6741

College Place, Walla Walla, Pop. 8,557
College Place SD 250 900/K-12
1755 S College Ave 99324 509-525-4827
Timothy Payne, supt. Fax 525-3741
www.cpps.org
Davis ES 500/K-5
31 SE Ash Ave 99324 509-525-5110
Mark Ferraro, prin. Fax 526-5662
Sager MS 300/6-8
1755 S College Ave 99324 509-525-5300
Dale Stopperan, prin. Fax 525-6005

Rogers Adventist S 300/K-8
200 SW Academy Way 99324 509-529-1850

Colton, Whitman, Pop. 412
Colton SD 306 200/K-12
706 Union St 99113 509-229-3385
Nathan Smith, supt. Fax 229-3374
www.colton.k12.wa.us
Colton S 200/K-12
706 Union St 99113 509-229-3306
Nathan Smith, prin. Fax 229-3374

Guardian Angel/St. Boniface S 50/K-8
PO Box 48 99113 509-229-3579
Lori Becker, prin.

Colville, Stevens, Pop. 4,534
Colville SD 115 1,800/K-12
217 S Hofstetter St 99114 509-684-7850
Pete Lewis, supt. Fax 684-7855
www.colsd.org
Colville JHS 400/6-8
990 S Cedar St 99114 509-684-7820
Paul Dumas, prin. Fax 684-7825
Fort Colville ES 400/3-5
1212 E Ivy Ave 99114 509-684-7830
Brian Cecil, prin. Fax 684-7831
Hofstetter ES 400/K-2
640 N Hofstetter St 99114 509-684-7690
Ann McKern, prin. Fax 684-7691

Onion Creek SD 30 50/PK-8
2006 Lotze Creek Rd 99114 509-732-4240
Rebekah Angus, supt. Fax 732-6114
www.ocsd30.org/
Onion Creek ES 50/PK-8
2006 Lotze Creek Rd 99114 509-732-4240
Patsy Guglielmino, prin. Fax 732-6114

Colville Valley SDA S 50/K-9
139 E Cedar Loop 99114 509-684-6830

Concrete, Skagit, Pop. 682
Concrete SD 11 400/PK-12
45389 Airport Way 98237 360-853-4000
Wayne Barrett, supt. Fax 853-4004
www.concrete.k12.wa.us
Concrete ES 300/PK-6
7838 S Superior Ave 98237 360-853-4110
Jaci Gallagher, prin. Fax 853-4149

Connell, Franklin, Pop. 4,122
North Franklin SD J 51-162 2,100/K-12
PO Box 829 99326 509-234-2021
Gregg Taylor, supt. Fax 234-9200
www.nfsd.org
Connell ES 500/K-6
PO Box 829 99326 509-234-4381
Nathan Schmutz, prin. Fax 234-4444
Olds JHS 300/7-8
PO Box 829 99326 509-234-3931
Jim Jacobs, prin. Fax 234-0525
Other Schools – See Mesa

Cook, Skamania
Mill A SD #31 50/K-12
1142 Jessup Rd, 509-538-2522
Bob Rogers, supt. Fax 538-2181
www.milla.k12.wa.us
Mill A S 50/K-8
1142 Jessup Rd, 509-538-2522
Bob Rogers, prin. Fax 538-2181

Cosmopolis, Grays Harbor, Pop. 1,610
Cosmopolis SD 99 100/PK-6
PO Box 479 98537 360-532-7181
Cherie Patterson, supt. Fax 532-1535
www.cosmopolisschool.com/
Cosmopolis ES 100/PK-6
PO Box 479 98537 360-532-7181
Cherie Patterson, supt. Fax 532-1535

North River SD 200 100/PK-12
2867 N River Rd 98537 360-532-3079
David Pickering, supt. Fax 532-1738
www.nr.k12.wa.us/
North River S 100/PK-12
2867 N River Rd 98537 360-532-3079
Sean Pierson, prin. Fax 532-1738

Coulee City, Grant, Pop. 541
Coulee-Hartline SD 151 200/K-12
PO Box 428 99115 509-632-5231
Dr. James Evans, supt. Fax 632-5166
www.achsd.org/chsd.htm
Coulee City ES 100/K-5
410 Locust W 99115 509-632-5231
Kelley Boyd, prin. Fax 632-5166

Coulee Dam, Okanogan, Pop. 1,042
Grand Coulee Dam SD 301J 500/PK-12
110 Stevens Ave 99116 509-633-2143
Paul Turner, supt. Fax 633-2530
www.gcdsd.org
Lake Roosevelt ES 300/PK-6
503 Crest Dr 99116 509-633-0730
Margo Piver, prin. Fax 633-2652

Coupeville, Island, Pop. 1,760
Coupeville SD 204 900/K-12
501 S Main St 98239 360-678-2400
Dr. Jim Shank, supt. Fax 678-4834
www.coupeville.k12.wa.us
Coupeville ES 400/K-5
6 S Main St 98239 360-678-2470
David Ebersole, prin. Fax 678-6810
Coupeville MS 200/6-8
501 S Main St 98239 360-678-2410
Geoff Kappes, prin. Fax 678-0540

Covington, King, Pop. 16,615
Kent SD 415
Supt. — See Kent
Cedar Heights MS 600/7-8
19640 SE 272nd St 98042 253-373-7620
Erika Wyn Hanson, prin. Fax 373-7628
Cedar Valley ES 300/K-6
26500 Timberlane Way SE 98042 253-373-7649
Brian Rosand, prin. Fax 373-7651
Covington ES 500/PK-6
17070 SE Wax Rd 98042 253-373-7652
Sarita Williams, prin. Fax 373-7654
Crestwood ES 500/K-6
25225 180th Ave SE 98042 253-373-7634
Ryan Preis, prin. Fax 373-7636
Jenkins Creek ES 300/K-6
26915 186th Ave SE 98042 253-373-7331
Michael Jackson, prin. Fax 373-7333
Mattson MS 600/7-8
16400 SE 251st St 98042 253-373-7670
James Schiechl, prin. Fax 373-7673

Tahoma SD 409
Supt. — See Maple Valley
Maple View MS 1,800/6-8
18200 SE 240th St 98042 425-413-5500
Sean Cassidy, prin. Fax 413-5555

Cowiche, Yakima, Pop. 418
Highland SD 203 1,200/K-12
PO Box 38 98923 509-678-8630
Mark Anderson, supt. Fax 678-4177
www.highland.wednet.edu/
Highland JHS 200/7-8
17000 Summitview Rd 98923 509-678-8800
Kelly Thorson, prin. Fax 678-4140
Whitman-Cowiche ES 400/K-3
1181 Thompson Rd 98923 509-678-8900
Mindy Schultz, prin. Fax 678-5494
Other Schools – See Tieton

Creston, Lincoln, Pop. 228
Creston SD 73 50/PK-12
485 SE E St 99117 509-636-2721
Charles Wyborney, supt. Fax 636-2910
www.creston.wednet.edu
Creston S 50/PK-12
485 SE E St 99117 509-636-2721
Glenn Arland, prin. Fax 636-2910

Curlew, Ferry, Pop. 114
Curlew SD 50 200/PK-12
PO Box 370 99118 509-779-4931
Dr. John Glenewinkel, supt. Fax 779-4938
www.curlew.wednet.edu
Curlew S 200/PK-12
PO Box 370 99118 509-779-4931
Dr. John Glenewinkel, admin. Fax 779-4938

Curtis, Lewis
Boistfort SD 234 100/PK-8
983 Boistfort Rd 98538 360-245-3343
Shannon Criss, supt. Fax 245-3451
Boistfort S 100/PK-8
983 Boistfort Rd 98538 360-245-3343
Shannon Criss, supt. Fax 245-3451

Cusick, Pend Oreille, Pop. 205
Cusick SD 59 300/K-12
305 Monumental Rd 99119 509-445-1125
Don Hawpe, supt. Fax 445-1598
www.cusick.wednet.edu/
Herian ES 100/K-5
305 Monumental Rd 99119 509-445-0361
Stephen Bollinger, admin. Fax 445-1598

Custer, Whatcom, Pop. 360
Ferndale SD 502
Supt. — See Ferndale
Custer ES 400/K-5
7660 Custer School Rd 98240 360-383-9500
John Fairbairn, prin. Fax 383-9502

Darrington, Snohomish, Pop. 1,303
Darrington SD 330 500/PK-12
PO Box 27 98241 360-436-1323
Dr. Buck Marsh, supt. Fax 436-2045
www.dsd.k12.wa.us
Darrington ES 300/PK-8
PO Box 27 98241 360-436-1313
Tracy Franke, prin. Fax 436-0592

Davenport, Lincoln, Pop. 1,697
Davenport SD 207 400/PK-12
801 7th St 99122 509-725-1481
Jim Kowalkowski, supt. Fax 725-2260
www.davenport.wednet.edu
Davenport ES 200/PK-5
601 Washington St 99122 509-725-1261
Courtney Strozyk, prin. Fax 725-2780
Davenport MS 6-8
601 Washington St 99122 509-725-0766
Chad Prewitt, prin. Fax 725-2780

Dayton, Columbia, Pop. 2,459
Dayton SD 2 400/PK-12
609 S 2nd St 99328 509-382-2543
Doug Johnson, supt. Fax 382-2081
www.daytonsd.org
Dayton ES 200/PK-5
302 E Park St 99328 509-382-2507
Denise Smith, prin. Fax 382-2081
Dayton MS 100/6-8
614 S 3rd St 99328 509-382-4775
Paul Shaber, prin. Fax 382-2081

Deer Park, Spokane, Pop. 3,505
Deer Park SD 414 2,100/PK-12
PO Box 490 99006 509-464-5500
Travis Hanson, supt. Fax 464-5510
www.dpsd.org
Arcadia ES 400/3-5
PO Box 610 99006 509-464-5700
Michele Miller, prin. Fax 464-5710
Deer Park Early Learning Center 50/PK-PK
1406 E D St 99006 509-464-5680
Cindy Ashworth, coord. Fax 464-5520
Deer Park ES 400/K-2
PO Box 609 99006 509-464-5600
Russ Lodge, prin. Fax 464-5610
Deer Park MS 500/6-8
PO Box 882 99006 509-464-5800
Tim Olietti, prin. Fax 464-5810

Deming, Whatcom, Pop. 349
Mt. Baker SD 507 1,500/K-12
PO Box 95 98244 360-383-2000
Charles Burleigh, supt. Fax 383-2009
www.mtbaker.wednet.edu
Other Schools – See Acme, Bellingham, Maple Falls

Des Moines, King, Pop. 27,680
Federal Way SD 210
Supt. — See Federal Way
Woodmont K-8 S 500/K-8
26454 16th Ave S 98198 253-945-4500
Dr. Jordanne Nevin, prin. Fax 945-4545

Highline SD 401
Supt. — See Burien
Des Moines ES 400/K-6
22001 9th Ave S 98198 206-631-3700
Rick Wisen, prin. Fax 631-3747
Midway ES 600/K-6
22447 24th Ave S 98198 206-631-4400
Rebekah Kim, prin. Fax 631-4499
Pacific MS 700/7-8
22705 24th Ave S 98198 206-631-5800
Vanessa Banner, prin. Fax 631-5860
Parkside ES 600/K-6
2104 S 247th St 98198 206-631-4700
Cindy Black, prin. Fax 631-4760

Grace Lutheran S 100/PK-K
22975 24th Ave S 98198 206-878-5048
Marilyn Russell, dir. Fax 878-2461
Holy Trinity Lutheran S 100/PK-8
2021 S 260th St 98198 253-839-6516
Jason Kelley M.S., prin. Fax 839-7921
St. Philomena S 200/PK-8
1815 S 220th St 98198 206-824-4051
Dr. Steve Morissette, prin. Fax 878-8646

Dixie, Walla Walla, Pop. 195
Dixie SD 101 50/PK-5
PO Box 40 99329 509-525-5339
Kevin Graffis, supt. Fax 525-1062
www.dixiesd.org
Dixie ES 50/PK-5
PO Box 40 99329 509-525-5339
Kevin Graffis, prin. Fax 525-1062

DuPont, Pierce, Pop. 7,501
Steilacoom Historical SD 1
Supt. — See Steilacoom
Clark ES 600/PK-3
1700 Palisade Blvd 98327 253-583-7100
Gary Yoho, prin. Fax 964-0935
Pioneer MS 800/6-8
1750 Bobs Hollow Ln 98327 253-583-7200
JoAnne Fernandes, prin. Fax 583-7292

Duvall, King, Pop. 6,458
Riverview SD 407 3,400/PK-12
PO Box 519 98019 425-844-4500
Dr. Anthony L. Smith, supt. Fax 844-4502
www.rsd407.org
Cherry Valley ES 500/K-5
26701 NE Cherry Valley Rd 98019 425-844-4750
Roxanne Luchini, prin. Fax 844-4752
Eagle Rock Multi-Age 100/K-5
29300 NE 150th St 98019 425-844-4900
Molly Lutz, prin. Fax 844-4902
Other Schools – See Carnation

Hillside Academy PK-8
PO Box 1344 98019 425-844-8608
Tim Foley, dir.

Easton, Kittitas, Pop. 472
Easton SD 28 100/PK-12
PO Box 8 98925 509-656-2317
Dr. Patrick Dehuff, supt. Fax 656-2585
www.easton.wednet.edu/
Easton S 100/PK-12
PO Box 8 98925 509-656-2317
Dr. Patrick Dehuff, supt. Fax 656-2585

Eastsound, San Juan
Orcas Island SD 137 900/K-12
557 School Rd 98245 360-376-2284
Eric Webb, supt. Fax 376-2283
www.orcasislandschools.org
Orcas Island ES 200/K-6
611 School Rd 98245 360-376-2286
Lorena Stankevich, prin. Fax 376-5410
Orcas Island MS 100/7-8
611 School Rd 98245 360-376-2287
Kyle Freeman, prin. Fax 376-6078
Other Schools – See Waldron

Orcas Christian Day S 100/K-12
PO Box 669 98245 360-376-6683

East Wenatchee, Douglas, Pop. 12,915
Eastmont SD 206 5,200/K-12
800 Eastmont Ave 98802 509-884-7169
Dr. Garn Christensen, supt. Fax 884-4210
www.eastmont206.org
Cascade ES 500/K-4
2330 N Baker Ave 98802 509-884-0523
Kim Browning, prin. Fax 886-1446
Clovis Point IS 700/5-7
1855 4th St SE 98802 509-888-1400
Bob Celebrezze, prin. Fax 888-1401
Grant ES 500/K-4
1430 1st St SE 98802 509-884-0557
Greg Loomis, prin. Fax 886-7219
Kenroy ES 500/K-4
601 N Jonathan Ave 98802 509-884-1443
Jon Abbott, prin. Fax 884-0732
Lee ES 500/K-4
1455 N Baker Ave 98802 509-884-1497
Jamea Connor, prin. Fax 886-1419
Sterling S 200/K-7
600 N James Ave 98802 509-884-7115
Chris Hall, prin. Fax 886-7503
Other Schools – See Rock Island

Eatonville, Pierce, Pop. 2,651
Eatonville SD 404 1,800/K-12
PO Box 698 98328 360-879-1000
Krestin Bahr, supt. Fax 879-1086
www.eatonville.wednet.edu/
Eatonville ES 400/K-5
PO Box 669 98328 360-879-1600
Diane Heersink, prin. Fax 879-1640
Eatonville MS 400/6-8
PO Box 910 98328 360-879-1400
Janna Rush, prin. Fax 879-1480
Weyerhaeuser ES 300/K-5
6105 365th St E 98328 360-879-1650
Amy Sturdivant, prin. Fax 879-1662
Other Schools – See Ashford

Edgewood, Pierce, Pop. 9,076
Fife SD 417
Supt. — See Tacoma
Hedden ES 500/2-5
11313 8th St E 98372 253-517-1500
Don Sims, prin. Fax 517-1505

Puyallup SD 3
Supt. — See Puyallup
Mountain View ES 300/K-6
3411 119th Ave E 98372 253-841-8739
Brian Curtis, prin. Fax 840-8949
Northwood ES 400/K-6
9805 24th St E 98371 253-841-8740
Melanie Helle, prin. Fax 840-8973

Salvation Christian Academy 200/PK-10
10622 8th St E 98372 253-952-7163
Vadim Hetman, prin. Fax 952-7164

Edmonds, Snohomish, Pop. 38,105
Edmonds SD 15
Supt. — See Lynnwood
Chase Lake Community S 400/K-6
21603 84th Ave W 98026 425-431-7495
Sean Silver, prin. Fax 431-7493
Edmonds ES 300/K-6
1215 Olympic Ave 98020 425-431-7374
Brett Hagen, prin. Fax 431-7372
Madrona S 600/K-8
9300 236th St SW 98020 425-431-7979
Kathleen Hodges, prin. Fax 431-7985
Seaview ES 300/K-6
8426 188th St SW 98026 425-431-7383
Heather Pickar, prin. Fax 431-7389
Sherwood ES 400/K-6
22901 106th Ave W 98020 425-431-7460
Christine Kessler, prin. Fax 431-7464
Westgate ES 500/K-6
9601 220th St SW 98020 425-431-7470
Jennifer Braile, prin. Fax 431-7473

Mukilteo SD 6
Supt. — See Everett
Picnic Point ES 600/K-5
5819 140th St SW 98026 425-366-3400
Ali Williams, prin. Fax 366-3402
Serene Lake ES 400/K-5
4709 Picnic Point Rd 98026 425-366-3500
Lori Bumstead, prin. Fax 366-3502

Holy Rosary S 200/PK-8
PO Box 206 98020 425-778-3197
Sue Venable, prin. Fax 771-8144

Edwall, Lincoln

Christian Heritage S 100/K-12
48009 Ida Ave E 99008 509-236-2224
Jonathan Belgarde, prin. Fax 236-2412

Ellensburg, Kittitas, Pop. 17,598
Damman SD 7 50/K-5
2681 Umptanum Rd 98926 509-962-9079
Marsha Smith, supt. Fax 925-2591
Damman ES 50/K-5
41 Manastash Rd 98926 509-962-9076
Rochelle Bierek, lead tchr. Fax 925-2591

Ellensburg SD 401 3,100/K-12
1300 E 3rd Ave 98926 509-925-8000
Mike Nollan, supt. Fax 925-8025
www.esd401.org
Lincoln ES 500/K-5
200 S Anderson St 98926 509-925-8052
John Graf, prin. Fax 925-8056
Morgan MS 700/6-8
400 E 1st Ave 98926 509-925-8200
Michelle Bibich, prin. Fax 925-8202
Mount Stuart ES 500/K-5
705 W 15th Ave 98926 509-925-8400
Dan Patton, prin. Fax 925-8406
Valley View ES 500/K-5
1508 E 3rd Ave 98926 509-925-7316
Rob Moffat, prin. Fax 925-8134

Ellensburg Christian S 100/K-8
407 S Anderson St 98926 509-925-2411
Tammie Lenz, prin.

Elma, Grays Harbor, Pop. 2,963
Elma SD 68 1,600/PK-12
1235 Monte Elma Rd 98541 360-482-2822
Kevin Acuff, supt. Fax 482-2092
www.eagles.edu
Elma ES 600/PK-5
1235 Monte Elma Rd 98541 360-482-2632
Mark Keating, prin. Fax 482-4565
Elma MS 300/6-8
1235 Monte Elma Rd 98541 360-482-2237
Sunshine Perry, prin. Fax 482-4872

Mary M. Knight SD 311 200/PK-12
2987 W Matlock Brady Rd 98541 360-426-6767
Dr. Ellen Perconti, supt. Fax 427-5516
www.marymknight.com
Knight ES 100/PK-6
2987 W Matlock Brady Rd 98541 360-426-6767
Dr. Ellen Perconti, admin. Fax 427-5516

Endicott, Whitman, Pop. 289
St. John-Endicott Cooperative SD 100/PK-8
308 School Dr 99125 509-657-3523
Suzanne Schmick, supt. Fax 657-3521
www.sje.wednet.edu/endicott.html
Endicott ES 50/PK-5
308 School Dr 99125 509-657-3523
Bruce Porubek, prin. Fax 657-3521
Other Schools – See Saint John

Entiat, Chelan, Pop. 1,090
Entiat SD 127 400/PK-12
2650 Entiat Way 98822 509-784-1800
Dr. Miles Caples, supt. Fax 784-2986
www.entiatschools.org
Rumburg ES 200/PK-5
2650 Entiat Way 98822 509-784-1314
Robin Kirkpatrick, prin. Fax 784-2986

Enumclaw, King, Pop. 10,407
Enumclaw SD 216 4,000/K-12
2929 McDougall Ave 98022 360-802-7100
Michael Nelson, supt. Fax 802-7140
www.enumclaw.wednet.edu/
Black Diamond ES 300/K-5
1640 Fell St 98022 360-802-7570
Gerrie Garton, prin. Fax 802-7610
Enumclaw MS 500/6-8
550 Semanski St 98022 360-802-7150
Jill Barrett, prin. Fax 802-7224
Kibler ES 400/K-5
2057 Kibler Ave 98022 360-802-7263
Mimi Brown, prin. Fax 802-7300
Southwood ES 300/K-5
3240 McDougall Ave 98022 360-802-7370
Andrew Means, prin. Fax 802-7374
Sunrise ES 400/K-5
899 Osceola St 98022 360-802-7425
Kyle Fletcher, prin. Fax 802-7427
Thunder Mountain MS 500/6-8
42018 264th Ave SE 98022 360-802-7492
Steven Stoker, prin. Fax 802-7500
Westwood ES 300/K-5
21200 SE 416th St 98022 360-802-7620
Scott Meyer, prin. Fax 802-7622

Ephrata, Grant, Pop. 7,502
Ephrata SD 165 2,300/K-12
499 C St NW 98823 509-754-2474
Dr. Jerry Simon, supt. Fax 754-4712
www.ephrataschools.org
Columbia Ridge ES 500/K-4
60 H St SE 98823 509-754-2882
Karla Williams, prin. Fax 754-4086
Ephrata MS 400/7-8
384 A St SE 98823 509-754-4659
Ken Murray, prin. Fax 754-5625
Grant ES 400/K-4
451 3rd Ave NW 98823 509-754-4676
Shannon Dahl, prin. Fax 754-4512
Parkway ES 300/5-6
1011 Parkway Blvd 98823 509-754-9729
Dawn Turley, prin. Fax 754-5429

New Life Christian S 100/PK-8
911 E Division Ave 98823 509-754-5558
St. Rose of Lima S 100/PK-6
520 Nat Washington Way 98823 509-754-4901
Amy Krautscheid, prin. Fax 754-9274

Everett, Snohomish, Pop. 98,083
Everett SD 2 18,800/PK-12
3900 Broadway 98201 425-385-4000
Dr. Gary Cohn, supt. Fax 385-4012
www.everettsd.org
Eisenhower MS 800/6-8
10200 25th Ave SE 98208 425-385-7500
Kevin Allen, prin. Fax 385-7502
Emerson ES 600/K-5
8702 7th Ave SE 98208 425-385-6200
Paul Edwards, prin. Fax 385-6202
Evergreen MS 1,000/6-8
7621 Beverly Ln 98203 425-385-5700
Christine Avery, prin. Fax 385-5702
Forest View ES 600/K-5
5601 156th St SE 98208 425-385-7900
Darren Larama, prin. Fax 385-7902
Garfield ES 400/K-5
2215 Pine St 98201 425-385-4700
Monique Beane, prin. Fax 385-4702
Gateway MS 800/6-8
15404 Silver Firs Dr 98208 425-385-6600
Shelley Petillo, prin. Fax 385-6602
Hawthorne ES 500/PK-5
1110 Poplar St 98201 425-385-4600
Celia O'Connor-Weaver, prin. Fax 385-4602
Jackson ES 400/K-5
3700 Federal Ave 98201 425-385-5600
Falicia Green, prin. Fax 385-5602
Jefferson ES 600/K-5
2500 Cadet Way 98208 425-385-7400
Elizabeth Kelley, prin. Fax 385-7402
Lowell ES 500/PK-5
5010 View Dr 98203 425-385-5300
Cindy Foster, prin. Fax 385-5302
Madison ES 400/PK-5
616 Pecks Dr 98203 425-385-5900
Amanda Overly, prin. Fax 385-5902
Monroe ES 500/K-5
10901 27th Ave SE 98208 425-385-7300
Gerard Holzman, prin. Fax 385-7302
North MS 700/6-8
2514 Rainier Ave 98201 425-385-4800
Mary O'Brien, prin. Fax 385-4802
Penny Creek ES 700/K-5
4117 132nd St SE 98208 425-385-7200
Maggie Heater, prin. Fax 385-7202
Silver Firs ES 500/K-5
5909 146th Pl SE 98208 425-385-6500
Kim Brenner, prin. Fax 385-6502
Silver Lake ES 500/PK-5
12815 Bothell Everett Hwy 98208 425-385-6900
Elizabeth Nunes, prin. Fax 385-6902
View Ridge ES 500/PK-5
202 Alder St 98203 425-385-5400
Katrina Farias, prin. Fax 385-5402
Whittier ES 400/PK-5
916 Oakes Ave 98201 425-385-4300
Tony Wentworth, prin. Fax 385-4302
Other Schools – See Bothell, Mill Creek

Mukilteo SD 6 15,700/PK-12
9401 Sharon Dr 98204 425-356-1274
Dr. Marci Larsen, supt. Fax 356-1310
www.mukilteo.wednet.edu
Challenger ES 600/K-5
9600 Holly Dr 98204 425-366-2500
Dirk Adkinson, prin. Fax 366-2502
Discovery ES 700/K-5
11700 Meridian Ave S 98208 425-366-2700
Shannon Koehnen, prin. Fax 366-2702
Explorer MS 900/6-8
9600 Sharon Dr 98204 425-366-5000
Kendrah Larson, prin. Fax 366-5002
Fairmount ES 700/K-5
11401 Beverly Park Rd 98204 425-366-2900
Janelle Phinney, prin. Fax 366-2902
Horizon ES 800/K-5
222 W Casino Rd 98204 425-366-3000
Edmund Wong, prin. Fax 366-3002
Odyssey ES 700/K-5
13025 17th Ave W 98204 425-366-3200
Rebecca Oren, prin. Fax 366-3202
Olivia Park ES 700/K-5
200 108th St SW 98204 425-366-3300
Katie Pence, prin. Fax 366-3302
Pathfinder K K-K
11401 Beverly Park Rd 98204 425-366-3800
Cheryl Boze, prin.
Voyager MS 800/6-8
11711 4th Ave W 98204 425-366-5300
Wes Bailey, prin. Fax 366-5302
Other Schools – See Edmonds, Lynnwood, Mukilteo

Snohomish SD 201
Supt. — See Snohomish
Seattle Hill ES 600/K-6
12711 51st Ave SE 98208 360-563-4675
Paula Nelson, prin. Fax 563-4680

Cedar Park Christian S - Mill Creek 200/PK-8
13000 21st Dr SE 98208 425-337-6992
Garron Smith, admin. Fax 357-9399
Everett Christian S 100/PK-8
2221 Cedar St 98201 425-259-3213
Joel Alberts, prin. Fax 259-0721
Forest Park Adventist Christian S 50/K-8
4120 Federal Ave 98203 425-258-6911
Immaculate Conception S 300/PK-8
2508 Hoyt Ave 98201 425-349-7777
Kathy Wartelle, prin. Fax 349-7048
Montessori S of Snohomish County 100/PK-12
1804 Puget Dr 98203 425-355-1311
Kathleen Gunnell, admin. Fax 347-1000

Northshore Christian Academy 800/PK-8
5700 23rd Dr W 98203 425-322-2301
Holly Leach, supt. Fax 322-2386
St. Mary Magdalen S 400/PK-8
8615 7th Ave SE 98208 425-353-7559
Zack Cunningham, prin. Fax 356-2687

Everson, Whatcom, Pop. 2,414
Meridian SD 505
Supt. — See Bellingham
Reither ES 500/PK-5
954 E Hemmi Rd 98247 360-398-2111
Patti Fouts, prin. Fax 398-8340

Nooksack Valley SD 506 1,500/PK-12
3326 E Badger Rd 98247 360-988-4754
Dr. Mark Johnson, supt. Fax 988-8983
www.nv.k12.wa.us/
Everson ES 200/PK-5
216 Everson Goshen Rd 98247 360-966-2030
Kevin DeVere, prin. Fax 966-0945
Nooksack ES 300/PK-5
3333 Breckenridge Rd 98247 360-966-3321
Cindy Tjoelker, prin. Fax 966-7512
Other Schools – See Nooksack, Sumas

Fairchild AFB, Spokane, Pop. 2,585
Medical Lake SD 326
Supt. — See Medical Lake
Anderson ES 500/PK-5
400 W Fairchild Hwy 99011 509-565-3600
Darlene Starr, prin. Fax 565-3601

Fall City, King, Pop. 1,940
Snoqualmie Valley SD 410
Supt. — See Snoqualmie
Chief Kanim MS 700/6-8
PO Box 639 98024 425-831-8225
Michelle Trifunovic, prin. Fax 831-8290
Fall City ES 600/K-5
PO Box 220 98024 425-831-4000
Katelyn Long, prin. Fax 831-4010

Summit Classical Christian S 100/PK-10
32725 SE 42nd St 98024 425-222-0564
Katie Ross, prin.

Federal Way, King, Pop. 82,130
Federal Way SD 210 22,100/PK-12
33330 8th Ave S 98003 253-945-2000
Dr. Tammy Campbell, supt. Fax 945-2001
www.fwps.org
Adelaide ES 400/K-5
1635 SW 304th St 98023 253-945-2300
Michelle Frank, prin. Fax 945-2323
Brigadoon ES 300/K-5
3601 SW 336th St 98023 253-945-2400
Debbie Audet, prin Fax 945-2424
Enterprise ES 500/PK-5
35101 5th Ave SW 98023 253-945-2600
Jeff Soltez, prin. Fax 945-2626
Green Gables ES 400/PK-5
32607 47th Ave SW 98023 253-945-2700
Margot Hightower, prin. Fax 945-2727
Hill ES 400/PK-5
5830 S 300th St 98001 253-945-3200
Diane Ellis, prin. Fax 945-3232
Illahee MS 700/6-8
36001 1st Ave S 98003 253-945-4600
Brianna Ward, prin. Fax 945-4646
Lake Grove ES 400/K-5
303 SW 308th St 98023 253-945-2900
Doug Rutherford, prin. Fax 945-2929
Lakota MS 800/6-8
1415 SW 314th St 98023 253-945-4800
Angela Williamson, prin. Fax 945-4848
Mirror Lake ES 400/K-5
625 S 314th St 98003 253-945-3300
Stephanie McPhail, prin. Fax 945-3333
Nautilus K-8 S 500/K-8
1000 S 289th St 98003 253-945-3400
Stacy Lucas, prin. Fax 945-3434
Olympic View ES 400/K-5
2626 SW 327th St 98023 253-945-3500
Chris McCrummen, prin. Fax 945-3535
Panther Lake ES 500/K-5
34424 1st Ave S 98003 253-945-3600
Julie Van Wijk, prin. Fax 945-3636
Rainier View ES 400/PK-5
3015 S 368th St 98003 253-945-3700
Kent Cross, prin. Fax 945-3737
Sacajawea MS 700/6-8
1101 S Dash Point Rd 98003 253-945-4900
Jeff Hunt, prin. Fax 945-4040
Sherwood Forest ES 500/K-5
34600 12th Ave SW 98023 253-945-3800
Alisa DeSart, prin. Fax 945-3838
Silver Lake ES 400/K-5
1310 SW 325th Pl 98023 253-945-3900
Kristi White, prin. Fax 945-3939
Twain ES 600/PK-5
2450 S Star Lake Rd 98003 253-945-3100
Shelley Habenicht, prin. Fax 945-3131
Twin Lakes ES 400/PK-5
4400 SW 320th St 98023 253-945-4200
Dr. Anne Plenkovich, prin. Fax 945-4242
Wildwood ES 500/PK-5
2405 S 300th St 98003 253-945-4400
Michael Swartz, prin. Fax 945-4444
Other Schools – See Auburn, Des Moines, Kent

Brooklake Christian S 200/PK-5
629 S 356th St 98003 253-517-8247
Kyle Ferguson, dir. Fax 517-8297
Christian Faith S 300/PK-12
33645 20th Ave S 98003 253-943-2500
Debbie Schindler, head sch Fax 200-1335
Evergreen Christian S 100/PK-8
3405 S 336th St 98001 253-880-1021
Angelina Nalivayko, head sch

Life Academy of Puget Sound 50/PK-12
414 SW 312th St 98023 253-839-7378
Rev. Sue Austin, admin. Fax 839-1031
St. Luke Lutheran S 100/PK-K
515 S 312th St 98003 253-941-3000
Stephanie Hagen, dir. Fax 941-8994
St. Vincent De Paul S 300/PK-8
30527 8th Ave S 98003 253-839-3532
Wanda Stewart, prin. Fax 946-1247

Ferndale, Whatcom, Pop. 10,997
Ferndale SD 502 4,800/PK-12
PO Box 698 98248 360-383-9200
Dr. Linda Quinn Ed.D., supt. Fax 383-9201
ferndalesd.org
Cascadia ES 500/PK-5
PO Box 2009 98248 360-383-2300
Kellie Larrabee, prin. Fax 383-2302
Central ES 300/K-5
PO Box 187 98248 360-383-9600
Georgia Dellinger, prin. Fax 383-9602
Eagleridge ES 500/PK-5
PO Box 1127 98248 360-383-9700
Mischa Burnett, prin. Fax 383-9702
Horizon MS 600/6-8
PO Box 1769 98248 360-383-9850
Dr. Faye Britt, prin. Fax 383-9852
Skyline ES 400/PK-5
PO Box 905 98248 360-383-9450
Bill Tipton, prin. Fax 383-9452
Vista MS 600/6-8
PO Box 1328 98248 360-383-9370
Heather Leighton, prin. Fax 383-9372
Other Schools – See Custer, Lummi Island

Pioneer Meadows Montessori S 100/PK-6
2377 Douglas Rd 98248 360-778-3681
Lee Smith, head sch

Forks, Clallam, Pop. 3,383
Queets-Clearwater SD 20 50/K-8
146000 Highway 101 98331 360-962-2395
Richard Rohlman, supt. Fax 962-2038
www.qcsd20.org
Queets-Clearwater ES 50/K-8
146000 Highway 101 98331 360-962-2395
Richard Rohlman, admin. Fax 962-2038

Quillayute Valley SD 402 2,900/PK-12
411 S Spartan Ave 98331 360-374-6262
Diana Reaume, supt. Fax 374-6990
www.qvschools.org
Forks ES 400/PK-3
301 S Elderberry Ave 98331 360-374-6262
Rob Shadle, prin. Fax 374-2363
Forks IS 200/4-6
121 S Spartan Ave 98331 360-374-6262
Caspar Van Haalen, prin. Fax 374-2362
Forks JHS, 191 S Spartan Ave 98331 7-8
Elena Velasquez, prin. 360-374-6262

Friday Harbor, San Juan, Pop. 2,106
San Juan Island SD 149 800/K-12
PO Box 458 98250 360-378-4133
Dr. Danna Diaz, supt. Fax 378-6276
www.sjisd.wednet.edu
Friday Harbor ES 400/K-6
PO Box 458 98250 360-378-5209
Diane Ball, prin. Fax 378-3405
Friday Harbor MS 100/7-8
PO Box 458 98250 360-378-5214
Fred Woods, prin. Fax 378-9750

Paideia Classical S 50/K-8
PO Box 1875 98250 360-378-8322

Garfield, Whitman, Pop. 585
Garfield SD 302 100/PK-8
PO Box 398 99130 509-635-1331
Zane Wells, supt. Fax 635-1332
www.garpal.net
Garfield ES 50/PK-5
PO Box 398 99130 509-635-1331
Zane Wells, prin. Fax 635-1332
Garfield-Palouse MS 50/6-8
PO Box 398 99130 509-635-1331
Zane Wells, prin. Fax 635-1332

Gifford, Stevens
Evergreen SD 205 50/PK-6
3341 Addy Gifford Rd 99131 509-722-6084
Bill Glidewell, supt. Fax 722-6085
www.evergreen.k12.wa.us
Evergreen ES 50/PK-6
3342 Addy Gifford Rd 99131 509-722-6384
Bill Glidewell, prin. Fax 722-6084

Gig Harbor, Pierce, Pop. 6,870
Peninsula SD 401 9,100/PK-12
14015 62nd Ave NW 98332 253-530-1000
Robert W. Manahan Ed.D., supt. Fax 530-1010
www.psd401.net/
Artondale ES 400/PK-5
6219 40th St NW 98335 253-530-1100
Jessica Rosendahl, prin. Fax 530-1120
Discovery ES 400/K-5
4905 Rosedale St NW 98335 253-530-1200
David Brooks, prin Fax 530-1220
Goodman MS 600/6-8
3701 38th Ave NW 98335 253-530-1600
D.J. Sigurdson, prin. Fax 530-1620
Harbor Heights ES 600/PK-5
4002 36th St NW 98335 253-530-1800
Stephanie Strader, prin. Fax 530-1820
Harbor Ridge MS 600/6-8
9010 Prentice Ave 98332 253-530-1900
Mike Benoit, prin. Fax 530-1920
Kopachuck MS 600/6-8
10414 56th St NW 98335 253-530-4100
Heidi Fedore, prin. Fax 530-4120

Minter Creek ES 400/K-5
12617 118th Ave NW 98329 253-530-4300
Tyrone Robuck, prin. Fax 530-4320
Purdy ES 700/PK-5
13815 62nd Ave NW 98332 253-530-4600
Kristi Rivera, prin. Fax 530-4620
Voyager ES 500/K-5
5615 Kopachuck Dr NW 98335 253-530-4800
Katja Rimmele, prin. Fax 530-4820
Other Schools – See Lakebay, Vaughn

Gig Harbor Academy 100/PK-5
6820 32nd St NW 98335 253-265-2150
Harbor Montessori 100/PK-8
5414 Comte Dr NW 98335 253-851-5722
Hosanna Christian S 100/PK-8
3114 45th Street Ct NW 98335 253-851-8952
Peggy Hobbs, prin. Fax 851-9971
Lighthouse Christian S 300/K-8
3008 36th St NW 98335 253-858-5962
Stephen Roddy, prin. Fax 858-8911
St. Nicholas S 100/PK-8
3555 Edwards Dr 98335 253-858-7632
Amy Unruh, prin. Fax 858-1597

Glenwood, Klickitat
Glenwood SD 401 50/K-12
PO Box 12 98619 509-364-3438
Heather Gimlin, supt. Fax 364-3689
www.glenwood.k12.wa.us/
Glenwood S 50/K-12
PO Box 12 98619 509-364-3438
Heather Gimlin, supt. Fax 364-3689

Gold Bar, Snohomish, Pop. 1,982
Sultan SD 311
Supt. — See Sultan
Gold Bar ES 300/K-5
419 Lewis Ave 98251 360-793-9840
Keith Buechler, prin. Fax 793-4158

Goldendale, Klickitat, Pop. 3,344
Goldendale SD 404 1,000/K-12
604 E Brooks Ave 98620 509-773-5177
Mark Heid, supt. Fax 773-6028
www.goldendaleschools.org
Goldendale MS 300/5-8
520 E Collins St 98620 509-773-4323
Dave Barta, prin. Fax 773-4579
Goldendale PS 300/K-4
820 S Schuster St 98620 509-773-4665
Chip Ferrell, prin. Fax 773-6602

Goldendale Adventist Christian S 50/1-8
PO Box 241 98620 509-773-3120

Graham, Pierce, Pop. 21,945
Bethel SD 403
Supt. — See Spanaway
Centennial ES 500/K-5
24323 54th Ave E 98338 253-683-7700
Chris Brauer, prin. Fax 683-7798
Cougar Mountain MS 600/6-8
5108 260th St E 98338 253-683-8000
Bethany Aoki, prin. Fax 683-8098
Frontier MS 800/6-8
22110 108th Ave E 98338 253-683-8300
Mark Barnes, prin. Fax 683-8398
Graham ES 600/K-5
10026 204th St E 98338 253-683-8500
Amy Low, prin. Fax 683-8598
Kapowsin ES 400/K-5
10412 264th St E 98338 253-683-8600
David Cordell, prin. Fax 683-8698
Nelson ES 600/PK-5
22109 108th Ave E 98338 253-683-6400
Tami Nelson, prin. Fax 683-6498
North Star ES 500/K-5
7719 224th St E 98338 253-683-8800
Stephen Rushing, prin. Fax 683-8898
Rocky Ridge ES 400/K-5
6514 260th St E 98338 253-683-5000
Lindsey Marquardt, prin. Fax 683-5098

Grandview, Yakima, Pop. 10,766
Grandview SD 200 3,600/PK-12
913 W 2nd St 98930 509-882-8500
Henry Strom, supt. Fax 882-2029
www.gsd200.org
Grandview MS 800/6-8
1401 W 2nd St 98930 509-882-8600
James Heinle, prin. Fax 882-3538
McClure ES 600/PK-5
811 W 2nd St 98930 509-882-7100
Jose Rivera, prin. Fax 882-5041
Smith ES 600/PK-5
205 Fir St 98930 509-882-8700
Jared Lind, prin. Fax 882-5871
Thompson ES 600/PK-5
1105 W 2nd St 98930 509-882-8550
Julie Wysong, prin. Fax 882-5947

Grandview Adventist Junior Academy 50/1-8
106 N Elm St 98930 509-882-3817

Granger, Yakima, Pop. 3,222
Granger SD 204 1,500/PK-12
701 E Ave 98932 509-854-1515
Margarita C. Lopez, supt. Fax 854-1126
www.gsd.wednet.edu
Granger MS 500/5-8
701 E Ave 98932 509-854-1003
Stephanie Funk, prin. Fax 854-1083
Roosevelt ES 600/PK-4
701 E Ave 98932 509-854-1420
Elizabeth Hockens, prin. Fax 854-1281

Granite Falls, Snohomish, Pop. 3,190
Granite Falls SD 332 1,600/K-12
205 N Alder St 98252 360-691-7717
Linda Hall, supt. Fax 691-4459
www.gfalls.wednet.edu
Granite Falls MS 400/6-8
405 N Alder Ave 98252 360-691-7710
Dave Bianchini, prin. Fax 283-4415
Monte Cristo ES 200/3-5
1201 100th St NE 98252 360-691-7718
Tori Thomas, prin. Fax 691-2673
Mountain Way ES 200/K-2
702 N Granite Ave 98252 360-691-7719
Cheryl Larsen, prin. Fax 283-4416

Grapeview, Mason, Pop. 922
Grapeview SD 54 200/K-8
822 E Mason Benson Rd 98546 360-426-4921
Bill Evans, supt. Fax 427-8975
gsd54.org
Grapeview ES 200/K-8
822 E Mason Benson Rd 98546 360-426-4921
Josie Bean, prin. Fax 427-8975

Harrah, Yakima, Pop. 600
Mount Adams SD 209
Supt. — See White Swan
Harrah ES 600/PK-6
PO Box 159 98933 509-848-2935
Rachel Leslie, prin. Fax 848-2770

Harrah Community Christian S 100/PK-8
PO Box 100 98933 509-848-2418
Marie Wegmuller, admin. Fax 848-2662

Harrington, Lincoln, Pop. 416
Harrington SD 204 100/PK-12
PO Box 204 99134 509-253-4331
Justin Bradford M.A., supt. Fax 456-6306
www.harrsd.k12.wa.us
Harrington ES 100/PK-6
PO Box 204 99134 509-253-4331
Justin Bradford M.A., admin. Fax 456-6306

Hoquiam, Grays Harbor, Pop. 8,401
Hoquiam SD 28 1,600/PK-12
325 W Chenault Ave 98550 360-538-8200
Mike Villarreal, supt. Fax 538-8202
hoquiam.net
Central ES 200/4-5
310 Simpson Ave 98550 360-538-8230
Denise Pearl, prin. Fax 538-8232
Emerson ES 200/K-1
101 W Emerson Ave 98550 360-538-8240
Marah Gannaway, prin. Fax 538-8242
Hoquiam MS 400/6-8
200 Spencer St 98550 360-538-8220
Jason Ihde, prin. Fax 538-8222
Lincoln ES 300/PK-PK, 2-
700 Wood Ave 98550 360-538-8250
Colin Nelson, prin. Fax 538-8252

Hunters, Stevens
Columbia SD 206 200/PK-12
PO Box 7 99137 509-722-3311
Dr. William Wadlington, supt. Fax 722-3310
www.columbia206.com
Columbia S 200/PK-12
PO Box 7 99137 509-722-3311
Matt McLain, prin. Fax 722-3310

Ilwaco, Pacific, Pop. 906
Ocean Beach SD 101
Supt. — See Long Beach
Hilltop S 5-8
PO Box F 98624 360-642-1234
Todd Carper, prin. Fax 642-1350

Inchelium, Ferry, Pop. 393
Inchelium SD 70 50/K-12
PO Box 285 99138 509-722-6181
Kim Spacek, supt. Fax 722-6192
www.inchelium.wednet.edu
Inchelium S 50/K-12
PO Box 285 99138 509-722-6181
Brian Myers, prin. Fax 722-6192

Index, Snohomish, Pop. 176
Index SD 63 50/PK-8
PO Box 237 98256 360-793-1330
Brad Jernberg, supt. Fax 793-2835
www.index.k12.wa.us
Index ES 50/PK-8
PO Box 237 98256 360-793-1330
Brad Jernberg, supt. Fax 793-2835

Issaquah, King, Pop. 29,272
Issaquah SD 411 18,500/PK-12
565 NW Holly St 98027 425-837-7000
Ron Thiele, supt. Fax 837-7005
www.issaquah.wednet.edu
Beaver Lake MS 900/6-8
25025 SE 32nd St 98029 425-837-4150
Stacy Cho, prin. Fax 837-4195
Challenger ES 600/K-5
25200 SE Klahanie Blvd 98029 425-837-7550
Sara Jo Pietrazewski, prin. Fax 837-5159
Clark ES 500/K-5
500 2nd Ave SE 98027 425-837-6300
Tod Wood, prin. Fax 837-6251
Endeavour ES 700/K-5
26205 SE Issqh Fall City Rd 98029 425-837-7350
Alaina Sivadasan, prin. Fax 837-7355
Grand Ridge ES 700/K-5
1739 NE Park Dr 98029 425-837-7925
Christy Otley, prin. Fax 837-7929
Issaquah MS 800/6-8
600 2nd Ave SE 98027 425-837-6800
Seth Adams, prin. Fax 837-6855
Issaquah Valley ES 600/K-5
555 NW Holly St 98027 425-837-6600
Michelle Pickard, prin. Fax 837-6605
Pacific Cascade MS 900/6-8
24635 SE Issaquah Fall City 98029 425-837-5900
Dana Bailey, prin. Fax 837-5910
Sunny Hills ES 600/K-5
3200 Issqah Pine Lake Rd SE 98075 425-837-7400
Leslie Lederman, prin. Fax 837-7402
Other Schools – See Bellevue, Newcastle, Renton, Sammamish

St. Joseph S 400/PK-8
220 Mt Park Blvd SW 98027 425-313-9129
Peg Johnston, prin. Fax 313-7296
Snoqualmie Springs S 100/PK-3
25237 SE Issaquah Fall City 98029 425-392-1196
Joe Drovetto, admin. Fax 427-9639

Joyce, Clallam
Crescent SD 313 200/K-12
PO Box 20 98343 360-928-3311
David Bingham, supt. Fax 928-3066
www.crescentschooldistrict.org
Crescent ES 100/K-5
PO Box 20 98343 360-928-3311
Fax 928-3066

Kahlotus, Franklin, Pop. 189
Kahlotus SD 56 100/PK-12
PO Box 69 99335 509-282-3338
Mark Bitzer, supt. Fax 282-3339
www.kahlotussd.org
Kahlotus S 100/PK-12
PO Box 69 99335 509-282-3338
Mark Bitzer, prin. Fax 282-3339

Kalama, Cowlitz, Pop. 2,270
Kalama SD 402 900/K-12
548 China Garden Rd 98625 360-673-5282
Eric Nerison, supt. Fax 673-5228
kalamaschools.org
Kalama ES 400/K-5
548 China Garden Rd 98625 360-673-5207
Dr. Kala Lougheed, prin. Fax 673-5265

Keller, Ferry, Pop. 212
Keller SD 3 50/K-6
PO Box 367 99140 509-634-4325
Wayne Massie, supt. Fax 634-4330
www.keller.k12.wa.us
Keller ES 50/K-6
PO Box 367 99140 509-634-4325
Wayne Massie, supt. Fax 634-4330

Kelso, Cowlitz, Pop. 11,473
Kelso SD 458 4,800/PK-12
601 Crawford St 98626 360-501-1900
Glenn Gelbrich, supt. Fax 501-1944
www.kelso.wednet.edu
Barnes ES 400/PK-5
401 Barnes St 98626 360-501-1500
Christine McDaniel, prin. Fax 501-1510
Butler Acres ES 400/K-5
1609 Burcham St 98626 360-501-1600
Cindy Cromwell, prin. Fax 501-1610
Carrolls ES 100/K-5
3902 Old Pacific Hwy S 98626 360-501-1380
Brooke Henley, prin. Fax 501-1370
Catlin ES 300/K-5
404 Long Ave 98626 360-501-1550
Tim Yore, prin. Fax 501-1589
Coweeman MS 600/6-8
2000 Allen St 98626 360-501-1750
Greg Gardner, prin. Fax 501-1782
Huntington MS 600/6-8
500 Redpath St 98626 360-501-1700
Chris Clark, prin. Fax 501-1723
Rose Valley ES 100/K-5
1502 Rose Valley Rd 98626 360-501-1400
Brooke Henley, prin. Fax 501-1420
Wallace ES 400/K-5
410 Elm St 98626 360-501-1650
Ray Cattin, prin. Fax 501-1660
Other Schools – See Longview

Journey Christian S 50/PK-8
96 Garden St 98626 360-423-9250

Kenmore, King, Pop. 19,563
Northshore SD 417
Supt. — See Bothell
Arrowhead ES 400/K-5
6725 NE Arrowhead Dr 98028 425-408-4000
Jesse Harrison, prin. Fax 408-4002
Kenmore ES 500/K-5
19121 71st Ave NE 98028 425-408-4800
Melissa Riley, prin. Fax 408-4802
Kenmore MS 700/6-8
20323 66th Ave NE 98028 425-408-6400
Bryan Stutz, prin. Fax 408-6402
Moorlands ES 600/K-5
15115 84th Ave NE 98028 425-408-5100
Talena Graff, prin. Fax 408-5102

Kennewick, Benton, Pop. 72,070
Finley SD 53 900/PK-12
224606 E Game Farm Rd 99337 509-586-3217
Lance Hahn, supt. Fax 586-4408
www.finleysd.org
Finley ES 400/PK-5
213504 E Cougar Rd 99337 509-586-7577
Pam Kinne, prin. Fax 586-8239
Finley MS 200/6-8
37208 S Finley Rd 99337 509-586-7561
Michael Harrington, prin. Fax 582-8452

Kennewick SD 17 17,100/PK-12
1000 W 4th Ave 99336 509-222-5000
Dave Bond, supt. Fax 222-5050
www.ksd.org
Amistad ES 600/K-5
930 W 4th Ave 99336 509-222-5100
Andy Woehler, prin. Fax 222-5101
Canyon View ES 600/K-5
1229 W 22nd Pl 99337 509-222-5200
Mark Stephens, prin. Fax 222-5201
Cascade ES 600/K-5
505 S Highland Dr 99337 509-222-5300
Chad Foltz, prin. Fax 222-5301
Chinook MS, 4891 W 27th Ave 99336 6-8
Kevin Pierce, prin. 509-222-7500
Cottonwood ES 600/K-5
16734 Cottonwood Creek Blvd 99338 509-222-6400
MaryAnn Kautzky, prin. Fax 222-6401
Desert Hills MS 1,000/6-8
1701 S Clodfelter Rd 99338 509-222-6600
Steve Jones, prin. Fax 222-6601
Eastgate ES 500/K-5
910 E 10th Ave 99336 509-222-5400
Brittany Gilson, prin. Fax 222-5401
Edison ES 500/K-5
201 S Dawes St 99336 509-222-5500
Mia Benjamin, prin. Fax 222-5501
Hawthorne ES 500/K-5
3520 W John Day Ave 99336 509-222-5600
Craig Miller, prin. Fax 222-5601
Highlands MS 900/6-8
425 S Tweedt St 99336 509-222-6700
Lori McCord, prin. Fax 222-6701
Horse Heaven Hills MS 1,000/6-8
3500 S Vancouver St 99337 509-222-6800
Diana Burns, prin. Fax 222-6801
Keewaydin Discovery Center 200/PK-PK
125 S Conway Pl 99336 509-222-5028
Becca Anderson, coord. Fax 222-5056
Lincoln ES 600/K-5
4901 W 20th Ave 99338 509-222-5700
Tony Langdon, prin. Fax 222-5701
Park MS 900/6-8
1011 W 10th Ave 99336 509-222-6900
Shaun Espe, prin. Fax 222-6901
Ridge View ES 500/K-5
7001 W 13th Ave 99338 509-222-5800
Lori Butler, prin. Fax 222-5801
Sage Crest ES K-5
6411 W 38th Ave 99338 509-222-6500
Rob Phillips, prin.
Southgate ES 500/K-5
3121 W 19th Ave 99337 509-222-5900
Bob Smart, prin. Fax 222-5901
Sunset View ES 500/K-5
711 N Center Pkwy 99336 509-222-6000
Heidi Reigsecker, prin. Fax 222-6001
Vista ES 600/K-5
1701 N Young St 99336 509-222-6100
Jennifer Behrends, prin. Fax 222-6101
Washington ES 500/K-5
105 W 21st Ave 99337 509-222-6200
Ryan Rettig, prin. Fax 222-6201
Westgate ES 500/K-5
2514 W 4th Ave 99336 509-222-6300
Dale Kern, prin. Fax 222-6301

Bethlehem Lutheran S 200/PK-8
2505 W 27th Ave 99337 509-582-5624
Lisa Stueve, prin. Fax 586-6702
St. Joseph S 300/PK-8
901 W 4th Ave 99336 509-586-0481
Perry Kelly, prin. Fax 585-9781

Kent, King, Pop. 85,961
Federal Way SD 210
Supt. — See Federal Way
Star Lake ES 500/K-5
4014 S 270th St 98032 253-945-4000
Kris Rennie, prin. Fax 945-4040
Sunnycrest ES 600/K-5
24629 42nd Ave S 98032 253-945-4100
Shana Watkins, prin. Fax 945-4141
Totem MS 600/6-8
26630 40th Ave S 98032 253-945-5100
Rudy Baca, prin. Fax 945-5151

Kent SD 415 27,500/PK-12
12033 SE 256th St 98030 253-373-7000
Dr. Calvin Watts, supt. Fax 373-7231
www.kent.k12.wa.us
Daniel ES 500/PK-6
11310 SE 248th St, 253-373-7615
Patricia Drobny, prin. Fax 373-7617
East Hill ES 500/K-6
9825 S 240th St 98031 253-373-7455
Dr. Brian Patrick, prin. Fax 373-7457
Emerald Park ES 500/K-6
11800 SE 216th St 98031 253-373-3850
Dean Ficken, prin. Fax 373-3852
Glenridge ES 500/K-6
19405 120th Ave SE 98031 253-373-7494
Scott Abernathy, prin. Fax 373-7495
Grass Lake ES 400/K-6
28700 191st Pl SE 98042 253-373-7661
Dan Irvine, prin. Fax 373-7663
Horizon ES 500/K-6
27641 144th Ave SE 98042 253-373-7313
Miles Erdly, prin. Fax 373-7324
Kent ES 700/PK-6
24700 64th Ave S 98032 253-373-7497
Rosa Villarreal, prin. Fax 373-7499
Kent Valley Early Learning Center PK-K
317 4th Ave S 98032 253-373-7600
Alice Humphres, coord. Fax 373-7601
Lake Youngs ES 500/K-6
19660 142nd Ave SE 98042 253-373-7646
Cathy Lendosky, prin. Fax 373-7648
Meadow Ridge ES 600/PK-6
27710 108th Ave SE, 253-373-7870
Aric Kooima, prin. Fax 373-7877
Meridian ES 600/K-6
25621 140th Ave SE 98042 253-373-7664
LySander Collins, prin. Fax 373-7666
Meridian MS 600/7-8
23480 120th Ave SE 98031 253-373-7383
Darice Johnson, prin. Fax 373-7395

Mill Creek MS 900/7-8
620 Central Ave N 98032 253-373-7446
Tammy Unruh, prin. Fax 373-7478
Millennium ES 600/K-6
11919 SE 270th St, 253-373-3900
Carla Janes, prin. Fax 373-3905
Neely-O'Brien ES 800/K-6
6300 S 236th St 98032 253-373-7434
Rosa Cabrera, prin. Fax 373-7458
Panther Lake ES 600/K-6
10200 SE 216th St 98031 253-373-7470
Beth Wallen, prin. Fax 373-7472
Park Orchard ES 500/K-6
11010 SE 232nd St 98031 253-373-7473
Patrick O'Connor, prin. Fax 373-7475
Pine Tree ES 500/K-6
27825 118th Ave SE, 253-373-7687
Dana Stiner, prin. Fax 373-7688
Scenic Hill ES 600/K-6
26025 Woodland Way S, 253-373-7479
Harjeet Sandhu-Fuller, prin. Fax 373-7481
Soos Creek ES 300/K-6
12651 SE 218th Pl 98031 253-373-7690
Brian Gauthier, prin. Fax 373-7692
Sortun ES 600/K-6
12711 SE 248th St, 253-373-7314
Greg Kroll, prin. Fax 373-7316
Springbrook ES 500/K-6
20035 100th Ave SE 98031 253-373-7485
Ashlie Short, prin. Fax 373-7487
Sunrise ES 500/K-6
22300 132nd Ave SE 98042 253-373-7630
Katharine Geiss, prin. Fax 373-7632
Other Schools – See Black Diamond, Covington, Renton

Sunbeams Lutheran S 100/PK-3
23810 112th Ave SE 98031 253-854-3240
Denise Pacilli, dir. Fax 854-2721

Kettle Falls, Stevens, Pop. 1,505
Kettle Falls SD 212 900/K-12
PO Box 458 99141 509-738-6625
Thaynan Knowlton, supt. Fax 738-6375
www.kfschools.org
Kettle Falls ES 300/K-4
PO Box 458 99141 509-738-6725
Valerie McKern, prin. Fax 738-4148
Kettle Falls MS 200/5-8
PO Box 458 99141 509-738-6014
Tracy Vining, prin. Fax 738-2401

Kingston, Kitsap, Pop. 2,022
North Kitsap SD 400
Supt. — See Poulsbo
Gordon ES 400/PK-5
26331 Barber Cut Off Rd NE 98346 360-396-3800
Karen Tollefson, prin. Fax 396-3950
Kingston MS 600/6-8
9000 NE West Kingston Rd 98346 360-396-3400
Craig Barry, prin. Fax 396-3945
Wolfle ES 400/PK-5
27089 Highland Rd NE 98346 360-396-3700
Ben Degnin, prin. Fax 396-3917

Kirkland, King, Pop. 46,527
Lake Washington SD 414
Supt. — See Redmond
Bell ES 300/K-5
11212 NE 112th St 98033 425-936-2510
Heidi Paul, prin. Fax 576-6342
Community ES 100/1-5
11133 NE 65th St 98033 425-936-2395
Margaret Kinney, prin. Fax 936-2398
Discovery Community S 100/K-5
12801 84th Ave NE 98034 425-936-2704
Lori Pierce, prin. Fax 814-0456
Environmental & Adventure S 100/6-8
8040 NE 132nd St 98034 425-936-2355
Victor Scarpelli, prin. Fax 825-0921
Finn Hill MS 600/6-8
8040 NE 132nd St 98034 425-936-2340
Victor Scarpelli, prin. Fax 814-2955
Franklin ES 400/K-5
12434 NE 60th St 98033 425-936-2550
Jimmy Cho, prin. Fax 739-0607
Frost ES 400/K-5
11801 NE 140th St 98034 425-936-2560
Toby Brenner, prin. Fax 821-4947
Juanita ES 300/K-5
9635 NE 132nd St 98034 425-936-2570
Dana Stairs, prin. Fax 820-2312
Kamiakin MS 500/6-8
14111 132nd Ave NE 98034 425-936-2400
Joe Joss, prin. Fax 823-2921
Keller ES 300/K-5
13820 108th Ave NE 98034 425-936-2580
Sandy Dennehy, prin. Fax 814-1540
Kirk ES 500/K-5
1312 6th St 98033 425-936-2590
Monica Garcia, prin. Fax 889-8359
Kirkland MS 600/6-8
430 18th Ave 98033 425-936-2420
Deborah McCarson, prin. Fax 889-1589
Lakeview ES 500/K-5
10400 NE 68th St 98033 425-936-2600
Heather Frazier, prin. Fax 827-2045
Muir ES 400/K-5
14012 132nd Ave NE 98034 425-936-2640
Jeff DeGallier, prin. Fax 814-1089
Northstar MS 100/6-8
10903 NE 53rd St 98033 425-936-2390
Nell Ballard-Jones, prin. Fax 936-2308
Rose Hill ES 400/K-5
8110 128th Ave NE 98033 425-936-2680
Jennifer Hodges, prin. Fax 822-7494
Sandburg ES 500/K-5
12801 84th Ave NE 98034 425-936-2700
Lori Pierce, prin. Fax 814-0456
Thoreau ES 300/K-5
8224 NE 138th St 98034 425-936-2720
Kerriann Levinson, prin. Fax 814-4986

Twain ES 600/K-5
9525 130th Ave NE 98033 425-936-2730
Craig Mott, prin. Fax 936-2736

Holy Family S 300/PK-8
7300 120th Ave NE 98033 425-827-0444
Jacqueline Degel, prin. Fax 827-0150
Kirkland SDA S 100/K-8
5320 108th Ave NE 98033 425-822-7554

Kittitas, Kittitas, Pop. 1,352
Kittitas SD 403 700/K-12
PO Box 599 98934 855-380-8844
Rich Stewart, supt. Fax 955-3120
www.ksd403.org
Kittitas ES 300/K-5
PO Box 599 98934 855-380-8843
Del Enders, prin. Fax 955-3130

Klickitat, Klickitat, Pop. 348
Klickitat SD 402 100/K-12
PO Box 37 98628 509-369-4145
Kevin Davis, supt. Fax 369-3422
www.klickitat.wednet.edu
Klickitat S 100/K-12
PO Box 37 98628 509-369-4145
Kevin Davis, admin. Fax 369-3422

La Center, Clark, Pop. 2,714
La Center SD 101 1,600/PK-12
PO Box 1840 98629 360-263-2131
David Holmes, supt. Fax 263-1140
www.lacenterschools.org
La Center ES 700/PK-5
PO Box 1810 98629 360-263-2134
Scott Lincoln, prin. Fax 263-2133
La Center MS 400/6-8
PO Box 1750 98629 360-263-2136
Lauri Landerholm, prin. Fax 263-5936

Lacey, Thurston, Pop. 39,269
North Thurston SD 3 13,900/PK-12
305 College St NE 98516 360-412-4400
Debra J. Clemens, supt. Fax 412-4410
www.nthurston.k12.wa.us
Aspire MS 300/6-8
5900 54th Ave SE 98513 360-412-4730
Courtney Crawford, prin. Fax 412-4739
Chambers Prairie ES 500/K-5
6501 Virginia St SE 98513 360-412-4720
Michael Suhling, prin. Fax 412-4729
Chinook MS 900/6-8
4301 6th Ave NE 98516 360-412-4760
Kirsten Rue, prin. Fax 412-4769
Evergreen Forest ES 500/K-5
3025 Marvin Rd SE 98503 360-412-4670
Stephanie Hollinger, prin. Fax 412-4679
Hawk ES 400/K-5
7600 5th Ave SE 98503 360-412-4610
Kathleen Delpino, prin. Fax 493-2801
Horizons ES 600/K-5
4601 67th Ave SE 98513 360-412-4710
Nate Grygorcewicz, prin. Fax 412-4719
Komachin MS 800/6-8
3650 College St SE 98503 360-412-4740
Deborah Sarver, prin. Fax 412-4749
Lacey ES 400/K-5
1800 Homann Dr SE 98503 360-412-4650
Gary Culbertson, prin. Fax 412-4659
Lakes ES 600/K-5
6211 Mullen Rd SE 98503 360-412-4600
Jami Roberts, prin. Fax 412-4609
Meadows ES 300/PK-5
836 Deerbrush Dr SE 98513 360-412-4690
Angie DeAguiar, prin. Fax 412-4699
Mountain View ES 600/PK-5
1900 College St SE 98503 360-412-4630
Heather McCarthy, prin. Fax 412-4639
Nisqually MS 600/6-8
8100 Steilacoom Rd SE 98503 360-412-4770
David Crane, prin. Fax 493-2756
Olympic View ES 700/K-5
1330 Horne St NE 98516 360-412-4660
Jason Greer, prin. Fax 412-4669
Pleasant Glade ES 500/K-5
1920 Abernethy Rd NE 98516 360-412-4620
Andrew Pitman, prin. Fax 412-4629
Salish MS 6-8
8605 Campus Glen Dr NE 98516 360-412-4780
Karen Owen, prin. Fax 412-4789
Seven Oaks ES 600/PK-5
1800 7 Oaks Rd SE 98503 360-412-4700
Rebecca Lee, prin. Fax 412-4709
South Bay ES 600/K-5
3845 Sleater Kinney Rd NE 98506 360-412-4640
Kate Cook, prin. Fax 412-4649
Woodland ES 500/K-5
4630 Carpenter Rd SE 98503 360-412-4680
Casey Crawford, prin. Fax 412-4689

Community Christian Academy 200/PK-8
4706 Park Center Ave NE 98516 360-493-2223
Kim DeLeon, prin. Fax 412-0910
Faith Lutheran S 200/PK-8
7075 Pacific Ave SE 98503 360-491-1733
Laura White, admin. Fax 292-6012
Holy Family S 100/PK-8
PO Box 3700 98509 360-491-7060
Monica Davis, prin. Fax 456-3725

La Conner, Skagit, Pop. 873
La Conner SD 311 600/K-12
PO Box 2103 98257 360-466-3171
Dr. Whitney Meissner, supt. Fax 466-3523
www.lcsd.wednet.edu
La Conner ES 300/K-5
PO Box 2103 98257 360-466-3172
Beverly Bowen, prin. Fax 466-2171
La Conner MS 100/6-8
PO Box 2103 98257 360-466-4113
Todd Torgeson, prin. Fax 466-0153

LaCrosse, Whitman, Pop. 304
LaCrosse SD 126 100/K-12
111 Hill Ave 99143 509-549-3591
Doug Curtis, supt. Fax 549-3529
www.lacrossesd.k12.wa.us
LaCrosse ES 50/K-5
111 Hill Ave 99143 509-549-3592
Jeff Pietila, prin. Fax 549-3529

Lakebay, Pierce
Peninsula SD 401
Supt. — See Gig Harbor
Evergreen ES 200/PK-5
1820 Key Peninsula Hwy S 98349 253-530-1300
Hugh Maxwell, prin. Fax 530-1320
Key Peninsula MS 400/6-8
5510 Key Peninsula Hwy N 98349 253-530-4200
Jeri Goebel, prin. Fax 530-4220

Lake Forest Park, King, Pop. 12,012
Shoreline SD 412
Supt. — See Shoreline
Brookside ES 500/K-6
17447 37th Ave NE, 206-393-4140
John Simard, prin. Fax 393-4149
Lake Forest Park ES 500/K-6
18500 37th Ave NE, 206-393-4130
Aimee Miner, prin. Fax 393-4139

Lake Stevens, Snohomish, Pop. 26,753
Lake Stevens SD 4 8,200/PK-12
12309 22nd St NE 98258 425-335-1500
Dr. Amy Beth Cook, supt. Fax 335-1549
www.lkstevens.wednet.edu
Early Learning Center PK-PK
9215 29th St NE 98258
Matt Wyant, dean
Glenwood ES 600/K-5
2221 103rd Ave SE 98258 425-335-1510
John Balmer, prin. Fax 335-1595
Highland ES 700/K-5
3220 113th Ave NE 98258 425-335-1585
Ryan Henderson, prin. Fax 335-1600
Hillcrest ES 800/K-5
9315 4th St SE 98258 425-335-1545
Steve Burleigh, prin. Fax 377-0453
Lake Stevens MS 600/6-7
1031 91st Ave SE 98258 425-335-1544
Lisa Sanchez, prin. Fax 335-1564
Mt. Pilchuck ES 600/PK-5
12806 20th St NE 98258 425-335-1525
Chris Larson, prin. Fax 397-0536
North Lake MS 700/6-7
2202 123rd Ave NE 98258 425-335-1530
Brad Abels, prin. Fax 335-1576
Skyline ES 500/K-5
1033 91st Ave SE 98258 425-335-1520
Dave Bartlow, prin. Fax 335-1587
Sunnycrest East ES 700/K-5
3411 99th Ave NE 98258 425-335-1535
Tim Haines, prin. Fax 377-0453

Zion Lutheran S 100/PK-8
3923 103rd Ave SE 98258 425-334-5064
Lynne Hereth, prin. Fax 334-4106

Lake Tapps, Pierce, Pop. 11,482
Dieringer SD 343 1,500/K-8
1320 178th Ave E, 253-862-2537
Dr. Judy Neumeier-Martinson, supt. Fax 862-8472
www.dieringer.wednet.edu
Dieringer Heights ES 500/K-K, 4-5
21727 34th St E, 253-826-4937
Kevin Anderson, prin. Fax 826-4908
Lake Tapps ES 500/1-3
1320 178th Ave E, 253-862-6600
Pat Webster, prin. Fax 862-3176
North Tapps MS 500/6-8
20029 12th St E, 253-862-2776
Nate Salisbury, prin. Fax 862-2587

Lakewood, Pierce, Pop. 52,506
Clover Park SD 400 10,700/PK-12
10903 Gravelly Lake Dr SW 98499 253-583-5000
Debbie LeBeau, supt. Fax 583-5198
www.cloverpark.k12.wa.us
Carter Lake ES 400/K-5
3420 Lincoln Blvd SW 98439 253-583-5210
Jeff Murrell, prin. Fax 583-5218
Custer ES 300/PK-5
7801 Steilacoom Blvd SW 98498 253-583-5230
Jane Al-Tamimi, prin. Fax 583-5238
Dower ES 300/PK-5
7817 John Dower Rd W 98499 253-583-5240
Megan Qualls, prin. Fax 583-5248
Four Heroes ES K-5
9101 Lakewood Dr SW 98499 253-583-5340
John Mitchell, admin. Fax 583-5348
Hudtloff MS 700/6-8
8102 Phillips Rd SW 98498 253-583-5400
Cindy Adams, prin. Fax 583-5408
Idlewild ES 400/K-5
10806 Idlewild Rd SW 98498 253-583-5290
Jim Pfeiffer, prin. Fax 583-5298
Lake Louise ES 300/K-5
11014 Holden Rd SW 98498 253-583-5310
Kristi Webster, prin. Fax 583-5318
Lakeview Hope Academy 500/K-5
10501 47th Ave SW 98499 253-583-5320
Meghan Eakin, prin. Fax 583-5328
Lochburn MS 600/6-8
5431 Steilacoom Blvd SW 98499 253-583-5420
Greg Wilson, prin. Fax 583-5428
Mann MS 400/6-8
11509 Holden Rd SW 98498 253-583-5440
Steve Seberson, prin. Fax 583-5448
Oakbrook ES 300/K-5
7802 83rd Ave SW 98498 253-583-5330
Sheri Warrick, prin. Fax 583-5338
Park Lodge ES 400/K-5
6300 100th St SW 98499 253-583-5350
Synette Melluzzo, prin. Fax 583-5358

Tillicum ES 300/PK-5
8514 Maple St SW 98498 253-583-5370
Jeff Miller, prin. Fax 583-5378
Tyee Park ES 500/K-5
11920 Seminole Rd SW 98499 253-583-5380
Sean Schoenfeldt, prin. Fax 583-5388
Woodbrook MS 500/6-8
14920 Spring St SW 98439 253-583-5460
Nancy LaChapelle, prin. Fax 583-5468
Other Schools – See Lewis McChord

St. Frances Cabrini S 200/PK-8
5621 108th St SW 98499 253-584-3850
Monica Des Jarlais, prin. Fax 584-3852

Lamont, Whitman, Pop. 66
Lamont SD 264 50/5-8
602 Main St 99017 509-257-2463
Joseph Whipple, supt. Fax 257-2316
www.spraguelamont.org
Lamont MS 50/5-8
602 Main St 99017 509-257-2463
Joseph Whipple, admin. Fax 257-2316

Langley, Island, Pop. 1,005
South Whidbey SD 206 1,400/K-12
5520 Maxwelton Rd 98260 360-221-6100
Dr. Josephine Moccia, supt. Fax 221-3835
www.sw.wednet.edu
South Whidbey ES 500/K-6
5380 Maxwelton Rd 98260 360-221-4600
Jeff Cravy, prin. Fax 221-6929
South Whidbey MS 300/7-8
5675 Maxwelton Rd 98260 360-221-4300
James Swanson, prin. Fax 221-5797

Island Christian Academy 100/PK-12
PO Box 1048 98260 360-221-0919
Brenda Chittim, dir. Fax 221-1653

Leavenworth, Chelan, Pop. 1,933
Cascade SD 228 1,300/PK-12
330 Evans St 98826 509-548-5885
Bill Motsenbocker, supt. Fax 548-6149
www.cascadesd.org
Beaver Valley ES 50/K-5
19265 Beaver Valley Rd 98826 509-763-3309
Kenny Renner-Singer Ed.D., prin. Fax 763-4347
Icicle River MS 300/6-8
10195 Titus Rd 98826 509-548-4042
Mike Janski, prin. Fax 548-6646
Osborn ES 300/3-5
225 Central Ave 98826 509-548-5839
Kenny Renner-Singer Ed.D., prin. Fax 548-6856
Other Schools – See Peshastin

Lewis McChord, Pierce, Pop. 10,018
Clover Park SD 400
Supt. — See Lakewood
Beachwood ES 600/K-5
8890 Concord Ave, 253-583-5260
Paula Gayson, prin. Fax 583-5268
Evergreen ES 600/PK-5
9020 Blaine St, 253-583-5250
Diana Dix, prin. Fax 583-5258
Hillside ES 400/K-5
61700 Garcia Blvd, 253-583-5280
David Young, prin. Fax 583-5288
Meriwether ES K-5
10285 Compass Ave, 253-583-5200
Leila Davis, prin. Fax 583-5208
Rainier ES K-5
2410 Stryker Ave, 253-583-5220
Kylie Danielson, prin. Fax 583-5228

Liberty Lake, Spokane, Pop. 7,369
Central Valley SD 356
Supt. — See Spokane Valley
Liberty Creek ES 200/K-3
23909 E Country Vista Dr 99019 509-558-5380
Kim Kyle, prin. Fax 558-5389
Liberty Lake ES 700/1-5
23606 E Boone Ave 99019 509-558-4300
Jen Tesky, prin. Fax 558-4311

Lind, Adams, Pop. 553
Lind-Ritzville SD 400/PK-12
PO Box 340 99341 509-677-3481
Matt Ellis, supt. Fax 677-3463
www.lrschools.org
Lind ES 100/PK-5
PO Box 340 99341 509-677-3481
Cindy Deska, prin. Fax 677-3463
Lind/Ritzville MS 50/6-8
PO Box 340 99341 509-677-3408
Cindy Deska, prin. Fax 677-3420
Other Schools – See Ritzville

Littlerock, Thurston
Tumwater SD 33
Supt. — See Tumwater
Littlerock ES 300/PK-5
PO Box 40 98556 360-709-7250
Glenn Spinnie, prin. Fax 709-7252

Long Beach, Pacific, Pop. 1,362
Ocean Beach SD 101 700/PK-12
PO Box 778 98631 360-642-3739
Jenny Risner, supt. Fax 642-1298
www.ocean.k12.wa.us
Long Beach ES 200/K-4
PO Box 758 98631 360-642-3242
Cathy Meinhardt, prin. Fax 642-1226
Ocean Beach ECC 50/PK-PK
PO Box 758 98631 360-642-4089
Dixie Miniken, coord. Fax 642-8970
Other Schools – See Ilwaco, Ocean Park

Longview, Cowlitz, Pop. 35,373
Kelso SD 458
Supt. — See Kelso
Beacon Hill ES 500/K-5
257 Alpha Dr 98632 360-501-1450
Jay Sparks, prin. Fax 501-1455

Longview SD 122 6,600/K-12
2715 Lilac St 98632 360-575-7000
Dr. Dan Zorn, supt. Fax 575-7022
www.longview.k12.wa.us
Cascade MS 500/6-8
2821 Parkview Dr 98632 360-577-2701
Chris Rugg, prin. Fax 577-2790
Columbia Heights ES 400/K-5
2820 Parkview Dr 98632 360-575-7461
Stephanie Casillas, prin. Fax 575-7465
Columbia Valley Gardens ES 400/K-5
2644 30th Ave 98632 360-575-7502
Aaron Whitright, prin. Fax 575-7503
Gray ES 500/K-5
4622 Ohio St 98632 360-575-7302
Dr. Lori Larson, prin. Fax 575-7350
Kessler ES 400/K-5
1902 E Kessler Blvd 98632 360-575-7580
Noma Hudson, prin. Fax 575-7544
Mint Valley ES 400/K-5
2745 38th Ave 98632 360-575-7581
Jean Merritt, prin. Fax 575-7596
Monticello MS 500/6-8
1225 28th Ave 98632 360-575-7050
Scott Merzoian, prin. Fax 575-7220
Mt. Solo MS 500/6-8
5300 Mt Solo Rd 98632 360-577-2800
Jay Opgrande, prin. Fax 577-2888
Northlake ES 400/K-5
2210 Olympia Way 98632 360-501-8700
Dr. Cora Lazo, prin. Fax 575-7633
Olympic ES 400/K-5
1324 30th Ave 98632 360-575-7084
Michael Mendenhall, prin. Fax 575-7088
St. Helens ES 300/K-5
431 27th Ave 98632 360-575-7362
Megan Shea, prin. Fax 575-7412

St. Rose S 200/PK-8
720 26th Ave 98632 360-577-6760
Catherine Strader, prin. Fax 577-3689
Three Rivers Christian S 100/PK-7
2610 Ocean Beach Hwy 98632 360-423-4510
Erin Hart, admin. Fax 423-4512

Loon Lake, Stevens, Pop. 761
Loon Lake SD 183 100/PK-6
4001 Maple St 99148 509-233-2212
Brad Van Dyne, supt. Fax 233-2537
www.loonlakeschool.org
Loon Lake ES 100/PK-6
4001 Maple St 99148 509-233-2212
Brad Van Dyne, admin. Fax 233-2537

Lopez Island, San Juan
Lopez Island SD 144 200/K-12
86 School Rd 98261 360-468-2202
Brian Auckland, supt. Fax 468-2212
www.lopezislandschool.org
Lopez Island ES 100/K-5
86 School Rd 98261 360-468-2202
Brian Auckland, prin. Fax 468-2235
Other Schools – See Anacortes

Lummi Island, Whatcom
Ferndale SD 502
Supt. — See Ferndale
Beach ES 50/K-5
3786 Centerview Rd 98262 360-383-9440
Mark Hall, prin. Fax 383-9442

Lyle, Klickitat, Pop. 484
Lyle SD 406 200/K-12
PO Box 368 98635 509-365-2191
Andrew Kelly, supt. Fax 365-2665
www.lyleschools.org
Dallesport ES 100/K-5
PO Box 368 98635 509-365-2211
Andrew Kelly, prin. Fax 365-2665
Lyle MS 50/6-8
PO Box 522 98635 509-365-2211
Andrew Kelly, prin. Fax 365-2665

Lyman, Skagit, Pop. 434
Sedro-Woolley SD 101
Supt. — See Sedro Woolley
Lyman ES 200/K-6
PO Box 1308 98263 360-855-3535
Scott McPhee, prin. Fax 855-3536

Lynden, Whatcom, Pop. 11,746
Lynden SD 504 2,700/K-12
1203 Bradley Rd 98264 360-354-4443
Jim Frey, supt. Fax 354-7662
www.lynden.wednet.edu
Fisher ES 300/K-5
501 14th St 98264 360-354-4291
Courtney Ross, prin. Fax 354-0952
Isom ES 400/K-5
8461 Benson Rd 98264 360-354-1992
Patrick McClure, prin. Fax 354-5494
Lynden MS 600/6-8
516 Main St 98264 360-354-2952
Molly Mitchell-Mumma, prin. Fax 354-6631
Vossbeck ES 500/K-5
1301 Bridgeview Dr 98264 360-354-0488
Becky Midboe, prin. Fax 318-8318

Meridian SD 505
Supt. — See Bellingham
Meridian MS 300/6-8
861 Ten Mile Rd 98264 360-398-2291
Gerald Sanderson, prin. Fax 398-8131

Cornerstone Christian S 100/1-12
8872 Northwood Rd 98264 360-318-0663
Darryn Kleyn, prin. Fax 318-8175
Ebenezer Christian S 100/PK-8
9390 Guide Meridian Rd 98264 360-354-2632
Jim Buss, prin. Fax 354-7093
Lynden Christian ES 500/PK-4
307 Drayton St 98264 360-354-5492
Don Van Maanen, prin. Fax 354-6690
Lynden Christian MS 300/5-8
503 Lyncs Dr 98264 360-354-3358
Aaron Bishop, prin. Fax 354-6690

Lynnwood, Snohomish, Pop. 34,119
Edmonds SD 15 19,700/PK-12
20420 68th Ave W 98036 425-431-7000
Kris McDuffy, supt. Fax 431-7006
www.edmonds.wednet.edu
Alderwood ECC PK-PK
2000 200th Pl SW 98036 425-431-7595
Dennis Burkhardt, admin. Fax 431-7591
Alderwood MS 700/7-8
1132 172nd St SW 98037 425-431-7579
Brian Stewart, prin. Fax 431-7580
Beverly ES 500/K-6
5221 168th St SW 98037 425-431-7732
Danielle Sanders, prin. Fax 431-7738
Cedar Valley Community ES 400/K-6
19200 56th Ave W 98036 425-431-7390
C.J. Gray, prin. Fax 431-7395
College Place ES 500/K-6
20401 76th Ave W 98036 425-431-7620
Scott Morrison, prin. Fax 431-7626
College Place MS 500/7-8
7501 208th St SW 98036 425-431-7451
Sam Yuhan, prin. Fax 431-7449
Hazelwood ES 500/K-6
3300 204th St SW 98036 425-431-7884
Dr. Tim Parnell, prin. Fax 431-7883
Hilltop ES 500/K-6
20425 Damson Rd 98036 425-431-7604
Janie O'Brien, prin. Fax 431-7608
Lynndale ES 400/K-6
19030 72nd Ave W 98036 425-431-7365
Chris Fulford, prin. Fax 431-7363
Lynnwood ES 600/K-6
18638 44th Ave W 98037 425-431-7615
Chris Lindblom, prin. Fax 431-7617
Martha Lake ES 600/K-6
17500 Larch Way 98037 425-431-7766
Tom Trexel, prin. Fax 431-7764
Meadowdale ES 500/K-6
6505 168th St SW 98037 425-431-7754
Daniel Davis, prin. Fax 431-7758
Meadowdale MS 700/7-8
6500 168th St SW 98037 425-431-7707
Joe Webster, prin. Fax 431-7714
Oak Heights ES 500/K-6
15500 18th Ave W, 425-431-7744
Susan Ardissono, prin. Fax 431-7747
Spruce ES 500/K-6
17405 Spruce Way 98037 425-431-7720
Emily Moore, prin. Fax 431-7726
Other Schools – See Brier, Edmonds, Mountlake Terrace

Mukilteo SD 6
Supt. — See Everett
Lake Stickney ES 700/K-5
1625 Madison Way, 425-366-3600
Lynn Olsen, prin. Fax 366-3602

Cedar Park Christian S - Lynwood 100/PK-6
17931 64th Ave W 98037 425-742-9518
Jan Isakson, prin. Fax 745-9306
Cypress Adventist S 100/K-8
21500 Cypress Way 98036 425-775-3578
St. Thomas More S 300/PK-8
6511 176th St SW 98037 425-743-4242
Teresa Fewel, prin. Fax 745-8367
Soundview S 100/PK-8
6515 196th St SW 98036 425-778-8572

Mabton, Yakima, Pop. 2,272
Mabton SD 120 800/K-12
PO Box 37 98935 509-894-4852
Minerva Morales, supt. Fax 894-4769
www.msd120.org
Artz-Fox ES 500/K-6
PO Box 40 98935 509-894-4941
Angie Ozuna, prin. Fax 894-5110

Mc Cleary, Grays Harbor, Pop. 1,608
McCleary SD 65 300/PK-8
611 S Main St 98557 360-495-3204
Dan Casler, supt. Fax 495-4589
www.mccleary.wednet.edu
McCleary S 300/PK-8
611 S Main St 98557 360-495-3204
Rick Brownell, prin. Fax 495-4589

Mc Kenna, Pierce, Pop. 685
Yelm Community SD 2
Supt. — See Yelm
McKenna ES 500/K-6
35120 State Route 507 S 98558 360-458-2400
Kari Martin, prin. Fax 458-6282

Mansfield, Douglas, Pop. 319
Mansfield SD 207 100/PK-12
PO Box 188 98830 509-683-1012
Mike Messenger, supt. Fax 683-1281
www.mansfield.wednet.edu/
Mansfield S 100/PK-12
PO Box 188 98830 509-683-1012
Shane Bird, admin. Fax 683-1281

Manson, Chelan, Pop. 1,456
Manson SD 19 700/PK-12
PO Box A 98831 509-687-3140
Matt Charlton, supt. Fax 687-9877
www.manson.org
Manson ES 300/PK-5
PO Box A 98831 509-687-9502
Keitlyn Watson, prin. Fax 687-9537

Manson MS 100/6-8
PO Box A 98831 509-687-9585
Todd Smith, prin. Fax 687-6109

Maple Falls, Whatcom, Pop. 316
Mt. Baker SD 507
Supt. — See Deming
Kendall ES 400/K-6
7547 Kendall Rd 98266 360-383-2055
Susan Gribble, prin. Fax 383-2059

Maple Valley, King, Pop. 21,591
Tahoma SD 409 7,800/PK-12
25720 Maple Valley Black Di 98038 425-413-3400
Rob Morrow, supt. Fax 413-3455
www.tahomasd.us
Cedar River ES 600/K-5
22615 Sweeney Rd SE 98038 425-413-5400
Fritz Gere, prin. Fax 413-5455
Glacier Park ES 900/K-5
23700 SE 280th St 98038 425-413-3700
Shelly Gaston, prin. Fax 413-3798
Lake Wilderness ES 1,100/PK-5
24216 Witte Rd SE 98038 425-413-3500
Dr. Audrey Meyers, prin. Fax 413-3555
Rock Creek ES 900/K-5
25700 Maple Valley Black Di 98038 425-413-3300
Chris Thomas, prin. Fax 413-3355
Shadow Lake ES 600/K-5
22620 Sweeney Rd SE 98038 425-413-6100
Mike Hanson, prin. Fax 413-6113
Tahoma ES 600/K-5
24425 SE 216th St 98038 425-413-3600
Jerry Gaston, prin. Fax 413-3655
Other Schools – See Covington, Ravensdale

Marysville, Snohomish, Pop. 56,950
Lakewood SD 306 2,400/PK-12
17110 16th Dr NE 98271 360-652-4500
Dr. Michael Mack, supt. Fax 652-4502
www.lwsd.wednet.edu
English Crossing ES 400/K-5
16728 16th Dr NE 98271 360-652-4515
Michelle Ricci, prin. Fax 654-2036
Lakewood ES 300/PK-5
17000 16th Dr NE 98271 360-652-4520
Susan Cotton, prin. Fax 654-2039
Lakewood MS 500/6-8
16800 16th Dr NE 98271 360-652-4510
Bryan Toutant, prin. Fax 652-4512
Other Schools – See Arlington

Marysville SD 25 10,600/PK-12
4220 80th St NE 98270 360-965-0000
Dr. Becky Berg, supt. Fax 965-0079
www.msd25.org
Allen Creek ES 500/K-5
6505 60th Dr NE 98270 360-965-1100
Janelle McFalls, prin. Fax 965-1104
Cascade ES 500/K-5
5200 100th St NE 98270 360-965-1200
Theresa Williams, prin. Fax 965-1204
Cedarcrest MS 900/6-8
6400 88th St NE 98270 360-965-0700
Stephanie Clark, prin. Fax 965-0704
Grove ES 500/K-5
6510 Grove St 98270 360-965-1700
Sharon Anderson, prin. Fax 965-1704
Kellogg Marsh ES 500/K-5
6325 91st St NE 98270 360-965-1900
Eneille Nelson, prin. Fax 965-1904
Liberty ES 500/PK-5
1919 10th St 98270 360-965-1800
Richard Middaugh, prin. Fax 965-1804
Marshall ES 400/PK-5
4407 116th St NE 98271 360-965-1600
Kelly Sheward, prin. Fax 965-1604
Marysville MS 800/6-8
4923 67th St NE 98270 360-965-0900
Angela Hansen, prin. Fax 965-0904
Pinewood ES 500/K-5
5115 84th St NE 98270 360-965-1300
Kathy Thornton, prin. Fax 965-1304
Quil Ceda & Tulalip ES 200/K-5
2415 74th St NE 98271 360-965-3100
Douglas Shook, prin. Fax 965-3104
Shoultes ES 500/PK-5
13525 51st Ave NE 98271 360-965-1400
Cory Taylor, prin. Fax 965-1404
Sunnyside ES 500/K-5
3707 Sunnyside Blvd 98270 360-965-1500
Brynn Marcum, prin. Fax 965-1504
Tenth Street MS 200/6-8
7204 27th Ave NE 98271 360-965-0400
Sonja Machovina, prin. Fax 965-0404
Totem MS 600/6-8
1605 7th St 98270 360-965-0500
Angela Deldago, prin. Fax 965-0504

Bethlehem Christian S 50/PK-1
7215 51st Ave NE 98270 360-653-2882
Kelly Stadum, dir. Fax 651-2772
Evangel Classical S 50/K-12
9015 44th Dr NE 98270 425-344-2789
Grace Academy 300/PK-12
8521 67th Ave NE 98270 360-659-8517
Timothy Lugg, prin. Fax 653-5899

Mattawa, Grant, Pop. 4,417
Wahluke SD 73 2,300/K-12
PO Box 907 99349 509-932-4565
Aaron Chavez, supt. Fax 932-4571
www.wsd73.wednet.edu
Mattawa ES 500/K-5
PO Box 907 99349 509-932-4433
Sean Langdon, prin. Fax 932-5265
Saddle Mountain ES 500/K-5
PO Box 907 99349 509-932-5693
Teri Davison, prin. Fax 932-4586
Schott ES 300/K-5
PO Box 907 99349 509-932-3877
Karl Edie, prin. Fax 932-3911
Wahluke JHS 500/6-8
PO Box 907 99349 509-932-4455
Andrew Harlow, prin. Fax 932-4282

Mead, Spokane, Pop. 7,091
Mead SD 354 9,100/K-12
2323 E Farwell Rd 99021 509-465-6000
Thomas Rockefeller, supt. Fax 465-6020
www.mead354.org
Meadow Ridge ES 600/K-6
15601 N Freya St 99021 509-465-6600
Shawn Worstell, prin. Fax 465-6620
Other Schools – See Colbert, Spokane

Medical Lake, Spokane, Pop. 4,877
Medical Lake SD 326 1,900/PK-12
PO Box 128 99022 509-565-3100
Timothy Ames, supt. Fax 565-3102
www.mlsd.org/
Hallett ES 400/K-5
PO Box 128 99022 509-565-3400
Cindy McSmith, prin. Fax 565-3401
Medical Lake MS 400/6-8
PO Box 128 99022 509-565-3300
Sylvia Campbell, prin. Fax 565-3301
Other Schools – See Fairchild AFB

Medina, King, Pop. 2,860
Bellevue SD 405
Supt. — See Bellevue
Medina ES 500/K-5
8001 NE 8th St 98039 425-456-5400
Laurie Harvey, prin. Fax 456-5404

Bellevue Christian Three Points ES 400/PK-6
7800 NE 28th St 98039 425-454-3977
Tony Bylenga, prin. Fax 454-5379
St. Thomas S 300/PK-8
8300 NE 12th St 98039 425-454-5880
Dr. Kirk Wheeler Ed.D., head sch Fax 454-1921

Mercer Island, King, Pop. 21,809
Mercer Island SD 400 4,400/PK-12
4160 86th Ave SE 98040 206-236-3300
Donna Colosky, supt. Fax 236-3333
www.mercerislandschools.org
Islander MS 1,100/6-8
7447 84th Ave SE 98040 206-236-3413
Mary Jo Budzius, prin. Fax 236-3408
Island Park ES 600/K-5
5437 Island Crest Way 98040 206-236-3410
David Hoffman, prin. Fax 230-6251
Lakeridge ES 600/K-5
8215 SE 78th St 98040 206-236-3415
Heidi Jenkins, prin. Fax 230-6232
Northwood ES K-5
4030 86th Ave SE 98040 206-275-5800
Aimee Batliner-Gillette, prin. Fax 275-5889
West Mercer ES 700/PK-5
4141 81st Ave SE 98040 206-236-3130
Carol Best, prin. Fax 230-6043

French-American S of Puget Sound 400/PK-8
3795 E Mercer Way 98040 206-275-3533
Eric Thuau, head sch Fax 812-0231
St. Monica S 200/PK-8
4320 87th Ave SE 98040 206-232-5432
Marybeth Bohm, prin. Fax 275-2874
Yellow Wood Academy 50/K-12
9655 SE 36th St Ste 101 98040 206-236-1095

Mesa, Franklin, Pop. 487
North Franklin SD J 51-162
Supt. — See Connell
Basin City ES 500/K-6
303 Bailie Blvd 99343 509-269-4224
Lisa Flatau, prin. Fax 269-4215
Mesa ES 200/K-6
200 E Pepiot Rd 99343 509-265-4229
Cara Morrill, prin. Fax 265-4238

Metaline Falls, Pend Oreille, Pop. 233
Selkirk SD 70 200/PK-12
PO Box 129 99153 509-446-2951
Nancy Lotze, supt. Fax 446-2929
www.selkirk.k12.wa.us
Selkirk ES 100/PK-5
PO Box 68 99153 509-446-4225
Nancy Lotze, admin. Fax 446-2929

Mill Creek, Snohomish, Pop. 17,443
Everett SD 2
Supt. — See Everett
Heatherwood MS 900/6-8
1419 Trillium Blvd SE 98012 425-385-6300
Laura Phillips, prin. Fax 385-6302
Mill Creek ES 700/K-5
3400 148th St SE 98012 425-385-6800
Brenda Fuglevand, prin. Fax 385-6802

Milton, Pierce, Pop. 6,594
Fife SD 417
Supt. — See Tacoma
Discovery PS 600/PK-1
1205 19th Ave 98354 253-517-1200
Julie Bartlett, prin. Fax 517-1205
Endeavour IS 600/2-5
1304 17th Ave 98354 253-517-1400
Joshua Goodman, prin. Fax 517-1405
Surprise Lake MS 500/6-7
2001 Milton Way 98354 253-517-1300
Jim Snider, prin. Fax 517-1305

Monroe, Snohomish, Pop. 16,699
Monroe SD 103 6,300/K-12
200 E Fremont St 98272 360-804-2500
Dr. Fredrika Smith, supt. Fax 804-2529
www.monroe.wednet.edu
Fryelands ES 500/K-5
15286 Fryelands Blvd SE 98272 360-804-3400
Jeff Presley, prin. Fax 804-3499
Park Place MS 800/6-8
1408 W Main St 98272 360-804-4300
Terry Cheshire, prin. Fax 804-4399
Salem Woods ES 500/K-5
12802 Wagner Rd 98272 360-804-3600
Janna Pope, prin. Fax 804-3699
Wagner ES 600/K-5
115 Dickinson Ave 98272 360-804-3200
Vikki Berard, prin. Fax 804-3299
Other Schools – See Snohomish

Monroe Christian S 100/PK-8
1009 W Main St 98272 360-794-8200
Elaine Obbink, admin. Fax 863-9270
Monroe Montessori S 100/PK-3
733 Village Way 98272 360-794-4622
Sky Valley Adventist S 50/PK-8
200 Academy Way 98272 360-794-7655

Montesano, Grays Harbor, Pop. 3,841
Montesano SD 66 1,200/PK-12
502 E Spruce Ave 98563 360-249-3942
Dan Winter, supt. Fax 841-7198
www.monteschools.org
Beacon Avenue ES 300/PK-2
1717 E Beacon Ave 98563 360-249-4528
Craig Loucks, prin. Fax 841-7526
Simpson IS 300/3-6
519 W Simpson Ave 98563 360-249-4331
Chris Cady, prin. Fax 841-7528

Grays Harbor Adventist Christian S 50/K-8
1216 US Highway 12 98563 360-249-1115

Morton, Lewis, Pop. 1,107
Morton SD 300/PK-12
PO Box 1219 98356 360-496-5300
John Hannah, supt. Fax 496-5399
www.morton.k12.wa.us
Morton ES 200/PK-6
PO Box 1299 98356 360-496-5143
Josh Brooks, prin. Fax 496-0327

Moses Lake, Grant, Pop. 19,890
Moses Lake SD 161 8,300/PK-12
920 W Ivy Ave 98837 509-766-2650
Dr. Josh Meek, supt. Fax 766-2678
www.mlsd161.org
Chief Moses MS 1,000/6-8
1111 E Nelson Rd 98837 509-766-2661
Vicki Swisher, prin. Fax 766-2680
Endeavor MS 300/6-8
6527 Patton Blvd NE 98837 509-766-2667
Ryan Pike, admin. Fax 766-2690
Frontier MS 800/6-8
517 W 3rd Ave 98837 509-766-2662
Greg Kittrell, prin. Fax 766-2663
Garden Heights ES 500/K-5
707 E Nelson Rd 98837 509-766-2651
Abe Ramirez, prin. Fax 766-3951
Knolls Vista ES 300/PK-5
454 W Ridge Rd 98837 509-766-2652
Nikki Mackey, prin. Fax 766-3955
Lakeview Terrace ES 400/K-5
780 S Clover Dr 98837 509-766-2653
Kristi Bateman, prin. Fax 766-3956
Larson Heights ES 300/PK-5
700 Lindberg Ln 98837 509-766-2655
Diana McFaul, prin. Fax 766-3960
Longview ES 400/K-5
9783 Apple Rd NE 98837 509-766-2656
Robbie Mason, prin. Fax 766-2665
Midway ES 400/PK-5
502 S C St 98837 509-766-2657
John Farley, prin. Fax 766-3952
North ES 300/K-5
1200 W Craig St 98837 509-766-2654
Kelly Frederick, prin. Fax 766-3958
Park Orchard ES 500/K-5
417 N Paxson Dr 98837 509-766-2699
Scott West, prin. Fax 766-2675
Peninsula ES 400/PK-5
2406 W Texas St 98837 509-766-2658
Sydney Richins, prin. Fax 766-3950
Sage Point ES 500/K-5
4000 W Peninsula Dr 98837 509-766-2444
Noreen Thomas, prin. Fax 766-2674

Crestview Christian S 50/K-9
1601 W Valley Rd 98837 509-765-4632
Moses Lake Christian Academy 200/PK-12
1475 Nelson Rd NE Ste A 98837 509-765-9704
Stephanie Voigt, dir. Fax 765-3693

Mossyrock, Lewis, Pop. 745
Mossyrock SD 206 500/K-12
PO Box 478 98564 360-983-3181
Dr. Lisa Grant, supt. Fax 983-8111
www.mossyrockschools.org
Mossyrock ES 300/K-6
PO Box 455 98564 360-983-3184
Randy Torrey, prin. Fax 983-8190

Mountlake Terrace, Snohomish, Pop. 18,701
Edmonds SD 15
Supt. — See Lynnwood
Cedar Way ES 400/K-6
22222 39th Ave W 98043 425-431-7864
Mary MacLean, prin. Fax 431-7862
Mountlake Terrace ES 500/K-6
22001 52nd Ave W 98043 425-431-7894
Doug Johnson, prin. Fax 431-7899
Terrace Park S 300/K-8
5409 228th St SW 98043 425-431-7482
Mary Freitas, prin. Fax 431-7486

Brighton S 300/PK-8
21705 58th Ave W 98043 425-640-7067
Dr. David Locke, prin. Fax 640-7445
St. Pius X S 100/PK-8
22105 58th Ave W 98043 425-778-9861
Clinton Parker, prin. Fax 776-2663

Mount Vernon, Skagit, Pop. 30,973
Conway SD 317 400/K-8
19710 State Route 534 98274 360-445-5785
Dr. Chris Pearson, supt. Fax 445-4511
www.conway.k12.wa.us
Conway S 400/K-8
19710 State Route 534 98274 360-445-5785
Brenda Naish, prin. Fax 445-4511

Mount Vernon SD 320 5,700/K-12
124 E Lawrence St 98273 360-428-6110
Carl Bruner, supt. Fax 428-6172
www.mountvernonschools.org/
Centennial ES 600/K-5
3100 E Martin Rd 98273 360-428-6138
Erwin Stroosma, prin. Fax 428-6158
Jefferson ES 500/K-5
1801 E Blackburn Rd 98274 360-428-6128
Tim Newall, prin. Fax 428-6159
LaVenture MS 400/6-8
1200 N Laventure Rd 98273 360-428-6116
Dave Riddle, prin. Fax 428-6189
Lincoln ES 300/K-5
1005 S 11th St 98274 360-428-6135
Henk Kruithof, prin. Fax 428-6170
Little Mountain ES 500/K-5
1514 S LaVenture Rd 98274 360-428-6125
Krista Paulson, prin. Fax 428-6164
Madison ES 600/K-5
907 E Fir St 98273 360-428-6131
Juan Gaona, prin. Fax 428-6171
Mount Baker MS 500/6-8
2310 E Section St 98274 360-428-6127
Evelyn Morse, prin. Fax 428-6155
Washington ES 400/K-5
1020 Mclean Rd 98273 360-428-6122
Marsha Hanson, prin. Fax 428-6162

Sedro-Woolley SD 101
Supt. — See Sedro Woolley
Big Lake ES 300/K-6
16802 Lake View Blvd 98274 360-855-3525
Jodee Anderson, prin. Fax 855-3526

Foothills Christian S 100/PK-8
PO Box 2537 98273 360-420-9749
Greg Wagner, prin.
Immaculate Conception Regional S 300/PK-8
1321 E Division St 98274 360-428-3912
Gwen Rodriguez, prin. Fax 424-8838
Mt. Vernon Christian S 300/PK-12
820 W Blackburn Rd 98273 360-424-9157
Jeffrey Droog, supt. Fax 424-9256

Moxee, Yakima, Pop. 3,240
East Valley SD 90
Supt. — See Yakima
Moxee ES 500/K-5
PO Box 69 98936 509-573-7700
Elizabeth Hockens, prin. Fax 573-7740

Mukilteo, Snohomish, Pop. 19,401
Mukilteo SD 6
Supt. — See Everett
Columbia ES 600/PK-5
10520 Harbour Pointe Blvd 98275 425-366-2600
Wendy Eidbo, prin. Fax 366-2602
Endeavour ES 500/K-5
12300 Harbour Pointe Blvd 98275 425-366-2800
Steve Raymond, prin. Fax 366-2802
Harbour Pointe MS 800/6-8
5000 Harbour Pointe Blvd 98275 425-366-5100
Kevin Rohrich, prin. Fax 366-5102
Mukilteo ES 700/K-5
2600 Mukilteo Speedway 98275 425-366-3100
Jack Sackett, prin. Fax 366-3102
Olympic View MS 800/6-8
2602 Mukilteo Speedway 98275 425-366-5200
Devin McLane, prin. Fax 366-5202

Naches, Yakima, Pop. 787
Naches Valley SD JT3 1,200/K-12
PO Box 99 98937 509-653-2220
Duane Lyons, supt. Fax 653-1211
www.nvsd.org
Naches Valley ES 300/K-4
151 Bonlow Dr 98937 509-653-1508
Allison Schnebly, prin. Fax 966-6004
Naches Valley MS 400/5-8
PO Box 39 98937 509-653-1599
Todd Hilmes, prin. Fax 653-2729

Napavine, Lewis, Pop. 1,693
Napavine SD 14 800/PK-12
PO Box 840 98565 360-262-3303
Geoff Parks, supt. Fax 262-9737
www.napavineschools.org
Napavine ES 400/PK-6
PO Box 837 98565 360-262-3345
Paul Lewis, prin. Fax 266-0452

Naselle, Pacific, Pop. 396
Naselle-Grays River Valley SD 155 200/K-12
793 State Route 4 98638 360-484-7121
Dr. Lisa Nelson, supt. Fax 484-3191
www.naselle.wednet.edu
Naselle-Grays River Valley S 100/K-12
793 State Route 4 98638 360-484-7121
Quinn Donlon, prin. Fax 484-3191

Neah Bay, Clallam, Pop. 795
Cape Flattery SD 401
Supt. — See Sekiu
Neah Bay ES 200/K-5
PO Box 86 98357 360-645-2382
Alice Murner, prin. Fax 645-2708

Nespelem, Okanogan, Pop. 227
Nespelem SD 14 100/PK-8
PO Box 291 99155 509-634-4541
Dr. Mary S. Hall, supt. Fax 634-4551
www.nsdeagles.org
Nespelem ES 100/PK-8
PO Box 291 99155 509-634-4541
Debra Pankey, prin. Fax 634-4551

Newcastle, King, Pop. 9,833
Issaquah SD 411
Supt. — See Issaquah
Newcastle ES 600/K-5
8400 136th Ave SE 98059 425-837-5800
Richard Mellish, prin. Fax 837-5850

Renton SD 403
Supt. — See Renton
Hazelwood ES 500/K-5
7100 116th Ave SE 98056 425-204-4550
Tracey Naylor-Tymczyszyn, prin. Fax 204-4561

Newman Lake, Spokane
East Valley SD 361
Supt. — See Spokane Valley
East Farms ES 400/K-6
26203 E Rowan Ave 99025 509-226-3039
Tammy Fuller, prin. Fax 226-3668

Newport, Pend Oreille, Pop. 2,055
Newport SD 56-415 1,000/PK-12
PO Box 70 99156 509-447-3167
Dave Smith, supt. Fax 447-2553
www.newport.wednet.edu
Halstead MS 300/5-8
PO Box 70 99156 509-447-2426
Tony Moser, prin. Fax 447-4914
Stratton ES 400/PK-4
PO Box 70 99156 509-447-0656
Jennifer Erickson, prin. Fax 447-2612

Nine Mile Falls, Spokane
Nine Mile Falls SD 325 1,500/PK-12
10110 W Charles Rd 99026 509-340-4300
Brian Talbott, supt. Fax 340-4301
www.9mile.org
Lakeside MS 400/6-8
6169 Highway 291 99026 509-340-4100
Jeff Baerwald, prin. Fax 340-4101
Lake Spokane ES 500/PK-5
6015 Highway 291 99026 509-340-4040
Kevin Simpson, prin. Fax 340-4041
Nine Mile Falls ES 200/K-5
10102 W Charles Rd 99026 509-340-4010
Keith Browning, prin. Fax 340-4011

Nooksack, Whatcom, Pop. 1,290
Nooksack Valley SD 506
Supt. — See Everson
Nooksack Valley MS 300/6-8
404 W Columbia St 98276 360-966-7561
Joel VanderYacht, prin. Fax 966-7805

Normandy Park, King, Pop. 6,064
Highline SD 401
Supt. — See Burien
Marvista ES 600/K-6
19800 Marine View Dr SW 98166 206-631-4200
Melissa Pointer, prin. Fax 631-4259

North Bend, King, Pop. 5,558
Snoqualmie Valley SD 410
Supt. — See Snoqualmie
North Bend ES 600/K-5
400 E 3rd St 98045 425-831-8400
Stephanie Shepherd, prin. Fax 831-8410
Opstad ES 600/PK-5
1345 Stilson Ave SE 98045 425-831-8300
Ryan Hill, prin. Fax 831-8333
Twin Falls MS 700/6-8
46910 SE Middle Fork Rd 98045 425-831-4150
Jeffrey D'Ambrosio, prin. Fax 831-4140

Northport, Stevens, Pop. 287
Northport SD 211 200/K-12
PO Box 1280 99157 509-732-4251
Don Baribault, supt. Fax 732-6606
www.northportschools.org
Northport ES 100/K-8
PO Box 1280 99157 509-732-4251
Terry Carlson, prin. Fax 732-6606

Oakesdale, Whitman, Pop. 413
Oakesdale SD 324 100/PK-12
PO Box 228 99158 509-285-5296
Dr. Jake Dingman, supt. Fax 285-5121
www.gonighthawks.net
Oakesdale ES 100/PK-5
PO Box 228 99158 509-285-5296
Dr. Jake Dingman, supt. Fax 285-5121

Oak Harbor, Island, Pop. 20,413
Oak Harbor SD 201 5,200/PK-12
350 S Oak Harbor St 98277 360-279-5000
Dr. Lance Gibbon, supt. Fax 279-5070
www.ohsd.net
Broad View ES 500/K-5
473 SW Fairhaven Dr 98277 360-279-5250
Jennifer Mouw, prin. Fax 279-5299
Crescent Harbor ES 500/K-5
330 E Crescent Harbor Rd 98277 360-279-5650
Kate Valenzuela, prin. Fax 279-5699
Hillcrest ES 600/K-5
1500 NW 2nd Ave 98277 360-279-5200
Paula Seaman, prin. Fax 279-5249
North Whidbey MS 500/6-8
67 NE Izett St 98277 360-279-5500
William Weinsheimer, prin. Fax 279-5516
Oak Harbor ES 500/PK-5
151 SE Midway Blvd 98277 360-279-5100
Dorothy Day, prin. Fax 279-5149
Oak Harbor MS 600/6-8
150 SW 6th Ave 98277 360-279-5300
Raenette Wood, prin. Fax 279-5399
Olympic View ES 400/K-5
380 NE Regatta Dr 98277 360-279-5150
Laura Aesoph, prin. Fax 279-5199

Oak Harbor Christian S 200/PK-6
675 E Whidbey Ave 98277 360-675-2831
Sherry Fakkema, admin. Fax 675-4216
Whidbey Christian S 50/1-8
31830 State Route 20 98277 360-279-1812

Oakville, Grays Harbor, Pop. 661
Oakville SD 400 300/K-12
PO Box H 98568 360-273-0171
Rich Staley, supt. Fax 273-6724
oakvilleschools.org
Oakville ES 100/K-6
PO Box H 98568 360-273-5946
Rich Staley, admin. Fax 858-1359

Ocean Park, Pacific, Pop. 1,545
Ocean Beach SD 101
Supt. — See Long Beach
Ocean Park ES 200/K-4
PO Box 1220 98640 360-665-4815
Kara Powell, prin. Fax 665-1275

Ocean Shores, Grays Harbor, Pop. 5,358
North Beach SD 64 600/PK-12
PO Box 159 98569 360-289-2447
Deborah Holcomb, supt. Fax 289-2492
www.northbeachschools.org
North Beach JHS 100/7-8
PO Box 969 98569 360-289-3888
Lynn Buedefeldt, prin. Fax 289-0996
Ocean Shores ES 200/PK-6
300 Mount Olympus Ave SE 98569 360-289-2147
Rhonda Ham, prin. Fax 289-0120
Other Schools – See Pacific Beach

Odessa, Lincoln, Pop. 895
Odessa SD 105-157-166 J 200/PK-12
PO Box 248 99159 509-982-2668
Dan Read, supt. Fax 982-0163
www.odessa.wednet.edu
Jantz ES 100/PK-6
PO Box 248 99159 509-982-2603
Jamie Nelson, prin. Fax 982-0163

Okanogan, Okanogan, Pop. 2,464
Okanogan SD 105 1,000/K-12
PO Box 592 98840 509-422-3629
Dr. Richard Johnson, supt. Fax 422-1525
www.oksd.wednet.edu
Grainger ES 500/K-5
PO Box 592 98840 509-422-3580
Ashley Goetz, prin. Fax 422-1639
Okanogan MS 300/6-8
PO Box 592 98840 509-422-2680
Brett Baum, prin. Fax 422-0068

Olalla, Kitsap
South Kitsap SD 402
Supt. — See Port Orchard
Olalla ES 300/K-5
6100 SE Denny Bond Blvd 98359 360-443-3350
Ted Macomber, prin. Fax 443-3399

Olympia, Thurston, Pop. 44,308
Griffin SD 324 700/K-8
6530 33rd Ave NW 98502 360-866-2515
Greg Woods, supt. Fax 866-9684
www.griffinschool.us
Griffin S 700/K-8
6530 33rd Ave NW 98502 360-866-2515
Greg Woods, supt. Fax 866-9684

Olympia SD 111 9,300/PK-12
1113 Legion Way SE 98501 360-596-6100
Dr. Patrick C. Murphy Ed.D., supt. Fax 596-6111
osd.wednet.edu
Boston Harbor ES 100/PK-5
7300 Zangle Rd NE 98506 360-596-6200
Jennifer Brotherton, prin. Fax 596-6201
Brown ES 300/PK-5
2000 26th Ave NW 98502 360-596-6800
Charleen Hayes, prin. Fax 596-6801
Centennial ES 500/K-5
2637 45th Ave SE 98501 360-596-8300
Shannon Ritter, prin. Fax 596-8301
Garfield ES 300/K-5
325 Plymouth St NW 98502 360-596-6900
Brendon Chertok, prin. Fax 596-6901
Hansen ES 500/K-5
1919 Road 65 NW 98502 360-596-7400
Ernie Rascon, prin. Fax 596-7401
Jefferson MS 400/6-8
2200 Conger Ave NW 98502 360-596-3200
Michael Cimino, prin. Fax 596-3201
Lincoln ES 300/K-5
213 21st Ave SE 98501 360-596-6400
Marcella Abadi, prin. Fax 596-6401
Madison ES 200/K-5
1225 Legion Way SE 98501 360-596-6300
Domenico Spatola-Knoll, prin. Fax 596-6301
Marshall MS 400/6-8
3939 20th Ave NW 98502 360-596-7600
Condee Wood, prin. Fax 596-7601
McKenny ES 400/PK-5
3250 Morse Merryman Rd SE 98501 360-596-8400
Michael Havens, prin. Fax 596-8401
McLane ES 300/PK-5
200 Delphi Rd SW 98502 360-596-6600
Monica West, prin. Fax 596-6601
Pioneer ES 400/K-5
1655 Carlyon Ave SE 98501 360-596-6500
Joel Lang, prin. Fax 596-6501

Reeves MS 400/6-8
2200 Quince St NE 98506 360-596-3400
Aaron Davis, prin. Fax 596-3401
Roosevelt ES 400/PK-5
1417 San Francisco Ave NE 98506 360-596-6700
Sean Shaughnessy, prin. Fax 596-6701
Washington MS 700/6-8
3100 Cain Rd SE 98501 360-596-3000
Paul Anders, prin. Fax 596-3001

Tumwater SD 33
Supt. — See Tumwater
Black Lake ES 500/PK-5
6345 Black Lake Blmre Rd SW 98512 360-709-7350
Misty Hinkle, prin. Fax 709-7352
East Olympia ES 500/PK-5
8700 Rich Rd SE 98501 360-709-7150
Patricia Kilmer, prin. Fax 709-7152

Cornerstone Christian S 100/PK-8
5005 Lacey Blvd SE 98503 360-923-0071
Tricia Davis, admin. Fax 923-9307
Evergreen Christian S 500/PK-8
1010 Black Lake Blvd SW 98502 360-357-5590
Cyndi Pollard, prin. Fax 596-5864
NOVA S 100/6-8
2020 22nd Ave SE 98501 360-491-7097
Barbara Hutton, head sch Fax 491-0775
Olympia Christian S 100/PK-8
1215 Ethel St NW 98502 360-352-1831
Sharron Schwartz, prin. Fax 352-1195
Olympia Waldorf S 200/PK-8
8126 Normandy St SE 98501 360-493-0906
St. Michael S 300/PK-8
1204 11th Ave SE 98501 360-754-5131
Connor Geraghty, prin. Fax 753-6090

Omak, Okanogan, Pop. 4,701
Omak SD 19 2,200/PK-12
PO Box 833 98841 509-826-0320
Dr. Erik Swanson, supt. Fax 826-7689
www.omaksd.org
East Omak ES 300/3-5
PO Box 833 98841 509-826-3003
Dr. Ryan Christoph, prin. Fax 826-8231
ECC PK-PK
PO Box 833 98841 509-826-4908
Sheila Crowder, coord. Fax 826-8166
North Omak ES 400/K-2
PO Box 833 98841 509-826-2380
Jack Schneider, prin. Fax 826-8166
Omak MS 300/6-8
PO Box 833 98841 509-826-2320
Dr. Chris Blackman, prin. Fax 826-7696

Omak Adventist Christian S 50/1-8
PO Box 3294 98841 509-826-5341

Onalaska, Lewis, Pop. 606
Onalaska SD 300 600/PK-12
540 Carlisle Ave 98570 360-978-4111
Jeff Davis, supt. Fax 978-4185
www.onysd.wednet.edu
Onalaska ES 300/PK-5
540 Carlisle Ave 98570 360-978-4111
Stephanie Teel, prin. Fax 978-6142
Onalaska MS 200/6-8
540 Carlisle Ave 98570 360-978-4111
Kristin Soderback, prin. Fax 978-6142

Orient, Ferry, Pop. 111
Orient SD 65 100/PK-8
365 Main St 99160 509-684-6873
Sherry Cowbrough, supt. Fax 684-3469
orientsd.org
Orient ES 50/PK-8
365 Main St 99160 509-684-6873
Sherry Cowbrough, admin. Fax 684-3469

Orondo, Douglas
Orondo SD 13 200/PK-8
100 Orondo School Rd 98843 509-784-2443
Ismael Vivanco, supt. Fax 784-0633
www.orondo.wednet.edu/
Orondo S 200/PK-8
100 Orondo School Rd 98843 509-784-1333
Millie Watkins, prin. Fax 784-0633

Oroville, Okanogan, Pop. 1,653
Oroville SD 410 600/PK-12
816 Juniper St 98844 509-476-2281
Jeff Hardesty, supt. Fax 476-2190
www.oroville.wednet.edu
Oroville ES 300/PK-6
816 Juniper St 98844 509-476-3332
Jamie Mikelson, prin. Fax 476-3832

Orting, Pierce, Pop. 6,443
Orting SD 344 2,300/PK-12
121 Whitesell St NE 98360 360-893-6500
Dr. Marci Shepard, supt. Fax 893-2300
www.ortingschools.org
Orting MS 600/6-8
111 Whitehawk Blvd NW 98360 360-893-3565
David Slagle, prin. Fax 893-2919
Orting PS 500/PK-3
316 Washington Ave N 98360 360-893-2248
Lisa Couch, prin. Fax 893-4409
Ptarmigan Ridge ES 500/K-5
805 Old Pioneer Way NW 98360 360-893-0595
Alicia Jensen, prin. Fax 893-0603

Othello, Adams, Pop. 7,325
Othello SD 147-163-55 4,000/K-12
1025 S 1st Ave 99344 509-488-2659
Dr. Chris Hurst, supt. Fax 488-5876
www.othelloschools.org
Hiawatha ES 500/K-5
506 N 7th Ave 99344 509-488-3389
John Wiseman, prin. Fax 488-6784

Lutacaga ES 500/K-5
795 S 7th Ave 99344 509-488-9669
Aurora Garza, prin. Fax 488-6783
McFarland MS 800/6-8
790 S 10th Ave 99344 509-488-3326
Dennis Adams, prin. Fax 488-6788
Scootney Springs ES 500/K-5
695 S 14th Ave 99344 509-488-9625
Jennifer Garza, prin. Fax 488-6785
Wahitis ES 500/K-5
905 S 14th Ave 99344 509-764-1200
Alejandro Vergara, prin. Fax 488-3002

Otis Orchards, Spokane, Pop. 5,811
East Valley SD 361
Supt. — See Spokane Valley
Otis Orchards ES 400/K-6
22000 E Wellesley Ave 99027 509-924-9823
Suzanne Savall, prin. Fax 926-0786

Outlook, Yakima, Pop. 285
Sunnyside SD 201
Supt. — See Sunnyside
Outlook ES 600/1-5
3800 Van Belle Rd 98938 509-837-3352
Maria Hernandez, prin. Fax 837-7895

Pacific, King, Pop. 6,168
Auburn SD 408
Supt. — See Auburn
Alpac ES 500/K-5
310 Milwaukee Blvd N 98047 253-931-4976
Jim Riley, prin. Fax 931-4720

Pacific Beach, Grays Harbor, Pop. 268
North Beach SD 64
Supt. — See Ocean Shores
Pacific Beach ES 100/PK-6
PO Box 338 98571 360-276-4512
Lynette Reime, prin. Fax 276-4510

Palisades, Douglas
Palisades SD 102 50/K-5
1114 Palisades Rd 98845 509-884-8071
Dr. Ismael Vivanco, supt. Fax 886-0615
www.palisades.wednet.edu
Palisades ES 50/K-5
1114 Palisades Rd 98845 509-884-8071
Dr. Ismael Vivanco, prin. Fax 886-0615

Palouse, Whitman, Pop. 974
Palouse SD 301 200/PK-12
600 E Alder St 99161 509-878-1921
Calvin Johnson, supt. Fax 878-1948
www.garpal.net
Palouse ES 100/PK-5
600 E Alder St 99161 509-878-1921
Mike Jones, prin. Fax 878-1675

Pasco, Franklin, Pop. 58,798
Pasco SD 1 15,800/K-12
1215 W Lewis St 99301 509-543-6700
Michelle Whitney, supt. Fax 546-6728
www.psd1.org
Angelou ES 900/K-6
6001 N Road 84 99301 509-543-6748
Diana Cissne, prin. Fax 543-6749
Chess ES 600/K-6
715 N 24th Ave 99301 509-543-6789
Dora Noble, prin. Fax 546-2897
Curie STEM ES 3-6
715 N California Ave 99301 509-416-7810
Valerie Aragon, prin.
Emerson ES 600/K-6
1616 W Octave St 99301 509-543-6792
Brooke Schuldheisz, prin. Fax 546-2698
Franklin STEM ES 800/K-6
6010 N Road 52 99301 509-416-7114
Deidre Holmberg, prin. Fax 416-7811
Frost ES 600/K-6
1915 N 22nd Ave 99301 509-543-6795
Nora Flores, prin. Fax 546-2837
Gray STEM ES 500/K-6
1102 N 10th Ave 99301 509-547-2474
Armando Castrellon, prin. Fax 546-2695
Livingston ES 900/K-6
2515 N Road 84 99301 509-546-2688
Scott Raab, prin. Fax 546-2690
Longfellow ES 600/K-6
301 N 10th Ave 99301 509-547-2429
Claudia Serrano, prin. Fax 543-6793
Markham ES 400/K-6
4031 Elm Rd 99301 509-543-6790
Kim Mahaffey, prin. Fax 543-6791
McClintock STEM ES K-6
5706 Road 60 99301 509-416-7808
Jaime Morales, prin.
McGee ES 1,000/K-6
4601 Horizon Dr 99301 509-547-6583
Wendy Locholt Polstor, prin. Fax 546-2841
McLoughlin MS 1,100/7-8
2803 N Road 88 99301 509-547-4542
Dominique Dennis, prin. Fax 543-6797
Ochoa MS 700/7-8
1801 E Sheppard St 99301 509-543-6742
Jackie Ramirez, prin. Fax 543-6744
Robinson ES, 125 S Wehe Ave 99301 800/K-6
Wendi Manthei, prin. 509-543-6086
Stevens MS 600/7-8
1120 N 22nd Ave 99301 509-543-6798
Raquel Martinez, prin. Fax 546-2854
Twain ES 800/K-6
1801 N Road 40 99301 509-543-6794
Barbara Pierce, prin. Fax 546-2847
Whittier ES 400/K-2
616 N Wehe Ave 99301 509-543-6750
Victor Silva, prin. Fax 543-6751

Star SD 54 50/K-6
24180 Pasco Kahlotus Rd 99301 509-547-6030
Rich Puryear, supt. Fax 586-6537
www.starsd.org
Star ES 50/K-6
24180 Pasco Kahlotus Rd 99301 509-547-2704
Rich Puryear, prin. Fax 586-6537

Kingspoint Christian S 200/PK-12
7900 W Court St 99301 509-547-6498
Georgia Perkins, admin. Fax 547-6788
St. Patrick S 300/PK-8
1016 N 14th Ave 99301 509-547-7261
Kristine Peugh, prin Fax 547-2352
Tri-City Adventist S 200/PK-10
4115 W Henry St 99301 509-547-8092
Spencer Hannah, prin. Fax 547-8516

Pateros, Okanogan, Pop. 658
Pateros SD 122 200/K-12
PO Box 98 98846 509-923-2343
Lois Davies, supt. Fax 923-2283
www.pateros.org
Pateros S 200/K-12
PO Box 98 98846 509-923-2343
Michael Hull, prin. Fax 923-2283

Paterson, Benton
Paterson SD 50 100/PK-8
PO Box 189 99345 509-875-2601
John Seaton, supt. Fax 875-2067
www.patersonschool.org
Paterson S 100/PK-8
PO Box 189 99345 509-875-2601
John Seaton, admin. Fax 875-2067

Pe Ell, Lewis, Pop. 610
Pe Ell SD 301 300/PK-12
PO Box 368 98572 360-291-3244
Kyle MacDonald, supt Fax 291-3823
www.peell.k12.wa.us/
Pe Ell S 300/PK-12
PO Box 368 98572 360-291-3244
Kyle MacDonald, supt. Fax 291-3823

Peshastin, Chelan
Cascade SD 228
Supt. — See Leavenworth
Peshastin-Dryden ES 300/PK-2
10001 School St 98847 509-548-5832
Emily Ross, prin. Fax 548-6752

Point Roberts, Whatcom, Pop. 1,296
Blaine SD 503
Supt. — See Blaine
Point Roberts PS 50/K-3
PO Box 910 98281 360-945-2223
Dr. Craig Baldwin, prin. Fax 945-2230

Pomeroy, Garfield, Pop. 1,407
Pomeroy SD 110 300/K-12
PO Box 950 99347 509-843-3393
Rachel Gwinn, supt. Fax 843-3046
www.psd.wednet.edu
Pomeroy ES 200/K-6
PO Box 950 99347 509-843-1651
Rachel Gwinn, prin. Fax 843-8246

Port Angeles, Clallam, Pop. 18,283
Port Angeles SD 121 3,700/PK-12
216 E 4th St 98362 360-457-8575
Dr. Marc Jackson, supt. Fax 457-4649
www.portangelesschools.org/
Dry Creek ES 400/K-6
25 Rife Rd 98363 360-457-5050
Brittane Hendricks, prin. Fax 417-8019
Franklin ES 400/K-6
2505 S Washington St 98362 360-457-1343
Amity Butler, prin. Fax 417-2066
Hamilton ES 300/PK-6
1822 W 7th St 98363 360-452-6819
Gary Pringle, prin. Fax 452-6359
Jefferson ES 400/PK-6
218 E 12th St 98362 360-457-4231
Joyce Mininger, prin. Fax 457-4296
Roosevelt ES 400/K-6
106 Monroe Rd 98362 360-452-8973
Michelle Olsen, prin. Fax 452-4011
Stevens MS 600/7-8
1139 W 14th St 98363 360-452-5590
Ryan Stevens, prin. Fax 457-5709

Olympic Christian S 200/PK-8
43 OBrien Rd 98362 360-457-4640
Queen of Angels S 100/PK-8
1007 S Oak St 98362 360-457-6903
Thomas McDonald, prin. Fax 457-6866

Port Hadlock, Jefferson, Pop. 2,742
Chimacum SD 49
Supt. — See Chimacum
Chimacum Creek PS 200/K-2
313 Ness Corner Rd 98339 360-302-5820
Kalie Enlow, prin. Fax 344-3271

Cedarbrook Adventist Christian S 50/1-8
PO Box 150 98339 360-385-4610
Sunfield Waldorf S, PO Box 85 98339 100/PK-8
Abra Derbis, admin. 360-385-3658

Port Orchard, Kitsap, Pop. 10,384
South Kitsap SD 402 8,900/K-12
2689 Hoover Ave SE 98366 360-874-7000
Karst Brandsma, supt. Fax 874-7068
www.skitsap.wednet.edu
Burley-Glenwood ES 400/K-5
100 SW Lakeway Blvd 98367 360-443-3110
Derek Grant, prin. Fax 874-3169
Cedar Heights JHS 400/6-8
2220 Pottery Ave 98366 360-874-6020
Andrew Cain, prin. Fax 874-6420

East Port Orchard ES 500/K-5
2649 Hoover Ave SE 98366 360-443-3170
Paul Hulbert, prin. Fax 443-3229
Glen ES 600/K-5
500 SW Birch Rd 98367 360-443-3400
Jason Shdo, prin. Fax 443-3469
Hidden Creek ES 500/K-5
5455 Converse Ave SE 98367 360-443-3050
Laura Smith, prin. Fax 443-3109
Manchester ES 400/K-5
1901 California Ave E 98366 360-443-3230
Rachelle Byrd, prin. Fax 443-3289
Mullenix Ridge ES 600/K-5
3900 SE Mullenix Rd 98367 360-443-3290
Barbara Pixton, prin. Fax 443-3349
Orchard Heights ES 500/K-5
2288 Fircrest Dr SE 98366 360-443-3530
Kris Kristenberry, prin. Fax 443-3604
Sedgewick JHS 700/6-8
8995 SE Sedgwick Rd 98366 360-874-6090
Daniel Novick, prin. Fax 874-6430
South Colby ES 400/K-5
3281 Banner Rd SE 98366 360-443-3000
Joe Riley, prin. Fax 443-3049
Sunnyslope ES 500/K-5
4183 Sunnyslope Rd SW 98367 360-443-3470
Lisa Fundanet, prin. Fax 443-3529
Whitman JHS 700/6-8
1887 Madrona Dr SE 98366 360-874-6160
Brian Carlson, prin. Fax 874-6440
Other Schools – See Olalla

Burley Christian S 100/PK-12
14687 Olympic Dr SE 98367 253-851-8619

Port Townsend, Jefferson, Pop. 8,812
Port Townsend SD 50 1,200/PK-12
1610 Blaine St 98368 360-379-4501
Dr. John Polm Ed.D., supt. Fax 385-3617
www.ptschools.org
Blue Heron MS 400/4-8
3939 San Juan Ave 98368 360-379-4540
Patrick Gaffney, prin. Fax 379-4548
Grant Street ES 400/PK-3
1637 Grant St 98368 360-379-4535
Lisa Condran, prin. Fax 379-4261

Poulsbo, Kitsap, Pop. 8,738
North Kitsap SD 400 6,100/PK-12
18360 Caldart Ave NE 98370 360-396-3000
Dr. Laurynn Evans, supt.
www.nkschools.org
Pearson ES 300/PK-5
15650 Central Valley Rd NW 98370 360-396-3750
Deb Foreman, prin. Fax 396-3918
Poulsbo ES 500/K-5
18531 Noll Rd NE 98370 360-396-3500
Andrew Crandall, prin. Fax 396-3909
Poulsbo MS 800/6-8
2003 NE Hostmark St 98370 360-396-3200
Josh Emmons, prin. Fax 396-3904
Vinland ES 600/K-5
22104 Rhododendron Ln NW 98370 360-396-3600
Brenda Ward, prin. Fax 396-3949
Other Schools – See Kingston, Suquamish

Gateway Christian S 100/K-5
18901 8th Ave NE 98370 360-779-9189
Donna Beaver, prin.
Poulsbo Adventist S 50/1-8
1700 NE Lincoln Rd 98370 360-779-6290

Prescott, Walla Walla, Pop. 314
Prescott SD 402-37 200/K-12
PO Box 65 99348 509-849-2215
Brett Cox, supt. Fax 849-2800
www.prescott.k12.wa.us/
Prescott ES 100/K-6
PO Box 65 99348 509-849-2217
Dr. Jodi Thew, prin. Fax 849-2800

Prosser, Benton, Pop. 5,618
Prosser SD 116 2,900/PK-12
1126 Meade Ave Ste A 99350 509-786-3323
Dr. Deanna Flores, supt. Fax 786-2062
www.prosserschools.org/
Housel MS 700/6-8
2001 Highland Dr 99350 509-786-1732
Michael Denny, prin. Fax 786-2814
Keene-Riverview ES 500/PK-2
832 Park Ave 99350 509-786-2020
Kris Moore, prin. Fax 786-4271
Prosser Heights ES 500/3-5
2008 Miller Ave 99350 509-786-2633
Sally Juzeler, prin. Fax 786-3121
Whitstran ES 300/K-5
102101 W Foisy Rd 99350 509-778-4434
Kevin Gilman, prin. Fax 973-2500

Pullman, Whitman, Pop. 28,533
Pullman SD 267 2,600/K-12
240 SE Dexter St 99163 509-332-3581
Bob Maxwell, supt. Fax 336-7202
www.psd267.org
Franklin ES 400/K-5
850 SE Klemgard St 99163 509-334-5641
Bill Holman, prin. Fax 332-0864
Jefferson ES 400/K-5
1150 NW Bryant St 99163 509-332-2617
Craig Nelson, prin. Fax 332-0680
Lincoln MS 600/6-8
315 SE Crestview St 99163 509-334-3411
Cameron Grow, prin. Fax 336-7203
Sunnyside ES 500/K-5
425 SW Shirley St 99163 509-334-1800
Pam Brantner, prin. Fax 332-0329

Pullman Christian S 100/K-12
345 SW Kimball Dr 99163 509-332-3545
Sherri Goetze, prin.

Puyallup, Pierce, Pop. 35,083
Bethel SD 403
Supt. — See Spanaway
Frederickson ES 600/PK-5
17418 74th Ave E 98375 253-683-6300
Ellen Eddy, prin. Fax 683-6398

Puyallup SD 3 20,700/K-12
PO Box 370 98371 253-841-1301
Dr. Timothy Yeomans, supt. Fax 840-8959
www.puyallup.k12.wa.us
Brouillet ES 700/K-6
17207 94th Ave E 98375 253-841-8670
Nancy Strobel, prin. Fax 840-8871
Carson ES 900/K-6
8615 184th St E 98375 253-840-8808
Abigail Chandler, prin. Fax 840-8987
Edgerton ES 700/K-6
16528 127th Avenue Ct E 98374 253-840-8809
Lisa Rowan, prin. Fax 840-8993
Firgrove ES 600/K-6
13918 Meridian S 98373 253-841-8733
Richard Lasso, prin. Fax 840-8948
Fruitland ES 500/K-6
1515 S Fruitland 98371 253-841-8734
Melayne Jones, prin. Fax 840-8915
Hunt ES 600/K-6
12801 144th St E 98374 253-841-8690
Rebecca Williams, prin. Fax 840-8939
Karshner ES 300/K-6
1328 8th Ave NW 98371 253-841-8736
LaShawnda Baldwin, prin. Fax 435-6278
Maplewood ES 400/K-6
1110 W Pioneer 98371 253-841-8737
Susan Walton, prin. Fax 840-8947
Meeker ES 400/K-6
409 5th St SW 98371 253-841-8738
Patrick McGregor, prin. Fax 435-2396
Pope ES 500/K-6
15102 122nd Ave E 98374 253-841-8755
Krista Bates, prin. Fax 841-8684
Ridgecrest ES 400/K-6
12616 Shaw Rd E 98374 253-841-8753
Michelle Fox, prin. Fax 840-8944
Shaw Road ES 500/K-6
1106 Shaw Rd 98372 253-841-8675
Michelle Cruckshank, prin. Fax 840-8945
Spinning ES 300/K-6
1306 E Pioneer 98372 253-841-8742
Kari Helling, prin. Fax 840-8942
Stewart ES 300/K-6
426 4th Ave NE 98372 253-841-8743
Elissa Dornan, prin. Fax 840-8955
Sunrise ES 500/K-6
2323 39th Ave SE 98374 253-841-8744
Lisa McNamara, prin. Fax 840-8972
Wildwood Park ES 500/K-6
1601 26th Ave SE 98374 253-841-8746
Jennifer Fox, prin. Fax 840-8940
Woodland ES 600/K-6
7707 112th St E 98373 253-841-8747
Heather McMullen, prin. Fax 840-8885
Zeiger ES 700/K-6
13008 94th Ave E 98373 253-841-8663
Angelo Mills, prin. Fax 841-8704
Other Schools – See Edgewood, Tacoma

All Saints S 400/PK-8
504 2nd St SW 98371 253-845-5025
Amy Orm, prin. Fax 435-9841
Cascade Christian/McAlder ES 100/K-6
15502 96th St E 98372 253-256-4382
Tim Lorenz, prin. Fax 881-1727
Cascade Christian/Puyallup ES 400/K-6
601 9th Ave SE 98372 253-841-2091
Terry Broberg, prin. Fax 841-2095
Northwest Christian S 100/PK-8
904 Shaw Rd 98372 253-845-5722

Quilcene, Jefferson, Pop. 571
Quilcene SD 48 300/K-12
PO Box 40 98376 360-765-3363
Wally Lis, supt. Fax 765-3015
www.quilcene.wednet.edu
Quilcene S 200/K-12
PO Box 40 98376 360-765-3363
Dr. Gary Stebbins, prin. Fax 765-4183

Quincy, Grant, Pop. 6,701
Quincy SD 144-101 2,700/K-12
119 J St SW 98848 509-787-4571
John Boyd, supt. Fax 787-4336
www.qsd.wednet.edu
George ES 200/K-4
401 Washington Way 98848 509-785-2244
William Schutzmann, prin. Fax 787-8955
Monument ES 600/4-6
1400 13th Ave SW 98848 509-787-9826
Lisa Navarro-Avila, prin. Fax 787-8974
Mountain View ES 400/K-3
119 D St NW 98848 509-787-4548
Colleen Frerks, prin. Fax 787-9025
Pioneer ES 400/K-3
224 J St SE 98848 509-787-1595
Ellen Hopkins, prin. Fax 787-2583
Quincy JHS 400/7-8
417 C St SE 98848 509-787-4435
Scott Ramsey, prin. Fax 787-8949

Rainier, Thurston, Pop. 1,719
Rainier SD 307 800/PK-12
PO Box 98 98576 360-446-2207
Bryon Bahr, supt. Fax 446-2918
www.rainier.wednet.edu
Rainier ES 400/PK-5
PO Box 98 98576 360-446-4020
Rita Meldrum, prin. Fax 446-4022
Rainier MS 200/6-8
PO Box 98 98576 360-446-2206
John Beckman, prin. Fax 446-7414

Randle, Lewis
White Pass SD 303 400/PK-12
PO Box 188 98377 360-497-3791
Fax 497-2560
www.whitepass.k12.wa.us
White Pass ES 200/PK-6
127 Kindle Rd 98377 360-497-7300
Nathan Coutsoubos, prin. Fax 497-2126

Ravensdale, King, Pop. 1,086
Tahoma SD 409
Supt. — See Maple Valley
Summit Trail MS 1,200/6-8
25600 SE Summit Landsburg 98051 425-413-5600
Andy McGrath, prin. Fax 413-5500

Raymond, Pacific, Pop. 2,787
Raymond SD 116 600/PK-12
1016 Commercial St 98577 360-942-3415
Dr. Stephen Holland, supt. Fax 942-3416
raymondk12.org
Raymond ES 300/PK-6
921 Commercial St 98577 360-942-3415
Mike Scott, prin. Fax 942-2503

Willapa Valley SD 160 300/PK-12
22 Viking Way 98577 360-942-5855
Rob Friese, supt. Fax 942-3216
www.willapavalley.org
Willapa ES 100/K-5
845 Willapa Fourth St 98577 360-942-3311
Jay Pearson, admin. Fax 942-3406

Reardan, Lincoln, Pop. 562
Reardan-Edwall SD 9 600/PK-12
PO Box 225 99029 509-796-2701
Marcus Morgan, supt. Fax 796-4954
www.reardan.net
Reardan ES 200/PK-5
PO Box 225 99029 509-796-2701
Dwight Cooper, prin. Fax 796-2161

Redmond, King, Pop. 51,981
Lake Washington SD 414 25,400/K-12
PO Box 97039 98073 425-936-1200
Dr. Traci Pierce, supt. Fax 936-1213
www.lwsd.org
Alcott ES 600/K-5
4213 228th Ave NE 98053 425-936-2490
Jon Hedin, prin. Fax 836-8903
Audubon ES 500/K-5
3045 180th Ave NE 98052 425-936-2500
Kimo Spray, prin. Fax 882-3422
Dickinson ES 500/K-5
7040 208th Ave NE 98053 425-936-2530
Karen Barker, prin. Fax 836-4658
Einstein ES 500/K-5
18025 NE 116th St 98052 425-936-2540
Robin Imai, prin. Fax 867-0797
Evergreen MS 800/6-8
6900 208th Ave NE 98053 425-936-2320
Robert Johnson, prin. Fax 868-0105
Explorer Community S 100/K-5
7040 208th Ave NE 98053 425-936-2530
Karen Barker, prin. Fax 836-4658
Mann ES 400/K-5
17001 NE 104th St 98052 425-936-2610
Megan Spaulding, prin. Fax 556-0874
Parks ES 600/K-5
22845 NE Cedar Park Cres 98053 425-936-2650
Kim Bilanko, prin. Fax 836-1350
Redmond ES 400/K-5
16800 NE 80th St 98052 425-936-2660
Kirsten Gometz, prin. Fax 882-0591
Redmond MS 1,000/6-8
10055 166th Ave NE 98052 425-936-2440
Jon Young, prin. Fax 556-9806
Rockwell ES 700/K-5
11125 162nd Ave NE 98052 425-936-2670
Michael Clark, prin. Fax 885-5528
Rose Hill MS 600/6-8
13505 NE 75th St 98052 425-936-2460
Erin Bowser, prin. Fax 576-6342
Rush ES 500/K-5
6101 152nd Ave NE 98052 425-936-2690
Lucy Davies, prin. Fax 556-0364
Stella Schola MS 100/6-8
13505 NE 75th St 98052 425-936-2475
Erin Bowser, prin. Fax 936-2476
Other Schools – See Kirkland, Sammamish, Woodinville

Northshore SD 417
Supt. — See Bothell
Sunrise ES 300/K-5
14075 172nd Ave NE 98052 425-408-5300
Steve Hopkins, prin. Fax 408-5302

Bear Creek S 800/PK-12
8905 208th Ave NE 98053 425-898-1720
Patrick Carruth, hdmstr. Fax 898-1430
Montessori Children's House 100/PK-6
5003 218th Ave NE 98053 425-868-7805
Jennifer McConnell, head sch Fax 516-7188
Sammamish Montessori S 300/PK-3
7655 178th Pl NE 98052 425-883-3271

Renton, King, Pop. 85,890
Issaquah SD 411
Supt. — See Issaquah
Apollo ES 600/K-5
15025 SE 117th St 98059 425-837-7500
Jane Harris, prin. Fax 837-7508
Briarwood ES 500/K-5
17020 SE 134th St 98059 425-837-5000
Steven Thatcher, prin. Fax 837-5037
Maple Hills ES 400/K-5
15644 204th Ave SE 98059 425-837-5100
JoEllen Tapper, prin. Fax 837-5108
Maywood MS 1,000/6-8
14490 168th Ave SE 98059 425-837-6900
Erin McKee, prin. Fax 837-6910

Kent SD 415
Supt. — See Kent
Carriage Crest ES 400/K-6
18235 140th Ave SE 98058 253-373-7597
Robert Gallagher, prin. Fax 373-7563
Fairwood ES 400/PK-6
16600 148th Ave SE 98058 253-373-7491
Patricia Hoyle, prin. Fax 373-7492
Meeker MS 700/7-8
12600 SE 192nd St 98058 253-373-7284
Shannon Nash, prin. Fax 373-7560
Northwood MS 600/7-8
17007 SE 184th St 98058 253-373-7780
Sherilyn Ulland, prin. Fax 373-7788
Ridgewood ES 500/K-6
18030 162nd Pl SE 98058 253-373-7482
Cynthia Green, prin. Fax 373-7483

Renton SD 403 14,900/K-12
300 SW 7th St 98057 425-204-2300
Damien Pattenaude, supt. Fax 204-2456
www.rentonschools.us
Benson Hill ES 500/K-5
18665 116th Ave SE 98058 425-204-3300
Martha Flemming, prin. Fax 204-3313
Cascade ES 600/K-5
16022 116th Ave SE 98058 425-204-3350
Rachel Lockhart, prin. Fax 204-3357
Highlands ES 500/K-5
2720 NE 7th St 98056 425-204-4600
Alfred Deblasio, prin. Fax 204-4616
Honey Dew ES 500/K-5
800 Union Ave NE 98059 425-204-4800
Misty Mbadugha, prin.
Kennydale ES 600/K-5
1700 NE 28th St 98056 425-204-4700
Nikki O'Brien, prin. Fax 204-4747
Maplewood Heights ES 600/K-5
130 Jericho Ave SE 98059 425-204-4750
Tamra Prince, prin. Fax 204-4798
McKnight MS 1,200/6-8
1200 Edmonds Ave NE 98056 425-204-3600
Brian Teppner, prin. Fax 204-3680
Nelsen MS 1,000/6-8
2403 Jones Ave S 98055 425-204-3000
Colin Falk, prin. Fax 204-3079
Renton Park ES 500/K-5
16828 128th Ave SE 98058 425-204-2950
Jo Kain, prin. Fax 204-2957
Risdon MS, 6928 116th Ave SE 98056 6-8
Craig Cooper, prin. 425-204-2345
Sierra Heights ES 600/K-5
2501 Union Ave NE 98059 425-204-4650
Laura Bohn, prin. Fax 204-4659
Talbot Hill ES 400/K-5
2300 Talbot Rd S 98055 425-204-4900
Holly Nielson, prin. Fax 204-4948
Tiffany Park ES 500/K-5
1601 Lake Youngs Way SE 98058 425-204-4850
Erin Morin, prin. Fax 204-4857
Other Schools – See Newcastle, Seattle

Cedar River Montessori S 100/PK-8
15828 SE Jones Rd 98058 425-271-9614
Melinda Woodard, admin. Fax 271-6934
King of Kings Lutheran Preschool & K 100/PK-K
18207 108th Ave SE 98055 425-255-8520
Debra Timm, dir. Fax 276-5327
RCS Maple Valley Christian S 100/PK-6
PO Box 58129 98058 425-226-4640
Weldo Melvin, admin. Fax 228-1934
Renton Christian S 500/PK-8
15717 152nd Ave SE 98058 425-226-0820
Randy McMillan, head sch Fax 970-3074
Renton Preparatory Christian S 100/3-12
200 Mill Ave Ste 110 98057 206-723-5526
Dr. David Zimmerman, head sch
St. Anthony S 500/PK-8
336 Shattuck Ave S 98057 425-255-0059
Michael Cantu, prin. Fax 235-6555

Republic, Ferry, Pop. 1,028
Republic SD 309 300/K-12
30306 E Highway 20 99166 509-775-3173
Dr. John Glenewinkel, supt. Fax 775-3712
www.republic.wednet.edu
Republic ES 200/K-6
30306 E Highway 20 99166 509-775-3327
Christopher Burch, prin. Fax 775-2674
Republic JHS 100/7-8
30306 E Highway 20 99166 509-775-3171
Christopher Burch, prin. Fax 775-1098

Richland, Benton, Pop. 46,846
Richland SD 400 11,900/K-12
615 Snow Ave 99352 509-967-6000
Dr. Rick Schulte, supt. Fax 942-2401
www.rsd.edu
Badger Mountain ES 700/K-5
1515 Elementary St 99352 509-967-6225
Gail Ledbetter, prin. Fax 628-2702
Carmichael MS 900/6-8
620 Thayer Dr 99352 509-967-6425
Brian Stadelman, prin. Fax 942-2471
Chief Joseph MS 700/6-8
504 Wilson St, 509-967-6400
Kevin Norris, prin. Fax 942-2492
Jefferson ES 400/K-5
1525 Hunt Ave, 509-967-6250
Bobbi Buttars, prin. Fax 942-2569
Lee ES 500/K-5
1750 McMurray Ave, 509-967-6475
Joe Jisa, prin. Fax 942-2556
Lewis & Clark ES 500/K-5
415 Jadwin Ave 99352 509-967-6275
Elizabeth Crider, prin. Fax 942-2377
Orchard ES K-5
1600 Gala Way 99352 509-967-6175
Alysia Arsanto, prin. Fax 820-3330

Sacajawea ES 500/K-5
535 Fuller St, 509-967-6325
Jim Bruce, prin. Fax 371-2681
White Bluffs ES 800/K-5
1250 Kensington Way 99352 509-967-6575
Paul Chartrand, prin. Fax 628-2982
Whitman ES 400/K-5
1704 Gray St 99352 509-967-6300
Brian Moore, prin. Fax 713-7029
Other Schools – See West Richland

Christ the King S 400/PK-8
1122 Long Ave, 509-946-6158
Sheila LaSalle, prin. Fax 943-8402
Coram Deo Academy 100/K-6
1632 George Washington Way,
Rev. Donald Van Dyken, hdmstr. 509-392-7420
Liberty Christian S of the Tri-Cities 400/PK-12
2200 Williams Blvd, 509-946-0602
Karen Bjur, prin. Fax 943-5623

Ridgefield, Clark, Pop. 4,650
Ridgefield SD 122 2,200/K-12
2724 S Hillhurst Rd 98642 360-619-1301
Dr. Nathan McCann, supt. Fax 619-1397
www.ridgefieldsd.org
South Ridge ES 500/K-6
502 NW 199th St 98642 360-619-1500
Todd Graves, prin. Fax 619-1559
Union Ridge ES 700/K-6
330 N 5th Ave 98642 360-750-7600
Kelly Macdonald, prin. Fax 750-7659
View Ridge MS 300/7-8
510 Pioneer St 98642 360-619-1400
Tony Smith, prin. Fax 619-1459

Cedar Tree Classical Christian S 200/K-12
20601 NE 29th Ave 98642 360-887-0190

Ritzville, Adams, Pop. 1,650
Lind-Ritzville SD
Supt. — See Lind
Ritzville ES 100/PK-5
401 E 6th Ave 99169 509-659-0232
Tom Arlt, prin. Fax 659-4119

Rochester, Thurston, Pop. 2,337
Rochester SD 401 2,200/K-12
10140 Highway 12 SW 98579 360-273-5536
Kimberly Fry, supt. Fax 273-5547
www.rochester.wednet.edu
Grand Mound ES 500/3-5
7710 James Rd SW 98579 360-273-5512
Kelley Bremgartner, prin. Fax 273-8917
Rochester MS 500/6-8
9937 Highway 12 SW 98579 360-273-5958
Will Maus, prin. Fax 273-2045
Rochester PS 500/K-2
7440 James Rd SW 98579 360-273-5161
Amy Nelson Roney, prin. Fax 273-2582

Rockford, Spokane, Pop. 465
Freeman SD 358 900/PK-12
15001 S Jackson Rd 99030 509-291-3695
Randy Russell, supt. Fax 291-3636
www.freemansd.org
Freeman ES 300/PK-5
14917 S Jackson Rd 99030 509-291-4791
Lisa Phelan, prin. Fax 291-7339
Freeman MS 200/6-8
15001 S Jackson Rd 99030 509-291-7301
Ben Ferney, prin. Fax 291-8009

Rock Island, Douglas, Pop. 780
Eastmont SD 206
Supt. — See East Wenatchee
Rock Island ES 300/K-4
5645 Rock Island Rd 98850 509-884-5023
Penny Brown, prin. Fax 884-1720

Roosevelt, Klickitat, Pop. 153
Roosevelt SD 403 50/K-6
PO Box 248 99356 509-384-5462
Kate Watson, supt. Fax 384-5621
Roosevelt ES 50/K-6
PO Box 248 99356 509-384-5462
Kate Watson, supt. Fax 384-5621

Rosalia, Whitman, Pop. 547
Rosalia SD 320 200/PK-12
916 S Josephine Ave 99170 509-523-3061
Larry Keller, supt. Fax 523-3861
www.rosaliaschools.org
Rosalia S 200/PK-12
916 S Josephine Ave 99170 509-523-3061
Darrell Kuhn, prin. Fax 523-3861

Roslyn, Kittitas, Pop. 872

Mayflower Christian S PK-2
300 N 2nd St 98941 509-649-2603
Jerry Ihrke, admin.

Roy, Pierce, Pop. 730
Bethel SD 403
Supt. — See Spanaway
Roy ES 300/K-5
PO Box 238 98580 253-683-5100
Stephanie Weinheimer, prin. Fax 683-5198

Royal City, Grant, Pop. 2,135
Royal SD 160 1,300/PK-12
PO Box 486 99357 509-346-2222
Roger W. Trail, supt. Fax 346-8746
www.royal.wednet.edu/
Red Rock ES 600/PK-3
PO Box 486 99357 509-346-2206
David Andra, prin. Fax 346-2207
Royal IS 4-6
PO Box 486 99357 509-346-2226
Linda Achondo, admin. Fax 346-2933

Royal MS 300/7-8
PO Box 486 99357 509-346-2268
David Jaderlund, prin. Fax 346-2269

Saint John, Whitman, Pop. 519
St. John SD 322 200/PK-12
301 W Nob Hill Rd 99171 509-648-3336
Suzanne Schmick, supt. Fax 648-3451
www.sje.wednet.edu
St. John ES 100/PK-5
301 W Nob Hill Rd 99171 509-648-3336
Mark Purvine, prin. Fax 648-3451

St. John-Endicott Cooperative SD
Supt. — See Endicott
Endicott-St. John MS 100/6-8
301 W Nob Hill Rd 99171 509-657-3523
Mark Purvine, prin. Fax 657-3521

Sammamish, King, Pop. 44,087
Issaquah SD 411
Supt. — See Issaquah
Cascade Ridge ES 600/K-5
2020 Trossachs Blvd SE 98075 425-837-5500
Tia Klienkopf, prin. Fax 837-5505
Creekside ES 700/K-5
20777 SE 16th St 98075 425-837-5200
Tera Coyle, prin. Fax 837-5210
Discovery ES 600/PK-5
2300 228th Ave SE 98075 425-837-4100
Marti Shefveland, prin. Fax 837-4044
Pine Lake MS 800/6-8
3200 228th Ave SE 98075 425-837-5700
Michelle Caponigro, prin. Fax 837-5762

Lake Washington SD 414
Supt. — See Redmond
Blackwell ES 400/K-5
3225 205th Pl NE 98074 425-936-2520
Jim Eaton, prin. Fax 868-0832
Carson ES 500/K-5
1035 244th Ave NE 98074 425-936-2750
Scott Power, prin. Fax 836-0834
Inglewood MS 1,100/6-8
24120 NE 8th St 98074 425-936-2360
Tim Patterson, prin. Fax 868-0628
McAuliffe ES 500/K-5
23823 NE 22nd St 98074 425-936-2620
Brady Howden, prin. Fax 836-4238
Mead ES 600/K-5
1725 216th Ave NE 98074 425-936-2630
Sandy Klein, prin. Fax 868-4721
Renaissance S of Art & Reasoning 100/6-8
400 228th Ave NE 98074 425-936-1544
Chris Bede, prin. Fax 836-6609
Smith ES 600/K-5
23305 NE 14th St 98074 425-936-2710
Jamie Warner, prin. Fax 836-8258

Arbor S 100/PK-6
1107 228th Ave SE 98075 425-392-3866
Sean O'Brien, head sch Fax 557-0176
TLC Montessori 100/PK-3
21512 NE 16th St 98074 425-868-1943

Satsop, Grays Harbor, Pop. 656
Satsop SD 104 100/K-6
PO Box 96 98583 360-482-5330
Marsha Hendrick, supt. Fax 482-5724
www.satsopschool.org
Satsop ES 100/K-6
PO Box 96 98583 360-482-5330
Marsha Hendrick, prin. Fax 482-5724

SeaTac, King, Pop. 24,721
Highline SD 401
Supt. — See Burien
Bow Lake ES 700/K-6
18237 42nd Ave S 98188 206-631-3500
Douglas Neufeld, prin. Fax 631-3573
Chinook MS 600/7-8
18650 42nd Ave S 98188 206-631-5700
Karin Jones, prin. Fax 631-5770
Madrona ES 600/K-6
20301 32nd Ave S 98198 206-631-4100
Kellie Hernandez, prin. Fax 631-4162
McMicken Heights ES 500/K-6
3708 S 168th St 98188 206-631-4300
Alexandria Haas, prin. Fax 631-4364
Valley View Early Learning Center 200/PK-PK
17622 46th Ave S 98188 206-631-5100
Kimberly Nelson, admin. Fax 631-5135

Seattle Christian S 500/K-12
18301 Military Rd S 98188 206-246-8241
Laird Leavitt, supt. Fax 246-9066

Seattle, King, Pop. 578,438
Highline SD 401
Supt. — See Burien
Beverly Park ES 500/K-6
1201 S 104th St 98168 206-631-3400
Robin Lamoureux, prin. Fax 631-3452
Cascade MS 600/7-8
11212 10th Ave SW 98146 206-631-5500
Daniel Calderon, prin. Fax 631-5568
Hilltop ES 600/K-6
12250 24th Ave S 98168 206-631-4000
Katherine Emerick, prin. Fax 631-4056
Mount View ES 700/PK-6
10811 12th Ave SW 98146 206-631-4500
Mike Fosberg, prin. Fax 631-4506
North Hill ES 600/K-6
19835 8th Ave S 98148 206-631-4600
Kimberly Gilmore, prin. Fax 631-4660
Southern Heights ES 300/K-6
11249 14th Ave S 98168 206-631-5000
Andrea Smith, prin. Fax 631-5042
White Center Heights ES 600/PK-6
10015 6th Ave SW 98146 206-631-5200
Anne Reece, prin. Fax 631-5261

Renton SD 403
Supt. — See Renton
Bryn Mawr ES 400/K-5
8212 S 118th St 98178 425-204-4150
Jaime Maxie, prin. Fax 204-4195
Campbell Hill ES 400/K-5
6418 S 124th St 98178 425-204-4000
DeeAnn Wells, prin. Fax 204-4013
Dimmitt MS 1,000/6-8
12320 80th Ave S 98178 425-204-2800
Gioia Pitts, prin. Fax 204-2812
Lakeridge ES 400/K-5
7400 S 115th St 98178 425-204-4100
Holly Megan Thompson, prin. Fax 204-4145

Seattle SD 1 49,300/PK-12
PO Box 34165 98124 206-252-0000
Dr. Larry Nyland, supt. Fax 252-0102
www.seattleschools.org
Adams ES 500/K-5
6110 28th Ave NW 98107 206-252-1300
Tim Moynihan, prin. Fax 252-1301
Addams MS 300/6-8
11051 34th Ave NE 98125 206-252-4500
Paula Montgomery, prin.
Alki ES 400/PK-5
3010 59th Ave SW 98116 206-252-9050
Rena Deese, prin. Fax 252-9051
Arbor Heights ES 400/K-5
3701 SW 104th St 98146 206-252-9250
Christy Collins, prin. Fax 252-9251
Bagley ES 400/K-5
7821 Stone Ave N 98103 206-252-5110
Carla Holmes, prin. Fax 252-5111
Beacon Hill International ES 500/K-5
2025 14th Ave S 98144 206-252-2700
Katie Virga, prin. Fax 252-2701
Blaine ES 600/K-8
2550 34th Ave W 98199 206-252-1920
Ryan LaDage, prin. Fax 252-1921
Boren STEM K-8 S 300/K-8
5950 Delridge Way SW 98106 206-252-8450
Ben Ostrom, prin.
Broadview-Thomson ES 700/K-8
13052 Greenwood Ave N 98133 206-252-4080
R.J. Sammons, prin. Fax 252-4081
Bryant ES 600/K-5
3311 NE 60th St 98115 206-252-5200
Dan Sanger, prin. Fax 252-5201
Cascadia ES, 1700 N 90th St 98103 1-5
Anna Birinyi, prin. 206-413-2000
Cedar Park ES PK-5
13224 37th Ave NE 98125 206-252-4300
Doug Ouellette, prin.
Coe ES 500/K-5
2424 7th Ave W 98119 206-252-2000
Virginia Turner, prin. Fax 252-2001
Concord International ES 400/K-5
723 S Concord St 98108 206-252-8100
Norma Zavala, prin. Fax 252-8101
Day ES 300/K-5
3921 Linden Ave N 98103 206-252-6010
Stan Jaskot, prin. Fax 252-6011
Dearborn Park ES 300/K-5
2820 S Orcas St 98108 206-252-6930
Jessica Conte, prin. Fax 252-6931
Decatur ES PK-5
7711 43rd Ave NE 98115 206-252-3230
Rina Geoghagan, prin. Fax 252-3231
Denny International MS 900/6-8
2601 SW Kenyon St 98126 206-252-9000
Jeff Clarke, prin. Fax 252-9001
Dunlap ES 400/PK-5
4525 S Cloverdale St 98118 206-252-7000
Winifred Todd, prin. Fax 252-7001
Eagle Staff MS 6-8
1330 N 90th St 98103 206-413-2300
Marni Campbell, prin. Fax 413-2301
Eckstein MS 1,200/6-8
3003 NE 75th St 98115 206-252-5010
Treena Sterk, prin. Fax 252-5011
Emerson ES 300/K-5
9709 60th Ave S 98118 206-252-7100
Erin Rasmussen, prin. Fax 252-7101
Fairmount Park ES 200/K-5
3800 SW Findlay St 98126 206-252-9300
Julie Breidenbach, prin.
Gatewood ES 500/K-5
4320 SW Myrtle St 98136 206-252-9400
Kyna Hogg, prin. Fax 252-9401
Gatzert ES 400/K-5
1301 E Yesler Way 98122 206-252-2810
Laurie Kazanjian, prin. Fax 252-2811
Genesee Hill ES K-5
5013 SW Dakota St 98116 206-252-9700
Gerrit Kischner, prin. Fax 252-9701
Graham Hill ES 400/PK-5
5149 S Graham St 98118 206-252-7140
Deena Russo, prin. Fax 252-7141
Green Lake ES 300/K-5
2400 N 65th St 98103 206-252-5320
Joanne Bowers, prin. Fax 252-5321
Greenwood ES 400/K-5
144 NW 80th St 98117 206-252-1400
Walter Trotter, prin. Fax 252-1401
Hamilton International MS 1,100/6-8
1610 N 41st St 98103 206-252-5810
Tip Blish, prin. Fax 252-5811
Hawthorne ES 300/PK-5
4100 39th Ave S 98118 206-252-7210
Sandra Scott, prin. Fax 252-7211
Hay ES 500/K-5
201 Garfield St 98109 206-252-2100
Tami Beach, prin. Fax 252-2101
Highland Park ES 400/K-5
1012 SW Trenton St 98106 206-252-8240
Chris Cronas, prin. Fax 252-8241
Kimball ES 400/K-5
3200 23rd Ave S 98144 206-252-7280
James Buckwalter, prin. Fax 252-7281
King ES 400/K-5
6725 45th Ave S 98118 206-252-6770
Chris Thomas, prin. Fax 252-6771
Kurose MS 700/6-8
3928 S Graham St 98118 206-252-7700
Mia Williams, prin. Fax 252-7701
Lafayette ES 600/K-5
2645 California Ave SW 98116 206-252-9500
Cindy Chaput, prin. Fax 252-9501
Laurelhurst ES 400/K-5
4530 46th Ave NE 98105 206-252-5400
Sarah Talbot, prin. Fax 252-5401
Lawton ES 400/K-5
4000 27th Ave W 98199 206-252-2130
Dorian Manza, prin. Fax 252-2131
Leschi ES 400/K-5
135 32nd Ave 98122 206-252-2950
Rhonda Claytor, prin. Fax 252-2951
Licton Springs K-8 S 200/K-8
1330 N 90th St 98103 206-413-2400
Lisa Allphin, prin.
Lowell ES 200/1-5
1058 E Mercer St 98102 206-252-3020
Colleen Stump, prin. Fax 252-3021
Loyal Heights ES 400/K-5
520 NE Ravenna Blvd 98115 206-252-1500
Geri Guerrero, prin. Fax 252-1501
Luke ES 400/K-5
3701 S Kenyon St 98118 206-252-7630
Davy Muth, prin. Fax 252-7631
Madison MS 800/6-8
3429 45th Ave SW 98116 206-252-9200
Robert Gary, prin. Fax 252-9201
Madrona ES 300/K-8
1121 33rd Ave 98122 206-252-3100
Mary McDaniel, prin. Fax 252-3101
Maple ES 400/K-5
4925 Corson Ave S 98108 206-252-8310
Elena Sanchez, prin. Fax 252-8311
Marshall ES 500/PK-5
2401 S Irving St 98144 206-252-2800
Katie May, prin. Fax 252-2801
McClure MS 500/6-8
1915 1st Ave W 98119 206-252-1900
Shannon Conner, prin. Fax 252-1901
McDonald International S 400/K-5
144 NE 54th St 98105 206-252-2900
Michelle Sushner, prin.
McGilvra ES 300/K-5
1617 38th Ave E 98112 206-252-3160
Maria Breuder, prin. Fax 252-3161
Meany MS, 301 21st Ave E 98112 6-8
Chanda Oatis, prin. 206-413-2100
Mercer MS 1,000/6-8
1600 S Columbian Way 98108 206-252-8000
Chris Carter, prin. Fax 252-8001
Montlake ES 200/K-5
2409 22nd Ave E 98112 206-252-3300
Melissa Gray, prin. Fax 252-3301
Muir ES 400/K-5
3301 S Horton St 98144 206-252-7400
Brenda Ball-Cuthbertson, prin. Fax 252-7401
North Beach ES 300/K-5
9018 24th Ave NW 98117 206-252-1510
Julie Cox, prin. Fax 252-1511
Northgate ES 200/K-5
11725 1st Ave NE 98125 206-252-4180
Deirdre Fauntleroy, prin. Fax 252-4181
Olympic Hills ES 300/K-5
13018 20th Ave NE 98125 206-413-2200
Elizabeth DeBell, prin.
Olympic View ES 500/K-5
504 NE 95th St 98115 206-252-5500
Andrew Bean, prin. Fax 252-5501
Orca K-8 S 500/K-8
5215 46th Ave S 98118 206-252-6900
Tonie Talbert, prin. Fax 252-6901
Pathfinder K-8 S 500/K-8
1901 SW Genesee St 98106 206-252-9710
David Dockendorf, prin. Fax 252-9711
Queen Anne ES, 411 Boston St 98109 300/K-5
Janine Roy, prin. 206-252-2480
Ranier View ES 200/PK-5
11650 Beacon Ave S 98178 206-252-6700
Anitra Pinchback-Jones, prin.
Rogers ES 300/K-5
4030 NE 109th St 98125 206-252-4320
Sara Mirabueno, prin. Fax 252-4321
Roxhill ES 400/PK-5
9430 30th Ave SW 98126 206-252-9570
Tarra Patrick, prin. Fax 252-9571
Sacajawea ES 200/K-5
9501 20th Ave NE 98115 206-252-5550
Rachel Friesen, prin. Fax 252-5551
Salmon Bay K-8 S 700/K-8
1810 NW 65th St 98117 206-252-1720
Neil Gerrans, prin. Fax 252-1721
Sand Point ES 300/K-5
6208 60th Ave NE 98115 206-252-4640
Kirsten Roberts, prin.
Sanislo ES 300/K-5
1812 SW Myrtle St 98106 206-252-8380
Erika Ayer, prin. Fax 252-8381
South Shore PK-8 S 600/PK-8
4800 S Henderson St 98118 206-252-7600
Kristin DeWitte, prin. Fax 252-6561
Stanford International ES 500/K-5
4057 5th Ave NE 98105 206-252-6080
Sarah Jones, prin. Fax 252-6081
Stevens ES 400/K-5
1242 18th Ave E 98112 206-252-3400
Brian Fitch, prin. Fax 252-3401
Thornton Creek ES 400/K-5
7712 40th Ave NE 98115 206-252-5300
John Miner, prin. Fax 252-5301
TOPS K-8 S 500/K-8
2500 Franklin Ave E 98102 206-252-3510
Amy Schwentor, prin. Fax 252-3511
Van Asselt ES 500/PK-5
8311 Beacon Ave S 98118 206-252-7500
Monique Manuel, prin. Fax 252-7501
Viewlands ES 300/K-5
10525 3rd Ave NW 98177 206-252-4400
Amy Klainer, prin.
View Ridge ES 600/PK-5
7047 50th Ave NE 98115 206-252-5600
Ed Roos, prin. Fax 252-5601
Washington MS 1,200/6-8
2101 S Jackson St 98144 206-252-2600
Susan Follmer, prin. Fax 252-2601
Wedgwood ES 500/K-5
2720 NE 85th St 98115 206-252-5670
Stephen Liu, prin. Fax 252-5671
West Seattle ES 400/K-5
6760 34th Ave SW 98126 206-252-9450
Pamela McCowan-Conyers, prin. Fax 252-9451
West Woodland ES 500/K-5
5601 4th Ave NW 98107 206-252-1600
Farah Thaxton, prin. Fax 252-1601
Whitman MS 1,000/6-8
9201 15th Ave NW 98117 206-252-1200
Susan Kleitsch, prin. Fax 252-1201
Whittier ES 500/PK-5
1320 NW 75th St 98117 206-252-1650
Melissa Schweitzer, prin. Fax 252-1651
Wolf K-8 STEM S 500/K-8
11530 12th Ave NE 98115 206-252-3580
Debbie Nelsen, prin. Fax 743-3131

Amazing Grace Christian S 200/PK-5
10056 Renton Ave S 98178 206-723-5526
Dr. Michelle Zimmerman, dir.
Assumption-St. Bridget S 500/PK-8
6220 32nd Ave NE 98115 206-524-7452
Kathleen Conklin, prin. Fax 524-6757
Bertschi S 200/PK-5
2227 10th Ave E 98102 206-324-5476
Rafael del Castillo, head sch Fax 329-4806
Billings MS 100/6-8
7217 Woodlawn Ave NE 98115 206-547-4614
Anne-Evan Williams, head sch Fax 545-8505
Bright Water Waldorf S 200/PK-8
1501 10th Ave E Ste 100 98102 206-624-6176
Bush S 600/K-12
3400 E Harrison St 98112 206-322-7978
Percy Abram Ph.D., head sch Fax 860-3876
Christ the King S 200/PK-8
415 N 117th St 98133 206-364-6890
Joanne Cecchini, prin. Fax 364-8325
Concordia Lutheran S 100/PK-8
7040 36th Ave NE 98115 206-525-7407
Christine Malone, admin. Fax 526-2082
Epiphany S 200/PK-5
3611 E Denny Way 98122 206-323-9011
Jenn Elkin, head sch Fax 324-2127
Explorer West MS 100/6-8
10015 28th Ave SW 98146 206-935-0495
Evan Hundley, head sch Fax 932-7113
Fairview Christian S 100/PK-8
844 NE 78th St 98115 206-526-0762
Kent Davis, admin. Fax 526-0763
Giddens S 200/PK-5
620 20th Ave S 98144 206-324-4847
Dr. Morva McDonald, head sch Fax 322-0923
Holy Family S 100/PK-8
9615 20th Ave SW 98106 206-767-6640
Larkin Temme, prin. Fax 767-9466
Holy Rosary S 500/K-8
4142 42nd Ave SW 98116 206-937-7255
Anna Horton, prin. Fax 937-2610
Hope Lutheran S 200/PK-8
4456 42nd Ave SW 98116 206-935-8500
Kristen Okabayashi, prin. Fax 937-9332
Lakeside MS 300/5-8
13510 1st Ave NE 98125 206-368-3630
Bernie Noe, hdmstr. Fax 368-3639
Lake Washington Girls MS 100/6-8
810 18th Ave 98122 206-709-3800
Patricia Hearn, head sch Fax 323-9860
Menachem Mendel Seattle Cheder Day S 100/PK-8
8420 Dayton Ave N 98103 206-523-9766
Meridian S 200/K-5
4649 Sunnyside Ave N # 242 98103 206-632-7154
Meghan Kimpton, head sch Fax 633-1864
Northwest Montessori S - Wedgewood 100/PK-6
7400 25th Ave NE 98115 206-524-4244
Northwest Montessori S - Woodland Park 100/PK-6
4910 Phinney Ave N 98103 206-634-1347
Northwest Montessori S - W Seattle PK-6
7344 35th Ave SW 98126 206-933-8557
Our Lady of Fatima S 300/K-8
3301 W Dravus St 98199 206-283-7031
Nicholas Ford, prin. Fax 352-4588
Our Lady of Guadalupe S 200/PK-8
3401 SW Myrtle St 98126 206-935-0651
Anton Kramer, prin. Fax 938-3695
Our Lady of the Lake S 300/PK-8
3520 NE 89th St 98115 206-525-9980
Vince McGovern, prin. Fax 523-2858
Pacific Crest S 200/PK-8
600 NW Bright St 98107 206-789-7889
St. Alphonsus S 200/PK-8
5816 15th Ave NW 98107 206-782-4363
Matthew Eisenhauer, prin. Fax 789-5709
St. Anne S 300/PK-8
101 W Lee St 98119 206-282-3538
Mary Sherman, prin. Fax 284-4191
St. Benedict S 200/PK-8
4811 Wallingford Ave N 98103 206-633-3375
Brian Anderson, prin. Fax 632-3236
St. Catherine S 200/PK-8
8524 8th Ave NE 98115 206-525-0581
Pam Schwartz, prin. Fax 985-0253
St. Edward S 200/PK-8
4200 S Mead St 98118 206-725-1774
Mary Lundeen, prin. Fax 725-4569
St. George S 200/PK-8
5117 13th Ave S 98108 206-762-0656
Monica Wingard, prin. Fax 763-3220

St. John S 500/PK-8
120 N 79th St 98103 206-783-0337
Bernadette O'Leary, prin. Fax 706-2704
St. Joseph S 600/K-8
700 18th Ave E 98112 206-329-3260
Patrick Fennessy, prin. Fax 324-7773
St. Matthew S 200/PK-8
1230 NE 127th St 98125 206-362-2785
Karen Herlihy, prin. Fax 440-9476
St. Paul S 100/PK-8
10001 57th Ave S 98178 206-725-0780
Elizabeth Kromer, prin. Fax 725-0781
St. Therese Academy 100/PK-8
900 35th Ave 98122 206-324-0460
Matthow DoBoor, prin. Fax 324 8464
Seattle Classical Christian S 100/PK-5
1013 8th Ave 98104 206-259-5831
Seattle Country Day S 300/K-8
2619 4th Ave N 98109 206-284-6220
Michael Murphy, head sch Fax 283-4251
Seattle Girls' S 100/5-8
2706 S Jackson St 98144 206-709-2228
Brenda Leaks, head sch Fax 329-1580
Seattle Hebrew Academy 200/PK-8
1617 Interlaken Dr E 98112 206-323-5750
Seattle Nativity S 6-8
2800 S Massachusetts St 98144 206-494-4708
Edward Nelson, dir.
Seattle Waldorf S 300/PK-8
2728 NE 100th St 98125 206-524-5320
Tracy Bennett, head sch Fax 523-3920
Shorewood Christian S 200/PK-8
10300 28th Ave SW 98146 206-933-1056
Rev. David Glass, prin. Fax 932-9002
Spruce Street S 100/K-5
914 Virginia St 98101 206-621-9211
Briel Schmitz, head sch Fax 624-2832
Torah Day S of Seattle 100/PK-8
1625 S Columbian Way 98108 206-722-1200
University Child Development S 300/PK-5
5062 9th Ave NE 98105 206-547-8237
Paula Smith, head sch Fax 547-3615
Valley S 100/PK-5
318 30th Ave E 98112 206-328-4475
Villa Academy 400/PK-8
5001 NE 50th St 98105 206-524-8885
John Milroy, head sch Fax 523-7131
West Seattle Montessori S & Academy 100/PK-8
11215 15th Ave SW 98146 206-935-0427
Westside S 300/PK-8
10404 34th Ave SW 98146 206-932-2511
Ted Kalmus, head sch Fax 935-2813

Sedro Woolley, Skagit, Pop. 10,288
Sedro-Woolley SD 101 4,300/PK-12
801 Trail Rd 98284 360-855-3500
Phil Brockman, supt. Fax 855-3574
www.swsd.k12.wa.us
Cascade MS 600/7-8
905 McGarigle Rd 98284 360-855-3520
Laura Davis, prin. Fax 855-3521
Central ES 400/K-6
601 Talcott St 98284 360-855-3560
Matt Mihelich, prin. Fax 855-3561
Evergreen ES 500/K-6
1007 McGarigle Rd 98284 360-855-3545
Brian Isakson, prin. Fax 855-3546
Good Beginnings Center 50/PK-PK
780 Cook Rd 98284 360-855-3863
Tony Smith, prin.
Purcell ES 400/K-6
700 Bennett St 98284 360-855-3555
Mike Cullum, prin. Fax 855-3556
Samish ES 200/K-6
23953 Prairie Rd 98284 360-855-3540
Mischelle Darragh, prin. Fax 855-3541
Other Schools – See Clearlake, Lyman, Mount Vernon

Sekiu, Clallam, Pop. 27
Cape Flattery SD 401 400/K-12
PO Box 109 98381 360-963-2249
Michelle Parkin, supt. Fax 963-2373
www.capeflattery.wednet.edu
Other Schools – See Clallam Bay, Neah Bay

Selah, Yakima, Pop. 6,994
Selah SD 119 1,600/PK-12
316 W Naches Ave 98942 509-698-8000
Shane Backlund, supt. Fax 698-8099
www.selah.k12.wa.us
Campbell PS 400/K-2
408 N 1st St 98942 509-698-8100
Rob Darling, prin. Fax 698-8101
Lince Early Learning Center PK-PK
308 W Naches Ave 98942 509-698-8023
Susan Petterson, dir.
Selah IS 200/3-5
1401 W Fremont Ave 98942 509-698-8300
Ryan Ranger, prin. Fax 698-8313
Selah MS 300/6-8
411 N 1st St 98942 509-698-8400
Marc Gallaway, prin. Fax 698-8399

Sequim, Clallam, Pop. 6,414
Sequim SD 323 2,700/K-12
503 N Sequim Ave 98382 360-582-3260
Gary Neal, supt. Fax 683-6303
sequimschools.org
Greywolf ES 500/K-5
171 Carlsborg Rd 98382 360-582-3300
Donna Hudson, prin. Fax 582-9555
Haller ES 600/K-5
350 W Fir St 98382 360-582-3200
Rebecca Stanton, prin. Fax 681-8543
Sequim MS 600/6-8
301 W Hendrickson Rd 98382 360-582-3500
Vince Riccobene, prin. Fax 582-9486

Mountain View Christian S 50/K-8
255 Medsker Rd 98382 360-683-6170

Shaw Island, San Juan
Shaw Island SD 10 50/K-8
PO Box 426 98286 360-468-2570
Jennifer Swanson, supt. Fax 468-2585
www.shaw.k12.wa.us
Shaw Island S 50/K-8
PO Box 426 98286 360-468-2570
Jennifer Swanson, supt. Fax 468-2585

Shelton, Mason, Pop. 9,392
Hood Canal SD 404 300/PK-8
111 N State Route 106 98584 360-877-5463
Shawn Batstone, supt. Fax 877-9123
www.hoodcanal.wednet.edu
Hood Canal ES 300/PK-8
111 N State Route 106 98584 360-877-5463
Shawn Batstone, admin. Fax 877-9123

Pioneer SD 402 700/PK-8
112 E Spencer Lake Rd 98584 360-426-9115
Martin A. Brewer, supt. Fax 426-1036
www.psd402.org
Pioneer ES 300/PK-5
112 E Spencer Lake Rd 98584 360-427-2737
Jodi Schaefer, admin. Fax 427-2933
Pioneer MS 400/6-8
112 E Spencer Lake Rd 98584 360-426-8291
Bracken Budge, prin. Fax 426-1036

Shelton SD 309 4,200/PK-12
700 S 1st St 98584 360-426-1687
Dr. Alex Apostle, supt. Fax 427-8610
www.sheltonschools.org
Bordeaux ES 500/K-5
350 E University Ave 98584 360-426-3253
Carey Murray, prin. Fax 462-7392
Evergreen ES 500/PK-5
900 W Franklin St 98584 360-426-8281
Adina Brito, prin. Fax 426-8576
Mountain View ES 700/PK-5
534 E K St 98584 360-426-8564
Jorge Nelson, prin. Fax 426-3446
Olympic MS 500/6-7
800 E K St 98584 360-462-6671
Eric Barkman, prin. Fax 462-6676

Southside SD 42 200/K-7
161 SE Collier Rd 98584 360-426-8437
Doris Bolender, supt. Fax 426 9970
www.southsideschool.org
Southside ES 200/K-7
161 SE Collier Rd 98584 360-426-8437
Doris Bolender, admin. Fax 426-9970

Shelton Valley Christian S 50/K-8
PO Box 773 98584 360-426-4198

Shoreline, King, Pop. 50,457
Shoreline SD 412 8,800/PK-12
18560 1st Ave NE 98155 206-393-4203
Dr. Rebecca Miner, supt. Fax 393-4204
www.shorelineschools.org
Briarcrest ES 500/K-6
2715 NE 158th St 98155 206-393-4170
Jonathan Nessan, prin. Fax 393-4174
Echo Lake ES 500/K-6
19345 Wallingford Ave N 98133 206-393-4338
Andrew Lohman, prin. Fax 393-4335
Einstein MS 700/7-8
19343 3rd Ave NW 98177 206-393-4730
Nyla Fritz, prin. Fax 393-4735
Highland Terrace ES 500/K-6
100 N 160th St 98133 206-393-4341
Gloria Henderson, prin. Fax 393-4348
Kellogg MS 600/7-8
16045 25th Ave NE 98155 206-393-4783
Heather Hiatt, prin. Fax 393-4780
Meridian Park ES 500/K-6
17077 Meridian Ave N 98133 206-393-4251
David Tadlock, prin. Fax 393-4259
Parkwood ES 500/K-6
1815 N 155th St 98133 206-393-4150
Ann Torres, prin. Fax 393-4158
Ridgecrest ES 500/K-6
16516 10th Ave NE 98155 206-393-4272
Dr. Sue McPeak, prin. Fax 393-4193
Shoreline Children's Center PK-PK
816 NE 190th St 98155 206-393-4256
Kelly Davidson, prin. Fax 393-4258
Syre ES 500/K-6
19545 12th Ave NW 98177 206-393-4165
Michelle Carroll, prin. Fax 393-4164
Other Schools – See Lake Forest Park

Evergreen S 400/PK-8
15201 Meridian Ave N 98133 206-364-2650
Ronnie Codrington-Cazeau, head sch Fax 365-1827
King's ES 500/PK-6
19531 Dayton Ave N 98133 206-546-7258
Evelyn Huling, prin. Fax 546-7586
King's JHS 200/7-8
19345 Crista Ln N 98133 206-546-7243
Jordana Halkett, prin. Fax 546-7250
St. Luke S 300/PK-8
17533 Saint Luke Pl N 98133 206-542-1133
Rick Boyle, prin. Fax 546-8693
St. Mark S 200/PK-8
18033 15th Pl NE 98155 206-364-1633
Kathryn Keck, prin. Fax 367-3919
Shoreline Christian S 200/PK-12
2400 NE 147th St 98155 206-364-7777
Timothy Visser, admin. Fax 364-0349

Silverdale, Kitsap, Pop. 17,925
Central Kitsap SD 401 9,200/K-12
PO Box 8 98383 360-662-1610
David McVicker, supt. Fax 662-1611
www.ckschools.org
Central Kitsap MS 500/6-8
PO Box 8 98383 360-662-2300
Scott McDaniel, prin. Fax 662-2301

Clear Creek ES 500/K-5
PO Box 8 98383 360-662-8100
Toby Tebo, prin. Fax 662-8101
Cougar Valley ES 400/K-5
PO Box 8 98383 360-662-8400
Jacque Crisman, prin. Fax 662-8401
Emerald Heights ES 500/K-5
PO Box 8 98383 360-662-8500
Greg Cleven, prin. Fax 662-8501
Ridgetop MS 400/6-8
PO Box 8 98383 360-662-2900
Rusty Willson, prin. Fax 662-2901
Silverdale ES 400/K-5
PO Box 8 98383 360-662-9400
Ninette Rivero, prin. Fax 662-9401
Silver Ridge ES 400/K-5
PO Box 8 98383 360-662-9500
Lisa Hawkins, prin. Fax 662-9501
Other Schools – See Bremerton

Skamania, Skamania
Skamania SD 2 100/K-8
122 Butler Loop Rd 98648 509-427-8239
Ralph Pruitt, supt. Fax 427-8921
skamania.k12.wa.us/
Skamania S 100/K-8
122 Butler Loop Rd 98648 509-427-8239
Sally Godwin, prin. Fax 427-8921

Skykomish, King, Pop. 197
Skykomish SD 404 50/K-12
PO Box 325 98288 360-677-2623
Thomas Jay, supt. Fax 677-2418
www.skykomish.wednet.edu
Skykomish S 50/K-12
PO Box 325 98288 360-677-2623
Thomas Jay, admin. Fax 677-2418

Snohomish, Snohomish, Pop. 8,810
Monroe SD 103
Supt. — See Monroe
Chain Lake ES 600/K-5
12125 Chain Lake Rd 98290 360-804-3100
Jef Lingelbach, prin. Fax 804-3199
Hidden River MS 400/6-8
9224 Paradise Lake Rd 98296 360-804-4100
Brett Wille, prin. Fax 804-4199
Maltby ES 400/K-5
9700 212th St SE 98296 360-804-3500
Bonnie McKerney, prin. Fax 804-3599

Snohomish SD 201 10,000/PK-12
1601 Avenue D 98290 360-563-7300
Kent Kultgen Ed.D., supt. Fax 563-7279
www.sno.wednet.edu
Cascade View ES 500/K-6
2401 Park Ave 98290 360-563-7000
Kert Lenseigne, prin. Fax 563-7004
Cathcart ES 400/K-6
8201 188th St SE 98296 360-563-7075
Mike Anderson, prin. Fax 563-7078
Centennial MS 800/7-8
3000 S Machias Rd 98290 360-563-4525
Dave Sage, prin. Fax 563-4585
Central ES 300/PK-2
221 Union Ave 98290 360-563-4600
Heidi Rothgeb, prin. Fax 563-4604
Dutch Hill ES 500/K-6
8231 131st Ave SE 98290 360-563-4450
Jack Tobin, prin. Fax 563-4455
Emerson ES 300/3-6
1103 Pine Ave 98290 360-563-7150
Craig Church, prin. Fax 563-7157
Little Cedars ES 700/K-6
7408 144th Pl SE 98296 360-563-2900
Lew Dickert, prin.
Machias ES 500/K-6
231 147th Ave SE 98290 360-563-4825
Shawn Ryan, prin. Fax 563-4828
Riverview ES 500/K-6
7322 64th St SE 98290 360-563-4375
Tammy Jones, prin. Fax 563-4378
Totem Falls ES 500/K-6
14211 Snohomish Cascade Dr 98296 360-563-4750
Hawk Cramer, prin. Fax 563-4756
Valley View MS 700/7-8
14308 Broadway Ave 98296 360-563-4225
Nancy Rhoades, prin. Fax 563-4236
Other Schools – See Everett

Cornerstone Academy 100/PK-9
16910 161st Ave SE 98290 425-892-3030
Michelle Jones, hdmstr.
St. Michael S 100/PK-8
1514 Pine Ave 98290 360-568-0821
Dr. Karen Matthews, prin. Fax 568-6426

Snoqualmie, King, Pop. 10,237
Snoqualmie Valley SD 410 6,400/PK-12
PO Box 400 98065 425-831-8000
Joel Aune, supt. Fax 831-8040
www.svsd410.org
Cascade View ES 700/K-5
34816 SE Ridge St 98065 425-831-4100
James Frazier, prin. Fax 831-4110
Snoqualmie ES 600/PK-5
39801 SE Park St 98065 425-831-8050
John Norberg, prin. Fax 831-8047
Timber Ridge ES K-5
34412 SE Swenson Dr 98065 425-831-3825
Amy Wright, prin. Fax 831-3810
Other Schools – See Fall City, North Bend

Soap Lake, Grant, Pop. 1,484
Soap Lake SD 156 500/K-12
410 Ginkgo St S 98851 509-246-1822
Rick Winters, supt. Fax 246-0669
www.slschools.org
Soap Lake ES 200/K-5
410 Ginkgo St S 98851 509-246-1323
Sunshine Rutherford, prin. Fax 246-0669

South Bend, Pacific, Pop. 1,566
South Bend SD 118 600/PK-12
PO Box 437 98586 360-875-6041
Dr. Jon Tienhaara, supt. Fax 875-6062
www.southbend.wednet.edu
Davis ES 300/K-6
PO Box 437 98586 360-875-5615
Kresta Byington, prin. Fax 875-6032
South Bend Early Learning Center 100/PK-PK
PO Box 437 98586 360-875-5327
Amy Nelson, dir. Fax 875-5379

Spanaway, Pierce, Pop. 24,048
Bethel SD 403 18,100/PK-12
516 176th St E 98387 253-683-6000
Tom Seigel, supt. Fax 683-6019
www.bethelsd.org
Bethel MS 700/6-8
22001 38th Ave E 98387 253-683-7200
Julie Schultz-Bartlett, prin. Fax 683-7298
Camas Prairie ES 600/K-5
320 176th St E 98387 253-683-7400
Cassandra Stephani, prin. Fax 683-7498
Cedarcrest MS 600/6-8
19120 13th Avenue Ct E 98387 253-683-7500
Scott Martin, prin. Fax 683-7598
Elk Plain S of Choice 500/PK-8
22015 22nd Ave E 98387 253-683-7900
Tom Mitchell, prin. Fax 683-7998
Evergreen ES 500/K-5
1311 172nd St E 98387 253-683-8200
Jamie Burnett, prin. Fax 683-8298
Liberty MS 800/6-8
7319 Eustis Hunt Rd 98387 253-683-6500
Seth Humphrey, prin. Fax 683-6598
Pioneer Valley ES 500/PK-5
7315 Eustis Hunt Rd 98387 253-683-8900
Christoph Green, prin. Fax 683-8998
Shining Mountain ES 600/PK-5
21615 38th Ave E 98387 253-683-5200
Paul Marquardt, prin. Fax 683-5298
Spanaway ES 400/PK-5
412 165th St S 98387 253-683-5300
Kim Kosa, prin. Fax 683-5398
Other Schools – See Graham, Puyallup, Roy, Tacoma

Spangle, Spokane, Pop. 277
Liberty SD 362 400/PK-12
29818 S North Pine Creek Rd 99031 509-624-4415
Kyle Rydell, supt. Fax 245-3288
www.libertysd.us
Liberty Elementary - JHS 300/PK-8
29818 S North Pine Creek Rd 99031 509-245-3211
Kyle Rydell, admin. Fax 245-3530

Upper Columbia Academy ES 50/1-8
3025 E Spangle Waverly Rd 99031 509-245-3629

Spokane, Spokane, Pop. 199,521
Cheney SD 360
Supt. — See Cheney
Westwood MS 500/6-8
6120 S Abbott Rd 99224 509-559-4150
Dr. Erika Burden, prin.
Windsor ES 400/PK-5
5504 W Hallett Rd 99224 509-559-4200
Vince Songaylo, prin. Fax 624-9107

Great Northern SD 312 50/K-6
3115 N Spotted Rd 99224 509-747-7714
Glenn Frizzell, supt. Fax 838-5670
www.gnsd.k12.wa.us
Great Northern ES 50/K-6
3115 N Spotted Rd 99224 509-747-7714
Fax 838-5670

Mead SD 354
Supt. — See Mead
Brentwood ES 500/K-6
406 W Regina Ave 99218 509-465-6200
Justin Valentine, prin. Fax 465-6220
Evergreen ES 600/K-6
215 W Eddy Ave 99208 509-465-6400
Michael Danford, prin. Fax 465-6420
Farwell ES 600/K-6
13005 N Crestline St 99208 509-465-6500
Barb Pybus, prin. Fax 465-6520
Northwood MS 700/7-8
13120 N Pittsburg St 99208 509-465-7500
Dave Stenersen, prin. Fax 465-7520
Prairie View ES 700/K-6
2606 W Johannsen Rd 99208 509-465-7800
Dr. Irene Gonzales, prin. Fax 465-7820
Shiloh Hills ES 500/K-6
505 E Stonewall Ave 99208 509-465-6800
Laura Duchow, prin. Fax 465-6820

Orchard Prairie SD 123 100/K-7
7626 N Orchard Prairie Rd 99217 509-467-9517
Howard King, supt. Fax 467-0590
www.orchardprairie.org
Orchard Prairie ES 100/K-7
7626 N Orchard Prairie Rd 99217 509-467-9517
Fax 467-0590

Spokane SD 81 29,300/PK-12
200 N Bernard St 99201 509-354-5900
Shelley Redinger Ph.D., supt. Fax 354-5959
www.spokaneschools.org
Adams ES 300/PK-6
2909 E 37th Ave 99223 509-354-2000
Beth Nye, prin. Fax 354-2020
Arlington ES 600/K-6
6363 N Smith St 99217 509-354-2100
Sue Unruh, prin. Fax 354-2121
Audubon ES 500/PK-6
2020 W Carlisle Ave 99205 509-354-2140
Kimberly Stretch, prin. Fax 354-2141
Balboa ES 400/K-6
3010 W Holyoke Ave 99208 509-354-2220
Stephanie Kubej, prin. Fax 354-2222
Bemiss ES 600/K-6
2323 E Bridgeport Ave 99207 509-354-2300
Janice Erickson, prin. Fax 354-2310
Browne ES 400/PK-6
5102 N Driscoll Blvd 99205 509-354-2400
Julia Lockwood, prin. Fax 354-2424
Chase MS 800/7-8
4747 E 37th Ave 99223 509-354-5000
John O'Dell, prin. Fax 354-5100
Cooper ES 500/PK-6
3200 N Ferrall St 99217 509-354-2500
Rona Williams, prin. Fax 354-2510
Finch ES 500/PK-6
3717 N Milton St 99205 509-354-2600
Shane O'Doherty, prin. Fax 354-2616
Franklin ES 400/K-6
3612 S Grand Blvd 99203 509-354-2620
Buz Hollingsworth, prin. Fax 354-2666
Garfield ES 500/PK-6
222 W Knox Ave 99205 509-354-2700
Jollene Vining, prin. Fax 354-2727
Garry MS 600/7-8
725 E Joseph Ave 99208 509-354-5200
Wendy Watson, prin. Fax 354-5212
Glover MS 600/7-8
2404 W Longfellow Ave 99205 509-354-5400
Mark Lund, prin. Fax 354-5399
Grant ES 400/K-6
1300 E 9th Ave 99202 509-354-2800
Ivan Corley, prin. Fax 354-2828
Hamblen ES 500/K-6
2121 E Thurston Ave 99203 509-354-2900
Stefanie Heinen, prin. Fax 354-2888
Holmes ES 400/K-6
2600 W Sharp Ave 99201 509-354-2990
Stephanie Lundberg, prin. Fax 354-2991
Hutton ES 500/K-6
908 E 24th Ave 99203 509-354-3030
Chuck Demarest, prin. Fax 354-3040
Indian Trail ES 300/PK-6
4102 W Woodside Ave 99208 509-354-3100
Brian Ormsby, prin. Fax 354-3110
Jefferson ES 600/PK-6
123 E 37th Ave 99203 509-354-3200
Nikki Golden, prin. Fax 354-3210
Lidgerwood ES 400/K-6
5510 N Lidgerwood St 99208 509-354-3225
Steve Barnes, prin. Fax 354-3235
Lincoln Heights ES 500/PK-6
3322 E 22nd Ave 99223 509-354-3300
Meghan Anderson, prin. Fax 354-3333
Linwood ES 400/PK-6
906 W Weile Ave 99208 509-354-3400
Gina Naccarato-Keele, prin. Fax 354-3404
Logan ES 500/PK-6
1001 E Montgomery Ave 99207 509-354-3434
Brent Perdue, prin. Fax 354-3499
Longfellow ES 600/PK-6
800 E Providence Ave 99207 509-354-3500
Ken Hermanson, prin. Fax 354-3535
Madison ES 300/K-6
319 W Nebraska Ave 99205 509-354-3600
Heather Jordan, prin. Fax 354-3636
Moran Prairie ES 500/PK-6
4224 E 57th Ave 99223 509-354-3700
Clint Price, prin. Fax 354-3666
Mullan Road ES 600/K-6
2616 E 63rd Ave 99223 509-354-3800
Mike McGinnis, prin. Fax 354-3777
Regal ES 500/K-6
2707 E Rich Ave 99207 509-354-3900
Tricia Kannberg, prin. Fax 354-3940
Ridgeview ES 400/K-6
5610 N Maple St 99205 509-354-4000
Matthew Beal, prin. Fax 354-3999
Roosevelt ES 500/PK-6
333 W 14th Ave 99204 509-354-4040
Debbie Oakley, prin. Fax 354-4080
Sacajawea MS 800/7-8
401 E 33rd Ave 99203 509-354-5500
Jeremy Ohse, prin. Fax 354-5505
Salk MS 700/7-8
6411 N Alberta St 99208 509-354-5600
Peter Elzey, prin. Fax 354-5542
Shaw MS 600/7-8
4106 N Cook St 99207 509-354-5800
Jon Swett, prin. Fax 354-5899
Sheridan ES 500/K-6
3737 E 5th Ave 99202 509-354-4100
Larry Quisano, prin. Fax 354-4101
Stevens ES 500/PK-6
1717 E Sinto Ave 99202 509-354-4200
Dan Jenkins, prin. Fax 354-4220
Westview ES 400/PK-6
3520 W Bismark Ave 99205 509-354-4300
Cathy Comfort, prin. Fax 354-4303
Whitman ES 600/K-6
5400 N Helena St 99207 509-354-4320
Jody Schmidt, prin. Fax 354-4323
Willard ES 600/K-6
500 W Longfellow Ave 99205 509-354-4444
Matt Truitt, prin. Fax 354-4474
Wilson ES 400/K-6
911 W 25th Ave 99203 509-354-4500
Tony Ressa, prin. Fax 354-4520
Woodridge ES 400/K-6
5100 W Shawnee Ave 99208 509-354-4600
Kale Colyar, prin. Fax 354-4604

West Valley SD 363
Supt. — See Spokane Valley
Millwood ECC 50/PK-PK
8818 E Grace Ave 99212 509-922-5478
Lisa Skay, dir. Fax 921-5259
West Valley Early Learning Center PK-PK
2523 N Park Rd 99212 509-922-5478
Dan Andrews, prin. Fax 921-5257

All Saints MS 300/PK-PK, 5-
1428 E 33rd Ave 99203 509-624-5712
Katherine Hicks, prin. Fax 624-7752
All Saints S 200/K-4
3510 E 18th Ave 99223 509-534-1098
Katherine Hicks, prin. Fax 534-1529
Assumption S 200/PK-8
3618 W Indian Trail Rd 99208 509-328-1115
T.J. Romano, prin. Fax 328-7872
Cataldo S 300/PK-8
455 W 18th Ave 99203 509-624-8759
Dr. Mark Selle, prin. Fax 624-8763
Countryside Adventist ES 50/1-8
12107 W Seven Mile Rd 99224 509-466-8982
Archie Harris, lead tchr.
First Presbyterian Christian S 200/PK-5
318 S Cedar St 99201 509-747-9192
Tracy Blue, prin.
North Wall S 50/PK-6
9408 N Wall St 99218 509-466-2695
Palisades Christian Academy 100/PK-10
1115 N Government Way 99224 509-325-1985
St. Aloysius S 300/PK-8
611 E Mission Ave 99202 509-489-7825
Angie Krauss, prin. Fax 487-0975
St. Charles S 300/PK-8
4515 N Alberta St 99205 509-327-9575
Fax 325-9353
St. George's S 400/K-12
2929 W Waikiki Rd 99208 509-466-1636
Jamie Tender, head sch Fax 467-3258
St. Matthew Lutheran S 100/PK-8
6917 N Country Homes Blvd 99208 509-327-5601
Jacob Biebert, prin. Fax 326-6751
St. Thomas More S 300/PK-8
515 W Saint Thomas Moore 99208 509-466-3811
Doug Banks, prin. Fax 466-0220
Southside Christian S 200/PK-8
401 E 30th Ave 99203 509-838-8139
Lorri Downs, prin. Fax 835-8050
Spokane Christian Academy 100/K-8
8909 E Bigelow Gulch Rd 99217 509-924-4888
Cheryl Gade, admin. Fax 924-0432
Spokane Classical Christian S 100/PK-12
7111 N Nine Mile Rd 99208 509-325-2252
Summit Christian Academy - Spokane 400/K-12
8913 N Nettleton Ln 99208 509-924-4618
Wes Evans M.Ed., admin. Fax 467-4942
Trinity S 200/PK-8
1306 W Montgomery Ave 99205 509-327-9369
Sandra Nokes, prin. Fax 328-4128

Spokane Valley, Spokane, Pop. 87,059
Central Valley SD 356 12,600/K-12
19307 E Cataldo Ave 99016 509-558-5400
Ben Small, supt. Fax 228-5439
www.cvsd.org
Adams ES 400/K-5
14707 E 8th Ave, 509-558-4000
Nicole Karaus, prin. Fax 558-4009
Bowdish MS 500/6-8
2109 S Skipworth Rd, 509-558-4700
Ty Larsen, prin. Fax 558-4714
Broadway ES 500/K-5
11016 E Broadway Ave, 509-558-4100
Lori Johnson, prin. Fax 558-4109
Chester ES 300/K-5
3525 S Pines Rd, 509-558-3150
Cindy Sothen, prin. Fax 558-3159
Evergreen MS 700/6-8
14221 E 16th Ave, 509-558-3700
John Parker, prin. Fax 558-3789
Greenacres ES 600/1-5
17915 E 4th Ave, 509-558-4200
Lindsay Kent, prin. Fax 558-4209
Greenacres MS 800/6-8
17409 E Sprague Ave, 509-558-4860
Vern DiGiovanni, prin. Fax 558-4869
Horizon MS 500/6-8
3915 S Pines Rd, 509-558-4940
Jesse Hardt, prin. Fax 558-4949
McDonald ES 300/K-5
1512 S McDonald Rd, 509-558-5350
Scott Krentel, prin. Fax 558-5359
North Pines MS 500/6-8
701 N Pines Rd, 509-558-5020
Lora Jackson, prin. Fax 558-5029
Opportunity ES 400/K-5
1109 S Wilbur Rd, 509-558-3550
Mandi Larson, prin. Fax 558-3559
Ponderosa ES 300/K-5
10105 E Cimmaron Dr, 509-558-6450
Sasha Deyarmin, prin. Fax 558-6459
Progress ES 400/K-5
710 N Progress Rd, 509-558-4500
Matthew Chisholm, prin. Fax 558-4509
South Pines ES 400/K-5
12021 E 24th Ave, 509-558-4400
Stan Koep, prin. Fax 558-4409
Summit S 300/K-8
13313 E Broadway Ave, 509-558-3250
Walt Clemons, prin. Fax 558-3259
Sunrise ES 600/K-5
14603 E 24th Ave, 509-558-3600
Sue McCollum, prin. Fax 558-3609
University ES 300/K-5
1613 S University Rd, 509-558-4650
Josh Wolcott, prin. Fax 558-4659
Other Schools – See Liberty Lake

East Valley SD 361 4,500/K-12
3830 N Sullivan Rd Bldg 1 99216 509-924-1830
Kelly Shea, supt. Fax 927-9500
www.evsd.org
Continuous Curriculum S 500/K-8
16924 E Wellesley Ave, 509-927-9501
Steve Pointer, prin. Fax 927-3211
East Valley MS 500/7-8
4920 N Progress Rd, 509-924-9383
Doug Kaplicky, admin. Fax 927-3214

Trent ES 500/K-6
3303 N Pines Rd, 509-924-2622
Ted Epperson, prin. Fax 927-3209
Trentwood ES 500/K-6
14701 E Wellesley Ave, 509-927-3215
Barbara Cruse, prin. Fax 927-3216
Other Schools – See Newman Lake, Otis Orchards

West Valley SD 363 3,600/PK-12
PO Box 11739 99211 509-924-2150
Dr. Gene Sementi, supt. Fax 922-5295
www.wvsd.org
Centennial MS 600/6-8
915 N Ella Rd, 509-922-5482
Karen Bromps, prin. Fax 891-9520
Ness ES 400/K-5
9612 E Cataldo Ave, 509-922-5470
Theresa Kendall, prin. Fax 927-1144
Orchard Center ES 300/K-5
7519 E Buckeye Ave, 509-922-5473
Barb Knauss, prin. Fax 927-1141
Pasadena Park ES 400/K-5
8508 E Upriver Dr, 509-922-5480
Brad Liberg, prin. Fax 891-9529
West Valley City MS 200/5-8
8920 E Valleyway Ave, 509-921-2836
Dusty Andres, prin. Fax 921-2849
Woodard ES 400/K-5
7401 E Mission Ave, 509-921-2160
Mike Lollar, prin. Fax 891-9524
Other Schools – See Spokane

Oaks-A Classical Christian Academy 300/K-12
PO Box 141146, 509-536-5955
Charlie Dowers, hdmstr. Fax 536-7877
St. John Vianney S 200/PK-8
501 N Walnut Rd, 509-926-7987
Sonia Flores-Davis, prin. Fax 922-5282
St. Mary's Catholic S 300/PK-8
14601 E 4th Ave, 509-924-4300
Laurene Nauditt, prin. Fax 922-8139
Spokane Valley Adventist S 50/K-8
1603 S Sullivan Rd, 509-926-0955
Valley Christian S 200/PK-12
10212 E 9th Ave, 509-924-9131
Derick Tabish, admin. Fax 924-2971

Sprague, Lincoln, Pop. 438
Sprague SD 8 100/K-12
PO Box 305 99032 509-257-2591
William Ressel, supt. Fax 257-2539
www.spraguelamont.org
Sprague ES 50/K-4
PO Box 305 99032 509-257-2591
William Ressel, prin. Fax 257-2539

Springdale, Stevens, Pop. 275
Mary Walker SD 207 400/PK-12
PO Box 159 99173 509-258-4534
Kevin Jacka, supt. Fax 258-4707
www.marywalker.org/
Springdale ES 200/PK-5
PO Box 159 99173 509-258-7357
Edwina Hargrave, prin. Fax 258-7756
Springdale MS 100/6-8
PO Box 159 99173 509-258-7357
Matthew Cobb, prin. Fax 258-7756

Stanwood, Snohomish, Pop. 6,009
Stanwood-Camano SD 401 4,500/K-12
26920 Pioneer Hwy 98292 360-629-1200
Dr. Jean Shumate, supt. Fax 629-1242
www.stanwood.wednet.edu
Cedarhome ES 600/K-5
27911 68th Ave NW 98292 360-629-1280
Jeff Lofgren, prin. Fax 629-1289
Port Susan MS 500/6-8
7506 267th St NW 98292 360-629-1360
Keri Von Moos, prin. Fax 629-1365
Stanwood ES 300/K-5
10227 273rd Pl NW 98292 360-629-1250
Barbara Marsh, prin. Fax 629-1252
Stanwood MS 500/6-8
9405 271st St NW 98292 360-629-1350
Tod Klundt, prin. Fax 629-1354
Twin City ES 300/K-5
26211 72nd Ave NW 98292 360-629-1270
Jennifer Allen, prin. Fax 629-1279
Other Schools – See Camano Island

Starbuck, Columbia, Pop. 121
Starbuck SD 35 50/K-8
PO Box 188 99359 509-399-2381
Kevin Grafftis, supt. Fax 399-2381
www.starbuck.k12.wa.us
Starbuck S 50/K-8
PO Box 188 99359 509-399-2381
Laura Christian, admin. Fax 399-2381

Stehekin, Chelan
Stehekin SD 69, PO Box 37 98852 50/K-8
Ron Scott, supt. 509-665-2610
stehekinschool.org
Stehekin ES, PO Box 37 98852 50/K-8
Ron Scott, supt. 509-665-2610

Steilacoom, Pierce, Pop. 5,521
Steilacoom Historical SD 1 3,100/PK-12
511 Chambers St 98388 253-983-2200
Kathi Weight, supt. Fax 584-7198
www.steilacoom.k12.wa.us
Cherrydale PS 300/PK-3
1201 Galloway St 98388 253-983-2500
Ryan Douglas, prin. Fax 583-8478
Salter's Point ES 500/4-5
908 3rd St 98388 253-983-2600
Alex Clauson, prin. Fax 581-9083
Other Schools – See Anderson Island, DuPont

Steptoe, Whitman, Pop. 175
Steptoe SD 304 50/PK-8
PO Box 138 99174 509-397-3119
Fax 397-6393
Steptoe S 50/PK-8
PO Box 138 99174 509-397-3119
Eric Patton, prin. Fax 397-6393

Stevenson, Skamania, Pop. 1,431
Stevenson-Carson SD 303 900/K-12
PO Box 850 98648 509-427-5674
Karen Douglass, supt. Fax 427-4028
www.scsd.k12.wa.us
Stevenson ES 200/K-2
PO Box 850 98648 509-427-5672
Karen Schreiber, prin. Fax 427-7413
Wind River MS 100/7-8
PO Box 850 98648 509-427-5631
Joe Randall, prin. Fax 427-5639
Other Schools – See Carson

Sultan, Snohomish, Pop. 4,514
Sultan SD 311 1,800/K-12
514 4th St 98294 360-793-9800
Dan Chaplik, supt. Fax 793-9890
www.sultanschools.org
Sultan ES 500/K-5
501 Date Ave 98294 360-793-9830
Aubrey Van Orden, prin. Fax 793-9836
Sultan MS 400/6-8
301 High Ave 98294 360-793-9850
Nathan Plummer, prin. Fax 793-9859
Other Schools – See Gold Bar

Sumas, Whatcom, Pop. 1,272
Nooksack Valley SD 506
Supt. — See Everson
Sumas ES 200/PK-5
1024 Lawson St 98295 360-988-9423
Megan Vigre, prin. Fax 988-0505

Sumner, Pierce, Pop. 9,086
Sumner SD 320 8,700/K-12
1202 Wood Ave 98390 253-891-6000
Keoni Smith, supt. Fax 891-6097
www.sumnersd.org
Daffodil Valley ES 500/K-5
1509 Valley Ave E 98390 253-891-4600
Jane Aronson, prin. Fax 891-4622
Maple Lawn ES 500/K-5
230 Wood Ave 98390 253-891-4400
Elli McDaniel, prin. Fax 891-4422
Sumner MS 700/6-8
1508 Willow St 98390 253-891-5000
Jennifer Williams, prin. Fax 891-5045
Other Schools – See Bonney Lake

Sunnyside, Yakima, Pop. 15,748
Sunnyside SD 201 6,400/K-12
1110 S 6th St 98944 509-837-5851
Jeri Paulakis, supt. Fax 837-0535
www.sunnysideschools.org
Chief Kamiakin ES 700/1-5
1700 E Lincoln Ave 98944 509-837-6444
Kim Frank, prin. Fax 836-8414
Harrison MS 800/6-8
810 S 16th St 98944 509-837-3601
Robert Bowman, prin. Fax 837-0450
Pioneer ES 800/1-5
2101 E Lincoln Ave 98944 509-836-2200
Kristine Diddens, prin. Fax 836-2220
Sierra Vista MS 700/6-8
916 N 16th St 98944 509-836-8500
Julie Perez, prin. Fax 836-8515
Sun Valley ES 500/K-K
1220 N 16th St 98944 509-836-7520
Jeri Paulakis, prin. Fax 515-3300
Washington ES 600/1-5
800 Jackson Ave 98944 509-837-3641
Gwyn Trull, prin. Fax 837-0454
Other Schools – See Outlook

Sunnyside Christian S 200/PK-8
811 North Ave 98944 509-837-3044
Brad Van Beek, prin. Fax 837-4086

Suquamish, Kitsap, Pop. 3,874
North Kitsap SD 400
Supt. — See Poulsbo
Suquamish ES 400/PK-5
18950 Park Blvd NE 98392 360-396-3850
Gwen Lyon, prin. Fax 396-3916

Tacoma, Pierce, Pop. 182,594
Bethel SD 403
Supt. — See Spanaway
Clover Creek ES 500/PK-5
16715 36th Ave E 98446 253-683-7800
Sara Olson, prin. Fax 683-7898
Naches Trail ES 500/K-5
15305 Waller Rd E 98446 253-683-8700
Sean McKenzie, prin. Fax 683-8798
Spanaway MS 700/6-8
15701 B St E 98445 253-683-5400
Shannon Leatherwood, prin. Fax 683-5408
Thompson ES 600/PK-5
303 159th St E 98445 253-683-5800
Ralph Wisner, prin. Fax 683-5898

Fife SD 417 3,600/PK-12
5802 20th St E 98424 253-517-1000
Kevin Alfano, supt. Fax 517-1055
www.fifeschools.com
Other Schools – See Edgewood, Milton

Franklin Pierce SD 402 7,500/PK-12
315 129th St S 98444 253-298-3000
Dr. Frank Hewins, supt. Fax 298-3015
www.fpschools.org
Brookdale ES 500/K-5
611 132nd St S 98444 253-298-3100
Connie Holman, prin. Fax 298-3115
Central Avenue ES 400/K-5
4505 104th St E 98446 253-298-3200
Tonya Middling, prin. Fax 298-3215
Christensen ES 400/K-5
10232 Barnes Ln S 98444 253-298-3300
Dr. Tim Enfield, prin. Fax 298-3315
Collins ES 400/K-5
4608 128th St E 98446 253-298-3400
Dr. Barbara Mondloch, prin. Fax 298-3415
Early Learning Center PK-PK
12223 S A St 98444 253-298-4675
Carol Miller, admin. Fax 537-3162
Elmhurst ES 500/K-5
420 133rd St E 98445 253-298-3500
Theresa Prather, prin. Fax 298-3515
Ford MS 900/6-8
1602 104th St E 98445 253-298-3600
Heather Renner, prin. Fax 298-3615
Harvard ES 400/K-5
1709 85th St E 98445 253-298-4100
Paul Elery, prin. Fax 298-4115
Keithley MS 700/6-8
12324 12th Ave S 98444 253-298-4300
Dr. Tom Edwards, prin. Fax 298-4315
Midland ES 500/K-5
2300 105th St E 98445 253-298-4500
Paula Dawson, prin. Fax 298-4515
Sales ES 400/K-5
11213 Sheridan Ave S 98444 253-298-4200
Brandy Nelson, prin. Fax 298-4215

Puyallup SD 3
Supt. — See Puyallup
Waller Road ES 300/K-6
6312 Waller Rd E 98443 253-841-8745
Rick Cox, prin. Fax 840-8941

Tacoma SD 10, PO Box 1357 98401 28,400/PK-12
Carla Santorno, supt. 253-571-1000
www.tacomaschools.org
Arlington ES 300/PK-5
3702 McKinley Ave E 98404 253-571-3200
Wendy Pye-Carter, prin. Fax 571-3201
Baker MS 700/6-8
8001 S J St 98408 253-571-5000
Scott Rich, prin. Fax 571-5091
Birney ES 400/PK-5
1202 S 76th St 98408 253-571-4600
James Neil, prin. Fax 571-4608
Blix ES 500/PK-5
1302 E 38th St 98404 253-571-7400
Jennifer Cooper, prin. Fax 571-7525
Boze ES 400/PK-5
1140 E 65th St 98404 253-571-4688
Arron Wilkins, prin. Fax 571-4690
Browns Point ES 500/K-5
1526 51st St NE 98422 253-571-7600
Dr. Forrest Griek, prin. Fax 571-7665
Bryant Montessori S 400/PK-8
717 S Grant Ave 98405 253-571-2800
Adam Kulass, prin. Fax 571-2801
Crescent Heights ES 500/K-5
4110 Nassau Ave NE 98422 253-571-5500
Sean McGeeney, prin. Fax 571-5546
DeLong ES 600/K-5
4901 S 14th St 98405 253-571-5800
Eric Konishi, prin. Fax 571-5803
Downing ES 300/PK-5
2502 N Orchard St 98406 253-571-7100
Olga Manos, prin. Fax 571-7151
Edison ES 500/PK-5
5830 S Pine St 98409 253-571-1700
Julia Bare, prin. Fax 571-1672
Fawcett ES 400/K-5
126 E 60th St 98404 253-571-4700
Christian Jordan, prin. Fax 571-4754
Fern Hill ES 400/PK-5
8442 S Park Ave 98444 253-571-3888
Mary Wilson, prin. Fax 571-3889
First Creek MS 800/6-8
1801 E 56th St 98404 253-571-2700
Tammy Larsen, prin. Fax 571-2717
Franklin ES 200/K-5
1402 S Lawrence St 98405 253-571-1400
Kecia Keller, prin. Fax 571-1790
Geiger Montessori S 400/K-5
7401 S 8th St 98465 253-571-6800
Neil O'Brien, prin. Fax 571-6850
Giaudrone MS 600/6-8
4902 S Alaska St 98408 253-571-5811
Billy Harris, prin. Fax 571-5812
Grant ES 400/PK-5
1018 N Prospect St 98406 253-571-5400
Steve Holmes, prin. Fax 571-5425
Gray MS 600/6-8
6229 S Tyler St 98409 253-571-5200
Shaun Martin, prin. Fax 571-5201
Jefferson ES 300/PK-5
4302 N 13th St 98406 253-571-4000
Avance Byrd, prin. Fax 571-3982
Larchmont ES 400/K-5
8601 E B St 98445 253-571-6200
Cynthia Horner, prin. Fax 571-6262
Lee MS 600/6-8
602 N Sprague Ave 98403 253-571-7700
Christi Brandt, prin. Fax 571-7710
Lister ES 500/PK-5
2106 E 44th St 98404 253-571-2900
Kristi Amrine, prin. Fax 571-2969
Lowell ES 400/K-5
810 N Mr Dahl Dr 98403 253-571-7200
Renee Rossman, prin. Fax 571-7202
Lyon ES 300/PK-5
101 E 46th St 98404 253-571-4800
Anita Roth, prin. Fax 571-4801
Manitou Park ES 600/PK-5
4330 S 66th St 98409 253-571-5300
Steven Mondragon, prin. Fax 571-5369
Mann ES 500/PK-5
1002 S 52nd St 98408 253-571-6300
Taj Jensen, prin. Fax 571-6301

Mason MS 800/6-8
3901 N 28th St 98407 253-571-7000
Patrice Sulkosky, prin. Fax 571-7091
McCarver ES 400/PK-5
2111 S J St 98405 253-571-4900
Becky Owens, prin. Fax 571-4950
Meeker MS 600/6-8
4402 Nassau Ave NE 98422 253-571-6500
Timothy Berndt, prin. Fax 571-6503
Northeast Tacoma ES 300/K-5
5412 29th St NE 98422 253-571-6933
Josh Zarling, prin. Fax 571-6934
Point Defiance ES 400/PK-5
4330 N Visscher St 98407 253-571-6900
Lisa Boyd, prin. Fax 571-6922
Reed ES 500/PK-5
1802 S 36th St 98418 253-571-6400
Kate Frazier, prin. Fax 571-6460
Roosevelt ES 200/PK-5
3550 E Roosevelt Ave 98404 253-571-4400
Autumn Foster, prin. Fax 571-4468
Sheridan ES 600/K-5
5317 McKinley Ave 98404 253-571-5900
Anna Griebel, prin. Fax 571-5929
Sherman ES 400/K-5
4415 N 38th St 98407 253-571-5488
Anne Tsuneishi, prin. Fax 571-5484
Skyline ES 400/PK-5
2301 N Mildred St 98406 253-571-7800
Regina Rainbolt, prin. Fax 571-7799
Stafford ES 500/K-5
1615 S 92nd St 98444 253-571-4300
Shannan Graves, prin. Fax 571-4301
Stanley ES 300/PK-5
1712 S 17th St 98405 253-571-4500
Cindy Johnson, prin. Fax 571-4555
Stewart MS 500/6-8
5010 S Pacific Ave 98408 253-571-4200
Zeek Edmond, prin. Fax 571-4244
Truman MS 700/6-8
5801 N 35th St 98407 253-571-5600
Andre Stout, prin. Fax 571-5680
Wainwright MS 200/4-8
130 Alameda Ave 98466 253-571-3444
Fax 571-3446
Washington ES 400/K-5
2615 N Adams St 98407 253-571-5700
Ed Schau, prin. Fax 571-5744
Whitman ES 400/PK-5
1120 S 39th St 98418 253-571-7272
Tracy Allen, prin. Fax 571-7270
Whittier ES 500/K-3
777 Elm Tree Ln 98466 253-571-7500
Donna Basil, prin. Fax 571-7586

Cascade Christian/Frederickson ES 200/PK-6
3425 176th St E 98446 253-537-9339
Tina deVries, prin. Fax 531-4699
Concordia Lutheran S 200/PK-8
202 E 56th St 98404 253-475-9513
Sherrie Gibleyou, prin. Fax 475-5445
Cor Deo S, 20 Tacoma Ave S 98402 100/PK-6
Matt Shuts, head sch 253-225-1721
Faith Lutheran S 100/PK-8
113 S 96th St 98444 253-537-2696
Paul Leifer, prin. Fax 537-2696
Holy Rosary S 100/PK-8
504 S 30th St 98402 253-272-7012
Katie Dempsey, prin. Fax 404-1804
Life Christian Academy 600/PK-12
1717 S Union Ave 98405 253-756-5300
Ross Hjelseth, hdmstr. Fax 761-9798
St. Charles Borromeo S 500/PK-8
7112 S 12th St 98465 253-564-5185
Brian Bradish, prin. Fax 566-5491
St. Patrick S 400/PK-8
1112 N G St 98403 253-272-2297
Chris Gavin, prin. Fax 383-2003
Tacoma Baptist S 300/PK-12
2052 S 64th St 98409 253-475-7226
Brad McCain, head sch Fax 471-9949
Tacoma Christian Academy 200/PK-10
2014 S 15th St 98405 253-234-5112
Alex Slobodyanik, prin. Fax 272-3413
Tacoma Waldorf S 100/PK-5
4301 N Stevens St 98407 253-383-8711
Chanin Escovedo, dean
Visitation STEM Academy 200/PK-8
3306 S 58th St 98409 253-474-6424
Marc Nuno, prin. Fax 474-6718
Wright Academy 700/PK-12
7723 Chambers Creek Rd W 98467 253-620-8300
Matt Culberson, head sch Fax 620-8431
Wright S 400/PK-12
827 N Tacoma Ave 98403 253-272-2216
Christian Sullivan, head sch Fax 572-3616

Taholah, Grays Harbor, Pop. 818
Taholah SD 77 100/K-12
PO Box 249 98587 360-276-4780
Lenora Hall M.Ed., supt. Fax 276-4370
www.taholah.org
Taholah S 100/K-12
PO Box 249 98587 360-276-4729
Patricia Larriva M.Ed., prin. Fax 276-4370

Tekoa, Whitman, Pop. 764
Tekoa SD 265 200/PK-12
PO Box 869 99033 509-284-3281
Dr. Connie Kliewer, supt. Fax 284-2045
www.tekoasd.org
Tekoa ES 100/PK-6
PO Box 869 99033 509-284-2781
Dr. Connie Kliewer, prin. Fax 284-4027

Tenino, Thurston, Pop. 1,631
Tenino SD 402 1,200/PK-12
PO Box 4024 98589 360-264-3400
Joe Belmonte, supt. Fax 264-3438
www.teninosd.org
Parkside ES 300/PK-2
PO Box 4024 98589 360-264-3800
Brock Williams, prin. Fax 264-3838
Tenino ES 300/3-5
PO Box 4024 98589 360-264-3700
Charles Harrington, prin. Fax 264-3738
Tenino MS 300/6-8
PO Box 4024 98589 360-264-3600
John Neal, prin. Fax 264-3638

Thorp, Kittitas, Pop. 235
Thorp SD 400 100/PK-12
PO Box 150 98946 509-964-2107
Dr. Linda Martin Ed.D., supt. Fax 964-2313
www.thorpschools.org/
Thorp S 100/PK-12
PO Box 150 98946 509-964-2107
Dr. Linda Martin Ed.D., prin. Fax 964-2313

Tieton, Yakima, Pop. 1,180
Highland SD 203
Supt. — See Cowiche
Tieton IS 300/4-6
PO Box 6 98947 509-678-8700
Kelly Thorson, prin. Fax 673-2771

Toledo, Lewis, Pop. 712
Toledo SD 237 800/PK-12
PO Box 469 98591 360-864-6325
Chris Rust, supt. Fax 864-6326
www.toledoschools.us
Toledo ES 300/PK-5
PO Box 549 98591 360-864-4761
Angela Bacon, prin. Fax 864-8146
Toledo MS 200/6-8
PO Box 668 98591 360-864-2395
Heather Ogden, prin. Fax 864-8147

Tonasket, Okanogan, Pop. 1,010
Tonasket SD 404 1,200/PK-12
35 Highway 20 98855 509-486-2126
Steve McCullough, supt. Fax 486-1263
www.tonasket.wednet.edu
Tonasket ES 500/PK-5
35 Highway 20 98855 509-486-4933
Jeremy Clark, prin. Fax 486-2164
Tonasket MS 200/6-8
35 Highway 20 98855 509-486-2147
Kristi Krieg, prin. Fax 486-1576

Peaceful Valley Christian S 50/1-8
PO Box 1062 98855 509-486-4345

Toppenish, Yakima, Pop. 8,831
Toppenish SD 202 3,700/PK-12
306 Bolln Dr 98948 509-865-4455
John M. Cerna, supt. Fax 865-2067
www.toppenish.wednet.edu
Garfield ES 400/K-5
505 Madison Ave 98948 509-865-4575
Debbie Whitney, prin. Fax 865-8407
Kirkwood ES 600/K-5
403 S Juniper St 98948 509-865-4750
Dawn Weddle, prin. Fax 865-3223
Lincoln ES 400/K-5
309 N Alder St 98948 509-865-4555
Patrisia Diaz, prin. Fax 865-7511
Toppenish MS 800/6-8
104 Goldendale Ave 98948 509-865-2730
Stephanie Wood, prin. Fax 865-7503
Toppenish Preschool 100/PK-PK
407 S Juniper St 98948 509-865-8179
Anastasia Sanchez, dir. Fax 865-2476
Valley View ES 400/K-5
515 Zillah Ave 98948 509-865-8240
Susan Rice, prin. Fax 865-8234

Touchet, Walla Walla, Pop. 415
Touchet SD 300 200/K-12
PO Box 135 99360 509-394-2352
Susan Bell, supt. Fax 394-2952
www.touchet.k12.wa.us
Touchet ES 100/K-5
PO Box 135 99360 509-394-2922
John Holcomb, prin. Fax 394-2924

Toutle, Cowlitz
Toutle Lake SD 130 600/K-12
5050 Spirit Lake Hwy 98649 360-274-6182
Scott Grabenhorst, supt. Fax 274-7608
www.toutlesd.k12.wa.us
Toutle Lake ES 300/K-6
5050 Spirit Lake Hwy 98649 360-274-6142
Jerry Johnson, prin. Fax 274-7608

Trout Lake, Klickitat, Pop. 545
Trout Lake SD R-400 100/K-12
PO Box 488 98650 509-395-2571
Doug Dearden, supt. Fax 395-2399
www.troutlake.k12.wa.us/
Trout Lake S 100/K-12
PO Box 488 98650 509-395-2571
Crystal Lanz, prin. Fax 395-2399

Tukwila, King, Pop. 17,643
Tukwila SD 406 2,900/K-12
4640 S 144th St 98168 206-901-8000
Dr. Nancy Coogan, supt. Fax 901-8016
tukwilaschools.org
Cascade View ES 500/K-5
13601 32nd Ave S 98168 206-901-7700
Fax 901-7707
Showalter MS 700/6-8
4628 S 144th St 98168 206-901-7800
Brett Christopher, prin. Fax 901-7807
Thorndyke ES 400/K-5
4415 S 150th St 98188 206-901-7600
Aaron Draganov, prin. Fax 901-7607
Tukwila ES 500/K-5
5939 S 149th St 98168 206-901-7500
Steve Salisbury, prin. Fax 901-7507

Tumwater, Thurston, Pop. 16,544
Tumwater SD 33 6,300/PK-12
621 Linwood Ave SW 98512 360-709-7000
John Bash, supt. Fax 709-7002
www.tumwater.k12.wa.us
Bush MS 500/6-8
2120 83rd Ave SW 98512 360-709-7400
Linda O'Shaughnessy, prin. Fax 709-7402
Schmidt ES 600/PK-5
237 Dennis St SE 98501 360-709-7200
Kim Doughty, prin. Fax 709-7202
Simmons ES 700/PK-5
1205 2nd Ave SW 98512 360-709-7100
Elliott Hedin, prin. Fax 709-7102
Tumwater Hill ES 400/PK-5
3120 Ridgeview Ct SW 98512 360-709-7300
Mandy Jessee, prin. Fax 709-7302
Tumwater MS 500/6-8
6335 Littlerock Rd SW 98512 360-709-7500
Jon Wilcox, prin. Fax 709-7502
Other Schools – See Littlerock, Olympia

Union Gap, Yakima, Pop. 5,960
Union Gap SD 2 600/PK-8
3201 4th St 98903 509-248-3966
Lisa Gredvig, supt. Fax 575-1876
uniongapschool.org
Union Gap S 600/PK-8
3201 4th St 98903 509-248-3966
Lisa Gredvig, prin. Fax 575-1876

University Place, Pierce, Pop. 28,698
University Place SD 83 5,600/K-12
3717 Grandview Dr W 98466 253-566-5600
Jeffery Chamberlin, supt. Fax 566-5607
www.upsd.wednet.edu
Chambers PS 400/K-4
9101 56th St W 98467 253-566-5650
Ali Shepard, prin. Fax 566-5698
Drum IS 600/5-7
4909 79th Ave W 98467 253-566-5660
Maile Carr, prin. Fax 566-5663
Evergreen PS 500/K-4
7102 40th St W 98466 253-566-5680
Clifford Schlattmann, prin. Fax 566-5684
Narrows View IS 700/5-7
7813 44th St W 98466 253-566-5630
Jennifer Wong, prin. Fax 566-5634
Sunset PS 400/K-4
4523 97th Ave W 98466 253-566-5640
Mary Godwin-Austen, prin. Fax 566-5642
University Place PS 500/K-4
2708 Grandview Dr W 98466 253-566-5620
William Keith, prin. Fax 566-5704

Heritage Christian S 200/PK-8
5412 67th Ave W 98467 253-564-6276
Ian Scott, prin. Fax 460-1695

Valley, Stevens, Pop. 135
Valley SD 070 1,000/PK-12
3030 Huffman Rd 99181 509-937-2791
Kevin Foster, supt. Fax 937-2691
www.valleysd.org/
Valley Early Learning Center PK-PK
3030 Huffman Rd 99181 509-937-2738
Candice Harris, dir. Fax 937-2691
Valley S 200/K-8
3034 Huffman Rd 99181 509-937-2413
Todd Smith, prin. Fax 937-2204

Vancouver, Clark, Pop. 153,919
Battle Ground SD 119
Supt. — See Brush Prairie
Glenwood Heights PS 600/K-4
9716 NE 134th St 98662 360-885-5250
Ken Evans, prin. Fax 885-5260
Laurin MS 600/5-8
13601 NE 97th Ave 98662 360-885-5200
Nick Krause, prin. Fax 885-5205
Pleasant Valley MS 500/5-8
14320 NE 50th Ave 98686 360-885-5500
Tamarah Grigg, prin. Fax 885-5510
Pleasant Valley PS 600/K-4
14320 NE 50th Ave 98686 360-885-5550
Michael Michaud, prin. Fax 885-5555

Evergreen SD 114 26,000/K-12
PO Box 8910 98668 360-604-4000
John Steach, supt. Fax 892-5307
www.evergreenps.org/
Burnt Bridge Creek ES 500/K-5
PO Box 8910 98668 360-604-6750
Darcy Mitchelson, prin. Fax 604-6751
Burton ES 400/K-5
PO Box 8910 98668 360-604-4975
Rebecca Chase, prin. Fax 604-4977
Cascade MS 900/6-8
PO Box 8910 98668 360-604-3600
Kristin White, prin. Fax 604-3602
Columbia Valley ES 500/K-5
PO Box 8910 98668 360-604-3375
James Fernandez, prin. Fax 604-3377
Covington MS 1,100/6-8
PO Box 8910 98668 360-604-6300
Charbonneau Gourde, prin. Fax 604-6302
Crestline ES 400/K-5
PO Box 8910 98668 360-604-3325
Bobbi Hite, prin. Fax 604-3327
Ellsworth ES 400/K-5
PO Box 8910 98668 360-604-6950
David Schaefer, prin. Fax 604-6952
Endeavour ES 600/K-5
PO Box 8910 98668 360-604-4920
Lauren Bradley, prin. Fax 604-4922
Fircrest ES 500/K-5
PO Box 8910 98668 360-604-6925
Scott Eppinger, prin. Fax 604-6927
Fisher's Landing ES 700/K-5
PO Box 8910 98668 360-604-6650
Judi DesRochers, prin. Fax 604-6652

Frontier MS 900/6-8
PO Box 8910 98668 360-604-3200
Griffin Peyton, prin. Fax 604-3202
Harmony ES 700/K-5
PO Box 8910 98668 360-604-6600
Laura Buno, prin. Fax 604-6602
Hearthwood ES 400/K-5
PO Box 8910 98668 360-604-6875
Tracy Schuster, prin. Fax 604-6877
Image ES 600/K-5
PO Box 8910 98668 360-604-6850
Kathleen Keller, prin. Fax 604-6852
Marrion ES 500/K-5
PO Box 8910 98668 360-604-6825
Mathew Hill, prin. Fax 604-6827
Mill Plain ES 500/K-5
PO Box 8910 98668 360-604-6800
Jennifer Dowell, prin. Fax 604-6802
Orchards ES 600/K-5
PO Box 8910 98668 360-604-6975
Elizabeth Brawley, prin. Fax 604-6977
Pacific MS 1,000/6-8
PO Box 8910 98668 360-604-6500
Heather Thiessen, prin. Fax 604-6502
Pioneer ES 600/K-5
PO Box 8910 98668 360-604-3300
Jenny Hayworth, prin. Fax 604-3302
Riverview ES 500/K-5
PO Box 8910 98668 360-604-6625
Stuart Anderson, prin. Fax 604-6627
Shahala MS 1,100/6-8
PO Box 8910 98668 360-604-3800
Gregg Brown, prin. Fax 604-3802
Sifton ES 500/K-5
PO Box 8910 98668 360-604-6675
Angela Mitchell, prin. Fax 604-6677
Silver Star ES 500/K-5
PO Box 8910 98668 360-604-6775
Mari Schauer, prin. Fax 604-6777
Sunset ES 500/K-5
PO Box 8910 98668 360-604-6900
Michael Martin, prin. Fax 604-6902
Wy' East MS 900/6-8
PO Box 8910 98668 360-604-6400
Caroline Garrett, prin. Fax 604-6402
York ES 500/K-5
PO Box 8910 98668 360-604-3975
Dawn Harris, prin. Fax 604-3977
Other Schools – See Camas

Vancouver SD 37 22,300/K-12
PO Box 8937 98668 360-313-1000
Dr. Steven Webb, supt. Fax 313-1001
www.vansd.org
Alki MS 700/6-8
1800 NW Bliss Rd 98685 360-313-3200
Darci Fronk, prin. Fax 313-3201
Anderson ES 800/K-5
2215 NE 104th St 98686 360-313-1500
Katie Arkoosh, prin. Fax 313-1501
Chinook ES 700/K-5
1900 NW Bliss Rd 98685 360-313-1600
Patrick Conners, prin. Fax 313-1601
Discovery MS 700/6-8
800 E 40th St 98663 360-313-3300
Mark Cain, prin. Fax 313-3301
Eisenhower ES 600/K-5
9201 NW 9th Ave 98665 360-313-1700
Jennifer Blechschmidt, prin. Fax 313-1701
Felida ES 700/K-5
2700 NW 119th St 98685 360-313-1750
Kris Janati, prin. Fax 313-1751
Franklin ES 400/K-5
5206 NW Franklin St 98663 360-313-1850
Woody Howard, prin. Fax 313-1851
Fruit Valley ES 200/K-5
3410 Fruit Valley Rd 98660 360-313-1900
Matthew Fechter, prin. Fax 313-1901
Gaiser MS 900/6-8
3000 NE 99th St 98665 360-313-3400
Abby Davis, prin. Fax 313-3401
Harney ES 600/K-5
3212 E Evergreen Blvd 98661 360-313-2000
Lucy Estrada-Guzman, prin. Fax 313-2001
Hazel Dell ES 500/K-5
511 NE Anderson St 98665 360-313-2050
Mychael Irwin, prin. Fax 313-2051
Hough ES 300/K-5
1900 Daniels St 98660 360-313-2100
Steve Vance, prin. Fax 313-2101
Jefferson MS 800/6-8
3000 NW 119th St 98685 360-313-3700
Tom Adams, prin. Fax 313-3701
King ES 500/K-5
4801 Idaho St 98661 360-313-2200
Janell Ephraim, prin. Fax 313-2201
Lake Shore ES 400/K-5
9300 NW 21st Ave 98665 360-313-2250
Starlet Heitz, prin. Fax 313-2251
Lee MS 600/6-8
8500 NW 9th Ave 98665 360-313-3500
Curt Scheidel, prin. Fax 313-3501
Lincoln ES 400/K-5
4200 NW Daniels St 98660 360-313-2300
Craig Homnick, prin. Fax 313-2301
Marshall ES 400/K-5
6400 MacArthur Blvd 98661 360-313-2400
Bobbi Geenty, prin. Fax 313-2401
McLoughlin MS 900/6-8
5802 MacArthur Blvd 98661 360-313-3600
Travis Boeh, prin. Fax 313-3601
Minnehaha ES 500/K-5
2800 NE 54th St 98663 360-313-2500
Troy Winzer, prin. Fax 313-2501
Ogden ES 500/K-5
8100 NE 28th St 98662 360-313-2550
April Whipple, prin. Fax 313-2551
Roosevelt ES 600/K-5
2921 Falk Rd 98661 360-313-2600
Megan Vickery, prin. Fax 313-2601
Sacajawea ES 400/K-5
700 NE 112th St 98685 360-313-2750
Travis Bond, prin. Fax 313-2751
Salmon Creek ES 500/K-5
1601 NE 129th St 98685 360-313-2800
Heath Angelbeck, prin. Fax 313-2801
Truman ES 500/K-5
4505 NE 42nd Ave 98661 360-313-2900
Theresa David-Turner, prin. Fax 313-2901
Walnut Grove ES 700/K-5
6103 NE 72nd Ave 98661 360-313-3000
Esteban Delgadillo, prin. Fax 313-3001
Washington ES 400/K-5
2908 S St 98663 360-313-3050
Kirsten Copeland, prin. Fax 313-3051

Cornerstone Christian Academy 500/PK-8
7708 NE 78th St Ste 100 98662 360-256-9715
Bill Gibbons, supt. Fax 882-7614
Hosanna Christian S 100/PK-12
4120 NE St Johns Rd 98661 360-906-0941
Sue Bishoprick, prin. Fax 694-0224
King's Way Christian S 700/PK-12
3300 NE 78th St 98665 360-574-1613
Our Lady of Lourdes S 300/PK-8
4701 NW Franklin St 98663 360-696-2301
Holly Rogers, prin. Fax 696-6700
St. Joseph S 400/PK-8
6500 Highland Dr 98661 360-696-2586
Mary Ellen LaRose, prin. Fax 696-0977

Vashon, King, Pop. 10,291
Vashon Island SD 402 1,500/PK-12
PO Box 547 98070 206-463-2121
Michael Soltman, supt. Fax 463-6262
www.vashonsd.org
Chautauqua ES 500/PK-5
9309 SW Cemetery Rd 98070 206-463-2882
Rebecca Goertzel, prin. Fax 463-0937
McMurray MS 400/6-8
9329 SW Cemetery Rd 98070 206-463-9168
Greg Allison, prin. Fax 463-9707

Vaughn, Pierce, Pop. 527
Peninsula SD 401
Supt. — See Gig Harbor
Vaughn ES 400/PK-5
17521 Hall Road KP N 98394 253-530-4700
Lillian Page, prin. Fax 530-4720

Waitsburg, Walla Walla, Pop. 1,189
Waitsburg SD 401-100 300/K-12
PO Box 217 99361 509-337-6301
Dr. Jon Mishra, supt. Fax 337-6042
www.waitsburgsd.org/
Preston Hall MS 50/6-8
PO Box 217 99361 509-337-9474
Stephanie Wooderchak, prin. Fax 337-6170
Waitsburg ES 100/K-5
PO Box 217 99361 509-337-6461
Jon Mishra, prin. Fax 337-6902

Waldron, San Juan
Orcas Island SD 137
Supt. — See Eastsound
Waldron Island S, 1 School Rd 98297 50/K-8
Kyle Freeman, prin. 360-588-3383

Walla Walla, Walla Walla, Pop. 30,829
Walla Walla SD 140 6,100/PK-12
364 S Park St 99362 509-527-3000
Wade Smith, supt. Fax 529-7713
www.wwps.org
Berney ES 400/K-5
1718 Pleasant St 99362 509-527-3060
Michelle Carpenter, prin. Fax 527-3096
Blue Ridge ES 400/PK-5
1150 W Chestnut St 99362 509-527-3066
Kim Doepker, prin. Fax 522-4480
Edison ES 500/K-5
1315 E Alder St 99362 509-527-3072
Julie Perron, prin. Fax 527-3062
Garrison MS 600/6-8
906 Chase Ave 99362 509-527-3040
Robert Elizondo, prin. Fax 527-3048
Green Park ES 400/K-5
1105 E Isaacs Ave 99362 509-527-3077
Gina Yonts, prin. Fax 522-4487
Pioneer MS 700/6-8
450 Bridge St 99362 509-527-3050
Kris Duncan, prin. Fax 526-5212
Prospect Point ES 500/K-5
55 Reser Rd 99362 509-527-3088
Dana Chandler, prin. Fax 522-4489
Sharpstein ES 500/K-5
410 Howard St 99362 509-527-3098
Maria Garcia, prin. Fax 527-3065

Assumption S 300/PK-8
2066 E Alder St 99362 509-525-9283
John Lesko, prin. Fax 527-0848
Liberty Christian S 100/PK-8
3172 Peppers Bridge Rd 99362 509-525-5082
Keala Hoe, prin. Fax 525-5073

Wapato, Yakima, Pop. 4,948
Wapato SD 207 3,400/PK-12
PO Box 38 98951 509-877-4181
Becky Imler, supt. Fax 877-6077
www.wapatosd.org
Adams ES 300/PK-5
1309 S Camas Ave 98951 509-877-4180
Ben Newell, prin. Fax 877-2761
Camas ES 700/K-5
1010 S Camas Ave 98951 509-877-3134
Maria Batarao, prin. Fax 877-3022
Satus ES 700/K-5
910 S Camas Ave 98951 509-877-2177
Irina Lupas, prin. Fax 877-7092
Wapato MS 800/6-8
1309 Kateri Ln 98951 509-877-2173
Scott Wells, prin. Fax 877-6232

Warden, Grant, Pop. 2,646
Warden SD 146-161 1,000/PK-12
101 W Beck Way 98857 509-349-2366
Dr. David LaBounty, supt. Fax 349-2367
www.warden.wednet.edu
Warden ES 400/PK-5
101 W Beck Way 98857 509-349-2311
Michele Cram, prin. Fax 349-2312
Warden MS 200/6-8
101 W Beck Way 98857 509-349-2902
Trever Summers, prin. Fax 349-2531

Washougal, Clark, Pop. 13,617
Mount Pleasant SD 29-93 100/K-8
152 Marble Rd 98671 360-835-3371
Vicki Prendergast, supt. Fax 835-0377
www.mtpleasantschool.org
Mount Pleasant S 100/K-8
152 Marble Rd 98671 360-835-3371
Vicki Prendergast, admin. Fax 835-0377

Washougal SD 112-6 3,200/PK-12
4855 Evergreen Way 98671 360-954-3000
Michael Stromme, supt. Fax 835-7776
www.washougal.k12.wa.us
Canyon Creek MS 300/6-8
9731 Washougal River Rd 98671 360-954-3500
Sandi Christensen, prin. Fax 837-1500
Cape Horn-Skye ES 400/PK-5
9731 Washougal River Rd 98671 360-954-3600
Penny Andrews, prin. Fax 837-3906
Gause ES 600/K-5
1100 34th St 98671 360-954-3700
Renae Burson, prin. Fax 954-3799
Hathaway ES 400/PK-5
630 24th St 98671 360-954-3800
Sarika Mosley, prin. Fax 335-0511
Jemtegaard MS 500/6-8
35300 SE Evergreen Hwy 98671 360-954-3400
David Cooke, prin. Fax 835-9145

Riverside Christian SDA S 50/PK-8
PO Box 367 98671 360-835-5600

Washtucna, Adams, Pop. 206
Washtucna SD 109-43 100/K-12
730 E Booth Ave 99371 509-646-3237
Vance Alan Wing, supt. Fax 646-3249
www.tucna.wednet.edu
Washtucna S 100/K-12
730 E Booth Ave 99371 509-646-3237
Vance Wing, prin. Fax 646-3249

Waterville, Douglas, Pop. 1,124
Waterville SD 209 300/K-12
PO Box 490 98858 509-745-8585
Fax 745-9073
www.waterville.wednet.edu/
Waterville ES 100/K-5
PO Box 490 98858 509-745-8585
Tabatha Mires, prin. Fax 745-9073

Wellpinit, Stevens
Wellpinit SD 49 400/K-12
PO Box 390 99040 509-258-4535
John Adkins, supt. Fax 258-4065
www.wellpinit.org
Wellpinit ES 200/K-5
PO Box 390 99040 509-258-4535
Kim Ewing, prin. Fax 258-4091
Wellpinit MS 100/6-8
PO Box 390 99040 509-258-4535
Kristopher Herda, prin. Fax 258-7378

Wenatchee, Chelan, Pop. 31,295
Wenatchee SD 246 7,700/K-12
PO Box 1767 98807 509-663-8161
Brian Flones, supt. Fax 663-3082
www.wenatcheeschools.org
Columbia ES 500/K-5
600 Alaska St 98801 509-662-7256
Si Stuber, prin. Fax 664-2910
Foothills MS 600/6-8
1410 Maple St 98801 509-664-8961
Mark Goveia, prin. Fax 663-6610
Lewis & Clark ES 500/K-5
1130 Princeton Ave N 98801 509-663-5351
Alfonso Lopez, prin. Fax 663-5601
Lincoln ES 500/K-5
1224 Methow St 98801 509-663-5710
Tim Sheppard, prin. Fax 662-6831
Mission View ES 500/K-5
60 Terminal Ave 98801 509-663-5851
Jeff Jaeger, prin. Fax 667-1117
Newbery ES 500/K-5
850 N Western Ave 98801 509-664-8930
Kevin Loomis, prin. Fax 664-8940
Orchard MS 500/6-8
1024 Orchard Ave 98801 509-662-7745
Taunya Brown, prin. Fax 663-8042
Pioneer MS 700/6-8
1620 Russell St 98801 509-663-7171
Rob Cline, prin. Fax 663-0453
Sunnyslope ES 300/K-5
3109 School St 98801 509-662-8803
Dave Perkins, prin. Fax 664-5094
Washington ES 600/K-5
1401 Washington St 98801 509-662-5504
Keith Collins, prin. Fax 662-9227

Cascade Christian Academy 200/PK-12
600 N Western Ave 98801 509-662-2723
River Academy 200/PK-12
PO Box 4485 98807 509-665-2415
Eric DeVries, hdmstr. Fax 662-9235
St. Joseph S 200/PK-5
600 Saint Joseph Pl 98801 509-663-2644
Sr. Olga Cano, prin. Fax 663-8474

St. Paul's Lutheran S 100/PK-5
PO Box 2219 98807 509-662-4757
Tara Breidert, admin.

Westport, Grays Harbor, Pop. 2,036
Ocosta SD 172 700/PK-12
2580 S Montesano St 98595 360-268-9125
Kurt Hilyard, supt. Fax 268-2540
www.ocosta.k12.wa.us
Ocosta ES 300/PK-6
2580 S Montesano St 98595 360-268-9125
Dr. David Dooley Ed.D., prin. Fax 268-6327

West Richland, Benton, Pop. 11,498
Richland SD 400
Supt. — See Richland
Enterprise MS 1,000/6-8
5200 Paradise Dr 99353 509-967-6200
Jennifer Klauss, prin. Fax 967-5685
Libby MS, 6200 Keene Rd 99353 6-8
Andre Hargunani, prin. 509-967-6000
Tapteal ES 600/K-5
705 N 62nd Ave 99353 509-967-6350
Rhonda Pratt, prin. Fax 967-4101
Wiley ES 600/K-5
2820 S Highlands Blvd 99353 509-967-6375
Marc Nelson, prin. Fax 967-4122

White Salmon, Klickitat, Pop. 2,180
White Salmon Valley SD 405-17 1,100/K-12
PO Box 157 98672 509-493-1500
Dr. Jerry Lewis, supt. Fax 493-2275
www.whitesalmonschools.org/
Henkle MS 200/7-8
PO Box 1309 98672 509-493-1502
Haley Ortega, prin. Fax 493-3385
Stevenson IS 100/4-6
PO Box 2550 98672 509-493-4028
Columba Jones, prin. Fax 494-1358
Whitson ES 400/K-3
PO Box 1279 98672 509-493-1560
Todd McCauley, prin. Fax 493-8214

White Swan, Yakima, Pop. 779
Mount Adams SD 209 1,000/PK-12
PO Box 578 98952 509-874-2611
Dr. Curt Guaglianone, supt. Fax 874-2960
www.masd209.org
Mount Adams MS 100/7-8
PO Box 578 98952 509-874-8626
Joey Castilleja, prin. Fax 874-2646
Other Schools – See Harrah

Wilbur, Lincoln, Pop. 857
Wilbur SD 200 300/K-12
PO Box 1090 99185 509-647-2221
Chuck Wyborney, supt. Fax 647-2509
www.wilbur.wednet.edu
Wilbur ES 100/K-6
PO Box 1090 99185 509-647-5892
Belinda Ross, prin. Fax 647-2509

Wilkeson, Pierce, Pop. 476
White River SD 416
Supt. — See Buckley
Wilkeson ES 200/PK-5
PO Box A 98396 360-829-3357
Laurie Gelinas, prin. Fax 829-3386

Wilson Creek, Grant, Pop. 198
Wilson Creek SD 167-202 100/K-12
PO Box 46 98860 509-345-2541
Laura Christian, supt. Fax 345-2288
www.wilsoncreek.org
Wilson Creek ES 100/K-6
PO Box 46 98860 509-345-2541
Sally Nelson, prin. Fax 345-2288

Winlock, Lewis, Pop. 1,291
Evaline SD 36 100/K-6
111 Schoolhouse Rd 98596 360-785-3460
Kyle MacDonald, supt. Fax 785-0951
www.evalinesd.k12.wa.us
Evaline ES 100/K-6
111 Schoolhouse Rd 98596 360-785-3460
Annie Robinson, lead tchr. Fax 785-0951

Winlock SD 232 700/PK-12
311 NW Fir St 98596 360-785-3582
Dr. Richard Serns, supt. Fax 262-6651
www.winlockschools.org
Winlock MS 200/6-8
241 N Military Rd 98596 360-785-3046
Brian Maley, prin. Fax 864-3105
Winlock-Miller ES 300/PK-5
405 NW Benton Ave 98596 360-785-3516
Boyd Calder, prin. Fax 864-3102

Winthrop, Okanogan, Pop. 390
Methow Valley SD 350 600/PK-12
18 Twin Lakes Rd 98862 509-996-9205
Tom Venable, supt. Fax 996-9208
www.methow.org
Methow Valley ES 300/PK-6
18 Twin Lakes Rd 98862 509-996-2186
Bob Winters, prin. Fax 996-9202

Wishram, Klickitat, Pop. 339
Wishram SD 94 100/PK-12
PO Box 8 98673 509-748-2551
Michael Roberts, supt. Fax 748-2127
www.wishramschool.org
Wishram S 100/PK-12
PO Box 8 98673 509-748-2551
Michael Roberts, supt. Fax 748-2127

Woodinville, King, Pop. 10,516
Lake Washington SD 414
Supt. — See Redmond
Wilder ES 500/K-5
22130 NE 133rd St, 425-936-2740
Steve Roetcisoender, prin. Fax 702-0114

Northshore SD 417
Supt. — See Bothell
Bear Creek ES 500/K-5
18101 Avondale Rd NE, 425-408-4100
Stephanie Penrod, prin. Fax 408-4102
Cottage Lake ES 300/K-5
15940 Avondale Rd NE, 425-408-4200
Jen Welch, prin. Fax 408-4202
East Ridge ES 400/K-5
22150 NE 156th Pl, 425-408-4400
Sarah White, prin. Fax 408-4402
Hollywood Hill ES 300/K-5
17110 148th Ave NE 98072 425-408-4700
JoAnn Todd, prin. Fax 408-4702
Kokanee ES 600/K-5
23710 57th Ave SE 98072 425-408-4900
Cathi Davis, prin. Fax 408-4902
Leota MS 700/6-8
19301 168th Ave NE 98072 425-408-6500
Audee Gregor, prin. Fax 408-6502
Timbercrest MS 800/6-8
19115 215th Way NE, 425-408-6900
Kristi Hannigan, prin. Fax 408-6902
Wellington ES 500/K-5
16501 NE 195th St 98072 425-408-5900
Bill Bagnall, prin. Fax 408-5902

Bellevue Christian Mack ES 200/PK-6
18250 168th Pl NE 98072 425-485-1824
Jennifer Smith, prin. Fax 481-1167
Chrysalis S 200/K-12
14241 NE Woodinville Duvall 98072 425-481-2228
Karen Fogle, dir. Fax 486-8107

Woodland, Cowlitz, Pop. 5,391
Green Mountain SD 103 100/K-8
13105 NE Grinnell Rd 98674 360-225-7366
Tyson Vogeler, supt. Fax 225-2217
www.greenmountainschool.us
Green Mountain S 100/K-8
13105 NE Grinnell Rd 98674 360-225-7366
Tyson Vogeler, supt. Fax 225-2217

Woodland SD 404 1,600/PK-12
800 2nd St 98674 360-841-2700
Michael Green, supt. Fax 841-2701
www.woodlandschools.org/
Woodland IS 200/2-4
2250 Lewis River Rd 98674 360-841-2750
Steve Carney, prin. Fax 841-2751
Woodland MS 300/5-8
755 Park St 98674 360-841-2850
James Johnston, prin. Fax 841-2851
Woodland PS 300/PK-1
600 Bozarth Ave 98674 360-841-2900
Ingrid Colvard, prin. Fax 841-2901
Other Schools – See Ariel

Yacolt, Clark, Pop. 1,536
Battle Ground SD 119
Supt. — See Brush Prairie
Yacolt PS 800/K-4
406 W Yacolt Rd 98675 360-885-6000
David Kennedy, prin. Fax 885-6010

Yakima, Yakima, Pop. 89,018
East Valley SD 90 3,000/K-12
2002 Beaudry Rd 98901 509-573-7300
John Schieche, supt. Fax 573-7340
www.evsd90.org
East Valley Central MS 700/6-8
2010 Beaudry Rd 98901 509-573-7500
Matt Toth, prin. Fax 573-7540
East Valley ES 500/K-5
1951 Beaudry Rd 98901 509-573-7600
Colleen Crowston, prin. Fax 573-7640
Terrace Heights ES 500/K-5
101 N 41st Ave 98908 509-573-7800
Tami Scrivner, prin. Fax 573-7840
Other Schools – See Moxee

West Valley SD 208 4,900/K-12
8902 Zier Rd 98908 509-972-6000
Dr. Michael Brophy, supt. Fax 972-6025
www.wvsd208.org
Ahtanum Valley ES 200/K-4
3006 S Wiley Rd 98903 509-972-5500
Richard Pryor, prin. Fax 966-7034
Apple Valley ES 300/K-4
7 N 88th Ave 98908 509-972-5510
Heidi Sutton, prin. Fax 972-5511
Cottonwood ES 400/K-4
1041 S 96th Ave 98908 509-972-5520
Sherry Adams, prin. Fax 972-5521
Mountainview ES 200/K-4
830 Stone Rd 98908 509-972-5530
Nick Hartman, prin. Fax 972-5531
Summitview ES 300/K-4
6305 W Chestnut Ave 98908 509-972-5540
Eva Lust, prin. Fax 972-5541
West Valley JHS 800/7-8
7505 Zier Rd 98908 509-972-5800
Russ Tuman, prin. Fax 972-5801
West Valley MS 800/5-6
1500 S 75th Ave 98908 509-972-5700
Russ Tuman, prin. Fax 972-5701
Wide Hollow ES 400/K-4
1000 S 72nd Ave 98908 509-972-5550
Rick Ferguson, prin. Fax 972-5551

Yakima SD 7 15,900/PK-12
104 N 4th Ave 98902 509-573-7000
Dr. Jack Irion, supt. Fax 573-7222
www.yakimaschools.org
Adams ES 700/PK-5
723 S 8th St 98901 509-573-5100
Bill Varady, prin. Fax 573-5151
Barge-Lincoln ES 600/PK-5
219 E I St 98901 509-573-5200
Stacey Drake, prin. Fax 573-5252
Discovery Lab S 200/1-8
2810 Castlevale Rd 98902 509-573-5400
Phil Vasquez, prin. Fax 573-5490
Franklin MS 900/6-8
410 S 19th Ave 98902 509-573-2100
Sherry Anderson, prin. Fax 573-2121
Garfield ES 600/K-5
612 N 6th Ave 98902 509-573-5700
Steve Brownlow, prin. Fax 573-5757
Gilbert ES 600/K-5
4400 Douglas Dr 98908 509-573-5800
Paul Voorhees, prin. Fax 573-5858
Hoover ES 700/PK-5
400 W Viola Ave 98902 509-573-5900
Luz Juarez-Stump, prin. Fax 573-5959
King ES 600/K-5
2000 S 18th St 98903 509-573-1100
Maria Lucero, prin. Fax 573-1111
Lewis & Clark MS 800/6-8
1114 W Pierce St 98902 509-573-2200
Victor Nourani, prin. Fax 573-2222
McClure ES 600/PK-5
1222 S 22nd Ave 98902 509-573-1300
Deb Lavis, prin. Fax 573-1313
McKinley ES 500/K-5
621 S 13th Ave 98902 509-573-1400
Amanda Voorhees, prin. Fax 573-1414
Nob Hill ES 500/K-5
801 S 34th Ave 98902 509-573-1500
Erin Thomas, prin. Fax 573-1515
Ridgeview ES 600/K-5
609 W Washington Ave 98903 509-573-1803
K.C. Mitchell, prin. Fax 573-1818
Robertson ES 500/K-5
2807 W Lincoln Ave 98902 509-573-1600
Mark Hummel, prin. Fax 573-1616
Roosevelt ES 500/K-5
120 N 16th Ave 98902 509-573-1700
Dan Williams, prin. Fax 573-1717
Washington MS 700/6-8
510 S 9th St 98901 509-573-2300
Bill Hilton, prin. Fax 573-2323
Whitney ES 500/K-5
4411 W Nob Hill Blvd 98908 509-573-1900
Kimberlee Newell, prin. Fax 573-1919
Wilson MS 800/6-8
902 S 44th Ave 98908 509-573-2400
Ernesto Araiza, prin. Fax 573-2424

Grace Lutheran S 50/PK-8
1207 S 7th Ave 98902 509-457-6611
Rebecca Hussman, prin. Fax 457-6611
Riverside Christian S 400/PK-12
721 Keys Rd 98901 509-965-2602
Rick Van Beek, admin. Fax 966-7031
St. Joseph - Marquette S 300/PK-8
202 N 4th St 98901 509-575-5557
Gregg Pleger, prin. Fax 457-5621
St. Paul Cathedral S 200/PK-8
1214 W Chestnut Ave 98902 509-575-5604
Heather Remillard, prin. Fax 577-8817
Yakima Adventist Christian S 100/PK-10
1200 City Reservoir Rd 98908 509-966-1933

Yelm, Thurston, Pop. 6,363
Yelm Community SD 2 5,700/PK-12
PO Box 476 98597 360-458-1900
Brian Wharton, supt. Fax 458-6178
www.ycs.wednet.edu
Fort Stevens ES 600/PK-6
PO Box 476 98597 360-458-4800
Lisa Crowell, prin. Fax 458-6315
Lackamas ES 300/K-6
PO Box 476 98597 360-894-6000
Kurt Fourre, prin. Fax 894-6002
Mill Pond ES 500/K-6
PO Box 476 98597 360-458-3400
Jeri Lipe, prin. Fax 458-8040
Southworth ES 600/K-6
PO Box 476 98597 360-458-2500
Charles Cook, prin. Fax 458-6303
Yelm Prairie ES 500/PK-6
PO Box 476 98597 360-458-3700
Debbie McLaren, prin. Fax 458-6326
Other Schools – See Mc Kenna

Eagle View Christian S 100/PK-12
13036 Morris Rd SE 98597 360-458-3090
Barbara Ballou, prin. Fax 458-4990

Zillah, Yakima, Pop. 2,907
Zillah SD 205 1,300/PK-12
213 4th Ave 98953 509-829-5911
Doug Burge, supt. Fax 829-6290
www.zillahschools.org/
Hilton ES 400/PK-3
211 4th Ave 98953 509-829-5400
Ryne Phillips, prin. Fax 829-6470
Zillah IS 300/4-6
303 2nd Ave 98953 509-829-5555
Paula Dasso, prin. Fax 829-3575
Zillah MS 200/7-8
1301 Cutler Way 98953 509-829-5511
Tracy Savage, prin. Fax 829-0754

WEST VIRGINIA

WEST VIRGINIA DEPARTMENT OF EDUCATION
1900 Kanawha Blvd E Rm 358, Charleston 25305-0330
Telephone 304-558-2681
Fax 304-558-0048
Website wvde.state.wv.us

State Superintendent of Schools Steven Paine

WEST VIRGINIA BOARD OF EDUCATION
1900 Kanawha Blvd E Rm 358, Charleston 25305-0009

President Thomas Campbell

REGIONAL EDUCATION SERVICE AGENCIES (RESA)

RESA I
Dr. Robin Lewis, dir. 304-256-4712
400 Neville St, Beckley 25801 Fax 256-4683
resa1.k12.wv.us/

RESA II
Jan Hanlon, dir 304-529-6205
2001 McCoy Rd, Huntington 25701 Fax 529-6209
www.resa2.com

RESA III
Kelly Watts, dir. 304-766-7655
501 22nd St, Dunbar 25064 Fax 766-7915
resa3.k12.wv.us

RESA IV
David Warvel, dir., 404 Old Main Dr 304-872-6440
Summersville 26651 Fax 872-6442
resa4.k12.wv.us/

RESA V
Joseph Oliverio, dir. 304-485-6513
2507 9th Ave, Parkersburg 26101 Fax 485-6515
resa5.k12.wv.us

RESA VII
Kathy Hypes, dir. 304-624-6554
1201 N 15th St, Clarksburg 26301 Fax 624-5223
resa7.k12.wv.us

RESA VIII
Lynn Aikens, dir., 109 S College St 304-267-3595
Martinsburg 25401 Fax 267-3599
www.resa8.org

RESA VI
Nick Zervos, dir. 304-243-0440
30 G C and P Rd, Wheeling 26003 Fax 243-0443
resa6.k12.wv.us/

PUBLIC, PRIVATE AND CATHOLIC ELEMENTARY SCHOOLS

Accoville, Logan, Pop. 569
Logan County SD
Supt. — See Logan
Buffalo ES 200/PK-4
2367 Buffalo Creek Rd 25606 304-583-9132
Debbie Holly, prin. Fax 583-7512

Alderson, Greenbrier, Pop. 1,157
Greenbrier County SD
Supt. — See Lewisburg
Alderson ES 200/PK-5
305 Elmwood Ave 24910 304-445-7241
Deborah Fairchild, prin. Fax 445-9718

Alum Creek, Lincoln, Pop. 1,747
Lincoln County SD
Supt. — See Hamlin
Midway ES 300/PK-5
267 Midway Rd 25003 304-756-3121
Don Davis, prin. Fax 756-1459

Anawalt, McDowell, Pop. 222
McDowell County SD
Supt. — See Welch
Anawalt S 100/PK-5
PO Box 230 24808 304-383-4849
Bonnie Campbell, prin. Fax 383-4674

Ansted, Fayette, Pop. 1,400
Fayette County SD
Supt. — See Fayetteville
Ansted ES 300/PK-5
PO Box 766 25812 304-658-5961
Amy McDonald, prin. Fax 658-5961
Ansted MS 200/6-8
PO Box 766 25812 304-658-5170
Richard Petitt, prin. Fax 658-3059

Arnoldsburg, Calhoun
Calhoun County SD
Supt. — See Mount Zion
Arnoldsburg S 200/PK-4
90 Spring Run Rd 25234 304-655-8616
Charles Thomas, prin. Fax 655-8618

Arthurdale, Preston
Preston County SD
Supt. — See Kingwood
West Preston S 500/PK-8
PO Box 700 26520 304-864-3835
Mark Graham, prin. Fax 864-4037

Artie, Raleigh
Raleigh County SD
Supt. — See Beckley
Clear Fork District ES 200/PK-5
4851 Clear Fork Rd 25008 304-854-1000
Debbra Black, prin. Fax 854-1151

Ashford, Boone
Boone County SD
Supt. — See Madison
Ashford-Rumble ES 100/PK-6
1649 Ashford Nellis Rd 25009 304-836-5381
Amy Pritt, prin. Fax 836-5381

Ashton, Mason
Mason County SD
Supt. — See Point Pleasant
Ashton ES 400/PK-6
997 Ashton Upland Rd 25503 304-576-9931
Aleisha Green, prin. Fax 576-9935

Athens, Mercer, Pop. 1,039
Mercer County SD
Supt. — See Princeton
Athens ES 300/PK-5
PO Box 568 24712 304-384-9229
Shelley Weiss, prin. Fax 384-7946

Augusta, Hampshire
Hampshire County SD
Supt. — See Romney
Augusta ES 300/PK-5
61 Pancione Loop 26704 304-496-7001
Brenda Omps, prin. Fax 496-7001

Aurora, Preston, Pop. 200
Preston County SD
Supt. — See Kingwood
Aurora ES 100/PK-8
125 Aurora School Dr 26705 304-735-3781
Debra Hibbs, prin. Fax 735-6805

Avondale, McDowell
McDowell County SD
Supt. — See Welch
Sandy River MS 300/6-8
PO Box 419 24811 304-938-2407
Sara Garrett, prin. Fax 938-2418

Baker, Hardy
Hardy County SD
Supt. — See Moorefield
East Hardy Early MS 500/PK-8
PO Box 260 26801 304-897-5970
Don Rhodes, prin. Fax 897-6653

Barboursville, Cabell, Pop. 3,916
Cabell County SD
Supt. — See Huntington
Barboursville MS 800/6-8
1400 Central Ave 25504 304-733-3003
Brent Jarrell, prin. Fax 733-3009
Davis Creek ES 300/PK-5
6330 Davis Creek Rd 25504 304-733-3024
R. Patrick O'Neal, prin. Fax 733-3049
Martha ES 200/PK-5
3067 Martha Rd 25504 304-733-3027
Boyd Mynes, prin. Fax 733-3016
Nichols ES 200/PK-5
3505 Erwin Rd 25504 304-733-3031
Serena Collins, prin. Fax 733-3054
Village of Barboursville ES 700/PK-5
718 Central Ave 25504 304-733-3000
Kelli Jordan, prin. Fax 733-3036

Barrackville, Marion, Pop. 1,289
Marion County SD
Supt. — See Fairmont
Barrackville ES 400/PK-8
PO Box 150 26559 304-367-2128
Vicki Bombard, prin. Fax 367-2173

Beaver, Raleigh, Pop. 1,300

Victory Baptist Academy 100/K-12
PO Box 549 25813 304-255-4535

Beckley, Raleigh, Pop. 17,086
Raleigh County SD 12,500/PK-12
105 Adair St 25801 304-256-4500
David Price, supt. Fax 256-4739
boe.rale.k12.wv.us

Beckley ES 400/PK-5
399 Grey Flats Rd 25801 304-256-4575
Meghan Houck, prin. Fax 256-4581
Beckley-Stratton MS 700/6-8
401 Grey Flats Rd 25801 304-256-4616
Rachel Pauley, prin. Fax 256-4763
Cranberry-Prosperity ES 300/PK-5
4575 Robert C Byrd Dr 25801 304-256-4588
Alicia Lett, prin. Fax 256-4574
Crescent ES 400/PK-5
205 Crescent Rd 25801 304-256-4585
Theresa Lewis, prin. Fax 256-4576
Hollywood ES 300/PK-5
412 Old Mill Rd 25801 304-256-4590
Tamber Hodges, prin. Fax 256-4579
Maxwell Hill ES 300/PK-5
1001 Maxwell Hill Rd 25801 304-256-4599
Amanda Richmond, prin. Fax 256-4584
Park MS 400/6-8
212 Park Ave 25801 304-256-4586
Jacquelin McPeake, prin. Fax 256-4709
Stanaford ES 300/PK-5
950 Stanaford Rd 25801 304-256-4626
Michelle Blankenship, prin. Fax 256-4587
Stratton ES 300/PK-5
1129 S Fayette St 25801 304-256-4604
Tammy Accord, prin. Fax 256-4627
Other Schools – See Artie, Coal City, Crab Orchard, Daniels, Fairdale, Ghent, Glen Daniel, Lester, Mabscott, Mount Hope, Rock Creek, Shady Spring, Sophia

---

St. Francis de Sales S 200/PK-8
622 S Oakwood Ave 25801 304-252-4087
Karen Wynne, prin. Fax 252-4087

Beech Bottom, Brooke, Pop. 521
Brooke County SD
Supt. — See Wellsburg
Beech Bottom PS 100/PK-4
PO Box 36 26030 304-394-5341
Michalene Mills, prin. Fax 394-5342

Belington, Barbour, Pop. 1,905
Barbour County SD
Supt. — See Philippi
Belington ES 400/PK-4
471 Morgantown Pike 26250 304-823-1411
Cindy Vance-Sigley, prin. Fax 823-2414
Belington MS 200/5-8
469 Morgantown Pike 26250 304-823-1281
Mary Hovatter, prin. Fax 823-2403

Belle, Kanawha, Pop. 1,248
Kanawha County SD
Supt. — See Charleston
Belle ES 300/PK-5
401 E 6th St 25015 304-949-2612
Amanda Mays, prin. Fax 949-5854
DuPont MS 400/6-8
1 Panther Dr 25015 304-348-1978
Romie Canterbury, prin. Fax 949-1793

Belmont, Pleasants, Pop. 892
Pleasants County SD
Supt. — See Saint Marys
Belmont ES 200/PK-4
512 Riverview Dr 26134 304-299-6274
Eric Croasmun, prin. Fax 665-2408

Pleasants County MS 400/5-8
510 Riverview Dr 26134 304-299-5275
Lori Barnhart, prin. Fax 665-2451

Berkeley Springs, Morgan, Pop. 614
Morgan County SD 2,500/PK-12
247 Harrison Ave 25411 304-258-2430
Erich May, supt. Fax 258-9146
www.morganschools.net
Warm Springs IS 400/3-5
575 Warm Springs Way 25411 304-258-0031
Dudley Cable, prin. Fax 258-0033
Warm Springs MS 500/6-8
271 Warm Springs Way 25411 304-258-1500
Gene Brock, prin. Fax 258-4600
Widmyer ES 500/PK-2
128 Widmyer Cir 25411 304-258-2024
Rhett Beckman, prin. Fax 258-7693
Other Schools – See Hedgesville, Paw Paw

Beverly, Randolph, Pop. 692
Randolph County SD
Supt. — See Elkins
Beverly ES 300/PK-5
505 Main St 26253 304-636-9162
Paul Zickefoose, prin. Fax 636-9163

Big Sandy, McDowell, Pop. 165
McDowell County SD
Supt. — See Welch
Fall River ES 200/PK-5
PO Box 179 24816 304-656-7665
Lori Howington, prin. Fax 656-7530

Birch River, Nicholas, Pop. 107
Nicholas County SD
Supt. — See Summersville
Birch River ES 100/PK-5
379 Birch River Rd 26610 304-649-2651
Bronlyn Morlan, prin. Fax 649-2651

Blacksville, Monongalia, Pop. 166
Monongalia County SD
Supt. — See Morgantown
Mason-Dixon ES 300/PK-5
7041 Mason Dixon Hwy 26521 304-662-6113
Denice Corder, prin. Fax 662-6167

Bluefield, Mercer, Pop. 10,213
Mercer County SD
Supt. — See Princeton
Bluefield IS 300/3-5
1301 Southview Dr 24701 304-327-8339
Jeff Johnson, prin. Fax 327-8348
Bluefield MS 600/6-8
2002 Stadium Dr 24701 304-325-2481
Kimberly Miller, prin. Fax 325-2156
Bluewell ES 200/PK-5
205 Bluewell School Rd 24701 304-589-5057
Sarah Grose, prin. Fax 589-3723
Brushfork ES 200/K-5
140 Brushfork School Rd 24701 304-325-7066
Krissy Zickafoose, prin. Fax 325-2574
Ceres ES 200/K-5
3716 Maple Acres Rd 24701 304-325-6786
Mary Terry, prin. Fax 327-5516
Cumberland Heights Early Learning Center 300/PK-PK
3318 E Cumberland Rd 24701 304-325-7316
Steve Hayes, prin. Fax 323-2591
Memorial PS 200/K-2
319 Memorial Ave 24701 304-327-8016
Rebecca Peery, prin. Fax 327-3933
Whitethorn PS 200/K-2
1919 Maryland Ave 24701 304-327-6217
Brittany Anderson, prin. Fax 324-3894

Bomont, Clay
Clay County SD
Supt. — See Clay
White ES 100/PK-5
501 Bomont Rd 25030 304-548-7101
April Kearns, prin. Fax 548-7548

Bradshaw, McDowell, Pop. 335
McDowell County SD
Supt. — See Welch
Bradshaw ES 300/PK-5
PO Box 40 24817 304-967-7700
Deborah Maxwell, prin. Fax 967-7701

Branchland, Lincoln
Lincoln County SD
Supt. — See Hamlin
Guyan Valley MS 300/6-8
5312 McClellan Hwy 25506 304-824-3235
Johnnalyn Davis, prin. Fax 824-3459

Brandywine, Pendleton, Pop. 211
Pendleton County SD
Supt. — See Franklin
Brandywine ES 100/PK-6
PO Box 247 26802 304-249-5381
Kathleen McDonald, prin. Fax 249-5226

Brenton, Wyoming, Pop. 241
Wyoming County SD
Supt. — See Pineville
Baileysville ES 300/K-8
PO Box 409 24818 304-732-6399
Lori Stewart, prin. Fax 732-8365

Bridgeport, Harrison, Pop. 8,059
Harrison County SD
Supt. — See Clarksburg
Bridgeport MS 600/6-8
413 Johnson Ave 26330 304-326-7142
Carole Crawford, prin. Fax 842-6275
Johnson ES 600/PK-5
531 Johnson Ave 26330 304-326-7109
Vicki Huffman, prin. Fax 842-6562
Simpson ES 400/PK-5
250 Worthington Dr 26330 304-326-7060
Jill Steele, prin. Fax 842-2568

Heritage Christian S 100/PK-12
225 Newton Ave 26330 304-842-1740
Linda Simms, admin. Fax 842-1750

Bruceton Mills, Preston, Pop. 85
Preston County SD
Supt. — See Kingwood
Bruceton S 600/PK-8
PO Box 141 26525 304-379-2593
Belinda Moss, prin. Fax 379-4079

Buckeye, Pocahontas
Pocahontas County SD
Supt. — See Marlinton
Marlinton MS 200/6-8
1 Copperhead Way 24924 304-799-6773
Dustin Lambert, prin. Fax 799-7278

Buckhannon, Upshur, Pop. 5,544
Upshur County SD 3,800/PK-12
102 Smithfield St 26201 304-472-5480
Roy Wager, supt. Fax 472-0258
www.upshurschools.com
Buckhannon Academy ES 600/PK-5
16 College Ave 26201 304-472-3310
Susanne Spiker Britton, prin. Fax 472-3790
Buckhannon-Upshur MS 900/6-8
553 Route 20 South Rd 26201 304-472-1520
Renee Warner, prin. Fax 472-6864
Hodgesville ES 200/PK-5
918 Teter Rd 26201 304-472-3212
Janet Phillips, prin. Fax 472-3932
Tennerton ES 300/PK-5
167 Gawthrop Rd 26201 304-472-1278
Tristen Gray, prin. Fax 472-8530
Union ES 300/PK-5
481 Heavner Grove Rd 26201 304-472-1394
Dr. Sara Stankus Ed.D., prin. Fax 472-2780
Washington District ES 100/PK-5
5078 Tallmansville Rd 26201 304-472-6599
Jeanne Bennett, prin. Fax 471-2044
Other Schools – See French Creek, Rock Cave

Bud, Wyoming, Pop. 478
Wyoming County SD
Supt. — See Pineville
Herndon Consolidated S 200/PK-8
PO Box 309 24716 304-294-7668
Virginia Calhoun-Lusk, prin. Fax 294-8474

Buffalo, Putnam, Pop. 1,223
Putnam County SD
Supt. — See Winfield
Buffalo ES 200/PK-5
19366 Buffalo Rd 25033 304-937-2651
Sherry Craigo, prin. Fax 937-3142

Bunker Hill, Berkeley
Berkeley County SD
Supt. — See Martinsburg
Bunker Hill ES 400/K-3
58 Happy School Ave 25413 304-229-1980
Tabitha Campbell, prin. Fax 229-1983
Mill Creek IS 500/3-5
8785 Winchester Ave 25413 304-229-4570
Elizabeth McCoy, prin. Fax 229-4793
Musselman MS 1,200/6-8
105 Pride Ave 25413 304-229-1965
James Holland, prin. Fax 229-1967

Burlington, Mineral, Pop. 182
Mineral County SD
Supt. — See Keyser
Burlington PS 100/PK-4
10474 Patterson Creek Rd 26710 304-289-3073
Joyce Malcolm, prin. Fax 289-5116

Burnsville, Braxton, Pop. 503
Braxton County SD
Supt. — See Sutton
Burnsville ES 100/PK-4
PO Box 35 26335 304-853-2523
Robin Lewis, prin. Fax 853-2431

Cameron, Marshall, Pop. 941
Marshall County SD
Supt. — See Moundsville
Cameron ES 300/K-6
12 Church St 26033 304-686-3305
Wendy Clutter, prin. Fax 686-3502

Capon Bridge, Hampshire, Pop. 353
Hampshire County SD
Supt. — See Romney
Capon Bridge ES 400/PK-5
99 Capon School St 26711 304-856-3329
John Ferraro, prin. Fax 856-2519
Capon Bridge MS 300/6-8
PO Box 147 26711 304-856-2534
Ann Downs, prin. Fax 856-3192

Cedar Grove, Kanawha, Pop. 982
Kanawha County SD
Supt. — See Charleston
Cedar Grove ES 300/PK-5
PO Box J 25039 304-949-1642
Deborah Mougaes, prin. Fax 595-2541
Cedar Grove MS 200/6-8
PO Box K 25039 304-949-1642
Melissa Lawrence, prin. Fax 949-3418

Ceredo, Wayne, Pop. 1,432
Wayne County SD
Supt. — See Wayne
Ceredo ES 200/PK-5
PO Box 635 25507 304-453-1511
Kim Hurley, prin. Fax 453-1502
Ceredo-Kenova MS 200/6-8
PO Box 705 25507 304-453-3588
Tonji Bowen, prin. Fax 453-4420

Chapmanville, Logan, Pop. 1,250
Logan County SD
Supt. — See Logan
Chapmanville MS 600/5-8
774 Crawley Creek Rd 25508 304-855-8378
Kristen Dingess, prin. Fax 855-1307
East Chapmanville ES 300/PK-4
PO Box 340 25508 304-855-3302
Darren Glandon, prin. Fax 855-7568
West Chapmanville ES 400/PK-4
100 W Tiger Ln 25508 304-855-3209
Fax 855-3376

Charleston, Kanawha, Pop. 49,755
Kanawha County SD 28,100/PK-12
200 Elizabeth St 25311 304-348-7770
Ronald Duerring Ed.D., supt. Fax 348-7735
kcs.kana.k12.wv.us
Adams MS 800/6-8
2002 Presidential Dr 25314 304-348-6652
John Moyers, prin. Fax 348-6592
Chamberlain ES 200/PK-5
4901 Venable Ave 25304 304-348-1969
Phoebe McCloud, prin. Fax 348-1970
Edgewood ES 400/PK-5
550 Hawks Rdg 25302 304-348-6631
Janet Scott, prin. Fax 348-6644
Elk Elementary Center 600/PK-5
3320 Pennsylvania Ave 25302 304-348-7776
Donna Chambers, prin. Fax 965-6921
Flinn ES 500/K-4
2006 McClure Pkwy 25312 304-348-1960
Maria Clendenin, prin. Fax 348-1959
Grandview ES 300/PK-5
959 Woodward Dr 25387 304-348-1928
Sharon Brooks, prin. Fax 746-0771
Holz ES 300/PK-5
1505 Hampton Rd 25314 304-348-1906
Lynn Davis, prin. Fax 345-0387
Jackson MS 600/6-8
812 Park Ave 25302 304-348-6123
Jessica Austin, prin. Fax 348-1999
Kanawha City ES 300/PK-5
3601 Staunton Ave SE 25304 304-348-1985
Cathi Bradley, prin. Fax 348-6537
Kenna ES 200/PK-5
198 Eureka Rd 25314 304-348-6104
Leah Earnest, prin. Fax 348-6107
Malden ES 200/PK-5
4001 Salines Dr 25306 304-348-1973
Julie Sayre, prin. Fax 348-1974
Mann MS 500/6-8
4300 MacCorkle Ave SE 25304 304-348-1971
Shandon Tweedy, prin. Fax 348-6591
Overbrook ES 500/PK-5
218 Oakwood Rd 25314 304-348-6179
Gerald Comer, prin. Fax 347-7494
Piedmont ES 300/PK-5
203 Bradford St 25301 304-348-1910
Fax 348-1911
Ruffner ES 400/PK-5
809 Litz Dr 25311 304-348-1130
Henry Nearman, prin. Fax 348-1131
Shoals ES 300/PK-5
100 Dutch Rd 25302 304-348-1900
David Anderson, prin. Fax 348-1901
Sissonville MS 600/5-8
100 Middle School Ln 25312 304-348-1993
Brian Eddy, prin. Fax 348-6594
Snow West Side ES 500/PK-5
100 Florida St 25302 304-348-1902
Cheryl Plear, prin. Fax 348-6681
Weberwood ES 200/PK-5
732 Gordon Dr 25303 304-348-1924
Mary Lou Munoz, prin. Fax 347-7421
Other Schools – See Belle, Cedar Grove, Chesapeake, Cross Lanes, Diamond, Dunbar, East Bank, Elkview, Marmet, Miami, Nitro, Pratt, Saint Albans, Sissonville, South Charleston, Tad, Tornado

---

Bible Center S 400/PK-8
1111 Oakhurst Dr 25314 304-941-1704
Lee Walker, admin. Fax 346-0433
Boulevard Adventist Academy 50/K-8
622 Kanawha Blvd W 25302 304-415-7461
Cross Lanes Christian S 300/K-12
5330 Floradale Dr 25313 304-776-5020
Mountaineer Montessori S 100/PK-8
308 20th St SE 25304 304-342-7870
Sacred Heart ES 400/PK-5
1035 Quarrier St 25301 304-346-5491
Susan Malinoski, prin. Fax 342-0870
St. Agnes S 100/PK-5
4801 Staunton Ave SE 25304 304-925-4341
Christopher Bulger, prin. Fax 925-4423

Charles Town, Jefferson, Pop. 5,074
Jefferson County SD 8,800/PK-12
110 Mordington Ave 25414 304-725-9741
Dr. Bondy Gibson, supt. Fax 725-6487
boe.jeff.k12.wv.us
Charles Town MS 700/6-8
193 High St 25414 304-725-7821
Tim Sites, prin. Fax 728-7526
Denny IS 400/3-5
209 W Congress St 25414 304-725-2513
Chris Walter, prin. Fax 725-1721
Page-Jackson ES 400/PK-2
370 Page Jackson School Rd 25414 304-728-9212
Amy Schmitt, lead tchr. Fax 725-2968
South Jefferson ES 500/K-5
4599 Summit Point Rd 25414 304-728-9216
Richard Jenkins, prin. Fax 725-6428
Other Schools – See Harpers Ferry, Kearneysville, Ranson, Shenandoah Junction, Shepherdstown

Chesapeake, Kanawha, Pop. 1,531
Kanawha County SD
Supt. — See Charleston
Chesapeake ES 200/PK-5
13620 MacCorkle Ave, 304-949-1121
Marianne Annie, prin. Fax 949-2351

Chester, Hancock, Pop. 2,567
Hancock County SD
Supt. — See New Cumberland

Allison ES 400/PK-4
605 Railroad St 26034 304-387-1915
Toni Hartung, prin. Fax 387-2114

Circleville, Pendleton
Pendleton County SD
Supt. — See Franklin
North Fork ES 100/PK-6
PO Box 186 26804 304-567-3193
Randolph West, prin. Fax 567-3196

Clarksburg, Harrison, Pop. 16,197
Harrison County SD 10,900/PK-12
PO Box 1370 26302 304-624-3325
Dr. Mark Manchin, supt. Fax 624-3361
www.harcoboe.net
Adamston ES 300/PK-5
1636 W Pike St 26301 304-624-3399
Tammy Leaseburg, prin. Fax 624-3270
Irving MS 600/6-8
443 Lee Ave 26301 304-326-7420
Susan Ferrell, prin. Fax 624-3388
Mountaineer MS 500/6-8
2 Mountaineer Dr 26301 304-326-7620
John Rogers, prin. Fax 326-7632
North View ES 300/PK-5
1400 N 19th St 26301 304-326-7650
Danielle Veltri, prin. Fax 624-3287
Wilsonburg ES 200/PK-5
1040 Wilsonburg Rd 26301 304-326-7640
Laura Dick, prin. Fax 624-3279
Other Schools – See Bridgeport, Lost Creek, Lumberport, Nutter Fort Stonewood, Salem, Shinnston, Stonewood, West Milford

---

Emmanuel Christian S 100/PK-12
1318 N 16th St 26301 304-624-6125
St. Mary Central S 200/PK-6
107 E Pike St 26301 304-622-9831
Nicole Folio, prin. Fax 622-9831

Clay, Clay, Pop. 483
Clay County SD 2,000/PK-12
PO Box 120 25043 304-587-4266
Fax 587-4181
clay-k12.wvnet.edu/boe/
Clay County MS 400/6-8
PO Box 489 25043 304-587-2343
Anita Stephenson, prin. Fax 587-2759
Clay ES 600/PK-5
PO Box 600 25043 304-587-4276
Michelle Paxton, prin. Fax 587-4279
Other Schools – See Bomont, Duck, Lizemores

Clay Christian Academy 50/K-12
11594 Triplett Ridge Rd 25043 304-587-2786
Gary Drake, head sch Fax 587-2786

Coal City, Raleigh, Pop. 1,761
Raleigh County SD
Supt. — See Beckley
Coal City ES 300/PK-5
PO Box 1240 25823 304-683-5001
David Null, prin. Fax 683-3165

Coalton, Randolph, Pop. 248
Randolph County SD
Supt. — See Elkins
Coalton ES 200/PK-5
278 Broadway Ave 26257 304-636-9164
Fax 636-9165

Colliers, Brooke
Brooke County SD
Supt. — See Wellsburg
Colliers PS 200/K-4
270 Pennsylvania Ave 26035 304-748-8188
JoEllen Goodall, prin. Fax 797-7242

Comfort, Boone, Pop. 306
Boone County SD
Supt. — See Madison
Sherman ES 500/PK-6
PO Box 369 25049 304-837-8310
Lisa Lowe, prin. Fax 837-8342

Cottageville, Jackson
Jackson County SD
Supt. — See Ripley
Cottageville ES 100/PK-5
100 School St 25239 304-372-7330
Tracy LeMasters, prin. Fax 372-7342

Cowen, Webster, Pop. 533
Webster County SD
Supt. — See Webster Springs
Glade ES 300/PK-6
25 Mill St 26206 304-226-5353
Stephen White, prin. Fax 226-3666

Crab Orchard, Raleigh, Pop. 2,635
Raleigh County SD
Supt. — See Beckley
Crab Orchard ES 300/PK-5
PO Box 727 25827 304-256-4577
Rose Kelly, prin. Fax 256-4573

Craigsville, Nicholas, Pop. 2,184
Nicholas County SD
Supt. — See Summersville
Gauley River ES 400/PK-5
100 School St 26205 304-872-5271
Heather Nutter, prin. Fax 872-5279

Crawley, Greenbrier
Greenbrier County SD
Supt. — See Lewisburg
Western Greenbrier MS 300/6-8
315 Timberwolf Dr 24931 304-392-6446
Christy Bailey, prin. Fax 392-6785

Cross Lanes, Kanawha, Pop. 9,816
Kanawha County SD
Supt. — See Charleston
Cross Lanes ES 400/PK-5
5525 Big Tyler Rd 25313 304-776-2022
Jodie Hypes, prin. Fax 776-2029
Jackson MS 600/6-8
5445 Big Tyler Rd 25313 304-776-3310
Rhonda Donohoe, prin. Fax 776-3305
Point Harmony ES 600/PK-5
5312 Big Tyler Rd 25313 304-776-3482
Jen Cummings-Cochran, prin. Fax 776-6476

Crum, Wayne, Pop. 179
Wayne County SD
Supt. — See Wayne
Crum MS 100/PK-8
PO Box 9 25669 304-393-3200
Nona Newsome, prin. Fax 393-4429

Culloden, Cabell, Pop. 3,038
Cabell County SD
Supt. — See Huntington
Culloden ES 200/PK-5
2100 US Highway 60 25510 304-743-7301
R. Keith Thomas, prin. Fax 743-7306

Cyclone, Wyoming
Wyoming County SD
Supt. — See Pineville
Road Branch S 200/PK-8
1165 Huff Creek Rd 24827 304-682-5916
Rebecca Stewart Cooke, prin. Fax 682-5916

Dailey, Randolph, Pop. 112
Randolph County SD
Supt. — See Elkins
Homestead ES 100/K-5
PO Box 158 26259 304-338-4903
Suzanne Cain, prin. Fax 338-4908

Dallas, Marshall
Marshall County SD
Supt. — See Moundsville
Sand Hill ES 50/K-6
169 Sand Hill Rd 26036 304-547-5041
K. Allender, prin. Fax 547-5041

Daniels, Raleigh, Pop. 1,865
Raleigh County SD
Supt. — See Beckley
Daniels ES 700/PK-5
351 4H Lake Rd 25832 304-256-4622
Alvin James, prin. Fax 256-4738

Danville, Boone, Pop. 688
Boone County SD
Supt. — See Madison
Ramage ES 200/PK-5
15908 Spruce River Rd 25053 304-369-0763
Amy Hale, prin. Fax 369-0765

Davisville, Wood
Wood County SD
Supt. — See Parkersburg
Kanawha ES 300/PK-5
6465 Staunton Tpke 26142 304-420-9557
Randy Edge, prin. Fax 420-9608

Delbarton, Mingo, Pop. 564
Mingo County SD
Supt. — See Williamson
Burch S 300/PK-8
275 Bulldog Blvd 25670 304-475-2700
Leah Wireman, prin. Fax 475-5106

Diamond, Kanawha
Kanawha County SD
Supt. — See Charleston
Midland Trail ES 200/PK-5
200 Ferry St 25015 304-949-1823
Grant Davis, prin. Fax 949-1016

Dingess, Mingo
Mingo County SD
Supt. — See Williamson
Dingess ES 200/PK-5
PO Box 34 25671 304-752-7036
Paula Hinkle Brown, prin. Fax 752-7036

Dixie, Nicholas, Pop. 286
Nicholas County SD
Supt. — See Summersville
Dixie ES 100/PK-5
PO Box 288 25059 304-632-1323
Monica Belmont, prin. Fax 623-1323

Duck, Clay
Clay County SD
Supt. — See Clay
Big Otter ES 300/PK-5
59 Ossia Rd 25063 304-286-3111
Anthony Boggs, prin. Fax 286-3112

Dunbar, Kanawha, Pop. 7,684
Kanawha County SD
Supt. — See Charleston
Dunbar IS 300/3-5
1300 Myers Ave 25064 304-766-1570
Jennifer Spencer, prin. Fax 766-1573
Dunbar MS 400/6-8
325 27th St 25064 304-766-0363
Donnell Gilliam, prin. Fax 766-0365
Dunbar PS 300/PK-2
2401 Myers Ave 25064 304-766-0367
Michelle Adams, prin. Fax 766-0368

Dunlow, Wayne
Wayne County SD
Supt. — See Wayne
Dunlow ES 100/PK-5
32800 Route 152 25511 304-385-4376
Kim Mills, prin. Fax 385-1026

East Bank, Kanawha, Pop. 953
Kanawha County SD
Supt. — See Charleston
East Bank MS 400/6-8
PO Box 897 25067 304-595-2311
Michael Wilkinson, prin. Fax 595-4676

East Lynn, Wayne
Wayne County SD
Supt. — See Wayne
East Lynn ES 200/PK-5
19594 E Lynn Rd 25512 304-849-3171
Melissa Maynard, prin. Fax 849-5608

Eleanor, Putnam, Pop. 1,501
Putnam County SD
Supt. — See Winfield
Washington ES 300/PK-5
PO Box 680 25070 304-586-2184
Twyla Melton, prin. Fax 586-4275
Washington MS 300/6-8
PO Box 660 25070 304-586-2875
Tiauna Slack, prin. Fax 586-3037

Elizabeth, Wirt, Pop. 816
Wirt County SD 1,000/PK-12
PO Box 189 26143 304-275-4279
Mary Jane Pope-Albin, supt. Fax 275-4581
www.edline.net/pages/wirtboe
Wirt County MS 300/5-8
PO Box 699 26143 304-275-3977
David Tupper, prin. Fax 275-4257
Wirt County PS 400/PK-4
PO Box 220 26143 304-275-4263
Melissa Emerson, prin. Fax 275-4277

Elk Garden, Mineral, Pop. 228
Mineral County SD
Supt. — See Keyser
Elk Garden PS 100/PK-4
PO Box 355 26717 304-446-5141
Michael Saturday, prin. Fax 446-5425

Elkins, Randolph, Pop. 7,020
Randolph County SD 4,100/PK-12
40 11th St 26241 304-636-9150
Pam Hewitt, supt. Fax 636-9157
boe.rand.k12.wv.us
Elkins MS 700/6-8
308 Robert E Lee Ave 26241 304-636-9176
Chris Hamrick, prin. Fax 636-9178
Elkins Third Ward ES 300/PK-5
111 Nathan St 26241 304-636-9183
Debbie Schmidlen, prin. Fax 636-9184
Jennings Randolph ES 300/PK-5
101 Scott Ford Rd 26241 304-636-9181
Rochelle Chenoweth, prin. Fax 636-9166
Midland ES 300/PK-5
150 Kennedy Dr 26241 304-636-9186
Teena Wallace, prin. Fax 636-9187
North ES 300/PK-5
RR 2 Box 320 26241 304-636-9188
Cindy Bodkin, prin. Fax 636-9189
Other Schools – See Beverly, Coalton, Dailey, Harman, Mill Creek, Pickens, Valley Head

---

Highland Adventist S 50/PK-12
1 Old Leadsville Rd 26241 304-636-4274

Elkview, Kanawha, Pop. 1,216
Kanawha County SD
Supt. — See Charleston
Bridge ES 200/PK-5
5120 Elk River Rd N 25071 304-965-5501
Maggie Holley, prin. Fax 348-1125
Clendenin ES 300/PK-5
5120 Elk River Rd N 25071 304-965-5311
Vanessa Brown, prin. Fax 548-7372
Elkview MS 800/6-8
5090 Elk River Rd N 25071 304-348-1947
Melissa Lovejoy, prin. Fax 348-6590
Pinch ES 400/PK-5
300 S Pinch Rd 25071 304-348-1943
Betty Moore, prin. Fax 348-1944

Elk Valley Christian S 100/PK-12
58 Mount Pleasant Dr 25071 304-965-7063

Ellenboro, Ritchie, Pop. 363
Ritchie County SD
Supt. — See Harrisville
Ellenboro ES 100/PK-5
PO Box 219 26346 304-869-3305
Katrina White, prin. Fax 869-3306
Ritchie County MS 300/6-8
105 Ritchie County School 26346 304-869-3512
Michael Dotson, prin. Fax 869-3519

Evans, Jackson
Jackson County SD
Supt. — See Ripley
Evans ES 200/PK-5
205 Schoolhouse Dr 25241 304-372-7333
Matt Howery, prin. Fax 372-7317

Fairdale, Raleigh
Raleigh County SD
Supt. — See Beckley
Fairdale ES 500/PK-5
PO Box 10 25839 304-934-7217
Shanna Alderman, prin. Fax 934-7835

Fairmont, Marion, Pop. 18,276
Marion County SD 8,000/PK-12
1516 Mary Lou Retton Dr 26554 304-367-2100
Gary Price, supt. Fax 367-2111
www.marionboe.com
East Dale ES 700/PK-6
57 E Dale Rd 26554 304-367-2132
Melissa Dewitt, prin. Fax 366-2522
East Fairmont MS 400/5-8
221 Mason St 26554 304-367-2123
Jay Michael, prin. Fax 367-2179
East Park ES 400/PK-4
1025 Fairfax St 26554 304-367-2134
Mark Hoffman, prin. Fax 367-2187
Jayenne ES 400/PK-4
1504 Country Club Rd 26554 304-367-2136
Scott Morris, prin. Fax 367-2178
Watson ES 400/PK-4
1579 Mary Lou Retton Dr 26554 304-367-2156
Cindy Keeling, prin. Fax 366-0107

West Fairmont MS 700/5-8
110 10th St 26554 304-366-5631
Lisa Lister, prin. Fax 366-5636
White Hall ES 200/PK-4
38 Emerald Ln 26554 304-367-2158
Karen Rhoades, prin. Fax 367-2181
Other Schools – See Barrackville, Fairview, Mannington, Monongah, Pleasant Valley, Rivesville

---

Fairmont Catholic Grade S 200/K-8
416 Madison St 26554 304-363-5313
Stacey Spadafore, prin. Fax 363-7701

Fairview, Marion, Pop. 404
Marion County SD
Supt. — See Fairmont
Fairview ES 200/PK-3
PO Box 39 26570 304-449-1752
Melvin Coleman, prin. Fax 449-1866
Fairview MS 100/4-8
17 Jesses Run Rd 26570 304-449-1312
Steve Rodriguez, prin. Fax 449-1305

Falling Waters, Berkeley, Pop. 849
Berkeley County SD
Supt. — See Martinsburg
Marlowe ES 200/PK-2
9580 Williamsport Pike 25419 304-274-2291
Amanda Stevens, prin. Fax 274-8939

Fayetteville, Fayette, Pop. 2,872
Fayette County SD 6,800/PK-12
111 Fayette Ave 25840 304-574-1176
Terrence George, supt. Fax 574-3643
www.boe.faye.k12.wv.us
Fayetteville ES 400/PK-6
200 W Wiseman Ave 25840 304-574-1011
Ellen Deel, prin. Fax 574-2942
Gatewood ES 100/PK-4
5094 Gatewood Rd 25840 304-574-2025
Paul Thompson, prin. Fax 574-2025
Other Schools – See Ansted, Gauley Bridge, Lookout, Meadow Bridge, Mount Hope, Oak Hill, Smithers

Flatwoods, Braxton, Pop. 276
Braxton County SD
Supt. — See Sutton
Flatwoods ES 300/PK-6
PO Box 130 26621 304-765-5821
Gregory Ball, prin. Fax 765-3586

Flemington, Taylor, Pop. 310
Taylor County SD
Supt. — See Grafton
Flemington ES 200/PK-4
824 Simpson Rd 26347 304-739-4749
Jeanne Gren, prin. Fax 739-4671
West Taylor ES 300/PK-4
200 Morrow Cross Rd 26347 304-842-0490
Jamison Fisher, prin. Fax 842-0492

Follansbee, Brooke, Pop. 2,935
Brooke County SD
Supt. — See Wellsburg
Follansbee MS 500/5-8
1400 Main St 26037 304-527-1942
Gregory Rothwell, prin. Fax 527-1954
Hooverson Heights PS 200/K-4
200 Rockdale Rd 26037 304-527-0870
Joseph Farran, prin. Fax 527-2440
Jefferson PS 200/K-4
1098 Jefferson St 26037 304-527-2250
Nadine Sweda, prin. Fax 527-2014

Fort Ashby, Mineral, Pop. 1,375
Mineral County SD
Supt. — See Keyser
Fort Ashby PS 200/PK-2
44 Fort Ashby Primary Sch 26719 304-298-3632
Dawn Burke, prin. Fax 298-3200
Frankfort IS 300/PK-PK, 3-
PO Box 427 26719 304-298-3616
Jackie Beverlin, prin. Fax 298-3557

Fort Gay, Wayne, Pop. 690
Wayne County SD
Supt. — See Wayne
Fort Gay S 200/PK-8
1 Viking Dr 25514 304-648-5404
Donita Webb, prin. Fax 648-7802

Foster, Boone
Boone County SD
Supt. — See Madison
Brookview ES 500/PK-5
1 Learning Way 25081 304-369-1012
Jason Hill, prin. Fax 369-1054

Frametown, Braxton
Braxton County SD
Supt. — See Sutton
Frametown ES 200/PK-6
65 Jeanie Ellis Dr 26623 304-364-5526
Linda Sears, prin. Fax 364-8620

Frankford, Greenbrier
Greenbrier County SD
Supt. — See Lewisburg
Frankford ES 300/PK-5
21692 Seneca Trl N 24938 304-497-2921
Linda King, prin. Fax 497-2963

Franklin, Pendleton, Pop. 713
Pendleton County SD 1,000/PK-12
PO Box 888 26807 304-358-2207
Charles Hedrick, supt. Fax 358-2936
pendletoncountyschools.com
Franklin ES 300/PK-6
PO Box 848 26807 304-358-2206
Sandra Simmons, prin. Fax 358-7628
Other Schools – See Brandywine, Circleville

French Creek, Upshur
Upshur County SD
Supt. — See Buckhannon
French Creek ES 300/PK-5
7619 Route 20 South Rd 26218 304-924-6381
Kasey Baisden, prin. Fax 924-6386

Gallipolis Ferry, Mason, Pop. 810
Mason County SD
Supt. — See Point Pleasant
Beale ES 300/PK-6
PO Box 27 25515 304-675-1260
Patricia Brumfield, prin. Fax 675-1261

Gassaway, Braxton, Pop. 900
Braxton County SD
Supt. — See Sutton
Davis ES 200/PK-6
113 5th St 26624 304-364-5291
Tony Minney, prin. Fax 364-8547

Gauley Bridge, Fayette, Pop. 609
Fayette County SD
Supt. — See Fayetteville
Gauley Bridge ES 200/PK-5
PO Box 519 25085 304-632-2661
Joseph Groom, prin. Fax 632-0297

Genoa, Wayne
Wayne County SD
Supt. — See Wayne
Genoa ES 100/PK-5
21269 Route 152 25517 304-385-4421
Tony Clay, prin. Fax 385-4427

Gerrardstown, Berkeley
Berkeley County SD
Supt. — See Martinsburg
Gerrardstown ES 200/K-2
15 Dominion Rd 25420 304-229-1985
Kevin McBee, prin. Fax 229-1988
Mountain Ridge IS 400/3-5
2691 Gerrardstown Rd 25420 304-229-6791
Autumne Frye, prin. Fax 222-6914
Mountain Ridge MS 6-8
2771 Gerrardstown Rd 25420 304-229-8833
Dr. Ron Branch, admin. Fax 229-8830

Ghent, Raleigh, Pop. 449
Raleigh County SD
Supt. — See Beckley
Ghent ES 200/PK-5
PO Box 350 25843 304-787-3631
Shanna Regester, prin. Fax 787-3474

Gilbert, Mingo, Pop. 447
Mingo County SD
Supt. — See Williamson
Gilbert ES 300/PK-4
PO Box 1900 25621 304-664-5042
Daniel Dean, prin. Fax 664-9723
Gilbert MS 200/5-8
1 Lion Country Way 25621 304-664-8197
Beverly Bailey, prin. Fax 664-8249

Darrin Christian Academy 100/K-12
PO Box 402 25621 304-664-3763
Kenny Pool, admin. Fax 664-3764

Glen Dale, Marshall, Pop. 1,510
Marshall County SD
Supt. — See Moundsville
Glen Dale ES 200/K-5
407 7th St 26038 304-843-4427
Kim Cain, prin. Fax 843-4464

Glen Daniel, Raleigh
Raleigh County SD
Supt. — See Beckley
Trap Hill MS 500/6-8
665 Coal River Rd 25844 304-934-5392
Jerry Bawgus, prin. Fax 934-5393

Glen Fork, Wyoming, Pop. 481
Wyoming County SD
Supt. — See Pineville
Glen Fork ES 200/K-8
PO Box 50 25845 304-682-6423
Brenda Shumate, prin. Fax 682-3160

Glenville, Gilmer, Pop. 1,501
Gilmer County SD 700/PK-12
809 Medical Dr 26351 304-462-7386
Gabriel DeVono, supt. Fax 462-5103
boe.gilmer.k12.wv.us
Gilmer County ES 200/PK-6
99 Fairground Rd 26351 304-462-7338
Toni Bishop, prin. Fax 462-5108

Grafton, Taylor, Pop. 5,091
Taylor County SD 2,400/PK-12
71 Utt Dr 26354 304-265-2497
Kathleen Green, supt. Fax 265-2508
www.taylorcountyboe.net
Jarvis ES 600/PK-4
650 N Pike St 26354 304-265-4090
Heather Mugnano, prin. Fax 265-2560
Taylor County MS 700/5-8
670 Spring Hills Rd 26354 304-265-0722
Matt Keener, prin. Fax 265-4623
Other Schools – See Flemington

Grantsville, Calhoun, Pop. 561
Calhoun County SD
Supt. — See Mount Zion
Pleasant Hill ES 200/PK-4
3254 N Calhoun Hwy 26147 304-354-6022
Amy Nicholas, prin. Fax 354-6070

Green Bank, Pocahontas, Pop. 140
Pocahontas County SD
Supt. — See Marlinton
Green Bank ES 300/PK-8
5917 Potomac Highlands Trl 24944 304-456-4865
Ricky Sharp, prin. Fax 456-5162

Griffithsville, Lincoln
Lincoln County SD
Supt. — See Hamlin
Duval S 500/PK-8
PO Box 67 25521 304-524-2101
Mary Patton, prin. Fax 524-2232

Hacker Valley, Webster
Webster County SD
Supt. — See Webster Springs
Hacker Valley S 100/PK-8
11 School Loop Rd 26222 304-493-6488
Kennetha Howes, prin. Fax 493-6489

Hambleton, Tucker, Pop. 231
Tucker County SD
Supt. — See Parsons
Tucker Valley S 500/PK-8
81 Tucker Valley School Rd 26269 304-478-3606
Teresa Brusak, prin. Fax 478-4888

Hamlin, Lincoln, Pop. 1,134
Lincoln County SD 3,400/PK-12
10 Marland Ave 25523 304-824-3033
Jeff Midkiff, supt. Fax 824-7947
boe.linc.k12.wv.us
Hamlin ES 600/PK-8
8130 Court Ave 25523 304-824-3036
Rebecca Ferguson, prin. Fax 824-5575
Other Schools – See Alum Creek, Branchland, Griffithsville, Harts, Ranger, West Hamlin

Hanover, Wyoming
Wyoming County SD
Supt. — See Pineville
Huff Consolidated S 300/PK-8
PO Box E 24839 304-938-3672
Carolyn Hatfield, prin. Fax 938-3672

Harman, Randolph, Pop. 143
Randolph County SD
Supt. — See Elkins
Harman S 200/PK-12
PO Box 130 26270 304-227-4114
April Senic, prin. Fax 227-3610

Harpers Ferry, Jefferson, Pop. 283
Jefferson County SD
Supt. — See Charles Town
Blue Ridge ES 300/2-5
18866 Charles Town Rd 25425 304-725-2995
Susan Zigler, prin. Fax 728-7041
Blue Ridge PS PK-1
175 Lowery Ln 25425 304-724-3300
Susan Zigler, prin. Fax 724-3307
Harpers Ferry MS 400/6-8
1710 W Washington St 25425 304-535-6357
Eric Vandell, prin. Fax 535-6986
Shipley ES 400/K-5
652 Shipley School Rd 25425 304-725-4395
Ian Hillman, prin. Fax 728-7388

Harrisville, Ritchie, Pop. 1,865
Ritchie County SD 1,500/PK-12
134 S Penn Ave 26362 304-643-2991
Ora Coffman, supt. Fax 643-2994
www.ritchieschools.com
Harrisville ES 300/PK-5
1201 E Main St 26362 304-643-2220
Laura Snodgrass, prin. Fax 643-2710
Other Schools – See Ellenboro, Pennsboro, Smithville

Harts, Lincoln, Pop. 652
Lincoln County SD
Supt. — See Hamlin
Harts ES 200/PK-8
1246 McClellan Hwy 25524 304-855-3173
Deborah Dingess, prin. Fax 855-8494

Logan County SD
Supt. — See Logan
Dingess ES 100/PK-4
25 Hugh Dingess School Rd 25524 304-855-3585
Sam Dalton, prin. Fax 855-6600

Hedgesville, Berkeley, Pop. 311
Berkeley County SD
Supt. — See Martinsburg
Back Creek Valley ES 100/K-2
1962 Back Creek Valley Rd 25427 304-229-1975
Steve Dellinger, prin. Fax 229-1978
Hedgesville ES 700/PK-2
88 School House Dr 25427 304-754-3341
Sonia Knipe, prin. Fax 754-6660
Hedgesville MS 700/6-8
334 School House Dr 25427 304-754-3313
Elizabeth Adams, prin. Fax 754-6613
Tomahawk IS 500/3-5
6665 Hedgesville Rd 25427 304-754-3171
Beth McCoy, prin. Fax 754-3201

Morgan County SD
Supt. — See Berkeley Springs
Pleasant View ES 100/K-5
10500 Martinsburg Rd 25427 304-258-2606
Keri Chilcote, prin. Fax 258-7993

Hillsboro, Pocahontas, Pop. 259
Pocahontas County SD
Supt. — See Marlinton
Hillsboro ES 100/PK-5
7724 Seneca Trl 24946 304-653-4221
Rebecca Spencer, prin. Fax 653-4212

Hilltop, Fayette, Pop. 613

Mountainview Christian S 100/PK-12
176 Mountain View Rd 25855 304-465-0502
Rev. Rudell Bloomfield, hdmstr. Fax 465-5484

Hinton, Summers, Pop. 2,623
Summers County SD 1,600/PK-12
116 Main St 25951 304-466-6000
Kimberly Rodes, supt. Fax 466-6008
boe.summers.k12.wv.us
Hinton Area ES 500/PK-4
121 Park Ave 25951 304-466-6024
Angela Gumm, prin. Fax 466-6008

Summers MS 400/5-8
400 Temple St 25951 304-466-6030
M. Susie Hudson, prin. Fax 466-2271
Other Schools – See Jumping Branch, Talcott

Holden, Logan, Pop. 872
Logan County SD
Supt. — See Logan
Holden Central ES 200/PK-4
1034 Copperas Fork Rd 25625 304-239-2771
Janice Williamson, prin. Fax 239-2514

Hometown, Putnam, Pop. 660
Putnam County SD
Supt. — See Winfield
Hometown ES 100/PK-5
107 School Ln 25109 304-586-2395
Barbara Black, prin. Fax 586-1014

Huntington, Cabell, Pop. 47,796
Cabell County SD 12,800/PK-12
2850 5th Ave 25702 304-528-5000
Ryan Saxe, supt. Fax 528-5080
www.cabellschools.com
Altizer ES 300/PK-5
250 3rd St 25705 304-528-5100
Carrie Smith, prin. Fax 528-5148
Central City ES 600/PK-5
2100 Washington Ave 25704 304-528-5231
Shannon Rayburn, prin. Fax 528-5245
Guyandotte ES 300/PK-5
605 5th Ave 25702 304-528-5128
Michael Krenzel, prin. Fax 528-5151
Highlawn ES 300/PK-5
2549 1st Ave 25703 304-528-5130
Robin Harmon, prin. Fax 528-5152
Hite-Saunders ES 200/PK-5
3708 Green Valley Rd 25701 304-528-5132
Brenda Horne, prin. Fax 528-5038
Huntington East MS 500/6-8
1 Campbell Dr 25705 304-528-9508
DeLois Perry, prin. Fax 528-5197
Huntington MS 600/6-8
925 3rd St 25701 304-528-5180
James Paxton, prin. Fax 528-5215
Meadows ES 300/PK-5
1601 Washington Blvd 25701 304-528-5166
Connie Mize, prin. Fax 528-5153
Southside ES 500/PK-5
930 2nd St 25701 304-528-5168
Carolyn Frye, prin. Fax 528-5154
Spring Hill ES 600/PK-5
1901 Hall Ave 25701 304-528-5175
Pamela Bailey, prin. Fax 528-5177
Other Schools – See Barboursville, Culloden, Lesage, Milton, Ona, Salt Rock

Wayne County SD
Supt. — See Wayne
Kellogg ES 500/PK-5
4415 Piedmont Rd 25704 304-429-4441
Rebecca Richards, prin. Fax 429-7200
Vinson MS 300/6-8
3851 Piedmont Rd 25704 304-429-1641
Tammy Forbush, prin. Fax 429-6162

Covenant S 200/K-12
2400 Johnstown Rd 25701 304-781-6741
Grace Christian S 200/PK-12
1111 Adams Ave 25704 304-522-8635
Dr. Dan Brokke, admin. Fax 522-3240
Our Lady of Fatima S 200/PK-8
535 Norway Ave 25705 304-523-2861
Jena Naswadi, prin. Fax 525-0390
St. Joseph Catholic S 400/PK-8
1326 6th Ave 25701 304-522-2644
Carol Templeton, prin. Fax 522-2512

Hurricane, Putnam, Pop. 6,205
Putnam County SD
Supt. — See Winfield
Conner Street ES 400/PK-5
445 Conner St 25526 304-562-9351
Kristi Barker, prin. Fax 562-3635
Hurricane MS 1,000/6-8
518 Midland Trl 25526 304-562-9271
Mary Allen, prin. Fax 562-7163
Hurricane Town ES 400/PK-5
300 Harbour Ln 25526 304-562-3610
Elizabeth Willis, prin. Fax 562-6625
Lakeside ES 300/PK-5
2554 US Route 60 25526 304-562-3630
Lisa Lewis, prin. Fax 562-9406
Mountain View ES 500/PK-5
4170 Teays Valley Rd 25526 304-757-5667
Jill Cox, prin. Fax 757-5664
West Teays ES 600/PK-5
3676 Teays Valley Rd 25526 304-757-6711
Valerie Fowler, prin. Fax 757-8098

Calvary Baptist Academy 200/K-12
3655 Teays Valley Rd 25526 304-757-6768
Milton Thompson, prin. Fax 757-6777

Iaeger, McDowell, Pop. 301
McDowell County SD
Supt. — See Welch
Iaeger ES 300/PK-5
PO Box 359 24844 304-938-2227
Sheena Ashby, prin. Fax 938-5289

Inwood, Berkeley, Pop. 2,871
Berkeley County SD
Supt. — See Martinsburg
Inwood PS 200/K-3
7864 Winchester Ave 25428 304-229-1990
Ryan Ott, prin. Fax 229-1992

Jane Lew, Lewis, Pop. 406
Lewis County SD
Supt. — See Weston
Jane Lew ES 400/PK-4
6536 Main St 26378 304-884-7836
Denise Sprouse, prin. Fax 884-7185

Jumping Branch, Summers
Summers County SD
Supt. — See Hinton
Jumping Branch ES 100/PK-5
6617 Beech Run Rd 25969 304-466-6025
Angela Miller, prin. Fax 466-6025

Junior, Barbour, Pop. 519
Barbour County SD
Supt. — See Philippi
Junior ES 100/PK-4
49 W 1st St 26275 304-823-1200
Ashley Workman, prin. Fax 823-2895

Kearneysville, Jefferson
Jefferson County SD
Supt. — See Charles Town
North Jefferson ES 300/PK-5
6996 Charles Town Rd 25430 304-725-9587
D. Nicole Johnson, prin. Fax 728-7331

Jefferson Academy 100/PK-5
449 Rose Hill Dr 25430 304-725-1438
Sara Howie, head sch

Kenna, Jackson
Jackson County SD
Supt. — See Ripley
Kenna ES 300/PK-5
275 Business Park Dr 25248 304-372-7343
Sonya White, prin. Fax 372-7313

Kenova, Wayne, Pop. 3,199
Wayne County SD
Supt. — See Wayne
Buffalo ES 500/PK-5
331 Buffalo Creek Rd 25530 304-429-2911
Stephanie May, prin. Fax 429-3269
Buffalo MS 300/6-8
298 Buffalo Creek Rd 25530 304-429-6062
Elizabeth Ryder, prin. Fax 429-7245
Kenova ES 400/PK-5
300 9th St 25530 304-453-1521
Deidre Farley, prin. Fax 453-4415

Kermit, Mingo, Pop. 404
Mingo County SD
Supt. — See Williamson
Kermit S 300/PK-8
300 Blue Devil Ln 25674 304-393-4130
Deborah Starr, prin. Fax 393-4137

Keyser, Mineral, Pop. 5,316
Mineral County SD 4,200/PK-12
1 Baker Pl 26726 304-788-4200
Shawn Dilly M.A., supt. Fax 788-4204
boe.mine.k12.wv.us
Fountain PS 100/PK-4
289 Fountain School Rd 26726 304-788-4215
Patricia Twigg, prin. Fax 788-4229
Keyser MS 700/5-8
700 Harley O Staggers Sr Dr 26726 304-788-4220
Julie McBee, prin. Fax 788-4225
Keyser PS 600/PK-4
590 Harley O Staggers Sr Dr 26726 304-788-4508
Barbara Kesner, prin. Fax 788-4510
Other Schools – See Burlington, Elk Garden, Fort Ashby, New Creek, Ridgeley, Wiley Ford

Kimball, McDowell, Pop. 184
McDowell County SD
Supt. — See Welch
Kimball ES 300/PK-5
PO Box 308 24853 304-585-7570
April Hedinger, prin. Fax 585-7165

Kingwood, Preston, Pop. 2,912
Preston County SD 4,400/PK-12
731 Preston Dr 26537 304-329-0580
Stephen Wotring, supt. Fax 329-0720
preston-k12.wvnet.edu/boe/
Central Preston MS 300/6-8
64 Wildcat Way 26537 304-329-0033
Karen Ovesney, prin. Fax 329-2389
Kingwood ES 600/PK-5
207 S Price St 26537 304-329-1034
Jill Zeigler, prin. Fax 329-1035
Other Schools – See Arthurdale, Aurora, Bruceton Mills, Rowlesburg, Terra Alta, Tunnelton

Lavalette, Wayne, Pop. 1,065
Wayne County SD
Supt. — See Wayne
Lavalette ES 300/PK-5
1150 Beech Fork Rd 25535 304-525-3221
Allison Brewer, prin. Fax 525-3245

Left Hand, Roane
Roane County SD
Supt. — See Spencer
Geary ES 300/PK-8
PO Box 89 25251 304-565-3721
Brenda Chadwell, prin. Fax 565-3741

Leon, Mason, Pop. 156
Mason County SD
Supt. — See Point Pleasant
Leon ES 200/PK-6
1226 Burdette St 25123 304-458-1710
Don Bower, prin. Fax 458-2049

Lerona, Mercer
Mercer County SD
Supt. — See Princeton
Sun Valley ES 100/K-5
PO Box 10 25971 304-384-7441
Ashley Smith, prin. Fax 384-3114

Lesage, Cabell, Pop. 1,331
Cabell County SD
Supt. — See Huntington
Cox Landing ES 200/PK-5
6358 Cox Ln 25537 304-733-3019
Kristin Giles, prin. Fax 733-3021

Lester, Raleigh, Pop. 341
Raleigh County SD
Supt. — See Beckley
Lester ES 100/PK-5
PO Box 727 25865 304-934-5885
Lisa Adkins, prin. Fax 934-6242

Levels, Hampshire
Hampshire County SD
Supt. — See Romney
Cornwell ES 100/PK-5
HC 60 Box 72 25431 304-492-5520
Pam Slocum, prin. Fax 492-5123

Lewisburg, Greenbrier, Pop. 3,773
Greenbrier County SD 5,200/PK-12
197 Chestnut St 24901 304-647-6470
Jeff Bryant, supt. Fax 647-6490
www.greenbriercountyschools.org
Lewisburg ES 500/PK-5
492 W Washington St 24901 304-647-6477
Leann Piercy-McMillian, prin. Fax 647-4838
Other Schools – See Alderson, Crawley, Frankford, Quinwood, Rainelle, Ronceverte, Rupert, Smoot, White Sulphur Springs

---

Greenbrier Episcopal S 50/PK-8
3100 Houfnaggle Rd 24901 304-793-2420
Gretchen Graves, head sch Fax 793-2421

Liberty, Putnam
Putnam County SD
Supt. — See Winfield
Confidence ES 200/PK-5
8786 McLane Pike 25124 304-586-2041
Colleen Huston, prin. Fax 586-9036

Linn, Gilmer
Lewis County SD
Supt. — See Weston
Leading Creek ES 200/PK-6
15300 US Highway 33 W 26384 304-462-7127
Kimberly Freelund, admin. Fax 462-4925

Lizemores, Clay
Clay County SD
Supt. — See Clay
Lizemore ES 100/PK-5
100 Lions Rd 25125 304-587-4823
Britni Ramsey, prin. Fax 587-2772

Logan, Logan, Pop. 1,749
Logan County SD 6,100/PK-12
PO Box 477 25601 304-792-2060
Patricia Lucas, supt. Fax 752-3711
logancs.schoolinsites.com
Justice ES 100/PK-4
407 Circle Dr 25601 304-752-3250
Whitney Ellis, prin. Fax 752-5456
Logan ES 400/K-4
18 Wildcat Way 25601 304-752-4180
Cheryl Deskins, prin. Fax 752-5463
Logan MS 700/5-8
14 Wildcat Way 25601 304-752-1804
Ernestine Sutherland, prin. Fax 752-0207
Other Schools – See Accoville, Chapmanville, Harts, Holden, Mallory, Man, Omar, Verdunville

Lookout, Fayette
Fayette County SD
Supt. — See Fayetteville
Divide ES 200/PK-5
PO Box 180 25868 304-574-1443
Steve Rhodes, prin. Fax 574-0693

Lost Creek, Harrison, Pop. 482
Harrison County SD
Supt. — See Clarksburg
Lost Creek ES 200/PK-5
PO Box 128 26385 304-326-7040
Laura Trent, prin. Fax 745-4393
South Harrison MS 300/6-8
3003 Hawk Hwy 26385 304-326-7460
Scott Hage, prin. Fax 745-5587

Lumberport, Harrison, Pop. 868
Harrison County SD
Supt. — See Clarksburg
Lumberport ES 300/PK-5
PO Box 417 26386 304-326-7020
Vickie Luchuck, prin. Fax 584-5943

Mabscott, Raleigh, Pop. 1,370
Raleigh County SD
Supt. — See Beckley
Mabscott ES 200/PK-5
PO Box 174 25871 304-256-4583
Beverly Weis, prin. Fax 256-4595

Mc Mechen, Marshall, Pop. 1,914
Marshall County SD
Supt. — See Moundsville
Center McMechen ES 200/K-5
800 Marshall St, 304-232-6530
Arica Holt, prin. Fax 232-6520

Madison, Boone, Pop. 3,064
Boone County SD 4,200/PK-12
69 Avenue B 25130 304-369-3131
Jeffrey Huffman, supt. Fax 369-0855
www.boonecountyboe.org
Madison ES 500/PK-5
150 Josephine Ave 25130 304-369-2241
Connie Napier, prin. Fax 369-2869
Madison MS 500/6-8
404 Riverside Dr W 25130 304-369-4464
Shann Elkins, prin. Fax 369-5800
Other Schools – See Ashford, Comfort, Danville, Foster, Seth, Van, Whitesville

Mallory, Logan, Pop. 1,628
Logan County SD
Supt. — See Logan
Man ES 200/PK-4
1 Pioneer Path 25634 304-583-8316
Doug Barrett, prin. Fax 583-7342

Man MS 500/5-8
PO Box 390 25634 304-583-8037
Cynthia Caldwell, prin. Fax 583-8253

Man, Logan, Pop. 759
Logan County SD
Supt. — See Logan
South Man ES 100/PK-4
301 E Mcdonald Ave 25635 304-583-7522
Danita Noel, prin. Fax 583-8046

Mannington, Marion, Pop. 2,054
Marion County SD
Supt. — See Fairmont
Blackshere ES 400/PK-4
77 Blackshere Dr 26582 304-986-2707
Jane DeVaul, prin. Fax 986-2715
Mannington MS 300/5-8
113 Clarksburg St 26582 304-986-1050
Richard Ott, prin. Fax 986-1747

Marlinton, Pocahontas, Pop. 1,050
Pocahontas County SD 1,100/PK-12
926 5th Ave 24954 304-799-4505
Terrence Beam, supt. Fax 799-4499
pocahontas-k12.wvnet.edu
Marlinton ES 200/PK-5
926 5th Ave 24954 304-799-6551
Phillip Anderson, prin. Fax 799-6552
Other Schools – See Buckeye, Green Bank, Hillsboro

Marmet, Kanawha, Pop. 1,480
Kanawha County SD
Supt. — See Charleston
Marmet ES 200/PK-5
408 94th St 25315 304-949-2382
Cynthia Schilling, prin. Fax 949-6116

Martinsburg, Berkeley, Pop. 16,642
Berkeley County SD 17,300/PK-12
401 S Queen St 25401 304-267-3500
Fax 267-3506
berkeleycountyschools.org
Bedington ES 200/K-2
149 Bedington Rd, 304-274-2535
Kim Agee, prin. Fax 274-3957
Berkeley Heights ES 600/K-3
726 Hack Wilson Way 25401 304-267-3520
Amber Boeckmann, prin. Fax 263-3798
Burke Street ES 100/PK-3
422 W Burke St 25401 304-267-3525
Todd Cutlip, prin. Fax 267-3527
Eagle IS 500/4-5
730 Eagle School Rd, 304-263-0422
Lewis Mullenax, prin. Fax 229-6506
Martinsburg North MS 600/6-8
250 East Rd, 304-267-3540
Rebekah Eyler, prin. Fax 264-5066
Martinsburg South MS 900/6-8
150 Bulldog Blvd 25401 304-267-3545
Rosa Clark, prin. Fax 264-5062
Opequon ES 500/K-2
395 East Rd, 304-267-3550
Tana Burkhart, prin. Fax 267-3552
Orchard View IS 600/3-5
1455 Delmar Orchard Rd, 304-263-4143
Dr. Luke Smith, prin. Fax 263-4148
Potomack IS 700/3-5
5308 Williamsport Pike, 304-274-6592
Amanda Billmeyer, prin. Fax 274-6876
Rosemont ES 500/K-3
301 S Alabama Ave 25401 304-267-3560
Erica Propst, prin. Fax 263-3838
Spring Mills MS 700/6-8
255 Campus Dr, 304-274-5030
Nancy Melonas, prin. Fax 274-3598
Spring Mills PS 400/K-2
401 Campus Dr, 304-274-5892
Drenna Reineck, prin. Fax 274-5807
Tuscarora ES 300/K-2
2000 Tavern Rd 25401 304-267-3565
Drenna Reineck, prin. Fax 264-5059
Valley View ES 500/K-2
140 Nadenbousch Ln, 304-229-1970
Fred Johnson, prin. Fax 229-1973
Winchester Avenue ES 300/PK-2
650 Winchester Ave 25401 304-267-3570
Dean Warrenfeltz, prin. Fax 267-3572
Other Schools – See Bunker Hill, Falling Waters, Gerrardstown, Hedgesville, Inwood

---

Faith Christian Academy 300/PK-12
138 Greensburg Rd, 304-263-0011
Eric Kerns, admin. Fax 267-0638
Rocky Knoll SDA S 100/PK-8
52 Advent Dr, 304-263-9894
St. Joseph S 300/PK-8
110 E Stephen St 25401 304-267-6447
Robert Edwards, prin. Fax 267-6573

Matewan, Mingo, Pop. 490
Mingo County SD
Supt. — See Williamson
Matewan S 500/PK-8
PO Box 568 25678 304-426-4719
Cynthia Calfee, prin. Fax 426-4732

Matoaka, Mercer, Pop. 227
Mercer County SD
Supt. — See Princeton
Lashmeet-Matoaka ES 300/PK-5
PO Box 408 24736 304-467-8282
Dina Smith, prin. Fax 467-7477

Maysville, Grant
Grant County SD
Supt. — See Petersburg
Maysville ES 200/PK-6
7 Elementary School Dr # 1 26833 304-749-7441
Megan DiBenedetto, prin. Fax 749-7446

Meadow Bridge, Fayette, Pop. 378
Fayette County SD
Supt. — See Fayetteville
Meadow Bridge ES 200/PK-6
804 Main St 25976 304-484-7914
Cheryl Altizer, prin. Fax 484-7599

Metz, Wetzel
Wetzel County SD
Supt. — See New Martinsville
Long Drain S 300/PK-8
3538 Long Drain Rd 26585 304-775-4221
Paul Huston, prin. Fax 775-4261

Miami, Kanawha
Kanawha County SD
Supt. — See Charleston
Dawes ES 200/PK-5
PO Box 149 25134 304-595-3323
Natalie Vaughan, prin. Fax 595-3361

Middlebourne, Tyler, Pop. 809
Tyler County SD 1,300/PK-12
PO Box 25 26149 304-758-2145
Robin Daquilante, supt. Fax 758-4566
www.tylercountypublicschools.com
Borman ES 400/PK-5
PO Box 299 26149 304-758-2152
Scott Wall, prin. Fax 758-2148
Other Schools – See Sistersville

Mill Creek, Randolph, Pop. 718
Randolph County SD
Supt. — See Elkins
Ward ES 300/PK-5
PO Box 278 26280 304-335-4975
Angie Wilson, prin. Fax 335-4976

Milton, Cabell, Pop. 2,401
Cabell County SD
Supt. — See Huntington
Milton ES 700/PK-5
1201 Pike St 25541 304-743-7303
Kim Alan Cooper, prin. Fax 743-7307
Milton MS 700/6-8
1 Panther Trl 25541 304-743-7308
Deborah Underwood, prin. Fax 743-7324

Mineral Wells, Wood, Pop. 1,918
Wood County SD
Supt. — See Parkersburg
Mineral Wells ES 600/PK-5
1776 Elizabeth Pike 26150 304-489-1670
Melissa Powers, prin. Fax 489-2637

Moatsville, Barbour
Barbour County SD
Supt. — See Philippi
Kasson ES 200/PK-8
19 Kasson Rd 26405 304-457-1485
Dr. Teresa Marsh, prin. Fax 457-6186

Monongah, Marion, Pop. 1,032
Marion County SD
Supt. — See Fairmont
Monongah ES 400/PK-4
628 Walnut St 26554 304-367-2159
Robert Moore, prin. Fax 367-2188
Monongah MS 200/5-8
550 Camden Ave 26554 304-367-2164
Steve Malnick, prin. Fax 367-2190

Moorefield, Hardy, Pop. 2,511
Hardy County SD 2,300/PK-12
510 Ashby St 26836 304-530-2348
Dr. Matthew Dotson, supt. Fax 530-2340
www.hardycountyschools.com
Moorefield ES 500/PK-2
400 N Main St 26836 304-530-6356
L. Wade Armentrout, prin. Fax 530-2536
Moorefield IS 400/3-5
345 Caledonia Heights Rd 26836 304-530-3450
Sheena VanMeter, prin. Fax 530-3451
Moorefield MS 300/6-8
303 Caledonia Heights Rd 26836 304-434-3000
Patrick McGregor, prin. Fax 434-3003
Other Schools – See Baker

Morgantown, Monongalia, Pop. 29,068
Monongalia County SD 10,900/PK-12
13 S High St 26501 304-291-9210
Dr. Frank Devono, supt. Fax 291-3015
boe.mono.k12.wv.us
Brookhaven ES 500/K-5
1215 Baker St 26508 304-291-9236
Davene Burks, prin. Fax 284-9355
Cheat Lake ES 800/PK-5
154 Crosby Rd 26508 304-594-2772
Dennis Gallon, prin. Fax 594-2283
Dorsey Center 50/PK-PK
1433 Dorsey Ave 26501 304-291-9330
Debbie Jones, prin. Fax 291-9324
Eastwood ES 600/PK-5
677 201st Memorial Hwy 26505 304-284-8226
DeAnn Hartshorn, prin. Fax 284-8235
Mountaineer MS 500/6-8
991 Price St 26505 304-594-1165
Crystal Nantz, prin. Fax 594-1677
Mountainview ES 700/K-5
661 Greenbag Rd 26508 304-291-9255
Karen Collins, prin. Fax 291-9254
Mylan Park ES 500/PK-5
901 Mylan Park Ln 26501 304-983-7700
Ann Lupo, prin. Fax 983-7705
North ES 800/K-5
825 Chestnut Ridge Rd 26505 304-291-9280
Natalie Webb, prin. Fax 291-9213
Ridgedale ES 400/K-5
1550 Goshen Rd 26508 304-291-9231
Sharon Petitte, prin. Fax 291-9215
Skyview ES 500/PK-5
668 River Rd 26501 304-284-2890
Jennifer Cox, prin. Fax 284-2894
South MS 700/6-8
500 E Parkway Dr 26501 304-291-9340
Sandra Brown, prin. Fax 291-9306
Suncrest ES 300/PK-5
3647 Collins Ferry Rd 26505 304-291-9347
Joanne Hines, prin. Fax 284-9388
Suncrest MS 500/6-8
360 Baldwin St 26505 304-291-9335
Dawna Hicks, prin. Fax 284-9362
Westwood MS 400/6-8
670 River Rd 26501 304-291-9300
Leonard Haney, prin. Fax 284-9368
Other Schools – See Blacksville

Alliance Christian S 100/PK-12
200 Trinity Way 26505 304-291-4659
Covenant Christian S 100/PK-8
PO Box 342 26507 304-292-6050
Rev. David Friend, hdmstr. Fax 292-9614
St. Francis de Sales Central S 400/PK-8
41 Guthrie Ln 26508 304-291-5070
Arthur Moore, prin. Fax 291-5104
Trinity Christian S 300/PK-12
200 Trinity Way 26505 304-291-4659
Michelle Stellato, supt. Fax 291-4660

Moundsville, Marshall, Pop. 9,248
Marshall County SD 4,500/PK-12
PO Box 578 26041 304-843-4400
Dr. Jeffrey Crook, supt. Fax 843-4409
boe.mars.k12.wv.us
Central ES 300/3-5
750 Tomlinson Ave 26041 304-843-4425
Erin Cuffaro, prin. Fax 843-4426
McNinch PS 400/PK-2
162 Middle Grave Creek Rd 26041 304-843-4431
Jane Duffy, prin. Fax 843-4461
Moundsville MS 500/6-8
223 Tomlinson Ave 26041 304-843-4440
Sandy McAllister, prin. Fax 843-4446
Washington Lands ES 300/K-5
116 School Rd 26041 304-843-4420
Michael Berner, prin. Fax 843-4459
Other Schools – See Cameron, Dallas, Glen Dale, Mc Mechen, Wheeling

Mount Hope, Fayette, Pop. 1,370
Fayette County SD
Supt. — See Fayetteville
Mount Hope ES 300/PK-5
408 Lincoln St 25880 304-877-2891
Marsha Bishop, prin. Fax 877-6105

Raleigh County SD
Supt. — See Beckley
Bradley ES 600/PK-5
210 Bradley School Rd 25880 304-256-4605
Mary McClung, prin. Fax 256-4624

Mount Lookout, Nicholas
Nicholas County SD
Supt. — See Summersville
Mount Lookout ES 100/K-5
1945 E Mount Lookout Rd 26678 304-872-2731
Joann Gainer, prin. Fax 872-2731

Mount Nebo, Nicholas
Nicholas County SD
Supt. — See Summersville
Mount Nebo ES 100/PK-5
PO Box 160 26679 304-872-2440
Glen Tyree, prin. Fax 872-2440

Mount Zion, Calhoun
Calhoun County SD 1,100/PK-12
540 Alan B Mollohan Dr 26151 304-354-7011
Kelli Whytsell, supt. Fax 354-7420
www.edline.net/pages/Calhoun_CSD
Other Schools – See Arnoldsburg, Grantsville

Mullens, Wyoming, Pop. 1,540
Wyoming County SD
Supt. — See Pineville
Mullens ES 200/K-4
2107 Caloric Rd 25882 304-294-5252
Carolyn Wilcox, prin. Fax 294-5252
Mullens MS 200/5-8
801 Moran Ave 25882 304-294-5757
Terri Lea Smith, prin. Fax 294-5762

Nettie, Nicholas, Pop. 567
Nicholas County SD
Supt. — See Summersville
Panther Creek ES 300/PK-5
PO Box 39 26681 304-846-6808
Angie Amick, prin. Fax 846-2144

New Creek, Mineral
Mineral County SD
Supt. — See Keyser
New Creek PS 100/PK-4
PO Box 97 26743 304-788-4249
Robin McDowell, prin. Fax 788-4208

New Cumberland, Hancock, Pop. 1,085
Hancock County SD 3,100/PK-12
PO Box 1300 26047 304-564-3411
Dr. Kathy Kidder-Wilkerson, supt. Fax 564-3990
boe.hancock.k12.wv.us
New Manchester ES 300/PK-4
128 Frankfort Rd 26047 304-564-3242
Cindy Virtue, prin. Fax 564-5084
Oak Glen MS 600/5-8
39 Golden Bear Dr 26047 304-387-2363
Virginia Greene, prin. Fax 387-4624
Other Schools – See Chester, Weirton

New Haven, Mason, Pop. 1,546
Mason County SD
Supt. — See Point Pleasant
New Haven ES 500/PK-6
PO Box 989 25265 304-882-2025
Walter Raynes, prin. Fax 882-2037

New Martinsville, Wetzel, Pop. 5,337
Wetzel County SD 2,700/PK-12
333 Foundry St 26155 304-455-2441
Edward Toman, supt. Fax 455-3446
www.wetzelcountyschools.com
New Martinsville S 800/K-8
20 E Benjamin Dr 26155 304-455-2291
M. Fay Pritchard, prin. Fax 455-6436

Other Schools – See Metz, Paden City, Reader

Nitro, Kanawha, Pop. 7,083
Kanawha County SD
Supt. — See Charleston
Nitro ES 400/PK-5
1921 19th St 25143 304-755-2451
Ashley Garrett, prin. Fax 755-9215

Putnam County SD
Supt. — See Winfield
Rock Branch ES 200/PK-5
4616 1st Ave 25143 304-755-1443
Beth Scott, prin. Fax 755-0019

Nutter Fort Stonewood, Harrison, Pop. 1,562
Harrison County SD
Supt. — See Clarksburg
Nutter Fort IS 500/3-5
1302 Buckhannon Pike 26301 304-326-7501
JoDee Decker, prin. Fax 624-3259
Nutter Fort PS 700/PK-2
1302 Buckhannon Pike 26301 304-326-7520
Joann Gilbert, prin. Fax 624-3382

Oak Hill, Fayette, Pop. 7,618
Fayette County SD
Supt. — See Fayetteville
Collins MS 900/5-8
320 W Oyler Ave 25901 304-469-3711
Cynthia Hedrick, prin. Fax 465-1352
New River ES 800/PK-4
262 Oyler Ave 25901 304-465-3806
Lee Jones, prin. Fax 465-3808
Rosedale ES 300/PK-4
4001 Summerlee Rd 25901 304-469-6661
Ted Dixon, prin. Fax 469-3569

SS. Peter & Paul S 100/PK-8
123 Elmore St 25901 304-465-5045
Ricky White, prin. Fax 465-8726

Oceana, Wyoming, Pop. 1,373
Wyoming County SD
Supt. — See Pineville
Berlin McKinney ES 400/PK-4
HC 65 Box 402 24870 304-682-6481
Robert Lyons, prin. Fax 682-5234
Oceana MS 300/5-8
309 Cook Pkwy 24870 304-682-6296
Shanda Lester, prin. Fax 682-6330

Omar, Logan, Pop. 551
Logan County SD
Supt. — See Logan
Omar ES 200/PK-4
PO Box 590 25638 304-946-2660
Martha Curry, prin. Fax 946-4236

Ona, Cabell
Cabell County SD
Supt. — See Huntington
Ona ES 400/PK-5
2701 Elementary Dr 25545 304-743-7318
Lisa Alexander, prin. Fax 743-7321

Paden City, Wetzel, Pop. 2,615
Wetzel County SD
Supt. — See New Martinsville
Paden City ES 200/PK-6
510 N 2nd Ave 26159 304-337-2221
Tammy Chambers, prin. Fax 337-9049

Parkersburg, Wood, Pop. 30,848
Wood County SD 13,300/PK-12
1210 13th St 26101 304-420-9663
John Flint, supt. Fax 420-9513
woodcountyschoolswv.com
Blennerhassett ES 400/PK-5
444 Jewell Rd 26101 304-863-5128
Justin Hartshorn, prin. Fax 863-5335
Blennerhassett MS 500/6-8
444 Jewell Rd 26101 304-863-3356
Clint Spencer, prin. Fax 863-3357
Criss ES 300/PK-5
2800 22nd St 26101 304-420-9522
Heather Grant, prin. Fax 420-9541
Edison MS 700/6-8
1201 Hillcrest St 26101 304-420-9525
Jean Mewshaw, prin. Fax 420-9527
Emerson ES 300/K-5
1605 36th St 26104 304-420-9528
Tabatha Efaw, prin. Fax 420-9632
Fairplains ES 200/PK-5
615 Broadway Ave 26101 304-420-9531
Liz Conrad, prin. Fax 420-9533
Franklin ES 300/PK-5
1511 Division Street Ext 26101 304-420-9534
Lee Cumpston, prin. Fax 420-9537
Gihon ES 300/PK-5
2000 Belmont Rd 26101 304-420-9539
Lori Lowers, prin. Fax 420-9540
Hamilton MS 600/6-8
3501 Cadillac Dr 26104 304-420-9547
Kevin Campbell, prin. Fax 420-9567
Jefferson ES 500/PK-5
1103 Plum St 26101 304-420-9554
Jodie Pierotti, prin. Fax 420-9507
Lubeck ES 400/PK-5
206 Lubeck Rd 26101 304-863-3321
Melanie Cutright, prin. Fax 863-3848
Madison ES 400/PK-5
1426 32nd St 26104 304-420-9563
Valissa Porter, prin. Fax 420-9564
Martin ES 300/PK-5
1301 Hillcrest St 26101 304-420-9625
Julie Gibson, prin. Fax 420-9578
McKinley ES 300/PK-5
1130 19th St 26101 304-420-9581
Allen Laugh, prin. Fax 420-9582
Van Devender MS 300/6-8
918 31st St 26104 304-420-9645
Darlene Murphy, prin. Fax 420-9647
Worthington ES 200/K-5
2500 36th St 26104 304-420-9660
Tom Wheeler, prin. Fax 420-2459
Other Schools – See Davisville, Mineral Wells, Vienna, Waverly, Williamstown

---

North Christian S 100/PK-5
3109 Emerson Ave 26104 304-485-0241
Teresa Carroll, prin. Fax 428-3231
Parkersburg Academy 50/PK-8
1800 38th St 26104 304-485-6901
Parkersburg Catholic ES 200/PK-6
810 Juliana St 26101 304-422-6694
Kevin Simonton, prin. Fax 422-2469

Parsons, Tucker, Pop. 1,472
Tucker County SD 1,000/PK-12
100 Education Ln 26287 304-478-2771
Eddie Campbell Ed.D., supt. Fax 478-3422
www.tuckercountyschools.com
Other Schools – See Hambleton, Thomas

Paw Paw, Morgan, Pop. 498
Morgan County SD
Supt. — See Berkeley Springs
Paw Paw ES 100/PK-6
60 Pirate Cir 25434 304-947-7425
Melinda Kasekamp, prin. Fax 947-5913

Pennsboro, Ritchie, Pop. 1,164
Ritchie County SD
Supt. — See Harrisville
Creed Collins ES 300/PK-5
512 Collins Ave 26415 304-659-2140
Debbie White, prin. Fax 659-3322

Petersburg, Grant, Pop. 2,438
Grant County SD 1,800/PK-12
204 Jefferson Ave 26847 304-257-1011
Douglas S. Lambert, supt. Fax 257-2453
grantcountyschools.org
Petersburg ES 700/PK-6
333 Rig St 26847 304-257-1110
Mitch Webster, prin. Fax 257-9658
Other Schools – See Maysville

Peterstown, Monroe, Pop. 646
Monroe County SD
Supt. — See Union
Peterstown ES 500/PK-4
108 College Dr 24963 304-753-4328
Fax 753-4786
Peterstown MS 300/5-8
36 College Dr 24963 304-753-4322
Angie Terry, prin. Fax 753-5376

Philippi, Barbour, Pop. 2,882
Barbour County SD 2,400/PK-12
45 School St 26416 304-457-3030
Jeffrey Woofter, supt. Fax 457-3559
www.wvschools.com/barbourcountyschools/
Philippi ES 400/PK-4
547 Cherry Hill Rd 26416 304-457-4229
Julie Bibey, prin. Fax 457-2287
Philippi MS 200/5-8
611 Cherry Hill Rd 26416 304-457-2999
David Neff, prin. Fax 457-2561
Other Schools – See Belington, Junior, Moatsville

Feed My Sheep Christian S 50/K-8
36 Sesame St 26416 304-457-1135
Sharon Arnett, admin. Fax 457-1135

Pickens, Randolph, Pop. 66
Randolph County SD
Supt. — See Elkins
Pickens S 50/K-12
PO Box 146 26230 304-924-5525
Christine Long, prin. Fax 924-6325

Pineville, Wyoming, Pop. 659
Wyoming County SD 4,200/PK-12
PO Box 69 24874 304-732-6262
Deirdre Cline, supt. Fax 732-7226
boe.wyom.k12.wv.us
Pineville ES 500/PK-4
PO Box 700 24874 304-732-7966
Donald Clay, prin. Fax 732-6767
Pineville MS 300/5-8
PO Box 470 24874 304-732-6442
Terry Shumate, prin. Fax 732-6737
Other Schools – See Brenton, Bud, Cyclone, Glen Fork, Hanover, Mullens, Oceana

Pleasant Valley, Marion
Marion County SD
Supt. — See Fairmont
Pleasant Valley ES 300/K-4
1858 Valley School Rd 26554 304-367-2148
Kim Middlemas, prin. Fax 367-2175

Poca, Putnam, Pop. 970
Putnam County SD
Supt. — See Winfield
Poca ES 300/PK-5
PO Box 430 25159 304-755-7561
Lauretta Ghavami, prin. Fax 755-3843
Poca MS 300/6-8
2884 Charleston Rd 25159 304-755-7343
Lynda Rumbaugh, prin. Fax 755-8930

Point Pleasant, Mason, Pop. 4,266
Mason County SD 4,300/PK-12
1 Education Ln 25550 304-675-4540
Jack Cullen, supt. Fax 675-7226
boe.maso.k12.wv.us
Point Pleasant IS 400/3-6
1 Walden Roush Way 25550 304-675-1430
Fax 675-2110
Point Pleasant PS 400/PK-2
2200 Lincoln Ave 25550 304-675-1420
Vickie Workman, prin. Fax 675-1474
Roosevelt ES 300/K-6
7953 Ripley Rd 25550 304-675-3337
Timothy Click, prin. Fax 675-7331

Other Schools – See Ashton, Gallipolis Ferry, Leon, New Haven

Pratt, Kanawha, Pop. 599
Kanawha County SD
Supt. — See Charleston
Pratt ES 300/PK-5
PO Box 278 25162 304-949-4838
Jacqueline Hersch, prin. Fax 442-4541

Prichard, Wayne, Pop. 524
Wayne County SD
Supt. — See Wayne
Prichard ES 200/PK-5
500 Prichard Rd 25555 304-486-5096
Stephanie McCloud, prin. Fax 486-5032

Princeton, Mercer, Pop. 6,324
Mercer County SD 9,900/PK-12
1403 Honaker Ave 24740 304-487-1551
Dr. Deborah Akers Ed.D., supt. Fax 425-5844
boe.merc.k12.wv.us
Glenwood S 800/K-8
1734 Glenwood Park Rd, 304-425-2445
Michael Morgan, prin. Fax 487-0047
Melrose ES 300/K-5
2121 Athens Rd, 304-425-3757
Edie Bennett, prin. Fax 487-0819
Mercer ES 300/3-5
1200 Mercer St 24740 304-425-3160
Kelli Stanley, prin. Fax 487-3617
Oakvale ES 100/PK-5
2503 Goodwyns Chapel Rd 24740 304-898-3731
LaCosta Hodges, prin. Fax 898-2031
Pikeview MS 600/6-8
3550 Eads Mill Rd, 304-384-3600
Joshua Riffe, prin. Fax 384-3605
Princeton MS 600/6-8
300 N Johnston St 24740 304-425-7517
David Lee, prin. Fax 487-2250
Princeton PS 600/K-2
180 Tiger Dr, 304-487-3904
Dr. Ernest Adkins, prin. Fax 487-2649
Silver Springs Early Learning Center 400/PK-PK
821 Broadway St 24740 304-425-4251
Steve Hayes, prin. Fax 425-5117
Straley ES 200/3-5
810 Straley Ave 24740 304-425-3173
Angela Damon, prin. Fax 487-2724
Other Schools – See Athens, Bluefield, Lerona, Matoaka, Rock, Spanishburg

---

Mercer Christian Academy 200/PK-12
314A Oakvale Rd 24740 304-425-5671

Prosperity, Raleigh, Pop. 1,474

Greater Beckley Christian S 200/PK-12
PO Box 670 25909 304-255-1571
Charles Atkins, admin. Fax 582-0341

Quinwood, Greenbrier, Pop. 282
Greenbrier County SD
Supt. — See Lewisburg
Crichton ES 100/PK-5
133 School St 25981 304-438-6958
Stephania Meadows, prin. Fax 438-5227

Rainelle, Greenbrier, Pop. 1,479
Greenbrier County SD
Supt. — See Lewisburg
Rainelle ES 200/PK-5
643 Kanawha Ave 25962 304-438-8861
Kimberly Tincher, prin. Fax 438-8875

Ranger, Lincoln
Lincoln County SD
Supt. — See Hamlin
Ranger ES 100/PK-5
59 Vanatters Crk 25557 304-778-3454
Christina Napier, prin. Fax 778-3454

Ranson, Jefferson, Pop. 2,891
Jefferson County SD
Supt. — See Charles Town
Ranson ES 400/PK-5
600 N Preston St 25438 304-725-7310
Debra Corbett, prin. Fax 725-1912

Ravenswood, Jackson, Pop. 3,825
Jackson County SD
Supt. — See Ripley
Kaiser ES 400/PK-2
803 Kaiser Ave 26164 304-273-2692
Amber Gill, prin. Fax 273-3029
Ravenswood ES 300/3-5
1 Grade School Rd 26164 304-273-5391
Jane Graham, prin. Fax 273-5392
Ravenswood MS 400/6-8
409 Sycamore St 26164 304-273-5480
Jeffrey Hopkins, prin. Fax 273-5740

Reader, Wetzel, Pop. 397
Wetzel County SD
Supt. — See New Martinsville
Short Line S 400/PK-8
9817 Shortline Hwy 26167 304-386-4115
Teresa Standiford, prin. Fax 386-4969

Richwood, Nicholas, Pop. 2,006
Nicholas County SD
Supt. — See Summersville
Cherry River ES 200/PK-5
190 Riverside Dr 26261 304-846-6646
C.C. Lester, prin. Fax 846-6897
Richwood MS 300/6-8
2 Valley Ave 26261 304-846-2638
Gene Collins, prin. Fax 846-9632

Ridgeley, Mineral, Pop. 658
Mineral County SD
Supt. — See Keyser
Frankfort MS 500/5-8
356 Golden Dr 26753 304-726-4339
Julie McBee, prin. Fax 726-4626

Ripley, Jackson, Pop. 3,223
Jackson County SD 4,900/PK-12
PO Box 770 25271 304-372-7300
Blaine C. Hess, supt. Fax 372-7312
jackson.wv.schoolwebpages.com
Fairplain ES 200/PK-5
51 Panther Dr 25271 304-372-7340
Melissa Browning, prin. Fax 372-7347
Ripley ES 700/PK-5
404 2nd Ave 25271 304-372-7345
Janet Postlethwaite, prin. Fax 372-7364
Ripley MS 700/6-8
1 W School St 25271 304-372-7350
Dr. Cathryn Carena, prin. Fax 372-7332
Other Schools – See Cottageville, Evans, Kenna, Ravenswood, Sandyville

Rivesville, Marion, Pop. 933
Marion County SD
Supt. — See Fairmont
Rivesville S 400/PK-8
229 Phillips Ave 26588 304-278-5331
Frank Moore, prin. Fax 278-5351

Roanoke, Lewis
Lewis County SD
Supt. — See Weston
Roanoke ES 100/PK-4
1176 Oil Creek Rd 26447 304-452-8887
Kristina Benedum, prin. Fax 452-0438

Rock, Mercer
Mercer County SD
Supt. — See Princeton
Montcalm ES 300/PK-6
838 Rock Rd 24747 304-589-5202
Jason Underwood, prin. Fax 589-7095

Rock Cave, Upshur
Upshur County SD
Supt. — See Buckhannon
Rock Cave ES 100/PK-5
12292 Route 20 South Rd 26234 304-924-6969
Amanda Craig, prin. Fax 924-5541

Rock Creek, Raleigh
Raleigh County SD
Supt. — See Beckley
Marsh Fork ES 200/K-5
5960 Coal River Rd 25174 304-854-1951
Melanie Morrison, prin. Fax 854-1054

Romney, Hampshire, Pop. 1,832
Hampshire County SD 3,400/PK-12
111 School St 26757 304-822-3528
Dr. Jeffrey Pancione, supt. Fax 822-3540
boe.hamp.k12.wv.us
Romney ES 400/PK-5
45 School St 26757 304-822-3018
Patty Lipps, prin. Fax 822-3018
Romney MS 400/6-8
296 Calvert Dr 26757 304-822-5014
John Watson, prin. Fax 822-5744
Other Schools – See Augusta, Capon Bridge, Levels, Slanesville, Springfield

Ronceverte, Greenbrier, Pop. 1,742
Greenbrier County SD
Supt. — See Lewisburg
Eastern Greenbrier MS 900/6-8
403 Knight Dr 24970 304-647-6498
Preston Modlin, prin. Fax 647-3087
Ronceverte ES 400/PK-5
879 Rocky Hill Rd 24970 304-647-6480
Andrea Stewart, prin. Fax 647-3086

Rowlesburg, Preston, Pop. 581
Preston County SD
Supt. — See Kingwood
Rowlesburg S 100/PK-8
46 Center St 26425 304-454-9311
Pete Pell, prin. Fax 454-9313

Rupert, Greenbrier, Pop. 937
Greenbrier County SD
Supt. — See Lewisburg
Rupert ES 200/PK-5
PO Box D 25984 304-392-5235
Jenny Harden, prin. Fax 392-5234

Saint Albans, Kanawha, Pop. 10,870
Kanawha County SD
Supt. — See Charleston
Alban ES 400/PK-5
2030 Harrison Ave 25177 304-722-0234
Johnna Jacobs, prin. Fax 722-0235
Bailey ES 300/PK-5
405 Winfield Rd 25177 304-722-0230
Robert Somerville, prin. Fax 722-0231
Central ES 400/PK-5
900 Helene St 25177 304-722-0226
Beth Sturgill, prin. Fax 722-0227
Hayes MS 500/6-8
830 Strawberry Rd 25177 304-722-0222
Scott Monty, prin. Fax 722-0247
Lakewood ES 300/PK-5
2089 Lakewood Dr 25177 304-722-0200
Evelyn Haynes, prin. Fax 722-0456
McKinley MS 400/6-8
3000 Kanawha Ter 25177 304-722-0218
Amy Scott, prin. Fax 722-0246
Weimer ES 200/PK-5
3040 Kanawha Ter 25177 304-722-0205
Pamela Snead, prin. Fax 722-0206

St. Francis of Assisi S 100/PK-5
525 Holley St 25177 304-727-5690
Erin Sikora, prin. Fax 727-5690

Saint Marys, Pleasants, Pop. 1,851
Pleasants County SD 1,200/PK-12
202 Fairview Ave 26170 304-684-2215
Mike Wells, supt. Fax 684-3569
www.pleasantscountyschools.com
Saint Marys ES 300/PK-4
317 Washington St 26170 304-684-3510
Tammy Haught, prin. Fax 684-2640
Other Schools – See Belmont

Salem, Harrison, Pop. 1,554
Harrison County SD
Supt. — See Clarksburg
Salem ES 300/PK-5
273 Education Way 26426 304-326-7180
David Decker, prin. Fax 782-1293

Salt Rock, Cabell, Pop. 382
Cabell County SD
Supt. — See Huntington
Salt Rock ES 200/PK-5
5570 Madison Creek Rd 25559 304-733-3037
Jennifer Ross, prin. Fax 733-3060

Sandyville, Jackson
Jackson County SD
Supt. — See Ripley
Gilmore ES 200/PK-5
7412 Parkersburg Rd 25275 304-273-3511
Jennifer Knopp, prin. Fax 273-9560

Scott Depot, Putnam
Putnam County SD
Supt. — See Winfield
Scott Teays ES 400/PK-5
6153 Teays Valley Rd 25560 304-757-7279
Melissa Isaacs, prin. Fax 757-4114

Teays Valley Christian S 400/K-12
6562 Teays Valley Rd 25560 304-757-9550
Jack Davis, supt. Fax 757-2560

Seth, Boone
Boone County SD
Supt. — See Madison
Sherman JHS 200/7-8
PO Box AA 25181 304-837-3694
Matthew Riggs, prin. Fax 837-7603

Shady Spring, Raleigh, Pop. 2,968
Raleigh County SD
Supt. — See Beckley
Shady Spring ES 500/PK-5
600 Flat Top Rd 25918 304-256-4633
Penny Carrico, prin. Fax 256-4592
Shady Spring MS 700/6-8
500 Flat Top Rd 25918 304-256-4570
Matthew Bell, prin. Fax 256-4612

Shenandoah Junction, Jefferson, Pop. 673
Jefferson County SD
Supt. — See Charles Town
Driswood ES 500/PK-5
75 Caspian Way 25442 304-885-5020
Kelly Osborne, prin. Fax 725-1936
Lowery ES 600/PK-5
103 Shenandoah Junction Rd 25442 304-728-7250
Kristen Martin, prin. Fax 728-7631
Wildwood MS 600/6-8
1209 Shenandoah Junction Rd 25442 304-728-4518
Patricia Brockway, prin. Fax 728-9521

Shepherdstown, Jefferson, Pop. 1,690
Jefferson County SD
Supt. — See Charles Town
Shepherdstown ES 400/PK-5
662 S Church St 25443 304-876-6270
Scott Jacobson, prin. Fax 876-6850
Shepherdstown MS 400/6-8
54 Minden St 25443 304-876-6120
Rebecca Horn, prin. Fax 876-6428

Shinnston, Harrison, Pop. 2,173
Harrison County SD
Supt. — See Clarksburg
Big Elm ES 700/PK-5
200 Tetrick Rd 26431 304-326-7280
Julie Mancini, prin. Fax 592-3255
Lincoln MS 400/6-8
78 Jerry Toth Dr 26431 304-326-7540
Lori Scott, prin. Fax 584-4602

Sissonville, Kanawha, Pop. 4,008
Kanawha County SD
Supt. — See Charleston
Sissonville ES 300/PK-4
8324 Sissonville Dr 25320 304-348-1961
David Agnew, prin. Fax 348-6147

Sistersville, Tyler, Pop. 1,391
Tyler County SD
Supt. — See Middlebourne
Sistersville ES 300/PK-5
651 Sistersville Ele School 26175 304-652-2601
Krista DeVaughn, prin. Fax 652-2603
Tyler Consolidated MS 300/6-8
1993 Silver Knight Dr 26175 304-758-9000
Suzette Miller, prin. Fax 758-9006

Slanesville, Hampshire
Hampshire County SD
Supt. — See Romney
Slanesville ES 200/PK-5
PO Box 308 25444 304-496-7069
Susan Brathwaite, prin. Fax 496-1139

Smithers, Fayette, Pop. 800
Fayette County SD
Supt. — See Fayetteville
Valley ES 400/PK-5
PO Box 215 25186 304-442-2321
Melissa Harrah, prin. Fax 442-2337

Smithville, Ritchie
Ritchie County SD
Supt. — See Harrisville
Smithville ES 100/PK-5
PO Box 30 26178 304-477-3273
C. Kerns, prin. Fax 477-3118

Smoot, Greenbrier
Greenbrier County SD
Supt. — See Lewisburg
Smoot ES 100/PK-5
PO Box 29 24977 304-392-5295
Molly Adkins-Judy, prin. Fax 392-2152

Sophia, Raleigh, Pop. 1,330
Raleigh County SD
Supt. — See Beckley
Independence MS 500/6-8
PO Box 1171 25921 304-683-4542
Teresa Lester, prin. Fax 683-4552
Sophia-Soak Creek ES 300/PK-5
PO Box 487 25921 304-683-4541
Becky Hendrick, prin. Fax 683-4525

South Charleston, Kanawha, Pop. 13,050
Kanawha County SD
Supt. — See Charleston
Alum Creek ES 200/PK-5
4540 Brounland Rd 25309 304-348-1935
Elizabeth Hoylman, prin. Fax 348-1936
Bridgeview ES 500/PK-5
5100 Ohio St 25309 304-766-0383
Mellow Lee, prin. Fax 766-0388
Montrose ES 300/K-5
631 Montrose Dr 25303 304-348-1930
Julie Hedge, prin. Fax 347-7409
Richmond ES 300/PK-5
4620 Spring Hill Ave 25309 304-766-0357
Jordan McBride, prin. Fax 766-0358
Ruthlawn ES 300/PK-5
736 Ruthdale Rd 25309 304-744-9481
Natalie Laliberty, prin. Fax 744-9482
South Charleston MS 400/6-8
400 3rd Ave 25303 304-348-1918
Henry Graves, prin. Fax 744-4869

Spanishburg, Mercer
Mercer County SD
Supt. — See Princeton
Spanishburg ES 200/PK-5
PO Box 7 25922 304-425-5854
Melissa Boothe, prin. Fax 425-1229

Spencer, Roane, Pop. 2,289
Roane County SD 2,300/PK-12
PO Box 609 25276 304-927-6400
Jerry Garner, supt. Fax 927-6412
www.roanecountyschools.com
Spencer ES 600/PK-4
85 Clay Rd 25276 304-927-6428
Kimberly Frum, prin. Fax 927-6429
Spencer MS 400/5-8
102 Chapman Ave 25276 304-927-6415
Jacqueline Durst, prin. Fax 927-6416
Other Schools – See Left Hand, Walton

Springfield, Hampshire, Pop. 470
Hampshire County SD
Supt. — See Romney
Springfield-Green Spring ES 100/PK-5
43 Education Ln 26763 304-822-4317
Pam Slocum, prin. Fax 822-4317

Stonewood, Harrison, Pop. 1,777
Harrison County SD
Supt. — See Clarksburg
Norwood ES 300/PK-5
208 Kidd Ave 26301 304-326-7050
Dora Stutler, prin. Fax 624-3262

Summersville, Nicholas, Pop. 3,550
Nicholas County SD 3,900/PK-12
400 Old Main Dr 26651 304-872-3611
Dr. Donna Burge-Tetrick, supt. Fax 872-4626
ncboe.ss8.sharpschool.com
Glade Creek ES 100/K-5
7950 Webster Rd 26651 304-872-2882
Tanya Martin, prin. Fax 872-2882
Summersville ES 400/PK-5
108 McKees Creek Rd 26651 304-872-1421
Pamela Butcher, prin. Fax 872-1444
Summersville MS 600/6-8
40 Grizzley Ln 26651 304-872-5092
Kristina Frame, prin. Fax 872-6314
Zela ES 100/PK-5
165 Country Rd 26651 304-872-1481
Teresa Morris, prin. Fax 872-1481
Other Schools – See Birch River, Craigsville, Dixie, Mount Lookout, Mount Nebo, Nettie, Richwood

---

New Life Christian Academy 100/PK-12
899 Broad St 26651 304-872-1148
Summersville Adventist S 50/K-8
70 Friends R Fun Dr 26651 304-872-0588

Sutton, Braxton, Pop. 987
Braxton County SD 2,100/PK-12
98 Carter Braxton Dr 26601 304-765-7101
David Dilly, supt. Fax 765-7148
boe.brax.k12.wv.us/
Braxton County MS 300/7-8
100 Carter Braxton Dr 26601 304-765-2644
Michelle Gorby-Tefft, prin. Fax 765-2696
Little Birch ES 100/PK-6
55 Little Birch Rd 26601 304-765-2042
Meredith Hoover, prin. Fax 765-2042
Sutton ES 300/PK-6
288 N Hill Rd 26601 304-765-5202
Kyre-Anna Minney, prin. Fax 765-5547
Other Schools – See Burnsville, Flatwoods, Frametown, Gassaway

Tad, Kanawha
Kanawha County SD
Supt. — See Charleston
Ingles ES 200/PK-5
PO Box 367 25201 304-348-1975
Melissa Rider-Wilfong, prin. Fax 348-1976

Talcott, Summers
Summers County SD
Supt. — See Hinton

Talcott ES 200/PK-5
PO Box 140 24981 304-466-6029
Carol Renae Jones, prin. Fax 466-6004

Terra Alta, Preston, Pop. 1,469
Preston County SD
Supt. — See Kingwood
Terra Alta/East Preston S 400/PK-8
1103 E State Ave 26764 304-789-2344
Cathern Reeves, prin. Fax 789-2596

Cranesville Christian Academy K-6
54 Camp Aldersgate Ln 26764 304-789-5252
Paige Dopson, dir.

Thomas, Tucker, Pop. 584
Tucker County SD
Supt. — See Parsons
Davis-Thomas S 200/PK-8
PO Box 250 26292 304-463-4422
Alicia Lambert, prin. Fax 463-4424

Tornado, Kanawha, Pop. 1,006
Kanawha County SD
Supt. — See Charleston
Andrews Heights ES 300/PK-5
PO Box 340 25202 304-722-0232
Suzanne Armstrong, prin. Fax 722-0233

Triadelphia, Ohio, Pop. 798
Ohio County SD
Supt. — See Wheeling
Middle Creek ES 300/K-5
579 Middle Creek Rd 26059 304-243-0369
Katrina Lewis, prin. Fax 243-0371

Tunnelton, Preston, Pop. 293
Preston County SD
Supt. — See Kingwood
Fellowsville ES 100/PK-5
139 Fellowsville School Rd 26444 304-892-3866
Gregory Cummings, prin. Fax 892-4456
South Preston S 200/PK-8
5258 S Preston Hwy 26444 304-568-2292
Jim Hoit, prin. Fax 568-2372

Union, Monroe, Pop. 551
Monroe County SD 1,800/PK-12
PO Box 330 24983 304-772-3094
Joetta Basile, supt. Fax 772-5020
boe.monroe.k12.wv.us
Mountain View ES 500/PK-8
620 School St 24983 304-772-4903
Sue Lee, admin. Fax 772-4907
Other Schools – See Peterstown

Valley Head, Randolph, Pop. 267
Randolph County SD
Supt. — See Elkins
Valley Head ES 50/K-5
Route 219 S 26294 304-339-4950
Melissa Wilfong, prin. Fax 339-4474

Van, Boone, Pop. 209
Boone County SD
Supt. — See Madison
Van ES 100/PK-5
PO Box 360 25206 304-245-8811
Pam Campbell, prin. Fax 245-8816

Verdunville, Logan, Pop. 684
Logan County SD
Supt. — See Logan
Verdunville ES 100/PK-4
PO Box 470 25649 304-752-1656
Eva Marcum, prin. Fax 752-2142

Vienna, Wood, Pop. 10,628
Wood County SD
Supt. — See Parkersburg
Greenmont ES 300/PK-5
209 58th St 26105 304-420-9544
Brett Ubbens, prin. Fax 420-9543
Jackson MS 500/6-8
1601 34th St 26105 304-420-9551
Richard Summers, prin. Fax 295-9954
Neale ES 400/PK-5
2305 Grand Central Ave 26105 304-420-9587
Linda Brunicardi, prin. Fax 420-9589
Vienna ES 300/PK-5
700 41st St 26105 304-420-9648
Doug Jones, prin. Fax 420-9693

Walton, Roane
Roane County SD
Supt. — See Spencer
Walton ES 400/PK-8
90 School Dr 25286 304-577-6731
Josh Holley, prin. Fax 577-6220

War, McDowell, Pop. 849
McDowell County SD
Supt. — See Welch
Southside S 400/K-8
PO Box 730 24892 304-875-2283
Florisha McGuire, prin. Fax 875-2238

Waverly, Wood, Pop. 391
Wood County SD
Supt. — See Parkersburg
Waverly ES 100/PK-6
422 Virginia St 26184 304-464-4250
Steve Taylor, prin. Fax 464-4263

Wayne, Wayne, Pop. 1,402
Wayne County SD 7,100/PK-12
PO Box 70 25570 304-272-5116
Dr. Steven Paine, supt. Fax 272-6500
boe.wayn.k12.wv.us
Wayne ES 600/PK-5
PO Box 308 25570 304-272-6342
William Preece, prin. Fax 272-6450
Wayne MS 600/6-8
200 Pioneer Rd 25570 304-272-3227
Beth Webb, prin. Fax 272-5811
Other Schools – See Ceredo, Crum, Dunlow, East Lynn, Fort Gay, Genoa, Huntington, Kenova, Lavalette, Prichard

Webster Springs, Webster, Pop. 772
Webster County SD 1,100/PK-12
315 S Main St 26288 304-847-5638
Scott Cochran, supt. Fax 847-2538
boe.webs.k12.wv.us/
Webster Springs S 300/PK-6
318 River Dr 26288 304-847-5321
Jeremy Pyle, prin. Fax 847-5364
Other Schools – See Cowen, Hacker Valley

Weirton, Hancock, Pop. 19,434
Brooke County SD
Supt. — See Wellsburg
Millsop PS 100/K-4
1401 Legion Rd 26062 304-748-7760
Brandi Reinacher, prin. Fax 748-8470

Hancock County SD
Supt. — See New Cumberland
Weir MS 600/5-8
125 Sinclair Ave 26062 304-748-6080
Sara Parsons, prin. Fax 748-0847
Wierton ES 400/PK-4
3428 Pennsylvania Ave 26062 304-748-8370
Frank Carey, prin. Fax 748-8383

St. Joseph the Worker S 200/PK-8
151 Michael Way 26062 304-723-1970
Recheal Fuscardo, prin. Fax 723-5122
St. Paul S 300/PK-8
140 Walnut St 26062 304-748-5225
Deena Tomshack, prin. Fax 748-4163

Welch, McDowell, Pop. 2,358
McDowell County SD 3,400/PK-12
30 Central Ave 24801 304-436-8441
Nelson Spencer, supt.
boe.mcdo.k12.wv.us
Welch ES 300/PK-5
1235 Stewart St 24801 304-436-4645
Fax 436-4049
Other Schools – See Anawalt, Avondale, Big Sandy, Bradshaw, Iaeger, Kimball, War

Wellsburg, Brooke, Pop. 2,772
Brooke County SD 3,100/PK-12
1201 Pleasant Ave 26070 304-737-3481
Toni Shute, supt. Fax 737-3480
brooke.schoolwires.net
Franklin PS 200/K-4
1305 Washington Pike 26070 304-737-1760
Scott Donohew, prin. Fax 737-1760
Wellsburg MS 400/5-8
1447 Main St 26070 304-737-2922
Jennifer Sisinni, prin. Fax 737-2976
Wellsburg PS 200/K-4
1448 Main St 26070 304-737-0133
Stephanie Zimmer, prin. Fax 737-0403
Other Schools – See Beech Bottom, Colliers, Follansbee, Weirton

West Hamlin, Lincoln, Pop. 765
Lincoln County SD
Supt. — See Hamlin
West Hamlin ES 600/PK-5
114 Dairy Rd 25571 304-824-3630
John Roy, prin. Fax 824-3638

West Milford, Harrison, Pop. 611
Harrison County SD
Supt. — See Clarksburg
West Milford ES 400/PK-5
182 School St 26451 304-326-7030
Patricia Kinney, prin. Fax 745-4488

Weston, Lewis, Pop. 4,051
Lewis County SD 2,500/PK-12
239 Court Ave 26452 304-269-8300
Dr. Joseph Mace, supt. Fax 269-8305
lewisboe.com
Bland MS 800/5-8
358 Court Ave 26452 304-269-8325
Julie Radcliff, prin. Fax 269-8310
Peterson Central ES 500/PK-4
509 Berlin Rd 26452 304-269-8330
Steven Hall, prin. Fax 269-8351
Other Schools – See Jane Lew, Linn, Roanoke

St. Patrick S 200/PK-7
224 Center Ave 26452 304-269-5547
Maureen Gildein, prin. Fax 269-5547

West Union, Doddridge, Pop. 823
Doddridge County SD 1,200/PK-12
1117 WV Route 18 N 26456 304-873-2300
Adam Cheeseman, supt. Fax 873-2210
www.dcschools.us
Doddridge County ES 400/K-4
182 Doddridge County School 26456 304-873-3294
D. Michelle Robey, prin. Fax 873-3297
Doddridge County MS 300/5-8
65 Doddridge County School 26456 304-873-2332
Dr. Deborah Kuhns, prin. Fax 873-2541
Doddridge County Preschool Center 100/PK-PK
2945 Smithton Rd 26456 304-873-3955
Wesley Ezell, dir. Fax 874-3956

Wheeling, Ohio, Pop. 27,794
Marshall County SD
Supt. — See Moundsville
Hilltop ES 300/K-5
1 Ram Dr 26003 304-232-8640
Cynthia McCutcheon, prin. Fax 232-1044
Sherrard MS 400/6-8
1000 Fairmont Pike 26003 304-233-3331
Jason Marling, prin. Fax 233-6418

Ohio County SD 5,400/PK-12
2203 National Rd 26003 304-243-0300
Dr. Kimberly S. Miller, supt. Fax 243-0328
boe.ohio.k12.wv.us
Bethlehem ES 100/K-5
22 Chapel Rd 26003 304-243-0350
Stacy Greer, prin. Fax 243-0351
Bridge Street MS 300/6-8
19 Junior Ave 26003 304-243-0381
Joseph Kolb, prin. Fax 243-0385
Elm Grove ES 400/PK-5
85 Mil Acres Dr 26003 304-243-0363
Richard Dunlevy, prin. Fax 243-0364
Madison ES 300/PK-5
91 Zane St 26003 304-243-0366
Andrea Trio, prin. Fax 243-0457
Ritchie ES 300/PK-5
3700 Wood St 26003 304-243-0372
John Jorden, prin. Fax 243-0373
Steenrod ES 300/PK-5
100 Clarks Ln 26003 304-243-0354
Michelle Dietrich, prin. Fax 243-0357
Triadelphia MS 400/6-8
1636 National Rd 26003 304-243-0387
Ann Coleman, prin. Fax 243-0392
Warwood S 500/PK-8
150 Viking Dr 26003 304-243-0394
Robb Bauer, prin. Fax 243-0395
West Liberty ES 100/K-5
745 Van Meter Way 26003 304-336-7221
Stacy Greer, prin. Fax 336-7222
Wheeling MS 200/6-8
3500 Chapline St 26003 304-243-0425
Richard McCardle, prin. Fax 243-0426
Woodsdale ES 500/PK-5
1 Bethany Pike 26003 304-243-0378
Ashlea Minch, prin. Fax 243-0379
Other Schools – See Triadelphia

Corpus Christi S 100/PK-8
1512 Warwood Ave 26003 304-277-1220
Dick Taylor, prin. Fax 277-2823
Our Lady of Peace S 200/PK-8
640 Old Fairmont Pike 26003 304-242-1383
Maureen Kerr, prin. Fax 243-5410
St. Michael S 400/PK-8
1221 National Rd 26003 304-242-3966
Jamie Kovalski, prin. Fax 214-6578
St. Vincent de Paul S 200/PK-8
127 Key Ave 26003 304-242-5844
Laurajenn Rossell, prin. Fax 243-1624
Wheeling Country Day S 200/PK-5
8 Park Rd 26003 304-232-2430
E. Hofreuter-Landini, hdmstr. Fax 232-2434

White Sulphur Springs, Greenbrier, Pop. 2,403
Greenbrier County SD
Supt. — See Lewisburg
White Sulphur Springs ES 300/PK-5
150 Reed St 24986 304-536-2244
Ann Smith, prin. Fax 536-1930

Whitesville, Boone, Pop. 505
Boone County SD
Supt. — See Madison
Whitesville ES 200/PK-6
37949 Coal River Rd 25209 304-854-1301
Christopher Duncan, prin. Fax 854-1301

Wiley Ford, Mineral, Pop. 1,024
Mineral County SD
Supt. — See Keyser
Wiley Ford PS 200/PK-2
71 Wiley Ford School Rd 26767 304-738-0400
Paula Athey, prin. Fax 738-3633

Williamson, Mingo, Pop. 3,116
Mingo County SD 4,400/PK-12
110 Cinderella Rd 25661 304-235-3333
Donald Spence, supt. Fax 235-3410
mingoboe.us
Lenore S 600/PK-8
100 Ranger Ave 25661 304-475-5231
Tamra Ferris, prin. Fax 475-2411
Williamson ES 500/PK-8
5 Parkway Dr 25661 304-235-2520
Shannon Blackburn, prin. Fax 235-2520
Other Schools – See Delbarton, Dingess, Gilbert, Kermit, Matewan

Williamstown, Wood, Pop. 2,880
Wood County SD
Supt. — See Parkersburg
Williamstown ES 600/PK-6
418 Williams Ave 26187 304-375-7675
Heather Mannix, prin. Fax 375-4894

Wood County Christian S 300/PK-12
113 W 9th St 26187 304-375-2000
Daryl Van Norman, head sch Fax 375-2000

Winfield, Putnam, Pop. 2,257
Putnam County SD 9,900/PK-12
77 Courthouse Dr 25213 304-586-0500
John Hudson, supt. Fax 586-0553
www.putnamschools.com
Eastbrook ES 300/PK-5
2092 Bills Creek Rd 25213 304-755-9835
Martica Dillon, prin. Fax 755-0012
Winfield ES 500/PK-5
75 Wall St 25213 304-586-2565
Candi Hatfield, prin. Fax 586-5351
Winfield MS 600/6-8
11883 Winfield Rd 25213 304-586-3072
Dan Rinick, prin. Fax 586-0920
Other Schools – See Buffalo, Eleanor, Hometown, Hurricane, Liberty, Nitro, Poca, Scott Depot

WISCONSIN

WISCONSIN DEPARTMENT PUBLIC INSTRUCTION
PO Box 7841, Madison 53707-7841
Telephone 608-266-3390
Fax 608-267-1052
Website dpi.wi.gov

Superintendent of Public Instruction Tony Evers PhD

COOPERATIVE EDUCATIONAL SERVICE AGENCIES (CESA)

CESA 1
Mary Gavigan, admin. 262-787-9500
N25W23131 Paul Rd Ste 100 Fax 787-9501
Pewaukee 53072
www.cesa1.k12.wi.us

CESA 2
Dan Hanrahan, admin. 262-473-1473
1221 Innovation Dr Fax 472-2269
Whitewater 53190
www.cesa2.org

CESA 3
Jamie Nutter, admin. 608-822-3276
1300 Industrial Dr Fax 822-3860
Fennimore 53809
www.cesa3.org

CESA 4
Cheryl Gullicksrud, admin. 800-514-3075
923 Garland St E Fax 786-4801
West Salem 54669
www.cesa4.k12.wi.us

CESA 5
Jeremy Biehl, admin. 608-742-8811
626 E Slifer St, Portage 53901 Fax 742-2384
www.cesa5.org/

CESA 6
Dr. Ted Neitzke, admin. 920-233-2372
2935 Universal Ct, Oshkosh 54904 Fax 236-0580
www.cesa6.org

CESA 7
Jeffery Dickert, admin. 920-492-5960
595 Baeten Rd, Green Bay 54304 Fax 492-5965
www.cesa7.k12.wi.us

CESA 8
David Honish, admin. 920-855-2114
223 W Park St, Gillett 54124 Fax 855-2299
www.cesa8.k12.wi.us

CESA 9
Dr. Karen Wendorf-Heldt, admin. 715-453-2141
PO Box 449, Tomahawk 54487 Fax 453-7519
www.cesa9.org

CESA 10
Mike Haynes, admin. 715-723-0341
725 W Park Ave Fax 720-2070
Chippewa Falls 54729
www.cesa10.k12.wi.us

CESA 11
Jerry Walters, admin. 715-986-2020
225 Ostermann Dr Fax 986-2040
Turtle Lake 54889
www.cesa11.k12.wi.us

CESA 12
Kenneth Kasinski, admin. 715-682-2363
618 Beaser Ave, Ashland 54806 Fax 682-7244
www.cesa12.org

PUBLIC, PRIVATE AND CATHOLIC ELEMENTARY SCHOOLS

Abbotsford, Clark, Pop. 2,301
Abbotsford SD 700/PK-12
510 W Hemlock St 54405 715-223-6715
Cheryl Baker, supt. Fax 223-4239
www.abbotsford.k12.wi.us
Abbotsford ES 400/PK-5
510 W Hemlock St 54405 715-223-4281
Gary Gunderson, prin. Fax 223-0691

Abrams, Oconto, Pop. 338
Oconto Falls SD
Supt. — See Oconto Falls
Abrams ES 300/PK-5
3000 Elm St 54101 920-826-5819
Joanne Michalski, prin. Fax 826-7858

Adams, Adams, Pop. 1,940
Adams-Friendship Area SD
Supt. — See Friendship
Adams-Friendship ES 500/PK-5
500 N Pierce St 53910 608-339-3016
Roxanne Irey, prin. Fax 339-0416
Adams-Friendship MS 300/6-8
420 N Main St 53910 608-339-4064
Michelle Johnson, prin. Fax 339-2434

Albany, Green, Pop. 1,005
Albany SD 300/PK-12
400 5th St 53502 608-862-3225
Amy Vesperman, supt. Fax 862-3230
www.albany.k12.wi.us
Albany Community MS 100/6-8
400 5th St 53502 608-862-3135
Connie Gregerson, prin. Fax 862-3230
Albany ES 200/PK-5
400 5th St 53502 608-862-3225
Connie Gregerson, admin. Fax 862-3230

Algoma, Kewaunee, Pop. 3,136
Algoma SD 700/PK-12
1715 Division St 54201 920-487-7001
Nicholas Cochart, supt. Fax 487-7016
algomawolves.org
Algoma ES 300/PK-6
514 Fremont St 54201 920-487-7001
Katie Servi, prin. Fax 487-7015

St. Mary S 100/PK-8
214 Church St 54201 920-487-5004
Margaret Hall, prin. Fax 487-5002
St. Paul Lutheran S 100/PK-8
1115 Division St 54201 920-487-5712
James Hussman, prin. Fax 487-9733

Allenton, Washington, Pop. 821
Slinger SD
Supt. — See Slinger
Allenton ES 400/PK-5
228 Weis St 53002 262-629-5546
Angela Wickus, prin. Fax 629-1821

Alma, Buffalo, Pop. 776
Alma SD 300/PK-12
S1618 State Road 35 54610 608-685-4416
Steven Sedlmayr, supt. Fax 685-4446
www.alma.k12.wi.us
Alma ES 200/PK-8
S1618 State Road 35 54610 608-685-4416
Jane Bremer, prin. Fax 685-4446

Alma Center, Jackson, Pop. 492
Alma Center-Humbird-Merrillan SD 600/PK-12
PO Box 308 54611 715-964-8271
Paul Fischer, supt. Fax 964-1005
www.lincolnhornets.org
Lincoln JHS 100/7-8
PO Box 308 54611 715-964-5311
Glenda Morgan, prin. Fax 964-1005
Other Schools – See Merrillan

Almena, Barron, Pop. 662
Barron Area SD
Supt. — See Barron
Almena ES 100/PK-4
PO Box 86 54805 715-357-3263
Jennifer Clemens, prin. Fax 357-6513

Almond, Portage, Pop. 447
Almond-Bancroft SD 200/PK-12
1336 Elm St 54909 715-366-2941
Richard Hanson, admin. Fax 366-2940
www.abschools.k12.wi.us
Almond-Bancroft S 200/PK-12
1336 Elm St 54909 715-366-2941
Jeff Rykal, prin. Fax 366-2943

Altoona, Eau Claire, Pop. 6,546
Altoona SD 1,600/PK-12
1903 Bartlett Ave 54720 715-839-6032
Dr. Connie Biedron, supt. Fax 839-6066
www.altoona.k12.wi.us
Altoona ES 600/PK-3
157 Bartlett Ave 54720 715-839-6050
Tara Betlach, prin. Fax 839-6166
Altoona IS 200/4-5
1903 Bartlett Ave 54720 715-839-6030
Andrea Steffen, prin. Fax 839-6099
Altoona MS 300/6-8
1903 Bartlett Ave 54720 715-839-6030
Dan Peggs, prin. Fax 839-6099

Otter Creek Christian Academy 50/1-8
919 10th St W 54720 715-834-1782
Mike Meadows, prin.
St. Mary S 100/PK-5
1828 Lynn Ave 54720 715-830-2278
Carisa Smiskey, prin. Fax 830-9573

Amery, Polk, Pop. 2,886
Amery SD 1,600/PK-12
543 Minneapolis Ave S 54001 715-268-9771
James Kuchta, admin. Fax 268-7300
www.amerysd.k12.wi.us
Amery IS 300/3-5
543 Minneapolis Ave S 54001 715-268-9771
Oralee Schock, prin. Fax 268-5612
Amery MS 300/6-8
501 Minneapolis Ave S 54001 715-268-9771
Thomas Bensen, prin. Fax 268-4967
Lien ES 400/PK-2
469 Minneapolis Ave S 54001 715-268-9771
Cheryl Meyer, prin. Fax 268-5633

Amherst, Portage, Pop. 1,031
Tomorrow River SD 1,000/PK-12
357 N Main St 54406 715-824-5521
Michael Toelle, supt. Fax 824-7177
www.amherst.k12.wi.us
Amherst ES 400/PK-4
357 N Main St 54406 715-824-5523
Sherry Oleson, prin. Fax 824-5474
Amherst MS 200/5-8
357 N Main St 54406 715-824-5524
Phillip Tubbs, prin. Fax 824-6354

Antigo, Langlade, Pop. 8,127
Antigo SD 2,200/PK-12
120 S Dorr St 54409 715-627-4355
Dr. Colleen Timm, supt. Fax 623-3279
www.antigo.k12.wi.us
Antigo MS 500/6-8
815 7th Ave 54409 715-623-4173
Amy Dahms, prin. Fax 627-4982
Crestwood ES 100/PK-5
W8464 County Road AA 54409 715-623-6557
Kelly Fassbender, prin. Fax 627-0805
East ES 200/PK-5
220 7th Ave 54409 715-623-2506
Tollef Wienke, prin. Fax 623-3948
North ES 200/K-5
506 Graham Ave 54409 715-623-3515
Donna Smith, prin. Fax 627-2612
Pleasant View ES 100/PK-5
W11141 County Road HH 54409 715-627-7700
Tollef Wienke, prin. Fax 627-0457
Spring Valley ES 100/K-5
N4754 County Road BB 54409 715-623-6900
Jeff Neufeld, prin. Fax 627-0460
West ES 200/PK-5
1232 7th Ave 54409 715-623-2508
Jeff Neufeld, prin. Fax 627-0906

All Saints S 200/PK-8
419 6th Ave 54409 715-623-4835
Paul Galuska, prin. Fax 623-3303
Peace Lutheran S 100/PK-8
300 Lincoln St 54409 715-623-2200
David Reineke, admin. Fax 627-4117

Appleton, Outagamie, Pop. 71,375
Appleton Area SD 15,900/PK-12
PO Box 2019 54912 920-832-6161
Dr. Judith Baseman Ph.D., supt. Fax 832-1725
www.aasd.k12.wi.us
Appleton Community 4K 900/PK-PK
313 S State St 54911 920-832-6209
Suzette Preston, admin. Fax 832-1746
Badger ES 300/PK-6
501 S Bluemound Dr 54914 920-832-6264
Tim Hopfensperger, prin. Fax 832-6149
Berry ES 500/PK-6
3601 S Telulah Ave 54915 920-832-5750
Rick Waters, prin. Fax 832-2986
Columbus ES 200/PK-6
913 N Oneida St 54911 920-832-6232
Joel Cannon, prin. Fax 832-6355

Edison ES 300/PK-6
412 N Meade St 54911 920-832-6235
James Donnellan, prin. Fax 993-7033
Einstein MS 500/7-8
324 E Florida Ave 54911 920-832-6240
Dave Mueller, prin. Fax 832-6164
Ferber ES 600/PK-6
515 E Capitol Dr 54911 920-832-5755
Paul Cooney, prin. Fax 993-7069
Franklin ES 400/PK-6
2212 N Jarchow St 54911 920-832-6246
Carrie Willer, prin. Fax 832-4464
Highlands ES 600/PK-6
2037 N Elinor St 54914 920-832-6250
Kristin Comerford, prin. Fax 832-4389
Horizons ES 400/PK-6
2101 Schaefer Cir 54915 920-832-4600
Karen Brice, prin. Fax 832-1592
Houdini ES 600/PK-6
2305 W Capitol Dr 54914 920-832-4608
Ryan Verrier, prin. Fax 993-7078
Huntley ES 700/PK-6
2224 N Ullman St 54911 920-832-6255
Kendra Vandertie, prin. Fax 832-6118
Jefferson ES 400/PK-6
1000 S Mason St 54914 920-832-6260
Lori Leschisin, prin. Fax 993-7060
Johnston ES 500/PK-6
2725 E Forest St 54915 920-832-6265
Doug Benz, prin. Fax 832-6199
Lincoln ES 400/PK-6
1000 N Mason St 54914 920-832-6270
William McClone, prin. Fax 832-6348
Madison MS 600/7-8
2020 S Carpenter St 54915 920-832-6276
David Torrey, prin. Fax 832-6337
McKinley ES 500/PK-6
1125 E Taft Ave 54915 920-832-6285
Andrea Vinje, prin. Fax 832-6326
Richmond ES 300/PK-6
1441 E John St 54915 920-832-5779
Jack Knaack, prin. Fax 993-7044
Wilson MS 400/7-8
225 N Badger Ave 54914 920-832-6226
Scott Werfal, prin. Fax 832-4857

Kimberly Area SD
Supt. — See Combined Locks
Sunrise ES 500/K-4
N9363 Exploration Ave 54915 920-954-1822
Sean Fitzgerald, prin. Fax 954-5945
Woodland ES 500/K-4
N9085 N Coop Rd 54915 920-730-0924
Timothy Doleysh, prin. Fax 423-4177
Woodland IS 300/5-6
N9085 N Coop Rd 54915 920-730-0924
Dave Lamers, prin. Fax 423-4177

Celebration Lutheran S 100/PK-8
3100 E Evergreen Dr 54913 920-734-8218
Jerry Jiter, dir. Fax 734-7890
Holy Spirit S 200/PK-8
W2796 County Road KK 54915 920-733-2651
Richard Krainz, prin. Fax 733-5440
Mt. Olive Evangelical Lutheran S 200/PK-8
930 E Florida Ave 54911 920-739-9194
Landon Zacharyasz, prin. Fax 739-9423
Riverview Lutheran S 100/PK-8
136 W Seymour St 54915 920-733-3728
Seth Zimmermann, prin. Fax 733-3728
St. Edward S 50/K-5
N2944 State Road 47 54913 920-733-6276
Renee Cowart, prin. Fax 733-1005
St. Francis Xavier MS 400/6-8
2626 N Oneida St 54911 920-730-8849
Robert Bires, prin. Fax 730-4147
St. Francis Xavier S - Marquette St Cmps 300/PK-5
500 W Marquette St 54911 920-733-4918
Laura Barnett, prin. Fax 733-7269
St. Francis Xavier S - McDonald St Cmps 200/PK-5
1810 N McDonald St 54911 920-739-7826
Carolyn Reuter, prin. Fax 739-2376
St. Paul Lutheran S 100/PK-8
225 E Harris St 54911 920-733-9061
Nathaniel Kallies M.Ed., prin. Fax 733-4200
St. Peter Lutheran S 100/PK-8
N2740 French Rd 54913 920-739-2009
Philip Punzel, prin. Fax 739-3615

Arcadia, Trempealeau, Pop. 2,912
Arcadia SD 1,200/PK-12
756 Raider Dr 54612 608-323-3315
Louie Ferguson, supt. Fax 323-2256
www.arcadia.k12.wi.us/
Arcadia ES 600/PK-4
358 E River St 54612 608-323-3315
Paul Halverson, prin. Fax 323-7015
Arcadia MS 300/5-8
725 Fairfield Ave 54612 608-323-3315
Michele Butler, prin. Fax 323-3188

Holy Family Catholic S 100/PK-8
532 Mc Kinley St 54612 608-323-3676
Nicole Michalak, prin. Fax 323-7386

Arena, Iowa, Pop. 827
River Valley SD
Supt. — See Spring Green
River Valley Arena ES 100/K-5
314 Willow St 53503 608-753-2361
Jaime Hegland, dir. Fax 753-2519

Argyle, Lafayette, Pop. 857
Argyle SD 300/PK-12
PO Box 256 53504 608-543-3318
Phillip Updike, supt. Fax 543-3868
www.argyle.k12.wi.us
Argyle ES 100/PK-5
PO Box 256 53504 608-543-3318
Phillip Updike, prin. Fax 543-3868

Arkdale, Adams, Pop. 158
Adams-Friendship Area SD
Supt. — See Friendship
Roche A Cri ES 100/PK-5
1501 18th Ave 54613 608-339-3228
Garrett Gould, prin. Fax 564-7714

Arlington, Columbia, Pop. 811
Poynette SD
Supt. — See Poynette
Arlington K 100/K-K
307 Bullen Rd 53911 608-635-4347
Jay Hausser, prin. Fax 635-9470

Arpin, Wood, Pop. 325

Bethel Jr. Academy 50/1-8
8054 Bethel Rd 54410 715-652-2763
Andrew Easley, prin.

Ashland, Ashland, Pop. 7,896
Ashland SD 2,200/PK-12
2000 Beaser Ave 54806 715-682-7080
Keith Hilts, supt. Fax 682-7097
www.ashland.k12.wi.us
Ashland MS 500/6-8
203 11th St E 54806 715-682-7087
Jake Levings, prin. Fax 682-7944
Lake Superior IS 300/3-5
1101 Binsfield Rd 54806 715-682-7083
Travis Powell, prin. Fax 682-7506
Lake Superior PS 400/PK-2
1101 Binsfield Rd 54806 715-682-7085
Chris Graff, prin. Fax 682-7946
Marengo Valley ES 200/K-5
62408 State Highway 112 54806 715-278-3286
Heidi Stricker, prin. Fax 278-3586

Our Lady of the Lake S 100/PK-8
215 Lake Shore Dr E 54806 715-682-7622
Betty Swiston, prin. Fax 682-7626

Athens, Marathon, Pop. 1,096
Athens SD 400/PK-12
PO Box F 54411 715-257-7511
Timothy Micke, supt. Fax 257-7502
www.athens1.org
Athens ES 100/PK-5
PO Box 190 54411 715-257-7571
Joy Redmann, prin. Fax 257-9026
Athens MS 100/6-8
PO Box F 54411 715-257-7511
Juli Gauerke-Peter, prin. Fax 257-7651

St. Anthony S 100/K-8
PO Box I 54411 715-257-7541
Lucas Knoedler, prin. Fax 257-7541
Trinity Lutheran S 50/PK-8
PO Box 100 54411 715-257-7526
Dean Frick, prin. Fax 257-7559

Auburndale, Wood, Pop. 703
Auburndale SD 900/PK-12
PO Box 139 54412 715-652-2117
Dr. William Greb, supt. Fax 652-2836
www.aubschools.com
Auburndale ES 500/PK-5
PO Box 139 54412 715-652-2812
Andrew Scharenbroch, prin. Fax 652-2836

Augusta, Eau Claire, Pop. 1,531
Augusta SD 500/PK-12
E19320 Bartig Rd 54722 715-286-2291
Ryan Nelson, supt. Fax 286-3336
www.augusta.k12.wi.us
Augusta ES 300/PK-5
E19320 Bartig Rd 54722 715-286-2291
Nicole Steinmetz, prin. Fax 286-3335

Baldwin, Saint Croix, Pop. 3,900
Baldwin-Woodville Area SD 1,700/PK-12
550 US Highway 12 54002 715-684-3411
Eric Russell, supt. Fax 684-3168
www.bwsd.k12.wi.us
Greenfield ES 700/PK-5
1160 14th Ave 54002 715-684-3334
Tiffanie Grodevant, prin. Fax 684-5109
Other Schools – See Woodville

Baldwin Christian S 100/PK-12
896 US Highway 63 54002 715-684-2656
Monte Knetter, head sch

Balsam Lake, Polk, Pop. 991
Unity SD 1,000/PK-12
1908 150th St 54810 715-825-3515
Brandon Robinson, supt. Fax 825-3517
www.unity.k12.wi.us/
Unity ES 400/PK-4
1908 150th St 54810 715-825-2101
Zachary Fugate, prin. Fax 825-4034
Unity MS 300/5-8
1908 150th St 54810 715-825-2101
Elizabeth Jorgensen, prin. Fax 825-4410

Bangor, LaCrosse, Pop. 1,446
Bangor SD 600/PK-12
PO Box 99 54614 608-486-2331
David Laehn, supt. Fax 486-4587
www.bangor.k12.wi.us
Bangor ES 300/PK-5
PO Box 99 54614 608-486-5205
Jacquelyn Lyga, prin. Fax 486-4045

St. Paul's Evangelical Lutheran S 100/PK-8
PO Box 257 54614 608-486-2641
Richard Bakken, prin.

Baraboo, Sauk, Pop. 11,882
Baraboo SD 2,900/PK-12
423 Linn St 53913 608-355-3950
Dr. Lori Mueller, supt. Fax 355-3960
www.baraboo.k12.wi.us
Behrman ES 400/PK-5
400 Mulberry St 53913 608-355-3910
John Blosenski, prin. Fax 355-3971
East ES 300/PK-5
815 6th St 53913 608-355-3920
Dr. Molly Fitzgerald, prin. Fax 355-4677
West K 100/PK-K
707 Center St 53913 608-355-3905
Dr. Chris Olson, prin. Fax 355-4679
Young MS 700/6-8
1531 Draper St 53913 608-355-3930
John Gunnell, prin. Fax 355-3998
Other Schools – See North Freedom, West Baraboo

St. John Lutheran S 100/PK-8
515 5th St 53913 608-355-3860
Craig Breitkreutz, prin. Fax 355-3861
St. Joseph S 100/PK-8
310 2nd St 53913 608-356-3083
Denise Brinker, prin. Fax 356-4024

Barneveld, Iowa, Pop. 1,221
Barneveld SD 400/K-12
PO Box 98 53507 608-924-4711
Brett Stousland, supt. Fax 924-1646
www.barneveld.k12.wi.us
Barneveld ES 200/K-5
PO Box 98 53507 608-924-4711
Erin Eslinger, prin. Fax 924-1646

Barron, Barron, Pop. 3,378
Barron Area SD 1,300/PK-12
100 W River Ave 54812 715-537-5612
Diane Tremblay, supt. Fax 637-5161
www.barron.k12.wi.us
Riverview MS 400/5-8
135 W River Ave 54812 715-537-5641
Scott Stralka, prin. Fax 637-5373
Woodland ES 300/PK-4
808 E Woodland Ave 54812 715-537-5621
Jennifer Clemens, prin. Fax 637-9353
Other Schools – See Almena, Ridgeland

Bayfield, Bayfield, Pop. 459
Bayfield SD 400/PK-12
300 N 4th St 54814 715-779-3201
Jeff Gordon, supt. Fax 779-5268
www.bayfield.k12.wi.us
Bayfield ES 200/PK-5
300 N 4th St 54814 715-779-3201
Melissa Giesregen, prin. Fax 779-5268
Bayfield MS 100/6-8
300 N 4th St 54814 715-779-3201
Shellie Swanson, prin. Fax 779-5268
La Pointe ES 50/K-5
300 N 4th St 54814 715-747-3605
Melissa Giesregen, prin. Fax 779-5226

Bayside, Milwaukee, Pop. 4,320
Fox Point Bayside SD
Supt. — See Fox Point
Bayside MS 400/5-8
601 E Ellsworth Ln 53217 414-247-4201
Jodi Hackl, prin. Fax 247-8963

Beaver Dam, Dodge, Pop. 16,040
Beaver Dam SD 3,400/PK-12
705 McKinley St 53916 920-885-7300
Stephen Vessey, supt. Fax 885-7306
www.bdusd.org
Beaver Dam MS 800/6-8
108 4th St 53916 920-885-7365
John Casper, prin. Fax 885-7415
Jefferson ES 300/K-5
301 Brook St 53916 920-885-7392
Mary Klawitter, prin. Fax 885-7395
Lincoln ES 200/K-5
210 Gould St 53916 920-885-7396
Kathy Lehman, prin. Fax 885-7399
Prairie View ES 500/PK-5
510 N Crystal Lake Rd 53916 920-885-7380
Jesse Peters, prin. Fax 885-7381
South Beaver Dam ES 100/K-5
W9787 County Road D 53916 920-885-7383
Christine Ziemann, prin. Fax 885-7384
Washington ES 300/K-5
600 Grove St 53916 920-885-7376
Laura Maron, prin. Fax 885-7379
Wilson ES 100/K-5
405 W 3rd St 53916 920-885-7373
Christine Ziemann, prin. Fax 885-7375

St. Katharine Drexel S 300/PK-8
503 S Spring St 53916 920-885-5558
Barbara Haase, prin. Fax 885-7610
St. Stephen Lutheran S 100/K-8
412 W Maple Ave 53916 920-885-6484
Jared Brennan, prin. Fax 885-3106

Belleville, Dane, Pop. 2,367
Belleville SD 1,000/PK-12
625 W Church St 53508 608-835-6120
Pam Yoder, supt. Fax 424-3486
www.belleville.k12.wi.us/
Belleville ES 200/PK-1
237 W Pearl St 53508 608-835-6120
Dr. William Conzemius, prin. Fax 424-1687

Belleville IS 400/2-6
101 S Grant St 53508 608-835-6120
Dr. William Conzemius, prin. Fax 424-1409
Belleville MS 100/7-8
625 W Church St 53508 608-835-6120
Nate Perry, prin. Fax 424-3692

Belmont, Lafayette, Pop. 980
Belmont Community SD 400/PK-12
PO Box 348 53510 608-762-5131
Christy Larson, supt. Fax 762-5129
www.belmont.k12.wi.us
Belmont ES 200/PK-5
PO Box 348 53510 608-762-5131
Mike Beranek, prin. Fax 762-5129

Beloit, Rock, Pop. 35,780
Beloit SD 6,500/K-12
1633 Keeler Ave 53511 608-361-4000
Dr. Thomas Johnson, supt. Fax 361-4122
www.sdb.k12.wi.us
Aldrich IS 600/4-8
1859 Northgate Dr 53511 608-361-3600
Joe Vrydaghs, prin. Fax 361-4122
Converse ES 400/K-3
1602 Townline Ave 53511 608-361-2100
Vicky Hamilton, prin. Fax 361-4122
Cunningham IS 300/4-8
910 Townline Ave 53511 608-361-2200
Devon LaRosa, prin. Fax 361-4122
Fruzen IS 700/4-8
2600 Milwaukee Rd 53511 608-361-2000
Mathew Kleinschmidt, prin. Fax 361-4122
Gaston ES 400/K-3
1515 W Grand Ave 53511 608-361-2300
Brandye Hereford, prin. Fax 361-4122
Hackett ES 400/K-3
625 8th St 53511 608-361-2400
Ryan McReynolds, prin. Fax 361-4122
McNeel IS 800/4-8
1524 Frederick St 53511 608-361-3800
Michelle Hendrix-Nora, prin. Fax 361-4122
Merrill ES 200/K-3
1635 Nelson Ave 53511 608-361-2600
Betsy Schroeder, prin. Fax 361-4122
Robinson ES 400/K-3
1801 Cranston Rd 53511 608-361-2800
Sam Carter, prin. Fax 361-4122
Todd ES 300/K-3
1621 Oakwood Ave 53511 608-361-4200
Melody Wirgau, prin. Fax 361-4122

School District of Beloit Turner 1,500/PK-12
1237 E Inman Pkwy 53511 608-364-6372
Dr. Dennis McCarthy, supt. Fax 364-6373
www.turnerschools.org/
Powers ES 300/PK-2
620 Hillside Ave 53511 608-364-6360
Vickie Smith, prin. Fax 364-6362
Townview ES 300/3-5
2442 W Beloit Newark Rd 53511 608-364-6365
Randall McClellan, prin. Fax 365-7549
Turner MS 400/6-8
1237 E Inman Pkwy 53511 608-364-6367
Cory Everson, prin. Fax 364-6369

Our Lady of Assumption S 200/PK-8
2222 Shopiere Rd 53511 608-365-4014
Trevor Seivert, prin. Fax 368-2832

Benton, Lafayette, Pop. 970
Benton SD 300/PK-12
PO Box 7 53803 608-759-4002
Fax 759-3805
www.benton.k12.wi.us
Benton ES 100/PK-6
PO Box 7 53803 608-759-4002
Lisa Lawrence, prin. Fax 759-3805

Berlin, Green Lake, Pop. 5,480
Berlin Area SD 1,700/PK-12
295 E Marquette St 54923 920-361-2004
Dr. Robert Eidahl Ed.D., supt. Fax 361-2170
www.berlin.k12.wi.us
Berlin MS 400/6-8
242 Memorial Dr 54923 920-361-2441
Mike Raether, prin. Fax 361-3379
Clay Lamberton ES 800/PK-5
259 E Marquette St 54923 920-361-2442
Scott Bartol, prin. Fax 361-4352

All Saints Catholic S 200/PK-8
151 S Grove St 54923 920-361-1781
Steven Zangl, prin. Fax 361-7379
St. John Lutheran S 100/PK-8
146 Mound St 54923 920-361-0555
Curtis Snow M.A., prin. Fax 361-0575

Big Bend, Waukesha, Pop. 1,275
Mukwonago SD
Supt. — See Mukwonago
Big Bend ES 400/K-6
W230S8695 Big Bend Dr 53103 262-662-4401
Shawn Waller, prin. Fax 662-1309

Christ Lutheran S 100/PK-8
W229S8930 Clark St 53103 262-662-3355
Steven Janke, prin. Fax 662-3370
St. Joseph S 100/PK-8
S89W22650 Milwaukee Ave 53103 262-662-2737
Jeff Van Rixel, prin. Fax 662-2684

Birchwood, Washburn, Pop. 440
Birchwood SD 400/PK-12
300 S Wilson St 54817 715-354-3471
Diane Johnson, supt. Fax 354-3469
www.birchwood.k12.wi.us
Birchwood ES 100/PK-5
300 S Wilson St 54817 715-354-3471
Jeff Stanley, prin. Fax 354-3469
Birchwood MS 50/6-8
300 S Wilson St 54817 715-354-3471
Jeff Stanley, prin. Fax 354-3469

Birnamwood, Shawano, Pop. 810
Wittenberg-Birnamwood SD
Supt. — See Wittenberg
Birnamwood S 400/PK-8
337 Main St 54414 715-449-2576
Guy Steckbauer, prin. Fax 449-2826

Black Creek, Outagamie, Pop. 1,299
Seymour Community SD
Supt. — See Seymour
Black Creek S 400/PK-8
PO Box 237 54106 920-984-3396
Jason Wesenberg, prin. Fax 984-9303

Black Earth, Dane, Pop. 1,326
Wisconsin Heights SD
Supt. — See Mazomanie
Black Earth ES 200/PK-2
1133 Center St 53515 608-767-2251
Deborah Winkler, prin. Fax 767-2545

Black River Falls, Jackson, Pop. 3,539
Black River Falls SD 1,600/PK-12
301 N 4th St 54615 715-284-4357
Dr. Shelly Severson, supt. Fax 284-7064
www.brf.org
Black River Falls MS 400/6-8
1202 Pierce St 54615 715-284-5315
David Roou, prin. Fax 284-0364
Forrest Street ES 400/PK-1
720 Forrest St 54615 715-284-9406
Chad Stanley, prin. Fax 284-7064
Red Creek ES 2-5
410 County Rd A 54615 715-284-4357
Richard Dobbs, prin. Fax 284-7064

Blair, Trempealeau, Pop. 1,358
Blair-Taylor SD 600/PK-12
PO Box 107 54616 608-989-2881
Jeff Eide, supt. Fax 989-2451
btsd.k12.wi.us
Blair-Taylor ES 300/PK-6
PO Box 107 54616 608-989-9835
Lynn Halvorson, prin. Fax 989-2451

Blanchardville, Lafayette, Pop. 822
Pecatonica Area SD 400/PK-12
PO Box 117 53516 608-523-4248
Jill Underly, supt. Fax 523-4286
www.pecatonica.k12.wi.us
Other Schools – See Hollandale

Bloomer, Chippewa, Pop. 3,508
Bloomer SD 1,200/PK-12
1310 17th Ave 54724 715-568-2800
Dr. Brian Misfeldt, supt. Fax 568-5315
www.bloomer.k12.wi.us
Bloomer ES 500/PK-4
401 8th Ave 54724 715-568-1042
Josh Hartman, prin. Fax 568-1045
Bloomer MS 300/5-8
600 Jackson St 54724 715-568-1025
Rhonda Herrick, prin. Fax 568-3687

St. Paul Lutheran S 50/PK-8
1319 Larson St 54724 715-568-4322
Tom Rosenow, prin. Fax 568-3472
St. Paul S 100/PK-8
1210 Main St 54724 715-568-3233
Jackie Peterson, prin. Fax 568-3244

Bloomington, Grant, Pop. 728
River Ridge SD
Supt. — See Patch Grove
River Ridge Upper ES 100/5-6
PO Box 97 53804 608-994-2711
Clay Koenig, prin. Fax 994-2714

St. Mary S 100/1-8
PO Box 35 53804 608-994-2435
Julie Zenz, prin. Fax 994-2551

Bonduel, Shawano, Pop. 1,465
Bonduel SD 800/PK-12
PO Box 310 54107 715-758-4860
Patrick Rau, supt. Fax 758-4869
www.bonduel.k12.wi.us
Bonduel ES 300/PK-5
PO Box 310 54107 715-758-4810
Brad Grayvold, prin. Fax 758-4819
Bonduel MS 200/6-8
PO Box 310 54107 715-758-4840
Mark Margelofsky, prin. Fax 758-4849

St. Paul Lutheran S 200/PK-8
PO Box 577 54107 715-758-8532
Gerald Schmidt, prin. Fax 758-6352

Boscobel, Grant, Pop. 3,210
Boscobel Area SD 800/PK-12
1110 Park St 53805 608-375-4164
Greg Bell, supt. Fax 375-2378
www.boscobel.k12.wi.us
Boscobel ES 500/PK-6
200 Buchanan St 53805 608-375-4165
Danelle Schmid, prin. Fax 375-4197
Boscobel MS 100/7-8
300 Brindley St 53805 608-375-4161
Rodney Lewis, prin. Fax 375-2640

Bowler, Shawano, Pop. 282
Bowler SD 400/PK-12
500 S Almon St 54416 715-793-4101
Dr. Randy Refsland, supt. Fax 793-1302
www.bowler.k12.wi.us
Bowler ES 200/PK-6
500 S Almon St 54416 715-793-4101
Wade Turner, prin. Fax 793-1302

Boyceville, Dunn, Pop. 1,080
Boyceville Community SD 800/PK-12
1003 Tiffany St 54725 715-643-3647
Kevin Sipple, supt. Fax 643-3127
www.boyceville.k12.wi.us
Boyceville MS 100/7-8
1003 Tiffany St 54725 715-643-3647
Steven Glocke, prin. Fax 643-2209
Tiffany Creek ES 400/PK-6
1003 Tiffany St 54725 715-643-3647
Nicholas Kaiser, prin. Fax 643-7805

Boyd, Chippewa, Pop. 549
Stanley-Boyd Area SD
Supt. — See Stanley
Boyd ES 100/PK-PK
303 E Park St 54726 715-667-3221
Dean Lew, prin. Fax 667-3094

St. Joseph S, PO Box 129 54726 50/PK-8
Sara Giza, prin. 708-703-1034

Brandon, Fond du Lac, Pop. 865
Rosendale-Brandon SD
Supt. — See Rosendale
Brandon ES 200/PK-8
200 W Bowen St 53919 920-346-2915
Leanne Greff, prin. Fax 346-5490

Briggsville, Marquette
Wisconsin Dells SD
Supt. — See Wisconsin Dells
Neenah Creek ES 100/K-5
PO Box 68 53920 608-981-2341
Felipe Armijo, prin. Fax 981-2104

Brillion, Calumet, Pop. 3,113
Brillion SD 1,000/PK-12
315 S Main St 54110 920-756-2368
Dominick Madison Ph.D., supt. Fax 756-3705
www.brillionsd.org
Brillion ES 400/PK-5
315 S Main St 54110 920-756-3624
Carrie Deiter, prin. Fax 756-3705
Brillion MS 200/6-8
315 S Main St 54110 920-756-2166
Bonnie Olson, prin. Fax 756-3705

Holy Family S 100/PK-8
209 N Custer St 54110 920-756-2502
Scott Smith, prin. Fax 756-9702
Trinity Evangelical Lutheran S 100/PK-8
601 E National Ave 54110 920-756-3738
Dane Mattes, prin. Fax 756-9189

Bristol, Kenosha
Bristol SD 1 600/K-8
20121 83rd St 53104 262-857-2334
Michael Juech, supt. Fax 857-6644
www.bristol.k12.wi.us
Bristol S 600/K-8
20121 83rd St 53104 262-857-2334
Jeff Terry, prin. Fax 857-6644

Brodhead, Green, Pop. 3,270
Brodhead SD 1,000/PK-12
2501 W 5th Ave 53520 608-897-2141
Leonard Lueck, supt. Fax 897-2770
www.brodhead.k12.wi.us
Albrecht ES 500/PK-5
1400 21st St 53520 608-897-2146
David Novy, prin. Fax 897-2212
Brodhead MS 200/6-8
2100 W 9th Ave 53520 608-897-2184
Dr. Lisa Semrow, prin. Fax 897-2789

Brookfield, Waukesha, Pop. 37,413
Elmbrook SD 6,900/PK-12
PO Box 1830 53008 262-781-3030
Mark Hansen, supt. Fax 790-4095
www.elmbrookschools.org
Brookfield ES 500/K-5
2530 N Brookfield Rd 53045 262-785-3930
Daniel Westfahl, prin. Fax 785-3934
Burleigh ES 700/PK-5
16185 Burleigh Pl 53005 262-781-5280
Christian Pleister, prin. Fax 790-0302
Dixon ES 400/K-5
2400 Pilgrim Square Dr 53005 262-785-3970
Jeanne Siegenthaler, prin. Fax 785-3904
Swanson ES 700/K-5
305 N Calhoun Rd 53005 262-789-2540
Kori Hartman, prin. Fax 789-3288
Wisconsin Hills MS 900/6-8
18700 W Wisconsin Ave 53045 262-785-3960
Lisa Rettler, prin. Fax 785-3967
Other Schools – See Elm Grove

Brookfield Academy 900/PK-12
3462 N Brookfield Rd 53045 262-783-3200
Brookfield Christian S 200/PK-8
14155 W Burleigh Rd 53005 262-782-4722
Kevin Vos, prin. Fax 782-0511
Christ the Lord Lutheran Evangelical S 100/PK-8
1650 N Brookfield Rd 53045 262-782-3040
John Melso, prin. Fax 782-3504
Immanuel Lutheran S 200/PK-8
13445 Hampton Rd 53005 262-781-4135
Sharon Wallace, prin. Fax 781-5460

St. Dominic Catholic S 400/PK-8
18105 W Capitol Dr 53045 262-783-7565
Jill Fischer, prin. Fax 781-3283
St. John Vianney S 400/K-8
17500 Gebhardt Rd 53045 262-796-3942
Dan Demeter, prin. Fax 796-3953

Brooklyn, Green, Pop. 1,387
Oregon SD
Supt. — See Oregon
Brooklyn ES 400/K-4
204 Division St 53521 608-455-4500
Kerri Modjeski, prin. Fax 455-2404

Brown Deer, Milwaukee, Pop. 11,652
Brown Deer SD 1,100/PK-12
8200 N 60th St 53223 414-371-6750
Dr. Deborah Kerr, supt. Fax 371-6751
www.browndeerschools.com
Brown Deer ES 200/PK-6
5757 W Dean Rd 53223 414-371-6800
Kortney Smith, prin. Fax 371-6801

Brownsville, Dodge, Pop. 579

St. Paul Lutheran S 50/PK-8
PO Box 370 53006 920-583-4242
Rev. William Carter, prin. Fax 583-4242

Bruce, Rusk, Pop. 772
Bruce SD 500/PK-12
104 W Washington Ave 54819 715-868-2533
Patrick Sturzl, supt. Fax 868-2534
www.bruce.k12.wi.us
Bruce ES 200/PK-5
104 W Washington Ave 54819 715-868-2585
Larry Villiard, prin. Fax 868-2534
Bruce MS 100/6-8
104 W Washington Ave 54819 715-868-2585
Larry Villiard, prin. Fax 868-2534

Brussels, Door
Southern Door SD 1,100/PK-12
2073 County Road DK 54204 920-825-7311
Patricia Vickman, supt. Fax 825-7155
www.southerndoor.k12.wi.us
Southern Door ES 500/PK-5
2073 County Road DK 54204 920-825-7321
Cory Vandertie, prin. Fax 825-7692
Southern Door MS 200/6-8
2073 County Road DK 54204 920-825-7321
Steve Bousley, prin. Fax 825-7692

Burlington, Racine, Pop. 10,361
Burlington Area SD 3,100/PK-12
100 N Kane St 53105 262-763-0210
Peter Smet, supt. Fax 763-0215
www.basd.k12.wi.us
Cooper ES 400/PK-4
249 Conkey St 53105 262-763-0180
Christine Anderson, prin. Fax 763-5384
Dyer IS 400/5-6
201 S Kendrick Ave 53105 262-763-0220
Scott Schimmel, prin. Fax 767-5583
Karcher MS 500/7-8
225 Robert St 53105 262-763-0190
Jill Oelslager, prin. Fax 767-5580
Lyons Center ES 100/K-4
1622 Mill St 53105 262-763-5380
Sue Mosher, prin. Fax 763-5382
Waller ES 400/PK-4
195 Gardner Ave 53105 262-763-0185
Victoria Libbey, prin. Fax 763-0187
Winkler ES 200/PK-4
34150 Fulton St 53105 262-539-2726
Jacqueline Syens, prin. Fax 539-2217

Randall J1 SD 700/PK-8
37101 87th St 53105 262-537-2211
John Gendron, supt. Fax 537-2280
www.randall.k12.wi.us
Randall S 700/PK-8
37101 87th St 53105 262-537-2211
Erin Zigler, prin. Fax 537-2280

Wheatland J1 SD 500/PK-8
6606 368th Ave 53105 262-537-2216
Marty McGinley, admin. Fax 537-4059
www.wheatland.k12.wi.us
Wheatland Center S 500/PK-8
6606 368th Ave 53105 262-537-2216
Drew Halbesma, prin. Fax 537-4059

St. Charles Borromeo S 200/K-8
449 Conkey St 53105 262-763-2848
Mary MacDonald, prin. Fax 763-3818
St. John's Lutheran S 200/PK-8
198 Westridge Ave 53105 262-763-2377
Chris Avery, prin. Fax 288-2089
St. Mary S 300/PK-8
225 W State St 53105 262-763-1515
Loretta Jackson, prin. Fax 763-1508

Butler, Waukesha, Pop. 1,820

St. Agnes Catholic S 100/K-8
12801 W Fairmount Ave 53007 262-781-4996
Nicole Kuehne, prin. Fax 781-3512

Butternut, Ashland, Pop. 367
Butternut SD 100/PK-12
PO Box 247 54514 715-769-3434
Joseph Zirngibl, supt. Fax 769-3712
www.lightatorch.info
Butternut S 100/PK-12
PO Box 247 54514 715-769-3434
Joseph Zirngibl, admin. Fax 769-3712

Cadott, Chippewa, Pop. 1,424
Cadott Community SD 900/PK-12
426 Myrtle St 54727 715-289-3795
Randal Rosburg, supt. Fax 289-3748
www.cadott.k12.wi.us
Cadott ES 500/PK-6
463 E Mills St 54727 715-289-3795
Terri Goettl, prin. Fax 289-3017
Cadott JHS 100/7-8
426 Myrtle St 54727 715-289-3795
Peter Apple, prin. Fax 289-3085

Caledonia, Racine, Pop. 24,349

Trinity Lutheran S 200/PK-8
7900 Nicholson Rd 53108 262-835-4326
David Habeck, prin. Fax 835-0707

Cambria, Columbia, Pop. 765
Cambria-Friesland SD 400/PK-12
410 E Edgewater St 53923 920-348-5548
Timothy Raymond, supt. Fax 348-5119
www.cf.k12.wi.us
Cambria-Friesland ES 200/PK-5
410 E Edgewater St 53923 920-348-5135
Timothy Raymond, prin. Fax 348-5119

Cambridge, Dane, Pop. 1,441
Cambridge SD 900/PK-12
403 Blue Jay Way 53523 608-423-4345
Bernard Nikolay, supt. Fax 423-9869
www.cambridge.k12.wi.us
Cambridge ES 400/PK-5
802 W Water St 53523 608-423-9727
Chris Holt, prin. Fax 423-7078
Nikolay MS 200/6-8
211 South St 53523 608-423-7335
Krista Jones, prin. Fax 423-4499

Cameron, Barron, Pop. 1,761
Cameron SD 1,100/PK-12
PO Box 378 54822 715-458-4560
Joe Leschisin, admin. Fax 458-4822
www.cameron.k12.wi.us
Cameron ES 400/PK-4
PO Box 378 54822 715-458-4560
Cory Martens, prin. Fax 458-0041
Cameron MS 300/5-8
PO Box 378 54822 715-458-4560
Hans Schmidt, prin. Fax 458-3436

Campbellsport, Fond du Lac, Pop. 1,998
Campbellsport SD 1,400/PK-12
114 W Sheboygan St 53010 920-533-8381
Paul A. Amundson, admin. Fax 533-5726
www.csd.k12.wi.us
Campbellsport ES 400/PK-5
751 Grandview Ave 53010 920-533-8032
Shanda Cerny, prin. Fax 533-3433
Campbellsport MS 300/6-8
114 W Sheboygan St 53010 920-533-4811
Todd Hencsik, prin. Fax 533-1268
Other Schools – See Eden

St. Matthew S 100/K-8
PO Box 639 53010 920-533-4103
Joan Schlaefer, prin. Fax 533-8078
Waucousta Lutheran S 50/PK-8
W2011 County Road F 53010 920-533-4792
David Wege, prin. Fax 533-4792

Camp Douglas, Juneau, Pop. 597
Tomah Area SD
Supt. — See Tomah
Camp Douglas ES 50/3-5
81 Junction St 54618 608-374-7091
Diana Lesneski, prin. Fax 372-5087

Casco, Kewaunee, Pop. 569
Luxemburg-Casco SD
Supt. — See Luxemburg
Luxemburg-Casco MS 300/7-8
619 Church Ave 54205 920-837-2205
Mike Snowberry, prin. Fax 837-7517

Holy Trinity S 100/PK-6
510 Church Ave 54205 920-837-7531
Gail Waterstreet, prin. Fax 837-2361

Cashton, Monroe, Pop. 1,094
Cashton SD 600/PK-12
PO Box 129 54619 608-654-5131
Ryan Alderson, supt. Fax 654-5136
www.cashton.k12.wi.us
Cashton ES 300/PK-5
PO Box 129 54619 608-654-7377
Kari Huth, prin. Fax 654-7390

Sacred Heart S 50/PK-8
710 Kenyon St 54619 608-654-7733
Michael Klos, lead tchr. Fax 654-7413

Cassville, Grant, Pop. 939
Cassville SD 200/PK-12
715 E Amelia St 53806 608-725-5116
John Luster, supt. Fax 725-2353
www.cassvillesd.k12.wi.us
Cassville ES 100/PK-6
715 E Amelia St 53806 608-725-5307
John Luster, prin. Fax 725-2353

St. Charles Borromeo S 50/1-8
PO Box 167 53806 608-725-5173
Julie Zelz, prin. Fax 725-5179

Cato, Manitowoc

St. Mary / St. Michael S 100/PK-8
19 S County Road J 54230 920-775-4366
George Smith, prin. Fax 775-4365

Cazenovia, Sauk, Pop. 314
Weston SD 300/PK-12
E2511A County Road S 53924 608-986-2151
Dr. Stephen Guenther, supt. Fax 986-2205
www.weston.k12.wi.us
Weston ES 200/PK-5
E2511A County Road S 53924 608-986-2151
Dr. Stephen Guenther, admin. Fax 986-2205
Weston MS 100/6-8
E2511A County Road S 53924 608-986-2151
Dr. Stephen Guenther, admin. Fax 986-2205

Cedarburg, Ozaukee, Pop. 11,308
Cedarburg SD 3,000/K-12
W68N611 Evergreen Blvd 53012 262-376-6100
Todd Bugnacki, supt. Fax 376-6110
www.cedarburg.k12.wi.us
Parkview ES 400/K-5
W72N853 Harrison Ave 53012 262-376-6800
Jayne Holck, prin. Fax 376-6810
Thorson ES 400/K-5
W51N932 Keup Rd 53012 262-376-6700
Angela Little, prin. Fax 376-6710
Webster MS 700/6-8
W75N624 Wauwatosa Rd 53012 262-376-6500
Tony DeRosa, prin. Fax 376-6510
Westlawn ES 300/K-5
W64N319 Madison Ave 53012 262-376-6900
Katie Ramos, prin. Fax 376-6992

First Immanuel Lutheran S 300/PK-8
W67N622 Evergreen Blvd 53012 262-377-6610
Dawn Walker, prin. Fax 377-9606
St. Francis Borgia S 400/PK-8
1425 Covered Bridge Rd 53012 262-377-2050
Kelly Swietlik, prin. Fax 377-4099

Cedar Grove, Sheboygan, Pop. 2,097
Cedar Grove-Belgium Area SD 1,100/PK-12
321 N 2nd St 53013 920-668-8686
Dr. Jeanne Courneene, supt. Fax 668-8605
www.cedargrovebelgium.k12.wi.us/
Cedar Grove-Belgium ES 400/PK-4
321 N 2nd St 53013 920-668-8518
Jeffrey Kondrakiewicz, prin. Fax 668-6933
Cedar Grove-Belgium MS 300/5-8
321 N 2nd St 53013 920-668-8518
Kelly Dzuriek, prin. Fax 668-8560

Chetek, Barron, Pop. 2,205
Chetek-Weyerhaeuser Area SD 900/PK-12
PO Box 6 54728 715-924-2226
Dr. Mark Johnson, supt. Fax 924-2376
www.cwasd.k12.wi.us
Chetek Weyerhaeuser Area MS 200/6-8
PO Box 6 54728 715-924-3136
Larry Zeman, prin. Fax 924-1794
Roselawn ES 500/PK-5
PO Box 6 54728 715-924-2244
Ceil Marc, prin. Fax 924-2279

Chilton, Calumet, Pop. 3,890
Chilton SD 1,200/PK-12
530 W Main St 53014 920-849-8109
Susan Kaphingst, supt. Fax 849-4539
www.chilton.k12.wi.us
Chilton ES 500/PK-4
530 W Main St 53014 920-849-9388
Pamela Schuster, prin. Fax 849-9457
Chilton MS 400/5-8
530 W Main St 53014 920-849-9152
Matthew Kiel, prin. Fax 849-7210

Chilton Area Catholic S 100/PK-6
60 E Washington St 53014 920-849-4141
Elisabeth Rollmann, prin. Fax 849-9092

Chippewa Falls, Chippewa, Pop. 13,496
Chippewa Falls Area USD 4,700/PK-12
1130 Miles St 54729 715-726-2417
Heidi Taylor-Eliopoulos, supt. Fax 726-2781
cfsd.chipfalls.k12.wi.us
Chippewa Falls MS 1,100/6-8
750 Tropicana Blvd 54729 715-726-2400
Susan Kern, prin. Fax 726-2789
Halmstad ES 400/K-5
565 E South Ave 54729 715-726-2415
Wade Pilloud, prin. Fax 720-3756
Hillcrest ES 400/K-5
1200 Miles St 54729 715-726-2405
Leslie Lancette, prin. Fax 720-3754
Parkview ES 500/K-5
501 Jefferson Ave 54729 715-720-3750
Melissa Olson, prin. Fax 720-3755
Southview ES 300/PK-5
615 A St 54729 715-726-2411
Sara Denure, prin. Fax 726-2798
Stillson ES 400/K-5
17250 County Highway J 54729 715-726-2412
Carol Wilczek, prin. Fax 720-3745
Other Schools – See Jim Falls

Holy Ghost ES 100/3-5
436 S Main St 54729 715-723-6478
Kayla Bahnub, prin. Fax 723-8990
Notre Dame MS 100/6-8
1316 Bel Air Blvd 54729 715-723-4777
Brian Schulner, prin. Fax 723-3353
St. Charles Borromeo PS 200/PK-3
429 W Spruce St 54729 715-723-5827
Kayla Bahnub, prin. Fax 723-2109

St. Peter S 100/1-8
11370 County Highway Q 54729 715-288-6250
Tammy Christopher, prin. Fax 288-6250

Clayton, Polk, Pop. 562
Clayton SD 400/PK-12
236 Polk Ave W 54004 715-948-2163
Cathleen Shimon, supt. Fax 948-2362
www.claytonschooldistrict.new.rschooltoday.com
Clayton ES 200/PK-5
236 Polk Ave W 54004 715-948-2163
Cathleen Shimon, prin. Fax 948-2362
Clayton MS 100/6-8
236 Polk Ave W 54004 715-948-2163
Edward Cerney, prin. Fax 948-2362

Clear Lake, Polk, Pop. 1,055
Clear Lake SD 600/PK-12
1101 3rd St SW 54005 715-263-2114
Josh Ernst, admin. Fax 263-2933
www.clwarriors.org
Clear Lake JHS 100/7-8
1101 3rd St SW 54005 715-263-2113
Nick Gilles, prin. Fax 263-3550
Nelson ES 400/PK-6
135 8th Ave 54005 715-263-2117
Chris Petersen, prin. Fax 263-3519

Cleveland, Manitowoc, Pop. 1,481
Sheboygan Area SD
Supt. — See Sheboygan
Cleveland ES 100/K-5
411 E Washington Ave 53015 920-693-8241
Jacqueline Iseler, prin. Fax 693-8357

Clinton, Rock, Pop. 2,131
Clinton Community SD 1,200/PK-12
PO Box 566 53525 608-676-5482
Dr. Jim Brewer, supt. Fax 676-4444
www.clinton.k12.wi.us
Clinton ES 500/PK-4
PO Box 70 53525 608-676-2211
Heidi Simms, prin. Fax 676-5717
Clinton MS 300/5-8
PO Box 559 53525 608-676-2275
Ben Simmons, prin. Fax 676-5176

Clintonville, Waupaca, Pop. 4,497
Clintonville SD 1,400/PK-12
45 W Green Tree Rd 54929 715-823-7215
David Dyb, supt. Fax 823-1315
www.clintonville.k12.wi.us
Clintonville MS 400/5-8
255 N Main St 54929 715-823-7215
Troy Kuhn, prin. Fax 823-1443
Dellwood Early Learning Center 100/PK-PK
238 Harriet St 54929 715-823-7215
Amy Bindas, prin. Fax 823-1401
Rexford/Longfellow ES 400/K-4
105 S Clinton Ave 54929 715-823-7215
Tami Bagstad, prin. Fax 823-7140

St. Martin Lutheran S 200/PK-8
100 S Clinton Ave 54929 715-823-6538
Mark Moran M.S., prin. Fax 823-1464
St. Rose - St. Mary S 100/PK-8
140 Auto St 54929 715-201-9913
Michelle Vosters, prin. Fax 823-3402

Colby, Clark, Pop. 1,841
Colby SD 900/PK-12
PO Box 110 54421 715-223-2301
Dr. Steven Kolden, supt. Fax 223-4539
www.colby.k12.wi.us
Colby ES 300/K-3
PO Box 80 54421 715-223-3939
Dr. Steven Kolden, prin. Fax 223-2123
Colby MS 200/4-8
PO Box 110 54421 715-223-8869
Jim Hagen, prin. Fax 223-6754
Little Stars Preschool 100/PK-PK
PO Box 140 54421 715-223-2044
Dr. Steven Kolden, prin. Fax 223-4388

St. Mary S 100/K-8
PO Box 408 54421 715-223-3033
Tina Feiten, prin. Fax 223-0223

Coleman, Marinette, Pop. 713
Coleman SD 600/PK-12
347 Business 141 N 54112 920-897-4011
Douglas Polomis, supt. Fax 897-4921
www.coleman.k12.wi.us
Coleman ES 400/PK-8
347 Business 141 N 54112 920-897-2525
Yvette Marshall, prin. Fax 897-4921

Colfax, Dunn, Pop. 1,143
Colfax SD 900/PK-12
601 University Ave 54730 715-962-3155
William Yingst, supt. Fax 962-4024
www.colfax.k12.wi.us/
Colfax ES 500/PK-6
601 University Ave 54730 715-962-3676
Trevor Hovde, prin. Fax 962-4024

Colgate, Washington
Germantown SD
Supt. — See Germantown
Belle ES 400/K-5
3294 Willow Creek Rd 53017 262-253-3470
Dr. Katie Kohel, prin. Fax 253-3490

Richfield J1 SD
Supt. — See Richfield
Plat ES 200/PK-2
4908 Monches Rd 53017 262-628-1778
Tara Villalobos, admin. Fax 628-9959

Coloma, Waushara, Pop. 450
Westfield SD
Supt. — See Westfield
Coloma ES 100/PK-6
210 N Linden St 54930 715-228-2851
Chase Gildenzoph, prin. Fax 228-2860

Columbus, Columbia, Pop. 4,934
Columbus SD 1,300/PK-12
200 W School St 53925 920-623-5950
Annette Deuman, supt. Fax 623-5958
www.columbus.k12.wi.us
Columbus ES 400/PK-3
200 Fuller St 53925 920-623-5950
Beth Hellpap, prin. Fax 623-6026
Columbus MS 400/4-8
400 S Dickason Blvd 53925 920-623-5950
Loren Glasbrenner, prin. Fax 623-5742

Petersen SDA S 50/K-8
W1004 Hall Rd 53925 920-623-4056
Pennie Wredberg, prin.
St. Jerome S 100/PK-8
1550 Farnham St 53925 920-623-5780
Jamie Cotter, prin. Fax 623-1115
Zion Lutheran S 100/K-8
822 Western Ave 53925 920-623-5180
Alex Vandenberg, prin. Fax 623-2352

Combined Locks, Outagamie, Pop. 3,308
Kimberly Area SD 4,600/PK-12
PO Box 159 54113 920-788-7900
Bob Mayfield Ed.D., supt. Fax 788-7919
www.kimberly.k12.wi.us
Janssen ES 400/K-4
420 Wallace St 54113 920-788-7915
Dr. Hercules Nikolaou, prin. Fax 788-7923
Other Schools – See Appleton, Kimberly

Coon Valley, Vernon, Pop. 762
Westby Area SD
Supt. — See Westby
Coon Valley ES 100/PK-4
300 Lien St 54623 608-452-3143
Mike Berg, prin. Fax 452-3155

Cornell, Chippewa, Pop. 1,446
Cornell SD 300/PK-12
PO Box 517 54732 715-861-6947
Dr. Paul Schley, supt. Fax 239-6587
www.cornell.k12.wi.us
Cornell ES 200/PK-5
PO Box 517 54732 715-861-6947
Dr. Paul Schley, prin. Fax 239-6587

Cottage Grove, Dane, Pop. 6,069
Monona Grove SD
Supt. — See Monona
Cottage Grove ES 400/2-4
470 N Main St 53527 608-839-4576
Reed Foster, prin. Fax 839-4439
Glacial Drumlin MS 800/5-8
801 Damascus Trl 53527 608-839-8437
Renee Tennant, prin. Fax 839-8984
Taylor Prairie ES 400/PK-1
900 N Parkview St 53527 608-839-8515
Connie Haessly, prin. Fax 839-8323

Crandon, Forest, Pop. 1,853
Crandon SD 900/PK-12
9750 US Highway 8 W 54520 715-478-3339
Theodore Kryder, supt. Fax 478-5130
www.crandon.k12.wi.us
Crandon ES 500/PK-5
9750 US Highway 8 W 54520 715-478-6123
Jamee Belland, prin. Fax 478-5130
Crandon MS 200/6-8
9750 US Highway 8 W 54520 715-478-6124
Andy Space, prin. Fax 478-5130

Crivitz, Marinette, Pop. 971
Crivitz SD 700/PK-12
400 South Ave 54114 715-854-2721
Patrick Mans, supt. Fax 854-3755
www.crivitz.k12.wi.us
Crivitz ES 400/PK-8
400 South Ave 54114 715-854-2721
Jeff Walsh, prin. Fax 854-2050

Cross Plains, Dane, Pop. 3,510
Middleton-Cross Plains Area SD
Supt. — See Middleton
Glacier Creek MS 600/5-8
2800 N Military Rd 53528 608-829-9420
Ken Metz, prin. Fax 798-5425
Park ES 300/PK-4
1209 Park St 53528 608-829-9250
Monica Schommer, prin. Fax 798-4943

St. Francis Xavier S 200/PK-8
2939 Thinnes St 53528 608-798-2422
Robert Abshire, prin. Fax 798-0898

Cuba City, Grant, Pop. 2,077
Cuba City SD 700/PK-12
101 N School St 53807 608-744-2847
Aaron Olson, admin. Fax 744-2324
www.cubacity.us
Cuba City ES 400/PK-8
518 W Roosevelt St 53807 608-744-2174
Rhonda Loeffelholz, prin. Fax 744-7469

St. Rose of Lima S 100/PK-8
218 N Jackson St 53807 608-744-2120
Mary Schneider, prin. Fax 744-8449

Cudahy, Milwaukee, Pop. 17,945
Cudahy SD 2,400/PK-12
2915 E Ramsey Ave 53110 414-294-7400
Dr. James Heiden, supt. Fax 294-4083
www.cudahy.k12.wi.us/
Cudahy MS 400/6-8
5530 S Barland Ave 53110 414-294-2830
Kim Berner, prin. Fax 489-3010
Jones ES 200/PK-5
5845 S Swift Ave 53110 414-294-7150
Jacqueline Santi, prin. Fax 489-3007
Kosciuszko ES 300/PK-5
5252 S Kirkwood Ave 53110 414-294-7200
Melissa Kostka, prin. Fax 769-1584
Lincoln ES 300/PK-5
4416 S Packard Ave 53110 414-294-2930
Matthew Orlowski, prin. Fax 489-3008
Mitchell ES 300/PK-5
5950 S Illinois Ave 53110 414-294-7100
Michael Moore, prin. Fax 489-3006
Park View ES 300/PK-5
5555 S Nicholson Ave 53110 414-294-7250
Gregory Burton, prin. Fax 489-3009

St. Paul's Lutheran S 100/PK-8
3766 E Cudahy Ave 53110 414-744-9771
Donald Kolander, prin. Fax 744-2717

Cumberland, Barron, Pop. 2,141
Cumberland SD 1,000/PK-12
1010 8th Ave 54829 715-822-5124
Dr. Barry Rose, supt. Fax 822-5136
www.cumberland.k12.wi.us
Cumberland ES 400/PK-4
1530 2nd Ave 54829 715-822-5123
Jim Richie, prin. Fax 822-5135
Cumberland MS 300/5-8
980 8th Ave 54829 715-822-5122
Colin Green, prin. Fax 822-5132

Custer, Portage

Sacred Heart S 50/PK-6
7379 Church St 54423 715-592-4902
Tom McCann, prin. Fax 592-4189

Dane, Dane, Pop. 990

Blessed Trinity S 50/K-8
109 Military Rd 53529 608-849-5619
Jeff Karls, prin. Fax 850-5610

Darien, Walworth, Pop. 1,571
Delavan-Darien SD
Supt. — See Delavan
Darien ES 200/4-5
125 S Walworth St 53114 262-728-2642
Kelly Pickel, prin. Fax 724-4147

Darlington, Lafayette, Pop. 2,431
Darlington Community SD 800/PK-12
11630 Center Hill Rd 53530 608-776-2006
Dr. Denise Wellnitz, supt. Fax 776-3407
www.darlington.k12.wi.us
Darlington S 600/PK-8
11630 Center Hill Rd 53530 608-776-4021
Michelle Savatski, prin. Fax 776-3510

Holy Rosary S 50/PK-4
744 Wells St 53530 608-776-3710
Tanya Horne, prin. Fax 776-4059

Deerfield, Dane, Pop. 2,294
Deerfield Community SD 800/PK-12
300 Simonson Blvd 53531 608-764-5431
Michelle Jensen, supt. Fax 764-2556
www.deerfield.k12.wi.us
Deerfield ES 400/PK-6
340 W Quarry St 53531 608-764-5442
Melinda Kamrath, prin. Fax 764-8652
Deerfield MS 100/7-8
300 Simonson Blvd 53531 608-764-5431
Brad Johnsrud, prin. Fax 764-5433

De Forest, Dane, Pop. 8,802
De Forest Area SD 3,600/PK-12
520 E Holum St 53532 608-842-6500
Eric Runez, supt. Fax 842-6592
www.deforest.k12.wi.us
De Forest Area MS 1,000/5-8
404 Yorktown Rd 53532 608-842-6000
Kurt Becker, prin. Fax 842-6015
Eagle Point ES 300/K-4
201 N Cleveland Ave 53532 608-842-6200
Dr. Ann Schoenberger, prin. Fax 842-6215
Holum Education Center 300/PK-PK
520 E Holum St 53532 608-842-6200
Dr. Pete Wilson, dir. Fax 842-6215
Yahara ES 400/K-4
234 N Lexington Pkwy 53532 608-842-6400
Mike Weisensel, prin. Fax 842-6415
Other Schools – See Morrisonville, Windsor

Delafield, Waukesha, Pop. 7,026
Kettle Moraine SD
Supt. — See Wales
Cushing ES 500/PK-5
227 Genesee St 53018 262-646-6700
Rebecca Toetz, prin. Fax 646-6730

Delavan, Walworth, Pop. 8,369
Delavan-Darien SD 2,400/PK-12
324 Beloit St 53115 262-233-6800
Dr. Robert Crist, supt. Fax 728-5954
www.ddschools.org
Phoenix MS 500/6-8
414 Beloit St 53115 262-728-2642
Henry Schmelz, prin. Fax 728-0359

Turtle Creek ES 600/1-3
1235 Creek Rd 53115 262-728-2642
Christopher Fountain, prin. Fax 728-6951
Wileman ES 300/PK-K
1001 E Geneva St 53115 262-728-2642
Rebecca Schneider, prin. Fax 728-6956
Other Schools – See Darien

Delavan Christian S 100/PK-8
848 Oak St 53115 262-728-5667
Grace Hirte, prin. Fax 728-0092
Our Redeemer Lutheran S 200/PK-8
416 W Geneva St 53115 262-728-6589
Kristi Collins, prin. Fax 728-5581
St. Andrew S 100/PK-8
115 S 7th St 53115 262-728-6211
Randy Green, prin. Fax 728-3683

Denmark, Brown, Pop. 2,098
Denmark SD 1,500/PK-12
450 N Wall St 54208 920-863-4000
Tony Klaubauf, supt. Fax 863-4015
www.denmark.k12.wi.us
Denmark ECC 200/PK-K
450 N Wall St 54208 920-863-4175
David Harper, contact Fax 863-1923
Denmark ES 500/1-5
450 N Wall St 54208 920-863-4050
Ann Birdsall, prin. Fax 863-8302
Denmark MS 300/6-8
450 N Wall St 54208 920-863-4100
Amy Gleeson, prin. Fax 863-3184

All Saints S 100/PK-8
PO Box 787 54208 920-863-2449
Jean VanderHeiden, prin. Fax 863-5425

De Pere, Brown, Pop. 23,399
De Pere SD 4,000/K-12
1700 Chicago St 54115 920-337-1032
Benjamin Villarruel, supt. Fax 337-1033
www.depere.k12.wi.us
Altmayer ES 500/K-4
3001 Ryan Rd 54115 920-338-1894
Dr. Emmy Mayer, prin. Fax 338-1360
De Pere MS 700/7-8
700 Swan Rd 54115 920-337-1024
Betty Hartman, prin. Fax 337-1049
Dickinson ES 500/K-4
435 S Washington St 54115 920-337-1027
Luke Herlache, prin. Fax 337-1043
Foxview IS 600/5-6
650 S Michigan St 54115 920-337-1036
Andy Bradford, prin. Fax 403-7390
Heritage ES 500/K-4
1250 Swan Rd 54115 920-337-1035
Kathleen Van Pay, prin. Fax 403-7381

West De Pere SD 3,100/PK-12
400 Reid St Ste W 54115 920-337-1393
John Zegers, supt. Fax 337-1398
www.wdpsd.com
Hemlock Creek ES 800/PK-5
1900 Williams Grant Dr 54115 920-425-1900
Kathleen Held, prin. Fax 425-1914
West De Pere MS 600/6-8
1177 S 9th St 54115 920-337-1099
Dr. James Finley, prin. Fax 337-1380
Westwood ES 800/PK-5
1155 Westwood Dr 54115 920-337-1087
Dr. Jason Lau, prin. Fax 337-1091

Notre Dame S 300/PK-8
221 S Wisconsin St 54115 920-337-1115
Gregory Balza, prin. Fax 337-1117
Our Lady of Lourdes S 200/PK-8
1305 Lourdes Ave 54115 920-336-3091
Jeff Young, prin. Fax 337-6806

De Soto, Vernon, Pop. 286
De Soto Area SD 600/PK-12
615 Main St 54624 608-648-0100
Linzi Gronning, supt. Fax 648-3959
www.desoto.k12.wi.us
De Soto MS 100/6-8
615 Main St 54624 608-648-0100
Linzi Gronning, prin. Fax 648-0117
Prairie View ES 100/PK-5
E3245 County Rd N 54624 608-648-2227
Kelly Olson, prin. Fax 648-2224
Other Schools – See Stoddard

Dickeyville, Grant, Pop. 1,058

Holy Ghost/Immaculate Conception S 200/PK-3
PO Box 40 53808 608-568-7790
Rita Hesseling, prin. Fax 568-3872

Dodgeville, Iowa, Pop. 4,656
Dodgeville SD 1,300/PK-12
307 N Iowa St 53533 608-935-3307
Dr. Jeffrey Jacobson, supt. Fax 935-3021
www.dsd.k12.wi.us
Dodgeville ES 400/PK-5
404 N Johnson St 53533 608-935-3307
Julie Piper, prin. Fax 935-2824
Dodgeville MS 300/6-8
951 W Chapel St 53533 608-935-3307
Sally Baxter, prin. Fax 935-9643
Other Schools – See Ridgeway

St. Joseph S 200/PK-8
305 E Walnut St 53533 608 935 3392
Dana Graber, prin. Fax 935-1722

Dousman, Waukesha, Pop. 2,279
Kettle Moraine SD
Supt. — See Wales
Dousman ES 500/PK-5
341 E Ottawa Ave 53118 262-965-6550
Jeremy Monday, prin. Fax 965-6559
Kettle Moraine MS 900/6-8
301 E Ottawa Ave 53118 262-965-6500
Michael Comiskey, prin. Fax 965-6506

St. Bruno S 100/PK-8
246 W Ottawa Ave 53118 262-965-2291
Ben Holzem, prin. Fax 965-4749

Downsville, Dunn, Pop. 146
Menomonie Area SD
Supt. — See Menomonie
Downsville ES 100/K-5
PO Box 78 54735 715-664-8546
Mary Begley, prin. Fax 664-8548

Dresser, Polk, Pop. 890
St. Croix Falls SD
Supt. — See Saint Croix Falls
Dresser ES 100/K-K
131 2nd St 54009 715-483-9823
Jeff Benoy, prin. Fax 483-3695

Drummond, Bayfield, Pop. 153
Drummond Area SD 400/PK-12
PO Box 40 54832 715-739-6669
John Knight, supt. Fax 739-6345
www.dasdk12.net
Drummond ES 200/PK-6
PO Box 40 54832 715-739-6731
John Knight, prin. Fax 739-6345
Drummond MS 100/7-8
PO Box 40 54832 715-739-6231
Kristine Lamb, prin. Fax 739-6345

Durand, Pepin, Pop. 1,916
Durand-Arkansaw SD 600/PK-12
PO Box 190 54736 715-672-8919
Greg Doverspike, supt. Fax 672-8930
www.durand.k12.wi.us
Woodlawn ES 100/PK-5
PO Box 190 54736 715-672-8977
Erika Johnson, prin. Fax 672-8930

Assumption Catholic S Durand Campus 100/4-8
901 W Prospect St 54736 715-672-5617
Mary Lansing, prin. Fax 672-3931
Assumption Catholic S Lima Campus 100/K-3
N6217 County Road V 54736 715-672-4276
Mary Lansing, prin. Fax 672-3485

Eagle, Waukesha, Pop. 1,944
Palmyra-Eagle Area SD
Supt. — See Palmyra
Eagle ES 200/PK-6
PO Box 550 53119 262-594-2148
Matthew Stich, prin. Fax 594-2820

Eagle River, Vilas, Pop. 1,377
Northland Pines SD 1,400/PK-12
1800 Pleasure Island Rd 54521 715-479-6487
Mike Richie Ed.D., supt. Fax 479-7633
www.npsd.k12.wi.us/
Northland Pines/Eagle River ES 400/PK-6
1700 Pleasure Island Rd 54521 715-479-6471
Karie Jo Bornberg, prin. Fax 477-6263
Northland Pines MS 300/7-8
1800 Pleasure Island Rd 54521 715-479-6479
Dan Marien, prin. Fax 479-7303
Other Schools – See Land O Lakes, Saint Germain

Christ Lutheran S 100/PK-8
201 N 3rd St 54521 715-479-8284
Jim Kuchenbecker, prin. Fax 479-8284

East Troy, Walworth, Pop. 4,231
East Troy Community SD 1,700/PK-12
2043 Division St 53120 262-642-6710
Dr. Christopher Hibner, supt.
www.easttroy.k12.wi.us
East Troy MS 400/6-8
3143 Graydon Ave 53120 262-642-6740
Peter Synes, prin. Fax 642-6743
Little Prairie PS 300/PK-2
2109 Townline Rd 53120 262-642-6730
Lindsey Harris, prin. Fax 642-6723
Prairie View ES 400/3-5
2131 Townline Rd 53120 262-642-6720
Mark Weerts, prin. Fax 642-6788

Good Shepherd Lutheran S 50/PK-5
1936 Emery St 53120 262-642-3310
Karl Sattler, admin. Fax 642-3310
St. Paul's Lutheran S 100/PK-8
2665 North St 53120 262-642-3202
Kenneth White, prin. Fax 642-4132
St. Peter S 100/PK-8
3001 Elm St 53120 262-642-5533
Sarah Halbesma, prin. Fax 642-5897

Eau Claire, Eau Claire, Pop. 64,812
Eau Claire Area SD 10,900/PK-12
500 Main St 54701 715-852-3000
Dr. Mary Ann Hardebeck, supt. Fax 852-3004
www.ecasd.us
Davey ES 400/K-5
3000 Starr Ave 54703 715-852-3200
William Giese, prin. Fax 852-3204
DeLong MS 900/6-8
2000 Vine St 54703 715-852-4900
Dr. Tim O'Reilly, prin. Fax 852-4904
Flynn ES 300/K-5
1430 Lee St 54701 715-852-3300
Adam Keeton, prin. Fax 852-3304
Lakeshore ES 400/K-5
711 Lake St 54703 715-852-3400
Colleen Miner, prin. Fax 852-3404
Locust Lane ES 300/K-5
3245 Locust Ln 54703 715-852-3700
Laura Schlichting, prin. Fax 852-3704
Longfellow ES 300/K-5
512 Balcom St 54703 715-852-3800
Sarah Lynch, prin. Fax 852-3804
Manz ES 400/K-5
1000 E Fillmore Ave 54701 715-852-3900
Heather Grant, prin. Fax 852-3904
Meadowview ES 400/K-5
4714 Fairfax St 54701 715-852-4000
Kurt Madsen, prin. Fax 852-4004
Northstar MS 600/6-8
2711 Abbe Hill Dr 54703 715-852-5100
Tim Skutley, prin. Fax 852-5104
Northwoods ES 400/K-5
3600 Northwoods Ln 54703 715-852-4100
Rob Modjeski, prin. Fax 852-4104
Prairie Ridge Early Learning S 700/PK-PK
3031 Epiphany Ln 54703 715-852-3600
Heidi White, prin. Fax 852-3604
Putnam Heights ES 400/K-5
633 W MacArthur Ave 54701 715-852-4200
Kim Koller, prin. Fax 852-4204
Robbins ES 500/K-5
3832 E Hamilton Ave 54701 715-852-4600
Andrew Thiel, prin. Fax 852-4604
Roosevelt ES 300/K-5
3010 8th St 54703 715-852-4700
Ben Dallman, prin. Fax 852-4704
Sherman ES 400/K-5
3110 Vine St 54703 715-852-4800
Fax 852-4804
South MS 800/6-8
2115 Mitscher Ave 54701 715-852-5200
Dianna Zeegers, prin. Fax 852-5204

Genesis Child Development Center 100/PK-PK
418 N Dewey St 54703 715-830-2275
Corissa McCoy, dir. Fax 830-2275
Immaculate Conception S 200/K-6
1703 Sherwin Ave 54701 715-830-2276
Renee Cassidy, prin. Fax 830-9846
Messiah Lutheran S 100/PK-8
2015 N Hastings Way 54703 715-834-2865
Seth Schaller, prin. Fax 834-8144
Regis Child Development Center 100/PK-PK
2114 Fenwick Ave 54701 715-830-2274
Julie Burhop, dir. Fax 830-2270
Regis MS 100/7-8
2100 Fenwick Ave 54701 715-830-2272
Paul Pedersen, prin. Fax 830-5461
St. James the Greater S 100/K-6
2502 11th St 54703 715-830-2277
Kelly Mechelke, prin. Fax 830-9861
St. Mark Lutheran S 100/PK-8
3307 State St 54701 715-834-5782
Peter Micheel, prin. Fax 777-5867

Eden, Fond du Lac, Pop. 864
Campbellsport SD
Supt. — See Campbellsport
Eden ES 300/PK-5
PO Box 38 53019 920-477-3291
Melinda Myers, prin. Fax 477-7203

Shepherd of the Hills S 100/K-8
W1562 County Road B 53019 920-477-3551
Amy Royes, prin. Fax 477-3030

Edgar, Marathon, Pop. 1,476
Edgar SD 600/PK-12
PO Box 196 54426 715-352-2351
Cari Guden, supt. Fax 352-3198
www.edgar.k12.wi.us
Edgar ES 300/PK-5
PO Box 198 54426 715-352-2727
Lisa Witt, prin. Fax 352-3022
Edgar MS 100/6-8
PO Box 198 54426 715-352-2352
David Duncan, prin. Fax 352-3022

St. John the Baptist S 100/PK-8
PO Box 66 54426 715-352-3000
Lynelle Cichon, prin. Fax 352-7517

Edgerton, Rock, Pop. 5,394
Edgerton SD 1,900/PK-12
200 Elm High Dr 53534 608-561-6100
Dr. Dennis Pauli, supt. Fax 884-9327
www.edgerton.k12.wi.us
Community ES 800/PK-5
100 Elm High Dr 53534 608-561-6010
Drew Wellman, prin. Fax 884-8548
Edgerton MS 400/6-8
300 Elm High Dr 53534 608-561-6030
Clark Bretthauer, prin. Fax 884-2279
Yahara Valley ES 100/1-5
100 Elm High Dr 53534 608-884-4931
Drew Wellman, prin. Fax 884-4975

Egg Harbor, Door, Pop. 201

Zion Lutheran S 50/K-8
3937 County Road V 54209 920-743-2325
Peter Lindemann, prin. Fax 743-2325

Elcho, Langlade, Pop. 333
Elcho SD 300/PK-12
PO Box 800 54428 715-275-3225
William Fisher, supt. Fax 275-4388
www.elchoschool.org
Elcho ES 200/PK-5
PO Box 800 54428 715-275-3707
Elizabeth Gruszynski, prin. Fax 275-4388

Eleva, Trempealeau, Pop. 667
Eleva-Strum SD
Supt. — See Strum
Eleva IS 100/4-6
26237 W Mondovi St 54738 715-287-4217
Marty Kempf, prin. Fax 287-3531

Elkhart Lake, Sheboygan, Pop. 964
Elkhart Lake - Glenbeulah SD 500/PK-12
PO Box 326 53020 920-876-3381
Dr. Ann Buechel-Haack, supt. Fax 876-3511
www.elgs.k12.wi.us/
Elkhart Lake - Glenbeulah ES 300/PK-8
PO Box 518 53020 920-876-3307
Debbie Hammann, prin. Fax 876-3105

Elkhorn, Walworth, Pop. 9,969
Elkhorn Area SD 3,000/K-12
3 N Jackson St 53121 262-723-3160
Jason Tadlock, supt. Fax 723-4652
www.elkhorn.k12.wi.us
Elkhorn Area MS 700/6-8
627 E Court St 53121 262-723-6800
Bryan Frost, prin. Fax 723-4967
Jackson ES 500/K-5
13 N Jackson St 53121 262-723-1200
Tammy Fisher, prin. Fax 723-3719
Tibbets ES 400/K-5
W5218 County Road A 53121 262-742-2585
Gregory Wells, prin. Fax 742-4582
West Side ES 500/K-5
222 Sunset Dr 53121 262-723-3297
Sara Stone, prin. Fax 723-6790

First Lutheran S 100/PK-8
415 Devendorf St 53121 262-723-1091
Benjamin Schramm, prin.

Elk Mound, Dunn, Pop. 858
Elk Mound Area SD 1,200/PK-12
405 University St 54739 715-879-5066
Eric Wright, supt. Fax 879-5846
www.elkmound.k12.wi.us
Elk Mound MS 400/5-8
302 University St 54739 715-879-5595
Christopher Hahn, prin. Fax 879-5886
Mound View ES 500/PK-4
455 University St 54739 715-879-5744
Eric Hanson, prin. Fax 879-5846

Ellsworth, Pierce, Pop. 3,234
Ellsworth Community SD 1,700/PK-12
300 Hillcrest St 54011 715-273-3900
Barry Cain, supt. Fax 273-5775
www.ellsworth.k12.wi.us
Ellsworth ES 400/PK-5
445 S Piety St 54011 715-273-3912
Mary Zimmerman, prin. Fax 273-6838
Ellsworth MS 500/5-8
312 Panther Dr 54011 715-273-3908
Jon Dodge, prin. Fax 273-6834

St. Francis S 100/K-5
PO Box 250 54011 715-273-4391
Chuck Buckel, prin. Fax 273-6374

Elm Grove, Waukesha, Pop. 5,869
Elmbrook SD
Supt. — See Brookfield
Pilgrim Park MS 800/6-8
1500 Pilgrim Pkwy 53122 262-785-3920
Mark Peperkorn, prin. Fax 785-3933
Tonawanda ES 400/K-5
13605 Underwood River Pkwy 53122 262-785-3950
Kristin Olson, prin. Fax 785-3956

Elm Grove Lutheran S 100/PK-8
945 Terrace Dr 53122 262-797-2970
David Koopman, prin. Fax 797-2977
St. Mary's Visitation S 300/PK-8
13000 Juneau Blvd 53122 262-782-7057
Mary Tretow, prin. Fax 782-3035

Elmwood, Pierce, Pop. 815
Elmwood SD 300/PK-12
213 S Scott St 54740 715-639-2711
Paul Blanford Ed.D., supt. Fax 639-3110
www.elmwood.k12.wi.us
Elmwood ES 200/PK-5
213 S Scott St 54740 715-639-2711
Paul Blanford Ed.D., admin. Fax 639-3110
Elmwood MS 100/6-8
213 S Scott St 54740 715-639-2721
Christopher Segerstrom, prin. Fax 639-3110

Elroy, Juneau, Pop. 1,424
Royall SD 500/PK-12
1501 Academy St 53929 608-462-2600
Mark Gruen, supt. Fax 462-2618
www.royall.k12.wi.us
Royall ES 200/PK-3
1501 Academy St 53929 608-462-2600
Darcy Uppena, prin. Fax 462-2618
Royall IS 100/4-6
1501 Academy St 53929 608-462-2600
Darcy Uppena, prin. Fax 462-2618

Endeavor, Marquette, Pop. 464
Portage Community SD
Supt. — See Portage
Endeavor ES 100/PK-5
414 S Church St 53930 608-587-2625
Salina Thistle, prin. Fax 587-2881

Ettrick, Trempealeau, Pop. 522
Galesville-Ettrick-Trempealeau SD
Supt. — See Galesville
Ettrick ES 100/PK-5
22750 Washington St 54627 608-525-4571
Pete Peterson, prin. Fax 525-8600

Evansville, Rock, Pop. 4,947
Evansville Community SD 1,700/PK-12
340 Fair St 53536 608-882-5224
Jerry Roth, supt. Fax 882-6564
www.ecsdnet.org
Leonard ES 400/PK-2
401 S 3rd St 53536 608-882-4606
Mark Schwartz, prin. Fax 882-5838
McKenna MS 400/6-8
307 S 1st St 53536 608-882-4780
Joanie Dobbs, prin. Fax 882-5744
Robinson IS 400/3-5
420 S 4th St 53536 608-882-3888
Barbara Dorn, prin. Fax 882-3889

Fall Creek, Eau Claire, Pop. 1,306
Fall Creek SD 800/PK-12
336 E Hoover Ave 54742 715-877-2123
Dr. Joseph Sanfelippo, supt. Fax 877-2911
www.fallcreek.k12.wi.us
Fall Creek ES 400/PK-5
336 E Hoover Ave 54742 715-877-3331
Brad LaPoint, prin. Fax 877-2911
Fall Creek MS 200/6-8
336 E Hoover Ave 54742 715-877-2511
Brad LaPoint, prin. Fax 877-2911

Fall River, Columbia, Pop. 1,685
Fall River SD 500/PK-12
PO Box 116 53932 920-484-3333
Dr. Michael Garrow, supt. Fax 484-3600
www.fallriver.k12.wi.us
Fall River ES 300/PK-5
PO Box 116 53932 920-484-3333
Daniel Grady, prin. Fax 484-3600

Fennimore, Grant, Pop. 2,489
Fennimore Community SD 700/PK-12
1397 9th St 53809 608-822-3243
Jane Wonderling, supt. Fax 822-3250
www.fennimore.k12.wi.us
Fennimore ES 400/PK-5
830 Madison St 53809 608-822-3285
Carmen Burkum, prin. Fax 822-3257

Fish Creek, Door
Gibraltar Area SD 600/PK-12
3924 State Highway 42 54212 920-868-3284
Tina Van Meer, supt. Fax 868-2714
www.gibraltar.k12.wi.us
Gibraltar ES 300/PK-6
3924 State Highway 42 54212 920-868-3284
Brian Annen, prin. Fax 868-2714
Gibraltar MS 100/7-8
3924 State Highway 42 54212 920-868-3284
Dr. Gereon Methner, prin. Fax 868-2714

Fitchburg, Dane, Pop. 24,633
Verona Area SD
Supt. — See Verona
Early Learning Center 50/PK-PK
5830 Devoro Rd 53711 608-845-4200
Emmett Durtsche, prin. Fax 845-4220
Savanna Oaks MS 500/6-8
5890 Lacy Rd 53711 608-845-4000
Sandy Eskrich, prin. Fax 845-4020
Stoner Prairie ES 400/K-5
5830 Devoro Rd 53711 608-845-4200
Mike Pisani, prin. Fax 845-4220

Florence, Florence, Pop. 589
Florence SD 400/PK-12
PO Box 440 54121 715-528-3215
Ben Niehaus, supt. Fax 528-5338
www.myflorence.org
Florence ES 200/PK-6
PO Box 350 54121 715-528-3262
Neil Hall, prin. Fax 528-5910
Florence MS 50/7-8
PO Box 440 54121 715-528-3217
Brandon Jerue, admin. Fax 528-5338

Fond du Lac, Fond du Lac, Pop. 42,372
Fond du Lac SD 7,400/PK-12
72 W 9th St 54935 920-929-2900
James Sebert Ed.D., supt. Fax 929-6804
www.fonddulac.k12.wi.us
Chegwin ES 400/PK-5
109 E Merrill Ave 54935 920-929-2820
Katie Moder, prin. Fax 929-7014
Evans ES 400/PK-5
140 S Peters Ave 54935 920-929-2828
Amy Rettler, prin. Fax 929-7060
Lakeshore ES 400/PK-5
706 N Prairie Rd 54935 920-929-2901
Kelly Barkovich-Smith, prin. Fax 929-6991
Parkside ES 400/PK-5
475 W Arndt St 54935 920-929-2840
Stacey Buchholz, prin. Fax 929-6156
Pier ES 500/PK-5
259 Old Pioneer Rd 54935 920-929-2868
Amy Jahn, prin. Fax 929-6910
Riverside ES 400/PK-5
396 Linden St 54935 920-929-2880
Timothy Schipper, prin. Fax 929-6912
Roberts ES 400/K-5
270 Candy Ln 54935 920-929-2835
Michelle Hagen, prin. Fax 929-6158
Rosenow ES 500/PK-5
290 Weis Ave 54935 920-929-2996
Michael Mockert, prin. Fax 929-6957
Sabish MS 500/6-8
100 N Peters Ave 54935 920-929-2800
Torrie Rochon-Luft, prin. Fax 929-2807
Theisen MS 500/6-8
525 E Pioneer Rd 54935 920-929-2850
Brad Nerat, prin. Fax 929-2854
Waters ES 400/PK-5
495 Wabash Ave 54935 920-929-2845
Catherine Daniels, prin. Fax 929-2944
Woodworth MS 500/6-8
101 Morningside Dr 54935 920-929-6900
Steven Hill, prin. Fax 929-6944

Faith Lutheran S, 55 Prairie Rd 54935 200/PK-8
Shawn Herkstroeter M.Ed., prin. 920-923-6313
Fond du Lac Christian S 100/PK-12
720 Rienzi Rd 54935 920-924-2177
Dr. Wendy Lundberg, admin. Fax 322-9459
Holyland S 100/PK-8
N9290 County Rd W 54937 920-795-4222
Dr. Rick Erickson, prin. Fax 795-4126
Redeemer Lutheran S 100/PK-8
606 Forest Ave 54935 920-921-4020
Jeremy Thiesfeldt, prin. Fax 921-4020
St. Mary's Springs Academy 200/PK-12
255 County Road K 54937 920-921-4870
Julie Shively, prin. Fax 921-2786
St. Peter's Lutheran S 100/K-8
1600 S Main St 54937 920-922-1160
Andrew Mildebrandt, prin.

Fontana, Walworth, Pop. 1,667
Fontana J8 SD 300/PK-8
450 S Main St 53125 262-275-6881
Dr. Sara Norton, admin. Fax 275-5360
www.fontana.k12.wi.us
Fontana S 300/PK-8
450 S Main St 53125 262-275-6881
Dr. Sara Norton, admin. Fax 275-5360

Fort Atkinson, Jefferson, Pop. 12,238
Fort Atkinson SD 2,800/PK-12
201 Park St 53538 920-563-7800
Dr. Lynn Brown, supt. Fax 563-7809
www.fortschools.org
Barrie ES 300/K-5
1000 Harriette St 53538 920-563-7817
Brent Torrenga, prin. Fax 563-7821
Fort Atkinson MS 600/6-8
310 S 4th St E 53538 920-563-7833
Robert Abbott, prin. Fax 563-7838
4K S PK-PK
201 Park St 53538 920-563-7800
Brent Torrenga, admin. Fax 563-7821
Luther ES 300/K-5
205 Park St 53538 920-563-7828
Dave Geiger, prin. Fax 568-7051
Purdy ES 400/PK-5
719 S Main St 53538 920-563-7822
Leigh Ann Scheuerell, prin. Fax 563-7837
Rockwell ES 300/K-5
821 Monroe St 53538 920-563-7818
Jennifer Walden, prin. Fax 568-3202

Faith Community Christian S 50/PK-12
W5949 Hackbarth Rd 53538 920-563-9954
Lacy Behringer, admin. Fax 563-4754
St. Joseph S 100/PK-8
1650 Endl Blvd 53538 920-563-3029
Kari Homb, prin. Fax 563-3150
St. Paul's Lutheran S 200/PK-8
309 Bluff St 53538 920-563-5349
William Hinz, prin. Fax 563-5061

Fountain City, Buffalo, Pop. 848
Cochrane-Fountain City SD 700/PK-12
S2770 State Road 35 54629 608-687-7771
Thomas Hiebert, supt. Fax 687-3312
www.cfc.k12.wi.us
Cochrane-Fountain City ES 400/PK-6
S2770 State Road 35 54629 608-687-4171
Steve Stoppelmoor, prin. Fax 687-6412

Fox Lake, Dodge, Pop. 1,514

St. John Lutheran S 100/PK-8
110 Edgelawn Dr 53933 920-928-3296
John Schlavensky, prin. Fax 928-3296

Fox Point, Milwaukee, Pop. 6,600
Fox Point Bayside SD 900/PK-8
7300 N Lombardy Rd 53217 414-247-4167
Dr. Robert Kobylski, supt. Fax 351-7164
www.foxbay.k12.wi.us
Stormonth ES 500/PK-4
7301 N Longacre Rd 53217 414-247-4102
Karen Grimm-Nilsen, prin. Fax 247-8970
Other Schools – See Bayside

Maple Dale-Indian Hill SD 500/PK-8
8377 N Port Washington Rd 53217 414-351-7380
Jennifer Wimmer, supt.
www.mapledale.k12.wi.us
Maple Dale S 300/3-8
8377 N Port Washington Rd 53217 414-351-7380
Tom Holtgreive, prin.
Other Schools – See River Hills

St. Eugene S 200/PK-8
7600 N Port Washington Rd 53217 414-918-1120
Rebecca Jones, prin. Fax 918-1122

Franklin, Milwaukee, Pop. 34,981
Franklin SD 4,400/PK-12
8255 W Forest Hill Ave 53132 414-529-8220
Dr. Judy Mueller, supt. Fax 529-8230
www.franklin.k12.wi.us
Country Dale ES 400/PK-6
7380 S North Cape Rd 53132 414-529-8240
Shaunna LaPlant, prin. Fax 529-8242

Forest Park MS 700/7-8
8225 W Forest Hill Ave 53132 414-529-8250
Erin King, prin. Fax 529-8249
Franklin ES 400/PK-6
7620 S 83rd St 53132 414-529-8270
Sarah Edbauer, prin. Fax 529-8274
Pleasant View ES 500/PK-6
4601 W Marquette Ave 53132 414-423-4650
Jamie Foeckler, prin. Fax 423-4653
Robinwood ES 500/PK-6
10705 W Robinwood Ln 53132 414-529-8255
Chad Nelson, prin. Fax 529-8256
Southwood Glen ES 400/PK-6
9090 S 35th St 53132 414-761-1181
Christine Cody, prin. Fax 761-1755

Indian Community S 300/PK-8
10405 W Saint Martins Rd 53132 414-525-6100
Jason Dropik, head sch Fax 525-6160
St. Martin of Tours S 100/PK-8
7933 S 116th St 53132 414-425-9200
Paul Hohl, prin. Fax 425-2527
St. Paul Lutheran S 200/PK-8
6881 S 51st St 53132 414-421-1930
Nathan Schulmeister, prin. Fax 421-4299

Franksville, Racine
North Cape SD 200/PK-8
11926 County Road K 53126 262-835-4069
John Lehnen, supt. Fax 835-2311
www.northcape.k12.wi.us
North Cape S 200/PK-8
11926 County Road K 53126 262-835-4069
John Lehnen, supt. Fax 835-2311

Norway J7 SD 100/PK-8
21016 W 7 Mile Rd 53126 414-425-6020
Carrie Reid, supt. Fax 425-6038
www.droughtschool.net
Drought ES 100/PK-8
21016 W 7 Mile Rd 53126 414-425-6020
Carrie Reid, admin. Fax 425-6038

Raymond SD 14 400/PK-8
2659 76th St 53126 262-835-2929
Joseph Dawidziak, supt. Fax 835-2087
raymond.k12.wi.us
Raymond S 400/PK-8
2659 76th St 53126 262-835-2929
Fax 835-2087

Frederic, Polk, Pop. 1,124
Frederic SD 500/PK-12
1437 Clam Falls Dr 54837 715-327-5630
Josh Robinson, admin. Fax 327-5609
www.frederic.k12.wi.us/
Frederic ES 200/PK-5
305 Birch St E 54837 715-327-4221
Kelly Steen, prin. Fax 327-8327

Fredonia, Ozaukee, Pop. 2,138
Northern Ozaukee SD 1,300/PK-12
401 Highland Dr 53021 262-692-2489
Dave Karrels, supt. Fax 692-6257
www.nosd.edu
Ozaukee ES 300/PK-5
401 Highland Dr 53021 262-692-2401
Lynn Kucharski, prin. Fax 692-2441
Ozaukee MS 200/6-8
401 Highland Dr 53021 262-692-2463
Charles Schwartz, prin. Fax 692-2313

Divine Savior S 100/K-6
PO Box 250 53021 262-692-2141
Lynn Sauer, prin. Fax 692-3085

Freedom, Outagamie
Freedom Area SD 1,600/PK-12
N4021 County Rd E, Kaukauna WI 54130
920-788-7944
Kevin Kilstofte, supt. Fax 788-7949
www.freedomschools.k12.wi.us
Freedom ES 700/PK-5
N3569 County Rd E, 920-788-7950
Tammy Lipsey, prin. Fax 788-7956
Freedom MS 400/6-8
N4021 County Rd E, Kaukauna WI 54130
920-788-7945
Ken Fisher, prin. Fax 788-7701

St. Nicholas S 100/PK-8
W2035 County Rd S, Kaukauna WI 54130
920-788-9371
Travis Gerritts, prin. Fax 788-1492

Fremont, Waupaca, Pop. 676
Weyauwega-Fremont SD
Supt. — See Weyauwega
Fremont ES 200/PK-5
PO Box 308 54940 920-867-8050
Doug Nowak, prin. Fax 867-8075

St. John Lutheran S 50/PK-8
N6199 37th Ave 54940 920-446-3836
Jacob Zimmermann, prin. Fax 446-3836

Friendship, Adams, Pop. 720
Adams-Friendship Area SD 1,600/PK-12
201 W 6th St 53934 608-339-3213
James Boebel, supt. Fax 339-6213
www.afasd.net
Other Schools – See Adams, Arkdale, Grand Marsh

Galesville, Trempealeau, Pop. 1,463
Galesville-Ettrick-Trempealeau SD 1,400/PK-12
PO Box 4000 54630 608-582-4657
Aaron Engel, supt. Fax 582-4961
www.getsd.org

Gale-Ettrick-Tremp MS 300/6-8
19650 Prairie Ridge Ln 54630 608-582-3500
Matt Wenthe, prin. Fax 582-3501
Galesville ES 300/PK-5
PO Box 4001 54630 608-582-2241
Lindsey Schubert, prin. Fax 582-4447
Other Schools – See Ettrick, Trempealeau

Genesee Depot, Waukesha
Kettle Moraine SD
Supt. — See Wales
Magee ES 300/PK-5
PO Box 37 53127 262-968-6450
Sue Sterner, prin. Fax 968-6471

St. Paul S 100/PK-8
PO Box 95 53127 262-968-3175
Ally Blonien, prin. Fax 968-5546

Genoa, Vernon, Pop. 251

St. Charles S 50/PK-8
PO Box 130 54632 608-689-2642
Aruldoss Sundaram, lead tchr. Fax 689-2811

Genoa City, Walworth, Pop. 3,006
Genoa City J2 SD 600/PK-8
PO Box 250 53128 262-279-1051
Kellie Bohn, supt. Fax 279-1052
www.genoacityschools.org
Brookwood ES 300/PK-3
PO Box 250 53128 262-279-6496
Luke Braden, prin. Fax 279-2098
Brookwood MS 300/4-8
PO Box 250 53128 262-279-1053
Pam Larson, prin. Fax 279-1052

Germantown, Washington, Pop. 19,491
Germantown SD 3,900/K-12
N104W13840 Donges Bay Rd 53022 262-253-3900
Jeff Holmes, supt. Fax 251-6999
www.germantown.k12.wi.us
County Line ES 500/K-5
W159N9939 Butternut Rd 53022 262-253-3465
Fax 253-3491
Kennedy MS 900/6-8
W160N11836 Crusader Ct 53022 262-253-3450
Susan Climer, prin. Fax 253-3499
MacArthur ES 400/K-5
W154N11492 Fond Du Lac Ave 53022
262-253-3468
Steven Williams, prin. Fax 253-3496
Rockfield ES 300/K-5
N132W18473 Rockfield Rd 53022 262-253-3472
Dr. Dana Croatt, prin. Fax 253-3497
Other Schools – See Colgate

Bethlehem Lutheran S - North 200/PK-4
N108W14290 Bel Aire Ln 53022 262-251-3120
Daryl Weber, prin. Fax 257-0407
St. Boniface S 200/PK-8
W204N11968 Goldendale Rd 53022 262-628-1955
Diana Erlandson, prin. Fax 628-1689

Gillett, Oconto, Pop. 1,370
Gillett SD 500/PK-12
PO Box 227 54124 920-855-2137
Todd Carlson, supt. Fax 855-1557
www.gillett.k12.wi.us
Gillett ES 200/PK-5
PO Box 230 54124 920-855-2119
Curt Angeli, prin. Fax 855-1502
Gillett MS 100/6-8
PO Box 227 54124 920-855-2137
Jason Dreier, prin. Fax 855-6600

Gilman, Taylor, Pop. 409
Gilman SD 400/PK-12
325 N 5th Ave 54433 715-447-8211
Wally Leipart, supt. Fax 447-8731
www.gilman.k12.wi.us
Gilman ES 200/PK-6
325 N 5th Ave 54433 715-447-8211
Wally Leipart, prin. Fax 447-8731

Gilmanton, Buffalo
Gilmanton SD 200/PK-12
PO Box 28 54743 715-946-3158
Glen Denk, supt. Fax 946-3474
www.ghs.k12.wi.us
Gilmanton ES 100/PK-4
PO Box 28 54743 715-946-3158
Kory Rud, prin. Fax 946-3474
Gilmanton MS 50/5-8
PO Box 28 54743 715-946-3158
Kory Rud, prin. Fax 946-3474

Glendale, Milwaukee, Pop. 12,578
Glendale-River Hills SD 1,000/PK-8
2600 W Mill Rd 53209 414-351-7170
Larry Smalley, supt. Fax 434-0109
www.glendale.k12.wi.us
Glen Hills MS 500/4-8
2600 W Mill Rd 53209 414-351-7160
Jeffrey Fleig, prin. Fax 351-8100
Parkway ES 500/PK-3
5910 N Milwaukee River Pkwy 53209 414-351-7190
Dr. Haydee Smith, prin. Fax 351-8103

St. John Lutheran S 100/PK-8
7877 N Port Washington Rd 53217 414-352-4150
Jennifer Comfort, prin. Fax 352-4221

Glenwood City, Saint Croix, Pop. 1,234
Glenwood City SD 700/PK-12
850 Maple St 54013 715-265-4757
Timothy Johnson, supt. Fax 265-4214
www.gcsd.k12.wi.us

Glenwood City ES 400/PK-5
850 Maple St 54013 715-265-4231
Betsy Haltinner, prin. Fax 265-7129
Glenwood City MS 200/6-8
850 Maple St 54013 715-265-4266
Patrick Gretzlock, prin. Fax 265-7129

Glidden, Ashland, Pop. 505
Chequamegon SD
Supt. — See Park Falls
Chequamegon MS 200/6-8
64 S Grant St 54527 715-264-2141
Kacey Hanson, prin. Fax 264-3413
Glidden ES 50/PK-3
64 S Grant St 54527 715-264-2141
Kacey Hanson, prin. Fax 264-3413

Goodman, Marinette, Pop. 271
Goodman-Armstrong Creek SD 100/PK-12
PO Box 160 54125 715-336-2575
Allison Space, supt. Fax 336-2576
www.goodman.k12.wi.us
Goodman-Armstrong ES 100/PK-5
PO Box 160 54125 715-336-2576
Allison Space, prin. Fax 336-2576

Grafton, Ozaukee, Pop. 11,349
Grafton SD 2,100/PK-12
1900 Washington St 53024 262-376-5400
Jeff S. Nelson, supt. Fax 376-5599
www.grafton.k12.wi.us
Grafton ES 300/PK-5
1800 Washington St 53024 262-376-5700
Karen Noel, prin. Fax 376-5727
Kennedy ES 300/PK-5
1629 11th Ave 53024 262-376-5650
Craig Gunderson, prin. Fax 376-5660
Long MS 500/6-8
700 Hickory St 53024 262-376-5800
Kevin Deering, prin. Fax 376-5810
Woodview ES 300/PK-5
600 5th Ave 53024 262-376-5750
Michael McMahon, prin. Fax 376-5760

Our Savior Lutheran S 100/PK-8
1332 Arrowhead Rd 53024 262-377-7780
Joel Grulke, prin. Fax 377-9045
St. Joseph S 200/PK-8
1619 Washington St 53024 262-375-6505
Mary Stallmann, prin. Fax 375-6509
St. Paul Lutheran S 300/PK-8
701 Washington St 53024 262-377-4659
Michael Yurk, prin. Fax 377-7808

Grand Marsh, Adams, Pop. 126
Adams-Friendship Area SD
Supt. — See Friendship
Grand Marsh ES 100/PK-5
620 County Rd E 53936 608-339-6556
Garrett Gould, prin. Fax 339-7306

Granton, Clark, Pop. 353
Granton Area SD 200/K-12
217 N Main St 54436 715-238-7292
Scott Woodington, supt. Fax 238-7288
www.granton.k12.wi.us
Granton ES 100/K-5
217 N Main St 54436 715-238-7292
Scott Woodington, prin. Fax 238-7288

Grantsburg, Burnett, Pop. 1,314
Grantsburg SD 1,400/PK-12
480 E James Ave 54840 715-463-5499
Joni Burgin, supt. Fax 463-2534
www.gk12.net/
Grantsburg ES 200/1-3
480 E James Ave 54840 715-463-2320
Elizabeth Olson, prin. Fax 463-5158
Grantsburg MS 300/4-8
480 E James Ave 54840 715-463-2455
Bill Morrin, prin. Fax 463-3209
Nelson ES 100/PK-K
480 E James Ave 54840 715-689-2421
Elizabeth Olson, prin. Fax 689-2421

Green Bay, Brown, Pop. 101,558
Ashwaubenon SD 3,300/PK-12
1055 Griffiths Ln 54304 920-492-2900
Brian Hanes, supt. Fax 492-2911
www.ashwaubenon.k12.wi.us
Cormier S & Early Learning Center 400/PK-K
2280 S Broadway 54304 920-448-2870
Maria Arena, prin Fax 448-2873
Parkview MS 700/6-8
955 Willard Dr 54304 920-492-2940
Kris Hucek, prin. Fax 492-2944
Pioneer ES 400/K-5
1360 Ponderosa Ave 54313 920-492-2920
Pete Marto, prin. Fax 492-2987
Valley View ES 700/1-5
2200 True Ln 54304 920-492-2930
Kurt Weyers, prin. Fax 492-2340

Green Bay Area SD 20,500/PK-12
PO Box 23387 54305 920-448-2000
Dr. Michelle Langenfeld, supt. Fax 448-3562
www.gbaps.org/
Baird ES 400/PK-5
539 Laverne Dr 54311 920-391-2410
Michael Sheean, prin. Fax 391-2532
Beaumont ES 300/PK-5
1505 Gatewood St 54304 920-492-2690
Jami Grall, prin. Fax 492-5565
Chappell ES 400/PK-5
205 N Fisk St 54303 920-492-2630
Kristen Worden, prin. Fax 492-5566
Danz ES 500/PK-5
2130 Basten St 54302 920-391-2440
Kelly Agen, prin. Fax 391-2533

Da Vinci S for Gifted Learners K-8
139 S Monroe Ave 54301 920-448-2135
Tammy VanDyke, prin. Fax 272-7007
Doty ES 400/PK-5
525 Longview Ave 54301 920-337-2360
Natalie Nienhuis, prin. Fax 337-2373
Early Learning Center 300/PK-K
312 Victoria St 54302 920-272-7075
Tammy Vann, prin. Fax 272-7079
Edison MS 1,100/6-8
442 Alpine Dr 54302 920-391-2450
Jonathan Wiebel, prin. Fax 391-2531
Eisenhower ES 500/PK-5
1770 Amy St 54302 920-391-2420
Annette Zernicke, prin. Fax 391-2534
Elmore ES 300/PK-5
615 Ethel Ave 54303 920-492-2615
Stacy Norman, prin. Fax 492-5567
Fort Howard ES 300/K-5
520 Dousman St 54303 920-448-2105
DeAnn Lehman, prin. Fax 448-3553
Franklin MS 700/6-8
1233 Lore Ln 54303 920-492-2670
Jackie Hauser, prin. Fax 492-5563
Froebel Garden of Early Learning 400/PK-K
3542 Finger Rd 54311 920-391-2447
Mary McCabe, prin. Fax 272-7063
Howe ES 500/PK-5
525 S Madison St 54301 920-448-2141
Amy Kallioinen, prin. Fax 448-3554
Jackson ES 400/PK-5
1306 S Ridge Rd 54304 920-492-2620
Jennifer Sipes, prin. Fax 492-5568
Jefferson ES 200/K-5
905 Harrison St 54303 920-448-2106
Kate Dolan, prin. Fax 448-3555
Keller ES 300/PK-5
1806 Bond St 54303 920-492-2685
Dan Malmberg, prin. Fax 492-5569
Kennedy ES Children's Ctr for Enginrng 300/PK-5
1754 9th St 54304 920-492-2640
Aaron Manders, prin. Fax 492-5570
King ES 400/PK-5
1601 Dancing Dunes Dr 54313 920-492-2771
Diane Stelmach, prin. Fax 492-5571
Langlade ES 300/PK-5
400 Broadview Dr 54301 920-337-2370
Jesse Brinkmann, prin. Fax 337-2374
Leopold S 500/PK-8
622 Eliza St 54301 920-448-2140
Trina Lambert, prin. Fax 448-3552
Lincoln ES 200/PK-5
105 S Buchanan St 54303 920-492-2675
Angela Hager, prin. Fax 492-5572
Lombardi MS 900/6-8
1520 S Point Rd 54313 920-492-2625
Jim Van Abel, prin. Fax 492-5564
MacArthur ES 300/PK-5
1331 Hobart Dr 54304 920-492-2680
Kim Spychalla, prin. Fax 492-5573
Martin ES 400/K-5
626 Pinehurst Ave 54302 920-391-2405
Carrie Shepherd, prin. Fax 391-2500
McAuliffe ES 600/PK-5
2071 Emerald Dr 54311 920-391-2436
Kelly Rollin, prin. Fax 391-2535
Nicolet ES 400/K-5
1309 Elm St 54302 920-448-2142
Matthew Heller, prin. Fax 448-3556
Smith S 1,000/PK-8
2765 Sussex Rd 54311 920-391-2425
William Birkholz, prin. Fax 391-2564
Sullivan ES 700/K-5
1567 Deckner Ave 54302 920-391-2470
Peggy Fisher, prin. Fax 391-2536
Tank ES 200/K-5
814 S Oakland Ave 54304 920-448-2104
Ellen VanPay, prin. Fax 448-3557
Washington MS 800/6-8
314 S Baird St 54301 920-448-2095
Dennis Christensen, prin. Fax 448-3551
Webster ES Center for Integrated Arts 300/PK-5
2101 S Webster Ave 54301 920-448-2143
Nancy Schultz, prin. Fax 448-3558
Wequiock ES 100/PK-5
3994 Wequiock Rd 54311 920-448-2477
Sarah Lange, prin. Fax 448-2234
Wilder ES 400/K-5
2590 Robinson Ave 54311 920-391-2460
Mark Allen, prin. Fax 391-2537

Howard-Suamico SD 5,900/PK-12
2706 Lineville Rd 54313 920-662-7878
Damian LaCroix, supt. Fax 662-9777
www.hssd.k12.wi.us
Bay View MS 800/7-8
1217 Cardinal Ln 54313 920-662-8196
Steve Meyers, prin. Fax 662-7979
Forest Glen ES 500/K-4
1935 Cardinal Ln 54313 920-662-7958
Angela Sorenson, prin. Fax 662-7900
4-K Collaborative 400/PK-PK
2706 Lineville Rd 54313 920-662-7941
Jennifer Trudell, coord. Fax 662-9777
Howard ES 300/K-4
631 W Idlewild Ct 54303 920-662-9700
Kristin Ashley, prin. Fax 662-9750
Lineville IS 800/5-6
2700 Lineville Rd 54313 920-662-7871
Phil Hart, prin. Fax 662-7822
Meadowbrook ES 500/K-4
720 Hillcrest Hts 54313 920-662-5000
Rebecca Zimmer, prin. Fax 662-5050
Suamico ES 300/K-4
2153 School Ln 54313 920-662-9800
Ryan Welnetz, prin. Fax 662-9888
Other Schools – See Suamico

Pulaski Community SD
Supt. — See Pulaski
Lannoye ES 200/PK-5
2007 County Road U 54313 920-865-6400
Jennifer Sommers, prin. Fax 865-6402

Father Allouez Catholic S 200/PK-4
2575 S Webster Ave 54301 920-432-5223
Kay Franz, prin. Fax 435-5139
Father Allouez Catholic S 200/5-8
333 Hilltop Dr 54301 920-336-3230
Kay Franz, prin. Fax 336-1949
Green Bay Adventist Junior Academy 50/K-10
1422 Shawano Ave 54303 920-494-2741
Kiana Roat, prin. Fax 494-6507
Green Bay Trinity Lutheran S 100/K-8
120 S Henry St 54302 920-655-4673
Kellie Meerstein, admin. Fax 468-5757
Holy Cross S 200/PK-8
3002 Bay Settlement Rd 54311 920-468-0625
Sharon Gast, prin. Fax 468-0625
Holy Family S 300/PK-8
1204 S Fisk St 54304 920-494-1931
Allison Moseng, prin. Fax 494-4942
Pilgrim Lutheran S 200/PK-8
1731 Saint Agnes Dr 54304 920-965-2244
John Schultz, prin. Fax 965-2255
Providence Academy 100/PK-12
1420 Division St 54303 920-592-0890
St. Bernard S 500/PK-8
2020 Hillside Ln 54302 920-468-5026
Crystal Blahnik, prin. Fax 468-3478
St John Paul II S, 1204 S Fisk St 54304 K-8
Frank Nicely, head sch 920-497-7042
St. John the Baptist S 300/PK-8
2561 Glendale Ave 54313 920-434-3822
Andrew Mulloy, prin. Fax 434-5016
St. Joseph S 100/PK-8
991 Pilgrim Way 54304 920-497-7085
Pamela Otto, prin. Fax 497-7240
St. Mark Lutheran S 200/PK-8
1167 Kenwood St 54304 920-494-9113
Kyle Gut, prin. Fax 494-3028
St. Paul Lutheran S 100/PK-8
514 S Clay St 54301 920-435-8468
Nate Reich, prin.
St. Thomas More S 100/PK-8
650 S Irwin Ave 54301 920-432-8242
Olgamar Amor, prin. Fax 432-1562

Greendale, Milwaukee, Pop. 13,859
Greendale SD 2,600/PK-12
6815 Southway 53129 414-423-2700
Dr. Gary Kiltz, supt. Fax 423-2723
www.greendale.k12.wi.us
Canterbury ES 300/K-5
7000 Enfield Ave 53129 414-423-2770
Michael Mullen, prin. Fax 423-2994
College Park ES 300/K-5
5701 W College Ave 53129 414-423-2850
Kerry Owens-Bur, prin. Fax 423-2852
Greendale MS 600/6-8
6800 Schoolway 53129 414-423-2800
John Weiss, prin. Fax 423-2806
Highland View ES 400/PK-5
5900 S 51st St 53129 414-423-2750
Tracy Flater, prin. Fax 423-0592

St. Alphonsus S 400/PK-8
6000 W Loomis Rd 53129 414-421-1760
Pat Wadzinski, prin. Fax 421-8744

Greenfield, Milwaukee, Pop. 36,124
Greenfield SD 3,900/PK-12
4850 S 60th St 53220 414-855-2050
Lisa Elliott, supt. Fax 855-2051
www.greenfield.k12.wi.us
Edgewood ES 400/PK-5
4711 S 47th St 53220 414-281-5750
Marget Boyd, prin. Fax 281-3909
Glenwood ES 400/PK-5
3550 S 51st St 53220 414-545-2280
Steven Newcomer, prin. Fax 545-5626
Greenfield MS 800/6-8
3200 W Barnard Ave 53221 414-282-4700
Brad Iding, prin. Fax 282-1017
Maple Grove ES 500/PK-5
6921 W Cold Spring Rd 53220 414-541-0600
Kenneth McCormick, prin. Fax 541-8070
Other Schools – See Milwaukee

Whitnall SD 2,400/PK-12
5000 S 116th St 53228 414-525-8400
Dr. Lisa Olson, supt. Fax 525-8401
www.whitnall.com
Whitnall MS 500/6-8
5025 S 116th St 53228 414-525-8650
Laura Jennaro, prin. Fax 525-8651
Other Schools – See Hales Corners

Our Father's Lutheran S 100/PK-8
6025 S 27th St 53221 414-282-7500
Nathan Wingfield, prin. Fax 282-9737
St. Jacobi Lutheran S 200/PK-8
8605 W Forest Home Ave 53228 414-425-2040
Brian Mensching, prin. Fax 425-0583
St. John the Evangelist S 100/K-8
8500 W Coldspring Rd 53228 414-321-8540
Mary Laidlaw-Otto, prin. Fax 321-4450

Green Lake, Green Lake, Pop. 956
Green Lake SD 300/PK-12
PO Box 369 54941 920-294-6411
Mary Allen, supt. Fax 294-6589
www.glsd.k12.wi.us
Green Lake ES 100/PK-6
PO Box 369 54941 920-294-6411
Gina Baxter, prin. Fax 294-6589

Peace Lutheran S 100/K-8
435 Walker Ave 54941 920-294-3509
Todd Stoltz, prin.

Greenleaf, Brown, Pop. 603

Zion Lutheran S 100/K-8
7373 County Rd W 54126 920-864-2349
Richard Muchka, prin.
Zion Lutheran S 100/PK-8
8374 County Rd W 54126 920-864-2468
Doug Jacoby, prin. Fax 864-2684

Greenville, Outagamie
Hortonville SD
Supt. — See Hortonville
Greenville ES 800/PK-4
W6822 Greenridge Dr 54942 920-757-7160
David Harris, prin. Fax 757-6972
Greenville MS 600/5-8
N1450 Fawn Ridge Dr 54942 920-757-7140
Travis Lawrence, prin. Fax 757-7141
North Greenville ES K-4
N2468 Learning Way 54942 920-757-7030
Janna Cochrane, prin. Fax 757-7031

Immanuel Evangelical Lutheran S 200/PK-8
W7265 School Rd 54942 920-757-6606
Richard Huebner, prin. Fax 757-1151
St. Mary S 200/PK-8
N2387 Municipal Dr 54942 920-757-6555
Debra Fuller, prin. Fax 757-6560

Greenwood, Clark, Pop. 1,021
Greenwood SD 400/PK-12
PO Box 310 54437 715-267-6101
Todd Felhofer, supt. Fax 267-6113
www.greenwood.k12.wi.us/
Greenwood ES 200/PK-6
PO Box 310 54437 715-267-7211
Todd Fischer, prin. Fax 267-7209

St. Mary S 50/1-6
PO Box 129 54437 715-267-6477
Jeannine Raycher, prin. Fax 267-4421

Gresham, Shawano, Pop. 545
Gresham SD 200/PK-12
501 Schabow St 54128 715-787-3211
Newell Haffner, supt. Fax 787-3951
www.gresham.k12.wi.us/
Gresham S 200/PK-8
501 Schabow St 54128 715 787 3211
Newell Haffner, admin. Fax 787-3951

Hales Corners, Milwaukee, Pop. 7,616
Whitnall SD
Supt. — See Greenfield
Edgerton ES 400/K-5
5145 S 116th St 53130 414-525-8900
Chris D'Acquisto, prin. Fax 525-8901
Hales Corners ES 600/K-5
11319 W Godsell Ave 53130 414-525-8800
Lori Komas, prin. Fax 525-8801

Hales Corners Lutheran S 600/PK-8
12300 W Janesville Rd 53130 414-529-6702
Albert Amling, supt. Fax 529-6710
St. Mary Parish S 400/PK-8
9553 W Edgerton Ave 53130 414-425-3100
Maria Schram, prin. Fax 425-6270

Hammond, Saint Croix, Pop. 1,895
St. Croix Central SD 1,600/PK-12
PO Box 118 54015 715-796-4500
Tim Widiker, supt. Fax 796-4510
www.scc.k12.wi.us
St. Croix Central MS 400/5-8
PO Box 118 54015 715-796-2256
Pete Nusbaum, prin. Fax 796-2460
Other Schools – See Roberts

Hartford, Washington, Pop. 14,070
Erin SD 300/PK-8
6901 County Road O 53027 262-673-3720
Dr. Keith Kriewaldt, admin. Fax 673-2659
www.erinschool.org
Erin S 300/PK-8
6901 County Road O 53027 262-673-3720
Joannie Kalina, prin. Fax 673-2659

Hartford J1 SD 1,800/PK-8
402 W Sumner St 53027 262-673-3155
Dr. Mark Smits, admin. Fax 673-3548
www.hartfordjt1.k12.wi.us
Central MS 500/6-8
1100 Cedar St 53027 262-673-8040
Joseph Viste, prin. Fax 673-7596
Lincoln ES 600/PK-5
755 S Rural St 53027 262-673-2100
Neil Hanlon, prin. Fax 673-0148
Rossman ES 700/PK-5
600 Highland Ave 53027 262-673-3300
Doan Bui, prin. Fax 673-3543

Slinger SD
Supt. — See Slinger
Addison ES 400/PK-5
5050 Indian Dr 53027 262-644-8037
Joel Dziedzic, prin. Fax 644-1936

Peace Lutheran S 200/PK-8
1025 Peace Lutheran Dr 53027 262-673-3811
Benjamin Washburn, prin. Fax 673-3897
St. Kilian S 200/PK-8
245 High St 53027 262-673-3081
Jenny Trimberger, prin. Fax 673-0412

Hartland, Waukesha, Pop. 8,992
Hartland-Lakeside J3 SD 1,200/PK-8
800 E North Shore Dr 53029 262-369-6700
Dr. Glenn Schilling, supt. Fax 369-6755
www.hartlake.org
Hartland North ES 400/PK-2
232 Church St 53029 262-369-6710
Heather Grindatti, prin. Fax 369-6711
Hartland S of Community Learning 100/3-5
651 E Imperial Dr 53029 262-369-6720
David Risch, prin. Fax 369-6722
Hartland South ES 200/3-5
651 E Imperial Dr 53029 262-369-6720
David Risch, prin. Fax 369-6722
North Shore MS 300/6-8
800 N Shore Dr 53029 262-369-6767
Michele Schmidt, prin. Fax 369-6766

Lake Country SD 500/PK-8
1800 Vettelson Rd 53029 262-367-3606
Mark Lichte, admin. Fax 367-3205
www.mylakecountryschool.org
Lake Country S 500/PK-8
1800 Vettelson Rd 53029 262-367-3606
Mark Lichte, admin. Fax 367-3205

Swallow SD 600/PK-8
W299N5614 County Rd E 53029 262-367-2000
Dr. Melissa Thompson, supt. Fax 367-5014
www.swallowschool.org
Swallow S 600/PK-8
W299N5614 County Rd E 53029 262-367-2000
Kyle Moore, prin. Fax 367-5014

Divine Redeemer Lutheran S 300/PK-8
31385 Hill St 53029 262-367-3664
Michael Oldenburg, prin. Fax 367-0824
St. Charles S 200/PK-8
526 Renson Rd 53029 262-367-2040
Laura Anderson, prin. Fax 367-6960
University Lake S 300/PK-12
PO Box 290 53029 262-367-6011
Ron Smyczek, head sch Fax 367-3146
Zion Lutheran S 50/PK-8
1023 E Capitol Dr 53029 262-367-3617
Dr. John Freese, prin.

Hatley, Marathon, Pop. 568
D.C. Everest Area SD
Supt. — See Weston
Hatley ES 100/PK-5
417 Emmonsville Rd 54440 715-446-3336
Craig Miller, prin. Fax 446-3171

Haugen, Barron, Pop. 276
Rice Lake Area SD
Supt. — See Rice Lake
Haugen ES 100/PK-4
615 5th St W 54841 715-234-7341
Natalie Springer, prin. Fax 236-7598

Hayward, Sawyer, Pop. 2,245
Hayward Community SD 1,900/PK-12
15930 W 5th St 54843 715-634-2619
Craig Olson, supt. Fax 634-3560
www.hayward.k12.wi.us
Hayward IS 400/3-5
15930 W 5th St 54843 715-634-2619
Ronda Lee, prin. Fax 934-2244
Hayward MS 400/6-8
15930 W 5th St 54843 715-634-2619
Hugh Duffy, prin. Fax 634-9953
Hayward PS 500/PK-2
15930 W 5th St 54843 715-634-2619
Ronda Lee, prin. Fax 934-2246

Hazel Green, Grant, Pop. 1,238
Southwestern Wisconsin SD 600/PK-12
PO Box 368 53811 608-854-2261
John Costello, supt. Fax 854-2305
www.swsd.k12.wi.us
Southwestern Wisconsin S 400/PK-8
PO Box 368 53811 608-854-2261
Angela Barth, prin. Fax 854-2305

St. Joseph S 100/PK-8
780 County Road Z 53811 608-748-4442
Barbara Wills, prin. Fax 748-5201

Helenville, Jefferson, Pop. 247

St. Peters Lutheran S 100/PK-8
PO Box 86 53137 262-582-3010
Craig Winkler, prin.

Hilbert, Calumet, Pop. 1,124
Hilbert SD 400/PK-12
PO Box 390 54129 920-853-3558
Anthony Sweere, supt. Fax 853-7030
www.hilbert.k12.wi.us
Hilbert ES 200/PK-4
PO Box 390 54129 920-853-3558
Amy Schmitz, prin. Fax 853-7030
Hilbert MS 100/5-8
PO Box 390 54129 920-853-3558
Anthony Sweere, prin. Fax 853-7030

St. Mary S 50/K-6
PO Box 249 54129 920-853-3216
Chandra Sromek, prin. Fax 853-3560
Trinity Lutheran S 100/PK-8
N6081 W River Rd 54129 920-853-3134
Susan Boeck, prin.

Hillsboro, Vernon, Pop. 1,405
Hillsboro SD 500/PK-12
PO Box 526 54634 608-489-2221
Curt Bisarek, supt. Fax 489-2811
www.hillsboro.k12.wi.us
Hillsboro ES 300/PK-5
PO Box 526 54634 608-489-2224
Melissa Herek, prin. Fax 489-3358

Pulaski Community SD
Supt. — See Pulaski
Hillcrest ES 300/PK-5
4193 Hillcrest Dr, 920-272-6900
Kris Wells, prin. Fax 272-6905

Holcombe, Chippewa, Pop. 266
Lake Holcombe SD 100/PK-12
27331 262nd Ave 54745 715-595-4241
Jeffrey Mastin, supt. Fax 595-6383
www.lakeholcombe.k12.wi.us
Lake Holcombe S 100/PK-12
27331 262nd Ave 54745 715-595-4241
Mark Porter, prin. Fax 595-6383

Hollandale, Iowa, Pop. 285
Pecatonica Area SD
Supt. — See Blanchardville
Pecatonica ES 200/PK-5
PO Box 128 53544 608-967-2372
Kyle Walsh, prin. Fax 967-1172

Holmen, LaCrosse, Pop. 8,875
Holmen SD 3,900/PK-12
1019 McHugh Rd 54636 608-526-6610
Dr. Kristin Mueller, supt. Fax 526-1333
www.holmen.k12.wi.us
Evergreen ES 400/K-5
510 Long Coulee Rd 54636 608-526-9080
Rachel Fawver, prin. Fax 526-9540
Holmen MS 800/6-8
502 N Main St 54636 608-526-3391
Ryan Vogler, prin. Fax 526-6716
Holmen Public Preschool 300/PK-PK
500 E Wall St 54636 608-526-1381
Sue Eilland, prin. Fax 526-1393
Prairie View ES 400/K-5
1201 Newport Ln 54636 608-526-1600
Patrice Tronstad, prin. Fax 526-1695
Sand Lake ES 500/K-5
3600 Sandlake Rd 54636 608-781-0974
Natalie Morgan, prin. Fax 781-2809
Viking ES 400/K-5
500 E Wall St 54636 608-526-3316
Bonnie Striegel, prin. Fax 526-9482

Horicon, Dodge, Pop. 3,609
Horicon SD 700/PK-12
611 Mill St 53032 920-485-2898
Richard Appel, supt. Fax 485-3601
www.horicon.k12.wi.us
Horicon JHS 100/7-8
841 Gray St 53032 920-485-4441
Teresa Graven, prin. Fax 485-3244
Van Brunt ES 400/PK-6
611 Mill St 53032 920-485-4423
Lisa Sawyer, prin. Fax 485-4318

Mountain Top Christian Academy 50/PK-12
W3941 State Road 33 53032 920-485-6630
Stacy Nummerdor, admin. Fax 485-0236
St. Stephen Lutheran S 100/PK-8
505 N Palmatory St 53032 920-485-6687
Joel M. Bahr, prin. Fax 485-2545

Hortonville, Outagamie, Pop. 2,685
Hortonville SD 3,400/PK-12
PO Box 70 54944 920-779-7921
Todd Timm, supt. Fax 779-7903
www.hasd.org
Hortonville ES 600/PK-4
240 Warner St 54944 920-779-7911
Larry Sikowski, prin. Fax 779-7915
Hortonville MS 400/5-8
220 Warner St 54944 920-779-7922
Steven Gromala, prin. Fax 779-7923
Other Schools – See Greenville

Bethlehem Evangelical Lutheran S 100/PK-8
PO Box 250 54944 920-779-6761
Mike Schulz, prin. Fax 779-4320

Houlton, Saint Croix, Pop. 374
Hudson SD
Supt. — See Hudson
Houlton ES 200/K-5
70 Houlton School Cir 54082 715-377-3850
Sue Hellmers, prin. Fax 549-5707

Howards Grove, Sheboygan, Pop. 3,170
Howards Grove SD 800/K-12
403 Audubon Rd 53083 920-565-4454
Christopher Peterson, supt. Fax 565-4461
www.hgsd.k12.wi.us
Howards Grove MS 300/5-8
506 Kennedy Ave 53083 920-565-4452
Andy Hansen, prin. Fax 565-4460
Northview ES 300/K-4
902 Tyler Rd 53083 920-565-4457
Jason Cole, prin. Fax 565-4458

St. Paul's Lutheran S 100/PK-8
441 Millersville Ave 53083 920-565-3780
Chad Marohn, prin. Fax 565-3781

Hubertus, Washington
Friess Lake SD 200/PK-8
1750 State Road 164 53033 262-628-2380
John Engstrom, admin. Fax 628-2546
www.friesslakeschool.org
Friess Lake S 200/PK-8
1750 State Road 164 53033 262-628-2380
John Engstrom, admin. Fax 628-2546

Crown of Life Lutheran S 100/PK-8
1292 Tally Ho Trl 53033 262-628-2550
Eric Troge, prin.
St. Gabriel S 100/PK-8
3733 Hubertus Rd 53033 262-628-1711
Steve Hamilton, prin. Fax 628-0280

Hudson, Saint Croix, Pop. 12,505
Hudson SD 5,600/PK-12
644 Brakke Dr 54016 715-377-3700
Dr. Nick Ouellette, supt. Fax 377-3726
www.hudsonraiders.org
Hudson MS 1,300/6-8
1300 Carmichael Rd 54016 715-377-3820
Jim Dalluhn, prin. Fax 377-3821
Hudson Prairie ES 500/PK-5
1400 Carmichael Rd 54016 715-377-3860
Joe Behnke, prin. Fax 377-3861
North Hudson ES 300/PK-5
510 Lemon St N 54016 715-377-3870
Dolf Schmidt, prin. Fax 377-3871
River Crest ES 600/PK-5
535 County Road F 54016 715-377-3890
Kathleen Coppenbarger, prin. Fax 377-3891
Rock ES 600/K-5
340 13th St S 54016 715-377-3840
Amy Hamborg, prin. Fax 377-3841
Willow River ES 400/K-5
1118 4th St 54016 715-377-3880
Kimberly Osterhues, prin. Fax 377-3881
Other Schools – See Houlton

St. Patrick S 300/PK-8
403 Saint Croix St 54016 715-386-3941
Dan Bell, prin. Fax 381-5125
Trinity Academy 300/PK-8
1205 6th St 54016 715-386-9349
Alison Johnson, dir. Fax 386-0137

Hurley, Iron, Pop. 1,529
Hurley SD 300/PK-12
5503 W Range View Dr 54534 715-561-4900
Christopher Patritto, supt. Fax 561-4953
www.hurley.k12.wi.us
Hurley S 300/PK-12
5503 W Range View Dr 54534 715-561-4900
Melissa Oja, prin. Fax 561-4953

Hustisford, Dodge, Pop. 1,121
Hustisford SD 400/PK-12
PO Box 326 53034 920-349-8109
Heather Cramer Ph.D., supt. Fax 349-3716
www.hustisford.k12.wi.us
Hustis ES 200/PK-5
PO Box 386 53034 920-349-3228
Margaret Bell, prin. Fax 349-3530

Bethany Lutheran S 50/PK-8
PO Box 518 53034 920-349-3244
William Fuerstenau, prin. Fax 349-3245

Independence, Trempealeau, Pop. 1,329
Independence SD 400/PK-12
23786 Indee Blvd 54747 715-985-3172
Barry Schmitt, supt. Fax 985-2303
www.indps.k12.wi.us
Independence ES 200/PK-8
23786 Indee Blvd 54747 715-985-3172
Rob Vanderloop, prin. Fax 985-2303

SS. Peter & Paul S 100/PK-8
36100 Osseo Rd 54747 715-985-3719
Tom Burkhalter, prin. Fax 985-2649

Iola, Waupaca, Pop. 1,297
Iola-Scandinavia SD 700/PK-12
450 Division St 54945 715-445-2411
Raymond Przekurat Ed.D., supt. Fax 445-4468
www.iola.k12.wi.us
Iola Scandinavia ES 400/PK-6
450 Division St 54945 715-445-2411
Stacey Wester, prin. Fax 445-4468

Iron Ridge, Dodge, Pop. 925

St. Matthew's Lutheran S 50/PK-8
308 Herman St 53035 920-625-6600
Kevin Lorge, prin.

Iron River, Bayfield, Pop. 747
Maple SD
Supt. — See Maple
Iron River ES 100/K-5
PO Box 128 54847 715-372-4334
Steven Gustafson, prin. Fax 372-4319

Ixonia, Jefferson, Pop. 1,596
Oconomowoc Area SD
Supt. — See Oconomowoc
Ixonia ES 200/K-4
N8425 North St 53036 262-560-8400
Stacy Yearling, prin. Fax 560-8418

St. Pauls Evangelical Lutheran S 100/K-8
W1956 Gopher Hill Rd 53036 920-261-5589
Jon Lindemann, prin. Fax 261-5589

Jackson, Washington, Pop. 6,685
West Bend SD
Supt. — See West Bend
Jackson ES 400/K-4
W204N16850 Jackson Dr 53037 262-335-5474
Leonard Hanson, prin. Fax 677-1594

Davids Star Lutheran S 100/PK-8
2740 Davids Star Dr 53037 262-677-2412
Timothy Gustafson, prin. Fax 677-8960

Morning Star Lutheran S 200/PK-8
N171W20131 Highland Rd 53037 262-677-9196
James Brohn, prin. Fax 677-9772

Janesville, Rock, Pop. 62,455
Janesville SD 10,400/PK-12
527 S Franklin St, 608-743-5000
Steven Pophal, supt. Fax 743-5110
www.janesville.k12.wi.us
Adams ES 400/PK-5
1138 E Memorial Dr 53545 608-743-6300
Dana Simmons, prin. Fax 743-6337
Edison MS 700/6-8
1649 S Chatham St 53546 608-743-5900
James Lemire, prin. Fax 743-5910
Franklin MS 600/6-8
450 N Crosby Ave, 608-743-6000
Charles Urness Ph.D., prin. Fax 743-6010
Harrison ES 300/K-5
760 Princeton Rd 53546 608-743-6400
Jessica Grandt-Turke, prin. Fax 743-6437
Jackson ES 300/PK-5
441 W Burbank Ave 53546 608-743-6500
Kristen Moisson, prin. Fax 743-6510
Jefferson ES 400/PK-5
1831 Mount Zion Ave 53545 608-743-6600
Kurt Krueger, prin. Fax 743-6610
Kennedy ES 400/K-5
3901 Randolph Rd 53546 608-743-7500
Jennifer Fanning, prin. Fax 743-7560
Lincoln ES 400/PK-5
1821 Conde St 53546 608-743-6700
Shawn Galvin, prin. Fax 743-6710
Madison ES 400/PK-5
331 N Grant Ave, 608-743-6800
Stephanie Filter, prin. Fax 743-6810
Marshall MS 900/6-8
25 S Pontiac Dr 53545 608-743-6200
Synthia Taylor, prin. Fax 743-6210
Monroe ES 400/PK-5
55 S Pontiac Dr 53545 608-743-6900
Sally Pope, prin. Fax 743-6937
P4J 500/PK-PK
527 S Franklin St, 608-743-5038
Angela Lynch, coord. Fax 743-5130
Roosevelt ES 400/PK-5
316 S Ringold St 53545 608-743-7000
Olga Hanna, prin. Fax 743-7010
Van Buren ES 400/PK-5
1515 Lapham St 53546 608-743-7100
Stephanie Pajerski, prin. Fax 743-7110
Washington ES 400/PK-5
811 N Pine St, 608-743-7200
Robert Conner, prin. Fax 743 7210
Wilson ES 300/PK-5
465 Rockport Rd, 608-743-7300
Ashley Wright, prin. Fax 743-7310

Milton SD
Supt. — See Milton
Consolidated ES 100/K-3
4838 N County Road F 53545 608-868-9595
Sarah Stuckey, prin. Fax 752-5136
Harmony ES 300/PK-3
4243 E Rotamer Rd 53546 608-868-9360
Sarah Stuckey, prin. Fax 868-5664

Rock County Christian ES 100/K-6
5122 S Driftwood Dr 53546 608-757-1000
Barb Waldner, prin. Fax 757-1058
Rock Prairie Montessori S 100/PK-6
5246 E Rotamer Rd 53546 608-868-4844
Martha Carver, head sch Fax 868-5965
St. John Vianney S 300/PK-8
1250 E Racine St 53545 608-752-6802
Christine Silha, prin. Fax 752-3095
St. Mary S 100/PK-8
307 E Wall St 53545 608-754-5221
Matthew Parish, prin. Fax 754-1871
St. Matthew's Lutheran S 100/PK-8
709 Milton Ave 53545 608-752-1304
Kevin Proeber, prin. Fax 757-9076
St. Patrick S 100/PK-8
305 Lincoln St, 608-752-2031
Nicole May, prin. Fax 754-0357
St. Paul's Lutheran S 300/PK-8
210 S Ringold St 53545 608-754-4471
Rob Lunak, prin. Fax 754-4050
St. William S 200/PK-8
1822 Ravine St, 608-755-5184
Diane Rebout, prin. Fax 755-5190

Jefferson, Jefferson, Pop. 7,891
Jefferson SD 1,900/PK-12
206 S Taft Ave 53549 920-675-1000
Mark Rollefsonm, supt. Fax 675-1020
www.sdoj.org
East ES 400/PK-5
120 S Sanborn Ave 53549 920-675-1400
Jake Wichman, prin. Fax 675-1420
Jefferson MS 400/6-8
501 S Taft Ave 53549 920-675-1300
David Wallace, prin. Fax 675-1320
West ES 300/K-5
900 W Milwaukee St 53549 920-675-1200
Mike Howard, prin. Fax 675-1220
Other Schools – See Sullivan

St. John's Evangelical Lutheran S 100/PK-8
232 E Church St 53549 920-674-2922
Peter Lemke, prin. Fax 674-5477
St. John the Baptist S 200/PK-8
333 E Church St 53549 920-674-5821
Terry Tinkle, prin. Fax 674-2521

Jim Falls, Chippewa, Pop. 235
Chippewa Falls Area USD
Supt. — See Chippewa Falls
Jim Falls ES 100/K-5
13643 198th St 54748 715-720-3260
Jenny Sarauer, prin. Fax 720-3262

Johnson Creek, Jefferson, Pop. 2,707
Johnson Creek SD 600/PK-12
PO Box 39 53038 920-541-4800
Michael Garvey Ph.D., supt. Fax 541-4852
www.johnsoncreek.k12.wi.us/
Johnson Creek ES 300/PK-4
PO Box 39 53038 920-541-4801
Kris Blakeley, prin. Fax 541-4851

Juda, Green, Pop. 357
Juda SD 300/PK-12
N2385 Spring St 53550 608-934-5251
Traci Davis, supt. Fax 934-5254
www.judaschool.com
Juda ES 200/PK-8
N2385 Spring St 53550 608-934-5251
Traci Davis, prin. Fax 934-5254

Junction City, Portage, Pop. 436
Stevens Point Area SD
Supt. — See Stevens Point
Kennedy ES 200/PK-6
616 W 2nd St 54443 715-345-5614
Clover Schmitt, prin. Fax 345-5606

Juneau, Dodge, Pop. 2,802
Dodgeland SD 800/PK-12
401 S Western Ave 53039 920-386-4404
Annette Thompson, supt. Fax 386-4498
www.dodgeland.k12.wi.us
Dodgeland ES 400/PK-5
401 S Western Ave 53039 920-386-4404
Jessica Johnson, prin. Fax 386-2602
Dodgeland MS 200/6-8
401 S Western Ave 53039 920-386-4404
Jeffrey Sauer, prin. Fax 386-0345

St. John's Lutheran S 100/PK-8
402 S Main St 53039 920-386-4644
Richard Cody, prin. Fax 386-9660

Kansasville, Racine
Brighton SD 1 200/K-8
1200 248th Ave 53139 262-878-2191
Dr. Penny Boileau, supt. Fax 878-2869
www.brightonschool.net
Brighton S 200/K-8
1200 248th Ave 53139 262-878-2191
Dr. Penny Boileau, admin. Fax 878-2869

Dover SD 1 100/PK-8
4101 S Beaumont Ave 53139 262-878-3773
Matt Stratton, admin. Fax 878-1231
kansasvillegradeschool.weebly.com
Kansasville S 100/PK-8
4101 S Beaumont Ave 53139 262-878-3773
Matt Stratton, admin. Fax 878-1231

Kaukauna, Outagamie, Pop. 15,244
Kaukauna Area SD 3,900/PK-12
1701 County Road CE 54130 920-766-6100
Mark Duerwaechter, admin. Fax 766-6104
www.kaukauna.k12.wi.us
Haen ES 300/1-4
1130 Haen Dr 54130 920-766-6134
Holly Magness, prin. Fax 766-6138
Quinney ES 400/2-4
2601 Sullivan Ave 54130 920-766-6116
Stacy Knapp, prin. Fax 766-6122
River View MS 1,100/5-8
101 Oak St 54130 920-766-6111
Daniel Joseph, prin. Fax 766-6109
Tanner ES 600/PK-1
2500 Fieldcrest Dr 54130 920-766-6150
Elizabeth Thoreson, prin. Fax 766-6550

St. Ignatuis S, 2020 Doty St 54130 100/PK-8
Larry Konetzke, hdmstr. 920-766-0186

Kenosha, Kenosha, Pop. 96,606
Kenosha SD 21,900/PK-12
3600 52nd St 53144 262-359-6300
Dr. Sue Savaglio-Jarvis, supt. Fax 359-7672
www.kusd.edu
Bain S of Creative Arts 500/PK-5
2600 50th St 53140 262-359-2300
Cherise Easley, prin. Fax 359-2400
Bain S of Dual Language 300/PK-5
2600 50th St 53140 262-359-2300
Betzaida Gomez, prin. Fax 359-2400
Bose ES 300/K-5
1900 15th St 53140 262-359-4044
Margaret Zei, prin. Fax 359-4005
Brass Community ES 500/PK-5
6400 15th Ave 53143 262-359-8000
Joel Kaufmann, prin. Fax 359-8050
Bullen MS 800/6-8
2804 39th Ave 53144 262-359-4460
Andy Baumgart, prin. Fax 359-4487
Chavez Learning Station 200/PK-PK
6300 27th Ave 53143 262-359-6078
Luanne Rohde, admin. Fax 359-6286
Forest Park ES 400/K-5
6810 45th Ave 53142 262-359-6319
Jody Cascio, prin. Fax 359-6170
Frank ES 400/K-5
1816 57th St 53140 262-359-6324
Heather Connolly, prin. Fax 359-6393
Grant ES 300/PK-5
1716 35th St 53140 262-359-6346
Shebaniah Muhammad, prin. Fax 359-6672
Grewenow ES 400/K-5
7714 20th Ave 53143 262-359-6362
Joseph Sellenheim, prin. Fax 359-7706
Harvey ES 300/PK-5
2012 19th Ave 53140 262-359-4040
Ursula Hamilton-Perry, prin. Fax 359-4020
Jefferson ES 300/K-5
1832 43rd St 53140 262-359-6390
Kathy Walsh, prin. Fax 359-7578
Jeffery ES 300/K-5
4011 87th St 53142 262-359-2100
Kurt Johnson, prin. Fax 359-2033
Lance MS 1,000/6-8
4515 80th St 53142 262-359-2240
Chad Dahlk, prin. Fax 359-2184
Lincoln MS 800/6-8
6729 18th Ave 53143 262-359-6296
Star Daley, prin. Fax 359-5966
Mahone MS 1,100/6-8
6900 60th St 53144 262-359-8100
Terri Huck, prin. Fax 359-6851
McKinley ES 400/PK-5
5520 32nd Ave 53144 262-359-6002
Theresa Giampietro, prin. Fax 359-7641
Nash ES 600/K-5
6801 99th Ave 53142 262-359-3500
Brett Basley, prin. Fax 359-3550
Roosevelt ES 400/K-5
3322 Roosevelt Rd 53142 262-359-6097
Jered Kotarak, prin. Fax 359-6107
Somers ES 500/PK-5
1245 72nd Ave 53144 262-359-3200
Wendy LaLonde, prin. Fax 359-3212
Southport ES 500/PK-5
723 76th St 53143 262-359-6309
Jacqueline Mellott-Graje, prin. Fax 359-5952
Stocker ES 500/PK-5
6315 67th St 53142 262-359-2143
April Nelson, prin. Fax 359-2012
Strange ES 500/K-5
5414 49th Ave 53144 262-359-6024
Jonathan Bar-Din, prin. Fax 359-6247
Vernon ES 400/PK-5
8518 22nd Ave 53143 262-359-2113
Alicia Hribal, prin. Fax 359-2169
Washington MS 600/6-8
811 Washington Rd 53140 262-359-6291
Curtiss Tolefree, prin. Fax 359-6056
Wilson ES 200/K-5
4520 33rd Ave 53144 262-359-6094
Yolanda Jackson-Lewis, prin. Fax 359-5993
Other Schools – See Pleasant Prairie

Paris J1 SD 300/PK-8
1901 176th Ave 53144 262-859-2350
Roger Gahart, supt. Fax 859-2641
www.paris.k12.wi.us
Paris ES 300/PK-8
1901 176th Ave 53144 262-859-2350
Roger Gahart, prin. Fax 859-2641

All Saints Catholic S North Campus 200/K-8
4400 22nd Ave 53140 262-652-2771
Dr. Jacqueline Lichter, prin. Fax 652-6179
All Saints Catholic S South Campus 300/K-8
7400 39th Ave 53142 262-925-4000
Dr. Jacqueline Lichter, prin. Fax 694-6048
Bethany Lutheran S 100/K-8
2100 75th St 53143 262-654-3234
Stephen Schultz, prin. Fax 654-3501
Christian Life S 800/PK-12
10700 75th St 53142 262-694-3900
Rev. Susan Nelson, supt. Fax 694-3312
Friedens Lutheran S 100/PK-8
5043 20th Ave 53140 262-652-3451
Bruce Babler, prin. Fax 654-1565
Kenosha Montessori S 100/PK-6
2401 69th St 53143 262-654-6950
Jo Ann Miller-Cole, prin.
St. Joseph Catholic Academy 100/PK-5
7207 14th Ave 53143 262-656-7360
Robert Freund, prin. Fax 654-1615

Keshena, Menominee, Pop. 1,238
Menominee Indian SD 800/PK-12
PO Box 1330 54135 715-799-3824
Wendell Waukau, supt. Fax 799-4659
www.misd.k12.wi.us
Keshena PS 500/PK-5
PO Box 1410 54135 715-799-3828
Laura Duggan, prin. Fax 799-1342
Other Schools – See Neopit

Kewaskum, Washington, Pop. 3,967
Kewaskum SD 1,800/PK-12
PO Box 37 53040 262-626-8427
James Smasal, supt. Fax 626-2961
www.kewaskumschools.org
Farmington ES 200/K-5
8736 Boltonville Rd 53040 262-626-3102
Jacob Flood, prin. Fax 692-6863
Kewaskum ES 500/PK-5
PO Box 127 53040 262-626-8427
Jody Heipp, prin. Fax 626-4151
Kewaskum MS 400/6-8
PO Box 432 53040 262-626-8427
Julie Skelton, prin. Fax 626-4214

Holy Trinity S 100/PK-8
PO Box 464 53040 262-626-2603
Jodi Casetta, prin. Fax 626-8863
St. Lucas Lutheran S 100/PK-8
PO Box 86 53040 262-626-2680
David Stoltz, prin. Fax 626-8451

Kewaunee, Kewaunee, Pop. 2,918
Kewaunee SD 1,000/PK-12
915 3rd St 54216 920-388-3230
Karen Treml, supt. Fax 388-5174
www.kewaunee.k12.wi.us

Kewaunee ES 500/PK-5
921 3rd St 54216 920-388-2458
Tracy Ledvina, prin. Fax 388-5696
Kewaunee MS 200/6-8
921 3rd St 54216 920-388-2458
Kacy Rohr, prin. Fax 388-5696

Holy Rosary S 100/PK-8
519 Kilbourn St 54216 920-388-2431
Kris Stollberg, prin. Fax 388-3822

Kiel, Manitowoc, Pop. 3,708
Kiel Area SD 1,300/PK-12
PO Box 201 53042 920-894-2266
Brad Ebert, supt. Fax 894-5100
www.kiel.k12.wi.us
Kiel MS 400/5-8
PO Box 197 53042 920-894-2264
Dr. Deborah Sixel, prin. Fax 894-5121
Zielanis ES 500/PK-4
PO Box 217 53042 920-894-2265
Chad Ramminger, prin. Fax 894-5104

Divine Savior S 100/PK-8
423 Fremont St 53042 920-894-3533
Kerry Sievert, prin. Fax 894-4959
Trinity Lutheran S 100/PK-8
387 Cemetery Rd 53042 920-894-3012
Adam Glodowski, prin. Fax 894-4742

Kieler, Grant, Pop. 494

Holy Ghost/Immaculate Conception S 50/4-8
PO Box 129 53812 608-568-7220
Rita Hesseling, prin. Fax 568-3811

Kimberly, Outagamie, Pop. 6,394
Kimberly Area SD
Supt. — See Combined Locks
4K Center for Literacy PK-PK
614 E Kimberly Ave 54136 920-423-4190
Sean Fitzgerald, prin. Fax 423-4191
Gerritts MS 700/7-8
545 S John St 54136 920-788-7905
Eric Brinkmann, prin. Fax 788-7914
Mapleview IS 400/5-6
125 E Kimberly Ave 54136 920-788-7910
John Schultz, prin. Fax 788-7760
Westside ES 400/K-4
746 W 3rd St 54136 920-739-3578
Jonathan Peterson, prin. Fax 739-6212

Knapp, Dunn, Pop. 458
Menomonie Area SD
Supt. — See Menomonie
Knapp ES 100/K-5
110 South St 54749 715-665-2131
Kristin Humphrey, prin. Fax 665-2344

Kohler, Sheboygan, Pop. 2,103
Kohler SD 800/PK-12
333 Upper Rd 53044 920-803-7200
Quynh Trueblood, supt. Fax 459-2930
www.kohlerpublicschools.org/
Kohler ES 500/PK-5
333 Upper Rd 53044 920-803-7210
Lisa Greene, prin. Fax 459-2930
Kohler MS 200/6-8
333 Upper Rd 53044 920-803-7202
Timothy Brown, prin. Fax 459-2930

Krakow, Oconto, Pop. 346
Pulaski Community SD
Supt. — See Pulaski
Fairview ES 100/PK-5
2840 State Highway 32 54137 920-899-6300
Nichole Napralla, prin. Fax 899-6302

Lac du Flambeau, Vilas, Pop. 1,932
Lac du Flambeau SD 1 500/PK-8
2899 State Highway 47 S 54538 715-588-3838
Larry Ouimette, supt. Fax 588-2618
www.ldf.k12.wi.us/
Lac du Flambeau S 500/PK-8
2899 State Highway 47 S 54538 715-588-3838
Ronald Grams, prin. Fax 588-2618

La Crosse, LaCrosse, Pop. 50,284
La Crosse SD 6,800/PK-12
807 East Ave S 54601 608-789-7600
Randy Nelson, supt. Fax 789-7960
www.lacrosseschools.org/
Emerson ES 400/PK-5
2101 Campbell Rd 54601 608-789-7990
Brian Oberweiser, prin. Fax 789-7171
Hamilton Early Learning Center 100/PK-5
1111 7th St S 54601 608-789-7695
Steve Michaels, prin. Fax 789-7030
Hintgen ES 400/PK-5
3505 28th St S 54601 608-789-7767
Amy Oliver, prin. Fax 789-7173
La Crosse Offsite Preschool 100/PK-PK
807 East Ave S 54601 608-789-7000
Curt Rees, prin. Fax 789-7960
Lincoln MS 400/6-8
510 9th St S 54601 608-789-7780
Melissa Murray, prin. Fax 789-7181
Logan MS 400/6-8
1450 Avon St 54603 608-789-7740
Jay Pica, prin. Fax 789-7754
Longfellow MS 500/6-8
1900 Denton St 54601 608-789-7670
Penny Reedy, prin. Fax 789-7975
Northside ES 300/PK-5
1611 Kane St 54603 608-789-7970
Laura Huber, prin. Fax 789-0035
North Woods International ES 400/PK-5
2541 Sablewood Rd 54601 608-789-7000
Sandy Brauer, prin. Fax 789-7010
Southern Bluffs ES 400/PK-5
4010 Sunnyside Dr 54601 608-789-7020
Lisa Schreiner, prin. Fax 789-7176
Spence ES 400/PK-5
2150 Bennett St 54601 608-789-7773
Shelley Shirel, prin. Fax 789-7174
State Road ES 300/K-5
3900 Pammel Creek Rd 54601 608-789-7690
Curt Rees, prin. Fax 789-7084
Summit Environmental S 400/PK-5
1800 Lakeshore Dr 54603 608-789-7980
Dirk Hunter, prin. Fax 789-7175

Aquinas MS South Campus 100/7-8
315 11th St S 54601 608-784-0156
Denise Ring, prin. Fax 784-0229
Blessed Sacrament S 200/3-6
2404 King St 54601 608-782-5564
Kay Berra, prin. Fax 782-7765
Cathedral S 100/PK-2
1319 Ferry St 54601 608-782-5998
Patty Gallagher-Kosmatka, prin. Fax 784-9933
First Evangelical Lutheran S 100/PK-8
520 West Ave S 54601 608-784-1050
Matt Meitner, prin. Fax 785-2417
Immanuel Lutheran S 100/K-8
806 Saint Paul St 54603 608-784-5712
Jonathan Mumm, prin.
Mt. Calvary-Grace Lutheran S 50/PK-8
1614 Park Ave 54601 608-784-8223
Jon Biedenbender, prin. Fax 784-7305
Providence Academy 100/PK-12
716 Windsor St 54603 608-784-6167
Amy Strom, hdmstr. Fax 784-1070

Ladysmith, Rusk, Pop. 3,376
Ladysmith SD 800/PK-12
1700 Edgewood Ave E 54848 715-532-5277
Paul Uhren, supt. Fax 532-7445
ladysmith.k12.wi.us
Ladysmith ES 300/PK-5
624 E 6th St S 54848 715-532-5464
Andrew Grimm, prin. Fax 532-3475
Ladysmith MS 200/6-8
1700 Edgewood Ave E 54848 715-532-5252
Robert Lecheler, prin. Fax 532-7455

Our Lady of Sorrows S 100/PK-8
105 Washington Ave 54848 715-532-3232
Megan Dieckman, prin. Fax 532-7368

La Farge, Vernon, Pop. 740
La Farge SD 200/PK-12
301 W Adams St 54639 608-625-0107
Shawn Donovan, supt. Fax 625-0118
www.lafarge.k12.wi.us/
La Farge ES 100/PK-5
301 W Adams St 54639 608-625-2400
Angela Egge, prin. Fax 625-0152
La Farge MS 50/6-8
301 W Adams St 54639 608-625-2400
Angela Egge, prin. Fax 625-0152

Lake Delton, Sauk, Pop. 2,882
Wisconsin Dells SD
Supt. — See Wisconsin Dells
Lake Delton ES 200/PK-5
PO Box 280 53940 608-253-4391
Felipe Armijo, prin. Fax 254-6765

Lake Geneva, Walworth, Pop. 7,583
Geneva J4 SD 200/PK-8
N2575 Snake Rd 53147 262-248-3816
Jeffrey Klaisner, supt. Fax 248-7021
www.woodsschool.com
Woods S 200/PK-8
N2575 Snake Rd 53147 262-248-3816
Jeffrey Klaisner, prin. Fax 248-7021

Lake Geneva J1 SD 2,200/PK-8
208 E South St 53147 262-348-1000
James Gottinger, supt. Fax 248-9704
www.lakegenevaschools.com
Central-Denison ES 700/PK-3
900 Wisconsin St 53147 262-348-4000
Becky Buhler, prin. Fax 248-7321
Eastview ES 300/4-5
507 Sage St 53147 262-348-6000
Tami Martin, prin. Fax 248-0456
Lake Geneva MS 700/6-8
600 N Bloomfield Rd 53147 262-348-3000
Anne Heck, prin. Fax 348-3092
Star Center ES 400/PK-5
W1380 Lake Geneva Hwy 53147 262-348-7000
Lidalyn Tennessen, prin. Fax 279-7938

Linn J4 SD 100/PK-8
W3490 Linton Rd 53147 262-248-4067
Dr. Mark Pienkos, admin. Fax 248-1050
www.traverschool.org
Traver S 100/PK-8
W3490 Linton Rd 53147 262-248-4067
Allyssa Andersen, prin. Fax 248-1050

Linn J6 SD 100/PK-8
W4094 S Lakeshore Dr 53147 262-248-4120
Dr. Samantha Polek, supt. Fax 248-5133
www.linn6.k12.wi.us
Reek S 100/PK-8
W4094 S Lakeshore Dr 53147 262-248-4120
Dr. Samantha Polek, prin. Fax 248-5133

First Evangelical Lutheran S 100/PK-8
1101 Logan St 53147 262-248-3374
Steve Haag, prin. Fax 248-3317
Mount Zion Christian S 50/PK-8
2330 State Road 120 53147 262-248-5255
Rob Micklinghoff, prin. Fax 248-7648
St. Francis DeSales S 200/PK-8
130 W Main St 53147 262-248-2778
Eric Gallagher, prin. Fax 248-7860

Lake Mills, Jefferson, Pop. 5,657
Lake Mills Area SD 1,500/PK-12
120 E Lake Park Pl 53551 920-648-2215
Pamela Streich, supt. Fax 648-5795
www.lakemills.k12.wi.us
Lake Mills ES 700/PK-4
155 E Pine St 53551 920-648-2338
Amanda Thompson, prin. Fax 648-5490
Lake Mills MS 400/5-8
318 College St 53551 920-648-2358
Jennifer Bower, prin. Fax 648-8928

St. Paul Evangelical Lutheran S 200/PK-8
1530 S Main St 53551 920-648-2918
Steven Gartner, prin. Fax 648-2250

Lancaster, Grant, Pop. 3,854
Lancaster Community SD 900/PK-12
925 W Maple St 53813 608-723-2175
Rob Wagner, supt. Fax 723-6397
www.lancastersd.k12.wi.us
Lancaster MS 200/6-8
802 E Elm St 53813 608-723-6425
Mark Uppena, prin. Fax 723-6731
Winskill ES 500/PK-5
861 W Maple St 53813 608-723-4066
Leah Whitford, prin. Fax 723-2608

St. Clement S 100/K-6
330 W Maple St 53813 608-723-7474
Josh Jensen, prin. Fax 723-4424

Land O Lakes, Vilas
Northland Pines SD
Supt. — See Eagle River
Northland Pines/Land O Lakes ES 100/PK-4
6485 Town Hall Rd 54540 715-547-3619
Carie Brock, prin. Fax 547-3903

Lannon, Waukesha, Pop. 1,100
Hamilton SD
Supt. — See Sussex
Lannon ES 300/K-5
7145 N Lannon Rd 53046 262-255-6106
Brian Balfany, prin. Fax 255-4185

St. John Lutheran S 100/PK-8
20813 W Forest View Dr 53046 262-251-2940
Bill Tomlin, prin. Fax 251-3612

Laona, Forest, Pop. 574
Laona SD 200/PK-12
5216 Forest Ave 54541 715-674-2143
Larry Palubicki, supt. Fax 674-5904
www.laona.k12.wi.us
Robinson ES 100/PK-6
5216 Forest Ave 54541 715-674-3801
Larry Palubicki, prin. Fax 674-5904

La Valle, Sauk, Pop. 367
SD of Reedsburg
Supt. — See Reedsburg
Ironton-La Valle ES 100/K-3
PO Box 329 53941 608-985-7716
Paul Bierman, prin. Fax 985-7719

Lena, Oconto, Pop. 558
Lena SD 400/PK-12
304 E Main St 54139 920-829-5703
Ben Pytleski, supt. Fax 829-5122
www.lena.k12.wi.us
Lena ES 200/PK-5
304 E Main St 54139 920-829-5959
Ben Pytleski, prin. Fax 829-5122
Lena MS 100/6-8
304 E Main St 54139 920-829-5244
James Torzala, prin. Fax 829-5122

Maranatha SDA S 50/1-8
5100 McCarthy Rd 54139 920-834-5247

Little Chute, Outagamie, Pop. 10,339
Little Chute Area SD 1,500/PK-12
325 Meulemans St Ste A 54140 920-788-7605
David Botz, supt. Fax 788-7603
www.littlechute.k12.wi.us
Little Chute ES 600/PK-4
901 Grand Ave 54140 920-788-7610
James Neubert, prin. Fax 788-7847
Little Chute IS 200/5-6
325 Meulemans St Ste B 54140 920-788-7607
Lori Van Handel, admin. Fax 788-7615
Little Chute MS 200/7-8
325 Meulemans St Ste B 54140 920-788-7607
Lori Van Handel, prin. Fax 788-7615

St. John Nepomucene S 300/PK-8
328 Grand Ave 54140 920-788-9082
Kevin Flottmeyer, prin. Fax 788-7046

Livingston, Iowa, Pop. 663
Iowa-Grant SD 800/PK-12
498 County Road IG 53554 608-943-6311
Linda Erickson, supt. Fax 943-8438
www.igs.k12.wi.us
Iowa-Grant S 500/PK-8
498 County Road IG 53554 608-943-6313
Robyn Oberfoell, prin. Fax 943-8438

Lodi, Columbia, Pop. 3,022
Lodi SD 1,500/PK-12
115 School St 53555 608-592-3851
Charles Pursell, supt. Fax 592-3852
www.lodi.k12.wi.us

Lodi ES 400/1-5
101 School St 53555 608-592-3842
Lyle Hendrickson, prin. Fax 592-2507
Lodi MS 400/6-8
900 Sauk St 53555 608-592-3854
Joe Prosek, prin. Fax 592-1035
Lodi PS 100/PK-K
103 Pleasant St 53555 608-592-3855
Sherri Endres-Lovell, prin. Fax 592-2496

Loganville, Sauk, Pop. 299
SD of Reedsburg
Supt. — See Reedsburg
Loganville ES 100/K-3
S5864 State Road 23 53943 608-727-3401
Tammy Hayes, prin. Fax 727-2715

Lomira, Dodge, Pop. 2,408
Lomira SD 1,000/PK-12
PO Box 919 53048 920-269-4396
Robert Lloyd, admin. Fax 269-4996
www.lomira.k12.wi.us/
Lomira ES 300/PK-5
PO Box 919 53048 920-269-4396
Sandy Schaefer, prin. Fax 269-4996
Lomira MS 300/6-8
PO Box 919 53048 920-269-4396
Robert Lloyd, prin. Fax 269-4996
Other Schools – See Theresa

St. John Lutheran S 100/PK-8
558 S Water St 53048 920-269-4514
Greg Obermiller, prin. Fax 269-7364

Loyal, Clark, Pop. 1,258
Loyal SD 500/PK-12
PO Box 10 54446 715-255-8552
Cale Jackson, supt. Fax 255-8553
www.loyal.k12.wi.us
Loyal ES 300/PK-6
PO Box 250 54446 715-255-8561
Christopher Lindner, prin. Fax 255-8553
Loyal JHS 100/7-8
PO Box 10 54446 715-255-8511
Christopher Lindner, prin. Fax 255-8553

St. Anthony S 50/PK-6
PO Box 189 54446 715-255-8636
Patrice Ann Billings, prin. Fax 255-8636

Luck, Polk, Pop. 1,101
Luck SD 500/PK-12
810 S 7th St 54853 715-472-2152
Cory Hinkel, supt. Fax 472-2159
www.lucksd.k12.wi.us
Luck ES 300/PK-6
810 S 7th St 54853 715-472-2153
Jason Harelson, prin. Fax 472-2159

Luxemburg, Kewaunee, Pop. 2,502
Luxemburg-Casco SD 1,900/PK-12
PO Box 70 54217 920-845-2391
Glenn Schlender, supt. Fax 845-5871
www.luxcasco.k12.wi.us
Luxemburg-Casco IS 500/3-6
PO Box 70 54217 920-845-2371
Jolene Hussong, prin. Fax 845-2232
Luxemburg-Casco PS 400/PK-2
PO Box 220 54217 920-845-2315
Peter Kline, prin. Fax 845-2503
Other Schools – See Casco

St. Mary S 100/K-6
1406 Main St 54217 920-845-2224
Marc Vandenhouten, prin. Fax 845-5581
St. Paul Lutheran S 100/PK-8
N4118 County Road AB 54217 920-845-2095
Rev. Daniel Olson, prin. Fax 845-9075

Lyndon Station, Juneau, Pop. 495
Mauston SD
Supt. — See Mauston
Lyndon Station ES 100/K-4
PO Box 405 53944 608-666-2341
Michele Yates-Wickus, prin. Fax 666-2510

Mc Farland, Dane, Pop. 7,692
Mc Farland SD 4,200/PK-12
5101 Farwell St 53558 608-838-3169
Andrew Briddell Ph.D., admin. Fax 838-3074
www.mcfarland.k12.wi.us
Elvehjem Early Learning Center 200/PK-K
6009 Johnson St 53558 608-838-3146
Kelley Novak, prin. Fax 838-4503
Indian Mound MS 500/6-8
6330 Exchange St 53558 608-838-8980
Erin Tarnutzer, prin. Fax 838-4588
Mc Farland PS 300/1-2
6103 Johnson St 53558 608-838-3115
Kelley Novak, prin. Fax 838-4612
Waubesa IS 500/3-5
5605 Red Oak Trl 53558 608-838-7667
Sue Murphy, prin. Fax 838-4613

Madison, Dane, Pop. 226,807
Madison Metro SD 25,300/PK-12
545 W Dayton St 53703 608-663-1879
Jennifer Cheatham, supt. Fax 204-0342
www.madison.k12.wi.us
Allis ES 400/K-5
4201 Buckeye Rd 53716 608-204-1056
Sue Abplanalp, prin. Fax 204-0364
Black Hawk MS 400/6-8
1402 Wyoming Way 53704 608-204-4360
Kenya Walker, prin. Fax 204-0368
Chavez ES 600/K-5
3502 Maple Grove Dr 53719 608-442-2000
Linda Allen, prin. Fax 442-2100
Cherokee Heights MS 500/6-8
4301 Cherokee Dr 53711 608-204-1240
Kevin Brown, prin. Fax 204-0378
Crestwood ES 400/K-5
5930 Old Sauk Rd 53705 608-204-1120
Britta Hanson, prin. Fax 204-0384
Elvehjem ES 500/PK-5
5106 Academy Dr 53716 608-204-1400
Sarah Larson, prin. Fax 204-0396
Emerson ES 400/PK-5
2421 E Johnson St 53704 608-204-2000
Karen Kepler, prin. Fax 204-0401
Falk ES 300/K-5
6323 Woodington Way 53711 608-204-2180
Grace Okoli, prin. Fax 204-0479
Franklin ES 400/PK-2
305 W Lakeside St 53715 608-204-2292
Sylla Zarov, prin. Fax 204-0405
Glendale ES 500/PK-5
1201 Tompkins Dr 53716 608-204-2400
Benjamin Ketterer, prin. Fax 204-0409
Gompers ES 300/K-5
1502 Wyoming Way 53704 608-204-4520
Sarah Chaja, prin. Fax 204-0413
Hamilton MS 800/6-8
4801 Waukesha St 53705 608-204-4620
Jessica Taylor, prin. Fax 204-0417
Hawthorne ES 400/PK-5
3344 Concord Ave 53714 608-204-2500
Beth Lehman, prin. Fax 204-0423
Huegel ES 500/K-5
2601 Prairie Rd 53711 608-204-3100
Aubree Potter, prin. Fax 204-0427
Jefferson MS 600/6-8
101 S Gammon Rd 53717 608-663-6403
Issac Kirkwood, prin. Fax 442-2193
Kennedy ES 600/K-5
221 Meadowlark Dr 53714 608-204-3420
Nancy Caldwell, prin. Fax 204-0431
Lake View ES 300/K-5
1802 Tennyson Ln 53704 608-204-4040
Kristi Kloos, prin. Fax 204-4099
Lapham ES 300/PK-2
1045 E Dayton St 53703 608-204-4140
Tammy Thompson-Kapp, prin. Fax 204-0447
Leopold ES 700/K-5
2602 Post Rd 53713 608-204-4240
Karine Sloan, prin. Fax 204-0451
Lincoln ES 400/3-5
909 Sequoia Trl 53713 608-204-4900
Deborah Hoffman, prin. Fax 204-0455
Lindbergh ES 200/K-5
4500 Kennedy Rd 53704 608-204-6500
Salvador Velasco, prin. Fax 204-0459
Lowell ES 400/PK-5
401 Maple Ave 53704 608-204-6600
John Burkholder, prin. Fax 204-0463
Marquette ES 200/3-5
1501 Jenifer St 53703 608-204-3220
Pam Wilson, prin. Fax 204-0467
Mendota ES 300/K-5
4002 School Rd 53704 608-204-7840
Carlettra Stanford, prin. Fax 204-0471
Midvale ES 500/PK-2
502 Caromar Dr 53711 608-204-6700
Becky Galvan, prin. Fax 204-0475
Muir ES 500/PK-5
6602 Inner Dr 53705 608-663-8170
Andrea Kreft, prin. Fax 442-2200
O'Keeffe MS 400/6-8
510 S Thornton Ave 53703 608-204-6820
Tony Dugas, prin. Fax 204-0561
Orchard Ridge ES 300/K-5
5602 Russett Rd 53711 608-204-2320
Becky Kundert, prin. Fax 204-0483
Randall ES 400/3-5
1802 Regent St 53726 608-204-3300
John Wallace, prin. Fax 204-0487
Sandburg ES 400/K-5
4114 Donald Dr 53704 608-204-7940
Brett Wilfrid, prin. Fax 204-0491
Schenk ES 400/PK-5
230 Schenk St 53714 608-204-1500
Emmett Durtschi, prin. Fax 204-0539
Sennett MS 600/6-8
502 Pflaum Rd 53716 608-204-1920
Tremayne Clardy, prin. Fax 204-0495
Sherman MS 400/6-8
1610 Ruskin St 53704 608-204-2100
Kristin Foreman, prin. Fax 204-0501
Shorewood Hills ES 500/K-5
1105 Shorewood Blvd 53705 608-204-1200
Anu Ebbe, prin. Fax 204-0505
Spring Harbor MS 300/6-8
1110 Spring Harbor Dr 53705 608-204-1100
Pam Waite, prin. Fax 204-0509
Stephens ES 500/K-5
120 S Rosa Rd 53705 608-204-1900
Sarah Galanter-Guziewski, prin. Fax 204-0516
Thoreau ES 400/PK-5
3870 Nakoma Rd 53711 608-204-6940
Kathleen Costello, prin. Fax 204-0519
Toki MS 500/6-8
5606 Russett Rd 53711 608-204-4740
Nicole Schaefer, prin. Fax 204-0523
Van Hise ES 400/K-5
4747 Waukesha St 53705 608-204-4800
Peg Keeler, prin. Fax 204-0419
Whitehorse MS 500/6-8
218 Schenk St 53714 608-204-4480
Deborah Ptak, prin. Fax 204-0538
Other Schools – See Verona

Abundant Life Christian S 300/K-12
4901 E Buckeye Rd 53716 608-221-1520
Doug Butler, prin. Fax 221-8572
Blessed Sacrament S 300/PK-8
2112 Hollister Ave 53726 608-233-6155
Steve Castrogiovanni, prin. Fax 238-4220
Charis Classical Academy 50/K-9
PO Box 5642 53705 608-250-0551
Kim Nielsen, head sch
Eagle S Of Madison 200/K-8
5454 Gunflint Trl 53711 608-273-0309
Eastside Evangelical Lutheran S 100/PK-8
2310 Independence Ln 53704 608-244-3045
Benjamin Rank, prin. Fax 244-2168
Edgewood Campus S 300/PK-8
829 Edgewood College Dr 53711 608-663-4100
Anne Palzkill, prin. Fax 663-4101
High Point Christian S 300/PK-8
7702 Old Sauk Rd 53717 608-836-7170
Dr. Charles Moore, prin. Fax 824-9135
Holy Cross Lutheran S 100/PK-8
2670 Milwaukee St 53704 608-249-3101
Chris Poetter, prin. Fax 249-0601
Kids Express Learning Center 200/PK-K
3276 High Point Rd 53719 608-845-3245
Dr. Sandra Dahl, dir. Fax 848-3028
Madison Waldorf S 100/PK-8
6510 Schroeder Rd 53711 608-270-9005
Ginny Buhr, admin. Fax 270-9337
Our Lady Queen of Peace S 500/K-8
418 Holly Ave 53711 608-231-4580
Mary Jo Vitale, prin. Fax 231-4589
Our Redeemer Lutheran S 100/PK-8
1701 McKenna Blvd 53711 608-274-2830
Randy Peck, prin. Fax 274-7606
St. Dennis S 200/K-8
409 Dempsey Rd 53714 608-246-5121
Matt Beisser, prin. Fax 246-5137
St. James S 200/PK-8
1204 Saint James Ct 53715 608-268-9935
Michael McCabe, prin.
St. Maria Goretti S 500/PK-8
5405 Flad Ave 53711 608-271-7551
Elizabeth Adams Young, prin. Fax 275-6625
Three Angels Christian S 50/PK-8
900 Femrite Dr 53716 608-222-5775
Jayme Denis, prin. Fax 222-2047
Wingra S 100/K-8
718 Gilmore St 53711 608-238-2525
Debbie Millon, head sch Fax 238-6316

Manawa, Waupaca, Pop. 1,362
Manawa SD 700/PK-12
800 Beech St 54949 920-596-2525
Dr. Melanie Oppor, supt. Fax 596-5308
www.manawaschools.org
Manawa ES 400/PK-6
800 Beech St 54949 920-596-5700
Michelle Pukita, prin. Fax 596-5339

St. Paul Lutheran S 100/PK-8
750 Depot St 54949 920-596-2815
Brian Elmhorst, prin. Fax 596-2851

Manitowish Waters, Vilas
North Lakeland SD 200/PK-8
12686 County Road K 54545 715-543-8417
Brent Jelinski, supt. Fax 543-8868
www.nles.us
North Lakeland S 200/PK-8
12686 County Road K 54545 715-543-8417
Brent Jelinski, prin. Fax 543-8868

Manitowoc, Manitowoc, Pop. 33,258
Manitowoc SD 5,200/PK-12
PO Box 1657 54221 920-686-4777
Mark Holzman, supt. Fax 686-4780
www.manitowocpublicschools.org
Franklin ES 400/1-6
800 S 35th St 54220 920-663-9510
Nathan Brunnbauer, prin. Fax 663-9511
Jackson ES 400/1-6
1201 N 18th St 54220 920-663-9520
Duane Simmons, prin. Fax 663-9521
Jefferson ES 400/1-6
1415 Division St 54220 920-663-9530
Stacie Cihlar, prin. Fax 663-9531
Madison ES 200/1-6
701 N 4th St 54220 920-663-9540
Matthew Malcore, prin. Fax 663-9541
Monroe ES 400/1-6
2502 S 14th St 54220 920-663-9550
William Bertsche, prin. Fax 663-9551
Riverview K 700/PK-K
4400 Michigan Ave 54220 920-663-9500
Catherine Burish, prin. Fax 663-9501
Stangel ES 400/1-6
1002 E Cedar Ave 54220 920-663-9560
Heidi Schroderus, prin. Fax 663-9561

Bethany Evangelical Lutheran S 100/K-8
3209 Meadow Ln 54220 920-684-9777
Aaron Krause, prin. Fax 684-9587
First German Evangelical Lutheran S 100/PK-8
1025 S 8th St 54220 920-682-7021
Ryan Klatt, prin. Fax 682-3538
Immanuel Evangelical Lutheran S 100/PK-8
916 Pine St 54220 920-684-3404
David Wilson, prin. Fax 684-6461
St. Francis of Assisi ES 200/PK-5
1408 Waldo Blvd 54220 920-683-6892
Kyle Kapinos, prin. Fax 683-6889
St. Francis of Assisi MS 200/6-8
2109 Marshall St 54220 920-683-6884
Steve Thiele, prin. Fax 683-6882
St. John Evangelical Lutheran S 100/PK-8
7531 English Lake Rd Ste A 54220 920-758-2633
Dave Backus, prin. Fax 758-3418

Maple, Douglas
Maple SD 1,400/PK-12
PO Box 188 54854 715-363-2431
Dr. Sara Croney, supt. Fax 363-2191
www.nw-tigers.org
Other Schools – See Iron River, Poplar

Marathon, Marathon, Pop. 1,520
SD of Marathon City 700/PK-12
PO Box 37 54448 715-443-2226
Richard Parks, supt. Fax 443-2611
www.marathon.k12.wi.us
Marathon Area ES 300/PK-5
PO Box 457 54448 715-443-2538
Sarah Budny, prin. Fax 443-2230

St. Mary S 200/K-8
PO Box 102 54448 715-443-3430
Joseph Koch, prin. Fax 443-3045

Maribel, Manitowoc, Pop. 349

St. John Lutheran S 100/PK-8
14323 Maribel Rd 54227 920-863-2850
Lance Waege, prin. Fax 863-2850

Marinette, Marinette, Pop. 10,850
Marinette SD 2,100/PK-12
2139 Pierce Ave 54143 715-735-1400
Dr. Wendy Dzurick, supt. Fax 732-7930
www.marinette.k12.wi.us
Garfield ES 200/1-4
1615 Carney Blvd 54143 715-735-2400
Cassandra Schultz, prin. Fax 732-3431
Marinette MS 600/5-8
1011 Water St 54143 715-735-1500
Michael Whisler, prin. Fax 732-7939
Merryman ES 200/1-4
611 Elizabeth Ave 54143 715-735-2500
Kathy Kostrova, prin. Fax 732-3433
Park ES 200/1-4
1225 Hockridge St 54143 715-735-2600
Beverly Schewe, prin. Fax 732-3434
Sunrise Early Learning Center 300/PK-K
115 Hancock St 54143 715-735-2700
Hollie Jersey, coord.

St. Thomas Aquinas Academy 100/PK-12
1200 Main St 54143 715-735-7481
Mike Cattani, prin. Fax 735-3375
Trinity Lutheran S 100/PK-8
1216 Colfax St 54143 715-732-2956
Nathan Deering, prin.

Marion, Waupaca, Pop. 1,253
Marion SD 500/PK-12
1001 N Main St 54950 715-754-2511
James Bena, supt. Fax 754-4508
www.marion.k12.wi.us
Marion ES 300/PK-6
1001 N Main St 54950 715-754-4501
James Bena, prin. Fax 754-4508

Markesan, Green Lake, Pop. 1,472
Markesan SD 700/PK-12
PO Box 248 53946 920-398-2373
Duane Bark, supt. Fax 398-3281
www.markesan.k12.wi.us
Markesan ES 300/PK-5
PO Box 248 53946 920-398-4301
Connie Hynnek, prin. Fax 398-3281
Markesan MS 200/6-8
PO Box 248 53946 920-398-4101
John Koopman, prin. Fax 398-3281

Marshall, Dane, Pop. 3,813
Marshall SD 1,200/PK-12
PO Box 76 53559 608-655-3466
Dr. Barb Sramek, supt. Fax 655-4481
www.marshall.k12.wi.us
Marshall Early Learning Center 300/PK-2
PO Box 76 53559 608-655-1588
Rich Peters, prin. Fax 655-1592
Marshall ES 300/3-6
PO Box 76 53559 608-655-4403
Becca Stein, prin. Fax 655-3425
Marshall MS 200/7-8
PO Box 76 53559 608-655-1571
Lisa Blochwitz, prin. Fax 655-1591

Marshfield, Wood, Pop. 18,924
Marshfield SD 3,800/PK-12
1010 E 4th St 54449 715-387-1101
Dr. Deirdre Wells, supt. Fax 387-0133
www.marshfieldschools.org
Grant ES 700/PK-6
425 W Upham St 54449 715-384-4747
Jeff Damrau, prin. Fax 384-2727
Lincoln ES 300/K-6
1621 S Felker Ave 54449 715-387-1296
Brooke Bargender, prin. Fax 389-9402
Madison ES 300/K-6
510 N Palmetto Ave 54449 715-384-8181
Dr. Tiffany Scheer, prin. Fax 486-1291
Marshfield MS 600/7-8
900 E 4th St 54449 715-387-1249
Mike Nicksic, prin. Fax 384-9269
Nasonville ES 300/K-6
11044 US Highway 10 54449 715-676-3611
Charmaine Ulrich, prin. Fax 676-8040
Washington ES 400/PK-6
1112 W 11th St 54449 715-387-1238
Peg Geegan, prin. Fax 389-9302

Columbus MS 100/6-8
710 S Columbus Ave 54449 715-387-1177
Steven VanWhye, prin. Fax 384-4535
Immanuel Lutheran S 100/PK-8
604 S Chestnut Ave 54449 715-384-5121
Dr. Karen Bahn, prin. Fax 389-2963
Our Lady of Peace IS 100/3-5
1300 W 5th St 54449 715-384-5474
Nancy Baierl, prin. Fax 387-8697
St. John the Baptist PS 100/PK-2
307 N Walnut Ave 54449 715-384-4989
Nancy Baierl, prin. Fax 384-5131
Trinity Evangelical Lutheran S 100/PK-8
9529 State Highway 80 54449 715-676-2121
Michael Wisniewski, admin. Fax 676-3771

Mauston, Juneau, Pop. 4,366
Mauston SD 1,500/PK-12
510 Grayside Ave 53948 608-847-5451
Dr. Christine M. Weymouth, supt. Fax 847-4635
www.maustonschools.org
Grayside ES 200/3-5
510 Grayside Ave 53948 608-847-5616
Bobbi Steele, prin. Fax 847-2496
Olson MS 300/6-8
508 Grayside Ave 53948 608-847-6603
Brian Bauer, prin. Fax 847-4925
West Side ES 300/PK-2
708 Loomis Dr 53948 608-847-1828
Jolene Routson, prin. Fax 847-6342
Other Schools – See Lyndon Station

St. Patrick S 200/PK-8
325 Mansion St 53948 608-847-5844
Linda Layer, prin. Fax 847-4103

Mayville, Dodge, Pop. 5,113
Mayville SD 1,300/PK-12
N8210 State Road 28 53050 920-387-7963
Scott Sabol, supt. Fax 387-7979
www.mayvilleschools.com
Mayville MS 500/3-8
445 N Henninger St 53050 920-387-7970
John Schlender, prin. Fax 387-7974
Parkview ES 300/PK-2
259 Oak St 53050 920-387-7973
Rebecca LeBouton, prin. Fax 387-7975

Immanuel Lutheran S 50/PK-8
N8092 County Road AY 53050 920-387-5363
Rev. Douglas Zahner, prin.
St. John Lutheran S 100/PK-8
520 Bridge St 53050 920-387-4310
Kay Koenitzer, prin. Fax 387-2321
St. Mary S 100/PK-2
28 Naber St 53050 920-387-2920
Kris Hies, prin. Fax 387-4037

Mazomanie, Dane, Pop. 1,638
Wisconsin Heights SD 700/PK-12
10173 US Highway 14 53560 608-767-2595
Jordan Sinz, supt. Fax 767-3579
www.wisheights.k12.wi.us
Mazomanie ES 100/3-5
314 Anne St 53560 608-767-2737
Dale Green, prin. Fax 767-2103
Wisconsin Heights MS 200/6-8
10173 US Highway 14 53560 608-767-2586
Chris Conohan, prin. Fax 767-2062
Other Schools – See Black Earth

Medford, Taylor, Pop. 4,279
Medford Area SD 2,200/PK-12
124 W State St 54451 715-748-4620
Patrick Sullivan, supt. Fax 748-6839
www.medford.k12.wi.us
Medford ES 600/PK-4
1065 W Broadway Ave 54451 715-748-2316
Dan Miller, prin. Fax 748-2570
Medford MS 600/5-8
509 Clark St 54451 715-748-2516
Al Leonard, prin. Fax 748-1213
Other Schools – See Stetsonville

Holy Rosary S 200/PK-7
215 S Washington Ave 54451 715-748-3336
Debbie Johnston, prin. Fax 748-5110
Immanuel Lutheran S 50/PK-8
420 Lincoln St 54451 715-748-2921
Joseph Hering, prin. Fax 748-2948

Mellen, Ashland, Pop. 725
Mellen SD 300/PK-12
PO Box 500 54546 715-274-3601
Michael Cox, supt. Fax 274-3715
www.mellendiggers.org
Mellen ES 200/PK-8
PO Box 500 54546 715-274-3601
Maija Alexandrou, prin. Fax 274-3715

Melrose, Jackson, Pop. 499
Melrose-Mindoro SD 800/PK-12
N181 State Hwy 108 54642 608-488-2201
Del DeBerg, supt. Fax 488-2805
www.mel-min.k12.wi.us
Melrose S 400/PK-8
805 2nd St 54642 608-488-2311
Corey Peterson, prin. Fax 488-4015
Other Schools – See Mindoro

Menasha, Winnebago, Pop. 17,081
Menasha JSD 3,600/PK-12
PO Box 360 54952 920-967-1400
Chris VanderHeyden, supt. Fax 751-5038
www.mjsd.k12.wi.us
Banta ES 200/K-5
PO Box 360 54952 920-967-1417
Gina Cornu-Zacharias, prin. Fax 751-1455
Butte Des Morts ES 400/PK-5
501 Tayco St 54952 920-967-1900
Bridget Mowbray, prin. Fax 751-4645
Clovis Grove ES 500/PK-5
974 9th St 54952 920-967-1955
Tammy Richter, prin. Fax 751-5261
Gegan ES 400/PK-5
675 W Airport Rd 54952 920-967-1360
Elizabeth LaNou, prin. Fax 751-4834
Jefferson ES 100/PK-2
105 Ice St 54952 920-967-1660
Kristi Gonzalez, prin. Fax 751-4831
Maplewood MS 800/6-8
1600 Midway Rd 54952 920-967-1600
Dr. Bev Sturke, prin. Fax 832-5837
Nicolet ES 100/3-5
449 Ahnaip St 54952 920-967-1710
Kristi Gonzalez, prin. Fax 751-4830

St. Mary ES 100/PK-5
540 2nd St 54952 920-725-5351
Patrick Batey, prin. Fax 725-7612
Shepherd of the Valley Lutheran S 100/PK-8
N8728 Coop Rd 54952 920-731-4001
Carl Weisheim, prin. Fax 731-4041
Trinity Lutheran S, 300 Broad St 54952 100/PK-8
Rev. Keith GeRue, prin. 920-725-1715

Menomonee Falls, Waukesha, Pop. 35,186
Hamilton SD
Supt. — See Sussex
Marcy ES 600/K-5
W180N4851 Marcy Rd 53051 262-781-8283
Michele Trawicki, prin. Fax 781-6028
Willow Springs Learning Center 300/PK-PK
W220N6660 Town Line Rd 53051 262-255-6190
Renae MacCudden Ph.D., prin. Fax 255-4149

Menomonee Falls SD 4,200/PK-12
W156N8480 Pilgrim Rd 53051 262-255-8440
Patricia Greco, supt. Fax 255-8461
www.fallsschools.org
Franklin ES 700/PK-2
N81W14701 Franklin Dr 53051 262-255-8470
Cassie Martin, prin. Fax 255-8482
North MS 900/6-8
N88W16750 Garfield Dr 53051 262-255-8450
Lynn Grimm, prin. Fax 255-8475
Riverside ES 400/3-5
W153N8681 Margaret Rd 53051 262-255-8484
Scott Walter, prin. Fax 255-8393
Shady Lane ES 400/K-2
W172N8959 Shady Ln 53051 262-255-8480
Brad Hoffman, prin. Fax 255-8448
Valley View ES 400/3-5
W180N8130 Town Hall Rd 53051 262-250-2620
Tina Posnanski, prin. Fax 255-8476

Aquinas Academy 100/PK-8
N72W15935 Good Hope Rd 53051 262-502-1540
Andrew Denten, prin. Fax 502-1750
Bethlehem Lutheran S - South 100/5-8
N84W15252 Menomonee Ave 53051 262-251-3120
Daryl Weber, prin. Fax 251-4679
Calvary Baptist S 200/PK-12
N84W19049 Menomonee Ave 53051 262-251-0328
Grace Lutheran S 200/PK-8
N87W16173 Kenwood Blvd 53051 262-251-7140
Deb Erdmann, prin. Fax 251-3460
Pilgrim Evangelical Lutheran S 100/PK-8
W156N5429 Bette Dr 53051 262-781-3520
Brett Kriese, prin. Fax 781-8287
St. Anthony Montessori S 200/PK-3
N74W13646 Appleton Ave 53051 262-251-4390
Anne Schramka, prin. Fax 251-2412
St. Mary S 300/K-8
N89W16215 Cleveland Ave 53051 262-251-1050
Linda Joyner, prin. Fax 502-1671
Zion Lutheran S 100/PK-8
N48W18700 Lisbon Rd 53051 262-781-7437
Matthew Pankow, prin. Fax 781-4656

Menomonie, Dunn, Pop. 15,977
Menomonie Area SD 3,100/K-12
215 Pine Ave NE 54751 715-232-1642
Joe Zydowsky, supt. Fax 232-1317
www.msd.k12.wi.us
Menomonie MS 700/6-8
920 21st St SE 54751 715-232-1673
Stacey Everson, prin. Fax 232-5486
Oaklawn ES 400/K-5
500 21st St SE 54751 715-232-3798
Lori Smith, prin. Fax 232-1091
River Heights ES 400/K-5
615 24th Ave W 54751 715-232-3987
Peg Kolden, prin. Fax 232-2321
Wakanda ES 400/K-5
1801 Wakanda St NE 54751 715-232-3898
Susan Mommsen, prin. Fax 232-3887
Other Schools – See Downsville, Knapp

St. Joseph S 100/K-6
910 Wilson Ave 54751 715-232-4922
Keila Drout, prin. Fax 232-4923
St. Paul's Lutheran S 100/PK-8
1100 9th St E 54751 715-235-9622
Robert Buss, prin. Fax 235-9625

Mequon, Ozaukee, Pop. 22,848
Mequon-Thiensville SD 3,500/PK-12
5000 W Mequon Rd 53092 262-238-8500
Matthew Joynt, supt. Fax 238-8520
www.mtsd.k12.wi.us
Donges Bay ES 400/K-5
2401 W Donges Bay Rd 53092 262-238-7920
Chris Gray, prin. Fax 238-7970
Lake Shore MS 400/6-8
11036 N Range Line Rd 53092 262-238-7613
Alli Rudich, prin. Fax 238-7650

Oriole Lane ES 400/PK-5
12850 N Oriole Ln 53097 262-238-4220
Mary Jo Tye, prin. Fax 238-4250
Range Line ECC PK-PK
11040 N Range Line Rd 53092 262-238-7535
Rachel Fellenz, prin.
Steffen MS 400/6-8
6633 W Steffen Dr 53092 262-238-4706
Deborah Anderson, prin. Fax 238-4740
Wilson ES 600/K-5
11001 N Buntrock Ave 53092 262-238-4600
Jocelyn Sulsberger, prin. Fax 238-4662

Lumen Christi S 200/PK-8
11300 N Saint James Ln 53092 262-242-7960
Kelly Fyfe, prin. Fax 512-8986
Trinity Lutheran S 100/PK-8
10729 W Freistadt Rd 53097 262-242-2045
Gene Ladendorf, prin. Fax 242-4407

Mercer, Iron, Pop. 516
Mercer SD 100/PK-12
2690 W Margaret St 54547 715-476-2154
Erik Torkelson, supt. Fax 476-2587
www.mercer.k12.wi.us
Mercer S 100/PK-12
2690 W Margaret St 54547 715-476-2154
Erik Torkelson, admin. Fax 476-2587

Merrill, Lincoln, Pop. 9,553
Merrill Area SD 3,500/PK-12
1111 N Sales St 54452 715-536-4581
John Sample, supt. Fax 536-1788
www.maps.k12.wi.us
Goodrich ES 300/K-5
505 W 10th St 54452 715-536-5233
Glenda Oginski, prin. Fax 539-3736
Jefferson ES 300/K-5
1914 Jackson St 54452 715-536-5432
Heather Skutak, prin. Fax 536-7260
Pine River S Young Learners 200/PK-PK
W4165 State Highway 64 54452 715-536-2392
Jill Seaman, dir. Fax 536-6328
Prairie River MS 600/6-8
106 N Polk St 54452 715-536-9593
Ryan Martinovici, prin. Fax 536-6378
Washington ES 300/K-5
1900 E 6th St 54452 715-536-2373
Trisha Detert, prin. Fax 536-1759

St. Frances Xavier S 100/PK-8
1708 E 10th St 54452 715-536-6083
Sonja Doughty, prin. Fax 536-7536
St. John Lutheran S 200/PK-8
1104 E 3rd St 54452 715-536-7264
Kathleen Hahn, prin. Fax 539-3381
Trinity Lutheran S 100/PK-8
611 W Main St 54452 715-536-7501
Kathy Yahr M.Ed., admin.

Merrillan, Jackson, Pop. 518
Alma Center-Humbird-Merrillan SD
Supt. — See Alma Center
Lincoln ES 300/PK-6
PO Box 270 54754 715-333-2911
Brad Rogers, prin. Fax 333-2914

Merton, Waukesha, Pop. 3,309
Merton Community SD 800/PK-8
PO Box 15 53056 262-538-2227
Ronald Russ, supt. Fax 538-4978
www.merton.k12.wi.us
Merton IS 400/5-8
PO Box 15 53056 262-538-1130
Jay Posick, prin. Fax 538-4978
Merton PS 400/PK-4
PO Box 15 53056 262-538-2227
Mike Budisch, prin. Fax 538-3937

Middleton, Dane, Pop. 17,031
Middleton-Cross Plains Area SD 5,900/PK-12
7106 South Ave 53562 608-829-9000
Dr. George Mavroulis, supt. Fax 836-1536
www.mcpasd.k12.wi.us
Elm Lawn ES 500/PK-4
6701 Woodgate Rd 53562 608-829-9070
Robert Schell, prin. Fax 831-4470
Kromrey MS 700/5-8
7009 Donna Dr 53562 608-829-9530
Steve Soeteber, prin. Fax 831-8388
Northside ES 400/PK-4
3620 High Rd 53562 608-829-9130
Roz Craney, prin. Fax 831-1355
Sauk Trail ES 400/PK-4
2205 Branch St 53562 608-829-9190
Chris Dahlk, prin. Fax 828-1678
Sunset Ridge ES 500/PK-4
8686 Airport Rd 53562 608-829-9300
Maria Dyslin, prin. Fax 827-1805
Other Schools – See Cross Plains, Verona

Madison Community Montessori S 100/PK-8
8406 Ellington Way 53562 608-827-6267
Vicki McCarthy, head sch Fax 827-6264
St. Peter S 50/K-5
7129 County Road K 53562 608-831-4846
Kathi Klaas, prin. Fax 831-6095
Westside Christian S 100/PK-8
6815 Schneider Rd 53562 608-831-8540
Hank Hoenecke, prin. Fax 824-6594

Milton, Rock, Pop. 5,493
Milton SD 3,400/PK-12
448 E High St 53563 608-868-9200
Timothy J. Schigur, supt. Fax 868-9215
www.milton.k12.wi.us
Milton East ES 300/PK-3
201 S Janesville St 53563 608-868-9380
Jennifer Cramer, prin. Fax 868-9256
Milton MS 500/7-8
20 E Madison Ave 53563 608-868-9350
Matt Biederwolf, prin. Fax 868-9269
Milton West ES 400/PK-3
825 W Madison Ave 53563 608-868-9230
Marcia Schwengels, prin. Fax 868-9225
Northside IS 800/4-6
159 Northside Dr 53563 608-868-9280
Jon Lyon, prin. Fax 868-9259
Other Schools – See Janesville

Milwaukee, Milwaukee, Pop. 580,512
Greenfield SD
Supt. — See Greenfield
Elm Dale ES 500/PK-5
5300 S Honey Creek Dr 53221 414-281-7100
Christine Brzycki, prin. Fax 281-2580

Milwaukee SD 75,400/PK-12
5225 W Vliet St 53208 414-475-8393
Dr. Darienne Driver, supt. Fax 475-8595
www.milwaukee.k12.wi.us
Academy of Accelerated Learning 600/PK-5
3727 S 78th St 53220 414-604-7300
Eric Rian, prin. Fax 604-7315
Alcott S 400/PK-8
3563 S 97th St 53228 414-604-7400
Marisol Alvarado-Patton, prin. Fax 604-7415
Allen-Field ES 700/PK-5
730 W Lapham Blvd 53204 414-902-9200
Fritz Blandon, prin. Fax 902-9215
Audubon Technology & Communication Ctr 600/6-8
3300 S 39th St 53215 414-902-7800
Leon Groce, prin. Fax 902-7815
Auer Avenue S 300/PK-8
2319 W Auer Ave 53206 414-875-4500
Zannetta Walker, prin. Fax 875-4515
Barbee Montessori S 200/K-6
4456 N Teutonia Ave 53209 414-874-5600
Catherine Loss, prin. Fax 874-5615
Barton ES 400/PK-5
5700 W Green Tree Rd 53223 414-393-3900
Shiron Posley, admin. Fax 393-3915
Bethune Academy 500/PK-8
1535 N 35th St 53208 414-934-4600
Paulette Chambers, prin. Fax 934-4615
Browning ES 300/PK-5
5440 N 64th St 53218 414-393-5200
Raymond Unanka, prin. Fax 393-5215
Brown Street Academy 300/PK-5
2029 N 20th St 53205 414-935-3100
Ava Morris, prin. Fax 935-3115
Bruce ES 300/PK-5
6453 N 89th St 53224 414-393-2100
Lisa Turner, prin. Fax 393-2115
Bryant ES 300/PK-5
8718 W Thurston Ave 53225 414-393-6500
Erik Conner, prin. Fax 393-6515
Burbank S 600/PK-8
6035 W Adler St 53214 414-256-8400
Angela Smith, prin. Fax 256-8415
Burdick S 700/PK-8
4348 S Griffin Ave 53207 414-294-1200
Theresa Russell, prin. Fax 294-1215
Carson Academy of Science 500/PK-8
4920 W Capitol Dr 53216 414-393-4800
Toni Straughter, prin. Fax 393-4815
Carver Academy 500/K-8
1900 N 1st St 53212 414-267-0500
Kristin Hinds, prin. Fax 267-0515
Cass Street S 400/PK-8
1647 N Cass St 53202 414-212-2700
Tyrone Nichols, prin. Fax 212-2715
Clarke Street S 300/PK-8
2816 W Clarke St 53210 414-267-1000
Shunda Davis, prin. Fax 267-1015
Clemens ES 300/PK-5
3600 W Hope Ave 53216 414-875-6300
Toni Dinkins, prin. Fax 875-6315
Clement Avenue ES 500/PK-8
3666 S Clement Ave 53207 414-294-1500
Steven Carnes, prin. Fax 294-1515
Congress S 900/PK-8
5225 W Lincoln Creek Dr 53218 414-616-5300
Lorraine Applewhite, prin. Fax 616-5315
Cooper S 400/PK-8
5143 S 21st St 53221 414-304-6300
Jennifer Doucette, prin. Fax 304-6315
Craig Montessori S 400/K-8
7667 W Congress St 53218 414-393-4200
Jason Galien, prin. Fax 393-4214
Curtin Leadership Academy 300/PK-8
3450 S 32nd St 53215 414-902-7700
Patricia Cifax, prin. Fax 902-7715
Doerfler S 800/PK-8
3014 W Scott St 53215 414-902-9500
Jessica Quindel, prin. Fax 902-9515
Douglas S, 3620 N 18th St 53206 K-8
Zerda Palmer, prin. 414-256-8200
Eighty First Street S 400/PK-5
2964 N 81st St 53222 414-874-5400
Ronald Cox, prin. Fax 874-5415
Elm Creative Arts ES 600/PK-5
900 W Walnut St 53205 414-267-1800
Tonya Love, prin. Fax 267-1815
Emerson ES 300/PK-5
9025 W Lawrence Ave 53225 414-393-4300
Joel Eul, prin. Fax 393-4315
Engleburg ES 400/PK-5
5100 N 91st St 53225 414-616-5600
Lisa Marion-Howard, prin. Fax 616-5615
Fernwood Montessori S 600/PK-8
3239 S Pennsylvania Ave 53207 414-294-1300
John Sanchez, prin. Fax 294-1315
Fifty Third Street S 400/PK-8
3618 N 53rd St 53216 414-874-5300
Stephanie Zollicoffer, prin. Fax 874-5315
Forest Home Avenue ES 800/PK-5
1516 W Forest Home Ave 53204 414-902-6200
Bradley Christensen, prin. Fax 902-6215
Franklin S 300/PK-8
2308 W Nash St 53206 414-875-4400
Sara Hmielewski, prin. Fax 875-4415
Fratney ES 500/PK-5
3255 N Fratney St 53212 414-267-1100
Sylvia Buckman, admin. Fax 267-1115
Gaenslen S 700/PK-8
1250 E Burleigh St 53212 414-267-5700
Cynthia Dismuke, prin. Fax 267-5715
Garland ES 500/PK-7
3120 W Green Ave 53221 414-304-6500
David Zech, prin. Fax 304-6515
Goodrich ES 300/PK-5
8251 N Celina St 53224 262-236-1500
Sharonda Harris, prin. Fax 236-1515
Grantosa Drive S 600/PK-8
4850 N 82nd St 53218 414-393-4400
Kristen Brown, prin. Fax 393-4415
Grant S 700/PK-8
2920 W Grant St 53215 414-902-8000
Thomas Bruno, prin. Fax 902-8015
Green Bay ES 400/K-5
3872 N 8th St 53206 414-252-0200
Richard Spates, prin. Fax 263-2902
Greenfield Bilingual S 600/K-8
1711 S 35th St 53215 414-902-8200
Adalberto Barreto, prin. Fax 902-8215
Hampton ES 300/PK-5
5000 N 53rd St 53218 414-393-5400
Bridget Araujo, prin. Fax 393-5415
Hartford Avenue University S 700/PK-8
2227 E Hartford Ave 53211 414-906-4700
Shannon Kilsdonk, prin. Fax 906-4715
Hawthorne ES 300/PK-5
6945 N 41st St 53209 414-247-7200
Jeri Agee, prin. Fax 247-7215
Hi-Mount Community S 400/PK-8
4921 W Garfield Ave 53208 414-875-2700
Jacqueline Richardson, prin. Fax 875-2715
Holmes S 300/PK-8
2463 N Buffum St 53212 414-267-1300
Patrick Chatman, prin. Fax 267-1315
Hopkins Lloyd Community S 400/PK-8
1503 W Hopkins St 53206 414-267-0600
Natosha Harris, admin. Fax 267-0615
Howard Avenue Montessori S PK-6
357 E Howard Ave 53207 414-935-0700
Heidi Panosh, prin.
Jackson ES 400/PK-5
2121 W Hadley St 53206 414-267-5500
Robert Hooks, prin. Fax 267-5515
Kagel ES 300/PK-5
1210 W Mineral St 53204 414-902-7400
Mary Saldana, prin. Fax 902-7415
Keefe Avenue S 400/PK-8
1618 W Keefe Ave 53206 414-267-4800
Christlyn Frederick-Stan, prin. Fax 267-4815
Kilbourn ES 300/PK-5
5354 N 68th St 53218 414-393-4500
Thresessa Childs, prin. Fax 393-4515
King International MS 400/6-8
121 E Hadley St 53212 414-616-5200
Tamara Ellis, prin.
King S 500/PK-8
3275 N 3rd St 53212 414-267-1500
Marcus Arrington, prin. Fax 267-1515
Kluge ES 400/PK-5
5760 N 67th St 53218 414-578-5000
Keushum Willingham, prin. Fax 578-5015
Lafollette S 300/PK-8
3239 N 9th St 53206 414-267-5200
Dr. Marny Gamble, prin. Fax 267-5215
Lancaster S 400/PK-8
4931 N 68th St 53218 414-393-5500
Justin Henze, prin. Fax 393-5515
Lincoln Avenue ES 600/PK-5
1817 W Lincoln Ave 53215 414-902-9700
Yaribel Rodriguez, prin. Fax 902-9715
Lincoln MS of the Arts 700/6-8
820 E Knapp St 53202 414-212-3300
Ramon Evans, prin. Fax 212-3315
Longfellow S 1,000/PK-8
1021 S 21st St 53204 414-902-9800
Rosa Cerda, prin. Fax 902-9815
Lowell ES 300/PK-5
4360 S 20th St 53221 414-304-6600
Pandora Bedford, prin. Fax 304-6615
MacDowell Montessori S 700/PK-12
6415 W Mount Vernon Ave 53213 414-935-1400
Andrea Corona, prin. Fax 935-1415
Manitoba S 500/PK-8
4040 W Forest Home Ave 53215 414-902-8600
Rhoda Goodwin, prin. Fax 902-8615
Maple Tree ES 300/PK-5
6644 N 107th St 53224 414-578-5100
Debra Rash, admin. Fax 578-5115
Maryland Avenue Montessori S 300/K-8
2418 N Maryland Ave 53211 414-906-4800
Joseph Di Carlo, prin. Fax 906-4815
Meir S 500/3-10
1555 N Martin Luther King 53212 414-212-3200
Michelle Carter, prin. Fax 212-3215
Metcalfe S 300/K-8
3400 W North Ave 53208 414-874-3600
Melinda Gladney, prin. Fax 874-3615
Milwaukee Academy of Chinese Language 400/PK-8
2430 W Wisconsin Ave 53233 414-934-4340
James Sayavong, admin. Fax 934-4345
Milwaukee French Immersion ES 400/PK-5
2360 N 52nd St 53210 414-874-8400
Gina Bianchi, prin. Fax 874-8415

Milwaukee German Immersion ES 600/PK-5
3778 N 82nd St 53222 414-393-5600
Frank Lammers, prin. Fax 393-5615
Milwaukee Parkside S for the Arts 700/PK-8
2969 S Howell Ave 53207 414-294-1800
Lila Hillman, admin. Fax 294-1815
Milwaukee Sign Language S 600/PK-8
7900 W Acacia St 53223 414-393-3800
Suzanne Gahan, prin. Fax 393-3815
Milwaukee Spanish Immersion ES 600/PK-5
2765 S 55th St 53219 414-604-7600
Marybell Nieves-Harris, prin. Fax 604-7615
Mitchell Integrated Arts S 700/PK-8
1728 S 23rd St 53204 414-902-8100
Kim Malacara, prin. Fax 902-8115
Morgandale S 600/PK-8
3635 S 17th St 53221 414-902-9900
Christina Flood, prin. Fax 902-9915
Morse S for Gifted and Talented 1,400/6-8
6700 N 80th St 53216 414-393-3500
Phyllis Anderson, prin. Fax 393-2315
Neeskara ES 400/PK-5
1601 N Hawley Rd 53208 414-256-8600
Erick Owens, prin. Fax 256-8615
Ninety Fifth Street ES 400/PK-5
3707 N 94th St 53222 414-393-4100
Sarah Sanders, prin. Fax 393-4115
Obama S of Career & Tech Educ 200/K-12
5075 N Sherman Blvd 53209 414-393-4900
Dr. Carol McKay, prin.
Parkview ES 400/PK-5
10825 W Villard Ave 53225 414-393-2700
Cheryl Colbert, prin. Fax 393-2715
Pierce ES 400/K-5
2765 N Fratney St 53212 414-267-4400
Leticia Washington, prin. Fax 267-4415
Pratt ES 300/PK-5
5131 N Green Bay Ave 53209 414-247-7300
Janice Carter, prin. Fax 247-7315
Riley ES 600/PK-5
2424 S 4th St 53207 414-902-7100
Harry Russo, prin. Fax 902-7115
River Trail S 500/PK-8
12021 W Florist Ave 53225 414-393-2200
Tiffany Fisher, prin. Fax 393-2215
Rogers Street Academy 700/PK-8
2430 W Rogers St 53204 414-902-1100
Ramon Cruz, prin. Fax 902-1115
Roosevelt Creative Arts MS 600/6-8
800 W Walnut St 53205 414-267-8800
Tiffany Fisher, prin. Fax 267-8815
Sherman Multicultural Arts S 500/PK-8
5110 W Locust St 53210 414-874-5800
Ebbie Wells, prin. Fax 874-5815
Siefert ES 300/PK-5
1547 N 14th St 53205 414-935-1500
Wanda Katz, prin. Fax 935-1515
Starms Discovery Learning Center 500/1-8
2035 N 25th St 53205 414-934-4900
Bryan Terry, prin. Fax 934-4915
Starms ECC 300/PK-K
2616 W Garfield Ave 53205 414-934-4700
Bryan Terry, prin. Fax 934-4715
Story S 400/K-8
3815 W Kilbourn Ave 53208 414-934-4800
Portia Ewing-Lipsey, prin. Fax 934-4815
Stuart ES 300/PK-5
7001 N 86th St 53224 414-393-3700
Nicole Jude, prin. Fax 393-3715
Thoreau S 500/PK-8
7878 N 60th St 53223 262-236-1800
Paula Boyd, prin. Fax 236-1815
Thurston Woods S 500/PK-8
5966 N 35th St 53209 414-393-2800
Felice Beal, prin. Fax 393-2815
Townsend Street S 300/PK-8
3360 N Sherman Blvd 53216 414-874-5900
Redona Williams, prin. Fax 874-5915
Trowbridge S of Discovery & Tech 300/PK-8
1943 E Trowbridge St 53207 414-294-1900
Thomas Matthews, prin. Fax 294-1915
Victory S 600/PK-8
2222 W Henry Ave 53221 414-304-6700
Janine Graber, prin. Fax 304-6715
Vieau S 700/PK-8
823 S 4th St 53204 414-902-6100
Eduardo Galvan, prin. Fax 902-6115
Webster MS, 6850 N 53rd St 53223 6-8
Dr. Carletta Noland, prin. 414-206-0500
Wedgewood Park International S 800/6-8
6506 W Warnimont Ave 53220 414-604-7800
Elhadji Ndaw, prin. Fax 604-7815
Whitman ES 200/PK-8
4200 S 54th St 53220 414-604-7700
Sally Schumacher, prin. Fax 604-7715
WI Consrv Lifelong Learning S 700/K-12
1017 N 12th St 53233 414-304-6800
Stanley McWilliams, prin. Fax 304-6815
Zablocki ES 500/PK-5
1016 W Oklahoma Ave 53215 414-294-2200
Chris Garza, admin. Fax 294-2215

West Allis SD 9,700/PK-12
1205 S 70th St Ste 500 53214 414-604-3000
Dr. Martin Lexmond, supt. Fax 256-6314
www.wawmsd.org
Other Schools – See New Berlin, West Allis, West Milwaukee

Atlas Preparatory Academy 900/PK-12
1039 E Russell Ave 53207 414-385-0771
Michelle Lukacs, dir. Fax 385-0773
Atonement Lutheran S 200/PK-8
4224 W Ruby Ave 53209 414-871-1224
Todd Gorsline, admin. Fax 871-0379
Bader Hillel Academy 100/K-8
6401 N Santa Monica Blvd 53217 414-962-9545
B. Devorah Shmotkin, prin. Fax 967-8373
Believers in Christ Christian Academy 200/PK-12
4065 N 25th St 53209 414-444-1146
Candace Covington, prin. Fax 444-5378
Blessed Sacrament S 200/PK-8
3126 S 41st St 53215 414-649-4730
Carol Degan, prin. Fax 649-4726
Blessed Savior Catholic S - East 200/PK-8
5140 N 55th St 53218 414-438-2745
Barbara O'Donnell, prin. Fax 438-9330
Blessed Savior Catholic S - North 200/PK-8
5501 N 68th St 53218 414-466-0470
Nadia Pope, prin. Fax 466-3740
Blessed Savior Catholic S - South 200/K-5
4059 N 64th St 53216 414-463-3878
Megan Prudom, prin. Fax 535-9265
Blessed Savior Catholic S - West 200/PK-8
8545 W Villard Ave 53225 414-464-5775
Sarah Helms, prin. Fax 464-5737
Bufkin Christian Academy 100/PK-12
827 N 34th St 53208 414-934-8885
Texas Bufkin, admin. Fax 934-8886
Carter's Christian Academy 200/PK-8
5268 N 35th St 53209 414-466-3284
Andre Carter, prin.
Catholic East S Holy Rosary Campus 100/PK-1
2038 N Bartlett Ave 53202 414-964-1770
Jennifer Jones, prin. Fax 988-8959
Catholic East S Sts. Peter & Paul Campus 100/2-8
2461 N Murray Ave 53211 414-964-1770
Jennifer Jones, prin. Fax 964-6578
Christian Faith Acad of Higher Learning 100/PK-8
3965 N 15 St 53206 414-234-7657
Gwen Mallory, prin. Fax 316-3719
Christ - St. Peter Lutheran S 200/PK-8
2229 W Greenfield Ave 53204 414-383-2055
Brett Baade, prin. Fax 383-2497
Cross Trainers Academy 100/PK-11
1530 W Center Ave 53206 414-935-0500
Jacquelyn Verhulst, admin. Fax 755-7620
Early View Academy of Excellence 400/PK-12
7132 W Good Hope Rd 53223 414-431-0001
Sr. Ella Hayes, prin. Fax 431-0046
Eastbrook Academy 400/PK-12
5375 N Green Bay Ave 53209 414-228-7905
Michael Maxson, head sch Fax 228-9854
Garden Homes Lutheran S 200/PK-8
2450 W Roosevelt Dr 53209 414-444-9050
David Dodge, prin. Fax 444-9105
Granville Lutheran S 200/PK-8
8242 N Granville Rd 53224 414-354-6601
Trenae Howard, prin. Fax 354-5586
Hickman Academy Preparatory S 400/PK-8
4200 N 51st Blvd 53216 414-578-1708
Bennie Hickman, dir.
Holy Redeemer Christian Academy 500/PK-12
3500 W Mother Daniels Way 53209 414-466-1800
Br. Jatiki Smith, prin. Fax 466-9294
Holy Wisdom Academy East 200/PK-3
3329 S 10th St 53215 414-744-7188
Julie Robinson, prin. Fax 744-8370
Holy Wisdom Academy West Campus 100/4-8
3344 S 16th St 53215 414-383-3453
Julie Ann Robinson, prin. Fax 672-2645
Hope Christian School: Fortis 200/K-8
3601 N Port Washington Rd 53212 414-264-6284
Brenna Prochnow, prin. Fax 264-6285
Hope Christian School: Prima 500/PK-8
2345 N 25th St 53206 414-931-0350
Chelsea Prochnow, prin. Fax 931-0702
Institute of Technology & Academics 200/K-8
8940 N 85th St 53224 414-365-9375
Kings Academy Christian S 200/PK-8
7798 N 60th St 53223 414-371-9100
Jennie Dorsey, prin. Fax 371-9200
Loving Shepherd Lutheran S 100/PK-8
3909 W Clinton Ave 53209 414-352-2662
Timothy Paschke, prin. Fax 352-3175
Messmer Preparatory S 400/K-8
3027 N Fratney St 53212 414-264-6070
Kristin Merry, prin. Fax 264-6430
Milwaukee Jewish Day S 200/PK-8
6401 N Santa Monica Blvd 53217 414-964-1499
Milwaukee Montessori S 400/PK-8
345 N 95th St 53226 414-259-0370
Dr. Monica Van Aken Ed.D., head sch Fax 259-0427
Milwaukee SDA S 100/PK-10
10900 W Mill Rd 53225 414-353-3520
Ken Smith, prin. Fax 353-1451
Mohammed S 200/PK-12
317 W Wright St 53212 414-263-6772
Halim Mahdi, dir. Fax 263-6852
Mother of Good Counsel S 200/PK-8
3001 N 68th St 53210 414-442-7600
Regina Shaw, prin. Fax 442-0644
Mt. Calvary Lutheran S 200/PK-8
2862 N 53rd St 53210 414-873-3466
Carrie Miller, prin. Fax 873-0567
Mt. Lebanon Lutheran S - Alpha Campus 100/K-4
6100 W Hampton Ave 53218 414-464-5410
Jonathan Winkel, dir. Fax 464-6210
Mt. Lebanon Lutheran S - Omega Campus 100/5-8
8444 W Melvina St 53222 414-463-5030
Jonathan Winkel, dir. Fax 463-5086
Mt. Olive Lutheran S 100/PK-8
5301 W Washington Blvd 53208 414-774-2200
Rosalie Meier, prin. Fax 774-2212
Nativity Jesuit MS 100/4-8
1515 S 29th St 53215 414-645-1060
John Meuler, pres. Fax 645-0505
New Testament Christian Academy 200/PK-8
10201 W Bradley Rd 53224 414-365-1677
Dr. Donna Childs, dir. Fax 365-5611
Northwest Catholic S - Lower Campus 200/PK-8
7140 N 41st St 53209 414-352-6927
Michelle Paris, prin. Fax 760-1037
Northwest Lutheran S 200/PK-8
4119 N 81st St 53222 414-463-4040
Trila Pitchford, prin. Fax 463-0524
Notre Dame ES K-4
1418 S Layton Blvd 53215 414-431-7950
Patrick Landry, prin.
Notre Dame MS 100/5-8
1420 W Scott St 53204 414-671-3000
Patrick Landry, prin. Fax 671-3170
Our Lady Queen of Peace S 200/K-8
2733 W Euclid Ave 53215 414-672-6660
Janet Orlowski, prin. Fax 672-2739
Prince of Peace ES 300/1-5
1114 S 25th St 53204 414-383-2157
Patricia Blaszczyk, prin. Fax 383-4940
Prince of Peace MS 300/PK-K, 6-8
1646 S 22nd St 53204 414-645-4922
Patricia Blaszczyk, prin. Fax 645-4940
Risen Savior Lutheran S 200/PK-8
9550 W Brown Deer Rd 53224 414-354-7320
Robert Dusseau, prin. Fax 354-6815
St. Adalbert S 400/PK-8
1913 W Becher St 53215 414-645-5450
Amy Jarmuz-Kluth, prin. Fax 645-5510
St. Anthony ES 800/K-2
1669 S 5th St 53204 414-384-1729
Brandy Hart, prin. Fax 384-6613
St. Anthony ES 800/3-5
1747 S 9th St 53204 414-384-1730
Teresa Reilly, prin. Fax 384-1733
St. Anthony MS 6-8
2156 S 4th St 53207 414-810-3858
Alfredo Velasquez, prin. Fax 810-3938
St. Catherine S 200/PK-8
2647 N 51st St 53210 414-445-2846
Michael Turner, prin. Fax 445-0448
St. Charles Borromeo S 200/PK-8
3100 W Parnell Ave 53221 414-282-0767
Courtney Albright, prin. Fax 817-9605
St. Gregory the Great S 200/K-8
3132 S 63rd St 53219 414-321-1350
Amy Schlegel, prin. Fax 328-3881
St. John Evangelical Lutheran S 100/PK-8
4001 S 68th St 53220 414-541-5881
David Rust, prin. Fax 541-7869
St. John Kanty S 200/PK-8
2840 S 10th St 53215 414-483-8780
Dan Jorgenson, prin. Fax 744-1846
St. Josaphat S 200/K-8
801 W Lincoln Ave 53215 414-645-4378
Kelly Savasta, prin. Fax 645-1978
St. Joseph Academy 400/PK-7
1600 W Oklahoma Ave 53215 414-645-5337
St. Lucas Lutheran S 200/PK-8
648 E Dover St 53207 414-483-8000
Andrew Baxter, prin. Fax 486-0591
St. Marcus Lutheran S 600/PK-8
2215 N Palmer St 53212 414-562-3163
Erin Johnson, prin. Fax 562-9188
St. Margaret Mary S 200/PK-8
3950 N 92nd St 53222 414-463-8760
Dr. Sabrina Claude, prin. Fax 463-2373
St. Martini Lutheran S 300/PK-8
1520 S Cesar E Chavez Dr 53204 414-383-7058
Julieane Cook, prin. Fax 383-0637
St. Matthias S 400/K-8
9300 W Beloit Rd 53227 414-321-0894
Kristin Lee, prin. Fax 321-9228
St. Peter Immanuel Lutheran S 200/PK-8
7801 W Acacia St 53223 414-353-6800
Amy Puechner, prin. Fax 353-5510
St. Philips Lutheran S 100/PK-8
3012 N Holton St 53212 414-263-7614
Jason Schapekahm, prin. Fax 263-7858
St. Rafael the Archangel S - North 100/PK-1
2075 S 32nd St 53215 414-643-6090
Terisa Folaron, prin. Fax 259-9285
St. Rafael the Archangel S - South 300/2-8
2251 S 31st St 53215 414-645-1300
Terisa Folaron, prin. Fax 645-1415
St. Roman Parish S 300/PK-8
1810 W Bolivar Ave 53221 414-282-7970
Susan Shawver, prin. Fax 282-5140
St. Rose and St. Leo Catholic S 400/PK-8
514 N 31st St 53208 414-933-6070
Kristin Merry, prin. Fax 933-3071
St. Sebastian S 300/K-8
1747 N 54th St 53208 414-453-5830
Heather Grams, prin. Fax 453-9449
St. Thomas Aquinas Academy 200/PK-8
341 E Norwich St 53207 414-744-1214
Dan Heding, prin. Fax 744-8340
St. Vincent Pallotti S 200/PK-8
201 N 76th St 53213 414-258-4165
Jeffrey Johnson, prin. Fax 258-9844
Salam S 700/PK-12
4707 S 13th St 53221 414-282-0504
Br. Wanis Shalaby, prin. Fax 282-6959
Salem Lutheran S 100/PK-8
6844 N 107th St 53224 414-353-8190
Nicholas Bush, prin. Fax 353-5819
Sharon Jr. Academy 50/K-8
1369 W Meinecke Ave 53206 414-265-9000
Maureen Nedd, prin. Fax 265-8390
Sherman Park Lutheran S 300/PK-8
2703 N Sherman Blvd 53210 414-447-0266
Sarah Weber, prin. Fax 445-6556
Siloah Lutheran S 200/K-8
3721 N 21st St 53206 414-873-8240
Scott Anthony, prin. Fax 873-8250
Tamarack Waldorf S 200/PK-12
1150 E Brady St 53202 414-277-0009
Jean Kacanek, admin. Fax 277-7799
University S 1,100/PK-12
2100 W Fairy Chasm Rd 53217 414-352-6000
Laura Fuller, admin. Fax 352-8076

Victory Christian Academy 100/K-8
6021 W Lincoln Ave 53219 414-384-0049
Christina Dyson, admin. Fax 384-0048
Word of Life Lutheran S 100/PK-8
3545 S 23rd St 53221 414-281-7808
Philip Krueger, prin. Fax 281-8823
Yeshiva ES 200/K-8
5115 W Keefe Ave 53216 414-871-9376
Rabbi Dovid Kossowsky, prin. Fax 871-9151

Mindoro, LaCrosse
Melrose-Mindoro SD
Supt. — See Melrose
Mindoro ES 200/K-K, 3-5
N8244 County Rd C 54644 608-857-3410
Corey Peterson, prin. Fax 857-3421

Mineral Point, Iowa, Pop. 2,475
Mineral Point SD 700/PK-12
705 Ross St 53565 608-987-0740
Luke Francois, supt. Fax 987-3766
www.mineralpointschools.org
Mineral Point ES 400/PK-5
611 Cothern St 53565 608-987-0710
Matt Renwick, prin. Fax 987-3904
Mineral Point MS 100/6-8
705 Ross St 53565 608-987-0720
Vickie Dahl, prin. Fax 987-3766

Minocqua, Oneida, Pop. 440
Minocqua J1 SD 600/PK-8
7450 Titus Dr 54548 715-356-5206
Dr. Jim Ellis, supt. Fax 356-1626
www.mhlt.org/
MHLT ES 500/PK-8
7450 Titus Dr 54548 715-356-5206
Brent Johnson, prin. Fax 356-1626

Trinity Lutheran S 50/PK-8
8781 Brunswick Rd 54548 715-356-2255
Michael Wieting, prin. Fax 356-2132

Mishicot, Manitowoc, Pop. 1,424
Mishicot SD 800/PK-12
PO Box 280 54228 920-755-4633
Lee Bush, supt. Fax 755-4068
www.mishicot.k12.wi.us
Mishicot MS 200/6-8
PO Box 280 54228 920-755-2808
Terri Risch, prin. Fax 755-2390
Schultz ES 400/PK-5
PO Box 280 54228 920-755-2041
Eric Nelson, prin. Fax 755-4463

Mondovi, Buffalo, Pop. 2,751
Mondovi SD, 337 N Jackson St 54755 1,000/K-12
Greg Corning, supt. 715-926-3684
www.mondovi.k12.wi.us
Mondovi ES 400/K-5
337 N Jackson St 54755 715-926-3645
Paul Franzwa, prin. Fax 926-4704
Mondovi MS, 337 N Jackson St 54755 200/6-8
Mike Bruning, prin. 715-926-3656

Monona, Dane, Pop. 7,407
Monona Grove SD 3,100/PK-12
5301 Monona Dr 53716 608-221-7660
Dr. Daniel Olson Ed.D., supt. Fax 221-7688
www.mononagrove.org
Winnequah ES 500/PK-5
800 Greenway Rd 53716 608-221-7677
Angie Fassl, prin. Fax 223-6514
Other Schools – See Cottage Grove

Immaculate Heart of Mary S 200/PK-8
4913 Schofield St 53716 608-222-8831
Callie Meiller, prin. Fax 221-4492

Monroe, Green, Pop. 10,726
Monroe SD 2,500/PK-12
925 16th Ave Ste 3 53566 608-328-7171
Rick Waski, supt. Fax 328-7214
www.monroeschools.com
Lincoln ES 400/PK-5
2625 14th Ave 53566 608-328-7172
Sara Latimer, prin. Fax 328-7228
Monroe MS 500/6-8
1510 13th St 53566 608-328-7120
Brian Boehm, prin. Fax 328-7224
Northside ES 400/K-5
3005 8 1/2 St 53566 608-328-7134
Amy Timmerman, prin. Fax 328-7226
Parkside ES 400/PK-5
920 4th St 53566 608-328-7130
Todd Paradis, prin. Fax 328-7222

St. Victor S 100/PK-5
1416 20th Ave 53566 608-325-3395
Joseph Peters, prin. Fax 325-3115

Montello, Marquette, Pop. 1,476
Montello SD 700/PK-12
222 Forest Ln 53949 608-297-7617
Dr. Margaret Banker, supt. Fax 297-7726
www.montelloschools.org
Forest Lane Community S 300/PK-5
222 Forest Ln 53949 608-297-2128
Elizabeth Tierney-Olson, prin. Fax 297-8075

St. John Lutheran S 100/K-8
313 E Montello St 53949 608-297-2866
Timothy Hemling, prin. Fax 297-9069

Monticello, Green, Pop. 1,208
Monticello SD 400/PK-12
334 S Main St 53570 608-938-4194
Allen Brokopp, supt. Fax 938-1062
www.monticello.k12.wi.us/
Monticello ES 200/PK-5
334 S Main St 53570 608-938-4194
Mark Gustafson, prin. Fax 938-1062
Monticello MS 100/6-8
334 S Main St 53570 608-938-4194
Mark Gustafson, prin. Fax 938-1062

Morrisonville, Dane
De Forest Area SD
Supt. — See De Forest
Morrisonville ES 50/K-4
4649 Willow St 53571 608-842-6200
Bill Huebsch, prin. Fax 846-6549

Mosinee, Marathon, Pop. 3,964
Mosinee SD 2,100/PK-12
591 W State Highway 153 54455 715-693-2530
Dr. Ann Schultz, supt. Fax 693-7272
www.mosineeschools.org
Mosinee ES 700/PK-3
600 12th St 54455 715-693-2810
Katie Colwell, prin. Fax 693-1974
Mosinee MS 800/4-8
700 High St 54455 715-693-3660
Joshua Sween, prin. Fax 693-6655

St. Paul S 100/PK-8
404 High St 54455 715-693-2675
JoAnn Sondelski, prin. Fax 693-1332

Mount Calvary, Fond du Lac, Pop. 757

St. Pauls Lutheran S 100/PK-8
W2090 Highway 23 53057 920-922-9056

Mount Horeb, Dane, Pop. 6,889
Mount Horeb Area SD 2,400/PK-12
1304 E Lincoln St 53572 608-437-7006
Dr. Steve Salerno, supt. Fax 437-5597
www.mhasd.k12.wi.us
Early Learning Center 200/PK-K
300 Spellman St 53572 608-437-7606
Rachael Johnson, prin. Fax 437-4027
Mount Horeb Area Community 4K PK-K
300 Spellman St 53572 608-437-7606
Nicole Tepe, coord.
Mount Horeb Intermediate Center 600/3-5
200 Hanneman Blvd 53572 608-437-7406
Stephen Guziewski, prin. Fax 437-8483
Mount Horeb MS 600/6-8
900 E Garfield St 53572 608-437-7306
Paul Christiansen, prin. Fax 437-6227
Mount Horeb Primary Center 400/1-2
207 Academy St 53572 608-437-7506
Rachael Johnson, prin. Fax 437-4620

Mukwonago, Waukesha, Pop. 7,291
Mukwonago SD 4,700/K-12
385 E Veterans Way 53149 262-363-6300
Shawn McNulty, supt. Fax 363-6272
www.masd.k12.wi.us
Clarendon Avenue ES 500/K-6
915 Clarendon Ave 53149 262-363-6286
Andrea Kaplan, prin. Fax 363-6289
Park View MS 800/7-8
930 N Rochester St 53149 262-363-6292
Mark Doome, prin. Fax 363-6320
Rolling Hills ES 500/K-6
W322S9230 Beulah Rd 53149 262-363-6318
Mike Marincic, prin. Fax 363-6343
Section ES 500/K-6
W318S8430 County Road EE 53149 262-363-6260
Robert Slane, prin. Fax 363-6341
Other Schools – See Big Bend, North Prairie

Nature's Classroom Inst & Montessori S 50/PK-12
PO Box 660 53149 800-574-7881
St. John's Lutheran S 100/PK-8
410 W Veterans Way 53149 262-363-4999
James Schneck M.A., prin. Fax 363-7383

Muscoda, Grant, Pop. 1,294
Riverdale SD 600/PK-12
PO Box 66 53573 608-739-3832
Bryce Bird, supt. Fax 739-3751
www.riverdale.k12.wi.us/
Riverdale ES 300/PK-6
800 N 6th St 53573 608-739-3101
Shari Hougan, prin. Fax 739-9118
Riverdale JHS 100/7-8
235 E Elm St 53573 608-739-3116
Jonathan Schmidt, prin. Fax 739-4486

Muskego, Waukesha, Pop. 23,915
Muskego-Norway SD 4,700/PK-12
S87W18763 Woods Rd 53150 262-971-1800
Dr. Kelly Thompson, supt. Fax 679-5790
www.muskegonorway.org/
Bay Lane MS 700/5-8
S75W16399 Hilltop Dr 53150 262-971-1810
Dawn Zandt, prin. Fax 422-2204
Country Meadows ES 300/PK-4
S75W16399 Hilltop Dr 53150 262-971-1815
Courtney Arntzen, prin. Fax 422-1672
Lake Denoon MS 700/5-8
W216S10586 Crowbar Dr 53150 262-971-1820
Linda O'Bryan, prin. Fax 662-1588
Mill Valley ES 300/K-4
W191S6445 Hillendale Dr 53150 262-971-1830
Robin Schrot, prin. Fax 679-4087
Muskego ES 200/K-4
S75W17476 Janesville Rd 53150 262-971-1840
Robin Schrot, prin. Fax 679-4085
Tess Corners ES 500/K-4
W147S6800 Durham Pl 53150 262-971-1860
Sara Stanley, prin. Fax 422-2223
Other Schools – See Wind Lake

St. Leonard S 200/PK-8
W173S7777 Westwood Dr 53150 262-679-0451
Lisa Ellis, prin. Fax 679-8519
St. Paul's Lutheran S 300/PK-8
S66W14325 Janesville Rd 53150 414-422-0320
Seth Fitzsimmons, prin. Fax 422-1711

Nashotah, Waukesha, Pop. 1,378

St. Joan of Arc S 100/PK-8
120 Nashotah Rd 53058 262-646-5821
Holly Cerveny, prin. Fax 646-5861

Necedah, Juneau, Pop. 904
Necedah Area SD 700/PK-12
1801 S Main St 54646 608-565-2256
Tanya Kotlowski, supt. Fax 565-3201
www.necedahschools.org
Necedah ES 300/PK-5
1801 S Main St 54646 608-565-2256
Wendy Horbinski, prin. Fax 565-7044

Neenah, Winnebago, Pop. 25,158
Neenah SD 6,200/PK-12
410 S Commercial St 54956 920-751-6800
Mary Pfeiffer Ph.D., supt. Fax 751-6809
www.neenah.k12.wi.us
Clayton ES 300/K-5
2916 W Fairview Rd 54956 920-751-6950
Amy McKeefry, prin. Fax 836-2881
Coolidge ES 300/K-5
321 Alcott Dr 54956 920-751-6955
April Keepers, prin. Fax 751-6857
Hoover ES 300/PK-5
950 Hunt Ave 54956 920-751-6960
Melissa Chrisman, prin. Fax 751-6858
Lakeview ES 300/K-5
1645 S Commercial St 54956 920-751-6965
Mary Renning, prin. Fax 751-6859
Mann MS 500/6-6
1021 Oak St 54956 920-751-6940
Jackie Munoz-Ellman, prin. Fax 751-7099
Roosevelt ES 100/K-5
215 E Forest Ave 54956 920-751-6970
Diane Luft, prin. Fax 751-6861
Shattuck MS 1,000/7-8
600 Elm St 54956 920-751-6850
Stephanie Phernetton, prin. Fax 751-6899
Spring Road ES 400/K-5
1191 County Road II 54956 920-751-6975
Michaela Neitzel, prin. Fax 751-6911
Taft ES 100/PK-5
133 S Western Ave 54956 920-751-6980
Lucille Hrib, prin. Fax 751-6912
Tullar ES 400/K-5
925 Tullar Rd 54956 920-751-6985
Diane Galow, prin. Fax 751-6913
Washington Early Learning Center 100/PK-PK
220 E Franklin Ave 54956 920-751-6990
Stacie Brethouwer, admin. Fax 751-6914
Wilson ES 400/PK-5
920 Higgins Ave 54956 920-751-6995
Ryan Hammerschmidt, prin. Fax 751-6984

Fox Valley Christian Academy 200/PK-8
PO Box 799 54957 920-725-7985
Ron Halma, admin. Fax 725-3236
Luther Lutheran S 100/PK-8
807 Adams St 54956 920-725-8047
Roger Kramp, prin. Fax 886-1266
New Hope Christian S 300/PK-8
1850 American Dr 54956 920-725-8797
Laurie Prewitt M.Ed., admin. Fax 886-8729
St. Gabriel ES 200/PK-5
900 Geiger St 54956 920-725-4161
Patrick Batey, prin. Fax 722-2566
St. Margaret Mary ES 300/PK-5
610 Division St 54956 920-729-4565
Patrick Batey, prin. Fax 729-4567
St. Mary Catholic MS 200/6-8
1000 Zephyr Dr 54956 920-727-0279
Patrick Batey, prin. Fax 727-1215
Trinity Lutheran S 100/PK-8
410 Oak St 54956 920-722-3051
Jason Gibson, prin. Fax 722-8297

Neillsville, Clark, Pop. 2,446
Neillsville SD 1,000/PK-12
614 E 5th St 54456 715-743-3323
John Gaier, supt. Fax 743-8718
www.neillsville.k12.wi.us
Neillsville ES 500/PK-6
504 E 5th St 54456 715-743-8712
Tim Rueth, prin. Fax 743-8715

St. John's Lutheran S 100/PK-8
805 W 5th St 54456 715-743-2501
Mike Allard, prin. Fax 743-2501

Nekoosa, Wood, Pop. 2,530
Nekoosa SD 1,300/PK-12
600 S Section St 54457 715-886-8000
Terry Whitmore, supt. Fax 886-8012
www.nekoosasd.net
Alexander MS 400/4-8
540 Birch St 54457 715-886-8040
Clint Rogers, prin. Fax 886-8097
Humke ES 400/PK-3
500 S Section St 54457 715-886-8010
Jon Sprehn, prin. Fax 886-8024

Neopit, Menominee, Pop. 682
Menominee Indian SD
Supt. — See Keshena
Menominee Indian MS 100/6-8
PO Box 9 54150 715-756-2324
Timothy Meyers, prin. Fax 756-2496

Neosho, Dodge, Pop. 566
Herman Neosho Rubicon SD 200/PK-8
201 Center St 53059 920-625-3531
Dennis Kaczor, supt. Fax 625-3536
www.hnrschools.org
Honor ES 100/PK-4
201 Center St 53059 920-625-3531
Dennis Kaczor, admin. Fax 625-3536
Other Schools – See Rubicon

New Auburn, Chippewa, Pop. 537
New Auburn SD 300/PK-12
PO Box 110 54757 715-237-2202
Scott Johnson, supt. Fax 237-2350
www.newauburn.k12.wi.us
New Auburn ES 200/PK-6
PO Box 110 54757 715-237-2505
David Hutzler, prin. Fax 237-2350

New Berlin, Waukesha, Pop. 39,208
New Berlin SD 4,600/K-12
4333 S Sunnyslope Rd 53151 262-789-6200
Joe Garza, supt. Fax 786-0512
www.nbexcellence.org/
Elmwood ES 600/K-6
5900 S Sunnyslope Rd 53151 262-789-6581
Katherine Williams, prin. Fax 427-7290
Orchard Lane ES 400/K-6
2015 S Sunnyslope Rd 53151 262-789-6500
Amy Fare, prin. Fax 789-6286
Poplar Creek ES 500/K-6
17401 W Cleveland Ave 53146 262-789-6520
Matt Stempniewski, prin. Fax 789-6234
Reagan ES 700/K-6
4225 S Calhoun Rd 53151 262-789-6550
Brady Reinke, prin. Fax 789-6205

West Allis SD
Supt. — See Milwaukee
Hoover ES 500/PK-5
12705 W Euclid Ave 53151 414-604-3810
Mike Elliott, prin. Fax 782-2231

Heritage Christian Schools 500/PK-12
3500 S West Ln 53151 262-432-0333
John Davis, pres. Fax 432-0542
Holy Apostles S 400/K-8
3875 S 159th St 53151 262-786-7331
Melissa Trepte, prin. Fax 786-0425
Star of Bethlehem Lutheran S 200/PK-8
3700 S Casper Dr 53151 262-786-2901
Tim Mueller, prin. Fax 786-2836

Newburg, Washington, Pop. 1,248

St. John's Lutheran S 100/PK-8
PO Box 169 53060 262-675-6852
Tim Payne, prin. Fax 675-0707

New Glarus, Green, Pop. 2,162
New Glarus SD 800/PK-12
PO Box 7 53574 608-527-2410
Dr. Jennifer Thayer, supt. Fax 527-5101
www.ngsd.k12.wi.us
New Glarus ES 400/PK-4
PO Box 37 53574 608-527-2410
Laura Eicher, prin. Fax 527-5101
New Glarus MS 100/5-8
PO Box 67 53574 608-527-2410
Mark Stateler, prin. Fax 527-5101

New Holstein, Calumet, Pop. 3,214
New Holstein SD 1,100/PK-12
1715 Plymouth St 53061 920-898-5115
Dan Nett, supt. Fax 898-4112
www.nhsd.k12.wi.us
New Holstein ES 500/PK-5
2226 Park Ave 53061 920-898-4208
Tanya Fenner, prin. Fax 898-9152
New Holstein MS 300/6-8
1717 Plymouth St 53061 920-898-4769
Amanda Jacobson, prin. Fax 898-4810

New Lisbon, Juneau, Pop. 2,524
New Lisbon SD 700/PK-12
500 S Forest St 53950 608-562-3700
Dennis Birr, supt. Fax 562-5333
www.newlisbon.k12.wi.us
New Lisbon ES 400/PK-6
500 S Forest St 53950 608-562-3700
Mark Toelle, prin. Fax 562-3062

New London, Waupaca, Pop. 7,241
New London SD 2,500/PK-12
901 W Washington St 54961 920-982-8530
Dennis Krueger, supt. Fax 982-8551
www.newlondon.k12.wi.us
Lincoln ES 300/PK-4
201 E Washington St 54961 920-982-8540
Kirk Delwiche, prin. Fax 982-8701
New London IS / MS 700/5-8
1000 W Washington St 54961 920-982-8532
Pete Schulz, prin. Fax 982-8605
Parkview ES 400/PK-4
1300 Werner Allen Rd 54961 920-982-8538
Jody Peterson, prin. Fax 982-8700
Sugar Bush ES 100/PK-4
W10736 County Road WW 54961 715-752-4135
Kristin Grable, prin. Fax 752-4010
Other Schools – See Readfield

Emanuel Lutheran S 100/PK-8
200 E Quincy St 54961 920-982-5444
Matt Foley, prin. Fax 982-0954
Most Precious Blood S 50/PK-4
120 E Washington St 54961 920-982-2134
Sandra Piotrowski, prin. Fax 982-8381

New Richmond, Saint Croix, Pop. 8,254
SD of New Richmond 3,200/PK-12
701 E 11th St 54017 715-243-7411
Patrick Olson, supt. Fax 246-3638
www.newrichmond.k12.wi.us
New Richmond Hillside ES 600/K-5
701 E 11th St 54017 715-243-1400
Frank Norton, prin. Fax 243-1418
New Richmond MS 700/6-8
701 E 11th St 54017 715-243-7472
Doug Hatch, prin. Fax 246-0580
Paperjack ES 300/K-5
701 E 11th St 54017 715-243-7400
Mike Ballard, prin. Fax 246-4278
Starr ES 500/PK-5
701 E 11th St 54017 715-243-7431
Nicholas Hall, prin. Fax 246-2898

St. Mary S 200/PK-8
257 S Washington Ave 54017 715-246-2469
Laura Jo Jarchow, prin. Fax 246-6195

Niagara, Marinette, Pop. 1,609
Niagara SD 500/PK-12
700 Jefferson Ave 54151 715-251-4541
Nathaniel Burklund, supt. Fax 251-4544
www.niagara.k12.wi.us
Niagara ES 300/PK-6
700 Jefferson Ave 54151 715-251-4541
Scott Trevillian, prin. Fax 251-3715

North Fond du Lac, Fond du Lac, Pop. 4,969
North Fond Du Lac SD 1,300/PK-12
225 McKinley St 54937 920-929-3750
Aaron Sadoff, supt. Fax 929-3696
www.nfdl.k12.wi.us
Allen MS 300/6-8
305 Mckinley St 54937 920-929-3754
Michael Gonzalez, prin. Fax 929-3747
Early Learning Center 200/PK-K
923 Minnesota Ave 54937 920-929-3762
Debra Ellingen, prin. Fax 322-9117
Friendship ES 400/1-5
1115 Thurke Ave 54937 920-929-3757
Kerri Jo Patten, prin. Fax 929-7020

St. Paul Lutheran S 100/PK-8
1010 Adams Ave 54937 920-922-1080
Aaron Hartwig, prin. Fax 922-1080

North Freedom, Sauk, Pop. 697
Baraboo SD
Supt. — See Baraboo
North Freedom ES 100/K-5
500 N Maple St 53951 608-522-4946
Kathleen Andreasen, prin. Fax 522-4506

North Lake, Waukesha
North Lake SD 400/PK-8
PO Box 188 53064 262-966-2033
Liesl R. Ackley, supt. Fax 966-3710
www.northlakeschool.org
North Lake S 400/PK-8
PO Box 188 53064 262-966-2033
Liesl R. Ackley, supt. Fax 966-3710

North Prairie, Waukesha, Pop. 2,131
Mukwonago SD
Supt. — See Mukwonago
Prairie View ES 400/K-6
W330S6473 County Rd E 53153 262-392-6310
Stephanie Blue, prin. Fax 392-6312

Oak Creek, Milwaukee, Pop. 33,834
Oak Creek-Franklin SD 6,400/PK-12
7630 S 10th St 53154 414-768-5880
Dr. Tim Culver, supt. Fax 768-6172
ocfsd.org
Carollton ES 400/PK-5
8965 S Carollton Dr 53154 414-768-6290
Paul Kenwood, prin. Fax 768-6286
Cedar Hills ES 400/PK-5
2225 W Sycamore Ave 53154 414-761-3020
Keith Ruffolo, prin. Fax 761-6301
Deerfield ES 400/PK-5
3871 E Bluestem Dr 53154 414-768-6220
James Arata, prin. Fax 768-6221
Edgewood ES 500/PK-5
8545 S Shepard Ave 53154 414-768-6285
John Krenek, prin. Fax 768-6287
Forest Ridge ES K-5
2200 W Drexel Ave 53154 414-574-4050
Ed Mittag, prin.
Meadowview ES 400/PK-5
10420 S McGraw Dr 53154 414-768-6240
Lisa Rezner, prin. Fax 768-6288
Oak Creek East MS 900/6-8
9330 S Shepard Ave 53154 414-768-6260
Sue Thompson, prin. Fax 768-6293
Oak Creek West MS 500/6-8
8401 S 13th St 53154 414-768-6250
Megan Arens, prin. Fax 768-6296
Shepard Hills ES 500/PK-5
9701 S Shepard Hills Dr 53154 414-768-6270
Lois Booth, prin. Fax 768-6289

Grace Lutheran S 100/PK-8
8537 S Pennsylvania Ave 53154 414-762-3655
Steven Gettleman, prin. Fax 762-8869
St. Matthew S 200/K-8
9329 S Chicago Rd 53154 414-762-6820
Kelly Stefanich, prin. Fax 762-4555

Oakfield, Fond du Lac, Pop. 1,057
Oakfield SD 500/PK-12
PO Box 99 53065 920-583-3141
Dr. Vance Dalzin, supt. Fax 583-4671
www.oakfield.k12.wi.us
Oakfield ES 300/PK-5
PO Box 99 53065 920-583-3146
Becky Doyle, prin. Fax 583-3820
Oakfield MS 100/6-8
PO Box 39 53065 920-583-3141
Carmen Klassy, prin. Fax 583-4673

St. Luke Lutheran S 50/PK-8
PO Box 277 53065 920-933-4707
Kaleb Buch, prin.

Oconomowoc, Waukesha, Pop. 15,586
Oconomowoc Area SD 4,900/K-12
W360N7077 Brown St 53066 262-560-1115
Dr. Roger Rindo, supt.
www.oasd.k12.wi.us
Greenland ES 300/K-4
440 Coolidge St 53066 262-560-8100
Shannon McCaffery, prin. Fax 560-8118
Meadow View ES 500/K-4
W360n7077 Brown St 53066 262-560-8000
Jason Schreiber, prin. Fax 560-8018
Nature Hill IS 800/5-8
850 N Lake Rd 53066 262-569-4945
Jason Curtis, prin. Fax 569-4958
Park Lawn ES 400/K-4
300 Parklawn St 53066 262-560-8200
Jennifer Jones, prin. Fax 560-8218
Silver Lake IS 700/5-8
555 Oconomowoc Pkwy 53066 262-560-4305
Jill Marr, prin. Fax 560-4318
Summit ES 500/K-4
1680 E Valley Rd 53066 262-560-8300
Brian Stuckey, prin. Fax 560-8318
Other Schools – See Ixonia

Stone Bank SD 300/K-8
N68W33866 County Road K 53066 262-966-2900
Lynn Davies Ph.D., supt. Fax 966-1828
www.stonebank.k12.wi.us
Stone Bank S 300/K-8
N68W33866 County Road K 53066 262-966-2900
Lynn Davies Ph.D., admin. Fax 966-1828

St. Jerome S 300/K-8
1001 S Silver Lake St 53066 262-569-3030
Mary Johnson, prin. Fax 569-3023
St. Matthew's Lutheran S 200/PK-8
818 W Wisconsin Ave 53066 262-912-6364
Eric Ziol, prin. Fax 737-0036
St. Paul's Lutheran S 100/PK-8
210 E Pleasant St 53066 262-567-5001
Jill George, prin. Fax 567-1207

Oconto, Oconto, Pop. 4,472
Oconto USD 1,000/PK-12
400 Michigan Ave 54153 920-834-7814
Emily Miller, supt. Fax 834-9884
www.oconto.k12.wi.us
Oconto ES 400/PK-4
810 Scherer Ave 54153 920-834-7808
Ben Bourassa, prin. Fax 834-9883
Oconto MS 200/5-8
400 Michigan Ave 54153 920-834-7806
Adam DeWitt, prin. Fax 834-9884

Oconto Falls, Oconto, Pop. 2,850
Oconto Falls SD 1,800/PK-12
200 N Farm Rd 54154 920-848-4471
Dr. Dean Hess, supt. Fax 848-4474
www.ocontofalls.k12.wi.us
Oconto Falls ES 600/PK-5
415 Maria Volk Dr 54154 920-848-4476
Dan Moore, prin. Fax 848-4454
Washington MS 400/6-8
102 S Washington St 54154 920-846-4463
Stephanie Landreman, prin. Fax 846-4453
Other Schools – See Abrams

St. Anthony S 50/K-5
253 N Franklin St 54154 920-846-2276
Alex Wolf, prin. Fax 846-2180

Okauchee, Waukesha

Holy Trinity Evangelical Lutheran S 100/PK-8
PO Box 146 53069 262-567-2737
Kevin Klug, prin. Fax 567-2615

Omro, Winnebago, Pop. 3,492
Omro SD 1,300/PK-12
455 Fox Trl 54963 920-303-2302
Dr. Kelly Rieckmann, admin. Fax 685-5757
www.omro.k12.wi.us
Omro ES 300/2-5
1000 N Webster Ave 54963 920-303-2312
David Wellhoefer, prin. Fax 685-3105
Omro MS 300/6-8
455 Fox Trl 54963 920-303-2311
Kari Strebig, prin. Fax 685-5757
Patch ES 200/PK-1
607 Tyler Ave 54963 920-303-2312
David Wellhoefer, prin. Fax 685-7042

Onalaska, LaCrosse, Pop. 17,449
Onalaska SD 2,800/PK-12
237 2nd Ave S 54650 608-781-9700
Dr. Francis E. Finco, supt. Fax 781-9712
www.onalaska.k12.wi.us
Eagle Bluff ES 400/PK-5
200 Eagle Bluff Ct 54650 608-783-2453
Todd Saner, prin. Fax 783-2068
Northern Hills ES 500/PK-5
910 East Ave N 54650 608-783-4542
Amy Russ, prin. Fax 779-4114
Onalaska MS 600/6-8
711 Quincy St 54650 608-783-5366
Jed Kees, prin. Fax 781-8030

Pertzsch ES 400/PK-5
524 Main St 54650 608-783-5644
Todd Antony, prin. Fax 783-1351

St. Patrick S 200/PK-6
127 11th Ave N 54650 608-783-5483
Susan Amble, prin. Fax 783-2128
St. Paul Evangelical Lutheran S 200/PK-8
PO Box 128 54650 608-783-4822
Benjamin Bain, prin. Fax 779-5942

Ontario, Vernon, Pop. 550
Norwalk-Ontario-Wilton SD 700/PK-12
PO Box 130 54651 608-337-4403
Dr. Kelly Burhop, supt. Fax 337-4348
www.now.k12.wi.us/
Norwalk-Ontario-Wilton ES 400/PK-6
PO Box 130 54651 608-337-4420
Dr. Gayle Luebke, prin. Fax 337-4348

Oostburg, Sheboygan, Pop. 2,866
Oostburg SD 1,000/PK-12
PO Box 700100 53070 920-564-2346
Kevin Bruggink, supt. Fax 564-6138
oostburg.k12.wi.us
Oostburg ES 500/PK-5
PO Box 700100 53070 920-564-2392
Aaron White, prin. Fax 564-6138
Oostburg MS 200/6-8
PO Box 700100 53070 920-564-2383
Sherri Stengel, prin. Fax 564-6138

Oostburg Christian S 200/PK-8
PO Box 700319 53070 920-564-2664
Paul Modahl, admin. Fax 564-3166

Oregon, Dane, Pop. 9,079
Oregon SD 3,600/K-12
123 E Grove St 53575 608-835-4000
Brian Busler, supt. Fax 835-9509
www.oregonsd.org
Netherwood Knoll ES 500/K-4
276 Soden Dr 53575 608-835-4100
Chris Kluck, prin. Fax 835-7827
Oregon MS 600/7-8
601 Pleasant Oak Dr 53575 608-835-4800
Shannon Anderson, prin. Fax 835-3849
Prairie View ES 500/K-4
300 Soden Dr 53575 608-835-4200
Dr. Dawn Goltz, prin. Fax 835-8037
Rome Corners IS 500/5-6
1111 S Perry Pkwy 53575 608-835-4700
Jason Zurawik, prin. Fax 835-2704
Other Schools – See Brooklyn

Orfordville, Rock, Pop. 1,432
Parkview SD 500/PK-12
PO Box 250 53576 608-879-2717
Dr. Steve Lutzke, supt. Fax 879-2732
www.parkview.k12.wi.us
Parkview ES 200/PK-6
PO Box 250 53576 608-879-2956
Dr. Karen Strandt-Conroy, prin. Fax 879-9971

Osceola, Polk, Pop. 2,529
Osceola SD 1,800/PK-12
PO Box 128 54020 715-294-4140
Mark Luebker, supt. Fax 294-2428
www.osceola.k12.wi.us
Osceola ES 400/PK-2
PO Box 128 54020 715-294-3457
Peggy Weber, prin. Fax 294-2428
Osceola IS 400/3-5
PO Box 128 54020 715-294-2800
Jake Dodge, prin. Fax 294-2428
Osceola MS 400/6-8
PO Box 128 54020 715-294-4180
Rebecca Styles, prin. Fax 294-2428

Oshkosh, Winnebago, Pop. 65,117
Oshkosh Area SD 10,000/PK-12
PO Box 3048 54903 920-424-0395
Stan Mack, supt. Fax 424-0466
www.oshkosh.k12.wi.us
Cook ES 300/PK-5
1600 Hazel St 54901 920-424-0152
Michael Ruhl, prin. Fax 424-7580
Franklin ES 400/PK-5
1401 W 5th Ave 54902 920-424-0078
Jami Kohl, prin. Fax 424-7581
Jefferson ES 200/PK-5
244 W 11th Ave 54902 920-424-0165
Rhonda Buchanan, prin. Fax 424-7583
Lakeside ES 300/PK-5
4991 S US Highway 45 54902 920-424-0131
Amy Ashton, prin. Fax 424-7584
Merrill ES 300/PK-5
108 W New York Ave 54901 920-424-0420
Sarah Poquette, prin. Fax 424-7504
Merrill MS 400/6-8
108 W New York Ave 54901 920-424-0177
Cindy Olson, prin. Fax 424-7512
Oaklawn ES 400/PK-5
112 Viola Ave 54901 920-424-0170
Scott Johan-Krecht, prin. Fax 424-7590
Oakwood ES 500/PK-5
1225 N Oakwood Rd 54904 920-424-0315
Susan Martin, prin. Fax 424-7591
Read ES 300/PK-5
1120 Algoma Blvd 54901 920-424-0172
Jacquelyn Kiffmeyer, prin. Fax 424-7592
Ready 4 Learning ES 600/PK-K
215 S Eagle St 54902 920-424-0077
Elizabeth Schendel, prin.
Roosevelt ES 300/PK-5
910 N Sawyer St 54902 920-424-0411
Kristin Burgert, prin. Fax 424-7593

Smith ES 200/PK-5
1745 Oregon St 54902 920-424-0174
Marlene Gundlach, prin. Fax 424-7595
South Park MS 400/6-8
1551 Delaware St 54902 920-424-0431
Lisa McLaughlin, prin. Fax 424-7513
Stanley ES 300/PK-5
915 Hazel St 54901 920-424-0460
Elizabeth Galeazzi, prin. Fax 424-7598
Stanley MS 400/6-8
915 Hazel St 54901 920-424-0442
Philip Marshall, prin. Fax 424-7515
Tipler MS 300/6-8
325 S Eagle St 54902 920-424-0320
Jay Jones, prin. Fax 424-7514
Traeger ES 500/PK-5
3000 W 20th Ave 54904 920-424-0221
Brenna Garrison-Bruden, prin. Fax 424-7586
Traeger MS 500/6-8
3000 W 20th Ave 54904 920-424-0065
Jill Pascarella, prin. Fax 424-7511
Washington ES 200/PK-5
929 Winnebago Ave 54901 920-424-0190
Kristi Levy, prin. Fax 424-7597

Grace Lutheran S 100/PK-8
913 Nebraska St 54902 920-231-8957
Benjamin Leibl, prin. Fax 231-8552
Lourdes Academy - Cabrini 200/PK-5
619 Merritt Ave 54901 920-235-0637
Amy Geffers, prin. Fax 426-6429
Lourdes Academy MS 200/6-8
110 N Sawyer St 54902 920-235-5670
Kyle Schleis, prin. Fax 235-7453
Lourdes Academy - Seton 200/PK-5
1207 Oregon St 54902 920-235-4060
Amy Geffers, prin. Fax 426-6430
Luther S 100/PK-8
1526 Algoma Blvd 54901 920-235-1612
Steven Hennig, prin. Fax 967-0447
Trinity Lutheran S 100/PK-8
819 School Ave 54901 920-235-1730
Joseph Reinl, admin. Fax 235-1734
Valley Christian S 200/PK-12
3450 Vinland St 54901 920-231-9704
Bradley Dunn, admin. Fax 231-9804

Osseo, Trempealeau, Pop. 1,691
Osseo-Fairchild SD 900/PK-12
50851 East St 54758 715-597-3141
William Tourdot Ed.D., supt. Fax 597-3606
www.ofsd.k12.wi.us
Osseo-Fairchild ES 300/PK-5
13025 15th St 54758 715-597-3196
Lori Whelan, prin. Fax 597-3406
Osseo-Fairchild MS 200/6-8
50851 East St 54758 715-597-3141
Drew Semingson, prin. Fax 597-3647

Owen, Clark, Pop. 936
Owen-Withee SD 500/PK-12
PO Box 417 54460 715-229-2151
Robert Houts, supt. Fax 229-4322
www.owen-withee.k12.wi.us
Owen-Withee ES 300/PK-6
PO Box 417 54460 715-229-4488
Lance Batchelor, prin. Fax 229-4981
Owen-Withee JHS 100/7-8
PO Box 417 54460 715-229-2151
Julie Van Ark, prin. Fax 229-4322

Oxford, Marquette, Pop. 604
Westfield SD
Supt. — See Westfield
Oxford ES 100/PK-6
222 S Franklin Ave 53952 608-586-5131
Chase Gildenzoph, prin. Fax 586-4521

Palmyra, Jefferson, Pop. 1,774
Palmyra-Eagle Area SD 1,000/PK-12
PO Box 901 53156 262-495-7101
Steven Bloom, supt. Fax 495-7151
www.palmyra.k12.wi.us
Palmyra-Eagle MS 200/7-8
PO Box 901 53156 262-495-7101
Kari Timm, prin. Fax 495-7146
Palmyra ES 300/PK-6
PO Box 901 53156 262-495-7103
Steven Greenquist, prin. Fax 495-7134
Other Schools – See Eagle

Pardeeville, Columbia, Pop. 2,095
Pardeeville Area SD 800/PK-12
PO Box 130 53954 608-429-2153
Gus Knitt, supt. Fax 429-2277
www.pardeeville.k12.wi.us
Pardeeville ES 400/PK-4
PO Box 130 53954 608-429-2151
Mary Kamrath, prin. Fax 429-4807
Pardeeville MS 200/5-8
PO Box 130 53954 608-429-2153
David Bell, prin. Fax 429-2277

St. John's Lutheran S 100/PK-8
PO Box 367 53954 608-429-3636
Fax 429-4876

Park Falls, Price, Pop. 2,367
Chequamegon SD 800/PK-12
420 9th St N 54552 715-762-2474
David Anderson, admin. Fax 762-5469
www.csdk12.net
Park Falls ES 300/PK-6
380 9th St N 54552 715-762-2474
Marilyn Brink, prin. Fax 762-2428
Other Schools – See Glidden

Patch Grove, Grant, Pop. 198
River Ridge SD 500/PK-12
PO Box 78 53817 608-994-2715
Dr. Jeff Athey, supt. Fax 994-2891
www.rrsd.k12.wi.us
River Ridge ES 200/PK-4
PO Box 78 53817 608-994-2715
Jeff Athey, prin. Fax 994-2891
Other Schools – See Bloomington

Pembine, Marinette, Pop. 189
Beecher-Dunbar-Pembine SD 300/PK-12
PO Box 247 54156 715-324-5314
Chris Metras, supt. Fax 324-5282
www.pembine.k12.wi.us/
Pembine ES 100/PK-6
PO Box 247 54156 715-324-5314
Julie Rittenhouse, admin. Fax 324-5282

Pepin, Pepin, Pop. 835
Pepin Area SD 200/PK-12
PO Box 128 54759 715-442-2391
Bruce Quinton, supt. Fax 442-3607
www.pepin.k12.wi.us
Pepin ES 100/PK-6
PO Box 128 54759 715-442-2391
Bruce Quinton, prin. Fax 442-3607

Peshtigo, Marinette, Pop. 3,466
Peshtigo SD 1,300/PK-12
341 N Emery Ave 54157 715-582-3677
Kim Eparvier, supt. Fax 582-3850
www.peshtigo.k12.wi.us
Peshtigo ES 700/PK-6
341 N Emery Ave 54157 715-582-3762
Kelly Collins, prin. Fax 582-4106

St. John Evangelical Lutheran S 50/PK-8
N1926 Church Rd 54157 715-582-4565
Lance List, prin.

Pewaukee, Waukesha, Pop. 8,065
Pewaukee SD 2,800/PK-12
404 Lake St 53072 262-691-2100
Mike Cady, supt. Fax 691-1052
pewaukee.schoolwires.net
Clark MS 400/7-8
472 Lake St 53072 262-691-2100
Randy Daul, prin. Fax 695-5004
Horizon ES 600/4-6
458 Lake St 53072 262-691-2100
Pete Gull, prin. Fax 695-5033
Pewaukee Lake ES 1,000/PK-3
436 Lake St 53072 262-691-2100
Robin Wilson, prin. Fax 695-5002

Prairie Hill Waldorf S 100/PK-8
N14W29143 Silvernail Rd 53072 262-646-7497
Jeanne Ring, admin. Fax 646-7495
St. Anthony on the Lake S 200/K-8
W280N2101 Prospect Ave 53072 262-691-0460
Ellen Knippel, prin. Fax 691-7376
Trinity Academy 100/PK-12
W225N3131 Duplainville Rd 53072 262-695-2933
Robin Mitchell Ph.D., hdmstr. Fax 695-2934

Phelps, Vilas
Phelps SD 100/K-12
4451 Old School Rd 54554 715-545-2724
Delnice Hill, supt. Fax 545-3728
www.phelps.k12.wi.us
Phelps ES 100/K-8
4451 Old School Rd 54554 715-545-2724
Jason Pertile, dean Fax 545-3728

Phillips, Price, Pop. 1,454
Phillips SD 800/PK-12
PO Box 70 54555 715-339-2419
Rick Morgan, supt. Fax 339-2416
www.phillips.k12.wi.us
Phillips ES 400/PK-5
400 Turner St 54555 715-339-3864
Dave Scholz, prin. Fax 339-2295
Phillips MS 200/6-8
PO Box 70 54555 715-339-2141
Colin Hoogland, prin. Fax 339-2144

Pine River, Waushara, Pop. 147
Wild Rose SD
Supt. — See Wild Rose
Pleasant View ES 100/PK-4
N5275 County Road NN 54965 920-987-5123
Matt Wilbert, prin. Fax 987-5136

Pittsville, Wood, Pop. 868
Pittsville SD 600/PK-12
5459 Elementary Ave Ste 2 54466 715-884-6694
Rodney Figueroa, supt. Fax 884-5218
www.pittsville.k12.wi.us
Pittsville ES 400/PK-8
5459 Elementary Ave Ste 1 54466 715-884-2517
Heather Friday, prin. Fax 884-5218

Plain, Sauk, Pop. 765
River Valley SD
Supt. — See Spring Green
River Valley Early Learning Center 100/PK-K
1370 Cherry St 53577 608-546-2228
Jaime Hegland, prin. Fax 546-4028

St. Luke S 100/PK-8
1290 Nachreiner Ave 53577 608-546-2963
Cindy Haag, prin. Fax 546-2616

Plainfield, Waushara, Pop. 852
Tri-County Area SD 500/PK-12
409 S West St 54966 715-335-6366
Anthony Marinack, supt. Fax 335-6365
tricounty.k12.wi.us

Tri-County ES 300/PK-6
409 S West St 54966 715-335-6366
Shawn Jepson, prin. Fax 335-6364

Platteville, Grant, Pop. 11,124
Platteville SD 1,500/PK-12
780 N 2nd St 53818 608-342-4000
Connie Valenza, supt. Fax 342-4412
www.platteville.k12.wi.us
Platteville MS 500/5-8
40 E Madison St 53818 608-342-4010
Jason Julius, prin. Fax 342-4497
Westview ES 200/1-4
1205 Camp St 53818 608-342-4050
ReNah Reuter, prin. Fax 342-4557
Wilkins Early Learning Center 300/PK-K
425 Broadway St 53818 608-342-4040
Tamara Haag, dir. Fax 342-4581

Pleasant Prairie, Kenosha, Pop. 19,418
Kenosha SD
Supt. — See Kenosha
Pleasant Prairie ES 700/PK-5
9208 Wilmot Rd 53158 262-359-2104
Shane Gayle, prin. Fax 359-2157
Prairie Lane ES 400/PK-5
10717 47th Ave 53158 262-359-3600
Camille Schroeder, prin. Fax 359-3650
Whittier ES 500/PK-5
8542 Cooper Rd 53158 262-359-2110
Teresa Curley, prin. Fax 359-2270

Good Shepherd Lutheran S 50/PK-5
4311 104th St 53158 262-694-4405
Jennifer Leinss, prin. Fax 694-0964

Plover, Portage, Pop. 11,981
Stevens Point Area SD
Supt. — See Stevens Point
Plover-Whiting ES 500/K-6
1400 Hoover Ave 54467 715-345-5424
Carl Coffman, prin. Fax 345-7354
Roosevelt ES 500/K-6
2200 Wisconsin Ave 54467 715-345-5425
Kelly Snyder-Chase, prin. Fax 345-7347

Pacelli Catholic S - St. Bronislava 100/PK-5
3301 Willow Dr 54467 715-342-2015
Gregg Hansel, admin. Fax 342-2016

Plum City, Pierce, Pop. 598
Plum City SD 300/PK-12
907 Main St 54761 715-647-2591
Dr. Ronald Walsh, supt. Fax 647-3015
www.plumcity.k12.wi.us
Plum City ES 100/PK-5
621 Main St 54761 715-647-2911
Dr. Mike Kennedy, prin. Fax 647-4002

Plymouth, Sheboygan, Pop. 8,357
Plymouth SD 2,100/PK-12
125 S Highland Ave 53073 920-892-2661
Carrie Dassow Ph.D., supt. Fax 892-6366
www.plymouth.k12.wi.us
Fairview ES 300/PK-5
300 Salem Dr 53073 920-892-2621
Nick O'Malley, prin. Fax 892-5071
Horizon ES 300/PK-5
411 S Highland Ave 53073 920-892-2225
Dena Budrecki, prin. Fax 892-5073
Parkview ES 300/PK-5
500 Parkview Dr 53073 920-892-4076
John Mather, prin. Fax 892-5077
Riverview MS 400/6-8
300 Riverside Cir 53073 920-892-4353
Todd Hunt, prin. Fax 892-5072

St. John Lutheran S 200/PK-8
222 N Stafford St 53073 920-893-5114
Jay Lindsey, prin. Fax 892-2845
St. John the Baptist S 200/PK-8
116 N Pleasant St 53073 920-893-5961
Amy Nelson, prin. Fax 893-3160

Poplar, Douglas, Pop. 589
Maple SD
Supt. — See Maple
Northwestern ES 500/PK-5
PO Box 76 54864 715-364-8465
Steve Gustafson, prin. Fax 364-2270
Northwestern MS 300/6-8
PO Box 46 54864 715-364-2218
T. Krieg, prin. Fax 364-2540

Portage, Columbia, Pop. 10,179
Portage Community SD 2,400/PK-12
305 E Slifer St 53901 608-742-4879
Charles Poches Ed.D., supt. Fax 742-4950
www.portage.k12.wi.us
Bartels MS 600/6-8
2505 New Pinery Rd 53901 608-742-2165
Fax 745-4884
Lewiston ES 100/K-5
W11195 State Road 127 53901 608 742 2524
Nicole Schoenborn, prin. Fax 742-2418
Muir ES 400/2-5
2600 Woodcrest Dr 53901 608-742-5531
Jason Meyer, prin. Fax 742-2525
Rusch ES 300/PK-5
117 W Franklin St 53901 608-742-7376
Nicole Schoenborn, prin. Fax 742-6987
Woodridge PS 200/K-1
333 E Slifer St 53901 608-742-3494
Salina Thistle, prin. Fax 742-5356
Other Schools – See Endeavor

St. John Lutheran S 100/PK-8
430 W Emmett St 53901 608-742-4222
Doug Jacoby, prin. Fax 745-4889
St. Marys Parochial S 100/PK-8
315 W Cook St 53901 608-742-4998
Jamie Hahn, prin. Fax 742-1039

Port Edwards, Wood, Pop. 1,802
Port Edwards SD 400/PK-12
801 2nd St 54469 715-887-9000
Kyle Cronan, supt. Fax 887-9040
www.pesd.k12.wi.us
Edwards MS 100/5-8
801 2nd St 54469 715-887-9000
Cara Christy, prin. Fax 887-9040
Port Edwards ES 100/PK-4
801 2nd St 54469 715-887-9000
Cara Christy, prin. Fax 887-9095

Port Washington, Ozaukee, Pop. 11,098
Port Washington-Saukville SD 2,700/PK-12
100 W Monroe St 53074 262-268-6000
Michael Weber Ph.D., supt. Fax 268-6020
www.pwssd.k12.wi.us
Dunwiddie ES 500/PK-4
1243 W Lincoln Ave 53074 262-268-5700
Joanna Bannon, prin. Fax 268-5720
Jefferson MS 700/5-8
1403 N Holden St 53074 262-268-6100
Steven Sukawaty, prin. Fax 268-6120
Lincoln ES 400/PK-4
1325 N Theis Ln 53074 262-268-5800
Jane Gennerman, prin. Fax 268-5820
Other Schools – See Saukville

St. John XXIII Catholic S 200/PK-4
1802 N Wisconsin St 53074 262-284-2441
Kristine Klein, prin. Fax 284-5408
St. John XXIII Catholic S 100/5-8
1802 N Wisconsin St 53074 262-284-2682
Kristine Klein, prin. Fax 284-4168

Port Wing, Bayfield, Pop. 160
South Shore SD 200/PK-12
PO Box 40 54865 715-774-3500
Clendon Gustafson, admin. Fax 774-3569
sshore.org
South Shore ES 100/PK-6
PO Box 40 54865 715-774-3500
Clendon Gustafson, prin. Fax 774-3569

Potosi, Grant, Pop. 686
Potosi SD 300/PK-12
128 US Highway 61 N 53820 608-763-2162
Ronald S. Saari, supt. Fax 763-2035
www.potosisd.k12.wi.us
Potosi ES 100/PK-5
128 US Highway 61 N 53820 608-763-2163
Mike Uppena, prin. Fax 763-2035
Potosi MS 100/6-8
128 US Highway 61 N 53820 608-763-2162
Mike Uppena, prin. Fax 763-2035

SS. Andrew & Thomas S 100/K-8
PO Box 160 53820 608-763-2120
Debra Pfab, prin. Fax 763-4064

Poynette, Columbia, Pop. 2,497
Poynette SD 1,100/PK-12
PO Box 10 53955 608-635-4347
Matt Shappell, supt. Fax 635-9200
www.poynette.k12.wi.us
Poynette ES 500/PK-PK, 1-
PO Box 10 53955 608-635-4347
Jay Hausser, prin. Fax 635-9233
Poynette MS 200/6-8
PO Box 10 53955 608-635-4347
Dr. Jerry Pritzl, prin. Fax 635-9233
Other Schools – See Arlington

Prairie du Chien, Crawford, Pop. 5,867
Prairie du Chien Area SD 1,000/PK-12
800 E Crawford St 53821 608-326-3700
Robert Smudde, supt. Fax 326-0000
www.pdc.k12.wi.us
Bluff View IS 400/2-8
1901 E Wells St 53821 608-326-3722
Aaron Amundson, prin. Fax 326-3708
Kennedy ES 200/PK-1
420 S Wacouta Ave 53821 608-326-3719
Laura Stuckey, prin. Fax 326-3707

Prairie Catholic S - St. Gabriel 100/PK-4
515 N Beaumont Rd 53821 608-326-8624
Mary Henry, prin. Fax 326-4876
Prairie Catholic S - St. John MS 100/5-8
720 S Wacouta Ave 53821 608-326-4400
Mary Henry, prin. Fax 326-4876

Prairie du Sac, Sauk, Pop. 3,923
Sauk Prairie SD 2,100/PK-12
440 13th St 53578 608-643-5990
Cliff Thompson, supt. Fax 643-6216
www.saukprairieschools.org
Bridges ES PK-2
1200 Broadway St 53578 608-643-1844
Chanda Kulow, prin. Fax 643-1849
Grand Avenue ES 400/3-5
225 Grand Ave 53578 608-643-1900
Craig Trautsch, prin. Fax 643-1957
Lower Rock ES 100/PK-5
S9033 Denzer Rd 53578 608-643-1997
Kelly Petrowski, prin. Fax 544-5801
Other Schools – See Sauk City

Prairie Farm, Barron, Pop. 472
Prairie Farm SD 300/PK-12
630 River Ave S 54762 715-455-1861
Tom Rich, admin. Fax 455-1869
www.prairiefarm.k12.wi.us
Prairie Farm ES 200/PK-5
630 River Ave S 54762 715-455-1615
Casey Fossum, prin. Fax 455-1869
Prairie Farm MS 100/6-8
630 River Ave S 54762 715-455-1841
Casey Fossum, prin. Fax 455-1869

Prentice, Price, Pop. 653
Prentice SD 300/PK-12
PO Box 110 54556 715-428-2811
Randall Bergman, supt. Fax 428-2815
www.prentice.k12.wi.us
Ogema ES 100/PK-3
PO Box 110 54556 715-428-2811
Randall Bergman, prin. Fax 428-2815
Prentice ES 100/PK-4
PO Box 110 54556 715-428-2812
Randall Bergman, prin. Fax 428-2815

Prescott, Pierce, Pop. 4,176
Prescott SD 1,200/PK-12
1220 Saint Croix St 54021 715-262-5782
Dr. Rick Spicuzza, supt. Fax 262-5091
www.prescott.k12.wi.us
Malone ES 600/PK-5
505 Campbell St N 54021 715-262-5463
Deanne Edlefsen, prin. Fax 262-0052
Prescott MS 300/6-8
125 Elm St N 54021 715-262-5054
Kyle Igou, prin. Fax 262-3965

St. Joseph Catholic S 100/K-6
281 Dakota St S 54021 715-262-5912
Chris Magee, prin. Fax 262-5901

Princeton, Green Lake, Pop. 1,208
Princeton SD 400/PK-12
PO Box 147 54968 920-295-6571
Sam Santacroce, supt. Fax 295-4778
www.princetonschooldistrict.org
Princeton S 400/PK-12
PO Box 147 54968 920-295-6571
Sam Santacroce, prin. Fax 295-4778

St. John the Baptist S 100/PK-8
125 Church St 54968 920-295-3541
Fr. Dale Grubba, prin. Fax 295-0178

Pulaski, Brown, Pop. 3,500
Pulaski Community SD 3,700/PK-12
PO Box 36 54162 920-822-6000
Bec Kurzynske, supt. Fax 822-6005
www.pulaskischools.org
Glenbrook ES 600/PK-5
PO Box 825 54162 920-822-6100
Kurtis Sufka, prin. Fax 822-6105
Pulaski Community MS 800/6-8
911 S Saint Augustine St 54162 920-822-6500
Patrick Fullerton, prin. Fax 822-6505
Other Schools – See Green Bay, , Krakow, Sobieski

Assumption of the BVM S 100/PK-5
109 E Pulaski St 54162 920-822-5650
Deanne Wilinski, prin. Fax 822-8003

Racine, Racine, Pop. 76,696
Racine USD 19,800/PK-12
3109 Mount Pleasant St 53404 262-635-5600
Dr. Lolli Haws, supt. Fax 631-7121
www.rusd.org
Brown ES 500/PK-5
2115 5 1/2 Mile Rd 53402 262-664-6650
Josh Hancock, prin. Fax 664-6680
Bull Fine Arts ES 300/K-5
815 De Koven Ave 53403 262-664-6800
Zach Jacobsmeier, prin. Fax 664-6810
Fratt ES 500/PK-5
3501 Kinzie Ave 53405 262-664-8150
Priscilla Marquez, prin. Fax 664-8160
Giese ES 300/PK-5
5120 Byrd Ave 53406 262-664-8250
Tom Hyland, prin. Fax 664-8270
Gifford ES 900/PK-8
8332 Northwestern Ave 53406 262-619-4550
Mary Cline, prin. Fax 619-4595
Gilmore MS 700/6-8
2330 Northwestern Ave 53404 262-619-4260
Amanda Jordan, prin. Fax 619-4272
Goodland ES 400/PK-5
4800 Graceland Blvd 53406 262-664-6850
Janet Colvin, prin. Fax 664-6870
Janes ES 400/PK-5
1425 N Wisconsin St 53402 262-664-6550
Dr. Evelyn Resto, prin. Fax 664-6553
Jefferson Lighthouse ES 600/K-5
1722 W 6th St 53404 262-664-6900
Heidi Williams, prin. Fax 664-6910
Jerstad-Agerholm ES 300/PK-5
3535 Lasalle St 53402 262-664-6050
Tom Tuttle, prin. Fax 664-6054
Jerstad-Agerholm MS 700/6-8
3601 Lasalle St 53402 262-664-6075
Tom Tuttle, prin. Fax 664-6120
Johnson ES 600/PK-5
2420 Kentucky St 53405 262-664-6950
Kim DeLaO, prin. Fax 664-6960
Jones ES 500/PK-5
3300 Chicory Rd 53403 262-664-8050
Sherrie Hopkins, prin. Fax 664-8060
Knapp ES 400/PK-5
2701 17th St 53405 262-664-8000
Richard Wytonick, prin. Fax 664-8010

McKinley MS 800/6-8
2340 Mohr Ave 53405 262-664-6150
Ellis Turrentine, prin. Fax 664-6196
Mitchell ES 500/PK-5
2701 Drexel Ave 53403 262-664-6350
Esteban Malacara, prin. Fax 664-6375
Mitchell MS 700/6-8
2701 Drexel Ave 53403 262-664-6400
Esteban Malacara, prin. Fax 664-6444
North Park ES 400/PK-5
4748 Elizabeth St 53402 262-664-6450
William Ticha, prin. Fax 664-6455
Racine Early Education Center 100/PK-PK
2015 Franklin St 53403 262-664-8200
Culleen Witthuhn, dir. Fax 664-8225
Red Apple ES 400/PK-5
914 Saint Patrick St 53402 262-619-4500
Dr. Kevin McCormick, prin. Fax 619-4505
Roosevelt ES 400/PK-5
915 Romayne Ave 53402 262-664-8300
Gabriel Lopez, prin. Fax 664-8310
Starbuck MS 800/6-8
1516 Ohio St 53405 262-664-6500
Andre Bennett, prin. Fax 664-6510
Thomas ES 600/PK-5
930 Martin Luther King Dr 53404 262-664-8400
Demetri Beekman, prin. Fax 664-8444
Wadewitz ES 600/PK-5
2700 Yout St 53404 262-664-6000
Chad Chapin, prin. Fax 664-6005
West Ridge ES 600/PK-5
1347 S Emmertsen Rd 53406 262-664-6200
Thomas George, prin. Fax 664-6225
Other Schools – See Sturtevant

John Paul II Academy 200/K-8
2023 Northwestern Ave 53404 262-637-2012
Gloria Schumacher, prin. Fax 637-5130
Our Lady of Grace Academy 300/K-8
1435 Grove Ave 53405 262-636-8044
Fax 636-8045
Racine Christian S 200/K-8
912 Virginia St 53405 262-634-0961
David Van Swol, admin. Fax 634-7467
Racine Montessori S 200/PK-8
2317 Howe St 53403 262-637-7892
Rita Lewis, admin.
Renaissance S 300/PK-8
6150 Taylor Ave 53403 262-554-6768
Tiffany Venegas, prin.
St. John's Lutheran S 100/PK-8
510 Kewaunee St 53402 262-633-2758
Kevin Charpentier, admin. Fax 637-7089
St. Joseph S 200/PK-8
1525 Erie St 53402 262-633-2403
Emily Knippel, prin. Fax 633-4423
St. Lucy S 200/K-8
3035 Drexel Ave 53403 262-554-1801
Rudee Koepke, prin. Fax 554-7618
St. Rita S 300/PK-8
4433 Douglas Ave 53402 262-639-3333
Gina Brown, prin. Fax 639-3346
Trinity Lutheran S 200/PK-8
2065 Geneva St 53402 262-632-1766
Pamela Amling, prin. Fax 632-3838
Wisconsin Lutheran S 100/PK-8
734 Villa St 53403 262-633-7143
Paul Patterson, prin. Fax 633-1121

Randolph, Columbia, Pop. 1,798
Randolph SD 500/PK-12
110 Meadowood Dr 53956 920-326-2427
Kevin Knudson, supt. Fax 326-2439
www.rsdwi.org
Randolph ES 400/PK-8
110 Meadowood Dr 53956 920-326-2431
Christy Fay, prin. Fax 326-5056

Randolph Christian S 100/PK-8
457 2nd St 53956 920-326-3320
Dr. Jeff Hoogeveen, prin. Fax 326-3001

Random Lake, Sheboygan, Pop. 1,574
Random Lake SD 900/PK-12
605 Random Lake Rd 53075 920-994-4342
Michael Trimberger, supt. Fax 994-4820
www.randomlake.k12.wi.us
Random Lake ES 300/PK-4
605 Random Lake Rd 53075 920-994-4344
Sandra Mountain, prin. Fax 994-4820
Random Lake MS 300/5-8
605 Random Lake Rd 53075 920-994-2498
Susan McDonald, prin. Fax 994-4820

St. John Lutheran S 100/PK-8
W5407 County Road SS 53075 920-994-9190
Cassandra Makela, prin. Fax 994-9721

Readfield, Waupaca
New London SD
Supt. — See New London
Readfield ES 200/PK-4
PO Box 40 54969 920-667-4265
Kristin Grable, prin. Fax 667-4295

Redgranite, Waushara, Pop. 2,122
Wautoma Area SD
Supt. — See Wautoma
Redgranite ES 100/K-5
PO Box 649 54970 920-566-2357
Clyde Simonson, prin. Fax 566-0490

Reedsburg, Sauk, Pop. 9,120
SD of Reedsburg 2,600/PK-12
501 K St 53959 608-524-2016
Thomas Benson, supt. Fax 768-8927
www.rsd.k12.wi.us
Pineview ES 600/PK-5
1121 8th St 53959 608-768-8932
Clint Beyer, prin. Fax 768-8933
South ES 200/K-3
420 Plum St 53959 608-768-8936
Tammy Hayes, prin. Fax 768-8937
Webb MS 600/6-8
707 N Webb Ave 53959 608-768-8930
Casey Campbell, prin. Fax 768-8931
Westside ES 300/PK-3
401 Alexander Ave 53959 608-768-8934
Paul Bierman, prin. Fax 768-8935
Other Schools – See La Valle, Loganville

Sacred Heart S 200/PK-8
545 N Oak St 53959 608-524-3611
Karen Marklein, prin. Fax 524-3831
St. Peter Lutheran S 200/PK-8
345 N Pine St 53959 608-524-4066
Roger Tessendorf, prin. Fax 524-8821

Reedsville, Manitowoc, Pop. 1,195
Reedsville SD 500/PK-12
340 Manitowoc St 54230 920-754-4341
Tony Butturini, supt. Fax 754-4344
www.reedsville.k12.wi.us
Reedsville ES 300/PK-8
350 Park St 54230 920-754-4345
Michael Nate, prin. Fax 754-4577

St. John - St. James Lutheran S 50/PK-8
223 Manitowoc St 54230 920-754-4432
Corey Marohn, prin. Fax 754-4568

Rhinelander, Oneida, Pop. 7,686
Rhinelander SD 2,300/K-12
665 Coolidge Ave Ste B 54501 715-365-9700
Kelli Jacobi, supt. Fax 365-9713
www.rhinelander.k12.wi.us
Central ES 300/4-5
418 N Pelham St 54501 715-365-9600
Paul Johnson, prin. Fax 365-9612
Crescent ES 300/K-3
3319 Boyce Dr 54501 715-365-9137
Gayle Daniel, prin. Fax 365-9124
Pelican ES 300/K-3
3350 V Hickey Rd 54501 715-365-9160
Martha Knudtson, prin. Fax 365-9177
Williams MS 400/6-8
915 Acacia Ln 54501 715-365-9220
Richard Gretzinger, prin. Fax 365-9296

Three Lakes SD
Supt. — See Three Lakes
Sugar Camp ES 100/PK-6
4066 Camp Four Rd 54501 715-272-1105
Staci Volkmann, prin. Fax 272-1299

Nativity of Our Lord S 300/PK-8
103 E King St 54501 715-362-5588
Melanie Nycz, prin. Fax 362-0952
Zion Lutheran S 100/PK-8
26 W Frederick St 54501 715-365-6300
Tim Ristow, admin. Fax 365-6329

Rib Lake, Taylor, Pop. 905
Rib Lake SD 500/PK-12
PO Box 278 54470 715-427-3222
Lori Manion, supt. Fax 427-3221
www.riblake.k12.wi.us
Rib Lake ES 200/PK-5
PO Box 278 54470 715-427-5818
Jon Dallmann, prin. Fax 427-3221
Rib Lake MS 100/6-8
PO Box 278 54470 715-427-5446
Rick Cardey, prin. Fax 427-3221

Rice Lake, Barron, Pop. 8,342
Rice Lake Area SD 2,000/PK-12
700 Augusta St 54868 715-234-9007
Randy Drost, supt. Fax 234-4552
www.ricelake.k12.wi.us
Hilltop Day Care & Preschool 50/PK-PK
104 Cameron Rd 54868 715-234-6671
Barbara Sparish, dir. Fax 234-8080
Hilltop ES 300/K-4
202 Cameron Rd 54868 715-234-4998
Natalie Springer, prin. Fax 736-0169
Rice Lake MS 600/5-8
204 Cameron Rd 54868 715-234-8156
Josh Tomesh, prin. Fax 234-9439
Tainter ES 200/PK-4
2201 Carrie Ave 54868 715-234-8065
Jill Bennett, prin. Fax 234-2081
Other Schools – See Haugen

Redeemer Lutheran S 50/PK-8
520 E Orchard Beach Ln 54868 715-234-2412
Jeffrey Seelow, prin. Fax 736-9357
St. Joseph S 200/PK-8
128 W Humbird St 54868 715-234-7721
Jerry Van Dyke, prin. Fax 234-5062

Richfield, Washington, Pop. 11,239
Richfield J1 SD 400/PK-8
PO Box 127 53076 262-628-1032
Tara Villalobos, admin. Fax 628-3013
www.richfield.k12.wi.us
Richfield ES 200/3-8
PO Box 127 53076 262-628-1032
Tara Villalobos, admin. Fax 628-3013
Other Schools – See Colgate

Richland Center, Richland, Pop. 5,137
Ithaca SD 400/PK-12
24615 State Hwy 58 53581 608-585-2311
Julie Prouty, admin. Fax 585-2505
www.ithaca.k12.wi.us/
Ithaca ES 200/PK-5
24615 State Hwy 58 53581 608-585-2311
Kathleen Schoen, prin. Fax 585-2505
Ithaca MS 100/6-8
24615 State Hwy 58 53581 608-585-2311
Paul Coenen, prin. Fax 585-2505

Richland SD 1,400/PK-12
1996 US Hwy 14 W 53581 608-647-6106
Jarred Burke, admin. Fax 647-8454
www.richland.k12.wi.us
Doudna ES 400/K-5
1990 Bohmann Dr 53581 608-647-8971
Amy Hardy, prin. Fax 647-7293
Jefferson ES 200/K-5
586 N Main St 53581 608-647-6351
Stephanie Moore, prin. Fax 647-9121
Lincoln ES 200/PK-K
678 S Park St 53581 608-647-2511
Stephanie Moore, prin. Fax 647-2303
Richland MS 300/6-8
1801 State Hwy 80 S 53581 608-647-6381
Ryan Meyer, prin. Fax 647-4735

St. Mary S 100/K-8
155 W 5th St 53581 608-647-2422
Vicki Faber, prin. Fax 647-6029

Ridgeland, Dunn, Pop. 268
Barron Area SD
Supt. — See Barron
Ridgeland ES 100/PK-4
PO Box 196 54763 715-949-1445
Jennifer Clemens, prin. Fax 949-1617

Ridgeway, Iowa, Pop. 652
Dodgeville SD
Supt. — See Dodgeville
Ridgeway ES 200/PK-5
208 Jarvis St 53582 608-924-3461
Julie Piper, prin. Fax 924-1362

Ringle, Marathon
D.C. Everest Area SD
Supt. — See Weston
Riverside ES 500/PK-5
R12231 River Rd 54471 715-359-2417
Kevin Kampmann, prin. Fax 355-3725

Rio, Columbia, Pop. 1,045
Rio Community SD 500/PK-12
411 Church St 53960 920-992-3141
Mark McGuire, supt. Fax 992-3157
www.rio.k12.wi.us
Rio ES 200/PK-5
355 Lowville Rd 53960 920-992-3143
Craig Vetter, prin. Fax 992-3012

Ripon, Fond du Lac, Pop. 7,674
Ripon Area SD 1,800/PK-12
PO Box 991 54971 920-748-4600
Dr. Mary Whitrock, supt. Fax 748-2715
www.ripon.k12.wi.us
Barlow Park ES 300/PK-2
PO Box 991 54971 920-748-1550
Tanya Sanderfoot, prin. Fax 748-1552
Murray Park ES 200/3-5
PO Box 991 54971 920-748-4695
Renee Bunge, prin. Fax 748-4698
Ripon MS 200/6-8
PO Box 991 54971 920-748-4638
Rick Bunge, prin. Fax 748-4653

River Falls, Pierce, Pop. 14,778
River Falls SD 3,200/PK-12
852 E Division St 54022 715-425-1800
Jamie Benson, supt. Fax 425-1804
www.rfsd.k12.wi.us
Greenwood ES 400/K-5
982 E Division St 54022 715-425-1810
Nate Schurman, prin. Fax 425-0783
Meyer MS 700/6-8
230 N 9th St 54022 715-425-1820
Mark Chapin, prin. Fax 425-1823
River Falls 4 Children 200/PK-PK
1007 W Pine St 54022 715-425-1815
Rita Humbert, admin. Fax 425-1801
Rocky Branch ES 400/PK-5
1415 Bartosh Ln 54022 715-425-1819
Charles Eaton, prin. Fax 425-0599
Westside ES 400/K-5
1007 W Pine St 54022 715-425-1815
Rita Humbert, prin. Fax 425-1805

Heartland Montessori S 50/PK-K
N8226 945th St 54022 715-426-0350
St. Bridget S 200/PK-8
135 E Division St 54022 715-425-1872
Jeanne McCoy, prin. Fax 425-1873

River Hills, Milwaukee, Pop. 1,562
Maple Dale-Indian Hill SD
Supt. — See Fox Point
Indian Hill S 100/PK-2
1101 W Brown Deer Rd 53217 414-351-7390
Laura Witkov, prin.

Roberts, Saint Croix, Pop. 1,631
St. Croix Central SD
Supt. — See Hammond
St. Croix Central ES 700/PK-4
PO Box 129 54023 715-749-3119
Shelly Clay, prin. Fax 749-3130

Rosendale, Fond du Lac, Pop. 1,054
Rosendale-Brandon SD 1,000/PK-12
300 W Wisconsin St 54974 920-872-2851
Wayne Weber, supt. Fax 872-2647
www.rbsd.k12.wi.us

Rosendale IS 200/4-8
200 S Main St 54974 920-872-2126
John Hokenson, prin. Fax 872-5481
Rosendale PS 200/PK-3
300 W Wisconsin St 54974 920-872-2151
John Hokenson, prin. Fax 872-2647
Other Schools – See Brandon

Rosholt, Portage, Pop. 506
Rosholt SD 600/PK-12
PO Box 310 54473 715-677-4542
Marc Christianson, supt. Fax 677-3543
www.rosholt.k12.wi.us
Rosholt ES 300/PK-5
PO Box 310 54473 715-677-4543
John Parks, prin. Fax 677-3543
Rosholt MS 100/6-8
PO Box 310 54473 715-677-4541
James Grygleski, prin. Fax 677-6767

St. Adalbert S 50/PK-8
3314 Saint Adalberts Rd 54473 715-677-4517
Tom McCann, prin. Fax 677-4517

Rothschild, Marathon, Pop. 5,209
D.C. Everest Area SD
Supt. — See Weston
Evergreen ES 500/PK-5
1610 Pine Rd 54474 715-359-6591
Richard Koepke, prin. Fax 355-3722
Rothschild ES 400/PK-5
810 1st St 54474 715-359-3186
Rena Sabey, prin. Fax 355-3723

Newman Catholic ES at St. Mark 100/PK-5
602 Military Rd 54474 715-359-9662
Tina Meyer, prin. Fax 355-8904

Rubicon, Dodge
Herman Neosho Rubicon SD
Supt. — See Neosho
Honor IS 100/5-8
N3501 County Road P 53078 262-673-2920
Karl Herrmann, prin. Fax 673-2975

Rudolph, Wood, Pop. 436
Wisconsin Rapids SD
Supt. — See Wisconsin Rapids
THINK Academy 200/PK-5
6950 Knowledge Ave 54475 715-424-6784
Roxanne Filtz, prin. Fax 435-2070

Saint Croix Falls, Polk, Pop. 2,110
St. Croix Falls SD 1,100/PK-12
PO Box 130 54024 715-483-2507
Mark Burandt, supt. Fax 483-3695
www.scf.k12.wi.us
St. Croix Falls ES 400/PK-PK, 1-
PO Box 130 54024 715-483-9823
Jeff Benoy, prin. Fax 483-3695
St. Croix Falls MS 300/5-8
PO Box 130 54024 715-483-2507
Joe Connors, prin. Fax 483-3695
Other Schools – See Dresser

Saint Francis, Milwaukee, Pop. 9,213
St. Francis SD 1,300/PK-12
4225 S Lake Dr 53235 414-747-3900
Blake Peuse, supt. Fax 482-7198
www.sfsd.k12.wi.us
Deer Creek IS 400/4-8
3680 S Kinnickinnic Ave 53235 414-482-8400
Anna Young, prin. Fax 482-8406
Willow Glen S 300/PK-3
2600 E Bolivar Ave 53235 414-486-6300
Laurie Pogorzelski, prin. Fax 486-6305

Saint Germain, Vilas
Northland Pines SD
Supt. — See Eagle River
Northland Pines/St Germain ES 100/PK-4
8234 State Highway 70 W 54558 715-542-3632
Tony Duffek, prin. Fax 542-3660

Saint Nazianz, Manitowoc, Pop. 779

St. Gregory S 100/PK-7
PO Box 199 54232 920-773-2530
Rita Steffen, prin. Fax 773-3086

Salem, Kenosha
Salem SD 1,000/PK-8
PO Box 160 53168 262-843-2356
Dr. David Milz, supt. Fax 843-4138
www.salem.k12.wi.us
Salem ES 1,000/PK-8
PO Box 160 53168 262-843-2356
Eileen Bruton, prin. Fax 843-4138

Sauk City, Sauk, Pop. 3,378
Sauk Prairie SD
Supt. — See Prairie du Sac
Sauk Prairie MS 600/6-8
207 Maple St 53583 608-643-5500
Ted Harter, prin. Fax 643-5503

St. Aloysius S 100/PK-5
608 Oak St 53583 608-643-6868
Daniela Saldana, prin. Fax 643-3472

Saukville, Ozaukee, Pop. 4,396
Port Washington-Saukville SD
Supt. — See Port Washington
Saukville ES 300/K-4
333 N Mill St 53080 262-268-5900
Chad Brakke, prin. Fax 268-5920

Ozaukee Christian S 50/PK-8
341 S Dries St 53080 262-284-6980
Krista Austin, admin. Fax 284-6938

Schofield, Marathon, Pop. 2,124

Newman Catholic ECC at St. Therese 50/PK-PK
112 Kort St W 54476 715-355-5254
Amy Faust, dir. Fax 359-9565
St. Peter Lutheran S 100/K-8
115 Eau Claire St 54476 715-359-3020
Scott Huebner, prin. Fax 241-6301

Seneca, Crawford
Seneca SD 300/PK-12
PO Box 34 54654 608-734-3411
David Boland, supt. Fax 734-3430
www.seneca.k12.wi.us
Seneca ES 100/PK-4
PO Box 34 54654 608-734-3411
David Boland, prin. Fax 734-3430
Seneca JHS 100/5-8
PO Box 34 54654 608-734-3411
David Boland, prin. Fax 734-3430

Seymour, Outagamie, Pop. 3,392
Seymour Community SD 2,400/PK-12
10 Circle Dr 54165 920-833-2304
Laurie Asher, supt. Fax 833-6037
www.seymour.k12.wi.us/
Rock Ledge IS 400/3-5
330 W Hickory St 54165 920-833-7380
Amy McKeefry, prin. Fax 833-9684
Rock Ledge PS 400/PK-2
330 W Hickory St 54165 920-833-5155
Jamie Inman, prin. Fax 833-5144
Seymour MS 500/6-8
10 Circle Dr 54165 920-833-7199
Judy Schenk, prin. Fax 833-9376
Other Schools – See Black Creek

Sharon, Walworth, Pop. 1,595
Sharon J11 SD 300/PK-8
104 E School St 53585 262-736-4477
Sara Andrus, supt. Fax 736-4457
www.sharon.k12.wi.us
Sharon S 300/PK-8
104 E School St 53585 262-736-4477
Sara Andrus, prin. Fax 736-4457

Shawano, Shawano, Pop. 9,050
Shawano SD 2,600/PK-12
218 County Road B 54166 715-526-3194
Gary Cumberland, supt. Fax 526-6072
www.shawanoschools.com
Brener IS 500/3-5
1300 S Union St 54166 715-524-2131
Terri Schultz, prin. Fax 524-9899
Hilcrest ES 700/PK-2
1410 Waukechon Rd 54166 715-524-2134
Troy Edwards, prin. Fax 526-4372
Shawano Community MS 500/6-8
1050 S Union St 54166 715-526-2192
Mary Kramer, prin. Fax 526-5037

Sacred Heart S 100/K-8
124 E Center St 54166 715-526-5328
Aleta Young, prin. Fax 526-4107
St. James Lutheran S 200/PK-8
324 S Andrews St 54166 715-524-4213
Susan Longmire, prin. Fax 524-4876

Sheboygan, Sheboygan, Pop. 48,427
Sheboygan Area SD 10,100/PK-12
830 Virginia Ave 53081 920-459-3500
Joseph Sheehan Ph.D., supt. Fax 459-6487
www.sheboygan.k12.wi.us
Cooper ES 300/K-5
2014 Cooper Ave 53083 920-459-3693
Kristin DeTroye, prin. Fax 459-4033
Early Learning Center 600/PK-PK
1227 Wilson Ave 53081 920-459-4330
Pam Kugi, prin. Fax 459-6708
Farnsworth MS 600/6-8
1017 Union Ave 53081 920-459-3655
Todd DeBruin, prin. Fax 459-3660
Grant ES 400/K-5
1528 N 5th St 53081 920-459-3626
James Renzelmann, prin. Fax 459-3719
Jackson ES 300/K-5
2530 Weeden Creek Rd 53081 920-459-3573
Lynn Walters, prin. Fax 459-6496
Jefferson ES 400/K-5
1515 Heller Ave 53081 920-459-3620
Zach Pethan, prin. Fax 453-5209
Lincoln-Erdman ES 400/K-5
4101 N 50th St 53083 920-459-3595
Amanda Schermetzler, prin. Fax 459-4049
Longfellow ES 400/K-5
819 Kentucky Ave 53081 920-459-3580
Paul DePagter, prin. Fax 459-0451
Madison ES 400/K-5
2302 David Ave 53081 920-459-3585
Jason Ledermann, prin. Fax 459-3589
Mann MS 600/6-8
2820 Union Ave 53081 920-459-3666
Vicki Ritchie, prin. Fax 459-3669
Pigeon River ES 300/K-5
3508 N 21st St 53083 920-459-3563
Kelly Blum, prin. Fax 459-4002
Sheridan ES 300/K-5
1412 Maryland Ave 53081 920-459-3550
Kelly Cvetan, prin. Fax 459-3833
Urban MS 700/6-8
1226 North Ave 53083 920-459-3680
Ted DiStefano, prin. Fax 459-4065
Wilson ES 500/K-5
1625 Wilson Ave 53081 920-459-3688
Chad Renzelmann, prin. Fax 803-7760
Other Schools – See Cleveland

Bethlehem Lutheran S 200/PK-8
1121 Georgia Ave 53081 920-452-5071
Patrick Vanic, prin. Fax 452-0209
Christ Child Academy 200/PK-8
2722 Henry St 53081 920-459-2660
Mark Ruedinger, prin. Fax 459-2665
Immanuel Lutheran S 100/PK-8
1626 Illinois Ave 53081 920-452-9681
Heidi Wallner, prin. Fax 452-0102
St. Elizabeth Ann Seton S 200/PK-8
814 Superior Ave 53081 920-452-1571
Stephanie Nardi, prin. Fax 208-4371
St. Paul Lutheran S 100/PK-8
1819 N 13th St 53081 920-452-6882
Wendy Kretschmar, prin. Fax 452-7893
Sheboygan Christian ES 200/PK-8
418 Geele Ave 53083 920-457-3060
Ann Steenwyk, dir. Fax 457-6441
Trinity Lutheran S 100/PK-8
824 Wisconsin Ave 53081 920-458-8248
Jenna Roeske, prin.

Sheboygan Falls, Sheboygan, Pop. 7,719
Sheboygan Falls SD 1,800/PK-12
220 Amherst Ave 53085 920-467-7893
Jean Born, supt. Fax 467-7899
www.sheboyganfalls.k12.wi.us
Sheboygan Falls ES 700/PK-4
1 Alfred Miley Ave 53085 920-467-7820
Lynn Bub, prin. Fax 467-7824
Sheboygan Falls MS 500/5-8
101 School St 53085 920-467-7880
Meloney Markofski, prin. Fax 467-7885

Shell Lake, Washburn, Pop. 1,340
Shell Lake SD 700/PK-12
271 Highway 63 S 54871 715-468-7816
David Bridenhagen, supt. Fax 468-7812
www.shelllake.k12.wi.us
Shell Lake ES 200/3-6
271 Highway 63 S 54871 715-468-7815
Laura Stunkel, prin. Fax 468-7476
Shell Lake PS 200/PK-2
271 Highway 63 S 54871 715-468-7889
Laura Stunkel, prin. Fax 468-4450

Sherwood, Calumet, Pop. 2,687

St. John - Sacred Heart S 100/PK-8
N361 Military Rd 54169 920-989-1373
Jaclyn Behnke, prin. Fax 989-1689

Shiocton, Outagamie, Pop. 910
Shiocton SD 600/PK-12
PO Box 68 54170 920-986-3351
Nichole Schweitzer, supt. Fax 986-3291
www.shiocton.k12.wi.us
Shiocton ES 400/PK-6
PO Box 68 54170 920-986-3351
Kim Griesbach, prin. Fax 986-3291

Shorewood, Milwaukee, Pop. 12,886
Shorewood SD 2,100/PK-12
1701 E Capitol Dr 53211 414-963-6901
Bryan Davis, supt. Fax 963-6904
www.shorewoodschools.org
Atwater ES 500/PK-6
2100 E Capitol Dr 53211 414-963-6962
Kayla Russick, prin. Fax 963-6970
Lake Bluff ES 600/PK-6
1600 E Lake Bluff Blvd 53211 414-963-6972
Angela Patterson, prin. Fax 961-2815
Shorewood IS 300/7-8
3830 N Morris Blvd 53211 414-963-6951
Michael Joynt, prin. Fax 963-6946

St. Robert S 400/PK-8
2200 E Capitol Dr 53211 414-332-1164
Lauren Beckmann, prin. Fax 332-7355

Shullsburg, Lafayette, Pop. 1,223
Shullsburg SD 400/PK-12
444 N Judgement St 53586 608-965-4427
Loras Kruser, admin. Fax 965-3794
www.shullsburg.k12.wi.us
Shullsburg ES 200/PK-5
444 N Judgement St 53586 608-965-4427
Mark Lierman, prin. Fax 965-3794
Shullsburg JHS 100/6-8
444 N Judgement St 53586 608-965-4427
Mark Lierman, prin. Fax 965-3794

Silver Lake, Kenosha, Pop. 2,381
Silver Lake J1 SD 600/PK-8
PO Box 69 53170 262-889-4384
Jon Schleusner, admin. Fax 889-8450
www.silverlakejt1.k12.wi.us
Riverview S 600/PK-8
PO Box 69 53170 262-889-4384
Andrea Zackery, prin. Fax 889-8450

Siren, Burnett, Pop. 776
Siren SD 400/PK-12
24022 4th Ave 54872 715-349-7392
Dr. Kevin Shetler, supt. Fax 349-7476
www.siren.k12.wi.us
Siren ES 200/PK-5
24022 4th Ave 54872 715-349-2278
Carrie Herman, prin. Fax 349-2001

Slinger, Washington, Pop. 5,014
Slinger SD 3,100/PK-12
207 Polk St 53086 262-644-9615
Daren Sievers, supt. Fax 644-7514
www.slinger.k12.wi.us
Slinger ES 600/PK-5
203 Polk St 53086 262-644-6669
Griffin Glapa, prin. Fax 644-6550
Slinger MS 700/6-8
521 Olympic Dr 53086 262-644-5226
Dean Goneau, prin. Fax 644-7353
Other Schools – See Allenton, Hartford

St. Peter S 100/PK-5
206 E Washington St 53086 262-644-8083
Cheryl Jaeger, prin. Fax 644-7951

Sobieski, Oconto, Pop. 257
Pulaski Community SD
Supt. — See Pulaski
Sunnyside ES 500/PK-5
720 County Road C 54171 920-822-6200
Marc Klawiter, prin. Fax 822-6205

Soldiers Grove, Crawford, Pop. 590
North Crawford SD 500/PK-12
47050 County Road X 54655 608-735-4318
Brandon Munson, supt. Fax 735-4317
www.northcrawford.com
North Crawford ES 300/PK-8
47050 County Road X 54655 608-624-5201
Julie Kruizenga, prin. Fax 735-4317

Solon Springs, Douglas, Pop. 597
Solon Springs SD 300/PK-12
8993 E Baldwin Ave 54873 715-378-2263
Frank Helquist, supt. Fax 378-2073
www.solonk12.net
Solon Springs S 300/PK-12
8993 E Baldwin Ave 54873 715-378-2263
Geraldine Muller, prin. Fax 378-2073

Somerset, Saint Croix, Pop. 2,588
Somerset SD 1,600/PK-12
PO Box 100 54025 715-247-3313
Dr. Mark Bezek, supt. Fax 247-5588
www.somerset.k12.wi.us
Somerset ES 700/PK-4
PO Box 100 54025 715-247-3311
Dr. Chris Kamrath, prin. Fax 247-3327
Somerset MS 500/5-8
PO Box 100 54025 715-247-4400
Sara Eichten, prin. Fax 247-4437

St. Anne S 100/PK-8
140 Church Hill Rd 54025 715-247-3762
Randall Stanke, prin. Fax 247-4335

South Milwaukee, Milwaukee, Pop. 20,823
South Milwaukee SD 3,300/PK-12
901 15th Ave 53172 414-766-5000
Dr. Rita Olson, supt. Fax 766-5005
www.sdsm.k12.wi.us
Blakewood ES 400/PK-5
3501 Blakewood Ave 53172 414-766-5900
David Newman, prin. Fax 766-5905
Lakeview ES 300/PK-5
711 Marion Ave 53172 414-766-5252
Cynthia Dennis, prin. Fax 766-5253
Luther ES 300/PK-5
718 Hawthorne Ave 53172 414-766-5326
Eric Wightman, prin. Fax 766-5327
Rawson ES 500/PK-5
1410 Rawson Ave 53172 414-766-2904
Nicole Horsley, prin. Fax 766-2905
South Milwaukee MS 700/6-8
1001 15th Ave 53172 414-766-5800
James Hendrickson, prin. Fax 766-5803

Divine Mercy S 100/PK-8
695 College Ave 53172 414-764-4360
Liz Dworak, prin. Fax 764-6740
Zion Evangelical Lutheran S 100/PK-8
3600 S Chicago Ave 53172 414-762-1258
Fonda Fischer, prin. Fax 762-1258

South Wayne, Lafayette, Pop. 489
Black Hawk SD 300/PK-12
PO Box 303 53587 608-439-5400
Dr. William Chambers, supt. Fax 439-1022
www.blackhawk.k12.wi.us
Black Hawk ES 200/PK-5
PO Box 303 53587 608-439-5444
Cory Milz, prin. Fax 439-1022

Sparta, Monroe, Pop. 9,396
Sparta Area SD 2,700/PK-12
201 E Franklin St 54656 608-269-3151
Dr. Amy Van Deuren, supt. Fax 366-3526
www.spartan.org
Cataract ES 100/PK-3
6070 State Highway 27 54656 608-366-3453
Toby Oswald, prin. Fax 366-3455
Lawrence-Lawson ES 300/K-3
429 N Black River St 54656 608-366-3438
Toby Oswald, prin. Fax 366-3437
Maplewood ES 200/PK-3
900 E Montgomery St 54656 608-366-3467
Patrick Olbert, prin. Fax 366-3461
Southside ES 200/PK-3
1023 Walrath St 54656 608-366-3450
Diane Everson-Riley, prin. Fax 366-3446
Sparta Meadowview IS 300/4-5
1225 N Water St 54656 608-366-3481
Michael Roddick, prin. Fax 366-3500
Sparta Meadowview MS 500/6-8
1225 N Water St 54656 608-366-3497
Jeffery Krull, prin. Fax 366-3500

St. John's Lutheran S 100/PK-8
419 Jefferson Ave 54656 608-269-6001
Chuck Lukasek, prin. Fax 269-6192
St. Patrick S 100/K-8
100 S L St 54656 608-269-4748
Jean Suttie, prin. Fax 269-4748

Spencer, Marathon, Pop. 1,903
Spencer SD 800/PK-12
300 N School St 54479 715-659-5347
Michael Endreas, supt. Fax 659-5470
www.spencer.k12.wi.us
Spencer ES 400/PK-5
300 N School St 54479 715-659-4642
Jill Schulz, prin. Fax 659-5470

Spooner, Washburn, Pop. 2,637
Spooner Area SD 1,200/PK-12
801 County Highway A 54801 715-635-2171
David Aslyn, supt. Fax 635-7174
www.spooner.k12.wi.us
Spooner ES 500/PK-4
1821 Scribner St 54801 715-635-2174
Luke Stordahl, prin. Fax 635-7074
Spooner MS 300/5-8
750 Oak St 54801 715-635-2171
Brad Larrabee, prin. Fax 635-7074

St. Francis De Sales S 100/PK-8
300 Oak St 54801 715-635-2774
Kathy Kurkiewicz, prin. Fax 635-7341

Spring Green, Sauk, Pop. 1,601
River Valley SD 1,300/PK-12
660 W Daley St 53588 608-588-2551
Tom Wermuth, supt. Fax 588-2558
www.rvschools.org
River Valley ES 200/K-5
830 W Daley St 53588 608-588-2559
Jaime Hegland, prin. Fax 588-2550
River Valley MS 300/6-8
660 W Daley St 53588 608-588-2556
James Radtke, prin. Fax 588-2026
Other Schools – See Arena, Plain

St. John Evangelist S 100/PK-5
PO Box 129 53588 608-588-2021
Terrie Feigl, prin. Fax 588-9372

Spring Valley, Pierce, Pop. 1,346
Spring Valley SD 600/PK-12
PO Box 249 54767 715-778-5551
Dr. Donald Haack, supt. Fax 778-4761
www.springvalley.k12.wi.us
Spring Valley ES 400/PK-5
PO Box 427 54767 715-778-5602
Daniel B. McGuire, prin. Fax 778-5615

Stanley, Chippewa, Pop. 3,592
Stanley-Boyd Area SD 1,000/PK-12
507 E 1st Ave 54768 715-644-5534
James Jones, supt. Fax 644-5584
www.stanleyboyd.k12.wi.us
Stanley-Boyd MS 200/6-8
507 E 1st Ave 54768 715-644-5715
Donna Goodman, prin. Fax 644-5584
Stanley ES 400/K-5
507 E 1st Ave 54768 715-644-5810
Dean Lew, prin. Fax 644-5584
Other Schools – See Boyd

Stetsonville, Taylor, Pop. 538
Medford Area SD
Supt. — See Medford
Stetsonville ES 200/PK-4
W5338 County Road A 54480 715-678-2600
Don Everhard, prin. Fax 678-2162

Stevens Point, Portage, Pop. 26,351
Stevens Point Area SD 6,800/PK-12
1900 Polk St 54481 715-345-5456
Craig Gerlach, supt. Fax 345-7302
www.pointschools.net
Bannach ES 400/PK-6
5400 Walter St, 715-345-5668
Jessica Champion, prin. Fax 345-7346
Jefferson ES 300/K-6
1800 East Ave 54481 715-345-5418
Molly Demrow, prin. Fax 345-7352
Madison ES 400/K-6
600 Maria Dr 54481 715-345-5419
Karl Bancker, prin. Fax 345-7349
McDill ES 400/K-6
2516 School St 54481 715-345-5420
Jeanne Koepke, prin. Fax 345-7345
McKinley Center ES 500/K-6
2926 Blaine St 54481 715-345-5421
Amanda Mayo, prin. Fax 345-7350
Washington ES 400/K-6
3500 Prais St 54481 715-345-5426
Ryan Ourada, prin. Fax 345-7353
Other Schools – See Junction City, Plover

Pacelli Catholic ECC 100/PK-PK
1901 Lincoln Ave 54481 715-341-2878
Lesley Lingofelt-Svihel, dir. Fax 342-2013
Pacelli Catholic MS 200/6-8
708 1st St 54481 715-344-1890
Ellen Lopas, prin. Fax 342-2005
Pacelli Catholic S - St. Stanislaus 100/PK-2
2150 High St 54481 715-344-3086
Gregg Hansel, prin. Fax 342-2014
Pacelli Catholic S - St. Stephen S 100/3-5
1335 Clark St 54481 715-344-3751
Gregg Hansel, prin. Fax 344-3766
St. Paul Lutheran S 200/PK-8
1919 Wyatt Ave 54481 715-344-5660
Jim Wegner, prin. Fax 344-5240

Stevens Point Christian Academy 50/K-12
801 County Road HH 54481 715-341-3275
Heidi Uitenbroek, prin. Fax 341-3275

Stockbridge, Calumet, Pop. 630
Stockbridge SD 200/PK-12
PO Box 188 53088 920-439-1782
Chad Marx, supt. Fax 439-1150
www.stockbridge.k12.wi.us/
Stockbridge ES 100/PK-5
PO Box 188 53088 920-439-1158
Chad Marx, prin. Fax 439-1150
Stockbridge MS 50/6-8
PO Box 188 53088 920-439-1158
Chad Marx, prin. Fax 439-1150

Stoddard, Vernon, Pop. 774
De Soto Area SD
Supt. — See De Soto
Stoddard ES 100/PK-5
300 N Cottage St 54658 608-457-2101
Michael Chapes, prin. Fax 457-2007

St. Matthew's Evangelical Lutheran S 50/PK-8
PO Box 208 54658 608-457-2700
James Otto, prin. Fax 457-2702

Stone Lake, Sawyer, Pop. 176

St. Francis Solanus S 50/PK-8
13885 W Mission Rd 54876 715-865-3662
Sr. Felissa Zander, prin. Fax 865-4055

Stoughton, Dane, Pop. 12,430
Stoughton Area SD 3,200/PK-12
320 North St 53589 608-877-5000
Tim Onsager, admin. Fax 877-5028
www.stoughton.k12.wi.us
Fox Prairie ES 400/K-5
1601 W South St 53589 608-877-5101
Krista Huntley-Rogers, prin. Fax 877-5184
Kegonsa ES 400/K-5
1400 Vernon St 53589 608-877-5201
Erin Conrad, prin. Fax 877-5278
River Bluff MS 700/6-8
235 N Forrest St 53589 608-877-5503
Trish Gates, prin. Fax 877-5508
Sandhill ES 600/PK-5
1920 Lincoln Ave 53589 608-877-5401
Jeff Fimreite, prin. Fax 877-5408

St. Ann S 100/PK-6
324 N Harrison St 53589 608-873-3343
Kara Roisum, prin. Fax 873-6425

Stratford, Marathon, Pop. 1,570
Stratford SD 900/PK-12
PO Box 7 54484 715-687-3130
Scott Winch, supt. Fax 687-4074
www.stratford.k12.wi.us
Stratford ES 400/PK-5
PO Box 7 54484 715-687-3535
Amy Schmitt, prin. Fax 687-4881
Stratford MS 200/6-8
PO Box 7 54484 715-687-4311
Janeen LaBorde, prin. Fax 687-4652

St. Joseph S 100/PK-8
430 E Larch St 54484 715-687-4145
Nancy Zygarlicke, prin. Fax 687-4343

Strum, Trempealeau, Pop. 1,111
Eleva-Strum SD 600/PK-12
W23597 US Highway 10 54770 715-695-2696
Kellie Manning, admin. Fax 695-3519
www.esschools.k12.wi.us/
Strum PS 200/PK-3
409 8th Ave S 54770 715-695-2916
Marty Kempf, prin. Fax 695-2690
Other Schools – See Eleva

Sturgeon Bay, Door, Pop. 9,041
Sevastopol SD 500/PK-12
4550 State Highway 57 54235 920-743-6282
Kyle Luedtke, supt. Fax 743-4009
www.sevastopol.k12.wi.us
Sevastopol ES 200/PK-5
4550 State Highway 57 54235 920-743-6282
Kathy Hoppe, prin. Fax 743-4009
Sevastopol MS 100/6-8
4550 State Highway 57 54235 920-743-6282
Adam Baier, prin. Fax 743-4009

Sturgeon Bay SD 1,200/PK-12
1230 Michigan St 54235 920-746-2800
Daniel Tjernagel, supt. Fax 746-3888
www.sturbay.k12.wi.us
Sawyer ES 200/1-2
60 Willow Dr 54235 920-746-1825
Ann Smejkal, prin. Fax 743-5493
Sunrise ES 200/3-5
1414 Rhode Island St 54235 920-746-1829
Ann Smejkal, prin. Fax 743-5823
Sunset ES 200/PK-K
827 N 8th Ave 54235 920-746-5855
Ann Smejkal, prin. Fax 743-6195
Walker MS 300/6-8
19 N 14th Ave 54235 920-746-2810
Randy Watermolen, prin. Fax 746-3885

St. John Bosco S 100/K-8
15 N Elgin Ave 54235 920-743-4144
Vickie Dassler, prin. Fax 743-3711
St. Peter's Evangelical Lutheran S 100/PK-8
108 W Maple St 54235 920-743-4432
Paul Lutze, prin. Fax 743-5388

Sturtevant, Racine, Pop. 6,857
Racine USD
Supt. — See Racine
Schulte ES 400/PK-5
8515 Westminster Dr 53177 262-664-6300
Damon Jackson, prin. Fax 664-6310

Concordia Lutheran S 100/PK-8
8500 Durand Ave 53177 262-884-0991
Jeannine Klein, prin. Fax 833-0322

Suamico, Brown, Pop. 11,263
Howard-Suamico SD
Supt. — See Green Bay
Bay Harbor ES 400/PK-4
1590 Harbor Lights Rd 54173 920-662-8800
Anthony Ebeling, prin. Fax 662-8899

Sullivan, Jefferson, Pop. 665
Jefferson SD
Supt. — See Jefferson
Sullivan ES 200/PK-5
618 Bakertown Rd 53178 920-675-1500
Nicholas Skretta, prin. Fax 675-1520

Sun Prairie, Dane, Pop. 28,546
Sun Prairie Area SD 7,100/PK-12
501 S Bird St 53590 608-834-6500
Dr. Brad Saron, supt. Fax 834-6555
www.spasd.k12.wi.us
Bird ES 500/PK-5
1170 N Bird St 53590 608-834-7300
Chris Sadler, prin. Fax 834-7392
Creekside ES 400/PK-5
1251 Okeeffe Ave 53590 608-834-7700
Jillian Block, prin. Fax 834-7792
Eastside ES 500/PK-5
661 Elizabeth Ln 53590 608-834-7400
Craig Coulthart, prin. Fax 834-7492
Horizon ES 500/PK-4
625 N Heatherstone Dr 53590 608-834-7900
Michelle Kelly, prin. Fax 834-7992
Marsh MS 500/5-7
1351 Columbus St 53590 608-834-7600
Corey Shefchik, prin. Fax 834-7692
Northside ES 500/PK-5
230 W Klubertanz Dr 53590 608-834-7100
Lexi Ballweg, prin. Fax 834-7192
Prairie View MS 500/5-7
400 N Thompson Rd 53590 608-834-7800
Nancy Hery, prin. Fax 834-7892
Royal Oaks ES 500/PK-5
2215 Pennsylvania Ave 53590 608-834-7200
James Ackley, prin. Fax 834-7292
Westside ES 400/PK-5
1320 Buena Vista Dr 53590 608-834-7503
Nicolle Burke, prin. Fax 834-7592

Peace Lutheran S 100/PK-8
1007 Stonehaven Dr 53590 608-834-1200
Kyle Raymond, prin. Fax 825-9806
Sacred Hearts Jesus and Mary S 500/PK-8
221 Columbus St 53590 608-837-8508
Kimberlee Frederick, prin. Fax 825-9585

Superior, Douglas, Pop. 26,443
Superior SD 4,600/PK-12
3025 Tower Ave 54880 715-394-8700
Janna Stevens, supt. Fax 394-8708
www.superior.k12.wi.us
Bryant ES 300/PK-5
1423 Central Ave 54880 715-394-8785
Kate Tesch, prin. Fax 394-8735
Cooper ES 400/PK-5
1807 Missouri Ave 54880 715-394-8790
Aaron Lieberz, prin. Fax 394-8793
Four Corners ES 200/PK-5
4465 E County Road B 54880 715-399-8911
Kim O'Donnell, prin. Fax 399-0119
Great Lakes ES 400/PK-5
129 N 28th St E 54880 715-395-8500
Ryan Haroldson, prin. Fax 395-8505
Lake Superior ES 200/K-5
6200 E 3rd St 54880 715-398-7672
Mark Howard, prin. Fax 398-3131
Northern Lights ES 600/PK-5
1201 N 28th St 54880 715-395-6066
Mike Matejka, prin. Fax 395-6072
Superior Community Preschool 200/PK-PK
3025 Tower Ave 54880 715-394-8700
Jennifer Willoughby, dir. Fax 394-8708
Superior MS 900/6-8
3626 Hammond Ave 54880 715-394-8740
Richard Flaherty, prin. Fax 395-8483

Cathedral S 300/PK-8
1419 Baxter Ave 54880 715-392-2976
Fax 392-2977
Maranatha A Christian Classical Academy 100/PK-12
4916 S State Road 35 54880 715-399-8757
Cheree Waring, admin. Fax 399-8758

Suring, Oconto, Pop. 532
Suring SD 400/PK-12
PO Box 158 54174 920-842-2178
Kelly Casper, supt. Fax 842-4570
www.suring.k12.wi.us
Suring S 300/PK-8
PO Box 158 54174 920-842-2181
Pamela Berg, prin. Fax 842-4570

St. John Lutheran S 50/PK-8
8905 Saint Johns Rd 54174 920-842-4443

Sussex, Waukesha, Pop. 10,416
Hamilton SD 4,700/PK-12
W220N6151 Town Line Rd 53089 262-246-1973
Dr. Paul Mielke, supt. Fax 246-6552
www.hamilton.k12.wi.us
Maple Avenue ES 500/K-5
W240N6059 Maple Ave 53089 262-246-4220
Kristin Koeper-Hamblin, prin. Fax 246-3914
Templeton MS 1,100/6-8
N59W22490 Silver Spring Dr 53089 262-246-6477
Brad Hoffmann, prin. Fax 246-0465
Woodside ES 600/K-5
W236N7465 Woodside Rd 53089 262-820-1530
Dr. James Edmond, prin. Fax 820-0314
Other Schools – See Lannon, Menomonee Falls

Richmond SD 500/PK-8
N56W26530 Richmond Rd 53089 262-538-1360
Dr. Jeff Weiss, admin. Fax 538-1572
www.richmond.k12.wi.us
Richmond S 500/PK-8
N56W26530 Richmond Rd 53089 262-538-1360
Dr. Jeff Weiss, admin. Fax 538-1572

Peace Lutheran Academy 50/PK-8
PO Box 123 53089 262-246-3200
Kimberly Hughes, hdmstr. Fax 246-8455

Theresa, Dodge, Pop. 1,256
Lomira SD
Supt. — See Lomira
Theresa ES 200/K-5
PO Box 157 53091 920-488-2181
Sandy Schaefer, prin. Fax 488-2722

Thiensville, Ozaukee, Pop. 3,175

Christ Alone Lutheran S 100/PK-8
110 Division St 53092 262-242-3870
Dan Aswege M.A., prin.

Thorp, Clark, Pop. 1,612
Thorp SD 600/PK-12
PO Box 449 54771 715-669-5401
John Humphries, admin. Fax 669-5403
www.thorp.k12.wi.us/
Thorp ES 400/PK-8
PO Box 449 54771 715-669-5548
Tyler Nelson, prin. Fax 669-5403

Thorp Catholic S 100/PK-8
411 E School St 54771 715-669-5530
Karen Lipinski, prin. Fax 669-5474

Three Lakes, Oneida, Pop. 604
Three Lakes SD 500/PK-12
6930 W School St 54562 715-546-3496
Dr. George Karling, supt. Fax 546-8125
www.threelakessd.k12.wi.us
Three Lakes ES 200/PK-6
6930 W School St 54562 715-546-3323
Steve Gruszynski, prin. Fax 546-4351
Other Schools – See Rhinelander

Tigerton, Shawano, Pop. 725
Tigerton SD 200/PK-12
PO Box 10 54486 715-535-4044
Benjamin Rayome, admin. Fax 535-4010
www.tigerton.k12.wi.us
Tigerton ES 100/PK-5
PO Box 370 54486 715-535-4051
Dr. Benjamin Rayome, admin. Fax 535-1301

Tomah, Monroe, Pop. 8,916
Tomah Area SD 2,900/PK-12
129 W Clifton St 54660 608-374-7004
Cindy Zahrte, supt. Fax 372-5087
www.tomah.k12.wi.us
La Grange ES 400/PK-5
600 Straw St 54660 608-374-7057
Michelle Clark, prin. Fax 372-5087
Lemonweir ES 300/PK-5
711 N Glendale Ave 54660 608-374-7847
Nicki Pope, prin. Fax 372-5087
Miller ES 300/PK-5
813 Oak Ave 54660 608-374-7026
Diana Lesneski, prin. Fax 372-5087
Oakdale ES 100/PK-2
217 S Oakwood St 54660 608-374-7081
Diana Lesneski, prin. Fax 372-5087
Tomah MS 600/6-8
612 Hollister Ave 54660 608-374-7885
Steven Buss, prin. Fax 374-7303
Other Schools – See Camp Douglas, Warrens, Wyeville

Queen of the Apostles S 200/K-8
315 W Monroe St 54660 608-372-5765
Sandra Murray, prin. Fax 372-4440
St. Paul Lutheran S 200/PK-8
505 Superior Ave 54660 608-372-4542
Geoff Hoffmann, prin. Fax 372-2335

Tomahawk, Lincoln, Pop. 3,356
Tomahawk SD 1,300/PK-12
1048 E King Rd 54487 715-453-5555
Terry Reynolds, supt. Fax 453-6736
www.tomahawk.k12.wi.us
Tomahawk ES 500/PK-5
1048 E King Rd 54487 715-453-2126
Penny Antell, prin. Fax 453-5903
Tomahawk MS 300/6-8
1048 E King Rd 54487 715-453-5371
Wendell Quesinberry, prin. Fax 453-9630

St. Mary S 100/PK-5
221 E Washington Ave 54487 715-453-3542
Rita Lee, prin. Fax 453-6678

Tony, Rusk, Pop. 113
Flambeau SD 500/PK-12
PO Box 86 54563 715-532-3183
Erica Schley, supt. Fax 532-5405
www.flambeau.k12.wi.us
Flambeau ES 300/PK-5
PO Box 86 54563 715-532-3183
Vince Ross, prin. Fax 532-5405

Trempealeau, Trempealeau, Pop. 1,518
Galesville-Ettrick-Trempealeau SD
Supt. — See Galesville
Trempealeau ES 300/PK-5
PO Box 277 54661 608-534-6394
Sam Ruud, prin. Fax 534-6395

Trevor, Kenosha
Trevor-Wilmot Consolidated SD 600/PK-8
26325 Wilmot Rd 53179 262-862-2356
Michelle Garven, supt. Fax 862-9226
trevorwilmotschool.net
Trevor-Wilmot S 600/PK-8
26325 Wilmot Rd 53179 262-862-2356
Ted Gavlin, prin. Fax 862-9226

Turtle Lake, Barron, Pop. 1,031
Turtle Lake SD 400/PK-12
205 Oak St 54889 715-986-2597
Kent Kindschy, admin. Fax 986-2444
www.turtlelake.k12.wi.us
Turtle Lake ES 300/PK-5
205 Oak St 54889 715-986-4470
Troy Wagner, prin. Fax 986-2444
Turtle Lake MS 100/6-8
205 Oak St 54889 715-986-4470
Kent Kindschy, admin. Fax 986-2444

Twin Lakes, Kenosha, Pop. 5,936
Twin Lakes SD 4 400/PK-8
1218 Wilmot Ave 53181 262-877-2148
Joseph Price, admin. Fax 877-4507
www.twinlakes.k12.wi.us/
Lakewood S 400/PK-8
1218 Wilmot Ave 53181 262-877-2148
Joseph Price, admin. Fax 877-4507

Two Rivers, Manitowoc, Pop. 11,594
Two Rivers SD 1,700/PK-12
4521 Lincoln Ave 54241 920-793-4560
Lisa Quistorf, supt. Fax 793-4014
www.trschools.k12.wi.us
Clarke MS 500/5-8
4608 Bellevue Pl 54241 920-794-1614
Tim Wester, prin. Fax 793-1819
Koenig ES 300/PK-4
1114 Lowell St 54241 920-794-7522
Dana McLinn, prin. Fax 794-6120
Magee ES 400/PK-4
3502 Glenwood St 54241 920-793-1118
Chad Bauknecht, prin. Fax 794-7449

St. John's Lutheran S 100/PK-8
3607 45th St 54241 920-793-5001
Ryan Jaeger, prin. Fax 793-8669

Union Grove, Racine, Pop. 4,851
Union Grove J1 SD 800/PK-8
1745 Milldrum St 53182 262-878-2015
Brenda Stevenson, supt. Fax 878-3133
www.uges.k12.wi.us
Union Grove ES 800/PK-8
1745 Milldrum St 53182 262-878-2015
Brenda Stevenson, admin. Fax 878-3133

Yorkville J2 SD 500/PK-8
18621 Washington Ave 53182 262-878-3759
Dave Alexander, admin. Fax 878-3794
www.yorkville.k12.wi.us
Yorkville ES 500/PK-8
18621 Washington Ave 53182 262-878-3759
Amy Foszpanczyk, prin. Fax 878-3794

All Saints Catholic S 100/K-8
1481 172nd Ave 53182 262-859-2007
Jackie Lichter, prin. Fax 878-3299
Union Grove Christian S 100/PK-12
417 15th Ave 53182 262-878-1265
Adam Love, admin. Fax 878-2085

Valders, Manitowoc, Pop. 958
Valders Area SD 1,000/K-12
138 E Wilson St 54245 920-775-9500
Debra Hunt, supt. Fax 775-9509
www.valders.k12.wi.us
Valders ES 300/K-4
331 W Wilson St 54245 920-775-9510
Jason Procknow, prin. Fax 775-9509
Valders MS 300/5-8
138 Jefferson St 54245 920-775-9520
Kelly Isselmann, prin. Fax 775-9509

Verona, Dane, Pop. 10,419
Madison Metro SD
Supt. — See Madison
Olson ES 400/K-5
801 Redan Dr 53593 608-442-2600
Deborah Lyons, prin. Fax 442-2699

Middleton-Cross Plains Area SD
Supt. — See Middleton
West Middleton ES 400/PK-4
7627 W Mineral Point Rd 53593 608-829-9360
Katrina Krych, prin. Fax 829-1147

Verona Area SD 5,200/PK-12
700 N Main St 53593 608-845-4300
Dean Gorrell, supt. Fax 845-4321
www.verona.k12.wi.us
Badger Ridge MS 500/6-8
740 N Main St 53593 608-845-4100
Michael Murphy, prin. Fax 845-4120

Country View ES — 500/K-5
710 Lone Pine Way 53593 — 608-845-4800
Michelle Nummerdor, prin. — Fax 845-4820
Glacier Edge ES — 500/K-5
800 Kimball Ln 53593 — 608-497-2100
Theresa Taylor, prin. — Fax 497-2120
Sugar Creek ES — 500/K-5
420 Church Ave 53593 — 608-845-4700
Todd Brunner, prin. — Fax 845-4720
Other Schools – See Fitchburg

Vesper, Wood, Pop. 572
Wisconsin Rapids SD
Supt. — See Wisconsin Rapids
Vesper Community Academy — 200/PK-5
6443 Virginia St 54489 — 715-424-6786
Jen Wilhorn, prin. — Fax 569-5300

Viola, Vernon, Pop. 694
Kickapoo Area SD — 500/PK-12
S6520 State Highway 131 54664 — 608-627-0101
Douglas Olsen, supt. — Fax 627-0118
www.kickapoo.k12.wi.us
Kickapoo ES — 300/PK-5
S6520 State Highway 131 54664 — 608-627-0107
Kimberly Johnson, prin. — Fax 627-0145

Viroqua, Vernon, Pop. 4,314
Viroqua Area SD — 1,200/PK-12
115 N Education Ave 54665 — 608-637-1186
Dr. Kehl Arnson, supt. — Fax 637-8554
www.viroqua.k12.wi.us
Viroqua ES — 400/PK-4
115 N Education Ave 54665 — 608-637-7071
Kate Moll, prin. — Fax 637-1211
Viroqua MS — 300/5-8
100 Blackhawk Dr 54665 — 608-637-3171
John Schneider, prin. — Fax 637-8034

Cornerstone Christian Academy — 50/PK-12
S3655 Duncan Ln 54665 — 608-634-4102
Nicholas Lavy, admin. — Fax 634-4162
Pleasant Ridge Waldorf S — 100/PK-8
431 E Court St 54665 — 608-637-7828
Amy Hazell, admin. — Fax 637-3952

Wabeno, Forest, Pop. 550
Wabeno Area SD — 500/PK-12
PO Box 460 54566 — 715-473-2592
Jennifer Vogler, supt. — Fax 473-5201
www.wabeno.k12.wi.us
Wabeno ES — 200/PK-6
PO Box 460 54566 — 715-473-3633
Eric Becker, prin. — Fax 473-5201

Wales, Waukesha, Pop. 2,532
Kettle Moraine SD — 4,000/PK-12
563 A J Allen Cir 53183 — 262-968-6300
Patricia Deklotz, supt. — Fax 968-6390
www.kmsd.edu/
Wales ES — 300/PK-5
219 N Oak Crest Dr 53183 — 262-968-6400
Christopher Otto, prin. — Fax 968-6405
Other Schools – See Delafield, Dousman, Genesee Depot

Walworth, Walworth, Pop. 2,799
Walworth JSD 1 — 600/PK-8
121 Beloit St 53184 — 262-275-6896
Dr. Mary Ann Kahl, supt. — Fax 275-2272
www.walworth.k12.wi.us
Walworth ES — 600/PK-8
121 Beloit St 53184 — 262-275-6896
Phill Klamm, supt. — Fax 275-2272

Warrens, Monroe, Pop. 356
Tomah Area SD
Supt. — See Tomah
Warrens ES — 100/PK-5
PO Box 8 54666 — 608-374-7800
Tim Gnewikow, prin. — Fax 372-5087

Washburn, Bayfield, Pop. 2,031
Washburn SD — 600/PK-12
PO Box 730 54891 — 715-373-6188
Dr. Thomas Wiatr, supt. — Fax 373-5877
www.washburn.k12.wi.us
Washburn ES — 300/PK-6
PO Box 730 54891 — 715-373-6199
Al Krause, prin. — Fax 373-0586
Washburn MS — 100/7-8
PO Box 730 54891 — 715-373-6188
Heidi King, prin. — Fax 373-0586

Washington Island, Door
Washington SD — 100/K-12
888 Main Rd 54246 — 920-847-2507
Mati Palm-Leis, supt. — Fax 847-2865
www.island.k12.wi.us
Washington Island S — 50/K-8
888 Main Rd 54246 — 920-847-2507
Dr. Mati M. Palm-Leis, admin. — Fax 847-2865

Waterford, Racine, Pop. 5,327
Washington-Caldwell SD — 200/K-8
8937 Big Bend Rd 53185 — 262-662-3466
Jill Saltzmann, supt. — Fax 662-9888
www.washcald.com
Washington S — 200/K-8
8937 Big Bend Rd 53185 — 262-662-3466
Jill Saltzmann, prin. — Fax 662-9888

Waterford Graded JSD 1 — 1,500/PK-8
819 W Main St 53185 — 262-514-8250
Ed Brzinski, supt. — Fax 514-8251
www.waterford.k12.wi.us
Evergreen ES — 400/PK-6
817 W Main St 53185 — 262-514-8210
Chris Multhauf, prin. — Fax 514-8211
Fox River MS — 400/7-8
921 W Main St 53185 — 262-514-8240
Jason Werchowski, prin. — Fax 514-8241
Trailside ES — 300/PK-6
615 N Milwaukee St 53185 — 262-514-8220
James Dembosky, prin. — Fax 514-8221
Woodfield ES — 400/PK-6
905 Barnes Dr 53185 — 262-514-8230
Tracey Conners, prin. — Fax 514-8231

St. Thomas Aquinas S — 200/PK-8
302 S 2nd St 53185 — 262-534-2265
Julianne Lobitz, prin. — Fax 534-5549

Waterloo, Jefferson, Pop. 3,304
Waterloo SD — 700/PK-12
813 N Monroe St 53594 — 920-478-3633
Brian Henning, admin. — Fax 478-3821
www.waterloo.k12.wi.us
Waterloo ES — 300/PK-4
813 N Monroe St 53594 — 920-478-2168
Maureen Adams, prin. — Fax 478-9589
Waterloo IS/MS — 100/5-8
813 N Monroe St 53594 — 920-478-2696
Shawn Bartelt, prin. — Fax 478-3987

Holy Family S — 50/PK-6
205 Milwaukee Ave 53594 — 920-478-3221
Fr. Jorge Miramontes, prin. — Fax 478-2032
St. John Lutheran S — 100/K-8
413 E Madison St 53594 — 920-478-2707
Mark Eternick, prin. — Fax 478-3745

Watertown, Jefferson, Pop. 23,579
Watertown Unified SD — 3,800/PK-12
111 Dodge St 53094 — 920-262-1460
Cassandra Schug, supt. — Fax 262-1469
www.watertown.k12.wi.us
Douglas ES — 500/PK-5
1101 Prospect St 53098 — 920-262-1495
Emily Lessner, prin. — Fax 262-7596
Lebanon ES — 100/K-5
W4712 County Road O 53098 — 920-925-3712
Melissa Hahn, prin. — Fax 262-1469
Lincoln ES — 200/PK-3
210 N Montgomery St 53094 — 920-262-1465
Emily Lessner, prin. — Fax 262-7581
Riverside MS — 800/6-8
131 Hall St 53094 — 920-262-1480
Jonathan Rouse, prin. — Fax 262-1468
Schurz ES — 300/K-5
1508 Neenah St 53094 — 920-262-1485
Andrew Bare, prin. — Fax 206-7438
Watertown 4 Kids Preschool — 200/PK-PK
111 Dodge St 53094 — 920-262-1460
Jennifer Borst, dir. — Fax 262-1469
Webster ES — 400/PK-5
634 S 12th St 53094 — 920-262-1490
Brad Clark, prin. — Fax 262-1493

Faith Lutheran S — 50/PK-8
626 Milford St 53094 — 920-261-8060
Judi Hoeppner, prin. — Fax 275-0932
Good Shepherd Lutheran S — 100/PK-8
1611 E Main St 53094 — 920-261-2579
Amy Gromowski, prin. — Fax 261-2574
Lebanon Lutheran S — 100/PK-8
N534 County Road R 53098 — 920-925-3791
Julia Wackt, prin. — Fax 925-3799
St. Henry S — 100/PK-8
300 E Cady St 53094 — 920-261-2586
Adrienne Van Norman, prin. — Fax 261-3681
St. John's Lutheran S — 100/PK-8
317 N 6th St 53094 — 920-261-3756
Christopher Mueller, prin.
St. Mark's Lutheran S — 300/PK-8
706 Jones St 53094 — 920-262-8501
Frederick Uttech, prin. — Fax 262-8517
Trinity-St. Luke's Lutheran S — 100/PK-4
801 S 5th St 53094 — 920-261-3615
James Moeller, prin. — Fax 261-5840
Trinity-St. Luke's Lutheran S — 100/5-8
303 Clark St 53094 — 920-206-1844
James Moeller, prin. — Fax 206-1750

Waukesha, Waukesha, Pop. 69,639
Waukesha SD — 13,200/PK-12
222 Maple Ave 53186 — 262-970-1000
Todd Gray, supt. — Fax 970-1021
www.waukesha.k12.wi.us
Banting ES — 500/PK-5
2019 Butler Dr 53186 — 262-970-1200
Mary Garcia-Valez, prin. — Fax 970-1220
Bethesda ES — 400/PK-5
730 S University Dr 53188 — 262-970-1305
Jeremy Martin, prin. — Fax 970-1320
Blair ES — 400/PK-5
301 Hyde Park Ave 53188 — 262-970-1400
Aida Cruz-Farin, prin. — Fax 970-1420
Butler MS — 900/6-8
310 N Hine Ave 53188 — 262-970-2900
Jason Sadowski, prin. — Fax 970-2920
Hadfield ES — 300/PK-5
733 Linden St 53186 — 262-970-1500
Al Busch, prin. — Fax 970-1520
Hawthorne ES — 300/PK-5
1111 Maitland Dr 53188 — 262-970-1600
Duy Nguyen, prin. — Fax 970-1620
Heyer ES — 400/PK-5
1209 Heyer Dr 53186 — 262-970-1700
Mark Schneider, prin. — Fax 970-1720
Hillcrest ES — 400/PK-5
2200 Davidson Rd 53186 — 262-970-1800
Faith Lincicum, prin. — Fax 970-1820
Horning MS — 800/6-8
2000 Wolf Rd 53186 — 262-970-3300
Robert Blessington, prin. — Fax 970-3320
Lowell ES — 300/PK-5
140 N Grandview Blvd 53188 — 262-970-1900
Rachel Hermann, prin. — Fax 970-1920
Meadowbrook ES — 300/PK-5
3130 Rolling Ridge Dr 53188 — 262-970-2000
Jessica Wagner, prin. — Fax 970-2020
Paul MS — 600/6-8
400 N Grand Ave 53186 — 262-970-3100
Rob Bennett, prin. — Fax 970-3120
Prairie ES — 400/PK-5
1801 Center Rd 53189 — 262-970-2200
Dennis Griffin, prin. — Fax 970-2220
Rose Glen ES — 500/PK-5
W273S3845 Brookhill Dr 53189 — 262-970-2400
Melissa Nikolic, prin. — Fax 970-2420
Summit View ES — 600/PK-5
2100 Summit Ave 53188 — 262-970-2600
Jeff Peterson, prin. — Fax 970-2620
Waukesha Early Learning Center — 700/PK-K
1150 Whiterock Ave 53186 — 262-970-2700
Laura Faust, coord. — Fax 970-2720
Whittier ES — 300/PK-5
1103 S East Ave 53186 — 262-970-2800
Cynthia Gannon, prin. — Fax 970-2820

Beautiful Savior Lutheran S — 100/PK-6
1205 S East Ave 53186 — 262-542-6558
Jennifer Wolff, prin. — Fax 542-8574
Montessori S of Waukesha — 200/PK-8
2600 Summit Ave 53188 — 262-547-2545
William Walsh, dir. — Fax 547-2715
Mount Calvary Lutheran S — 100/PK-8
1941 Madison St 53188 — 262-547-6740
Robert Frick, prin. — Fax 522-3234
St. Joseph MS — 200/6-8
818 N East Ave 53186 — 262-896-2930
Lisa Kovaleski, prin. — Fax 896-2935
St. Mary S — 300/1-5
520 E Newhall Ave 53186 — 262-896-2932
Lisa Kovaleski, prin. — Fax 896-2931
St. William S — 200/PK-K
444 N Moreland Blvd 53188 — 262-896-2920
Lisa Kovaleski, prin. — Fax 896-2931
Trinity Lutheran S — 200/PK-8
1060 Whiterock Ave 53186 — 262-547-8020
Justin Gut, prin. — Fax 547-7331

Waumandee, Buffalo, Pop. 68

St. Boniface S — 50/PK-8
S2026 County Road U 54622 — 608-626-2611
Brian Jazdzewski, lead tchr.

Waunakee, Dane, Pop. 11,963
Waunakee Community SD — 3,800/PK-12
905 Bethel Cir 53597 — 608-849-2000
Randy Guttenberg, supt. — Fax 849-2350
www.waunakee.k12.wi.us
Arboretum ES — 500/PK-4
1350 Arboretum Dr 53597 — 608-849-1800
Sheila Weihert, prin. — Fax 849-1810
Waunakee Heritage ES — 300/PK-4
501 South St 53597 — 608-849-2030
Dan Carter, prin. — Fax 849-2265
Waunakee IS — 600/5-6
6273 Woodland Dr 53597 — 608-849-2176
Christine Hetzel, prin. — Fax 849-2198
Waunakee MS — 600/7-8
1001 South St 53597 — 608-849-2060
Marcy Peters-Felice, prin. — Fax 849-2088
Waunakee Prairie ES — 500/PK-4
700 N Madison St 53597 — 608-849-2200
Dean Kaminski, prin. — Fax 849-2255

Madison Country Day S — 300/PK-12
5606 River Rd 53597 — 608-850-6000
Ben Hebebrand, head sch — Fax 850-6006
St. John the Baptist S — 200/PK-8
114 E 3rd St 53597 — 608-849-5325
Constance Stark, prin. — Fax 849-5342

Waupaca, Waupaca, Pop. 6,011
Waupaca SD — 2,200/PK-12
515 School St 54981 — 715-258-4121
Gregory Nyen, supt. — Fax 258-4125
www.waupaca.k12.wi.us/
Chain O'Lakes ES — 100/K-2
N3160 Silver Lake Dr 54981 — 715-258-4151
Rhonda Hare, prin. — Fax 258-4512
Waupaca Learning Center ES — 700/PK-4
1515 Shoemaker Rd 54981 — 715-258-4141
John Erspamer, prin. — Fax 258-4138
Waupaca MS — 700/5-8
1149 Shoemaker Rd 54981 — 715-258-4140
Carl Eggebrecht, prin. — Fax 256-5681

Waupun, Dodge, Pop. 11,240
Waupun Area SD — 1,600/PK-12
950 Wilcox St 53963 — 920-324-9341
Dr. Tonya Olson, supt. — Fax 324-2630
www.waupun.k12.wi.us
Meadow View PS — 400/PK-1
601 Grandview Ave 53963 — 920-324-3361
Wendy Sallam, prin. — Fax 324-0490
Rock River IS — 600/2-6
451 E Spring St 53963 — 920-324-9322
Sarah Leisses, prin. — Fax 324-2929

Central Wisconsin Christian S — 300/PK-12
301 Fox Lake Rd 53963 — 920-324-4233
Mark Buteyn, admin. — Fax 324-5036

Wausau, Marathon, Pop. 38,312
Wausau SD — 8,100/PK-12
PO Box 359 54402 — 715-261-0500
Dr. Michael Schwei, supt. — Fax 261-2503
www.wausauschools.org/

Franklin ES 300/K-5
1509 N 5th St 54403 715-261-0000
Elizabeth White, prin. Fax 261-2144
Grant ES 200/K-5
500 N 4th Ave 54401 715-261-0190
Christopher Nyman, prin. Fax 261-2223
Hawthorn Hills ES 200/K-5
1600 Kickbusch St 54403 715-261-0045
Angela Lloyd, prin. Fax 261-2291
Hewitt-Texas ES 100/K-5
T10331 Quarry Rd 54403 715-261-0015
Philip Beck, prin. Fax 261-2305
Jefferson ES 400/PK-5
500 W Randolph St 54401 715-261-0175
Cathy Wenzel Prozanski, prin. Fax 261-3100
Jones ES 300/PK-5
1018 S 12th Ave 54401 715-261-0950
Robin Franks, prin. Fax 261-2157
Lincoln ES 300/K-5
720 S 6th Ave 54401 715-261-0965
Colleen Whooley Jepson, prin. Fax 261-2690
Maine ES 200/K-5
5901 N 44th Ave 54401 715-261-0250
Marie Northup, prin. Fax 675-6852
Mann MS 800/6-8
3101 N 13th St 54403 715-261-0725
Rob Phelps, prin. Fax 261-2035
Marshall ES 300/K-5
1918 Lamont St 54403 715-261-0060
Amanda Patterson, prin. Fax 261-2355
Muir MS 900/6-8
1400 Stewart Ave 54401 715-261-0100
Larry Mancl, prin. Fax 261-2461
Rib Mountain ES 300/K-5
2701 Robin Ln 54401 715-261-0220
Tammy Steckbauer, prin. Fax 261-2752
Riverview ES 400/PK-5
4303 Troy St 54403 715-261-0030
Andrew Place, prin. Fax 261-3905
South Mountain ES 200/K-5
5400 Bittersweet Rd 54401 715-261-0235
Deb Heilman, prin. Fax 261-3930
Stettin ES 300/K-5
109 N 56th Ave 54401 715-261-0205
Kelly Halvorsen, prin. Fax 261-2801

Faith Christian Academy 100/PK-12
225 S 28th Ave 54401 715-842-0797
Clint Steinke, admin. Fax 842-1042
Hillside Christian S K-8
6300 Bittersweet Rd 54401 715-241-7722
Newman Catholic ECC at St. Michael 50/PK-PK
615 Stark St 54403 715-848-0206
Jacci LePak, dir. Fax 845-6852
Newman Catholic ES at St. Anne 200/K-5
604 N 6th Ave 54401 715-845-5754
Terry Vechinski, prin. Fax 842-4021
Our Savior's Evangelical Lutheran S 50/PK-8
703 Flieth St 54401 715-845-3253
Ethan Hutchinson, prin. Fax 849-8139
St. John Lutheran S 50/PK-8
E10723 County Road Z 54403 715-842-5212
Mary Jo Prahl, admin. Fax 849-9558
Trinity Lutheran S 200/PK-8
501 Stewart Ave 54401 715-848-0166
Bill Zuelsdorff, admin. Fax 843-7278

Wausaukee, Marinette, Pop. 563
Wausaukee SD 500/PK-12
PO Box 258 54177 715-856-5153
Bob Berndt, supt. Fax 856-6592
www.wausaukee.k12.wi.us
Wausaukee ES 300/PK-6
PO Box 258 54177 715-856-5152
Katey Ambrose, prin. Fax 856-6592
Wausaukee JHS 100/7-8
PO Box 258 54177 715-856-5151
Jared Deschane, prin. Fax 856-6592

Wautoma, Waushara, Pop. 2,182
Wautoma Area SD 1,400/PK-12
PO Box 870 54982 920-787-7112
Jeff Kasuboski, supt. Fax 787-1389
www.wautomasd.org
Parkside MS 500/4-8
PO Box 870 54982 920-787-4577
Deb Premo, prin. Fax 787-7336
Riverview ES 400/PK-3
PO Box 870 54982 920-787-4590
Ann Fajfer, prin. Fax 787-1556
Other Schools – See Redgranite

Wauwatosa, Milwaukee, Pop. 45,454
Wauwatosa SD 7,100/PK-12
12121 W North Ave 53226 414-773-1000
Phil Ertl, supt. Fax 773-1019
www.wauwatosaschools.org
Eisenhower ES 400/PK-5
11600 W Center St 53222 414-773-1100
Stephanie Calarco, prin. Fax 773-1120
Jefferson ES 300/PK-5
6927 Maple Ter 53213 414-773-1200
Jenny Schultz, prin. Fax 773-1220
Lincoln ES 300/PK-5
1741 N Wauwatosa Ave 53213 414-773-1300
Michelle Miner, prin. Fax 773-1320
Longfellow MS 800/6-8
7600 W North Ave 53213 414-773-2400
SethLarson, prin. Fax 773-2420
Madison ES 400/PK-5
9925 W Glendale Ave, 414-773-1400
Lori Lester, prin. Fax 773-1420
McKinley ES 400/PK-5
2435 N 89th St 53226 414-773-1500
Jean Hoffman, prin. Fax 773-1520
Roosevelt ES 500/PK-5
2535 N 73rd St 53213 414-773-1600
Mark Supa, prin. Fax 773-1620
Underwood ES 300/PK-5
11132 W Potter Rd 53226 414-773-1700
Jenny Keats, prin. Fax 773-1720
Washington ES 400/PK-5
2166 N 68th St 53213 414-773-1800
Joe Russell, prin. Fax 773-1820
Wauwatosa Montessori S 100/PK-8
12121 W North Ave 53226 414-773-3300
Ashley Imperiale, prin. Fax 773-1089
Whitman MS 700/6-8
11100 W Center St 53222 414-773-2600
Jeff Keranen, prin. Fax 773-2620
Wilson ES 200/PK-5
1060 Glenview Ave 53213 414-773-1900
Mike Heun, prin. Fax 773-1920

Christ King S 400/K-8
2646 N Swan Blvd 53226 414-258-4160
Dr. Kevin Hughes, prin. Fax 258-0916
Our Redeemer Lutheran S 300/PK-8
10025 W North Ave 53226 414-258-4558
Jim Van Dellen, prin. Fax 258-5775
Pilgrim Lutheran S 200/PK-8
6717 W Center St 53210 414-259-0190
Cassandra Neiman, prin. Fax 259-0113
St. John's Evangelical Lutheran S 200/PK-8
1278 Dewey Ave 53213 414-258-4214
Scott Uecker, prin. Fax 453-9322
St. Joseph S 200/PK-8
2750 N 122nd St 53222 414-771-4626
Linda Cooney, prin. Fax 771-9826
St. Jude the Apostle S 400/K-8
800 Glenview Ave 53213 414-771-1520
Catherine LaDien, prin. Fax 771-3748
Wauwatosa Catholic S 100/PK-8
1500 N Wauwatosa Ave 53213 414-258-9977
Heidi Hernandez, prin. Fax 258-9972

Wauzeka, Crawford, Pop. 697
Wauzeka-Steuben SD 200/PK-12
301 E Main St 53826 608-875-5311
Robert Sailer, supt. Fax 875-5100
www.wauzeka.k12.wi.us
Wauzeka-Steuben S 200/PK-12
301 E Main St 53826 608-875-5311
Tiffany Dums, prin. Fax 875-5100

Webster, Burnett, Pop. 634
Webster SD 700/PK-12
PO Box 9 54893 715-866-4391
Jim Erickson, supt. Fax 866-4283
www.webster.k12.wi.us
Webster ES 300/PK-4
PO Box 9 54893 715-866-8210
Martha Anderson, prin. Fax 866-8262
Webster MS 200/5-8
PO Box 9 54893 715-866-4282
Diana Lesneski, prin. Fax 866-4377

West Allis, Milwaukee, Pop. 59,182
West Allis SD
Supt. — See Milwaukee
Franklin ES 300/PK-5
2060 S 86th St 53227 414-604-3710
Leslie Connors, prin. Fax 546-5682
Irving ES 500/PK-5
10230 W Grant St 53227 414-604-4010
Chris Gosch, prin. Fax 546-5641
Jefferson ES 600/PK-5
7229 W Becher St 53219 414-604-4110
Lynn Wall, prin. Fax 546-5683
Lane IS 6-8
1300 S 109th St 53214 414-329-6610
Bob Antholine, prin. Fax 259-0306
Longfellow ES 300/PK-5
2211 S 60th St 53219 414-604-4310
Jessica Moe, prin. Fax 546-5540
Madison ES 200/PK-5
1117 S 104th St 53214 414-604-4410
Breanne Willms, prin. Fax 256-6782
Mann ES 600/PK-5
6213 W Lapham St 53214 414-604-3900
Chad Krupar, prin. Fax 546-5554
Mitchell ES 500/PK-5
10125 W Montana Ave 53227 414-604-4510
Ryan Johnson, prin. Fax 546-5684
Walker ES 400/PK-5
900 S 119th St 53214 414-604-4710
Tracy Fischer-Tubbs, prin. Fax 479-3481
Wilson ES 500/PK-5
8710 W Orchard St 53214 414-604-4810
Mary Gottinger, prin. Fax 256-6781
Wright IS 1,100/6-8
9501 W Cleveland Ave 53227 414-604-3410
Jeff Thomson, prin. Fax 546-5785

Good Shepherds Evangelical Lutheran S 100/PK-8
1337 S 100th St 53214 414-774-8520
Mike Henning, prin. Fax 443-9947
Grace Christian Academy 200/PK-12
8420 W Beloit Rd 53227 414-327-4200
Cynthia Hummitzsch, admin. Fax 327-4386
Lamb of God Lutheran S 100/PK-8
2217 S 99th St 53227 414-321-8780
Jay Schwall, prin. Fax 321-4184
Mary Queen of Saints Academy 200/PK-8
1435 S 92nd St 53214 414-476-0751
Nicole Kuehne, prin. Fax 259-9285
St. Paul Lutheran S 100/PK-8
7821 W Lincoln Ave 53219 414-541-6251
Rick Schneider, prin. Fax 541-2205

West Baraboo, Sauk, Pop. 1,400
Baraboo SD
Supt. — See Baraboo
Willson ES 300/K-5
146 Berkley Blvd 53913 608-355-3925
Amy Fassbender, prin. Fax 355-4678

West Bend, Washington, Pop. 30,669
West Bend SD 5,400/PK-12
735 S Main St 53095 262-335-5435
Erik Olson, supt. Fax 335-5470
www.west-bend.k12.wi.us
Badger MS 600/7-8
727 S 6th Ave 53095 262-335-5456
Dave Uelmen, prin. Fax 306-4380
Decorah ES 400/K-4
1225 Sylvan Way 53095 262-335-5476
Adrienne Schneider, prin. Fax 335-5192
Fair Park ES 500/K-4
519 N Indiana Ave 53090 262-335-5516
Jodee Stahmer, prin. Fax 335-6196
Green Tree ES 400/K-4
1330 Green Tree Rd 53090 262-335-5521
John Graf, prin. Fax 335-8243
McLane ES 500/K-4
833 Chestnut St 53095 262-335-5487
Andy Kasik, prin. Fax 335-8245
Rolfs Education Center 100/Alt
737 S 3rd Ave 53095 262-335-5471
Sharon Kailas, coord. Fax 335-6182
Silverbrook IS 200/5-6
120 N Silverbrook Dr 53095 262-335-5499
Lance Roell, prin. Fax 335-5610
Other Schools – See Jackson

Good Shepherd Lutheran S 300/PK-8
777 S Indiana Ave 53095 262-334-7881
James Sievert, prin. Fax 334-8039
Holy Angels S 300/PK-8
230 N 8th Ave 53095 262-338-1148
Michael Sternig, prin. Fax 334-6116
St. Frances Cabrini S 400/PK-8
529 Hawthorn Dr 53095 262-334-7142
Aaron Hilts, prin. Fax 334-8168
St. John Lutheran S 200/K-8
899 S 6th Ave 53095 262-334-3077
Dawn Oldenettel, prin. Fax 334-3591

Westby, Vernon, Pop. 2,182
Westby Area SD 1,100/PK-12
206 West Ave S 54667 608-634-0101
John Burnett, supt. Fax 634-0118
www.westby.k12.wi.us
Westby Area MS 300/5-8
206 West Ave S 54667 608-634-0200
Mike Weninger, prin. Fax 634-0218
Westby ES 400/PK-4
122 Nelson St 54667 608-634-0500
Bruce Peterson, prin. Fax 634-0518
Other Schools – See Coon Valley

Westfield, Marquette, Pop. 1,241
Westfield SD 1,100/PK-12
N7046 County Road M 53964 608-296-2141
Robert Meicher, supt. Fax 296-2938
www.westfield.k12.wi.us
Westfield Area MS 200/7-8
N7046 County Road M 53964 608-296-2141
David Moody, prin. Fax 296-2293
Westfield ES 400/PK-6
329 Hawk Ln 53964 608-296-2224
Cory Parman, prin. Fax 296-4001
Other Schools – See Coloma, Oxford

West Milwaukee, Milwaukee, Pop. 4,109
West Allis SD
Supt. — See Milwaukee
Pershing ES 300/PK-5
1330 S 47th St 53214 414-604-4610
Steve Harris, prin. Fax 649-4981
West Milwaukee IS 500/6-8
5104 W Greenfield Ave 53214 414-604-3310
Tom Blair, prin. Fax 389-3815

Weston, Marathon, Pop. 12,921
D.C. Everest Area SD 5,600/PK-12
6300 Alderson St 54476 715-359-4221
Kristine Gilmore, supt. Fax 359-2056
www.dce.k12.wi.us
D.C. Everest MS 800/6-7
9302 Schofield Ave 54476 715-241-9700
Gina Lehman, prin. Fax 241-9697
D.C. Everest Multi-Age ES K-5
4704 Camp Phillips Rd 54476 715-359-1040
Casey Nye, prin.
Mountain Bay ES 500/PK-5
8602 Schofield Ave 54476 715-355-0302
Patrick Phalen, prin. Fax 355-0307
Weston ES 600/K-5
5200 Camp Phillips Rd 54476 715-359-4181
Sarah Trimner, prin. Fax 355-3726
Other Schools – See Hatley, Ringle, Rothschild

West Salem, LaCrosse, Pop. 4,740
West Salem SD 1,800/PK-12
405 Hamlin St E 54669 608-786-0700
Troy Gunderson, supt. Fax 786-2960
www.wsalem.k12.wi.us
West Salem ES 900/PK-5
475 Mark St N 54669 608-786-1662
Ryan Rieber, prin. Fax 786-3415
West Salem MS 400/6-8
450 Mark St N 54669 608-786-2090
Ben Wopat, prin. Fax 786-1081

Christ-St. John's Lutheran S 100/PK-8
500 Park St 54669 608-786-1250
Stephen Berg, prin. Fax 432-9863
Coulee Christian S 200/PK-12
230 Garland St W 54669 608-786-3004
Dr. Tammy Chandler, admin. Fax 786-3005

Weyauwega, Waupaca, Pop. 1,882
Weyauwega-Fremont SD 900/PK-12
PO Box 580 54983 920-867-8800
Scott Bleck, supt. Fax 867-8815
www.wegafremont.k12.wi.us
Weyauwega ES 300/K-5
PO Box 580 54983 920-867-8150
Douglas Nowak, prin. Fax 867-8175
Weyauwega-Fremont MS 200/6-8
PO Box 580 54983 920-867-8850
Jeremy Schroeder, prin. Fax 867-8875
Other Schools – See Fremont

Christ Evangelical Lutheran S 50/PK-8
N6412 State Road 49 54983 920-867-3263
Colleen Boelter, prin. Fax 867-3263
St. Peter Lutheran S 100/PK-8
312 W Main St 54983 920-867-2200
Jeffrey Miller, prin. Fax 867-3160

Whitefish Bay, Milwaukee, Pop. 13,847
Whitefish Bay SD 3,100/PK-12
1200 E Fairmount Ave 53217 414-963-3921
John Thomsen, supt. Fax 963-3959
www.wfbschools.com
Cumberland ES 800/PK-5
4780 N Marlborough Dr 53211 414-963-3943
Jayne Heffron, prin. Fax 963-3945
Richards ES 700/PK-5
5812 N Santa Monica Blvd 53217 414-963-3951
Alix Kasmarick, prin. Fax 963-3946
Whitefish Bay MS 600/6-8
1144 E Henry Clay St 53217 414-963-6800
Mike O'Connor, prin. Fax 963-6808

Holy Family S 200/PK-8
4849 N Wildwood Ave 53217 414-332-8175
Amy Kern, prin. Fax 961-7396
St. Monica S 400/PK-8
5635 N Santa Monica Blvd 53217 414-332-3660
Michael Landgraf, prin. Fax 332-8649

Whitehall, Trempealeau, Pop. 1,550
Whitehall SD 500/PK-12
19121 Hobson St 54773 715-538-4374
Michael Beighley, supt. Fax 538-4639
www.whitehallsd.k12.wi.us
Whitehall Memorial ES 300/PK-6
PO Box 37 54773 715-538-4316
Damon Lisowsky, prin. Fax 538-2350

White Lake, Langlade, Pop. 352
White Lake SD 200/PK-12
PO Box 67 54491 715-882-8421
William Fisher, supt. Fax 882-2914
www.whitelake.k12.wi.us
White Lake ES 100/PK-6
PO Box 67 54491 715-882-2361
Glenda Boldig, prin. Fax 882-2914

Whitewater, Walworth, Pop. 14,180
Whitewater USD 1,800/PK-12
419 S Elizabeth St 53190 262-472-8700
Dr. Mark Elworthy, supt. Fax 472-8710
www.wwusd.org
Lakeview ES 200/PK-5
W8363 R and W Townline Rd 53190 262-472-8400
David Brokopp, prin. Fax 472-8410
Lincoln ES 400/PK-5
242 S Prince St 53190 262-472-8500
Mary Kilar, prin. Fax 472-8510
Washington ES 300/PK-5
506 E Main St 53190 262-472-8600
Tom Grosinske, prin. Fax 472-8610
Whitewater MS 400/6-8
401 S Elizabeth St 53190 262-472-8300
Dr. Tanya Wojciechowicz, prin. Fax 472-8310

Wild Rose, Waushara, Pop. 719
Wild Rose SD 600/PK-12
PO Box 276 54984 920-622-4203
Craig Hayes, supt. Fax 622-4604
www.wildroseschools.org
Wild Rose ES 200/PK-5
PO Box 119 54984 920-622-4204
Matt Wilbert, prin. Fax 622-4601
Other Schools – See Pine River

Williams Bay, Walworth, Pop. 2,540
Williams Bay SD 600/PK-12
PO Box 1410 53191 262-245-1575
Dr. Wayne Anderson, supt. Fax 245-5877
www.williamsbayschool.org
Williams Bay ES 300/PK-5
250 Theatre Rd 53191 262-245-5571
Ali Bond, prin. Fax 245-1839
Williams Bay MS 100/6-8
PO Box 1410 53191 262-245-6224
Dr. William White, prin. Fax 245-5877

Faith Christian S 200/PK-12
PO Box 1230 53191 262-245-9404
Jim McCormick M.Ed., head sch Fax 245-0128

Wind Lake, Racine, Pop. 5,282
Muskego-Norway SD
Supt. — See Muskego
Lakeview ES 300/K-4
26335 Fries Ln 53185 262-971-1850
Alyson Eisch, prin. Fax 895-7631

Wind Point, Racine, Pop. 1,708

Prairie S 700/PK-12
4050 Lighthouse Dr, 262-752-2500
Dr. Nat Coffman, head sch Fax 752-2517

Windsor, Dane, Pop. 3,527
De Forest Area SD
Supt. — See De Forest
Windsor ES 500/K-4
4352 Windsor Rd 53598 608-842-6300
Roy Bernards, prin. Fax 842-6315

Winneconne, Winnebago, Pop. 2,364
Winneconne Community SD 1,500/PK-12
PO Box 5000 54986 920-582-5802
Margaret Larson, supt. Fax 582-5816
www.winneconne.k12.wi.us
Winneconne ES 600/PK-5
PO Box 5000 54986 920-582-5803
Lisa Hughes, prin. Fax 582-5816
Winneconne MS 400/6-8
PO Box 5000 54986 920-582-5800
Todd Schroeder, prin. Fax 582-5812

Winter, Sawyer, Pop. 305
Winter SD 300/PK-12
PO Box 310 54896 715-266-3301
Kurt Lindau, admin. Fax 266-2216
www.winter.k12.wi.us/
Winter ES 100/PK-5
PO Box 310 54896 715-266-6701
Kurt Lindau, admin. Fax 266-2216
Winter MS 100/6-8
PO Box 310 54896 715-266-6701
Kurt Lindau, admin. Fax 266-2216

Wisconsin Dells, Columbia, Pop. 2,648
Wisconsin Dells SD 1,800/PK-12
811 County Road H 53965 608-254-7769
Terrance Slack, supt. Fax 254-8058
www.sdwd.k12.wi.us
Spring Hill ES 600/PK-5
300 Vine St 53965 608-253-2468
Julie Ennis, prin. Fax 254-6397
Spring Hill MS 300/6-8
300 Vine St 53965 608-253-2467
Julie Ennis, prin. Fax 254-6397
Other Schools – See Briggsville, Lake Delton

Trinity Lutheran S 50/PK-6
728 Church St 53965 608-253-3241
Kyle Motzkus, prin.

Wisconsin Rapids, Wood, Pop. 18,141
Wisconsin Rapids SD 5,300/PK-12
510 Peach St 54494 715-424-6700
Craig Broeren, supt. Fax 422-6070
www.wrps.org
Grant ES 200/PK-5
8511 County Road WW 54494 715-424-6766
Timothy Bruns, prin. Fax 422-6384
Grove ES 300/PK-5
471 Grove Ave 54494 715-424-6769
Tina Wallner, prin. Fax 422-6325
Howe ES 400/K-5
221 8th St N 54494 715-424-6772
Tina Miller, prin. Fax 422-6385
Washington ES 300/PK-5
2911 Washington St 54494 715-424-6788
Kelly Schaeffer, prin. Fax 422-6315
Wisconsin Rapids Area MS 700/6-7
1921 27th Ave S 54495 715-424-6740
Tracy Ginter, prin. Fax 422-6187
Woodside ES 400/PK-5
611 Two Mile Ave 54494 715-424-6793
Paul Mann, prin. Fax 422-6338
WRPS Four-year-old K 200/PK-PK
510 Peach St 54494 715-424-6700
Kelly Schaeffer, prin. Fax 422-6070
Other Schools – See Rudolph, Vesper

Assumption MS 100/6-8
440 Mead St 54494 715-422-0950
Joan Bond, prin. Fax 422-0955
Good Shepherd Lutheran S 50/1-8
10611 State Highway 13 S 54494 715-325-3355
Donna Tullberg, prin.
Immanuel Lutheran S 100/PK-8
111 11th St N 54494 715-423-0272
Brian Betts, prin. Fax 423-2853
Our Lady Queen of Heaven S 100/K-2
750 10th Ave S 54495 715-422-0980
Rebecca Gudelis, prin. Fax 424-2972
St. Lawrence ECC 100/PK-K
551 10th Ave N 54495 715-422-0990
Tara Biebl, dir. Fax 422-0993
St. Paul's Evangelical Lutheran S 100/PK-8
311 14th Ave S 54495 715-421-3634
Jon Engelbrecht, prin. Fax 421-3643
St. Vincent De Paul S 100/3-5
831 12th St S 54494 715-422-0960
Pam Fochs, prin. Fax 422-0963

Wittenberg, Shawano, Pop. 1,064
Wittenberg-Birnamwood SD 1,200/PK-12
400 W Grand Ave 54499 715-253-2213
Garrett Rogowski, supt. Fax 253-3588
www.wittbirn.k12.wi.us/
Wittenberg S 400/PK-8
300 S Prouty St 54499 715-253-2221
Vicky Haas, prin. Fax 253-3210
Other Schools – See Birnamwood

Wonewoc, Juneau, Pop. 810
Wonewoc-Union Center SD 300/PK-12
101 School Rd 53968 608-464-3165
Dr. Sharon Ennis, supt. Fax 464-3325
www.wc.k12.wi.us
Wonewoc ES 200/PK-5
101 School Rd 53968 608-464-3165
Dr. Sharon Ennis, prin. Fax 464-3325
Wonewoc JHS 50/6-8
101 School Rd 53968 608-464-3165
Michelle Noll, prin. Fax 464-3325

St. Paul's Evangelical Lutheran S 100/PK-8
PO Box 325 53968 608-464-3212
Rick Zimmerman, prin. Fax 464-3258

Woodruff, Oneida, Pop. 943
Woodruff J1 SD 500/PK-8
11065 Old 51 N 54568 715-356-3282
Jocelyn Smith, supt. Fax 358-2933
www.avwschool.org
Arbor Vitae-Woodruff ES 500/PK-8
11065 Old 51 N 54568 715-356-3282
Richard Fortier, prin. Fax 358-2933

Woodville, Saint Croix, Pop. 1,320
Baldwin-Woodville Area SD
Supt. — See Baldwin
Viking MS 500/6-8
500 Southside Dr 54028 715-698-2456
Scott Benoy, prin. Fax 698-3315

Wrightstown, Brown, Pop. 2,803
Wrightstown Community SD 1,400/PK-12
PO Box 128 54180 920-532-5551
Carla Buboltz, supt. Fax 532-4664
www.wrightstown.k12.wi.us
Wrightstown ES 500/PK-4
PO Box 128 54180 920-532-4818
Kendilyn Brockman, prin. Fax 532-4664
Wrightstown MS 400/5-8
PO Box 128 54180 920-532-5553
Lee Mierow, prin. Fax 532-3869

St. Clare S 100/PK-8
425 Main St 54180 920-532-4833
Lisa Gruber, prin. Fax 532-0458
St. John Lutheran S 50/PK-8
261 Clay St 54180 920-532-4361
Timothy Raddatz, prin. Fax 532-4413

Wyeville, Monroe, Pop. 145
Tomah Area SD
Supt. — See Tomah
Wyeville ES 100/PK-5
225 W Tomah Rd 54660 608-374-7826
Tim Gnewikow, prin. Fax 372-5087

WYOMING

WYOMING DEPARTMENT OF EDUCATION
2300 Capitol Ave, Cheyenne 82001-3644
Telephone 307-777-7673
Fax 307-777-6234
Website edu.wyoming.gov

Superintendent of Public Instruction Jillian Balow

WYOMING BOARD OF EDUCATION
2300 Capitol Ave, Cheyenne 82001-3644

Chairperson Walt Wilcox

BOARDS OF COOPERATIVE EDUCATIONAL SERVICES (BOCES)

Big Horn County SD 2 BOCES
Rhonda Savage, dir. 307-548-6466
502 Hampshire Ave, Lovell 82431
Carbon Co. Higher Education Center BOCES
David Throgmorton Ph.D., dir. 307-328-9274
812 E Murray St, Rawlins 82301 Fax 324-9273
www.cchec.org
Carbon County SD 2 BOCES
Melissa Donough, dir. 307-326-5271
PO Box 1530, Saratoga 82331 Fax 326-8089
www.crb2.k12.wy.us/boces/
Central Wyoming BOCES 307-268-3309
, 125 College Dr, Casper 82601 Fax 268-2611
www.caspercollege.edu/boces/index.html
Eastern Wyoming BOCES
Roger Humphrey, dir. 307-532-8346
3200 W C St, Torrington 82240 Fax 532-8229
Fremont County BOCES
Sandy Barton, dir. 307-856-2028
320 W Main St, Riverton 82501 Fax 856-4058
www.fcboces.org

Northeast Wyoming BOCES
Julie Cudmore, dir. 307-682-0231
410 N Miller Ave, Gillette 82716 Fax 686-7628
www.newboces.com/
Northwest Wyoming BOCES
Carolyn Conner, dir. 307-864-2171
PO Box 112, Thermopolis 82443 Fax 864-9463
www.nwboces.com/
Oyster Ridge BOCES
Bridget Stewart, dir. 307-877-6958
20 Adaville Dr, Diamondville 83116 Fax 828-9040
www.kemmereroutreach.com
Powell Valley Community Education BOCES
Anna Sapp, coord. 307 754 6460
231 W 6th St Bldg 25, Powell 82435 Fax 754-7839
nwc.edu/pvce
Region V BOCES
Dan Mayer, dir. 307-733-8210
PO Box 899, Wilson 83014 Fax 733-8462
boces5.org

Sublette BOCES
Ward Wise, dir. 307-367-6873
PO Box 977, Pinedale 82941 Fax 367-6634
www.subletteboces.com
Sweetwater BOCES
Bernadine Craft Ph.D., dir. 307 382 1607
PO Box 428, Rock Springs 82902 Fax 382-1875
www.sweetwaterboces.com
Teton BOCES
Scott Crisp, prin. 307-732-3700
PO Box 568, Jackson 83001
Uinta BOCES
Michael Williams, dir. 307-789-5742
1013 W Cheyenne Dr Unit A Fax 789-7975
Evanston 82930
www.uintaeducation.org
Uinta County SD #4 & #6 BOCES
Karla Behunin, dir. 307-782-6401
PO Box 130, Mountain View 82939 Fax 782-7410
www.westernwyoming.edu/distance/vlc/
Western Sublette 9 BOCES
Angie Clifford, dir. 307-276-5522
PO Box 706, Big Piney 83113 Fax 276-3480
www.sublette9boces.org

PUBLIC, PRIVATE AND CATHOLIC ELEMENTARY SCHOOLS

Afton, Lincoln, Pop. 1,881
Lincoln County SD 2 2,600/K-12
222 E 4th Ave 83110 307-885-3811
Alan Allred, supt. Fax 885-9562
www.lcsd2.org
Afton ES 400/K-3
333 E 1st Ave 83110 307-885-8002
Layne Parmenter, prin. Fax 885-8010
Osmond ES 300/4-6
3120 State Highway 241 83110 307-885-9457
Matt Erickson, prin. Fax 886-5789
Star Valley MS 400/7-8
999 Warrior Way 83110 307-885-5208
Steve Burch, prin. Fax 885-0472
Other Schools – See Cokeville, Etna, Thayne

Albin, Laramie, Pop. 181
Laramie County SD 2
Supt. — See Pine Bluffs
Albin ES 100/K-6
PO Box 38 82050 307-245-4090
Dr. LeAnn Smith, prin. Fax 246-3261

Alcova, Natrona, Pop. 73
Natrona County SD 1
Supt. — See Casper
Alcova ES 50/K-6
PO Box 106 82620 307-472-2079
Tammy Creger, prin. Fax 472-3105

Alta, Teton, Pop. 388
Teton County SD 1
Supt. — See Jackson
Alta ES 100/K-6
15 School Rd, 307-353-2472
Jenna Beck, prin. Fax 353-2473

Arapahoe, Fremont, Pop. 1,626
Fremont County SD 38 400/PK-12
445 Little Wind Rvr Bottom 82510 307-856-9333
Kenneth Crowson, supt. Fax 857-4327
www.fcsd38.org
Arapahoe ES 400/PK-8
445 Little Wind Rvr Bottom 82510 307-856-9333
Jeffry Fuller, prin. Fax 857-4327

Baggs, Carbon, Pop. 438
Carbon County SD 1
Supt. — See Rawlins
Little Snake River Valley S 200/K-12
PO Box 9 82321 307-383-2185
Joel Thomas, prin. Fax 383-2184

Bar Nunn, Natrona, Pop. 2,176
Natrona County SD 1
Supt. — See Casper
Bar Nunn ES 300/PK-5
2050 Siebke Dr 82601 307-253-4000
Rene Rickabaugh, prin. Fax 253-4033

Basin, Big Horn, Pop. 1,274
Big Horn County SD 4 300/K-12
PO Box 151 82410 307-568-2684
David Kerby, supt. Fax 568-2654
www.bgh4.org
Irwin ES 100/K-5
PO Box 151 82410 307-568-2488
Tony Anson, prin. Fax 568-9307

Big Horn, Sheridan, Pop. 487
Sheridan County SD 1
Supt. — See Ranchester
Big Horn ES 200/K-5
PO Box 490 82833 307-672-3497
Kathy Powers, prin. Fax 672-5396
Big Horn MS 100/6-8
PO Box 490 82833 307-674-8190
Richard Welch, prin. Fax 672-5306

Big Piney, Sublette, Pop. 550
Sublette County SD 9 700/K-12
PO Box 769 83113 307-276-3322
Steve Loyd, supt. Fax 276-3731
www.sublette9.org
Big Piney ES 200/K-5
PO Box 769 83113 307-276-3313
Amy Bell, prin. Fax 276-3314
Big Piney MS 200/6-8
PO Box 769 83113 307-276-3315
Stanley Dodds, prin. Fax 276-5209
Other Schools – See La Barge

Bondurant, Sublette, Pop. 93
Sublette County SD 1
Supt. — See Pinedale
Bondurant ES 50/K-5
14224 US Highway 191 S 82922 307-367-2828
Greg Legerski, prin. Fax 367-4706

Buffalo, Johnson, Pop. 4,536
Johnson County SD 1 1,300/K-12
601 W Lott St 82834 307-684-9571
Gerry Chase, supt. Fax 684-5182
www.jcsd1.k12.wy.us
Clear Creek MS 200/6-8
361 W Gatchell St 82834 307-684-5594
Darren Schmidt, prin. Fax 684-9096
Cloud Peak ES 300/3-5
100 Conrad 82834 307-684-0153
Craig Anderson, prin. Fax 684-0156
Meadowlark ES 300/K-2
550 S Burritt Ave 82834 307-684-9518
Craig Kitto, prin. Fax 684-5386
Other Schools – See Kaycee

Buffalo Christian Academy 50/K-7
6 Barstaad Ln 82834 307-267-4758
Kristen Crago, prin.

Burlington, Big Horn, Pop. 287
Big Horn County SD 1
Supt. — See Cowley
Burlington ES 100/PK-5
PO Box 9 82411 307-762-3334
Matt Davidson, prin. Fax 762-3604
Burlington MS 50/6-8
PO Box 9 82411 307-762-3334
Matt Davidson, prin. Fax 762-3604

Burns, Laramie, Pop. 295
Laramie County SD 2
Supt. — See Pine Bluffs
Burns ES 200/K-6
PO Box 10 82053 307-245-4150
Jerry Burkett, prin. Fax 547-3721

Carpenter, Laramie, Pop. 94
Laramie County SD 2
Supt. — See Pine Bluffs
Carpenter ES 100/K-6
PO Box L 82054 307-245-4180
Wes Woodward, prin Fax 649-2247

Casper, Natrona, Pop. 54,284
Natrona County SD 1 12,800/PK-12
970 N Glenn Rd 82601 307-253-5200
Steve Hopkins, supt. Fax 253-5330
www.natronaschools.org/
Centennial JHS 600/6-8
1421 Waterford 82609 307-253-2900
Mike Britt, prin. Fax 253-2891
Cottonwood ES 300/PK-5
1230 W 15th St 82604 307-253-4700
Brian Doner, prin. Fax 253 4760
Crest Hill ES 300/K-5
4445 S Poplar St 82601 307-253-4200
Nicole Rapp, prin. Fax 253-4230
Ft. Caspar Academy 500/K-5
4100 W 38th St 82604 307-253-3400
Richard Edwards, prin. Fax 253-3450
Frontier MS 100/6-8
900 S Beverly St 82609 307-253-2300
Casey Cloninger, prin. Fax 253-2280
Grant ES 200/PK-5
1536 S Oakcrest Ave 82601 307-253-1300
Shawna Smith, prin. Fax 253-1311

James ES 400/K-5
701 Carriage Ln 82609 307-253-1100
Kevin Pagett, prin. Fax 253-1150
Lincoln ES, 945 N Jane St 82601 K-5
Phil Hubert, prin. 307-253-6100
Manor Heights ES 300/K-5
3201 E 15th St 82609 307-253-1800
Dr. Kent Thompson, prin. Fax 253-1844
Morgan JHS 800/6-8
1440 S Elm St 82601 307-253-2500
Steve Ellbogen, prin. Fax 253-2411
Mountain View ES 200/PK-5
400 N 3rd Ave 82604 307-253-6500
Coebie Taylor-Logan, prin. Fax 253-6545
Oregon Trail ES 300/K-5
6332 Buckboard Rd 82604 307-253-6200
Randall Harris, prin. Fax 253-6202
Paradise Valley ES 400/PK-5
22 Magnolia St 82604 307-253-1200
Aaron Wilson, prin. Fax 253-1275
Park ES 300/K-5
140 W 9th St 82601 307-253-3200
Gib Ostheimer, prin. Fax 253-3230
Pineview ES 400/PK-5
639 Payne Ave 82609 307-253-6000
Christine Carruth-Britt, prin. Fax 253-6040
Poison Spider S 200/K-8
14200 W Poison Spider Rd 82604 307-253-6900
Tammy Creger, prin. Fax 253-6931
Red Creek ES 50/K-6
15651 State Highway 487 82604 307-473-1224
Tammy Creger, prin. Fax 473-2475
Sagewood ES 300/K-5
2451 Shattuck Ave 82601 307-253-3300
Tyler Hartl, prin. Fax 253-3303
Southridge ES 300/K-5
1600 W 29th St 82604 307-253-1900
Doug Smith, prin. Fax 253-1903
Summit ES 400/K-5
2210 Waterford 82609 307-253-3000
Anne Laplante-Miles, prin. Fax 253-3050
University Park ES 200/PK-5
600 N Huber Dr 82609 307-253-3800
Julie Hornby, prin. Fax 253-3840
Willard ES 200/PK-5
129 N Elk St 82601 307-253-6300
Angie Hayes, prin. Fax 253-6328
Woods Learning Center 200/K-8
500 S Walsh Dr 82609 307-253-3900
Melissa Noah, contact Fax 253-3950
Other Schools – See Alcova, Bar Nunn, Evansville, Midwest, Mills, Powder River

---

Mountain Road Christian Academy 50/K-8
2657 Casper Mountain Rd 82601 307-235-2859
Mount Hope Lutheran S 100/PK-8
2300 S Hickory St 82604 307-234-6865
Angela Hill, hdmstr.
Paradise Valley Christian S 100/PK-8
3041 Paradise Dr 82604 307-234-2450
Larry Berlin, admin. Fax 577-0763
St. Anthony's S 300/PK-8
1145 W 20th St 82604 307-234-2873
Cyndy Novotny, prin. Fax 235-4946

Centennial, Albany, Pop. 269
Albany County SD 1
Supt. — See Laramie
Centennial ES 50/K-6
PO Box 326 82055 307-745-9585
Barb Farley, prin. Fax 721-0105

Cheyenne, Laramie, Pop. 58,048
Laramie County SD 1 13,600/K-12
2810 House Ave 82001 307-771-2100
John Lyttle, supt. Fax 771-2364
www.laramie1.org
Afflerbach ES 400/K-6
400 W Wallick Rd 82007 307-771-2300
Matthew Schlagel, prin. Fax 771-2304
Alta Vista ES 300/K-6
1514 E 16th St 82001 307-771-2310
Brent Young, prin. Fax 771-2212
Anderson ES 500/K-6
2204 Plain View Rd 82009 307-771-2606
Sean Gorman, prin. Fax 771-2609
Arp ES 400/K-6
1216 E Reiner Ct 82007 307-771-2365
Don Brantz, prin. Fax 771-2368
Baggs ES 400/K-6
3705 Cheyenne St 82001 307-771-2385
Brooke Kelly, prin. Fax 771-2388
Bain ES 300/K-6
903 Adams Ave 82001 307-771-2525
Todd Burns, prin. Fax 771-2540
Buffalo Ridge ES 300/K-6
5331 Pineridge Ave 82009 307-771-2595
Lori Peeples, prin. Fax 771-2429
Carey JHS 700/7-8
1780 E Pershing Blvd 82001 307-771-2580
Derek Nissen, prin. Fax 771-2578
Cole ES 200/K-6
615 W 9th St 82007 307-771-2480
Margee Robertson, prin. Fax 771-2483
Davis ES 300/K-6
6309 Yellowstone Rd 82009 307-771-2600
Mary Beth Emmons, prin. Fax 771-2599
Deming ES 100/K-3
715 W 5th Ave 82001 307-771-2400
Tina Hunter, prin. Fax 771-2402
Dildine ES 500/K-6
4312 Van Buren Ave 82001 307-771-2320
Mike Wortman, prin. Fax 771-2521
Fairview ES 100/3-6
2801 E 10th St 82001 307-771-2610
Cara Ogirima, prin. Fax 771-2478
Freedom ES 300/K-6
4500 Happy Jack Rd 82009 307-771-2305
Chad Delbridge, prin. Fax 771-2306
Gilchrist ES 100/K-6
1108 Happy Jack Rd 82009 307-771-2285
Harry Petty, prin. Fax 771-2287
Goins ES 400/K-6
224 Dey Ave 82007 307-771-2620
Amanda Hall, prin. Fax 771-2623
Hebard ES 200/K-6
413 Seymour Ave 82007 307-771-2450
Donna Adams, prin. Fax 771-2453
Henderson ES 300/K-6
2820 Henderson Dr 82001 307-771-2550
Karen Brooks-Lyons, prin. Fax 771-2554
Hobbs ES 400/K-6
5710 Syracuse Rd 82009 307-771-2560
Mark Hurd, prin. Fax 771-2568
Jessup ES 400/K-6
6113 Evers Blvd 82009 307-771-2570
Barbara Leiseth, prin. Fax 771-2574
Johnson JHS 700/7-8
1236 W Allison Rd 82007 307-771-2640
Brian Cox, prin. Fax 771-2660
Lebhart ES 100/K-2
807 Coolidge St 82001 307-771-2614
Cara Ogirima, prin. Fax 771-2393
McCormick JHS 600/7-8
6000 Education Dr 82009 307-771-2650
Jeff Conine, prin. Fax 771-2661
Meadowlark ES 5-6
6325 Chief Washakie Ave 82009 307-771-2260
Jim Fraley, prin. Fax 771-2261
Miller ES 100/4-6
3501 Evans Ave 82001 307-771-2376
Christine Hunter, prin. Fax 771-2378
Pioneer Park ES 300/K-6
1407 Cosgriff Ct 82001 307-771-2316
April Gates, prin. Fax 771-2319
Prairie Wind ES K-6
11400 Yellowstone Rd 82009 307-771-2340
Michael Fullmer, prin. Fax 771-2345
Rossman ES 400/K-6
916 W College Dr 82007 307-771-2544
Maurice Darnell, prin. Fax 771-2549
Saddle Ridge ES 400/K-6
6815 Wilderness Trl 82001 307-771-2360
Eric Jackson, prin. Fax 771-2395
Sunrise ES 400/K-6
5021 E 13th St 82001 307-771-2280
John Broda, prin. Fax 771-2281
Other Schools – See Granite Canon, Horse Creek

Mason Christian Academy 50/K-8
723 Storey Blvd 82009 307-638-2457
St. Mary S 200/PK-8
2200 ONeil Ave 82001 307-638-9268
Patrick Lane, prin. Fax 635-2847
Trinity Lutheran S 100/PK-8
1111 E 22nd St 82001 307-635-2802
Fax 778-0799

Chugwater, Platte, Pop. 210
Platte County SD 1
Supt. — See Wheatland
Chugwater ES 50/K-6
406 5th St 82210 307-422-3501
Tom Waring, prin. Fax 422-3433
Chugwater JHS 50/7-8
406 5th St 82210 307-422-3501
Tom Waring, prin. Fax 422-3433

Clearmont, Sheridan, Pop. 141
Sheridan County SD 3 100/K-12
PO Box 125 82835 307-758-4412
Charles Auzqui, supt. Fax 758-4444
www.sheridan3.com
Arvada ES 50/K-6
PO Box 125 82835 307-751-0832
Charles Auzqui, admin. Fax 751-0832
Clearmont K-12 S 50/K-12
PO Box 125 82835 307-758-4412
Charles Auzqui, admin. Fax 758-4444

Cody, Park, Pop. 9,367
Park County SD 6 2,100/K-12
919 Cody Ave 82414 307-587-4253
Ray Schulte, supt. Fax 527-5762
www.park6.org
Cody MS 500/6-8
919 Cody Ave 82414 307-587-4273
Kelly Merager, prin. Fax 587-3547
Eastside ES 300/K-5
919 Cody Ave 82414 307-587-4275
Nick Gallagher, prin. Fax 587-9464
Livingston ES 300/K-5
919 Cody Ave 82414 307-587-4271
Mike Wood, prin. Fax 587-9742
Sunset ES 300/K-5
919 Cody Ave 82414 307-587-4279
Jay McCarten, prin. Fax 587-6405
Valley ES 50/K-5
919 Cody Ave 82414 307-587-3287
Mike Wood, prin. Fax 587-9464
Other Schools – See Wapiti

Veritas Academy 50/PK-7
PO Box 1581 82414 307-250-5167

Cokeville, Lincoln, Pop. 533
Lincoln County SD 2
Supt. — See Afton
Cokeville ES 100/K-6
PO Box 400 83114 307-279-3233
Brian Toomer, prin. Fax 279-3280

Cowley, Big Horn, Pop. 654
Big Horn County SD 1 1,000/PK-12
PO Box 688 82420 307-548-2254
Shon Hocker, supt. Fax 548-7610
bighorn1.com
Rocky Mountain ES 300/K-5
PO Box 38 82420 307-548-2211
Karma Sanders, prin. Fax 548-9350
Rocky Mountain MS 200/6-8
PO Box 280 82420 307-548-2723
Tim Winland, prin. Fax 548-6452
Other Schools – See Burlington

Crowheart, Fremont, Pop. 135
Fremont County SD 6
Supt. — See Pavillion
Crowheart ES 50/K-3
8434 US Highway 26 82512 307-486-2202
Barney Lacock, prin. Fax 486-2373

Diamondville, Lincoln, Pop. 720
Lincoln County SD 1 400/K-12
PO Box 335 83116 307-877-9095
Teresa Chaulk, supt. Fax 877-9638
www.lcsd1.k12.wy.us
Other Schools – See Kemmerer

Douglas, Converse, Pop. 6,039
Converse County SD 1 1,700/K-12
615 Hamilton St 82633 307-358-2942
Dr. Paige Hughes, supt. Fax 358-3934
converse1schools.org
Douglas IS 300/2-3
615 Hamilton St 82633 307-358-5250
Brent Notman, prin. Fax 358-2528
Douglas MS 400/6-8
615 Hamilton St 82633 307-358-9771
Ryan Mackey, prin. Fax 358-5315
Douglas PS 300/K-1
615 Hamilton St 82633 307-358-3502
Tanya Seeds, prin. Fax 358-3552
Douglas Upper ES 300/4-5
615 Hamilton St 82633 307-358-0025
Brent Notman, prin. Fax 358-2528
Dry Creek S 50/K-8
615 Hamilton St 82633 307-358-2351
Wes Gamble, prin. Fax 358-2528
Moss Agate S 50/K-8
615 Hamilton St 82633 307-358-3221
Wes Gamble, prin. Fax 358-2528
Shawnee S 50/K-8
615 Hamilton St 82633 307-358-3278
Wes Gamble, prin. Fax 358-2528
Walker Creek S 50/K-8
615 Hamilton St 82633 307-358-8001
Wes Gamble, prin. Fax 358-4891
White S 50/K-8
615 Hamilton St 82633 307-358-0842
Wes Gamble, prin. Fax 358-2528

Dubois, Fremont, Pop. 957
Fremont County SD 2 200/K-12
PO Box 188 82513 307-455-5545
Martha Gale, supt. Fax 455-2178
www.fremont2.org
Dubois ES 100/K-5
PO Box 188 82513 307-455-5524
Brandon Farris, prin. Fax 455-2654
Dubois MS 50/6-8
PO Box 188 82513 307-455-5524
Brandon Farris, prin. Fax 455-2654

Elk Mountain, Carbon, Pop. 191
Carbon County SD 2
Supt. — See Saratoga
Elk Mountain ES 50/K-6
PO Box 20 82324 307-348-7731
Mark Shipp, prin. Fax 348-7321

Encampment, Carbon, Pop. 445
Carbon County SD 2
Supt. — See Saratoga
Encampment S 200/K-12
PO Box 277 82325 307-327-5442
Michael Erickson, prin. Fax 327-5142

Ethete, Fremont, Pop. 1,530
Fremont County SD 14 600/PK-12
638 Blue Sky Hwy 82520 307-332-3904
Owen St. Clair, supt. Fax 332-7567
www.fremont14.k12.wy.us
Wyoming Indian ES 300/PK-5
638 Blue Sky Hwy 82520 307-332-2053
Scott Morrow, prin. Fax 332-6739
Wyoming Indian MS 100/6-8
638 Blue Sky Hwy 82520 307-332-2992
Scott Gion, prin.

Etna, Lincoln, Pop. 163
Lincoln County SD 2
Supt. — See Afton
Etna ES 200/4-6
PO Box 5068 83118 307-885-2472
Keith Klein, prin. Fax 883-3051

Evanston, Uinta, Pop. 12,128
Uinta County SD 1 2,900/K-12
PO Box 6002 82931 307-789-7571
Ryan Thomas, supt. Fax 789-6225
www.uinta1.com
Aspen ES 300/K-5
PO Box 6002 82931 307-789-3106
Steve Peterson, prin. Fax 789-6338
Clark ES 200/K-5
PO Box 6002 82931 307-789-2833
Kimber Fessler, prin. Fax 789-7759
Davis MS 300/6-8
PO Box 6002 82931 307-789-8096
Chris Brown, prin. Fax 789-3386

Evanston MS 300/6-8
PO Box 6002 82931 307-789-5499
Eric Christenot, prin. Fax 789-7972
North Evanston ES 300/K-5
PO Box 6002 82931 307-789-7658
Diane Gardner, prin. Fax 789-2046
Uinta Meadows ES 500/K-5
PO Box 6002 82931 307-789-8098
Jerrod Dastrup, prin. Fax 789-3426

Evansville, Natrona, Pop. 2,496
Natrona County SD 1
Supt. — See Casper
Evansville ES 300/PK-5
PO Box E 82636 307-253-6400
Wayne Tuttle, prin. Fax 253-6440

Farson, Sweetwater, Pop. 309
Sweetwater County SD 1
Supt. — See Rock Springs
Farson-Eden ES 100/K-5
PO Box 400 82932 307-273-9301
Michael Estes, prin. Fax 273-9313
Farson-Eden MS 50/6-8
PO Box 400 82932 307-273-9301
Michael Estes, prin. Fax 273-9313

Fort Washakie, Fremont, Pop. 1,730
Fremont County SD 21 500/PK-12
90 Ethete Rd 82514 307-332-5983
H. Terry Ebert, supt. Fax 332-7267
www.fortwashakieschool.com
Fort Washakie ES 400/PK-6
90 Ethete Rd 82514 307-332-2380
George Mirich, prin. Fax 332-3597
Fort Washakie MS 100/7-8
90 Ethete Rd 82514 307-332-2380
George Mirich, prin. Fax 332-3597

Gillette, Campbell, Pop. 28,659
Campbell County SD 1 8,800/K-12
PO Box 3033 82717 307-682-5171
Dr. Boyd Brown, supt. Fax 682-6619
www.campbellcountyschools.net/
Buffalo Ridge ES 400/K-6
4501 Tanner Dr 82718 307-686-3058
Kevin Sinclair, prin. Fax 682-6645
Conestoga ES 400/K-6
4901 Sleepy Hollow Blvd 82718 307-686-2373
Steve Anderson, prin. Fax 687-0350
4-J ES 50/K-6
2830 State Highway 50 82718 307-682-3076
David Hardesty, prin. Fax 687-7286
Hillcrest ES 400/K-6
1500 Butler Spaeth Rd 82716 307-682-7291
Bradley Winter, prin. Fax 686-5032
Lakeview ES 400/K-6
1017 Gabriel Dr 82716 307-682-7293
Dale Petersen, prin. Fax 682-5843
Meadowlark ES 300/K-6
816 E 7th St 82716 307-682-4740
Brandon Crosby, prin. Fax 682-4649
Paintbrush ES 400/K-6
1001 W Lakeway Rd 82718 307-686-1778
Brian Knox, prin. Fax 686-2767
Prairie Wind ES 500/K-6
200 Overdale Dr 82718 307-682-7289
Rory Williams, prin. Fax 682-6236
Pronghorn ES 400/K-6
3005 Oakcrest Dr 82718 307-682-1676
Clay Cates, prin. Fax 682-0061
Rawhide ES 300/K-6
200 Prospector Pkwy 82716 307-682-0774
Bertine Bahige, prin. Fax 682-7301
Stocktrail ES 200/K-6
800 Stocktrail Ave 82716 307-682-7289
Keri Shannon, prin. Fax 682-6236
Sunflower ES 400/K-6
2500 Dogwood Ave 82718 307-686-0631
Troy Claycomb, prin. Fax 686-0251
Wagonwheel ES 400/K-6
800 Hemlock Ave 82716 307-686-1060
Eric Stremcha, prin. Fax 686-4045
Other Schools – See Recluse, Rozet, Weston, Wright

Heritage Christian S 100/PK-12
510 Wall Street Ct 82718 307-686-1392
Jenn VerBurg, head sch Fax 257-7256
John Paul II S 200/PK-8
1000 Butler Spaeth Rd 82716 307-682-3319
Melanie Sylte, prin. Fax 682-6386

Glendo, Platte, Pop. 203
Platte County SD 1
Supt. — See Wheatland
Glendo JHS 50/7-8
305 N Paige Ave 82213 307-735-4471
Kathy Morsett, prin. Fax 735-4220
Glendo S 50/K-6
305 N Paige Ave 82213 307-735-4471
Kathy Morsett, prin. Fax 735-4220

Glenrock, Converse, Pop. 2,551
Converse County SD 2 600/K-12
PO Box 1300 82637 307-436-5331
Coley Shadrick, supt. Fax 436-8235
www.cnv2.k12.wy.us/
Boxelder Rural S 50/K-6
1866 Boxelder Rd 82637 307-436-8953
Deborah Brown, prin.
Glenrock Intermediate MS 100/5-8
PO Box 1300 82637 307-436-9258
Scott James, prin. Fax 436-7507
Grant ES 300/K-4
PO Box 1300 82637 307-436-2774
Deborah Brown, prin. Fax 436-7589

Granger, Sweetwater, Pop. 139
Sweetwater County SD 2
Supt. — See Green River
Granger ES 50/K-4
50 N Granger Rd 82934 307-875-4840
Cathy Hemker, prin. Fax 875-9313

Granite Canon, Laramie
Laramie County SD 1
Supt. — See Cheyenne
Willadsen ES 50/K-6
645 Road 102 82059 307-771-2295
Harry Petty, prin. Fax 771-2296

Green River, Sweetwater, Pop. 12,356
Sweetwater County SD 2 2,700/K-12
320 Monroe Ave 82935 307-872-5500
Donna Little-Kaumo, supt. Fax 872-5518
www.swcsd2.org
Harrison ES 300/K-4
1825 Alabama St 82935 307-872-1700
Steven Lake, prin. Fax 872-1888
Jackson ES 300/K-4
2200 E Teton Blvd 82935 307-872-1800
Sheryl Wilson, prin. Fax 872-5532
Lincoln MS 400/7-8
350 Monroe Ave 82935 307-872-4400
Matt Mikkelsen, prin. Fax 872-4477
Monroe IS 400/5-6
250 Monroe Ave 82935 307-872-4000
Anne Marie Covey, prin. Fax 872-5542
Truman ES 300/K-4
1055 W Teton Blvd 82935 307-872-1900
Gregory Figenser, prin. Fax 872-5579
Washington ES 200/K-4
750 W 5th North St 82935 307-872-2000
Gayle Kendall, prin. Fax 872-5578
Other Schools – See Granger, Kemmerer, Mc Kinnon

Greybull, Big Horn, Pop. 1,834
Big Horn County SD 3 500/K-12
640 8th Ave N 82426 307-765-4756
Dr. Barry Bryant, supt. Fax 765-4617
www.greybullschools.com
Greybull ES 200/K-5
640 8th Ave N 82426 307-765-2311
Brett Suiter, prin. Fax 765-9424
Greybull MS 100/6-8
640 8th Ave N 82426 307-765-4492
Joel Rogers, prin. Fax 765-2586

Guernsey, Platte, Pop. 1,136
Platte County SD 2 200/K-12
PO Box 189 82214 307-836-2735
Mike Beard, supt. Fax 836-2450
www.guernseysunrise.org
Guernsey-Sunrise ES 100/K-6
PO Box 189 82214 307-836-2733
Glen Suppes, prin. Fax 836-2450
Guernsey-Sunrise JHS 50/7-8
PO Box 189 82214 307-836-2745
Glen Suppes, prin. Fax 836-2450

Hanna, Carbon, Pop. 829
Carbon County SD 2
Supt. — See Saratoga
Hanna ES 100/K-6
PO Box 1000 82327 307-325-6523
Mark Shipp, prin. Fax 325-9811

Horse Creek, Laramie
Laramie County SD 1
Supt. — See Cheyenne
Clawson ES 50/K-6
376 Road 228A 82061 307-771-2291
Harry Petty, prin. Fax 771-2292

Hulett, Crook, Pop. 375
Crook County SD 1
Supt. — See Sundance
Hulett S 200/K-12
PO Box 127 82720 307-467-5231
Linda Wolfskill, prin. Fax 467-5280

Jackson, Teton, Pop. 9,432
Teton County SD 1 2,600/K-12
PO Box 568 83001 307-733-2704
Gillian Chapman Ed.D., supt. Fax 733-6443
www.tcsd.org
Colter ES 500/K-5
PO Box 568 83001 307-733-9651
Bo Miller, prin. Fax 739-1452
Jackson ES 600/K-5
PO Box 568 83001 307-733-5302
Scott Eastman, prin. Fax 739-2116
Jackson Hole MS 600/6-8
PO Box 568 83001 307-733-4234
Matt Hoelscher, prin. Fax 733-4254
Other Schools – See Alta, Kelly, Moran, Wilson

Jackson Hole Classical Academy K-9
3255 W High School Rd 83001 307-201-5040
Journeys S 200/PK-12
700 Coyote Canyon Rd 83001 307-733-1313
Nancy Lang, head sch Fax 733-7560
Timber Ridge Academy 50/PK-8
PO Box 1924 83001 307-200-9564
Tami Koerber, head sch

Jeffrey City, Fremont, Pop. 57
Fremont County SD 1
Supt. — See Lander
Jeffrey City ES 50/K-5
375 Bob Adams 82310 307-332-6690
Andrew Lanz-Ketcham, prin. Fax 332-5878

Kaycee, Johnson, Pop. 260
Johnson County SD 1
Supt. — See Buffalo
Kaycee K-12 S 100/K-12
PO Box 6 82639 307-738-2573
Andrea Gilbert, prin. Fax 738-2495

Kelly, Teton, Pop. 138
Teton County SD 1
Supt. — See Jackson
Kelly ES 50/K-5
PO Box 128 83011 307-733-2955
Stephanie Hardeman, prin. Fax 733-7845

Kemmerer, Lincoln, Pop. 2,635
Lincoln County SD 1
Supt. — See Diamondville
Canyon ES 100/3-6
1310 Antelope St 83101 307-877-2286
Brad Meyer, prin. Fax 877-3365
Kemmerer ES 200/K-2
1401 Lincoln Heights Dr 83101 307-877-5584
Shawn Rogers, prin. Fax 877-9522

Sweetwater County SD 2
Supt. — See Green River
Thoman Ranch ES 50/K-8
38622 State Highway 372 83101 307-877-3426
Jamie Christensen, prin. Fax 877-3426

La Barge, Lincoln, Pop. 542
Sublette County SD 9
Supt. — See Big Piney
La Barge ES 100/K-5
PO Box 36 83123 307-386-2227
Stanley Dodds, prin. Fax 386-2284

LaGrange, Goshen, Pop. 446
Goshen County SD 1
Supt. — See Torrington
La Grange ES 50/K-6
PO Box 188 82221 307-834-2311
Cory Gilchriest, prin. Fax 834-2312

Lance Creek, Niobrara, Pop. 39
Niobrara County SD 1
Supt. — See Lusk
Lance Creek S, PO Box 334 82222 50/K-8
Rodney Wilhelm, prin. 307-334-3403

Lander, Fremont, Pop. 7,311
Fremont County SD 1 1,700/K-12
863 Sweetwater St 82520 307-332-4711
Dave Barker, supt. Fax 332-6671
www.landerschools.org
Baldwin Creek ES 300/4-5
350 Smith St 82520 307-332-0967
Jade Morton, prin. Fax 332-3475
Gannett Peak ES 600/K-3
615 Popo Agie St 82520 307-332-6690
Leslie Voxland, prin. Fax 332-5878
Lander MS 400/6-8
755 Jefferson St 82520 307-332-4040
Julie Shanley, prin. Fax 332-0435
Other Schools – See Jeffrey City

Cornerstone Christian S 50/K-8
80 Mortimore Ln 82520 307-332-6000
Bryce Roberts, admin. Fax 332-0350

Laramie, Albany, Pop. 30,183
Albany County SD 1 3,500/PK-12
1948 E Grand Ave 82070 307-721-4400
Dr. Jubal C. Yennie, supt. Fax 721-4408
www.acsd1.org
Beitel ES 300/K-5
811 S 17th St 82070 307-721-4436
Loren Engel, prin. Fax 721-4498
Harmony ES 50/K-6
20 Lewis Rd 82070 307-745-5720
Barb Farley, prin. Fax 745-5858
Indian Paintbrush ES 300/K-5
1653 N 28th St 82072 307-721-4490
Teresa Ross, prin. Fax 721-4568
Laramie MS 600/6-8
1355 N 22nd St 82072 307-721-4430
Kevin O'Dea, prin. Fax 721-4435
Linford ES 400/PK-5
120 S Johnson St 82070 307-721-4439
David Hardesty, prin. Fax 721-4443
Slade ES 300/PK-5
1212 E Baker St 82072 307-721-4446
Heather Moro, prin. Fax 721-4497
Spring Creek ES 300/K-5
1203 Russell St 82070 307-721-4410
Liann Brenneman, prin. Fax 721-4418
UW Laboratory S 200/K-8
1000 E University Ave 82071 307-721-2155
Margaret Hudson, prin. Fax 742-5765
Valley View ES 50/K-6
16 Mandel Ln 82070 307-721-4525
Loren Engel, prin. Fax 721-4408
Other Schools – See Centennial, Rock River, Wheatland

Lingle, Goshen, Pop. 467
Goshen County SD 1
Supt. — See Torrington
Lingle-Ft. Laramie ES 100/K-5
PO Box 379 82223 307-837-2296
Cory Gilchriest, prin. Fax 837-3026
Lingle-Ft. Laramie MS 100/6-8
PO Box 379 82223 307-837-2296
Lane Stratton, prin. Fax 837-3025

Lovell, Big Horn, Pop. 2,347
Big Horn County SD 2 700/K-12
502 Hampshire Ave 82431 307-548-2259
Dr. Rick Woodford, supt. Fax 548-7555
www.bgh2.org
Lovell ES 300/K-5
520 Shoshone Ave 82431 307-548-2247
Deanna Martineau, prin. Fax 548-2593
Lovell MS 100/6-8
325 W 9th St 82431 307-548-6553
Douglas Hazen, prin. Fax 548-6136

Lusk, Niobrara, Pop. 1,541
Niobrara County SD 1 700/PK-12
PO Box 629 82225 307-334-3793
Aaron Carr, supt. Fax 334-0126
www.lusk.k12.wy.us
Lusk S 400/PK-8
PO Box 1239 82225 307-334-2224
Rodney Wilhelm, prin. Fax 334-0126
Other Schools – See Lance Creek

Lyman, Uinta, Pop. 2,090
Uinta County SD 6 700/K-12
PO Box 1090 82937 307-786-4100
Colby Gull, supt. Fax 787-3241
www.uinta6.k12.wy.us
Lyman IS 200/5-8
PO Box 1090 82937 307-786-4100
Justin Smith, prin. Fax 787-6149
Urie ES 300/K-4
PO Box 1090 82937 307-786-4100
Anthony Lott, prin. Fax 787-2129

Mc Kinnon, Sweetwater, Pop. 56
Sweetwater County SD 2
Supt. — See Green River
McKinnon ES 50/K-5
US Highway 414 82938 307-874-6199
Cathy Hemker, prin. Fax 874-6190

Medicine Bow, Carbon, Pop. 281
Carbon County SD 2
Supt. — See Saratoga
Medicine Bow ES 50/K-6
PO Box 185 82329 307-379-2345
Mark Shipp, prin. Fax 379-2283

Meeteetse, Park, Pop. 325
Park County SD 16 100/K-12
PO Box 218 82433 307-868-2501
Shane Ogden, supt. Fax 868-9264
www.park16.k12.wy.us
Meeteetse S 100/K-12
PO Box 218 82433 307-868-2501
Shane Ogden, prin. Fax 868-9264

Midwest, Natrona, Pop. 395
Natrona County SD 1
Supt. — See Casper
Midwest S 200/PK-12
256 Lewis 82643 307-253-3500
Chris Tobin, prin. Fax 253-3520

Mills, Natrona, Pop. 3,419
Natrona County SD 1
Supt. — See Casper
Mills ES 200/PK-5
PO Box 268 82644 307-253-3700
Coebie Taylor-Logan, prin. Fax 253-3791

Moorcroft, Crook, Pop. 998
Crook County SD 1
Supt. — See Sundance
Moorcroft K-8 S 300/K-8
PO Box 40 82721 307-756-3781
Teresa Brown, prin. Fax 756-3681

Moran, Teton
Teton County SD 1
Supt. — See Jackson
Moran ES 50/K-5
2 Central St 83013 307-543-2438
Sandra Dudzik, prin. Fax 543-2809

Mountain View, Uinta, Pop. 1,273
Uinta County SD 4 600/K-12
PO Box 130 82939 307-782-3377
Jeff Newton, supt. Fax 782-6879
www.uinta4.com
Mountain View ES 200/K-8
PO Box 130 82939 307-782-6202
Bill Erickson, prin. Fax 782-6422

Newcastle, Weston, Pop. 3,468
Weston County SD 1 800/K-12
116 Casper Ave 82701 307-746-4451
Brad LaCroix, supt. Fax 746-3289
www.weston1.k12.wy.us
Newcastle 3-5 ES 200/3-5
116 Casper Ave 82701 307-746-2717
Brandy Holmes, prin. Fax 746-2718
Newcastle K-2 ES 200/K-2
116 Casper Ave 82701 307-746-2717
Brandy Holmes, prin. Fax 746-2718
Newcastle MS 200/6-8
116 Casper Ave 82701 307-746-2746
Kyle Gunderson, prin. Fax 746-4983

Parkman, Sheridan, Pop. 151
Sheridan County SD 1
Supt. — See Ranchester
Slack ES 50/K-5
562 County Road 144 82838 307-655-2460
Annie Griffin, prin. Fax 655-2447

Pavillion, Fremont, Pop. 225
Fremont County SD 6 400/PK-12
PO Box 10 82523 307-856-7970
Diana Clapp, supt. Fax 856-3385
www.fre6.k12.wy.us/
Wind River ES 200/PK-5
PO Box 10 82523 307-856-7970
Barney Lacock, prin. Fax 856-7745
Wind River MS 100/6-8
PO Box 10 82523 307-856-7970
Orvin Jenks, prin. Fax 856-8641
Other Schools – See Crowheart

Pine Bluffs, Laramie, Pop. 1,114
Laramie County SD 2 1,000/K-12
PO Box 489 82082 307-245-4050
Jon Abrams, supt. Fax 245-3561
laramie2.org
Pine Bluffs ES 100/K-6
PO Box 430 82082 307-245-4070
Andrea Verosky, prin. Fax 245-3091
Other Schools – See Albin, Burns, Carpenter

Pinedale, Sublette, Pop. 1,999
Sublette County SD 1 1,000/K-12
PO Box 549 82941 307-367-2139
Jay Harnack, supt. Fax 367-4626
www.sub1.org
Pinedale ES 500/K-5
PO Box 549 82941 307-367-2828
Greg Legerski, prin. Fax 367-4706
Pinedale MS 200/6-8
PO Box 549 82941 307-367-2821
Jeryl Fluckiger, prin. Fax 367-4217
Other Schools – See Bondurant

Powder River, Natrona, Pop. 44
Natrona County SD 1
Supt. — See Casper
Powder River ES 50/K-6
35462 Notches Rd 82648 307-472-3939
Tammy Creger, prin. Fax 472-5882

Powell, Park, Pop. 6,232
Park County SD 1 1,700/K-12
160 N Evarts St 82435 307-764-6186
Jay Curtis, supt. Fax 764-6156
www.park1.net
Clark ES 50/K-5
160 N Evarts St 82435 307-645-3241
Jason Hillman, prin. Fax 645-3340
Parkside ES 200/K-5
160 N Evarts St 82435 307-764-6182
Jason Hillman, prin. Fax 764-6152
Powell MS 400/6-8
160 N Evarts St 82435 307-764-6185
Jason Sleep, prin. Fax 764-6155
Southside ES 300/K-5
160 N Evarts St 82435 307-764-6183
Scott Schiller, prin. Fax 764-6153
Westside ES 300/K-5
160 N Evarts St 82435 307-764-6184
Angie Woyak, prin. Fax 764-6154

Ranchester, Sheridan, Pop. 853
Sheridan County SD 1 1,000/K-12
PO Box 819 82839 307-655-9541
Marty Kobza, supt. Fax 655-9477
www.sheridan.k12.wy.us/
Tongue River ES 200/K-5
PO Box 849 82839 307-655-2206
Annie Griffin, prin. Fax 655-2447
Tongue River MS 100/6-8
PO Box 879 82839 307-655-9533
Pete Kilbride, prin. Fax 655-9894
Other Schools – See Big Horn, Parkman

Rawlins, Carbon, Pop. 9,144
Carbon County SD 1 1,800/K-12
615 Rodeo St 82301 307-328-9200
Mike Hamel, supt. Fax 328-9258
www.crb1.net
Rawlins ES 800/K-5
1301 Darnley Rd 82301 307-328-7900
Darrin Jennings, prin. Fax 328-7901
Rawlins MS 400/6-8
1001 Brooks St 82301 307-328-9205
Kevin O'Dea, prin. Fax 328-9226
Other Schools – See Baggs

Recluse, Campbell
Campbell County SD 1
Supt. — See Gillette
Recluse S 50/K-8
31 Greenough Rd 82725 307-682-9612
Christopher Rashleigh, prin. Fax 682-9619

Riverton, Fremont, Pop. 10,330
Fremont County SD 25 2,600/K-12
121 N 5th St W 82501 307-856-9407
Terry Snyder, supt. Fax 856-3390
www.fremont25.org
Ashgrove ES 200/1-3
121 N 5th St W 82501 307-856-2626
Alleta Baltes, prin. Fax 856-4318
Aspen Early Learning Center 300/K-3
121 N 5th St W 82501 307-856-2625
Sheryl Esposito, prin. Fax 857-7164
Jackson ES 200/1-3
121 N 5th St W 82501 307-856-9495
Jeffrey Sandlian, prin. Fax 857-1825
Rendezvous ES 600/4-5
121 N 5th St W 82501 307-857-7070
Karly Ward, prin. Fax 857-6124
Riverton MS 500/6-8
121 N 5th St W 82501 307-856-9443
Brant Nyberg, prin. Fax 857-1695
Willow Creek ES 1-3
1200 W Monroe Ave 82501 307-856-6004
Jeremy Hill, prin. Fax 856-6732

St. Margaret S 100/PK-5
220 N 7th St E 82501 307-856-5922
Josephine Laux, prin. Fax 857-5892
Trinity Lutheran S 100/PK-8
419 E Park Ave 82501 307-857-5710
Susan Tucker, lead tchr. Fax 857-5710

Rock River, Albany, Pop. 236
Albany County SD 1
Supt. — See Laramie
Rock River S 50/K-12
PO Box 128 82083 307-378-2271
Wade Fiscus, prin. Fax 378-2505

Rock Springs, Sweetwater, Pop. 22,670
Sweetwater County SD 1 5,500/K-12
PO Box 1089 82902 307-352-3400
Kelly McGovern, supt. Fax 352-3411
www.sweetwater1.org
Desert View ES 400/K-4
PO Box 1089 82902 307-352-3200
Barbara Rezzonico, prin. Fax 316-1388
Eastside ES 400/5-6
PO Box 1089 82902 307-352-3425
Brent McMurtrey, prin. Fax 391-5947
Northpark ES 300/K-4
PO Box 1089 82902 307-352-3235
Carrie Ellison, prin. Fax 503-2836
Overland ES 300/K-4
PO Box 1089 82902 307-352-3260
Ryan Allen, prin. Fax 503-3189
Pilot Butte ES 400/5-6
PO Box 1089 82902 307-352-3464
Susan Dickman, prin. Fax 316-5768
Rock Springs JHS 800/7-8
PO Box 1089 82902 307-352-3474
Tina Johnson, prin. Fax 316-5634
Sage ES 400/K-4
PO Box 1089 82902 307-352-3270
Tina Searle, prin. Fax 316-1781
Stagecoach ES K-4
PO Box 1089 82902 307-352-3265
Jennifer Martin-Palacios, prin. Fax 512-1098
Walnut ES 300/K-4
PO Box 1089 82902 307-352-3225
Kristeen Cundall, prin. Fax 316-8506
Westridge ES 400/K-4
PO Box 1089 82902 307-352-3250
Dr. Karl Wells, prin. Fax 503-6519
Other Schools – See Farson, Wamsutter

Holy Spirit Catholic S 100/PK-6
210 A St 82901 307-362-6077
Linda Marcos, prin. Fax 362-3228

Rozet, Campbell
Campbell County SD 1
Supt. — See Gillette
Rozet ES 300/K-6
PO Box 200 82727 307-682-3133
Nate Cassidy, prin. Fax 682-7850

Saratoga, Carbon, Pop. 1,658
Carbon County SD 2 700/K-12
PO Box 1530 82331 307-326-5271
Dr. Jim Copeland, supt. Fax 326-8089
www.crb2.k12.wy.us
Saratoga ES 100/K-6
PO Box 1590 82331 307-326-8365
Darrin Jennings, prin. Fax 326-5720
Other Schools – See Elk Mountain, Encampment, Hanna, Medicine Bow

Sheridan, Sheridan, Pop. 17,182
Sheridan County SD 2 3,300/K-12
PO Box 919 82801 307-674-7405
Craig Dougherty, supt. Fax 674-5041
www.scsd2.com/
Coffeen ES 300/K-5
1053 S Sheridan Ave 82801 307-674-9333
Brad Gregorich, prin. Fax 464-3101
Highland Park ES 400/K-5
2 Mydland Rd 82801 307-672-2113
Scott Cleland, prin. Fax 939-7087
Meadowlark ES 300/K-5
1410 De Smet Ave 82801 307-672-3786
Casey O'Connor, prin. Fax 464-3105
Sagebrush ES 400/K-5
1685 Hillpond Dr 82801 307-672-9059
Brett Dahl, prin.
Sheridan JHS 700/6-8
500 Lewis St 82801 307-672-9745
Nicki Thomas, prin. Fax 939-7091
Woodland Park ES 300/K-5
1010 E Woodland Park Rd 82801 307-674-7937
Paige Sanders, prin. Fax 241-5971
Other Schools – See Story

Holy Name S 100/PK-8
121 S Connor St 82801 307-672-2021
Mary Drake, prin. Fax 673-4474
Luther Grammar S & Immanuel Acad 50/K-8
1300 W 5th St 82801 307-674-6434
Rev. Paul Cain, hdmstr.

Shoshoni, Fremont, Pop. 645
Fremont County SD 24 400/PK-12
404 Wrangler Way 82649 307-876-2583
Bruce Thoren, supt. Fax 876-2469
www.fremont24.com/
Shoshoni ES 200/PK-6
404 Wrangler Way 82649 307-876-2563
Mark Rose, prin. Fax 876-2542
Shoshoni JHS 100/7-8
404 Wrangler Way 82649 307-876-2576
Carl Rice, prin. Fax 876-9325

Story, Sheridan, Pop. 822
Sheridan County SD 2
Supt. — See Sheridan
Story ES, PO Box 129 82842 50/K-5
Brad Gregorich, prin. 307-683-2316

Sundance, Crook, Pop. 1,174
Crook County SD 1 1,000/K-12
PO Box 830 82729 307-283-2299
Mark Broderson, supt. Fax 283-1810
www.crook1.com
Sundance ES 200/K-6
PO Box 870 82729 307-283-1227
Brian Hartwig, prin. Fax 283-1717
Other Schools – See Hulett, Moorcroft

Ten Sleep, Washakie, Pop. 257
Washakie County SD 2 — 100/K-12
PO Box 105 82442 — 307-366-2223
Jimmy Phelps, supt. — Fax 366-2304
www.wsh2.k12.wy.us
Ten Sleep ES — 50/K-6
PO Box 105 82442 — 307-366-2233
Russell Budmayr, prin. — Fax 366-2304
Ten Sleep MS — 50/7-8
PO Box 105 82442 — 307-366-2233
Russell Budmayr, prin. — Fax 366-2304

Thayne, Lincoln, Pop. 361
Lincoln County SD 2
Supt. — See Afton
Thayne ES — 400/K-3
PO Box 520 83127 — 307-885-2380
Justin Pierantoni, prin. — Fax 883-2032

Thermopolis, Hot Springs, Pop. 2,973
Hot Springs County SD 1 — 600/K-12
415 Springview St 82443 — 307-864-6515
Dustin Hunt, supt. — Fax 864-6615
www.hotsprings1.org
Thermopolis MS — 200/5-8
415 Springview St 82443 — 307-864-6551
Breez Daniels, prin. — Fax 864-6608
Witters ES — 200/K-4
415 Springview St 82443 — 307-864-6561
Laurie Graves, prin. — Fax 864-6605

Torrington, Goshen, Pop. 6,432
Goshen County SD 1 — 1,700/K-12
626 W 25th Ave 82240 — 307-532-2171
Jean Chrostoski, supt. — Fax 532-7085
www.goshen1.org
Lincoln ES — 300/K-2
1402 E P St 82240 — 307-532-4003
Tim Williams, prin. — Fax 532-2669
Torrington MS — 300/6-8
2742 W E St 82240 — 307-532-7014
Marvin Haiman, prin. — Fax 532-8402
Trail ES — 300/3-5
1601 E M St 82240 — 307-532-5429
Tyler Floerchinger, prin. — Fax 532-3451
Other Schools – See LaGrange, Lingle, Yoder

Valley Christian S — 100/PK-5
2441 E E St 82240 — 307-532-3133
Cheryl Stoeger, admin. — Fax 532-3144

Upton, Weston, Pop. 1,090
Weston County SD 7 — 300/K-12
PO Box 470 82730 — 307-468-2461
Dr. Summer Stephens, supt. — Fax 468-2797
www.weston7.org
Upton ES — 100/K-5
PO Box 470 82730 — 307-468-9331
Clark Coberly, prin. — Fax 468-2832
Upton MS — 100/6-8
PO Box 470 82730 — 307-468-9331
Clark Coberly, prin. — Fax 468-2832

Wamsutter, Sweetwater, Pop. 442
Sweetwater County SD 1
Supt. — See Rock Springs
Desert ES — 50/K-5
PO Box 10 82336 — 307-324-7811
Jared Hardman, prin. — Fax 589-1164
Desert MS — 50/6-8
PO Box 10 82336 — 307-324-7811
Jared Hardman, prin. — Fax 589-1164

Wapiti, Park
Park County SD 6
Supt. — See Cody
Wapiti ES — 50/K-5
3167 Northfork Hwy 82450 — 307-587-3947
Patrick Couture, prin. — Fax 587-4426

Weston, Campbell
Campbell County SD 1
Supt. — See Gillette
Little Powder ES — 50/K-8
15902 State Highway 59 N 82731 — 307-682-2725
Laurie Davis, prin. — Fax 682-7096

Wheatland, Platte, Pop. 3,590
Albany County SD 1
Supt. — See Laramie
Notch Peak ES — 50/K-5
2612 Palmer Canyon Rd 82201 — 307-721-0106
Wade Fiscus, admin. — Fax 378-2505

Platte County SD 1 — 1,000/K-12
1350 Oak St 82201 — 307-322-3175
Dennis Fischer, supt. — Fax 322-2084
platte1.org
Libbey ES — 200/K-2
1350 Oak St 82201 — 307-322-3836
Shane Schaffner, prin. — Fax 322-2517
West ES — 200/3-5
1350 Oak St 82201 — 307-322-4180
Vicki Begin, prin. — Fax 322-4606
Wheatland MS — 200/6-8
1350 Oak St 82201 — 307-322-1518
Cory Dziowgo, prin. — Fax 322-1560
Other Schools – See Chugwater, Glendo

Wilson, Teton, Pop. 1,473
Teton County SD 1
Supt. — See Jackson
Wilson ES — 200/K-5
5200 HHR Ranch Rd 83014 — 307-733-3077
Kathleen Milburn, prin. — Fax 733-8431

Worland, Washakie, Pop. 5,424
Washakie County SD 1 — 1,400/K-12
1900 Howell Ave 82401 — 307-347-9286
David Nicholas, supt. — Fax 347-8116
www.wsh1.k12.wy.us
East Side ES — 200/K-5
203 N 15th St 82401 — 307-347-4662
Kenneth Dietz, prin. — Fax 347-3783
South Side ES — 200/K-5
1229 Howell Ave 82401 — 307-347-3306
Wade Sanford, prin. — Fax 347-6150
West Side ES — 200/K-5
810 S 6th St 82401 — 307-347-4298
Bruce Miller, prin. — Fax 347-4927
Worland MS — 300/6-8
2150 Howell Ave 82401 — 307-347-3233
Ryan Clark, prin. — Fax 347-3710

Worland Adventist Christian S — 50/K-8
PO Box 433 82401 — 307-347-2026

Wright, Campbell, Pop. 1,786
Campbell County SD 1
Supt. — See Gillette
Cottonwood ES — 300/K-6
PO Box 330 82732 — 307-464-0584
Derek Barnhurst, prin. — Fax 464-1304

Yoder, Goshen, Pop. 151
Goshen County SD 1
Supt. — See Torrington
Southeast ES — 100/K-6
PO Box 160 82244 — 307-532-3679
Cory Gilchrest, prin. — Fax 532-5771
Southeast JHS — 100/7-8
PO Box 160 82244 — 307-532-7176
Randy Epler, prin. — Fax 532-5771

CHARTER SCHOOLS

School	Address	City,State	Zip code	Telephone	Fax	Grade	Contact
Alaska							
Academy Charter S	801 E Arctic Ave	Palmer, AK	99645	907-746-2358	746-2368	PK-8	Barbara Gerard
Alaska Native Cultural Charter S	550 Bragaw St	Anchorage, AK	99508	907-742-1370	742-1373	K-8	Bongi Agerter
American Charter Academy	244 S Sylvan Rd Ste 110	Wasilla, AK	99654	907-352-0150	352-0180	2-12	Becky Huggins
Anvil City Science Academy	PO Box 131	Nome, AK	99762	907-443-6207	443-5144	5-8	Lisa Leeper
Aquarian Charter S	1705 W 32nd Ave	Anchorage, AK	99517-2002	907-742-4900	742-4919	K-6	Lucas Saltzman
Aurora Borealis Charter S	705 Frontage Rd Ste A	Kenai, AK	99611-7740	907-283-0292	283-0293	K-8	Cody McCanna
Birchtree Charter S	7107 E Palmer Wasilla Hwy	Palmer, AK	99645	907-745-1831	745-1843	K-8	Cathy Busbey
Chinook Charter S	3002 International St	Fairbanks, AK	99701-7391	907-452-5020	452-5048	K-8	Wendy Demers
Eagle Academy Charter S	10901 Mausel St	Eagle River, AK	99577-8065	907-742-3025	742-3035	K-6	Kitty Logan
Family Partnership Charter S	401 E Fireweed Ln Ste 100	Anchorage, AK	99503-2100	907-742-3700	742-3710	K-12	Deanne Carroll
Fireweed Academy	995 Soundview Ave Ste 2	Homer, AK	99603	907-235-9728	235-8561	K-6	Todd Hindman
Fronteras Spanish Immersion S	2315 N Seward Meridian Pky	Wasilla, AK	99654	907-745-2223	376-2227	K-8	Jennifer Hutchins
Frontier Charter S	400 W Northern Lights Blvd	Anchorage, AK	99503-3877	907-742-1180	742-1188	K-12	Gerald Finkler
Highland Academy Charter S	5530 E Northern Lights Blvd	Anchorage, AK	99504	907-742-1700	742-1711	6-12	Dr. Michael Shapiro
Juneau Community Charter S	10014 Crazy Horse Dr	Juneau, AK	99801-8529	907-586-5699	586-3543	K-8	Cynthia McFeeters
Kaleidoscope S	549 N Forest Dr	Kenai, AK	99611-7410	907-283-0804	283-3786	K-5	Robin Dahlman
Ketchikan Charter S	410 Schoenbar Rd	Ketchikan, AK	99901-6218	907-225-8568	247-8568	PK-8	Julie Espinosa
Kokrine Charter S	601 Loftus Rd	Fairbanks, AK	99709-3430	907-474-0958	479-2104	7-12	Josh Snow
Midnight Sun Family Learning Center	7362 W Parks Hwy # 714	Wasilla, AK	99623	907-357-6786	373-6786	K-8	Jeanne Troshynski
PAIDEIA Cooperative S	616 W 10th Ave	Anchorage, AK	99501	907-742-4164	742-4165	K-12	Cheryl Huber
Rilke Schule German Schl of Arts & Sci	1846 E 64th Ave	Anchorage, AK	99507	907-742-0900	742-0945	K-8	Christopher Barr
Soldotna Montessori Charter S	162 E Park Ave	Soldotna, AK	99669-7552	907-260-9221	260-9032	K-6	John DeVolld
Star of the North Secondary S	2945 Monk Ct	North Pole, AK	99705-6129	907-490-9025	490-9021	7-12	Diana Childs
STrEaM Academy	7801 E 32nd Ave	Anchorage, AK	99504	907-742-9000	742-9010	6-8	Adam Mokelke
Tongass S of Arts & Sciences	410 Schoenbar Rd Ste 202	Ketchikan, AK	99901	907-225-5720	225-8822	PK-6	Dr. Marian Gonzales
Twindly Bridge Charter S	141 E Seldon Rd Ste C	Wasilla, AK	99654-3351	907-376-6680	746-6683	K-12	John Weetman
Watershed Charter S	4975 Decathlon Ave	Fairbanks, AK	99709	907-374-9350	374-9360	K-8	Jarrod Decker
Winterberry Charter S	4802 Bryn Mawr Ct	Anchorage, AK	99508	907-742-0139	742-0189	K-8	Eric Anderson
Arizona							
AAEC - Estrella Mountain HS	3400 N Dysart Rd	Avondale, AZ	85392-1003	623-535-0754	535-1210	9-12	Dale Nicol
AAEC - Mesa	1833 W Southern Ave	Mesa, AZ	85202	480-833-8899	833-1266	9-12	Eric Stevens
AAEC - Paradise Valley	3775 E Union Hills Dr	Phoenix, AZ	85050-3214	602-569-1101	569-6372	9-12	Jeremy Hendrix
AAEC - Prescott Valley	7500 E Civic Cir	Prescott Valley, AZ	86314	928-775-3200	775-3201	9-12	Patrick Welert
AAEC - Red Mountain Early College HS	2165 N Power Rd	Mesa, AZ	85215-2971	480-854-1504	854-3564	9-12	Ray Gless
AAEC - South Mountain	2002 E Baseline Rd	Phoenix, AZ	85042	602-323-9890	323-9869	9-12	Linda LaFontain
Acacia ES	12955 E Colossal Cave Rd	Vail, AZ	85641-9091	520-879-2200	879-2201	K-5	Terri Brooks
Academy Adventures Midtown ES	3025 N Winstel Blvd	Tucson, AZ	85716	520-777-3757	207-6489	K-5	John Penczar
Academy Adventures PS	3902 N Flowing Wells Rd	Tucson, AZ	85705-2403	520-407-1200	407-1201	K-5	Dayna Arnold
Academy Del Sol	7102 W Valley Crest Pl	Tucson, AZ	85757	520-789-7731		K-8	Jason Reigart
Academy Del Sol	732 W Roger Rd	Tucson, AZ	85705	520-624-7169		K-8	Aaron Davis
Academy of Building Industries	1547 E Lipan Blvd	Fort Mohave, AZ	86426-6031	928-788-2601	788-2610	9-12	Jean Thomas
Academy of Excellence	425 N 36th St	Phoenix, AZ	85008-6303	602-389-4271	389-4278	K-8	Dr. Eula Dean
Academy of Math & Science	1557 W Prince Rd	Tucson, AZ	85705-3023	520-293-2676	888-1732	K-12	Sandra Lomeland
Academy of Math & Science Camelback	6633 Camelback Rd	Phoenix, AZ	85033	520-547-5587		K-8	Shirley Ortega
Academy of Mathematics and Science South	3335 W Flower St	Phoenix, AZ	85017	520-888-9572	888-1732	K-8	Brynn Embley
Academy of Tucson ES	9209 E Wrightstown Rd	Tucson, AZ	85715-5514	520-886-6076	886-6575	K-4	Carole Rostash M.Ed.
Academy of Tucson HS	10720 E 22nd St	Tucson, AZ	85748-7029	520-733-0096	733-0097	9-12	Wendi Allardice M.Ed.
Academy of Tucson MS	7310 E 22nd St	Tucson, AZ	85710	520-749-1413	749-2824	5-8	Larry Speta
Academy With Community Partners	433 N Hall	Mesa, AZ	85203-7407	480-833-0068	833-8966	9-12	Margaret Williamson M.A.
Accelerated Learning Center	4105 E Shea Blvd	Phoenix, AZ	85028	602-485-0309	485-9356	9-12	Frank Canady Ed.D.
Accelerated Learning Laboratory	5245 N Camino De Oeste	Tucson, AZ	85745-8925	520-743-2256	743-2417	PK-12	David Jones
ACCLAIM Academy	7624 W Indian School Rd	Phoenix, AZ	85033-3009	623-691-0919	691-6091	K-8	Jose Martinez
ACE Charter HS - North	1929 N Stone Ave	Tucson, AZ	85705-5642	520-623-5843	628-2820	9-12	Jay Slauter
Acorn Montessori Charter S	8556 E Loos Dr	Prescott Valley, AZ	86314-6455	928-772-5778	775-8654	2-8	Cynthia Johnson
Acorn Montessori Charter S - West	7555 E Long Look Dr	Prescott Valley, AZ	86314-5507	928-775-0238	775-8654	PK-1	Dawn Grantham
Adams Traditional Academy	2323 W Parkside Ln	Phoenix, AZ	85027	602-938-5517	938-1179	PK-8	
Adventure S	5757 E Pima St	Tucson, AZ	85712-5609	520-296-0656	721-4472	K-5	Stacey Martinez
Aim Higher College Prep Academy	4848 S 2nd St	Phoenix, AZ	85040	602-243-7788	243-7799	7-12	Xochitl Ramirez
Air and Space Academy	730 W Calle Arroyo Sur	Green Valley, AZ	85614	520-399-4700		K-8	Mary Lou Klem
Air and Space Academy	3295 W Orange Grove Rd	Tucson, AZ	85741-2937	520-544-0220	544-0220	K-8	Mary Lou Klem
All Aboard Charter S	5827 N 35th Ave	Phoenix, AZ	85017-1915	602-433-0500	973-8208	K-5	Rhonda Newton
Alta Vista Charter HS	5040 S Campbell Ave	Tucson, AZ	85706-1510	520-294-4922	294-4933	9-12	Alicia Alvarez
American Heritage Academy	2030 E Cherry St	Cottonwood, AZ	86326-6963	928-634-2144	634-9053	K-12	Eric Evans
American Heritage Academy	132 W General Crook Trl	Camp Verde, AZ	86322	928-567-0462	567-0464	K-8	Lance Barnes
American Leadership Academy	4507 S Mountain Rd	Mesa, AZ	85212	480-420-2110	420-2109	K-6	Angi Coleman
American Leadership Academy	650 W Combs Rd	Queen Creek, AZ	85140	480-344-9899	420-2103	K-6	Nikole Disney
American Leadership Academy	1070 S Higley Rd	Gilbert, AZ	85296	480-344-9895		7-12	Erik Huso
American Leadership Academy	23908 S Hawes Rd	Queen Creek, AZ	85142	480-987-4500	882-1330	7-12	Chris Moss
American Leadership Academy	850 W Combs Rd	Queen Creek, AZ	85140	480-344-9898	344-9849	7-12	Raymond Turley
American Leadership Academy	1010 S Higley Rd	Gilbert, AZ	85296	480-344-9892		K-6	Cristina Schubert
American Leadership Academy	1750 E Riggs Rd	Gilbert, AZ	85298	480-344-9894		K-6	Sheila Frame
American Leadership Academy	22512 S Signal Butte Rd	Queen Creek, AZ	85142	480-344-9893		K-6	Ryan Taylor
American Leadership Academy	4380 N Hunt Hwy	Florence, AZ	85132	480-344-9800	518-5245	K-6	Bryan Foster
American Leadership Academy	19843 E Chandler Hts Rd	Queen Creek, AZ	85142	480-420-2150	987-4527	K-6	Dan Provonsha
American Leadership Academy	34696 N Village Ln	San Tan Valley, AZ	85142	480-420-2100	729-6003	K-6	Chad McLeod
American Leadership Academy	3155 S San Tan Village Pkwy	Gilbert, AZ	85295	480-988-3204	988-3280	K-6	Robert Brown
Amerischools Academy - Camelback	1333 W Camelback Rd	Phoenix, AZ	85013-2106	602-532-0100	532-9964	K-8	Lori Eastep
Amerischools Academy - Country Club	1150 N Country Club Rd	Tucson, AZ	85716-3942	520-620-1100	624-4376	PK-8	Claudio Bravo
Amerischools Academy - Yuma North	1220 S 4th Ave	Yuma, AZ	85364	928-919-7203	919-7205	PK-6	Linda McCormack
Amerischools Academy - Yuma South	2098 S 3rd Ave	Yuma, AZ	85364-6425	928-329-1100	329-9177	PK-6	Ashley Fox
Anthem Preparatory Academy	39808 N Gavilan Peak Pkwy	Anthem, AZ	85086	623-465-4776	465-4832	K-12	Alison Westerlind
Apache Trail HS	945 W Apache Trl	Apache Junction, AZ	85120	480-288-0337	288-0340	9-12	Terra Kasapo
Archway Classical Academy - Arete	4525 E Baseline Rd	Gilbert, AZ	85234	480-422-4233	424-1795	K-5	Neil Gillingham
Archway Classical Academy - Chandler	1951 N Alma School Rd	Chandler, AZ	85224	480-855-6474	855-7475	K-5	Leanne Fawcett
Archway Classical Academy - Cicero	7205 N Pima Rd Suite B	Scottsdale, AZ	85258	480-424-1790	434-6614	K-5	Matthew Vlahovich
Archway Classical Academy - Glendale	23276 N 83rd Ave Suite 2	Peoria, AZ	85383	623-866-4710	866-4711	K-5	Jack Kersting
Archway Classical Academy - Lincoln	2250 S Gilbert Rd	Chandler, AZ	85286	480-424-1798	424-1799	K-6	Robby Kuhlman
Archway Classical Academy - N Phoenix	14100 N 32nd St	Phoenix, AZ	85032	602-996-4355	889-0187	K-6	Joy Hanks
Archway Classical Academy - Scottsdale	7496 E Tierra Buena Ln	Scottsdale, AZ	85260	480-776-0413	889-7014	K-4	Lisa Armstrong
Archway Classical Academy - Trivium East	14130 W McDowell Rd #222	Goodyear, AZ	85395	623-866-4718	866-4719	K-5	Heather Washburn
Archway Classical Academy - Trivium West	2001 N Bullard Ave	Goodyear, AZ	85395	623-414-4883	889-6286	K-5	Jamee Twardeck
Archway Classical Academy - Veritas	3102 N 56th St Ste 100	Phoenix, AZ	85018	602-489-7341	759-1300	K-5	Dr. Mary Frances Jeffries
Arete Preparatory Academy	4525 E Baseline Rd	Gilbert, AZ	85234	480-222-4233	222-4234	6-12	Julia Gillingham
Arizona Academy of Science	2920 N 7th St	Phoenix, AZ	85014	602-222-9278	801-3871	K-8	
AZ Call-A-Teen Center of Excellence	649 N 6th Ave	Phoenix, AZ	85003-1659	602-252-6721	252-2952	9-12	
Arizona Charter Academy	16025 N Dysart Rd	Surprise, AZ	85374	623-974-4959	974-4840	K-12	Jordan Beckmam
Arizona College Prep Academy	3434 E Broadway Blvd	Tucson, AZ	85716	520-722-1200	722-0052	9-12	Charlene Mendoza
Arizona Collegiate HS	3161 N 33rd Ave	Phoenix, AZ	85017	623-498-8200	269-2970	9-12	Amy Eveleth
AZ Compass Prep and Arts S	2020 N Arizona Ave	Chandler, AZ	85225	877-225-2118	821-5462	7-12	Phil Willson M.Ed.
AZ Connections Academy	335 E Germann Rd Ste 140	Gilbert, AZ	85297	480-782-5842	323-2905	K-12	Kerri Wright
AZ Conservatory for Arts & Academics	16454 N 28th Ave	Phoenix, AZ	85053	623-878-0986	776-7956	K-5	Christopher Lalley
AZ Conservatory for Arts & Academics	2820 W Kelton Ln	Phoenix, AZ	85053-3028	602-266-4278	978-2764	6-12	Holly Foged
Arizona Language Preparatory	4645 E Marilyn Rd	Phoenix, AZ	85032	602-996-1595	344-9560	K-4	Tawnie Weaver
Arizona Prep Academy	4200 N 99th Ave	Phoenix, AZ	85037	623-907-2661	907-2501	9-12	Kurt Huzar
Arizona School for the Arts	1410 N 3rd St	Phoenix, AZ	85004	602-257-1444	252-7795	5-12	Dr. Leah Fregulia
Arizona Virtual Academy	99 E Virginia Ave Ste 200	Phoenix, AZ	85004	866-476-1320	595-6874	K-12	Kelly Van Sande
Arroyo ES	4535 W Cholla St	Glendale, AZ	85304-3535	602-896-5100	896-5120	K-8	Philip Liles
Arts Academy at Estrella Mountain	2504 S 91st Ave	Tolleson, AZ	85353-8921	623-474-2120		PK-8	Vicki Higgins
Arts Academy at Scottsdale	6140 E Thunderbird Rd	Scottsdale, AZ	85254	480-951-3190	998-4029	K-6	Carolyn Repetto
ASU Prep Academy Casa Grande HS	2612 W Gila Bend Hwy	Casa Grande, AZ	85193	520-374-4200		9-12	Sylvia Mejia
ASU Preparatory Academy	735 E Fillmore St	Phoenix, AZ	85006	602-496-3100	257-4852	K-8	

School	Address	City,State	Zip code	Telephone	Fax	Grade	Contact
ASU Prep Polytechnic HS	7350 E Innovation Way S	Mesa, AZ	85212	480-727-5769	727-3737	9-12	Chrystal Keller
ASU Prep Tempe at Compadre	500 W Guadalupe Rd	Tempe, AZ	85283	480-752-3560		9-12	
Avalon Charter School	1045 S San Marcos Dr	Apache Junction, AZ	85120	480-671-4584	671-4586	K-8	
AZTEC HS	2330 W 28th St	Yuma, AZ	85364-6954	928-314-1900	726-2826	9-12	Molly Kelly
BASIS Ahwatukee	10210 S 50th Pl	Phoenix, AZ	85044	480-659-2294	696-3607	4-12	Becky Ratliff
BASIS Chandler	4825 S Arizona Ave	Chandler, AZ	85248	480-907-6072	907-6624	5-12	Stephanie Terrell
BASIS Chandler Primary North	1800 E Chandler Blvd	Chandler, AZ	85225	480-798-6447		K-4	Dania Gold
BASIS Chandler Primary South	204 W Chandler Hts Rd	Chandler, AZ	85248	480-494-2200	895-0074	K-4	Sharon Elisco
BASIS Flagstaff	1700 N Gemini Dr	Flagstaff, AZ	86001	928-774-5502	774-5503	3-12	Corey Hartman
BASIS Goodyear	15800 W Sherman St	Goodyear, AZ	85338	480-276-8592		K-9	Jacqueline Jones
BASIS Mesa	5010 S Eastmark Pkwy	Mesa, AZ	85212	602-239-4807	822-1259	3-12	Kristen Ramos
BASIS Oro Valley	11155 N Oracle Rd	Oro Valley, AZ	85737	520-308-5220	308-5078	K-12	Elizabeth Thies
BASIS Peoria	9902 W Yearling Rd	Peoria, AZ	85383	623-566-9100	566-9109	5-12	Jayme Dunn
BASIS Peoria Primary	25950 N Lake Pleasant Pkwy	Peoria, AZ	85383	623-251-1504		K-4	Melissa Fields-Koerper
BASIS Phoenix	11850 N 32nd St	Phoenix, AZ	85028	602-595-9870	595-9820	5-12	Stovon Villafuorto
BASIS Phoenix Central PS	201 E Indianola Ave	Phoenix, AZ	85012	602-559-5399	283-7500	K-8	Rosalind Thompson
BASIS Phoenix South Primary	5700 S19th Ave	Phoenix, AZ	85041	480-447-1795		K-4	Brian Jones
BASIS Prescott	1901 Prescott Lakes Pkwy	Prescott, AZ	86301	928-277-0334	458-5562	K-12	Abby McCarty
BASIS Scottsdale	10400 N 128th St	Scottsdale, AZ	85259	480-451-7500	451-4555	4-12	Kristen Jordison
BASIS Scottsdale PS	11440 N 136th St	Scottsdale, AZ	85259	480-391-1099		K-3	Monica Morris
BASIS Tucson North	5740 E River Rd	Tucson, AZ	85750	520-207-0076	207-6606	5-12	Erin Paradis
BASIS Tucson PS	3825 E 2nd St	Tucson, AZ	85716-4368	520-326-6367	326-6359	K-4	Roberto Ramirez
Benchmark S	4120 E Acoma Dr	Phoenix, AZ	85032-4753	602-765-3582	765-1932	K-6	Barbara Darroch
Bennett Academy	2930 W Bethany Home Rd	Phoenix, AZ	85017-1615	602-943-1317	943-0280	K-8	Dr. Nancy Bennett
Bennett Academy - Venture	1535 W Dunlap Ave	Phoenix, AZ	85021	602-242-4220		K-5	Dr. Nancy Bennett
Berean Academy	1169 N Colombo Ave	Sierra Vista, AZ	85635	520-459-4113	459-4121	K-12	Beverly Enriquez
Blueprint HS	670 N Arizona Ave Ste 1	Chandler, AZ	85225	480-892-0235	892-0236	9-12	Robert Rodenbaugh
Bright Beginnings S	400 N Andersen Blvd	Chandler, AZ	85224-8273	480-821-1404	821-1463	PK-6	Dr. Sophia Patterson
Brighton Charter S	8632 W Northern Ave	Glendale, AZ	85305	623-271-9518	328-8958	K-12	Katryn Goodwin
Burke Basic S	131 E Southern Ave	Mesa, AZ	85210-5355	480-964-4602	964-6566	K-6	Glen Gaddie
Butterfield ES	44150 W Maricopa Casa Grand	Maricopa, AZ	85138	520-568-6100	568-6109	K-5	Janel Hildick
Calibre Academy Surprise	15688 W Acoma Dr	Surprise, AZ	85379-5652	623-556-2179	556-2806	K-8	Rebecca Venegas
Cambridge Academy - Mesa Campus	9412 E Brown Rd	Mesa, AZ	85207-4338	480-641-2828	325-2365	K-6	Amy Monarrez
Cambridge Academy - Queen Creek	20365 E Ocotillo Rd	Queen Creek, AZ	85142	480-987-3577	926-2791	K-8	Heidi Goleman
Camelback Academy	7634 W Camelback Rd	Glendale, AZ	85303-5627	623-247-2204	247-1113	K-8	Karen Kordon
Camino Montessori	44301 W Maricopa Ave	Maricopa, AZ	85138	520-868-6145	868-6149	PK-6	Judith Webster
Candeo Schools	9965 W Calle Lejos	Peoria, AZ	85383	623-979-6500	979-6510	K-8	Dr. Stephanie Musser Ed.D.
Canyon Pointe Academy	4941 W Union Hills Dr	Glendale, AZ	85308-1486	602-896-1166	896-1164	K-6	Dawn Adams
Canyon Rose Academy	2401 S Wilmot Rd	Tucson, AZ	85711	520-797-4884	797-8868	9-12	Christopher Golston
Canyon Rose East	8981 E Tanque Verde Rd	Tucson, AZ	85749	520-448-3700		9-12	Kimberly McNally
Canyon View Prep Academy	9030 E Florentine Rd	Prescott Valley, AZ	86314	928-775-5115	775-6253	9-12	Sean Anderson
Carden of Tucson S	5260 N Royal Palm Dr	Tucson, AZ	85705 1148	520-293-6661	408-7366	K-8	Belle Jeppson
Career Success HS - Duffy Campus	2550 E Jefferson St	Phoenix, AZ	85034	602-393-4200	393-4205	8-12	Mike McCarthy
Career Success HS - Main Campus	3816 N 27th Ave	Phoenix, AZ	85017-4703	602-285-5525	285-0026	9-12	Kelly Sheick
Career Success JSHS - North Phoenix	2325 E Bell Rd	Phoenix, AZ	85022	602-687-8282	687-8283	7-12	Eric Pawlak
Career Success S - Sage Campus	3120 N 32nd St	Phoenix, AZ	85018-6202	602-955-0355	955-4805	PK-8	Kurt Walker
Carpe Diem E-Learning Community S	3777 W 22nd Ln	Yuma, AZ	85364-5905	928-317-3113	317-0828	6-12	Roger Sciarretta
CASA Academy	1500 W Maryland Ave	Phoenix, AZ	85015	602-892-5022	892-5023	K-3	Tacey Clayton
Caurus Academy	41900 N 42nd Ave	Anthem, AZ	85086-1595	623-551-5083	551-5679	K-8	Dameon Blair M.S.
Center for Academic Success #3	919 3rd St	Douglas, AZ	85607	520-805-1558	805-1549	K-5	
Center for Academic Success ES	900 Carmelita Dr	Sierra Vista, AZ	85635	520-458-4200	458-1409	K-8	Stephen Huff
Center for Academic Success HS	900 Carmelita Dr	Sierra Vista, AZ	85635	520-458-4200	458-6396	9-12	Stephen Huff
Center for Academic Success HS	510 N G Ave	Douglas, AZ	85607-2822	520-364-2616	417-0973	9-12	Marcela Munguia
Center for Academic Success MS	1415 F Ave	Douglas, AZ	85607-1655	520-805-1558	458-1409	6-8	Marcela Munguia
Center for Educational Excellence	1700 E Elliot Rd Ste 9	Tempe, AZ	85284-1631	480-632-1940	632-1398	K-8	Stacey Cochran
Challenge Charter S	5801 W Greenbriar Dr	Glendale, AZ	85308-3847	602-938-5411	938-5393	K-6	Wendy Miller
Challenger Basic S	1315 N Greenfield Rd	Gilbert, AZ	85234-2813	480-830-1750	830-1763	K-6	Brad Tobin
Champion S	250 S McQueen Rd	Chandler, AZ	85225	480-664-3379	656-6445	K-8	
Champion S	1846 E Bella Vista	San Tan Valley, AZ	85142	480-765-2223		K-8	
Champion Schools	7900 S Jesse Owens Pkwy	Phoenix, AZ	85042	602-341-6527	341-6529	K-8	Carolyn Sawyer
Chandler Preparatory Academy	1951 N Alma School Rd	Chandler, AZ	85224	480-855-5410	855-7789	6-12	John-Paul Poppleton
Changemaker HS	1300 S Belvedere Ave	Tucson, AZ	85711	520-615-2200	615-2112	9-12	Luis Perales
Children First Leadership Academy	1648 S 16th St	Phoenix, AZ	85034	602-712-0500	712-0506	K-8	Karen Crang
Children Reaching for the Sky Prep	1844 S Alvernon Way	Tucson, AZ	85711-5607	520-790-8400	620-6570	K-5	Lee Griffin
Cicero Preparatory Academy	7205 N Pima Rd	Scottsdale, AZ	85250	480-424-1790	434-0014	6-9	Dr. Mark Discher
City HS	48 E Pennington St	Tucson, AZ	85701-1535	520-623-7223	547-0680	9-12	Brett Goble
Civano Community S	10625 E Drexel Rd	Tucson, AZ	85747	520-879-1700	879-1701	K-5	B.J. Madsen
Colegio Petite S	850 N Morley Ave	Nogales, AZ	85621	520-222-9213		K-4	Deedrick Martinez
Compass HS	PO Box 17810	Tucson, AZ	85731-7810	520-296-4070	296-4103	9-12	Kerk Ferguson
Concordia Charter S	142 N Date	Mesa, AZ	85201-6419	480-461-0555	461-0556	K-6	Margaret Roush-Meier
Cooley MS	1100 S Recker Rd	Gilbert, AZ	85296	480-279-8300	279-8305	7-8	Shawn Varner
Copper Canyon Academy	7785 W Peoria Ave	Peoria, AZ	85345-5922	623-930-1734	930-8709	K-8	Ed MacDonald
Copper Point HS	732 W Roger Rd	Tucson, AZ	85705	520-624-7169	624-7169	6-12	Dustie Gunn-Ader
Cornerstone Charter S	7107 N Black Canyon Hwy	Phoenix, AZ	85021-7619	602-595-2198	242-2398	9-12	Casey Weiss
Country Gardens Charter S	6313 W Southern Ave	Laveen, AZ	85339	602-237-3741	237-3892	K-12	Catherine Gerber
Create Academy	2645 N 24th St	Phoenix, AZ	85008	602-710-1101	714-5345	K-5	
Crestview College Prep HS	2616 E Greenway Rd	Phoenix, AZ	85032-4320	602-765-8470	765-8471	7-12	Jon Kronstedt
Crown Charter S	PO Box 363	Litchfield Park, AZ	85340-0363	623-535-9300	535-5410	K-6	James Shade
Crown Point HS	4802 N 59th Ave	Phoenix, AZ	85033	623-845-0781	848-4065	9-12	Claudia Ramirez
Deer Valley Academy	18424 N 51st Ave	Glendale, AZ	85308-1443	602-467-6874	467-6955	9-12	Barbara Dalicandro
Desert Cove ES	11020 N 28th St	Phoenix, AZ	85028-2500	602-449-3400	449-3405	K-6	Stacey Orest
Desert Heights Charter S	5821 W Beverly Ln	Glendale, AZ	85306-1801	602-896-2900	467-9540	K-4	Katherine Miller M.A.
Desert Heights Preparatory Academy	3540 W Union Hills Dr	Glendale, AZ	85308	602-896-2900	547-4576	5-12	Chelsey Peitz
Desert Hills HS	1515 S Val Vista Dr	Gilbert, AZ	85296-3854	480-813-1151	813-1161	9-12	David Miller M.Ed.
Desert Marigold S	6210 S 28th St	Phoenix, AZ	85042-4715	602-243-6909	243-6933	PK-12	Charles Burkum
Desert Mirage Preparatory Academy	13226 N 113th Ave	Youngtown, AZ	85363			K-6	Mary Berg
Desert Pointe Academy	7785 W Peoria Ave	Peoria, AZ	85345-5922	623-930-1734	930-8709	9-12	Ed McDonald
Desert Rose Academy	326 W Fort Lowell Rd	Tucson, AZ	85705	520-797-4884	797-8868	9-12	Richard Connet
Desert Sky Community S	1350 N Arcadia Ave	Tucson, AZ	85712	520-745-3888	745-5110	K-5	Shelly Adrian
Desert Springs Academy	10129 E Speedway Blvd	Tucson, AZ	85748	520-321-1709	321-9316	K-5	Ellie Wray
Desert Springs Preparatory ES	6010 E Acoma Dr	Scottsdale, AZ	85254-2599	602-449-7100	449-7105	PK-6	Raquel Scott
Desert Star Academy	5635 Highway 95	Fort Mohave, AZ	86426	928-770-4523		PK-6	Margie Montgomery
Desert Star Community S	1240 S Recycler Rd	Cornville, AZ	86325-5224	928-282-0171	284-9565	K-8	Cheryl LeBlanc
Desert View Academy	3777 W 16th St	Yuma, AZ	85364	928-314-1102		K-5	Jon Larson
Desert View Academy	2363 S Kennedy Ln	Yuma, AZ	85365	928-314-1102	314-1086	K-5	Deb Weigel
Destiny S	798 E Prickly Pear Dr	Globe, AZ	85501-2395	928-425-0925	425-0927	K-8	Scott Williamson
Discovery Plus Academy	PO Box 1089	Pima, AZ	85543	928-485-2498	485-2508	K-5	DeeAnn Williams
Dobson Academy	PO Box 6070	Chandler, AZ	85246-6070	480-855-6325	855-6323	K-8	Dawne Winn
EAGLE College Prep: Maryvale	3950 N 53rd Ave	Phoenix, AZ	85031	602-638-0820	429-8177	K-5	Yesenia Fitzhugh
EAGLE College Prep: Mesa	1619 E Main St	Mesa, AZ	85203	602-638-0802	638-0806	K-5	Tracy Allen
EAGLE College Prep S	2450 W South Mountain Ave	Phoenix, AZ	85041	602-323-5400	323-5401	K-8	Crystal Danzy
EAGLE Harmony S	2435 E Pecan Rd	Phoenix, AZ	85040	602-268-1212	237-5140	K-8	Sarka White
Eastpointe HS	8495 E Broadway Blvd	Tucson, AZ	85710-4009	520-731-8180	731-8179	9-12	
East Valley Academy	1858 E Brown Rd	Mesa, AZ	85203	480-610-1711		K-6	Janet Stoeppelmann
East Valley HS	7420 E Main St	Mesa, AZ	85207	480-981-2008	641-1342	9-12	Kathy Tolman
Edge Charter S - Himmel Park	2555 E 1st St	Tucson, AZ	85716-4152	520-881-1389	881-0852	9-12	Rob Pecharich
Edge Charter S - Northwest	231 W Giaconda Way	Tucson, AZ	85704-4341	520-877-9179	881-0852	9-12	Rob Pecharich
EdOptions Preparatory Academy	2021 N Grand Ave Unit B	Nogales, AZ	85621	520-281-9179	761-0927	7-12	
Educational Opportunity Center	3810 W 16th St	Yuma, AZ	85364	928-329-0990	783-0886	9-12	
EduPreneurship Student Center	7310 N 27th Ave	Phoenix, AZ	85051	602-973-8998	973-5510	K-8	Deborah Salas
Edu-Prize S	580 W Melody Ave	Gilbert, AZ	85233-1418	480-813-9537	813-6742	PK-12	Lynn Robershotte
EDUPRIZE S - Queen Creek Campus	4567 W Roberts Rd	Queen Creek, AZ	85142	480-888-1610	888-1655	K-8	
E-Institute at Avondale	1035 E Van Buren St	Avondale, AZ	85323	623-760-9061	760-9068	9-12	William Burke
E-Institute at Metro	9640 N Metro Pkwy W	Phoenix, AZ	85051	602-943-2236	944-1248	9-12	Eric Luthi
E-Institute at Surprise	16578 W Greenway Rd Ste 204	Surprise, AZ	85388-2184	623-544-9285	546-9540	9-12	Casey Robertson
E-Institute at Union Hills	3515 W Union Hills Dr	Glendale, AZ	85308-2429	602-843-3891	843-4375	9-12	Rick Wolff
E-Institute Charter HS at Grovers	4744 W Grovers Ave	Glendale, AZ	85308	602-621-4398	889-0351	9-12	Rick Wolff M.Ed.
E-Institute HS at Buckeye	6213 S Miller Rd	Buckeye, AZ	85326	623-505-7118	760-9068	9-12	Marty Acosta
El Dorado HS	2200 N Arizona Ave Ste 17	Chandler, AZ	85225-3452	480-726-9536	726-9543	9-12	Bahja Ali M.Ed.
Empower College Prep HS	2411 W Colter St	Phoenix, AZ	85015	602-283-5720	535-5409	8-12	Sarah Caffee
Empower Collegiate Prep	5757 N Central Ave	Phoenix, AZ	85012	602-283-5720		3-8	Brian Holman
Envision HS	351 W Prince Rd	Tucson, AZ	85705	520-887-0045		9-12	Daniel Morales
Estrella HS	510 N Central Ave	Avondale, AZ	85323-1909	623-932-6561	932-1263	9-12	Laura Perry
Ethos Academy	8840 N 43rd Ave	Glendale, AZ	85302	623-249-3211	249-3209	K-7	Tim Boykin
Farm at Mission Montessori Academy	4530 E Gold Dust Ave	Phoenix, AZ	85028	602-466-1153		4-8	
Fireside ES	3725 E Lone Cactus Dr	Phoenix, AZ	85050	602-449-4700	449-4705	K-6	Teresa Simmons
Flagstaff Arts and Leadership Academy	3401 N Fort Valley Rd	Flagstaff, AZ	86001	928-779-7223	779-7041	7-12	Deidre Crawley

School	Address	City,State	Zip code	Telephone	Fax	Grade	Contact
Flagstaff Junior Academy	306 W Cedar Ave	Flagstaff, AZ	86001-1413	928-774-6007	774-7268	PK-8	Thomas Drumm
Foothills Academy	7191 E Ashler Hills Dr	Scottsdale, AZ	85266-9300	480-488-5583	488-6902	K-12	Dr. Donald Senneville
Fountain Hills Charter S	PO Box 18419	Fountain Hills, AZ	85269	480-837-0046	837-0024	PK-8	
Franklin Charter S - Crismon	22120 E Queen Creek Rd	Queen Creek, AZ	85142	480-987-0722	987-3517	K-6	John Baker
Franklin Charter S - Gilbert	13717 S Val Vista Dr	Gilbert, AZ	85296	480-632-0722	632-8716	K-6	Diana Dana
Franklin Charter S - Power	22951 S Power Rd	Queen Creek, AZ	85142	480-677-8400	677-8555	K-6	Adrienne Lamb
Franklin HS	18864 E Germann Rd	Queen Creek, AZ	85142	480-558-1197	659-5354	7-12	Mark McAfee
Franklin Phonetic PS Sunnyslope	9317 N 2nd St	Phoenix, AZ	85020	602-870-6674		PK-5	Joseph Gubbins
Franklin Phonetic S	6116 E State Route 69	Prescott Valley, AZ	86314-2806	928-775-6747	775-6740	K-8	Cindy Franklin
Freedom Academy - Paradise Campus	3916 E Paradise Ln	Phoenix, AZ	85032	602-424-0771	424-0773	K-8	Linda Hoffman
Freedom Academy - Pima Campus	28700 N Pima Rd	Scottsdale, AZ	85266	480-419-8200	419-8215	K-8	Linda Hoffman
Freire Freedom S	47 E Pennington St	Tucson, AZ	85701	520-352-0057	352-0058	6-8	Joann Groh
Freire Freedom S	300 E University Blvd	Tucson, AZ	85705-6929	520-624-7552	624-7518	6-8	Chad Blair
Friendly House Academia Del Pueblo S	201 E Durango St	Phoenix, AZ	85004-2913	602-258-4353		K-8	Frank Lomeli
Future Investment MS	1854 S Alvernon Way	Tucson, AZ	85711	520-747-3733	745-2848	6-8	Lee Griffin
GateWay Early College HS	108 N 40th St	Phoenix, AZ	85034-1704	602-286-8759	286-8752	9-12	Lisa Smith
GEM Charter S / Good Earth Montessori	1704 N Center St	Mesa, AZ	85201-2223	480-833-2622	833-2655	PK-5	Nelleke van Savooyen
Genesis Academy	525 E McDowell Rd	Phoenix, AZ	85004-1537	602-254-8090	254-8094	9-12	Karen Callahan
Gervin Prep Academy	2801 E Southern Ave	Phoenix, AZ	85040	480-219-2121	633-6787	PK-8	D. Mendoza
Gilbert Arts Academy	862 E Elliot Rd	Gilbert, AZ	85234-6912	480-325-6100	632-2077	PK-6	Lauren Arnold
Girls Leadership Academy	715 W Mariposa St	Phoenix, AZ	85013-2449	602-288-4518	288-4118	9-12	Kellie Warren
Glendale Preparatory Academy	23276 N 83rd Ave Ste 1	Peoria, AZ	85383	623-889-0822	889-0825	6-12	Brandon Crowe
Glenview College Prep HS	3802 W Maryland Ave	Phoenix, AZ	85019	602-841-1221	841-1364	9-12	Chris Ecton
Grande Innovation Academy	950 N Peart Rd	Casa Grande, AZ	85122	520-381-2360	413-9397	K-5	Patty Messer
Great Expectations Academy	1466 W Camino Antigua	Sahuarita, AZ	85629-9720	520-399-2121	399-2123	K-8	Mark Phillips
Ha:San Prep & Leadership Charter S	1333 E 10th St	Tucson, AZ	85719-5808	520-882-8826	882-8651	9-12	James Merino
Happy Valley S	7140 W Happy Valley Rd	Peoria, AZ	85383-3255	623-376-2900	376-9030	K-6	James Born
Happy Valley S East	266 E Westbrooke Rd	San Tan Valley, AZ	85140	480-888-1342	888-8450	K-6	Jared Palmer
Harvest Preparatory Academy	350 E 18th St	Yuma, AZ	85364-5723	928-782-2052	819-5976	K-12	
Harvest Preparatory Academy	1044 N 10th Ave	San Luis, AZ	85349	928-627-5008		K-7	
Harvest Preparatory Academy	14900 W Van Buren St	Goodyear, AZ	85338	602-708-2334	236-3248	K-8	
Havasu Preparatory Academy	3155 Maricopa Ave	Lk Havasu Cty, AZ	86406	928-854-4011	453-4042	K-8	Amy Hanon
Haven Montessori S	621 W Clay Ave	Flagstaff, AZ	86001	928-522-0985	774-7412	K-6	Christy Zeller
Hearn Academy	17606 N 7th Ave	Phoenix, AZ	85023-1567	602-896-9160	896-1997	K-8	Gaye Leo
Heritage Academy Gateway	19705 Germann Rd	Queen Creek, AZ	85242	480-461-4400	452-0833	7-12	Spencer Bowers
Heritage Academy - Laveen	4275 W Baseline Rd	Laveen, AZ	85339	602-290-8546	926-2656	7-12	Kim Ellsworth
Heritage Academy Mesa	32 S Center St	Mesa, AZ	85210-1306	480-969-5641	969-6972	7-12	Dr. Travis Moore
Heritage ES - Glendale Campus	6805 N 125th Ave	Glendale, AZ	85307	623-742-3956	742-3957	K-8	Justin Dye
Heritage ES - Williams Campus	790 E Rodeo Rd	Williams, AZ	86046-9653	928-635-3998	635-3999	K-5	Kaytie Thies
Hermosa Montessori Charter S	12051 E Fort Lowell Rd	Tucson, AZ	85749-9702	520-749-5518	749-6087	PK-8	Sheila Stolov
Hiaki HS	4747 W Calle Vicam	Tucson, AZ	85757-8860	520-883-5051	879-5877	9-12	
Highland Free S	510 S Highland Ave	Tucson, AZ	85719-6427	520-623-0104	903-1318	K-6	Nicholas Sofka
Hirsch Academy	6535 E Osborn Rd	Scottsdale, AZ	85251	480-488-9362		K-5	
Holsteiner Agricultural S	44400 W Honeycutt Rd	Maricopa, AZ	85138	520-568-8620		K-6	Tanya Graysmark
Hope HS	7620 W Lower Buckeye Rd	Phoenix, AZ	85043	623-772-8013	772-8021	9-12	Krissyn Sumare
Hope HS Online	5651 W Talavi Blvd Ste 170	Glendale, AZ	85306	602-674-8344	943-9700	7-12	Erin Horn
Horizon Community Learning Center	16233 S 48th St	Phoenix, AZ	85048-0801	480-659-3000	659-3022	K-12	Betsy Fera
Huachuca Mountain ES	3555 E Fry Blvd	Sierra Vista, AZ	85635-2972	520-515-2960	515-2966	K-6	Karen Kukuchka
Humanities & Sciences Academy	1105 E Broadway Rd	Tempe, AZ	85282-1505	480-317-5900	829-4999	9-12	
Humanities & Sciences HS	5201 N 7th St	Phoenix, AZ	85014-2802	602-650-1333	650-1777	9-12	Michael Curd
Imagine Avondale ES	950 N Eliseo Felix Jr Way	Avondale, AZ	85323	602-344-1730	344-1740	PK-8	Kim Agnew
Imagine Charter S at Bell Canyon	18052 N Black Canyon Hwy	Phoenix, AZ	85053-1715	602-547-7920	547-7923	PK-8	Joshua Jordan
Imagine Charter S at Camelback	5050 N 19th Ave	Phoenix, AZ	85015-3205	602-344-4620	344-4630	K-8	Freddie Villalon
Imagine Charter S at Cortez Park	3535 W Dunlap Ave	Phoenix, AZ	85051-5303	602-589-9840	589-9841	K-8	Jason Whitaker
Imagine Charter S at Desert West	6738 W McDowell Rd	Phoenix, AZ	85035-4642	602-344-7150	344-7160	K-8	Bill Heintz
Imagine Charter S at East Mesa	9701 E Southern Ave	Mesa, AZ	85209-3769	480-355-6830	355-6840	PK-8	Melynda Hache
Imagine Charter S at Rosefield	12050 N Bullard Ave	Surprise, AZ	85379-6325	623-344-4300	344-4310	PK-5	James Mecca
Imagine Charter S at Tempe	1538 E Southern Ave	Tempe, AZ	85282-5687	480-355-1640	355-1650	PK 6	Selethia Benn
Imagine Charter S at West Gilbert	2061 S Gilbert Rd	Gilbert, AZ	85295-4620	480-855-2700	855-2701	PK-8	Jon Gentile
Imagine Coolidge ES	1290 W Vah Ki Inn Rd	Coolidge, AZ	85128	520-723-5391	723-5491	K-6	Clara Thigpen
Imagine Prep at Surprise	14850 N 156th Ave	Surprise, AZ	85379-5653	623-344-1770	344-1780	7-12	Chris McComb
Imagine Prep Coolidge	1290 W Vah Ki Inn Rd	Coolidge, AZ	85128	520-424-2790	723-6315	6-12	Angela West
Imagine Prep - Superstition	1843 W 16th Ave	Apache Junction, AZ	85120	480-355-0530	355-0540	6-12	Frank Stirpe
Incito S	PO Box 7470	Goodyear, AZ	85338	623-398-6868		K-8	April Black
Integrity Education Centre	515 E Continental Dr	Tempe, AZ	85281	480-731-4829	394-0711	K-12	
Intelli School - Chandler	1727 N Arizona Ave Ste 5	Chandler, AZ	85225	602-564-7230	564-7231	9-12	Kenny DeLoera
Intelli School - Glendale	13806 N 51st Ave	Glendale, AZ	85306-4834	602-564-7210	564-7301	9-12	Issac Barrio
Intelli School - Metro Center	3327 W Peoria Ave	Phoenix, AZ	85029	602-564-7240	564-7241	9-12	Jeff Graves
Intelli School - Paradise Valley	1427 E Bell Rd Ste 102	Phoenix, AZ	85022	602-564-7280	564-7281	9-12	Jason Swingler
International Commerce HS	5201 N 7th St	Phoenix, AZ	85014-2802	602-650-1333	650-1777	9-12	
International Commerce HS	1105 E Broadway Rd	Tempe, AZ	85282-1505	480-317-5900	829-4999	9-12	
iSchool 2020	3777 W 22nd Ln	Yuma, AZ	85364	928-317-3113	783-3473	7-12	Ryan Hackmann
Jefferson Preparatory	16635 N 51st Ave	Glendale, AZ	85306	602-595-2990	595-2440	7-12	Tawnya Mecham
Keystone Montessori Charter S	1025 E Liberty Ln	Phoenix, AZ	85048-8462	480-460-7312	283-8402	K-9	Cindy Maschoff
Khalsa Montessori S	2536 N 3rd St	Phoenix, AZ	85004-1308	602-252-3759	252-9244	K-6	Keerat Giordano
Khalsa Montessori S	3701 E River Rd	Tucson, AZ	85718-6633	520-529-3611	615-0625	K-8	Nirvair Khalsa
Kingman Academy of Learning HS	3420 N Burbank St	Kingman, AZ	86409-3105	928-681-2900	681-2922	9-12	Eric Lillis
Kingman Academy of Learning IS	3419 Harrison St	Kingman, AZ	86409-3604	928-681-3200	681-3210	3-5	Jeff Martin
Kingman Academy of Learning MS	3269 Harrison St	Kingman, AZ	86409-3679	928-692-5265	692-3444	6-8	Tony Victory
Kingman Academy of Learning PS	3400 N Burbank St	Kingman, AZ	86409-3105	928-692-2500	692-2505	K-2	Trudi Bradley
La Paloma Academy - Central	2050 N Wilmot Rd	Tucson, AZ	85712-3039	520-721-4205	721-4263	K-8	Brendan Ewald
La Paloma Academy - Lakeside	8140 E Golf Links Rd	Tucson, AZ	85730	520-733-7373	733-7392	K-8	Sean Watins
La Paloma Academy South	5660 S 12th Ave	Tucson, AZ	85706	520-807-9668		K-8	Paul Bummer
Larkspur ES	2430 E Larkspur Dr	Phoenix, AZ	85032	602-449-3300	449-3305	K-6	Jamie Roberson
Las Puertas Community S	100 W 37th St	Tucson, AZ	85713	520-546-9296		6-11	
La Tierra Community S	124 N Virginia St	Prescott, AZ	86301-3224	928-445-5100	445-4802	K-6	Lenka Studnicka Ph.D.
Leading Edge Academy at East Mesa	10115 E University Dr	Mesa, AZ	85207	480-984-5645	627-3634	K-6	Chad Kobold
Leading Edge Academy - Gilbert	717 W Ray Rd	Gilbert, AZ	85233	480-545-6646	558-7038	K-6	Dr. Gerald Slemmer
Leading Edge Academy - Glbrt Early Coll	717 W Ray Rd	Gilbert, AZ	85233	480-545-8011	558-7038	7-12	Dr. Gerald Slemmer
Leading Edge Academy - Maricopa	18700 N Porter Rd	Maricopa, AZ	85138	520-568-7800	448-6865	K-12	Mat Reese
Leading Edge Academy - Mountain View	4815 W Hunt Hwy	Queen Creek, AZ	85142	480-655-6787	655-6788	K-8	Steve Butcher
Learning Foundation & Performing Arts S	3939 E Warner Rd	Gilbert, AZ	85296	480-240-8025	248-9429	K-6	Chris Paulson
Learning Foundation & Performing Arts S	4055 E Warner Rd	Gilbert, AZ	85296	480-635-9400	635-1907	7-12	Robert Villa
Learning Foundation & Performing Arts S	851 N Stapley Dr	Mesa, AZ	85203-5644	480-834-6202	834-3991	K-6	Missy Aitken
Learning Foundation & Performing Arts S	5761 E Brown Rd	Mesa, AZ	85205-4400	480-807-1100	807-1190	K-8	Nikki Triggs-Valle
Legacy Traditional S - Avondale Campus	12320 W Van Buren St	Avondale, AZ	85323-5238	623-344-0330	932-7848	K-8	Michelle Hart
Legacy Traditional S - Casa Grande	1274 E ONeil Dr	Casa Grande, AZ	85122	520-421-2323	421-4443	K-8	
Legacy Traditional S - Chandler	3201 S Gilbert Rd	Chandler, AZ	85286	480-270-5422	237-5780	K-8	
Legacy Traditional S- Gilbert	2747 S Recker Rd	Gilbert, AZ	85295	480-397-9260	212-9893	K-8	
Legacy Traditional S - Glendale	13901 N 67th Ave	Glendale, AZ	85306	623-219-4300	219-4301	K-8	
Legacy Traditional S - Laveen Campus	7900 S 43rd Ave	Laveen, AZ	85339	623-344-0472	298-0196	K-8	
Legacy Traditional S - Maricopa	17760 Regent Dr	Maricopa, AZ	85138	520-423-9999	423-9997	K-8	Amy Sundeen M.Ed.
Legacy Traditional S - North Chandler	1900 N McQueen Rd	Chandler, AZ	85225	480-757-5400	757-5401	K-8	
Legacy Traditional S - Northwest Tucson	3500 W Cortaro Farms Rd	Tucson, AZ	85742-7808	520-505-3640	579-6833	K-8	Christine Fitzsimmons
Legacy Traditional S - Peoria	7877 W Hillcrest Blvd	Peoria, AZ	85383	623-299-9825	299-9826	K-6	
Legacy Traditional S - Queen Creek	41800 N Barnes Pkwy	San Tan Valley, AZ	85140	480-655-5553	655-5558	K-8	
Legacy Traditional S - Surprise	14506 W Sweetwater Ave	Surprise, AZ	85379	623-299-9820	299-9821	K-8	Brandi Adams-Bressler
Leman Academy of Excellence	7720 N Silverbell Rd	Tucson, AZ	85743	520-639-8080	395-1352	K-8	Dennis O'Reilly
Leman Academy of Excellence	1000 E Wilcox Dr	Sierra Vista, AZ	85635	520-352-7780	459-4387	K-7	Dennis O'Reilly
Leman Academy of Excellence	3761 S Power Rd	Mesa, AZ	85212	877-235-3626	395-1352	K-6	Bethany Papajohn
Liberty Arts Academy	3015 S Power Rd	Mesa, AZ	85212-3000	480-830-3444	830-4335	PK-8	Brady Wald
Liberty HS	1300 E Cedar St	Globe, AZ	85501	928-402-8024	402-8328	9-12	Colleen DeRose
Liberty Traditional Charter S	4027 N 45th Ave	Phoenix, AZ	85031-2840	602-442-8791	353-9270	K-8	Jeremy Parker
Liberty Traditonal S - Saddleback	3715 N Washington Ave	Douglas, AZ	85607	520-364-6311	364-6312	K-8	Oscar Romero
Life Skills Center of Arizona	8123 N 35th Ave Ste 2	Phoenix, AZ	85051	602-242-6400	242-6823	9-12	
Lincoln Preparatory Academy	2250 S Gilbert Rd	Chandler, AZ	85286	480-424-1796	424-1797	6-9	Dr. Benjamin Mitchell
Lincoln Traditional S	10444 N 39th Ave	Phoenix, AZ	85051-1179	602-896-6300	896-6320	K-8	Emmit Phok
Madison Highland Prep S	1431 E Campbell Ave	Phoenix, AZ	85014	602-745-3800	745-3899	9-12	Dr. Kerry Clark
Madison Preparatory S	5815 S Mcclintock Dr	Tempe, AZ	85283-3227	480-345-2306	345-0059	6-12	David Batchelder
Maricopa ES	44150 W Maricopa Casa Grand	Maricopa, AZ	85138	520-568-5160	568-5166	K-5	Dr. Jennifer Robinson
Maricopa Institute of Technology	3900 S 55th Ave	Phoenix, AZ	85043	602-272-0006		9-12	Ramona Gonzales
Maricopa Wells MS	44150 W Maricopa Casa Grand	Maricopa, AZ	85138	520-568-7100	568-7104	6-8	Rick Abel
Maryvale Preparatory Academy	6301 W Indian School Rd	Phoenix, AZ	85033	602-247-6095	889-6282	K-8	Mac Esau
Masada Charter S	PO Box 2277	Colorado City, AZ	86021-2277	928-875-2525	875-2526	K-9	Leanne Timpson
Math & Science Success Academy	434 W Lerdo Rd	Tucson, AZ	85756	520-889-1504		K-12	Norma Derby
Maya HS	3660 W Glendale Ave	Phoenix, AZ	85051-8335	602-242-3442	242-5255	9-12	John Anderson
Mesa Arts Academy	221 W 6th Ave	Mesa, AZ	85210-2446	480-844-3965	844-0205	K-8	Michael Dillon

School	Address	City,State	Zip code	Telephone	Fax	Grade	Contact
Mesquite ES	9455 E Rita Rd	Tucson, AZ	85747-6300	520-879-2100	879-2101	K-5	Diane Samorano
Metropolitan Arts Institute	1700 N 7th Ave	Phoenix, AZ	85007	602-258-9500	258-9504	7-12	Matthew Baker
Mexicayotl Academy	667 N 7th Ave	Tucson, AZ	85705	520-624-4018	287-0037	K-4	Ivonne Ferreira
Midtown HS	7318 W Lynwood St	Phoenix, AZ	85035-4542	623-936-8682	936-8559	9-12	John White
Midtown PS	4735 N 19th Ave	Phoenix, AZ	85015-3725	602-265-5133	604-2337	K-5	Judy White
Milestones Charter S	4707 E Robert E Lee St	Phoenix, AZ	85032-9529	602-404-1009	404-5456	K-8	Tara Cabardo
Mingus Springs Charter S	3600 Sunset Dr	Chino Valley, AZ	86323	928-636-4766	636-5149	K-8	Dawn Gonzales
Mission Heights Prep HS	1376 E Cottonwood Ln	Casa Grande, AZ	85122	520-836-9383	836-9662	9-12	Amanda Mace
Mission Montessori Academy	4530 E Gold Dust Ave	Phoenix, AZ	85028-4221	602-466-1153		7-8	Joslyn Maike
Mission Montessori del Cielo	5550 E Mercer Ln	Scottsdale, AZ	85254-4737	480-284-8000	284-8875	PK-K	
Mission Montessori del Jardin	5550 E Mercer Ln	Scottsdale, AZ	85254-4737	480-699-4950	314-3346	1-3	
Mission Montessori del Norte	5550 E Mercer Ln	Scottsdale, AZ	85254-4737	480-840-1609	840-1676	4-6	Dr. Lalit Ecka
Mission Montessori on the Desert	5550 E Mercer Ln	Scottsdale, AZ	85254	480-860-4330	657-3715	PK-K	
Mohave Accelerated ES	625 Marina Blvd	Bullhead City, AZ	86442	928-704-9345	704-4977	K-5	Sandy Smith
Mohave Accelerated ES East	945 Thumb Butte Rd	Bullhead City, AZ	86442	928-704-9345	704-4977	K-5	Jeremy Klingonsmith
Mohave Accelerated Learning Center	625 Marina Blvd	Bullhead City, AZ	86442-5414	928-704-9345	704-4977	6-12	Valorie Merrigan
Montessori Academy	6050 N Invergordon Rd	Paradise Valley, AZ	85253	480-945-1121	874-2928	K-8	Juli Newman
Montessori Charter S of Flagstaff	850 N Locust St	Flagstaff, AZ	86001	928-226-1212	774-0337	K-6	Kim Loaiza
Montessori Day Charter S - Mountainside	9215 N 14th St	Phoenix, AZ	85020-2713	602-943-7672	395-0271	K-8	Pat Freeman
Montessori Day S - Chandler Lakeshore	1700 W Warner Rd	Chandler, AZ	85224-2676	480-730-8886	730-9072	PK-6	Theresa Averill
Montessori de Santa Cruz Charter S	PO Box 4706	Tubac, AZ	85646-4706	520-398-0536	398-0776	PK-6	Mary Gilbert
Montessori Education Centre Main Campus	2834 E Southern Ave	Mesa, AZ	85204-5517	480-926-8375	503-0515	PK-6	
Montessori Education Centre North	815 N Gilbert Rd	Mesa, AZ	85203-5805	480-964-1381	668-5457	PK-6	
Montessori House Charter S	2415 N Terrace Cir	Mesa, AZ	85203-1220	480-464-2800	464-2836	K-6	Sherie Richardson
Montessori Schoolhouse	1301 E Fort Lowell Rd	Tucson, AZ	85719-2239	520-319-8668	881-4096	K-5	Regine Ebner
Mountain Oak Charter S	1455 Willow Creek Rd	Prescott, AZ	86301	928-541-7700	445-1301	K-8	Cynthia Roe
Mountain Rose Academy	3686 W Orange Grove Rd	Tucson, AZ	85741	520-797-4884	797-8868	9-12	Jennifer Haley
Mountain S	311 W Cattle Drive Trl	Flagstaff, AZ	86005	928-779-2392	773-3246	PK-5	Gina Andress
Mountain View Preparatory S	2939 E Del Rio Dr	Cottonwood, AZ	86326	928-649-8144	649-8145	K-8	Stephanie Jones
Mt. Turnbull Academy	PO Box 129	Bylas, AZ	85530	928-475-3050	475-3051	9-12	Jayson Stanley
New Horizon S for the Performing Arts	446 E Broadway Rd	Mesa, AZ	85204-2020	480-655-7444	655-8220	K-6	Jim Wyler
New School for the Arts	1216 E Apache Blvd	Tempe, AZ	85281-6005	480-481-9235	970-6625	6-12	Katy Cardenas
New World Educational Center Charter S	5818 N 7th St	Phoenix, AZ	85014	602-238-9577	238-9210	K-12	Jesus Armenta
NFL YET College Prep Academy	222 E Olympic Dr	Phoenix, AZ	85042	602-243-7788	243-7799	7-12	Arlahee Ruiz
Northern AZ Academy for Career Dev.	PO Box 125	Taylor, AZ	85939-0125	928-536-4222	536-4441	9-12	Scott Moore
Northland Preparatory Academy	3300 E Sparrow Ave	Flagstaff, AZ	86004-6703	928-214-8776	214-8778	6-12	Toni Keberlein
North Phoenix Preparatory Academy	14100 N 32nd St	Phoenix, AZ	85032	602-996-4355	889-0161	7-12	Paul Weinhold
North Pointe Preparatory S	10215 N 43rd Ave	Phoenix, AZ	85051-1025	623-209-0017	209-0021	7-12	Suzanne Smailagic
Northpoint Expeditionary Learning Acad	551 1st St	Prescott, AZ	86301-2501	928-717-3272	541-2294	7-12	Charles Mentken
Nosotros Academy	440 N Grande Ave	Tucson, AZ	85745-2703	520-624-1023	624-7999	K-12	Paul Felix
Odyssey Institute for Advanced Studies	1495 S Verrado Way	Buckeye, AZ	85326	623-327-1757		6-12	Bryan Pratt
Odyssey Prep Academy - Apache	6500 S Apache Rd	Buckeye, AZ	85326	623-327-3111	327-0554	K-5	Angie Price
Odyssey Preparatory Academy	17532 W Harrison St	Goodyear, AZ	85338	623-882-1140	882-1196	K-5	Liz Douglass
Odyssey Preparatory Academy-Sienna Hills	2400 N Sienna Hills Pkwy	Buckeye, AZ	85396	623-444-9934	444-9654	K-5	Lorrese Roer
Old Vail MS	13299 E Colossal Cave Rd	Vail, AZ	85641-9090	520-879-2400	879-2401	6-8	Michael Fester
Ombudsman Charter S - East	3943 E Thomas Rd	Phoenix, AZ	85018-7511	602-840-2997	840-1402	9-12	Dorothy Cohen
Ombudsman Charter S - East II	4041 E Thomas Rd Ste 210	Phoenix, AZ	85018	602-667-7759	667-7793	9-12	Lisa Thomas
Ombudsman Charter S - Metro	7910 N 43rd Ave	Glendale, AZ	85301	602-840-2997	842-6157	9-12	Lupita Ingram
Ombudsman Charter S - Northeast	1290 N Scottsdale Rd #130	Tempe, AZ	85281	602-485-9872	367-0367	9-12	Sara Garcia
Ombudsman Charter S - Northwest	9516 W Peoria Ave	Peoria, AZ	85345-6139	602-840-2997	840-1402	9-12	Jessica De La Cruz
Ombudsman Charter S - Valencia	1660 W Valencia Rd	Tucson, AZ	85746	520-573-5858	807-9333	6-12	Patricia Wood
Ombudsman Charter S - West	2909 W Bell Rd	Phoenix, AZ	85053	602-840-2997	840-1402	9-12	Stephen Myers
Omega Alpha Academy	1402 N San Antonio Ave	Douglas, AZ	85607-2434	520-805-1261	805-1272	K-12	Jose Frisby
Open Doors Community S	13644 N Sandario Rd	Marana, AZ	85653	520-744-2484		K-8	Mary Franco
Orangewood S	7337 N 19th Ave	Phoenix, AZ	85021-7998	602-347-2900	347-2920	K-8	Colleen Mahoney
PACE Preparatory Academy	6711 E 2nd St	Prescott Valley, AZ	86314	928-775-9675	775-9673	9-12	Mary Augustinovich
Paideia Academy of South Phoenix	7777 S 15th Ter	Phoenix, AZ	85042	602-343-3040	381-9029	PK-8	Dr. Brian Winsor
Painted Desert Montessori	2400 S 247th Ave	Buckeye, AZ	85326	623-900-5132		K-8	Michael Bartlett
Painted Rock Academy	14800 N 25th Dr	Phoenix, AZ	85023	623-466-8855		K-8	Joshua Bauer
Pan-American Charter ES	3001 W Indian School Rd	Phoenix, AZ	85017-4151	602-266-3989	266-3979	K-12	Marta Pasos
Paradise Education Center	15533 W Paradise Ln	Surprise, AZ	85374-5851	623-975-2646	975-2841	K-8	Allison Gonzales
Paradise Honors HS	12775 N 175th Ave	Surprise, AZ	85388	623-546-7200	975-4380	9-12	Jessica Alessio
Paragon Science Academy	2975 W Linda Ln	Chandler, AZ	85224	480-814-1600	814-1661	K-12	Selim Tanyeri M.Ed.
Paramount Academy	11039 W Olive Ave	Peoria, AZ	85345-9200	623-977-0614	977-0615	K-8	Ron Painter
Park View MS	9030 E Florentine Rd	Prescott Valley, AZ	86314	928-775-5115	775-6253	6-8	Sean Anderson
Patagonia Montessori S	PO Box 628	Patagonia, AZ	85624	520-394-9530	394-2864	PK-8	Jessi Beebe
Pathfinder Academy	2906 N Boulder Canyon	Mesa, AZ	85207-1066	480-986-7071	986-9858	K-8	Susan Stradling
Pathways in Education	2226 N 7th St	Phoenix, AZ	85006	602-626-7057		9-12	George Barnes
Patriot Academy	19023 E San Tan Blvd	Queen Creek, AZ	85142	480-279-4780	807-1209	K-8	Jay Brown
Paulden Community S	24850 N Naples St	Paulden, AZ	86334	928-636-1430	636-3087	K-8	James Sexton
Peak S	2016 N 1st St Ste A	Flagstaff, AZ	86004-4241	928-779-0771	779-0774	K-8	Paula Drossman
Pensar Academy	6135 N Black Canyon Hwy	Phoenix, AZ	85015	602-383-4013	858-2737	4-8	Sandra Zupetz
Peoria Accelerated HS	8885 W Peoria Ave	Peoria, AZ	85345-6442	623-979-0031	979-0113	9-12	Amanda Bachler
Performing Arts HS	25 E Drachman St	Tucson, AZ	85705	520-917-7880		9-12	April Rubasch
Phoenix Advantage Charter S	3738 N 16th St	Phoenix, AZ	85016-5915	602-263-8777		K-8	Leanne Bowley
Phoenix College Prep Academy	3310 N 10th Ave	Phoenix, AZ	85013	602-285-7998	285-7697	9-12	Keith Brown
Phoenix Collegiate Academy	5610 S Central Ave	Phoenix, AZ	85040	602-551-6594	268-9911	5-8	Thai Nguyen
Phoenix Collegiate Academy	40 E Hidalgo Ave	Phoenix, AZ	85040	602-492-1722	535-8861	K-4	Kristine Morris
Phoenix Collegiate Academy	4445 S 12th St	Phoenix, AZ	85040	602-842-1722	441-0570	9-12	Rebecca Halada
Phoenix School of Academic Excellence	5308 N 12th St	Phoenix, AZ	85014	602-241-7876	424-0281	7-12	Julie Palma
Pillar Academy of Business & Finance	8433 N Black Canyon Hwy	Phoenix, AZ	85021	602-920-8253		9-12	
Pima Partnership S	1346 N Stone Ave	Tucson, AZ	85705-7338	520-326-2528	326-2527	6-12	Ian Kidd
Pima Rose Academy	1690 W Irvington Rd	Tucson, AZ	85746	520-797-4884	797-8868	9-12	Joanne Vigilant
Pima Vocational HS	175 W Irvington Rd	Tucson, AZ	85714	520-724-9740		9-12	
Pima Vocational HS	5025 W Ina Rd	Tucson, AZ	85743	520-724-9400		9-12	
Pine Forest Charter S	2257 E Cedar Ave	Flagstaff, AZ	86004	928-779-9880	779-9792	K-8	Kelly Smith
Pinnacle HS - Casa Grande	2510 N Trekell Rd	Casa Grande, AZ	85122	520-423-2380	423-2383	9-12	Molly Ryan-Smith
Pinnacle HS - Mesa	151 N Centennial Way	Mesa, AZ	85201-6734	480-233-3362	785-7778	9-12	
Pinnacle HS - Nogales	2055 N Grand Ave	Nogales, AZ	85621-1038	520-281-5109	281-5132	9-12	
Pinnacle HS - Tempe E	810 S Alma School Rd Ste 4	Mesa, AZ	85210	480-668-5003	668-5005	9-12	
Pinnacle HS - Tempe W	2224 W Southern Ave Ste 1	Tempe, AZ	85282	480-755-8222	755-8223	9-12	
Pinnacle Peak Preparatory S	7690 E Williams Dr	Scottsdale, AZ	85255-4801	602-449-6700	449-6705	K-7	Lora Herbein
Pinnacle Pointe Academy	6753 W Pinnacle Peak Rd	Glendale, AZ	85310-5301	623-537-3535	537-4433	K-6	Dawn Adams
Pinnacle Virtual HS	2224 W Southern Ave Ste 1	Tempe, AZ	85282	480-755-8222	755-8223	6-12	Beth Cirulis
Pioneer Preparatory S	6510 W Clarendon Ave	Phoenix, AZ	85033	623-933-3733	252-0022	K-6	Tony Best
Polytechnic STEM Academy	6950 E Williams Field Rd	Mesa, AZ	85212	480-727-5700	727-5701	K-8	Claudia Mendoza
PPEP TEC - Chavez Learning Center	PO Box 6779	San Luis, AZ	85349	928-627-8550	627-8980	9-12	Angelica Sanchez
PPEP TEC - Fernandez Learning Center	1840 E Benson Hwy	Tucson, AZ	85714-1770	520-889-8276	616-0176	9-12	
PPEP TEC - Paul Learning Center	409 W McMurray Blvd	Casa Grande, AZ	85122	520-836-6549	836-0290	9-12	
PPEP TEC - Powell Learning Center	4116 Avenida Cochise Ste F	Sierra Vista, AZ	85635-5843	520-458-8205	458-8293	9-12	
PPEP TEC - Raul H. Castro Learning Ctr	1122 N G Ave	Douglas, AZ	85607	520-364-4405	364-1405	9-12	Raul Torrez
PPEP TEC - Yepez Learning Center	201 N Bingham Ave	Somerton, AZ	85350	928-627-9648	627-9197	9-12	
Precision Academy	7318 W Lynwood St	Phoenix, AZ	85035-4542	623-936-8682	936-8559	9-12	Dr. Caroline White
Premier Charter HS	7544 W Indian School Rd	Phoenix, AZ	85033-3030	623-245-1500	245-1506	9-12	Debbie Petersen
Prescott Valley S	PO Box 27348	Prescott Valley, AZ	86312	928-772-8744	775-4457	K-12	Monika Fuller
Presidio S	1695 E Fort Lowell Rd	Tucson, AZ	85719-2319	520-881-5222	881-5522	K-12	Dr. Mark Saliba
Primavera Online HS	2471 N Arizona Ave Ste 1	Chandler, AZ	85225	480-456-6678	355-2100	7-12	Donald Mitchell
Pueblo Del Sol ES	3555 E Fry Blvd	Sierra Vista, AZ	85635-2972	520-515-2970	515-2973	K-6	Dr. Christine Tucker
Quail Run ES	3303 E Utopia Rd	Phoenix, AZ	85050-3900	602-449-4400	449-4405	K-6	Marta Maynard
Quest HS	217 E Olympic Dr	Phoenix, AZ	85042	602-243-8496	276-5244	9-12	Michael Johnson
RCB College Preparatory Academy	7033 W Cactus Rd	Peoria, AZ	85381	623-500-2853		9-12	
RCB Medical Arts Academy	6049 N 43rd Ave	Phoenix, AZ	85019-1641	602-973-6018	589-1349	7-12	Russel Sperati
Reyes Maria Ruiz Leadership Academy	4848 S 2nd St	Phoenix, AZ	85040	602-243-7788	243-7799	K-6	Armando Ruiz
Ridgeline Academy	33625 N North Valley Pkwy	Phoenix, AZ	85085	623-223-1335	488-2079	K-8	Keven Barker
Rincon Vista MS	10770 E Bilby Rd	Tucson, AZ	85747	520-879-3200	879-3201	6-8	Cristela Cardenas
Rising S	7444 E Broadway Blvd	Tucson, AZ	85710	520-730-2657		6-12	George Rising Ph.D.
Riverbend Preparatory S	5625 S 51st Ave	Laveen, AZ	85339	602-285-3003	285-5560	K-8	John Paquin
Royal Palm MS	8520 N 19th Ave	Phoenix, AZ	85021-4293	602-347-3200	347-3220	6-8	Will Ambos
RSD HS - Blended Learning Academy	13615 N 35th Ave	Phoenix, AZ	85029	602-993-5225	993-0506	9-12	
SABIS International	1903 E Roeser Rd	Phoenix, AZ	85040-3341	602-305-8865	323-5526	K-8	Will Henry
Saddleback ES	44150 W Maricopa Casa Grand	Maricopa, AZ	85138	520-568-6110	568-6119	PK-5	Felicia Williams
Sage Academy	1055 E Hearn Rd	Scottsdale, AZ	85254	602-485-3402		K-8	Neilee Weber
Sandpiper ES	6724 E Hearn Rd	Scottsdale, AZ	85254-3332	602-449-6300	449-6305	K-6	Diana Cameron
San Pedro Valley HS	360 S Patagonia St	Benson, AZ	85602	520 720 6726	720-6702	9-12	Shannon Sherman
Santa Cruz ES	44150 W Maricopa Casa Grand	Maricopa, AZ	85138	520-568-5170	568-5176	K-5	Dr. Loraine Conley
San Tan Charter S	3959 E Elliot Rd	Gilbert, AZ	85234	480-222-0811	471-5990	PK-12	Dr. Kristofer Sippel
Santa Rosa ES	44150 W Maricopa Casa Grand	Maricopa, AZ	85138	520-568-6152	568-6155	K-5	Eva Safranek

School	Address	City,State	Zip code	Telephone	Fax	Grade	Contact
Satori Charter S	3727 N 1st Ave	Tucson, AZ	85719-1609	520-293-7555	293-7020	2-8	Jesse Ramos
Scottsdale Country Day S	10460 N 56th St	Scottsdale, AZ	85253	480-452-5777		K-8	Steve Prahcharov
Scottsdale Preparatory Academy	16537 N 92nd St	Scottsdale, AZ	85260	480-776-1970	776-1975	5-12	Alison Chaney
Sedona Charter S	165 Kachina Dr	Sedona, AZ	86336-4303	928-204-6464	204-6486	K-8	Alice Madar
Self Development Charter S	1515 E Indian School Rd	Phoenix, AZ	85014	602-274-1910		K-8	
Self Development Charter S	1709 N Greenfield Rd	Mesa, AZ	85205-3103	480-641-2640	641-2678	K-8	
Sequoia Charter ES	1460 S Horne	Mesa, AZ	85204	480-890-4002	890-4107	K-6	Altrena Anderson
Sequoia Charter Secondary S	1460 S Horne	Mesa, AZ	85204-5760	480-649-7737	649-0711	9-12	Jevon Lewis
Sequoia Choice Precision S	3906 E Broadway Rd	Phoenix, AZ	85040-2996	602-453-3661	453-3669	9-12	Jaime Tejada
Sequoia Choice S - AZ Distance Learning	2331 N Horne	Mesa, AZ	85203	480-461-3222	890-4106	K-12	Cindy Chleborad
Sequoia Deaf S	1460 S Horne	Mesa, AZ	85204-5760	480-890-4001	890-4113	K-12	Heather Laine
Sequoia Lehi ES	2331 N Horne	Mesa, AZ	85203	480-397-9890	397-4003	PK-6	Matthew Metcalf
Sequoia Pathfinder Academy	4816 S Eastmark Pkwy	Mesa, AZ	85212	480-351-8070	351-8407	K-8	Sue Paschal
Sequoia Pathway Academy	19265 N Porter Rd	Maricopa, AZ	85138	520-568-2112	505-3665	K-12	Dr. Alfonso Alva
Sequoia Village S	982 Full House Ln	Show Low, AZ	85901	928-537-1208	537-4275	K-12	Mindy Savoia M.Ed.
Shelby S	249 W Standage Dr	Payson, AZ	85541	928-478-4706	478-0681	K-10	Ezra Stuyvesant
Sky Islands S	6000 E 14th St	Tucson, AZ	85711	520-382-9210	382-5888	9-12	Dr. Shari Popen
Skyline District 5 S	PO Box 10858	Bapchule, AZ	85121-0104	520-315-3236	315-3233	5-12	Vaughn Flannigan
Skyline Prep HS	7500 S 40th St	Phoenix, AZ	85042	602-343-4980	343-4996	9-12	Tonya Bridges-Brown M.A.
Skyview HS	4290 S Miller Rd	Buckeye, AZ	85326	623-386-6799	327-9636	9-12	Danielle Calderon
Skyview S	125 S Rush St	Prescott, AZ	86303-4432	928-776-1730	776-1742	K-8	Scott McCreery
Sonoran Desert S	6724 S Kings Ranch Rd	Gold Canyon, AZ	85118	480-396-5463	396-4980	5-12	Patricia Dalman
Sonoran Science Academy - Broadway	6880 E Broadway Blvd	Tucson, AZ	85710	520-751-2401	751-2451	K-8	Erdal Kocak
Sonoran Science Academy - Davis Monthan	5741 E Ironwood St	Tucson, AZ	85708	520-300-5699	207-7698	6-12	Peggy Fontenot M.Ed.
Sonoran Science Academy - Peoria	17667 N 91st Ave	Peoria, AZ	85382	623-776-9344	933-8001	K-8	Deb Hofmeier
Sonoran Science Academy - Phoenix	4837 E McDowell Rd	Phoenix, AZ	85008-4225	602-244-9855	244-9856	K-12	Jim Satterlee
Sonoran Science Academy - Tucson	2325 W Sunset Rd	Tucson, AZ	85741-3809	520-665-3400	665-3420	K-12	Dr. Adnan Doyuran Ph.D.
Sonoran Sky ES	12990 N 75th St	Scottsdale, AZ	85260-4746	602-449-6500	449-6505	PK-6	Robert Dawson
Southern Arizona Community Academy	2470 N Tucson Blvd	Tucson, AZ	85716-2469	520-319-6113	319-6115	9-12	Abelardo Cubillas
Southgate Academy	7842 E Wrightstown Rd	Tucson, AZ	85715	520-741-7900	741-7901	K-12	Delia McCraley
South Phoenix Prep and Arts School	7450 S 40th St	Phoenix, AZ	85042	877-225-8711		PK-4	Jessica Carlstson M.Ed.
South Pointe Charter ES	2033 E Southern Ave	Phoenix, AZ	85040	602-276-1943	276-2726	K-6	Delores Jones-Bell
South Pointe HS	8325 S Central Ave	Phoenix, AZ	85042-6576	602-243-0600	243-0800	9-12	Larry McGill
South Pointe JHS	217 E Olympic Dr	Phoenix, AZ	85042	602-243-8496	276-5244	6-8	Melissa Barnett
South Ridge HS	1122 S 67th Ave	Phoenix, AZ	85043-4417	623-247-0106	247-0527	9-12	Jim Sigman
Southside Community S	2701 S Campbell Ave	Tucson, AZ	85713-5080	520-623-7102	623-7125	K-9	Laura LaFave
South Valley Prep and Arts Academy	7500 S 40th St	Phoenix, AZ	85042	877-225-2118	437-2901	5-8	Tasha Gant M.Ed.
South Verde Technology Magnet S	462 S Main St	Camp Verde, AZ	86322	928-567-8076	567-8093	9-12	Marie Zawel
Southwest Leadership Academy	4301 W Fillmore St	Phoenix, AZ	85043	602-265-2000		9-12	Dr. Gregory Fowler
STAR S	145 Leupp Rd	Flagstaff, AZ	86004-8501	928-415-4157	225-2179	K-8	Dr. Mark Sorenson
StarShine Academy Creative Community	3535 E McDowell Rd	Phoenix, AZ	85008	602-957-9557	956-0065	K-12	Todd Peapenburg
Stepping Stones Academy	35812 N 7th St	Phoenix, AZ	85086-7410	623-465-4910	587-8514	PK-8	Dedre Stewart-Alliger
Step Up S	44 E 5th St	Mesa, AZ	85201	480-344-2600	850-0004	K-8	Diane Fernichio
Student Choice HS	1833 N Scottsdale Rd	Tempe, AZ	85281-1563	480-947-9511	947-9624	9-12	Peggy Lynam
Student Choice HS - Peoria	8194 W Deer Valley Rd	Peoria, AZ	85382	623-242-2722	566-1634	9-12	Joy McCain
Summit HS	728 E McDowell Rd	Phoenix, AZ	85006	602-258-8959	258-8953	9-12	James Sigman
Sun Valley Charter S	5806 S 35th Ave	Phoenix, AZ	85041	602-692-4914	276-6298	K-6	Tanae Morrison M.Ed.
Sun Valley HS	1143 S Lindsay Rd	Mesa, AZ	85204-6298	480-497-4800	497-1314	9-12	Telleny Gilliam
Sweetwater S	4602 W Sweetwater Ave	Glendale, AZ	85304-1505	602-896-6500	896-6520	K-8	Luanne Herman
SySTEM Phoenix	1301 E Almeria Rd	Phoenix, AZ	85006	602-710-1873	714-5068	6-12	Angelica Cruz
Taylion Virtual Academy	4744 W Grovers Ave	Glendale, AZ	85308-3453	623-688-2296	889-7806	9-12	Paul Dahl
Teleos Preparatory Academy	1401 E Jefferson St	Phoenix, AZ	85034	602-275-5455	275-5954	K-8	Christina Lucas
Telesis Preparatory Academy	2598 Starlite Ln	Lk Havasu Cty, AZ	86403-4946	928-855-8661	855-9302	K-12	Sandra Breece Ed.D.
Tempe Preparatory Academy	1251 E Southern Ave	Tempe, AZ	85282-5605	480-839-3402	755-0546	6-12	Dr. Wayne Porter
Toltecali Academy	251 W Irvington Rd	Tucson, AZ	85714	520-882-3029	882-3041	9-12	Lori Mejia
Tri-City College Prep HS	5522 Side Rd	Prescott, AZ	86301-8483	928-777-0403	777-0402	9-12	Keri Milliken
Triumphant Learning Center	201 E Main St	Safford, AZ	85546-2051	928-348-8422	348-8423	K-8	Robin Dutt
Trivium Preparatory Academy	2001 N Bullard Ave	Goodyear, AZ	85395	623-866-4730	866-4729	6-12	Heidi Vasiloff
Tucson Collegiate Prep	40 W Fort Lowell Rd	Tucson, AZ	85705	520-870-1670		6-8	Steve Campbell
Tucson Country Day S	9239 E Wrightstown Rd	Tucson, AZ	85715-5514	520-296-0883	290-1521	K-8	Adrian Hannah
Tucson International Academy - Broadway	2700 W Broadway Blvd	Tucson, AZ	85745	520-792-3255	792-3245	K-12	Mike Montemayor
Tucson International Academy East Tucson	2700 W Broadway Blvd	Tucson, AZ	85745	520-792-3255	792-3245	K-12	Peter Meehan
Tucson International Academy - Midvale	2700 W Broadway Blvd	Tucson, AZ	85745	520-792-3255	792-3245	K-12	Valerie Enriquez
Tucson International Academy West Tucson	2700 W Broadway Blvd	Tucson, AZ	85745	520-792-3255	792-3245	K-12	Valerie Enriquez
Tucson Preparatory S	104 E Prince Rd	Tucson, AZ	85705	520-622-4185	622-4755	9-12	Jody Sullivan
Vail Academy and HS	7762 E Science Park Dr	Tucson, AZ	85747	520-879-1900	879-1901	K-12	Dennis Barger
Valiant Academy	3738 N 16th St	Phoenix, AZ	85016	480-529-5533		9-12	Justin Schmitt
Valley Academy	1520 W Rose Garden Ln	Phoenix, AZ	85027-3529	623-516-7747	516-2703	PK-8	Victoria Wilber M.Ed.
Valley Preparatory Academy	2150 E Southern Ave	Tempe, AZ	85282	480-621-5382	621-3383	9-12	Jon Owen
Val Vista Academy	4120 S Val Vista Dr	Gilbert, AZ	85297	480-656-5555	689-5952	K-8	Debbie Baca
Vector Prep and Arts Academy	2020 N Arizona Ave	Chandler, AZ	85225	480-779-2000	779-2100	K-6	Deborah Coleman M.Ed.
Verde Valley Montessori Charter S	PO Box 2678	Cottonwood, AZ	86326	928-634-3288	634-9781	PK-8	Maryann Green
Veritas Preparatory Academy	3102 N 56th St Ste 100	Phoenix, AZ	85018	602-263-1128	263-7997	6-12	David Dean
Victory Collegiate Academy	3535 N 63rd Ave	Phoenix, AZ	85033	623-810-9781		K-6	Nick Schuerman
Victory HS	PO Box 8374	Phoenix, AZ	85066-8374	602-243-7583	243-7563	9-12	Dr. Shirley Branham
Villa Montessori - Phoenix	2802 E Meadowbrook Ave	Phoenix, AZ	85016	602-955-2210	957-4017	K-8	Margo O'Neill
Vision Charter S	5901 S Santa Cruz Calle	Tucson, AZ	85709-0001	520-741-8419	741-8123	9-12	Dr. Wilma Soroosh
Vista College Prep	4520 W McDowell Rd	Phoenix, AZ	85035	623-601-7069		K-5	Sarah Mertz
Vista College Preparatory S	812 S 6th Ave	Phoenix, AZ	85003	602-374-7159	374-8201	K-5	Julia Meyerson
Vista Grove Preparatory Academy	2929 E McKellips Rd	Mesa, AZ	85213	480-924-1500	924-0552	K-8	Abelardo Batista
Washington Academy	1945 S 1st St E	Snowflake, AZ	85937	928-440-6228		K-8	D. Benson Wallace
Webster Basic S	5399 N Pima Rd	Scottsdale, AZ	85250	480-291-6900	291-6901	K-6	Heidi Simms
Webster Basic S	7301 E Baseline Rd	Mesa, AZ	85209-4907	480-986-2335	373-9176	PK-6	Jessica Friedermann
Western S of Science and Technology	6515 W Indian School Rd	Phoenix, AZ	85033	623-249-3900	243-9030	7-12	Charles Kaplan
Westland S	4141 N 67th Ave	Phoenix, AZ	85033-3314	623-247-6456	247-6520	K-12	Kathryn Couch
West Phoenix HS	3835 W Thomas Rd	Phoenix, AZ	85019-4434	602-269-1110	269-1112	9-12	Alex Horton
Whispering Wind Academy	15844 N 43rd St	Phoenix, AZ	85032-4124	602-449-7300	449-7305	K-6	Johnny Brownlie
Willow Creek Charter S	2100 Willow Creek Rd	Prescott, AZ	86301-5391	928-776-1212	776-0009	K-8	Terese Soto
Young Scholars Academy	1501 E Valencia Rd	Bullhead City, AZ	86426	928-704-1100	704-1177	K-8	Tonnie Smith
YouthWorks Charter HS	1915 E 36th St	Tucson, AZ	85713	520-495-4113	628-2820	9-12	Kelvin Strozier
Arkansas							
Academic Center of Excellence	21 Funtastic Dr	Cabot, AR	72023-6005	501-743-3520	843-0283	7-12	Michele Evans
Arkansas Arts Academy	1110 W Poplar St	Rogers, AR	72756	479-636-2272	636-5447	K-8	Matt Young
Arkansas Arts Academy	1110 W Poplar St	Rogers, AR	72756	479-631-2787	899-6479	9-12	Barbara Padgett
Arkansas Connections Academy	1009 Beau Terre Dr	Bentonville, AR	72712	501-386-3419		K-12	
Arkansas Virtual Academy	4702 W Commercial Dr Ste B3	No Little Rock, AR	72116	501-664-4225	664-4226	K-12	Dr. Scott Sides
Brunson New Vision Charter S	PO Box 1210	Warren, AR	71671-1210	870-226-2351	226-8541	4-5	Regina Scroggins
Capital City Lighthouse Charter S	3901 Virginia Dr	No Little Rock, AR	72118	501-313-2901	313-2910	K-6	Eric Dailey
Cloverdale Magnet MS	6300 Hinkson Rd	Little Rock, AR	72209-4712	501-447-2500	447-2501	6-8	Wanda Ruffins
Covenant Keepers Charter S	5615 Geyer Springs Rd	Little Rock, AR	72209-1812	501-682-7550	682-7577	6-8	Dr. Valerie Tatum
Cross County Elementary Technology Acad	2622 Highway 42	Cherry Valley, AR	72324-8674	870-588-3337	588-4454	K-6	Mindy Searcy
Cross County HS A New Tech S	21 County Road 215	Cherry Valley, AR	72324-8957	870-588-3337	588-4606	7-12	Stephen Prince
Eastside New Vision Charter S	PO Box 1210	Warren, AR	71671-1210	870-226-6761	226-8538	K-3	Sara Weaver
eStem Public Charter ES	112 W 3rd St	Little Rock, AR	72201	501-748-9200	975-4092	K-6	Jessi Forster
eStem Public Charter HS	2801 S University Dr	Little Rock, AR	72204	501-478-2800	748-9370	10-12	Johnecia Howard
eStem Public Charter JHS	123 W 3rd St	Little Rock, AR	72201	501-748-1347	975-4092	7-9	Jarrod DuPriest
Exalt Academy Of Southwest Little Rock	6111 W 83rd St	Little Rock, AR	72209	501-568-3279	568-3286	K-4	Terri Guy
Farmington Career Academies	12329 N Highway 170	Farmington, AR	72730	479-266-1860	267-6065	10-12	Jon Purifoy
Flightline Upper Academy	1030 Cannon Dr	No Little Rock, AR	72114	501-988-1085	988-1090	5-8	Evan McGrew
Forrest City College Preparatory	637 S Washington St	Forrest City, AR	72335	870-667-6766	633-0602	5-8	Kenisha Hawthorne
Future S of Fort Smith	622 N 7th St	Fort Smith, AR	72901	479-431-8695	424-2623	9-12	Mitchel Logan
Haas Hall Academy	2600 SE J St	Bentonville, AR	72712	479-268-3424	250-9292	7-12	Dr. Rod Wittenberg
Haas Hall Academy	3880 N Front St	Fayetteville, AR	72703-5130	479-966-4930	966-4932	7-12	Dr. Martin Schoppmeyer
Hope Academy of Public Services	601 W 6th St	Hope, AR	71801	870-777-3454		5-8	Carol Duke
Imboden Area Charter S	PO Box 297	Imboden, AR	72434-0297	870-869-3015	869-3016	K-8	Judy Warren
Jacksonville Lighthouse Charter S	251 N 1st St	Jacksonville, AR	72076	501-985-1200	985-1201	K-6	Adriane Smith
Jacksonville Lighthouse Coll Prep Acad	251 N 1st St	Jacksonville, AR	72076	501-985-1228	985-1233	7-12	Ralph Cosio
Jacksonville Lighthouse Flightline S	Bldg 1030 Cannon Dr	Jacksonville, AR	72099	501-988-1085	988-1090	5-8	Evan McGrew
KIPP Blytheville College Preparatory S	1124 Moultrie Dr	Blytheville, AR	72315	870-776-8833	762-7763	4-8	Alice Goldsberry
KIPP Blytheville Collegiate HS	1200 Byrum Rd	Blytheville, AR	72315-8119	870-780-6333	780-6310	9-12	Maisie Wright
KIPP Delta College Preparatory S	514 Missouri	Helena, AR	72342-3751	870-753-9444	753-9450	5-8	Heather Johnson
KIPP Delta Collegiate High School	320 Missouri	Helena, AR	72342-3709	870-338-8138	338-8623	9-12	Stephanie Bennetts
KIPP Delta Elementary Literacy Academy	215 Cherry St	Helena, AR	72342	870-753-9800	753-9801	K-4	Todd Dixon
Lisa Academy	21 Corporate Hill Dr	Little Rock, AR	72205-4537	501-227-4942	227-4952	6-12	Ilker Fidan
Lisa Academy Chenal	12200 Westhaven Dr	Little Rock, AR	72211	501-476-3309	476-3310	K-6	

School	Address	City,State	Zip code	Telephone	Fax	Grade	Contact
Lisa Academy-North Little Rock	5410 Landers Rd	No Little Rock, AR	72117-1935	501-945-2727	945-2728	K-12	Fatih Bogrek
Little Rock Prep Academy	6711 W Markham St	Little Rock, AR	72205	501-683-1855	683-1847	5-8	Anitra Rogers
Little Rock Prep Academy	1616 Spring St	Little Rock, AR	72205	501-683-1855	683-1847	K-4	
Maumelle Charter ES	900 Edgewood Dr	Maumelle, AR	72113	501-803-0666	803-9748	K-6	Paula Newton
Maumelle Charter HS	600 Edgewood Dr	Maumelle, AR	72113	501-851-3333	851-2599	6-12	Kimberly Willis
Miner Academy	800 School St	Bauxite, AR	72011-9143	501-557-5453	557-2235	6-12	Joshua Harrison
Northwest Arkansas Classical Academy	1302 Melissa Dr Ste 100	Bentonville, AR	72712	479-715-6676	821-7385	K-8	Susan Provenza
Osceola STEM Academy	112 N School St	Osceola, AR	72370-2413	870-563-2150	622-1025	5-8	Christel Smith
Ozark Montessori Academy	301 S Holcomb St	Springdale, AR	72764	479-935-9992	439-9235	K-8	Thomas Gourd
Pea Ridge Manufacturing & Business Acad	781 W Pickens Rd	Pea Ridge, AR	72751	800-451-1241	431-6332	11-12	Charley Clark
Pine Bluff Lighthouse Charter S	708 W 2nd Ave	Pine Bluff, AR	71601	870-534-0277	534-0263	K-8	Renea Smith
Premier HS of Little Rock	1621 Dr Martin Luther King	Little Rock, AR	72202-6068	501-246-3161	677-0271	9-12	Mia Meadows
Quest MS of Pine Bluff	308 S Blake St	Pine Bluff, AR	71601-3622	870-536-1009		5-8	Arnold Robertson
Quest MS of West Little Rock	1815 Rahling Rd	Little Rock, AR	72223	501-821-0382	437-0487	6-8	Dave Bobbitt
Rockbridge Montessori Charter S	108 W Roosevelt Rd	Little Rock, AR	72206-2246	501-404-9549	508-5740	K-8	Shannon Nuckols
Scott Charter S	15306 Alexander Rd	Scott, AR	72142-9781	501-961-1744		K-6	
SIATech Little Rock	6724 Interstate 30	Little Rock, AR	72209-3157	501-562-0039	562-7671	9-12	Katie Tatum
Warren HS A Conversion Charter S	PO Box 1210	Warren, AR	71671-1210	870-226-6736	226-8527	9-12	Bryan Cornish
Warren MS A Conversion Charter S	PO Box 1210	Warren, AR	71671-1210	870-226-2484	226-8511	6-8	Kathryn Cornish
Washington Academy Charter S	3512 Grand Ave	Texarkana, AR	71854-2232	870-772-4792	774-2185	7-12	Terry Taylor
California							
Abraxis Charter HS	PO Box 2587	Santa Rosa, CA	95405-0587	707-539-2897	539-2778	9-12	Christopher Paige
Academia Avance Charter S	PO Box 42095	Los Angeles, CA	90042-0095	323-230-7270	652-0994	6-12	Ricardo Mireles
Academia Moderna	2410 Broadway	Walnut Park, CA	90255-6342	323-923-0383	923-0380	K-5	Carrie Checca
Academies of the Antelope Valley	6300 W Avenue L	Lancaster, CA	93536	661-943-3031		7-12	Stephen Ford
Academy for Academic Excellence	17500 Mana Rd	Apple Valley, CA	92307-2181	760-946-5414	242-6398	K-12	Lisa Lamb
Academy of Alameda ES	401 Pacific Ave	Alameda, CA	94501	510-748-4017	523-5304	K-2	Nora Bullock
Academy of Alameda MS	401 Pacific Ave	Alameda, CA	94501-1837	510-214-2460	523-5801	6-8	Matt Huxley
Academy of Business Law & Education	6515 Inglewood Ave	Stockton, CA	95207-3871	209-478-1600	235-2986	9-12	Matthew George
Academy of Careers & Exploration	PO Box 249	Helendale, CA	92342-0249	760-952-2396	952-1178	7-12	Chet Richards
Accelerated Achievement Academy	1059 N State St	Ukiah, CA	95482-3413	707-463-7080	463-7085	4-12	Selah Sawyer
Accelerated Charter ES	3914 S Main St	Los Angeles, CA	90011	323-846-6694	846-0686	K-6	Susan Raudry
Accelerated Charter HS	4136 N Mooney Blvd	Tulare, CA	93274	559-688-2021	687-7317	9-12	Wendi Powell
Accelerated S	4000 S Main St	Los Angeles, CA	90037-1022	323-235-6343	235-6346	K-8	Francis Reading
ACE Charter HS	1776 Educational Park Dr	San Jose, CA	95133-1703	408-251-1362	251-1366	9-12	Keyur Shah
ACE Charter HS	570 Airport Way	Camarillo, CA	93010-8500	805-437-1410	437-1491	9-12	Joseph Clausi
ACE Charter S	1665 Santee Dr	San Jose, CA	95122	408-426-6361		5-7	Cesar Torrico
ACE I Empower Academy	625 S Sunset Ave	San Jose, CA	95116	408-729-3920		5-8	Greg Lippman
ACE Inspire Axademy	1155 E Julian St	San Jose, CA	95112	408-295-6008	295-3584	5-8	Raymond Andrade
Achieve Academy	1700 28th Ave	Oakland, CA	94601	510-904-6440	904-6771	4-5	Shawna Myers
Achieve Charter S of Paradise	771 Elliott Rd	Paradise, CA	95969-3913	530-872-4100	872-4105	K-8	Casey Taylor
Adams Academy	4250 Town Center Blvd	El Dorado Hills, CA	95762	916-260-4800		K-12	Jordan Zacharia
Adams Academy	1 Sierra Gate Plz	Roseville, CA	95678	916-780-6800	888-1343	K-12	Heather Brown
Adams Academy - Lincoln	280 Oak Tree Ln	Lincoln, CA	95648	916-209-5540		K-6	Heather Brown
Adelante Charter S of Santa Barbara	1102 E Yanonali St	Santa Barbara, CA	93103	805-966-7392	966-7243	PK-6	David Bautista
Advanced Learning Academy	335 E Walnut St	Santa Ana, CA	92701-5928	714-480-4300	480-4399	K-8	Kimberly Garcia
Alameda Community Learning Center	1900 3rd St	Alameda, CA	94501-1851	510-521-7123	521-7350	6-12	Patti Wilczek
Alder Grove Charter S	714 F St	Eureka, CA	95501-1036	707-268-0854	268-0813	K-12	Tim Warner
Alexander Science Center	3737 S Figueroa St	Los Angeles, CA	90007-4366	213-746-1995	746-7443	K-5	Norma Spencer
Alianza Charter S	115 Casserly Rd	Watsonville, CA	95076-8645	831-728-6333	728-6947	K-8	Rafael Ramirez
Alliance 6-12 College Ready Academy	11933 Allegheny St	Sun Valley, CA	91352	747-223-2649		6-12	Jonathan Tiongco
Alliance Alice Baxter College-Ready HS	461 W 9th St	San Pedro, CA	90731-3211	310-221-0430		9-12	Robert Canosa Carr
Alliance Bloomfield Technology HS	7907 Santa Fe Ave	Huntington Park, CA	90255-6630	323-537-2060	537-2044	9-12	Ani Meymerian
Alliance College-Ready Middle Academy 12	100 E 49th St	Los Angeles, CA	90011	323-238-7270		6-8	Robin Manly
Alliance College-Ready Middle Academy 8	113 S Rowan Ave	Los Angeles, CA	90063	323-269-2156		6-8	Melissa Chew
Alliance College-Ready Middle Academy 9	5006 Compton Ave	Los Angeles, CA	90001-1345	323-484-0450		6-8	Omar Reyes
Alliance Collins Family College-Ready HS	2071 Saturn Ave	Huntington Park, CA	90255-3635	323-923-1588	923-1589	9-12	Robert Delfino
Alliance Gertz-Ressler HS	2023 S Union Ave	Los Angeles, CA	90007-1326	213-745-8141	745-8142	9-12	Stephanie Tsai
Alliance Health Services Academy HS	10616 S Western Ave	Los Angeles, CA	90047	323-972-9010	905-1578	9-12	Carla McCullough
Alliance Leadership Middle Academy	2941 W 70th St	Los Angeles, CA	90043-4420	323-920-4388		6-8	Joy May-Harris
Alliance Morgan McKinzie HS	110 S Townsend Ave	Los Angeles, CA	90063	323-526-8198	526-8438	9-12	Arthur Sanchez
Alliance Neuwirth Leadership Academy	4610 S Main St	Los Angeles, CA	90037-2736	323-342-2874	342-2875	9-12	Miguel Gamboa
Alliance Ouchi-O'Donovan 6-12 Complex	5356 5th Ave	Los Angeles, CA	90043-2622	323-596-2290	596-2295	6-12	Doa Tramblo
Alliance Ted Tajima HS	1552 W Rockwood St	Los Angeles, CA	90026	213-241-8533	943-4931	9-12	Carmen Vazquez-Mancini
All Tribes American Indian Charter S	PO Box 1432	Valley Center, CA	92082-1432	760-749-5982	749-4153	PK-12	Mary Ann Donohue
Almond Acres Charter Academy	1601 L St	San Miguel, CA	93451-9107	805-467-2095	467-2098	K-8	Bob Bourgault
Alpha: Cindy Avitia HS	1881 Cunningham Ave	San Jose, CA	95122-1712	408-758-1195	791-1558	9-10	Will Eden
Alpha: Jose Hernandez MS	1601 Cunningham Ave	San Jose, CA	95122	408-780-1551		6-8	Samantha Hanlon
Alpha Charter S	7900 Eloise Ave	Elverta, CA	95626-9217	916-991-2244	991-0271	9-12	Michael Borgaard
Alpha I Blanca Alvarado MS	1601 Cunningham Ave	San Jose, CA	95122	408-780-0831		6-7	John Glover
Alta Vista Community Charter S	173 Oak St	Auburn, CA	95603	530-885-7067	885-7066	PK-5	Camille Taylor
Alternatives in Action	6221 E 17th St	Oakland, CA	94621	510-285-6290	285-6294	9-12	Patricia Murillo
Alvarado Academy	26247 Ellis St	Madera, CA	93638-0813	559-675-2070	675-2074	K-8	Dr. Nicolas Retana
Alvina Charter ES	295 W Saginaw Ave	Caruthers, CA	93609-9710	559-864-9411	864-1808	K-8	Mike Iribarren
Ambassador Sanchez Charter S	5659 E Kings Canyon Rd	Fresno, CA	93727-4641	559-470-8222		9-12	David Petropulos
American Indian Charter HS	746 Grand Ave	Oakland, CA	94607	510-482-6000	482-6002	9-12	Tareyton Russ
American Indian Charter S II	171 12th St	Oakland, CA	94607-4900	510-893-8701	893-0345	K-8	Peter Holmquist
American River Charter S	6620 Wentworth Springs Rd	Georgetown, CA	95634	530-333-8340	333-8346	K-12	Sally Dyck
Americas Finest Charter S	730 45th St	San Diego, CA	92102-3619	619-694-4790	794-2762	K-8	Jan Perry
Anahuacalmecac Intl University Prep S	4736 Huntington Dr S	Los Angeles, CA	90032-1942	323-352-3148	352-8758	K-12	
Anderson New Technology HS	2098 North St	Anderson, CA	96007-3477	530-365-3100	365-2957	9-12	Carol Germano
Animo College Preparatory Academy	2265 E 103rd St	Los Angeles, CA	90002-3132	323-568-4136	568-4190	9-12	James Marin
Animo Ellen Ochoa Charter MS	725 S Indiana St	Los Angeles, CA	90023	323-565-3245		6-8	Cynthia Ybarra
Animo Florence-Firestone Charter MS	155 W 69th St	Los Angeles, CA	90003	323-585-3312	565-1610	6-8	Josh Hartford
Animo Inglewood Charter HS	3425 W Manchester Blvd	Inglewood, CA	90305-2101	323-565-2100	565-2109	9-12	Sue Jean Hong
Animo Jackie Robinson Charter HS	3500 S Hill St	Los Angeles, CA	90007-4333	323-846-5800	846-8760	9-12	Kristine Botello
Animo James B. Taylor Charter MS	810 E 111th Pl	Los Angeles, CA	90059	323-568-8613	568-8617	6-8	Michelle Ahn
Animo Jefferson Charter MS	1655 E 27th St	Los Angeles, CA	90011	323-232-1857	232-6505	6-8	Edgar Flota
Animo Leadership Charter HS	11044 S Freeman Ave	Inglewood, CA	90304-2418	323-565-4420	565-4421	9-12	Julio Murcia
Animo Mae Jemison Charter MS	12700 Avalon Blvd	Los Angeles, CA	90061-2730	323-565-4450	754-1382	6-8	Nathan Geller
Animo Pat Brown Charter HS	8255 Beach St	Los Angeles, CA	90001	323-585-3312	585-8985	9-12	Brian Thomas-Reed
Animo Phillis Wheatley Charter MS	12226 S Western Ave	Los Angeles, CA	90047-5240	323-600-6099		6-8	Wendy Perez
Animo Ralph Bunche Charter HS	1655 E 27th St	Los Angeles, CA	90011-2202	323-232-9436	232-9440	9-12	Nancy Padilla-Flores
Animo South Los Angeles HS	11100 S Western Ave	Los Angeles, CA	90047-4845	323-779-0544	779-0565	9-12	Taiala Carvalho
Animo Venice HS	820 Broadway St	Venice, CA	90291-3408	310-392-8751	392-8752	9-12	Julio Murcia
Animo Watts Charter HS	12628 Avalon Blvd	Los Angeles, CA	90061-2728	323-756-3930	756-3947	9-12	Abraham Devilliers
Animo Western Charter MS	12226 S Western Ave	Los Angeles, CA	90047-5240	323-600-6000	652-1849	6-8	Sonja Johnson
Animo Westside Charter MS	5456 McConnell Ave	Los Angeles, CA	90066-2056	323-565-3251	227-9739	6-8	Lemuel Mossel
Annenberg HS	4000 S Main St	Los Angeles, CA	90037-1022	323-235-6343	235-6346	9-12	Rene Quon
Antelope Valley Learning Academy	1240 Commerce Center Dr	Lancaster, CA	93534-5841	661-952-5520	940-9908	K-12	Erin Wade
Antioch Charter Academy	3325 Hacienda Way	Antioch, CA	94509-5407	925-755-7311	755-7313	K-8	Todd Heller
Antioch Charter Academy II	1201 W 10th St	Antioch, CA	94509-1406	925-755-1252	755-7527	K-8	Todd Heller
Aptitud Community Academy at Goss	2475 Van Winkle Ln	San Jose, CA	95116-3758	408-928-7650	928-7651	PK-8	Maria Manzanedo
Ararat Charter S	6555 Sylmar Ave	Van Nuys, CA	91401-6202	818-994-2904	994-8096	K-5	Eduardo Villela
ARISE HS	3301 E 12th St Ste 205	Oakland, CA	94601-2940	510-436-5487	436-5493	9-12	Soo Jin Kim
Arroyo Paseo Charter HS	3773 El Cajon Blvd	San Diego, CA	92105	619-677-3017	677-3018	9-12	Brian Wickersham
Arroyo Vista Charter S	2491 School House Rd	Chula Vista, CA	91915-2534	619-656-9676	656-1858	K-8	Patricia Roth
Arts in Action Community Charter S	1241 S Soto St	Los Angeles, CA	90023	323-266-4371	266-4371	K-8	Kalin Balcomb
Arundel ES	200 Arundel Rd	San Carlos, CA	94070-1945	650-508-7311	508-7314	PK-4	Ray Dawley
ASA Charter S	3512 N E St	San Bernardino, CA	92405-2110	909-475-3322	883-2708	K-12	Susan Lucey
Aspen Valley Prep Academy	4221 N Hughes Ave	Fresno, CA	93705-1611	559-225-7737	225-0976	K-8	Corrie Sands
Aspire Alexander Twilight College Prep S	2360 El Camino Ave	Sacramento, CA	95821-5611	916-979-1788	979-1796	K-5	Jamie Wallen
Aspire Alexander Twilight Secondary Acad	2360 El Camino Ave	Sacramento, CA	95821-5611	916-979-1788	979-1796	6-12	Lisa Geigle
Aspire APEX Academy	444 N American St	Stockton, CA	95202-2129	209-466-3861	466-4290	K-5	Melissa Brookens
Aspire Berkley Maynard Academy	6200 San Pablo Ave	Oakland, CA	94608-2228	510-658-2900	658-1013	K-8	Jay Stack
Aspire Capitol Heights Academy	2520 33rd St	Sacramento, CA	95817-1943	916-739-8520	739-8529	K-8	Steph Sanders
Aspire College Academy	8030 Atherton St	Oakland, CA	94605	510-562-8030	562-8013	K-5	Jessica Newburn
Aspire East Palo Alto Charter S	1286 Runnymede St	East Palo Alto, CA	94303-1332	650-614-9100	614-9183	K-5	Maricela Wilson
Aspire East Palo Alto Phoenix Academy	1039 Garden St	East Palo Alto, CA	94303	650-325-1460	325-1327	6-12	Kaleesha Washington
Aspire Eres Academy	1936 Courtland Ave	Oakland, CA	94601	510-436-9760	436-9765	K-8	Jenna Ogur-Managella
Aspire Firestone Academy	8929 Kauffman Ave	South Gate, CA	90280-3422	323-249-5740	568-2017	K-5	Dustin Katch
Aspire Gateway Academy	8929 Kauffman Ave	South Gate, CA	90280	323-249-5740	249-5759	K-5	Semi Park
Aspire Golden State College Prep Academy	1009 66th Ave	Oakland, CA	94621	510-567-9631	632-1569	6-12	Greg Dutton
Aspire Inskeep Academy	123 W 59th St	Los Angeles, CA	90003-1103	323-235-8400	232-8030	K-6	Amy Coventry
Aspire Junior Collegiate Academy	6724 S Alameda St	Huntington Park, CA	90255-3617	323-583-5421		K-5	Rachel Garfield

School	Address	City,State	Zip code	Telephone	Fax	Grade	Contact
Aspire Langston Hughes Academy	2050 West Ln	Stockton, CA	95205-3358	209-943-2389	943-2901	6-12	Anthony Solina
Aspire Lugo Academy	6100 Carmelita Ave	Huntington Park, CA	90255-4603	323-585-1153	585-1283	K-5	Sandra Kim
Aspire Monarch Academy	1445 101st Ave	Oakland, CA	94603-3207	510-568-3101	655-1222	K-5	Jennifer Green
Aspire Ollin University Prep Academy	2540 E 58th St	Huntington Park, CA	90255-2659	323-277-2901		6-12	Jennifer Garcia
Aspire Pacific College Prep Academy	2565 E 58th St	Huntington Park, CA	90255-2606	323-589-2800	589-2802	10-12	John Zapata
Aspire Port City Academy	2040 West Ln	Stockton, CA	95205-3358	209-943-2389	943-2901	K-5	Shelby Scheideman
Aspire Richmond CA College Prep Academy	3040 Hilltop Mall Rd	Richmond, CA	94806	510-646-1696		6-12	Javier Cabra
Aspire Richmond Technology Academy	3040 Hilltop Mall Rd	Richmond, CA	94806	510-480-0660		K-5	Arlena Ford
Aspire River Oaks Charter S	1801 Pyrenees Ave	Stockton, CA	95210-5207	209-956-8100	956-8102	K-5	Kris Jamison
Aspire Slauson Academy	123 W 59th St	Los Angeles, CA	90003-1103	323-235-8400	232-8030	K-6	Paul Delgado
Aspire Summit Charter Academy	2036 E Hatch Rd	Modesto, CA	95351-5142	209-538-8082	538-1620	K-5	Kimberly Chastain
Aspire Tate Academy	123 W 59th St	Los Angeles, CA	90003-1103	323-235-8400	583-7271	K-6	Ana Martinez
Aspire Titan Academy	6720 S Alameda St	Huntington Park, CA	90255-3617	323-583-5421	588-7342	K-5	Leilani Lafaurie
Aspire Triumph Technology Academy	3200 62nd Ave	Oakland, CA	94605	510-638-9445	638-0744	K-5	Jessica Chacon
Aspire University Charter S	3313 Coffee Rd	Modesto, CA	95355-1534	209-544-8722	544-8864	K-5	Laura Thompson
Aspire Vanguard College Prep Acad	5255 1st St	Empire, CA	95319	209-269-9977	538-1620	6-12	Salvador Padilla M.A.
Aspire Vincent Shalvey Academy	10038 N Highway 99	Stockton, CA	95212-2127	209-931-5399	931-5185	K-5	Karla Fachner
Assurance Learning Academy	43145 Business Center	Lancaster, CA	93535	661-272-1225	269-0849	K-12	Jeffrey Martineau
Atkinson Academy Charter S	4718 Engle Rd	Carmichael, CA	95608	916-977-3790	977-3793	K-12	James Atkinson
Audeo Charter S	10170 Huennekens St	San Diego, CA	92121-2964	858-678-2050	552-9394	6-12	Tim Tuter
Audeo Charter S II	2525 El Camino Real	Carlsbad, CA	92008	858-678-2050	552-6660	K-12	Veronica Ballman
Aveson Global Leadership Acadmey	1919 Pinecrest Dr	Altadena, CA	91001-2116	626-797-1440	797-1918	6-12	Kate Bean
Aveson School of Leaders	1919 Pinecrest Dr	Altadena, CA	91001-2116	626-797-1440	797-1918	K-5	Kate Bean
Bachrodt Charter Academy	102 Sonora Ave	San Jose, CA	95110-1457	408-535-6211	535-6588	K-5	Rigo Palacios
Ballington Academy for Arts and Science	799 E Rialto Ave	San Bernardino, CA	92408	619-228-2054	282-1300	K-5	Doreen Mulz
Ballington Academy for the Arts/Sciences	1525 W Main St	El Centro, CA	92243-2211	760-353-0140	353-0745	K-6	Doreen Mulz
Banks Charter S	PO Box 80	Pala, CA	92059-0080	760-742-3300	742-3102	K-5	Eric Kosch
Barona Indian Charter S	1095 Barona Rd	Lakeside, CA	92040-1516	619-443-0948	443-7280	K-8	Austin McKeever
Bay Area Technology S	8251 Fontaine St	Oakland, CA	94605-4109	510-382-9932	382-9934	6-12	Hayri Hatipoglu
Baypoint Preparatory Academy	26089 Girard St	Hemet, CA	92544-8701	951-658-1700	658-0723	K-12	Nancy Spencer
Bayshore Prep Charter S	1175 Linda Vista Dr	San Marcos, CA	92078-3811	760-471-0847	736-0275	K-12	Nancy Spencer
Bayside Community Day S	24501 Cactus Ave	Moreno Valley, CA	92553	951-571-7890	571-7891	6-12	Dr. Henry Herreras
Bay View Academy	222 Casa Verde Way	Monterey, CA	93940	831-717-4630		K-5	Karina Barger
Beckford Charter S for Enriched Studies	19130 Tulsa St	Northridge, CA	91326-2645	818-360-1924	832-9831	K-5	Shelly Brower
Bella Mente Montessori Academy	1737 W Vista Way	Vista, CA	92083-2112	760-621-8948	639-0611	K-8	Erin Feeley
Bellevue-Sante Fe Charter S	1401 San Luis Bay Dr	San Luis Obispo, CA	93405-8003	805-595-7169	595-9013	K-6	Brian Getz
be.tech Academies	2271 W Louise Ave	Manteca, CA	95337	209-858-7460	858-7524	11-12	Carey Simoni
Big Picture HS - Fresno	1207 S Trinity St	Fresno, CA	93706-2611	559-420-1234		7-12	Pasquale Catanzarite
Big Sur Charter S	304 Foam St	Monterey, CA	93940	831-324-4573	884-5454	K-12	Aimee Alling
Binkley ES	4965 Canyon Dr	Santa Rosa, CA	95409-3204	707-539-6060	539-4862	PK-6	Kelly Lister
Birmingham Community HS	17000 Haynes St	Van Nuys, CA	91406-5420	818-758-5200	342-5877	9-12	Elena Paul
Bitney College Prep HS	135 Joerschke Dr	Grass Valley, CA	95945-5249	530-477-1235	272-1091	9-12	Russ Jones
Blue Oak Academy	PO Box 1189	Visalia, CA	93279	559-622-3236	622-3237	K-3	Dana Stinson
Blue Oak Charter S	450 W East Ave	Chico, CA	95926-7238	530-879-7483	879-7490	K-8	Susan Domenighini
Bowling Green Chacon Language & Science	6807 Franklin Blvd	Sacramento, CA	95823	916-433-7321	433-7388	PK-6	Sylvia Silva-Torres
Bowling Green McCoy Academy	4211 Turnbridge Dr	Sacramento, CA	95823-1929	916-433-5426	433-5429	K-6	Susan Gibson
Bowman Charter S	13777 Bowman Rd	Auburn, CA	95603-3147	530-885-1974	888-8175	K-8	Mr. Kelly Graham
Bridges Academy	1702 McLaughlin Ave	San Jose, CA	95122-2936	408-283-6400	283-6419	7-8	Ann-Marie Cobarrubias
BRIDGES Charter S	1335 Calle Bouganvilla	Thousand Oaks, CA	91360	805-492-3560		K-8	Dr. Kelly Simon
Bright Star Secondary Academy	2636 S Mansfield Ave	Los Angeles, CA	90016-3512	424-789-8337		9-12	Corey Taylor
Brittan Acres ES	2000 Belle Ave	San Carlos, CA	94070-3798	650-508-7307	508-7310	PK-3	Jessica Blumen
Buckingham Charter Magnet HS	188 Bella Vista Rd Ste B	Vacaville, CA	95687-5413	707-453-7300	453-7303	9-12	Paul Tytler
Bullis Charter S	102 W Portola Ave	Los Altos, CA	94022-1210	650-947-4939	947-4989	K-8	Wanny Hersey
Burton Pathways Charter Academy	1414 W Olive Ave	Porterville, CA	93257-3062	559-782-4748	782-4708	9-12	Matt McCracken
Burton Technology Academy HS	10101 S Broadway	Los Angeles, CA	90003	323-920-6125	920-6950	9-12	Rogelio Sanchez M.Ed.
Butterfield Charter HS	600 W Grand Ave	Porterville, CA	93257-2029	559-782-7057	782-7090	9-12	Staci Phipps
Cain MS	150 Palm Ave	Auburn, CA	95603-3712	530-823-6106	823-0943	6-8	Cindy Giove
Calahan Community Charter S	18722 Knapp St	Northridge, CA	91324-3027	818-886-4612	886-0760	K-6	Michelle Wells
Caliber: Beta Academy	4301 Berk Ave	Richmond, CA	94804	510-685-9886		K-6	Ashlee Gutierrez
Caliber: ChangeMakers Academy	1357 Colusa St	Vallejo, CA	94590	707-563-9827		K-6	Rachael Weingarten
Cali Calmecac Language Academy	9491 Starr Rd	Windsor, CA	95492-9460	707-837-7747	837-7752	K-8	Jeanne Acuna
California Academy for Liberal Studies	7350 N Figueroa St	Los Angeles, CA	90041	213-239-0063	254-4099	6-12	Connie Rivas
California Collegiate Charter S	2009 W Martin Luther King B	Los Angeles, CA	90062	323-450-7290		6-10	Sue Marie Louise Brown
CA Connections Academy @ North Bay	20932 Big Canyon Rd	Middletown, CA	95461	949-306-8498		K-12	Richard Savage
California Connections Academy @ Ripon	580 N Wilma Ave	Ripon, CA	95366	209-253-1208	253-0406	PK-12	Amy Hunt
CA Heritage Youthbuild Academy II	8544 Airport Rd	Redding, CA	96002	530-378-5254	378-5256	9-12	Cathy Clouse-Taylor
California Military Institute	755 N A St	Perris, CA	92570	951-443-2731	943-0473	5-12	Michael Rhodes
California Montessori Project-Amer River	6838 Kermit Ln	Fair Oaks, CA	95628-3048	916-864-0081	864-0084	K-8	Julie Miller
California Montessori Project-Capitol	2635 Chestnut Hill Dr	Sacramento, CA	95826-2912	916-325-0910	325-0912	K-8	Bernie Evangelista
California Montessori Project-Carmichael	5325 Engle Rd Ste 810	Carmichael, CA	95608	916-971-2430	971-2435	K-8	Kim Aldridge
California Montessori Project-Elk Grove	8828 Elk Grove Blvd Ste 4	Elk Grove, CA	95624-1875	916-714-9699	714-9703	K-8	Kathleen Merz
California Montessori Project-Orangevale	6545 Beech Ave	Orangevale, CA	95662	916-673-9389	989-1584	K-6	Kim Aldridge
California Montessori Project-Shingl Spr	4645 Buckeye Rd	Shingle Springs, CA	95682-9505	530-672-3095	672-3097	K-8	Kim Aldridge
California Pacific Charter S	1200 Quail St Ste 250	Newport Beach, CA	92660	855-225-7227		K-12	Kurt Madden
California Prep Sutter 8-12	15898 Central St	Meridian, CA	95957-9517			8-12	Deanna Nguyen
California Prep Sutter K-7	15898 Central St	Meridian, CA	95957-9517			K-7	Deanna Nguyen
California S of the Arts - SGV	1401 Highland Dr	Duarte, CA	91010	657-321-4000		7-12	William Wallace
California STEAM San Bernardino	83600 Trona Rd	Trona, CA	93562	310-527-1741		K-12	Eli Johnson
California STEAM Sonoma	170 Liberty School Rd	Petaluma, CA	94952	707-527-1741		K-12	Eli Johnson
California Virtual Academy @ San Joaquin	50 Moreland Rd	Simi Valley, CA	93065	805-581-0202		K-12	April Warren
Calvert Charter S for Enriched Studies	19850 Delano St	Woodland Hills, CA	91367-3898	818-347-2681	347-5301	K-5	Amanda Evans
Camarillo Academy of Progressive Educ	777 Aileen St	Camarillo, CA	93010	805-384-1415	385-1473	K-8	MaryEllen Lang
Camino Nuevo Academy #2	3400 W 3rd St	Los Angeles, CA	90020	213-736-5542	736-5664	K-8	Nicole Brown
Camino Nuevo Academy - Cisneros	1018 Mohawk St	Los Angeles, CA	90026-3131	213-353-5300	596-3878	K-8	Melissa Mendoza
Camino Nuevo Charter Academy	697 S Burlington Ave	Los Angeles, CA	90057-3743	213-736-5542	736-5664	PK-8	Mark Healy
Camino Nuevo Charter HS	1215 Miramar St	Los Angeles, CA	90026-6115	213-240-8700		9-12	Marisol Pineda-Conde
Camino Nuevo Charter HS 2	3500 W Temple St	Los Angeles, CA	90004-3620	213-736-5566	736-5066	9-12	Julie Jhun
Camino Nuevo Charter S Burlington Campus	697 S Burlington Ave	Los Angeles, CA	90057-3743	213-413-4245	413-8553	K-8	Mark Healy
Camino Nuevo ES - Jose Castellanos	1723 Cordova St	Los Angeles, CA	90007	323-730-7165	737-5626	K-5	James Lee
Camino Science & Natural Rsrcs Charter S	3060 Snows Rd	Camino, CA	95709-9578	530-644-2204	644-5412	K-8	Matthew Smith
Camptonville Academy	321 16th St	Marysville, CA	95901-4223	530-742-2786	742-6067	K-12	Christopher Mahurin
Canyon ES	421 Entrada Dr	Santa Monica, CA	90402-1303	310-454-7510	454-7543	K-5	Nicole Sheard
Capistrano Connections Academy	33272 Valle Rd	San Juan Capo, CA	92675-4842	949-461-1667		K-12	Richard Savage
Capitol Collegiate Academy	2118 Meadowview Rd	Sacramento, CA	95832	916-476-5796		K-8	Cristin Fiorelli
Capitol Heights Academy	2520 33rd St	Sacramento, CA	95817	916-739-8520	739-8529	K-5	Dr. Stephan Sanders
Carpenter Community Charter S	3909 Carpenter Ave	Studio City, CA	91604-3732	818-761-4363	508-6724	K-5	Joseph Martinez
Carver S of Arts & Sciences	10101 Systems Pkwy	Sacramento, CA	95827-3007	916-228-5751	228-5760	9-12	Allegra Alessandri
Casa Ramona Academy for Technology	1524 W 7th St	San Bernardino, CA	92411-2508	909-888-3132		K-12	Esther Ramos Estrada
Castle Rock Charter S	1260 Glenn St	Crescent City, CA	95531-2113	707-464-0390	464-9606	K-12	Jeff Slayton
Cecil Avenue Math & Science Academy	1430 Cecil Ave	Delano, CA	93215-1444	661-721-5030	721-5097	6-8	Micah Wilson
Ceiba College Preparatory Academy	260 W Riverside Dr	Watsonville, CA	95076	831-740-8800	464-3213	6-12	Annie Millar
Celerity Achernar Charter S	310 E El Segundo Blvd	Compton, CA	90222	310-764-1234	868-2517	K-5	Jason Rios
Celerity Cardinal Charter S	7330 Bakman Ave	Sun Valley, CA	91352	323-223-9184	688-3835	K-5	Wilburd Estrada
Celerity Himalia Charter S	4501 S Wadsworth Ave	Los Angeles, CA	90011	323-231-1202	231-1255	K-5	Patrick Stickley
Celerity Nascent Charter S	3417 W Jefferson Blvd	Los Angeles, CA	90018-3235	323-732-6613	733-2977	K-8	Sergio Alvarez Ruiz
Celerity Octavia Charter S	3010 Estara Ave	Los Angeles, CA	90065	310-904-2012	843-9912	K-8	Adriana Mungia
Celerity Palmati Charter S	6501 Laurel Canyon Blvd	North Hollywood, CA	91606	818-753-2712	301-2278	K-6	Titchamroeun Son
Celerity Rolas Charter S	1495 Colorado Blvd	Los Angeles, CA	90041	323-904-2012	290-9845	K-8	Karina Solis
Centennial College Preparatory Academy	2079 Saturn Ave	Huntington Park, CA	90255-3635	323-826-9616	588-7342	6-7	Jesicah Rolapp
Center for Advanced Learning	4016 S Central Ave	Los Angeles, CA	90011-2708	323-232-0245	233-3675	K-5	Brooke Jackson
Center for Advanced Research Technology	2555 Clovis Ave	Clovis, CA	93612-3901	559-248-7400	248-7423	11-12	Rick Watson
Central California Connections Academy	4020 S Demaree St Ste B	Visalia, CA	93277-9476	559-713-1324	713-1330	K-12	Richard Savage
Central City Value S	221 N Westmoreland Ave	Los Angeles, CA	90004-4815	213-471-4686	385-5127	9-12	Joaquin Arroyo
Century Academy for Excellence	2400 W 85th St	Inglewood, CA	90305-1816	323-752-8834	752-8874	6-8	Giselle Edman
Century Community Charter S	901 Maple St	Inglewood, CA	90301-3823	310-412-2286	412-4085	6-8	Dana Means
Century HS Integrated Global Studies	1860 Sierra Gardens Dr	Roseville, CA	95678	916-677-6497		9-12	Sybil Healy
Cesar Chavez Language Academy	2750 W Steele Ln	Santa Rosa, CA	95403	707-528-5011	528-5012	K-8	Rebekah Rocha
Charter Alternatives Academy	31411 Road 160	Visalia, CA	93292	559-730-7491	730-7490	7-12	Carlos Peralta
Charter Alternative S	6520 Oak Dell Rd	El Dorado, CA	95623-4322	530-622-6984	621-2543	K-8	David Publicover
Charter Community S and Home Study Acad	6767 Green Valley Rd	Placerville, CA	95667-8984	530-295-2259	642-0492	7-12	David Publicover
Charter HS of Arts Multimedia/Performing	6842 Van Nuys Blvd	Van Nuys, CA	91405-4650	818-994-7614	994-0099	9-12	Linda Pierce Ph.D.
Charter Home School Academy	211 W Tulare Ave	Visalia, CA	93277-4813	559-730-7916	735-8060	K-8	Steve Rodriguez
Charter S of Morgan Hill	9530 Monterey Rd	Morgan Hill, CA	95037-9356	408-463-0618	463-0267	K-8	Paige Cisewski
Charter S of San Diego	10170 Huennekens St	San Diego, CA	92121-2964	858-678-2020	552-6660	7-12	Ginese Quann
Chatsworth Charter HS	10027 Lurline Ave	Chatsworth, CA	91311-3153	818-678-3400	709-6952	9-12	Dr. Timothy Guy Ed.D.
Chawanakee Academy	PO Box 210	O Neals, CA	93645-0210	559-868-4200	868-4222	K-12	Gary Talley
Chicago Park Community Charter S	15725 Mount Olive Rd	Grass Valley, CA	95945	530-346-2153	346-8559	K-8	Katie Kohler

School	Address	City,State	Zip code	Telephone	Fax	Grade	Contact
Chico Country Day S	102 W 11th St	Chico, CA	95928-6006	530-895-2650	895-9159	K-8	Suzanne Michelony
Children of Promise Preparatory Academy	3130 W 111th Pl	Inglewood, CA	90303	310-677-3014	677-1599	K-3	Carleton Lincoln
Children's Community Charter S	6830 Pentz Rd	Paradise, CA	95969-2902	530-877-2227	872-1396	K-8	Steve Hitchco
CHIME Institute's Schwarzenegger Cmnty S	19722 Collier St	Woodland Hills, CA	91364-3618	818-346-5100	346-5120	K-8	Jennifer Hill
Choices Charter S	4425 Laurelwood Way	Sacramento, CA	95864-0881	916-979-8378		6-12	Tony Oddo
Chrysalis Charter S	PO Box 709	Palo Cedro, CA	96073-0709	530-547-9726	547-9734	K-8	Irene Salter
Chula Vista Learning Comm Charter HS	3730 Arey Dr	San Diego, CA	92154	619-423-2211	423-3007	9-12	Francisco Lopez
Chula Vista Learning Comm Charter MS	380 3rd Ave	Chula Vista, CA	91910	619-946-4200	946-4201	7-8	Dr. Jorge Ramirez
Chula Vista Learning Comm Charter PS	590 K St	Chula Vista, CA	91911-1118	619-426-2885	426-3048	PK-6	Lydia Burgos
Cielo Vista Charter S	650 S Paseo Dorotea	Palm Springs, CA	92264-1406	760-416-8250	416-8253	K-6	Devlin Clinton
Cinnabar Charter ES	286 Skillman Ln	Petaluma, CA	94952-1226	707-765-4345	765-4349	PK-8	Sandy Doyle
Circle of Independent Learning	4700 Calaveras Ave	Fremont, CA	94538-1124	510-797-0100	797-0118	K-12	Stephanie Walton
Citizens of the World Charter S	1516 Carlton Way	Los Angeles, CA	90028	323-464-4063	372-3847	PK-4	Dr. Ramona Patrick
Citizens of the World Charter S	11561 Gateway Blvd	Los Angeles, CA	90064	424-248-0544		K-5	Meline Sarkissian
Citizens of the World Charter S	1316 N Bronson Ave	Hollywood, CA	90028	323-464-4292	464-8292	K-5	Marissa Berman
Citrus Springs Charter S	2121 N Grand Ave	Santa Ana, CA	92705	951-252-8800		K-10	Monica Lopez
City Arts & Technology HS	325 La Grande Ave	San Francisco, CA	94112-2866	415-841-2200	695-5326	9-12	Brianna Winn
City Heights Preparatory Academy	3770 Altadena Ave	San Diego, CA	92105-3007	619-795-3137		6-12	Dr. Marnie Nair
City HS	11625 W Pico Blvd	Los Angeles, CA	90064-2908	310-273-2489	273-2499	9-12	Sheri Werner
City Honors Charter HS	120 W Regent St	Inglewood, CA	90301-1225	310-680-4880	680-5144	9-12	Kiwiana Cain
City Language Immersion Charter S	4001 Venice Blvd	Los Angeles, CA	90019	323-294-4937	294-4938	K-5	Raul Alarcon
City S	11625 W Pico Blvd	Los Angeles, CA	90064	310-273-2489	273-2499	6-8	Sheri Werner
Civicorps Academy	101 Myrtle St	Oakland, CA	94607-2543	510-992-7800	992-7950	9-12	Tyfahra Singleton
Classical Academy	2950 Bear Valley Pkwy S	Escondido, CA	92025-7446	760-546-0101	739-8289	K-8	Cameron Curry
Classical Academy HS	207 E Pennsylvania Ave	Escondido, CA	92025-2808	760-480-9845	739-8289	9-12	Dana Moen
Clayton Valley Charter HS	1101 Alberta Way	Concord, CA	94521-3747	925-682-7474	825-7859	9-12	Jeff Anderson
Clear Passage Educational Center	1471 Martin Luther King Jr	Long Beach, CA	90813-2162	888-502-1116		9-12	Vivianna Trujillo
Clemente Charter S	5701 Fishburn Ave	Maywood, CA	90270-2819	323-984-9008		PK-5	Ann Smith
Cleveland HS	8140 Vanalden Ave	Reseda, CA	91335-1199	818-885-2300	727-0964	9-12	Cindy Duong
Clovis Online S / Enterprise	1655 David E Cook Way	Clovis, CA	93611-0581	559-327-4400	327-4490	K-12	Rees Warne
Coastal Academy Charter	4096 Calle Platino	Oceanside, CA	92056-5805	760-631-4020	631-4027	K-8	Marcy Cashin
Coastal Grove Charter S	PO Box 510	Arcata, CA	95518-0510	707-825-8804	825-1761	K-8	Bettina Eipper
Cole Academy	333 E Walnut St	Santa Ana, CA	92701-5928	714-836-9023	836-9041	K-5	Kimberly Saguilan
Colfax Charter ES	11724 Addison St	North Hollywood, CA	91607-3202	818-761-5115	985-6017	K-5	Robyn Friedman
College and Career Preparatory Academy	1669 E Wilshire Ave Ste 603	Santa Ana, CA	92705-4508	714-547-9986		9-12	Byron Fairchild
College Bridge Academy	1827 E 103rd St	Los Angeles, CA	90007	323-285-1111	285-1333	9-12	Noel Trout
College Preparatory MS	5150 Jackson Dr	La Mesa, CA	91942-9001	619-303-2782	303-3759	5-8	Christina Callaway
College Ready Middle Academy #4	9719 S Main St	Los Angeles, CA	90003-4135	323-451-3009	455-1655	6-8	Darron Evans
College Ready Middle Academy #5	211 S Avenue 20	Los Angeles, CA	90031-2508	323-352-8034	352-8980	6-8	Laura Galvan
Collegiate Charter HS	312 N Record Ave	Los Angeles, CA	90063-1824	213-304-7077		9-12	Camille Einstein
Collins School at Cherry Valley	1001 Cherry St	Petaluma, CA	94952-2065	707-778-4740	778-4839	K-8	Fran Hansell
Come Back Butte Charter S	1860 Bird St	Oroville, CA	95965	530-532-5767		9-12	Barbara Mandelbaum
Come Back Kids Charter S	3939 13th St	Riverside, CA	92501-3505	951-826-6454		9-12	Janice Delagrammatikas
Community Charter Early College HS	11500 Eldridge Ave	Lake View Ter, CA	91342-6522	818-485-0933	485-0940	6-8	Dr. Akilah Lyons-Moore
Community Charter MS	11500 Eldridge Ave	Lake View Ter, CA	91342-6522	818-485-0933	485-0940	6-8	Akilah Lyons-Moore
Community Collaborative Charter S	32248 Crown Valley Rd	Acton, CA	93510-2620	760-494-9646	897-7558	K-12	Kurt Madden
Community Collaborative Charter S	5715 Skvarla Ave	McClellan, CA	95652	916-286-5161	643-2031	K-12	Jon Campbell
Community Magnet ES	11301 Bellagio Rd	Los Angeles, CA	90049-1705	310-476-2281	472-6391	K-5	Carla Cretaro
Community Outreach Academy	5640 Dudley Blvd	McClellan, CA	95652-1034	916-286-1950	640-0227	K-6	Larissa Gonchar
Community Outreach Academy	3800 Bolivar Ave	North Highlands, CA	95660	916-286-1908	286-1992	7-8	Scott Jonard
Community Preparatory Academy	7511 Raymond Ave	Los Angeles, CA	90044-2430	323-751-1460	704-3045	K-5	Janis Bucknor
Community Roots Academy	29292 Crown Valley Pkwy	Laguna Niguel, CA	92677	949-831-4272		K-8	Jeremy Cavallaro
Community S for Creative Education	2111 International Blvd	Oakland, CA	94606	510-517-0331		PK-8	Dr. Monique Brinson
Compass Charter S	850 Hampshire Rd Ste P	Thousand Oaks, CA	91361	855-937-4227		K-12	J.J. Lewis
Competitive Edge Charter Academy	34450 Stonewood Dr	Yucaipa, CA	92399-6852	909-790-3207	790-8364	K-8	Joe Mead
Connect Community Charter S	635 Oakside Ave	Redwood City, CA	94063-3863	650-562-7190	562-7191	K-8	Alicia Yamashita
Connecting Waters Charter S	12420 Bentley St	Waterford, CA	95386-9158	209-874-9463	874-9531	K-12	Sherri Nelson
Connections VPA Academy	17555 Tuolumne Rd	Tuolumne, CA	95379-9701	209-928-4228	928-1422	7-12	Diana Harford
Conservatory of Vocal/Instrumental Arts	3800 Mountain Blvd	Oakland, CA	94619	510-285-7511		K-8	Valerie Abad
Conservatory Vocal Instrumental Arts HS	12500 Campus Dr	Oakland, CA	94619	510-328-1119		9-12	Valerie Abad
Contra Costa S of Performing Arts	150 N Wiget Ln Ste 203	Walnut Creek, CA	94598	925-690-8600		6-12	Neil McChesney
CORE Butte Charter S	260 Cohasset Rd Ste 120	Chico, CA	95926-2282	530-894-3952	566-9819	K-12	Mary Cox
CORE Placer Charter S	1033 S Auburn St	Colfax, CA	95713-9703	530-346-8340	346-2446	K-12	Alison Garcia
Cornerstone Academy Preparatory	1598 Lucretia Ave	San Jose, CA	95122	408-361-3876		K-6	Valerie Douglass
Corona Charter S	9400 Remick Ave	Pacoima, CA	91331-4223	818-834-5805	834-0075	6-8	Larry Simonsen
Cottonwood Creek Charter S	PO Box 1648	Cottonwood, CA	96022	530-347-7200	347-9375	K-8	Mark Boyle
County Collaborative Charter S	3291 Buckman Springs Rd	Pine Valley, CA	91962	858-472-5222		K-12	Dawn Zwibel
Cox Academy	9860 Sunnyside St	Oakland, CA	94603-2750	510-904-6300	904-6730	K-5	David Norris
Creative Arts Charter S	1601 Turk St	San Francisco, CA	94115-4527	415-749-3509	749-3437	K-8	Jenny Kipp
Creative Connections Arts Academy	7201 Arutas Dr	North Highlands, CA	95660-2809	916-566-1870	566-1871	K-6	Edward Delgado
Creative Connections Arts Academy	6444 Walerga Rd	North Highlands, CA	95660-3945	916-566-3470	566-3505	7-12	Edward Delgado
Credo HS	1300 Valley House Dr # 100	Rohnert Park, CA	94928	707-664-0600		9-12	Chip Romer
Creekside Charter S	PO Box 2891	Olympic Valley, CA	96146-2891	530-581-1036	581-2012	K-8	Jeff Kraunz
Crenshaw Arts-Technology Charter HS	4120 11th Ave	Los Angeles, CA	90008-3712	323-778-7700	778-7712	9-12	Patricia Smith
Crescent Valley Public Charter S	116 E Main St	Visalia, CA	93291	559-316-4210	713-1432	K-12	Shellie Hanes
Crescent View Charter West HS	1901 E Shields Ave	Fresno, CA	93726-5318	559-470-8822	225-1205	9-12	Abby Sipes
Crescent View South Charter S	4348 W Shaw Ave Ste 5	Fresno, CA	93722	559-389-7270	276-2543	K-12	David Petropulos
Crete Academy	5125 Crenshaw Blvd	Los Angeles, CA	90043	323-791-1600	496-2089	PK-6	Hattie Mitchell
Crossroads Charter S	418 W 8th St	Hanford, CA	93230-4536	559-583-5060	585-7298	K-12	Laurie Blue
Crown Preparatory Academy	2055 W 24th St	Los Angeles, CA	90018-1925	213-448-9747	410-2271	5-8	Amy Fulinara
Cruz Leadership Academy	14265 Story Rd	San Jose, CA	95127-3823	408-729-2281		9-12	Yesenia Marquez
Cypress Charter HS	2039 Merrill St	Santa Cruz, CA	95062-4176	831-477-0302	477-7659	9-12	Megan Thresham
Dailey Charter ES	3135 N Harrison Ave	Fresno, CA	93704-5240	559-248-7060	227-5530	K-5	Jeanne Pentorali
Dantzler Preparatory Academy	5940 S Budlong Ave	Los Angeles, CA	90044	323-290-6968	459-7813	K-5	Akeysha Allen-Goods
Darby Avenue Charter S	10818 Darby Ave	Northridge, CA	91326-3112	818-360-1824	832-9761	K-5	Lucy Lee
Darnall Charter S	6020 Hughes St	San Diego, CA	92115-6520	619-582-1822	287-4732	K-8	Consuelo Manriquez
DaVinci Academy JSHS	1400 E 8th St	Davis, CA	95616	530-757-7154	759-2178	7-12	Tyler Millsap
DaVinci Communications S	12495 Isis Ave	Hawthorne, CA	90250	310-725-5800	643-7659	9-12	Dr. Scott Weatherford
DaVinci Design S	12501 Isis Ave	Hawthorne, CA	90250-4149	310-725-5800	643-7659	9-12	Kate Parsons
DaVinci Health Sciences Charter S	PO Box 8830	Chula Vista, CA	91912-8830	619-420-0066	420-0677	K-8	Josh Stepner
DaVinci Innovation Academy	13500 Aviation Blvd	Hawthorne, CA	90250-6462	310-725-5800	643-7659	K-8	Michelle Rainey
DaVinci Science S	13500 Aviation Blvd	Hawthorne, CA	90250-6462	310-725-5800	643-3013	K-12	Steve Wallis
DCP Alum Rock MS	2800 Ocala Ave	San Jose, CA	95148	408-942-7000	942-7007	6-8	Leticia Villa
Dearborn Elementary Charter Academy	9240 Wish Ave	Northridge, CA	91325-2533	818-349-4381	886-2149	K-5	Kimberly Estrada
Dehesa Charter S	1441 Montiel Rd Ste 143	Escondido, CA	92026-2242	760-743-7880	743-7919	K-12	Terri Novacek
De La Hoya Animo Charter HS	1114 S Lorena St	Los Angeles, CA	90023-2915	323-780-1259	780-4862	9-12	Kathya Arriaran-Buono
Delta Bridges Charter S	703 E Swain Rd	Stockton, CA	95207	209-830-9219		K-7	Jeff Tilton
Delta Charter ES	PO Box 127	Clarksburg, CA	95612-0127	916-744-1200	744-1246	K-6	Vanessa Belair
Delta Charter S	343 Soquel Ave	Santa Cruz, CA	95062-2355	831-477-5213	479-6173	9-12	Angela Meeker
Delta Charter S	31400 S Koster Rd	Tracy, CA	95304-8824	209-830-6363	830-9707	K-12	George Vierra
Delta Home Charter S	1301 Durham Ferry Rd	Tracy, CA	95304	209-937-4227	329-4227	K-12	Kellyann Reis
Delta Keys Charter S	16988 S Harlan Rd	Lathrop, CA	95330	209-830-6363		K-12	
Delta Keys Charter S	722 W March Ln	Stockton, CA	95207	209-830-6363		K-12	Dr. Jeff Tilton
Delta Launch Charter S	16988 Harlan Rd	Lathrop, CA	95330	209-830-9370		K-12	Jeff Tilton
Del Vista Math & Science Academy	710 Quincy St	Delano, CA	93215-3044	661-721-5040	721-5087	PK-5	Ana Ruiz
Denair Charter Academy	3460 Lester Rd	Denair, CA	95316-9502	209-634-0917	669-9282	K-12	David Naranjo
Denair Elementary Charter Academy	3460 Lester Rd	Denair, CA	95316	209-632-8887	632-8442	K-5	Kelly Beard
Desert Sands Charter HS	44130 20th St W	Lancaster, CA	93534-4045	661-942-3357	944-4857	9-12	Jessica Sherlock
Desert Trails Prep Academy	14350 Bellflower St	Adelanto, CA	92301	760-530-7680	246-6131	K-6	Debbie Tarver
Design Tech HS	1800 Rollins Rd	Burlingame, CA	94010	650-231-2701		9-12	Ken Montgomery
Diamond Technology Institute	112 Diamond Dr	Watsonville, CA	95076-3184	831-728-6225	728-6233	11-12	Marci Keller
Diego Hills Charter S	4585 College Ave	San Diego, CA	92115	619-286-0312	286-0791	8-12	Lindsay Reese
Diego Springs Academy	2281 Diegueno Rd	Borrego Springs, CA	92004	877-360-5327		K-12	
Diego Valley Charter S	511 N 2nd St	El Cajon, CA	92021	619-286-0312	286-0791	K-12	Jonelle Godfrey
Discovery Charter Preparatory S	13570 Eldridge Ave	Sylmar, CA	91342	818-897-1187	897-1295	9-12	Karen Smith
Discovery Charter S	1100 Camino Biscay	Chula Vista, CA	91910-7737	619-656-0797	656-3899	K-8	Sandy Du-Song
Discovery Charter S	51 E Beverly Pl	Tracy, CA	95376-3191	209-831-5240	831-5243	5-8	Virginia Stewart
Discovery Charter S	4021 Teale Ave	San Jose, CA	95117-3433	408-243-9800	243-9812	K-8	Debby Perry
Discovery Charter S II	762 Sunset Glen Dr	San Jose, CA	95123	408-300-3158	972-9114	PK-8	Debby Perry
Dixie Canyon Community Charter S	4220 Dixie Canyon Ave	Sherman Oaks, CA	91423-3904	818-784-6283	788-3340	K-5	Gloria Yniguez
Dixon Montessori Charter S	355 N Almond St	Dixon, CA	95620-2702	707-678-8953	676-5215	K-8	Joanne Green
Downtown Charter Academy	2000 Dennison St	Oakland, CA	94606	510-535-1580	535-1597	6-8	Angela Ortega
Downtown College Preparatory	1402 Monterey Hwy	San Jose, CA	95110	408-271-1730	271-1734	9-12	Andria Plasencia
Downtown College Preparatory MS	1155 E Julian St	San Jose, CA	95116-1005	408-271-8120	271-8855	6-8	Pedro Cuevas
Downtown College Prep S	2888 Ocala Ave	San Jose, CA	95148	408-942-7000	742-9000	6-8	Brandon Jones
Downtown Value S	950 W Washington Blvd	Los Angeles, CA	90015-3312	213-748-8062	748-8868	K-8	Claudia Godlewski
Dunham Charter S	4111 Roblar Rd	Petaluma, CA	94952	707-795-5050	795-5166	PK-6	Christin Barkas

School	Address	City,State	Zip code	Telephone	Fax	Grade	Contact
Dunlap Leadership Academy	39500 Dunlap Rd	Dunlap, CA	93621	559-305-7320	338-2026	9-12	Ron Pack
e3 Civic HS	395 11th Ave 6th Floor	San Diego, CA	92101	619-241-4306		9-12	Helen Griffith
Eagle Peak Montessori S	800 Hutchinson Rd	Walnut Creek, CA	94598-4505	925-946-0994	946-9409	1-8	Michelle Hammons
Early College Acad for Leaders/Scholars	2050 N San Fernando Rd	Los Angeles, CA	90065-1267	323-276-5525	276-5534	9-12	Chanel Young-Smith
East Bay Innovation Academy	3400 Malcolm Ave	Oakland, CA	94605-5353	510-577-9557		6-12	Devin Krugman
East Oakland Leadership Academy	2614 Seminary Ave	Oakland, CA	94605-1570	510-562-5238	562-5239	K-8	Dr. Laura Armstrong
East Palo Alto Academy	1050 Myrtle St	East Palo Alto, CA	94303	650-839-8900	839-8902	9-12	Amika Guillaume
eCademy Charter	1100 Cahill Ave	Turlock, CA	95380	209-669-3410	669-0180	K-12	Tim Norton
Edison-Bethune Charter Academy	1616 S Fruit Ave	Fresno, CA	93706-2819	559-457-2530	498-0711	PK-6	Rodolfo Garcia
Edison Charter Academy	3531 22nd St	San Francisco, CA	94114-3405	415-970-3330	285-0527	K-8	Anastasia Shattner
Ednovate - USC College Prep Pico Union	600 S La Fayette Park Pl	Los Angeles, CA	90057	323-446-2570	446-2571	9-12	Jeanie Cho
Eel River Charter S	PO Box 218	Covelo, CA	95428-0218	707-983-6946	983-6197	K-6	Betty Tuttle
Einstein Academy	3035 Ash St	San Diego, CA	92102-1718	619-795-1190	795-1180	K-5	Greta Bouterse
Einstein Academy Letters Arts Science	11311 Frascati St	Agua Dulce, CA	91390	661-268-1660	268-0209	K-12	Stefanie Council
Einstein Academy MS	458 26th St	San Diego, CA	92102-3026	619-795-1190	795-1180	6-8	David Sciarretta
Einstein Acad for Letters Art & Sciences	8844 Burton Way	Beverly Hills, CA	90211	310-409-2940		K-12	Michael Fishler
EJE Academy Charter ES	851 S Johnson Ave	El Cajon, CA	92020-5811	619-401-4150	401-4151	K-8	Delia Pacheco
El Camino Real Charter HS	5440 Valley Circle Blvd	Woodland Hills, CA	91367-5949	818-595-7500	710-9023	9-12	David Hussey
Elevate ES	2285 Murray Ridge Rd	San Diego, CA	92123-3934	858-751-4774	839-3700	K-5	Robert Elliott
Elk Grove Charter S	10065 Atkins Dr	Elk Grove, CA	95757-4309	916-714-1653	714-1721	K-12	Marc Levine
El Oro Way Charter S	12230 El Oro Way	Granada Hills, CA	91344-1609	818-360-2288	360-3264	K-5	SooJoon Choi
El Rancho Charter S	181 S Del Giorgio Rd	Anaheim, CA	92808-1307	714-997-6238	281-8791	7-8	Michele Walker
El Sol Santa Ana Science & Arts Academy	1010 N Broadway	Santa Ana, CA	92701-3408	714-543-0023	543-0026	K-8	Monique Daviss
Emelita Academy Charter S	17931 Hatteras St	Encino, CA	91316-1037	818-342-6353	774-9352	K-5	Elizabeth Mayorga
Emerson MS	1650 Selby Ave	Los Angeles, CA	90024-5716	310-234-3100	474-6517	6-8	Dimone Watson
Emerson Parkside Academy	2625 Josie Ave	Long Beach, CA	90815-1511	562-420-2631	420-7642	K-5	Adilis Vitetta
Empire Springs Charter S	15350 Riverview Rd	Helendale, CA	92342	951-242-8800	252-8801	K-12	Tanya Rogers
Empower Charter S	2230 E Jewett St	San Diego, CA	92111-6013	858-292-1304	292-1358	K-6	Demetria Brown
Enadia Way Technology Charter S	22944 Enadia Way	West Hills, CA	91307	818-595-3900	716-7738	K-5	Heather Jeanne
Encino Charter ES	16941 Addison St	Encino, CA	91316-3433	818-784-1762	995-7110	K-5	Christine Chun
Encore HS for Performing & Visual Arts	16955 Lemon St	Hesperia, CA	92345-5139	760-956-2632	956-7052	7-12	Denise Griffin
Encore HS for the Arts - Riverside	3800 Main St	Riverside, CA	92501-3624	951-824-1358		7-12	Denise Griffin
Endeavor College Prep Charter S	126 Bloom St	Los Angeles, CA	90012-1902	323-947-7311	843-9502	K-8	Edward Morris
Environmental Charter HS	16315 Grevillea Ave	Lawndale, CA	90260-2858	310-214-3400	214-3410	9-12	Alison Diaz
Environmental Charter MS	3600 W Imperial Hwy	Inglewood, CA	90303-2714	310-793-0157	680-9843	6-8	Beth Bernstein-Yamashiro
Environmental Charter MS	812 W 165th Pl	Gardena, CA	90247-5105	310-425-1605	217-1096	6-8	Robert Gloria
Environmental Science & Technology HS	2930 Fletcher Dr	Los Angeles, CA	90065-1407	323-739-0560	739-0565	9-12	Andres Versage
Envision Academy for Arts & Technology	1515 Webster St	Oakland, CA	94612	510-596-8901	596-8905	9-12	Eve Gordon
Epic Charter S	100 S Anaheim Blvd	Anaheim, CA	92805	657-220-1000	749-4540	K-12	Paul MacGregor
Epic Charter S	1112 29th Ave	Oakland, CA	94601-2212	510-689-2035	904-6751	6-8	Michael McCaffrey
EPIC de Cesar Chavez	122 E Tehachapi Blvd	Tehachapi, CA	93561	661-822-4381	822-4703	9-12	David Villarino
EPIC S	2945 Ramco St	West Sacramento, CA	95691	916-286-1960		K-8	Erin Marston
Epiphany Prep Charter S	725 N Escondido Blvd	Escondido, CA	92025	760-440-8199		K-4	David Rivera
Epiphany Prep Charter S	6785 Imperial Ave	San Diego, CA	92114	619-677-2180		K-8	Lucille Real Ed.D.
Equitas Academy	1700 W Pico Blvd	Los Angeles, CA	90015	213-201-0440		K-4	Mallory Kochmann
Equitas Academy 2	2723 W 8th St	Los Angeles, CA	90005	213-201-5940		5-8	April Adams
Equitas Academy 3	631 S Commonwealth Ave	Los Angeles, CA	90005	213-204-0344		K-2	Cristina Lowry
Equitas Academy 4	631 S Commonwealth Ave	Los Angeles, CA	90005	213-271-5454		5-8	Corrie Janssens
Escondido Charter HS	1868 E Valley Pkwy	Escondido, CA	92027-2525	760-737-3154	738-8996	9-12	Denny Snyder
Escuela Popular Accelerated Family Lrng	467 N White Rd	San Jose, CA	95127-1441	408-275-7190	275-7192	K-12	Patricia Reguerin
Escuela Popular HS Academy	149 N White Rd	San Jose, CA	95127-1936	408-275-7191	259-1595	9-12	Patricia Reguerin
Everest Public HS	455 5th Ave	Redwood City, CA	94063-3727	650-366-1050	366-1892	9-12	Christopher Lewine
Everest Value S	668 S Catalina St	Los Angeles, CA	90005-1708	213-487-7736		K-8	Christopher Medinger
Evergreen Institute of Excellence	19500 Learning Way	Cottonwood, CA	96022	530-347-3411	347-7954	PK-12	Leila Dumore
Excel Charter Academy	1855 N Main St	Los Angeles, CA	90031-3227	323-222-5010	222-5148	6-8	Dr. Gloria Gasca
Excel Prep Charter S	25560 Alessandro Blvd	Moreno Valley, CA	92553	951-601-6620	472-2003	K-6	Mason Patterson
Excelsior Education Center Charter S	18422 Bear Valley Rd # 11	Victorville, CA	92395-5850	760-245-4262	245-4009	7-12	William Flynn
Executive Preparatory Academy of Finance	2814 Manhattan Beach Blvd	Gardena, CA	90249	310-467-4175		9-12	Monique Woodley
Extera Public School	2226 E 3rd St	Los Angeles, CA	90033	323-780-8300	780-8301	K-5	Jim Kennedy Ed.D.
Extera Public S # 2	1015 S Lorena St	Los Angeles, CA	90023-2222	323-263-3600	263-3633	K-5	Lucrecia Villamar
Fairmont Charter ES	1355 Marshall Rd	Vacaville, CA	95687-5519	707-453-6240	447-0759	K-6	Deanna Brownlee
Family First Charter S	4953 Marine Ave	Lawndale, CA	90260-1250	310-263-3204		9-12	Paul Guzman
Family Partnership Home Study Charter S	625 S McClelland	Santa Maria, CA	93454	805-686-5339	686-4658	K-12	Kathy Grbac
Fammatre Charter ES	2800 New Jersey Ave	San Jose, CA	95124-1556	408-377-5480	377-8751	K-5	Lisa MacFarland
Farnham Charter S	15711 Woodard Rd	San Jose, CA	95124-2697	408-377-3321	377-7237	K-5	Matt Hill
Feaster Charter S	670 Flower St	Chula Vista, CA	91910-1327	619-422-8397	422-4780	K-8	Francisco Velasco
Fenton Avenue Charter S	11828 Gain St	Sylmar, CA	91342-7132	818-896-7482	890-9986	2-5	Stacy Hutter
Fenton Leadership Academy	8926 Sunland Blvd	Sun Valley, CA	91352	818-962-3636		K-2	Cary Rabinowitz
Fenton Primary Center	11351 Dronfield Ave	Pacoima, CA	91331-1404	818-896-7482	890-9986	K-1	Richard Parra
Fenton STEM Academy	8926 Sunland Blvd	Sun Valley, CA	91352	818-962-3636		3-5	Jennifer Miller
Finch S	PO Box 428	Orland, CA	95963-0428	530-865-1683	865-1688	K-12	Lisa Morgan
Folsom Cordova Community Charter S	4420 Monhegan Way	Mather, CA	95655	916-294-9190	985-3665	K-8	Jim Cagney
Foothill Leadership Academy	19401 Susan Way	Sonora, CA	95370	209-213-6065		K-8	Ian McVey
Forest Charter S	470 Searls Ave	Nevada City, CA	95959-3030	530-265-4823	265-5037	K-12	Peter Sagebiel
Forest Ranch Charter S	15815 Cedar Creek Rd	Forest Ranch, CA	95942	530-891-3154	891-3155	K-6	Christia Marasco
Forestville Academy	6321 Hwy 116	Forestville, CA	95436	707-887-2279	887-2185	2-6	Phyllis Parisi
Fortune S	6829 Stockton Blvd Ste 380	Sacramento, CA	95823-2396	916-287-4470	287-4477	K-8	Kim Howard
Francophone Charter S of Oakland	9736 Lawlor St	Oakland, CA	94605-4735	510-394-4110		K-8	Heidi Hughes
Freshwater Charter MS	75 Greenwood Heights Dr	Eureka, CA	95503-9441	707-442-2969	442-9527	7-8	Si Talty
Frontier ES	1854 Mustang Dr	Hanford, CA	93230-9811	559-585-2430	585-2440	K-5	John Raven
Fuenta Nueva Charter S	1730 Janes Rd	Arcata, CA	95521	707-822-3348	822-5862	K-5	Beth Wylie
Fuerte S	119 W Palm St	Altadena, CA	91001	858-472-2245		K-8	Anne Lee
Fusion Charter S	441 W Linwood Ave	Turlock, CA	95380	209-667-9047	667-9205	7-12	Susan Nisan
Futures HS	3701 Stephen Dr	North Highlands, CA	95660-4532	916-286-1902	263-6059	7-12	Nataliya Burko
Futuro Academy	2351 Olivera Rd	Concord, CA	94520	925-246-5537	270-0326	K-2	Jason Colon
Gabriella Charter S	1435 Logan St	Los Angeles, CA	90026	213-413-5741	413-5874	K-8	Liza Bercovici
Gabriella Charter S 2	3736 Trinity St	Los Angeles, CA	90011	213-413-5828		K-8	Lindi Williams
Gardner Community Charter S	647 E St	Chula Vista, CA	91910	619-934-0300	207-0300	K-6	Beverly Bautista
GARR Academy of Math & Entrepreneurial	2506 W Imperial Hwy	Hawthorne, CA	90250	323-421-6092	294-2004	K-5	Reginald Brunson
Gates ES	23882 Landisview Ave	Lake Forest, CA	92630-5199	949-837-2260	837-5013	K-6	Yvonne Estling
Gateway Academy	1520 Yosemite Ave	Escalon, CA	95320-1753	209-838-7177	838-6703	K-8	Jennifer Klopatek-Drisco
Gateway College and Career Academy	4800 Magnolia Ave	Riverside, CA	92506	951-222-8934		9-12	Miguel Contreras
Gateway HS	1430 Scott St	San Francisco, CA	94115-3510	415-749-3600	749-2716	9-12	Michael Fuller
Gateway International S	900 Morse Ave	Sacramento, CA	95864	916-286-1985	550-5328	K-8	Joi Tikoi
Gateway MS	1512 Golden Gate Ave	San Francisco, CA	94115-4515	415-922-1001	922-1055	6-8	Aaron Watson
Gateway to College Academy	680 Sonoma Mountain Pkwy	Petaluma, CA	94954	707-778-4621	778-4822	9-12	Vanessa Shannon
Germain Charter Academy	20730 Germain St	Chatsworth, CA	91311-2418	818-341-5821	882-3599	K-5	Luis Lopez
Gilroy Prep Charter S	277 I00F Ave	Gilroy, CA	95020	408-337-5445		1-7	Christin Barkas
Girls Athletic Leadership S	8755 Woodman Ave	Arleta, CA	91331	818-389-1184		6-8	Vanessa Garza
Glacier Charter HS	41267 Highway 41	Oakhurst, CA	93644-9403	559-642-1422	642-1592	9-12	Michael Cox
Global Education Academy	4141 S Figueroa St	Los Angeles, CA	90037-2038	323-232-9588	232-9587	K-5	Craig Merrill
Global Education Academy 2	2020 Oak St	Los Angeles, CA	90007-1307	323-537-7225	232-9587	K-5	David Warken
Global Education Academy MS	1374 W 35th St	Los Angeles, CA	90007	323-641-7283	641-7314	6-8	Rosalind Mickels-Miller
Global Learning Charter S	1051 Robin Dr	Visalia, CA	93291	559-730-7768	730-7439	K-8	Karen Aure
GOALS Academy	412 W Carl Karcher Way	Anaheim, CA	92801	714-563-2390	563-2401	PK-6	Dr. Debra Schroeder Ed.D.
Goethe International Charter S	12500 Braddock Dr	Los Angeles, CA	90066-6808	310-306-3484	306-3245	K-8	Gwenis Laura
Golden Eagle Charter S	2226 S Mount Shasta Blvd #C	Mount Shasta, CA	96067	530-926-5800	926-5826	K-12	Shelly Adams
Golden Oak Montessori S of Hayward	2652 Vergil Ct	Castro Valley, CA	94546-6402	510-931-7868		1-8	Maria Omari
Golden Valley Charter S	3585 Maple St Ste 101	Ventura, CA	93003-3507	805-642-3435	642-3468	K-12	Terri Schiavone
Golden Valley Orchard S	6550 Filbert Ave	Orangevale, CA	95662	916-987-1490	987-1102	K-8	John Baker
Golden Valley River S	9601 Lake Natoma Dr	Orangevale, CA	95662-5099	916-987-6141	987-6741	K-8	Caleb Buckley
Gold Rush Charter S	16331 Hidden Valley Rd	Sonora, CA	95370-7926	209-532-9781	532-9234	K-12	Ron Hamilton
Gompers Preparatory Academy	1005 47th St	San Diego, CA	92102-3626	619-263-2171	264-4342	6-12	Vince Riveroll
Gorman Learning Center	1826 Orange Tree Ln	Redlands, CA	92374-2821	909-307-6312	793-5964	K-12	Denice Burchett
Granada Hills Charter HS	10535 Zelzah Ave	Granada Hills, CA	91344-5999	818-360-2361	363-9504	9-12	Brian Bauer
Grass Valley Charter S	225 S Auburn St	Grass Valley, CA	95945-7229	530-273-8723	271-0557	PK-8	Scott Maddock
Gratton ES	4500 S Gratton Rd	Denair, CA	95316-9762	209-632-0505	632-7810	K-8	Shannon Sanford
Greater San Diego Academy	14567 Lyons Valley Rd	Jamul, CA	91935	619-669-3050	669-3066	K-12	Catherine Bowes
Great Valley Academy	3200 Tully Rd	Modesto, CA	95350	209-576-2283	576-2838	K-8	Russell Howell
Great Valley Academy - Salida	5901 Sisk Rd	Modesto, CA	95356	209-545-7500	545-7712	K-8	Russell Howell
Greene Academy	2950 W River Dr	Sacramento, CA	95833-3767	916-567-5560		7-12	Leslie Sargent
Grimmway Academy	471 W Los Angeles	Shafter, CA	93263	661-630-7220		K-4	Joanna Kendrick
Grimmway Academy	901 Nectarine Ct	Arvin, CA	93203	661-855-8200		K-6	Cole Sampson
Grizzly ChalleNGe Charter S	PO Box 3209	San Luis Obispo, CA	93403-3209	805-782-6882	594-6341	10-12	Paul Piette
Grove S	200 Nevada St	Redlands, CA	92373-5385	909-798-7831	307-6464	7-12	Ben Moudry
Growth S	9320 Tech Center Dr	Sacramento, CA	95826	916-394-5007	642-1087	K-8	Audria Johnson
Guajome Park Academy	2000 N Santa Fe Ave	Vista, CA	92083-1534	760-631-8500	631-8504	K-12	Kevin Hampton

School	Address	City,State	Zip code	Telephone	Fax	Grade	Contact
Guidance Charter HS	37230 37th St E	Palmdale, CA	93550	661-285-1600	285-1601	7-12	Kamal Al-Khatib
Guidance Charter S	1125 E Palmdale Blvd Ste B	Palmdale, CA	93550-4867	661-272-1701	272-1728	K-6	Kamal Al-Khatib
Hale Charter Academy	23830 Califa St	Woodland Hills, CA	91367-2922	818-313-7400	346-7517	6-8	Christopher Perdigao
Hallmark Charter S	2445 9th St	Sanger, CA	93657-2780	559-524-7170	875-3573	K-12	Alfred Sanchez
Hamlin Charter Academy	22627 Hamlin St	West Hills, CA	91307-3603	818-348-4741	348-3506	K-5	Dana Carter
Harbor Springs Charter S	43466 Business Park Dr	Temecula, CA	92590	866-252-8800	252-8801	K-12	Dr. Kathleen Hermsmeyer
Hardy Brown College Prep	PO Box 1590	San Bernardino, CA	92402	909-884-1410	889-5002	K-8	Toiya Allen
Harmony Magnet Academy	19429 Road 228	Strathmore, CA	93267	559-568-0347	568-1929	9-12	Jeff Brown
Hart-Ransom Academic Charter S	3920 Shoemake Ave	Modesto, CA	95358-8577	209-523-0401	523-1064	PK-12	David Cline M.Ed.
Harvest Ridge Cooperative Charter S	9050 Old State Hwy	Newcastle, CA	95658-9515	916-259-1425	259-1428	K-8	Janet Sutton
Hawking II Charter S	1411 27th St	San Diego, CA	92154	619-628-2650		9-12	Lorena Chavez
Hawking STEAM Charter S	1355 2nd Ave	Chula Vista, CA	91911	619-498-8830		K-12	Lorena Chavez
Hawthorne Math & Science Academy	4467 W Broadway	Hawthorne, CA	90250-3819	310-973-8620	973-8167	9-12	Esau Berumen
Haynes Charter for Enriched Studies	6624 Lockhurst Dr	West Hills, CA	91307-3135	818-716-7310	716-7249	K-5	Barbara Meade
Healdsburg Charter S @ Healdsburg ES	400 1st St	Healdsburg, CA	95448-3939	707-431-3440	431-3592	K-2	Stephanie Feith
Healdsburg Charter S - Fitch Mountain	520 Monte Vista Ave	Healdsburg, CA	95448	707-473-4449	473-4483	3-5	Erika McGuire
Health Careers Academy	931 E Magnolia St	Stockton, CA	95202	209-933-7360	941-0687	9-12	Aaron Mata
Health Sciences HS & Middle College	3910 University Ave Ste 100	San Diego, CA	92105-7302	619-528-9070	528-9084	10-12	Dr. Sheri Johnson
Health Sciences MS	3910 University Ave Ste 100	San Diego, CA	92105-7302	619-528-9070		6-9	Sheri Johnson
Hearthstone S	2280 6th St	Oroville, CA	95965-3261	530-532-5644	532-5794	K-12	Barbara Mandelbaum
Heather ES	2757 Melendy Dr	San Carlos, CA	94070-3604	650-508-7303	508-7306	PK-4	Pam Jasso
Heights Charter S	2710 Alpine Blvd	Alpine, CA	91901-2276	619-792-9000		K-8	Diana Whyte
Helix Charter HS	7323 University Ave	La Mesa, CA	91942-0555	619-644-1940	462-9266	9-12	Kevin Osborn
Henry HS	1402 Marina Way S	Richmond, CA	94804	510-235-2439	235-2487	9-12	Jeff Clinton
Heritage Charter S	1855 E Valley Pkwy	Escondido, CA	92027-2517	760-737-3111	737-9322	K-8	Shawn Roner
Heritage Peak Charter S	6450 20th St	North Highlands, CA	95660	866-992-9033	348-4325	K-12	Dr. Paul Keefer
Hesby Oaks Leadership Charter S	15530 Hesby St	Encino, CA	91436-1519	818-528-7000	907-0788	K-8	Movses Tarakhchyan
Hickman Charter S	13306 4th St	Hickman, CA	95323-9634	209-874-9070	874-1457	K-8	Paul Gardner
Hickman ES	13306 4th St	Hickman, CA	95323-9634	209-874-1816	874-3721	K-5	Candetta Holdren
Hickman MS	13306 4th St	Hickman, CA	95323-9634	209-556-6540	874-3721	6-8	Candetta Holdren
Higher Learning Academy	2625 Plover St	Sacramento, CA	95815	916-286-5183	643-9893	K-8	Cindy Petersen
Highlands Community Charter S	1333 Grand Ave	Sacramento, CA	95838-3654	916-844-2283	471-0552	1-12	Michael Roessler
High Tech ES	2150 Cushing Rd	San Diego, CA	92106-6189	619-564-6700		K-5	Anne Worrall
High Tech ES Chula Vista	1949 Discovery Falls Dr	Chula Vista, CA	91915-2037	619-591-2550	591-2553	K-5	Stacey Lopaz
High Tech ES North County	1460 W San Marcos Blvd	San Marcos, CA	92078-4017	760-759-2785	759-2788	K-5	Karen Feitelberg
High Tech Explorer ES	2230 Truxtun Rd Ste A	San Diego, CA	92106	619-795-3600	795-3090	K-5	Briony Chown
High Tech High Media Arts	2230 Truxtun Rd Ste B	San Diego, CA	92106-6128	619-398-8620	758-9568	9-12	Isaac Jones
High Tech HS Chula Vista	1945 Discovery Falls Dr	Chula Vista, CA	91915-2037	619-591-2500	591-2503	9-12	Tim McNamara
High Tech HS North County	1420 W San Marcos Blvd	San Marcos, CA	92078-4017	760-759-2700	759-2799	9-12	Emilio Torres
High Tech International HS	2855 Farragut Rd	San Diego, CA	92106-6029	619-398-4900	758-1960	9-12	Brett Peterson
HighTech LA	17111 Victory Blvd	Van Nuys, CA	91406-5455	818-609-2640	881-1754	9-12	Mathew McClenahan
High Tech Middle Media Arts	2230 Truxtun Rd Ste B	San Diego, CA	92106-6128	619-398-8640	758-0668	6-8	Cassy Salmon
High Tech MS	2359 Truxtun Rd	San Diego, CA	92106-6049	619-814-5060	243-5050	6-8	Nicole Hinostro
High Tech MS Chula Vista	1949 Discovery Falls Dr	Chula Vista, CA	91915-2037	619-591-2530	591-2533	6-8	Melissa Daniels
High Tech MS North County	1460 W San Marcos Blvd	San Marcos, CA	92078-4017	760-759-2750	759-2779	6-8	Juliet Mohnkern
Hollister Prep S	881 Line St	Hollister, CA	95023	831-313-0772		K-8	Heather Parsons
Holly Drive Leadership Academy	4801 Elm St	San Diego, CA	92102-1354	619-266-7333	266-7330	K-8	Alysia Smith
Holt College Prep Academy	3293 Morada Ln	Stockton, CA	95212-3110	209-955-1477	955-1472	6-8	Joseph Williams
Holt College Prep Academy	3201 Morada Ln	Stockton, CA	95212-3110	209-955-1477	955-1472	9-12	Jeff Palmquist
HomeTech Charter S	6249 Skyway	Paradise, CA	95969	530-872-1171	872-1172	K-12	Michael Ervin
Hopper STEM Academy	601 Grace Ave	Inglewood, CA	90301-1306	310-910-0230		6-8	Adell Walker
Horizon Charter S	PO Box 489000	Lincoln, CA	95648-9000	916-408-5200	408-5223	K-12	Cynthia Wood Ph.D.
Hume Lake Charter S	64144 Hume Lake Rd	Hume, CA	93628-9600	559-305-7565	305-7707	K-12	Hollie Carroll
ICEF Inglewood Elementary Charter Acad	434 S Grevillea Ave	Inglewood, CA	90301	323-290-6420	293-9092	K-5	Shuron Owens-Lincoln
ICEF Inglewood Middle Charter Academy	304 E Spruce Ave	Inglewood, CA	90301-2711	323-298-6425	293-9092	6-8	Shuron Owens-Lincoln
ICEF Innovation Los Angeles Charter	5029 S Vermont Ave	Los Angeles, CA	90037	323-290-6997		K-5	Charles Lemle
ICEF Vista Academy	4471 Inglewood Blvd	Los Angeles, CA	90066	323-298-6400	317-2839	K-5	Kristen Buczek
ICEF Vista Middle Academy	4471 Inglewood Blvd	Los Angeles, CA	90066-6209	323-298-6400	317-2839	6-8	Kristen Buczek
I Empire Academy	25560 Alessandro Blvd	Moreno Valley, CA	92553	800-940-3918		K-8	Jacquet Dumas
IFTIN Charter S	5465 El Cajon Blvd	San Diego, CA	92115-3620	619-265-2411	265-2484	K-8	Jama Yacub
iLEAD Hybrid	3720 Sierra Highway Suite A	Acton, CA	93510	661-755-6621		K-12	Dawn Evenson
iLEAD Lancaster Charter S	254 E Ave K-4	Lancaster, CA	93535	661-722-4287	323-8394	K-8	Kim Etter
Imagine School at Imperial Valley	1150 N Imperial Ave	El Centro, CA	92243-1740	760-592-7250	592-7251	K-7	Grace Jiminez
Imagine S Coachella Valley	84090 Ave 50	Coachella, CA	92236	760-391-9200		K-2	Luisa Fuller
Impact Academy of Arts & Technology	2560 Darwin St	Hayward, CA	94545	510-300-1560	300-1565	9-12	Clare Green
Imperial Beach Charter S	650 Imperial Beach Blvd	Imperial Beach, CA	91932-2706	619-628-5600	628-5680	2-8	Melissa Griffith
Imperial Beach Charter School West	525 3rd St	Imperial Beach, CA	91932-1101	619-628-8900	628-8980	PK-1	Michelle Syverson
Imperial Pathways Charter S	253 E Ross Ave	El Centro, CA	92243	760-312-5500		9-12	Monalisa Vitela
Independence Charter Academy	PO Box 249	Helendale, CA	92342-0249	760-952-1760	245-1034	K-12	Michael Esposito
Independence Charter S	3920 Blue Bird Dr	Modesto, CA	95356-0254	209-545-4415	545-2682	K-8	Agustin Mireles
Ingenium Charter MS	7330 Winnetka Ave	Canoga Park, CA	91306	818-309-2777	309-2779	6-8	Cindy Guardado
Ingenium Charter S	22250 Elkwood St	Canoga Park, CA	91304	818-456-4590		K-5	Cindy Guardado
Ingenuity Charter S	6130 Skyline Dr	San Diego, CA	92114-5620	619-487-1163	487-9682	6-12	Dr. Jonathan Dean
Inland Leaders Charter S	12375 California St	Yucaipa, CA	92399	909-446-1100	446-1125	K-8	Michael Gordon
Innovations Academy	10380 Spring Canyon Rd	San Diego, CA	92131-3699	619-271-1414	271-1418	K-8	Christine Kuglen
Innovative Horizons Charter S	1461 N A St	Perris, CA	92570-1968	951-657-0728	940-5103	K-8	Sharill Cortez
Inspire Charter S	32248 Crown Valley Rd	Acton, CA	93510	760-269-2214	269-2216	K-12	Cris Alcala
Inspire Charter S - Central	1781 E Fir Ave Ste 101	Fresno, CA	93720	559-754-1442	335-4089	K-12	Janell Gaertig
Inspire Charter S - Kern	955 Stanislaus St	Maricopa, CA	93252	661-932-1802	932-1804	K-12	Herbert Nichols
Inspire Charter S - North	4305 S Meridian Rd	Meridian, CA	95957	626-932-1802	932-1804	K-12	Herbert Nichols
Inspire Charter S - South	4612 Dehesa Rd	El Cajon, CA	92019-2922	619-784-7481	784-7482	K-12	Herbert Nichols
Inspire School of Arts and Sciences	335 W Sacramento Ave	Chico, CA	95926	530-891-3090	891-3089	9-12	Eric Nilson
Integrity Charter S	701 National City Blvd	National City, CA	91950	619-336-0808	336-0807	K-8	Susie Fahey
Intellectual Virtues Acad of Long Beach	3601 Linden Ave	Long Beach, CA	90807	562-912-7017		6-8	Armine Movsisyan
International S of Monterey	1720 Yosemite St	Seaside, CA	93955-3914	831-583-2165	899-7653	K-8	Sean Madden
Ipakanni Early College Charter HS	1459 Downer St	Oroville, CA	95965	530-532-1165		6-12	Walter Gramps
IQ Academy California Los Angeles	50 Moreland Rd	Simi Valley, CA	93065	888-997-4722	398-5515	K-12	Cathy Andrew
Island Community Day S	1776 6th Avenue Dr	Kingsburg, CA	93631-1701	559-897-1046	897-1265	4-8	Misti Jennings
Island S	7799 21st Ave	Lemoore, CA	93245-9673	559-924-6424	924-0247	K-8	Charlotte Hines
Ivy Academia Entrepreneurial Charter S	7353 Valley Circle Blvd	West Hills, CA	91304-6706	818-449-5900	914-3674	7-12	Joe Herzog
Ivy Academia Entrepreneurial Charter S	5461 Winnetka Ave	Winnetka, CA	91364	818-716-0771	348-8339	PK-6	Joe Herzog Ed.D.
Ivy Bound Academy	15355 Morrison St	Sherman Oaks, CA	91403-1514	818-808-0158	808-0157	5-8	Adam Gaunt
Ivy Bound Academy MST Charter MS	20040 Parthenia St	Northridge, CA	91324-3222	818-646-4992	646-4993	5-8	Sean Tessier
IvyTech Charter S	6591 Collins Dr	Moorpark, CA	93021-1492	805-222-5188	426-8245	7-12	Jacqueline Gardner
Jacobs High Tech HS	2861 Womble Rd	San Diego, CA	92106-6025	619-243-5000	243-5050	9-12	Kaleb Rashad
Jacoby Creek Charter S	1617 Old Arcata Rd	Bayside, CA	95524-9301	707-822-4896	822-4898	K-8	Melanie Nannizzi
Jardin De la Infancia	307 E 7th St	Los Angeles, CA	90014-2209	213-614-1745	614-2047	K-1	Zuzy Chavez
Jew Academy	1944 Flint Ave	San Jose, CA	95148	408-223-3750	223-7346	K-8	Joseph Nuno
Johnson JHS	1300 Stroud Ave	Kingsburg, CA	93631-1000	559-897-1091	897-6867	7-8	Bobby Rodriguez
Jordan MS	7911 Winnetka Ave	Winnetka, CA	91306	818-882-2496	882-1798	6-8	Dr. Maria Alvarado
Journey S	27102 Foxborough	Aliso Viejo, CA	92656-3377	949-448-7232	448-7256	K-5	Gavin Keller
Juan Bautista de Anza Charter S	2101 S Marina Dr	Salton City, CA	92274-8509	760-767-5850	759-1221	1-12	Dr. Sandra Thorpe
Juarez ES	1450 Marina Way S	Richmond, CA	94804	510-215-7009	215-7016	PK-5	Rocio Gonzalez
Julian Charter S	PO Box 2470	Julian, CA	92036	866-853-0003	765-3849	K-12	Jennifer Cauzza
Justice Street Academy Charter	23350 Justice St	West Hills, CA	91304-4402	818-346-4388	346-4649	K-5	Cynthia Hernandez Morris
Kairos Public School Vacaville Academy	129 Elm St	Vacaville, CA	95688-6925	707-356-9210		K-8	Jared Austin
Kavod Charter ES	3201 Marathon Dr	San Diego, CA	92123-2638	858-386-0887		K-5	Alexa Greenland
Kawana Springs ES	2121 Moraga Dr	Santa Rosa, CA	95404-6114	707-545-4283	573-9065	PK-6	Carolina Castro
Keiller Leadership Academy MS	7270 Lisbon St	San Diego, CA	92114-3007	619-263-9266	262-2217	K-8	Joel Christman
Kenny Charter S	3525 M L King Blvd	Sacramento, CA	95817	916-395-4570	277-6507	K-8	Gail Johnson
Kenter Canyon ES	645 N Kenter Ave	Los Angeles, CA	90049-1999	310-472-5918	472-9738	K-5	Dr. Terry Moren
Kepler Neighborhood S	1462 Broadway St	Fresno, CA	93721	559-495-0849		K-8	Christine Montanez
Kern Workforce 2000 Academy	5801 Sundale Ave	Bakersfield, CA	93309-2924	661-827-3158	396-2987	10-12	Roman Aguilar
Keyes To Learning Charter S	PO Box 519	Keyes, CA	95328-0519	209-634-6467	669-7121	PK-12	Rusty Wynn
Kid Street Learning Center	PO Box 6784	Santa Rosa, CA	95406-0784	707-525-9223	525-9432	K-6	Linda Conklin
Kimme Charter Academy	1949 Peabody Rd	Vacaville, CA	95687	707-449-2305		K-12	Lois Chancellor
Kinetic Academy	721 Utica Ave	Huntingtn Bch, CA	92648	714-465-4565		K-8	Breanne Lionetti
King-Chavez Academy of Excellence	2716 Marcy Ave	San Diego, CA	92113	619-232-2825	232-2943	K-8	Jorge Collins
King/Chavez Arts Academy	415 31st St	San Diego, CA	92102-4236	619-525-7320	696-7459	3-5	Sr. Shelley Baca
King/Chavez Athletics Academy	415 31st St	San Diego, CA	92102-4236	619-525-7320	744-3817	3-5	Shelley Baca
King-Chavez Community HS	201 A St	San Diego, CA	92101-4003	619-704-1020	704-1021	9-12	Dr. Kevin Bradshaw
King/Chavez Preparatory Academy	500 30th St	San Diego, CA	92102-3090	619-744-3828	744-3829	6-8	Scott Worthing
King/Chavez Primary Academy	415 31st St	San Diego, CA	92102-4236	619-525-7320	696-7459	K-2	Gerry Guevara
Kings River Hardwick S	10300 Excelsior Ave	Hanford, CA	93230-0108	559-584-4475	585-1422	K-8	Cathlene Anderson
Kings Valley Academy	312 W 7th st	Hanford, CA	93230	559-470-8822		9-12	Shellie Hanes
KIPP Academy of Innovation	5156 Whittier Blvd	Los Angeles, CA	90022	323-406-8000	406-8002	5-8	Alice Lai
KIPP Academy of Opportunity	7019 S Van Ness Ave	Los Angeles, CA	90047-1659	323-778-0125	778-0162	5-8	Aisha Bonner

School	Address	City,State	Zip code	Telephone	Fax	Grade	Contact
KIPP Adelante Preparatory Academy	1475 6th Ave Ste 100	San Diego, CA	92101-3245	619-233-3242	233-3212	5-8	Monique McKeown
KIPP Bayview Academy	1060 Key Ave	San Francisco, CA	94124-3563	415-467-2522	467-9522	5-8	Neil Davis
KIPP Bridge Charter S	1700 Market St	Oakland, CA	94607	510-874-7255	874-6796	5-8	Lolita Jackson
KIPP Comienza Community Prep S	6410 Rita Ave	Huntington Park, CA	90255	323-589-1450	589-1716	K-8	Hadley Huberman
KIPP Corazon Academy	2728 Liberty Blvd	South Gate, CA	90280	323-457-5051		K-8	Colleen Kennedy
KIPP Empower Academy	8466 S Figueroa St	Los Angeles, CA	90003-2729	323-750-2279	750-7902	K-4	Neela Parasnis
KIPP Excelencia Charter S	656 Laurel St	Redwood City, CA	94063	650-465-3616		K-8	Kyle Shaffer
KIPP Heritage Academy	423 Los Arboles St	San Jose, CA	95111	408-283-6260	283-6258	5-8	Amy Tran
KIPP Ignite Academy	9110 S Central Ave	Los Angeles, CA	90002	323-486-6402	486-6403	K-1	Cassandra Cope
KIPP I Heartwood Academy	1250 S King Rd	San Jose, CA	95122-2146	408-926-5477	926-5478	5-8	Susana Mena
Kipp II Prize Preparatory Academy	1250 S King Rd	San Jose, CA	95122-2146	408-251-5600	251-5602	5-8	Autumn Zangrilli
KIPP Iluminar Academy	4800 E Cesar Chavez Ave	Los Angeles, CA	90022	323-800-5218	489-4471	K-4	Mara Bond
KIPP King Collegiate HS	2005 Via Barrett	San Lorenzo, CA	94580-1315	510-828-9509	317-2333	9-12	Ben Thompson
KIPP Los Angeles College Preparatory	2810 Whittier Blvd	Los Angeles, CA	90023-1527	323-264-7737	264-7730	5-8	Carlos Lanuza
KIPP Philosophers Academy	8300 S Central Ave	Los Angeles, CA	90001-3707	323-584-6664	584-6666	5-8	Heidi Kunkel
KIPP Promesa Prep S	207 S Dacotah St	Los Angeles, CA	90063	323-486-6400	486-6401	K-4	Adriana Rodriguez
KIPP Raices Academy	668 S Atlantic Blvd	Los Angeles, CA	90022-3212	323-780-3900	780-3939	K-4	Yesenia Castro
KIPP San Francisco Bay Academy	1430 Scott St	San Francisco, CA	94115-3510	415-440-4306	440-4308	5-8	Ellen Bray
KIPP San Francisco College Preparatory	1195 Hudson Ave	San Francisco, CA	94124-2488	415-643-6951	826-9182	9-12	Savina Woodyard
KIPP San Jose Collegiate Charter S	1790 Educational Park Dr	San Jose, CA	95133-1703	408-937-3752	937-3755	9-12	Tom Ryan
KIPP Scholar Academy	1729 W MLK Jr Blvd	Los Angeles, CA	90062	323-292-2272	292-2555	5-8	Tiffany Moore
KIPP Sol Academy	4800 E Cesar Chavez Ave	Los Angeles, CA	90022	323-800-5220	800-5221	5-8	
KIPP Summit Academy	2005 Via Barrett	San Lorenzo, CA	94580-1315	510-258-0106	258-0097	5-8	Salome Portugal
KIPP Valiant Community Prep	2033-A Pulgas Ave	East Palo Alto, CA	94303	650-422-4022		K-8	Kate Belden
KIPP Vida Preparatory Academy	5101 S Western Ave	Los Angeles, CA	90062	323-406-8007	406-8008	K-4	Erendira Flores
Knowledge Enlightens You (KEY) Academy	1570 Ward St	Hayward, CA	94541	510-397-2524	363-8542	K-8	Krista Kastriotis
Lake County International Charter S	PO Box 984	Middletown, CA	95461-0984	707-987-3063	825-9344	K-8	Gwendolyn Maupin-Ahern
Lakeview Charter Academy	11465 Kagel Canyon St	Lake View Ter, CA	91342-6505	818-485-0340	485-0342	6-8	Melisa Serio
Lakeview Charter HS	13361 Glenoaks Blvd	Sylmar, CA	91342-2110	818-356-2591	356-2581	9-12	Jorge Beas
Language Academy	2850 49th St	Sacramento, CA	95817-2303	916-277-7137	277-7141	K-8	Eduardo De Leon
Larchmont Charter ES	1265 N Fairfax Ave	West Hollywood, CA	90046-5205	323-656-6418	656-6407	K-10	Mersedeh Emrani
Lashon Academy	7477 Kester Ave	Van Nuys, CA	91405-1722	818-514-4566	337-0102	K-6	Sara Garcia
La Sierra Academy	1735 E Houston Ave	Visalia, CA	93292-2349	559-733-6963	733-6845	7-12	Anjelica Zermeno
LA's Promise Charter HS 1	1755 W 52nd St	Los Angeles, CA	90062	323-375-5273		9-12	Qiana O'Leary
LA's Promise Charter MS 1	1755 W 52nd St	Los Angeles, CA	90062	323-745-4928		6-8	David Carr
La Tijera Academy of Excellence	1415 N La Tijera Blvd	Inglewood, CA	90302	310-680-5260	419-2537	K-8	Ugema James
Latino College Preparatory Academy	14271 Story Rd	San Jose, CA	95127	408-729-2281	285-5324	9-12	Jesus Rios
Laurel Preparatory Academy	10170 Huennekens St	San Diego, CA	92121-2964	858-678-4812		6-12	Lynne Alipio
Laurel Tree Charter S	4555 Valley West Blvd	Arcata, CA	95521-4683	707-822-5626	822-5654	K-12	Brenda Sutter
LAVA Charter S	1660 Monroe St	Red Bluff, CA	96080	530-727-9495	727-9498	5-8	John Sheffield
Laverne Elementary Preparatory Academy	PO Box 400880	Hesperia, CA	92340	760-948-4333	948-9333	K-8	Debbie Tarver
LaVerne Science & Technology Charter S	250 W La Verne Ave	Pomona, CA	91767-2375	909-397-4684	392-0191	K-6	Dolores Lobaina
La Vida Charter S	16201 N Highway 101	Willits, CA	95490-8724	707-459-6344	459-6377	K-12	Ann Kelly
Lazear Charter Academy	824 29th Ave	Oakland, CA	94601-2205	510-689-2000		K-8	Sarah Morrill
Leadership HS	350 Seneca Ave	San Francisco, CA	94112-3248	415-841-8910	841-8925	9-12	Beth Silbergeld
Leadership Public S - Hayward	28000 Calaroga Ave	Hayward, CA	94545-4600	510-300-1340	372-0396	9-12	Michael DeSousa
Leadership Public S - Richmond	251 S 12th St	Richmond, CA	94801	510-235-4522	588-4593	9-12	Shawn Benjamin
Learning Choice Academy	9950 Scripps Lake Dr	San Diego, CA	92131-1082	619-463-8811	463-8339	K-12	Debi Gooding
Learning for Life Charter S	3180 Imjin Rd	Marina, CA	93933	831-582-9820	582-9825	7-12	Kenneth Emanuel
Learning Works!	88 N Daisy Ave	Pasadena, CA	91107-3704	626-564-2871	564-2870	7-12	Mikala Rhn
Lemoore Middle College HS	555 College Dr	Lemoore, CA	93245-9248	559-925-3552	925-6059	9-12	Charles Gent
Lemoore Online College Prep HS	555 College Ave	Lemoore, CA	93245	559-925-3552	925-6059	9-12	Charles Gent
Lemoore University Charter S	100 Vine St	Lemoore, CA	93245-3418	559-924-6890	924-6839	5-8	Crescenciano Camarena
Lennox Math Science & Technology Academy	10319 Firmona Ave	Lennox, CA	90304-1419	310-680-5600	671-5029	9-12	Armando Mena
Libertas College Preparatory Charter S	3875 Dublin Ave	Los Angeles, CA	90008-1945	310-902-6808		4-8	Allison Metz
Liberty Charter HS	8425 Palm St	Lemon Grove, CA	91945	619-668-2131	668-2133	9-12	Debbie Beyer
Liberty ES	170 Liberty School Rd	Petaluma, CA	94952	707-795-4380	795-6468	PK-6	Chris Rafanelli
Life Learning Academy	651 8th St	San Francisco, CA	94130-1901	415-397-8957	397-9274	9-12	Teri Delane
Lifeline Education Charter S	225 S Sante Fe Ave	Compton, CA	90221	310-605-2510	764-4890	6-12	Paula DeGroat
Life Source International Charter S	44339 Beech Ave	Lancaster, CA	93534	661-579-2970	579-2977	K-8	Deberae Culpepper
Lighthouse Community Charter S	444 Hegenberger Rd	Oakland, CA	94621	510-562-8801	562-8803	K-12	Steve Sexton
Lincoln ES	1900 Mariposa St	Kingsburg, CA	93631-2044	559-897-5141	897-3537	2-3	Matt Stovall
Lincoln Street S	1135 Lincoln St	Red Bluff, CA	96080	530-528-7301	529-4120	K-8	Michelle Barnard
Linscott Charter S	220 Elm St	Watsonville, CA	95076-5025	831-728-6301	761-5478	K-8	Julie Wiley
Literacy First Charter S	799 E Washington Ave	El Cajon, CA	92020-5327	619-579-7232	579-5730	K-12	Debbie Beyer
Live Oak Charter S	PO Box 2054	Petaluma, CA	94953-2054	707-762-9020	762-9019	K-8	Matthew Morgan
Locke College Prep Academy	325 E 111th St	Los Angeles, CA	90061	323-420-2067		9-12	Dr. Peggy Gutierrez
Lockhurst Drive Charter ES	6170 Lockhurst Dr	Woodland Hills, CA	91367-1299	818-888-5280	346-0283	K-5	Susan Dacorsi
Lodestar: a Lighthouse Charter S	2433 Coolidge Ave	Oakland, CA	94601	510-209-2166	271-8803	K-12	Yanira Canizales
Loma Vista Charter S	467 E Honolulu St	Lindsay, CA	93247	559-562-5111	562-4637	9-12	Dennis Doane
Loma Vista Immersion Academy	207 Maria Dr	Petaluma, CA	94954-2301	707-765-4302	765-4343	K-6	Jorge Arvizu
Long Valley Charter S	PO Box 7	Doyle, CA	96109-0007	530-827-2395	827-3562	K-12	Sherri Morgan
Loomis Basin Charter S	5438 Laird Rd	Loomis, CA	95650-8916	916-652-2642	652-1809	K-8	Kati Messerli
Los Angeles Academy of Arts & Enterprise	1200 W Colton St Ste 3-320	Los Angeles, CA	90026	213-487-0600	487-0500	6-12	Yolanda Jimenez
Los Angeles International Charter S	625 Coleman Ave	Los Angeles, CA	90042-4903	323-257-1499	257-1497	9-12	Angelique Sims
Los Angeles Leadership Academy	2670 Griffin Ave	Los Angeles, CA	90031-2311	323-381-8484	381-8489	K-8	Antonio Sanchez
Los Angeles Leadership Academy - HS	234 E Avenue 33	Los Angeles, CA	90031-1937	323-227-7719	227-7721	9-12	Roger Lowenstein
Los Feliz Charter S for the Arts	2709 Media Center Dr	Los Angeles, CA	90065-1700	323-539-2810	539-2815	K-6	Linda Lee
LPS College Park Charter S	8601 MacArthur Blvd	Oakland, CA	94605-4037	510-633-0750	291-9783	9-12	Ellen Digiacomo
Luskin Academy	2941 W 70th St	Los Angeles, CA	90043-4420	213-905-1210	905-1215	9-12	Donna Jacobson
MAAC Community Charter S	1385 3rd Ave	Chula Vista, CA	91911-4302	619-476-0749	476-0913	9-12	Debbie VanEnkevort
Madera County Independent Academy	1105 S Madera Ave	Madera, CA	93637	559-662-4640	675-4968	K-12	Brett Salinas
Magnolia Science Academy	18238 Sherman Way	Reseda, CA	91335-4550	818-609-0507	609-0534	6-12	Mustafa Sahin M.Ed.
Magnolia Science Academy	2840 W 1st St	Santa Ana, CA	92703	714-479-0115	242-1449	K-12	Laura Schlottman
Magnolia Science Academy 2	17125 Victory Blvd	Van Nuys, CA	91406	818-758-0300	758-0333	6-12	Steven Keskinturk
Magnolia Science Academy 3	1254 E Helmick St	Carson, CA	90746	310-637-3806	933-4767	6-12	Shandrea Daniel
Magnolia Science Academy 4	11330 Graham Pl	Los Angeles, CA	90064-3725	310-473-2464	473-2416	6-12	Lisa Ross
Magnolia Science Academy 5	18230 Kittridge St	Reseda, CA	91335	818-705-5676	705-5627	6-10	Brad Plonka
Magnolia Science Academy 6	3754 Dunn Dr	Los Angeles, CA	90034-5805	310-842-8555	842-8558	6-8	John G. Terzi
Magnolia Science Academy 7	18355 Roscoe Blvd	Northridge, CA	91325-4104	818-886-0585	975-5215	K-5	Fatih Metin
Magnolia Science Academy 8	6411 Orchard Ave	Bell, CA	90201-2222	310-826-3925	826-3926	6-8	Jason Hernandez
Magnolia Science Academy - San Diego	6525 Estrella Ave	San Diego, CA	92120	619-644-1300	644-1600	6-8	Gokhan Serce
Making Waves Academy	4123 Lakeside Dr	Richmond, CA	94806-1942	510-262-1511	262-1518	5-12	Evangelia Ward-Jackson
Manzanita Charter MS	461 33rd St	Richmond, CA	94804	510-222-3500	222-3555	6-8	Jim Trombley
Manzanita Public Charter S	991 Mountain View Blvd	Vandenberg AFB, CA	93437-1209	805-734-5600	734-3572	K-6	Suzanne Nicastro
Mare Island Technology Academy HS	2 Positive Pl	Vallejo, CA	94589-1825	707-552-6482	552-0288	6-12	Matt Smith
Maria Montessori Charter Academy	1850 Wildcat Blvd	Rocklin, CA	95765-5471	916-630-1510	624-7305	K-8	Brent Boothby
Marquez Charter S	16821 Marquez Ave	Pacific Plsds, CA	90272-3243	310-454-4019	573-1532	K-5	Benjamin Meritt
Marysville Charter Academy for the Arts	1917 B St	Marysville, CA	95901-3731	530-749-6157	741-7892	7-12	Tim Malone
Math and Science College Preparatory	3200 W Adams Blvd	Los Angeles, CA	90018	323-821-1393	607-1453	9-12	Lisa Marcelino
Mattole Valley Charter S	PO Box 211	Petrolia, CA	95558	707-629-3634	629-3649	PK-12	Shari Lovett
McCandless STEM Charter S	2020 W Swain Rd	Stockton, CA	95207-4055	209-953-8740		K-8	Phyllis Kahl
McGill School of Success	3025 Fir St	San Diego, CA	92102-1123	619-239-0632	239-1318	K-3	Kimberly Lopez
Meadows Arts & Technology ES	2000 La Granada Dr	Thousand Oaks, CA	91362-2016	805-495-7037	374-1160	K-5	Brenda Olshever
Merced Scholars Charter S	1850 Wardrobe Ave	Merced, CA	95341-6407	209-381-5165	381-5166	6-12	Mark Pintor
Merkin MS	2023 S Union Ave	Los Angeles, CA	90007-1326	213-748-0141	748-0142	6-8	Meghan Van Pelt
Method Charter S	24620 Jefferson St	Murrieta, CA	92562	951-461-4620		K-12	Jessica Venezia
Method S	317 E Foothill Blvd	Arcadia, CA	91006-2510	626-408-5882		K-12	Jessica Venezia
Metro Charter S	320 W 15th St	Los Angeles, CA	90015-3091	213-377-5708	943-1502	K-5	Kim Clerx
MET Sacramento Charter HS	810 V St	Sacramento, CA	95818-1330	916-395-5417	264-4701	9-12	Vince Wolfe
Mid Valley Alternative Charter S	9895 7th Ave	Hanford, CA	93230-8802	559-583-1149	582-7565	K-8	Todd Barlow
Milagro Charter S	1855 N Main St	Los Angeles, CA	90031-3227	323-223-1786	223-8593	K-5	Sascha Robinett
Millennium Charter HS	51 E Beverly Pl	Tracy, CA	95376-3191	209-831-5240	831-5243	9-12	Virginia Stewart
Millennium Charter HS	901 Blanco Circle	Salinas, CA	93901	831-755-0830		9-12	Richard Diaz
Minarets Charter HS	PO Box 208	O Neals, CA	93645	559-868-8689	868-8686	9-12	Daniel Ching
Mirus Secondary S	14073 Main St Ste 103	Hesperia, CA	92345-4675	760-947-7100	947-7135	7-12	Mary Bixby
Mission Preparatory S	1050 York St	San Francisco, CA	94110	415-508-9626		K-8	Kristine MacDonald
Mission View Charter S	20655 Soledad Canyon Rd #12	Santa Clarita, CA	91351	661-272-1225	945-2430	7-12	Taera Childers
Miwok Valley Language Academy	1010 Saint Francis Dr	Petaluma, CA	94954-5322	707-765-4304	765-4380	K-6	Brett Wilson
Mohan High School	644 W 17th St	Los Angeles, CA	90015-3400	213-342-2870	342-2871	9-12	Loreen Riley
Mojave River Academy	PO Box 386	Oro Grande, CA	92368	760-245-3222	245-7260	K-12	Kari Hemsley
Monarch Learning Center	PO Box 992418	Redding, CA	96099-2418	530-247-7307	243-4819	K-8	Ethan Cohen
Montague Charter Academy	13000 Montague St	Pacoima, CA	91331-4146	818-899-0215	834-9782	K-5	Leonidas Tarca
Monterey Bay Charter S	1004B David Ave	Pacific Grove, CA	93950-5443	831-655-4638	655-4815	K-8	Cassandra Bridge
Monterey County Home Charter S	PO Box 80851	Salinas, CA	93912-0851	831-755-0331	755-0837	K-12	Justin McCollum
Mountain Academy Charter S	201 Memorial Dr	Weaverville, CA	96093	530-623-2861	623-4489	K-12	Fabio Robles
Mountain Home Charter S	41267 Highway 41	Oakhurst, CA	93644-9403	559-642-1422	642-1592	K-8	Michael Cox

School	Address	City,State	Zip code	Telephone	Fax	Grade	Contact
Mountain Oaks S	PO Box 1209	San Andreas, CA	95249-1209	209-754-0532	754-3556	K-12	Anne Colman
Mountain View Montessori Charter S	12219 Second Ave	Victorville, CA	92395	760-843-3303	843-1074	K-6	Tanya Newell
Mt Lassen Charter S	100 David S Hall St	Herlong, CA	96113	530-252-4313	252-4314	K-6	Michael Altenburg
Mueller Bayfront Charter HS	830 Bay Blvd	Chula Vista, CA	91911	619-934-7000	422-0356	9-12	Kevin Riley
Mueller Charter S	715 I St	Chula Vista, CA	91910-5199	619-422-6192	422-0356	K-9	Dr. Maureen DeLuca
Muir Charter S	117 New Mohawk Drive	Grass Valley, CA	95949	530-272-4008	366-7349	9-12	Richard Guess
Multicultural Learning Center	7510 De Soto Ave	Canoga Park, CA	91303-1430	818-716-5783	716-1085	K-8	Shirley Aragon
Museum S	211 Maple St	San Diego, CA	92103-6527	619-236-8712	236-8906	K-8	Phil Beaumont
Napa Valley Language Academy	2700 Kilburn Ave	Napa, CA	94558-5623	707-253-3678	259-8427	K-6	Alejandra Uribe
Natomas Charter S	4600 Blackrock Dr	Sacramento, CA	95835-1250	916-928-5353	928-5333	PK-12	Ting Sun Ph.D.
Natomas-Pacific Pathways Prep	3700 Del Paso Rd	Sacramento, CA	95834	916-567-5740	567-5749	9-12	Tom Rutten
Natomas Pacific Pathways Prep ES	4400 E Commerce Way	Sacramento, CA	95834	916-567-5741	567-5749	K-5	Marcie Dart
Natomas Pacific Pathways Prep MS	3700 Del Paso Rd	Sacramento, CA	95834	916-567-5741	567-5749	6-8	David Hunt
NAVA College Preparatory Academy	1319 E 41st St	Los Angeles, CA	90011	213-235-6800	521-1668	9-12	Gustavo Barrientos
Nea Community Learning Center	1900 3rd St	Alameda, CA	94501-1851	510-748-4008	864-4281	K-12	Annalisa Moore
Nestle Avenue ES	5060 Nestle Ave	Tarzana, CA	91356-4399	818-342-6148	609-9864	K-5	Cheryl Gray-Sortino
Nestor Language Academy Charter S	1455 Hollister St	San Diego, CA	92154-4063	619-628-0900	628-0980	K-8	Guadalupe Avilez
Nevada City Charter S	750 Hoover Ln	Nevada City, CA	95959-2910	530-265-1885	265-1889	K-8	Brynn Bourke
Nevada City S for the Arts	13032 Bitney Springs Rd # 8	Nevada City, CA	95959-9017	530-273-7736	273-1378	PK-8	Holly Pettitt
NEW Academy Canoga Park	21425 Cohasset St	Canoga Park, CA	91303-1450	818-710-2640	710-2654	PK-5	Patricia Gould
NEW Academy of Science & Arts	379 Loma Dr	Los Angeles, CA	90017-1149	213-413-9183	413-9187	PK-5	Dr. Eric Todd Ed.D.
Newcastle Charter S	8951 Valley View Dr	Newcastle, CA	95658-9723	916-663-3307	663-3524	PK-8	David Cory
New Day Academy	214 W 1st St	Alturas, CA	96101	530-233-3861	233-3864	K-12	Laura Van Acker
New Designs Charter S	2303 Figueroa Way	Los Angeles, CA	90007-2504	213-765-9084	765-0214	6-12	Stephen Gyesaw
New Designs Charter S - Watts	12714 Avalon Blvd	Los Angeles, CA	90061-2730	323-418-0600	418-1600	6-12	Joseph Ntung
New Heights Charter S	2202 W Martin Luther King	Los Angeles, CA	90008-2723	323-508-0155	508-0156	K-8	Amy Berfield
New Horizons Charter Academy	5955 Lankershim Blvd	North Hollywood, CA	91601-1006	818-655-9602	655-9607	K-8	Richard Thomas
New Jerusalem ES	31400 S Koster Rd	Tracy, CA	95304-9543	209-835-2597	835-2613	K-8	Donald Patzer
New Joseph Bonnheim Community Charter S	7300 Marin Ave	Sacramento, CA	95820	916-277-6294	691-9858	K-6	Christie Wells-Artman
New Los Angeles Charter ES	5421 Rodeo Rd	Los Angeles, CA	90016	323-556-9500	939-6411	K-5	Kate O'Brien
New Los Angeles Charter S	1919 S Burnside Ave	Los Angeles, CA	90016-1114	323-939-6400	939-6411	6-8	Daryl Brook
Newman Leadership Academy	1314 E Date St	San Bernardino, CA	92404-4234	909-522-4461		K-6	Michelle Braswell
New Millenium Secondary S	1301 W 182nd St Ste B	Gardena, CA	90248-3322	310-999-6162	999-6163	9-12	Samantha Navarro
New Opportunities Charter S	110 S La Brea Ave Ste 305A	Inglewood, CA	90301	310-946-0399		9-12	Paul Guzman
New S of San Francisco	655 De Haro St	San Francisco, CA	94107	415-401-8489		K-5	Ryan Chapman
New Technology HS	1400 Dickson St	Sacramento, CA	95822-3437	916-395-5254	433-2840	9-12	Kenneth Durham
New Village Girls Academy	147 N Occidental Blvd	Los Angeles, CA	90026-4601	213-385-4015	385-4020	9-12	Dr. Andrea Purcell
New Vision MS	2050 Pacific St	San Bernardino, CA	92404-6179	909-888-8390	888-8470	6-8	Alex Lucero
New West Charter S	1905 Armacost Ave	Los Angeles, CA	90025-5210	310-943-5444	231-3399	6-12	Dr. Sharon Weir
NextGeneration STEAM Academy	18001 Commercial St	Lathrop, CA	95330-8543	209-229-4736		K-8	Leslie Pombo
Nightingale S	1721 Carpenter Rd	Stockton, CA	95206-3809	209-933-7260	234-1850	K-8	Myra Machuca
Nobel MS	9950 Tampa Ave	Northridge, CA	91324-1142	818-773-4700	701-9480	6-8	Derek Horowitz
Nord Country Charter S	5554 California St	Chico, CA	95973-9795	530-891-3138	891-3273	K-8	Kathleen Dahlgren
Northcoast Prep and Performing Arts Acad	PO Box 276	Arcata, CA	95518-0276	707-822-0861	822-0878	6-12	Michael Bazemore
North County Trade Tech HS	1126 N Melrose Dr	Vista, CA	92083-3467	760-598-0782	598-0895	9-12	Doreen Quinn
Northern Summit Academy	2877 Childress Dr	Anderson, CA	96007	530-949-0154		K-12	Julia Knight
North Oakland Community Charter S	1000 42nd St	Oakland, CA	94608-3621	510-655-0540	655-1222	K-8	Stephen Ajani
North Valley Pivot Charter School	2550 Lakewest Dr	Chico, CA	95928	877-544-1423		6-12	Jayne Gaskell
Northwest Prep Charter S	2590 Piner Rd	Santa Rosa, CA	95401-4035	707-522-3320	522-3101	7-12	Joyce Hamilton
Norton Science and Language Academy	503 E Central Ave	San Bernardino, CA	92408	909-386-2300	386-7855	K-12	Fausto Barragan
NOVA Academy - Coachella	52780 Frederick St	Coachella, CA	92236	714-543-5437	543-5463	9-12	Lisa Hernandez
Nova Academy Early College HS	500 W Santa Ana Blvd	Santa Ana, CA	92706	714-569-0948	569-1693	9-12	Andrea Brumbaugh
Novato Charter S	940 C St	Novato, CA	94949-5060	415-883-4254	883-1859	K-8	Nikki Lloyd
Nueva Esperanza Charter Academy	1218 4th St	San Fernando, CA	91340-2314	818-256-1951	256-2397	6-12	Fidel Ramirez
Nueva Vista Language Academy	120 Garces Hwy	Delano, CA	93215-3328	661-721-5070	721-3638	PK-5	Anamarie Sanchez
Nuview Bridge Early College HS	30401 Reservoir Ave	Nuevo, CA	92567-9361	951-928-8498	928-0186	9-12	Dr. Jason Fowler Ed.D.
N Valley Military Institute Coll Prep	12105 Allegheny St	Sun Valley, CA	91352	818-368-1557	368-1935	6-12	Dr. Mark Ryan
Oakdale Charter HS	1235 E D St	Oakdale, CA	95361-3223	209-848-4361	848-4363	9-12	Craig Redman
Oak Grove ES	8760 Bower St	Sebastopol, CA	95472-2450	707-823-5225	829-2614	K-5	Paige Gardner
Oakland Charter Academy	4215 Foothill Blvd	Oakland, CA	94601	510-532-6751	532-6753	6-8	Joel Julien
Oakland Charter HS	2433 Coolidge Ave	Oakland, CA	94601	510-893-8700	893-8705	9-12	Sam Pasarow
Oakland Military Institute College Prep	3877 Lusk St	Oakland, CA	94608	510-594-3900	597-9886	6-12	Johnna Grell
Oakland S for the Arts	530 18th St	Oakland, CA	94612-1512	510-873-8800	873-8816	6-12	Brian Kohn
Oakland Unity HS	6038 Brann St	Oakland, CA	94605-1544	510-635-7170	635-3830	9-12	William Nee
Oakland Unity MS	6038 Brann St	Oakland, CA	94605	510-969-5302		6-8	Damon Grant
Oak Park Preparatory Academy	2315 34th St	Sacramento, CA	95817	916-533-4861		7-8	Annie Cervenka
Oasis Charter S	1135 Westridge Pkwy	Salinas, CA	93907-2529	831-424-9003	424-9005	K-6	Dr. Juanita Perea
Obama Charter S	PO Box 72028	Los Angeles, CA	90002	323-566-1965	566-1418	PK-5	Chaleese Norman
Ocean Charter S	12606 Culver Blvd	Los Angeles, CA	90066-6506	310-827-5511	827-2012	K-3	Stephanie Edwards
Ocean Charter S	7400 W Manchester Ave	Los Angeles, CA	90045	310-348-9050	348-9085	4-8	Stephanie Edwards
Ocean Grove Charter S	1166 Broadway Ste Q	Placerville, CA	95667-5745	800-979-4436	295-3583	K-12	Randy Gaschler
Odyssey Charter S	725 W Altadena Dr	Altadena, CA	91001-4103	626-229-0993	229-0586	K-8	Lauren O'Neill
O'Farrell Charter S	6130 Skyline Dr	San Diego, CA	92114-5620	619-263-3009	263-4339	PK-12	Dr. Jonathan Dean
Old Adobe ES	2856 Old Adobe Rd	Petaluma, CA	94954-9546	707-765-4301	765-4334	K-6	Jeff Williamson
Old Town Academy	2120 San Diego Ave	San Diego, CA	92110-2901	619-574-6225	683-2096	K-8	Jon Centofranchi
Olive Grove Charter S	PO Box 370	New Cuyama, CA	93254	805-623-1111	623-8512	K-12	Laura Mudge
Olivet Elementary Charter S	1825 Willowside Rd	Santa Rosa, CA	95401-3923	707-522-3045	522-3047	K-6	Mary Reynolds
one.Charter	800 Douglas Rd	Stockton, CA	95207-3607	209-468-9079	468-4651	7-12	Janine Kaeslin
OnePurpose S	PO Box 24509	San Francisco, CA	94124	415-657-0277		K-5	Antonio Tapia
Open Charter Magnet S	5540 W 77th St	Los Angeles, CA	90045-3214	310-568-0735	568-0904	K-5	Antoinette Cass
Opportunities for Learning	12731 Ramona Blvd Ste 201	Irwindale, CA	91706	626-814-0161	814-0686	K-12	Richard Moreno
Opportunities for Learning Charter S	18824 Soledad Canyon Rd	Canyon Country, CA	91351	661-424-1337	424-1129	7-12	Candice Varner
Opportunities for Learning - Duarte	806 E Huntington Dr	Monrovia, CA	91016	626-303-2022	303-2223	7-12	Richard Moreno
Opportunities for Learning S	33621 Del Obispo St Ste E	Dana Point, CA	92629-2100	949-248-1282	248-2450	K-12	Christian Cutter
Opportunity Charter S	2300 International Blvd	Oakland, CA	94601	510-670-4157		K-12	Tracey Burns
Opportunity Youth Academy	1290 Ridder Park Dr	San Jose, CA	95131	844-692-4888		10-12	Philip Morales
Optimist Charter S	6957 N Figueroa St	Los Angeles, CA	90042-1245	323-443-3100		7-12	Lynn DeYoung
Options for Youth - Apple Valley	13675 Niabi Rd	Apple Valley, CA	92308	760-247-6078	961-1723	7-12	Ami Popineau
Options for Youth - Arden	2125 Fulton Ave Ste 100	Sacramento, CA	95825	916-971-3175	971-3186	7-12	Jocelyn Baldwin
Options for Youth Carmichael	5825 Windmill Way	Carmichael, CA	95608	916-485-5155	485-5484	7-12	Jocelyn Baldwin
Options for Youth Charter S	405 S San Gabriel Blvd	San Gabriel, CA	91776	626-282-0390	282-0391	7-12	Bill Tynan
Options for Youth - Chino 1	7011 Schaefer Ave Ste E	Chino, CA	91710	909-465-9529	465-9809	7-12	Wendy Gillespie
Options for Youth - Chino 2	5475 Philadelphia St Ste B	Chino, CA	91710	909-591-6559	591-8438	7-12	Maricela Frymark
Options for Youth - Fontana 1	16981 Foothill Blvd	Fontana, CA	92335	909-357-3168	357-2875	7-12	Wendy Gillespie
Options for Youth - Fontana 2	17216 Slover Ave	Fontana, CA	92337	909-429-0482	429-9212	7-12	Wendy Gillespie
Options for Youth - Hesperia 1	15461 Main St	Hesperia, CA	92345	760-948-3355		7-12	
Options for Youth Highland Park	5926 Monterey Rd	Los Angeles, CA	90042	323-478-7334		7-12	
Options for Youth Irwindale	16023 Arrow Hwy Ste C	Baldwin Park, CA	91706	626-337-9352	337-4503	7-12	Zitlaly Marin
Options for Youth La Crescenta	2626 Foothill Blvd	La Crescenta, CA	91214	626-236-2060	236-2062	7-12	Bill Tynan
Options for Youth Moreno Valley	23080 Alessandro Blvd	Moreno Valley, CA	92553	951-653-3085		7-12	Ileana Arroyo
Options for Youth North Highlands	3542 A St	North Highlands, CA	95660	916-338-2375	338-2417	7-12	Jocelyn Baldwin
Options for Youth - Ontario	3130 Inland Empire Blvd	Ontario, CA	91764	909-476-5959	476-3636	7-12	Maricela Frymark
Options for Youth Orangevale	9470 Madison Ave	Orangevale, CA	95662	916-988-4138	988-4176	7-12	Jocelyn Baldwin
Options for Youth Oxnard	1731 E Ventura Blvd	Oxnard, CA	93036	888-389-9992		7-12	
Options for Youth Pomona	695 E Foothill Blvd	Pomona, CA	91767	909-593-2163	596-5627	7-12	Maricela Frymark
Options for Youth - Rancho	9849 Foothill Blvd	Rch Cucamonga, CA	91730	909-466-9082	466-9083	7-12	Jocelyn Baldwin
Options for Youth Rancho Cordova	11088 Olson Dr	Rancho Cordova, CA	95670-5650	916-631-8113	631-8121	7-12	Jocelyn Baldwin
Options for Youth San Bernardino I	985 S E St Ste A	San Bernardino, CA	92408	909-381-6260	381-6230	7-12	Ileana Arroyo
Options for Youth San Bernardino II	1148 E Highland Ave	San Bernardino, CA	92404	909-882-8500	882-8315	7-12	Ileana Arroyo
Options for Youth - Upland	1438 W 7th St	Upland, CA	91786	909-946-0500	946-0506	7-12	Wendy Gillespie
Options for Youth Victorville - 1	14725 7th St	Victorville, CA	92395	760-955-5525	955-1107	7-12	
Options for Youth Victorville - 2	11975 Hesperia Rd	Hesperia, CA	92345	760-955-5900	955-5919	7-12	Bryan Gillespie
Options for Youth Victorville - 3	15378 Ramona Ave	Victorville, CA	92392	760-245-9086		7-12	
Options for Youth Victorville - 4	14120 Bear Valley Rd # 104	Victorville, CA	92392	760-241-8300	241-8879	7-12	
Orange County Academy Science and Arts	29292 Crown Valley Pkwy	Laguna Niguel, CA	92677	949-269-3290		K-8	Doreen Fioretto
Orange County Educational Arts Academy	825 N Broadway	Santa Ana, CA	92701-3423	714-558-2787	558-2775	K-8	Kristin Collins
Orange County HS of the Arts	1010 N Main St	Santa Ana, CA	92701-3602	714-560-0900	664-0463	7-12	Steven Wagner
Orange County Workforce Innovation High	505 N Euclid St	Anaheim, CA	92805	714-576-2714		9-12	Julie Parra
Orchard View Charter S	700 Watertrough Rd	Sebastopol, CA	95472-3917	707-823-4709	823-6187	K-12	Cathy Stroud
Orcutt Academy	610 Pinal Ave	Orcutt, CA	93455	805-938-8550		K-8	Joe Dana
Orcutt Academy	610 Pinal Ave	Orcutt, CA	93455	805-938-8550	938-8995	9-12	Rhett Carter
Our Community Charter S	10045 Jumilla Ave	Chatsworth, CA	91311	818-350-5000	350-5007	K-8	Lynn Izakowitz
Oxford Day Academy	1001 Beech St	East Palo Alto, CA	94303	650-260-3152		9-12	Mallory Dwinal Ph.D.
Oxford Preparatory Academy	23000 Via Santa Maria	Mission Viejo, CA	92691-1827	949-305-6111	297-4747	K-8	Denise Pascoe
Oxford Preparatory Academy	22882 Loumont Dr	Lake Forest, CA	92630	949-916-5672	692-2102	K-8	Jeff Rich
Pacific Coast Charter S	294 Green Valley Rd	Watsonville, CA	95076-1300	831-786-2180	786-2192	K-12	Suzanne Smith
Pacific Collegiate Charter S	3004 Mission St	Santa Cruz, CA	95060-5733	831-479-7785	427-5254	7-12	Archie Douglas

School	Address	City,State	Zip code	Telephone	Fax	Grade	Contact
Pacific Community Charter S	PO Box 984	Point Arena, CA	95468-0984	707-882-4131	882-4132	K-12	Sigrid Hillscan
Pacific Law Academy	1621 Brookside Rd	Stockton, CA	95207	209-933-7475	472-7841	9-12	Carol Sanderson
Pacific View Charter S	3670 Ocean Ranch Blvd	Oceanside, CA	92056-2669	760-757-0161	435-2666	K-12	Gina Campbell
Pacoima Charter S	11016 Norris Ave	Pacoima, CA	91331-2598	818-899-0201	890-3812	K-5	Sylvia Fajardo
Pajaro Valley HS	500 Harkins Slough Rd	Watsonville, CA	95076	831-728-8102	728-6944	9-12	Alison Niizawa
Palisades Charter ES	800 Via De La Paz	Pacific Plsds, CA	90272-3617	310-454-3700	459-5627	K-5	Gary Saunders
Palisades Charter HS	15777 Bowdoin St	Pacific Plsds, CA	90272-3523	310-230-6623	454-6076	9-12	Dr. Pamela Magee
Palmdale Aerospace Academy	3300 E Palmdale Blvd	Palmdale, CA	93550	661-273-3680	273-0850	7-12	Dr. Laura Herman
Palm Desert Charter MS	74200 Rutledge Way	Palm Desert, CA	92260-2646	760-862-4320	862-4327	6-8	Sallie Fraser
Paradise Charter MS	6473 Clark Rd	Paradise, CA	95969-3501	530-872-7277	872-2924	6-8	Chris Reid
Paradise Charter S	3361 California Ave	Modesto, CA	95358-8337	209-524-0184	524-0363	K-8	Heath Thomason
Paragon Collegiate Academy	1608 Sampson St	Marysville, CA	95901-4314	530-742-2505	763-5772	K-8	Laura Cotney
Para Los Ninos Charter S	1617 E 7th St	Los Angeles, CA	90021-1207	213-239-6605		K-5	Santa Acuna
Para Los Ninos - Gratts ECC	474 Hartford Ave	Los Angeles, CA	90017-1306	213-481-3200	977-5449	PK-2	Dr. Juan Ramirez
Para Los Ninos MS	835 Stanford Ave	Los Angeles, CA	90021-1847	213-896-2640	896-2660	6-8	Hassan Dornayi
Paramount Collegiate Academy	4010 El Camino Ave	Sacramento, CA	95821	916-484-1480		6-12	Dawn Douglas
Pasadena Rosebud Academy	3544 Canon Blvd	Altadena, CA	91001	626-797-7704	797-0788	K-8	Shawn Brumfield Ed.D.
Paseo Grande S	2444 Marconi Ave	Sacramento, CA	95821	916-974-7307		K-12	Dave Petropulos
Pathways Academy Charter	1782 La Costa Meadows # 102	San Marcos, CA	92078	760-494-9646	897-7558	K-12	Kurt Madden
Pathways Charter S	150 Professional Center Dr	Rohnert Park, CA	94928	707-585-6510	585-6515	K-12	Sara Jordan
Pathways Community S	8800 S San Pedro St	Los Angeles, CA	90003-3541	323-481-2334		9-12	Erica Hamilton
Pathways ICare Charter S	1020 Sun Down Way	Roseville, CA	95661-4473	916-784-6107	771-0893	K-8	Christina Smith
Pathways to College Charter S	PO Box 402672	Hesperia, CA	92340-2672	760-949-8002	947-9648	K-8	Dr. Sonya Joyner
Peabody Charter S	3018 Calle Noguera	Santa Barbara, CA	93105-2848	805-563-1172	569-7042	K-6	Demian Barnett
Peak to Peak Mountain Charter S	19009 Cerro Noroeste Rd	Pine Mountain C, CA	93222	661-242-3811		K-8	Tamara Trost
Penngrove ES	365 Adobe Rd	Penngrove, CA	94951	707-778-4755	778-4831	K-6	Amy Fadeji
Petaluma Accelerated Charter S	110 Ellis St	Petaluma, CA	94952	707-778-4750	778-4789	7-8	Matthew Harris
Phoenix Academy	PO Box 4925	San Rafael, CA	94913-4925	415-491-0581	491-0981	9-12	Raquel Rose
Phoenix Charter Academy	2195 Larkspur Ln	Redding, CA	96002	530-222-9275		K-12	Patricia Dougherty
Piner-Olivet Charter S	2707 Francisco Ave	Santa Rosa, CA	95403-1869	707-522-3310	522-3317	7-8	Susan Donner
Pinnacle Academy Charter Program	760 Broadway St	King City, CA	93930	831-385-4661	385-0643		Dr. Steve James
Pioneer ES	1888 Mustang Dr	Hanford, CA	93230-9811	559-584-8831	584-7049	PK-5	Sharon Cronk
Pioneer MS	101 W Pioneer Way	Hanford, CA	93230-9489	559-584-0112	584-0118	6-8	Jamie Rogers
Pioneer Technical Center	1105 S Madera Ave	Madera, CA	93637-5576	559-664-1600	673-5569	9-12	Leslie Neumeier
Pittman S	701 E Park St	Stockton, CA	95202-2207	209-933-7496	942-2769	K-8	Emilio Junez
Pivot Charter S	1030 La Bonita Dr	San Marcos, CA	92078	760-591-0217	891-0562	6-12	Craig Hobart
Pivot Online Charter - North Bay	2999 Cleveland Ave Ste D	Santa Rosa, CA	95403-2761	707-843-4676	544-2908	K-12	Jayna Gaskell
Plainview Academic Charter Academy	10819 Plainview Ave	Tujunga, CA	91042-1633	818-353-1730	353-6658	K-5	Kenneth Johnson
Plumas Charter S	175 N Mill Creek Rd	Quincy, CA	95971-9678	530-283-3851	283-3841	K-12	Taletha Washburn
Pomelo Community Charter S	7633 March Ave	West Hills, CA	91304-5233	818-887-9700	887-1744	K-5	Andrea Ferber
Port of Los Angeles HS	250 W 5th St	San Pedro, CA	90731-3304	310-832-9201	832-1605	9-12	Gaetano Scotti
Prepa Tec Los Angeles	2665 Clarendon Ave	Walnut Park, CA	90255	323-800-2741	923-0380	6-7	
Preuss S	9500 Gilman Dr	La Jolla, CA	92093-5004	858-822-3000	822-1620	6-12	Scott Barton
Price Charter MS	2650 New Jersey Ave	San Jose, CA	95124-1520	408-377-2532	377-7406	6-8	Natalie Gioco
Primary Charter S	51 E Beverly Pl	Tracy, CA	95376-3191	209-831-5240	831-5243	K-4	Virginia Stewart
Provisional Accelerated Learning Academy	PO Box 7100	San Bernardino, CA	92411-0100	909-887-7002	887-8942	9-12	Dwaine Radden
Public Policy Charter S	1701 Browning Blvd	Los Angeles, CA	90062-1302	323-205-7920		5-8	Sonali Tucker
Public Safety Academy	1482 E Enterprise Dr	San Bernardino, CA	92408-0161	909-382-4574		6-12	Jennifer Stickel
PUC Community Charter ES	14019 Sayre St	Sylmar, CA	91342-4265	818-492-1890	492-1881	K-5	Jocelyn Velez
PUC Inspire Charter Academy	12550 Van Nuys Blvd	Pacoima, CA	91331	818-492-1880		6-8	Megan McGarry
PUC iPrep Charter Academy	1800 Colorado Blvd	Los Angeles, CA	90041	323-287-8479		K-8	Yvonne Carillo
Puente Charter S	501 S Boyle Ave	Los Angeles, CA	90033-3816	323-780-8900		K-K	Jerome Greening
Quail Lake Charter S	4087 N Quail Lake Dr	Clovis, CA	93619-4646	559-524-6720	292-1276	K-8	Kim Labosky
REACH	708 Gravenstein Hwy N	Sebastopol, CA	95472-2808	707-823-8618	829-6285	K-8	Julie Heinsen
REACH Leadership STEAM Academy	4850 Jurupa Ave	Riverside, CA	92504	951-275-8820	275-8829	PK-6	Dr. Virgie Rentie
Reagan ES	1180 Diane Ave	Kingsburg, CA	93631-2830	559-897-6986	897-6987	4-6	Amy Winchell
REALM Charter HS	1222 University Ave	Berkeley, CA	94702-1766	510-665-8300	809-9899	9-12	Victor Diaz
REALM Charter MS	2023 8th St	Berkeley, CA	94710-2026	510-809-9800	809-9899	6-8	Victor Diaz
Redding School of the Arts	955 Inspiration Pl	Redding, CA	96003	530-243-7145	243-4318	K-8	Margaret Johnson
Redding STEM Academy	3711 Oasis Rd	Redding, CA	96003	530-275-5480	275-5416	K-8	John Husome
Redwood Academy of Ukiah	PO Box 1383	Ukiah, CA	95482-1383	707-467-0500	467-4942	7-12	Rod Logan
Redwood Coast Montessori	1611 Peninsula Dr	Arcata, CA	95521	707-832-4194	832-4194	K-9	Bryan Little
Redwood Preparatory Charter S	1480 Ross Hill Rd	Fortuna, CA	95540	707-682-6149		PK-8	Krista Croteau
Renaissance Arts Academy	2558 N San Fernando Rd	Los Angeles, CA	90065	323-259-5700	259-5718	K-12	P.K. Candaux
Resolute Academy Charter	1265 E 112th St	Los Angeles, CA	90059	323-559-6284		5-8	Natasha Sperstein
Revere Charter MS	1450 Allenford Ave	Los Angeles, CA	90049-3614	310-917-4800	576-7957	6-8	Thomas Iannucci
Richmond Charter Academy	1450 Marina Way S	Richmond, CA	94804	510-235-2465	235-2487	6-8	Randy Taylor
Richmond College Prep S	PO Box 2814	Richmond, CA	94802-2814	510-235-2066		K-6	Jennifer Tester
Ridgecrest Charter S	325 S Downs St	Ridgecrest, CA	93555-4531	760-375-1010	375-7766	K-8	Steve Martinez
Riebli ES	315 Mark West Springs Rd	Santa Rosa, CA	95404-1101	707-524-2980	524-2986	K-6	Patty Dineen
Rincon Valley Charter S	5305 Dupont Dr	Santa Rosa, CA	95409-3843	707-539-3410	537-1791	7-8	Amy Wiese
Rio Valley Charter S	1110 W Kettleman Ln	Lodi, CA	95240	209-368-4934	368-4953	K-12	Leslie Leedy
Rise Kohyang HS	1575 W 2nd St	Los Angeles, CA	90026	213-284-2553	256-3974	9-12	Elias Pappas
Rise Kohyang MS	3020 Wilshire Blve Ste 2	Los Angeles, CA	90010	424-789-8338	256-3974	6-8	Eliza Kim
Rising Sun Montessori S	7006 Rossmore Ln	El Dorado Hills, CA	95762	916-936-2333		PK-8	Karl Zierhut
Riverbank Language Academy Charter S	2400 Stanislaus St	Riverbank, CA	95367-2233	209-869-8093	869-0430	K-8	Vanessa Rojas
River Charter S Lighthouse Charter	1500 Park Blvd	West Sacramento, CA	95691	916-744-1212		K-8	Steve Lewis
River Islands Technology Academy	1175 Marina Dr	Lathrop, CA	95330-8586	209-229-4700		K-7	Brenda Scholl
River MS	2447 Old Sonoma Rd	Napa, CA	94558-6006	707-253-6813	258-2800	6-8	Celeste Akiu
River Montessori Charter S	3880 Cypress Dr	Petaluma, CA	94954-5613	707-778-6414	773-5800	1-6	Kelly Mannion
River Oak Charter S	555 Leslie St	Ukiah, CA	95482-5507	707-467-1855	467-1857	K-8	Rima Meechan
River Oaks Academy Charter S	920 Hampshire Rd Ste X	Westlake Vlg, CA	91361	805-777-7999	777-7998	PK-12	Claudia Weintraub
Riverside County Education Academy	44-801 Golf Center Pkwy	Indio, CA	92201	760-863-3111	863-3110	9-12	Santos Campos
Riverside County Education Academy	13730 Perris Blvd	Moreno Valley, CA	92553	951-826-4905		9-12	Santos Campos
Riverside Drive ES	13061 Riverside Dr	Sherman Oaks, CA	91423-2199	818-990-4525	789-4835	K-5	Erin Haynes
Riverside Preparatory S	PO Box 386	Oro Grande, CA	92368	760-243-5884	843-3766	K-12	JoAnn Baeten
River Springs Charter S	43466 Business Park Dr	Temecula, CA	92590-5526	951-252-8800	252-8801	K-12	Tanya Rogers
River Valley Charter S	9707 1/2 Marilla Dr	Lakeside, CA	92040-2868	619-390-2579	390-2581	7-12	Brooke Faigin
Roberts Ferry Charter School Academy	101 Roberts Ferry Rd	Waterford, CA	95386-9502	209-874-2331		6-8	Bob Loretelli
Rocketship Academy Brilliant Minds	2960 Story Road	San Jose, CA	95127	408-708-5650	618-8637	PK-4	Chioma Ellis
Rocketship Alma Academy	198 W Alma Ave	San Jose, CA	95110-3631	877-931-6838	982-3691	K-5	Samantha Turner
Rocketship Discovery Prep S	370 Wooster Ave	San Jose, CA	95116-1095	408-217-8951	217-9251	K-6	Chaka Hajii
Rocketship Fuerza Community Prep	70 S Jackson Ave	San Jose, CA	95116-2506	408-708-5744		K-4	Juan Mateos
Rocketship Los Suenos Academy	331 S 34th St	San Jose, CA	95116-2905	877-684-4028	935-6084	K-5	Judy Lavi
Rocketship Mateo Sheedy ES	788 Locust St	San Jose, CA	95110	408-286-3330	286-3331	K-5	Jason Fromoltz
Rocketship Mosaic ES	950 Owsley Ave	San Jose, CA	95122-3109	408-899-2607	899-2613	K-5	Danny Etcheverry
Rocketship Rising Stars	3167 Senter Rd	San Jose, CA	95111	301-677-4879		K-5	Kylie Alsofrom
Rocketship Si Se Puede Academy	2249 Dobern Ave	San Jose, CA	95116-3405	408-286-3344	286-3331	K-12	Heidy Shinn
Rocketship Spark Academy	683 Sylvandale Ave	San Jose, CA	95111	408-622-6651	622-5748	K-5	Annie Tran
Rocklin Academy	6532 Turnstone Way	Rocklin, CA	95765-5865	916-632-6580	784-3034	K-6	Laura Regan
Rocklin Academy at Meyers Street	5035 Meyers St	Rocklin, CA	95677-2811	916-632-6580	784-3034	K-6	Wendy Mitchell
Rocklin Academy Gateway	6550 Lonetree Blvd	Rocklin, CA	95765-5874	916-632-6580	784-3034	PK-8	Jillyane Antoon
Rocklin Independent Charter Academy	3250 Victory Dr	Rocklin, CA	95765	916-632-3195		K-12	Chuck Thibideau A.B.
Rocky Point Charter S	3500 Tamarack Dr	Redding, CA	96003-1747	530-225-0456	225-0499	K-8	Shawna Norris
Romero Charter S	1157 S Berendo St	Los Angeles, CA	90006	213-413-9600	413-9699	6-8	Kevin Myers
Roosevelt Community Learning Center	31191 Road 180	Visalia, CA	93292-9585	559-592-9160	592-2927	K-12	Daniel Huecker
Roosevelt ES	1185 10th Ave	Kingsburg, CA	93631-2100	559-897-5193	897-6865	1-1	Shawn Marshall
Rosa Parks Academy	1930 S D St	Stockton, CA	95206-2489	209-944-5590	465-2690	K-5	Natalie June
Roseland Accelerated MS	1934 Biwana Rd	Santa Rosa, CA	95407	707-546-7089	546-0434	7-8	Haley Piazza
Roseland Collegiate Prep	80 Ursuline Rd	Santa Rosa, CA	95403	707-528-1764	528-8605	7-12	Danielle Yount
Roseland University Prep	1931 Biwana Dr	Santa Rosa, CA	95407	707-566-9990	566-9992	9-12	Sue Reese
Roses in Concrete Community S	4551 Steele St	Oakland, CA	94619-2743	510-698-3794		K-8	Jeff Duncan-Andrade
Ross Valley Charter S	PO Box 791	Fairfax, CA	94978	415-534-6970		PK-5	Luke Duchene
Sacramento HS	2315 34th St	Sacramento, CA	95817-1299	916-277-6200	277-6370	9-12	Shannon Wheatley
Sacramento Valley Charter S	2399 Sellers Way	West Sacramento, CA	95691	916-596-6422	372-7249	K-8	Dr. Amrik Singh
Sage Oak Charter S	1473 Ford St Ste 105	Redlands, CA	92373	888-435-4445		K-12	Kurt Madden
St. HOPE Public School 7	5201 Strawberry Ln	Sacramento, CA	95820-4815	916-649-7850	277-7039	K-8	Kari Wehrly
Salmon Creek S	1935 Bohemian Hwy	Occidental, CA	95465-9100	707-874-1205	874-1226	2-8	Rene McBride
Samueli Academy	1901 N Fairview St	Santa Ana, CA	92706	714-619-0245	619-0252	9-12	Rocio Gomez
San Carlos Charter Learning Center	750 Dartmouth Ave	San Carlos, CA	94070-1769	650-508-7343	508-7341	K-8	Stacy Emory
San Diego Cooperative Charter S	7260 Linda Vista Rd	San Diego, CA	92111-6128	858-496-1613	467-9741	K-8	Dr. Sarah Saluta
San Diego Cooperative Charter S 2	PO Box 13926	San Diego, CA	92170	619-840-6993		K-8	Anthony Villasenor
San Diego Cooperative Charter S 2	3550 Logan Ave	San Diego, CA	92113-2712	619-840-6993		K-8	Anthony Vissasenor
San Diego Global Vision Academy	3430 School St	San Diego, CA	92116-3423	619-600-5321	550-3637	K-5	Christine Kane
San Diego Neighborhood Homeschools	3548 Seagate Way Ste 140	Oceanside, CA	92056-2676	760-295-1117	509-4691	K-12	Salvador Leon
San Diego Virtual Charter S	7950 University Ave	La Mesa, CA	91942-5579	619-713-7271	308-6007	7-12	Brennan McLaughlin
Sanger Academy Charter S	2207 9th St	Sanger, CA	93657-2711	559-524-6840	875-8045	K-8	Mark Coleman

School	Address	City,State	Zip code	Telephone	Fax	Grade	Contact
San Jacinto Valley Academy	480 N San Jacinto Ave	San Jacinto, CA	92583-2729	951-654-6113	644-5083	K-12	Penny Harrison
San Joaquin Building Futures Academy	PO Box 213030	Stockton, CA	95213-9030	209-468-8140	468-4951	9-12	Janine Kaeslin
San Jose Charter Academy	2021 W Alwood St	West Covina, CA	91790-3259	626-856-1693	480-7125	K-8	Erin Shiroma
San Jose Conservation Corps Charter S	1560 Berger Dr	San Jose, CA	95112-2703	408-283-7171		12-12	Stephanie Ogden
San Lorenzo Valley USD Charter S	325 Marion Ave	Ben Lomond, CA	95005	831-335-0932	336-0131	K-12	Rhonda Schlosser
San Miguel ES	5350 Faught Rd	Santa Rosa, CA	95403-1205	707-524-2960	524-2968	K-6	Patrick Eagle
Santa Barbara Charter S	6100 Stow Canyon Rd	Goleta, CA	93117-1705	805-967-6522	967-6382	PK-8	Laura Donner
Santa Clarita Valley International S	28060 Hasley Canyon Rd	Castaic, CA	91384-4572	661-705-4820	607-0295	K-12	Kimberly Matthes
Santa Monica Blvd Community Charter S	1022 N Van Ness Ave	Los Angeles, CA	90038-3252	323-469-0971	462-4093	K-6	David Riddick
Santa Rosa Academy	27587 La Piedra Rd	Menifee, CA	92584	951-672-2400	672-6060	K-12	Nick Stearns
Santa Rosa Accelerated Charter	4650 Badger Rd	Santa Rosa, CA	95409-2633	707-528-5319	528-5644	5-6	Ed Navarro
Santa Rosa Charter Academy	3838 Eagle Rock Blvd	Los Angeles, CA	90065-3638	323-254-1703	254-0958	6-8	Melody Morris
Santa Rosa Charter S for the Arts	2230 Lomitas Ave	Santa Rosa, CA	95404	707-522-3170	522-3172	K-8	Kristen Vogel
Santa Rosa French-American Charter S	1350 Sonoma Ave	Santa Rosa, CA	95405	707-522-3161		K-6	Richard Johnstone
Santa Ynez Valley Charter S	PO Box 59	Santa Ynez, CA	93460-0059	805-686-7360	686-7383	K-8	Mark Palmerston
Santiago Charter MS	515 N Rancho Santiago Blvd	Orange, CA	92869-2724	714-997-6366	532-4758	7-8	Dr. James D'Agostino
Sartorette Charter S	3850 Woodford Dr	San Jose, CA	95124-3736	408-264-4380	264-1758	K-5	John Hayes
SAVA: Sacramento Academic and Vocational	3141 Dwight Rd Ste 400	Elk Grove, CA	95758-6473	916-428-3200	428-3232	7-12	Morri Elliott
SAVA: Sacramento Academic and Vocational	5330 Power Inn Rd Ste D	Sacramento, CA	95820-6757	916-387-8063	387-0139	7-12	Morri Elliott
SCALE Leadership Academy	14816 Central Ave	Chino, CA	91710	888-315-4660		K-12	Lawrence Wynder
Schaefer Charter S	1370 San Miguel Rd	Santa Rosa, CA	95403-1986	707-522-3015	522-3017	K-6	Gina Silveira
Scholarship Prep Charter S	1010 W 17th St	Santa Ana, CA	92706	714-795-3498		K-8	Matthew Bragman
Scholarship Prep Charter S	4070 Mission Ave	Oceanside, CA	92057	442-262-3249		K-12	Dr. Erci Beam
S for Entrepreneurship and Technology	3540 Aero Ct	San Diego, CA	92123	858-874-4338	874-5645	9-12	Dr. Neil McCurdy
School of Arts and Enterprise	295 N Garey Ave	Pomona, CA	91767-5429	909-622-0699	620-1018	6-12	Lucille Berger
School of Extended Educational Options	1460 E Holt Ave Ste 100	Pomona, CA	91767-5851	909-397-4900	622-2496	7-12	Tom Sweeney
S of Universal Learning	533 Lomas Santa Fe Dr	Solana Beach, CA	92075	858-345-1888		7-9	Marisa Bruyneel
School of Unlimited Learning	2336 Calaveras St	Fresno, CA	93721-1104	559-498-8543	237-0956	9-12	Dr. Mark Wilson
Science and Technology Charter S	PO Box 458	Knights Landing, CA	95645-0458	530-735-6435	735-6155	K-6	Barbara Herms
Sebastopol Independent Charter S	PO Box 1170	Sebastopol, CA	95473-1170	707-824-9700	824-1432	K-8	Chris Topham
Sequoia Charter ES	PO Box 44260	Lemon Cove, CA	93244-0260	559-564-2106	564-2126	K-8	Perry D. Jensen
Serna Charter S	19 S Central Ave	Lodi, CA	95240-2901	209-331-7809	331-7997	K-6	Maria Cervantes
Serrania Charter for Enriched Studies	5014 Serrania Ave	Woodland Hills, CA	91364-3350	818-340-6700	592-0565	K-5	Sr. Luis Alvarado M.Ed.
Shasta Charter Academy	307 Park Marina Cir	Redding, CA	96001	530-245-2600	245-2611	9-12	Ben Claassen M.A.
Shasta Co. Independent Study Charter S	1644 Magnolia Ave	Redding, CA	96001	530-225-0163		7-12	Mary Lord
Shenandoah HS	6540 Koki Ln	El Dorado, CA	95623-4328	530-622-6212	622-1071	9-12	Chuck Palmer
Shenandoah Valley MS	10010 Shenandoah Rd	Plymouth, CA	95669	209-257-5334		5-8	Tia Peters
Sherman Oaks Charter S	14755 Greenleaf St	Sherman Oaks, CA	91403-4199	818-784-8283	981-8258	K-5	Carla Miller
Sherwood Montessori S	1010 Cleveland Ave	Chico, CA	95928	530-345-6600	345-6620	K-8	Michelle Yezbick
Shiloh Charter School	6633 Paradise Rd	Modesto, CA	95358	209-522-2261	522-2261	3-12	Seth Ehrler
SIATech Charter S	1949 Avenida del Oro	Oceanside, CA	92056-5820	760-945-1227	631-3411	9-12	Dr. Linda Dawson
Sierra Academy of Expeditionary Learning	340 Buena Vista St	Grass Valley, CA	95945-7210	530-268-2200		9-12	Erica Crane
Sierra Charter S	1931 N Fine Ave	Fresno, CA	93727-1534	559-490-4290	490-4292	K-12	Lisa Marasco
Sierra Expeditionary Learning	11603 Donner Pass Rd	Truckee, CA	96161-4953	530-582-3701	582-3703	K-8	David Manahan
Sierra Foothill Charter S	4952 School House Rd	Catheys Valley, CA	95306-9710	209-742-6222	742-6922	K-8	Mindy Bolar
Sierra Montessori Academy	16229 Duggans Rd	Grass Valley, CA	95949-8520	530-268-9990	268-0613	K-8	Henry Bietz
Sierra Vista Charter HS	351 N K St	Tulare, CA	93274	559-687-7384	687-7388	9-12	Tammy Aldaco
Silver Oak HS	951 Palisade St	Hayward, CA	94542-1048	510-370-3334		9-12	Elaine Blasi
Simon Technology Acad HS	10720 Wilmington Ave	Los Angeles, CA	90059-1236	323-744-2122	744-2123	9-12	Dr. Christopher Carr
Six Rivers Charter HS	1720 M St	Arcata, CA	95521-5741	707-825-2428	825-2034	9-12	Ron Perry
Sixth Grade Academy	700 Bantam Way	Petaluma, CA	94952-1709	707-778-4724		6-6	Renee Semik
Sixth Street Prep-STREAM S	12219 Second Ave	Victorville, CA	92395	760-241-0962	241-2497	K-6	Collin Rowe
Skirball MS	603 E 115th St	Los Angeles, CA	90059-2322	323-905-1377	905-1378	6-8	Marco Ibarra
Sky Mountain Charter S	4535 Missouri Flat Rd	Placerville, CA	95667-6846	530-295-3566	295-3583	K-12	Susan Clark
Smidt Technology HS	211 S Avenue 20	Los Angeles, CA	90031-2508	323-352-3206		9-12	Dr. Dean Marolla-Turner
Smythe Academy of Arts & Sciences	2781 Northgate Blvd	Sacramento, CA	95833-2208	916-566-2740	566-3584	PK-6	Ken Dandurand
Smythe Academy of Arts & Sciences	700 Dos Rios St	Sacramento, CA	95811	916-566-3430	566-3531	7-8	Melissa Jewell M.Ed.
SOAR Charter Academy	198 W Mill St	San Bernardino, CA	92408-1402	909-888-3300	888-3310	K-8	Trisha Lancaster
Sol Aureus College Prep Charter S	6620 Gloria Dr	Sacramento, CA	95831	916-421-0600	421-0601	K-8	Norman Hernandez
Soledad Enrichment Action Charter S	222 N Virgil Ave	Los Angeles, CA	90004-3622	213-480-4200	480-4199	9-12	Margaret Godinez
Sonoma Charter S	17202 Highway 12	Sonoma, CA	95476	707-935-4232	935-4207	K-8	
Sonoma Mountain ES	1900 Rainier Cir	Petaluma, CA	94954-2543	707-765-4305	765-4385	K-6	Michele Gochberg
South Bay Charter S	6077 Loma Ave	Eureka, CA	95503-6869	707-443-4828	444-3690	K-8	Gary Storts
South Sutter Charter S	4535 Missouri Flat Rd Ste1A	Placerville, CA	95667	800-979-4436	295-3583	K-12	Cynthia Rachel
Spark Charter S	739 Morse Ave	Sunnyvale, CA	94085-3010	408-752-2631		K-8	Christopher Mahoney Ed.D.
Spring Creek Matanzas Charter S	1687 Yulupa Ave	Santa Rosa, CA	95405-7778	707-546-6183	528-8027	4-6	Kate Westrich
Spring Creek Matanzas Charter S	4675 Mayette Ave	Santa Rosa, CA	95405-7331	707-545-1771	545-6926	PK-3	Joan Boyce
Squaw Valley Preparatory	PO Box 2891	Olympic Valley, CA	96146-2891	530-581-1036	581-2012	6-12	Jeff Kraunz
Stallworth Charter S	1610 E Main St	Stockton, CA	95205	209-948-4511	943-5218	PK-8	Alice Stallworth
Stanislaus Alternative Charter S	1120 13th St	Modesto, CA	95354-0950	209-238-6801	238-4216	9-12	Julie Moore
Steele Canyon Charter HS	12440 Campo Rd	Spring Valley, CA	91978-2331	619-660-3500	660-7198	9-12	Don Hohimer
Stella Middle Charter Academy	2636 S Mansfield Ave	Los Angeles, CA	90016-3512	323-406-7155	954-6415	5-6	Darryl Garris
Stellar Charter School	5885 E Bonnyview Rd	Redding, CA	96001-4535	530-245-7730	245-7731	K-12	Heidi Schuler
Stern Math and Science S	5151 State Univ Dr Lot 7	Los Angeles, CA	90032	323-987-2144	987-2149	9-12	Kirsten Woo Ph.D.
Stockton Collegiate International ES	PO Box 2286	Stockton, CA	95201-2286	209-390-9861	390-9862	K-5	Scott Luhn
Stockton Collegiate International S	PO Box 2286	Stockton, CA	95201	209-390-9861	390-9862	6-12	Scott Luhn
Stockton Early College Academy	349 E Vine St	Stockton, CA	95202-1107	209-933-7370	939-9504	9-12	Joshaua Thom
Stockton HS	22 S Van Buren St	Stockton, CA	95203-3118	209-933-7365	465-5822	9-12	Maryann Santella
Stone Bridge S	1680 Los Carneros Ave	Napa, CA	94559-9741	707-252-5522	251-9767	K-8	Maria Martinez
Stony Point Academy	3223 Primrose Ave	Santa Rosa, CA	95407	707-568-7504		K-10	
STREAM Charter S	455 Oro Dam Blvd E	Oroville, CA	95965	530-534-1633		K-8	Dr. Donald Phillips
Success One Charter S	451 S Villa Ave	Willows, CA	95988-2964	530-934-6575		K-5	Susan Domenighini
Summit Charter Academy - Lombardi Campus	1509 Lombardi St	Porterville, CA	93257	559-788-6445	783-9400	K-6	Stacie Fleischman
Summit Charter Academy - Mathew Campus	175 S Mathew St	Porterville, CA	93257-2710	559-782-5902	782-5907	K-6	Lily Shimer
Summit Charter Collegiate Academy	15550 Redwood St	Porterville, CA	93257	559-788-6440	788-6444	6-12	Jorge Ramos
Summit K2 Charter S	1800 Elm St	El Cerrito, CA	94530	510-374-4093		7-12	Abbie Ridenour
Summit Leadership Academy High Desert	12850 Muscatel St	Hesperia, CA	92344-5566	760-949-9202	949-9257	9-12	Shannon Brandner
Summit Preparatory Charter HS	890 Broadway St	Redwood City, CA	94063-3105	650-556-1110	556-1121	9-12	Penelope Pak
Summit Preparatory Charter S	5100 S Broadway Ave	Los Angeles, CA	90037	323-642-8806		4-8	Arianna Haut
Summit Public S: Rainier	1750 S White Rd	San Jose, CA	95127-4760	408-831-3104	831-3105	9-12	Edwin Avarca
Summit Public S: Shasta	699 Serramonte Blvd	Daly City, CA	94015-4132	650-799-4719	799-4721	9-12	Wren Maletsky
Summit Public S: Tahoma	285 Blossom Hill Rd	San Jose, CA	95123-2048	408-729-1981	729-3853	9-12	Jonathan Stewart
Summit Public School: Denali	495 Mercury Dr	Sunnyvale, CA	94085-4707	669-600-5697		6-12	Kevin Bock
SunRidge Charter S	7285 Hayden Ave	Sebastopol, CA	95472-4359	707-824-2844	824-2861	K-8	Kalen Wood
Sunrise MS	1149 E Julian St	San Jose, CA	95116-1005	877-659-4785		6-8	Teresa Robinson
Sutter Peak Charter Academy	6450 20th St	Rio Linda, CA	95673-3718	866-992-9033		K-12	Heather Marshall
Sycamore Academy Science & Cultural Arts	23151 Palomar St	Wildomar, CA	92595	951-678-5217	678-5932	K-8	Barbara Hale
Sycamore Valley Academy	4230 W Tulare Ave	Visalia, CA	93277	559-622-3236	622-3237	K-8	Ruth Dutton
Sylmar Charter HS	13050 Borden Ave	Sylmar, CA	91342-4299	818-833-3700	364-1037	9-12	James Lee
Synergy Charter Academy	PO Box 78999	Los Angeles, CA	90016-0999	323-235-7960	235-7970	K-5	Kristine Miklos
Synergy Kinetic Academy	PO Box 78999	Los Angeles, CA	90016	323-846-2225	846-2234	6-8	Christine Bradford
Synergy Quantum Academy	PO Box 78999	Los Angeles, CA	90016-0999	323-846-4716	846-4729	9-12	Dr. Phillip Gedeon
Taft Charter HS	5461 Winnetka Ave	Woodland Hills, CA	91364-2548	818-227-3600	592-0877	9-12	Daniel Steiner
Taylion Academy	1184 W 2nd St Ste 101	San Bernardino, CA	92410	909-889-5152	723-1131	K-12	Amy Riggs
Taylion High Desert Academy	11336 Bartlett Ave Ste 9	Adelanto, CA	92301	760-843-6622		K-12	Timothy Smith
Taylion San Diego Academy	100 N Rancho Santa Fe Rd	San Marcos, CA	92069-1280	760-295-5564	295-5614	K-12	Timothy Smith
TEACH Academy of Technologies	10045 S Western Ave	Los Angeles, CA	90047	323-777-2068	777-7143	5-8	Dr. Greg Perez
TEACH Tech Charter HS	10000 S Western Ave	Los Angeles, CA	90047-4254	323-750-8471	750-8477	9-12	Frank Williams
TEAM Charter S	600 E Main St	Stockton, CA	95202	209-462-2282	462-5262	PK-8	Lynn Lysko
Tehama eLearning Academy	715 Jackson St Ste B	Red Bluff, CA	96080-3771	530-527-0188	527-0273	6-12	Michelle Barnard
Temecula International Academy	31530 La Serena Way	Temecula, CA	92591	951-816-5506	380-8588	K-6	Gina Wickwire
Temecula Preparatory S	35777 Abelia St	Winchester, CA	92596-8450	951-926-6776	926-6797	K-12	Dr. Michael Agostini
Temecula Valley Charter S	35755 Abelia St	Winchester, CA	92596-8450	951-294-6775	294-6780	K-8	Lois Hastings
Tennenbaum Family Technology HS	2050 N San Fernando Rd	Los Angeles, CA	90065-1267	323-276-5545		9-12	Dr. Abigail Nunez
Thomas Charter HS	101 W Adell St	Madera, CA	93638	559-675-6626	675-6612	9-12	Jessica Montemayor
Thomas Charter S	101 W Adell St	Madera, CA	93638	559-674-1192	674-8955	K-8	Jamie Brock
Thomas STEM Academy	101 W Adell St	Madera, CA	93638	559-871-5490		6-8	Jamie Brock
Three Rivers Charter S	1211 Del Mar Dr	Fort Bragg, CA	95437-5641	707-964-1128	964-1003	K-12	Roger Coy
Thrive Public Charter S	4260 54th St	San Diego, CA	92115-6009	619-839-9543		K-8	Carmina Osuna
Tierra Linda MS	750 Dartmouth Ave	San Carlos, CA	94070-1769	650-508-7370	508-7341	5-8	Steven Kaufman
Tierra Pacifica Charter S	986 Bostwick Ln	Santa Cruz, CA	95062	831-462-9404	477-0936	K-8	Linda Lambdin
Today's Fresh Start Charter S	4513 Compton Blvd	Compton, CA	90221	310-631-1502		K-8	Tanya Goff
Today's Fresh Start Charter S	4476 Crenshaw Blvd	Los Angeles, CA	90043	323-293-9826		K-8	
Today's Fresh Start Charter S	3405 W Imperial Hwy	Inglewood, CA	90303	424-227-9200		K-8	Jeanette Parker
Topanga Charter ES	22075 Topanga School Rd	Topanga, CA	90290-3835	310-455-3711	455-3517	K-6	Steven Gediman
Topeka Charter S for Advanced Studies	9815 Topeka Dr	Northridge, CA	91324-1800	818-886-2266	885-7682	K-5	Josephine Stevens
Tree of Life International Charter S	19415 Jacqueline St	Anderson, CA	96007	530-378-7040		K-4	Deborah Wallace

School	Address	City,State	Zip code	Telephone	Fax	Grade	Contact
Tree of Life Montessori Charter S	PO Box 966	Ukiah, CA	95482-0966	707-462-0913	462-0914	PK-8	Celeste Beck
Trillium Charter S	1464 Spear Ave	Arcata, CA	95521-4882	707-822-4721	822-7054	PK-5	Marianne Keller
Triumph Charter S	13361 Glenoaks Blvd	Sylmar, CA	91342-2110	818-356-2795	979-6579	6-12	Christine Graves
Trivium Charter S	1600 Berkeley Dr	Lompoc, CA	93436-7105	805-291-1303		K-12	Trisha Vais
Tubman Village Charter S	6880 Mohawk St	San Diego, CA	92115-1728	619-668-8635	668-2480	K-8	Ryan Woodard
Twin Hills Charter MS	1685 Watertrough Rd	Sebastopol, CA	95472-4647	707-823-7446	823-6470	6-8	Catherine Bosch
Twin Ridges Home Study Charter S	111 New Mohawk Rd	Nevada City, CA	95959-3270	530-478-1815	478-0266	K-8	Jenny Travers
Twin Rivers Charter S	2510 Live Oak Blvd	Yuba City, CA	95991	530-755-2872	673-1847	K-8	Karen Villalobos
Uncharted Shores Academy	330 E St	Crescent City, CA	95531-3945	707-464-9828	464-1428	PK-8	Margie Rouge
Union Street Charter S	470 Union St	Arcata, CA	95521-6429	707-822-4845	825-9025	K-5	Rea Erickson
Unity Middle College HS	815 S Esplanade St	Orange, CA	92869	714-473-0723		9-12	William Gray
University HS	2611 E Matoian Way MS/UH134	Fresno, CA	93740-0001	559-278-8263	278-0447	9-12	Dr. James Bushman
University Preparation S	550 Temple Ave	Camarillo, CA	93010-4833	805-482-4608	388-5814	PK-8	Charmon Evans
University Preparatory Academy	2315 Canoas Garden Ave	San Jose, CA	95125-2005	408-723-1839	779-0519	7-12	Daniel Ordaz
University Preparatory HS	915 S Mooney Blvd	Visalia, CA	93277-2214	559-730-2529	737-4378	9-12	Eric Thiessen
University Preparatory S	2200 Eureka Way	Redding, CA	96001-0337	530-245-2790	245-2791	6-12	Shelle Peterson
University Preparatory Value HS	700 Wilshire Blvd Fl 4	Los Angeles, CA	90017	213-335-3730		9-12	David Doyle
Urban Corps of San Diego County Charter	3127 Jefferson St	San Diego, CA	92110	619-235-6884		9-12	Dan Thomas
Urban Discovery Academy	840 14th St	San Diego, CA	92101	619-788-4668	688-9796	K-8	Jenni Owen
Urban Montessori Charter S	5328 Brann St	Oakland, CA	94619	510-842-1181	535-3841	PK-6	David Castillo
USC College Prep Santa Ana	1010 W 17th St	Santa Ana, CA	92706	714-988-2775	242-1337	9-12	Evelyn Castro
USC East College Prep	3825 N Mission Rd	Los Angeles, CA	90031-3137	323-285-1441		9-12	Andrew Goltermann
USC Esperanza College Prep	319 N Humphreys Ave	Los Angeles, CA	90022	323-457-0050	457-0051	9-12	Rosa Alanis
Valdez Leadership Academy	1855 Lucretia Ave	San Jose, CA	95122-3730	408-384-4015	936-3095	9-12	Jeffrey Camarillo
Vallejo Charter S	2833 Tennessee St	Vallejo, CA	94591	707-556-8620	556-8624	K-8	Dr. Carla Galbraith
Valley Charter ES	16514 Nordhoff St	North Hills, CA	91343-3724	818-810-6713	810-9667	K-5	Leslie Lainer
Valley Charter HS	108 Campus Way	Modesto, CA	95350-5803	209-238-6800	238-6897	9-12	Michael Berhorst
Valley Charter MS	6952 Van Nuys Blvd	Van Nuys, CA	91405	818-988-9128	988-9265	6-8	Matthew Rubin
Valley Life Charter S	3737 W Walnut Ave	Visalia, CA	93277-3947	559-761-1299		K-12	Lori Lackey
Valley Oak Charter S	PO Box 878	Ojai, CA	93024-0878	805-640-4421	646-4700	K-12	Laura Fulmer
Valley Oaks Charter S	1300 17th St	Bakersfield, CA	93301-4504	661-852-6750	633-5287	K-12	Deanna Downs
Valley View Charter Montessori	1665 Blackstone Pkwy	El Dorado Hills, CA	95762	916-939-9640	939-5015	K-5	Paul Stewart
Valley View Charter Prep	2453 Grand Canal Blvd	Stockton, CA	95207-8259	916-866-9033	991-5770	K-12	John Mittan
Valor Academy Charter HS	8015 Van Nuys Blvd	Panorama City, CA	91402-6009	323-934-8910	934-8916	9-12	Evelyn Licea
Valor Academy Charter S	9034 Burnet Ave	North Hills, CA	91343	818-830-1700	830-1799	5-8	Maurice Regalado
Valor Academy ES	17081 Devonshire St	Northridge, CA	91325	818-217-2733	934-8916	K-4	May Oey
Van Gogh Charter S	17160 Van Gogh St	Granada Hills, CA	91344-1299	818-360-2141	831-9081	K-5	Pamela Merloni
Vantage Point Charter S	10862 Spenceville Rd	Penn Valley, CA	95946-9625	530-432-5312	432-8744	K-12	Torie F. England
Vaughn Next Century Learning Center	13330 Vaughn St	San Fernando, CA	91340-2216	818-896-7461	834-9036	PK-12	Anita Zepeda
Ventura S of Arts & Global Education	PO Box 392	Ventura, CA	93002-0392	805-648-5503	648-5539	K-8	Mary Galvin
Venture Academy	PO Box 213030	Stockton, CA	95213-9030	209-468-5940	468-9000	K-12	Kathleen Focacci
View Park Accelerated MS	5311 S Crenshaw Blvd	Los Angeles, CA	90043	323-290-6970	676-3462	6-8	AyEsha McLaughlin
View Park Prep Accelerated Charter ES	5311 S Crenshaw Blvd	Los Angeles, CA	90043	323-290-6975	508-2837	K-5	AyEsha McLaughlin
View Park Prep Accelerated HS	5701 Crenshaw Blvd	Los Angeles, CA	90043-2409	323-290-6975	881-4924	9-12	Dr. Traci Porter
Village Charter Academy	7357 Jordan Ave	Canoga Park, CA	91303-1238	818-716-2887		K-5	Jennifer Clark
Village Charter S	2590 Piner Rd	Santa Rosa, CA	95401-4035	707-524-2848		K-8	Rebecca Ivanoff
Village ES	900 Yulupa Ave	Santa Rosa, CA	95405-7018	707-545-5754	573-0951	K-6	Cecilia Holt
Vincent Academy	2501 Chestnut St	Oakland, CA	94607	510-452-2100	452-2101	K-5	Monica Rasmussen
Visalia Charter Independent Study	1821 W Meadow Ave	Visalia, CA	93277	559-735-8055	622-3170	7-12	Michele Reid
Visions in Education Charter S	5030 El Camino Ave	Carmichael, CA	95608	877-971-7037	293-4610	K-12	
Vista Charter MS	2900 W Temple St	Los Angeles, CA	90026-4516	213-201-4000	201-5861	6-8	Jose Miguel Kubes
Vista Heritage Charter MS	2609 W Fifth St	Santa Ana, CA	92703	714-988-2720	201-5861	6-8	Lauri Martin
Vista Oaks Charter S	14301 Byron Hwy	Byron, CA	94514-2515	925-420-6616		K-8	Joy Groen
Vista Real Charter HS	401 S A St Ste 3	Oxnard, CA	93030-5278	805-486-5449	486-5455	9-12	Corrine Manley
Voices Academy at Morgan Hill	16870 Murphy Ave	Morgan Hill, CA	95037	408-763-5770		K-8	Juan Carlos Villasenor
Voices Academy at Mt. Pleasant	14271 Story Rd	San Jose, CA	95127	408-684-3503		K-8	Maria Madrigal
Voices College-Bound Language Academy	715 Hellyer Ave	San Jose, CA	95111	408-361-1960	361-1979	K-8	Charles Miller
Walden Academy	1149 W Wood St	Willows, CA	95988-2614	530-361-6480		PK-5	
Washington Charter S	45768 Portola Ave	Palm Desert, CA	92260-4861	760-862-4350	862-4356	K-5	Allan Lehmann
Washington ES	1501 Ellis St	Kingsburg, CA	93631-1896	559-897-2955	897-6863	PK-K	Laura North M.Ed.
Washington Middle College HS	1504 Fallbrook St	West Sacramento, CA	95691	916-375-7680	375-0920	9-12	Sean O'Neil
Watsonville Charter S of the Arts	75 Whiting Rd	Watsonville, CA	95076-1421	831-728-8123	728-6286	K-8	Amy Thomas
Watts Learning Center	310 W 95th St	Los Angeles, CA	90003-4012	323-754-9900	754-0935	K-5	Kelly Baptiste
Watts Learning Ctr Charter MS	8800 S San Pedro St	Los Angeles, CA	90003-3541	323-565-4800	750-5051	6-8	Gayle Windom
W.E.B. DuBois Charter S	2604 Martin Luther King Blv	Fresno, CA	93706	559-486-1166	486-1199	K-12	Linda Washington
Welby Way Charter ES & Gifted Magnet Ctr	23456 Welby Way	West Hills, CA	91307-3328	818-348-1975	704-8726	K-5	Helen Kim
West Charter S	4600 Lavell Rd	Santa Rosa, CA	95403	707-524-2741	524-2782	K-8	Tracy Kendall
West County Charter MS	6321 Highway 116	Forestville, CA	95436	707-887-1037		7-8	Kirsten Sanft
Western Center Academy	2345 Searl Pkwy	Hemet, CA	92543	951-791-0033	791-0032	6-12	Paul Bailey
Western Sierra Collegiate Academy	660 Menlo Dr	Rocklin, CA	95765-3713	916-778-4544	626-5540	7-12	Gregg Moses
Westlake Charter S	2680 Mabry Dr	Sacramento, CA	95834	916-567-5760	567-5769	K-7	John Eick
West Park Charter Academy	2695 S Valentine Ave	Fresno, CA	93706-9042	559-233-6501	497-1944	K-12	Ramiro Elizondo
Westside Innovative School House	6550 W 80th St	Los Angeles, CA	90045	310-642-9474	598-7770	K-8	Shawna Draxton
Westside Prep Charter S - Eastside	6469 Guthrie St	North Highlands, CA	95660-3944	916-566-1860	566-1861	7-8	Renee Scott-Femenella
Westside Prep Charter S - Frontier	6691 Silverthorne Cir	Sacramento, CA	95842-2654	916-566-1840	566-1841	7-8	Ellen Giffin
Westside Prep Charter S - Westside	6537 W 2nd St	Rio Linda, CA	95673	916-566-1990	566-1991	7-8	Laura Lofgren
Westwood Charter ES	2050 Selby Ave	Los Angeles, CA	90025-6311	310-474-7788	475-1295	K-5	Kathy Flores
Wheatland Charter Academy	123 Beale Hwy	Beale AFB, CA	95903	530-788-0248	788-0518	K-5	Jodie Jacklett
White Oaks ES	1901 White Oak Way	San Carlos, CA	94070-4747	650-508-7317	508-7320	PK-3	Allison Liner
Whitmore Charter HS	PO Box 307	Ceres, CA	95307-0307	209-556-1617	538-7931	9-12	Sarah Olson
Whitmore Charter S	PO Box 307	Ceres, CA	95307-0307	209-556-1610	538-7931	K-8	Sarah Olson
Wilbur Charter S for Enriched Academics	5213 Crebs Ave	Tarzana, CA	91356-4010	818-345-1090	881-8128	K-5	Deborah Rubenacker
Wilder's Preparatory Academy Charter S	830 N La Brea Ave	Inglewood, CA	90302-2206	310-671-5578	671-2424	K-8	Rosalyn S. Robinson
Wildflower Open Classroom	2414 Cohasset Rd	Chico, CA	95926	530-892-1676	892-9317	K-8	Tom Hicks
Willits Charter ES	405 E Commercial St	Willits, CA	95490	707-459-1400	455-6650	K-5	Kara McClellan
Willits Charter S	1431 S Main St	Willits, CA	95490-4309	707-459-5506	459-5576	6-12	Jennifer Lockwood
Willow Creek Academy	636 Nevada St	Sausalito, CA	94965-1654	415-331-7530	331-1622	K-8	Tara Seekins
Willowside MS	5285 Hall Rd	Santa Rosa, CA	95401-5566	707-542-3322	525-4439	6-8	Linsey Gannon
Wilson College Prep S	400 105th Ave	Oakland, CA	94603-2968	510-635-7737	635-7727	6-12	Michelle Cortez
WISH Academy HS	7400 W Manchester Ave	Los Angeles, CA	90045	310-743-6990		9-12	Kellie Mowll
Wonderful College Prep Academy	2070 Veneto St	Delano, CA	93215	661-454-3000	454-3099	6-12	Ricardo Esquivel
Wonderful College Prep Acad - Lost Hills	20767 Highway 46	Lost Hills, CA	93249	661-709-1355		K-12	Alesha Hixon
Woodlake ES	23231 Hatteras St	Woodland Hills, CA	91367-3199	818-347-7097	883-3953	K-5	Mario Thompson
Woodland Hills Charter S	22201 San Miguel St	Woodland Hills, CA	91364-3039	818-347-9220	347-2365	K-5	Yvonne Dix
Woodland Star Charter S	17811 Arnold Dr	Sonoma, CA	95476-4019	707-996-3849	996-4369	K-8	Jamie Lloyd
Woodson Charter S	3333 N Bond Ave	Fresno, CA	93726-5712	559-229-3529	229-0459	7-12	Victor Martinez
Woodward Leadership Academy	1777 W Base Line St	San Bernardino, CA	92411-1648	909-266-1762		K-6	Jaqueline Johnson
Wright Charter S	4389 Price Ave	Santa Rosa, CA	95407-6550	707-542-0556	542-0418	K-8	Michael Waters
Yav Pem Suab Academy	7555 S Land Park Dr	Sacramento, CA	95831-3863	916-433-5057	433-5289	K-6	Vince Xiong
Yosemite-Wawona Elementary Charter	7925 Chilnualna Falls Rd	Yosemite NtPk, CA	95389	209-375-6383	375-1029	1-5	Esme McCarthy
Youthbuild Charter S	155 W Washington St	Los Angeles, CA	90015	213-741-2600	741-2628	9-12	Phil Matero
Youth Opportunities Unlimited S	915 W Manchester Ave	Los Angeles, CA	90044	323-789-4731	778-4612	9-12	Christina Green
Yuba City Charter S	256 Wilbur Ave	Yuba City, CA	95991	530-822-9667	822-9629	PK-12	James Ferreira
Yuba County Career Prep Charter S	1104 E St	Marysville, CA	95901-4825	530-749-4000		K-12	Jennifer Morrison
Yuba Environmental Science Charter Acad	PO Box 430	Oregon House, CA	95962	530-692-2210	692-3241	PK-8	Louise Miller
Yuba River Charter S	505 Main St	Nevada City, CA	95959-2218	530-265-6060	265-6070	K-8	Ron Charles
Yu Ming Charter S	1086 Alcatraz Ave	Emeryville, CA	94608	415-452-2063	452-2095	K-6	Sue Park

Colorado

School	Address	City,State	Zip code	Telephone	Fax	Grade	Contact
Academy 360	12000 E 47th Ave	Denver, CO	80239	303-574-1360		PK-5	Eric Brucz
Academy Charter S	1551 Prairie Hawk Dr	Castle Rock, CO	80109-7900	303-660-4881	660-6385	K-8	Yvette Brown
Academy for Advanced & Creative Learning	2510 N Chestnut St	Colorado Spgs, CO	80907	719-434-6566	434-9696	K-8	Nikki Myers
Academy of Advanced Learning	441 N Sable Blvd	Aurora, CO	80011	303-500-5252		K-6	Mike Miles
Academy of Urban Learning Charter S	2417 W 29th Ave	Denver, CO	80211-3709	303-282-0900	282-0902	9-12	Michelle Kennard
Academy	11800 Lowell Blvd	Westminster, CO	80031-5097	303-289-8088	289-8087	K-12	Tony Fontana
ACE Community Challenge Charter S	948 Santa Fe Dr	Denver, CO	80204-3937	303-436-9588	436-0919	8-10	Rachel Ramirez
Addenbrooke Classical Academy	3940 S Teller St	Lakewood, CO	80235	303-989-1336	986-5509	K-12	Charles Wright
Alta Vista Charter ES	PO Box 449	Lamar, CO	81052-0449	719-336-2154	336-0170	K-6	Talara Coen
American Academy	10260 Twenty Mile Rd	Parker, CO	80134	720-292-5300	841-9121	K-8	Sarah Miller
American Academy	11155 Motsenbocker Rd	Parker, CO	80134	720-292-5600	805-9901	K-8	Amanda Cline
American Academy	6971 Mira Vista Ln	Castle Pines, CO	80108	720-292-5200	660-5550	K-8	Amanda Cline
Animas HS	PO Box 4414	Durango, CO	81302	970-247-2474	247-2483	9-12	Sean Woytek
Aspen Community Charter S	PO Box 336	Woody Creek, CO	81656-0336	970-923-4080	923-6207	K-8	Jim Gilchrist
Aspen Ridge Prep S	705 Austin Ave	Erie, CO	80516	720-242-6225	294-0573	K-5	Charla Salmeron
Aspen View Academy	2131 Low Meadow Blvd	Castle Rock, CO	80109-8032	720-733-3436	660-5959	PK-8	Jason Edwards
Atlas Preparatory S	1602 S Murray Blvd	Colorado Spgs, CO	80916	719-358-7196	355-1819	5-12	Adam Lenzmeier

School	Address	City,State	Zip code	Telephone	Fax	Grade	Contact
Aurora Academy Charter S	10251 E 1st Ave	Aurora, CO	80010-4308	303-367-5983	367-5820	K-8	Pat Leger
Axl Academy	14100 E Jewell Ave	Aurora, CO	80012	303-377-0758	597-1547	PK-8	Dan Cohen
Banning Lewis Prep Academy	9433 Vista Del Pico Blvd	Colorado Spgs, CO	80927	719-638-3040	638-3050	6-9	Brandon Monson
Banning Lewis Ranch Academy	7094 Cottonwood Tree Dr	Colorado Spgs, CO	80927-5000	719-570-0075	522-2900	K-5	Shannon Molnar
Battle Rock Charter S	11351 Road G	Cortez, CO	81321	970-565-3237	564-1140	K-6	Justine Bayles
Belle Creek Charter S	9290 E 107th Ave	Henderson, CO	80640-8964	303-468-0160	468-0164	K-8	Jackie Fields
Blair Edison Charter S	4905 Cathay St	Denver, CO	80249-8376	303-371-9570	371-8348	K-8	Kristen Lee
Boulder Prep Charter HS	5075 Chaparral Ct	Boulder, CO	80301-3589	303-545-6186	545-6187	9-12	Lili Adeli
Boys S of Denver	2401 Alcott St	Denver, CO	80211	720-688-3842		6-8	Nick Jackson
Bromley East Charter S	356 Longspur Dr	Brighton, CO	80601-8700	720-685-3297	685-9513	K-8	David Shadwell
Caprock Academy	714 24 1/2 Rd	Grand Junction, CO	81505	970-243-1771	243-3612	K-12	Kristin Trezise
Carbondale Community S	PO Box 365	Carbondale, CO	81623-0365	970-963-9647	704-0501	K-8	Sam Germain
Carbon Valley Academy	4040 Coriolis Way	Frederick, CO	80504-5449	303-774-9555	774-9592	PK-8	Julie Johnson
Cardinal Community Academy	3101 County Road 65	Keenesburg, CO	80643-8604	303-732-9312	732-9314	K-8	April Dowdy
Career Building Academy	1120 Court St	Pueblo, CO	81003	719-546-1740		7-12	Dr. Dana Lambert
Challenge to Excellence Charter S	16995 Carlson Dr	Parker, CO	80134-8000	303-841-9816	840-3246	K-8	Donna Mitchell
Chavez Academy	2500 W 18th St	Pueblo, CO	81003-1152	719-295-1623	295-1625	K-8	Lori Montanez
Chavez Academy	3752 Tennyson St	Denver, CO	80212-1914	303-455-0848	855-7252	K-8	MaryAnn Mahoney
Cherry Creek Academy Charter	6260 S Dayton St	Englewood, CO	80111-5203	303-779-8988	779-8817	K-8	Jay Cerny
Children's Kiva Montessori S	25 N Beech St	Cortez, CO	81321	970-564-9377		K-8	Susan Likes
CIVA Charter S	4635 Northpark Dr	Colorado Spgs, CO	80918-3813	719-633-1306	633-1691	9-12	Randy Zimmerman
Classical Academy Central	1655 Springcrest Rd	Colorado Spgs, CO	80920-1545	719-265-9766	265-1751	K-6	Rebecca DeMeyer
Classical Academy East	12201 Cross Peak Vw	Colorado Spgs, CO	80921	719-282-1181	260-9743	K-6	Amy Nelson
Classical Academy HS	975 Stout Rd	Colorado Spgs, CO	80921-3801	719-484-0091	484-0085	9-12	Sean Shields
Classical Academy JHS	975 Stout Rd	Colorado Spgs, CO	80921-3801	719-484-0091	487-2339	7-8	Hugh DiPretore
Classical Academy North	975 Stout Rd	Colorado Spgs, CO	80921-3801	719-484-0081	484-0078	K-6	Don Stump
Collegiate Academy of Colorado	8420 Sangre De Cristo Rd	Littleton, CO	80127-4201	303-972-7433	932-0695	K-12	Christian Becker
Colorado Calvert Academy	6170 Lehman Dr	Colorado Spgs, CO	80918	719-258-1550	258-1591	K-8	Donna Heinrich
Colorado Charter HS	1175 Osage St Ste 100	Denver, CO	80204-3445	303-892-8475	825-3011	10-12	Clark Callahan
Colorado Charter HS - GES	3037 E 42nd Ave	Denver, CO	80216	303-955-5309		9-12	Liz Feldhusen
Colorado Early Colleges Douglas County	10235 Parkglenn Way	Parker, CO	80138	720-638-6824		9-12	Dr. Alex Tuel
Colorado Early Colleges Fort Collins	4424 Innovation Dr	Fort Collins, CO	80525	970-377-0044	377-1144	9-12	Sandi Brown
Colorado Springs Charter Academy	2577 N Chelton Rd	Colorado Spgs, CO	80909-1302	719-636-2722	636-2726	K-8	Dan Ajamian
Colorado Springs Early Colleges	4405 N Chestnut St # E	Colorado Spgs, CO	80907	719-955-4675	260-1253	9-12	Jennifer Daugherty
Colorado Virtual Academy	165 S Union Blvd Ste 777	Lakewood, CO	80228	303-255-4650	504-4072	9-12	Melissa Lambrecht
Community Leadership Academy	6880 Holly St	Commerce City, CO	80022-2536	303-288-2711	288-2714	PK-5	Ron Jajdelski
Community Prep Charter S	332 E Willamette Ave	Colorado Spgs, CO	80903-1116	719-227-8836	227-8897	9-12	Marty Schneider
Compass Academy	2285 S Federal Blvd	Denver, CO	80219	720-424-0096		6-8	Marcia Fulton
Compass Montessori Charter S	10399 W 44th Ave	Wheat Ridge, CO	80033-2701	303-420-8288	420-0139	PK-6	Cameron Gehlen
Compass Montessori Charter S	4441 Salvia St	Golden, CO	80403-1698	303-271-1977	271-1984	PK-12	Seth Webb
Connect Charter S	104 W 7th St	Pueblo, CO	81003	719-542-0224	583-9799	6-8	Jeff Hawkins
Crest Academy	220 W 12th St	Salida, CO	81201	719-539-2977	530-5234	5-8	Jill Davis
Crestone Charter S	PO Box 400	Crestone, CO	81131-0400	719-256-4907	256-4908	K-12	Marie-Louise Baker
Crown Pointe Academy	2900 W 86th Ave	Westminster, CO	80031	303-428-1882	428-1938	K-8	Keith Ouweneel
DCS Montessori Charter S	311 E Castle Pines Pkwy	Castle Pines, CO	80108	720-531-3311		PK-8	Jeromy Johnson
Denver Justice HS	300 E 9th Ave	Denver, CO	80203	303-480-5610	480-5613	9-12	Stephen Parce
Denver Language S	451 Newport St	Denver, CO	80220	303-557-0852	393-6805	K-8	Kathy Benzel
Denver S of Science & Tech-Henry MS	3005 S Golden Way	Denver, CO	80227	303-802-4130		6-8	Lisa Richardson
Denver S of Science & Technology	2000 Valentia St	Denver, CO	80238	303-320-5570	377-5101	9-12	Jeff Desserich
Denver S of Science & Technology	150 S Pearl St	Denver, CO	80209	303-524-6350		9-9	Brad White
Denver S of Science & Technology	2000 Valentia St	Denver, CO	80238	303-320-5570		6-8	Jessica Heesacker
Denver S of Science & Technology-Byers	150 S Pearl St	Denver, CO	80209	303-524-6350	524-6355	6-8	Brad White
Denver S of Science & Technology - CG	8499 Stoll Pl	Denver, CO	80238	303-802-4120	802-4205	6-8	John Clark
Denver S of Science & Technology-Cole HS	3240 N Humboldt St	Denver, CO	80205	303-524-6354		9-12	Rebecca Bloch
Denver S of Science & Technology-Cole MS	1350 E 33rd Ave	Denver, CO	80205	303-524-6354	524-6309	6-8	Rebecca Bloch
Denver S of Science & Technology CV HS	3111 W Dartmouth Ave	Denver, CO	80236-2842	303-524-6320		9-12	Rebecca Meyer
Denver S of Science & Technology CV MS	3111 W Dartmouth Ave	Denver, CO	80236	720-524-6374		6-8	Erin Dillon
Denver S of Science & Technology - GVR	4800 Telluride St	Denver, CO	80249	303-524-6300	389-7398	9-12	Jenna Kalin
Denver S of Science & Technology - GVR	4800 Telluride St	Denver, CO	80249	303-524-6300		6-8	Caroline Gaudiani
Doral Academy of Colorado	9050 Field St	Westminster, CO	80021	303-428-8443	389-9367	K-8	Arley Blanco
Downtown Denver Expeditionary S	1860 N Lincoln St	Denver, CO	80203	720-424-2350		K-5	Erin Sciscione
DSST: Conservatory Green HS	11200 E 45th Ave	Denver, CO	80239	303-802-4127		9-12	Adeel Khan
Eagle County Charter Academy	1105 Miller Ranch Rd	Edwards, CO	81632-6425	970-926-0656	926-0786	K-8	Kim Walter
Eagle Ridge Academy	3551 E Southern St	Brighton, CO	80601-0015	303-655-0773	655-9155	9-12	Mary Nell Stringer
Early College of Arvada	4905 W 60th Ave	Arvada, CO	80003	720-473-4400	308-4701	6-12	Ryan Conrad
Excel Academy	11500 W 84th Ave	Arvada, CO	80005-5272	303-467-2295	467-2291	K-8	Lisa Gjellum
Flagstaff Academy	2040 Miller Dr	Longmont, CO	80501-6748	303-651-7900	651-7922	PK-8	Robin Lowe
Fort Collins Montessori S	1900 S Taft Hill Rd	Fort Collins, CO	80526-1227	970-631-8612		PK-3	Frank Vincent
Foundations Academy	340 S 45th Ave	Brighton, CO	80601	303-659-9519	835-7151	K-8	Jerry Martinez
Franklin Academy	2270 Plaza Dr	Highlands Ranch, CO	80129	720-383-4519	974-1738	PK-8	Diana Simpson
Free Horizon Montessori S	581 Conference Pl	Golden, CO	80401-5615	303-231-9801	231-9983	PK-8	Kresta Vuolo
Frontier Academy Charter S	2560 W 29th St	Greeley, CO	80631-8507	970-330-1780	330-4334	K-5	Dr. Bradford Every
Frontier Academy Charter S	6530 W 16th St	Greeley, CO	80634-8675	970-339-9153	339-5631	6-12	Dr. Stephen Seedorf
Frontier Charter Academy	418 Yoder St	Calhan, CO	80808	719-347-3156	347-3054	K-8	Karin Gurokovich
Georgetown Community S	PO Box 129	Georgetown, CO	80444	303-569-3277	569-2761	PK-6	Sharon Warren
Girls Athletic Leadership S	750 Galapago St	Denver, CO	80204	303-282-6437	282-6815	6-12	Carrie Donovan
Global Village Academy	555 W 112th Ave	Northglenn, CO	80234	303-446-7100	446-7101	K-8	Nicole Caldwell
Global Village Academy	18451 Ponderosa Dr	Parker, CO	80134	720-476-8044		K-8	Stacy Bush
Global Village Academy Colorado Springs	1702 N Murray Blvd	Colorado Spgs, CO	80915	719-645-8063	591-6784	K-4	Alicia Welch
Global Village Academy East	403 S Airport Blvd Unit A	Aurora, CO	80017	303-309-6657	317-6538	K-2	Courtney Black
Global Village Academy Fort Collins	2130 W Horsetooth Rd	Fort Collins, CO	80526	970-282-3767	282-3766	K-4	David Finley
Global Village Academy West	16401 E Alameda Dr	Aurora, CO	80017	303-248-4242	248-4241	3-8	Courtney Black
GLOBE Charter S	3302 Alpine Pl	Colorado Spgs, CO	80909	719-630-0577	630-0395	K-6	Heidi Breakey
Goal HS	304 S Victoria Ave	Pueblo, CO	81003	855-695-3354		6-12	
Golden View Classical Academy	601 Corporate Cir	Golden, CO	80401-5609	303-598-6700	598-6698	K-12	Robert Garrow
Guffey Community Charter S	PO Box 147	Guffey, CO	80820-0147	719-689-2093	689-3407	PK-8	Martine Walker
Heritage Heights Academy	20050 E Smoky Hill Rd	Centennial, CO	80015	720-870-9541		K-6	Natalia Miller-Forrest
Highline Academy Northeast	19451 E Maxwell Pl	Denver, CO	80249	303-454-2706		K-5	Andria Hinman
Highline Academy Southeast	2170 S Dahlia St	Denver, CO	80222	303-759-7808	759-7809	K-8	Kali Garofoli
High Point Academy	6750 N Dunkirk St	Aurora, CO	80019	303-217-5152	217-5153	PK-8	Keri Melmed
Hope Online Learning Academy Co-op	373 Inverness Pkwy Ste 205	Englewood, CO	80112	720-402-3000	675-3013	K-12	Heather O'Mara
Horizons K-8 School	4545 Sioux Dr	Boulder, CO	80303-3732	720-561-3600	561-3601	K-8	Lauren Tracy
Huerta Preparatory HS	2727 W 18th St	Pueblo, CO	81003	719-583-1030	545-2389	9-12	Fred Segura
Imagine Charter S at Firestone	5753 Twilight Ave	Firestone, CO	80504	303-772-3711	772-3977	PK-8	Nancy Box
Imagine Classical Academy - Indigo Ranch	6464 Peterson Rd	Colorado Spgs, CO	80923	719-495-7360	495-4239	PK-8	Frank Fowler
Independence Academy	651 29 Rd	Grand Junction, CO	81504	970-254-6850	241-2064	K-8	
Indian Peaks Charter S	PO Box 1819	Granby, CO	80446-1819	970-887-3805	887-3829	K-8	Allison Beauvais
Irwin Charter ES - Astrozon Cmpc	5525 Astrozon Blvd	Colorado Spgs, CO	80916	719-302-9107	884-0992	K-5	Elizabeth Berg
Irwin Charter ES - Howard Campus	1801 Howard Ave	Colorado Spgs, CO	80909	719-302-9100	632-4178	K-5	Saadia Dumas
Irwin Charter HS	5525 Astrozon Blvd	Colorado Spgs, CO	80916-4226	719-302-9109	576-8071	9-12	Alex Marquez
Irwin Charter MS	5525 Astrozon Blvd	Colorado Spgs, CO	80916-4226	719-302-9108	591-9993	6-8	Michelle Prusinowski
Jefferson Academy	11251 Reed Way	Broomfield, CO	80020-2720	303-887-1992	887-2435	7-12	Heather Grantham
Jefferson Academy	9955 Yarrow St	Broomfield, CO	80021-4048	303-438-1011	438-1046	K-6	Michael Nolan
Juniper Ridge Charter S	640 24 1/2 Rd	Grand Junction, CO	81505	970-639-0884		K-9	Patrick Ebel
Juniper S	PO Box 655	Durango, CO	81302	970-764-4185		K-5	Katie McCullough
Justice HS	805 Excalibur St	Lafayette, CO	80026	720-277-6480	328-4865	9-12	Tijani Cole
KIPP Denver Collegiate HS	451 S Tejon St	Denver, CO	80223	303-922-5324	922-9910	9-12	Kurt Pusch
KIPP Northeast Denver Leadership Academy	18250 E 51st Ave	Denver, CO	80249	720-452-2570		9-10	Grant Erwin
KIPP Northeast Denver MS	4635 Walden St	Denver, CO	80249	303-307-1970		5-8	Stephani Olson
KIPP Northeast ES	4635 Walden St	Denver, CO	80249	720-452-2551	492-1031	PK-2	Lindsey Lorehn
KIPP Sunshine Peak Academy	375 S Tejon St	Denver, CO	80223-1961	303-623-5772	623-0410	5-8	Kristie Servis
Knowledge Quest Academy	705 School House Dr	Milliken, CO	80543-3154	970-587-5742	587-5750	K-8	Linda Spreitzer
Lake George Charter S	PO Box 420	Lake George, CO	80827-0420	719-748-3911	748-8151	PK-6	Natalie Sardi
Landmark Academy at Reunion	10566 Memphis St	Commerce City, CO	80022	303-287-2901	379-2050	K-8	Jennifer Stengel
Legacy Academy	1975 Legacy Cir	Elizabeth, CO	80107	303-646-2636	646-2366	K-8	Kurt Naber
Liberty Common ES	1725 Sharp Point Dr	Fort Collins, CO	80525-4424	970-482-9800	482-8007	K-6	Keith Churchill
Liberty Common HS	2745 Minnesota Dr	Fort Collins, CO	80525-6794	970-672-5500	672-5499	7-12	Bob Schaffer
Life Skills Center of Colorado Springs	1810 Eastlake Blvd	Colorado Spgs, CO	80910-3422	719-471-0684	471-4392	9-12	Mary Ruben-Clapper
Lincoln Academy	7180 Oak St	Arvada, CO	80004-1416	303-467-5363	467-5367	PK-8	Janelle Johnson
Littleton Academy Charter S	1200 W Mineral Ave	Littleton, CO	80120-4536	303-798-5252	798-0298	K-8	Shelly Russell
Littleton Preparatory Charter S	5301 S Bannock St	Littleton, CO	80120-1742	303-734-1995	734-3620	K-8	Kimberly Ash
Lotus S for Excellence	11001 E Alameda Ave Ste A	Aurora, CO	80012-1034	303-360-0052	360-0071	K-12	Eray Idil
Loveland Classical Charter S	3835 14th St SW	Loveland, CO	80537-6675	970-541-1507	776-9227	K-12	Ian Stout
Maclaren Charter S	1702 N Murray Blvd	Colorado Spgs, CO	80915	719-313-4488	313-4491	6-12	Mary Faith Hall
Madison Charter Academy	660 Syracuse St	Colorado Spgs, CO	80911-2546	719-391-3977	391-1744	K-6	Dr. Anne Shineman
Magon Academy	5301 Lowell Blvd	Denver, CO	80221	303-412-7610	412-7658	K-8	Kaye Taavialma
Marble Charter S	418 W Main St	Marble, CO	81623	970-963-9550	963-8435	K-10	Amy Rusby

School	Address	City,State	Zip code	Telephone	Fax	Grade	Contact
Mesa Valley Community S	2387 Patterson Rd	Grand Junction, CO	81505-1219	970-254-7202	243-3075	K-12	Laurajean Downs
Monarch Montessori of Denver	4895 Peoria St	Denver, CO	80239	303-712-2001	500-0646	K-5	Rob Clemens
Montessori del Mundo	15503 E Mississippi Ave # B	Aurora, CO	80017	720-863-8629		PK-4	Karen Farquharson
Montessori Peaks Academy	9904 W Capri Ave	Littleton, CO	80123-3535	303-972-2627	933-4182	PK-6	Shannon Aasheim
Monument Academy	1150 Village Ridge Pt	Monument, CO	80132-8992	719-481-1950	481-1948	PK-8	Dr. Don Griffin
Mountain MS	108 W 31st St	Durango, CO	81301-4231	970-828-5600		6-8	Shane Voss
Mountain Phoenix Community S	4725 Miller St	Wheat Ridge, CO	80033	303-728-9100	728-9801	PK-8	Dirk Angevine
Mountain Sage Community S	2310 E Prospect Rd Ste A	Fort Collins, CO	80525-9770	970-568-5456	797-1202	K-8	Liv Helmericks
Mountain Song Community S	2904 W Kiowa St	Colorado Spgs, CO	80904	719-203-6364	375-0180	K-8	Donald Samson
Mountain View Core Knowledge S	890 Field Ave	Canon City, CO	81212-9250	719-275-1980	275-1998	K-8	Karen Sartori
New America S - Jeffco	5806 W Alameda Ave	Lakewood, CO	80226	303-894-3171	237-4119	9-12	Jon Berninzoni
New America S - Lowry	9125 E 7th Pl	Denver, CO	80230-7111	303-320-9854	363-8083	9-12	Annie Trujillo
New America S - Thornton	8978 Washington St	Thornton, CO	80229	303-991-0130	252-9254	9-12	Mike Epke
New Legacy Charter S	2091 Dayton St	Aurora, CO	80010	303-340-7880		9-12	Jennifer Douglas
New Vision Charter S	2366 E 1st St	Loveland, CO	80537-5906	970-593-6827	461-1947	K-8	Tim Bishop
North Routt Charter S	26990 Eagle Ln	Clark, CO	80428-9702	970-871-6062	871-6067	K-8	Brandon LaChance
North Star Academy	16700 Keystone Blvd	Parker, CO	80134-3544	720-851-7827	851-0976	K-8	Kendra Hossfeld
Odyssey S of Denver	6550 E 21st Ave	Denver, CO	80207	303-316-3944	316-4016	K-8	Marnie Cooke
Paradox Valley Charter S	PO Box 420	Paradox, CO	81429-0420	970-859-7236	859-7235	PK-12	Jon Orris
Parker Core Knowledge Charter S	11661 N Pine Dr	Parker, CO	80138-8022	303-840-7070	840-9785	PK-8	Teri Aplin
Parker Performing Arts S	15035 Compark Blvd	Parker, CO	80134	720-709-7400	709-7401	K-8	Jennifer Burgess
Paul Academy of Arts & Knowledge	4800 Wheaton Dr	Fort Collins, CO	80525	970-226-2800	226-2806	PK-5	Shannon Keigan
Peak to Peak Charter S	800 Merlin Dr	Lafayette, CO	80026-2146	303-453-4600	453-4613	K-12	Melissa Christensen
Pikes Peak Prep S	525 E Costilla St	Colorado Spgs, CO	80903-3764	719-570-7575	475-0831	K-12	Janet Nace
Pikes Peak S of Expeditionary Learning	11925 Antlers Ridge Dr	Falcon, CO	80831	719-522-2580	522-2585	PK-8	Don Knapp
Pinnacle Charter S	1001 W 84th Ave	Federal Heights, CO	80260-4717	303-450-3985	255-6305	K-12	Craig Pierce
Platte River Academy	4085 Lark Sparrow St	Highlands Ranch, CO	80126-5209	303-221-1070	221-1069	K-8	Mike Munier
Power Technical Early College	2525 Canada Dr	Colorado Spgs, CO	80922	719-301-6200		6-12	Rob Daugherty
Prospect Ridge Academy	2555 Preble Creek Pkwy	Broomfield, CO	80023-8096	720-399-0300	545-2163	K-12	April Wilkin
Pueblo S for the Arts and Sciences	1411 Santa Rosa St	Pueblo, CO	81006	719-225-1107	569-4407	K-5	Brian Repola
Pueblo S for the Arts & Sciences	2415 Jones Ave	Pueblo, CO	81004	719-404-2680	404-2681	K-8	Charles Maglia
REACH	940 Fillmore St	Denver, CO	80206	720-668-9691		PK-3	Dr. Moira Coogan
Ridge View Academy	28101 E Quincy Ave	Watkins, CO	80137-9502	303-766-3000	766-2151	9-12	Ed Cope
Ridgeview Classical S	1800 S Lemay Ave	Fort Collins, CO	80525-1240	970-494-4620	494-4625	K-12	Derek Anderson
RiseUp Community HS	1801 Federal Blvd	Denver, CO	80204	303-587-4713		9-12	Lucas Ketzer
Rocky Mountain Academy of Evergreen	2959 Royale Elk Way	Evergreen, CO	80439	303-670-1070	670-1253	PK-8	Ann Hudson
Rocky Mountain Classical Academy	4620 Antelope Ridge Dr	Colorado Spgs, CO	80922-2497	719-622-8000	622-8004	K-8	Christianna Fogler
Rocky Mountain Deaf S	10300 W Nassau Ave	Denver, CO	80235	303-984-5749	984-7290	PK-12	Amy Novotny
Rocky Mountain Prep	7808 Cherry Creek South Dr	Denver, CO	80231	720-863-8920	863-8940	PK-5	Austen Kassinger
Rocky Mountain Prep S	10455 E 25th Ave	Aurora, CO	80010	720-863-8922	863-8940	PK-5	Caitlin Vaughan
Rocky Mountain Prep Southwest S	911 S Hazel Ct	Denver, CO	80219	720-863-8920		PK-5	Jennifer Reese
Roosevelt Charter Academy	205 Byron Dr	Colorado Spgs, CO	80910-2508	719-637-0311	380-0176	K-5	Steve Tompkins
Roots ES	3350 Hudson St	Denver, CO	80207	720-593-1338		K-5	Eve Bunevich
Ross Montessori S	109 Lewies Ln	Carbondale, CO	81623	970-963-7199	963-7342	K-8	Sonya Hemmen M.A.
St. Vrain Community Montessori Charter S	1055 Delaware Ave	Longmont, CO	80501	303-682-4339	682-8925	PK-6	Katie Torres
Salida Del Sol Academy	111 E 26th St	Greeley, CO	80631	970-347-8223		K-8	Paul Kirkpatrick
Salida Montessori Charter S	PO Box 1080	Salida, CO	81201	719-539-4887		K-8	Rafe Quinton
SkyView Academy	6161 Business Center Dr	Highlands Ranch, CO	80130	303-471-8439	470-1903	PK-12	Jon Ail
SOAR	4800 Telluride St	Denver, CO	80249	720-287-5100	287-5119	K-5	Laurie Godwin
Southwest Early College Charter S	3001 S Federal Blvd	Denver, CO	80236-2711	303-935-5473	935-5591	9-12	Halley Joseph
Southwest Open Charter S	410 N Dolores Rd	Cortez, CO	81321	970-565-1150	565-8770	9-12	Charlotte Wolf Ph.D.
Stargate Charter S	14530 Washington St	Thornton, CO	80023	303-450-3936	450-3941	K-12	Josh Cochran
STEM S Highlands Ranch	8773 Ridgeline Blvd	Highlands Ranch, CO	80129	303-683-7836	683-2099	K-12	Dr. Penny Eucker
Stone Creek Charter S	33520 Highway 6	Edwards, CO	81632	970-569-3327	569-3492	K-8	Jason Mills
STRIVE Prep - Excel	2960 N Speer Blvd	Denver, CO	80211	303-630-0360		9-12	Ben Lewis
STRIVE Prep - Federal	2626 W Evans Ave	Denver, CO	80219	303-573-2017		6-8	Rebecca Riopelle
STRIVE Prep - GVR	4800 Telluride St	Denver, CO	80249	303-999-2893		6-8	Jessica Savage
STRIVE Prep - Kepner	911 S Hazel Ct	Denver, CO	80219	720-485-6394		6-6	Katie Ryan
STRIVE Prep - Lake	1820 Lowell Blvd	Denver, CO	80204	303-551-7200	551-7207	6-8	Susan Morris
STRIVE Prep - Montbello	5000 Crown Blvd	Denver, CO	80239	303-999-3825		6-8	Tara Byers
STRIVE Prep - Rise	18250 E 51st Ave	Denver, CO	80249	720-485-6393		9-9	Elisha Roberts
STRIVE Prep - Ruby Hill	2626 W Evans Ave	Denver, CO	80219	720-460-2800		K-3	Alexa Mason
STRIVE Prep - SMART	3201 W Arizona Ave	Denver, CO	80219	303-962-9880	962-9885	9-12	Joshua Smith
STRIVE Prep - Sunnyside	4735 Pecos St	Denver, CO	80211	720-723-2000		6-8	Jessica Tillis
STRIVE Prep - Westwood	3201 W Arizona Ave	Denver, CO	80219	303-962-9880	962-9886	6-8	Kathleen Esparza
Summit MS	4655 Hanover Ave	Boulder, CO	80305-6036	720-561-3900	561-3901	6-8	Adam Galvin
Swallows Charter Academy	278 S McCulloch Blvd	Pueblo West, CO	81007-2844	719-547-1627	547-2509	K-12	Dr. Cindy Compton
TCA College Pathways	12201 Cross Peak Vw	Colorado Spgs, CO	80921	719-487-2000	260-9742	7-12	Justin Peterson
Tjardes S of Innovation	717 6th St	Greeley, CO	80631	970-348-4800		K-8	
Twin Peaks Charter Academy	340 S Sunset St	Longmont, CO	80501	303-772-7286	494-3611	K-12	Joe Mehsling
Two Rivers Community S	PO Box 188	Glenwood Spgs, CO	81602	970-384-5200	384-5201	K-8	Adriana Ayala-Hire Ed.D.
Two Roads Charter S	6980 Pierce St	Arvada, CO	80003-3646	303-423-3377	467-6955	K-12	Wendy Noel
Union Colony Prep ES	1051 29th Street Rd	Evans, CO	80620	970-673-4997	353-2271	K-6	Ken Wildenstein
Union Colony Prep S	2000 Clubhouse Dr	Greeley, CO	80634-3643	970-673-4546	330-7604	7-12	Kevin Rouse
University Preparatory S	2409 Arapahoe St	Denver, CO	80205	303-292-0463	296-2844	K-3	John Argue
University Prep - Steele St	3230 E 38th Ave	Denver, CO	80205-3726	303-292-0463		K-5	Jessica Valsechi
University Schools	6525 W 18th St	Greeley, CO	80634	970-506-7000	506-7070	K-12	Dr. Sherry Gerner
Vanguard Classical S	801 Yosemite St	Denver, CO	80230	303-691-2384	226-5529	K-8	Peggy Downs
Vanguard Classical S	17101 E Ohio Dr	Aurora, CO	80017	303-338-4110	338-4129	K-12	Peggy Downs
Vanguard Lower S	1832 S Wahsatch Ave	Colorado Spgs, CO	80905-2341	719-471-1999	799-6149	K-3	Renee Henslee
Vanguard Upper S	1605 S Corona Ave	Colorado Spgs, CO	80905	719-471-1999	634-4180	4-12	Colin Mullaney
Vega Collegiate Academy	1345 Macon St	Aurora, CO	80010	303-828-6217		K-8	Kathryn Mullins
Venture Prep Charter S	2900 Richard Allen Ct	Denver, CO	80205	303-893-0805	320-7665	9-12	Erin Quigley
Victory Prep Academy	5701 Quebec St	Commerce City, CO	80022	303-288-6111		6-12	Ron Jajdelski
Vision Charter Academy	1080 Pioneer Rd	Delta, CO	81416	970-874-8226	874-8336	K-8	Willyn Webb
Vista Charter S	PO Box 10000	Montrose, CO	81402-9701	970-249-4470	252-3354	9-12	Emily MacNiven
Westgate Community S	12500 Washington St	Thornton, CO	80241	303-425-0967	452-4519	K-12	Sharon Collins
West Ridge Academy	6905 W 8th St	Greeley, CO	80634	970-330-3671	330-3679	K-9	Russ Spicer
Wilson Academy	8300 W 94th Ave	Westminster, CO	80021-4590	303-431-3694	423-4388	PK-8	Carole Bartusiak
Windsor Charter Academy	680 Academy Ct	Windsor, CO	80550-3101	970-674-5020	674-5017	K-12	Rebecca Teeples
World Compass Academy	2490 S Perry St	Castle Rock, CO	80104	303-814-5200	688-9543	PK-5	Lance Howard
Wyatt Academy	3620 N Franklin St	Denver, CO	80205	303-292-5515	292-5111	K-8	Karen Craig

Connecticut

School	Address	City,State	Zip code	Telephone	Fax	Grade	Contact
Achievement First Amistad HS	580 Dixwell Ave	New Haven, CT	06511	203-772-1092	772-1784	9-12	Morgan Barth
Achievement First Bridgeport Academy	529 Noble Ave	Bridgeport, CT	06608	203-333-9128	333-9142	5-8	Challa Flemming
Achievement First Bridgeport Academy	655 Stillman St	Bridgeport, CT	06608	203-338-0593	338-0714	K-4	Christina Pares
Achievement First Hartford Academy ES	305 Greenfield St	Hartford, CT	06112-1826	860-695-6560	242-6457	K-4	Ernest Peterson
Achievement First Hartford Academy HS	305 Greenfield St	Hartford, CT	06112-1826	860-695-6680	722-8138	9-12	Emily Banks
Achievement First Hartford Academy MS	305 Greenfield St	Hartford, CT	06112-1826	860-695-6760	242-6457	5-8	Sorby Grant
Achievement First Summit S	85 Edwards St	Hartford, CT	06120	860-695-6200	722-8805	5-8	Benjamin Cruse
Amistad Academy ES	130 Edgewood Ave	New Haven, CT	06511	203-772-7000	772-2520	K-4	Christine Paris
Amistad Academy MS	130 Edgewood Ave	New Haven, CT	06511	203-772-7000	776-0229	5-8	Katie Poynter
Bridge Academy	160 Pulaski St	Bridgeport, CT	06608	203-336-9999	336-9852	7-12	Timothy Dutton
Common Ground HS	358 Springside Ave	New Haven, CT	06515-1024	203-389-4333	389-7458	9-12	Lizanne Cox
Dickerson's Jumoke Academy ES	250 Blue Hills Ave	Hartford, CT	06112	860-527-0575		PK-4	Dr. Michael Finley
Elm City College Preparatory ES	407 James St	New Haven, CT	06513	203-772-7010	498-0712	K-6	Andrew Poole
Elm City College Preparatory MS	794 Dixwell Ave	New Haven, CT	06511	203-772-5332	772-3641	7-8	Robert Hawke
Elm City Montessori S	375 Quinnipiac Ave	New Haven, CT	06513	203-903-4031	490-2316	PK-5	Dr. Alissa Levy
Explorations Charter S	71 Spencer St	Winsted, CT	06098-1128	860-738-9070	738-9092	9-12	Jill Johnson
Great Oaks Charter S	510 Barnum Ave	Bridgeport, CT	06608	203-870-8188	870-8189	6-8	Monica Filppu
Highville Charter S	1 Science Park	Hamden, CT	06511	203-287-0528	497-9899	PK-12	Craig Drazek
Integrated Day Charter S	68 Thermos Ave	Norwich, CT	06360-6957	860-892-1900	892-1902	PK-8	Anna James
Interdistrict S for Arts & Communication	190 Governor Winthrop Blvd	New London, CT	06320-6612	860-447-1003	447-0470	6-8	David C. Howes
Jumoke Academy Honors SMaRT	339 Blue Hills Ave	Hartford, CT	06112	860-527-0575	286-1137	5-8	Iris Gomero
Jumokoe Academy Honors	875 Asylum Ave	Hartford, CT	06105	860-527-0575	286-1137	5-8	Nichelle Woodson
Milner S	104 Vine St	Hartford, CT	06112-2295	860-695-4380	278-4694	PK-8	Karen Lott
New Beginnings Family Academy	184 Garden St	Bridgeport, CT	06605-1213	203-384-2897	384-2898	PK-8	Ronelle Swagerty
Odyssey Community S	579 Middle Tpke W	Manchester, CT	06040-2728	860-645-1234	533-0324	K-8	Annie Busby
Park City Prep Charter S	1550 State St	Bridgeport, CT	06605	203-953-3766	953-3771	5-8	Bruce Ravage
Side by Side Charter S	10 Chestnut St	Norwalk, CT	06854-2928	203-857-0306	838-2666	PK-8	Matthew Nittoly
Stamford Academy	229 North St	Stamford, CT	06901-1112	203-324-6300	324-6310	9-12	Andrea Weller
Trailblazers Academy	83 Lockwood Ave	Stamford, CT	06902	203-977-5690	977-5688	6-8	Miguel Pickering
Washington Academy	804 State St	New Haven, CT	06511	203-691-6535	684-2744	K-4	John Taylor

Delaware

School	Address	City,State	Zip code	Telephone	Fax	Grade	Contact
Academia Antonia Alonso	1200 N French St	Wilmington, DE	19884	302-660-4760	660-4761	K-2	Dr. Mark Phelps
Academy of Dover Charter S	104 Saulsbury Rd	Dover, DE	19904-2705	302-674-0684	674-3894	K-5	Cheri Marshall
Campus Community S	350 Pear St	Dover, DE	19904	302-736-0403	736-5330	K-8	Leroy Travis
Charter S of Wilmington	100 N DuPont Rd	Wilmington, DE	19807-3106	302-651-2727	652-1246	9-12	Samuel Paoli
Delaware Acad of Pub Safety & Security	801 N DuPont Hwy	New Castle, DE	19720	302-322-6050	322-4029	9-12	Herbert Sheldon
Delaware Design-Lab HS	179 Stanton Christiana Rd	Newark, DE	19702	302-292-5450	368-3460	9-12	Dr. Cristina C. Alvarez
Delaware Military Academy	112 Middleboro Rd	Wilmington, DE	19804-1621	302-998-0745	998-3521	9-12	Anthony Pullella
Early College HS at DE State University	1570 N DuPont Hwy	Dover, DE	19901	302-678-3247	857-4456	9-12	Dr. Evelyn Edney
East Side Charter S	3000 N Claymont St	Wilmington, DE	19802-2807	302-762-5834	762-3864	PK-8	Aaron Bass
Edison Charter S	2200 N Locust St	Wilmington, DE	19802-4429	302-778-1101	778-2232	K-8	Salome Thomas-El
Family Foundations Academy	170 Lukens Dr	New Castle, DE	19720	302-324-8901	324-8908	K-8	Aaron Bass
First State Military Academy	355 W Duck Creek Rd	Clayton, DE	19938	302-223-2150		9-10	Patrick Gallucci
First State Montessori Academy	1000 N French St	Wilmington, DE	19801	302-576-1500	576-1501	K-5	Courtney Fox
Freire Charter S	201 W 14th St	Wilmington, DE	19801	302-407-4800	654-1125	8-10	Paul Ramirez
Gateway Lab S	2501 Centerville Rd	Wilmington, DE	19808	302-633-4091	633-5680	3-8	Tim Griffiths
Great Oaks Charter S - Wilmington	1200 N French St	Wilmington, DE	19001	302-660-4790	660-4788	6-8	Kia Johnson
Kuumba Academy Charter S	1200 N French St	Wilmington, DE	19801	302-472-6450	472-6452	K-5	Sally Maldonado
Las Americas Aspira Academy	326 Ruthar Dr	Newark, DE	19711	302-292-1463	292-1291	K-8	Margaret Lopez Waite
MOT Charter S	1156 Levels Rd	Middletown, DE	19709-7700	302-376-5125	376-5120	K-10	Ned Southworth
Newark Charter S	2001 Patriot Way	Newark, DE	19711	302-369-2001	368-3460	K-12	Gregory Meece
Odyssey Charter HS	4319 Lancaster Pike	Wilmington, DE	19805	302-516-8000	780-5962	9-12	Dr. Nick Manolakos
Odyssey Charter S Lower Campus	4319 Lancaster Pike	Wilmington, DE	19805	302-994-6490	780-5962	K-5	Dr. Nick Manolakos
Odyssey Charter S Upper Campus	4319 Lancaster Pike	Wilmington, DE	19805	302-655-6490	780-5962	6-8	Dr. Nick Manolakos
Positive Outcomes Charter S	3337 S Dupont Hwy	Camden, DE	19934	302-697-8805	697-8813	6-12	Edward Emmett
Prestige Academy	1121 Thatcher St	Wilmington, DE	19802	302-762-3240	762-4782	5-8	Cordie Greenlea
Providence Creek Academy Charter S	PO Box 265	Clayton, DE	19938-0265	302-653-6276	653-5238	K-8	Audrey Erschen
Sussex Academy of Arts and Sciences	21150 Airport Rd	Georgetown, DE	19947	302-856-3636	856-3376	6-12	Patricia Oliphant Ed.D.

District Of Columbia

School	Address	City,State	Zip code	Telephone	Fax	Grade	Contact
Academy of Hope	421 Alabama Ave SE	Washington, DC	20032	202-373-0246		Adult	Lecester Johnson
Academy of Hope S	2315 18th Pl	Washington, DC	20018	202-269-6623	269-6632	Adult	Lecester Johnson
Angelou Charter HS	5600 E Capitol St NE	Washington, DC	20019-6739	202-379-4335	506-5749	9-12	Tameika Ashford
Angelou Charter S - Young Adult	5600 E Capitol St NE	Washington, DC	20019	202-289-8898	289-8897	Adult	Dr. Sean Yisrael
AppleTree Early Learning - Columbia Hts	2750 14th St NW	Washington, DC	20009	202-667-9490		PK-8	Karen Stona
AppleTree Early Learning-Douglass Knoll	2017 Savannah Ter SE	Washington, DC	20020	202-629-2545	629-2548	PK-PK	Charlie Crabtree
AppleTree Early Learning - Lincoln Park	138 12th St NE	Washington, DC	20002	202-621-6581	621-6584	PK-PK	Megan Marrinan
AppleTree Early Learning - Oklahoma Ave	330 21st St NE	Washington, DC	20002	202-629-2179	629-2189	PK-8	Terica Alleyne
AppleTree Early Learning - Parklands	2011 Savannah St SE	Washington, DC	20020	202-506-1890		PK-4	Niesha Cumberpatch
AppleTree Early Learning - Southwest	801 7th St SW	Washington, DC	20024	202-646-0500	646-0510	PK-5	Shontice McKenzie
BASIS Washington DC	410 8th St NW	Washington, DC	20004	202-393-5437	393-5438	5-12	Jill Garrett
Bethune Day Academy	1404 Jackson St NE	Washington, DC	20017	202-459-4710	318-7588	PK-8	Linda McKay
Breakthrough Montessori Charter S	1244 Taylor St NW	Washington, DC	20011	202-407-7022		PK-PK	Keith Whitescarver
Bridges Public Charter S	100 Gallatin St NE	Washington, DC	20011	202-545-0515	545-0517	PK-5	Kristine Rigley
Briya Charter S	100 Gallatin St	Washington, DC	20011	202-232-7777		PK-Ad	Christie McKay
Briya Charter S	4300 13th St NW	Washington, DC	20011	202-797-7337		PK-Ad	Christie McKay
Briya Charter S	3912 Georgia Ave NW	Washington, DC	20011-5861	202-545-2020	797-8470	PK-12	Christie McKay
Briya Charter S	2333 Ontario Rd NW	Washington, DC	20009	202-420-7200		PK-12	Christie McKay
Capital City Public Charter S	100 Peabody St NW	Washington, DC	20011	202-808-9800	733-1812	PK-12	Karen Dresden
Cedar Tree Academy	701 Howard Rd SE	Washington, DC	20020	202-610-4193	610-2845	PK-K	Dr. Latonya Henderson
Center City Pub Charter S - Brightwood	6008 Georgia Ave NW	Washington, DC	20011	202-723-3322	291-0219	PK-8	Rachel Tommelleo
Center City Pub Charter S - Capitol Hill	1503 E Capitol St SE	Washington, DC	20003-1508	202-547-7556	547-5686	PK-8	Valery Dragon
Center City Pub Charter S - Congress Hts	220 Highview Pl SE	Washington, DC	20032	202-562-7070	574-5829	PK-8	Niya White
Center City Public Charter S - Petworth	510 Webster St NW	Washington, DC	20011	202-726-9212	726-3378	PK-8	Nazo Burgy
Center City Public Charter S - Shaw	711 N St NW	Washington, DC	20001	202-234-1093	462-6875	PK-8	Alicia McCloud
Center City Public Charter S - Trinidad	1217 W Virginia Ave NE	Washington, DC	20002	202-397-1614	398-4832	PK-8	Charlotte Hansen
Chavez - Capitol Hill HS	709 12th St SE	Washington, DC	20003	202-547-3424	547-2507	9-12	Sarah Lehar
Chavez - Parkside MSHS	3701 Hayes St NE	Washington, DC	20019-1702	202-398-2230	398-2535	6-12	William Massey
Chavez Prep MS	770 Kenyon St NW	Washington, DC	20010	202-723-3975	723-3976	6-9	Dr. Courtney Miller
Children's Guild DC	2146 24th Pl NE	Washington, DC	20018	202-774-5442		K-8	Nakia Nicholson
City Arts & Prep Charter S	705 Edgewood St NE Fl 2	Washington, DC	20017-3341	202-269-4646	403-3222	PK-8	Lanette Dailey-Reese
Community College Prep Academy	2405 Martin L King Ave SE	Washington, DC	20020	202-610-5780		Adult	Connie Spinner
Community College Prep Academy	3301 Wheeler Rd SE	Washington, DC	20032	202-770-3252		Adult	Connie Spinner
Creative Minds International Charter S	3700 N Capitol St NW	Washington, DC	20011	202-588-0370	588-0263	PK-8	Dr. Golnar Abedin
Democracy Prep Congress Hts Charter S	3100 Martin L King Ave SE	Washington, DC	20032	202-561-0860	561-0864	PK-8	Shukurat Adamoh-Faniyan
DC Bilingual Public Charter S	33 Riggs Rd NE	Washington, DC	20011	202-750-6674	750-6733	PK-5	Daniela Anello
DC Prep Charter ES - Anacostia	1409 V St SE	Washington, DC	20020	202-729-3500	889-2785	PK-3	Maria-Teresa Duvall
DC Prep Charter ES - Benning	100 41st St NE	Washington, DC	20019-3308	202-398-2838	398-2839	PK-6	Maura Englender
DC Prep Charter ES - Edgewood	707 Edgewood St NE	Washington, DC	20017	202-635-4411	635-4412	PK-3	Avise Hayes
DC Prep Charter MS - Edgewood	701 Edgewood St NE	Washington, DC	20017	202-832-5700	832-5701	4-8	Rachel McClam
DC Scholars Charter S	5601 E Capitol St SE	Washington, DC	20019	202-559-6138	618-9396	PK-8	Jessica Hiltabidel
Eagle Academy Charter S - Capital Rvrft	1017 New Jersey Ave SE	Washington, DC	20003	202-459-6825	479-6796	PK-3	Sabrina Ogilvie
Eagle Academy Charter S - Congress Hts.	3400 Wheeler Rd SE	Washington, DC	20032	202-544-2646	544-0187	PK-3	Royston Lyttle
Early Childhood Academy	4025 9th St SE	Washington, DC	20032-6051	202-373-0035	373-5586	PK-3	Wendy Edwards
Excel Academy Public Charter S	2501 Martin L King Jr SE	Washington, DC	20020	202-373-0097	373-0477	PK-8	Deborah Lockhart
Friendship Charter S - Armstrong	111 O St NW	Washington, DC	20001	202-518-3928	518-3924	PK-5	Khabria Hundley
Friendship Charter S - Blow-Pierce	725 19th St NE	Washington, DC	20002-4713	202-572-1070	399-6157	PK-8	Dr. Jeffrey Grant
Friendship Charter S - Chamberlain	1345 Potomac Ave SE	Washington, DC	20003-4411	202-547-5800	547-4554	PK-8	Morrise Harbour
Friendship Charter S - Collegiate Acad	4095 Minnesota Ave NE	Washington, DC	20019	202-396-5500	396-8229	9-12	Curtis Lawrence
Friendship Charter S - Online	1351 Nicholson St NW	Washington, DC	20011	202-729-8287		K-8	John Sloane
Friendship Charter S - Southeast	645 Milwaukee Pl SE	Washington, DC	20032-2606	202-562-1980	562-0726	PK-5	David Lawery
Friendship Charter S - Technology Prep	2705 Martin Luther King Ave	Washington, DC	20032	202-552-5700		6-12	Peggy Jones
Friendship Charter S - Woodridge	2959 Carlton Ave NE	Washington, DC	20018-2615	202-635-6500	635-6481	PK-8	Felicia Owo
Goodwill Excel Center	1776 G St NW	Washington, DC	20006	202-839-3650		9-12	
Harmony DC Public Charter S	62 T St NE	Washington, DC	20002	202-529-7500	529-7501	K-5	Emin Cavusoglu
Haynes Public Charter S	4501 Kansas Ave NW	Washington, DC	20011	202-706-5838	706-5832	PK-12	Phyllis Hedlund
Haynes Public Charter S	3600 Georgia Ave NW	Washington, DC	20010	202-667-4446	667-8811	5-8	Myron Long
Howard University MS of Math & Science	405 Howard Pl NW	Washington, DC	20059-0001	202-806-7725	865-0271	6-8	Kathryn Procope
Ideal Academy	6130 N Capitol St NW	Washington, DC	20011-1405	202-729-6660	729-6677	PK-8	George Rutherford Ph.D.
IDEA Public Charter HS	1027 45th St NE	Washington, DC	20019-3802	202-399-4750	399-4387	9-12	Nicole McCrae
Imagine Hope Community Charter - Lamond	6200 Kansas Ave NE	Washington, DC	20011	202-722-4421	722-4431	PK-6	Diana Tharpe
Imagine Hope Community Charter - Tolson	2917 8th St NE	Washington, DC	20017-1669	202-832-7370	832-7644	PK-8	Chloe Marshall
Ingenuity Prep Charter S	4600 Livingston Rd SE	Washington, DC	20032	202-562-0391		PK-4	Aaron Cuny
Inspired Teaching S	200 Douglas St NE	Washington, DC	20002	202-248-6825	248-6939	PK-8	Latisha Coleman
Kingsman Academy	1375 E St NE	Washington, DC	20002-5429	202-547-1028	503-9913	6-12	Shannon Hodge
KIPP DC: AIM Academy	2600 Douglass Pl SE	Washington, DC	20020	202-678-5477	678-4383	5-8	Aliesha Maye
KIPP DC: Arts and Technology Academy	5300 Blaine St NE	Washington, DC	20019	202-398-6811		PK-K	Allison Artis
KIPP DC: College Preparatory	1401 Brentwood Pkwy NE	Washington, DC	20002	202-678-2627	678-0082	9-12	Andhra Lutz
KIPP DC: Connect Academy	1375 Mount Olivet Rd NE	Washington, DC	20002	202-396-5477	223-4504	PK-K	Amy Drake
KIPP DC: Discover Academy	2600 Douglass Pl SE	Washington, DC	20020	202-678-7735	678-0085	PK-K	Sommer Wynn
KIPP DC: Grow Academy	421 P St NW	Washington, DC	20001	202-986-4769	986-1625	PK-K	Lauren Ellis
KIPP DC: Heights Academy	2600 Douglass Pl SE	Washington, DC	20020	202-610-5323	610-6555	1-4	Gaelen Gallagher
KIPP DC: KEY Academy	4801 Benning Rd SE	Washington, DC	20019-6145	202-582-5477	582-0152	5-8	John Barnhardt
KIPP DC: LEAD Academy	421 P St NW	Washington, DC	20001	202-469-3300		1-4	Mekia Love
KIPP DC: LEAP Academy	4801 Benning Rd SE	Washington, DC	20019-6145	202-582-5327	582-4680	PK-PK	Abraham Clayman
KIPP DC: Northeast Academy	1375 Mount Olivet Rd NE	Washington, DC	20002	202-398-5477		5-8	Caitlin Maxwell
KIPP DC: Promise Academy	4801 Benning Rd SE	Washington, DC	20019	202-265-7766	582-4686	1-4	Erin Huseby
KIPP DC: Quest Academy	5300 Blaine St NE	Washington, DC	20019	202-397-5477		1-4	John Petersen
KIPP DC: Spring Academy	1375 Mount Olivet Rd NE	Washington, DC	20002-2509	202-397-5477	223-4504	1-4	Donny Tiengtum
KIPP DC: Valor Academy	5300 Blaine St NE	Washington, DC	20019	202-398-6811		5-8	Gillian Connor
KIPP DC: WILL Academy	421 P St NW	Washington, DC	20001-2417	202-328-9455	328-9457	5-8	Jerry Jellig
Latin American Montessori Bilingual S	1375 Missouri Ave NW	Washington, DC	20011-1862	202-726-6200	722-4125	PK-5	Cristina Encinas
Latin American Montessori Bilingual S	1800 Perry St NE	Washington, DC	20018	202-525-5105	621-8621	PK-5	Cristina Encinas
LAYC Career Academy	3047 15th St NW	Washington, DC	20009	202-319-2228	319-2250	Adult	Angola Stopancic
Lee Montessori Public Charter S	3025 4th St NE	Washington, DC	20017	202-779-9740	318-0763	PK-6	Megan Hubbard
Marshall Academy	2427 M L K Jr Ave SE	Washington, DC	20020	202-563-6862	563-6946	9-12	Melanie Sala
Meridian Public Charter S	3029 14th St NW	Washington, DC	20009	202-793-2667	793-2668	7-8	Candice Bobo
Meridian Public Charter S	2120 13th St NW	Washington, DC	20009	202-387-9830	238-0036	PK-6	Candice Bobo
Monument Academy	500 19th St NE	Washington, DC	20002	202-545-3180	478-2824	5-7	Marlene Magrino
Mundo Verde Bilingual Charter S	30 P St NW	Washington, DC	20001	202-750-7060	667-4811	PK-5	Kristin Scotchmer
National Collegiate Prep Charter HS	4600 Livingston Rd SE	Washington, DC	20032	202-832-7737	832-7736	9-12	Jennifer Ross
Next Step Public Charter S	3047 15th St NW	Washington, DC	20009	202-319-2249	234-0001	Adult	Arturo Martinez
Paul Charter S	5800 8th St NW	Washington, DC	20011-1900	202-291-7499	291-7495	6-12	Charlotte Spann
Perry Street Preparatory S	1800 Perry St NE	Washington, DC	20018	202-529-4400	526-2214	PK-8	Rachel Crouch
Rocketship Rise Academy	2335 Raynolds Pl SE	Washington, DC	20020	202-750-7177		PK-3	Joshua Pacos
Roots Public Charter S	15 Kennedy St NW	Washington, DC	20011	202-882-8073	882-8075	PK-5	Dr. Bernida Thompson
Rosario International Public Charter S	1100 Harvard St NW	Washington, DC	20009-5356	202-797-4700	232-6442	Adult	Holly-Ann Freso-Moore

School	Address	City,State	Zip code	Telephone	Fax	Grade	Contact
Rosario International Public Charter S	514 V St NE	Washington, DC	20002	202-734-4900		Adult	Karen Rivas
St. Coletta Special Education Charter S	1901 Independence Ave SE	Washington, DC	20003-1733	202-350-8680	350-8699	PK-12	Janice Corazza
SEED S of Washington DC	4300 C St SE	Washington, DC	20019-4100	202-248-7773	204-5766	6-12	Mecha Inman
Sela Charter S	6015 Chillum Pl NE	Washington, DC	20011	202-670-7352		PK-3	Jenifer Moore
Shining Stars Montessori Academy	1240 Randolph St NE	Washington, DC	20017	202-723-1467	319-2309	PK-6	Regina Rodriguez
Somerset Prep Academy	3301 Wheeler Rd SE	Washington, DC	20032	202-562-9170	562-9105	6-12	Lauren Catalano
Stokes Charter S	3700 Oakview Ter NE	Washington, DC	20017	202-265-7237	265-4656	PK-5	Erika Bryant
Two Rivers Public Charter S	1234 4th St NE	Washington, DC	20002	202-543-8477	543-8479	6-8	Jennifer McCormick
Two Rivers Public Charter S	1227 4th St NE	Washington, DC	20002-3431	202-546-4477	546-0869	PK-5	Caroline Mwendwa-Baker
Two Rivers Public Charter S - Young	820 26th St NE	Washington, DC	20002	202-388-1360		PK-3	Guye Turner
Wahler Place ES	908 Wahler Pl SE	Washington, DC	20032-4000	202-562-1307	748-5970	PK-3	Rebeccah Brooking
Wahler Place MS	908 Wahler Pl	Washington, DC	20032	202-562-1214	562-1219	4-8	Shantelle Wright
Washington Global Charter S	525 School St SW	Washington, DC	20024	202-796-2415		6-8	Howard Mebane
Washington Latin Public Charter S	5200 2nd St NW	Washington, DC	20011	202-223-1111	723-1171	5-12	Peter Anderson
Washington Leadership Academy	3015 4th St NE	Washington, DC	20017	202-580-3371		9-12	Stacy Kane
Washington MST Public Charter HS	1920 Bladensburg Rd NE	Washington, DC	20002-1812	202-636-8011	636-8022	9-12	Dr. N'Deye Diagne
Washington Yu Ying Public Charter S	220 Taylor St NE	Washington, DC	20017	202-635-1950	635-1960	PK-5	Maquita Alexander
Wright Charter S	770 M St SE	Washington, DC	20003	202-388-1011	388-5197	8-12	Dr. Marco Clark
YouthBuild Public Charter S	3220 16th St NW	Washington, DC	20010	202-319-0141	518-0618	Adult	Andrew Touchette

Florida

School	Address	City,State	Zip code	Telephone	Fax	Grade	Contact
Academic Solutions Academy	4099 N Pine Island Rd	Sunrise, FL	33351-6548	954-572-6600	572-6444	9-12	Andrew Kinlock
Academic Solutions Academy	2000 W Commercial Blvd	Fort Lauderdale, FL	33309	954-572-6600	572-6444	9-12	Andrew Kinlock
AcadeMir Charter MS	5800 SW 135th Ave	Miami, FL	33183	305-967-8492	392-1928	6-8	Karla Rodriguez
AcadeMir Charter S Preparatory	19185 SW 127th Ave	Miami, FL	33177	305-964-7542	964-7458	K-5	Dr. Mary Gonzalez-Ledo
AcadeMir Charter S West	14880 SW 26th St	Miami, FL	33185	305-485-9911	485-9944	K-5	Olivia Bernal
AcadeMir Prep Academy	5800 SW 135th Ave	Miami, FL	33176	305-967-8492	392-1928	K-5	Karla Rodriguez
Academy at the Farm	9500 Alex Lange Way	Dade City, FL	33525-8213	352-588-9737	588-0508	K-8	Ray Polk
Academy Da Vinci	1060 Keene Rd	Dunedin, FL	34698-6300	727-298-2778	502-6065	K-5	Lucy Foran
Academy for Positive Learning Charter S	1200 N Dixie Hwy	Lake Worth, FL	33460-2123	561-585-6104	585-7849	K-8	Renatta Adan-Espinoza
Academy of Environmental Science	12695 W Fort Island Trl	Crystal River, FL	34429-5290	352-795-8793	249-2100	9-12	Zachary Leonard
Academy of International Education	1080 La Baron Dr	Miami Springs, FL	33166-6064	305-883-3900	883-3901	K-8	Vera Hirsh
Acceleration MS	3365 Seminole Ave	Fort Myers, FL	33916	239-400-1818	689-8511	6-8	Dr. Patricia Lightner
Access Charter S	6000 E Colonial Dr	Orlando, FL	32807	321-319-0640	319-0643	6-12	Roger Watkins
Achievement Academy - Bartow	695 E Summerlin St	Bartow, FL	33830-4848	863-533-0690	534-0798	PK-PK	Cindi Parker-Pearson
Achievement Academy - Lakeland	716 E Bella Vista St	Lakeland, FL	33805-3009	863-683-6504	688-9292	PK-PK	Cindi Parker-Pearson
Achievement Academy - Winter Haven	2211 28th St NW	Winter Haven, FL	33881-1807	863-965-7586	968-5016	PK-PK	Cindi Parker-Pearson
Adler ES	4515 38th Ave N	St Petersburg, FL	33713	727-329-9545	522-2854	K-6	Yuri Yamashita
Advantage Academy	350 W Prosser Dr	Plant City, FL	33563	813-567-0801	441-0272	K-8	Keith Miller
Advantage Academy Santa Fe	9790 SW 107th Ct	Miami, FL	33176	786-228-5309	718-1921	K-5	Teresita Nieves
Alachua Learning Center	PO Box 1389	Alachua, FL	32616	386-418-2080	418-4116	K-8	Krishna Rivera
Alee Academy Charter S	1705 E County Road 44	Eustis, FL	32736	352-357-9426	357-8426	9-12	Robin Valentino
Aloma Charter HS	495 N Semoran Blvd Ste 8	Winter Park, FL	32792	407-657-4343	657-4317	9-12	Jacqueline Evans
Alpha Charter S of Excellence	1223 SW 4th St	Miami, FL	33135	305-643-2132	642-3717	K-5	Isabel Navas
Alpha International Academy	121 S 24th Ave	Hollywood, FL	33020	954-505-7974	505-7976	K-5	Wayne Neunie
Altoona S	42630 State Road 19	Altoona, FL	32702	352-669-3444	669-3407	K-5	Walter Schmidt
AMI Kids Emerald Coast	207 4th St SE	Ft Walton Bch, FL	32548-5636	850-244-2711	244-2171	6-12	Audra Ray
Andrews HS	3500 N Andrews Ave Ext	Pompano Beach, FL	33064	954-944-4123	784-3681	9-12	Eunice Casey
Apalachicola Bay Charter S	98 12th St	Apalachicola, FL	32320-2003	850-653-1222	653-1857	K-8	Chimene Johnson
Archimedean Academy	12425 SW 72nd St	Miami, FL	33183-2513	305-279-6572	675-8448	K-5	Christina Briz
Archimedean Middle Conservatory	12425 SW 72nd St	Miami, FL	33183-2513	305-279-6572	675-8448	6-8	Vasiliki Moysidis
Archimedean Upper Conservatory	12425 SW 72nd St	Miami, FL	33183	305-279-6572	675-8448	9-12	Demetrios Demopoulos
Arts Academy of Excellence	780 Fisherman St	Opa Locka, FL	33054	786-534-4528	452-9349	6-12	Angela Kemp
Ascend Career Academy	5251 Coconut Creek Pkwy	Margate, FL	33063-3962	954-978-4555		9-12	Vincent Alessi
ASPIRA Arts DECO	1 NE 19th St	Miami, FL	33132-1030	305-576-1512	576-0810	6-8	Maria Caceres
ASPIRA Leadership and College Prep	13330 SW 288th St	Homestead, FL	33033	305-246-1111	246-1433	K-8	Antonio Cejas
ASPIRA Raul Martinez Charter S	13300 Memorial Hwy	North Miami, FL	33161-3940	305-893-8050	891-6055	6-9	Denovilee Richardson
Aspire Charter Academy	928 Malone Dr	Orlando, FL	32810	407-297-9955	297-9944	K-5	Pamela Schenkel
Athenian Academy of Pasco	3118 Seven Springs Blvd	New Port Richey, FL	34655-3340	727-372-0200	376-1916	K-8	Evan Markowitz
Athenian Academy	2289 N Hercules Ave	Clearwater, FL	33763-2326	727-298-2718	298-2719	K-8	Kathy Hershelman
Atlantic Montessori Charter S	9893 Pines Blvd	Pembroke Pines, FL	33024-6164	754-263-2700	263-2596	K-3	Juana Garcia
Atlantic Montessori Charter S	2550 S Flamingo Rd	Davie, FL	33325	954-790-8943	399-9787	PK-5	Juana Garcia
Avant Garde Academy	2025 McKinley St	Hollywood, FL	33020	954-816-6153	800-2715	K-12	Frank Bolanos
Avant Garde Academy	13901 Sheldon Rd	Tampa, FL	33626	813-551-0395		K-6	Deedra Copeland
Avant Garde Academy	3540 Pleasant Hill Rd	Kissimmee, FL	34746	407-944-4464	368-6048	K-8	Pamela Chapman
Avant Garde Academy of Osceola	2880 N Orange Blossom Trl	Kissimmee, FL	34741	321-697-3800	386-7357	6-12	Ivonne Sardinas
Aventura City of Excellence Charter S	3333 NE 188th St	Aventura, FL	33180-2933	305-466-1499	466-1339	K-8	Julie Alm
Bay Haven Charter Academy	2501 Hawks Landing Blvd	Panama City, FL	32405-6658	850-248-3500	248-3514	PK-8	Jamie Vickers
Beacon College Preparatory	13400 NW 28th Ave	Opa Locka, FL	33054-4842	786-353-6109		PK-5	Patrick Evans
Beasley Technical Academy	60 Bell Blvd N	Lehigh Acres, FL	33936	239-476-9100	561-9864	9-12	Dr. Joseph Torregrasso
Believers Academy	5840 Corporate Way Ste 100	West Palm Beach, FL	33407-2040	561-340-2507	340-2510	9-12	Lori Dyer
Bellalago Charter Academy	3651 Pleasant Hill Rd	Kissimmee, FL	34746-2935	407-933-1690	933-2143	K-8	Jonathan Rasmussen
Bell Creek Academy	13221 Boyette Rd	Riverview, FL	33569	813-793-6075	413-2985	6-12	Dr. Margaret Fahringer
Belle Glade Excel	555 SW 16th St	Belle Glade, FL	33430	561-257-5210	983-8020	K-5	Altoria Henley
Belmont Academy	496 SW Ring Ct	Lake City, FL	32025	386-487-0487	755-7989	PK-12	Ron Barker
Berkley Accelerated MS	5316 Berkley Rd	Auburndale, FL	33823-8493	863-984-2400	984-2411	6-8	Jill Bolender
Berkley ES	5240 Berkley Rd	Auburndale, FL	33823-8491	863-968-5024	968-5026	K-5	Gayle Thomas
Beulah Academy of Science	8633 Beulah Rd	Pensacola, FL	32526-5203	850-944-2822	944-2848	6-8	Sherry Bailey
Big Pine Academy	30220 Overseas Hwy	Big Pine Key, FL	33043-3357	305-872-1266	872-1265	PK-8	Cathy Hoffman
Biscayne HS	1680 Dunn Ave Ste 8	Jacksonville, FL	32218	904-423-8855		9-12	Erica Williams
Boca Raton Charter S	269 NE 14th St	Boca Raton, FL	33432	561-750-0437	750-7880	K-5	Louise Nelson
Bok Academy	13901 Hwy 27	Lake Wales, FL	33859-2570	863-638-1010	638-1212	6-8	Damien Moses
Bonita Springs Charter S	25380 Bernwood Dr	Bonita Springs, FL	34135-7850	239-992-6932	992-7359	K-8	Carissa Carroll
Boulware Springs Charter S	1303 NE 23rd Ave	Gainesville, FL	32609-3822	352-215-2175		K-5	Kay Abbitt
Bridgeprep Academy Greater Miami	137 NE 19th St	Miami, FL	33132	786-477-4372	446-8714	K-5	Ana Natali
Bridgeprep Academy Interamerican	621 SW 22nd Ave	Miami, FL	33135	305-643-4833	643-4832	K-8	Guillermo Gonzalez
Bridgeprep Academy of Arts & Minds	3138 Commodore Plz	Miami, FL	33133-5814	305-448-1100	448-9737	9-12	Antonietta DiGirolamo
Bridge Prep Academy of Broward	7595 NW 61st St	Tamarac, FL	33321	954-417-3813		K-8	Niesha Mack
BridgePrep Academy of Hollywood Hills	1400 N 46th Ave	Hollywood, FL	33021	954-362-8268	362-8271	K-5	Ronald Marcelo
BridgePrep Academy of Palm Beach	9085 Happy Hollow Rd	Delray Beach, FL	33446	561-406-0709		K-8	Paul Sirota
Bridgeprep Academy of Tampa	2418 W Swann Ave	Tampa, FL	33609-4712	813-258-5652	258-5654	K-8	Christine Harris
Bridgeprep Academy of Village Green	13300 SW 120th St	Miami, FL	33186	305-253-8775	554-7611	K-8	Patty Garcia
BridgePrep Academy - Orlando	5710 La Costa Dr	Orlando, FL	32807	321-775-2119		K-7	Dr. Joy Gordon Fernandez
Bridgeprep Academy Riverview	6309 S US Hwy 301	Riverview, FL	33578	813-405-1770		K-8	Keith Jacobs
Bridgeprep Academy South	10700 SW 56th St	Miami, FL	33165	305-271-3109	271-5315	K-8	Yvette Rodriguez
BridgePrep Preparatory of Sunset	12001 Sunset Dr	Miami, FL	33183	305-595-8822	595-5487	PK-8	Elizabeth Altare M.Ed.
Bright Futures Academy	10350 Riverside Dr	Palm Bch Gdns, FL	33410	561-253-7504	658-0565	K-8	Ashley Slone
Brooks-DeBartolo Collegiate HS	10948 N Central Ave	Tampa, FL	33612	813-971-5600	971-5656	9-12	Kristine Bennett
Brooksville Engineering Science Tech.	835 School St	Brooksville, FL	34601-4006	352-544-2373		9-12	Andre Buford
Broward Math and Science S	6101 NW 31st St	Margate, FL	33063	954-969-8488	756-8053	K-12	Ali Gumus
Burns Science & Technology Charter S	160 Ridge Rd	Oak Hill, FL	32759-9773	386-210-4915	210-4922	K-8	Dr. Janet McGee
Byrneville Charter S	1600 Byrneville Rd	Century, FL	32535-3640	850-256-6350	256-6357	K-5	Dee Wolfe-Sullivan
Campus Charter S	3815 Curtis Blvd	Port Saint Joe, FL	32927	321-633-8234	848-0989	K-6	Trisha Leitem
Canoe Creek Charter Academy	3600 Canoe Creek Rd	Saint Cloud, FL	34772-9132	407-891-7320	891-7330	PK-8	Julie Ramirez
Cape Coral Charter S	76 Mid Cape Ter	Cape Coral, FL	33991-2008	239-995-0904	995-0369	PK-8	Sara Abraham
Capstone Academy	4901 W Fairfield Dr	Pensacola, FL	32506-4111	850-458-7735	455-7754	PK-K	Aileen Ilano
Capstone Academy Milton Charter S	5308 Stewart St	Milton, FL	32570-4736	850-626-3091	626-3093	PK-PK	Claire Errington
Caring & Sharing Charter S	PO Box 5936	Gainesville, FL	32627-5936	352-372-1004	372-0894	PK-6	Curtis Peterson
Central Charter S	4515 N State Road 7	Laud Lakes, FL	33319-5883	954-735-6295	735-6232	K-8	Tonya Dix
Central Florida Leadership Academy	427 N Primrose Dr	Orlando, FL	32803	407-480-2352	289-5224	6-12	Joanne Goubourn
Central HS	1250 W 17th St	Panama City, FL	32405	850-866-4148	615-0552	9-12	Jeremy Knapp
Chain of Lakes Collegiate HS	999 Avenue H NE	Winter Haven, FL	33881-4256	863-298-6800	298-6801	11-12	Bridget Fetter
Chambers HS of South Miami-Dade County	698 N Homestead Blvd	Homestead, FL	33030	305-909-6307	248-2913	9-12	Daniel Walke
Championship Academy	3367 N University Dr	Davie, FL	33328	954-362-3415	640-9678	K-8	Paulina Reyna
Championship Academy	1100 Hillcrest Dr	Hollywood, FL	33021	954-924-8006	924-8044	K-12	Savitria Guthrie
Championship Academy of Distinction	7100 W Oakland Park Blvd	Sunrise, FL	33313	954-514-7323		K-8	Marilyn Davis
Chancery High Charter	7001 S Orange Blossom Trl	Orlando, FL	32809	407-850-9791	850-9856	9-12	Michael Showalter
Channelside Academy of Math & Science	1029 E Twiggs St	Tampa, FL	33602	813-579-9649	463-2439	K-8	Cristina Fuentes
Charter HS of the Americas	970 W Flagler St	Miami, FL	33130	305-325-1001	324-9934	9-12	Barbara Sanchez
Charter S at Waterstone	855 Waterstone Way	Homestead, FL	33033-5941	305-248-6206	248-6208	K-5	Nancy Roque
Charter S of Excellence - Davie	2801 N University Dr	Pembroke Pines, FL	33024	954-433-8838	433-8636	K-5	Rosa Dyer
Chautauqua Learn & Serve Charter S	1118 Magnolia Ave	Panama City, FL	32401-2815	850-785-5056	785-5071	9-Adu	Cynthia McCauley
Children's Reading Center	7901 Saint Johns Ave	Palatka, FL	32177	386-328-9990	328-9949	K-5	Jacqueline England
Chiles Academy	868 George W Engram Blvd	Daytona Beach, FL	32114-1859	386-322-6102	258-4681	6-12	Anne Ferguson
Choices in Learning Charter S	1100 E State Road 434	Winter Springs, FL	32708	407-302-1005	542-5553	K-5	Dr. Janet Kearney
City of Hialeah Education Academy	2590 W 76th St	Hialeah, FL	33016-6888	305-362-4006	362-7006	6-12	Carlos Alvarez

School	Address	City,State	Zip code	Telephone	Fax	Grade	Contact
City of Palms Charter HS	2830 Winkler Ave Ste 201	Fort Myers, FL	33916	239-561-6611	561-6230	9-12	Sarah White
City of Pembroke Pines Central ES	12350 Sheridan St	Pembroke Pines, FL	33026-3813	954-322-3330	322-3389	K-8	Sean Chance
City of Pembroke Pines Charter HS	17189 Sheridan St	Pembroke Pines, FL	33331-1934	954-538-3700	538-3715	6-12	Peter Bayer
City of Pembroke Pines East ES	10801 Pembroke Rd	Pembroke Pines, FL	33025-1707	954-443-4800	443-4811	K-5	Kenneth Bass
City of Pembroke Pines West ES	1680 SW 184th Ave	Pembroke Pines, FL	33029-6120	954-450-6990	443-4820	K-5	Michael Castellano
City of Pembroke Pines West MS	18500 Pembroke Rd	Pembroke Pines, FL	33029-6108	954-443-4847	447-1691	6-8	Michael Castellano
Clark Advanced Learning Center	2400 SE Salerno Rd	Stuart, FL	34997-6505	772-419-5750	419-5760	10-12	Debra Kohuth
Classical Preparatory Charter S	16500 Lyceum Way	Spring Hill, FL	34610	727-803-7903		K-12	Ben Davis
Clay Charter Academy	1417 Red Apple Rd	Middleburg, FL	32068	904-406-1607	406-1608	K-8	Talya Taylor
C.O.A.S.T. Charter S	PO Box 338	Saint Marks, FL	32355-0338	850-925-6344	925-6396	PK-8	Alyssa Higgins
Collaboratory Preparatory Academy	6406 E Chelsea St	Tampa, FL	33610	844-702-3123		K-2	Heather Jenkins
Collegiate HS at NW FL State College	100 College Blvd E	Niceville, FL	32578-1347	850-729-4949	729-4950	10-12	Anthony Boyer
Collier Charter Academy	12101 Immokalee Rd	Naples, FL	34120	239-330-3810	330-3811	K-6	Kimberly Zambito
Community Charter S of Excellence	11604 N 15th St	Tampa, FL	33612	813-931-5500	971-5232	K-8	Matthew Torano M.Ed.
Compass Middle Charter S	550 E Clower St	Bartow, FL	33830-6403	863-519-8701	519-8704	5-8	Anita Fine
Connections Educ Ctr of the Palm Beaches	1310 Old Congress Ave	West Palm Beach, FL	33409	561-328-6044	584-6868	K-8	Debra Johnson
Coral Reef Montessori Academy	10853 SW 216th St	Cutler Ridge, FL	33170	305-255-0064	255-4085	K-8	Lucy Canzoneri-Golden
Coral Springs Charter S	3205 N University Dr	Coral Springs, FL	33065-4115	954-340-4100	340-4111	6-12	Gary Springer
Cornerstone Academy Charter S	5903 Randolph Ave	Orlando, FL	32809	407-608-7171	608-7172	K-8	Renee Pancoast
Cornerstone Academy HS	5903 Randolph Ave	Orlando, FL	32809	407-608-7171	608-7172	9-12	Renee Pancoast
Coronado HS	3057 Cleveland Ave	Fort Myers, FL	33901	239-337-9140	337-9141	9-12	Joelle Lyman
Countryside Montessori Charter S	5852 Ehren Cutoff	Land O Lakes, FL	34639-3428	813-996-0991	996-0993	1-8	Dr. Michael Rom
Crossroad Academy Charter S	470 Strong Rd	Quincy, FL	32351-6006	850-875-9626	875-1403	PK-12	Kevin Forehand
Cypress Junction Montessori	PO Box 102	Winter Haven, FL	33882	863-259-1490		K-8	Karen Winningham
Dayspring Academy	9509 Palm Ave	Port Richey, FL	34668-4647	727-847-9003	848-8774	6-12	Tim Greenier
Dayspring Academy	8911 Timber Oaks Ave	Port Richey, FL	34668-2426	727-862-8600	868-5175	K-5	Wendy Finlay
Discovery Academy at Lake Alfred	1000 N Buena Vista Dr	Lake Alfred, FL	33850-2031	863-295-5955	956-5089	6-8	Kevin Warren
Discovery Academy of Science	1120 Curlew Rd	Dunedin, FL	34698	727-369-6361	499-6828	2-6	Emre Akbaba
Discovery Academy of Science	1380 Pinehurst Rd	Dunedin, FL	34698	727-330-2424	499-6828	K-1	Megan Holland
Discovery HS	640 Evenhouse Rd	Lake Alfred, FL	33850	863-268-7178	956-5089	9-12	Carol Fulks
Doctors Charter S	11301 NW 5th Ave	Miami Shores, FL	33168-3343	305-754-2381	751-5833	6-12	Dr. Kelly Andrews
Dolphin Park HS	3206 S University Dr	Miramar, FL	33025	954-433-1573	433-1589	9-12	Sharard Walker
Doral Academy	2450 NW 97th Ave	Doral, FL	33172-2308	305-597-9999	591-2669	K-5	Eleonora Cuesta
Doral Academy HS	11100 NW 27th St	Doral, FL	33172-5001	305-597-9950	477-6762	9-12	Carlos Ferrals
Doral Academy Preparatory MS	2601 NW 112th Ave	Doral, FL	33172-1804	305-591-0020	591-9251	6-8	Carlos Ferrals
Doral International Academy	6700 NW 104th Ave	Doral, FL	33178	786-270-2088	221-2238	K-8	Victoria Gomez
Downtown Doral Charter ES	8390 NW 53rd St	Doral, FL	33166	305-569-2223	569-2226	PK-5	Jeanette Isenberg
Downtown Miami Charter S	305 NW 3rd Ave	Miami, FL	33128-1606	305-579-2112	579-2115	K-6	Dr. Rebecca Dinda
Duval Charter Scholars Academy	100 Scholars Way	Jacksonville, FL	32216	904-724-1536	721-5381	K-8	Carin White
Duval Charter S at Baymeadows	7510 Baymeadows Way	Jacksonville, FL	32256	904-638-7947	466-4101	K-12	Kim Stidham
Duval Charter S at Flagler Center	12755 Flagler Center Blvd	Jacksonville, FL	32258-2610	904-899-1010	899-1011	K-8	Adam Cross
Duval Charter S at Mandarin	5209 Shad Rd	Jacksonville, FL	32257-2005	904-440-2901	440-2902	K-8	Dawn Lamb
Duval Charter S at Southside	8680 A C Skinner Pkwy	Jacksonville, FL	32256-6985	904-423-5348	423-5349	K-8	Ashley Doty
Duval Charter S at Westside	9238 103rd St	Jacksonville, FL	32210-8610	904-421-0250	423-2601	K-8	Tania Woods
Eagle Arts Academy	1000 Wellington Trce	Wellington, FL	33414	561-412-4087		K-8	Gregory Blount
Eagles Nest Charter Academy	3698 NW 15th St	Lauderhill, FL	33311	954-635-2308	990-6921	K-8	Christine Mentis
Early Beginnings Academy	1411 NW 14th Ave	Miami, FL	33125-1616	305-325-1080	325-1044	PK-2	Makeesha Coleman
Early Childhood Learning Center	4309 N 34th St	Tampa, FL	33610	813-816-2100		K-1	Frances McCrimmon
Easter Seals Charter S	1219 Dunn Ave	Daytona Beach, FL	32114-2405	386-255-4568	258-7677	PK-PK	April Leopold
Econ River Charter HS	14180 E Colonial Dr	Orlando, FL	32826	407-641-1062		9-12	Isabel Villanueva
Educational Horizons Charter S	1281 S Wickham Rd	West Melbourne, FL	32904-2450	321-729-0786	802-6823	K-6	Cynthia Thomas
Ed Venture Charter S	117 East Coast Ave	Hypoluxo, FL	33462	561-582-1454	547-9682	9-12	Barbara Fitz
Einstein S	5910 SW Archer Rd	Gainesville, FL	32608	352-335-4321	335-1575	2-8	Christine Aurelio
Enterprise HS	2461 N McMullen Booth Rd	Clearwater, FL	33759-1305	727-474-1237	725-3470	9-12	Donna Hulbert
Escambia Charter S	391 90 9 Ranch Rd	Cantonment, FL	32533	850-937-0500	968-5605	9-12	Taravell McKinnies
Everest Charter S	10044 W McNab Rd	Tamarac, FL	33321	954-532-3015	876-1696	K-8	Dr. Marsha Reece
Everglades Preparatory Academy	360 E Main St Bldg C	Pahokee, FL	33476	561-924-3002	924-3013	9-12	Edna Stephens M.Ed
Everglades Preparatory Academy	2251 E Mowry Dr	Homestead, FL	33033	786-601-1969	377-5759	6-12	Aimee Leyva
Excelsior Charter Academy	18200A NW 22nd Ave	Miami Gardens, FL	33056	786-565-9188	621-8960	K-9	Janell Ferguson
Excelsior Charter S of Broward	10066 W McNab Rd	Tamarac, FL	33321	954-726-5227	722-2451	K-5	Cristina Reynolds
Excelsior Language Academy of Hialeah	369 E 10th St	Hialeah, FL	33010	305-887-9004	883-5279	PK-8	
Excelsior Prep Charter S	2156 University Square Mall	Tampa, FL	33612	813-644-9060	200-1113	K-3	Rosalyn Williams-Palmer
Expressions Learning Arts Academy	5408 SW 13th St	Gainesville, FL	32608-5038	352-373-5223	373-6327	K-5	Juniper DiGiovanni M.Ed.
Fair Babson Park ES	815 N Scenic Hwy	Babson Park, FL	33827-9795	863-678-4664	678-4669	PK-5	Elizabeth Tyler
Flagler HS	1951 W Copans Rd	Pompano Beach, FL	33064	754-220-7899	973-3199	9-12	Stuart Morgan-Graham
Florida Autism Center of Excellence	6310 E Sligh Ave	Tampa, FL	33617-9107	813-985-3223	985-3199	PK-12	Annie Russell
Florida Cyber Charter Academy	9143 Philips Hwy Ste 590	Jaxville Bch, FL	32256	904-247-3268	719-1645	9-12	Warren Buck
Florida Futures Academy North	1760 N Congress Ave	West Palm Beach, FL	33409	561-215-0933		9-12	Carolyn Taylor
Florida Futures Academy South	8160 Okeechobee Blvd	West Palm Beach, FL	33411	561-215-0933		9-12	Carolyn Taylor
Florida International Academy	13400 NW 28th Ave	Opa Locka, FL	33054-4842	305-685-8190	688-1745	K-8	Sonia Mitchell
Florida SIA Tech at Gainesville	7022 NW 10th Pl	Gainesville, FL	32605	352-333-7952	333-7953	9-12	Dr. William Scott
Florida Southwestern Collegiate HS	8099 College Pkwy	Fort Myers, FL	33919-5566	239-432-6767	433-6912	9-12	Dr. Brian Botts
Focus Academy	304 Druid Hills Rd	Temple Terrace, FL	33617	813-443-5558	443-5630	9-12	Elisabeth Kraft
Forman Downtown Campus	1217 SE 3rd Ave	Fort Lauderdale, FL	33316-1905	954-522-2997	522-3159	K-5	Lisa Castro
Four Corners Charter S	9100 Teacher Ln	Davenport, FL	33897-6212	407-787-4300	787-4331	K-5	Denise Thompson
Four Courners Upper S	9160 Bella Citta Blvd	Davenport, FL	33896	407-589-4600	589-4601	6-12	Denise Thompson
Franklin Academy	7882 S Military Trl	Boynton Beach, FL	33436	561-767-4700	432-3200	K-8	Rena Tornopsky
Franklin Academy	4500 NW 103rd Ave	Sunrise, FL	33351	954-206-0850	497-3296	K-8	Sergio Delgado
Franklin Academy	18800 Pines Blvd	Pembroke Pines, FL	33029-1310	954-703-2294	436-2861	K-8	Elena Diaz
Franklin Academy	5651 Hood Rd	Palm Bch Gdns, FL	33418	561-348-2525		K-8	Margaret Ellis
Franklin Academy	6301 S Flamingo Rd	Cooper City, FL	33330	954-780-5533	252-8147	K-8	Alexandra LeRose
Galileo S for Gifted Learning	3900 E State Road 46	Sanford, FL	32771	321-249-9221	878-0791	K-8	Michelle Nunez
Gamla Charter S	8600 Jog Rd	Boynton Beach, FL	33472	561-742-8017	742-8018	K-8	Elanit Weizman
Gamla Charter S	11155 SW 112th Ave	Miami, FL	33176	305-596-6266	596-6964	K-8	Dr. Gur Berman
Gamla Charter S North Broward	2620 Hollywood Blvd	Hollywood, FL	33020-4807	954-342-4064	342-4107	K-6	Sharon Miller
Gamla Charter School South Broward	6511 W Sunrise Blvd	Plantation, FL	33313	954-587-8348	587-8347	K-8	Christine Cardoso
Gamla Preparatory Academy	2650 Van Buren St	Hollywood, FL	33020	954-924-6495	924-6496	7-12	Monique Machado
Gardens S of Technology Arts	9153 Roan Ln	Palm Bch Gdns, FL	33403	561-290-7661	449-3470	K-8	Dr. Kevin Kovacs
Gateway Charter ES	12850 Commonwealth Dr	Fort Myers, FL	33913-8039	239-768-5048	768-5710	K-8	Angela Carter
Gateway Charter HS	12770 Gateway Blvd	Fort Myers, FL	33913-8654	239-768-3350	768-3874	9-12	Amber Jensen
Genesis Preparatory S	207 NW 23rd Ave	Gainesville, FL	32609-3604	352-379-1188	379-1142	K-3	Charmaine Henry
Gibson Charter S	1682 NW 4th Ave	Miami, FL	33136	305-438-0895	438-0896	K-6	Jennifer DeSousa
Glades Academy	7368 State Road 15	Pahokee, FL	33476	561-924-9402	924-9279	K-8	Vinnisha Jones
Global Outreach Charter Academy	9570 Regency Square Blvd	Jacksonville, FL	32225-9104	904-551-7104	551-7120	K-8	Tangia Anderson
Governors Charter Academy	4351 Mahan Dr	Tallahassee, FL	32308	850-391-5259	391-5260	K-8	James Simpson
Greentree Preparatory Charter S	6301 SW 160 Ave	Southwest Ranch, FL	33331	954-780-8733	430-7706	K-5	Rosa Pou
G-STAR School of the Arts	2030 S Congress Ave	Palm Springs, FL	33406	561-967-2023	963-8975	9-12	Kim Collins M.Ed.
Gulf Coast Acad of Science & Technology	10444 Tillery Rd	Spring Hill, FL	34608-3700	352-600-5092	600-5095	6-8	Nevin Siefert
Gulf Coast Charter Academy South	215 Airport Pulling Rd N	Naples, FL	34104	239-784-1539	263-4443	K-8	William Staros
Gulf Coast MS	2139 Deborah Dr	Spring Hill, FL	34609-3827	352-666-5790	666-5792	6-8	Dave Schoelles
Gulfstream Goodwill LIFE Academy	3800 S Congress Ave	Boynton Beach, FL	33426-8424	561-259-1000	259-1011	9-12	Cindy Maunder
Harlem Heights Community Charter S	15570 Hagie Dr	Fort Myers, FL	33908	239-482-7706	204-3009	K-3	Debra Mathinos
Harris Preparatory Academy	8190 Pensacola Blvd	Pensacola, FL	32534	850-432-2273	432-4624	K-5	Celestine Lewis
Hartridge Academy	1400 US Highway 92	Winter Haven, FL	33881-8137	863-956-4434	956-3267	K-5	Debra Richards
Hawn Charter School of the Arts	565 S Lakeview Dr Unit 110	Lake Helen, FL	32744	386-228-3900	228-3901	K-8	Kelly Conway M.A.
Healthy Learning Academy	13505 W Newberry Rd	Newberry, FL	32669-2752	352-372-2279	372-1665	K-5	Anni Egan
Henderson Hammock Charter S	10322 Henderson Rd	Tampa, FL	33625	813-739-6633	739-6681	K-8	Jami Shetter
Hillcrest ES	1051 State Road 60 E	Lake Wales, FL	33853-4258	863-678-4216	678-4086	PK-5	Jennifer Barrow
Hillsborough Academy of Math & Science	9659 W Waters Ave	Tampa, FL	33635	813-793-6085	413-2984	K-8	Brittany Deen
HIVE Prep S	5855 NW 171st St	Miami, FL	33015	305-231-4888	231-4881	K-8	Carlos Gonzalez
Hollywood Academy of Arts & Science	1705 Van Buren St	Hollywood, FL	33020-5125	954-925-6404	925-8123	K-8	Mark Hage
Hope Center for Autism Charter S	1695 SE Indian St	Stuart, FL	34997	772-334-3288	872-7229	PK-2	Joanne Sweazey
Hope Charter S	1550 E Crown Point Rd	Ocoee, FL	34761-3722	407-656-4673	264-6960	K-6	Allen Quain
Horizon Charter S of Tampa	7235 W Hillsborough Ave	Tampa, FL	33634	813-887-3800	885-9626	K-8	Sheila Thornley
Imagine Charter S at Broward	9001 Westview Dr	Coral Springs, FL	33067	954-255-0020	255-1336	K-8	Debra Darling
Imagine Charter S at Lakewood Ranch	10535 Portal Xing	Bradenton, FL	34211	941-750-0900	750-0966	PK-8	Selenia Quinones
Imagine Charter S at North Lauderdale	1395 S State Road 7	N Lauderdale, FL	33068-4023	954-973-8900	974-5588	K-5	Erin Kelly
Imagine Charter S at North Manatee	9275 49th Ave E	Palmetto, FL	34221	941-981-5345	981-5349	K-8	Dawn Patterson
Imagine Charter S at Town Center	775 Town Center Blvd	Palm Coast, FL	32164-2520	386-586-0100	586-2784	PK-8	James Menard
Imagine Charter S at West Melbourne	3355 Imagine Way	West Melbourne, FL	32904	321-768-6200	768-6300	K-6	Brian DeGonzague
Imagine Charter S at Weston	2500 Glades Cir	Weston, FL	33327-2253	954-659-3600	659-3620	K-8	Nadine Laham
Imagine MSHS at North Port	2757 Sycamore St	North Port, FL	34289	941-426-2050	423-8252	6-12	Cher Gardner
Imagine S at Land O' Lakes	2940 Sunlake Blvd	Land O Lakes, FL	34638	813-428-7444	428-7445	K-8	Aimee Williams
Imagine S at North Port	1000 Innovation Ave	North Port, FL	34289-9308	941-426-2050	423-8252	K-5	Aleischa Coover
Imagine S at Palmer Ranch	6220 McIntosh Rd	Sarasota, FL	34238	941-923-1125	923-1124	PK-8	Alisa Wright
Imagine S - Chancellor Campus	3333 High Ridge Rd	Boynton Beach, FL	33426-8745	561-585-1189	585-1166	K-8	Susan Onori
Imagine S Plantation Campus	8200 Peters Rd	Plantation, FL	33324-3201	954-358-4200	472-1994	K-8	Ethiel Calvo

School	Address	City,State	Zip code	Telephone	Fax	Grade	Contact
Imagine South Lake Charter S	2750 Hartwood Marsh Rd	Clermont, FL	34711	352-243-2960	243-2967	K-8	Kathleen Dial
Imagine South Vero Charter S	6000 4th St	Vero Beach, FL	32968	772-567-2728	410-0329	K-8	Chris Rock
IMater Academy	600 W 20th St	Hialeah, FL	33010	305-884-6320	884-6321	PK-5	Elizabeth Poveda
iMater Academy MSHS	651 W 20th St	Hialeah, FL	33010	305-805-5722	805-5723	6-12	Teresa M. Santalo
Immokalee Community S	123 N 4th St	Immokalee, FL	34142	239-867-3223	867-3224	K-6	Dr. Zulaika Quintero
Independence Academy	12902 E US Highway 92	Dover, FL	33527	813-473-8600	441-7160	K-8	Shane Clark
Indian River Charter HS	6055 College Ln	Vero Beach, FL	32966-1285	772-567-6600	567-6338	9-12	Cynthia Trevino-Aversa
Inlet Grove Community HS	600 W 28th St	Riviera Beach, FL	33404	561-881-4600	881-4668	9-12	John Myszkowski
Innovation Charter S	600 SW 3rd St	Pompano Beach, FL	33060	954-715-1777		K-5	
Innovation Montessori Ocoee	1610 N Lakewood Ave	Ocoee, FL	34761			PK-8	
Innovations MS	2768 N Hiawassee Rd	Orlando, FL	32818	407-440-2846	440-2852	6-8	Dr. Patricia Lightner
Integrated Science and Asian Culture	301 Westward Dr	Miami Springs, FL	33166	305-863-8030	863-8031	K-8	Eleonora Cuesta
International S of Broward	3100 NW 75th Ave	Hollywood, FL	33024-2355	954-987-2026	987-7261	6-12	Dr. Jacquelyne Hoy
International Studies Charter S	2480 SW 8th St	Miami, FL	33135-3016	305-643-2955	643-2956	6-12	Victoriano Rodriguez
International Studies Virtual Academy	807 SW 25th Ave	Miami, FL	33135	305-643-2955	643-2956	6-12	Victorino Rodriguez
Island Park HS	16520 S Tamiami Trl Ste 190	Fort Myers, FL	33908-5349	239-204-5965	243-0043	9-12	A.J. Nauss
Island S	PO Box 1090	Boca Grande, FL	33921-1090	941-964-8016	964-8017	K-5	Jean Thompson
Island Village Montessori S Sarasota	11011 Clark Rd	Sarasota, FL	34241	941-954-4999	925-0267	K-8	Cindy Hoffman
Island Village Montessori S Venice	2001 Pinebrook Rd	Venice, FL	34292-1560	941-484-4999	484-2150	K-8	Jason Hunter
Jackson Preparatory S	546 Mary Esther Blvd	Ft Walton Bch, FL	32548	850-833-3321	833-3292	K-8	Kaye McKinley
Jewel Charter Academy	705 Blake Ave	Cocoa, FL	32922	321-634-5462	634-5465	K-8	Thomas Cole
Just Arts and Management Charter MS	2450 NW 97th Ave	Doral, FL	33172	305-597-9999	591-2669	6-8	Eleonara Cuesta
Just for Girls Academy	1011 21st St E	Bradenton, FL	34208	941-747-5757	251-4913	K-5	
Keys Gate Charter HS	2325 SE 28th Ave	Homestead, FL	33035	786-272-9600	272-9602	9-12	Rodney Hull
Keys Gate Charter S	2000 SE 28th Ave	Homestead, FL	33035-2102	305-230-1616	230-1347	K-8	Corinne Baez
Key West Collegiate Charter S	5901 College Rd	Key West, FL	33040	305-296-5927	809-3191	9-12	Thomas Rompella
Kids Community College Charter HS	10550 Johanna Ave	Riverview, FL	33654	813-699-5751	551-7193	9-10	La-Keshia Cook
Kids Community College Charter S -Orange	1475 E Silver Star Rd	Ocoee, FL	34761	407-982-2421	203-3867	K-5	Keri Hefferin
Kids Community College - Riverview South	10030 Mathog Rd	Riverview, FL	33578	813-671-1440	553-1719	K-8	Karen Seder
Kids Community College SE Charter MS	11513 Mcmullen Rd	Riverview, FL	33569	813-699-5752	511-7193	6-8	Amy Brown
Kids Community College SE Charter S	11519 McMullen Rd	Riverview, FL	33569	813-699-4600	671-1245	K-6	Amy Brown
Kidz Choice Charter S	1800 N Douglas Rd	Pembroke Pines, FL	33024	954-251-2419	260-5935	K-5	Lilly Swanson
Kings Kids Academy of Health Sciences	3000 N 34th St	Tampa, FL	33605-2250	813-238-4900	238-6700	K-5	Lillia Stroud
KIPP Impact MS	1440 McDuff Ave N	Jacksonville, FL	32254-2035	904-683-6643	683-9895	5-8	Warren Buck
KIPP Jacksonville	1440 McDuff Ave N	Jacksonville, FL	32254	904-683-6643	683-9895	K-2	Kim Davidson
KIPP VOICE ES	1440 McDuff Ave N	Jacksonville, FL	32254-2035	904-683-6643	683-9895	K-4	Kimberly Davidson
Kissimmee Charter Academy	2850 Bill Beck Blvd	Kissimmee, FL	34744-4073	407-847-1400	847-1401	PK-8	Lori McCarley
Lake Eola Charter S	135 N Magnolia Ave	Orlando, FL	32801-2301	407-246-0900	246-6334	K-8	
Lakeland Montessori MS	800 E Palmetto St	Lakeland, FL	33801-5529	863-413-0003	812-4689	7-8	Heather Manrow
Lakeland Montessori Schoolhouse	1124 N Lake Parker Ave	Lakeland, FL	33805-4725	863-413-0003	413-0006	PK-6	Heather Manrow
Lake Wales HS	1 Highlander Way	Lake Wales, FL	33853-3334	863-678-4222	678-4064	9-12	Donna Dunson
Lauderhill HS	4131 NW 16th St	Lauderhill, FL	33313	954-731-2585	731-2587	9-12	Eboni Grant-Burts
LBA Academy	11093 NW 138th St Ste 207	Hialeah, FL	33018	305-802-8455	827-5729	9-12	Jennifer Jaynes
Learning Academy	5880 Stewart St	Milton, FL	32570	850-983-3495	983-8098	6-12	Kara Whitney
Learning Center at the Els Center	18370 Limestone Creek Rd	Jupiter, FL	33458	561-640-0270		PK-8	Stacie Routt
Learning Gate Community S	16215 Hanna Rd	Lutz, FL	33549-5701	813-948-4190	948-7587	K-8	Michelle Mason
Learning Lodge Academy	5844 Pine Hill Rd	Port Richey, FL	34668-6616	727-389-0067		K-5	Kerrie Cuffe
Legacy Charter HS	1550 E Crown Point Rd	Ocoee, FL	34761	407-656-4673	264-6960	7-12	Roberta VanHouten
Legacy Preparatory Academy	302 E Linebaugh Ave	Tampa, FL	33612	813-253-0053	253-0182	K-8	Yolanda Capers
Legends Academy Charter S	3032 Monte Carlo Trl	Orlando, FL	32805	407-985-5195	650-8355	K-8	
Lincoln-Marti Charter S	3500 W 84th St	Hialeah, FL	33018	305-827-8080	827-8004	K-12	Yaimy Fernandez
Lincoln-Marti Charter S	970 W Flagler St	Miami, FL	33130	305-325-1001	324-9934	K-12	Barbara Sanchez
Lincoln-Marti Charter S	2244 Fortune Rd	Kissimmee, FL	34744	407-530-5000	518-9047	K-2	Andria Hoyos
Lincoln-Marti Charter S - International	103 E Lucy St	Florida City, FL	33034	305-242-3330	242-3331	K-8	Barbara Sanchez
Literacy Leadership Technology Academy	6771 Madison Ave	Tampa, FL	33619-6836	813-234-0940	234-0946	K-8	Lesley Logan
Lone Star HS	8050 Lone Star Rd Ste 1	Jacksonville, FL	32211-6227	904-725-5998	724-3172	9-12	LaShanda Roberts
Lutz Preparatory S	17951 N US Highway 41	Lutz, FL	33549	813-428-7100	428-7061	K-8	Bonnie Guertin
Madison Creative Arts Academy	PO Box 690	Madison, FL	32341-0690	850-973-2529	973-8974	PK-8	Janna Barrs
Magnolia Montessori Academy	1540 New Jersey Rd	Lakeland, FL	33803	863-797-4991		K-5	Kate Harris
Main Street HS	1100 N Main St	Kissimmee, FL	34744	321-250-1871	846-0816	9-12	Veronica Torres
Manatee Charter S	4550 30th St E	Bradenton, FL	34203	941-465-4296	465-4297	K-12	Bonnie Brett
Manatee S for the Arts	700 Haben Blvd	Palmetto, FL	34221-4173	941-721-6800	721-6805	6-12	Dr. Bill Jones
Manatee S of Arts and Sciences	3700 32nd St W	Bradenton, FL	34205-2708	941-755-5012	755-7934	PK-6	Richard Ramsey
Marco Island Academy	2255 San Marco Rd	Marco Island, FL	34145	239-393-5133	393-5143	9-12	Melissa Scott
Marco Island Charter MS	1401 Trinidad Ave	Marco Island, FL	34145-3949	239-377-3200	377-3201	6-8	George Abounader
Marion Charter MS	3233 SE Maricamp Rd	Ocala, FL	34471	352-264-9940		6-8	Elias Posth
Marion Charter S	39 Cedar Rd	Ocala, FL	34472-8331	352-687-2100	687-2700	K-5	Michelle Axson
Marion Military Academy	5895 SE 83rd St	Ocala, FL	34472	352-291-6600	291-6602	9-12	Tom Adair
Mascotte Conversion Charter ES	460 Midway Ave	Mascotte, FL	34753-8800	352-429-2294	429-4836	PK-5	Radean Johnson
Mason Classical Academy	3073 Horseshoe Dr S Ste 104	Naples, FL	34104-6145	239-227-2838	201-2056	K-12	David Hull
Mater Academy	8003 NW 103rd St	Hialeah Gardens, FL	33016	305-698-9900	698-3822	3-5	Cecilia Guilarte
Mater Academy	8625 Byron Ave	Miami Beach, FL	33141-4834	305-864-2889	864-2890	K-12	Marisol Gomez
Mater Academy at Mount Sinai	4300 Alton Rd	Miami Beach, FL	33140-2948	305-604-1453	604-1454	K-8	Eileen Hernandez
Mater Academy Bay	22025 SW 87th Ave	Cutler Bay, FL	33190	305-269-5989	969-5990	K-8	Brenda Cruz
Mater Academy Charter MSHS	7901 NW 103rd St	Hialeah Gardens, FL	33016-2419	305-828-1886	828-6175	6-12	Jose Nunez
Mater Academy East Charter HS	998 SW 1st St	Miami, FL	33130-1112	305-324-6963	324-6966	6-12	Jenney Aguirre
Mater Academy East Charter S	450 SW 4th St	Miami, FL	33130-1410	305-324-4667	324-6580	K-5	Beatrice Riera
Mater Academy HS International Studies	795 NW 32nd St	Miami, FL	33127-3645	305-634-0445	634-0446	9-12	Ileana Melian
Mater Academy Lakes HS	17300 NW 87th Ave	Hialeah, FL	33015-3516	305-698-8000	698-1800	6-12	Rene Rovirosa
Mater Academy of International Studies	795 NW 32nd St	Miami, FL	33127-3645	305-634-0445	634-0446	K-8	Ileana Melian
Mater Academy PS	7700 NW 98th St	Hialeah Gardens, FL	33016	305-698-9900	698-3822	PK-2	Cecilia Guilarte
Mater Brighton Lakes Academy	3200 Pleasant Hill Rd	Kissimmee, FL	34746	407-931-0325	931-0326	K-8	Carmen Cangemi
Mater Gardens Academy	9010 NW 178th Ln	Hialeah, FL	33018-6548	305-512-9775	512-3708	K-8	Lourdes Isla-Marrero
Mater Grove Academy	2805 SW 32nd Ave	Miami, FL	33133-3431	305-442-4992	442-4993	K-8	Sheila Caleo-Gonzalez
Mater International Academy	3405 NW 27th Ave	Miami, FL	33142	305-638-8016	638-8017	K-3	Olga Camarena
Mater Performing Arts Academy	7901 NW 103rd St	Hialeah Gardens, FL	33016-2419	305-828-1886	828-6175	9-12	Judith Marty
Mater Virtual Academy	17300 NW 87th Ave	Hialeah, FL	33015	305-512-3917	512-3712	6-12	Ofelia Alvarez
Mavericks HS at Palm Springs	3525 S Congress Ave	Palm Springs, FL	33461	561-623-6935	641-6370	9-12	DeAnna Allen
Mavericks HS of North Miami-Dade County	16150 NE 17th Ave	N Miami Beach, FL	33162	786-629-7053	949-5604	9-12	Alejandro Madrigal
May Sands Montessori S	1400 United St	Key West, FL	33040	305-293-1400		K-8	Lynn Barras
McAuliffe Charter S	2817 SW 3rd Ln	Cape Coral, FL	33991-1151	239-283-4511	282-0376	PK-5	Kevin Brown
Mc Intosh Area Charter S	PO Box 769	Mc Intosh, FL	32664-0769	352-591-9797	591-9747	K-5	Cindy Roach
McKeel Academy of Technology	1810 W Parker St	Lakeland, FL	33815-1243	863-499-2818	603-6339	6-12	Joyce Powell
McKeel Central Academy	411 N Florida Ave	Lakeland, FL	33801-4803	863-499-1287	688-1607	K-5	Michele Spurgeon
Melrose HS	2744 Davie Blvd	Fort Lauderdale, FL	33312	954-681-4096	797-4446	9-12	Tona Coley
Miami Arts Charter S	95 NW 23rd St	Miami, FL	33127	305-763-6257	573-5622	6-12	Alfredo de la Rosa
Miami Childrens Museum Charter S	980 MacArthur Cswy	Miami, FL	33132-1604	305-329-3758	329-3767	K-5	Christina Carmona
Miami Community Charter HS	18720 SW 352nd St	Florida City, FL	33034	786-243-9981	217-6804	9-12	Dr. Jila Rezaie
Miami Community Charter MS	18720 SW 352nd St	Florida City, FL	33034	786-243-9981	217-6804	6-8	Dr. Jila Rezaie
Miami Community Charter S	101 S Redland Rd	Florida City, FL	33034-4630	305-245-2552	245-2527	K-5	Dr. Jila Rezaie
Micanopy Area Cooperative S	802 NW Seminary Ave	Micanopy, FL	32667-8500	352-466-0990	466-4090	PK-5	Brenda Maynard
Micanopy MS	PO Box 109	Micanopy, FL	32667-0109	352-466-1090	466-1030	6-9	Tara Lowe-Phillips
Milburn Academy - Deland	913 E New York Ave	DeLand, FL	32724	386-738-9150	738-9151	9-12	Art Sands
Milburn Academy	1031 Mason Ave	Daytona Beach, FL	32117	386-304-0086	304-0087	9-12	Art Sands
Minneola Conversion Charter ES	320 E Pearl St	Minneola, FL	34715	352-394-2600	394-2079	PK-5	Sherry Watts
Montessori Academy of Early Enrichment	6300 Lake Worth Rd	Greenacres, FL	33463-3006	561-649-0004	649-0964	PK-5	Jean Ranck
MYcroSchool Citrus Charter HS	3612 W Educational Path	Lecanto, FL	34461	352-527-0900	527-0814	9-12	Dawna Boley
MYcroSchool Gainesville	2209 NW 13th St	Gainesville, FL	32609-3426	352-379-2902	379-2956	9-12	Randy Starling
MYcroSchool Jacksonville	1584 Normandy Village Pkwy	Jacksonville, FL	32221	904-783-3611	783-3703	9-12	Randy Hudspeth
MYcroSchool Pinellas HS	840 3rd Ave S	St Petersburg, FL	33701	727-825-3710	825-3751	9-12	Steven Humphries
Nature Coast MS	6830 NW 140th St	Chiefland, FL	32626-8271	352-490-0700	490-0702	6-8	Charles Bowe
New Beginnings HS	3425 Lake Alfred Rd	Winter Haven, FL	33881	863-298-5666	298-5675	6-12	Terri Nelson
New Dimensions HS	4900 Old Pleasant Hill Rd	Kissimmee, FL	34759-3430	407-870-9949	870-8976	9-12	Dr. Jacqueline Grimm
New Life Charter Academy	3550 Davie Blvd	Fort Lauderdale, FL	33312	954-381-5199	734-6408	K-5	Shirley Brunache
New Springs S	2410 E Busch Blvd	Tampa, FL	33612	813-933-5025	527-9982	K-8	Oguz Tekin
Nixon Academy	1780 Mercy Dr	Orlando, FL	32808	407-412-6968	930-5754	K-5	Melanie Harp
North Bay Haven Charter Academy	1 Buccaneer Dr	Panama City, FL	32404	850-248-0205	215-0644	K-5	Michael McLaughlin
North Bay Haven Charter MSHS	1 Buccaneer Dr	Panama City, FL	32404	850-248-0801	248-1201	6-12	Michael McLaughlin
North Broward Academy of Excellence	8200 SW 17th St	N Lauderdale, FL	33068	954-718-2211	718-2215	K-5	Robin Sandler
North Broward Academy of Excellence MS	8200 SW 17th St	N Lauderdale, FL	33068-4101	954-718-2211	718-2215	6-8	Robin Sandler
North County Charter S	6640 Old Dixie Hwy	Vero Beach, FL	32967	772-794-1941	794-1945	K-5	Dr. Jessica Keaton
Northern Palms Charter HS	13251 N Cleveland Ave	N Ft Myers, FL	33903	239-997-9987	997-9981	9-12	Bernadette Graham
North Gardens HS	4692 NW 183rd St	Miami Gardens, FL	33055	786-528-6308	621-1611	9-12	Porshia Jones
North Nicholas HS	428 SW Pine Island Rd	Cape Coral, FL	33991-1916	239-242-4230	242-4231	9-12	Janet Morris
North Park HS	3400 NW 135th St	Opa Locka, FL	33054-4708	305-720-2995	953-3289	9-12	Stacey Frater
North University HS	4800 N University Dr	Lauderhill, FL	33351-5746	954-746-4483	741-8113	9-12	Frank Gaines
Oak Creek Charter S of Bonita Springs	28011 Performance Ln	Bonita Springs, FL	34135	239-498-6864	495-7178	K-8	Jose Rubio

School	Address	City,State	Zip code	Telephone	Fax	Grade	Contact
Oakland Avenue Charter S	PO Box 949	Oakland, FL	34760	407-877-2039	877-6222	K-5	Pamela Dwyer
Oasis Charter ES	3415 Oasis Blvd	Cape Coral, FL	33914-4924	239-542-1577	549-7662	K-5	Jacquelin Collins
Oasis Charter HS	3519 Oasis Blvd	Cape Coral, FL	33914	239-541-1167	541-1590	9-12	Amanda Sanford
Oasis Charter MS	3507 Oasis Blvd	Cape Coral, FL	33914	239-945-1999	540-7677	6-8	Donnie Hopper
Oasis MS	4304 32nd St W	Bradenton, FL	34205	941-749-1979	714-7333	6-8	
Oasis Preparatory Academy	5200 W South St	Orlando, FL	32811	407-930-2581		K-5	Tiffany Ward
Ocean Studies Charter S	92295 Overseas Hwy	Tavernier, FL	33070	305-852-7700		K-5	Abbie Freeman
Odyssey Charter ES	1755 Eldron Blvd SE	Palm Bay, FL	32909-6832	321-733-0442	733-1178	K-6	Wendi Nolder
Odyssey Charter JSHS	1350 Wyoming Dr SE	Palm Bay, FL	32909-5757	321-345-4117	327-7261	7-12	Dr. Monica Knight
Odyssey Preparatory Academy	1350 Wyoming Dr SE	Palm Bay, FL	32909	321-345-4117		K-6	Dr. Monica Knight
Okaloosa Academy	720 Lovejoy Rd NW	Ft Walton Bch, FL	32548-3833	850-864-3133	834-4305	6-12	Ray Sansom
One Room S House Project	4180 NE 15th St	Gainesville, FL	32609-2011	352-376-4014	376-3345	K-8	Sarah Sonberg
Orange County Preparatory Academy	10250 University Blvd	Orlando, FL	32817	407-440-9293	960-2662	K-8	Jack Burkett
Orlando Science Charter ES	2011 Technology Dr	Orlando, FL	32804	407-299-6595	299-6594	PK-7	Michael Singleton
Orlando Science Charter MSHS	2427 Lynx Ln	Orlando, FL	32804	407-253-7304	253-7305	8-12	Abdulaziz Yalcin
Osceola Science Charter S	2880 N Orange Blossom Trl	Kissimmee, FL	34744	407-864-8296	253-7305	K-8	Murat Cetin
Palm Acres Charter HS	507 Sunshine Blvd	Lehigh Acres, FL	33971	239-333-3300	368-1330	9-12	Sarah White
Palm Bay Academy	2112 Palm Bay Rd NE	Palm Bay, FL	32905-2915	321-984-2710	984-0799	K-5	Madhu Longani
Palm Bay Charter MS	635 Community College SE	Palm Bay, FL	32909	321-726-9005	726-3938	6-8	Madhu Longani
Palm Bay Language Immersion S	1465 Troutman Blvd NE	Palm Bay, FL	32905	321-723-4218	953-5160	K-5	Madhu Longani
Palm Bay Preparatory Academy	1104 Balboa Ave	Panama City, FL	32401	850-215-0770	818-0486	K-12	Kathy Fontaine
Palm Beach Maritime Academy	600 S East Coast Ave	Lantana, FL	33462	561-578-5700	540-5177	K-8	Marie Turchiaro
Palm Beach Maritime Academy HS	1518 Lantana Rd	Lantana, FL	33462	561-547-3775	540-5177	9-12	Marie Turchiaro
Palm Beach S for Autism	8480 Lantana Rd	Lake Worth, FL	33467	561-533-9917	533-9918	PK-12	Olive Balbosa
Palmetto Charter S	1601 17th St W	Palmetto, FL	34221-6151	941-723-3711	729-5805	K-8	Brian Bustle
Palm Glades Preparatory Academy	22655 SW 112th Ave	Miami, FL	33170	786-272-2269	441-2177	6-12	Archalena Coats
Palm Harbor Academy	95 Old Kings Rd N	Palm Coast, FL	32137	386-447-9692		K-5	Taylor Croot
Palm Pointe Educ Research S at Tradition	10680 SW Academic Way	Port St Lucie, FL	34987	772-345-3245	345-3244	K-8	Kathleen Perez
Panacea Prep\Eagles Nest Charter S	201 N University Dr	Coral Springs, FL	33071	954-341-5550	341-5557	K-8	Latoya Tucker-Robinson
Paragon Academy of Technology	502 N 28th Ave	Hollywood, FL	33020	954-925-0155	925-0209	6-12	Dr. Steven Montes
Pasco MYcroSchool	3565 Universal Pl	New Port Richey, FL	34652	727-359-2183	255-5172	9-12	Sandra Sonberg
Passport S	5221 Curry Ford Rd	Orlando, FL	32812-8741	407-658-9900	658-9911	K-8	Dr. Osvaldo Garcia
Pemayetv Emahakv Charter S	100 E Harney Pond Rd NE	Okeechobee, FL	34974	863-467-2501	467-8610	PK-8	Brian Greseth
Pembroke Academy Pines MSHS	5000 SW 207th Ter	Pembroke Pines, FL	33332	954-315-0770	315-0769	6-12	Dr. Arlene Valdes
Pembroke Pines FSU Charter ES	601 SW 172nd Ave	Pembroke Pines, FL	33029	954-499-4244	499-3016	K-5	Dr. Lisa Libidinsky
Pensacola Beach ES	900 Via De Luna Dr	Pensacola Beach, FL	32561-2262	850-934-4020	934-4040	K-5	Jeff Castleberry
Pepin Academies	9304 Camden Field Pkwy	Riverview, FL	33578	813-533-2999	533-2966	3-12	Dr. Craig Butz
Pepin Academies	3916 E Hillsborough Ave	Tampa, FL	33610-4542	813-236-1755	236-1195	3-12	Dr. Craig Butz
Pepin Academies - Pasco	9804 Little Rd	New Port Richey, FL	34654	727-233-2961	233-2963	3-12	Celeste Kellar
Pineapple Cove Classical Academy	6162 Minton Rd NW	Palm Bay, FL	32907	321-802-9500	802-9933	K-8	Dr. Kelly Gunter
Pinecrest Academy North Charter S	10207 W Flagler St	Miami, FL	33174	305-553-9762	553-9760	K-6	Victoria Larrauri
Pinecrest Academy - South Campus	15130 SW 80th St	Miami, FL	33193-1302	305-386-0800	386-6298	K-5	Elaine Clemente
Pinecrest Cove Academy	4101 SW 107th Ave	Miami, FL	33165-4814	305-480-2097	207-1897	K-8	Susie Dopico
Pinecrest Creek Charter S	1100 Lee Rd	Orlando, FL	32810	407-757-2706	757-2710	K-5	Ericka Briones
Pinecrest Glades Academy	15250 SW 8th St	Miami, FL	33194	305-229-6949		K-12	Carrie Montano
Pinecrest Lakes Academy	14012 Old Highway 50	Minneola, FL	34711	352-223-4482		PK-8	Christina Alcalde
Pinecrest Preparatory Academy	14301 SW 42nd St	Miami, FL	33175-7832	305-207-1027	207-1897	K-5	Ana Diaz
Pinecrest Preparatory Academy HS	14901 SW 42nd St	Miami, FL	33185-4535	305-559-8583	559-8584	6-12	Maria Nunez
Pinecrest Preparatory S Orlando	8503 Daetwyler Dr	Orlando, FL	32827	407-856-8359	856-8361	K-8	Desiree Lumpuy
Pinellas Academy of Math and Science	1775 S Highland Ave	Largo, FL	33756-1847	727-330-9449	581-9205	K-8	Linda Schwerer
Pinellas Preparatory Academy	2300 Belcher Rd S Ste 100	Largo, FL	33771-4257	727-536-3600	536-3661	4-8	Amanda Matsumoto
Pinellas Primary Academy	2300 Belcher Rd S	Largo, FL	33771-4257	727-536-3600	536-3661	PK-3	Nancy Walker
Pivot Charter S	3020 S Falkenburg Rd	Riverview, FL	33578-2562	813-626-6724	626-6712	6-12	Elizabeth Bretz
Plato Academy	8812 Old County Road 54	New Port Richey, FL	34653	727-877-2437	799-0200	K-3	Jennifer Perez
Plato Academy Charter S	4903 Ehrlich Rd	Tampa, FL	33624	813-437-2867		K-2	Matthew Gunderson
Plato Academy Clearwater	2045 Palmetto St	Clearwater, FL	33765	727-228-9517	228-9518	PK-8	Dawn Parker
Plato Academy Largo	7100 142nd Ave	Largo, FL	33771	727-228-9952	228-9953	K-8	Veronica Han-G
Plato Academy Palm Harbor	1601 Curlew Rd	Palm Harbor, FL	34683	727-228-6850	228-6851	K-8	Stephen Donnelly
Plato Academy Pinellas Park	9200 49th St N	Pinellas Park, FL	33782	727-521-7260	521-7261	K-3	Carrie Aranzabal
Plato Academy St. Petersburg	3901 Park St N	St Petersburg, FL	33709	727-521-7258	521-7259	K-8	Michelle West
Plato Academy Seminole	10888 126th Ave	Largo, FL	33778	727-228-9950	228-9951	K-8	Karen Staab
Plato Academy Tarpon Springs	2795 Keystone Rd	Tarpon Springs, FL	34688	727-939-6413	939-6414	K-8	Danielle Turro
Polk Avenue ES	110 E Polk Ave	Lake Wales, FL	33853-4199	863-678-4244	678-4680	PK-5	Gail Quam
Polk Pre-Collegiate Academy	5316 Berkley Rd	Auburndale, FL	33823-8493	863-984-2400	984-2411	9-10	Cathy Carver
Polk State College Collegiate HS	3425 Winter Lake Rd	Lakeland, FL	33803	863-669-2322	669-2944	11-12	Rick Jeffries
Polk State Lakeland Gateway to Coll HS	3425 Winter Lake Rd	Lakeland, FL	33803	863-669-2923	669-4983	11-12	Corey Barnes
Potentials Charter S	1201 Australian Ave	Riviera Beach, FL	33404-6635	561-842-3213	863-4352	PK-8	Bairbre Flood
Princeton House Charter S	1166 Lee Rd	Orlando, FL	32810-5847	407-523-7121	523-7187	PK-5	Kim Gelalia
Prosperitas Leadership Academy Charter	4504 S Orange Blossom Trl	Orlando, FL	32839	407-854-3945	854-3955	9-12	
Putnam Academy of Arts and Sciences	310 S Palm Ave	Palatka, FL	32177-4161	386-326-4212	326-6235	6-8	Curtis Ellis
Putnam EDGE HS	PO Box 1258	Palatka, FL	32178	386-385-7292		9-12	Keith Smith
Quantum HS	1275 Gateway Blvd	Boynton Beach, FL	33426-8302	561-293-2971	277-0590	9-12	Dr. Joy Hicks-Gomez
RCMA Leadership Academy	18236 S US Highway 301	Wimauma, FL	33598-4307	813-672-5159	633-6119	6-8	Mark Haggett
RCMA Wimauma Academy	18240 S US Highway 301	Wimauma, FL	33598-4307	813-672-5159	633-6119	K-5	Mark Haggett
Reading Edge Academy	2975 Enterprise Rd	DeBary, FL	32713-2708	386-668-8911	668-8443	K-5	Margaret Comardo
Renaissance Charter S	300 NW Cashmere Blvd	Port St Lucie, FL	34986	772-344-5982	344-5985	K-8	Christiana Coburn
Renaissance Charter S at Central Palm	6696 S Military Trl	Lake Worth, FL	33463-7501	561-209-7106	209-7107	K-8	Jackson Self
Renaissance Charter S at Chickasaw Trail	8203 Valencia College Ln	Orlando, FL	32825-3242	321-206-0662	206-0664	K-8	Cindy Townsend
Renaissance Charter S at Cooper City	2800 N Palm Ave	Cooper City, FL	33026	954-668-2500	668-2980	K-8	Jacob Goldberg
Renaissance Charter S at Coral Springs	6250 W Sample Rd	Coral Springs, FL	33067-3176	954-369-1179	780-5411	K-8	Diana Sierra-Krumrie
Renaissance Charter S at Crown Point	83 West Rd	Ocoee, FL	34761	407-573-1080	573-1081	K-8	Brett Taylor
Renaissance Charter S at Cypress	8151 Okeechobee Blvd	West Palm Beach, FL	33411	561-282-5860		K-8	Dr. Tony Stewart
Renaissance Charter S at Goldenrod	6004 S Goldenrod Rd	Orlando, FL	32822	321-536-2952	536-2953	K-8	Nate Mariano
Renaissance Charter S at Hunter's Creek	4140 Town Center Blvd	Orlando, FL	32837	321-206-3103	206-3104	K-8	Roberto Acosta
Renaissance Charter S at Palms West	12031 Southern Blvd	Ryl Palm Bch, FL	33470-4994	561-214-6782	214-6783	K-8	Steve Epstein
Renaissance Charter S at Pines	10501 Pines Blvd	Pembroke Pines, FL	33026-6006	954-862-1283	862-1284	K-8	Daniel Verdier
Renaissance Charter S at Plantation	6701 W Sunrise Blvd	Plantation, FL	33313	954-556-9700	556-9701	K-8	Sheriffee Humphrey
Renaissance Charter S at Poinciana	5125 Robert McLane Blvd	Kissimmee, FL	34758	407-569-0639	569-0640	K-8	Bianca Washington-Brown
Renaissance Charter S at Summit	2001 Summit Blvd	West Palm Beach, FL	33406-4439	561-228-5240	228-5241	K-8	Heather Czeskleba
Renaissance Charter S at Tapestry	2510 W Carroll St	Kissimmee, FL	34741	407-569-0163	569-0164	K 8	Jodi Evans
Renaissance Charter S at Tradition	10900 SW Tradition Pkwy	Fort Pierce, FL	34987	772-236-2180	236-2181	K-8	Stacy Schmit
Renaissance Charter S at University	8399 N University Dr	Tamarac, FL	33321-1711	954-414-0996	414-0998	K-8	LaShonda White
Renaissance Charter S at Wellington	3220 S State Road 7	Wellington, FL	33449	561-228-5242		K-8	Mary Beth Greene
Renaissance Charter S at West Palm Beach	1889 Palm Beach Lakes Blvd	West Palm Beach, FL	33409-3501	561-839-1994	839-1995	K-8	Michael Lupton
Renaissance Elementary Charter S	10651 NW 19th St	Doral, FL	33172-2536	305-591-2225	591-2984	K-5	Maria Torres
Renaissance Learning Academy	18370 Limestone Creek Rd	Jupiter, FL	33458	561-296-1776	296-1791	9-12	Toby Honsberger
Renaissance Middle Charter S	8360 NW 33rd St	Doral, FL	33122	305-728-4622	401-1978	6-8	Maria Torres
Resilience Charter S	1717 NE 9th St Bldg A	Gainesville, FL	32609	352-745-3690		6-12	Jenny Hill
Ridgeview Global Studies Academy	1000 Dunson Rd	Davenport, FL	33896-8383	863-419-3171	419-3172	K-5	Sam Johnson
RISE Academy S of Science and Technology	6101 NW 31st St	Margate, FL	33063	954-968-7977	968-8386	K-8	Dr. Carmella Morton
Rising Leaders Academy	1527 Lincoln Ave	Panama City, FL	32405	850-215-0844	215-1711	K-8	Suha Jaber
River City Science Academy	7565 Beach Blvd	Jacksonville, FL	32216-3003	904-855-8010	855-8014	6-12	Ozan Sipahioglu
River City Science Academy Elementary	7555 Beach Blvd	Jacksonville, FL	32216	904-855-8010	727-9245	K-5	Jamey Hough
River City Science Academy - Innovations	8313 Baycenter Rd	Jacksonville, FL	32256-7415	904-647-5110	551-0821	K-8	Mesut Erdogan
River City Science at Mandarin	10911 Old St	Jacksonville, FL	32257	904-440-5339		K-8	Alaaddin Akgul
Round Lake Conversion Charter ES	31333 Round Lake Rd	Mount Dora, FL	32757-9599	352-385-4399	735-1860	PK-5	Linda Bartberger
Rowlett Academy for Arts & Communication	3500 9th St E	Bradenton, FL	34208-4516	941-708-6100	708-6109	K-5	Kim Penman
Royal Palm Charter S	7135 Babcock St SE	Palm Bay, FL	32909	321-723-0650	722-1117	PK-8	Shannon Shupe
St. Augustine Public Montessori S	7 Williams St	Saint Augustine, FL	32084	904-342-5350	342-5354	1-6	Ann Johnson
St. Cloud Prep Academy	3101 Progress Ln	Saint Cloud, FL	34769	407-593-6601	891-0145	K-8	Michele Quinn
St. Johns Community Campus	62 Cuna St	Saint Augustine, FL	32084-3684	904-209-6842		9-12	Lynne Funcheon
Saint Peter's Academy	4250 38th Ave	Vero Beach, FL	32967-1711	772-562-1963	567-8361	PK-6	Ruth Jefferson
St. Petersburg Collegiate HS	PO Box 13489	St Petersburg, FL	33733-3489	727-341-4610	341-4226	10-12	Starla Metz
SALTech Charter HS	4811 Payne Stewart Dr	Jacksonville, FL	32209	904-328-5001	768-8618	9-12	Michael LaRoche
Samsula Academy	248 N Samsula Dr	New Smyrna, FL	32168-8762	386-423-6650	423-6651	K-5	Peggy Comardo
San Jose Academy	4072 Sunbeam Rd	Jacksonville, FL	32257	904-425-1725	683-9101	6-12	Alan Hall
Sarasota Academy of the Arts	4466 Fruitville Rd	Sarasota, FL	34232-1926	941-377-2278	404-4492	K-8	Cecilia Blankenship
Sarasota Military Academy	801 Orange Ave	Sarasota, FL	34236-4116	941-926-1700	926-1701	9-12	Robin Livingston
Sarasota Military Academy Prep	3101 Bethel Ln	Sarasota, FL	34240	941-877-7737	877-7738	6-8	Thomas Vara
Sarasota S of Arts & Sciences	717 Central Ave	Sarasota, FL	34236	941-330-1855	330-1835	6-8	Tara Tahmosh-Newell
Sarasota Suncoast Academy	8084 Hawkins Rd	Sarasota, FL	34241	941-924-4242	924-8282	K 8	Steve Crump
S for Accelerated Lrng & Technologies	4751 Walgreen Rd	Jacksonville, FL	32209	904-328-5001	768-8618	9-12	Michael LaRoche
School of Arts & Sciences	3208 Thomasville Rd	Tallahassee, FL	32308-7904	850-386-6566	386-8183	K-8	Eirin Lombardo
S of Arts & Sciences	2415 N Monroe St Ste 2700	Tallahassee, FL	32303	850-999-8267		K-4	Lindsey Merrick
School of Success Academy	6974 Wilson Blvd	Jacksonville, FL	32210-3663	904-573-0880	573-0889	6-8	Genell Mills
Sculptor Charter S	1301 Armstrong Dr	Titusville, FL	32780-7907	321-264-4000	264-4011	K-8	Renee Bernhard
Seacoast Collegiate HS	109 Greenway Trl	Santa Rsa Bch, FL	32459-5415	850-200-4170		9-11	Jonathan Davignon

School	Address	City,State	Zip code	Telephone	Fax	Grade	Contact
Seacost Charter Academy	9100 Regency Square Blvd N	Jacksonville, FL	32211-8103	904-562-4780	726-0249	K-5	Marla Stremmel
Seagull Academy for Independent Living	6250 N Military Trl	Riviera Beach, FL	33404	561-540-8110	540-8331	6-12	Linda Moore
Seaside Community Charter S	2630 State Road A1A	Jacksonville, FL	32233	904-853-6287	485-8448	K-5	Sharon Sanders
Seaside Neighborhood S	PO Box 4610	Santa Rsa Bch, FL	32459-4610	850-231-0396	231-4725	5-8	Kim Mixon
Sebastian Charter JHS	782 Wave St	Sebastian, FL	32958-5049	772-388-8838	388-8815	6-8	Bill Dodds
Seed S of Miami	1901 NW 127th St	Miami, FL	33167	855-818-7333	503-7033	6-12	Kara Locke
Seminole Heights Charter HS	4006 N Florida Ave	Tampa, FL	33603	813-234-0809	236-2406	9-12	Robert Schodt
Seminole Science Charter S	3580 N US Highway 17/92	Lake Mary, FL	32746	407-864-8296	253-7305	K-8	
Sheeler Charter HS	871 E Semoran Blvd	Apopka, FL	32703	407-886-1825	886-7482	9-12	Johnathan Owens
Sigsbee Charter S	939 Felton Rd	Key West, FL	33040-6798	305-294-1861	292-6869	PK-8	Elisa Jannes
Six Mile Charter Academy	6851 Lancer Ave	Fort Myers, FL	33912-4334	239-768-9375	225-2477	K-8	Jaime Trotter
Sky Academy Englewood	881 S River Rd	Englewood, FL	34223	941-999-4775	999-4796	6-8	John Bailey
Sky Academy Venice	705 Center Rd	Venice, FL	34285	941-244-2626	244-2319	6-8	Steve Smith
Somerset Academy	305 NE 2nd Rd	Homestead, FL	33030	305-242-8992	242-8993	6-12	Alina Lopez
Somerset Academy	20801 Johnson St	Pembroke Pines, FL	33029	954-442-0233	442-0813	K-5	Bernardo Montero
Somerset Academy	18491 SW 134th Ave	Miami, FL	33177-2923	305-969-6074	969-6077	K-5	Suzette Ruiz
Somerset Academy Bay	9500 SW 97th Ave	Miami, FL	33176-2827	305-274-0682	274-0683	K-8	Salli Hernandez
Somerset Academy Boca	333 SW 4th Ave	Boca Raton, FL	33432	561-393-1091	393-1092	K-8	Daniel Shourds
Somerset Academy Canyons HS	9385 Boynton Beach Blvd	Boynton Beach, FL	33472	561-732-8252	732-8253	6-12	George Groezinger
Somerset Academy Central Miramar Campus	9300 Pembroke Rd	Miramar, FL	33025-1640	954-435-1570	435-1571	K-12	Athena Guillen
Somerset Academy Davie	3788 Davie Rd	Davie, FL	33314	954-584-5528	584-5598	K-5	Dina Miller
Somerset Academy Eagle Campus	8711 Lone Star Rd	Jacksonville, FL	32211	904-551-3292	551-3293	K-5	LaTatia Ray
Somerset Academy East Prep & Hollywood	2000 S State Road 7	Miramar, FL	33023	954-987-7890	987-7891	K-5	Dr. Mary Stuart
Somerset Academy HS	20805 Johnson St	Pembroke Pines, FL	33029-1916	954-442-0233	442-0813	9-12	Bernardo Montero
Somerset Academy JFK	4696 Davis Rd	Lake Worth, FL	33461-5204	561-868-6100	963-4697	K-8	Sharon Hench
Somerset Academy Key	959 SE 6th Ave	Deerfield Beach, FL	33441	954-481-0602	481-0603	6-12	Dennis Mulrooney
Somerset Academy Lakes	2845 Summit Blvd	West Palm Beach, FL	33406	561-641-4449	360-2452	K-2	Clint Duvo
Somerset Academy MS	18491 SW 134th Ave	Miami, FL	33177	305-969-6074	969-6077	6-8	Suzette Ruiz
Somerset Academy MS	20803 Johnson St	Pembroke Pines, FL	33029-1916	954-442-0233	442-0813	6-8	Bernardo Montero
Somerset Academy Miramar	12601 Somerset Blvd	Miramar, FL	33027-5898	305-829-2406	829-4477	PK-8	Alexandra Prieto
Somerset Academy Pompano	1101 NW 33rd St	Pompano Beach, FL	33064	954-946-4144	946-4005	K-8	Dr. Donna Kaye
Somerset Academy Prep	11155 SW 12th Ave	Miami, FL	33176	305-274-5696	274-5697	K-5	Angela Nunez
Somerset Academy St. Lucie	4402 SW Yamada Dr	Port St Lucie, FL	34953	772-281-2300		K-5	Erika Rains
Somerset Academy Silver Palms	23255 SW 115th Ave	Homestead, FL	33032-4505	305-257-3737	257-3751	K-12	Kerri Rodriguez
Somerset Academy South Homestead	300 SE 1st Dr	Homestead, FL	33030	305-245-6108	245-6109	K-5	Layda Morales
Somerset Academy South Miami	5876 SW 68th St	South Miami, FL	33143-3693	305-740-0509	740-0510	K-8	Kim Guilarte
Somerset Arts Conservatory	20807 Johnson St	Pembroke Pines, FL	33029	954-442-0233	442-0813	9-12	Bernardo Montero
Somerset City Arts Conservatory	47 NW 16 St	Homestead, FL	33030	305-246-4949	249-4919	K-6	Idalia Suarez
Somerset College Prep Academy	725 NW California Blvd	Port St Lucie, FL	34986	772-343-7028	343-7029	6-12	Erika Rains
Somerset Gables Academy	624 Anastasia Ave	Coral Gables, FL	33134-6404	305-442-8626	442-8627	K-8	Suzette Ruiz
Somerset Miramar South S	12425 SW 53rd St	Miramar, FL	33027-5493	305-829-2406	829-4477	K-5	Alexandra Prieto
Somerset Oaks Academy	1000 Old Dixie Hwy	Homestead, FL	33030	305-247-3993	247-3994	K-8	Idalia Suarez
Somerset Pines Academy	901 NE 33rd St	Pompano Beach, FL	33064-5231	954-786-5980	786-5981	K-8	Dr. Donna Kaye
Somerset Preparatory Academy	1429 Broward Rd	Jacksonville, FL	32218-5315	904-503-0661	379-5936	PK-10	David Cook
Somerset Prep North Lauderdale	7101 Kimberly Blvd	N Lauderdale, FL	33068	954-718-5065	718-5066	K-12	Donyale McGhee
Somerset Village Academy	225 NW 29th St	Wilton Manors, FL	33311	954-390-0971	390-0972	K-8	Anthony Marruci
Somerset Virtual Academy	305 NE 2nd Rd	Homestead, FL	33030	305-258-7497	258-7498	6-12	Alina Lopez
South Broward Montessori Charter S	520 NW 5th St	Hallandale Bch, FL	33009-3314	954-251-1443	251-1820	K-5	Elaine Padron
South Florida Autism Charter S	18305 NW 75th Pl	Hialeah, FL	33015	305-823-2700	823-2705	K-12	Dr. Tamara Moodie
South McKeel Academy	2222 Edgewood Dr S	Lakeland, FL	33803-3631	863-510-0044	510-0021	K-7	Kim Benson
Southshore Charter Academy	11667 Big Bend Rd	Riverview, FL	33578	813-769-1209	769-2161	K-8	Kristen Storm-Taylor
South Tech Academy	1300 SW 30th Ave	Boynton Beach, FL	33426-9099	561-369-7004	369-7024	9-12	Jay Boggess
South Tech Preparatory Academy	1325 Gateway Blvd	Boynton Beach, FL	33426-8304	561-318-8087	369-7024	6-8	Nicole Handy
Sports Leadership Academy of Miami	604 NW 12th Ave	Miami, FL	33136	305-326-0003	326-0004	6-12	Francisco Jimenez
Sports Leadership Academy of Miami MS	16551 NE 16th Av	Miami, FL	33162	305-333-5702		6-8	Francisco Jimenez
Sports Leadership and Management Academy	7116 Gunn Hwy	Tampa, FL	33625	813-920-8802		6-12	James Griffin
Sports Leadership and Management MS	2845 Summit Blvd	West Palm Beach, FL	33406	561-434-2162	360-2452	6-8	Clint Duvo
Spring Creek Conversion Charter ES	44440 Spring Creek Rd	Paisley, FL	32767-9063	352-669-3275	669-3762	PK-8	Wesley Locke
State College of Florida Collegiate S	5840 26th St W	Bradenton, FL	34207	941-752-5494	758-4801	6-12	Kelly Monod
Stellar Leadership Academy	7900 NW 27th Ave Ste F-1	Miami, FL	33147-4909	305-693-2273	693-8016	9-12	Dr. Angel Chaisson
Student Leadership Academy	200 Field Ave E	Venice, FL	34285-3936	941-485-5551	485-2694	6-8	Vickie Marble
Summerville Advantage Academy	11575 SW 243rd St	Homestead, FL	33032-7163	305-253-2123	253-4304	K-8	Mary March
Suncoast S for Innovative Studies	845 S School Ave	Sarasota, FL	34237-8039	941-953-4433	953-4435	PK-8	Stephen Evans
SunEd HS	2360 W Oakland Park Blvd	Oakland Park, FL	33311-1410	954-678-3939	485-6243	9-12	DeeEtte Naukana
SunEd HS of North Broward	1121 Banks Rd	Margate, FL	33063-6702	954-246-4004	379-2722	9-12	Tammy Lara
Sunlake Academy of Math and Science	18681 N Dale Mabry Hwy	Lutz, FL	33548	813-616-5099	343-6099	K-8	Suzanne Elder
Sunrise HS	424 W Sunrise Blvd	Fort Lauderdale, FL	33311	954-446-9234	522-1539	9-12	Martie Lovely
Sunshine ES	502 N 28th Ave	Hollywood, FL	33020	954-925-0155	925-0209	K-5	Dr. Steven Montes
Sunshine High Charter	6600 Old Winter Garden Rd	Orlando, FL	32835	407-641-4156	886-7482	9-12	Ian Dye
Tallahassee S of Math & Science	3434 N Monroe St	Tallahassee, FL	32303	850-681-7827	325-6706	K-8	Ahmet Temel
Team Success S of Excellence	202 13th Ave E	Bradenton, FL	34208-3246	941-714-7260	714-7333	K-12	Armando Viota
Terrace Community MS	11734 Jefferson Rd	Thonotosassa, FL	33592-2101	813-987-6555	324-8974	6-8	Tahvia Shaw
Therapeutic Learning Center	2109 ARC Dr	Saint Augustine, FL	32084-0512	904-824-8932	824-8063	PK-PK	Paulette Hudson
Tiger Academy	6079 Bagley Rd	Jacksonville, FL	32209-1805	904-309-6840	309-6867	PK-5	Charles McWhite
Toussaint L'Ouverture HS	2601 S Military Trl	West Palm Beach, FL	33415	561-266-1200	266-1286	9-12	Mandy Freeman
Town and Country Charter HS	7555 W Waters Ave	Tampa, FL	33615	813-902-2858	884-7807	9-12	Rufus Floyd
Treasure Village Montessori Charter S	86731 Overseas Hwy	Islamorada, FL	33036-3129	305-852-3482	852-2432	PK-8	Kelly Mangel
Trinity S for Children	2402 W Osborne Ave	Tampa, FL	33603-1434	813-874-2402	874-2412	K-8	Dr. Madeline O'Dea
True North Classical Academy	9393 Sunset Dr	Miami, FL	33173	305-749-5725	271-9052	K-8	Dr. Mark Snyder
UCP Bailes Campus	12702 Science Dr	Orlando, FL	32826	407-852-3300	270-9253	PK-5	Dr. Jennifer Holbrook
UCP Charter S Downtown Campus	4680 Lake Under Hill	Orlando, FL	32807	407-852-3300	381-0907	PK-5	Lillian Flores
UCP Osceola Campus	1820 Armstrong Blvd	Kissimmee, FL	34741	407-852-3300	932-3480	PK-3	Elizabeth Morris
UCP Pine Hills Campus	5800 Golf Club Pkwy	Orlando, FL	32808-4800	407-852-3300	412-5356	PK-5	Dr. Karyn Hawkins-Scott
UCP Seminole Campus	756 N Sun Dr	Lake Mary, FL	32746	407-852-3300	915-5078	PK-3	Marife Gomez
UCP Transitional Learning Academy	3305 S Orange Ave	Orlando, FL	32806	407-852-3300	412-5975	6-12	David DeAmato
UCP West Orange Campus	1297 Winter Garden Vineland	Winter Garden, FL	34787	407-852-3300	614-2011	PK-5	Tracy Stockwell
Unity Charter S of Cape Coral	2107 Santa Barbara Blvd	Cape Coral, FL	33991	239-829-5134	242-0477	K-8	Stephan Terebieniec
Unity Charter S of Fort Myers	4740 S Cleveland Ave	Fort Myers, FL	33907	239-333-0766	333-0768	K-8	George Coates M.Ed.
University Academy	1980 Discovery Loop	Panama City, FL	32405	850-481-4410		K-8	Elizabeth Crowe Ph.D.
University Preparatory Academy	2101 N Australian Ave	West Palm Beach, FL	33407-5630	561-670-1138		K-8	Richard Ledgister
Valor Academy of Leadership	4819 Soutel Dr	Jacksonville, FL	32208	904-469-8195	524-8440	6-12	John Taylor
Valrico Lake Advantage Academy	13306 Boyette Rd	Riverview, FL	33569-5741	813-699-5049	413-5191	K-5	Lauren Herbert
Victory Ridge Academy	555 Burns Ave	Lake Wales, FL	33853-3335	863-679-3338	679-3944	PK-12	Debra Johnson
Viera Charter S	6206 Breslay Dr	Viera, FL	32940-8418	321-541-1434	608-2322	K-8	Dr. Julie Cady
Village of Excellence Academy	8718 N 46th St	Temple Terrace, FL	33617-6002	813-988-8632	983-0683	K-5	Dr. Cametra Edwards
Village of Excellence Academy MS	4600 E Busch Blvd	Tampa, FL	33617	813-374-9972	304-2202	6-8	Lakeisha Walker
Villages Charter HS	251 Buffalo Trl	The Villages, FL	32162-7176	352-259-3777	259-3850	9-12	Jason Spencer
Villages Charter Intermediate Center	521 Old School Rd	The Villages, FL	32162-7170	352-259-2300	259-2056	2-3	LeAnne Yerk
Villages Charter MS	450 Village Campus Cir	The Villages, FL	32162-7169	352-259-0044	753-1113	6-8	Dr. Peggy Irwin
Villages Charter Primary Center	420 Village Campus Cir	The Villages, FL	32162-7169	352-259-7700	259-7707	K-1	LeAnne Yerk
Virtue Arts & Science Academy	1824 Dean Rd	Jacksonville, FL	32216	904-379-0004	619-1531	6-12	Michelle Knapp
Visible Men Academy Charter S	921 63rd Ave E	Bradenton, FL	34203	941-758-7588	761-5375	K-5	Neil Phillips
Walton Academy	389 Dorsey Ave	Defuniak Spgs, FL	32435-3013	850-892-3999	892-7854	6-12	David Schmidt
Walton Academy for the Performing Arts	4817 N Florida Ave	Tampa, FL	33603-2117	813-231-9272	231-9271	K-5	Tanika Walton
Waterset Charter S	6540 Knowledge Ln	Apollo Beach, FL	33572	813-602-0622	602-0623	K-8	Sara Capwell
Waverly Academy	5710 Wesconnett Blvd	Jacksonville, FL	32244	904-647-8552	515-5353	6-8	Fernette Moore
Wayman Academy of the Arts	1176 Labelle St	Jacksonville, FL	32205-6487	904-695-9995	693-1127	K-5	Simaran Bakshi
Wells Charter Academy	2426 Remington Blvd	Kissimmee, FL	34744-8467	407-697-1020	697-1021	K-8	Alan Ramos
West Broward Academy	5281 Coconut Creek Pkwy	Margate, FL	33063	754-702-2320	263-5900	K-8	Donna Baggs
Western Academy Charter S	650 Royal Palm Blvd Ste 300	Ryl Palm Bch, FL	33411	561-792-4123	422-0674	K-8	Linda Terranova
West University Charter HS	11602 N 15th St	Tampa, FL	33612	813-774-4396	971-5011	9-12	Jeffrey Mitchell
Whispering Winds Charter S	2480 NW Old Fannin Rd	Chiefland, FL	32626	352-490-5799	490-7242	K-8	Kimberly Bartley
Wilson ES	306 Florida Ave	Lake Wales, FL	33853-3121	863-678-4211	678-4217	PK-5	Linda Ray
Winthrop Charter S	6204 Scholars Hill Ln	Riverview, FL	33578-4298	813-235-4811	315-4403	K-8	Terry Johnson
Woodmont Charter S	10402 N 56th St	Temple Terrace, FL	33617	813-708-1596	739-7301	K-8	Lane Morris
Workforce Advantage Academy	2113 E South St	Orlando, FL	32803-6502	407-898-7228	898-6448	11-12	
Worthington HS	1711 Worthington Rd	West Palm Beach, FL	33409	561-537-5696	697-4366	9-12	Cassandra Oliver
Youth Co-Op Preparatory Charter S	7700 W 20th Ave	Hialeah Gardens, FL	33016	305-819-8855	826-9212	K-12	Maritza Aragon

Georgia

School	Address	City,State	Zip code	Telephone	Fax	Grade	Contact
Academies of Creative Education	1130 Dahlonega Hwy	Cumming, GA	30040	770-781-3141	888-1193	9-12	Betty Pope
Academy for Advanced Studies	401 E Tomlinson St	McDonough, GA	30253	770-320-7997	610-5853	9-12	John Uesseler
Academy for Classical Education	5665 New Forsyth Rd	Macon, GA	31210	478-238-5757		K-12	Laura Perkins
Amana Academy	285 S Main St	Alpharetta, GA	30009-1937	678-624-0989	624-0892	K-8	Cherisse Campbell
Athens Community Career Academy	PO Box 1708	Athens, GA	30603	706-357-5244	353-3877	10-12	Lawrence Harris
Atlanta Classical Academy	3260 Northside Dr NW	Atlanta, GA	30305	404-369-3500	795-1049	K-12	Stephen Lambert

School	Address	City,State	Zip code	Telephone	Fax	Grade	Contact
Atlanta Heights Charter S	3712 Martin Luther King Jr	Atlanta, GA	30331-3674	404-472-3003	264-2132	K-8	Nicole Bullen
Atlanta Neighborhood Charter ES	688 Grant St SE	Atlanta, GA	30315-1420	404-624-6226	624-9093	K-5	Lara Zelski
Atlanta Neighborhood Charter MS	820 Essie Ave SE	Atlanta, GA	30316-2425	678-904-0051	904-0052	6-8	Cathey Goodgame
Baconton Community Charter S	260 E Walton St	Baconton, GA	31716-7706	229-787-9999	787-0077	PK-12	Lynn Pinson
Baldwin College and Career Academy	155 GA Highway 49 W	Milledgeville, GA	31061	478-453-6429	453-5060	7-12	Natalie Stowe
Bartow County College & Career Academy	738 Grassdale Rd NW	Cartersville, GA	30121	770-606-5182	606-5890	9-12	Dr. Paul Sabin
Berrien Academy Performance Learning Ctr	1015 Exum Rd	Nashville, GA	31639-2730	229-686-6576	686-6580	9-12	Michele Garner
Bishop Hall Charter S	220 N Pinetree Blvd	Thomasville, GA	31792-3915	229-227-1397	558-9420	9-12	Chris Huckans
Brighten Academy	3264 Brookmont Pkwy	Douglasville, GA	30135	770-615-3680	575-3614	K-8	Lisa McDonald
Brookhaven Innovation Academy	3159 Campus Dr	Norcross, GA	30071	770-538-1550		K-8	Laurie Kimbrel
Cairo HS	455 5th St SE	Cairo, GA	39828-2399	229-377-2222	377-2812	9-12	Christopher Lokey
Carroll County College and Career Acad	1075 Newnan Rd	Carrollton, GA	30116-6435	770-832-8380	830-5037	9-12	Cindy Clanton
Centennial Academy	531 Luckie St NW	Atlanta, GA	30313-2401	404-802-8550	853-4089	K-8	Carol Santos
Central Educational Center	160 Martin Luther King Dr	Newnan, GA	30263-2331	678-423-2000	423-2008	8-12	Mark Ballou
Chamblee Charter HS	3688 Chamblee Dunwoody Rd	Chamblee, GA	30341-2143	678-676-6902	676-6910	9-12	Rebecca Braaten
Chattahoochie Hills Charter S	9670 Rivertown Rd	Fairburn, GA	30213	678-466-7300	466-7305	K-5	Walt Buttler
Cherokee Charter Academy	2126 Sixes Rd	Canton, GA	30114	678-385-7322	385-7323	K-8	April Wallis
Chesnut ES Charter	4576 N Peachtree Rd	Dunwoody, GA	30338-5809	678-676-7102	676-7110	PK-5	Veronica Williams
Chestatee Academy	2740 Fran Mar Dr	Gainesville, GA	30506-1136	770-297-6270	297-6275	6-8	Jennifer Kogod
Chestnut Mountain Creative S of Inquiry	4841 Union Church Rd	Flowery Branch, GA	30542-5202	770-967-3121	967-4891	K-5	Wade Pearce
Cirrus Charter Academy	1870 Pio Nono Ave	Macon, GA	31204	478-250-1376		K-8	Dr. Gail Fowler
Clear Creek MS	1020 Clear Creek Rd	Ellijay, GA	30536-7898	706-276-5150	276-5151	7-8	David Mashburn
Clubview ES	2836 Edgewood Rd	Columbus, GA	31906-1225	706-565-3017	565-3022	PK-5	Teresa Lawson
Coastal Empire Montessori Charter S	301 Buckhalter Rd	Savannah, GA	31405-6111	912-395-4070	201-5051	PK-5	Stephanie Babcock-Wright
Coastal Plains Charter HS	2900 Albany St	Brunswick, GA	31520	912-280-6777		9-12	Robert Pope
Coastal Plains Charter HS	210 S College St	Metter, GA	30439	912-685-5713		9-12	Ronnie Doolittle
Coweta Charter Academy	6675 Highway 16	Senoia, GA	30276-3345	770-599-0228	599-0556	K-8	Gene Dunn
Dekalb Academy of Tech & Environment	1492 Kelton Dr	Stone Mountain, GA	30083	678-999-9290	999-9294	K-8	Dr. Maury Wills
DeKalb PATH Academy	3007 Hermance Dr NE	Atlanta, GA	30319-2627	404-846-3242	846-3243	5-8	Crystal Clarke
DeKalb Prepatory Academy	1402 Austin Dr	Decatur, GA	30032	404-937-2000	937-2020	K-8	Christopher Estes
Destiny Achievers Academy of Excellence	3595 Linecrest Rd	Ellenwood, GA	30294-1839	404-328-0898	328-1294	9-12	Kelvin Griffin
Douglas Co. College & Career Institute	4600 Timber Ridge Dr	Douglasville, GA	30135	770-947-7690	947-3896	9-12	Gary Morris
Drew Charter S	300 E Lake Blvd SE	Atlanta, GA	30317	404-355-1200	687-0480	PK-12	Don Doran
Dubois Integrity Academy	6479 Church St	Riverdale, GA	30274	770-997-4860		K-5	Dr. Stephanie Payne
Effingham Career Academy	2940 GA Highway 21 S	Rincon, GA	31326	912-754-5610	754-5611	10-12	Ashley Kieffer
Ellijay ES	32 McCutchen St	Ellijay, GA	30540-3302	706-276-5020	276-5022	2-4	Lauree Pierce
Ellijay PS	196 McCutchen St	Ellijay, GA	30540-3393	706-276-5010	276-5013	PK-1	Stephanie Burnette
Flowery Branch HS	6603 Spout Springs Rd	Flowery Branch, GA	30542	770-967-8000	967-1218	9-12	Dr. Jason Carter
Floyd County College and Career Academy	100 Tom Poe Dr SW	Rome, GA	30161	706-236-1860	236-1862	9-12	Eric Waters
Foothills Charter HS	600 Madison St	Danielsville, GA	30633-7030	706-795-2197		9-12	Renee Padgett
Fulton Academy of Science and Technology	11365 Crabapple Rd	Roswell, GA	30075	678-321-1100		K-6	Annette Higgins M Ed
Fulton Leadership Academy	2575 Dodson Dr	East Point, GA	30344	404-472-3529	472-3520	6-12	Douglas Ward
Furlow Charter S	63 Valley Dr	Americus, GA	31709	229-931-8667		K-12	Elizabeth Kuipers
Futral Road ES	180 Futral Rd	Griffin, GA	30224-7454	770-229-3735	233-6001	PK-5	Ben Steele
Genesis Innovation Academy	1049 Custer Ave SE	Atlanta, GA	30316	404-990-3844		K-8	Gavin Samms
Georgia Connections Academy	2763 Meadow Church Rd # 208	Duluth, GA	30097	678-825-3258		K-12	Heather Robinson
Georgia Cyber Academy	1745 Phoenix Blvd Ste 100	Atlanta, GA	30349-5534	404-334-4790	684-8816	K-12	Matt Arkin
Georgia S for Innovation & the Classics	5073 Storey Mill Rd	Hephzibah, GA	30815	706-434-8085	434-8086	K-8	Mary Abbott
Gilmer HS	408 Bobcat Trl	Ellijay, GA	30540-5406	706-276-5080	276-5088	9-12	Carla Foley
Gilmer MS	1860 S Main St	Ellijay, GA	30540-5407	706-276-5030	276-5035	5-6	Larry Walker
Glascock County Consolidated S	1230 Panther Way	Gibson, GA	30810-4238	706-598-2121	598-2611	PK-12	Danny Lovering
GLOBE Academy	2225 Heritage Dr NE	Atlanta, GA	30345	404-464-7040		K-6	Christi Elliott-Earby
Golden Isles Career Academy	4404 Glynco Pkwy	Brunswick, GA	31525	912-280-4000	261-2205	9-12	Randal Harvey
Graduation Achievement Charter HS	100 Edgewood Ave NE Ste 915	Atlanta, GA	30303-3070	404-937-5735	577-9023	9-12	Dr. Monica Henson
Gwinnett S of Math Science and Tech	970 McElvaney Ln	Lawrenceville, GA	30044	678-518-6700	518-6702	9-12	I.V. Bray
Hampton ES	10 Central Ave	Hampton, GA	30228-2100	770-946-4345	946-3472	PK-5	Brian Keefer
Hapeville Charter Career Academy	6045 Buffington Rd	College Park, GA	30349	404-766-0101	941-1102	9-12	Jarnard Rainey
Hapeville Charter MS	3535 S Fulton Ave	Hapeville, GA	30354-1701	404-767-7730	767-7706	6-8	Marcia Lowe
Harris Elementary Charter S	2300 Danielsville Rd	Athens, GA	30601-1038	706-357-5203	357-5209	PK-5	Xernona Thomas
Heart of Georgia College & Career Acad	338 W Laurens School Rd	Dublin, GA	31021	478-278-7760		9-12	Eric Cannada
Hickory Flat ES	841 Brannan Rd	McDonough, GA	30253-4749	770-898-0107	898-0114	K-5	Marla Surette
Hillcrest ES	1100 Edgewood Dr	Dublin, GA	31021-5599	478-353-8200	353-8201	PK-4	Sherrell Edmond
Houston County Career Academy	1311 Corder Rd	Warner Robins, GA	31088-7117	478-322-3280	322-3294	9-12	Sabrina Phelps
Hutchings College & Career Academy	1780 Anthony Rd	Macon, GA	31204	478-779-2550	779-2540	9-12	Barbara Alston
International Academy of Smyrna	2144 S Cobb Dr SE Ste A	Smyrna, GA	30080	678-370-0980	370-0981	K-6	Kari Schrock
International Charter S of Atlanta	1335 Northmeadow Pkwy # 100	Roswell, GA	30076	470-222-7420	561-7516	K-7	Pamela Spalla
International Community S	2418 Wood Trail Ln	Decatur, GA	30033	404-499-8969	499-8968	K-5	Chad Velde-Cabrera
International Studies Magnet ES	2237 Cutts Dr	Albany, GA	31705-3810	229-431-3384	431-3381	PK-5	Dr. Zeda George
Ivy Preparatory Academy	3705 Engineering Dr	Norcross, GA	30092	770-342-0089	342-0088	6-8	Wayne Dennis
Ivy Preparatory Academy at Kirkwood	1807 Memorial Dr SE	Atlanta, GA	30317	404-622-2727	622-2725	K-8	Charcia Nichols
Jenkins-White Charter ES	800 15th Ave	Augusta, GA	30901-4145	706-737-7320	731-7651	PK-5	Vanessa Darling
Kennesaw Charter Science & Math Academy	3010 Cobb Pkwy NW	Kennesaw, GA	30152	678-290-9628	290-9638	K-5	James McNealey
Kindezi S	386 Pine St NE	Atlanta, GA	30308	404-719-4005		K-8	Gilberte Pascal
Kindezi S	897 Welch St SW	Atlanta, GA	30310	404-802-7700		PK-5	Danielle Washington
Kindezi S	286 Wilson Mill Rd SW	Atlanta, GA	30331	404-802-8251		K-8	Shombai Strond
Kingsley ES	2051 Brendon Dr	Dunwoody, GA	30338-4599	678-874-8902	874-8910	PK-5	Melanie Pearch
KIPP Atlanta Collegiate S	98 Anderson Ave NW	Atlanta, GA	30314	404-574-5126	574-5129	9-12	David Howland
KIPP South Fulton Academy	1286 Washington Rd	East Point, GA	30344	678-278-0160	278-0165	5-8	Siobhan Gardner
KIPP STRIVE Academy	1444 Lucile Ave SW	Atlanta, GA	30310	404-753-1530	753-1532	5-8	Kim Karacalidis
KIPP STRIVE Primary Academy	1448 Lucile Ave SW	Atlanta, GA	30310	404-585-4192	585-4191	K-4	Lakeesha Ramdhanie
KIPP Vision Academy	660 McWilliams Rd SE	Atlanta, GA	30315	404-537-5252	671-4882	5-8	Alison Irons
KIPP Vision PS	660 McWilliams Rd SE	Atlanta, GA	30315	404-537-5252	671-4882	K-4	Kristi Reaves
KIPP WAYS Academy	350 Temple St NW	Atlanta, GA	30314-2721	404-475-1941	475-1946	5-8	Dwight Ho-Sang
KIPP WAYS PS	350 Temple St NW	Atlanta, GA	30314	404-475-1941	475-1946	K-4	Tandi Prillerman
Lake Oconee Academy	1021 Titan Cir	Greensboro, GA	30642	706-454-1562	453-1773	PK-12	Otho Tucker Ph.D.
Lamar County College and Career Academy	1 Trojan Way	Barnesville, GA	30204	770-358-8641	358-8649	9-12	Dr. David Boland
Lanier Charter Career Academy	2719 Tumbling Creek Rd	Gainesville, GA	30504	770-531-2330	450-5978	9-12	David Moody
Latin College Prep	2626 Hogan Rd	East Point, GA	30344	404-669-8060	393-1491	6-8	Christian Harden
Latin Grammar S	2626 Hogan Rd	East Point, GA	30344	404-669-8060	393-1491	K-5	Alka Franceschi
Leadership Preparatory Academy	6400 Woodrow Rd	Lithonia, GA	30038	678-526-2589	526-2581	K-8	Lonnie Hall
Liberty College and Career Academy	245 Darsey Rd	Hinesville, GA	31313	912-876-4904		9-12	Karisa Young
Liberty Tech Charter S	119 Price Rd	Brooks, GA	30205	678-456-5673		K-8	Mike Stewart
Main Street Academy	2861 Lakeshore Dr	College Park, GA	30337	404-768-0081	767-2491	K-8	Cheryl Parker
Martin Technology Acad of Math & Science	4216 Martin Rd	Flowery Branch, GA	30542-3509	770-965-1578	965-1668	K-5	Dr. Ley Hathcock
McEver Arts Academy	3265 Montgomery Dr	Gainesville, GA	30504-5515	770-534-7473	531-3055	K-5	Matthew Alexander
Morgan County ES	1640 Buckhead Rd	Madison, GA	30650	706-752-4750	752-4751	3-5	Lara Still
Morgan County HS	1231 College Dr	Madison, GA	30650-1499	706-752-4900	752-4901	9-12	Dr. Miki Edwards
Morgan County MS	920 Pearl St	Madison, GA	30650-1056	706-752-4800	752-4801	6-8	Hillary Meeler
Morgan County PS	993 East Ave	Madison, GA	30650-1498	706-752-4700	752-4701	PK-2	Lisa Daniel
Mountain Education Charter HS	901 Fairview School Rd	Demorest, GA	30535	706-754-4461	754-5181	9-12	Sherrie Whiten
Mountain Education Charter HS	218 School St	Blairsville, GA	30512	706-745-9575	745-3588	9-12	Roy Perren
Mountain Education Charter HS	4560 Old Highway 76	Blue Ridge, GA	30513	706-632-6100	632-0461	9-12	Betsy Hyde
Mountain Education Charter HS	175 Primary School Rd	Ellijay, GA	30540	706-276-4444	276-5008	9-12	Lori Chastain
Mountain Education Charter HS	65 Kenimer St	Cleveland, GA	30528	706-219-4664	219-4665	9-12	Darren Sledge
Mountain Education Charter HS	136 Elm St	Cumming, GA	30040	678-965-4971	965-4972	9-12	Frank Gordy
Mountain Education Charter HS	328 Old Blairsville Rd	Cleveland, GA	30528	706-348-4599	348-4498	9-12	Darren Sledge
Mountain Education Charter HS	121 D B Carroll St	Jasper, GA	30143	706-253-1750	253-1755	9-12	Scott Perkins
Mountain Education Charter HS	86 Adams Cir	Bowman, GA	30624	706-213-4300	245-0407	9-12	Renee Padgett
Mountain Education Charter HS	1130 Dahlonega Hwy	Cumming, GA	30040	678-965-4971	965-5022	9-12	Kimberly Barnes
Mountain Education Charter HS	2723 Tumbling Creek Rd	Gainesville, GA	30504	770-531-2330	297-2399	9-12	Harold Williams
Mountain Education Charter HS	963 Tiger Connector Rd	Tiger, GA	30576	706-212-4390	782-2188	9-12	Tomy Short
Mountain Education Charter HS	50 Eastanollee Livestock Rd	Eastanollee, GA	30538	706-886-3114	886-3127	9-12	Debbie Gurley
Mountain View ES	350 Calvin Jackson Dr	Ellijay, GA	30540-5589	706-276-5100	276-5102	K-4	Charles Walker
Mount Vernon Exploratory S	4844 Jim Hood Rd	Gainesville, GA	30506-2834	770-983-1759	983-1663	K-5	Jennifer Westbrook
Murphey MS	1921 Eagles Way	Augusta, GA	30904	706-737-7350	737-7353	6-8	D'Andrea Jackson
Museum S of Avondale Estates	923 Forrest Blvd	Decatur, GA	30030	404-289-0320		PK-8	Katherine Kelbaugh
New Life Academy of Excellence	4725 River Green Pkwy	Duluth, GA	30096	678-720-9870	720-9875	K-8	Alphonsa Foward
Newton College & Career Academy	144 Ram Dr	Covington, GA	30014	678-625-6769	625-6041	9-12	Chad Walker
North Metro Academy of Performing Arts	182 Hunter St	Norcross, GA	30071	770-903-3400	903-2950	K-5	Rodriguez Johnson
Northwest Georgia College & Career Acad	2300 Maddox Chapel Rd NE	Dalton, GA	30721-6645	706-876-3600	876-3602	9-12	David Moeller
Odyssey Charter S	14 Saint John Cir	Newnan, GA	30265	770-251-6111	251-6606	K-8	Scot Hooper
Oglethorpe Charter S	7202 Central Ave	Savannah, GA	31406-4203	912-395-5075	201-7626	6-8	Dr. Kevin Wall
Pataula Charter Academy	PO Box 332	Edison, GA	39846	229-354-4001	835-2233	PK-12	Kylie Holley
Peachtree Charter MS	4664 N Peachtree Rd	Atlanta, GA	30338-5811	678-676-7702	676-7710	6-8	Scott Heptinstall
Polk College and Career Academy	612 S College St	Cedartown, GA	30125-3522	770-748-3821		9-12	Dr. Katie Thomas
Putnam County ES	314 S Washington Ave	Eatonton, GA	31024-1126	706-485-5312	923-2808	3-5	Scott Sauls
Putnam County HS	300 War Eagle Rd	Eatonton, GA	31024-2304	706-485-9971	485-3128	9-12	Marc Dastous

School	Address	City,State	Zip code	Telephone	Fax	Grade	Contact
Putnam County MS	140 Sparta Hwy	Eatonton, GA	31024-8493	706-485-8547	485-7090	6-8	Jay Homan
Putnam County PS	162 Old Glenwood Springs Rd	Eatonton, GA	31024-6525	706-485-5141	485-4147	PK-2	Dr. Fernando Aker
Resurgence Hall Charter S	1743 Hardin Ave	College Park, GA	30337	404-382-8512		K-8	Tori Hines
Rockdale Career Academy	1064 Culpepper Dr SW	Conyers, GA	30094-5985	770-388-5677	388-5678	9-12	Jill Oldham
SAIL Charter Academy	4575 Blanchard Woods Dr	Evans, GA	30809	762-585-1400		K-8	Kristy Zgol
Sardis Enrichment School	2805 Sardis Rd	Gainesville, GA	30506-2228	770-532-0104	531-3057	PK-5	Neil Yarrington
Savannah Classical Academy	705 E Anderson St	Savannah, GA	31401	912-395-4040		K-12	Benjamin Payne
Sawyer Road ES	840 Sawyer Rd	Marietta, GA	30062-2263	770-429-9923	429-9936	K-5	Susan Graves
Scintilla Charter Academy	2171 E Park Ave	Valdosta, GA	31602-4436	229-244-5750	333-0283	K-5	Stephanie Mullis
Sedalia Park ES	2230 Lower Roswell Rd	Marietta, GA	30068-3359	770-509-5162	509-5342	K-5	Tiffany Jackson
Skyview HS	5134 Old National Hwy	College Park, GA	30349	404-418-8812		9-12	Byron Foster
Smoke Rise ES	1991 Silver Hill Rd	Stone Mountain, GA	30087-1699	678-874-3602	874-3610	PK-5	Pamela McCloud
South Eastern Early College & Career Acd	413 Pete Phillips Dr	Vidalia, GA	30474	912-538-3248		9-12	Shelly Smith
Southwest Georgia STEM Charter S	185 Pecan St	Shellman, GA	39886	229-679-5555	648-5253	PK-7	Amy Foster
Spout Springs S of Enrichment	6640 Spout Springs Rd	Flowery Branch, GA	30542-5575	770-967-4860	967-4883	K-5	Arlene Thomas
Statesboro STEAM Academy	1718 Northside Dr E	Statesboro, GA	30458	912-764-5888	489-8493	6-12	Corliss Reese
Taliaferro County S	557 Broad St NW	Crawfordville, GA	30631-2918	706-456-2575	456-2689	PK-12	Ronald Lewis
Tapestry Charter Public S	3130 Raymond Dr	Atlanta, GA	30340	470-268-6403	268-6403	6-12	Barbara Boone
Tapestry Charter S	3130 Raymond Dr	Atlanta, GA	30340	470-268-6403	268-6854	6-9	Barbara Boone
Taylor Community S	1709 Bull St	Savannah, GA	31401	912-395-4200		K-8	Latrisha Chattin
THINC Academy	1 College Cir	LaGrange, GA	30240	706-443-5826	523-0266	10-12	Dr. Chris Williams
Tybee Island Maritime Academy	PO Box 1519	Tybee Island, GA	31328-1519	912-395-4060		K-5	Patrick Rossiter
Unidos Dual Language Charter S	4475 Hendrix Dr	Forest Park, GA	30297-1244	678-827-7947	827-7948	PK-5	Dr. Prince Bowie
Union Point STEAM Academy	1401 Highway 77 N	Union Point, GA	30669-1109	706-486-4117	486-4974	K-8	Ashlie Miller
Utopian Academy for the Arts Charter S	6630 Camp St	Riverdale, GA	30274	770-892-1644	234-6707	6-8	Dr. Artesius Miller
Walton HS	1590 Bill Murdock Rd	Marietta, GA	30062-5999	770-578-3225	578-3227	9-12	Judith McNeill
Wauka Mtn Multiple Intelligences Academy	5850 Brookton Lula Rd	Gainesville, GA	30506-2909	770-983-3221	983-1019	PK-5	Pam Doig
Webster County HS	7168 Washington St	Preston, GA	31824	229-828-3365	828-2014	9-12	Janie Downer
Wesley International Academy	211 Memorial Dr SE	Atlanta, GA	30312	678-904-9137	904-9138	K-8	Jason Marshall
Westside Atlanta Charter S	1903 Drew Dr NW	Atlanta, GA	30318	404-228-9678		K-8	Delana Reeves
World Language Academy	4670 Winder Hwy	Flowery Branch, GA	30542-3611	770-967-5854	967-3496	PK-4	Britney Bennett
World Language Academy	3215 Poplar Springs Rd	Gainesville, GA	30507	770-533-4004	533-4018	5-8	Laurie Hitzges
Wynnton Arts Academy	2303 Wynnton Rd	Columbus, GA	31906-2540	706-748-3147	748-3151	K-5	Carolyn Mull

Hawaii

School	Address	City,State	Zip code	Telephone	Fax	Grade	Contact
Connections New Century Charter S	174 Kamehameha Ave	Hilo, HI	96720-2865	808-961-3664	961-2665	K-12	John Thatcher
Hakipu'u Learning Center	PO Box 1159	Kaneohe, HI	96744-1159	808-235-9155	235-9160	4-12	Charlene Hoe
Halau Ku Mana Charter S	2101 Makiki Heights Dr	Honolulu, HI	96822	808-945-1600	945-1604	4-12	Keoni Bunag
Hawaii Academy of Arts & Science	PO Box 1494	Pahoa, HI	96778-1494	808-965-3730	965-3733	K-12	Steve Hirakami
Hawaii Technology Academy	94-450 Mokuola St Ste 200	Waipahu, HI	96797	808-676-5444	676-5470	K-12	Leigh Fitzgerald M.Ed.
Innovations Public Charter S	75-5815 Queen Kaahumanu Hwy	Kailua Kona, HI	96740-2013	808-327-6205	327-6209	K-8	Jennifer Hiro
Kamaile Academy	85-180 Ala Akau St	Waianae, HI	96792-2323	808-697-7110	697-7115	PK-12	Anna Winslow
Kamalani Academy	1403 California Ave	Wahiawa, HI	96786	808-203-2993		K-8	Jeffery Vilardi
Kanuikapono Charter S	4333 Kukuihale Rd	Anahola, HI	96703	808-822-9032	482-3055	K-12	Ku'uipo Torio-Kauhane
Kanu 'o Ka 'Aina Charter S	64-1043 Hiiaka St	Kamuela, HI	96743	808-887-8144	887-8146	K-12	Allyson Tamura
Kapolei Charter S	2140 Lauwiliwili St	Kapolei, HI	96707	808-690-9909		9-9	Wanda Villareal
Ka'u Learning Academy	PO Box 89	Naalehu, HI	96772	808-498-0761	498-0763	3-6	Kathryn Tydlacka-McKow
Ka 'Umeke Ka'eo Public Charter S	222 Desha Ave	Hilo, HI	96720-4815	808-933-3482	933-3488	K-10	Olani Lilly
Ka Waihona O Ka Na'auao Charter S	89-195 Farrington Hwy	Waianae, HI	96792-4102	808-620-9030	620-9036	K-8	Alvin Parker
Kawaikini Charter S	3-1821 Kaumualii Hwy Ste J	Lihue, HI	96766	808-632-2032	246-4635	K-12	Jessell Tanaka
Ke Ana La'ahana Public Charter S	PO Box 4997	Hilo, HI	96720	808-961-6228	961-6229	7-12	Mapuana Waipa
Ke Kula Ni'ihau o Kekaha Charter S	PO Box 129	Kekaha, HI	96752	808-337-0481	337-1289	PK-12	Tia Koerte
Ke Kula 'O Nawahiokalani'opu'u Charter S	16-120 Opukahaia St	Keaau, HI	96749-8135	808-982-4260	966-7821	K-8	Dr. Kauanoe Kamana
Ke Kula 'o Samuel Kamakau Lab Charter S	46-500 Kuneki St	Kaneohe, HI	96744	808-235-9175	235-9173	PK-12	Dr. Meahilahila Kelling
Kihei Charter S	PO Box 1098	Kihei, HI	96753	808-875-0700	874-6745	K-12	John Colson
Kona Pacific Public Charter S	PO Box 115	Kealakekua, HI	96750	808-322-4900	322-4906	K-8	Deann Canuteson
Kualapu'u Charter ES	PO Box 260	Kualapuu, HI	96757-0260	808-567-6900	567-6906	K-6	Lydia Trinidad
Kua 'O Ka La Public Charter S	14-5322 Kalapana Kapoho Rd	Pahoa, HI	96778	808-965-5098	965-9618	K-12	
Kula Aupuni Niihau A Kahelelani Aloha	PO Box 610	Kekaha, HI	96752	808-337-2022	337-2033	K-12	Hedy Sullivan
Lanikai ES	140 Alala Rd	Kailua, HI	96734-3199	808-266-7844	266-7848	PK-6	Ed Noh
Malama Honua Charter S	41-054 Ehukai St	Waimanalo, HI	96795	808-259-5522	259-5525	K-2	Denise Espania
Na Wai Ola Public Charter S	181355 Volcano Rd	Mountain View, HI	96771	808-968-2318	968-0778	K-6	Jason Wong
SEEQS Charter S	845 22nd Ave	Honolulu, HI	96816-4521	808-677-3377		6-12	Buffy Cushman-Patz
Thompson Academy	1040 Richards St Ste 220	Honolulu, HI	96813-2920	808-441-8000	683-7062	K-12	Diana Oshiro
University Laboratory S	1776 University Ave #121	Honolulu, HI	96822	808-956-7833	956-7260	K-12	Keoni Jeremiah
Volcano S of Arts & Sciences	PO Box 845	Volcano, HI	96785-0845	808-985-9800	985-9898	K-8	Kalima Cayir
Voyager Charter S	2428 Wilder Ave	Honolulu, HI	96822	808-521-9770	521-9772	K-8	Evan Anderson
Wai'alae ES	1045 19th Ave	Honolulu, HI	96816-4699	808-733-4880	733-4886	K-5	Kapono Ciotti
Waimea Charter MS	67-1229 Mamalahoa Hwy	Kamuela, HI	96743-8429	808-887-6090	887-6087	6-8	Amy Kendziorski M.Ed.
West Hawaii Explorations Academy	73-4460 Queen Kaahumanu Hwy	Kailua Kona, HI	96740-2632	808-327-4751	327-4750	6-12	Heather Nakakura

Idaho

School	Address	City,State	Zip code	Telephone	Fax	Grade	Contact
Academy	1295 Alpine Ave	Pocatello, ID	83202-3100	208-232-1447	232-1448	K-8	Joel Lovstedt
American Heritage Charter S	1736 S 35th W	Idaho Falls, ID	83402	208-529-6570	529-3344	K-9	Shawn Rose
Another Choice Virtual Charter S	1014 W Hemingway Blvd	Nampa, ID	83651-1733	208-475-4255	475-4274	K-12	Dr. Kelsey Williams
ANSER Charter S	202 E 42nd St	Garden City, ID	83714	208-426-9840	426-9863	K-8	Michelle Dunstan
Bird Charter S	614 S Madison Ave	Sandpoint, ID	83864-8724	208-255-7771	263-9441	6-12	Alan Millar
Blackfoot Charter Community Learning Ctr	2801 Hunters Loop	Blackfoot, ID	83221-6206	208-782-0744	782-1330	K-8	Debbie Steele
Chief Tahgee Elementary Academy	PO Box 217	Fort Hall, ID	83203	208-237-2710	237-1734	K-6	Joel Weaver
Coeur D'Alene Charter Academy	4904 N Duncan Dr	Coeur d Alene, ID	83815-8329	208-676-1667	930-4215	6-12	Dan Nicklay
Compass Charter S	2511 W Cherry Ln	Meridian, ID	83642-1135	208-855-2802	895-0197	K-12	Kelly Trudeau
Connor Academy	1295 Alpine Ave	Chubbuck, ID	83202	208-232-1447		K-8	Joel Lovstedt
Falcon Ridge Charter S	278 S Ten Mile Rd	Kuna, ID	83634	208-922-9228	922-4198	K-8	Mark Green
Gem Prep S	5226 Southside Blvd	Nampa, ID	83686	208-468-2848		K-12	Stacey Walker
Heritage Academy	500 S Lincoln Ave	Jerome, ID	83338	208-595-1617	595-1618	K-8	Dr. Christine Ivie
Heritage Community Charter S	1803 E Ustick Rd	Caldwell, ID	83605	208-453-8070	453-8077	K-8	Javier Castaneda
Idaho Arts Charter S	1220 5th St N	Nampa, ID	83687	208-463-4324	468-0572	K-12	Jackie Collins
Idaho College & Career Readiness Academy	1965 S Eagle Rd Ste 150	Meridian, ID	83642	866-917-2420	917-2416	9-12	Monti Pittman
Idaho Connects Online S	12639 W Explorer Dr Ste 185	Boise, ID	83713	208-287-3668	287-3671	6-12	Vickie McCullough
Idaho Digital Learning Academy	PO Box 10017	Boise, ID	83707	208-342-0207	577-4034	K-12	Dr. Cheryl Charlton
Idaho Distance Education Academy	PO Box 338	Deary, ID	83823-0338	208-877-1513	877-1713	K-12	Tera Reeves
Idaho Science and Technology Charter S	21 N 550 W	Blackfoot, ID	83221	208-785-7827	785-9913	6-8	Devin Larsen
Idaho Virtual Academy	1965 S Eagle Rd Ste 190	Meridian, ID	83642-9246	208-322-3559	322-3688	K-12	Kelly Edgington
Inspire Virtual Charter S	600 N Steelhead Way Ste 164	Boise, ID	83704	208-322-4002	322-4008	K-12	
iSucceed Virtual HS	6148 N Discovery Way # 120	Boise, ID	83713	208-375-3116	375-3117	9-12	Katie Allison
Jefferson Charter S	1209 Adam Smith Ave	Caldwell, ID	83605-5487	208-455-8772	455-8713	K-12	Chuck Ward
Kootenai Bridge Academy	606 River Ave	Coeur D Alene, ID	83814	208-930-4515	930-4791	11-12	Charles Kenna
Legacy Charter S	4015 Legacy Way	Nampa, ID	83686	208-467-0947	467-0948	K-6	Seth Stallcop
Liberty Charter S	9955 Kris Jensen Ln	Nampa, ID	83686	208-466-7952	466-7961	K-12	Rebecca Stallcop
McKenna Charter HS	675 S Haskett St	Mountain Home, ID	83647	208-580-2449	580-2450	9-12	Eric Freed
McKenna Montessori S	1305 E 8th N	Mountain Home, ID	83647	208-580-2347		PK-3	Eric Freed
Meridian Medical Arts Charter HS	1789 E Heritage Park Ln	Meridian, ID	83646	208-855-4075	895-1996	9-12	Scott Hill
Meridian Technical Charter HS	3800 N Locust Grove Rd	Meridian, ID	83646-5510	208-288-2928	288-5685	9-12	Randy Yadon
Monticello Montessori Charter S	4707 Sweetwater Way	Ammon, ID	83406	208-419-0742	419-0765	K-6	Erica Kemery
Moscow Charter S	1723 E F St	Moscow, ID	83843-9571	208-883-3195	892-3855	K-8	Tony Bonuccelli
North Idaho STEM Charter Academy	PO Box 434	Rathdrum, ID	83858	208-687-8002		K-9	Scott Thomson
North Star Charter S	839 N Linder Rd	Eagle, ID	83616	208-939-9600	939-6090	K-12	Melissa Andersen
North Valley Academy	906 Main St	Gooding, ID	83330	208-934-4567	934-4522	K-12	Gayle DeSmet
Palouse Prairie Charter S	PO Box 9511	Moscow, ID	83843	208-882-3684	882-3689	K-8	Jeneille Branen
Pathways in Education Charter S	124 Holly St	Nampa, ID	83686	208-505-4800	473-0320	9-12	Susan Lux
Payette River Technical Academy	721 W 12th St Ste A	Emmett, ID	83617	208-365-0985	365-7800	9-12	Patrick Goff
Pocatello Community Charter S	995 S Arthur Ave	Pocatello, ID	83204-3400	208-478-2522	478-2622	K-8	Michael Mendive
Rolling Hills Charter S	8900 Horseshoe Bend Rd	Boise, ID	83714-3859	208-939-5400	939-5401	K-8	Shane Pratt M.Ed.
Sage International S of Boise	431 E Parkcenter Blvd	Boise, ID	83706	208-343-7243	287-0829	K-12	Micah Doramus
Syringa Mountain S	4021 Glenbrook Dr	Hailey, ID	83333	208-806-2880		K-8	Christine Fonner
Taylors Crossing Charter S	1445 N Wood River Dr	Idaho Falls, ID	83401	208-552-0397	904-3814	K-12	Daniel Wendt
Upper Carmen Charter S	PO Box 33	Carmen, ID	83462	208-756-4590	756-6695	K-12	Sue Smith
Victory Charter S	9779 Kris Jensen Ln	Nampa, ID	83686-4741	208-442-9400	442-9401	K-12	Dr. Marianne Saunders
Village Charter S	8444 W Fairview Ave	Boise, ID	83706	208-336-2000	367-1234	K-8	Tony Richard
Vision Charter S	19291 Ward Ln	Caldwell, ID	83605	208-455-9220	455-9121	K-12	Wendy Oldenkamp
White Pine Charter S	2959 John Adams Pkwy	Ammon, ID	83406-4508	208-522-4432	522-4452	K-8	Jeremy Clarke
Xavier Charter S	1218 N College Rd W	Twin Falls, ID	83301	208-734-3947	733-1348	K-12	Gary Moon

Illinois

School	Address	City,State	Zip code	Telephone	Fax	Grade	Contact
Academy for Global Citizenship	4647 W 47th St	Chicago, IL	60632	773-582-1100	582-1101	K-8	Dr. Jennifer Moore

School	Address	City,State	Zip code	Telephone	Fax	Grade	Contact
Acero Charter S - Brighton Park	4420 S Fairfield Ave	Chicago, IL	60632	773-455-5434	455-5435	K-8	Luke Corry
Acero Charter S - Carlos Fuentes Campus	2845 W Barry Ave	Chicago, IL	60618-7015	312-279-9826	279-9852	K-8	Joanne Tanner
Acero Charter S - Cruz	7416 N Ridge Blvd	Chicago, IL	60645	312-455-5440	455-5441	K-12	Molly Robinson
Acero Charter S - De Las Casas	1641 W 16th St	Chicago, IL	60608-2039	312-432-3224	432-1066	K-8	Courtney Mix-Binish
Acero Charter S - Garcia HS	4248 W 47th St	Chicago, IL	60632	773-579-3480	376-5785	9-12	Lindsay Ahlgren-Blythe
Acero Charter S - Idar	5050 S Homan Ave	Chicago, IL	60632	312-455-5450	455-5451	PK-8	Sandra Medina-Alba
Acero Charter S - Octavio Paz	2651 W 23rd St	Chicago, IL	60608-3609	773-890-1054	890-1069	K-8	Karem Gomez
Acero Charter S - Officer Donald Marquez	2916 W 47th St	Chicago, IL	60632-1907	773-321-2200	321-2250	K-8	Allison Hansen
Acero Charter S - Omar Torres	4248 W 47th St	Chicago, IL	60632	773-579-3475	376-5645	K-8	Christopher Allen
Acero Charter S - Roberto Clemente	2050 N Natchez Ave	Chicago, IL	60707	312-455-5425	455-5456	K-8	Maisha Copeland
Acero Charter S - Rufino Tamayo Campus	5135 S California Ave	Chicago, IL	60632-2124	773-434-6355	434-5036	K-8	Matthew Katz
Acero Charter S - Sandra Cisneros	2744 W Pershing Rd	Chicago, IL	60632	773-376-8830	376-8825	K-8	Adams Sparks
Acero Charter S - Santiago	2510 W Cortez St	Chicago, IL	60622	312-455-5410	455-5411	K-8	Melissa Sweazy
Acero Charter S - Soto	5025 S Saint Louis Ave	Chicago, IL	60632	312-455-5446	455-5447	9-12	Kelly Smith
Acero Charter S - SPC Daniel Zizumbo	4248 W 47th St	Chicago, IL	60632	773-579-3470	376-5005	K-8	Christopher Allen
ACE Technical Charter HS	5410 S State St	Chicago, IL	60609-6342	773-548-8705	548-8706	9-12	Marvin Talley
Amandla Charter S	6820 S Washtenaw Ave	Chicago, IL	60629	773-535-7150	535-7151	6-12	Alyssa Nickow
Asian Human Services - Passages Charter	1643 W Bryn Mawr Ave	Chicago, IL	60660	773-433-3530	769-3229	PK-8	Maritza Francois
ASPIRA - Antonia Pantoja Alternative HS	3121 N Pulaski Rd	Chicago, IL	60641	773-252-0970	427-0872	9-12	Dr. Martha Zurita
ASPIRA Business and Finance HS	2989 N Milwaukee Ave	Chicago, IL	60618	773-252-0970		9-12	Hector Freytas
ASPIRA - Early College HS	3986 W Barry Ave	Chicago, IL	60618	773-252-0970	267-3568	9-12	Brenda Stolle
ASPIRA Haugan MS	3729 W Leland Ave	Chicago, IL	60625-5706	773-252-0970	267-3568	6-8	Ricardo Garcia
Cambridge Lakes S	900 Wester Blvd	Pingree Grove, IL	60140-2050	847-464-4300	464-0318	PK-8	Julie Skaggs
Catalyst Charter - Maria	6727 S California Ave	Chicago, IL	60629	773-993-1770	993-1771	K-12	Jasmia Fowler
Catalyst Charter S - Circle Rock	5608 W Washington Blvd	Chicago, IL	60644	773-945-5025	626-2345	K-8	Elizabeth Jamison-Dunn
Chicago Collegiate Charter S	11816 S Indiana Ave	Chicago, IL	60628	773-536-9098	264-5792	4-9	Tracie Sanlin
Chicago International Charter S - Avalon	1501 E 83rd Pl	Chicago, IL	60619-6501	773-721-0858	731-0142	K-8	Lindsay Robinson
Chicago International Charter S - Basil	1816 W Garfield Blvd	Chicago, IL	60609-5606	773-778-9455	778-9456	K-8	Robert Curry
Chicago International Charter S - Bond	13300 S Langley Ave	Chicago, IL	60827	773-468-1300	253-0988	K-6	Lloyd Knight
Chicago International Charter S Longwood	1309 W 95th St	Chicago, IL	60643-1496	773-238-5330	238-5350	3-12	Kenyatta Stansberry
Chicago International Charter S - Loomis	9535 S Loomis St	Chicago, IL	60643	773-429-8955	429-8441	K-2	Lindsey Girard
Chicago International Charter S Prairie	11530 S Prairie Ave	Chicago, IL	60628-5612	773-928-0480	928-6971	K-8	Jessica Christopher
Chicago International Charter S - Quest	1443 N Ogden Ave	Chicago, IL	60610	773-565-2100	951-2906	6-12	Ayanna Gore
Chicago International Charter S W Belden	2245 N McVicker Ave	Chicago, IL	60639-2766	773-637-9430	637-9791	K-8	Colleen Collins
Chicago Intl Charter S - Bucktown	2235 N Hamilton Ave	Chicago, IL	60647-3303	773-645-3321	645-3327	K-8	Sophia Halkias
Chicago Intl Charter S - Irving Park	3820 N Spaulding Ave	Chicago, IL	60618-4413	773-433-5000	433-5009	K-8	J.W. Kuebler
Chicago Intl Charter S Northtown	3900 W Peterson Ave	Chicago, IL	60659-3162	773-478-3655	478-6029	9-12	Torry Bennett
Chicago Intl Charter S Ralph Ellison	1817 W 80th St	Chicago, IL	60620	773-478-4434	224-2594	9-12	Dr. Kimberly Hinton
Chicago Intl Charter S Washington Park	110 E 61st St	Chicago, IL	60637	773-324-3300	324-3302	K-8	Sarah Horn
Chicago Intl Charter S Wrightwood	8130 S California Ave	Chicago, IL	60652-2716	773-434-4575	434-2026	K-8	Jillian Carew
Chicago Math and Science Academy	7212 N Clark St	Chicago, IL	60626	773-761-8960	761-8961	6-12	Ali Kuran
Chicago Virtual Charter S	38 S Peoria St	Chicago, IL	60607-2628	312-267-4486	676-3689	K-12	Dr. Richard Lebron
Christopher House Charter ES	5235 W Belden St	Chicago, IL	60639	773-922-7542	922-7559	K-4	Kristin Novy
EPIC Academy	8255 S Houston Ave	Chicago, IL	60617-2191	773-535-7930	535-7934	9-12	Matthew King
Erie Charter S	1405 N Washtenaw Ave	Chicago, IL	60622	773-486-7161	486-7234	K-8	Eleanor Nicholson
Excel Academy - Woodlawn	7530 S South Shore Dr	Chicago, IL	60649	773-902-7800	902-7615	9-12	Renee Carter
Foundations College Prep S	1233 W 109th Pl	Chicago, IL	60643	773-298-5800		6-12	Sarah Hunko-Baker
Frazier Preparatory Academy	3711 W Douglas Blvd	Chicago, IL	60623	773-521-1303	521-1365	PK-8	Dr. Patrice Payne
Galapagos Charter S	2605 School St	Rockford, IL	61101-5264	815-708-7946	708-7966	K-8	Michael Lane
Great Lakes Academy Charter S	8401 S Saginaw Ave	Chicago, IL	60617	773-530-3040	530-3039	K-3	Katherin Myers
Horizon Science Academy - SW Charter	5401 S Western Blvd	Chicago, IL	60609	773-498-3355	498-4984	K-10	Matt Yildiz
HSA Belmont Charter S	2456 N Mango Ave	Chicago, IL	60639	773-237-2702	237-2726	K-8	Serdar Kartal
HSA McKinley Park Charter S	2245 W Pershing Rd	Chicago, IL	60609-2211	773-247-8400	247-8401	K-12	Cafer Cengiz
Instituto Health Sciences Career Academy	2520 S Western Ave	Chicago, IL	60608	773-890-8020	376-8573	9-12	Hillyn Sennholtz
Instituto - Justice Lozano	2570 S Blue Island Ave	Chicago, IL	60608-4817	773-890-8060	890-1537	9-12	Christine Diaz
Intrinsic Charter HS	4540 W Belmont Ave	Chicago, IL	60641	708-887-2735	887-2812	7-12	Melissa Zaikos
Jackson Charter S	315 Summit St	Rockford, IL	61107	815-316-0093	316-0170	K-8	Angelique Watson
KIPP Ascend MS	1616 S Avers Ave	Chicago, IL	60623	773-521-4399	521-4766	5-8	Lauren Henley
KIPP Ascend PS	1440 S Christiana Ave	Chicago, IL	60623	773-522-1261	522-1185	K-4	Jacob Boesch
KIPP Bloom College Prep S	5515 S Lowe Ave	Chicago, IL	60621	773-938-8565	783-6910	5-8	Ellen Sale
KIPP Create College Prep S	4818 W Ohio St	Chicago, IL	60644	773-938-8553	287-4548	5-8	Billy Warden
KIPP One Academy	730 N Pulaski Rd	Chicago, IL	60624	773-938-8578	589-4441	K-6	Rashid Bell
LEARN 6 Charter S	601 D St Bldg 130H	Great Lakes, IL	60088	847-473-3845	473-2988	K-8	Kelly Tyson
LEARN 7 Charter ES	3021 W Carroll Ave	Chicago, IL	60612	773-584-4350	826-7918	K-5	Margie Smagacz
LEARN 8 Charter MS	3021 W Carroll Ave	Chicago, IL	60612	773-584-4300	826-7933	6-8	Ryan Rampelsreiter
LEARN 9 Campus in Waukegan	1200 W Glen Flora Ave	Waukegan, IL	60085	847-377-0690		K-4	Maytee Diez
LEARN 10 Charter S	1811 Morrow Ave	North Chicago, IL	60064-3206	847-693-5021		K-4	Christian Cigan
Learn 10 in North Chicago	1811 Morrow Ave	North Chicago, IL	60064	847-473-3845		K-3	Christian Cigan
LEARN Charter S Campbell Campus	212 S Francisco Ave	Chicago, IL	60612	773-826-0370	826-0109	K-5	Karin McGuire
LEARN Charter S Excel Campus	3021 W Carroll Ave	Chicago, IL	60612	312-243-7001	243-7160	K-5	Sekou Robertson
LEARN Charter S Hunter Perkins Campus	1700 W 83rd St	Chicago, IL	60620	773-488-1634	488-1753	K-7	Jon Bennett
LEARN Charter S - Romano Butler Campus	1132 S Homan Ave	Chicago, IL	60624-4344	773-722-0200	826-0015	PK-8	Robin Johnson
LEARN Charter S - South Chicago Campus	8914 S Buffalo Ave	Chicago, IL	60617	773-722-8577		K-8	David Lewis
Legacy Academy for Excellence Charter S	4029 Prairie Rd	Rockford, IL	61102-4501	815-961-1100		K-12	Barbara Forte
Legacy Charter S	4217 W 18th St	Chicago, IL	60623-2325	773-542-1640	542-1699	PK-8	Richard Glass
Legal Prep Charter Academy	4319 W Washington Blvd	Chicago, IL	60624	773-922-7800	386-5796	9-12	Samuel Finkelstein
Little Black Pearl Art and Design Center	1060 E 47th St	Chicago, IL	60653	773-285-1211	285-1633	9-12	Monica Haslip
Locke Charter Academy	3141 W Jackson Blvd	Chicago, IL	60612-2729	773-265-7232	265-7258	PK-8	Patrick Love
Montessori S of Englewood	6936 S Hermitage Ave	Chicago, IL	60636	773-535-9255	535-9590	K-6	Rita Nolan
Morgan ES	420 N Colfax St	Byron, IL	61010-1438	815-234-5491	234-4094	PK-5	Buster Barton
Moving Everest Charter S	416 N Laramie Ave	Chicago, IL	60644	312-683-9695	674-7221	K-2	Mika Krause
Namaste Charter S	3737 S Paulina St	Chicago, IL	60609-2047	773-715-9558	376-6495	K-8	Stephanie Bloom
Noble Academy	1443 N Ogden Ave	Chicago, IL	60610	312-574-1527	575-4217	9-12	Lauren Boros
Noble - Baker College Prep	2710 E 89th St	Chicago, IL	60617	773-535-6340	913-0346	9-12	Mary Arrigo
Noble - Butler College Prep	821 E 103rd St	Chicago, IL	60628	773-535-5490	442-0343	9-12	Christopher Goins
Noble - Chicago Bulls College Prep S	2040 W Adams St	Chicago, IL	60612	773-534-7599	850-0192	9-12	Wendy Erskine
Noble - DRW College Prep	931 S Homan Ave	Chicago, IL	60624	773-893-4500	893-4501	9-12	Matthew Kelley
Noble - Gary Comer College Prep	7131 S South Chicago Ave	Chicago, IL	60619	773-729-3969	729-3960	9-12	Estee Kelly
Noble - Golder College Prep	1454 W Superior St	Chicago, IL	60642	312-265-9925	243-8402	9-12	Stephanie Hernandez
Noble - Hansberry College Prep	8748 S Aberdeen St	Chicago, IL	60620	773-729-3400	304-1995	9-12	Kashawndra Wilson
Noble - ITW David Speer Academy	5321 W Grand Ave	Chicago, IL	60639	773-622-7484	304-2700	9-12	Tom Mulder
Noble - Johnson College Prep	6350 S Stewart Ave	Chicago, IL	60621	312-348-1888	278-0449	9-12	Matthew Brown
Noble - Mansueto HS	2911 W 47th St	Chicago, IL	60632	773-349-8200	409-0440	9-12	Darko Simunovic
Noble - Muchin College Prep	1 N State St	Chicago, IL	60602	312-445-4680	332-0058	9-12	Emily Mason
Noble - Pritzker College Prep	4131 W Cortland St	Chicago, IL	60639-4923	773-394-2848	394-2931	9-12	Pablo Sierra
Noble - Rauner College Prep	1337 W Ohio St	Chicago, IL	60642-6430	312-226-5345	226-3552	9-12	Jennifer Reid
Noble - Rowe - Clark Math & Science Acad	3645 W Chicago Ave	Chicago, IL	60651-3934	773-242-2212	826-6936	9-12	Brenda Cora
Noble Street College Prep	1010 N Noble St	Chicago, IL	60642	773-862-1449	278-0421	9-12	Ellen Metz
Noble - UIC College Prep	1231 S Damen Ave	Chicago, IL	60608	312-768-4858	496-7149	9-12	Tressie McDonough
North Lawndale College Prep - Christiana	1615 S Christiana Ave	Chicago, IL	60623	773-542-1490	542-1492	9-12	Senita Murphy
North Lawndale College Prep - Collins	1313 S Sacramento Dr	Chicago, IL	60623-2218	773-542-6766	542-6995	9-12	Senita Murphy
Perspectives Charter MS	8131 S May St	Chicago, IL	60620	773-358-6300	358-6399	6-8	Sauda Porter
Perspectives - HS of Technology	8131 S May St	Chicago, IL	60620	773-358-6120	358-6129	9-12	Eron Powell
Perspectives - Joslin HS	1930 S Archer Ave	Chicago, IL	60616-6505	312-225-7400	225-7411	6-12	Stephen Todd
Perspectives - Leadership Academy	8131 S May St	Chicago, IL	60620-3007	773-358-6100	358-6199	6-12	Sarah Severson
Perspectives - Math & Science Academy	3663 S Wabash Ave	Chicago, IL	60653	773-358-6800	358-6055	6-12	Stephen Todd
Plato Learning Academy	5545 W Harrison St	Chicago, IL	60644	773-413-3090	413-3095	K-8	Charles Williams
Polaris Charter Academy	620 N Sawyer Ave	Chicago, IL	60624-1528	773-534-0820	534-6645	K-8	Michelle Navarre
Prairie Crossing Charter S	1571 Jones Point Rd	Grayslake, IL	60030-3536	847-543-9722	543-9744	K-8	Geoff Doigan
Providence Englewood Charter S	6515 S Ashland Ave	Chicago, IL	60636-3003	773-434-0202	434-0196	K-8	Angela Johnson-Williams
Quest Charter Academy	2503 N University St	Peoria, IL	61604-2601	309-402-0030	685-3001	5-12	Dr. Nicole Woods
Robertson Charter S	2240 E Geddes Ave	Decatur, IL	62526-5127	217-428-7072	428-9214	K-8	Niki Fenderson
Rowe ES	1424 N Cleaver St	Chicago, IL	60642	312-445-5870	445-5875	K-8	Tony Sutton
Shabazz Academy	7823 S Ellis Ave	Chicago, IL	60619-3213	773-651-1221	651-0302	K-8	Shannon Mason
SIU East St. Louis Charter S	601 James R Thompson Blvd	E Saint Louis, IL	62201-1129	618-482-8370	482-8372	9-12	Veronica Washington
Sizemore Academy of B Shabazz	6547 S Stewart Ave	Chicago, IL	60621	773-651-1661	651-4125	K-8	Danielle Robinson
Southland College Prep	4601 Sauk Trl	Richton Park, IL	60471-1470	708-748-8105		9-12	Dr. Blondean Davis
Springfield Ball Charter S	2530 E Ash St	Springfield, IL	62703-5600	217-525-3275	525-3316	PK-8	Matthew Fraas
UCCS - Carter Woodson Campus	4444 S Evans Ave	Chicago, IL	60653	773-624-0700	624-0707	6-8	Jarred Brown
UCCS - Donoghue Campus	707 E 37th St	Chicago, IL	60653-1406	773-285-5301	268-2088	PK-5	Erin Slack
UCCS - North Kenwood/Oakland Campus	1119 E 46th St	Chicago, IL	60653-4403	773-536-2399	536-2435	PK-5	Tonya Howell
UCCS - Woodlawn Campus	6420 S University Ave	Chicago, IL	60637-3659	773-752-8101	324-0653	6-12	Kioran Palmer-Klein
Urban Prep Academy - Englewood HS	6201 S Stewart Ave	Chicago, IL	60621-3247	773-535-9724	535-0012	9-12	Dion Steele
Urban Prep - Bronzeville	521 E 35th St	Chicago, IL	60616	773-624-3444	624-3405	9-12	Conrad Timbers-Ausar
Urban Prep - West HS	1326 W 14th Pl	Chicago, IL	60608	773-534-8860	534-1050	9-12	Patrick Robinson
West Town Academy	534 N Sacramento Blvd	Chicago, IL	60612	312-563-9044	563-9672	10-12	Alicia Schutter
YCCS-Academy of Scholastic Achievement	4651 W Madison St	Chicago, IL	60644-3646	773-921-1315	854-8397	10-12	Nicole Simpson Ed.D.

School	Address	City,State	Zip code	Telephone	Fax	Grade	Contact
YCCS-Addams HS	1814 S Union Ave	Chicago, IL	60616-1045	312-563-1746	563-1756	9-12	Theresa Comparini
YCCS-Albizu Campos HS	2739 W Division St	Chicago, IL	60622-2854	773-342-8022	342-6609	10-12	Dr. Carmen Rodriguez
YCCS-Association House HS	1116 N Kedzie Ave	Chicago, IL	60651-4152	773-772-7170	772-8617	10-12	David Piper
YCCS-Austin Career Education Center	5352 W Chicago Ave	Chicago, IL	60651-2857	773-626-6988	626-2641	10-12	Dr. Anne Gottlieb
YCCS-CCA Academy	1231 S Pulaski Rd	Chicago, IL	60623	773-762-2272	762-2065	10-12	Genessa Schultz
YCCS-Chatham Academy	9035 S Langley Ave	Chicago, IL	60619	773-651-1500	651-1523	10-12	Lisa Williams
YCCS-Community Youth Development Inst	7836 S Union Ave	Chicago, IL	60620-2409	773-224-2273	224-2214	10-12	Keena Robinson
YCCS-Harvey Middle College S	10001 S Woodlawn Ave	Chicago, IL	60628-1645	773-291-6518	291-6199	10-12	Matthew Trujillo
YCCS-Houston HS	7847 S Jeffery Blvd	Chicago, IL	60649	773-723-9630	723-9022	10-12	Dr. Dionne Kirksey
YCCS-Innovation HS	17 N State St Fl 3	Chicago, IL	60602	312-999-9360	999-9361	10-12	Melissa Cortirla
YCCS-Latino Youth HS	2001 S California Ave	Chicago, IL	60608-2486	773-648-2130	648-2098	10-12	
YCCS-McKinley Lakeside Academy	2920 S Wabash Ave	Chicago, IL	60616	312-949-5010	949-5015	10-12	
YCCS-Sullivan House Alternative HS	8164 S South Chicago Ave	Chicago, IL	60617-1041	773-978-8680	375-1482	9-12	Dr. Thomas Gattuso
YCCS-Truman Middle College HS	1145 W Wilson Ave	Chicago, IL	60640-6063	773-907-4840	907-4844	9-12	Michelle Yoo
YCCS Virtual HS	1900 W Van Buren St Rm 2417	Chicago, IL	60612	312-429-0027	243-5733	10-12	Mary Bradley
YCCS-Westside Holistic Leadership Acad	4909 W Division St	Chicago, IL	60651-3161	773-261-0994	261-1029	9-12	Early King
YCCS-Youth Connection Leadership Acdmy	3424 S State St	Chicago, IL	60616-5000	312-225-4668	225-4862	9-12	Keisha Davis-Johnson
Young Womens Leadership S	2641 S Calumet Ave	Chicago, IL	60616-2901	312-949-9400	949-9142	8-12	Dr. Vanesa Thompson
YouthBuild McLean County Charter S	360 Wylie Dr Ste 305	Normal, IL	61761	309-454-3898	454-3913	9-12	Suzanne Fitzgerald

Indiana

School	Address	City,State	Zip code	Telephone	Fax	Grade	Contact
ACE Prep Academy	5326 Hillside Ave	Indianapolis, IN	46220	317-744-9847	744-9836	K-5	Anna Shults
Anderson Preparatory Academy	101 W 29th St	Anderson, IN	46016-5209	765-649-8472		K-12	Jill Barker
Aspire Charter Academy	4900 W 15th Ave	Gary, IN	46406	219-944-7400	359-2175	K-8	ReNae Robinson
Avondale Meadows Academy	3980 Meadows Dr	Indianapolis, IN	46205-3114	317-803-3182	803-2367	K-5	Chrystal Westerhaus
Bloomington Project S	349 S Walnut St	Bloomington, IN	47401	812-558-0041	334-5873	K-8	Catherine Diersing
Bowman Leadership Academy	975 W 6th Ave	Gary, IN	46402-1708	219-883-4826	883-1331	K-12	Sarita Stevens
Brown Charter Academy	3600 N German Church Rd	Indianapolis, IN	46235-8504	317-891-0730	891-0908	K-8	James Hill
Campagna Academy Charter S	7403 Cline Ave	Schererville, IN	46375-2645	219-322-8614	322-8436	9-12	Elena Dwyre
Canaan Community Academy	8775 N Canaan Main St	Canaan, IN	47224	812-839-0003		K-6	Donna Taylor
Career Academy South Bend	3801 Crescent Cir	South Bend, IN	46628	574-299-9800	288-6125	6-12	Lydia Jagger
Carpe Diem - Northwest	5435 W Pike Plaza Rd	Indianapolis, IN	46254	317-808-8749		6-12	Rosalie Pettigrew
Charter School of the Dunes	7300 Melton Rd	Gary, IN	46403	219-939-9690	939-9031	K-8	Justin Stok
Christel House Academy South	2717 S East St	Indianapolis, IN	46225-2104	317-783-4690	783-4693	K-12	Jenny Reynolds
Christel House Academy West	55 N Tibbs Ave	Indianapolis, IN	46222	317-783-4901	951-2182	K-5	Richard Hunt
Circle City Prep	4002 N Franklin Rd	Indianapolis, IN	46226	317-721-8515	947-1329	K-1	Megan Murphy
Community Montessori S	4102 Saint Joseph Rd	New Albany, IN	47150-9750	812-948-1000	948-0441	PK-12	Barbara Burke-Fondren
Damar Charter Academy	5125 Decatur Blvd	Indianapolis, IN	46241-7511	317-455-2400	455-2447	K-12	Aimee Brown
Decatur Township S for Excellence	5106 S High School Rd	Indianapolis, IN	46221-3606	317-856-0900	856-0143	7-12	Tim VanWanzeele
Discovery Charter S	800 Canonie Dr	Chesterton, IN	46304	219-983-9800	929-5723	K-8	Ernesto Martinez
Donnan Elementary & MS	1202 E Troy Ave	Indianapolis, IN	46203	317-217-1979		PK-8	Michael Dunagan
East Chicago Lighthouse Charter S	3916 Pulaski St	East Chicago, IN	46312	219-378-7450	378-9070	K-7	Jessica Beasley
East Chicago Urban Enterprise Academy	1402 E Chicago Ave	East Chicago, IN	46312-3587	219-392-3650	392-3652	K-8	Veronica Eskew
Enlace Academy	3725 Kiel Ave	Indianapolis, IN	46107	317-383-0607		K-7	Bernice Armstrong
Enlace Academy	3725 Kiel Ave	Indianapolis, IN	46224	317-383-0607	383-0605	K-7	Kevin Kubacki
Excel Center South Bend	2721 Kenwood Ave	South Bend, IN	46628	574-314-5570	314-5571	9-12	Justin Zobrosky
Excel Center	1329 Applegate Ln	Clarksville, IN	47129	812-283-7908	645-3885	9-12	Lakia Osborne
Excel Center	630 Nichol Ave	Anderson, IN	46016-1247	317-524-3930	374-0047	9-12	Brandon Marks
Excel Center	2855 N Franklin Rd	Indianapolis, IN	46219	317-524-3910	429-1015	9-12	Corey Emery
Excel Center	300 N 17 St	Noblesville, IN	46060	317-524-4410	565-5284	9-12	Dr. Steve Dillon
Excel Center	3919 Madison Ave	Indianapolis, IN	46227	317-524-4420	275-7879	9-12	Khalilah Palmer
Excel Center	1635 W Michigan St	Indianapolis, IN	46222	317-524-4141	524-4337	9-12	Khalilah Palmer
Excel Center	101 W Superior St	Kokomo, IN	46901-4658	317-524-3642	457-3367	9-12	Tom Pengelly
Excel Center	615 N 18th St	Lafayette, IN	47904-3413	317-524-3641	420-7916	9-12	Danielle White
Excel Center	1215 S J St	Richmond, IN	47374	317-524-3734	935-7511	9-12	Tyler Stewart
Faulkner Academy	1111 W 2nd St	Marion, IN	46952-3674	765-662-9910	662-9918	K-6	Janice Adams
Gary Lighthouse Charter S	3201 Pierce St	Gary, IN	46408	219-884-2407	884-4858	K-7	Rodney Bly
Gary Middle College	131 E 5th Ave	Gary, IN	46402	219-888-7120	886-6646	9-12	Joseph Arredondo
Geist Montessori S	13942 E 96th St	Mc Cordsville, IN	46055-9811	317-335-1158	335-1265	K-8	Dr. Susan Fries
Global Preparatory Academy	2033 Sugar Grove Ave	Indianapolis, IN	46202	317-226-4244	226-3469	K-8	Mariama Carson
Hammond Academy of Science & Tech	33 Muenich Ct	Hammond, IN	46320-1706	219-852-0500	852-4153	6-12	Dr. Sean Egan
Herron HS	110 E 16th St	Indianapolis, IN	46202-2404	317-231-0010	231-3759	9-12	Janet McNeal
Higher Institute of Arts & Technology	5861 Harrison St	Merrillville, IN	46410	219-359-1522	239-2863	K-6	Erica Brownfield M.Ed.
Hoosier Academy	2855 N Franklin Rd	Indianapolis, IN	46219	317-547-1400	547-1500	K-6	Dr. Byron Ernest
Hoosier Academy	2855 N Franklin Rd	Indianapolis, IN	46219	317-495-6494	454-0670	7-12	Christopher Chalker
Hope Academy	8102 Clearvista Pkwy	Indianapolis, IN	46256-1661	317-572-9356	849-1455	9-12	Linda Gagyi
Howe Community HS	4900 Julian Ave	Indianapolis, IN	46201-3755	317-693-1980		7-12	Tyler Small
Ignite Achievement Academy	1002 W 25th St	Indianapolis, IN	46208	317-226-4242		K-6	Brooke Beavers
Indiana College Preparatory S	4050 E 38th St	Indianapolis, IN	46218-1444	317-914-5868		K-8	Ashely Green
Indiana Connections Academy	6640 Intech Blvd Ste 250	Indianapolis, IN	46278	317-550-3188	818-6000	K-12	Stephanie Chi
Indiana Math and Science Academy	4575 W 38th St	Indianapolis, IN	46254-3313	317-298-0025	282-0505	K-8	Murat Atlihan
Indiana Math and Science Academy North	7435 N Keystone Ave	Indianapolis, IN	46240-4377	317-259-7300	259-7363	K-12	Onder Secen
Indianapolis Academy of Excellence	1145 E 22nd St	Indianapolis, IN	46202	317-653-4009	653-4008	K-6	Tara Gustin
Indianapolis Lighthouse Charter S	1780 Sloan Ave	Indianapolis, IN	46203-3640	317-351-1534	351-1804	PK-12	Kim Randall
Indianapolis Lighthouse Charter S East	4002 N Franklin Rd	Indianapolis, IN	46226-5297	317-897-2472	897-0302	7-12	Jeremy Wolley
Indianapolis Metropolitan HS	1635 W Michigan St	Indianapolis, IN	46222-3852	317-524-4638	524-4114	9-12	Christina Lear
Indiana Virtual S	500 E 96th St Ste 400	Indianapolis, IN	46240	317-581-5355	581-5399	6-12	Lora Feeser
Insight S of Indiana	2855 N Franklin Rd	Indianapolis, IN	46219	317-495-6494	454-0670	7-12	Kathy Coe
Inspire Academy - A S of Inquiry	2801 E 16th St	Muncie, IN	47302	765-216-7980	216-7798	PK-8	Leslie Draper
Irvington Community S	6705 Julian Ave	Indianapolis, IN	46219-6642	317-357-5359	357-9752	K-12	Tim Mulherin
Johnson Academy	4625 Werling Dr	Fort Wayne, IN	46806-3410	260-441-8727	441-9357	K-5	Dawn Starks
Joshua Academy	1230 E Illinois St	Evansville, IN	47711-5745	812-401-6300	401-6307	K-6	Pamela Decker
Kindezi Academy	3421 N Keystone Ave	Indianapolis, IN	46218-1133	317-226-4269	226-3338	K-6	Kevin Kubacki
KIPP Indy College Prep MS	1740 E 30th St	Indianapolis, IN	46218	317-547-5477	547-5499	6-8	Nick Perry
KIPP Indy Unite ES	1740 E 30th St	Indianapolis, IN	46218	317-547-5477	547-5499	K-3	Ellen Reuter
Lighthouse College Preparatory Academy	725 Clark Rd	Gary, IN	46406-1822	219-977-9583	977-9725	8-12	Rodney Bly
Manual HS	2405 Madison Ave	Indianapolis, IN	46225-2106	317-217-1983	396-5399	9-12	Misty Ndiritue
Marion Academy	2107 N Riley Ave	Indianapolis, IN	46218-3925	317-983-1300	225-4174	6-12	LaToya Black
Marshall Leadership Academy	2310 Weisser Park Ave	Fort Wayne, IN	46803-3462	260-755-0193		K-8	Tameka Wilson
Mays Community Academy	929 E South St	Mays, IN	46155	765-645-5577	645-5230	K-6	Shannon New
Miller Academy	9958 E County Road 150 N	Otwell, IN	47564	812-354-0800		PK-5	Rick Fears
Mind Program HS	3698 Dubarry Rd	Indianapolis, IN	46226	317-531-4737		8-12	Tiffany Thomas
Neighbors New Vistas HS	5201 US Highway 6	Portage, IN	46368	219-850-4448	850-4445	9-12	Anna Swope
Nexus Academy of Indianapolis	6101 N Keystone Ave Ste 302	Indianapolis, IN	46220-2493	317-252-5919	252-5917	9-12	Jamie Brady
Options Charter S	530 W Carmel Dr	Carmel, IN	46032	317-815-2098	846-3806	9-12	Camille Scott
Options Charter S Noblesville	9945 Cumberland Pointe Blvd	Noblesville, IN	46060	317-773-8659	773-9017	6-12	Jacob Brandau
Paramount S of Excellence	3020 Nowland Ave	Indianapolis, IN	46201-1422	317-775-6660	423-0569	K-8	Scott Frye
Phalen @ Francis Scott Key S	3920 Baker Dr	Indianapolis, IN	46235-1619	317-226-4103	226-3730	PK-6	Agnes Ikhiobe Aleobua
Phalen Leadership Academy	7151 E 35th St	Indianapolis, IN	46226-5745	317-226-4293	226-3663	K-6	Javaris Carrion
Phalen Leadership Academy	2323 N Illinois St	Indianapolis, IN	46208	317-333-6980	924-8383	K-6	Amanda Rinehart
Renaissance Academy	4093 W US Highway 20	La Porte, IN	46350-8269	219-878-8711	311-8321	PK-8	Kieran McHugh
Riverside HS	110 E 16th St	Indianapolis, IN	46202	317-231-0010	231-3759	9-12	Katie Dorsey
Rock Creek Community Academy	11525 Highway 31	Sellersburg, IN	47172	812-246-9271	246-0722	K-12	Sara Hauselman
Rural Community Academy	2385 N State Road 63	Sullivan, IN	47882-7152	812-382-4500	382-4055	K-8	Ginger Hathaway
Seven Oaks Classical S	200 E Association St	Ellettsville, IN	47429	812-935-5003	935-5040	K-8	Dr. Stephen Shipp
Signature S	610 Main St	Evansville, IN	47708-1618	812-421-1820	421-9189	9-12	Jean Hitchcock
Smith Academy for Excellence	725 W Washington Blvd	Fort Wayne, IN	46802	260-579-6939	424-3846	4-12	Corey Smith
Southeast Neighborhood S of Excellence	1601 Barth Ave	Indianapolis, IN	46203-2743	317-423-0204	631-4401	K-8	Dr. Kristie Sweeney
Steel City Academy	2650 W 35th Ave	Gary, IN	46408	219-750-1010	654-2284	7-10	Katie Kirley
Success Academy	3408 Ardmore Trl	South Bend, IN	46628-1302	574-288-5333		PK-4	Dean Fecher
Tindley Accelerated S	3960 Meadows Dr	Indianapolis, IN	46205-3114	317-545-1745	547-4323	9-12	Marcus Robinson
Tindley Collegiate Academy	4020 Meadows Pkwy	Indianapolis, IN	46205	317-777-7740	377-1435	6-8	Erica Goodridge
Tindley Genesis Academy	2540 N Capitol Ave	Indianapolis, IN	46208	317-777-6832	926-0673	K-5	Todd Hawks
Tindley Preparatory Academy	4010 N Sherman Dr	Indianapolis, IN	46226	317-777-6290	546-7224	6-8	Luke Lennon
Tindley Renaissance Academy	4020 Sherman Dr	Indianapolis, IN	46226	317-777-7290	377-1808	K-5	Edward Rangel
Tindley Summit Academy	3698 Dubarry Rd	Indianapolis, IN	46226	317-777-6830	273-2820	K-5	Sondra Towne
21st Century Charter S	556 Washington St	Gary, IN	46402	219-886-9339	886-0869	PK-12	Anthony Cherry
Vision Academy	1751 E Riverside Dr	Indianapolis, IN	46202	317-632-2006	662-3792	K-8	Ian Yearwood
Xavier S of Excellence	3423 S Michigan St	South Bend, IN	46614	574-231-6600	231-6640	K-8	Samantha Smith

Iowa

School	Address	City,State	Zip code	Telephone	Fax	Grade	Contact
Prescott ES	1151 White St	Dubuque, IA	52001-5005	563-552-4200	552-4201	PK-5	Vicki Sullivan
Vista Early College S	621 Tornado Dr	Storm Lake, IA	50588-2277	712-732-8065	732-8068	9-12	Beau Ruleaux
West Central Charter HS	PO Box 54	Maynard, IA	50655-0054	563-637-2283	637-2294	9-12	Josh Bahr

School	Address	City,State	Zip code	Telephone	Fax	Grade	Contact
Kansas							
Abilene Virtual S	213 N Broadway St	Abilene, KS	67410-2648	785-263-2630		6-12	B. Roth
Caney Valley Charter Academy	601 E Bullpup Blvd	Caney, KS	67333-2543	620-879-9232	879-9232	10-12	Ron Oyler
Erie HS	1400 N Main St	Erie, KS	66733-5006	620-244-3287	244-3290	9-12	Noah Francis
Greeley County JSHS	400 W Lawrence St	Tribune, KS	67879-9636	620-376-4265	376-2465	6-12	Mark Lackey
Hope Street Charter Academy	1900 SW Hope St	Topeka, KS	66604-3984	785-438-4280	271-3684	9-12	Dale Noll
Hugoton Learning Academy	215 W 11th St	Hugoton, KS	67951	620-428-6374	428-6378	7-12	Jennifer Burrows
Insight S of Kansas	16740 W 175th St	Olathe, KS	66062-8984	800-260-0438	664-2796	K-12	Cassandra Barton
Kinsley-Offerle JSHS	716 Colony Ave	Kinsley, KS	67547-1155	620-659-2126	659-2180	7-12	William King
Lawrence Virtual HS	1104 E 1000 Rd	Lawrence, KS	66047-9409	785-832-5620	832-5621	9-12	Keith Wilson
Lawrence Virtual S	1104 E 1000 Rd	Lawrence, KS	66047-9409	785-832-5620	832-5621	K-8	Keith Wilson
Service Valley Charter Academy	PO Box 129	Oswego, KS	67356-0129	620-421-3449	421-3640	K-8	Theresa Farris
Smoky Valley Virtual Charter S	121 S Main St	Lindsborg, KS	67456	785-227-4292	227-3610	K-12	Glen Suppes
21st Century Learning Academy	730 S Main St	Greensburg, KS	67054	620-548-2280	548-2389	6-12	Brian Deterding
Walton Rural Life ES	PO Box 140	Walton, KS	67151-0140	620-837-3161	837-5669	K-4	Jason Chalashtari
West Franklin Learning Center	PO Box 407	Williamsburg, KS	66095-0407	785-746-5766		9-12	Braden Anshutz
Yoder Charter S	PO Box 78	Yoder, KS	67585-0078	620-465-2605	465-2307	K-8	Delon Martens
Louisiana							
Acadiana Renaissance Charter Academy	600 Savoy Rd	Youngsville, LA	70592	337-374-1209	374-1210	K-8	Christine Stoudt
Advantage Charter Academy	14740 Plank Rd	Baker, LA	70714	225-774-3111	208-1962	K-7	Dr. Clifford Wallace
Akili Academy of New Orleans	3811 N Galvez St	New Orleans, LA	70117-5503	504-355-4172	355-4176	K-8	Allison Lowe
Algiers Technology Academy	6501 Berkley Dr	New Orleans, LA	70131-5513	504-302-7071	324-6998	9-12	Nia Mitchell
Apex Collegiate Academy Charter S	9700 Scenic Hwy	Baton Rouge, LA	70807	225-304-6162	341-3254	6-12	Eric Lewis
ARISE Academy	3819 Saint Claude Ave	New Orleans, LA	70117-5735	504-615-6354	456-2087	PK-8	Krista Brown
Ashe Charter S	1456 Gardena Dr	New Orleans, LA	70122-1914	504-373-6267	896-4003	K-8	Ryan Bennett
Audubon Charter S	428 Broadway St	New Orleans, LA	70118-3514	504-324-7100	866-1691	PK-3	Latoye Brown
Audubon Charter S	1111 Milan St	New Orleans, LA	70115-2760	504-324-7110	866-1691	4-8	Latoye Brown
Avoyelles Charter S	201 Longfellow Rd	Mansura, LA	71350-4292	318-240-9991	253-4198	K-12	Julie Roy
Baton Rouge College Prep Charter S	5300 Monarch Ave Bldg 8	Baton Rouge, LA	70811	225-257-9180		5-12	Kathryn Rice
Baton Rouge University Prep ES	7802 Howell Blvd	Baton Rouge, LA	70807	225-364-9805		K-2	Meghan Turner
Bayou Community Academy	800 E 7th St	Thibodaux, LA	70301-3607	985-446-3011		PK-8	Dr. Melanie Becnel
Beekman Charter S	15190 A M Baker Rd	Bastrop, LA	71220-6408	318-281-1743	283-5100	PK-12	Roy McCoy
Behrman S	715 Opelousas Ave	New Orleans, LA	70114-2449	504-302-7090	309-8042	PK-8	Brian Young
Belle Chasse Academy	100 5th St	Belle Chasse, LA	70037-1002	504-433-5850	433-5590	K-8	Rene Thompson
Bricolage Academy	3368 Esplanade Ave	New Orleans, LA	70119-3132	504-539-4505		K-3	Josh Densen
Capdau Charter S	4621 Canal St	New Orleans, LA	70119-5807	504-872-9257	280-2312	PK-8	Rulonda Green
Capitol HS	1000 N 23rd St	Baton Rouge, LA	70802-3398	225-239-7506	227-2420	9-12	Brian Beck
Carver Collegiate Academy	3059 Higgins Rd	New Orleans, LA	70126	504-308-3660	754-7980	9-12	Jerel Bryant
Carver Preparatory Academy	3059 Higgins Blvd	New Orleans, LA	70126	504-308-3660	754-7980	9-12	Jerel Bryan
Celerity Crestworth Charter S	10650 Avenue F	Baton Rouge, LA	70807	225-308-3274	341-6779	6-8	Jaquita Sims
Celerity Dalton Charter S	3605 Ontario St	Baton Rouge, LA	70805	225-357-0244	341-6779	PK-8	Melissa Landry
Celerity Lanier Charter S	4705 Lanier Dr	Baton Rouge, LA	70812-4020	225-308-3273	341-6679	PK-8	Kimberly Boudreaux
Celerity Woodmere Charter S	3191 Alex Kornman Blvd	Harvey, LA	70058	504-348-2410	371-0517	PK-5	Ericka Jones
Children's Charter S	1143 North St	Baton Rouge, LA	70802-4547	225-387-9273	387-9272	PK-5	Eddie Greenup
Clark Leadership Academy	1517 Statesman Rd	Opelousas, LA	70570	337-418-4222	942-4273	5-12	Tiffanie Lewis
Clark Prep HS	1301 N Derbigny St	New Orleans, LA	70116-2213	504-373-6202	827-4538	9-12	Margaret Leaf
Coghill Accelerated Academy	4617 Mirabeau Ave	New Orleans, LA	70126	504-373-6237	308-3661	PK-8	Alnita Porea
Cohen College Prep MSHS	3520 Dryades St	New Orleans, LA	70115	504-335-0400	617-7200	6-12	Michael George
Collegiate Baton Rouge	282 Lobdell Blvd	Baton Rouge, LA	70806	225-225-9775		9-12	Kelsey Lambrecht
Community S for Apprenticeship Learning	1555 Madison Ave	Baton Rouge, LA	70802-3460	225-336-1410	336-1414	6-8	LaMont Cole
Craig Charter S	1423 Saint Philip St	New Orleans, LA	70116-2933	504-940-2115		PK-8	Ann Ford
Crescent Leadership Academy	2701 Lawrence St	New Orleans, LA	70114	504-702-5790	702-5791	7-12	Nicholas Dean
Crocker College Prep	2301 Marengo St	New Orleans, LA	70115	504-335-0404	285-9980	PK-8	Nicole Boykins
Cypress Academy	4217 Orleans Ave	New Orleans, LA	70119	504-383-3337		K-2	Bob Berk
D'Arbonne Woods Charter S	9560 Highway 33	Farmerville, LA	71241	318-368-8051	368-8053	K-12	Heath Murry
Delhi Charter S	6940 Highway 17	Delhi, LA	71232-7021	318-878-0433	878-0434	K-12	Brett Raley
Delta Charter S	300 Lynwood Dr	Ferriday, LA	71334	318-757-3202	757-6497	K-12	Monica Miller
Democracy Prep Baton Rouge	4055 Prescott Rd	Baton Rouge, LA	70805	225-372-2037	389-6587	K-7	Michelle Gieg
Downsville Charter S	4787 Highway 151	Downsville, LA	71234-5145	318-982-5318	982-5737	PK-12	Tony Cane
Easton Charter HS	3019 Canal St	New Orleans, LA	70119-6305	504-324-7400	324-7946	9-12	Alexina Medley
Einstein Charter MSHS @Sarah Towles Reed	5316 Michoud Blvd	New Orleans, LA	70129	504-503-0470		6-12	Nathan Stockman
Einstein Charter S @ Village de l'Est	5100 Cannes St	New Orleans, LA	70129-1203	504-324-7450	254-4121	PK-5	Teisha Goudeau
Einstein Charter S Sherwood Forest	4801 Maid Marion	New Orleans, LA	70128	504-503-0110		PK-5	Shimon Ancker
Eisenhower ES	3700 Tall Pines Dr	New Orleans, LA	70131-8499	504-302-7109	398-7129	PK-5	Cherie Goins
Elan Academy	709 Park Blvd	New Orleans, LA	70119	504-019-9720		K-3	Melanie Askew
Encore Academy	4217 Orleans Ave	New Orleans, LA	70119-4605	504-444-2224		PK-8	Terri Smith
Encore Academy	2518 Arts St	New Orleans, LA	70117	504-444-2224	754-7665	K-8	Terri Smith
Esperanza Charter S	4407 S Carrollton Ave	New Orleans, LA	70119-6823	504-373-6272	488-1813	K-8	Nicole Saulny
Fischer Academy	1801 L B Landry Ave	New Orleans, LA	70114-6166	504-302-7111	363-1016	PK-8	Beverly Johnson
Foundation Prep Charter S	7301 Dwyer Rd	New Orleans, LA	70126	504-434-0521		K-6	Myrialis King
Franklin HS	2001 Leon C Simon Dr	New Orleans, LA	70122-3524	504-286-2600	286-2642	9-12	Dr. Pat Widhalm
GEO Prep Academy of Greater Baton Rouge	4006 Platt Dr	Baton Rouge, LA	70814	225-927-1500		K-4	Sandra Douglas
Geo Prep Mid City	1900 Lobdell Blvd	Baton Rouge, LA	70806	225-236-9933		K-8	Sandra Douglas
Glencoe Charter S	4491 Highway 83	Franklin, LA	70538-7500	337-923-6900	923-0982	K-8	Kimberly Roberts
Greater Grace Charter Academy	PO Box 1002	Vacherie, LA	70090	225-624-2113		K-8	Dr. Claudette Aubert
Green Charter S	2319 Valence St	New Orleans, LA	70115-5959	504-304-3532	896-4147	K-8	Ava Lee
Habans Charter ES	3501 Seine St	New Orleans, LA	70114	504-941-1810		PK-8	Elisabeth Mitchell
Harney Spirit of Excellence Acad	2503 Willow St	New Orleans, LA	70113-3234	504-373-6230	891-6919	PK-8	Aisha Jones
Harte Charter S	5300 Berkley Dr	New Orleans, LA	70131-7204	504-373-6281	304-1817	K-8	Jamar McKneely
Haynes Charter ES	8600 Elmgrove Garden Dr	Baton Rouge, LA	70807	225-774-1311	774-1323	PK-6	Diana Haynes
Hughes Academy	3519 Trafalgar St	New Orleans, LA	70119-2041	504-373-6251	267-9760	PK-8	Kamisha Gray
Hynes Charter S	990 Harrison Ave	New Orleans, LA	70124-3833	504-324-7160	488-0213	PK-8	Michelle Douglas
Iberville Charter Academy	24360 Enterprise Blvd	Plaquemine, LA	70764	225-238-7346	238-7347	K-8	John McCrary
Impact Charter ES	4815 Lavey Ln	Baker, LA	70714	225-308-9565	308-4239	PK-6	Chakesha Scott
Inspire Charter Academy	5454 N Foster Dr	Baton Rouge, LA	70805	225-356-3936		K-8	Lorna Davis
International HS	727 Carondelet St	New Orleans, LA	70130-3705	504-613-5703	566-1142	9-12	Sean Wilson
International S of Louisiana	1400 Camp St	New Orleans, LA	70130-4208	504-654-1088	654-1086	K-8	Melanie Tennyson
Jeff Community S	PO Box 19227	New Orleans, LA	70179	504-373-6258	308-3620	PK-8	Patricia Perkins
Jefferson Chamber Foundation Acad-East	3410 Jefferson Hwy	Jefferson, LA	70121	504-410-3280		8-12	Mille Harris
Jefferson Chamber Foundation Academy	475 Manhattan Blvd	Harvey, LA	70058	504-410-3121	410-3120	9-12	Anne Lene
Jefferson RISE Charter S	501B Lapalco Blvd	Gretna, LA	70056	504-410-5905		6-7	Kathleen Sullivan
Karr Charter HS	3332 Huntlee Dr	New Orleans, LA	70131-7046	504-302-7135	301-2721	9-12	Harold Clay
Kenilworth Science & Technology Charter	7600 Boone Ave	Baton Rouge, LA	70808-6716	225-766-8111	767-9061	6-8	Hasan Suzuk
Kenner Discovery Health Sciences Academy	2504 Maine Ave	Metairie, LA	70003	504-233-4720	229-2151	PK-9	Patty Glaser Ph.D.
King Charter S for Science & Tech	1617 Caffin Ave	New Orleans, LA	70117-2909	504-940-2243	940-2276	PK-12	Dr. Doris Hicks Ed.D.
KIPP Believe College Prep S	9330 Forshey St	New Orleans, LA	70118	504-304-8857	304-8862	5-8	Anthony Cognata
KIPP Believe PS	421 Burdette St	New Orleans, LA	70118	504-266-2050	264-9363	K-4	Sarah Beth Greenberg
KIPP Booker T. Washington HS	2514 3rd St	New Orleans, LA	70113	504-609-2283		9-10	Alex Jarrell
KIPP Central City Academy	2514 3rd St	New Orleans, LA	70113	504-609-2283	708-5334	5-8	Alex Jarrell
KIPP Central City PS	2625 Thalia St	New Orleans, LA	70113	504-373-6290	302-9737	K-4	Theresa Schmitt
KIPP East Community PS	5500 Piety Dr	New Orleans, LA	70126-2308	504-301-2964		K-4	Jennifer Carey
KIPP Leadership Academy	2300 Saint Claude Ave	New Orleans, LA	70117-8307	504-373-6256	322-3924	K-8	Herneshia Dukes
KIPP Morial MS	5500 Piety Dr	New Orleans, LA	70126	504-609-2280	264-5598	5-8	Deanna Reddick
KIPP Morial PS	7701 Grant St	New Orleans, LA	70126	504-592-8520	592-8515	PK-4	Mark Burton
KIPP Renaissance HS	3820 Saint Claude Ave	New Orleans, LA	70117-5736	504-373-6255	322-3924	9-12	Towana Pierre-Floyd
Lafayette Academy	2727 S Carrollton Ave	New Orleans, LA	70118-4338	504-861-8370	861-8369	PK-8	Monica Boudouin
Lafayette Renaissance Charter Academy	205 Vienne Ln	Lafayette, LA	70507	337-706-0066	706-0068	K-8	Tale Lockett
Lake Area New Tech Early College HS	6026 Paris Ave	New Orleans, LA	70122-2726	504-267-8811	267-8833	9-12	Dr. Bethel Cager
Lake Charles Charter Academy	3160 Power Center Pkwy	Lake Charles, LA	70607	337-475-7900	475-7901	K-8	Dr. Pamela Quebodeaux
Lake Charles College Prep S	2750 Power Center Pkwy	Lake Charles, LA	70607	337-419-2868	419-2867	9-12	Ken Roebuck
Lake Forest Charter ES	11110 Lake Forest Blvd	New Orleans, LA	70128	504-826-7140	248-7020	PK-8	Mardele Early
Landry - O.P. Walker HS	1200 L B Landry Ave	New Orleans, LA	70114	504-302-7170	302-7229	9-12	Tyrone Casby
Laureate Academy Charter S	3400 6th St	Harvey, LA	70058	504-503-0170		K-8	Claire Heckerman
Laurel Oaks Charter S	440 N Foster Dr	Baton Rouge, LA	70806	225-394-5490		K-1	Rashid Young
Lincoln Preparatory S	PO Box 16	Grambling, LA	71245	318-436-9598		K-12	Gordan Ford
Linwood Public Charter S	401 W 70th St	Shreveport, LA	71106	318-683-2500	865-0542	K-8	Staughton Jennings
Livingston Collegiate Academy	7301 Dwyer Rd	New Orleans, LA	70126	504-503-0004		9-10	Evan Stoudt
Louisiana Key Academy	3172 Government St	Baton Rouge, LA	70806	225-298-1223		K-5	Heather Bourgeois
Louisiana S for Agricultural Sciences	5303 Highway 115	Bunkie, LA	71322-4301	318-346-8029	346-4479	7-12	Dexter Compton
Louisiana Virtual Charter Academy	4962 Florida Blvd	Baton Rouge, LA	70806	877-490-3596		K-12	Danielle Scott-Johnson
Lusher Charter Lower S	7315 Willow St	New Orleans, LA	70118-5232	504-862-5110	866-4292	K-5	Kathleen Riedlinger
Lusher Charter MSHS	5624 Freret St	New Orleans, LA	70115-6547	504-304-3960	861-1839	6-12	Kathleen Riedlinger
Lycee Francais de la Nouvelle Orleans	5951 Patton St	New Orleans, LA	70115	504-620-5500	875-2441	PK-6	Keith Bartlett
Madison Preparatory Academy	1555 Madison Ave	Baton Rouge, LA	70802-3460	225-636-5865	336-1414	9-12	Alisa Welsh

School	Address	City,State	Zip code	Telephone	Fax	Grade	Contact
Magnolia S of Excellence	2290 Clyde Fant Pkwy Servc	Shreveport, LA	71104	318-402-4220	402-4230	K-12	Pamela Barker
MAX Charter S	PO Box 2072	Thibodaux, LA	70310-0001	985-227-9500	227-9515	1-8	Linda Musson Ed.D.
McDonogh 32 S	800 De Armas St	New Orleans, LA	70114-4414	504-302-7144	363-1058	PK-8	Beverly Johnson
McDonogh 42 S	1651 N Tonti St	New Orleans, LA	70119	504-942-3660	942-0731	PK-8	Jeremy Geary
McMain Magnet JSHS	5712 S Claiborne Ave	New Orleans, LA	70125	504-324-7500	862-5123	7-12	John Green
Mentorship Academy	339 Florida St	Baton Rouge, LA	70801	225-346-5180		9-12	Robert Webb
Moton Charter S	6800 Chef Menteur Hwy	New Orleans, LA	70126	504-245-4400	248-7300	PK-7	Paulette Bruno
Moton Charter S	8550 Curran Blvd	New Orleans, LA	70127	504-245-4400		PK-8	Paulette Bruno
Nelson Charter S	3121 Saint Bernard Ave	New Orleans, LA	70119-1916	504-943-1311	304-5160	PK-8	Freda Smith
NET Charter HS	1614 Oretha Castle Haley Bl	New Orleans, LA	70113	504-267-9060	267-9059	9-12	Elizabeth Ostberg
NET Charter HS Gentilly	6601 Franklin Ave	New Orleans, LA	70122	504-267-9765		9-12	Elizabeth Ostberg
New Orleans Charter Science and Math HS	5625 Loyola Ave	New Orleans, LA	70115-5014	504-324-7061	309-4178	9-12	Chana Benenson
New Orleans Military & Maritime Academy	425 OBannon St	New Orleans, LA	70114	504-227-3810	875-4326	9-12	Dr. Cecilia Garcia
New Vision Learning Academy	507 Swayze St	Monroe, LA	71201-8130	318-338-9995	338-9987	PK-12	Dr. Andrea Miller
Noble Minds	3819 Herschel St	New Orleans, LA	70014	504-962-7286		K-3	Vera Triplett
Northshore Charter S	111 Walker St	Bogalusa, LA	70427	985-732-0005	732-0580	K-12	Dee Dee McCullough
Osborne ES	6701 Curran Blvd	New Orleans, LA	70126	504-400-0614	708-4556	PK-8	Jolene Galpin
Pathways in Education - North Market	1909 N Market St	Shreveport, LA	71107	318-424-8138		9-12	Martin McGreal
Pathways in Education - Southern Hills	8999 Mansfield Rd	Shreveport, LA	71118	318-688-2301		9-12	Martin McGreal
Plessy Community S	2021 Pauger St	New Orleans, LA	70116	504-503-0055	503-0056	PK-5	Joan Reilly
ReNEW Aaron ES	10200 Curran Blvd	New Orleans, LA	70127	504-570-6354		PK-8	John Gravier
ReNEW Accelerated HS	3649 Laurel St	New Orleans, LA	70115	504-367-3307		9-12	Emily Perhamus
ReNEW Cultural Arts Academy	3128 Constance St	New Orleans, LA	70115-2337	504-324-4207	267-4741	PK-8	Jared Lamb
ReNEW McDonogh City Park Academy	2733 Esplanade Ave	New Orleans, LA	70119-3332	504-940-1740	940-1780	K-8	Jonathan Mccarty
ReNEW Schaumburg ES	9501 Grant St	New Orleans, LA	70127-4256	504-304-1532	304-1390	PK-8	Laci Blondell
ReNEW SciTech Academy	820 Jackson Ave	New Orleans, LA	70130	504-267-4574	267-0572	PK-8	Monica Supak
Rooted S	4238 St Charles Ave	New Orleans, LA	70115	504-383-4654		9-10	Jonathan Johnson
Sci Academy	5552 Read Blvd	New Orleans, LA	70127	504-373-6264	324-0171	9-12	Rhonda Dale
Singleton Charter S	2220 Oretha C Haley Blvd	New Orleans, LA	70113	504-568-3466	569-3378	PK-6	Rosemary Martin
Slaughter Community Charter S	2944 Highway 412 W	Slaughter, LA	70777	225-570-8682	570-8694	7-12	Clint Ebey
Smothers Academy	2012 Jefferson Hwy	Jefferson, LA	70121	504-302-1089	404-5872	K-6	Averil Sanders
South Baton Rouge Charter Academy	9211 Parkway Dr	Baton Rouge, LA	70810	225-349-7489	349-7490	K-8	Monique Smith
Southwest Louisiana Charter Academy	1700 E McNeese St	Lake Charles, LA	70607	337-475-7910	475-7911	PK-8	Dr. LaTonia Harris
Success Preparatory Academy	2011 Bienville St	New Orleans, LA	70112-3313	504-909-6275	571-6317	K-8	Niloy Gangopadhyay
Tallulah Charter S	1206 N Cedar St	Tallulah, LA	71282-2710	318-574-0029	574-0073	PK-5	Keith Wolfe
Tangi Academy Charter S	43052 Yokum Rd	Hammond, LA	70403	985-269-7695		K-6	Pamela Prescott
Thrive Baton Rouge	2585 Brightside Dr	Baton Rouge, LA	70820	225-726-3355		6-12	
Tubman ES	2832 General Meyer Ave	New Orleans, LA	70114-3012	504-227-3800	227-3801	PK-8	Julie Lause
University View Academy	4664 Jamestown Ave	Baton Rouge, LA	70808	225-421-2900	421-2901	K-12	Alonzo Luce
Virtual Academy of Lafourche	639 Harrison St	Thibodaux, LA	70301-2739	985-446-2877	446-2993	K-12	Julie Bourgeois
Vision Academy	1411 Sherrouse St	Monroe, LA	71203	318-651-3984		9-12	Latoya Jackson
Wheatley Community S	2300 Dumaine St	New Orleans, LA	70119-3512	504-373-6205	488-4091	PK-8	Diana Archuleta
Williams ES	11755 Dwyer Rd	New Orleans, LA	70128-3454	504-373-6288	245-2796	PK-8	Kelly Batiste
Williams ES	3127 Martin Luther King Jr	New Orleans, LA	70125-3328	504-522-0100	910-1045	PK-8	Erin LaBostrie
Willow Charter Academy	1818 NE Evangeline Thruway	Lafayette, LA	70501	337-534-8218	205-6195	K-8	Ronnie Harrison
Wilson Charter S	3617 General Pershing St	New Orleans, LA	70125-4530	504-373-6274	308-3615	PK-8	Lee Green
Wright Charter S	1426 Napoleon Ave	New Orleans, LA	70115-3958	504-304-3916	896-4095	6-12	Sharon Clark
Young Audiences Charter S	1407 Virgil St	Gretna, LA	70053	504-304-6332	267-4667	PK-6	Brandon House

Maine

School	Address	City,State	Zip code	Telephone	Fax	Grade	Contact
Acadia Academy	12 Westminster St	Lewiston, ME	04240	207-333-3765	333-3767	PK-6	Julie Colello
Baxter Academy for Technology & Science	54 York St	Portland, ME	04101	207-699-5500	331-4831	9-12	Michele LaForge
Cornville Regional Charter S	1192 W Ridge Rd	Cornville, ME	04976-6214	207-474-8503	474-8515	PK-9	Travis Works
Fiddlehead S of Arts & Sciences	25 Shaker Rd	Gray, ME	04039	207-657-2244		PK-5	Jacinda Cotton-Castro
Harpswell Coastal Academy	9 Ash Point Rd	Harpswell, ME	04079	207-233-6125		6-12	Matt Hamilton
Harpswell Coastal Academy	8 Leavitt Dr	Brunswick, ME	04011	207-833-3229	833-3231	6-12	Scott Barksdale
Maine Academy of Natural Sciences	PO Box 159	Hinckley, ME	04944	207-238-4100	238-4107	9-12	Tonya Arnold
Maine Connections Academy	75 John Roberts Rd Ste 11B	South Portland, ME	04106	207-805-3254	541-3990	7-12	Chad Strout
Maine Virtual Academy	6 E Chestnut St	Augusta, ME	04330	207-613-8900		7-12	Dr. Melinda Browne
Snow Pond Arts Academy	8 Goldenrod Ln	Sidney, ME	04330	844-476-6976		9-12	Heather King

Maryland

School	Address	City,State	Zip code	Telephone	Fax	Grade	Contact
AFYA Charter MS	2800 Brendan Ave	Baltimore, MD	21213-1213	410-485-2102		6-8	Tiffany Halsey
Baltimore Collegiate S for Boys	900 Woodbourne Ave	Baltimore, MD	21212	443-642-5320		4-8	John Snowdy
Baltimore International Academy	4410 Frankford Ave	Baltimore, MD	21206	410-426-3650	426-3651	K-8	Elena Lokounia
Baltimore Leadership S for Young Women	128 W Franklin St	Baltimore, MD	21201-4504	443-642-2048	338-2684	6-12	Chevonne Hall
Baltimore Montessori Charter S	1600 Guilford Ave	Baltimore, MD	21202-2823	410-528-5393	528-8126	PK-8	Allison Shecter
Banneker Blake Academy Arts & Sciences	PO Box 11311	Baltimore, MD	21239	443-642-5420		6-8	Lisa Harvin
Carroll Creek Montessori Charter S	7215 Corporate Ct	Frederick, MD	21703	301-663-7970	663-6107	PK-5	Marilyn Horan
Chesapeake Charter S	20945 Great Mills Rd	Lexington Park, MD	20653-4370	301-863-9585	863-9586	K-8	Angela Funya
Chesapeake Math & IT Academy North	6100 Frost Pl	Laurel, MD	20707	301-350-6051	560-3461	6-8	Mehmet Gunes
Chesapeake Math & IT Academy South	9822 Fallard Ct	Upper Marlboro, MD	20772	240-573-7250	823-9326	6-10	Omolara Asafa
Chesapeake Math & IT ES	6151 Chevy Chase Dr	Laurel, MD	20707	240-573-7240	776-2322	K-5	Gonul Ozturk
Chesapeake Math & IT North HS	14800 Sweitzer Ln	Laurel, MD	20707	240-767-4080		9-12	Mehmet Gunes
Chesapeake Science Point Charter S	7321 Parkway Dr	Hanover, MD	21076	410-757-5277	757-5280	6-12	Erkan Derin
City Neighbors Charter S	4301 Raspe Ave	Baltimore, MD	21206-1913	410-325-2627	325-2489	K-8	Mary Seidel
City Neighbors Hamilton S	5609 Sefton Ave	Baltimore, MD	21214	443-642-2052	426-0190	K-8	Mike Chalupa
City Neighbors HS	5609 Sefton Ave	Baltimore, MD	21214	443-642-2119		9-12	Cheyanne Zahrt
City Springs ES	100 S Caroline St	Baltimore, MD	21231-1798	410-396-9165	396-9113	PK-8	Rhonda Richetta
College Park Academy	5751 Rivertech Ct	Riverdale Park, MD	20737	240-696-3206	422-0510	6-12	Gordon Libby
ConneXions: A Community Based Arts S	2801 N Dukeland St	Baltimore, MD	21216	410-984-1418	669-4418	6-12	Sidney Brooks
Coppin Academy	2500 W North Ave	Baltimore, MD	21216-3633	443-642-5060	951-2610	9-12	Aisha Almond
Creative City Charter S	2810 Shirley Ave	Baltimore, MD	21215	443-642-3600		K-5	Traci Mathena
Crossroads S	802 S Caroline St	Baltimore, MD	21231	410-276-4924		6-8	Matthew Ebert
Empowerment Academy	851 Braddish Ave	Baltimore, MD	21216-4723	443-984-2381	362-2454	PK-8	Ashley Moore
Excel Academy	7910 Scott Rd	Landover, MD	20785	301-925-2320		K-8	Chien Hwa Nee
Frederick Classical Charter S	8455 Spires Way Ste CC	Frederick, MD	21701	240-236-1200		K-7	Erica Cummins
Govans ES	5801 York Rd	Baltimore, MD	21212-3616	410-396-6396	547-7840	PK-5	Linda Taylor
Green S	2851 Kentucky Ave	Baltimore, MD	21213-1215	410-488-5312	488-5314	K-5	Kate Primm
Green Street Academy	125 N Hilton St	Baltimore, MD	21229	443-642-2068		6-12	Crystal Harden-Lindsey
Hampstead Hill Academy	500 S Linwood Ave	Baltimore, MD	21224-3856	410-396-9146	396-3637	PK-8	Matthew Hornbeck
Imagine Andrews Charter S	4701 San Antonio Blvd	Andrews AFB, MD	20762	301-350-6002	599-5620	K-8	H. Douglas Rice
Imagine - Foundations at Leeland	14111 Oak Grove Rd	Upper Marlboro, MD	20774-8424	301-383-1899	218-1454	K-8	Lance Pace
Imagine Foundations at Morningside	6900 Ames St	Morningside, MD	20746-3504	301-817-0544	817-0956	K-8	Jessica Johnson
Imagine - Lincoln Public Charter S	4207 Norcross St	Temple Hills, MD	20748	301-808-5600	808-5611	K-8	Benjamin Roberts
Independence S Local I HS	2801 N Dukeland St	Baltimore, MD	21226	443-642-2504	467-1091	9-12	Dimitric Roseboro
Jackson Charter S	900 Woodbourne Ave	Baltimore, MD	21212	443-320-9499	320-9036	5-8	Damia Thomas
KIPP Harmony Academy	4701 Greenspring Ave	Baltimore, MD	21209	443-642-2027		K-8	Samantha Pugh
Midtown Academy	1398 W Mount Royal Ave	Baltimore, MD	21217-4134	410-225-3257	225-3514	K-8	Suzanne Penny
Monarch Academy	2525 Kirk Ave	Baltimore, MD	21218	443-642-2402	254-0201	K-8	Kiara Hargrove
Monarch Academy Charter S	6730 Baymeadow Dr	Glen Burnie, MD	21060-6412	410-760-2072	760-1321	K-8	Maurine Larkin
Monocacy Valley Montessori S	217 Dill Ave	Frederick, MD	21701-4905	301-668-5013	668-5015	K-8	Nancy Radkiewicz
Northwood Appold Community Academy	4417 Loch Raven Blvd	Baltimore, MD	21218-1554	410-323-9546	323-1836	K-5	Charlene Whilby
Patterson Park Charter S	27 N Lakewood Ave	Baltimore, MD	21224-1155	410-558-1230	558-1003	PK-8	Dr. Charles Kramer
Roots and Branches S	1807 Harlem Ave	Baltimore, MD	21217	443-642-2320		K-5	Anne Rossi
Rosemont ES	2777 Presstman St	Baltimore, MD	21216-4025	410-396-0574	545-3298	PK-8	Dwayne Wheeler
Southwest Baltimore Charter S	1300 Herkimer St	Baltimore, MD	21223	443-984-3385	244-0410	K-8	Iffeisha Gordon-Toppin
Templeton Preparatory Academy	1200 Pennsylvania Ave	Baltimore, MD	21217-3045	410-396-0882		PK-5	Evelyn Perry
Tunbridge ES	5504 York Rd	Baltimore, MD	21212	410-323-8692		PK-8	Sheila Adams
Turning Point Academy	7800 Good Luck Rd	Lanham Seabrook, MD	20706-3505	301-552-0164	552-7307	K-8	Rhonda Clomax
Wolfe Street Academy	245 S Wolfe St	Baltimore, MD	21231-2622	410-396-9140	396-8064	PK-5	Mark Gaither

Massachusetts

School	Address	City,State	Zip code	Telephone	Fax	Grade	Contact
Academy of Pacific Rim Charter S	1 Westinghouse Plz	Hyde Park, MA	02136-2077	617-361-0050	361-0045	5-12	Spencer Blasdale
Advanced Math & Science Academy	201 Forest St	Marlborough, MA	01752-3012	508-597-2400	597-2499	6-12	Ellen Linzey
Alma del Mar Charter S	515 Belleville Ave	New Bedford, MA	02746	774-206-6827	206-6833	K-8	Will Gardner
Amesbury: Amesbury Innovation HS	71 Friend St	Amesbury, MA	01913-2723	978-388-8037	388-8073	9-12	Eryn Maguire
Argosy Collegiate Charter S	263 Hamlet St	Fall River, MA	02724-3342	508-567-4725		6-8	Kristen Pavao
Atlantis Charter S	37 Park St	Fall River, MA	02721-1712	508-672-3537	672-2474	K-12	Robert Beatty
Banneker Charter Public S	21 Notre Dame Ave	Cambridge, MA	02140-2505	617-497-7771	497-4223	PK-6	Sherley Bretous
Barnstable Comm Horace Mann Charter S	165 Bearses Way	Hyannis, MA	02601	508-790-6485	790-6432	K-3	Dr. Sheila Kukstis
Baystate Academy	2001 Roosevelt Ave	Springfield, MA	01104-1657	413-366-5100	366-5101	6-12	Tim Sneed
Bentley Academy Charter S	25 Memorial Dr	Salem, MA	01970-5651	978-740-1260	740-1164	K-5	Marlena Afonso
Berkshire Arts & Technology Charter S	PO Box 267	Adams, MA	01220-0267	413-743-7311	743-7327	6-12	April West
Boston Collegiate Charter S	11 Mayhew St	Dorchester, MA	02125-1628	617-265-1172	265-1176	5-12	Sarah Morland

School	Address	City,State	Zip code	Telephone	Fax	Grade	Contact
Boston Day & Evening Academy	20 Kearsarge Ave	Roxbury, MA	02119-2318	617-635-6789	635-6380	9-12	Alison Hramiec
Boston Green Academy	20 Warren St	Brighton, MA	02135-3602	617-635-9860	635-9858	9-12	Matthew Holzer
Boston Preparatory Charter S	885 River St	Hyde Park, MA	02136	617-333-6688	333-6689	6-12	Sharon Liszanckie
Boston Renaissance Charter S	1415 Hyde Park Ave	Hyde Park, MA	02136	617-357-0900	357-0949	K-6	Alexandra Buckmire
Bridge Boston Charter S	2 McLellan St	Dorchester, MA	02121-4011	857-229-1601	674-0861	PK-5	Jennifer Daly
Brooke East Boston Charter S	94 Horace St	East Boston, MA	02128	617-409-5150	567-5295	K-8	Molly Cole
Brooke Mattapan Charter S	150 American Legion Hwy	Dorchester, MA	02124	617-268-1006	474-4612	K-8	Abby Waldman
Brooke Roslindale Charter S	190 Cummins Hwy	Roslindale, MA	02131-3722	617-325-7977	325-2260	K-8	Meghan Parquette
Cape Cod Lighthouse Charter S	195 Route 137	Harwich, MA	02645-1320	774-408-7994	237-9041	6-8	Paul Niles
City on a Hill Charter S	58 Circuit St	Roxbury, MA	02119-1925	617-445-1515	445-9153	9-12	DeOtis Williams
City on a Hill Charter S	384 Acushnet Ave	New Bedford, MA	02740	508-985-6400	985-6422	9-12	Gail Keith
City on a Hill Charter S	2179 Washington St	Roxbury, MA	02119	617-516-5888	533-9421	9-12	Sonya Pratt
Codman Academy	637 Washington St	Dorchester, MA	02124-3510	617-287-0700	287-9064	K-12	Thabiti Brown
Collegiate Charter S of Lowell	1857 Middlesex St	Lowell, MA	01851	978-458-1399	458-1300	K-8	Frederick Randall
Community Charter S of Cambridge	245 Bent St	Cambridge, MA	02141-2001	617-354-0047	354-3624	6-12	Caleb Hurst-Hiller
Community Day Arlington ES	150 Arlington St	Lawrence, MA	01841	978-722-8311	722-8514	K-4	Tiffany Goddard
Community Day Charter S	190 Hampshire St	Lawrence, MA	01840-1251	978-722-2583	682-1013	PK-8	Mary Chance
Community Day Charter S Gateway	9 Ballard Way	Lawrence, MA	01843	978-688-4283	688-4370	K-8	
Community Day S R. Kingman Webster	50 Pleasant St	Lawrence, MA	01841	978-686-9327		K-8	
Conservatory Lab Charter S	2120 Dorchester Ave	Dorchester, MA	02124	617-254-8904	254-8909	PK-8	Nicole Mack
Davis Leadership Academy Charter S	23 Leonard St	Dorchester, MA	02122-2718	617-474-7950	474-7957	6-8	Karmala Sherwood
Dudley Street Neighborhood S	6 Shirley St	Roxbury, MA	02119-2726	617-227-8055		K-5	Dawn Lewis
Excel Academy Charter S	1150 Saratoga St	East Boston, MA	02128-1228	617-561-1371	963-7162	5-8	Nina Cronan
Excel Academy - Chelsea	180 2nd St	Chelsea, MA	02150	617-336-9970	516-1676	5-8	Katherine Pereira
Excel Academy - East Boston	58 Moore St	East Boston, MA	02128	617-874-4080	516-1603	5-8	Jocelyn Foulke
Foster Charter S	10 New Bond St	Worcester, MA	01606-2699	508-854-8400	854-8484	K-12	Brian Haas
Four Rivers Charter S	248 Colrain Rd	Greenfield, MA	01301-9701	413-775-4577	775-4578	7-12	Peter Garbus
Foxborough Regional Charter S	131 Central St	Foxboro, MA	02035-2458	508-543-2508	543-7982	K-12	Ronald Griffin
Franklin Classical Charter S	201 Main St	Franklin, MA	02038-1933	508-541-3434	541-5396	K-8	Heather Zolnowski
Freire Social Justice Charter S	PO Box 1009	Holyoke, MA	01041	413-536-3201	536-3206	9-12	Melissa Mirhej
Global Learning Charter S	190 Ashley Blvd	New Bedford, MA	02746-1752	508-991-4105	991-4110	5-12	Dr. Stephen Furtado
Hampden Charter S of Science	20 Johnson Rd	Chicopee, MA	01022	413-593-9090	294-2648	6-12	Tarkan Topcuoglu
Hilltown Cooperative Charter S	1 Industrial Pkwy	Easthampton, MA	01027	413-529-7178	527-1530	K-8	Daniel Klatz
Hill View Montessori Charter S	75 Foundation Ave	Haverhill, MA	01835-6926	978-521-2616	521-2656	K-8	Debra Diggins
Holyoke Community Charter S	2200 Northampton St	Holyoke, MA	01040-3430	413-533-0111	536-5444	K-8	Sonia Pope
Innovation Academy Charter S	72 Tyng Rd	Tyngsboro, MA	01879-2044	978-649-0432	649-6337	5-12	Gregory Orpen
Kennedy Academy for Health Careers	360 Huntington Ave	Boston, MA	02115-5005	617-373-8576	373-7850	9-12	Dr. Caren Walker-Gregory
King Charter S of Excellence	285 Dorset St	Springfield, MA	01108-2821	413-214-7806	214-7838	K-5	Juraye Pierson
KIPP Academy Boston Charter S	37 Babson St	Mattapan, MA	02126	617-393-5682	652-7461	K-8	Nikki Barnes
KIPP Academy Lynn Charter S	90 High Rock St	Lynn, MA	01902	781-598-1609	598-1639	5-12	Drea DeAngelo
KIPP Academy Lynn ES	20 Wheeler St	Lynn, MA	01902	781-558-9263	598-1639	K-2	Eveleen Hsu
Lawrence Family Development Charter S	34 West St	Lawrence, MA	01841-3426	978-689-9863	689-8133	PK-8	Susan Earabino
Leominster Center for Excellence	98 Adams St	Leominster, MA	01453	978-537-3222	537-3232	9-12	Carrie Duff
Libertas Academy Charter S	146 Chestnut St	Springfield, MA	01103	413-342-5510		6-12	Modesto Montero
Lowell Community Charter S	206 Jackson St	Lowell, MA	01852-2106	978-323-0800	323-4600	K-8	Nicholas Leonardos
Lowell Middlesex Academy Charter S	67 Middle St	Lowell, MA	01852-1868	978-656-3165	459-0456	9-12	Margaret McDevitt
Marblehead Community Charter S	17 Lime St	Marblehead, MA	01945-2530	781-631-0777	631-0500	4-8	Helena Cullen-Hamzeh
Martha's Vineyard Charter S	PO Box 1150	West Tisbury, MA	02575-1150	508-693-9900	696-9008	K-12	Robert Moore
MATCH Charter S	1001 Commonwealth Ave	Boston, MA	02215-1308	617-232-0300	232-2838	PK-12	Hannah Larkin
McAuliffe Regional Charter S	139 Newbury St Ste 1	Framingham, MA	01701-4591	508-879-9000	879-1066	6-8	Kristin Harrison
Mystic Valley Regional Charter S	770 Salem St	Malden, MA	02148-4415	781-388-0222	321-5688	K-12	Martin Trice
Neighborhood House Charter S	21 Queen St	Dorchester, MA	02122-2509	617-825-0703	825-1829	PK-8	Kate Scott
New Heights Charter S of Brockton	1690 Main St	Brockton, MA	02301	508-857-4633	857-5721	6-8	Janice Manning
New Liberty Innovation S	2 East India Square	Salem, MA	01970	978-825-3470	825-3475	9-12	Jennifer Winsor
Old Sturbridge Academy	1 Old Sturbridge Village Rd	Sturbridge, MA	01566	508-347-0271		K-8	Jim Donahue
Parker Charter Essential S	49 Antietam St	Ayer, MA	01434-5230	978-772-3293	772-3295	7-12	Todd Sumner
Phoenix Academy	15 Union St	Lawrence, MA	01840	978-722-8410	686-3613	9-12	Tamara Soraluz
Phoenix Charter Academy	175 Hawthorne St	Chelsea, MA	02150	617-889-3100	889-3144	9-12	Kevin Dean
Phoenix Charter Academy Springfield	65 Lincoln St	Springfield, MA	01105	413-273-1236		9-12	Jacqueline Adam-Taylor
Pioneer Charter S of Science	51 Summer St	Everett, MA	02149-3741	617-389-7277	389-7278	K-12	Sanela Jonuz
Pioneer Charter S of Science II	97 Main St	Saugus, MA	01906	781-666-3907	666-3910	7-12	Vahit Sevinc
Pioneer Valley Chinese Immrsn Charter S	317 Russell St	Hadley, MA	01035	413-582-7040	582-7068	K-12	Kathleen Wang
Pioneer Valley Performing Arts Charter S	15 Mulligan Dr	South Hadley, MA	01075-7511	413-552-1580	552-1594	7-12	George Simpson
Prospect Hill Academy Charter S	50 Essex St	Cambridge, MA	02139-2602	617-284-7800	284-7980	K-12	Angela Allen Ph.D.
Rising Tide Charter S	6 Resnik Rd	Plymouth, MA	02360-4873	508-747-2620	830-9441	5-12	Tyler Post
River Valley Charter S	2 Perry Way	Newburyport, MA	01950-4001	978-465-0065	465-0119	K-8	Andrew Willemsen
Roxbury Prep HS	86 Wachusett St	Jamaica Plain, MA	02130	617-858-2288	275-4004	9-12	Shradha Patel
Roxbury Prep Mission Hill Campus	120 Fisher Ave	Roxbury, MA	02120-3320	617-566-2361	566-2373	5-8	Ryan Kelly
Roxbury Prep S Dorchester Campus	206 Magnolia St	Dorchester, MA	02121	617-858-2300	275-5760	5-8	Dan Cosgrove
Roxbury Prep S Lucy Stone Campus	22 Regina Rd	Dorchester, MA	02124	617-979-0115	822-7527	5-8	Nikhil Bhatia
SABIS International Charter S	160 Joan St	Springfield, MA	01129-1530	413-783-2600	783-2555	K-12	Karen Reuter
Salem Academy Charter S	45 Congress St	Salem, MA	01970-5579	978-744-2105	744-7246	6-12	Stephanie Callahan
Seven Hills Charter S	51 Gage St	Worcester, MA	01605-3014	508-799-7500	713-0956	K-8	Michael Barth
Silver Hill Horace Mann Charter S	675 Washington St	Haverhill, MA	01832-4523	978-374-3448	374-3461	K-5	Margaret Shepherd
Sizer S	500 Rindge Rd	Fitchburg, MA	01420	978-345-2701	345-9127	7-12	David Perrigo
South Shore Charter S	100 Longwater Cir	Norwell, MA	02061-1650	781-982-4202	982-4201	K-12	Angie Pepin
Springfield Prep Charter S	370 Pine St	Springfield, MA	01105	413-231-2722	215-0004	K-8	Bill Spirer
Sturgis Charter Public S	427 Main St	Hyannis, MA	02601-3905	508-778-1782	771-6785	9-12	Paul Marble
UP Academy	215 Dorchester St	South Boston, MA	02127-2876	617-635-8819	635-8820	6-8	Katy Buckland
UP Academy	60 Allen St	Lawrence, MA	01840-1806	978-722-8159	722-8533	6-8	Komal Bhasin
UP Academy Dorchester	35 Westville St	Dorchester, MA	02124	617-635-8810	635-8815	PK-8	Jabari Peddie
UP Academy Holland	85 Olney St	Dorchester, MA	02121-3535	617-635-8832	220-3023	PK-5	Hillary Casson
UP Academy Kennedy MS	1385 Berkshire Ave	Springfield, MA	01151	413-787-7510	787-7561	6-8	Desmond Caldwell
UP Academy Oliver MS	233 Haverhill St	Lawrence, MA	01840	978-242-7446	722-8527	6-8	Kelsey Lebuffe
Veritas Preparatory Charter S	370 Pine St	Springfield, MA	01105	413-539-0055	306-5076	5-8	Rachel Romano

Michigan

School	Address	City,State	Zip code	Telephone	Fax	Grade	Contact
Abney Academy	1435 Fulton St E	Grand Rapids, MI	49503-3853	616-454-5541	454-5598	K-6	Paul Adams
Academic and Career Education Academy	884 E Isabella Rd	Midland, MI	48640-8326	989-631-5202	631-4541	9-12	Michelle Zielinski
Academy of Business and Technology	19625 Wood St	Melvindale, MI	48122-2201	313-382-3422	382-3906	6-12	Carmen Willingham
Academy of Business and Technology ES	5277 Calhoun St	Dearborn, MI	48126-3203	313-581-2223	581-2247	K-5	Dr. Paul Merritt
Academy of International Studies	2609 Poland St	Hamtramck, MI	48212	313-873-9900	262-6440	K-8	Dawn Lynk-Jones
Academy of Warren	13943 E 8 Mile Rd	Warren, MI	48089-3351	586-552-8010	552-8014	K-8	Jim Perry
Achieve Charter Acadmey	3250 Denton Rd	Canton, MI	48188-2110	734-397-0960	397-0968	K-7	Jen Conley
Advanced Technology Academy	4801 Oakman Blvd	Dearborn, MI	48126-3755	313-625-4700	582-9407	K-12	Cynthia Anderson
A.G.B.U. Alex & Marie Manoogian S	22001 Northwestern Hwy	Southfield, MI	48075-4081	248-569-2988	569-1346	K-12	Dyana Kezelian
Alternative Educational Acad Ogemaw Co.	2389 S M 76	West Branch, MI	48661	989-362-3006	362-9076	6-12	Dana McGrew
American International Academy	27100 Avondale	Inkster, MI	48141	734-713-5525	713-9007	6-10	Tom White
American International Academy	300 S Henry Ruff	Westland, MI	48186	734-713-5525	713-9007	K-5	Tom White
American Montessori Academy	14800 Middlebelt Rd	Livonia, MI	48154-4031	734-525-7100	525-8952	K-2	Andrea Curd
American Montessori Academy Upper ES	17175 Olympia	Redford, MI	48240	313-533-0000	533-0005	3-8	Renee Arnot
Ann Arbor Learning Community	3980 Research Park Dr	Ann Arbor, MI	48108-2220	734-477-0340	929-6505	K-8	Abby Kuhn
Arbor Academy	55 Arbor St	Battle Creek, MI	49015-2903	269-963-5851	964-2643	K-8	Brandy Resman
Arbor Preparatory HS	6800 Hitchingham Rd	Ypsilanti, MI	48197-8998	734-961-9700	961-9701	9-12	Aquan Grant
Arts Academy in the Woods	32101 Caroline	Fraser, MI	48026-3209	586-294-0391	294-0617	9-12	Michael Mitchell
Arts & Technology Academy of Pontiac	888 Enterprise Dr	Pontiac, MI	48341-3167	248-452-9309	452-9312	PK-12	Septembra Williams
Augusta Academy	600 W Michigan Ave	Augusta, MI	49012	269-731-5454		K-5	Meadow Nuyen
Bahweting Charter S	1301 Marquette Ave	Sault S Marie, MI	49783-9533	906-635-5055	635-3805	K-8	Lynn Methner
Battle Creek Area Learning Center	15 Arbor St	Battle Creek, MI	49015-2903	269-565-2460	565-2468	9-12	Timothy Allard
Battle Creek Montessori Academy	399 20th St N	Springfield, MI	49037-4815	269-339-3308	339-3309	PK-8	Jessica Eldridge
Bay-Arenac Community HS	805 Langstaff St	Essexville, MI	48732-1367	989-893-8811	895-7749	9-12	Ryan Donlan
Bay City Academy - Farragut Campus	301 N Farragut St	Bay City, MI	48708	989-414-8254	321-2225	K-10	Darci Long
Benton Harbor Charter S	455 Riverview Dr	Benton Harbor, MI	49022-5080	269-925-3807	927-3673	PK-8	Tim Harris
Black River Public S	491 Columbia Ave	Holland, MI	49423-4838	616-355-0055	355-0057	K-12	Shannon Brunink
Blended Lrng Acad Credit Recovery HS	1754 E Clark Rd	Lansing, MI	48906-1020	517-574-4667		9-12	Dr. Tim Brannan
Blue Water Middle College Academy	323 Erie St	Port Huron, MI	48060-3812	810-989-5805	989-5848	9-12	Pete Spencer
Boggs S	4141 Mitchell St	Detroit, MI	48207-1620	313-923-2301	923-2300	K-6	Julia Putnam
Bradford Academy	24218 Garner St	Southfield, MI	48033-2900	248-351-0000	356-4770	K-12	Cheryl Paull
Branch Line S	16360 Hubbard St	Livonia, MI	48154-6100	734-335-0663		K-8	Jennifer Wilkins
Bridge Academy - East	9600 Buffalo St	Hamtramck, MI	48212-3323	313-624-6100	624-6200	PK-8	Mohammed Alsanai
Bridge Academy - West	3105 Carpenter Rd	Detroit, MI	48212	313-462-6200	462-6201	6-8	Mohammad Alsanai
Burton Glen Charter Academy	4171 E Atherton Rd	Burton, MI	48519-1435	810-744-2300	744-2400	K-8	Aaron Williams
Byron Center Charter S	9930 Burlingame Ave SW	Byron Center, MI	49315-8631	616-878-4852	878-7196	K-12	Thomas Berriman
Caniff Liberty Academy	2650 Caniff St	Hamtramck, MI	48212-3033	313-872-2000	338-3344	K-8	Rebecca Snoblin
Canton Charter Academy	49100 Ford Rd	Canton, MI	48187-5415	734-453-9517	453-9551	K-8	Kelie Fuller
Canton Preparatory HS	46610 Cherry Hill Rd	Canton, MI	48187	734-656-0003	656-0009	9-10	Stephanie Roberts

School	Address	City,State	Zip code	Telephone	Fax	Grade	Contact
Capstone Academy	3500 John R St	Detroit, MI	48201-2402	313-202-6082	831-3510	4-12	Brian Serafino
Carleton Academy	2001 W Hallett Rd	Hillsdale, MI	49242-1959	517-437-2000	437-2919	K-12	Colleen Vogt
Carver Academy	14510 2nd Ave	Highland Park, MI	48203-5715	313-865-6024	865-6658	K-8	Dez'arae Adams
CASMAN Alternative Academy	225 9th St	Manistee, MI	49660-3109	231-723-4981	723-1555	7-12	Michelle VanVoorst
Central Academy	2459 S Industrial Hwy	Ann Arbor, MI	48104-6129	734-822-1100	822-1101	PK-12	Dr. Luay Shalabi
Cesar Chavez Academy - Elementary East	4130 Maxwell St	Detroit, MI	48214-1109	313-924-0317	924-0425	K-5	Adasina Philyaw
Chandler Park Academy ES	20200 Kelly Rd	Harper Woods, MI	48225-1203	313-884-8830	884-9130	K-5	Marian Flaggs
Chandler Park Academy HS	20234 Kelly Rd	Harper Woods, MI	48225	313-499-3010	499-3052	9-12	Shaun Black
Chandler Park Academy MS	20100 Kelly Rd	Harper Woods, MI	48225-1201	313-839-9886	839-3221	6-8	Kenneth Williams
Chandler Woods Charter Academy	6895 Samrick Ave NE	Belmont, MI	49306-8844	616-866-6000	866-6001	PK-8	Joe Hammond
Charlevoix Montessori Academy for Arts	115 W Hurlbut St	Charlevoix, MI	49720-1510	231-547-9000	547-9464	K-12	Kali Kondrat
Chatfield S	231 Lake Dr	Lapeer, MI	48446-1661	810-667-8970	667-8983	K-8	Matt Young
Chavez HS	1761 Waterman St	Detroit, MI	48209-2194	313-551-0611	552-0552	9-12	Juan Martinez
Chavez Lower Academy	8126 W Vernor Hwy	Detroit, MI	48209-1524	313-843-9440	297-6948	K-2	Gabriela Jaime
Chavez MS	6782 Goldsmith St	Detroit, MI	48209-2089	313-842-0006	842-0167	6-8	April Jenkins
Chavez Upper ES	4100 Martin St	Detroit, MI	48210-2806	313-361-1083	361-1095	3-5	Thomas Goodley
Cole Academy	1915 W Mount Hope Ave	Lansing, MI	48910-2434	517-372-0038	372-1446	K-6	Brian Shaughnessy
Commonwealth Community Development Acad	13477 Eureka St	Hamtramck, MI	48212-1754	313-366-9470	366-9471	K-8	Angela Moore
Concord Academy - Boyne	401 E Dietz Rd	Boyne City, MI	49712-9653	231-582-0194	582-4214	K-12	Rebekah Leist
Concord Academy-Petoskey	2468 Atkins Rd	Petoskey, MI	49770-9003	231-439-6800	439-6803	K-12	Robert Ollar
Conner Creek Academy East	16911 Eastland St	Roseville, MI	48066-2078	586-779-8055	498-8734	K-6	Karen Smith
Cornerstone Health and Technology S	17351 Southfield Rd	Detroit, MI	48235	313-486-4260		9-12	Jared Davis
Cornerstone Jefferson-Douglass Academy	6861 E Nevada Ave	Detroit, MI	48234	313-314-1300		K-8	Kalyani Bhatt
Countryside Academy	4821 North St	Benton Harbor, MI	49022	269-944-5655	944-5695	K-2	Nathaniel Smith
Countryside Academy	4800 Meadowbrook Rd	Benton Harbor, MI	49022-9629	269-944-3319	944-0242	3-12	Sean Deiters
Covenant House Academy Central	2959 Martin Luther King Jr	Detroit, MI	48208-2475	313-899-6900	899-6910	9-12	Anna West
Covenant House Academy East	7600 Goethe St	Detroit, MI	48214-1762	313-267-4315	267-4320	9-12	Nathaniel King
Covenant House Academy - Grand Rapids	50 Antoine St SW	Grand Rapids, MI	49507	616-364-2000		9-12	Markeith Large
Covenant House Academy SW	1450 25th St	Detroit, MI	48216	313-297-8720	297-8730	9-12	Eric George
Creative Montessori Academy	15100 Northline Rd	Southgate, MI	48195-2408	734-284-5600	281-2637	PK-8	Carol Hutton
Creative Technologies Academy	350 Pine St	Cedar Springs, MI	49319-8680	616-696-4905	696-4920	K-12	Dan George
Crescent Academy	17570 W 12 Mile Rd	Southfield, MI	48076-1905	248-423-4581	423-1027	PK-12	Dr. Cherise Cupidore M.Ed.
Crockett Academy	4851 14th St	Detroit, MI	48208-2204	313-896-6078	896-1363	K-12	Monique Woodland-Phillip
Cross Creek Charter Academy	7701 Kalamazoo Ave SE	Byron Center, MI	49315-9534	616-656-4000	656-4001	PK-8	Joe Nieuwkoop
Crossroads Charter Academy	215 N State St	Big Rapids, MI	49307-1444	231-796-6589	796-9874	K-6	Ross Meads
Crossroads Charter Academy	215 Spruce St W	Big Rapids, MI	49307-1471	231-796-9041	796-9790	7-12	Ross Meads
da Vinci HS	2255 Emmons Rd	Jackson, MI	49201-8335	517-796-0031	796-0320	9-12	Sandy Maxson
da Vinci PS	559 Murphy St	Jackson, MI	49202	517-780-9980	780-9747	K-8	Kristi Neelis
Dearborn Academy	19310 Ford Rd Ste 2	Dearborn, MI	48128-2403	313-982-1300	982-9087	K-8	Afrin Alavi
DeTour Arts & Technology Academy	202 Division St	De Tour Village, MI	49725-5006	906-297-2011	297-3403	K-12	Brooke Maciag
Detroit Academy of Arts & Sciences	2985 E Jefferson Ave	Detroit, MI	48207-4288	313-259-1744	393-0404	K-5	Gabriela Chulevski
Detroit Academy of Arts & Sciences MS	2985 E Jefferson Ave	Detroit, MI	48207	313-259-1744	393-0404	6-8	Janocus Sanders
Detroit Achievement Academy	7000 W Outer Dr	Detroit, MI	48235	313-468-9518		K-5	Sharon Yaecker-Roesser
Detroit Collegiate HS	3111 Elmwood St	Detroit, MI	48207	313-977-9178	977-9623	9-12	Edwynn Bell
Detroit Community ES	12675 Burt Rd	Detroit, MI	48223-3314	313-537-3570	537-6904	K-8	Sharon McPhail
Detroit Community HS	12675 Burt Rd	Detroit, MI	48223-3314	313-537-3570	537-6904	9-12	Sharon McPhail
Detroit Delta Prep Acad Social Justice	3550 John C Lodge Fwy	Detroit, MI	48201	313-638-1444		9-12	William Tandy
Detroit Edison Academy	1903 Wilkins St	Detroit, MI	48207-2112	313-833-1100	833-8653	K-12	Ralph Bland
Detroit Enterprise Academy	11224 Kercheval St	Detroit, MI	48214-3323	313-823-5799	823-0342	K-8	Chanavia Patterson
Detroit Innovation Academy	18211 Plymouth Rd	Detroit, MI	48228	313-736-5537	242-1527	K-8	Sherie Manthiram
Detroit Leadership Academy ES	13550 Virgil St	Detroit, MI	48223	313-242-1500	241-1527	K-5	Jill Mackellar
Detroit Leadership Academy HS	5845 Auburn St	Detroit, MI	48228	313-769-2015	791-7994	6-12	Edwynn Bell
Detroit Merit Academy	1091 Alter Rd	Detroit, MI	48215-2861	313-331-3328	331-3278	PK-8	Sandra Terry-Martin
Detroit Premier Academy	7781 Asbury Park	Detroit, MI	48228-3685	313-945-1472	945-1744	K-8	James Kinsey
Detroit Prep	2411 Iroquois Ave	Detroit, MI	48214	313-343-1495		K-2	Jen McMillan
Detroit Public Safety Academy	1250 Rosa Parks Blvd	Detroit, MI	48216-1950	313-965-6916	965-6938	7-12	Isaiah Pettway
Detroit Service Learning Academy	21605 W 7 Mile Rd	Detroit, MI	48219-1810	313-541-7619	541-7656	PK-8	Shannon Smith
Distinctive College Prep	19360 Harper Ave	Harper Woods, MI	48225	313-969-7671		K-3	Cassie Williams
Douglass International Acad	21700 Marlow St	Oak Park, MI	48237-2604	248-953-2003		PK-6	Robert Davis
Dove Academy of Detroit	20001 Wexford St	Detroit, MI	48234-1807	313-366-9110	366-9130	PK-8	Brandon Slone M.Ed.
Eagle Crest Charter Academy	11950 Riley St	Holland, MI	49424-8553	616-786-2400	786-4692	K-8	Jack DeLeeuw Ed.D.
Eagle's Nest Academy	5005 Cloverlawn Dr	Flint, MI	48504	810-869-6495	853-6404	K-6	Dr. Brigitte Jackson
East Arbor Charter Academy	6885 Merritt Rd	Ypsilanti, MI	48197-8958	734-484-5506	547-3078	K-8	Tanesha Newby
East Shore Leadership Academy	1403 7th St	Port Huron, MI	48060	810-247-0687		K-8	Nancy Gardner
Eaton Academy	21450 Universal Ave	Eastpointe, MI	48021-2969	586-777-1519	777-1527	K-8	Maria E. (Kenis) Walleva
Edgewood Elementary Academy	3028 Howden St	Muskegon Hts, MI	49444	231-830-3250	830-3576	PK-1	James Russell
El-Hajj Malik El-Shabazz Academy	1028 W Barnes Ave	Lansing, MI	48910-1308	517-267-8474	484-0095	PK-6	Vincent Price
Ellis Academy	18977 Schaefer Hwy	Detroit, MI	48235-1762	313-927-5395	927-5376	K-8	Michael Johnson
Ellis Academy West	19800 Beech Daly Rd	Redford, MI	48240-1348	313-450-0300	450-0305	PK-8	Tyron Hurd
Endeavor Charter Academy	380 Helmer Rd N	Springfield, MI	49037-7776	269-962-9300	962-9393	K-8	Angela Wyckoff
Excel Charter Academy	4201 Breton Rd SE	Grand Rapids, MI	49512-3857	616-281-9339	281-6707	K-8	Daniel Bartels
Faxon Language Immersion Academy	28555 Middlebelt Rd	Farmingtn Hls, MI	48334-4104	248-702-6272	702-6376	K-8	Rosalie Cohen
Flagship Charter Academy	13661 Wisconsin St	Detroit, MI	48238-2356	313-933-7933	933-9061	K-8	Faren D'Abell
Flat River Academy	9481 Jordan Rd	Greenville, MI	48838-9437	616-754-9360	754-9363	K-12	Elizabeth Kreiner
FlexTech HS	7707 Conference Center Dr	Brighton, MI	48114-7334	810-844-3366	229-2331	9-12	Ryan Gillis
FlexTech HS Novi	24245 Karim Blvd	Novi, MI	48375	248-426-8530	426-8557	9-12	Sarah Pazur
Ford Academy: S for Creative Studies	10225 3rd St	Detroit, MI	48202-1287	313-826-1159	731-0400	K-5	Felicia Brimage
Ford Academy	20651 W Warren St	Dearborn Hts, MI	48127-2622	313-436-0020	441-9169	5-12	Dr. Beverly Baroni
Ford Academy	PO Box 1148	Dearborn, MI	48121-1148	313-982-6200	982-6195	9-12	Cora Christmas
Ford Academy/Schl for Creative Studies	485 W Milwaukee St	Detroit, MI	48202-3220	313-481-4000	481-4001	6-12	Dr. Curtis Lewis
Forest Academy	5196 Comstock Ave	Kalamazoo, MI	49048	269-488-2315	488-2317	K-8	Amanda Brown
Fortis Academy	3875 Golfside Rd	Ypsilanti, MI	48197-3726	734-572-3623	572-5792	K-8	Ira Kleiman
Four Corners Montessori Academy	1075 E Gardenia Ave	Madison Heights, MI	48071-3433	248-542-7001	542-7901	PK-8	Chris Schoenherr
Francis Street PS	PO Box 1562	Jackson, MI	49204	734-719-0024		K-2	Laura Wyble
Frontier International Academy	28111 Imperial Dr	Warren, MI	48093	586-354-2044		K-5	Dr. Rana Khalaf
Frontier International Academy	13200 Conant St	Hamtramck, MI	48212	313-462-6300	316-4554	9-12	Adnan Aabed
Gateway to Success Academy	526 N Scottville Rd	Scottville, MI	49454	231-845-0922	258-8162	6-12	James Bandstra
GEE Edmonson Academy	1300 W Canfield St	Detroit, MI	48201-1006	313-228-0910	447-2533	PK-8	Domini Nailer
GEE White Academy	5161 Charles St	Detroit, MI	48212-2462	313-228-0911		PK-8	Thomas Talmadge M.Ed.
Genesee STEM Academy	5240 Calkins Rd	Flint, MI	48532	810-600-6466	600-6445	K-9	Rita Cheek
Global Heights Academy	23713 Joy Rd	Dearborn Hts, MI	48127-1408	313-624-3400	624-3401	PK-5	Shawn Robson
Global Preparatory Academy	26200 Ridgemont St	Roseville, MI	48066	586-575-9500	575-9483	PK-6	Robert Hooper
Global Tech Academy	1715 E Forest Ave	Ypsilanti, MI	48198-4160	734-390-9625		K-5	Robin Tolbert
Grand Blanc Academy	5135 E Hill Rd	Grand Blanc, MI	48439-7637	810-953-3140	953-3165	K-8	Patty Wood
Grand Rapids Child Discovery Center	409 Lafayette Ave SE	Grand Rapids, MI	49503-5329	616-459-0330	732-4437	K-5	Sarah Cooper
Grand River Academy	28111 8 Mile Rd	Livonia, MI	48152-2359	248-893-6100	479-1996	K-8	Alan Harper
Grand River Prep HS	650 52nd St SE	Kentwood, MI	49548-5837	616-261-1800	261-1853	9-12	Koree Woodward
Grand Traverse Academy	1245 Hammond Rd E	Traverse City, MI	49686-9000	231-995-0665	995-0880	PK-12	Susan Dameron
Greater Heights Academy	3196 W Pasadena Ave	Flint, MI	48504-2330	810-768-3860	768-3865	K-5	Lisa Leimeister
Great Lakes Academy	46312 Woodward Ave	Pontiac, MI	48342-5006	248-334-6434	334-6457	K-8	Sean Waters
Great Lakes Cyber Academy	2140 University Park # 270	Okemos, MI	48864	517-381-5062	381-5090	6-12	Heather Ballien
Great Oaks Academy	4257 Bart Ave	Warren, MI	48091-1977	586-427-4540	427-4541	K-8	Damon Williams
Greenspire S	1026 Red Dr	Traverse City, MI	49684-4593	231-421-5905	805-1327	6-8	Kevin Kelly
Hamilton Academy	14223 Southampton St	Detroit, MI	48213-3744	313-866-4505	344-7981	K-8	Dr. P. Bilbrew
Hamtramck Academy	11420 Conant St	Hamtramck, MI	48212-3134	313-368-7312	368-7376	K-8	Michael Griffie
Hanley International Academy	2400 Denton St	Hamtramck, MI	48212-3616	313-875-8888	875-8889	PK-8	Shameka McPherson
Heston Academy	1350 N Saint Helen Rd	Saint Helen, MI	48656-9521	989-632-3390	632-3393	PK-12	David Patterson
Highland Park Renaissance Academy	45 E Buena Vista St	Highland Park, MI	48203-3343	313-957-3005	868-0345	PK-12	Carmen Willingham
Highpoint Virtual Academy of Michigan	PO Box 596	Mesick, MI	49668	855-831-0145		K-9	Mary Moorman
Hillsdale Preparatory S	160 Mechanic Rd	Hillsdale, MI	49242-1053	517-437-4625	437-3830	K-8	Stephen Philipp
Holly Academy	820 Academy Rd	Holly, MI	48442-1546	248-634-5554	634-5564	K-8	Julie Kildee
Honey Creek Community S	PO Box 1406	Ann Arbor, MI	48106-1406	734-994-2636	994-2341	K-8	Al Waters
Hope Academy	12121 Broadstreet Ave	Detroit, MI	48204-1550	313-934-0054	934-0074	K-8	Dr. Ronald E. Williams
Hope Academy of West Michigan	240 Brown St SE	Grand Rapids, MI	49507-2502	616-301-8458	264-3346	K-12	Phil Haack
Hope of Detroit Academy	4444 35th St	Detroit, MI	48210	313-897-8720	897-5142	5-11	Ali Abdel
Hope of Detroit Academy	4443 N Campbell St	Detroit, MI	48210-2520	313-897-8720	897-5142	K-4	Ali Abdel
Huron Academy	36301 Utica Rd	Clinton Twp, MI	48035	586-690-8180		3-8	Mark Talbot
Huron Academy	11401 Metropolitan Pkwy	Sterling Hts, MI	48312-2937	586-446-9170	446-9173	PK-2	Mark Talbot
ICademy Global	8485 Homestead Dr	Zeeland, MI	49464	616-748-5637	772-0373	K-12	Tyler Huizenga
Inkster Preparatory Academy	27355 Woodsfield St	Inkster, MI	48141	313-278-3825		K-4	Shawn Hurt
Innocademy	8485 Homestead Dr	Zeeland, MI	49464-8969	616-748-5637	772-0373	K-12	kelli Gunn
Innocademy Allegan Campus	2611 56th St	Fennville, MI	49408	269-561-4050	772-0373	K-8	Marty Lappe
Insight S of Michigan	6512 Centurion Dr Ste 320	Lansing, MI	48917-8248	877-842-3793		6-12	Teresa Boardman
International Academy of Flint	2820 S Saginaw St	Flint, MI	48503-5708	810-600-5000	600-5300	K-12	Reginald Kirkland
International Academy of Saginaw	1944 Iowa Ave	Saginaw, MI	48601-5213	989-921-1000	921-1001	K-8	Christopher Matheson
Island City Academy	6421 S Clinton Trl	Eaton Rapids, MI	48827-9698	517-663-0111	663-0167	PK-8	William Aaron Warren
Jackson Preparatory & Early College S	2111 Emmons Rd	Jackson, MI	49201	517-768-7093	795-2735	6-12	Shane Malmquist

School	Address	City,State	Zip code	Telephone	Fax	Grade	Contact
Jefferson International Academy	825 Golf Dr	Pontiac, MI	48341	248-338-2787		4-8	Dr. Elizabeth Herron-Ruff
Jefferson International Academy	60 S Lynn Ave	Waterford, MI	48328	248-682-5000	481-2053	PK-3	Dr. Elizabeth Herron-Ruff
Joy Preparatory Academy	15055 Dexter Ave	Detroit, MI	48238-2124	313-340-0023	340-0678	PK-8	Frances Gardulescu
Kalamazoo Covenant Academy	400 W Crosstown Pkwy	Kalamazoo, MI	49001	269-226-2100	226-2114	9-12	Jerri Williams-Harper
Kensington Woods HS	PO Box 206	Lakeland, MI	48143-0206	517-545-0828	545-7588	6-12	Markus Muennix
Keys Grace Academy	27321 Hampden St	Madison Heights, MI	48071	248-629-7700	629-7708	K-8	Lisa Mansour
Keystone Academy	47925 Bemis Rd	Belleville, MI	48111-9760	734-697-9470	697-9471	K-8	Keturah Godfrey
King Education Center	16827 Appoline St	Detroit, MI	48235-4205	313-341-4944	341-7014	K-8	Dr. Constance Price
King Jr. Academy	55 E Sherman Blvd	Muskegon Hts, MI	49444	231-830-3600	830-3572	2-6	Vanessa Marble
Kingsbury Country Day S	5000 Hosner Rd	Oxford, MI	48370-1000	248-628-2571	628-3612	PK-8	David Poirier
Knapp Charter Academy	1759 Leffingwell Ave NE	Grand Rapids, MI	49525-4531	616-364-1100	364-9780	PK-8	Dave Turcotte
Lakeside Charter S	3921 Oakland Dr	Kalamazoo, MI	49008-4820	269-202-5536	381-5332	4-12	Steven Laidacker
Lake Superior Academy	8936 S Mackinac Trl	Sault S Marie, MI	49783	906-259-1168		K-3	Susie Schlehuber
Landmark Academy	4800 Lapoor Rd	Kimball, MI	48074-1517	810-982-7210	982-0679	K-12	Debby Wilton
Lansing Charter Academy	3300 Express Ct	Lansing, MI	48910-4370	517-882-9585	882-9587	K-6	Erin Melcher
Laurus Academy	24590 Lahser Rd	Southfield, MI	48033-6040	248-799-8401	799-8404	K-8	Dr. Carolyn Boyer
Leelanau Montessori Academy	PO Box 838	Suttons Bay, MI	49682-0838	231-271-8609	271-8689	PK-6	Rebecca Creighton
Legacy Charter Academy	4900 E Hildale St	Detroit, MI	48234-2225	313-368-2215	432-2807	K-8	Letoskey Carey
Life Skills Center of Pontiac	142 Auburn Ave	Pontiac, MI	48342-3008	248-322-1163	322-1164	9-12	Keisha Palmer
Life Tech Academy	3101 Technology Blvd Ste A	Lansing, MI	48910	517-325-5469	325-5468	7-12	Thomas Ackerson
Lighthouse Academy	3330 36th St SE	Grand Rapids, MI	49512-2810	616-949-2287	949-2379	K-12	Jamie San Miguel
Lighthouse Academy - North Campus	1260 Ekhart St NE	Grand Rapids, MI	49503-1380	616-965-9700	965-9701	3-12	Todd Penning
Light of the World Academy	550 E Hamburg St	Pinckney, MI	48169	734-720-9760	720-9763	PK-8	Kathy Moorehouse
Lincoln-King Academy	13436 Grove St	Detroit, MI	48235-4222	313-862-2352	862-2462	PK-8	Carolyn Brown
Linden Charter Academy	3244 N Linden Rd	Flint, MI	48504-1753	810-720-0515	720-0626	K-8	Deonna Washington
Livingston Classical Cyber Academy	8877 Main St	Whitmore Lake, MI	48189	734-839-6307		K-9	DeNesha Rawls-Smith
MacDowell Preparatory Academy	4201 W Outer Dr	Detroit, MI	48221	313-494-8141	494-8142	PK-7	Lindsie Boykin
Macomb Academy	39092 Garfield Rd	Clinton Twp, MI	48038-2790	586-228-2201	228-2210	12-12	Andrew Wise
Macomb Montessori Academy	14057 E 9 Mile Rd	Warren, MI	48089	586-359-2138	533-2812	K-6	Ashley Ogonowski
Madison Academy	6170 Torrey Rd	Flint, MI	48507-5954	810-655-2949	655-2931	K-6	Tricai Osborne
Madison Academy - HS	3266 S Genesee Rd	Burton, MI	48519	810-875-9050	877-6255	9-12	Tamiko Powell-Johnson
Madison-Carver Academy	19900 McIntyre St	Detroit, MI	48219-1263	313-486-4626		K-8	Pamela Farris
Marshall Academy	18203 Homer Rd	Marshall, MI	49068-8718	269-781-6330	781-8749	K-12	Brent Swan
Merritt Academy	59900 Havenridge Rd	New Haven, MI	48048-1915	586-749-6000	749-8582	PK-12	Nathan Seiferlein
Metro Charter Academy	34800 Ecorse Rd	Romulus, MI	48174-1642	734-641-3200	641-6530	K-8	Shelli Wildfong
Michigan Collegiate MSHS	31300 Ryan Rd	Warren, MI	48092	586-777-5792	698-0392	7-12	Vergil Smith
Michigan Connections Academy	3950 Heritage Ave Ste 100	Okemos, MI	48864-3389	517-507-5390	507-5389	K-12	Bryan Klochack
Michigan Great Lakes Virtual Academy	50 Filer St Ste F	Manistee, MI	49660-2788	855-380-2480	794-6416	K-12	Kendall Schroeder
Michigan Mathematics & Science Academy	27300 Dequindre Rd	Warren, MI	48092	586-353-2108	353-2109	K-12	Oguzhan Yildiz M.Ed.
Michigan Virtual Academy	678 Front Ave NW	Grand Rapids, MI	49504-5325	877-794-9427	843-5871	K-12	Andrei Nichols
Midland Acad Advanced & Creative Studies	4653 E Bailey Bridge Rd	Midland, MI	48640-8542	989-496-2404	496-2466	K-12	Dr. Katherine Jock
Mid-Michigan Leadership Academy	730 W Maple St	Lansing, MI	48906-5086	517-485-5379	485-5892	K-8	Tim Tenneriello
Momentum Academy	99 E Woodward Heights Blvd	Hazel Park, MI	48030-1450	248-336-5600	808-6478	PK-8	LaMonte Fondren
Mt. Clemens Montessori Academy	1070 Hampton Rd	Mount Clemens, MI	48043-2955	586-465-5545	465-2283	PK-5	Stelgene P'sachoulias
Multicultural Academy	5550 Platt Rd	Ann Arbor, MI	48108-9762	734-677-0732	677-0740	PK-8	Dr. Naji Shalabi
Murphy Academy	23901 Fenkell St	Detroit, MI	48223-1431	313-409-8453	494-7550	K-8	Jason Drain
Muskegon Covenant Academy	125 Catherine Ave	Muskegon, MI	49442-3331	231-720-3100		9-12	Jim VanBergen
Muskegon Heights Academy	2441 Sanford St	Muskegon Hts, MI	49444-1438	231-830-3700	830-3534	7-12	Calvin Sims
Muskegon Montessori Academy	2950 McCracken St	Norton Shores, MI	49441-3623	231-766-7500	766-7215	K-6	Ali DuBois
New Bedford Academy	6315 Secor Rd	Lambertville, MI	48144-9411	734-854-5437	854-1573	K-8	Greg Sauter
New Beginnings Academy	211 E Michigan Ave	Ypsilanti, MI	48198-5677	734-481-9001	544-2706	K-6	Kenya Crockett
New Branches Charter Academy	3662 Poinsettia Ave SE	Grand Rapids, MI	49508	616-243-6221	243-6221	PK-8	Terry Larkin
New Paradigm College Prep S	2450 S Beatrice St	Detroit, MI	48217	313-406-7060		K-5	Luvonia Perkins
New Paradigm Glazer Academy	2001 La Belle St	Detroit, MI	48238-2941	313-852-1500	852-1499	PK-7	Stanley Wheeler
New Paradigm Loving Academy	1000 Lynn St	Detroit, MI	48211-1081	313-252-3028	866-0989	PK-8	Thea Marsh
New School High	46250 Ann Arbor Rd W	Plymouth, MI	48170	734-386-6601	892-2107	9-12	Cynthia Burnstein
New Standard Academy	2040 W Carpenter Rd	Flint, MI	48505-1908	810-787-3330		PK-8	Calvin Sims
NexTech HS of Grand Rapids	801 Broadway Ave NW Ste 225	Grand Rapids, MI	49504	616-458-4992	458-6088	9-12	Daniel McMinn
NexTech HS of Lansing	2175 University Park Dr	Okemos, MI	48864	517-347-7793	347-7864	9-12	Charles Carver
NexTech HS of Metro Detroit	31333 Southfield Rd Ste 200	Beverly Hills, MI	48025	248-593-8440	593-8264	9-12	Diane Mayse
Noor International Academy	37412 Dequindre Rd	Sterling Hts, MI	48310	586-365-5000	365-5001	PK-6	Nawal Hamadeh
North Central Academy	5055 Corey Rd	Mancelona, MI	49659-9467	231-584-2080	356-5916	K-12	Tina McNeely
Northridge Academy	4100 W Coldwater Rd	Flint, MI	48504	810-785-8811	785-9844	K-8	Latricia Brown M.Ed.
North Saginaw Charter Academy	2332 Trautner Dr	Saginaw, MI	48604-9593	989-249-5400	249-5800	K-8	Sarah Simpson
North Star Academy	3030 Wright St	Marquette, MI	49855-9649	906-226-0156	226-0167	K-12	Joseph Kukulski
Oakland Academy	6325 Oakland Dr	Portage, MI	49024-2589	269-324-8951	324-8974	K-7	Shawn Boris
Oakland International Academy	4001 Miller St	Detroit, MI	48211	313-925-1000	925-1133	2-4	Mahasti Mafee
Oakland International Academy	6111 Miller St	Detroit, MI	48211	313-923-0790	923-0927	PK-1	Mahasti Mafee
Oakland International Academy - HS	2619 Florian St	Hamtramck, MI	48212-3452	313-285-8990	784-9438	9-12	Ahmed Saber
Oakland International Academy Middle	8228 Conant St	Detroit, MI	48211-1407	313-347-0246	347-0250	5-8	Ghassan Taha
Oakside Scholars Charter Academy	355 Summit Dr	Waterford, MI	48328-3366	248-706-2000	920-0351	K-8	Kathleen Grinwis
Ojibwe Charter S	11507 W Industrial Dr	Brimley, MI	49715-9087	906-248-2530	248-2532	K-12	Stephanie Vittitow
Old Redford Academy ES	17195 Redford St	Detroit, MI	48219-3259	313-532-7510	543-2055	K-5	Tomeka Dixon
Old Redford Academy MS	22122 W McNichols Rd	Detroit, MI	48219	313-412-2137	412-2162	6-8	Jennifer Neal
Old Redford Academy Prep HS	8001 W Outer Dr	Detroit, MI	48235-3293	313-543-3080	543-3129	9-12	Charles Davis M.Ed.
Outlook Academy	2879 116th Ave	Allegan, MI	49010-9004	269-673-2161	673-2361	5-12	Rick Cain
Pansophia Academy	52 Abbott Ave	Coldwater, MI	49036-1430	517-279-4686	279-0089	K-12	Jamie Mueller
Paragon Charter Academy	3750 McCain Rd	Jackson, MI	49201-7675	517-750-9500	750-9501	K-8	Ben Kriesch
Paramount Charter Academy	3624 S Westnedge Ave	Kalamazoo, MI	49008-2969	269-553-6400	553-6401	PK-8	Jodi Donkin
Paris Academy	PO Box 5142	Saginaw, MI	48603	989-401-9101	401-9105	K-12	
Pathways Academy	11340 E Jefferson Ave	Detroit, MI	48214	734-221-0977		7-12	Michelle Parham
Pathways Global Leadership Academy	30053 Parkwood St	Inkster, MI	48141	313-355-0952	731-0177	9-12	
Plymouth Educational Center	1460 E Forest Ave	Detroit, MI	48207-1000	313-831-3280	831-5766	PK-8	LaShanda Thomas
Plymouth Scholars Charter Academy	48484 N Territorial Rd	Plymouth, MI	48170	734-459-6149	864-0341	K-8	Walter Reese
Pollack Academic Center of Excellence	23777 Southfield Rd	Southfield, MI	48075-3458	248-569-1060	569-1403	K-8	Dr. Jamila Whitaker
Pontiac Academy for Excellence	196 Cesar E Chavez Ave	Pontiac, MI	48342	248-745-9420	745-4898	K-12	Nada Makki-Berry
Presque Isle Academy	20830 Cedar St	Onaway, MI	49765-8600	989-733-6708	733-6701	9-12	Earl Bassett
Prevail Academy	353 Cass Ave	Mount Clemens, MI	48043-2112	586-783-0173	783-0179	K-8	Colleen Furman
Quest Charter Academy	24745 Van Born Rd	Taylor, MI	48180-1221	734-299-0534	299-0577	K-8	Ralph Garza
Reach Academy	25275 Chippendale St	Roseville, MI	48066	586-498-9171	498-9173	K-8	Lorianne DeDomenico
Redford Service Learning Academy	25940 Grand River Ave	Redford, MI	48240-1435	313-539-4115	539-4660	K-8	Robert Warmack
Regent Park Scholars Charter Academy	15865 E 7 Mile Rd	Detroit, MI	48205-2545	313-371-1300	221-9942	K-8	Crystal Byse
Regents Academy	17715 Brady	Redford, MI	48240	888-473-2408	884-8266	K-12	Dr. Paula Watkins
Reh Academy	2201 Owen St	Saginaw, MI	48601-3466	989-753-2349	753-1819	PK-8	Kate Scheid
Renaissance Public S Academy	2797 S Isabella Rd	Mount Pleasant, MI	48858-2067	989-773-9889	772-4503	K-8	Lisa Bergman
Richfield Public School Academy	3807 N Center Rd	Flint, MI	48506-2642	810-736-1281	736-2326	PK-8	Pamela Haldy
Ridge Park Charter Academy	4120 Camelot Ridge Dr SE	Grand Rapids, MI	49546-2432	616-222-0093	222-0138	K-8	Hector Ulloa
Rising Stars Academy	23855 Lawrence	Center Line, MI	48015-1083	586-806-6455	806-6967	12-12	John Commyn
River City Scholars Charter Academy	944 Evergreen St	Grand Rapids, MI	49507	616-248-3390	723-0128	K-8	Holly Hillary
Riverside Academy East	7124 Miller Rd	Dearborn, MI	48126-1918	313-624-3200	624-3201	K-5	Eman Radha
Riverside Academy ECC	7050 Pinehurst St	Dearborn, MI	48126	313-624-3500	624-3599	PK-PK	
Riverside Academy West	6409 Schaefer Rd	Dearborn, MI	48126-2212	313-624-3600	624-3601	6-12	Ramzi Saab
Rose Leadership Academy	15000 Trojan St	Detroit, MI	48235	313-397-3333	397-4155	9-12	Wendie Lewis
Rutherford Winans Academy	16411 Curtis St	Detroit, MI	48235-3202	313-852-0709	852-0702	PK-5	Karen Abbott
Saginaw Learn to Earn Academy	1000 Tuscola St	Saginaw, MI	48607-1421	989-399-8775		9-12	Brad Gomoluch
Saginaw Preparatory Academy	5173 Lodge St	Saginaw, MI	48601-6829	989-752-9600	752-9618	PK-8	Molly Rundell
St. Clair County Intervention Academy	1170 Michigan Rd	Port Huron, MI	48060-4658	810-966-1649	966-4312	6-12	Troy Peyerk
SER Metro Learning Academy	9215 Michigan Ave	Detroit, MI	48210	313-846-2240		9-12	
South Arbor Charter Academy	8200 Carpenter Rd	Ypsilanti, MI	48197-9173	734-528-2821	528-2829	K-8	Kim Bondy
South Canton Scholars Charter Academy	3085 S Canton Center Rd	Canton, MI	48188-2452	734-398-5658	547-3077	K-8	Sabrina Terenzi
South Pointe Scholars Charter Academy	10550 Geddes Rd	Ypsilanti, MI	48198	734-484-0118	864-0353	K-8	Jamie Sheldon
Southwest Detroit Community S	4001 29th St	Detroit, MI	48210	313-782-4422	782-4469	K-8	Frank Donner
Star International Academy	24425 Hass St	Dearborn Hts, MI	48127-3275	313-724-8990	724-8994	PK-12	Ali Bazzi
State Street Academy	1110 State St	Bay City, MI	48706-3669	989-684-6484	684-6202	K-6	Nick Meldrum
Stewart Academy	13120 Wildemere St	Detroit, MI	48238-3336	313-409-8453		K-8	Detra Coleman
Stockwell Academy	9758 E Highland Rd	Howell, MI	48843-9098	810-632-2200	632-2201	K-8	Jessica Moceri
Stockwell Preparatory Academy	1032 Karl Greimel Dr	Brighton, MI	48116-9471	810-225-9940	225-9941	9-12	Steven Beyer
Success Academy	1620 Ludington St	Escanaba, MI	49829	906-553-7979	553-7981	9-12	Laura Bartel
Success Mile Academy	27300 Dequindre Rd	Warren, MI	48092-2870	586-353-2108	353-2109	K-8	Thomas Gladieux
Success Virtual Learning Centers	7188 Avenue B	Vestaburg, MI	48891	989-268-3090	268-3092	9-12	Brian Barber
Summit Academy	PO Box 310	Flat Rock, MI	48134-0310	734-379-6810	379-6745	K-8	Leann Hedke
Summit Academy HS	18601 Middlebelt Rd	Romulus, MI	48174-9290	734-955-1730	955-1737	9-12	Erin Avery
Summit Academy MS	18601 Middlebelt Rd	Romulus, MI	48174-9290	734-955-1712	955-1729	6-8	Leann Hedke
Summit Academy North ES	28697 Sibley Rd	Romulus, MI	48174-9736	734-789-1428	789-1431	K-5	Michael Bravo
Taylor Exemplar Academy	26727 Goddard Rd	Taylor, MI	48180-3912	734-941-7742	941-9641	K-8	Melissa Nickel
Taylor Preparatory HS	9540 Telegraph Rd	Taylor, MI	48180-3356	734-668-2100	668-2101	9-12	Aquan Miles
Three Lakes Academy	W17352 Main St	Curtis, MI	49820	906-586-6631	586-6573	K-7	Susan Pann

School	Address	City,State	Zip code	Telephone	Fax	Grade	Contact
Three Oaks Public School Academy	1212 Kingsley St	Muskegon, MI	49442-4025	231-767-3365	777-9815	K-6	Monecia Vasbinder
Timberland Charter Academy	2574 McLaughlin Ave	Muskegon, MI	49442-4439	231-767-9700	767-9710	K-8	Angelia Coleman
Timbuktu Academy	10800 E Canfield St	Detroit, MI	48214-1601	313-823-6000	823-9748	K-8	ChaRhonda Edgerson
Tipton Academy	1615 Belton St	Garden City, MI	48135	734-261-0500	956-6360	PK-8	Suzanne March
Trillium Academy	15740 Racho Blvd	Taylor, MI	48180-5211	734-374-8222	374-5025	K-12	Angela Romanowski
Triumph Academy	3000 Vivian Rd	Monroe, MI	48162-8600	734-240-2610	240-2785	K-8	Amy Tansel
Trix Academy	13700 Bringard Dr	Detroit, MI	48205-1156	313-409-8453		K-8	Emily Piccoli
Universal Academy	4833 Ogden St	Detroit, MI	48210-2011	313-581-5006	581-5514	PK-12	Uzma Anjum
Universal Learning Academy	28015 Joy Rd	Westland, MI	48185-5525	734-402-5900	402-5901	PK-12	Layal Boussi
University Prep Academy Murray ES	435 Amsterdam St	Detroit, MI	48202	313-309-0552	309-0555	PK-5	Kimberly Llorens
University Preparatory Academy HS	600 Antoinette St	Detroit, MI	48202-3457	313-874-4340	874-4470	9-12	Derrick Kellam
University Preparatory Academy MS	5310 Saint Antoine St	Detroit, MI	48202-4131	313-831-0100	831-4197	6-8	Aisha Scott
University Preparatory Acad Thompson ES	957 Holden St	Detroit, MI	48202-3443	313-874-9800	874-9822	K-5	Tamara Johnson
University Prep Science & Math ES	2251 Antietam Ave	Detroit, MI	48207	313-782-4400		K-5	Kimberly Phillips
University Prep Science & Math HS	2664 Franklin St	Detroit, MI	48207	313-393-9166	393-9165	9-12	Zetia Hogan M.Ed.
University Prep Science & Math MS	5100 John R St	Detroit, MI	48202-4061	313-832-8400	833-4816	6-8	Jennifer Spencer
University Yes Academy	PO Box 2716	Detroit, MI	48202	313-270-2556	646-6887	K-12	Robert Hines
Vanderbilt Charter Academy	301 W 16th St	Holland, MI	49423-3417	616-820-5050	820-5051	PK-8	Holly Hillary
Vanguard Charter Academy	1620 52nd St SW	Wyoming, MI	49519-9629	616-538-3630	538-3646	K-8	Mark DeJong
Virtual Learning Academy of St. Clair	1520 Michigan Rd	Port Huron, MI	48060	810-364-1362	364-3347	9-12	Denice Lapish
Vista Charter Academy	711 32nd St SE	Grand Rapids, MI	49548-2307	616-246-6920	246-6930	K-8	Heather Guerra M.Ed.
Vista Meadows Academy	20651 W Warren St	Dearborn Hts, MI	48127	313-240-4347	441-9169	9-12	Dr. Darryln Harrison
Voyageur Academy	4321 Military St	Detroit, MI	48210-2451	313-361-4180	361-4770	K-8	Kimberly Pressley
Voyageur College Prep	4366 Military St	Detroit, MI	48210	313-748-4000	897-1760	9-12	Jeff Maxwell
Voyageur College Preparatory HS	4366 Military St	Detroit, MI	48210	313-748-4000	897-1760	5-12	Jeffrey Maxwell
Walden Green Montessori S	17339 Roosevelt Rd	Spring Lake, MI	49456-1253	616-842-4523	842-4522	K-8	Mark Neidlinger
Walker Charter Academy	1801 3 Mile Rd NW	Grand Rapids, MI	49544-1445	616-785-2700	785-0894	K-8	Steve Bagley
Walton Charter Academy	744 E Walton Blvd	Pontiac, MI	48340-1361	248-371-9300	371-1642	K-8	Mona Boersma
Warrendale Charter Academy	19400 Sawyer St	Detroit, MI	48228-3330	313-240-4200	240-4203	K-8	Vondra Glass
Washington-Parks Academy	11685 Appleton	Redford, MI	48239-1445	313-592-6061	242-5156	K-8	Kalyani Bhatt
Washtenaw Technical Middle College	4800 E Huron River Dr	Ann Arbor, MI	48105-9481	734-973-3410	973-3464	10-12	Dr. Karl Covert
Waterford Montessori Academy	4860 Midland Ave	Waterford, MI	48329	248-674-2400	674-2424	PK-7	Theo Papatheodoropoulos
W-A-Y Academy	8701 W Vernor	Detroit, MI	48209	313-444-8082		7-12	Jennifer Hernandez
W-A-Y Academy - Flint	817 E Kearsley St	Flint, MI	48503	810-412-8655	820-2642	6-12	Scott Henwood
W-A-Y Academy - Roseville Site	15900 Common Rd	Roseville, MI	48066	586-806-9031	879-6504	7-12	Paul Tregembo
W-A-Y Academy West Campus	19321 W Chicago St	Detroit, MI	48228	313-444-9398		7-12	Madeline Black
W-A-Y Michigan	407 E Fort St	Detroit, MI	48226	313-444-9292		6-12	Steven Beaulieu
Wells Academy	281 S Fair Ave	Benton Harbor, MI	49022-7219	269-926-2885	926-2923	K-7	Esther Dowdell
Wellspring Preparatory HS	1031 Page St NE	Grand Rapids, MI	49505-5544	616-235-9500	235-2526	9-12	Jessica Knoth
West MI Academy Environmental Science	4463 Leonard St NW	Grand Rapids, MI	49534-2138	616-791-7454	791-7453	PK-12	Kerri Barrett
West Michigan Acad of Arts & Academics	17350 Hazel St	Spring Lake, MI	49456-1222	616-844-9961	844-9941	PK-8	Cathy Cantu
West Michigan Aviation Academy	5363 44th St SE	Grand Rapids, MI	49512-4093	616-446-8886	957-0491	9-12	Patrick Cwayna
Weston Preparatory Academy	22930 Chippewa St	Detroit, MI	48219-1161	313-387-6038	387-6180	K-8	Yvonne McClean
West Village Academy - South Campus	3530 Westwood St	Dearborn, MI	48124-3100	313-274-9200	274-0062	K-8	Carletta Counts
White Pine Academy	510 Russell St	Leslie, MI	49251-9478	517-589-8961	589-9194	K-8	Marianne Horner
Winans Academy of Performing Arts ES	9740 McKinney St	Detroit, MI	48224-2503	313-640-4610	640-4611	K-8	Randy Hayward
Windemere Park Charter Academy	3100 W Saginaw St	Lansing, MI	48917-2307	517-327-0700	327-0800	PK-8	Yvonne Thomas
Windover HS	919 Smith Rd	Midland, MI	48640-4164	989-832-0852	839-7699	9-12	Gina Wilson
Woodland Park Academy	2083 E Grand Blanc Rd	Grand Blanc, MI	48439-2700	810-695-4710	695-1658	K-8	Jeremy Brown
Woodland S	7224 Supply Rd	Traverse City, MI	49696-9400	231-947-7474	947-7667	K-8	Jeremiah Stieve
WSC Academy	855 Jefferson St	Ypsilanti, MI	48197-5209	734-794-0218	794-0216	9-12	Portia Davis-Mann
Youth Advancement Academy	6750 Chime St	Kalamazoo, MI	49009	269-353-4193	353-4214	9-12	Amber Long

Minnesota

School	Address	City,State	Zip code	Telephone	Fax	Grade	Contact
Academia Cesar Chavez S	1801 Lacrosse Ave	Saint Paul, MN	55119	651-778-2940	778-2942	PK-7	Bondo Nyembwe
Academic Arts HS	60 Marie Ave E	West Saint Paul, MN	55118-5932	651-457-7427	554-7611	9-12	Samantha Kavilhaug
Achieve Language Academy	2169 Stillwater Ave E	Saint Paul, MN	55119-3508	651-738-4875	738-8268	PK-8	Paul McGlynn
AFSA HS	100 Vadnais Blvd	Vadnais Heights, MN	55127	651-209-3910	209-3911	8-12	Becky Meyer
AFSA MS	1435 Midway Pkwy	Saint Paul, MN	55108	612-260-2662	493-2088	5-7	Becky Meyer
Agamim Classical Academy	1503 Boyce St	Hopkins, MN	55343	952-856-2531	856-2728	K-6	Miranda Morton
Arcadia Charter S	1719 Cannon Rd	Northfield, MN	55057	507-663-8806	663-8802	6-12	Dr. Barbara Wornson
Art and Science Academy	903 6th Avenue Ct NE	Isanti, MN	55040	763-568-4091		K-8	Jill Arendt
Aspen Academy	14825 Zinran Ave	Savage, MN	55378-4557	952-226-5940	226-5949	K-8	Mike McNulty
Athlos Academy St. Cloud	3701 33rd St S	Saint Cloud, MN	56301	320-281-4430		K-6	Dan McKeon
Athlos Leadership Academy	10100 Noble Pkwy N	Brooklyn Park, MN	55443-1311	763-777-8942	315-0601	PK-8	Dr. Jennifer Geraghty
Augsburg Fairview Academy	2504 Columbus Ave	Minneapolis, MN	55404	612-333-1614	339-2229	9-12	Heidi Anderson
Aurora Charter S	2101 E 26th St	Minneapolis, MN	55404	612-722-1999	870-4287	PK-8	Matthew Cisewski
Avalon Charter S	700 Glendale St	Saint Paul, MN	55114-1782	651-649-5495	649-5462	6-12	Carrie Bakken
Banaadir Academy - North Campus	1130 N 7th St	Minneapolis, MN	55411	612-326-7200	521-4007	K-9	Shawn Fondow
Banaadir Academy - South Campus	2526 27th Ave S	Minneapolis, MN	55406	612-518-8176	521-4007	K-6	Rani Hayden
Banaadir Math & Science	2872 26th Ave S	Minneapolis, MN	55406	612-722-3294	724-4763	7-9	Christine Schnaser
Bdote Learning Center	3216 E 29th St	Minneapolis, MN	55406	612-279-6380		K-5	Dr. Cynthia Thompson
Beacon Academy	3415 Louisiana Ave N	Crystal, MN	55427	763-546-9999	416-3682	K-8	Mike Reeder
Best Academy	1300 Olson Memorial Hwy	Minneapolis, MN	55411	612-876-4105		K-8	Fatou Diahame
Big Picture Twin Cities	5929 Brooklyn Blvd	Minneapolis, MN	55429	763-310-1255	374-8831	6-8	Rachel Ngendakuriyo
Birch Grove Community S	PO Box 2383	Tofte, MN	55615-2383	218-663-0170	663-7904	PK-5	Diane Blanchette
Bluesky Online Charter S	33 Wentworth Ave E Ste 100	West Saint Paul, MN	55118-3432	651-642-0888	642-0435	7-12	Amy Larsen
Bluffview Montessori S	1321 Gilmore Ave	Winona, MN	55987-2459	507-452-2807	452-6869	K-8	Henry Schantzen
Bright Water ES	5140 Fremont Ave N	Minneapolis, MN	55430	612-302-3410	302-5911	K-6	Ann Johnson
Cannon River STEM S	1800 14th St NE	Faribault, MN	55021	507-331-7836		K-8	Nalani McCutcheon
Cedar Riverside Community Charter S	1610 S 6th St Ste 100	Minneapolis, MN	55454-1102	612-339-5767	339-2951	K-8	Randy Vetsch
CHOICE Technical Academy	315 S Grove Ave	Owatonna, MN	55060	507-400-4009		7-12	Sara Baird
City Academy	958 Jessie St	Saint Paul, MN	55130-4058	651-298-4624	292-6511	9-12	Milo Cutter
Clarkfield Charter S	301 13th St	Clarkfield, MN	56223	320-669-1995	669-1997	K-6	Kathy Koetter
College Prep Elementary S	355 Randolph Ave	Saint Paul, MN	55102	651-605-2360	605-2369	K-6	Mary Yakibchuk
Cologne Academy	1221 Village Pkwy	Cologne, MN	55322-9248	952-466-2276	466-4030	K-8	Lynn Gluck-Peterson
Community of Peace Academy	471 Magnolia Ave E	Saint Paul, MN	55130-3849	651-776-5151	771-4841	PK-12	Cara Quinn
Community School of Excellence	170 Rose Ave W	Saint Paul, MN	55117-4437	651-917-0073	917-3717	K-8	Kazoua Kong-Thao
Cornerstone Montessori ES	1611 Ames Ave	Saint Paul, MN	55106-2903	651-774-5000		K-6	Liesl Taylor
Crosslake Community Charter S	36974 County Road 66	Crosslake, MN	56442-2527	218-692-5437	692-5437	K-8	Todd Lyscio
Crosslake Community Online HS	36974 County Road 66	Crosslake, MN	56442-2527	218-692-5437	692-5437	9-12	Todd Lyscio
Cyber Village Academy	768 Hamline Ave S	Saint Paul, MN	55116-2224	651-523-7170	523-7113	K-12	Dave Glick
DaVinci Academy of Arts and Science	532 Bunker Lake Blvd NE	Ham Lake, MN	55304	763-754-6577	767-7817	K-8	Debra Lach
Discovery Charter S	4100 66th St E	Inver Grove, MN	55076	651-444-8464	444-8468	K-5	Heather Lines
Discovery Public S	126 8th St NW	Faribault, MN	55021-4241	507-331-5423	331-2618	6-12	Jim Severson
Discovery Woods Montessori Charter S	604 N 7th St	Brainerd, MN	56401	218-828-8200		K-6	Kristi Crocker
DREAM Technical Academy	1705 16th Street NE	Willmar, MN	56201	320-262-5640		7-12	Jaime Larson
Dugsi Academy	1091 Snelling Ave N	Saint Paul, MN	55108	651-642-0667	642-0668	K-8	Mary Stafford
Eagle Ridge Academy	11111 Bren Rd W	Minnetonka, MN	55343	952-746-7760	746-7765	K-12	Erica Powell
East Range Academy of Tech & Science	2000 Siegel Blvd	Eveleth, MN	55734	218-744-7965	744-2349	10-12	Judy Youso
E.C.H.O. Charter S	PO Box 158	Echo, MN	56237-0158	507-925-4143	925-4165	K-12	Helen Blue-Redner
Edvisions Off Campus S	PO Box 307	Henderson, MN	56044-0307	507-248-3101	665-2752	7-12	Gigi Dobosenski
El Colegio Charter S	4137 Bloomington Ave	Minneapolis, MN	55407-3332	612-728-5728	728-5790	9-12	Norma C. Garces
Excell Academy for Higher Learning	6510 Zane Ave N	Brooklyn Park, MN	55429-1571	763-533-0500	533-0508	PK-8	Sabrina Williams
Face to Face Academy	1165 Arcade St	Saint Paul, MN	55106-2615	651-772-5544	772-5621	9-12	Jim Gitar
FIT Academy	7200 147th St W	Apple Valley, MN	55124	952-847-3798		K-8	Claud Allaire
Friendship Academy of the Arts	2600 E 38th St	Minneapolis, MN	55406	612-879-6703	879-6707	K-6	Dr. Charvez Russell
Glacial Hills ES	PO Box 189	Starbuck, MN	56381-0189	320-239-3840	239-2803	K-6	Deb Mathias
Global Academy	4065 Central Ave NE	Columbia Hts, MN	55421-2917	763-404-8200	781-5260	K-8	Helen Fisk
Goodall Environmental Science Academy	8008 83rd St NW	Maple Lake, MN	55358-2454	952-852-0129	679-7617	6-12	Craig Wignes
Great Expectations S	PO Box 310	Grand Marais, MN	55604-0310	218-387-9322	387-9344	K-8	Peter James
Great River S	1326 Energy Park Dr	Saint Paul, MN	55108-5202	651-305-2780	305-2781	1-12	Samuel O'Brien
Green Isle Community S	PO Box 277	Green Isle, MN	55338-0277	507-326-7144	326-5434	PK-6	Brandy Barrett
Harbor City International HS	332 W Michigan St Ste 300	Duluth, MN	55802-1644	218-722-7574	625-6068	9-12	Anne Wise
Harvest Prep S - Seed Academy	1300 Olson Memorial Hwy	Minneapolis, MN	55411-3968	612-876-4105		K-4	Rachelle Larson
Hennepin ES	2123 Clinton Ave	Minneapolis, MN	55404	612-843-5050	871-2406	K-6	Dr. Julie Henderson
Hiawatha College Prep	3800 Pleasant Ave	Minneapolis, MN	55409	612-353-4324	886-2850	5-8	Rochelle Van Dijk
Hiawatha Collegiate HS	4640 17th Ave	Minneapolis, MN	55407-4790	612-547-9056		9-12	Nicole Cooley
Hiawatha Leadership Academy	1611 E 46th St	Minneapolis, MN	55407-3669	612-455-4004	248-8947	K-4	Daniela Vasan
Hiawatha Leadership Academy	3810 E 56th St	Minneapolis, MN	55417-2218	612-987-5688	825-4777	PK-4	Eli Kramer
Higher Ground Academy	1381 Marshall Ave	Saint Paul, MN	55104-6353	651-645-1000	645-2100	K-12	Bill Wilson
High School for Recording Arts	1166 University Ave W	Saint Paul, MN	55104-4169	651-287-0890	287-0891	9-12	Anthony Simmons
Hmong College Prep Academy	1515 Brewster St	Saint Paul, MN	55108-2612	651-209-8002	289-1802	K-8	Dr. Christianna Hang
Hmong College Prep Academy HS	1515 Brewster St	Saint Paul, MN	55108-2612	612-209-8002	209-8003	9-12	Dr. Christianna Hang
Hope Community Academy	720 Payne Ave	Saint Paul, MN	55130-4127	651-796-4500	796-4599	K-8	MayChy Vu
International Spanish Language Academy	5959 Shady Oak Rd S	Minnetonka, MN	55343	952-746-6020	746-6023	K-6	Jeremy Perrin

School	Address	City,State	Zip code	Telephone	Fax	Grade	Contact
Jeffrey Academy	1550 Summit Ave	Saint Paul, MN	55105-2274	651-414-6000	414-6006	5-8	Jennifer Schiller
Jennings Community Learning Center	2455 University Ave W	Saint Paul, MN	55114-1507	651-649-5403	649-5490	7-12	Bill Zimneiwicz
Kaleidoscope Charter S	7525 Kalland Ave NE	Otsego, MN	55301-9690	763-428-1890	428-1691	K-12	Dr. Brett Wedlund
Kato Public Carter S	110 N 6th St	Mankato, MN	56001-4443	507-387-5524	387-5680	7-12	Claudia Madrigal
KIPP North Star Academy	5034 Oliver Ave N	Minneapolis, MN	55430	612-287-9700	287-9702	5-8	Jamie Scherle
La Crescent Montessori & STEM S	1116 S Oak St	La Crescent, MN	55947	507-895-4054	895-4064	PK-12	Stephanie Wehman
Lafayette Charter S	PO Box 125	Lafayette, MN	56054-0125	507-228-8943	228-8288	PK-8	Peter Roufs
Lakes International Language Academy	246 11th Ave SE	Forest Lake, MN	55025	651-464-0771	464-4429	PK-5	Cam Hedlund
Lakes International Language Academy	19850 Fenway Ave N	Forest Lake, MN	55025	651-464-8989	464-8990	6-12	Shannon Peterson
Learning for Leadership Charter	3300 5th St NE	Minneapolis, MN	55418-1165	612-789-9598	789-0547	K-12	Jit Kundan
Level Up Academy	2600 Co Rd E East	White Bear Lake, MN	55110	651-408-5559		K-8	Molly Dandelet
LIFE Prep	930 Geranium Ave E	Saint Paul, MN	.55106-2610	651-793-6624	793-6633	PK-6	Leah Jones
Lincoln International S	2520 Minnehaha Ave	Minneapolis, MN	55404-4118	612-872-8690	879-9557	9-12	Manyi Tambe
Lionsgate Academy	5605 Green Cir Dr	Minnetonka, MN	55343	612-351-4507	707-4007	7-12	Diano Halpin Ph.D.
Loveworks Academy for Arts	2225 Zenith Ave N	Golden Valley, MN	55422-3852	763-522-6830	522-6840	K-8	April Shaw
Mastery S	4021 Thomas Ave N	Minneapolis, MN	55412	612-876-4105		K-4	Paula Bump
Math & Science Academy	8430 Woodbury Xing	Woodbury, MN	55125-9433	651-578-8061	578-7532	6-12	John Gawarecki
Metro Deaf S	1471 Brewster St	Saint Paul, MN	55108-2612	651-224-3995	222-0939	PK-12	Dr. Susan Lane-Outlaw
Metro Schools of MN	2600 E 26th St	Minneapolis, MN	55406-1201	612-722-2555	729-2274	6-12	Farhan Hussein
Milroy Area Charter S	PO Box 10	Milroy, MN	56263	507-336-2563	336-2568	K-4	Heidi Sachariason
Minisinaakwaang Leadership Academy	20930 367th Ln	McGregor, MN	55760	218-768-5320	768-3357	K-12	Mary Sue Anderson
Minnesota Connections Academy	1336 Energy Park Dr Ste 100	Saint Paul, MN	55108	651-523-0888	726-2917	K-12	Melissa Gould
Minnesota Excellence in Learning Academy	9060 Zanzibar Ln N	Maple Grove, MN	55311	763-205-4396	999-6988	K-6	Jennifer Mitchell
Minnesota International MS	277 12th Ave N	Minneapolis, MN	55401	612-465-8465		5-8	Faysal Ali
Minnesota Internship Center Charter	2507 Fremont Ave N	Minneapolis, MN	55411	612-238-3022		9-12	James Morehouse
Minnesota Internship Center Charter	2507 Fremont Ave N	Minneapolis, MN	55411	612-238-0758		9-12	Jim Morehouse
Minnesota Internship Center Charter	2507 Fremont Ave N	Minneapolis, MN	55411	612-588-1449		9-12	Tracy Eberlein
Minnesota Internship Center Charter	1821 University Ave W # 271	Saint Paul, MN	55104	651-288-3152		9-12	Fatima Fisher
Minnesota Math and Science Academy	169 Jenks Ave	Saint Paul, MN	55117	651-246-0845	330-1984	K-9	Murat Oguz
Minnesota New Country S	PO Box 488	Henderson, MN	56044-0488	507-248-3353	248-3604	K-12	Nancy Pfarr
Minnesota Online HS	2314 University Ave W	Saint Paul, MN	55114-1863	800-764-8166	586-2870	9-12	Elissa Raffa
Minnesota Virtual HS	180 5th St E # M10A	Saint Paul, MN	55101-2672	612-746-7977	746-7989	6-12	Bill Glenz
MTS ES	1800 2nd St NE	Minneapolis, MN	55418	612-729-9140	789-0446	K-6	Suzette Dornfeld
MTS HS	2872 26th Ave S	Minneapolis, MN	55406	612-722-9013	724-4763	7-12	Christine Schnaser
MTS P.E.A.S.E. Academy	601 13th Ave SE	Minneapolis, MN	55414-1437	612-378-1377	378-4886	9-12	Michael Durchslag
Nasha Shkola Charter S	6717 85th Ave N	Brooklyn Park, MN	55445	763-496-5550	432-5435	K-8	Paul Kinsley
Natural Science Academy	920 Holley Ave Ste 3	Saint Paul Park, MN	55071-1558	651-925-5050	925-5051	K-5	Kendra Hunding
Naytahwaush Community S	PO Box 8	Naytahwaush, MN	56566-0008	218-935-5025	935-5263	K-6	Terri Anderson
Nerstrand Charter S	PO Box 156	Nerstrand, MN	55053-0156	507-333-6850	333-6870	K-5	Maggie Kiley
New Century Academy	950 School Rd SW	Hutchinson, MN	55350	320-234-3660	234-3668	7-12	Jason Becker
New Century S	1380 Energy Ln Ste 108	Saint Paul, MN	55108	612-478-4535	305-0891	K-8	Dr. Dido Kotile
New City S	229 13th Ave NE	Minneapolis, MN	55413-1117	612-623-3309	623-3319	K-8	Todd Bartholomay
New Discoveries Montessori Academy	1000 5th Ave SE	Hutchinson, MN	55350	320-234-6362	234-6300	K-8	Dave Conrad
New Heights Charter S	614 Mulberry St W	Stillwater, MN	55082-4858	651-439-1962	439-0716	K-12	Thomas Kearney
New Millennium Academy	5105 Brooklyn Blvd	Minneapolis, MN	55429	763-235-7900	235-7979	K-8	Bao Vang
Noble Academy	9477 Decatur Dr N	Minneapolis, MN	55445-3400	763-592-7706	592-7707	K-5	Neal Thao
Northeast College Prep Charter S	300 Industrial Blvd NE	Minneapolis, MN	55413	612-248-8240		K-6	Carl Phillips
Northern Lights Community S	PO Box 2829	Warba, MN	55793-2829	218-492-4400	492-4402	6-12	Michael Hamernick
North Lakes Academy	308 15th St SW	Forest Lake, MN	55025-1303	651-982-2688	464-6409	9-12	Cam Stottler
North Lakes Academy	255 7th Ave NW Ste B	Forest Lake, MN	55025-1177	651-982-2773	464-6409	5-8	Andrew Brandt
North Metro Flex Academy	2350 Helen St	North St Paul, MN	55109	612-900-4435		K-4	Therese Privette
North Shore Community S	5926 Ryan Rd	Duluth, MN	55804-9672	218-525-0663	525-0024	K-6	Kristi Lounsberry
North Star Academy	3301 Technology Dr	Duluth, MN	55811	218-728-9556	728-2075	K-8	Bonnie Jorgenson
Northwest Passage HS	11345 Robinson Dr NW	Coon Rapids, MN	55433-4061	763-862-9223	862-9250	9-12	Peter Wieczorek
Nova Classical Academy	1455 Victoria Way	Saint Paul, MN	55102-4213	651-209-6320	209-6325	K-12	Dr. Eric Williams
Odyssey Academy	6201 Noble Ave N	Brooklyn Center, MN	55429	763-971-8200	549-2380	K-8	Melinda Crowley
Oshki Ogimaag Charter S	PO Box 320	Grand Portage, MN	55605	218-475-2112	475-2119	K-6	Carmen Keyport
PACT Charter S	7250 E Ramsey Pkwy	Ramsey, MN	55303-6902	763-712-4200	712-4201	K-12	Emily Mertes
Paladin Career & Technical HS	308 Northtown Dr NE	Blaine, MN	55434-1039	763-786-4799	786-4798	9-12	Brandon Wait
Parnassus Preparatory S	11201 96th Ave N	Maple Grove, MN	55369-3676	763-496-1416	898-3977	K-12	Constance Ford
Partnership Academy	305 E 77th St	Richfield, MN	55423-4312	612-866-3630	866-3640	K-5	Lisa Hendricks
Pillager Area Charter S	PO Box 130	Pillager, MN	56473-0130	218-746-3875	746-3876	9-12	Greg Zimmerman
PIM Arts HS	7255 Flying Cloud Dr	Eden Prairie, MN	55344	952-224-1340	224-2955	9-12	Matt McFarlane
Prairie Creek Community S	27695 Denmark Ave	Northfield, MN	55057-5333	507-645-9640	645-8234	K-5	Simon Tyler
Prairie Seeds Academy	6200 W Broadway Ave	Minneapolis, MN	55428-2826	763-450-1388	450-1389	K-12	Choua Yang
Prodeo Academy	1555 40th Ave NE	Columbia Hts, MN	55421-3103	612-559-4881		K-8	Richard Campion
Raleigh Academy	5905 Raleigh St	Duluth, MN	55807	218-628-0697	628-9924	K-5	Danielle Perich
Ridgeway Community S	35564 County Road 12	Houston, MN	55943-4006	507-454-9566	454-9567	PK-5	Jodi Dansingburg
River Grove S	14189 Ostlund Trail N	Marine St Crx, MN	55047	651-409-3122	538-1022	K-6	Drew Goodson
River's Edge Academy	188 Plato Blvd W	Saint Paul, MN	55107-2021	651-234-0150	234-0159	9-12	Meghan Cavalier
Riverway Learning Community Charter S	1733 W Service Dr Ste 18	Winona, MN	55987-2286	507-474-6120	474-6190	PK-12	Katey Wadewitz
Rochester Beacon Academy	974 Skyline Dr SW	Rochester, MN	55902	507-258-5351		6-12	Kari Weiss
Rochester Math and Science Academy	415 16th St SW	Rochester, MN	55902-2125	507-252-5995		K-8	Abdulkadir Abdulle
Rochester STEM Academy	415 16th St SW	Rochester, MN	55902-2125	507-281-2381		9-12	Dr. Bryan Rossi Ph.D.
Rosa Parks Charter HS	2364 Valleyhigh Dr NW	Rochester, MN	55901-7641	507-282-3325	282-0976	9-12	Jay Martini
SAGE Academy Charter S	3900 85th Ave N	Brooklyn Park, MN	55443-1908	763-315-4020	315-4028	9-12	Kimberly Turitto
Saint Cloud Math and Science Academy	1025 18th St N	Saint Cloud, MN	56303	320-774-2201	774-2204	K-5	Tammy Bengtson
St. Croix Preparatory Academy	4260 Stagecoach Trl N	Stillwater, MN	55082-1197	651-395-5900	395-5901	K-12	Andrew Sachariason
Saint Paul City S	260 Edmund Ave	Saint Paul, MN	55103-1783	651-225-9177	487-7551	PK-8	Justin Tiarks
Saint Paul Conservatory Performing Art	16 5th St W	Saint Paul, MN	55102	651-290-2225	290-9000	9-12	Callie Jacobs
Sankofa Underground North Academy	1711 W Broadway Ave	Minneapolis, MN	55411	612-547-6617	208-0382	K-1	AsaleSol Young
Schoolcraft Learning Community S	PO Box 1685	Bemidji, MN	56619-1685	218-586-3284	586-3285	K-8	Adrienne Eickman
Sejong Academy of Minnesota	1330 Blair Ave N	Saint Paul, MN	55104	651-330-6944	330-7011	PK-8	Brad Tipka
Seven Hills Preparatory Academy	8600 Bloomington Ave	Minneapolis, MN	55425	952-426-6000	426-6020	K-5	
Seven Hills Preparatory Academy	1401 W 76th St	Richfield, MN	55423	612-314-7600	314-7609	K-8	Carolyn Farrell
Seven Hills Preparatory Academy	1401 W 76th St	Richfield, MN	55423-3852	612-314-7600		6-8	Carl Schlueter
Sojourner Truth Academy	3820 Emerson Ave N	Minneapolis, MN	55412-2039	612-588-3599	588-0217	PK-8	Julie Guy
Southside Family Charter S	4500 Clinton Ave	Minneapolis, MN	55419-5143	612-872-8322	872-0612	K-8	David Nunez
Spectrum 6th Grade Center	11044 Industrial Circle NW	Elk River, MN	55330	763-241-8703		6-6	Dan DeBruyn
Spectrum HS	17796 Industrial Cir NW	Elk River, MN	55330	763-241-8703	633-1380	7-12	Dan DeBruyn
Spero Academy	1534 6th St NE	Minneapolis, MN	55413	612-465-8600	465-8603	K-6	Curtis Windham
Star of the North Academy Charter S	1562 Viking Blvd NE	East Bethel, MN	55011	763-812-1367		K-8	Lulzim Axhijaj
STEP Academy	835 5th St E	Saint Paul, MN	55106	651-289-6120	457-4692	6-12	Mustafa Ibrahim
Stonebridge World S	4530 Lyndale Ave S	Minneapolis, MN	55419-4802	612-877-7400	877-7444	K-6	Barbara Novy
Stride Academy	3241 Oakham Ln	Saint Cloud, MN	56301	320-230-5340	217-6318	K-3	Eric Williams
Stride Academy South Campus	3241 Oakham Ln	Saint Cloud, MN	56301-6373	320-230-5340	217-6318	4-8	Diane Moeller
Summit Charter S	8201 Park Ave S	Bloomington, MN	55420	612-876-3050		K-6	Madgy Rabeaa
Swan River Montessori Charter S	500 Maple St	Monticello, MN	55362-8878	763-271-7926	295-0075	PK-6	Katie Curtis
TEAM Academy	220 17th Ave NE	Waseca, MN	56093-2753	507-833-8326	833-8327	K-6	Jill Courtney
Tesfa International S	1745 University Ave 1st Fl	Saint Paul, MN	55104	651-717-4844	641-4052	K-6	Jonas Beugen
TrekNorth HS	2400 Pine Ridge Ave NW	Bemidji, MN	56601	218-444-1888	444-1893	6-12	Kristin Gustafson
Trio Wolf Creek Distance Learning	10363 Liberty Ln	Chisago City, MN	55013-5418	651-213-2017	257-0576	4-12	Tracy Quarnstrom
Twin Cities Academy	690 Birmingham St	Saint Paul, MN	55106	651-205-4797	205-4799	6-8	Betsy Lueth
Twin Cities Academy HS	690 Birmingham St	Saint Paul, MN	55106	651-205-4797	205-4799	9-12	Betsy Lueth
Twin Cities German Immersion S	1031 Como Ave	Saint Paul, MN	55103-1021	651-492-7106	330-2270	K-8	Ted Anderson
Twin Cities International ES	277 12th Ave N	Minneapolis, MN	55401-1026	612-821-6470	821-6477	K-4	Abdirashid Warsame
Ubah Medical Academy Charter S	1600 Mainstreet	Hopkins, MN	55343-7409	952-540-2942	540-2950	9-12	Musa Farah
Universal Academy Charter S	2919 27th Ave S	Minneapolis, MN	55406	651-442-3124	202-3904	PK-8	Farhiya Einto
Upper Mississippi Academy	426 Osceola Ave S	Saint Paul, MN	55102-3535	651-528-8091	683-2042	6-12	Harry Adler
Urban Academy Charter S	133 E 7th St	Saint Paul, MN	55101	651-215-9419	215-9571	K-6	Mongsher Ly
Venture Academy	315 27th Ave SE	Minneapolis, MN	55414	612-345-9040	294-6737	6-12	Jon Bacal
Vermilion Country S	PO Box 629	Tower, MN	55790-0629	218-753-1246		7-12	Kevin Fitton
Voyageurs Expeditionary S	3724 Bemidji Ave N	Bemidji, MN	56601	218-444-3130	444-3126	6-12	Scott Anderson
Watershed HS	6541 16th Ave S	Minneapolis, MN	55423-1751	612-871-4363	871-1004	9-12	Destiny Sparks
West Side Summit Charter S	497 Humboldt Ave	Saint Paul, MN	55107	651-200-4543		K-8	Sarah Hanson
Woodbury Leadership Academy	600 Weir Dr	Woodbury, MN	55125	651-539-2641	656-3031	K-8	Dr. Kathleen Mortensen
World Learner Charter S	112050 Hundertmark Rd	Chaska, MN	55318-2817	952-368-7398	368-6094	1-8	Deana Siekmann
Yinghua Academy	1616 Buchanan St NE	Minneapolis, MN	55413-1609	612-788-9095	788-9079	K-8	Susan Berg
Mississippi							
Hayes Cooper Center for Math & Science	500 N Martin Luther King	Merigold, MS	38759-9632	662-748-2734	748-2735	PK-6	Renee Lamastus
Midtown Public Charter S	301 Adelle St	Jackson, MS	39202	601-354-7770	487-9319	5-6	Josalyn Filkins
ReImagine Prep	309 W McDowell Rd	Jackson, MS	39204	601-941-0844	510-2231	6-12	Christina McDonald
Smilow Prep S	787 E Northside Dr	Jackson, MS	39206	769-524-5330	510-2231	5-6	Lynzie Jackson
Missouri							

School	Address	City,State	Zip code	Telephone	Fax	Grade	Contact
Academie Lafayette S	3421 Cherry St	Kansas City, MO	64109-2269	816-888-7400	888-7410	K-3	Heather Royce
Academie Lafayette S	6903 Oak St	Kansas City, MO	64113-2530	816-361-7735	361-5788	4-8	Elimane Mbengue
Academy for Integrated Arts	7910 Troost Ave	Kansas City, MO	64131	816-444-1720	444-1721	PK-6	Tricia DeGraff
Academy of Envrnmntl Sci & Math ES	3325 Bell Ave	Saint Louis, MO	63106-1602	314-932-1464		K-5	Jennene Anthony
Academy of Envrnmntl Sci & Math MS	3021 Hickory St	Saint Louis, MO	63104-1818	314-345-5673		6-8	CeAndre Perry
Allen Village HS	4251 Bridger Rd	Kansas City, MO	64111	816-931-0177	561-4640	9-12	Rhonda Reddick
Allen Village S	706 W 42nd St	Kansas City, MO	64111-3120	816-931-0177	561-4640	K-8	Amy Washington
Arch Community S	2153 Salisbury St	Saint Louis, MO	63107	314-267-8191		K-3	Bill Schiller
Aspire Academy	5421 Thekla Ave	Saint Louis, MO	63120-2513	314-383-8900	383-8925	PK-6	Sheldon McAfee
Banneker Charter Academy Technology	6401 Rockhill Rd	Kansas City, MO	64131-1122	816-926-9110	363-8721	PK-8	Dr. Marian Brown
Biome S	4471 Olive St	Saint Louis, MO	63108	314-531-0982	737-7187	K-3	Dr. Michele Mosley
Brookside Charter S	1815 E 63rd St	Kansas City, MO	64130	816-531-2192	756-3055	K-8	Roger Offield
Carondelet Leadership Academy	7604 Michigan Ave	Saint Louis, MO	63111-3332	314-802-8744	802-8721	K-8	Apryll Mendez
Citizens of the World Charter S	3435 Broadway Blvd	Kansas City, MO	64111	816-499-8000		K-2	Dr. Kristin Droege
City Garden Montessori Charter S	1618 Tower Grove Ave	Saint Louis, MO	63110-2206	314-664-7646	664-4997	PK-8	Dr. Nicole Evans Ed.D.
Confluence Academy-Old North St. Louis	3017 N 13th St	Saint Louis, MO	63107-3924	314-241-1110	241-1115	K-6	Sonya Murray
Confluence Academy-South City Campus	4235 S Compton Ave	Saint Louis, MO	63111	314-481-4700	351-0240	PK-8	Pam Davenport
Confluence Prep Academy	310 N 15th St	Saint Louis, MO	63103-2378	314-588-1247	588-1296	9-12	Mike Powers
Crossroads Academy - Central Street	1015 Central St	Kansas City, MO	64105	816-221-2600	221-2601	K-8	Laura LaCroix
Crossroads Academy - Quality Hill	1080 Washington St	Kansas City, MO	64105	816-221-3191	221-3192	K-4	Lindsay Yates
Crossroads HS	911 Main St	Kansas City, MO	64105	816-369-0090		9-9	Kirsten Brown
DeLaSalle Charter S	3737 Troost Ave	Kansas City, MO	64109-2658	816-561-4445	561-6106	9-12	Mark Williamson
EAGLE College Preparatory S	2617 Shenandoah Ave	Saint Louis, MO	63104	314-664-7627	735-4471	K-4	Shawn Williams
EAGLE College Preparatory S	3630 Ohio Ave	Saint Louis, MO	63118	314-664-7627		K-4	Aaron Massey
EAGLE College Preparatory S	2900 S Grand Blvd	Saint Louis, MO	63118	314-664-7627	930-2452	K-4	Emily Dittmer
EAGLE College Preparatory S	3716 Morganford Rd	Saint Louis, MO	63116	314-664-7627	664-6250	K-8	TarynAnn Barry
Frontier S of Excellence	5605 Troost Ave	Kansas City, MO	64110	816-822-1331	822-1332	6-12	
Frontier S of Innovation	6700 Corporate Dr	Kansas City, MO	64120	816-363-1907	363-1165	4-8	Kristin Snyder
Frontier S of Innovation	6700 Corporate Dr	Kansas City, MO	64120	816-363-1907	363-1165	K-3	Mark Barber
Frontier STEM HS	6455 E Commerce Ave	Kansas City, MO	64120	816-541-8200	399-2747	9-12	Serkan Kilic
Gateway Science Academy	5049 Fyler Ave	Saint Louis, MO	63139-1103	314-261-4361	261-4364	6-12	Matt Sagnak
Gateway Science Academy	6651 Gravois Ave	Saint Louis, MO	63116	314-669-9000	669-9944	K-5	Wendy Gilliam
Gateway Science Academy of St. Louis	6576 Smiley Ave	Saint Louis, MO	63139	314-932-7513	932-7514	K-5	Nuh Celik
Genesis Promise Academy	3800 E 44th St	Kansas City, MO	64130-2168	816-921-0775	921-4268	K-8	Kevin Foster
Grand Center Arts Academy	711 N Grand Blvd	Saint Louis, MO	63103	314-533-1791	371-4630	6-12	Gina Bell-Moore
Guadalupe Centers HS	1524 Paseo Blvd	Kansas City, MO	64127	816-471-2582	221-0012	9-12	Eduardo Mendez
Guadalupe Centers MS	2640 Belleview Ave	Kansas City, MO	64108	816-472-4120	960-4913	6-8	Claudia Meyer
Guadalupe ES	5123 E Truman Rd	Kansas City, MO	64127	816-994-0396	472-1471	PK-5	Marentes Elizabeth
Hawthorn Leadership S for Girls	1901 N Kingshighway Blvd	Saint Louis, MO	63113-1123	314-361-5323		6-8	Dr. Robyn Wiens
Hogan Preparatory Academy	6409 Agnes Ave	Kansas City, MO	64132	816-444-4479	444-4268	6-8	Zac Coughlin
Hogan Preparatory Academy	1221 E Meyer Blvd	Kansas City, MO	64131-1207	816-444-3464	363-0473	9-12	Shannon North
Hogan Preparatory Academy	5000 E 17th St	Kansas City, MO	64127	816-444-5010	361-2410	K-5	Amber White
Hope Leadership Academy	2800 E Linwood Blvd	Kansas City, MO	64128-1544	816-921-1213	332-6296	K-4	Sean Saunders
Kansas City International Academy	414 Wallace Ave	Kansas City, MO	64125	816-242-4206	842-7727	K-8	Joe Palmer
Kansas City Neighborhood Academy	1619 E 24th Ter	Kansas City, MO	64108	816-418-1500		PK-3	Dr. Robin Henderson
Kauffman S	6401 Paseo Blvd	Kansas City, MO	64131-1213	816-268-5660	268-5645	5-12	Hannah Lofthus
KIPP Endeavor Academy	PO Box 22624	Kansas City, MO	64113	816-241-3994	241-3339	K-8	Jana Cooper
KIPP Inspire S	1212 N 22nd St	Saint Louis, MO	63106	314-296-3502	696-8925	5-8	Joseph Olwig
KIPP St. Louis HS	706 N Jefferson	Saint Louis, MO	63103	314-349-1388		9-12	Nicole Niewald
KIPP Triumph Academy	955 Arcade Ave	Saint Louis, MO	63112-2702	314-454-9255	249-4328	5-8	Elizabeth Valerio
KIPP Victory Academy	955 Arcade Ave	Saint Louis, MO	63112	314-454-9255		K-4	Altepeter Cetera
KIPP Wisdom Academy	2647 Ohio Ave	Saint Louis, MO	63118	314-384-9561	975-0072	K-4	Jacob Shiffrin
Lafayette Preparatory Academy	1900 Lafayette Ave	Saint Louis, MO	63104	314-880-4458	880-4459	K-6	Sarah Ranney
La Salle MS	1106 N Jefferson Ave	Saint Louis, MO	63106	314-531-9820	531-4820	5-8	LaShanda Boone
Lift for Life Academy	1731 S Broadway	Saint Louis, MO	63104-4050	314-231-2337	231-1299	6-12	David LeMay
North Side Community S	3033 N Euclid Ave	Saint Louis, MO	63115-1632	314-385-4500	385-9538	PK-5	John Grote
Parks ES	3715 Wyoming St	Kansas City, MO	64111-3945	816-753-6700	753-3436	K-4	Joe Palmer
Pathway Academy	2015 E 72nd St	Kansas City, MO	64132	816-631-7100	621-7101	PK-4	Ally Heiserman
Preclarus Mastery Academy	620 N Grand Blvd	Saint Louis, MO	63103	314-454-0815	338-7435	4-8	Dr. Tonya Harris
Premier Charter S	5279 Fyler Ave	Saint Louis, MO	63139-1300	314-645-9600	645-9700	K-8	Julie Frugo
St. Louis College Prep	1224 Grattan St	Saint Louis, MO	63104-2922	314-561-3440	667-3477	5-8	Fleischer Lauren
St. Louis College Prep HS	1224 Grattan St	Saint Louis, MO	63104	314-561-3440	667-3477	9-12	Lauren Chaney
St. Louis Language Immersion S	4011 Papin St	Saint Louis, MO	63110	314-533-0975	533-0974	K-8	Dr. Lilith Werner
Scuola Vita Nuova	535 Garfield Ave	Kansas City, MO	64124-1513	816-231-5788	231-5181	K-8	Nicole Goodman
Tolbert Community Academy	3400 Paseo Blvd	Kansas City, MO	64109-2429	816-561-0114	561-1015	K-8	Dr. LaQuanda Carpenter
University Academy	6801 Holmes Rd	Kansas City, MO	64131-1382	816-412-5900	410-0322	K-12	Tony Kline

Nevada

School	Address	City,State	Zip code	Telephone	Fax	Grade	Contact
Academy for Career Education	2800 Vassar St	Reno, NV	89502-3214	775-324-3900	324-3901	9-12	Bob DeRuse
Alpine Academy	605 Boxington Way Ste 112	Sparks, NV	89434-6918	775-356-1166	356-1168	9-12	Jill Ross
American Preparatory Academy	8377 W Patrick Ln	Las Vegas, NV	89113	702-970-6800	248-0454	K-11	Christie Olivieri M.S.
Bailey Charter ES	210 Gentry Way	Reno, NV	89502-4209	775-323-6767	323-6799	K-6	Michelle Engebretson
Beacon Academy of Nevada	7360 W Flamingo Rd	Las Vegas, NV	89147-5404	702-726-8600	538-9500	9-12	Tambre Tondryk
Carson Montessori S	2263 Mouton Dr	Carson City, NV	89706-0446	775-887-9500	887-9502	K-6	Jessica Daniels
Coral Academy of Science Charter S	1701 Valley Rd	Reno, NV	89512	775-322-0274	322-1378	K-4	Feyzi Tandogan
Coral Academy of Science Charter S	6275 Neil Rd	Reno, NV	89511	775-829-4601	829-4612	9-12	Feyzi Tandogan
Coral Academy of Science Charter S	1350 E 9th St	Reno, NV	89512-2904	775-323-2332	323-2366	5-8	Feyzi Tandogan
Coral Academy of Science - Las Vegas	8185 Tamarus St	Las Vegas, NV	89123-2464	702-269-8512	269-3258	K-2	Ercan Aydogdu
Coral Academy of Science - Las Vegas	7951 Deer Springs Way	Las Vegas, NV	89131	702-685-4333	385-7525	K-5	
Coral Academy of Science - Las Vegas	42 Baer Dr	Las Vegas, NV	89115	702-643-5121	643-5138	K-5	
Coral Academy of Science - Las Vegas	2150 Windmill Pkwy	Henderson, NV	89074	702-485-3410	722-2718	3-5	Ercan Aydogdu
Coral Academy of Science - Las Vegas	1051 Sandy Ridge Ave	Henderson, NV	89052	702-776-8800	776-8803	6-12	
Delta Academy	818 W Brooks Ave	Las Vegas, NV	89030	702-396-2252	396-0848	7-12	Dr. Kyle Konold
Discovery Charter S	3883 E Mesa Vista Ave	Las Vegas, NV	89120-2036	702-547-5682	547-5685	K-8	Clark Price
Doral Academy Cactus Campus	9025 W Cactus Ave	Las Vegas, NV	89178	702-960-7500	960-7960	K-8	Danielle Marshall
Doral Academy - Fire Mesa	2568 Fire Mesa St	Las Vegas, NV	89128	702-901-4950		K-12	Bridget Bilbray-Phillips
Doral Academy - Red Rock	626 Crossbridge Dr	Las Vegas, NV	89138	702-776-8530		K-12	Bridget Bilbray-Phillips
Doral Academy Saddle Campus	9625 W Saddle Ave	Las Vegas, NV	89147	702-776-6491	802-2638	K-9	Debbie Tomasetti
Elko Institute for Academic Achievement	1031 Railroad St Ste 107	Elko, NV	89801-3975	775-738-3422	738-3488	K-8	Connie Zeller
enCompass Academy	1300 Foster Dr	Reno, NV	89509	775-322-5566	322-5509	9-12	Toby Weidenmayer
Equipo Academy	4131 E Bonanza Rd	Las Vegas, NV	89110-2280	702-907-0432		6-12	Ben Salkowe
Explore Knowledge Academy	5871 Mountain Vista St	Las Vegas, NV	89120-2308	702-870-5032	871-5032	K-12	Abbe Mattson
Founders Academy	4025 N Rancho Dr	Las Vegas, NV	89130-3492	702-998-8368	998-1328	K-10	Timm Petersen
High Desert Montessori Charter S	2590 Orovada St	Reno, NV	89512-2119	775-624-2800	624-2801	PK-9	Tammie Stockton
Honors Academy of Literature	195 N Arlington Ave	Reno, NV	89501	775-737-4084	737-4533	K-8	Dr. Andi Morency
I Can Do Anything Charter HS	1195 Corporate Blvd Ste C	Reno, NV	89502-2363	775-857-1544	857-6825	9-12	Dawn Reid
Imagine S at Mountain View	6610 Grand Montecito Pkwy	Las Vegas, NV	89149	702-253-0251	253-0254	K-6	Dr. Eve Breier
Innovations International Charter S	1600 E Oakey Blvd	Las Vegas, NV	89104-3334	702-216-4337	216-4353	K-6	Dr. Connie Malin
Innovations International Charter S	950 E Sahara Ave	Las Vegas, NV	89104-3022	702-216-4337	216-4353	7-12	Dr. Connie Malin
Leadership Academy of Nevada	7495 W Azure Dr	Las Vegas, NV	89130-4416	702-350-1472	825-2684	6-12	Bryon Richardson
Learning Bridge	505 S Pioche Hwy	Ely, NV	89301	775-289-3500	289-3516	K-8	Kristy Sedlacek
Mariposa Dual Language Academy	3875 Glen St	Reno, NV	89502	775-826-4040	826-4030	PK-5	Chris McBride
Mater Academy of Nevada	3445 Mountain Vista St	Las Vegas, NV	89121	702-485-2400	485-3322	PK-8	Renee Fairless
Nevada Connections Academy	555 Double Eagle Ct #2000	Reno, NV	89521	775-826-4200	826-4288	K-12	Steve Werlein
Nevada State HS	233 N Stephanie St	Henderson, NV	89074-8060	702-953-2600	953-2608	11-12	Mark Schumm
Nevada Virtual Academy	4801 S Sandhill Rd	Las Vegas, NV	89121	702-514-4025	407-5055	K-12	Yolanda Hamilton
Oasis Academy	920 W Williams Ave Ste 100	Fallon, NV	89406-2615	775-423-5437	423-5433	K-12	Melissa Mackedon
Odyssey Charter S	2251 S Jones Blvd	Las Vegas, NV	89146-3145	702-257-0578	259-7793	K-12	Tim Lorenz
One Hundred Academy of Excellence	2341 Comstock Dr	North Las Vegas, NV	89032-3512	702-636-2551	636-9475	K-8	Rachelle Conner
Pinecrest Academy	2840 Via Contressa	Henderson, NV	89044	702-473-5777		K-8	Michael O'Dowd
Pinecrest Academy	1385 E Cactus Ave	Las Vegas, NV	89183	702-750-9150	570-6360	K-8	Lucy Keaton
Pinecrest Academy	1360 S Boulder Hwy	Henderson, NV	89015-6958	702-749-3500	749-9995	K-8	Dr. Carrie Buck
Quest Preparatory Academy	7550 W Alexander Rd	Las Vegas, NV	89149	702-631-4751		K-K	Janelle Veith
Quest Preparatory Academy	1300 E Bridger Ave	Las Vegas, NV	89101	702-631-4751		K-5	Janelle Veith
Quest Preparatory Academy	4025 N Rancho Dr	Las Vegas, NV	89130	702-631-4751	548-2225	K-8	Janelle Veith
Rainbow Dreams Academy	950 W Lake Mead Blvd	Las Vegas, NV	89106-2339	702-638-0222	638-0220	K-6	King Duncan
Sierra Nevada Academy	13880 Stead Blvd	Reno, NV	89506-1579	775-677-4500	677-4441	K-8	Dr. Kim Regan
Silver Sands Montessori Charter S	1841 Whitney Mesa Dr	Henderson, NV	89014-2070	702-522-6220	522-6218	K-8	Denise Crosby
Silver State Charter S	788 Fairview Dr	Carson City, NV	89701	775-883-7900	883-9130	9-12	Krystal Hoefling
Somerset Academy of Las Vegas	385 W Centennial Pkwy	North Las Vegas, NV	89084-5801	702-633-5616	633-5628	K-8	Dr. Francine Mayfield
Somerset Academy of Las Vegas	50 N Stephanie St	Henderson, NV	89074	702-998-0500	998-0503	K-8	Reggie Farmer
Somerset Academy of Las Vegas	4650 Losee Rd	North Las Vegas, NV	89081-4208	702-902-5466	902-5444	K-10	Dan Phillips
Somerset Academy of Las Vegas	7058 Sky Pointe Dr	Las Vegas, NV	89131	702-478-8888	776-7216	K-12	Dr. Andre Denson
Sports Leadership & Management Academy	1095 Fielders St	Henderson, NV	89015	702-473-5735	473-5753	6-9	Dan Triana

New Hampshire

School	Address	City,State	Zip code	Telephone	Fax	Grade	Contact
Academy for Science & Design	486 Amherst St Unit 1	Nashua, NH	03063-1282	603-595-4705	262-9163	6-12	Jennifer Cava
Birches Academy of Academics and Art	419 S Broadway	Salem, NH	03079	603-458-6399		K-8	Ruth Templeton
Cocheco Academy of the Arts	40 Hampshire Cir	Dover, NH	03820	603-742-0700	742-7207	9-12	James Friel M.Ed.
Compass Classical Academy	15 Elkins St	Franklin, NH	03235	603-729-3370		K-8	Judy Tilton
CSI Charter S	26 Washington St	Penacook, NH	03303-1519	603-753-0194	753-0009	11-12	James Gorman
Founders Academy	5 Perimeter Rd	Manchester, NH	03103-3305	603-952-4705	624-0057	6-12	Maureen Mooney
Frost Charter S	110 Main St	Conway, NH	03818	603-356-6332		K-8	Janine McLauchlan
Gate City Charter S for the Arts	7 Henry Clay Dr	Merrimack, NH	03054-4847	603-943-5273		K-8	Richard Boardman
Granite State Arts Academy	19 Keewaydin Dr	Salem, NH	03079	603-912-4944		9-12	Anthony Polito
Great Bay eLearning Charter S	30 Linden St	Exeter, NH	03833-2622	603-775-8638	775-8528	7-12	Peter Stackhouse
LEAF Charter S	6A Baine Rd	Alstead, NH	03602	603-252-1829		9-12	Dakota Benedetto
Ledyard Charter S	PO Box 327	Lebanon, NH	03766	603-727-4772		9-12	John Higgins
Making Community Connections Charter S	60 Rogers St	Manchester, NH	03103	603-935-7488		6-12	Conor Sands
MC2 Charter S	149 Emerald St Ste UP3	Keene, NH	03431	603-283-0844		9-12	Chris O'Reilly
MicroSociety Academy Charter S	591 W Hollis St	Nashua, NH	03062	603-595-7077		K-7	Amy Bottomley
Mill Falls Charter S	100 William Loeb Dr	Manchester, NH	03109-5309	603-232-5176	518-7489	K-6	Meryl Levin
Mountain Village Charter S	13 Old Route 25	Plymouth, NH	03264	603-536-3900	947-0189	K-8	Katy Gautsch
Next Charter S	5 Hood Rd	Derry, NH	03038	603-437-6398	437-6398	9-12	Joseph Crawford
North Country Charter Academy	260 Cottage St Ste A	Littleton, NH	03561-4137	603-444-1535	444-9843	7-12	Lisa Lavoie
PACE Career Academy	65 Pinewood Rd	Allenstown, NH	03275	603-210-1882	210-2341	9-12	Martin Castle
Polaris Charter S	100 Coolidge Ave	Manchester, NH	03102-3208	603-634-0034	634-0041	K-6	Jennifer Murdock - Smith
Seacoast Charter S	171 Watson Rd	Dover, NH	03820-5820	603-842-5764	842-5415	K-8	Peter Sweet
Strong Foundations Charter S	715 Riverwood Dr	Pembroke, NH	03275-3701	603-225-2715	225-2738	K-8	Beth McClure
Surry Village Charter S	449 Route 12A	Surry, NH	03431	603-357-9700	357-9701	K-8	Dr. Matora Fiorey
Virtual Learning Academy	30 Linden St	Exeter, NH	03833-2622	603-778-2500	651-5038	6-12	Stephen Kossakoski

New Jersey

School	Address	City,State	Zip code	Telephone	Fax	Grade	Contact
Academy Charter HS	1725 Main St	South Belmar, NJ	07719-3051	732-681-8377	681-8375	9-12	Dr. Mary Jo McKinley
Academy for Urban Leadership Charter S	612 Amboy Ave	Perth Amboy, NJ	08861	848-203-3742	203-3948	7-12	Dr. Nestor Collazo
Achieve Community Charter S	352 S 7th St	Newark, NJ	07112	973-556-7070		PK-12	
Atlantic Community Charter S	112 S New York Road	Galloway, NJ	08205	609-428-4300		K-6	Jeanine Bethel
Banneker Preparatory Charter S	PO Box 128	Willingboro, NJ	08046-0128	609-531-0158		6-8	Richard Wilson M.A.
BelovED Community Charter S	508 Grand St	Jersey City, NJ	07302	201-630-4700	918-6137	K-7	Kelly Convery
Bergen Arts and Science Charter ES	30 Madonna Pl	Garfield, NJ	07026	862-247-8510	247-8511	K-3	
Bergen Arts and Science Charter HS	43 Maple Ave	Hackensack, NJ	07601	201-968-5039	968-5044	9-12	
Bergen Arts and Science Charter MS	200 MacArthur Ave	Garfield, NJ	07026-1214	973-253-0002	253-0110	4-8	Nihat Guvercin
Bridgeton Charter S	790 E Commerce St	Bridgeton, NJ	08302	856-497-8202		K-3	Ja'Shanna Jones-Booker
Burch Charter S of Excellence	100 Linden Ave	Irvington, NJ	07111-2560	973-373-3223	373-3228	PK-5	Dr. Theodore Boler
Camden Academy Charter HS	879 Beideman Ave	Camden, NJ	08105-4227	856-365-1000	365-1005	9-12	Dr. Marvin Jones
Camden Prep Bonsall ES	1575 Mount Ephraim Ave	Camden, NJ	08104-1678	856-966-5088	756-0294	PK-4	Tyrone Richards
Camden Prep Charter S	1500 S 8th St	Camden, NJ	08104	856-379-4488		K-6	Michael Ambriz
Camden's Pride Charter S	897 N 31st St	Camden, NJ	08105	856-365-1000	966-5383	K-4	Christa Hahn
Camden's Promise Charter S	879 Beideman Ave	Camden, NJ	08105-4227	856-365-1000	365-1005	5-8	Dr. Joseph Conway
Central Jersey College Prep Charter S	101 Mettlers Rd	Somerset, NJ	08873	732-302-9991	302-9992	K-12	Dr. Namik Sercan
ChARTer-TECHnical HS for Performing Arts	413 New Rd	Somers Point, NJ	08244-2143	609-926-7694	926-8472	9-12	Dr. Brian McGuire
Classical Academy Charter S of Clifton	20 Valley Rd	Clifton, NJ	07013-1030	973-278-7707	277-7720	6-8	Sandra Giordano
College Achieve Charter S	21 Market St	Paterson, NJ	07501	862-257-1423		K-9	Henry McNair
College Achieve Charter S	700 Grand Ave	Asbury Park, NJ	07712	732-890-7338		K-6	Daniel Simon
College Achieve Charter S	365 Emerson Ave	Plainfield, NJ	07062	908-625-1879	441-9877	K-8	Mike Piscal
Community Charter S of Paterson	75 Spruce St	Paterson, NJ	07501	973-413-2057	345-7623	K-8	Mark Valli
Compass Academy Charter School	23 W Chestnut Ave	Vineland, NJ	08360	856-899-5570	431-7971	K-5	Susan Little
Cramer Hill ES	1033 Cambridge Ave	Camden, NJ	08105	856-726-0027		K-8	Jesse Gismondi
Cresthaven Academy	530 W 7th St	Plainfield, NJ	07060	908-756-1234		K-1	Monica Villafuerte
Discovery Charter S	240 Halsey St	Newark, NJ	07102	973-623-0222	623-0024	4-8	Barbara Weiland
Early Learning Academy	501 Cooper St	Camden, NJ	08102	856-614-3246		PK PK	
East Orange Community Charter S	99 Washington St	East Orange, NJ	07017-1006	973-996-0400	996-0398	K-4	Harvin Dash
Edison Energysmart Charter S	150 Pierce St 2nd Fl	Somerset, NJ	08873	732-412-7643	412-7645	K-9	Oguz Yildiz
Edwards Academic Charter S	509 Bramhall Ave	Jersey City, NJ	07304-2730	201 433 5300		K-8	James Brewer
Elysian Charter S	1460 Garden St	Hoboken, NJ	07030	201-876-0102	876-9576	K-8	Harry Laub Ph.D.
Empowerment Academy Charter S	508 Grand St	Jersey City, NJ	07302	201-630-4798		K-3	Carly Gigl
Englewood on the Palisades Charter S	65 W Demarest Ave	Englewood, NJ	07631-2316	201-569-9765	568-9576	K-7	Shirl Burns M.Ed.
Environment Comm Opportunity Charter S	817 Carpenter St	Camden, NJ	08102-1132	856-963-2627	963-2628	K-5	Dr. Antoinette Dendtler
Ethical Community Charter S	95 Broadway	Jersey City, NJ	07306	201-984-4151	200-9931	K-8	Marta Bergamini
Foundation Academy Charter IS	363 W State St	Trenton, NJ	08618-5705	609-920-9200	920-9205	3-8	Graig Weiss
Foundation Collegiate Academy	22 Grand St	Trenton, NJ	08611	609-920-9200	920-9205	9-12	Shavonne McMillan
Freedom Prep Charter S	1000 Atlantic Ave	Camden, NJ	08104	856-962-0766	962-0769	K-12	Ronald Brady
Golden Door Charter S	3044 John F Kennedy Blvd	Jersey City, NJ	07306-3604	201-795-4400	795-3308	K-8	Brian Stiles
Gray Charter S	55 Liberty St	Newark, NJ	07102-4815	973-824-6661	824-2296	K-8	Verna Gray
Greater Brunswick Charter S	429 Joyce Kilmer Ave	New Brunswick, NJ	08901	732-448-1052	448-1055	K-8	Vanessa Jones
Great Futures Charter HS	225 Morris Blvd	Jersey City, NJ	07302	201-716-1520	716-1530	9-12	Kevin Ahearn
Great Oaks Legacy Charter S	24 Maiden Ln	Newark, NJ	07102	973-565-9170		K-12	Jared Taillefer
Hatikvah International Academy Charter S	7 Lexington Ave	East Brunswick, NJ	08816	732-254-8300	254-8380	K-8	Dr. Marcia Grayson
Hoboken Charter S	4 Garden St	Hoboken, NJ	07030	201-963-3280	963-0695	PK-12	Deirdra Grode
Hoboken Dual Language Charter S	123 Jefferson St	Hoboken, NJ	07030	201-427-1458	706-4491	K-8	Jennifer Sargent
Holland Charter S	190 Oliver St	Paterson, NJ	07501	973-345-2212	345-2233	PK-8	Christina Scano
Hope Academy Charter S	601 Grand Ave	Asbury Park, NJ	07712-6656	732-988-4227	988-9125	K-8	DaVisha Pratt
Hope Community Charter S	836 S 4th St	Camden, NJ	08103	856-379-3448		K-5	Robin Ruiz
Hudson Arts & Science Charter S	131 Midland Ave	Kearny, NJ	07032	201-955-1818	955-1817	K-6	Nihat Guvercin
International Academy of Atlantic City	25 W Black Horse Pike	Pleasantville, NJ	08232	609-498-6350		K-5	Dr. Natakie Chestnut
International Academy of Trenton	500 Perry St	Trenton, NJ	08618	609-759-2005	288-8461	K-6	Dr. Jermaine Kamau
International Charter S of Trenton	105 Grand St	Trenton, NJ	08611-2417	609-394-3111	394-3116	K-4	Melissa Benford
Jersey City Community Charter S	128 Danforth Ave	Jersey City, NJ	07305-2626	201-433-2288	433-5803	K-8	Ayana Williams
Jersey City Global Charter S	255 Congress St	Jersey City, NJ	07307	201-636-8540	636-8543	K-6	Dr. Nadira Jack
Kingdom Charter S of Leadership	121 W Church St	Blackwood, NJ	08012	856-232-0100		K-5	Wandria McCall-Hampton
KIPP Cooper Norcross	525 Clinton St	Camden, NJ	08103	856-966-9600		K-1	Joanna Belcher
Knowledge A to Z Charter S	3098 Pleasant St	Camden, NJ	08105	856-375-1140	963-1980	K-4	
Lady Liberty Academy Charter S	746 Sandford Ave	Newark, NJ	07106	973-623-9005	483-0807	K-8	Dr. James Catalano
LEAD Charter S	201 Bergan St	Newark, NJ	07103	862-772-1724		9-12	Juan Acevedo
Learning Community Charter S	2495 John F Kennedy Blvd	Jersey City, NJ	07304-2007	201-332-0900	332-4981	K-8	Colin Hogan
Link Community Charter S	23 Pennsylvania Ave	Newark, NJ	07114-2007	973-642-0529	642-1978	5-8	Kathleen Hester J.D.
M.E.T.S. Charter S	211 Sherman Ave	Jersey City, NJ	07307	201-526-8500	526-7630	6-12	
Millville Public Charter S	1101 Wheaton Ave Ste 220	Millville, NJ	08332	856-506-8143		K-8	Valerie James-Kemp
Molina Lower ES	415 N 9th St	Camden, NJ	08102	856-993-7004		K-2	
Molina Upper ES	601 Vine St	Camden, NJ	08102-1801	856-966-8970	342-6930	3-8	Rickia Reid
Newark Educators Community Charter S	9-11 Hill St	Newark, NJ	07102-2642	973-732-3848	732-3847	PK-5	Dina Velez
New Horizons Community Charter S	45 Hayes St	Newark, NJ	07103	973-848-0400	596-0984	K-7	Andre Hollis
North Star Academy Charter S	10 Washington Pl	Newark, NJ	07102-3106	973-642-0101	642-5800	K-12	Michael Ambriz
Obama Green Charter HS	35 Watchung Ave	Plainfield, NJ	07060-1207	877-643-4064		9-12	Steven King
Ocean Academy Charter S	678 5th St	Lakewood, NJ	08701	732-987-6525		K-2	Cindy Coughlin
PACE Charter School of Hamilton	1949 Hamilton Ave	Hamilton, NJ	08619-3736	609-587-2288	587-8483	K-5	Debbie Pontoriero
Passaic Arts and Science Charter S	7 Saint Francis Way	Passaic, NJ	07055	973-928-5544	928-5545	K-10	Nihat Guvercin
Paterson Arts and Science Charter S	225 Grand St	Paterson, NJ	07501	862-336-1550	336-1551	K-9	Nihat Guvercin
Paterson Charter S for Science and Tech	276 Wabash Ave	Paterson, NJ	07503	973-345-4400	345-4636	K-6	Ali Riza Gurcanli M.Ed.
Paterson Charter S for Science and Tech	196 W Railway Ave	Paterson, NJ	07503	973-247-0600	247-9924	7-12	
People's Preparatory HS	321 Bergen St	Newark, NJ	07103-2639	973-622-1790	622-1453	9-12	Jess Rooney
Phillip's Academy Charter S	47 State St	Paterson, NJ	07501	973-247-8920	624-0102	K-1	Regina Lauricella
Phillip's Academy Charter S	342 Central Ave	Newark, NJ	07103-2808	973-624-0644	624-0102	K-9	Mark Shultz
Pride Academy Charter S	117 Elmwood Ave	East Orange, NJ	07018-2420	973-672-3200	672-3207	5-8	Fiona Thomas
Princeton Charter S	100 Bunn Dr	Princeton, NJ	08540-2821	609-924-0575	924-0282	K-8	Lawrence Patton
Queen City Academy Charter S	815 W 7th St	Plainfield, NJ	07063-1449	908-753-4700	753-4816	K-8	Danielle West
Red Bank Charter S	58 Oakland St	Red Bank, NJ	07701-1104	732-450-2092	936-1923	PK-8	Meredith Pennotti
Ridge & Valley Charter S	1234 State Route 94	Blairstown, NJ	07825-4115	908-362-1114	362-6680	K-8	Nanci Dvorsky
Riverbank Charter S of Excellence	1300 Hornberger Ave	Roebling, NJ	08554-1313	609-499-4321	447-0350	K-3	Beth Kelley
Robeson Charter S for the Humanities	643 Indiana Ave	Trenton, NJ	08638-3821	609-394-7721	394-7720	4-8	Freya Lund
Roseville Community Charter S	540 Orange St	Newark, NJ	07107	973-483-4400	483-0770	K-1	Marshae Newkirk
Soaring Heights Charter S	1 Romar Ave	Jersey City, NJ	07305-1713	201-434-4800	434-7474	K-8	Claudia Zuorick
STEM ES	639 Cooper St	Camden, NJ	08102	856-614-2088		K-3	
STEM IS	532 Cooper St	Camden, NJ	08102	856-614-3292		7-8	
STEM/STEAM HS	130 N Broadway	Camden, NJ	08102	856-614-5640		9-12	
STEM Upper ES	549 Cooper St	Camden, NJ	08102	856-614-0400		4-6	
Sussex Co. Charter S for Technology	385 N Church Rd	Sparta, NJ	07871-3307	973-383-3250	383-2901	6-8	Noreen Lazariuk
TEAM Academy Charter S	60 Park Pl Ste 802	Newark, NJ	07102-5508	973-705-8326	556-1238	K-12	Joanna Belcher
Teaneck Community Charter S	563 Chestnut Ave	Teaneck, NJ	07666	201-833-9600	833-9225	K-8	Ralph Gallo
Thomas Charter MS	570 Broad St	Newark, NJ	07103	973-621-0060	792-0066	6-8	Genique Hamilton
Thomas Charter S	370 S 7th St	Newark, NJ	07103-2047	973-621-0060	621-0061	PK-5	Lisa Finn-Bruce
Treat Academy Charter S - North	443 Clifton Ave	Newark, NJ	07104-1339	973-482-8811	482-7681	K-8	Theresa Adubato

School	Address	City,State	Zip code	Telephone	Fax	Grade	Contact
Treat Academy Chartr S - Central	180 William St	Newark, NJ	07103	973-286-1020	286-1050	K-8	Theresa Adubato
Trenton Stem-to-Civics Charter S	1555 Pennington Rd	Ewing, NJ	08618-1301	609-503-1103		9-12	Dr. Leigh Byron
Union County TEAMS Charter S	515 W 4th St	Plainfield, NJ	07060-4225	908-754-9043	754-7790	K-12	Sheila Thorpe
Unity Charter S	1 Evergreen Pl	Morristown, NJ	07960	973-292-1808	267-9288	K-8	Connie Sanchez
University Academy Charter HS	275 W Side Ave	Jersey City, NJ	07305-1130	201-200-3200	200-3262	9-12	Erie Lugo
University Heights Charter S	74 Hartford St	Newark, NJ	07103-2832	973-623-1965	623-8511	K-8	Tamara Cooper
Varisco-Rogers Charter S	233 Woodside Ave	Newark, NJ	07104-3113	973-481-9001	481-9009	K-8	Teresa Segarra
Village Charter S	101 Sullivan Way	Trenton, NJ	08628-3425	609-695-0110	695-1880	K-8	Keoke Wooten-Johnson
Vineland Public Charter S	1480 Pennsylvania Ave	Vineland, NJ	08361	856-691-1611		PK-10	Dr. Ann Garcia

New Mexico

School	Address	City,State	Zip code	Telephone	Fax	Grade	Contact
ABQ Charter Academy	405 Dr Martin Luther King	Albuquerque, NM	87102	505-242-6640	242-6872	9-12	Amy Roble
Academy for Technology and the Classics	74 A Van NU PO	Santa Fe, NM	87508	505-473-4282	467-6513	7-12	Susan Lumley
Academy of Trades & Technology	2551 Karsten Ct SE	Albuquerque, NM	87102	505-765-5517	765-5898	9-12	Dr. Karen Griego-Sanchez
ACE Leadership HS	1240 Bellamah Ave NW	Albuquerque, NM	87104	505-242-4733	242-2220	9-12	Tori Stephens-Shauger
Albuquerque Institute of Math & Science	933 Bradbury Dr SE	Albuquerque, NM	87106-4374	505-559-4249	243-9235	6-12	Kathy Sandoval-Snider
Albuquerque School of Excellence	13201 Lomas Blvd NE	Albuquerque, NM	87112	505-312-7711	312-7712	1-12	Salih Aykac
Albuquerque Sign Language Academy	620 Lomas Blvd NW	Albuquerque, NM	87102	505-247-1701	247-1704	K-12	Raphael Martinez M.A.
Albuquerque Talent Development Academy	1800 Atrisco Dr NW	Albuquerque, NM	87120	505-503-2465	831-7031	9-12	Gloria Garza
Alma D Arte Charter HS	402 W Court Ave	Las Cruces, NM	88005-2596	575-541-0145	527-5329	9-12	Mark Harshorne
Anansi Charter S	PO Box 1709	El Prado, NM	87529-1709	575-776-2256	776-5561	K-8	Michele Hunt
Anthony Charter S	780 Landers Rd	Anthony, NM	88021	575-882-0600	882-2116	7-12	Abe Armendariz
ASK Academy	4550 Sundt Rd NE	Rio Rancho, NM	87124	505-891-0757	891-2115	6-12	Dan Busse
Biehl Charter HS	123 4th St SW	Albuquerque, NM	87102-3201	505-299-9409	299-9493	9-12	Frank McCulloch
Carinos De Los Ninos S	714 Calle Don Diego	Espanola, NM	87532	505-753-1128	747-3932	K-8	Vernon Jaramillo
Chavez Community S	1325 Palomas Dr SE	Albuquerque, NM	87108	505-877-0558	242-1466	9-12	Tani Arness
Cien Aguas International S	2000 Randolph Rd SE	Albuquerque, NM	87106	505-255-0001	255-0400	K-8	Casey Benavidez
Coral Community Charter S	4401 Silver Ave SE	Albuquerque, NM	87108	505-292-6725	200-0440	K-4	Lori Bachman
Corrales International S	5500 Wilshire Ave NE	Albuquerque, NM	87113	505-344-9733	338-1409	K-12	Mark Tolley
Cottonwood Classical Preparatory S	7801 Jefferson St NE	Albuquerque, NM	87109	505-998-1021	341-9510	6-12	Sam Obenshain
Cottonwood Valley Charter S	PO Box 1829	Socorro, NM	87801-1829	575-838-2026	838-2420	K-8	Kim Schaffer
Deming Cesar Chavez Charter HS	315 E 1st St	Deming, NM	88030	575-544-8404	544-8755	9-12	Stan Lyons
Digital Arts and Technology Academy	1011 Lamberton Pl NE	Albuquerque, NM	87107-1641	505-341-0888	341-0658	9-12	Lisa Myhre
Dorn Community Charter S	1119 Edith Blvd SE	Albuquerque, NM	87102	505-243-1434	243-6943	K-5	Ellen Esquibel-Bellamy
Dream Dine	PO Box 4386	Shiprock, NM	87420	505-368-2500		PK-8	
Duncan Heritage Academy	1900 Atrisco Dr NW	Albuquerque, NM	87120	505-839-4971	831-9027	PK-8	Jesus Moncada
Dzil Dit Looi S of Empowerment	PO Box 156	Navajo, NM	87328	505-777-2053		6-12	Kayla Begay
East Mountain HS	PO Box 340	Sandia Park, NM	87047-0340	505-281-7400	281-4173	9-12	Monique Siedschlag
El Camino Real Charter S	3713 Isleta Blvd SW	Albuquerque, NM	87105-5919	505-314-2212	314-2216	K-12	Paym Greene
Estancia Valley Classical Academy	PO Box 2340	Moriarty, NM	87035	505-832-2223	832-5006	K-12	Tim Thiery
Explore Academy	5100 Masthead St NE	Albuquerque, NM	87109	505-336-1466		9-12	Justin Baiardo
GREAT Academy	6001A San Mateo Blvd NE	Albuquerque, NM	87109	505-792-0306	792-0225	6-12	Jasper Matthews M.Ed.
Gutierrez MS	69 Gail Harris Blvd	Roswell, NM	88203	575-347-9703	347-9707	6-8	Joe Andreis
Health Leadership HS	1900 Randolph Rd SE	Albuquerque, NM	87106	505-750-4547		9-12	Blanca Lopez
Horizon Academy - West	3021 Todos Santos St NW	Albuquerque, NM	87120	505-998-0459	998-0463	PK-5	Cynthia Carter
International S at Mesa del Sol	2660 Eastman Ave SE	Albuquerque, NM	87106	505-508-3295	508-3328	K-12	Barbra Langmaid
Jefferson Montessori Academy	500 W Church St	Carlsbad, NM	88220	575-234-1703	887-9391	K-12	Stacey Frakes
Kennedy HS	4300 Blake Rd SW	Albuquerque, NM	87121-5179	505-873-1165	242-7444	9-12	Robert Baade
King Community S	8100 Mountain Rd NE	Albuquerque, NM	87110	505-344-0746	344-0789	K-8	Tonya Newton
La Academia de Esperanza	1401 Old Coors SW	Albuquerque, NM	87121	505-764-5500	764-5501	6-12	Steve Wood
La Academia Dolores Huerta	1480 N Main St	Las Cruces, NM	88001-1106	575-526-2984	523-5407	6-8	Octavio Casillas
La Promesa Early Learning Center	7500 La Morada NW	Albuquerque, NM	87120-1765	505-268-3274	268-3276	PK-8	Dr. Analee Maestas
La Resolana Leadership Academy	230 Truman St NE	Albuquerque, NM	87108	505-243-8114	243-8385	6-8	Justina Montoya
Las Montanas Charter S	1405 S Solano Dr	Las Cruces, NM	88001-4235	575-636-2100	527-7686	9-12	Richard Robinson
La Tierra Montessori S of the Arts & Sci	PO Box 1399	Espanola, NM	87532	505-852-0200	367-3544	K-8	Christie Berg
Learning Community Charter S	5555 McLeod Rd NE	Albuquerque, NM	87109	505-332-3200	332-8780	6-12	Viola Martinez
Leopold Charter S	1422 Highway 180 E	Silver City, NM	88061-7837	575-538-2547	388-4970	6-12	Wayne Sherwood
Lindrith Area Heritage Charter S	PO Box 119	Lindrith, NM	87029	575-774-6669		K-8	Rebecca Gibson M.A.
Los Puentes Charter S	4012 4th St NW	Albuquerque, NM	87107	505-342-5959	341-0836	7-12	Micaela Smith
MASTERS Program	6401 S Richards Ave	Santa Fe, NM	87508	505-428-7320	428-7322	10-12	Anne Salzmann
McCurdy Charter S	PO Box 2250	Espanola, NM	87532	505-692-6090	692-6095	K-12	Janette Archuleta
Media Arts Collaborative Charter S	4401 Central Ave NE	Albuquerque, NM	87108-1209	505-243-1957	268-1651	6-12	Glenna Voigt M.A.
Middle College HS	705 Gurley Ave	Gallup, NM	87301	505-722-9945	722-9946	10-12	Dr. Robert Hunter
Mission Achievement & Success Charter S	1718 Yale Blvd SE	Albuquerque, NM	87106	505-242-3118	243-3062	K-12	JoAnn Myers
Monte Del Sol Charter S	4157 Walking Rain Rd	Santa Fe, NM	87507-0825	505-982-5225	982-5321	7-12	Dr. Robert Jessen
Montessori ES	1730 Montano Rd NW	Albuquerque, NM	87107	505-796-0149	796-0147	K-8	Mary Jane Besante
Montessori of the Rio Grande Charter S	1650 Gabaldon Dr NW	Albuquerque, NM	87104	505-842-5993	242-2907	PK-6	Dr. Deborah Henwood
Moreno Valley HS	PO Box 1037	Angel Fire, NM	87710-1037	575-377-3100	377-7263	9-12	Greg Vincent
Mosaic Academy	450 Llano St	Aztec, NM	87410	505-334-6364	334-3948	K-8	Diane Mittler
Mountain Mahogany Community S	5014 4th St NW	Albuquerque, NM	87107-3908	505-341-1424	341-1428	K-8	Amy Chase
Native American Community Academy	1000 Indian School Rd NW	Albuquerque, NM	87104	505-266-0992	266-2905	6-12	Kara Bobroff
New America S - Las Cruces	PO Box 16680	Las Cruces, NM	88004	575-527-9085	527-9153	9-12	Margarita Porter
New America School	1734 Isleta Blvd SW	Albuquerque, NM	87105	505-222-4360	873-2602	9-12	LaTricia Mathis
New Mexico Connections Academy	4001 Office Court Dr # 201	Santa Fe, NM	87507	505-428-2130	424-9092	4-12	Jodie Dean
New Mexico International School	8650 Alameda Blvd NE	Albuquerque, NM	87122	505-503-7670	503-7989	K-5	Todd Knouse
New Mexico School for the Arts	275 E Alameda St	Santa Fe, NM	87501	505-310-4194	820-3529	9-12	Cindy Montoya
New Mexico Virtual Academy	845 Sullivan Ave	Farmington, NM	87401	855-718-7724	258-4080	6-12	Deborah Jackson
North Valley Academy	7939 4th St NW	Los Ranchos, NM	87114	505-998-0501	998-0505	PK-8	Susan McConnell
Nuestros Valores Charter S	6800 Gonzales Rd SW	Albuquerque, NM	87121	505-873-7758	873-3567	9-12	Monica Aguilar
Public Academy for Performing Arts	11800 Princess Jeanne NE	Albuquerque, NM	87112	505-830-3128	830-9930	6-12	Doreen Winn
Red River Valley Charter S	PO Box 742	Red River, NM	87558-0742	575-754-6117	754-3258	PK-8	Karen Phillips
Rio Gallinas S for Ecology and the Arts	1107 Montezuma St	Las Vegas, NM	87701	505-454-8687	454-8688	K-8	Kirk Ludi
Roots & Wings Community S	35 La Lama Rd	Questa, NM	87556	575-586-2076	586-2087	K-8	Nancy Gonzalez
Sage Montessori Charter S	3831 Midway Pl NE	Albuquerque, NM	87109	505-344-7447	797-4294	K-6	Felix Garcia
SAMS Academy	4100 Aerospace Pkwy NW	Albuquerque, NM	87120	505-338-8601	296-0510	7-12	Coreen Carrillo
San Diego Riverside Charter S	PO Box 99	Jemez Pueblo, NM	87024-0099	575-834-7419	834-9167	K-8	
Sandoval Academy of Bilingual Education	4321 Fulcrum Way NE	Rio Rancho, NM	87144	505-771-0555	771-9071	K-8	Pedro Vallejo
School of Dreams Academy	906 Juan Perea Rd	Los Lunas, NM	87031	505-804-7639	804-7639	PK-12	Michael Ogas
Sena Charter HS	69 Hotel Cir NE	Albuquerque, NM	87123-1202	505-237-2374	237-2380	9-12	Nadine Torres
Siembra Leadership HS	524 Central Rd SW	Albuquerque, NM	87102	505-681-0284	243-3308	9-12	Moises Padilla
South Valley Academy	3426 Blake Rd SW	Albuquerque, NM	87105-5009	505-452-3132	452-3133	9-12	Julie Radoslovich
South Valley Preparatory S	2813 Gun Club Rd SW	Albuquerque, NM	87105	505-222-5642	222-5647	6-8	Charlotte Trujillo
Southwest Intermediate Learning Center	10301 Candelaria Rd NE	Albuquerque, NM	87112-1504	505-296-7677	296-0510	7-8	Robert Pasztor
Southwest Primary Learning Center	10301 Candelaria Rd NE	Albuquerque, NM	87112-1504	505-296-7677	296-0510	4-6	Robert Pasztor
Southwest Secondary Learning Center	10301 Candelaria Rd NE	Albuquerque, NM	87112-1504	505-296-7677	296-0510	7-12	Kirk Hartom
Taos Academy	110 Paseo Del Canon W	Taos, NM	87571	575-751-3109	751-3394	5-12	Traci Filiss
Taos Charter S	1303 Paseo Del Canon East	Taos, NM	87571	575-751-7222	751-7546	K-8	Jeremy Jones
Taos Integrated School of the Arts	PO Box 668	Taos, NM	87571	575-758-7755	758-7766	K-8	Rich Greywolf
Taos International S	118 Este Es Rd	Taos, NM	87571	575-751-7115	751-3642	K-8	Nadine Vigil M.A.
Taylor Academy	402 W Court Ave Bldg 2	Las Cruces, NM	88005	575-652-4006	652-4621	K-8	Eric Ahner
Technology Leadership HS	10500 Research Rd SE	Albuquerque, NM	87123	505-338-2266		9-12	Kara Cortazzo
Tierra Adentro - NM Sch Acedemics/Art	1511 Central Ave NE	Albuquerque, NM	87106-4408	505-967-4720	967-4721	6-12	Veronica Torres
Tierra Encantada Charter S	551 Alarid St	Santa Fe, NM	87501	505-983-3337	983-6637	7-12	Danny Pena
Turqoise Trail ES	13A San Marcos Loop	Santa Fe, NM	87508-7083	505-986-4000	474-7862	PK-6	Dr. Ray Griffin
21st Century Public Academy	4300 Cutler Ave NE	Albuquerque, NM	87110	505-254-0280	254-8507	5-8	Mary Tarango
Vista Grande HS	213 Paseo Del Canon E	Taos, NM	87571	575-758-5100	758-5102	9-12	Isabelle St. Onge

New York

School	Address	City,State	Zip code	Telephone	Fax	Grade	Contact
Academic Leadership Charter S	677 E 141st St	Bronx, NY	10454	718-585-4215	585-4837	K-4	Leena Varghese
Academic Leadership Charter S	470 Jackson Ave	Bronx, NY	10454	718-993-1870	993-1875	5-8	Jaime Kennedy
Academy Charter S	117 N Franklin St	Hempstead, NY	11550	516-408-2200	292-2329	K-6	C. Morris
Academy MS	159 N Franklin St	Hempstead, NY	11550	516-408-2200		5-8	D. Mattison
Academy of the City Charter S	3614 12th St	Astoria, NY	11106	718-487-9857	785-9592	K-5	Richard Lee
Achievement First Apollo Charter S	350 Linwood St	Brooklyn, NY	11208-2116	718-235-2647	235-2649	K-4	Jesse Balis-Harris
Achievement First Apollo MS	301 Vermont St	Brooklyn, NY	11207	347-471-2680	235-2649	5-8	Michael Hendricks
Achievement First Aspire Charter S	982 Hegeman Ave	Brooklyn, NY	11208	347-471-2055	228-8839	K-4	Sarah Kasok Iannucci
Achievement First Brooklyn HS	1485 Pacific St	Brooklyn, NY	11216	718-363-2260	363-2262	9-12	Cristina del Castillo
Achievement First Brownsville Charter S	2021 Bergen St	Brooklyn, NY	11233	347-471-2600	402-2900	K-8	Jesse Balis-Harris
Achievement First Bushwick S	1300 Greene Ave	Brooklyn, NY	11237	718-471-2560	453-0428	K-12	Riley Bauling
Achievement First Crown Heights Charter	790 E New York Ave	Brooklyn, NY	11203-1212	347-471-2580	228-9141	K-8	Roseann Basile
Achievement First East New York ES	557 Pennsylvania Ave	Brooklyn, NY	11207-5727	718-485-4924	228-6028	K-4	Lucy Volkmar
Achievement First Endeavor S	510 Waverly Ave	Brooklyn, NY	11238	718-622-4786	789-1649	K-12	Caroline Roth
Achievement First E NY MS	158 Richmond St	Brooklyn, NY	11208	347-471-2570	228-9141	5-8	Max Milliken
Achievement First Linden ES	800 Van Siclen Ave	Brooklyn, NY	11207	718-471-2700	789-1649	K-4	Amanda Hageman
Achievement First North Brooklyn Prep S	200 Woodbine St	Brooklyn, NY	11221	718-471-2690	402-1818	K-4	Elena Knappen

School	Address	City,State	Zip code	Telephone	Fax	Grade	Contact
Achievement First Voyager Charter S	601 Parkside Ave	Brooklyn, NY	11226	347-471-2640		5-6	Priam Dutta
Albany Community Charter S	65 Krank St	Albany, NY	12202	518-433-1500	433-1501	K-8	S. Neal Currie
Albany Leadership Charter HS for Girls	19 Hackett Blvd	Albany, NY	12208	518-694-5300	694-5307	9-12	William Rivers
Amani Charter S	60 S 3rd Ave Ste 1	Mount Vernon, NY	10550-3313	914-668-6450	699-0839	5-8	Debra Stern
Amber Charter S	220 E 106th St	New York, NY	10029-4020	212-534-9667	534-6225	K-5	Dr. Vasthi Acosta
Amber Charter S II	3120 Corlear Ave	Bronx, NY	10463	646-802-1140		K-2	Veronica Almedina
American Dream Charter S	510 E 141st St	Bronx, NY	10454-2753	718-585-3071	227-2760	6-8	Melissa Melkonian
Atmosphere Academy	22 Marble Hill Ave	Bronx, NY	10463	718-696-0493		6-8	Colin Greene
Bedford Stuyvesant Collegiate Charter S	800 Gates Ave	Brooklyn, NY	11221	718-669-7460	669-7771	5-8	Mabel Lajes-Guiteras
Bed-Stuy New Beginnings Charter S	82 Lewis Ave	Brooklyn, NY	11206	718-453-1001	452-2090	K-8	Nicholas Tishuk
Beginning With Children Charter S II	215 Heyward St	Brooklyn, NY	11206	718-302-7700	302-7701	PK-8	Esosa Ogbahon
Boys Prep Charter S of New York	1695 Seward Ave	Bronx, NY	10473-4249	646-783-3589	346-9096	K-5	Kristin Norgrove
Brighter Choice Charter MS for Boys	116 Lake Ave	Albany, NY	12206	518-694-8200	694-8201	5-8	Karen McLean
Brighter Choice Charter MS for Girls	250 Central Ave	Albany, NY	12206	518-694-5550	694-5551	5-8	Marcus Puccioni
Brighter Choice Charter S for Boys	116 N Lake Ave	Albany, NY	12206-2710	518-694-8200	694-8201	K-5	Karen McLean
Brighter Choice Charter S for Girls	250 Central Ave	Albany, NY	12206-2639	518-694-4100	694-4123	K-5	Marcus Puccioni
Brilla College Preparatory Charter S	413 E 144th St	Bronx, NY	10454	347-273-8439		K-5	Alexandra Apfel
Brilla College Prep Charter S	500 Courtlandt Ave	Bronx, NY	10451	347-273-8439		K-4	Sheila Mulcahy
Bronx Academy of Promise Charter S	1349 Inwood Ave	Bronx, NY	10452-3222	718-293-6950	681-8225	K-8	Catherine Jackvony
Bronx Charter S 2 for Better Learning	2545 Gunther Ave	Bronx, NY	10469	718-655-6660	794-9816	K-1	Nysheria Sims
Bronx Charter S for Better Learning	3740 Baychester Ave	Bronx, NY	10466-5031	718-655-6660	655-5555	K-5	Shubert Jacobs
Bronx Charter S for Children	388 Willis Ave	Bronx, NY	10454-1303	718-402-3300	402-3258	K-5	Doreen Land
Bronx Charter S for Excellence	1960 Benedict Ave	Bronx, NY	10462-4402	718-828-7301	828-7302	K-8	Charlene Reid
Bronx Charter S for Excellence 2	1804 Holland Ave	Bronx, NY	10462	718-828-7301		K-5	Charlene Reid
Bronx Charter S for Excellence 3	3956 Carpenter Ave	Bronx, NY	10466	718-308-1082		K-5	
Bronx Charter S for the Arts	950 Longfellow Ave	Bronx, NY	10474-4809	718-893-1042	893-7910	K-5	Miriam Raccah
Bronx Community Charter S	3170 Webster Ave	Bronx, NY	10467-4902	718-584-1400	944-1405	K-5	Martha Andrews
Bronx Global Learning Institute	750 Concourse Vlg W	Bronx, NY	10451	718-993-1740	993-1965	K-8	Mary Cordero
Bronx Lighthouse Charter S	1001 Intervale Ave	Bronx, NY	10459-3151	646-915-0025	915-0037	K-12	Travis Brown
Bronx Preparatory Charter S	3872 3rd Ave	Bronx, NY	10457-8222	718-294-0841	294-2381	5-12	Lourdes Flores
Brooklyn Ascend Lower S	205 Rockaway Pkwy	Brooklyn, NY	11212	718-907-9147	240-9140	K-4	Johana Andujar
Brooklyn Ascend MS	123 E 98th St	Brooklyn, NY	11212	347-289-9000		5-8	Marsha Gadsden
Brooklyn Charter S	545 Willoughby Ave	Brooklyn, NY	11206-6815	718-218-2300	302-2426	K-5	Omigbade Escayg
Brooklyn Dreams Charter S	259 Parkville Ave	Brooklyn, NY	11230	718-859-8400	586-0347	K-8	Omar Thomas
Brooklyn East Collegiate Charter S	80 Underhill Ave	Brooklyn, NY	11238	718-250-5760	250-5761	5-8	Rodolpho Loureiro
Brooklyn Emerging Leaders Academy	125 Stuyvesant Ave	Brooklyn, NY	11221	347-491-8320		9-12	Nicia Fullwood
Brooklyn Excelsior Charter S	856 Quincy St	Brooklyn, NY	11221-3612	718-246-5681	246-5864	K-8	Christopher Petty
Brooklyn LAB Charter S	240 Jay St	Brooklyn, NY	11201-1937	347-429-8439	612-9127	6-8	Eric Tucker Ph.D.
Brooklyn Prospect Charter S	300 Willoughby Ave	Brooklyn, NY	11205	718-783-1570		6-8	Daniel Rub
Brooklyn Prospect Charter S	3002 Fort Hamilton Pkwy	Brooklyn, NY	11218-1608	347-889-7041	889-7038	6-12	LaNolia Omowanile
Brooklyn Scholars Charter S	2635 Linden Blvd	Brooklyn, NY	11208-4907	718-348-9360	348-9362	K-8	Desiree Kirton
Brooklyn S of Inquiry	50 Avenue P	Brooklyn, NY	11204	718-621-5730	621-5735	K-8	Eric Havlik
Brooklyn Urban Garden Charter S	500 19th St	Brooklyn, NY	11215-6204	212-437-8318		6-8	Susan Tenner
Broome Street Academy	121 Avenue of the Americas	New York, NY	10013	212-453-0295	966-7253	9-12	Louise Grotenhuis
Brownsville Ascend Charter S	1501 Pitkin Ave	Brooklyn, NY	11212	347-294-2600	342-1082	K-8	Erica Murphy
Brownsville Collegiate Charter S	364 Sackman St	Brooklyn, NY	11212	718-636-0370	296-8321	5-9	Joel Tracy
Buffalo Academy of Science Charter S	190 Franklin St	Buffalo, NY	14202	716-854-2490	854-5039	5-12	Joseph Polat
Buffalo Collegiate Charter S	375 Summer St	Buffalo, NY	14213	716-713-2162		4-12	Brian Pawloski
Buffalo United Charter S	325 Manhattan Ave	Buffalo, NY	14214-1809	716-835-9862	835-6272	K-8	Tammy Messmer
Bushwick Ascend Charter S	751 Knickerbocker Ave	Brooklyn, NY	11221	718-240-9162	484-0498	K-4	Dellianna Burrows
Bushwick Ascend MS	2 Aberdeen St	Brooklyn, NY	11207	718-744-6100		5-8	Emily McGraw
CAMPA Charter S	1962 Linden Blvd	Brooklyn, NY	11207	347-619-6800		6-8	George Leonard
Canarsie Ascend Charter S	9719 Flatlands Ave	Brooklyn, NY	11236	718-907-0153		K-4	Anastasia Michals
Capital Prep Harlem Charter S	1 E 104th St	New York, NY	10029	212-328-9370	400-0930	6-9	Danita Jones
Cardinal McCloskey Community Charter S	629 Courtland Ave	Bronx, NY	10451	718-402-0081		K-1	
Central Brooklyn Ascend Charter S	465 E 29th St	Brooklyn, NY	11226-7825	718-246-4800		K-5	Michelle Flowers
Central Queens Academy	8824 Myrtle Ave	Glendale, NY	11385	718-850-3111		7-8	Ashish Kapadia
Central Queens Academy Charter S	5530 Junction Blvd	Elmhurst, NY	11373	718-271-6200	271-6900	5-6	Jesse Tang
Challenge Preparatory Charter S	710 Hartman Ln	Far Rockaway, NY	11691	718-327-1352	327-1361	K-8	Nicole Griffin
Charter HS for Law and Social Justice	1960 University Ave	Bronx, NY	10453	347-696-0042		9-12	Courtney Crawford
Charter S for Applied Technologies	2303 Kenmore Ave	Buffalo, NY	14207-1311	716-876-7505	876-9758	K-12	Efrain Martinez
Charter S of Educational Excellence	260 Warburton Ave	Yonkers, NY	10701-2226	914-476-5070	476-2858	K-8	Cindy Lopez
Charter S of Inquiry	404 Edison St	Buffalo, NY	14215	716-833-3250		K-8	
Children's Aid Society Charter S	1919 Prospect Ave	Bronx, NY	10457	347-871-9002	583-6238	K-5	Casey Vier
Citizens of the World Charter S	424 Leonard St	Brooklyn, NY	11222	718-384-1386		K-5	Jonoa Thomas
Citizens of the World Charter S	791 Empire Blvd	Brooklyn, NY	11213	718-221-5095		K-5	Andrea Dozier
City Polytechnic HS	105 Tech Pl	Brooklyn, NY	11201	718-875-1473	875-1947	9-12	Judie Cherenfant
Community Partnership Charter S	241 Emerson Pl	Brooklyn, NY	11205-3808	718-399-3824	399-1495	PK-8	Nicole Blair-Barzey
Community Roots Charter S	51 Saint Edwards St	Brooklyn, NY	11205-2932	718-858-1629	858-1754	K-6	Allison Keil
Compass Charter S	300 Adelphi St	Brooklyn, NY	11205-4601	718-310-3588	852-4682	K-5	Brooke Peters
Comp Sci HS	1300 Boynton Ave	Bronx, NY	10472	646-421-4523		9-12	David Noah
Coney Island Prep Public Charter S	501 West Ave	Brooklyn, NY	11224-4220	718-513-6951	513-6955	5-8	Jacob Mnookin
Cultural Arts Academy at Spring Creek	1400 Linden Blvd	Brooklyn, NY	11212	718-683-3300	272-1330	K-5	Dr. Laurie B. Midgette
de Hostos Charter S	27 Zimbrich St	Rochester, NY	14621	585-544-6170	544-3848	K-10	Maycanitza Perez
Democracy Preparatory Harlem HS	212 W 120th St	New York, NY	10027	212-932-7791	666-3706	9-12	Steve Popper
Democracy Prep Charter HS	222 W 134th St	New York, NY	10030	212-281-3061	281-3064	9-12	Natasha Trivers
Democracy Prep Charter MS	207 W 133rd St	New York, NY	10030	212-281-1248	283-4202	6-8	Zach Siegel
Democracy Prep Charter MS	2230 5th Ave	New York, NY	10037	212-281-8247	281-5359	6-8	Tanya Nunez
Democracy Prep Endurance Charter S	250 W 127th St	New York, NY	10027	212-316-7602	316-7022	6-8	Katherine Perez
Democracy Prep Endurance HS	240 E 123rd St	New York, NY	10035	646-490-3693	316-7022	9-12	Pia Dandiya
Democracy Prep Harlem ES	2005 Madison Ave	New York, NY	10035	212-348-3795	348-3796	K-3	Theresa Walsh
Discovery Charter S	133 Hoover Dr	Rochester, NY	14615	585-342-4032	342-4003	K-6	Joseph Saia
DREAM Charter S	1991 2nd Ave	New York, NY	10029	212-722-0232	348-5979	K-8	Eve Colavito
Eagle Academy for Young Men III	17110 Linden Blvd	Jamaica, NY	11434	718-480-2600	723-4709	6-8	Cedric Hall
East Harlem Scholars Academy	2050 2nd Ave	New York, NY	10029	212-348-2518	348-2848	K-8	Desree Cabrall-Njenga
East Harlem Scholars Academy II	1573 Madison Ave	New York, NY	10029	212-831-0650	289-7967	K-8	Nick West
Elm Community Charter S	3325 92nd St	Jackson Heights, NY	11372	917-669-4212		K-5	Priscilla Walton
Elmwood Village Charter S	665 Hertel Ave	Buffalo, NY	14207	716-424-0555		K-8	Kathy Jamil
Elmwood Village Charter S	40 Days Park	Buffalo, NY	14201	716-886-4581	348-3707	K-8	Danielle Bruno
Ember Charter S	616 Quincy St	Brooklyn, NY	11221	718-285-3787	919-0486	K-12	Rafiq Kalam Id-Din
Emblaze Academy	424 E 147th St	Bronx, NY	10455	347-977-1342		5-8	Kristen Shroff
Enterprise Charter S	275 Oak St	Buffalo, NY	14203-1643	716-855-2114	855-2967	K-8	Julie Schwab
Equality Charter HS	2141 Seward Ave	Bronx, NY	10473	718-459-9597		9-12	Favrol Philemy
Equality Charter S	4140 Hutchinson River Pkwy	Bronx, NY	10475	718-320-3032	320-3721	6-8	Caitlin Franco
Equity Project Charter S	549 Audubon Ave	New York, NY	10040	646-254-6451	202-3584	K-K,	Zeke Vanderhoek
Evergreen Charter S	605 Peninsula Blvd	Hempstead, NY	11550	516-292-2060		K-5	Edwin Irizarry
Excellence Boys Charter S	225 Patchen Ave	Brooklyn, NY	11233	718-638-1830	638-2548	K-8	Felix Li
Excellence Girls Charter S	794 Monroe St	Brooklyn, NY	11221-3501	718-638-1875	228-6670	K-4	Nikki Bowen
Exploration Elementary Charter S	1001 Lake Ave	Rochester, NY	14613	585-498-4700	498-4719	K-5	Lisa Clark
Explore Charter S	655 Parkside Ave	Brooklyn, NY	11226	718-703-4484	703-8550	K-8	Anwar Abdul-Rahman
Explore Empower Charter S	188 Rochester Ave	Brooklyn, NY	11213-3102	718-771-2090	771-2128	K-5	Christina Cotter
Explore Exceed Charter S	443 Saint Marks Ave	Brooklyn, NY	11238	718-989-6702	701-8328	K-8	Loretta Hickman
Explore Excel Charter S	1077 Remsen Ave	Brooklyn, NY	11236	347-303-3245	272-1827	K-8	Karen Francois
Family Life Academy Charter S	14 W 170th St	Bronx, NY	10452-3227	718-410-8100	410-8800	K-8	Evelyn Centeno
Family Life Academy Charter S II	296 E 140th St	Bronx, NY	10454	718-410-8100		K-5	Kathy Ortiz
Family Life Academy Charter S III	370 Gerard Ave	Bronx, NY	10451	718-585-6580		K-5	Andrea Hernandez
Finn Academy	610 Lake St	Elmira, NY	14901	607-737-8040		K-5	Aimee Ciarlo
Forte Preparatory Academy	3220 108th St	Elmhurst, NY	11369	929-666-4430		5-8	Graham Browne
Future Leaders Institute	134 W 122nd St	New York, NY	10027-5501	212-678-2868	866-2367	K-8	Dani McPartlin
Genesee Community Charter S	657 East Ave	Rochester, NY	14607-2101	585-697-1960	271-5904	K-6	Lisa Wing
Girls Preparatory Charter S	442 E Houston St	New York, NY	10002	212-388-0241	388-1086	K-8	Elyse Reed
Girls Preparatory Charter S of the Bronx	681 Kelly St Rm 205	Bronx, NY	10455	718-292-2113	292-5586	PK-5	Sharon Stephens
Girls Prep Bronx Charter MS	890 Cauldwell Ave	Bronx, NY	10456	718-665-6090	665-6095	6-8	Josie Carbone
Global Community Charter S	2350 5th Ave	New York, NY	10037	646-360-2363	390-6036	K-5	Bill Holmes
Global Concepts Charter S	1001 Ridge Rd	Lackawanna, NY	14218-1755	716-821-1903	821-9563	K-12	Tracy McGee
Grand Concourse Academy Charter S	925 Hutchinson River Pkwy	Bronx, NY	10465	718-684-6505	684-6514	K-7	Ira Victor
Great Oaks Charter S	38 Delancey St	New York, NY	10002	212-233-5152	267-4357	6-8	Antonio Vance
Green Tech High Charter S	99 Slingerland St	Albany, NY	12202	518-694-3400	694-3401	9-12	Dr. Paul Miller
Growing Up Green Charter S	3927 28th St	Long Is City, NY	11101-3728	347-642-4306	642-4310	K-4	Matthew Greenberg
Growing Up Green Charter S	8435 152nd St	Jamaica, NY	11432	347-642-4306	642-4310	K-2	Nancy Wong
Hahn Expeditionary Learning S	5800 Tilden Ave	Brooklyn, NY	11203	718-629-1204	629-1076	9-12	Veronica Coleman
Harbor Science & Arts Charter S	132 E 111th St	New York, NY	10029	917-261-2700	360-7429	K-8	Mark Johnson
Harlem Childrens Zone Promise Academy I	245 W 129th St	New York, NY	10027	646-556-6290	368-3621	K-12	Zahida Aminy
Harlem Childrens Zone Promise Academy II	2005 Madison Ave	New York, NY	10035-1294	646-556-6205	492-1542	K-5	Sheryl Ragland
Harlem Childrens Zone Promise Acad II MS	35 E 125th St	New York, NY	10035-1816	646-437-1481		6-8	Judy Palacios
Harlem Hebrew Language Academy Charter S	147 Saint Nicholas Ave	New York, NY	10026	212-866-4608	537-0280	K-5	Lindsay Malanga
Harlem Link Charter S	20 W 112th St	New York, NY	10026-3902	212-289-3249	289-3686	K-5	Steven Evangelista

School	Address	City,State	Zip code	Telephone	Fax	Grade	Contact
Harlem Prep Charter S	240 E 123rd St Frnt 1	New York, NY	10035	212-876-9953	876-9926	K-5	Kevin Shrum
Harlem Village Academy Charter HS	35 W 124th St	New York, NY	10027	646-812-9200		9-12	Meg Lembo
Harlem Village Academy West MS	244 W 144th St	New York, NY	10030	646-812-9300	548-9576	5-8	
Harlem Village Acad Ldrshp Charter S	2351 1st Ave	New York, NY	10035	646-812-9490	996-1626	5-8	Megan Ou-Yang
Health Sciences Charter S	1140 Ellicott St	Buffalo, NY	14209-1934	716-888-4080	464-7623	9-12	Dr. Hank Stopinski
Hebrew Language Academy Charter S	2186 Mill Ave	Brooklyn, NY	11234	718-377-7200	377-7220	K-4	Peter Katcher
Hebrew Language Academy II	1870 Stillwell Ave	Brooklyn, NY	11223	718-682-5610		K-5	Ashley Furan
Heketi Community Charter S	403 Concord Ave	Bronx, NY	10454	718-260-6002	292-7154	K-5	David Rosas
Hellenic Classical Charter S	646 5th Ave	Brooklyn, NY	11215-5401	718-499-0957	499-0959	K-8	Christine Tettonis
Hyde Leadership Charter S	730 Bryant Ave	Bronx, NY	10474-6006	718-991-5500	842-8616	K-12	Betsy Olney
Hyde Leadership Charter S	330 Alabama Ave	Brooklyn, NY	11207-4005	718-495-5620	495-5827	K-2	Sandra DuPree
Icahn Charter S 1	1525 Brook Ave	Bronx, NY	10457-8005	718-716-8105	214-6596	K-8	Lawford Cunningham
Icahn Charter S 2	1640 Bronxdale Ave	Bronx, NY	10462-3302	212-828-6107	828-7308	K-7	Brenda Carrasquillo
Icahn Charter S 3	1500 Pelham Pkwy S	Bronx, NY	10461-1100	718-828-0034	794-2357	K-6	Midga Agosto
Icahn Charter S 4	1500 Pelham Pkwy S	Bronx, NY	10461	718-828-0034	828-0664	K-8	Michelle Allen
Icahn Charter S 5	1500 Pelham Pkwy S	Bronx, NY	10461	718-828-0034	794-2359	K-8	Danielle Masi
Icahn Charter S 6	1701 Fulton Ave	Bronx, NY	10457	718-294-1706	583-6194	K-8	Brian Geelan
Icahn Charter S 7	1535 Story Ave	Bronx, NY	10473	718-328-5480	328-5483	K-7	Naudia Bethany
Imagine Me Leadership Charter S	818 Schenck Ave	Brooklyn, NY	11207	347-985-2140	985-2145	K-4	Bevon Thompson
International Charter S of New York	55 Willoughby St	Brooklyn, NY	11201	718-305-4199		K-3	Ellen Borenstein
International Leadership Charter HS	3030 Riverdale Ave	Bronx, NY	10463	718-562-2300	562-2235	9-12	Dr. Elaine Lopez
Invictus Preparatory Charter S	370 Fountain Ave	Brooklyn, NY	11208	718-235-1682	235-1685	5-8	Briana Sadler
Inwood Academy for Leadership Charter S	108 Cooper St	New York, NY	10034	212-304-0103	303-0370	5-12	Christina Reyes
Izquierdo Health & Science Charter S	800 Home St	Bronx, NY	10456	718-378-0490	378-0492	6-12	Richard Burke
Johnson Charter S	15 Jewett Pkwy	Buffalo, NY	14214	716-856-4390	856-4391	K-4	Jerry Linder
Johnson Charter S	15 Jewett Pkwy	Buffalo, NY	14214-2319	716-856-4390		K-4	Wendy Richards
Johnson Charter S	30 Watervliet Ave	Albany, NY	12206-1983	518-432-4300	432-4311	K-4	Gregory Mott
Key Collegiate Charter S	257 Chester St	Brooklyn, NY	11212	347-633-6059		K-5	Katie Mazer
King Center Charter S	156 Newburgh Ave	Buffalo, NY	14211-1826	716-891-7912	895-2058	K-8	Antoinette Rhodes
King's Collegiate Charter S	1084 Lenox Rd	Brooklyn, NY	11212-1930	718-342-6047	342-6727	5-8	Scott Schuster
KIPP Academy Charter MS	250 E 156th St	Bronx, NY	10451	718-665-3555	585-7982	5-8	Frank Corcoran
Kipp Academy ES	730 Concourse Vlg W	Bronx, NY	10451	718-943-3737	292-7199	K-4	Tyritia Groves
KIPP A.M.P. Charter S	1224 Park Pl	Brooklyn, NY	11213-2703	718-943-3740	774-3673	5-12	Antoine Lewis
KIPP Freedom ES	2246 Jerome Ave	Bronx, NY	10453			K-5	Sarah English
KIPP Infinity Charter S	625 W 133rd St	New York, NY	10027-7303	212-991-2600	234-8396	K-8	Glenn Davis
KIPP STAR MS	433 W 123rd St	New York, NY	10027-5002	212-991-2650	666-4723	5-8	Chrystal Griffin
KIPP Tech Valley Charter S	321 Northern Blvd	Albany, NY	12210	518-694-9494	694-9411	5-8	Don Applyrs
KIPP Washington Heights MS	21 Jumel Pl	New York, NY	10032-4316	212-991-2620	342-2521	5-5	Danny Swersky
La Cima Charter S	800 Gates Ave	Brooklyn, NY	11221-2203	718-443-2136	443-7291	K-5	Andrea Zayas
Launch Expeditionary Learning Charter S	1580 Dean St	Brooklyn, NY	11213-1713	718-221-1064	604-6915	6-8	Geoffrey Roehm
Lavelle Preparatory Charter S	1 Teleport Dr	Staten Island, NY	10311	347-855-2238	466-5746	3-12	Christopher Zilinski
Leadership Preparatory Ocean Hill S	51 Christopher Ave	Brooklyn, NY	11212-8014	718-250-5767	881-9666	K-3	Rachel King
Leadership Prep Bedford Stuy Charter S	141 Macon St	Brooklyn, NY	11216-2206	718-636-0360	636-0747	K-7	Owen Losse
Leadership Prep Brownsville Charter S	985 Rockaway Ave	Brooklyn, NY	11212	718-669-7461	228-6496	K-4	Elizabeth Jimenez
Leadership Prep Canarsie Charter S	1001 E 100th St	Brooklyn, NY	11236-4415	347-390-0570	534-3881	K-8	Katie Thaeder
Legacy College Prep S	416 Willis Ave	Bronx, NY	10454	347-746-1558		6-12	Summer Schneider
Lindsay Wildcat Academy Charter S	17 Battery Pl	New York, NY	10004-1207	212-209-6006	635-3874	9-12	Ronald Tabano
Manhattan Charter S	100 Attorney St	New York, NY	10002-3405	212-533-2743	533-2820	K-5	Genie DePolo
Manhattan Charter S II	220 Henry St	New York, NY	10002	212-964-3792	964-3795	K-5	Amy Salazar
Merrick Academy-Queens Public Charter S	13625 218th St	Sprngfld Gdns, NY	11413	718-479-3753	479-8108	K-5	Dr. Karen Valbrun
MESA Charter HS	231 Palmetto St	Brooklyn, NY	11221	917-257-6876	227-2763	9-12	Arthur Samuels
Metropolitan Lighthouse Charter S	180 E 165th St	Bronx, NY	10452	718-893-0640	893-0675	K-5	Tyra Williams
Middle Village Prep Charter S	6802 Metropolitan Ave	Middle Village, NY	11379	718-869-2933	821-2498	6-8	Nancy Velez
Mott Hall Charter S	1260 Franklin Ave	Bronx, NY	10456	718-991-9139	991-9150	6-8	Connie Lobdell
Mott Haven Academy Charter S	170 Brown Pl	Bronx, NY	10454-4140	718-292-7015	292-7823	K-5	Jessica Nauiokas
Neighborhood Charter S of Harlem	132 W 124th St	New York, NY	10027	646-701-7117	484-6652	3-6	Brett Gallini
New American Academy Charter S	9301 Avenue B	Brooklyn, NY	11236	718-385-1709	385-1856	K-4	Lisa Silva
Newburgh Preparatory Charter HS	471 Broadway	Newburgh, NY	12550-5332	845-565-4040	565-4033	9-12	Wendy Wright
New Dawn Charter HS	242 Hoyt St	Brooklyn, NY	11217-2913	347-505-9103	505-2516	9-12	Dr. Sara Asmussen
New Heights Academy Charter S	1818 Amsterdam Ave	New York, NY	10031-1715	212-283-5400	507-9314	5-12	Robert Parkes
New Hope Academy Charter S	475 E 57th St	Brooklyn, NY	11203	718-337-8303	504-3883	K-5	Dr. Temica Francis
New Roots Charter S	PO Box 936	Ithaca, NY	14851-0936	607-882-9220	882-9230	9-12	Tina Nilsen-Hodges
New Ventures Charter S	1 Teleport Dr	Staten Island, NY	10311	347-855-2238	466-5746	9-12	Ron Gorsky
New Vision Aim Charter HS I	1495 Herkimer St	Brooklyn, NY	11233	718-269-7090	498-0604	9-12	Kristin Greer
New Vision Aim Charter HS II	1010 Rev James A Polite Ave	Bronx, NY	10459	718-861-7515	861-7518	9-12	Tameka Jackson
New Vision Charter HS Humanities IV	10000 Beach Channel Dr	Rockaway Park, NY	11694	718-734-3350		9-12	Hannah Kehn
New Visions Charter HS for Humanities	99 Terrace View Ave	Bronx, NY	10463-5079	718-817-7686	817-7688	9-12	Seth Levin
New Visions Charter HS Humanities III	3000 Avenue X	Brooklyn, NY	11235-1232	718-368-4145		9-12	Porsche Cox
New Visions Charter HS Humanities II	455 Southern Blvd	Bronx, NY	10455	718-665-5380	665-5383	9-12	Melisha Jackman
New Visions Charter HS II	900 Tinton Ave	Bronx, NY	10456-7411	718-665-3671	645-7409	9-12	Stacey King
New Visions Charter HS Math & Sci III	3000 Avenue X	Brooklyn, NY	11235	718-934-9240	934-9171	9-12	Nissi Jonathan
New Visions Charter HS Math & Sci IV	156-10 Baisley Blvd	Jamaica, NY	11434	718-525-2041	525-2636	9-12	Sharon John
New Visions Charter HS Math & Science	99 Terrace View Ave	Bronx, NY	10463-5079	718-817-7683	817-7685	9-12	Robert Hiller
New World Preparatory Charter S	26 Sharpe Ave	Staten Island, NY	10302-1234	718-705-8990	442-1583	6-8	Amanda Ainley
NY Center for Autism Charter S	977 Fox St	Bronx, NY	10459	718-991-1340		9-12	Jennifer Connelly
NY Charter S of the Arts	440 W 53rd St	New York, NY	10019	646-793-6320	787-9427	6-6	Jamie Davidson
New York City Montessori Charter S	423 E 138th St	Bronx, NY	10454-3041	347-226-9094	226-9097	PK-5	Abeku Hayes
New York French American Charter S	311 W 120th St	New York, NY	10027-6128	212-666-4134		K-5	Marc Maurice
Niagara Charter S	2077 Lockport Rd	Niagara Falls, NY	14304-1109	716-297-4520	297-4617	K-6	Darci Novak
Nicotra Early College Charter S	2 Teleport Dr	Staten Island, NY	10311	347-855-2238		8-12	
Northside Charter HS	424 Leonard St	Brooklyn, NY	11222-3908	347-390-1273	390-1274	9-12	Suzanne Curran
North Side S	1650 Utopia Pkwy	Whitestone, NY	11357	718-229-5050	402-2028	PK-3	
NYC Autism Charter S	433 E 100th St	New York, NY	10029-6606	212-860-2580	860-2960	K-12	Julie Fisher
NYC Charter HS for AECI	838 Brook Ave	Bronx, NY	10451-4620	646-400-5566	585-4780	9-12	Charles Gallo
Ocean Hill Collegiate Charter S	1137 Herkimer St	Brooklyn, NY	11233	718-250-5765	250-5766	5-12	Hannah Solomon
OnTECH Charter HS	312 Sedgwick Dr	Syracuse, NY	13203	315-256-2461		9-12	
Opportunity Charter S	240 W 113th St	New York, NY	10026-3306	212-866-6137	665-7436	6-12	Jacqueline King-Robins
Oracle Charter S	888 Delaware Ave	Buffalo, NY	14209-2008	716-362-3188	362-3187	9-12	Janet Barnes
Our World Neighborhood Charter S	3612 35th Ave	Astoria, NY	11106-1227	718-392-3405	392-2840	K-8	Brian Ferguson
PAVE Academy	732 Henry St	Brooklyn, NY	11231-3229	718-858-7813	858-7814	K-5	Spencer Robertson
Peninsula Prep Academy Charter S	611 Beach 19th St	Far Rockaway, NY	11691	347-403-9231	327-2580	K-5	Karen Jones
Persistence Prep Academy	104 York St	Buffalo, NY	14213	716-909-3666		K-8	Joelle Formato
PUC Achieve Charter S	14 Mark St	Rochester, NY	14605	585-471-6219	232-1316	5-8	Bob Zimmerli
Reach Academy Charter S	115 Ash St	Buffalo, NY	14204	716-248-1485	248-2833	K-5	Linda Marszalek
Renaissance Charter HS for Innovation	410 E 100th St	New York, NY	10029-6604	212-722-5871	430-8555	9-12	Stephen Riff
Renaissance Charter S	3559 81st St	Jackson Heights, NY	11372-5033	718-803-0060	803-3785	K-12	Stacey Gauthier
Riverhead Charter S	3685 Middle Country Rd	Calverton, NY	11933-1807	631-369-5800	369-6687	K-8	Raymond Ankrum
Riverton Street Charter S	11834 Riverton St	Saint Albans, NY	11412	718-481-8200	923-3315	K-8	Andrea Whitehurst
Rochdale Early Advantage Charter S	12205 Smith St	Jamaica, NY	11434-2522	718-978-0075	978-0110	K-3	Derrick Dunlap
Rochester Academy Charter S	1777 Latta Rd	Rochester, NY	14612	585-467-9201	467-9250	7-12	Mehmet Demirtas
Rochester Academy Charter S of the Arts	299 Kirk Rd	Rochester, NY	14612	585-225-4200		K-2	Donna Cozine
Rochester Prep ES	899 Jay St	Rochester, NY	14611	585-235-0008	235-0014	K-4	Jaimie Brillante
Rochester Prep ES - West Campus	85 Saint Jacob St	Rochester, NY	14621	585-368-5100	368-5091	K-4	Emily Volpe
Rochester Prep MS - Brooks Campus	630 Brooks Ave	Rochester, NY	14619-2255	585-436-8629	436-5985	5-8	Patrick Pastore
Rochester Prep MS - West Campus	432 Chili Ave	Rochester, NY	14611	585-368-5090	368-5091	5-8	Adrienne Sopinski
Roosevelt Childrens Academy Charter S	201 Debevoise Ave	Roosevelt, NY	11575	516-867-6202	867-6206	K-8	Darryl Wilson
St. Hope Leadership Academy	222 W 134th St	New York, NY	10030-3002	212-283-1204	283-1207	5-8	Constance Bond
School in the Square	120 Wadsworth Ave	New York, NY	10033	718-916-7683		6-8	Carrie Amon
Sisulu-Walker Charter S	125 W 115th St	New York, NY	10026-2908	212-663-8216	866-5793	K-5	Michelle Haynes
South Bronx Charter S Intl Culture/Arts	164 Bruckner Blvd	Bronx, NY	10454	718-292-5737	292-1205	K-5	Evelyn Hey
South Bronx Classical Charter S	977 Fox St	Bronx, NY	10459-3320	718-860-4340	860-4125	K-5	Lester Long
South Bronx Classical Charter S II	333 E 135th St	Bronx, NY	10454-4301	718-860-4340	860-4125	K-5	Leena Gyftopoulos
South Bronx Classical Charter S III	3490 3rd Ave	Bronx, NY	10456	929-285-3025	232-2025	K-2	Rebecca Geary
South Bronx Community Charter HS	890 Washington Ave 5th Flr	Bronx, NY	10451	646-470-5594		9-12	Harvey Chism
South Bronx Early College Academy	423 E 138th St	Bronx, NY	10454	929-291-7700	291-7721	6-8	Ric Campbell
South Buffalo Charter S	154 S Ogden St	Buffalo, NY	14210	716-826-7213	826-7168	K-8	David Ehrle
Southside Academy Charter S	2200 Onondaga Creek Blvd	Syracuse, NY	13207-2361	315-476-3019	476-6639	K-8	Dr. Ronald Large
Storefront Academy	423 E 138th St	Bronx, NY	10454	646-476-1400	476-1409	K-5	Dr. Nicole Garcia
Stradford Prep Charter S	2023 Burr Ave	Bronx, NY	10461	917-539-3154		5-8	
Success Academy Bed-Stuy 3	787 Lafayette Ave	Brooklyn, NY	11221	646-790-2125		K-2	Molly Gortz
Success Academy Bushwick	139 Menahan St	Brooklyn, NY	11221	646-790-2173		K-4	Katherine Haves
Success Academy Charter Harlem 1	34 W 118th St	New York, NY	10026-1937	646-747-7170	457-5659	K-4	Danique Loving
Success Academy Charter Harlem 2	144 E 128th St Ste 3	New York, NY	10035	646-442-6600	281-4638	K-4	Lavinia Mackall
Success Academy Charter Harlem 3	141 E 111th St	New York, NY	10029-2641	646-747-6700	478-9492	K-5	Richard Seigler
Success Academy Charter Harlem 4	240 W 113th St	New York, NY	10026	646-442-6500	478-9493	K-5	Francesca Vanin
Success Academy Charter Harlem 5	301 W 140th St	New York, NY	10030	646-380-2580	961-4731	K-3	Molly Cohen
Success Academy Charter S Bed-Stuy 2	211 Throop Ave	Brooklyn, NY	11206	718-704-1439		K-4	Alisha Neptune

School	Address	City,State	Zip code	Telephone	Fax	Grade	Contact
Success Academy Charter S Bed-Stuy 1	70 Tompkins Ave	Brooklyn, NY	11206	718-635-3294	964-6598	K-4	Marni Aronson
Success Academy Charter S Bensonhurst	99 Avenue P	Brooklyn, NY	11204-6119	347-514-7082		K-4	Jonathan Dant
Success Academy Charter S Bergen Beach	1420 E 68th St	Brooklyn, NY	11234	347-817-2017		K-4	Regina Loftus
Success Academy Charter S Bronx 3	968 Cauldwell Ave	Bronx, NY	10456	646-790-2145		K-2	Kim Schacht
Success Academy Charter S Bronx 4	885 Bolton Ave	Bronx, NY	10473-2737	646-558-0043		K-12	Shea Reeder
Success Academy Charter S Bronx 1	339 Morris Ave	Bronx, NY	10451-6122	347-286-7950	479-1192	K-5	Elizabeth Vandlik
Success Academy Charter S Bronx 2	450 Saint Pauls Pl	Bronx, NY	10456	347-286-7965	479-1194	K-4	Angela Inslee
Success Academy Charter S Cobble Hill	284 Baltic St	Brooklyn, NY	11201	718-704-1460		K-4	Alissa Bishop
Success Academy Charter S Crown Hts	330 Crown St	Brooklyn, NY	11225	646-790-2129		K-4	Libby Ashton
Success Academy Charter S Fort Greene	101 Park Ave	Brooklyn, NY	11205	646-790-2137		K-4	Jennifer Loving
Success Academy Charter S Harlem Central	461 W 131st St	New York, NY	10027	646-569-5900		6-8	Kiah Hufane
Success Academy Charter S Harlem West	215 W 114th St Fl 5	New York, NY	10026	646-569-5920		5-8	Khari Shabazz
Success Academy Charter S Hell's Kitchen	439 W 49th St	New York, NY	10019-7235	646-790-2153		K-5	Michael LaFrancis
Success Academy Charter S Prospect Hts	760 Prospect Pl	Brooklyn, NY	11216	646-790-2121		K-4	Sydney Chernoff
Success Academy Charter S - Rosedale	14765 249th St	Laurelton, NY	11422-2400	347-514-7060		K-4	Christina Danielsen
Success Academy Charter S Springfield Gd	13255 Ridgedale St	Laurelton, NY	11413-1500	347-602-4335		K-4	Michelle Cooper
Success Academy Charter S Upper West	145 W 84th St Fl 2	New York, NY	10024-4614	646-274-1580		K-2	Carrie Roby
Success Academy Charter S Williamsburg	183 S 3rd St Fl 4	Brooklyn, NY	11211	718-704-1419		K-5	Alison Levy
Success Academy Charter Washington Hts	701 Fort Washington Ave	New York, NY	10040-3702	646-558-0027		K-4	Kelsey DePalo
Success Academy Far Rockaway	1045 Nameoke St	Far Rockaway, NY	11691	718-704-1421		K-4	Ty Redmond
Success Academy Flatbush	15 Snyder Ave	Brooklyn, NY	11226	646-790-2150		K-4	Wintanna Abai
Success Academy Hudson Yards	500 W 41st St	New York, NY	10036	212-845-9683		K-4	Will Loskoch
Success Academy South Jamaica	12027 141st St	Jamaica, NY	11436	718-704-1441		K-4	Meghan Daly
Success Academy Union Square	40 Irving Pl	New York, NY	10003	646-790-2161		K-4	Dan Rojas
Summit Academy Charter S	27 Huntington St	Brooklyn, NY	11231-1824	718-875-1403	875-1891	6-9	Natasha Campbell
Syracuse Academy	301 Valley Dr	Syracuse, NY	13207	315-671-0270	671-0275	K-12	
Syracuse Academy of Science Charter S	1001 Park Ave	Syracuse, NY	13204-2125	315-428-8997	428-9109	K-12	Dr. Tolga Hayali Ed.D.
Tapestry Charter S	65 Great Arrow Ave	Buffalo, NY	14216	716-204-5883	204-5887	K-12	Eric Klapper
True North Troy Preparatory S	2 Polk St	Troy, NY	12180-5512	518-445-3100	445-3101	K-8	Paul Powell
Tubman Charter S	3565 3rd Ave	Bronx, NY	10456-3403	718-537-9912	537-9858	K-8	Cleveland Person
UFT Charter S	800 Van Siclen Ave	Brooklyn, NY	11207	718-927-5540		9-12	Justin Davis
Uncommon Charter HS	1485 Pacific St	Brooklyn, NY	11216	718-638-1868	296-8322	9-12	Thomas O'Brien
Unity Prep S of Brooklyn	432 Monroe St	Brooklyn, NY	11221	212-437-8372		6-12	Joshua Beauregard
University Preparatory Charter HS	1290 Lake Ave	Rochester, NY	14613-1230	585-672-1280	458-2732	7-12	Dr. Connie Lucchese
University Prep Charter HS	600 Saint Anns Ave	Bronx, NY	10455-2800	718-292-6543	220-8110	9-12	Andrea d'Amato
Urban Choice Charter S	545 Humboldt St	Rochester, NY	14610-1221	585-288-5702	654-9882	K-8	Nicole Berg
Urban Dove Charter S	600 Lafayette Ave	Brooklyn, NY	11216	718-783-8232	783-8239	9-10	Amit Bahl
Utica Academy of Science Charter S	1214 Lincoln Ave	Utica, NY	13502-4532	315-266-1072	266-1073	6-12	Mustafa Ersoy
Vertus Charter S	21 Humboldt St	Rochester, NY	14609	585-747-8911		9-12	Dr. Leigh McGuigan
VOICE Charter S of NY	3624 12th St	Long Is City, NY	11106-5002	718-786-6213		K-5	Frank Headley
West Buffalo Charter S	113 Lafayette Ave	Buffalo, NY	14213	716-923-1534	768-0980	K-6	Andrea Todoro
Western NY Maritime Charter S	266 Genesee St	Buffalo, NY	14204-1453	716-842-6289	842-4241	9-12	Catherine Oldenburg
Westminster Community Charter S	24 Westminster Ave	Buffalo, NY	14215-1614	716-816-3450	838-7458	K-8	Robert Hoss
WHIN Music Community Charter S	401 W 164th St	New York, NY	10032	844-489-0817		K-2	Charles Ortiz
Williamsburg Charter S	198 Varet St	Brooklyn, NY	11206	718-782-9830	782-9834	9-12	Tanishia Williams
Williamsburg Collegiate Charter S	157 Wilson St	Brooklyn, NY	11211-7706	718-302-4018	881-9978	5-12	Alex Bronson
Yalow Charter S	116 E 169th St	Bronx, NY	10452	347-735-5480		K-8	Alec Diacou
Young Women's College Prep Charter S	133 Hoover Dr	Rochester, NY	14615	585-254-0320		7-12	Barbara Zelazny
Zeta Bronx 1 ES	222 Alexander Ave	Bronx, NY	10454	929-376-9987		K-2	
Zeta Inwood 1 ES	652 W 187th St	New York, NY	10033	929-376-9987		K-1	

North Carolina

School	Address	City,State	Zip code	Telephone	Fax	Grade	Contact
Academy of Moore County	12588 US Highway 15 501	Aberdeen, NC	28315	910-757-0401	757-0403	K-5	Allyson Schoen
A.C.E. Academy Charter S	7807 Caldwell Rd	Harrisburg, NC	28075	704-456-7153	626-2655	K-8	Lalla Minott
Alpha Academy	8030 Raeford Rd	Fayetteville, NC	28304	910-223-7711	678-9011	K-9	Eugene Slocum
American Renaissance ES	132 E Broad St	Statesville, NC	28677	704-924-8870	873-1398	K-8	James Duffey
Anderson Creek Club Charter S	4940 Ray Rd	Spring Lake, NC	28390	910-814-9001	814-9002	K-5	Mary Majors
Arapahoe Charter S	9005 NC Highway 306 S	Arapahoe, NC	28510-9699	252-249-2599	249-1316	K-12	Dr. Dennis Sawyer
Aristotle Preparatory Academy	8101 Fallsdale Dr	Charlotte, NC	28214	980-237-0371		K-4	Charlie French
Arts Based S	1380 N Martin Luther King	Winston Salem, NC	27101-3035	336-748-4116	748-4117	K-8	Robin Hollis
ArtSpace Charter S	2030 US 70 Hwy	Swannanoa, NC	28778-8211	828-298-2787	298-6221	K-8	Lori Cozzi
Bear Grass Charter S	6344 E Bear Grass Rd	Williamston, NC	27892-8434	252-789-1010	789-1014	6-12	Donna Moore
Bethany Community MS	1288 Hudson Rd	Summerfield, NC	27358	336-951-2500	951-0087	6-9	Vicky Bethel
Bethel Hill Charter S	401 Bethel Hill School Rd	Roxboro, NC	27574-7503	336-599-2823	599-9299	K-5	Stephen Hester
Bradford Preparatory S	2502 Salome Church Rd	Charlotte, NC	28262	704-549-0080	549-0085	K-12	Kelly Painter
Brevard Academy	1110 Hendersonville Hwy	Pisgah Forest, NC	28768	828-885-2665	862-3497	K-8	Ted Duncan
Bridges Academy	2587 Pleasant Ridge Rd	State Road, NC	28676-9318	336-874-2721	874-3804	K-8	Merry Lowe
Brown Leadership Academy	PO Box 1433	Elizabethtown, NC	28337-1433	910-862-2965	862-3054	6-12	Roland McKoy
Cabarrus Charter Academy	7550 Ruben Linker Rd	Concord, NC	28027	704-886-2158	886-2159	6-11	Lloyd Knight
Cabarrus Charter Academy	355 Poplar Crossing Dr NW	Concord, NC	28027	704-789-2500	789-2501	K-5	De'Shaunda Hampton
Cape Fear Center for Inquiry	2525 Wonder Way	Wilmington, NC	28401-8014	910-362-0000	362-0048	K-8	Lori Roy
Capitol Encore Academy	126 Hay St	Fayetteville, NC	28301-5650	910-849-0888	491-6786	K-5	Sylvia Adamczyk
Cardinal Charter S	1020 Saint Charles Pl	Cary, NC	27513	919-653-5000	653-6000	K-6	Dr. Becky Draper
Carolina International S	9545 Poplar Tent Rd	Concord, NC	28027-9512	704-455-3847	455-4672	K-12	David Kukielski
Carter Community Charter S	1955 W Cornwallis Rd	Durham, NC	27705	919-797-2340	797-2343	K-8	LaManda Pryor
Casa Esperanza Montessori Charter S	2600 Sumner Blvd Ste 130	Raleigh, NC	27616-5146	919-855-9811	855-9813	PK-8	Ibis Nunez
Central Park S for Children	724 Foster St	Durham, NC	27701-2111	919-682-1200	680-6381	K-8	John Heffernan
Central Wake Charter HS	1425 Rock Quarry Rd	Raleigh, NC	27610	919-521-5067	890-3286	9-12	Thomas Hanley
Charlotte Choice Charter S	PO Box 44065	Charlotte, NC	28215	980-272-8306		K-8	Cassandra Gregory
Charlotte Lab S	301 E 9th St Ste 100	Charlotte, NC	28202	704-464-3830	223-5005	K-6	Dr. Mary Moss Brown
Charlotte Learning Academy	800 Briar Creek Rd	Charlotte, NC	28205	980-355-2077		6-10	Stacey Rose
Charlotte Secondary S	8601 McAlpine Park Dr	Charlotte, NC	28211	704-295-0137	295-0156	6-12	Anthony Hall
Charter Day S	7055 Bacons Way NE	Leland, NC	28451-7960	910-655-1214	655-1549	K-8	Steve Smith
Chatham Charter S	PO Box 245	Siler City, NC	27344-0245	919-742-4550	742-2518	K-12	Dr. John Eldridge
Children's Village Academy	PO Box 2206	Kinston, NC	28502-2206	252-939-1958	939-1242	K-8	Jessica Jones
CIS Academy	818 W 3rd St	Pembroke, NC	28372-7307	910-521-1669	521-1670	6-8	Billy Haggans
Clover Garden S	2454 Altamahaw Union Ridge	Burlington, NC	27217-7965	336-586-9440	586-9477	K-12	Walter Finnigan
Coastal Preparatory Academy	1135 Pandion Dr	Wilmington, NC	28411	910-839-0012	839-0014	K-8	Jamie Getz
College Preparatory & Leadership Academy	5700 Riverdale Dr	Jamestown, NC	27282	336-884-0131	883-0109	K-12	Dr. Michelle Johnson
Columbus Charter S	35 Bacons Way	Whiteville, NC	28472-6225	910-641-4042	641-4043	K-8	Steven Smith
Commonwealth HS	5112 Central Ave	Charlotte, NC	28205	704-899-4998	469-4661	9-12	Sydney Culver
Community S of Davidson	404 Armour St	Davidson, NC	28036-6905	704-896-6262	896-2025	K-12	Joy Warner
Connections Academy	1280 Buck Jones Rd	Cary, NC	27606	919-694-8910		K-12	Janet Roberts
Cornerstone Charter Academy	7800 Airport Center Dr	Greensboro, NC	27409	336-482-3855	482-3857	K-12	Joe Caraher
Corvian Community School	9501 David Taylor Dr	Charlotte, NC	28262	704-717-7550	717-7558	K-8	Stacey Haskell
Crosscreek Charter S	306 Sandalwood Ave	Louisburg, NC	27549-2650	919-497-3198	497-0232	K-8	Robin Jackson
Delany New S for Children	119 Brevard Rd	Asheville, NC	28806-2922	828-236-9441	236-9442	K-8	Buffy Fowler
Dillard Academy	PO Box 1188	Goldsboro, NC	27533-1188	919-581-0166	581-0122	K-6	Hilda Hicks
Douglass Academy	507 N 6th St	Wilmington, NC	28401	910-763-1976	763-1974	K-5	Carla Fisher
East Wake Academy	821 Charter School Way	Zebulon, NC	27597	919-404-0444	404-2377	K-12	Stephen Gay
Emereau: Bladen	995 Airport Rd	Elizabethtown, NC	28337	910-247-6595	247-6643	K-6	Kate Dunaway
Endeavor Charter S	4879 One World Way	Wake Forest, NC	27587-5902	919-848-0333	848-8716	K-8	Christi Whiteside
Eno River Academy	920 Corporate Dr	Hillsborough, NC	27278-8557	919-644-6272	644-6275	K-8	Lisa Bair
Eno River Academy	1220 NC Hwy 57 N	Hillsborough, NC	27278	919-644-6272		9-12	
Envision Science Academy	590 Traditions Grande Blvd	Wake Forest, NC	27587	919-435-4002	307-4308	K-8	Charles Fuller
Evergreen Community Charter S	50 Bell Rd	Asheville, NC	28805-1538	828-298-2173	298-2269	K-8	Dr. Susan Mertz
Excelsior Classical Academy	4100 N Roxboro St	Durham, NC	27704	919-213-8585	219-2610	K-6	Cynthia Gadol
Expedition S	437 Dimmocks Mill Rd Ste 33	Hillsborough, NC	27278	919-245-8432		K-8	Tammy Finch
Exploris S: K-8 Learning Community	401 Hillsborough St	Raleigh, NC	27603-1791	919-715-3690	715-2042	K-8	Ellio Schollmeyer
Falls Lake Academy	1701 E Lyon Station Rd	Creedmoor, NC	27522	919-964-9003	964-9008	K-12	Amy Hobgood
FernLeaf Community Charter S	58 Howard Gap Rd	Fletcher, NC	28732	828-398-9268	575-5402	K-8	Michael Luplow
Forsyth Academy	5426 Shattalon Dr	Winston Salem, NC	27106-1919	336-922-1121	922-1033	K-8	Wendy Barajas
Franklin Academy	1127 Chalk Rd	Wake Forest, NC	27587	919-570-8262	570-8241	3-8	Denise Kent
Franklin Academy	604 S Franklin St	Wake Forest, NC	27587	919-554-4911	554-2340	K-2	Denise Kent
Franklin Academy HS	648 Flaherty Ave	Wake Forest, NC	27587	919-453-5090	453-5099	9-12	James Kornegay
Franklin S of Innovation	21 Innovation Dr	Asheville, NC	28806	828-318-8140	318-8125	5-12	Michelle Vruwink
Gaston College Preparatory S	320 Pleasant Hill Rd	Gaston, NC	27832-9511	252-308-6932	308-6936	K-12	Tammi Sutton
Gate City Charter Academy	123 Flemingfield Rd	Greensboro, NC	27405	336-617-5900	232-1734	K-8	Corey Moore
Girls Leadership Academy of Wilmington	PO Box 7621	Wilmington, NC	28406	910-338-5258		6-12	Laura Hunter
Global Scholars Academy	311 Dowd St	Durham, NC	27701-2443	919-682-5903	956-8535	K-8	Jason Jowers
Grandfather Academy	PO Box 98	Banner Elk, NC	28604	800-395-2591	898-8513	K-12	Michelle Griffin
Gray Stone Day S	PO Box 650	Misenheimer, NC	28109	704-463-0567	463-0569	6-12	Helen Nance
Greensboro Academy	4049 Battleground Ave	Greensboro, NC	27410-8410	336-286-8404	286-8403	K-8	Doug Hower
Guilford Preparatory Academy	2210 E Cone Blvd	Greensboro, NC	27405	336-954-1344	954-1965	K-8	Dr. Robin Duckrham
Haliwa-Saponi Tribal S	130 Haliwa Saponi Trl	Hollister, NC	27844-9390	252-257-5853	257-1093	K-12	Warren Bell
Hawbridge S	PO Box 40	Saxapahaw, NC	27340	336-376-1122	376-6996	4-12	Dr. Kenneth Moles

School	Address	City,State	Zip code	Telephone	Fax	Grade	Contact
Healthy Start Academy	807 W Chapel Hill St	Durham, NC	27701-3112	919-956-5599	688-9027	K-8	Dr. Alex Quigley
Henderson Collegiate	1071 Old Epsom Rd	Henderson, NC	27536	252-598-1038	598-1037	4-8	Frank Terranova
Henderson Collegiate HS	906 Health Center Rd	Henderson, NC	27536	252-598-1039		9-12	Jackson Olsen
Heritage Collegiate Leadership Academy	PO Box 1170	Windsor, NC	27983	252-794-0597	794-0598	K-8	Kashi Bazemore-Hall
Hope Elementary Charter S	1116 N Blount St	Raleigh, NC	27604-1302	919-834-0941	834-9338	K-5	Clarissa Fleming
Howard S for the Arts & Educ	1004 Herring Ave E	Wilson, NC	27893-3311	252-293-4150	293-4151	K-8	Dr. JoAnne Woodard
Ignite Innovation Academy	901 Staton Rd Ste 204	Greenville, NC	27834	252-689-6744	689-6693	K-7	Matthew Lococo
Institute for Development Young Leaders	4300 S Miami Blvd	Durham, NC	27703	919-973-4178	401-8005	K-8	Yvette Munroe
Invest Collegiate	2045 Suttle Ave	Charlotte, NC	28208	704-370-4000	973-7876	K-7	Danah Telfaire
Invest Collegiate-Imagine	1000 Brevard Rd Ste 175	Asheville, NC	28806-2276	828-633-6491	633-6494	K-10	Laura Townley
Iredell Charter Academy	251 Home Improvement St	Troutman, NC	28166	704-508-0104	508-0105	K-8	Dr. Andrea LoPresti
Island Montessori Charter S	6339 Carolina Beach Rd	Wilmington, NC	28412	910-795-4860	707-1201	K-8	Brian Corrigan
Jefferson Classical Academy	2527 US 221A Hwy	Mooresboro, NC	28114-7698	828-657-9998	202-5135	K-12	Joseph Maimone
Joy Charter S	107 S Driver St	Durham, NC	27703-4133	919-908-1600	402-4263	K-8	Mark Bailey
Kannapolis Charter Academy	1911 Concord Lake Rd	Kannapolis, NC	28083	704-273-5310	273-5326	K-8	Katrina Samuels
Kestrel Heights S	4900 Prospectus Dr	Durham, NC	27713	919-484-1300	484-1355	K-8	Dr. Mark Tracy
KIPP Academy Charlotte	931 Wilann Dr	Charlotte, NC	28215-2147	704-537-2044	537-2855	K-K,	Tiffany Flowers
KIPP Durham College Preparatory S	1107 Holloway St	Durham, NC	27701	919-973-0285		5-7	Anders Campbell
KIPP Halifax College Prep	9986 Hwy 903	Halifax, NC	27839	252-410-0277	308-9656	5-8	Marlow Wilkins
Lake Lure Classical Academy	PO Box 6	Lake Lure, NC	28746	828-625-9292	625-9298	K-12	Thomas Keever
Lake Norman Charter ES	10019 Hambright Rd	Huntersville, NC	28078	704-948-8600	948-3773	K-2	
Lake Norman Charter S	12435 S Old Statesville Rd	Huntersville, NC	28078	704-948-8600	948-8778	5-12	Shannon Stein
Langtree Charter Academy	185 W Waterlynn Rd	Mooresville, NC	28117	704-235-0865	235-0866	6-12	
Langtree Charter Academy	154 Foundation Ct	Mooresville, NC	28117	704-705-1698	360-3026	K-5	Christopher Scholl
Learning Center	945 Connahetta St	Murphy, NC	28906-3524	828-835-7240	835-9471	K-8	Mary Jo Dyre
Lincoln Charter S Denver	7834 Galway Ln	Denver, NC	28037	704-483-6611	483-6611	K-12	Jonathan Bryant
Lincoln Charter S Lincolnton	133 Eagle Nest Rd	Lincolnton, NC	28092-7383	704-736-9888		K-8	Jonathan Bryant
Longleaf School of the Arts	322 Chapanoke Rd	Raleigh, NC	27603	919-896-8164	516-0923	9-12	Rachel Davis
Magellan Charter S	9324 Baileywick Rd	Raleigh, NC	27615-1909	919-844-0277	844-3882	3-8	Mary Griffin
Mallard Creek STEM Academy	9142 Browne Rd	Charlotte, NC	28269	980-288-4811	799-3166	K-7	Deanna Smith
Matthews Charter Academy	2332 Mount Harmony Church	Matthews, NC	28105	980-339-5449	321-7058	K-7	Christy Morrin
Metrolina Regional Scholars Academy	5225 77 Center Dr	Charlotte, NC	28217-0708	704-503-1112	503-1183	K-8	Jessica Cuneo
Millennium Charter Academy	500 Old Springs Rd	Mount Airy, NC	27030-3034	336-789-7570	789-8445	K-12	Kirby McCrary
Mountain Community S	613 Glover St	Hendersonville, NC	28792-5451	828-696-8480	696-8451	K-8	Denise Pesce
Mountain Discovery Charter S	890 Jenkins Branch Rd N	Bryson City, NC	28713-4514	828-488-1222	488-0526	K-8	Carter Petty
Mountain Island Charter S	13440 Lucia Riverbend Hwy	Mount Holly, NC	28120-9766	704-827-8840	827-8675	K-12	Justin Matthews
Movement S	2701C Freedom Dr	Charlotte, NC	28208	704-585-1356	549-4635	K-2	Jamie Sumter
Neuse Charter S	909 E Booker Dairy Rd	Smithfield, NC	27577	919-938-1077	938-1079	K-12	Susan Pullium
New Dimensions S	550 Lenoir Rd	Morganton, NC	28655-2697	828-437-5753	437-2980	K-8	Jeffrey Mayo
NC Connections Academy	PO Box 12052	Durham, NC	27709	919-224-4040	361-6321	K-12	Dr. Nathan Currie
North Carolina Leadership Academy	PO Box 1728	Kernersville, NC	27285	336-992-2710	992-2714	K-12	Dottie Heath
North Carolina Virtual Academy	4220 NC Highway 55	Durham, NC	27713	919-346-0121	324-6597	K-12	Joel Medley
Northeast Academy of Aerospace Tech	PO Box 2889	Elizabeth City, NC	27906	252-562-0653	338-8546	7-11	Andrew Harris
North East Carolina Prep S	274 Husky Trl	Tarboro, NC	27886	252-641-0464	641-1816	K-12	William Etheridge
Notheast Regional S of Biotech Ag	1215 Saint Andrews St	Jamesville, NC	27846-9772	252-792-0241	792-0245	9-12	Hallet Davis
Oxford Preparatory S	6041 Landis Rd	Oxford, NC	27565-7411	919-690-0360	690-0230	8-12	Andrew Swanner
PAVE SE Raliegh Charter S	3420 Idlewood Village Dr	Raleigh, NC	27610	919-446-4777	800-3054	K-3	Benjamin Pierce
Peak Charter Academy	1601 Orchard Villas	Apex, NC	27502	919-377-1552	589-4860	PK-8	Steve Pond
Phoenix Academy	4020 Meeting Way	High Point, NC	27265	336-869-0079	464-2070	K-8	Kimberly Norcross M.Ed.
Piedmont Classical HS	1401 Lees Chapel Rd	Greensboro, NC	27405	336-701-2271	283-5340	9-12	Hannah Cobb
Piedmont Community Charter S	PO Box 3706	Gastonia, NC	28054-0038	704-853-2428	853-3689	K-12	Jennifer Purdee
Pine Lake Preparatory S	104 Yellow Wood Cir	Mooresville, NC	28115-6100	704-237-5300	237-5398	K-12	Andrew Moceri
Pine Springs Prep Academy	220 Rosewood Centre Dr	Holly Springs, NC	27540	919-439-9448	439-9416	K-8	Christina Womble
Pinnacle Classical Academy	2401 Joes Lake Rd	Shelby, NC	28152	704-740-4040	482-5527	K-12	Robert Brown
Pioneer Springs Community S	9300 Bob Beatty Rd	Charlotte, NC	28269	704-494-0777		K-6	Dr. Rebecca Friend
PreEminent Charter S	3815 Rock Quarry Rd	Raleigh, NC	27610-5123	919-235-0511	235-0514	K-8	Melanie Butler-Williams
Quality Education Academy	5012 Lansing Dr Ste D	Winston Salem, NC	27105-3026	336-744-0804	293-0617	K-12	Simon Johnson
Queen City STEM S	PO Box 480064	Charlotte, NC	28269	980-299-6633	299-6634	K-8	Atila Akyurek
Queen's Grant Community S	6400 Matthews Mint Hill Rd	Mint Hill, NC	28227-9323	704-573-6611	943-2395	K-12	Krista Tolchin
Quest Academy	10908 Strickland Rd	Raleigh, NC	27615-1873	919-841-0441	841-0443	K-8	Elizabeth Readmond
Raleigh Charter HS	1307 Glenwood Ave	Raleigh, NC	27605-1216	919-715-1155	715-1176	9-12	Dr. Lisa Huddleston
Reaching All Minds Academy	2703 Holloway St	Durham, NC	27703	919-596-1899	882-8339	K-6	Thomas McKoy
Research Triangle Charter Academy	2418 Ellis Rd	Durham, NC	27703-5543	919-957-7108	957-9698	K-8	Dr. Wayne Muhammad
Research Triangle HS	PO Box 13453	Durham, NC	27709-3453	919-998-6757	998-3402	9-12	Eric Grunden
River Mill Academy	235 Cheeks Ln	Graham, NC	27253	336-229-0909	229-9975	K-12	Jeffrey Dishmon
Rocky Mount Prep S	3334 Bishop Rd	Rocky Mount, NC	27804	252-443-9923	443-9932	K-12	Todd Pipkin
Roxboro Community S	115 Lake Dr	Roxboro, NC	27573-5672	336-597-0020	597-3152	6-12	Donna Ingram
Sandhills Theatre Arts Renaissance S	140 Southern Dunes Dr	Vass, NC	28394-9218	910-695-1004	695-7322	K-10	Dr. Wesley Graner
Shining Rock Classical Academy	1023 Dellwood Rd	Waynesville, NC	28786	828-738-2665		K-8	Bonnie Brown
Socrates Academy	3909 Weddington Rd	Matthews, NC	28105	704-321-1711	321-1714	K-8	Sandra Brighton
South Brunswick Charter S	2260 Achievement Ave SE	Bolivia, NC	28422	910-338-4178	338-4179	K-5	Michelle Mena
Southeastern Academy	12251 NC Highway 41 N	Lumberton, NC	28358-6892	910-738-7828	671-8067	PK-8	Kristen Stone
Southern Wake Academy	5108 Old Powell Rd	Holly Springs, NC	27540-9200	919-567-9955	567-9956	6-12	David Thomas
Sterling Montessori Academy	202 Treybrooke Dr	Morrisville, NC	27560-9300	919-462-8889	462-8890	PK-8	Frank Brainard
Stewart Creek HS	2701F Freedom Dr	Charlotte, NC	28208	704-755-5112	960-1726	9-12	Dr. Jonathan Kay
Success Institute Charter S	PO Box 1332	Statesville, NC	28687	704-881-0441	881-0870	K-8	Tenna Williams
Sugar Creek Charter S	4101 N Tryon St	Charlotte, NC	28206-2066	704-509-5470	921-1004	K-10	Cheryl Turner
Summerfield Charter Academy	5300 N US 220	Summerfield, NC	27358	336-643-1974	217-8367	K-6	Rudy Swofford
Summit Charter S	370 Mitten Ln	Cashiers, NC	28717-4511	828-743-5755	743-9157	K-8	Danny Howell
Thomas Academy	PO Box 300	Lake Waccamaw, NC	28450	910-646-2237	356-0028	6-12	Geraldine Bradshaw
Thunderbird Preparatory S	17609 Old Statesville Rd	Cornelius, NC	28031	704-412-1024	445-7754	K-7	Janice Davidson
Tiller S	1950 Live Oak St	Beaufort, NC	28516	252-728-1995	728-3711	K-5	Kelly Riley
Torchlight Academy	3211 Bramer Dr	Raleigh, NC	27604-1603	919-850-9960	850-9961	K-8	Dr. Cynthia McQueen
Triad Math and Science Academy	700 Creek Ridge Rd	Greensboro, NC	27406	336-621-0061	621-0072	K-12	Dr. Guray Taysever
Triangle Math and Science Academy	312 Gregson Dr	Cary, NC	27511-6444	919-388-0077	651-1418	K-12	Mithat Karabulut
Two Rivers Community S	1018 Archie Carroll Rd	Boone, NC	28607-8506	828-262-5411	262-5412	K-8	Dr. David Rizor
Union Academy	675 N M L King Jr Blvd	Monroe, NC	28110-8119	704-283-8883	283-8823	K-12	Dr. Ann Walters
Union Day S	PO Box 1005	Waxhaw, NC	28173	704-256-1494	256-5567	K-4	John Westberg
Union Prep Academy at Indian Trail	2324 Younts Rd	Indian Trail, NC	28079	704-893-3607	893-3608	K-8	Alison Simpson
United Community S	1406 Suther Rd	Charlotte, NC	28213	980-819-0555	819-0663	K-5	Erika Hedgepeth
Unity Classical Charter S	1929 W Arrowood Rd	Charlotte, NC	28217	980-202-5899		K-3	Sheila Goad
UpROAR Leadership Academy	5500 N Tryon St	Charlotte, NC	28213	980-585-3722		5-8	LaToya Purvis
Uwharrie Charter Academy	PO Box 1282	Asheboro, NC	27204	336-610-0813	610-0815	5-12	Heather Soja
Vance Charter S	2090 Ross Mill Rd	Henderson, NC	27536	252-431-0440	436-0688	K-10	Sean Connolly
Veritas Community S	2600 Grimes St	Charlotte, NC	28206	980-677-0101	228-3028	K-5	Katy Ridnouer M.Ed.
Voyager Academy ES	4210 Ben Franklin Blvd	Durham, NC	27704	919-433-3301	471-3932	K-3	Leslie Paynter M.Ed.
Voyager Academy HS	4302 Ben Franklin Blvd	Durham, NC	27704	919-433-3301	620-0554	9-12	Dr. Charles Nolan
Voyager Academy MS	101 Hock Parc	Durham, NC	27704	919-433-3301	433-3305	4-8	Gwen Johnson
Wake Forest Charter Academy	1851 Friendship Chapel Rd	Wake Forest, NC	27587	919-263-8673	882-9038	K-8	Amanda Brown
Washington Montessori S	2330 Old Bath Hwy	Washington, NC	27889	252-946-1977	946-5938	K-12	Austin Smigel
Water's Edge Village S	PO Box 215	Corolla, NC	27927	252-453-4502	453-3154	K-8	Meghan Agresto
Wayne Preparatory Academy	600 Tommys Rd	Goldsboro, NC	27530	919-734-8085		K-8	John Twitty
Williams Academy	PO Box 309	Crossnore, NC	28616-0309	828-733-5241	737-7915	K-12	Dr. Cyndi Austin Ed.D.
Willow Oak Montessori S	50101 Governors Dr	Chapel Hill, NC	27517	919-240-7787		1-7	Peter Rubinas
Wilmington Preparatory Academy	134 Cinema Dr	Wilmington, NC	28403-1490	910-799-6776	338-1834	K-8	Kevin Johnson
Wilson Preparatory Academy	2755 Tilghman Rd N	Wilson, NC	27896	252-294-2533	294-2534	K-11	Daryl Woodard
Winterville Charter Academy	4160 Bays Water Rd	Winterville, NC	28590	252-689-6153	360-4576	K-8	Glenn Reaves
Woods Charter S	160 Woodland Grove Ln	Chapel Hill, NC	27516-4085	919-960-8353	960-0133	K-12	Cotton Bryan
Woodson S	437 Goldfloss St	Winston Salem, NC	27127-3125	336-723-6838	723-6425	K-12	Ruth Hopkins
Youngsville Academy	PO Box 250	Youngsville, NC	27596	919-556-3609	556-3498	K-5	Larry Henson
Z.E.C.A. School of Arts & Technology	1249 Hargett St	Jacksonville, NC	28540	910-219-8603	219-8604	K-6	Stacey Owens-Howard
Ohio							
A+ Arts Academy	2633 Maybury Rd	Columbus, OH	43205	614-626-2250	626-2258	K-6	Renee Craft
A+ Arts Academy	270 S Napoleon Ave	Columbus, OH	43213	614-338-0767	338-0787	7-8	Vicki Washington
A+ Arts Academy	1395 Fair Ave	Columbus, OH	43205	614-725-1305	725-2305	PK-6	Dr. David Fant
A+ Children's Academy	100 Obetz Rd	Columbus, OH	43207-4031	614-491-3270	492-0035	PK-2	
Academy For Urban Scholars HS	1808 E Broad St	Columbus, OH	43203	614-545-9890	545-9889	9-12	
Academy of Arts & Sciences	3038 N Leavitt Rd	Lorain, OH	44052	440-244-0156	244-3935	K-12	James Sinclair
Academy of Educational Excellence	728 Parkside Blvd	Toledo, OH	43607-3858	330-382-2280		K-3	Israel Irizarry-Koppisch
Academy of Urban Scholars	1350 5th Ave Ste 100	Youngstown, OH	44504	330-774-9070	776-9636	9-12	Sabrina Jones
Achieve Career Preparatory Academy	3891 Martha Ave	Toledo, OH	43612	419-243-8559	243-8583	8-12	Cindy Wilson
Akron Digital Academy	133 Merriman Rd	Akron, OH	44303	330-237-2200	237-2207	K-12	Teresa Sayles
Akron Preparatory S	1200 E Market St Ste 3360	Akron, OH	44305	330-247-6232	299-7173	K-8	Donald Gordon
Akros MS	265 Park St	Akron, OH	44304	330-374-6704	374-6713	6-8	Faith Decesare
Allen Academy III	1206 Shuler Ave	Hamilton, OH	45011	513-795-6549	805-7723	K-6	Erin Ramsey

School	Address	City,State	Zip code	Telephone	Fax	Grade	Contact
Allen Academy II	184 Salem Ave	Dayton, OH	45406	937-951-2800		2-6	Gabrielle Billingsley
Allen Academy	700 Heck Ave	Dayton, OH	45417	937-586-9815	586-0271	7-9	Gabrielle Billingsley
Allen Preparatory S	627 Salem Ave	Dayton, OH	45406	937-723-7721	723-7738	K-1	Yolanda Clark
Alliance Academy of Cincinnati	1712 Duck Creek Rd	Cincinnati, OH	45207-1644	513-751-5555	751-5072	K-8	Elizabeth King
Alternative Education Academy	1830 Adams St	Toledo, OH	43604	330-253-8680	514-8227	K-12	Dr. David Bowlin Ph.D.
Apex Academy	16005 Terrace Rd	East Cleveland, OH	44112-2001	216-451-1725	451-1765	K-8	Jennifer Littlefield
Arts & College Preparatory Academy	4401 Hilton Corporate Dr	Columbus, OH	43232-3303	614-986-9974	986-9976	9-12	Anthony Gatto
Ashland County Community Academy	716 Union St	Ashland, OH	44805	419-903-0295	903-0341	7-12	Allen Wilson
Auglaize County Educational Academy	1130 E Albert St	Lima, OH	45804	419-738-4572	738-4591	K-12	Jen Korte
Aurora Academy	824 6th St	Toledo, OH	43605	419-693-6841	693-4799	K-8	
Autism Academy of Learning	110 Arco Dr Ste 1	Toledo, OH	43607	419-865-7487	865-8360	K-12	James Jones
Autism Model S	3020 Tremainsville Rd	Toledo, OH	43613	419-897-4400	897-4403	K-12	Mary Walters
Beacon Academy	1379 Garfield Ave SW	Canton, OH	44706	330-941-5852		K-8	Danielle Artl
Beacon Hill Academy	10470 Winesburg Rd	Dundee, OH	44624	330-359-5600		6-12	Bradley Herman
Bella Academy of Excellence	19114 Bella Dr	Cleveland, OH	44119-3007	216-481-1500	481-4515	K-6	Arun Dutt
Bennett Venture Academy	5130 Bennett Rd	Toledo, OH	43612-3422	419-269-2247	269-2257	K-8	Nicolette Whitson
Berwyn East Academy	1850 Bostwick Rd	Columbus, OH	43227-3374	614-564-9548		PK-3	Shannan Enoch
Bridge Gate Community S	4060 Sullivant Ave	Columbus, OH	43228	614-501-3820		6-12	Dr. Brian Collier Ph.D.
Bridges Community Academy	190 Saint Francis Ave	Tiffin, OH	44883-4012	419-455-9295	455-9296	K-12	Catherine Smith
Broadway Academy	3398 E 55th St	Cleveland, OH	44127-1691	216-271-7747	271-6438	PK-8	Sherree Ray-Dillions
Brookwood Academy	2685 E Livingston Ave	Columbus, OH	43209-2961	614-231-1199	235-2280	9-12	
Buckeye On-Line School for Success	119 E 5th St	East Liverpool, OH	43920	330-385-1987	385-4535	K-12	Andrea Dobbins
Buckeye Preparatory Academy	1414 Gault St	Columbus, OH	43205	614-300-3685	252-7083	K-8	David Mounts
Canton College Preparatory S	101 Cleveland Ave NW	Canton, OH	44702	330-455-0498		K-8	Darryl Lindsay
Canton Harbor HS	1731 Grace Ave NE	Canton, OH	44705	330-452-8414	452-8452	9-12	Joseph Cole
Capella HS	5130 Warrensville Center Rd	Maple Heights, OH	44137	216-587-5282		9-12	Shana Black
Capital HS	640 Harrisburg Pike	Columbus, OH	43223	614-228-2854	228-4679	9-12	Monica Scott-Matthews
CASTLE HS	3950 Prospect Ave E	Cleveland, OH	44115	216-583-5210	443-9017	9-12	Jaeda Dancy
Central Academy of Ohio	2727 Kenwood Blvd	Toledo, OH	43606-3216	419-205-9800	205-9899	K-6	Mariam Saleh
Central HS	840 W State St	Columbus, OH	43222	614-362-7530		9-12	Thomas Rogan
Chapelside Cleveland Academy	3845 E 131st St	Cleveland, OH	44120-4661	216-283-6589	283-3087	K-8	Anna Turner
Charles S at Ohio Dominican	1270 Brentnell Ave	Columbus, OH	43219	614-258-8588	258-8584	9-12	Gregory Brown
Chavez College Prep ES	2400 Mock Rd	Columbus, OH	43219	614-294-3020	299-3680	K-5	
Cincinnati College Prep Academy	1425 Linn St	Cincinnati, OH	45214	513-684-0777	684-8888	K-12	Guyton Mathews M.Ed.
Cincinnati Learning S	5641 Belmont Ave	Cincinnati, OH	45224	513-783-1025	783-1026	6-12	Yolanda Cooper
Cincinnati Technology Academy	3800 Glenway Ave	Cincinnati, OH	45205	513-471-7323	386-7931	9-12	
Citizens Academy	10118 Hampden Ave	Cleveland, OH	44108-3538	216-791-4195	791-3013	K-5	Kimberly Peterlin
Citizens Academy East	12523 Woodside Ave	Cleveland, OH	44108	216-367-9392	761-7398	K-3	Jennifer Taylor
Citizens Academy Southeast	17900 Harvard Ave	Cleveland, OH	44128	216-586-3887	561-1121	K-5	Lachelle Dixon-Harris
Citizens Leadership Academy	9711 Lamont Ave	Cleveland, OH	44106-4124	216-229-8185	229-8516	6-8	Sydney Gruhin
City Day Community S	320 S Main St	Dayton, OH	45402	937-223-8130	223-8136	K-8	Crystal Gilbert-Mosley
Clark Preparatory Academy	501 S Wittenberg Ave	Springfield, OH	44506	937-504 1175		K-8	Stefanie Page
Clay Avenue Community S	1030 Clay Ave	Toledo, OH	43608-2167	419-727-9900	727-9902	K-8	Sarah Bennett
Cleveland Art & Social Science Academy	10701 Shaker Blvd	Cleveland, OH	44104-3752	216-229-3000	229-3182	K-8	Debroah Mays
Cleveland College Preparatory S	4906 Fleet Ave	Cleveland, OH	44105	216-341-1347	341-4466	K-8	Phillip Penn
Cliff Park HS	821 N Limestone St	Springfield, OH	45503-3609	937-342-3006		9-12	Jeffrey Waechter
Collinwood Village Academy	716 E 156th St	Cleveland, OH	44110	216-451-4022	451-4040	9-12	Bethany Scott
Colonial Preparatory Academy	2199 5th St SW	Akron, OH	44314-2405	330-752-2792		K-8	Leeanna Simmons
Columbus Arts & Tech Academy	2255 Kimberly Pkwy E	Columbus, OH	43232-7210	614-577-0900	866-0300	K-9	Derrick Shelton
Columbus Collegiate Academy	1469 E Main St	Columbus, OH	43205	614-299-5284	299-5303	6-8	Melissa Barrett
Columbus Collegiate Academy - Dana	300 Dana Ave	Columbus, OH	43223	614-545-9570	375-1702	6-8	Nathan Parker
Columbus Humanities Arts & Tech Academy	1333 Morse Rd	Columbus, OH	43229-6322	614-261-1200	261-1201	K-8	Latasha Morgan M.Ed.
Columbus Performance & Fitness Academy	274 E 1st Ave Ste 200	Columbus, OH	43201	614-318-0720	375-1995	K-8	Tony Cochren
Columbus Prep & Fitness Academy	1258 Demorest Rd	Columbus, OH	43204	614-318-0606	351-9804	K-8	Jeff Luelleman
Columbus Preparatory Academy	3330 Chippewa St	Columbus, OH	43204-1653	614-275-3600	275-3601	K-8	Brian Carlton
Cornerstone Academy	6015 E Walnut St	Westerville, OH	43081-9620	614-775-0615	775-0633	K-8	Natalee Long
Coshocton Opportunity S	1205 Cambridge Rd	Coshocton, OH	43812-2741	740-622-3600	623-6860	9-12	Roger Moore
Dayton Business Technology HS	348 W 1st St	Dayton, OH	45402	937-225-3989	225-3998	9-12	Greg Stone
Dayton Early College Academy	1529 Brown St	Dayton, OH	45469	937-229-5780	229-5786	7-12	Katy Jo Bull
Dayton Leadership Academies	1416 W Riverview Ave	Dayton, OH	45402-6217	937-567-9426	567-9446	K-8	Tess Asinjo
Dayton Liberty Campus	4401 Dayton Liberty Rd	Dayton, OH	45417	937-262-4080	262-4091	K-8	Dr. Theodore Wallace
Dayton SMART Bilingual Academy	601 S Keowee St	Dayton, OH	45410	937-222-2812	222-2594	K-4	Jason Clark
DECA PREP	200 Homewood Ave	Dayton, OH	45405	937-610-0110	260-4478	K-6	Aileen Ernst
Discovery Academy	2740 W Central Ave	Toledo, OH	43623	419-214-3266		K-6	Noah Campbell
Dohn Community HS	608 E McMillan St	Cincinnati, OH	45206-1926	513-281-6100	281-6103	9-12	Leando Davenport
Douglass Reclamation Academy	3167 Fulton Rd	Cleveland, OH	44109-1465	216-961-5631	961-5637	9-12	Gamal Brown M.Ed.
Eagle Academy	1430 Idaho St	Toledo, OH	43605	419-697-2760	697-2763	6-12	Julie Jacobs
Eagle Learning Center HS	2665 Navarre Ave	Oregon, OH	43616	419-720-2003	720-2007	9-12	Dean Sandwisch
Early College Academy	345 E 5th Ave	Columbus, OH	43201-2819	614-298-4742	298-9107	9-12	Jonathan Stevens
East Academy	15720 Kipling Ave	Cleveland, OH	44110-3105	216-383-1214		K-8	Nehemiah Thomas
East Bridge Academy of Excellence	2323 Lake Club Dr	Columbus, OH	43232	614-501-3822		K-6	
East Preparatory Academy	4129 Superior Ave	Cleveland, OH	44103-1129	216-539-0595		K-8	Joy Beasley
Eastside Arts Academy	6700 Lansing Ave	Cleveland, OH	44105	216-441-9830	441-9834	K-5	Katherine Rybak
Edge Academy	92 N Union St	Akron, OH	44304-1347	330-535-4581	535-5074	K-5	Faith DeCesare
Educational Academy for Boys & Girls	35 Midland Ave	Columbus, OH	43223	614-351-9397	351-1968	K-5	Christina Burchfield
Einstein Academy	3550 Crocker Rd	Westlake, OH	44145	440-471-4982	617-6809	4-12	Kristen Thomas
Electronic Classroom of Tomorrow	3700 S High St Ste 95	Columbus, OH	43207-4083	614-492-8884	492-8894	K-12	James Condron
Elyria Community MS	336 S Logan St	Elyria, OH	44035	440-365-0390	365-0397	6-8	Eric Fortuna
Elyria Community S	300 Abbe Rd N	Elyria, OH	44035-3724	440-366-5225	366-6280	K-5	Eric Fortuna
Emerson Academy of Dayton	501 Hickory St	Dayton, OH	45410-1232	937-223-2889	660-6386	K-8	Allison Foreman
E Prep & Village Prep Charter S	1415 E 36th St	Cleveland, OH	44114	216-456-2080	361-9717	K-8	Dr. Randy Yates
E Prep & Village Prep Charter S	9201 Crane Ave	Cleveland, OH	44105	216-298-1164	341-0106	K-8	Chris O'Brien
Euclid Preparatory S	23001 Euclid Ave	Euclid, OH	44117	216-750-2070		K-8	Darlene Montague
Everest HS	1555 Graham Rd	Reynoldsburg, OH	43068	614-367-1980		9-12	Mark Fullen
Fairborn Digital Academy	700 Black Ln	Fairborn, OH	45324-5844	937-879-0511	879-8160	9-12	Erik Tritsch
Findlay Digital Academy	1219 W Main Cross St # 101	Findlay, OH	45840	419-425-3598	425-3588	9-12	Rosemary Rooker
Flex HS	115 S Gift St	Columbus, OH	43215	614-610-9749		9-12	Jason Morton
Focus Learning Academy East	4480 Refugee Rd	Columbus, OH	43232-4459	614-269-0150	269-0151	9-12	Joseph Paulauskas
Focus Learning Academy North	4807 Evanswood Dr	Columbus, OH	43229-6285	614-310-0430	310-0469	9-12	Kelley Straight
Focus Learning Academy West	190 Southwood Ave	Columbus, OH	43207-1133	614-545-2000	545-1995	9-12	Kerry Hill
Focus Learning Acad of Northern Columbus	1880 E Dublin Granville Rd	Columbus, OH	43229-3523	614-547-0920	547-0924	K-8	Travis Budd
Foundation Academy	1050 Wyandotte Ave	Mansfield, OH	44906	419-526-9540	526-9542	K-10	Mitzi Kimani
Fox Academy	1505 Jefferson Ave	Toledo, OH	43604	419-720-4500	720-4502	7-12	Jodi Johns
Foxfire ES	2805 Pinkerton Ln	Zanesville, OH	43701	740-453-4509	455-4084	K-4	Todd Whiteman
Foxfire HS	PO Box 1818	Zanesville, OH	43702	740-453-4509	455-4084	9-12	Jason Lee
Foxfire IS	2805 Pinkerton Ln	Zanesville, OH	43701	740-453-4509		5-8	Todd Whiteman
Franklin Local Community S	PO Box 95	Roseville, OH	43777-0095	740-697-7317	697-0793	7-12	Jennifer Woodard
Franklinton Preparatory Academy	40 Chicago Ave	Columbus, OH	43222-1132	614-636-3721		9-12	Martin Griffith
Glass City Academy	1000 Monroe St	Toledo, OH	43604-5954	419-720-6311	720-6315	11-12	Stewart Joooo
Global Ambassadors Language Academy	13442 Lorain Ave	Cleveland, OH	44111	216-315-7942		K-8	Michael Salwiesz
Global Village Academy	5720 State Rd	Parma, OH	44134	216-767-5956	767-5653	K-7	Oleh Holowatyj
Goal Digital Academy	890 W 4th St Ste 400	Mansfield, OH	44906	419-521-9008	529-2970	K-12	Patricia Jenkins
Graham Elementary and Middle School	140 E 16th Ave	Columbus, OH	43201	614-253-4000	643-5146	K-8	Gregory Brown
Graham S	3950 Indianola Ave	Columbus, OH	43214-3167	614-262-1111	262-5878	9-12	Gregory Brown
Greater Ohio Virtual S	1879 Deerfield Rd	Lebanon, OH	45036	513-695-2924	695-2588	7-12	Shawn E. Lenney
Greater Summit County Early Learning Ctr	1651 Massillon Rd	Akron, OH	44312	234-718-2626		PK-4	Teresa Graves
Great Western Academy	310 N Wilson Rd	Columbus, OH	43204-6221	614-276-1028	276-1049	K-8	Kathryn Kountz
Green Inspiration Academy	4265 Northfield Rd	Highland Hills, OH	44128	216-378-9573	882-0554	K-8	Donna Kolb
Groveport Community S	4485 S Hamilton Rd	Groveport, OH	43125-9334	614-574-4100	574-4107	K-8	Dair Foster
Haley S	4901 Galaxy Pkwy	Cleveland, OH	44128	216-591-9190	591-9199	K-6	Constance Williams
Hamilton County Math & Science S	2675 Civic Center Dr	Cincinnati, OH	45231-1311	513-728-8620	728-8623	K-8	Dwan Moore M.Ed.
Hardin Community S	400 Decatur St	Kenton, OH	43326-2043	419-673-3210		6-12	Wade Melton
Harrisburg Pike Community S	680 Harrisburg Pike	Columbus, OH	43223	614-223-1510	223-1584	K-6	Dreama Carroll
Harvard Avenue Performance Academy	12000 Harvard Ave	Cleveland, OH	44105-5444	216-283-5100	283-5762	K-8	Brittiany Sanford
Heir Force Community S	150 W Grand Ave	Lima, OH	45801-4006	419-228-9241	228-1555	K-8	Darwin Lofton
Hollingworth S for Talented & Gifted	653 Miami St	Toledo, OH	43605-2277	419-705-3411	720-4923	K-9	Terrence Franklin
Hope Academy for Autism	1628 Niles Rd SE	Warren, OH	44484	330-469-9501	369-2455	K-12	Kimberly Clinkscale
Hope Academy Northcoast	4310 E 71st St	Cleveland, OH	44105-5759	216-429-0232	429-0249	K-8	Martin Ngom
Hope Learning Academy of Toledo	4234 Monroe St	Toledo, OH	43606-1938	419-297-6313	725-9184	K-8	Justin Bryson
Horizon Science Academy Cincinnati	1055 Laidlaw Ave	Cincinnati, OH	45237-5005	513-242-0099	242-2467	K-8	John Adams
Horizon Science Academy Cleveland HS	6000 S Marginal Rd	Cleveland, OH	44103	216-432-3660	432-3670	9-12	Mehmet Gurbuz
Horizon Science Academy Cleveland MS	6100 S Marginal Rd	Cleveland, OH	44103-1043	216-432-9940	432-9941	6-8	
Horizon Science Academy Columbus ES	2835 Morse Rd	Columbus, OH	43231	614-475-4585	475-4587	K-5	Jessica Shoaf
Horizon Science Academy Columbus HS	1070 Morse Rd	Columbus, OH	43229-6290	614 846-7616	846-7696	9-12	
Horizon Science Academy Columbus MS	2350 Morse Rd	Columbus, OH	43229	614-428-6564	428-6574	6-8	Hasan Akkaya
Horizon Science Academy Dayton	4751 Sue Ann Blvd	Dayton, OH	45415-1171	937-277-1177	277-3090	K-4	Kellie Berlean
Horizon Science Academy Dayton Downtown	121 S Monmouth St	Dayton, OH	45403-2127	937-281-1980	281-1979	K-8	Mustafa Ada

School	Address	City,State	Zip code	Telephone	Fax	Grade	Contact
Horizon Science Academy Dayton HS	250 Shoup Mill Rd	Dayton, OH	45415-3517	937-281-1480	281-1481	5-12	Hakan Bagcioglu
Horizon Science Academy - Denison	1700 Denison Ave	Cleveland, OH	44109-2945	216-739-9911	739-9913	K-8	Bulent Akbenlioglu M.Ed.
Horizon Science Academy Denison ES	2261 Columbus Rd	Cleveland, OH	44113	216-661-8840	661-8850	K-5	Tracy Hammond
Horizon Science Academy of Lorain	760 Tower Blvd	Lorain, OH	44052-5223	440-282-4277	282-4278	K-12	Fatih Sumer
Horizon Science Academy Springfield	630 S Reynolds Rd	Toledo, OH	43615-6314	419-535-0524	535-0525	K-8	Erin Schreiner
Horizon Science Academy Youngstown	3403 Southern Blvd	Youngstown, OH	44507-2044	330-782-3003	782-3356	K-8	Ferhat Kapki
iLEAD Spring Meadows	1615 Timberwolf Dr	Holland, OH	43528	419-491-7423		PK-8	
IMAC HS	445 Bowman St	Mansfield, OH	44903	567-247-4475	525-0106	9-12	Deborah Franklin
Imagine Akron Academy	1585 Frederick Blvd	Akron, OH	44320	330-379-1034	379-0489	K-K	Audrea Pettaway
Imagine Columbus Primary Academy	4656 Heaton Rd	Columbus, OH	43229-6612	614-433-7510	433-7515	K-8	Melissa Hackett
Imagine Hill Academy	6145 Hill Ave	Toledo, OH	43615	419-867-8167		K-5	Daphne Williams
Imagine Leadership Academy	2405 Romig Rd	Akron, OH	44320-3826	330-848-1100		1-6	Audrea Pettaway
Imagine Woodbury Academy	100 E Woodbury Dr	Dayton, OH	45415	937-277-1710		K-5	Jennifer Keller
Insight School of Ohio	2760 Airport Dr Ste 135	Columbus, OH	43219-2294	614-300-2766	448-2739	9-12	Amanda Conley
Intergenerational S	11327 Shaker Blvd Ste 200	Cleveland, OH	44104	216-721-0120	721-0126	K-8	Silvia Kruger
International Academy of Columbus	2439 Fuji Dr	Columbus, OH	43229	614-794-0643	794-0697	K-8	Dr. Mouhamed Tarazi
Invictus HS	3122 Euclid Ave	Cleveland, OH	44115-2508	216-539-7200	361-3090	9-12	Dean Manke
King Academy Community S	224 W Liberty St	Cincinnati, OH	45202	513-421-7519	421-1770	K-8	Andrea Martinez
KIPP Columbus	2900 INSPIRE Dr	Columbus, OH	43224	614-263-6137	263-6207	5-8	Hannah Powell
Klepinger Road Community S	3650 Klepinger Rd	Dayton, OH	45416-1919	937-610-1710	610-1730	K-8	Melissa McManaway
Lake Erie College Preparatory S	14405 Saint Clair Ave	Cleveland, OH	44110	216-453-4556	268-4951	K-8	Denecia Dillard
Lake Erie International HS	11650 Detroit Ave	Cleveland, OH	44102	216-539-7229	651-6174	9-12	Larry Burt
Lakeland Academy Community S	101 E Main St	Freeport, OH	43973	740-658-1042	658-1062	K-12	Scott Bardall
Lakeshore Intergenerational S	18025 Marcella Rd	Cleveland, OH	44119	216-586-3872	486-7324	K-3	Robin Bartley
Lakewood City Academy	1470 Warren Rd	Lakewood, OH	44107-3918	216-529-4037	227-5975	6-12	Terrilynn Bornino-Elwell
Liberty HS	140 N Keowee St	Dayton, OH	45402	937-701-7945		9-12	Sean Fadden
Liberty Preparatory S	PO Box 374	Smithville, OH	44677	330-669-0055	669-0055	9-12	Brian Hessey
LifeSkills Center Columbus North	1900 E Dublin Granville Rd	Columbus, OH	43229-3553	614-891-9041	891-8571	9-12	Sharon Watkins
Life Skills Center of Cincinnati	2612 Gilbert Ave	Cincinnati, OH	45206-1205	513-475-0222	475-0444	9-12	
Life Skills Center of Dayton	1721 N Main St	Dayton, OH	45405-4143	937-274-2841	274-2873	9-12	Lanicka Shepherd-Masey
Life Skills Center of Elyria	2015 W River Rd N	Elyria, OH	44035-2309	440-324-1755	324-1723	9-12	Crystal Garmon
Life Skills Center of North Akron	1458 Brittain Rd	Akron, OH	44310-3641	330-633-5990	633-7005	9-12	Monica Speights
Life Skills Center of Toledo	1830 Adams St	Toledo, OH	43604-4428	419-241-5504	241-9176	9-12	Vanice Williams
Life Skills Center of Youngstown	3405 Market St	Youngstown, OH	44507-2009	330-743-6698	743-6702	9-12	Denise Otteni-Jones
LifeSkills Columbus Southeast	2400 S Hamilton Rd	Columbus, OH	43232-4963	614-452-4379		9-12	Eunique Seifullah
Life Skills HS of Cleveland	4600 Carnegie Ave	Cleveland, OH	44103	216-431-7571		9-12	Tim Spencer
Life Skills HS of Cleveland	12201 Larchmere Blvd	Shaker Heights, OH	44120-1101	216-421-7587	421-8189	9-12	Ryan Demro
Lighthouse Community S	6100 Desmond St	Cincinnati, OH	45227-1897	513-561-7888	561-7818	6-12	Alexander Quigley
Lincoln Park Academy	3185 W 41st St	Cleveland, OH	44109	216-263-7008	263-7007	K-8	Alissa Clugh
Lincoln Preparatory S	4215 Robert Ave	Cleveland, OH	44109-1255	216-772-1336	961-5378	K-8	Lisa Lyons
Lorain Community ES	1110 W 4th St	Lorain, OH	44052	440-204-2130	204-2134	K-4	Melisa Shady
Lorain Community MS	1110 W 4th St	Lorain, OH	44052	440-242-2023	204-2134	5-8	Melisa Shady
Lorain K-12 Digital Academy	401 Broadway Ave	Lorain, OH	44052	440-204-1095	204-1167	K-12	Karen Mahan
Lorain Preparatory Academy	4125 Leavitt Rd # 2	Lorain, OH	44053-2341	440-282-3127	282-3179	3-8	James Sinclair
Madison Ave School of the Arts	1511 Madison Ave	Toledo, OH	43604-4433	419-259-4000	243-1513	K-5	Lindsey Day
Madison Community S	2015 W 95th St	Cleveland, OH	44102-3791	216-651-5212	651-9040	K-8	Louis Marconi
Madisonville SMART ES	4324 Homer Ave	Cincinnati, OH	45227	513-241-1101		K-6	Jamal Maxsam
Mahoning County HS	940 Bryn Mawr Ave	Youngstown, OH	44505	330-702-7890	702-7891	9-12	Jennifer Merritt
Mahoning Unlimited Classroom	7401 Market St Rm 519	Youngstown, OH	44512	330-533-8755	729-9349	4-12	Brad Justice
Mahoning Valley Opportunity S	496 Glenwood Ave	Youngstown, OH	44502-1509	330-744-7656	743-9757	9-12	David Macali
Main Preparatory Academy	1035 Clay St	Akron, OH	44301	234-738-1925		6-8	Nikita Tidwell
Mansfield Elective Academy	445 Bowman St	Mansfield, OH	44903-1201	567-247-4475	247-3392	K-9	Deborah Franklin
Maritime Academy of Toledo	803 Water St	Toledo, OH	43604-1831	419-244-9999	244-9898	5-12	Aaron Lusk
Marshall HS	4720 Roosevelt Blvd	Middletown, OH	45044-6250	513-318-7078	425-6951	9-12	Chuck Hall
Mason Run HS	923 S James Rd	Columbus, OH	43227	614-362-7540		9-12	Aaron Butler
Massillon Digital Academy	930 17th St NE	Massillon, OH	44646	330-830-3900	830-0953	K-12	Dr. Amy Hollingsworth
Menlo Park Academy	2149 W 53rd St	Cleveland, OH	44102	440 925 6365	925-0698	K-8	Stacy Stuhldreher M.Ed.
Miamisburg Secondary Academy	540 Park Ave	Miamisburg, OH	45342-2854	937-866-3381	865-5250	7-12	Greg Whitehead
Miami Valley Academies	5656 Springboro Pike	Dayton, OH	45449-2806	937-294-4522	294-4545	K-12	Marvis Meeks
Middlebury Academy	88 Kent St	Akron, OH	44305-2544	330-752-2766	940-1339	K-5	Alvin McDaniel
Middletown Prep & Fitness Academy	816 2nd Ave	Middletown, OH	45044-4201	513-424-6110	424-6121	K-8	Eric Oliver
Midnimo Cross Cultural MS	1567 Loretta Ave	Columbus, OH	43211	614-261-7480	261-7481	6-9	Dr. Robert Stephens
Millenium Community ES	3500 Refugee Rd	Columbus, OH	43232-4862	614-255-5585	255-5580	K-8	Tijuana Russell
Monroe Prep Academy	328 E Monroe St	Sandusky, OH	44870	567-998-7522		K-5	Dr. Erik Thorson
Mound Street Health Careers Academy	354 Mound St	Dayton, OH	45402-8325	937-223-3041	223-5867	9-12	Ron Cothran
Mound Street IT Careers Academy	354 Mound St	Dayton, OH	45402-8325	937-223-3041	223-5867	9-12	Ron Cothran
Mound Street Military Careers Academy	354 Mound St	Dayton, OH	45402-8325	937-223-3041	223-5867	9-12	Ron Cothran
Mt. Auburn International Academy	244 Southern Ave	Cincinnati, OH	45219-3023	513-241-5500	241-5501	K-12	Claudia Ehrle
Mt. Healthy Prep & Fitness Academy	7601 Harrison Ave	Mount Healthy, OH	45231-3107	513-587-6280	521-4509	K-8	Timothy Baggs
Near West Intergenerational S	3805 Terrett Ave	Cleveland, OH	44113	216-961-4308	961-4606	K-6	Molly Toussant
Newark Digital Academy	255 Woods Ave	Newark, OH	43055-4436	740-328-2022	328-2270	K-12	John Lutz
New Beginnings Academy	4707 Hilton Corporate Dr	Columbus, OH	43232	614-367-0589	367-0921	8-12	Aaron Butler
NewBridge Academy	3850 Sullivant Ave	Columbus, OH	43228	614-279-6000		K-5	Andrew Carr
New Day Academy	291 E 222nd St Ste 205	Euclid, OH	44123	216-516-0866	797-1604	K-12	Terrance Walton
Noble Academy - Cleveland	1200 E 200th St	Euclid, OH	44117-1111	216-486-8866	486-2846	K-8	
Noble Academy - Columbus	1329 Bethel Rd	Columbus, OH	43220-2611	614-326-0687	326-0691	K-8	Abdulkadir Parlar
North Central Academy	928 W Market St Ste B	Tiffin, OH	44883	419-448-5786	448-5789	6-12	Matt Wolph
North Dayton S of Discovery	3901 Turner Rd	Dayton, OH	45415-3654	937-278-6671	278-6964	K-8	Renaldo O'Neal
Northeast Ohio College Preparatory S	2357 Tremont Ave	Cleveland, OH	44113	216-965-0580	394-0364	K-12	Jennifer Sullivan
Northland Prep & Fitness ES	1875 Morse Rd	Columbus, OH	43229-6603	614-318-0600	262-9111	K-8	Lynn Hursey
Northpointe Academy	3648 Victory Ave	Toledo, OH	43607-2564	419-535-1997	244-4205	K-8	Nicholas Jacobs
Northwest Academy	1441 W 116th St	Cleveland, OH	44102-2301	216-226-6800	226-6805	K-8	Julio Alarcon
Oakstone Community S	5747 Cleveland Ave	Columbus, OH	43231-2831	614-865-9643	865-9649	PK-12	Erik Wilson
Ohio College Preparatory S	21100 Southgate Park Blvd	Maple Heights, OH	44137	216-453-4550		K-8	Robert Williams
Ohio Connections Academy	3615 Superior Ave E	Cleveland, OH	44114	216-361-9460		K-12	Marie Hanna
Ohio Construction Academy	1725 Jetway Blvd	Columbus, OH	43219	614-532-1863		9-12	Jennifer Johnston
Ohio Virtual Academy	1690 Woodlands Dr Ste 200	Maumee, OH	43537-4045	419-482-0948	482-0955	K-12	Dr. Kristin Stewart Ph.D.
Old Brook HS	4877 Pearl Rd	Cleveland, OH	44109	440-319-3370	661-2298	9-12	Jamila Smith
Old Brooklyn Community ES	4430 State Rd	Cleveland, OH	44109	216-661-7888	661-5975	K-4	Cherie Kaiser
Old Brooklyn Community MS	4430 State Rd	Cleveland, OH	44109-4779	216-351-0280	661-5975	5-8	Cherie Kaiser
Orchard Park Academy	14440 Triskett Rd	Cleveland, OH	44111	440-340-3202		K-8	Anthony Ligon
Orion Academy	1798 Queen City Ave	Cincinnati, OH	45214-1427	513-251-6000	251-3851	K-8	Kendell Dorsey
Par - Excellence Academy	1350 Granville Rd	Newark, OH	43055	740-344-7279	344-7272	PK-5	Gisele James
Parma Community ES	7667 Day Dr	Parma, OH	44129	440-888-5490	888-5890	K-3	Brian Belmont
Parma Community HS	5983 W 54th St	Parma, OH	44129	440-887-0319	845-2834	9-12	Linda Geyer
Parma Community IS	3421 Snow Rd	Parma, OH	44134	440-340-4654	340-4668	4-6	Linda Geyer
Parma Community MS	5983 W 54th St	Parma, OH	44129	440-845-2587	845-2834	7-8	Linda Geyer
Pathway S of Discovery	173 Avondale Dr	Dayton, OH	45404-2123	937-235-5498	235-5569	K-8	Keith Colbert
Patriot Preparatory Academy	4938 Beatrice Dr	Columbus, OH	43227	614-864-5332	864-5381	K-12	Brenda Williams
Performance Academy of Eastland	2220 S Hamilton Rd	Columbus, OH	43232	614-314-6301	577-1933	K-8	Norbert Tate
Phoenix Academy Community S	1505 Jefferson Ave	Toledo, OH	43604	419-720-4500		7-12	Jodi Johns
Phoenix Community Learning Center	3595 Washington Ave	Cincinnati, OH	45229	513-351-5801	351-5809	K-8	Dr. Elaine Wilson
Pinnacle Academy	860 E 222nd St	Euclid, OH	44123	216-731-0127	731-0688	K-8	Charlena Dykes-Hunt
Pleasant Community Digital S	1105 Owens Rd W	Marion, OH	43302	740-389-4815	389-6985	K-K	Dr. Shelly Dason
Promise Academy	1701 E 13th St	Cleveland, OH	44114-3227	216-443-0500	443-0506	9-12	Dr. Cordelia Harris
Puritas Community ES	15204 Puritas Ave	Cleveland, OH	44135-2716	216-688-0680	688-0609	K-4	Margaret Colwell
Puritas Community MS	15204 Puritas Ave	Cleveland, OH	44135	216-251-1596	251-3540	5-8	Meg Colwell
QDA HS	400 Mill Ave SE Ste 901	New Phila, OH	44663-3878	330-364-0618	364-0618	K-12	Stephen Eckert
REACH Academy	2014 Consaul St	Toledo, OH	43605	419-691-4876	691-5184	K-5	Dawn Milner
Regent HS	5806 Broadway Ave	Cleveland, OH	44127	216-512-0076	441-0208	9-12	Jason Windon
Renaissance Academy	4300 Kimberly Pkwy N	Columbus, OH	43232	614-866-7277		9-12	Sharice Martin
Richland S of Academic Arts	75 N Walnut St	Mansfield, OH	44902	419-522-8224		K-8	Sandra Sutherland
Rise & Shine Academy	3248 Warsaw St	Toledo, OH	43608	419-244-9900	244-9906	K-6	Tashlai Burney
Rittman Academy	100 Saurer St	Rittman, OH	44270-1259	330-927-7162	927-7405	9-12	Kent Smith
River Gate HS	458 Franklin St SE	Warren, OH	44483	330-647-6500		9-12	Jason Cooper
Riverside Academy	3280 River Rd	Cincinnati, OH	45204-1214	513-921-7777	921-7704	K-8	Arnez Gray
Road to Success Academy	3377 Cleveland Ave	Columbus, OH	43224	614-252-4656		9-12	Kimberly Jones
Rushmore Academy	2222 Marion-Mount Gilead Rd	Marion, OH	43302	740-387-2043	387-2169	9-12	Steve Vanderhoff
Schnee Learning Center	2222 Issaquah St	Cuyahoga Falls, OH	44221-3704	330-922-1966	945-4059	9-12	Tony Pallija
Sciotoville Elementary Academy	5523 3rd St	Sciotoville, OH	45662	740-776-2920	776-2916	K-5	Foresta Shope
Sciotoville HS	224 Marshall St	Sciotoville, OH	45662-5549	740-776-6777	776-6812	6-12	James Mahlmeister
South Columbus Prep Academy	3220 Groveport Rd	Columbus, OH	43207	614-986-0116	986-0118	K-4	Kyle Glispie
Southern Ohio Academy	522 Glenwood Ave	Sciotoville, OH	45662	740-354-0215	354-0288	9-12	Patricia Ciraso
South Scioto Academy	2200 Winslow Dr	Columbus, OH	43207	614-445-7684	445-7688	K-8	Courtney Watters
Southside Academy	1400 Oak Hill Ave	Youngstown, OH	44507	330-774-5562	742-9095	K-8	Stephanie Groscost
Southwest Ohio Preparatory S	5555 Little Flower Ave	Cincinnati, OH	45239	513-508-2275		K-8	John Dickinson
Springfield Prep & Fitness Academy	1615 Selma Rd	Springfield, OH	45505-4245	937-323-6250	323-6252	K-8	Darren Fansler

School	Address	City,State	Zip code	Telephone	Fax	Grade	Contact
Stambaugh Charter Academy	2420 Donald Ave	Youngstown, OH	44509-1306	330-792-4806	787-0278	K-8	Landon Brown
Star Academy of Toledo	5025 Glendale Ave	Toledo, OH	43614-1855	419-720-6330	720-7372	K-8	Vincent Riccardi
Stark HS	1379 Garfield Ave SW	Canton, OH	44706	234-214-4140		9-12	Carly Hart
STEAM Academy of Akron	1338 Virginia Ave	Akron, OH	44306	330-773-1100	773-1102	K-7	Nova O'Callaghan
STEAM Academy of Dayton	545 Odlin Ave	Dayton, OH	45405	937-262-7063	262-7136	K-8	Debra A. Johnson M.Ed.
STEAM Academy of Warren	261 Elm Rd NE	Warren, OH	44483-5003	330-394-3200	394-3600	K-8	Jonathan Natko
STEAM Academy of Warrensville Heights	4700 Richmond Rd	Warrensvl Hts, OH	44128-5984	216-595-2866	595-3180	K-6	Gary Lane
Steel Academy	1570 Creighton Ave	Akron, OH	44310	330-633-1383		7-12	Stephanie Eafford
Stepstone Academy	2121 E 32nd St	Cleveland, OH	44115	440-260-6400	431-7897	K-5	Kelly Krupa
Stockyard Community ES	3200 W 65th St	Cleveland, OH	44102-5510	216-651-5143	651-9515	K-6	Amber Steele
Stockyard Community MS	3224 W 65th St	Cleveland, OH	44102	216-961-5052	651-9227	7-8	Amber Steele
Stonebrook Montessori	975 East Blvd	Cleveland, OH	44108	216-644-3012		PK-3	Jacqui Miller
Sullivant Avenue Community S	3435 Sullivant Ave	Columbus, OH	43204	614-308-5991	308-5622	K-6	Jamie Lama
Summit Academy Akron ES	2503 Leland Ave	Akron, OH	44312-2426	330-253-7441	253-7457	K-6	Dawn Presley
Summit Academy Akron HS	464 S Hawkins Ave	Akron, OH	44320-1228	330-434-2343	434-5295	9-12	Ralph Grant
Summit Academy Akron MS	464 S Hawkins Ave	Akron, OH	44320	330-252-1510	784-8347	7-8	Crystal Phillips
Summit Academy - Canton HS	2400 Cleveland Ave NW	Canton, OH	44709-3613	330-453-8547	453-8924	9-12	Lisa Cook
Summit Academy - Canton S	1620 Market Ave S	Canton, OH	44707	330-458-0393	458-0518	K-8	Robert Housel
Summit Academy Columbus	2521 Fairwood Ave Ste 100	Columbus, OH	43207-2712	614-237-5497	237-6519	K-5	Cheryl Elliott
Summit Academy Community S Cincinnati	1660 Sternblock Ln	Cincinnati, OH	45237-3805	513-321-0561	321-0795	K-8	Sharon Jones
Summit Academy Community S Dayton	4128 Ceder Ridge Rd	Dayton, OH	45414	937-278-4298	278-4613	K-8	Megan Fagan
Summit Academy Community S for Alt Lrnrs	2140 E 36th St	Lorain, OH	44055-2756	440-277-4110	277-4112	K-5	Albert Charpentier
Summit Academy Community S Warren	2106 Arbor Ave SE	Warren, OH	44484-5225	330-369-4233	369-4299	K-6	Allison Glass
Summit Academy Community S Xenia	1694 Pawnee Dr	Xenia, OH	45385-4126	937-372-5210	372-5250	K-8	Cassy Stidham
Summit Academy MS Columbus	2521 Fairwood Ave Ste 200	Columbus, OH	43207	614-237-5497	237-6519	6-8	Cheryl Elliott
Summit Academy - Middletown	4700 Central Ave	Middletown, OH	45044-5354	513-422-8540	423-6352	K-6	Megan Bockelman
Summit Academy Middletown HS	7 S Marshall Rd	Middletown, OH	45044-5375	513-420-9767	727-1520	7-12	Beth Varley
Summit Academy MSHS - Lorain	346 Illinois Ave	Lorain, OH	44052	440-288-0448	288-0997	6-12	Diane Solomon
Summit Academy Painesville	268 N State St	Painesville, OH	44077-4009	440-358-0877	358-0397	K-9	Frank Cheraso
Summit Academy Parma	5868 Stumph Rd	Parma, OH	44130-1736	440-888-5407	888-5417	K-12	Charlotte Ray
Summit Academy S for Alt Learners	1461 Moncrest Dr NW	Warren, OH	44485-1928	330-399-1692	399-1768	7-12	Erin Bradley
Summit Academy - Toledo	301 Collingwood Blvd	Toledo, OH	43604	419-243-1815	392-9810	K-12	Abby Spangler
Summit Academy Transition HS - Cinci	5800 Salvia Ave	Cincinnati, OH	45224-3029	513-541-4000	541-4075	9-12	Stephen Geresy
Summit Academy Transition HS Columbus	2521 Fairwood Ave	Columbus, OH	43207	614-880-0714	880-0732	9-12	Trina Moore
Summit Academy Transition HS Dayton	251 Erdiel Dr	Dayton, OH	45415	937-813-8592	813-8596	9-12	Gary Miller
Summit Academy - Youngstown	1400 Oak Hill Ave	Youngstown, OH	44507-1018	330-228-8235	747-0957	8-12	Kevin Sheely
Summit Academy Youngstown	144 N Schenley Ave	Youngstown, OH	44509-2041	330-259-0421	259-0424	K-7	Michael Majzun
Sunbridge S	2105 N McCord Rd	Toledo, OH	43615	419-725-5437	754-2073	9-12	Aaron Grizaniuk
T2 Honors Academy	18450 S Miles Rd	Warrensvl Hts, OH	44128	216-510-5458		7-12	Dr. India Ford
T.C.P. World Academy	6000 Ridge Ave	Cincinnati, OH	45213-1624	513-531-9500	531-2406	K-6	Karen French
Toledo Prep & Fitness Academy	3001 Hill Ave	Toledo, OH	43607-2932	419-535-3700	535-3701	K-8	Valerie Sandy
Toledo S for the Arts	333 14th St	Toledo, OH	43604-7713	419-246-8732	244-3979	6-12	Michelle Hiser
Toledo SMART ES	1850 Airport Hwy	Toledo, OH	43609	419-214-3290	214-3294	K-3	Jessica Molina
Tomorrow Center	3700 County Road 168	Cardington, OH	43315	419-718-4242	718-4246	6-12	Jamie Byrne
Tooba Academy	1950 Morse Rd	Columbus, OH	43229	614-888-8536	888-8496	K-8	Mahmoud shaheen
Townsend North Community S	305 S Washington St	Castalia, OH	44824-9263	419-684-5402		9-12	Peter Bartkowiak
Towpath Trail HS	275 W Market St	Akron, OH	44303-2159	234-542-0102		9-12	Christina Fraser
TRECA Digital Academy	100 Executive Dr	Marion, OH	43302-6306	740-389-4798	389-4517	K-12	Adam Clark
Trotwood Preparatory & Fitness Academy	3100 Shiloh Springs Rd	Trotwood, OH	45426-2247	937-854-4100	837-9759	K-8	Caitlin Stevens
United Preparatory Academy	1469 E Main St	Columbus, OH	43205	614-557-3574		K-K	Kenya Brooks
University Academy	107 S Arlington St	Akron, OH	44306	330-535-7728		K-8	Willie Banks
University of Cleveland Preparatory S	1906 E 40th St	Cleveland, OH	44103	216-361-9720	431-3375	K-8	Kenan Bishop
Utica Shale Academy of Ohio	38095 State Route 39	Salineville, OH	43945	330-420-5353		9-12	Eric Sampson
Village Preparatory S Willard	2220 W 95th St	Cleveland, OH	44102	216-586-3892	691-1959	K-6	Cherrelle Turner
Washington Park Community S	4000 Washington Park Blvd	Newburgh Hts, OH	44105-3211	216-271-6055	271-6099	K-8	Helene Jasinski
West Academy	12913 Bennington Ave	Cleveland, OH	44135-3761	216-251-5450	251-6410	K-8	Michael Jaissle
West Central Learning Academy	522 W North St	Lima, OH	45801	419-227-9252	227-2511	7-12	Mindy Schulz
Westpark Community ES	16210 Lorain Ave	Cleveland, OH	44111-5521	216-688-0271	688-0273	K-4	Sheila Delzani
Westpark Community MS	16210 Lorain Ave	Cleveland, OH	44111	216-251-7200	251-0355	5-8	Mindy Kidd
West Preparatory Academy	13111 Crossburn Ave	Cleveland, OH	44135-5017	216-772-1340	898-5894	K-5	Jennifer Heyman
Westside Academy	4330 Clime Rd N	Columbus, OH	43228	614-272-9392	272-8940	K-8	Heather O'Bannon
Westside Community S of the Arts	3727 Bosworth Rd	Cleveland, OH	44111	216-688-1900	688-1902	K-8	Deborah Rotolo
Westwood Preparatory Academy	840 W State St	Columbus, OH	43222	330-510-5400		9-12	Christopher Antjas
Whitehall Prep & Fitness S	3474 E Livingston Ave	Columbus, OH	43227-2219	614-324-4585	238-3184	K-8	Matthew Dolan
Wildwood Environmental Academy	1546 Dartford Rd	Maumee, OH	43537-1374	419-868-9885	868-9981	K-8	Elizabeth Lewin
Wings Academy	10615 Lamontier Ave	Cleveland, OH	44104	216-812-0244	812-0234	K-12	Timothy Roberts
Winterfield Venture Academy	305 Wenz Rd	Toledo, OH	43615-6244	419-531-3285	531-3637	K-8	Nate Preston
Winton Preparatory Academy	4750 Winton Rd	Cincinnati, OH	45232	513-276-4166		K-8	Duane Crowe
Youngstown Academy of Excellence	1408 Rigby St	Youngstown, OH	44506-1617	330-746-3970	746-3965	K-8	Lawrence Reeves
Youngstown Community ES	50 Essex St	Youngstown, OH	44502-1838	330-746-2240	746-6618	K-6	Heidi Cope-Barker
YouthBuild Columbus Comm S	1183 Essex Ave	Columbus, OH	43201-2925	614-291-0805	291-0890	9-12	Nkenge Jacobs
Zanesville Community S	920 Moxahala Ave	Zanesville, OH	43701-5533	740-588-5685	455-4331	9-12	Jeffrey Moore
Zenith Academy East	2261 S Hamilton Rd	Columbus, OH	43232-4301	614-577-0997	577-0995	K-8	Tia Lamar
Zenith Academy North	4606 Heaton Rd	Columbus, OH	43229	614-888-9997	888-6689	K-7	
Zenith Academy West	3385 South Blvd	Columbus, OH	43204	614-272-6300	272-6301	K-9	Tina Bennett

Oklahoma

School	Address	City,State	Zip code	Telephone	Fax	Grade	Contact
ASTEC Charter S	2401 NW 23rd St Ste 39A	Oklahoma City, OK	73107	405-947-6274	947-0035	6-12	Ronald Grant
Brown Community S	2 S Elgin Ave	Tulsa, OK	74120-1808	918-425-1407	425-6693	K-5	Deborah Brown
Carlton Landing Academy	10 Boulevard	Eufaula, OK	74432	918-452-3572		PK-12	Lindsay Ward
College Bound Academy	2525 S 103rd E Ave	Tulsa, OK	74129	918-925-1580		PK-4	Chelsea Vanacore
Collegiate Hall	1142 E 56th St	Tulsa, OK	74105	918-925-1620		4-8	Nikhil Kawlra
Discovery School of Tulsa	4821 S 72nd East Ave	Tulsa, OK	74145-6502	918-960-3131	960-3130	K-8	Maureen Brown
Dove Science Academy	280 S Memorial Dr	Tulsa, OK	74112-2202	918-834-3936	834-3352	6-12	
Dove Science Academy	919 NW 23rd St	Oklahoma City, OK	73106-5691	405-524-9762	524-9471	6-12	Barbaros Aslan
Dove Science Academy	4901 N Lincoln Blvd	Oklahoma City, OK	73105	405-605-5566	605-5578	K-5	Jason Mack
Epic One on One S	4101 NW 122nd St Ste B	Oklahoma City, OK	73120-8816	405-749-4550	749-4540	PK-12	David Chaney
Greenwood Leadership Academy	1789 W Seminole St	Tulsa, OK	74127	918-833-8760		K-8	Kojo Asamora-Caesar
Harding Charter Preparatory HS	3333 N Shartel Ave	Oklahoma City, OK	73118-7277	405-606-8742	609-1677	9-12	Dr. Mylo Miller
Harding Fine Arts Academy	PO Box 18895	Oklahoma City, OK	73154-0895	405-702-4322	601-0904	9-12	Barry Schmelzenbach
M.Ed.							
Hughes Academy	1821 E 66th St	Tulsa, OK	74130	918-728-8588		9-12	Dr. Rodney Clark
Hupfeld Academy at Western Village	1508 NW 106th St	Oklahoma City, OK	73114-5214	405-751-1774	752-6833	PK-5	Ruthie Rayner
Independence Charter MS	3232 NW 65th St	Oklahoma City, OK	73116-3512	405-767-3000	767-3007	6-8	Jill Rumbaugh
Insight S of Oklahoma	1156 S Douglas Blvd	Midwest City, OK	73130-5237	877-637-2614		7-12	Sheryl Tatum
KIPP Reach College Preparatory	PO Box 776	Oklahoma City, OK	73101	405-425-4622	425-4624	5-8	Tracy McDaniel
KIPP Tulsa Academy	1661 E Virgin St	Tulsa, OK	74106	918-794-8652	794-8712	5-8	Andrew McRae
Oklahoma Connections Academy	2425 Nowata Pl	Bartlesville, OK	74006-4741	918-977-3285	331-3629	K-12	Tammy Shepherd
Oklahoma Virtual Charter Academy	1160 S Douglas Blvd	Midwest City, OK	73130	866-467-0848	259-8332	K-12	Sheryl Tatum
Rex Charter ES	500 W Sheridan Ave	Oklahoma City, OK	73102-5001	405-587-8100		PK-3	Joseph Pierce Ed.D.
Sankofa Charter S	111 E 1st St	Tulsa, OK	74103	918-425-1407		6-8	Richard Patterson
Santa Fe South ECC	2222 SW 44th St	Oklahoma City, OK	73119	405-600-1986		PK-1	Sue Schlosser
Santa Fe South ES	301 SE 38th St	Oklahoma City, OK	73129	405-606-3916	606-3952	K-5	Carma Barlow
Santa Fe South ES	5325 S Pennsylvania Ave	Oklahoma City, OK	73119	405-681-7480	681-7484	2-5	Kim Figueroa
Santa Fe South ES	4906 S Santa Fe Ave	Oklahoma City, OK	73129	405-600-7038		K-6	Amanda Kissling
Santa Fe South HS	6921 Plaza Mayor Blvd	Oklahoma City, OK	73149	405-631-6100	681-6993	9-12	Lance Seeright
Santa Fe South MS	4712 S Santa Fe Ave	Oklahoma City, OK	73109-7545	405-635-1053	635-0423	7-8	Michael Figueroa
Santa Fe South Pathways Middle College S	7777 S May Ave	Oklahoma City, OK	73159-4419	405-682-7840	685-7883	9-12	Chris McAdoo
SeeWorth Academy	12600 N Kelley Ave	Oklahoma City, OK	73131-1869	405-475-6400	475-8566	3-12	Arthur Schofield
Tsunadeloquasdi Cherokee Immersion S	17675 S Muskogee Ave	Tahlequah, OK	74465	918-453-5400	467-4746	PK-8	Holly Davis
Tulsa Honor Academy	2525 S 101st E Ave	Tulsa, OK	74129	918-833-9420		5-8	Elsie Urueta
Tulsa Legacy Charter S	105 E 63rd St N	Tulsa, OK	74126	918-794-1442	794-1480	PK-4	Carlisha Williams
Tulsa Legacy Charter Upper Academy	6001 N Peoria AVE	Tulsa, OK	74126	918-576-6129		5-7	Carlisha Williams
Tulsa S of Arts and Sciences	1202 W Easton St	Tulsa, OK	74127	918-828-7727	828-7747	7-12	Liesa Smith

Oregon

School	Address	City,State	Zip code	Telephone	Fax	Grade	Contact
Academy for Character Education	195 N 6th St	Cottage Grove, OR	97424-1602	541-942-9707	942-7884	K-12	Starr Sahnow
Academy of Arts and Academics	615 Main St	Springfield, OR	97477	541-744-6728	744-6713	9-12	Mike Fisher
Alliance Charter Academy	16075 Front Ave	Oregon City, OR	97045	503-785-8556	722-4113	1-12	Nic Chapin
Alsea Charter S	PO Box B	Alsea, OR	97324-0120	541-487-4305	487-4089	K-12	Marc Thielman
Annex Charter S	402 Annex Rd	Ontario, OR	97914-8010	541-262-3280	262-3578	K-8	Steve Bishop
Arco Iris Spanish Immersion S	13600 SW Allen Blvd	Beaverton, OR	97005	503-473-0416		1-6	Martha Diaz
Arlington Community Charter S	PO Box 10	Arlington, OR	97812-0010	541-454-2727	454-2335	K-12	Kevin Hunking
Armadillo Technical Institute	PO Box 1560	Phoenix, OR	97535-1560	541-535-3287		4-12	Summer Brandon
Arthur Academy	13717 SE Division St	Portland, OR	97236-2841	503-252-3753	760-1204	K-5	Jon Luebke

School	Address	City,State	Zip code	Telephone	Fax	Grade	Contact
Bend International S	63020 OB Riley Rd	Bend, OR	97703	541-797-7038	797-7039	K-8	Meera Rupp
Bethany Charter S	11824 Hazelgreen Rd NE	Silverton, OR	97381-9626	503-873-4300	873-0143	K-8	Kathy Frank
Bridge Charter Academy	60 S Pioneer St	Lowell, OR	97452	541-937-5200	937-5201	K-11	John VonDoloski
Bridge Charter Academy Bend	21300 Bear Creek Rd	Bend, OR	97702	458-202-0114	937-5201	K-11	John VonDoloski
Burnt River S	PO Box 9	Unity, OR	97884	541-446-3336	446-3581	K-12	Lorrie Andrews
Butte Falls Charter S	PO Box 228	Butte Falls, OR	97522-0228	541-865-3563	865-3217	K-12	Dianne Gorman
Camas Valley S	PO Box 57	Camas Valley, OR	97416-0057	541-445-2131	445-2041	PK-12	Patrick Lee
Career Technical HS	801 SW Highway 101 Ste 404	Lincoln City, OR	97367-2752	541-351-8551	994-7592	9-12	Sean Larson
Cascade Heights Charter S	15301 SE 92nd Ave	Clackamas, OR	97015	503-653-3996	343-4500	K-8	Kristin Macy
Center for Advanced Learning	1484 NW Civic Dr	Gresham, OR	97030-5564	503-667-4978	492-1572	11-12	Carol Eagan
Childs Way Charter S	37895 Row River Rd	Culp Creek, OR	97434-9610	541-946-1821	946-2007	6-12	Michael Kerns
City View Charter S	PO Box 1808	Hillsboro, OR	97123	503-844-9424	844-9425	K-8	Nicole Kopacz
Clackamas Academy of Industrial Science	1306 SE 12th St	Oregon City, OR	97045	503-785-7860	785-8396	8-12	Scott Curtis
Clackamas Middle College HS	12021 SE 82nd Ave	Happy Valley, OR	97086	503-518-5925	518-5928	9-12	Dr. Brian Sien Ed.D.
Clackamas Web Academy	8740 SE Sunnybrook Blvd	Clackamas, OR	97015-5737	503-659-4664	659-4994	1-12	Brad Linn
Coburg Community Family Charter S	91274 N Coburg Rd	Coburg, OR	97408	541-790-3408	790-3532	K-5	Shara MonDragon
Community Roots S	229 Eureka Ave	Silverton, OR	97381	503-874-4107	874-4108	K-6	Miranda Pickner
Cottonwood S of Civics and Science	0640 SW Bancroft St	Portland, OR	97239	503-244-1697	244-1709	K-8	Amanda McAdoo
Cove S	PO Box 68	Cove, OR	97824-0068	541-568-4424	568-4231	K-12	Mat Miles
Dallas Community S	788 SW Birch St	Dallas, OR	97338	503-420-4360		K-8	Bill Conlon
Days Creek Charter S	PO Box 10	Days Creek, OR	97429-0010	541-825-3296	825-3052	K-12	Dr. Mark Angle
EAGLE Charter S	999A Locust St NE	Salem, OR	97301	503-339-7114	990-6909	K-5	John Trotta
EagleRidge Charter HS	677 S 7th St	Klamath Falls, OR	97601-6223	541-884-7627	871-7054	9-12	Donald Peterson
Eddyville Charter S	1 Eddyville School Rd	Eddyville, OR	97343	541-875-2942	875-2491	K-12	Jennifer Johnson
Elkton Charter S	PO Box 390	Elkton, OR	97436-0390	541-584-2228	584-2227	K-12	Mike Hughes
Emerson Charter S	105 NW Park Ave	Portland, OR	97209-3315	503-525-6124	223-4875	K-5	Sunita Sandoz
Eola Hills Charter S	PO Box 69	Amity, OR	97101	503-843-2537	843-2080	1-12	Nicole Wollenweber
Forest Grove Community S	1914 Pacific Ave	Forest Grove, OR	97116	503-359-4600	359-4622	1-8	Vanessa Gray
Fossil Charter S	PO Box 206	Fossil, OR	97830-0206	541-763-4384	763-4010	K-12	Brad Sperry
Four Rivers Community S	2449 SW 4th Ave	Ontario, OR	97914	541-889-3715	889-3718	K-8	Chelle Robins
Glendale Community Charter S	PO Box E	Glendale, OR	97442-0605	541-832-1801	832-2486	9-12	Brenyl Swanson
Goodall Environmental MS	999B Locust St NE	Salem, OR	97301	503-399-7070	391-4070	6-8	Lorelei Gilmore
Gresham Arthur Academy	1890 NE Cleveland Ave	Gresham, OR	97030-4210	503-667-4900	667-4933	K-5	Kandace Burton
Harper Charter S	2987 Harper Westfall Rd	Harper, OR	97906-2008	541-358-2473	358-2488	K-12	Ron Talbot
Hope Chinese Charter S	3500 SW 104th Ave	Beaverton, OR	97005	971-226-7500		K-5	Julie Rickman M.Ed.
Howard Street Charter S	710 Howard St SE	Salem, OR	97302-3098	503-399-3408	375-7861	6-8	Christina Tracy
Imbler Charter S	PO Box 164	Imbler, OR	97841-0164	541-534-5331	534-9560	K-12	Angie Lakey-Campbell
Ione Community Charter S	PO Box 167	Ione, OR	97843-0167	541-422-7131	422-7555	K-12	Rollie Marshall
Ivy S	4212 NE Prescott St	Portland, OR	97218	503-288-8820	288-8711	1-8	Liz Caravaca
Joseph Charter S	PO Box 787	Joseph, OR	97846-2023	541-432-7311	432-1100	K-12	Sherri Kilgore
KairosPDX Learning Academy Charter S	PO Box 12190	Portland, OR	97212	503-567-9820		K-5	Zalika Gardner
Kids Unlimited Academy	821 N Riverside Ave	Medford, OR	97501	541-774-3900	772-3443	K-6	Jani Hale
Kings Valley Charter S	38840 Kings Valley Hwy	Philomath, OR	97370-9750	541-929-2134	929-8179	K-12	Jamon Ellingson
Le Monde French Immersion ES	2044 E Burnside St	Portland, OR	97214	503-467-7529	548-2190	K-6	Dr. Chantal Martel Ph.D.
Lewis & Clark Montessori Charter S	15600 SE 232nd Dr	Damascus, OR	97089-8172	503-427-0803	855-3017	PK-3	Melissa Harbert
Lighthouse S	62868 School Rd	Coos Bay, OR	97420	541-751-1649	751-1659	K-8	Wade Lester
Logos Public Charter S	400 Earhart St	Medford, OR	97501-7828	541-842-3658	842-1927	K-12	Jason Winningham
Lourdes Charter S	39059 Jordan Rd	Scio, OR	97374-9330	503-394-3340		1-8	Linda Duman
Luckiamute Valley Charter S	17475 Bridgeport Rd	Dallas, OR	97338-9458	503-838-1933	606-9879	K-8	Christie Wilkins
Madrone Trail Charter S	3070 Ross Ln	Central Point, OR	97502	541-842-3657		K-8	Karen Bailey
Metro East Web Academy	1394 NW Civic Dr	Gresham, OR	97030	503-258-4790	258-4791	6-12	David Gray
Milwaukie Academy of the Arts	2301 SE Willard	Milwaukie, OR	97222	503-353-5843	353-5845	9-12	Tim Taylor
M.I.T.C.H. Charter S	19550 SW 90th Ct	Tualatin, OR	97062-7505	503-639-5757		K-8	Melissa Meyer
Molalla River Academy	16897 S Callahan Rd	Molalla, OR	97038	503-829-6672	759-6672	K-8	Shelley Urben
Mosier Community S	PO Box 307	Mosier, OR	97040-0307	541-478-3321	478-2536	K-8	Kieran Connolly
Mountain View Academy	PO Box 485	Lowell, OR	97452	541-735-1709		K-8	Laurie Cardwell
Muddy Creek Charter S	30252 Bellfountain Rd	Corvallis, OR	97333	541-752-0377	752-9481	K-5	Bryan Traylor
Multisensory Learning Academy	22565 NE Halsey St	Fairview, OR	97024	503-405-7868	405-7869	K-8	Sheri Fitzsimmons
Network Charter S	2550 Portland St	Eugene, OR	97405	541-344-1229	344-5118	7-12	Stephanie Ford
Nixyaawi Community S	PO Box 638	Pendleton, OR	97801-0638	541-429-7900	966-2671	9-12	Ryan Heinrich
North Columbia Academy	28168 Old Rainier Rd	Rainier, OR	97048-3017	503-556-3777	556-3778	7-12	Anne Montgomery
North Powder Charter S	PO Box 10	North Powder, OR	97867-0010	541-898-2244	898-2046	PK-12	Lance Dixon
Opal Charter S	4015 SW Canyon Rd	Portland, OR	97221-2759	503-471-9902	223-6600	K-5	Beth Hutchins
Optimum Learning Environments Charter S	7905 June Reid Pl NE	Keizer, OR	97303-2559	503-399-5548	399-3469	1-5	Tom Charboneau
Oregon City Service Learning Academy	995 S End Rd	Oregon City, OR	97045	503-785-8445	650-5483	7-12	Josh Bryan
Oregon Trail Academy	36225 SE Proctor Rd	Boring, OR	97009	503-668-5541	668-7906	K-11	Ginger Redlinger
Oregon Virtual Academy	400 Virginia Ave Ste 210	North Bend, OR	97459	541-751-8060	751-8016	K-12	Brandy Osborn
Paisley S	PO Box 97	Paisley, OR	97636-0097	541-943-3111	943-3129	K-12	Paul Hauder M.S.
Phoenix S of Roseburg	3131 NE Diamond Lake Blvd	Roseburg, OR	97470-3632	541-673-3036	957-5906	8-12	Ron Breyne
Pine Eagle Charter S	375 N Main St	Halfway, OR	97834-8153	541-742-2811	742-2810	K-12	Morgan Gover
Portland Arthur Academy	7507 SE Yamhill St	Portland, OR	97215-2284	503-257-3936	257-3929	K-5	Susan Spreadborough
Portland Village ES	7654 N Delaware Ave	Portland, OR	97217-6417	503-445-0056	445-0058	K-8	Paul Berg
Powell Butte Community Charter S	13650 SW Highway 126	Powell Butte, OR	97753	541-548-1166	548-7635	K-8	Jennifer Berry-O'Shea
Prospect Charter S	PO Box 40	Prospect, OR	97536-0040	541-560-3653	560-3644	PK-12	Brian Purnell
Redmond Proficiency Academy-HS	657 SW Glacier Ave	Redmond, OR	97756	541-526-0882		9-12	Dr. Jon Bullock
Redmond Proficiency Academy-MS	639 SW Forest Ave	Redmond, OR	97756	541-526-0882	516-1160	6-8	Dr. Jon Bullock
Reedsport Community Charter S	2260 Longwood Dr	Reedsport, OR	97467-1167	541-271-2141	271-2143	7-12	Vincent Swagerty
Renaissance Public Academy	PO Box 208	Molalla, OR	97038	503-759-7002	759-7004	4-12	Darrel Camp
Resource Link Charter S	1255 Hemlock Ave	Coos Bay, OR	97420-1298	541-267-1499	266-7314	K-12	Dale Inskeep
Reynolds Arthur Academy	123 SW 21st St	Troutdale, OR	97060	503-465-8882	465-8883	K-6	Chris Arnold
Ridgeline Montessori Public Charter S	4500 W Amazon Dr	Eugene, OR	97405	541-681-9662	681-4394	K-8	Sharon Martin
Rockwood Preparatory Academy	740 SE 182nd Ave	Portland, OR	97233	503-907-1023	907-1024	K-6	John Nelsen
Sage Community S	PO Box 655	Chiloquin, OR	97624-0655	541-783-2533	783-2544	K-8	Anna Fowler
Saint Helens Arthur Academy	33035 Pittsburg Rd	Saint Helens, OR	97051-3305	503-366-7030		K-8	Michael Arthur
Sand Ridge Charter S	30581 Sodaville Mtn Home Rd	Lebanon, OR	97355	541-258-2416	258-1898	K-8	Audrey Cota
Sauvie Island Academy	14445 NW Charlton Rd	Portland, OR	97231-1402	503-621-3426	621-3384	K-8	Darla Meeuwsen
SEI Academy Charter S	3920 N Kerby Ave	Portland, OR	97227-1255	503-249-1721	284-4456	6-8	Timothy Rodgers
Sheridan Allprep Online Academy	PO Box 583	Sheridan, OR	97378-0583	503-843-9330	758-1982	K-12	Jesse Eisenschmidt
Sheridan Japanese S	PO Box 446	Sheridan, OR	97378-0446	503-843-3400	843-7438	4-12	
Sherwood Charter S	PO Box 1342	Sherwood, OR	97140-1342	503-925-8007	925-8172	K-8	Joy Raboli
Siletz Valley S	PO Box 247	Siletz, OR	97380-0247	541-444-1100	444-2368	K-12	Sam Tupou
Silvies River Charter S	39235 Highway 205	Frenchglen, OR	97736	541-589-2401	722-7129	K-12	Eric Nichols
South Columbia Family S	33589 High School Way	Warren, OR	97053	503-366-9009	366-9010	K-12	Ray Brown
Springwater Environmental Sciences S	PO Box 3010	Oregon City, OR	97045-0301	503-631-7700	631-7720	K-8	Dawn Bolotow
Summit Community College HS	PO Box 2631	Estacada, OR	97023	503-630-5001	630-5206	10-12	Joni Tabler
Summit Learning Charter	30391 SE Highway 211	Eagle Creek, OR	97022	503-630-5001	630-5206	K-12	Sean Gallagher
Sunny Wolf Charter S	PO Box 438	Wolf Creek, OR	97497-0438	541-866-2735	866-2738	K-5	Penelope DiGennaro
Sweet Home Charter S	28721 Liberty Rd	Sweet Home, OR	97386-9776	541-367-1833	367-1839	K-6	Tavia Thornton
Three Rivers Charter S	2565 SW Ek Rd	West Linn, OR	97068	503-673-7850	723-1060	4-8	Katherine Holtgraves
Triangle Lake Charter S	20264 Blachly Grange Rd	Blachly, OR	97412-9714	541-925-3262	925-3062	K-12	James Brookins
Trillium Charter S	5420 N Interstate Ave	Portland, OR	97217-4569	503-285-3833	249-0348	K-12	Patrice Mats
Twin Rivers Charter S	2621 Augusta St	Eugene, OR	97403	541-349-5055		9-12	Jay Breslow
Valley Inquiry Charter S	5774 Hazelgreen Rd NE	Salem, OR	97305	503-399-3150	391-4091	K-5	Lisa Sundseth
Valley S	PO Box 1225	Medford, OR	97501	541-842-3914		6-8	
Village S	3411 Willamette St	Eugene, OR	97405	541-345-7285	242-6874	K-8	Carla LaFleur
West Lane Technology Learning Center	24967 Highway 126	Veneta, OR	97487	541-935-2101	935-8345	9-12	Ron Osibov
Willamette Leadership Academy	34020 B St	Eugene, OR	97405	541-246-2842	246-2841	6-12	Steve Brandom
Woodburn Arthur Academy	575 Gatch St	Woodburn, OR	97071-4927	503-981-5746	981-5742	K-5	Glenn Izer
Woodland Charter S	PO Box 740	Murphy, OR	97533	541-846-4246		1-8	Phil Centers
Pennsylvania							
Achievement House Charter S	600 Eagleview Blvd Ste 1	Exton, PA	19341-1121	484-615-6200	458-1204	7-12	Don Asplen
ACT Academy Cyber Charter S	7301 Germantown Ave	Philadelphia, PA	19119	267-297-1668		9-12	Joanne Hill
Ad Prima Charter S	3556 Frankford Ave	Philadelphia, PA	19134	215-288-7062	288-8673	K-6	Dr. Julliette Pennyman
Ad Prima Charter S	1922 N 63rd St	Philadelphia, PA	19151	215-883-0638	292-4058	K-8	Dr. Julliette Pennyman
Agora Cyber Charter S	590 N Gulph Rd	King of Prussia, PA	19406	844-402-4672	254-8939	K-12	Dr. Michael Conti
Allen Preparatory Charter S	2601 S 58th St	Philadelphia, PA	19143-6146	215-878-1544	727-0711	5-8	Lawrence Jones
Alliance for Progress Charter S	1630 N 16th St	Philadelphia, PA	19121	215-232-4892	232-4894	4-8	Joanna Hightower
Alliance for Progress Charter S	1821 Cecil B Moore Ave	Philadelphia, PA	19121-3135	215-232-4892	232-4893	K-3	Joanna Hightower
Architecture & Design Charter HS	105 S 7th St	Philadelphia, PA	19106-3324	215-351-2900	351-9458	9-12	Gregory Wright
Arts Academy Charter ES	601 W Union St	Allentown, PA	18101	610-657-5388		K-5	Jacqueline Vogel
Arts Academy Charter S	1610 E Emmaus Ave	Allentown, PA	18103-8307	610-351-0234	351-0307	5-8	Jan Labellarte
ASPIRA Bilingual Cyber Charter S	4332 N 5th St	Philadelphia, PA	19140	215-455-1300	455-1300	K-12	Cynthia Cruz-Vega
ASPIRA Olney HS	100 W Duncannon Ave	Philadelphia, PA	19120	215-456-3014	456-3064	9-12	James Thompson
Attucks Youth Build Charter S	605 S Duke St	York, PA	17401-3111	717-848-3610	843-3914	9-12	Jacquie Martino-Miller
Avon Grove Charter S	110 State Rd	West Grove, PA	19390-8908	484-667-5000		K-12	Kristen Bishop

School	Address	City,State	Zip code	Telephone	Fax	Grade	Contact
Baden Academy Charter S	1016 W State St	Baden, PA	15005	855-590-2227	869-4269	K-6	
Bear Creek Community Charter S	30 Charter School Way	Wilkes Barre, PA	18702	570-820-4070	270-6149	K-8	Brian Dugas
Belmont Academy Charter S	907 N 41st St	Philadelphia, PA	19104-1278	215-386-5768	386-5769	K-K	Claire Cohen
Belmont Charter S	4030 Brown St	Philadelphia, PA	19104-4844	215-823-8208	823-8209	1-8	Claire Cohen
Birney Charter S	900 Lindley Ave	Philadelphia, PA	19141-3920	215-456-3000	456-3113	K-8	Kareem Thomas
Boys Latin of Philadelphia Charter S	5501 Cedar Ave	Philadelphia, PA	19143-1929	215-387-5149	387-5159	6-12	Dr. Noah Tennant
Bracetti Academy Charter S	1840 Torresdale Ave	Philadelphia, PA	19124-4418	215-291-4436	291-4985	K-12	Jana Somma
Bucks County Montessori Charter S	219 Tyburn Rd	Fairless Hills, PA	19030-4403	215-428-6700	428-6702	K-6	Brian Long
Byers Charter S	1911 Arch St	Philadelphia, PA	19103-1403	215-972-1700	972-1701	PK-6	Jesse Bean
Capital Area School for the Arts	150 Strawberry Sq	Harrisburg, PA	17101-1815	717-732-8450	732-8451	9-12	Timothy Wendling
Center for Student Learning Charter S	345 Lakeside Dr	Levittown, PA	19054-3933	215-269-7390	269-7395	6-12	Dr. Charles Bonner
Central Pennsylvania Digital Charter S	580 Foot of Ten Rd	Duncansville, PA	16635	814-682-5258	946-8526	K-12	Angela Boutiller
Centre Learning Community Charter S	2643 W College Ave	State College, PA	16801-2604	814-861-7980	861-8030	5-8	Kosta Dussias
Chester Charter S for the Arts	1500 Highland Ave	Chester, PA	19013	610-859-3010		K-11	Akosua Watts
Chester Community Charter S	214 E 5th St	Chester, PA	19013-4510	610-447-0400	876-5716	K-6	Dr. David Clark
Chester County Family Academy	530 E Union St	West Chester, PA	19382-4206	610-696-5910	696-6324	K-2	Susan Flynn
Circle of Seasons Charter S	8380 Mohr Ln	Fogelsville, PA	18051	610-285-6267		K-5	Alison Saeger
City Charter HS	201 Stanwix St	Pittsburgh, PA	15222-1350	412-690-2489	690-2316	9-12	Dr. Ron Sofo
Clemente Charter S	136 S 4th St	Allentown, PA	18102-5445	610-439-5181	435-4731	6-12	Damian Romero
Clemente ES - Charter	850 N 5th St	Allentown, PA	18102	610-435-5334		K-6	Samuel Polanco
Collegium Charter S	435 Creamery Way Ste 300	Exton, PA	19341	610-903-1300	903-1317	K-12	Dr. Antoinette Rath
Columbus Charter S	1242 S 13th St	Philadelphia, PA	19147	215-389-6000	389-3732	6-8	Rosemary Dougherty
Columbus Charter S	916 Christian St	Philadelphia, PA	19147-3808	215-925-7400	925-7491	K-5	Rosemary Dougherty
Commonwealth Charter Academy	4050 Crums Mill Rd	Harrisburg, PA	17112	717-651-7200	651-0670	K-12	Dr. Maurice Flurie
Community Academy of Philadelphia	1100 E Erie Ave	Philadelphia, PA	19124-5424	215-533-6700	533-6722	K-12	Joe Proietta
DeHostos Charter S	6301 N 2nd St	Philadelphia, PA	19120-1522	215-455-2300	455-6312	K-8	
Discovery Charter S	4700 Parkside Ave	Philadelphia, PA	19131	215-879-8182	879-9510	K-8	Khailiah Canada
Douglass Mastery Charter S	2118 W Norris St	Philadelphia, PA	19121-2100	215-684-5063	684-8916	K-8	Tom Weishaupt
Eastern University Academy Charter S	3300 Henry Ave Ste 2	Philadelphia, PA	19129-1121	215-769-3131	769-3112	7-12	Omar Barlow
Easton Arts Academy	30 N 4th St	Easton, PA	18042	484-546-4230		K-5	Johanna Hughes
Environmental Charter S at Frick Park	829 Milton St	Pittsburgh, PA	15218-1005	412-247-7970	247-7971	K-6	Jon McCann
Erie Rise Leadership Academy Charter S	2501 Plum St	Erie, PA	16502-2570	814-520-6468		K-6	Terry Lang
Esperanza Academy Charter S	301 W Hunting Park Ave	Philadelphia, PA	19140-2625	215-457-3667	457-4381	1-12	David Rossi
Esperanza Cyber Charter S	4261 N 5th St	Philadelphia, PA	19140-2615	215-967-9703		6-12	
Evergreen Community Charter S	PO Box 523	Mountainhome, PA	18342-0523	570-595-6355	595-6038	6-12	Jill Shoesmith
Executive Education Academy Charter S	555 Union Blvd	Allentown, PA	18109	484-841-7044		K-12	Robert Lysek
Fell Charter S	777 Main St	Simpson, PA	18407-1236	570-282-5199	282-0930	K-8	Mary Jo Walsh
First Philadelphia Charter S	4300 Tacony St	Philadelphia, PA	19124-4134	215-743-3100	743-9877	K-12	Myra Mezei
Folk Arts-Cultural Treasures Charter S	1023 Callowhill St	Philadelphia, PA	19123-3704	215-569-2600	569-3985	K-8	Pheng Lim
Franklin Towne Charter ES	4259 Richmond St	Philadelphia, PA	19137-1930	215-289-3389	288-4041	K-8	Patrick Field
Franklin Towne Charter HS	5301 Tacony St	Philadelphia, PA	19137-2345	215-289-5000	535-8910	9-12	Dr. Joseph Venditti Esq.
Freire Charter HS	2027 Chestnut St	Philadelphia, PA	19103-3307	215-592-4252	557-9051	9-12	Dr. Kelly Davenport
Freire Charter S	1026 Market St	Philadelphia, PA	19107-4205	267-670-7499	670-7740	5-8	Dr. Kelly Davenport
Gardner Multiple Intelligence S	1615 E Elm St	Scranton, PA	18505	570-941-4100	941-7699	K-8	Maria Rozaieski
Gettysburg Montessori Charter S	888 Coleman Rd	Gettysburg, PA	17325	717-334-1120		K-6	Faye Pleso
Gillingham Charter S	915 Howard Ave	Pottsville, PA	17901	570-955-3830		K-12	
Global Leadership Academy	4601 W Girard Ave	Philadelphia, PA	19131-4615	267-295-5700	295-5701	K-8	Dr. Naomi Johnson-Booker
Global Leadership Academy Southwest	5200 Pine St	Philadelphia, PA	19143			PK-8	Tamika Evans
Gratz Prep MS	1798 W Hunting Park Ave	Philadelphia, PA	19140	215-227-4408	227-3694	7-8	Raymond Fields
Green Woods Charter S	468 Domino Ln	Philadelphia, PA	19128	215-482-6337		K-8	Stephani Finnin
Harambee Institute of Science Technology	640 N 66th St	Philadelphia, PA	19151-3606	215-472-8770	472-9611	K-8	
Hill House Passport Academy Charter S	510 Heldman St	Pittsburgh, PA	15219	412-376-3724		9-12	
HOPE for Hyndman Charter S	130 School Dr	Hyndman, PA	15545-8125	814-842-3918	842-6246	K-12	Dr. Thomas Otis
I-Lead Charter S	401 Penn St	Reading, PA	19601-3974	855-453-2327		9-12	Angel Figueroa
Imhotep Institute Charter HS	6201 N 21 St	Philadelphia, PA	19138	215-438-4140	438-4160	9-12	Jury Segers
Independence Charter S	1600 Lombard St	Philadelphia, PA	19146-1507	215-238-8000	545-2924	K-8	Ramzy Andrawos
Independence Charter S West	5600 Chester Ave	Philadelphia, PA	19143	215-724-5600		K-4	Julio Nunez
Infinity Charter S	5405 Locust Ln	Harrisburg, PA	17109	717-200-1000		K-8	Suzanne Gausman
Innovative Arts Academy	330 Howerton Rd	Catasauqua, PA	18032	610-403-2787	403-2687	6-12	Douglas Taylor
Insight PA Cyber Charter S	350 Eagleview Blvd	Exton, PA	19341	855-667-4536		K-10	Patti Dahl
Ketterer Charter S	1133 Village Way	Latrobe, PA	15650-5201	724-537-9110	537-9114	1-12	Eric Guldin
Keystone Academy Charter S	4521 Longshore Ave	Philadelphia, PA	19135	215-332-2111	332-2840	K-8	
Keystone Education Center Charter S	425 S Good Hope Rd	Greenville, PA	16125-8629	724-588-2511	588-2545	6-12	Mike Gentile
Khepera Charter S	926 W Sedgley Ave	Philadelphia, PA	19140	215-843-1700	644-9432	K-8	Mwlimu Waset
KIPP Dubois Collegiate Academy	5070 Parkside Ave	Philadelphia, PA	19131	215-307-3465	307-3271	9-12	Melissa Poorman
KIPP Philadelphia Charter S	2539 N 16th St	Philadelphia, PA	19132	215-227-1728	827-5942	5-8	Kazmir Davis
KIPP Philadelphia ES	2409 W Westmoreland St	Philadelphia, PA	19129	267-687-7283	687-7295	K-4	Ivana Gasiorowski
KIPP West Philadelphia Prep Charter S	5900 Baltimore Ave	Philadelphia, PA	19143	215-294-2973	294-8707	5-8	Cheshonna Miles
La Academia Charter S	30 N Ann St	Lancaster, PA	17602-3063	717-295-7763	399-6456	6-12	Guillermo Barroso
Laboratory Charter S	5339 Lebanon Ave	Philadelphia, PA	19131	215-877-9881	877-9882	2-8	
Laboratory Charter S	800 N Orianna St	Philadelphia, PA	19123	215-574-1680	574-0622	K-8	Stacey Cruise
Lancaster County Academy	1202 Park City Ctr	Lancaster, PA	17601	717-295-2499	392-8603	9-12	Emily Fields
Lehigh Valley Academy	1560 Valley Center Pkwy	Bethlehem, PA	18017-2276	610-866-9660		K-12	Susan Mauser
Lehigh Valley Charter HS for the Arts	321 E 3rd St	Bethlehem, PA	18015-1309	610-868-2971	868-1446	9-12	Diane LaBelle
Lehigh Valley Dual Language Charter S	675 E Broad St	Bethlehem, PA	18018	610-419-3120	419-3968	K-8	Lisa Pluchinsky
Lincoln Charter S	559 W King St	York, PA	17401-3776	717-699-1573	846-4031	K-5	Leonard Hart
Lincoln Leadership Academy Charter S	1414 E Cedar St	Allentown, PA	18109-2308	484-860-3300		K-12	Sandra Figueroa-Torres
Lincoln Park Performing Arts Charter S	1 Lincoln Park	Midland, PA	15059-1535	724-643-9004	643-0769	7-12	Patrick Poling
Manchester Academic Charter S	1214 Liverpool St	Pittsburgh, PA	15233-1304	412-322-0585	322-2176	K-8	Vasilios Scoumis
Maritime Academy Charter S	2275 Bridge St	Philadelphia, PA	19137-1300	215-535-4555	535-4398	4-12	Edward Poznek
MaST Community Charter S	1800 Byberry Rd	Philadelphia, PA	19116-3012	215-348-1100	348-1217	K-12	John Swoyer
Mastery Charter HS Hardy Williams Campus	5400 Warrington Ave	Philadelphia, PA	19143-4810	267-499-2100	729-1892	7-10	Lisa Bellamy
Mastery Charter HS - Lenfest Campus	35 S 4th St	Philadelphia, PA	19106-2710	215-922-1902	922-1903	7-12	Steven Kollar
Mastery Charter HS - Pickett Campus	5700 Wayne Ave	Philadelphia, PA	19144-3314	215-866-9000	866-9001	6-12	Jason Kegel
Mastery Charter HS - Shoemaker Campus	5301 Media St	Philadelphia, PA	19131-4035	267-296-7111	296-7112	7-12	Sharif El-Mekki
Mastery Charter HS - Thomas Campus	927 Johnston St	Philadelphia, PA	19148-5016	267-236-0036	236-0030	7-12	Kristy Fruit
Mastery Charter S Clymer Campus	1201 W Rush St	Philadelphia, PA	19133	215-223-2243	227-3697	K-6	Tiffany Holmes
Mastery Charter S Grover Cleveland Cmps	3701 N 19th St	Philadelphia, PA	19140-3555	215-227-5042	893-5290	K-8	Charmaine Collins
Mastery Charter S -Hardy Williams Campus	5400 Warrington St	Philadelphia, PA	19143	215-724-2343	724-2374	K-12	
Mastery Charter S Harrity Campus	5601 Christian St	Philadelphia, PA	19143-2805	215-471-2908	471-3807	PK-8	Stuart Warshawer
Mastery Charter S Mann Campus	5376 W Berks St	Philadelphia, PA	19131-3229	215-581-5616	581-5610	K-6	Stan Bobowski
Mastery Charter S Pastorius	5650 Sprague St	Philadelphia, PA	19138	215-951-5689		K-8	
Mastery Charter S Simon Gratz Campus	1798 W Hunting Park Ave	Philadelphia, PA	19140-3408	215-227-4408	227-3694	9-12	Rickia Reid
Mastery Charter S Smedley Campus	1790 Bridge St	Philadelphia, PA	19124-1359	215-537-2523	537-3694	K-6	Brian McLaughlin
Mastery Charter S - Thomas Campus	814 Bigler St	Philadelphia, PA	19148-5023	267-296-7000	236-0030	K-6	Michael Farrell
Mastery Charter Wister ES	67 E Bringhurst St	Philadelphia, PA	19144-2338	215-951-4003	951-4534	K-5	
Math Civics & Sciences Charter S	447 N Broad St	Philadelphia, PA	19123-3643	215-923-4880	923-4859	1-12	Frank Devine
Memphis Street Academy Charter S	2950 Memphis St	Philadelphia, PA	19134-4314	215-291-4709	291-4754	5-8	Antoinette Powell
Montessori Regional Charter S	2910 Sterrettania Rd	Erie, PA	16506	814-833-7771	833-1030	K-6	Mark Zielinski
Multicultural Academy Charter S	3821 N Broad St	Philadelphia, PA	19140	215-227-0513	227 0415	9-12	James Higgins
New Day Charter S	256 S 5th St	Huntingdon, PA	16652	814-643-7112	643-7116	7-12	Joshua Hicks
New Foundations Charter S	8001 Torresdale Ave	Philadelphia, PA	19136-2917	215-624-8100	624 0600	K-8	Paul Stadelberger
New Foundations Charter S	4850 Rhawn St	Philadelphia, PA	19136-2935	215-344-6410	624-6817	9-12	Paul Stadelberger
Nittany Valley Charter S	1612 Norma St	State College, PA	16801-6228	814-867-3842	231-0795	K-8	Kara Martin
Northwood Academy	4621 Castor Ave	Philadelphia, PA	19124-3024	215-289-5606	289-5464	K-8	Amy Hollister
Pan American Academy Charter S	2830 N American St	Philadelphia, PA	19133	215-425-1212	423-0871	K-8	Dr. Darcy Russotto
Pantoja Community Charter S	4101 N American St	Philadelphia, PA	19140-2606	215-329-2733	329-2433	K-8	Sandra Gonzalez
Penn Hills Charter S Entrepreneurship	2501 Main St	Pittsburgh, PA	15235	412-793-6471	793-6473	K-8	Tamara Allen
Pennsylvania Cyber Charter S	652 Midland Ave	Midland, PA	15059	724-643-1180	643-1963	K-12	Brian Hayden
Pennsylvania Distance Learning Charter S	2100 Corporate Dr Ste 500	Wexford, PA	15090-7647	724-933-7300	933-7655	K-12	Dr. Ed Mandell
Pennsylvania Leadership Charter S	1332 Enterprise Dr	West Chester, PA	19380-5996	610-701-3333		K-12	Dr. James Hanak
PA Learners Online Cyber Charter S	475 E Waterfront Dr	Homestead, PA	15120	412-394-5733		9-12	Dr. David Martin
Pennsylvania Virtual Charter S	630 Park Ave	King of Prussia, PA	19406	610-275-8501	275-1719	K-12	Dr. John Chandler
People for People Charter S	800 N Broad St	Philadelphia, PA	19130-2202	215-763-7060	763-6210	K-12	Pri Seebadri
Perseus House Charter S of Excellence	1511 Peach St	Erie, PA	16501-2104	814-480-5914	454-9859	7-12	Dana LaFata
Philadelphia Academy Charter S	1700 Tomlinson Rd	Philadelphia, PA	19116-3848	215-673-3990	673-3341	9-12	Megan Simmons
Philadelphia Academy Charter S	11000 Roosevelt Blvd	Philadelphia, PA	19116-3903	215-676-8320	676-8340	K-8	Allyssa Schmitt
Philadelphia Charter S for the Arts/Sci	1197 Haworth St	Philadelphia, PA	19124-2505	215-537-2520	537-2861	K-8	Ayanna Johnson
Philadelphia Electrical & Tech Charter S	1420 Chestnut St	Philadelphia, PA	19102-2505	267-514-1823	514-1834	9-12	Erin Dougherty
Philadelphia Montessori Charter S	2227 Island Rd	Philadelphia, PA	19142-1009	215-365-4011	365-4367	K-6	Paulla Jones
Philadelphia Performing Arts Charter S	2600 S Broad St	Philadelphia, PA	19145-4616	215-551-4000	551-1113	K-5	Angela Puleio
Philadelphia Performing Arts Charter S	2407 S Broad St	Philadelphia, PA	19148-3508	215-551-4000	551-1113	K-1	Angela Puleio
Premier Arts and Science Charter S	500 N 17th St	Harrisburg, PA	17103-1423	717-234-3200		K-5	Steven Rayzer
Preparatory Charter S	1928 Point Breeze Ave	Philadelphia, PA	19145-2612	215-334-6144	334-6147	9-12	Dr. Chadwick Antonio
Propel Charter HS - Andrew Street	605 E 10th Ave	Munhall, PA	15120	412-462-4625	462-6980	9-12	Lauren Reiber
Propel Charter HS - Braddock Hills	1500 Yost Blvd	Pittsburgh, PA	15221	412-271-4929	271-4905	9-12	Bob Bischoff
Propel Charter HS - Montour	5501 Steubenville Pike	Mc Kees Rocks, PA	15136	412-470-6998		6-12	Mark McClinchie

School	Address	City,State	Zip code	Telephone	Fax	Grade	Contact
Propel Charter S - Braddock Hills	1500 Yost Blvd	Braddock Hills, PA	15221-4822	412-271-3061	271-0865	K-8	Jocelyn Artinger
Propel Charter S - East	1611 Monroeville Ave	Turtle Creek, PA	15145-1652	412-823-0347	823-0924	K-8	Bethany Thomas
Propel Charter S - Hazelwood	5401 Glenwood Ave	Pittsburgh, PA	15207	412-325-7105		K-6	Tina Chekan
Propel Charter S - Homestead	129 E 10th Ave	Homestead, PA	15120-1608	412-464-2604		K-8	Robert Powell
Propel Charter S - Mc Keesport	2412 Versailles Ave	McKeesport, PA	15132-2037	412-678-7215		K-8	Mike Evans
Propel Charter S - Montour	340 Bilmar Dr	Pittsburgh, PA	15205	412-539-0100	539-0109	K-8	Matt Strine
Propel Charter S - Northside	1805 Buena Vista St	Pittsburgh, PA	15212-3914	412-325-1412	325-1428	K-8	Ariane Watson
Propel Charter S - Pitcairn	435 Agatha St	Pitcairn, PA	15140-1310	412-457-0020		K-8	Robert Bischoff
Provident Charter S	1400 Troy Hill Rd	Pittsburgh, PA	15212	412-709-5160		2-8	Brett Marcoux
REACH Cyber Charter S	750 East Park Dr	Harrisburg, PA	17111	717-704-8437		K-12	Jane Swan
Renaissance Academy	413 Fairview St	Phoenixville, PA	19460	610-983-4080	983-4096	K-12	Gina Guarino-Buli
Sankofa Freedom Academy	2501 Kensington Ave	Philadelphia, PA	19125-1321	215-228-2001	228-2099	K-12	Dr. Ayesha Imani
School Lane Charter S	2400 Bristol Pike	Bensalem, PA	19020-5263	215-245-6055	245-6058	K-10	Karen Schade
Science Leadership Academy MS	3509 Spring Garden St	Philadelphia, PA	19104	215-400-8320		5-6	Timothy Boyle
Seven Generations Charter S	154 E Minor St	Emmaus, PA	18049	610-421-8844		K-8	Paul Hunter
Souderton Charter S Collaborative	110 E Broad St	Souderton, PA	18964-1276	215-721-4560	721-4071	K-8	Jennifer Arevalo
Southwest Leadership Academy	7101 Paschall Ave	Philadelphia, PA	19142-1031	215-729-1939	729-1976	K-8	Leigh Purnell
Spectrum Charter S	4369 Northern Pike	Monroeville, PA	15146-2807	412-374-8130	374-9629	9-12	Michelle Johnson
Stetson Charter S	3200 B St	Philadelphia, PA	19134-2202	215-291-4720	291-4168	5-8	Thomas Mullin
Stone Valley Community Charter S	13006 Greenwood Rd	Huntingdon, PA	16652-6030	814-667-2705	667-2231	K-5	Dr. Kim Connelly
Sugar Valley Rural Charter S	236 E Main St	Loganton, PA	17747-9502	570-725-7822	725-7825	K-12	Tracie Kennedy
SusQ-Cyber Charter S	240 Market St Box 1A	Bloomsburg, PA	17815	866-370-1226	245-0246	9-12	Patricia Leighow
Sylvan Heights Science Charter S	915 S 13th St	Harrisburg, PA	17104-3402	717-232-9220	232-9221	K-4	Timothy Hess M.Ed.
Tacony Academy Charter S	1330 Rhawn St	Philadelphia, PA	19111-2802	215-742-5100	742-5200	K-8	Ashley Redfearn-Neswick
Tacony Academy Charter S	6201 Keystone St	Philadelphia, PA	19135	267-388-8656	388-8666	9-12	Naimah Holliday
Thackston Charter MS	625 E Philadelphia St	York, PA	17403	717-846-6160	848-2856	5-8	Melissa Achuff
Tidioute Community Charter S	241 Main St	Tidioute, PA	16351-1222	814-484-3550	484-3977	K-12	Dr. Doug Allen
21st Century Cyber Charter S	126 Wallace Ave	Downingtown, PA	19335-2600	484-875-5400	875-5404	6-12	Kim McCully
Universal Alcorn Charter S	3200 Dickinson St	Philadelphia, PA	19146-3316	215-952-6219	952-0853	K-8	Sheila Mallory
Universal Audenried Charter HS	3301 Tasker St	Philadelphia, PA	19145-1021	215-952-4801	952-4805	9-12	Blanchard Diavua
Universal Bluford Charter S	5720 Media St	Philadelphia, PA	19131	215-581-5502	581-5725	K-6	Crystal Gary-Nelson
Universal Creighton Charter S	5401 Tabor Ave	Philadelphia, PA	19120-2130	215-537-2531	537-8398	K-8	Wendy Baldwin
Universal Daroff Charter S	5630 Vine St	Philadelphia, PA	19139-1301	215-471-2905	471-3159	K-8	Anna Smith
Universal Institute Charter S	801 S 15th St	Philadelphia, PA	19146-2215	215-732-2876	732-8066	K-8	Jeffrey Williams
Universal Vare Charter MS	2100 S 24th St	Philadelphia, PA	19145-3222	215-952-8611	952-8520	5-8	Craig Metcalfe
Urban Academy Greater Pittsburgh Charter	437 Turrett St	Pittsburgh, PA	15206	412-361-1008	361-1042	K-5	Dr. Gail Edwards
Urban Pathways Charter S	925 Penn Ave	Pittsburgh, PA	15222	412-325-4075	392-4602	K-5	Kimberly Fitzgerald
Vida Charter S	120 E Broadway	Gettysburg, PA	17325	717-334-3643	334-9806	K-6	Martha Davis
Vision Academy Charter S	41 E Baltimore Ave	Lansdowne, PA	19050	484-466-2124	441-1366	K-6	Isik Durmus
Westinghouse Arts Academy	320 Marguerite Ave	Wilmerding, PA	15148	412-518-0907		9-12	Sal Aloe
West Oak Lane Charter S	7115 Stenton Ave	Philadelphia, PA	19138-1136	215-927-7995	927-7980	K-8	Dr. Debbera Peoples-Lee
West Philadelphia Achievement Charter S	6701 Callowhill St	Philadelphia, PA	19151-3603	215-476-6471	476-6481	K-5	Christine Godfrey
Widener Partnership Charter S	1450 Edgmont Ave	Chester, PA	19013-3943	610-872-1358	872-1794	K-7	Dr. Darlene Davis
Wiley Community Charter S	1446 E Lake Rd	Erie, PA	16507-1936	814-461-9600	461-0226	K-8	Peter Russo
Wissahickon Charter S	4700 Wissahickon Ave	Philadelphia, PA	19144-4252	267-338-1020	338-1030	K-8	Kristi Littell
Wonderland Charter S	2112 Sandy Dr	State College, PA	16803-2282	814-234-5886		K-K	Kelly Raudabaugh
York Academy Regional Charter S	32 W North St	York, PA	17401-2403	717-801-3900	718-1092	K-6	
Young Scholars Charter S	900 N Marshall St	Philadelphia, PA	19123	215-232-9727	232-4542	6-8	Melissa Campbell
Young Scholars of Central PA Charter S	1530 Westerly Pkwy	State College, PA	16801-2848	814-237-9727	237-1517	K-8	Levent Kaya
Young Scholars of Western PA	600 Newport Dr	Pittsburgh, PA	15234	412-668-2064	668-2068	K-8	Kasim Biyikli
YouthBuild Charter S	1231 N Broad St Fl 3	Philadelphia, PA	19122	215-627-8671	763-5774	12-12	Scott Emerick

Rhode Island

School	Address	City,State	Zip code	Telephone	Fax	Grade	Contact
Academy for Career Exploration	155 Harrison St	Providence, RI	02907	401-456-1738	521-0653	9-12	Mario Cirillo Ph.D.
Achievement 1st Providence Mayoral Acad	370 Hartford Ave	Providence, RI	02909	401-347-1106	633-6677	K-5	Morgan Carter
BEACON Charter HS for the Arts	320 Main St	Woonsocket, RI	02895-3138	401-671-6261	671-6264	9-12	Michael Skeldon
Blackstone Academy	334 Pleasant St	Pawtucket, RI	02860-5289	401-726-1750	726-1753	9-12	Kyleen Carpenter
Blackstone Valley Prep ES 1	291 Broad St	Cumberland, RI	02864	401-335-3133	305-3185	K-4	Kyle Quadros
Blackstone Valley Prep ES 2	52 Broad St	Cumberland, RI	02864	401-305-6860	305-6866	K-4	
Blackstone Valley Prep Mayoral Acad HS	65 Macondray St	Cumberland, RI	02864	401-405-0320	405-0440	9-12	
Blackstone Valley Prep Mayoral Acad MS	3 Fairlawn Way	Lincoln, RI	02865	401-475-8829	475-8931	5-8	Marielle Emet
Blackstone Valley Prep S 3	3 Fairlawn Way	Lincoln, RI	02865	401-475-2680	475-2415	K-6	Josh Falk
Compass S	537 Old North Rd	Kingston, RI	02881-1220	401-788-8322	788-8326	K-8	
Cuffee S	459 Promenade St	Providence, RI	02908-5601	401-453-2711	453-4964	K-12	Eric Charlesworth
Founders Academy	1 Social St	Woonsocket, RI	02895	401-671-6261		6-8	Amanda Turcotte
Greene S	94 John Potter Rd	West Greenwich, RI	02817	401-397-8600	397-8392	9-12	Joshua Laplante
Highlander Charter S	42 Lexington Ave	Providence, RI	02907	401-277-2600	277-2603	PK-12	Rose Grant
Hope Academy	1000 Eddy St	Providence, RI	02905	401-533-9192	533-9101	K-2	Angela Holt
International Charter S	334 Pleasant St	Pawtucket, RI	02860-5289	401-721-0824	721-0976	K-5	Darlene Pugnali
Kingston Hill Academy	850 Stony Fort Rd	Saunderstown, RI	02874-1003	401-783-8282	783-5656	K-5	Linda Paolillo
Learning Community S	21 Lincoln Ave	Central Falls, RI	02863-2012	401-722-9998	722-0990	K-8	Meg O'Leary
NEL/CPS Construction Career Academy	4 Sharpe Dr	Cranston, RI	02920-4410	401-270-8692	270-8697	9-12	Dennis Curran
Nowell Leadership Academy II	133 Delaine St	Providence, RI	02909	401-751-0405	751-0020	9-12	Toby Shepherd
Nowell Leadership Academy I	43 Hawes St	Central Falls, RI	02863	401-751-0405	751-0020	9-12	Toby Shepherd
RI Nurses Institute Middle College	150 Washington St	Providence, RI	02903	401-680-4900	331-5646	10-12	Colleen Hitchings
RISE Prep Mayoral Academy	1 Social St	Woonsocket, RI	02895	401-765-5127		K-8	Rosalind DaCruz
Segue Institute for Learning	325 Cowden St	Central Falls, RI	02863	401-721-0964	721-0984	6-8	Melissa Lourenco
SouthSide Elementary Charter S	135 Prairie Ave	Providence, RI	02905	401-270-9007		K-3	Wendy Randle
Times2 STEM Academy	50 Fillmore St	Providence, RI	02908-3105	401-272-5094	272-0555	K-12	Carrie McWilliams
Trinity Academy for the Performing Arts	150 Washington St	Providence, RI	02903	401-432-7968	432-7882	7-12	Elizabeth Hegnauer
Village Green Virtual Charter S	135 Weybosset St	Providence, RI	02903	401-831-2878		9-12	Robert Pilkington

South Carolina

School	Address	City,State	Zip code	Telephone	Fax	Grade	Contact
Academy for Teaching and Learning	109 Hinton St	Chester, SC	29706-2022	803-385-6334	385-6335	PK-8	Robyn Brakefield
Academy of Hope Charter S	3521 Juniper Bay Rd	Conway, SC	29527-4227	843-397-5719	397-5712	K-8	Melissa McCloud
Aiken Performing Arts Academy	130 Avery Ln	Aiken, SC	29801	803-644-4824	641-1155	9-12	Keisha Lloyd-Kennedy
Allegro Charter S of Music	120 Broad St	Charleston, SC	29401	843-297-8033	207-4701	6-12	Daniel Neikirk
Anderson V Charter S	1225 S McDuffie St	Anderson, SC	29624-2746	864-260-5538	260-5911	9-12	Katie Brown
Brashier Middle College HS	1830 W Georgia Rd	Simpsonville, SC	29680-7212	864-757-1800	757-1850	9-12	Michael Sinclair
Bridges Preparatory S	PO Box 120	Beaufort, SC	29901	843-982-7737	982-7707	K-9	Dr. Nick Ithomitis
Bridgewater Academy	191 River Landing Blvd	Myrtle Beach, SC	29579-9502	843-236-3689	236-4921	K-8	Steve Wilson
Calhoun Falls Charter S	205 Edgefield St	Calhoun Falls, SC	29628-1018	864-418-8014	418-9379	6-12	Deirdre McCullough
Cape Romain Environmental Educ Charter S	1011 Old Cemetery Rd	Mc Clellanville, SC	29458-9735	843-887-3323	887-3525	PK-8	Margaret Crouch M.Ed.
Carolina School for Inquiry	PO Box 2484	Columbia, SC	29202	803-691-1250	691-1247	PK-6	Victoria Dixon-Mokeba
Carolina Voyager Charter S	721 Wappoo Rd	Charleston, SC	29407	843-203-3891	718-2903	K-4	Dr. Harry Walker
Charleston Charter S for Math & Science	1002 King St	Charleston, SC	29403	843-720-3085	720-3196	6-12	Mary Carmichael
Charleston Development Academy	233 Line St	Charleston, SC	29403-8100	843-722-2689	722-2694	PK-8	Dr. Shaun Johnson
Coastal Leadership Academy	3710 Palmetto Pointe Blvd	Myrtle Beach, SC	29588	843-788-9898	410-4826	9-12	Renee Mathews
Coastal Montessori Charter S	111 Old Plantation Dr	Pawleys Island, SC	29585	843-235-0413	235-0418	1-8	Dr. Nathalie Hunt
Cooper Charter S	4568 Seaboard Rd	Salters, SC	29590-3365	843-387-5426	387-5444	PK-8	Dr. Kerry Singleton
Cyber Academy of South Carolina	330 Pelham Rd Ste 101	Greenville, SC	29615	855-611-2830	558-0535	K-12	David Crook
Discovery S	302 W Dunlap St	Lancaster, SC	29720-2405	803-285-8430	416-8907	K-5	Tom McDuffie
East Cooper Montessori Charter S	1120 Rifle Range Rd	Mount Pleasant, SC	29464-4229	843-216-2883	216-8880	PK-8	Jody Swanigan
East Point Academy	1401 Leaphart St	West Columbia, SC	29169	803-926-0520		PK-8	Dr. Winnie Johnson
Felton Laboratory Charter S	PO Box 2349	Orangeburg, SC	29116	803-536-7034	533-3635	K-8	Dr. Gloria Winkler
Fox Creek HS	165 Shortcut Rd	North Augusta, SC	29860-9123	803-613-9435	613-1533	9-12	Josh Trahan
Gray Collegiate Academy	3833 Leaphart Rd	West Columbia, SC	29169	803-951-3321	381-9764	9-12	Dr. Brian Newsome
GREEN Charter S	1440 Pelham Rd	Greenville, SC	29615	864-288-4134	288-0826	K-10	Adem Dokmeci
GREEN Charter S of the Midlands	7820 Broad River Rd	Irmo, SC	29063	803-563-5387	563-5438	K-6	Osman Demirel
Greenville Technical Charter HS	PO Box 5616	Greenville, SC	29606-5616	864-250-8845	250-8846	9-12	Dr. J. Brodie Bricker
Greer Middle College Charter HS	138 W McElhaney Rd	Taylors, SC	29687	864-469-7571	469-7573	9-12	Jimmy Armstrong Ph.D.
High Point Academy	6655 Pottery Rd	Spartanburg, SC	29303	864-316-9788	249-1516	K-12	Christy Junkins
Horse Creek Academy	1200 Toolebeck Rd	Aiken, SC	29803	803-226-0160	226-0202	PK-8	Dr. Frank Roberson
James Island Charter HS	1000 Fort Johnson Rd	Charleston, SC	29412-8898	843-762-2754	762-5228	9-12	Timothy Thorn
Kennedy Charter S	130 Avery Ln	Aiken, SC	29801	803-644-4824	641-1155	3-8	Keisha Lloyd-Kennedy
Langston Charter MS	1950 Woodruff Rd	Greenville, SC	29607	864-286-9700	286-9699	6-8	Greg Abel
Lead Academy	804 Mauldin Rd	Greenville, SC	29607	864-770-1790	302-1278	K-8	Chase Willingham
Legacy Early College ES	1613 W Washington St	Greenville, SC	29601	864-214-1600	451-7023	K-4	Virginia Burrows
Legacy Early College S Parker Campus	900 Woodside Ave	Greenville, SC	29611	864-248-0646	283-6444	5-12	Stephen Hampton
Lowcountry Leadership Charter S	5139 Gibson Rd	Hollywood, SC	29449	843-889-5527	889-5529	K-12	Wes Harris
Lowcountry Montessori S	749 Broad River Dr	Beaufort, SC	29906	843-322-0577	322-0925	PK-12	Amy Horn
Mathis Charter HS	2872 Azalea Dr	N Charleston, SC	29405	843-557-1611	747-5810	9-12	Natrice Henriques
Mevers S of Excellence	7750 Henry E Brown Jr Blvd	Goose Creek, SC	29445	843-806-5909	806-5910	K-6	John Spagnolia
Meyer Center for Special Children	1132 Rutherford Rd	Greenville, SC	29609-3927	864-250-0005	250-0028	PK-2	Chris Neeley
Midlands Middle College	1260 Lexington Dr	West Columbia, SC	29170-2176	803-822-7043	822-7039	11-12	Courtney Girolamo

School	Address	City,State	Zip code	Telephone	Fax	Grade	Contact
Midlands STEM Institute	112 Crane St	Winnsboro, SC	29180-6941	803-815-1524	815-0072	K-12	Marie Milam
NEXT HS	2000 Wade Hampton Blvd	Greenville, SC	29615	864-735-7260		6-12	Zachary Eikenberry
Oceanside Collegiate Academy	580 Faison Rd	Mount Pleasant, SC	29466	843-936-7128		9-12	Brenda Corley
OCSD5 HS for Health Professions	770 Stilton Rd	Orangeburg, SC	29115	803-535-1693	535-1635	9-12	Angel Malone
Odyssey Online Learning S	200 Arbor Lake Dr Ste 301	Columbia, SC	29223	803-735-9110	701-9024	9-12	Stephanie Cagle
Orange Grove Charter S	1225 Orange Branch Rd	Charleston, SC	29407	843-763-1520	769-2245	PK-8	John Clendaniel
PALM Charter HS	136 Rodeo Dr	Myrtle Beach, SC	29579	843-903-6600	903-6602	9-12	Avery Moore
Palmetto Academy of Learning and Success	3021 Fred Nash Blvd	Myrtle Beach, SC	29577	843-293-1725		K-8	Courtney Fancher
Palmetto Scholar's Academy	7499 Dorchester Rd	N Charleston, SC	29418-3310	843-300-4118	300-4123	6-12	Dr. Tim Gott
Palmetto S at Children's Attention Home	PO Box 2892	Rock Hill, SC	29732	803-328-6555	327-8618	K-8	Dr. Hugh Wilson
Palmetto Youth Academy	1209 N Douglas St	Florence, SC	29501-0600	843-679-7070	679-7046	1-6	Yvonne Burgess
Pattison's Academy for Comprehensive Ed.	2014 Bees Ferry Rd	Charleston, SC	29414	843-556-1070	556-6742	K-12	J. Elaine Fort
Pee Dee Math Science Technology Academy	101 Docs Dr	Bishopville, SC	29010	803-428-8400	883-8736	K-8	E. Keith Bailey
Phoenix Charter HS	PO Box 170	Alcolu, SC	29001-0170	803-505-6800	505-6801	9-12	Elease Fulton
Prestige Preparatory Academy	2415 Avenue F	N Charleston, SC	29405	843-900-7722		K-4	Joyce Coleman
Quest Leadership Academy	29 Ridgeway Dr	Greenville, SC	29605	864-277-7575	277-7404	PK-5	Kristin White M.Ed.
Richland One Middle College S	316 Beltline Blvd	Columbia, SC	29205-3624	803-738-7114	738-7117	11-12	Dr. Tinicoo Javis
Richland Two Charter HS	7900 Brookmont Ln	Columbia, SC	29203	803-419-1348	935-1212	9-12	Bobby Cunningham
Riverview Charter S	81 Savannah Hwy	Beaufort, SC	29906	843-379-0123	379-0133	K-8	Alison Thomas
Riverwalk Academy	5750 Mount Gallant Rd	Rock Hill, SC	29732	803-327-8400	454-9031	K-8	Cori Stepp
Royal Live Oaks Academy Arts & Sciences	PO Box 528	Hardeeville, SC	29927-0528	843-784-2630	784-2623	K-12	Karen Wicks
SC Connections Academy	220 Stoneridge Dr Ste 403	Columbia, SC	29210-8018	803-212-4712	212-4946	K-12	Amanda Ebel
South Carolina Science Academy	2015 Marion St	Columbia, SC	29201	803-227-6422	391-4902	6-12	Kalu Kalu
SC Virtual Charter School	140 Stoneridge Dr Ste 420	Columbia, SC	29210-8200	803-253-6222	253-6279	K-12	Dr. Cherry Daniel
South Carolina Whitmore S	501 Commerce Dr NE	Columbia, SC	29223	866-476-6416	476-1646	9-12	John Loveday
Spartanburg Preparatory S	385 S Spring St	Spartanburg, SC	29306	864-621-3882	804-6404	K-9	Dr. Gerald Edwards
Tall Pines STEM Academy	82 Camp Long Rd	Aiken, SC	29805	803-502-1692	459-1092	5-7	Kathy Griffin
York Preparatory Academy	1047 Golden Gate Ct	Rock Hill, SC	29732-8878	803-324-4400	496-2083	K-12	Dr. Lionel Kennedy
Youth Leadership Academy	698 Concord Church Rd	Pickens, SC	29671	864-898-4511	898-5784	6-8	Sandee Blankenship

Tennessee

School	Address	City,State	Zip code	Telephone	Fax	Grade	Contact
Arrow Academy of Excellence	645 Semmes St	Memphis, TN	38111	901-207-1891		K-3	Dr. Andrea Mayfield
Aspire Coleman ES	3210 Raleigh Millington Rd	Memphis, TN	38128-3395	901-416-4306		PK-7	Owen Ricciardi
Aspire East Academy	6870 Winchester Rd	Memphis, TN	38115	901-567-7086		K-3	Monique Cincore
Aspire Hanley ES	680 Hanley St	Memphis, TN	38114	901-416-5958	416-5961	K-5	Steven Ward
Aspire Hanley MS	680 Hanley St	Memphis, TN	38114	901-416-5958	416-5961	6-8	Steven Ward
Aurora Collegiate Academy	3804 Given Ave	Memphis, TN	38122	901-249-4615	274-4019	K-5	Teneicesia White
Bluff City HS	4100 Ross Rd	Memphis, TN	38115	901-730-8157		9-12	Jonas Cleaves
Brick Church College Prep S	2835 Brick Church Pike	Nashville, TN	37207	615-806-6317		5-8	Dr. Katrina Frazier
Cameron College Prep S	1034 1st Ave S	Nashville, TN	37210-2616	615-806-6320		5-8	Tait Danhausen
Chattanooga Charter School of Excellence	5600 Brainerd Rd	Chattanooga, TN	37411	423-710-1121	710-3180	K-8	Susan Brown
Chattanooga Girls Leadership Academy	1802 Bailey Ave	Chattanooga, TN	37404-3005	423-702-7230		6-12	Maryo Beck Ed.D.
Circles of Success Learning Academy	867 S Parkway E	Memphis, TN	38106-5605	901-322-7978	322-7993	K-5	Sheri Catron-Cooper
City University S Boys Preparatory	1475 E Shelby Dr	Memphis, TN	38116-7225	901-775-2219	775-2044	6-8	Wanda Hannah
City University S Girls Preparatory	1475 E Shelby Dr	Memphis, TN	38116	901-775-2219	526-1945	6-8	Wanda Hannah
City University S of Independence	1475 E Shelby Dr	Memphis, TN	38116	901-775-2219	775-2044	9-12	Tracie Greer
City University S of Liberal Arts	1475 E Shelby Dr	Memphis, TN	38116	901-775-2219	775-2044	9-12	Equan Ashe
Cornerstone Prep - Denver Campus	1940 Frayser Blvd	Memphis, TN	38127	901-416-3938		PK-5	Michelle Lyons
Cornerstone Prep - Lester Campus	320 Carpenter St	Memphis, TN	38112	901-416-5969	416-5971	PK-6	Dr. Melinda Harper
DuBois S of Arts & Technology	817 Brownlee Rd	Memphis, TN	38116	901-801-6171	801-6170	K-12	
DuBois S of Leadership & Public Policy	817 Brownlee Rd	Memphis, TN	38116	901-505-6833		K-12	Angela Holloway
East End Preparatory S	1460 McGavock Pike	Nashville, TN	37216	615-630-7470	630-7490	K-7	Jim Leckrone
Fairley HS	4950 Fairley Rd	Memphis, TN	38109-7399	901-730-8160	416-3908	9-12	Michael Bates
Freedom Prep Academy	964 Fields Rd	Memphis, TN	38109	901-425-2019		K-1	Ayanna Grey
Freedom Prep Academy - Westwood	778 Parkrose Rd	Memphis, TN	38109	901-259-5959		PK-8	Kyle Kucharski
Freedom Preparatory Academy	5132 Jonetta St	Memphis, TN	38109	901-259-5959	259-5950	9-12	Kyle Kucharski
Gateway University	6165 Stage Rd	Bartlett, TN	38134	901-509-7140		9-12	Sosepriala Dede
GRAD Academy	1880 Prospect St	Memphis, TN	38106-6710	901-206-8848		9-12	Dr. Noah Gordan
Hillcrest HS	4184 Graceland Dr	Memphis, TN	38116-2655	901-730-4098		9-12	Meredith Davis
Humes Preparatory Academy - Upper S	659 N Manassas St	Memphis, TN	38107	901-310-1332		6-8	Dr. Lakishia Robinson
Independence Academy	5221 Hickory Hollow Pwky	Antioch, TN	37013	615-334-0070		9-9	Bryan Kariuki
Ivy Academy Environmental Charter S	8520 Dayton Pike	Soddy Daisy, TN	37379	423-305-7494	305-7496	6-12	Scott Grisar
Kaleidoscope S of Memphis	110 N Court Ave	Memphis, TN	38103	901-623-1888		6-8	Alice Henry
King Preparatory HS	1530 Dellwood Ave	Memphis, TN	38127	901-567-9224		9-12	Marcus Shead
KIPP: Kirkpatrick ES	1000 Sevier St	Nashville, TN	37206	615-226-4484		K-4	Amy Galloway
KIPP Academy Nashville MS	123 Douglas Ave	Nashville, TN	37207	615-226-4484		5-8	Hada Flores
KIPP Memphis Academy ES	2248 Shannon Ave	Memphis, TN	38108	901-881-5130		K-2	
KIPP Memphis Academy MS	2110 Howell Ave	Memphis, TN	38108	901-791-9793		5-8	Andrea Criollo
KIPP Memphis Collegiate ES	230 Henry Ave	Memphis, TN	38107	901-791-9391	791-9394	K-4	Jeff Jenifer
KIPP Memphis Collegiate HS	2110 Howell Ave	Memphis, TN	38108-2268	901-791-9792	791-9796	9-10	Sharifa Edwards
KIPP Memphis Collegiate MS	230 Henry Ave	Memphis, TN	38107	901-791-9390	791-9392	5-8	Brian Seay
KIPP Memphis Preparatory ES	2230 Corry Rd	Memphis, TN	38106	901-577-3330		K-3	Grace Bailey
KIPP Memphis Preparatory MS	2230 Corry Rd	Memphis, TN	38106	901-881-5128		5-7	
KIPP Nashville College Prep	3410 Knight Dr	Nashville, TN	37207	615-226-4484	226-4401	5-8	Nikki Olszewski
KIPP Nashville College Prep ES	3410 Knight Dr	Nashville, TN	37207	615-226-4484		K-2	Christa Thomas
KIPP Nashville Collegiate HS	123 Douglas Ave	Nashville, TN	37207	615-226-4484		9-12	Jake Ramsey
Kirby MS	6670 E Raines Rd	Memphis, TN	38115-6610	901-416-1980	416-0974	6-8	Deadre Ussery
Knowledge Academies	5320 Hickory Hollow Pkwy	Antioch, TN	37013	615-810-8370	887-0502	5-8	Edon Katz
Knowledge Academies HS	5320 Hickory Hollow Pkwy	Antioch, TN	37013	615-800-6814	887-0502	9-12	Ariel McCallum
LEAD Academy	2835 Brick Church Pike	Nashville, TN	37207	615-352-1253	327-5425	5-8	Nic Frank
LEAD Academy HS	1034 1st Ave S	Nashville, TN	37210	615-327-5422		9-12	Nic Frank
Leadership Prep Charter S	4190 Elliston Rd	Memphis, TN	38111	901-512-4495	240-8040	K-5	Valissia Allen
LEAD Prep Southeast	531 Metroplex Dr	Nashville, TN	37211	615-678-0543	800-8272	5-8	Chris Elliott
Legacy Leadership Academy	3333 N Old Brownsville Rd	Memphis, TN	38134	901-343-0832		6-12	Danielle Berry-Leach
Lester Prep	320 Carpenter St	Memphis, TN	38112	901-416-3640		6-8	Koai Matthews
Libertas S at Brookmeade	3777 Edenburg Dr	Memphis, TN	38127	901-609-3611		PK-3	Bob Nardo
Liberty Collegiate Academy	3515 Gallatin Pike	Nashville, TN	37216	615-564-1965	650-0912	5-8	Macy Bennett
Memphis Academy of Health Sciences	3925 Chelsea Avenue Ext	Memphis, TN	38108-2612	901-382-1441	382-1944	6-12	Reginald Williams
Memphis Academy of Science & Engineering	1254 Jefferson Ave	Memphis, TN	38104-7229	901-333-1580	333-1582	6-12	Rodrick Gaston
Memphis Business Academy	1082 Berclair Rd	Memphis, TN	38122	901-591-7267	680-5375	K-5	Marsharee Shaw
Memphis Business Academy HS	3306 Overton Crossing St	Memphis, TN	38127	901-357-8680	357-8681	9-12	Shunskis Hamilton
Memphis Business Academy MS	3306 Overton Crossing St	Memphis, TN	38127	901-357-2708	357-2442	6-8	Shunskis Hamilton
Memphis College Prep S	1500 Dunn Ave	Memphis, TN	38106	901-620-6475	620-6476	K-5	Brittany Monda
Memphis Delta Prep Charter S	1299 E McLemore Ave	Memphis, TN	38106	901-251-1010		K-5	Michael McKenna
Memphis Grizzlies Prep Charter S	168 Jefferson Ave	Memphis, TN	38103-2219	901-474-0955	474-9049	9-12	Parker Couch
Memphis Rise Academy	5130 Raleigh Lagrange Rd	Memphis, TN	38134	901-379-5750		6-12	Jack Vuylsteke
Memphis Scholars Caldwell-Guthrie S	951 Chelsea Ave	Memphis, TN	38107-2034	901-236-0105	416-3211	PK-5	Janai Douglas
Memphis Scholars Florida-Kansas	90 W Olive St	Memphis, TN	38106	901-305-9983		K-5	Molicca McCall
Memphis Scholars Raleigh-Egypt MS	1380 Pennsylvania Ave	Memphis, TN	38106	901-236-0110	416-4110	6-8	Heather Johnson
Memphis School of Excellence	4450 S Mendenhall Rd	Memphis, TN	38141	901-367-7814	367-7816	6-12	Alise Pruitt
Memphis School of Excellence ES	4450 S Mendenhall Rd	Memphis, TN	38141	901-367-7814	367-7816	K-5	Irfan Demir
Memphis STEM Academy	2450 Frayser Blvd	Memphis, TN	38127	901-353-1475	308-1430	K-1	LaWanda Clark
Nashville Academy of Computer Science	3230 Brick Church Pike	Nashville, TN	37207	615-921-5000		5-8	Stephanie Jarrett-Thorpe
Nashville Classical Charter S	1310 Ordway Pl	Nashville, TN	37206	615-538-5841		K-4	Charlie Friedman
Nashville Prep Academy	1300 56th Ave N	Nashville, TN	37209	615-921-8440	921-8460	5-8	Arlyn Ilgenfritz
Neelys Bend ES	1300 Neelys Bend Rd	Madison, TN	37115-5515	615-860-1471		K-4	Dr. Derrick Salter
Neelys Bend MS	1251 Neelys Bend Rd	Madison, TN	37115-5471	615-645-6461		5-8	Dr. Tait Danhausen
New Vision Academy	297 Plus Park Blvd	Nashville, TN	37217	615-360-1115	361-8545	5-8	Tim Malone
Nexus STEM Academy MS	8220 Shelby Dr	Memphis, TN	38125	901-352-6226		6-8	Angela Joyner
Opportunity Academy	5432 Bell Forge Ln E	Antioch, TN	37013	615-810-8443		5-8	Lizzie Stewart
Partners Community Prep S	1506 Mary St	Nashville, TN	37208	615-489-4243		K-3	Dennis Wolff
Power Center Academy ES	6120 Winchester Rd	Memphis, TN	38115	901-310-2999	367-9682	K-5	Matthew Martinez
Power Center Academy ES Southeast	8220 E Shelby Dr	Memphis, TN	38125	901-602-5530	432-5443	K-5	Emily Higgins
Power Center Academy HS	5390 Mendenhall Mall	Memphis, TN	38115	901-310-1331	367-0039	9-12	Antonio Ryan
Power Center Academy MS	5449 Winchester Rd	Memphis, TN	38115	901-333-6874	367-9682	6-8	Michelle Jones-Wright
Promise Academy	1346 Bryan St	Memphis, TN	38108-2401	901-324-4456	324-4457	K-4	Dr. Kiasi Malone
Promise Academy Spring Hill	3796 Frayser Raleigh Rd	Memphis, TN	38128	901-410-0284	324-4457	PK-4	Patrick Washington
Purpose Preparatory S	220 Venture Cir	Nashville, TN	37228	615-724-0705		K-4	Lagra Newman
RePublic HS	3307 Brick Church Pike	Nashville, TN	37207	615-921-6620		9-12	Scott Campbell
Rocketship Nashville Northeast ES	2526 Dickerson Pike	Nashville, TN	37207	615-650-5560		K-4	Jermaine Gassaway
Rocketship United Academy	320 Plus Park Blvd	Nashville, TN	37217	615-712-7499		K-4	James Robinson
Smithson-Craighead Academy	730 Neelys Bend Rd	Madison, TN	37115	615-228-9886	865-6308	K-4	Ahmed White
Soulsville Charter S	1115 College St	Memphis, TN	38106	901-261-6366	261-6398	6-12	NeShante Brown
Southern Avenue Charter S	2221 Democrat Rd	Memphis, TN	38132	901-743-7335	743-7677	K-2	Katie Jones
Southwest Early College HS	737 Union Ave	Memphis, TN	38103	901-333-5681	333-5699	9-12	Curtis Weathers
STAR Academy Charter S	3260 James Rd	Memphis, TN	38128-5351	901-387-5050	387-0798	K-5	James Johnson

School	Address	City,State	Zip code	Telephone	Fax	Grade	Contact
STEM Prep Academy	1162 Foster Ave	Nashville, TN	37210	615-921-2200		5-8	Dr. Kristin McGraner
STEM Prep HS	1162 Foster Ave	Nashville, TN	37210	615-921-2200		9-12	
Strive Collegiate Academy	3055 Lebanon Pike	Nashville, TN	37214	615-645-6440		5-8	LaKendra Butler
Valor Flagship Academy	4527 Nolensville Pike	Nashville, TN	37211	615-823-7982		5-8	Jamie Gutter
Valor Voyager Academy	4527 Nolensville Pike	Nashville, TN	37211	615-823-7982		5-8	Sarah Giblin
Veritas College Preparatory Charter S	1500 Dunn Ave	Memphis, TN	38106	901-526-1900	322-4201	6-8	Nick Getschman
Vision Preparatory Charter S	260 Joubert Ave	Memphis, TN	38109-1828	901-775-1018		K-5	Megan Salemi
Whitney Achievement ES	1219 Whitney Ave	Memphis, TN	38127-7754	901-416-3949	416-3953	PK-5	Dr. LaSandra Young
Wooddale MS	3467 Castleman St	Memphis, TN	38118-4538	901-730-4086	794-9002	6-8	Marysa Utley
Woods Academy of Innovation	3824 Austin Peay Hwy	Memphis, TN	38128-3722	901-800-1209	627-6081	K-8	Pam Brown

Texas

School	Address	City,State	Zip code	Telephone	Fax	Grade	Contact
A+ Academy ES	10327 Rylie Rd	Dallas, TX	75217-8240	972-557-5578	557-4128	PK-6	Christy Drekaj
A+ Academy Secondary S	445 S Masters Dr	Dallas, TX	75217	469-667-1000		7-12	Jimmy Trotter
Academy of Accelerated Learning	6025 Chimney Rock Rd	Houston, TX	77081-4011	713-773-4766	666-2532	PK-5	Doris Robins
Academy of Accelerated Learning	6711 Bellfort St	Houston, TX	77087-6457	713-645-0336	640-2435	PK-5	Doris Robins
Academy of Dallas	1030 Oak Park Dr	Dallas, TX	75232-1238	214-371-9600	371-1053	PK-8	Conrad Hargest
Accelerated Learning Center	721 Omaha Dr	Corpus Christi, TX	78408-2839	361-887-7766	887-6035	PK-12	Maria Garza
Advantage Academy - Grand Prairie East	300 W Pioneer Pkwy	Grand Prairie, TX	75051	214-276-5800	276-5890	8-12	Roy Watts
Advantage Academy - Grand Prairie West	955 Freetown Rd	Grand Prairie, TX	75051	214-451-2120	602-2212	PK-8	Dr. Lisa Hill
Advantage Academy - North Duncanville	4009 Joseph Hardin Dr	Dallas, TX	75236	214-276-5800	467-9131	PK-8	Donita White
Advantage Academy - Waxahachie	701 W Highway 287 Byp	Waxahachie, TX	75165-5163	972-451-2107	937-9876	PK-8	Deb Garten
AIA Houston ES	PO Box 20589	Houston, TX	77225-0589	713-728-9330	283-6190	PK-6	LaShawn Hoskins
AIA Lancaster ES	901 E Belt Line Rd	Lancaster, TX	75146	972-227-2105	283-6190	PK-6	LaShawn Hoskins
AIM College & Career Prep	5200 Avenue N 1/2	Galveston, TX	77551	409-761-6302	770-0918	6-12	Cheryl Rutledge
Alief Montessori Community S	4215 H St	Houston, TX	77072	281-530-9406	530-2233	PK-6	Nancy Chieu
Allen Charter S	5220 Nomas St	Dallas, TX	75212-3229	972-794-5100	794-5101	PK-5	Sheila Ortiz Espinell
Altamira Academy	220 Foremost Dr	Austin, TX	78745	512-953-8301	842-9308	PK-4	Dan Horn
Amarillo Collegiate Academy	6000 S Georgia St	Amarillo, TX	79118	806-352-0171	367-5449	K-12	Michael Griffin
Ambassadors Preparatory Academy	5001 Avenue U	Galveston, TX	77551	409-762-1115	762-1114	PK-8	Dr. Patricia Williams
Amigos Por Vida-Friends for Life Charter	5503 El Camino Del Rey St	Houston, TX	77081-1805	713-349-9945	349-0671	PK-8	Freddy Delgado
Annunciation Home	3610 Shell Rd	Georgetown, TX	78628-9246	512-864-7755		6-12	Holly Engleman
Aristoi Classical Academy	5618 11th St	Katy, TX	77493-1971	281-391-5003	391-5010	K-12	Brenda Davidson
Arlington Classics Academy	2800 W Arkansas Ln	Arlington, TX	76016-5819	817-274-2008	274-8768	K-2	Melissa Fambrough
Arlington Classics Academy Intermediate	2800 W Arkansas Ln Ste B	Arlington, TX	76016	817-303-1553	549-0246	3-5	Teri Rodgers
Arlington Classics Academy Middle	5200 S Bowen Rd	Arlington, TX	76017-3756	817-987-1819	549-0246	6-8	Kurtis Flood
Austin Achieve Public S	5908 Manor Rd	Austin, TX	78723-3631	512-522-4190	727-3788	6-12	John Armbrust
Austin Can Academy Charter S	2406 Rosewood Ave	Austin, TX	78702-2408	512-477-4226	931-8034	9-12	Frank Oakes
Austin Discovery S	9303 FM 969	Austin, TX	78724	512-674-0700	674-3133	K-8	Leigh Moss
Austin State University Charter S	PO Box 6072	Nacogdoches, TX	75962-0001	936-468-5899	468-7015	K-5	Lysa Hagan
Baker-Ripley Charter S	6500 Rookin St	Houston, TX	77074	713-273-3731	273-3797	K-5	Roel Saldivar
Barkley/Ruiz ES	1111 S Navidad St	San Antonio, TX	78207-6000	210-978-7940	227-4029	PK-5	Jackie Ibarra-Lanford
BASIS San Antonio North Central	318 E Ramsey Rd	San Antonio, TX	78216	210-775-4125	877-9214	K-5	Geneva Ricowatson
BASIS San Antonio Primary Medical Center	8519 Floyd Curl Dr	San Antonio, TX	78240	210-319-5525	877-9214	K-5	David King
BASIS San Antonio Shavano Campus	2220 NW Military Hwy	San Antonio, TX	78213	210-874-9250		6-12	David King
Beta Academy	9701 Almeda Genoa Rd	Houston, TX	77075	832-331-2460		K-8	Latisha Andrews
Bexar County Academy	1485 Hillcrest Dr	San Antonio, TX	78228-3900	210-432-8600	432-8667	PK-8	Linda Sleeper
Bonham Academy	925 S Saint Marys St	San Antonio, TX	78205-3410	210-228-3300	223-3899	K-8	Will Webber
Brazos River Charter S	PO Box 949	Nemo, TX	76070-0949	254-898-9226	898-2297	K-12	Bengie Laning
Brazos S for Inquiry & Creativity	1055 W Tidwell Rd	Houston, TX	77091	713-681-1960	681-1979	K-6	Dr. John Bean
Brazos S for Inquiry & Creativity	1101 Pinemont Dr Ste P	Houston, TX	77018	713-290-0146	290-0103	PK-K	Margarie Bradford
Brazos S for Inquiry & Creativity	410 Bethel Ln	Bryan, TX	77802-1005	979-774-5032	774-5039	PK-8	Christopher Osgood
Brewer Academy	906 Merida St	San Antonio, TX	78207	210-438-6825	228-3091	6-12	Mary Olison
Bridgeway Prep Academy	4100 Alpha Rd Ste 1150	Dallas, TX	75244	214-257-8883		K-8	Dr. Natalie Davenport
Briscoe ES	2015 S Flores St	San Antonio, TX	78204-1936	210-228-3305	222-0822	PK-6	D'Les Herron
Brooks Academy of Science & Engineering	3803 Lyster Rd	San Antonio, TX	78235-5152	210-633-9006	633-9990	K-12	Sam De La Rosa
Brooks Collegiate Academy	4802 Vance Jackson Rd	San Antonio, TX	78230	210-850-3002	388-0293	K-12	Nammie Itchilov
Brooks Lone Star Academy	134 E Lambert St	San Antonio, TX	78204	210-998-4452		K-7	Patricia Lozano-Landry
Brooks Oaks Academy	6070 Babcock Rd	San Antonio, TX	78240	210-627-6013	627-6016	PK-5	Talisa Williams
Brown Leadership Academies Quest	5701 Red Bird Center Dr	Dallas, TX	75237-1917	972-709-4700	339-2273	K-8	Michelle Neely
Brown Leadership Academy Genesis	6901 S Westmoreland Rd	Dallas, TX	75237	972-709-4700	330-8686	PK-5	Chavalla Arnold
Brune Charter S	PO Box 399	Leakey, TX	78873-0399	830-232-7101	232-4279	1-12	Dr. Carmen Boatright
Burnham ES	7310 Bishop Flores Dr	El Paso, TX	79912-1429	915-584-9499	585-8814	K-5	Audrey Shetty
Buzbee Vocational HS	143 Forest Service Road 233	New Waverly, TX	77358	936-344-7235	344-6396	9-12	Will Gollihar
Cailloux-Najim S	PO Box 609	Ingram, TX	78025	830-367-6100	367-2611	1-12	Kelly Bluemel
Calallen Charter HS	46 Cornett Dr	Corpus Christi, TX	78410	361-242-5980	242-5682	10-12	Larissa Duke
Carpe Diem Innovative S	8038 W Military Dr	San Antonio, TX	78227	210-774-9284		6-12	Valerie Robertson
Carrollton Classical Academy	2400 N Josey Ln	Carrollton, TX	75006	972-245-2900	245-2999	K-5	Yvette Iglinsky
Cedar Hill Collegiate HS	1533 High Pointe Ln	Cedar Hill, TX	75104	469-272-2021	293-2652	9-12	Niki Edwards
Cedar Park Charter Academy	201 Buttercup Creek Blvd	Cedar Park, TX	78613	512-331-2980	590-8721	PK-12	Michele Kelsay
Cedars International Academy	8416 N Interstate 35	Austin, TX	78753-6438	512-419-1551	419-1581	PK-8	Heather Rauls
Cedars International HS	6700 Middle Fiskville Rd	Austin, TX	78752	512-956-4406		8-12	Steven Zipkes
Champions Academy	2113 Cypress Landing Dr	Houston, TX	77090	832-446-6762		K-5	Venora Goodie
Chaparral Star Academy	14046 Summit Dr	Austin, TX	78728-7115	512-989-2672	251-9799	K-12	Marsha Hagin
Chapel Hill Academy	4640 Sycamore School Rd	Fort Worth, TX	76133-7356	817-289-0242	289-3657	PK-5	Victoria Sendejo M.Ed.
Chavez Academy	4613 S Padre Island Dr	Corpus Christi, TX	78411-4413	361-561-5651	561-5654	9-12	Sandra Valencia
Cityscape S	6211 E Grand Ave	Dallas, TX	75223-1425	214-824-4747	824-4447	PK-5	Carol Thorne
Clay Classical Academy	3303 Potters House Way	Dallas, TX	75236-3037	469-251-5419		K-8	Jacqueline Owens
Clear Horizons Early College HS	13735 Beamer Rd Box 913	Houston, TX	77089	281-929-4657	284-9960	9-12	Dr. Brett Lemley
Clear View HS	400 S Walnut St	Webster, TX	77598-5120	281-284-1500	284-1505	9-12	Michael Houston
Coastal Village ES	721 10th St	Galveston, TX	77550	409-761-6800	765-5674	PK-4	Cherie Spencer
Collegiate HS	101 Baldwin Blvd	Corpus Christi, TX	78404-3805	361-698-2425	698-2427	9-12	Tracie Rodriguez
Compass Academy Charter S	5530 Billy Hext Rd	Odessa, TX	79765	432-272-1836		K-8	Dr. Ann Moore
Compass Rose Academy	8005 Outer Cir Dr	San Antonio, TX	78235	210-540-9265		6-12	Paul Morrissey
Comquest Academy	207 Peach St	Tomball, TX	77375-4733	281-516-0611	516-9807	7-12	Tanis Stanfield
Coppell Classical Academy	140 S Hertz Rd	Coppell, TX	75019	972-393-3077		K-8	Chris Sisk
Corinth Classical Academy	3600 Meadowview Dr	Corinth, TX	76210	940-497-0148		K-7	Aimee Giacumakis
Corinth Classical Academy	800 Point Vista Dr Ste 518	Hickory Creek, TX	75065	940-321-1144	708-0153	8-9	Kimberly Powell
Cornerstone Academy	9016 Westview Dr	Houston, TX	77055	713-251-1600	251-1615	6-8	Jill Wright
Corpus Christi College Prep HS	3501 S Padre Island Dr	Corpus Christi, TX	78415-2908	361-225-4240	561-5654	9-12	Stephen Mora
Corpus Christi Montessori S	822 Ayers St	Corpus Christi, TX	78404	361-852-0707	653-2340	PK-8	Cerise Weeks
Cove Charter Academy	2205 FM 3046	Copperas Cove, TX	76522	254-238-8231	247-3931	PK-12	Dr. Mike Anderson
Crosstimbers Academy	PO Box 1327	Weatherford, TX	76086-1327	817-594-6220	594-6227	9-12	Dr. Kendra Nelson
Cumberland Academy	1340 Shiloh Rd	Tyler, TX	75703	903-581-2890	581-1476	K-5	Andrew Griffith
Cumberland Academy HS	7200 Paluxy Dr	Tyler, TX	75703	903-630-7670		9-12	Kathy Parker
Cumberland Academy MS	1040 Shiloh Rd	Tyler, TX	75703	903-581-2890	581-1476	6-8	Timothy Schodowski
Dallas Can Academy Carrollton/Farmers	2720 Hollandale Ln	Farmers Branch, TX	75234-2035	972-243-2178	243-2669	9-12	Amparo Hakemack
Dallas Can Academy - Grant East	2901 Morgan Dr	Dallas, TX	75241-6516	972-228-4226		9-12	Rodney Milliner
Dallas Can Academy - Oak Cliff	325 W 12th St	Dallas, TX	75208-6502	214-943-2244	946-4427	9-12	Faustino Rivas
Dallas Can Academy - Pleasant Grove	1227 N Masters Dr	Dallas, TX	75217-3722	972-225-1194	225-1164	9-12	Mene Khepera
Dallas Can Academy Ross Avenue	4621 Ross Ave	Dallas, TX	75204-4994	214-824-4226	841-7951	9-12	Fernando Vadillo
Da Vinci S for Science and the Arts	785 Southwestern Dr	El Paso, TX	79912-1240	915-584-4024	581-9840	6-12	Richard Harrid
Denton Classical Academy	4420 Country Club Rd	Denton, TX	76210	940-565-8333	919-5316	K-1	Susan Thomas
Discovery MS	6400 Westpark Dr Ste 200	Houston, TX	77057	713-954-9528	953-0119	6-8	Albert Fernandez
Draw Academy	3920 Stoney Brook Dr	Houston, TX	77063-6406	713-706-3729	706-3711	PK-8	Fernando Donatti
Early College HS	3939 Valley View Ln	Farmers Branch, TX	75244-4906	972-968-6200	968-6210	9-12	Timothy Isaly
East Austin College Prep Academy	6002 Jain Ln	Austin, TX	78721	512-287-5000	928-1440	PK-5	Maria Cavazos
East Austin College Prep - MLK Campus	5800 E MLK Blvd	Austin, TX	78721	512-287-5050		6-12	Dr. Erica Gonzales
East Fort Worth Montessori Academy	501 Oakland Blvd	Fort Worth, TX	76103-1014	817-496-3003	496-3004	PK-5	Shello Tabb
East Texas Charter S Chadwick Campus	2402 Alpine Rd	Longview, TX	75601	903-753-9400	753-0285	9-12	Terry Lapic
Eden Park Academy	6215 Manchaca Rd Bldg D	Austin, TX	78745-4927	512-383-1800	383-0665	K-6	Lisa Drummond
Edinburg Classical Academy	2110 S McColl Rd	Edinburg, TX	78539	956-720-4361	720-4361	K-8	Dr. Alicia Luna
Education Center International Academy	201 N Erby Campbell Blvd	Royse City, TX	75189	972-636-2600	628-9124	K-8	Tonya Harris
Education Center International Academy	302 N Town East Blvd	Sunnyvale, TX	75182	214-628-9152	628-9124	K-8	Laverna Greenlee
Education Center International Academy	8200 Schrade Rd	Rowlett, TX	75088-4716	972-412-8080	628-9124	K-8	Lisa Hiatt
Ehrhart S	PO Box 7733	Beaumont, TX	77726-7733	409-839-8200	839-8242	PK-8	Corina Long
El Paso Academy East	11000 Argal Ct	El Paso, TX	79935-3712	915-590-8589	590-0052	9-12	Lionel Rubio
El Paso Academy West	201 W Redd Rd	El Paso, TX	79932-1903	915-845-7997	845-7522	9-12	Toni Kreye
El Paso Leadership Academy	1918 Texas Ave	El Paso, TX	79901-1917	915-298-3900		6-8	Omar Yanar
Empowerment HS	6400 Westpark Dr Ste 200	Houston, TX	77057	713-954-9528	953-0119	9-12	Jorge Martin
Energized For Excellence Academy ES	6201 Bissonnet St	Houston, TX	77081	713-773-3600	773-3630	K-5	Jose Cintron
Energized For Excellence ECC	6400 Southwest Fwy	Houston, TX	77074	281-779-4410	779-4414	PK-PK	Ada Cooper
Energized For Excellence ES	6107 Bissonnet St	Houston, TX	77081	713-773-3600	773-3630	K-5	Jose Cintron
Energized for STEM Academy HS	9220 Jutland Rd	Houston, TX	77033	713-641-1630	773-3630	9-12	Dr. Shavon Clark
Energized for STEM Academy MS	6107 Bissonnet	Houston, TX	77081	713-773-3600	773-3630	5-8	Adrienne Henderson
Etoile Academy Charter S	230 T C Jester Blvd Ste 242	Houston, TX	77007	713-201-5714		5-8	Kayleigh Colombero

School	Address	City,State	Zip code	Telephone	Fax	Grade	Contact
Evolution Academy Charter S	2414 Spring Cypress Rd	Spring, TX	77388	972-907-3755	907-3605	9-12	Julia Askew
Evolution Academy Charter S	3920 W Cardinal Dr	Beaumont, TX	77705	409-239-5553	347-7135	9-12	Cynthia Trigg
Evolution Academy Charter S	1101 S Sherman St	Richardson, TX	75081-4852	972-907-3755	907-3605	9-12	Veronica Durden
Excel Center	1015 Norwood Park Blvd	Austin, TX	78753	512-531-5500		9-12	Theresa Terlik
Excellence in Leadership Academy	915 W Expressway 83	Mission, TX	78572	956-424-9504	585-4673	PK-6	Elizabeth B. Lopez
Fallbrook Academy	12512 Walters Rd	Houston, TX	77014	281-880-1360		K-8	Demetris White
Ford Academy Alameda S for Art & Design	318 W Houston St	San Antonio, TX	78205-2427	210-226-4031	271-0125	9-12	Wayne Boggs
Fort Worth Academy of Fine Arts	3901 S Hulen St	Fort Worth, TX	76109-3321	817-924-1482	926-9932	3-12	Randy Dean
Fort Worth Can Academy	6620 Westcreek Dr	Fort Worth, TX	76133	817-531-3223		9-12	Ku-Masi Lewis
Fort Worth Can Academy South Campus	1316 E Lancaster Ave	Fort Worth, TX	76102-6634	817-735-1515	735-1465	9-12	William Arevelo
Founders Classical Academy	500 Parker Sq	Flower Mound, TX	75028-7431	972-899-2521		K-5	Sam Vanderplas
Founders Classical Academy	790 Windbell Cir	Mesquite, TX	75149-3116	214-444-7255		K-8	Dr. Ferrell Yeokum
Founders Classical Academy in Dallas	8510 Military Pkwy	Dallas, TX	75227	469-607-6277		K-6	Oscar Ortiz
Founders Classical Academy in Lewisville	1010 Bellaire Blvd	Lewisville, TX	75067-5650	469-464-3415	524-9980	K-12	Jason Caros
Founders Classical Academy of Leander	1303 Leander Dr	Leander, TX	78641-2037	512-259-0103	532-6503	K-12	Kathleen O'Toole
Founders Classical Academy of Schertz	8453 F 1518 N	Schertz, TX	78154	210-510-2618		K-7	Nathanael Rea
Frank Inspire Academy	11216 Bandera Rd	San Antonio, TX	78250	210-638-5900	638-5975	K-12	Nino Etienne
Garcia Early College HS	5241 University Blvd	Laredo, TX	78041	956-273-7700	795-8185	9-12	Israel Castilla
Garland Can Academy	2256 Arapaho Rd	Garland, TX	75044	972-441-7202		9-12	Dr. Daniel Johnson
Garza-Gonzales Charter S	4129 Greenwood Dr	Corpus Christi, TX	78416-1841	361-881-9988	881-9994	PK-12	Adolfo Chapa
Gateway Academy Sierra Vista	4620 S Lucy	Laredo, TX	78046	956-723-0345	712-1112	9-12	Odie Arambula
Gateway Academy Townlake	1230 Townlake Dr	Laredo, TX	78041-3786	956-722-0747	722-0767	9-12	Olga Trevino
Gateway Charter Academy	1015 E Wheatland Rd	Dallas, TX	75241	214-375-1921	375-1842	PK-12	Raymond Edward
Gateway College Prep S	3360 Westinghouse Rd	Georgetown, TX	78626	512-868-4947	868-4946	K-12	Alan Santucci
Gateway Tech HS	2951 Williams Dr	Georgetown, TX	78628	512-868-5299	869-3030	9-12	Jolene Bruce
GCCLR Institute of Technology	4125 Greenwood Dr	Corpus Christi, TX	78416	361-881-9988	814-1687	PK-12	Adolfo Chapa
Georgetown Charter Academy	302 Serenada Dr	Georgetown, TX	78628	512-863-9236	863-9290	PK-8	Josiah Perkins
Gervin Academy	6944 S Sunbelt Dr	San Antonio, TX	78218-3335	210-568-8800	568-8897	PK-12	Jesse Villanueva M.Ed.
Gervin Technology Center	3030 E Commerce St	San Antonio, TX	78220-1013	210-587-3576	587-3587	10-12	Keith Thomas
Golden Rule Charter S DeSoto	135 W Wintergreen Rd	DeSoto, TX	75115	469-248-4463	248-4471	PK-5	Tonja Frazier
Golden Rule Charter S Grand Prairie	1729 Avenue B	Grand Prairie, TX	75051	214-988-3257		PK-2	Jim Wright
Golden Rule Charter S Illinois	2602 W Illinois Ave	Dallas, TX	75233-1002	214-333-9330	333-9325	PK-8	Vicente Delgado
Golden Rule Charter S Pleasant Grove	2602 W Illinois Ave	Dallas, TX	75233	469-341-5780		PK-4	Diana Lara
Golden Rule Charter S Sunnyside	2602 W Illinois Ave	Dallas, TX	75233	214-393-6911		PK-4	Jim Wright
Goodwater Montessori Charter S	710 Stadium Dr	Georgetown, TX	78626	512-966-5484		PK-8	Nancy Gribble-Tay M.Ed.
Grand Prairie Collegiate Institute	401 E Grand Prairie Rd	Grand Prairie, TX	75051	972-343-3120	343-3159	6-12	Darnisha Carreathers
Great Hearts Irving	3350 W Story Rd	Irving, TX	75038	469-759-3030		K-9	Philip Althage
Great Hearts Monte Vista North	319 E Mulberry Ave	San Antonio, TX	78212	210-888-9485		6-12	Peter Crawford
Great Hearts Monte Vista South	211 Belknap Pl	San Antonio, TX	78212	210-888-9484		K-5	Mandi Cannon
Great Hearts Northern Oaks	17223 Jones Maltsberger Rd	San Antonio, TX	78247	210-888-9843		K-9	Trinette Keffer
Great Hearts Western Hills	8702 Ingram Rd	San Antonio, TX	78245			K-4	Robby Kuhlman
Harmony S of Achievement	16209 Kieth Harrow Blvd	Houston, TX	77084	281-855-2500	858-2505	K-5	Melissa Knight
Harmony S of Advancement	3171 N Sam Houston Pkwy W	Houston, TX	77038	281-741-8899	741-8006	9-12	Faith Oner
Harmony S of Business-Dallas	8080 President George Bush	Dallas, TX	75252	214-321-0100	919-4352	K-12	Muhammed Gecit
Harmony S of Discovery	6270 Barker Cypress Rd	Houston, TX	77084-1628	281-861-5105	656-8525	K-10	Adnan Karanci
Harmony S of Enrichment	3207 N Sam Houston Pkwy W	Houston, TX	77038	281-999-0606		K-5	Brent Bardo
Harmony S of Excellence	2015 SW Loop 410	San Antonio, TX	78227-2534	210-645-7166	645-7178	K-12	Bambi Teaff
Harmony School of Excellence	7340 Gessner Rd	Houston, TX	77040	713-983-8668	983-8667	K-12	Hasan Sazci
Harmony S of Excellence - Austin	2100 E Saint Elmo Rd	Austin, TX	78744	512-693-0000	693-0008	K-12	Engin Dogan
Harmony S of Excellence El Paso	9435 Betel Dr	El Paso, TX	79907	915-307-4412	307-4772	K-8	
Harmony S of Excellence-Endeavor	5668 W Little York Rd	Houston, TX	77091	281-999-8400	999-8404	K-12	Kamil Yilmaz
Harmony S of Exploration	9305 W Sam Houston Pkwy S	Houston, TX	77099	713-831-7406	831-7408	K-3	Nora Morales
Harmony S of Fine Arts and Technology	9115 Kirby Dr	Houston, TX	77054	832-433-7001	433-7083	K-9	Atila Akyurek
Harmony S of Ingenuity	10555 Stella Link Rd	Houston, TX	77025	713-664-1020	664-1025	K-12	Recep Yilmaz
Harmony S of Innovation	13522 W Airport Blvd	Sugar Land, TX	77478	713-302-6445	302-6745	7-12	
Harmony S of Innovation	3451 Dana Ave	Brownsville, TX	78526	956-544-1348	544-1349	6-12	Leyla Trevino
Harmony S of Innovation	1110 S Valley Mills Dr	Beverly Hills, TX	76711	254-235-0321	235-1373	6-12	Serkan Beyhan
Harmony S of Innovation	13522 W Airport Blvd	Sugar Land, TX	77498	281-302-6445	302-0745	7-12	Alpaslan Uzgoren
Harmony S of Innovation	9421 W Sam Houston Pkwy S	Houston, TX	77099-1898	713-541-3030	541-3032	PK-8	Ali Yilmaz
Harmony S of Innovation - Austin	2124 E Saint Elmo Rd	Austin, TX	78744	512-300-0895	330-4225	K-5	Tiffany Molina
Harmony S of Innovation - Dallas	1024 W Rosemeade Pkwy	Carrollton, TX	75007	469-892-5556	892-5667	K-12	Clinton Barnes
Harmony S of Innovation - El Paso	5210 Fairbanks Dr	El Paso, TX	79924	915-757-2929	757-2202	K-12	Riza Gurlek
Harmony S of Innovation - Euless	701 S Industrial Blvd # 115	Euless, TX	76040	817-554-2800	684-9405	K-4	Crystal McAnalley
Harmony S of Innovation-Fort Worth	8100 S Hulen St	Fort Worth, TX	76123	817-386-5505	977-1727	6-12	Mehmet Basoglu
Harmony S of Innovation - Garland	2250 Firewheel Pkwy	Garland, TX	75040	469-814-0059	814-0579	6-12	Murat Tunca
Harmony S of Innovation-Laredo	4608 Daugherty Ave	Laredo, TX	78041	956-568-9495	568-9490	K-12	Gelaldine Salas
Harmony S of Innovation - San Antonio	8125 Glen Mont	San Antonio, TX	78239	210-265-1715	265-5364	K-8	Mert Aykanat
Harmony S of Nature & Athletics	8120 W Camp Wisdom Rd	Dallas, TX	75249-4402	972-296-1000	296-2125	K-12	Bilal Ozen
Harmony S of Political Science	13415 Ranch Road 620 N	Austin, TX	78717	512-284-9880	284-9632	5-12	Waydon Stengler
Harmony S of Science - Austin	11800 Stonehollow Dr # 100	Austin, TX	78758	512-821-1700	821-1702	K-8	Allanur Agaberdiyev
Harmony S of Science - Houston	5435 S Braeswood Blvd	Houston, TX	77096-4001	713-729-4400	729-6600	K-8	Celal Giret
Harmony S of Technology	3203 N Sam Houston Pkwy W	Houston, TX	77038	281-444-1555	444-1015	K-8	Sezgin Aydi
Harmony Science Academy	13415 W Bellfort Ave	Sugar Land, TX	77478	713-265-2525	265-2565	PK-6	Afreem Merchant
Harmony Science Academy	12200 Anderson Mill Rd	Austin, TX	78726	512-494-5151	494-5177	PK-4	Yilker Yilmaz
Harmony Science Academy - Austin	930 E Rundberg Ln	Austin, TX	78753-4826	512-835-7900	835-7901	6-12	Agil Sharifov
Harmony Science Academy - Beaumont	4055 Calder Ave	Beaumont, TX	77706-4925	409-838-4000	838-4009	PK-12	Klediol Murati
Harmony Science Academy - Brownsville	1124 Central Blvd	Brownsville, TX	78520	956-574-9555	574-9558	PK-12	Mustafa Altindag
Harmony Science Academy - Bryan	2031 S Texas Ave	Bryan, TX	77802-1834	979-779-2100	779-2110	PK-8	Laura Mattingly
Harmony Science Academy - Carrollton	1024 W Rosemeade Pkwy	Carrollton, TX	75007	972-394-9560		6-12	
Harmony Science Academy - Dallas	12005 Forestgate Dr	Dallas, TX	75243	214-954-7277	954-7277	PK-12	Serif Mercan
Harmony Science Academy - El Paso	9405 Betel Dr	El Paso, TX	79907-3457	915-859-4620	859-4630	K-12	Selcuk Bakir
Harmony Science Academy - Euless	701 S Industrial Blvd # 115	Euless, TX	76040	817-354-3000	354-3008	5-12	Maksat Altiyev
Harmony Science Academy - Fort Worth	5651 Westcreek Dr	Fort Worth, TX	76133-2248	817-263-0700	263-0705	K-12	Serena Jackson
Harmony Science Academy - Garland	2302 Firewheel Pkwy	Garland, TX	75040	972-212-4777	212-4778	K-5	Jennifer Hornsby
Harmony Science Academy - Grand Prairie	1102 NW 7th St	Grand Prairie, TX	75050	972-642-9911	642-9922	K-12	Angela Knapp
Harmony Science Academy HS	9431 W Sam Houston Pkwy S	Houston, TX	77099	713-492-0214	383-2839	9-12	
Harmony Science Academy - Katy	22400 Grand Corner Dr	Katy, TX	77494	832-437-3926	437-3927	K-5	Jasmeen Kohli
Harmony Science Academy - Laredo	4401 San Francisco Ave	Laredo, TX	78041	956-712-1177	712-1188	6-8	Mustafa Ayik
Harmony Science Academy - Lubbock	1516 53rd St	Lubbock, TX	79412-2916	806-747-1000	747-1005	K-12	Hakan Simsek
Harmony Science Academy - North Austin	1421 Wells Branch Pkwy #200	Pflugerville, TX	78660	512-251-5000	251-5001	6-12	Fr. Engin Dogan
Harmony Science Academy - Odessa	2755 N Grandview Ave	Odessa, TX	79762-6952	432-363-6000	363-6001	K-12	Cetin Demir
Harmony Science Academy - San Antonio	8505 Lakeside Pkwy	San Antonio, TX	78245	210-674-7788	674-7766	K-12	Yasar Cakir
Harmony Science Academy - Waco	1900 N Valley Mills Dr	Waco, TX	76710-2559	254-751-7878	751-7877	K-12	Serkan Beyhan
Harris MS	325 Pruitt Ave	San Antonio, TX	78204-2598	210-228-1220	226-9448	6-8	Dr. Carol Velazquez
Harvest Preparatory Academy	17770 Imperial Valley Dr	Houston, TX	77060	832-446-3138	446-6362	K-6	Michael Blackshire
Harvey College Prep Harvey E Najim	926 S WW White Rd	San Antonio, TX	78220	210-239-4900		6-6	Yvonne Anglada
Hawthorne Academy	115 W Josephine St	San Antonio, TX	78212-4125	210-738-9795	733-1495	K-8	Guadalupe Rodriguez
Helping Hands Charter S	2200 E 6th St	Austin, TX	78702-3457	512-538-0177	232-9177	K-7	Holly Engleman
Heritage Academy	8750 Fourwinds Dr	San Antonio, TX	78239	210-510-4640	615-3954	PK-8	Eric Davis
Heritage Academy	709 Kings Way	Del Rio, TX	78840	830-774-6230	774-6235	6-12	Judy Galindo
Highland Park ES	635 Rigsby Ave	San Antonio, TX	78210-3099	210-228-3335	533-8132	PK-5	Dr. Rose Engelbrecht
High Point Academy	1256 N Jim Wright Fwy	Wht Settlemt, TX	76108-1048	817-600-6401		K-10	Katie Stellar
Hope ES	4301 32nd St	Port Arthur, TX	77642	409-983-3244	983-6408	PK-5	Bobby Lopez
Hope S	2849 9th Ave	Port Arthur, TX	77642-3961	409-983-3244	983-6408	6-12	Bobby Lopez
Horizon Montessori III - Harlingen	2802 S 77 Sunshine Strip	Harlingen, TX	78550	956-423-8200	423-8207	PK-7	Dr. Patricia Quesada
Horizon Montessori II - Weslaco	1222 W Sugar Cane Dr	Weslaco, TX	78599-3892	956-969-0044	969-0065	PK-8	Valerie Uresti-Reyes
Horizon Montessori I - Mc Allen	221 N Main St	McAllen, TX	78501	956-668-1400	668-1404	PK-8	John Gonzalez
Houston A+ Challenge	2700 Southwest Frwy Ste B	Houston, TX	77098	832-519-9590	840-5616	6-8	Dr. Scott Van Beck
Houston A+ Up University	2700 Southwest Frwy Ste B	Houston, TX	77098	832-519-9590	840-5616	6-8	Gabrielle Gunn
Houston Can Academy - Hobby	9020 Gulf Fwy	Houston, TX	77017-7007	832-379-4226	944-6736	9-12	Yardley Williams
Houston Can Academy - North	3401 Hardy St	Houston, TX	77009-5928	713-659-4226	651-1493	9-12	Roslyn Philpott
Houston Can Academy Southwest	9745 Bissonett Dr Bldg D	Houston, TX	77036	281-931-4324		9-12	Dr. James Troutman
Houston Gateway Acad - Elite Coll Prep	7310 Bowie St	Houston, TX	77012-2904	832-649-2700	649-3092	PK-8	Tiffany Wright
Houston Gateway Academy - Coral Campus	1020 Coral St	Houston, TX	77012-2906	832-649-2700	649-3092	PK-12	Ignacio Arroyo
Houston Gateway Academy - Evergreen	3400 Evergreen Dr	Houston, TX	77087-3715	713-644-8292	649-3092	PK-8	Yuridia Lublano
Houston Heights HS	1125 Lawrence St	Houston, TX	77008-6651	713-868-9797	868-9750	9-12	Richard Mik
Houston State Univ Charter S	22801 Aldine Westfield Rd	Spring, TX	77373	936-294-1103	294-1102	PK-6	Dr. Stacey Edmonson
Huston Academy	680 Peach Orchard Rd	Stephenville, TX	76401-4938	254-965-8883	965-8654	7-12	Carol Taylor
IDEA Academy Alamo	325 State Highway 495	Alamo, TX	78516-6877	956-588-4005	588-4006	K-5	Ana Garza
IDEA Academy Allan	1701 Vargas Rd	Austin, TX	78741	512-646-2800	646-2801	PK-12	Disha Jain
IDEA Academy Brackenridge	5555 Old Pearsall Rd	San Antonio, TX	78242	210-239-4300	239-4301	PK-1	Elisha McCardell
IDEA Academy Brownsville	4395 Paredes Line Rd	Brownsville, TX	78526-1296	956-832-5150	832-5716	K-5	Erica Matamoros
IDEA Academy Carver	217 Robinson Pl	San Antonio, TX	78202-2751	210-223-8885	223-8970	K-5	Guadalupe Diaz
IDEA Academy Donna	401 S 1st St	Donna, TX	78537-3055	956-464-0203	464-8532	PK-5	Sylvia Verdooran
IDEA Academy Eastside	2519 Martin Luther King Dr	San Antonio, TX	78203	210-239-4800	239-4801	K-8	Janie Gomez
IDEA Academy Edinburg	2553 N Roegiers Rd	Edinburg, TX	78541-8602	956-287-6100	287-6101	PK-5	Nora Perez
IDEA Academy Ewing Halsell	2523 W Ansley Blvd	San Antonio, TX	78224	210-239-4850	239-4851	PK-1	Pam Ray

School	Address	City,State	Zip code	Telephone	Fax	Grade	Contact
IDEA Academy Frontier	2800 S Dakota Ave	Brownsville, TX	78521-6133	956-541-2002	541-5561	K-5	Dora Villegas
IDEA Academy Harvey E Najim	926 S WW White Rd	San Antonio, TX	78220	210-239-4900		PK-1	Hope Walker
IDEA Academy McAllen	201 N Bentsen Rd	McAllen, TX	78501-8297	956-429-4100	429-4126	K-5	Darlene Espinoza
IDEA Academy Mission	1600 S Schuerbach Rd	Mission, TX	78572	956-583-8315	424-3248	K-5	C. Cavazos-Escamilla
IDEA Academy Monterrey Park	222 SW 39th St	San Antonio, TX	78237	210-239-4200	239-4201	K-5	Martha Short
IDEA Academy North Mission	2706 N Holland Ave	Mission, TX	78572	956-424-4300	424-4301	PK-8	Adrianna Villarreal
IDEA Academy Pharr	600 E Las Milpas Rd	Pharr, TX	78577-9864	956-283-1515	783-1557	PK-5	Sonia Aguilar
IDEA Academy Rio Grande City	2803 W Monarch Ln	Rio Grande City, TX	78582	956-263-4900		PK-1	Fernando Salinas
IDEA Academy Riverview	30 Palm Blvd	Brownsville, TX	78520	956-832-5900	832-5901	PK-8	Radha Guajardo
IDEA Academy Rundberg	9504 N IH 35	Austin, TX	78753	512-822-4800	822-4801	K-8	Karen Weissinger
IDEA Academy San Benito	2151 Russell Ln	San Benito, TX	78586-8969	956-399-5252	361-9478	K-5	Christina Villarreal
IDEA Academy San Juan	200 N Nebraska Ave	San Juan, TX	78589	956-702-5150	702-4497	K-5	Melissa Finch
IDEA Academy South Flores	6919 S Flores St	San Antonio, TX	78221-1943	210-239-4150		K-5	Hailey McCarthy
IDEA Academy Tres Lagos	5200 Tres Lagos Blvd	McAllen, TX	78504	956-287-6900		PK-2	Benigna Carcano
IDEA Academy Walzem	6445 Walzem Rd	San Antonio, TX	78239	210-239-4600	239-4601	K-5	Ryane Burke
IDEA Academy Weslaco	2931 E Sugar Cane Dr	Weslaco, TX	78599-2723	956-351-4100	351-4101	K-5	Sylvia Mejia
IDEA Academy Weslaco Pike	1000 E Pike Blvd	Weslaco, TX	78596	956-351-4850	351-4851	PK-5	Silvia Martinez
IDEA Bluff Springs Academy	1700 E Slaughter Ln	Austin, TX	78744	512-822-4200	822-4201	K-3	Jayne Pocquette
IDEA College Prep Alamo	325 State Highway 495	Alamo, TX	78516-6877	956-588-4005	588-4006	6-12	Mayra Martinez
IDEA College Prep Allan	220 Foremost Dr	Austin, TX	78745	512-646-2800	646-2801	6-12	Nathan Lowry
IDEA College Prep Bluff Springs	1700 E Slaughter Ln	Austin, TX	78744	512-822-4200		6-7	DeAnna Bruce
IDEA College Prep Brackenridge	5555 Old Pearsall Rd	San Antonio, TX	78242	210-239-4300	239-4301	6-6	Zachary Stingl
IDEA College Prep Brownsville	4395 Paredes Line Rd	Brownsville, TX	78526	956-832-5150	832-5716	6-12	Virginia Callaway
IDEA College Prep Carver	217 Robinson Pl	San Antonio, TX	78202-2751	210-223-8885	223-8970	6-12	Chang John Yu
IDEA College Prep Donna	401 S 1st St	Donna, TX	78537-3055	956-464-0203	464-8532	6-12	Amanda Canales
IDEA College Prep Edinburg	2553 N Roegiers Rd	Edinburg, TX	78541-8602	956-287-6100	287-6101	6-12	Ramiro Gomez
IDEA College Prep Ewing Halsell	2523 W Ansley Blvd	San Antonio, TX	78224	210-239-4850	239-4851	6-6	William Chermak
IDEA College Prep Frontier	2800 S Dakota Ave	Brownsville, TX	78521	956-541-2002	541-5561	6-12	Virginia Callaway
IDEA College Prep Judson	13427 Judson Rd	San Antonio, TX	78233	210-529-3600	529-3601	6-7	Joaquin Hernandez
IDEA College Prep Mays	1210 Horal Rd	San Antonio, TX	78245	210-529-3200		6-7	Gerald Boyd
IDEA College Prep McAllen	201 N Bentsen Rd	McAllen, TX	78501-8297	956-429-4100	429-4126	6-12	Jon Alvarez
IDEA College Prep Mission	1600 S Schuerbach Rd	Mission, TX	78572-1217	956-583-8315	424-3248	6-12	Matthew Kyle
IDEA College Prep Monterrey Park	222 SW 39th St	San Antonio, TX	78237	210-239-4200	239-4201	6-9	Jonathan Tyrrell
IDEA College Prep Pharr	600 E Las Milpas Rd	Pharr, TX	78577-9864	956-283-1515	783-1557	6-12	Claudia Ash
IDEA College Prep Rio Grande City	2803 W Monarch Ln	Rio Grande City, TX	78582	956-263-4900		6-6	Fernando Salinas
IDEA College Prep San Benito	2151 Russell Ln	San Benito, TX	78586-8969	956-399-5252	361-9478	6-12	Janet Crenshaw
IDEA College Prep San Juan	600 E Sioux Rd	San Juan, TX	78589-3491	956-588-4021	588-4030	6-12	Lindsey Campbell
IDEA College Prep South Flores	6919 S Flores St	San Antonio, TX	78221	210-239-4150		6-10	Constantine Polites
IDEA College Prep Toros	315 E Palm Dr	Edinburg, TX	78539	956-351-4350		6-12	Brad Scott
IDEA College Prep Tres Lagos	5200 Tres Lagos Blvd	McAllen, TX	78504	956-287-6900		6-6	Megan Arenas-Goossen
IDEA College Prep Walzem	6445 Walzem Rd	San Antonio, TX	78239	210-239-4600	239-4601	6-9	Dr. Andrea Fernandez
IDEA College Prep Weslaco	2931 E Sugar Cane Dr	Weslaco, TX	78599	956-351-4100	351-4101	6-12	Leanna Sarinana
IDEA College Prep Weslaco Pike	1000 E Pike Blvd	Weslaco, TX	78596	956-351-4850	351-4851	6-9	Stephanie Sullenger
IDEA Judson Academy	13427 Judson Rd	San Antonio, TX	78233	210-529-3600	529-3601	K-3	Hope Williams
IDEA Mays Academy	1210 Horal Dr	San Antonio, TX	78245	210-529-3200		K-3	Maria Sepulveda
IDEA Quest Academy	14001 N Rooth Rd	Edinburg, TX	78541-4194	956-287-1003	287-2737	K-5	Rosa Chapa
IDEA Quest College Prep S	14001 N Rooth Rd	Edinburg, TX	78541-4194	956-287-1003	287-2737	6-12	Jose De Leon
Imagine International Academy	2860 Virginia Pkwy	Mc Kinney, TX	75071	214-491-1500	491-1504	K-12	Don Menzies
Innovation Academy	3900 University Blvd	Tyler, TX	75799	903-730-3988	705-4330	K-12	Aimee Dennis
Innovation Academy	3201 N Eastman Rd	Longview, TX	75605	903-663-8219	705-4380	1-12	Angela Ladine
Innovation Academy	100 University Blvd	Palestine, TX	75801	903-727-2326		1-12	Becky Rutledge
Inspired for Excellence Academy West	12525 Fondren Rd	Houston, TX	77035	832-834-5295	641-1669	5-8	Pamela Caviel
Inspired Vision Academy Secondary S	8501 Bruton Rd	Dallas, TX	75217-1909	972-285-5758	285-0061	7-12	Nick Kongamnach
Inspired Vision Charter ES	8421 Bohannon Dr	Dallas, TX	75217-1917	214-391-7964	391-7954	PK-4	Sherqueena Myles
Inspired Vision Elementary 5-6	8301 Bruton Rd	Dallas, TX	75217	214-391-7964		5-6	Clayton Claridy
International Leadership of Texas ES	3501 S Great Southwest Pkwy	Grand Prairie, TX	75052	469-348-7960		K-8	Valerie Layne
International Leadership of Texas ES	4131 Rufe Snow Dr	N Richlnd Hls, TX	76180	817-345-0926		K-8	Gerald Doyle
International Leadership of Texas ES	24406 Franz Rd	Katy, TX	77493	281-394-9417		K-8	Dr. Melanie De Sautu
International Leadership of Texas ES	5901 Boca Raton Blvd	Fort Worth, TX	76112	817-395-1776	446-4270	K-8	Nikia Smith
International Leadership of Texas ES	1900 W Pleasant Run Rd	Lancaster, TX	75146	469-862-4237		K-8	Senta Wilson
International Leadership of Texas ES	500 Old Decatur Rd N	Saginaw, TX	76179	682-250-3600		K-8	Nanette Coleman
International Leadership of Texas ES	15300 Bellaire Blvd	Houston, TX	77083	346-203-4126	933-8129	K-8	Charlie Butler Ed.D.
International Leadership of Texas ES	9898 Windmill Lakes Blvd	Houston, TX	77075	832-667-0453		K-8	Dr. Leonard Brown
International Leadership of Texas ES	2301 Heritage Trace Pkwy	Fort Worth, TX	76177	817-665-0646	232-8220	K-8	Dr. Dora Renaud
International Leadership of Texas ES	3301 N Shiloh Rd	Garland, TX	75044	972-414-8000	495-2405	K-8	Jade Esquivel
International Leadership of Texas ES	4950 S Bowen Rd	Arlington, TX	76017	817-419-9281		K-8	Dionel Waters
International Leadership of Texas HS	10537 NW Highway 287	Fort Worth, TX	76131	682-250-3701	306-6039	9-12	Rodney Cooksy
International Leadership of Texas HS	20055 Beechnut St	Richmond, TX	77407	832-222-9470	222-9112	9-12	Mark Hemphill
International Leadership of Texas HS	4413 N Shiloh Rd	Garland, TX	75044	972-414-3414		9-12	Karen Marx
International Leadership of Texas HS	2851 Ragland Rd	Grand Prairie, TX	75052	682-808-5960		9-12	Quentyn Seamster
Irving MS	1300 Delgado St	San Antonio, TX	78207-1467	210-738-9740	734-0941	6-8	Dr. Olivia Almanza-Pena
iSchool at Amarillo	6000 S Georgia St	Amarillo, TX	79118	806-352-0171	397-5456	K-12	Michael Griffin
iSchool High at Houston University Park	20515 State Highway 249	Houston, TX	77070	281-251-5770	643-9673	9-12	Stacy Bare
iSchool High at Montgomery The Woodlands	3232 College Park Dr	The Woodlands, TX	77384	936-231-8594	861-3810	9-12	Guamma Goff
iSchool High of Hickory Creek	800 Point Vista Rd Ste 518	Hickory Creek, TX	75065	940-321-1144		9-12	Marci Stapp
iSchool High of Lewisville	1800 Lakeway Dr Ste 100	Lewisville, TX	75057-6438	972-317-2470	397-1633	9-12	Gary Wilhelmi
Jubilee Aspire to Lead	201 N 19th St	Kingsville, TX	78363	361-516-0840		PK-3	Noemy Garcia
Jubilee Brownsville	4955 Pablo Kisel Blvd	Brownsville, TX	78520	956-509-2690	509-2326	PK-12	Yolanda Cantu
Jubilee Destiny	2601 Brothwell Rd	Harlingen, TX	78552	956-440-8447		PK-5	Dr. Cindy Sadler
Jubilee Harlingen	4501 W Expressway 83	Harlingen, TX	78552	956-364-2456	364-2453	PK-6	Dr. Cindy Sadler
Jubilee Highland Hills	1515 Goliad Rd	San Antonio, TX	78223	210-634-7590		PK-8	Trina Cardenas
Jubilee Highland Park	501 E Drexel Ave	San Antonio, TX	78210	210-801-8030	801-8043	PK-8	Martha Kizer
Jubilee Kingsville	1727 Senator Carlos Truan	Kingsville, TX	78363	210-221-2591	221-2594	4-8	Noemy Garcia
Jubilee - Lake View University Prep	325 Castroville Rd	San Antonio, TX	78207	210-431-7355		PK-12	Diana Wagner
Jubilee Leadership Academy	4150 Jaime J Zapata Ave	Brownsville, TX	78521	956-410-8165		PK-12	
Jubilee Livingway	350 Ruben M Torres Blvd	Brownsville, TX	78520	956-554-0999	554-9701	PK-5	Cecilia Septimo
Jubilee San Antonio	4427 Chandler	San Antonio, TX	78222	210-278-3880	278-3929	PK-12	Hector Gomez
Jubilee Wells Branch	3711 Shoreline Dr	Austin, TX	78728	512-872-8400	872-8445	PK-8	William Ihlenfeldt
Kandy Stripe Academy	8701 Delilah St	Houston, TX	77033-3827	713-734-4909	731-7890	PK-8	Cassandra Anderson
Kauffman Leadership Academy	314 W Wilson St	Cleburne, TX	76033	682-459-2800		6-12	Dr. Theresa Kauffman
Kelley Charter S	802 Oblate Dr	San Antonio, TX	78216-7330	210-431-9881	253-2198	PK-6	Cristen Martens
KI Charter Academy	120 Bert Brown St	San Marcos, TX	78666-5803	512-396-8500	754-3894	1-12	Jerry Lager
King Academy	3501 Martin Luther King Dr	San Antonio, TX	78220-2325	210-978-7935	223-6907	K-8	Natasha Pinnix
Kingsland S	136 Real St	Kingsland, TX	78639	325-388-0020	388-0021	K-6	Meloni Puishes
KIPP 3D Academy	500 Tidwell Rd	Houston, TX	77022-2122	832-230-0566		5-8	Alison Cumbley
KIPP: Climb Academy	8805 Ferndale	Houston, TX	77017	832-230-0578		K-2	Lindsey Smith
KIPP: Pleasant Grove MS	2200 N Saint Augustine Rd	Dallas, TX	75227	972-323-4235	323-4236	5-8	Delshon Henry
KIPP: Pleasant Grove PS	2200 Saint Augustine	Dallas, TX	75227	972-323-4230		PK-4	Dexter Chaney
KIPP: Prime College Preparatory	8805 Ferndale	Houston, TX	77017	832-230-0578		5-6	Robbie Gill
KIPP Academy MS	10711 Kipp Way Dr	Houston, TX	77099-2675	832-328-1051	328-0178	5-8	Steven Khadam
KIPP Academy MS West	8500 Highway 6 S	Houston, TX	77083	832-230-0573		5-8	Steven Khadam-Hir
KIPP Aspire Academy	239 Stark St	San Antonio, TX	78204	210-735-7300	735-7305	5-8	Bradley Tarrance
KIPP Austin Academy of Arts & Letters	8509 FM 969 Ste A	Austin, TX	78724-5702	512-501-3640	501-3641	5-8	Kevin Newman
KIPP Austin Beacon Prep	5107 I-35 S Ste A	Austin, TX	78744	512-651-1918	924-2872	5-8	Katie Hayes
KIPP Austin Brave HS	8509 FM 969 Building 676	Austin, TX	78724	512-651-2225		9-12	Stephanie Burns
KIPP Austin College Prep S	8004 Cameron Rd	Austin, TX	78754	512-501-4969	637-6899	5-8	Katie Shapiro
KIPP Austin Collegiate	8509 FM 969 Ste 676	Austin, TX	78724	512-501-3586	501-3587	9-12	Carrie Donovan
KIPP Austin Comunidad	8004 Cameron Rd	Austin, TX	78754	512-501-3911	870-9224	K-4	Justin Scott
KIPP Austin Connections	8509 FM 969 Ste 629	Austin, TX	78724-5713	512-651-5537	870-9537	K-4	Bethany Blevins
KIPP Austin Leadership Elementary	5107 I-35 S Ste A	Austin, TX	78744	512-651-2168		K-4	Nicole Seltman
KIPP Austin Obras	5107 I-35 S Ste A	Austin, TX	78744	512-651-2069		K-4	Matthew Frank
KIPP Austin Vista MS	5107 I-35 S Ste A	Austin, TX	78744	512-651-1921	461-8086	5-8	Laura Farber
KIPP Camino Academy	4343 W Commerce St	San Antonio, TX	78237	210-829-4200	829-4207	5-8	Juan Juarez
KIPP CONNECT S	6700 Bellaire Blvd	Houston, TX	77074	281-879-3023		PK-4	Lisa Williams
KIPP Destiny ES	3663 W Camp Wisdom Rd	Dallas, TX	75237	972-708-8500		K-4	Katie Gilleland
KIPP Destiny MS	3663 W Camp Wisdom Rd	Dallas, TX	75237-2507	972-708-8500		5-8	Esmeralda Cardoso
KIPP DREAM Prep	500 Tidwell Rd	Houston, TX	77022	832-230-6082		PK-4	Haley Simonton-Bonilla
KIPP Esperanza Dual Language Academy	103 Tuleta Dr	San Antonio, TX	78212-3176	210-317-2731		K-K	Michael Shay
KIPP Explore Academy	5402 Lawndale St	Houston, TX	77023	832-230-0547	924-5046	PK-4	Amy Stabile
KIPP Generations Collegiate	500 Tidwell Rd	Houston, TX	77022-2122	832-230-0566	328-0178	9-12	Nancy Flores
KIPP Houston HS	10711 Kipp Way Dr	Houston, TX	77099-2675	832-328-1082	838-4293	9-12	Mohamad Maarouf
KIPP Intrepid Preparatory S	5402 Lawndale St	Houston, TX	77023	281-879-3100	463-7318	6-8	Joy Taluyo
KIPP Legacy Preparatory S	9606 Mesa Dr	Houston, TX	77078-3024	832-230-0567	491-7311	PK-3	Monique Payton
KIPP Liberation College Preparatory S	5400 Martin Luther King	Houston, TX	77021-3010	832-230-0565	842-6689	5-8	Tai Ingram
KIPP Nexus S	4211 Watonga Blvd	Houston, TX	77092	832-230-0553		K-8	Lisa McClinton
KIPP Northeast College Preparatory	9680 Mesa Dr	Houston, TX	77078-3015	832-230-0567		9-12	Gillian Quinn-Pineda
KIPP PEACE ES	5400 Martin Luther King	Houston, TX	77021	832-230-0565		PK-4	Precious Parks

School	Address	City,State	Zip code	Telephone	Fax	Grade	Contact
KIPP Poder Academy	128 S Audubon Dr	San Antonio, TX	78212-1520	210-888-6513	888-6515	5-5	Rachel Obermeier
KIPP Polaris Academy for Boys	9636 Mesa Dr	Houston, TX	77078-3024	832-230-0567	633-4783	5-8	Aaron Green
KIPP SHARP College Preparatory Lower S	8430 Westglen Dr	Houston, TX	77063-6312	281-879-3000	915-0074	PK-4	Michelle Bennett
KIPP Sharpstown College Prep	8440 Westpark Dr	Houston, TX	77063	281-879-3005	915-0074	5-8	Rebecca Easterby
KIPP Shine Prep	10711 Kipp Way Dr	Houston, TX	77099-2675	832-328-1051	328-0178	PK-5	Deborah Shifrine
KIPP Spirit College Preparatory S	11000 Scott St	Houston, TX	77047	832-230-0562	731-1644	5-8	Tiffany George-Prados
KIPP Sunnyside HS	11000 Scott St	Houston, TX	77047	832-230-0562	230-0570	9-12	Rian Wright
KIPP Truth Academy	1545 S Ewing Ave	Dallas, TX	75216	214-375-8326	375-2990	4-8	Michael Horne
KIPP Truth ES	3663 W Camp Wisdom Rd	Dallas, TX	75237	214-893-4377		PK-4	Katie Hill
KIPP Unity PS	8500 Highway 6 S	Houston, TX	77083-5709	832-230-0572		PK-4	Kaleena Rosenbauer
KIPP University Prep HS	239 Stark St	San Antonio, TX	78204	210-290-8720	290-9427	9-12	Abbey Morton-Garland
KIPP Un Mundo Dual Language Academy	4343 W Commerce St	San Antonio, TX	78237-1625	210-824-1905	485-1393	K-2	Nancy Ocasio
KIPP Voyage Academy for Girls	9616 Mesa Dr	Houston, TX	77078	832-230-0567	491-7311	5-8	Celeste Barretto
KIPP ZENITH Academy	11000 Scott St	Houston, TX	77047	832-230-0562		PK-4	Cassandra Cotman
Kolitz Academy	12500 NW Military Hwy	San Antonio, TX	78231	210-302-6900	302-6913	K-8	Kathryn Davis
Kometzky S	2200 E 6th St	Austin, TX	78723	512-791-2270	232-9177	PK-12	Nicole Whetstone
La Academia de Estrellas	111 S Beckley Ave	Dallas, TX	75203	214-946-8908	946-8777	PK-8	Kemlyn Stephens
La Fe Preparatory S	616 E Father Rahm Ave	El Paso, TX	79901-2912	915-533-4560	533-4175	PK-8	Amy O'Rourke
Laurel Ridge	17720 Corporate Woods Dr	San Antonio, TX	78259-3500	210-491-9400		PK-12	Sally Arnold
Lawson Academy	5220 Scott St Ste 108	Houston, TX	77004	713-741-3600	741-3603	6-8	Marthea Raney
Leadership Academy	6720 Oak Hill Blvd	Tyler, TX	75703	903-561-1002		PK-6	Louise Dyer
Leadership Prep S	8500 Teel Pkwy	Frisco, TX	75034	972-294-6921	294-3416	K-12	Audra Floyd
Lee Academy	1826 Basse Rd	San Antonio, TX	78213	210-431-9881	582-2547	9-12	Valarie Walker
Legacy Preparatory Academy	8510 Military Pkwy	Dallas, TX	75227	469-287-8530	461-0794	K-12	Rebecca Good
Legacy Preparatory Academy	601 Accent Dr	Plano, TX	75075	469-206-2250	461-0794	K-12	Amelia Ahmed
Legacy S of Sport Sciences	4301 Roseneath Dr	Houston, TX	77021	512-203-3747		9-12	Kerrie Patterson-Brown
Liberation Academy	11600 W Airport Blvd	Meadows Place, TX	77477	346-754-5867		K-6	Audrey Sanders
Life S - Cedar Hill ES	129 W Wintergreen Rd	Cedar Hill, TX	75104	972-293-2825	291-2877	K-6	Candace Johnson
Life S - Lancaster ES	950 S Interstate 35 E	Lancaster, TX	75146-3304	972-274-7950	274-7991	K-6	DeWayne Parker
Life S - Mountain Creek ES	5525 W Illinois Ave	Dallas, TX	75211-6612	214-623-0012	467-2857	K-3	Lloyd Ashcraft
Life S - Oak Cliff ES	4400 S R L Thornton Fwy	Dallas, TX	75224-5110	214-376-8200	371-0297	K-6	Anne Beckman
Life S - Oak Cliff HS	4400 S R L Thornton Fwy	Dallas, TX	75224	214-413-1612	371-0193	7-12	Anne Beckman
Life S - Red Oak ES	777 S Interstate 35 Rd	Red Oak, TX	75154	469-552-9200	617-5767	K-6	Joy Shepherd
Life S - Waxahachie HS	170 Butcher Rd	Waxahachie, TX	75165-6016	469-708-4444	708-4445	9-12	Patrick Harvell
Life S - Waxahachie MS	3295 Highway 77	Waxahachie, TX	75165	972-937-0715	937-0503	7-8	Kim Riepe
Lighthouse Charter S	2718 Frontier Dr	San Antonio, TX	78227-4069	210-674-4100	674-4108	PK-8	Mary Salinas
Lighthouse Charter S	8138 Westshire Dr	San Antonio, TX	78227	210-236-7693	254-9284	PK-12	
Lindsley Park Community S	7130 Lindsley Ave	Dallas, TX	75223	214-321-9155	321-0702	PK-3	Jan Mallett
Lone Star Language Academy	5301 Democracy Dr	Plano, TX	75024	972-244-7220		K-6	Staci Weaver
Lowell MS	919 Thompson Pl	San Antonio, TX	78226-1494	210-228-1225	223-6248	6-8	Maribel Rodriguez
Madla Early College HS	1400 W Villaret Blvd	San Antonio, TX	78224-2417	210-486-3686		9-12	Jeff Flores
Magnolia Montessori For All	5100 Pecan Brook Dr	Austin, TX	78724	512-522-2429	291-6242	PK-8	Sara Cotner
Mainland Preparatory Academy	319 Newman Rd	La Marque, TX	77568-3440	409-934-9100	934-9130	K-8	Diana Merchant
Manara Academy	8201 Tristar Dr	Irving, TX	75063	972-304-1155	304-1150	K-6	Dr. Monica Hall
Manara Leadership Academy	8001 Jetstar Dr Ste 100	Irving, TX	75063	972-304-1155	304-1150	7-12	Adam Flores
Manara STEM Academy	6101 S Collins St	Arlington, TX	76018	972-304-1155	304-1150	K-7	Luis Valdez
Mangum ES	4315 Mangum Rd	Houston, TX	77092	713-688-0505	688-3286	PK-5	Ruben Gomez
Massieu Academy	823 N Center St	Arlington, TX	76011-5859	817-460-0396	460-9867	PK-12	Monica Fox
Mayes Institute	5807 Calhoun Rd	Houston, TX	77021-3301	713-747-5629	747-5683	K-8	Beatrice Mayes
Meadowland Charter S	121 Old San Antonio Rd	Boerne, TX	78006	830-331-4094	331-4096	7-12	Geoff Knitt
Meridian Preparatory S	1001 S Beach St	Fort Worth, TX	76105	817-288-1700	288-1692	K-5	Ginger Cole-Leffel
Meridian S	2555 N Interstate 35	Round Rock, TX	78664-2015	512-660-5230	660-5231	K-12	Rick Fernandez
Methodist Children's Home	1111 Herring Ave	Waco, TX	76708-3642	254-750-2601	755-4683	6-12	Michelle Arocha
Meyer HS	1020 Elm St Bldg 100	Waco, TX	76704-2277	254-754-2288	754-8002	9-12	Tara Spence
Meyerpark Charter S	PO Box 35616	Houston, TX	77235-5616	713-729-9712	729-9720	K-5	Julia Hutcherson
Midland Academy Charter S	500 N Baird St	Midland, TX	79701-4704	432-686-0003	686-0845	PK-8	Janet Wallace
Mid-Valley Academy	1785 W US Highway 77	San Benito, TX	78586	956-276-9930	276-9943	9-12	Nancy Ramirez
Mid-Valley Academy	200 N 17th St	McAllen, TX	78501	956-618-2303	618-2323	9-12	Francene Phoenix
Mid-Valley Academy	103 E 2nd St	Mercedes, TX	78570-2701	956-565-5417	565-8439	9-12	Jennifer McLelland
Milburn Academy - Amarillo	4106 SW 51st Ave	Amarillo, TX	79109-6132	806-463-2284	463-2231	9-12	Jolane Maddox
Milburn Academy -Corpus Christi	5333 Everhart Rd Bldg C	Corpus Christi, TX	78411	361-225-4424	225-4945	9-12	Mary Ann Peres
Milburn Academy - Fort Worth	6785 Camp Bowie Blvd	Fort Worth, TX	76116-7158	817-731-7627	731-7628	9-12	Susan Richey
Milburn Academy - Houston	713 E Airtex Dr	Houston, TX	77073	281-209-3505	209-9475	9-12	Gregory Tod Nix
Milburn Academy - Killeen	802 N 8th St	Killeen, TX	76541	254-634-4444	634-4044	9-12	Jerrod Barton
Milburn Academy - Lubbock	2333 50th St	Lubbock, TX	79412	806-740-0811	740-0804	9-12	Shawn Haseloff
Milburn Academy - Midland	503 E Interstate 20 Ste 110	Midland, TX	79701	432-203-9829	704-5520	9-12	Leticia Flores
Milburn Academy - Odessa	2419 N County Rd W	Odessa, TX	79763-2677	432-550-7833	550-7884	9-12	Mary Janssen
Milburn Academy - Pasadena	171 Pasadena Town Sq # 353	Pasadena, TX	77506	832-730-4570		9-12	Sonja Williams
Mount Carmel Academy	7155 Ashburn St	Houston, TX	77061-2611	713-643-2008	645-0078	9-12	Maureen Giacchino
Nelms Charter HS	20625 Clay Rd	Katy, TX	77449-5593	281-398-8031	398-8032	9-12	Michael Dean
Nelms Charter MS	20625 Clay Rd	Katy, TX	77449-5593	281-398-8031	398-8032	6-8	Michael Dean
New Frontiers Charter S	4018 S Presa St	San Antonio, TX	78223-1005	210-533-3655	533-5077	K-8	Ruben Pesina
New Horizons S	850 Highway 574 W	Goldthwaite, TX	76844	325-938-5513	938-5512	1-12	Shelley Williams
Newman International Academy Arlington	2011 S Fielder Rd	Arlington, TX	76013	682-207-5175	207-5175	PK-12	Donna Hart
Newman International Academy at Grace	308 W Park Row Dr	Arlington, TX	76010	817-655-2156		K-5	Dr. Wendy Dansby
Newman International Academy Cedar Hill	1114 FM 1382	Cedar Hill, TX	75104	682-207-5061		PK-12	Subhas Mathew
Newman International Acad of Fort Worth	6801 Meadowbrook Dr	Fort Worth, TX	76112	817-655-2255		PK-3	Miriam Dale Duncan
Newman International Acad of Mansfield	1201 N State Highway 360	Mansfield, TX	76063	682-400-4010	207-5175	K-4	Keith Shull
New Neighbor Campus	6500 Rookin St	Houston, TX	77074-5019	713-273-3731		K-5	Roel Saldivar
Nolan Creek S	505 E Avenue C	Belton, TX	76513	254-939-4491		K-5	Ken Wiseman
Northwest Early College HS	6701 S Desert Blvd	El Paso, TX	79932-8501	915-877-1700	877-7033	9-12	Tracy Speaker
Nova Academy	PO Box 170127	Dallas, TX	75217-0127	214-381-3422	381-3499	PK-4	Donna Houston-Woods
Nova Academy Southeast - Cedar Hill	820 E Wintergreen Rd	Cedar Hill, TX	75104	972-291-1900		PK-6	Donna Houston-Woods
Nova Academy Southeast - Prichard	PO Box 170127	Dallas, TX	75217	972-808-7470	381-8235	PK-8	Donna Houston-Woods
NYOS Charter S	1605 Kramer Ln	Austin, TX	78758-4284	512-275-1593	287-5258	PK-3	Terry Berkenhoff
NYOS Charter S	12301 N Lamar Blvd	Austin, TX	78753-1314	512-583-6967	583-6973	4-12	Curtis Wilson
Oak Cliff Faith Family Academy	300 W Kiest Blvd	Dallas, TX	75224	214-375-7682	375-7681	PK-12	Kermit Ward
Odyssey Academy Bay Area ES	2600 Stanley Ln	El Lago, TX	77586	281-326-4555		K-6	Aimee Felchak
Odyssey Academy Bay Area HS	201 Houston Ave	League City, TX	77573	281-316-0001		7-12	Heather Nielson
Odyssey Academy - Galveston	2412 61st St	Galveston, TX	77551	409-750-9289	740-3735	PK-12	Jennifer Goodman
Olive Tree Montessori Academy	8601 Randol Mill Rd	Fort Worth, TX	76120	817-460-5000	460-5003	PK-5	Sadia Haq
Olympic Hills Charter S	2200 E 6th St	Austin, TX	78702	512-633-0795	462-6665	K-12	Dottie Goodman
Panola Charter S	PO Box 610	Carthage, TX	75633-0610	903-693-6355	693-6391	8-12	Keith Koonce
Panola Early College HS	PO Box 610	Carthage, TX	75633	903-693-6355	694-2208	8-12	Bryan Tarjick
PARAMUS Early College HS	602 S Raguet St	Lufkin, TX	75904	936-634-5515	634-5518	9-12	Dr. Merilyn Session
Paseo Del Norte Academy	1599 George Dieter Dr	El Paso, TX	79936	915-298-3637	298-3644	9-12	Luis Liano
Paseo Del Norte Academy - Ysleta	711 N Mesa St	El Paso, TX	79902-3925	915-532-7216	532-2251	9-12	Jamie Sanchez
Pathfinder Camp	20800 FM 150 W	Driftwood, TX	78619-9202	512-791-2270	232-9177	K-12	Nicole Whetstone
Pathways 3H Ranch	110 Youth Ranch Rd # 3H	Mountain Home, TX	78058	512-560-8132	232-9177	6-12	Sally Arnold
Pegasus Charter HS	601 N Akard St Ste 203	Dallas, TX	75201-3303	214-740-9991	740-9799	K-12	Virginia Hart
Phoenix S	3333 Bering Dr	Houston, TX	77057-6718	713-784-6345		K-12	Tonya Sanders-Woods
Pioneer Technology & Arts Academy	3100 Oates Dr	Mesquite, TX	75150	972-375-9672	301-2135	6-8	
Pioneer Technology & Arts Academy	300 Aerobic Ln	Greenville, TX	75402	903-257-3920		6-8	
Porter S	PO Box 2053	Wimberley, TX	78676-6953	512-847-6867	847-0737	9-12	Kenn Peters
Por Vida Academy	1135 Mission Rd	San Antonio, TX	78210-4505	210-775-1132	390-1744	9-12	Loren Franckowiak
Positive Solutions Charter S	1325 N Flores St	San Antonio, TX	78212-4900	210-299-1025	299-1052	9-12	Ruby Torres
Premier HS CTE Edinburg	4701 Sugar Rd	Edinburg, TX	78539	956-386-1793		9-12	Nelda Garza
Premier HS of Abilene	3161 S 23rd St	Abilene, TX	79605-5861	325-698-8111	695-5620	9-12	Sue Pond
Premier HS of Amarillo	3242 Hobbs Rd	Amarillo, TX	79109-3213	806-367-5447	315-9506	9-12	Mimi Allen
Premier HS of Arlington	551 Ryan Plaza Dr	Arlington, TX	76011	817-717-4874		9-12	
Premier HS of Austin	1701 W Ben White Blvd #100A	Austin, TX	78704	512-444-8442	673-0058	9-12	Jennifer Kasapi
Premier HS of Beaumont	209 N 11th St	Beaumont, TX	77702-2213	409-835-4303	835-2882	9-12	Jennifer Kasapi
Premier HS of Brownsville	955 Paredes Line Rd	Brownsville, TX	78521-2659	956-550-0084	554-0890	9-12	Maria Alvarado
Premier HS of Brownwood/Early	819 Early Blvd	Early, TX	76802	325-643-3735	363-4987	7-12	Michelle Welch
Premier HS of Comanche	1008 S Austin St	Comanche, TX	76442	325-356-9673	794-8319	6-12	
Premier HS of Dayton	1709 County Road 611	Dayton, TX	77535-8561	936-257-8017	449-6775	9-12	Suzanne Thomas
Premier HS of Del Rio	1701 Kings Way	Del Rio, TX	78840	830-298-2100	573-0849	9-12	Carol Mirles
Premier HS of East El Paso	8720 Gateway Blvd E Ste E	El Paso, TX	79907	915-633-1598	693-5206	9-12	Dr. Eduardo Servin
Premier HS of Fort Worth	6411 Camp Bowie Blvd Ste B	Fort Worth, TX	76116-5449	817-731-2028	728-0824	9-12	Tawaiua Mitchell
Premier HS of Granbury	919 E US Highway 377 Ste 1	Granbury, TX	76048-1436	817-573-0435	895-9616	9-12	Marsha Grissom
Premier HS of Huntsville	2407 Sam Houston Ave Ste C	Huntsville, TX	77340-5862	936-439-5204	622-9113	9-12	Kevin Nichols
Premier HS of Irving South	1081 W Shady Grove Rd	Irving, TX	75060-5868	972-254-1016	565-1157	9-12	Matthew Cannon
Premier HS of Laredo	2201 Chihuahua St	Laredo, TX	78043-3737	956-723-7788	284-0175	9-12	Berta Martinez
Premier HS of Lewisville	1800 Lakeway Dr	Lewisville, TX	75057-6429	972-316-4160		9-12	Lisa Ehrke
Premier HS of Lubbock	2002 W Loop 289 Ste 121	Lubbock, TX	79407-7701	806-763-1518	763-9310	9-12	Thomas Martin
Premier HS of Midland	4320 W Illinois Ave Ste A	Midland, TX	79703-5591	432-682-0384	682-0897	9-12	Tanya Bell
Premier HS of Mission	1203 St Claire Blvd	Mission, TX	78572-8465	956-424-9290	859-0140	9-12	Laura Thatcher

School	Address	City,State	Zip code	Telephone	Fax	Grade	Contact
Premier HS of New Braunfels	1928 S Seguin Ave Unit 100A	New Braunfels, TX	78130	830-609-6606	319-4382	9-12	Richard Ramirez
Premier HS of North Austin	13801 Burnet Rd Ste 100	Austin, TX	78727	512-832-0965	563-6438	9-12	Carolyn Griego
Premier HS of North Houston	14314 Walters Rd	Houston, TX	77014	281-918-4044		9-12	Alexis DelGado
Premier HS of Palmview	406 W Veterans Blvd	Palmview, TX	78572-8327	956-584-8458	584-9807	9-12	Selma Femat
Premier HS of Pflugerville	616 FM 685 Ste 204B	Pflugerville, TX	78660-3681	512-969-5100		6-12	Paulita Zuniga
Premier HS of Pharr	200 E Expressway 83 Ste E	Pharr, TX	78577	956-781-8800	781-7464	9-12	Rosie Zamora
Premier HS of San Antonio East	8220 Windsor Cross	Windcrest, TX	78239	210-650-0944		9-12	Luis Gonzalez
Premier HS of San Antonio West	6218 NW Loop 410	San Antonio, TX	78230	210-920-0010		9-12	
Premier HS of San Juan	1200 E Business 83	San Juan, TX	78589-4758	956-961-4721	961-4724	9-12	Alma Prado
Premier HS of Texarkana	3448 Summerhill Rd	Texarkana, TX	75503	430-200-4385		9-12	Heather McNeill
Premier HS of Tyler	1106 N Glenwood Blvd	Tyler, TX	75702-5059	903-592-5222	592-0324	9-12	Chris Chambers
Premier HS of Waco	4720 N 19th St	Waco, TX	76708-1213	254-752-0441	752-0445	9-12	Lisa Linton
Premier HS of West El Paso	1035 Belvidere St Ste 116	El Paso, TX	79912	915-581-4300	581-4378	9-12	Dr. Laura Dominguez
Pro-Vision S	4590 Wilmington St	Houston, TX	77051	713-748-0030	748-0037	3-12	Andrea Credit
Quinn Campus MS	1020 Elm St Bldg 100	Waco, TX	76704-2277	254-754-8000	754-8009	5-8	Tyler Ellis
Ramirez Charter S	702 Avenue T	Lubbock, TX	79401-2303	806-219-6500	766-1825	K-5	Nancy Parker
Ranch Academy	3120 VZ County Road 2318	Canton, TX	75103-4671	903-939-8000	200-2918	6-12	Melissa Pardue
Rapoport Academy East	2000 J J Flewellen Rd	Waco, TX	76704-1642	254-799-4191	799-4525	PK-1	Cindy Kubacak
Rapoport Academy North	2200 MacArthur Dr	Waco, TX	76708	254-313-1313		2-4	Amy Taylor
Real Learning Academy	6405 S IH 35	Austin, TX	78744	512-438-7325	842-9308	PK-4	Michelle Stahl
Rhodes MS	3000 Tampico St	San Antonio, TX	78207-6498	210-978-7925	433-7299	6-8	Moises Ortiz
Rhodes S - Channelview	1215 Pecan St	Channelview, TX	77530	281-864-7015		K-5	
Rhodes S - Northeast	600 Charles St	Humble, TX	77338	281-319-9300	446-2898	PK-8	
Rhodes S - Northshore	12818 Tidwell Rd	Houston, TX	77044	281-459-9797	459-9702	PK-5	
Rhodes S - Northwest	6601 Antoine Dr	Houston, TX	77091	832-562-2822		K-5	Deoniara Parrish
Richardson Classical Academy	2101 E Renner Rd	Richardson, TX	75082	972-479-9584	679-0860	K-8	Ashley Cooper
Richland Collegiate HS	12800 Abrams Rd	Dallas, TX	75243-2104	972-761-6888	761-6890	11-12	Donna Walker
Ripley House Charter S	4410 Navigation Blvd	Houston, TX	77011-1036	713-315-6429	547-8201	PK-5	Angela Wedlick
Ripley House MS	4414 Navigation Blvd	Houston, TX	77011	713-315-6430		6-8	
Rise Academy	PO Box 2837	Lubbock, TX	79408-2837	806-744-0438	201-7088	PK-8	Richard Baumgartner
Riverside Park ES	202 School St	San Antonio, TX	78210-3940	210-228-3355	534-6987	PK-5	Dr. Cassie McClung
Robbins MS	602 S Raguet St	Lufkin, TX	75904	936-634-5515	634-5518	6-8	JoDee Woodcock
Saenz JHS	1826 Basse Rd	San Antonio, TX	78213	210-431-9881	582-2587	7-8	Valarie Walker
St. Anthony S	3732 Myrtle St	Dallas, TX	75215-3849	214-421-3645	421-7416	K-5	David Ray
St. Mary's Academy Charter S	507 N Filmore St	Beeville, TX	78102-5000	361-358-5601	358-5704	K-8	Hirma Elizondo
San Antonio Can Academy	1807 Centennial Blvd	San Antonio, TX	78211-1205	210-923-1226	928-3366	9-12	Mark Tribett
Sanchez HS	6001 Gulf Fwy	Houston, TX	77023-5425	713-926-1112	926-8129	6-12	Giselle Easton
Sanchez HS North	406 E Rittenhouse St	Houston, TX	77076	713-742-0947	742-0874	6-12	
Save Our Streets Learning Center	1700 Groesbeck St	Bryan, TX	77803	979-703-1810	703-1834	K-5	Becky Tucker
School for the Highly Gifted	2990 S State Highway 161	Grand Prairie, TX	75052-7247	972-343-7864		1-3	Holly Mohler
School of Science and Technology	4737 Saratoga Blvd	Corpus Christi, TX	78413-2117	361-851-2450	851-2475	K-12	Ekrem Demirci
S of Science & Technology Advancement	10550 Westoffice Dr	Houston, TX	77042	713-266-2522	266-2494	PK-8	
School of Science and Technology Alamo	12200 Crownpoint Dr	San Antonio, TX	78233	210-657-6400	657-6401	K-8	Mustafa Kililioglu
School of Science & Technology Discovery	5707 Bandera Rd	Leon Valley, TX	78238	210-543-1111	543-1112	K-8	Yvette Alvarez
S of Science & Technology Excellence	330 N Sam Houston Pkwy E	Houston, TX	77060	832-672-6671	672-7842	K-6	Mehmet Okumus M.Ed.
School of Science and Technology HS	1450 NE Loop 410	San Antonio, TX	78209-1513	210-804-0222	822-3422	6-12	Celal Keskin
S of Science and Technology Houston	16200 State Highway 249	Houston, TX	77086	346-270-2101	270-2187	K-8	
Sci-Tech Preparatory	6405 S IH-35	Austin, TX	78744	512-220-9120	842-9308	6-12	Ulrike Puryear M.Ed.
Seashore Learning Center	14493 S Padre Isl PMB 307A	Corpus Christi, TX	78418	361-949-1222	949-6762	PK-4	Genger Holt
Seashore Middle Academy	14493 S Padre Isl PMB 307A	Corpus Christi, TX	78418	361-654-1134	654-1139	5-8	Barbara Beeler
Seguin ES	2400 E Walnut St	Seguin, TX	78155	830-549-5930	433-4534	PK-5	Christine Wilmoth
SER-Ninos Charter S	5815 Alder Dr	Houston, TX	77081-2708	713-667-6145	667-0645	PK-8	Charmaine Constantine
Settlement Home	1600 Payton Gin Rd	Austin, TX	78758-6506	512-751-4534	232-9177	K-12	Holly Engleman
Shoreline Academy	1220 Gregory St	Taft, TX	78390-3044	361-528-3959	528-2143	7-12	DeAnn Phillips
South Plains Academy	4008 Avenue R	Lubbock, TX	79412-1603	806-744-0330	741-1089	9-12	Jennifer McLelland
Southwest ES	8440 Bissonnet St	Houston, TX	77074-3908	713-988-5839	270-0076	PK-5	Pamela Sailors
Southwest Preparatory ES NW Campus	4151 Culebra Rd	San Antonio, TX	78228	210-819-7860	438-8253	PK-6	Cheryl Wills-Pacheco
Southwest Preparatory HS NW Campus	6535 Culebra Rd	San Antonio, TX	78238	210-432-2634	432-5482	7-12	Lesley Carr
Southwest Preparatory S NE Campus	1258 Austin Hwy Ste 220	San Antonio, TX	78209-4820	210-829-8017	829-8514	PK-5	Carolyn Martinez
Southwest Preparatory S SE Campus	735 S WW White Rd	San Antonio, TX	78220-2524	210-333-1403	333-3024	6-12	Javier Garcia
Southwest Prep S New Directions Campus	1258 Austin Hwy Bldg 2	San Antonio, TX	78209-4891	210-828-2161	826-9962	6-12	Veronica Champion
Steele Montessori Academy	722 Haggin St	San Antonio, TX	78210-5218	210-438-6870	533-5394	PK-K	Laura Christenberry
Stem Academy of Lewisville	650 Bennett Ln	Lewisville, TX	75057	972-829-4492		6-12	Marci Stapp
Step Charter S	11250 S Wilcrest Dr	Houston, TX	77099	281-988-7797		K-8	
Storm ES	435 Brady Blvd	San Antonio, TX	78207-8001	210-978-8005	224-1998	PK-5	Claudia Ramos-Coto
Strinden ES	602 S Raguet St	Lufkin, TX	75904	936-634-5515	634-5518	PK-5	Jennifer Shaw
Tekoa Academy of Accelerated Studies	1408 W Park Ave	Orange, TX	77630-4951	409-886-9864		PK-5	Rhonda Orebo
Tekoa Academy of Accelerated Studies	326 Thomas Blvd	Port Arthur, TX	77640-5242	409-982-5400	982-8498	PK-5	Dr. Paula Richardson
Tekoa Academy of Accelerated Studies	327 Thomas Blvd	Port Arthur, TX	77640	409-985-4738		6-12	Dr. Paula Richardson
Temple Charter Academy	7177 Airport Rd	Temple, TX	76502-7142	254-778-8682	853-4144	PK-12	Jason Osburn
Texas Connections Academy at Houston	10550 Richmond Ave Ste 140	Houston, TX	77042-5112	281-661-8293	780-2487	3-12	Lea Ann Lockard
Texas Early College HS	3714 E End Blvd S	Marshall, TX	75672	903-935-4109	935-4067	8-12	Robert Bruce
Texas Education Centers at Aubrey	1851 Oak Grove Pkwy	Little Elm, TX	75068	972-292-3562	292-3563	PK-8	Debbie Foster
Texas Education Centers at Denton	4601 IH 35 N	Denton, TX	76210	940-383-1972	383-7655	PK-8	James Gandy
Texas Education Centers in Lewisville	968 Raldon St	Lewisville, TX	75067-5229	972-221-3564	221-3576	PK-8	Donica Hill
Texas Empowerment Academy	3613 Bluestein Dr	Austin, TX	78721	512-494-1076	494-1009	K-5	David Nowlin
Texas Empowerment Academy	6414 N Hampton Dr	Austin, TX	78723	512-928-0118	928-0128	5-12	David Nowlin
Texas Leadership Charter Acad Arlington	2001 Brown Blvd	Arlington, TX	76006	817-385-9338	861-1242	K-9	Ron Carroll
Texas Leadership Charter Academy Abilene	1840 N 8th St	Abilene, TX	79603	325-480-3500		K-7	Carmen Crane
Texas Leadership Charter Academy Midland	3300 Thomas Ave	Midland, TX	79703	432-242-7117	262-0994	K-9	Becky Rejon
Texas NeuroRehabilitation Center	1106 W Dittmar Rd	Austin, TX	78745-6328	512-444-4835	462-6665	K-12	Dottie Goodman
Texas Preparatory S	7540 Ed Bluestein Rd	Austin, TX	78723	512-928-3000		K-6	Daphne McDole
Texas Preparatory S	PO Box 1643	San Marcos, TX	78667-1643	512-928-3000	928-3005	K-6	Daphne McDole
Texas S of the Arts	6025 Village Pkwy	Fort Worth, TX	76134-3430	817-732-8372	732-8373	K-8	Natalie Texada
Texas Serenity Academy	8787 N Houston Rosslyn Rd	Houston, TX	77088	281-820-9540	820-6204	K-8	Michelle Foreman
Texas Serenity Academy - Gano	4637 Gano St	Houston, TX	77009	281-258-7700		K-5	Danielle Johnson
Texas Virtual Academy	1955 Lakeway Dr Ste 250B	Lewisville, TX	75057-6436	866-360-0161	506-6777	3-12	Lonnie Morgan
TLC Academy	PO Box 61726	San Angelo, TX	76906	325-652-3200	942-6795	K-12	Johnny Burleson
Travis Early College HS	1915 N Main Ave	San Antonio, TX	78212	210-738-9830	733-5486	9-12	Adrianna Arredondo
Treetops School International	12500 S Pipeline Rd	Euless, TX	76040-5853	817-283-1771	684-0892	PK-12	Lou Blanchard
Trinity Basin S - 10th St Campus	831 W 10th St	Dallas, TX	75208	214-296-9302	296-9306	PK-4	
Trinity Basin S - Ewing Campus	808 N Ewing Ave	Dallas, TX	75203-1524	214-942-8846	942-8864	PK-4	Kyla Jaramillo
Trinity Basin S - Jefferson Campus	855 E 8th St	Dallas, TX	75203	214-941-4881	941-4866	5-8	
Trinity Basin S - Pafford Campus	101 E Pafford St	Fort Worth, TX	76110	817-840-7501	840-7502	PK-8	
Trinity Basin S - Panola Campus	4400 Panola Ave	Fort Worth, TX	76103	817-458-4222	946-9194	PK-3	Natasha Forge
Trinity Charter S - Big Sandy Campus	15892 County Road 26	Tyler, TX	75707-2728	512-459-1000	705-2447	6-12	Nicki Cornejo
Trinity Charter S - Bokenkamp Campus	5517 S Alameda St	Corpus Christi, TX	78412	361-992-1412		K-12	Hilda Vega
Trinity Charter S - Chapel Hill Campus	15892 County Road 26	Tyler, TX	75707-2728	903-459-1000	705-2447	K-12	Nicki Cornejo
Trinity Charter S - Krause Center Campus	25752 Kingsland Blvd	Katy, TX	77494-2086	281-392-7505	392-6887	6-12	Sandra Flores
Trinity Charter S - New Hope Campus	1000 N McColl Rd	McAllen, TX	78501	956-435-0700	705-2447	3-12	Hilda Vega
Trinity Charter S - New Life Campus	650 Scarbourough	Canyon Lake, TX	78133-4529	830-964-4390	964-4376	4-12	Kellie Ragland
Trinity Charter S - Pegasus Campus	896 Robin Ranch Rd	Lockhart, TX	78644-4578	512-432-1652	705-2447	3-12	Keely Reynolds
Trinity Charter S - Willow Bend Campus	2902 Highway 31 E	Tyler, TX	75702-8613			K-12	Nicki Cornejo
Trinity Environmental Academy	PO Box 570975	Dallas, TX	75357-0975	972-920-6558	767-0494	PK-12	Michael Hooten
Trivium Academy	2205 E Hebron Pkwy	Carrollton, TX	75010	469-854-9007	907-2533	K-6	Sheryl Bradley
TSU Charter Lab S	3100 Cleburne St	Houston, TX	77004	713-313-6754	313-6745	K-5	Debbra Collins
Two Dimensions Preparatory Academy	12121 Veterans Memorial Dr	Houston, TX	77067-5237	281-227-4708	232-0032	PK-5	DeAteria Akan
Two Dimensions Preparatory Academy	901 E 10th Ave	Corsicana, TX	75110-6726	281-227-4700	872-2858	PK-K	Shirley Harris
Two Dimensions Preparatory Academy	12330 Vickery St	Houston, TX	77039-3608	281-227-4700	987-7306	PK-4	Jamal Adams
Tyler Classical Academy	3405 E Grande Blvd	Tyler, TX	75707	903-504-5690	567-2247	K-9	Keith Garcia
UME Preparatory Academy	3838 Spur 408	Dallas, TX	75236	214-545-6243	709-7951	K-12	Kayla Smith
UME Preparatory Academy	415 N Cedar Ridge Dr	Duncanville, TX	75116	972-296-0084	296-0084	K-5	Shannan Horton
Universal Academy	2616 N MacArthur Blvd	Irving, TX	75062-5401	972-255-1800	255-6122	PK-12	
Universal Academy - Flower Mound	1001 E Sandy Lake Rd	Coppell, TX	75019-3112	972-393-5834	255-6122	PK-12	Diane Moshier
University Charter S	2200 E 6th St	Austin, TX	78702-3457	512-495-3300	495-9631	PK-5	Nicole Whetstone
University HS	2007 University Ave	Austin, TX	78705	512-741-4553	232-9177	9-12	Holly Engleman
University of Houston Charter S of Tech	3855 Holman St	Houston, TX	77204-6056	713-743-9111	743-9121	K-5	Dr. Carolyn Black
Uplift Gradus Prep	121 Seahawk Dr	DeSoto, TX	75115	214-451-5551		K-3	Sharon Duplantier
Uplift Grand Preparatory S	300 E Church St	Grand Prairie, TX	75050	972-854-6000		K-12	Allen Anderson
Uplift Hampton Preparatory	8915 S Hampton Rd	Dallas, TX	75232-6002	972-421-1982	421-1986	K-12	Kecia Clark
Uplift Heights Preparatory	2806 Canada Dr	Dallas, TX	75212	214-442-7094	442-7099	K-12	Kristen Algier
Uplift Infinity Preparatory S	1401 S MacArthur Blvd	Irving, TX	75060	469-621-9200		PK-12	Sarah Hobson
Uplift Lee Prep	401 E Grand Prairie Rd	Grand Prairie, TX	75051	972-262-6785		K-3	Priscilla Parhms
Uplift Lee Preparatory	401 E Grand Prairie Rd	Grand Prairie, TX	75051	972-262-6785		K-2	Dani Erbert
Uplift Luna Preparatory HS	2625 Elm St	Dallas, TX	75226	214-445-3300	445-3299	6-12	Chloe LaFrance
Uplift Luna Preparatory PS	2020 N Lamar St	Dallas, TX	75202	214-442-7882		K-5	Alieshia Baisy
Uplift Mighty Prep S	3700 Mighty Mite Dr	Fort Worth, TX	76105	817-288-3800		K-12	Wes Seaton

School	Address	City,State	Zip code	Telephone	Fax	Grade	Contact
Uplift North Hills Preparatory	606 E Royal Ln	Irving, TX	75039-3503	972-501-0645	501-9439	K-12	George Rutzen
Uplift Peak Academy	4600 Bryan St	Dallas, TX	75204	214-821-7325	370-3972	PK-12	Carlos de la Garza
Uplift Pinnacle HS	301 W Camp Wisdom Rd	Dallas, TX	75232	214-453-6900		6-12	Katie Leinenkugel
Uplift Pinnacle Preparatory S	2510 S Vernon Ave	Dallas, TX	75224	214-442-6100	442-6181	K-5	Katie Leinenkugel
Uplift Summit International Preparatory	1305 N Center St	Arlington, TX	76011	817-287-5121	287-5132	K-12	Jason Smith
Uplift Triumph Preparatory S	9411 Hargrove Dr	Dallas, TX	75220-6034	972-590-5100		K-5	Christine Denison
Uplift White Rock Hills Prep S	7370 Valley Glen Dr	Dallas, TX	75228	469-914-7500	914-7502	PK-2	Kaitlin McDermott
Uplift Williams Preparatory S	1750 Viceroy Dr	Dallas, TX	75235-2308	214-276-0352	637-6393	K-12	Molly Salomon
Vanguard Academy Beethoven ES	2215 S Veterans Blvd	Edinburg, TX	78539	956-318-0211	318-0220	PK-4	Norma Espino
Vanguard Academy Charter School	1200 E Kelly Ave	Pharr, TX	78577-5033	956-781-1701	781-8055	PK-12	Charlene Rodriguez
Vanguard Academy II	901 S Athol St	Pharr, TX	78577	956-702-0134	702-0166	PK-5	Angelica Martinez
Vanguard Mozart ES	155 E Business Highway 83	Alamo, TX	78516	956-702-2548	702-2731	PK-5	Fred Gonzalez
Varnett S - East	PO Box 1457	Houston, TX	77251-1457	713-637-6574	637-8319	PK-6	Gayle Voltz
Varnett S - Northeast	PO Box 1457	Houston, TX	77251-1457	713-631-4396	491-3597	PK-6	Toni Fisher
Varnett S - Southeast	PO Box 1457	Houston, TX	77251	713-667-4051	726-7685	PK-6	
Varnett S - Southwest	PO Box 1457	Houston, TX	77251-1457	713-723-4699	283-1728	PK-6	Jese Arps
Victory Preparatory Academy	6011 W Orem Dr	Houston, TX	77085	832-547-2524		9-12	Winston Stoolo
Victory Preparatory Academy	2903 Jensen Dr	Houston, TX	77026-6019	713-229-0560	250-7074	PK-8	Shawanna Jasper
Village Tech S	1010 E Parkerville Rd	Cedar Hill, TX	75104	469-454-4441		PK-12	Robert Johansen
Vista Academy of Austin	1504 E 51st St	Austin, TX	78723-3012	512-371-8933	433-9225	K-5	Miriam Spiller
Vista Academy of Beaumont	10255 Eastex Fwy Ste 100	Beaumont, TX	77708-1061	409-434-4549	316-2728	K-5	Sherry Hanson
Vista Academy of Crockett	1303 E Houston Ave	Crockett, TX	75835-1749	936-546-0493	546-0034	K-5	Deborah Kelly M.S.
Vista Academy of Garland	3024 Anita Dr	Garland, TX	75041-2708	972-840-1100	840-1105	K-8	Tiffany Linwood
Vista Academy of Humble	901 Wilson Rd	Humble, TX	77338-5104	281-913-5107	655-1476	K-5	Alyson Kelly
Vista Academy of Huntsville	2407 Sam Houston Ave	Huntsville, TX	77340-5862	936-291-0203	293-8096	K-6	Sherrie Sheppard
Vista Academy of Jasper	1501B S Wheeler St	Jasper, TX	75951-5103	409-489-9222	489-9272	K-8	Laura McMillon
Vista Academy of North Garland	1600 W Campbell Rd	Garland, TX	75044-2300	972-530-7373	679-0860	K-5	Matthew Stone
Vista Academy of Pasadena Beta Academy	6109 Fairmont Pkwy	Pasadena, TX	77505-4024	281-372-8999	345-6895	K-4	Gwen Abshire
Vista Academy of The Woodlands	6565 Research Forest Dr	The Woodlands, TX	77381-6030	936-242-1541	688-8037	K-8	Hanh Perzigian
Vista Academy of Willis	202 S Thomason St	Willis, TX	77378-8987	936-890-0100	890-0110	K-8	Russell Shafer
Vista del Futuro Charter S	7310 Bishop Flores Dr	El Paso, TX	79912-1429	915-855-8143	855-8179	K-6	Yvonne Whitman
Waco Charter S	615 N 25th St	Waco, TX	76707-3443	254-754-8169	754-7389	PK-5	Sabrina Gray
Walker IS	6500 N Interstate 35	San Antonio, TX	78218	210-654-4411	590-0376	PK-6	Tamiko Askew M.Ed.
Wallace Accelerated HS	312 E 12th St	Colorado City, TX	79512	325-728-2392	728-1025	8-12	Steven Reese
Waxahachie Faith Family Academy	701 Ovilla Rd	Waxahachie, TX	75167-9430	972-937-3704	383-3075	PK-8	Monica Kramer
Westchester Acad International Studies	901 Yorkchester Dr	Houston, TX	77079-3446	713-251-1800	251-1815	6-12	Valerie Muniz
Westlake Academy	2600 J T Ottinger Rd	Westlake, TX	76262-8012	817-490-5757	490-5758	K-12	Dr. Mechelle Bryson
Whittier MS	2101 Edison Dr	San Antonio, TX	78201-3499	210-738-9755	735-0704	6-8	Irene Talamantes
Winfree Academy Charter S	2985 S State Highway 360	Grand Prairie, TX	75052-7615	214-204-2030	204-2034	9-12	Corrine Johnson
Winfree Academy Charter S	2550 Beckleymeade Ave # 150	Dallas, TX	75237	469-930-5199	930-5206	9-12	Brad Landis
Winfree Academy Charter S	1661 Gateway Blvd	Richardson, TX	75080-3530	972-234-9855	234-9975	9-12	David Stubblefield
Winfree Academy Charter S	3110 Skyway Cir S	Irving, TX	75038-4207	972-251-2010	251-4301	9-12	Ridwan Williams
Winfree Academy Charter S	341 Bennett Ln	Lewisville, TX	75057-4801	214-222-2200	222-0201	9-12	Madge Ennis
Winfree Academy Charter S	6311 Boulevard 26 Ste 300	N Richlnd Hls, TX	76180-1595	817-590-2240	590-8724	9-12	Troy Gray
Wood Charter S at Afton Oaks	620 E Afton Oaks Blvd	San Antonio, TX	78232-1236	210-638-5000	638-5575	5-12	Asa Cuellar
Wood Charter S at Granbury	1300 Crossland Rd	Granbury, TX	76048-5208	210-638-5600	638-5675	4-12	Marc Malloy
Wood Charter S at Hays County	2250 Clovis R Barker Rd	San Marcos, TX	78666	210-638-5400	638-5475	5-12	Kayla Heyward
Wood Charter S at Meridell	12550 W State Highway 29	Liberty Hill, TX	78642	512-528-2462		K-12	Wendy Rollins
Wood Charter S at Rockdale	696 N FM 487	Rockdale, TX	76567-6005	210-638-5700	638-5775	4-12	Tamra Vance
Wood Charter S - Legacy Ranch	13326 N Highway 183	Gonzales, TX	78629	830-638-5300		K-12	Patsy Smith
Wood Charter S - Williams House	107 W Railway St	Lometa, TX	76853	210-638-5800	638-5875	K-12	Stephanie House
Yes Prep S - Brays Oaks	9000 W Bellfort St	Houston, TX	77031-2410	713-967-8400	778-0917	6-12	Chris Claflin
Yes Prep S - East End	8329 Lawndale St	Houston, TX	77012-3707	713-967-7800	921-2305	6-12	Leah Peters
Yes Prep S - Fifth Ward	1305 Benson St	Houston, TX	77020-4044	713-924-0602	670-0032	6-12	Barbara Campbell
Yes Prep S - Gulfton	6565 De Moss Dr	Houston, TX	77074-5099	713-967-9800	774-1808	6-12	Hugh Guill
Yes Prep S - Northbrook	3030 Rosefield Dr	Houston, TX	77080	713-251-4200	251-4214	6-8	Jeremy Jones
Yes Prep S - North Central	13703 Aldine Westfield Rd	Houston, TX	77039-2001	281-227-2044	227-2090	6-12	Bryan Reed
Yes Prep S - North Forest	6602 Winfield Rd	Houston, TX	77050	713-967-8600	636-7806	6-12	James Mosley
Yes Prep S - Northline	5815 Airline Dr	Houston, TX	77076	713-842-5400		6-6	Brittany McGruder
Yes Prep S - Northside	5215 Jensen Dr	Houston, TX	77026-2514	713-924-0400	589-2502	6-8	Maureen Israel
Yes Prep S - Southeast	353 Crenshaw Rd	Houston, TX	77034-1543	713-967-9400	910-2350	6-12	Antonio Castillo
Yes Prep S - Southside	5515 S Loop E	Houston, TX	77033	713-924-5500		6-6	Chris Claflin
Yes Prep S - Southwest	4411 Anderson Rd	Houston, TX	77053-2307	713-967-9200	413-0003	6-12	Eric Newcomer
Yes Prep S - West	10535 Harwin Dr	Houston, TX	77036	713-967-8200	541-8518	6-12	Ashleigh Fritz
Yes Prep S - White Oak	5620 W Tidwell Rd	Houston, TX	77091-4638	713-924-5200	589-2502	6-12	
Young Learners Charter S	3333 Bering Dr	Houston, TX	77057-6718	713-784-1215	780-2338	PK-K	Lillian Conway
Young Learners S	8432 Bissonnet St	Houston, TX	77074	713-772-7100	772-7104	PK-2	Lillian Conway
Young Scholars Academy of Excellence	1809 Louisiana St	Houston, TX	77002-8013	713-654-1404	654-1401	PK-8	Anella Coleman
Young Womens Leadership Academy	2123 W Huisache Ave	San Antonio, TX	78201-4809	210-438-6525	732-7999	6-12	Delia McLerran
Yzaguirre S for Success	2950 Broadway St	Houston, TX	77017	713-640-3763	454-0893	6-8	Philip Cano
Yzaguirre S for Success	2950 Broadway St	Houston, TX	77017	713-640-3734	454-0893	PK-5	Luisa Martinez
Yzaguirre S for Success	2950 Broadway St	Houston, TX	77017-1706	713-649-6201	641-1853	9-12	Alma Perez-Silva
Yzaguirre S for Success	2255 N Coria St	Brownsville, TX	78520	956-544-7103	542-2667	PK-8	Maria Knosel

Utah

School	Address	City,State	Zip code	Telephone	Fax	Grade	Contact
Academy for Math Engineering & Science	5715 S 1300 E	Salt Lake City, UT	84121-1023	801-278-9460	277-3527	9-12	Brett Wilson
American Academy of Innovation	5410 W South Jordan Pkwy	South Jordan, UT	84009	801-810-4786		6-12	Scott Jones
American International S of Utah	4998 S Galleria Dr	Murray, UT	84123	801-989-7191		K-12	Nathan Justis
American Leadership Academy	898 W 1100 S	Spanish Fork, UT	84660-5654	801-794-2226	794-2130	K-12	Richard Morley
American Prep Academy - Accelerated S	3636 W 3100 S	West Valley, UT	84120	385-351-3090	351-3089	K-12	Carolyn Sharette
American Prep Academy - New Americas	1255 W Crystal Ave	West Valley, UT	84119	801-839-3613	839-3626	K-9	Carolyn Sharette
American Preparatory Academy Draper	11938 S Lone Peak Pkwy	Draper, UT	84020	801-810-3590	810-3589	K-12	Kevin McVicar
American Preparatory Academy Draper 1	12892 S Pony Express Rd	Draper, UT	84020	801-553-8500	576-9300	K-6	Carolyn Sharette
American Preparatory Academy - Salem	1195 Elk Ridge Dr	Salem, UT	84653-5521	801-465-4434	465-7808	K-9	Richard Fillerup
Ascent Academies of Utah - Farmington	22 S 650 W	Farmington, UT	84025	801-220-2200		K-9	Janice Newton
Ascent Academies of Utah - Lehi	1999 W 900 N	Lehi, UT	84043	801-374-9641		K-9	Tricia Remington
Ascent Academies of Utah - West Jordan	5662 W 8200 S	West Jordan, UT	84081	385-275-0909		K-9	Michael Clark
Athenian Eacademy	765 E 340 S	American Fork, UT	84003	385-715-5400	265-4308	K-12	Matt Throckmorton
Athlos Academy of Utah	12309 S Mustang Trail Way	Herriman, UT	84096	801-809-5206		K-9	Esther Thompson
Bear River Charter S	75 S 400 W	Logan, UT	84321	435-753-8811	661-6118	K-8	Janet Adams
Beehive Science & Technology Academy	830 E 9400 S	Sandy, UT	84094	801-576-0070	618-4115	6-12	Hanifi Oguz
Bowen Laboratory ES	6700 Old Main Hl	Logan, UT	84322-6700	435-797-3085	797-3668	K-5	Dan Johnson
Canyon Grove Academy	588 W 3300 N	Pleasant Grove, UT	84062	801-785-9300	785-8997	K-9	Kim Goates
Canyon Rim Academy	3005 S 2900 E	Salt Lake City, UT	84109	801-474-2066	474-2085	K-6	Merry Fusselman
Channing Hall Charter S	13515 S 150 E	Draper, UT	84020-8602	801-572-2709	571-8786	K-8	Heather Shepherd
City Academy	555 E 200 S	Salt Lake City, UT	84102-2007	801-596-8489	521-4181	7-12	Sonja Woodbury
DaVinci Academy of Science and the Arts	2033 Grant Ave	Ogden, UT	84401-0409	801-409-0700	334-8533	K-12	Fred Donaldson
Dixie Montessori Academy	1160 N 645 W	Washington, UT	84780	435-251-8539	578-0718	K-7	Julie Wand
Dual Immersion Academy	1155 S Glendale Dr	Salt Lake City, UT	84104	801-972-1425	972-9482	PK-8	Angela Fanjul
Early Light Academy	11709 S Vadania Dr	South Jordan, UT	84009	801-302-5988	727-0773	K-9	Sydney Young
East Hollywood HS	2185 S 3600 W	West Valley, UT	84119-1121	801-886-8181	972-9585	9-12	Katrina Walker
Edison Charter S - North	180 E 2600 N	North Logan, UT	84341-1551	435-787-2820	787-0299	K-9	Scott Jackson
Edison Charter S - South	1275 W 2350 S	Nibley, UT	84321-6181	435-752-0123	787-4350	K-9	Melani Kirk
Endeavor Hall Charter S	2614 S Decker Lake Ln	West Valley, UT	84119	801-972-1153	972-1163	K-8	Simon Raubenheimer
Entheos Academy-Kearns	4710 W 6200 S	Kearns, UT	84118	801-417-5444	417-5448	K-9	Eric Robins
Entheos Academy-Magna	2606 S 7200 W	Magna, UT	84044	801-250-5233	250-5240	K-9	Mat Edvik
Esperanza ES	4956 W 3500 S	West Valley, UT	84120	801-305-1450	722-8252	K-6	Eulogio Alejandre
Excelsior Academy	124 E Erda Way	Tooele, UT	84074-9735	435-882-3062	882-4997	K-8	Stephanie Eccles
Fast Forward Charter HS	875 W 1400 N	Logan, UT	84321-6804	435-713-4255	753-9615	9-12	Jill Lowe
Franklin Discovery Academy	320 E Gammon Rd	Vineyard, UT	84058	801-785-6500		K-6	Kris Hatch
Freedom Preparatory Academy	1190 W 900 N	Provo, UT	84604-3171	801-437-3100	437-3149	K-5	Lynne Herring
Freedom Preparatory Academy Secondary	1761 W 820 N	Provo, UT	84604	801-437-3100	437-3149	7-12	Buddy Ivie M.Ed.
Freedom Preparatoy Academy	426 N 100 W	Vineyard, UT	84058	801-437-3100	437-3149	K-5	Jonathan Kano
Gateway Preparatory Academy	201 E Thoroughbred Way	Enoch, UT	84721	866-867-5558	867-5497	K-8	Andrew Burt
Good Foundations Academy	5101 S 1050 W	Riverdale, UT	84405	801-393-2950	393-2953	K-6	Brent Petersen
Greenwood Charter S	840 N US 89	Harrisville, UT	84404	801-590-2972	689-0331	K-8	Jessie Kidd
Guadalupe S	1385 N 1200 W	Salt Lake City, UT	84116	801-531-6100	531-6106	K-6	Richard Pater
Hancock Charter S	125 N 100 E	Pleasant Grove, UT	84062-2355	801-796-5646	785-4934	K-8	Julie Adamic
Hawthorn Academy - South Jordan Campus	1137 W 11400 S	South Jordan, UT	84095	801-260-3040	254-6677	K-6	Spencer Jacobs
Hawthorn Academy - West Jordan Campus	9062 S 2200 W	West Jordan, UT	84088	801-282-9066	727-0836	K-9	Ryan Dubois
HighMark Charter S	2467 E South Weber Dr	South Weber, UT	84405	801-476-4627	475-5803	K-9	Mary Johnston
Intech Collegiate HS	1787 Research Park Way	North Logan, UT	84341-5600	435-753-7377	753-3775	9-12	Jason Stanger
Itineris Early College HS	8714 S Roy Del Cir	West Jordan, UT	84088	385-800-2140	800-2141	10-12	Renee Edwards
Jefferson Academy	1425 S Angel St	Kaysville, UT	84037	801-593-8200	660-6996	K-6	Nicole Jones
Kairos Academy	1325 W 2200 S	West Valley, UT	84119	385-355-1640		9-12	Brad Lester
Lakeview Academy	527 W 400 N	Saratoga Spgs, UT	84045	801-331-6788	331-6792	K-9	Rick Veasey

School	Address	City,State	Zip code	Telephone	Fax	Grade	Contact
Leadership Learning Academy	100 W 2675 N	Layton, UT	84041	801-593-9552	784-5174	K-6	Heidi Bauerle
Legacy Preparatory Academy	1375 W Center St	North Salt Lake, UT	84054-2952	801-936-0555	936-1038	K-4	Karen Holman
Legacy Preparatory Academy	2214 S 1250 W	Woods Cross, UT	84087	801-294-2801		5-9	Priscilla Stringfellow
Lewis Academy	364 N State Road 198	Santaquin, UT	84655	801-754-3376	754-3102	K-6	Diane Nelson
Lincoln Academy	1582 W 3300 N	Pleasant Grove, UT	84062-9041	801-756-2039	785-2109	K-9	Jake Hunt
Lumen Scholar Institute	2342 Coyote St	Eagle Mountain, UT	84005	801-987-9497		K-12	Rebecca Harrison
Maeser Prep Academy	320 W 600 S	Lindon, UT	84042	801-235-9000	235-9010	7-12	Robyn Ellis
Mana Aademy Charter S	2355 S Technology Dr	West Valley, UT	84119	801-972-6262	401-7135	K-12	Fr. Anapesi Kaili
Maria Montessori Academy	2505 N 200 E	Ogden, UT	84414	801-827-0150	827-0145	K-9	Stephanie Speicher
Merit College Prep Academy	1440 W Center St	Springville, UT	84663	801-491-7600	491-7650	7-12	Kim Mitchell
Moab Charter S	358 E 300 S	Moab, UT	84532-2624	435-259-2277	259-6652	K-6	
Monticello Academy	2782 S Corporate Park Dr	West Valley, UT	84120	801-417-8040	417-8041	K-9	Dr. Gregory Cox
Mountain Heights Academy	9067 S 1300 W Ste 204	West Jordan, UT	84088	801-721-6329	670-0032	7-12	DeLaina Tonks
Mountainville Academy	195 S Main St	Alpine, UT	84004-1630	801-756-9805	763-9823	K-9	Janese Vance
Mountain West Montessori Academy	4125 S Foxview Dr	South Jordan, UT	84095	801-566-6962	727-7109	K-9	Amy Pilkington
Navigator Pointe Academy	6844 S Navigator Dr	West Jordan, UT	84084	801-840-1210	840-1236	K-9	Judy Farris
North Davis Preparatory Academy	1765 W Hill Field Rd	Layton, UT	84041-7323	801-547-1809	547-1649	K-9	Ryan Robinson
Northern Utah Acad for Math Engnrg & Sci	2750 University Park Blvd	Layton, UT	84041-9099	801-395-3350	395-3351	10-12	Kelli Booth
North Star Academy	2920 W 14000 S	Bluffdale, UT	84065	801-302-9579	302-9578	K-9	Tana Archer
Odyssey Charter S	738 Quality Dr	American Fork, UT	84003-3309	801-492-8105	763-8743	K-6	Russell Schellhous
Ogden Preparatory Academy	1415 Lincoln Ave	Ogden, UT	84404	801-627-2066	394-2267	K-6	Amie Campbell
Ogden Preparatory Academy	1435 Lincoln Ave	Ogden, UT	84404	801-627-3066	395-2267	7-9	Amie Campbell
Open Classroom	134 D St	Salt Lake City, UT	84103-2640	801-578-8144	578-8218	PK-8	Christine Marriott
Pacific Heritage Academy	1755 W 1100 N	Salt Lake City, UT	84116	801-363-1892	364-4735	K-8	Dirk Matthias
Paradigm HS	11577 S 3600 W	South Jordan, UT	84095	801-676-1018	676-1036	9-12	Fernando Seminario
Pinnacle Canyon Academy	210 N 600 E	Price, UT	84501-2613	435-613-8102	613-8105	K-12	Roberta Hardy
Pioneer HS for the Performing Arts	704 S 600 E	American Fork, UT	84003	801-768-8787		9-12	Shari Bradley
Promontory S of Expeditionary Learning	1051 W 2700 S	Perry, UT	84302	435-919-1900	919-1902	K-8	Jamie McKay
Providence Hall ES	4795 W Patriot Ridge Dr	Herriman, UT	84096	801-727-8260	727-8282	K-6	
Providence Hall HS	4557 W Patriot Ridge Dr	Herriman, UT	84096	801-727-8260		9-12	Nate Marshall
Providence Hall JHS	4558 W Patriot Ridge Dr	Herriman, UT	84096	801-727-8260	432-8496	6-8	Brian Fauver
Quest Academy	4862 W 4000 S	West Haven, UT	84401	801-731-9859	731-9860	K-9	Dr. David Bullock
Ranches Academy	7789 N Tawny Owl Cir	Eagle Mountain, UT	84005	801-789-4000	789-4001	K-6	Susie Scherer
Reagan Academy	1143 W Center St	Springville, UT	84663-3028	801-489-7828	491-2829	K-8	Justin Riggs
Renaissance Academy	3435 N 1120 E	Lehi, UT	84043-6538	801-768-4202	768-4295	K-9	Mark Ursic
Rockwell Charter HS	3435 Stonebridge Ln	Eagle Mountain, UT	84005	801-789-7625	789-7628	7-12	Darren Beck
Roots Charter HS	2250 S 1300 W	West Valley, UT	84119	801-573-8719		9-12	Tyler Bastian
Salt Lake Arts Academy	844 S 200 E	Salt Lake City, UT	84111-4203	801-531-1173	531-7726	5-8	Amy Wadsworth
Salt Lake Center for Science Education	1400 W Goodwin Ave	Salt Lake City, UT	84116	801-578-8226	578-8677	6-12	Gina Sanzenbacher
Salt Lake School for the Performing Arts	2291 S 2000 E	Salt Lake City, UT	84106-4138	801-466-6700	485-1707	9-12	Ronald Litteral
Scholar Academy	928 N 100 E	Tooele, UT	84074	435-566-6957	882-6641	K-6	Sandy Shepard
Soldier Hollow Charter S	2002 Olympic Dr	Midway, UT	84049-6216	435-654-1347	654-1349	K-6	Brenda Hedden
Spectrum Academy	665 Cutler Dr	North Salt Lake, UT	84054	801-936-0318	936-0209	7-12	Christina Guevera
Spectrum Academy	575 Cutler Dr	North Salt Lake, UT	84054	801-936-0318	936-0568	K-6	Christine Manning
Spectrum Academy - Pleasant Grove	867 S 800 W	Pleasant Grove, UT	84062	801-785-9019	899-1635	K-10	Liz Banner
Stegner Academy	980 S Bending River Rd	Salt Lake City, UT	84104	801-884-7950		K-8	Adam Gerlach
Success Academy at SUU	351 W University Blvd	Cedar City, UT	84720	435-865-8790	865-8795	9-12	John Tripp
Success Academy DSU	225 S 700 E	Saint George, UT	84770-3875	435-652-7830	656-4149	10-12	John Tripp
Summit Academy	1285 E 13200 S	Draper, UT	84020-9000	801-572-4166	572-4169	K-8	Tyler Whittle
Summit Academy - Bluffdale	1940 W 14400 S	Bluffdale, UT	84065	801-254-9488		K-8	Odila Conica
Summit Academy HS	14942 S 560 W	Bluffdale, UT	84065	801-495-3272	495-3275	9-12	Ted Mecham
Summit Academy - Independence	15327 S Noell Nelson Dr	Bluffdale, UT	84065	801-987-8755	987-8733	K-8	Lisa Cutler
Syracuse Arts Academy - Antelope	2893 W 1700 S	Syracuse, UT	84075-9838	801-779-2066	779-2087	K-9	Jan Whimpey
Syracuse Arts Academy - North	357 S 1550 W	Syracuse, UT	84075	801-827-0540	774-9270	K-6	Judy Nixon
Terra Academy	267 Aggie Blvd	Vernal, UT	84078	844-322-6562	887-9006	K-12	Cassie Hays
Timpanogos Academy	70 S 100 E	Lindon, UT	84042	801-785-4979	785-9690	K-6	Errol Porter
Tuacahn HS for the Performing Arts	1100 Tuacahn	Ivins, UT	84738-4701	435-652-3201	652-3306	9-12	Dr. Drew Williams
Uintah River HS	PO Box 235	Fort Duchesne, UT	84026-0235	435-725-4088	722-0811	9-12	Ben Pugh
Utah Career Path HS	450 S Simmons Way	Kaysville, UT	84037	801-593-2440	593-2140	9-12	Robyn Bagley
Utah Connections Academy	687 W 700 S Ste E	Woods Cross, UT	84087	801-298-6660	298-6670	K-12	Jeffrey Herr
Utah County Academy of Science	940 W 800 S	Orem, UT	84058-5915	801-863-2222	225-2214	10-12	Dr. Anna Trevino
Utah International Charter S	350 E Baird Cir	Salt Lake City, UT	84115	385-290-1306		7-12	Angela Rowland
Utah Military Academy - Riverdale	5120 S 1050 W	Riverdale, UT	84405	801-689-3013	689-3325	7-12	Matt Throckmorton
Utah Virtual Academy	310 E 4500 S Ste 620	Murray, UT	84107	801-262-4922	262-5086	K-12	Stacey Hutchings
Valley Academy Charter S	539 N 870 W	Hurricane, UT	84737	435-635-0772		K-8	Kevin Dunkley
Vanguard Academy	2650 S Decker Lake Lane	West Valley, UT	84119	801-327-8724	327-8725	7-12	Suzanne Owen
Venture Academy	495 N 1500 W	Ogden, UT	84404	801-393-3900	393-2006	K-12	Dr. Mark Child
Vista at Entrada S	585 E Center St	Ivins, UT	84738	435-673-4110	256-6433	K-8	Samuel Gibbs
Voyage Academy	1891 N 1500 W	Clinton, UT	84015	801-776-4900	776-1966	K-6	Stacee Phillips
Walden S of Liberal Arts	4230 N University Ave	Provo, UT	84604	801-374-1545	374-3397	PK-12	Dr. Lois Bobo
Wasatch Peak Academy	414 Cutler Dr	North Salt Lake, UT	84054-2951	801-936-3066	936-0887	K-6	Emily Swan
Wasatch Waldorf Charter S	1458 E Murray Holladay Rd	Murray, UT	84117	801-871-3950		K-8	Emily Merchant
Washington Academy	2277 S 3000 E	Saint George, UT	84790-8510	435-673-2232	673-0142	K-8	Anya Yeager M.S.
Weber State University Charter Academy	1351 Edvalson St	Ogden, UT	84408	801-626-6271	626-7427	K-K	Camie Bearden M.Ed.
Webster Academy	205 E 400 S	Orem, UT	84058-6311	801-426-6624		K-6	Angela Rasmussen M.Ed.
Weilenmann S of Discovery	4199 Kilby Rd	Park City, UT	84098	435-575-5411	575-5412	K-8	Cindy Phillips
Winter Sports S in Park City	4251 Shadow Mountain Dr	Park City, UT	84098	435-649-8760	649-9087	9-12	Tess Miner-Farra
Virginia							
Community Public Charter S	1200 Forest St	Charlottesville, VA	22903	434-972-1607	984-4975	6-8	Chad Ratliff
Green Run Collegiate Charter S	1700 Dahlia Dr	Virginia Beach, VA	23453	757-648-5393	965-3089	9-12	Barbara Winn
Henry S of Science and Arts	3411 Semmes Ave	Richmond, VA	23225	804-888-7061	888-7064	K-5	Eileen Atkinson
Hillsboro Charter Academy	37110 Charles Town Pike	Purcellville, VA	20132-2942	540-751-2560	771-6732	K-5	Mark Wertheimer
Middleburg Community Charter S	101 N Madison St	Middleburg, VA	20117-2645	540-687-5048	542-1257	K-5	David Larson
York River Academy	11201 George Washington Mem	Yorktown, VA	23690-9701	757-898-0516	890-1045	9-12	Walter Cross
Washington							
Destiny MS	1301 E 34th St	Tacoma, WA	98404	253-772-5883	382-2402	6-8	Cheryl Sullivan
Excel Charter S	19300 108th Ave SE	Kent, WA	98031	253-487-7530		7-9	Kristina Howard
Pride Prep	811 E Sprague Ave	Spokane, WA	99202	509-309-7680	309-7686	6-12	Brenda McDonald
Rainier Prep	10211 12th Ave S	Seattle, WA	98168	206-494-5979	494-5979	5-8	
Rainier Valley Leadership Academy	3900 S Holly Park Dr	Seattle, WA	98118	206-659-0956		6-6	Walter Chen
Rainier Valley Leadership Academy HS	6020 Rainier Ave S	Seattle, WA	98118	206-773-3234		9-12	
SOAR Academy	2136 Martin Luther King Jr	Tacoma, WA	98405	253-444-6759		K-8	Lihi Rosenthal
Spokane International Academy	2706 E Queen Ave	Spokane, WA	99217	509-209-8730		K-3	Morgen Flowers
Spokane International Academy	4224 E 4th Ave	Spokane, WA	99202	509-321-8950		5-8	Melissa Pettey
Summit Atlas	9601 35th Ave SW	Seattle, WA	98126	253-987-1535		6-9	Katie Bubalo
Summit Olympus	409 Puyallup Ave	Tacoma, WA	98421	253-444-9781	444-9778	9-12	Greg Ponikvar
Summit Sierra	1025 S King St	Seattle, WA	98104	206-453-2520		9-12	Malia Burns
Wisconsin							
Advanced Learning Academy of WI	100 W River Ave	Barron, WI	54812	715-537-5612	637-5161	K-12	Jessica Mullikin
A L B A	1712 S 32nd St	Milwaukee, WI	53215-2104	414-902-7525	902-7526	PK-5	Brenda Martinez
Alliance Charter ES	215 E Forest Ave	Neenah, WI	54956-2765	920-751-6970	751-6861	K-5	Diane Luft
Alliance HS	850 W Walnut St	Milwaukee, WI	53205	414-267-5400	267-5415	9-12	Allan Laird
ALPS Charter S	325 S Eagle St	Oshkosh, WI	54902	920-424-0320	424-7514	5-8	Jay Jones
Andrews Academy	1225 4th St	Beloit, WI	53511	608-361-3000	361-4122	6-12	Darrell Williams
Appleton Bilingual S	913 N Oneida St	Appleton, WI	54911	920-832-6232	832-6355	K-6	Joel Cannon
Appleton Central HS	PO Box 2019	Appleton, WI	54912-2019	920-832-6136	993-7074	6-12	Justin Heitl
Appleton eSchool	2121 E Emmers Dr	Appleton, WI	54915-3802	920-832-6212	832-4880	7-12	Matt Mineau
Appleton Public Montessori S	1545 E Broadway Dr	Appleton, WI	54915	920-832-6325	832-6322	K-6	Dom Ferrito
Appleton Technical Academy	610 N Badger Ave	Appleton, WI	54914	920-832-6234	832-4198	9-12	Mark McQuade
ARISE Virtual Academy	450 N Crosby Ave	Janesville, WI	53548-3340	608-743-6654	743-5130	K-12	David Parr
Ashland Charter HS	1900 Beaser Ave	Ashland, WI	54806	715-682-7089	682-2075	9-12	Brian Trettin
Badger Rock MS	501 E Badger Rd	Madison, WI	53713	608-442-1335	442-1347	6-8	Timothy Bubon
Barron Area Montessori S	808 E Woodland Ave	Barron, WI	54812-1759	715-537-5621	637-9353	PK-4	Tawnee Glinski
Bayshore Community Academy	400 Michigan Ave	Oconto, WI	54153	920-834-7406	834-9884	5-8	Adam DeWitt
Birchwood Blue Hills Charter HS	201 E Birch Ave	Birchwood, WI	54817	715-354-3471	354-3469	7-12	Jeffrey Stanley
Birchwood Public Montessori S	201 E Birch Ave	Birchwood, WI	54817	715-354-3471	354-3469	K-6	Jeffrey Stanley
Bobcat Virtual Academy	300 S Wilson St	Birchwood, WI	54817	715-354-3471		K-12	Jeffrey Stanley
Bridges Virtual S	1201 N Sales St	Merrill, WI	54452	866-539-8560		K-12	John Hagemeister
Brompton S	7951 36th Ave	Kenosha, WI	53142-2119	262-359-2191	359-2194	K-8	Suzanne Loewen
Bruce - Guadalupe Community S	1028 S 9th St	Milwaukee, WI	53204-1335	414-643-6441	649-9022	K-8	Pascual Rodriguez
Capitol West Academy	3939 N 88th St	Milwaukee, WI	53222-2748	414-465-1302	465-1319	PK-8	Donna Niccolai-Weber
C.A.R.E. Charter S	2031 Porter Rd	Plover, WI	54467	715-342-0614	342-0614	7-9	Steve Prokop

School	Address	City,State	Zip code	Telephone	Fax	Grade	Contact
Carmen HS of Science & Tech - Southeast	2500 W Oklahoma Ave	Milwaukee, WI	53215	414-509-7800	509-7850	9-12	Shenora Jordan
Carmen HS of Science and Tech - South	1712 S 32nd St	Milwaukee, WI	53215-2104	414-384-4444	384-4455	9-12	Patricia Hoben
Carmen MSHS of Science & Tech - NW	5496 N 72nd St	Milwaukee, WI	53218	414-837-4000		6-12	Dr. Patricia Hoben
Catalyst Academy	709 S Shawano St	New London, WI	54961-1754	920-982-8686		7-12	Anna Krueger
Catalyst Charter MS	PO Box 991	Ripon, WI	54971	920-748-4638	748-4653	6-8	Rick Bunge
CAVE	PO Box 378	Cameron, WI	54822	715-458-4560	458-4236	PK-12	Jon Griffith
Central City Cyberschool	4301 N 44th St	Milwaukee, WI	53216-1473	414-444-2330	444-2435	K-8	Christine Faltz
Central HS	621 S Water St	Sheboygan, WI	53081-4431	920-459-6746	803-7756	9-12	Bill Klein
Central Wisconsin STEM Academy	540 Birch St	Nekoosa, WI	54457	715-886-8040	886-8097	4-8	Clint Rogers
Chippewa Valley Montessori Charter S	400 Cameron St	Eau Claire, WI	54703-5101	715-852-6950	852-6995	PK-5	Todd Johnson
Cirrus Charter HS	301 W Division St	Rosendale, WI	54974	920-872-2161	872-5482	9-12	Nate Roets
Clark Street Community S	2429 Clark St	Middleton, WI	53562	608-829-9640	831-5160	9-12	Jill Gurtner
Class ACT Charter S	400 9th St N	Park Falls, WI	54552-1384	715-762-2474	762-5674	9-12	Timothy Kief
Classical Charter S	3310 N Durkee St	Appleton, WI	54911-1215	920-832-4968	997-1390	K-8	Thomas Boman
Community HS	6700 N 80th St	Milwaukee, WI	53223	414-256-8200	256-8215	9-12	Joel Eul
Connects Learning Center	6201 S Barland Ave	Cudahy, WI	53110-2951	414-766-5090	766-5095	9-12	Stacey Adamczyk
CORE 4-Edgerton ES	5145 S 116th St	Hales Corners, WI	53130-1001	414-525-8900	525-8901	PK-PK	Lori Komas
CORE 4-Hales Corners ES	11319 W Godsell Ave	Hales Corners, WI	53130	414-525-8800	525-8801	PK-PK	Lori Komas
Coulee Montessori Charter S	1611 Kane St	La Crosse, WI	54603	608-789-7970	789-0035	PK-5	Laura Huber
Creative Minds Charter S	7450 Titus Dr	Minocqua, WI	54548-9139	715-356-5206	356-1626	3-5	Brent Johnson
Daniels University Preparatory Academy	4834 N Mother Daniels Way	Milwaukee, WI	53209-5981	414-466-1650		K-8	Mondell Mayfield
D.C. Everest Idea S	4704 Camp Phillips Rd	Weston, WI	54476	715-359-1040		6-12	Casey Nye
Denmark Community Charter S	450 N Wall St	Denmark, WI	54208-9416	920-863-4153	863-4036	7-12	Melissa Dupke
De Soto Virtual S	615 Main St	De Soto, WI	54624-8644	608-648-0102		K-12	Scott Kelly
Destinations Career Academy of WI	4709 Dale Curtin Dr	Mc Farland, WI	53558	855-475-3218		K-12	Nicholaus Sutherland
Dewey Academy of Learning	1420 Harvey St	Green Bay, WI	54302	920-272-7074	272-7093	9-12	Jen Agamaite
Dimensions of Learning Academy	6218 25th Ave	Kenosha, WI	53143-4370	262-359-6849	359-3134	K-8	Diana Pearson
Discovery Charter S	200 Fuller St	Columbus, WI	53925-1647	920-623-5950	623-6026	K-3	Beth Hellpap
Downtown Montessori Academy	2507 S Graham St	Milwaukee, WI	53207-1609	414-744-6005	744-6007	K-8	Virginia Flynn
eAchieve Academy of Wisconsin	222 Maple Ave	Waukesha, WI	53186-4725	262-970-1074	970-1148	K-12	Rick Nettesheim
Eagleville Elementary Charter S	S101W34511 County Road LO	Eagle, WI	53119	262-363-6258	594-5495	K-6	Ron Schlicht
Elkhorn Options Virtual Charter S	3 N Jackson St	Elkhorn, WI	53121-1905	262-723-3160	723-4652	K-12	Trisha Spende
Endeavor Charter S	825 Endeavour Dr	Watertown, WI	53098	920-262-7525		9-12	Bob Logan
Enrich Excel Achieve Learning Academy	2607 N 18th St	Wausau, WI	54403	715-261-0636	845-2913	6-12	Dr. Shannon Young
Escuela Verde	3628 W Pierce St	Milwaukee, WI	53215-1030	414-988-7960	988-7961	7-12	Joella Zocher
Etude ES	3508 N 21st St	Sheboygan, WI	53083	920-459-0947		K-5	Susan Griffiths
Etude HS	834 Virginia Ave	Sheboygan, WI	53081	920-459-0950		9-12	Ted Hamm
Etude MS	843 Jefferson Ave	Sheboygan, WI	53081	920-459-0946		6-8	Ted Hamm
Exploration Academy	400 N Main St	Verona, WI	53593-1147	608-845-4550		9-12	Pheng Lee
Fairview S	6500 W Kinnickinnic River	Milwaukee, WI	53219-3099	414-546-7700	546-7715	PK-8	Ebbie Wells
Fond du Lac STEM Academy	401 S Military Rd	Fond du Lac, WI	54935	920-906-6722		3-5	Timothy Scottberg
Fond du Lac STEM Institute	401 S Military Rd	Fond du Lac, WI	54935	920-906-6722		6-10	Timothy Scottberg
Foster ES	305 W Foster St	Appleton, WI	54915-1515	920-832-6288	832-4831	K-6	Matt Zimmerman
Fox Cities Leadership Academy	5000 N Ballard Rd	Appleton, WI	54913-8942	920-832-4300	832-4301	9-12	Patrick Lee
Fox River Academy	1000 S Mason St	Appleton, WI	54914-5457	920-832-6260	993-1390	1-8	Lori Leschisin
Fox West Academy	220 Warner St	Hortonville, WI	54944-8559	920-779-7929	779-7923	6-8	Steven Gromala
Grandview HS	2745 S 13th st	Milwaukee, WI	53215-3875	414-672-1168	672-1273	9-12	Debi Harry
HACIL	15930 W 5th St	Hayward, WI	54843	715-934-2112	934-8080	PK-12	Crystal Hexum
Harborside Academy	714 49th St	Kenosha, WI	53140-3353	262-359-8400	359-8450	6-12	William Haithcock
Hartland Fine Arts Leadership Academy	232 Church St	Hartland, WI	53029-1704	262-369-6710	369-6711	K-2	Heather Grindatti
Hawley Environmental S	5610 W Wisconsin Ave	Milwaukee, WI	53213-4258	414-256-8500	256-8515	PK-5	Richard Bukosky
Highland Community ES	1030 Cardinal Dr	Highland, WI	53543-9791	608-929-4525	929-4527	PK-5	Josh Tarrell
Highland Community HS	1030 Cardinal Dr	Highland, WI	53543-9791	608-929-4525	929-4527	9-12	Josh Tarrell
Highland Community MS	1030 Cardinal Dr	Highland, WI	53543-9791	608-929-4525	929-4527	6-8	Josh Tarrell
Highland Community S	1706 W Highland Ave	Milwaukee, WI	53233	414-342-1412	342-1408	PK-8	Dr. Mark Joerres
High Marq Environmental Charter S	222 Forest Ln	Montello, WI	53949-9390	608-297-2126	297-7726	7-12	Chuck Harsh
HS of Health Sciences	349 N Oak Crest Dr	Wales, WI	53183	262-968-6273		9-12	Stephen Plum
Hines Academy	7151 N 86th St	Milwaukee, WI	53224-4861	414-358-3542	760-3501	PK-8	Precious Washington
Hmong American Peace Academy	4601 N 84th St	Milwaukee, WI	53225-4958	414-383-4944	383-4950	PK-12	Chris Her-Xiong
Honey Creek Continuous Progess Charter S	6701 W Eden Pl	Milwaukee, WI	53220-1335	414-604-7900	604-7915	PK-5	Gitanjali Chawla
Humboldt Park ES	3230 S Adams Ave	Milwaukee, WI	53207-2700	414-294-1700	294-1715	PK-8	Georgia Becker
i4Learning Community S	5760 Mohawk Rd	Campbellsport, WI	53010	262-626-3102	626-4401	PK-5	Jacob Flood
IDEAL Charter S	1420 W Goldcrest Ave	Milwaukee, WI	53221	414-267-1600	267-1615	K-8	Jennifer Carter
IForward: Wisconsin's Online Charter S	480 E James Ave	Grantsburg, WI	54840	855-447-4723	463-6677	6-12	Billy Beesley
iLEAD Charter S	510 Grayside Ave	Mauston, WI	53948	608-847-4410	847-4635	7-12	Gil Saylor
Innovations STEM Academy	1225 N Water St	Sparta, WI	54656-4303	608-366-3497		6-8	Kurt Sanders
Island City Academy	980 8th Ave	Cumberland, WI	54829-9188	715-822-5122	822-5132	7-12	Colin Green
Island City Virtual Academy	1010 8th Ave	Cumberland, WI	54829	715-822-5124	822-5136	PK-12	Dr. Barry Rose
JEDI Virtual HS	1221 Innovation Dr	Whitewater, WI	53190	262-473-1469	472-2269	PK-12	Leslie Steinhaus
Journey Charter S	PO Box 991	Ripon, WI	54971	920-748-1550	748-1552	K-2	Tanya Sanderfoot
Juneau County Charter S	N11003 17th Ave	Necedah, WI	54646	608-565-7494	565-7559	7-12	Amy McMillen
Kaleidoscope Academy	318 E Brewster St	Appleton, WI	54911-3702	920-832-6294	832-4605	6-8	Al Brant
Kenosha e-School	1808 41st Pl	Kenosha, WI	53140-5612	262-359-7715	359-5933	K-12	Dan Tenuta
Kenosha Schl of Enhanced Tech/Curriculum	6811 18th Ave	Kenosha, WI	53143-4932	262-359-3800	359-3850	K-8	Angela Andersson
Kiel eSchool	PO Box 201	Kiel, WI	53042-0201	920-894-5169	894-5100	7-12	Heidi Dorner
KM Explore Charter S	219 N Oak Crest Dr	Wales, WI	53183-9705	262-968-6300		PK-5	Laura Dahm
KM Global S	349 N Oak Crest Dr	Wales, WI	53183	262-968-6273	968-6390	9-12	Erica Bardon
KM Perform	349 N Oak Crest Dr	Wales, WI	53183	262-968-6273	968-6217	9-12	Kevin Erickson
La Casa de Esperanza Charter S	410 Arcadian Ave	Waukesha, WI	53186	262-547-0887	547-0735	K-K	Lashawnda Holland
La Causa Charter S	PO Box 4188	Milwaukee, WI	53204	414-902-1660	902-1676	K-8	Maria Ayala
La Crosse Design Institute	1900 Denton St	La Crosse, WI	54601	608-789-7670	789-7975	6-8	Penny Reedy
LaCrossroads Charter HS	1801 Losey Blvd S	La Crosse, WI	54601	608-789-7700	789-7711	9-12	Jeff Axness
Lake Country Academy	4101 Technology Pkwy	Sheboygan, WI	53083-6049	920-208-3020	208-3022	PK-8	Shawn Dzwonkowski
Laker Online Virtual Charter S	205 Oak St	Turtle Lake, WI	54889-8929	715-986-4470	986-2444	K-12	Kent Kindschy
Lake Superior IS	1101 Binsfield Rd	Ashland, WI	54806	715-682-7083	682-7506	3-5	Travis Powell
Lakeview Montessori S	711 Pine St	Sparta, WI	54656	608-366-3468	366-3473	PK-6	Patrick Olbert
Laurel HS	100 Blackhawk Dr	Viroqua, WI	54665-1315	608-637-3191	637-8034	9-12	Katherine Klos
LEADS Primary Charter S	1410 Waukechon Rd	Shawano, WI	54166	715-524-2134	526-4372	PK-2	Troy Edwards
LIFE Entrepreneurial S	800 N Shore Dr	Hartland, WI	53029-2713	262-369-6767	369-3766	6-8	Michele Schmidt
Lighthouse Learning Academy	4521 Lincoln Ave	Two Rivers, WI	54241	920-793-4560		K-12	Lisa Quistorf
Link2Learn Virtual Charter S	PO Box 6	Chetek, WI	54728	715-924-2226	924-2376	PK-12	Kim Ruda
Little Chute Career Pathways	325 Meulemans St Ste A	Little Chute, WI	54140	920-788-7600	788-7841	9-12	Tony Bird
Little Chute FLEX Academy	325 Meulemans St Ste B	Little Chute, WI	54140	920-380-9250	788-7603	K-7	Kent Swanson
Lumen Charter HS	PO Box 991	Ripon, WI	54971-0991	920-748-4616	748-4622	9-12	Randy Hatlen
Magellan Charter MS	225 N Badger Ave	Appleton, WI	54914-3832	920-832-6226	832-4857	7-8	Debra Moreland
Maple Grove Charter S	290 County Road F	Hamburg, WI	54411-9141	715-536-7684	536-4221	K-5	Dawn Nonn
Marathon Venture Academy	100 Spring Valley Dr	Marathon, WI	54448-3400	715-443-2538		6-8	Sarah Budny
Marshall Charter S	PO Box 76	Marshall, WI	53559-0076	608-655-1310	655-3046	11-12	Brian Sniff
Mauston Montessori Charter S	708 Loomis Dr	Mauston, WI	53948	608-847-1828		PK-3	Jolene Routson
McKinley Academy	1010 Huron St	Manitowoc, WI	54220-3314	920-686-4700	686-4701	9-12	Luke Valitchka
McKinley Charter S	1266 McKinley Rd	Eau Claire, WI	54703-2220	715-852-6900	852-6904	6-12	Peter Riley
Mead Charter S	241 17th Ave S	Wisc Rapids, WI	54495-2408	715-424-6777	422-6333	PK-6	Margie Dorshorst
Merrill Adult Diploma Academy	1101A N Mill St	Merrill, WI	54452-1179	715-536-1431	539-2769	10-12	Shannon Murray
Merrimac Community Charter S	360 School St	Merrimac, WI	53561-9584	608-643-1995	493-2895	PK-5	Sid Malek
Mighty River Acad of Virtual Education	800 E Crawford St	Pr du Chien, WI	53821-2327	608-326-3703		K-12	Mike Liddell
Milwaukee Academy of Science	2000 W Kilbourn Ave	Milwaukee, WI	53233-1625	414-933-0302	933-1426	PK-12	Anthony McHenry
Milwaukee College Prep - 38th St	2623 N 38th St	Milwaukee, WI	53210-2502	414-445-1000	445-1005	K-8	Maggy Olson
Milwaukee College Prep - Lloyd St	1228 W Lloyd St	Milwaukee, WI	53205	414-264-6000	264-2004	K-8	Mark Ketterhagen
Milwaukee College Prep S - 36th St	2449 N 36th St	Milwaukee, WI	53210-3040	414-445-8020	445-8167	K-8	Kristen Foster
Milwaukee College Prep S North Campus	1350 W North Ave	Milwaukee, WI	53205-1257	414-264-6600	264-6607	K-8	Michael Morgan
Milwaukee Collegiate Academy	4030 N 29th St	Milwaukee, WI	53216-1816	414-873-4014	873-4344	9-12	Judith Parker
Milwaukee Community Cyber HS	131 S 1st St	Milwaukee, WI	53204	414-308-1230	308-1231	9-12	Colleen Stuckart
Milwaukee Environmental Sciences Charter	6600 W Melvina St	Milwaukee, WI	53216	414-353-3830	353-3834	PK-8	Michael Morgan
Milwaukee Excellence Charter S	4950 N 24th St	Milwaukee, WI	53209	414-403-5892	464-7173	6-12	Maurice Thomas
Milwaukee Math & Science Academy	110 W Burleigh St	Milwaukee, WI	53212-2046	414-263-6400	263-6403	PK-8	Huseyin Alper Akyurek
Milwaukee Scholars Charter S	7000 W Florist Ave	Milwaukee, WI	53218-1855	414-393-0197		K-8	Nikole Laskov
Monona Grove Liberal Arts Charter S	5301 Monona Dr	Monona, WI	53716-3126	608-316-1924	221-7688	9-12	Kristen Langer
Montello JSHS	222 Forest Ln	Montello, WI	53949-9390	608-297-2126	297-9390	6-12	Chuck Harsh
Montello Virtual S	222 Forest Ln	Montello, WI	53949	608-297-2128	297-8075	K-12	Elizabeth Tierney-Olson
New Century Charter S	401 W Verona Ave	Verona, WI	53593	608-845-4900	845-4920	K-5	Ann Princl
New Directions Learning Community	2601 Sullivan Ave	Kaukauna, WI	54130-3564	920-766-6116	766-6122	K-4	Abbey Frischmann
New Horizons for Learning	1701 E Capitol Dr	Shorewood, WI	53211-1911	414-963-6921	961-2819	9-12	Tim Kenney
New Path Charter S	512 Caldwell Ave	Oconto Falls, WI	54154-1138	920-848-4455	848-3899	7-12	Mark Trepanier
Next Door Charter S	2545 N 29th St	Milwaukee, WI	53210-3116	414-562-2929	562-1979	PK-K	Tanya Johnson
Next Generation Academy	1700 Klatt Rd	New London, WI	54961-8603	920-982-8420	982-8440	6-12	Anne Ferge
North Division Charter HS	1011 W Center St	Milwaukee, WI	53206-3262	414-267-4900	267-5015	9-12	Keith Carrington
Northeast Wisconsin Montessori S	411 E Washington Ave	Cleveland, WI	53015-1517	920-693-8241	693-8357	1-6	Jacqueline Iseler

School	Address	City,State	Zip code	Telephone	Fax	Grade	Contact
Northern Lakes Regional Academy	33 Ann St	Rice Lake, WI	54868-2265	715-234-9007		9-12	Curt Pacholke
Northern Waters Environmental S	15930 W 5th St	Hayward, WI	54843	715-634-2619	634-9953	6-11	Brittany Roberts
Northland Pines Montessori Learning Ctr	8234 Highway 70 W	Saint Germain, WI	54558-9749	715-542-3632		PK-4	Tony Duffek
North Star Academy	207 N 1st St	Cameron, WI	54822	715-537-5612	637-5161	9-12	
NorthStar Community Charter S	N14463 Highway 53	Minong, WI	54859	715-466-2297	466-5149	4-8	Tammie Denninger
Northwood ES	N14463 Highway 53	Minong, WI	54859	715-466-2297		PK-5	Tammie Denninger
Northwood MSHS	N14463 Highway 53	Minong, WI	54859-9483	715-466-2297	466-5149	6-12	Tammie Denninger
Northwoods Community ES	9086 County K	Harshaw, WI	54529-9731	715-282-8200	282-8218	K-5	Timothy Howell
Northwoods Community Secondary S	665 Coolidge Ave	Rhinelander, WI	54501	715-365-9500	365-9687	6-12	Will Losch
Northwood Virtual Charter S	N14463 Highway 53	Minong, WI	54859	715-466-2297	466-2297	PK-12	Dana Lucius
NOVA Tech	225 W Capitol Dr	Milwaukee, WI	53212	414-301-6592	301-6593	9-12	Nancy DeYoung
NR4Kids Charter S	701 E 11th St	New Richmond, WI	54017-2399	715-243-7403	246-4278	PK-PK	Mike Ballard
Nuestro Mundo Community S	902 Nichols Rd	Monona, WI	53716-2565	608-663-1079	204-0364	K-5	Josh Forehand
Oconto Falls Alternative Learning Site	320 E Central Ave	Oconto Falls, WI	54154-1456	920-848-4455	848-3899	10-12	Mark Trepanier
Odyssey Charter S	2037 N Elinor St	Appleton, WI	54914-2255	920-832-6250	832-4389	3-6	Kristin Comerford
Oredocker Project S	203 11th St E	Ashland, WI	54806	715-682-7087	682-7944	6-8	Laura Comer
Osceola Charter Preschool	PO Box 128	Osceola, WI	54020-0128	715-294-3457	294-2428	PK-PK	Peggy Weber
Ouisconsing S of Collaboration	103 Pleasant St	Lodi, WI	53555	608-592-3855	592-2496	3-5	Sherri Endres-Lovell
Park Community Charter S	509 Lawe St	Kaukauna, WI	54130-2021	920-766-6129	766-6544	K-4	Kenneth Kortens
Pathways Charter S	1043 S Main St	West Bend, WI	53095	262-306-7125	335-6190	7-9	Anton Balzar
Pathways HS	336 W Walnut St	Milwaukee, WI	53212	414-943-2891		9-12	John Tharp
Penfield Montessori S	1441 N 24th St	Milwaukee, WI	53205	414-999-2330	488-3967	PK-8	Dr. Kathy Ronco
Phantom Knight S of Opportunity	400 Reid St Ste W	De Pere, WI	54115-2164	920-425-1915	429-1919	7-12	Dr. Jason Lau
Point of Discovery S	1900 W Zinda Dr	Stevens Point, WI	54481	715-345-5566	245-0203	6-8	Dan Lathrop
Portage Academy of Achievement	117 W Franklin St	Portage, WI	53901-1755	608-742-8545	745-0887	9-12	Matt Paulsen
Promethean Charter S	PO Box 247	Butternut, WI	54514-0247	715-769-3434	769-3712	9-12	Joseph Zirngibl
Quest ES	PO Box 991	Ripon, WI	54971-0991	920-748-4695	748-4698	3-5	Renee Bunge
REAL S	10116 Stellar Ave	Sturtevant, WI	53177	262-664-8100	664-8110	6-12	Curt Shircel
Renaissance Charter Alternative Academy	1107 S Wasson Ln	River Falls, WI	54022-2726	715-425-7687	425-7693	9-12	Kit Luedtke
Renaissance S for the Arts	610 N Badger Ave	Appleton, WI	54914-3405	920-832-5708	832-4198	9-12	Todd Kadolph
Richland Online Academy	1996 US Hwy 14 W	Richland Center, WI	53581	608-647-6106	647-8454	6-12	Jamie Johnson
River Falls Montessori ES	421 W Maple St	River Falls, WI	54022	715-425-7645	425-5380	PK-6	Nate Schurman
Rocketship Southside Community Prep	3003 W Cleveland Ave	Milwaukee, WI	53215	414-455-3539	918-8999	K-5	Jordan Blanton
Rock River Charter S	31 W Milwaukee St	Janesville, WI	53548-2911	608-743-5070	752-8430	9-12	Dr. Lisa Peterson
Rock University HS	2909 Kellogg Ave	Janesville, WI	53546-5606	608-758-6512		10-12	Tina Johnson
Rural Virtual Academy	624 College St	Medford, WI	54451	888-801-2666		PK-12	Charlie Heckel
St. Croix Academy of Virtual Education	PO Box 118	Hammond, WI	54015	715-796-4500	796-4510	K-12	Stephani Posta
S for AGricultural & Environmental Study	200 S Depot St	Fox Lake, WI	53933	920-928-3136	324-2630	PK-6	Jewel Mucklin
School for Early Developmnt & Achievment	2020 W Wells St	Milwaukee, WI	53233-2720	414-937-2024	937-2021	PK-2	Michelle Jenkins
School of Sci Engineering & Technology	PO Box 107	Blair, WI	54616	608-989-9835	989-2451	1-6	Lynn Halvorson
School of Technology & Arts I	1111 7th St S	La Crosse, WI	54601-5474	608-789-7695	789-7030	K-5	Steve Michaels
School of Technology & Arts II	510 9th St S	La Crosse, WI	54601	608-789-7780	789-7181	6-8	Melissa Murray
Shapiro STEM Academy	1050 W 18th Ave	Oshkosh, WI	54902-6602	920-424-0164	424-7594	PK-5	Trina Anderson
Shared Journeys Charter S	9004 W Lincoln Ave	West Allis, WI	53227-2452	414-328-6535	545-6230	7-12	Lisa Colla
Sheboygan Leadership Academy	1305 Saint Clair Ave	Sheboygan, WI	53081-3233	920-208-5930		PK-8	Laura Studee
SOAR Charter HS	1700 Pleasure Island Rd	Eagle River, WI	54521	715-479-5701	479-5808	9-12	Carie Brock
SOAR Charter S	6485 Town Hall Rd	Land O Lakes, WI	54540	715-547-3619	547-3903	5-12	Carie Brock
Sparta Area Independent Learning S	201 E Franklin St	Sparta, WI	54656	608-366-3430	366-3529	9-12	John Blaha
Sparta Charter Preschool	201 E Franklin St	Sparta, WI	54656	608-269-3151	366-3529	PK-PK	Diane Everson-Riley
Sparta High Point Charter S	201 E Franklin St	Sparta, WI	54656-1803	608-366-3400	366-3529	6-12	Peggy Jadack
Spooner Area Virtual Academy	801 County Highway A	Spooner, WI	54801	715-635-2171	635-7174	K-12	Kurt Kunkel
Stellar Collegiate S	1115 S 7th St	Milwaukee, WI	53204	414-210-5707		PK-2	Melissa McGonegle
TAGOS Leadership Academy	1350 N Parker Dr	Janesville, WI	53545-0719	608-743-5071	743-5095	7-12	Dr. Lisa Peterson
Tenor High S	840 N Jackson St	Milwaukee, WI	53202-3807	414-431-4371	431-4376	9-12	Tyson Tlachac
Tesla Engineering Charter S	2121 E Emmers Dr	Appleton, WI	54915-3802	920-997-1399	832-4880	9-12	Paul Weisse
Time 4 Learning Charter S	5900 S 51st St	Greendale, WI	53129-2634	414-423-2750		PK-PK	Tracy Flater
Tomah Area Montessori S	1720 Academy Ave	Tomah, WI	54660	608-374-5406	372-5087	PK-6	Tim Gnewikow
Tomorrow River Community Charter S	10186 County Road MM	Amherst Jct, WI	54407	715-281-4776	346-2730	PK-6	Chamomile Nusz
Transitional Skills Center	850 Maple St	Glenwood City, WI	54013-4346	715-265-4266	265-7129	10-12	Timothy Johnson
21st Century eSchool	2429 Clark St	Middleton, WI	53562	608-829-9991	831-5160	K-12	Jill Gurtner
21st Century Prep S	1220 Mound Ave	Racine, WI	53404-3350	262-598-0026	598-0031	PK-8	Valencia Koker
UCC Acosta MS	615 W Washington St	Milwaukee, WI	53204	414-384-3100	649-1920	6-8	Santiago Navarro
Valley New S	10 E College Ave Ste 228	Appleton, WI	54911	920-993-7037	832-1725	7-12	Ben Vogel
Veritas HS	3025 W Oklahoma Ave	Milwaukee, WI	53215-4347	414-389-5574	389-5576	9-12	Sherry Tolkan
Vernon County Area Better Futures HS	100 Blackhawk Dr	Viroqua, WI	54665-1315	608-637-3191	637-8034	10-12	Katherine Klos
Verona Area Core Knowledge Charter S	740 N Main St	Verona, WI	53593-1153	608-845-4130	845-4961	K-8	Rick Kisting
Verona Area International S	5830 Devoro Rd	Fitchburg, WI	53711	608-845-4024	845-4220	K-5	Ann Princl
Viroqua Area Montessori S	115 N Education Ave	Viroqua, WI	54665	608-637-7071	637-1211	PK-6	Kate Moll
Walworth County Education Alternative HS	400 County Road H	Elkhorn, WI	53121-2035	262-741-8138	741-8131	9-12	Kelly Demerath
Warriner MSHS for Personalized Learning	712 Riverfront Dr Ste 101	Sheboygan, WI	53081	920-459-0945	459-0950	6-12	Corey Butters
Waukesha Academy of Health Professions	401 E Roberta Ave	Waukesha, WI	53186-6637	262-970-3710	970-3720	9-12	Ryan Galante
Waukesha East Alternative S	1150 Whiterock Ave	Waukesha, WI	53186-4101	262-970-4355	970-4380	9-12	Tiara Chambers
Waukesha Engineering Preparatory Academy	401 E Roberta Ave	Waukesha, WI	53186-6637	262-970-3880	970-3720	9-12	Ryan Galante
Waukesha STEM Academy	114 S Charles St	Waukesha, WI	53186-6202	262-970-2300	970-2320	K-5	James Murray
Waukesha STEM Academy	130 Walton Ave	Waukesha, WI	53186	262-970-2500	970-2520	6-8	James Murray
Waupaca County Charter S	PO Box 457	Weyauwega, WI	54983-0457	920-867-4744		6-12	Wendy Cartledge
Wausau Area Montessori Charter S	3101 N 13th St	Wausau, WI	54403-2317	715-261-0795	261-2035	K-6	Elizabeth Channel
Wausau EGL Academy	2607 N 18th St	Wausau, WI	54403	715-261-0625	845-5341	9-12	Mike Schwei
Wauwatosa STEM	1060 Glenview Ave	Wauwatosa, WI	53213-3034	414-773-1900	773-1920	K-5	Mike Heun
Westside Academy	1940 N 36th St	Milwaukee, WI	53208-1927	414-934-4400	934-4415	K-8	Renee Drane
Whittier ES	4382 S 3rd St	Milwaukee, WI	53207-4968	414-294-1400	294-1415	PK-5	Peggy Mystrow
Wildlands Research Charter S	S1 County Road K	Fall Creek, WI	54742	715-286-4400	877-2234	7-12	Paul Tweed
Windlake Academy	1445 S 32nd St	Milwaukee, WI	53215	414-672-0726	672-2019	4-8	Jim Kotsonis
Windlake ES	2433 S 15th St	Milwaukee, WI	53215-3132	414-643-9052	643-0162	K-3	Jim Kotsonis
Wisconsin Connections Academy	350 W Capitol Dr	Appleton, WI	54911	920-993-7076	832-6284	K-12	Michelle Mueller
Wisconsin Virtual Learning	401 Highland Dr	Fredonia, WI	53021-9491	262-692-3988	692-3952	PK-12	Michael Leach
WIVA	4709 Dale Curtin Dr	Mc Farland, WI	53558-8958	608-838-9482	838-9483	K-12	Nicholaus Sutherland
Woodland Progressive Charter S	7450 Titus Dr	Minocqua, WI	54548-9139	715-356-5206	358-2649	6-8	Brent Johnson
Woodlands S	5510 W Blue Mound Rd	Milwaukee, WI	53208-3012	414-475-1600	475-9575	PK-8	Patty Rogers
Woodlands S East	3121 W State St	Milwaukee, WI	53208-3494	414-937-2000	937-3730	PK-4	Tommie Myles
Wright Charter MS	1717 Fish Hatchery Rd	Madison, WI	53713-1244	608-204-1340	204-0547	6-8	Angela Crawford

Wyoming

School	Address	City,State	Zip code	Telephone	Fax	Grade	Contact
Arapahoe Charter HS	445 Little Wind Rvr Bottom	Arapahoe, WY	82510	307-856-3795		9-12	Elberta Monroe
Laramie Montessori Charter School	608 S 4th St	Laramie, WY	82070	307-742-9964	201-6965	K-6	Mark Crawford
Poder Academy	2201 Morrie Ave	Cheyenne, WY	82001	307-632-2248		K-8	Dr. Jayne Smith
Snowy Range Academy	4037 E Grand Ave Ste A	Laramie, WY	82070-5128	307-745-9930	745-9931	K-8	Dawn Wilson

BUREAU OF INDIAN AFFAIRS SCHOOLS

Agency/School	Address	City,State	Zip code	Telephone	Fax	Grade	Enr	Superintendent/Principal
Education Resource Center - Albuquerque	1011 Indian School NW	Albuquerque, NM	87104	505-563-5180	563-5281	K-12	3,300	Charlotte Garcia
Education Resource Center - Belcourt	School St #16	Belcourt, ND	58316			PK-12	400	
Education Resource Center - Bismarck	3315 University Dr	Bismarck, ND	58504			K-12	300	
Education Resource Center - Chinle	PO Box 6003	Chinle, AZ	86503-6003	928-674-5130	674-5134	K-12	600	
Education Resource Center - Crownpoint	PO Box 848	Crownpoint, NM	87313	505-786-6151	786-6016	K-12	3,800	
Education Resource Center - Flandreau	1132 N Crescent St	Flandreau, SD	57028			K-12	800	
Education Resource Center - Kyle	PO Box 333	Pine Ridge, SD	57770-0333	605-867-1306	867-5610	K-12	1,700	
Education Resource Center - Minneapolis	2001 Killebrew Dr Ste 122	Bloomington, MN	55425	952-851-5427	851-5439	K-12	1,200	Joel Longie
Education Resource Center - Nashville	545 Marriott Dr Ste 700	Nashville, TN	37214	615-564-6500	564-6701	PK-12	2,100	
Education Resource Center - Phoenix	2600 N Central Ave Ste 800	Phoenix, AZ	85004	602-265-1592	265-0293	K-12	100	Jim Hastings
Education Resource Center - Seattle	909 1st Ave Ste 192	Seattle, WA	98104	206-220-7976	220-7981	K-12	1,100	

Agency/School	Address	City,State	Zip code	Telephone	Fax	Grade	Enr	Superintendent/Principal
Education Resource Center - Shiprock	PO Box 3229	Shiprock, NM	87420	505-368-3400	368-3409	K-12	1,800	
Education Resource Center - Tuba City	PO Box 746	Tuba City, AZ	86045-0746	928-871-5932	871-5945	K-12	200	Veronica Klain
Education Resource Center - Window Rock	PO Box 1449	Window Rock, AZ	86515	928-871-5932	871-5945	K-12	1,200	John McIntosh
Bureau of Indian Affairs	1849 C St NW	Washington, DC	20240-0002	202-208-6123	208-3312			Tony Dearman
Blackwater Community S	3652 E Blackwater School Rd	Coolidge, AZ	85128	520-215-5859	215-5862	K-5		Jagdish Sharma
Casa Blanca Community S	PO Box 10940	Bapchule, AZ	85121	520-315-3489	315-3505	K-4	300	Patricia Avalos
Chemawa Indian S	3700 Chemawa Rd NE	Salem, OR	97305-1199	503-399-5721	399-5870	9-12		Lora Braucher
Dishchii'bikoh Community S	PO Box 80068	Cibecue, AZ	85911-0068	928-332-2444	332-2341	K-12		Juan Aragon
First Mesa ES	PO Box 750	Polacca, AZ	86042-0750	928-737-2581	737-2323	K-6		Alma Shinquah
Flandreau Indian HS	1132 N Crescent St	Flandreau, SD	57028	605-997-3773	997-2601	9-12		Everall Fox
Gila Crossing S	4665 W Pecos Rd	Laveen, AZ	85339	520-550-4834	550-4252	PK-8		Dr. Gregory Sackos
Hopi Day S	PO Box 42	Kykotsmovi, AZ	86039-0042	928-734-2467	734-2470	K-6		
Hopi JSHS	PO Box 337	Keams Canyon, AZ	86034-0356	928-738-5111	738-5333	7-12	500	Alban Naha
Hotevilla-Bacavi Community S	PO Box 48	Hotevilla, AZ	86030-0048	928-734-2462	734-2225	K-8		
Isleta ES	1000 Moonlight Dr SW	Albuquerque, NM	87105	505-869-2321	869-1625	K-6	200	Rebecca Vesley
Jemez Day S	PO Box 139	Jemez Pueblo, NM	87024-0139	575-834-7304	834-7081	K-6	100	Freddie Cardenas
Jicarilla Dormitory	PO Box 1009	Dulce, NM	87528-1009	575-759-3101	759-3338	1-12		David Montoya
Keams Canyon ES	PO Box 397	Keams Canyon, AZ	86034-0385	928-738-2385	738-5519	K-6	100	Gary Polacca
Laguna ES	PO Box 191	Laguna, NM	87026-0191	505-552-9200	552-7294	K-5	200	Holly Gurule
Laguna MS	PO Box 268	Laguna, NM	87026-0268	505-552-9091	552-6466	6-8	100	Thomas Trujillo
Mescalero Apache S	PO Box 230	Mescalero, NM	88340-0230	575-464-4431	464-0053	PK-12	500	Charlie Savedra
Moencopi Day S	PO Box 185	Tuba City, AZ	86045-0185	928-283-5361	283-4662	K-6		Aaron Hornbuckle
Ohkay Owingeh Community S	PO Box 1077	San Juan Pueblo, NM	87566-1077	505-852-2154	852-4305	K-8	100	Maxine Ortiz
Pine Hill S	PO Box 220	Pinehill, NM	87357-0220	505-775-3242	775-3241	K-12	300	Grant Clawson
Riverside Indian S	101 Riverside Dr	Anadarko, OK	73005	405-247-6670	247-5529	4-12		Amber Wilson
Roosevelt S, Theodore	PO Box 567	Fort Apache, AZ	85926-0567	928-338-4464	338-1009	6-8		
Salt River S	10005 E Osborn Rd	Scottsdale, AZ	85256	480-362-2500	362-2501	PK-12		Dr. Louis Laffitte
San Felipe Pueblo S	PO Box 4343	San Felipe Pb, NM	87001	505-867-3364	867-6253	K-7	400	Ruby Montoya
San Ildefonso Day S	36 Tunyo Po	Santa Fe, NM	87506-7258	505-455-2366	455-2155	K-6	50	Julianna Trujillo
Santa Clara Day S	625 Kee St	Espanola, NM	87532	505-753-4406	753-8866	K-6	100	Steve Marsh
Santa Fe Indian S	PO Box 5340	Santa Fe, NM	87502-5340	505-989-6300	989-6317	7-12		Roy Herrera
Second Mesa Day S	PO Box 98	Second Mesa, AZ	86043-0098	928-737-2571	737-2565	K-6	300	Marie Morales
Sherman Indian HS	9010 Magnolia Ave	Riverside, CA	92503-4431	951-276-6325	276-6336	9-12		Mary Yarger
Sky City Community S	PO Box 349	Pueblo of Acoma, NM	87034-0349	505-552-6671	552-6672	K-8	200	Yvonne Haven
Taos Day S	PO Box 1850	Taos, NM	87571	575-758-3652	758-1566	K-8	200	Andrew Hartwitz
Te Tsu Geh Oweenge S	RR 42 Box 2	Santa Fe, NM	87506	505-982-1516	982-2090	K-6	50	Veronica Martinez
T'siya S, Zia	1000 Borrego Canyon Rd	Zia Pueblo, NM	87053-6104	505-867-3553	867-5079	K-7		Dr. Melanie Haskin
Blackfeet Dormitory	PO Box 627	Browning, MT	59417	406-338-7441	338-5725	1-12		Eric North
Cheyenne-Eagle Butte S	PO Box 672	Eagle Butte, SD	57625-0672	605-964-8777	964-8776	K-12		Dr. Kathie Bowker
Dunseith Day S	PO Box 759	Dunseith, ND	58329-0759	701-263-4636	263-4200	K-8		Michelle Thomas
Ojibwa Indian S	PO Box 600	Belcourt, ND	58316-0600	701-477-3108	477-6039	K-8		Michael Blue
Pine Ridge S	PO Box 1202	Pine Ridge, SD	57770-1202	605-867-5193	867-5482	K-12	400	Michael Carlow
Jamerson S, Theodore	3315 University Dr	Bismarck, ND	58504-7565	701-530-0677	530-0601	K-8		Laura Hoerner
Little Eagle Grant S	PO Box 26	Little Eagle, SD	57639-0026	605-823-4235	823-2292	K-8		Jessie Fisher
Rock Creek Grant S	PO Box 127	Bullhead, SD	57621-0127	605-823-4971	823-4350	K-8		Clyde Naasz
Standing Rock Community S	PO Box 377	Fort Yates, ND	58538-0377	701-854-3461	854-2078	K-12	200	Bernadette Dauenhauer
Tate Topa Tribal S	PO Box 199	Fort Totten, ND	58335-0199	701-766-1400	766-1457	K-8		Byron Engberg
Twin Buttes S	7997 7A St NW	Halliday, ND	58636-4004	701-938-4396	938-4398	K-8	50	Sandra Starr
White Shield S	2 2nd Ave W	Roseglen, ND	58775-6009	701-743-4350	743-4501	K-12	100	Wayne Fox
Black Mesa Community S	PO Box 97	Pinon, AZ	86510-0097	928-674-3632	659-8187	K-8	50	Marie Rose
Cottonwood Day S	Navajo Route 4	Chinle, AZ	86503	928-725-3256	725-3243	K-8		Dr. Leclare Gishey
Dennehotso Boarding S	PO Box 2570	Dennehotso, AZ	86535-2570	928-658-3201	658-3221	K-8		James Brown
Greasewood Springs Community S	HC 58 Box 60	Ganado, AZ	86505-9706	928-654-3331	654-3384	PK-8	200	Lucinda Godinez
Jeehdeez'a ES	PO Box 1073	Pinon, AZ	86510-1073	928-725-3308	725-3306	K-5		Sylvia Largo
Lukachukai Community S	PO Box 230	Lukachukai, AZ	86507	928-787-4400	787-4434	K-8		Charlotte Begay
Many Farms Community S	PO Box 70	Many Farms, AZ	86538-3070	928-781-6221	781-6376	K-8		Mary James-Goy
Many Farms HS	PO Box 307	Many Farms, AZ	86538	928-781-6226	781-6355	9-12		Dr. Carmelia Becenti
Nazlini Community S	HC 58 Box 35	Ganado, AZ	86505-9704	928-755-6125	755-3729	K-6	50	Ronald Arias
Pinon Community S	PO Box 159	Pinon, AZ	86510-0159	928-725-3234	725-3232	K-12		Lorraine Yazzie
Rock Point Community S	PO Box 560	Rock Point, AZ	86545	928-659-4221	659-4235	K-12	300	Deanna Dugi
Rough Rock Community S	PO Box 5000-PTT	Chinle, AZ	86503	928-728-3550	728-3502	K-12	300	Mary Keyonnie-Cly
Alamo Navajo Community S	PO Box 5907	Alamo, NM	87825	575-854-2543	854-2545	K-12	300	Susan Comisky
Baca/Dlo'ay Azhi Community S	PO Box 509	Prewitt, NM	87045	505-972-2769	972-2310	K-6	300	Timothy Nelson
Borrego Pass S	PO Box 679	Crownpoint, NM	87313-0679	505-786-5237	786-7078	K-8	1,200	John Bach
Ch'ooshgai Community S	PO Box 321	Tohatchi, NM	87325-0321	505-733-2700	733-2703	K-8	400	Leon Oosahwe
Lake Valley Navajo S	PO Box 748	Crownpoint, NM	87313-0748	505-786-5392	786-5956	K-8	100	Dr. Tonya Sturgess
Mariano Lake Community S	PO Box 787	Crownpoint, NM	87313-0787	505-786-5265	786-5203	PK-6	100	Charles Sherman
Na NeelZhiin Ji'Olta S	HC 79 Box 9	Cuba, NM	87013-9701	575-731-2272	731-2252	K-8		Kenneth Toledo
Ojo Encino S	HC 79 Box 7	Cuba, NM	87013-9701	505-731-2333	731-2361	K-8	100	Vickie Blackwater
Pueblo Pintado Community S	HC 79 Box 80	Cuba, NM	87013-9600	575-655-3341	655-3342	PK-8	300	Irowena Whitehair
T'iis Ts'ozi Bi'Olta' S	PO Box 178	Crownpoint, NM	87313-0178	505-786-6159	786-6163	K-8	400	Virginia Jumbo
Tohaali' Community S	PO Box 9857	Newcomb, NM	87455-9857	505-789-3201	789-3202	K-8	200	Delores Bitsilly
To'Hajiilee'He S	PO Box 3438	Canoncito, NM	87026-3438	505-908-2426	908-2914	PK-12	300	Keri Jojola Ed.D.
Tse'ii'ahi' Community S	PO Box 828	Crownpoint, NM	87313-0828	505-786-5389	726-5635	K-4	100	Donald Pine
Chickasaw Children's Village	12998 Village Rd	Kingston, OK	73439	580-564-3060	564-3605	1-12		Sallie Wallace
Crow Creek Sioux Tribal S	101 Crow Creek Loop	Stephan, SD	57346	605-852-2455	852-2140	K-12		Cody Russell
Enemy Swim S	13525 446th Ave	Waubay, SD	57273-5715	605-947-4605	947-4188	PK-8	200	Virginia Dolney
Eufaula Dormitory	716 Swadley Dr	Eufaula, OK	74432	918-689-2522	689-2438	1-12		Tony York
Jones Academy	HC 74 Box 102-5	Hartshorne, OK	74547	918-297-2518	297-2364	1-12	100	Jay McAdams
Kickapoo Nation S	PO Box 106	Powhattan, KS	66527-0106	785-474-3365	474-3530	K-12	100	Debra Turner
Lower Brule Day S	PO Box 245	Lower Brule, SD	57548-0245	605-473-0216	473-0217	PK-6		Wildmike Pada
Lower Brule HS	PO Box 245	Lower Brule, SD	57548-0245	605-473-5510	473-5207	7-12		Berle Johnson
Marty Indian S	PO Box 187	Marty, SD	57361-0187	605-384-5431	384-5933	K-12		Gina Curran
Meskwaki Settlement S	1610 305th St	Tama, IA	52339	641-484-9000	484-3264	K-12		Francine Hall
Sequoyah HS	PO Box 520	Tahlequah, OK	74465	918-453-5400	456-0634	9-12		Leroy Qualls
Takini S	HC 77 Box 537	Howes, SD	57748-9511	605-538-4399	538-4315	K-12		Linda Hunter
Tiospaye Topa S	PO Box 300	Ridgeview, SD	57652-0300	605-733-2290	733-2299	K-12		Brent Mareska
Tiospa Zina Tribal S	PO Box 719	Agency Village, SD	57262-0719	605-698-3953	698-7686	K-12	500	Dr. Jen Heath
American Horse S	PO Box 660	Allen, SD	57714-0660	605-455-1209	455-2249	PK-8	300	Jodi Richards
Crazy Horse S	PO Box 260	Wanblee, SD	57577-0260	605-462-6836	462-6510	K-12	300	Silas Blaine
Isna Wica Owayawa-Loneman S	PO Box 50	Oglala, SD	57764-0050	605-867-6875	867-5109	K-8	200	Charles Cuny
Little Wound S	PO Box 500	Kyle, SD	57752-0500	605-455-6150	455-2703	PK-12	900	Charles Cuny
Pierre Indian Learning Center	3001 E Sully Ave	Pierre, SD	57501-4403	605-224-8661	224-8465	1-8		Dr. Veronica Pietz
Porcupine S	PO Box 180	Porcupine, SD	57772-0180	605-455-6450	867-5480	K-8		Wilbert Buckman
St. Francis Indian S	PO Box 379	Saint Francis, SD	57572-0379	605-747-2299	747-2379	K-12		Richard Bad Milk
St. Stephens Indian S	PO Box 345	Saint Stephens, WY	82524-0345	307-856-4147	856-3742	K-12		Frank No Runner
Sicangu Owaye Oti	PO Box 69	Mission, SD	57555	605-856-4486	856-4490	1-12		Nancy Hernandez
Wounded Knee S	PO Box 350	Manderson, SD	57756-0350	605-867-4350	867-5156	K-8		Alice Phelps
Bug-O-Nay-Ge-Shig S	15353 Silver Eagle Dr NW	Bena, MN	56626-1012	218-665-3000	665-3024	K-12	300	Mary Trapp
Circle of Life S	PO Box 447	White Earth, MN	56591-0447	218-983-4180	983-3767	K-12		Ricky White
Circle of Nations Indian Boarding S	832 8th St N	Wahpeton, ND	58075-3642	701-642-3796	642-1984	1-8		Charles Morin
Fond du Lac Ojibwe S	49 University Rd	Cloquet, MN	55720	218-878-7242	878-7263	K-12		Jennifer Johnson
Lac Courte Oreilles Ojibwa S	8575 N Trepania Rd	Hayward, WI	54843	715-634-8924	634-6058	K-12		Jessica Hutchison
Lumsden Bahweting Anishinabe S, J.K.	1301 Marquette Ave	Sault S Marie, MI	49783-9533	906-635-5055	635-3805	K-8	500	Susan Palmer
Menominee Tribal S	PO Box 39	Neopit, WI	54150-0039	715-756-2354	756-2364	K-8		Lori Corn
Nah Tah Wahsh Public S Academy	N14911 Hannahville Road B 1	Wilson, MI	49896-9612	906-466-2952	466-2556	K-12	200	Tom Miller
Nay Ah Shing S	43651 Oodena Dr	Onamia, MN	56359-2320	320-532-4695	532-4675	K-12		Noah Johnson
Oneida Nation S	PO Box 365	Oneida, WI	54155-0365	920-869-1676	869-1684	PK-12	300	Sharon Mousseau
Ahafachkee S	30290 Josie Billie Hwy	Clewiston, FL	33440	863-983-6348	983-6535	PK-12		Dorothy Cain
Bogue Chitto S	13241 Highway 491 N	Philadelphia, MS	39350-5463	601-389-1000	389-1002	K-8		Skyla Hailey
Cherokee Central ES	1582 Ravensford Dr	Cherokee, NC	28719	828-554-5020	554-5035	K-5		Paula Coker
Cherokee Central HS	1582 Ravensford Dr	Cherokee, NC	28719	828-554-5030	554-5033	9-12		Fredrick Hickman
Cherokee Central MS	1582 Ravensford Dr	Cherokee, NC	28719	828-554-5026	554-5029	6-8		Deborah Foerst
Chitimacha Day S	3613 Chitimacha Trl	Jeanerette, LA	70544-8317	337-923-9960	923-7346	K-8	100	Tanya Rosamond
Choctaw Central HS	150 Recreation Rd	Choctaw, MS	39350-7180	601-663-7777	656-7776	9-12	400	Dr. Fredrick Hickmon
Choctaw Central MS	150 Recreation Rd	Choctaw, MS	39350-7180	601-656-8938	656-1558	7-8	200	Lula Townsend
Conehatta S	851 Tushka Rd	Conehatta, MS	39057-2804	601-775-8254	775-9229	PK-8	300	Brian Parkman
Indian Island S	10 Wabanaki Way	Indian Island, ME	04468-1254	207-827-4285	827-3599	PK-8	100	Annemarie Swanson
Indian Township S	13 School Dr	Princeton, ME	04668-5000	207-796-2362	796-2726	PK-8	100	Matthew Harvey
Miccosukee Indian S	PO Box 440021	Miami, FL	33144-0021	305-894-2364	894-2365	K-12	100	Manuel Varela
Pearl River ES	470 Industrial Rd	Choctaw, MS	39350-4256	601-656-9051	656-9054	PK-6	700	Suzanne Hyatt
Rafferty S, Beatrice	22 Bayview Dr	Pleasant Point, ME	04667-4111	207-853-6085	853-2483	PK-8	100	Mike Chadwick
Red Water S	107 Braves Blvd	Carthage, MS	39051	601-267-8500	267-5193	PK-8		Presley Tate
Standing Pine ES	538 Highway 487 E	Carthage, MS	39051-0031	601-267-9225	267-9129	PK-6		Linda Peoples
Tucker S	126 E Tucker Cir	Philadelphia, MS	39350-8351	601-650-9039	656-9341	PK-8		Lari York
Havasupai S	PO Box 40	Supai, AZ	86435-0040	928-448-2901	448-2108	K-8		Coleen Maldonado

Agency/School	Address	City,State	Zip code	Telephone	Fax	Grade	Enr	Superintendent/Principal
Kennedy S, John F.	PO Box 130	Whiteriver, AZ	85941-0130	928-338-4591	338-4592	K-8		Susan Higgins M.Ed.
San Simon S	HC 1 Box 8292	Sells, AZ	85634-9711	520-362-2231	362-2405	K-8		Frank Rogers
Santa Rosa Day S	HC 1 Box 8400	Sells, AZ	85634-9713	520-361-2276	361-2511	K-8		Maxine Roanhorse-Dineyaz
Santa Rosa Ranch S	HC 2 Box 7570	Sells, AZ	85634-9741	520-383-2359	383-3960	K-8		Jim Hastings
Tohono O'Odham HS	HC 1 Box 8513	Sells, AZ	85634-9735	520-362-2400	362-2265	9-12	100	Michael Krug
Chief Leschi S	5625 52nd St E	Puyallup, WA	98371-3610	253-445-6000	445-2352	PK-12		Michelle Zimnisky
Couer D'Alene Tribal S	PO Box 338	Desmet, ID	83824-0338	208-686-5808	686-5080	K-8	100	Donavan Chase
Duckwater Shoshone S	PO Box 140002	Duckwater, NV	89314	775-863-0242		K-8	50	
Lummi Nation S	2334 Lummi View Dr	Bellingham, WA	98226-9277	360-758-4330	758-3152	K-12		Bernie Thomas
Muckleshoot Tribal S	15209 SE 376th St	Auburn, WA	98092	253-931-6709	939-5568	K-12	300	John Lombardi
Noli S	PO Box 700	San Jacinto, CA	92581-0700	951-654-5596	654-7198	6-12	100	Donovan Post
Northern Cheyenne Tribal S of Busby	PO Box 150	Busby, MT	59016-0150	406-592-3646	592-3645	K-12		Loverty Erickson
Paschal Sherman Indian S	169 N End Omak Lake Rd	Omak, WA	98841	509-422-7590	422-7539	PK-9	200	Marcy Horne
Pyramid Lake HS	PO Box 267	Nixon, NV	89424	775-574-1016	574-1037	7-12		Jake Chapin
Quileute Tribal S	PO Box 39	La Push, WA	98350	360-374-5609	374-5648	K-12		Sheri Crippen
Shoshone Bannock S	PO Box 790	Pocatello, ID	83204	208-238-4200	238-2628	7-12	100	Jonathan Braack
Two Eagle River S	PO Box 160	Pablo, MT	59855-0160	406-675-0292	675-0294	K-12		Rollie Sullivan
Wa He Lut Indian S	11110 Conine Ave SE	Olympia, WA	98513-9603	360-456-1311	456-1319	K-8	100	Harvey Whitford
Yakama Nation Tribal S	PO Box 151	Toppenish, WA	98948	509-865-4478		8-12	100	Relyn Storm
Aneth Community S	PO Box 600	Montezuma Creek, UT	84534-0600	435-651-3271	651-3272	K-6	200	Brenda Whitehorse
Atsa'Biya'a'zh Community S	PO Box 1809	Shiprock, NM	87420-1809	505-368-2100	368-2076	K-6		Freda Nells
Beclabito Day S	PO Box 1200	Shiprock, NM	87420-1200	928-656-3556	656-3557	K-4		Dr. Gladys Tracy
Cove Day S	PO Box 2000	Red Valley, AZ	86544	928-653-4457	653-4415	K-6	50	Dr. Leo Johnson
Dzilth-Na-O-Dith-Hle Comm S	35 Road 7585 Ste 5003	Bloomfield, NM	87413-4936	505-960-0356	960-8563	K-8	200	Mike Walker
Hanaa'dli Community S	PO Box 639	Bloomfield, NM	87413	505-325-3411	327-3591	K-12		Janice Yazzie-Montoya
Kayenta Community S	PO Box 188	Kayenta, AZ	86033-0188	928-697-3439	697-3490	K-8		Veronica Klain
Kinteel Residential Academy	1600 Lydia Rippey Rd	Aztec, NM	87410	505-334-6565	334-8630	9-12		Farrell Begay
Navajo Prep S	1220 W Apache St	Farmington, NM	87401-3886	505-326-6571	564-8099	9-12	300	Betty Ojaye
Nenahnezad Community S	PO Box 337	Fruitland, NM	87416-0337	505-960-6922	598-0970	K-6	200	Nolan Johnson
Red Rock Day S	PO Box 2007	Red Valley, AZ	86544-2007	928-653-4456	863-5711	K-8	200	Dr. Leo Johnson
Sanostee Day S	PO Box 159	Sanostee, NM	87461-0159	505-723-2476	723-2425	K-3	100	David Smith
Shiprock HS	PO Box 1809	Shiprock, NM	87420-1809	505-368-2157	368-2076	7-12	600	Albert Madera
T'iis Nazbas Community S	PO Box 2002	Teec Nos Pos, AZ	86514	928-656-3252	656-3486	K-8	200	Dr. Karina Roessel
Chilchinbeto Community S	PO Box 740	Kayenta, AZ	86033-0740	928-697-3800	697-3448	K-8		Vee Brown
Dilcon Community S	HC 63 Box G	Winslow, AZ	86047-9414	928-657-3211	657-3213	K-8		Bill Wachunas
Greyhills Academy HS	PO Box 160	Tuba City, AZ	86045-0160	928-283-6271	283-6604	9-12		Dr. Loren Hudson
Kaibeto Boarding S	PO Box 1420	Kaibeto, AZ	86053	928-673-3480	673-3489	K-8		Phyllis N. Yazzie
KinLani Bordertown Dormitory	901 N Kinlani Dr	Flagstaff, AZ	86001-1585	928-774-5270	556-9683	9-12		Theresa Boone-Schular
Leupp S	Highway 99	Leupp, AZ	86035	928-686-6211	686-6216	K-12		Tommy Yonnie
Little Singer Community S	PO Box AQ	Winslow, AZ	86047	928-686-6108	686-6150	K-6		Etta Shirley
Naa Tsis 'Aan Community S	PO Box 10010	Tonalea, AZ	86044	928-672-2335	672-2609	K-8		Lolita Paddock
Richfield Residential Hall	765 W 1st Ave	Richfield, UT	84701	435-896-6121		9-12		Cody Workman
Rocky Ridge Boarding S	PO Box 299	Kykotsmovi, AZ	86039-0299	928-725-3650	725-3655	K-8		Kimberly Dominguez
Seba Dalkai Boarding S	HC 63 Box H	Winslow, AZ	86047-9415	928-657-3208	657-3224	K-9	100	Maye Bigboy
Shonto Preparatory S	PO Box 7900	Shonto, AZ	86054-7900	928-672-3528	672-3505	K-12	100	Lemual Adson
Tonalea Day S	PO Box 39	Tonalea, AZ	86044-0039	928-283-6325	283-5158	K-8		Cheryl Kaye
Tuba City Boarding S	PO Box 187	Tuba City, AZ	86045-0187	928-283-2330	283-2362	K-8		Donald Coffland
Bread Springs Day S	PO Box 1117	Gallup, NM	87305-1117	505-778-5665	778-5692	K-3	100	Nancy Taranto
Chi-Chil'tah Community S	PO Box 278	Vanderwagen, NM	87326-0278	505-778-5574	778-5575	K-8	100	Marlene Tsosie
Crystal Boarding S	PO Box 1288	Navajo, NM	87328	505-777-2385	777-2648	K-6		Alberto Castruita
Hunters Point Boarding S	PO Box 99	Saint Michaels, AZ	86511-0099	928-871-4439	871-4435	K-5	100	Dr. Berdina Tsosie
Kin Dah Lichi'i Olta	PO Box 800	Ganado, AZ	86505-0800	928-755-3430	755-3448	K-6	200	Ora James
Pine Springs Day S	PO Box 4198	Houck, AZ	86505	928-871-4311	871-4341	K-4	100	Lou Ann Jones
Tiisyaakin Residential Hall	1100 W Buffalo St	Holbrook, AZ	86025-2330	928-524-6222	524-2231	9-12		Renee White-Alcott
Wide Ruins Community S	PO Box 309	Chambers, AZ	86502-0309	928-652-3251	652-3286	K-6	100	Dr. Catherine Begay
Wingate ES	PO Box 1	Fort Wingate, NM	87316-0001	505-488-6300	488-6300	PK-8		Dr. Edie Morris
Wingate HS	PO Box 2	Fort Wingate, NM	87316-0002	505-488-6400	488-6444	9-12	500	Gloria Arviso
Winslow Residential Hall	600 N Alfred Ave	Winslow, AZ	86047-3130	928-289-4488	289-2821	7-12		Isabel Britton

DEPARTMENT OF DEFENSE DEPENDENT SCHOOLS

DODEA AMERICAS REGION OFFICE
700 Westpark Dr, Peachtree City, GA 30269
Telephone 678-364-8000
Website http://www.dodea.edu/Americas/schools-by-area.cfm

District/School	Address	City,State	Zip code	Telephone	Fax	Grade	Enr	Superintendent/Principal
Americas Mid-Atlantic District	**PO Box 70089**	**Fort Bragg, NC**	**28307-0089**	**910-907-0200**	**907-1405**	**PK-9**	**4,300**	**Dr. Emily Marsh**
Americas Southeast District	**7441 Custer Rd Bldg 2670**	**Fort Benning, GA**	**31905-9647**	**706-545-7276**	**545-8227**	**PK-8**	**400**	**Dr. Christy Huddleston**
Albritton MS	PO Box 70089	Fort Bragg, NC	28307-0089	910-907-0201	432-4072	6-8	600	Pat Schob
Bitz IS	2028 Bevin St	Camp Lejeune, NC	28547-1436	910-451-2575	451-1475	3-5	400	Dewanda Sholar
Bowley ES	PO Box 70089	Fort Bragg, NC	28307-0089	910-907-0202	907-3513	PK-5	300	Mike Thornburg
Brewster MS	883 Stone St	Camp Lejeune, NC	28547-2501	910-451-2561	451-2600	6-8		Emilio Garza
Butner PS	PO Box 70089	Fort Bragg, NC	28307-0089	910-907-0203	432-8400	PK-2	500	Kim McBroom
Crossroads ES	3315 Purvis Rd	Quantico, VA	22134	703-630-7065		PK-5	700	Kathy Downs
Dahlgren S	6117 Sampson Rd Ste 206	Dahlgren, VA	22448-5121	540-653-8822	653-4591	PK-8		Tracey Fairfax
Delalio ES	1500 Curtis Rd	Jacksonville, NC	28540-3406	910-449-0601	449-0677	PK-5		Wyonia Chevis
Devers ES	PO Box 70089	Fort Bragg, NC	28307-0089	910-907-0204	396-7374	PK-5	500	Cassandra White
Gordon ES	4200 Percy Blvd	Cameron, NC	28326-9832	910-907-1300	908-3504	PK-5	500	Joel Grim
Hampton PS	PO Box 70089	Fort Bragg, NC	28307	910-907-0205	908-1190	PK-2		Priscilla Joiner
Heroes ES	100 Barnett Way	Camp Lejeune, NC	28547-2552	910-449-8000		PK-5		Kendra White
Irwin IS	PO Box 70089	Fort Bragg, NC	28307-0089	910-907-0206	907-1247	2-5	500	Miriam Breece
Johnson PS	2027 Stone St	Camp Lejeune, NC	28547-2506	910-451-2431	451-2433	PK-2		Andrea Mial
Lejeune HS	835 Stone St	Camp Lejeune, NC	28547-2520	910-451-2451	451-3130	9-12		Eric Steimel
Quantico MSHS	3307 Purvis Rd	Quantico, VA	22134-2198	703-630-7055	784-4851	6-12		Michael Johnson
Shughart ES	4800 Camel Rd	Cameron, NC	28326-5056	910-907-0210		PK-5	600	Dr. Carolyn Carr
Shughart MS	4800 Camel Rd	Cameron, NC	28326-5056	910-907-0211	907-2150	6-8	500	Karen Jones
Tarawa Terrace ES	84 Iwo Jima Blvd	Tarawa Terrace, NC	28543-1231	910-450-1635	450-1637	PK-5		Leigh Anne Faulkner
West Point ES	705A Barry Rd	West Point, NY	10996-1110	845-938-2313	938-3352	PK-4		Denise Cochenour
West Point MS	705 Barry Rd	West Point, NY	10996-1110	845-938-2923	938-2568	5-8		Miles Shea
Barkley ES	3708 Polk Rd	Fort Campbell, KY	42223	270-640-1205	439-1901	PK-5	600	Ted Turnipseed
Barsanti ES	7409 McAuliffe Loop	Fort Campbell, KY	42223	270-640-1213	431-0519	PK-5	600	Hugh McKinnon
Bolden S, Charles Frank	2 Albacore St	Beaufort, SC	29906	843-846-6112	846-9283	3-8	4,000	Dr. Angela Stephens
Dexter ES, Herbert J.	99 Yeager Ave	Fort Benning, GA	31905-6522	706-545-3424	545-9106	PK-5		Edwina Smith
Diamond ES	2493 Hero Rd	Fort Stewart, GA	31315	912-876-1451	876-8350	PK-6		Rachel Brumbaugh
Elliott ES, Middleton Stuart	345 Elliott Dr	Beaufort, SC	29906	843-846-6982	846-6720	PK-2	300	Carol Lee Kipp Caldwell
Faith MS, Don C.	1375 Ingersoll St	Fort Benning, GA	31905-7200	706-545-0310	545-7800	6-8		Dr. Joan Islas
Fort Campbell HS	902 Bastogne Ave	Fort Campbell, KY	42223	270-640-1219	431-9386	9-12	600	Kimberly Butts
Fort Knox HS	266 Maine St	Fort Knox, KY	40121	502-624-6647	624-6171	9-12	400	Brian Perry
Fort Rucker ES	PO Box 620279	Fort Rucker, AL	36362-0279	334-255-1607	268-7482	3-6	300	Dr. Vicki Gilmer
Fort Rucker PS	PO Box 620279	Fort Rucker, AL	36362-0279	334-255-2822	268-7483	PK-2	300	Dr. Deborah Deas
Kessler ES, Patrick	1127 Austin Rd	Fort Stewart, GA	31315	912-368-3958	368-5048	PK-6	100	Dr. Djuna Crowder
Kingsolver ES		Fort Knox, KY	40121			K-8		Linda Gibson
Lucas ES, Andre	2115 Airborne St	Fort Campbell, KY	42223-5333	270-640-1208	431-5842	PK-5	500	Steven Gardner
Mahaffey MS	71 S Carolina Ave	Fort Campbell, KY	42223	270-640-1215	439-3472	6-8	400	Linda Haberman
Marshall ES	70 Texas Ave	Fort Campbell, KY	42223	270-640-1214	439-4382	PK-5	500	Suzanne Jones
Maxwell AFB ES	800 Magnolia Blvd	Maxwell AFB, AL	36112-5922	334-953-7804	953-4339	PK-8	300	Paul Hernandez
McBride ES, Morris R.	700 Custer Rd	Fort Benning, GA	31905-7402	706-544-9411	544-9299	PK-5		William Pollard
Murray ES, Charles P.	24 Murray Ave	Fort Stewart, GA	31315	912-369-1576	767-3600	PK-6	200	Talisha Thompson
Pierce Terrace ES	5715 Adams Ct	Columbia, SC	29206-5379	803-782-1772	738-8895	PK-1	200	Dr. Raymond Burk

District/School	Address	City,State	Zip code	Telephone	Fax	Grade	Enr	Superintendent/Principal
Pinckney ES, Charles C.	5900 Chesnut Rd	Columbia, SC	29206-5365	803-787-6815	790-2169	2-6	200	Dr. Theresa Harvey
Scott MS	266 Mississippi St	Fort Knox, KY	40121-6814	502-624-2236	624-5433	6-8	300	Youlanda Washington
Ph.D.								
Stowers ES, Freddie	7791 Stowers Dr	Fort Benning, GA	31905-3130	706-544-2312	544-2349	PK-5		Debbie Parks
Van Voorhis ES	120 Folger St	Fort Knox, KY	40121-6086	502-624-5854	624-7267	PK-5	500	Angelique Joyner
Wassom MS	175 Forest Rd	Fort Campbell, KY	42223	270-640-1218	439-0249	6-8	300	Linda Haberman
White ES, Edward A.	300 1st Division Rd	Fort Benning, GA	31905-6627	706-545-4623	545-5469	PK-5	300	Dr. Renee Mallory
Wilson ES, Richard G.	112 Lavoie Ave	Fort Benning, GA	31905-7523	706-545-5723	545-9505	PK-5		Michelle Allen

CATHOLIC SCHOOL SUPERINTENDENTS

NATIONAL CATHOLIC EDUCATIONAL ASSOC.

1005 N Glebe Rd Ste 525, Arlington, VA 22201-5792
Telephone 800-711-6232
Fax 243-0025
Website ncea.org

Archdiocese/Diocese	Address	City,State	Zip code	Telephone	Fax	Grade	Enr	Superintendent
Diocese of Albany	40 N Main Ave	Albany, NY	12203-1481	518-453-6602	453-6667	PK-12	6,500	Giovanni Virgiglio
Diocese of Alexandria	PO Box 7417	Alexandria, LA	71306-0417	318-445-2401	448-6121	PK-12	2,500	Thomas Roque
Diocese of Allentown	1425 Mountain Dr N	Bethlehem, PA	18015-4722	610-866-0581	867-8702	PK-12	11,900	Philip Fromuth
Diocese of Altoona-Johnstown	933 S Logan Blvd	Hollidaysburg, PA	16648	814-693-1401	696-6725	PK-12	4,400	Sr. Donna Leiden
Diocese of Amarillo	PO Box 5644	Amarillo, TX	79107	806-383-2243	383-8452	PK-12	700	Fr. Robert Busch Ph.D.
Archdiocese of Anchorage	225 Cordova St	Anchorage, AK	99501-2409	907-297-7700	297-3885	PK-12	500	
Diocese of Arlington	200 N Glebe Rd Ste 503	Arlington, VA	22203	703-841-2519	524-8670	PK-12	17,100	Jennifer Bigelow
Archdiocese of Atlanta	2401 Lake Park Dr SE	Smyrna, GA	30080	404-920-7700	920-7701	PK-12	11,900	Dr. Diane Starkovich Ph.D.
Diocese of Austin	6225 E Highway 290	Austin, TX	78723	512-949-2400	949-2520	PK-12	5,100	Misty Poe
Diocese of Baker	2450 NE 27th St	Bend, OR	97701	541-382-4701	312-9111	PK-8	600	Dr. Dennis Dempsey
Archdiocese of Baltimore	320 Cathedral St	Baltimore, MD	21201-4421	410-547-5515	547-5566	PK-12	27,400	James Sellinger
Diocese of Baton Rouge	PO Box 2028	Baton Rouge, LA	70821-2028	225-336-8735	336-8711	PK-12	14,900	Dr. Melanie Verges
Diocese of Beaumont	PO Box 3948	Beaumont, TX	77704-3948	409-924-4328	838-4511	PK-12	1,600	Marcia Stevens
Diocese of Belleville	2620 Lebanon Ave	Belleville, IL	62221-3002	618-235-9601	235-7115	PK-12	5,900	Thomas Posnanski
Diocese of Biloxi	1790 Popps Ferry Rd	Biloxi, MS	39532-2118	228-702-2130	702-2178	PK-12	4,100	Dr. Mike Ladner
Diocese of Birmingham	PO Box 12047	Birmingham, AL	35202-2047	205-838-8303	838-8330	PK-12	5,900	Frances Lawlor
Diocese of Bismarck	218 1st St SE	Minot, ND	58701	701-838-1026		PK-12	2,700	Fr. Justin Waltz
Diocese of Boise	1501 S Federal Way Ste 400	Boise, ID	83705-2591	208-342-1311	342-0224	PK-12	3,000	Dr. Sarah Quilici
Archdiocese of Boston	66 Brooks Dr	Braintree, MA	02184	617-779-3601	746-5702	PK-12	40,200	Kathleen Mears
Diocese of Bridgeport	238 Jewett Ave	Bridgeport, CT	06606-2892	203-416-1638	372-1961	PK-12	11,100	Dr. Steven Cheeseman
Diocese of Brooklyn	310 Prospect Park W	Brooklyn, NY	11215	718-965-7300	965-7353	PK-12	40,200	Dr. Thomas Chadzutko
Diocese of Brownsville	700 Virgen de San Juan	San Juan, TX	78589-3030	956-784-5051	784-5081	PK-12	3,900	Sr. Cynthia A. Mello M.A.
Diocese of Buffalo	795 Main St	Buffalo, NY	14203-1215	716-847-5520	847-5593	PK-12	14,100	Sr. Carol Cimino Ed.D.
Diocese of Burlington	55 Joy Dr	S Burlington, VT	05403	802-658-6110	658-6112	PK-12	2,100	Lisa Lorenz
Diocese of Camden	631 Market St	Camden, NJ	08102	856-583-6103	756-0225	PK-12	13,800	Mary Boyle M.Ed.
Diocese of Charleston	901 Orange Grove Rd	Charleston, SC	29407	843-261-4096		PK-12	7,000	Sandra Leatherwood
Diocese of Charlotte	1123 S Church St	Charlotte, NC	28203-4003	704-370-6299		PK-12	7,800	Dr. Janice Ritter
Diocese of Cheyenne	PO Box 1468	Cheyenne, WY	82003	307-638-1530	637-7936	PK-12	1,000	Vernon Dobelmann
Archdiocese of Chicago	PO Box 1979	Chicago, IL	60690-1979	312-534-5200	534-5295	PK-12	81,700	Jim Rigg Ph.D.
Archdiocese of Cincinnati	100 E 8th St	Cincinnati, OH	45202	513-421-3131	421-6271	PK-12	43,000	Susan Gibbons
Diocese of Cleveland	1404 E 9th St	Cleveland, OH	44114-1735	216-696-6525	579-9655	PK-12	43,900	Christopher Knight
Diocese of Colorado Springs	228 N Cascade Ave	Colorado Spgs, CO	80903-1324	719-636-2345	636-1216	PK-12	1,700	Holly Goodwin
Diocese of Columbus	197 E Gay St	Columbus, OH	43215	614-221-5829	241-2563	PK-12	17,200	Dr. Joe Brettnacher Ph.D.
Diocese of Corpus Christi	PO Box 2620	Corpus Christi, TX	78403-2620	361-882-6191	693-6798	PK-12	3,600	Dr. Rosemary Henry
Diocese of Covington	1125 Madison Ave	Covington, KY	41011	859-392-1500	392-1500	K-12	10,000	Michael Clines
Diocese of Crookston	PO Box 610	Crookston, MN	56716	218-281-4533	281-3328	PK-12	1,300	Tina Stanger
Diocese of Dallas	PO Box 190507	Dallas, TX	75219-0507	214-379-2830	522-1753	PK-12	14,600	Matthew Vereecke Ed.D.
Diocese of Davenport	780 W Central Park Ave	Davenport, IA	52804-1901	563-324-1911	324-5811	PK-12	4,800	Dr. Lee Morrison
Archdiocese of Denver	1300 S Steele St	Denver, CO	80210-2599	303-715-3200	715-2007	PK-12	10,400	Kevin Kijewski J.D.
Diocese of Des Moines	601 Grand Ave	Des Moines, IA	50309-2501	515-237-5013	237-5070	PK-12	6,400	Dr. Tracy Bonday
Archdiocese of Detroit	12 State St	Detroit, MI	48226	313-237-4661	237-5857	PK-12	31,900	Dr. Brian Dougherty
Diocese of Dodge City	PO Box 137	Dodge City, KS	67801	620-227-1513	227-1570	PK-8	900	Trina Delgado
Archdiocese of Dubuque	1229 Mount Loretta Ave	Dubuque, IA	52003-8787	563-556-2580	556-5464	PK-12	11,700	Kimberly Hermsen
Diocese of Duluth	2830 E 4th St	Duluth, MN	55812-1501	218-724-9111	724-1056	PK-8	1,500	Cynthia Zook
Diocese of El Paso	499 Saint Matthews St	El Paso, TX	79907-4214	915-872-8426	872-8464	PK-12	4,100	Sr. Elizabeth Swartz
Diocese of Erie	PO Box 10397	Erie, PA	16514-0397	814-824-1241	824-1239	PK-12	8,100	Dr. Samuel Signorino
Diocese of Evansville	PO Box 4169	Evansville, IN	47724-0169	812-424-5536	424-0973	PK-12	6,700	Dr. Daryl Hagan
Diocese of Fairbanks	PO Box 71620	Fairbanks, AK	99701	907-456-4574	452-5978	K-12	500	Nancy Hanson
Diocese of Fall River	423 Highland Ave	Fall River, MA	02720-3718	508-678-2828	674-4218	PK-12	6,800	Stephen Perla
Diocese of Fargo	5201 Bishops Blvd S Ste A	Fargo, ND	58104	701-356-7900	356-7994	PK-12	2,200	Mike Hagstrom
Diocese of Fort Worth	800 W Loop 820 S	Fort Worth, TX	76108-2936	817-560-3300	244-8839	PK-12	5,900	Jennifer Pelletier
Diocese of Fresno	1550 N Fresno St	Fresno, CA	93703	559-488-7420	488-7422	PK-12	6,100	Mona Faulkner
Diocese of Ft. Wayne-South Bend	PO Box 390	Fort Wayne, IN	46801-0390	260-422-4611	426-3077	PK-12	12,800	Marsha Jordan
Diocese of Gallup	PO Box 1338	Gallup, NM	87305-1338	505-863-4406	863-2269	PK-12	1,300	Jeanette Suter
Archdiocese of Galveston-Houston	2403 Holcombe Blvd	Houston, TX	77021-2023	713-741-8704	741-7379	PK-12	18,000	Dr. Julie Vogel
Diocese of Gary	9292 Broadway	Merrillville, IN	46410-7088	219-769-9292	738-9034	PK-12	6,200	Dr. Joe Majchrowicz
Diocese of Gaylord	611 W North St	Gaylord, MI	49735-8349	989-732-5147	705-3589	PK-12	3,000	Frank Sander
Diocese of Grand Island	PO Box 996	Grand Island, NE	68802-0996	308-382-6565	382-6569	PK-12	1,500	Gregory Logsdon
Diocese of Grand Rapids	360 Division Ave S Ste 3A	Grand Rapids, MI	49503	616-246-0590	551-5650	PK-12	6,600	David Faber
Diocese of Great Falls-Billings	PO Box 1399	Great Falls, MT	59403	406-442-5761	442-9047	PK-12	2,900	Dr. Timothy Uhl
Diocese of Green Bay	PO Box 23825	Green Bay, WI	54305-3825	920-272-8309	272-8273	PK-12	9,600	Todd Blahnik
Diocese of Greensburg	723 E Pittsburgh St	Greensburg, PA	15601-2697	724-837-0901	837-0857	PK-12	3,300	Dr. Maureen Marsteller
Diocese of Harrisburg	4800 Union Deposit Rd	Harrisburg, PA	17111-3710	717-657-4804	657-3790	PK-12	11,300	Livia Riley
Archdiocese of Hartford	467 Bloomfield Ave	Bloomfield, CT	06002-2903	860-242-5573		PK-12	14,700	Dr. Michael Griffin
Diocese of Helena	PO Box 1708	Helena, MT	59601	406-442-5761	442-9047	PK-12	1,200	Dr. Timothy Uhl
Diocese of Honolulu	6301 Pali Hwy	Kaneohe, HI	96744-5224	808-203-6761	261-7022	PK-12	8,600	Michael Rockers Ed.D.
Diocese of Houma-Thibodaux	PO Box 505	Schriever, LA	70395-0505	985-850-3114	850-3225	PK-12	5,600	Suzanne Troxclair
Archdiocese of Indianapolis	1400 N Meridian St	Indianapolis, IN	46202-2305	317-236-1430	261-3364	PK-12	22,000	Gina Kuntz Fleming
Diocese of Jackson	PO Box 2248	Jackson, MS	39225-2248	601-960-8470	960-8469	PK-12	4,000	Catherine Cook
Diocese of Jefferson City	PO Box 104900	Jefferson City, MO	65110-4900	573-635-9127	635-2286	PK-12	6,900	Sr. Elizabeth Youngs
Diocese of Joliet	16555 Weber Rd	Crest Hill, IL	60403	815-838-2181	838-2182	PK-12	21,700	Rev. John Belmonte Ph.D.
Diocese of Juneau	415 6th St Ste 300	Juneau, AK	99801-1091	907-586-2227	463-3237	PK-6	100	
Diocese of Kalamazoo	215 N Westnedge Ave	Kalamazoo, MI	49007-3760	269-903-0165	349-6440	PK-12	3,100	Margaret Erich
Archdiocese of Kansas City	12615 Parallel Pkwy	Kansas City, KS	66109-3718	913-721-1570	721-5598	PK-12	15,100	Dr. Kathleen O'Hara
Diocese of Kansas City-Saint Joseph	PO Box 419037	Kansas City, MO	64141-6037	816-756-1850	756-1571	PK-12	11,300	Dr. Dan Peters
Diocese of Knoxville	805 S Northshore Dr	Knoxville, TN	37919	865-584-3307	584-4319	PK-12	3,500	Sr. Mary Marta Abbott
Diocese of La Crosse	PO Box 4004	La Crosse, WI	54602	608-788-7707	788-7709	PK-12	7,500	Thomas Reichenbacher
Diocese of Lafayette	PO Box 3387	Lafayette, LA	70502	337-261-5529	261-5572	PK-12	14,400	Anna Larriviere
Diocese of Lafayette-in-Indiana	2300 S 9th St	Lafayette, IN	47909-2400	765-269-4670	269-4671	PK-12	5,100	Peg Dispenzieri
Diocese of Lake Charles	1112 Bilbo St	Lake Charles, LA	70601-5226	337-433-9640	433-9685	PK-12	2,500	Kimberlee Gazzolo
Diocese of Lansing	228 N Walnut St	Lansing, MI	48933	517-342-2482	342-2468	PK-12	9,000	Sean Costello
Diocese of Laredo	1201 Corpus Christi St	Laredo, TX	78040-5354	956-753-5208	753-5203	K-12	2,100	Fred Valle
Diocese of Las Cruces	1280 Med Park Dr	Las Cruces, NM	88005-3239	575-523-7577	524-3874	PK-8	600	Julie Fracker
Diocese of Las Vegas	PO Box 18316	Las Vegas, NV	89114-8316	702-697-3903	735-8941	K-12	3,900	Catherine Thompson
Diocese of Lexington	1310 W Main St	Lexington, KY	40508-2048	859-253-1993	253-0111	PK-12	3,800	Dr. James Conneely Ph.D.
Diocese of Lincoln	PO Box 80328	Lincoln, NE	68501-0328	402-473-0610	488-6525	K-12	6,900	Msgr. John Perkinton
Diocese of Little Rock	PO Box 7565	Little Rock, AR	72217-7565	501-664-0340	603-0518	K-12	6,900	Vernell Bowen M.Ed.
Archdiocese of Los Angeles	3424 Wilshire Blvd	Los Angeles, CA	90010-2241	213-637-7300	637-6140	PK-12	79,000	Dr. Kevin Baxter
Archdiocese of Louisville	1935 Lewiston Dr	Louisville, KY	40216-2523	502-448-8581	448-5518	PK-12	20,000	Leisa Schulz
Diocese of Lubbock	PO Box 98700	Lubbock, TX	79499-8700	806-792-3943	792-8109	PK-12	400	Christine Wanjura
Diocese of Madison	PO Box 44983	Madison, WI	53744-4983	608-821-3180	821-3181	PK-12	7,200	Michael Lancaster

Archdiocese/Diocese	Address	City,State	Zip code	Telephone	Fax	Grade	Enr	Superintendent
Diocese of Manchester	153 Ash St	Manchester, NH	03104-4396	603-669-3100	669-0377	PK-12	6,700	David Thibault
Diocese of Marquette	1004 Harbor Hills Dr	Marquette, MI	49855	906-227-9127	225-0437	PK-8	1,300	Mark Salisbury
Diocese of Memphis	5825 Shelby Oaks Dr	Memphis, TN	38134-7316	901-373-1200	373-1269	PK-12	6,600	Janet M. Donato
Diocese of Metuchen	146 Metlars Ln	Piscataway, NJ	08854-4303	732-562-2446	562-1016	PK-12	10,300	Ellen Ayoub
Archdiocese of Miami	9401 Biscayne Blvd	Miami Shores, FL	33138-2970	305-762-1076	762-1115	PK-12	33,500	Kim Pryzbylski Ph.D.
Archdiocese of Milwaukee	PO Box 070912	Milwaukee, WI	53207	414-758-2256	769-3408	PK-12	29,800	Dr. Kathleen Cepelka
Archdiocese of Mobile	352 Government St	Mobile, AL	36602	251-438-4611	438-4612	PK-12	6,200	Gwen Byrd
Diocese of Monterey	485 Church St	Monterey, CA	93940-3207	831-373-1608	373-0173	PK-12	4,900	Kimberly Cheng
Diocese of Nashville	2800 McGavock Pike	Nashville, TN	37214	615-383-6393	353-7972	PK-12	6,100	Dr. Therese Williams
Archdiocese of Newark	PO Box 9500	Newark, NJ	07104-0500	973-497-4260	497-4249	PK-12	31,900	Dr. Margaret Dames
Archdiocese of New Orleans	7887 Walmsley Ave	New Orleans, LA	70125-3496	504-866-7916	861-6260	PK-12	36,900	Dr. RaeNell Houston
Diocese of New Ulm	1421 6th St N	New Ulm, MN	56073	507-359-2966	354-0268	PK-12	2,200	Karla Cross
Archdiocese of New York	1011 1st Ave Fl 18	New York, NY	10022	212-371-1000	758-3018	PK-12	70,100	Dr. Timothy McNiff
Diocese of Norwich	43 Perkins Ave	Norwich, CT	06360-3643	860-887-4086	887-9371	PK-12	4,400	Henry Fiore
Diocese of Oakland	2121 Harrison St	Oakland, CA	94612	510-628-2154	451-5331	PK-12	17,500	Kathleen Radecke
Diocese of Ogdensburg	PO Box 369	Ogdensburg, NY	13669-0369	315-393-2920	314-7296	PK-12	1,900	Sr. Ellen Rose Coughlin
Archdiocese of Oklahoma City	PO Box 32180	Oklahoma City, OK	73123-0380	405-721-5651	709-2811	PK-12	5,000	Diane Floyd
Archdiocese of Omaha	3300 N 60th St	Omaha, NE	68104	402-557-5600	827-3792	PK-12	18,900	Michael Ashton
Diocese of Orange	13280 Chapman Ave	Garden Grove, CA	92840	714-282-3000	282-5059	PK-12	19,200	Gregory Dhuyvetter
Diocese of Orlando	PO Box 1800	Orlando, FL	32802-1800	407-246-4800	246-4942	PK-12	13,400	Henry Fortier
Diocese of Owensboro	600 Locust St	Owensboro, KY	42301-2130	270-683-1545	683-6883	PK-12	3,900	Ann Flaherty
Diocese of Palm Beach	9995 N Military Trl	West Palm Beach, FL	33410-5497	561-775-9500	775-9556	PK-12	6,100	Gary Gelo
Diocese of Paterson	777 Valley Rd	Clifton, NJ	07013-2205	973-777-8818	779-0083	PK-12	10,300	Mary Baier
Diocese of Pensacola-Tallahassee	11 N B St	Pensacola, FL	32502-4601	850-435-3540	436-6424	PK-12	2,700	Michael P. Juhas
Diocese of Peoria	419 NE Madison Ave	Peoria, IL	61603	309-671-1550	671-1579	PK-12	11,200	Sharon Weiss Ed.D.
Archdiocese of Philadelphia	222 N 17th St	Philadelphia, PA	19103-1202	215-587-3700	587-5644	PK-12	69,400	Mary Rochford
Diocese of Phoenix	400 E Monroe St	Phoenix, AZ	85004-2336	602-354-2345	354-2436	PK-12	14,000	Harry Plummer
Diocese of Pittsburgh	111 Blvd of the Allies	Pittsburgh, PA	15222-1618	412-456-3090	456-3098	PK-12	18,900	Michael Latusek Ed.D.
Archdiocese of Portland	2838 E Burnside St	Portland, OR	97214-1895	503-233-8300	236-3683	PK-12	13,400	Br. William Dygert
Diocese of Portland	510 Ocean Ave	Portland, ME	04103-4900	207-773-6471	773-0182	PK-12	2,700	Jim King
Diocese of Providence	1 Cathedral Sq	Providence, RI	02903-3695	401-278-4550	278-4596	PK-12	13,500	Daniel Ferris
Diocese of Pueblo	101 N Greenwood St	Pueblo, CO	81003	719-544-9861	561-2251	PK-12	900	John Brainard M.Ed.
Diocese of Raleigh	7200 Stonehenge Dr	Raleigh, NC	27613	919-821-9749	522-1695	PK-12	8,800	Dr. Michael Fedewa
Rapid City Catholic School System	424 Fairmont Blvd	Rapid City, SD	57701	605-348-1477	342-4367	K-12	1,000	Barb Honeycutt
Diocese of Reno	290 S Arlington Ave Ste 200	Reno, NV	89501-1713	775-326-9430	372-6247	PK-12	1,700	Karen Barreras
Diocese of Richmond	7800 Carousel Ln	Richmond, VA	23294-4201	804-359-5661	358-9159	PK-12	9,200	Ray Honeycutt
Diocese of Rochester	1150 Buffalo Rd	Rochester, NY	14624-1890	585-328-3228	328-3149	PK-12	7,700	Dr. Anthony Cook Ed.D.
Diocese of Rockford	PO Box 7044	Rockford, IL	61125-7044	815-399-4300	399-6278	PK-12	14,000	Michael Kagan
Diocese of Rockville Centre	128 Cherry Ln	Hicksville, NY	11801	516-678-5800	764-3316	PK-12	29,400	Dr. Kathleen Walsh
Diocese of Sacramento	2110 Broadway	Sacramento, CA	95818-2518	916-733-0110	733-0120	PK-12	13,500	Lincoln Snyder
Diocese of Saginaw	5800 Weiss St	Saginaw, MI	48603-2762	989-799-7910	399-2257	PK-12	2,700	Mary Ann Deschaine
Diocese of St. Augustine	11625 Old St Augustine Rd	Jacksonville, FL	32258-2056	904-262-3200	596-1042	PK-12	10,200	Rev. Scott Conway
Diocese of St. Cloud	305 7th Ave N Ste 201	Saint Cloud, MN	56303-3633	320-251-0111	251-0259	PK-12	4,900	Linda Kaiser
Archdiocese of St. Louis	20 Archbishop May Dr	Saint Louis, MO	63119	314-792-7300	792-7350	PK-12	41,300	Sr. Nathalie Meyer
Archdiocese of St. Paul	777 Forest St	Saint Paul, MN	55106	651-291-4494	290-1628	PK-12	31,700	Jason Slattery
Diocese of St. Petersburg	PO Box 40200	St Petersburg, FL	33743-0200	727-347-5539	341-6848	PK-12	12,400	Chris Pastura
Diocese of Salina	PO Box 825	Salina, KS	67402-0825	785-827-8746	827-6133	PK-12	2,400	Dr. Nick Compagnone
Diocese of Salt Lake City	27 C St	Salt Lake City, UT	84103-2302	801-328-8641	328-8643	PK-12	5,500	Mark Longe
Diocese of San Angelo	2000 W Texas Ave	Midland, TX	79701	432-684-4563	687-2468	PK-8	700	Joan Wilmes
Archdiocese of San Antonio	2718 W Woodlawn Ave	San Antonio, TX	78228-5195	210-734-2620	734-9112	PK-12	12,700	Marti West
Diocese of San Bernardino	1201 E Highland Ave	San Bernardino, CA	92404-4641	909-475-5437	475-5477	PK-12	7,700	Patricia Vesely
Diocese of San Diego	PO Box 85728	San Diego, CA	92186-5728	858-490-8240	490-8272	PK-12	16,100	John Galvan
Archdiocese of San Francisco	1 Peter Yorke Way	San Francisco, CA	94109-6602	415-614-5660	614-5664	PK-12	24,600	Pamela Lyons
Diocese of San Jose	1150 N 1st St Ste 100	San Jose, CA	95112	408-983-0185	983-0192	PK-12	16,000	Katherine Almazol
Archdiocese of Santa Fe	4000 Saint Josephs Pl NW	Albuquerque, NM	87120-1714	505-831-8173	831-8107	PK-12	5,000	Susan Murphy
Diocese of Santa Rosa	PO Box 1297	Santa Rosa, CA	95402	707-566-3311	566-3382	PK-12	4,500	Dr. Linda Norman
Diocese of Savannah	2170 E Victory Dr	Savannah, GA	31404	912-201-4100	201-4101	K-12	5,000	Michelle Kroll
Diocese of Scranton	300 Wyoming Ave	Scranton, PA	18503-1243	570-207-2251	207-2261	PK-12	5,900	Msgr. David L. Tressler
Archdiocese of Seattle	710 9th Ave	Seattle, WA	98104-2017	206-382-4861	654-4651	PK-12	22,700	Kristin Dixon
Diocese of Shreveport	3500 Fairfield Ave	Shreveport, LA	71104-4108	318-868-4441	868-5057	PK-12	2,000	Sr. Carol Shively
Diocese of Sioux City	PO Box 3379	Sioux City, IA	51102-3379	712-233-7527	233-7598	PK-12	5,900	Patty Lansink
Diocese of Sioux Falls	523 N Duluth Ave	Sioux Falls, SD	57104-2714	605-988-3761	988-3746	PK-12	5,000	Katie Mellor
Diocese of Spokane	PO Box 1453	Spokane, WA	99210-1453	509-358-7330	358-7302	PK-12	4,300	Dr. Duane Schafer Ph.D.
Diocese of Springfield-Cape Girardeau	601 S Jefferson Ave	Springfield, MO	65806-3107	417-866-0841	866-1140	PK-12	4,400	Leon Witt
Diocese of Springfield	1615 W Washington St	Springfield, IL	62702-4757	217-698-8500	897-5855	PK-12	10,700	Brandi Borries
Diocese of Springfield	PO Box 1730	Springfield, MA	01102-1730	413-452-0830	452-0555	PK-12	3,200	Sr. M. Andrea Ciszewski
Diocese of Steubenville	PO Box 969	Steubenville, OH	43952-5969	740-282-3631	282-3327	PK-12	2,000	Paul Ward
Diocese of Stockton	212 N San Joaquin St	Stockton, CA	95202	209-466-0636	463-5937	PK-12	4,100	Marian Graham
Diocese of Superior	PO Box 969	Superior, WI	54880	715-392-2937	392-2015	PK-8	2,400	Peggy Schoenfuss
Diocese of Syracuse	240 E Onondaga St	Syracuse, NY	13202-2668	315-470-1450	470-1470	PK-12	5,900	William Crist
Diocese of Toledo	1933 Spielbusch Ave	Toledo, OH	43604-5360	419-244-6711	255-8269	PK-12	18,400	Dr. Vincent Schmidt
Diocese of Trenton	PO Box 5147	Trenton, NJ	08638-0147	609-406-7400	406-7429	PK-12	19,400	JoAnn Tier
Diocese of Tucson	PO Box 31	Tucson, AZ	85702-0031	520-838-2547	838-2589	PK-12	6,700	Sheri Dahl
Diocese of Tulsa	820 S Boulder Ave	Tulsa, OK	74119-1624	918-582-9177	582-1851	PK-12	4,600	Jim Pohlman
Diocese of Tyler	1015 E Southeast Loop 323	Tyler, TX	75701-9656	903-534-1077	534-1370	PK-12	1,000	Dr. James Klassen
Diocese of Venice in Florida	1000 Pinebrook Rd	Venice, FL	34285-6426	941-484-9543	484-1121	PK-12	4,200	Dr. Kristy Swol
Diocese of Victoria	PO Box 4070	Victoria, TX	77903-4070	361-573-0828	573-5725	PK-12	2,900	Dr. John Quary
Archdiocese of Washington DC	5001 Eastern Ave	Hyattsville, MD	20782-3447	301-853-4500	853-7672	PK-12	27,600	William Ryan
Diocese of Wheeling-Charleston	PO Box 230	Wheeling, WV	26003-0010	304-233-0880	233-8551	PK-12	5,800	Rick Barnabei
Diocese of Wichita	424 N Broadway Ave	Wichita, KS	67202	316-269-3950	269-2486	PK-12	10,400	Bob Voboril
Diocese of Wilmington	1626 N Union St	Wilmington, DE	19806-2540	302-573-3133	573-6945	PK-12	11,600	Louis De Angelo Ed.D.
Diocese of Winona	PO Box 588	Winona, MN	55987-0588	507-454-4643	454-8106	PK-12	5,000	Marsha Stenzel
Diocese of Worcester	49 Elm St	Worcester, MA	01609-2514	508-929-4317	929-4386	PK-12	7,400	David Perda Ph.D.
Diocese of Yakima	5301 Tieton Dr Ste B	Yakima, WA	98908-3479	509-965-7117	966-8334	PK-12	1,700	Rev. Thomas Bunnell
Diocese of Youngstown	144 W Wood St	Youngstown, OH	44503-1030	330-744-8451	744-5099	PK-12	6,900	Mary Fiala

LUTHERAN SCHOOL SUPERINTENDENTS

LUTHERAN CHURCH MISSOURI SYNOD
1333 S Kirkwood Rd, Saint Louis, MO 63122-7295
Telephone 800-248-1930

Website http://www.lcms.org

Region	Address	City,State	Zip code	Telephone	Fax	Superintendent
Atlantic	171 White Plains Rd	Bronxville, NY	10708-1923	914-337-5700	337-7471	Jessica Hinsch Raba
California-Nevada-Hawaii	2772 Constitution Dr Ste A	Livermore, CA	94551-7571	925-245-4000	245-1107	Dr. Robert Newton
Central Illinois	1850 N Grand Ave W	Springfield, IL	62702-1626	217-793-1802	793-1822	Glenn Goeres
Eastern	5111 Main St	Williamsville, NY	14221-5203	716-634-5111	634-5452	Dr. Chris Wicher
English	33100 Freedom Rd	Farmington, MI	48336-4030	248-476-0039	476-0188	Rev. Jamison Hardy
Florida-Georgia	5850 T G Lee Blvd Ste 500	Orlando, FL	32822	407-857-5556	857-5665	Mark Brink
Indiana	1145 Barr St	Fort Wayne, IN	46802-3135	260-423-1511	423-1514	Dr. Daniel May
Iowa East	1100 Blairs Ferry Rd	Marion, IA	52302-3092	319-373-2112	373-9827	Dr. Brian Saunders
Iowa West	409 Kenyon Rd Ste B	Fort Dodge, IA	50501	515-576-7666	576-2323	Dr. Steve Turner
Kansas	1000 SW 10th Ave	Topeka, KS	66604-1104	785-357-4441	357-5071	Jim Bradshaw
Michigan	3773 Geddes Rd	Ann Arbor, MI	48105-3098	888-225-2111	665-0255	Dr. Bruce Braun
Mid-South	1675 Wynne Rd	Cordova, TN	38016-4905	866-373-1343	373-4826	Dr. Roger Paavola
Minnesota North	PO Box 604	Brainerd, MN	56401-0604	218-829-1781	829-0037	Rev. Donald Fondow
Minnesota South	14301 Grand Ave	Burnsville, MN	55306-5707	952-435-2550	435-2581	Sean Martens
Missouri	660 Mason Ridge Center Dr	Saint Louis, MO	63141-8557	314-590-6200	590-6201	Alan Freeman

Region	Address	City,State	Zip code	Telephone	Fax	Superintendent
Montana	30 Broadwater Ave	Billings, MT	59101-1826	406-259-2908	259-1305	Rev. Terry Forke
Nebraska	PO Box 407	Seward, NE	68434-0407	888-643-2961	643-2990	Bob Ziegler
New England	400 Wilbraham Rd	Springfield, MA	01109-2723	413-783-0131	783-0909	Rev. Tim Yeadon
New Jersey	1168 Springfield Ave	Mountainside, NJ	07092-2906	908-233-8111	233-3883	Caren Vogt
North Dakota	413 E Avenue D	Bismarck, ND	58501	701-751-3424		Rev. Arie Bertsch
Northern Illinois	2301 S Wolf Rd	Hillside, IL	60162-2211	708-449-3020	449-3026	Mike Zimmer
Northwest	1700 NE Knott St	Portland, OR	97212-3301	503-288-8383	284-2785	Jim Scriven
North Wisconsin	3103 Seymour Ln	Wausau, WI	54401-4049	715-845-8241	845-3836	Rev. Dwayne Lueck
Ohio	PO Box 38277	Olmsted Falls, OH	44138-0277	440-235-2297	235-1970	Rev. Terry Cripe
Oklahoma	308 NW 164th St	Edmond, OK	73013	405-348-7600	384-7601	Rev. Barrie Henke
Pacific Southwest	1540 Concordia	Irvine, CA	92612-3203	949-854-3232	854-8140	Rachel Klitzing
Rocky Mountain	14334 E Evans Ave	Aurora, CO	80014-1408	303-695-8001	695-4047	Rev. Allen Anderson
SELC	559 Raritan Rd	Clark, NJ	07066	732-382-7320	382-7512	Rev. Andrew Dzurovcik
South Dakota	PO Box 89110	Sioux Falls, SD	57109-9110	605-361-1514	361-7959	Rev. Scott Sailer
Southeastern	6315 Grovedale Dr	Alexandria, VA	22310-2501	703-971-9371	922-6047	Rev. John Denninger
Southern	100 Mission Dr	Slidell, LA	70460	504-282-2632	871-9696	Glenn Gerber
Southern Illinois	2408 Lebanon Ave	Belleville, IL	62221-2529	618-234-4767	234-4830	Roger Sprengel
South Wisconsin	8100 W Capitol Dr	Milwaukee, WI	53222-1981	414-464-8100	464-0602	Dr. Chris Cody
Texas	7900 E Highway 290	Austin, TX	78724-2402	512-926-4272	926-1006	Dr. William Hinz
Wyoming	2400 S Hickory St	Casper, WY	82604-3471	307-265-9000	234-6629	Rev. John Hill

GENERAL CONFERENCE OF SEVENTH-DAY ADVENTISTS SUPERINTENDENTS

NORTH AMERICAN DIV. OFFICE OF EDUCATION

12501 Old Columbia Pike, Silver Spring, MD 20904-6601
Telephone 301-680-6400
Fax 680-6464
Website http://www.nadadventist.org

Conference	Address	City,State	Zip code	Telephone	Fax	Superintendent
Atlantic Union	**PO Box 1189**	**South Lancaster, MA**	**01561-1189**	**978-368-8333**	**368-7948**	**Jerrell Gilkeson**
Greater New York Conference	7 Shelter Rock Rd	Manhasset, NY	11030-3222	516-627-9350	627-9272	Marlene Romeo
New York Conference	4930 W Seneca Tpke	Syracuse, NY	13215-2225	315-469-6921	469-6924	Jeremy Garlock
Northeastern Conference	11550 Merrick Blvd	Jamaica, NY	11434-1852	718-291-8006	739-5133	Viola Chapman
Northern New England Conference	479 Main St	Westbrook, ME	04092	207-797-3760	797-2851	Trevor Schlisner
Southern New England Conference	PO Box 1169	South Lancaster, MA	01561-1169	978-365-4551	365-3838	
Columbia Union Conference	**5427 Twin Knolls Rd**	**Columbia, MD**	**21045-3247**	**410-997-3414**	**596-6758**	**Donovan Ross**
Allegheny East Conference	767 Douglass Dr	Boyertown, PA	19512	610-326-4610	326-3946	Judy Dent
Allegheny West Conference	1339 E Broad St	Columbus, OH	43205-1503	614-252-5271	252-3246	Brenda Arthurs
Chesapeake Conference	6600 Martin Rd	Columbia, MD	21044-3999	410-995-1910	917-2920	Janesta Walker
Mountain View Conference	1400 Liberty St	Parkersburg, WV	26101-4124	304-422-4581	422-4582	Cheryl Jacko
New Jersey Conference	2303 Brunswick Ave	Lawrenceville, NJ	08648	609-802-0840	396-9273	Sadrail Saint-Ulysse
Ohio Conference	PO Box 1230	Mount Vernon, OH	43050-8230	740-397-4665	397-1648	Richard Bianco
Pennsylvania Conference	720 Museum Rd	Reading, PA	19611-1420	610-374-8331	374-9331	Jeff Dovee
Potomac Conference	606 Greenville Ave	Staunton, VA	24401-4881	540-886-0771	886-5734	Keith Hallam
Lake Union Conference	**PO Box 287**	**Berrien Springs, MI**	**49103**	**269-473-8200**	**471-7920**	**Linda Fuchs**
Illinois Conference	619 Plainfield Rd	Willowbrook, IL	60527	630-856-2890	734-0929	Ron Huff
Indiana Conference	15205 Westfield Blvd	Carmel, IN	46032	317-844-6201	571-9281	Nicole Mattson
Lake Region Conference	8517 S State St	Chicago, IL	60619-5697	773-846-2661	846-5309	Renee Humphreys
Michigan Conference	PO Box 24187	Lansing, MI	48909	517-316-1550	316-1501	Diane Barlow
Wisconsin Conference	PO Box 100	Fall River, WI	53932	920-484-6555	484-6550	Linda Rosen
Mid-America Union Conference	**PO Box 6128**	**Lincoln, NE**	**68506-0128**	**402-484-3000**	**483-4453**	**LouAnn Howard**
Central States Conference	3301 Parallel Pkwy	Kansas City, KS	66104-4354	913-371-1071	371-1609	Kimberly Douglas
Dakota Conference	7200 N Washington St	Bismarck, ND	58503	701-751-6177	751-6178	Gerard Ban
Iowa-Missouri Conference	PO Box 65665	West Des Moines, IA	50265-0665	515-223-1197	223-5692	Dr. Joseph Allison
Kansas-Nebraska Conference	3440 SW Urish Rd	Topeka, KS	66614-4601	785-478-4726	478-1000	Gary Kruger
Minnesota Conference	7384 Kirkwood Ct	Maple Grove, MN	55369	763-424-8923	424-9576	John Bedell
Rocky Mountain Conference	2520 S Downing St	Denver, CO	80210-5818	303-282-3650	733-1843	Lonnie Hetterle
North Pacific Union Conference	**5709 N 20th St**	**Ridgefield, WA**	**98642-7724**	**360-857-7027**	**857-7127**	**Dennis Plubell**
Alaska Conference	6100 OMalley Rd	Anchorage, AK	99507-6958	907-346-1004	346-3279	Kevin Miller
Idaho Conference	7777 W Fairview Ave	Boise, ID	83704-8418	208-375-7524	375-7526	Patrick Frey
Montana Conference	175 Canyon View Rd	Bozeman, MT	59715-0607	406-587-3101	587-1598	Phil Hudema
Oregon Conference	19800 Oatfield Rd	Gladstone, OR	97027	503-850-3500	654-5657	Gale Crosby
Upper Columbia Conference	3715 S Grove Rd	Spokane, WA	99224	509-838-2761	838-4882	Larry Marsh
Washington Conference	32229 Weyerhaeuser Way S	Federal Way, WA	98001	253-681-6008	681-6009	Archie Harris
Pacific Union Conference	**PO Box 5005**	**Westlake Vlg, CA**	**91359-5005**	**805-413-7319**	**413-7319**	**Berit von Pohle**
Arizona Conference	PO Box 12340	Scottsdale, AZ	85267-2340	480-991-6777	991-4833	Gus Martin
Central California Conference	PO Box 770	Clovis, CA	93613-0770	559-347-3000	347-3054	Ken Bullington
Hawaii Conference	2728 Pali Hwy	Honolulu, HI	96817-1485	808-595-7591	595-2345	Miki Akeo Nelson
Nevada-Utah Conference	10475 Double R Blvd	Reno, NV	89521	775-322-6929	322-9371	Eileen White
Northern California Conference	PO Box 23165	Pleasant Hill, CA	94523-0165	925-603-5061	599-1304	Bill Keresoma
Southeastern California Conference	PO Box 79990	Riverside, CA	92513	951-509-2307	509-2392	Donald Dudley
Southern California Conference	PO Box 969	Glendale, CA	91209-0969	818-546-8400	546-8454	Dr. Harold Crook
Southern Union Conference	**PO Box 923868**	**Norcross, GA**	**30010**	**770-408-1800**	**408-1801**	**Debra Fryson**
Carolina Conference	PO Box 44270	Charlotte, NC	28215	704-596-3200	596-5775	Gary Rouse
Florida Conference	351 S State Rd 434	Altamonte Spg, FL	32714	407-644-5000	644-7550	Frank Runnels Ed.D.
Georgia-Cumberland Conference	PO Box 12000	Calhoun, GA	30703-7001	706-629-7951	625-3684	Kevin Kossick
Gulf States Conference	PO Box 240249	Montgomery, AL	36124-0249	334-272-7493	272-7987	Stan Hobbs
Kentucky-Tennessee Conference	PO Box 1088	Goodlettsville, TN	37070-1088	615-859-1391	859-2120	Stephen Bralley
South Atlantic Conference	3978 Memorial Dr	Decatur, GA	30032	404-792-0535	792-7817	Kim Gaiter
South Central Conference	PO Box 78767	Nashville, TN	37207	615-226-6500	262-9141	Johnny Holliday
Southeastern Conference	1701 Robie Ave	Mount Dora, FL	32757-6339	352-735-3142	735-3562	Barbara Davis
Southwestern Union Conference	**PO Box 4000**	**Burleson, TX**	**76097-1630**	**817-295-0476**	**447-2443**	**Randy Gilliam**
Arkansas-Louisiana Conference	PO Box 31000	Shreveport, LA	71130-1000	318-631-6240	631-7611	Stephen Burton
Oklahoma Conference	PO Box 32098	Oklahoma City, OK	73123-0298	405-721-6110	721-7594	Jack Francisco
Southwest Region Conference	PO Box 226289	Dallas, TX	75222-6289	214-943-4491	946-2528	Buford Griffith
Texas Conference	PO Box 800	Alvarado, TX	76009-0800	817-790-2255	783-5266	John Hopps
Texico Conference	PO Box 1366	Corrales, NM	87048-1366	505-244-1611	244-1811	Derral Reeve